BROADCASTING CABLE
YEARBOOK 2006

UNIVERSITY LIBRARY
UW-STEVENS POINT

Y0-CTE-069

BROADCASTING & CABLE YEARBOOK 2006
was prepared by R.R. Bowker's Serials Editorial Department
in collaboration with the Information Technology Department

Michael Cairns, President
Gary Aiello, Executive Vice President and General Manager, Retail and Publisher Division
Belinda Tseo, Senior Vice President, Chief Financial Officer
Boe Horton, Senior Vice President and General Manager, Library Division
Angela D'Agostino, Vice President, Business Development and Marketing
Mark Heinzelman, Chief Information Officer
Doreen Gravesande, Senior Director, ISBN/SAN, and Production
Galen Strazza, Director, Marketing and Creative Services

Product Development
Yvette Diven, Director, Product Management, Serials

Editorial
Laurie Kaplan, Director, Serials
Valerie Mahon, Senior Editor
Nancy Bucenec, Managing Editor
Joseph A. Esser, Associate Editor
Sara Curtiss, Patricia Farrell, and Carolyn Hamilton, Assistant Editors

Data Acquisition
O'Sheila Delgado, Coordinator
Jennifer Williams, Assistant Editor

Production & Manufacturing Services
Ralph Coviello, Manager, Manufacturing Services
Myriam Nunez, Project Manager, Content Integrity
Kennard McGill, Production Systems Analyst
Jocelyn Kwiatkowski, Senior Associate Editor

Editorial Systems, Information Technology Group
Frank Morris, Project Manager
Dina Dvinyanova, Chris Voser, Tim Helck, Programmer Analysts

Sales
Charlie Friscia, Director, Inside Sales
Richard Lorenzo, Director, Advertising Sales

Computer Operations Group
John Nesselt, UNIX Administrator
Daniel O'Malley, Manager, Network Administration and Operations

BROADCASTING CABLE
YEARBOOK 2006

Published by
R.R. Bowker LLC
630 Central Avenue
New Providence, NJ 07974 USA

Michael Cairns, President

Copyright© 2005 by R.R. Bowker LLC
Broadcasting & Cable Yearbook is a registered trademark of Reed Publishing (Nederland) B.V., used under license.

No part of this publication may be reproduced or transmitted in any form or by any means, or stored in any information storage and retrieval system, without prior written permission of R.R. Bowker, 630 Central Avenue, New Providence, New Jersey 07974 USA.

Telephone: 908-286-1090, Toll-free: 1-888-BOWKER2 (1-888-269-5372); Fax: 908-219-0182
E-mail address: info@bowker.com; URL: http://www.bowker.com

International Standard Book Number
ISBN 10: 0-8352-4777-5
ISBN 13: 978-0-8352-4777-1

International Standard Serial Number
0000-1511

Library of Congress Control Number
71-649524

Printed and Bound in the United States of America

No payment is either solicited or accepted for the inclusion of entries in this publication. R.R. Bowker has used its best efforts in collecting and preparing material for inclusion in this publication, but does not warrant that the information herein is complete or accurate, and does not assume, and hereby disclaims, any liability to any person for any loss or damage caused by errors or omissions in this publication, whether such errors or omissions result from negligence, accident, or any other cause.

ISBN 0-8352-4777-5

Ref.
HE
8664
.B76
2006

Table of Contents

Index to Sections..vi
Index to Advertisers..xii
Glossary of Terms..xiii
List of Abbreviations...xv

Section A
Industry Overview A-1

Television Markets Ranked by Number of TV Homes............A-2
Top 25 TV Station Groups..A-6
Top 25 TV Station Groups..A-7
Top 25 Cable/Satellite Operators................................A-8
Top 100 Cable Clusters/Systems.................................A-9
U.S. Sales of Television Receivers 1983-2003.................A-11
Television Sets in Use...A-12
51 Years of Station Transactions...............................A-13
Record of Television Station Growth Since Television Began....A-14
Top 10 Cable Networks..A-15
Top 100 Television Programs....................................A-16
Television Advertising Shares..................................A-19
Top 25 TV Advertisers..A-20
Top 25 TV Advertising Categories...............................A-21
A Brief History of Broadcasting and Cable......................A-22
A Chronology of the Electronic Media...........................A-24
The FCC and the Rules of Broadcasting..........................A-29

Section B
Broadcast Television B-1

TV Group Ownership...B-2
Key to Television Listings....................................B-13
Directory of Television Stations in the United States and
    Canada..B-14
U.S. Television Stations by Call Letters.....................B-114
Canadaian Television Stations by Call Letters................B-119
U.S. Television Stations by Analog Channel...................B-120
Canadain Television Stations by Channel......................B-125
U.S. Television Stations by Digital Channel..................B-126
Spanish-Language Television Stations.........................B-128
U.S. TV Stations Providing News Programming..................B-129
Nielsen DMA Market Atlas.....................................B-132
Multi-City DMA Cross-Reference...............................B-216

Section C
Cable C-1

Top 25 Cable/Satellite Operators..............................C-2
The Top 25 Cable/Satellite TV Operators.......................C-3
Top 100 Cable Clusters/Systems................................C-4
Top 100 Cable Clusters/Systems, by Owner......................C-6
Cable Penetration by DMA......................................C-7
Top 50 DMA by Cable Penetration..............................C-11
Bottom 50 DMA by Cable Penetration...........................C-13
Top 50 DMA by Cable Households...............................C-15

Section D
Radio D-1

Radio Group Ownership..D-2
Key to Radio Listings...D-32
Directory of Radio Stations in the United States and Canada...D-33
Miscellaneous Radio Services.................................D-605
Satellite Services...D-607
U.S. AM Stations by Call Letters.............................D-608
U.S. FM Stations by Call Letters.............................D-620
Canadian AM Stations by Call Letters.........................D-642
Canadian FM Stations by Call Letters.........................D-643
U.S. AM Stations by Frequency................................D-645
U.S. FM Stations by Frequency................................D-657
Canadian AM Stations by Frequency............................D-679
Canadian FM Stations by Frequency............................D-680
Radio Formats Defined..D-682
U.S. and Canada Radio Programming Formats....................D-684

Programming on Radio Stations in the United States and
    Canada..D-686
Special Programming on Radio Stations in the United States and
    Canada..D-733
U.S. Radio Markets..D-753
U.S. Radio Markets: Arbitron Metro Survey Area Ranking......D-764

Section E
Programming E-1

Major Broadcast TV Networks....................................E-2
Major TV Program Syndicators/Distributors......................E-3
Regional Broadcast TV Networks.................................E-4
National Cable Networks..E-5
Regional Cable News Networks..................................E-12
Regional Cable Sports Networks................................E-14
Cable Audio Services..E-16
Major National TV News Organizations..........................E-17
TV News Services..E-19
National Radio Programming Services...........................E-21
Regional Radio Programming Services...........................E-25
Radio News Services...E-27
Radio Format Providers..E-30
Music Licensing...E-32
Canadian Broadcast Networks...................................E-33
Canadian Cable Networks.......................................E-34
Canadian Radio Networks and Services..........................E-37
Producers, Distributors, and Production Services Alphabetical
    Index..E-38
Producers, Distributors, and Production Services Subject Index..E-68

Section F
Technology F-1

Equipment Manufacturers and Distributors Alphabetical Index....F-2
Equipment Manufacturers and Distributors Subject Index........F-33
Satellite Owners and Transmission Services....................F-54
Teleports...F-57

Section G
Professional Services G-1

Station and Cable System Brokers...............................G-2
Management and Marketing Consultants...........................G-6
Station Financing Services....................................G-14
Research Services...G-16
Engineering and Technical Consultants.........................G-20
Law Firms...G-24
Talent Agents and Managers....................................G-33
Employment and Executive Search Services......................G-34

Section H
Associations, Events, H-1
Education, and Awards

Major National Associations....................................H-2
National Associations..H-5
State and Regional Broadcast Associations......................H-9
State and Regional Cable Associations.........................H-11
Union/Labor Groups..H-12
Trade Shows...H-14
Vocational and Career Development Schools.....................H-16
Universities and Colleges with Broadcasting or Journalism
    Programs...H-18
Major Broadcasting and Cable Awards...........................H-23

Section I
Government I-1

Federal Communications Commission Executives and Staff.........I-2
U.S. Government Agencies.......................................I-8
U.S. State Cable Regulatory Agencies...........................I-9

Broadcasting & Cable Yearbook 2006

Index to Sections

Abbreviations．．．．．．．．．．．．．．．．．．．．．．．．．．． xx	Arabic	Brief History of Broadcasting and Cable ．．．．．． A-22
ABC	Format, Canada ．．．．．．．．．．．．．．．． D-684	Broadcast History ．．．．．．．．．．．．．．．．．．．．．．．．． A-22
Executives and Staff ．．．．．．．．．．．．． E-2, E-21	Format, U.S. ．．．．．．．．．．．．．．．．．．．．． D-684	Broadcasters State and Regional Associations ．． H-9
Networks, Radio ．．．．．．．．．．．．．．．．．．．．．．． E-21	Special Programming, U.S. ．．．．．．．．．．． D-735	Broadcasting
Networks, TV．．．．．．．．．．．．．．．．．．．．．．．．．．． E-2	Arbitron Metro Survey Area	Degrees in ．．．．．．．．．．．．．．．．．．．．．．． H-18
Academy of Television Arts & Sciences．．．．．．． H-2	Ranking of Radio Markets．．．．．．．．．．．．． D-764	History of．．．．．．．．．．．．．．．．．．．．．．．．．．． A-22
Adult Contemporary	Armed Forces Radio & TV Service (AFRTS) ． D-605	Major Awards ．．．．．．．．．．．．．．．．．．．．．．． H-23
Definition of Format．．．．．．．．．．．．．．．．． D-682	Artists Representatives ．．．．．．．．．．．．．．．．．．． G-33	Brokers．．．．．．．．．．．．．．．．．．．．．．．．．．．．．．．．．．． G-2
Format, Canada ．．．．．．．．．．．．．．．．． D-684	Assignments of	
Format, U.S. ．．．．．．．．．．．．．．．．．．．．． D-684	AM Stations, U.S. ．．．．．．．．．．．．．．．．． D-608	**C**
Programming, Canada ．．．．．．．．．．．．．．． D-729	FM Stations, U.S. ．．．．．．．．．．．．．．．．． D-620	CAB (Cabletelevision Advertising Bureau Inc.) ． H-2
Programming, U.S. ．．．．．．．．．．．．．．．．． D-686	TV Channels, U.S．．．．．．．．．．．．．．．．．．． B-120	Cable
Special Programming, U.S．．．．．．．．．．．．． D-733	Associated Press (AP) Radio Networks．．．．．．． E-21	Brokers．．．．．．．．．．．．．．．．．．．．．．．．．．．．． G-2
Advertisers Index ．．．．．．．．．．．．．．．．．．．．．．． xiii	Associated Press Broadcast Services ．．．．．．．． E-21	History of．．．．．．．．．．．．．．．．．．．．．．．．．．． A-22
Advertising	Associations	National Services．．．．．．．．．．．．．．．．．．．． E-5
Associations, Media Societies．．．．．．．．．．． H-5	Major National．．．．．．．．．．．．．．．．．．．．．．． H-2	Penetration by DMA ．．．．．．．．．．．．．．．．． C-7
Professional Cards ．．．．．．．．．．．．．．．．． G-35	National．．．．．．．．．．．．．．．．．．．．．．．．．．．． H-5	Regional Associations ．．．．．．．．．．．．．．．． H-9
Affiliates (see appropriate network)	State and Regional Broadcast．．．．．．．．．．． H-9	Regional Cable News Networks ．．．．．．．． E-12
AFRTS (Armed Forces Radio	State and Regional Cable ．．．．．．．．．．．． H-11	Regional Cable Sports Networks．．．．．．．． E-14
and Television Service)．．．．．．．．．．．．．．． D-605	Associations, Events, Education and Awards ．．． H-1	Regulatory Agencies, State．．．．．．．．．．．．． I-9
Agencies	Attorneys, Communications．．．．．．．．．．．．．．． G-24	Schools．．．．．．．．．．．．．．．．．．．．．．．．．．． H-16
State Cable Regulatory．．．．．．．．．．．．．．．．． I-9	Awards, Major Broadcasting and Cable ．．．．．． H-23	State Associations．．．．．．．．．．．．．．．．．．． H-9
U.S. Government ．．．．．．．．．．．．．．．．．．．． I-8		Systems, Top 100 by Ownership ．．．．．．．．． C-6
Agents, Talent ．．．．．．．．．．．．．．．．．．．．．．．．．． G-33	**B**	Systems, Top 100 by Subscribers．．．．．．．．． C-4
Agriculture	Beautiful Music	Cable Audio Services ．．．．．．．．．．．．．．．．．．．． E-16
Definition of Format．．．．．．．．．．．．．．．．． D-682	Definition of Format．．．．．．．．．．．．．．．．． D-682	Cable News Network (CNN) ．．．．．．．．．． E-6, E-17
Format, Canada ．．．．．．．．．．．．．．．．． D-684	Format, Canada ．．．．．．．．．．．．．．．．． D-684	Cabletelevision Advertising Bureau Inc. (CAB) ． H-2
Format, U.S. ．．．．．．．．．．．．．．．．．．．．． D-684	Format, U.S. ．．．．．．．．．．．．．．．．．．．．． D-684	Call Letters
Programming, Canada ．．．．．．．．．．．．．．． D-729	Programming, Canada ．．．．．．．．．．．．．．． D-729	Radio, Canadian AM by ．．．．．．．．．．．．． D-642
Programming, U.S. ．．．．．．．．．．．．．．．．． D-690	Programming, U.S. ．．．．．．．．．．．．．．．．． D-691	Radio, Canadian FM by．．．．．．．．．．．．．． D-643
Special Programming, Canada ．．．．．．．．． D-751	Special Programming, U.S. ．．．．．．．．．．． D-735	Radio, U.S. AM by ．．．．．．．．．．．．．．．．． D-608
Special Programming, U.S．．．．．．．．．．．．． D-733	Big Band	Radio, U.S. FM by．．．．．．．．．．．．．．．．．． D-620
Album-Oriented Rock (AOR)	Definition of Format．．．．．．．．．．．．．．．．． D-682	TV, Canadian by ．．．．．．．．．．．．．．．．．．． B-119
Definition of Format．．．．．．．．．．．．．．．．． D-682	Format, Canada ．．．．．．．．．．．．．．．．． D-684	TV, U.S. by ．．．．．．．．．．．．．．．．．．．．．．． B-114
Format, Canada ．．．．．．．．．．．．．．．．． D-684	Format, U.S. ．．．．．．．．．．．．．．．．．．．．． D-684	Canada
Format, U.S. ．．．．．．．．．．．．．．．．．．．．． D-684	Programming, Canada ．．．．．．．．．．．．．．． D-729	AM Stations by Call Letters．．．．．．．．．．． D-642
Programming, Canada ．．．．．．．．．．．．．．． D-729	Programming, U.S. ．．．．．．．．．．．．．．．．． D-691	AM Stations by Frequency ．．．．．．．．．．． D-679
Programming, U.S. ．．．．．．．．．．．．．．．．． D-690	Special Programming, Canada ．．．．．．．．． D-751	FM Stations by Call Letters ．．．．．．．．．． D-643
Alternative	Special Programming, U.S. ．．．．．．．．．．． D-735	FM Stations by Frequency ．．．．．．．．．．． D-680
Definition of Format．．．．．．．．．．．．．．．．． D-682	Black	Radio Station Directory ．．．．．．．．．．．．．． D-574
Format, Canada ．．．．．．．．．．．．．．．．． D-684	Definition of Format．．．．．．．．．．．．．．．．． D-682	TV by Channel．．．．．．．．．．．．．．．．．．．． B-125
Format, U.S. ．．．．．．．．．．．．．．．．．．．．． D-684	Format, Canada ．．．．．．．．．．．．．．．．． D-684	TV Station Directory ．．．．．．．．．．．．．．．． B-103
Programming, Canada ．．．．．．．．．．．．．．． D-729	Format, U.S. ．．．．．．．．．．．．．．．．．．．．． D-684	Canadian Broadcasting Corp. ．．．．．．．．． E-33, E-37
Programming, U.S. ．．．．．．．．．．．．．．．．． D-690	Programming, Canada ．．．．．．．．．．．．．．． D-729	Canadian Broadcasting Networks ．．．．．．．．．．． E-33
Special Programming, U.S．．．．．．．．．．．．． D-735	Programming, U.S. ．．．．．．．．．．．．．．．．． D-691	Canadian Cable Television Assn. (CCTA) ．．．．． H-2
AM Stations	Special Programming, Canada ．．．．．．．．． D-751	Canadian Radio
By Call Letters, Canada ．．．．．．．．．．．．． D-642	Special Programming, U.S. ．．．．．．．．．．． D-735	Formats, Canada．．．．．．．．．．．．．．．．．．． D-684
By Call Letters, U.S. ．．．．．．．．．．．．．．． D-608	Bluegrass	Programming．．．．．．．．．．．．．．．．．．．．．． D-729
By Frequencies, Canada．．．．．．．．．．．．．． D-679	Definition of Format．．．．．．．．．．．．．．．．． D-682	Programming Formats．．．．．．．．．．．．．．． D-684
By Frequencies, U.S．．．．．．．．．．．．．．．．． D-645	Format, Canada ．．．．．．．．．．．．．．．．． D-684	Special Programming ．．．．．．．．．．．．．．． D-751
American Broadcasting Co. (see ABC)	Format, U.S. ．．．．．．．．．．．．．．．．．．．．． D-684	CBS Corp.
American Indian	Programming, U.S. ．．．．．．．．．．．．．．．．． D-691	Executives and Staff ．．．．．．．．．．．．． E-2, E-21
Definition of Format．．．．．．．．．．．．．．．．． D-682	Special Programming, Canada ．．．．．．．．． D-751	Networks, Radio ．．．．．．．．．．．．．．．．．．． E-21
Format, Canada ．．．．．．．．．．．．．．．．． D-684	Special Programming, U.S. ．．．．．．．．．．． D-736	Networks, TV．．．．．．．．．．．．．．．．．．．．．．．． E-2
Format, U.S. ．．．．．．．．．．．．．．．．．．．．． D-684	Blues	CCTA (Canadian Cable Television Assn.) ．．．．． H-2
Programming, Canada ．．．．．．．．．．．．．．． D-729	Definition of Format．．．．．．．．．．．．．．．．． D-682	Channels
Programming, U.S. ．．．．．．．．．．．．．．．．． D-691	Format, Canada ．．．．．．．．．．．．．．．．． D-684	TV by, Canadian ．．．．．．．．．．．．．．．．．．． B-125
Special Programming, Canada ．．．．．．．．． D-751	Format, U.S. ．．．．．．．．．．．．．．．．．．．．． D-684	TV by, United States ．．．．．．．．．．．．．．．． B-120
Special Programming, U.S．．．．．．．．．．．．． D-735	Programming, Canada ．．．．．．．．．．．．．．． D-729	Charts
American Urban Radio Networks ．．．．．．．．．．． E-21	Programming, U.S. ．．．．．．．．．．．．．．．．． D-691	Bottom 50 Market Areas Ranked by
AOR (see Album-Oriented Rock)	Special Programming, Canada ．．．．．．．．． D-751	
AP Radio Networks (Associated Press) ．．．．．． E-21	Special Programming, U.S．．．．．．．．．．．．． D-737	

Index to Sections

Percentage of Cable Penetration C-11
Cable Penetration by Market............. C-7
Comparable Record of TV Station Growth
    Since TV Began A-14
Federal Communications Commission Staff .. I-2
History of Station Sales Transactions A-13
Multi-City DMA Cross-Reference........ B-216
Nielsen DMA Market Atlas.............. B-132
Radio Markets Ranked by Arbitron
    Metro Survey Area D-764
Top 25 Station Groups A-6
Top 50 Market Areas Ranked by
    Cable TV Households C-15
Top 50 Market Areas Ranked by
    Percentage of Cable Penetration C-11
Top 50 Market Areas Ranked by
    TV Households C-15
Top 100 Cable Systems by Ownership..... C-6
Top 100 Cable Systems Ranked by
    Basic Subscribers C-4
U.S. and Canadian Radio
    Programming Formats................ D-684
U.S. Sales of Television
    Receivers 1983-2003................. A-11

Children
    Definition of Format.................. D-682
    Format, Canada D-684
    Format, U.S........................ D-684
    Programming, U.S................... D-692
    Special Programming, Canada D-751
    Special Programming, U.S............ D-737

Chinese
    Format, Canada D-684
    Format, U.S........................ D-684
    Programming, Canada D-729
    Programming, U.S................... D-692
    Special Programming, Canada D-751
    Special Programming, U.S............ D-737

Christian
    Definition of Format.................. D-682
    Format, Canada D-684
    Format, U.S........................ D-684
    Programming, Canada D-729
    Programming, U.S................... D-692
    Special Programming, Canada D-751
    Special Programming, U.S............ D-737

Citations and Awards..................... H-23

Classic Rock
    Definition of Format.................. D-682
    Format, Canada D-684
    Format, U.S........................ D-684
    Programming, Canada D-729
    Programming, U.S................... D-694
    Special Programming, Canada D-751
    Special Programming, U.S............ D-738

Classical
    Definition of Format.................. D-682
    Format, Canada D-684
    Format, U.S........................ D-684
    Programming, Canada D-729
    Programming, U.S................... D-696
    Special Programming, Canada D-751
    Special Programming, U.S............ D-738

CNN (Cable News Network) E-6, E-17

Colleges Offering Radio-TV-Cable Courses ... H-18

Colleges Offering Broadcasting Degrees...... H-18

Colleges Offering Two-Year Programs........ H-18

Comedy
    Definition of Format.................. D-682
    Format, Canada D-684

Format, U.S........................ D-684
Programming, Canada D-730
Programming, U.S................... D-697
Special Programming, U.S............ D-738

Commerce Committees, House and Senate..... I-8

Communications Law, Firms Active in G-24

Congressional Committees................... I-8

Consultants
    Management....................... G-6
    Technical, Engineering G-20

Contemporary Hit/Top-40
    Definition of Format.................. D-682
    Format, Canada D-684
    Format, U.S........................ D-684
    Programming, Canada D-730
    Programming, U.S................... D-697
    Special Programming, Canada D-751
    Special Programming, U.S............ D-738

Country
    Definition of Format.................. D-682
    Format, Canada D-684
    Format, U.S........................ D-684
    Programming, Canada D-730
    Programming, U.S................... D-699
    Special Programming, U.S............ D-738

Croatian
    Special Programming, U.S............ D-738

Cross-Ownership, Station B-2

Czech
    Special Programming, U.S............ D-738

D

Definition of Radio Formats............... D-682

Degrees in Broadcasting H-18

Digital TV Assignments B-126

Directories
    Canadian Radio Stations.............. D-574
    Canadian TV Stations B-103
    Miscellaneous Radio Services D-605
    U.S. Radio Stations D-33
    U.S. TV Stations B-14

Disco
    Definition of Format.................. D-682
    Format, Canada D-684
    Format, U.S........................ D-684
    Programming, U.S................... D-704
    Special Programming, U.S............ D-738

Discussion
    Special Programming, U.S............ D-739

Distributors
    Equipment F-2, F-33

Diversified
    Definition of Format.................. D-682
    Format, Canada D-684
    Format, U.S........................ D-684
    Programming, Canada D-730
    Programming, U.S................... D-704
    Special Programming, U.S............ D-739

DMA
    Bottom 50 by % Cable Penetration....... C-13
    By % Penetration C-7
    Multi-City DMA Cross-Reference B-216
    Nielsen Market Atlas B-132
    Top 50 by TV Households............. C-15

Drama/Literature

Definition of Format.................. D-682
Format, Canada D-684
Format, U.S........................ D-684
Programming, Canada D-730
Special Programming, U.S............ D-739

E

Eastern Public Radio..................... E-22

Easy Listening
    Definition of Format.................. D-682
    Format, Canada D-684
    Format, U.S........................ D-684
    Programming, Canada D-730
    Programming, U.S................... D-704

Education
    Schools Specializing in Radio-TV-Cable ... H-16
    Universities and Colleges Offering
    Degrees in Broadcasting.............. H-18

Educational
    Definition of Format.................. D-682
    Format, Canada D-684
    Format, U.S........................ D-684
    Programming, Canada D-730
    Programming, U.S................... D-704
    Special Programming, U.S............ D-739

Electronic Media, Chronology A-24

Employment Services G-34

Engineering Consultants G-20

Equipment Manufacturers, Distributors.... F-2, F-33

Eskimo
    Format, Canada D-684
    Format, U.S........................ D-684
    Programming, Canada D-730

Ethnic (also see Foreign/Ethnic)
    Definition of Format.................. D-682
    Format, Canada D-684
    Format, U.S........................ D-684
    Programming, Canada D-730
    Special Programming, Canada D-751

Events
    Trade Show........................ H-14

Executive Search Services G-34

F

Farm (See Agriculture)

Farsi
    Programming, U.S................... D-705
    Special Programming, U.S............ D-739

Federal Communications Commission
    Executives & Staff.................... I-2
    Organization Chart I-3

Filipino
    Format, Canada D-684
    Format, U.S........................ D-684
    Programming, Canada D-739
    Programming, U.S................... D-705
    Special Programming, Canada D-751
    Special Programming, U.S............ D-739

Financial Consultants G-6, G-14

Financing, Station G-14

Finnish
    Special Programming, Canada D-751
    Special Programming, U.S............ D-739

FM Stations

Index to Sections

By Call Letters, Canada D-643
By Call Letters, U.S. D-620
By Frequency, Canada D-680
By Frequency, U.S. D-657

Folk
   Definition of Format D-682
   Format, Canada D-684
   Format, U.S. D-684
   Programming, Canada D-730
   Programming, U.S. D-705
   Special Programming, Canada D-751
   Special Programming, U.S. D-739

Foreign/Ethnic
   Definition of Format D-682
   Format, Canada D-684
   Format, U.S. D-684
   Programming, Canada D-730
   Programming, U.S. D-705
   Special Programming, Canada D-751
   Special Programming, U.S. D-739

Formats
   Canadian for Radio D-684
   Canadian Radio Programming D-729
   Definition for Radio D-682
   U.S. for Radio D-684
   U.S. Radio Programming D-686

Fox Broadcasting Company E-2

French
   Format, Canada D-684
   Format, U.S. D-684
   Programming, Canada D-730
   Programming, U.S. D-705
   Special Programming, Canada D-751
   Special Programming, U.S. D-740

Frequencies
   Canadian AM D-679
   Canadian FM D-680
   United States AM D-643
   United States FM D-645

Full Service
   Definition of Format D-682
   Format, Canada D-684
   Format, U.S. D-684
   Programming, U.S. D-705
   Special Programming, U.S. D-740

G

German
   Programming, Canada D-730
   Special Programming, Canada D-751
   Special Programming, U.S. D-740

Global Television Network E-33

Glossary of Terms xix

Golden Oldies
   Definition of Format D-682
   Format, Canada D-684
   Format, U.S. D-684
   Programming, Canada D-731
   Programming, U.S. D-705
   Special Programming, U.S. D-740

Gospel
   Definition of Format D-682
   Format, Canada D-684
   Format, U.S. D-684
   Programming, Canada D-731
   Programming, U.S. D-705
   Special Programming, Canada D-751
   Special Programming, U.S. D-740

Government Agencies
   Federal Communications Commission I-8
   House Committee on Commerce I-8
   Senate Committee on Commerce I-8
   Supreme Court I-8

Greek
   Format, Canada D-684
   Format, U.S. D-684
   Programming, U.S. D-707
   Special Programming, Canada D-751
   Special Programming, U.S. D-742

Group Ownership of Stations B-2

Groups, Labor & Unions H-12

H

Hardcore
   Special Programming, U.S. D-742

Hebrew
   Special Programming, Canada D-751
   Special Programming, U.S. D-742

Hindi
   Programming, Canada D-731
   Special Programming, Canada D-751
   Special Programming, U.S. D-742

History of Broadcasting and Cable A-22

House Committee on Commerce I-8

Hungarian
   Special Programming, Canada D-751
   Special Programming, U.S. D-742

I

Index
   Advertisers xiii
   Equipment Manufacturers and Distributors
      Alphabetical F-2
   Equipment Manufacturers and Distributors
      Subject F-33
   Producers, Distributors, and
      Production Services Subject E-68
   Sections iv

Inspirational
   Format, Canada D-684
   Format, U.S. D-684
   Programming, Canada D-731
   Programming, U.S. D-707
   Special Programming, U.S. D-742

International Stations in the U.S. D-605

Irish
   Programming, U.S. D-707
   Special Programming, Canada D-751
   Special Programming, U.S. D-742

Italian
   Format, Canada D-684
   Format, U.S. D-684
   Programming, U.S. D-707
   Special Programming, Canada D-751
   Special Programming, U.S. D-742

J

Japanese
   Programming, U.S. D-707
   Special Programming, Canada D-751
   Special Programming, U.S. D-742

Jazz
   Definition of Format D-682
   Format, Canada D-685
   Format, U.S. D-685
   Programming, Canada D-731
   Programming, U.S. D-707
   Special Programming, Canada D-751
   Special Programming, U.S. D-742

Jewish
   Special Programming, U.S. D-743

Jones Radio Network E-22

K

Key to Radio Listings D-32
Key to Television Listings B-13

Korean
   Programming, U.S. D-708
   Special Programming, U.S. D-743

L

Labor Groups & Unions H-12

Law and Regulation & Government Agencies I-1

Law Firms G-24

Lawyers, Communications G-24

Licensing, Music E-32

Light Rock
   Format, Canada D-685
   Format, U.S. D-685
   Programming, Canada D-731
   Programming, U.S. D-708
   Special Programming, U.S. D-743

Lithuanian
   Special Programming, U.S. D-743

M

Magazine or Newspaper
   Cross-Ownership with Stations B-2
   Ownership of Stations B-2

Major Broadcasting and Cable Awards H-23

Major National Associations
   Cabletelevision Advertising
      Bureau Inc. (CAB) H-2
   Canadian Cable Television Assn. (CCTA) . . . H-2
   Media Rating Council H-2
   National Association of Broadcasters (NAB) . H-2
   National Association of Farm Broadcasters . . H-2
   NATPE International (National Association of
      Television Program Executives) H-2
   National Cable and Telecommunications
      Association Inc. (NCTA) H-3
   National Cable Television Cooperative Inc. . . H-3
   Radio Advertising Bureau H-3
   Radio-Television News Directors Assn. H-3
   Television Bureau of Advertising (TVB) H-4

Major Networks, Radio
   ABC Radio Networks E-21
   American Urban Radio Networks E-21
   AP Radio Networks E-21
   CBS E-21
   Eastern Public Radio E-22
   Jones Radio Network E-22
   National Public Radio E-22
   Public Radio International E-23
   United Press International E-23
   USA Radio Networks E-23
   Westwood One E-24

Index to Sections

Major Networks, TV
   ABC.................................... E-2
   CBS.................................... E-2
   Fox..................................... E-2
   NBC.................................... E-2
   PAX.................................... E-2
   UPN.................................... E-2
   The WB................................. E-2

Management Consultants G-6

Managers, Talent............................ G-33

Manufacturers of Equipment F-2, F-33

Maps of TV Markets B-132

Market Research Services G-16

Markets
   Bottom 50 Ranked by Percentage of
   Cable Penetration C-7
   DMA TV, Multi-City B-216
   DMA TV, Nielsen Market Atlas B-132
   Radio by Arbitron Metro Survey Area D-753
   Top 50 Ranked by Cable TV Households .. C-15
   Top 50 Ranked by Percentage of
   Cable Penetration C-7
   Top 50 Ranked by TV Households C-15
   TV (Maps) B-132

Media Rating Council H-2

Media Societies, Groups H-2, H-5

Middle-of-the-Road (see MOR)

MOR (Middle-of-the-Road)
   Definition of Format................... D-682
   Format, Canada D-685
   Format, U.S. D-685
   Programming, Canada D-731
   Programming, U.S. D-708
   Special Programming, U.S............. D-743

Music Licensing Groups E-32

N

NAB (National Assocation of Broadcasters) H-3

National Associations................... H-2, H-5

National Association of Broadcasters (NAB) H-2

National Association of Farm Broadcasters..... H-2

National Association of Television Program
   Executives (NATPE International) H-2

National Broadcasting Co. (see NBC)

National Cable and Telecommunications
   Association Inc. (NCTA) H-3

National Cable Services E-5

National Cable Television Cooperative Inc...... H-3

National Networks, Radio
   ABC Radio Networks.................. E-21
   American Urban Radio Networks E-21
   AP Radio Networks................... E-21
   CBS E-21
   Eastern Public Radio................. E-22
   Jones Radio Network E-22
   National Public Radio E-22
   Public Radio International E-23
   United Press International E-23
   USA Radio Networks................. E-23
   Westwood One E-24

National Networks, TV
   ABC.................................. E-2
   CBS.................................. E-2
   Fox................................... E-2

NBC.................................... E-2
PAX.................................... E-2
UPN.................................... E-2
The WB................................. E-2

NATPE International (National Association
   of Television Program Executives) H-2

National Public Radio (NPR) E-22

Native American
   Programming, Canada D-731
   Programming, U.S. D-709
   Special Programming, U.S............ D-743

NBC.................................... E-2

NCTA (National Cable and Telecommunications
   Association Inc.) H-3

Networks, Radio
   ABC Radio Networks................. E-21
   American Urban Radio Networks E-21
   AP Radio Networks.................. E-21
   Canadian............................ E-37
   CBS.................................. E-21
   CNN Radio Networks E-22
   Eastern Public Radio............... E-22
   Family Stations Inc. E-22
   Jones Radio Network E-22
   Moody's Broadcasting Network E-22
   National Public Radio E-22
   Public Radio International E-23
   Radio Program E-21
   Regional Radio E-25
   Superadio Network E-23
   USA Radio Network E-23
   United Press International E-23
   Westwood One E-24

Networks, TV
   ABC.................................. E-2
   Canadian........................... E-33
   CBS.................................. E-2
   Fox................................... E-2
   NBC.................................. E-2
   Regional TV E-4
   TV Program........................ E-2

New Age
   Definition of Format................ D-682
   Format, Canada D-685
   Format, U.S. D-685
   Programming, U.S. D-709
   Special Programming, Canada D-751
   Special Programming, U.S......... D-743

New Wave
   Definition of Format................ D-682
   Format, U.S. D-685
   Special Programming, U.S......... D-744

News
   Definition of Format................ D-682
   Format, Canada D-685
   Format, U.S. D-685
   Programming, Canada D-731
   Programming, U.S. TV Stations Providing. B-129
   Programming, U.S. D-709
   Special Programming, Canada D-751
   Special Programming, U.S......... D-744

News Directors, Radio-TV Association H-3

News Services
   Radio............................... E-27
   TV E-17

News/Talk
   Definition of Format................ D-682
   Format, Canada D-685
   Format, U.S. D-685

Programming, Canada D-731
Programming, U.S. D-710
Special Programming, Canada D-751
Special Programming, U.S.......... D-744

Newspaper or Magazine
   Cross-Ownership with Stations B-2
   Ownership of Stations B-2

Nostalgia
   Definition of Format................ D-682
   Format, Canada D-685
   Format, U.S. D-685
   Programming, Canada D-731
   Programming, U.S. D-713
   Special Programming, Canada D-751
   Special Programming, U.S......... D-744

NPR (National Public Radio) E-22

O

Oldies
   Definition of Format................ D-682
   Format, Canada D-685
   Format, U.S. D-685
   Programming, Canada D-731
   Programming, U.S. D-714
   Special Programming, Canada D-751
   Special Programming, U.S......... D-744

Other (Program Format)
   Definition of Format................ D-682
   Format, Canada D-685
   Format, U.S. D-685
   Programming, Canada D-731
   Programming, U.S. D-716
   Special Programming, Canada D-751
   Special Programming, U.S......... D-744

Owners and Operators, Satellite F-54

Ownership
   Group Stations B-2
   Magazine of Broadcast Station B-2
   Newspaper of Broadcast Station B-2

P

Placement Services G-34

Polish
   Format, U.S. D-685
   Programming, U.S. D-717
   Special Programming, Canada D-752
   Special Programming, U.S......... D-745

Polka
   Definition of Format................ D-682
   Format, U.S. D-685
   Programming, U.S. D-717
   Special Programming, U.S......... D-745

Portuguese
   Format, U.S. D-685
   Programming, U.S. D-717
   Special Programming, Canada D-752
   Special Programming, U.S......... D-745

Production Services E-38, E-68

Professional Cards (Advertising)............ G-35

Professional Societies H-2, H-5

Program
   Consultants........................ G-6
   Distribution..................... E-38, E-68
   Producers...................... E-38, E-68

Programming, Canada
   Adult Contemporary................ D-729

Index to Sections

Agriculture & Farm D-729
Album-Oriented Rock D-729
Alternative D-729
American Indian D-729
Beautiful Music D-729
Big Band D-729
Black D-729
Blues D-729
Chinese D-729
Christian D-729
Classic Rock D-729
Classical D-729
Comedy D-731
Contemporary Hit/Top-40 .... D-731
Country D-731
Diversified D-731
Drama/Literature D-731
Easy Listening D-731
Educational D-731
Eskimo D-731
Ethnic D-731
Foreign/Ethnic D-731
French D-731
Golden Oldies D-731
Gospel D-731
Inspirational D-731
Jazz D-731
Light Rock D-731
MOR (Middle-of-the-Road) D-731
Native American D-731
News D-731
News/Talk D-731
Nostalgia D-731
Oldies D-731
Other D-731
Progressive D-731
Public Affairs D-731
Religious D-731
Rock/AOR D-731
Smooth Jazz D-732
Sports D-732
Talk D-732
Top-40 .... D-732
Urban Contemporary D-732
Variety/Diverse D-732

Programming, U.S. Radio
Adult Contemporary D-686
Agriculture D-690
Album-Oriented Rock D-690
Alternative D-690
American Indian D-691
Arabic D-691
Beautiful Music D-691
Big Band D-691
Black D-691
Bluegrass D-691
Blues D-691
Children D-692
Chinese D-692
Christian D-692
Classic Rock D-694
Classical D-696
Comedy D-697
Contemporary Hit/Top-40 .... D-697
Country D-699
Disco D-704
Diversified D-704
Easy Listening D-704
Educational D-704
Farsi D-705
Filipino D-705
Folk D-705
Foreign/Ethnic D-705
French D-705

Full Service D-705
Golden Oldies D-705
Gospel D-705
Greek D-707
Inspirational D-707
Irish D-707
Italian D-707
Japanese D-707
Jazz D-707
Korean D-708
Light Rock D-708
MOR (Middle-of-the Road) D-708
Native American D-709
New Age D-709
News D-709
News/Talk D-710
Nostalgia D-713
Oldies D-714
Other D-716
Polish D-717
Polka D-717
Portuguese D-717
Progressive D-717
Public Affairs D-717
Reggae D-717
Religious D-717
Rock/AOR D-719
Russian D-721
Smooth Jazz D-721
Soul D-721
Spanish D-721
Sports D-722
Talk D-725
Tejano D-726
Top-40 .... D-726
Triple A D-727
Underground D-727
Urban Contemporary D-727
Variety/Diverse D-728
Vietnamese D-728

Programming Services E-1

Progressive
Definition of Format D-682
Format, Canada D-685
Format, U.S. D-685
Programming, Canada D-731
Programming, U.S. D-717
Special Programming, U.S. D-745

Promotion
Consultants G-6

Public Affairs
Definition of Format D-682
Format, Canada D-685
Format, U.S. D-685
Programming, Canada D-731
Programming, U.S. D-717
Special Programming, Canada D-752
Special Programming, U.S. D-745

R

Radio
Advertising Bureau H-3
Armed Forces D-605
Assignments of FM Stations D-620
Call Letters, AM D-608
Call Letters, FM D-620
Canadian AM-FM Stations D-642, D-643
Directory of Stations D-33
Equipment Manufacturers F-2, F-33
Format Providers E-30
Formats, U.S. D-684

Formats, Canada D-684
Formats, Defined D-682
Frequencies, AM D-645
Frequencies, FM D-657
Group Ownership D-2
International Stations D-605
Listings, Key to D-32
Markets D-753
Miscellaneous Services D-605
Networks, Regional E-25
Newspaper Ownership B-2
News Services E-27
Program Distributors E-38, E-68
Program Producers E-38, E-68
Programming, Canada D-729
Programming, U.S. D-686
Programming Formats Defined D-682
Schools H-16
Special Programming, Canada D-751
Special Programming, U.S. D-733
Stations on Air, by Market D-753
U.S. AM Stations D-608
U.S. FM Stations D-620

Radio Advertising Bureau H-3
Radio Free Asia D-605
Radio Free Europe D-605
Radio Liberty D-605
Radio-TV News Directors Association . H-3

Reggae
Definition of Format D-682
Format, U.S. D-685
Programming, U.S. D-717
Special Programming, Canada D-752
Special Programming, U.S. D-746

Regional Radio Networks E-25
Regional TV Networks E-4

Religious
Definition of Format D-682
Format, Canada D-685
Format, U.S. D-685
Programming, Canada D-731
Programming, U.S. D-717
Special Programming, Canada D-752
Special Programming, U.S. D-746

Representatives of Artists G-33
Research Services, Radio-TV G-16

Rock/AOR
Definition of Format D-682
Format, Canada D-685
Format, U.S. D-685
Programming, Canada D-731
Programming, U.S. D-719
Special Programming, Canada D-752
Special Programming, U.S. D-748

Russian
Format, U.S. D-685
Programming, U.S. D-721
Special Programming, U.S. D-748

S

Sacred
Special Programming, U.S. D-748
Sales
Consultants G-6
of U.S. TV Receivers A-11
Satellites Owners and Operators F-54

Index to Sections

Scottish
    Special Programming, Canada D-752
    Special Programming, U.S. D-748

Sections, Index to v

Senate Committee on Commerce I-8

Serbian
    Special Programming, U.S. D-748

Services
    Brokers, Station and Cable System G-2
    Cable Audio Services E-16
    Canadian Cable Networks E-34
    Communications Law, Firms Active in..... G-24
    Consulting G-6
    Distribution E-38, E-68
    Employment G-34
    Engineering Consultation G-20
    Executive Search G-34
    Financing, of Stations G-14
    Market Research G-16
    Music Licensing Groups E-32
    National Cable E-5
    National Cable E-5
    Production E-38, E-68
    Radio Format Providers E-30
    Radio News E-27
    Rating & Research G-16
    Regional Cable Sports E-14
    Research G-16
    Talent Agents and Managers G-33
    Technical Consultation G-20
    TV News Service E-19

Shows, Trade H-14

Slovak
    Special Programming, U.S. D-748

Slovenian
    Special Programming, U.S. D-748

Smooth Jazz
    Programming, Canada D-732
    Programming, U.S. D-721

Societies, Professional, Radio-TV H-2, H-5

Soul
    Programming, U.S. D-721
    Special Programming, U.S. D-748

Spanish
    Format, U.S. D-685
    Programming, U.S. D-721
    Special Programming, Canada D-752
    Special Programming, U.S. D-748

Spanish-Language Stations, TV B-128

Special Programming, Canada
    Agriculture D-751
    Album-Oriented Rock D-751
    American Indian D-751
    Arabic D-751
    Big Band D-751
    Black D-751
    Bluegrass D-751
    Blues D-751
    Children D-751
    Chinese D-751
    Christian D-751
    Classical D-751
    Contemporary Hit/Top-40 .... D-751
    Country D-751
    Croation D-751
    Disco D-751
    Educational D-751
    Ethnic D-751
    Farsi D-751

    Filipino D-751
    Finnish D-751
    Folk D-751
    Foreign/Ethnic D-751
    French D-751
    German D-751
    Gospel D-751
    Greek D-751
    Hebrew D-751
    Hindi D-751
    Hungarian D-751
    Irish D-751
    Italian D-751
    Japanese D-751
    Jazz D-751
    New Age D-751
    News D-751
    News/Talk D-751
    Nostalgia D-751
    Oldies D-751
    Other D-751
    Polish D-752
    Portuguese D-752
    Public Affairs D-752
    Reggae D-752
    Religious D-752
    Rock/AOR D-752
    Scottish D-752
    Spanish D-752
    Sports D-752
    Talk D-752
    Ukrainian D-752
    Urban Contemporary D-752
    Vietnamese D-752

Special Programming, U.S.
    Adult Contemporary D-733
    Agriculture D-733
    Alternative D-735
    American Indian D-735
    Arabic D-735
    Armenian D-735
    Beautiful Music D-735
    Big Band D-735
    Black D-735
    Bluegrass D-736
    Blues D-737
    Children D-737
    Chinese D-737
    Christian D-737
    Classic Rock D-738
    Classical D-738
    Comedy D-738
    Contemporary Hit/Top-40 .... D-738
    Country D-738
    Croation D-738
    Czech D-738
    Disco D-738
    Discussion D-739
    Diversified D-739
    Drama/Literature D-739
    Easy Listening D-753
    Educational D-739
    Eskimo D-753
    Ethnic D-753
    Farsi D-739
    Filipino D-739
    Finnish D-739
    Folk D-739
    Foreign/Ethnic D-739
    French D-740
    Full Service D-740
    German D-740
    Golden Oldies D-740
    Gospel D-740

    Greek D-742
    Hardcore D-742
    Hebrew D-742
    Hindi D-742
    Hungarian D-742
    Inspirational D-742
    Irish D-742
    Italian D-742
    Japanese D-742
    Jazz D-742
    Jewish D-743
    Korean D-743
    Light Rock D-743
    Lithuanian D-743
    MOR (Middle-of-the-Road) D-743
    Native American D-743
    New Age D-743
    New Wave D-744
    News D-744
    News/Talk D-744
    Nostalgia D-744
    Oldies D-744
    Other D-744
    Polish D-745
    Polka D-745
    Portuguese D-745
    Progressive D-745
    Public Affairs D-745
    Reggae D-746
    Religious D-746
    Rock/AOR D-748
    Russian D-748
    Sacred D-748
    Scottish D-748
    Serbian D-748
    Slovak D-748
    Slovenian D-748
    Smooth Jazz D-748
    Soul D-748
    Spanish D-748
    Sports D-749
    Talk D-750
    Tejano D-750
    Top-40 .... D-750
    Triple A D-750
    Ukrainian D-750
    Underground D-750
    Urban Contemporary D-750
    Variety/Diverse D-750
    Vietnamese D-750
    Women D-750

Sports
    Definition of Format D-682
    Format, Canada D-685
    Format, U.S. D-685
    Programming, Canada D-732
    Programming, U.S. D-722
    Special Programming, Canada D-752
    Special Programming, U.S. D-749

State
    Broadcast Associations H-9
    Cable Associations H-11
    Cable Regulatory Agencies I-9

Station
    Brokers G-2
    Cross-Ownership B-2
    Financing G-14
    Groups, Top 25 .... A-6
    Transactions, 51 Years of A-13

Stations
    Directory of Canadian Radio D-574
    Directory of U.S. Radio D-33
    Group Ownership of B-2

Index to Advertisers

- Miscellaneous Radio D-605
- Newspaper/Magazine Cross-Ownership with B-2
- Newspaper/Magazine Ownership of B-2
- Programming on Canadian Radio D-729
- Programming on U.S. Radio D-686
- Spanish-Language TV B-128
- Special Programming on Canadian Radio. D-751
- Special Programming on U.S. Radio D-733
- TV by Channel, Canadian B-125
- TV by Channel, U.S. B-120
- TV Providing News Programming B-129

Surveys & Market Research G-16

T

Talent Agents and Managers G-33

Talk
- Definition of Format D-682
- Format, Canada D-685
- Format, U.S. D-685
- Programming, Canada D-732
- Programming, U.S. D-725
- Special Programming, Canada D-752
- Special Programming, U.S. D-750

Technical Consultants G-20

Tejano
- Definition of Format D-683
- Format, U.S. D-685
- Programming, U.S. D-726
- Special Programming, U.S. D-750

Teleports F-57

Television
- Advertising Bureau H-4
- Analog Channels, U.S. B-120
- Bureau of Advertising H-4
- Call Letters, Canada B-119
- Call Letters, U.S. B-114
- Channels, Canada B-125
- Channels, U.S. B-120
- Commercial Producers E-38, E-68
- DMA Markets B-132
- Digital TV Assignments B-126
- Directory, Canadian B-103
- Directory, U.S. B-14
- Equipment Manufacturers E-38, E-68
- Group Ownership B-2

- Listings, Key to B-13
- Markets, by DMA B-14
- Networks, Major National E-2
- Networks, Regional E-4
- News Services E-19
- Newspaper Ownership B-2
- Program Distributors E-38, E-68
- Program Production Services E-38, E-68
- Program Services E-38, E-68
- Regional Networks E-4
- Schools H-16
- Spanish-Language Stations B-128
- Station Transactions A-13
- Stations, Canadian B-103
- Stations, U.S. B-14

Television Bureau of Advertising (TVB) H-4

Television Quatre Saisons E-33

Terms, Glossary of xiii

Top-40 (also see Contemporary Hit)
- Format, Canada D-685
- Format, U.S. D-685
- Programming, Canada D-732
- Programming, U.S. D-726
- Special Programming, U.S. D-750

Trade Shows H-14

Transactions, 51 Years of Station A-13

Triple A (AAA)
- Definition of Format D-683
- Format, U.S. D-685
- Programming, U.S. D-727
- Special Programming, U.S. D-750

TVA (Network) E-33

TVB (Television Bureau of Advertising) H-4

U

Ukrainian
- Special Programming, Canada D-752
- Special Programming, U.S. D-750

Underground
- Definition of Format D-683
- Programming, U.S. D-727
- Special Programming, U.S. D-750

Union/Labor Groups H-12

- United Press International (UPI) E-23

United States
- Government Agencies I-8
- International Radio D-605
- Radio Markets D-753
- Radio Programming Formats D-684
- Radio Station Directory D-33
- Special Programming D-733
- TV Station Directory B-14
- TV Stations by Call Letters B-114

Universities Offering Broadcasting Degrees ... H-18

Universities Offering Radio-TV Cable Courses . H-18

Universities Offering Two-Year Programs H-18

UPI (United Press International) E-23

Urban Contemporary
- Definition of Format D-683
- Format, Canada D-685
- Format, U.S. D-685
- Programming, Canada D-732
- Programming, U.S. D-727
- Special Programming, Canada D-752
- Special Programming, U.S. D-750

USA Radio Networks E-23

V

Variety/Diverse
- Definition of Format D-683
- Format, Canada D-685
- Format, U.S. D-685
- Programming, Canada D-732
- Programming, U.S. D-728
- Special Programming, U.S. D-750

Vietnamese
- Format, U.S. D-685
- Programming, U.S. D-728
- Special Programming, Canada D-752
- Special Programming, U.S. D-750

Voice of America D-606

W

Westwood One E-24

Women
- Definition of Format D-683
- Special Programming, U.S. D-750

Index to Advertisers

- **John P. Allen** G-35
- **Altronic Research Inc.** F-3
- **American Media Services LLC** .D-35 to D-573 (every right-hand page); Spine; G-2
- **Associated Broadcasters** G-2
- **The Austin Company** G-6
- **Avid Technology** .... Inside front cover, E-38, F-5
- **Battery Pros** F-6
- **BMI** E-32
- **Bond & Pecaro** G-6, G-7
- **John F.X. Browne & Associates, PC** .G-20, G-35
- **Cavell, Mertz & Davis** G-20, G-35
- **Coaxial Dynamics** F-9
- **Cobb Corp.** .. Inside Back Cover; Back Cover; G-2
- **Cohen, Dippell & Everist PC** G-20, G-21
- **Lauren A. Colby, Esq.** G-25, G-26

- **Communications Technologies Inc.** ..G-20, G-35
- **Cox & Cox LLC** G-2
- **Denny & Associates, PC** G-35
- **du Treil, Lundin & Rackley Inc.** G-35
- **Eatman Media Services** G-33
- **Evans Associates** G-35
- **Evertz** F-12
- **The Exline Company** G-3
- **FirstCom Music** E-45
- **Fischer Broadcast Services** E-45
- **Hammett & Edison, Inc.** G-21, G-22, G-35
- **Hatfield & Dawson** G-21, G-35
- **Independent Broadcast Consultants, Inc.** . G-35
- **VIR James, P.C.** G-22, G-35
- **Carl T. Jones Corporation** G-35
- **Jones Radio Networks** E-49

- **Kagan Research** C-1
- **H.B. LaRue, Media Brokers** G-3
- **Marsand, Inc.** G-35
- **Meintel, Sgrignoli, & Wallace** G-35
- **Mullaney Engineering, Inc.** G-35
- **Munn-Reese, Inc.** G-20, G-22, G-35
- **NorthStar Studios Inc.** E-20
- **Ohio News Network** E-12
- **Omnimusic** E-54
- **Patrick Communications** ..Front cover, G-4, G-15
- **Carl E. Smith Consulting Engineers** G-35
- **Smith and Fisher** G-35
- **Snowden Associates** G-4
- **Sundance** F-27
- **teletech.ca** F-28
- **United Scenic Artists General Fund** H-13

Broadcasting & Cable Yearbook 2006

Glossary of Terms Used in *Broadcasting & Cable Yearbook*

AM—Amplitude modulation. Also referring to audio service broadcast over 535 khz-1705 khz.

Analog—A continuous electrical signal that carries information in the form of variable physical values, such as amplitude or frequency modulation.

Basic cable service—Package of programming on cable systems eligible for regulation by local franchising authorities under 1992 Cable Act, including all local broadcast signals and PEG (public, educational and government) access channels.

Cable television—System that transmits original programming, and programming of broadcast television stations, to consumers over wired network (see page xvii).

CC—Closed captioning. Method of transmitting textual information over television channel's vertical blanking interval; transmissions are deciphered with decoders; decoded transmissions appear as text superimposed over television image.

CED—Capacitance electronic disk (RCA videodisk).

Clear channel—AM radio station allowed to dominate its frequency with up to 50 kw of power; their signals are generally protected for distance of up to 750 miles at night.

Closed circuit—The method of transmission of programs or other material that limits its target audience to a specific group rather than the general public.

Coaxial cable—Cable with several common axis lines under protective sheath used for television signal transmissions.

Common carrier—Telecommunication company that provides communications transmission services to the public.

DAB—Digital audio broadcasting. Modulations for sending digital rather than analog audio signals by either terrestrial or satellite transmitter with audio response up to compact disc quality (20 khz).

DBS—Direct broadcast satellite. High powered satellite authorized to broadcast direct to homes (see page xxviii).

Digital—A discontinuous electrical signal that carries information in binary fashion. Data is represented by a specific sequence of off-on electrical pulses.

Directional antenna—An antenna that directs most of its signal strength in a specific direction rather than at equal strength in all directions. Used chiefly in AM radio operation.

Downlink—Earth station used to receive signals from satellites.

Earth station—Equipment used for transmitting or receiving satellite communications.

EDTV—Enhanced-definition television. Proposed intermediate systems for evolution to full HDTV, usually including slightly improved resolution and sound, with a wider (16:9) aspect ratio.

Effective competition—Market status under which cable TV systems are exempt from regulation of basic tier rates by local franchising authorities, as defined in 1992 Cable Act. To claim effective competition, a cable system must compete with at least one other multichannel provider that is available to at least 50%of an area's households and is subscribed to by more than 15% of the households.

EM—Electronic mail (commonly referred to as E-mail).

Encryption—System for scrambling signals to prevent unauthorized reception.

ENG—Electronic news gathering.

ETV—Educational television.

Fiber-optic cable—Wires made of glass fiber used to transmit video, audio, voice or data providing vastly wider bandwidth than standard coaxial cable.

Field—Half of the video information in the frame of a video picture. The NTSC system displays 59.94 fields per second.

FM—Frequency modulation. Also referring to audio service broadcast over 88 mhz-108 mhz.

Footprint—Area on earth within which a satellite's signal can be received.

Frame—A full video picture. The NTSC system displays 29.97 525-line frames per second.

Frequency—The number of cycles a signal is transmitted per second, measured in hertz.

Geostationary orbit—Orbit 22,300 miles above earth's equator where satellites circle earth at same rate earth rotates.

ghz—Gigahertz. One billion hertz (cycles) per second.

HDTV—High-definition television (see page xxviii).

Headend—Facility in cable system from which all signals originate. (Local and distant television stations, and satellite programming, are picked up and amplified for retransmission through system.)

Hertz—A measurement of frequency. One cycle per second equals one hertz (hz).

HUT—Households using television.

Independent television—Television stations that are not affiliated with networks and that do not use the networks as a primary source of their programming.

Information services—Broad term used to describe full range of audio, video and data transmission services that can be transmitted over the air or by cable.

Interactive—Allowing two-way data flow.

Interlaced scanning—Television transmission technique in which each frame is divided into two fields. NTSC system interleaves odd-numbered lines with even-numbered lines at a transmission rate of 59.94 fields per second.

ITFS—Instructional Television Fixed Service (see page xxvii).

khz—Kilohertz. One thousand hertz (cycles) per second.

LED—Light emitting diode. Type of semiconductor that lights up when activated by voltage.

LO—Local origination channel.

LPTV—Low-power television (see page xxvii).

LV—LaserVision (optical videodisk).

MDS—Multipoint distribution service (see page xxvii).

mhz—Megahertz. One million hertz (cycles) per second.

Microwave—Frequencies above 1,000 mhz.

MSO—Multiple cable systems operator.

Must carry—Legal requirement that cable operators carry local broadcast signals. Cable systems with 12 or fewer channels must carry at least three broadcast signals; systems with 12 or more channels must carry up to one-third of their capacity; systems with 300 or fewer subscribers are exempt. The 1992 Cable Act requires broadcast station to waive must-carry rights if it chooses to negotiate retransmission compensation (see "Retransmission consent").

NTSC-National Television System Committee. Committee that recommended current American standard color television.

PCM—Pulse code modulation. Conversion of voice signals into digital code.

PPV—Pay-per-view.

Program access—Prohibition on exclusive programming contracts between cable operators and program services controlled by cable operators, designed to give alternative multichannel distributors (such as wireless cable and DBS) the opportunity to bid for established cable services (such as CNN or Nickelodeon). The rule expires in 2002.

Progressive scanning—TV system where video frames are transmitted sequentially, unlike interlaced scanning in which frames are divided into two fields.

PSA—Public service announcement.

PTV—Public television.

Public radio—Radio stations and networks that are operated on a noncommercial basis.

Public television-Television stations and networks that operate as noncommercial ventures.

RCC—Radio common carrier. Common carriers whose major businesses include radio paging and mobile telephone services.

Retransmission consent—Local TV broadcasters' right to negotiate a carriage fee with local cable operators, as provided in 1992 Cable Act.

SCA—Subsidiary communications authorizations. Authorizations granted to FM broadcasters for using subcarriers on their channels for other communications services.

Shortwave—Transmissions on frequencies of 6-25 mhz.

SHF—Super high frequency.

Signal-to-noise ratio—The ratio between the strength of an electronically produced signal to interfering noises in the same bandwidth.

SMATV—Satellite master antenna television (see page xxviii).

STV—Subscription television (see page xxvii).

Superstation—Local television station whose signal is retransmitted via satellite to cable systems beyond reach of over-the-air signal.

Teletext—A one-way electronic publishing service that can be transmitted over the vertical blanking interval of a standard television signal or the full channel of a television station or cable television system. The major use today is for closed-captioning.

Translator—Broadcast station that rebroadcasts signals of other stations without originating its own programming.

Glossary of Terms

Transponder—Satellite transmitter/receiver that picks up signals transmitted from earth, translates them into new frequencies and amplifies them before retransmitting them back to ground.

UHF—Ultra high frequency band (300 mhz-3,000 mhz), which includes TV channels 14-83.

Uplink—Earth station used for transmitting to satellite.

VCR—Videocassette recorder.

VHF—Very high frequencies (30 mhz-300 mhz), which include TV channels 2-13 and FM radio.

Videotext—Two-way interactive service that uses either two-way cable or telephone lines to connect a central computer to a television screen.

VTR—Videotape recorder.

List of Abbreviations Used in *Broadcasting & Cable Yearbook*

*	noncommercial
a	annual
A&E	Arts & Entertainment
actg	acting
admin	administrative
adv	advertising
affil	affiliate
affrs	affairs
AFRTS	Armed Forces Radio and TV Service
alt	alternate
ant	antenna
AOR	album-oriented rock
AP	Associated Press
assn	association
assoc	associate
asst	assistant
atty	attorney
aur	aural
aux	auxiliary
bcst	broadcast
bcstg	broadcasting
bcstr	broadcaster
bd	board
BET	Black Entertainment Television
bi-m	every two months
bk rev	book reviews
bldg	building
bor	borough
btfl	beautiful
C-SPAN	Cable Satellite Public Affairs Network
CATV	community antenna television
CBC	Canadian Broadcasting Corp.
CEO	chief executive officer
ch	channel
CH	critical hours
chg	charge
CHR	contemporary hit radio
chmn	chairman
circ	circulation
coml	commercial
contemp	contemporary
COO	chief operating officer
coord	coordinator
CP	construction permit
CRTC	Canadian Radio-television and Telecommunications Commission
C&W	country & western
D	day
d	daily
DA	directional antenna
dance rev	dance reviews
DBS	direct broadcast satellite
dev	development
dir	director
div	diverse
DMA	Designated Market Area
dups	duplicates
Eds	editors
Ed Bd	Editorial Board
educ	educational
engr	engineer
engrg	engineering
EPG	Electronic Program Guide
ERP	effective radiated power
ESPN	Entertainment & Sports Programming Network
ETV	educational television
exec	executive
FCC	Federal Communications Commission
film rev	film reviews
fortn	fortnightly
Fr	French
g	ground
gen	general
Ger	German
govt	government
HAAT	height above average terrain
HBO	Home Box Office
horiz	horizontal polarization
hqtrs	headquarters
ind	independent
info	information
instal	installation
ISBN	International Standard Book Number
ISSN	International Standard Serial Number
illus	illustrations
irreg	irregular
It	Italian
khz	kilohertz
kw	kilowatts
loc	local
LPTV	low power television
LS	local sunset
lstng	listening
lw	long wave
m	meters
MDS	Multipoint Distribution Service
mdse	merchandising
mfg	manufacturing
mgng	managing
mgr	manager
mgmt	management
mhz	megahertz
mi	miles
mktg	marketing
MMDS	Multichannel Multipoint Distribution Service
mo	month
mod	modification
MOR	middle of the road
MSO	multiple system operator
mthy	monthly
MTV	Music Television
mus	music
music rev	music reviews
mw	medium wave
N	night
na	not available
NAB	National Association of Broadcasters
natl	national
net	network
NPR	National Public Radio
nwspr	newspaper
off	officer
opns	operations
per	personnel
play rev	play reviews (theatre reviews)
Pol	Polish
pop	population
PR	public relations
pres	president
PRI	Public Radio International
progmg	programming
progsv	progressive
prom	promotion
PSA	presunrise authority, public service announcement
ptnr	partner
pub affrs	public affairs
publ	publicity
q	quarterly
quad	quadraphonic
record rev	record reviews
rel	relations
relg	religion
rep	representative
RFE	Radio Free Europe
rgn	region
rgnl	regional
RL	Radio Liberty
rsch	research
s-a	twice annually
s-m	twice monthly
s-w	twice weekly
sec	secretary
sep	separate
sh	shares
SH	specified hours
sls	sales
SMATV	satellite master antenna television
Sp	Spanish
sr	senior
ST	shares time
stn	station
sub	subscriber
supt	superintendent
supvr	supervisor
svcs	services
sw	short wave
t	terrain
tech	technical
tele rev	television reviews
3/m	three times a month
3/y	three times a year
TNN	The Nashville Network
traf	traffic
trans	translators
treas	treasurer
twp	township
TWX	Teletypewriter Exchange
U	unlimited
UHF	ultra high frequency
UPI	United Press International
UPN	United Paramount Network
var	variety
vert	vertical polarization
VHF	very high frequency
video rev	video reviews
vis	visual
VOA	Voice of America
vp	vice president
w	watts
wkly	weekly

Section A
Industry Overview

Television Markets Ranked by Number of TV Homes	A-2
Top 25 TV Station Groups	A-6
Top 25 TV Station Groups Ranked by FCC	A-7
Top 25 Cable/Satellite Operators	A-8
Top 100 Cable Systems	A-9
U.S. Sales of Television Receivers 1983-2003	A-11
Television Sets in Use	A-12
51 Years of Station Transactions	A-13
Record of Television Station Growth Since Television Began	A-14
Top 10 Cable Networks	A-15
Top 100 Television Programs	A-16
Top 10 Cable Programs	A-18
Television Advertising Shares	A-19
Top 25 TV Advertisers	A-20
Top 25 TV Advertising Categories	A-21
A Brief History of Broadcasting and Cable	A-22
A Chronology of the Electronic Media	A-24
The FCC and the Rules of Broadcasting	A-29

Television Markets Ranked by Number of TV Homes

Listed below are the Nielsen Media Research Designated Market Areas (DMAs) ranked by the number of television households. The estimates are from September 2004.

Rank	Designated Market Area	TV Households
1	New York	7,355,710
2	Los Angeles	5,431,140
3	Chicago	3,417,330
4	Philadelphia	2,919,410
5	Boston (Manchester)	2,391,840
6	San Francisco-Oakland-San Jose	2,359,870
7	Dallas-Fort Worth	2,292,760
8	Washington, DC (Hagerstown)	2,241,610
9	Atlanta	2,059,450
10	Detroit	1,943,930
11	Houston	1,902,810
12	Seattle-Tacoma	1,690,640
13	Tampa-St. Petersburg, Sarasota	1,671,040
14	Minneapolis-St. Paul	1,665,540
15	Phoenix (Prescott)	1,596,950
16	Cleveland-Akron (Canton)	1,556,670
17	Miami-Fort Lauderdale	1,496,810
18	Denver	1,401,760
19	Sacramento-Stockton-Modesto	1,315,030
20	Orlando-Daytona Beach-Melbourne	1,303,150
21	St. Louis	1,216,700
22	Pittsburgh	1,186,010
23	Baltimore	1,087,730
24	Portland, OR	1,086,900
25	Indianapolis	1,053,020
26	San Diego	1,025,730
27	Hartford & New Haven	1,017,530
28	Charlotte	1,004,440
29	Raleigh-Durham (Fayetteville)	966,720
30	Nashville	916,170
31	Kansas City	894,580
32	Milwaukee	886,770
33	Cincinnati	883,230
34	Columbus, OH	867,490
35	Greenville-Spartanburg-Asheville-Anderson	813,210
36	Salt Lake City	800,000
37	San Antonio	748,950
38	Grand Rapids-Kalamazoo-Battle Creek	732,600
39	West Palm Beach-Fort Pierce	729,010
40	Birmingham (Anniston, Tuscaloosa)	717,300
41	Norfolk-Portsmouth-Newport News	707,750
42	Harrisburg-Lancaster-Lebanon-York	702,590
43	New Orleans	675,760
44	Memphis	658,250
45	Oklahoma City	655,250
46	Buffalo	651,970
47	Albuquerque-Santa Fe	649,680
48	Greensboro-High Point-Winston Salem	648,860
49	Providence-New Bedford	644,980
50	Louisville	637,680
51	Las Vegas	614,150
52	Jacksonville, Brunswick	613,000
53	Wilkes Barre-Scranton	592,560

Broadcasting & Cable Yearbook 2006

Television Markets Ranked by Number of TV Homes

Rank	Designated Market Area	TV Households
54	Austin	567,870
55	Albany-Schenectady-Troy	555,640
56	Dayton	537,710
57	Little Rock-Pine Bluff	531,770
58	Fresno-Visalia	527,770
59	Knoxville	513,630
60	Tulsa	510,960
61	Richmond-Petersburg	509,860
62	Charleston-Huntington	508,750
63	Mobile-Pensacola (Fort Walton Beach)	492,070
64	Lexington	481,120
65	Flint-Saginaw-Bay City	479,520
66	Wichita-Hutchinson Plus	445,690
67	Roanoke-Lynchburg	445,670
68	Fort Myers-Naples	444,130
69	Green Bay-Appleton	433,640
70	Toledo	432,430
71	Honolulu	417,120
72	Tucson (Sierra Vista)	417,070
73	Des Moines-Ames	412,230
74	Portland-Auburn	409,060
75	Rochester, NY	396,880
76	Omaha	396,460
77	Syracuse	395,400
78	Springfield, MO	388,530
79	Paducah-Cape Girardeau-Harrisburg-Mt. Vernon	384,860
80	Spokane	384,060
81	Shreveport	382,700
82	Champaign & Springfield-Decatur	382,460
83	Columbia, SC	374,680
84	Huntsville-Decatur, Florence	370,160
85	Madison	364,000
86	Chattanooga	353,210
87	South Bend-Elkhart	332,860
88	Cedar Rapids-Waterloo & Dubuque	331,610
89	Tri-Cities, TN-VA	329,910
90	Burlington-Plattsburgh	329,200
91	Jackson, MS	327,670
92	Colorado Springs-Pueblo	313,170
93	Harlingen-Weslaco-Brownsville-McAllen	312,300
94	Davenport-Rock Island-Moline	309,900
95	Waco-Temple-Bryan	308,970
96	Baton Rouge	306,910
97	Johnstown-Altoona	300,850
98	Savannah	293,170
99	Evansville	289,840
100	El Paso (Las Cruces)	288,440
101	Charleston, SC	282,740
102	Youngstown	281,340
103	Lincoln & Hastings-Kearney	275,230
104	Fort Wayne	271,890
105	Greenville-New Bern-Washington	270,200
106	Springfield-Holyoke	267,500
107	Fort Smith-Fayetteville-Springdale-Rogers	267,030
108	Myrtle Beach-Florence	265,370
109	Tallahassee-Thomasville	259,720
110	Lansing	259,240
111	Tyler-Longview (Lufkin & Nacogdoches)	254,170

Television Markets Ranked by Number of TV Homes

Rank	Designated Market Area	TV Households
112	Traverse City-Cadillac	249,450
113	Montgomery (Selma)	247,800
114	Reno	246,700
115	Augusta	246,620
116	Sioux Falls (Mitchell)	242,930
117	Peoria-Bloomington	242,020
118	Fargo-Valley City	235,490
119	Macon	230,000
120	Eugene	229,360
121	Santa Barbara-Santa Maria-San Luis Obispo	224,710
122	Boise	223,890
123	Lafayette, LA	220,740
124	Monterey-Salinas	218,450
125	Columbus, GA	208,860
126	Yakima-Pasco-Richland-Kennewick	207,180
127	La Crosse-Eau Claire	206,490
128	Bakersfield	194,180
129	Corpus Christi	193,290
130	Amarillo	190,120
131	Chico-Redding	189,310
132	Columbus-Tupelo-West Point	187,650
133	Wausau-Rhinelander	181,780
134	Rockford	181,180
135	Monroe-El Dorado	176,380
136	Duluth-Superior	175,030
137	Topeka	171,470
138	Beaumont-Port Arthur	168,740
139	Columbia-Jefferson City	167,390
140	Wilmington	163,560
141	Medford-Klamath Falls	162,260
142	Erie	158,910
143	Sioux City	157,340
144	Wichita Falls & Lawton	156,300
145	Lubbock	152,620
146	Joplin-Pittsburg	152,310
147	Albany, GA	151,970
148	Bluefield-Beckley-Oak Hill	148,760
149	Terre Haute	146,860
150	Salisbury	146,510
151	Bangor	144,740
152	Wheeling-Steubenville	144,330
153	Rochester-Mason City-Austin	142,570
154	Binghamton	141,350
155	Anchorage	139,960
156	Biloxi-Gulfport	137,590
157	Minot-Bismarck-Dickinson	135,760
158	Odessa-Midland	135,450
159	Palm Springs	135,190
160	Panama City	134,770
161	Sherman, TX-Ada, OK	123,540
162	Gainesville	116,670
163	Abilene-Sweetwater	112,950
164	Idaho Falls-Pocatello	112,700
165	Clarksburg-Weston	109,480
166	Utica	106,690
167	Quincy-Hannibal-Keokuk	105,070
168	Hattiesburg-Laurel	104,800
169	Missoula	103,810

Broadcasting & Cable Yearbook 2006

Television Markets Ranked by Number of TV Homes

Rank	Designated Market Area	TV Households
170	Billings	102,370
171	Yuma-El Centro	99,490
172	Dothan	98,850
173	Elmira	98,270
174	Jackson, TN	94,770
175	Watertown	94,390
176	Alexandria, LA	94,350
177	Lake Charles	94,240
178	Rapid City	93,220
179	Jonesboro	93,100
180	Marquette	91,100
181	Harrisonburg	85,550
182	Bowling Green	81,470
183	Greenwood-Greenville	78,160
184	Meridian	72,280
185	Charlottesville	69,930
186	Lafayette, IN	65,060
187	Parkersburg	64,790
188	Great Falls	64,650
189	Grand Junction-Montrose	63,650
190	Laredo	62,720
191	Twin Falls	59,940
192	Eureka	58,380
193	Butte-Bozeman	57,680
194	Lima	54,200
195	Cheyenne-Scottsbluff	53,920
196	San Angelo	53,530
197	Bend, OR	52,550
198	Casper-Riverton	51,850
199	Mankato	51,390
200	Ottumwa-Kirksville	51,190
201	St. Joseph	48,740
202	Zanesville	33,240
203	Presque Isle	31,840
204	Fairbanks	31,640
205	Victoria	30,180
206	Helena	25,360
207	Juneau	25,070
208	Alpena	17,930
209	North Platte	15,590
210	Glendive	5,150

© 2004 Nielsen Media Research: Reprinted with permission.

Top 25 TV Station Groups

Ranked by Total Coverage*

In this list, the Top 25 TV Station Groups are ranked according to the percentage of the 109.6 million U.S. TV homes that they reach. If a group owns or manages other stations in a market, those stations are not counted in its total, nor are low-power and satellite stations and translators.

Rank	Group	% of U.S. TV Homes
1	Paxson Communications Corporation	64.29
2	FOX Television Stations, Inc.	44.48
3	Viacom Television Stations Group	42.80
4	Univision Television Group, Inc.	42.14
5	Tribune Broadcasting Company	40.13
6	NBC/General Electric	38.09
7	Trinity Broadcasting Network, Inc.	33.83
8	ABC, Inc./Disney	23.54
9	Sinclair Broadcast Group, Inc.	23.06
10	Scripps Howard Broadcasting	21.85
11	Hearst-Argyle Television, Inc.	18.17
12	Gannett Company, Inc.	17.86
13	Daystar TV Network	14.52
14	Belo	13.83
15	Entravision Communications Corporation	12.64
16	Clear Channel Communications	12.45
17	Pappas Telecasting Companies	12.41
18	LIN Television Corporation (1)	10.51
19	Raycom Media, Inc. (2)	10.42
20	Cox Television	10.15
21	Meredith Corporation	8.97
22	Liberman Broadcasting	8.78
23	Media General Broadcast Group	7.87
24	Post-Newsweek Stations, Inc.	7.31
25	Nexstar Broadcasting Group	7.15

* As of June 30, 2005.
** Coverage is % of 50 states only; does not include Puerto Rico
Note: LPTVs and satellite stations are not counted towards the national cap per the FCC. In this table, Kagan assumes all LMAs have the requisite 33% financial interest to be counted toward ownership.
(1) Table does not include the Emmis divestiture of five stations to LIN TV, three to Journal Comm. and one to Gray Television
(2) Does not include the planned Liberty Corp./Raycom merger.
© 2005 Kagan Research, LLC. Reprinted with permission.

Top 25 TV Station Groups

Ranked by FCC Coverage*

In this list, the Top 25 TV Station Groups are ranked according to the percentage of the 109.6 million U.S. TV homes they reach as calculated by the FCC, which discounts the reach of UHF stations (chs. 14-83) by half. If a group owns or manages other stations in a market, those stations are not counted in its total, nor are low-power and satellite stations and translators.

Rank	Group	FCC % of U.S. TV Homes
1	Viacom Television Stations Group	38.39
2	FOX Television Stations, Inc.	37.85
3	NBC/General Electric	33.34
4	Paxson Communications Corporation	32.15
5	Tribune Broadcasting Company	29.91
6	ABC, Inc./Disney	23.29
7	Univision Television Group, Inc.	21.99
8	Gannett Company, Inc.	17.69
9	Trinity Broadcasting Network, Inc.	16.91
10	Hearst-Argyle Television, Inc.	16.51
11	Scripps Howard Broadcasting	13.99
12	Belo	13.11
13	Sinclair Broadcast Group, Inc.	13.09
14	Cox Television	10.02
15	Daystar TV Network	8.86
16	LIN Television Corporation (1)	8.74
17	Clear Channel Communications	8.58
18	Raycom Media, Inc. (2)	7.77
19	Meredith Corporation	7.50
20	Post-Newsweek Stations, Inc.	7.31
21	Media General Broadcast Group	7.05
22	Entravision Communications Corporation	6.83
23	Pappas Telecasting Companies	6.60
24	Emmis Broadcasting Corporation (1)	6.05
25	Young Broadcasting, Inc.	5.77

* As of June 30, 2005.
** Coverage is % of 50 states only; does not include Puerto Rico
Note: LPTVs and satellite stations are not counted towards the national cap per the FCC. In this table, Kagan assumes all LMAs have the requisite 33% financial interest to be counted toward ownership.
(1) Table does not include the Emmis divestiture of five stations to LIN TV, three to Journal Comm. and one to Gray Television
(2) Does not include the planned Liberty Corp./Raycom merger.
© 2005 Kagan Research, LLC. Reprinted with permission.

Top 25 Cable/Satellite Operators

Ranked by Basic Subscribers*

Rank	Company	Subscribers
1	Comcast Cable Comm.	21,448,000
2	DIRECTV	14,670,000
3	EchoStar	11,455,000
4	Time Warner Cable	10,905,000
5	Cox Communications	6,283,100
6	Charter Communications	5,943,100
7	Adelphia Comm. (1)	5,130,900
8	Cablevision Systems	3,005,600
9	Bright House Networks (e)	2,180,000
10	Mediacom LLC	1,446,000
11	Insight Communications	1,257,200
12	CableOne	702,800
13	Cebridge Connection (e)	449,200
14	RCN Corp.	371,000
15	Bresnan (e)	300,100
16	WideOpenWest (e)	292,500
17	Service Electric (e)	285,000
18	Atlantic Broadband	249,200
19	Armstrong Group of Cos.	227,300
20	Susquehanna Cable	226,100
21	Midcontinent Communications	195,000
22	Pencor Services (e)	181,900
23	Knology Holdings	179,800
24	Northland Communications	160,100
25	Millennium Digital Media (e)	156,300

* As of June 30, 2005.
(e) Estimate.
(1) Includes Non-Filing Entities and Rigas Entities, including customers in Brazil and Puerto Rico.
© 2005 Kagan Research, LLC. Reprinted with permission.

Top 100 Cable Clusters/Systems

Ranked by Basic Subscribers*

Rank	System	Subscribers
1	Cablevision Systems Corp., Greater New York Area, NY	2,963,001
2	Comcast, Boston, MA	1,937,608
3	Time Warner Cable, Los Angeles, CA	1,918,746
4	Comcast, Philadelphia, PA	1,906,925
5	Comcast, Chicago, IL	1,760,735
6	Comcast, San Francisco Bay Area, CA	1,608,716
7	Time Warner Cable, New York, NY	1,379,086
8	Comcast, Seattle, WA	1,030,982
9	Bright House Networks, Tampa Bay, FL	1,011,169
10	Comcast, Detroit, MI	981,693
11	Comcast, Washington, DC	959,979
12	Time Warner Cable, Cleveland-Akron (Canton), OH	854,077
13	Cox Comm., Middle America Cox	777,629
14	Bright House Networks, Central FL	776,651
15	Cox Comm., AZ	774,216
16	Comcast, Atlanta, GA	769,072
17	Time Warner Cable, Houston, TX	753,857
18	Mediacom, South Central Region	746,000
19	Comcast, Miami, FL	739,534
20	Comcast, New York, NY	720,139
21	Mediacom, North Central Region	712,000
22	Comcast, Denver, CO	665,945
23	Comcast, Baltimore, MD	649,301
24	Comcast, Pittsburgh, PA	606,967
25	Comcast, Hartford & New Haven, CT	546,759
26	Cox Comm., San Diego, CA	542,222
27	Comcast, St. Paul & Minneapolis, MN	539,088
28	Comcast, Sacramento, CA	535,240
29	Cox Comm., OK	501,020
30	Time Warner Cable, Raleigh-Durham, NC	471,280
31	Cox Comm., New England	456,647
32	Charter Comm., St. Louis Metro, MO	447,400
33	Time Warner Cable, Charlotte, NC	426,081
34	Cox Comm., Hampton Roads, VA	420,805
35	Time Warner Cable, Milwaukee, WI	416,684
36	Comcast, Portland, OR	407,139
37	Cox Comm., Las Vegas, NV	403,259
38	Time Warner Cable, HI	397,253
39	Time Warner Cable, Cincinnati, OH	388,981
40	Time Warner Cable, San Antonio, TX	384,016
41	Time Warner Cable, Albany, NY	380,700
42	Comcast, Harrisburg-Lancaster-Lebanon-York, PA	377,823
43	Comcast, Grand Rapids-Kalamazoo-Battle Creek, MI	369,623
44	Comcast, West Palm Beach-Ft. Pierce, FL	368,374
45	Time Warner Cable, Columbus, OH	364,973
46	Charter Comm., New England	358,700
47	Comcast, Jacksonville & Brunswick, FL	357,671
48	Charter Comm., AL	354,800
49	Time Warner Cable, Greensboro, NC	351,808
50	Comcast, Nashville, TN	334,612

Broadcasting & Cable Yearbook 2006

Top 100 Cable Clusters/Systems

Rank	System	Subscribers
51	Time Warner Cable, Austin, TX	316,594
52	Cox Comm., KS	309,425
53	Charter Comm., SC	305,100
54	Charter Comm., GA	304,800
55	Time Warner Cable, Kansas City, MO	303,350
56	Time Warner Cable, San Diego, CA	301,355
57	Charter Comm., Los Angeles Metro, CA	297,300
58	Charter Comm., Northwest Region	293,400
59	Time Warner Cable, Syracuse, NY	280,128
60	Charter Comm., Southern MN	279,300
61	Comcast, Richmond-Petersburg, VA	278,389
62	Charter Comm., East TN/KY	276,000
63	Cox Comm., Orange County, CA	273,541
64	Insight Comm., Louisville, KY	271,700
65	Comcast, Indianapolis, IN	270,728
66	Cox Comm., New Orleans, LA	270,171
67	Charter Comm., WV	267,900
68	Time Warner Cable, Rochester, NY	264,868
69	Comcast, Ft. Myers-Naples, FL	259,726
70	Cox Comm., Northern VA	257,425
71	Time Warner Cable, Portland-Auburn, ME	255,182
72	Charter Comm., NC/VA	245,800
73	Comcast, Salt Lake City, UT	244,436
74	Cox Comm., West TX	229,423
75	Charter Comm., Southern WI	226,500
76	Charter Comm., West TN/KY	222,700
77	Charter Comm., Mid-America	215,000
78	Comcast, Fresno-Visalia, CA	208,365
79	Comcast, Tampa/Sarasota, FL	203,743
80	Comcast, Wheeling-Steubenville, WV	201,694
81	Comcast, Memphis, TN	201,000
82	Charter Comm., Eastern MI	198,800
83	Charter Comm., Northern MI	197,200
84	Charter Comm., Central CA	197,000
85	Charter Comm., Western MI	194,800
86	Charter Comm., Eastern WI	190,800
87	Cox Comm., Omaha, NE	190,382
88	Comcast, Albuquerque-Santa Fe, NM	186,514
89	Cox Comm., Baton Rouge, LA	179,011
90	Charter Comm., LA/MS	178,200
91	Cox Comm., Gulf Coast/FL	167,955
92	Charter Comm., Ft. Worth, TX	167,300
93	Comcast, Eugene, OR	164,600
94	Time Warner Cable, Columbia, SC	163,619
95	Comcast, Salisbury, MD	162,441
96	Charter Comm., MN/WI	162,000
97	Comcast, Knoxville, TN	160,911
98	Time Warner Cable, Green Bay, WI	147,981
99	Charter Comm., NV	146,500
100	Charter Comm., Inland Empire	137,800

* As of December 2004.
© 2005 Kagan Research, LLC. Reprinted with permission.

U.S. Sales of Television Receivers 1983-2003

Data compiled by Consumer Electronics Association

	Analog Color TV		Digital TV		LCD TV		TV/VCR/DVD Combinations		Projection TV	
Year	Units	Dollars	Units	Dollars	Units	Dollars	Units	Dollars	Units	Dollars
1983	11,179	3,443	n/a	n/a	n/a	n/a	n/a	n/a	n/a	n/a
1984	13,092	3,875	n/a	n/a	n/a	n/a	n/a	n/a	n/a	n/a
1985	13,993	4,114	n/a	n/a	n/a	n/a	n/a	n/a	266	488
1986	15,399	4,481	n/a	n/a	n/a	n/a	n/a	n/a	304	530
1987	16,805	4,890	n/a	n/a	n/a	n/a	n/a	n/a	293	527
1988	17,768	4,691	n/a	n/a	n/a	n/a	n/a	n/a	302	529
1989	19,557	5,359	n/a	n/a	n/a	n/a	n/a	n/a	265	478
1990	18,453	5,148	n/a	n/a	n/a	n/a	424	178	351	626
1991	17,951	5,134	n/a	n/a	n/a	n/a	662	265	380	683
1992	21,056	6,591	n/a	n/a	n/a	n/a	936	375	404	714
1993	23,005	7,316	n/a	n/a	n/a	n/a	1,629	599	465	841
1994	24,715	7,225	n/a	n/a	n/a	n/a	2,017	710	636	1,117
1995	23,231	6,798	n/a	n/a	n/a	n/a	2,205	723	820	1,417
1996	22,384	6,492	n/a	n/a	n/a	n/a	2,199	697	887	1,426
1997	21,293	6,036	n/a	n/a	n/a	n/a	2,311	684	917	1,361
1998	22,204	6,122	14	43	n/a	n/a	3,147	832	1,070	1,577
1999	23,218	6,199	121	295	n/a	n/a	4,148	1,014	1,232	1,632
2000	24,175	6,503	648	1,426	832	107	4,964	968	1,216	1,481
2001	21,167	5,130	1,460	2,648	845	101	4,630	790	933	1,060
2002	22,469	5,782	2,536	4,281	935	246	4,870	733	681	733
2003	20,791	4,756	4,102	6,521	1,253	664	4,373	778	276	293

Dollar figure in millions and represent factory sales price multiplied by unit sales to dealers.
Unit figures include distributor sales and factory direct sales to dealers. All unit figures are in thousands (add 000).
n/a=not available
© 2005 Consumer Electronics Association. Reprinted with permission.

Television Sets in Use

Year	In Home (000)	Avg. Sets Per HH
1970	81,040	1.39
1971	85,290	1.42
1972	89,770	1.45
1973	95,330	1.47
1974	100,020	1.51
1975	105,460	1.54
1976	108,890	1.56
1977	113,440	1.59
1978	118,630	1.63
1979	124,570	1.67
1980	128,190	1.68
1981	132,260	1.70
1982	142,460	1.75
1983	148,910	1.79
1984	149,180	1.78
1985	155,410	1.83
1986	157,500	1.83
1987	162,750	1.86
1988	168,260	1.90
1989	175,580	1.94
1990	193,320	2.10
1991	193,200	2.08
1992*	192,480	2.09
1993	200,565	2.15
1994	211,443	2.24
1995	217,067	2.28
1996	222,753	2.32
1997	228,740	2.36
1998	235,010	2.40
1999	240,320	2.42
2000	244,990	2.43
2001	248,160	2.43
2002	254,360	2.41
2003	260,230	2.44
2004	268,260	2.47
2005	287,000	2.62

* Reflects adjustments to conform to the 1990 census; 1970-79, as of September of prior year; 1980 to date as of January of calendar year; excludes Alaska and Hawaii prior to 1989.
Source: Television Bureau of Advertising, Nielsen Media Research.

51 Years of Station Transactions

Dollar volume of transactions (number of stations changing hands)

YEAR	RADIO ONLY*	GROUPS*	TV ONLY	TOTAL
1954	$10,224,047 (187)	$26,213,323 (18)	$23,906,760 (27)	$60,344,130
1955	27,333,104 (242)	22,351,602 (11)	23,394,660 (29)	73,079,366
1956	32,563,378 (316)	65,212,055 (24)	17,830,395 (21)	115,605,828
1957	48,207,470 (357)	47,490,884 (28)	28,489,206 (38)	124,187,660
1958	49,868,123 (407)	60,872,618 (17)	16,796,285 (23)	127,537,026
1959	65,544,653 (436)	42,724,727 (15)	15,227,201 (21)	123,496,581
1960	51,763,285 (345)	24,648,400 (10)	22,930,225 (21)	99,341,910
1961	55,532,516 (282)	42,103,708 (13)	31,167,943 (24)	128,804,167
1962	59,912,520 (306)	18,822,745 (8)	23,007,638 (16)	101,742,903
1963	43,457,584 (305)	25,045,726 (3)	36,799,768 (16)	105,303,078
1964	52,296,480 (430)	67,185,762 (20)	86,274,494 (36)	205,756,736
1965	55,933,300 (389)	49,756,993 (15)	29,433,473 (32)	135,123,766
1966	76,633,762 (367)	28,510,500 (11)	30,574,054 (31)	135,718,316
1967	59,670,053 (316)	32,086,297 (9)	80,316,223 (30)	172,072,573
1968	71,310,709 (316)	47,556,634 (9)	33,588,069 (20)	152,455,412
1969	108,866,538 (343)	35,037,000 (5)	87,794,032 (32)	231,697,570
1970	86,292,899 (268)	1,038,465 (3)	87,454,078 (19)	174,785,442
1971	125,501,514 (270)	750,000 (2)	267,296,410 (27)	393,547,924
1972	114,424,673 (239)	0 (0)	156,905,864 (37)	271,330,537
1973	160,933,557 (352)	2,812,444 (4)	66,635,144 (25)	230,381,145
1974	168,998,012 (369)	19,800,000 (5)	118,983,462 (24)	307,781,474
1975	131,065,860 (363)	0 (0)	128,420,101 (22)	259,485,961
1976	180,663,820 (413)	1,800,000 (3)	108,459,657 (32)	290,923,477
1977	161,236,169 (344)	0 (0)	128,635,435 (25)	289,871,604
1978	331,557,239 (586)	30,450,000 (5)	289,721,159 (51)	651,728,398
1979	335,597,000 (546)	463,500,000 (52)	317,581,000 (47)	1,116,648,000
1980	339,634,000 (424)	27,000,000 (3)	534,150,000 (35)	876,084,000
1981	447,838,060 (625)	78,400,000 (6)	227,950,000 (24)	754,188,067
1982	470,722,833 (597)	0 (0)	527,675,411 (30)	998,398,244
1983	621,077,876 (669)	332,000,000 (10)	1,902,701,830 (61)	2,854,895,356
1984	977,024,266 (782)	234,500,000 (2)	1,252,023,787 (82)	2,118,056,053
1985	1,414,816,073 (1,558)	962,450,000 (218)	3,290,995,000 (99)	5,668,261,073
1986	1,490,131,426 (959)	1,993,021,955 (192)	2,709,516,490 (128)	6,192,669,871
1987	1,236,355,748 (775)	4,610,965,000 (132)	1,661,832,724 (59)	7,509,154,473
1988	1,841,630,156 (845)	1,326,250,000 (106)	1,779,958,042 (70)	4,947,838,198
1989	1,148,524,765 (663)	533,599,078 (40)	1,541,055,033 (84)	3,235,436,376
1990	868,636,700 (1,045)	411,037,150 (60)	696,952,350 (75)	1,976,626,100
1991	534,694,500 (793)	206,995,500 (61)	273,365,000 (38)	1,014,579,000
1992	603,192,980 (667)	318,176,050 (24)	124,004,000 (41)	1,045,373,000
1993	815,450,000 (633)	756,722,000 (NA)	1,728,711,000 (101)	3,300,883,000
1994	970,400,000 (494)	1,800,000,000 (154)	2,200,000,000 (89)	4,970,400,000
1995	792,440,000 (524)	2,790,000,000 (213)	4,740,000,000 (112)	8,322,440,000
1996	2,840,820,000 (671)	12,034,000,000 (345)	10,488,000,000 (99)	25,362,820,000
1997	2,461,570,000 (630)	14,580,000,000 (329)	6,400,000,000 (108)	23,441,570,000
1998	1,596,210,000 (589)	14,080,000,000 (271)	7,120,000,000 (90)	22,796,210,000
1999	1,718,000,000 (382)	26,880,000,000 (196)	4,720,000,000 (86)	33,318,000,000
2000	24,900,000,000 (1,794)	0 (0)	8,800,000,000 (154)	33,700,000,000
2001	3,800,000,000 (1,000)	0 (0)	4,900,000,000 (108)	8,700,000,000
2002	5,594,141,000 (836)	0 (0)	2,529,039,000 (249)	8,123,180,000
2003	2,400,000,000 (950)	0 (0)	520,000,000 (97)	2,920,000,000
2004	1,897,422,000 (901)	0 (0)	871,923,000 (66)	2,769,345,000
TOTAL	$62,708,233,175	$84,585,715,066	$73,400,106,153	$220,694,054,394

Note: Dollar volume figures represent total considerations reported for all transactions with exception of minority interest transfers in which control of stations did not change hands and stations sold as part of larger company transactions. Although all states have been approved by the FCC, they may not necessarily have reached final closing. Prior to 1978, combined AM-FM facilities were counted as one station in computing total number of stations traded. Now AM-FM combinations are counted as two stations.
*Starting in 1993, the Radio only column includes only stand alone AM and FM deals and the Groups column contains AM-FM combos and all other multiple station deals. In previous years the AM-FM combos were included under Radio only.
**Figures for 2000, 2001, 2002, 2003, and 2004 courtesy of BIA Financial Network.

Broadcasting & Cable Yearbook 2006

Record of Television Station Growth Since Television Began

	TV Authorized	On Air
Jan. 1, 1946*	9	6
Jan. 1, 1947*	52	
Jan. 1, 1948*	73	17
Jan. 1, 1949	124	50
Jan. 1, 1950	111	97
Jan. 1, 1951	109	107
Jan. 1, 1952	108	108
Jan. 1, 1953*	273	129
Jan. 1, 1954	567	356
Jan. 1, 1955	576	439 [1]
Jan. 1, 1956	590	482 [2]
Jan. 1, 1957	631	511
Jan. 1, 1958	657	544 [3]
Jan. 1, 1959	666	562 [4]
Jan. 1, 1960	673	573 [5]
Jan. 1, 1961	634	583
Jan. 1, 1962	654	563
Jan. 1, 1963	662	579
Jan. 1, 1964	661	582
Jan. 1, 1965	676	586
Jan. 1, 1966	702	596
Jan. 1, 1967	769	623
Jan. 1, 1968	818	644
Jan. 1, 1969	834	672
Jan. 1, 1970	1,038	872
Jan. 1, 1971	1,025	892
Jan. 1, 1972	1,004	905
Jan. 1, 1973	1,001	922
Jan. 1, 1974	1,002	938
Jan. 1, 1975	1,010	952
Jan. 1, 1976	1,030	962
Jan. 1, 1977	1,029	984
Jan. 1, 1978	1,045	986
Jan. 1, 1979	1,059	992
Jan. 1, 1980	1,094	1,013
Jan. 1, 1981	1,143	1,019
Jan. 1, 1982	1,168	1,020
Jan. 1, 1983	1,276	1,090
Jan. 1, 1984	1,318	1,149
Jan. 1, 1985	1,505	1,194
Oct. 30, 1986	1,493	1,220
Oct. 31, 1987	1,558	1,285
Jan. 1, 1988	1,615	1,342
Jan. 1, 1989	1,683	1,395
Jan. 1, 1990	1,684	1,436
Jan. 1, 1991	1,690	1,469
Jan. 1, 1992	1,688	1,488
Jan. 1, 1993	1,688	1,505
Jan. 1, 1994		1,518
Jan. 1, 1995		1,520
Jan. 1, 1996		1,544
Jan. 1, 1997		1,554
Jan. 1, 1998		1,564
Jan. 1, 1999		1,589
Jan. 1, 2000		1,616
Jan. 1, 2001		1,663
Jan. 1, 2002		1,686
Jan. 1, 2003		1,719
Jan. 1, 2004		1,733
Jan. 1, 2005		1,748

*Comparable figures for all services not available at this date.

[1] Includes stations with Special Temporary Authorizations (STAs), which either had not started operations as of this date, had started but had gone dark, or had received authorizations but turned them back with or without operating.

[2] Includes 2 licenses that had suspended operation and 37 stations with STAs in same category as footnote 1.

[3] Includes 7 licenses that had suspended operation and 40 stations with STAs in same category as footnote 1

[4] Includes 6 licenses that had suspended operation and 38 stations with STAs in same category as footnote 1.

[5] Includes 10 licenses that had suspended operation and 38 stations with STAs in same category as footnote 1.

Top 10 Cable Networks

Primetime

	Rating	Total homes (000)
Nickelodeon	1.8	1981
TNT	1.8	1998
Nick-At-Nite	1.5	1659
USA	1.5	1680
Lifetime	1.4	1489
Disney Channel	1.3	1472
Cartoon	1.3	1379
TBS	1.2	1291
Fox News	1.1	1223
ESPN	1.0	1051

Total day

	Rating	Total homes (000)
Nickelodeon	1.5	1634
Nick-At-Nite	1.2	1318
TNT	1.0	1135
Cartoon	1.0	1071
Disney Channel	0.9	941
Lifetime	0.8	920
USA	0.8	909
TBS	0.7	783
Fox News	0.6	700
A&E	0.5	510

2005 Year-To-Date 1/1/05 to 7/3/05.
Source: Nielsen Media Research.

Top 100 Television Programs

Full Season: 9/20/04-5/25/05

Rank	Program	Network	% U.S. Households
1	Super Bowl XXXIX (6:39p): New England vs Philadelphia	FOX	41.13
2	Academy Awards	ABC	25.43
3	Fox MLB ALCS Game 7: Boston at New York Yankees	FOX	19.41
4	Fox World Series Game 4: Boston at St Louis	FOX	18.18
5	Oscar Countdown 2005	ABC	17.39
6	CSI	CBS	16.46
7	AFC/NFC Playoff Gm2: NY Jets at San Diego	ABC	16.02
8	ABC Premiere Event-3/6: Their Eyes Were Watching God	ABC	15.93
9	Fox World Series Game 2: St Louis at Boston	FOX	15.87
10	American Idol-Tuesday	FOX	15.74
11	Numb3rs Preview	CBS	15.68
12	Fox World Series Game 3: Boston at St Louis	FOX	15.65
12	Fox MLB ALCS Game 6: Boston at New York Yankees	FOX	15.65
14	Raymond: Last Laugh	CBS	15.34
14	American Idol-Wednesday	FOX	15.34
16	CBS NCAA Bskbl Champshps: Illinois vs North Carolina	CBS	15.00
17	Desperate Housewives	ABC	14.49
18	Fox NFC Playoff-Sat: St Louis at Atlanta	FOX	14.00
19	American Idol Sp-3/7 8p	FOX	13.99
20	Fox World Series Game 1: St Louis at Boston	FOX	13.71
21	Orange Bowl: USC vs Oklahoma	ABC	13.68
22	American Idol Sp-2/28 8p	FOX	13.52
23	CSI - Thanksgiving	CBS	13.46
24	American Idol Sp-2/21 8p	FOX	13.34
25	Fox MLB NLCS Game 7: Houston at St Louis	FOX	13.04
26	Law and Order 9/22	NBC	12.52
27	Happy Days 30 Anv Reunion	ABC	12.48
28	CSI: Miami	CBS	12.42
29	Without a Trace	CBS	12.31
30	Survivor: Palau	CBS	12.22
31	Amer Idol-Thu Rslt Show	FOX	12.06
32	Without a Trace-Thnks	CBS	11.94
33	Survivor: Vanuatu	CBS	11.68
34	Grey's Anatomy	ABC	11.64
35	Grammy Awards: 47th Annual	CBS	11.59
36	Law & Order:Trial/Jury 3/3	NBC	11.57
37	CMA Awards: 38th Annual	CBS	11.47
38	Survivor: Palau Finale	CBS	11.43
39	Golden Globe Awards	NBC	11.32
40	Dateline NBC Special 1/4	NBC	11.25
41	Everybody Loves Raymond	CBS	11.22

Top 100 Television Programs

Rank	Program	Network	% U.S. Households
42	ABC Premiere Event-12/5: M.Albom 5 People U Meet Heaven	ABC	11.21
43	BC: 10 Most Fascinating People '04	ABC	10.94
44	Survivor: Vanuatu Finale	CBS	10.92
45	CBS NCAA Bskbl Champ Sa-2: North Carolina vs Mich State	CBS	10.89
46	Survivor: Palau Wed Spcl	CBS	10.88
47	CSI Special	CBS	10.85
48	Survivor: Palau Wed Sp	CBS	10.84
49	NFL Monday Night Football	ABC	10.83
50	CSI Thu 8p-Special	CBS	10.78
51	Two and a Half Men	CBS	10.64
52	Apprentice 2	NBC	10.43
53	E.R.	NBC	10.41
54	Fox MLB LCS: Gms 1&2: Boston at NYY/Hou at Stl	FOX	10.07
55	CSI-Wed Special	CBS	10.03
56	Fox MLB ALCS Game 1: Boston at New York Yankees	FOX	9.96
57	Law & Order:CI 5/25	NBC	9.91
58	Lost	ABC	9.84
59	60 Minutes Special	CBS	9.81
60	Cold Case	CBS	9.74
61	Two and a Half Men-Spcl	CBS	9.73
62	Sugar Bowl: Auburn vs Virginia Tech	ABC	9.52
62	Fox MLB ALCS Game 4: New York Yankees at Boston	FOX	9.52
64	Decision '04 Prime	NBC	9.51
65	Apprentice 2 9/29	NBC	9.33
66	Primetime Lv Sp Edtn-5/4	ABC	9.30
67	Fox World Series Gm3-Pre: Boston at St Louis	FOX	9.29
68	Law And Order:SVU	NBC	9.22
69	60 Minutes	CBS	9.18
70	Apprentice 3	NBC	9.10
71	Extreme Makeover:Hm Ed-8p	ABC	9.09
71	Medium	NBC	9.09
73	Survivor: Palau Reunion	CBS	9.06
74	CSI: Miami - Spcl	CBS	9.02
75	CSI - Thu 8p Special	CBS	8.99
76	CBS NCAA Bskbl-Bridge Shw	CBS	8.97
76	Survivor: Vanuatu Reunion	CBS	8.97
76	Dr. Phil Primetime Spcl	CBS	8.97
79	24 Prvw Sp-1/9 8p	FOX	8.95
80	Extrm Makeover:Hm Ed-1/30	ABC	8.94
81	CSI: NY	CBS	8.93
81	Decision '04:Pres Analys-	NBC	8.93
83	CSI: NY Sunday Spcl	CBS	8.92
84	Law and Order	NBC	8.88
85	NCIS 9p Special	CBS	8.82
86	Survivor: Vanuatu-Thnks	CBS	8.77
87	CBS Wednesday Movie Sp	CBS	8.75
88	NYPD Blue:A Final Tribute	ABC	8.70
89	Jake in Progress Sp1-3/13	ABC	8.53
90	Cold Case - Special	CBS	8.49
91	Dallas Reunion:Ret Sthfrk	CBS	8.47
92	24 Prvw Sp-1/9 9p	FOX	8.43

Broadcasting & Cable Yearbook 2006

Top 100 Television Programs

Rank	Program	Network	% U.S. Households
93	Desperate Housewives Spl	ABC	8.29
93	House	FOX	8.29
95	Everybdy Loves Raymnd-Spc	CBS	8.28
96	SNL Presidential Bash '04	NBC	8.23
97	NCIS 9p Special	CBS	8.22
98	Seinfeld Story	NBC	8.19
99	Amazing Race: 5	CBS	8.16
100	Rudolph-Red-Nose-Reindeer	CBS	8.15

Top 10 Cable Programs

Rank	Program	Network	% U.S. Households
298	NFL Regular Season	ESPN	6.06
342	Trading Spaces: 100 Grand	TLC	5.61
390	2004 NBA All-Star Game	TNT	5.10
510	NBA All-Star Pre-Game Show	TNT	4.23
524	MLB Divisional Series	ESPN	4.13
549	Holiday Bowl	ESPN	3.97
560	AFC/NFC Pro Bowl	ESPN	3.91
606	Budweiser Shootout	TNT	3.59
612	NCAA Women's Bsktbll Tour.	ESPN	3.51
621	Alamo Bowl	ESPN	3.44

Source: Television Bureau of Advertising, based on data from Nielsen Media Research and Galaxy Explorer. A household rating is the percentage of the 109.6 million homes in the U.S. with TV sets.

Note: Shows identified by date or as specials were one-time programs, programs that aired outside the regular time slot, or episodes that extended beyond regularly scheduled time periods.

Ad-Supported Cable only

Programming under 25 minutes excluded

Television Advertising Shares

	Network*	Spot	Local	Synd.*	Cable	Total
1970	$1,658	$1,234	$704	-		$3,596
1971	1,593	1,145	796	-		3,534
1972	1,804	1,318	969	-		4,091
1973	1,968	1,377	1,115	-		4,460
1974	2,145	1,497	1,212	-		4,854
1975	2,306	1,623	1,334	-		5,263
1976	2,857	2,154	1,710	-		6,721
1977	3,460	2,204	1,948	-		7,612
1978	3,975	2,607	2,373	-		8,955
1979	4,599	2,873	2,682	-		10,154
1980	5,130	3,269	2,967	50	72	11,488
1981	5,540	3,746	3,368	75	160	12,889
1982	6,144	4,364	3,765	150	290	14,713
1983	6,955	4,827	4,345	300	452	16,879
1984	8,318	5,488	5,084	420	733	20,043
1985	8,060	6,004	5,714	520	989	21,287
1986	8,342	6,570	6,514	600	1,173	23,199
1987	8,500	6,846	6,833	762	1,321	24,262
1988	9,172	7,147	7,270	901	1,641	26,131
1989	9,110	7,354	7,612	1,288	2,095	27,459
1990	9,863	7,788	7,856	1,109	2,631	29,247
1991	9,533	7,110	7,565	1,253	3,145	28,606
1992	10,249	7,551	8,079	1,370	3,830	31,079
1993	10,209	7,800	8,435	1,576	4,451	32,471
1994	10,942	8,993	9,464	1,734	5,209	36,342
1995	11,600	9,119	9,985	2,016	6,166	38,886
1996	13,081	9,803	10,944	2,218	7,778	43,824
1997	13,020	9,999	11,436	2,438	8,750	45,643
1998	13,736	10,659	12,169	2,609	10,340	49,513
1999	13,961	10,500	12,680	2,870	12,570	52,581
2000	15,888	12,264	13,542	3,108	15,455	60,257
2001	14,300	9,223	12,256	3,102	15,736	54,617
2002	15,000	10,920	13,114	3,034	16,297	58,365
2003	15,030	9,948	13,520	3,434	18,814	60,746

all figures in millions
*Fox is included in syndication prior to 1990; it's included in network starting in 1990.
Source: Television Bureau of Advertising and Universal McCann.

Top 25 TV Advertisers

Jan. 1, 2004-Dec. 31, 2004

1	Procter & Gamble Co	$2,433,387,381
2	General Motors Corp	$1,860,281,793
3	Daimlerchrysler Ag	$1,390,932,926
4	PSA Parent	$1,192,267,774
5	Ford Motor Co	$1,080,672,746
6	Time Warner Inc	$1,023,166,726
7	Johnson & Johnson	$1,006,412,749
8	Walt Disney Co	$985,646,719
9	SBC Communications Inc	$917,450,664
10	Pfizer Inc	$824,959,632
11	Nissan Motor Co Ltd	$806,634,859
12	Pepsico Inc	$747,647,615
13	Toyota Motor Corp	$744,479,341
14	Glaxosmithkline Plc	$740,089,319
15	Yum! Brands Inc	$719,903,058
16	Honda Motor Co Ltd	$711,850,764
17	Altria Group Inc	$701,395,491
18	Sears Holding Corp	$657,731,418
19	Verizon Communications Inc	$641,184,685
20	McDonalds Corp	$626,061,127
21	Sony Corp	$621,807,615
22	US Government	$611,239,983
23	General Mills Inc	$608,267,258
24	General Electric Co	$602,955,568
25	Ford Motor Co-Da	$599,786,204
	Grand Total	**$22,856,213,415**

Source: Nielsen Monitor-Plus.

Top 25 TV Advertising Categories

Jan. 1, 2004-Dec. 31, 2004

Autos	$9,970,769,012
Restaurant-Quick Service	$3,250,339,824
Prescription Drugs-Human	$2,983,868,783
Motion Picture	$2,674,400,119
Store-Dept.	$2,138,690,466
Telephone Svcs.-Wireless	$1,758,089,737
Credit Card Svcs.	$1,465,910,453
Dir. Resp. Prod.	$1,109,325,004
Restaurant	$978,986,516
Beer	$969,493,528
Recordings-Video	$959,855,832
Internet Svc. Provider	$862,698,044
Auto Dealership	$824,329,686
Political Campaign	$804,610,641
Store-Furniture	$733,076,048
Auto Insurance	$728,330,606
Cerial	$663,675,037
Reg. Soft Drink	$659,226,386
Financial-Investment Svcs.	$635,770,734
Store-Home Improvement	$563,376,730
Store-Electronics	$494,353,083
Professional Organization	$466,215,033
Bank Svcs.	$461,525,250
Store-apparel	$439,820,903
Pain Reliever	$437,671,800
Satellite Comm. Svcs.	$422,749,165
Total	**$37,457,158,420**

Source: Nielsen Monitor-Plus.

A Brief History of Broadcasting and Cable

By Mark K. Miller, freelance writer and former managing editor, *Broadcasting & Cable* magazine

We could start our history of the electronic media in many places. We chose November 2, 1920. On that day, in Pittsburgh, Westinghouse Electric and Manufacturing Co.'s KDKA, generally acknowledged as the first licensed commercial radio station in the United States, broadcast the results of the Harding-Cox presidential elections. The broadcast demonstrated that radio was more than a novelty, that it could have real impact on our culture and our politics. The broadcast touched off a revolution that continues to this day. To give you a clear sense of the history, our history takes it decade by decade, assigning a theme to each.

1920s: Radio Begins Finding its Way

Although we begin with that KDKA broadcast in 1920, there had been a lot of radio activity prior to that. Inventors and hobbyists had been filling the airwaves with signals, often on a very haphazard basis, for years. And government experiments during World War I contributed much to the growing volume of radio knowledge.

On August 20, 1920, WWJ(AM) Detroit/Mowned by the Detroit News/Mbegan what it claimed to be the first regular broadcasting schedule when it inaugurated daily broadcasts.

In 1922 the superheterodyne circuit as a broadcast receiver is demonstrated by its inventor, Edwin H. Armstrong, and will prove to become the industry standard. By May, there are 80 licensed radio stations in the United States; by year's end the number has grown to 569.

The rest of the decade is filled with examples of radio's surging growth and the unfettered vision of inventors around the world. In 1923 Dr. Vladimir K. Zworykin files for a U.S. patent for an all-electronic television system.

Stations begin to link themselves into "chains" or networks via telephone lines and numerous experiments test the feasibility of transmitting short-wave signals across the oceans, from airplanes and ships.

The 1924 Republican convention in Cleveland and the Democratic convention in New York are broadcast over networks, and in 1925 President Calvin Coolidge's inaugural ceremony is broadcast by 24 stations in a transcontinental network. The government was taking notice of the burgeoning industry; in 1926 the Federal Radio Commission is created in response to the chaos caused by the explosive growth of broadcasting.

But it was the launch of the National Broadcasting Co. on November 15, 1926, that marked the beginning of the network system of broadcasting that exists to this day. NBC was a joint venture of radio equipment manufacturers RCA (30 percent), General Electric (50 percent), and Westinghouse (20 percent). The initial broadcast was carried by 25 stations ranging from the East Coast to St. Louis and Kansas City, Missouri, and was estimated to have been heard by almost half of the nation's five million homes equipped with radios. In 1928 NBC would establish a permanent coast-to-coast radio network.

NBC's entry was followed in 1927 by that of the Columbia Broadcasting System, which debuted with a basic network of 16 stations. Two years later, William S. Paley, 27, purchases a controlling interest and is elected president.

There is also continuing activity on the television front. In 1927 Philo T. Farnsworth applies for a patent on his image dissector television camera tube and in 1929 Russian inventor Vladimir Zworykin demonstrates his kinescope, or cathode ray television receiver, before a meeting of the Institute of Radio Engineers.

1930s: The Rise of Radio Entertainment

It was in the 1930s that the "American Plan" of advertising-supported radio flourished, making it extremely unlikely that proponents (and there were many) of the "European Plan" of a government-operated medium would prevail. The attractiveness of free, high-quality entertainment during the Great Depression resulted in larger and larger audiences for the networks, exactly what companies needed to advertise their products.

As listening skyrocketed (about 12 million U.S. homes had a radio in 1930, by 1940 the figure was 28.5 million and car radios were becoming standard equipment), so too did the fortunes of the major networks: NBC's Red and Blue, CBS and Mutual (plus numerous regional nets). With radio personalities such as Jack Benny, Charles Correll, and Freeman Gosden (Amos 'n' Andy), Eddie Cantor, Burns and Allen, and Major Bowes attracting larger and larger audiences, advertisers wanted more precise listening figures. So in 1936 A.C. Nielsen Co. proposed its Audimeter, which would be attached to a sampling of radio sets and measure audience size.

Work continued on television. By 1937 there were 17 experimental TV stations operating and President Franklin D. Roosevelt was seen on TV when he opened the 1939 New York World's Fair.

1940s: The Rise of Radio News

As Europe was engulfed in war and the United States appeared headed toward the conflict, Americans turned to their radios to stay informed. During 1940, the networks' typical weekly schedules contained 56 quarter hours during the day as opposed to only 33 in evening programming in 1939 and none during daytime hours. CBS had Edward R. Murrow in London and his team of correspondents across Europe, while NBC had Fred Bate, Max Jordan, William Kierker, and many others. When the United States was attacked by Japan on December 7, 1941, network news reporting preempted regular programming. And the audience for President Roosevelt's broadcast to the nation on December 9, the day after war was declared, attracted the largest audience to that time/Mabout 90 million. By the end of the week, all the networks and most stations were operating around the clock. For the first time, a war was heard by the people back home.

In addition to war reporting, coverage of domestic news was on the rise. With a tremendous amount of public interest in the 1944 presidential campaign, the networks canceled all commercial programs that would have interfered with their coverage of the Republican and Democratic conventions and used more than 300 reporters, technicians, and officials at each.

When the war ended and the era of the atomic bomb and the cold war began, the networks put their news departments to work on radio documentaries. CBS established a documentary unit that later resulted in a separate series, Ed Murrow and Fred Friendly's Hear It Now.

1950s: The Rise of Television Entertainment

While television had been in development since the 1920s and there had been experimental broadcasts since the 1930s, it wasn't until after World War II that the networks were able to concentrate on developing programming, manufacturers were able to return to making sets, and the public was able to afford them. (At the beginning of 1952 about 19 million U.S. homes had a TV set, and by the end of the decade that number was about 46.5 million.) The post-war economy was booming and the country's optimism was reflected in many of those early TV shows. Some of radio's stars made the transition to TV, as did many of the radio show formats. Soap operas (*The Guiding Light* on CBS), comedies (*Life of Riley* on NBC), westerns (*Gunsmoke* on CBS), dramas (*Kraft Television Theater* on NBC and ABC), variety (*Toast of the Town with Ed Sullivan* on CBS), and quiz shows (*Twenty One* on NBC) emerged as early favorites.

And the TV syndication business was born when Frederic W. Ziv began selling shows such as 1951's *Bold Venture* with Humphrey Bogart and Lauren Bacall to local and regional advertisers and stations.

At the beginning of the decade RCA and CBS were in a battle: the companies each wanted FCC approval of a system for color TV. RCA eventually prevailed in 1953 because programs broadcast in its "compatible color" could still be watched on existing black and white sets. Another innovation that was to change television programming dramatically was unveiled in 1956 when Ampex Corp. demonstrated its videotape recorder at the National Association of Radio and Television Broadcasters convention and received $4 million in orders.

1960s: The Rise of Television News

Television journalism came of age in the 1960s. As the decade began, the FCC suspended its equal-time requirement for presidential and vice presidential candidates (following the suggestion of CBS President Frank Stanton), paving the way for the four "Great Debates" between Vice President Richard Nixon and Senator John F. Kennedy. The first debate, broadcast from Chicago on September 26, was seen by 75 million viewers, a record at that time. It changed the course of political campaigning and, quite probably, the course of the election. In 1961, the newly elected President Kennedy, recognizing the influence of the medium, allowed television to cover his press conferences. In 1963 the networks expanded their evening newscasts from 15 minutes to a half-hour. The nation was stunned when President Kennedy was assassinated in November 1963 and it's been said that television news came of age with its coverage. For four days following, the networks suspended normal programming and commercials with NBC-TV on the air for more than 71 hours, CBS-TV for 55, and ABC-TV for 60. The network coverage cost an unprecedented $32 million and CBS research showed that 93 percent of U.S. homes watched coverage of JFK's burial and that the average set was in use for more than 13 consecutive hours.

Americans were transfixed by coverage of the space race, beginning with Alan Shepard's suborbital flight in 1961 and culminating in live pictures of the moon landing in 1969. Americans were also presented with almost nightly images not so uplifting, with coverage of the civil rights movement and the Vietnam war (the networks established news bureaus in Saigon in 1965) becoming almost nightly subjects. The decade ended on two disappointing notes for broadcasters. Shortly after the election of Richard Nixon in 1968, Vice President Spiro Agnew began a series of speeches attacking the media and accusing the press of bias against the administration. And in 1969 the Supreme Court's decision in the Red Lion case upheld the FCC's fairness doctrine and personal attack rules, saying they "enhance rather than abridge the freedoms of speech and press protected by the First Amendment."

1970s: The Rise of FM and Satellites

While the technique of broadcasting using frequency modulation was patented by Edwin Armstrong in 1933, the first station built in 1939, and an FM band allocated by the FCC in 1940, growth of the new radio service was very slow. Delayed by World War II and a suspicion by many AM station owners that the new service would offer unwanted competition, it wasn't until the late 1960s that large numbers of consumers began buying FM receivers. Another handicap was beginning to be resolved in 1971 when car manufacturers began to include FM-equipped radios as standard equipment in about 20 percent of the new models (that number would rise to 50 percent within five years).

To differentiate FM stations from those on the AM band/Mand to take advantage of FM's higher fidelity/Mprogrammers developed new formats. One

A Brief History of Broadcasting and Cable

of the most innovative was the "underground" or "progressive" sound introduced by Tom Donahue at KMPX(FM) San Francisco in the late 1960s that played album tracks not heard on the tightly formatted top 40 AM stations. But "underground" wasn't the only sound to be heard on FM or even the predominant one. There was also the very aboveground sound of carefully researched syndicated formats. Coupled with the increased use of automation equipment, services like Drake-Chenault's "Solid Gold" and Bonneville's easy listening formats turned many money-losing FM stations into profit centers. This success was translated into value as multimillion-dollar prices for FM stations became common. And for the first time industry observers began predicting that FM would overtake AM as the band for music, with AM becoming primarily a news and information medium.

The phenomenon of the 1970s was the development of international broadcasting live via satellites. RCA inaugurated the nation's first domestic satellite communications service in 1974, using a Canadian satellite, later launching its Satcom series of birds. But the breakthrough came in 1975 when Home Box Office/MTime Inc.'s pay cable subsidiary/Mannounced plans to extend its service from the Northeast to nationwide via satellite.

The next year, 1976, Ted Turner, owner of two TV stations, begins using the satellite to distribute the signal of his Atlanta UHF station, WTCG, to cable systems across the country, dubbing it the "superstation." Buoyed by his success, in 1978 Turner announced plans to sell his other station, WRET-TV Charlotte, North Carolina, and use the money to start CNN, a 24-hour cable news service to be distributed by satellite.

Later in 1978, the FCC moved to enhance the competitive environment of satellite-distributed TV superstations by endorsing an "open entry" policy for the resale carriers that wished to feed local stations to cable television systems. Then in April 1979, a former Nixon administration staffer and cable trade reporter, Brian Lamb, persuaded a critical mass of the cable industry to support the Cable Satellite Public Affairs Network (C-SPAN). The new service provided satellite gavel-to-gavel television coverage of the House of Representatives proceedings.

1980s: The Rise of Cable Television

Building on the innovation of satellite delivery pioneered by HBO, the cable industry began to be viewed as more than just a relay service for TV stations. Now it could offer alternative channels. (The strategy paid off in increased demand: in 1980 cable had 20 percent penetration of U.S. TV households and by the end of the decade it was seen in 60 percent.) Ted Turner launched his Cable News Network on June 1, 1980, sending 24-hour-a-day news to 172 cable systems from its Atlanta studios.

Innovations and new cable channels appeared in almost every year of the decade. Most pay cable channels begin to scramble their satellite signals and in 1998 AT&T demonstrates laser-modulated fiber optics offering wider bandwidth and greater signal quality than coaxial cable.

1990s: The Rise of Mega-Media Companies

The modern media era really began in 1989 with the announcement that Time Inc. and Warner Communications Inc. had agreed to swap stock and merge into what would be the largest media and entertainment company in the world. The media landscape would only continue to change, and at an accelerating pace. A deregulatory wind was blowing through Washington in the 1990s.

In 1992 the FCC raised the cap on the number of radio stations a company could own from 12 AM and 12 FM to 18 of each and also permitted two of each service to be co-located in the same large market. A flurry of duopoly deals followed. The next year, the commission gave the big three TV networks a conditional OK to enter the lucrative network rerun business, when it lifts its financial interest and syndication rules (full repeal comes in 1995).

The year 1994 sees the radio caps raised again, to 20 AM and 20 FM. The FCC also said that it was time to acknowledge the dramatic changes in the video marketplace with equally dramatic deregulation of its TV ownership policies. The commission proposed new rules that would allow broadcasters to own as many stations as they want as long as they remain within the cap on total national audience reach. At the same time, the commission proposed raising that cap of 25 percent of the nation's TV households by 5 percent every three years to a maximum of 50 percent.

In another mega-merger, Viacom buys Paramount Communications. This is quickly followed in 1995 by announcements of Disney's $18.5 billion purchase of ABC, Time Warner's purchase of Turner Broadcasting System in an $8 billion stock swap, Westinghouse's $5.4 billion purchase of CBS, and Comcast's $1.6 billion purchase of the Scripps cable holdings. The big four TV networks get more competition in 1995 as The WB and United Paramount Network debut.

More deregulation appears with the Telecommunications Act of 1996, which eliminated cable rate regulation and the bar to telephone company-cable competition, resulting in AT&T and other phone companies offering packages that included cable, telephone, and Internet services and cable companies offering phone service. (This resulted in AT&T becoming the country's largest cable operator in 1999 when it bought TCI for $50 billion.) The 1996 act also eliminated the cap on radio station ownership and companies wasted no time in expanding their portfolios both through acquisitions and mergers (including Westinghouse/CBS-Infinity, which merged in 1996 in a $4.9 billion deal).

In 1997, TV group owner Bud Paxson began the seventh broadcast TV network with his PAX TV. Radio deals continued to proliferate, with a huge upsurge in station sales in 1998 and the mega-merger of Clear Channel's $6.35 billion purchase of Jacor.

The decade ends in a flurry of activity in 1999 with the FCC allowing ownership of two TV and up to six radio stations in top markets. AT&T bought Media One, Viacom spent $36 billion for CBS and the two largest radio groups/MClear Channel and AMFM/Mcombined, leaving the merged Clear Channel owning 830 stations.

2000s: The Rise of Digital

Digital technology began to make a major impact. Cable used it to increase significantly the number of channels it offered/Mto justify higher monthly fees and to meet the competition from channel-rich satellite technology. In contrast to cable, TV broadcasting has been slow to put digital technology to work. With digital, TV broadcasters could offer multiple channels of conventional TV, HDTV, or a little bit of both. But digital TV broadcasting has been mired in standards disputes and the resulting chicken-and-egg problem of receivers and programming: consumers are slow to replace their analog sets if there is little digital programming to watch and producers are hesitant to invest in new production equipment if few viewers are watching. But the transition continues.

The first digital TV station, WRAL-DT Raleigh, North Carolina, went on the air in 1996 and the FCC made digital channel assignments to all analog stations in 1997. All TV stations must be broadcasting digitally by 2006. There were 1,508 digital stations in 211 markets as of August 30, 2005, according to the National Association of Broadcasters.

The first push for digital audio (other than that delivered by DBS or digital cable) is satellite-delivered radio. Two players/MXM Satellite Radio and Sirius Satellite Radio/Moffer nationwide subscription service to receivers in cars and homes. Terrestrial radio is just beginning to make the digital transition. In-band, on-channel (IBOC) technology developed by iBiquity Digital Corp. allows radio stations to overlay their analog service with a digital one. As of September 2005, 512 stations are on the air with HD technology developed by iBiquity Digital Corp. JVC, Kenwood, and Panasonic are among the companies offering consumer IBOC receivers.

A Chronology of the Electronic Media

From Isaac Newton to Janet Jackson: A Chronology of the Electronic Media

Mark K. Miller
freelance writer and former managing editor, *Broadcasting & Cable* magazine

1666
Sir Isaac Newton performs basic experiments on the spectrum.

1794
Allessandro Volta of Italy invents the voltaic cell, a primitive battery.

1827
George Ohm of Germany shows the relationship between resistance, amperage and voltage. Sir Charles Wheatstone of England invents an acoustic device to amplify sounds that he calls a "microphone."

1844
Samuel F.B. Morse tests the first telegraph with "What hath God wrought?" message sent on link between Washington and Baltimore.

1858
First trans-Atlantic cable completed. President James Buchanan and Queen Victoria exchange greetings.

1867
James Clerk Maxwell of Scotland develops the electromagnetic theory.

1875
George R. Carey of Boston proposes a system that would transmit and receive moving visual images electrically.

1876
Alexander Graham Bell invents the telephone.

1877
Thomas A. Edison applies for a patent on a "phonograph or talking machine."

1878
Sir William Cooke of England passes high voltage through a wire in a sealed glass tube, causing a pinkish glow—evidence of cathode rays. It's the first step toward the development of the vacuum tubes.

1884
Paul Nipkow of Germany patents a mechanical, rotating facsimile scanning disk.

1886
Heinrich Hertz of Germany proves that electromagnetic waves can be transmitted through space at the speed of light and can be reflected and refracted.

1895
Wilheim Conrad Roentgen of Germany discovers X-rays.

Guglielmo Marconi sends and receives his first wireless signals across his father's estate at Bologna, Italy.

1896
Marconi applies for British patent for wireless telegraphy. He receives an American patent a year later.

1899
Marconi flashes the first wireless signals across the English Channel.

1900
Constantin Perskyi (France) coins the word television at the International Electricity Congress, part of the 1900 Paris Exhibition.

1901
Marconi at Newfoundland, Canada, receives the first trans-Atlantic signal, the letter "S," transmitted from Poldhu, England.

1906
Dr. Lee de Forest invents the audion, a three-element vacuum tube, having a filament, plate and grid, which leads to the amplification of radio signals.

1910
Enrico Caruso and Emmy Destinn, singing backstage at the Metropolitan Opera House in New York, broadcast through the De Forest radiophone and are heard by an operator on the SS Avon at sea and by wireless amateurs in Connecticut.

United States approves an act requiring certain passenger ships to carry wireless equipment and operators.

1912
The *Titanic* disaster proves the value of wireless at sea; 705 lives saved. Jack Phillips and Harold Bride are the ship's wireless operators.

1920
On August 20, 8MK (later, WWJ) in Detroit, owned by the Detroit News, starts what is later claimed to be regular broadcasting.

The Westinghouse Co.'s KDKA(AM) Pittsburgh broadcasts the Harding-Cox election on returns November 2 as the country's first licensed commercial radio station.

1921
The Dempsey-Carpentier fight is broadcast from Boyle's Thirty Acres in Jersey City through a temporarily installed transmitter at Hoboken, New Jersey. Major J. Andrew White was the announcer. This event gave radio a tremendous boost.

1922
The superheterodyne circuit is demonstrated by its inventor, Edwin H. Armstrong. It dramatically improves AM radio reception.

WEAF(AM) New York broadcasts what is claimed to be the first commercially sponsored program on September 7. The advertiser is the Queensborough Corp., a real estate organization.

WOI(AM) Ames, Iowa, goes on air as the country's first licensed educational station.

1923
Dr. Vladimir K. Zworykin files for a U.S. patent for an all-electronic television system.

A "chain" broadcast features a telephone tie-up between WEAF(AM) New York and WNAC(AM) Boston.

1924
The Republican convention in Cleveland and the Democratic convention in New York are broadcast over networks.

1925
President Calvin Coolidge's inaugural ceremony is broadcast by 24 stations in a transcontinental network.

1926
President Coolidge signs the Dill-White Radio Bill creating the Federal Radio Commission and ending the chaos on the radio dial caused by the wild growth of broadcasting.

National Broadcasting Co. is organized on November 1 with WEAF(AM) and WJZ(AM) in New York as key stations and Merlin Hall Aylesworth as president. Headquarters are at 711 Fifth Ave., New York.

1927
The Columbia Broadcasting System goes on the air with a basic network of 16 stations. Major J. Andrew White is president.

Philo T. Farnsworth applies for a patent on his image dissector television camera tube.

1928
NBC establishes a permanent coast-to-coast radio network.

1929
William S. Paley, 27, is elected president of the Columbia Broadcasting System.

Vladimir Zworykin demonstrates his kinescope or cathode ray television receiver before a meeting of the Institute of Radio Engineers on November 19.

1930
Experimental TV station W2XBS is opened by National Broadcasting Co. in New York.

1931
Experimental television station W2XAB is opened by Columbia Broadcasting System in New York.

The first issue of *Broadcasting* magazine appears on October 15.

The National Association of Broadcasters reports that more than half of the nation's radio stations are operating without a profit.

1932
CBS, NBC, and New York area stations, notably WOR(AM), go into round-the-clock operations to cover the Lindbergh kidnapping, radio's biggest spot-news reporting job to date.

NBC lifts its ban on recorded programs for its owned-and-operated stations, but continues to bar them from network use.

NBC withdraws prohibitions against price mentions on the air during daytime hours; two months later, both NBC and CBS allow price mentions at nighttime as well.

1933
Associated Press members vote to ban network broadcasts of AP news and to restrict local broadcasts to bulletins to stipulated times with air credit to member newspapers.

The American Newspaper Publishers Association

A Chronology of the Electronic Media

declares radio program schedules are advertising and should be published only if paid for.

CBS assigns publicity director Paul White to organize a nationwide staff to collect news for network broadcast. General Mills agrees to sponsor twice-daily newscasts.

1934
Congress passes the Communication Act, which, among other things, replaces the Federal Radio Commission with the Federal Communications Commission.

1935
RCA announces that it is taking television out of the laboratory for a $1 million field-test program.

1936
A year of TV demonstrations begins in June with the Don Lee Broadcasting System's first public exhibition of cathode ray television in the U.S., using a system developed by Don Lee TV director Harry Lubcke. One month later, RCA demonstrates its system of TV with transmissions from the Empire State Building, and Philco follows with a seven-mile transmission in August.

FM (frequency modulation) broadcasting, a new radio system invented by Major Edwin H. Armstrong, is described at an FCC hearing as static-free, free from fading and cross-talk, having uniformity day and night in all seasons and greater fidelity of reproduction.

A.C. Nielsen, revealing his firm's acquisition of the MIT-developed "Audimeter," proposes a metered tuning method of measuring radio audience size.

1937
WLS(AM) Chicago recording team of Herb Morrison, announcer, and Charles Nehlsen, engineer, on a routine assignment at Lakehurst, New Jersey, records an on-the-spot account of the explosion of the German dirigible Hindenburg. NBC breaks its rigid rule against recordings to put it on the network.

1938
Broadcasting publishes the first facsimile newspaper in a demonstration at the National Association of Broadcasters convention.

1939
After 15 years of litigation, the patent for iconoscope-kinescope tubes, the basis for electronic television, is granted to Dr. Vladimir Zworykin.

A telecast of the opening ceremonies of the New York World's Fair marks the start of a regular daily television schedule by RCA-NBC in New York.

The first baseball game ever televised—Princeton vs. Columbia—appears on NBC.

1940
The FCC authorizes commercial operation of FM, but puts TV back into the laboratory until the industry reaches an agreement on technical standards.

CBS demonstrates a system of color TV developed by its chief TV engineer, Dr. Peter Goldmark.

1941
Bulova Watch Co., Sun Oil Co., Lever Bros. and Procter & Gamble sign as sponsors of the first commercial telecasts on July 1 over NBC's WNBT(TV) New York (until then W2XBS).

President Roosevelt's broadcast to the nation on December 9, the day after war is declared, has the largest audience in radio history—about 90 million listeners.

1942
The Advertising Council is organized by advertisers, agencies, and media to put the talents and techniques of advertising at the disposal of the government to inspire and instruct the public concerning the war effort.

1943
Edward J. Noble buys the Blue Network from RCA for $8 million in cash. RCA had two networks, NBC Red and NBC Blue.

1944
With the FCC approval of the transfer of owned stations, the Blue Network assumes the name of its holding company, the American Broadcasting Co.

1945
Pooled coverage of the Nazi surrender in May brings the American people full details of the end of the war in Europe. Peace heralds a communications boom: Not only will programming restrictions end, but new station construction, frozen for the duration, will proceed at an explosive pace soon after V-J Day in August.

1946
A telecast of the Louis-Conn heavyweight title fight, sponsored by Gillette Safety Razor Co. on a four-city hookup, reaches an estimated 100,000 viewers and convinces skeptics that television is here to stay.

RCA demonstrates its all-electronic system of color TV.

Bristol-Myers is the first advertiser to sponsor a television network program—Geographically Speaking—which debuted October 27 on NBC TV's two-station network.

1947
Radio comedian Fred Allen uses a gag, which NBC had ruled out, about network vice presidents, and is cut off the air while he tells it. The story is front-page news across the country as the sponsor's ad agency demands a rebate for 35 seconds of dead air.

1948
Texaco puts an old-style vaudeville show on NBC TV; the hour-long series stars Milton Berle.

1949
The Academy of Television Arts & Sciences presents the first Emmy Awards at ceremonies televised by KTSL(TV) Los Angeles.

1950
General Foods drops actress Jean Muir, who denies any communist affiliations or sympathies, from the cast of The Aldrich Family (NBC TV) after protests against her appearance by "a number of groups." The Joint Committee Against Communism claims credit for her removal, announcing a drive to "cleanse" radio and television of pro-communist actors, directors, and writers.

The FCC approves CBS's color TV system, effective November 20. The network promises 20 hours of color programming a week within two months. TV set manufacturers are divided, however, over whether to make sets, since the CBS system is incompatible with black-and-white broadcasts. In the meantime, RCA continues work on its color system.

1951
Witness Frank Costello's hands provide TV's picture of the week as he refuses to expose his face to cameras covering New York hearings on organized crime of the Senate Crime Investigation Committee, chaired by Senator Estes Kefauver (D-Tenn.)

Sixteen advertisers sponsor the first commercial color telecast, an hour-long program on a five-station East Coast CBS TV hook-up.

Bing Crosby Enterprises announces the development of a system for recording video and audio programs on magnetic tape. The pictures shown at demonstrations are described as "hazy" but "viewable." A year later the images are described as improved "more than 20-fold."

1952
By rushing equipment across the country, from Bridgeport, Connecticut, to Portland, Oregon, KPTV(TV) Portland goes on the air as the first commercial UHF TV station.

1953
With the end of daylight-saving time, CBS TV and NBC TV inaugurate "hot kinescope" systems to put programs on the air on the West Coast at the same clock hour as in the East.

RCA demonstrates black-and-white and color TV programs recorded on magnetic tape. RCA-NBC Board Chairman David Sarnoff says two years of finishing touches are needed before the system is ready for market.

The FCC approves RCA's compatible (with black-and-white transmission) color TV standards. System supplants the incompatible CBS system.

1954
CBS President Frank Stanton broadcasts the first network editorial, urging that radio and TV be allowed to cover congressional hearings.

1955
A contract between the DuMont TV network and Jackie Gleason Enterprises calls for Gleason's The Honeymooners to be done as a filmed program for CBS TV on Saturday nights.

1956
Ampex Corp. unveils the first practical videotape recorder at the National Association of Radio and Television Broadcasters convention in Chicago. The company takes in $4 million in orders.

1957
Videotape recorders are seen as the solution to the TV networks' daylight-saving time problems.

1958
Subliminal TV messages are put under the spotlight at hearings in Los Angeles and Washington.

The BBDO ad agency converts live commercials to videotape.

1959
Sixty-eight TV stations defy the broadcasters' code of conduct by refusing to drop Preparation H commercials.

The quiz show scandal climaxes when famed Twenty-One prizewinner Charles Van Doren admits to a House committee that he had been provided with answers and strategies in advance. The sad ending to the quiz show era prompts cancellation of big-prize shows and vows by NBC and CBS to end deceptive practices.

1960
A satellite sends weather reports back from a 400-mile-high orbit.

RKO-Zenith plans a $10 million test of an on-air pay TV system in Hartford, Connecticut.

Sam Goldwyn offers a package of movies to television.

The last daytime serial on network radio ends.

The opening Kennedy-Nixon debate attracts the largest TV audience to date.

1961
FCC Chairman Newton Minnow shakes up the National Association of Broadcasters convention with his assessment of TV programming: Although it occasionally shines with programs like Twilight Zone and CBS Reports, it is, more than anything, from sign-on to sign-off "a vast wasteland."

Off-network shows become popular as syndicated fare.

The Ampex "electronic editor" permits inserts and additions to be made in videotape without physical splices.

ABC TV engineers develop a process for the immediate playback of videotape recordings in slow motion.

1962
John Glenn's orbital space flight is seen by 135 million TV viewers.

Telstar, AT&T's orbiting satellite, provides a glamorous debut for global television.

1963
Astronaut Gordon Cooper sends back the first TV pictures from space.

Broadcasting & Cable Yearbook 2006

A Chronology of the Electronic Media

All radio and TV network commercials and entertainment programming are canceled following the assassination of President Kennedy. In the same week, the first trans-Pacific broadcast via satellite previews live TV coverage of the 1964 Olympics in Tokyo.

1964

The government and the tobacco companies each ponder their next move after the surgeon general's report links cigarette smoking and lung cancer. Within weeks, American Tobacco drops sports broadcasts, radio stations begin to ban cigarette ads and CBS TV orders a de-emphasis of cigarette use on programs.

1965

Early Bird, the first commercial communications satellite, goes into stationary orbit, opening trans-Atlantic circuits for TV use.

1966

Fred W. Friendly quits as president of CBS News when his new boss, John Schneider, CBS group vice president for broadcasting, cancels coverage of a Senate hearing on the Vietnam War and runs a rerun of *I Love Lucy* instead.

Network TV viewers see live close-up pictures of the moon—sent back by Surveyor I—as they come into the Jet Propulsion Laboratory.

1967

ABC Radio introduces a radical plan: four networks instead of one, each tailored to suit different station formats.

President Johnson signs the Public Broadcasting Act into law, establishing the Corporation for Public Broadcasting, federal funding mechanism.

1968

The Children's Television Workshop is created by the Ford Foundation, the Carnegie Corp., and the Office of Education to develop a 26-week series of hour-long color programs for preschool children. *Sesame Street* is the result.

The U.S. Supreme Court gives the FCC jurisdiction over all cable TV systems.

Pictures taken inside Apollo 7 in flight and sent back to Earth revive public interest in the space program.

NBC TV earns the life-long ire of sports fans when it cuts off the end of a Jets-Raiders game to air its made-for-TV movie *Heidi*. Viewers miss the Raiders' two-touchdowns-in-nine-seconds defeat of the Jets.

1969

The Corporation for Public Broadcasting plans the creation of the Public Broadcasting Service to distribute programming to noncommercial TV stations.

In the same week that ABC-TV announces its $8 million *Monday Night Football* deal (games to begin in 1970), Apollo 10 sends back the first color TV pictures of the moon and of Earth from the moon.

The world watches live coverage of Neil Armstrong's walk on the moon.

1970

House and Senate conferees agree on legislation to outlaw cigarette advertising on radio and TV, but change the bill's effective date from January 1, 1971, to January 2, so commercials can appear on New Year's Day football telecasts.

The FCC rules that TV stations in the top 50 markets cannot accept more than three hours of network programming between 7 and 11 p.m., and bars them from domestic syndication and from acquiring subsidiary rights in independently produced programs.

1971

National Public Radio debuts with a 90-station interconnected lineup.

1972

Judge Benjamin Hooks of Memphis, Tennessee, is nominated to the FCC. He becomes the first black to serve on a federal regulatory agency.

Home Box Office Inc., New York, is formed as a subsidiary of Sterling Communications to provide pay-cable TV systems with live and film programming.

1973

Western Union becomes the first company to receive federal permission to launch a commercial communications satellite in the U.S.

Broadcast media around the world open their coverage of the Senate select committee's investigation of the Watergate scandal.

1974

RCA inaugurates the nation's first domestic satellite communications service, using a Canadian satellite.

More than 110 million viewers watch President Nixon announce his resignation.

1975

Home Box Office, Time Inc.'s pay cable subsidiary, announces that it will inaugurate a satellite delivery network in the fall.

1976

Ampex Corp. and CBS develop the electronic still-store system, which uses a digital recording technique to store 1,500 frames in random mode, each accessible in 100 milliseconds.

Cable network launches include Showtime and Univision.

1977

ABC's eight-day telecast of the miniseries *Roots* becomes the most watched program in television history, with ratings in the mid-40s and shares in the mid-60s. Eighty million people watch at least some part of the final episode.

Sony unveils its Betamax videocassette in August and later the same month RCA introduces its SelectaVision home videotape recorder.

1978

The U.S. Supreme Court upholds the FCC in the "seven dirty words" case involving Pacifica's WBAI(FM) New York. The ruling says the FCC may regulate and punish for the broadcasting of "indecent material."

1979

Ampex demonstrates its digital videotape recorder at the Society of Motion Picture and Television Engineers conference in San Francisco in February. Sony unveils its version two months later.

Cable network launches include C-SPAN, ESPN, The Movie Channel, and Nickelodeon.

1980

"Who Shot J.R.?" episode of *Dallas* garners the highest rating for any program in modern TV history, with a 53.3 rating and a 76 share.

Cable network launches include Cable News Network, Black Entertainment Television, the Learning Channel, Bravo, and USA Network.

1981

With five ENG cameras rolling, the shooting of President Reagan becomes history's most heavily covered assassination attempt.

The first U.S. demonstration of high-definition television (HDTV) takes place at the annual convention of the Society of Motion Picture and Television Engineers. The Japanese Broadcasting Corp.'s (NHK) 1,125-line analog system draws raves from engineers and filmmakers.

Cable network launches include MTV: Music Television and the Eternal Word Television Network.

1982

Having reached a settlement with the Justice Department to divest itself of its 23 local telephone companies, communications giant AT&T hopes to lead the country into the "information age." The National Cable Television Association, Congress, and the FCC wonder what the agreement has wrought.

Cable network launches include the Weather Channel and the Playboy Channel.

1983

Reagan appointee Mark Fowler, chairman of the FCC, tells a common carrier conference that the U.S. is heading toward a regulation-free telecommunications marketplace.

In February, the two-and-a-half-hour final episode of CBS's *M*A*S*H* is the most watched program in TV history, garnering a 60.3 rating and a 77 share.

Cable network launches include the Disney Channel and Country Music Television.

1984

The U.S. Supreme Court rules that home videotaping is legal.

Congress passes the Cable Telecommunications Act of 1984, landmark legislation deregulating cable. Law accelerates the growth of cable.

Cable network launches include the Arts & Entertainment Network (A&E), American Movie Classics, and Lifetime.

1985

Ted Turner makes inquiries at the FCC about a possible takeover of CBS. Later, in March, media company Capital Cities Communications purchases ABC for $3.5 billion. Turner's efforts to acquire CBS fail by the end of July, when a federal judge approves the network's stock buyback plan.

The Advanced Television Services Committee (ATSC) votes in favor of the NHK HDTV standard: 1,125 lines, 60 fields, 2:1 interlace, 5.33:3 ratio. This standard is put forward by the U.S. to the International Radio Consultative Committee (CCIR) for consideration as the international standard. The CCIR adopts the recommendation later in the year.

Having lost his bid to buy CBS, Ted Turner makes a $1.5 billion offer for MGM/UA.

Cable network launches include The Discovery Channel, Home Shopping Network, and VH-1.

1986

MGM and Color Systems Technology sign an agreement for the conversion of 100 of the studio's black-and-white films to color.

Cable network launches include C-SPAN2 and QVC.

1987

Fox Broadcasting Co. introduces its primetime lineup with 108 affiliates in its bid to become the fourth major U.S. commercial television network.

The National Association of Broadcasters and the Association for Maximum Service Television broadcast HDTV over standard TV channels during public demonstrations in Washington.

President Reagan vetoes legislation to write the fairness doctrine into law. The doctrine required broadcast stations to allow opposing views of issues, but critics claimed that it discouraged open debate.

Cable network launches include Movietime (renamed E! Entertainment Television in 1990), The Travel Channel, and Telemundo.

1988

The FCC adopts preliminary ground rules for HDTV. It tentatively decides to require HDTV broadcasts to be compatible with NTSC sets and says it will not make additional spectrum available outside the VHF and UHF bands for HDTV because there is enough already available to accommodate the service.

Cable network launches include Turner Network Television.

1989

Time Inc. and Warner Communications agree to swap stock and merge into what will be world's largest media and entertainment company.

Broadcasting & Cable Yearbook 2006

A Chronology of the Electronic Media

1990

Digital audio broadcasting is demonstrated at the National Association of Broadcasters convention and is heralded as the HDTV of radio.

General Instrument revolutionizes the development of high-definition television by proposing an all-digital system. The video compression system also has implications for satellite transmissions.

Cable network launches include CNBC and The Inspiration Network (INSP).

1991

The U.S. air attack on Iraq begins January 16 with dramatic live coverage from network reporters in Baghdad. CNN is the lone network to maintain contact with its Baghdad reporters through the night.

Free to move around Moscow and ready to commit resources to coverage, television and radio provide gripping details of the short-lived Soviet coup and the collapse of communism in the Soviet Union. During his detention in the Crimea, Soviet President Mikhail Gorbachev keeps track of events by listening to the BBC, Voice of America, and Radio Liberty.

Cable network launches include Court TV, Comedy Central, and Encore.

1992

In March, the Supreme Court let stand an appeals court ruling that struck down the FCC's around-the-clock ban on broadcast indecency as unconstitutional and requiring the commission to establish a safe harbor—a part of the day when few children are tuning in and during which radio and TV stations may broadcast without fear of FCC sanctions for indecency.

General Instrument and MIT show the first over-the-air digital HDTV transmission to Washington lawmakers and regulators. The 12-minute transmission of 1,050-line video was broadcast by noncommercial WETA-TV Washington.

The FCC raises the limit on radio stations a single company may own from 12 AM and 12 FM to 30 of each, then backpedals and lowers the caps to 18 each, with no more than two AMs and two FMs in large markets and three stations—only two in the same service—in small markets.

Fox expands its programming lineup to seven nights a week, ending its status as a "weblet" and becoming the fourth full-fledged commercial TV network in the U.S.

The FCC unanimously approves allowing broadcast TV networks to purchase cable systems that serve no more than 10 percent of U.S. homes and up to 50 percent of a particular market's homes.

The FCC tells TV broadcasters they will have five years to begin broadcasting in HDTV once the agency adopts a standard and makes channels available.

Cable network launches include The Cartoon Network and the Sci Fi Channel.

1993

Warner Bros. announces it will launch a fifth broadcast TV network in 1994.

The FCC expands the AM band's upper limit from 1605 kHz to 1705 kHz.

General Instrument, Zenith, AT&T, and the ATRC join forces as the "Grand Alliance" to develop a single HDTV system. Later in the year, the Grand Alliance announces its support of the emerging MPEG-2 digital compression HD system: six-channel, CD-quality Dolby AC-3 music system; 1,920-pixel by 1,080-line interlaced scanning picture; and progressive scanning.

Paramount Communications begins talks with TV stations about forming a fifth broadcast TV network.

Southwestern Bell and Cox Cable form a $4.9-billion partnership.

Cable network launches include ESPN2 and the Television Food Network.

1994

Two companies, Hubbard's United States Satellite Broadcasting and Hughes's DirecTV, begin direct broadcast satellite transmissions to 18-inch home dish antennas from a shared satellite.

Paramount and Viacom merge in a deal worth $9.2 billion, forming the world's most powerful entertainment company. Viacom's Sumner Redstone becomes the new company's chairman. Later in the year, Viacom adds Blockbuster Entertainment to its portfolio.

Cable network launches include FX, Home & Garden TV, the International Film Channel, Starz!, Trio, the Game Show Network, and Turner Classic Movies.

1995

Seagram pays $7 billion for the 80 percent of Hollywood studio MCA Inc. owned by Matsushita Electric Industrial Co. Seagram is controlled by the Bronfman family and is headed by President/CEO Edgar Bronfman Jr.

The Megamedia Age begins when, in the same week, Walt Disney Co. announces it is buying Capital Cities/ABC for $18.5 billion and then Westinghouse Electric Co. releases word of its purchase of CBS Inc. for $5.4 billion.

Time Warner and Turner Broadcasting System agree to merge in an $8 billion stock swap deal.

Live television coverage of the verdict in the O.J. Simpson murder trial sets viewing records when 150 million people watch the jury return a "not guilty" verdict.

Microsoft buys 50 percent stake in NBC's cable channel *America's Talking* for $250 million. AT's talk format will be dropped and the network will become a news operation after being rechristened MSNBC.

The FCC repeals its Prime Time Access and Fin-Syn rules. These rules restricted the major broadcast networks from owning interest in their own primetime programming.

Cable network launches include CNN/fn, The Golf Channel, Great American Country, the History Channel, and the Outdoor Life Network.

1996

Congress passes—and President Clinton signs—the Telecommunications Act of 1996, the first major overhaul of telecommunication legislation since 1934. Its key provisions include: replacing the 12-station TV ownership limit with a national home coverage cap of 35 percent; eliminating the national ownership limits on radio stations and allowing one company to own different numbers of stations locally, depending on the market size; requiring TV sets sold in the U.S. to be equipped with a V-chip to enable blocking of channels based on encoded ratings; deregulating cable rates.

Westinghouse/CBS buys Infinity Broadcasting for $4.9 billion, creating the country's largest radio station group in terms of earnings. The deal results in Westinghouse/CBS owning 83 radio stations in 15 markets.

The FCC releases its first list of proposed digital TV channel assignments for all U.S. analog television stations.

In July, WRAL-HD Raleigh, North Carolina, begins HDTV transmission on channel 32 under an experimental FCC license, making it the first HDTV station to broadcast in the U.S.

The Washington-based Model HDTV Station Project demonstrates live, over-the-air digital TV transmission and reception. A few months later, it bounces digital signals off a satellite and displays them on a receiver.

Cable network launches include Animal Planet, Fox News Channel, MSNBC, the Sundance Channel, and TVLand.

1997

After several starts and stops, the TV industry unveils content-based V-chip ratings to mixed reviews. Recalcitrant NBC maintains it will not implement the new ratings.

Paxson Communications chief Bud Paxson announces plans to launch a new television network, Pax Net, using his 73 owned UHF stations as a base and airing family friendly off-network programming.

ABC Television Network President Preston Padden and Sinclair Broadcasting President David Smith say broadcasters ought to consider using DTV channels for broadcasting multiple channels of conventional TV rather than a single channel of HDTV.

Hearst Corp. (8 TVs) and Argyle Television (6 TVs) join their TV stations and create a new company, Hearst-Argyle Television Inc., that is valued at $1.8 billion.

The FCC gives TV broadcasters a second channel for the delivery of HDTV and other digital services and said that all network affiliates in the top 10 markets have 24 months to start broadcasting a digital signal; those in markets 11-30 have 30 months; all other commercial stations have five years. Noncommercial broadcasters have six.

DTV service provider EchoStar plans to launch two satellites that will give it the ability to provide local broadcast TV signals to about 43 percent of the U.S.

Cable network launches include WE.

1998

The National Association of Broadcasters agrees to support plans by satellite TV providers to retransmit local TV station signals into their markets as long as the satellite services carry all a market's signals.

At 2:17 p.m. on February 27, WFAA-TV Dallas broadcast what it claims is the first non-experimental HDTV signal (in 1080i, 16:9 format). The broadcast began with a half-hour of taped HD programming, followed by a live simulcast of the station's NTSC programming that was upconverted to HDTV. The next month, Sinclair Broadcasting becomes the first TV group owner to broadcast multiple digital channels.

AT&T pays $50 billion for cable system giant Tele-Communications Inc.

Paxson Communications launches its broadcast television network, now called Pax TV, with a lineup of 90 stations covering about 75 percent of U.S. TV homes.

Radio group owner Clear Channel Communications purchases competitor Jacor Communications for $4.4 billion. The deal gives Clear Channel 453 stations in 101 markets. The year's other big deals include: Chancellor Media's purchase of Capstar Broadcasting for $3.9 billion; Hearst-Argyle Television's purchase of Pulitzer Broadcasting for $1.85 billion; Chancellor's purchase of LIN Television for $1.5 billion; and Sinclair Broadcast Group's purchase of Sullivan Broadcasting for $1 billion.

CBS is the first broadcast TV network to air a live HDTV sports event with its Nov. 8 telecast of the New York Jets-Buffalo Bills NFL game. It is carried by CBS stations in New York; Philadelphia; Washington; Cincinnati; Charlotte, North Carolina; Raleigh, North Carolina; and Columbus, Ohio.

Hughes Electronics Corp., parent of DBS provider DirecTV, announces deal to buy rival U.S. Satellite Broadcasting from Hubbard Broadcasting for $1.3 billion. The DBS business now has three providers: DirecTV, EchoStar, and Primestar.

Cable network launches include BBC America, the Biography Channel, Cinemax, Tech TV, and Toon Disney.

1999

Hughes Electronics Corp., parent of DBS provider DirecTV, buys rival Primestar for $1.1 billion plus stock. The DBS business now has two providers: DirecTV and EchoStar.

Paxson Broadcasting sells its 30 percent interest in The Travel Channel to the cable channel's 70 percent owner, Discovery Channel.

MSO Comcast offers $58 billion for MediaOne Group's cable systems. AT&T then comes in with a $69 billion offer that has AT&T swapping and selling Comcast systems with 2 million subscribers for roughly $9 billion. In return, Comcast agrees to withdraw its $58 billion offer.

CBS pays $2.5 billion for syndication giant King World Productions, whose properties include the hit shows *Oprah, Wheel of Fortune,* and *Jeopardy!*

FCC votes to allow a broadcaster to own two TV stations in a market under certain conditions and liberalizes its radio/TV cross-ownership restrictions. A flood of station deals follow.

Viacom Inc. buys CBS Corp. for $36 billion, merging Viacom's Paramount Station Group, UPN network, cable networks, and other properties, with those of CBS.

Clear Channel Communications pays $23.5 billion in stock and assumption of debt for the 443 radio stations of AMFM Inc., the country's largest radio broadcaster. Clear Channel will have to divest about 100 stations to comply with FCC and Justice Department regulations. Those spinoffs will bring Clear Channel $4.3 billion.

Legislation takes affect allowing satellite delivery of local television stations in their markets, increasing DBS providers' ability to compete with cable.

A Chronology of the Electronic Media

2000

America Online Inc. and Time Warner merge in a deal worth $181 billion. The merged company, AOL Time Warner, combines the company that serves the largest number of Internet users with the largest producer of TV shows and movies and cable programming, plus cable systems passing 20 percent of U.S. homes.

Tribune Co. buys Times Mirror Co. for $6.5 billion, acquiring seven daily newspapers and various magazines. The deal will give Tribune co-ownership of TV stations and major daily newspapers in the top three markets and the assets to sell packages of multimedia advertising to clients on national, regional, and local levels.

Harry Pappas, head of Pappas Television, the country's largest privately held TV station group, announces plans to launch Azteca America, the third U.S. Hispanic television network (Univision and Telemundo are the others) in 2001.

Cable network launches include Oxygen.

2001

FCC approves the $5.4-billion sale of Chris-Craft Broadcasting's ten TV stations to Fox Television.

DBS operator EchoStar Communications engineers a $26-billion bid for competitor DirecTV, owned by GM's Hughes Corp. The move follows attempts by Rupert Murdoch's News Corp. to acquire DirecTV. But regulatory reviews keep the deal in limbo.

XM Satellite Radio begins broadcasting a nationwide radio service of 200 channels from two satellites—"Rock" and "Roll"—in orbit above the equator. The Washington-based company charges subscribers $9.95 a month for the service. A rival, New York-based Sirius Satellite Radio, plans to launch a similar service later in the year.

The September 11 terrorist attacks on New York and Washington result in around-the-clock news coverage, dropping commercials. It's estimated that the networks lost $200 million-$300 million in the first four days of coverage. Four FM and nine New York TV stations whose antennas were on top of the World Trade Center are knocked off the air and several stations lost employees who had been manning the transmitters in Tower 1. Across the country, broadcasters raised money and arranged blood drives. The fall TV season is delayed, late-night talk/comedy shows are put on hiatus, the Emmy Awards are postponed, and several industry gatherings are canceled.

NBC buys Telemundo, the No. 2 U.S. Spanish-language TV network, for $2.7 billion.

Comcast negotiates $72 billion merger with rival cable operator AT&T Broadband, topping bids by AOL Time Warner and Cox Communications.

Cable network launches include ABC Family, Hallmark Channel, and National Geographic Television.

2002

Sirius Satellite Radio launches its satellite-delivered subscription radio service in four markets in February, then rolls out nationally in July. Sirius follows XM Satellite Radio to become the second U.S. satellite radio programmer.

Prompted by lawsuits from Fox, Viacom, NBC, and Time Warner, a three-judge panel of the federal appeals court in Washington refuses to uphold an FCC rule limiting a TV station group owner's audience reach to 35 percent of U.S. TV households and strikes down a rule barring a cable system from owning TV stations in its market. The court orders the FCC to rewrite or justify the ownership limit rule.

Tom Brokaw of NBC News announces he will step down as evening news anchor after the 2004 presidential election, to be succeeded by NBC's Brian Williams. Brokaw will then focus on in-depth reporting projects.

The Securities and Exchange Commission begins a formal investigation into the accounting practices of cable MSO Adelphia Communications. Five of Adelphia's top executives—including founder John Rigas and his two sons, Michael and Tim—are arrested on fraud charges, alleging that the family used the company as a "personal piggy bank," financing various personal transactions, including $3.1 billion in loans for stock and family businesses.

The FCC mandates that all TV sets must be equipped with digital tuners by 2007 and proposes strong copy-protection measures intended to prevent widespread copying and streaming of content over the Internet.

Lifestyle diva Martha Stewart, whose media empire included TV, magazines, and books, is investigated by the Justice Department for allegedly lying to federal authorities looking into insider trading involving Stewart's sale of ImClone Systems stock the day before it became public that the Food and Drug Administration had denied the company's application to market a new cancer drug.

In October, both the FCC and the Department of Justice reject DBS operator EchoStar Communications' proposed $26-billion purchase of competitor DirecTV, and a revised agreement fails to sway either agency. In December, EchoStar withdrew its merger request from the FCC. Rupert Murdoch's News Corp., whose previous bid for DirecTV had been rebuffed, puts together a new deal.

2003

Rupert Murdoch's News Corp. receives FCC and Justice Department approval of its deal to acquire 34 percent of DBS operator DirecTV's parent company Hughes Electronics for $6.6 billion in cash and stock.

New York City's Metropolitan Television Alliance agrees to place a new broadcast tower for New York-area television stations on top of the Freedom Tower, a 1,776-foot office tower that will be built on the site of the World Trade Center, where the stations' towers were located prior to 9/11. The MTVA comprises all the city's major TV broadcasters. After the terrorist attacks, most of the stations operated from backup facilities atop the Empire State Building. Ground is expected to be broken on the Freedom Tower in the summer of 2004, and broadcasters should begin operating from the tower by 2008.

The FCC releases new media ownership rules in response to a federal appeals court ruling in 2002. Among the changes: raising the national coverage cap for TV groups from 35 percent to 45 percent; allowing ownership of two TV stations (duopoly) in markets with five or more commercial stations; allowing ownership of three TV stations (triopoly) in markets with at least 18 stations; newspaper-TV cross-ownership is permitted in markets with at least four TV stations; radio-TV cross-ownership now include newspapers in the formula—owners in markets with nine or more TV stations face no cross-ownership restrictions per se but are limited by individual radio and TV limits applicable to specific markets. TV-duopoly owners would not be permitted to own newspapers in markets with fewer than nine TV stations. In markets with three or fewer TV stations, no cross-ownership of TV, radio, or newspapers is permitted. In markets with four to eight TV stations, an owner may form one of the following combos: (1) A daily newspaper, one TV station, up to one-half the number of radio stations permitted to one owner in that market. (2) A daily newspaper, the total number of radio stations permitted to one owner there, no TV stations. (3) Two TV stations and the total number of radio stations permitted there. Congress quickly reacts with legislation introduced by Rep. John Dingell (D-Mich.), which would restore the 35 percent cap. Other critics of the new rules challenge them in federal court.

Liberty Media pays $7.9 billion for Comcast's 56 percent stake in home shopping giant QVC. With 2002 sales of $4.4 billion, QVC is not just the largest shopping network, it's the second-largest television network of any kind.

A panel of federal appeals court judges in Philadelphia agrees with public advocacy groups and imposes a stay of the FCC's new broadcast-ownership rules scheduled to take effect on September 4. The stay will remain in effect until lawsuits to overturn the new rules are settled. The Philadelphia court then decides to retain the case attacking the new FCC broadcast-ownership limits rather than granting broadcast networks' pleas to transfer it to a court in Washington.

The Bush White House brokered a surprise compromise over media deregulation by agreeing to permanently set the national TV station ownership cap at 39 percent of U.S. television households. That percentage allows Fox and Viacom to retain all their stations. Wielding a threat to veto a catch-all spending bill over a provision that would roll the limit back to 35 percent, aides to President Bush persuaded Senate Appropriations Committee Chairman Ted Stevens (R-Alaska) to back down from the tighter limit. Stevens's action came less than a week after he had persuaded reluctant House leadership to go along with the old level. The compromise splits the difference between the 45 percent limit set by the FCC in June and the previous 35 percent level that rank-and-file lawmakers on both sides of Capitol Hill had been pushing to reinstate. The agreement is part of a spending bill that funds the FCC and many other agencies in fiscal 2004.

After a 36-year run, the California Cable Telecommunications Association's annual Western Cable Show makes its curtain call in December, citing consolidation in the cable industry and economic pressure.

Cable network launches include Spike TV.

2004

NBC gets Federal Trade Commission approval for its $14 billion purchase of Vivendi Universal Entertainment, its last regulatory hurdle. The FCC was not required to review the deal because it involved no station licenses. Among other things, NBC acquires USA Network and the Sci Fi Network. The new entity will be called NBC Universal.

Congress and the FCC react swiftly to the "wardrobe malfunction" that bared Janet Jackson's breast during the MTV-produced half-time entertainment in CBS TV's Super Bowl broadcast. Congress passes legislation that dramatically increases the limits on FCC fines for indecency violations.

Congress and the FCC take the first steps toward punishing stations that air "excessively" violent shows. Under orders from leaders of the House Commerce Committee, FCC Chairman Michael Powell by the end of the year will start investigating whether the commission should restrict onscreen violence. Cable can't count on immunity either. Growing ranks of lawmakers say cable must do more to make sure that children aren't exposed to potentially traumatizing content.

A panel of federal appeals court judges in Philadelphia concludes that the FCC wasn't justified in its June 2003 decision relaxing ownership restrictions in the newspaper, television, and radio industries. The rules, which were blocked from taking effect in September 2003, have been sent back to the FCC for a rewrite. A frustrated FCC Chairman Michael Powell criticized the decision, claiming that it created a "clouded and confused state of media law" and makes it nearly impossible for his agency to design standards for ownership limits.

Cable network launches include TV One.

The FCC and the Rules of Broadcasting

The following is the FCC's own overview of the laws and regulations that govern TV and radio stations. It is edited and printed here with the permission of the FCC. The agency invites those with questions about its rules and how it operates to visit its web site (www.fcc.gov) or to call 1-888-CALLFCC (1-888-225-5322).

THE FCC AND ITS REGULATORY AUTHORITY

The Communications Act

The FCC was created by Congress in the Communications Act of 1934 for the purpose, in part, of "regulating interstate and foreign commerce in communication by wire and radio so as to make available, so far as possible, to all the people of the United States a rapid, efficient, Nation-wide, and worldwide wire and radio communications service...." The Communications Act authorizes the FCC to "make such regulations not inconsistent with law as it may deem necessary to prevent interference between stations and to carry out the provisions of [the] Act.

How the FCC Adopts Regulations

Like most other federal agencies, the FCC cannot adopt regulations without first notifying and seeking comment from the public. The agency releases a document called a Notice of Proposed Rulemaking, where it explains the specific regulations being proposed and set a deadline for public comment. After receiving the comments, the FCC has several options: (1) adopt the proposed rules; (2) adopt a modified version of the proposed rules; (3) ask for public comment on additional issues relating to the proposals; or (4) end the rulemaking proceeding without adopting any rules at all. The FCC also establishes broadcast regulatory policies through individual cases that it decides.

The FCC and the Media Bureau

The FCC has five commissioners who are appointed by the President and confirmed by the Senate. Under the commissioners are various operating bureaus, one of which is the Media Bureau. The Media Bureau has day-to-day responsibility for developing, recommending and administering the rules governing radio and television stations. These rules are in Title 47 of the Code of Federal Regulations ("CFR"), Parts 73 and 74. The rules of practice and procedure are in Part 1 of Title 47.

FCC REGULATION OF BROADCAST TV AND RADIO

The FCC allocates new stations based both on the relative needs of communities for additional broadcast outlets and on engineering standards that prevent interference between stations. Whenever it looks at a broadcast station application/Mwhether to build, modify, renew or sell/Mit must determine if granting it would serve the public interest. The FCC expects stations to be aware of the important problems or issues in their communities and to foster public understanding by presenting some programs and/or announcements about local issues. However, broadcasters/Mnot the FCC or any other government agency/Mare responsible for selecting all the material they air. The Communications Act prohibits the FCC from censoring broadcast matter and, therefore, its role in overseeing the content of programming is limited. It is authorized to fine a station or revoke its license if it has, among other things, aired obscene language, broadcast indecent language when children are likely to be in the audience, broadcast some types of lottery information, or solicited money under false pretenses.

THE LICENSING OF TV AND RADIO STATIONS

Commercial and Noncommercial-Educational Stations

The FCC licenses radio and TV stations to be either commercial or noncommercial-educational. Commercial stations generally support themselves by advertising. In contrast, noncommercial-educational stations (including public stations) generally support themselves by contributions from listeners and viewers, and they may also receive government funding. Noncommercial-educational stations may also receive contributions from for-profit entities, and they may acknowledge such contributions or underwriting donations with announcements naming and generally describing the entity. However, noncommercial-educational stations may not broadcast promotional announcements or commercials on behalf of for-profit entities.

Applications to Build New Stations; Length of the License Period

To build a new TV or radio station, a citizen must first apply to the FCC for a construction permit. The applicant must demonstrate that he is qualified to construct and operate as proposed in the application. After the applicant has built the station, he must file a license application, where he certifies that he has constructed the station consistently with the construction permit. The FCC licenses radio and TV stations for a period of up to eight years. Before the FCC renews a station's license, it must first determine whether it has served the public interest. In addition, to have its license renewed, a station must certify that: (1) it has sent us certain specified reports that we require; (2) its ownership is consistent with Section 310(b) of the Communications Act, which restricts interests held by foreign governments and non-citizens; (3) there has not been a judgment against it by a court or administrative body under federal, state, or local law; and (4) it has placed certain specified material in its public inspection file (see below).

Employment Discrimination and Equal Employment Opportunity (EEO)

The FCC requires all radio and TV stations to afford equal opportunity in employment. We also prohibit employment discrimination on the basis of race, color, religion, national origin, or sex.

Public Participation in Licensing Process

Renewal Applications. Citizens can file a formal protest against a station by filing a formal petition to deny its renewal application, or by sending us an informal objection to the application. The citizen must file a petition to deny the application by the end of the first day of the last full calendar month of the expiring license term. (For example, if the license expires on December 31, the petition must be filed by the end of the day on December 1.) Before a citizen files a petition to deny an application, he should check the FCC's rules and policies to make sure that the petition complies with the procedural requirements. Before their licenses expire, stations have to broadcast announcements giving the date the license will expire, the date on which a renewal application must be filed, and the date by which formal petitions against it must be filed. A citizen can file an informal objection at any point until the FCC grant or deny the application.

Other Types of Applications. Citizens may also participate formally in the application process when a station is sold (technically called an assignment of the license), undergoes a major stock transfer (technically called a transfer of control), or proposes major construction. The station owner is required to run a series of advertisements in the closest local newspaper when it files these types of applications. Later, the FCC will also run a Public Notice (all FCC Public Notices are placed on our Internet home page at www.fcc.gov) and open a 30-day period during which you may file petitions to deny these applications. As with renewal applications, you can also file an informal objection at any point until we either grant or deny the application.

BROADCAST PROGRAMMING

The FCC and Freedom of Speech

The First Amendment and federal law generally prohibit us from censoring broadcast material and from interfering with freedom of expression in broadcasting. Individual radio and TV stations are responsible for selecting everything they broadcast and for determining how they can best serve their communities. Stations are responsible for choosing their entertainment programming, as well as their programs concerning local issues, news, public affairs, religion, sports events, and other subjects. They also decide how their programs (including call-in shows) will be conducted and whether to edit or reschedule material for broadcasting. The FCC does not substitute its judgment for that of the station, and it does not advise stations on artistic standards, format, grammar, or the quality of their programming. This also applies to a station's commercials, with the exception of commercials for political candidates during an election (see below).

Access to Station Facilities

Stations are not required to broadcast everything that is offered or suggested to them. Except as required by the Communications Act, stations have no obligation to have any particular person participate in a broadcast or to present that person's remarks. Further, no federal law or rule requires stations to broadcast "public service announcements" of any kind. The FCC generally does not require stations to keep the material they broadcast.

Station Identification

Stations must make identification announcements when they sign on and off for the day. They must also make the announcements hourly, as close to the hour as possible, at a natural programming break. TV stations may make these announcements on-screen or by voice only. Official station identification includes the station's call letters followed by the community or communities specified in its license as the station's location. Between the call letters and its community, the station may insert the name of the licensee, the station's channel number, and/or its frequency. However, we do not allow any other insertion.

Broadcast Journalism

Under the First Amendment and the Communications Act, the FCC cannot tell stations how to select material for news programs, and we cannot prohibit the broadcasting of an opinion on any subject. We also do not review anyone's qualifications to gather, edit, announce, or comment on the news; these decisions are the station's responsibility.

Broadcasts by Candidates for Public Office (Equal Time)

When a qualified candidate for public office has been permitted to use a station, the law requires the station to "afford equal opportunities to all other such candidates for that office." The Act also states that the station "shall have no power of censorship over the material broadcast" by the candidate. The FCC exempts the following: (1) An appearance by a legally qualified candidate on a bona fide newscast,

The FCC and the Rules of Broadcasting

interview or documentary (if the appearance of the candidate is incidental to the presentation of the subject covered by the documentary); or (2) on-the-spot coverage of bona fide news events, including political conventions and related incidental activities.

Children's Television Programming

Throughout its license term, every TV station must serve the educational and informational needs of children both through its overall programming. It must also broadcast programming that is specifically designed to serve those needs. The FCC considers programming to be educational and informational if it furthers the educational and informational needs of children 16 years old and under (this includes their intellectual/cognitive or social/emotional needs). A program is considered to be "specifically designed to serve educational and information needs of children" if (1) that it its principal purpose; (2) it is aired between the hours of 7:00 a.m. and 10:00 p.m.; (3) it is a regularly scheduled weekly program; and (4) it is at least 30 minutes in length. Commercial TV stations must identify programs specifically designed to educate and inform children at the beginning of the program, in a form left to their discretion, and must provide information identifying such programs to publishers of program guides. Additionally, in TV programs aimed at children 12 and under, advertising may not exceed 10.5 minutes an hour on weekends and 12 minutes an hour on weekdays.

Criticism, Ridicule, and Humor Concerning Individuals, Groups, and Institutions

The First Amendment's guarantee of freedom of speech protects programming that stereotypes or otherwise offends people with regard to their religion, race, national background, gender, or other characteristics. It also protects broadcasts that criticize or ridicule established customs and institutions, including the government and its officials.

Clear and Present Danger

The First Amendment protects advocacy of using force or of violating the law. However, the Supreme Court has said that the government may curtail speech if it is both: (1) intended to incite or produce dangerous activity; and (2) likely to succeed in achieving that result. Even where this "clear and present danger" test is met, the FCC believes that any review that might lead to a curtailment of speech should be performed by the appropriate criminal law enforcement authorities, and not by the FCC.

Obscenity and Indecency

Federal law prohibits the broadcasting of obscene programming and regulates the broadcasting of "indecent" language and images. Obscene speech is not protected by the First Amendment and cannot be broadcast at any time. To be obscene, material must have all three of the following characteristics: (1) an average person, applying contemporary community standards, must find that the material, as a whole, appeals to the prurient interest; (2) the material must depict or describe, in a patently offensive way, sexual conduct specifically defined by applicable law; and (3) the material, taken as a whole, must lack serious literary, artistic, political, or scientific value. Indecent speech is protected by the First Amendment and cannot be outlawed. However, the courts have upheld Congress's prohibition of the broadcast of indecent speech during times of the day when there is a reasonable risk that children may be in the audience. The FCC has decided that those times fall between 6:00 a.m. and 10:00 p.m. In other words, stations may only broadcast indecent material between 10 p.m. and 6 a.m. Indecent speech is defined as "language or material that, in context, depicts or describes, in terms patently offensive as measured by contemporary community standards for the broadcast medium, sexual or excretory organs or activities." Profanity that does not fall under one of the above two categories is fully protected by the First Amendment and cannot be regulated.

Violent Programming

Neither the law nor FCC rules regulate violent programming. However, the law requires TV sets with screens 13 inches or larger to be equipped with V-chip technology, which allows parents to program their TV sets to block display of TV programming that carries a certain rating. The rating system, voluntarily created by the television industry, tags programming that contains sexual, violent, or other indecent material programmers believe may be harmful to children.

Station-Conducted Contests

Stations that broadcast or advertise information about a contest that they conduct must fully and accurately disclose the material terms of the contest, and they must conduct the contest substantially as announced or advertised. Contest descriptions may not be false, misleading, or deceptive with respect to any material term. Material terms include the factors that define the operation of the contest and affect participation.

Broadcast Hoaxes

Broadcasting false information concerning a crime or a catastrophe violates the FCC's rules if: (1) the station knew the information was false; (2) broadcasting the false information directly caused substantial public harm; (3) and it was foreseeable that broadcasting the false information would cause substantial public harm. In this context, a "crime" is an act or omission that makes the offender subject to criminal punishment by law, and a "catastrophe" is a disaster or imminent disaster involving violent or sudden events affecting the public. "Public harm" must begin immediately; it must cause direct and actual damage to property or to the health or safety of the general public, or diversion of law enforcement or other public health and safety authorities from their duties.

Lotteries

The law prohibits broadcasting any advertisement for a lottery or any information concerning a lottery. A lottery is any game, contest, or promotion that contains the elements of prize, chance, and "consideration" (a legal term that means an act or promise that is made to induce someone into an agreement). There are a number of exceptions to this prohibition. Some of the exceptions are: (1) lotteries conducted by a state acting under the authority of state law, where the advertisement or information is broadcast by a radio or TV station licensed to a location in that state or in any other state that conducts such a lottery; (2) gaming conducted by an Indian Tribe under the Indian Gaming Regulatory Act; (3) lotteries authorized or not otherwise prohibited by the state in which they are conducted, and which are conducted by a not-for-profit organization or a governmental organization; and (4) lotteries conducted as a promotional activity by commercial organizations that are clearly occasional and ancillary to the primary business of that organization, as long as the lotteries are authorized or not otherwise prohibited by the state in which they are conducted.

Soliciting Funds

No federal law prohibits broadcast requests for funds for legal purposes (including appeals by stations for contributions to meet their operating expenses) if the money or other valuable things contributed are used for the announced purposes. It is up to an individual station to decide whether to permit fund solicitations. Fraud by wire, radio or television is prohibited by federal law and may lead to FCC sanctions, as well as to criminal prosecution by the U.S. Department of Justice.

Broadcasting Telephone Conversations

Before recording a telephone conversation for broadcast, or broadcasting a telephone conversation live, a station must inform any party to the call of its intention to broadcast the conversation. However, this does not apply to conversations whose broadcast can reasonably be presumed (for example, telephone calls to programs where the station customarily broadcasts the calls).

BROADCASTING AND ADVERTISING

Business Practices, Advertising Rates, and Profits

Except with respect to political advertisements, the FCC does not regulate a station's advertising rates or its profits. Rates charged for broadcast time are matters for negotiation between sponsors and stations. Further, except for certain classes of political advertisements, stations are free to accept or reject any advertising.

Sponsorship Identification

Sponsorship identification or disclosure must accompany any material that is broadcast in exchange for money, service, or anything else of value paid to a station, either directly or indirectly. This announcement must clearly say that the time was purchased and by whom. In the case of advertisements for commercial products or services, it is sufficient to announce the sponsor's corporate or trade name, or the name of the sponsor's product when it is clear that the mention of the product constitutes a sponsorship identification.

Underwriting Announcements on Noncommercial-Educational Stations

Noncommercial educational stations may acknowledge contributions over the air, but they may not promote the goods and services of for-profit donors or underwriters. Acceptable "enhanced underwriting" acknowledgements may include (1) logograms and slogans that identify but do not promote; (2) location information; (3) value-neutral descriptions of a product line or service; and (4) brand names, trade names, and product service listings. However, such acknowledgements may not interrupt a noncommercial station's regular programming.

Amount of Advertising

Except with respect to children's television programming, no law or regulation limits the amount of commercial matter that a station may broadcast. In TV programs aimed at children 12 and under, advertising may not exceed 10.5 minutes an hour on weekends and 12 minutes an hour on weekdays.

Loud Commercials

In surveys and technical studies of broadcast advertising, the FCC has found that loudness is a judgment that varies with each listener and is influenced by many factors (such as an announcement's content and style). We have also found no evidence that stations deliberately raise audio and modulation levels to emphasize commercial messages. Broadcast licensees have primary responsibility for the adoption of equipment and procedures to avoid objectionably loud commercials. Citizens should address any complaint about such messages to the station. They should identify each message by the sponsor or product's name and by the date and time of the broadcast.

False or Misleading Advertising

The Federal Trade Commission has primary responsibility for determining whether an advertisement is false or deceptive and for taking action against the sponsor. Also, the Food and Drug Administration has primary responsibility for the safety of food and drug products. Citizens should contact these agencies regarding advertisements that they believe may be false or misleading.

Offensive Advertising

Unless a broadcast advertisement is found to be in violation of a specific law or regulation, the government cannot take action against it. If a citizen thinks that an advertisement is offensive because of the kind of item advertised, the scheduling of the announcement, or the way the message is presented, then he should address his complaint directly to the stations and networks involved. This will help them become better informed about audience opinion.

Tobacco and Alcohol

The FCC and the Rules of Broadcasting

The law prohibits advertising for cigarettes, little cigars, smokeless tobacco, or chewing tobacco on radio, TV, or any other medium of electronic communication under the FCC's jurisdiction. The law does not ban the advertising of smoking accessories, cigars, pipes, pipe tobacco, or cigarette-making machines. Congress has not enacted any law prohibiting broadcast advertising for any kind of alcoholic beverage. Also, the FCC does not have a rule or policy regulating advertisements for alcoholic beverages. Most broadcasters have voluntarily abstained from advertising hard liquor, although they accept beer and wine advertising.

Subliminal Programming

The FCC sometimes receives complaints regarding the alleged use of subliminal techniques in radio and TV programming. Subliminal programming is designed to be perceived on a subconscious level only. Regardless of whether it is effective, the use of subliminal perception is inconsistent with a station's obligation to serve the public interest because the broadcast is intended to be deceptive. However, it is not specifically prohibited.

INTERFERENCE

Blanketing Interference

Some people who are close to a radio station's transmitting antenna may experience impaired reception of other stations. This is called "blanketing" interference. The FCC requires the station causing the interference to resolve most interference complaints received within the first year of operation at no cost to the person complaining. However, stations are not required to resolve interference complaints based on malfunctioning or mistuned receivers, improperly installed antenna systems, or the use of high gain antennas or antenna booster amplifiers. Mobile receivers and non-radio frequency (RF) devices such as tape recorders or CD players are also excluded. Stations are not financially responsible for resolving interference complaints located outside the blanketing contour.

THE LOCAL PUBLIC INSPECTION FILE

Requirement to Maintain a Public Inspection File

The FCC requires all TV and radio stations and applicants for new stations to maintain a file available for public inspection containing documents relevant to the station's operation. The public inspection file generally must be maintained at the station's main studio. The station must make its public inspection file available at its main studio at any time during regular business hours. A station that chooses to maintain all or part of its public file in a computer database must provide a computer terminal to those who wish to review the file. Stations must keep the following materials in their public inspection file:

The License. Stations must keep a copy of their current FCC license in the public file, together with any material documenting FCC-approved modifications to the license. The license reflects the station's technical parameters (authorized frequency, call letters, operating power, transmitter location, etc.), as well as any special conditions imposed by the FCC on the station's operation. The license also indicates when it was issued and when it will expire.

Applications and Related Materials. The public file must contain copies of all applications that are pending before either the FCC or the courts. These include applications to sell the station or to modify its facilities (for example, to increase power, change the antenna system, or change the transmitter location); copies of any construction or sales application whose grant required the FCC to waive our rules; applications that required the FCC to waive its rules; renewal applications granted for less than a full license term (the FCC grants short-term renewals when it is concerned about the station's performance over the previous term).

Citizen Agreements. Stations must keep a copy of any written agreements they make with local viewers or listeners. These "citizen agreements" deal with programming, employment, or other issues of community concern. The station must keep these agreements in the public file for as long as they are in effect.

Contour Maps. The public file must contain copies of any service contour maps or other information submitted with any application filed with the FCC that reflects the station's service area and/or its main studio and transmitter location. These documents must stay in the file for as long as they remain accurate.

Material Relating to an FCC Investigation or a Complaint. The station must keep this material until the FCC notifies it that the material may be discarded. Since the FCC is not involved in disputes regarding matters unrelated to the Communications Act or our rules, stations do not have to keep material relating to such matters in the public file.

Ownership Reports and Related Material. The public file must contain a copy of the most recent, complete Ownership Report filed for the station. This report has the names of the owners of the station and their ownership interests, lists any contracts related to the station that are required to be filed with the FCC, and identifies any interest held by the station licensee in other broadcast stations.

List of Contracts Filed with the FCC. Stations have to keep either a copy of all the contracts that they have to file with the FCC, or an up-to-date list identifying all such contracts. If the station keeps a list and you ask to see copies of the actual contracts, the station must give them to you within seven days. Such contracts include network affiliation contracts; contracts relating to ownership or control of the licensee or permittee or its stock. Examples include articles of incorporation, bylaws, agreements providing for the assignment of a license or permit or affecting stock ownership or voting rights (stock options, pledges, or proxies), and mortgage or loan agreements that restrict the licensee or permittee's freedom of operation; management consultant agreements with independent contractors, and station management contracts that provide for a percentage of profits or sharing of losses.

Political File. Stations must keep a file containing records of all requests for broadcast time made by or for a candidate for public office. The file must identify how the station responded to such requests and (if the request was granted) the charges made, a schedule of the time purchased, the times the spots actually aired, the rates charged, and the classes of time purchased. The file must also reflect any free time provided to a candidate. The station must keep the political records for two years after the spot airs. You can find the political broadcasting rules elsewhere in this manual.

Letters and E-Mail from the Public. Commercial stations must keep written comments and suggestions received from the public regarding their operation for at least three years. Noncommercial stations are not subject to this requirement.

Issues/Programs List. Every three months, all stations must prepare and place in their file a list of programs that have provided their most significant treatment of community issues during the preceding three months. The list must briefly describe both the issue and the programming where the issue was discussed. The stations must keep these lists for the entire license term.

Children's Television Programming Reports. The Children's Television Act of 1990 and our rules require all TV stations to air programming that serves the educational and informational needs of children 16 and under, including programming that is specifically designed to serve such needs. In addition, commercial TV stations must make and retain Children's Television Programming Reports identifying the educational and informational programming for children aired by the station. (Noncommercial stations are not required to prepare these reports.) The report must include the name of the person at the station responsible for collecting comments on the station's compliance with the law. The station has to prepare these reports each calendar quarter, and it must place them in the public file separately from the file's other material. Stations must keep the reports for the remainder of their license terms. You can also view each station's reports on our web site at http://www.fcc.gov/mb/policy/kidstv.html.

Records Regarding Children's Programming Commercial Limits. The Children's Television Act of 1990 and our rules limit the type and amount of advertising that may be aired in TV programming directed to children 12 and under. On weekends, commercial television stations may air no more than 10.5 minutes of commercials per hour during children's programming, and no more than 12 minutes on weekdays. Stations must keep records that substantiate compliance with these limits.

Radio Time Brokerage Agreements. A time brokerage agreement is a type of contract that generally involves a station's sale of discrete blocks of air time to a broker, who then supplies the programming to fill that time and sells the commercial spot announcements to support the programming. Commercial radio stations must keep a copy of every agreement involving: (1) time brokerage of that station; or (2) time brokerage by any other station owned by the same licensee.

List of Donors. Noncommercial TV and radio stations must keep a list of donors supporting specific programs for two years after the program airs.

Local Public Notice Announcements. When someone files an application to build a new station or to renew, sell, or modify an existing station, the FCC often requires the applicant to make a series of local announcements to inform the public of the application's existence and nature.

Must-Carry or Retransmission Consent Election. There are two ways that a broadcast TV station can choose to be carried on a cable TV system: "must-carry" and "retransmission consent." All TV stations are generally entitled to be carried on cable television systems in their local markets. A station that chooses to exercise this must-carry right receives no compensation from the cable system. Instead of exercising their must-carry rights, TV stations may choose to receive compensation from a cable system in return for granting permission to the cable system to carry the station. This option is available only to commercial TV stations. Every three years, commercial TV stations must decide whether their relationship with each local cable system will be governed by must-carry or by retransmission consent agreements. Each commercial station must keep a copy of its decision in the public file for the three-year period to which it pertains. Noncommercial stations are not entitled to compensation in return for carriage on a cable system, but they may request mandatory carriage on the system. A noncommercial station making this request must keep a copy of the request in the public file for the duration of the period to which it applies.

Broadcasting & Cable Yearbook 2006

Section B
Television

Section B
Broadcast Television

TV Group Ownership B-2
TV Station Listings by DMA
    Key to Television Listings B-13
    Directory of Television Stations in the U.S. B-14
    Directory of Television Stations in Canada B-103
    U.S. Television Stations by Call Letters B-114
    Canadian Television Stations by Call Letters B-119
    U.S. Television Stations by Analog Channel B-120
    Canadian Television Stations by Channel B-125
    U.S. Television Stations by Digital Channel. B-126
    Spanish-Language Television Stations B-128
    U.S. TV Stations Providing News Programming B-129
    Nielsen DMA Market Atlas B-132
    Multi-City DMA Cross-Reference B-216

Broadcasting & Cable Yearbook 2006

TV Group Ownership

A

ABC Inc. 77 W. 66th St., New York, NY 10023-6298. Phone: (212) 456-7777. Web Site: www.abc.com. Ownership: ABC Enterprises Inc., 100%. Note: ABC Enterprises Inc. is 100% owned by Disney Enterprises Inc. Disney Enterprises Inc. is 100% owned by The Walt Disney Co.

Stns: 10 TV. WLS, Chicago; WJRT-TV, Flint-Saginaw-Bay City, MI; KFSN-TV, Fresno-Visalia, CA; KTRK, Houston; KABC, Los Angeles; WABC-TV, New York; WPVI, Philadelphia; WTVD, Raleigh-Durham (Fayetteville), NC; KGO, San Francisco-Oakland-San Jose; WTVG, Toledo, OH

Stns: 50 AM. 15 FM. KDIS-FM Little Rock, AR; KMIK Tempe, AZ; KLOS-FM Los Angeles, CA; KABC Los Angeles, CA; KSPN(AM) Los Angeles, CA; KMKY Oakland, CA; KDIS(AM) Pasadena, CA; KIID(AM) Sacramento, CA; KGO San Francisco, CA; KDDZ Arvada, CO; WDZK Bloomfield, CT; WMAL Washington, DC; WBWL Jacksonville, FL; WMYM(AM) Miami, FL; WDYZ(AM) Orlando, FL; WMNE(AM) Riviera Beach, FL; WWMI Saint Petersburg, FL; WDWD Atlanta, GA; WYAY-FM Gainesville, GA; WSDZ Belleville, IL; WZZN(FM) Chicago, IL; WMVP Chicago, IL; WLS Chicago, IL; WRDZ La Grange, IL; WPJX(AM) Zion, IL; WRDZ-FM Plainfield, IN; KQAM Wichita, KS; WDRD(AM) Newburg, KY; WBYU New Orleans, LA; WMKI(AM) Boston, MA; WDRQ-FM Detroit, MI; WJR Detroit, MI; WFDF Flint, MI; WGVY(FM) Cambridge, MN; WGVZ(FM) Eden Prairie, MN; KQRS-FM Golden Valley, MN; WGVX(FM) Lakeville, MN; KXXR-FM Minneapolis, MN; KPHN Kansas City, MO; WGFY Charlotte, NC; WWJZ Mount Holly, NJ; KALY Los Ranchos de Albuquerque, NM; WDDY(AM) Albany, NY; WEPN(AM) New York, NY; WABC(AM) New York, NY; WPLJ(FM) New York, NY; WWMK Cleveland, OH; KMUS(AM) Sperry, OK; KDZR(AM) Lake Oswego, OR; KKSL(AM) Lake Oswego, OR; WEAE Pittsburgh, PA; WDDZ(AM) Pawtucket, RI; KESN(FM) Allen, TX; KTYS(FM) Flower Mound, TX; WBAP Fort Worth, TX; KMIC(AM) Houston, TX; KMKI Plano, TX; KRDY(AM) San Antonio, TX; KWDZ(AM) Salt Lake City, UT; WDZY Colonial Heights, VA; WHKT Portsmouth, VA; WRJR(AM) Portsmouth, VA; WJZW-FM Woodbridge, VA; KKDZ Seattle, WA; WKSH(AM) Sussex, WI

Robert A. Iger, pres; Phillip J. Meek, pres; Lawrence J. Pollock, chmn owned TV stns.

ACME Communications Inc. 2101 E. Fourth St., Suite 202A, Santa Ana, CA 92705. Phone: (714) 245-9499. Fax: (714) 245-9494. E-mail: t.allen@acmecomm.com. Web Site: www.acmecommunications.com. Ownership: Alta Cpmmunications; Seaport Capital.

Stns: 10 TV. KASY, Albuquerque-Santa Fe, NM; KWBQ, Albuquerque-Santa Fe, NM; KRWB-TV, Albuquerque-Santa Fe, NM; WBUI, Champaign & Springfield-Decatur, IL; WBDT, Dayton, OH; WTVK, Ft. Myers-Naples, FL; WIWB, Green Bay-Appleton, WI; WBXX, Knoxville, TN; WBUW, Madison, WI; KUWB, Salt Lake City, UT

Jamie Kellner, chmn/CEO; Doug Gealy, pres/COO; Tom Allen, exec VP & CFO.

Access.1 Communications Corp. 11 Penn Plaza, 16th Fl., New York, NY 10001. Phone: (212) 714-1000. Fax: (212) 714-1563. Ownership: Sydney L. Small, 54.12%; Black Enterprise/Greenwich Street Capital Partners, 19.47%; MESBIC Ventures Inc., 5.54%; Chesley Maddox-Dorsey, 2.84%; and Adriane Gaines, 1.85%.

Stns: 1 TV. WMGM, Philadelphia

Stns: 7 AM. 11 FM. KSYR(FM) Benton, LA; KDKS-FM Blanchard, LA; KBTT(FM) Haughton, LA; KLKL(FM) Minden, LA; KOKA Shreveport, LA; WMGM-FM Atlantic City, NJ; WGYM(AM) Hammonton, NJ; WTKU-FM Ocean City, NJ; WOND Pleasantville, NJ; WUSS(AM) Pleasantville, NJ; WWRL New York, NY; KOYE(FM) Frankston, TX; KOOI-FM Jacksonville, TX; KFRO Longview, TX; KYKX-FM Longview, TX; KCUL Marshall, TX; KTAL-FM Texarkana, TX; KKUS(FM) Tyler, TX

Chesley Maddox-Dorsey, pres/COO; Sydney L. Small, chmn/CEO.

Allbritton Communications Co. 808 17th St. N.W., Suite 300, Washington, DC 20006. Phone: (202) 789-2130. Fax: (202) 822-6749.

Stns: 8 TV. WCFT, Birmingham (Anniston, Tuscaloosa), AL; WJSU, Birmingham (Anniston, Tuscaloosa), AL; WCIV, Charleston, SC; WHTM, Harrisburg-Lancaster-Lebanon-York, PA; KATV, Little Rock-Pine Bluff, AR; WSET, Roanoke-Lynchburg, VA; KTUL, Tulsa, OK; WJLA-TV, Washington, DC (Hagerstown, MD)

Allbritton Communications, through affiliated company, publishes the *Enfield* (CT) *Press*, *The Longmeadow* (MA) *News*, *Westfield* (MA) *Evening News* & *The Penny Saver*, Westfield, MA.

Also owns Cable-NewsChannel 8, Arlington, VA. All 100% owned.

Frederick Ryan, pres; Robert L. Allbritton, CEO.

AsianMedia Group LLP 1990 S. Bundy Dr., c/o KSCI, Suite 850, Los Angeles, CA 90025. Phone: (310) 478-1818. Fax: (310) 479-8118. E-mail: info@kscitv.com. Web Site: www.kscitv.com. Ownership: Leonard Green & Partners, LLP.

Stns: 2 TV. KIKU, Honolulu, HI; KSCI, Los Angeles

Peter Mathes, chmn/CEO.

B

Bahakel Communications Box 32488, Charlotte, NC 28232. Phone: (704) 372-4434. Fax: (704) 335-9904. Ownership: The Cy N. Bahakel Trust Dated January 12, 2005, 100%.

Stns: 5 TV. WCCU, Champaign & Springfield-Decatur, IL; WRSP-TV, Champaign & Springfield-Decatur, IL; WCCB, Charlotte, NC; WABG, Greenwood-Greenville, MS; WAKA, Montgomery (Selma), AL

Stns: 4 AM. 5 FM. KILO-FM Colorado Springs, CO; KYZX(FM) Pueblo West, CO; KOKZ-FM Waterloo, IA; KWLO Waterloo, IA; KXEL Waterloo, IA; KFMW-FM Waterloo, IA; WABG(AM) Greenwood, MS; WDEF-FM Chattanooga, TN; WDOD Chattanooga, TN

Cy N. Bahakel, pres; Beverly Poston, exec VP/COO; Stephen Bahakel, Sr VP radio div; Russell Schwartz, Sr VP business affrs/gen counsel; Ed Conrad, V VP finance; Bill Napier, VP eng/tech; Anna Rufty, VP Hum Res.

Banks Broadcasting Inc. 1124 Merrill St., Winnetka, IL 60093. Phone: (847) 446-9995. Fax: (847) 446-9997. Ownership: LIN Television; Banc of America; 21st Century Group.

Stns: 2 TV. KNIN, Boise, ID; KWCV, Wichita-Hutchinson Plus, KS

Lyle Banks, pres/CEO.

Barrington Broadcasting LLC. 2500 W. Higgins Rd., Suite 880, Hoffman Estates, IL 60195. Phone: (847) 884-1877. Ownership: Pilot Group LP, 100% of votes.

Stns: 7 TV. KVIH, Amarillo, TX; KVII, Amarillo, TX; KRCG, Columbia-Jefferson City, MO; WBSF, Flint-Saginaw-Bay City, MI; WEYI, Flint-Saginaw-Bay City, MI; WHOI, Peoria-Bloomington, IL; KHQA, Quincy, IL-Hannibal, MO-Keokuk, IA

Paul M. McNicol, sr VP.

Beach TV Properties Inc. Box 9556, Panama City Beach, FL 32417. Phone: (850) 234-2773.

Stns: 2 TV. WAWD, Mobile, AL-Pensacola (Ft. Walton Beach), FL; WPCT, Panama City, FL

Byron J. Colley, pres.

Bela LLC 7500 N.W. 72 Ave., Medley, FL 33166. Phone: (305) 530-1322. Ownership: Star Studios LLC, 51%; Cranston LLC, 44%; and Leibowitz Family Broadcasting LLC, 5%.

Stns: 2 TV. KMOH, Phoenix, AZ; KBEH, Santa Barbara-Santa Maria-San Luis Obispo, CA

Robert Behar, pres; Matthew L. Leibowitz, VP.

Belo Corp (Television Group). 400 S. Record St., Dallas, TX 75202. Phone: (214) 977-6600. Fax: (214) 977-6603. Web Site: www.belo.com. Ownership: Belo Corp.

Stns: 19 TV. KVUE, Austin, TX; KTVB, Boise, ID; WCNC, Charlotte, NC; WFAA-TV, Dallas-Ft. Worth; KHOU-TV, Houston; WHAS, Louisville, KY; WWL, New Orleans, LA; WVEC, Norfolk-Portsmouth-Newport News, VA; KTVK, Phoenix, AZ; KASW, Phoenix, AZ; KGW, Portland, OR; KENS, San Antonio, TX; KING, Seattle-Tacoma, WA; KONG, Seattle-Tacoma, WA; KREM, Spokane, WA; KSKN, Spokane, WA; KMOV, St. Louis, MO; KMSB, Tucson (Sierra Vista), AZ; KTTU, Tucson (Sierra Vista), AZ

The publishing division of Belo Corp., publishes the following dailies: *The Dallas* (TX) *Morning News* and *The Press-Enterprise*, Riverside, CA; *Denton Record Chronicle*, Denton, TX; *The Providence Journal*, Providence, RI; *Arlington Morning News*, Arlington, VA. Other interests: News cable channels (100% owned): Northwest Cable News, Texas Cable News, 24/7 Newschannel (distribution in ID from Boise, ID). News cable channel partnerships in the following DMAs: Phoenix, AZ; New Orleans; and Norfolk-Portsmouth-Newport News, VA.

Robert W. Decherd, chmn.

Block Communications Inc. 541 N. Superior St., Toledo, OH 43660. Phone: (419) 724-6000. Fax: (419) 724-6167. Web Site: www.blockcommunications.com. Ownership: William Block, Allan Block, John R. Block.

Stns: 4 TV. KTRV, Boise, ID; WLIO, Lima, OH; WDRB, Louisville, KY; WFTE, Louisville, KY

Block Communications Inc. publishes the *Toledo* OH *Blade* & *Pittsburgh* (PA) *Post-Gazette*.

Allan Block, mng dir; Gary J. Blair, VP.

Bonneville International Corporation Broadcast House, Box 1160, Salt Lake City, UT 84110-1160. Phone: (801) 575-7500. Fax: (801) 575-7521. Web Site: www.bonnint.com. Ownership: Deseret Management Corp. Deseret Management Corp. owns *The Deseret Morning News*, a Salt Lake City, UT, daily.

Stns: 1 TV. KSL, Salt Lake City, UT

Stns: 14 AM. 24 FM. KPKX(FM) Phoenix, AZ; KMVP Phoenix, AZ; KTAR(AM) Phoenix, AZ; KZBR(FM) San Francisco, CA; KOIT San Francisco, CA; KOIT-FM San Francisco, CA; KDFC-FM San Francisco, CA; WTOP Washington, DC; WGMS-FM Washington, DC; KBLI Blackfoot, ID; KCVI(FM) Blackfoot, ID; KLCE-FM Blackfoot, ID; KSLJ(AM) Blackfoot, ID; KFTZ-FM Idaho Falls, ID; KSSL(AM) Idaho Falls, ID; KTHK(FM) Idaho Falls, ID; WDRV(FM) Chicago, IL; WILV(FM) Chicago, IL; WVRV-FM East St. Louis, IL; WARH(FM) Granite City, IL; WTMX-FM Skokie, IL; WWDV(FM) Zion, IL; WIL(AM) Saint Louis, MO; WIL-FM Saint Louis, MO; KREC(FM) Brian Head, UT; KQMB(FM) Midvale, UT; KSNN-FM Saint George, UT; KDXU Saint George, UT; KRSP-FM Salt Lake City, UT; KSFI-FM Salt Lake City, UT; KSL Salt Lake City, UT; KUTR(AM) Taylorsville, UT; KUNF(AM) Washington, UT; WTOP-FM Warrenton, VA; WWVZ-FM Braddock Heights, MD; WXTR Frederick, MD; WFED(AM) Silver Spring, MD; WWZZ(FM) Waldorf, MD

Bruce T. Reese, pres/CEO; Robert A. Johnson, exec VP & COO.

C

CHUM Ltd. 1331 Yonge St., Toronto, ON M4T 1Y1. Canada. Phone: (416) 925-6666. Fax: (416) 926-1380. Web Site: www.chumlimited.com. Ownership: Alan Waters, controlling shareholder.

Stns: 13 TV. CKVR, Barrie, ON; CKX, Brandon, MB; CKAL, Calgary, AB; CKEM, Edmonton, AB; CJAL, Edmonton, AB; CKX-1, Foxwarren, MB; CFPL-TV, London, ON; CHMI, Portage la Prairie, MB; CITY-TV, Toronto, ON; CKVU, Vancouver, BC; CIVI-TV, Victoria, BC; CHWI-TV, Windsor, ON; CKNX, Wingham, ON

Stns: 12 AM. 8 FM. CHBN-FM Edmonton, AB; CHQM-FM Vancouver, BC; CKST Vancouver, BC; CHBE-FM Victoria, BC; CFAX Victoria, BC; CFWM-FM Winnipeg, MB; CFRW(AM) Winnipeg, MB; CJCH Halifax, NS; CJPT-FM Brockville, ON; CFJR-FM Brockville, ON; CKKW Kitchener, ON; CKLY-FM Lindsay (city of Kawartha Lakes), ON; CHST-FM London, ON; CFGO Ottawa, ON; CFRA Ottawa, ON; CKPT Peterborough, ON; CHUM Toronto, ON; CKLW Windsor, ON; CKWW Windsor, ON; CKGM Montreal, PQ

Stephen Tapp, exec VP; Paul Ski, exec VP; Jay Switzer, pres/CEO; Peter Miller, VP; David Kirkwood, exec VP; Sarah Crawford, VP; Mary Powers, VP; Denise Cooper, VP; Alan Mayne, CFO.

CTV Inc. Box 9, Station O, Scarborough, ON M4A 2M9. Canada. Phone: (416) 332-5000. Fax: (416) 332-5283. Web Site: www.ctv.ca. Ownership: Bell Globemedia, 100%.

Stns: 40 TV. CKYB, Brandon, MB; CJCH-6, Caledonia, NS; CFCN, Calgary, AB; CKCD, Campbellton, NB; CJCH-1, Canning, NS; CKCW-1, Charlottetown, PE; CKCK-1, Colgate, SK; CJOH-8, Cornwall, ON; CJOH-6, Deseronto, ON; CFRN, Edmonton, AB; CICI-1, Elliot Lake, ON; CKMC-1, Golden Prairie, SK; CJCH, Halifax, NS; CITO-2, Kearns, ON; CKCO, Kitchener, ON; CFCN-5, Lethbridge, AB; CKBQ, Melfort, SK; CKCW, Moncton, NB; CFCF, Montreal, PQ; CKNY, North Bay, ON; CJOH-TV, Ottawa, ON; CIPA, Prince Albert, SK; CKCK, Regina, SK; CKCW-TV-2, Saint Edward, PE; CKLT, Saint John, NB; CKCO-3, Sarnia, ON; CFQC, Saskatoon, SK; CHBX, Sault Ste. Marie, ON; CICI, Sudbury, ON; CKMC, Swift Current, SK; CJCB, Sydney, NS; CITO, Timmins, ON; CFTO, Toronto, ON; CKAM,

Broadcasting & Cable Yearbook 2006

B-2

Upsalquitch Lake, NB; CIVT, Vancouver, BC; CIEW, Warmley, SK; CKCO-2, Wiarton, ON; CKCK-2, Willow Bunch, SK; CKY, Winnipeg, MB; CICC, Yorkton, SK

Ivan Fecan, CEO; Rick Brace, pres.

California Oregon Broadcasting Inc. Box 1489, Medford, OR 97501. Phone: (541) 779-5555. Fax: (541) 779-1151. E-mail: cobiadmin@kobi5.com. Ownership: Patricia C. Smullin and Carol Anne Smullin Brown. Other interests: Cable TV: Crestview Cable TV (systems in Oregon).

Stns: 3 TV. KLSR, Eugene, OR; KOBI, Medford-Klamath Falls, OR; KOTI, Medford-Klamath Falls, OR

Patricia C. Smullin, owner.

CanWest Global Communications Corp. 201 Portage Ave., 31st Fl., Winnipeg, MB R3B 3L7. Canada. Phone: (204) 956-2025. Fax: (204) 947-9841. E-mail: bleslie@canwest.com. Web Site: www.canwestglobal.com. Ownership: Asper Family 85% voting shares, 45% of equity.

Stns: 13 TV. CHEK-5, Campbell River, BC; CKRD-1, Coronation, AB; CITV, Edmonton, AB; CIHF, Halifax, NS; CHCH, Hamilton, ON; CHBC, Kelowna, BC; CISA-TV, Lethbridge, AB; CJNT, Montreal, PQ; CKRD, Red Deer, AB; CFRE, Regina, SK; CHAN, Vancouver, BC; CHEK, Victoria, BC; CKND-TV, Winnipeg, MB

Stns: 3 FM. CJZZ-FM Winnipeg, MB; CHAL-FM Halifax, NS; CKBT-FM Kitchener-Waterloo, ON

Leonard Asper, pres/CEO.

Capitol Broadcasting Co. Inc. Box 12000, Raleigh, NC 27605. Phone: (919) 821-8555. Fax: (919) 821-8733. Ownership: Capitol Holding Co. Inc.

Stns: 4 TV. WWWB, Charlotte, NC; WJZY, Charlotte, NC; WRAL-TV, Raleigh-Durham (Fayetteville), NC; WRAZ, Raleigh-Durham (Fayetteville), NC

Stns: 2 FM. WRAL(FM) Raleigh, NC; WFXQ-FM Chase City, VA

James F. Goodmon, pres/CEO.

Cascade Broadcasting Group L.L.C. 60 E. Sir Francis Drake Blvd., Suite 300, Larkspur, CA 94939. Phone: (415) 925-6500.

Stns: 3 TV. WBKI-TV, Louisville, KY; KWBA, Tucson (Sierra Vista), AZ; KWBT, Tulsa, OK

Catamount Broadcast Group 71 East St., Norwalk, CT 06851. Phone: (203) 852-7164. Fax: (203) 852-7163. Web Site: www.catamounttv.com. Ownership: BCI Partners Inc.; Becker Television, Inc.

Stns: 2 TV. KHSL-TV, Chico-Redding, CA; KXJB, Fargo-Valley City, ND

Daniel J. Duman, sec/treas; Ralph E. Becker, pres/CEO.

Chambers Communications Corp. Box 7009, Eugene, OR 97401. Phone: (541) 485-5611. Fax: (541) 342-1568. Web Site: www.cmc.net/chambers. Ownership: Carolyn S. Chambers. Other interests: Oregon cable TV.

Stns: 3 TV. KEZI, Eugene, OR; KDKF, Medford-Klamath Falls, OR; KDRV, Medford-Klamath Falls, OR

Scott Chambers, pres; Carolyn Chambers, CEO.

Chelsey Broadcasting Co. 712 Fifth Ave., 45th Fl., New York, NY 10019. Phone: (212) 586-3010.

Stns: 4 TV. KGWC, Casper-Riverton, WY; KGWL, Casper-Riverton, WY; KGWR, Salt Lake City, UT; WYTV, Youngstown, OH

Stuart Feldman, pres.

Christian Faith Broadcasting Inc. 3809 Maple Ave., Castalia, OH 44824. Phone: (419) 684-5311. Fax: (419) 684-5378. E-mail: wggn@lrbcg.com.

Stns: 2 TV. WGGN, Cleveland, OH; WLLA, Grand Rapids-Kalamazoo-Battle Creek, MI

Stns: 3 FM. WJKW-FM Athens, OH; WGGN-FM Castalia, OH; WLRD(FM) Willard, OH

Shelby Gillam, pres; Rusty Yost, VP.

Christian Television Corporation Inc. 6922 142nd Ave. N., Largo, FL 33771. Phone: (727) 535-5622. Fax: (727) 531-2497. Web Site: www.ctnonline.com. Ownership: Robert D'Andrea, 25% of votes; Virginia Oliver, 25% of votes; Jimmy Smith, 25% of votes; and Wayne Wetzel, 25% of votes.

Stns: 2 TV. KFXB, Cedar Rapids-Waterloo & Dubuque, IA; WCLF, Tampa-St. Petersburg (Sarasota), FL

Robert D'Andrea, pres.

Citadel Communications Co. LTD. (Coronet Communications, Capital Communications, Citadel Comm. LLC.). 99 Pondfield Rd., Bronxville, NY 10708. Phone: (914) 793-3400. Fax: (914) 793-3693. E-mail: citnyltd@aol.com. Ownership: (Coronet Communications, Capital Communications, Citadel Comm. LLC.)

Stns: 5 TV. WHBF-TV, Davenport, IA-Rock Island-Moline, IL; WOI, Des Moines-Ames, IA; KLKE, Lincoln & Hastings-Kearney, NE; KLKN, Lincoln & Hastings-Kearney, NE; KCAU, Sioux City, IA

Philip J. Lombardo, pres.

Clear Channel Communications Inc. 200 E. Basse Rd., San Antonio, TX 78209. Phone: (210) 822-2828. Fax: (210) 822-2299. E-mail: markpmays@clearchannel.com. Web Site: www.clearchannel.com. Ownership: Thomas O. Hicks, 6.5%; L. Lowry Mays, 5.2%. Publicly traded company with the majority of its shares owned by the investing public.

Stns: 35 TV. WXXA-TV, Albany-Schenectady-Troy, NY; KGET-TV, Bakersfield, CA; WIVT, Binghamton, NY; WKRC, Cincinnati, OH; WETM, Elmira, NY; KMTR, Eugene, OR; KMTX, Eugene, OR; KMTZ, Eugene, OR; KVIQ, Eureka, CA; KTVF, Fairbanks, AK; KGPE, Fresno-Visalia, CA; WHP-TV, Harrisburg-Lancaster-Lebanon-York, PA; WJKT, Jackson, TN; WTEV-TV, Jacksonville, FL; WAWS, Jacksonville, FL; KLRT, Little Rock-Pine Bluff, AR; KASN, Little Rock-Pine Bluff, AR; WPTY, Memphis, TN; WLMT, Memphis, TN; WPMI-TV, Mobile, AL-Pensacola (Ft. Walton Beach), FL; WJTC, Mobile, AL-Pensacola (Ft. Walton Beach), FL; KION-TV, Monterey-Salinas, CA; WHAM-TV, Rochester, NY; KTVX, Salt Lake City, UT; WOAI-TV, San Antonio, TX; KFTY, San Francisco-Oakland-San Jose; KCOY, Santa Barbara-Santa Maria-San Luis Obispo, CA; KVOS, Seattle-Tacoma, WA; WSYR-TV, Syracuse, NY; KTFO, Tulsa, OK; KOKI, Tulsa, OK; WWTI, Watertown, NY; KSAS-TV, Wichita-Hutchinson Plus, KS; KAAS, Wichita-Hutchinson Plus, KS; KBDK, Wichita-Hutchinson Plus, KS

Stns: 339 AM. 688 FM. KASH-FM Anchorage, AK; KBFX(FM) Anchorage, AK; KENI Anchorage, AK; KGOT-FM Anchorage, AK; KTZN Anchorage, AK; KYMG-FM Anchorage, AK; KFBX(AM) Fairbanks, AK; KIAK-FM Fairbanks, AK; KKED-FM Fairbanks, AK; KAKQ-FM Fairbanks, AK; WSTH-FM Alexander City, AL; WMJJ-FM Birmingham, AL; WRTR(FM) Brookwood, AL; WZBQ-FM Carrollton, AL; WDRM-FM Decatur, AL; WHOS Decatur, AL; WTXT-FM Fayette, AL; WAGH-FM Fort Mitchell, AL; WAAX Gadsden, AL; WQEN(FM) Gadsden, AL; WGMZ-FM Glencoe, AL; WTAK-FM Hartselle, AL; WENN(FM) Hoover, AL; WBHP Huntsville, AL; WDXB(FM) Jasper, AL; WHLW(FM) Luverne, AL; WXQW-FM Meridianville, AL; WWMG(FM) Millbrook, AL; WPMI(AM) Mobile, AL; WKSJ-FM Mobile, AL; WRKH-FM Mobile, AL; WHAL(AM) Phenix City, AL; WGSY-FM Phenix City, AL; WBFA-FM Smiths, AL; WWXQ-FM Trinity, AL; WZHT-FM Troy, AL; WACT Tuscaloosa, AL; WLAY-FM Tuscumbia, AL; KMJI(FM) Ashdown, AR; KHKN(FM) Benton, AR; KMJX-FM Conway, AR; KKIX-FM Fayetteville, AR; KEZA-FM Fayetteville, AR; KMAG-FM Fort Smith, AR; KWHN(AM) Fort Smith, AR; KWHF(FM) Harrisburg, AR; KDJE(FM) Jacksonville, AR; KIYS(FM) Jonesboro, AR; KNEA(AM) Jonesboro, AR; KFIN(FM) Jonesboro, AR; KSSN-FM Little Rock, AR; KMXF-FM Lowell, AR; KMSX(FM) Maumelle, AR; KOSY(AM) Texarkana, AR; KYGL-FM Texarkana, AR; KFXR-FM Chinle, AZ; KTZR-FM Green Valley, AZ; KOHT-FM Marana, AZ; KZZP-FM Mesa, AZ; KYOT-FM Phoenix, AZ; KOY Phoenix, AZ; KNIX-FM Phoenix, AZ; KMXP-FM Phoenix, AZ; KGME(AM) Phoenix, AZ; KESZ-FM Phoenix, AZ; KXEW South Tucson, AZ; KNST Tucson, AZ; KRQQ-FM Tucson, AZ; KWFM(AM) Tucson, AZ; KWMT-FM Tucson, AZ; KTTI-FM Yuma, AZ; KQSR(FM) Yuma, AZ; KZXY-FM Apple Valley, CA; KIXW Apple Valley, CA; KHYL-FM Auburn, CA; KDFO(AM) Bakersfield, CA; KGET(AM) Bakersfield, CA; KUSS(FM) Carlsbad, CA; KSBL-FM Carpinteria, CA; KDFO-FM Delano, CA; KRDU Dinuba, CA; KHTS-FM El Cajon, CA; KSPE-FM Ellwood, CA; KEZL-FM Fowler, CA; KCBL Fresno, CA; KALZ(FM) Fresno, CA; KATJ-FM George, CA; KURQ(FM) Grover Beach, CA; KRZR-FM Hanford, CA; KAVL Lancaster, CA; KSMY(FM) Lompoc, CA; KBIG-FM Los Angeles, CA; KFI Los Angeles, CA; KOST-FM Los Angeles, CA; KIIS-FM Los Angeles, CA; KHHT(FM) Los Angeles, CA; KLAC Los Angeles, CA; KYSR-FM Los Angeles, CA; KTLK(AM) Los Angeles, CA; KSTT-FM Los Osos-Baywood Park, CA; KIXA-FM Lucerne Valley, CA; KMRQ(FM) Manteca, CA; KTOM-FM Marina, CA; KJSN-FM Modesto, CA; KFIV Modesto, CA; KTPI(AM) Mojave, CA; KVVS(FM) Mojave, CA; KQKE(AM) Oakland, CA; KNEW Oakland, CA; KOCN-FM Pacific Grove, CA; KOSO-FM Patterson, CA; KSTE Rancho Cordova, CA; KGGI-FM Riverside, CA; KDIF Riverside, CA; KOSS-FM Rosamond, CA; KGBY-FM Sacramento, CA; KFBK Sacramento, CA; KDON-FM Salinas, CA; KZFX(AM) Salinas, CA; KPRC-FM Salinas, CA; KABL(AM) Salinas, CA; KKDD San Bernardino, CA; KTDD(AM) San Bernardino, CA; KGB-FM San Diego, CA; KMYI(FM) San Diego, CA; KIOZ-FM San Diego, CA; KOGO(AM) San Diego, CA; KLSD(AM) San Diego, CA; KIOI-FM San Francisco, CA; KISQ-FM San Francisco, CA; KMEL-FM San Francisco, CA; KKSF-FM San Francisco, CA; KYLD-FM San Francisco, CA; KUFX-FM San Jose, CA; KSJO-FM San Jose, CA; KSLY-FM San Luis Obispo, CA; KVEC San Luis Obispo, CA; KTYD-FM Santa Barbara, CA; KIST-FM Santa Barbara, CA; KBKO Santa Barbara, CA; KIST(AM) Santa Barbara, CA; KUYL(AM) Stockton, CA; KQOD-FM Stockton, CA; KCNL(FM) Sunnyvale, CA; KTPI-FM Tehachapi, CA; KMYT(FM) Temecula, CA; KTMQ(FM) Temecula, CA; KBOS-FM Tulare, CA; KFSO-FM Visalia, CA; KVBL Visalia, CA; KRSX-FM Yermo, CA; KBCO-FM Boulder, CO; KBPI(FM) Denver, CO; KRFX-FM Denver, CO; KOA Denver, CO; KHOW Denver, CO; KMGG(FM) Denver, CO; KTCL-FM Fort Collins, CO; KIIX(AM) Fort Collins, CO; KIBT(FM) Fountain, CO; KSME(FM) Greeley, CO; KVUU-FM Pueblo, CO; KCCY(FM) Pueblo, CO; KDZA-FM Pueblo, CO; KCSJ Pueblo, CO; KGHF Pueblo, CO; KPHT(FM) Rocky Ford, CO; KKZN(AM) Thornton, CO; KCOL(AM) Wellington, CO; KKLI-FM Widefield, CO; WPKX-FM Enfield, CT; WHCN-FM Hartford, CT; WKSS-FM Hartford, CT; WAVZ New Haven, CT; WELI New Haven, CT; WWYZ-FM Waterbury, CT; WPHH(FM) Waterbury, CT; WMZQ-FM Washington, DC; WWDC-FM Washington, DC; WBIG-FM Washington, DC; WASH-FM Washington, DC; WIHT(FM) Washington, DC; WWRC(AM) Washington, DC; WTEM Washington, DC; WFUS(FM) Bradenton, FL; WPLA-FM Callahan, FL; WBTP(FM) Clearwater, FL; WXTB-FM Clearwater, FL; WMMV Cocoa, FL; WJRR-FM Cocoa Beach, FL; WTKS-FM Cocoa Beach, FL; WSRZ-FM Coral Cove, FL; WTZB(FM) Englewood, FL; WHYI-FM Fort Lauderdale, FL; WBGG-FM Fort Lauderdale, FL; WMIB(FM) Fort Lauderdale, FL; WOLZ-FM Fort Myers, FL; WKGR-FM Fort Pierce, FL; WLDI-FM Fort Pierce, FL; WSYR-FM Gifford, FL; WJBT-FM Green Cove Springs, FL; WOLL-FM Hobe Sound, FL; WFXJ(AM) Jacksonville, FL; WROO-FM Jacksonville, FL; WQIK-FM Jacksonville, FL; WKEY-FM Key West, FL; WEOW-FM Key West, FL; WAIL-FM Key West, FL; WZJZ(FM) Lehigh Acres, FL; WMMB Melbourne, FL; WPBH(FM) Mexico Beach, FL; WINZ(AM) Miami, FL; WIOD Miami, FL; WLVE-FM Miami Beach, FL; WMGE(FM) Miami Beach, FL; WBWT(FM) Midway, FL; WMGF-FM Mount Dora, FL; WBTT(FM) Naples Park, FL; WFKS(FM) Neptune Beach, FL; WQTM(AM) Orlando, FL; WRUM(FM) Orlando, FL; WPAP-FM Panama City, FL; WDIZ Panama City, FL; WFBX(FM) Parker, FL; WTKX-FM Pensacola, FL; WYCL-FM Pensacola, FL; WFLF(AM) Pine Hills, FL; WCTH-FM Plantation Key, FL; WFKZ-FM Plantation Key, FL; WCKT(FM) Port Charlotte, FL; WEBZ-FM Port St. Joe, FL; WCCF(AM) Punta Gorda, FL; WXSR-FM Quincy, FL; WZZR(FM) Riviera Beach, FL; WSRQ(AM) Sarasota, FL; WCVU(FM) Solana, FL; WAVW(FM) Stuart, FL; WTNT-FM Tallahassee, FL; WHNZ(AM) Tampa, FL; WFLA(AM) Tampa, FL; WXXL-FM Tavares, FL; WKEZ-FM Tavenier, FL; WLTQ-FM Venice, FL; WDDV(AM) Venice, FL; WZTA(AM) Vero Beach, FL; WCZR(FM) Vero Beach, FL; WQOL-FM Vero Beach, FL; WRLX-FM West Palm Beach, FL; WJNO(AM) West Palm Beach, FL; WBZT(AM) West Palm Beach, FL; WJYZ Albany, GA; WKLS(FM) Atlanta, GA; WGST Atlanta, GA; WBBQ-FM Augusta, GA; WIBL(FM) Augusta, GA; WRAK-FM Bainbridge, GA; WBZY(FM) Bowdon, GA; WSOL-FM Brunswick, GA; WWVA-FM Canton, GA; WQMT-FM Chatsworth, GA; WDAK Columbus, GA; WSHE(AM) Columbus, GA; WVRK-FM Columbus, GA; WDAL Dalton, GA; WBLJ(AM) Dalton, GA; WMWR(AM) Dry Branch, GA; WQBZ-FM Fort Valley, GA; WIBB-FM Fort Valley, GA; WYNF(FM) Gray, GA; WMGP(FM) Hogansville, GA; WLCG Macon, GA; WCOH Newnan, GA; WVWA(FM) Peachtree City, GA; WTUN(FM) Ringgold, GA; WUUS(AM) Rossville, GA; WRXR-FM Rossville, GA; WTKS(AM) Savannah, GA; WAEV-FM Savannah, GA; WSOK Savannah, GA; WTLY(FM) Thomasville, GA; WOBB-FM Tifton, GA; WRBV-FM Warner Robins, GA; WEBL(FM) Warner Robins, GA; KDNN(FM) Honolulu, HI; KHBZ(AM) Honolulu, HI; KHVH Honolulu, HI; KSSK(AM) Honolulu, HI; KUCD(FM) Pearl City, HI; KSSK-FM Waipahu, HI; KASI Ames, IA; KCCQ(FM) Ames, IA; KDRB(FM) Ankeny, IA; KBUR Burlington, IA; KGRS-FM Burlington, IA; KMJM(AM) Cedar Rapids, IA; WMT Cedar Rapids, IA; WMT-FM Cedar Rapids, IA; KCHA Charles City, IA; KCHA-FM Charles City, IA; KLKK-FM Clear Lake, IA; KMXG(FM) Clinton, IA; KCQQ(FM) Davenport, IA; WOC Davenport, IA; WLLR-FM Davenport, IA; WHO(AM) Des Moines, IA; KXNO(AM) Des Moines, IA; KKDM-FM Des Moines, IA; KKEZ-FM Fort Dodge, IA; KWMT Fort Dodge, IA; KBKB Fort Madison, IA; KBKB-FM Fort Madison, IA; KXKT(FM) Glenwood, IA; KXIC Iowa City, IA; KKRQ-FM Iowa City, IA; KGLO(AM) Mason City, IA; KIAI(FM) Mason City, IA; KCZE(FM) New Hampton, IA; KSMA-FM Osage, IA; KSEZ-FM Sioux City, IA; KMNS Sioux City, IA; KGLI-FM Sioux City, IA; KWSL Sioux City, IA; KFXD(AM) Boise, ID; KSAS-FM Caldwell, ID; KLLP-FM Chubbuck, ID; KXLT-FM Eagle, ID; KCIX(FM) Garden City, ID; KID Idaho Falls, ID; KID-FM Idaho Falls, ID; KIDO(AM) Nampa, ID; KWIK Pocatello, ID; KCDA(FM) Post Falls, ID; KEZJ-FM Twin

TV Group Ownership Clear Channel Communications Inc.

Falls, ID; KLIX Twin Falls, ID; KATZ-FM Alton, IL; WKSC-FM Chicago, IL; WGRB(AM) Chicago, IL; WGCI-FM Chicago, IL; WLIT-FM Chicago, IL; WNUA-FM Chicago, IL; KMJM-FM Columbia, IL; KUUL(FM) East Moline, IL; WVZA-FM Herrin, IL; WXAJ(FM) Hillsboro, IL; WRLL(AM) Johnston City, IL; WDDD Johnston City, IL; WDDD-FM Marion, IL; WFXN(AM) Moline, IL; WTAO-FM Murphysboro, IL; WVAZ-FM Oak Park, IL; WFMB(AM) Springfield, IL; WCVS-FM Virden, IL; WFRX West Frankfort, IL; WQUL-FM West Frankfort, IL; WTFX-FM Clarksville, IN; WRZX-FM Indianapolis, IN; WFBQ-FM Indianapolis, IN; WNDE Indianapolis, IN; WQMF-FM Jeffersonville, IN; WZKF(FM) Salem, IN; KZCH(FM) Derby, KS; KZSN-FM Hutchinson, KS; KRBB-FM Wichita, KS; KTHR(FM) Wichita, KS; WSFE(AM) Burnside, KY; WSEK(FM) Burnside, KY; WKED-FM Frankfort, KY; WFKY Frankfort, KY; WXRA(AM) Georgetown, KY; WBUL-FM Lexington, KY; WMXL-FM Lexington, KY; WLKT-FM Lexington-Fayette, KY; WKRD(AM) Louisville, KY; WKJK Louisville, KY; WLUE(FM) Louisville, KY; WMKJ(FM) Mt. Sterling, KY; WUBT(FM) Russellville, KY; WCND Shelbyville, KY; WJZO(FM) Shelbyville, KY; WKEQ-FM Somerset, KY; WSFC Somerset, KY; WLLK-FM Somerset, KY; WKQQ-FM Winchester, KY; KZMZ-FM Alexandria, LA; KDBS Alexandria, LA; WJBO Baton Rouge, LA; WPYR(AM) Baton Rouge, LA; WYNK-FM Baton Rouge, LA; KRVE-FM Brusly, LA; WSKR Denham Springs, LA; KHEV(FM) Houma, LA; WRNO-FM New Orleans, LA; WODT New Orleans, LA; WYLD New Orleans, LA; WNOE-FM New Orleans, LA; KKST-FM Oakdale, LA; KVKI-FM Shreveport, LA; KWKH(AM) Shreveport, LA; KEEL(AM) Shreveport, LA; WJMN-FM Boston, MA; WXKS Everett, MA; WKOX Framingham, MA; WHYN Springfield, MA; WSNE-FM Taunton, MA; WNNZ Westfield, MA; WTAG Worcester, MA; WKCG-FM Augusta, ME; WABI Bangor, ME; WLKE-FM Bar Harbor, ME; WBFB-FM Belfast, ME; WCME-FM Boothbay Harbor, ME; WQSS-FM Camden, ME; WGUY(FM) Dexter, ME; WKSQ-FM Ellsworth, ME; WFAU Gardiner, ME; WVOM-FM Howland, ME; WIGY-FM Madison, ME; WRKD Rockland, ME; WFZX(FM) Searsport, ME; WTOS-FM Skowhegan, ME; WUBB-FM York Center, ME; WTKA Ann Arbor, MI; WWWW(FM) Ann Arbor, MI; WBCK Battle Creek, MI; WRCC Battle Creek, MI; WNIC-FM Dearborn, MI; WDTW(AM) Dearborn, MI; WDTW-FM Detroit, MI; WMXD-FM Detroit, MI; WDFN Detroit, MI; WJLB-FM Detroit, MI; WKQI-FM Detroit, MI; WBCT-FM Grand Rapids, MI; WTKG Grand Rapids, MI; WOOD Grand Rapids, MI; WVTI-FM Holland, MI; WWKN-FM Marshall, MI; WKBZ(AM) Muskegon, MI; WMUS(FM) Muskegon, MI; WSNX-FM Muskegon, MI; WSHZ(FM) Muskegon, MI; WMRR-FM Muskegon Heights, MI; WLBY(AM) Saline, MI; KQQL-FM Anoka, MN; KNFX Austin, MN; KQHT-FM Crookston, MN; KRVI(FM) Detroit Lakes, MN; KLDJ-FM Duluth, MN; WEBC Duluth, MN; KMFX-FM Lake City, MN; KYSM Mankato, MN; KTCZ-FM Minneapolis, MN; KFXN Minneapolis, MN; KFAN Minneapolis, MN; KJZI(FM) Minneapolis, MN; KVOX Moorhead, MN; KXLP(FM) New Ulm, MN; KBMX(FM) Proctor, MN; KDWB-FM Richfield, MN; KWEB(AM) Rochester, MN; KRCH(FM) Rochester, MN; KEEY-FM Saint Paul, MN; KSNR-FM Thief River Falls, MN; KMFX Wabasha, MN; KSWF(FM) Aurora, MO; KTOZ-FM Pleasant Hope, MO; KSLZ-FM Saint Louis, MO; KSD-FM Saint Louis, MO; KLOU-FM Saint Louis, MO; KATZ Saint Louis, MO; KIGL(FM) Seligman, MO; KGMY Springfield, MO; KXUS-FM Springfield, MO; WESE-FM Baldwyn, MS; WMJY-FM Biloxi, MS; WBVV(FM) Booneville, MS; WWKZ(FM) Columbus, MS; WJKX-FM Ellisville, MS; WFOR Hattiesburg, MS; WUSW-FM Hattiesburg, MS; WHER-FM Heidelberg, MS; WHAL-FM Horn Lake, MS; WJDX Jackson, MS; WHLH(FM) Jackson, MS; WMSI-FM Jackson, MS; WZRX Jackson, MS; WQJQ-FM Kosciusko, MS; WNSL-FM Laurel, MS; WEEZ Laurel, MS; WYYW-FM Marion, MS; WJDQ-FM Meridian, MS; WFFX Meridian, MS; WBUV(FM) Moss Point, MS; WWZD-FM New Albany, MS; WMSO(FM) Newton, MS; WQYZ-FM Ocean Springs, MS; WKNN-FM Pascagoula, MS; WZLD(FM) Petal, MS; WKMQ(AM) Tupelo, MS; WTUP Tupelo, MS; WZKS-FM Union, MS; WSTZ-FM Vicksburg, MS; KISN(FM) Belgrade, MT; KKBR-FM Billings, MT; KBBB(FM) Billings, MT; KBUL Billings, MT; KCTR-FM Billings, MT; KMMS Bozeman, MT; KMMS-FM Bozeman, MT; KZMY(FM) Bozeman, MT; KLCY East Missoula, MT; KLYQ Hamilton, MT; KBAZ(FM) Hamilton, MT; KMHK-FM Hardin, MT; KPRK Livingston, MT; KXLB(FM) Livingston, MT; KYSS-FM Missoula, MT; KGVO Missoula, MT; KSEN Shelby, MT; KZIN-FM Shelby, MT; KLTC-FM Superior, MT; WWNC Asheville, NC; WRSN-FM Burlington, NC; WDCG-FM Durham, NC; WGBT(FM) Eden, NC; WPEK(AM) Fairview, NC; WQNQ(FM) Fletcher, NC; WMYI(FM) Hendersonville, NC; WLYT-FM Hickory, NC; WMAG(FM) High Point, NC; WVBZ(FM) High Point, NC; WRFX-FM Kannapolis, NC; WCDG(FM) Moyock, NC; WRVA-FM Rocky Mount, NC; WEND-FM Salisbury, NC; WIBT(FM) Shelby, NC; WKKT-FM Statesville, NC; WSIC Statesville, NC; WMXF(AM) Waynesville, NC; WRDU-FM Wilson, NC; WTQR-FM Winston-Salem, NC; KBMR Bismarck, ND; KFYR Bismarck, ND; KQDY(FM) Bismarck, ND; KSSS-FM Bismarck, ND; KXMR Bismarck, ND; KZRX-FM Dickinson, ND; KCAD(FM) Dickinson, ND; KFGO Fargo, ND; WDAY-FM Fargo, ND; KJKJ-FM Grand Forks, ND; KKXL Grand Forks, ND; KDAM(FM) Hope, ND; KFAB-FM Kindred, ND; KMXA-FM Minot, ND; KRRZ Minot, ND; KIZZ-FM Minot, ND; KCJB Minot, ND; KTGL-FM Beatrice, NE; KHUS(FM) Bennington, NE; KIBZ(FM) Crete, NE; KLMY(FM) Lincoln, NE; KMCX-FM Ogallala, NE; KOGA Ogallala, NE; KOGA-FM Ogallala, NE; KGOR-FM Omaha, NE; KEFM-FM Omaha, NE; KFAB Omaha, NE; KZKX-FM Seward, NE; KSFT-FM South Sioux City, NE; WERZ-FM Exeter, NH; WGIP Exeter, NH; WGXL-FM Hanover, NH; WTSL Hanover, NH; WXXK-FM Lebanon, NH; WGIR Manchester, NH; WGIR-FM Manchester, NH; WVRR-FM Newport, NH; WHEB-FM Portsmouth, NH; WQSO-FM Rochester, NH; WHCY-FM Blairstown, NJ; WSUS-FM Franklin, NJ; WHTZ-FM Newark, NJ; WNNJ Newton, NJ; KZRR-FM Albuquerque, NM; KABQ Albuquerque, NM; KBQI(FM) Albuquerque, NM; KPEK-FM Albuquerque, NM; KCQL Aztec, NM; KKFG-FM Bloomfield, NM; KTEG(FM) Bosque Farms, NM; KSYU-FM Corrales, NM; KTRA-FM Farmington, NM; KDAG(FM) Farmington, NM; KFMQ-FM Gallup, NM; KGLX(FM) Gallup, NM; KAZX(FM) Kirtland, NM; KBAC(FM) Las Vegas, NM; KABQ-FM Santa Fe, NM; KXTC-FM Thoreau, NM; KSFQ-FM White Rock, NM; KWNR-FM Henderson, NV; KQOL-FM Las Vegas, NV; KSNE-FM Las Vegas, NV; KWID(FM) Las Vegas, NV; WPYX-FM Albany, NY; WHRL-FM Albany, NY; WPHR(FM) Auburn, NY; WKKF(FM) Ballston Spa, NY; WINR Binghamton, NY; WISY-FM Canandaigua, NY; WCTW-FM Catskill, NY; WWDG(FM) DeRuyter, NY; WALK(AM) East Patchogue, NY; WRWD(AM) Ellenville, NY; WFKP(FM) Ellenville, NY; WENE(AM) Endicott, NY; WBBI(FM) Endwell, NY; WCPV-FM Essex, NY; WBBS-FM Fulton, NY; WRWD-FM Highland, NY; WFXF(FM) Honeoye Falls, NY; WHUC Hudson, NY; WZCR(FM) Hudson, NY; WKGS-FM Irondequoit, NY; WGHQ Kingston, NY; WKTU(FM) Lake Success, NY; WIXT(AM) Little Falls, NY; WSKU(FM) Little Falls, NY; WBWZ-FM New Paltz, NY; WAXQ-FM New York, NY; WLTW-FM New York, NY; WWPR-FM New York, NY; WEAV Plattsburgh, NY; WVTK(FM) Port Henry, NY; WKIP Poughkeepsie, NY; WPKF(FM) Poughkeepsie, NY; WRNQ-FM Poughkeepsie, NY; WOKR(FM) Remsen, NY; WADR Remsen, NY; WHTK Rochester, NY; WHAM Rochester, NY; WRNY Rome, NY; WTRY-FM Rotterdam, NY; WBPM(FM) Saugerties, NY; WGY Schenectady, NY; WNVE(FM) South Bristol Township, NY; WYYY-FM Syracuse, NY; WHEN Syracuse, NY; WSYR Syracuse, NY; WOFX(AM) Troy, NY; WUTQ Utica, NY; WMXW-FM Vestal, NY; WSKS(FM) Whitesboro, NY; WXZO(FM) Willsboro, NY; WHLO Akron, OH; WARF(AM) Akron, OH; WNCO Ashland, OH; WYBL(FM) Ashtabula, OH; WFUN Ashtabula, OH; WXEG-FM Beavercreek, OH; WNUS-FM Belpre, OH; WKDD(FM) Canton, OH; WLZT(FM) Chillicothe, OH; WCHI Chillicothe, OH; WBEX Chillicothe, OH; WSAI(AM) Cincinnati, OH; WKRC Cincinnati, OH; WLW Cincinnati, OH; WVMX-FM Cincinnati, OH; WCKY(AM) Cincinnati, OH; WTAM Cleveland, OH; WMMS-FM Cleveland, OH; WMJI-FM Cleveland, OH; WGAR-FM Cleveland, OH; WMJK(FM) Clyde, OH; WBVB-FM Coal Grove, OH; WCOL-FM Columbus, OH; WNCI-FM Columbus, OH; WTVN(AM) Columbus, OH; WLWD(FM) Columbus Grove, OH; WMMX-FM Dayton, OH; WTUE-FM Dayton, OH; WONE Dayton, OH; WONW Defiance, OH; WZOM-FM Defiance, OH; WDFM-FM Defiance, OH; WJER-FM Dover, OH; WZOO-FM Edgewood, OH; WDKF(FM) Englewood, OH; WZRX-FM Fort Shawnee, OH; WXXR(FM) Fredericktown, OH; WFXN-FM Galion, OH; WDSJ(FM) Greenville, OH; WFJX(FM) Hilliard, OH; WSRW Hillsboro, OH; WSRW-FM Hillsboro, OH; WBKS(FM) Ironton, OH; WIRO Ironton, OH; WLQT-FM Kettering, OH; WIMA Lima, OH; WXXF(FM) Loudonville, OH; WMAN Mansfield, OH; WLTP(AM) Marietta, OH; WRVB-FM Marietta, OH; WMRN Marion, OH; WDIF-FM Marion, OH; WKFS-FM Milford, OH; WMVO(AM) Mount Vernon, OH; WQIO-FM Mount Vernon, OH; WNDH-FM Napoleon, OH; WBBG(FM) Niles, OH; WPFX-FM North Baltimore, OH; WFXJ-FM North Kingsville, OH; WBUK(FM) Ottawa, OH; WMLX-FM Saint Mary's, OH; WCPZ(FM) Sandusky, OH; WVKF(FM) Shadyside, OH; WIZE Springfield, OH; WTTF Tiffin, OH; WVKS-FM Toledo, OH; WSPD Toledo, OH; WRVF(FM) Toledo, OH; WIOT(FM) Toledo, OH; WCWA Toledo, OH; WYNT-FM Upper Sandusky, OH; WCHO(AM) Washington Court House, OH; WKBN Youngstown, OH; WNIO(AM) Youngstown, OH; KIZS(FM) Broken Arrow, OK; KTBT(FM) Collinsville, OK; KLAW(FM) Lawton, OK; KVRW-FM Lawton, OK; KZCD(FM) Lawton, OK; KXXY-FM Oklahoma City, OK; KTST-FM Oklahoma City, OK; KTOK(AM) Oklahoma City, OK; KHBZ-FM Oklahoma City, OK; KQLL-FM Owasso, OK; KZBB-FM Poteau, OK; KKBD(FM) Sallisaw, OK; KMOD-FM Tulsa, OK; KTBZ(AM) Tulsa, OK; KAKC(AM) Tulsa, OK; KTHH(AM) Albany, OR; KRKT-FM Albany, OR; KIFS(FM) Ashland, OR; KKCW-FM Beaverton, OR; KLOO Corvallis, OR; KEJO Corvallis, OR; KZZE-FM Eagle Point, OR; KPNW Eugene, OR; KDUK-FM Florence, OR; KRWQ-FM Gold Hill, OR; KMED Medford, OR; KLDZ(FM) Medford, OR; KPOJ(AM) Portland, OR; KEX Portland, OR; WAEB Allentown, PA; WKAP Allentown, PA; WZZO-FM Bethlehem, PA; WTKT(AM) Harrisburg, PA; WKBO Harrisburg, PA; WHP Harrisburg, PA; WRBT-FM Harrisburg, PA; WRKK Hughesville, PA; WLAN Lancaster, PA; WVRT(FM) Mill Hall, PA; WSNI(FM) Philadelphia, PA; WIOQ-FM Philadelphia, PA; WJJZ-FM Philadelphia, PA; WDAS Philadelphia, PA; WUSL-FM Philadelphia, PA; WKST-FM Pittsburgh, PA; WDVE-FM Pittsburgh, PA; WPGB(FM) Pittsburgh, PA; WXDX-FM Pittsburgh, PA; WBGG(AM) Pittsburgh, PA; WRAW Reading, PA; WBYL(FM) Salladasburg, PA; WBLJ-FM Shamokin, PA; WAKZ(FM) Sharpsville, PA; WKGB-FM Susquehanna, PA; WRAK Williamsport, PA; WHJJ Providence, RI; WHJY-FM Providence, RI; WWBB-FM Providence, RI; WKSP(FM) Aiken, SC; WYKZ(FM) Beaufort, SC; WLTY-FM Cayce, SC; WEZL-FM Charleston, SC; WALC-FM Charleston, SC; WLTQ(AM) Charleston, SC; WVOC Columbia, SC; WCOS Columbia, SC; WNOK(FM) Columbia, SC; WSCC-FM Goose Creek, SC; WLFJ(AM) Greenville, SC; WESC-FM Greenville, SC; WGVL Greenville, SC; WLVH-FM Hardeeville, SC; WBZT-FM Mauldin, SC; WRFQ-FM Mt. Pleasant, SC; WPCH(AM) North Augusta, SC; WXLY-FM North Charleston, SC; WXBT(FM) West Columbia, SC; WUSY-FM Cleveland, TN; WPTN Cookeville, TN; WHUB Cookeville, TN; WTJS Jackson, TN; WRVW-FM Lebanon, TN; WBMC McMinnville, TN; WAKI McMinnville, TN; WDIA Memphis, TN; WEGR(FM) Memphis, TN; WREC(AM) Memphis, TN; KJMS-FM Memphis, TN; WYNU-FM Milan, TN; WLAC Nashville, TN; WSIX-FM Nashville, TN; WKXJ(FM) Signal Mountain, TN; WMAX-FM South Pittsburg, TN; WTZX Sparta, TN; WSMT Sparta, TN; WKZP(FM) Spencer, TN; KYYW(AM) Abilene, TX; KEYJ-FM Abilene, TX; KSLI(AM) Abilene, TX; KFGL(FM) Abilene, TX; KULL-FM Abilene, TX; KIXZ Amarillo, TX; KMML-FM Amarillo, TX; KMXJ-FM Amarillo, TX; KATP(FM) Amarillo, TX; KASE-FM Austin, TX; KVET-FM Austin, TX; KPEZ-FM Austin, TX; KLVI Beaumont, TX; KYKR-FM Beaumont, TX; KLUB-FM Bloomington, TX; KVNS(AM) Brownsville, TX; KTEX-FM Brownsville, TX; KKYS-FM Bryan, TX; KNFX-FM Bryan, TX; KTUX-FM Carthage, TX; KUNO Corpus Christi, TX; KRYS-FM Corpus Christi, TX; KMXR-FM Corpus Christi, TX; KFXR(AM) Dallas, TX; KDMX(FM) Dallas, TX; KZPS-FM Dallas, TX; KHKS-FM Denton, TX; KRPT(FM) Devine, TX; KAFX-FM Diboll, TX; KBFM(FM) Edinburg, TX; KHEY(AM) El Paso, TX; KPRR-FM El Paso, TX; KTSM(AM) El Paso, TX; KDGE(FM) Fort Worth, TX; KEGL-FM Fort Worth, TX; KHFI-FM Georgetown, TX; KCOL-FM Groves, TX; KBRQ(FM) Hillsboro, TX; KPWW-FM Hooks, TX; KPRC Houston, TX; KODA-FM Houston, TX; KTRH Houston, TX; KHMX-FM Houston, TX; KTBZ-FM Houston, TX; KKRW-FM Houston, TX; KBME Houston, TX; KBGE(AM) Kilgore, TX; KKTX-FM Kilgore, TX; KIIZ-FM Killeen, TX; KKCL-FM Lorenzo, TX; KKAM Lubbock, TX; KQBR(FM) Lubbock, TX; KFYO Lubbock, TX; KYKS-FM Lufkin, TX; KAGG(FM) Madisonville, TX; KHKZ(FM) Mercedes, TX; KCRS(AM) Midland, TX; KCHX(FM) Midland, TX; KQXX-FM Mission, TX; KFZX-FM Monahans, TX; KSFA Nacogdoches, TX; KLFX-FM Nolanville, TX; KMRK-FM Odessa, TX; KKMY-FM Orange, TX; KIOC-FM Orange, TX; KSAB-FM Robstown, TX; KFMK-FM Round Rock, TX; WOAI San Antonio, TX; KQXT-FM San Antonio, TX; KTKR San Antonio, TX; KXXM-FM San Antonio, TX; KNCN-FM Sinton, TX; KKYR-FM Texarkana, TX; KTYL-FM Tyler, TX; KNUE(FM) Tyler, TX; KQVT(FM) Victoria, TX; KIXS-FM Victoria, TX; KBGO(FM) Waco, TX; KWTX Waco, TX; KWTX-FM Waco, TX; WACO-FM Waco, TX; KISX-FM Whitehouse, TX; KNIN-FM Wichita Falls, TX; KWFS Wichita Falls, TX; KBZS(FM) Wichita Falls, TX; KJMY(FM) Bountiful, UT; KXRV(FM) Centerville, UT; KALL(AM) North Salt Lake City, UT; KNRS Salt Lake City, UT; KODJ-FM Salt Lake City, UT; KZHT(FM) Salt Lake City, UT; KOSY-FM Spanish Fork, UT; WYYD-FM Amherst, VA; WSNZ(FM) Appomattox, VA; WCHV Charlottesville, VA; WKAV Charlottesville, VA; WCJZ(FM) Charlottesville, VA; WSUH(FM) Crozet, VA; WACL-FM Elkton, VA; WFQX-FM Front Royal, VA; WKCY Harrisonburg, VA; WVGM Lynchburg, VA; WROV-FM Martinsville, VA; WOWI-FM Norfolk, VA; WKUS(FM) Norfolk, VA; WRVQ-FM Richmond, VA; WRVA Richmond, VA; WRNL Richmond, VA; WBTJ(FM) Richmond, VA; WTVR-FM Richmond, VA; WZBL(FM) Roanoke, VA; WGMN Roanoke, VA; WHTE-FM Ruckersville, VA; WSNV(FM) Salem, VA; WKDW Staunton, VA; WCYK-FM Staunton, VA; WKSI-FM Stephens City, VA; WJJS-FM Vinton, VA; WKCI(AM) Waynesboro, VA; WTFX(AM) Winchester, VA; WJCD(FM) Windsor, VA; WAZR-FM Woodstock, VA; WEZF-FM Burlington, VT; WCVR-FM Randolph, VT; WWWT Randolph, VT; WSYB Rutland, VT; WTSM(FM) Springfield, VT; WMXR-FM Woodstock, VT; KNBQ(FM) Centralia, WA;

KELA Centralia-Chehalis, WA; KMNT(FM) Chehalis, WA; KFNK(FM) Eatonville, WA; KQSN(FM) Naches, WA; KIXZ-FM Opportunity, WA; KOLW(FM) Othello, WA; KEYW-FM Pasco, WA; KFLD Pasco, WA; KJR Seattle, WA; KUBE-FM Seattle, WA; KPTQ(AM) Spokane, WA; KKZX-FM Spokane, WA; KQNT(AM) Spokane, WA; KHHO Tacoma, WA; KDBL(FM) Toppenish, WA; KRVO(FM) Vancouver, WA; KXRX-FM Walla Walla, WA; KUTI(AM) Yakima, WA; KIT Yakima, WA; WISM-FM Altoona, WI; WQRB-FM Bloomer, WI; WATQ(FM) Chetek, WI; WBIZ Eau Claire, WI; WIBA Madison, WI; WTSO Madison, WI; WMEQ(AM) Menomonie, WI; WQBW(FM) Milwaukee, WI; WISN Milwaukee, WI; WRIT-FM Milwaukee, WI; WOKY Milwaukee, WI; WKKV-FM Racine, WI; WMAD(FM) Sauk City, WI; WXXM(FM) Sun Prairie, WI; WMIL-FM Waukesha, WI; WMRE Charles Town, WV; WVHU(AM) Huntington, WV; WTCR-FM Huntington, WV; WTCR Kenova, WV; WAMX-FM Milton, WV; WZZW Milton, WV; WHNK(AM) Parkersburg, WV; WDMX-FM Vienna, WV; WEGW-FM Wheeling, WV; WBBD Wheeling, WV; WWVA(AM) Wheeling, WV; KIGN(FM) Burns, WY; KKTL Casper, WY; KTWO Casper, WY; KTRS-FM Casper, WY; KWYY-FM Casper, WY; KLEN-FM Cheyenne, WY; KQLF(FM) Cheyenne, WY; KOWB Laramie, WY; KCGY(FM) Laramie, WY; KRVK(FM) Midwest, WY; KGAB Orchard Valley, WY; WSMJ(FM) Baltimore, MD; WPOC-FM Baltimore, MD; WCAO Baltimore, MD; WTNT(AM) Bethesda, MD; WFMD(AM) Frederick, MD; WFRE(FM) Frederick, MD; WWFG-FM Ocean City, MD; WDKZ(FM) Salisbury, MD; WTGM Salisbury, MD; WSBY-FM Salisbury, MD; WOSC-FM Bethany Beach, DE; WDOV Dover, DE; WLBW-FM Fenwick Island, DE; WDSD-FM Smyrna, DE; WILM Wilmington, DE; WWTX(AM) Wilmington, DE; XETRA Tijuana, MEX

L. Lowry Mays, chmn; Mark P. Mays, pres/CEO; Randall T. Mays, exec VP; Kenneth E. Wyker, sr VP; Herbert W. Hill Sr., sr VP; Don Perry, exec VP.

Cocola Broadcasting Companies 706 W. Herndon Ave., Fresno, CA 93650. Phone: (559) 435-7000. Fax: (559) 435-3201. E-mail: info@cocolatv.com. Web Site: www.cocolatv.com. Ownership: Gary M. Cocola, owner

Stns: 2 TV. KKJB, Boise, ID; KGMC, Fresno-Visalia, CA

Gary M. Cocola, pres/CEO.

Cogeco Radio-Television Inc. 612 St. Jacques, Suite 100, Montreal, PQ H3C 5R1. Canada. Phone: (514) 390-6035. Fax: (514) 390-6070. Ownership: Cogeco Inc., 100%.

Stns: 1 TV. CFAP, Quebec City, PQ

Stns: 4 FM. CJMF-FM Quebec, PQ; CJEC-FM Quebec, PQ; CFGE-FM Sherbrooke, PQ; CJEB-FM Trois Rivieres, PQ

Rene Guimond, pres/CEO; Luc Doyon, VP; Therese David, VP; Guy Meunier, sls VP; Jacques Boiteau, gen mgr; Geoffrey O. Brow, gen mgr.

Communications Corp. of America Box 53708, Lafayette, LA 70505-3708. Phone: (337) 237-1142. Fax: (337) 237-1373. Ownership: Apollo Capital Management II & T. Galloway, jointly.

Stns: 10 TV. WGMB, Baton Rouge, LA; KTSM-TV, El Paso, TX; WEVV, Evansville, IN; KVEO, Harlingen-Weslaco -Brownsville-McAllen, TX; KADN, Lafayette, LA; KPEJ, Odessa-Midland, TX; KMSS, Shreveport, LA; KETK, Tyler-Longview (Lufkin & Nacogdoches), TX; KWKT, Waco-Temple-Bryan, TX; KYLE, Waco-Temple-Bryan, TX

Thomas R. Galloway, chmn; Wayne Elmore, pres/CEO.

Cordillera Communications Inc. 600 E. Superior St., Suite 203, Duluth, MN 55802. Phone: (218) 625-3045. Fax: (218) 625-3047. Web Site: www.cordillera.tv. Ownership: Evening Post Publishing Co., 100%.

Stns: 11 TV. KTVQ, Billings, MT; KXLF-TV, Butte-Bozeman, MT; KBZK, Butte-Bozeman, MT; KOAA, Colorado Springs-Pueblo, CO; KRIS, Corpus Christi, TX; KRTV, Great Falls, MT; KATC, Lafayette, LA; WLEX, Lexington, KY; KPAX, Missoula, MT; KSBY, Santa Barbara-Santa Maria-San Luis Obispo, CA; KVOA, Tucson (Sierra Vista), AZ

Terrance Hurley, pres.

Cornerstone TeleVision Inc. 1 Signal Hill Dr., Wall, PA 15148-1499. Phone: (412) 824-3930. Fax: (412) 824-5442. E-mail: info@ctvn.org. Web Site: www.ctvn.org. Ownership: Nonprofit.

Stns: 2 TV. WKBS, Johnstown-Altoona, PA; WPCB, Pittsburgh, PA

Ron Hembree, pres.

Corus Entertainment Inc. 630 3rd Ave. S.W., Suite 105, Calgary, AB T2P 4L4. Canada. Phone: (403) 444-4244. Fax: (403) 444-4242. Web Site: www.corusent.com. Ownership: J.R. Shaw controls an aggregate of 80% of the voting rights.

Stns: 3 TV. CKWS, Kingston, ON; CHEX-TV-2, Oshawa, ON; CHEX, Peterborough, ON

Stns: 20 AM. 20 FM. CFGQ-FM Calgary, AB; CKRY-FM Calgary, AB; CKNG-FM Edmonton, AB; CISN-FM Edmonton, AB; CHED Edmonton, AB; CKNW New Westminster, BC; CHMJ(AM) Vancouver, BC; CJOB Winnipeg, MB; CIQB-FM Barrie, ON; CHAY-FM Barrie, ON; CFNY-FM Brampton, ON; CJXY-FM Burlington, ON; CJDV-FM Cambridge, ON; CKCB-FM Collingwood, ON; CJSS-FM Cornwall, ON; CFLG-FM Cornwall, ON; CJUL(AM) Cornwall, ON; CJOY Guelph, ON; CHML Hamilton, ON; CFMK-FM Kingston, ON; CFFX(AM) Kingston, ON; CFPL London, ON; CILQ-FM North York, ON; CKRU Peterborough, ON; CFHK-FM St. Thomas, ON; CFMJ(AM) Toronto, ON; CKDK-FM Woodstock, ON; CJRC(AM) Gatineau, PQ; CFOM-FM Levis, PQ; CHMP-FM Longueuil, PQ; CFEL-FM Montmagny, PQ; CINW(AM) Montreal, PQ; CKAC Montreal, PQ; CHRC Quebec, PQ; CKRS(AM) Saguenay, PQ; CIME-FM Saint Jerome, PQ; CHLT Sherbrooke, PQ; CKTS Sherbrooke, PQ; CHLN Trois Rivieres, PQ; CINF(AM) Verdun, PQ

John M. Cassaday, pres.

Cox Enterprises Inc. 6205 Peachtree Dunwoody Rd., Atlanta, GA 30328. Phone: (678) 645-0000. Web Site: www.coxenterprises.com. Ownership: Dayton Cox Trust-A, Barbara Cox Anthony, Anne Cox Chambers and Richard L. Braunstein, trustees, 41.06368% votes; Anne Cox Chambers Atlanta Trust, Barbara Cox Anthony, trustee, 28.94032% votes; and Barbara Cox Anthony Atlanta Trust, Anne Cox Chambers, trustee, 28.94032% votes.

Stns: 13 TV. WSB, Atlanta; WSOC-TV, Charlotte, NC; WAXN-TV, Charlotte, NC; WHIO, Dayton, OH; KFOX, El Paso, TX; WJAC, Johnstown-Altoona, PA; WRDQ, Orlando-Daytona Beach-Melbourne, FL; WFTV, Orlando-Daytona Beach-Melbourne, FL; WPXI, Pittsburgh, PA; KTVU, San Francisco-Oakland-San Jose; KICU, San Francisco-Oakland-San Jose; KIRO, Seattle-Tacoma, WA; WTOV-TV, Wheeling, WV-Steubenville, OH

Stns: 13 AM. 64 FM. WZZK-FM Birmingham, AL; WBPT(FM) Birmingham, AL; WAGG(AM) Birmingham, AL; WZZK(AM) Birmingham, AL; WNCB(FM) Homewood, AL; WBHJ-FM Tuscaloosa, AL; WBHK-FM Warrior, AL; WEZN-FM Bridgeport, CT; WPLR-FM New Haven, CT; WNLK(AM) Norwalk, CT; WEFX-FM Norwalk, CT; WKHL-FM Stamford, CT; WFYV-FM Atlantic Beach, FL; WHQT-FM Coral Gables, FL; WCFB-FM Daytona Beach, FL; WSUN-FM Holiday, FL; WMXQ-FM Jacksonville, FL; WOKV Jacksonville, FL; WAPE-FM Jacksonville, FL; WJGL(FM) Jacksonville, FL; WPYO(FM) Maitland, FL; WHDR(FM) Miami, FL; WFLC-FM Miami, FL; WEDR-FM Miami, FL; WDUV-FM New Port Richey, FL; WDBO Orlando, FL; WHTQ-FM Orlando, FL; WMMO-FM Orlando, FL; WXGL(FM) Saint Petersburg, FL; WPOI(FM) Saint Petersburg, FL; WHPT(FM) Sarasota, FL; WWRM(FM) Tampa, FL; WSB Atlanta, GA; WSB-FM Atlanta, GA; WBTS(FM) Doraville, GA; WFOX(FM) Gainesville, GA; WALR-FM La Grange, GA; KCCN-FM Honolulu, HI; KRTR(AM) Honolulu, HI; KINE-FM Honolulu, HI; KRTR-FM Kailua, HI; KPHW(FM) Kaneohe, HI; KKNE(AM) Waipahu, HI; WSFR-FM Corydon, IN; WVEZ(FM) Louisville, KY; WPTI(FM) Louisville, KY; WRKA-FM Saint Matthews, KY; WBAB(FM) Babylon, NY; WGBB Freeport, NY; WBLI-FM Patchogue, NY; WHFM-FM Southampton, NY; WHIO Dayton, OH; WHKO-FM Dayton, OH; WDPT(FM) Piqua, OH; WZLR(FM) Xenia, OH; KRTQ-FM Sand Springs, OK; KRAV-FM Tulsa, OK; KRMG Tulsa, OK; KJSR-FM Tulsa, OK; KWEN-FM Tulsa, OK; WJMZ-FM Anderson, SC; WHZT(FM) Seneca, SC; KTHT(FM) Cleveland, TX; KHPT(FM) Conroe, TX; KONO-FM Helotes, TX; KLDE(FM) Lake Jackson, TX; KKBQ-FM Pasadena, TX; KKYX San Antonio, TX; KONO San Antonio, TX; KISS-FM San Antonio, TX; KCYY(FM) San Antonio, TX; KSMG(FM) Seguin, TX; KELZ-FM Terrell Hills, TX; WDYL-FM Chester, VA; WKHK-FM Colonial Heights, VA; WKLR-FM Fort Lee, VA; WMXB-FM Richmond, VA

Cox Enterprises Inc. owns the following daily newspapers: The (Grand Junction, CO) *Daily Sentinel; Palm Beach* (FL) *Daily News* and *The Palm Beach* (FL) *Post; The Atlanta* (GA) *Journal & Constitution; The Daily Advance* (Elizabeth City), *The* (Greenville) *Daily Reflector* and the *Rocky Mount Telegram*, all NC; *Dayton Daily News* and the *Springfield News-Sun*, both OH; *Austin American-Statesman, Longview News-Journal, The Lufkin Daily News, News Messenger* (Marshall), *The* (Nacogdoches) *Daily Sentinel* and the *Waco Tribune-Herald*, all TX. Cox also owns weekly newspapers and shoppers in CO, FL, NC, OH, and TX.

James C. Kennedy, chmn/CEO; Dennis Berry, pres; Andrew S. Fisher, pres & Cox Television; Robert F. Neil, pres/CEO & Cox Radio Inc.

Cunningham Broadcasting Corporation 2000 W. 41st St., Baltimore, MD 21211. Phone: (410) 662-9688. Fax: (410) 662-0816.

Stns: 6 TV. WNUV, Baltimore, MD; WTAT, Charleston, SC; WVAH, Charleston-Huntington, WV; WTTE, Columbus, OH; WRGT, Dayton, OH; WBSC, Greenville-Spartanburg, SC-Asheville, NC-Anderson, SC

The Curators of the University of Missouri (Business Services Division). University of Missouri, 316 University Hall, Columbia, MO 65211. Phone: (573) 882-2388. Fax: (573) 882-0010. Web Site: www.umsystem.edu. Ownership: (Business Services Division).

Stns: 1 TV. KOMU, Columbia-Jefferson City, MO

Stns: 5 FM. KBIA(FM) Columbia, MO; KCUR-FM Kansas City, MO; KMNR-FM Rolla, MO; KUMR-FM Rolla, MO; KWMU-FM Saint Louis, MO

Michael Dunn, gen mgr; Martin Siddall, gen mgr.

D

Dispatch Broadcast Group 770 Twin Rivers Dr., Columbus, OH 43215. Phone: (614) 460-3700. Fax: (614) 460-2809. Web Site: www.10tv.com. Ownership: Dispatch Printing Company

Stns: 2 TV. WBNS, Columbus, OH; WTHR, Indianapolis, IN

Stns: 1 AM. 1 FM. WBNS Columbus, OH; WBNS-FM Columbus, OH

Owns *The Columbus* (OH) *Dispatch, This Week* & *Ohio Magazine.*

Tamara J. Clapsaddle, controller; Michael J. Fiorile, pres.

Diversified Communications 121 Free St., Box 7437, Portland, ME 04112-7437. Phone: (207) 842-5400. Fax: (207) 842-5405. Web Site: www.divbusiness.com. Ownership: Horace A. Hildreth Jr., Josephine H. Detmer. See Cross-Ownership, Sect. A. Cable TV: New England Cablevision Inc.

Stns: 3 TV. WABI, Bangor, ME; WPDE, Florence-Myrtle Beach, SC; WCJB, Gainesville, FL

David H. Lowell, pres.

R.H. Drewry Group Box 708, Lawton, OK 73502. Phone: (580) 353-0820. Phone: (580) 355-7000. Fax: (580) 357-3811. Ownership: R.H. Drewry owns 69% of KSWO-TV. KFDA-TV is a joint venture owned by Lawton Cablevision (50%), KSWD-TV (45%), KSWO(AM) (2 1/2%) and KRHD-AM-FM (2 1/2%). KWAB(TV) and KWES-TV are owned by KSWO Television Inc. (50%) and Lawton Cablevision Inc. (50%). KXXV(TV) is owned by Centrex Television L.P. Cable TV.

Stns: 4 TV. KFDA, Amarillo, TX; KWES, Odessa-Midland, TX; KXXV, Waco-Temple-Bryan, TX; KSWO, Wichita Falls, TX & Lawton, OK

Robert H. Drewry, pres; Larry Patton, VP.

Duhamel Broadcasting Enterprises Box 1760, Rapid City, SD 57709. Phone: (605) 342-2000. Fax: (605) 342-7305. Web Site: www.kotatv.com. Ownership: William F. Duhamel, 63%; Peter A. and Lois G. Duhamel, 37%.

Stns: 4 TV. KDUH, Cheyenne, WY-Scottsbluff, NE; KHSD-TV, Rapid City, SD; KOTA-TV, Rapid City, SD; KSGW-TV, Rapid City, SD

Stns: 1 AM. 1 FM. KOTA Rapid City, SD; KDDX(FM) Spearfish, SD

William F. Duhamel, pres.

E

Eagle Creek Broadcasting LLC 2193 Association Dr., Suite 300, Okemos, MI 48864. Phone: (517) 347-4141.

Stns: 2 TV. KZTV, Corpus Christi, TX; KVTV, Laredo, TX

Emmis Communications Corp. 3500 W. Olive Ave., Suite 1450, Burbank, CA 91436. Phone: (818) 238-9154. Fax: (818) 238-9158. Web Site: www.emmis.com. Ownership: Jeffrey H. Smulyan, approximately 61% votes.

Stns: 25 TV. KBIM, Albuquerque-Santa Fe, NM; KREZ, Albuquerque-Santa Fe, NM; KRQE, Albuquerque-Santa Fe, NM; WSAZ-TV, Charleston-Huntington, WV; WFTX, Ft. Myers-Naples, FL; WLUK-TV, Green Bay-Appleton, WI; KGMD, Hilo, HI; KHAW, Hilo, HI; KHON-TV, Honolulu, HI; KGMB, Honolulu, HI; WALA-TV, Mobile, AL-Pensacola (Ft. Walton Beach), FL; WBPG, Mobile, AL-Pensacola (Ft. Walton Beach), FL; WVUE, New Orleans, LA; KMTV, Omaha, NE; WKCF, Orlando-Daytona Beach-Melbourne, FL; KOIN, Portland, OR; WTHI, Terre Haute, IN; KSNT, Topeka, KS; KGUN, Tucson (Sierra Vista), AZ; KAII,

Wailuku, HI; KGMV, Wailuku, HI; KSNW, Wichita-Hutchinson Plus, KS; KSNC, Wichita-Hutchinson Plus, KS; KSNG, Wichita-Hutchinson Plus, KS; KSNK, Wichita-Hutchinson Plus, KS

Stns: 2 AM. 21 FM. KKFR-FM Glendale, AZ; KPWR-FM Los Angeles, CA; KZLA-FM Los Angeles, CA; WKQX-FM Chicago, IL; WLUP-FM Chicago, IL; WRDA(FM) Jerseyville, IL; WYXB(FM) Indianapolis, IN; WIBC(AM) Indianapolis, IN; WLHK(FM) Shelbyville, IN; WTHI-FM Terre Haute, IN; WWVR-FM West Terre Haute, IN; KSHE(FM) Crestwood, MO; KFTK(FM) Florissant, MO; KIHT-FM Saint Louis, MO; KPNT-FM Sainte Genevieve, MO; WRKS(FM) New York, NY; WQHT-FM New York, NY; WQCD(FM) New York, NY; KLBJ Austin, TX; KGSR-FM Bastrop, TX; KROX-FM Buda, TX; KDHT(FM) Cedar Park, TX; KBPA(FM) San Marcos, TX

The publishing unit of Emmis Communications publishes seven magazines: *Atlanta Magazine, Cincinnati Magazine, Los Angeles Magazine, Wildlife Journal, Indianapolis Monthly* and *Texas Monthly*.

Rick Cummings, pres; Randy Bongarten, pres.

Entravision Communications Corp. 2425 Olympic Blvd., Suite 6000W, Santa Monica, CA 90404. Phone: (310) 447-3872. Fax: (310) 447-3899. E-mail: kthompson@entravision.com. Web Site: www.entravision.com. Ownership: Walter F. Ulloa, Philip W. Wilkinson, Paul Zevnik.

Stns: 17 TV. KLUZ, Albuquerque-Santa Fe, NM; WUNI, Boston (Manchester, NH); KORO, Corpus Christi, TX; KCEC, Denver, CO; KINT, El Paso, TX; KTFN, El Paso, TX; KNVO, Harlingen-Weslaco-Brownsville-McAllen, TX; WUVN, Hartford & New Haven, CT; KLDO, Laredo, TX; KINC, Las Vegas, NV; KSMS, Monterey-Salinas, CA; KUPB, Odessa-Midland, TX; WVEN-TV, Orlando-Daytona Beach-Melbourne, FL; KPMR, Santa Barbara-Santa Maria-San Luis Obispo, CA; WVEA-TV, Tampa-St. Petersburg (Sarasota), FL; WJAL, Washington, DC (Hagerstown, MD); KVYE, Yuma, AZ-El Centro, CA

Stns: 13 AM. 41 FM. KVVA-FM Apache Junction, AZ; KMIA(AM) Black Canyon City, AZ; KDVA(FM) Buckeye, AZ; KLNZ-FM Glendale, AZ; KZLZ-FM Kearny, AZ; KRRN(FM) Kingman, AZ; KSSE(FM) Arcadia, CA; KSEH(FM) Brawley, CA; KCVR-FM Columbia, CA; KXSE(FM) Davis, CA; KWST(AM) El Centro, CA; KSSD(FM) Fallbrook, CA; KLOK-FM Greenfield, CA; KMXX-FM Imperial, CA; KCVR Lodi, CA; KRCX-FM Marysville, CA; KDLE(FM) Newport Beach, CA; KTSE-FM Patterson, CA; KLYY(FM) Riverside, CA; KBMB(FM) Sacramento, CA; KBRG(FM) San Jose, CA; KLOK San Jose, CA; KDLD(FM) Santa Monica, CA; KSES-FM Seaside, CA; KCCL-FM Shingle Springs, CA; KMBX(AM) Soledad, CA; KLOB-FM Thousand Palms, CA; KMIX-FM Tracy, CA; KSSC(FM) Ventura, CA; KPVW(FM) Aspen, CO; KMXA Aurora, CO; KJMN-FM Castle Rock, CO; KXPK-FM Evergreen, CO; WLQY Hollywood, FL; KRZY Albuquerque, NM; KRZY-FM Santa Fe, NM; KQRT(FM) Las Vegas, NV; KRNV-FM Reno, NV; KTCY(FM) Azle, TX; KKPS-FM Brownsville, TX; KVLY-FM Edinburg, TX; KINT-FM El Paso, TX; KHRO(AM) El Paso, TX; KYSE(FM) El Paso, TX; KOFX-FM El Paso, TX; KFRQ-FM Harlingen, TX; KGOL Humble, TX; KBZO Lubbock, TX; KZZA(FM) Muenster, TX; KZMP-FM Pilot Point, TX; KNVO-FM Port Isabel, TX; KZMP(AM) University Park, TX; KAIQ(FM) Wolfforth, TX; WACA Wheaton, MD

Walter F. Ulloa, chmn/CEO; Philip Wilkinson, pres/COO; Larry Safir, exec VP.

Equity Broadcasting Corp. 1 Shackleford Dr., Suite 400, Little Rock, AR 72211. Phone: (501) 219-2400. Fax: (501) 221-1101. Web Site: www.ebcorp.net.

Stns: 26 TV. WNGS, Buffalo, NY; KBTZ, Butte-Bozeman, MT; KTWO-TV, Casper-Riverton, WY; KWWF, Cedar Rapids-Waterloo & Dubuque, IA; KDEV, Cheyenne, WY-Scottsbluff, NE; KTUW, Cheyenne, WY-Scottsbluff, NE; KTVC, Eugene, OR; KLMN, Great Falls, MT; KYPX, Little Rock-Pine Bluff, AR; KWBF, Little Rock-Pine Bluff, AR; WMQF, Marquette, MI; KMMF, Missoula, MT; WBMM, Montgomery (Selma), AL; KEYU, Oklahoma City, OK; KUOK, Oklahoma City, OK; WPXS, Paducah, KY-Cape Girardeau, MO-Harrisburg-Mount Vernon, IL; WBIF, Panama City, FL; KPOU, Portland, OR; KEGS, Reno, NV; KBNY, Salt Lake City, UT; KBCJ, Salt Lake City, UT; KUTF, Salt Lake City, UT; KQUP, Spokane, WA; KWBM, Springfield, MO; KWFT, Springfield, MO; WNYI, Syracuse, NY

Larry Morton, pres; Greg Fess, VP; Max Hooper, VP; James Hearnsberger, VP; Lori Withrow, sec; Emilia Chastain, treas.

F

Family Stations Inc. 290 Hegenberger Rd., Oakland, CA 94621. Phone: (510) 568-6200. Fax: (510) 568-6190. Ownership: Nonprofit corporation.

Stns: 1 TV. WFME, New York

Stns: 12 AM. 50 FM. WBFR-FM Birmingham, AL; KPHF-FM Phoenix, AZ; KFRB-FM Bakersfield, CA; KHAP(FM) Chico, CA; KFRJ(FM) China Lake, CA; KFRP(FM) Coalinga, CA; KECR El Cajon, CA; KFNO-FM Fresno, CA; KEFR-FM Le Grand, CA; KFRN Long Beach, CA; KEBR Rocklin, CA; KEDR-FM Sacramento, CA; KFRC San Francisco, CA; KHFR(FM) Santa Maria, CA; KFRS-FM Soledad, CA; KPRA-FM Ukiah, CA; KFRY(FM) Pueblo, CO; WCTF Vernon, CT; WMFL-FM Florida City, FL; WFTI-FM Saint Petersburg, FL; WWFR(FM) Stuart, FL; WFRC-FM Columbus, GA; KDFR(FM) Des Moines, IA; KEGR(FM) Fort Dodge, IA; KYFR Shenandoah, IA; WJCH-FM Joliet, IL; WQLZ(FM) Taylorville, IL; KPOR-FM Emporia, KS; WOFR(FM) Schoolcraft, MI; KFRD(FM) Butte, MT; KFRW(FM) Great Falls, MT; KBFR(FM) Bismarck, ND; WKDN-FM Camden, NJ; WFME-FM Newark, NJ; WFBF-FM Buffalo, NY; WFRH-FM Kingston, NY; WFRS-FM Smithtown, NY; WFRW-FM Webster, NY; WCUE Cuyahoga Falls, OH; WOTL-FM Toledo, OH; WYTN-FM Youngstown, OH; KYOR(FM) Newport, OR; KPFR(FM) Pine Grove, OR; KQFE-FM Springfield, OR; WUFR(FM) Bedford, PA; WEFR-FM Erie, PA; WFRJ-FM Johnstown, PA; WXFR(FM) State College, PA; WFCH-FM Charleston, SC; KKAA Aberdeen, SD; KQFR(FM) Rapid City, SD; KQKD Redfield, SD; KFRT(FM) Bay City, TX; KTXB-FM Beaumont, TX; KUFR-FM Salt Lake City, UT; KARR Kirkland, WA; KJVH-FM Longview, WA; WMWK-FM Milwaukee, WI; WJJO-FM Watertown, WI; WFSI-FM Annapolis, MD; WBGR Baltimore, MD; WBMD Baltimore, MD

Harold Camping, pres.

Fisher Broadcasting Company 100 4th Ave. N., Suite 440, Suite 1525, Seattle, WA 98109. Phone: (206) 404-7000. Fax: (206) 404-7050. Web Site: www.fisherbroadcasting.com. Ownership: Fisher Commmunications Inc., 100%.

Stns: 10 TV. KBCI-TV, Boise, ID; KCBY, Eugene, OR; KPIC, Eugene, OR; KVAL, Eugene, OR; KIDK, Idaho Falls-Pocatello, ID; KATU, Portland, OR; KOMO, Seattle-Tacoma, WA; KLEW-TV, Spokane, WA; KIMA-TV, Yakima-Pasco-Richland-Kennewick, WA; KEPR, Yakima-Pasco-Richland-Kennewick, WA

Stns: 8 AM. 19 FM. KRQS(FM) Alberton, MT; KYYA-FM Billings, MT; KBLG Billings, MT; KRZN(FM) Billings, MT; KRKX(FM) Billings, MT; KXTL Butte, MT; KAAR(FM) Butte, MT; KMBR-FM Butte, MT; KIKF(FM) Cascade, MT; KINX(FM) Great Falls, MT; KXGF Great Falls, MT; KAAK(FM) Great Falls, MT; KQDI Great Falls, MT; KQDI-FM Great Falls, MT; KXDR-FM Hamilton, MT; KYLT Missoula, MT; KGGL-FM Missoula, MT; KGRZ Missoula, MT; KZOQ-FM Missoula, MT; KBQQ(FM) Pinesdale, MT; KZPH-FM Cashmere, WA; KYSN-FM East Wenatchee, WA; KWWW-FM Quincy, WA; KAAP(FM) Rock Island, WA; KOMO Seattle, WA; KPLZ-FM Seattle, WA; KWWX Wenatchee, WA

Benjamin Tucker, pres.

Fort Myers Broadcasting Co. 2824 Palm Beach Blvd., Fort Myers, FL 33916. Phone: (239) 334-1111. Fax: (239) 334-0744. Ownership: Brian A. McBride.

Stns: 1 TV. WINK-TV, Ft. Myers-Naples, FL

Stns: 2 AM. 2 FM. WINK(AM) Fort Myers, FL; WINK-FM Fort Myers, FL; WPTK(AM) Pine Island Center, FL; WTLQ-FM Punta Rassa, FL

Forum Communications Co. Box 2020, Fargo, ND 58107. Phone: (701) 235-7311. Fax: (701) 241-5406. Web Site: www.in-forum.com.

Stns: 4 TV. WDAY, Fargo-Valley City, ND; WDAZ, Fargo-Valley City, ND; KBMY, Minot-Bismarck-Dickinson, ND; KMCY, Minot-Bismarck-Dickinson, ND

Stns: 1 AM. 1 FM. WZUU-FM Allegan, MI; WDAY Fargo, ND

Forum Communications Co. owns the *Alexandria* (MN) *Echo Press; The Pioneer*, Bemidji, MN; *Detroit Lakes* (MN) *Tribune; The Becker County Record*, Detroit Lakes, MN; *Park Rapids* (MN) *Enterprise; The Wadena* (MN) *Pioneer Journal; West Central Daily Tribune*, Willmar, MN; *The Daily Globe;* Worthington, MN; *The Daily Republic*, Mitchell SD; *The Dickinson Press*, Dickinson, ND & *The* (ND) *Forum*.

William C. Marcil, pres.

Fox Television Stations Inc. 1999 S. Bundy Dr., Los Angeles, CA 90025-5235. Phone: (310) 584-2000. Web Site: www.newscorp.com.

Stns: 37 TV. WAGA, Atlanta; KTBC, Austin, TX; WUTB, Baltimore, MD; WBRC, Birmingham (Anniston, Tuscaloosa), AL; WFXT, Boston (Manchester, NH); WFLD, Chicago; WJW, Cleveland, OH; KDFI, Dallas-Ft. Worth; KDFW, Dallas-Ft. Worth; KDVR, Denver, CO; KFCT, Denver, CO; WJBK, Detroit; WOGX, Gainesville, FL; WPWR-TV, Gary, IN; WGHP, Greensboro-High Point-Winston Salem, NC; KRIV, Houston; KTXH, Houston; WDAF-TV, Kansas City, MO; KTTV, Los Angeles; KCOP, Los Angeles; WHBQ, Memphis, TN; WITI, Milwaukee, WI; KFTC, Minneapolis-St. Paul, MN; KMSP, Minneapolis-St. Paul, MN; WFTC, Minneapolis-St. Paul, MN; WNYW, New York; WWOR, New York; WRBW, Orlando-Daytona Beach-Melbourne, FL; WOFL, Orlando-Daytona Beach-Melbourne, FL; WTXF, Philadelphia; KUTP, Phoenix, AZ; KSAZ-TV, Phoenix, AZ; KSTU, Salt Lake City, UT; KTVI, St. Louis, MO; WTVT, Tampa-St. Petersburg (Sarasota), FL; WTTG, Washington, DC (Hagerstown, MD); WDCA, Washington, DC (Hagerstown, MD)

Kevin Hale, gen mgr; Jack Abernethy, CEO; Roger Ailes, chmn.

Freedom Communications Inc., Broadcast Division Box 19549, Irvine, CA 92623-9549. Phone: (949) 253-2315. Fax: (949) 798-3527. Web Site: www.freedom.com. Ownership: Freedom Communications Holdings Inc., 100%.

Stns: 3 TV. WRGB, Albany-Schenectady-Troy, NY; WWMT, Grand Rapids-Kalamazoo-Battle Creek, MI; WLAJ, Lansing, MI

Freedom Communications Inc., publishes 28 daily & 37 wkly nwsprs in 12 states.

Doreen Wade, pres.

G

Gannett Broadcasting (Division of Gannett Co. Inc.). 7950 Jones Branch Dr., Mclean, VA 22107. Phone: (703) 854-6760. Fax: (703) 854-2005. Web Site: www.gannett.com. Ownership: (Division of Gannett Co. Inc.)

Stns: 21 TV. WXIA, Atlanta; WLBZ, Bangor, ME; WGRZ, Buffalo, NY; WKYC, Cleveland, OH; WLTX, Columbia, SC; KUSA, Denver, CO; WZZM, Grand Rapids-Kalamazoo-Battle Creek, MI; WFMY-TV, Greensboro-High Point-Winston Salem, NC; WJXX, Jacksonville, FL; WTLV, Jacksonville, FL; WBIR, Knoxville, TN; KTHV, Little Rock-Pine Bluff, AR; WMAZ-TV, Macon, GA; KARE, Minneapolis-St. Paul, MN; KNAZ, Phoenix, AZ; KPNX, Phoenix, AZ; WCSH, Portland-Auburn, ME; KXTV, Sacramento-Stockton-Modesto, CA; KSDK, St. Louis, MO; WTSP, Tampa-St. Petersburg (Sarasota), FL; WUSA, Washington, DC (Hagerstown, MD)

Gannett owns 101 daily newspapers, including the national newspaper *USA Today*, and non-daily newspapers throughout the country.

Roger Ogden, pres/CEO.

Glenwood Communications Corp. 222 Commerce St., Kingsport, TN 37660. Phone: (423) 246-9578. Fax: (423) 246-6261. E-mail: golz@wkpttv.com. Web Site: www.wkpttv.com. Ownership: William M. Boyd; Hugh N. Boyd Trust.

Stns: 1 TV. WKPT-TV, Tri-Cities, TN-VA

Stns: 4 AM. WOPI Bristol, TN; WKTP Jonesborough, TN; WKPT Kingsport, TN; WMEV Marion, VA

George E. DeVault Jr., pres.

Global BC (A Division of Global Communications Ltd.). 7850 Enterprise St., Burnaby, BC V5A 1V7. Canada. Phone: (604) 420-2288. Fax: (604) 422-6427. Web Site: www.canada.com. Ownership: CanWest Global Communications Corp., 100% (see listing).

Stns: 6 TV. CHAN-2, Bowen Island, BC; CHAN-5, Brackendale, BC; CHAN-1, Chilliwack, BC; CHKM-1, Pritchard, BC; CHAN-3, Squamish, BC; CHAN-7, Whistler, BC

Brett Manlove, VP sls; Roy Gardner, gen mgr; Fatbir Nijjar, VP finance; John O'Connor, VP.

Global Television Network (CanWest Global Communications Corp.). 81 Barber Greene Rd., Don Mills, ON M3C 2A2. Canada. Phone: (416) 446-5311. Fax: (416) 446-5447. Web Site: www.canada.com. Ownership: CanWest Global Communications Corp., 100% (see listing).

Stns: 9 TV. CIII-2, Bancroft, ON; CIII-7, Midland, ON; CIII-29, Oil Springs, ON; CIII-6, Ottawa, ON; CIII-4, Owen Sound, ON; CIII, Paris, ON; CIII-27, Peterborough, ON; CIII-22, Stevenson, ON; CIII-41, Toronto, ON

Rick Camilleri, CEO.

Good Life Broadcasting Inc. 653 W. Michigan St., Orlando, FL 32805. Phone: (407) 423-5200. Fax: (407) 422-0120. Web Site: www.goodlifebroadcasting.org.

Stns: 2 TV. WTGL-TV, Orlando-Daytona Beach-Melbourne, FL; WLCB-TV, Orlando-Daytona Beach-Melbourne, FL

Ken Mikesall, pres.

Granite Broadcasting Corp. 767 Third Ave., 34th Fl., New York, NY 10017. Phone: (212) 826-2530. Fax: (212) 826-2858. Web Site: www.granitetv.com.

Stns: 9 TV. WKBW, Buffalo, NY; WDWB, Detroit;

LIN Television Corporation

KBJR-TV, Duluth, MN-Superior, WI; KRII, Duluth, MN-Superior, WI; KSEE, Fresno-Visalia, CA; WISE-TV, Ft. Wayne, IN; WEEK, Peoria-Bloomington, IL; KBWB, San Francisco-Oakland-San Jose; WTVH, Syracuse, NY

W. Don Cornwell, chmn/CEO; Larry Willis, CFO; Stuart Beck, pres; Ellen McClain, CEO; John Deushane, COO.

Grant Broadcasting System II Inc. Box 2127, Roanoke, VA 24009. Phone: (540) 344-2127. Fax: (540) 345-1912. Web site: www.fox2127.com. Ownership: Milton Grant.

Stns: 2 TV. WZDX, Huntsville-Decatur (Florence), AL; WFXR, Roanoke-Lynchburg, VA

Milton Grant, pres/sec & pres.

Grant Media LLC 915 Middle River Dr., Suite 409, Fort Lauderdale, FL 33304. Phone: (954) 568-2000. Fax: (954) 568-2015. Ownership: Milton Grant.

Stns: 2 TV. WEUX, La Crosse-Eau Claire, WI; WLAX, La Crosse-Eau Claire, WI

Milton Grant, CEO; Mark Ryan, CFO.

Gray Television Inc. Box 1867, Albany, GA 31702-1867. Phone: (229) 888-9390. Fax: (229) 888-9374. Web Site: www.graytvinc.com. E-mail: cindy.holden@gcslink.com. Ownership: Bull Run Corp., Datasouth Computer Corp. and affiliated companies. Other interests: Porta Phone Paging Inc. and Lynqx.

Stns: 31 TV. WRDW-TV, Augusta, GA; WBKO, Bowling Green, KY; WCAV, Charlottesville, VA; KKTV, Colorado Springs-Pueblo, CO; WTVY, Dothan, AL; KKCO, Grand Junction-Montrose, CO; WITN-TV, Greenville-New Bern-Washington, NC; WHSV, Harrisonburg, VA; WVLT, Knoxville, TN; WEAU-TV, La Crosse-Eau Claire, WI; WILX, Lansing, MI; WKYT-TV, Lexington, KY; WYMT-TV, Lexington, KY; KGIN, Lincoln & Hastings-Kearney, NE; KOLN, Lincoln & Hastings-Kearney, NE; WMTV, Madison, WI; WTOK, Meridian, MS; WOWT, Omaha, NE; WJHG, Panama City, FL; WTAP-TV, Parkersburg, WV; KOLO, Reno, NV; WIFR, Rockford, IL; KXII, Sherman, TX-Ada, OK; WCTV, Tallahassee, FL-Thomasville, GA; WIBW, Topeka, KS; KWTX-TV, Waco-Temple-Bryan, TX; KBTX-TV, Waco-Temple-Bryan, TX; WSAW, Wausau-Rhinelander, WI; KAKE, Wichita-Hutchinson Plus, KS; KUPK, Wichita-Hutchinson Plus, KS; KLBY, Wichita-Hutchinson Plus, KS

Gray Communications publishes, through Albany Herald Publishing Co., *The Albany (GA) Herald* & publishes, through The Rockdale Citizen Publishing Co., *The Rockdale Citizen*, Conyers, GA & *The Gwinnett Daily Post*, Lawrenceville, GA. Gray Communications also publishes *The Goshen News*, Goshen, IN.

James Ryan, VP/CFO; J. Mack Robinson, chmn/CEO; Robert A. Beizer, VP law & dev; Wayne Martin, rgnl VP TV; Robert S. Prather Jr., pres/COO.

Greater Nebraska Television Inc. Box 749, North Platte, NE 69103. Phone: (308) 532-2222. Fax: (308) 532-9579. E-mail: knop@knoptv.com. Web Site: www.knop.msnbc.com. Ownership: Bank of America, N.A., Personal Representative of Estate of Richard F. Shively, 73.57%; Ulysses A. Carlini Sr., 3.58%.

Stns: 2 TV. KHAS, Lincoln & Hastings-Kearney, NE; KNOP-TV, North Platte, NE

Ulysses A. Carlini, VP; Lewys Carlini, gen mgr.

Groupe TVA Inc. Tele-4/CFCM-TV, 1000 Myrand Ave., Ste.-Foy, PQ G1V 2W3. Canada. Phone: (418) 688-9330. Fax: (418) 681-4239. Ownership: Quebecor Media Inc., 99.91%.

Stns: 6 TV. CJPM, Chicoutimi, PQ; CFCM, Quebec City, PQ; CFER, Rimouski, PQ; CFER-TV-2, Sept-Iles, PQ; CHLT, Sherbrooke, PQ; CHEM, Trois-Rivieres, PQ

Serge Gouin, pres.

H

Hearst-Argyle Television Inc. 888 7th Ave., 27th Fl., New York, NY 10106. Phone: (212) 887-6800. Fax: (212) 887-6875. Web Site: www.hearstargyle.com. Ownership: The Hearst Corp., 65%.

Stns: 33 TV. KOAT, Albuquerque-Santa Fe, NM; KOCT, Albuquerque-Santa Fe, NM; KOVT, Albuquerque-Santa Fe, NM; WBAL, Baltimore, MD; WCVB, Boston (Manchester, NH); WMUR, Boston (Manchester, NH); WNNE, Burlington, VT-Plattsburgh, NY; WPTZ, Burlington, VT-Plattsburgh, NY; WLWT, Cincinnati, OH; KCCI, Des Moines-Ames, IA; KHBS, Ft. Smith-Fayetteville-Springdale-Rogers, AR; KHOG, Ft. Smith-Fayetteville-Springdale-Rogers, AR; WXII, Greensboro-High Point-Winston Salem, NC; WYFF, Greenville-Spartanburg, SC-Asheville, NC-Anderson, SC; WGAL, Harrisburg-Lancaster-Lebanon-York, PA; KHVO, Hilo, HI; KITV, Honolulu, HI; WAPT, Jackson, MS; KMBC-TV, Kansas City, MO; WLKY, Louisville, KY; WISN, Milwaukee, WI; KSBW, Monterey-Salinas, CA; WDSU, New Orleans, LA; KOCO, Oklahoma City, OK; KETV, Omaha, NE; WESH, Orlando-Daytona Beach-Melbourne, FL; WTAE-TV, Pittsburgh, PA; WMTW-TV, Portland-Auburn, ME; KQCA, Sacramento-Stockton-Modesto, CA; KCRA, Sacramento-Stockton-Modesto, CA; WMOR, Tampa-St. Petersburg (Sarasota), FL; KMAU, Wailuku, HI; WPBF, West Palm Beach-Ft. Pierce, FL

KHOG-TV Fayetteville and KHBS(TV) Fort Smith, both AR; KCRA-DT Sacramento, KCRA-TV Sacramento and KSBW(TV) Salinas, all CA; WESH(TV) and WESH-DT Daytona Beach, FL; KHVO(TV) Hilo, KHVO-DT Hilo, KITV(TV) Honolulu, KITV-DT Honolulu, KMAU(TV) Wailuku and KMAU-DT Wailuku, all HI; KCCI(TV) Des Moines, IA; WLKY-TV Louisville, KY; WDSU(TV) New Orleans, LA; WBAL-TV and WBAL-DT Baltimore, MD; WCVB-DT and WCVB-TV Boston, MA; WAPT(TV) Jackson, MS; KMBC-TV Kansas City, MO; KETV(TV) Omaha, NE; KOAT-TV Albuquerque, KOCT(TV) Carlsbad, KOFT(TV) Farmington and KOVT(TV) Silver City, all NM; WPTZ(TV) North Pole, NY; WXII(AM) Kernersville and WXII-TV Winston-Salem, both NC; WLWT(TV) and WLWT-DT Cincinnati, OH; KOCO-TV Oklahoma City, OK; WGAL(TV) Lancaster, WTAE-DT Pittsburgh and WTAE-TV Pittsburgh, all PA; WYFF(TV) Greenville, SC; WNNE-TV Hartford, VT; WISN-DT and WISN-TV Milwaukee, WI. Stns managed by Hearst-Argyle Television, owned by The Hearst Corp.: WWWB(TV) Lakeland and WPBF(TV) Tequesta, both FL.

David J. Barrett, pres/CEO.

Heritage Broadcasting Co of MI Box 627, Cadillac, MI 49601. Phone: (231) 775-3478. Fax: (231) 775-3671. Web Site: www.9and10news.com. Ownership: Heritage Broadcasting Group Inc., 100%.

Stns: 2 TV. WWTV, Traverse City-Cadillac, MI; WWUP, Traverse City-Cadillac, MI

Mario F. Lacobelli, pres; William E. Kring, VP/gen mgr.

Hoak Media Corporation 500 Crescent Ct., Suite 220, Dallas, TX 75201. Phone: (972) 960-4848. Fax: (972) 960-4899.

Stns: 4 TV. KREG, Denver, CO; KREX, Grand Junction-Montrose, CO; KREY, Grand Junction-Montrose, CO; KAUZ, Wichita Falls, TX & Lawton, OK

Eric Van den Branden, pres.

Hubbard Broadcasting Inc. 3415 University Ave., St. Paul, MN 55114. Phone: (651) 646-5555. Fax: (651) 642-4103. E-mail: jmahoney@hbi.com.

Stns: 13 TV. WNYT, Albany-Schenectady-Troy, NY; KOBG-TV, Albuquerque-Santa Fe, NM; KOB, Albuquerque-Santa Fe, NM; KOBF, Albuquerque-Santa Fe, NM; KOBR, Albuquerque-Santa Fe, NM; WDIO, Duluth, MN-Superior, WI; WIRT, Duluth, MN-Superior, WI; KRWF, Minneapolis-St. Paul, MN; KSAX, Minneapolis-St. Paul, MN; KSTP, Minneapolis-St. Paul, MN; KSTC-TV, Minneapolis-St. Paul, MN; KAAL, Rochester, MN-Mason City, IA-Austin, MN; WHEC, Rochester, NY

Stns: 2 AM. 2 FM. WFMP(FM) Coon Rapids, MN; KSTP Saint Paul, MN; KSTP-FM Saint Paul, MN; WIXK(AM) New Richmond, WI

Stanley S. Hubbard, chmn/pres/CEO; Stanley E. Hubbard II, VP; Virginia H. Morris, VP; Robert W. Hubbard, VP; Julia D. Coyte, VP; Gerald D. Deeney, sr VP/treas/CFO; Harold C. Crump, VP; C. Thomas Newberry, VP; Linda S. Tremere, VP; Sue J. Cook, VP; Edward J. Aiken, VP; Kari Rominski, sec; Gary R. Macomber, asst sec.

I

International Broadcasting Corp. 1554 Bori St., San Juan, PR 00927-6113. Phone: (787) 274-1800. Fax: (787) 281-9758. Ownership: Pedro Roman Collazo, 100%. Note: Pedro Roman Collazo, as an individual, owns WVOZ(AM) San Juan, PR.

Stns: 3 TV. WVEO, Aguadilla, PR; WVOZ, Ponce, PR; WTCV, San Juan, PR

Stns: 7 AM. 1 FM. WRSJ(AM) Bayamon, PR; WGIT(AM) Canovanas, PR; WVOZ-FM Carolina, PR; WIBS Guayama, PR; WXRF Guayama, PR; WTIL Mayaguez, PR; WEKO(AM) Morovis, PR; WCHQ(AM) Quebradillas, PR

Pedro Roman Collazo, pres; Margarita Nazario, gen mgr.

J

Jefferson-Pilot Communications Co. 3350 Peachtree Rd., Penthouse Suite, Atlanta, GA 30326. Phone: (404) 261-2970. Fax: (404) 365-9020. Web site: www.jpcc.com. Ownership: Jefferson-Pilot Corp., 100%.

Stns: 2 TV. WBTV, Charlotte, NC; WWBT, Richmond-Petersburg, VA

Stns: 5 AM. 9 FM. KSOQ-FM Escondido, CA; KIFM-FM San Diego, CA; KBZT(FM) San Diego, CA; KSON-FM San Diego, CA; KKFN Denver, CO; KCKK Lakewood, CO; KJCD(FM) Longmont, CO; WLYF(FM) Miami, FL; WMXJ-FM Pompano Beach, FL; WAXY South Miami, FL; WQXI Atlanta, GA; WSTR-FM Smyrna, GA; WBT Charlotte, NC; WBT-FM Chester, SC

Clark Brown, pres.

Journal Communications Inc. 333 W. State St., Milwaukee, WI 53203. Phone: (414) 224-2616. Fax: (414) 224-2469. Web Site: www.jc.com. Ownership: Journal Communications Inc., 100%.

Stns: 6 TV. KIVI, Boise, ID; WGBA, Green Bay-Appleton, WI; WSYM, Lansing, MI; KTNV, Las Vegas, NV; WTMJ, Milwaukee, WI; KMIR-TV, Palm Springs, CA

Stns: 10 AM. 20 FM. KGMG-FM Oracle, AZ; KMXZ-FM Tucson, AZ; KZPT-FM Tucson, AZ; KGEM Boise, ID; KCID Caldwell, ID; KRVB(FM) Nampa, ID; KQXR-FM Payette, ID; KYQQ-FM Arkansas City, KS; KFXJ(FM) Augusta, KS; KMXW(FM) Newton, KS; KFTI(AM) Wichita, KS; KICT-FM Wichita, KS; KSGF-FM Ash Grove, MO; KZRQ-FM Mount Vernon, MO; KSPW(FM) Sparta, MO; KSGF(AM) Springfield, MO; KBBX-FM Nebraska City, NE; KOMJ(AM) Omaha, NE; KKCD-FM Omaha, NE; KEZO-FM Omaha, NE; KXSP(AM) Omaha, NE; KQCH(FM) Omaha, NE; KHLP(AM) Omaha, NE; KXBL(FM) Henryetta, OK; KFAQ(AM) Tulsa, OK; WMYU(FM) Karns, TN; WKHT(FM) Knoxville, TN; WQBB Powell, TN; WWST(FM) Sevierville, TN; WTMJ Milwaukee, WI

Journal Communications Inc., publisher of the morning *Milwaukee (WI) Journal Sentinel*, owns 100% of Journal Broadcast Corp.

Douglas G. Kiel, pres.

K

KB Prime Media L.L.C. 1320 Lafayette Rd., Gladwyne, PA 19035. Phone: (610) 526-2927. Fax: (610) 526-0679. E-mail: guyonturner@compuserve.com. Ownership: W.W. Keen Butcher, 80%; Guyon W. Turner, 20%.

Stns: 2 TV. WTLF, Tallahassee, FL-Thomasville, GA; WSWB, Wilkes Barre-Scranton, PA

W.W. Keen Butcher, member/CEO; Guyon W. Turner, pres/member.

KEVN Inc. Box 677, Rapid City, SD 57709. Phone: (605) 394-7777. Fax: (605) 348-9128. E-mail: news@kevn.com. Web Site: www.kevn.com.

Stns: 2 TV. KEVN-TV, Rapid City, SD; KIVV-TV, Rapid City, SD

Cindy McNeill, gen mgr; Robert Slocum, CFO; Bill Reyner, pres.

KHQ Inc. Box 600, Spokane, WA 99210-4102. Phone: (509) 448-6000. Fax: (509) 448-3231. Ownership: Cowles Publishing Company, 100%.

Stns: 3 TV. KHQ, Spokane, WA; KNDO, Yakima-Pasco-Richland-Kennewick, WA; KNDU, Yakima-Pasco-Richland-Kennewick, WA

Cowles Publishing owns *Spokesman-Review*, Spokane, WA.

Lon C. Lee, pres.

KM Communications Inc. 3654 Jarvis Ave., Skokie, IL 60076. Phone: (847) 674-0864. Fax: (847) 674-9188. Web Site: www.kmcommunications.com.

Stns: 2 TV. KWKB, Cedar Rapids-Waterloo & Dubuque, IA; KEJB, Monroe, LA-El Dorado, AR

Stns: 1 AM. 5 FM. WPNG(FM) Pearson, GA; KTKB(FM) Hagatna, GU; KQMG Independence, IA; KQMG-FM Independence, IA; WLCN(FM) Atlanta, IL; WMKB(FM) Earlville, IL

Myoung Hwa Bae, pres; Kevin J. Bae, VP/gen mgr.

L

LIN Television Corporation 4 Richmond Sq., Providence, RI 02906. Phone: (401) 454-2880. Fax: (401) 454-2817. E-mail: deborah.jacobson@lintv.com. Web Site: www.lintv.com. Ownership: Hicks, Muse, Tate & Furst 47%.

Stns: 27 TV. KXAM, Austin, TX; KXAN-TV, Austin, TX; WIVB, Buffalo, NY; WNLO, Buffalo, NY; WAND, Champaign & Springfield-Decatur, IL; WWHO, Columbus, OH; WDTN, Dayton, OH; WANE-TV, Ft. Wayne, IN; WOOD, Grand Rapids-Kalamazoo-Battle Creek, MI; WOTV, Grand Rapids-Kalamazoo-Battle Creek, MI; WTNH, Hartford & New Haven, CT; WCTX, Hartford & New Haven, CT; WNDY, Indianapolis, IN; WISH-TV, Indianapolis, IN; WLFI, Lafayette, IN; WNJX, Mayaguez, PR; WAVY-TV,

Norfolk-Portsmouth-Newport News, VA; WVBT, Norfolk-Portsmouth-Newport News, VA; WTIN, Ponce, PR; WKPV, Ponce, PR; WPRI, Providence, RI-New Bedford, MA; WJPX, San Juan, PR; WAPA, San Juan, PR; WJWN, San Sebastian, PR; WWLP, Springfield-Holyoke, MA; WUPW, Toledo, OH; WIRS, Yauco, PR

Gary Chapman, pres/CEO.

Lake Superior Community Broadcasting Corp. 1390 Bagley St., Alpena, MI 49707. Phone: (989) 356-3434. Ownership: Stephen A. Marks, 100%.

Stns: 2 TV. WBKP, Marquette, MI; WBUP, Marquette, MI

Lamco Communications Inc. 460 Market St., Suite 150, Williamsport, PA 17701. Phone: (570) 323-2252. Fax: (570) 323-2298. Ownership: Ann Y. Lamade, 9.62%; Howard J. Lamade Jr., 11.11%; James H. Lamade, 7.16%; J. Robert Lamade, 7.19%.

Stns: 7 TV. KTXS, Abilene-Sweetwater, TX; KTVM, Butte-Bozeman, MT; KRCR, Chico-Redding, CA; KAEF, Eureka, CA; KCFW, Missoula, MT; KECI, Missoula, MT; WCYB, Tri-Cities, TN-VA

Andrew W. Stabler Jr., pres/CEO.

Landmark Communications Inc. (Landmark Broadcast Division.). 150 W. Brambleton Ave., Norfolk, VA 23510. Phone: (757) 446-2000. Fax: (757) 446-2179. Web Site: www.landmarkcommunications.com. Ownership: (Landmark Broadcast Division.)

Stns: 2 TV. KLAS, Las Vegas, NV; WTVF, Nashville, TN

Landmark Communications Inc. publishes the following daily newspapers: *Citrus County Crhonicle*, Crystal River, FL; *News-Enterprise*, Elizabethtown, KY; *The Carroll County Times*, Westminster, MD; *Los Alamos Monitor*, Los Alamos, NM; *News & Record*, Greensboro, NC; *The Virginian-Pilot*, Norfolk, VA; *Roanoke Times*, Roanoke, VA. Landmark Community Newspapers, Shelbyville, KY, publishes four community dailies, four tri-wklys, nine semi-wklys, 29 wklys, 39 shoppers & free newspapers, & 38 special-interest publications. Landmark Communications owns 49.9% of Capital-Gazette Communications Inc., publisher of *The Capital* (a daily newspaper in Annapolis, MD), *The Maryland Gazette* (a twice-weekly newspaper in Glen Burnie, MD), *Washingtonian Magazine* & weekly newspapers in Bowie & Crofton, MD.

Frank Batten Jr., chmn; Decker Anstrom, pres.

Le Sea Broadcasting Box 12, South Bend, IN 46624. Phone: (574) 291-8200. Fax: (574) 291-9043. E-mail: leseabroadcasting@lesea.com. Web Site: www.lesea.com.

Stns: 8 TV. KWHD, Denver, CO; KWHH, Hilo, HI; KWHE, Honolulu, HI; WHMB-TV, Indianapolis, IN; WHNO, New Orleans, LA; WHME, South Bend-Elkhart, IN; KWHB, Tulsa, OK; KWHM, Wailuku, HI

Stns: 1 AM. 3 FM. WHPZ-FM Bremen, IN; WHME-FM South Bend, IN; WDOW-FM Dowagiac, MI; WDOW Dowagiac, MI

Peter Sumrall, pres/CEO.

Liberman Broadcasting Inc. 1845 Empire Ave., Burbank, CA 91504. Phone: (818) 729-5300. Fax: (818) 729-5678. E-mail: LBImedia@aol.com. Ownership: Lenard D. Liberman, 47.5-49% votes, 40-42.5% equity; Jose Liberman 2003 Annuity Trust, 23.75-24.5% votes, 20-21.25% equity; Esther Liberman 2003 Annuity Trust, 23.75-24.5% votes, 20-21.25% equity; public shareholders of Liberman Broadcasting Inc., 2-5% votes, 15-20% equity.

Stns: 3 TV. KMPX, Dallas-Ft. Worth; KZJL, Houston; KRCA, Los Angeles

Stns: 5 AM. 10 FM. KEBN(FM) Garden Grove, CA; KBUE(FM) Long Beach, CA; KHJ(AM) Los Angeles, CA; KBUA(FM) San Fernando, CA; KWIZ-FM Santa Ana, CA; KXGJ-FM Bay City, TX; KQQK(FM) Beaumont, TX; KJOJ Conroe, TX; KIOX-FM El Campo, TX; KJOJ-FM Freeport, TX; KQUE Houston, TX; KEYH Houston, TX; KNOR(FM) Krum, TX; KTJM-FM Port Arthur, TX; KSEV Tomball, TX

Lenard Liberman, pres; Brett Zane, CEO.

Liberty Corp. Box 502, Greenville, SC 29602-0502. Phone: (864) 241-5400. Fax: (864) 241-5401. Web Site: www.libertycorp.com. Ownership: The Liberty Corp., Greenville, SC (W. Hayne Hipp and families, principals).

Stns: 15 TV. WALB, Albany, GA; WLOX, Biloxi-Gulfport, MS; WIS, Columbia, SC; WFIE, Evansville, IN; KGBT-TV, Harlingen-Weslaco-Brownsville-McAllen, TX; WLBT, Jackson, MS; KAIT, Jonesboro, AR; KPLC, Lake Charles, LA; WAVE, Louisville, KY; KCBD, Lubbock, TX; WSFA, Montgomery (Selma), AL; WTOL, Toledo, OH; KLTV, Tyler-Longview (Lufkin & Nacogdoches), TX; KTRE, Tyler-Longview (Lufkin & Nacogdoches), TX; WWAY, Wilmington, NC

James M. Keelor, pres/COO; Howard Schrott, CFO.

M

MAX Media L.L.C. 900 Laskin Rd., Virginia Beach, VA 23451. Phone: (757) 437-9800. Fax: (757) 437-0034. Web Site: www.maxmedia.com. Ownership: MBG-GG LLC, 34.90%; MBG Quad-C Investors I Inc., 34.39%; Aardvarks Also LLC, 10.77%; Colonnade Max Investors Inc., 9.71%; Quad-C Max Investors Inc., 9.34%; MBG Quad-Investors II Inc., 0.52%; and Quad-C Max Investors II Inc., 0.37%.

Stns: 9 TV. KULR-TV, Billings, MT; WNKY, Bowling Green, KY; KWYB, Butte-Bozeman, MT; WVIF, Christiansted, VI; KTMF, Missoula, MT; WPFO, Portland-Auburn, ME; WGTQ, Traverse City-Cadillac, MI; WGTU, Traverse City-Cadillac, MI; KYTX, Tyler-Longview (Lufkin & Nacogdoches), TX

Stns: 11 AM. 23 FM. KVLD(FM) Atkins, AR; KCAB Dardanelle, AR; KVOM Morrilton, AR; KVOM-FM Morrilton, AR; KWKK-FM Russellville, AR; WCIL Carbondale, IL; WUEZ(FM) Carterville, IL; WXLT(FM) Christopher, IL; WOOZ-FM Harrisburg, IL; WJPF Herrin, IL; KEZS-FM Cape Girardeau, MO; KGIR Cape Girardeau, MO; KCGQ-FM Gordonville, MO; KLSC(FM) Malden, MO; KMAL(AM) Malden, MO; KWOC Poplar Bluff, MO; KJEZ-FM Poplar Bluff, MO; KKLR-FM Poplar Bluff, MO; KGKS-FM Scott City, MO; KSIM Sikeston, MO; WQDK-FM Ahoskie, NC; WGAI(AM) Elizabeth City, NC; WWOC(FM) Hatteras, NC; WCXL(FM) Kill Devil Hills, NC; WFYY(FM) Bloomsburg, PA; WYGL-FM Elizabethville, PA; WWBE-FM Mifflinburg, PA; WLGL-FM Riverside, PA; WYGL Selinsgrove, PA; WCMS(AM) Newport News, VA; WGH-FM Newport News, VA; WXMM(FM) Norfolk, VA; WFOG(FM) Suffolk, VA; WXEZ-FM Yorktown, VA

John A. Trinder, pres.

Malara Broadcast Group Inc. 5880 Midnight Pass Rd., Suite 701, Siesta Key, FL 34242. Phone: (941) 312-0214. Ownership: TCM Media Associates LLC, 100%.

Stns: 2 TV. KDLH, Duluth, MN-Superior, WI; WPTA, Ft. Wayne, IN

Manship Stations Box 2906, Baton Rouge, LA 70821. Phone: (225) 387-2222. Fax: (225) 336-2246. Web Site: www.2theadvocate.com. Ownership: WBRZ Richard Manship, 25%; Douglas Manship Jr., 25%; David Manship 25%; Dina Manship Planche 25%; and KRGV-TV is licensed to Mobile Video Tapes Inc.

Stns: 2 TV. WBRZ, Baton Rouge, LA; KRGV, Harlingen-Weslaco-Brownsville-McAllen, TX

Also owns Baton Rouge *Morning Advocate* & Saturday & Sunday *Advocate*.

Richard F. Manship, pres.

McGraw-Hill Broadcasting Co. c/o KGTV(TV), 4600 Air Way, San Diego, CA 92102. Phone: (619) 237-6212. Fax: (619) 262-2275. E-mail: equinn@kgtv.com. Web Site: www.mcgraw-hill.com. Ownership: The McGraw-Hill Companies, 100%.

Stns: 4 TV. KERO, Bakersfield, CA; KMGH, Denver, CO; WRTV, Indianapolis, IN; KGTV, San Diego, CA

McGraw-Hill Inc., owner of the McGraw-Hill Broadcasting Co., publishes *Business Week* magazine & various trade publications.

Edward J. Quinn, pres; Tim Boling, engrg dir.

McKinnon Broadcasting Co. 5002 S. Padre Island Dr., Corpus Christi, TX 78411. Phone: (361) 986-8300. Fax: (361) 986-8411. Ownership: Michael McKinnon.

Stns: 3 TV. KBMT, Beaumont-Port Arthur, TX; KIII, Corpus Christi, TX; KUSI, San Diego, CA

Michael McKinnon, pres/CEO.

Media General Broadcast Group 111 N. 4th St., Richmond, VA 23219. Phone: (804) 775-4600. Fax: (804) 775-4601. Web Site: www.mgbg.com. Ownership: Media General Inc.

Stns: 26 TV. KALB, Alexandria, LA; WJBF, Augusta, GA; WIAT, Birmingham (Anniston, Tuscaloosa), AL; WCBD, Charleston, SC; WDEF, Chattanooga, TN; WRBL, Columbus, GA; WBTW, Florence-Myrtle Beach, SC; WNCT, Greenville-New Bern-Washington, NC; WNEG, Greenville-Spartanburg, SC-Asheville, NC-Anderson, SC; WSPA-TV, Greenville-Spartanburg, SC-Asheville, NC-Anderson, SC; WASV, Greenville-Spartanburg, SC-Asheville, NC-Anderson, SC; WHLT, Hattiesburg-Laurel, MS; WJTV, Jackson, MS; WJWB, Jacksonville, FL; WTVQ, Lexington, KY; WKRG, Mobile, AL-Pensacola (Ft. Walton Beach), FL; WMBB, Panama City, FL; WSLS, Roanoke-Lynchburg, VA; KIMT, Rochester, MN-Mason City, IA-Austin, MN; WSAV, Savannah, GA; WFLA-TV, Tampa-St. Petersburg (Sarasota), FL; WJHL, Tri-Cities, TN-VA; KWCH, Wichita-Hutchinson Plus, KS; KBSD, Wichita-Hutchinson Plus, KS; KBSH, Wichita-Hutchinson Plus, KS; KBSL, Wichita-Hutchinson Plus, KS

The Dothan Eagle, Opelika-Auburn News, The Enterprise Ledger, all AL; *The Denver Post* (20% ownership), CO; *The Tampa Tribune*, (Sebring) *Highlands Today*, (Brooksville) *Hernando Today, Jackson County Floridan*, FL; *Winston-Salem Journal*, (Concord & Kannapolis) *Independent Tribune, Hickory Daily Record, Statesville Record & Landmark, The* (Morganton) *News Herald, The Reidsville Review, The* (Eden) *Daily News, The* (Marion) *McDowell News*, NC; *The* (Florence) *Morning News*, SC; *Richmond Times-Dispatch, Bristol Herald Courier, The* (Lynchburg) *News & Advance, The* (Charlottesville) *Daily Progress, Potomac* (Woodbridge) *News, Danville Register & Bee, The* (Waynesboro) *News Virginian, Manassas Journal Messenger, Culpeper Star-Exponent, Virginia Business (monthly magazine)*, VA. *Media General also owns nearly 100 weeklies and other periodicals and Media General News Service, DC.*

James A. Zimmerman, pres; Edward H. Deichman Jr., VP finance; Richard W. Roberts, VP; Ardell Hill, VP; Peter McCampbell, VP/dir sls; Daniel Bradley, VP; Steve Gleason, progmg VP; Catherine Gugerty, dir mktg; James Conschafter, VP; Tom Conway, VP; Paul Gaulke, mktg VP.

Mercury Broadcasting Co. Inc. 115 E. Travis, Suite 533, San Antonio, TX 78205. Phone: (210) 222-0973. Fax: (210) 222-0975. Ownership: Van H. Archer III.

Stns: 1 TV. KSCC, Wichita-Hutchinson Plus, KS

Stns: 1 AM. 1 FM. WKBF Rock Island, IL; WFMX-FM Statesville, NC

Van H. Archer III, pres/CEO.

Meredith Broadcasting Group, Meredith Corp. 1716 Locust St., Des Moines, IA 50309-3023. Phone: (515) 284-2159. Fax: (515) 284-2514. Web Site: www.meredith.com. Ownership: Meredith Broadcasting is an operating group of Meredith Corp., Des Moines, IA.

Stns: 11 TV. WGCL-TV, Atlanta; WFLI, Chattanooga, TN; WNEM-TV, Flint-Saginaw-Bay City, MI; WHNS, Greenville-Spartanburg, SC-Asheville, NC-Anderson, SC; WFSB, Hartford & New Haven, CT; KCTV, Kansas City, MO; KVVU, Las Vegas, NV; WSMV, Nashville, TN; KPHO, Phoenix, AZ; KPTV, Portland, OR; KPDX, Portland, OR

Stns: 1 AM. WNEM(AM) Bridgeport, MI

The publishing group includes:

Magazines: *American Baby, American Patchwork & Quilting, Better Homes & Gardens, Country Home, Country Home Country Gardens, Creative Home, Decorating, Do It Yourself, Garden, Deck, and Landscape, Garden Shed, Ladies' Home Journal, Midwest Living, MORE, Renovation Style, Successful Farming, Traditional Home,* and *Wood*, along with more than 170 special interest titles.

Paul Karpowic, pres; Douglas Lowe, exec VP.

Mission Broadcasting Inc. 7650 Chippewa Rd., Suite 305, Brecksville, OH 44141. Phone: (440) 526-2227. Fax: (330) 336-8454. Fax: (440) 546-1903. E-mail: dpthatcher@sbcglobal.net.

Stns: 13 TV. KRBC, Abilene-Sweetwater, TX; KCIT, Amarillo, TX; KHMT, Billings, MT; WFXP, Erie, PA; KODE, Joplin, MO-Pittsburg, KS; KAMC, Lubbock, TX; WTVO, Rockford, IL; KSAN-TV, San Angelo, TX; KOLR, Springfield, MO; WFXW, Terre Haute, IN; WUTR, Utica, NY; KJTL, Wichita Falls, TX & Lawton, OK; WYOU, Wilkes Barre-Scranton, PA

David Smith, pres; Nancie Smith, VP; Dennis Thatcher, COO.

Morris Multimedia Inc. 27 Abercorn St., Savannah, GA 31401. Phone: (912) 233-1281. Fax: (912) 238-2059. Web Site: www.morrismultimedia.com. Ownership: Charles H. Morris.

Stns: 3 TV. WXXV, Biloxi-Gulfport, MS; WCBI, Columbus-Tupelo-West Point, MS; WMGT-TV, Macon, GA

Daily newspapers, weekly newspapers.

Charles H. Morris, pres.

Morgan Murphy Stations (Evening Telegram Co) Box 44965, Madison, WI 53744-4965. Phone: (608) 271-4321. Fax: (608) 271-6111. E-mail: talkback@wisctv.com. Web Site: www.channel3000.com. Ownership: Evening Telegram Co. owns 100% of KVEW(TV), KXLY-AM-FM-TV, KXLY-DT and KAPP(TV). Evening Telegram Co. owns 84.4% of Television Wisconsin Inc., with an additional 15.2% of the stn held by Evening Telegram stockholders.

Stns: 5 TV. WKBT, La Crosse-Eau Claire, WI; WISC, Madison, WI; KXLY, Spokane, WA; KAPP, Yakima-Pasco -Richland-Kennewick, WA; KVEW, Yakima-Pasco -Richland-Kennewick, WA

Stns: 4 AM. 3 FM. KXLX(AM) Airway Heights, WA; KXLY Spokane, WA; KZZU-FM Spokane, WA; KEZE-FM Spokane, WA; WGLR Lancaster, WI; WPVL Platteville, WI; WPVL-FM Platteville, WI

The Evening Telegram principals own *Madison Magazine*, Madison, WI.

Elizabeth Murphy Burns, pres; George Nelson, exec VP; David Sanks, exec VP; Steve Herling, exec VP; Darrell Blue, VP/gen mgr; Scott Chorski, VP/gen mgr.

N

NBC TV Stations Division 30 Rockefeller Plaza, New York, NY 10112. Phone: (212) 664-4444. Fax: (212) 664-5830. Web Site: www.nbci.com.

Stns: 14 TV. WVTM, Birmingham (Anniston, Tuscaloosa), AL; WMAQ, Chicago; WCMH, Columbus, OH; KXTX, Dallas-Ft. Worth; WVIT, Hartford & New Haven, CT; KNBC, Los Angeles; WTVJ, Miami-Ft. Lauderdale, FL; WNBC, New York; WCAU, Philadelphia; WJAR, Providence, RI-New Bedford, MA; WNCN, Raleigh-Durham (Fayetteville), NC; KNSD, San Diego, CA; KNTV, San Francisco-Oakland-San Jose; WRC, Washington, DC (Hagerstown, MD)

Jay Ireland, pres.

Neuhoff Family L.P. 1501 N. Washington, Danville, IL 61832. Phone: (217) 442-1700. Phone: (217) 787-9200. Fax: (217) 431-1489. Web Site: www.wdnlfm.com. Ownership: Neuhoff Corp., North Palm Beach, FL, 100% of votes.

Stns: 1 TV. KMVT, Twin Falls, ID

Stns: 1 AM. 1 FM. WRHK-FM Danville, IL; WDAN(AM) Danville, IL

Mike Hulvey, gen mgr; Geoff Neuhoff, pres.

The New York Times Co. 229 W. 43rd St., New York, NY 10036. Phone: (212) 556-1234. Web Site: www.nytco.com. Ownership: (See also Cross-Ownership, Sect. A.)

Stns: 8 TV. WQAD, Davenport, IA-Rock Island-Moline, IL; WHO-TV, Des Moines-Ames, IA; KFSM-TV, Ft. Smith-Fayetteville-Springdale-Rogers, AR; WHNT, Huntsville-Decatur (Florence), AL; WREG, Memphis, TN; WTKR, Norfolk-Portsmouth-Newport News, VA; KFOR, Oklahoma City, OK; WNEP, Wilkes Barre-Scranton, PA

Stns: 1 FM. WQXR-FM New York, NY

The New York Times Co. publishes *The New York Times*, *The Boston* (MA) *Globe* and the *Worcester Telegram & Gazette*, Worcester, MA, and fifteen regional newspapers located throughout the southeast and in California.

Cynthia Augustine, pres.

NewCap Inc. 745 Windmill Rd., Dartmouth, NS B3B1C2. Canada. Phone: (902) 468-7557. Fax: (902) 468-7558. Web Site: www.ncc.ca. Ownership: H.R. Steele, Blavin & Company.

Stns: 2 TV. CITL, Lloydminster, AB; CKSA, Lloydminster, AB

Stns: 25 AM. 22 FM. CKBA Athabasca, AB; CJPR-FM Blairmore, AB; CIBQ Brooks, AB; CIQX-FM Calgary, AB; CFCW Camrose, AB; CKDQ Drumheller, AB; CKRA-FM Edmonton, AB; CIRK-FM Edmonton, AB; CJYR(AM) Edson, AB; CJXK-FM Grand Centre (Cold Lake), AB; CKVH High Prairie, AB; CIYR-FM Hinton, AB; CKSA-FM Lloydminster, AB; CKGY-FM Red Deer, AB; CIZZ-FM Red Deer, AB; CHLW Saint Paul, AB; CKWA Slave Lake, AB; CKSQ Stettler, AB; CKKY Wainwright, AB; CKWY-FM Wainwright, AB; CFOK(AM) Westlock, AB; CKJR Wetaskiwin, AB; CFRK-FM Fredericton, NB; CKIM Baie Verte, NF; CHVO Carbonear, NF; CFLC-FM Churchill Falls, NF; CKVO Clarenville, NF; CKXX-FM Corner Brook, NF; CFCB Corner Brook, NF; CKGA Gander, NF; CKXD-FM Gander, NF; CFLN Goose Bay, NF; CKCM Grand Falls, NF; CKXG-FM Grand Falls-Windsor, NF; CHCM Marystown, NF; CFNW Port au Choix, NF; CFCV-FM Saint Andrews, NF; CKIX-FM Saint John's, NF; VOCM(AM) Saint John's, NF; CFSX Stephenville, NF; CFLW Wabush, NF; CKUL-FM Halifax, NS; CIHT-FM Ottawa, ON; CHNO-FM Sudbury, ON; CJUK-FM Thunder Bay, ON; CKTG-FM Thunder Bay, ON; CHTN Charlottetown, PE

H.R. Steele, chmn; Scott Weatherby, CEO; R.G. Steele, pres/CEO.

Newfoundland Broadcasting Co. (NTV & OZ Networks). Box 2020, St. John's, NF A1C 5S2. Canada. Phone: (709) 722-5015. Fax: (709) 726-5107. E-mail: ozfm@ozfm.com. Web Site: www.ntv.ca. Ownership: Geoffrey W. Stirling, 89.95%; G. Scott Stirling, 10%; and others, 0.05%.

Stns: 6 TV. CJOM, Argentia, NF; CJWB, Bonavista, NF; CJWN, Corner Brook, NF; CJOX-1, Grand Bank, NF; CJCN, Grand Falls, NF; CJSV, Stephenville, NF

Stns: 8 FM. CJOZ-FM Bonavista Bay, NF; CJKK-FM Clarenville, NF; CKOZ-FM Corner Brook, NF; CIOZ-FM Marystown, NF; CHOS-FM Rattling Brook, NF; CKSS-FM Red Rocks, NF; CHOZ-FM Saint John's, NF; CIOS-FM Stephenville, NF

Scott G. Stirling, pres/CEO; Doug Neal, engrg dir.

News-Press & Gazette Co. Box 29, St. Joseph, MO 64502. Phone: (816) 271-8500. Fax: (816) 271-8695. Ownership: David R. Bradley Jr., Henry H. Bradley, Lyle E. Leimkuhler. Cable TV: NPG Cable of Arizona.

Stns: 4 TV. KTVZ, Bend, OR; KVIA-TV, El Paso, TX; KIFI, Idaho Falls-Pocatello, ID; KESQ-TV, Palm Springs, CA

Stns: 1 AM. 1 FM. KESQ Indio, CA; KUNA-FM La Quinta, CA

News-Press & Gazette Co. publishes the *St. Joseph News-Press*, St. Joseph, MO.

John Kueneke, pres.

Newsweb Corp. 1645 W. Fullerton Ave., Chicago, IL 60614. Phone: (773) 975-0401. Fax: (773) 975-1301. Ownership: Fred Eychaner, 100%.

Stns: 2 TV. KTVD, Denver, CO; KUPN, Denver, CO

Stns: 5 AM. 4 FM. WKIE-FM Arlington Heights, IL; WAIT(AM) Chicago, IL; WSBC(AM) Chicago, IL; WCFJ Chicago Heights, IL; WCPT(AM) Crystal Lake, IL; WDEK-FM De Kalb, IL; WKIF-FM Kankakee, IL; WRZA(FM) Park Forest, IL; WNDZ Portage, IN

Fred Eychaner, CEO; Charley Gross, COO.

Nexstar Broadcasting Group Inc. 909 Lake Carolyn Pkwy., Suite 1450, Irving, TX 75039. Phone: (972) 373-8800. Fax: (972) 373-8888. Web Site: www.nexstar.tv.

Stns: 29 TV. KTAB, Abilene-Sweetwater, TX; KAMR, Amarillo, TX; KBTV, Beaumont-Port Arthur, TX; KSVI, Billings, MT; WCFN, Champaign & Springfield-Decatur, IL; WCIA, Champaign & Springfield-Decatur, IL; WDHN, Dothan, AL; WJET-TV, Erie, PA; WTVW, Evansville, IN; KFTA-TV, Ft. Smith-Fayetteville-Springdale-Rogers, AR; KNWA-TV, Ft. Smith-Fayetteville-Springdale-Rogers, AR; WFFT-TV, Ft. Wayne, IN; KSNF, Joplin, MO-Pittsburg, KS; KARK, Little Rock-Pine Bluff, AR; KLBK, Lubbock, TX; KARD, Monroe, LA-El Dorado, AR; KMID, Odessa-Midland, TX; WMBD, Peoria-Bloomington, IL; WROC-TV, Rochester, NY; WQRF, Rockford, IL; KLST, San Angelo, TX; KTAL, Shreveport, LA; KSFX-TV, Springfield, MO; KQTV, St. Joseph, MO; WTWO, Terre Haute, IN; WFXV, Utica, NY; WHAG, Washington, DC (Hagerstown, MD); KFDX, Wichita Falls, TX & Lawton, OK; WBRE, Wilkes Barre-Scranton, PA

Perry Sook, pres.

Northwest Broadcasting Inc. 2111 University Park Dr., Suite 650, Okemos, MI 48864. Phone: (517) 347-4141. Fax: (517) 347-4675. E-mail: bradybw1@comcast.net.

Stns: 4 TV. WICZ, Binghamton, NY; KMVU, Medford-Klamath Falls, OR; KAYU-TV, Spokane, WA; KFFX-TV, Yakima-Pasco-Richland-Kennewick, WA

Brian Brady, pres/CEO.

P

Pappas Telecasting Companies 500 S. Chinowth Rd., Visalia, CA 93277. Phone: (559) 733-7800. Fax: (559) 733-7878. Ownership: Harry J. Pappas.

Stns: 18 TV. WLGA, Columbus, GA; KPWB, Des Moines-Ames, IA; KDBC, El Paso, TX; KMPH, Fresno-Visalia, CA; KFRE-TV, Fresno-Visalia, CA; WWAZ-TV, Green Bay-Appleton, WI; WTWB-TV, Greensboro-High Point-Winston Salem, NC; KAZH, Houston; KWNB, Lincoln & Hastings-Kearney, NE; KHGI, Lincoln & Hastings-Kearney, NE; KAZA-TV, Los Angeles; KPTM, Omaha, NE; KREN, Reno, NV; KTNC, San Francisco-Oakland-San Jose; KUNO-TV, San Francisco-Oakland-San Jose; KPTH, Sioux City, IA; KAZW-TV, Yakima-Pasco-Richland-Kennewick, WA; KSWT, Yuma, AZ-El Centro, CA

Stns: 2 AM. 1 FM. KVBE(FM) Hanford, CA; KTRB Modesto, CA; KPMP(AM) Modesto, CA

Harry J. Pappas, pres/CEO.

The Jim Pattison Broadcast Group 460 Pemberton Terrace, Kamloops, BC V2C 1T5. Canada. Phone: (250) 372-3322. Fax: (250) 374-0445. Web Site: www.jpbroadcast.com. Ownership: Jim Pattison Group.

Stns: 4 TV. CFJC-TV, Kamloops, BC; CHAT, Medicine Hat, AB; CHAT-1, Pivot, AB; CKPG, Prince George, BC

Stns: 3 AM. 17 FM. CIBW-FM Drayton Valley, AB; CJXX-FM Grande Prairie, AB; CHLB-FM Lethbridge, AB; CFMY-FM Medicine Hat, AB; CHAT Medicine Hat, AB; CHUB-FM Red Deer, AB; CFDV-FM Red Deer, AB; CHBW-FM Rocky Mountain House, AB; CJBZ-FM Taber, AB; CHBZ-FM Cranbrook, BC; CHDR-FM Cranbrook, BC; CJDR-FM Fernie, BC; CKBZ-FM Kamloops, BC; CIFM-FM Kamloops, BC; CKLZ-FM Kelowna, BC; CKOV Kelowna, BC; CKDV-FM Prince George, BC; CKKN-FM Prince George, BC; CJJR-FM Vancouver, BC; CKBD Vancouver, BC

Rick Arnish, pres.

Paxson Communications Corp. 601 Clearwater Park Rd., West Palm Beach, FL 33401-6233. Phone: (561) 659-4122. Fax: (561) 655-7246. Fax: (561) 659-4252. E-mail: sethgrossman@paxson.com. Web Site: www.pax.tv. Ownership: Publicly traded company on the Amex ticker (PXN). Note: Paxson Communications also owns Infomall TV Network, three state radio networks (Alabama Radio Network, Florida Radio Network, Tennessee Radio Network), three rgnl sports networks (University of Florida Sports Network, University of Miami Sports Network, Penn State Sports Network), outdoor adv.

Stns: 55 TV. WYPX, Albany-Schenectady-Troy, NY; WPXA, Atlanta; WPXH, Birmingham (Anniston, Tuscaloosa), AL; WPXG, Boston (Manchester, NH); WBPX, Boston (Manchester, NH); KPXR, Cedar Rapids-Waterloo & Dubuque, IA; WLPX, Charleston-Huntington, WV; WCPX, Chicago; WVPX, Cleveland, OH; KPXD, Dallas-Ft. Worth; KPXC, Denver, CO; KFPX, Des Moines-Ames, IA; WPXD, Detroit; WZPX, Grand Rapids-Kalamazoo-Battle Creek, MI; WGPX, Greensboro-High Point-Winston Salem, NC; WEPX, Greenville-New Bern-Washington, NC; WPXU-TV, Greenville-New Bern-Washington, NC; WHPX, Hartford & New Haven, CT; KPXB, Houston; WIPX, Indianapolis, IN; WPXC-TV, Jacksonville, FL; KPXO, Kaneohe, HI; KPXE, Kansas City, MO; WPXK, Knoxville, TN; WUPX-TV, Lexington, KY; KPXN, Los Angeles; WPXM, Miami-Ft. Lauderdale, FL; WPXE, Milwaukee, WI; KPXM, Minneapolis-St. Paul, MN; WNPX, Nashville, TN; WPXN, New York; WPXV, Norfolk-Portsmouth-Newport News, VA; KPXK, Odessa-Midland, TX; KOPX, Oklahoma City, OK; WOPX, Orlando-Daytona Beach-Melbourne, FL; WPPX, Philadelphia; KPPX, Phoenix, AZ; KPXG, Portland, OR; WDPX, Providence, RI-New Bedford, MA; WPXQ, Providence, RI-New Bedford, MA; WRPX, Raleigh-Durham (Fayetteville), NC; WFPX, Raleigh-Durham (Fayetteville), NC; WPXR, Roanoke-Lynchburg, VA; KSPX, Sacramento-Stockton-Modesto, CA; KUPX, Salt Lake City, UT; KPXL, San Antonio, TX; KKPX, San Francisco-Oakland-San Jose; KWPX, Seattle-Tacoma, WA; WXPX, Tampa-St. Petersburg (Sarasota), FL; KTPX, Tulsa, OK; WPXW, Washington, DC (Hagerstown, MD); WWPX, Washington, DC (Hagerstown, MD); WTPX, Wausau-Rhinelander, WI; WPXP, West Palm Beach-Ft. Pierce, FL; WQPX, Wilkes Barre-Scranton, PA

Lowell Paxson, pres.

Pegasus Broadcast Television Inc. 225 City Line Ave., Suite 200, Bala Cynwyd, PA 19004. Phone: (610) 934-7000. Fax: (610) 934-7072. Web Site: www.pgtv.com. Ownership: Marshall W. Pagon, 100%.

Stns: 5 TV. WDSI, Chattanooga, TN; WPXT, Portland-Auburn, ME; WTLH, Tallahassee, FL-Thomasville, GA; WILF, Wilkes Barre-Scranton, PA; WOLF, Wilkes Barre-Scranton, PA

Howard E. Verlin, exec VP; Marshall Pagon, chmn/CEO; Denise Rolfe, VP.

Piedmont Television Holdings LLC 7621 Little Ave., Suite 506, Charlotte, NC 28226. Phone: (704) 341-0944. Fax: (704) 341-0945. Web Site: www.piedmonttv.com. Ownership: Richard L. Gorman, Kathy R. Gorman.

Stns: 9 TV. KTBY, Anchorage, AK; WFXI, Greenville-New Bern-Washington, NC; WYDO, Greenville-New Bern-Washington, NC; WAAY-TV, Huntsville-Decatur (Florence), AL; WGXA, Macon, GA; KTVE, Monroe, LA-El Dorado, AR; WJCL, Savannah, GA; KSPR, Springfield, MO; WKBN, Youngstown, OH

Paul Brissette, pres/CEO; Bill Fielder, CFO.

Pikes Peak Broadcasting Co. Box 1457, Colorado Springs, CO 80901. Phone: (719) 632-1515. Fax: (719) 475-0815. Web Site: www.krdotv.com. Ownership: The Harry Hoth family.

Stns: 2 TV. KRDO-TV, Colorado Springs-Pueblo, CO; KJCT, Grand Junction-Montrose, CO

Stns: 1 AM. KRDO(AM) Colorado Springs, CO

Patti L. Hoth, pres; Neil D. Klockziem, gen mgr.

Pollack Broadcasting Co. 6699 Wild Berry Lane, Memphis, TN 38119. Phone: (901) 753-0768. Fax: (901) 753-0868. Ownership: William H. Pollack, 33 l/3%; Martin S. Belz, 33 l/3%; David L. Pollack, 33 l/3%.

Stns: 2 TV. KLAX, Alexandria, LA; KIEM, Eureka, CA

Stns: 3 AM. 3 FM. KBOA-FM Piggott, AR; KCRV Caruthersville, MO; KCRV-FM Caruthersville, MO; KBOA Kennett, MO; KTMO(FM) New Madrid, MO; KMIS Portageville, MO

William H. Pollack, pres.

Post-Newsweek Stations Inc. 550 W. Lafayette, Detroit, MI 48226. Phone: (313) 223-2260. Fax: (313) 223-2263. Ownership: Post-Newsweek Stations is a subsidiary of the publicly traded Washington Post Co.

Stns: 6 TV. WDIV, Detroit; KPRC, Houston; WJXT, Jacksonville, FL; WPLG, Miami-Ft. Lauderdale, FL; WKMG, Orlando-Daytona Beach-Melbourne, FL; KSAT, San Antonio, TX

The Washington Post Co. publishes the *Washington* DC *Post*, the *Everett* (WA) *Herald*, *Newsweek* magazine,

TV Group Ownership

Newsweek International (New York, NY), *Newsweek Japan* & *Newsweek Korea*.

Q

Quincy Newspapers Inc. 130 S. Fifth St., Quincy, IL 62301. Phone: (217) 223-5100. Fax: (217) 223-5019. Web Site: www.qni.biz.

Stns: 11 TV. WVVA, Bluefield-Beckley-Oak Hill, WV; WXOW, La Crosse-Eau Claire, WI; WQOW, La Crosse-Eau Claire, WI; WKOW, Madison, WI; WGEM-TV, Quincy, IL-Hannibal, MO-Keokuk, IA; KTTC, Rochester, MN-Mason City, IA-Austin, MN; WREX-TV, Rockford, IL; KTIV, Sioux City, IA; WSJV, South Bend-Elkhart, IN; WYOW, Wausau-Rhinelander, WI; WAOW, Wausau-Rhinelander, WI

Stns: 1 AM. 1 FM. WGEM Quincy, IL; WGEM-FM Quincy, IL

Quincy Newspapers Inc. owns the *Quincy* (IL) *Herald-Whig*, and the *New Jersey Herald*, Newton, NJ.

Thomas A. Oakley, pres.

R

Radio Nord Communications Inc. 380 Murdoch, Rowyn-Norando, PQ J9X 1G5. Canada. Phone: (514) 866-8686. Fax: (514) 866-8056. Web Site: www.radionord.com.

Stns: 5 TV. CKRN-3, Bearn-Fabre, PQ; CFGS-TV, Gatineau, PQ; CHOT-TV, Gatineau, PQ; CKRN-TV, Rouyn-Noranda, PQ; CFVS, Val d'Or, PQ

Stns: 8 FM. CHPR-FM Hawkesbury, ON; CFIX-FM Chicoutimi, PQ; CHVD-FM Dolbeau-Mistassini, PQ; CHLX-FM Gatineau, PQ; CJLA-FM Lachute, PQ; CKLX-FM Montreal, PQ; CHOA-FM Rouyn-Noranda, PQ; CHGO-FM Val d'Or, PQ

Pierre R. Brosseau, pres.

Ramar Communications II Ltd. Box 3757, Lubbock, TX 79452. Phone: (806) 745-3434. Fax: (806) 748-1949. Web Site: www.ramarcom.com. E-mail: bmoran@ramarcom.com. Ownership: Ray Moran, 51%; Brad Moran, 49%.

Lubbock, TX 79423, 9800 University Ave.

Stns: 4 TV. KTTL-TV, Albuquerque-Santa Fe, NM; KHFT, Albuquerque-Santa Fe, NM; KTEL-TV, Albuquerque-Santa Fe, NM; KJTV-TV, Lubbock, TX

Stns: 1 AM. 3 FM. KLZK(FM) Brownfield, TX; KJTV(AM) Lubbock, TX; KXTQ-FM Lubbock, TX; KSTQ-FM Plainview, TX

Ray Moran, chmn; Brad Moran, pres.

Rapid Broadcasting Co. Box 2860, Rapid City, SD 57709. Phone: (605) 355-0024. Fax: (605) 355-9274. Ownership: Scott Barbour, 11%; Leeann Rieman, 11%; Gilbert D. Moyle, 9.8%; Gilbert D. Moyle III, 9.8%; Clark D. Moyle, 9.8%; W.R. Barbour, 7.4%; William F. Turner, 3.8%; Suzanne M. Gabrielson, 2.9%; Charles H. Lien, 2.9%; James F. Simpson, 1.6%; and David M. Simpson, 1.6%.

Stns: 2 TV. KNBN, Rapid City, SD; KWSD, Sioux Falls (Mitchell), SD

Gilbert D. Moyle, pres; Gilbert D. Moyle III, exec VP; Clark D. Moyle, sec/treas.

Raycom Media Inc. 201 Monroe St., RSA Tower, 20th Fl, Montgomery, AL 36104. Phone: (334) 206-1400. Fax: (334) 206-1555. Web Site: www.raycommedia.com. Ownership: Raycom Media Inc. Other interests: Raycom Sports, New York, NY; Charlotte, NC; Ft. Lauderdale, FL; Nashville, TN; and Chicago, IL.

Stns: 33 TV. WFXL, Albany, GA; KASA, Albuquerque-Santa Fe, NM; WAFB, Baton Rouge, LA; KWWL, Cedar Rapids-Waterloo & Dubuque, IA; WXIX, Cincinnati, OH; WUAB, Cleveland, OH; WOIO, Cleveland, OH; KXRM, Colorado Springs-Pueblo, CO; WACH, Columbia, SC; WTVM, Columbus, GA; WDFX, Dothan, AL; WDAM, Hattiesburg-Laurel, MS; KHBC, Hilo, HI; KHNL, Honolulu, HI; KFVE, Honolulu, HI; WAFF, Huntsville-Decatur (Florence), AL; WTNZ, Knoxville, TN; KTVO, Ottumwa, IA-Kirksville, MO; KFVS-TV, Paducah, KY-Cape Girardeau, MO-Harrisburg-Mount Vernon, IL; WPGX, Panama City, FL; WTVR, Richmond-Petersburg, VA; WTOC, Savannah, GA; KSLA, Shreveport, LA; WSTM, Syracuse, NY; WNWO, Toledo, OH; WTOM, Traverse City-Cadillac, MI; WPBN, Traverse City-Cadillac, MI; KOLD, Tucson (Sierra Vista), AZ; KOGG, Wailuku, HI; WFLX, West Palm Beach-Ft. Pierce, FL; WECT, Wilmington, NC

Paul McTear, pres/CEO.

Red River Broadcast Co. L.L.C. Box 9115, Fargo, ND 58106. Phone: (701) 277-1515. Fax: (701) 277-1830. Ownership: Curtis Squire Inc., 100%. Myron Kunin owns 100% of Curtis Squire Inc.

Stns: 7 TV. KQDS-TV, Duluth, MN-Superior, WI; KVRR, Fargo-Valley City, ND; KBRR, Fargo-Valley City, ND; KJRR, Fargo-Valley City, ND; KNRR, Fargo-Valley City, ND; KDLT-TV, Sioux Falls (Mitchell), SD; KDLV, Sioux Falls (Mitchell), SD

Ro Grignon, pres; Kathy M. Lau, VP/gen mgr.

Reiten Television Inc. Box 1686, Minot, ND 58702-1686. Phone: (701) 852-2104. Fax: (701) 838-9360. Web Site: www.kxmc.com.

Stns: 4 TV. KXMA, Minot-Bismarck-Dickinson, ND; KXMB, Minot-Bismarck-Dickinson, ND; KXMC, Minot-Bismarck-Dickinson, ND; KXMD, Minot-Bismarck-Dickinson, ND

David Reiten, pres.

Roberts Broadcasting Co. 1408 N. Kingshighway Blvd., St. Louis, MO 63113. Phone: (314) 367-4600. Fax: (314) 367-0174. Web Site: www.upn46stl.com. Ownership: St. Louis/Denver LLC.

Stns: 4 TV. WZRB, Columbia, SC; KTFD-TV, Denver, CO; WRBJ, Jackson, MS; WRBU, St. Louis, MO

Michael Roberts, CEO; Steven C. Roberts, pres.

Rockfleet Broadcasting Inc. 575 Madison Ave., 10th Fl., New York, NY 10022. Phone: (212) 605-0401. Fax: (212) 605-0402. Ownership: Rockfleet Holdings, 100%.

Stns: 4 TV. WVII, Bangor, ME; WFQX-TV, Traverse City-Cadillac, MI; WFUP, Traverse City-Cadillac, MI; WJFW-TV, Wausau-Rhinelander, WI

R. Joseph Fuchs, pres.

Rogers Broadcasting Ltd. 777 Jarvis St., Toronto, ON M4Y 3B7. Canada. Phone: (416) 935-8200. Web Site: www.rogers.com. Ownership: Rogers Media Inc., 100%. Note: Rogers Media Inc. is 100% owned by Rogers Communications Inc.

Stns: 2 TV. CHNU-TV, Fraser Valley, BC; CJMT-TV, Toronto, ON

Stns: 5 AM. 29 FM. CFFR Calgary, AB; CHMN-FM Canmore, AB; CFRV-FM Lethbridge, AB; CJRX-FM Lethbridge, AB; CKQC-FM Abbotsford, BC; CKGO-FM-1 Boston Bar, BC; CKCL-FM Chilliwack, BC; CKSR-FM Chilliwack, BC; CFSR-FM Hope, BC; CISP-FM Pemberton, BC; CKKS-FM Sechelt, BC; CKWX Vancouver, BC; CKIZ-FM Vernon, BC; CHTT-FM Victoria, BC; CIOC-FM Victoria, BC; CISW-FM Whistler, BC; CITI-FM Winnipeg, MB; CKY-FM Winnipeg, MB; CKNI-FM Moncton, NB; CHNI-FM Saint John, NB; CJNI-FM Halifax, NS; CKAT North Bay, ON; CHUR-FM North Bay, ON; CICX-FM Orillia, ON; CHAS-FM Sault Ste. Marie, ON; CJQM-FM Sault Ste. Marie, ON; CKBY-FM Smiths Falls, ON; CIGM Sudbury, ON; CJMX-FM Sudbury, ON; CJRQ-FM Sudbury, ON; CKGB-FM Timmins, ON; CJQQ-FM Timmins, ON; CJCL Toronto, ON; CJAQ-FM Toronto, ON

Rael Merson, pres.

S

Saga Communications Inc. 73 Kercheval Ave., Suite 201, Grosse Pointe Farms, MI 48236. Phone: (313) 886-7070. Fax: (313) 886-7150. E-mail: chapsburg@sagacom.com. Web Site: www.sagacommunications.com. Ownership: Edward K. Christian, 56.5% of the voting stock. Other Interests: Illinois Radio Network, Michigan Radio Network, Michigan Farm Radio Network.

Stns: 3 TV. WXVT, Greenwood-Greenville, MS; KOAM, Joplin, MO-Pittsburg, KS; KAVU, Victoria, TX

Stns: 25 AM. 50 FM. KDEZ(FM) Jonesboro, AR; KDXY-FM Lake City, AR; KJBX(FM) Trumann, AR; KLTI-FM Ames, IA; KSTZ(FM) Des Moines, IA; KIOA(FM) Des Moines, IA; KAZR(FM) Pella, IA; KICD Spencer, IA; KICD-FM Spencer, IA; KLLT(FM) Spencer, IA; WIXY-FM Champaign, IL; WLRW-FM Champaign, IL; WXTT(FM) Danville, IL; WYMG(FM) Jacksonville, IL; WABZ(FM) Sherman, IL; WTAX(AM) Springfield, IL; WQQL(FM) Springfield, IL; WDBR(FM) Springfield, IL; WCFF(FM) Urbana, IL; WCVQ-FM Fort Campbell, KY; WJQI(AM) Fort Campbell, KY; WVVR(FM) Hopkinsville, KY; WZZP(FM) Hopkinsville, KY; WEGI(FM) Oak Grove, KY; WHNP(AM) East Longmeadow, MA; WPVQ(FM) Greenfield, MA; WHMQ(FM) Greenfield, MA; WHMP Northampton, MA; WLZX(FM) Northampton, MA; WAQY-FM Springfield, MA; WRSI(FM) Turners Falls, MA; WOQL(FM) Winchendon, MA; WVAE(AM) Biddeford, ME; WBAE Portland, ME; WGAN(AM) Portland, ME; WPOR(FM) Portland, ME; WZAN Portland, ME; WMGX(FM) Portland, ME; WYNZ-FM Westbrook, ME; WOXL-FM Biltmore Forest, NC; WLZR(AM) Canton, NC; WMLL(FM) Bedford, NH; WKBK(AM) Keene, NH; WKNE(FM) Keene, NH; WZBK(AM) Keene, NH; WFEA Manchester, NH; WZID(FM) Manchester, NH; WINQ(FM) Winchester, NH; WYXL-FM Ithaca, NY;

Quincy Newspapers Inc.

WNYY(AM) Ithaca, NY; WQNY-FM Ithaca, NY; WHCU Ithaca, NY; WBCO Bucyrus, OH; WSNY-FM Columbus, OH; WODB(FM) Delaware, OH; WJZA-FM Lancaster, OH; WJZK(FM) Richwood, OH; KMIT-FM Mitchell, SD; KUQL(FM) Wessington Springs, SD; WKFN(AM) Clarksville, TN; WINA Charlottesville, VA; WQMZ(FM) Charlottesville, VA; WWWV-FM Charlottesville, VA; WJOI Norfolk, VA; WAFX-FM Suffolk, VA; WKVT Brattleboro, VT; WRSY(FM) Marlboro, VT; KGMI Bellingham, WA; KBAI(AM) Bellingham, WA; KPUG Bellingham, WA; WFMR(FM) Brookfield, WI; WJMR-FM Menomonee Falls, WI; WKLH-FM Milwaukee, WI; WJYI Milwaukee, WI; WHQG(FM) Milwaukee, WI

Edward K. Christian, pres/CEO; Marcia Lobaito, VP business affrs; Sam Bush, CFO; Warren Lada Sr., VP opns.

SagamoreHill Broadcasting of Wyoming/Northern Colorado LLC Two Embarcadero Center, 23rd Fl., San Francisco, CA 94111. Phone: (415) 788-2755. Fax: (415) 788-7311. Ownership: SagamoreHill Broadcasting LLC, 100%.

Stns: 2 TV. KGWN, Cheyenne, WY-Scottsbluff, NE; KSTF, Cheyenne, WY-Scottsbluff, NE

Sage Broadcasting Corp. 406 S. Irving, San Angelo, TX 76903. Phone: (325) 655-6006. Fax: (325) 655-8461. Ownership: Suzanne S. Brown, 32%; Sherry S. Hawk, 32%; Paris R. Schindler, 32%; Anne Marie Carter, 3%; and Timothy R. Brown, 0.33%.

Stns: 2 TV. KXVA, Abilene-Sweetwater, TX; KIDY, San Angelo, TX

Sainte Partners II L.P. Box 4159, Modesto, CA 95352-4159. Phone: (209) 523-0777. Fax: (209) 523-0839. E-mail: csmith@sainte.tv. Ownership: Chester Smith, gen ptnr, & Naomi Smith, gen ptnr; & other limited ptnrs.

Stns: 2 TV. KCVU, Chico-Redding, CA; KBVU, Eureka, CA

Schurz Communications Inc. 225 W. Colfax Ave., South Bend, IN 46626. Phone: (219) 287-1001. Fax: (219) 287-2257. E-mail: mburdick@schurz.com. Ownership: Franklin D. Schurz Jr., James M. Schurz, Scott C. Schurz and Mary Schurz, trustees.

Stns: 4 TV. WAGT, Augusta, GA; WDBJ, Roanoke-Lynchburg, VA; WSBT, South Bend-Elkhart, IN; KYTV, Springfield, MO

Stns: 2 AM. 3 FM. WASK-FM Battle Ground, IN; WKOA-FM Lafayette, IN; WASK Lafayette, IN; WSBT South Bend, IN; WNSN-FM South Bend, IN

Schurz Communications publishes the following nwsprs: *Imperial Valley Press, Southside Times-Beech, Times; Bedford Times-Mail, Bloomington Herald-Times* , & *South Bend Tribune, Martinsville Reporter, Danville Advocate-Messenger, The Herald Mail Co.; Daily American, Somerset, PA.*

Marcia K. Burdick, sr VP bcstg; Franklin D. Schurz Jr., pres.

Scripps Howard Broadcasting Co. Box 5380, 312 Walnut St., 28th Fl., Cincinnati, OH 45201. Phone: (513) 977-3000. Fax: (513) 977-3728. Web Site: www.scripps.com. Ownership: The E.W. Scripps Co.

Stns: 15 TV. WMAR, Baltimore, MD; WMFP, Boston (Manchester, NH); WCPO, Cincinnati, OH; WEWS, Cleveland, OH; WOAC, Cleveland, OH; WXYZ, Detroit; KSHB-TV, Kansas City, MO; KMCI, Kansas City, MO; WSAH, New York; KNXV, Phoenix, AZ; WRAY, Raleigh-Durham (Fayetteville), NC; KCNS, San Francisco-Oakland-San Jose; WFTS, Tampa-St. Petersburg (Sarasota), FL; KJRH, Tulsa, OK; WPTV, West Palm Beach-Ft. Pierce, FL

Newspapers include: *Abilene Reporter-News; The Albuquerque Tribune; Anderson Independent-Mail; Birmingham Post-Herald; The Cincinnati Post; The Commercial Appeal* (Memphis); *Corpus Christi Caller-Times; Daily Camera* (Boulder); *Evansville Courier & Press; The Gleaner* (Henderson); *The Knoxville News-Sentinel; Naples Daily News; Redding Record Searchlight; Rocky Mountain News* (Denver); *San Angelo Standard-Times; The Stuart News; The Sun* (Bremerton); *The Tribune* (Ft. Pierce); *Ventura County Star; Vero Beach Press Journal; Wichita Falls Times Record News.*

William B. Peterson, sr VP, TV station group & The E.W. Scripps Co.

Sinclair Broadcast Group Inc. 10706 Beaver Dam Rd., Hunt Valley, MD 21030. Phone: (410) 568-1500. Fax: (410) 568-1533. E-mail: ir@sbgnet.com. Web Site: www.sbgi.net. Ownership: Smith brothers (major shareholders).

Stns: 49 TV. WBFF, Baltimore, MD; WABM, Birmingham (Anniston, Tuscaloosa), AL; WNYO, Buffalo, NY; WUTV, Buffalo, NY; KGAN, Cedar Rapids-Waterloo & Dubuque, IA; WICD, Champaign & Springfield-Decatur, IL; WICS, Champaign & Springfield-Decatur, IL; WMMP, Charleston, SC; WCHS, Charleston-Huntington, WV; WSTR-TV,

Cincinnati, OH; WSYX, Columbus, OH; WKEF, Dayton, OH; KDSM-TV, Des Moines-Ames, IA; WSMH, Flint-Saginaw-Bay City, MI; WUPN, Greensboro-High Point-Winston Salem, NC; WXLV, Greensboro-High Point-Winston Salem, NC; WLOS, Greenville-Spartanburg, SC-Asheville, NC-Anderson, SC; KSMO-TV, Kansas City, MO; KVWB, Las Vegas, NV; KFBT, Las Vegas, NV; WDKY, Lexington, KY; WMSN, Madison, WI; WCGV, Milwaukee, WI; WVTV, Milwaukee, WI; KMWB, Minneapolis-St. Paul, MN; WEAR, Mobile, AL-Pensacola (Ft. Walton Beach), FL; WFGX, Mobile, AL-Pensacola (Ft. Walton Beach), FL; WUXP, Nashville, TN; WZTV, Nashville, TN; WTVZ, Norfolk-Portsmouth-Newport News, VA; KOCB, Oklahoma City, OK; KOKH, Oklahoma City, OK; KBSI, Paducah, KY-Cape Girardeau, MO-Harrisburg-Mount Vernon, IL; WYZZ, Peoria-Bloomington, IL; WCWB, Pittsburgh, PA; WPGH, Pittsburgh, PA; WGME, Portland-Auburn, ME; WRDC, Raleigh-Durham (Fayetteville), NC; WLFL, Raleigh-Durham (Fayetteville), NC; WRLH, Richmond-Petersburg, VA; WUHF, Rochester, NY; KABB, San Antonio, TX; KRRT, San Antonio, TX; WGGB, Springfield-Holyoke, MA; KDNL, St. Louis, MO; WSYT, Syracuse, NY; WTWC-TV, Tallahassee, FL-Thomasville, GA; WTTA, Tampa-St. Petersburg (Sarasota), FL; WEMT, Tri-Cities, TN-VA

David D. Smith, pres/CEO; J.Duncan Smith, sec; Frederick Smith, treas; David B. Amy, exec VP.

Smith Media License Holdings LLC 1215 Cole St., St. Louis, MO 63106. Phone: (314) 853-7736. Ownership: Smith Media LLC, 100%.

Stns: 6 TV. KIMO, Anchorage, AK; WFFF, Burlington, VT-Plattsburgh, NY; KATN, Fairbanks, AK; KJUD, Juneau, AK; KEYT, Santa Barbara-Santa Maria-San Luis Obispo, CA; WKTV, Utica, NY

South Central Communications Corp. Box 3848, Evansville, IN 47736. Phone: (812) 424-8284. Fax: (812) 426-7925. Web Site: www.wiky.com. Ownership: John D. Engelbrecht, 80%, J.P. Engelbrecht, 20%.

Stns: 2 TV. WAZE-TV, Evansville, IN; WMAK, Knoxville, TN

Stns: 1 AM. 10 FM. WYXY(FM) Boonville, IN; WLFW(FM) Chandler, IN; WEOA Evansville, IN; WABX-FM Evansville, IN; WSTO-FM Owensboro, KY; WIMZ-FM Knoxville, TN; WJXB-FM Knoxville, TN; WTXM-FM Maryville, TN; WCJK(FM) Murfreesboro, TN; WJXA-FM Nashville, TN; WRMX-FM Norris, TN

John D. Engelbrecht, pres; J.P. Engelbrecht, VP.

Southeastern Media Holdings Inc. 3500 Colonnade Pkwy., Suite 600, Birmingham, AL 35243. Phone: (205) 298-7100. Fax: (205) 298-7104. Ownership: Community Newspaper Holdings Inc., 100%. Web site: www.cnhi.com

Stns: 2 TV. WFXG, Augusta, GA; WXTX, Columbus, GA

Community Newspaper Holdings Inc. is the parent company for daily, wkly and semiweekly newspapers published in more than 200 communities throughout the U.S.

Michael E. Reed, pres/CEO.

Standard Broadcasting Corp. 2 St. Clair Ave. W., Suite 1100, Toronto, ON M4V 1L6. Canada. Phone: (416) 960-9911. Fax: (416) 323-6828. Ownership: Slaight Communications Inc., 100%.

Stns: 2 TV. CJDC, Dawson Creek, BC; CFTK, Terrace, BC

Stns: 22 AM. 20 FM. CKMX Calgary, AB; CIBK-FM Calgary, AB; CFRN Edmonton, AB; CFMG-FM Saint Albert, AB; CFKC Creston, BC; CJDC Dawson Creek, BC; CKRX-FM Fort Nelson, BC; CHRX-FM Fort St. John, BC; CKNL-FM Fort St. John, BC; CKGR Golden, BC; CKIR Invermere, BC; CKFR(AM) Kelowna, BC; CKTK-FM Kitimat, BC; CKKC Nelson, BC; CKZX-FM New Denver, BC; CJOR Osoyoos, BC; CKOR Penticton, BC; CHTK Prince Rupert, BC; CKCR Revelstoke, BC; CISL Richmond, BC; CKXR Salmon Arm, BC; CFTK Terrace, BC; CJAT-FM Trail, BC; CKZZ-FM Vancouver, BC; CICF-FM Vernon, BC; CKXA-FM Brandon, MB; CKX-FM Brandon, MB; CFQX-FM Selkirk, MB; CKMM-FM Winnipeg, MB; CKOC Hamilton, ON; CHAM Hamilton, ON; CJBK(AM) London, ON; CJBX-FM London, ON; CKSL London, ON; CIQM-FM London, ON; CHVR-FM Pembroke, ON; CHRE-FM Saint Catharines, ON; CKTB Saint Catharines, ON; CFRB Toronto, ON; CJEZ-FM Toronto, ON; CJAD Montreal, PQ; CHOM-FM Montreal, PQ

Gary Slaight, pres/CEO.

Sunbelt Communications Co. c/o KVBC(TV), 1500 Foremaster Ln., Las Vegas, NV 89101. Phone: (702) 642-3333. Fax: (702) 657-3423. E-mail: ch3@kvbc.com. Web Site: www.kvbc.com. Ownership: James E. Rogers.

Stns: 12 TV. KCWY, Casper-Riverton, WY; KBAO, Great Falls, MT; KBBJ, Great Falls, MT; KTVH, Helena, MT; KPVI, Idaho Falls-Pocatello, ID; KSWY, Rapid City, SD; KRNV, Reno, NV; KBJN, Salt Lake City, UT; KENV, Salt Lake City, UT; KJWY, Salt Lake City, UT; KXTF, Twin Falls, ID; KYMA, Yuma, AZ-El Centro, CA

Ralph Toddre, pres.

Surtsey Media LLC 73 Kercheval Ave., Suite 100, Grosse Pointe Farms, MI 48236. Phone: (313) 884-7878. Ownership: Dana C. Raymant, 100%.

Stns: 2 TV. KFJX, Joplin, MO-Pittsburg, KS; KVCT, Victoria, TX

T

Sarkes Tarzian Inc. Box 62, Bloomington, IN 47402. Phone: (812) 332-7251. Fax: (812) 331-4575. Ownership: Tom Tarzian; Mary Tarzian estate.

Stns: 2 TV. WRCB-TV, Chattanooga, TN; KTVN, Reno, NV

Stns: 1 AM. 3 FM. WTTS-FM Bloomington, IN; WGCL Bloomington, IN; WLDE-FM Fort Wayne, IN; WAJI(FM) Fort Wayne, IN

Tom Tarzian, chmn.

Tele Inter-Rives Ltee. 298 Boulevard Theriault, Riviere-du-Loup, PQ G5R 4C2. Canada. Phone: (418) 867-1341. Fax: (418) 867-4710. Web Site: www.cimt.ca. Ownership: 101885 Canada Ltee., 54.37%; Groupe TVA Inc., 44.66% (see listing); and Marc Simard, 0.97%.

Stns: 4 TV. CHAU, Carleton, PQ; CIMT, Riviere-du-Loup, PQ; CKRT, Riviere-du-Loup, PQ; CFTF-TV, Riviere-du-Loup, PQ

Marc Simard, pres.

Telemundo Group Inc. 2290 W. 8th Ave., Hialeah, FL 33010. Phone: (305) 884-8200. Fax: (305) 889-7950. Web Site: www.telemundo.com. Ownership: TN Acquisition Corp., 100%. Note: General Electric Co, is 100% shareholder of TN Acquisition Corp. General Electric Co. also own NBC TV Stations Division (see listing).

Stns: 14 TV. WNEU, Boston (Manchester, NH); WSNS, Chicago; KMAS-TV, Denver, CO; KNSO, Fresno-Visalia, CA; KTMD, Houston; KVEA, Los Angeles; KWHY, Los Angeles; WSCV, Miami-Ft. Lauderdale, FL; WNJU, New York; KPHZ, Phoenix, AZ; KVDA, San Antonio, TX; KSTS, San Francisco-Oakland-San Jose; WKAQ, San Juan, PR; KHRR, Tucson (Sierra Vista), AZ

Richard Blangiardi, pres/CEO/chmn; Vincent Sadusky, CFO/treas; Juan Antunez, VP gen counsel/sec. VP/finance.

Tele-Quebec 1000 rue Fullum, Montreal, PQ H2K 3L7. Canada. Phone: (514) 521-2424. Fax: (514) 873-4413. E-mail: info@telequebec.qc.ca. Web Site: www.telequebec.qc.ca. Ownership: La Societe de radio-television du Quebec is a para-governmental organization. Its mandate is to manage an educ TV net throughout the province of Quebec.

Stns: 10 TV. CIVF, Baie-Trinite, PQ; CIVP, Chapeau, PQ; CIVV, Chicoutimi, PQ; CIVO-TV, Gatineau, PQ; CIVQ, Quebec City, PQ; CIVB, Rimouski, PQ; CIVA, Rouyn, PQ; CIVG, Sept-Iles, PQ; CIVS, Sherbrooke, PQ; CIVC, Trois-Rivieres, PQ

Paul Beaugrand Champagne, pres/dir gen; Mario Clement, dir mgr programming; Line Simoneau, dir mgr admin/fianances/human resources; Denis Belisle, dir sec gen; Cecile Bellemare, dir dev projects; Jacques Legace, dir dev institutional; Danielle Beaudry, dir production.

Television Station Group LLC 560 Columbia Dr., Johnson City, NY 13790-0012. Phone: (607) 729-8812. Fax: (607) 797-6211.

Stns: 3 TV. WBNG, Binghamton, NY; WLYH-TV, Harrisburg-Lancaster-Lebanon-York, PA; WTAJ-TV, Johnstown-Altoona, PA

Joe McNamara, gen mgr; Michael Granados, pres; Ian Guthrie, CFO.

Tri-State Christian Television Box 1010, Marion, IL 62959. Phone: (618) 997-9333. Fax: (618) 997-1859. Web Site: www.tct.tv. Ownership: Nonprofit corporation.

Stns: 6 TV. WNYB, Buffalo, NY; WAQP, Flint-Saginaw-Bay City, MI; WINM, Ft. Wayne, IN; WTLJ, Grand Rapids-Kalamazoo-Battle Creek, MI; WLXI, Greensboro-High Point-Winston Salem, NC; WTCT, Paducah, KY-Cape Girardeau, MO-Harrisburg-Mount Vernon, IL

Garth W. Coonce, pres; Shane Chaney, CFO.

Tribune Broadcasting Co. 435 N. Michigan Ave., Suite 1800, Chicago, IL 60611. Phone: (312) 222-3333. Fax: (312) 329-0611. Web Site: www.tribune.com. Ownership: Robert R. McCormick Tribune Foundation, 13.3%; The Chandler Trusts, 11.6%; Vanguard Fiduciary Trust Co., 6.9%.

Stns: 27 TV. WEWB, Albany-Schenectady-Troy, NY; WATL, Atlanta; WLVI, Boston (Manchester, NH); WGN, Chicago; KDAF, Dallas-Ft. Worth; KWGN, Denver, CO; WXMI, Grand Rapids-Kalamazoo-Battle Creek, MI; WPMT, Harrisburg-Lancaster-Lebanon-York, PA; WTIC, Hartford & New Haven, CT; WTXX, Hartford & New Haven, CT; KHWB, Houston; WXIN, Indianapolis, IN; WTTK, Indianapolis, IN; WTTV, Indianapolis, IN; KTLA, Los Angeles; WBZL, Miami-Ft. Lauderdale, FL; WGNO, New Orleans, LA; WNOL, New Orleans, LA; WPIX, New York; WPHL, Philadelphia; KWBP, Portland, OR; KTXL, Sacramento-Stockton-Modesto, CA; KSWB, San Diego, CA; KCPQ, Seattle-Tacoma, WA; KTWB, Seattle-Tacoma, WA; KPLR, St. Louis, MO; WBDC, Washington, DC (Hagerstown, MD)

Stns: 1 AM. WGN(AM) Chicago, IL

Patrick J. Mullen, pres.

Trinity Broadcasting Network 2442 Michelle Dr., Tustin, CA 92780. Phone: (714) 832-2950. Fax: (714) 730-0657. E-mail: comments@tbn.org. Web Site: www.tbn.org. Ownership: Nonprofit corporation.

Stns: 23 TV. KNAT, Albuquerque-Santa Fe, NM; WHSG-TV, Atlanta; WTJP-TV, Birmingham (Anniston, Tuscaloosa), AL; WELF-TV, Chattanooga, TN; WWTO, Chicago; WDLI-TV, Cleveland, OH; KDTX, Dallas-Ft. Worth; WKOI-TV, Dayton, OH; KAAH-TV, Honolulu, HI; WCLJ-TV, Indianapolis, IN; KTBN, Los Angeles; WBUY-TV, Memphis, TN; WHFT-TV, Miami-Ft. Lauderdale, FL; WMPV, Mobile, AL-Pensacola (Ft. Walton Beach), FL; WMCF, Montgomery (Selma), AL; WPGD-TV, Nashville, TN; WTBY-TV, New York; KTBO, Oklahoma City, OK; WGTW-TV, Philadelphia; KPAZ, Phoenix, AZ; KTBW, Seattle-Tacoma, WA; KTAJ-TV, St. Joseph, MO; KDOR-TV, Tulsa, OK

Paul F. Crouch, pres; Rod Henke, VP sls; Ben Miller, VP engrg; Janice Crouch, VP progmg.

Tyler Media Broadcasting Corp. 5101 S. Shields Blvd., Oklahoma City, OK 73129. Phone: (405) 616-5500. Fax: (405) 616-5505. Web Site: www.kkng.com. Ownership: Ty A. Tyler, Tony J. Tyler and Tony J. Tyler 2000 Irrevocable Trust, Tony J. Tyler, trustee.

Stns: 1 TV. KTUZ-TV, Oklahoma City, OK

Stns: 2 AM. 2 FM. KOCY(AM) Del City, OK; KKNG-FM Newcastle, OK; KTUZ-FM Okarche, OK; KTLR(AM) Oklahoma City, OK

Skip Stow, market mgr; Robert De Negri, CFO.

U

United Communications Corp. 5800 7th Ave., Kenosha, WI 53140. Phone: (262) 657-1000. Fax: (262) 657-1617. E-mail: hjb@kenoshanews.com. Web Site: www.kenoshanews.com. Ownership: Howard J. Brown. Note: Group also owns LPTV stn WNYF-CA Watertown, NY.

Stns: 2 TV. KEYC-TV, Mankato, MN; WWNY, Watertown, NY

Other media: Dailies: *Kenosha News,* Kenosha, WI; *Sun Chronicle,* Attleboro, MA; *Public Opinion,* Watertown, SD. Weeklies: *Zion-Benton News,* Zion, IL; *Foxboro Reporter,* Foxboro, MA; *Lake Geneva Regional News,* Lake Geneva, WI. Shoppers: *Bulletin,* Kenosha, WI; *News-Bargaineer,* Zion, IL; *Coteau Shopper,* Watertown, SD.

Howard J. Brown, pres; Kenneth Dowdell, VP; Ronald Montemurro, VP.

Univision Communications Inc. 5999 Center Dr., Los Angeles, CA 90045. Phone: (310) 216-3434. Fax: (310) 556-3568. Web Site: www.univision.com. Ownership: Perenchio Communications Inc., 78.5% voting stock. Perenchio Communications Inc. is headed by A. Jerrold Perenchio.

Stns: 38 TV. KTFQ-TV, Albuquerque-Santa Fe, NM; WUVG-TV, Atlanta; KUVI-TV, Bakersfield, CA; WUTF-TV, Boston (Manchester, NH); WLII, Caguas, PR; WXFT-TV, Chicago; WGBO, Chicago; WQHS, Cleveland, OH; KUVN-TV, Dallas-Ft. Worth; KSTR, Dallas-Ft. Worth; KFTV, Fresno-Visalia, CA; KTFF-TV, Fresno-Visalia, CA; KXLN, Houston; KFTH-TV, Houston; KMEX, Los Angeles; KFTR-TV, Los Angeles; WAMI, Miami-Ft. Lauderdale, FL; WLTV, Miami-Ft. Lauderdale, FL; WFTY-TV, New York; WFUT-TV, New York; WXTV, New York; WOTF-TV, Orlando-Daytona Beach-Melbourne, FL; WUVP-TV, Philadelphia; KFPH-TV, Phoenix, AZ; KTVW, Phoenix, AZ; WSUR, Ponce, PR; WUVC-TV, Raleigh-Durham (Fayetteville), NC; KUVS-TV, Sacramento-Stockton-Modesto, CA; KTFK-TV, Sacramento-Stockton-Modesto, CA; KUTH, Salt Lake City, UT; KWEX, San Antonio, TX; KFSF-TV, San Francisco-Oakland-San Jose; KDTV, San Francisco-Oakland-San Jose; WFTT-TV, Tampa-St. Petersburg (Sarasota), FL; KFTU-TV, Tucson

TV Group Ownership

(Sierra Vista), AZ; KUVE-TV, Tucson (Sierra Vista), AZ; KAKW-TV, Waco-Temple-Bryan, TX; WFDC-TV, Washington, DC (Hagerstown, MD)

Ray Rodriguez, pres/COO.

V

VCY America Inc. 3434 W. Kilbourn Ave., Milwaukee, WI 53208. Phone: (414) 935-3000. Fax: (414) 935-3015. E-mail: vcy@vcyamerica.com. Web Site: www.vcyamerica.org.

Stns: 1 TV. WVCY, Milwaukee, WI

Stns: 1 AM. 14 FM. KVCY-FM Fort Scott, KS; KCVS(FM) Salina, KS; WVCN(FM) Baraga, MI; WVCM(FM) Iron Mountain, MI; WJIC-FM Zanesville, OH; KVCF(FM) Freeman, SD; KVCX-FM Gregory, SD; KVFL(FM) Pierre, SD; WVCF-FM Eau Claire, WI; WVFL(FM) Fond du Lac, WI; WVCY-FM Milwaukee, WI; WVCY Oshkosh, WI; WVCX(FM) Tomah, WI; WEGZ(FM) Washburn, WI; WVRN(FM) Wittenberg, WI

Vic Eliason, VP/gen mgr.

Viacom Television Stations Group 524 W. 57th St., 3rd Fl., New York, NY 10019. Phone: (212) 975-4321. Web Site: www.viacom.com. Ownership: Viacom Inc., 100%.

Stns: 38 TV. WUPA, Atlanta; KEYE, Austin, TX; WJZ, Baltimore, MD; WSBK, Boston (Manchester, NH); WBZ, Boston (Manchester, NH); WBBM, Chicago; KTVT, Dallas-Ft. Worth; KTXA, Dallas-Ft. Worth; KCNC, Denver, CO; WKBD, Detroit; WWJ, Detroit; WFRV, Green Bay-Appleton, WI; KCAL, Los Angeles; KCBS, Los Angeles; WJMN, Marquette, MI; WFOR-TV, Miami-Ft. Lauderdale, FL; WBFS, Miami-Ft. Lauderdale, FL; WCCO, Minneapolis-St. Paul, MN; KCCO, Minneapolis-St. Paul, MN; KCCW, Minneapolis-St. Paul, MN; WUPL, New Orleans, LA; WCBS-TV, New York; WGNT, Norfolk-Portsmouth-Newport News, VA; KAUT-TV, Oklahoma City, OK; KYW, Philadelphia; WPSG, Philadelphia; WNPA, Pittsburgh, PA; KDKA, Pittsburgh, PA; WLWC, Providence, RI-New Bedford, MA; KMAX, Sacramento-Stockton-Modesto, CA; KOVR, Sacramento-Stockton-Modesto, CA; KUSG, Salt Lake City, UT; KUTV, Salt Lake City, UT; KPIX, San Francisco-Oakland-San Jose; KBHK-TV, San Francisco-Oakland-San Jose; KSTW, Seattle-Tacoma, WA; WTOG, Tampa-St. Petersburg (Sarasota), FL; WTVX, West Palm Beach-Ft. Pierce, FL

Fred Reynolds, pres.

The Victory Television Network Box 22007, Little Rock, AR 72221-2007. Phone: (501) 223-2525. Fax: (501) 221-3837. E-mail: jim.grant@vtntv.com. Web Site: www.vtntv.com. Ownership: Agape Church Inc.

Stns: 3 TV. KVTJ, Jonesboro, AR; KVTN, Little Rock-Pine Bluff, AR; KVTH, Little Rock-Pine Bluff, AR

Jim Grant, gen mgr; Pastor Happy Caldwell, pres.

W

WTVA Inc. Box 350, Tupelo, MS 38802. Phone: (662) 842-7620. Fax: (662) 844-7061. Web Site: www.wtva.com. Ownership: WTVA Inc. ownership: Mary Jane Spain, 51%; Margaret Spain, 40%; and Frank K. Spain, 9%. Note: Frank K. Spain owns 100% of WMDN Inc., licensee of WMDN(TV) Meridian, MS.

Stns: 3 TV. WTVA, Columbus-Tupelo-West Point, MS; WMDN, Meridian, MS; KTFL, Phoenix, AZ

Waitt Broadcasting Inc. 1125 S. 103rd St., Suite 200, Omaha, NE 68124-1071. Phone: (402) 330-2520. Fax: (402) 330-2445. Web Site: www.waittmedia.com.

Stns: 1 TV. KMEG, Sioux City, IA

Stns: 8 AM. 9 FM. KLGA Algona, IA; KLGA-FM Algona, IA; KWBG Boone, IA; KQWC Webster City, IA; KQWC-FM Webster City, IA; KKYY(FM) Whiting, IA; KQLS-FM Colby, KS; KXXX Colby, KS; KZRD(FM) Dodge City, KS; KGNO Dodge City, KS; KZLS-FM Great Bend, KS; KGTR-FM Larned, KS; KNNS Larned, KS; KSLS-FM Liberal, KS; KYUU Liberal, KS; KILS-FM Minneapolis, KS; KWLS Pratt, KS

Norman Waitt Jr., CEO.

Waterman Broadcasting Corp. Box 7578, Fort Myers, FL 33911-7578. Phone: (239) 939-2020. Fax: (239) 939-7903. Web Site: www.water.net. Ownership: Bernard Waterman, Edith Waterman.

Stns: 2 TV. WVIR-TV, Charlottesville, VA; WBBH, Ft. Myers-Naples, FL

Bernard Waterman, pres; Steve Pontius, exec VP; Joe Ernest, VP.

Weigel Broadcasting Co. 26 N. Halsted St., Chicago, IL 60661. Phone: (312) 705-2600. Fax: (312) 705-2656. Web Site: www.wciu.com. Ownership: Weigel Broadcasting Co., limited ptnr; Madison Halsted LLC, gen ptnr.

Stns: 2 TV. WCIU, Chicago; WDJT, Milwaukee, WI

Norman H. Shapiro, pres.

West Virginia Media Holdings LLC Box 11848, Charleston, WV 25339-1848. Phone: (304) 720-6527. Fax: (304) 345-7280. Ownership: West Virginia Medio Partners, LP.

Stns: 4 TV. WVNS-TV, Bluefield-Beckley-Oak Hill, WV; WOWK, Charleston-Huntington, WV; WBOY, Clarksburg-Weston, WV; WTRF-TV, Wheeling, WV-Steubenville, OH

Bray Cary, pres/CEO; Marty Becker, chmn.

Mel Wheeler Inc. 5009 S. Hulen, Suite 101, Fort Worth, TX 76132-1989. Phone: (817) 294-7644. Fax: (817) 294-8519. Ownership: Estate of Mel Wheeler, 68%; Clark Wheeler, 10.2%; Leonard Wheeler, 11.1%; Steve Wheeler, 10.6%.

Stns: 2 TV. KPOB, Paducah, KY-Cape Girardeau, MO-Harrisburg-Mount Vernon, IL; WSIL-TV, Paducah, KY-Cape Girardeau, MO-Harrisburg-Mount Vernon, IL

Stns: 2 AM. 3 FM. WVBE-FM Lynchburg, VA; WXLK-FM Roanoke, VA; WVBE(AM) Roanoke, VA; WSLQ-FM Roanoke, VA; WFIR(AM) Roanoke, VA

Leonard Wheeler, pres; Clark Wheeler, VP.

White Knight Holdings Inc. Box 3058, Lafayette, LA 70502. Phone: (337) 237-9965. Fax: (337) 235-5872.

Stns: 4 TV. WVLA, Baton Rouge, LA; WNTZ, Jackson, MS; KSHV, Shreveport, LA; KFXK, Tyler-Longview (Lufkin & Nacogdoches), TX

Sheldon Galloway, pres.

Wicks Television L.L.C. 405 Park Ave., Suite 702, New York, NY 10022-4405. Phone: (212) 407-2205. Fax: (212) 223-2109. Web Site: www.wicksgroup.com. Ownership: Wicks Communications & Media Partners L.P., 97.46%; and Wicks Parallel (Limited) Partnership I L.P., 2.54%.

Stns: 8 TV. KVLY, Fargo-Valley City, ND; KUMV, Minot-Bismarck-Dickinson, ND; KFYR, Minot-Bismarck-Dickinson, ND; KMOT, Minot-Bismarck-Dickinson, ND; KQCD, Minot-Bismarck-Dickinson, ND; KSFY, Sioux Falls (Mitchell), SD; KPRY, Sioux Falls (Mitchell), SD; KABY, Sioux Falls (Mitchell), SD

Robert Gluck, CEO; Matthew E. Gormly III, dir.

Withers Broadcasting Co. Box 1508, Mount Vernon, IL 62864. Phone: (618) 242-3500. Fax: (618) 242-4444. Ownership: W. Russell Withers Jr., 100%.

Stns: 2 TV. WDTV, Clarksburg-Weston, WV; WDHS, Marquette, MI

Stns: 9 AM. 7 FM. KOKX Keokuk, IA; WKIB(FM) Anna, IL; WILY Centralia, IL; WEBQ-FM Eldorado, IL; WISH-FM Galatia, IL; WEBQ Harrisburg, IL; WMOK Metropolis, IL; WZZT-FM Morrison, IL; WMIX Mount Vernon, IL; WMIX-FM Mount Vernon, IL; WSSQ-FM Sterling, IL; WSDR Sterling, IL; WZZL-FM Reidland, KY; KAPE Cape Girardeau, MO; KUGT Jackson, MO; KRHW Sikeston, MO

W. Russell Withers Jr., pres.

Woods Communications Corp. One WCOV Ave., Montgomery, AL 36111. Phone: (334) 288-7020. Fax: (334) 288-5414. Web Site: www.wcov.com. Ownership: David D. Woods, 100%.

Stns: 2 TV. KUPT, Lubbock, TX; WCOV, Montgomery (Selma), AL

David Woods, pres/CEO.

Wooster Republican Printing Co. (dba Dix Communications). 212 E. Liberty St., Wooster, OH 44691. Phone: (330) 264-3511. Fax: (330) 263-5013. Web Site: www.dixcom.com. Ownership: (dba Dix Communications).

Stns: 1 TV. KFBB, Great Falls, MT

Stns: 3 AM. 6 FM. WNDT(FM) Alachua, FL; WOGK(FM) Ocala, FL; WNDD-FM Silver Springs, FL; WKVX Wooster, OH; WQKT(FM) Wooster, OH; WTBO Cumberland, MD; WKGO-FM Cumberland, MD; WFRB Frostburg, MD; WFRB-FM Frostburg, MD

Wooster Republican Printing Co. publishes *The Daily Record*, Wooster, OH.

Robert C. Dix, TV div chmn; G. Charles Dix, VP; Dale E. Gerber, CFO.

Word Broadcasting Network Inc. Box 19229, Louisville, KY 40259. Phone: (502) 964-3304. Fax: (502) 966-9692. Web Site: www.wbna21.com. Ownership: Robert W. Rodgers, 20%; Gregory A. Holt, 20%; Melissa Fraser, 20%; Cleddie Kieth, 20%; and Margaret A. Rodgers, 20%.

Stns: 1 TV. WBNA, Louisville, KY

Stns: 3 AM. WYMM(AM) Jacksonville, FL; WVHI Evansville, IN; WYRM(AM) Norfolk, VA

Bob Rogers, pres; Greg Holt, VP.

Y

Young Broadcasting Inc. 599 Lexington Ave., 47th Fl., New York, NY 10022. Phone: (212) 754-7070. Fax: (212) 758-1229. Web Site: www.youngbroadcasting.com. Ownership: Vincent J. Young, Gabelli Asset Management Inc., New South Capital Management Inc.

Stns: 14 TV. WCDC, Albany-Schenectady-Troy, NY; WTEN, Albany-Schenectady-Troy, NY; KWQC, Davenport, IA-Rock Island-Moline, IL; WBAY, Green Bay-Appleton, WI; WATE, Knoxville, TN; KLFY, Lafayette, LA; WLNS, Lansing, MI; WKRN, Nashville, TN; KCLO, Rapid City, SD; WRIC, Richmond-Petersburg, VA; KRON-TV, San Francisco-Oakland-San Jose; KDLO, Sioux Falls (Mitchell), SD; KELO, Sioux Falls (Mitchell), SD; KPLO, Sioux Falls (Mitchell), SD

Vincent Young, chmn; James Morgan, exec VP & CFO.

Key to Television Listings

Television listings include TV stations in the United States, its territories and Canada. All collected data for these listings include information current to January 2002. To use the television key, see boldface numbers and corresponding explanations.

(1) **WOF-TV**—**(2)** Analog channel: 17. Digital Channel: 53. **(3)** On air date: Apr 13, 1952. **(4)** Box 100, Dothan, AL 36301. Phone: (909) 555-1000. FAX: (909) 999-9999. Web Site: www.wof.tv. **(5)** Licensee: WOF Broadcasting Co. **(6)** Group owner: Acme Stations (acq 7-20-69; $2 million; **(6a)** FTR 7-29-69). **(7)** Network: CBS. **(8)** Rep: Jones, Tri-State. Washington Atty: Goltz & Stick.
(9) Key Personnel
Jud Jones . . . . pres & gen mgr
D. Spark . . . . chief engr

(1) Station call letters as assigned by the Federal Communications Commission (FCC) or Canadian Radio-television and Telecommunications Commission (CRTC).

(2) Analog channel and digital channel, where applicable.

(3) Date station first went on the air (regardless of subsequent ownership changes).

(4) Address and zip code, telephone and fax number, web site and e-mail address.

(5) Licensee name.

(6) Ownership and date of acquisition (if not original owner). If a station has been sold, any available sale information is listed following the acquisition date. WOF-TV is owned by Acme Stations.

(6a) FTR date refers to Broadcasting & Cable magazine's weekly "For the Record" column that appeared in the magazine until June 8, 1998, where station sales were recorded as received from the FCC.

(7) Network programming. WOF-TV's national network is CBS.

(8) Representatives and Washington attorney. Sales representatives are listed with the national rep first, then regional.

(9) Key Personnel.

An asterisk (*) preceding station call letters indicates noncommercial stations.

Directory of TV Stations in the United States

Alabama

Anniston

see Birmingham (Anniston, Tuscaloosa), AL market

Birmingham (Anniston, Tuscaloosa), AL (DMA 40)

WABM—Analog channel: 68. On air date: January 1986. 651 Beacon Pkwy. W., Suite 105, Birmingham, AL 35209. Phone: (205) 943-2168. Fax: (205) 290-2114. Web Site: www.wabm68.com. Licensee: Birmingham (WABM-TV) Licensee Inc. **Group owner:** Glencairn Ltd. (acq 2-1-2002). Network: UPN.
Key Personnel:
Steve Marks . . . CFO
Scott Campbell . . . gen mgr
Charlie Slaight . . . gen sls mgr & adv dir
Lucrecia Rubio . . . progmg dir & engrg dir
Peggy Johnson . . . news dir
John Batspm . . . chief of engrg

***WBIQ**—Analog channel: 10. Digital channel: 53. On air date: Apr 28, 1955. 2112 11th Ave. S., Suite 400, Birmingham, AL 35205. Phone: (205) 328-8756. Fax: (205) 251-2192. Web Site: www.aptv.org. Licensee: Alabama ETV Commission. Network: PBS.
Key Personnel:
Allan Pizzato . . . CEO
Dr. John Mosley . . . chmn
Pauline Howland . . . CFO
Alan Pizzato . . . opns dir
Polly Anderson . . . dev dir
Mike McKenzie . . . prom dir & adv dir
Jamie Lewis . . . progmg mgr
Jon Beans . . . news dir
Windell Wood . . . engrg dir

WBRC—Analog channel: 6. On air date: July 1, 1949. Box 6, Birmingham, AL 35201. 1720 Valley View Dr., Mooresville, AL 35209. Phone: (205) 322-6666. Fax: (205) 583-4386. Web Site: www.wbrc.com. Licensee: Fox Television Stations Inc. Group owner: (group owner; acq 7-21-95). Network: Fox. Rep: TeleRep. News staff: 53; News: 21 hrs wkly.
Key Personnel:
Mike McClain . . . VP & news dir
Dennis Leonard . . . gen mgr
Roy Gardner . . . opns mgr
Mike Lewis . . . sls VP & gen sls mgr
Sonya Ridderhoff . . . natl sls mgr
Wayne Farr . . . progmg dir
Jerry Thorn . . . chief of engrg

WCFT-TV—Analog channel: 33. On air date: Oct 27, 1965. 800 Concourse Pkwy., Suite 200, Birmingham, AL 35244. 4000 37th St. E., Tuscaloosa, AL 35405. Phone: (205) 403-3340. Fax: (205) 403-3329. Web Site: www.abc3340.com. Licensee: TV Alabama Inc. Group owner: Allbritton Communications Co. (acq 1996; $20 million). Network: ABC. Rep: Katz Radio. Washington Atty: Hogan & Hartson.
Key Personnel:
Mike Murphy . . . gen mgr
Gary Watkins . . . opns dir

***WCIQ**—Analog channel: 7. Digital channel: 56. On air date: Jan 7, 1955. 2112 11th Ave. S., Suite 400, Birmingham, AL 35205. Phone: (205) 328-8756. Fax: (205) 251-2192. Web Site: www.aptv.org. Licensee: Alabama ETV Commission. Network: PBS.
Key Personnel:
Allan Pizzato . . . pres
Pauline Howland . . . exec VP & gen mgr
Polly Anderson . . . dev VP
Cindy Crowther . . . dev mgr
Donna Baker . . . mktg mgr

WDBB—Analog channel: 17. On air date: Oct 1, 1984. 651 Beacon Pkwy. W., Suite 105, Birmingham, AL 35209. Phone: (205) 943-2168. Fax: (205) 290-2114. Licensee: WDBB-TV Inc.. Ownership: Cecil Heftel; H. Carl Parmer; D&C L.L.C. (acq 1-19-95; $1.5 million). Rep: Adam Young. Washington Atty: Fletcher, Heald & Hildreth. News staff: 20; News: 15 hrs wkly.
Key Personnel:
Scott Campbell . . . gen mgr
Steve Marks . . . CEO & opns mgr
Amy Hughes . . . sls dir & rgnl sls mgr
Lucrecia Rubio . . . mktg dir & progmg dir
Mary Ann Huie . . . adv dir
Peggy Johnson . . . progmg dir & news dir
John Batson . . . engrg mgr & chief of engrg

WIAT—Analog channel: 42. On air date: Oct 17, 1965. 2075 Goldencrest Dr., Birmingham, AL 35209. Phone: (205) 322-4200. Fax: (205) 320-2710. Web Site: www.wiat.com. Licensee: Media General Communications Inc. Group owner: Media General Broadcast Group (acq 1997; grpsl). Network: CBS. Rep: MMT. Washington Atty: Dow, Lohnes & Albertson. News: 6 hrs wkly.
Key Personnel:
Bill Ballard . . . pres, VP & gen mgr
Phil Smith . . . opns dir & opns mgr
Dave Parker . . . gen sls mgr
Larry Ragan . . . news dir

WJSU-TV—Analog channel: 40. Digital channel: 9. On air date: Oct 26, 1969. 800 Concourse Pkwy., Suite 200, Birmingham, AL 35244. 1330 Noble St., Suite 40 Radio Bldg., Mooresville, AL 36202. Phone: (205) 403-3340. Fax: (205) 403-3329. Web Site: www.abc3340.com. Licensee: TV Alabama Inc. Group owner: Allbritton Communications Co. (acq 1-24-00). Network: ABC. Rep: Katz Radio. Washington Atty: Haley, Bader & Potts. News staff: 16; News: 9 hrs wkly.
Key Personnel:
Mike Murphy . . . gen mgr
Gary Watkins . . . opns mgr

WLDM—Analog channel: 23. On air date: 2000. 651 Beacon Pkwy. W., Suite 105, Birmingham, AL 35209. Phone: (205) 943-2168. Fax: (205) 290-2114. Licensee: The Board of Trustees of the University of Alabama. (acq 11-30-2004; donation).
Key Personnel:
Scott Campbell . . . gen mgr
Ron Snyder . . . natl sls mgr
Lucrecia Romeo . . . progmg dir
Peggy Johnson . . . news dir
John Batson . . . chief of engrg

WPXH—Analog channel: 44. Digital channel: 45. On air date: Apr 26, 1986. 2085 Goldencrest Dr., Birmingham, AL 35209. Phone: (205) 870-4404. Fax: (205) 870-0744. Licensee: Paxson Communications License Co. L.L.C. Group owner: Paxson Communications Corp. Network: PAX TV. Washington Atty: Fletcher, Heald & Hildreth. News: 8 hrs wkly.

WTJP-TV—Analog channel: 60. On air date: July 22, 1986. 313 Rosedale Ave., Gadsden, AL 35901-5361. Phone: (256) 546-8860. Fax: (256) 543-8623. Web Site: www.tbn.org. Licensee: Trinity Christian Center of Santa Ana Inc. dba Trinity Broadcasting Network. Group owner: Trinity Broadcasting Network (acq 5-8-00).
Key Personnel:
Paul F. Crouch . . . CEO & pres
Terry Hickey . . . exec VP
Gary Hodges . . . gen mgr & gen sls mgr
Curtiss Kemp . . . chief of engrg

WTTO—Analog channel: 21. On air date: Apr 21, 1982. 651 Beacon Pkwy. W., Suite 105, Huntsville, AL 35209. Phone: (205) 943-2168. Fax: (205) 290-2114. Web Site: www.wtto21.com. Licensee: WTTO Licensee L.L.C. (acq 12-21-90). Network: WB. Rep: Millennium Sales & Marketing. Washington Atty: Arter & Hadden.
Key Personnel:
Chris Hummel . . . CEO & CFO
Scott Campbell . . . gen mgr
Amy Hughes . . . rgnl sls mgr & prom dir
Lucrecia Rubio . . . adv dir & progmg dir
Peggy Johnson . . . news dir
John Batson . . . engrg dir & chief of engrg

WVTM-TV—Analog channel: 13. On air date: May 1949. 1732 Valley View Dr., Birmingham, AL 35209. Phone: (205) 558-7300 (news). Fax: (205) 933-7516 (sales). E-mail: newscomments@nbc13.com. Web Site: www.nbc13.com. Licensee: NBC Telemundo License Co. Group owner: NBC TV Stations Division (acq 1996; $425 million. plus working capital with KNSD(TV San Diego, CA). Network: NBC. News staff: 70; News: 24 hrs wkly.
Key Personnel:
Clark Dumornay . . . opns mgr
Joe Tracy . . . sls VP
Ed Moran . . . natl sls mgr
Mike Sherry . . . mktg mgr & prom dir
Yuette Miley . . . progmg dir
Yvette M. Miley . . . news dir
Terese Messick . . . pub affrs dir
Chuck Blackwood . . . engrg dir

Decatur

see Huntsville-Decatur (Florence), AL market

Dothan, AL (DMA 172)

WDFX-TV—Analog channel: 34. On air date: Feb 23, 1991. 2221 Ross Clark Cir., Dothan, AL 36301. Phone: (334) 794-3434. Fax: (334) 794-0034. Licensee: Raycom America License Subsidiary LLC. Group owner: Raycom Media Inc. (acq 10-14-2003; grpsl). Network: Fox. Washington Atty: Borsari & Paxson.
Key Personnel:
Melinda Chaney . . . gen mgr & rgnl sls mgr
Terri Bodiford . . . gen mgr
Misty Shingler . . . mktg mgr & prom dir
Wes Roten . . . chief of engrg

WDHN—Analog channel: 18. On air date: Aug 7, 1970. Box 6237, Dothan, AL 36302. 5274 E. Hwy. 52, Webb, AL 36302. Phone: (334) 793-1818. Fax: (334) 793-2623. Web Site: www.wdhn.com. Licensee: Nexstar Broadcasting Inc. Group owner: Nexstar Broadcasting Group Inc. (acq 8-1-2003; $40 million. with KARK-TV Little Rock, AR). Network: ABC. Rep: Katz Radio. Washington Atty: Fletcher, Heald & Hildreth. News staff: 8; News: 7 hrs wkly.
Key Personnel:
Mike Smith . . . VP, gen mgr & progmg dir
Janie Hinson . . . gen sls mgr
Yolanda Everett . . . prom dir
Mike Quinn . . . news dir
Edna Darrow . . . pub affrs dir
Neal Riddle . . . chief of engrg

WTVY—Analog channel: 4. Digital channel: 36. On air date: Feb 12, 1955. Box 1089, Dothan, AL 36302. 285 N. Foster St., Dothan, AL 36303. Phone: (334) 792-3195. Fax: (334) 793-3947. Web Site: www.wtvynews4.com. Licensee: Gray Television Licensee Inc. Group owner: Gray Television Inc. (acq 8-29-2002; grpsl). Network: CBS. Rep: Continental Television Sales. News staff: 20; News: 16 hrs wkly.
Key Personnel:
Patrick Dalbey . . . VP & gen mgr
Richard Morgan . . . gen sls mgr
Millicent Smith . . . natl sls mgr & prom dir
Judy Calhoun . . . rgnl sls mgr
Mike Doherty . . . prom mgr
Katie McManus . . . news dir
Wade Thomaston . . . chief of engrg

Florence

see Huntsville-Decatur (Florence), AL market

Huntsville-Decatur (Florence), AL (DMA 84)

WAAY-TV—Analog channel: 31. On air date: Aug 1, 1959. 1000 Monte Sano Blvd., Huntsville, AL 35801. Phone: (256) 533-3131. Fax: (256) 533-6616. Web Site: www.waaytv.com. Licensee: Piedmont Television of Huntsville License LLC. Group owner: Piedmont Television Holdings LLC (acq 7-19-99; $52 million).. Network: ABC. Washington Atty: Cohn & Marks.
Key Personnel:
Peter O'Brien . . . VP & gen mgr
Ben Boles . . . opns mgr & prom mgr
Chris Kidd . . . gen sls mgr
Dave Keller . . . progmg dir
Al Carl . . . news dir
Jim Bowman . . . chief of engrg

Broadcasting & Cable Yearbook 2006

B-14

WAFF—Analog channel: 48. Digital channel: 49. On air date: July 4, 1954. 1414 N. Memorial Pkwy., Huntsville, AL 35801. Phone: (256) 533-4848. Fax: (256) 533-1337. E-mail: webmaster@waff.com. Web Site: www.waff.com. Licensee: Raycom America License Subsidiary LLC. Group owner: Raycom Media Inc. (acq 3-16-97; grpsl). Network: NBC. Rep: Harrington, Righter & Parsons. Washington Atty: Covington & Burling. News staff: 43; News: 26 hrs wkly.
Key Personnel:
Lee Meredith . . . VP & gen mgr
Dale Stafford . . . gen sls mgr
Susan Craft . . . rgnl sls mgr
Becky Nichols . . . mktg mgr
Tracey Gallien . . . news dir
J.T. Harriman. . . . engrg dir

***WFIQ**—Analog channel: 36. Digital channel: 22. On air date: Aug 16, 1967. 2112 11th Ave. S., Suite 400, Birmingham, AL 35205. Phone: (205) 328-8756. Fax: (205) 251-2192. Web Site: www.aptv.org. Licensee: Alabama ETV Commission. Network: PBS.
Key Personnel:
Allan Pizzato . . . CEO & pres
Pauline Howland . . . exec VP
Polly Anderson. . . . dev VP
Cindy Crowther . . . dev mgr
Donna Baker . . . mktg mgr
Jamie Lewis . . . progmg dir
Tommy Weir . . . progmg dir
Jon Beans. . . . news dir & pub affrs dir
Windell Wood . . . chief of engrg

WHDF—Analog channel: 15. On air date: Oct 29, 1957. 200 Andrew Jackson Way, Huntsville, AL 35801. 840 Cypress Mill Rd., Florence, AL 35630. Phone: (256) 767-1515. Fax: (256) 764-7750. Web Site: www.upntv.tv. Licensee: Huntsville TV L.L.C.. Ownership: James L. Lockwood Jr., 100% Network: UPN. Rep: Blair Television.
Key Personnel:
Shanda Love . . . CEO & gen sls mgr
Louann Thomson . . . gen mgr
Brian Capaldo. . . . stn mgr
Tim Rovere . . . chief of engrg

***WHIQ**—Analog channel: 25. Digital channel: 24. On air date: November 1965. 2112 11th Ave. S., Suite 400, Birmingham, AL 35205. Phone: (205) 328-8756. Fax: (205) 251-2192. Web Site: www.aptv.org. Licensee: Alabama ETV Commission. Network: PBS.
Key Personnel:
Alan Pizzato. . . . CEO & pres
Pauline Howland. . . . exec VP & gen mgr
Polly Anderson. . . . dev VP
Cindy Crowther . . . dev mgr
Donna Baker . . . mktg mgr

WHNT-TV—Analog channel: 19. On air date: Nov 28, 1963. 200 Holmes Ave., Huntsville, AL 35801. Box 19, Huntsville, AL 35801. Phone: (256) 533-1919. Fax: (256) 533-4503. Fax: (256) 536-9468 (news). E-mail: feedback@whnt19.com. Web Site: www.whnt.com. Licensee: New York Times Management Services. Group owner: The New York Times Co. (acq 2-2-80; $12 million;. FTR: 3-27-80). Network: CBS. Rep: Katz Radio. Washington Atty: Koteen & Naftalin.
Key Personnel:
Tharon Honeycutt . . . gen mgr
Robert Alverson. . . . opns mgr & progmg dir
Stan Pylant . . . sls VP
Heather Carlton . . . rgnl sls mgr
Holy Griggs. . . . mktg dir
Kevin Osgood . . . news dir
Steve King. . . . engrg dir

WYLE—Analog channel: 26. On air date: Apr 19, 1986. Box 850, 801 W. Montgomery Ave., Sheffield, AL 35660. 700 W. Montgomery Ave., Sheffield, AL 35660. Phone: (256) 381-2600. Fax: (256) 383-3157. E-mail: etccom@bellsouth.net. Web Site: www.wyletv.com. Licensee: ETC Communications Inc.. Ownership: Les White, 100%. (acq 6-93). Washington Atty: Irwin, Campbell & Tannenwood. News staff: 9; News: 15 hrs wkly.
Key Personnel:
Karen Snead . . . gen mgr & progmg dir
Bud Hayle. . . . gen sls mgr
Les White . . . CEO & film buyer
Donna Kemp . . . engrg mgr

WZDX—Analog channel: 54. On air date: Apr 14, 1985. Box 3889, Huntsville, AL 35810. Phone: (256) 533-5454. Fax: (256) 533-5315. Web Site: www.fox54.com. Licensee: Huntsville Television Acquisition Corp. Group owner: Grant Communications (acq 4-90; $6.1 million). Network: Fox.
Key Personnel:
Milton Grant . . . pres & gen mgr
Rolfe Grover. . . . gen sls mgr
Brett Brooks. . . . prom mgr

Linda Jones . . . progmg dir
Shannon Ridinger . . . pub affrs dir
Harry Wilkins. . . . chief of engrg

Louisville

see Columbus, GA market

Mobile, AL-Pensacola (Ft. Walton Beach), FL (DMA 63)

WALA-TV—Analog channel: 10. Digital channel: 9. On air date: Jan 14, 1953. 1501 Satchel Paige Dr., Mobile, AL 36606. Phone: (251) 434-1010. Fax: (251) 434-1073. E-mail: fox10@wala.emmis.com. Web Site: www.fox10tv.com. Licensee: Emmis Television License LLC. Group owner: Emmis Communications Corp. (acq 7-16-98; grpsl). Network: Fox. Rep: TeleRep. Washington Atty: Fisher, Wayland, Cooper, Leader & Zaragoza. News staff: 45; News: 23 hrs.
Key Personnel:
Vanessa Oubre . . . VP
Venessa Oubre . . . gen mgr
Matt Pumo . . . gen sls mgr
Mike Kelly. . . . natl sls mgr
Kristen Mosley. . . . mktg mgr & prom mgr
Bob Cashen . . . news dir
Roland Fields . . . chief of engrg

WAWD—Analog channel: 58. Digital channel: 49. On air date: Aug 1, 1998. 8317 Front Beach Rd., Suite 23, Panama City, FL 32407. Phone: (850) 234-2773. Fax: (850) 234-1179. Licensee: Beach TV Properties Inc. Group owner: Beach TV Properties Inc. (acq 10-29-99; $175,000).. Washington Atty: Baraff, Koerner, Olender & Hochberg.
Key Personnel:
Robin Quinlan . . . gen mgr
Mike Hartzog . . . stn mgr

WBPG—Analog channel: 55. On air date: Sept 1, 2001. 1501 Satchel Paige Dr., Mobile, AL 36606. Phone: (251) 434-1010. Fax: (251) 434-1073. Web Site: www.thegulfcoast.wb. Licensee: Emmis Television License LLC. Group owner: Emmis Communications Corp. (acq 3-1-2003; $11.5 million).. Network: WB. Rep: TeleRep.
Key Personnel:
Vanessa Oubre . . . VP & gen mgr
Carey Golden . . . gen sls mgr
Mike Kelly. . . . natl sls mgr
Kristen Mosley . . . mktg mgr
Roland Fields . . . chief of engrg

WEAR-TV—(Pensacola).FL Analog channel: 3. On air date: Jan 13, 1954. Box 12278, Pensacola, FL 32581. 4990 Mobile Hgwy, Pensacola, FL 32506. Phone: (850) 456-3333. Fax: (850) 455-0159. E-mail: comments@wear.sbjnet.com. Web Site: www.weartv.com. Licensee: WEAR Licensee L.L.C. Group owner: Sinclair Broadcast Group Inc. (acq 10-8-97). Network: ABC. Washington Atty: Shaw Pittman LLP. News staff: 30; News: 14 hrs wkly.
Key Personnel:
Carl Leahy . . . pres
Peter Neuman . . . news dir
Sue Straughn . . . pub affrs dir
David Brown. . . . chief of engrg

***WEIQ**—Analog channel: 42. Digital channel: 41. On air date: Nov 6, 1964. 2112 11th Ave. S., Suite 400, Birmingham, AL 35205. Phone: (205) 328-8756. Fax: (205) 251-2192. Web Site: www.aptv.org. Licensee: Alabama ETV Commission. Network: PBS.
Key Personnel:
Alan Pizzato. . . . CEO & pres
Pauline Howland. . . . exec VP & gen mgr
Polly Anderson. . . . dev VP
Cindy Crowther . . . dev mgr
Donna Baker . . . mktg mgr

WFBD—Analog channel: 48. Digital channel: 48.Not on air, target date: unknown:. Stn currently dark 118 S. Bellevue, Suite 222, Memphis, TN 38104. Phone: (901) 516-8970. Permittee: George S. Flinn Jr.. Ownership: George S. Flinn Jr., 100%.

WFGX—Analog channel: 35. Digital channel: 25. On air date: Apr 7, 1987. PO Box 12278, Pensacola, FL 32581. 4990 Mobile Hgwy., Fort Walton Beach, FL 32506. Phone: (850) 456-3333. Fax: (850) 453-4335. E-mail: wfgx@wfgxtv.com. Web Site: www.wfgxtv.com. Licensee: WFGX Licensee LLC. Group owner: Sinclair Broadcast Group Inc. (acq 3-31-2004; $520,000).. Washington Atty: Shaw Pittman LLP.
Key Personnel:
David D. Smith. . . . pres
Carl Leahy . . . gen mgr
Joe Smith . . . opns mgr & progmg mgr
Deb Marks . . . gen sls mgr
John Merrill . . . natl sls mgr
Denise Dyson . . . rgnl sls mgr
Stephanie Yancey. . . . mktg mgr
Kathy Dunagan . . . prom mgr & adv mgr
David Brown. . . . chief of engrg

WHBR—Analog channel: 33. On air date: Jan 27, 1986. Box 2633, Pensacola, FL 32513. 6500 Pensacola Blvd., Saint Martinville, FL 32505. Phone: (850) 473-8633. Fax: (850) 473-8671. E-mail: dmayo@whbr.org. Web Site: www.whbr.org. Licensee: Christian Television of Pensacola/Mobile Inc.. Ownership: David C. Gibbs III, Wayne Wetzel , Bill Anderson and Ginny Oliver. (acq 12-16-97). Washington Atty: Gammon & Grange.
Key Personnel:
Bob D'Andrea . . . pres
Wayne Wetzel. . . . VP
David Mayo . . . gen mgr

WJTC—Analog channel: 44. On air date: December 1984. 661 Azalea Rd., Mobile, AL 36609. Phone: (251) 602-1544. Fax: (251) 602-1547. Web Site: www.wjtc.com. Licensee: Clear Channel Broadcasting Licenses Inc. Group owner: Clear Channel Communications Inc. (acq 3-21-01). Network: UPN.
Key Personnel:
Sharon Moloney. . . . gen mgr
Tim Woodard . . . opns mgr
Chris Kalifeh. . . . gen sls mgr
Bob Herron . . . natl sls mgr
Jean Stanley . . . prom mgr
Nona Simmons . . . pub affrs dir
Tim Reid . . . chief of engrg

WKRG-TV—Analog channel: 5. Digital channel: 27. On air date: Sept 5, 1955. 555 Broadcast Dr., Mobile, AL 36606. Phone: (251) 479-5555. Fax: (251) 473-8130. Fax: TWX: 810-741-4263. Web Site: www.krg.com. Licensee: Media General Communications Inc. Group owner: Media General Broadcast Group (acq 3-27-2000; grpsl). Network: CBS. Rep: Katz Radio. Washington Atty: Wiley, Rein & Fielding.
Key Personnel:
Joe Goleniowski . . . pres, VP & gen mgr
Warren Fiihr. . . . gen sls mgr
Robin Delaney . . . mktg dir
Darrel Taylor. . . . progmg mgr
Dan Cates. . . . news dir
Jim Richard . . . chief of engrg

WMPV-TV—Analog channel: 21. On air date: Dec 19, 1985. 1668 S. Beltline Hwy., Mobile, AL 36693. Phone: (251) 661-2101. Fax: (251) 661-7121. Web Site: www.tbn.org. Licensee: Trinity Broadcasting Network. Group owner: (group owner; acq 5-8-00; grpsl). Washington Atty: Fisher, Wayland, Cooper, Leader & Zaragoza.
Key Personnel:
Linda Dixon . . . gen mgr
Heather McCollum . . . progmg dir
LaTroynnda Cunningham. . . . pub affrs dir
Alvin Goins . . . chief of engrg

WPAN—Analog channel: 53. On air date: Feb 14, 1984. Box 18126, Pensacola, FL 32523. 2105 W. Gregory St., Pensacola, FL 32523. Phone: (850) 433-1766. Fax: (850) 433-1641. Licensee: Franklin Media Inc.. Ownership: John L. Franklin, 20%; Delores A. Franklin, 20%; Joseph C. Denison, 20%; Robert Gatlin, 20%; Glyn Lowery, 20% (acq 5-23-88). Washington Atty: Pepper & Corazzini.

WPMI-TV—Analog channel: 15. Digital channel: 47. On air date: Mar 12, 1982. 661 Azalea Rd., Mobile, AL 36609-1515. Phone: (251) 602-1500. Fax: (251) 602-1547. Web Site: www.wpmi.com. Licensee: Clear Channel Broadcasting Licenses Inc. Group owner: Clear Channel Communications Inc. Network: NBC. Rep: Millennium Sales & Marketing. Washington Atty: Wiley, Rein & Fielding. News staff: 50; News: 5 hrs wkly.
Key Personnel:
Sharon Moloney . . . VP & gen mgr
Tim Woodward. . . . opns mgr
Chris Kahifeh . . . gen sls mgr
Robert Herron . . . natl sls mgr
Ric Phillips . . . rgnl sls mgr
Jean Stanley . . . prom mgr
Betty Gurley . . . progmg dir & pub affrs dir
Joe Raia. . . . news dir
Tim Reid . . . chief of engrg

***WSRE**—Analog channel: 23. Digital channel: 31. On air date: Sept 11, 1967. Bldg. 23, 1000 College Blvd., Pensacola, FL 32504-8998.

Phone: (850) 484-1200. Fax: (850) 484-1255. E-mail: rolandphillips@wsre.pbs.org. Web Site: www.wsre.org. Licensee: District Board of Trustees of Pensacola Junior College. (acq 8-31-71). Network: PBS.

Key Personnel:
Sandy Cesartiray . . . gen mgr
Jean Norman . . . dev dir
Janie Stewart . . . prom mgr
Jim Bailip . . . progmg dir
Roland Phillips . . . chief of engrg

Montgomery (Selma), AL (DMA 113)

***WAIQ**—Analog channel: 26. Digital channel: 27. On air date: Dec 18, 1962. 2112 11th Ave. S., Suite 400, Birmingham, AL 35205. Phone: (205) 328-8756. Fax: (205) 251-2192. Web Site: www.aptv.org. Licensee: Alabama ETV Commission. Network: PBS. Washington Atty: Hogan & Hartson.

Key Personnel:
Alan Pizzato. . . . CEO & pres
Pauline Howland . . . pres & exec VP
Polly Anderson . . . gen mgr & dev VP
Cindy Crowther . . . dev dir & prom dir
Donna Baker . . . mktg mgr
Jamie Lewis . . . progmg dir
Tommy Weir . . . progmg dir
Jon Beans. . . . news dir & pub affrs dir
Windell Wood . . . engrg dir & chief of engrg

WAKA—Analog channel: 8. On air date: Mar 17, 1960. Box 230667, Montgomery, AL 36123. 3020 East Blvd., Montgomery, AL 36123. Phone: (334) 271-8888. Fax: (334) 272-6444. Web Site: www.waka.com. Licensee: Alabama Broadcasting Partners. Group owner: Bahakel Communications (acq 8-85). Network: CBS. Rep: Katz Radio. News staff: 22; News: 9 hrs wkly.

Key Personnel:
Jim Caruthers. . . . gen mgr
Steffanie Patterson . . . gen sls mgr & rgnl sls mgr
Mark Smith. . . . progmg dir
Rob Martin. . . . news dir
Thomas Mayberry. . . . chief of engrg

WBIH—Analog channel: 29. On air date: 2002. 225 N. Memorial, Suite 222, Prattville, AL 36067. Phone: (334) 491-2900. Fax: (334) 491-2929. Licensee: Flinn Broadcasting Corp.

WBMM—Analog channel: 22. On air date: June 1, 2002. 1 Shackleford Dr., Little Rock, AR 72211. Phone: (501) 219-2400. Fax: (501) 219-1210. Licensee: Montgomery 22, Inc. Group owner: Equity Broadcasting Corp. (acq 12-27-2000).

Key Personnel:
Steve Soldinger . . . gen mgr
Angie Hughes . . . gen sls mgr
Nathan Stamp . . . progmg mgr
Doug Krile . . . news dir
Paul Brondenburg . . . chief of engrg

WCOV-TV—Analog channel: 20. On air date: Apr 23, 1953. c/o WCOV-TV, One WCOV Ave., Montgomery, AL 36111. Box 250045, Montgomery, AL 36125. Phone: (334) 288-7020. Fax: (334) 288-5414. E-mail: mail@wcov.com. Web Site: www.wcov.com. Licensee: Woods Communications Corp. Group owner: (group owner; acq 12-1-85; $4 million; 6-10-85). Network: Fox. Rep: Millennium Sales & Marketing. Washington Atty: Kenkel, Barnard & Edmundson.

***WDIQ**—Analog channel: 2. Digital channel: 11. On air date: Aug 8, 1956. 2112 11th Ave. S., Suite 400, Birmingham, AL 35205. Phone: (205) 328-8756. Fax: (205) 251-2192. Web Site: www.aptv.org. Licensee: Alabama ETV Commission. Network: PBS.

Key Personnel:
Allan Pizzato . . . CEO & pres
Pauline Howland. . . . exec VP & gen mgr
Polly Anderson. . . . dev VP
Cindy Crowther . . . dev mgr

***WIIQ**—Analog channel: 41. Digital channel: 19. On air date: Sept 13, 1971. 2112 11th Ave. S., Suite 400, Birmingham, AL 35205-2884. Phone: (205) 328-8756. Fax: (205) 251-2192. Web Site: www.aptv.org. Licensee: Alabama ETV Commission. Network: PBS.

Key Personnel:
Allan Pizzato . . . CEO & pres
Pauline Howland . . . exec VP
Polly Anderson. . . . dev dir
Cindy Crowther . . . dev mgr
Donna Baker . . . mktg mgr
Jamie Lewis . . . progmg dir
Tommy Weir . . . progmg dir
Jon Beans. . . . news dir & pub affrs dir
Windell Wood . . . chief of engrg

WMCF-TV—Analog channel: 45. On air date: Oct 12, 1985. 300 Mendel Pkwy. W., Montgomery, AL 36117. Phone: (334) 272-0045. Fax: (334) 277-6635. Licensee: Trinity Broadcasting Network. Group owner: (group owner; acq 5-8-00; grpsl). Washington Atty: Baraff, Keorner, Olender & Hochberg.

Key Personnel:
P. Crouch . . . pres
Aaron Motley . . . gen mgr, opns mgr & progmg mgr
John Lee. . . . opns dir & progmg dir
Randi Hughey . . . pub affrs dir
Larry Dean . . . chief of engrg

WNCF—Analog channel: 32. Digital channel: 51. On air date: Mar 12, 1964. 3251 Harrison Rd., Montgomery, AL 36109. Phone: (334) 270-3200. Fax: (334) 271-2972. E-mail: gsingleton@wncftv.com. Web Site: www.wncftv.com. Licensee: Channel 32 Montgomery L.L.C.. Ownership: SagamoreHill Broadcasting L.L.C., 100% (acq 1999; $8 million).. Network: ABC. Rep: Blair Television. Washington Atty: Wiley, Rein & Fielding. News staff: 2; News: one hr wkly.

Key Personnel:
George Singleton . . . gen mgr
Katy Hodges. . . . gen sls mgr
Laura Balentine. . . . rgnl sls mgr & prom dir
Lois Crenshaw . . . progmg dir
Mack Paulk . . . chief of engrg

WRJM-TV—Analog channel: 67. Digital channel: 48. On air date: Dec. 5, 2000. Josie Park Broadcasting Inc., 285 E. Broad St., Ozark, AL 36360. 1014 S. Brundadge St., Troy, AL 36081. Phone: (334) 670-6766. Fax: (334) 670-6717. E-mail: wrjm67@troycable.net. Web Site: www.wrjm.com. Permittee: Josie Park Broadcasting Inc.. Ownership: H. Jack Misell, 67%; Walter P. Lunsford, 33% Washington Atty: Borsari and Assoc, PLC.

Key Personnel:
Jack Misell . . . CEO & gen mgr
Walter P. Lunsford . . . VP
Vincent Hodges . . . stn mgr & prom mgr
Boyd Mizell . . . opns mgr
Buddy Johnson. . . . natl sls mgr
Sonny Strassburger. . . . rgnl sls mgr
Don Hess . . . progmg dir
Jenny Dykes . . . pub affrs dir
Dan Mizell . . . engrg VP

WSFA—Analog channel: 12. On air date: Dec 25, 1954. 12 E. Delano Ave., Montgomery, AL 36105. Phone: (334) 288-1212. Fax: (334) 613-8301. Fax: (334) 613-8303. Web Site: www.wsfa.com. Licensee: Libco Inc. Group owner: Liberty Corp. (acq 9-2-59; $2.22 million;. FTR: 9-14-59). Network: NBC. Rep: Harrington, Righter & Parsons. Washington Atty: Dow, Lohnes & Albertson.

Key Personnel:
Hoyt Andres . . . gen mgr & stn mgr
Mark Wilder . . . opns dir
James Belton . . . natl sls mgr
Lewis Fryer . . . rgnl sls mgr
Edith Parten . . . mktg dir
Denise Vickers . . . news dir
Craig Young . . . engrg mgr
Ken Thayer . . . chief of engrg

Opelika

see Columbus, GA market

Selma

see Montgomery (Selma), AL market

Tuscaloosa

see Birmingham (Anniston, Tuscaloosa), AL market

Alaska

Anchorage, AK (DMA 155)

***KAKM**—Analog channel: 7. On air date: May 7, 1975. 3877 University Dr., Anchorage, AK 99508. Phone: (907) 563-7070. Fax: (907) 273-9192. E-mail: questions@kakm.org. Web Site: www.kakm.org. Licensee: Alaska Public Telecommunications Inc. Network: PBS. Washington Atty: Dow, Lohnes & Albertson.

Key Personnel:
Paul Stankovich. . . . gen mgr
Will Peterson . . . dev dir & dev mgr

KDMD—Analog channel: 33. On air date: February 1990. 1310 E. 66th Ave., Anchorage, AK 99518-1915. Phone: (907) 562-5363. Fax: (907) 562-5346. E-mail: stationmail@kdmd.tv. Web Site: www.kdmd.tv. Licensee: Ketchikan TV LLC. (acq 6-19-02).

Key Personnel:
David Drucker . . . CEO
Bill Vanderpoel . . . pres
Andy Tierney . . . gen mgr & sls VP
Don Nelson . . . chief of engrg

KIMO—Analog channel: 13. On air date: Oct 31, 1967. 2700 E. Tudor Rd., Anchorage, AK 99507. Phone: (907) 561-1313. Fax: (907) 561-1377. E-mail: info@aksuperstation.com. Web Site: www.aksuperstation.com. Licensee: Smith Media License Holdings LLC. Group owner: Smith Broadcasting Group Inc. (acq 11-8-2004; grpsl). Network: ABC. Rep: Katz Radio.

Key Personnel:
Sean Bradley . . . VP & gen mgr
Jeff Glaser. . . . sls dir
Rita Corwin. . . . mktg dir
Jim Filley . . . prom mgr
Terri Bradley . . . progmg dir
Ty Hardt. . . . news dir
George Heacock . . . chief of engrg

KTBY—Analog channel: 4. On air date: Dec 2, 1983. 440 E. Benson Blvd., Anchorage, AK 99503. Phone: (907) 274-0404. Fax: (907) 264-5180. Licensee: Piedmont Television of Anchorage License LLC. Group owner: Piedmont Television Holdings LLC Network: Fox. Washington Atty: Cohn & Marks.

Key Personnel:
Sean Bradley. . . . gen mgr
Jeff Glaser . . . gen sls mgr
Terri Bradley . . . progmg dir

KTUU-TV—Analog channel: 2. On air date: December 1953. Tudor Park, 701 E. Tudor Rd., Suite 220, Delta, AK 99503. Phone: (907) 762-9202. Fax: (907) 561-0882. Fax: (907) 563-3318. E-mail: ktuu@ktuu.com. Web Site: www.ktuu.com. Licensee: Channel 2 Broadcasting Co.. Ownership: Residential and Z&L Trust. (acq 3-9-01). Network: NBC. News staff: 40; News: 12 hrs wkly.

Key Personnel:
Greg D. Zaser . . . pres
Al Bramstedt Jr.. . . . gen mgr
Trent McNelly . . . opns mgr
Andy MacLeod . . . gen sls mgr
Nancy Johnson. natl sls mgr, mktg dir, prom mgr, progmg mgr & film buyer
Dianna Rowedder . . . adv dir & adv mgr
John Tracy. . . . news dir
Barry Sowinski. . . . pub affrs dir
Leland Verschueren . . . chief of engrg

KTVA—Analog channel: 11. On air date: Dec 11, 1953. 1007 W. 32nd Ave., Anchorage, AK 99503. Phone: (907) 273-3192. Fax: (907) 273-3189. E-mail: 11news@ktva.com. Web Site: www.ktva.com. Licensee: Alaska Broadcasting Company Inc.. Ownership: MediaNews Group Inc. (acq 5-25-00; grpsl). Network: CBS. Art Moore Washington Atty: Wilkinson, Barker, Knauer & Quinn. News staff: 16; News: 7 hrs wkly.

Key Personnel:
Jerry Bever . . . gen mgr & stn mgr
Bush Houston . . . opns mgr
Laurie Bruce. . . . gen sls mgr
Cyd Terhune . . . progmg dir
Staci Chil . . . news dir
Tom Lambert. . . . chief of engrg

KYES—Analog channel: 5. On air date: November 1989. 3700 Woodland Dr., Suite 800, Anchorage, AK 99517. Phone: (907) 248-5937. Fax: (907) 339-3889. Web Site: www.yestv.com. Licensee: Fireweed Communications LLC.. Ownership: Jeremy Lansman, 51%; Carol Schatz, 49% (acq 12-11-91; $100. & assumption of debt; FTR: 1-6-92). Washington Atty: Benjamin Perez. News: one hr wkly.

Key Personnel:
Jeremy Lansman . . . pres & chief of engrg
Carol Schatz. . . . gen mgr & progmg mgr
Roy Nederbrock . . . chief of opns
Lori Erickson . . . gen sls mgr, natl sls mgr & rgnl sls mgr
Maryann Spinella. . . . prom mgr

Bethel

***KYUK-TV**—Analog channel: 4. On air date: August 1973. Pouch 468, Bethel, AK 99559. Phone: (907) 543-3131. Fax: (907) 543-3130. Web

Site: www.kyuk.org. Licensee: Bethel Broadcasting Inc. Network: Network: Network: PBS, ABC, CBS. Washington Atty: Wilkinson, Barker, Knauer & Quinn. News staff: 5; News: 3 hrs wkly.

Key Personnel:
Joan Hamilton . . . . . chmn
Ron Daugherty . . . . . gen mgr
Jose Seibert . . . . . progmg dir & engrg dir

Fairbanks, AK (DMA 204)

KATN—Analog channel: 2. On air date: Mar 1, 1955. 516 2nd Ave., Suite 400, Fairbanks, AK 99701. Phone: (907) 452-2125. Fax: (907) 456-8225. E-mail: info@aksuperstation.com. Web Site: www.aksuperstation.com. Licensee: Smith Media License Holdings LLC. Group owner: Smith Broadcasting Group Inc. (acq 11-8-2004; grpsl). Network: ABC. Rep: Katz Radio. News: 6p - 11p wkly.

Key Personnel:
Sean Bradley . . . . . VP & gen mgr
Mike Hammer . . . . . opns VP
Jeff Glaser . . . . . sls VP
Rita Corwin . . . . . mktg dir & prom dir
Terri Bradley . . . . . progmg dir
Ty Hardt . . . . . news dir
Gerilynne Buonocore . . . . . pub affrs dir
George Heacock . . . . . engrg dir

KFXF—Analog channel: 7. On air date: Feb 27, 1995. 3650 Bradock St., Fairbanks, AK 99701. Phone: (907) 452-3697. Fax: (907) 456-3428. Web Site: www.TVTV.com. Licensee: Tanana Valley Television Co.. Ownership: Bill St. Pierre 60%, Mike Young, Dave Wike. Network: Fox. Washington Atty: Baker & Hostetler. News staff: 4; News: 10 hr wkly.

Key Personnel:
Christine Fry . . . . . opns mgr & progmg dir
John Hoff . . . . . gen mgr & gen sls mgr
Darryl Lewis . . . . . news dir
Dave Sala . . . . . chief of engrg

KJNP-TV—Analog channel: 4. Digital channel: 20. On air date: Dec 7, 1981. Box 56359, 2501 Mission Rd., North Pole, AK 99705-1359. Phone: (907) 488-2216. Fax: (907) 488-5246. E-mail: kjnp@mosquitonet.com. Web Site: www.mosquitonet.com/~kjnp. Licensee: Evangelistic Alaska Missionary Fellowship. Washington Atty: Fletcher, Heald & Hildreth.

Key Personnel:
Genevieve Nelson . . . . . CEO
Yvonne Carriker . . . . . pres
Richard T. Olson . . . . . VP
Julie Beaver . . . . . stn mgr

KTVF—Analog channel: 11. Digital channel: 26. On air date: Feb 17, 1955. 3528 International Way, Fairbanks, AK 99701. Phone: (907) 458-1800. Fax: (907) 458-1820. Web Site: www.webcenter11.com. Licensee: Ackerley Media Group Inc. Group owner: Clear Channel Communications Inc. (acq 6-14-02; grpsl). Network: NBC. Rep: Adam Young. Washington Atty: Wilkinson, Barker, Knauer & Quinn. News staff: 6; News: 5 hrs wkly.

Key Personnel:
Bill Wright . . . . . gen mgr
Richard Port . . . . . stn mgr & opns mgr
Deedee Caciari . . . . . gen sls mgr
Celia Vissers . . . . . progmg dir
Bob Miller . . . . . news dir
William Tanner . . . . . chief of engrg

***KUAC-TV**—Analog channel: 9. Digital channel: 24. On air date: Dec 22, 1971. Box 755620, Univ. of Alaska-Fairbanks, 312 Tanana Dr., Fairbanks, AK 99775-5620. Phone: (907) 474-7491. Fax: (907) 474-5064. E-mail: web@kuac.org. Web Site: www.kuac.org. Licensee: University of Alaska. Network: PBS.

Key Personnel:
Greg Petrowich . . . . . pres & sls dir
Gretchen Gordon . . . . . dev dir
Simon Phillips . . . . . gen mgr & progmg dir
Joseph Forgue . . . . . chief of engrg

Juneau, AK (DMA 207)

KJUD—Analog channel: 8. On air date: Feb 19, 1956. 175 S. Franklin St., Senate Bldg., Juneau, AK 99801. Phone: (907) 561-1313. Fax: (907) 561-1377. E-mail: info@aksuperstation.com. Web Site: www.aksuperstation.com. Licensee: Smith Media License Holdings LLC. Group owner: Smith Broadcasting Group Inc. (acq 11-8-2004; grpsl). Network: Network: ABC, NBC. Rep: Katz Radio. Washington Atty: Kaye, Scholer, Fierman, Hays & Handler. News staff: 9; News: 5 hrs wkly.

Key Personnel:
John Bradley . . . . . gen mgr
Jeff Glaser . . . . . gen sls mgr
Terri Bradley . . . . . progmg dir
Ty Hardt . . . . . news dir
Gerilynne Buonocore . . . . . pub affrs dir
George Heacock . . . . . chief of engrg

KTNL—Analog channel: 13. On air date: Sept 1, 1966. 9109 Mendenhall Loop Rd., Suite 3A, Juneau, AK 99801. Phone: (907) 586-2455. Fax: (907) 586-2495. E-mail: stationmail@ktnl.tv. Licensee: Ketchikan TV LLC. (acq 6-19-2002). Network: CBS. Rep: Tacher. Washington Atty: Wilkinson, Barker, Knauer L.L.P..

Key Personnel:
David Drucker . . . . . CEO
Bill Vanderpoel . . . . . VP
Charlene Nelson . . . . . gen mgr
Garrett Leighton . . . . . opns mgr
Amanda McMellon . . . . . sls dir

***KTOO-TV**—Analog channel: 3. Digital channel: 6. On air date: Oct 1, 1978. 360 Egan Dr., Juneau, AK 99801. Phone: (907) 586-1670. Fax: (907) 586-3612. E-mail: ktoo@ktoo.org. Web Site: www.ktoo.org. Licensee: Capital Community Broadcasting Inc. Network: PBS. Washington Atty: Schwartz, Woods & Miller. News staff: one; News: one hr wkly.

Key Personnel:
Bill Legere . . . . . pres & gen mgr
Jim Mahan . . . . . stn mgr
Cheryl Levitt . . . . . dev dir
William Judy . . . . . engrg dir

Ketchikan

KUBD—Analog channel: 4. On air date: Feb 11, 2000. 516 Stedman St., Ketchikan, AK 99901. Phone: (907) 225-4613. Fax: (907) 247-5365. Licensee: Ketchikan TV LLC.. Ownership: David M. Drucker, 100% (acq 6-19-02).

Arizona

Phoenix, AZ (DMA 15)

***KAET**—Analog channel: 8. Digital channel: 29. On air date: Jan 30, 1961. Box 871405, Tempe, AZ 85287. Stauffer Hall B-Wing, Arizona State Uni., Tempe, AZ 85287. Phone: (480) 965-8888. Fax: (480) 965-1000. Web Site: www.kaet.asu.edu. Licensee: Arizona Board of Regents. Network: PBS. Washington Atty: Covington & Burling. News staff: 7; News: 3 hrs wkly.

Key Personnel:
Greg Giczi . . . . . gen mgr
Beth Vershure . . . . . stn mgr
John Martinez . . . . . opns mgr
Kelly McCullough . . . . . dev dir, dev mgr, mktg dir & mktg mgr
John Menzies . . . . . prom mgr
Michael Philipsen . . . . . news dir
Joseph Manning . . . . . engrg mgr

KASW—Analog channel: 61. On air date: September 1995. c/o TV Stn KTVK, 5555 N. 7th Ave., Phoenix, AZ 85013. Phone: (602) 207-3333. Fax: (602) 207-3477. Web Site: www.azfamily.com. Licensee: KASW-TV Inc. Group owner: Belo Corp., Broadcast Division (acq 1-24-00).

Key Personnel:
Dean Apostalides . . . . . gen mgr
Skip Cass . . . . . stn mgr
Rick Soltesz . . . . . gen sls mgr
Brock Kruzie . . . . . natl sls mgr
Scott Rein . . . . . rgnl sls mgr
Mark Demopoulos . . . . . progmg dir
Mike Stone . . . . . chief of engrg

KAZT-TV—Analog channel: 7. On air date: Sept 5, 1982. 4343 E. Camelback Rd., Suite 130, Phoenix, AZ 85018. 3211 Tower Rd, Prescott, AZ 86305. Phone: (602) 224-0027. Fax: (602) 224-2214. E-mail: rbergamo@kaz.tv. Web Site: www.kaz.tv. Licensee: KAZT L.L.C.. Ownership: Londen Media Group L.L.C., 99%; and Ron Bergamo, 1% (acq 4-1-2002; $7.336 million).. Rep: Petry Television Inc.. Washington Atty: Shaw Pittman.

Key Personnel:
Ron Bergamo . . . . . gen mgr
Richard Howe . . . . . stn mgr
Michael Hagerty . . . . . prom dir, progmg dir & progmg mgr

KCFG—Analog channel: 9. On air date: 2001. 3654 W. Jarvis Ave., Skokie, IL 60076. 2616 North Steves Blvd., Flagstaff, AZ 86004. Phone: (928) 526-5234. Phone: (847) 674-0864. Fax: (928) 526-1172. Fax: (847) 674-9188. Web Site: www.kcfg.net. Licensee: KM Television of Flagstaff L.L.C.

***KDTP**—Analog channel: 39. On air date: 2001. Box 6102066, Dallas, TX 75261. Phone: (602) 207-3939. Fax: (623) 536-8449. Web Site: www.daystar.com. Licensee: Community Television Educators Inc.

Key Personnel:
Roger Crawford . . . . . gen mgr
Brenda Crawford . . . . . progmg dir
Dave Thompson . . . . . chief of engrg

KFPH-TV—Analog channel: 13. On air date: 1991. 2158 N. 4th St., Flagstaff, AZ 86004. Phone: (928) 527-1300. Fax: (928) 527-1394. Web Site: www.univision.com. Licensee: Univision Partnership of Flagstaff. Group owner: Univision Communications Inc. (acq 10-2-01; $19.113 million. plus assumption of liabilities with KFTU-TV Douglas).

Key Personnel:
Romon Pineda . . . . . gen mgr
Jose Luis Padilla . . . . . gen sls mgr
Michael Goldman . . . . . natl sls mgr
Javier Ramis . . . . . mktg dir, prom dir & adv dir
Virginia Luna . . . . . pub affrs dir
Tom Foy . . . . . chief of engrg

KMOH-TV—Analog channel: 6. On air date: Feb 22, 1988. 950 Flynn Rd., Camarillo, CA 93012. Phone: (805) 388-0081. Fax: (305) 863-5701. Licensee: Phoenix 6 TV LLC. Group owner: (group owner; (acq 12-8-2004).

KNAZ-TV—Analog channel: 2. On air date: May 2, 1970. 2201 N. Vickey St., Flagstaff, AZ 86004. Box 3360, Flagstaff, AZ 86004. Phone: (928) 526-2232. Fax: (928) 526-8110. E-mail: 2news@knaztv2.com. Licensee: Multimedia Cablevision Inc. Group owner: Gannett Broadcasting (acq 1997; $6.25 million with KMOH-TV Kingman). Network: NBC. Rep: Katz Radio. Washington Atty: Dow, Lohnes & Albertson.

Key Personnel:
Jerome Parra . . . . . gen mgr
Scott Jones . . . . . opns mgr & sls dir
Stan Pierce . . . . . gen sls mgr
Marge Divine . . . . . progmg dir
Kim Smith . . . . . news dir
Jon Koger . . . . . chief of engrg

KNXV-TV—Analog channel: 15. On air date: Sept 9, 1979. 515 N. 44th St., Phoenix, AZ 85008. Phone: (602) 273-1500. Fax: (602) 685-3000. E-mail: news15@abc15.com. Web Site: www.abc15.com. Licensee: Scripps Howard Broadcasting Co. Group owner: (group owner, see Cross-Ownership; acq 1-9-85; $26.6 million). Network: ABC. Washington Atty: Baker & Hostetler.

Key Personnel:
John M. Culliton . . . . . gen mgr
Ryan Steward . . . . . opns mgr, engrg mgr & chief of engrg
Janice Todd . . . . . gen sls mgr
Kimberly Steele . . . . . natl sls mgr
Jim Hart . . . . . prom mgr
Amy Wilson . . . . . progmg mgr
Bob Sullivan . . . . . news dir
Colleen Reid . . . . . pub affrs dir
Will Bruner . . . . . chief of engrg

***KPAZ-TV**—Analog channel: 21. Digital channel: 20. On air date: Sept 16, 1967. 3551 E. McDowell, Bristol, AZ 85008. Phone: (602) 273-1477. Fax: (602) 267-9427. Licensee: Trinity Broadcasting of Arizona Inc. Group owner: Trinity Broadcasting Network (acq 1977). Washington Atty: Joseph E. Dunne III.

Key Personnel:
Dralena Valero . . . . . progmg dir
Gary Nichols . . . . . gen mgr & chief of engrg

KPHO-TV—Analog channel: 5. Digital channel: 17. On air date: Dec 4, 1949. 4016 N. Black Canyon Hwy., Phoenix, AZ 85017. Phone: (602) 264-1000. Fax: (602) 650-5510. Fax: (602) 650-5545. Web Site: www.news5.tv. Licensee: Meredith Corp. Group owner: Meredith Broadcasting Group, Meredith Corp., see Cross-Ownership (acq 6-25-52; grpsl; 6-30-52). Network: CBS. Rep: Harrington, Righter & Parsons. Washington Atty: Garvey, Schubert & Barer. News staff: 60; News: 11 hrs wkly.

Key Personnel:
Steve Hammel . . . . . gen mgr
Mitch Nye . . . . . gen sls mgr
Seth Parker . . . . . progmg VP & progmg dir
Tom Bell . . . . . news dir & engrg dir

KPHZ—Analog channel: 11. On air date: July 4, 2000. 222 Navajo Blvd., Holbrook, AZ 85040. Phone: (928) 524-1652. Fax: (928) 524-6459. Licensee: NBC Telemundo License Co. Group owner: Telemundo Group Inc. (acq 8-23-02; $7.5 million. with KPHZ-LP Phoenix and KPSW-LP Phoenix). Washington Atty: Wiley, Rein, Fielding..

Key Personnel:
Thelma Abril . . . gen mgr
Phillip Williams . . . stn mgr
David Carr. . . . chief of engrg

KPNX—(Mesa).Analog channel: 12. Digital channel: 36. On air date: Apr 23, 1953. Box 711, Phoenix, AZ 85004. 1101 N. Central Ave., Phoenix, AZ 85001. Phone: (602) 257-1212. Fax: (602) 261-6135. Fax: (602) 257-6619 (news). E-mail: webmaster@12news.com. Licensee: Multimedia Holdings Corp. Group owner: Gannett Broadcasting (acq 6-7-79; grpsl; FTR: 6-11-79). Network: NBC. News staff: 70.

Key Personnel:
John Misner . . . gen mgr
Dan Mayasich . . . gen sls mgr

KPPX—Analog channel: 51. On air date: Feb 15, 1999. 1101 N. Central Ave., Phoenix, AZ 85004. Phone: (602) 808-0729. Fax: (602) 808-8864. Web Site: www.pax.tv. Licensee: America 51 L.P. Group owner: Paxson Communications Corp. (acq 1-2-01; $6.6 million for 51%). Washington Atty: Skadden, Arps, Slate, Meagher & Flom.

KSAZ-TV—Analog channel: 10. Digital channel: 31. On air date: Oct 24, 1953. 511 W. Adams St., Phoenix, AZ 85003. Phone: (602) 257-1234. Fax: (602) 262-0177. Fax: (602) 262-0456 (sales). Licensee: KSAZ License Inc. Group owner: Fox Television Stations Inc. (acq 11-96; grpsl). Network: Fox. Rep: Fox Stations Sales. Washington Atty: Koteen & Naftalin. News staff: 96; News: 38 hrs wkly.

Key Personnel:
Patrick Nevin . . . gen mgr
Paul Austill . . . opns mgr
Mellynda Hartel. . . . natl sls mgr
David Saline . . . progmg dir
Doug Bannard . . . news dir
Jim Kauffman . . . chief of engrg

KTFL—Analog channel: 4. On air date: 2002. Box 350, Tupelo, MS 38802. 1359 Rd. 681, Tupelo, MS 38802. Phone: (662) 842-7620. Fax: (662) 844-7061. Licensee: WTVA Inc. Group owner: (group owner). Washington Atty: Garvey, Schubert & Barer.

Key Personnel:
Frank Spain . . . pres
Mark Ledbetter . . . gen mgr
David Dillard. . . . opns mgr

KTVK—Analog channel: 3. On air date: Feb 28, 1955. 5555 N. 7th Ave., Phoenix, AZ 85013. Phone: (602) 207-3333. E-mail: feedback@azfamily.com. Web Site: www.azfamily.com. Licensee: KTVK Inc. Group owner: Belo Corp., Broadcast Division (acq 9-3-99; $315 million cash including 50% of Arizona News Channel). Rep: TeleRep.

KTVW-TV—Analog channel: 33. On air date: Sept 2, 1979. 6006 30th St., Phoenix, AZ 85042. Phone: (602) 243-3333. Fax: (602) 276-8658. Licensee: KTVW License Partnership G.P. Group owner: Univision Communications Inc. (acq 5-17-89; $23 million;. FTR: 6-5-89). Network: Univision (Spanish).

Key Personnel:
Ramon Pineda. . . . VP & gen mgr
Carlos Flys. . . . opns VP
Jose Luis Padilla . . . gen sls mgr
Andrew Deschapelles . . . rgnl sls mgr
Laura De La Mata . . . rgnl sls mgr
Javier Ramis . . . mktg dir & prom dir
Virginia Luna . . . progmg dir
Marco Flores . . . news dir
Tom Foy . . . chief of engrg

KUTP—Analog channel: 45. Digital channel: 26. On air date: Dec 23, 1985. 511 W. Adam St., Phoenix, AZ 85003. Phone: (602) 257-1234. Fax: (602) 262-0177. Web Site: www.kutp.com. Licensee: Fox Television Stations Inc. Group owner: (group owner; acq 7-31-01; grpsl). Washington Atty: Wilmer, Cutler & Pickering.

Key Personnel:
Patrick Nevin . . . gen mgr
Jim Kauffman . . . opns dir, opns mgr & chief of engrg
David Saline . . . gen sls mgr & progmg dir
Mellynda Hartel . . . gen sls mgr
Doug Bannard. . . . progmg dir & news dir

Sierra Vista

see Tucson (Sierra Vista), AZ market

Tucson (Sierra Vista), AZ (DMA 72)

KFTU-TV—Analog channel: 3. On air date: 2001. 1111 G Ave., Douglas, AZ 85607. Phone: (520) 805-1773. Fax: (520) 805-1768. Licensee: Univision Partnership of Douglas. Group owner: Univision Communications Inc. (acq 10-2-01; $19.113 million. plus assumption of liabilities with KFPH-TV Flagstaff).

Key Personnel:
Ramon J. Pineda . . . gen mgr
Carlos Flys . . . opns mgr
Jose Luis Padilla . . . gen sls mgr
Alfonso Romero . . . rgnl sls mgr
Javier Ramis . . . prom dir & adv dir
Salvador Ocano . . . progmg dir
Marco Flores . . . news dir
Tom Foy . . . chief of engrg

KGUN—Analog channel: 9. Digital channel: 35. On air date: June 3, 1956. 7280 E. Rosewood St., Tucson, AZ 85710. Phone: (520) 722-5486. Fax: (520) 733-7099. Fax: (520) 733-7070. Web Site: www.kgun9.com. Licensee: Emmis Television License LLC. Group owner: Emmis Communications Corp. (acq 9-25-2000; grpsl). Network: ABC. Rep: MMT. Washington Atty: Reed Smith LLP. News staff: 47; News: 22 hrs wkly.

Key Personnel:
Ray Depa . . . gen mgr & progmg mgr
Andrew Stewart . . . stn mgr & sls dir
Kelly Donnell . . . opns dir, opns mgr & prom mgr
Kara Quintela . . . natl sls mgr
Thor Wasbotten . . . news dir
Stephen Somerville . . . chief of engrg

KHRR—Analog channel: 40. Digital channel: 42. On air date: Jan 1, 1985. 2919 E. Broadway, Suite 100, Tucson, AZ 85716. Phone: (520) 322-6888. Fax: (520) 319-9148. Web Site: www.telemundo.com. Licensee: NBC Telemundo License Co. Group owner: Telemundo Group Inc. (acq 1-1-2003; $20 million. with KDRX-CA Phoenix). Network: Telemundo (Spanish). News staff: 7; News: 5 hrs wkly.

Key Personnel:
Thelma Abril. . . . VP & gen mgr
Lupita Celaya . . . opns dir & progmg dir
Martha Muniz . . . prom dir & prom mgr
Sergio Pedroza. . . . news dir & pub affrs dir

KMSB-TV—Analog channel: 11. Digital channel: 26. On air date: Feb 1, 1967. 1855 N. 6th Ave., Tucson, AZ 85705-5061. Phone: (520) 770-1123. Fax: (520) 629-7185. Web Site: www.kmsb.com. Licensee: Belo TV Inc. Group owner: Belo Corp., Broadcast Division (acq 2-28-97; grpsl). Network: Fox. Rep: TeleRep. Washington Atty: Wiley, Rein & Fielding.

Key Personnel:
Diane Frisch . . . gen mgr
Lou Medran . . . opns dir
Claudia Montgomery . . . gen sls mgr
Jim Ferreira . . . rgnl sls mgr
Betsy Green . . . mktg dir
Harry West . . . prom dir, progmg dir & film buyer
Bob Lee . . . pub affrs dir
Roy Mitchell . . . chief of engrg

KOLD-TV—Analog channel: 13. On air date: Jan 13, 1953. 7831 N. Business Park Dr., Tucson, AZ 85743. Phone: (520) 744-1313. Fax: (520) 744-5233. Web Site: www.kold.com. Licensee: Raycom America License Subsidiary LLC. Group owner: Raycom Media Inc. (acq 9-12-96). Network: CBS. Rep: Harrington, Righter & Parsons. Washington Atty: Covington & Burling. News: 27 hrs wkly.

Key Personnel:
Jim Arnold . . . VP & gen mgr
Bob Gaff . . . opns mgr
Adam Weyne . . . gen sls mgr
Bob Duffy. . . . rgnl sls mgr
Lec Coble . . . mktg dir
Michelle Germano . . . news dir
Stewart Roman. . . . chief of engrg

KTTU-TV—Analog channel: 18. On air date: Dec 31, 1984. 1855 N. 6th Ave., Tucson, AZ 85705. Phone: (520) 624-0180. Fax: (520) 629-7185. Web Site: www.kttu.com. Licensee: KTTU-TV Inc. Group owner: Belo Corp., Broadcast Division (acq 2-28-02; $18 million).. Network: UPN. Rep: TeleRep. Washington Atty: Hogan & Hartson.

Key Personnel:
Lou Medran . . . pres & opns mgr
Diane Frisch . . . gen mgr
Jim Watson . . . gen mgr & natl sls mgr
Michael Hornfeck. . . . rgnl sls mgr
Bob Richardson . . . progmg dir & news dir
Roy Mitchell . . . chief of engrg

***KUAS-TV**—Analog channel: 27. On air date: January 1986. Box 210067, University of Arizona, Carthage, AZ 85721-0067. Phone: (520) 621-5828. Fax: (520) 621-4122 (news). Web Site: www.kuat.org. Licensee: Arizona Board of Regents, University of Arizona. Network: PBS. Washington Atty: Dow, Lohnes & Albertson.

Key Personnel:
Jack Parris. . . . gen mgr
Rudy Casillas . . . progmg dir & progmg mgr
Rebecca Kunsberg . . . film buyer
Hector Gonzalez . . . news dir
John Anderson . . . chief of engrg

***KUAT-TV**—Analog channel: 6. On air date: Mar 8, 1959. Box 210067, University of Arizona, Tucson, AZ 85721-0067. Phone: (520) 621-5828. Fax: (520) 621-4122 (news). Web Site: www.kuat.org. Licensee: Arizona Board of Regents, University of Arizona. Network: PBS. Washington Atty: Dow, Lohnes & Albertson.

Key Personnel:
Jack Parris. . . . gen mgr
Michael Serres. . . . prom mgr
Rudy Casillas . . . progmg dir & film buyer
Hector Gonzalez . . . news dir
David Ross . . . chief of engrg

KUVE-TV—Analog channel: 46. On air date: 2002. 2301 N. Forbes Blvd., Suite 103, Tucson, AZ 85745. Phone: (520) 204-1245. Fax: (520) 204-1247. Licensee: Univision Television Group Inc. Group owner: Univision Communications Inc. (acq 9-24-03; $12.3 million). Network: Univision (Spanish).

Key Personnel:
Ramon J. Pineda . . . gen mgr
Bernarda Duarte . . . stn mgr
Carlos Flys . . . opns mgr

KVOA—Analog channel: 4. Digital channel: 23. On air date: Sept 15, 1953. Box 5188, Tucson, AZ 85703-0188. 209 W. Elm St., Tucson, AZ 85705-6538. Phone: (520) 792-2270. Fax: (520) 620-1309. Web Site: www.kvoa.com. Licensee: KVOA Communications Inc. Group owner: Cordillera Communications Inc. (acq 12-31-93; $13.25 million;. FTR: 11-15-93). Network: NBC. Rep: Millennium Sales & Marketing. Washington Atty: Dow, Lohnes & Albertson. News: 22 hrs wkly.

Key Personnel:
Gary R. Nielsen. . . . pres & gen mgr
Ed Ortelli . . . stn mgr & sls dir
Dave Kerrigan . . . opns mgr
Lisa Contreras . . . news dir

KWBA—Analog channel: 58. On air date: Jan 1, 1999. 3481 E. Michigan St., Tucson, AZ 85714. Phone: (520) 889-5800. Fax: (520) 889-5855. E-mail: soundoff@kwba.com. Web Site: www.kwba.com. Licensee: Tucson Communications L.L.C. Group owner: Cascade Broadcasting Group L.L.C. (acq 12-20-01; grpsl). Network: WB. Washington Atty: Shaw Pittman.

Key Personnel:
Greg Kunz . . . CEO
Carol La Fever . . . COO
Tom Hettle . . . CFO
Doug McClure. . . . VP & sls VP
Jackie Anderson. . . . VP & natl sls mgr
Jay Clifford . . . rgnl sls mgr
Gene Steinberg . . . mktg VP & progmg VP
Ken Cummings. . . . prom dir & progmg mgr
Alicia Knighton. . . . prom mgr
Mac Powas . . . chief of engrg

Yuma, AZ-El Centro, CA (DMA 171)

KAJB—Analog channel: 54. On air date: 2002. 1803 N. Imperial Ave., El Centro, CA 92243. Phone: (760) 482-7777. Fax: (760) 482-0099. Licensee: Calipatria Broadcasting Com. L.L.C.. Ownership: Kenneth D. Pollin. (acq 12-16-97; $30,000)..

Key Personnel:
Eric Chavez . . . gen mgr
Albert Valdez . . . stn mgr

KECY-TV—Analog channel: 9. On air date: Dec 11, 1968. 1965-B S. 4th Ave., Yuma, AZ 85364. Phone: (928) 539-9990. Fax: (928) 343-0218. Licensee: Pacific Media Corp.. Ownership: Robinson O. Everett, 50%; and Estate of Kathrine Everett, 50% (acq 5-97). Network: Fox. Rep: Millennium Sales & Marketing. Washington Atty: Baraff, Koerner, Olender & Hochberg.

Key Personnel:
Christopher T. Gallu . . . gen mgr
Deborah Weeks . . . gen sls mgr & natl sls mgr
Jesus Corona . . . prom mgr
Adriana Sanchez. . . . progmg mgr

KSWT—Analog channel: 13. Digital channel: 16. On air date: Dec 1, 1963. 1301 S. 3rd Ave., Yuma, AZ 85364. Phone: (928) 782-5113. Fax: (928) 783-0866. Fax: kswt@adelphia.net. Web Site: www.kswt.com. Licensee: Pappas Arizona License LLC. Group owner: Pappas Telecasting Companies (acq 9-8-00; $5.375 million). Network: CBS. Rep: Katz Radio. Washington Atty: Paul, Hastings, Janofsky & Walker. News staff: 8; News: 5 hrs wkly.

KVYE—Analog channel: 7. On air date: July 1996. 1803 N. Imperial Ave., El Centro, CA 92243. Phone: (760) 482-7777. Fax: (760) 482-0099. Web Site: www.entravision.com. Licensee: Entravision Holdings L.L.C. Group owner: Entravision Communications Co. L.L.C. (acq 2-19-98; $500,000. for CP). Network: Univision (Spanish). Washington Atty: Thompson, Hine & Flory L. News staff: 8; News: 5 hrs wkly.

Key Personnel:
Walter Ulloa . . . . . CEO
Philip Wilkinson . . . . . CFO
Albert Valdez . . . . . gen mgr & opns mgr
Eric Chavez . . . . . gen mgr

KYMA—Analog channel: 11. On air date: January 1988. Box 550, Yuma, AZ 85366. 1385 S. Pacific Ave., Yuma, AZ 85365. Phone: (928) 782-1111. Fax: (928) 782-5401. Web Site: www.kyma.com. Licensee: Yuma Broadcasting Co. Group owner: Sunbelt Communications Co. (acq 6-6-89; $60,000; 6-26-89). Network: NBC. Washington Atty: Dow, Lohnes & Albertson. News staff: 24; News: 12 hrs wkly.

Key Personnel:
Paul Heebink . . . . . gen mgr
Barbara Monroy . . . . . progmg dir
Luis Cruz . . . . . news dir
Robbie Decorse . . . . . chief of engrg

Arkansas

El Dorado

see Monroe, LA-El Dorado, AR market

Eureka Springs

see Springfield, MO market

Fayetteville

see Ft. Smith-Fayetteville-Springdale-Rogers, AR market

Ft. Smith-Fayetteville -Springdale-Rogers, AR (DMA 107)

***KAFT**—Analog channel: 13. On air date: Sept 18, 1976. Box 1250, Conway, AR 72033. 350 S. Donaghey, Conway, AR 72034. Phone: (501) 450-1727. Phone: (501) 682-2386. Fax: (501) 682-4122. Web Site: www.aetn.org. Licensee: Arkansas Educational Television Commission. Network: PBS. Washington Atty: Dow, Lohnes & Albertson.

Key Personnel:
Allen Weatherly . . . . . gen mgr
Tony Brooks . . . . . stn mgr
Robert Bland . . . . . opns dir
Mona Dixon . . . . . dev dir

KFSM-TV—Analog channel: 5. Digital channel: 18. On air date: Dec 3, 1956. Box 369, 318 N. 13th St., Fort Smith, AR 72902. Phone: (479) 783-3131. Fax: (479) 783-3295. Web Site: www.5newsonline.com. Licensee: New York Times Management Services. Group owner: The New York Times Co. (acq 8-6-79; $17.5 million;. FTR: 8-13-79). Network: CBS. Rep: Katz Radio. Washington Atty: Covington & Burling. News staff: 36; News: 28 hrs wkly.

Key Personnel:
Debby Etzkorn . . . . . pres & progmg dir
Van Comer . . . . . pres & gen mgr
Mark LaCrue . . . . . gen sls mgr
Rose Smith . . . . . prom mgr
Dale Cox . . . . . news dir
Larry Duncan . . . . . chief of engrg

KFTA-TV—Analog channel: 24. Digital channel: 27. On air date: Nov 12, 1978. 15 South Block Ave., Fayetteville, AR 72701. Phone: (479) 571-5100. Fax: (479) 571-8914. E-mail: news@knwa.com. Web Site: www.knwa.com. Licensee: Nexstar Broadcasting Inc. (acq 12-21-2004; $10 million. with KNWA-TV Rogers). Network: NBC. Rep: TeleRep. Washington Atty: Holland & Knight. News staff: 45; News: 20.5 hrs wkly.

Key Personnel:
Blake Russell . . . . . VP & gen mgr
Cheryl Gwym . . . . . opns mgr

KHBS—Analog channel: 40. On air date: July 28, 1971. 2415 N. Albert Pike, Fort Smith, AR 72904-5698. Phone: (479) 783-4040. Fax: (479) 785-5375. E-mail: comments@thehometownchannel.com. Web Site: www.thehometownchannel.com. Licensee: KHBS Hearst-Argyle Television Inc. Group owner: Hearst-Argyle Television Inc. (acq 7-16-97; grpsl). Network: ABC. Washington Atty: Wiley, Rein & Fielding. News staff: 30; News: 15 hrs wkly.

KHOG-TV—Analog channel: 29. On air date: December 1977. 2415 N. Albert Pike, Fort Smith, AR 72904. Phone: (479) 783-4040. Fax: (479) 785-5375. E-mail: comments@thehometownchannel.com. Web Site: www.thehometownchannel.com. Licensee: KHBS Hearst-Argyle Television Inc. Group owner: Hearst-Argyle Television Inc. (acq 7-16-97; grpsl). Network: ABC. Washington Atty: Wiley, Rein & Fielding.

KNWA-TV—Analog channel: 51. Digital channel: 50. On air date: Aug 23, 1989. 15 South Block St., Suite 101, Fayetteville, AR 72701. Phone: (479) 571-5100. Fax: (479) 571-8914. Web Site: www.knwa.com. Licensee: Nexstar Broadcasting Inc. (acq 12-21-2004; $10 million. with KFTA-TV Fort Smith). Network: NBC. Rep: Blair Television. Washington Atty: Drinker, Biddle & Reath. News staff: 27; News: 17 hrs wkly.

Key Personnel:
Blake Russell . . . . . VP & gen mgr
Mike Vaughn . . . . . gen sls mgr
Chad Beckham . . . . . natl sls mgr
Rob Heverling . . . . . news dir
Lisa Kelsey . . . . . sls

KSBN-TV—Analog channel: 57. On air date: Dec 11, 1995. Box 6968, Springdale, AR 72766. 3556 Liberty Ave., Springdale, AR 72762. Phone: (479) 361-2900. Phone: (888) 777-9392. Fax: (479) 361-2323. E-mail: ksbntv@safetv.org. Web Site: www.safetv.org. Licensee: Total Life Community Educational Foundation.

Key Personnel:
Carlos Pardeiro . . . . . CEO, pres, gen mgr & chief of engrg
Harold Harris . . . . . CFO

Harrison

see Springfield, MO market

Jonesboro, AR (DMA 179)

KAIT—Analog channel: 8. On air date: July 15, 1963. Box 790, Jonesboro, AR 72403-0790. 472 Craig 766, Jonesboro, AR 72401. Phone: (870) 931-8888. Fax: (870) 933-8058 (news). Fax: (870) 931-1371(sales). Web Site: www.kait8.com. Licensee: Libco Inc. Group owner: Liberty Corp. (acq 11-12-86; grpsl). Network: ABC. Rep: Harrington, Righter & Parsons. Washington Atty: Dow, Lohnes & Albertson. News staff: 24; News: 17 hrs wkly.

Key Personnel:
Clyde Anderson . . . . . VP & gen mgr
Ronnie Weston . . . . . opns dir
Ted Fortenberry . . . . . sls dir & gen sls mgr
Ralph Caudill . . . . . natl sls mgr
John Sheridan . . . . . prom mgr
Randy Parrott . . . . . news dir
Tory Beaver . . . . . mktg mgr & pub affrs dir
Gerald Erickson . . . . . chief of engrg

***KTEJ**—Analog channel: 19. On air date: May 1, 1976. Box 1250, Conway, AR 72033. 350 S. Donaghey, Conway, AR 72034. Phone: (501) 450-1727. Phone: (501) 682-2386. Fax: (501) 682-4122. Web Site: www.aetn.org. Licensee: Arkansas Educational Television Commission. Network: PBS. Washington Atty: Dow, Lohnes & Albertson.

Key Personnel:
Allen Weatherly . . . . . gen mgr
Tony Brooks . . . . . stn mgr
Robert Bland . . . . . opns dir
Mona Dixon . . . . . dev dir

KVTJ—Analog channel: 48. On air date: June 6, 1998. 701 Napa Valley Dr., Little Rock, AR 72211. Phone: (501) 223-2525. Fax: (501) 221-3837. E-mail: jim.grant@vtntv.com. Licensee: Agape Church Inc. Group owner: The Victory Television Network (acq 1995).

Little Rock-Pine Bluff, AR (DMA 57)

KARK-TV—Analog channel: 4. Digital channel: 32. On air date: Apr 15, 1954. 1401 W. Capitol Ave., Suite 104, North Las Vegas, AR 72201. Phone: (501) 340-4444. Fax: 501 376-1852. Web Site: www.kark.com. Licensee: Nexstar Broadcasting Inc. Group owner: Nexstar Broadcasting Group Inc. (acq 8-1-2003; $40 million. with WDHN(TV) Dothan, AL). Network: NBC. Rep: Petry Television Inc.. News staff: 40; News: 22 hrs wkly.

Key Personnel:
Perry Chester . . . . . VP & gen mgr
Craig Castrellon . . . . . gen sls mgr
Cindy Rochelle . . . . . natl sls mgr
Ed Tudor . . . . . prom dir
Mary Mobbs . . . . . progmg dir
Rick Iler . . . . . news dir
Bill Addington . . . . . chief of engrg

KASN—Analog channel: 38. On air date: June 17, 1986. 10800 Colonel Glenn, Little Rock, AR 72204. Phone: (501) 225-0038. Fax: (501) 225-0428. Web Site: www.upn38tv.com. Licensee: Clear Channel Broadcasting Licenses Inc. Group owner: (group owner; acq 12-24-91; $14,299,652; 2-3-92). Rep: Katz Radio.

Key Personnel:
Chuck Spohn . . . . . gen mgr
Vickie McRae . . . . . gen sls mgr
Holly Rose . . . . . rgnl sls mgr
Jim Hays . . . . . mktg dir
Miranda Morris . . . . . progmg dir
Michael Fabac . . . . . news dir
Alan Finne . . . . . chief of engrg

KATV—Analog channel: 7. On air date: Dec 18, 1953. Box 77, Little Rock, AR 72203. Phone: (501) 324-7777. Fax: (501) 324-7899. Web Site: www.katv.com. Licensee: KATV L.L.C. Group owner: Allbritton Communications Co. (acq 2-14-83; grpsl). Network: ABC. Washington Atty: Hogan & Hartson.

Key Personnel:
Dale Nicholson . . . . . pres & gen mgr
Mark Rose . . . . . gen sls mgr
Richard Farrester . . . . . progmg dir
Randy Dixon . . . . . news dir
Fred Anderson . . . . . chief of engrg

***KEMV**—Analog channel: 6. On air date: Nov 11, 1980. Box 1250, Conway, AR 72033. 350 S. Donaghey, Conway, AR 72034. Phone: (501) 450-1727. Phone: (501) 682-2386. Fax: (501) 682-4122. Web Site: www.aetn.org. Licensee: Arkansas Educational Television Commission. Network: PBS. Washington Atty: Dow, Lohnes & Albertson.

Key Personnel:
Allen Weatherly . . . . . gen mgr
Tony Brooks . . . . . stn mgr
Robert Bland . . . . . opns dir
Mona Dixon . . . . . dev dir & dev mgr

***KETG**—Analog channel: 9. On air date: Oct 2, 1976. Box 1250, Conway, AR 72033. 350 S. Donaghey St., Conway, AR 72034. Phone: (501) 450-1727. Phone: (501) 682-2386. Fax: (501) 682-4122. Web Site: www.aetn.org. Licensee: Arkansas Educational Television Commission. Network: PBS. Washington Atty: Dow, Lohnes & Albertson.

Key Personnel:
Allen Weatherly . . . . . gen mgr
Tony Brooks . . . . . stn mgr
Robert Bland . . . . . opns dir
Mona Dixon . . . . . dev dir

***KETS**—Analog channel: 2. Digital channel: 5. On air date: Dec 4, 1966. Box 1250, Conway, AR 72033. 350 S. Donaghey, Conway, AR 72034. Phone: (501) 450-1727. Phone: (501) 682-2386. Fax: (501) 682-4122. Web Site: www.aetn.org. Licensee: Arkansas Eucational Television Commission. Network: PBS. Washington Atty: Dow, Lohnes & Albertson.

Key Personnel:
Allen Weatherly . . . . . gen mgr
Tony Brooks . . . . . stn mgr
Robert Bland . . . . . opns dir
Mona Dixon . . . . . dev dir

***KKAP**—Analog channel: 36. On air date: 2001. 3901 Hwy 121, Bedford, TX 76034. Phone: (817) 571-1229. Fax: (817) 571-7458. Web Site: www.daystart.com. Licensee: Educational Broadcasting Corp.. Ownership: Dr. Tracy Harris, 14%; Eric S. Erickson, 14%;

Gregory Fess, 14%; Joni T. Lamb, 14%; Larry Morton, 14%; Marcus Lamb, 14%; and Max Hooper, 14% (acq 7-6-01; $1 million)..

***KLEP**—Analog channel: 17. On air date: Jan 1, 1985. 1502 N. Hill St., Newark, AR 72562. Phone: (870) 799-8969. Phone: (870) 799-8691. Fax: (870) 799-8647. Licensee: Newark Public School System.

KLRT—Analog channel: 16. On air date: June 26, 1983. 10800 Colonel Glenn, Little Rock, AR 72204. Phone: (501) 225-0016. Fax: (501) 225-0428. Web Site: www.fox16.com. Licensee: Clear Channel Radio Licenses Inc. Group owner: Clear Channel Communications Inc. (acq 6-19-91; $6.6 million; 7-8-91). Network: Fox. Rep: Katz Radio. Washington Atty: Crowell & Moring.
Key Personnel:
Chuck Spohn . . . gen mgr
Vicki McRae . . . gen sls mgr
Jim Hays. . . . mktg dir
Logan Wilcoxson . . . prom dir
Miranda Morris . . . progmg dir
Michael Fabac . . . news dir & pub affrs dir
Alan Finne. . . . chief of engrg

KTHV—Analog channel: 11. On air date: Nov 27, 1955. Box 269, Little Rock, AR 72203. 720 Izard St., Little Rock, AR 72201. Phone: (501) 376-1111. Fax: (501) 376-3324. Web Site: www.todaysthv.com. Licensee: Arkansas Television Co. Group owner: Gannett Broadcasting (acq 11-30-94; $27 million;. FTR: 1-16-95). Network: CBS. Rep: Blair Television. Washington Atty: Wiley, Rein & Fielding. News staff: 55; News: 20 hrs wkly.
Key Personnel:
Larry Audas. . . . chmn, pres & gen mgr
Alison Fletcher . . . opns mgr, chief of opns & chief of engrg
Leslie Heizman. . . . gen sls mgr
Chad Kelley . . . natl sls mgr
Joanne Canelli . . . rgnl sls mgr
David Craft . . . mktg VP, mktg dir, prom VP & prom dir
Bobbie Rawlins . . . progmg dir
Mark Raines . . . news dir
Theba Lolley . . . pub affrs dir

KVTH—Analog channel: 26. On air date: 1991. 701 Napa Valley Dr., Little Rock, AR 72211. Phone: (501) 223-2525. Fax: (501) 221-3837. E-mail: jimgrant@vtntv.com. Web Site: www.vtntv.com. Licensee: Agape Church. Group owner: The Victory Television Network (acq 1994).

KVTN—Analog channel: 25. On air date: Dec 1, 1988. 701 Napa Valley Dr., Little Rock, AR 72211. Phone: (501) 223-2525. Fax: (501) 221-3837. Web Site: www.vtntv.com. Licensee: Agape Church Inc. Group owner: The Victory Television Network (acq 6-87; $41,000; 5-1-87). Washington Atty: John Fiorini.

KWBF—Analog channel: 42. On air date: Dec 1, 1997. 1 Shackleford Dr., Suite 400, Little Rock, AR 72211. Phone: (501) 219-2400. Fax: (501) 219-1210. Licensee: River City Broadcasting Inc. Group owner: Equity Broadcasting Corp. (acq 7-28-00; $7.5 million)..
Key Personnel:
Angie Hughes . . . gen mgr & opns mgr
Steve Soldinger. . . . gen mgr
Nathan Stamp . . . progmg dir
Doug Krile. . . . news dir & pub affrs dir
Paul Brandenburg. . . . chief of engrg

KYPX—Analog channel: 49. Digital channel: 49. On air date: 1997. 1 Shackelford Dr., Little Rock, AR 72211. Phone: (501) 219-2400. Fax: (501) 604-8004. Permittee: Arkansas 49 Inc. Group owner: Equity Broadcasting Corp. (acq 8-23-99).

Pine Bluff

see Little Rock-Pine Bluff, AR market

Rogers

see Ft. Smith-Fayetteville-Springdale-Rogers, AR market

Springdale

see Ft. Smith-Fayetteville-Springdale-Rogers, AR market

California

Bakersfield, CA (DMA 128)

KBAK-TV—Analog channel: 29. Digital channel: 33. On air date: Aug 23, 1953. Box 2929, Bakersfield, CA 93303. 1901 Westwind Dr., Bakersfield, CA 93301. Phone: (661) 327-7955. Fax: (661) 327-5603. E-mail: news@cbs-29.com. Web Site: bakersfield.com. Licensee: Westwind Communications L.L.C. (acq 12-7-95). Network: CBS. Rep: Continental Television Sales. Washington Atty: Brooks, Pierce, McLendon, Humphrey & Leonard. News staff: 30; News: 27 hrs wkly.
Key Personnel:
Peter Desnoes . . . chmn
Pete Capra . . . opns mgr & chief of engrg
Mike Knotek . . . gen sls mgr
Tracy Peoples. . . . prom dir & engrg dir
Wayne Lansche. . . . CEO, pres, gen mgr & prom mgr
Nancy Clarke. . . . progmg dir & progmg mgr
Meaghan St.Pierre. . . . news dir

KERO-TV—Analog channel: 23. On air date: Sept 26, 1953. 321 21st St., Bakersfield, CA 93301. Phone: (661) 637-2323. Fax: (661) 322-1701. Web Site: www.thebakersfieldchannel.com. Licensee: McGraw-Hill Broadcasting Co. Group owner: (group owner; acq 3-8-72; grpsl; 3-13-72). Network: ABC. Rep: Harrington, Righter & Parsons. Washington Atty: Holland & Knight.
Key Personnel:
Craig Jahelka . . . VP, gen mgr, progmg VP & progmg dir
Steve McEvoy . . . gen sls mgr
Steve Taylor. . . . prom mgr
Todd Karli . . . news dir
Tom Wimberly. . . . engrg mgr & chief of engrg

KGET-TV—Analog channel: 17. On air date: Nov 8, 1959. 2120 L St., Bakersfield, CA 93301. Phone: (661) 283-1700. Fax: (661) 283-1794. Web Site: www.kget.com. Licensee: Ackerley Media Group Inc. Group owner: Clear Channel Communications Inc. (acq 6-14-02; grpsl). Network: NBC. News staff: 33; News: 27 hrs wkly.
Key Personnel:
Tom Randour . . . VP & gen mgr
Teri Brown . . . gen sls mgr
Jim Tripeny . . . prom mgr
Shirley Sanford . . . progmg dir
John Pilios . . . news dir
Kathleen McNeil . . . pub affrs dir
Tom Ballew . . . chief of engrg

KUVI-TV—Analog channel: 45. On air date: Dec 18, 1988. 5801 Truxtun Ave., Bakersfield, CA 93309. Phone: (661) 324-0045. Fax: (661) 334-2693. Licensee: KUVI License Partnership G.P. Group owner: Univision Communications Inc. (acq 2-4-98; $14,010,800).. Washington Atty: Shaw Pittman.
Key Personnel:
Denise Snanoudt . . . natl sls mgr
Maritere Alvarez-Jackson. . . . rgnl sls mgr
Teresa Ford . . . gen mgr, opns mgr, progmg dir & film buyer
Maria Herrandez . . . pub affrs dir
Ken Richter . . . chief of engrg

Calipatria

see Yuma, AZ-El Centro, CA market

Chico-Redding, CA (DMA 131)

KCVU—Analog channel: 30. Digital channel: 20. On air date: November 1990. 300 Main St., Chico, CA 95928-5438. Phone: (530) 893-1234. Fax: (530) 899-5475. E-mail: info@fox30.com. Web Site: www.fox30.com. Licensee: Sainte Partners II L.P. Group owner: (group owner) Network: Fox. Rep: Millennium Sales & Marketing. Washington Atty: Fletcher, Heald & Hildreth. News: 2.5 hrs wkly.
Key Personnel:
Doug Holroyd . . . VP & gen mgr
Bert Westhoff . . . natl sls mgr
Glenn Taylor. . . . rgnl sls mgr
Paula Murphy . . . progmg mgr
Ken Rice . . . chief of engrg
Betsy Brewer . . . prom

KHSL-TV—Analog channel: 12. On air date: Aug 29, 1953. 3460 Silverbell Rd., Chico, CA 95973. Phone: (530) 342-0141. Fax: (530) 342-4905. E-mail: khsltv@khsltv.com. Web Site: www.khsltv.com. Licensee: Catamount Broadcasting of Chico-Redding Inc. Group owner: Catamount Broadcast Group (acq 7-30-98; $10 million).. Network: CBS. Rep: Continental Television Sales. Washington Atty: Haley, Bader & Potts. News staff: 34; News: 20 hrs wkly.
Key Personnel:
John Stall . . . gen mgr
Cliff Nagler . . . gen sls mgr
Morgan Schmidt . . . mktg dir & prom dir
Shannon Bowman. . . . progmg dir & progmg mgr
Scott Howard. . . . news dir
Steve Burt. . . . chief of engrg

***KIXE-TV**—Analog channel: 9. On air date: Oct 5, 1964. Box 9, Redding, CA 96099. 603 N. Market, Redding, CA 96003. Phone: (530) 243-5493. Fax: (530) 243-7443. E-mail: channel9@kixe.org. Web Site: www.kixe.org. Licensee: Northern California Educational TV Association Inc. Network: PBS. Washington Atty: Schwartz, Woods & Miller.
Key Personnel:
Myron A. Tisdel . . . pres & gen mgr
Nancy Tucker . . . CFO
Mike Lampella . . . opns dir
Anne Kerns . . . dev dir
Fred Gebstadt . . . rgnl sls mgr
Denise B. Ross . . . prom mgr
Brad Fay . . . progmg dir & film buyer
Brian Anderson. . . . chief of engrg

KNVN—Analog channel: 24. On air date: Sept 24, 1985. 3460 Silverbell Rd., Chico, CA 95973. Phone: (530) 894-6397. Fax: (530) 342-2405. E-mail: news@knvn.com. Web Site: www.knvn.com. Licensee: Chico License L.L.C. (acq 6-00; $9.2 million). Network: NBC. Rep: Katz Radio. Washington Atty: Leventhal, Senter & Lerman.
Key Personnel:
John Stall . . . gen mgr
Scott Howard. . . . news dir

KRCR-TV—Analog channel: 7. Digital channel: 34. On air date: Aug 1, 1956. Box 992217, 755 Auditorium Dr., Redding, CA 96001. Phone: (530) 243-7777. Fax: (530) 243-0217. Web Site: www.krcrtv.com. Licensee: BlueStone License Holdings Inc. Group owner: Lamco Communcations Inc. (acq 1995; grpsl). Network: ABC. Rep: Petry Television Inc.. News staff: 21; News: 16 hrs wkly.
Key Personnel:
Sarah Smith . . . gen mgr
Dennis Siewert. . . . gen sls mgr
Danae Thompson . . . prom dir
Debbie Burke. . . . progmg dir
Gary Gunter . . . news dir

El Centro

see Yuma, AZ-El Centro, CA market

Eureka, CA (DMA 192)

KAEF—Analog channel: 23. On air date: Aug 1, 1987. 540 E St., Eureka, CA 95501. Phone: (707) 444-2323. Fax: (707) 445-9451. E-mail: kaeftv@kadf.com. Web Site: www.kaef23.com. Licensee: BlueStone License Holdings Inc. Group owner: Lamco Communications Inc. (acq 1995; grpsl). Network: ABC. Washington Atty: Koteen & Naftalin. News staff: 2; News: 2 hrs wkly.

KBVU—Analog channel: 29. On air date: July 20, 1994. 730 7th St., Suite 201, Eureka, CA 95501. Phone: (707) 442-2999. Fax: (707) 441-0111. Web Site: www.eurekatelevision.tv. Licensee: Sainte Partners II L.P. Group owner: (group owner; acq 7-24-97). Network: Fox. Rep: Millennium Sales & Marketing. Washington Atty: Womble, Carlyle, Sandrige & Rice.
Key Personnel:
Chester Smith . . . CEO
Don Smullin . . . gen mgr

***KEET**—Analog channel: 13. Digital channel: 11. On air date: Apr 14, 1969. Box 13, Eureka, CA 95502. 7246 Humboldt Hill Rd., Eureka, CA 95502. Phone: (707) 445-0813. Fax: (707) 445-8977. E-mail: letters@keet.pbs.org. Web Site: www.keet.com. Licensee: Redwood Empire Pub TV Inc. Network: PBS.
Key Personnel:
Ronald L. Schoenherr. . . . CEO & pres
Seth Frankel . . . opns dir
Karen Barnes. . . . dev dir & progmg dir
Claire Reynolds . . . prom dir
Joel Householter . . . chief of engrg

Broadcasting & Cable Yearbook 2006

B-20

KIEM-TV—Analog channel: 3. On air date: Oct 25, 1953. 5650 S. Broadway, Eureka, CA 95503. Phone: (707) 443-3123. Fax: (707) 442-6084. Web Site: www.kiem-tv.com. Licensee: Pollack/Belz Broadcasting Co. L.L.C. Group owner: Pollack Broadcasting Co. (acq 5-1-96; $3 million). Network: NBC. Rep: Katz Radio.
Key Personnel:
Robert Browning . . . gen mgr
Phil Wright . . . opns mgr & prom mgr
Hank Ingham . . . gen sls mgr
Shawna Brisco . . . progmg dir
Bob Brown . . . news dir
Bob Mottaz . . . chief of engrg

KVIQ—Analog channel: 6. Digital channel: 17. On air date: Apr 1, 1958. 1800 Broadway, Eureka, CA 95501. Phone: (707) 443-3061. Fax: (707) 443-4435. Web Site: www.kviq.com. Licensee: Ackerley Media Group Inc. Group owner: Clear Channel Communications Inc. (acq 6-14-02; grpsl). Network: CBS.
Key Personnel:
John Burgess . . . gen mgr
Penny King . . . stn mgr & gen sls mgr
Rick St. Charles . . . prom dir
Lauren Faucett . . . progmg dir
Deve Silurrbrand . . . news dir
Jim Mixou . . . chief of engrg

Fresno-Visalia, CA (DMA 58)

KAIL—Analog channel: 53. Digital channel: 7. On air date: Dec 18, 1961. 1590 Alluvial Ave., Clovis, CA 93611. Phone: (559) 299-9753. Fax: (559) 299-1523. Web Site: www.kail.tv. Licensee: Trans-America Broadcasting Corp.. Ownership: Albert J. Williams, 79.9%; Jack M. Reeder, 20.1%. (acq 12-23-66; $236,500; 12-26-66). Network: UPN. Washington Atty: Miller & Fields. News staff: 3; News: 3 hrs wkly.
Key Personnel:
Albert J. Williams . . . pres
Charles Williams . . . gen mgr
Mike Nicassio . . . opns mgr & chief of opns
Dave Hetrick . . . gen sls mgr
Robert Jenkins . . . progmg dir
Terrence Kendrials . . . prom VP & prom

KFRE-TV—(Sanger).Analog channel: 59. On air date: July 17, 1985. 5111 E. McKinley Ave., Fresno, CA 93727. Phone: (559) 435-5900. Fax: (559) 255-0275. Web Site: www.kfre.com. Licensee: KFRE(TV) License LLC. Group owner: Pappas Telecasting Companies (acq 12-22-2003; $25 million).. Network: WB. Washington Atty: Cohn & Marks. News staff: 5; News: 2 hrs wkly.
Key Personnel:
Charles Pfaff . . . stn mgr
Ken Felder . . . stn mgr & gen sls mgr
Mark Hodorowski . . . mktg dir, progmg dir & progmg mgr

KFSN-TV—Analog channel: 30. Digital channel: 9. On air date: May 10, 1956. 1777 G St., Fresno, CA 93706. Phone: (559) 442-1170. Fax: (559) 233-5844 (sls). Fax: (559) 266-5024 (news). Web Site: www.abc30.com. Licensee: KFSN Television LLC. Group owner: (group owner). Network: ABC. Rep: ABC National Television Sales. Washington Atty: ABC Legal. News staff: 50; News: 30 hrs wkly.
Key Personnel:
Eric Lerner . . . pres & gen mgr
Bob Hall . . . opns mgr & gen sls mgr
Jeff Aiello . . . mktg mgr & progmg dir
Charlene Ciavaglia . . . progmg mgr
Joel Davis . . . news dir
Beth Marney . . . pub affrs dir
Ron Neil . . . rgnl sls mgr & engrg dir

KFTV—Analog channel: 21. Digital channel: 20. On air date: July 1972. 3239 W. Ashlan Ave., Fresno, CA 93722. Phone: (559) 222-2121. Fax: (559) 222-2890. Fax: (559) 222-0917. Web Site: www.univision.net. Licensee: KFTV L.P., G.P. Group owner: Univision Communications Inc. (acq 8-87). Network: Univision (Spanish). Washington Atty: Shaw Pittman LLP. News staff: 58; News: 8 hrs wkly.
Key Personnel:
Maria L. Gutierrez . . . gen mgr
Brett Covish . . . opns mgr & gen sls mgr
Ken Holden . . . chief of engrg

KGMC—(Clovis).Analog channel: 43. Digital channel: 44. On air date: Sept 11, 1992. 706 W. Herndon Ave., Fresno, CA 93650. Phone: (559) 432-4300. Phone: (559) 435-7000. Fax: (559) 435-3201. E-mail: info@cocolatv.com. Web Site: www.cocolatv.com. Licensee: Gary M. Cocola. Group owner: Cocola Broadcasting Companies (acq 11-19-92). Washington Atty: Dow, Lohnes & Albertson.
Key Personnel:
Gary M. Cocola . . . CEO & pres
Todd Lopes . . . exec VP & gen mgr
Nick Giotto . . . opns dir
Kevin Mosesian . . . natl sls mgr
Nick Giotto . . . rgnl sls mgr & adv dir
James K. Zahn . . . progmg VP
Terry Dolph . . . engrg mgr

KGPE—Analog channel: 47. Digital channel: 34. On air date: Oct 1, 1953. 4880 N. First St., Fresno, CA 93720. Phone: (559) 222-2411. Fax: (559) 222-5593. Web Site: www.cbs47.tv. Licensee: Ackerley Broadcasting-Fresno LLC. Group owner: Clear Channel Communications Inc. (acq 6-14-02; grpsl). Network: CBS. Rep: Millennium Sales & Marketing. Washington Atty: Wiley, Rein & Fielding. News staff: 50; News: 28hrs wkly.
Key Personnel:
Steve Stendlove . . . exec VP
Diana Wilkin-Zapata . . . sr VP, VP & gen mgr
Mike Snyder . . . chief of opns & gen sls mgr
Patrice Coulter-Dos . . . sls dir
Jason Drilling . . . natl sls mgr
Scott Saldinger . . . rgnl sls mgr
Jim Holland . . . news dir

KMPH—(Visalia).Analog channel: 26. On air date: Oct 11, 1971. 5111 E. McKinley Ave., Fresno, CA 93727. Phone: (559) 255-2600. Fax: (559) 255-0275. E-mail: viewercomments@kmph.com. Web Site: www.kmph.com. Licensee: KMPH(TV) License LLC. Group owner: Pappas Telecasting Companies (acq 6-1-78; $3,105,550).. Network: Fox. Rep: TeleRep. Washington Atty: Fletcher, Heald & Hildreth. News staff: 21; News: 7 hrs wkly.
Key Personnel:
Harry J. Pappas . . . pres
LeBon Abercrombie . . . exec VP
John Carpenter . . . VP
Charlie Pfaff . . . gen mgr
Ken Felder . . . gen sls mgr
Mark Hodorowski . . . prom mgr
Debbie Sweeney . . . progmg dir
Roger Gadley . . . news dir
Jim Boston . . . chief of engrg

KNSO—Analog channel: 51. Digital channel: 5. On air date: Mar 22, 1996. 30 River Park Pl. W., Suite 200, Fresno, CA 93720. Phone: (559) 252-5101. Web Site: www.kcso33.com. Licensee: NBC Telemundo License Co. Group owner: Telemundo Group Inc. (acq 4-30-03; $33 million). Network: Telemundo (Spanish).

***KNXT**—Analog channel: 49. Digital channel: 50. On air date: Nov 2, 1986. 1550 N. Fresno St., Fresno, CA 93703. Phone: (559) 488-7440. Fax: (559) 488-7444. E-mail: knxt49@hotmail.com. Web Site: www.dioceseoffresno.org. Licensee: Board of Directors Diocese of Fresno Education Corp.
Key Personnel:
Bishop John T. Steinback . . . pres
Marvin Harrison . . . gen mgr

KSEE—Analog channel: 24. Digital channel: 38. On air date: June 1, 1953. 5035 E. McKinley Ave., Fresno, CA 93727-1964. Phone: (559) 454-2424. Fax: (559) 454-2487. Web Site: www.ksee24.com. Licensee: Ksee License, Inc. Group owner: (group owner; acq 12-93; $32 million with WTVH(TV) Syracuse, NY; 8-30-93). Network: NBC. Rep: Harrington, Righter & Parsons. Washington Atty: Akin, Gump, Strauss, Hauer & Feld.
Key Personnel:
Todd McWilliams . . . pres & gen mgr
George Hillis . . . chief of opns, progmg mgr & chief of engrg
Jan Katzenberger . . . gen sls mgr & prom dir
Kathleen Goble . . . natl sls mgr
Chris Zanghi . . . rgnl sls mgr
Julie Akins . . . news dir

KTFF-TV—Analog channel: 61. Digital channel: 48. On air date: May 6, 1992. 6715 N. Palm Ave., Suite 201, Fresno, CA 93707. Phone: (559) 439-6100. Fax: (559) 439-5950. Web Site: www.telefutura.com. Licensee: TeleFutura Fresno LLC. Group owner: Univision Communications Inc. acq 2-7-03; $35 million). Network: TeleFutura (Spanish).
Key Personnel:
Maria L. Gutierrez . . . gen mgr
Brett Covish . . . opns mgr
Jose Elgorriga . . . gen sls mgr
Darrell Jennings . . . rgnl sls mgr
Samuel Belilty . . . progmg dir & news dir
Ken Holden . . . chief of engrg

***KVPT**—Analog channel: 18. On air date: Apr 10, 1977. 1544 Van Ness Ave., Fresno, CA 93721. Phone: (559) 266-1800. Fax: (559) 650-1880. E-mail: info@kvpt.org. Web Site: www.kvpt.org. Licensee: Valley Public Television Inc. (acq 11-1-87). Network: PBS. Washington Atty: Fletcher, Heald & Hildreth. News staff: 35.
Key Personnel:
Paula Castadio . . . CEO & mktg dir
Douglas E. Noll . . . chmn
Jerry Lee . opns VP, opns mgr, prom VP, progmg VP & progmg dir
Eva Torres . . . dev dir & sls dir
Rodger Hixon . . . chief of engrg

Los Angeles (DMA 2)

KABC-TV—Analog channel: 7. Digital channel: 53. On air date: Sept 16, 1949. 500 Circle Seven Dr., Glendale, CA 91201. Phone: (818) 863-7777. Fax: (818) 863-7080. E-mail: abc7@abc.com. Web Site: www.abc.7.com. Licensee: ABC Inc. Group owner: (group owner; acq 1-6-86; grpsl; 7-15-85). Network: ABC.

KAZA-TV—Analog channel: 54. On air date: July 28, 2001. 500 S. Chinowth Rd., Visalia, CA 93277. Phone: (559) 733-7800. Phone: (818) 241-5400. Fax: (559) 733-7878. Web Site: pappastv.com. Licensee: Pappas Southern California License LLC. Group owner: Pappas Telecasting Companies.
Key Personnel:
Harry J. Pappas . . . CEO
Eduardo Urbiola . . . gen mgr
Fernando Acosta . . . gen mgr & opns mgr
Alberto Ezquerro . . . gen sls mgr
Ramon Delgado . . . progmg dir
Oscar Salcedo . . . news dir
Joe Berardi . . . chief of engrg

KCAL—Analog channel: 9. Digital channel: 43. On air date: Oct 6, 1948. 6121 Sunset Blvd., Hollywood, CA 90028. Phone: (323) 467-9999. Fax: (323) 464-2526. E-mail: kcalnews@cbs.com. Web Site: www.kcal.com. Licensee: Viacom Television Stations Group of Los Angeles LLC. Group owner: Viacom Television Stations Group (acq 5-3-2002; $650 million).. Network: CBS. Rep: Adam Young.

KCBS-TV—Analog channel: 2. Digital channel: 60. On air date: May 6, 1948. 6121 Sunset Blvd., Los Angeles, CA 90028. Phone: (323) 460-3000. Fax: (323) 460-3733. Web Site: www.cbs2.com. Licensee: CBS Inc. Group owner: CBS (acq 12-27-50; $3.6 million; 1-1-51). Network: CBS. News staff: 104; News: 26 hrs wkly.
Key Personnel:
Paul Latham . . . CFO
Don Corsini . . . gen mgr
Melanie Steensland . . . opns dir
Garen Vandebeek . . . prom dir
Virginia Hunt . . . progmg dir
Nancy Bauer Gonzalez . . . news dir
Craig Harrison . . . engrg dir

***KCET**—Analog channel: 28. Digital channel: 59. On air date: Sept 28, 1964. 4401 Sunset Blvd., Los Angeles, CA 90027. Phone: (323) 666-6500. Fax: (323) 953-5523. Web Site: www.kcet.org. Licensee: Community TV of Southern California. Network: PBS. Washington Atty: Arent, Fox, Kintner, Plotkin & Kahn.
Key Personnel:
Al Jerome . . . CEO, pres & gen mgr
Debbie Hinton . . . CFO
Roger Terracina . . . opns mgr & dev VP

KCOP—Analog channel: 13. Digital channel: 66. On air date: Sept 17, 1948. 1919 S. Bundy Dr., Asheville, CA 90025. Phone: (310) 584-2000. Fax: (310) 584-2024. Web Site: www.upn13.com. Licensee: Fox Television Stations Inc. Group owner: (group owner; acq 7-31-01; grpsl). Network: UPN. Washington Atty: Wilmer, Cutler & Pickering.

KDOC-TV—Analog channel: 56. On air date: Oct 1, 1982. 18021 Cowan, Irvine, CA 92614-6023. Phone: (949) 442-9800. Fax: (949) 261-5956. E-mail: mmerker@kdoctv.net. Web Site: www.kdoctv.net.. Stn video via satellite: directtv-echostar I-l Licensee: Golden Orange Broadcasting Co. Inc.. Ownership: Pat Boone, 36.42%; Calvin C. Brack, 19.05%. Washington Atty: Cohn & Marks.
Key Personnel:
Calvin Brack . . . CEO & VP
Pat Boone . . . pres
John Davis . . . gen mgr
Tom Jimenez . . . gen sls mgr
Dale Foshee . . . rgnl sls mgr
Michelle Merker . . . mktg dir, prom VP & pub affrs dir
John Atkinson . . . progmg mgr
Roger Knipp . . . chief of engrg

KFTR-TV—(Ontario).Analog channel: 46. On air date: Apr 21, 1984. 5999 Center Dr., Los Angeles, CA 90045. Phone: (310) 348-3411. Fax: (310) 348-4849. Licensee: Univision Partnership of Southern

California. Group owner: Univision Communications Inc. (acq 5-21-01; grpsl). Network: TeleFutura (Spanish). Washington Atty: Wiley, Rein & Fielding.

Key Personnel:
Jorge Delgado . . . gen mgr
Mark Dante . . . gen sls mgr
Luis De La Parra . . . mktg dir & prom dir
Amy Rico . . . progmg mgr
Chris Homer . . . chief of engrg

KHIZ—Analog channel: 64. Digital channel: 44. On air date: 1987. Box 1468, Victorville, CA 92393-1468. 15605 Village Dr., Victorville, CA 92394. Phone: (760) 241-6464. Fax: (760) 241-0056. Web Site: www.khiztv.com. Licensee: Sunbelt Television Inc.. Ownership: Mary Ellen Zenz, conservator (acq 12-27-01). Washington Atty: Wilkinson, Barker & Knauer. News staff: 10; News: 5 hrs wkly.

Key Personnel:
Peter White . . . pres
Garrett Law . . . gen mgr
Stella Montoya . . . progmg dir

KJLA—Analog channel: 57. Digital channel: 49. On air date: October 1990. 2323 Corinth Ave., West Los Angeles, CA 90064. Phone: (310) 943-5288. Fax: (310) 943-5299. E-mail: kjlainfo@kjla.com. Web Site: www.kjla.com. Licensee: KJLA LLC.. Ownership: LATV LLC (acq 11-14-94; FTR: 1-2-95). Washington Atty: Thompson Hine & Flory.

Key Personnel:
Walter Ulloa . . . pres
Ed Safa . . . CFO
Daniel Crowe . . . exec VP
Francis Wilkinson . . . exec VP & gen mgr
Mike Seros . . . opns dir
Richard Deanda . . . dev dir & rgnl sls mgr

***KLCS**—Analog channel: 58. On air date: Nov 5, 1973. 1061 W. Temple St., Los Angeles, CA 90012. Phone: (213) 625-6958. Fax: (213) 481-1019. E-mail: info@klcs.org. Web Site: www.klcs.org. Licensee: Los Angeles Unified School District.. Ownership: Los Angeles Unified School Dist. Network: PBS. Washington Atty: Cohn & Marks. News: 5 hrs wkly.

Key Personnel:
Dr. Janalyn W. Glymph . . . gen mgr & stn mgr
Myles Jang . . . dev dir
Sabrina Thomas . . . opns dir, progmg dir & progmg mgr

KMEX-TV—Analog channel: 34. On air date: Sept 30, 1962. 1999 Center Dr., Los Angeles, CA 90045. Phone: (310) 216-3434. Fax: (310) 348-3459. Web Site: www.univision.com (keyword: Los Angeles). Licensee: KMEX License Partnership G.P. Group owner: Univision Communications Inc. Network: Univision (Spanish). News: 17 hrs wkly.

Key Personnel:
A. Jerrold Perenchio . . . CEO & chmn
Jose Delgado . . . pres
George Blank . . . CFO
Jorge Delgado . . . gen mgr & opns mgr
Mark Dante . . . gen sls mgr
Luis De la Parra . . . mktg dir
Antoinette Gill . . . progmg dir
Jorge Mattey . . . news dir
Christina Sanchez-Camino . . . pub affrs dir
Chris Homer . . . engrg mgr & chief of engrg

KNBC—Analog channel: 4. Digital channel: 36. On air date: 1998. 3000 W. Alameda Ave., Burbank, CA 91523. Phone: (818) 840-4444. Fax: (818) 840-3003. Web Site: www.nbc4.tv. Licensee: NBC Telemundo License Co. Group owner: NBC TV Stations Division (acq 6-5-86). Network: NBC. Rep: NBC TV Stations Sales.

Key Personnel:
Paula Madison . . . pres
Paul Madison . . . gen mgr
Robert Long . . . stn mgr
Mike McCarthy . . . sls VP & gen sls mgr
Robert L. Long . . . news dir

***KOCE-TV**—Analog channel: 50. Digital channel: 48. On air date: November 1972. Box 2476, 15751 Gothard St., Huntington Beach, CA 92647. Phone: (714) 895-5623. Fax: (714) 895-0852. E-mail: koce@cccd.edu. Web Site: www.koce.org. Licensee: KOCE-TV Foundation. (acq 11-1-2004; $25.5 million).. Network: PBS. Washington Atty: Vorys, Sater, Seymour & Pease. News: 3 hrs wkly.

Key Personnel:
Robert Brown . . . chmn
Michael Taylor . . . VP & news dir
Mel Rogers . . . gen mgr
Nancy Weed . . . stn mgr
Bette Kain . . . dev dir
Judith Schaefer . . . prom dir & pub affrs dir
Patricia Petric . . . progmg dir
Roger Yoakum . . . chief of engrg

KPXN—Analog channel: 30. On air date: Jan 7, 1994. 3000 W. Alameda Ave., Suite 32622, Burbank, CA 91523. Phone: (818) 840-4444. Fax: (818) 840-2129. Web Site: www.pax.tv. Licensee: Paxson Los Angeles License Inc. Group owner: Paxson Communications Corp. (acq 3-22-95; $18 million; 6-19-95).

Key Personnel:
Alisha Wofford . . . VP
Paula Madison . . . gen mgr & chief of engrg
Rob Word . . . stn mgr & progmg dir
Mark Douglas . . . gen sls mgr
Steve Vinke . . . chief of engrg

KRCA—Analog channel: 62. Digital channel: 68. On air date: Dec 17, 1988. 1813 Victory Pl., Burbank, CA 91504. Phone: (818) 563-5722. Fax: (818) 972-2694. E-mail: info@lbimedia.com. Licensee: KRCA License Corp. Group owner: Liberman Broadcasting Inc. (acq 6-18-90).

Key Personnel:
Ivan Stoickovich . . . gen mgr
Ozzie Mendoza . . . gen sls mgr
Miguel Ban . . . progmg dir
Victor Zeladita . . . engrg VP
Chris Buchanan . . . chief of engrg

KSCI—Analog channel: 18. Digital channel: 61. On air date: June 30, 1977. 1990 S. Bundy Dr., Suite 850, Los Angeles, CA 90025. Phone: (310) 478-1818. Fax: (310) 479-8118. E-mail: info@kscitv.com. Web Site: www.kscitv.com. Licensee: KSLS Inc. Group owner: Asian Media Group (acq 1-18-01; $165 million cash. for 69.4%). Washington Atty: Wilkinson, Barker, Knauer LLP. News staff: 12; News: 12 hrs wkly.

Key Personnel:
Peter Mathes . . . chmn
Marna Grantham . . . pres & gen mgr
Loren Michaels . . . CFO

KTBN-TV—(Santa Ana).Analog channel: 40. On air date: Jan 5, 1967. Box A, Santa Ana, CA 92711. 2442 Michelle Dr., Tustin, CA 92780. Phone: (714) 832-2950. Fax: (714) 665-2191. Web Site: www.tbn.org. Licensee: Trinity Broadcasting Network. Group owner: (group owner; acq 8-2-74; $1,266,400; 8-19-74). Washington Atty: Joseph E. Dunne III.

KTLA—Analog channel: 5. Digital channel: 31. On air date: Jan 22, 1947. 5800 Sunset Blvd., Los Angeles, CA 90028. Phone: (323) 460-5500. Fax: (323) 460-5405. Web Site: www.ktla.com. Licensee: KTLA Inc. Group owner: Tribune Broadcasting Co. (acq 12-23-85; $510 million). Network: WB. Rep: TeleRep. Washington Atty: Sidley & Austin. News: 22 hrs wkly.

Key Personnel:
Vinnie Malcolm . . . VP, gen mgr & stn mgr
Gordon Peppars . . . gen sls mgr
Jymm Adams . . . prom dir
Gracelyn Brown . . . progmg dir
Jeff Wald . . . news dir
Ray Gonzales . . . pub affrs dir
Chris Neuman . . . engrg dir
Dave Cox . . . chief of engrg

KTTV—Analog channel: 11. Digital channel: 65. On air date: Jan 1, 1949. 1999 S. Bundy Dr., Los Angeles, CA 90025. Phone: (310) 584-2000. Fax: (310) 584-2024. Web Site: www.fox11la.com. Licensee: Fox Television Stations Inc. Group owner: (group owner; acq 11-14-86; grpsl). Network: Fox. News: 25 hrs wkly.

Key Personnel:
Jack Abernathy . . . CEO
Kevin Hale . . . gen mgr

***KVCR-TV**—Analog channel: 24. Digital channel: 26. On air date: Sept 11, 1962. 701 S. Mt. Vernon Ave., San Bernardino, CA 92410. Phone: (909) 384-4444. Fax: (909) 885-2116. E-mail: info@kvcr.pbs.org. Web Site: www.kvcr.org. Licensee: San Bernardino Community College District. Network: PBS.

Key Personnel:
Larry R. Ciecalone . . . gen mgr
Al Gondos . . . opns dir
Richard Dulock . . . dev dir
Lillian Vasquez . . . prom dir
Don Leiffer . . . progmg dir
Patty Littlejohn . . . pub affrs dir
Thomas Guptill . . . chief of engrg

KVEA—(Corona).Analog channel: 52. On air date: June 29, 1966. 3000 W. Alameda, Burbank, CA 91523. Phone: (818) 260-5700. Fax: (818) 260-5222. Web Site: www.kvea.com. Licensee: NBC Telemundo License Co. Group owner: Telemundo Group Inc. (acq 4-12-02; grpsl). Network: Telemundo (Spanish).

KVMD—Analog channel: 31. Digital channel: 23. 6448 Hallee Rd., Suite 3, Joshua Tree, CA 92252. Phone: (760) 366-9881. Fax: (760) 366-1342. Licensee: KVMD Licensee Co. LLC.. Ownership: Ronald L. Ulloa, 100% (acq 4-5-01; $900,000)..

Key Personnel:
Larry Peterson . . . gen mgr, stn mgr, opns mgr & gen sls mgr
Ken Brown . . . chief of engrg

KWHY-TV—Analog channel: 22. Digital channel: 42. On air date: Mar 25, 1963. 1100 Airway, Glendale, CA 91201. Phone: (818) 409-5255. Fax: (818) 409-5228. Licensee: NBC Telemundo License Co. Group owner: Telemundo Group Inc. (acq 4-12-2002; grpsl). Washington Atty: Cohn & Marks. News staff: 6; News: 12 hrs wkly.

KXLA—Analog channel: 44. Digital channel: 51. On air date: 2001. 2323 Corinth Ave., Los Angeles, CA 90064. Phone: (310) 478-0055. Fax: (310) 478-8070. Licensee: Rancho Palos Verdes Broadcasters Inc.. Ownership: RPVB Lender Inc. (acq 8-27-01; up to $40 million. for stock with KXLA-DT Rancho Palos Verdes).

Key Personnel:
Ron Ulloa . . . pres, gen mgr & progmg dir
Ken Brown . . . chief of engrg

Modesto

see Sacramento-Stockton-Modesto, CA market

Monterey-Salinas, CA (DMA 124)

***KCAH**—Analog channel: 25. On air date: November 1989. c/o KTEH, 1585 Schallenburger Rd., San Jose, CA 95110-1301. Phone: (408) 795-5400. Fax: (408) 995-5446. Web Site: www.kteh.org. Licensee: KTEH-TV Foundation. (acq 8-17-99; $300,000). Network: PBS.

Key Personnel:
Tom Fanella . . . CEO
Judy Armstrong . . . gen mgr & dev dir

KCBA—Analog channel: 35. On air date: Nov 1, 1981. 1550 Moffat St., Salinas, CA 93905. Phone: (831) 422-3500. Fax: (831) 754-1120. Web Site: www.iknowcentralcoast.com. Licensee: Seal Rock Broadcasters L.L.C.. Ownership: George V. Kristie and Lance W. Anderson, mgng members (acq 1-5-00; $11 million).. Network: Fox. Washington Atty: Rubin, Winston, Diercks, Harris & Cooke. News: 10 hrs wkly.

Key Personnel:
Mark Faylor . . . VP & gen mgr
Chris Chidlaw . . . gen mgr & stn mgr
Camilla Boolootian . . . gen sls mgr & prom mgr
Eric Casalla . . . progmg dir
Monica Escobedo . . . film buyer
Denise Clodjeaux . . . news dir
Adam Perez . . . engrg dir & chief of engrg

KION-TV—(Monterey).Analog channel: 46. On air date: Feb 2, 1969. 1550 Moffett St., Salinas, CA 93905. Phone: (831) 784-1702. Fax: (831) 784-6395. Web Site: www.kion46.com. Licensee: Ackerley Media Group Inc. Group owner: Clear Channel Communications Inc. (acq 6-14-02; grpsl). Network: CBS. Rep: Katz Radio. Washington Atty: Wiley, Rein & Fielding. News staff: 25; News: 8 hrs wkly.

KSBW—Analog channel: 8. On air date: Sept 11, 1953. 238 John St., Salinas, CA 93901. Phone: (831) 758-8888. Fax: (831) 424-3750. Web Site: www.theksbwchannel.com. Licensee: Hearst-Argyle Stations Inc. Group owner: Hearst-Argyle Television Inc. (acq 6-1-98). Network: NBC. Washington Atty: Brooks, Pierce, McLendon, Humphrey & Leonard. News staff: 31; News: 26 hrs wkly.

Key Personnel:
Joseph W. Heston . . . pres & gen mgr
Jose Camacho . . . opns mgr, mktg mgr & engrg mgr
Wendy Hillan . . . gen sls mgr & natl sls mgr
Dave Butta . . . mktg dir, prom dir & adv dir
Britt Govea . . . mktg mgr
Becky Jackson . . . progmg mgr
Lawton Dodd . . . news dir
Theresa Wright . . . pub affrs dir
Jim Grimes . . . engrg dir

KSMS-TV—(Monterey).Analog channel: 67. On air date: Sept 1, 1986. 67 Garden Ct., Monterey, CA 93940. Phone: (831) 373-6767. Fax: (831) 373-6700. Web Site: www.entravision.com. Licensee: Entravision Holdings L.L.C. Group owner: Entravision Communications Co. L.L.C. (acq 4-25-97). Network: Univision (Spanish).

Key Personnel:
Philip Wilkinson . . . pres & VP

Aaron Scoby . . . . . gen mgr
Alejandro Sanchez . . . . . gen sls mgr

Oakland

see San Francisco-Oakland-San Jose market

Palm Springs, CA (DMA 159)

KESQ-TV—Analog channel: 42. Digital channel: 52. On air date: Oct 5, 1968. 42-650 Melanie Pl., Palm Desert, CA 92211. Phone: (760) 773-0342. Fax: (760) 773-5107. Web Site: www.kesq.com. Licensee: Gulf-California Broadcast Co. (acq 4-24-96; $19.4 million). Network: ABC. Rep: Continental Television Sales. Washington Atty: Smithwick & Belendiuk. News staff: 40; News: 17 hrs wkly.
Key Personnel:
Bob Allen . . . . . pres, exec VP & gen mgr
Todd Graham . . . . . opns mgr
Barry Gorfine . . . . . sls dir & gen sls mgr
Ken Spalding . . . . . progmg dir & progmg mgr
Tony Ballew . . . . . news dir
Dave Swartz . . . . . engrg dir & chief of engrg

KMIR-TV—Analog channel: 36. On air date: Oct 26, 1968. 72-920 Parkview Dr., Palm Desert, CA 92260. Phone: (760) 568-3636/(760) 340-1623. Fax: (760) 568-1176. E-mail: news@kmir6.com. Web Site: www.kmir6.com. Licensee: Journal Broadcast Corp. Group owner: Journal Broadcast Group Inc. (acq 6-11-99; $28.1 million).. Network: NBC. Washington Atty: Koteen & Naftalin. News staff: 30; News: 8 hrs wkly.
Key Personnel:
Dianne Downey . . . . . VP & gen mgr
Manuel Dela Rosa . . . . . opns dir & prom dir
Bob Ruderman . . . . . gen sls mgr & natl sls mgr
Scott Johnson . . . . . rgnl sls mgr & adv dir
Mayra Mancilla . . . . . progmg mgr
Greg Green . . . . . film buyer
Davida Vanderploeg . . . . . news dir
Joe Pandolfo . . . . . chief of engrg

Redding

see Chico-Redding, CA market

Sacramento-Stockton-Modesto, CA (DMA 19)

***KBSV**—Analog channel: 23.Not on air, target date: unknown: Box 4116, Modesto, CA 95352. Phone: (209) 538-9801. Fax: (209) 538-2795. E-mail: kssv@aol.com. Licensee: Bet-Nahrain.
Key Personnel:
Dr. Sargon Dadesho . . . . . pres
Shemiran Daniel . . . . . VP & gen mgr

KCRA-TV—Analog channel: 3. Digital channel: 35. On air date: Sept 3, 1955. 3 Television Cir., Sacramento, CA 95814-0794. Phone: (916) 446-3333. Fax: (916) 441-4050 (news). Web Site: www.thekcrachannel.com. Licensee: Hearst-Argyle Stations Inc. Group owner: Hearst-Argyle Television Inc. (acq 2-18-99). Network: NBC. Rep: Petry Television Inc.. Washington Atty: Koteen & Naftalin. News: 55 hrs wkly.

KMAX-TV—Analog channel: 31. Digital channel: 21. On air date: Oct 5, 1974. 500 Media Pl., Sacramento, CA 95815. Phone: (916) 925-3100. Fax: (916) 920-1078. Web Site: www.upn31.com. Licensee: WVIT Inc. Group owner: Viacom Television Stations Group (acq 3-24-98; $100 million).. Network: UPN.
Key Personnel:
Bruno Cohen . . . . . VP & gen mgr
Matthew Aaron . . . . . gen sls mgr
Gavin Joe . . . . . natl sls mgr
Jeff Schneider . . . . . rgnl sls mgr
Jennifer Nicholson . . . . . prom mgr
Rita Gazitano . . . . . progmg mgr
Brent Baader . . . . . news dir
Bob Hess . . . . . chief of engrg

KOVR—(Stockton).Analog channel: 13. Digital channel: 25. On air date: Sept 5, 1954. 2713 KOVR Dr., West Sacramento, CA 95605. Phone: (916) 374-1313. Fax: (916) 374-1459. Web Site: www.kovr13.com. Licensee: SCI - Sacramento Licensee L.L.C. Group owner: Sinclair Broadcast Group Inc. Network: CBS. Rep: Harrington, Righter & Parsons. Washington Atty: Shaw Pittman LLP. News staff: 60; News: 22 hrs wkly.
Key Personnel:
Dan Mellon . . . . . gen mgr
J.R. Jackson . . . . . gen sls mgr
Joanne Jackson . . . . . progmg dir & progmg mgr
Jim Lemon . . . . . news dir
Denise Dituri . . . . . pub affrs dir
Bob Olson . . . . . chief of engrg

KQCA—(Stockton).Analog channel: 58. Digital channel: 46. On air date: Apr 13, 1986. 3 Television Cir., Sacramento, CA 95814-0794. Phone: (916) 446-3333. Fax: (916) 554-4658. Web Site: www.thekcrachannel.com. Licensee: Hearst-Argyle Stations Inc. Group owner: Hearst-Argyle Television Inc. (acq 1-24-2000; less than $1 million).. Network: NBC. Washington Atty: Skadden, Arps, Slate, Meagher & Flom.
Key Personnel:
Elliot Troshinsky . . . . . gen mgr
Jerry Brehm . . . . . sls dir & natl sls mgr
Patrick Donnelly . . . . . gen sls mgr
Jim Caselli . . . . . mktg dir & progmg dir
Gene Robinson . . . . . prom mgr
Dan Weiser . . . . . news dir
Stefan Hadl . . . . . pub affrs dir & engrg dir

KSPX—Analog channel: 29. Digital channel: 48. On air date: Aug 27, 1990. 3352 Mather Field Rd., Rancho Cordova, CA 95670. Phone: (916) 368-2929. Fax: (916) 368-0225. Licensee: Paxson Sacramento License Inc. Group owner: Paxson Communications Corp. (acq 5-25-00; $17.725 million). Washington Atty: Wiley, Rein & Fielding. News staff: 75; News: 7 hrs wkly.
Key Personnel:
Jim Eaton . . . . . gen sls mgr
Lee Roberts . . . . . gen mgr & pub affrs dir
Frank Ernandes . . . . . engrg dir & chief of engrg

KTFK-TV—Analog channel: 64. On air date: July 11, 1988. 1710 Arden Way, Sacramento, CA 95815. Phone: (916) 927-1900. Fax: Licensee: TeleFutura Sacramento LLC. Group owner: Univision Communications Inc. (acq 12-1-2003; $65 million). Network: TeleFutura (Spanish).
Key Personnel:
Diego Ruiz . . . . . gen mgr & stn mgr
Steve Stuck . . . . . gen sls mgr

KTXL—Analog channel: 40. On air date: Oct 26, 1968. 4655 Fruitridge Rd., Sacramento, CA 95820-5299. Phone: (916) 454-4422. Fax: (916) 739-1079. Web Site: www.ktxl.com. Licensee: Channel 40 Inc. Group owner: Tribune Broadcasting Co. (acq 3-25-97; grpsl). Network: Fox. Rep: TeleRep. News: 7 hrs wkly.
Key Personnel:
Audrey L. Farrington . . . . . VP & gen mgr
Bill Gee . . . . . opns mgr, progmg dir & progmg mgr
Mike Armstrong . . . . . gen sls mgr
Eric Byers . . . . . rgnl sls mgr
Pam Schoen . . . . . prom dir
Steve Kraycik . . . . . news dir
Elyse Dietrich . . . . . pub affrs dir
Jack Davis . . . . . chief of engrg

KUVS-TV—(Modesto).Analog channel: 19. Digital channel: 18. On air date: Aug 26, 1966. 1710 Arden Way, Sacramento, CA 95815. 1150 9th St., Suite 1505, Modesto, CA 95354. Phone: (916) 927-1900. Fax: (916) 614-1902. Web Site: www.univision.com. Licensee: KUVS License Partnership G.P. Group owner: Univision Communications Inc. (acq 3-6-97; $40 million). Network: Univision (Spanish). Washington Atty: Shaw Pittman. News staff: 30; News: 12 hrs wkly.

***KVIE**—Analog channel: 6. Digital channel: 53. On air date: Feb 23, 1959. 2595 Capitol Oaks Dr., Sacramento, CA 95833. Phone: (916) 929-5843. Fax: (916) 929-7215. E-mail: publicinfo@kvie.org. Web Site: www.kvie.org. Licensee: KVIE Inc. Network: PBS. Washington Atty: Dow, Lohnes & Albertson.
Key Personnel:
David Hosley . . . . . pres & gen mgr
David Lowe . . . . . mktg VP
Jan Tilmon . . . . . progmg VP
Michael Wall . . . . . chief of engrg

KXTV—Analog channel: 10. Digital channel: 61. On air date: Mar 20, 1955. 400 Broadway, Sacramento, CA 95818-2041. Phone: (916) 441-2345. Fax: (916) 321-3380. Web Site: www.news10.net. Licensee: KXTV Inc. Group owner: Gannett Broadcasting (acq 1999; swap with KVUE-TV Austin, TX). Network: ABC. Rep: Blair Television. Washington Atty: Wiley, Rein & Fielding.
Key Personnel:
Russell Postell . . . . . pres & gen mgr
Kelly Bradley . . . . . gen sls mgr
Dustin Snyder . . . . . natl sls mgr & rgnl sls mgr
Ron Comings . . . . . news dir
Rod Robinson . . . . . chief of engrg

Salinas

see Monterey-Salinas, CA market

San Diego, CA (DMA 26)

KFMB-TV—Analog channel: 8. Digital channel: 55. On air date: May 16, 1949. 7677 Engineer Rd., San Diego, CA 92111. Box 85888, San Diego, CA 92186. Phone: (858) 571-8888. Fax: (858) 495-9363. Web Site: www.kfmb.com. Licensee: Midwest Television Inc.. Ownership: August C. Meyer Jr., 100% of votes Group owner: (group owner; (acq 2-19-64; grpsl). Network: CBS. Rep: TeleRep. Washington Atty: Covington & Burling.
Key Personnel:
Ed Trimble . . . . . pres & gen mgr
Rich Lochmann . . . . . opns mgr & engrg mgr
John Marquiss . . . . . sls dir
Sheri Kowalke . . . . . rgnl sls mgr

KGTV—Analog channel: 10. Digital channel: 25. On air date: Sept 13, 1953. Box 85347, San Diego, CA 92186. Phone: (619) 237-1010. Fax: (619) 262-1302. Web Site: www.thesandiegochannel.com. Licensee: McGraw-Hill Broadcasting Co. Group owner: (group owner; acq 6-1-72; grpsl; FTR: 3-13-72). Network: ABC. Rep: Harrington, Righter & Parsons. Washington Atty: Koteen & Naftalin.
Key Personnel:
Derek Dalton . . . . . gen mgr
Mike Biltucci . . . . . opns dir & opns mgr
Ken Rycyzn . . . . . gen sls mgr
Mike Stutz . . . . . news dir
Pam Smith . . . . . engrg mgr
Ron Eden . . . . . chief of engrg

KNSD—Analog channel: 39. Digital channel: 40. On air date: Nov 14, 1965. 225 Broadway, San Diego, CA 92101. Phone: (619) 231-3939. Fax: (619) 578-0225. E-mail: feedback@nbcsandiego.com. Web Site: www.nbcsandiego.com. Licensee: Station Venture Operations LP. Group owner: NBC TV Stations Division (acq 3-2-98; with KXAS-TV Fort Worth, TX). Network: NBC. Washington Atty: Pepper & Corazzini.
Key Personnel:
Phylliss Schwartz . . . . . gen mgr
Randy Mickler . . . . . opns mgr

***KPBS**—Analog channel: 15. Digital channel: 30. On air date: June 25, 1967. 5200 Campanile Dr., Hickory, CA 92182-5400. Phone: (619) 594-1515. Fax: (619) 594-3812. E-mail: letters@kpbs.org. Web Site: www.kpbs.org. Licensee: Board of Trustees, California State University for San Diego State University. Network: PBS. Washington Atty: Bryan Cave.
Key Personnel:
Doug Myrland . . . . . gen mgr
Keith York . . . . . progmg dir
Michael Marcotte . . . . . news dir

KSWB-TV—Analog channel: 69. Digital channel: 19. On air date: Oct 1, 1984. 7191 Engineer Rd., San Diego, CA 92111. Phone: (858) 492-9269. Fax: (858) 268-0401. Web Site: www.kswbtv.com. Licensee: KSWB Inc. Group owner: Tribune Broadcasting Co. (acq 1996; $70.5 million). Network: WB. Rep: MMT. Washington Atty: Sidley & Austin. News: 3 hrs wkly.

KUSI-TV—Analog channel: 51. Digital channel: 18. On air date: Sept 13, 1982. Box 719051, San Diego, CA 92171. 4575 Viewridge Ave., San Diego, CA 92171. Phone: (858) 571-5151. Fax: (858) 505-5050. E-mail: flaherty@kusi.com. Web Site: www.kusi.com. Licensee: Channel 51 of San Diego Inc. Group owner: McKinnon Broadcasting Co. (acq 6-29-90; 4-30-90). Rep: Katz Radio. Washington Atty: Cohn & Marks. News staff: 50; News: 25 hrs wkly.
Key Personnel:
Mike McKinnon . . . . . pres, gen mgr & opns VP
Steve Cohen . . . . . news dir
Richard Large . . . . . engrg dir & chief of engrg

XETV—(Tijuana).MEX Analog channel: 6. On air date: Jan 29, 1953. 8253 Ronson Rd., San Diego, CA 92111. Phone: (858) 279-6666. Fax: (858) 268-9388. E-mail: comments@fox6.com. Web Site: www.fox6.com. Licensee: Radio-Television S.A.. Ownership: Grupo Televisa, 100%. Network: Fox. Washington Atty: Leventhal, Senter & Lerman. News: 20 hrs wkly.
Key Personnel:

Rodrigo Salazar . . . . . CFO
Richard Doutre Jones . . . . . VP & gen mgr
Bob Anderson . . . . . opns dir & opns mgr
Chuck Dunning . . . . . gen sls mgr
Harry Melkerson . . . . . natl sls mgr
Lynda DiLorenzo . . . . . rgnl sls mgr
Scott Dillon . . . . . rgnl sls mgr
Cheri Olsen . . . . . mktg mgr
Judy Albrecht . . . . . prom dir & prom mgr
Deirdre Keane . . . . . progmg dir & progmg mgr
Albert Pando . . . . . news dir
Raphael Ahlgren . . . . . pub affrs dir
Dennis Doty . . . . . chief of engrg

XEWT-TV—(Tijuana).MEX Analog channel: 12. On air date: July 12, 1960. Box 434537, San Diego, CA 92143. 637 Third Ave., Suite B, Chulavista, CA 91910. Phone: (800) TELEV 12. Phone: (619) 585-9398. Fax: (619) 585-9463. Web Site: www.televisa.com. Licensee: Televisora de Calimex, S.A.. Ownership: Televisa, S.A. Washington Atty: Leventhal, Senter & Lerman. News staff: 50; News: 11 hrs wkly.
Key Personnel:
Ricardo Azcarraga . . . . . gen mgr
Lourdes Numez . . . . . opns mgr

San Francisco-Oakland-San Jose (DMA 6)

KBHK-TV—Analog channel: 44. Digital channel: 45. On air date: Jan 2, 1968. 855 Battery St., San Francisco, CA 94111-1509. Phone: (415) 249-4444. Fax: (415) 765-8916. Web Site: www.bayarea.com. Licensee: Viacom Television Stations Group of San Francisco Inc. Group owner: Viacom Television Stations Group (acq 11-6-2001; swap with WDCA(TV) Washington, DC; and KTXH(TV) Houston, TX). Network: UPN. Washington Atty: Hogan & Hartson.
Key Personnel:
Steve Poitras . . . . . VP
Steve Poitres . . . . . VP & stn mgr

KBWB—Analog channel: 20. Digital channel: 19. On air date: Apr 1, 1968. 2500 Marin St., San Francisco, CA 94124. Phone: (415) 821-2020. Fax: (415) 821-1518. Web Site: www.wb20.com. Licensee: KBWB License Inc. Group owner: Granite Broadcasting Corp. (acq 7-20-98; $173.75 million. which includes $30 million for a five-year non-compete agreement). Network: WB. Rep: MMT.
Key Personnel:
Bob Anderson . . . . . pres, CFO & gen mgr
Dennis McNamara . . . . . stn mgr & sls VP
Dave Figura . . . . . opns mgr & mktg dir
Steve Jones . . . . . gen sls mgr & natl sls mgr
Jennifer King . . . . . prom mgr
Michele Ball . . . . . progmg dir
Frank Brucks . . . . . chief of engrg

KCNS—Analog channel: 38. On air date: Jan 3, 1986. 1550 Bryant St., Suite 740, San Francisco, CA 94103. Phone: (415) 863-3800. Fax: (415) 863-3998. E-mail: kcnstv@pacbell.net. Web Site: www.kcnstv.com. Licensee: WRAY Inc. Group owner: Scripps Howard Broadcasting Co. (acq 2-27-2004; grpsl).
Key Personnel:
Russell Brown . . . . . stn mgr
Douglas Benson . . . . . pub affrs dir

***KCSM-TV**—Analog channel: 43. On air date: Oct 12, 1964. 1700 W. Hillsdale Blvd., San Mateo, CA 94402. Phone: (650) 574-6586. Fax: (650) 524-6975. Web Site: www.kcsm.org. Licensee: San Mateo County Community College District. Network: PBS. Washington Atty: Tierney & Swift.
Key Personnel:
Marilyn Lawrence . . . . . gen mgr
Alisa Clancy . . . . . opns mgr
Shelly Rogers . . . . . dev dir
Michelle Muller . . . . . engrg dir

KDTV—Analog channel: 14. On air date: Aug 13, 1975. 41st Fl., 50 Fremont St., San Francisco, CA 94105. Phone: (415) 538-8000. Fax: (415) 538-8053. Web Site: www.univison.com. Licensee: KDTV L.P. Group owner: Univision Communications Inc. Network: Univision (Spanish). Washington Atty: Fisher, Wayland, Cooper, Leader & Zaragoza. News staff: 15; News: 5 hrs wkly.
Key Personnel:
Jim VanTassell . . . . . VP & opns mgr
Marcela Medina . . . . . gen mgr
Ernie Rizzuti . . . . . gen sls mgr
Maria Rodriquez . . . . . progmg dir
Sandra Thomas . . . . . news dir
Mike Roberts . . . . . chief of engrg

KFSF-TV—Analog channel: 66. Digital channel: 34. On air date: Nov 25, 1986. 50 Fremont St., 4th Fl., San Francisco, CA 94105. Phone: (415) 538-6466. Fax: (415) 538-8053. Licensee: Univision Spanish Media Inc. Group owner: Univision Communications Inc. (acq 12-18-2001; $39 million). Network: TeleFutura (Spanish).
Key Personnel:
Jim VanTassell . . . . . CFO & opns mgr
Marcela Medina . . . . . gen mgr
Ernie Rizzuto . . . . . stn mgr & gen sls mgr
Maria S. Rodriguez . . . . . dev VP & progmg dir
Sandra Thomas . . . . . news dir
Mike Roberts . . . . . chief of engrg

KFTY—Analog channel: 50. On air date: May 1, 1981. 533 Mendocino Ave., Santa Rosa, CA 95401. Phone: (707) 526-5050. Fax: (707) 526-7429. Web Site: www.kfty.com. Licensee: Ackerley Media Group Inc. Group owner: Clear Channel Communications Inc. (acq 6-14-02; grpsl). Washington Atty: Rubin, Winston, Diercks, Harris & Cooke. News staff: 14; News: 7 hrs wkly.
Key Personnel:
John Burgess. VP, gen mgr, rgnl sls mgr, mktg VP, mktg dir, prom VP, prom dir, progmg VP, progmg dir & news dir
Richard Starkey . . . . . opns mgr & chief of opns
Rob Rector . . . . . gen sls mgr
Eric Casella . . . . . progmg dir & news dir
Brad Thompson . . . . . chief of engrg

KGO-TV—Analog channel: 7. Digital channel: 24. On air date: May 5, 1949. 900 Front St., San Francisco, CA 94111-1450. Phone: (415) 954-7777. Fax: (415) 956-6402. Web Site: www.abc7news.com. Licensee: KGO-TV Inc. Group owner: ABC Inc. (acq 6-27-86; grpsl; FTR: 7-15-85). Network: ABC.

KICU-TV—Analog channel: 36. On air date: Oct 3, 1967. 2102 Commerce Dr., San Jose, CA 95131-1804. Phone: (408) 953-3636. Web Site: www.kicu.com. Licensee: KTVU Partnership. Group owner: Cox Broadcasting (acq 2-18-00; $130 million). Washington Atty: Leventhal, Senter & Lerman. News staff: 3; News: .5 hr wkly.
Key Personnel:
Tom Raponi . . . . . gen mgr
Robert Martinez . . . . . sls VP & gen sls mgr
Carolyn Chang . . . . . progmg dir & progmg mgr
Frank Foge . . . . . chief of engrg

KKPX—Analog channel: 65. On air date: Nov 12, 1986. 2450 N. 1st St., San Jose, CA 95131. 848 Battery St., San Francisco, CA 94111. Phone: (415) 276-1400. Fax: (415) 276-1401. Web Site: www.pax.tv. Licensee: Paxson San Jose License Inc. Group owner: Paxson Communications Corp. (acq 3-22-95; $5 million; 6-19-95). Network: PAX TV. Washington Atty: Joseph E. Dunne III.
Key Personnel:
Carol Denham . . . . . gen mgr
Bob Getsla . . . . . chief of engrg

***KMTP-TV**—Analog channel: 32. On air date: Aug 31, 1991. 1504 Bryant St., 1st Fl., San Francisco, CA 94103. Phone: (415) 777-3232. Fax: (415) 552-3209. E-mail: kmtpgm@pacbell.net. Web Site: www.kmtp.org. Licensee: Minority Television Project. Network: PBS.
Key Personnel:
Arlene Stevens . . . . . opns dir, progmg dir & news dir
Booker T. Wade Jr. . . . . . gen mgr & dev dir

KNTV—Analog channel: 11. Digital channel: 12. On air date: Sept 12, 1955. 2450 N. 1st St., San Jose, CA 95131. Phone: (408) 286-1111. Fax: (408) 422-4425. Web Site: www.nbc11.com. Licensee: NBC Telemundo License Co. Group owner: NBC TV Stations Division (acq 4-30-02; $230 million).. Network: NBC. Rep: Harrington, Righter & Parsons. Washington Atty: Akin, Gump, Strauss, Hauer & Feld. News: 20 hrs wkly.
Key Personnel:
Linda Sullivan . . . . . gen mgr
Caroline Chang . . . . . progmg dir
Jim Sanders . . . . . news dir

KPIX-TV—Analog channel: 5. Digital channel: 29. On air date: Dec 22, 1948. 855 Battery St., San Francisco, CA 94111-1597. Phone: (415) 362-5550. Fax: (415) 765-8916. Web Site: www.kpix.com. Licensee: CBS Broadcasting Inc. Group owner: Viacom Television Stations Group (acq 5—4-2000; grpsl). Network: CBS. Rep: CBS Spot Sales. Washington Atty: Wilkes, Artis, Hedrick & Lane. News staff: 87; News: 20 hrs wkly.
Key Personnel:
Ron Longinotti . . . . . VP & gen mgr
John Satterfield . . . . . stn mgr & rgnl sls mgr
Robin Magyar . . . . . gen sls mgr
Maddie Griggs . . . . . natl sls mgr
Dee Joyce . . . . . mktg dir
Jerry Wagley . . . . . prom mgr
Tom Spitz . . . . . progmg dir
Dan Rosenheim . . . . . news dir
Rosemary Roach . . . . . pub affrs dir
Mike Englehaupt . . . . . chief of engrg

***KQED**—Analog channel: 9. Digital channel: 30. On air date: June 10, 1954. 2601 Mariposa St., San Francisco, CA 94110-1426. Phone: (415) 864-2000. Fax: (415) 553-2241. E-mail: (name)@kqed.org. Web Site: www.kqed.org. Licensee: KQED Inc. Network: PBS. Washington Atty: Arnold & Porter. News staff: 8; News: 1/2 hr wkly.
Key Personnel:
Jeff Clarke . . . . . CEO & pres
John Boland . . . . . exec VP
Michael Isip . . . . . stn mgr & progmg dir
Traci Eckels . . . . . dev VP
Donald Derheim . . . . . sls VP

***KRCB**—Analog channel: 22. On air date: Dec 2, 1984. 5850 Labath Ave., Rohnert Park, CA 94928. Phone: (707) 585-8522. Fax: (707) 585-1363. Web Site: www.krcb.org. Licensee: Rural California Broadcasting Corp. Network: PBS. News staff: 2; News: one hr wkly.
Key Personnel:
Nancy Dobbs . . . . . CEO, pres & gen mgr
Stan Marvin . . . . . progmg dir

KRON-TV—Analog channel: 4. Digital channel: 57. On air date: Nov 15, 1949. 1001 Van Ness Ave., San Francisco, CA 94109. Phone: (415) 441-4444. Fax: (415) 561-8142. Web Site: www.kron.com. Licensee: Young Broadcasting of San Francisco Inc. Group owner: Young Broadcasting Inc. (acq 6-26-2000; $823 million).. Rep: Adam Young. Washington Atty: Brooks, Pierce. News: 42 hrs wkly.
Key Personnel:
Mark Antonitis . . . . . pres & gen mgr
Mary Kennedy . . . . . stn mgr
Mark Mano . . . . . opns dir & opns mgr
Sarah Squiers . . . . . dev dir & rgnl sls mgr
Karen Orofino . . . . . sls VP & gen sls mgr
Ben Holland . . . . . natl sls mgr
Jeffrey Weinstock . . . . . mktg dir, prom dir & adv dir
Pat Patton . . . . . progmg VP
Stacy Owen . . . . . news dir
Javier Valeucia . . . . . pub affrs dir
Craig Porter . . . . . chief of engrg

KSTS—Analog channel: 48. Digital channel: 49. On air date: May 31, 1981. 2349 Bering Dr., San Jose, CA 95131. Phone: (408) 435-8848. Fax: (408) 433-5921. Web Site: www.ksts.com. Licensee: NBC Telemundo License Co. Group owner: Telemundo Group Inc. (acq 4-12-02; grpsl). Network: Telemundo (Spanish). Washington Atty: Hogan & Hartson. News staff: 10; News: 3 hrs wkly.

***KTEH**—Analog channel: 54. Digital channel: 50. On air date: October 1964. 1585 Schallenburger Rd., San Jose, CA 95110-1301. Phone: (408) 795-5400. Fax: (408) 995-5446. Web Site: www.kteh.org. Licensee: KTEH-TV Foundation. (acq 8-10-87). Network: PBS. Washington Atty: Schwartz, Woods & Miller.
Key Personnel:
Thomas Fanella . . . . . CEO
Judy Armstrong . . . . . pres & dev dir

KTLN-TV—Analog channel: 68. On air date: Aug 31, 1998. 400 Tamal Plaza, Suite 428, Corte Madera, CA 94925. Phone: (415) 924-7500. Fax: (415) 924-0264. E-mail: ktln@tln.com. Web Site: www.ktln.tv. Licensee: Christian Communications of Chicagoland Inc. (acq 12-10-98; $500,000)..
Key Personnel:
Jerry K. Rose . . . . . CEO & pres
James Nichols . . . . . CFO
Debra Fraser . . . . . gen mgr
Brian Avery . . . . . stn mgr

KTNC-TV—Analog channel: 42. Digital channel: 63. On air date: June 19, 1983. 1700 Montgomery St., Suite 400, San Francisco, CA 94111. Phone: (415) 398-4242. Fax: (415) 352-1800. E-mail: rpineda@ktnc.com. Web Site: www.ktnc.com. Licensee: KTNC License LLC. Group owner: Pappas Telecasting Companies (acq 10-29-97). Washington Atty: Fletcher, Heald & Hildreth.
Key Personnel:
Dennis Davis . . . . . CEO
Harry Pappas . . . . . chmn & pres
Fernando Acosta . . . . . gen mgr
LeBon Abercrombie . . . . . dev dir
Roberto Pineda . . . . . gen sls mgr

KTSF—Analog channel: 26. Digital channel: 27. On air date: Sept 4, 1976. 100 Valley Dr., Brisbane, CA 94005-1350. Phone: (415) 468-2626. Fax: (415) 467-7559. E-mail: genmgr@ktsftv.com. Web Site: www.ktsf.com.. Stn video via satellite: DirecTV & EchoStar in

Local Market Licensee: Lincoln Broadcasting Co., a California L.P. News staff: 40; News: 15 hrs wkly.
Key Personnel:
Lillian L. Howell . . . chmn
Lincoln C. Howell . . . pres
Michael Sherman . . . gen mgr
Mike Fusaro . . . chief of opns
Jack Soo Hoo . . . natl sls mgr
Lisa Yokota . . . mktg dir
Victor Marino . . . progmg dir
Rose Shirinian . . . news dir

KTVU—(Oakland).Analog channel: 2. Digital channel: 56. On air date: Mar 3, 1958. Box 22222, Oakland, CA 94623. Phone: (510) 834-1212. Fax: (510) 272-9957. Web Site: www.ktvu.com. Licensee: KTVU Partnership. Group owner: Cox Enterprises (acq 10-16-63; $12.36 million; 10-21-63). Network: Fox. Rep: TeleRep. Washington Atty: Dow, Lohnes & Albertson.
Key Personnel:
Jeff Block . . . VP, gen mgr & stn mgr
Tom Raponi . . . gen mgr & sls dir
Greg Bilte . . . gen sls mgr
Dan Haass . . . natl sls mgr
Phil Adams . . . natl sls mgr
Cesar Chavez . . . prom mgr
Caroline Chang . . . progmg mgr
Ed Chapuis . . . news dir
Rosy Chu . . . pub affrs dir
Don Thompson . . . engrg mgr
Ken Manley . . . chief of engrg

KUNO-TV—Analog channel: 8. Digital channel: 15. On air date: Feb 1, 1990. 303-B N. Main, Fort Bragg, CA 95437. Phone: (707) 964-8888. Fax: (707) 964-8150. Licensee: Concord License LLC. Group owner: Pappas Telecasting Companies (acq 6-12-97; $1.75 million).. Rep: Blair Television.
Key Personnel:
Ricardo Pineda . . . gen mgr, opns VP, gen sls mgr & progmg dir
Robbie Robinson . . . news dir
Norm Wright . . . chief of engrg

San Jose

see San Francisco-Oakland-San Jose market

San Luis Obispo

see Santa Barbara-Santa Maria-San Luis Obispo, CA market

Santa Barbara-Santa Maria-San Luis Obispo, CA (DMA 121)

KBEH—Analog channel: 63. Digital channel: 24. On air date: Aug 17, 1985. 950 Flynn Rd., Camarillo, CA 93012. Phone: (805) 388-0081. Fax: (305) 863-5701. Licensee: Bela TV LLC. Group owner: Bela LLC (acq 12-11-2003; $23 million).. Washington Atty: Wiley, Rein & Fielding. News: 3 hrs wkly.
Key Personnel:
Lou Bardfield . . . gen mgr & chief of engrg
Mara Rankin . . . gen sls mgr
Marie Pouget . . . progmg dir

KCOY-TV—Analog channel: 12. On air date: Mar 16, 1964. 1211 W. McCoy Ln., Santa Maria, CA 93455. Phone: (805) 925-1200. Fax: (805) 349-2740. E-mail: daveulrickson@clearchannel.com. Web Site: www.kcoy.com. Licensee: Ackerley Media Group Inc. Group owner: Clear Channel Communications Inc. (acq 2002; grpsl). Network: CBS. Rep: Continental Television Sales. Washington Atty: Covington & Burling. News staff: 42; News: 28 hrs wkly.
Key Personnel:
Steve Spendlove . . . VP
Dave Ulrickson . . . gen mgr
Larry Barnes . . . sls dir & gen sls mgr
Tracy Reiner . . . rgnl sls mgr
Laurie Pipan . . . prom mgr
Shirley Stanford . . . progmg mgr
Jimmy Sprague . . . chief of engrg

KEYT-TV—Analog channel: 3. On air date: July 24, 1953. 730 Miramonte Dr., Santa Barbara, CA 93109. Phone: (805) 882-3933. Fax: (805) 882-3934. E-mail: keyt@aol.com. Web Site: www.keyt.com.. Stn video via satellite: Dish TV, Direct TV in April '04 Licensee: Smith Media License Holdings LLC. Group owner: Smith Broadcasting Group Inc. (acq 11-8-2004; grpsl). Network: ABC. Rep: Blair Television. Washington Atty: Hogan & Hartson. News staff: 25; News: 21 hrs wkly.
Key Personnel:
Bob Grissom . . . VP, gen mgr & natl sls mgr
Dave Fete . . . opns mgr
Jim Valice . . . gen sls mgr
Jeff Martin . . . prom mgr & pub affrs dir
Renee Foley . . . progmg dir
Paul Vercammen . . . news dir
Dave Williams . . . chief of engrg

KPMR—Analog channel: 38. On air date: April 1, 2001. Entravision Communications Corp., 2425 Olympic Blvd., Suite 6000W, Santa Monica, CA 90404. Phone: (805) 685-3800. Fax: (805) 685-6892. Web Site: www.entravision.com. Permittee: Entravision Holdings LLC. Group owner: Entravision Communications Corp. (acq 11-2-00; $4.75 million). Network: Univision (Spanish).
Key Personnel:
Chris Roman . . . gen mgr
Michael Scanlon . . . gen sls mgr
Andres Angulo . . . news dir

KSBY—Analog channel: 6. Digital channel: 15. On air date: May 1953. 1772 Calle Joaquin, San Luis Obispo, CA 93405. Phone: (805) 541-6666. Fax: (805) 541-5142. E-mail: ksby@ksby.com. Web Site: www.ksby.com. Licensee: KSBY Communications Inc. Group owner: New Vision Group LLC (acq 2-18-2005; $67.75 million).. Network: NBC. Rep: TeleRep. Washington Atty: Latham & Watkins.
Key Personnel:
Wade O'Hagen . . . CFO
Tim Perry . . . gen mgr & gen sls mgr
Carl Edge . . . opns dir, progmg dir & progmg mgr
Madeline Palaszeuski . . . prom dir & prom mgr
Madeline Palaszewski . . . pub affrs dir
Aaron Klohs . . . chief of engrg

KTAS—Analog channel: 33. Digital channel: 34. On air date: 1990. Box 172, Santa Maria, CA 93456. 1138 W. Church St., Santa Maria, CA 93458. Phone: (805) 928-7700. Fax: (805) 928-8606. E-mail: ktastv@fix.net. Licensee: Raul and Consuelo Palazuelos. (acq 7-3-97). Network: Telemundo (Spanish). Washington Atty: Womble, Carlyle, Saudride & Rice. News staff: 6; News: 3 hrs wkly.

Santa Maria

see Santa Barbara-Santa Maria-San Luis Obispo, CA market

Stockton

see Sacramento-Stockton-Modesto, CA market

Visalia

see Fresno-Visalia, CA market

Yreka City

see Medford-Klamath Falls, OR market

Colorado

Colorado Springs-Pueblo, CO (DMA 92)

KKTV—Analog channel: 11. On air date: Dec 7, 1952. Box 2110, Colorado Springs, CO 80901. 3100 N. Nevada Ave., Colorado Springs, CO 80901. Phone: (719) 634-2844. Fax: (719) 632-0808. Fax: (719) 442-6981. Web Site: www.kktv.com. Licensee: WEAU Licensee Corp. Group owner: Gray Television Inc. (acq 10-25-02; grpsl). Network: CBS. Rep: Continental Television Sales. News staff: 42; News: 27 hrs wkly.
Key Personnel:
Robert Prather . . . pres
Charles Hogetvedt . . . VP, gen mgr, progmg dir & progmg mgr
Dave McCarty . . . opns mgr
Mark Puckett . . . gen sls mgr
Michelle Hughes . . . mktg dir & prom mgr
Nick Matesi . . . news dir
Tim Timora . . . chief of engrg

KOAA-TV—(Pueblo).Analog channel: 5. On air date: June 13, 1953. Box 195, 2200 7th Ave., Pueblo, CO 81003. 530 Communications Cir., Colorado Springs, CO 81003. Phone: (719) 544-5781. Phone: (719) 632-5030. Fax: (719) 228-6277. Fax: (719) 228-6265. Web Site: www.koaa.com. Licensee: Sangre De Cristo Communications Inc. Group owner: Evening Post Publishing Co. (acq 8-6-76; $4.5 million; 8-30-76). Network: NBC. Washington Atty: Dow, Lohnes & Albertson. News staff: 23; News: 7 hrs wkly.
Key Personnel:
David Whitaker . . . pres & gen mgr
Ron Eccher . . . opns mgr, progmg dir & film buyer
Tom Wright . . . natl sls mgr
Richard A. Bouchez . . . prom dir & prom mgr
Cindy Aubrey . . . news dir
Patricia Vaughan . . . pub affrs dir
Quentin Henry . . . chief of engrg

KRDO-TV—Analog channel: 13. On air date: Sept 21, 1953. Box 1457, Colorado Springs, CO 80901. 399 S. 8th St., Colorado Springs, CO 80905. Phone: (719) 632-1515. Fax: (719) 475-0815. Web Site: www.krdotv.com. Licensee: Pikes Peak Broadcasting Co. Group owner: (group owner) Network: ABC. Rep: Airtime TV. Blair Television Washington Atty: Fletcher, Heald & Hildreth.
Key Personnel:
Harry W. Hoth Jr. . . . chmn
Patti L. Hoth . . . pres
Neil Klockziem . . . gen mgr
Lori Rockwell . . . opns mgr

***KTSC**—Analog channel: 8. On air date: Feb 3, 1971. 2200 Bonforte Blvd., Pueblo, CO 81001-4901. Phone: (719) 543-8800. Fax: (719) 549-2208. E-mail: ktsc@rmpbs.org. Web Site: www.rmpbs.org. Licensee: Rocky Mountain Public Broadcasting Network Inc. (acq 1999; $2.375 million). Network: PBS.
Key Personnel:
Tom Scheel . . . chmn & dev dir
James Morgese . . . pres
Wynona Sullivan . . . stn mgr
Tiffany Q. Tyson . . . mktg dir
Donna Sanford . . . progmg dir
Ian Hartley . . . chief of engrg

KXRM-TV—Analog channel: 21. On air date: Dec 24, 1984. 560 Wooten Rd., Colorado Springs, CO 80915. Phone: (719) 596-2100. Fax: (719) 591-4180. E-mail: info@kxrm.com. Web Site: www.yourfavoritestation.com. Licensee: Raycom National License Subsidiary LLC. Group owner: Raycom Media Inc. (acq 2-15-2000; $45.8 million).. Network: Fox. Rep: TeleRep. Washington Atty: Covington & Durling. News: 3.5 hrs wkly.
Key Personnel:
Paul McTear . . . CEO
Marty Edelman . . . exec VP
Steve Dant . . . VP & gen mgr
Donna D'Amico . . . gen sls mgr & natl sls mgr
Dan Corken . . . rgnl sls mgr
Susan Corbin . . . mktg mgr
Patti Clements . . . progmg dir
Larry W. Douglas . . . film buyer
Joe Duckett . . . chief of engrg

Denver, CO (DMA 18)

***KBDI-TV**—(Broomfield).Analog channel: 12. On air date: Feb 22, 1980. 2900 Welton St., Denver, CO 80205. Phone: (303) 296-1212. Fax: (303) 296-6650. Web Site: www.kbdi.org. Licensee: Front Range Educational Media Corp. Network: PBS. Washington Atty: Mintz, Levin, Cohn, Ferris, Glovsky & Popeo.
Key Personnel:
Scott Shirai . . . chmn
Dr. Willard D. Rowland . . . pres
Kim Johnson . . . opns VP
Paula Roth . . . dev dir, mktg dir & adv mgr
Darrow "Dutch" Hodges . . . mktg VP
Darrow Hodges . . . adv VP
Kirby McClure . . . progmg dir
Richard Eversley . . . chief of engrg

KCEC—Analog channel: 50. On air date: Oct 19, 1990. 777 Grant St., 5th Fl., Monroe, CO 80203. Phone: (303) 832-0050. Fax: (303) 832-3410. Licensee: Entravision Holdings L.L.C. Group owner: Entravision Communications Co. L.L.C. (acq 4-25-97). Network: Univision (Spanish). Washington Atty: Kaye, Scholer, Fierman, Hays & Handler.
Key Personnel:
Walter Ulloa . . . pres
Mario M. Carrera . . . gen mgr
Gayle Shaw . . . gen sls mgr
Chris Matthews . . . natl sls mgr
Luis Canela . . . prom dir
Erma Atencio . . . progmg mgr
Rodolfo Cardenas . . . news dir
Jamie Moreno . . . pub affrs dir
Azael Villanueva . . . engrg mgr

Broadcasting & Cable Yearbook 2006
B-25

KCNC-TV—Analog channel: 4. Digital channel: 35. On air date: Dec 24, 1953. 1044 Lincoln St., Denver, CO 80203. Phone: (303) 861-4444. Fax: (303) 830-6537. Web Site: news4colorado.com. Licensee: CBS Television Stations Inc. Group owner: Viacom Television Stations Group (acq 9-10-95; grpsl). Network: CBS. Rep: CBS Spot Sales.

Key Personnel:
Walt DeHaven . . . gen mgr
David Layne . . . opns mgr
Kevin Dorsey . . . sls dir & gen sls mgr
Roxanne Marati . . . mktg dir
Wendy Holmes . . . progmg dir

KDEN—Analog channel: 25. On air date: 1999. 1175 S. Pennsylvania St., Denver, CO 80210. Phone: (303) 833-2525. Licensee: Longmont Channel 25 Inc.. Ownership: George S. Flinn Jr.

Key Personnel:
George S. Flinn Jr. . . . pres
Dirk Freeman II . . . gen mgr

KDVR—Analog channel: 31. Digital channel: 32. On air date: Aug 10, 1983. 100 E. Speer Blvd., Denver, CO 80203. Phone: (303) 595-3131. Fax: (303) 566-2931. Web Site: www.kdvr.com. Licensee: Fox Television Stations Inc. Group owner: (group owner; acq 1995; $70 million).. Network: Fox.

Key Personnel:
Bill Schneider . . . gen mgr
Ray Dowdle . . . gen sls mgr
John Hirsch . . . progmg dir & film buyer
Bill Dallman . . . news dir

KFCT—Analog channel: 22. On air date: October 1994. c/o TV Stn KDVR, 100 E. Speer Blvd., Denver, CO 80203. Phone: (303) 595-3131. Fax: (303) 566-2931. Web Site: www.kdvr.com. Licensee: Fox Television Stations Inc. Group owner: (group owner; acq 1995). Network: Fox.

Key Personnel:
Ray Dowdle . . . sr VP & gen sls mgr
William Schneider . . . gen mgr
Catherine Andrey . . . natl sls mgr
Sheryl Personett . . . rgnl sls mgr
Clyde Becker . . . prom VP & prom mgr
John Hirsch . . . progmg mgr
Bill Dallman . . . news dir
Jon Takayama . . . pub affrs dir
Skip Erickson . . . engrg VP & engrg mgr

KFNR—Analog channel: 11. On air date: Apr 16, 1986. 1856 Skyview Dr., Suite One, Casper, WY 82601. Phone: (307) 577-5923/5924. Fax: (307) 577-5928. E-mail: klwy@coffey.com. Licensee: First National Broadcasting Corp. Network: Fox. Washington Atty: Irwin, Campbell & Tannenwald.

Key Personnel:
Mark Nalbone . . . gen mgr
Terry Lane . . . opns mgr & progmg dir
Tina Nalbone . . . gen sls mgr & rgnl sls mgr
Joe Lownden . . . prom dir
Dave Ericson . . . chief of engrg

KMAS-TV—Analog channel: 24. On air date: May 1988. 1120 Lincoln St., Suite 800, Denver, CO 80203. Phone: (303) 832-0402 (Denver). Fax: (303) 832-0777. Web Site: www.kmas.tv. Licensee: NBC Telemundo License Co. Group owner: Telemundo Group Inc. (acq 4-12-2002; grpsl). Network: Telemundo (Spanish). Washington Atty: Borsari & Paxson. News staff: one; News: one hr wkly.

Key Personnel:
Don Brown . . . CEO & pres
Giovanni Mercia . . . VP & gen mgr

KMGH-TV—Analog channel: 7. On air date: Nov 1, 1953. 123 Speer Blvd., Denver, CO 80203. Phone: (303) 832-7777. Fax: (303) 832-0119. Web Site: www.thedenverchannel.com. Licensee: McGraw-Hill Broadcasting Co. Inc. Group owner: McGraw-Hill Broadcasting Co. (acq 6-1-72; grpsl; FTR: 3-13-72). Network: ABC. Rep: Harrington, Righter & Parsons.

Key Personnel:
Darrell K. Brown . . . gen mgr
Barry Edmond . . . opns mgr
John Curry . . . gen sls mgr
Laura Horgis . . . natl sls mgr

KPXC-TV—Analog channel: 59. On air date: Sept 10, 1987. 3001 S. Jamaica Ct., Suite 200, Aurora, CO 80014. Phone: (303) 751-5959. Fax: (303) 751-5993. Web Site: www.paxdenver.tv. Licensee: Paxson Denver License Inc. Group owner: Paxson Communications Corp. (acq 7-1-96; grpsl). Washington Atty: Cole, Raywid & Braverman. News: 24 hrs wkly.

Key Personnel:
Bud Paxson . . . pres
Christy Bradford . . . rgnl sls mgr
Mark Cornetta . . . gen sls mgr & progmg mgr
Brian Schauer . . . chief of engrg

KREG-TV—Analog channel: 3. Digital channel: 23. On air date: Dec 15, 1983. Box 789, Grand Junction, CO 81502. Phone: (970) 963-3333. Fax: (970) 242-0886. Web Site: www.kregtv.com. Licensee: Hoak Media of Colorado LLC. Group owner: Hoak Media Corporation (acq 10-10-2003; grpsl). Network: CBS. Rep: Petry Television Inc.. Washington Atty: Gardner, Carton & Douglas.

***KRMA-TV**—Analog channel: 6. Digital channel: 18. On air date: Jan 30, 1956. 1089 Bannock St., Denver, CO 80204. Phone: (303) 892-6666. Fax: (303) 620-5600. Web Site: www.rmpbs.org. Licensee: Rocky Mountain Public Broadcasting Network Inc. Network: PBS. Washington Atty: Dow, Lohnes & Albertson. News: one hr wkly.

Key Personnel:
James N. Morgese . . . pres & gen mgr
Charles Goldsmith . . . dev dir & dev mgr
Karen Hill . . . dev dir
Donna Sanford . . . progmg dir
James Schoedler . . . engrg dir & chief of engrg

***KRMT**—Analog channel: 41. Digital channel: 40. On air date: Jan 4, 1994. 12014 W. 64th Ave., Arvada, CO 80004. Phone: (303) 423-4141. Fax: (303) 424-0571. Web Site: www.daystar.com. Licensee: Word of God Fellowship Inc. dba Lamb of God Educators. (acq 5-29-97; $1.95 million).. Washington Atty: Hogan & Hartson.

Key Personnel:
Marcus D. Lamb . . . CEO & pres
Joni Lamb . . . exec VP
Dr. Dick Newman . . . gen mgr
Janice Smith . . . natl sls mgr, progmg VP & progmg dir
Trish Lord . . . mktg dir
Heather McComis . . . mktg mgr
Jenny Newman . . . pub affrs dir
Bob Saraduke . . . chief of engrg

KTFD-TV—Analog channel: 14. On air date: March 1986. 777 Grant St., 5th Fl., Denver, CO 80203. Phone: (303) 832-1414. Fax: (303) 832-3410. Licensee: Spanish Television of Denver Inc. Group owner: Roberts Broadcasting Co. (acq 2-27-03). Network: TeleFutura (Spanish).

Key Personnel:
Mario Carrera . . . gen mgr
Chris Matthews . . . opns mgr & natl sls mgr
Luis Caneda . . . prom dir & progmg dir

KTVD—Analog channel: 20. Digital channel: 19. On air date: Dec 1, 1988. 11203 E. Peakview Ave., Centennial, CO 80111. Phone: (303) 792-2020. Fax: (303) 790-4633. E-mail: feedback@upn20.tv. Web Site: www.upn20.tv. Licensee: Twenver Broadcast Inc. Group owner: Newsweb Corp. Network: UPN. Washington Atty: Fletcher, Heald & Hildreth.

KUPN—Analog channel: 3. On air date: Jan 1, 1964. c/o KTVD(TV), 11203 E. Peakview Ave., Centennial, CO 80111. Phone: (303) 792-2020. Fax: (303) 790-4633. Licensee: Channel 20 TV Co. Group owner: Newsweb Corp. (acq 8-31-99; $240,000).. Washington Atty: Covington & Burling. News: 17 hrs wkly.

Key Personnel:
Greg Armstrong . . . gen mgr
Hilary Castine . . . prom mgr
Rita McCoy . . . pub affrs dir
Michael Dant . . . chief of engrg

KUSA-TV—Analog channel: 9. Digital channel: 16. On air date: Oct 12, 1952. 500 Speer Blvd., Denver, CO 80203. Phone: (303) 871-9999. Fax: (303) 698-4719 (sales). E-mail: kusa@9news.com. Web Site: www.9news.com. Licensee: Multimedia Cablevision Inc. Group owner: Gannett Broadcasting (Division of Gannett Co. Inc.) (acq 6-7-79; grpsl; 6-11-79). Network: NBC. Washington Atty: Wiley, Rein & Fielding.

Key Personnel:
Roger Ogden . . . pres & gen mgr
Mark Cornetta . . . gen sls mgr
Steve Carter . . . mktg mgr & prom dir
Kathy McDonald . . . progmg dir
Patti Dennis . . . news dir
Don Perez . . . chief of engrg
Mercedes Cregar . . . chief of engrg

KWGN-TV—Analog channel: 2. Digital channel: 34. On air date: July 18, 1952. 6160 S. Wabash Way, Greenwood Village, CO 80111. Phone: (303) 740-2222. Fax: (303) 740-2847. Web Site: www.wb2.com. Licensee: KWGN Inc. Group owner: Tribune Broadcasting Co., see Cross-Ownership (acq 3-3-66; $3.5 million). Network: WB. Rep: TeleRep. Washington Atty: Sidley & Austin. News: 25 hrs wkly.

Key Personnel:
James D. Zerwekh . . . VP & gen mgr
Don Rooney . . . opns dir, engrg dir & engrg dir
Matt Mansi . . . gen sls mgr
Natalie Grant . . . progmg dir
Tom Sides . . . news dir
Beverly Martinez . . . pub affrs dir
Les Jensen . . . chief of engrg

KWHD—Analog channel: 53. Digital channel: 46. On air date: July 1, 1990. 12999 E. Jamison Cir., Englewood, CO 80112. Phone: (303) 799-8853. Fax: (303) 792-5303. Web Site: www.kwhdtv53.com. Licensee: LeSea Broadcasting. Group owner: (group owner)

Key Personnel:
Pete Sumrall . . . CEO
Mark Walker . . . gen mgr

***KWYP-TV**—Analog channel: 8.Not on air, target date: unknown: Wyoming Public Television, 2660 Peck Ave., Riverton, WY 82501. Phone: (307) 856-6944. Fax: (307) 856-3893. Web Site: wyoptv.org. Permittee: Central Wyoming College. Network: PBS.

Key Personnel:
JoAnne McFarland . . . pres
Dan Schiedel . . . gen mgr

Durango

see Albuquerque-Santa Fe, NM market

Grand Junction-Montrose, CO (DMA 189)

KFQX—Analog channel: 4. Digital channel: 15. On air date: 2000. 345 Hillcrest Manor, Grand Junction, CO 81501. Phone: (970) 242-5285. Fax: (970) 242-0886. Licensee: Parker Broadcasting Inc.. Ownership: Barry J.C. Parker, 100% (acq 12-27-2004). Network: Fox.

Key Personnel:
Dennis Adkins . . . gen mgr
Shawna Greiger . . . sls VP & mktg VP
Maranda Wolter . . . prom VP
Shelley Nelson . . . progmg VP
Keira Bresnalhan . . . news dir
Maranda Wolter . . . pub affrs dir
Don May . . . engrg VP

KJCT—Analog channel: 8. On air date: Oct 22, 1979. Box 3788, Grand Junction, CO 81502. 8 Foresight Cir., Grand Junction, CO 81505. Phone: (970) 245-8880. Fax: (970) 245-8249. Web Site: www.kjct8.com. Licensee: Pikes Peak Broadcasting Co. Group owner: (group owner) Network: ABC. Rep: Blair Television. Blair Television Washington Atty: Fletcher, Heald & Hildreth.

Key Personnel:
Harry Hoth . . . chmn
Patti Hoth . . . pres
Neil Klockziem . . . gen mgr

KKCO—Analog channel: 11. Digital channel: 12. On air date: July 19, 1996. 2325 Interstate Ave., Grand Junction, CO 81505. Phone: (970) 243-1111. Fax: (970) 243-1770. Web Site: www.nbc11news.com. E-mail: billv@nbc11news.com. Licensee: Gray Television Licensee Inc. (acq 1-14-2005; $13.5 million. with translator K50EZ Montrose). Network: NBC. Rep: Millennium Sales & Marketing. Washington Atty: Wood, Maines & Brown, Chartered. News staff: 35; News: 28 hrs wkly.

Key Personnel:
J. Mack Robinson . . . pres
Debbie Varecha . . . CFO
Paul Varecha . . . opns VP & prom dir
Sandy Moore . . . progmg dir
Peter Franklin . . . mus dir
Jean Reynolds . . . news dir
William Varecha. gen mgr, dev VP, sls VP, mktg VP, film buyer & engrg dir
Roger LaFrance . . . chief of engrg

KREX-TV—Analog channel: 5. Digital channel: 2. On air date: May 22, 1954. Box 789, 345 Hillcrest Manor, Grand Junction, CO 81502. Phone: (970) 242-5000. Fax: (970) 242-0886. Web Site: www.krextv.com. Licensee: Hoak Media of Colorado LLC. Group owner: Hoak Media Corporation (acq 11-12-2003; grpsl). Network: CBS. Rep: Petry Television Inc.. News staff: 15; News: 30 hrs wkly.

Key Personnel:
Dennis Adkins . . . gen mgr
Shelly Nelson . . . opns mgr

KREY-TV—Analog channel: 10. On air date: Aug 26, 1956. 614 N. First, Montrose, CO 81401. Phone: (970) 249-9601. Fax: (970) 249-9610. E-mail: kreytv@gwe.net. Licensee: Hoak Media of Colorado LLC. Group owner: Hoak Media Corporation (acq 10-10-2003; grpsl). Network: Network: CBS, NBC. Rep: Katz Radio.

***KRMJ**—Analog channel: 18. Digital channel: 17. On air date: January 1997. c/o KRMA-TV, 1089 Bannock St., Denver, CO 80204. Phone: (303) 892-6666. Fax: (303) 620-5600. Web Site: www.rmpbs.org. Licensee: Rocky Mountain Broadcasting Network Inc. Network: PBS.
Key Personnel:
James Morgese . . . pres & gen mgr
Angie Salazar . . . stn mgr
Charlies Goldsmith . . . dev dir
Donna Sanford . . . progmg dir
James Schoedler . . . engrg dir & chief of engrg

Montrose

see Grand Junction-Montrose, CO market

Pueblo

see Colorado Springs-Pueblo, CO market

Connecticut

Bridgeport

see New York market

Hartford & New Haven, CT (DMA 27)

WCTX—Analog channel: 59. On air date: Apr 3, 1995. 8 Elm St., New Haven, CT 06510. Phone: (203) 782-5900. Fax: (203) 782-5995. Web Site: www.wctx.com. Licensee: WTNH Broadcasting Inc. Group owner: LIN Television Corporation (acq 3-2002). Network: UPN. Rep: Petry Television Inc.. News: 4 hrs wkly.
Key Personnel:
Jon Hitchcock . . . gen mgr
Ed Bassler . . . stn mgr
Ryan Mahoney . . . natl sls mgr
Sem Dietrich . . . rgnl sls mgr
Connie Fitch . . . mktg mgr
Deanna Banas-Kluk . . . progmg dir
Kirk Varner . . . news dir
Francine DuVerger . . . engrg dir & chief of engrg

***WEDH**—Analog channel: 24. On air date: Oct 1, 1962. 1049 Asylum Ave., Hartford, CT 06105. Phone: (860) 278-5310. Fax: (860) 275-7403. Web Site: www.cptv.org. Licensee: Connecticut Public Broadcasting Inc. Network: PBS. Washington Atty: Schwartz, Woods & Miller.
Key Personnel:
Jerry Franklin . . . CEO, pres & gen mgr
Meg Sakellarides . . . CFO
Larry Rifkin . . . exec VP
Haig Papasian . . . opns VP
Joseph Zareski . . . opns dir
Christopher Flynn . . . dev dir & progmg dir

***WEDN**—Analog channel: 53. Digital channel: 45. On air date: Mar 5, 1967. 1049 Asylum Ave., Hartford, CT 06105. Phone: (860) 278-5310. Fax: (860) 275-7403. Web Site: www.cptv.org. Licensee: Connecticut Public Broadcasting. Network: PBS.
Key Personnel:
Jerry Franklin . . . CEO, pres & gen mgr
Meg Sakellarides . . . CFO
Larry Rifkin . . . exec VP
Haig Papasian . . . opns VP & opns dir
Christopher Flynn . . . dev VP

***WEDY**—Analog channel: 65. On air date: November 1974. 1049 Asylum Ave., Hartford, CT 06105. Phone: (860) 278-5310. Fax: (860) 275-7403. Web Site: www.cptv.org. Licensee: Connecticut Public Broadcasting Inc. Network: PBS.
Key Personnel:
Jerry Franklin . . . CEO, pres & gen mgr
Meg Sakellarides . . . CFO
Larry Rifkin . . . exec VP
Haig Papasian . . . opns VP
Joseph Zareski . . . opns dir
Christopher Flynn . . . dev VP

WFSB—Analog channel: 3. Digital channel: 33. On air date: Sept 23, 1957. 3 Constitution Plaza, Hartford, CT 06103-1821. Phone: (860) 728-3333. Fax: (860) 247-8940. Fax: (860) 728-0263 (News Room). Web Site: www.wfsb.com. Licensee: Meredith Corp. dba WFSB. Group owner: Meredith Broadcasting Group, Meredith Corp. (acq 9-4-97; $159 million). Network: CBS. Rep: Harrington, Righter & Parsons. Washington Atty: Garvey, Schubert & Barer. News: 36 hrs wkly.
Key Personnel:
Elden Hale . . . gen mgr
John Ahearn . . . opns mgr
Klarn De Palma . . . sls dir
Jim Messina . . . natl sls mgr
Lisa Brady . . . rgnl sls mgr
Rob Montesi . . . mktg dir
Chris Gallagher . . . prom mgr
Mary Moonen . . . progmg mgr
Lyn Tolan . . . news dir
Elijah Young . . . pub affrs dir
Chris Potwin . . . chief of engrg

WHPX—Analog channel: 26. On air date: Sept 15, 1986. 3 Shaws Cove, Suite 226, New London, CT 06320. Phone: (860) 444-2626. Fax: (860) 440-2601. Web Site: www.paxtv.com. Licensee: Paxson Hartford License Inc. Group owner: Paxson Communications Corp. (acq 2-25-00; grpsl). Network: PAX TV.
Key Personnel:
Bruce Fox . . . gen mgr
Anthony Polzaro . . . progmg dir
Glenn Peltier . . . film buyer

WTIC-TV—Analog channel: 61. On air date: Sept 17, 1984. One Corporate Ctr., Hartford, CT 06103. Phone: (860) 527-6161. Fax: (860) 727-0158. Web Site: www.fox61.com. Licensee: 61 Licensee Inc. Group owner: Tribune Broadcasting Co. (acq 7-15-97; grpsl). Network: Fox. Rep: TeleRep. News staff: 31; News: 6 hrs wkly.

WTNH-TV—Analog channel: 8. Digital channel: 10. On air date: June 15, 1948. Box 1859, 8 Elm St., New Haven, CT 06510. Phone: (203) 784-8888. Fax: (203) 789-2010. E-mail: wtnh@wtnh.com. Web Site: www.wtnh.com. Licensee: LIN Television Inc. Group owner: LIN Television Corporation (acq 12-94; $120.17 million;. FTR: 1-2-95). Network: ABC. Rep: Petry Television Inc.. Washington Atty: Lin Legal. News staff: 77; News: 32 hrs wkly.
Key Personnel:
Jon Hitchcock . . . gen mgr
Jerry Min . . . opns dir
Roger Hess . . . gen sls mgr
Roger Megroz . . . natl sls mgr
Phil Jermain . . . rgnl sls mgr
Mary Lee Weber . . . mktg dir & pub affrs dir
Deanna Barns-Kluk . . . progmg mgr
Kirk Varner . . . news dir
Francine DuVerger . . . engrg dir

WTXX—Analog channel: 20. Digital channel: 12. On air date: Sept 4, 1953. One Corporate Ctr., Hartford, CT 06103. Phone: (860) 520-6573. Phone: (203) 758-3900. Fax: (860) 727-0158. Licensee: WTXX Inc. (acq 8-6-2001). Network: WB. Rep: MMT.

WUVN—Analog channel: 18. On air date: Sept 25, 1954. 1 Constitution Plaza, Suite 7, Hartford, CT 06103. Phone: (860) 278-1818. Fax: (860) 278-1811. Web Site: www.wuvntv.com. Licensee: Entravision Holdings LLC. Group owner: Entravision Communications Corp. (acq 1-4-01; $18 million). Network: Univision (Spanish). Washington Atty: Wiley, Rein & Fielding.
Key Personnel:
Alexander Von Lichtenberg . . . gen mgr
Robert Smith . . . opns mgr
Alexander von Lichtenberg . . . gen sls mgr
Eydie Palmieri . . . natl sls mgr
Meg Godin . . . mktg mgr, prom mgr & adv mgr
Heather Robinson . . . progmg mgr
Dania Alexandrino . . . mus dir
Sara Suarez . . . news dir
Fran Vaccain . . . chief of engrg

WVIT—(New Britain).Analog channel: 30. On air date: Feb 13, 1953. 1422 New Britain Ave., West Hartford, CT 06110. Phone: (860) 521-3030. Fax: (860) 521-4860. Fax: (860) 521-3110. Licensee: NBC Telemundo License Co. Group owner: NBC TV Stations Division (acq 12-07-97; trade). Network: NBC. Rep: NBC TV Stations Sales.
Key Personnel:
Dave Doebler . . . pres & gen mgr
David Bondanza . . . opns dir & engrg dir
Bill Nandi . . . opns mgr & chief of opns
Steve Smith . . . sls VP
Eric Bloom . . . natl sls mgr
Marcie Miller . . . mktg mgr
Maria Famicielli . . . prom dir & adv dir
Ronni Attenello . . . progmg dir
B.J. Finnell . . . news dir
LaVerne Jefferys . . . pub affrs dir

New Haven

see Hartford & New Haven, CT market

Delaware

Seaford

see Salisbury, MD market

Wilmington

see Philadelphia market

District of Columbia

Washington, DC (Hagerstown, MD) (DMA 8)

WBDC-TV—Analog channel: 50. Digital channel: 51. On air date: November 1981. 2121 Wisconsin Ave. N.W., Suite 350, Washington, DC 20007. Phone: (202) 965-5050. Fax: (202) 965-0050. Web Site: www.wbdc.com. Licensee: WBDC Broadcasting Inc. Group owner: Tribune Broadcasting Co. (acq 11-16-99). Network: WB. Rep: Harrington, Righter & Parsons.
Key Personnel:
Dennis Fitzsimons . . . CEO
Eric Meyrowitz . . . VP & gen mgr
Chip Shenkan . . . gen sls mgr
Brett Burke . . . natl sls mgr
Jim Byrne . . . mktg dir & prom mgr
John Handley . . . chief of engrg

WDCA—Analog channel: 20. On air date: Apr 20, 1966. 5151 Wisconsin Ave. N.W., Truro, DC 20016-4124. Phone: (202) 895-3050. Fax: (202) 895-3340. E-mail: upn20wdca@paramount.com. Web Site: www.upn20wdca.com. Licensee: Fox Television Stations Inc. Group owner: (group owner; acq 11-6-01; with KTXH(TV) Houston, TX in swap for KBHK-TV San Francisco, CA). Network: UPN. Rep: Fox Stations Sales. Washington Atty: Leventhal, Senter & Lerman.

***WETA-TV**—Analog channel: 26. Digital channel: 27. On air date: Oct 2, 1961. 2775 S. Quincy St., Arlington, VA 22206. Phone: (703) 998-2600. Fax: (703) 998-3401. Web Site: www.weta.org. Licensee: Greater Washington Educational Telecommunications Association Inc. Network: PBS. Washington Atty: Dow, Lohnes & Albertson.
Key Personnel:
John W. Hechinger Jr. . . . chmn
Sharon Rockefeller . . . pres
Joe Bruns . . . CFO, exec VP & chief of opns
Karen Fritz . . . gen mgr
Chad Davis . . . progmg dir

WFDC-TV—Analog channel: 14. Digital channel: 15. On air date: Aug 3, 1993. 962 Wayne Ave., Suite 900, Silver Spring, MD 20910. Phone: (301) 589-0030. Fax: (301) 495-9556. E-mail: rguemica@entravisiondc.com. Web Site: www.wmto.washingtondcc.com. Licensee: TeleFutura D.C. LLC. Group owner: Univision Communications Inc. (acq 6-1-01; $30 million). Network: TeleFutura (Spanish).

***WFPT**—Analog channel: 62. Digital channel: 28. On air date: 1986. 11767 Owings Mills Blvd., Owings Mills, MD 21117-1499. Phone: (410) 356-5600. Fax: (410) 581-6579. E-mail: comments@mpt.org. Web Site: www.mpt.org. Licensee: Maryland Public Broadcasting Commission. Network: PBS. Washington Atty: Schwartz, Woods & Miller.
Key Personnel:
Robert Shuman . . . CEO & pres
Larry Unger . . . CFO
George Benaman . . . opns VP

WHAG-TV—Analog channel: 25. On air date: Jan 3, 1970. 13 E. Washington St., Hagerstown, MD 21740. Phone: (301) 797-4400. Fax: (301) 733-1735. Fax: (301) 745-4093. E-mail: hbreslin@ nbc25.com. Web Site: www.nbc25.com. Licensee: Nexstar Broadcasting Inc. Group owner: Nexstar Broadcasting Group Inc. (acq 12-31-2003; grpsl). Network: NBC. Rep: Petry Television Inc.. Washington Atty: Arter & Hadden. News: 20 hrs wkly.

*WHUT-TV—Analog channel: 32. On air date: Nov 17, 1980. 2222 4th St. N.W., Washington, DC 20059. Phone: (202) 806-3200. Fax: (202) 806-3300. Licensee: Howard University. Network: PBS. Washington Atty: Arnold & Porter.
Key Personnel:
Jennifer Lawson . . . . . gen mgr
Cassandra Ortega-Beckford . . . . . opns dir
Connie Harold . . . . . dev dir
Eric Richardson . . . . . progmg dir
William Kirkland. . . . . engrg dir

WJAL—Analog channel: 68. Digital channel: 16. On air date: May 5, 1987. Box 190, Chambersburg, PA 17201-0190. 262 Swamp Fox Rd., Chambersburg, PA 17201. Phone: (717) 375-4000. Fax: (717) 375-4052. E-mail: comments@wjal.com. Web Site: www.wjal.com. Licensee: Entravision Holdings LLC. Group owner: Entravision Communications Corp. (acq 6-20-01; $10.7 million. including $400,000 bridge loan). Washington Atty: Leventhal, Senter & Lerman. News: 5 hrs local news wkly.
Key Personnel:
Rudy Guernica . . . . . gen mgr
Steve Ullom. . . . . stn mgr
C. Griffen . . . . . opns mgr

WJLA-TV—Analog channel: 7. Digital channel: 39. On air date: Oct 3, 1947. 1100 Wilson Blvd., 6th Fl., Arlington, VA 22209. Phone: (703) 236-9552. Fax: (703) 236-2311. Web Site: www.wjla.com. Licensee: ACC Licensee Inc. Group owner: Allbritton Communications Co. (acq 1-76; grpsl). Network: ABC. Rep: Continental Television Sales. Washington Atty: Hogan & Hartson. News: 24 hrs wkly.

*WNVC—Analog channel: 56. On air date: June 1, 1983. 8101A Lee Hwy., Falls Church, VA 22042. Phone: (703) 698-9682. Fax: (703)770-7112. Licensee: Central Virginia Educational Telecommunications Corp. Washington Atty: Wiley, Rein & Fielding. News: one hr wkly.

*WNVT—Analog channel: 53. Digital channel: 30. On air date: Mar 1, 1972. 8101A Lee Hwy., Falls Church, VA 22042. Phone: (703) 770-7100. Fax: (703) 770-7112. Licensee: Commonweath Public Broadcasting Corp. (acq 7-3-74; $550,000;. FTR: 7-22-74). Network: PBS. Washington Atty: Wiley, Rein & Fielding.

WPXW—Analog channel: 66. Digital channel: 43. On air date: Mar 26, 1978. 6199 Old Arrington Ln., Fairfax Stn., VA 22039. Phone: (703) 503-7966. Fax: (703) 503-1225. Web Site: www.pax.tv. Licensee: Paxson Washington License Inc. Group owner: Paxson Communications Corp. (acq 4-16-97; $30 million). Network: PAX TV. Washington Atty: Wilmer, Cutler & Pickering.

WRC-TV—Analog channel: 4. Digital channel: 48. On air date: June 27, 1947. 4001 Nebraska Ave. N.W., Washington, DC 20016. Phone: (202) 885-4000. Fax: (202) 885-4104. Web Site: www.nbc4.com. Licensee: NBC Telemundo License Co. Group owner: NBC TV Stations Division. Network: NBC. Rep: NBC TV Stations Sales.

WTTG—Analog channel: 5. Digital channel: 36. On air date: Jan 1, 1947. 5151 Wisconsin Ave. N.W., Washington, DC 20016. Phone: (202) 244-5151. Fax: (202) 244-1745. Web Site: www.fox5dc.com. Licensee: Fox Television Stations Inc. Group owner: (group owner; acq 3-86; grpsl). Network: Fox. Rep: TeleRep. Washington Atty: Hogan & Hartson.

WUSA—Analog channel: 9. Digital channel: 34. On air date: Jan 16, 1949. 4100 Wisconsin Ave. N.W., Washington, DC 20016. Phone: (202) 895-5999. Fax: (202) 364-6163. E-mail: 9news@wusatv9.com. Web Site: www.wusatv9.com. Licensee: The Detroit News Inc. Group owner: Gannett Broadcasting (Division of Gannett Co. Inc.) (acq 2-18-86). Network: CBS. Washington Atty: Reed Smith LLP. News: 39 hrs wkly.
Key Personnel:
Darryll Green . . . . . pres
Cheryl Savastano. . . . . natl sls mgr & rgnl sls mgr
Sarah Lasio . . . . . mktg dir & news dir
David Jones . . . . . engrg dir

*WVPY—Analog channel: 42. On air date: Aug 22, 1996. c/o WVPT, 298 Port Republic Rd., Harrisonburg, VA 22801. Phone: (540) 434-5391. Fax: (540) 434-7084. E-mail: wvpt@wvpt.pbs.org. Web Site: www.wvpt.net. Licensee: Shenandoah Valley Educational TV Corp. Network: PBS. Washington Atty: Covington & Burling.
Key Personnel:
Jeffrey G. Lenhart . . . . . chmn
Bert Schmidt . . . . . pres & gen mgr
Tony Mancari. . . . . exec VP & engrg VP
Wanda Zimmerman . . . . . progmg dir

*WWPB—Analog channel: 31. Digital channel: 44. On air date: 1986. 11767 Owings Mills Blvd., Owings Mills, MD 21117-1499. Phone: (410) 356-5600. Fax: (410) 581-6579. E-mail: comments@mpt.org. Web Site: www.mpt.org. Licensee: Maryland Public Broadcasting Commission. Network: PBS. Washington Atty: Schwartz, Woods & Miller.
Key Personnel:
Robert Shuman . . . . . CEO & pres
Larry Unger . . . . . CFO

WWPX—Analog channel: 60. Digital channel: 12. On air date: Oct 1, 1991. 211 Discovery Rd., Suite One, Martinsburg, WV 25401. Phone: (304) 267-4950. Web Site: www.pax.tv. Licensee: Paxson Martinsburg License Inc. Group owner: Paxson Communications Corp. (acq 6-1-00). Network: PAX TV. Washington Atty: Cohn & Marks.

Florida

Daytona Beach

see Orlando-Daytona Beach-Melbourne, FL market

Destin

see Mobile, AL-Pensacola (Ft. Walton Beach), FL market

Fort Walton Beach

see Mobile, AL-Pensacola (Ft. Walton Beach), FL market

Ft. Lauderdale

see Miami-Ft. Lauderdale, FL market

Ft. Myers-Naples, FL (DMA 68)

WBBH-TV—Analog channel: 20. Digital channel: 15. On air date: Dec 19, 1968. 3719 Central Ave., Fort Myers, FL 33901. Phone: (239) 939-2020. Fax: (239) 939-3244. E-mail: comments@nbc-2.com. Web Site: www.nbc-2.com. Licensee: Waterman Broadcasting Corp. of Fla. Group owner: Waterman Broadcasting Corp. Network: NBC. Rep: Katz Radio. Washington Atty: Cohn & Marks. News staff: 80; News: 32 hrs wkly.
Key Personnel:
Bernard Waterman . . . . . pres
Gerry Poppe. . . . . CFO
Steven Pontius . . . . . exec VP & gen mgr
Bob Beville. . . . . sls dir
Gayla Wright. . . . . rgnl sls mgr
Lori Grimaldi . . . . . mktg dir
Deborah Abbott . . . . . progmg dir
Darrel Adams. . . . . news dir
Dan Billings . . . . . engrg dir

WFTX—(Cape Coral).Analog channel: 36. Digital channel: 35. On air date: Oct 14, 1985. 621 S.W. Pine Island Rd., Cape Coral, FL 33991. Phone: (239) 574-3636. Fax: (239) 574-2025. Web Site: www.fox4florida.com. Licensee: Emmis Television License LLC. (acq 1998; grpsl). Network: Fox. Washington Atty: Dow, Lohnes & Albertson.
Key Personnel:
Jeff Smulyan . . . . . CEO & chmn
Randy Bongarten . . . . . pres
Walter Berger . . . . . CFO
Ray Schonbak . . . . . sr VP
Donita Todd . . . . . VP & gen mgr
Tom Stemlar . . . . . sls dir
Carole Nelson . . . . . gen sls mgr
Jamie Ricks . . . . . rgnl sls mgr

Mary McCrork . . . . . prom mgr
Dave Ward . . . . . progmg VP
Geoffrey Roth. . . . . news dir
Marty Draper . . . . . engrg VP
Rick Carroll . . . . . chief of engrg

*WGCU—Analog channel: 30. On air date: Aug 15, 1983. 10501 FGCU Blvd., Fort Myers, FL 33965. Phone: (239) 590-2300. Fax: (239) 590-2310. Web Site: www.wgcu.org. Licensee: Board of Trustees, Florida Gulf Coast University. (acq 11-16-01). Network: PBS. Washington Atty: Cohn & Marks.
Key Personnel:
Kathleen Davey . . . . . stn mgr
Michael Stepp . . . . . opns mgr
Joseph Maggio . . . . . chief of opns & progmg mgr
Amy Tardiff . . . . . rgnl sls mgr & news dir

WINK-TV—Analog channel: 11. On air date: Mar 18, 1954. 2824 Palm Beach Blvd., Fort Myers, FL 33916. Phone: (239) 334-1111. Fax: (239) 334-0744. E-mail: webmaster@winktv.com. Web Site: www.winktv.com. Licensee: Fort Myers Broadcasting Co. Group owner: (group owner) Network: CBS. Rep: Blair Television. Washington Atty: Leibowitz & Associates. News staff: 55; News: 29 hrs wkly.
Key Personnel:
Brian A. McBride . . . . . CEO & pres
Gary W. Gardner . . . . . VP & gen mgr
Wayne Simons . . . . . sls dir
Jesse Daniels . . . . . natl sls mgr & rgnl sls mgr
Robert Voelker. . . . . natl sls mgr & rgnl sls mgr
Mark Gilson . . . . . prom dir
Greg Stetson . . . . . progmg dir
John Emmert . . . . . news dir
Keith Stuhlmann . . . . . engrg dir

WRXY-TV—Analog channel: 49. On air date: Jan 29, 1995. Box 50490, Ft. Myers, FL 33994-0490. 40000 Horseshoe Rd., Punta Gorda, FL 33982. Phone: (239) 543-7200. Fax: (239) 543-6800. E-mail: wrxy@skycasters.net. Licensee: West Coast Christian Television Inc.. Ownership: David C. Gibbs III, Wayne Wetzel and Bill Anderson. (acq 12-16-97).
Key Personnel:
Al Stropparo . . . . . chief of opns
Ken Griffith. . gen mgr, sls dir, mktg mgr, prom mgr & progmg mgr
Keith Grant . . . . . engrg dir & chief of engrg

WTVK—Analog channel: 46. On air date: Oct 22, 1990. 3451 Bonita Bay Blvd., Suite 101, Bonita Springs, FL 34134. Phone: (239) 498-4600. Fax: (239) 498-0146. Web Site: www.wb6tv.com. Licensee: Acme Television Licenses of Florida L.L.C. Group owner: Acme Communications Inc. (acq 5-15-98; $15.5 million). Washington Atty: Dickstein Shapiro Morin & Oshinsky L.L.P..
Key Personnel:
Bill Scaffide . . . . . gen mgr
Jack Spiess . . . . . chief of opns

WZVN-TV—Analog channel: 26. Digital channel: 41. On air date: Aug 21, 1974. 3719 Central Ave., Fort Myers, FL 33901. Phone: (239) 939-2020. Fax: (239) 939-3244 (news). Fax: (239) 939-4801. Web Site: abc-7.com. Licensee: Montclair Communications Inc.. Ownership: Lara Kunkler. (acq 10-10-96; $21.3 million). Network: ABC. Rep: Continental Television Sales. Washington Atty: Irwin, Campbell & Tannenwald. News staff: 85; News: 19.5 hrs wkly.
Key Personnel:
Lara Kunkler. . . . . pres
Steve Pontius. . . . . gen mgr
Laura Mickler . . . . . opns dir
Bob Beville. . . . . sls dir
Ron Stevens. . . . . natl sls mgr
Lori Grimaldi . . . . . mktg dir & prom dir
Deborah Abbott . . . . . progmg dir
Darrel Adams. . . . . news dir
David McKelvey . . . . . chief of engrg

Ft. Pierce

see West Palm Beach-Ft. Pierce, FL market

Ft. Walton Beach

see Mobile, AL-Pensacola (Ft. Walton Beach), FL market

Gainesville, FL
(DMA 162)

WCJB—Analog channel: 20. On air date: Apr 7, 1971. 6220 N.W. 43rd St., Gainesville, FL 32653. Phone: (352) 377-2020. Fax: (352) 373-6516. E-mail: tv20news@wcjb.com. Web Site: www.wcjb.com. Licensee: Diversified Broadcasting Inc. Group owner: Diversified Communications (acq 12-1-76; 11-1-76). Network: ABC. Washington Atty: Irwin, Campbell & Tannenwald. News staff: 35; News: 17 hrs wkly.

Key Personnel:
Carolyn Barrett . . . . pres & gen mgr
Alan Chatman . . . . gen sls mgr & adv mgr
Tim Smith . . . . natl sls mgr
Karen Woolfstead . . . . mktg mgr & progmg mgr
Adam Henning . . . . news dir
Steve Ingram . . . . chief of engrg

WGFL—Analog channel: 53. Digital channel: 28. On air date: Sept 20, 1997. 4190 N.W. 93 Ave., Gainesville, FL 32653. Phone: (352) 375-5300. Fax: (352) 371-9353. Web Site: www.wgfl.com. Licensee: WGFL License Corp.. Ownership: Pegasus Satellite Communications Inc., debtor-in-possession (acq 1-12-2004; $4.075 million. with WYPN-CA Gainesville and WLCF-LP Lake City). Network: CBS.

Key Personnel:
Todd Senter . . . . gen mgr
Sue Edwards . . . . opns dir & progmg dir
Joe Grant . . . . prom mgr
Terry Blakeney . . . . chief of engrg

WOGX—Analog channel: 51. On air date: Nov 1, 1983. 1551 S.W. 37th Ave., Ocala, FL 34474. 35 Skyline Drive, Orlando, FL 34474. Phone: (352) 873-6951. Phone: (407) 644-3535. Fax: (352) 237-5423. Licensee: Fox Television Stations Inc. Group owner: (group owner; acq 5-14-02; with WOFL(TV) Orlando). Network: Fox. Rep: TeleRep. Washington Atty: Skadden, Arps, Slate, Meagher & Flom. News staff: 35; News: 7 hrs wkly.

***WUFT**—Analog channel: 5. On air date: Nov 10, 1958. 2200 Weimer Hall, Univ. of Florida, Gainesville, FL 32611. Phone: (352) 392-5551. Fax: (352) 392-5731. E-mail: info@wuft.org. Web Site: www.wuft.org. Licensee: Board of Trustees, University of Florida. Network: PBS. Washington Atty: Schwartz, Woods & Miller. News: 3 hrs wkly.

Key Personnel:
Richard Lehner . . . . gen mgr
Titus Rush . . . . stn mgr
Brent Williams . . . . dev dir
Rob Carr . . . . chief of engrg

Jacksonville, FL
(DMA 52)

WAWS—Analog channel: 30. On air date: Feb 15, 1981. 11700 Central Pkwy., Jacksonville, FL 32224. Phone: (904) 642-3030. Fax: (904) 642-5665. E-mail: fox30news@ccjax.com. Web Site: www.fox30online.com. Licensee: Clear Channel Radio Licenses Inc. Group owner: Clear Channel Communications Inc. (acq 8-5-92). Network: Fox. Rep: Katz Radio. Washington Atty: Holland & Knight.

Key Personnel:
Susan Adams Loyd . . . . gen mgr
Marc Hefner . . . . gen sls mgr
Anne Baudeaux . . . . mktg mgr & pub affrs dir
Buffy Walsh . . . . prom mgr
Doug Crall . . . . chief of engrg

***WJCT**—Analog channel: 7. On air date: Sept 10, 1958. 100 Festival Park Ave., Jacksonville, FL 32202. Phone: (904) 353-7770. Fax: (904) 358-6331. E-mail: wjct@wjct.org. Web Site: www.wjct.org. Licensee: WJCT Inc. Network: PBS. Washington Atty: Schwartz, Woods & Miller.

Key Personnel:
Michael T. Boylan . . . . CEO & pres
Steven Wallace . . . . chmn
Jocelyn Enriquez . . . . CFO
Rick Johnson . . . . sr VP & opns VP
Jeri Cirillo . . . . dev VP

***WJEB-TV**—Analog channel: 59. On air date: May 29, 1991. Box 5219, Jacksonville, FL 32277. 3101 Emerson Expwy., Jacksonville, FL 32277. Phone: (904) 399-8413. Fax: (904) 399-8423. E-mail: prayer@wjeb.org. Web Site: www.wjeb.org. Licensee: Jacksonville Educators Broadcasting Inc. Network: PBS.

Key Personnel:
Collette D. Snowden . . . . gen mgr & stn mgr
Carolyn Rentrope . . . . pub affrs dir
Clayton Roney . . . . engrg mgr

WJWB—Analog channel: 17. On air date: Feb 19, 1966. Box 17000, Jacksonville, FL 32216. 9117 Hogan Rd., Jacksonville, FL 32216. Phone: (904) 641-1700. Fax: (904) 641-0306. Web Site: www.wjwb.com. Licensee: Media General Broadcasting Inc. Group owner: Media General Broadcast Group (acq 12-23-82; $18 million; 11-8-82). Network: WB. Washington Atty: Dow, Lohnes & Albertson.

Key Personnel:
Mike Liff . . . . pres & gen mgr
George Birnbaum . . . . . . opns dir, opns mgr & chief of engrg
Cheri Goetze . . . . natl sls mgr
Tom Cassaro . . . . gen sls mgr & natl sls mgr
Andre Boyd . . . . mktg dir
Dakota Neufville . . . . prom mgr & progmg dir

WJXT—Analog channel: 4. On air date: Sept 15, 1949. Box 5270, Jacksonville, FL 32247. 4 Broadcast Pl., Jacksonville, FL 32207. Phone: (904) 399-4000. Fax: (904) 399-1828. E-mail: jaxnews@news4jax.com. Web Site: www.news4jax.com. Licensee: Post-Newsweek Stations, Fla. Inc. Group owner: Post-Newsweek Stations Inc. (acq 1-28-53; grpsl; 2-2-53). Rep: MMT. Washington Atty: Covington & Burling. News staff: 65; News: 51 hrs wkly.

Key Personnel:
Ann Sutton . . . . VP, stn mgr & natl sls mgr
Larry Blackerby . . . . VP, gen mgr & gen mgr
Tina Schultz . . . . opns mgr
John Rafferty . . . . gen sls mgr
Greg MacGregor . . . . natl sls mgr
Rusty Wolfe . . . . prom mgr
Mo Ruddy . . . . news dir

WJXX—Analog channel: 25. On air date: Feb 9, 1997. 1070 East Adam St., Jacksonville, FL 32202. Phone: (904) 354-1212. Fax: (904) 353-3455. E-mail: news@firstcoastnews.com. Web Site: www.firstcoastnews.com. Licensee: Gannett River States Publishing Corp. Group owner: Gannett Broadcasting (acq 3-15-00; $81 million). Network: ABC.

Key Personnel:
Ken Tonning . . . . pres, gen mgr & opns dir
Sam Folley . . . . natl sls mgr
Glenn Sebold . . . . progmg dir
Mike McCormick . . . . news dir
Bishop Ellison . . . . engrg dir & chief of engrg

WPXC-TV—Analog channel: 21. On air date: Apr 2, 1990. 7434 Blythe Island Hwy., Brunswick, GA 31523. Phone: (912) 267-0021. Fax: (912) 261-9582. Web Site: www.paxtv.com. Licensee: Paxson Jax License Inc. Group owner: Paxson Communications Corp. (acq 12-6-00; $3.07 million).. Network: PAX TV. Washington Atty: Fleischman & Walsh.

WTEV-TV—Analog channel: 47. On air date: Aug 1, 1980. 11700 Central Pkwy., Jacksonville, FL 32224. Phone: (904) 642-3030. Fax: (904) 642-5665. E-mail: cbs47news@ccjax.com. Web Site: cbs47.com. Licensee: Clear Channel Broadcasting Licenses Inc. Group owner: Clear Channel Communications Inc. (acq 2-13-01; grpsl). Network: CBS. Rep: Millennium Sales & Marketing. Washington Atty: Holland & Knight. News staff: 72; News: 22 hrs wkly.

Key Personnel:
Susan Adams Loyd . . . . gen mgr
Marc Hefner . . . . gen sls mgr
Anne Baudeaux . . . . mktg mgr & pub affrs dir
Buffy Hammond . . . . prom dir
Doug Crall . . . . news dir & chief of engrg

WTLV—Analog channel: 12. On air date: Sept 1, 1957. 1070 E. Adams St., Jacksonville, FL 32202. Phone: (904) 354-1212. Fax: (904) 633-8899. E-mail: news@firstcoastnews.com. Web Site: www.firstcoastnews.com. Licensee: Multimedia Cablevision Inc. Group owner: Gannett Broadcasting (Division of Gannett Co. Inc.) (acq 5-12-75; $11,401,217; 4-14-75). Network: NBC. Washington Atty: Reed, Smith, Shaw & McClay. News staff: 54; News: 17 hrs wkly.

Key Personnel:
Ken Tonning . . . . pres & gen mgr
Sam Folley . . . . natl sls mgr
Mike McCormick . . . . news dir
Bishop Ellison . . . . engrg dir

***WXGA-TV**—Analog channel: 8. On air date: Dec 4, 1961. 6433 TV-Tower Rd., Milwood, GA 31552. Phone: (912) 338-5200. Web Site: www.gbp.org. Licensee: Georgia Public Telecommunications Commission. Network: PBS.

Melbourne

see Orlando-Daytona Beach-Melbourne, FL market

Miami-Ft. Lauderdale, FL
(DMA 17)

WAMI-TV—Analog channel: 69. Digital channel: 47. On air date: Aug 10, 1988. 1900 N.W.89th Pl., Miami, FL 33172. Phone: (305) 421-1900. Fax: (305) 463-9154. Web Site: www.univision.com. Licensee: TeleFutura Miami LLC. Group owner: Univision Communications Inc. (acq 6-6-01; grpsl). Network: TeleFutura (Spanish). Washington Atty: Hogan & Hartson. News staff: 35; News: 3 hrs wkly.

WBFS-TV—Analog channel: 33. Digital channel: 32. On air date: Dec 9, 1984. 8900 N.W. 18th Terr., Miami, FL 33172. Phone: (305) 621-3333. Fax: (305) 628-3900. E-mail: upn33@wbfs.com. Web Site: www.upn33.com. Licensee: Viacom Television Stations Group of Miami Inc. Group owner: Viacom Television Stations Group. Network: UPN.

Key Personnel:
Brian Kennedy . . . . pres & CFO
Brien Kennedy . . . . gen mgr
Tracy Letize . . . . progmg dir

WBZL—Analog channel: 39. Digital channel: 19. On air date: Oct 16, 1982. 2055 Lee St., Hollywood, FL 33020. Phone: (954) 925-3939. Phone: (305) 949-3900. Fax: (954) 922-3965. Web Site: www.wb39.com. Licensee: Channel 39 Inc. Group owner: Tribune Broadcasting Co. (acq 7-15-97; grpsl). Network: WB. Rep: MMT. News: 3.5 hrs wkly.

Key Personnel:
Patrick Mullen . . . . pres
Rich Engberg . . . . VP & gen mgr
Steve Sloane . . . . gen sls mgr
Allyson Di Palma . . . . natl sls mgr
Robert Venusti . . . . prom dir & prom mgr
Wendy Logsdon . . . . progmg dir & progmg mgr
Tatiana Liendo . . . . pub affrs dir
Ronald Rowe . . . . chief of engrg

WDLP-TV—Analog channel: 22. Digital channel: 3. On air date: June 1, 1993. 527 Southard St., Key West, FL 33040. Phone: (305) 296-1669. Fax: (305) 296-4969. Web Site: www.tvhola.com. Licensee: WDLP Broadcasting Co. LLC.. Ownership: De La Pena Family Trust Dated November 26, 2001, 100% (acq 1-15-2003; $7 million)..

Key Personnel:
Penny Drucker . . . . pres
David Drucker . . . . exec VP
Alberto Monge . . . . gen mgr
Oscar Ibarra . . . . sls dir & gen sls mgr
Drew Lassiter . . . . chief of engrg

WFOR-TV—Analog channel: 4. Digital channel: 22. On air date: Mar 21, 1949. 8900 N.W. 18th Terr., Miami, FL 33172. Phone: (305) 591-4444. Fax: (305) 639-4444. Web Site: www.cbs4news.com. Licensee: CBS Television Stations Inc. Group owner: Viacom Television Stations Group. Network: CBS. Rep: CBS Spot Sales. News staff: 90; News: 30 hrs wkly.

Key Personnel:
Brien Kennedy . . . . pres & gen mgr
Michael Applebaum . . . . gen mgr & gen sls mgr
Grace Vgarte . . . . mktg mgr
John Branco . . . . prom mgr
Tracy Letize . . . . progmg dir
Shannon High-Bassalik . . . . news dir
Juan Andrea . . . . engrg dir
Franklin Anderson . . . . chief of engrg

WGEN-TV—Analog channel: 8. Digital channel: 12. On air date: Jan 1, 1995. 16502 N.W. 52nd Ave., Miami, FL 33014. Phone: (305) 621-3688. Fax: (305) 621-5181. E-mail: tvch8@aol.com. Licensee: Sonia Licensed Subsidiary LLC.. Ownership: Community Property Trust under the De La Pena Family Trust of 11/26/01, 50%; and Husband's Separate Trust under the De La Pena Family Trust of 11/26/01, 50% (acq 4-16-2004; $2.75 million)..

Key Personnel:
John C. Bailie . . . . gen mgr & gen sls mgr
Bobby Quintero . . . . rgnl sls mgr
Robert Thompson . . . . stn mgr, dev mgr & progmg mgr
Ricardo Castellanos . . . . news dir
Raul Alfonso . . . . pub affrs dir
Ralph Johnson . . . . chief of engrg

***WHFT-TV**—Analog channel: 45. On air date: Mar 17, 1975. 3324 Pembroke Rd., Pembroke Park, FL 33021. Phone: (954) 962-1700. Fax: (954) 962-2817. Web Site: www.tbn.org. Licensee: Trinity Broadcasting of Florida Inc. Group owner: Trinity Broadcasting Network (acq 5-14-80; $10 million). Washington Atty: Joseph E. Dunne III.

Key Personnel:
Paul F. Crouch . . . . pres
Laurie Quinn . . . . gen mgr

***WLRN-TV**—Analog channel: 17. Digital channel: 20. On air date: June 26, 1962. 172 N.E. 15th St., Miami, FL 33135. Phone: (305) 995-1717. Fax: (305) 995-2299. E-mail: info@wlrn.org. Web Site: www.wlrn.org.. Stn video via satellite: Yes Licensee: The School Board of Miami-Dade County, FL. Network: PBS. Washington Atty: Leibowitz & Associates.

Key Personnel:
Karen Echols . . . . . CFO
John LaBonia . . . . . gen mgr
Bernadette Siy . . . . . stn mgr & dev mgr
Clyde Pinder . . . . . opns dir
Michael Peyton . . . . . sls dir
Jeneissey Azcuy . . . . . prom mgr & adv mgr
Steve Weisberg . . . . . progmg dir
Jack F. Yaghdjian . . . . . chief of engrg

WLTV—Analog channel: 23. On air date: Nov 15, 1967. 9405 N.W. 41st St., Miami, FL 33178. Phone: (305) 470-2323. Fax: (305) 471-3959. Web Site: www.univision.net. Licensee: WLTV L.P. Group owner: Univision Communications Inc. (acq 8-7-88). Network: Univision (Spanish). Washington Atty: Wiley, Rein & Fielding.

Key Personnel:
Lois Fernandez-Rocha . . . . . VP & gen mgr
Raul Perez-Liste . . . . . opns dir
Matt Chandler . . . . . dev mgr
Marilyn Hansen . . . . . gen sls mgr
Maura Calzadilla . . . . . mktg dir & mktg mgr
Evisabel Fabrega . . . . . prom mgr
Angela Ramos . . . . . progmg dir & pub affrs dir
Helga Silva . . . . . news dir
Douglas Peterson . . . . . chief of engrg

***WPBT**—Analog channel: 2. On air date: Aug 12, 1955. Box 2, Miami, FL 33261-0002. 14901 N.E. 20th Ave., Miami, FL 33261-0002. Phone: (305) 949-8321. Fax: (305) 944-4211. E-mail: channel2@wpbt.org. Web Site: www.channel2.org. Licensee: Community Television Foundation of South Florida Inc. Network: PBS. Washington Atty: Wilmer, Cutler & Pickering.

Key Personnel:
Rick Schneider . . . . . CEO, pres & gen mgr
Dave Mullins . . . . . mktg VP
Jody Rafkind . . . . . prom mgr

WPLG—Analog channel: 10. Digital channel: 9. On air date: Nov 20, 1961. 3900 Biscayne Blvd., Miami, FL 33137. Phone: (305) 576-1010. Fax: (305) 325-2381. Web Site: www.local10.com. Licensee: Post-Newsweek Stations, Fla. Inc. Group owner: Post-Newsweek Stations Inc. (acq 9-27-69; grpsl; 10-6-69). Network: ABC. Rep: MMT. Washington Atty: Covington & Burling.

Key Personnel:
David Boylan . . . . . VP & gen mgr
Sharon Harrison . . . . . opns mgr
Mimi Del Ca . . . . . progmg mgr

WPXM—Analog channel: 35. On air date: Oct 15, 1992. One Datran Ctr., 9100 S. Dadeland Blvd., Miami, FL 33156. 15000 S.W. 27th St., Miramar, FL 33027. Phone: (954) 622-6835. Fax: (954) 622-6843. Web Site: www.pax.tv. Licensee: Paxson Communications License Co. L.L.C. Group owner: Paxson Communications Corp. (acq 12-12-97).

Key Personnel:
Doug Barker . . . . . pres
Cynthia DeRose . . . . . gen mgr

WSCV—Analog channel: 51. On air date: Dec 6, 1968. 15000 S.W. 27th St., Miramar, FL 33027. Phone: (954) 622-6000. Fax: (954) 622-6107. E-mail: info@t51.com. Web Site: www.t51.com. Licensee: NBC Telemundo License Co. Group owner: Telemundo Group Inc. (acq 4-12-02; grpsl). Network: Telemundo (Spanish). News staff: 70; News: 3 hrs wkly.

Key Personnel:
Don Browne . . . . . CEO
Vince Sadusky . . . . . CFO
Michael Rodriguez . . . . . gen mgr
Jorge Carballo . . . . . gen sls mgr
Alan Brydger . . . . . mktg mgr
Maria Christina Barros . . . . . progmg dir

WSVN—Analog channel: 7. Digital channel: 8. On air date: July 29, 1956. 1401 79th St. Causeway, Miami, FL 33141. Phone: (305) 751-6692. Fax: (305) 757-2266. Fax: TWX: (810) 848-6151. Web Site: www.wsvn.com. Licensee: Sunbeam TV Corp.. Ownership: Edmund N. Ansin. (acq 10-4-67; 10-16-67). Network: Fox. Rep: Harrington, Righter & Parsons. Washington Atty: Koteen & Naftalin.

Key Personnel:
Edmund N. Ansin . . . . . pres
Steven Cejas . . . . . exec VP
Robert W. Leider . . . . . gen mgr

WTVJ—Analog channel: 6. On air date: Sept 20, 1967. 15000 S. 27th St., Miami, FL 33027. Phone: (954) 622-6702. Fax: (954) 622-6107. Web Site: www.nbc6.net. Licensee: NBC Telemundo License Co. Group owner: NBC TV Stations Division (acq 1995). Network: NBC. Rep: NBC TV Stations Sales.

Key Personnel:
Ardyth R. Diercks . . . . . pres, gen mgr, gen mgr & sls VP
Meg Green . . . . . pres & CFO

Naples

see Ft. Myers-Naples, FL market

Orlando-Daytona Beach-Melbourne, FL

(DMA 20)

WACX—(Leesburg).Analog channel: 55. On air date: Mar 6, 1982. Box 608040, Orlando, FL 32860. 4520 Parkbreeze Ct., Orlando, FL 32808. Phone: (407) 298-5555. E-mail: superchannel@wacxtv.com. Web Site: www.wacxtv.com. Licensee: Associated Christian Television System Inc. (acq 6-8-83; 7-4-83).

***WBCC**—Analog channel: 68. On air date: Jan 12, 1988. 1519 Clearlake Rd., Cocoa, FL 32922. Phone: (321) 632-1111. Fax: (321) 634-3724. E-mail: wbcc@brevardcc.edu. Web Site: www.brevardcc.edu/wbcc. Licensee: Brevard Community College. Network: PBS.

Key Personnel:
Dr. Tom Gamble . . . . . pres
Joe Williams . . . . . gen mgr
Phillip Wallace . . . . . stn mgr

***WCEU**—Analog channel: 15. Digital channel: 33. On air date: Feb 1, 1988. Box 2811, Daytona Beach, FL 32120-2811. 1200 W. International Speedway Blvd., Daytona Beach, FL 32114. Phone: (386) 506-4415. Fax: (386) 506-4427. E-mail: wceu@wceu-pbs.org. Web Site: www.wceu.org. Licensee: Daytona Beach Community College. (acq 6-30-2002). Network: PBS. Washington Atty: Fletcher, Heald & Hildreth.

Key Personnel:
Sandra Session-Robertson . . . . . gen mgr & gen sls mgr
Michael Dietz . . . . . progmg dir
Bill Schwartz . . . . . chief of engrg

WESH—(Daytona Beach).Analog channel: 2. Digital channel: 11. On air date: June 11, 1956. 1021 N. Wymore Rd., Winter Park, FL 32854. Phone: (407) 645-2222. Fax: (407) 539-7812. Fax: (407) 539-7948 (news). Web Site: www.wesh.com. Licensee: WESH-TV Broadcasting. Group owner: Hearst-Argyle Television Inc. (acq 1999; grpsl). Network: NBC. Washington Atty: Brooks, Pierce, McLendon, Humphrey & Leonard.

Key Personnel:
Wliam P. Bauman . . . . . pres & VP
William Bauman . . . . . gen mgr
Rick Scharf . . . . . opns mgr
Joseph Chaplinski . . . . . gen sls mgr
Jessica A. Derle . . . . . natl sls mgr
Claudia Wickham . . . . . rgnl sls mgr
Suzanne Grethen . . . . . mktg dir, prom dir & pub affrs dir
Linda Kitchens . . . . . progmg dir
Ed Trauschke . . . . . news dir
Richard Monn . . . . . chief of engrg

WFTV—Analog channel: 9. Digital channel: 39. On air date: Feb 1, 1958. Box 999, Orlando, FL 32802. 490 E. South St., Orlando, FL 32801-2841. Phone: (407) 841-9000. Fax: (407) 422-1887. Fax: (407) 481-2891 (news). Web Site: www.wftv.com. Licensee: WFTV-TV Holdings Inc. Group owner: Cox Communications Inc. (acq 8-85; $185 million).. Network: ABC. News staff: 80; News: 25 hrs wkly.

Key Personnel:
Bill Hoffman . . . . . VP & gen mgr
Chip Reif . . . . . opns mgr
Bob Jordan . . . . . news dir

WKCF—(Clermont).Analog channel: 18. Digital channel: 17. On air date: December 1988. 31 Skyline Dr., Lake Mary, FL 32746. Phone: (407) 645-1818. Fax: (407) 647-4163. E-mail: wb18wkcf@wb18.com. Web Site: www.wb18.com. Licensee: Emmis Television License LLC. Group owner: Emmis Communications Corp. (acq 10-28-99; $191.5 million).. Network: WB. Washington Atty: Bechtel & Cole. News: 3 hrs wkly.

Key Personnel:
Randy Bongarten . . . . . pres
Mark Lass . . . . . VP
Wayne Spracklin Valgen . . . . . gen mgr & stn mgr
Dave Ward . . . . . opns dir, progmg VP & progmg dir
Julie Brafford . . . . . opns mgr & prom dir
John Soapes . . . . . gen sls mgr
Chris Nurse . . . . . natl sls mgr
Steve Rickin . . . . . mktg dir
Greg Thomas . . . . . prom mgr
Tracy Moore . . . . . pub affrs dir
Joseph M. Addalia Jr. . . . . . engrg dir

WKMG-TV—Analog channel: 6. On air date: July 1, 1954. 4466 N. John Young Pkwy., Orlando, FL 32804. Phone: (407) 291-6000. Fax: (407) 521-1204. Fax: (407) 298-2122 (news). Web Site: www.local6.com. Licensee: Post-Newsweek Stations Orlando Inc. Group owner: Post-Newsweek Stations Inc. (acq 9-4-97). Network: CBS. Rep: MMT. Washington Atty: Covington & Burling. News staff: 80; News: 24 hrs wkly.

Key Personnel:
Alan Frank . . . . . pres & gen sls mgr
Henry Maldonado . . . . . VP & gen mgr
David Ware . . . . . rgnl sls mgr

WLCB-TV—Analog channel: 45. On air date: December 2000. 653 W. Michigan St., Orlando, FL 32805. Phone: (407) 423-5200. Fax: (407) 422-0120. E-mail: ed@tv52.org. Web Site: www.tv52.org. Licensee: Good Life Broadcasting Inc. Group owner: (group owner; acq 11-19-01; with WTGL-TV Cocoa). Washington Atty: Leventhal, Senter & Lerman.

Key Personnel:
Gene Polino . . . . . chmn
Ken Mikesell . . . . . pres & gen mgr
Ed Griffis . . . . . opns VP, sls VP & progmg VP
Kathy Wood . . . . . dev dir
Eileen Edwards . . . . . progmg dir
Kristen Mikesell . . . . . pub affrs dir
Marshall Royalty . . . . . chief of engrg

***WMFE-TV**—Analog channel: 24. Digital channel: 23. On air date: Mar 25, 1965. 11510 E. Colonial Dr., Orlando, FL 32817-4699. Phone: (407) 273-2300. Fax: (407) 206-2791. Web Site: wmfe.org. Licensee: Community Communications Inc.. Ownership: Community Licensee, 100%. Network: PBS. Washington Atty: Schwartz, Woods & Miller.

Key Personnel:
Joy Barrett Sebol . . . . . chmn
Stephen McKenney Steck . . . . . CEO & pres
Jose A. Fajardo . . . . . exec VP
Aldo Vivona . . . . . sr VP

WOFL—Analog channel: 35. Digital channel: 22. On air date: Oct 15, 1979. 35 Skyline Dr., Lake Mary, FL 32746. Phone: (407) 644-3535. Fax: (407) 333-3535. Licensee: Fox Television Stations Inc. Group owner: (group owner; acq 5-14-02; with WOGX(TV) Ocala). Network: Fox. Rep: TeleRep. Washington Atty: Skadden, Arps, Slate, Meagher & Flom.

Key Personnel:
Stan Knott . . . . . gen mgr
Lou Supowitz . . . . . sls VP & sls dir
Alan Sawyer . . . . . natl sls mgr
Ken Freedman . . . . . rgnl sls mgr
Rick Snyder . . . . . prom VP
Dawn Tevekelian . . . . . prom mgr
Kim Strickland . . . . . progmg mgr
Lena Sadiwskyj . . . . . news dir
Ken Preston . . . . . chief of engrg

WOPX—Analog channel: 56. Digital channel: 48. On air date: June 1986. 1021 N. Wymore Rd., Winter Park, FL 32789. Phone: (407) 370-5600. Fax: (407) 691-7728. Web Site: www.pax.tv. Licensee: Paxson Orlando License Inc. Group owner: Paxson Communications Corp. (acq 12-12-97; $13,161,274).. Network: PAX TV. Washington Atty: Dow, Lohnes & Albertson.

Key Personnel:
Bill Bowman . . . . . gen mgr
Joe Chaplinski . . . . . gen sls mgr
Allan Pullman . . . . . chief of engrg

WOTF-TV—Analog channel: 43. On air date: July 5, 1982. 739 C North Dr., Melbourne, FL 32934. Phone: (321) 254-4343. Fax: (321) 254-9343. Licensee: Univision of Melbourne Inc. Group owner: Univision Communications Inc. (acq 5-21-01; grpsl). Washington Atty: Dow, Lohnes & Albertson.

Key Personnel:
Sylvia Willis . . . . . VP
Francisco Banos . . . . . gen mgr
Bob Guzman . . . . . chief of opns
Sonja Mithcel . . . . . gen sls mgr
Delores McLaughlin . . . . . pub affrs dir
Frank Banos . . . . . chief of engrg

WRBW—Analog channel: 65. Digital channel: 41. On air date: June 6, 1994. 35 Skyline Dr., Lake Mary, FL 32746. Phone: (407) 644-3535.

Broadcasting & Cable Yearbook 2006

B-30

Fax: (407) 741-5048. E-mail: wrbw@wrbw.com. Web Site: www.wrbw.com. Licensee: Fox Television Stations Inc. Group owner: (group owner; acq 7-31-01; grpsl). Network: UPN.

Key Personnel:
Stan Knott . . . . . gen mgr
Terry Walden . . . . . opns dir & progmg mgr

WRDQ—Analog channel: 27. Digital channel: 14. On air date: 2000. 490 E. South St., Orlando, FL 32801. Phone: (407) 841-9000. Fax: (407) 422-1414. Web Site: www.wrdq.com. Licensee: WFTV-TV Holdings Inc. Group owner: Cox Communications Inc. (acq 2-1-2001).

WTGL-TV—Analog channel: 52. On air date: Aug 16, 1982. 653 W. Michigan St., Orlando, FL 32805. Phone: (407) 423-5200. Fax: (407) 423-8153. E-mail: ed@tv52.org. Web Site: www.tv52.org. Licensee: Good Life Broadcasting Inc. Group owner: (group owner; acq 11-19-01; with WLCB-TV Leesburg). Washington Atty: Gammon & Grange.

Key Personnel:
Gene Polino . . . . . chmn
Ken Mikesell . . . . . pres & gen mgr
Ed Griffis . . . . . opns VP
Eileen Kelly . . . . . progmg dir & progmg
Marshall Royalty . . . . . chief of engrg

WVEN-TV—(Daytona Beach).Analog channel: 26. On air date: October 1988. 523 Douglas Ave., Suite 100, Altamonte Springs, FL 32714. Phone: (407) 774-2626. Fax: (407) 774-3384. Licensee: Entravision Holdings L.L.C. Group owner: Entravision Communications Corp. (acq 9-15-00; $22.55 million). Network: Univision (Spanish).

Panama City, FL (DMA 160)

WBIF—Analog channel: 51. On air date: 2002. Tiger Eye Broadcasting Corp., 3400 Lakeside Dr., Suite 500, Miramar, FL 33027. Phone: (954) 431-3144. Fax: (954) 431-3591. Licensee: EBC Panama City Inc. Group owner: Equity Broadcasting Corp. (acq 3-23-2004; $1.2 million)..

***WFSG**—Analog channel: 56. Digital channel: 38. On air date: July 11, 1988. Public TV Ctr., 1600 Red Barber Plaza, Tallahassee, FL 32310. Phone: (850) 487-3170. Fax: (850) 487-3093. Web Site: www.wfsu.org. Licensee: Board of Regents of Florida. (acq 2-28-86). Network: PBS. Washington Atty: Cohn & Marks.

Key Personnel:
Patrick Keating . . . . . gen mgr
Charles Allen . . . . . dev dir
Jannie Whitt . . . . . prom dir & prom mgr
Mike Dunn . . . . . progmg dir
Jim McDaniel . . . . . pub affrs dir & engrg dir
David Lauther . . . . . chief of engrg

WJHG-TV—Analog channel: 7. On air date: Dec 1, 1953. 8195 Front Beach Rd., Panama City Beach, FL 32407. Phone: (850) 234-7777. Fax: (850) 233-6647. Licensee: WEAU Licensee Corp. Group owner: Gray Television Inc. (acq 6-29-60; $340,000;. FTR: 7-4-60). Network: NBC. Rep: Continental Television Sales. Washington Atty: Venable, Baetjer, Howard & Civiletti.

Key Personnel:
Jon McKee . . . . . opns mgr
Tracy Connors . . . . . gen mgr, gen sls mgr & adv dir
Kathy Fultz . . . . . progmg dir
Joe Moore . . . . . news dir
Sean Dixon . . . . . pub affrs dir
Mark Gilland . . . . . chief of engrg

WMBB—Analog channel: 13. On air date: Oct 3, 1973. Box 1340, Panama City, FL 32402. 613 Harrison Ave., Panama City, FL 32401. Phone: (850) 769-2313. Fax: (850) 769-8231. Web Site: www.wmbb.com. Licensee: Media General Communications Inc. Group owner: Media General Broadcast Group (acq 3-27-00; grpsl). Network: ABC. Washington Atty: Covington & Burling. News staff: 24; News: 143 hrs wkly.

Key Personnel:
Bill Byrd . . . . . gen mgr
Ray Hundley . . . . . gen sls mgr
George Baker . . . . . natl sls mgr
Cerise Roberts . . . . . mktg dir & prom dir
Larche' Hardy . . . . . news dir
Mark Gilland . . . . . chief of engrg

WPCT—Analog channel: 46. On air date: 1997. Box 9556, Panama City Beach, FL 32417. Phone: (850) 234-2773. Fax: (850) 234-1179. Licensee: Beach TV Properties Inc. Group owner: (group owner)

Key Personnel:
Jud Colley . . . . . pres
Mike Hartzog . . . . . gen mgr

WPGX—Analog channel: 28. On air date: May 21, 1988. Fox TV Ctr., 637 Luverne Ave., Panama City, FL 32401. Box 208, Panama City, FL 32402. Phone: (850) 784-0028. Fax: (850) 784-1773. Licensee: Raycom National Inc. Group owner: Raycom Media Inc. (acq 12-15-03; grpsl). Network: Fox. Rep: Millennium Sales & Marketing. Washington Atty: Leventhal, Senter & Lerman.

Key Personnel:
David Cavileer . . . . . VP & chief of engrg
Tim Cabrey . . . . . gen mgr
Sue Stewart . . . . . opns mgr & prom mgr

Pensacola

see Mobile, AL-Pensacola (Ft. Walton Beach), FL market

Sarasota

see Tampa-St. Petersburg (Sarasota), FL market

St. Petersburg

see Tampa-St. Petersburg (Sarasota), FL market

Tallahassee, FL-Thomasville, GA (DMA 109)

WCTV—(Thomasville).GA Analog channel: 6. On air date: Sept 15, 1955. 4000 Country Rd. 12, Tallahassee, FL 32312. Phone: (850) 893-6666. Fax: (850) 893-5193. Web Site: www.wctv6.com. Licensee: Gray Television Licensee Inc. Group owner: Gray Television Inc. (acq 1996; $165 million. with WVLT-TV Knoxville, TN). Network: CBS. Rep: Continental Television Sales.

Key Personnel:
Nick Waller . . . . . pres & gen mgr
Chris Mossman . . . . . sls dir & gen sls mgr
Ella Paris . . . . . natl sls mgr
Heather Pryor . . . . . rgnl sls mgr
Mike Smith . . . . . news dir

***WFSU-TV**—Analog channel: 11. On air date: Sept 20, 1960. 1600 Red Barber Plaza, Tallahassee, FL 32310. Phone: (850) 487-3170. Fax: (850) 487-3093. E-mail: mail@wfsu.org. Web Site: www.wfsu.org. Licensee: Florida Board of Regents & Florida State University. Network: PBS.

Key Personnel:
Patrick Keating . . . . . gen mgr
Beckie Hamilton . . . . . progmg dir
Jim McDaniel . . . . . engrg dir
Leo Barfield . . . . . chief of engrg

WFXU—Analog channel: 57. Digital channel: 48. On air date: July 1998. Box 949, Midway, FL 32343. Phone: (850) 576-4990. Fax: (850) 576-0200. E-mail: fox49@fox49.com. Web Site: www.fox49.com. Licensee: WFXU License Corp.. Ownership: Pegasus Communications Corp., 100% (acq 3-29-02; $250,914).. Network: UPN. Washington Atty: Shaw Pittman LLP.

Key Personnel:
Mark Pagon . . . . . CEO
Jack Paris . . . . . sr VP
David Hinterschied . . . . . gen mgr
Tyrone Hayes . . . . . opns mgr & chief of opns
Tana Kenny . . . . . gen sls mgr
Nathan Mears . . . . . natl sls mgr
Don Abel. mktg mgr, prom dir, progmg dir, progmg mgr & film buyer
Chuck Lindsey . . . . . pub affrs dir
Lee Carpenter . . . . . engrg VP
Mike Brown . . . . . chief of engrg

WTLF—Analog channel: 24. On air date: 2004. Box 949, Midway, FL 32343. 950 Commerce Blvd., Midway, FL 32343. Phone: (850) 576-4990. Fax: (850) 576-0200. Licensee: KB Prime Media L.L.C. Group owner: (group owner). Network: UPN.

Key Personnel:
Guyon W. Turner . . . . . pres
Jim Shaw . . . . . gen mgr

WTLH—(Bainbridge).GA Analog channel: 49. Digital channel: 50. On air date: 1989. 950 Commerce Blvd., Box 949, Midway, FL 32343. Phone: (850) 576-4990. Fax: (850) 576-0200. E-mail: fox49@fox49.com. Web Site: www.fox49.com. Licensee: WTLH License Corp., debtor-in-possession. Group owner: Pegasus Broadcast Television Inc. (acq 1996; $5.595 million).. Network: Fox. Washington Atty: Shaw Pittman LLP.

Key Personnel:
Mark Pagon . . . . . CEO
Jack Paris . . . . . exec VP & sr VP
David Hinterschied . . . . . gen mgr
Tyrone Hayes . . . . . opns mgr & chief of opns
Tana Kenny . . . . . gen sls mgr
Nathan Mears . . . . . natl sls mgr
Don Abel . . . . . mktg dir, prom dir & progmg dir
Tonya Herron . . . . . prom mgr
Craig Moody . . . . . adv mgr
Chuck Lindsey . . . . . pub affrs dir
Lee Carpenter . . . . . engrg VP
Mike Brown . . . . . chief of engrg

WTWC-TV—Analog channel: 40. On air date: Apr 21, 1983. 8440 Deerlake Rd. S., Tallahassee, FL 32312. Phone: (850) 893-4140. Fax: (850) 893-6974. Licensee: WTWC Licensee L.L.C. Group owner: Sinclair Broadcast Group Inc. (acq 1999; grpsl). Network: NBC. Rep: Millennium Sales & Marketing. Washington Atty: Dow, Lohnes & Albertson. News staff: 30; News: 14 hrs wkly.

Key Personnel:
Bob W. Franklin . . . . . gen mgr
Mike Plumber . . . . . stn mgr

WTXL-TV—Analog channel: 27. Digital channel: 22. On air date: Sept 16, 1976. 8440 Deer Lake Rd., Tallahassee, FL 32312. Phone: (850) 893-4140. Fax: (850) 668-1460. Web Site: www.wtxl.com. Licensee: Media Venture Management Inc.. Ownership: Brian E. Cobb; Denise L. Cobb Revocable Trust et al (acq 5-26-93; $5 million;. FTR: 7-14-93). Network: ABC. Washington Atty: Keck, Mahin & Cate. News staff: 26; News: 24 hrs wkly.

Key Personnel:
Brian E. Cobb . . . . . CEO
Mike Plummer . . . . . stn mgr
Steve Rollison . . . . . gen mgr & news dir

WVAG—Analog channel: 44. Digital channel: 43. On air date: Sept 1, 1995. Box 1987, Moultrie, GA 31776. Phone: (229) 985-1340. Fax: (229) 985-7549. E-mail: traffic@wvagtv.com. Web Site: wvagtv.com. Licensee: P.D. Communications LLC.. Ownership: Dr. Paul E. Shok, 66%; and Donald E. Meinke, 33% (acq 6-10-2003). Network: UPN. Washington Atty: Leventhal, Senter & Lerman.

Key Personnel:
Don Meinke . . . . . CEO & pres
Dr. Paul Shok . . . . . chmn
Jared Yost . . . . . gen mgr
Roger Terracina . . . . . opns mgr

Tampa-St. Petersburg (Sarasota), FL (DMA 13)

WCLF—Analog channel: 22. On air date: October 1979. Box 6922, Clearwater, FL 33758. 6922 142nd Ave. N., Largo, FL 33771. Phone: (727) 535-5622. Fax: (727) 531-2497. Web Site: www.ctnonline.com. Licensee: Christian Television Corporation Inc. Group owner: (group owner; acq 12-16-97). Washington Atty: Gammon & Grange.

***WEDU**—(Tampa).Analog channel: 3. On air date: Oct 27, 1958. Box 4033, Tampa, FL 33677-4033. 1300 North Blvd., Tampa, FL 33607. Phone: (813) 254-9338. Fax: (813) 253-0826. Web Site: www.wedu.org. Licensee: Florida West Coast Pub Broadcasting Inc. Network: PBS. Washington Atty: Dow, Lohnes & Albertson.

Key Personnel:
Patrick Perkins . . . . . CFO
Richard M. Lobo . . . . . CEO, pres & stn mgr
Frank Wolynski . . . . . opns VP & engrg VP
Darlene Armbruster . . . . . dev VP
Larry Jopek . . . . . sls dir
Paul Grove . . . . . progmg VP

WFLA-TV—(Tampa).Analog channel: 8. Digital channel: 7. On air date: Feb 14, 1955. 200 South Parker St., Tampa, FL 33606. Phone: (813) 228-8888. Fax: (813) 221-5787. Web Site: www.wfla.com. Licensee: Media General Communications Inc. Group owner: Media General Broadcast Group, see Cross-Ownership (acq 1965; $17.5 million).. Network: NBC. Rep: Harrington, Righter & Parsons. Washington Atty: Dow, Lohnes & Albertson.

Key Personnel:
Eric Land . . . . . pres & gen mgr
S. Rick McEwen . . . . . opns dir
Joe Pomilla . . . . . sls dir & gen sls mgr
Mark Overstreet . . . . . natl sls mgr
Carol Wald . . . . . rgnl sls mgr
Brad Moses . . . . . mktg dir & prom dir

Joyce Lueders . . . . progmg mgr & film buyer
Forrest Carr . . . . news dir
Mark Schaefer . . . . chief of engrg

WFTS—(Tampa).Analog channel: 28. Digital channel: 29. On air date: Dec 14, 1981. 4045 N. Himes Ave., Tampa, FL 33607. Phone: (813) 354-2828. Fax: (813) 878-2828. Web Site: www.abcactionnews.com. Licensee: Tampa Bay Television Inc. Group owner: Scripps Howard Broadcasting Co., see Cross-Ownership (acq 1-2-86; grpsl). Network: ABC. Rep: Katz Radio. Washington Atty: Baker & Hostetler.
Key Personnel:
Bill Carey . . . . VP & gen mgr
Jack Winter . . . . opns mgr
Larry Jopek . . . . gen sls mgr
Marsha Kidd-Collins . . . . natl sls mgr
Dave Balmer. . . . . rgnl sls mgr
Chris Raynor . . . . prom mgr
Chris Jadick . . . . news dir
Joy Petit . . . . pub affrs dir

WFTT-TV—(Tampa).Analog channel: 50. Digital channel: 47. On air date: Feb 1, 1988. 2610 W. Hillsborough Ave., Tampa, FL 33614. Phone: (813) 872-6262. Fax: (813) 998-3600. Web Site: univision.com. Licensee: TeleFutura Tampa LLC. Group owner: Univision Communications Inc. (acq 5-21-01; grpsl). Network: TeleFutura (Spanish). Washington Atty: Wiley, Rein & Fielding.

WMOR-TV—Analog channel: 32. On air date: Apr 24, 1986. 7201 E. Hillsborough Ave., Tampa, FL 33610-4126. Phone: (813) 626-3232. Fax: (813) 622-7732. Web Site: www.moretv32.com. Licensee: WMOR-TV Company. Group owner: Hearst-Argyle Television Inc. (acq 1996; $25.5 million).. Rep: MMT. Washington Atty: Brooks, Pierce, McLendon, Humphrey & Leonard.
Key Personnel:
Ken Lucas . . . . VP, gen mgr & gen sls mgr
Marilu Hernandez. . . . . opns mgr
Roy Tym . . . . natl sls mgr
Bonita Elias . . . . rgnl sls mgr
Lynne C. Conlan . . . . prom dir
Pete George . . . . prom mgr
Lynne Conlan . . . . progmg VP & pub affrs dir
Joseph Pauly . . . . progmg mgr
Gary Blais . . . . chief of engrg

WTOG—(Saint Petersburg).Analog channel: 44. On air date: Nov 4, 1968. 365 105th Terr. N.E., Saint Petersburg, FL 33716. Phone: (727) 576-4444. Fax: (727) 570-4458. E-mail: upn44@wtogtv.com. Web Site: www.upn44tv.com. Licensee: Viacom International Inc. Group owner: Viacom Television Stations Group (acq 9-19-96). Network: UPN. Rep: TeleRep. Washington Atty: Fletcher, Heald & Hildreth. News staff: 25; News: 5 hrs wkly.
Key Personnel:
Frank Detillio . . . . exec VP & gen mgr
Barbara Buriey . . . . prom dir & progmg dir
John Kays. . . . . chief of engrg

WTSP—(Saint Petersburg).Analog channel: 10. Digital channel: 24. On air date: July 17, 1965. 11450 Gandy Blvd., Saint Petersburg, FL 33702. Phone: (727) 577-1010. Fax: (727) 578-7637. Web Site: www.wtsp.com. Licensee: Pacific and Southern Co. Group owner: Gannett Broadcasting (acq 12-31-96). Network: CBS. Rep: Blair Television. Washington Atty: Wiley, Rein & Fielding.
Key Personnel:
Sam Rosenwasser. gen mgr
Lee Griffin. . . . . opns mgr
Anthony Diaz . . . . gen sls mgr
Dave Griscavage . . . . natl sls mgr
Pete Nikiel . . . . mktg mgr & prom mgr
Ellen Lasher . . . . progmg mgr & pub affrs dir
Jerry Michel . . . . engrg dir

WTTA—(Saint Petersburg).Analog channel: 38. On air date: June 21, 1991. 7622 Bald Cypress Pl., Tampa, FL 33614. Phone: (813) 886-9882. Fax: (813) 880-8100. E-mail: comments@wtta38.com. Licensee: Bay Television Inc. Network: WB. Washington Atty: Fisher, Wayland, Cooper, Leader & Zaragoza.

WTVT—(Tampa).Analog channel: 13. Digital channel: 12. On air date: April 1955. Box 31113, Tampa, FL 33631-3113. 3213 W. Kennedy Blvd., Tampa, FL 33609. Phone: (813) 876-1313. Fax: (813) 871-3135. E-mail: news@wtvt.com. Web Site: www.wtvt.com. Licensee: New World Communications of Tampa Inc. Group owner: Fox Television Stations Inc. (acq 11-96; grpsl). Network: Fox. Washington Atty: Hogan & Hartson. News staff: 100; News: 46 hrs wkly.
Key Personnel:
Bob Linger . . . . exec VP, gen mgr & sls dir
Jim Benedict . . . . opns dir
Jeff Maloney . . . . sls VP
Carrie Schroeder . . . . mktg mgr

Mike House . . . . prom VP
Brian Fields . . . . progmg dir
Phil Metlin . . . . VP & news dir
Cary Williams . . . . engrg dir

***WUSF-TV**—(Tampa).Analog channel: 16. On air date: Sept 12, 1966. Univ. of South Florida, 4202 Fowler Ave., Tampa, FL 33620. Phone: (813) 974-4000. Fax: (813) 974-4806. E-mail: pholley@wusf.org. Web Site: www.wusf.org. Licensee: University of South Florida. Network: PBS. Washington Atty: Cohn & Marks.
Key Personnel:
Jo Ann Urofsky . . . . gen mgr
Pat Holly . . . . stn mgr
Jeff Hammel. . . . . opns mgr
Cathy Coccia . . . . dev dir
Dale Thompson . . . . dev dir
Andy Latimer . . . . sls dir
Susan Geiger. progmg dir
Art Wilson . . . . chief of engrg

WVEA-TV—Analog channel: 62. Digital channel: 25. On air date: May 3, 1991. 2610 W. Hillsborough Ave., Tampa, FL 33614-6132. Phone: (813) 872-6262. Fax: (813) 998-3600. Web Site: www.wvea.entravision.com. Licensee: Entravision Holdings L.L.C. Group owner: Entravision Communications Corp. (acq 1999; $17 million). Network: Univision (Spanish). Washington Atty: Thompson Hine, LLP. News staff: 12; News: 2.5 hrs wkly.
Key Personnel:
Lilly Gonzalez. . . . . gen mgr
Nelson Castillo . . . . gen sls mgr
Pilar Ortiz . . . . news dir
Bill Mierisch . . . . chief of engrg

WWSB—Analog channel: 40. On air date: Oct 23, 1971. 1477 10th St., Sarasota, FL 34236. Phone: (941) 552-0777. Fax: (941) 924-3971. E-mail: generalmanager@wwsb.tv. Web Site: www.wwsb.tv. Licensee: Southern Broadcast Corp. of Sarasota.. Ownership: Calkins Newspapers Inc., 100%. (acq 3-26-86; $40,500). Network: ABC. Washington Atty: Leibowitz & Associates. News staff: 45; News: 21 hrs wkly.
Key Personnel:
Gary Shorts . . . . CEO
J. Manuel Calvo. . . . . pres & gen mgr
Jason Wildanstein . . . . opns dir

WXPX—Analog channel: 66. Digital channel: 42. On air date: Aug 1, 1994. 200 S. Parker St., Tampa, FL 33606. Phone: (813) 314-5462. Fax: (813) 314-5464. Web Site: www.pax.tv. Licensee: Paxson Communications License Co. L.L.C. Group owner: Paxson Communications Corp. (acq 12-15-97). Network: PAX TV.
Key Personnel:
Joe Pomilla . . . . gen sls mgr
Mike Dudich . . . . rgnl sls mgr
Joe Clary . . . . chief of engrg

West Palm Beach-Ft. Pierce, FL (DMA 39)

WFGC—Analog channel: 61. On air date: May 21, 1993. 1900 S. Congress Ave., Suite B, West Palm Beach, FL 33406. Phone: (561) 642-3361. Fax: (561) 967-5961. E-mail: comments@wfgc.com. Web Site: www.wfgc.com. Licensee: Christian TV of Palm Beach County Inc.. Ownership: David C. Gibbs III, Wayne Wetzel and Bill Anderson. (acq 12-16-97). Washington Atty: Gammon & Grange.
Key Personnel:
Wayne Wetzel . . . . pres
Neville Chankersingh . . . . CFO
Mike Gonzales . . . . gen mgr
Chris Mavrois . . . . chief of engrg

WFLX—Analog channel: 29. Digital channel: 28. On air date: Aug 14, 1982. 4119 W. Blue Heron Blvd., West Palm Beach, FL 33404. Phone: (561) 845-2929. Fax: (561) 863-1238. Web Site: www.wflx.com. Licensee: Raycom National Inc. Group owner: Raycom Media Inc. (acq 1998). Network: Fox. Washington Atty: Kaye, Scholer, Fierman, Hays & Handler.
Key Personnel:
John Spinola . . . . VP & gen mgr
John Heislman. . . . . gen sls mgr & natl sls mgr
Brian Correll . . . . mktg dir & prom mgr
Barb Billens . . . . progmg dir
Steve Hunsicker. . . . . news dir
Angelo Figurella . . . . chief of engrg

WPBF—Analog channel: 25. On air date: Jan 1, 1989. 3970 RCA Blvd., Suite 7007, Palm Beach Gardens, FL 33410. Phone: (561) 694-2525. Fax: (561) 627-6738. Web Site: www.thewpbfchannel.com. Licensee: WPBF-TV Co. Group owner: Hearst-Argyle Television Inc. (acq 8-1-97). Network: ABC. Rep: Katz Radio. News staff: 40; News: 20 hrs wkly.
Key Personnel:
Caroline Scollard . . . . gen sls mgr
Ryan Rothstein. . . . . natl sls mgr
Jeff Klayman. rgnl sls mgr
Mark Prutisto . . . . mktg mgr
Russ Larish . . . . progmg dir
Victoria Regan . . . . VP, gen mgr & film buyer
Joe Coscia. . . . . news dir
Cliff Thomas . . . . chief of engrg

WPEC—Analog channel: 12. Digital channel: 13. On air date: Jan 1, 1955. Box 198512, West Palm Beach, FL 33419-8512. 1100 Fairfield Dr., West Palm Beach, FL 33419-8512. Phone: (561) 844-1212. Fax: (561) 842-1212. Web Site: www.wpecnews12.com. Licensee: Freedom Broadcasting of Florida Licensee L.L.C. Group owner: Freedom Broadcasting Inc. (acq 2-1-96; $150 million).. Network: CBS. Rep: TeleRep. Washington Atty: Latham & Watkins. News: 24 hrs wkly.
Key Personnel:
Doreen Wade . . . . pres & VP
Donn Colee . . . . stn mgr & progmg mgr
Doug Wolfmueller. . . . . gen sls mgr
Mary Gregg . . . . natl sls mgr
Jim Posey. . . . . rgnl sls mgr
Steve Hunsicker. . . . . news dir
Keith Betts. . . . . engrg dir & chief of engrg

***WPPB-TV**—Analog channel: 63. On air date: 2001. Broward Education Communications Network, 6600 S.W. Nova Dr., Fort Lauderdale, FL 33317. Phone: (754) 321-1000. Fax: (754) 321-1180. E-mail: feedback@becon.tv. Web Site: www.becon.tv. Licensee: The School Board of Broward County, Florida. (acq 3-31-00).

WPTV—Analog channel: 5. On air date: Aug 22, 1954. 100 Banyan Blvd., West Palm Beach, FL 33401. Phone: (561) 655-5455. Fax: (561) 655-8947. E-mail: newstips@scripps.com. Web Site: www.wptv.com. Licensee: Scripps Howard Broadcasting Co. Group owner: (group owner; acq 12-27-61; $2 million; 12-25-61). Network: NBC. Rep: Harrington, Righter & Parsons. Washington Atty: Baker & Hostetler. News staff: 75; News: 27 hrs wkly.
Key Personnel:
Kenneth W. Lowe . . . . CEO
Joseph G. Ne Castro . . . . CFO
Bill Peterson . . . . sr VP
Brian Lawlor . . . . gen mgr
Donna Lane . . . . gen sls mgr
Cynthia Camacho . . . . natl sls mgr & rgnl sls mgr
Rich Martinez . . . . natl sls mgr & rgnl sls mgr
Bernadette O'Grady. . . . . prom dir & progmg dir
Peter Roghaar . . . . news dir
Dave McKinley . . . . engrg mgr

WPXP—Analog channel: 67. On air date: 1998. 1100 Banyan Blvd., West Palm Beach, FL 33401. Phone: (561) 653-5653. Fax: (561) 653-5711. Web Site: www.pax.tv. Licensee: Hispanic Broadcasting Inc.. Ownership: Paxson Communications Corp., 90%; Betti Lidsky, 10%. Group owner: Paxson Communications Corp. (acq 1998).
Key Personnel:
Bob Hanown. . . . . gen sls mgr
Greg Welch . . . . prom mgr
Debra Burdick . . . . pub affrs dir
Fred Shuler . . . . chief of engrg

***WTCE-TV**—Analog channel: 21. On air date: May 1990. 3601 N. 25th St., Fort Pierce, FL 34946. Phone: (772) 489-2701. Fax: (772) 489-6833. Licensee: Jacksonville Educators Broadcasting Inc. (acq 7-6-90; $630,089)..

WTVX—Analog channel: 34. Digital channel: 50. On air date: Apr 5, 1966. Majestic Plaza, 4411 Beacon Cir., West Palm Beach, FL 33407. Phone: (561) 841-3434. Fax: (561) 848-9150. Web Site: www.wtvx.com. Licensee: C-34 FCC Licensee Subsidiary L.L.C. Group owner: Viacom Television Stations Group (acq 11-13-2001). Network: Network: UPN, WB. Washington Atty: Haley, Bader & Potts.

***WXEL-TV**—Analog channel: 42. Digital channel: 27. On air date: July 7, 1982. Box 6607, West Palm Beach, FL 33405. 3401 South Congress Ave., Boynton Beach, FL 33426. Phone: (561) 737-8000. Fax: (561) 369-3067. Licensee: Barry Telecommunications Inc. (acq 4-16-97). Network: PBS. Washington Atty: Schwartz, Woods & Miller.
Key Personnel:
Jerry Carr. . . . . CEO
Bernard Henneberg . . . . CFO
Jerry Carr . . . . gen mgr
Fred Flaxman . . . . dev VP
Ross Cooper . . . . sls dir, mktg dir, mktg mgr & adv mgr
Lee Rowand . . . . prom dir
Lee Rowland. . . . . progmg VP

Toni May . . . . . pub affrs dir
Mike Maville . . . . . engrg VP

Georgia

Albany, GA
(DMA 147)

***WABW-TV**—Analog channel: 14. On air date: Jan 1, 1967. 260 14th St. N.W., Atlanta, GA 30318. Phone: (404) 685-2400. Fax: (404) 685-2431. Web Site: www.gpb.org. Licensee: Georgia Public Telecommunications Commission. Network: PBS.
Key Personnel:
Melvin Jones . . . . . pub affrs dir
Mark Fehlig . . . . . engrg dir
Richard W. Harrell . . . . . chmn & chief of engrg

***WACS-TV**—Analog channel: 25. On air date: Mar 6, 1967. 260 14th St. N.W., Atlanta, GA 30318. Phone: (404) 685-2400. Fax: (404) 685-2431. Web Site: www.gpb.org. Licensee: Georgia Public Telecommunications Commission. Network: PBS. Washington Atty: Arent, Fox, Kintner, Plotkin & Kahn.
Key Personnel:
Richard W. Harrell . . . . . CEO & chmn
Melvin Jones . . . . . gen mgr & pub affrs dir
Mark Fenlign . . . . . engrg dir & chief of engrg

WALB—Analog channel: 10. On air date: Apr 7, 1954. Box 3130, 1709 Stuart Ave., Albany, GA 31706. Phone: (229) 446-1010. Fax: (229) 446-4000. E-mail: walb@walb.com. Web Site: www.walb.com. Licensee: Libco Inc. Group owner: Liberty Corp. (acq 7-30-98; $78 million).. Network: NBC. Rep: Katz Radio. News staff: 5; News: 15 hrs wkly.
Key Personnel:
James Wilcox . . . . . pres
Dawn Hobby . . . . . news dir

WFXL—Analog channel: 31. Digital channel: 12. On air date: Feb 14, 1982. Box 4050, Albany, GA 31706. 1201 Stuart Ave., Albany, GA 31707. Phone: (229) 435-3100. Fax: (229) 903-8240. Web Site: www.wfxl.com. Licensee: Raycom America License Subsidiary LLC. Group owner: Raycom Media Inc. (acq 10-14-2003; grpsl). Network: Fox. Washington Atty: Fletcher, Heald & Hildreth. News staff: 7; News: 2.5 hrs wkly.
Key Personnel:
Jenny Collins . . . . . gen mgr
Deborah Owens . . . . . stn mgr
Pat Coffman . . . . . opns mgr

WSST-TV—Analog channel: 55. On air date: May 22, 1989. Box 917, 112 S. 7th St., Cordele, GA 31015. Phone: (229) 273-0001. Fax: (229) 273-8894. E-mail: wsst@sowega.net. Web Site: www.wsst.com. Licensee: Sunbelt-South Telecommunications Ltd.. Ownership: William B. Goodson, 65%; Phillip A. Streetman, 35%. Washington Atty: Law Offices of Scott Cinnamon.
Key Personnel:
Phillip Streetman . . . . . sr VP, VP, stn mgr & news dir
Sara J. Howell . . . . . gen sls mgr
Lee W. Wright . . . . . progmg dir
William B. Goodson . . . . CEO, pres, gen mgr & chief of engrg

Atlanta
(DMA 9)

WAGA—Analog channel: 5. Digital channel: 27. On air date: April 1949. 1551 Briarcliff Rd. N.E., Atlanta, GA 30306. Phone: (404) 875-5555. Fax: (404) 898-0238. Web Site: www.fox5atlanta.com. Licensee: Fox Television Stations Inc. Group owner: (group owner; acq 11-96; grpsl). Network: Fox. News: 38 hrs wkly.
Key Personnel:
Gene McHugh . . . . . gen mgr
Neil Mazur . . . . . opns VP, opns dir, engrg VP & engrg dir
Paul Antoci . . . . . natl sls mgr
Sant Perez . . . . . sls VP & rgnl sls mgr
Kathy Soifer . . . . . prom VP, progmg VP & progmg dir
Budd McEntee . . . . . news dir
Linda Torrence . . . . . pub affrs dir

***WATC**—Analog channel: 57. On air date: Apr 14, 1996. 1862 Enterprise Dr., Norcross, GA 30093. Phone: (770) 300-9828. Fax: (770) 300-9838. Web Site: www.watctv.net. Licensee: Community Television Inc. (acq 6-3-93; $79,866; 6-28-93).
Key Personnel:
James Thompson . . . . . pres & gen mgr
Joanne Thompson . . . . . VP
Greg West . . . . . prom dir & progmg dir

WATL—Analog channel: 36. Digital channel: 25. On air date: July 5, 1976. One Monroe Pl., Atlanta, GA 30324. Phone: (404) 881-3600. Fax: (404) 881-3749. Web Site: www.wb36.com. Licensee: Qwest Broadcasting L.L.C. dba WATL 36. Group owner: Tribune Broadcasting Co. (acq 1-12-00; approximately $95 million. for remaining 67% of WATL(TV) and WNOL-TV New Orleans, LA). Network: WB. Rep: TeleRep. Washington Atty: Leventhal, Senter & Lerman.

WGCL-TV—Analog channel: 46. Digital channel: 19. On air date: June 6, 1971. PO Box 93524, Atlanta, GA 30377. 425 14th St. NW, Atlanta, GA 30318. Phone: (404) 325-4646. Fax: (404) 327-3003. Fax: (404) 327-3004. E-mail: wgcltvnews@wgcltv.com. Web Site: www.wgcltv.com. Licensee: Meredith Corp. Group owner: Meredith Broadcasting Group, Meredith Corp. (acq 2-22-99; $370 million swap with KCPQ(TV) Tacoma, WA). Network: CBS. Rep: Harrington, Righter & Parsons. Washington Atty: Garvey, Schubert & Barer. News staff: 80; News: 29 hrs wkly.
Key Personnel:
Andy Alford . . . . . VP & gen mgr
Craig Nichols . . . . . opns dir
Joanna Hemleb . . . . . natl sls mgr
Nadra Scott . . . . . mktg dir
Kelly Makes . . . . . mktg mgr
Paul Sherno . . . . . prom mgr
Patti Cohen . . . . . progmg mgr
Micah Johnson . . . . . news dir
James Stanley . . . . . chief of engrg

***WGTV**—Analog channel: 8. On air date: May 23, 1960. 260 14th St. N.W., Atlanta, GA 30318. Phone: (404) 685-2400. Fax: (404) 685-2431. Web Site: www.gpb.org. Licensee: Georgia Public Telecommunications Commission.. Ownership: Ga. Public TV Net. Network: PBS. Washington Atty: Arent, Fox, Kintner, Plotkin & Kahn.

***WHSG-TV**—Analog channel: 63. On air date: Feb 22, 1991. 1550 Agape Way, Decatur, GA 30035. Phone: (404) 288-1156. Fax: (404) 288-5613. Web Site: www.tbn.org. Licensee: Trinity Broadcasting Network Inc. Group owner: (group owner; acq 11-21-89).
Key Personnel:
Dorothy Casoria . . . . . gen mgr
Nikki Taylor . . . . . pub affrs dir
Lloyd Holloway . . . . . chief of engrg

***WPBA**—Analog channel: 30. On air date: Feb 17, 1958. 740 Bismark Rd. N.E., Atlanta, GA 30324-4102. Phone: (678) 686-0321. Fax: (678) 686-0356. Web Site: www.WPBA.org. Licensee: Board of Education of the City of Atlanta. Network: PBS. Washington Atty: Schwartz, Woods & Miller. News: 1.5 hrs wkly.
Key Personnel:
Karen Bell . . . . . progmg dir
John York . . . . . chief of engrg

WPXA—Analog channel: 14. On air date: Jan 15, 1988. 1611 W. Peach Tree St. N.E., Ste. 100, Atlanta, GA 30309. Phone: (404) 885-7646. Fax: (404) 881-9553. Web Site: www.pax.tv. Licensee: TV-14 Inc. Group owner: Paxson Communications Corp. (acq 7-13-94; $9.5 million). Washington Atty: Dow, Lohnes & Albertson.
Key Personnel:
Lowell Paxson . . . . . CEO
James Bocock . . . . . pres
Scott Jolles . . . . . gen mgr

WSB-TV—Analog channel: 2. On air date: Sept 29, 1948. 1601 W. Peachtree St. N.E., Atlanta, GA 30309. Phone: (404) 897-7000. Fax: (404) 897-6246 (gen mgr). E-mail: talk2us@wsbtv.com. Web Site: www.wsbtv.com. Licensee: WSB-TV Holdings Inc. Group owner: Cox Broadcasting Network: ABC. Rep: TeleRep. Washington Atty: Dow, Lohnes & Albertson.
Key Personnel:
Gregory Stone . . . . . VP & gen mgr
David Lamothe . . . . . opns dir
Tim McVay . . . . . gen sls mgr
Jane Williams . . . . . rgnl sls mgr
Steve Riley . . . . . mktg dir
Barry Sinnock . . . . . prom mgr
Art Rogers . . . . . progmg dir
Jennifer Rigby . . . . . news dir
Jocelyn Dorsey . . . . . pub affrs dir
Gene Faulkner . . . . . engrg dir

WTBS—Analog channel: 17. On air date: Sept 1, 1967. 1050 Techwood Dr. N.W., Atlanta, GA 30318. Phone: (404) 827-1717. Fax: (404) 885-2148. Web Site: www.tbssuperstation.com. Licensee: Superstation Inc., div of Turner Broadcasting System.. Ownership: R.E. Turner III, 32.03%; TCI, 24.43%; Time-Warner, 20.34%. (acq 1-70). Rep: TBS.

WUPA—Analog channel: 69. Digital channel: 43. On air date: Aug 22, 1981. Phoenix Business Park, 2700 Northeast Expwy., Atlanta, GA 30345. Phone: (404) 325-6969. Fax: (404) 633-4567. Web Site: www.upnatlanta.com. Licensee: Viacom Stations Group of Atlanta Inc. Group owner: Viacom Television Stations Group (acq 5-4-2000; grpsl). Network: UPN. Washington Atty: Wiley, Rein & Fielding.

WUVG-TV—Analog channel: 34. On air date: April 1989. 3350 Peach Tree Rd., Suite 1250, Atlanta, GA 33026. Phone: (404) 926-2300. Fax: (404) 926-2320. Licensee: Univision Partnership of Atlanta. Group owner: Univision Communications Inc. (acq 6-6-01; grpsl). Network: Univision (Spanish). Washington Atty: William M. Barnard.

WXIA-TV—Analog channel: 11. Digital channel: 10. On air date: Sept 30, 1951. 1611 W. Peachtree St. N.E., Atlanta, GA 30309. Phone: (404) 892-1611. Fax: (404) 881-0675. Web Site: www.11alive.com. Licensee: Gannett Georgia L.P. Group owner: Gannett Broadcasting, division of Gannett Co. Inc. (acq 6-7-79; grpsl; 6-11-79). Network: NBC. Washington Atty: Reed Smith LLP.
Key Personnel:
Robert Walker . . . . . pres, VP & gen mgr
Laura Hale . . . . . prom mgr & progmg dir
Cal Callaway . . . . . chief of engrg

Augusta, GA
(DMA 115)

WAGT—Analog channel: 26. On air date: Dec 24, 1968. Box 1526, Augusta, GA 30903-1526. 905 Broad St., Augusta, GA 30901. Phone: (706) 826-0026. Fax: (706) 724-4028. Fax: (706) 724-7491. Web Site: www.wagt.com. Licensee: WAGT Television Inc. Group owner: Schurz Communications Inc. (acq 7-1-80; $5 million). Network: NBC. Washington Atty: Hogan & Hartson. News staff: 28; News: 8 hrs wkly.
Key Personnel:
John Mann . . . . . pres & gen mgr
Mary Mixon . . . . . gen sls mgr
Buddy Miller . . . . . natl sls mgr
Bryan Timmerman . . . . . rgnl sls mgr
Don Mathews . . . . . prom mgr & progmg dir
Greg Schieferstein . . . . . news dir
Rick Wood . . . . . pub affrs dir
Ronald Davis . . . . . chief of engrg

***WCES-TV**—Analog channel: 20. On air date: Sept 12, 1966. Box 525, Wrens, GA 30833. Phone: (706) 547-2107. Fax: (706) 547-7290. E-mail: viewerservices@gpb.org. Web Site: www.gpb.org. Licensee: Georgia Public Telecommunications Commission. Network: PBS.
Key Personnel:
Mike Klein . . . . . opns mgr
Melvin Jones . . . . . pub affrs dir
Mark Fenning . . . . . engrg dir

***WEBA-TV**—Analog channel: 14. On air date: Sept 5, 1967. 1101 George Rogers Blvd., Columbia, SC 29201. Phone: (803) 737-3545. Fax: (803) 737-3495. E-mail: mail@myetv.org. Web Site: www.myetv.org. Licensee: South Carolina ETV Commission. Network: PBS.
Key Personnel:
Maurice "Moss" Bresnahan . . . . . CEO, pres & sr VP
L.W. Griffin Jr. . . . . . engrg VP

WFXG—Analog channel: 54. On air date: May 23, 1991. Box 204540, Augusta, GA 30917-4540. 3933 Washington Rd., Augusta, GA 30907. Phone: (706) 650-5400. Fax: (706) 650-8411. E-mail: richj@wfxg.com. Web Site: www.wfxg.com. Licensee: Southeastern Media Holdings Inc. Group owner: (group owner; (acq 12-1-2003; $40 million. with WXTX(TV) Columbus). Network: Fox. Washington Atty: Miller & Fields.

WJBF—Analog channel: 6. Digital channel: 42. On air date: Nov 23, 1953. Box 1404, Augusta, GA 30903. 1001 Reynolds St., Augusta, GA 30901. Phone: (706) 722-6664. Fax: (706) 722-0022. Web Site: www.wjbf.com. Licensee: Media General Broadcasting of South Carolina Holdings Inc. Group owner: Media General Broadcast Group (acq 3-27-2000; grpsl). Network: ABC. Washington Atty: Dow, Lohnes & Albertson, PLLC. News: 22 hrs wky.
Key Personnel:
Gene Kirkconnell . . . . . gen mgr
Bill Stewart . . . . . gen sls mgr
Charles Coleman . . . . . natl sls mgr
Scot Seabolt . . . . . rgnl sls mgr
Cil Frazier . . . . . mktg dir
Mary Jones . . . . . progmg dir & progmg

Mark Rosen . . . . . news dir
Cary Hale . . . . . chief of engrg

WRDW-TV—Analog channel: 12. Digital channel: 31. On air date: Feb 14, 1954. Box 1212, Augusta, GA 30903-1212. 1301 Georgia Ave., North Augusta, SC 29841. Phone: (803) 278-1212. Fax: (803) 279-8316. Licensee: Gray Television Licensee Inc. Group owner: Gray Television Inc. (acq 1-4-96; $34 million).. Network: Network: CBS, UPN. Rep: Continental Television Sales. News staff: 35; News: 20 hrs wkly.
Key Personnel:
John Ray . . . . . pres & gen mgr
Shalanda Priester. . . . . opns mgr
Joe Tonsing . . . . . gen sls mgr
Michael Oates . . . . . natl sls mgr
Estelle Parsley . . . . . news dir
Edward Elser. . . . . chief of engrg

Bainbridge

see Tallahassee, FL-Thomasville, GA market

Brunswick

see Jacksonville, FL market

Chatsworth

see Chattanooga, TN market

Columbus, GA (DMA 125)

***WGIQ**—Analog channel: 43. Digital channel: 44. On air date: Sept 9, 1968. 2112 11th Ave. S., Suite 400, Birmingham, AL 35205. Phone: (205) 328-8756. Fax: (205) 251-2192. Web Site: www.aptv.org. Licensee: Alabama ETV Commission. Network: PBS.
Key Personnel:
Alan Pizzato. . . . . CEO & pres
Pauline Howland. . . . . exec VP & gen mgr
Polly Anderson . . . . . dev dir

***WJSP-TV**—Analog channel: 28. On air date: Aug 10, 1964. 609 Whitehouse Pkwy, Warm Springs, GA 31830. Phone: (706) 655-2145. Fax: (404) 685-2431. Web Site: www.gpb.org. Licensee: Georgia Public Telecommunications Commission. Network: PBS.

WLGA—Analog channel: 66. Digital channel: 31. On air date: May 16, 1982. 1800 Pepperell Pkwy., Opelika, AL 36801. Phone: (334) 745-0066. Fax: (334) 749-5768. E-mail: mbrooks@pappastv.com. Web Site: www.wswstv.com. Licensee: Pappas Telecasting of Opelika L.P. (a Delaware limited partnership). Group owner: (group owner; (acq 1996; $1.6 million).. Network: UPN. Washington Atty: Paul, Hastings, Janofsky & Walker.
Key Personnel:
Harry J. Pappas . . . . . pres
Mike Brooks . . . . . gen mgr
Walter Dix. . . . . opns mgr

WLTZ—Analog channel: 38. Digital channel: 35. On air date: Oct 29, 1970. 6140 Buena Vista Rd., Columbus, GA 31907. Box 12289, Columbus, GA 31917. Phone: (706) 561-3838. Fax: (706) 563-8467. Fax: (706) 561-3880 (sales). E-mail: wltz@wltz.com. Web Site: www.wltz.com. Licensee: Lewis Broadcasting Corp.. Ownership: J.C. Lewis Jr., 100%. (acq 7-1-81; $3.25 million). Network: NBC. Rep: Blair Television. Washington Atty: Wiley, Rein & Fielding.
Key Personnel:
J. Curtis Lewis Jr.. . . . . pres
Charles Izlar. . . . . CFO
Tom Breazeale. . . . . VP & gen mgr
Charles Collins . . . . . opns dir

WRBL—Analog channel: 3. On air date: Nov 15, 1953. Box 270, Columbus, GA 31902-0270. 1350 13th Ave., Columbus, GA 31902-0270. Phone: (706) 323-3333. Fax: (706) 327-6655. Fax: (706) 323-0841. Licensee: Media General Communications Inc. Group owner: Media General Broadcast Group (acq 3-27-00; grpsl). Network: CBS. Washington Atty: Dow, Lohnes & Albertson.
Key Personnel:
Matt Browning . . . . . gen mgr
Darlene Kittrel. . . . . mktg dir
Darlene Hughes . . . . . prom mgr
Kay Stringfellow . . . . . progmg dir & film buyer

Mark Wildman . . . . . news dir
Jim Barnes . . . . . chief of engrg

WTVM—Analog channel: 9. On air date: Oct 6, 1953. Box 1848, Columbus, GA 31902-1848. Phone: (706) 324-6471. Fax: (706) 322-7527. Web Site: www.wtvm.com. Licensee: Raycom America License Subsidiary LLC. Group owner: Raycom Media Inc. (acq 1996; grpsl). Network: ABC. Rep: Harrington, Righter & Parsons. Washington Atty: Powell, Goldstein, Frazer & Murphy.
Key Personnel:
Lee Brantley. . . . . VP & gen mgr
Rick Moll . . . . . news dir

WXTX—Analog channel: 54. On air date: June 17, 1983. Box 1848, Columbus, GA 31907. Phone: (706) 324-6471. Fax: (706) 322-7527. E-mail: programming@wxtx.com. Web Site: www.wxtx.com. Licensee: Southeastern Media Holdings Inc. Group owner: (group owner; (acq 12-1-2003; $40 million. with WFXG(TV) Augusta). Network: Fox. Washington Atty: Fisher, Wayland, Cooper, Leader & Zaragoza.
Key Personnel:
Lee Brantley . . . . . gen mgr
Rick Moll . . . . . news dir

Dalton

see Chattanooga, TN market

Macon, GA (DMA 119)

***WDCO-TV**—Analog channel: 29. On air date: Jan 1, 1968. Box 269, Salem Cary Rd., Cochran, GA 31014. Phone: (478) 934-3095. Fax: (478) 934-3646. Licensee: Georgia Public Telecommunications Commission. Network: PBS.

WGNM—Analog channel: 64. On air date: Nov 30, 1990. 178 Steven Dr., Macon, GA 31210. Phone: (478) 474-8400. Fax: (478) 474-4777. E-mail: recet@wgnm.com. Web Site: www.wgnm.com. Licensee: Christian Television Network Inc.. Ownership: Jimmy Smith, 25%; Robert T. D'Andrea, 25%; Virginia Oliver, 25%; and Wayne Wetzel, 25% (acq 12-31-2003; $3 million).. Washington Atty: Allen & Harold.
Key Personnel:
Robert D'Andrea . . . . . pres
Rip Kenley . . . . . gen mgr
Dan Jaskuld . . . . . opns mgr

WGXA—Analog channel: 24. On air date: Apr 21, 1982. Box 340, 599 Martin Luther King Blvd., Macon, GA 31201. Phone: (478) 745-2424. Fax: (478) 745-6057 (news). Web Site: www.fox24.com. Licensee: Piedmont Television of Macon License LLC. Group owner: GOCOM Communications (acq 1-27-2000). Network: Fox. Washington Atty: Leibowitz & Spencer.

WMAZ-TV—Analog channel: 13. Digital channel: 4. On air date: Sept 27, 1953. Box 5008, Macon, GA 31208. 1314 Gray Hwy., Macon, GA 31211. Phone: (478) 752-1313. Fax: (478) 752-1331. Web Site: www.13wmaz.com. Licensee: Gannett Georgia L.P. Group owner: Gannett Broadcasting (acq 12-4-95). Network: CBS. Washington Atty: Wiley, Rein & Fielding. News staff: 39; News: 27 hrs wkly.
Key Personnel:
Don McGouirk. . . . . pres, VP & gen mgr
Dodie Cantrell . . . . . VP & news dir
Frank Shurling . . . . . gen sls mgr
Jeff Dudley . . . . . mktg dir

WMGT-TV—Analog channel: 41. On air date: Aug 26, 1968. Box 4328, Macon, GA 31208-4328. 301 Poplar St., Macon, GA 31201. Phone: (478) 745-4141. Fax: (478) 742-2626. E-mail: info@wmgt.com. Web Site: www.wmgt.com. Licensee: Morris Network Inc. Group owner: Morris Multi-Media (acq 11-30-78; $2.8 million;. FTR: 12-18-78). Network: NBC. Washington Atty: McFadden, Evans & Sill.
Key Personnel:
Dean Hinson. . . . . pres
George Jobin . . . . . gen mgr
Greg Oliver . . . . . natl sls mgr
Cheryl Palmer . . . . . prom dir
Debbie Wright . . . . . progmg dir
Chris McLendon . . . . . engrg dir

WPGA-TV—Analog channel: 58. On air date: March 1995. 1691 Forsyth St., Macon, GA 31201. Phone: (478) 745-5858. Fax: (478) 745-5800. Web Site: www.58abc.com. Licensee: Radio Perry Inc. Network: ABC. Washington Atty: Brown, Nietert & Kaufman. News: 3 hrs wkly.
Key Personnel:
Debbie Hart . . . . . gen mgr
Len Register. . . . . opns mgr
Julie Register . . . . . prom mgr
Veronica Duhart. . . . . progmg dir
Hal Sutton. . . . . chief of engrg

Savannah, GA (DMA 98)

WGSA—Analog channel: 34. On air date: May 1, 1992. 401 Mall Blvd., Suite 202A, Savannah, GA 31406. Phone: (912) 692-8000. Fax: (912) 692-0400. Licensee: Southern TV Corp.. Ownership: Dan L. and Betty Jo Johnson, 42.5%. (acq 6-3-98; $3.2 million). Network: UPN. Washington Atty: Irwin, Campbell & Tannenwald.
Key Personnel:
Dan L. Johnson . . . . . CEO, chmn & pres
Charles E. Robb . . . . . CFO
Jo Johnson . . . . . exec VP
Fred Pierce . . . . . gen mgr

WJCL—Analog channel: 22. Digital channel: 23. On air date: July 18, 1970. 10001 Abercorn St., Savannah, GA 31406. Phone: (912) 925-0022. Fax: (912) 921-2235. E-mail: comments@wjcl.com. Web Site: www.abc22tv.com. Licensee: Piedmont Television of Savannah License LLC. Group owner: Piedmont Television Holdings LLC (acq 12-8-99; grpsl). Network: ABC. Washington Atty: Cohn & Marks. News staff: 14; News: 5 hrs wkly.
Key Personnel:
Paul Brissette . . . . . CEO
Mitchell Maund . . . . . gen mgr
Dave German . . . . . opns mgr
Jennifer Burns . . . . . natl sls mgr
Kurt Hetager . . . . . prom dir & pub affrs dir
Michael Sullivan. . . . . news dir
Ed Youmans . . . . . chief of engrg

***WJWJ-TV**—Analog channel: 16. On air date: Sept 19, 1976. Box 1165, Beaufort, SC 29901. 925 Ribaut Rd., Beaufort, SC 29902. Phone: (843) 524-0808. Fax: (843) 524-1016. E-mail: wjwj@hargray.com. Web Site: www.wjwj.org. Licensee: South Carolina ETV Commission. Network: PBS. News staff: 6; News: 2.5 hrs wkly.
Key Personnel:
John Brunelli. . . . stn mgr, adv mgr, progmg mgr & pub affrs dir
Juan Singleton . . . . . news dir
Mike Milburn . . . . . chief of engrg

WSAV-TV—Analog channel: 3. On air date: Feb 1, 1956. 1430 E. Victory Dr., Savannah, GA 31404. Phone: (912) 651-0300. Fax: (912) 651-0304. Web Site: www.wsav.com. Licensee: Media General Broadcasting Inc. Group owner: Media General Broadcast Group (acq 7-25-97; grpsl). Network: NBC. Washington Atty: Dow, Lohnes & Albertson.
Key Personnel:
Drew Rhodes . . . . . CFO & gen sls mgr
Jim Berman . . . . . VP & gen mgr
Tara Midkiff . . . . . natl sls mgr
Kris Hummer . . . . . mktg dir
Dave Stagnitto . . . . . progmg dir
Kevin Brennan . . . . . news dir
Jim Stembridge. . . . . chief of engrg

WTGS—Analog channel: 28. On air date: Sept 1, 1985. 10001 Abercorn St., Savannah, GA 31406. Phone: (912) 925-2287. Fax: (912) 925-7026. E-mail: ssimonson@wjcl.com. Web Site: www.fox28tv.com. Licensee: Bluenose Broadcasting of Savannah L.L.C.. Ownership: Stephen C. Brissette (acq 10-31-01). Network: Fox. Washington Atty: Goldberg, Godles, Wiener & Wright. News: 5 hrs wkly.
Key Personnel:
Mitchell Maund . . . . . gen mgr
Stephen C. Brissette . . . . . pres & gen mgr
Dave German . . . . . opns mgr
Jennifer Burns . . . . . natl sls mgr
Bernie Farris. . . . . rgnl sls mgr
Kurt Hetager . . . . . prom mgr & pub affrs dir
Michael Sullivan. . . . . news dir
Chris Schmidt . . . . . chief of engrg

WTOC-TV—Analog channel: 11. On air date: Feb 14, 1954. Box 8086, Savannah, GA 31412. 11 The News Place, Savannah, GA 31405. Phone: (912) 234-1111. Fax: (912) 238-5133. Web Site: www.wtoc.com. Licensee: Raycom America License Subsidiary LLC. Group owner: Raycom Media Inc. (acq 4-15-97; grpsl). Network: CBS. Rep: Harrington, Righter & Parsons. Washington Atty: Gardner, Carton & Douglas.
Key Personnel:
William Cathcart . . . . . VP & gen mgr
Craig Harney . . . . . opns mgr & progmg dir
Randy Peltier . . . . . gen sls mgr

Broadcasting & Cable Yearbook 2006

B-34

Jim Clayton . . . natl sls mgr
Kate Freeman . . . mktg mgr & prom dir
Larry Silbermann . . . news dir
Neil Pedersen . . . chief of engrg

***WVAN-TV**—Analog channel: 9. On air date: Sept 16, 1963. Box 367, 86 Vandiver St., Pembroke, GA 31321-0367. Phone: (912) 653-4996. Fax: (800) 222-6006. Web Site: www.gpb.org. Licensee: Georgia Public Telecommunications Commission. Network: PBS.

Thomasville

see Tallahassee, FL-Thomasville, GA market

Toccoa

see Greenville-Spartanburg, SC-Asheville, NC-Anderson, SC market

Valdosta

see Tallahassee, FL-Thomasville, GA market

Waycross

see Jacksonville, FL market

Hawaii

Hilo

KGMD-TV—Analog channel: 9. Digital channel: 8. On air date: May 15, 1955. c/o KGMB, 1534 Kapiolani Blvd., Honolulu, HI 96814. Phone: (808) 973-5462. Fax: (808) 941-8153. Fax: (808) 941-9889 (news). E-mail: kgmbnews@pixi.com. Web Site: www.kgmb.com. Licensee: Emmis Television License LLC. Group owner: Emmis Communications Corp. (acq 9-25-2000; grpsl). Network: CBS.

KHAW-TV—Analog channel: 11. Digital channel: 21. On air date: Nov 27, 1961. c/o KHON-TV, 88 Piikoi St., Honolulu, HI 96814. Phone: (808) 591-2222. Fax: (808) 591-9085. E-mail: khan@khon.emmis.com. Web Site: www.khon.com. Licensee: Emmis Television License LLC. Group owner: Emmis Communications Corp. (acq 8-98; grpsl). Network: Fox. Washington Atty: Gardner, Carton & Douglas. News staff: 45; News: 25 hrs wkly.
Key Personnel:
Rick Blangiardi . . . gen mgr
Rick Langardy . . . stn mgr
Stephen Hiromoto . . . gen sls mgr & natl sls mgr
Cheryl Oncea . . . rgnl sls mgr
Linda Brock . . . mktg dir, mktg mgr & prom dir
Jamie Inayoshi . . . progmg dir & progmg mgr
Dan Dennison . . . news dir
Kenny Elcock . . . engrg dir & chief of engrg

KHBC-TV—Analog channel: 2. On air date: Aug 22, 1983. c/o KHNL, 150-B Puuhale Rd., Honolulu, HI 96819. Phone: (808) 847-3246. Fax: (808) 845-3616. Web Site: www.khnl.com. Licensee: Raycom National Inc. Group owner: Raycom Media Inc. (acq 9-2-99; grpsl). Network: NBC. Washington Atty: Baraff, Koerner, Olender & Hochberg.
Key Personnel:
John Fink . . . pres, VP & gen mgr
Stuart Chang . . . gen sls mgr
Dan Chinn . . . natl sls mgr
Mike Langley . . . mktg dir & prom dir
Dan Schmidt . . . progmg dir
Sue Levine . . . news dir
Maelee Buenconsejo . . . pub affrs dir
Keith Aotaki . . . engrg dir

KHVO—Analog channel: 13. Digital channel: 18. On air date: May 15, 1960. 801 S. King St., Honolulu, HI 96813. Phone: (808) 535-0400. Licensee: Hearst-Argyle Stations Inc. Group owner: Hearst-Argyle Stations Inc. (acq 7-16-97; grpsl). Network: ABC.

KWHH—Analog channel: 14. On air date: Oct 1, 1989. 1188 Bishop St., Suite 502, Honolulu, HI 96813. Phone: (808) 538-1414. Fax: (808) 526-0326. E-mail: kwhe@lesea.com. Web Site: www.lesea.com. Licensee: Le Sea Broadcasting Corp. Group owner: (group owner; acq 10-1-89; $8,277; 12-26-89). Rep: Landin. Washington Atty: Gardner, Carton & Douglas.

Honolulu, HI (DMA 71)

***KAAH-TV**—Analog channel: 26. On air date: Dec 23, 1982. 1152 Smith St., Honolulu, HI 96817. Phone: (808) 521-5826. Fax: (808) 599-6238. E-mail: tbnkaahtv26@hotmail.com. Web Site: www.tbn.org. Licensee: Trinity Christian Center of Santa Ana Inc. dba Trinity Broadcasting Network. Group owner: Trinity Broadcasting Network (acq 7-1-00; grpsl). Washington Atty: Colby May.
Key Personnel:
Paul F. Crouch . . . pres
Paul Crouch Jr. . . . exec VP
Jan Crouch . . . VP & progmg VP
Cheryl Rzonca . . . gen mgr & pub affrs dir
Rod Henke . . . gen sls mgr & adv VP
Ben Miller . . . engrg VP

***KALO**—Analog channel: 38. On air date: 2000. Box 8969, Honolulu, HI 96830. Phone: (808) 596-8897. Fax: (808) 591-1250. Licensee: Pacifica Broadcasting Co.

KBFD—Analog channel: 32. On air date: Mar 7, 1986. Century Sq., 1188 Bishop St., Honolulu, HI 96813. Phone: (808) 521-8066. Fax: (808) 521-5233. Web Site: www.kbfd.com. Licensee: Allen Broadcasting Corp.. Ownership: Kea Sung Chung, 65%; Ok Soon Chung, 10%; Jaeh Hoon Chung, 15%; June Ho Chung, 10%. (acq 1-7-86; $35,000; 12-16-85). Washington Atty: Wilkinson, Barker, Knauer L.L.P.. News staff: 4; News: 6 hrs wkly.
Key Personnel:
Kea Sung Chung . . . CEO & pres
June Ho Chung . . . exec VP

KFVE—Analog channel: 5. On air date: Feb 7, 1988. 315 Sand Island, Access Rd., Honolulu, HI 96819. 150 B Puuhale Rd., Honolulu, HI 96819. Phone: (808) 847-3246. Phone: (808) 847-1112. Fax: (808) 847-3298. E-mail: news8@khnl.com. Web Site: www.k5thehometeam.com. Licensee: Raycom National Inc. Group owner: Raycom Media Inc. (acq 12-28-99). Network: WB. Washington Atty: Brown, Nietert & Kaufman. News: 3 hrs wkly.
Key Personnel:
John Fink . . . VP & gen mgr
Stuart Chang . . . gen sls mgr
Michael Langley . . . prom mgr
Dan Schmidt . . . progmg dir
Sue Levine . . . news dir
Maelee Buenconsejo . . . pub affrs dir
Keith Aotaki . . . chief of engrg

KGMB—Analog channel: 9. Digital channel: 22. On air date: Dec 1, 1962. 1534 Kapiolani Blvd., Honolulu, HI 96814. Phone: (808) 973-5462. Fax: (808) 941-8153. E-mail: kgmbnews@pixi.com. Web Site: www.kgmb.com. Licensee: Emmis Television License LLC. Group owner: Emmis Communications Corp. (acq 9-25-2000; grpsl). Network: CBS. Rep: Harrington, Righter & Parsons.
Key Personnel:
Rick Blangiardi . . . gen mgr
Phyllis Kihara . . . gen sls mgr
Tauna Lange . . . news dir

***KHET**—Analog channel: 11. On air date: Apr 15, 1966. 2350 Dole St., Honolulu, HI 96822. Box 11599, Honolulu, HI 96822. Phone: (808) 973-1000. Fax: (808) 973-1090. Web Site: www.khet.org. Licensee: Hawaii Public Broadcasting Authority. Network: PBS. Washington Atty: Wilkes, Artis, Hedrick & Lane.

KHNL—Analog channel: 13. On air date: July 4, 1962. 150 B. Puuhale Rd., Honolulu, HI 96819. Phone: (808) 847-3246. Fax: (808) 845-3616. E-mail: news8@khnl.com. Web Site: www.khnl.com. Licensee: Raycom National Inc. Group owner: Raycom Media Inc. (acq 9-2-99; grpsl). Network: NBC. Rep: TeleRep. Washington Atty: Covington & Burling. News staff: 40; News: 168 hrs wkly.
Key Personnel:
John Fink . . . VP & gen mgr
Stuart Chang . . . sls dir
Dan Chinn . . . natl sls mgr
Mike Langley . . . mktg mgr & prom mgr
Dan Schmidt . . . progmg dir
Sue Levine . . . news dir
Keith Aotaki . . . engrg dir

KHON-TV—Analog channel: 2. Digital channel: 8. On air date: Dec 15, 1952. 88 Piikoi St., Honolulu, HI 96814. Phone: (808) 591-2222. Fax: (808) 591-9085. E-mail: khon@khon.emmis.com. Web Site: www.khon.com. Licensee: Emmis Television License LLC. Group owner: Emmis Communications Corp. (acq 8-98; grpsl). Network: Fox. Washington Atty: Gardner, Carton & Douglas. News staff: 45; News: 25 hrs wkly.
Key Personnel:
Kent Baker . . . VP
Rick Blangiardi . . . gen mgr
Rick Langardy . . . gen mgr & stn mgr
Steve Hiromoto . . . gen sls mgr
Cheryl Oncea . . . rgnl sls mgr
Linda Brock . . . mktg dir
Jamie Inayoshi . . . progmg mgr
Dan Dennison . . . news dir
Kenny Elcock . . . engrg dir

KIKU—Analog channel: 20. Digital channel: 19. On air date: Dec 30, 1983. 737 Bishop St., Suite 1430, Honolulu, HI 96813. Phone: (808) 847-2021. Fax: (808) 841-3326. Web Site: www.kikutv.com. Licensee: KHLS Inc. Group owner: Asian Media Group (acq 1-18-01; $165 million cash. for 69.4%). Network: UPN. Washington Atty: Leventhal, Senter & Lerman.
Key Personnel:
Jon Yasuda . . . pres
Jason Hagiwara . . . stn mgr
Bill Daubner . . . opns dir
Phyllis Kihara . . . gen mgr & progmg mgr
Gail Oshita . . . chief of engrg

KITV—Analog channel: 4. Digital channel: 40. On air date: Apr 16, 1954. 801 S. King St., Honolulu, HI 96813. Phone: (808) 535-0400. Fax: (808) 536-8777. Web Site: www.thehawaiichannel.com. Licensee: Hearst-Argyle Stations Inc. Group owner: Hearst-Argyle Television Inc. (acq 7-16-97; grpsl). Network: ABC. Washington Atty: Brooks, Pierce, McLendon, Humphrey & Leonard. News staff: 40; News: 20 hrs wkly.

KKAI—Analog channel: 50.Not on air, target date: unknown: 3901 Hwy. 121, Bedford, TX 76021. Phone: (817) 571-1229. Fax: (817) 571-7458. Permittee: Kailua Television LLC.

KMGT—Analog channel: 56. On air date: 2004. c/o Donald F. Laidlaw, 2525 Date St., Suite 2503, Honolulu, HI 96826. Phone: (808) 259-3477. Permittee: Waimanalo Television Partners.

***KWBN**—Analog channel: 44. On air date: 2000. 3901 Hwy. 121, Bedford, TX 76021. Phone: (817) 571-1229. Fax: (817) 571-7458. Web Site: www.daystar.com. Licensee: Ho'ona'auao Community Television Inc.

KWHE—Analog channel: 14. On air date: Mar 7, 1988. Century Sq., 1188 Bishop St., Suite 502, Honolulu, HI 96813. Phone: (808) 538-1414. Fax: (808) 526-0326. E-mail: KWHE@lesea.com. Web Site: KWHE.com. Licensee: LeSea Broadcasting Corp. Group owner: (group owner; acq 8-15-86; $825,000; 6-16-86). Rep: Landin. Washington Atty: Gardner, Carton & Douglas.
Key Personnel:
Peter Sumrall . . . CEO
Anthony Hale . . . CFO
Tony Boquer . . . gen mgr
Stephen Agee . . . stn mgr
Mauro Pena . . . chief of engrg

Kailua-Kona

KLEI—Analog channel: 6. On air date: 1988. Box 8969, Honolulu, HI 96830. Phone: (808) 262-2000. Fax: (808) 254-1313. Licensee: Aina'e Co. Ltd. (acq 9-14-94; FTR: 9-26-94). Network: PAX TV.

Kaneohe

KPXO—Analog channel: 66. On air date: 1998. 875 Waimanu St., Suite 630, Honolulu, HI 96813. Phone: (808) 591-1275. Fax: (808) 591-1409. Web Site: www.paxhawaii.tv. Licensee: Paxson Hawaii License Inc. Group owner: Paxson Communications Corp. (acq 8-12-98; $6.9 million).

Wailuku

KAII-TV—Analog channel: 7. Digital channel: 36. On air date: Nov 17, 1958. 88 Piikoi St., Honolulu, HI 96814. Phone: (808) 591-2222. Fax: (808) 593-8479. E-mail: khon@khon.emmis.com. Web Site: www.khon.com.

Directory of Television Idaho

Licensee: Emmis Television License LLC. Group owner: Emmis Communications Corp. (acq 8-98; grpsl). Network: Fox. Washington Atty: Gardner, Carton & Douglas.
Key Personnel:
Rick Blangiardi . . . gen mgr
Rick Langardy . . . stn mgr
Stephen Hiramoto . . . gen sls mgr
Stephen Hiromoto . . . natl sls mgr
Cheryl Oncea . . . rgnl sls mgr
Linda Brock . . . mktg dir & prom dir
Jamie Inayoshi . . . progmg mgr
Dan Dennison . . . news dir
Jon Yoshimura . . . pub affrs dir
Kenny Elcock . . . engrg dir & chief of engrg

KGMV—Analog channel: 3. Digital channel: 24. On air date: Apr 24, 1955. c/o KGMB, 1534 Kapiolani Blvd., Honolulu, HI 96814. Phone: (808) 973-5462. Fax: (808) 941-8153. E-mail: kmbnews@pixi.com. Web Site: www.kgmb.com. Licensee: Emmis Television License LLC. Group owner: Emmis Communications Corp. (acq 9-25-2000; grpsl). Network: CBS.

KMAU—Analog channel: 12. Digital channel: 29. On air date: Nov 28, 1955. 801 S. King St., Honolulu, HI 96813. Phone: (808) 535-0400. Licensee: Hearst-Argyle Stations Inc. Group owner: Hearst-Argyle Television Inc. (acq 7-16-97; grpsl). Network: ABC.

***KMEB**—Analog channel: 10. On air date: Sept 22, 1966. 2350 Dole St., Honolulu, HI 96822. Box 11599, Honolulu, HI 96822. Phone: (808) 973-1000. Fax: (808) 973-1090. Web Site: www.knet.org. Licensee: Hawaii Public Broadcasting Authority. Network: PBS.

KOGG—Analog channel: 15. On air date: Aug 22, 1989. c/o KHNL, 150-B Puuhale Rd., Honolulu, HI 96819. Phone: (808) 847-3246. Fax: (808) 845-3616. Web Site: www.khnl.com. Licensee: Raycom National Inc. Group owner: Raycom Media Inc. (acq 9-2-99; grpsl). Network: NBC.
Key Personnel:
John Fink . . . pres, VP & gen mgr
Stuart Chang . . . gen sls mgr
Dan Chinn . . . natl sls mgr
Mike Langley . . . mktg dir & prom dir
Dan Schmidt . . . progmg dir
Sue Levine . . . news dir
Maelee Buenconsejo . . . pub affrs dir
Keith Aotaki . . . engrg dir

KWHM—Analog channel: 21. On air date: 1993. Century Square, 1188 Bishop St., Suite 502, Honolulu, HI 96813. Phone: (808) 538-1414. Fax: (808) 526-0326. Web Site: www.lesea.com. Licensee: Le Sea Broadcasting Corp. Group owner: (group owner) Rep: Landin. Washington Atty: Gardner, Carton & Douglas.
Key Personnel:
Peter Sumrall . . . CEO
Anthony Hale . . . CFO
Tony Boquer . . . gen mgr
Stephen Agee . . . stn mgr
Mauro Pena . . . chief of engrg

Idaho

Boise, ID (DMA 122)

***KAID**—Analog channel: 4. On air date: Dec 31, 1971. 1455 N. Orchard St., Boise, ID 83706. Phone: (208) 373-7220. Fax: (208) 373-7245. E-mail: idptv@idahoptv.org. Web Site: www.idahoptv.org. Licensee: Idaho State Board of Education. Network: PBS. Washington Atty: Fletcher, Heald & Hildreth. News staff: 5; News: 3 hrs wkly.
Key Personnel:
Peter Morrill . . . gen mgr
Kim Philipps . . . dev dir
Anne Peterson . . . prom mgr
Ron Pisaneschi . . . progmg dir
Bruce Reichert . . . news dir
Rich Van Genderen . . . engrg dir
Ted Poe . . . chief of engrg

KBCI-TV—Analog channel: 2. Digital channel: 28. On air date: Nov 26, 1953. Box 2, Boise, ID 83707. 140 N. 16th St., Boise, ID 83707. Phone: (208) 472-2222. Fax: (208) 472-2212. E-mail: comments@kbcitv.com. Web Site: www.kbcitv.com. Licensee: Fisher Broadcasting - Idaho TV L.L.C. Group owner: Fisher Broadcasting Company (acq 7-1-99; grpsl). Network: CBS. Rep: Katz Radio. Washington Atty: Shaw Pittman. News staff: 37; News: 15.5 hrs wkly.
Key Personnel:
Ben Tucker . . . CEO
Jeff Anderson . . . VP & gen mgr
Jeff Bishop . . . opns mgr
Steven Miller . . . news dir
Walt Baker . . . progmg dir & pub affrs dir

KIVI—(Nampa).Analog channel: 6. On air date: Feb 1, 1974. 1866 E. Chisholm Dr., Nampa, ID 83687. Phone: (208) 336-0500. Phone: (208) 336-6681. Fax: (208) 381-6682. Web Site: www.6onourside.com. Licensee: Journal Broadcast Corp. Group owner: Journal Communications Inc. (acq 11-15-2001). Network: ABC. Washington Atty: Dow, Lohnes & Albertson. News staff: 37; News: 16 hrs wkly.
Key Personnel:
Scott Eymer . . . VP & gen mgr
Ken Ritchie . . . sls dir & gen sls mgr
Fran Valentine . . . prom mgr
Brian Perkins . . . progmg dir & progmg mgr
Andy Apericio . . . news dir
Jerry Madsen . . . chief of engrg

KKJB—Analog channel: 39. On air date: 2005. Cocola Broadcasting Companies, 706 W. Herndon Ave., Fresno, CA 93650. Phone: (559) 435-7000. Fax: (559) 435-3201. Licensee: Boise Telecasters L.P. Group owner: Cocola Broadcasting Companies (acq 5-7-2004; $3 million. for CP).

KNIN-TV—Analog channel: 9. Digital channel: 10. On air date: 1993. 816 W. Bannock St., Suite 402, Boise, ID 83702. Phone: (208) 331-0909. Fax: (208) 344-0119. Web Site: www.knin.com. Licensee: Banks-Boise Inc. Group owner: Banks Broadcasting Inc. (acq 5-7-01). Network: UPN. Rep: Blair Television. Washington Atty: Covington & Burling.
Key Personnel:
Lyle Banks . . . CEO
Lyle Banks . . . pres & VP
Tom Keithly . . . natl sls mgr
Roger Ayers . . . rgnl sls mgr
Jim Stoner . . . prom mgr
Toni Gillette . . . progmg dir & progmg mgr
David Smith . . . chief of engrg

KTRV—Analog channel: 12. On air date: Oct 18, 1981. Box 1212, Nampa, ID 83653. 1 6th St. N., Monroe, ID 83687. Phone: (208) 466-1200. Fax: (208) 467-6958. Web Site: www.fox12news.com. Licensee: Idaho Independent Television Inc. Group owner: Block Communications Inc. (acq 4-23-85; $4.9 million;. FTR: 3-25-85). Network: Fox. Washington Atty: Dow, Lohnes & Albertson. News staff: 12; News: 3 hrs wkly.
Key Personnel:
Allan Block . . . chmn
Dave Huey . . . pres
Jim McKenna . . . CFO
Ed Crampton . . . opns mgr
Bruce Wetten . . . sls dir, natl sls mgr & natl sls mgr
Mary Shaner . . . prom mgr & pub affrs dir
Ricky Joseph . . . exec VP, VP, gen mgr, progmg dir & film buyer
Bob Jaundalderis . . . news dir
Kelly Cross . . . news dir
Lance Hankins . . . chief of engrg

KTVB—Analog channel: 7. Digital channel: 28. On air date: July 12, 1953. 5407 Fairview Ave., Boise, ID 83706. Phone: (208) 375-7277. Fax: (208) 378-1762. Web Site: www.ktvb.com. Licensee: KTVB-TV Inc. Group owner: Belo Corp., Broadcast Division (acq 1997; grpsl). Network: NBC. Rep: TeleRep. Washington Atty: Wiley, Rein & Fielding. News: 27 hrs wkly.
Key Personnel:
Douglas L. Armstrong . . . pres, progmg dir & film buyer
Douglas Armstrong . . . gen mgr
Paul Budell . . . opns mgr
Kristi Edmunds . . . gen sls mgr
Brad Bond . . . natl sls mgr
P.J. Laws . . . prom mgr
Mark Danielson . . . news dir
Sally Craven . . . pub affrs dir
Richard Strack . . . engrg dir

Coeur d'Alene

see Spokane, WA market

Idaho Falls-Pocatello, ID (DMA 164)

KFXP—Analog channel: 31. On air date: July 17, 1998. 902 E. Sherman St., Pocatello, ID 83201. Phone: (208) 232-6666. Fax: (208) 232-6678. Web Site: www.kpvi.com. Licensee: Compass Communications of Idaho Inc. Network: Fox.
Key Personnel:
Ralph Toddre . . . CFO
Bill Fouch . . . gen mgr
Steven Farrell . . . opns mgr

KIDK—Analog channel: 3. On air date: Dec 20, 1953. Box 1255 E. 17 th St., Idaho Falls, ID 83404. Phone: (208) 522-5100. Fax: (208) 522-5103. Web Site: www.kidk.com. Licensee: Fisher Broadcasting - S.E. Idaho TV L.L.C. Group owner: Fisher Broadcasting Company (acq 12-4-01 grpsl). Network: CBS. Rep: Katz Radio. Washington Atty: Shaw, Pittman. News staff: 20; News: 15 hrs wkly.
Key Personnel:
Gina Berger . . . dev dir
Terry Miller . . . news dir

KIFI-TV—Analog channel: 8. Digital channel: 9. On air date: Jan 21, 1961. Box 2148, Idaho Falls, ID 83401. Phone: (208) 525-2520. Fax: (208) 522-1930. Fax: (208) 529-2443 (news). E-mail: localnews8@aol.com. Web Site: www.localnews8.com. Licensee: NPG of Idaho Inc. Group owner: (group owner) (acq 6-15-2005; $12.5 million). Network: ABC. Washington Atty: Shaw Pittman LLP. News staff: 15; News: 30 hrs wkly.
Key Personnel:
David Bradley Jr. . . . pres
Rickie Brady . . . gen mgr
Monte Young . . . gen sls mgr

***KISU-TV**—Analog channel: 10. On air date: July 7, 1971. Campus Box 8111, Pocatello, ID 83209. Phone: (208) 282-2857. Fax: (208) 282-2848. E-mail: idptv@idptv.pbs.org. Web Site: www.idahoptv.org. Licensee: Idaho State Board of Education. Network: PBS.

KPIF—Analog channel: 15.Not on air, target date: unknown: KM Communications Inc., 3654 W. Jarvis Ave., Skokie, IL 60076. Phone: (847) 674-0864. Fax: (847) 674-9188. Permittee: Pocatello Channel 15 L.L.C.. Ownership: Myoung Hwa Bae, 100% (acq 12-1-03).

KPVI—(Pocatello).Analog channel: 6. On air date: Apr 26, 1974. Box 667, Pocatello, ID 83204. Phone: (208) 232-6666. Fax: (208) 233-6678. Web Site: www.kpvi.com. Licensee: Oregon Trail Broadcasting Co. Group owner: Sunbelt Communications Co. (acq 11-15-95). Network: NBC. Rep: Blair Television. News staff: 23; News: 17 hrs wkly.

Lewiston

see Spokane, WA market

Moscow

see Spokane, WA market

Pocatello

see Idaho Falls-Pocatello, ID market

Twin Falls, ID (DMA 191)

***KBGH**—Analog channel: 19. On air date: 1997. Box 1238, Twin Falls, ID 83303-1238. 315 Falls Ave., Twin Falls, ID 83301. Phone: (208) 736-3046. Fax: (208) 736-2188. Web Site: www.radio.boisestate.edu. Licensee: College of Southern Idaho.

KIDA—Analog channel: 5. On air date: 2003. Turner Enterprises, 3141 Beach View Ct., Las Vegas, NV 89117. Phone: (702) 256-8030. E-mail: mturnerco@aol.com. Licensee: Marcia T. Turner dba Turner Enterprises.

***KIPT**—Analog channel: 13. On air date: Jan 18, 1992. c/o KAID, 1455 N. Orchard St., Boise, ID 83706. Phone: (208) 373-7220. Fax: (208) 373-7245. E-mail: idptv@idahoptv.org. Web Site: www.idahoptv.org. Licensee: State Board of Education, State of Idaho. Network: PBS. Washington Atty: Fletcher, Heald & Hildreth.
Key Personnel:
Peter Morrill . . . gen mgr
Kim Philipps . . . dev dir
Anne Peterson . . . prom mgr
Ron Pisaneschi . . . progmg dir

Rich Van Genderen . . . . engrg dir
Ted Poe. . . . . chief of engrg

KMVT—Analog channel: 11. On air date: May 30, 1955. 1100 Blue Lakes Blvd. N., Twin Falls, ID 83301. Phone: (208) 733-1100. Fax: (208) 733-4649. Web Site: www.kmvt.com. Licensee: Neuhoff Family L.P. Group owner: (group owner; acq 8-3-2004; $17.3 million).. Network: CBS. Rep: Continental Television Sales. Washington Atty: Cohn & Marks. News staff: 14; News: 10 hrs wkly.
Key Personnel:
Lee Wagner. . . . . gen mgr & progmg dir
Mason Diedrich . . . . opns mgr
Lisa Collins . . . . gen sls mgr
Joe Martin . . . . news dir

KXTF—Analog channel: 35. On air date: Jan 31, 1989. 1061 Blue Lakes Blvd. N., Twin Falls, ID 83301. Phone: (208) 733-0035. Fax: (208) 733-0160. Licensee: Sunbelt Broadcasting Co. Group owner: Sunbelt Communications Co. Network: Fox. Washington Atty: Hamel & Park. News: 2 hrs wkly.
Key Personnel:
Bill Fouch . . . . gen mgr
Joe Nielsen. . . . . stn mgr

Illinois

Bloomington

see Peoria-Bloomington, IL market

Carbondale

see Paducah, KY-Cape Girardeau, MO-Harrisburg-Mount Vernon, IL market

Champaign & Springfield-Decatur, IL (DMA 82)

WAND—Analog channel: 17. On air date: Aug 16, 1953. 904 Southside Dr., Decatur, IL 62521. Phone: (217) 424-2500. Fax: (217) 424-2583. Web Site: www.wandtv.com. Licensee: WAND Television Inc. Group owner: LIN Television Corporation (acq 2-27-95; FTR: 5-22-95). Network: ABC. Washington Atty: Schwartz, Woods & Miller.
Key Personnel:
T. J. Vaughan. . . . . pres & gen mgr
Larry Katt . . . . sls dir
Carol Thomas . . . . prom mgr
Tracey Cole . . . . progmg dir
Jon McCall. . . . . news dir
Ken Frye . . . . pub affrs dir
Hal Campbell. engrg dir

WBUI—Analog channel: 23. On air date: May 14, 1984. 2510 Pkwy Ct., Decatur, IL 62526. Phone: (217) 428-2323. Fax: (217) 428-6455. E-mail: promotions@wb23tv.com. Web Site: www.wb23tv.com. Licensee: Acme TV Licenses of Illinois L.L.C. Group owner: Acme Communications Inc. (acq 6-14-99; $13.3 million).. Network: WB. Rep: MMT.
Key Personnel:
Angie Cardinal . . . . CFO
Bill Snider. . . . . VP & gen mgr
Dean Davidson. . . . . opns mgr

WCCU—Analog channel: 27. Digital channel: 26. On air date: 1987. 201 W. Springfield, Champaign, IL 61820. Phone: (217) 403-1002. Fax: (217) 403-1007. Web Site: www.wccutv.com. Licensee: Urbana-Champaign Broadcasting Partners. Group owner: Bahakel Communications (acq 7-20-92). Network: Fox.

WCFN—Analog channel: 49. On air date: 1987. Box 20, 509 S. Neil St., Champaign, IL 61824-0020. Phone: (217) 356-8333. Fax: (217) 373-3680. E-mail: vpgm@wcia.com. Web Site: www.wcia.com. Licensee: Nexstar Finance Inc. Group owner: Nexstar Broadcasting Group Inc. (acq 5-19-00; grpsl). Network: UPN. Rep: Blair Television. Washington Atty: Drinker-Biddle-Reath.
Key Personnel:
Perry Chester . . . . VP, gen mgr & progmg dir
Ross Hamilton. . . . . stn mgr
Tammy Graham-Dietert . . . . sls dir
David Nagel . . . . natl sls mgr
Ed Tudor . . . . prom dir
Jim Gee. . . . . news dir
Brad Hampton . . . . engrg dir

WCIA—Analog channel: 3. On air date: Nov 14, 1953. Box 20, 509 S. Neil, Champaign, IL 61824-0020. Phone: (217) 356-8333. Fax: (217) 373-3680. E-mail: webmaster@wcia.com. Web Site: www.wcia.com. Licensee: Nexstar Finance Inc. Group owner: Nexstar Broadcasting Group Inc. (acq 5-19-00; grpsl). Network: CBS. Washington Atty: Covington & Burling.

***WEIU-TV**—Analog channel: 51. On air date: July 1, 1986. Radio & TV Ctr., Eastern Illinois Univ., Charleston, IL 61920. Phone: (217) 581-5956. Fax: (217) 581-6650. Licensee: Eastern Illinois University. Network: PBS. Washington Atty: Cohn & Marks. News staff: 25; News: 3 hrs wkly.
Key Personnel:
Rick Sailors . . . . gen mgr
Amanda Gibson. . . . . dev dir & sls dir
Ke'an Rogers. . . . . prom dir, prom mgr & adv mgr
Linda Kingery . . . . progmg mgr
Kelly Runyon . . . . news dir
Rodd Boyken . . . . pub affrs dir
Kevin Armstrong . . . . engrg dir

WICD—Analog channel: 15. On air date: Apr 24, 1959. 250 S. Country Fair Dr., Champaign, IL 61821. Phone: (217) 351-8500. Fax: (217) 351-6056. Web Site: www.wicd15.com. Licensee: WICD License L.L.C. Group owner: Sinclair Broadcast Group Inc. (acq 7-2-99; $81 million with WICS(TV) Springfield). Network: NBC. Rep: Katz Radio. Washington Atty: Wiley, Rein & Fielding. News staff: 20; News: 17 hrs wkly.
Key Personnel:
David Smith. CEO & pres
Jack Connors. . . . . gen mgr
Gary Hackler . . . . stn mgr
Alvin Francis. . . . . opns mgr
Johnny Faith. . . . . gen sls mgr
Alan Edwards . . . . rgnl sls mgr
Holly Jones . . . . prom mgr
Ray Wilck . . . . news dir
Doug Quick . . . . pub affrs dir
Del Parks. . . . . engrg VP
Harvey Arnold . . . . engrg dir
Jim Wnek . . . . engrg mgr

WICS—Analog channel: 20. On air date: Oct 30, 1953. Box 3920, 2680 E. Cook St., Springfield, IL 62703. Phone: (217) 753-5620. Fax: (217) 753-8177. Licensee: WICS Licensee L.L.C. Group owner: Sinclair Broadcast Group Inc. (acq 7-1-99). Network: NBC. Washington Atty: Dow, Lohnes & Albertson. News staff: 32; News: 22 hrs wkly.
Key Personnel:
Jack Connors . . . . gen mgr & film buyer
Jim Waldeck . . . . opns dir
Johnny Faith. . . . . gen sls mgr
Cindy Larsen . . . . natl sls mgr
Steve Cramblit . . . . rgnl sls mgr
Mark Wilson . . . . prom dir & prom mgr
Alaina Marx . . . . progmg dir & progmg mgr
Susan Finzen. . . . . news dir
Jen Tibbs . . . . pub affrs dir
John Wamsley . . . . chief of engrg

***WILL-TV**—Analog channel: 12. On air date: Aug 1, 1955. Campbell Hall for Public Telecommunications, 300 N. Goodwin Ave., Urbana, IL 61801-2316. Phone: (217) 333-1070. Fax: (217) 244-6386. Web Site: www.will.uiuc.edu. Licensee: University of Illinois Board of Trustees. Network: PBS. Washington Atty: Dow, Lohnes & Albertson.
Key Personnel:
Dr. Donald Mullally. . . . . gen mgr
Carl Caldwell . . . . stn mgr
Deborah Day . . . . dev dir
Kate Dobrovolny . . . . prom VP
David Thiel. . . . . progmg dir
Ed West . . . . chief of engrg

WRSP-TV—Analog channel: 55. Digital channel: 44. On air date: June 1, 1979. 3003 Old Rochester Rd., Springfield, IL 62703. Phone: (217) 523-8855. Fax: (217) 523-4410. Web Site: www.wrsptv.com. Licensee: Springfield Independent Television Inc. Group owner: Bahakel Communications (acq 7-20-92). Network: Fox.
Key Personnel:
Beverly Bahakel-Poston . . . . pres
Jim Babb. . . . . VP
David A. Harbert . . . . gen mgr
Jeri Waldeck . . . . opns dir
Greg Watkins . . . . natl sls mgr
Tim Klasinski . . . . mktg dir
Ken Theobald . . . . chief of engrg

***WSEC**—Analog channel: 14. On air date: Aug 21, 1984. Box 6248, Springfield, IL 62708. Phone: (217) 483-7887. Fax: (217) 483-1112. Licensee: West Central Illinois Educational Telecommunication Corp. Network: PBS. Washington Atty: Dow, Lohnes & Albertson.
Key Personnel:
Jerold Gruebel. . . . . CEO, pres & gen mgr
Richard Plotkin . . . . opns VP, opns dir & engrg VP
Dawn Kuhn . . . . dev dir
Jack Dunn . . . . sls dir
Stephanie Cole . . . . progmg dir & progmg mgr
Gus Wills. . . . . engrg mgr

Chicago (DMA 3)

WBBM-TV—Analog channel: 2. Digital channel: 3. On air date: August 1940. 630 N. McClurg Ct., Chicago, IL 60611. Phone: (312) 202-2222. Fax: (312) 943-7193. Web Site: www.cbs.com. Licensee: CBS Broadcasting Inc. Group owner: Viacom Television Stations Group (acq 2-9-53; $6 million;. FTR: 2-16-53). Network: CBS. Rep: CBS Spot Sales.
Key Personnel:
Joseph Ahern. . . . . pres & gen mgr
Fran Preston . . . . VP, stn mgr & progmg dir
Joe Kopesky . . . . opns dir
Jim Sullivan . . . . sls dir
Vickie Bouchard. . . . . prom dir & adv dir
Shawnelle Richie . . . . pub affrs dir
Tim Schnecke . . . . engrg dir
Mike Wilken. . . . . engrg mgr

WCIU-TV—Analog channel: 26. On air date: Feb 6, 1964. 26 N. Halsted St., Chicago, IL 60661. Phone: (312) 705-2600. Fax: (312) 705-2656. Web Site: www.wciu.com. Licensee: WCIU-TV L.P. Group owner: Weigel Broadcasting Co. Washington Atty: Cohn & Marks.
Key Personnel:
Howard Shapiro . . . . CEO
Norman Shapiro . . . . pres
Neal Sabin. . . . . exec VP
Fred Weintraub . . . . stn mgr
Brad Lesak . . . . gen sls mgr
Kyle Walker . . . . chief of engrg

WCPX—Analog channel: 38. Digital channel: 43. On air date: May 31, 1976. 454 N. Columbus Dr., Chicago, IL 60611. Phone: (312) 836-5605. Fax: (312) 595-9813. Web Site: www.pax.tv. Licensee: Paxson Chicago License Inc. Group owner: Paxson Communications Corp. (acq 8-11-98; $120 million. including all interest in KWOK(TV) Novato, CA and other telecasting progmg rights) Washington Atty: Dow, Lohnes & Albertson.

WFLD—Analog channel: 32. Digital channel: 31. On air date: Jan 6, 1966. 205 N. Michigan Ave., Chicago, IL 60601. Phone: (312) 565-5532. Fax: (312) 819-0420. Web Site: www.foxchicago.com. Licensee: Fox Television Stations Inc. Group owner: (group owner; acq 11-14-86; grpsl). Network: Fox.
Key Personnel:
Debbie Carpenter . . . . gen mgr
Deborah Juarez-West . . . . news dir

WGBO-TV—Analog channel: 66. On air date: Sept 17, 1981. 541 N. Fairbanks Ct., Suite 1100, Chicago, IL 60611. Phone: (312) 670-1000. Fax: (312) 494-6492. Web Site: www.univision.com. Licensee: Combined Broadcasting of Chicago Inc. Group owner: Univision Communications Inc. (acq 2-27-95; 5-22-95). Network: Univision (Spanish). Washington Atty: Shaw Pittman LLP. News staff: 18.
Key Personnel:
Bert Medina . . . . sr VP & stn mgr
Vincent Cordero . . . . VP & gen mgr

WGN-TV—Analog channel: 9. On air date: Apr 5, 1948. 2501 Bradley W. Pl., Watertown, IL 60618-4718. Phone: (773) 528-2311. Fax: (773) 528-6857 (main). Web Site: wgntv.trb.com (Chicago). Licensee: WGN Continental Broadcasting Co. Group owner: Tribune Broadcasting Co., see Cross-Ownership Network: WB. Rep: TeleRep. Washington Atty: Sidley & Austin. News staff: 88; News: 32 hrs wkly.
Key Personnel:
Dennis Fitzsimons . . . . CEO & chmn
Pat Mullen. . . . . pres
Peter Walker . . . . sr VP
Tom Ehlmann . . . . VP & gen mgr
Dominic Mancuso . . . . stn mgr
Marc Schacher. . . . . dev VP & progmg VP
John Hendricks. . . . . sls VP
Marty Wilke . . . . sls dir
Carla Dregnolato . . . . natl sls mgr
Marissa Rudman . . . . natl sls mgr
Errol Gerber. . . . . rgnl sls mgr
Jeff Shaw . . . . rgnl sls mgr
Joanne Stern . . . . prom dir
Ken Reiner. . . . . progmg dir
Tom Boyd. . . . . progmg mgr
Greg Caputo . . . . news dir
Merri Dee. . . . . pub affrs dir

Ira Goldstone . . . . . engrg VP
Marc Drazin . . . . . engrg dir

WJYS—Analog channel: 62. Digital channel: 36. On air date: Mar 2, 1991. 18600 S. Oak Park Ave., Tinley Park, IL 60477. Phone: (708) 633-0001. Fax: (708) 633-0040. Licensee: Jovon Broadcasting Corp.

WLS-TV—Analog channel: 7. Digital channel: 52. On air date: Sept 17, 1948. 190 N. State St., Chicago, IL 60601. Phone: (312) 750-7777. Fax: (312) 750-7015. Web Site: www.abc7chicago.com. Licensee: WLS Television Inc. Group owner: ABC Inc. (acq 6-27-86; grpsl; 7-15-85). Network: ABC. News staff: 151; News: 8 hrs wkly.

Key Personnel:
Emily L. Barr . . . . . pres & gen mgr
Joseph Trimarco . . . . . opns mgr
Ed Pearson . . . . . gen sls mgr
John Idler . . . . . natl sls mgr
Nancy Sergey . . . . . rgnl sls mgr
Chris Reller . . . . . mktg mgr
Tom Hebel . . . . . prom dir & adv dir
Ellen Crawley . . . . . progmg dir
Fran Preston . . . . . film buyer
Jennifer Graves . . . . . news dir
Diana Palomar . . . . . pub affrs dir
Kal Hassan . . . . . engrg dir

WMAQ-TV—Analog channel: 5. On air date: January 1948. 454 N. Columbus Dr., Chicago, IL 60611-5555. Phone: (312) 836-5555. Web Site: www.nbc5.com. Licensee: NBC Telemundo License Co. Group owner: NBC TV Stations Division (acq 6-5-86). Network: NBC. Rep: NBC TV Stations Sales.

WPWR-TV—(Gary).IN Analog channel: 50. On air date: Jan 18, 1987. 205 N. Michigan Ave., Chicago, IL 60614. Phone: (219) 882-1507. Fax: (312) 819-0421. Licensee: Fox Television Stations Inc. Group owner: (group owner; acq 8-21-02; $425 million).. Network: UPN. Washington Atty: Holland & Knight.

WSNS—Analog channel: 44. On air date: Apr 5, 1970. 454 N. Columbus Dr., Chicago, IL 60611. Phone: (312) 836-3000. Fax: (312) 836-3034. Web Site: www.telemundochicago.com. Licensee: NBC Telemundo License Co. Group owner: Telemundo Group Inc. (acq 4-12-2002; grpsl). Network: Telemundo (Spanish). Washington Atty: Cohn & Marks. News staff: 12; News: 5 hrs wkly.

***WTTW**—Analog channel: 11. Digital channel: 47. On air date: Sept 6, 1955. 5400 N. St. Louis Ave., Chicago, IL 60625. Phone: (773) 583-5000. Fax: (773) 583-3046. Web Site: www.networkchicago.com. Licensee: Window to the World Communications Inc. Network: PBS. Washington Atty: Schwartz, Woods & Miller. News staff: 15; News: 5 hrs wkly.

Key Personnel:
Daniel Schmidt. . . . . CEO & pres
Reese Marcusson. . . . . CFO & opns VP
Farrell Frentress. . . . . exec VP
Randy King . . . . . exec VP
Jerry Glover . . . . . sr VP
Donna Davies . . . . . dev VP
Mary Beth Hughes. . . . . mktg VP
Joanie Bayhack . . . . . prom dir
Dan Rozkuszka . . . . . prom mgr
Anders Yocom . . . . . progmg VP
Daniel Soles . . . . . progmg dir
Phil Ponce. . . . . news dir & pub affrs dir
V.J. MacAleer. . . . . news dir
Larry Ocker . . . . . engrg VP

WWTO-TV—Analog channel: 35. On air date: Dec 1, 1986. 420 E. Stevenson Rd., Ottawa, IL 61350. Phone: (815) 434-2700. Fax: (815) 434-2458. Licensee: Trinity Broadcasting Network. Group owner: (group owner; acq 7-1-00; grpsl). Washington Atty: Joseph E. Dunne III.

Key Personnel:
Paul Crouch . . . . . pres
Marlene Zepeda . . . . . gen mgr & stn mgr
Emily Young. . . . . pub affrs dir
Charlie Boyd . . . . . chief of engrg

WXFT-TV—Analog channel: 60. On air date: Apr 20, 1982. 541 N. Fairbanks Ct. 9th Fl., Chicago, IL 60611. Phone: (312) 670-1000. Fax: (312) 467-5821. Licensee: TeleFutura Chicago LLC. Group owner: Univision Communications Inc. (acq 5-21-01; grpsl). Network: TeleFutura (Spanish). Washington Atty: Wiley, Rein & Fielding.

Key Personnel:
Vincent Cordero. . . . . gen mgr
Andrew Wallace . . . . . gen sls mgr
Brian Walsh . . . . . natl sls mgr
Don Daboub. . . . . rgnl sls mgr
Juanita Davis . . . . . mktg dir
Melanie Bretts . . . . . mktg mgr
Edgar Vargas. . . . . prom dir
Charles Fisher . . . . . chief of engrg

***WYCC**—Analog channel: 20. On air date: Sept 20, 1965. 7500 S. Pulaski Rd., Chicago, IL 60652. Phone: (773) 838-7878. Fax: (773) 581-2071. E-mail: comments@wycc.org. Web Site: www.wycc.org. Licensee: College Dist. #508, County of Cook. (acq 11-3-81). Network: PBS. Washington Atty: Dow, Lohnes & Albertson.

Key Personnel:
Maria Moore . . . . . gen mgr
Arthur Wood . . . . . stn mgr, opns VP & prom dir
James Belcher . . . . . rgnl sls mgr
James Brown . . . . . prom mgr
Cynthia Syperek . . . . . progmg mgr
Larry Eskridge . . . . . engrg VP
Tc Hill . . . . . chief of engrg

***WYIN**—Analog channel: 56. On air date: Nov 15, 1987. 8625 Indiana Pl., Merrillville, IN 46410. Phone: (219) 756-5656. Fax: (219) 755-4312. Web Site: www.wyin.tv.. Stn video via satellite: Echo Star Licensee: Northwest Indiana Public Broadcasting Inc. Network: PBS.

Key Personnel:
Thomas Carroll . . . . . CEO & pres
Renee Golas . . . . . opns mgr & rgnl sls mgr
Katherine Prochno . . . . . dev mgr & progmg dir
Kevin Maci. . . . . news dir
Carmen Segura . . . . . pub affrs dir
Henry Ruhwiedel . . . . . chief of engrg

Decatur

see Champaign & Springfield-Decatur, IL market

East St. Louis

see St. Louis, MO market

Harrisburg

see Paducah, KY-Cape Girardeau, MO-Harrisburg-Mount Vernon, IL market

Marion

see Paducah, KY-Cape Girardeau, MO-Harrisburg-Mount Vernon, IL market

Moline

see Davenport, IA-Rock Island-Moline, IL market

Mount Vernon

see Paducah, KY-Cape Girardeau, MO-Harrisburg-Mount Vernon, IL market

Olney

see Terre Haute, IN market

Peoria-Bloomington, IL (DMA 117)

WAOE—Analog channel: 59.Not on air, target date: unknown: 331 Fulton St., Suite 100, Peoria, CA 61602. Phone: (309) 674-5900. Fax: (309) 674-5959. Licensee: Four Seasons Peoria LLC.. Ownership: Venture Technologies Group LLC, 48.5%; Malibu Broadcasting LLC, 48.5%; and Paul H. Koplin, 3% (acq 9-15-99).

WEEK-TV—Analog channel: 25. On air date: Feb 1, 1953. 2907 Springfield Rd., East Peoria, IL 61611. Phone: (309) 698-2525. Fax: (309) 698-9663 (sales). Web Site: www.week.com. Licensee: WEEK-TV License Inc. Group owner: Granite Broadcasting Corp. (acq 10-31-88; $33 million). Network: NBC. Rep: Katz Radio. Washington Atty: Akin, Gump, Strauss, Hauer & Feld. News staff: 26; News: 16 hrs wkly.

Key Personnel:
Mark DeSantis. . . . . gen mgr & progmg dir
Pete Russell . . . . . sls dir
Lynn Dziedzie . . . . . natl sls mgr
Timm Campbell . . . . . prom dir
Jim Garrott. . . . . news dir
Dennis Riley . . . . . engrg dir

WHOI—Analog channel: 19. On air date: Oct 20, 1953. 500 N. Stewart St., Creve Coeur, IL 61610. Phone: (309) 698-1919. Fax: (309) 698-4819/(309) 698-4817. Web Site: www.hoinews.com. Licensee: Barrington Broadcasting Peoria Corp. Group owner: Barrington Broadcasting Corp. acq 4-30-2004; $23.5 million. with KHQA-TV Hannibal, MO). Network: ABC. Rep: Harrington, Righter & Parsons. Washington Atty: Covington & Burling. News: 7 hrs wkly.

Key Personnel:
Ron Pulera . . . . . VP & gen mgr
Christine Bateman . . . . . natl sls mgr
Val Bricka. . . . . gen sls mgr & rgnl sls mgr
Scott Shambley . . . . . prom mgr
Donna Thompson . . . . . progmg dir
Amanda Wozniak . . . . . news dir
Mike Seaver . . . . . chief of engrg

WMBD-TV—Analog channel: 31. On air date: Jan 1, 1958. 3131 N. University St., Peoria, IL 61604. Phone: (309) 688-3131. Fax: (309) 686-8650. Fax: TWX: 910-652-0139. Web Site: www.wmbd.com. Licensee: Nexstar Finance Inc. Group owner: Nexstar Broadcasting Group Inc. (acq 1999). Network: CBS. Washington Atty: Covington & Burling.

Key Personnel:
Kevin Harlan. . . . . VP & gen mgr
Barry Allentuck . . . . . sls dir
Nancy Linebaugh. . . . . gen sls mgr & natl sls mgr
Marty Monical . . . . . rgnl sls mgr
Kirby Matthews . . . . . prom mgr
Carol French . . . . . progmg mgr & pub affrs dir
Chris Manson. . . . . news dir
Herman Marvel . . . . . chief of engrg

***WTVP**—Analog channel: 47. Digital channel: 46. On air date: June 23, 1971. Box 1347, Peoria, IL 61654. 101 State St., Peoria, IL 61602. Phone: (309) 677-4747. Fax: (309) 677-3518. E-mail: wtvpmail@wtvp.pbs.org. Web Site: www.wtvp.org. Licensee: Illinois Valley Public Telecommunication Corp. Network: PBS. Washington Atty: Dow, Lohnes & Albertson.

Key Personnel:
Chet Tomczyk . . . . . CEO, pres & gen mgr
Jon Cecil . . . . . chmn & VP
Jackie Luebcke. . . . . opns mgr
Stacey Tomczyk . . . . . mktg mgr
Linda Miller. . . . . progmg dir
David Schenk . . . . . engrg dir

WYZZ-TV—Analog channel: 43. On air date: Oct 18, 1982. 2714 E. Lincoln, Bloomington, IL 61704. Phone: (309) 661-4343. Fax: (309) 663-6943. Licensee: WYZZ Licensee Inc. Group owner: Sinclair Broadcast Group Inc. (acq 1996; $23 million). Network: Fox. Rep: Harrington, Righter & Parsons. Washington Atty: Shaw Pittman LLP.

Key Personnel:
Kevin Harlan. . . . . VP & gen mgr
Barry Allentuck . . . . . sls dir
Kirby Matthews . . . . . prom dir
Chris Manson. . . . . news dir
Herman Manvel. . . . . engrg dir

Quincy, IL-Hannibal, MO-Keokuk, IA (DMA 167)

KHQA-TV—(Hannibal).MO Analog channel: 7. On air date: Sept 23, 1953. 301 S. 36th St., Quincy, IL 62301. Phone: (217) 222-6200. Fax: (217) 228-3164/(217) 222-5078. Web Site: www.khqa.com. Licensee: Barrington Broadcasting Quincy Corp. Group owner: Barrington Broadcasting Corp. (acq 4-30-2004; $23.5 million. with WHOI(TV) Peoria, IL). Network: CBS. Washington Atty: Covington & Burling. News staff: 12; News: 13 hrs wkly.

Key Personnel:
Robert B. Sherman . . . . . CEO
Frank Brady . . . . . gen mgr
Tracy Hagman . . . . . gen sls mgr & natl sls mgr
Carol Rees . . . . . mktg mgr
Paul Robinson . . . . . prom dir
Kathy McCarthy . . . . . progmg dir
Michael Seaver. . . . . chief of engrg

WGEM-TV—Analog channel: 10. Digital channel: 54. On air date: Sept 4, 1953. Box 80, 513 Hampshire, Quincy, IL 62306. Phone: (217) 228-6600. Fax: (217) 228-6670. E-mail: manger@wgem.com. Web Site: wgem.com. Licensee: Quincy Broadcasting Co. Group owner: Quincy Newspapers Inc. Network: NBC. Rep: Blair Television. Washington Atty: Wilkinson, Barker, Knauer & Quinn. News staff: 25; News: 25 hrs wkly.

Key Personnel:

Thomas A. Oakley . . . . CEO
Ralph M. Oakley . . . . COO & VP
Tomas A. Oakley . . . . pres
Leo T. Henning. . . . . VP & gen mgr

***WMEC**—Analog channel: 22. On air date: Oct 1, 1984. Box 6248, Springfield, IL 62708. Phone: (217) 483-7887. Fax: (217) 483-1112. Licensee: West Central Illinois Educational Telecommunications Corp. Network: PBS. Washington Atty: Dow, Lohnes & Albertson.
Key Personnel:
Jerold Gruebel. . . . . CEO, pres & gen mgr
Richard Plotkin . . . . opns VP & opns dir
Ed Strong. . . . . adv dir

***WQEC**—Analog channel: 27. On air date: Mar 11, 1985. Box 6248, Springfield, IL 62708. Phone: (217) 483-7887. Fax: (217) 483-1112. Licensee: West Central Illinois Educational Telecommunications Corp. Network: PBS. Washington Atty: Dow, Lohnes & Albertson.
Key Personnel:
Jerold Gruebel. . . . . CEO, pres & gen mgr
Richard Plotkin . . . . opns VP & opns dir
Ed Strong. . . . . adv dir

WTJR—Analog channel: 16. On air date: Jan 1, 1986. Box 1189, Quincy, IL 62306. 220 N. 6th St., Quincy, IL 62301. Phone: (217) 228-1616. E-mail: tv16@wtjr.org. Web Site: www.wtjr.org. Licensee: Believer's Broadcasting Corp.
Key Personnel:
Mike Wortman . . . . gen mgr
Rick Aston . . . . opns mgr

Rock Island

see Davenport, IA-Rock Island-Moline, IL market

Rockford, IL (DMA 134)

WIFR—(Freeport).Analog channel: 23. On air date: Sept 12, 1965. Box 123, Rockford, IL 61105. 2523 N. Meridian Rd., Rockford, IL 61101. Phone: (815) 987-5300. Fax: (815) 965-0981. E-mail: talkto23@wifr.com. Web Site: www.wifr.com. Licensee: WEAU Licensee Corp. Group owner: Gray Television Inc. (acq 8-29-02; grpsl). Network: CBS. Rep: Continental Television Sales. Washington Atty: Covington & Burling. News staff: 19; News: 19 hrs wkly.
Key Personnel:
Greg Graber. . . . . VP & gen mgr
Rich McBride . . . . opns mgr
Tim Myers . . . . sls dir
Davidia Williams . . . . natl sls mgr
Dan Bartlett . . . . prom mgr
Carol Comella . . . . progmg dir
Dave Smith . . . . news dir
Arles Hendershott . . . . pub affrs dir
Mark Olson . . . . chief of engrg

WQRF-TV—Analog channel: 39. On air date: Nov 27, 1978. 401 S. Main St., Rockford, IL 61101. Phone: (815) 987-3950. Fax: (815) 964-9974. Web Site: www.fox39.com. Licensee: Nexstar Finance Inc. Group owner: Nexstar Broadcasting Group Inc. (acq 12-31-03; grpsl). Network: Fox. Washington Atty: Arter & Hadden.
Key Personnel:
Terry McHugh. gen mgr
Julia Johnson . . . . gen sls mgr
Dale Hazlewood . . . . prom mgr
Jose Cabezas . . . . progmg mgr
Dean Turman . . . . chief of engrg

WREX-TV—Analog channel: 13. Digital channel: 54. On air date: Oct 1, 1953. Box 530, Rockford, IL 61105. 10322 W. Auburn Rd., Rockford, IL 61103. Phone: (815) 335-2213. Fax: (815) 335-2055. E-mail: wrex@wrex.com. Web Site: www.wrex.com. Licensee: WREX Television LLC. Group owner: Quincy Newspapers Inc., see Cross-Ownership (acq 5-22-01; grpsl). Network: NBC. Rep: Blair Television. Washington Atty: Wilkinson, Barker & Knauer.
Key Personnel:
Ralph M. Oakley . . . . COO & prom dir
John Chadwick. . . . . VP & gen mgr
Jon Skorburg . . . . stn mgr
Jay Meyers. . . . . opns dir
Thomas A. Oakley . . . . CEO & progmg dir
Maggie Hradecky . . . . news dir

WTVO—Analog channel: 17. Digital channel: 16. On air date: May 3, 1953. Box 470, Rockford, IL 61105. 1917 N. Meridian Rd., Rockford, IL 61101. Phone: (815) 963-5413. Fax: (815) 963-6113. Web Site: www.wtvo.com. Licensee: Mission Broadcasting Inc. Group owner: (group owner; (acq 11-22-2004; $20,750,000).. Network: ABC. Washington Atty: Wiley, Rein & Fielding. News staff: 16; News: 7 hrs wkly.

Springfield

see Champaign & Springfield-Decatur, IL market

Indiana

Elkhart

see South Bend-Elkhart, IN market

Evansville, IN (DMA 99)

WAZE-TV—Analog channel: 19. On air date: September 1997. 1277 N. St. Joseph Ave., Evansville, IN 47720. Phone: (812) 425-1900. Fax: (812) 423-3405. Web Site: www.wazetv.com. Licensee: South Central Communications Corp. Group owner: (group owner; acq 9-18-97; $5 million). Network: WB. Washington Atty: Fletcher, Heald & Hildreth.
Key Personnel:
John D. Engelbrecht. . . . . pres
Lyle Schulze . . . . gen mgr
Greg Pittman . . . . gen sls mgr
Brian Tornatta . . . . rgnl sls mgr
Rudy Winderlich . . . . opns dir & prom mgr

WEHT—Analog channel: 25. On air date: Sept 11, 1953. 800 Marywood Dr., Henderson, KY 42420. Phone: (800) 879-8542. Fax: (270) 826-6823. Web Site: www.news25.us. Licensee: Gilmore Broadcasting Corp.. Ownership: National City Bank of Michigan/Illinois, directed by G. Lennon & M. Lemieux (acq 1-15-03). Network: ABC. Washington Atty: Wiley, Rein & Fielding.
Key Personnel:
Doug Padchett . . . . gen mgr
Mike Riley . . . . stn mgr

WEVV—Analog channel: 44. On air date: Nov 17, 1983. 44 Main St., Evansville, IN 47708-1450. Phone: (812) 464-4444. Fax: (812) 465-4559. Fax: (812) 465-9450. Web Site: www.wevv.com. Licensee: Comcorp of Indiana License Corp. Group owner: Communications Corp. of America (acq 1999; $27.5 million). Network: CBS. Rep: Katz Radio. Washington Atty: Leventhal, Senter & Lerman. News staff: 30; News: 9 hrs wkly.
Key Personnel:
Dan Robbins . . . . gen mgr
Brent Zerby . . . . opns mgr

WFIE—Analog channel: 14. Digital channel: 46. On air date: Nov 9, 1953. Box 1414, 1115 Mt. Auburn Rd., Evansville, IN 47720. Phone: (812) 426-1414. Fax: (812) 426-1945. E-mail: 14wfie@.com. Web Site: www.14wfie.com. Licensee: Libco Inc. Group owner: Liberty Corp. (acq 7-19-56; $586,937;. FTR: 7-30-56). Network: NBC. Washington Atty: Dow, Lohnes & Albertson. News staff: 35.

***WKMA**—Analog channel: 35. On air date: Sept 23, 1968. c/o WKLE, 600 Cooper Dr., Lexington, KY 40502. Phone: (606) 258-7000. Fax: (606) 258-7399. Web Site: www.ket.org. Licensee: Kentucky Authority for Educational TV.
Key Personnel:
Malcolm Wall . . . . CEO, chmn & gen mgr
Linda Hume . . . . pres & CFO
Bob Ball . . . . opns dir & engrg dir
Craig Cornwell . . . . opns mgr & progmg dir
Michele Ripley. . . . . dev VP & dev dir

***WKOH**—Analog channel: 31. Digital channel: 30. On air date: Mar 1, 1979. c/o WKLE, 600 Cooper Dr., Lexington, KY 40502. Phone: (606) 258-7000. Fax: (606) 258-7399. Web Site: www.ket.org. Licensee: Kentucky Authority for Educational TV. Network: PBS. Washington Atty: Kenkel, Barnard & Edmundson.
Key Personnel:
Malcolm Wall . . . . CEO, chmn & gen mgr
Bob Bell . . . . opns mgr
Craig Cornwell . . . . opns mgr & progmg dir

***WNIN**—Analog channel: 9. Digital channel: 12. On air date: Mar 16, 1970. 405 Carpenter St., Evansville, IN 47708. Phone: (812) 423-2973. Fax: (812) 428-7548. E-mail: wnin@wnin.org. Web Site: www.wnin.org. Licensee: Tri-State Public Teleplex Inc. (acq 9-12-73). Network: PBS. Washington Atty: Dow, Lohnes & Albertson.
Key Personnel:
David Dial . . . . pres & gen mgr
Bonnie Rheinhardt . . . . opns VP & prom mgr
Rosi Weatherwax . . . . dev VP & mktg VP
Bonnie Reinhardt . . . . progmg VP & progmg mgr

WTVW—Analog channel: 7. On air date: Aug 26, 1956. 477 Carpenter St., Evansville, IN 47708. Phone: (812) 424-7777. Fax: (812) 421-4040. Web Site: www.wtvw.com. Licensee: Nexstar Broadcasting Inc. Group owner: Nexstar Broadcasting Group Inc. (acq 10-30-2003; grpsl). Network: Fox. Rep: Blair Television. Washington Atty: Arter & Hadden. News: 22.5 hrs wkly.
Key Personnel:
John Satterfield. . . . . VP, gen mgr & adv mgr
Jerry Hogan . . . . gen sls mgr
Steve Parkinson . . . . natl sls mgr
Pam Miller . . . . progmg mgr
Bob Walters . . . . news dir
Gary Maier . . . . chief of engrg

Ft. Wayne, IN (DMA 104)

WANE-TV—Analog channel: 15. On air date: Sept 26, 1954. Box 1515, Fort Wayne, IN 46801. 2915 W. State Blvd., Fort Wayne, IN 46808. Phone: (260) 424-1515. Fax: (260) 424-1428. Web Site: www.wane.com. Licensee: Indiana Broadcasting L.L.C. Group owner: LIN Television Corporation (acq 11-14-94; FTR: 12-12-94). Network: CBS. Washington Atty: Covington & Burling. News staff: 35; News: 22 hrs wkly.
Key Personnel:
Nancy Applegate . . . . pres & progmg dir
Alan Riebe. . . . . stn mgr, gen sls mgr & natl sls mgr
Jim Riecken . . . . opns mgr
Jerry Grider . . . . prom mgr
Rick Moll . . . . news dir
Mark Johnson . . . . engrg dir

WFFT-TV—Analog channel: 55. On air date: Dec 21, 1977. 3707 Hillegas Rd., Fort Wayne, IN 46808. Box 8655, Fort Wayne, IN 46898. Phone: (260) 471-5555. Fax: (260) 484-4331. E-mail: fox55@wfft.com. Web Site: www.wfft.com. Licensee: Nexstar Finance Inc. Group owner: Nexstar Broadcasting Group Inc. (acq 12-31-03; grpsl). Network: Fox. Rep: Blair Television. Washington Atty: Arter & Hadden.
Key Personnel:
Perry A. Sook . . . . CEO & pres
Bob Thompson. . . . . CFO
Tim Busch . . . . sr VP
Robert M. Blacher . . . . VP & gen mgr
Bill Ritchhart. . . . . gen sls mgr

***WFWA**—Analog channel: 39. Digital channel: 40. On air date: Dec 1, 1989. 2501 E. Coliseum Blvd., Fort Wayne, IN 46805-1562. Phone: (260) 484-8839. Fax: (260) 482-3632. E-mail: info@wfwa.org. Web Site: www.wfwa.org. Licensee: Fort Wayne Public Television. Network: PBS. News: 2 hrs wkly.
Key Personnel:
Roger Rhodes. . . . . pres, gen mgr & stn mgr
Claudia Johnson . . . . opns VP & opns mgr
Toni Kayumi. . . . . gen sls mgr & mktg mgr
Matt Kyle . . . . chief of engrg & engr

WINM—Analog channel: 63. On air date: Mar 10, 1983. Box 159, Butler, IN 46721. Phone: (419) 298-3703. Fax: (419) 298-3707. E-mail: winm@tct.tv. Licensee: Tri-State Christian TV. Group owner: (group owner; acq 1-24-91; $400,000; 2-11-91).
Key Personnel:
Leo Vogt. . . . . gen mgr
Lee Gilbert . . . . chief of engrg

WISE-TV—Analog channel: 33. Digital channel: 19. On air date: Nov 21, 1953. 2633 W. State Blvd., Fort Wayne, IN 46808. Phone: (260) 422-7474. Fax: (260) 422-7702. Web Site: www.wise33.com. Licensee: WISE-TV License LLC. Group owner: New Vision Group LLC (acq 3-8-2005; $44.2 million).. Network: NBC. Washington Atty: Drinker, Biddle & Reath, LLP. News staff: 32; News: 14 hrs wkly.

WPTA—Analog channel: 21. Digital channel: 24. On air date: Sept 28, 1957. 3401 Butler Rd., Fort Wayne, IN 46808. Phone: (260) 483-0584. Fax: (260) 483-2568. Web Site: www.wpta.com. Licensee: Malara Broadcast Group of Fort Wayne License LLC. Group owner: (group owner; (acq 12-8-2004; $45.9 million).. Network: ABC. Rep: Katz Radio. Washington Atty: Akin, Gump, Strauss, Hauer & Feld. News

staff: 31; News: 31 hrs wkly.
Key Personnel:
Tony Malara . . . . pres
Chris Fedele . . . . gen mgr
Doug Barrow . . . . gen sls mgr
Lynn Dziedzic . . . . natl sls mgr, rgnl sls mgr & mktg dir
Adrian Geunther . . . . prom dir
Don Bradley . . . . news dir
Bret Angel . . . . engrg dir

Gary

see Chicago market

Hammond

see Chicago market

Indianapolis, IN
(DMA 25)

WCLJ-TV—Analog channel: 42. Digital channel: 56. On air date: August 1987. 2528 U.S. 31 S., Greenwood, IN 46143. Phone: (317) 535-5542. Fax: (317) 535-8584. Licensee: Trinity Broadcasting of Indiana Inc. Group owner: Trinity Broadcasting Network.

***WDTI**—Analog channel: 69. Digital channel: 44. On air date: April 1992. Indianapolis Community Television Inc., 3901 Hwy. 121 S., Bedford, TX 76021. Phone: (817) 571-1229. Phone: (817) 571-7458. Web Site: www.daystar.com/schedules.htm. Licensee: Indianapolis Community Television Inc.. Ownership: Dr. Alan Bullock, 14.3%; Joni T. Lamb, 14.3%; Marcus D. Lamb, 14.3%; Peter Keenan, 14.3%; Rob Price, 14.3%; and Vernon Piercey, 14.3% (acq 8-2-2004; $4 million).. Washington Atty: Koerner & Olender.

***WFYI**—Analog channel: 20. On air date: Oct 4, 1970. 1401 N. Meridian, Indianapolis, IN 46202. Phone: (317) 636-2020. Phone: (317) 633-7410. Fax: (317) 633-7418. Web Site: www.wfyi.org. Licensee: Metropolitan Indianapolis Public Broadcasting. Network: PBS.
Key Personnel:
Lloyd Wright . . . . pres & gen mgr
Anthony Lorenz . . . . CFO
Alan Cloe . . . . exec VP & sr VP
Jeanelle Adamak . . . . exec VP & dev VP
Alan Coe . . . . opns VP
Susanne McAlister . . . . sls VP, mktg VP & mktg mgr
Rena Barraclough . . . . prom VP & adv VP
Lisa Liebschutz . . . . prom mgr
Richard Miles . . . . progmg dir
Steve Jensen . . . . engrg VP & engrg dir
Nate Pass . . . . chief of engrg

WHMB-TV—Analog channel: 40. On air date: Jan 25, 1971. Box 50450, Indianapolis, IN 46250. 10511 Greenfield Ave., Noblesville, IN 46250. Phone: (317) 773-5050. Fax: (317) 776-4051. E-mail: kpasson@lesea.com. Web Site: www.whmbtv.com. Licensee: LeSea Broadcasting Corp. Group owner: (group owner; acq 8-15-72; $354,618; 9-4-72). Washington Atty: Gardner, Carton & Douglas. News: one hr wkly.
Key Personnel:
Pete Sumrall . . . . CEO & VP
Tony Hale . . . . pres & CFO
Keith Passon . . . . gen mgr
Steve Butler . . . . gen sls mgr

***WIPB**—Analog channel: 49. On air date: May 8, 1953. Edmund F. Ball Bldg., Ball State Univ., Muncie, IN 47306. Phone: (765) 285-1249. Fax: (765) 285-5548. E-mail: wipb@bsu.edu. Web Site: www.bsu.edu/wipb. Licensee: Ball State University. (acq 10-31-71; $125,000; 12-6-71). Network: PBS. Washington Atty: Schwartz, Woods & Miller.
Key Personnel:
Blaine Brownell . . . . pres
Alice Cheney . . . . gen mgr

WIPX—Analog channel: 63. On air date: Dec 27, 1988. 1000 N. Meridian St., Indianapolis, IN 46204. Phone: (317) 636-1313. Fax: (317) 594-0630. E-mail: wipx@pax.net. Web Site: www.paxtv.com. Licensee: Paxson Indianapolis License Inc. Group owner: Paxson Communications Corp. (acq 2-18-00; grpsl). Washington Atty: Fisher, Wayland, Cooper, Leader & Zaragoza.
Key Personnel:
Mark Dunlap . . . . gen mgr & stn mgr
Rich Pegram . . . . gen mgr

WISH-TV—Analog channel: 8. Digital channel: 9. On air date: July 1, 1954. 1950 N. Meridian St., Indianapolis, IN 46202. Phone: (317) 923-8888. Fax: (317) 926-1144. Web Site: www.wishtv.com. Licensee: Indiana Broadcasting L.L.C. Group owner: LIN Television Corporation (acq 11-14-94; FTR: 12-12-94). Network: CBS. Washington Atty: Covington & Burling.
Key Personnel:
Scott Blumenthal . . . . pres & gen mgr
Jeff White . . . . stn mgr & gen sls mgr
Carol Sergi . . . . mktg mgr
Scott Hainey . . . . prom dir
Deirdre Conley . . . . prom mgr
Rick Thedwall . . . . progmg dir & progmg mgr
Tom Cochrun . . . . news dir
Tina Cosby . . . . pub affrs dir
Terry VanBibber . . . . chief of engrg

WNDY-TV—Analog channel: 23. On air date: Nov 1, 1987. Brickyard Plaza, 4551 W. 16th St., Indianapolis, IN 46222. 13044 E. 246th St., Noblesville, IN 46060. Phone: (317) 241-2388. Phone: (317) 552-0804. Fax: (317) 381-6975. Fax: (317) 552-0977. Web Site: www.upnindiana.com. Licensee: UPN Stations Group Inc. Group owner: Viacom Television Stations Group (acq 1-21-98; $34.99 million).. Network: UPN. Rep: Katz Radio. Washington Atty: Dow, Lohnes & Albertson.

WRTV—Analog channel: 6. Digital channel: 25. On air date: May 30, 1949. 1330 N. Meridian St., Indianapolis, IN 46202. Phone: (317) 635-9788. Phone: (317) 269-1440 (news). Fax: (317) 269-1400. E-mail: newstips@theindychannel.com. Web Site: www.theindychannel.com. Licensee: McGraw-Hill Broadcasting Co. Inc. Group owner: McGraw-Hill Broadcasting Co. (acq 6-1-72). Network: ABC. Rep: Harrington, Righter & Parsons. Washington Atty: Holland & Knight.
Key Personnel:
Ed Quinn . . . . pres & gen sls mgr
Mark Limbach . . . . CFO
Don Lundy . . . . gen mgr
Kurt Swadener . . . . opns mgr
William Byrd . . . . gen sls mgr
Brad Wood . . . . natl sls mgr
Monte Costes . . . . rgnl sls mgr
Paul Montgomery . . . . prom mgr
Brian Vetor . . . . chief of engrg

WTHR—Analog channel: 13. Digital channel: 46. On air date: Oct 30, 1957. Box 1313, Indianapolis, IN 46206. 1000 N. Meridian St., Indianapolis, IN 46204. Phone: (317) 636-1313. Fax: (317) 636-3717. Fax: (317) 632-6720 (news). Web Site: www.wthr.com. Licensee: VideoIndiana Inc. Group owner: Dispatch Broadcast Group (acq 10-1-75; $17.65 million; 9-1-75). Network: NBC. Washington Atty: Sidley & Austin.
Key Personnel:
Michael J. Fiorile . . . . pres
Rich Pegram . . . . gen mgr

***WTIU**—Analog channel: 30. On air date: March 1969. Radio-TV Bldg., Indiana Univ., 1229 E. 7th St., Bloomington, IN 47405. Phone: (812) 855-5900. Phone: (812) 855-8000. Fax: (812) 855-0729. E-mail: wtiu@indiana.edu. Web Site: www.wtiu.indiana.edu. Licensee: Trustees of Indiana University. Network: PBS. Washington Atty: Crowell & Moring. News staff: 2; News: 3 hrs wkly.
Key Personnel:
Perry Metz . . . . CEO & gen mgr
Virginia Metzger . . . . CFO
Phil Meyer . . . . stn mgr, progmg dir & progmg mgr
Barrie Zimmerman . . . . opns dir
Thomas Dukeman . . . . dev dir
Ann Wesley . . . . mktg dir & pub affrs dir
Brent Molnar . . . . progmg dir
Chuck Carney . . . . news dir
Bradley Howard . . . . chief of engrg

WTTK—Analog channel: 29. On air date: May 1988. 6910 Network Place, Indianapolis, IN 46278. 6910 network Place, Indianapolis, IN 46278. Phone: (317) 632-3900. Fax: (317) 687-6531, (317) 687-6534. Web Site: www.wb4.com. Licensee: Tribune Denver Radio Inc. Group owner: Tribune Broadcasting Co. (acq 7-12-02; $125 million. with WTTV(TV) Bloomington). Rep: TeleRep.
Key Personnel:
Rick Rogala . . . . VP & gen mgr
Rob Gordon . . . . opns mgr
Dan O'Sullivan . . . . dev dir
Tim McNamara . . . . sls dir
Greg Osborne . . . . natl sls mgr
Kurt Tovey . . . . mktg mgr & prom mgr
Michele Jarvis . . . . prom dir
Rusty Ricketts . . . . progmg mgr
Mary Kramer . . . . pub affrs mgr
Rich Kittilstved . . . . engrg dir

WTTV—(Bloomington).Analog channel: 4. Digital channel: 48. On air date: Nov 11, 1949. 6910 Network Pl., Indianapolis, IN 46278. Phone: (317) 632-5900. Fax: (317) 687-6532. E-mail: wb4@wb4.com. Web Site: www.wb4.com. Licensee: Tribune Denver Radio Inc. Group owner: Tribune Broadcasting Co. (acq 7-12-02; $125 million. with WTTK(TV) Kokomo). Network: WB. Rep: TeleRep. Washington Atty: Dow, Lohnes & Albertson.

WXIN—Analog channel: 59. Digital channel: 45. On air date: Feb 1, 1984. 6910 Network Pl., Indianapolis, IN 46278. Phone: (317) 632-5900. Fax: (317) 687-6532. Web Site: www.fox59.com. Licensee: Tribune Television Comp. Group owner: Tribune Broadcasting Co. (acq 7-15-97; grpsl). Network: Fox. Rep: TeleRep. Washington Atty: Koteen & Naftalin. News: 19 hrs wkly.

Lafayette, IN
(DMA 186)

WLFI-TV—Analog channel: 18. Digital channel: 11. On air date: June 15, 1953. Box 2618, West Lafayette, IN 47996. 2605 Yeager Rd., West Lafayette, IN 47906. Phone: (765) 463-1800. Fax: (765) 463-7979. Web Site: www.wlfi.com. Licensee: Primeland Television Inc. Group owner: LIN Television Corporation (acq 4-1-2000; in exchange for 67% of WAND(TV) Decatur, IL). Network: CBS. Rep: Petry Television Inc.. News staff: 30; News: 22 hrs wkly.
Key Personnel:
Mike Johnston . . . . gen mgr
Chris Hilgendorf . . . . opns mgr
Tom Combs . . . . sls dir
Terry Glaser . . . . natl sls mgr
Deb McMahan . . . . prom mgr
Rick Thedwall . . . . progmg mgr
Chris Morisse . . . . news dir
Carl Booker . . . . engrg mgr & chief of engrg

Richmond

see Dayton, OH market

Salem

see Louisville, KY market

South Bend-Elkhart, IN
(DMA 87)

WHME-TV—Analog channel: 46. On air date: July 27, 1974. 61300 S. Ironwood Rd., South Bend, IN 46614. Phone: (574) 291-8200. Fax: (574) 291-9043. Web Site: www.lesea.com. Licensee: Lester Sumrall Evangelistic Association. Group owner: Le Sea Broadcasting (acq 6-10-77; $496,000; 7-27-77). Rep: Landin. Washington Atty: Gardner, Carton & Douglas.
Key Personnel:
Peter Sumrall . . . . CEO, VP & gen mgr
Tony Hale . . . . CFO
Mike Swinehart . . . . opns mgr

WNDU-TV—Analog channel: 16. Digital channel: 42. On air date: July 15, 1955. Box 1616, South Bend, IN 46634. 54516 State Rd. 933, Delta, IN 46637. Phone: (574) 631-1616. Fax: (574) 631-1600. E-mail: newscenter16@wndu.com. Web Site: www.wndu.com. Licensee: Michiana Telecasting Corp.. Ownership: Univ. of Notre Dame du Lac, 100%. Network: NBC.
Key Personnel:
Jim Behling . . . . pres & gen mgr
Mike Leyes . . . . gen sls mgr
Howard Voss . . . . rgnl sls mgr
Karl Kirbie . . . . prom dir & progmg dir
Norm Stangland . . . . news dir
George Molnar . . . . chief of engrg

***WNIT-TV**—Analog channel: 34. On air date: Feb 14, 1974. Box 3434, Elkhart, IN 46515. 2300 Charger Blvd., Elkhart, IN 46514. Phone: (574) 674-5961. Phone: (574) 675-9648. Fax: (574) 262-8497. E-mail: wnit@wnit.org. Web Site: www.wnit.org. Licensee: Michiana Public Broadcasting Corp. Network: PBS. Washington Atty: Dow, Lohnes & Albertson.
Key Personnel:
Greg Lintjer . . . . chmn
Amy Cassidy . . . . CFO
Mary Pruess . . . . pres & gen mgr
Brian Hoover . . . . opns dir
Mark Chamberg . . . . dev VP & dev dir

WSBT-TV—Analog channel: 22. On air date: Dec 21, 1952. 300 W. Jefferson Blvd., South Bend, IN 46601. Phone: (574) 233-3141. Fax: (574) 288-6630/(574) 289-0622. Fax: (219) 289-0622. Web Site: www.wsbt.com. Licensee: WSBT Inc. Group owner: Schurz Communications Inc., see Cross-Ownership Network: CBS. Rep: Harrington, Righter & Parsons. Washington Atty: Hogan & Hartson. News staff: 40; News: 22 hrs wkly.

Key Personnel:
Todd F. Schurz . . . pres & gen mgr
Robert Johnson . . . opns dir & progmg dir
Thomas Labuzienski . . . gen sls mgr
Scott Leiter . . . prom dir & prom mgr
Meg Sauer . . . news dir
Mary Dunbar . . . pub affrs dir
Eugene Hale . . . chief of engrg

WSJV—(Elkhart).Analog channel: 28. On air date: Mar 15, 1954. Box 28, South Bend, IN 46624. Phone: (574) 679-9758. Fax: (574) 294-1267. E-mail: fox28@fox28.com. Web Site: www.fox28.com. Licensee: WSJV Television Inc. Group owner: Quincy Newspapers Inc., see Cross-Ownership (acq 3-31-75; $3.2 million;. FTR: 4-14-75). Network: Fox. Washington Atty: Wilkinson, Barker, Knauer & Quinn. News staff: 22; News: 16 hrs wkly.

Key Personnel:
Thomas A. Oakley . . . pres
Kevin Sargent . . . VP & gen mgr

Terre Haute, IN
(DMA 149)

WFXW—Analog channel: 38. Digital channel: 39. On air date: Apr 3, 1973. Box 299, Terre Haute, IN 47808. 10849 US Hwy. 41, Terre Haute, IN 47850. Phone: (812) 696-2121. Fax: (812) 696-2755. Web Site: www.fox38.com. Licensee: Mission Broadcasting Inc. Group owner: (group owner). Network: Fox. News: 2 hrs wkly.

Key Personnel:
Frank Forgie . . . gen mgr
Lois Mathes . . . stn mgr

WTHI-TV—Analog channel: 10. Digital channel: 24. On air date: July 22, 1954. Box 1486, 918 Ohio St., Terre Haute, IN 47808. Phone: (812) 232-9481. Fax: (812) 232-8953. Web Site: www.wthitv.com. Licensee: Emmis Television License LLC. Group owner: Emmis Communications Corp. (acq 1998; grpsl). Network: CBS. Rep: Katz Radio. Washington Atty: Gardner, Carton & Douglas.

Key Personnel:
Jeff Smulyan . . . CEO
Walter Berger . . . CFO
Todd Weber . . . VP, gen mgr & gen sls mgr

WTWO—Analog channel: 2. On air date: Sept 1, 1965. Box 299, Terre Haute, IN 47808. 10849 N. U.S. Hwy. 41, Farmersburg, IN 47850. Phone: (812) 696-2121. Fax: (812) 696-2755. E-mail: Station@nbga.net. Web Site: www.wtwo.com. Licensee: Nexstar Broadcasting Inc. Group owner: Nexstar Broadcasting Inc. (acq 2-14-97; with KQTV(TV) Saint Joseph, MO). Network: NBC. Washington Atty: Drinker, Biddle & Reath LLP. News staff: 25; News: 20 hrs wkly.

Key Personnel:
Frank Forgey . . . gen mgr & progmg mgr
Richard Haddox . . . opns mgr
Chris O'Neal . . . prom mgr & pub affrs dir
Kathy Dash . . . news dir
Bruce Yowell . . . chief of engrg

***WUSI-TV**—Analog channel: 16. Digital channel: 19. On air date: Aug 19, 1968. 1003 Communications Bldg., Carbondale, IL 62901-6602. Phone: (618) 453-6191. Fax: (618) 453-6186. Web Site: www.wsiu.org. Licensee: Board of Trustees, Southern Illinois University. Network: PBS. Washington Atty: Cohn & Marks.

Key Personnel:
Candis Isberner . . . gen mgr & stn mgr
Robert Henderson . . . opns mgr

***WVUT**—Analog channel: 22. On air date: Feb 15, 1968. Davis Hall, 1200 N. 2nd St., Vincennes, IN 47591. Phone: (812) 888-4345. Fax: (812) 882-2237. Licensee: Board of Trustees for the Vincennes Univ. (acq 9-16-76; FTR: 10-11-76). Network: PBS. Washington Atty: Fletcher, Heald & Hildreth. News staff: 4; News: 5 hrs wkly.

Key Personnel:
Al Rerko . . . gen mgr
Jill Ballinger . . . opns mgr
Sharon Keifer . . . progmg dir

Iowa

Ames

see Des Moines-Ames, IA market

Cedar Rapids-Waterloo & Dubuque, IA
(DMA 88)

KCRG-TV—Analog channel: 9. On air date: Oct 15, 1953. Box 816, Cedar Rapids, IA 52406-0816. 501 2nd Ave. S.E., Berlin, IA 52406-0816. Phone: (319) 395-9999. Fax: (319) 398-8378. Web Site: www.kcrg.com. Licensee: Cedar Rapids TV Co.. Ownership: The Gazette Co., 100% Group owner: The Gazette Co. (acq 8-12-54; $101,500; 8-23-54). Network: ABC. Washington Atty: Wiley, Rein & Fielding.

Key Personnel:
Joseph F. Hladky III. . . . CEO & pres
John Phelan III . . . gen mgr & gen sls mgr
David Welsh . . . prom dir
Dan Austin . . . progmg dir
Becky Lutgen Garoner . . . news dir
Karen Ultis . . . pub affrs dir
Kirk Schroeder . . . chief of engrg

KFXA—Analog channel: 28. On air date: August 1995. Box 3131, Cedar Rapids, IA 52406-3131. Phone: (319) 393-2800. Fax: (319) 395-7028. Licensee: Second Generation of Iowa Ltd.. Ownership: Tom Embrescia, Larry Blum. Network: Fox. News staff: 3; News: 4 hrs wkly.

Key Personnel:
Larry Blum . . . pres & progmg mgr
Joe Denk . . . gen mgr & gen sls mgr
Greg Stuart . . . opns mgr
Ted Baugh . . . natl sls mgr
Tim Atterberg . . . rgnl sls mgr
Tim Looney . . . prom mgr & pub affrs dir
Gary Haverland . . . chief of engrg

KFXB—Analog channel: 40. On air date: Sept 12, 1976. 600 Old Marion Rd., Cedar Rapids, IA 52402. Phone: (563) 556-4040. Fax: (563) 585-0108. E-mail: fox2840@fox2840.com. Web Site: www.fox2840.com. Licensee: Christian Television Corporation Inc. Group owner: (group owner; acq 8-2-2004). Network: Fox. Rep: Millennium Sales & Marketing. News staff: 12; News: 5 hrs wkly.

Key Personnel:
Jim Stoos . . . gen mgr & rgnl sls mgr
Joe Denk . . . gen mgr & gen sls mgr
Ted Baugh . . . natl sls mgr
Scott Davidson . . . prom mgr & progmg dir
Gary Haverland . . . chief of engrg

KGAN—Analog channel: 2. On air date: Sept 30, 1953. Box 3131, Cedar Rapids, IA 52406. 600 Old Marion Rd. N.E., Cedar Rapids, IA 52406. Phone: (319) 395-9060. Fax: (319) 395-0987. Web Site: www.kgan.com. Licensee: KGAN Licensee L.L.C. Group owner: Sinclair Broadcast Group Inc. (acq 1999; grpsl). Network: CBS. Rep: Millennium Sales & Marketing. Washington Atty: Shaw Pittman. News staff: 35; News: 12 hrs wkly.

Key Personnel:
Michael Sullivan . . . gen mgr & stn mgr
Ruth Barnett . . . opns dir
Mark Classon . . . gen sls mgr, natl sls mgr & prom mgr
Melissa Hubbard . . . progmg dir
Rod Peterson . . . news dir
Randy Schildmeyer . . . chief of engrg

***KIIN-TV**—Analog channel: 12. On air date: Feb 8, 1970. Box 6450, 6450 Corporate Dr., c/o Iowa Public TV, Johnston, IA 50131-6450. Phone: (515) 242-3100. E-mail: public_information@iptv.org. Web Site: www.iptv.org. Licensee: Iowa Public Broadcasting Board. Network: PBS. Washington Atty: Dow, Lohnes & Albertson.

KPXR—Analog channel: 48. On air date: May 3, 1997. 1957 Blairs Ferry Rd. N.E., Cedar Rapids, IA 52402-5819. Phone: (319) 378-1260. Fax: (319) 378-0076. Web Site: www.pax.tv. Licensee: Paxson Communications License Co. L.L.C. Group owner: Paxson Communications Corp. (acq 7-15-97; $5 million).

Key Personnel:
Vikki Steele . . . stn mgr
Joe Roberts . . . chief of engrg

***KRIN**—Analog channel: 32. On air date: Dec 15, 1974. Box 6450, 6450 Corporate Dr., c/o Iowa Public TV, Johnston, IA 50131-6450. Phone: (515) 242-3100. Fax: (515) 242-1451. E-mail: public_information@iptv.org. Web Site: www.iptv.org. Licensee: Iowa Public Broadcasting Board. Network: PBS. Washington Atty: Dow, Lohnes & Albertson.

KWKB—Analog channel: 20. On air date: 1999. 1547 Baker Ave., West Branch, IA 52358. Phone: (319) 643-5952. Fax: (319) 643-3124. E-mail: wb20@kwkb.com. Web Site: www.kwkb.com. Permittee: KM Television of Iowa L.L.C.

Key Personnel:
Mark Robbins. . . . gen mgr
Jeff Martin. . . . opns mgr
Robin McAllister . . . natl sls mgr
Dennis Doyle . . . rgnl sls mgr
Aaron Spears. . . . mktg mgr & prom dir
April Wright . . . prom mgr
Trish Juchter . . . progmg dir
Jeff Hoffman . . . engrg dir

KWWF—Analog channel: 22. On air date: April 4, 2003. 9279 Dutch Hill Rd., West Valley, NY 14171. Phone: (319) 287-5841. E-mail: bills@wngstv.com. Licensee: EBC Waterloo Inc. Group owner: Equity Broadcasting Corp. (acq 8-6-2004; $5 million. with WNYI(TV) Ithaca, NY).

KWWL—(Waterloo).Analog channel: 7. On air date: November 1953. 500 E. 4th St., Huntsville, IA 50703. Phone: (319) 291-1200. Fax: (319) 291-1255. Web Site: www.kwwl.com. Licensee: Raycom America License Subsidiary LLC. Group owner: Raycom Media Inc. (acq 4-15-97; grpsl). Network: NBC. Rep: Harrington, Righter & Parsons. Washington Atty: Covington & Burling. News staff: 40; News: 22 hrs wkly.

Council Bluffs

see Omaha, NE market

Davenport, IA-Rock Island-Moline, IL
(DMA 94)

KGWB-TV—Analog channel: 26. On air date: Jan 6, 1988. 937 E. 53rd St., Davenport, IA 52807. Phone: (563) 386-1818. Fax: (563) 386-8543. Web Site: www.kgwb.com. Licensee: Burlington Television Acquisition Corp.. Ownership: Quad Cities Television Acquisition Corp., 100%. (acq 1995; $400,000). Network: WB. Rep: Blair Television. Washington Atty: Wilkinson, Barker, Knauer & Quinn.

Key Personnel:
Milton Grant . . . pres & gen mgr
Kathy DeBoeuf . . . stn mgr
Randy Stone . . . gen sls mgr
Tony Wilkins. . . . natl sls mgr & rgnl sls mgr
Tim Emmerson. . . . prom mgr
John Bain. . . . progmg mgr

KLJB-TV—Analog channel: 18. On air date: July 28, 1985. 937 E. 53rd St., Suite D, Davenport, IA 52807. Phone: (563) 386-1818. Fax: (563) 386-8543. Web Site: www.kljb.com. Licensee: Quad Cities Television Acquisition.. Ownership: Milton Grant & Huntsville Television Holdings Corp. Network: Fox. Rep: Blair Television. Washington Atty: Wilkinson, Barker, Knauer & Quinn. News: 3 hrs wkly.

Key Personnel:
Milton Grant . . . pres & gen mgr
Kathy DeBoeuf . . . stn mgr & opns mgr
Randy Stone . . . gen sls mgr
Tony Wilkins. . . . natl sls mgr & rgnl sls mgr
Tim Emmerson. . . . prom mgr
John Bain. . . . progmg mgr

***KQCT**—Analog channel: 36. On air date: December 1991. 6600 34th Ave., Moline, IA 61265. Phone: (309) 796-2424. Fax: (309) 796-2484. E-mail: wqpt@bhc.edu. Web Site: www.wqpt.org. Licensee: Iowa Public Broadcasting Board. (acq 7-2-02; $200,000)..

Key Personnel:
Rick Best . . . gen mgr
Cathryn Lass . . . opns mgr
Lona Adams . . . mktg dir
Jerry Myers . . . progmg mgr
Susan McPeters . . . pub affrs dir
Steve Ellis. . . . chief of engrg

KWQC-TV—Analog channel: 6. Digital channel: 56. On air date: Oct 31, 1949. 805 Brady St., Davenport, IA 52803. Phone: (563) 383-7000. Fax: (563) 383-7129. Web Site: www.kwqc.com. Licensee: Young Broadcasting of Davenport Inc. Group owner: Young Broadcasting Inc. (acq 4-15-96; $55 million). Network: NBC. Rep: Adam Young. Washington Atty: Wiley, rein & Fielding.

Directory of Television | Iowa

Key Personnel:
Jim Graham . . . . . . VP & gen mgr
Cathie Whiteside . . . . . . stn mgr
John Hegeman . . . . . . opns mgr
Jeff Glass . . . . . . rgnl sls mgr
Trish Tague . . . . . . mktg dir
Jeff Bilyeu . . . . . . prom mgr
Doug Retherford . . . . . . news dir
Doug Bierman . . . . . . chief of engrg

WHBF-TV—Analog channel: 4. On air date: July 1, 1950. 231 18th St., Rock Island, IL 61201. Phone: (309) 786-5441. Fax: (309) 788-4975. Web Site: www.whbf.com. Licensee: Coronet Communications Co. Group owner: Citadel Communications Co. Ltd. (acq 3-16-87; grpsl; 11-17-86). Network: CBS. Rep: Continental Television Sales. Washington Atty: Latham & Watkins. News staff: 22; News: 7 hrs wkly.
Key Personnel:
Phillip J. Lombardo . . . . . . CEO
Raymond Cole. . . . . . COO & pres
Colleen Roach-Gally . . . . . . CFO
Tom Heston . . . . . . gen mgr
J. D. Walls . . . . . . opns dir
Steve Garman . . . . . . natl sls mgr
Michael German . . . . . . rgnl sls mgr
Patty Dietz . . . . . . prom mgr
J.D. Walls . . . . . . progmg dir
Arthur Steadman . . . . . . news dir
Dan Ackerman . . . . . . engrg VP
Troy Hollner . . . . . . chief of engrg

WQAD-TV—Analog channel: 8. On air date: Aug 1, 1963. 3003 Park 16th St., Moline, IL 61265. Phone: (309) 764-8888. Fax: (309) 764-5763. E-mail: wqad@wqad.com. Web Site: www.wqad.com. Licensee: New York Times Management Services. Group owner: The New York Times Co. (see Cross-Ownership). Network: ABC. Rep: Katz Radio. News staff: 75; News: 22.5 hrs wkly.
Key Personnel:
F. Marion Meginnis . . . . . . pres & gen mgr
Trent Poindexter . . . . . . sls VP
Tonya Terrell. . . . . . mktg dir
C.J. Beutien. . . . . . progmg dir & news dir
Rick Serre . . . . . . chief of engrg

***WQPT-TV**—Analog channel: 24. Digital channel: 23. On air date: Nov 3, 1983. 6600 34th Ave., Moline, IL 61265. Phone: (309) 796-2424. Fax: (309) 796-2484. E-mail: bestr@bhc.edu. Web Site: www.wqpt.org. Licensee: Black Hawk College. Network: PBS. Washington Atty: Drinker, Biddle & Reath.
Key Personnel:
Rick Best . . . . . . gen mgr
Michael Woods . . . . . . dev dir
Lora Adams . . . . . . mktg dir
Jerry Myers . . . . . . progmg mgr
Steve Ellis . . . . . . chief of engrg

Des Moines-Ames, IA (DMA 73)

KCCI—Analog channel: 8. Digital channel: 31. On air date: July 31, 1955. 888 9th St., Des Moines, IA 50309. Phone: (515) 247-8888. Fax: (515) 244-0202. Fax: (515) 471-8910. E-mail: dbusiek@hearst.com. Web Site: www.theiowachannel.com. Licensee: KCCI Television Inc. Group owner: Hearst-Argyle Television Inc. (acq 1999; grpsl). Network: CBS. Washington Atty: Verner, Liipfert, Bernhard, McPherson & Hand. News staff: 43; News: 17 hrs wkly.
Key Personnel:
Paul Fredericksen . . . . . . pres & gen mgr
John Pascuzzi . . . . . . opns dir
Dave Porepp . . . . . . gen sls mgr
Pam Kulik . . . . . . mktg dir
Mike Cunningham . . . . . . prom dir
Robert Day . . . . . . progmg mgr & pub affrs dir
Dave Busiek . . . . . . news dir
Steve Houg . . . . . . chief of engrg

***KDIN-TV**—Analog channel: 11. Digital channel: 50. On air date: Apr 27, 1959. Box 6450, 6450 Corporate Dr., c/o Iowa Public TV, Johnston, IA 50131-6450. Phone: (515) 242-3100. Fax: (551) 242-4151. E-mail: public_information@iptv.org. Web Site: www.iptv.org. Licensee: Iowa Public Broadcasting Board. Network: PBS. Washington Atty: Dow, Lohnes & Albertson.

KDMI—Analog channel: 56.Not on air, target date: unknown: 9279 Dutch Hill Rd., West Valley, NY 14171. Phone: (716) 942-3000. Fax: (716) 942-3010. Permittee: Caroline K. Powley.
Key Personnel:
Caroline K. Powley . . . . . . gen mgr
Donna McBonough . . . . . . opns mgr

KDSM-TV—Analog channel: 17. Digital channel: 16. On air date: 1983. 4023 Fleur Dr., Des Moines, IA 50321. Phone: (515) 287-1717. Fax: (515) 287-0064. E-mail: programming@kdsm17.com. Web Site: www.kdsm.com. Licensee: KDSM Licensee L.L.C. Group owner: Sinclair Broadcast Group Inc. Network: Fox. Rep: Millennium Sales & Marketing. Washington Atty: Dow, Lohnes & Albertson. News staff: 7; News: 4 hrs wkly.
Key Personnel:
Mike Wilson . . . . . . VP & gen mgr
Beth Grant. . . . . . opns VP
Eric Johnson . . . . . . gen sls mgr
Carolyn Lawrence. . . . . . natl sls mgr
Julie Quick-Alcorn . . . . . . progmg dir
Doug Hammond . . . . . . chief of engrg

KFPX—Analog channel: 39. On air date: 1998. 1801 Grand Ave., Des Moines, IA 50309. Phone: (515) 331-3939. Fax: (515) 242-3784. Web Site: www.pax.tv. Licensee: Paxson Des Moines License Inc. Group owner: Paxson Communications Corp. News: 2.5 hrs wkly.
Key Personnel:
Ross Reardon . . . . . . gen sls mgr
Dave Ohmstede . . . . . . chief of engrg

KPWB-TV—Analog channel: 23. On air date: Jan 20, 2001. 2701 S.E. Convenience Blvd., Suite 1, Ankeny, IA 50021-9433. Phone: (515) 964-2323. Fax: (515) 965-6900. E-mail: yourstation@kpwb.com. Web Site: www.kpwb.com. Licensee: Pappas Telecasting of Iowa L.L.C. Group owner: Pappas Telecasting Companies. Network: WB.
Key Personnel:
Ted Stephens. . . . . . gen mgr
Jim Cordero. . . . . . opns mgr & progmg mgr
David Presler . . . . . . rgnl sls mgr
Jeff Wamser. . . . . . prom mgr
Dan Sommers . . . . . . chief of engrg

***KTIN**—Analog channel: 21. On air date: Apr 8, 1977. Box 6450, 6450 Corporate Dr., c/o Iowa Public TV, Johnston, IA 50131-6450. Phone: (515) 242-3100. E-mail: public_information@iptv.org. Web Site: www.iptv.org. Licensee: Iowa Public Broadcasting Board. Network: PBS. Washington Atty: Dow, Lohnes & Albertson.

WHO-TV—Analog channel: 13. On air date: Apr 15, 1954. 1801 Grand Ave., Des Moines, IA 50309. Phone: (515) 242-3500. Fax: (515) 242-3743. Fax: (515) 242-3796 (news). Web Site: www.whotv.com. Licensee: New York Times Management Services. Group owner: The New York Times Co. (acq 1996; $71 million).. Network: NBC. Washington Atty: Holland & Knight LLC. News staff: 41; News: 29 hrs wkly.
Key Personnel:
James L. Boyer . . . . . . gen mgr
Brian Anstoetter . . . . . . gen sls mgr & rgnl sls mgr
John Duffin . . . . . . gen sls mgr
Bill Mucksch . . . . . . natl sls mgr
Mandy Zook . . . . . . mktg dir
Dave Peterson. . . . . . progmg mgr
Mark Ginther . . . . . . news dir
Tim Gardner . . . . . . prom mgr & pub affrs dir
Brad Olk . . . . . . chief of engrg

WOI-TV—(Ames).Analog channel: 5. On air date: Feb 21, 1950. 3903 Westown Pkwy., West Des Moines, IA 50266. Phone: (515) 457-9645. Fax: (515) 457-1034. Web Site: www.woi-tv.com. Licensee: Capital Communications Co. Inc. Group owner: Citadel Communications Company Ltd., Coronet Communications Co. (acq 3-1-94; $12.7 million). Network: ABC. Rep: Continental Television Sales. Washington Atty: Latham & Watkins. News staff: 25; News: 15 hrs wkly.
Key Personnel:
Philip J. Lombardo. . . . . . CEO & chmn
Ray Cole . . . . . . pres & gen mgr
Randy Shelton . . . . . . opns dir

Dubuque

see Cedar Rapids-Waterloo & Dubuque, IA market

Keokuk

see Quincy, IL-Hannibal, MO-Keokuk, IA market

Mason City

see Rochester, MN-Mason City, IA-Austin, MN market

Ottumwa, IA-Kirksville, MO (DMA 200)

KTVO—(Kirksville).MO Analog channel: 3. On air date: Nov 21, 1955. Box 949, Hwy. 63 N., Kirksville, MO 63501. 111 S. Market, Ottumwa, IA 52501. Phone: (660) 627-3333. Phone: (641) 682-3333. Fax: (660) 627-1885. Fax: (641) 682-1572. Web Site: www.ktov.com. Licensee: KTVO License Subsidiary Inc. Group owner: Raycom Media Inc. (acq 9-24-96; grpsl). Network: ABC. Rep: Harrington, Righter & Parsons. Washington Atty: Covington & Burling. News staff: 16; News: 14 hr wkly.
Key Personnel:
Marty Edelman . . . . . . sr VP
Crystal Amini-Rad . . . . . . gen mgr
Merle Snyder . . . . . . gen sls mgr, prom mgr & adv mgr
Melissa Billington . . . . . . progmg dir & progmg mgr
Teresa Johnson. . . . . . mktg mgr & news dir
John Wise. . . . . . chief of engrg

KYOU-TV—Analog channel: 15. Digital channel: 14. On air date: June 29, 1987. 820 W. 2nd St., Ottumwa, IA 52501. Phone: (641) 684-5415. Fax: (641) 682-5173. E-mail: reception@kyoutv.com. Licensee: Ottumwa Media Holdings LLC. (acq 10-31-03; $4 million).. Network: Fox. Rep: MMT. Washington Atty: Covington & Burling.
Key Personnel:
Eric Wertheim. . . . . . gen mgr
Dave Cecil . . . . . . opns mgr
Dianne Little. . . . . . gen sls mgr
Phil Benjamin . . . . . . chief of engrg

Red Oak

see Omaha, NE market

Sioux City, IA (DMA 143)

KCAU-TV—Analog channel: 9. On air date: Mar 28, 1953. 625 Douglas St., Sioux City, IA 51101. Phone: (712) 277-2345. Fax: (712) 277-3733. Web Site: www.kcautv.com. Licensee: Citadel Communications Co. Ltd. Group owner: Citadel Communications Co. Ltd., Coronet Communications Co. (acq 10-1-85; $15 million). Network: ABC. Rep: Katz Radio. Washington Atty: Latham & Watkins.
Key Personnel:
Will Meyl . . . . . . VP, VP & gen mgr
Brent Nelson . . . . . . opns mgr & progmg dir
Leah Brouillette . . . . . . rgnl sls mgr
Daniele Feenstra . . . . . . prom mgr
Tiffany Coleman. . . . . . news dir
Bob Van Vleet . . . . . . chief of engrg

KMEG—Analog channel: 14. On air date: Sept 5, 1967. 100 Gold Cir., Dakota Dunes, SD 57049. Phone: (712) 277-3554. Fax: (712) 277-4732. Web Site: www.kmeg.com. Licensee: Waitt Broadcasting Inc. Group owner: (group owner; acq 6-23-98; $12.25 million).. Network: CBS. Washington Atty: Wilkinson, Barker, Knauer & Quinn.
Key Personnel:
Norman Waitt Jr. . . . . . . CEO & pres
Steve Seline . . . . . . chmn
Mike Delich . . . . . . pres
John Schuele . . . . . . CFO
Brian McDonough . . . . . . gen mgr
Fritz Miller . . . . . . stn mgr, opns mgr & progmg dir
Brett Beach . . . . . . natl sls mgr
Tim Poppen . . . . . . mktg dir
Darrin Fullerton . . . . . . prom mgr
Tedd O'Connell . . . . . . news dir
Dick Herr . . . . . . chief of engrg

KPTH—Analog channel: 44. On air date: May 9, 1999. 3220 Plaza Dr., Suite E, South Sioux City, NE 68776. Phone: (402) 241-4400. Fax: (402) 241-4444/(402) 241-4046. E-mail: yourstation@kpth.com. Web Site: kpth.com. Licensee: Pappas Telecasting of Sioux City L.P. (a DE limited partnership). Group owner: Pappas Telecasting Companies Network: Fox. Rep: Harrington, Righter & Parsons.
Key Personnel:
Howard Shrier . . . . . . CEO
Harry Pappas . . . . . . chmn
Mary Ann Johnson . rgnl sls mgr, mktg mgr, gen mgr & gen sls mgr
Tim Hess . . . . . . prom mgr
Dale Scherbring . . . . . . chief of engrg
Gina Dierks . . . . . . chief of engrg

***KSIN**—Analog channel: 27. Digital channel: 28. On air date: Jan 4, 1975. Box 6450, 6450 Corporate Dr., c/o Iowa Public TV, Johnston, IA 50131-6450. Phone: (515) 242-3100. Fax: (515) 242-4151. E-mail:

Broadcasting & Cable Yearbook 2006

B-42

public_information@iptv.org. Web Site: www.iptv.org. Licensee: Iowa Public Broadcasting Board. Network: PBS. Washington Atty: Dow, Lohnes & Albertson.

KTIV—Analog channel: 4. On air date: Oct 9, 1954. 3135 Floyd Blvd., Sioux City, IA 51108. Phone: (712) 239-4100. Fax: (712) 239-2621. Web Site: www.ktiv.com. Licensee: KTIV Television Inc. Group owner: Quincy Newspapers Inc., see Cross-Ownership (acq 11-20-89). Network: NBC. Rep: Blair Television. Washington Atty: Wilkinson, Barker, Knauer & Quinn. News: 19 hrs wkly.
Key Personnel:
Jerry Watson . . . . VP
Adrian Wisner . . . . gen mgr & gen sls mgr
David Madsen . . . . stn mgr
Bridget Breen . . . . news dir

***KXNE-TV**—Analog channel: 19. Digital channel: 16. On air date: Nov 10, 1967. Box 83111, Lincoln, NE 68501. 1800 N. 33rd St., Lincoln, NE 68503. Phone: (402) 472-3611. Fax: (402) 472-1785. E-mail: net1@unl.edu. Web Site: www.netnebraska.org. Licensee: Nebraska Educational Telecommunications Commission. Network: PBS. Washington Atty: Dow, Lohnes & Albertson.

Waterloo

see Cedar Rapids-Waterloo & Dubuque, IA market

Kansas

Hutchinson Plus

see Wichita-Hutchinson Plus, KS market

Lawrence

see Kansas City, MO market

Pittsburg

see Joplin, MO-Pittsburg, KS market

Topeka, KS (DMA 137)

KSNT—Analog channel: 27. On air date: Dec 28, 1967. Box 2700, Topeka, KS 66601. 6835 N.W. Hwy. 24, Topeka, KS 66618. Phone: (785) 582-4000. Fax: (785) 582-5283. Fax: (785) 582-4783. Web Site: www.ksnt.com. Licensee: Emmis Television License Corp. of Topeka. Group owner: Emmis Communications Corp. (acq 10-1-00; grpsl). Network: NBC. Rep: Harrington, Righter & Parsons. News staff: 24; News: 17 hrs wkly.
Key Personnel:
Ken Selvaggi . . . . VP & gen mgr
Tim Bentley . . . . gen sls mgr
Phil Maddern . . . . natl sls mgr
Keith Walberg . . . . prom dir
Doug Overla . . . . chief of engrg

KTKA-TV—Analog channel: 49. Digital channel: 48. On air date: June 19, 1983. Box 4949, Topeka, KS 66604. 2121 S.W. Chelsea Dr., Topeka, KS 66614. Phone: (785) 273-4949. Fax: (785) 273-7811. E-mail: 49email@ktka.tv. Web Site: www.ktka.tv. Licensee: Northeast Kansas Broadcast Service Inc.. Ownership: Berl Brechner, 100%. (acq 5-1-86; $6.5 million;. FTR: 4-7-86). Network: ABC. Rep: Millennium Sales & Marketing. Washington Atty: Cohn & Marks. News staff: 21; News: 15 hrs wkly.
Key Personnel:
Marion Brechner . . . . chmn
Berl Brechner . . . . pres
Bob Fulmer . . . . gen mgr
Rudy Guzman . . . . opns mgr & progmg dir
Steve Drain . . . . prom mgr
Mike Caudle . . . . engrg mgr

***KTWU**—Analog channel: 11. On air date: Oct 21, 1965. 1700 S.W. College St., Topeka, KS 66621. Phone: (785) 231-1111. Fax: (785) 231-1112. E-mail: ktwu-press@lists.washburn.edu. Web Site: www.ktwu.washburn.edu. Licensee: Washburn University of Topeka. Network: PBS.
Key Personnel:
Eugene Williams . . . . gen mgr
Cindy Barry . . . . dev dir
Kevin Goodman . . . . mktg dir
David Pomeroy . . . . progmg dir
Duane Loyd . . . . chief of engrg

WIBW-TV—Analog channel: 13. On air date: Nov 15, 1953. 631 S.W. Commerce Pl., Topeka, KS 66615. Phone: (785) 272-6397. Fax: (785) 272-0117. E-mail: 13news@wibw.com. Web Site: www.wibw.com. Licensee: WEAU Licensee Corp. Group owner: Gray Television Inc. (acq 8-29-02; grpsl). Network: CBS. Rep: Continental Television Sales. Washington Atty: Covington & Burling. News staff: 22; News: 22.5 hrs wkly.
Key Personnel:
Steve Cornwell . . . . gen mgr
Mike Turner . . . . opns dir & opns mgr
Jon Janes . . . . news dir

Wichita-Hutchinson Plus, KS (DMA 66)

KAAS-TV—Analog channel: 18. On air date: April 1988. 316 N. West St., Wichita, KS 67203. Phone: (316) 942-2424. Fax: (316) 942-8927. E-mail: programming@foxkansas.com. Web Site: www.foxkansas.com. Licensee: Clear Channel Broadcasting Licenses Inc. Group owner: Clear Channel Communications Inc. (acq 8-2-90). Network: Fox. Washington Atty: Wiley, Rein & Fielding.
Key Personnel:
Kent Cornish . . . . gen mgr
Jon Deeble . . . . chief of opns
Todd Murphy . . . . natl sls mgr
David Hill . . . . rgnl sls mgr
Michael Truman . . . . prom mgr
Linda Madzey . . . . progmg mgr
Dave Caruso . . . . chief of engrg

KAKE-TV—Analog channel: 10. Digital channel: 21. On air date: Oct 19, 1954. 1500 North West St., Wichita, KS 67203. Phone: (316) 943-4221. Fax: (316) 943-5493. Web Site: www.kake.com. Licensee: Gray Television Licensee, Inc. Group owner: Gray Television Inc. (acq 8-29-02; grpsl). Network: ABC. Rep: Continental Television Sales. Washington Atty: Covington & Burling. News staff: 40; News: 16 hrs wkly.
Key Personnel:
Terry Cole . . . . pres & gen mgr
Glen Horn . . . . stn mgr & news dir
Patrick Myers . . . . opns dir
Dan Wall . . . . gen sls mgr
Bryan Frye . . . . mktg dir & prom mgr

KBDK—Analog channel: 14. On air date: 2001. 316 N. West St., Wichita, KS 67203. Phone: (316) 942-2424. Fax: (316) 942-8927. E-mail: programming@foxkansas.com. Web Site: www.foxkansas.com. Licensee: Clear Channel Broadcasting Licenses Inc. Group owner: Clear Channel Communications Inc. Network: Fox. Washington Atty: Wiley, Rein & Fielding.
Key Personnel:
Kent Cornish . . . . gen mgr
Jon Deeble . . . . opns dir
Jeff McCousland . . . . gen sls mgr
Michael Truman . . . . prom dir
Linda Madzey . . . . progmg dir
David Caruso . . . . engrg dir

KBSD-TV—Analog channel: 6. On air date: July 24, 1957. Box 157, Dodge City, KS 67801. Phone: (620) 227-3121. Fax: (620) 225-1675. Licensee: Media General Communications Inc. Group owner: Media General Broadcast Group (acq 3-27-00; grpsl). Network: CBS.
Key Personnel:
Kathy Mohn . . . . gen mgr
Cliff Walker . . . . stn mgr
Kerri Baker . . . . rgnl sls mgr
Don Vest . . chief of engrgRebroadcasts KWCH-(TV) Wichita 95%

KBSH-TV—Analog channel: 7. On air date: Sept 1, 1958. 2300 Hall St., Hays, KS 67601. Phone: (785) 625-5277. Fax: (785) 625-1161. Web Site: www.kwch.com. Licensee: Media General Communications Inc. Group owner: Media General Broadcast Group (acq 3-27-00; grpsl). Network: CBS. Rep: Harrington, Righter & Parsons. Washington Atty: Dow, Lohnes & Albertson. News staff: 1; News: 24 hrs wkly.
Key Personnel:
Stewart Bryan . . . . pres
Jim Zimmerman . . . . exec VP
Kathy Mohn . . . . VP
Joan Ballett . . . . gen mgr
Gary Sotir . . . . natl sls mgr
Deirdre Treacy . . . . mktg mgr
Laverne Goering . . . . prom dir
Jon North . . . . progmg VP & news dir
Don Vest . . . . chief of engrg

KBSL-TV—Analog channel: 10. On air date: Apr 28, 1959. Box 629, Goodland, KS 67735. 3023 W. 31 St., Goodland, KS 67735. Phone: (785) 899-2321. Fax: (785) 899-3138. E-mail: kbsltv@eaglecom.net. Licensee: Media General Communications Inc. Group owner: Media General Broadcast Group (acq 3-27-00; grpsl). Network: CBS.
Key Personnel:
Rafi Archilla . . . . gen mgr
Cliff Walker . . . . stn mgr
Don Newell . . . . gen sls mgr
Don McKenzie . . . . adv mgr
Trish Ayers . . . . news dir
Dennis Massier . . . . chief of engrg

***KDCK**—Analog channel: 21. On air date: March 1998. Box 9, 604 Elm St., Bunker Hill, KS 67626. Phone: (785) 483-6990. Fax: (785) 483-4605. E-mail: shptv@shptv.org. Web Site: www.pbs.org/shptv. Licensee: Smoky Hills Public Television. Network: PBS.
Key Personnel:
Lawrence Holden . . . . CEO & gen mgr
Mary-Pat Waymaster . . . . progmg dir
Robert Roe . . . . chief of opns & news dir
Jerry Cutler . . . . chief of engrg

KLBY—Analog channel: 4. Digital channel: 17. On air date: July 4, 1984. 2900 E. Schulman Ave., Garden City, KS 67846. Phone: (620) 275-1560. Web Site: www.kake.com. Licensee: Gray Television Licensee Inc. Group owner: Gray Television Inc. (acq 8-29-2002; grpsl). Network: ABC. Washington Atty: Covington & Burling. News staff: 2.

***KOOD**—Analog channel: 9. On air date: Nov 10, 1982. Box 9, 604 Elm St., Bunker Hill, KS 67626. Phone: (785) 483-6990. Fax: (785) 483-4605. Web Site: www.shptv.org. Licensee: Smoky Hills Public Television Corp. Network: PBS. Washington Atty: Dow, Lohnes & Albertson.
Key Personnel:
Larry Holden . . . . gen mgr
Wayne Roberts . . . . CEO & dev mgr
Kristy Nyp . . . . mktg dir
Mary-Pat Waymaster . . . . progmg dir
Lloyd E. Mintzmyer . . . . chief of engrg

***KPTS**—Analog channel: 8. On air date: Jan 7, 1970. 320 W. 21st St. N., Wichita, KS 67203. Phone: (316) 838-3090. Fax: (316) 838-8586. Web Site: www.tv8kpts.org. Licensee: Kansas Public Telecommunications Service Inc. (acq 1979). Network: PBS. Washington Atty: Dow, Lohnes & Albertson.
Key Personnel:
Andrew Nolan . . . . chmn
Don Checots . . . . pres & gen mgr
Dave McClintock . . . . opns dir & engrg dir
David Brewer . . . . progmg mgr
Dale Goter . . . . pub affrs dir

KSAS-TV—Analog channel: 24. On air date: Aug 24, 1985. 316 N. West St., Wichita, KS 67203. Phone: (316) 942-2424. Fax: (316) 942-8927. Web Site: www.foxkansas.com. Licensee: Clear Channel Broadcasting Licenses Inc. Group owner: Clear Channel Communications Inc. (acq 8-5-92). Network: Fox. Rep: Millennium Sales & Marketing. Washington Atty: Wiley, Rein & Fielding.
Key Personnel:
Kent Cornish . . . . gen mgr
Jon Deeble . . . . chief of opns

KSCC—Analog channel: 36. On air date: Jan 6, 2001. 316 N. W. St., Wichita, KS 67203. Phone: (316) 941-1036. Fax: (316) 942-5188. E-mail: upnfeedback@upnkanas.com. Web Site: www.upnkansas.com. Licensee: Mercury Broadcasting Co. Inc. Group owner: (group owner; acq 7-1-01). Network: UPN. Rep: Millennium Sales & Marketing. Washington Atty: Fletcher, Heald & Hildreth.
Key Personnel:
Kent Cornish . . . . VP & gen mgr
Tom Gdisis . . . . stn mgr
Jeff Causland . . . . sls dir
Michael Truman . . . . prom mgr
Linda Madzey . . . . progmg mgr
David Caruso . . . . chief of engrg

KSNC—Analog channel: 2. Digital channel: 22. On air date: Nov 28, 1954. 482 N. Hwy. 281, Great Bend, KS 67530. Phone: (620) 793-7868. Fax: (620) 793-3079. E-mail: ksnc@ksn.com. Web Site: www.ksn.com. Licensee: Emmis Television License Corp. of Wichita. Group owner: Emmis Communications Corp. (acq 12-29-00; grpsl). Network: NBC.

Key Personnel:
Shawn Oswald . . . gen mgr
Betty Erickson . . . opns dir & progmg dir
Becky Swann . . . gen sls mgr
Terry Weathers. . . . prom mgr
Jan Westfall. . . . adv VP
Dave Rickels . . . engrg VP

KSNG—Analog channel: 11. Digital channel: 16. On air date: Nov 5, 1958. 204 Fulton Terr., Garden City, KS 67846. Phone: (620) 276-2311. Fax: (620) 275-0576. Web Site: www.ksn.com. Licensee: Emmis Television License Corp. of Wichita. Group owner: Emmis Communications Corp. (acq 12-6-00; grpsl). Network: NBC. Rep: Katz Radio. Washington Atty: Latham & Watkins.
Key Personnel:
Shawn Oswald . . . gen mgr
Allison Toepperwein . . . news dir
Matthew Wellbrock . . . pub affrs dir
Dave Rickels. . . . chief of engrg

KSNK—Analog channel: 8. Digital channel: 12. On air date: Nov 28, 1959. Box 238, Oberlin, KS 67749. W. Hwy. 36, Oberlin, KS 67749. Phone: (785) 475-2248. Fax: (785) 475-3944. Web Site: www.ksn.com. Licensee: Emmis Television License Corp. of Wichita. Group owner: Emmis Communications Corp. (acq 12-29-00; grpsl). Network: NBC. Rep: Katz Radio. Washington Atty: Latham & Watkins.
Key Personnel:
Shawn Oswald . . . gen mgr
Terry Stover . . . gen sls mgr
Betty Erickson . . . progmg dir
David Rickles . . . chief of engrg

KSNW—Analog channel: 3. Digital channel: 45. On air date: Sept 1, 1955. 833 N. Main St., Wichita, KS 67201. Phone: (316) 265-3333. Phone: 316265-1111. Fax: (316) 292-1197. E-mail: news@ksn.com. Web Site: www.ksn.com. Licensee: Emmis Television License Corp. of Wichita. Group owner: Emmis Communications Corp. (acq 12-29-00; grpsl). Network: NBC. Rep: Katz Radio. Washington Atty: Wiley, Rein & Fielding.
Key Personnel:
Shawn Oswald. . . . VP & gen mgr
Jerome Biggars . . . opns mgr
Bryan Frye . . . prom mgr
Betty Erickson . . . progmg dir
Jim Tellus . . . news dir
Todd Spessard . . . news dir
David Rickels . . . chief of engrg

***KSWK**—Analog channel: 3. On air date: Mar 15, 1989. Box 9, 604 Elm St., Bunker Hill, KS 67626. Phone: (785) 483-6990. Fax: (785) 483-4605. Web Site: www.pbs.org/shptv. Licensee: Smoky Hills Public Television Corp.
Key Personnel:
Richard A. Hicks . . . CEO
Richard Hicks. . . . gen mgr
Richard D. Stanley . . . dev dir
Mary-Pat Waymaster . . . progmg dir
Les Kinderknecht . . . news dir
Lloyd Mintzmyer . . . chief of engrg

KUPK-TV—Analog channel: 13. Digital channel: 18. On air date: Nov 8, 1964. 2900 E. Schulman Ave., Garden City, KS 67846-9064. Phone: (620) 275-1560. Web Site: www.kake.com. Licensee: Gray Television Licensee Inc. Group owner: Gray Television Inc. (acq 8-29-2002; grpsl). Network: ABC. Washington Atty: Fletcher, Heald & Hildreth. News staff: 2; News: 7 hrs wkly.

KWCH-TV—(Hutchinson).Analog channel: 12. On air date: July 1, 1953. 2815 E. 37th St. N., Wichita, KS 67219. Box 12, Wichita, KS 67201. Phone: (316) 838-1212. Fax: (316) 831-6198. Web Site: www.kwch.com. Licensee: Media General Communications Inc. Group owner: Media General Broadcast Group (acq 3-27-00; grpsl). Network: CBS. Rep: Harrington, Righter & Parsons. Washington Atty: Dow, Lohnes & Albertson. News staff: 42; News: 24 hrs wkly.
Key Personnel:
Stewart Bryan . . . CEO & pres
Marshall Morton . . . CFO
Jim Zimmerman. . . . exec VP
Joan Barrett. . . . VP & gen mgr
Tony Thompson . . . gen sls mgr
Gary Sotir. . . . natl sls mgr
Deirdre Treacy. . . . prom mgr & pub affrs dir
Laverne Goering . . . progmg dir & film buyer
Don North . . . news dir
Don Vest . . . chief of engrg

KWCV—Analog channel: 33. Digital channel: 31. On air date: 2000. 200 W. Douglas, 7th Fl., Wichita, KS 67202. Phone: (316) 303-0700. Fax: (316) 303-0160 (sales; traffic). Fax: (316) 303-9807. E-mail: programming@wbkansas.com. Web Site: www.wbkansas.com. Licensee: WLBB Broadcasting L.L.C. Group owner: Banks Broadcasting Inc. (acq 12-8-2000). Network: WB.
Key Personnel:
Lyle Banks . . . CEO & pres
Eric Lassberg . . . gen mgr, gen sls mgr & natl sls mgr
Mike Haden . . . opns mgr
Marty Heffner. . . . chief of opns & engrg VP
Amy McClany . . . rgnl sls mgr
Sean Genosky . . . mktg dir, prom dir, progmg dir & pub affrs dir

Kentucky

Ashland

see Charleston-Huntington, WV market

Bowling Green, KY (DMA 182)

WBKO—Analog channel: 13. Digital channel: 33. On air date: June 3, 1962. Box 13000, Bowling Green, KY 42102-9800. 2727 Russellville Rd., Bowling Green, KY 42102-9800. Phone: (270) 781-1313. Fax: (270) 781-1814. Web Site: www.wbko.com. Licensee: WEAU Licensee Corp. Group owner: Gray Television Inc. (acq 8-29-02; grpsl). Network: ABC. Rep: Continental Television Sales. Washington Atty: Covington & Burling. News staff: 22; News: 17 hrs wkly.
Key Personnel:
J. Mack Robinson . . . CEO
Robert S. Prather Jr.. . . . COO, pres & CFO
Brad Odil. . . . sr VP, stn mgr, sls VP & gen sls mgr
Rick McCue . . . VP & gen mgr
Heath Myrick . . . prom mgr
Barbara Powell. . . . progmg mgr
John Preston . . . news dir
Dave Chumley . . . engrg dir

***WKGB-TV**—Analog channel: 53. Digital channel: 48. On air date: Sept 23, 1968. c/o WKLE, 600 Cooper Dr., Lexington, KY 40502. Phone: (859) 258-7000. Fax: (859) 258-7399. Web Site: www.ket.org. Licensee: Kentucky Authority for Educational TV. Network: PBS.
Key Personnel:
Linda Hume . . . CFO
Malcolm Wall . . . CEO, stn mgr & opns dir
Bob Ball . . . opns mgr
Craig Cornwell . . . progmg dir

***WKYU-TV**—Analog channel: 24. Digital channel: 18. On air date: Jan 17, 1989. Academic Complex 153, Western Kentucky Univ., Bowling Green, KY 42101. Phone: (270) 745-2400. Fax: (270) 745-2084. Web Site: www.pbs.org. Licensee: Western Kentucky University. Network: PBS. Washington Atty: Leventhal, Senter & Lerman. News staff: one; News: one hr wkly.
Key Personnel:
Gary Ransdell . . . pres
Linda Gerossky . . . stn mgr

WNKY—Analog channel: 40. On air date: Dec 15, 1991. 325 Emmett Ave., Bowling Green, KY 42101. Phone: (270) 781-2140. Fax: (270) 842-7140. E-mail: wnky@nbc40.tv. Web Site: www.nbc40.tv. Licensee: MMK License LLC. Group owner: MAX Media L.L.C. (acq 3-1-2003; $7 million).. Network: NBC. Rep: Millennium Sales & Marketing. Washington Atty: Williams & Mullen, P.C..
Key Personnel:
Ed Groves . . . pres & gen mgr
Greg Fotos . . . gen sls mgr
Gerald Keith . . . prom dir
Donna Groves . . . progmg dir & pub affrs dir
Tom White. . . . chief of engrg

Covington

see Cincinnati, OH market

Harlan

see Knoxville, TN market

Lexington, KY (DMA 64)

WDKY-TV—Analog channel: 56. On air date: Feb 10, 1986. Chevy Chase Plaza, 836 Euclid Ave., Lexington, KY 40502. Phone: (859) 269-5656. Fax: (859) 269-3774. Web Site: www.wdky56.com. Licensee: WDKY Licensee L.L.C. Group owner: Sinclair Broadcast Group Inc. (acq 1996; $63 million with KOCB(TV) Oklahoma City, OK). Network: Fox. Rep: Millennium Sales & Marketing. Washington Atty: Fisher, Wayland, Cooper, Leader & Zaragoza. News: 4 hrs wkly.
Key Personnel:
David Smith . . . CEO
Darren Shapiro . . . sls VP & natl sls mgr
Jeff Sleete . . . mktg VP & mktg dir

***WKHA**—Analog channel: 35. Digital channel: 16. On air date: June 6, 1968. c/o WKLE, 600 Cooper Dr., Lexington, KY 40502. Phone: (859) 258-7000. Fax: (859) 258-7399. Web Site: www.ket.org. Licensee: Kentucky Authority for Educational TV. Network: PBS.
Key Personnel:
Malcolm Wall . . . CEO, chmn & gen mgr
Linda Hume . . . pres & CFO
Bob Ball . . . opns mgr & engrg dir
Craig Cornwell . . . opns mgr & progmg dir
Michele Ripley. . . . dev VP & dev dir

***WKLE**—Analog channel: 46. Digital channel: 42. On air date: Sept 23, 1968. 600 Cooper Dr., Lexington, KY 40502. Phone: (859) 258-7000. Fax: (859) 258-7399. Web Site: www.ket.org. Licensee: Kentucky Authority for Educational TV. Network: PBS. Washington Atty: Kenkel, Barnard & Edmundson.
Key Personnel:
Linda Hume . . . CFO
Malcolm Wall. . . . CEO & gen mgr
Bob Ball. . . . opns mgr & progmg dir
Craig Cornwell . . . opns mgr & progmg dir

***WKMR**—Analog channel: 38. Digital channel: 38. On air date: Sept 23, 1968. c/o WKLE, 600 Cooper Dr., Lexington, KY 40502. Phone: (859) 258-7000. Fax: (606) 258-7399. Web Site: www.ket.org. Licensee: Kentucky Authority for Educational TV. Network: PBS.
Key Personnel:
Malcolm Wall. . . . CEO & gen mgr
Linda Hume . . . CFO
Bob Ball . . . opns mgr & engrg dir
Craig Cornwell . . . opns mgr & progmg dir
Michele Ripley . . . dev dir

***WKSO-TV**—Analog channel: 29. Digital channel: 14. On air date: Sept 23, 1968. c/o WKLE, 600 Cooper Dr., Lexington, KY 40502. Phone: (606) 258-7000. Fax: (606) 258-7399. Web Site: www.ket.org. Licensee: Kentucky Authority for Educational TV. Network: PBS.
Key Personnel:
Malcolm Wall. . . . CEO & gen mgr
Linda Hume . . . CFO
Bob Ball . . . opns mgr & engrg dir
Craig Cornwell . . . opns mgr & progmg dir
Michele Ripley . . . dev dir

WKYT-TV—Analog channel: 27. Digital channel: 59. On air date: Sept 30, 1957. Box 55037, Lexington, KY 40555-5037. 2851 Winchester Rd., Lubbock, KY 40509. Phone: (859) 299-0411. Fax: (859) 299-5531. E-mail: wmartin@wkyt.com. Web Site: www.wkyt.com. Licensee: Gray Television Licensee, Inc. Group owner: Gray Television Inc. (acq 1-21-76; FTR: 2-9-76). Network: CBS. Rep: Harrington, Righter & Parsons. Washington Atty: Venable, Baetjer, Howard & Civiletti. News staff: 50; News: 43 hrs wkly.
Key Personnel:
Wayne Martin. . . . pres, exec VP & gen mgr
Michael D. Kanarek . . . opns VP

WLEX-TV—Analog channel: 18. On air date: Mar 15, 1955. Box 1457, Lexington, KY 40588-1457. 1065 Russell Cave Rd., Lexington, KY 40505. Phone: (859) 259-1818. Fax: (859) 255-2418. Fax: TWX: 510-476-8896. E-mail: wlextv@wlextv.com. Web Site: www.wlextv.com. Licensee: WLEX Communications L.L.C. Group owner: Cordillera Communications Inc. (acq 7-8-99; $99.1 million). Network: NBC. Rep: Katz Radio. Washington Atty: Dow, Lohnes & Albertson.
Key Personnel:
Sandra Byron . . . CFO
Tim Gilbert . . . chmn, pres & gen mgr
Sean Franklin . . . opns mgr
Andrew Shenkan . . . sls VP & sls dir
Mary West . . . gen sls mgr
Sandy Stevenson. . . . natl sls mgr
Chip Al-Fred . . . prom dir & pub affrs dir
Teresa Cassidy. . . . progmg dir & progmg

Bruce Carter . . . . . news dir
David Powell. . . . . chief of engrg

WLJC-TV—Analog channel: 65. Digital channel: 7. On air date: Oct 16, 1982. Box Y, 219 Radio Station Loop, Beattyville, KY 41311. Phone: (606) 464-3600. Fax: (606) 464-5021. E-mail: wljc@wljc.com. Web Site: www.wljc.com. Licensee: Hour of Harvest Inc. Rep: Rgnl Reps. Washington Atty: Reddy, Begley & McCormick.
Key Personnel:
Margaret Drake. . . . . pres
Jonathan Drake. . . . . gen mgr, opns mgr & chief of engrg
Rachel Drake. . . . . gen sls mgr & progmg dir

WTVQ-TV—Analog channel: 36. Digital channel: 40. On air date: June 2, 1968. 6940 Man-O-War Blvd., Lexington, KY 40509-9493. Phone: (859) 294-3636. Fax: (859) 293-5002. E-mail: 36onyourside@wtvq.com. Web Site: www.wtvq.com. Licensee: Media General Communications Inc. Group owner: Media General Broadcast Group (acq 3-21-97; grpsl). Network: ABC. Rep: MMT. Washington Atty: Dow, Lohnes & Albertson. News staff: 45; News: 22 hrs wkly.
Key Personnel:
Mark Pimentel . . . . . VP & gen mgr
Blair Payne. . . . . mktg dir
Tai Takahashi. . . . . news dir

WUPX-TV—Analog channel: 67. Digital channel: 21. On air date: June 1998. 2166 McCausey Ridge Rd., Frenchburg, KY 40322. Phone: (606) 784-7932. Fax: (606) 768-9278. Web Site: www.pax.tv. Licensee: Paxson Lexington License Inc. Group owner: Paxson Communications Corp. (acq 4-27-01; $8 million)..

WYMT-TV—Analog channel: 57. Digital channel: 12. On air date: Oct 20, 1969. Box 1299, 199 Black Gold Blvd., Hazard, KY 41702. Phone: (606) 436-5757. Fax: (606) 439-3760. Web Site: www.wymtnews.com. Licensee: Gray Television Licensee Inc. Group owner: Gray Television Inc. (acq 9-2-94). Network: CBS. Rep: Harrington, Righter & Parsons. News staff: 15.
Key Personnel:
Ernestine Cornett . . . . . gen mgr
James Boggs . . . . . gen sls mgr
Edna Eldridge . . . . . prom dir, prom mgr & progmg dir
Neil Middleton . . . . . news dir
Phillip Hayes . . . . . adv mgr & chief of engrg

Louisville, KY (DMA 50)

WAVE—Analog channel: 3. On air date: Nov 24, 1948. Box 32970, 725 S. Floyd St., Louisville, KY 40203. Phone: (502) 585-2201. Fax: (502) 561-4115. Web Site: www.wave3.com. Licensee: Libco Inc. Group owner: Liberty Corp. (acq 10-16-81). Network: NBC. Rep: Harrington, Righter & Parsons. Washington Atty: Dow, Lohnes & Albertson.
Key Personnel:
Steve Langford. . . . . VP & gen mgr
Dan Foos . . . . . opns mgr & progmg dir
Nick Ulmer . . . . . gen sls mgr
Bob Mack . . . . . mktg dir
Bill Eschbach. . . . . chief of engrg

WBKI-TV—Analog channel: 34. On air date: Apr 6, 1983. 1601 Alliant Ave., Louisville, KY 40299. Phone: (502) 809-3400. Fax: (502) 266-6262. E-mail: hr@wb34.com. Web Site: www.wbki.tv. Licensee: Louisville Communications L.L.C. Group owner: Cascade Broadcasting Group L.L.C. (acq 6-9-00). Washington Atty: Shaw Pittman.
Key Personnel:
Greg Kunz . . . . . CEO
Carol LaFever. . . . . COO
Tom Hettle . . . . . CFO
Richard Williams . . . . . exec VP

WBNA—Analog channel: 21. Digital channel: 8. On air date: Apr 2, 1986. 3701 Fern Valley Rd., Louisville, KY 40219. Phone: (502) 964-2121. Fax: (502) 966-9692. Web Site: www.pax.tv. Licensee: Word Broadcasting Network Inc. Group owner: (group owner) Network: PAX TV. Washington Atty: Pepper & Corazzini.
Key Personnel:
Joseph Koker. . . . . pres, VP & gen mgr
Sally Lawler . . . . . gen sls mgr

WDRB—Analog channel: 41. Digital channel: 49. On air date: Feb 28, 1971. 624 W. Muhammad Ali Blvd., Louisville, KY 40203. Phone: (502) 584-6441. Fax: (502) 589-5559. Web Site: www.fox41.com. Licensee: Independence TV Co. Group owner: Block Communications Inc. (acq 3-84; $10 million;. FTR: 1-2-84). Network: Fox. Rep: TeleRep. Washington Atty: Dow, Lohnes & Albertson. News staff: 45; News: 33.5 hrs wkly.
Key Personnel:
Bill Lamb . . . . . pres & gen mgr
Harry Beam . . . . . opns mgr
Marti Hazel . . . . . gen sls mgr
Steve Ballard . . . . . CFO & natl sls mgr
Gary Schroder . . . . . chief of engrg

WFTE—Analog channel: 58. On air date: Mar 15, 1994. 624 W. Muhammed Ali Blvd., Louisville, KY 40203. Phone: (502) 584-6441. Fax: (502) 589-5559. Web Site: www.great58.com. Licensee: Independence Television Co. Group owner: Block Communications Inc. (acq 3-30-2001). Network: UPN.
Key Personnel:
Bill Lamb . . . . . pres & gen mgr
Marti Hazel. . . . . gen mgr
Harry Beam . . . . . opns mgr & progmg dir
Kim Erau . . . . . natl sls mgr
Shannon Stewart. . . . . rgnl sls mgr
David Jewell . . . . . prom dir
Kathy Lehmann. . . . . news dir
Gary Schroder . . . . . chief of engrg

WHAS-TV—Analog channel: 11. Digital channel: 55. On air date: Mar 27, 1950. Box 1100, Louisville, KY 40201. 520 W. Chestnut St., Louisville, KY 40201. Phone: (502) 582-7711. Fax: (502) 582-7279. Web Site: www.whas11.com. Licensee: Belo Kentucky Inc. Group owner: Belo Corp., Broadcast Division (acq 2-97; grpsl). Network: ABC. Washington Atty: Covington & Burling.
Key Personnel:
Robert Klingle. . . . . pres, VP & gen mgr
Neal Metersky . . . . . opns dir, engrg dir & chief of engrg
Lori Morgan . . . . . sls dir
Doug Roberts . . . . . natl sls mgr
Kirk Szesny . . . . . mktg dir, prom dir & pub affrs dir
Joy Pritchett . . . . . progmg dir & progmg mgr
Scott Diener . . . . . news dir

WKMJ—Analog channel: 68. Digital channel: 38. On air date: Aug 31, 1970. c/o WKLE, 600 Cooper Dr., Lexington, KY 40502. Phone: (859) 258-7000. Fax: (859) 258-7399. Web Site: www.ket.org. Licensee: Kentucky Authority for Educational TV. Network: PBS.
Key Personnel:
Malcolm Wall. . . . . CEO & gen mgr
Sally Hamilton . . . . . pres & CFO
Craig Cornwell . . . . . opns mgr
Michele Ripley . . . . . dev dir & dev mgr
Ron Griffin. . . . . sls dir & rgnl sls mgr
Mary Campbell . . . . . prom dir
Tona Barkley . . . . . prom mgr
Dick Hoffman . . . . . progmg dir
Bill Goodman . . . . . pub affrs dir
Robert Ball . . . . . engrg dir

***WKPC-TV**—Analog channel: 15. Digital channel: 17. On air date: Sept 5, 1958. c/o WKLE, 600 Cooper Dr., Lexington, KY 40502. Phone: (859) 258-7000. Fax: (859) 258-7399. Web Site: www.ket.org. Licensee: Kentucky Authority for Educational Television. Network: PBS. Washington Atty: Schwartz, Woods & Miller.
Key Personnel:
Malcolm Wall. . . . . CEO & gen mgr
Sally Hamilton . . . . . pres & CFO
Craig Cornwell . . . . . opns mgr
Michele Ripley. . . . . dev VP & dev dir
Ron Griffin. . . . . sls dir & rgnl sls mgr
Mary Campbell . . . . . prom dir
Tona Barkley. . . . . prom dir & prom mgr
Dick Hoffman . . . . . progmg VP & progmg dir
Robert Hall . . . . . chief of engrg

***WKZT-TV**—Analog channel: 23. Digital channel: 43. On air date: Sept 23, 1968. 600 Cooper Dr., Lexington, KY 40502. Phone: (859) 258-7000. Fax: (859) 258-7399. Web Site: www.ket.org. Licensee: Kentucky Authority for Educational TV. Network: PBS.
Key Personnel:
Malcolm Wall . . . . . CEO & stn mgr
Linda Hume . . . . . pres & CFO
Bob Ball . . . . . opns mgr & engrg dir
Craig Cornwell . . . . . opns mgr & progmg dir
Michele Ripley . . . . . dev dir & dev mgr

WLKY-TV—Analog channel: 32. On air date: Sept 18, 1961. Box 6205, 1918 Mellwood Ave., Louisville, KY 40206. Phone: (502) 893-3671. Fax: (502) 897-2384. Web Site: www.thelouisvillechannel.com. Licensee: Hearst-Argyle Properties Inc. Group owner: Hearst-Argyle Television Inc. (acq 3-18-99; grpsl). Network: CBS. Washington Atty: Brooks, Pierce, McLendon, Humphrey & Leonard. News: 37.5 hrs wkly.
Key Personnel:
Jim Carter . . . . . pres & gen mgr
David Levy . . . . . opns mgr

Madisonville

see Evansville, IN market

Newport

see Cincinnati, OH market

Owensboro

see Evansville, IN market

Owenton

see Cincinnati, OH market

Paducah, KY-Cape Girardeau, MO-Harrisburg-Mount Vernon, IL (DMA 79)

KBSI—Analog channel: 23. On air date: Sept 10, 1983. 806 Enterprise, Cape Girardeau, MO 63703. Phone: (573) 334-1223. Fax: (573) 334-1208. Web Site: www.kbsi23.com. Licensee: KBSI Licensee L.P. Group owner: Sinclair Broadcast Group Inc. (acq 1998; grpsl). Network: Fox. Rep: Millennium Sales & Marketing. News staff: one; News: 2 hrs wkly.
Key Personnel:
Ted Stephens. . . . . gen mgr
Rob Chronister . . . . . opns dir
Jennifer Chronister . . . . . gen sls mgr
Jean Graham . . . . . natl sls mgr
Wanda Evans . . . . . rgnl sls mgr
Chuck Moffitt . . . . . prom mgr
Alan Muster . . . . . progmg dir
Chris Girard . . . . . chief of engrg

KFVS-TV—Analog channel: 12. On air date: Oct 3, 1954. 310 Broadway, Cape Girardeau, MO 63701. Box 100, Cape Girardeau, MO 63702. Phone: (573) 335-1212. Fax: (573) 335-6303. E-mail: manager@kfvs12.com. Web Site: www.kfvs.com. Licensee: Raycom America License Subsidiary LLC. Group owner: Raycom Media Inc. (acq 4-97; grpsl). Network: CBS. Rep: Harrington, Righter & Parsons. Washington Atty: Covington & Burling. News staff: 45; News: 28 hrs wkly.
Key Personnel:
Mike Smythe . . . . . gen mgr
Mike Wunderlich. . . . . opns dir
Joe Trepasso . . . . . gen sls mgr
Brad Zaruba. . . . . natl sls mgr
David Stockard. . . . . rgnl sls mgr
Paul Keener . . . . . mktg dir
Dan Timpe . . . . . prom dir
Kathy Cowan. . . . . progmg dir & pub affrs dir
Mark Little . . . . . news dir
Arnold Killian. . . . . chief of engrg

KPOB-TV—Analog channel: 15. On air date: Sept 15, 1967. 1416 Country Air Dr., Carterville, IL 62918. Phone: (618) 985-2333. Fax: (618) 985-3709. Licensee: Mel Wheeler Inc. Group owner: (group owner; acq 5-12-83; $6.6 million; 6-6-83). Network: ABC. Rep: Katz Radio. Washington Atty: Pepper & Corazzini.
Key Personnel:
Leonard Wheeler . . . . . pres
Steve Wheeler . . . . . gen mgr
Harold McDaniel . . . . . opns mgr
Dave Cisco . . . . . gen sls mgr
Mike Snuffer . . . . . news dir
Pat Victorie . . . . . chief of engrg

WDKA—Analog channel: 49. On air date: June 1997. 806 Enterprise St., Cape Girardeau, MO 63703. Phone: (573) 334-1223. Fax: (573) 334-1208. Web Site: www.wdka49.com. Licensee: WDKA Acquisition Corp.
Key Personnel:
Dee Rose . . . . . gen mgr
Rob Chronister . . . . . opns dir
Jennifer Chonister . . . . . gen sls mgr
Jean Graham . . . . . natl sls mgr
Wanda Evans . . . . . rgnl sls mgr
Chuck Moffitt . . . . . prom dir
Alan Master . . . . . progmg dir
Chris Girard . . . . . chief of engrg

***WKMU**—Analog channel: 21. Digital channel: 36. On air date: Oct 9, 1968. c/o KET, 600 Cooper Dr., Lexington, KY 40502. Phone: (859) 258-7000. Fax: (859) 258-7399. Web Site: www.ket.org. Licensee: Kentucky Authority for Educational TV. Network: PBS.

Key Personnel:
Malcolm Wall . . . . . CEO & gen mgr
Linda Hume . . . . . CFO
Craig Cornwell . . . . . opns dir
Bob Ball . . . . . opns mgr & engrg dir
Michele Ripley . . . . . dev dir

***WKPD**—Analog channel: 29. Digital channel: 41. On air date: May 31, 1971. c/o WKLE, 600 Cooper Dr., Lexington, KY 40502. Phone: (859) 258-7000. Fax: (859) 258-7399. Web Site: www.ket.org. Licensee: Kentucky Authority for Educational TV. (acq 2-28-78). Network: PBS. Washington Atty: Kenkel, Barnard & Edmundson.

Key Personnel:
Malcolm Wall . . . . . CEO & gen mgr
Linda Hume . . . . . CFO
Bob Ball . . . . . opns mgr & engrg dir
Craig Cornwell . . . . . opns mgr & progmg dir
Michele Ripley . . . . . dev dir

WPSD-TV—Analog channel: 6. Digital channel: 32. On air date: May 28, 1957. Box 1197, Paducah, KY 42002-1197. 100 Television Ln., Edmonton, KY 42003. Phone: (270) 415-1900. Fax: (270) 415-2020. E-mail: bevans@wpsdtv.com. Web Site: www.wpsdtv.com. Licensee: WPSD-TV LLC.. Ownership: Paxton Media Group Inc., see Cross-Ownership. (acq 12-3-01). Network: NBC. Washington Atty: Covington & Burling. News staff: 49; News: 23 hrs wkly.

Key Personnel:
Richard Paxton . . . . . gen mgr
Bill Evans . . . . . opns VP
Mark Hall . . . . . opns mgr
David Jernigan . . . . . sls VP & progmg VP
Bob Crosno . . . . . rgnl sls mgr
Cathy Crecelius . . . . . prom mgr
Andrea Underwood . . . . . news dir
Cathy Crelelius . . . . . pub affrs dir
Joey Gill . . . . . chief of engrg

WPXS—Analog channel: 13. Digital channel: 21. On air date: Mar 1, 1983. 4751 Cartter Rd., Kell, IL 62853. Phone: (618) 822-6900. Fax: (618) 822-6526. Licensee: EBC St. Louis Inc. Group owner: Equity Broadcasting Corp. (acq 4-26-01; $17.75 million. with KDUO(TV) Flagstaff, AZ).

WSIL-TV—Analog channel: 3. On air date: December 1953. 1416 Country Aire Rd., Carterville, IL 62918. Phone: (618) 985-2333. Fax: (618) 985-3709. Web Site: www.wsiltv.com. Licensee: WSIL TV Inc. Group owner: Mel Wheeler Inc. (acq 5-12-83; grpsl; 6-6-83). Network: ABC. Rep: Continental Television Sales. Washington Atty: Brooks, Pierce, McLendon, Humprey & Leonard.

***WSIU-TV**—Analog channel: 8. Digital channel: 40. On air date: November 1961. 1003 Communications Bldg., Southern Illinois Univ., Carbondale, IL 62901-6602. Phone: (618) 453-4343. Fax: (618) 453-6186. Web Site: www.wsiu.org. Licensee: Board of Trustees of Southern Illinois University. Network: PBS. Washington Atty: Cohn & Marks. News staff: one; News: 2 hrs wkly.

Key Personnel:
Candis Isberner . . . . . CEO & gen mgr
Delores Kerstein . . . . . CFO
Robert Henderson . . . . . opns dir
Tom Godell . . . . . dev dir & gen sls mgr
Renee Dillard . . . . . mktg dir
Leyla Goodsell . . . . . prom dir
Monica Tichenor . . . . . adv dir
Trina Lyons . . . . . progmg dir & film buyer
Richard Kuenneke . . . . . news dir & pub affrs dir
Jack L. Hammer . . . . . engrg dir

WTCT—Analog channel: 27. Digital channel: 17. On air date: Aug 16, 1981. Box 698, 11717 Rt. 37 N., Marion, IL 62959. Phone: (618) 997-4700. Fax: (618) 993-9778. Licensee: Tri-State Christian TV. Group owner: (group owner; acq 5-29-84; $1.2 million).

Pikeville

see Charleston-Huntington, WV market

Louisiana

Alexandria, LA (DMA 176)

KALB-TV—Analog channel: 5. Digital channel: 35. On air date: Sept 29, 1954. Box 951, Alexandria, LA 71309. Phone: (318) 445-2456. Fax: (318) 442-7427. E-mail: news@kalb.com. Web Site: www.kalb.com. Licensee: Media General Communications Inc. Group owner: Media General Broadcast Group (acq 3-21-97; grpsl). Network: NBC. Washington Atty: Dow, Lohnes & Albertson.

Key Personnel:
Les Golmon . . . . . gen mgr
Gary Coullard . . . . . opns dir & chief of engrg
Tom Pears III . . . . . gen sls mgr
Keith Holt . . . . . mktg dir
Shannon Tassin . . . . . progmg dir

KBCA—Analog channel: 41. On air date: June 1, 2005. Delta Media Corp., 3501 Northwest Evangeline Thruway, Carencro, LA 70520. Phone: (337) 896-1600. Fax: (337) 896-2695. Permittee: Dimension Broadcasting Co. LLC.. Ownership: Delta Media Corp., 100%. Network: WB. Washington Atty: Fletcher, Heald & Hildreth.

Key Personnel:
Charles Chatelain . . . . . pres
Eddie Blanchard . . . . . gen mgr

KLAX-TV—Analog channel: 31. Digital channel: 32. On air date: Mar 3, 1983. Box 8818, 1811 England Dr., Alexandria, LA 71303. Phone: (318) 473-0031. Fax: (318) 442-4646. Web Site: www.klax.tv. Licensee: Pollack-Belz Communication Co. Inc. (acq 6-3-88; $1.1 million). Network: ABC. Rep: Blair Television. Washington Atty: Wood, Maines & Brown. News staff: 4; News: 4 hrs wkly.

Key Personnel:
William H. Pollack . . . . . pres
David Carlson . . . . . CFO
Ken Nolan . . . . . gen mgr
Carol Ulmer . . . . . gen sls mgr
Mike Mule . . . . . prom dir & prom mgr
Frances Yeager . . . . . progmg dir
Wes Fussell . . . . . chief of engrg

***KLPA-TV**—Analog channel: 25. On air date: July 1, 1983. 7733 Perkins Rd., Baton Rouge, LA 70810. Phone: (225) 767-5660. Phone: (800) 272-8161. Fax: (225) 767-4299. Web Site: www.lpb.org. Licensee: Louisiana Educational Television Authority. Network: PBS. Washington Atty: Schwartz, Woods & Miller.

Key Personnel:
Beth Corthey . . . . . CEO
Tonja Normand . . . . . opns dir & opns mgr

Baton Rouge, LA (DMA 96)

WAFB—Analog channel: 9. On air date: Apr 19, 1953. 844 Government St., Baton Rouge, LA 70802. Phone: (225) 383-9999. Fax: (225) 379-7891. Fax: TWX: 510-993-3406. E-mail: news@wafb.com. Web Site: www.wafb.com. Licensee: WAFB License Subsidiary LLC. Group owner: Raycom Media Inc. (acq 12-31-96; grpsl). Network: CBS. Rep: Harrington, Righter & Parsons. Washington Atty: Covington & Burling.

Key Personnel:
Nick Simonette . . . . . VP, gen mgr & progmg mgr
Vicki Kellum . . . . . gen sls mgr
Denise Murrell . . . . . rgnl sls mgr
Andree Boyd . . . . . prom mgr
Vicki Zimmerman . . . . . news dir
Dale Russell . . . . . chief of engrg

WBRZ—Analog channel: 2. On air date: Apr 14, 1955. Box 2906, Baton Rouge, LA 70821. 1650 Highland Rd., Baton Rouge, LA 70821. Phone: (225) 387-2222. Fax: (225) 336-2246. E-mail: news@2theadvocate.com. Web Site: www.2theadvocate.com. Licensee: Louisiana Television Broadcasting LLC. Group owner: Manship Stations (acq 1958; $548,000).. Network: ABC. News staff: 47; News: 22 hrs wkly.

Key Personnel:
Richard F. Manship . . . . . pres
Kim Manship . . . . . CFO
Rocky Daboval . . . . . gen mgr
Clyde Pierce . . . . . opns dir & engrg dir
Dave Brangan . . . . . sls dir
Jim "Rocky" Daboval . . . . . sls dir
Dan Penny . . . . . natl sls mgr
Denise Akers . . . . . mktg dir, mktg dir, prom dir & adv dir
Chuck Bark . . . . . news dir
Russ Kilgore . . . . . news dir
Suzanne Marva . . . . . progmg dir & pub affrs dir

WGMB—Analog channel: 44. On air date: Aug 11, 1991. Box 82959, Baton Rouge, LA 70884. 10000 Perkins Rd., Baton Rouge, LA 70810. Phone: (225) 769-0044. Fax: (225) 769-9462. Web Site: www.fox44.com. Licensee: Comcorp of Baton Rouge. Group owner: Communications Corp. of America (acq 2-13-95; 5-8-95). Network: Fox. Washington Atty: Fletcher, Heald & Hildreth.

Key Personnel:
Tom R. Galloway Sr. . . . . . pres
Wayne Elmore . . . . . CFO
Clark White . . . . . VP
Cheri Jacks . . . . . natl sls mgr
Thom Postema . . . . . rgnl sls mgr & adv dir
Terry Freeman . . . . . chief of engrg

***WLPB-TV**—Analog channel: 27. On air date: Sept 6, 1975. 7733 Perkins Rd., Baton Rouge, LA 70810. Phone: (225) 767-5660. Fax: (225) 767-4277. Fax: (225) 767-4299. Web Site: www.lpb.org. Licensee: Louisiana Educational Television Authority. Network: PBS. Washington Atty: Schwartz, Woods & Miller. News staff: 3; News: one hr wkly.

Key Personnel:
Beth Corthey . . . . . CEO
Tonja Normand . . . . . opns dir & opns mgr

WVLA—Analog channel: 33. Digital channel: 34. On air date: Oct 16, 1971. Box 82359, Baton Rouge, LA 70884-2359. 10000 Perkins Rd., Baton Rouge, LA 70810. Phone: (225) 766-3233. Fax: (225) 768-9191. Web Site: www.nbc33tv.com. Licensee: Knight Broadcasting of Baton Rouge. Group owner: White Knight Holdings Inc. (acq 1996; $23.975 million). Network: NBC. Rep: Katz Radio. Washington Atty: Dow, Lohnes & Albertson. News staff: 3; News: 6 hrs wkly.

Key Personnel:
David Brangan . . . . . gen mgr
Sheldon Galloway . . . . . opns VP
Damian Calato . . . . . sls VP
Fran McRae . . . . . natl sls mgr
Nils Breckoff . . . . . mktg mgr
Denise O'Neil . . . . . progmg dir
Pamela Matassa . . . . . news dir
Elaine Harrison . . . . . pub affrs dir
Terry Freeman . . . . . engrg VP

Lafayette, LA (DMA 123)

KACB-TV—Analog channel: 50.Not on air, target date: unknown: 516 St. Landry St., Lafayette, LA 70506. Phone: (337) 234-2020. Fax: (337) 234-8230. Permittee: Iberia Communications LLC.

KADN—Analog channel: 15. Digital channel: 16. On air date: Feb 28, 1980. 125 N. Easy St., Lafayette, LA 70506. Phone: (337) 237-1500. Fax: (337) 237-2237. Web Site: www.kadn.com. Licensee: Comcorp of Louisiana License Corp. (acq 12-9-2004; $13,125,000).. Network: Fox. Washington Atty: Fletcher, Heald & Hildreth.

KATC—Analog channel: 3. On air date: Sept 19, 1962. Box 63333, Lafayette, LA 70596-3333. 1103 Eraste Landry Rd., Lafayette, LA 70596-3333. Phone: (337) 235-3333. Fax: (337) 235-9363. E-mail: webmaster@katctv.com. Web Site: www.katc.com. Licensee: KATC Communications Inc. Group owner: Cordillera Communications Inc. (acq 1995; $24.5 million). Network: ABC. Rep: Continental Television Sales. Washington Atty: Dow, Lohnes. News staff: 45; News: 19.5 hrs wkly.

Key Personnel:
Nannette Frye . . . . . gen mgr
Bonnie R. Will . . . . . gen sls mgr
Arte Richard . . . . . mktg dir & mktg mgr
James Warner . . . . . news dir
Pat O'Brien . . . . . chief of engrg

KLFY-TV—Analog channel: 10. Digital channel: 56. On air date: June 3, 1955. Box 90665, 1808 Eraste Landry Rd., Lafayette, LA 70509. Phone: (337) 981-4823. Fax: (337) 981-6533. Web Site: www.klfy.com. Licensee: Young Broadcasting of Louisiana Inc. Group owner: Young Broadcasting Inc. (acq 5-28-88; $51 million; 12-14-87). Network: CBS. Rep: Adam Young. Washington Atty: Wiley, Rein & Fielding. News staff: 24; News: 14 hrs wkly.

***KLPB-TV**—Analog channel: 24. On air date: May 2, 1981. 7733 Perkins Rd., Baton Rouge, LA 70810. Phone: (225) 767-5660. Phone: (800) 272-8161. Fax: (225) 767-4299. Web Site: www.lpb.org. Licensee: Louisiana Educational Television Authority. Network: PBS. Washington Atty: Schwartz, Woods & Miller.

Key Personnel:
Beth Corthey . . . . . CEO & gen mgr
Bob Danidge . . . . . chmn

Lake Charles, LA (DMA 177)

***KLTL-TV**—Analog channel: 18. Digital channel: 20. On air date: May 5, 1981. 7733 Perkins Rd., Baton Rouge, LA 70810. Phone: (225) 767-5660. Phone: (800) 272-8161. Fax: (225) 767-4277. Web Site:

www.lpb.org. Licensee: Louisiana Educational Television Authority. Network: PBS. Washington Atty: Schwartz, Woods & Miller.

KPLC—Analog channel: 7. On air date: September 1954. Box 1490, Lake Charles, LA 70602. 320 Division St., Lake Charles, LA 70602. Phone: (337) 439-9071. Phone: (337) 437-7568 (news). Fax: (337) 437-7600. Fax: (337) 437-7546 (sales). Web Site: www.kplctv.com. Licensee: Libco Inc. Group owner: Liberty Corp. (acq 11-13-86; grpsl). Network: NBC. Rep: Harrington, Righter & Parsons. Washington Atty: Dow, Lohnes & Albertson. News staff: 28.
Key Personnel:
Jim Serra . . . . . gen mgr
Diana Mayo . . . . . opns mgr
Jim Reardon . . . . . gen sls mgr
Robin Daugereau . . . . . progmg dir
David Williams . . . . . news dir
John Scott . . . . . chief of engrg

KVHP—Analog channel: 29. Digital channel: 30. On air date: Dec 12, 1982. 129 W. Prien Lake Rd., Lake Charles, LA 70601. Phone: (337) 474-1316. Fax: (337) 477-0715. E-mail: info@watchfox.com. Web Site: www.watchfox.com. Licensee: National Communications Inc. (acq 10-3-96). Network: Fox. Washington Atty: Baraff, Koerner, Olender & Hochberg. News staff: 20; News: 9 hrs wkly.
Key Personnel:
Leslie Bass . . . . . gen mgr
Ken Smith . . . . . gen sls mgr
Mary Stevens . . . . . natl sls mgr
Nadia Matar . . . . . prom dir & prom mgr
Kim Anderson . . . . . progmg dir
John Korbel . . . . . news dir
Brett Thibodeaux . . . . . chief of engrg

Monroe, LA-El Dorado, AR
(DMA 135)

KAQY—Analog channel: 11. On air date: Dec 10, 1998. Box 4309, Monroe, LA 71211. Phone: (318) 325-3011. Fax: (318) 327-7519. Fax: (318) 327-7500. Web Site: www.abc-11.com. Licensee: Monroe Broadcasting Inc.. Ownership: Charles H. Chatelain, 100% (acq 11-98). Network: ABC.
Key Personnel:
Joe Currie . . . . . gen mgr, stn mgr & natl sls mgr
Kimberly Halverson . . . . . rgnl sls mgr
Larry Clifton . . . . . prom mgr
Doyg Ginn . . . . . progmg dir
Jerry Wimberty . . . . . chief of engrg

KARD—Analog channel: 14. On air date: Oct 6, 1974. 200 Pavilion Rd., West Monroe, LA 71292. Phone: (318) 323-1972. Fax: (318) 322-0926. Web Site: www.regionio.com. Licensee: Nexstar Finance Inc. Group owner: Nexstar Broadcasting Group Inc. (acq 12-31-03; grpsl). Network: Fox. Washington Atty: Arter & Hadden.
Key Personnel:
Lydia Guillory . . . . . gen mgr
Bob Douwden . . . . . gen sls mgr

KEJB—Analog channel: 43. On air date: October 2003. 1001 N. 11th St., Monroe, LA 71201. Phone: (318) 322-4188. Fax: (318) 322-9567. Licensee: KM Television of El Dorado L.L.C. Group owner: KM Communications Inc. Network: UPN.
Key Personnel:
John Wilson . . . . . gen mgr & gen sls mgr
Terri Egloff . . . . . progmg dir

***KETZ**—Analog channel: 30.Not on air, target date: unknown: Box 1250, Conway, AR 72033. Phone: (501) 682-2386. Fax: (501) 682-4122. Web Site: www.aetn.org. Permittee: Arkansas Educational Television Commission. Network: PBS.

***KLTM-TV**—Analog channel: 13. On air date: Sept 8, 1976. 7733 Perkins Rd., Baton Rouge, LA 70810. Phone: (225) 767-5660. Phone: (800) 272-8161. Fax: (225) 767-4219. Web Site: www.lpb.org. Licensee: Louisiana Educational Television Authority. Network: PBS. Washington Atty: Schwartz, Woods & Miller.
Key Personnel:
Beth Courtney . . . . . CEO
Tonja Normand . . . . . opns dir & prom mgr

KMCT-TV—Analog channel: 39. On air date: Apr 7, 1986. 701 Parkwood Dr., West Monroe, LA 71291-5435. Phone: (318) 322-1399. Fax: (318) 323-3783. E-mail: lamb@lambbroadcasting.org. Web Site: www.lambbroadcasting.org. Licensee: Louisiana Christian Broadcasting Inc.. Ownership: Lamb Broadcasting Inc., 100% Group owner: (group owner; (acq 7-13-2004). Washington Atty: Shaw Pittman. News: 6 hrs wkly.

KNOE-TV—Analog channel: 8. On air date: Sept 27, 1953. Box 4067, Monroe, LA 71211. 1400 Oliver Rd., Monroe, LA 71201. Phone: (318) 388-8888. Fax: (318) 388-0070. Fax: (318) 322-8774. E-mail: knoetv@bayou.com. Web Site: www.knoe.com. Licensee: Noe Corp. L.L.C.. Ownership: James A. Noe Jr., 100%. Network: CBS. Rep: Blair Television. Washington Atty: Cohn & Marks. News staff: 28; News: 22 hrs wkly.
Key Personnel:
James A. Noe Jr. . . . . . pres
George Noe . . . . . exec VP
Roy Frostenson . . . . . gen mgr
Ed Rayner . . . . . opns mgr
John Matherne . . . . . gen sls mgr
Andy Pontz . . . . . news dir
Jerry Harkins . . . . . chief of engrg

KTVE—Analog channel: 10. On air date: Dec 3, 1955. 200 Pavillion Rd., W. Monroe, LA 71292. Phone: (318) 323-1972. Fax: (318) 322-9718. Web Site: www.region10.com. Licensee: Piedmont Television of Monroe/El Dorado License LLC. Group owner: Piedmont Television Holdings LLC. Network: NBC. Rep: Katz Radio. Washington Atty: Cohn & Marks. News staff: 26; News: 13 hrs wkly.
Key Personnel:
Jim Prestwood . . . . . gen mgr
Mark McGeary . . . . . gen sls mgr
John Livingston . . . . . prom dir
Tim Bass . . . . . progmg dir
Mike Courington . . . . . news dir
Stew Romain . . . . . chief of engrg

New Orleans, LA
(DMA 43)

WDSU—Analog channel: 6. On air date: Dec 18, 1948. 846 Howard Ave., New Orleans, LA 70113. Phone: (504) 679-0600. Fax: (504) 679-0745. E-mail: feedback6@wdsu.com. Web Site: www.theneworleanschannel.com. Licensee: New Orleans Hearst-Argyle Television Inc. Group owner: Hearst-Argyle Television Inc. (acq 1999; grpsl). Network: NBC. Rep: Eagle Television Sales. Washington Atty: Verner, Liipfert, Bernhard, McPherson & Hand. News staff: 51; News: 18 hrs wkly.
Key Personnel:
Mason Granger . . . . . pres & gen mgr
Frank Raterman . . . . . gen sls mgr
Jason Ferguson . . . . . natl sls mgr
Giovana Smith . . . . . rgnl sls mgr
Randy Foulds . . . . . mktg dir & prom dir
Anzio Williams . . . . . progmg dir & news dir
Lenora Boutte . . . . . pub affrs dir
Chet Guillot . . . . . chief of engrg

WGNO—Analog channel: 26. On air date: Oct 16, 1967. 1400 Poydras St., Suite 745, New Orleans, LA 70112. Phone: (504) 525-3838. Fax: (504) 569-0908. E-mail: wgno-tv@tribune.com. Web Site: www.abc26.com. Licensee: WGNO Inc. Group owner: Tribune Broadcasting Co. (acq 9-1-83; $21 million; 8-8-83). Network: ABC. Rep: TeleRep. Washington Atty: Schnader, Harrison, Segal & Lewis.
Key Personnel:
Larry Delia . . . . . gen mgr
Michael LaBonia . . . . . gen sls mgr
Kathleen Quinn . . . . . prom dir & progmg dir
Paula Pendarvis . . . . . news dir
Joe Connolly . . . . . chief of engrg

WHNO—Analog channel: 20. On air date: October 1994. 1100 S. Jefferson Davis Pkwy., New Orleans, LA 70125. Phone: (504) 822-1920. Fax: (504) 822-2060. E-mail: whno@lesea.com. Web Site: www.whno.com. Licensee: Le Sea Broadcasting Corp. Group owner: Le Sea Broadcasting Network: CBS. News: 10 hrs wkly.

***WLAE-TV**—Analog channel: 32. On air date: July 8, 1984. 3330 N. Causeway Blvd., Metairie, LA 70002-3573. Phone: (504) 866-7411. Fax: (504) 840-9838. Web Site: www.pbs.cbs.org/wlae. Licensee: Educational Broadcasting Foundation Inc. Network: PBS. Washington Atty: Marmet & McCombs.

WNOL-TV—Analog channel: 38. On air date: Mar 25, 1984. 1400 Poydras St., Suite 745, New Orleans, LA 70112-5100. Phone: (504) 525-3838. Fax: (504) 569-0908. E-mail: wnoltv@tribune.com. Licensee: WGNO Inc. Group owner: Tribune Broadcasting Co. (acq 1-12-00; approximately $95 million. for remaining 67% with WATL(TV) Atlanta, GA) Rep: MMT.
Key Personnel:
Quincy Jones . . . . . pres
Larry Deira . . . . . gen mgr

WPXL—Analog channel: 49. On air date: Mar 19, 1989. 846 Howard Ave., New Orleans, LA 70113. Phone: (504) 679-0600. Fax: (504) 679-0849. Web Site: www.pax.tv. Licensee: Flinn Broadcasting Corp. (acq 4-30-93; $135,000; 5-24-93).
Key Personnel:
Ami Jenkins . . . . . opns mgr & progmg dir
Lynn Long . . . . . gen mgr & rgnl sls mgr
Joy Maurice . . . . . pub affrs dir
Ernie Harvey . . . . . chief of engrg

WUPL—Analog channel: 54. On air date: June 1, 1995. 3850 N. Causeway Blvd., Suite 454, Metairie, LA 70002. Phone: (504) 828-5454. Fax: (504) 828-5455. Web Site: www.upn54.com. Licensee: Infinity Radio Inc. Group owner: Viacom Television Stations Group. Network: UPN.
Key Personnel:
Gary Wordlaw . . . . . gen mgr
Ron Bartholomew . . . . . dev dir

WVUE—Analog channel: 8. Digital channel: 29. On air date: Feb 1, 1959. 1025 S. Jefferson Davis Pkwy., New Orleans, LA 70125. Phone: (504) 486-6161. Fax: (504) 483-1105. E-mail: info@fox8live.com. Web Site: www.fox8live.com. Licensee: Emmis Television License LLC. Group owner: Emmis Communications Corp. (acq 7-16-98; grpsl). Network: Fox. Rep: Katz Radio. Washington Atty: Brooks, Pierce, McLendon, Humphrey & Leonard.

WWL-TV—Analog channel: 4. On air date: Sept 7, 1957. 1024 N. Rampart St., New Orleans, LA 70116. Phone: (504) 529-4444. Fax: (504) 529-6483. Web Site: www.wwltv.com. Licensee: WWL-TV Inc. Group owner: Belo Corp. (acq 1994). Network: CBS. Rep: TeleRep. Washington Atty: Holland & Knight.
Key Personnel:
Jimmie B. Phillips . . . . . VP & gen mgr
Donna LeBlanc . . . . . opns mgr
Mike Zikmund . . . . . sls dir
Billie Bonnett . . . . . natl sls mgr
Tod Smith . . . . . rgnl sls mgr
Weezie Porter . . . . . rgnl sls mgr
Jimmie Phillips . . . . . progmg mgr
Sandy Breland . . . . . news dir
Laura Murphy . . . . . pub affrs dir
Rick Barber . . . . . chief of engrg

***WYES-TV**—Analog channel: 12. On air date: Apr 1, 1957. 916 Navarre Ave., New Orleans, LA 70124. Box 24026, New Orleans, LA 70184. Phone: (504) 486-5511. Fax: (504) 483-8408. E-mail: info@wyes.org. Web Site: www.wyes.org. Licensee: Greater New Orleans Educational TV Foundation. Network: PBS. Washington Atty: Schwartz, Woods & Miller.
Key Personnel:
Randall Feldman . . . . . CEO, pres & gen mgr
Joseph S. Exnicios . . . . . chmn
Victor Giancola . . . . . CFO
Linda Delaney . . . . . opns mgr
Robin Cooper . . . . . dev VP
Elizabeth Utterback . . . . . prom dir
Fred Barrett . . . . . engrg dir

Shreveport, LA
(DMA 81)

***KLTS-TV**—Analog channel: 24. On air date: Aug 9, 1978. 7733 Perkins Rd., Baton Rouge, LA 70810. Phone: (225) 767-5660. Fax: (225) 767-4219. Web Site: www.lpb.org. Licensee: Louisiana Education Television Authority. Network: PBS. Washington Atty: Schwartz, Woods & Miller.
Key Personnel:
Beth Courtney . . . . . CEO
Tonja Normand . . . . . opns dir & opns mgr

KMSS-TV—Analog channel: 33. On air date: Oct 6, 1985. 3519 Jewella Ave., Shreveport, LA 71109. Phone: (318) 631-5677. Fax: (318) 631-4195. Web Site: www.kmsstv.com. Licensee: Comcorp of Texas License Corp. Group owner: Communications Corp. of America (acq 10-94). Network: Fox. Washington Atty: Semmes, Bowen & Semmes.
Key Personnel:
Mark Cummings . . . . . gen mgr
Susan Newman . . . . . gen sls mgr
Margie Bueche . . . . . rgnl sls mgr
Cheryl May . . . . . prom dir

Directory of Television Maine

Doug Ginn. . . . . progmg dir & pub affrs dir
Erik Peterson. . . . . chief of engrg

KPXJ—Analog channel: 21. On air date: 1999. Box 4066, Shreveport, LA 71104. 312 E. Kings Hwy, Shreveport, LA 71104. Phone: (318) 861-5800. Fax: (318) 219-4634. Web Site: www.upn-21.com. Licensee: Minden Television Corp.. Ownership: Lauren B. Wray, 100% of votes, 88% of total assets (acq 4-14-2004; $10 million).. Network: Network: UPN, PAX TV.
Key Personnel:
Lauren Wray-Ostendorff. . . . . pres & gen mgr
George Sirven. . . . . stn mgr

KSHV—Analog channel: 45. On air date: Apr 15, 1994. 3519 Jewella Ave., Shreveport, LA 71109. Phone: (318) 631-4545. Fax: (318) 621-9688. Web Site: www.kshv.com. Licensee: White Knight Broadcasting of Shreveport License Corp. Group owner: White Knight Holdings Inc. (acq 1995; $3.8 million). Washington Atty: Gammon & Grange.
Key Personnel:
Sheldon Galloway . . . . pres & gen mgr
Issac Turner . . . . sls dir & progmg dir
Cindy Gleason. . . . . gen sls mgr & rgnl sls mgr
Cheryl May . . . . mktg dir & prom mgr
Eric Peterson. . . . . chief of engrg

KSLA-TV—Analog channel: 12. On air date: Jan 1, 1954. 1812 Fairfield Ave., Shreveport, LA 71101. Phone: (318) 222-1212. Fax: (318) 677-6703. E-mail: ksla@ksla.com. Licensee: KSLA License Subsidiary LLC. Group owner: Raycom Media Inc. (acq 9-1-96; grpsl). Network: CBS. Rep: TeleRep.
Key Personnel:
Edward Bradley . . . . VP & gen mgr
Cindy Delaney . . . . sls dir
Sandy Jones . . . . prom dir
Bob Cashell . . . . news dir
Mike Murphy . . . . chief of engrg

KTAL-TV—(Texarkana).TX Analog channel: 6. On air date: Aug 16, 1953. 3150 N. Market St., Shreveport, LA 71107. Box 7428, Shreveport, LA 71107. Phone: (318) 629-6000. Fax: (318) 629-6001. E-mail: news@newschannel6.tv. Web Site: www.newschannel6.tv. Licensee: Nexstar Finance Inc. Group owner: Nexstar Broadcasting Group Inc. (acq 9-11-00; $35.25 million).. Network: NBC. Washington Atty: Covington & Burling.

KTBS-TV—Analog channel: 3. On air date: Sept 3, 1955. Box 44227, Shreveport, LA 71134-4227. 312 E. Kings Hwy., Shreveport, LA 71104-3554. Phone: (318) 861-5800. Fax: (318) 219-4680. E-mail: ktbsnews@ktbs.com. Web Site: www.ktbs.com. Licensee: KTBS Inc.. Ownership: Helen H. Wray, Florence H. Wray, George D. Wray Jr. Network: ABC. Washington Atty: Fletcher, Heald & Hildreth.
Key Personnel:
Edwin Wray . . . . pres & gen mgr
George Sirven . . . . stn mgr & progmg mgr
Judy Meller . . . . rgnl sls mgr
Joe Todaro . . . . prom mgr
Melissa Parkerson . . . . pub affrs dir
David Hendricks . . . . chief of engrg

Maine

Auburn

see Portland-Auburn, ME market

Bangor, ME (DMA 151)

WABI-TV—Analog channel: 5. On air date: Jan 25, 1953. 35 Hildreth St., Bangor, ME 04401. Phone: (207) 947-8321. Fax: (207) 941-9378. E-mail: wabi@wabi.tv. Web Site: www.wabi.tv. Licensee: Community Broadcasting Service. Group owner: Diversified Communications (acq 10-7-53; $125,000; 10-12-53). Network: CBS. Rep: Continental Television Sales. Washington Atty: Irwin, Campbell & Tannenwald. News staff: 30; News: 25 hrs wkly.
Key Personnel:
David Lowell . . . . CEO
Carolin Barrett . . . . pres
Paul Clancy . . . . CFO
Michael Young . . . . VP
Horace Hildreth Jr. . . . . stn mgr
Brian Carter . . . . opns mgr
Tom Gass. . . . . gen sls mgr
Steve Hiltz . . . . progmg mgr

Jim Morris . . . . news dir
Dale Carter . . . . chief of engrg

WLBZ—Analog channel: 2. On air date: Sept 12, 1954. Box 415, Bangor, ME 04402-0415. 329 Mt. Hope Ave., Bangor, ME 04402-0415. Phone: (207) 942-4821. Fax: (207) 945-6816. Fax: (207) 942-2109 (news). Web Site: www.wlbz.com. Licensee: Pacific and Southern Co. Inc. Group owner: Gannett Broadcasting (acq 1998; $110 million with WCSH(TV) Portland). Network: NBC. Washington Atty: Wiley, Rein & Fielding. News staff: 22; News: 33 hrs wkly.
Key Personnel:
Judy Haran. . . . . gen mgr
Mark Parent . . . . prom dir
Mike Marshall. . . . . progmg dir
Heather Seavey. news dir
Dave Mundee . . . . engrg dir & chief of engrg

***WMEB-TV**—Analog channel: 12. On air date: Sept 23, 1963. 1450 Lisbon St., Lewiston, ME 04240. 65 Texas Ave., Bangor, ME 04401. Phone: (800) 884-1717. Phone: (207) 783-9101. Fax: (207) 783-5193. Fax: (207) 942-2857. Web Site: www.mpbc.org. Licensee: Maine Public Broadcasting Corp. (acq 6-23-92; 7-13-92). Network: PBS. Washington Atty: Dow, Lohnes & Albertson.
Key Personnel:
Mary Anne Alhadeff . . . . pres & sls dir
Mary Anne Anne Alhadeff . . . . gen mgr
John Likshis . . . . prom dir

***WMED-TV**—Analog channel: 13. On air date: September 1965. 1450 Lisbon St., Lewiston, ME 04240. 65 Texas Ave., Bangor, ME 04401. Phone: (207) 783-9101. Phone: (800) 884-1717. Fax: (207) 783-5193. Fax: (207) 942-2857. Web Site: www.mpbc.org. Licensee: Maine Public Broadcasting Corp. (acq 6-23-92; 7-13-92). Network: PBS. Washington Atty: Dow, Lohnes & Albertson.

WVII-TV—Analog channel: 7. On air date: Oct 15, 1965. 371 Target Industrial Cir., Bangor, ME 04401. Phone: (207) 945-6457. Fax: (207) 942-0511. Web Site: www.wvii.com. Licensee: Bangor Communications LLC. Group owner: Rockfleet Broadcasting Inc. Network: ABC. Rep: Katz Radio. Washington Atty: Mullin, Rhyne, Emmons & Topel. News staff: 15; News: 6 hrs wkly.
Key Personnel:
R. Joseph Fuchs . . . . CEO
Michael Palmer . . . . gen mgr & progmg dir
George Thomas . . . . opns mgr
Keryn Smith . . . . natl sls mgr
Jan Smith . . . . news dir
Gene Hardin. . . . . pub affrs dir
Mike Staples . . . . chief of engrg

Portland-Auburn, ME (DMA 74)

***WCBB**—Analog channel: 10. Digital channel: 17. On air date: Nov 13, 1961. 1450 Lisbon St., Lewiston, ME 04240. 65 Texas Ave., Bangor, ME 04401. Phone: (207) 783-9101. Phone: (800) 884-1717. Fax: (207) 783-5193. Fax: (207) 942-2857. E-mail: comments@mpbn.net. Web Site: www.mpbn.net. Licensee: Maine Public Broadcasting Corp. (acq 6-23-92; 7-13-92). Network: PBS. Washington Atty: Dow, Lohnes & Albertson.

WCSH—Analog channel: 6. On air date: Dec 1, 1953. One Congress Sq., Portland, ME 04101. Phone: (207) 828-6666. Fax: (207) 828-6620. E-mail: wcsh6@wcsh6.com. Web Site: www.wcsh6.com. Licensee: Pacific and Southern Co. Inc. Group owner: Gannett Broadcasting (acq 1-98). Network: NBC. Washington Atty: Wiley, Rein & Fielding.
Key Personnel:
Steve Thaxton . . . . pres & gen mgr
Debbie Briggs . . . . opns mgr
Stu Pruzansky . . . . gen sls mgr
Pat Archambault . . . . natl sls mgr
Mike Marshall . . . . prom mgr & progmg mgr
Mike Curry . . . . news dir
Charlene Belanger . . . . pub affrs dir
Dave Mundee . . . . chief of engrg

WGME-TV—Analog channel: 13. On air date: May 16, 1954. 1335 Washington Ave., Conroe, ME 04103. Phone: (207) 797-1313. Fax: (207) 878-3505. E-mail: tvmail@wgme.com. Web Site: www.wgme.com. Licensee: WGME Licensee L.L.C. Group owner: Sinclair Broadcast Group Inc. (acq 5-3-99; grpsl). Network: CBS. Rep: Katz Radio. Washington Atty: Dow, Lohnes & Albertson. News staff: 55; News: 25 hrs wkly.
Key Personnel:
Alan Cartwright . . . . pres & gen mgr

Mike Pendergast . . . . gen sls mgr
Dave Kaplas . . . . rgnl sls mgr & news dir

***WLED-TV**—Analog channel: 49. On air date: Feb 7, 1968. 268 Mast Rd., Durham, NH 03824-4601. Phone: (603) 868-1100. Fax: (603) 868-7552. E-mail: themailbox@nhptv.org. Web Site: www.nhptv.org. Licensee: University of New Hampshire. Network: PBS. Washington Atty: Schwartz, Woods & Miller.
Key Personnel:
Peter A. Frid . . . . gen mgr
Dennis Malloy . . . . dev dir & sls dir
Jeff Moris. . . . . prom mgr
Mercedes Sabio. . . . . progmg dir
Brian Shepperd. . . . . engrg dir & chief of engrg

***WMEA-TV**—Analog channel: 26. On air date: March 1975. 65 Texas Ave., Bangor, ME 04401. 65 Texas Ave., Bangor, ME 04401. Phone: (207) 783-9101. Fax: (207) 942-2857. Fax: (207) 783-5193. Web Site: www.mpbn.net. Licensee: Maine Public Broadcastig Corp. (acq 6-23-92; 7-13-92). Network: PBS. Washington Atty: Dow, Lohnes & Albertson.
Key Personnel:
Christopher Amann . . . . CFO
Mary Anne Alhadeff . . . . pres & gen mgr

WMTW-TV—(Poland Spring).Analog channel: 8. Digital channel: 46. On air date: Aug 31, 1954. Box 8, 99 Danville Cor Rd., Auburn, ME 04210. Box 9501, 477 Congress St., Portland, ME 04112-9501. Phone: (207) 782-1800. Phone: (207) 775-1800. Fax: (207) 783-7371. Fax: (207) 782-2165. E-mail: wmtw@wmtw.com. Web Site: www.wmtw.com. Licensee: Hearst-Argyle Properties Inc. Group owner: Hearst-Argyle Television Inc. (acq 5-11-2004; $37.5 million).. Network: ABC. Rep: Harrington, Righter & Parsons. Washington Atty: Wiley, Rein & Fielding. News: 13.5 hrs wkly.
Key Personnel:
David Kaufman . . . . exec VP, gen mgr & progmg dir
David Baer . . . . stn mgr & news dir
John Gregory . . . . opns mgr
Bill Hahn . . . . gen sls mgr
Cary O'Neill . . . . prom dir
Jack Conner . . . . engrg dir

WPFO—Analog channel: 23. On air date: Apr 24, 2003. 233 Oxford St., Portland, ME 04101. Phone: (207) 828-0023. Fax: (207) 347-7323. Licensee: CMCG Portland License LLC. Group owner: MAX Media L.L.C. (acq 4-7-2003; $10 million. with WVIF(TV) Christiansted, VI). Network: Fox.
Key Personnel:
Mitchell Lambert. gen mgr
Tom McCarka . . . . gen sls mgr
Michael Grant . . . . rgnl sls mgr

WPME—Analog channel: 35. On air date: Aug 1, 1997. 4 Ledgeview Dr., Westbrook, ME 04092. Phone: (207) 772-3535. Fax: (207) 774-6849. E-mail: upn35@ourmaine.com. Web Site: www.ourmaine.com. Licensee: Pegasus Satellite Communications Inc., debtor-in-possession.. Ownership: Pegasus Communications Corp., 100% Group owner: (group owner; (acq 2-10-2005; $3,775,523).. Washington Atty: Drinker, Biddle & Reath L. News: 3.5 hrs wkly.

WPXT—Analog channel: 51. Digital channel: 4. On air date: 1986. 4 Ledgeview Dr., Westbrook, ME 04092. Phone: (207) 774-0051. Fax: (207) 774-6849. E-mail: wb51@ourmaine.com. Web Site: www.ourmaine.com. Licensee: HMW Inc., debtor-in-possession. Group owner: Pegasus Broadcast Television Inc. (acq 5-17-96; $17.5 million).. Washington Atty: Drinker, Biddle & Reath L. News staff: 25; News: 3.5 hrs wkly.
Key Personnel:
Ann C. Gagne . . . . gen mgr & stn mgr
Dennis Holland . . . . stn mgr

Presque Isle, ME (DMA 203)

WAGM-TV—Analog channel: 8. On air date: Oct 13, 1956. Box 1149, 12 Brewer Rd., Presque Isle, ME 04769. Phone: (207) 764-4461. Fax: (207) 764-5329. E-mail: wagmtv@wagmtv.com. Web Site: www.wagmtv.com. Licensee: NEPSK Inc.. Ownership: Peter P. Kozloski, 100%. (acq 3-8-91; grpsl; 4-1-91). Network: Network: CBS, NBC. Rep: Katz Radio. Washington Atty: Koteen & Naftalin. News staff: 12; News: 14 hrs wkly.
Key Personnel:
Gordon Wark. . . . . pres, prom VP & prom dir
Peter Kozloski . . . . CEO, chmn & pres
Carole M. Kozloski. . . . . sr VP
Catherine Donovan. . . . . VP
Linda Connolly. gen sls mgr, natl sls mgr, rgnl sls mgr & progmg mgr

Broadcasting & Cable Yearbook 2006

B-48

Jon Gulliver . . . news dir
Gene Brewer. . . . chief of engrg

***WMEM-TV**—Analog channel: 10. Digital channel: 12. On air date: Feb 17, 1964. 1450 Lisbon St., Lewiston, ME 04240. 65 Texas Ave., Bangor, ME 04401. Phone: (800) 884-1717. Phone: (207) 783-9101. Fax: (207) 783-5193. Fax: (207) 942-2857. Web Site: www.mpbc.org. Licensee: Maine Public Broadcasting Corp. (acq 6-23-92; 7-13-92). Network: PBS. Washington Atty: Dow, Lohnes & Albertson.
Key Personnel:
Mary Anne Alnedeff . . . pres
Mary Anne Alhadeff . . . gen mgr

Maryland

Baltimore, MD (DMA 23)

WBAL-TV—Analog channel: 11. Digital channel: 59. On air date: Mar 11, 1948. 3800 Hooper Ave., Baltimore, MD 21211. Phone: (410) 467-3000. Fax: (410) 338-6460. Web Site: www.thewbalchannel.com. Licensee: WBAL Hearst-Argyle Television Inc. Group owner: (group owner) Network: NBC. Rep: Eagle Television Sales. Washington Atty: Brooks, Pierce, McLendon, Humphrey & Leonard. News staff: 63; News: 24 hrs wkly.
Key Personnel:
Jordan Wertlieb . . . gen mgr
Michelle Butt . . . news dir
Wanda Draper . . . progmg dir & pub affrs dir
Hank Volpe . . . engrg mgr & chief of engrg

WBFF—Analog channel: 45. On air date: Apr 11, 1971. 2000 W. 41st St., Baltimore, MD 21211. Phone: (410) 467-4545. Fax: (410) 467-5090. Web Site: www.foxbaltimore.com. Licensee: Chesapeake Television Licensee L.L.C. Group owner: Sinclair Broadcast Group Inc. (acq 9-10-90; grpsl; 10-15-90). Network: Fox. Rep: TeleRep. Washington Atty: Fisher, Wayland, Cooper, Leader & Zaragoza.
Key Personnel:
David D. Smith. . . . pres
Bill Fanshawe. . . . gen mgr
Russell Lucas. . . . opns dir & opns mgr
Mike Cobb. . . . sls dir & gen sls mgr
Peter Ferraro . . . prom mgr
Scott Livingston. . . . news dir
Sharon Wylie . . . mktg dir, mktg mgr & pub affrs dir
David Hackney . . . engrg mgr
Dennis Winters . . . chief of engrg

WJZ-TV—Analog channel: 13. Digital channel: 38. On air date: Nov 2, 1948. 3725 Malden Ave., Baltimore, MD 21211. Phone: (410) 466-0013. Fax: (410) 578-7502. E-mail: ness@wjz.com. Web Site: www.wjz.com. Licensee: Viacom Inc. Group owner: Viacom Television Stations Group (acq 6-28-57; $4.4 million;. FTR: 7-1-57). Network: CBS. Washington Atty: Wilkes, Artis, Hedrick & Lane.
Key Personnel:
Jay B. Newman . . . VP & gen mgr
Rick Seaby. . . . opns dir & engrg dir
David Morris . . . sls dir
Gail Bertling . . . progmg dir
Christine Coreman. . . . news dir
Susan Otradovec. . . . pub affrs dir

WMAR-TV—Analog channel: 2. Digital channel: 52. On air date: Oct 27, 1947. 6400 York Rd., Baltimore, MD 21212. Phone: (410) 377-2222. Fax: (410) 377-0493. E-mail: berry@wmar.com. Web Site: insidebaltimore.com. Licensee: Scripps-Howard Broadcasting Co. Group owner: (group owner; acq 1991; $125 million; 9-3-90). Network: ABC. Rep: Harrington, Righter & Parsons. Washington Atty: Baker & Hostetler.
Key Personnel:
Drew Berry. . . . gen mgr
Michael Draman . . . stn mgr
Steve Weinstein . . . opns mgr

***WMPB**—Analog channel: 67. Digital channel: 29. On air date: 1986. 11767 Owings Mills Blvd., Owings Mills, MD 21117-1499. Phone: (410) 356-5600. Fax: (410) 581-6579. E-mail: comments@mpt.org. Web Site: www.mpt.org. Licensee: Maryland Public Broadcasting Commission. Network: PBS. Washington Atty: Schwartz, Woods & Miller.
Key Personnel:
Robert J. Shuman . . . CEO & pres
Larry D. Unger. . . . CFO
George Beneman . . . opns VP

***WMPT**—Analog channel: 22. Digital channel: 42. On air date: 1986. 11767 Owings Mills Blvd., Owings Mills, MD 21117-1499. Phone: (410) 356-5600. Fax: (410) 581-6579. E-mail: comments@mpt.org. Web Site: www.mpt.org. Licensee: Maryland Public Broadcasting Commission. Network: PBS. Washington Atty: Schwartz, Woods & Miller.
Key Personnel:
Robert Shuman . . . CEO & pres
Larry Unger . . . CFO
George Benaman . . . opns VP

WNUV—Analog channel: 54. On air date: July 1, 1982. 2000 W. 41st St., Baltimore, MD 21211. Phone: (410) 467-8854. Fax: (410) 467-5093. Licensee: Baltimore (WNUV-TV) Licensee Inc. Group owner: Cunningham Broadcasting Corporation (acq 1-9-2002). Network: WB. Washington Atty: Arter & Hadden.
Key Personnel:
Bill Sanshaw . . . gen mgr
Russell Lucas . . . opns mgr
DuJuan McCoy . . . sls dir & rgnl sls mgr
Sharon Wylie . . . mktg mgr
Mark Bulla. . . . chief of engrg

WUTB—Analog channel: 24. Digital channel: 41. On air date: December 1985. 4820 Seton Dr., Suite M-N, Baltimore, MD 21215. Phone: (410) 358-2400. Fax: (410) 764-7232. E-mail: wttg-hr@foxtv.com. Web Site: www.upn24.com.. Stn video via satellite: Direct TV/Echo Star Licensee: Fox Television Stations Inc. Group owner: (group owner; acq 7-31-01; grpsl). Network: UPN. Washington Atty: Law Offices of Hogan & Hartson.
Key Personnel:
Kerry Toland . . . VP
Brian Knopp . . . natl sls mgr
Shirley Pridgean . . . gen sls mgr & rgnl sls mgr

Frederick

see Washington, DC (Hagerstown, MD) market

Hagerstown

see Washington, DC (Hagerstown, MD) market

Oakland

see Pittsburgh, PA market

Salisbury, MD (DMA 150)

WBOC-TV—Analog channel: 16. Digital channel: 21. On air date: July 15, 1954. Box 2057, Salisbury, MD 21802-2057. 1729 N. Salisbury Blvd., Salisbury, MD 21801. Phone: (410) 749-1111. Fax: (410) 749-2361. E-mail: wboc@wboc.com. Web Site: www.wboc.com. Licensee: WBOC Inc.. Ownership: Draper Holdings Business Trust (acq 9-80; $8 million).. Network: CBS. Rep: Katz Radio. Washington Atty: Covington & Burling. News staff: 40; News: 31 hrs wkly.
Key Personnel:
Thomas Draper . . . CEO, chmn, pres & pres
Laura Backer . . . CFO
Rick Jordan . . . VP & gen mgr
Danny Panicella . . . chief of opns
Bill Hahn . . . gen sls mgr
Dave Spencer . . . natl sls mgr
Betty-Ann Dailey . . . progmg dir
Jennifer Furbay . . . pub affrs dir

***WCPB**—Analog channel: 28. Digital channel: 56. On air date: 1986. 11767 Owings Mills Blvd., Owings Mills, MD 21117-1499. Phone: (410) 356-5600. Fax: (410) 581-6579. E-mail: comments@mpt-org. Web Site: www.mpt.org. Licensee: Maryland Public Broadcasting Commission. Network: PBS. Washington Atty: Schwartz, Woods & Miller.
Key Personnel:
Robert Shuman . . . CEO & pres
Larry Unger . . . CFO
George Benaman . . . opns VP

***WDPB**—Analog channel: 64. On air date: December 1982. The Linden Bldg., 625 Orange St., Wilmington, DE 19801. Phone: (302) 888-1200. Fax: (302) 575-0346. E-mail: whyydbc@whyy.org. Web Site: www.whyy.org. Licensee: WHYY Inc. (acq 2-28-86). Network: PBS. Washington Atty: Schwartz, Woods & Miller. News staff: 10; News: 3 hrs wkly.
Key Personnel:
Molly Dickinson Shephard. . . . CEO & chmn
William J. Marrazzo . . . pres & stn mgr

David A. Othmer. . . . VP
Allen Murphy . . . sls dir
David Rubinsohn . . . progmg dir
Cindy Balan . . . news dir
William J. Weber . . . engrg VP

WMDT—Analog channel: 47. On air date: Apr 11, 1980. 202 Downtown Plaza, Salisbury, MD 21801. Box 4009, Salisbury, MD 21803-4009. Phone: (410) 742-4747. Fax: (410) 742-5767. E-mail: wmdt@wmdt.com. Web Site: www.wmdt.com. Licensee: Delmarva Broadcast Service G.P.. Ownership: Marion B. Brechner, 80%; Berl M. Brechner, 20%. (acq 1982). Network: Network: Network: ABC, Fox, NBC. Washington Atty: Cohn & Marks. News staff: 23; News: 12 hrs wkly.
Key Personnel:
Kathleen McLain . . . gen mgr, prom mgr, adv mgr & pub affrs dir
Terry Monahan. gen sls mgr, natl sls mgr, rgnl sls mgr & progmg mgr
Dawn Mitchell. . . . news dir
Bill Hoctor . . . chief of engrg

Massachusetts

Adams

see Albany-Schenectady-Troy, NY market

Boston (Manchester, NH) (DMA 5)

WBPX—Analog channel: 68. On air date: January 1979. 1120 Soldiers Field Rd., Boston, MA 02134. Phone: (617) 787-6868. Fax: (617) 787-4114. Web Site: www.paxtv.net. Licensee: Paxson Boston-68 License Inc. Group owner: Paxson Communications Corp. (acq 5-2-00; grpsl). Network: PAX TV. News: 20 hrs wkly.
Key Personnel:
Robert Gilbert. . . . gen mgr & sls VP
William Spitzer. . . . dev VP

WBZ-TV—Analog channel: 4. On air date: June 9, 1948. 1170 Soldiers Field Rd., Boston, MA 02134. Phone: (617) 787-7000. Fax: (617) 787-5969. Web Site: www.wbs4boston.com. Licensee: Viacom Inc. Group owner: Viacom Television Stations Group. Network: CBS. Rep: CBS Spot Sales. Washington Atty: Wilkes, Artis, Hedrick & Lane. News staff: 81; News: 20 hrs wkly.

WCVB-TV—Analog channel: 5. Digital channel: 20. On air date: Mar 19, 1972. 5 TV Pl., Needham, MA 02494. Phone: (781) 449-0400. Fax: (781) 433-4490/(781) 433-4022. Web Site: www.thebostonchannel.com. Licensee: WCVB Hearst-Argyle Television Inc. Group owner: Hearst-Argyle Television Inc. (acq 7-16-97; grpsl). Network: ABC. Rep: Eagle Television Sales. Washington Atty: Brooks, Pierce, McLendon, Humphrey & Leonard. News staff: 100; News: 26 hrs wkly.
Key Personnel:
Bill Fine . . . pres & gen mgr
Gloria Spence . . . CFO
Elizabeth Cheng . . . VP
Joseph Rebelo. . . . opns mgr
Peter Hennessey . . . gen sls mgr

***WEKW-TV**—Analog channel: 52. On air date: May 21, 1968. 268 Mast Rd., Durham, NH 03824-4601. Phone: (603) 868-1100. Fax: (603) 868-7552. E-mail: themailbox@nhptv.org. Web Site: www.nhptv.org. Licensee: University of New Hampshire. Network: PBS. Washington Atty: Schwartz, Woods & Miller.
Key Personnel:
Peter A. Frid . . . gen mgr
Dennis Malloy . . . sls dir
Jeff Morris . . . adv mgr
Mercedes Sabio. . . . progmg dir
Brian Shepperd. . . . chief of engrg

***WENH-TV**—Analog channel: 11. Digital channel: 57. On air date: July 6, 1959. 268 Mast Rd., Durham, NH 03824-4601. Phone: (603) 868-1100. Fax: (603) 868-7552. E-mail: themailbox@nhptv.org. Web Site: www.nhptv.org. Licensee: University of New Hampshire. Network: PBS. Washington Atty: Schwartz, Woods & Miller. News: 2 hrs wkly.

WFXT—Analog channel: 25. Digital channel: 31. On air date: Oct 10, 1977. Box 9125, 25 Fox Dr., Dedham, MA 02027. Phone: (781) 467-2525. Fax: (781) 467-7201. Web Site: www.fox25.com. Licensee: Fox Television Stations Inc. Group owner: (group owner; acq 7-95; 3-6-95). Network: Fox. News staff: 70; News: 7 hrs wkly.

Key Personnel:
Lisa Graham . . . . VP
Gregg Kelley . . . . gen mgr

***WGBH-TV**—Analog channel: 2. Digital channel: 19. On air date: May 2, 1955. Box 200, 125 Western Ave., Boston, MA 02134. Phone: (617) 300-5400. Phone: (617) 300-2000. Fax: (617) 300-1026. Web Site: www.wgbh.org. Licensee: WGBH Educational Foundation. Network: PBS. Washington Atty: Covington & Burling.
Key Personnel:
Marita Rivero . . . . gen mgr
Tom Apone . . . . opns dir
Ira Miller . . . . opns mgr
Susan Schneider . . . . mktg dir

***WGBX-TV**—Analog channel: 44. Digital channel: 43. On air date: Sept 25, 1967. Box 200, 125 Western Ave., Boston, MA 02134. Phone: (617) 300-2000. Fax: (617) 300-1013. Web Site: www.wgbh.org. Licensee: WGBH Educational Foundation. Network: PBS. Washington Atty: Covington & Burling.
Key Personnel:
Henry P. Becton Jr. pres
Tom Apone . . . . gen mgr & opns dir
Ira Miller . . . . opns mgr & prom VP
Susan Schneider. . . . . mktg dir & progmg dir

WHDH-TV—Analog channel: 7. Digital channel: 42. On air date: June 21, 1948. 7 Bulfinch Pl., Boston, MA 02114. Phone: (617) 725-0777. Fax: (617) 248-5420. Web Site: www.whdh.com. Licensee: WHDH-TV Co.. Ownership: Sunbeam Television Corp. (acq 6-3-93; $204 million; 6-21-93). Network: NBC. Rep: TeleRep. Washington Atty: Koteen & Naftalin.
Key Personnel:
Edmund Ansin. . . . . chmn
Michael Carson . . . . VP & gen mgr
Jim Shultis . . . . opns dir & engrg dir
Michelle Dempsey Dubrow . . . . gen sls mgr
Marc Fauci . . . . natl sls mgr
Steve Donald . . . . mktg dir & prom VP
Joan McCready . . . . progmg mgr
Ed Kosowski . . . . news dir
Ro Dooley . . . . pub affrs dir

WLVI-TV—(Cambridge).Analog channel: 56. Digital channel: 41. On air date: Aug 31, 1953. 75 Morrissey Blvd., Boston, MA 02125. Phone: (617) 265-5656. Fax: (617) 265-2538. Fax: (617) 265-0063. E-mail: wb56@tribune.com. Web Site: www.wb56.com. Licensee: WLVI Inc. Group owner: Tribune Broadcasting Co. (acq 4-6-94; 2-7-94). Network: WB. Rep: Harrington, Righter & Parsons. News staff: 44; News: 7 hrs wkly.
Key Personnel:
Neal Davis . . . . VP
Vincent Manzi . . . . VP & gen mgr
Card French. . . . . opns mgr
Rich Graziano . . . . gen sls mgr
James Norton . . . . mktg mgr
Steven Ratner. . . . . prom dir & progmg dir
Pamela Johnston . . . . news dir
Kristen Holgerson . . . . pub affrs dir
Franco LaPietra. . . . . engrg dir

WMFP—Analog channel: 62. On air date: Oct 16, 1987. 35th Fl., One Beacon St., Boston, MA 02108. Phone: (617) 720-1062. Licensee: WSAH License Inc. Group owner: Scripps Howard Broadcasting Co. (acq 2-27-2004; grpsl). Washington Atty: Hopkins & Sutter.

WMUR-TV—Analog channel: 9. Digital channel: 59. On air date: Mar 9, 1954. 100 S. Commercial St., Manchester, NH 03101. Phone: (603) 641-9000. Fax: (603) 641-9005 (admin). Web Site: www.thewmurchannel.com. Licensee: Hearst-Argyle Properties Inc. Group owner: Hearst-Argyle Properties Inc. (acq 3-28-01; $185 million).. Network: ABC. Washington Atty: Arent, Fox, Kintner, Plotkin & Kahn.

WNDS—Analog channel: 50. On air date: Sept 5, 1983. 50 TV Pl., Derry, NH 03038. Phone: (603) 434-8850. Fax: (603) 434-8627. Web Site: www.wnds.com. Licensee: ShootingStar Broadcasting of New England LLC.. Ownership: ShootingStar Inc., 100% of votes; Alta ShootingStar Corp., approximately 98% of the nonvoting preferred membership units (acq 9-15-2004; $28 million).. Rep: Blair Television. Washington Atty: Leventhal, Senter & Lerman. News: 5 hrs wkly.
Key Personnel:
Diane Sutter. CEO & pres
Judy Carlough . . . . gen sls mgr
Alisha Doucette . . . . mktg dir
Martin Morenz . . . . news dir
Leo Demers . . . . chief of engrg
Gene Steinberg . . . . progmg

WNEU—Analog channel: 60. On air date: 1987. One Sundial Ave., Suite 501, Manchester, NH 03103. Phone: (603) 647-6060. E-mail: wneu.donna@comcast.net. Licensee: NBC Telemundo License Co. Group owner: Telemundo Group Inc. (acq 10-22-02; $26 million).. Network: Network: NBC, Telemundo (Spanish). Washington Atty: Davis Wright Tremaine L.L.P..

WPXG—Analog channel: 21. On air date: Apr 16, 1984. 1120 Soldiers Field Rd., Boston, MA 02134. Phone: (617) 787-6868. Fax: (617) 787-4114. E-mail: jenniedibartolomeo@pax.net. Web Site: www.paxtv.net. Licensee: Paxson Boston-68 License Inc. Group owner: Paxson Communications Inc. (acq 5-2-00; grpsl).
Key Personnel:
Robert Gilbert. . . gen mgr, gen sls mgr, mktg mgr & progmg mgr
Paul Strieby . . . . chief of engrg

WSBK-TV—Analog channel: 38. Digital channel: 39. On air date: Oct 12, 1964. 1170 Soldiers Field Rd., Boston, MA 02134. Phone: (617) 787-7000. Fax: (617) 787-5969. E-mail: webmaster@upn38.com. Web Site: www.upn38.com. Licensee: Viacom Inc. Group owner: Viacom Television Stations Group (acq 2-27-95; FTR: 5-22-95). Network: UPN. News: 4 hrs wkly.
Key Personnel:
Julio Marenghi . . . . gen mgr & opns dir
Angie Kucharski . . . . stn mgr
Scott McGomick . . . . gen sls mgr
Lee Kinberg . . . . prom dir
Matt Ellis . . . . news dir
Pat Kueger . . . . pub affrs dir
Jack Berry. . . . . chief of engrg

WUNI—Analog channel: 27. Digital channel: 29. On air date: Jan 2, 1970. 33 Fourth Ave., Needham, MA 02494. Phone: (781) 433-2727. Fax: (781) 433-2750. Fax: (781) 433-2701. E-mail: feedback@wunitv.com. Web Site: www.wunitv.com. Licensee: Entravision 27 L.L.C. Group owner: Entravision Communications Corp. (acq 1-4-01; $47.5 million). Network: Univision (Spanish). Washington Atty: Fletcher, Heald & Hildreth. News staff: 13; News: 3 hrs wkly.
Key Personnel:
Alexander Von Lichtenberg . . . . gen mgr
Bob Kerrigan . . . . opns mgr
Tina Castano . . . . gen sls mgr
Meg Godin . . . . mktg mgr & prom mgr
Sara Suarez . . . . news dir
Fran Vaccari . . . . chief of engrg

WUTF-TV—Analog channel: 66. Digital channel: 23. On air date: Feb 12, 1985. 71 Parmenter Rd., Hudson, MA 01749. Phone: (978) 562-0660. Fax: (978) 562-1166. Web Site: univision.com. Licensee: Univision Partnership of Massachusetts. Group owner: Univision Communications Inc. (acq 5-21-01; grpsl). Network: TeleFutura (Spanish). Washington Atty: Shaw Pittman.
Key Personnel:
David Reiten . . . . chmn
Rolo Duartas . . . . gen mgr
Richard A. Peper . . . . chief of engrg & chief of engrg

WWDP—Analog channel: 46. Digital channel: 52. On air date: Sept 15, 1996. 6740 Shady Oak Rd., Eden Prairie, MN 55344. Phone: (952) 943-6000. Fax: (952) 943-6566. Web Site: www.shopnbc.com. Licensee: Norwell Television LLC.. Ownership: ValueVision Media Acquisition Inc. (acq 4-1-03).

***WYDN**—Analog channel: 48. On air date: 2000. Box 612066, Dallas, TX 75261-2066. Phone: (817) 571-1229. Fax: (817) 571-7458. E-mail: comments@daystar.com. Web Site: www.daystar.com. Licensee: Educational Public TV Corp.

Holyoke

see Springfield-Holyoke, MA market

New Bedford

see Providence, RI-New Bedford, MA market

Pittsfield

see Albany-Schenectady-Troy, NY market

Springfield-Holyoke, MA (DMA 106)

***WGBY-TV**—Analog channel: 57. On air date: Sept 26, 1971. 44 Hampden St., Springfield, MA 01103. Phone: (413) 781-2801. Fax: (413) 731-5093. E-mail: feedback@wgby.org. Web Site: www.wgby.org. Licensee: WGBH Educational Foundation. Network: PBS. Washington Atty: Covington & Burling.
Key Personnel:
Russell Peotter . . . . VP
Russell J. Peotter . . . . gen mgr
Daren Winckel . . . . mktg dir
Ray Miller . . . . chief of engrg

WGGB-TV—Analog channel: 40. On air date: Apr 14, 1953. Box 40, Springfield, MA 01102-0040. 1300 Liberty St., Springfield, MA 01104. Phone: (413) 733-4040. Fax: (413) 781-1363. Web Site: www.wggb.com. Licensee: WGGB Licensee L.L.C. Group owner: Sinclair Broadcast Group Inc. (acq 1999; grpsl). Network: ABC. Rep: Katz Radio. Washington Atty: Dow, Lohnes & Albertson.
Key Personnel:
Christopher Westerkamp . . . . gen mgr
Mike Hayes . . . opns dir, rgnl sls mgr, engrg dir & chief of engrg
Patrick Berry . . . . opns dir & natl sls mgr
Kathy Tobin . . . . news dir

WWLP—Analog channel: 22. On air date: Mar 17, 1953. Box 2210, Springfield, MA 01102-2210. One Broadcast Ctr., Chicopee, MA 01013. Phone: (413) 377-2200. Fax: (413) 377-2261. Web Site: www.wwlp.com. Licensee: WWLP Broadcasting L.L.C. Group owner: LIN Television Corporation (acq 10-20-2000; about $128 million). Network: NBC. Washington Atty: Covington & Burling.
Key Personnel:
William Pepin. gen mgr
John Baran . . . . stn mgr
Fred Steinman . . . . gen sls mgr
Maripat Jordan . . . . natl sls mgr
Anna Giza . . . . prom dir
Michael Garreffi . . . . news dir
Dave Cote. . . . . chief of engrg

Vineyard Haven

see Providence, RI-New Bedford, MA market

Michigan

Alpena, MI (DMA 208)

WBKB-TV—Analog channel: 11. On air date: Sept 22, 1975. 1390 Bagley St., Alpena, MI 49707. Phone: (989) 356-3434. Fax: (989) 356-4188. E-mail: wbkbtv@speednetllc.com. Licensee: Thunder Bay Broadcasting Corp.. Ownership: Stephen A. Marks, 88.56%. Network: CBS. Rep: Millennium Sales & Marketing. Washington Atty: Cohn & Marks. News staff: 6; News: 5.5 hrs wkly.
Key Personnel:
Stephen A. Marks. pres
Curt Smith . . . . gen mgr
Robert Race . . . . stn mgr
Barbara Bowen . . . . gen sls mgr & rgnl sls mgr
Cher Allen. gen sls mgr

***WCML-TV**—Analog channel: 6. On air date: 1975. Central Michigan Univ., 1999 E. Campus Dr., Mt. Pleasant, MI 48859. Phone: (989) 774-3105. Fax: (989) 774-4427. Web Site: www.wcmu.org. Licensee: Central Michigan University. Network: PBS. Washington Atty: Dow, Lohnes & Albertson.
Key Personnel:
Ed Grant . . . . stn mgr
Jim Arneson. . . . . gen sls mgr & prom mgr
Tim Little. . . . . progmg dir
Greg Surma . . . . engrg dir & chief of engrg

Battle Creek

see Grand Rapids-Kalamazoo-Battle Creek, MI market

Bay City

see Flint-Saginaw-Bay City, MI market

Cadillac

see Traverse City-Cadillac, MI market

Detroit (DMA 10)

WADL—Analog channel: 38. Digital channel: 39. On air date: May 20, 1989. 22590 15 Mile Rd., Clinton Twp, MI 48035-2814. Phone: (586) 790-3838. Fax: (586) 790-3841. Licensee: Adell Broadcasting Corp.. Ownership: Franklin Z. Adell Trust (acq 9-3-03).
Key Personnel:
Kevin Adell . . . . . gen mgr, gen sls mgr, adv mgr & progmg dir
Nicole Harris . . . . . gen mgr & gen sls mgr
Louis Gibbs . . . . . mktg mgr
Tom Ponsart . . . . . chief of engrg

WDIV—Analog channel: 4. Digital channel: 45. On air date: Mar 4, 1947. 550 W. Lafayette Blvd., Detroit, MI 48226. Phone: (313) 222-0500. Fax: (313) 222-0592. Web Site: www.clickondetroit.com. Licensee: Post-Newsweek Stations, Michigan Inc. Group owner: Post-Newsweek Stations Inc. (acq 6-24-78). Network: NBC. Rep: MMT. Washington Atty: Covington & Burling.
Key Personnel:
Joseph Berwanger . . . . . VP & gen mgr
Bob Weed . . . . . mktg dir
Deborah Collura . . . . . news dir
Marcus Williams . . . . . chief of engrg

WDWB—Analog channel: 20. Digital channel: 21. On air date: Sept 15, 1968. 27777 Franklin Rd., Suite 1220, Southfield, MI 48034. Phone: (248) 355-2020. Fax: (248) 355-0368. Web Site: www.wb20detroit.com. Licensee: WXON License Inc. Group owner: Granite Broadcasting Corp. (acq 1-31-97; $175 million).. Network: WB. Washington Atty: Smithwick & Belendiuk.
Key Personnel:
Sarah Norat-Phillips . . . . . pres & gen mgr
Ken Murphy . . . . . stn mgr & sls VP
Carolyn Worford . . . . . opns mgr, progmg dir & news dir
Ken Frieison . . . . . natl sls mgr
Dan Riley . . . . . chief of engrg

WJBK—Analog channel: 2. Digital channel: 58. On air date: Oct 24, 1948. Box 2000, Southfield, MI 48037. 16550 W. Nine Mile Rd., Southfield, MI 48075. Phone: (248) 557-2000. Fax: (248) 557-6343. E-mail: contact@fox2detroit.com. Web Site: www.fox2detroit.com. Licensee: WJBK License Inc. Group owner: Fox Television Stations Inc. (acq 1-22-97; grpsl). Network: Fox. News staff: 140; News: 36 hrs wkly.
Key Personnel:
Jeff Murri . . . . . VP & gen mgr
Jon Best . . . . . VP
Sheila Bruce . . . . . opns mgr & sls VP
Richard Renko . . . . . natl sls mgr
Terry D'Esposito . . . . . mktg dir
Keith Stironek . . . . . prom dir
Connie Davis . . . . . progmg dir & progmg mgr
Dana McDaniel . . . . . news dir
Lee Thomas . . . . . news dir
Katie Fehr . . . . . pub affrs dir
Tim Redmond . . . . . chief of engrg

WKBD—Analog channel: 50. Digital channel: 14. On air date: Jan 10, 1965. 26905 W. 11 Mile Rd., Southfield, MI 48034. Phone: (248) 355-7000. Fax: (248) 355-2692. E-mail: shows@wkbdtv.com. Web Site: www.upndetroit.com. Licensee: Viacom Stations Group of Detroit Inc. Group owner: Viacom Television Stations Group (acq 9-1-93; $105 million;. FTR: 9-13-93). Network: UPN.
Key Personnel:
Linda Danna . . . . . exec VP & sr VP
Michael J. Michell . . . . . VP & stn mgr
David Bangura . . . . . sls dir & gen sls mgr
Tom Zito . . . . . natl sls mgr
Judy Paluso . . . . . prom mgr
Paul A. Prange . . . . . progmg dir
Edward Foxworth . . . . . pub affrs dir
Chuck Davis . . . . . engrg dir & chief of engrg

WPXD—Analog channel: 31. On air date: Jan 12, 1981. 20300 Civic Ctr. Dr., Suite 401, Lompoc, MI 48076. Phone: (248) 304-4493. Fax: (248) 304-8906. Web Site: www.pax.tv. Licensee: Paxson Communications License Co. L.L.C. Group owner: Paxson Communications Corp. (acq 12-11-97; $35 million. including LPTV ch). Washington Atty: Verner, Liipfert, Bernhard, McPherson & Hand.
Key Personnel:
Lowell Paxson . . . . . pres
Sandy Henry . . . . . gen mgr
Henry Sandee . . . . . gen sls mgr

***WTVS**—Analog channel: 56. Digital channel: 43. On air date: Oct 3, 1955. 7441 Second Blvd., Detroit, MI 48202. Phone: (313) 873-7200. Fax: (313) 876-8118. E-mail: email@dptv.org. Web Site: www.detroitpublictv.org. Licensee: Detroit Educational Television Foundation. Network: PBS. Karole White Washington Atty: Schwartz, Woods & Miller.
Key Personnel:
John Wenzel . . . . . CFO
Steve Antoniotti . . . . . gen mgr
Daniel Alpert . . . . . stn mgr
Karyn Hertel . . . . . sls dir & mktg dir
Dave Devereaux . . . . . prom VP
Daniel Gaitens . . . . . film buyer
John O'Donnell . . . . . pub affrs dir
Helge Blucher . . . . . engrg VP & chief of engrg

WWJ-TV—Analog channel: 62. Digital channel: 44. On air date: September 1975. 26905 W. 11-Mile Rd., Southfield, MI 48034. Phone: (248) 350-5050. Fax: (248) 352-5855. E-mail: shows@wwjtv.com. Web Site: www.wwjtv.com. Licensee: CBS Broadcasting Inc. Group owner: Viacom Television Stations Group (acq 1995; $24 million).. Network: CBS. Rep: CBS Spot Sales. Washington Atty: Hogan & Hartson.
Key Personnel:
Linda Danna . . . . . sr VP & gen mgr
Michael J. Michell . . . . . VP & stn mgr
Jaime Horowitz . . . . . gen sls mgr
Darren Pich . . . . . natl sls mgr
Scott Cote . . . . . rgnl sls mgr
Judy Paluso . . . . . prom dir
Paul Preange . . . . . progmg dir
Edward Foxworth . . . . . pub affrs dir
Chuck Davis . . . . . engrg dir & chief of engrg

WXYZ-TV—Analog channel: 7. Digital channel: 41. On air date: Oct 9, 1948. Box 789, 20777 W. 10 Mile Rd., Southfield, MI 48037. Phone: (248) 827-7777. Fax: (248) 827-4454. Web Site: www.detnow.com. Licensee: Channel 7 Detroit Inc. Group owner: Scripps Howard Broadcasting Co., see Cross-Ownership (acq 1-2-86; grpsl). Network: ABC. Rep: Katz Radio. Washington Atty: Baker & Hostetler.
Key Personnel:
Grace Gilchrist . . . . . VP & gen mgr
Chris Allen . . . . . opns dir
Mike Murri . . . . . gen sls mgr
Steve Kopicki . . . . . natl sls mgr
Mike MacLean . . . . . rgnl sls mgr
Keith Stironek . . . . . prom dir
Marla Drutz . . . . . progmg dir
Lewis C. Stokes . . . . . pub affrs dir
Ray Thurber . . . . . engrg dir & chief of engrg

Flint-Saginaw-Bay City, MI (DMA 65)

WAQP—Analog channel: 49. On air date: Mar 26, 1985. 2865 Trautner Dr., Saginaw, MI 48604-9483. Phone: (989) 249-5969. E-mail: waqp@tct.tv. Web Site: www.tct.tv. Licensee: TCT of Michigan Inc. Group owner: Tri-State Christian Television.
Key Personnel:
Garth W. Coonce . . . . . pres
Shane Chaney . . . . . CFO
Tina Coonce . . . . . sr VP
Michael Socier . . . . . gen mgr

WBSF—Analog channel: 46.Not on air, target date: unknown: Barrington Michigan Corp., 2500 W. Higgins Rd., Suite 880, Hoffman Estates, IL 60195. Phone: (847) 884-1877. Fax: (810) 687-4925. Permittee: Barrington Michigan Corp. (acq 4-14-2005; $4.5 million. for CP).

***WCMU-TV**—Analog channel: 14. On air date: Mar 29, 1967. Central Michigan Univ., 1999 E. Campus Dr., Mount Pleasant, MI 48859. Phone: (989) 774-3105. Fax: (989) 774-4427. Web Site: www.wcmu.org. Licensee: Central Michigan University. Network: PBS. Washington Atty: Dow, Lohnes & Albertson.
Key Personnel:
Ed Grant . . . . . gen mgr & stn mgr
Linda Dielman . . . . . sls dir, prom mgr & progmg dir
Randy Kapenga . . . . . chief of engrg

***WDCP-TV**—Analog channel: 19. On air date: Oct 12, 1964. 1961 Delta Rd., University Center, MI 48710. Phone: (877) 472-7677. Fax: (989) 686-0155. E-mail: wdcq@alpha.delta.edu. Web Site: www.delta.edu/broadcasting. Licensee: Delta College. Network: PBS. Washington Atty: Cohn & Marks.
Key Personnel:
Dr. Peter Boyse . . . . . pres
Barry Baker . . . . . gen mgr
Pam Clark . . . . . stn mgr
Tom Garnett . . . . . chief of engrg

***WDCQ-TV**—Analog channel: 35. On air date: Dec 12, 1986. University Ctr., 1961 Delta Rd., University Ctr, MI 48710. Phone: (877) 472-7677. Fax: (989) 686-0155. E-mail: wdcq@alpha.delta.edu. Web Site: www.delta.edu/broadcasting. Licensee: Delta College. Network: PBS. Washington Atty: Cohn & Marks.
Key Personnel:
Dr. Peter Boyse . . . . . pres
Barry Baker . . . . . gen mgr
Pam Clark . . . . . stn mgr
Diane Palm-Osantowski . . . . . dev mgr
Tom Garnett . . . . . chief of engrg

WEYI-TV—(Saginaw).Analog channel: 25. On air date: Apr 5, 1953. 2225 W. Willard Rd., Clio, MI 48420. Phone: (810) 687-1000. Fax: (810) 687-4925. E-mail: mail@nbc25.net. Web Site: www.nbc25.net. Licensee: Barrington Broadcasting Flint Corp. Group owner: Barrington Broadcasting Corp. acq 5-14-2004; $24 million).. Network: NBC. Rep: Petry Television Inc.. Washington Atty: Hogan & Hartson. News: 8 hrs wkly.
Key Personnel:
Jeff Gulbert . . . . . gen mgr & opns mgr
Jim Hanning . . . . . gen sls mgr
Kyle Pierson . . . . . prom mgr
Becky Butcher . . . . . adv dir

***WFUM**—Analog channel: 28. On air date: Aug 23, 1980. WFUM TV-28, Michigan-Television, Univ. of Michigan-Flint, 303 E. Kearsley St., Flint, MI 48502. Phone: (810) 762-3028. Fax: (810) 233-6017. E-mail: infor@wfum.org. Web Site: michigantelevision.org. Licensee: Board of Regents, University of Michigan. Network: PBS. Washington Atty: Dow, Lohnes & Albertson.
Key Personnel:
Kathy Bonds . . . . . CFO
Jay Nelson . . . . . stn mgr
Justin Ebeight . . . . . dev dir
Christopher Williams . . . . . mktg dir
Jim Gaver . . . . . progmg dir
Wayne Henderson . . . . . opns mgr & chief of engrg

WJRT-TV—Analog channel: 12. Digital channel: 36. On air date: Oct 12, 1958. 2302 Lapeer Rd., Flint, MI 48503. Phone: (810) 233-3130. Fax: (810) 257-2834. E-mail: wjrt@abc.com. Web Site: www.abc12.com.. Stn video via satellite: Dish Network Licensee: Flint License Subsidiary Corp., a wholly owned subsidiary of WJRT Inc. Group owner: ABC Inc. (acq 1995; $155 million with WTVG(TV) Toledo, OH). Network: ABC. Rep: ABC National Television Sales. News staff: 45; News: 27 hrs wkly.
Key Personnel:
Thomas Bryson . . . . . pres & gen mgr
Daniel C. Aube . . . . . gen sls mgr
Ray Scott . . . . . natl sls mgr
Cheri Foss . . . . . rgnl sls mgr
Sara Jo Gallock . . . . . mktg dir & progmg dir
James Bleicher . . . . . news dir

WNEM-TV—(Bay City).Analog channel: 5. On air date: Feb 16, 1954. Box 531, Saginaw, MI 48606. 107 N. Franklin St., Saginaw, MI 48607. Phone: (989) 758-8191. Fax: (989) 758-2111. E-mail: wnem@wnem.com. Web Site: www.wnem.com. Licensee: Meredith Corp. Group owner: Meredith Broadcasting Group, Meredith Corp. (acq 4-16-69; $11.5 million;. FTR: 4-21-69). Network: CBS. Rep: TeleRep. Washington Atty: Haley, Bader & Potts.
Key Personnel:
Al Blinke . . . . . VP & gen mgr
Jim Arneson . . . . . gen sls mgr
Tim Little . . . . . progmg dir & news dir
Terri Peck . . . . . pub affrs dir
Greg Surma . . . . . engrg dir & chief of engrg

WSMH—Analog channel: 66. On air date: Dec 15,1984. G-3463 W. Pierson Rd., Flint, MI 48504. Phone: (810) 785-8866. Fax: (810) 785-8963. Web Site: www.wsmh66.com. Licensee: WSMH Licensee L.L.C. Group owner: Sinclair Broadcast Group Inc. (acq 2-28-96; $33 million). Network: Fox. Rep: Harrington, Righter & Parsons.

Grand Rapids-Kalamazoo-Battle Creek, MI (DMA 38)

***WGVK**—Analog channel: 52. On air date: Oct 1, 1984. 301 W. Fulton St., Grand Rapids, MI 49504-6492. Phone: (616) 331-6666. Fax: (616) 331-6625. E-mail: wgvu@gvsu.edu. Web Site: www.wgvu.org. Licensee:

Broadcasting & Cable Yearbook 2006

B-51

Grand Valley State University. Network: PBS. Washington Atty: Cohn & Marks. News staff: 15; News: one hr wkly.
Key Personnel:
Michael T. Walenta. . . . . gen mgr
Ken Kolbe . . . . . opns VP & opns mgr
Michael Haiftey . . . . . dev mgr
Richard Nelson . . . . . sls dir
Pamela Holtz . . . . . prom mgr
Carrie Corbin . . . . . progmg dir
Fred Martino . . . . . news dir
Robert Lumbert. . . . . engrg dir

***WGVU-TV**—Analog channel: 35. Digital channel: 11. On air date: Dec 17, 1972. 301 W. Fulton St., Grand Rapids, MI 49504-6492. Phone: (616) 331-6666. Fax: (616) 331-6625. E-mail: wgvu@gvsu.edu. Web Site: www.wgvu.org. Licensee: Board of Control, Grand Valley State University. Network: PBS. Washington Atty: Arter & Hadden.
Key Personnel:
Michael Walenta. . . . . gen mgr
Ken Kolbe. . . . . opns mgr
Michael Haifley . . . . . dev mgr
Richard Nelson . . . . . sls dir & gen sls mgr
Pamela Holtz . . . . . prom mgr
Carrie Corbin . . . . . progmg mgr
Bob Lumbert. . . . . engrg dir

WLLA—Analog channel: 64. On air date: June 30, 1987. Box 3157, Kalamazoo, MI 49003. 7048 E. Kilgore Rd., Kalamazoo, MI 49003. Phone: (269) 345-6421. Fax: (269) 345-5665. E-mail: deloris@wlla.com. Web Site: www.wlla.com. Licensee: Christian Faith Broadcasting Inc. Group owner: (group owner; acq 1-13-86; $35,000; 12-9-85). Washington Atty: Joseph E. Dunne III.
Key Personnel:
Kelly Popplewell . . . . . gen sls mgr
Richard Hawkins . gen mgr, mktg mgr, progmg dir & chief of engrg

WOOD-TV—Analog channel: 8. Digital channel: 7. On air date: Aug 15, 1949. Box B, Grand Rapids, MI 49501. 120 College Ave. S.E., Grand Rapids, MI 49503. Phone: (616) 456-8888. Fax: (616) 771-9676. Fax: (616) 456-1413. E-mail: woodtv@woodtv.com. Web Site: www.woodtv.com. Licensee: Wood License Co. LLC. Group owner: LIN Television Corporation (acq 6-30-99). Network: NBC. Washington Atty: Covington & Burling.
Key Personnel:
Diane Kniowski . . . . . pres & gen mgr
Craig Cole . . . . . opns mgr & progmg dir
Marc Elliott . . . . . sls dir & gen sls mgr
Ann Marie Young . . . . . natl sls mgr
Ethan Beute. . . . . mktg mgr, prom mgr & adv mgr
Jim Loy . . . . . news dir
Eva Cooper . . . . . pub affrs dir
Ken Selvig. . . . . engrg dir & chief of engrg

WOTV—Analog channel: 41. On air date: July 24, 1971. Box 1616, Battle Creek, MI 49016-1616. 5200 W. Dickman Rd., Battle Creek, MI 49015. Phone: (269) 968-9341. Fax: (269) 660-1222. E-mail: wotv@wotv.com. Web Site: wotv.com. Licensee: Wood License Co. LLC. Group owner: LIN Television Corporation (acq 12-6-2001; $2.25 million).. Network: ABC. Washington Atty: Covington & Burling. News staff: 25; News: 13 hrs wkly.

WTLJ—Analog channel: 54. Digital channel: 24. On air date: Nov 1, 1986. 10290 48th Ave., Allendale, MI 49401. Phone: (616) 895-4154. Fax: (616) 892-4401. E-mail: wtlj@tct.tv. Web Site: www.tct.tv. Licensee: TCT of Michigan Inc. Group owner: Tri-State Christian Television (acq 1-15-92; $1.5 million;. FTR: 2-10-92).
Key Personnel:
Vic Van Deventer . . . . . gen mgr & stn mgr
Vic VanDeventer . . . . . natl sls mgr, mktg mgr & progmg dir
Frank Ayre. . . . . chief of engrg

WWMT—Analog channel: 3. Digital channel: 2. On air date: June 1, 1950. 590 W. Maple St., Kalamazoo, MI 49008. Phone: (269) 388-3333. Fax: (269) 388-8228. E-mail: news@wwmt.com. Web Site: www.wwmt.com. Licensee: Freedom Broadcasting of Michigan Licensee L.L.C. Group owner: Freedom Communications Inc., Broadcast Division (acq 7-18-98; $170 million. with WLAJ(TV) Lansing). Network: CBS. Rep: TeleRep. Washington Atty: Akin, Gump, Strauss, Hauer & Feld. News: 25 hrs wkly.
Key Personnel:
Thomas M. Long . . . . . VP & gen mgr
James Wagner. . . . . gen sls mgr
Noel Sederstrom . . . . . news dir
Jim Steffey . . . . . chief of engrg

WXMI—Analog channel: 17. Digital channel: 19. On air date: March 1982. 3117 Plaza Dr. N.E., Grand Rapids, MI 49525. Phone: (616) 364-8722. Fax: (616) 364-8506. E-mail: feedback@wxmi.com. Web Site: www.wxmi.com. Licensee: Tribune Television Holdings Inc. Group owner: Tribune Broadcasting Co. (acq 6-5-98; grpsl). Network: Fox. Rep: Harrington, Righter & Parsons. News staff: 30; News: 4 hrs wkly.
Key Personnel:
Bonnie Hunter . . . . . CFO
Patricia Hamilton. . . . . VP & gen mgr
Jeff Cartwright. . . . . sls dir & progmg dir
Pennie Westers . . . . . adv dir & adv dir
Tim Dye . . . . . sls dir & news dir
Dale Scholten . . . . . chief of engrg

WZPX—Analog channel: 43. Digital channel: 44. On air date: 1996. 2610 Horizon Dr. S.E., Grand Rapids, MI 49546. Phone: (616) 222-6443. Fax: (616) 493-2677. Web Site: www.pax.tv. Licensee: Paxson Battle Creek License Inc. Group owner: Paxson Communications Corp. (acq 3-13-00; grpsl). Network: PAX TV.

WZZM-TV—Analog channel: 13. On air date: Nov 1, 1962. Box Z, Grand Rapids, MI 49501. 645 Three Mile Rd., N.W., Grand Rapids, MI 49544. Phone: (616) 785-1313. Fax: (616) 785-1301. E-mail: management@wzzm13.com. Web Site: www.wzzm13.com. Licensee: Combined Communications Corp. of Oklahoma Inc. Group owner: Gannett Broadcasting (acq 1-27-97; grpsl). Network: ABC. Rep: Blair Television. News: 22 hrs wkly.
Key Personnel:
Janet Mason . . . . . pres & gen mgr
Chuck Mikowski . . . . . VP & prom dir
Kim Krause . . . . . gen sls mgr
Tim Geraghty. . . . . news dir
Catherine Behrendt. . . . . progmg

Kalamazoo

see Grand Rapids-Kalamazoo-Battle Creek, MI market

Lansing, MI (DMA 110)

WHTV—Analog channel: 18. On air date: 1999. 5815 S. Pennsylvania Ave., Lansing, MI 48911. Phone: (517) 393-9488. Fax: (517) 393-9499. E-mail: info@upn18.com. Web Site: www.upn18.com. Licensee: Spartan-TV L.L.C. Network: UPN.
Key Personnel:
Lori Harper . . . . . stn mgr, mktg mgr & adv dir
Katy Till . . . . . progmg dir

WILX-TV—Analog channel: 10. Digital channel: 57. On air date: Mar 15, 1959. 500 American Rd., Lansing, MI 48911. Phone: (517) 393-0110. Fax: (517) 393-8555/(517) 393-9180. E-mail: news@wilx.com. Web Site: www.wilx.com. Licensee: Gray Television Licensee Inc. Group owner: Gray Television Inc. (acq 8-29-02; grpsl). Network: NBC. Rep: Continental Television Sales. News staff: 45.
Key Personnel:
Mike King . . . . . gen mgr
Tom Dolata . . . . . opns mgr
John O'Brien . . . . . gen sls mgr
Sandy Carson . . . . . natl sls mgr
Kevin Vanderkolk. . . . . prom mgr
Kevin Ragan . . . . . news dir
Gary King . . . . . chief of engrg

***WKAR-TV**—Analog channel: 23. On air date: Jan 15, 1954. 212 Communication Arts Bldg., East Lansing, MI 48824-1212. Phone: (517) 355-2300. Fax: (517) 353-7124. E-mail: mail@wkar.org. Web Site: www.wkar.org. Licensee: Michigan State University. Network: PBS. Washington Atty: Schwartz, Woods & Miller.
Key Personnel:
De Ann Hamilton . . . . . gen mgr
Jayne Marsh . . . . . dev dir & gen sls mgr
Cindy Herfindahl . . . . . mktg mgr & film buyer
Jeanie Croope . . . . . prom mgr & adv mgr
Mary Jane Wilson . . . . . progmg dir
Gary Blievernicht . . . . . engrg dir & chief of engrg

WLAJ—Analog channel: 53. On air date: Oct 13, 1990. 5815 S. Pennsylvania Ave., Lansing, MI 48911-5230. Phone: (517) 394-5300. Fax: (517) 887-0077. Web Site: www.wlaj.com. Licensee: WLAJ License Inc. Group owner: Freedom Communications Inc., Broadcast Division (acq 6-22-98; $170 million with WWMT(TV) Kalamazoo). Network: ABC. News staff: 10; News: 5 hrs wkly.
Key Personnel:
Doreen Wade . . . . . pres
Jim Wareham . . . . . VP & gen mgr
Chuck Tonner . . . . . opns mgr

WLNS-TV—Analog channel: 6. On air date: May 1, 1950. 2820 E. Saginaw St., Lansing, MI 48912. Phone: (517) 372-8282. Fax: (517) 374-7610. E-mail: wlns@wlns.com. Web Site: www.wlns.com. Licensee: Young Broadcasting of Lansing Inc. Group owner: Young Broadcasting Inc. (acq 9-15-86; $72 million; 4-14-86). Network: CBS. Washington Atty: Wiley, Rein & Fielding.
Key Personnel:
Mark Arminio . . . . . VP & gen mgr
Doug Powers . . . . . stn mgr
Gene Shanahan . . . . . opns mgr
Toni Finelli . . . . . gen sls mgr
Robert Serve . . . . . natl sls mgr
Tim Sharky . . . . . rgnl sls mgr
Dan Clark . . . . . prom dir
Teresa Morton . . . . . progmg dir
Cory Cumming . . . . . chief of engrg

WSYM-TV—Analog channel: 47. On air date: Dec 1, 1982. 600 W. St. Joseph St., Suite 47, Lansing, MI 48933. Phone: (517) 484-7747. Fax: (517) 484-3144. E-mail: fox47news@fox47news.com. Web Site: www.fox47news.com. Licensee: Journal Broadcast Corp. Group owner: Journal Broadcast Group Inc. (acq 11-9-85; 12-3-84). Network: Fox. Rep: Harrington, Righter & Parsons. Washington Atty: Crowell & Moring. News staff: 22; News: 8.5 hrs wkly.
Key Personnel:
Judy Kenney . . . . . gen mgr
Gary Baxter . . . . . gen sls mgr, natl sls mgr & adv mgr
Kip Bohne . . . . . mktg mgr & prom mgr
Bill Shipley. . . . . progmg dir & pub affrs dir
Gary Williams . . . . . chief of engrg

Marquette, MI (DMA 180)

WBKP—Analog channel: 5. On air date: Oct 30, 1996. 2025 U.S. 41 W., Suite 5, Marquette, MI 49855. Phone: (906) 225-5700. Fax: (906) 225-5598. E-mail: wbkp@wbkp.com. Web Site: www.wbkp.com. Licensee: Lake Superior Community Broadcasting Corp. Group owner: (group owner; acq 1-15-2004; $500,000. with WBUP(TV) Ishpeming). Network: ABC. Rep: Katz Radio. News staff: 7; News: 10 hrs wkly.
Key Personnel:
Curt Smith . . . . . chmn & gen mgr
Dan Laithen. . . . . stn mgr
Ken Lindeman . . . . . opns dir
Bob McDonald . . . . . gen sls mgr
Gary Langrey . . . . . chief of engrg

WBUP—Analog channel: 10. On air date: Jan 30, 2003. 2025 US Hwy. 41 W., Marquette, MI 49855. Phone: (906) 225-5700. Fax: (906) 225-5598. E-mail: opwbkp@hotmail.com. Web Site: www.wbkp.com. Licensee: Lake Superior Community Broadcasting Corp. Group owner: (group owner; acq 1-15-2004; $500,000. with WBKP(TV) Calumet). Network: ABC. Washington Atty: Latham and Watkins.
Key Personnel:
Stephen A. Marks. . . . . pres
Dean Laitinen . . . . . gen mgr, mktg dir & progmg dir
Lucia Shyiak. . . . . gen sls mgr
Dawn Garner. . . . . news dir
Gary Langley. . . . . chief of engrg

WDHS—Analog channel: 8. On air date: September 1986. Box 303, 1500 W. B St., Iron Mountain, MI 49801. Phone: (906) 776-8888. Fax: (906) 776-8888. Licensee: W. Russell Withers Jr. Group owner: Withers Broadcasting Co.

WJMN-TV—Analog channel: 3. On air date: Oct 7, 1969. Box 19055, 1181 E. Mason St., Green Bay, WI 54307. Phone: (920) 437-5411. Phone: (906) 786-7767 (sales). Fax: (920) 437-5769 (news). E-mail: wfru@netnet.net. Licensee: CBS Broadcasting Inc. Group owner: Viacom Television Stations Group. Network: CBS. Rep: TeleRep.
Key Personnel:
R. Perry Kidder . . . . . VP & gen mgr
David Stewart. . . . . opns dir
Jackie Stewart . . . . . sls dir
Mike Smith . . . . . natl sls mgr
Kit Overlock . . . . . rgnl sls mgr
Monica Zegers . . . . mktg mgr, prom dir, adv mgr & pub affrs dir
Jay Schabow . . . . . progmg mgr
H. Lee Hitter . . . . . news dir
Dale Mitchell . . . . . engrg dir

WLUC-TV—Analog channel: 6. On air date: Apr 29, 1956. 177 U.S. Hwy. 41 E., Negaunee, MI 49866. Phone: (906) 475-4161. Phone: (906) 475-4141 (news). Fax: (906) 475-4824. Fax: (906) 475-5070 (news). E-mail: tv6@wluctv6.com. Web Site: www.wluctv6.com. Licensee: WLUC License Subsidiary Inc. Group owner: Raycom Media Inc. (acq 9-24-96; grpsl). Network: NBC. Rep: Harrington, Righter & Parsons. Washington Atty: Covington & Burling. News staff: 24; News: 15 hrs

Minnesota Stations in the U.S.

wkly.
Key Personnel:
Brad Van Sluyters . . . . . VP & gen mgr
Sonny Reschka . . . . . opns mgr & chief of engrg

WMQF—Analog channel: 19. On air date: 2003. Equity Broadcasting Corp., 1 Shackleford Dr., Suite 400, Little Rock, AR 72211. Phone: (501) 219-2400. Fax: (501) 604-8004. Permittee: Marquette Broadcasting Inc. Group owner: Equity Broadcasting Corp. (acq 7-18-01). Network: Fox.

***WNMU-TV**—Analog channel: 13. On air date: Dec 28, 1972. Northern Michigan Univ., 1401 Presque Isle Ave., Marquette, MI 49855. Phone: (906) 227-1300. Fax: (906) 227-2905. Licensee: Board of Control of Northern Michigan University. Network: PBS. Washington Atty: Cohn & Marks. News: one hr wkly.
Key Personnel:
Eric Smith . . . . . gen mgr
Bruce Turner . . . . . stn mgr

Saginaw

see Flint-Saginaw-Bay City, MI market

Traverse City-Cadillac, MI (DMA 112)

***WCMV**—Analog channel: 27. On air date: Sept 7, 1984. Central Michigan Univ., 1999 E. Campus Dr., Mt. Pleasant, MI 48859. Phone: (989) 774-3105. Fax: (989) 774-4427. Web Site: www.wcmu.org. Licensee: Central Michigan University. Network: PBS. Washington Atty: Dow, Lohnes & Albertson.
Key Personnel:
Edwards Grant . . . . . gen mgr & stn mgr
Kim Walters . . . . . opns dir & prom mgr
Rick Schudiske . . . . . progmg dir

***WCMW**—Analog channel: 21. On air date: Sept 7, 1984. Central Michigan Univ., 1999 E. Campus Dr., Mt. Pleasant, MI 48859. Phone: (989) 774-3105. Fax: (989) 774-4427. Web Site: www.wcmu.org. Licensee: Central Michigan University. Network: PBS. Washington Atty: Dow, Lohnes & Albertson.
Key Personnel:
Ed Grant . . . . . stn mgr
Linda Dielman . . . . . sls dir, prom mgr & progmg dir
Randy Kapenga . . . . . chief of engrg

WFQX-TV—Analog channel: 33. On air date: Oct 12, 1989. 7669 S. 45 Rd., Cadillac, MI 49601. Phone: (231) 775-9813. Phone: (231) 775-0330. Fax: (231) 775-1898. Web Site: www.fox33.com. Licensee: Rockfleet Broadcasting II L.L.C. Group owner: Rockfleet Broadcasting Inc. (acq 2-1-2000; with WFUP(TV) Vanderbilt). Network: Fox. Rep: Katz Radio. Washington Atty: Fletcher, Heald & Hildreth. News: 3 hrs wkly.
Key Personnel:
Joseph Fuchs . . . . . CEO & pres
Robert Farrow . . . . . exec VP
Bruce Pfeiffer . . . . . gen mgr & sls VP
Greg Buzzell . . . . . opns mgr, engrg VP & chief of engrg
Dean Bushor . . . . . sls dir
Ginny Buzzell . . . . . prom mgr
Julia Horchner . . . . . progmg VP & progmg mgr
Quentin Parker . . . . . news dir

WFUP—Analog channel: 45. On air date: Sept 24, 1992. 7669 S. 45 Rd., Cadillac, MI 49601. Phone: (231) 775-9813. Phone: (231) 775-0330. Fax: (231) 775-1898. E-mail: kimbel@fox33.com. Web Site: www.fox33.com. Licensee: Rockfleet Broadcasting II L.L.C. Group owner: Rockfleet Broadcasting Inc. (acq 2-1-00; with WFQX-TV Cadillac). Network: Fox. Rep: Katz Radio. Washington Atty: Fletcher, Heald & Hildreth. News staff: 5; News: 3 hrs wkly.
Key Personnel:
Joseph Fuchs . . . . . CEO & pres
Robert Farrow . . . . . exec VP
Bruce Pfeiffer . . . . . gen mgr, sls VP & natl sls mgr
Greg Buzzell . . . . . opns VP, opns mgr & engrg VP
Dean Bushor . . . . . gen sls mgr & rgnl sls mgr
Ginny Buzzell . . . . . prom VP & prom mgr
Julia Horchner. . . . . progmg VP & progmg dir
Quentin Parker . . . . . news dir & chief of engrg

WGTQ—Analog channel: 8. On air date: Nov 3, 1976. 201 East Font St., Traverse City, MI 49684. Phone: (231) 946-2900. Fax: (231) 946-1600. Web Site: www.wgtu.com. Licensee: MTC License LLC. Group owner: MAX Media L.L.C. (acq 8-13-03; $7.75 million. with WGTU(TV) Traverse City). Network: ABC. Washington Atty: Latham and Watkins.
Key Personnel:
John A. Trinder. . . . . pres
Jeff Cash . . . . . gen mgr
Chris Web. . . . . gen sls mgr
Lori Puckett . . . . . prom dir
Jay Zacharias . . . . . chief of engrg

WGTU—Analog channel: 29. Digital channel: 31. On air date: Aug 23, 1971. 201 E. Front St., Traverse City, MI 49684. Phone: (231) 946-2900. Fax: (231) 946-1600. E-mail: wgtu@wgtu.com. Web Site: www.wgtu.com. Licensee: MTC License LLC. Group owner: MAX Media L.L.C. Network: ABC. Washington Atty: Latham & Watkins.
Key Personnel:
Jeff Cash . . . . . pres & gen mgr
Ron Stark. . . . . opns mgr

WPBN-TV—Analog channel: 7. On air date: Sept 13, 1954. Box 546, Traverse City, MI 49685. 8518 M-72W, Traverse City, MI 49685. Phone: (231) 947-7770. Fax: (231) 947-0354. Fax: (231) 947-1229. E-mail: tv7-4@tv7-4.com. Web Site: www.tv7-4.com. Licensee: WPBN/WTOM License Subsidiary Inc. Group owner: Raycom Media Inc. (acq 9-24-96; grpsl). Network: NBC. Rep: Harrington, Righter & Parsons. Washington Atty: Hogan & Hartson.
Key Personnel:
John Llewellyn . . . . . gen mgr
Greg Johnson . . . . . prom dir
Kim Fox . . . . . prom mgr
Thom Pritz. . . . . gen sls mgr & adv mgr
Mary Speck . . . . . progmg dir
Rick Finnie . . . . . chief of engrg

WTOM-TV—Analog channel: 4. On air date: May 16, 1959. Box 546, Traverse City, MI 49685. 8518 M-72W, Traverse City, MI 49684. Phone: (231) 947-7770. Fax: (231) 947-1229. Fax: (231) 947-0354. E-mail: tv7-4@tv7-4.com. Web Site: www.tv7-4.com. Licensee: WPBN/WTOM License Subsidiary Inc. Group owner: Raycom Media Inc. (acq 9-24-96; grpsl). Network: NBC. Rep: Katz Radio. Washington Atty: Hogan & Hartson.
Key Personnel:
Jill Wellyn . . . . . gen mgr
T. Pritz . . . . . gen sls mgr

WWTV—Analog channel: 9. Digital channel: 40. On air date: Dec 11, 1953. Box 627, Cadillac, MI 49601. 22320 130th Ave., Tustin, MI 49688. Phone: (231) 775-3478. Fax: (231) 775-3671. Web Site: www.9and10news.com. Licensee: Heritage Broadcasting Co. of Michigan.. Ownership: . (acq 3-3-89; grpsl; 3-20-89). Network: CBS. Washington Atty: Pepper & Corazzini.
Key Personnel:
William Kring. . . . . CFO & gen mgr
Pete Ludviksen . . . . . opns VP & opns dir
Pete Iacobelli . . . . . dev VP
Mark Featherston. . . . . sls VP
Jennifer Reagan. . . . . mktg dir
Sherri Magiera . . . . . progmg dir
Kevin Dunaway . . . . . news dir
Lowell Shore. . . . . chief of engrg

WWUP-TV—Analog channel: 10. Digital channel: 49. On air date: June 15, 1962. Box 627, Cadillac, MI 49601. Phone: (231) 775-3478. Fax: (231) 775-3671. Web Site: www.9and10news.com. Licensee: Heritage Broadcasting Co. of Michigan. (acq 3-3-89; grpsl; 3-20-89). Network: CBS. Washington Atty: Pepper & Corazzini.
Key Personnel:
Mario Iacobelli . . . . . gen mgr
Mark Featherston. . . . . gen sls mgr
Jennifer Reagan . . . . . mktg mgr
Sherri Megiera . . . . . progmg dir
Lowell Shore. . . . . chief of engrg

Minnesota

Austin

see Rochester, MN-Mason City, IA-Austin, MN market

Crookston

see Fargo-Valley City, ND market

Duluth, MN-Superior, WI (DMA 136)

KBJR-TV—(Superior).WI Analog channel: 6. On air date: Mar 11, 1954. 246 S. Lake Ave., Duluth, MN 55802-2304. Phone: (218) 720-9600. Fax: (218) 720-9699. E-mail: news6@kbjr.com. Web Site: www.news6.com. Licensee: KBJR License, Inc. Group owner: Granite Broadcasting Corp. (acq 11-1-88; $12.8 million; 9-23-74). Network: NBC. Rep: Katz Radio. Washington Atty: Akin, Gump, Strauss, Hauer & Feld. News staff: 21; News: 10 hrs wkly.
Key Personnel:
Robert Wilmers . . . . . gen mgr
David Jensch . . . . . stn mgr

KDLH—Analog channel: 3. Digital channel: 33. On air date: Mar 14, 1954. 425 W. Superior St., Duluth, MN 55802. Phone: (218) 733-0303. Fax: (218) 727-7515. Web Site: www.kdlh.com. Licensee: Malara Broadcast Group of Duluth Licensee LLC. Group owner: New Vision Group LLC (acq 3-14-2005; $10.8 million).. Network: CBS. Rep: Blair Television. Washington Atty: Covington & Burling. News staff: 17; News: 12 hrs wkly.
Key Personnel:
Anthony C. Malara . . . . . pres
Deb Messer. . . . . gen mgr & progmg dir
Wendy Gustofson . . . . . sls dir & natl sls mgr
Jeff Reinarz. . . . . mktg dir, mktg mgr, prom mgr & adv dir
Rob Heverling . . . . . news dir
Terry Van Dell . . . . . engrg dir

KQDS-TV—Analog channel: 21. Digital channel: 17. On air date: November 1994. 2001 London Rd., Duluth, MN 55812. Phone: (218) 728-1622. Fax: (218) 728-1557. E-mail: dhileman@kqdsfox21.tv. Licensee: KQDS Acquisition Corp. Group owner: Red River Broadcast Co. LLC (acq 10-21-98; grpsl). Network: Fox.
Key Personnel:
Ro Grignon . . . . . pres
Kathy Lau. . . . . VP & opns dir
Dave Hileman . . . . . gen mgr, gen sls mgr & natl sls mgr

KRII—Analog channel: 11. On air date: Nov 27, 2002. 246 South Lake Ave., Duluth, MN 55802-2304. Phone: (218) 720-9600. Fax: (218) 720-9699. E-mail: news6@kbjr.com. Web Site: www.news6.tv. Licensee: Channel 11 License Inc. Group owner: Granite Broadcasting Corp. (acq 5-9-01; grpsl). Network: NBC.
Key Personnel:
Robert Wilmers . . . . . gen mgr
David Jensch . . . . . stn mgr
Vincent Nelson . . . . . sls dir
Todd Wentworth . . . . . gen sls mgr
Carl Keller. . . . . natl sls mgr
Derrick Hinds. . . . . news dir
Larry Erickson . . . . . engrg dir

WDIO-TV—Analog channel: 10. On air date: Jan 24, 1966. Box 16897, Duluth, MN 55816-0897. 10 Observation Rd., Duluth, MN 55811-3506. Phone: (218) 727-6864. Fax: (218) 727-4415. E-mail: news@wdio.com. Licensee: WDIO-TV L.L.C. Group owner: Hubbard Broadcasting Inc. (acq 12-87; grpsl). Network: ABC. Washington Atty: Fletcher, Heald & Hildreth. News staff: 18; News: 9 hrs wkly.

***WDSE-TV**—Analog channel: 8. On air date: Sept 1, 1964. 632 Niagara Ct., Duluth, MN 55811-3098. Phone: (218) 724-8567. Fax: (218) 724-4269. E-mail: wdse@pbs.org. Web Site: www.wdse.org. Licensee: Duluth-Superior Area Educ TV Corp. Network: PBS. Washington Atty: Arent, Fox, Kintner, Plotkin & Kahn.
Key Personnel:
Allan D. Harmon . . . . . gen mgr
Cheryl Leeper . . . . . gen sls mgr & mktg mgr
Beth Lyden . . . . . prom mgr
Jodi Hagen . . . . . prom mgr
Ronald Anderson . . . . . progmg dir
Rex Greenwell . . . . . chief of engrg

WIRT—Analog channel: 13. On air date: Sept 1, 1967. Box 16897, Duluth, MN 55816. 10 Observation Rd., Duluth, MN 55811. Phone: (218) 727-6864. Fax: (218) 727-4415. E-mail: news@wdio.com. Web Site: www.wdio.com. Licensee: WDIO-TV L.L.C. Group owner: Hubbard Broadcasting Inc. (acq 12-87; grpsl). Network: ABC.

Mankato, MN (DMA 199)

KEYC-TV—Analog channel: 12. On air date: Oct 5, 1960. Box 128, Mankato, MN 56002. 1570 Lookout Dr., N. Mankato, MN 56003. Phone: (507) 625-7905. Fax: (507) 625-5745. E-mail: keyc@keyc.com.

Broadcasting & Cable Yearbook 2006

B-53

Web Site: www.keyc.tv. Licensee: United Communications Corp. Group owner: (group owner; acq 10-14-77; $5 million). Network: CBS. Washington Atty: Wood, Maines & Brown. News staff: 12; News: 10 hrs wkly.
Key Personnel:
Dennis M. Wahlstrom . . . . VP, gen mgr & natl sls mgr
Sharon Freitag . . . . opns mgr
John Ginther. rgnl sls mgr
Jan Ellanson . . . . prom mgr, progmg dir & progmg mgr
Merv Steffen . . . . chief of engrg

Minneapolis-St. Paul, MN (DMA 14)

KARE—(Minneapolis).Analog channel: 11. Digital channel: 35. On air date: Sept 1, 1953. 8811 Olson Memorial Hwy., Minneapolis, MN 55427. Phone: (763) 546-1111. Fax: (763) 546-8590. Web Site: www.kare11.com. Licensee: Multimedia Holdings Corp. Group owner: Gannett Broadcasting (division of Gannett Co. Inc.) (acq 4-13-83; $75 million;. FTR: 5-7-83). Network: NBC.

***KAWB**—Analog channel: 22. On air date: Mar 1, 1988. BSU Box 9, 1500 Birchmont Dr. N.E., Bemidji, MN 56601-2699. Phone: (218) 751-3407. Fax: (218) 751-3142. E-mail: viewerservices@lakelandptv.org. Web Site: www.lacklandptv.org. Licensee: Northern Minnesota Public TV Inc. Network: PBS. Washington Atty: Dow, Lohnes & Albertson. News: 2.5 hrs wkly.
Key Personnel:
Rebecca Anderson . . . . pres
Bill Sanford. . . . . gen mgr
Dan Hegstad . . . . stn mgr
Jess Skala . . . . opns mgr
Deb McGregor-Pfleger . . . . dev dir & dev mgr

***KAWE**—Analog channel: 9. On air date: June 1, 1980. BSU Box 9, 1500 Birchmont Dr. N.E., Bemidji, MN 56601-2699. Phone: (218) 751-3407. Fax: (218) 751-3142. E-mail: viewerservices@lakelandptv.org. Web Site: www.lacklandptv.org. Licensee: Northern Minnesota Public TV Inc. Network: PBS. Washington Atty: Dow, Lohnes & Albertson. News staff: 7; News: 2.5 hrs wkly.
Key Personnel:
Rebecca Anderson . . . . pres
Bill Sanford. . . . . gen mgr
Jess Skala . . . . opns mgr
Deb McGregor-Pfleger . . . . dev dir & dev mgr

KCCO-TV—Analog channel: 7. Digital channel: 24. On air date: Oct 8, 1958. 90 S. 11th St., Minneapolis, MN 55403. Phone: (612) 339-4444. Fax: (612) 330-2767. E-mail: wcconewstips@wcco.com. Web Site: www.wcco.com. Licensee: CBS Broadcasting Inc. Group owner: Viacom Television Stations Group. Network: CBS. Rep: TeleRep. Washington Atty: Rosenman & Colin.

KCCW-TV—Analog channel: 12. Digital channel: 20. On air date: Jan 1, 1964. 90 S. 11th St., Minneapolis, MN 55403. Phone: (612) 339-4444. Fax: (612) 330-2682. Web Site: www.wcco.com. Licensee: CBS Broadcasting Inc. Group owner: Viacom Television Stations Group. Network: CBS. Washington Atty: Rosenman & Colin.
Key Personnel:
Edward Piette . . . . gen mgr & stn mgr
Gary Kroger . . . . engrg mgr

KFTC—Analog channel: 26.Not on air, target date: 2000: 11358 Viking Dr., Eden Prairie, MN 55344. Phone: (952) 944-9999. Fax: (952) 942-0455. Web Site: www.kftc.com. Licensee: Fox Television Stations Inc. Group owner: (group owner; acq 9-21-01; grpsl).

KMSP-TV—(Minneapolis).Analog channel: 9. Digital channel: 26. On air date: Jan 9, 1955. 11358 Viking Dr., Eden Prairie, MN 55344-7258. Phone: (952) 944-9999. Fax: (952) 942-0455. Web Site: www.fox9.com. Licensee: Fox Television Stations Inc. Group owner: (group owner; acq 7-31-01; grpsl). Network: Fox. News staff: 64; News: 19.5 hrs wkly.

KMWB—(Minneapolis).Analog channel: 23. Digital channel: 22. On air date: Sept 22, 1982. 1640 Como Ave., St. Paul, MN 55108. Phone: (651) 646-2300. Fax: (651) 646-1220. Web Site: www.kmwb23.com. Licensee: KLGT Licensee L.L.C. Group owner: Sinclair Broadcast Group Inc. (acq 3-16-98; $52.5 million).
Key Personnel:
Art Lanham . . . . gen mgr
Bob Weinstein . . . . gen sls mgr
Camille Sims-Scheel . . . . rgnl sls mgr
Steve Lunde . . . . chief of engrg

KPXM—Analog channel: 41. Digital channel: 40. On air date: Nov 24, 1982. 22601 176th St., Big Lake, MN 55309. 10700 Old County Rd. 15, Suite 285, Plymouth, MN 55441. Phone: (763) 263-8666. Phone: (763) 417-0041. Fax: (763) 263-6600. Fax: (763) 417-0841. Web Site: www.pax.tv. Licensee: Paxson Communications of Minneapolis/41 Inc. Group owner: Paxson Communications Corp. (acq 10-1-96; $12 million). Washington Atty: Mullin, Rhyne, Emmons & Topel.
Key Personnel:
Lowell Paxson. . . . . chmn
John F. DeLorenzo . . . . CFO
Dawn Hoglund. . . . . stn mgr
Jerry Bodine . . . . sls dir & gen sls mgr
Dave Petersen . . . . rgnl sls mgr
Cori Ziegler . . . . progmg mgr & pub affrs dir
Steve Buyze . . . . engrg VP
Bill Canning . . . . chief of engrg

KRWF—Analog channel: 43. On air date: Apr 14, 1987. Box 189, 415 Fillmore, Alexandria, MN 56308. Phone: (320) 763-5729. Fax: (320) 763-4627. E-mail: ksax@ksax.com. Web Site: ksax.com. Licensee: KSAX-TV Inc. Group owner: Hubbard Broadcasting Inc. Network: ABC. Washington Atty: Holland & Knight.
Key Personnel:
Robert Hubbard . . . . pres
Ed Piette. . . . . sr VP
Edward Smith . . . . gen mgr & stn mgr
Terri Shatek . . . . gen sls mgr
Corliss Stark. . . . . prom mgr
Nat Leding . . . . progmg dir
Mark Vanderwerf . . . . news dir
Larry Eckblad . . . . chief of engrg

KSAX—Analog channel: 42. On air date: Sept 15, 1987. Box 189, 415 Fillmore St., Alexandria, MN 56308. Phone: (320) 763-5729. Fax: (320) 763-4627. E-mail: ksax@ksax.com. Web Site: ksax.com. Licensee: KSAX-TV Inc. Group owner: Hubbard Broadcasting Inc. Network: ABC. Washington Atty: Holland & Knight.
Key Personnel:
Edward Smith. . . . . gen mgr, gen sls mgr & progmg dir
Corliss Stark. . . . . prom mgr
Larry Eckblad . . . . chief of engrg

KSTC-TV—(Minneapolis).Analog channel: 45. Digital channel: 44. On air date: 1995. 3415 University Ave., St. Paul, MN 55114-2099. Phone: (651) 645-4500. Fax: (651) 523-7320. Web Site: www.kstc45.com. Licensee: KSTC.TV LLC. Group owner: Hubbard Broadcasting Inc. (acq 4-24-2000). Washington Atty: Holland & Knight LLP.
Key Personnel:
Stanley Hubbard. . . . . chmn
Robert Hubbard . . . . pres
Susan Anderson . . . . stn mgr
Andy Stavast . . . . gen sls mgr
Fran Perpich-Hedtke . . . . rgnl sls mgr
Joe Johnston . . . . mktg dir
Michael E. Smith. . . . . . progmg dir, progmg mgr & film buyer
Dayna Deutsch . . . . pub affrs dir
Dick Rice . . . . engrg dir & chief of engrg

KSTP-TV—(Saint Paul).Analog channel: 5. Digital channel: 50. On air date: Apr 23, 1948. 3415 University Ave., Saint Paul, MN 55114. Phone: (651) 646-5555. Fax: (651) 642-4172. Web Site: www.kstp.com. Licensee: KSTP-TV LLC. Group owner: Hubbard Broadcasting Inc. Network: ABC. Rep: Petry Television Inc.. Washington Atty: Holland and Knight. News: 27.5 hrs wkly.
Key Personnel:
Robert Hubbard. . . . . pres & gen mgr
John McCormick . . . . gen sls mgr
Andrea Kreech. . . . . prom mgr
Michael Smith . . . . progmg dir & progmg mgr
Dick Rice . . . . chief of engrg

***KTCA-TV**—(Saint Paul).Analog channel: 2. Digital channel: 34. On air date: Sept 3, 1957. 172 E. 4th St., St. Paul, MN 55101. Phone: (651) 222-1717. Fax: (651) 229-1282. Web Site: www.tpt.org. Licensee: Twin Cities Public TV Inc. Network: PBS.
Key Personnel:
Jim Pagliarini . . . . CEO
Stephen Usery. . . . . exec VP, mktg mgr, prom mgr & news dir
Tom Holter . . . . progmg dir
Bruce Jacobs . . . . chief of engrg

***KTCI-TV**—(Saint Paul).Analog channel: 17. Digital channel: 16. On air date: May 3, 1965. 172 E. 4th St., Saint Paul, MN 55101. Phone: (651) 222-1717. Fax: (651) 229-1282. Web Site: www.tpt.org. Licensee: Twin Cities Public Television Inc. Network: PBS.
Key Personnel:
Jim Pagliarini . . . . CEO
Stephen Usery. . . . . mktg mgr & prom mgr
Tom Holter . . . . progmg dir
Bruce Jacobs . . . . chief of engrg

***KWCM-TV**—Analog channel: 10. On air date: Feb 7, 1966. 120 W. Schlieman Ave., Appleton, MN 56208. Phone: (320) 289-2622. Fax: (320) 289-2634. E-mail: yourtv@pioneer.org. Web Site: www.pioneer.org. Licensee: West Central Minnesota Educational TV Co. Network: PBS. Washington Atty: Fletcher, Heald & Hildreth.
Key Personnel:
Glen Cerny. . . . . pres & gen mgr
Jon Panzer. . . . . stn mgr, engrg VP & chief of engrg
Shirley Schwarz . . . . progmg dir

WCCO-TV—(Minneapolis).Analog channel: 4. Digital channel: 32. On air date: July 1, 1949. 90 S. 11th St., Minneapolis, MN 55403. Phone: (612) 339-4444. Fax: (612) 330-2682. Web Site: www.wcco.com. Licensee: CBS Broadcasting Inc. Group owner: Viacom Television Stations Group (acq 2-92; grpsl; FTR: 7-26-76). Network: CBS. Rep: CBS Spot Sales. News staff: 75; News: 23 hrs wkly.
Key Personnel:
Edward Piette . . . . VP & gen mgr
Trey Fabacher. . . . . stn mgr
Jeff Kiernan . . . . news dir
Gary Kroger . . . . engrg dir

WFTC—(Minneapolis).Analog channel: 29. Digital channel: 21. On air date: October 1982. 11358 Viking Dr., Eden Prairie, MN 55344. Phone: (952) 944-9999. Fax: (952) 942-0455. E-mail: fox9news@foxtv.com. Web Site: www.upn29.com. Licensee: Fox Television Stations Inc. Group owner: (group owner; acq 10-1-01; grpsl). Network: Fox. News: 3.5 hrs wkly.

***WHWC-TV**—Analog channel: 28. Digital channel: 27. On air date: Nov 18, 1973. 3319 W. Beltline Hwy., Madison, WI 53713. Phone: (608) 264-9600. Fax: (608) 264-9664. Web Site: www.ecb.org. Licensee: State of Wisconsin-Educational Communications Board. Network: PBS. Washington Atty: Dow, Lohnes & Albertson.
Key Personnel:
Byron Knight. . . . . gen mgr & stn mgr
Mike Edgette . . . . opns dir
Jon Miskowski . . . . dev dir & chief of engrg
Michael Bridgeman . . . . prom mgr
Mary Clare Sorenson . . . . adv dir & progmg mgr
Kathy Bissen . . . . news dir
Dick Taugher. . . . . chief of engrg

Rochester, MN-Mason City, IA-Austin, MN (DMA 153)

KAAL—Analog channel: 6. On air date: Aug 17, 1953. 1701 10th Pl. N.E., Austin, MN 55912. Phone: (507) 437-6666. Fax: (507) 433-9560. Web Site: www.kaaltv.com. Licensee: KAAL-TV LLC. Group owner: Hubbard Broadcasting Inc. (acq 12-13-00; $9.5 million).. Network: ABC. Washington Atty: Schwartz, Woods & Miller. News staff: 18; News: 11 hrs wkly.
Key Personnel:
Patrick St. George . . . . gen mgr
Jeff Bowers . . . . gen sls mgr
Dan Collado . . . . prom mgr & adv mgr
Leo Coyle . . . . progmg dir
Gary Peterson . . . . news dir
Wendell Nelson. . . . . chief of engrg

KIMT—Analog channel: 3. On air date: May 15, 1954. 112 N. Pennsylvania Ave., Mason City, IA 50401. Phone: (641) 423-2540. Fax: (641) 423-9309. E-mail: mail@kimt.com. Web Site: www.kimt.com. Licensee: Media General Communications Inc. Group owner: Media General Broadcast Group (acq 3-27-00; grpsl). Network: Network: CBS, UPN. Rep: Harrington, Righter & Parsons. Washington Atty: Covington & Burling. News staff: 21; News: 19 hrs wkly.
Key Personnel:
Steve Martinson . . . . VP & gen mgr
Michael Fitzgerald . . . . gen sls mgr
Wayne Kohlhaas . . . . rgnl sls mgr
Jerome Risting . . . . prom mgr & progmg dir
Dave Wertheimer . . . . news dir
Steve Reiter . . . . chief of engrg

***KSMQ-TV**—Analog channel: 15. On air date: Oct 17, 1972. 2000 8th Ave. N.W., Austin, MN 55912. Phone: (507) 433-0678. Fax: (507) 433-0670. E-mail: ksmq@ksmq.org. Web Site: www.ksmq.org. Licensee: Independent School District 492. Network: PBS. Washington Atty: Schwartz, Woods & Miller.
Key Personnel:
Cindy Samuel . . . . gen mgr & mktg mgr
Danielle Heiny. . . . . stn mgr
Shawn Weitzel . . . . chief of engrg

KTTC—Analog channel: 10. On air date: July 16, 1953. 6301 Bandel Rd. N.W., Hickory, MN 55901. Phone: (507) 288-4444. Fax: (507) 288-6324. Fax: (507) 288-6278 (news). E-mail: kttc@kttc.com. Web Site: www.kttc.com. Licensee: KTTC TV Inc. Group owner: Quincy Newspapers Inc. (acq 7-1-76; $4.25 million; 5-24-76). Network: NBC. Rep: Blair Television. Washington Atty: Wilkinson, Barker, Knauer & Quinn. News staff: 15; News: 11 hrs wkly.
Key Personnel:
Jerry Watson . . . gen mgr
Elizabeth Dahlen . . . stn mgr, gen sls mgr & mktg dir
Dave Ferber . . . natl sls mgr
Jim Schmeichel . . . rgnl sls mgr
Vickie Broughton . . . progmg dir & progmg mgr
Dennis Grant . . . news dir
Bonnie Bickel . . . pub affrs dir
Tim Morgan . . . engrg dir & chief of engrg

KXLT-TV—Analog channel: 47. On air date: Aug 1, 1987. 6301 Bandel Rd. N.W., Rochester, MN 55901. Phone: (507) 252-4747. Fax: (507) 252-5050. E-mail: comments@fox47kxlt.com. Web Site: www.fox47kxlt.com. Licensee: Shockley Broadcasting LLC. (acq 4-17-01; grpsl). Network: Fox. Washington Atty: Rosenman & colin. News: 7 hrs wkly.
Key Personnel:
Sandy Shockley . . . pres
Terry Shockley . . . pres
Robert Epstein. . . . gen mgr, gen sls mgr, mktg VP & adv VP
Brendan Ford . . . opns mgr
Kris Lake . . . natl sls mgr
Rita Duda . . . prom dir & prom mgr
Carrie Thiesse . . . progmg mgr
Dennis Grant . . . news dir
Tim Morgan . . . chief of engrg

***KYIN**—Analog channel: 24. On air date: May 14, 1977. Box 6450, 6450 Corporate Dr., c/o Iowa Public TV, Johnston, IA 50131. Phone: (515) 242-3100. Phone: (515) 242-4151. E-mail: public_information@iptv.org. Web Site: www.iptv.org. Licensee: Iowa Public Broadcasting Board. Network: PBS. Washington Atty: Dow, Lohnes & Albertson.

St. Paul

see Minneapolis-St. Paul, MN market

Thief River Falls

see Fargo-Valley City, ND market

Worthington

see Sioux Falls (Mitchell), SD market

Mississippi

Biloxi-Gulfport, MS (DMA 156)

WLOX—Analog channel: 13. On air date: Sept 15, 1962. Box 4596, 208 De Buys Rd., Biloxi, MS 39535-4596. Phone: (228) 896-1313. Fax: (228) 896-0749. E-mail: wlox@wlox.com. Web Site: www.wlox.com. Licensee: Libco Inc. Group owner: Liberty Corp. (acq 3-1-95; $41 million;. FTR: 2-27-95). Network: ABC. Rep: Katz Radio. Washington Atty: Dow, Lohnes & Albertson. News staff: 44; News: 18 hrs wkly.
Key Personnel:
Leon Long . . . VP & gen mgr
Dave Vincent . . . stn mgr
Roger Garrett . . . opns mgr
Linda Sherman . . . gen sls mgr
Don Moore . . . rgnl sls mgr
Darlene Duffano . . . progmg dir
David Vincent . . . news dir
John Armstrong . . . chief of engrg

***WMAH-TV**—Analog channel: 19. Digital channel: 16. On air date: Jan 14, 1972. 3825 Ridgewood Rd., Jackson, MS 39211. Phone: (601) 432-6565. Fax: (601) 432-6392. Web Site: www.mpbonline.org. Licensee: Mississippi Authority for Educational TV. Network: PBS. Washington Atty: Schwartz, Woods & Miller.
Key Personnel:
Marie Antoon . . . exec VP & gen mgr
Gene Edwards . . . opns dir
Ty Warren . . . dev dir
Ron Evans . . . gen sls mgr & engrg dir
Art Starkey . . . progmg dir

WXXV-TV—Analog channel: 25. Digital channel: 48. On air date: Feb 14, 1987. Box 2500, Gulfport, MS 39505. 14351 Hwy. 49 N., Gulfport, MS 39503. Phone: (228) 832-2525. Fax: (228) 832-4442. E-mail: info@wxxv25.com. Web Site: www.wxxv25.com. Licensee: Morris Network of Mississippi Inc. Group owner: Morris Network Inc. (acq 5-22-97; $17.475 million).. Network: Network: Fox, UPN. Rep: Millennium Sales & Marketing. Washington Atty: Fletcher, Heald.
Key Personnel:
Dean Hinson . . . pres
Phil Cox . . . gen mgr
Ray Luke . . . opns dir
Mike Travis . . . gen sls mgr
Shiren Brown . . . natl sls mgr
Michele Gibbs . . . prom dir

Columbus-Tupelo-West Point, MS (DMA 132)

WCBI-TV—Analog channel: 4. On air date: July 13, 1956. Box 271, Columbus, MS 39703. 201 5th St. S., Columbus, MS 39701. Phone: (662) 327-4444. Fax: (662) 329-1004. Web Site: www.wcbi.com. Licensee: WCBI-TV LLC. Group owner: Morris Multi-Media (acq 12-31-03; $20 million).. Network: CBS. Washington Atty: Latham & Watkins.
Key Personnel:
Carl V. Bruce Jr. . . . gen mgr
Bobby Berry . . . sls dir & gen sls mgr
Charles Hill Morris . . . natl sls mgr
Nell Thomas . . . prom mgr
Derek Rogers . . . progmg dir & progmg mgr
Dale Cox . . . news dir
Gary Savage . . . pub affrs dir & engrg dir

WKDH—Analog channel: 45. On air date: June 2002. Box 1645, Tupelo, MS 38802. Phone: (662) 842-7620. Fax: (662) 842-6342. Fax: (662) 844-7061. Web Site: www.wkda.com. Licensee: Southern Broadcasting Inc. Network: ABC. Washington Atty: Garvey, Schubert & Barer.
Key Personnel:
Walter Spain . . . pres
David Dillard . . . opns mgr
Larry Harris . . . gen sls mgr
Ed Bishop . . . progmg dir
Wendell Robinson . . . chief of engrg

WLOV-TV—Analog channel: 27. On air date: May 29, 1983. Box 1732, Tupelo, MS 38802. Phone: (662) 842-2227. Fax: (662) 844-7061. E-mail: manager@wlov.com. Web Site: www.wlov.com. Licensee: Lingard Broadcasting Corp.. Ownership: Jack Lingard, 100%. (acq 4-12-94). Network: Fox. Rep: Continental Television Sales. Washington Atty: Law Office of Robert E. Levine. News: 2.5 hrs wkly.
Key Personnel:
Jennifer Dennington . . . stn mgr
David Dillard . . . opns dir
Larry Harris . . . gen sls mgr
Ed Bishop . . . progmg dir
Terry Smith . . . news dir
Marty Davis . . . chief of engrg
Josh Ward . . . mktg

***WMAA**—Analog channel: 43.Not on air, target date: unknown: 3825 Ridgewood Rd., Jackson, MS 39211. Phone: (601) 432-6565. Fax: (601) 432-6392. Web Site: www.mpbonline.org. Permittee: Mississippi Authority for Educational Television. Network: PBS.
Key Personnel:
Marie Antoon . . . gen mgr
Ron Evans . . . gen sls mgr & mktg mgr
Jennifer Griffin . . . adv mgr
Art Starkey . . . progmg dir
Keith Martin . . . chief of engrg

***WMAB-TV**—Analog channel: 2. Digital channel: 24. On air date: July 4, 1971. 3825 Ridgewood Rd., Jackson, MS 39211. Phone: (601) 432-6565. Fax: (601) 432-6654. Fax: (601) 432-6311. Web Site: www.mpbonline.org. Licensee: Mississippi Authority for Educational TV. Washington Atty: Schwartz, Woods & Miller. News staff: 4.
Key Personnel:
Marie Antoon . . . exec VP & gen mgr
Gene Edwards . . . opns dir
Ty Warren . . . dev dir
Ron Evans . . . mktg mgr
Randy Tinney . . . prom dir
Art Starkey . . . progmg dir
Dick Rizzo . . . news dir & pub affrs dir
Keith Martin . . . engrg dir

***WMAE-TV**—Analog channel: 12. Digital channel: 55. On air date: Aug 11, 1974. 3825 Ridgewood Rd., Jackson, MS 39211. Phone: (601) 432-6565. Fax: (601) 432-6654. Fax: (601) 432-6311. Web Site: www.mpbonline.org. Licensee: Mississippi Authority for Educational TV. Washington Atty: Schwartz, Woods & Miller.
Key Personnel:
Marie Antoon . . . gen mgr
Gene Edwards . . . opns dir
Ty Warren . . . dev dir
Ron Evans . . . mktg mgr
Jennifer Griffin . . . prom dir
Art Starkey . . . progmg dir

WTVA—Analog channel: 9. Digital channel: 27. On air date: Mar 18, 1957. Box 350, Tupelo, MS 38801. 1359 Rd. 681, Tupelo, MS 38802. Phone: (662) 842-7620. Fax: (662) 844-7061. E-mail: manager@wtva.com. Web Site: www.wtva.com. Licensee: WTVA Inc. Group owner: (group owner). Network: NBC. Washington Atty: Garvey, Schubert & Barer. News: 21 hrs wkly.
Key Personnel:
Frank K. Spain . . . pres
Mark Ledbetter . . . gen mgr
David Dillard . . . opns mgr

Greenville

see Greenwood-Greenville, MS market

Greenwood-Greenville, MS (DMA 183)

WABG-TV—Analog channel: 6. On air date: Oct 20, 1959. Box 1243, 849 Washington Ave., Greenville, MS 38701. Box 720, 2001 Garrard Ave., Greenwood, MS 38930. Phone: (662) 332-0949. Fax: (601) 378-3055. Web Site: www.wabg.com. Licensee: Mississippi Broadcasting Partners. Group owner: Bahakel Communications Network: ABC. Rep: Continental Television Sales. News staff: 16; News: 13 hrs wkly.
Key Personnel:
Cy Bahakel . . . pres
Sherry Nelson . . . stn mgr
Donnie Reid . . . opns mgr & progmg dir
Larry Cazavan . . . gen sls mgr
Pat Chatman . . . news dir
Larry Nixon . . . chief of engrg

***WMAI**—Analog channel: 31.Not on air, target date: unknown: 3825 Ridgewood Rd., Jackson, MS 39211. Phone: (601) 432-6565. Fax: (610) 432-6392. Web Site: www.mpbonline.org. Permittee: Mississippi Authority for Educational Television. Network: PBS.
Key Personnel:
Marie Antoon . . . gen mgr
Ron Evans . . . gen sls mgr & mktg mgr
Jennifer Griffin . . . adv mgr
Art Starkey . . . progmg dir
Keith Martin . . . chief of engrg

***WMAO-TV**—(Greenwood).Analog channel: 23. Digital channel: 25. On air date: Sept 15, 1972. 3825 Ridgewood Rd., Jackson, MS 39211. Phone: (601) 432-6565. Fax: (601) 432-6654. Fax: (601) 432-6311. Web Site: www.mpbonline.org. Licensee: Mississippi Authority for Educational TV. Washington Atty: Schwartz, Woods & Miller.
Key Personnel:
Marie Antoon . . . exec VP & gen mgr
Gene Edwards . . . opns dir
Ty Warren . . . dev dir
Ron Evans . . . mktg mgr
Art Starkey . . . progmg dir

WXVT—Analog channel: 15. Digital channel: 17. On air date: Nov 7, 1980. 3015 E. Reed Rd., Greenville, MS 38703. Phone: (662) 334-1500. Fax: (662) 378-8122. Web Site: www.wxvt.com. Licensee: Saga Broadcasting LLC. Group owner: Saga Communications Inc. (acq 7-1-99; $5.2 million).. Network: CBS.

Gulfport

see Biloxi-Gulfport, MS market

Hattiesburg-Laurel, MS (DMA 168)

WDAM-TV—(Laurel).Analog channel: 7. On air date: June 8, 1956. Box 16269, Hattiesburg, MS 39404. Hwy. 11 N., Hattiesburg, MS 39459. Phone: (601) 544-4730. Fax: (601) 584-9302. Web Site: www.wdam.com. Licensee: WDAM License Subsidiary Inc. Group owner: Raycom Media Inc. (acq 9-24-96; grpsl). Network: NBC. Rep: Harrington, Righter & Parsons. Washington Atty: Covington & Burling.

News staff: 26; News: 20 hrs wkly.
Key Personnel:
Jim Cameron . . . . VP & gen mgr
Ted Palmer . . . . gen sls mgr
Wanda Morrison . . . . natl sls mgr
Brenda Parker . . . . mktg mgr & prom dir
Betty Young . . . . progmg dir
Jim Wilkinson . . . . engrg mgr & chief of engrg

WHLT—Analog channel: 22. On air date: Jan 12, 1987. 5912 Hwy. 49, The Cloverleaf Mall Suite A, Hattiesburg, MS 39401. Phone: (601) 545-2077. Fax: (601) 545-3589. Web Site: www.mediageneral.com. Licensee: Media General Broadcasting Inc. Group owner: Media General Broadcast Group (acq 7-25-97; grpsl). Network: CBS. Rep: MMT.
Key Personnel:
Robert Romine . . . . gen mgr
Fred Howard . . . . gen sls mgr
Gary Wolverton . . . . prom mgr
Jackie McDonald . . . . progmg dir
Gary Wright. . . . . engrg mgr & chief of engrg

Holly Springs

see Memphis, TN market

Jackson, MS
(DMA 91)

WAPT—Analog channel: 16. On air date: Oct 3, 1970. 7616 Channel 16 Way, Jackson, MS 39209. Phone: (601) 922-1607. Fax: (601) 922-1663. Web Site: www.thejacksonchannel.com. Licensee: WAPT Hearst-Argyle Television Inc. Group owner: Hearst-Argyle Televison Inc. (acq 7-16-97; grpsl). Network: ABC. Rep: Katz Radio. News staff: 26; News: 14 hrs wkly.
Key Personnel:
David Barrett . . . . CEO
Stuart Kellogg . . . . pres & gen mgr
Jeff Miller . . . . gen sls mgr
Jeff Wolfe. . . . . natl sls mgr & rgnl sls mgr
Abigail Flanders . . . . prom mgr
Linda Bozone . . . . progmg mgr
Bruce Barkley. . . . . news dir
Tom Bondurant . . . . chief of engrg

WDBD—Analog channel: 40. Digital channel: 41. On air date: Nov 30, 1984. One Great Pl., Jackson, MS 39209. Phone: (601) 922-1234. Fax: (601) 922-0268. Web Site: www.gomiss.com. Licensee: Jackson Television L.L.C. (acq 5-2-03; $13.4 million. with WXMS-LP Jackson). Washington Atty: Fisher, Wayland, Cooper, Leader & Zaragoza.
Key Personnel:
Mike Dunlop . . . . gen mgr
Mike Garza . . . . sls dir
Robert Flanagan. . . . . chief of opns & chief of engrg

WJTV—Analog channel: 12. On air date: Mar 15, 1954. 1820 TV Rd., Jackson, MS 39204-4148. Phone: (601) 372-6311. Fax: (601) 372-8798. Web Site: www.wjtv.com. Licensee: Media General Broadcasting Inc. Group owner: Media General Broadcast Group (acq 7-25-97; grpsl). Network: CBS. Washington Atty: Wiley, Rein & Fielding. News staff: 34; News: 21 hrs wkly.
Key Personnel:
Bob Romine . . . . gen mgr
David Bunger . . . . opns dir
Ron Romines. . . . . sls dir & gen sls mgr
Gary Wolverton . . . . mktg dir
Jackie McDonald . . . . progmg dir
Rick Russell . . . . news dir
Steve Schrader . . . . chief of engrg

WLBT—Analog channel: 3. On air date: Dec 28, 1953. 715 S. Jefferson St., Jackson, MS 39205. Box 1712, Jackson, MS 39205. Phone: (601) 948-3333. Fax: (601) 960-4412. E-mail: news@wlbt.com. Web Site: www.wlbt.com. Licensee: Civco Inc. Group owner: Liberty Corp. (acq 9-25-00; grpsl). Network: NBC. Rep: Continental Television Sales. Washington Atty: Dow, Lohnes & Albertson.
Key Personnel:
Dan Modisett . . . . VP & gen mgr
Steve Lavin . . . . opns mgr
Frankie Thomas . . . . gen sls mgr
James Belton. . . . . natl sls mgr & progmg dir
Jackie Ellens . . . . prom mgr
Dennis Smith . . . . news dir
Curtis McKnight. . . . . chief of engrg

***WMAU-TV**—Analog channel: 17. Digital channel: 18. On air date: Jan 14, 1972. 3825 Ridgewood Rd., Jackson, MS 39211. Phone: (601) 432-6565. Fax: (610) 432-6392. Web Site: www.mpbonline.org. Licensee: Mississippi Authority for Educational TV. Network: PBS. Washington Atty: Schwartz, Woods & Miller.
Key Personnel:
Gene Edwards. . . . . exec VP & opns dir
Marie Antoon . . . . gen mgr
Ron Evans. . . . . . dev dir, gen sls mgr, mktg mgr & engrg dir
Ty Warren. . . . . dev dir
Art Starkey . . . . progmg dir

***WMPN-TV**—Analog channel: 29. On air date: Feb 1, 1970. 3825 Ridgewood Rd., Jackson, MS 39211. Phone: (601) 432-6565. Fax: (601) 432-6654. Fax: (601) 432-6311. Web Site: www.mpbonline.org. Licensee: Mississippi Authority for Educational TV. Network: PBS. Washington Atty: Schwartz, Woods & Miller.
Key Personnel:
Marie Antoon . . . . gen mgr
Gene Edwards . . . . opns dir
Ty Warren. . . . . dev dir
Ron Evans . . . . mktg mgr
Jennifer Griffin . . . . prom dir

***WMYC**—Analog channel: 32.Not on air, target date: unknown: 3825 Ridgewood Rd., Jackson, MS 39211. Phone: (601) 432-6565. Fax: (601) 432-6311. Web Site: www.mpbonline.org. Permittee: Mississippi Authority for Educational Television. Network: PBS.
Key Personnel:
Marie Antoon . . . . gen mgr
Ty Warren. . . . . natl sls mgr
Jennifer Griffin . . . . mktg mgr
Shirley Mixon . . . . progmg dir
Keith Martin . . . . chief of engrg

WNTZ—Analog channel: 48. On air date: Nov 16, 1985. 1777 Jackson St., Alexandria, LA 71301. Phone: (318) 443-4700. Fax: (318) 443-4899. Web Site: fox48tv.com. Licensee: White Knight Broadcasting of Natchez License Corp. Group owner: White Knight Holdings Inc. (acq 6-22-98). Network: Fox. Rep: Millennium Sales & Marketing. Washington Atty: Shaw Pittman L.L.P..
Key Personnel:
Sharon Carter . . . . gen mgr
Sheldon Galloway. . . . . CEO & gen mgr
Noah Authement . . . . prom mgr

WRBJ—Analog channel: 34.Not on air, target date: unknown: Roberts Broadcasting Co., 1408 N. Kingshighway Blvd. #300, St. Louis, MO 63113. Phone: (314) 367-0090. Fax: (314) 367-0174. Permittee: Roberts Broadcasting of Jackson, MS, LLC. Group owner: Roberts Broadcasting Co.

WUFX—Analog channel: 35.Not on air, target date: unknown: Mississippi Television LLC, 700 St. John, Suite 300, Lafayette, LA 70501. Phone: (337) 237-9965. Fax: (337) 235-5872. Permittee: Mississippi Television LLC.. Ownership: Sheldon H. Galloway, 100% voting control (acq 10-3-03).

Laurel

see Hattiesburg-Laurel, MS market

Meridian, MS
(DMA 184)

***WGBC**—Analog channel: 30. On air date: Sept 15, 1991. Box 2424, Meridian, MS 39302. 1151 Crestview Cir., Meridian, MS 39301. Phone: (601) 485-3030. Fax: (601) 693-9889. Web Site: www.wgbctv.com. Licensee: Global Communications Inc.. Ownership: Estate of H. Alex Shields Jr., Phyllis Shields administratrix (acq 3-7-02). Network: NBC. Washington Atty: Wiley, Rein & Fielding.
Key Personnel:
Charles Young . . . . pres & sls dir
Bruce Martin. . . . . VP & progmg dir
Ray Denton . . . . stn mgr
Jet Scarbrough. . . . . opns mgr & chief of engrg

***WMAW-TV**—Analog channel: 14. Digital channel: 44. On air date: Jan 14, 1972. 3825 Ridgewood Rd., Jackson, MS 39211. Phone: (601) 432-6565. Fax: (601) 432-6654. Fax: (601) 432-6311. Web Site: www.mpbonline.org. Licensee: Mississippi Authority for Educational TV. Washington Atty: Schwartz, Woods & Miller. News staff: 4.
Key Personnel:
Marie Antoon . . . . exec VP & gen mgr
Gene Edwards . . . . opns dir
Ty Warren. . . . . dev dir
Ron Evans . . . . mktg mgr
Randy Tinney. . . . . prom dir
Art Starkey. . . . . progmg dir
Dick Rizzo. . . . . news dir & pub affrs dir
Keith Martin . . . . engrg dir

WMDN—Analog channel: 24. Digital channel: 26. On air date: June 10, 1968. Box 2424, Meridian, MS 39302. 1151Crestwood Cir., Meridian, MS 39301. Phone: (601) 693-2424. Fax: (601) 693-7126. E-mail: administration@wmdn.net. Web Site: www.wmdntv.com. Licensee: WMDN Inc. (acq 2-28-86; $4 million). Network: CBS. Washington Atty: Garvey, Schubert & Barer. News staff: 12; News: 7.5 hrs wkly.
Key Personnel:
Mark Ledbetter. . . . . VP, gen mgr, progmg dir & chief of engrg
Susan Ross . . . . stn mgr & gen sls mgr

WTOK-TV—Analog channel: 11. On air date: Sept 27, 1953. Box 2988, Meridian, MS 39302. 815 23rd Ave., Meridian, MS 39301. Phone: (601) 693-1441. Fax: (601) 483-3266. Web Site: www.wtok.com. Licensee: Gray Television Licensee Corp. Group owner: Gray Television Inc. (acq 8-29-2002; grpsl). Network: ABC. Rep: Continental Television Sales. Washington Atty: Covington & Burling. News staff: 15; News: 15 hrs wkly.
Key Personnel:
Ray Chumley . . . . gen mgr
Tim Walker . . . . opns mgr
Larry Torgerson . . . . gen sls mgr
Julie Walker . . . . prom mgr
Cassandra Turney . . . . progmg dir
John Johnson . . . . news dir & pub affrs dir
Brad LeBrun . . . . chief of engrg

Oxford

see Memphis, TN market

Tupelo

see Columbus-Tupelo-West Point, MS market

West Point

see Columbus-Tupelo-West Point, MS market

Missouri

Cape Girardeau

see Paducah, KY-Cape Girardeau, MO-Harrisburg-Mount Vernon, IL market

Columbia-Jefferson City, MO
(DMA 139)

KMIZ—Analog channel: 17. On air date: Dec 5, 1971. 501 Business Loop 70 E., Columbia, MO 65201. Phone: (573) 449-0917. Fax: (573) 875-7078. E-mail: info@kmiz.com. Web Site: www.kmiz.com. Licensee: JW Broadcasting LLC.. Ownership: Alta/JW Broadcasting Investor Corp., 52.38%; and DJ Broadcasting LLC, 47.62% (acq 10-21-03). Network: Network: ABC, Fox. Rep: Petry Television Inc.. Washington Atty: Covington & Burling. News staff: 12; News: 19 hrs wkly.
Key Personnel:
David Joseph . . . . CEO
Jim Woods . . . . CFO
Randy Wright . . . . VP & gen mgr
Eric Holmes . . . . opns dir & opns mgr
Mark Hotchkiss . . . . sls dir & gen sls mgr
Jeff Page . . . . natl sls mgr & rgnl sls mgr
Mark Kunkel . . . . natl sls mgr
Michelle Linn . . . . prom dir
Darin Eidson . . . . prom mgr
Donna Farmer . . . . film buyer
Curtis Varns . . . . news dir
DeWayne Roberts . . . . chief of engrg

KNLJ—Analog channel: 25. On air date: Mar 30, 1986. Box 2525, New Bloomfield, MO 65603-2525. 9810 State Rd. AE, New Bloomfield, MO 65603-2525. Phone: (573) 896-5105. Fax: (573) 896-4376. Web Site: www.hereshelpnet.org. Licensee: New Life Evangelistic Center Inc. Washington Atty: John H. Midlen Jr.
Key Personnel:
Larry Rice. . . . . pres
Penny Rice . . . . gen mgr, gen sls mgr & progmg dir
Jeffrey Davis . . . . opns dir & natl sls mgr
Shawn Baker. . . . . chief of engrg

KOMU-TV—Analog channel: 8. On air date: Dec 21, 1953. 5550 Hwy. 63 S., Columbia, MO 65201. Phone: (573) 882-8888. Fax: (573) 884-8888. Web Site: www.komu.com. Licensee: The Curators of the University of Missouri. Group owner: (group owner) Network: NBC. Rep: Millennium Sales & Marketing. Washington Atty: Shaw Pittman. News: 20 hrs wkly.
Key Personnel:
Martin Siddall . . . gen mgr
Al Leitl . . . gen sls mgr
Tom Dugan . . . natl sls mgr
Matt Garrett . . . prom dir
Stacey Woelfel . . . news dir
Chris Swisher . . . chief of engrg

KRCG—Analog channel: 13. Digital channel: 12. On air date: Feb 13, 1955. Box 659, Jefferson City, MO 65102. Old Hwy. 54, Holts Summit, MO 65102. Phone: (573) 896-5144. Fax: (573) 896-5193. E-mail: info@krcg.com. Web Site: www.krcg.com. Licensee: Barrington Broadcasting Missouri Corp. Group owner: (group owner; (acq 12-27-2004; $38 million).. Network: Network: CBS, Fox. Rep: Katz Radio. Washington Atty: Pepper & Corazzini. News staff: 14; News: 14 hrs wkly.
Key Personnel:
Betsy Farris . . . gen mgr
Kevin O'Neill . . . prom mgr
Lee Gordon Jr. . . . progmg dir
Roger Hulett . . . gen sls mgr, rgnl sls mgr, mktg mgr & news dir
Jim Malone . . . chief of engrg

Hannibal

see Quincy, IL-Hannibal, MO-Keokuk, IA market

Jefferson City

see Columbia-Jefferson City, MO market

Joplin, MO-Pittsburg, KS (DMA 146)

KFJX—Analog channel: 14. On air date: 2003. Box 659, Pittsburg, KS 66762-0659. Phone: (417) 782-1414. Fax: (417) 206-4081. E-mail: ddishman@fox14tv.com. Web Site: www.fox14pb.com. Licensee: Surtsey Media LLC. Group owner: (group owner; acq 3-7-2003). Network: Fox. News staff: 4; News: 3 hrs wkly.

KOAM-TV—Analog channel: 7. Digital channel: 13. On air date: Dec 13, 1953. Box 659, Pittsburg, KS 66762-0659. 2950 N.E. Hwy. 69, Pittsburg, KS 66762-0659. Phone: (417) 624-0233. Fax: (417) 624-3115, sls & admin. E-mail: email@koamtv.com. Web Site: www.koamtv.com. Licensee: Saga Quad States Communications LLC. Group owner: Saga Communications Inc. (acq 10-12-94; $8.55 million;. FTR: 9-5-94). Network: CBS. Rep: Continental Television Sales. News: 19 hrs wkly.
Key Personnel:
Danny Thomas . . . pres, gen mgr & film buyer
Kate McNulty . . . prom dir
Kristi Spencer. . . . news dir
Larry White . . . chief of engrg

KODE-TV—Analog channel: 12. On air date: Sept 26, 1954. Box 46, Joplin, MO 64802. 1928 W. 13th St., Joplin, MO 64802. Phone: (417) 623-7260. Fax: (417) 623-3736. Web Site: www.kode-tv.com. Licensee: Mission Broadcasting of Joplin Inc. Group owner: Mission Broadcasting Inc. (acq 2-27-02; $6 million).. Network: Network: ABC, Fox. Washington Atty: Cohn. News staff: 18; News: 16 hrs wkly.
Key Personnel:
Gary Hood . . . gen mgr, gen sls mgr, adv mgr & news dir
Dean Edwards . . . natl sls mgr, mktg mgr & prom mgr
Janice Rohman . . . progmg dir
Jeff Hadley . . . chief of engrg

***KOZJ**—Analog channel: 26. On air date: June 1, 1986. Box 1226, Joplin, MO 64802. 403 S. Main St., Joplin, MO 64801. Phone: (417) 782-2226. Fax: (417) 782-7222. E-mail: kozj@joplin.com. Web Site: www.kozj.com. Licensee: Board of Governors of Southwest Missouri State University. (acq 4-25-01; $1.3 million. assumption of debt with KOZK(TV) Springfield). Network: PBS.

KSNF—Analog channel: 16. On air date: Sept 2, 1967. Box 1393, Joplin, MO 64802. 1502 Cleveland, Joplin, MO 64802. Phone: (417) 781-2345. Fax: (417) 782-2417. Fax: TWX: 910-774-4520. Web Site: www.ksntv.com. Licensee: Nexstar Finance Inc. Group owner: Nexstar Broadcasting Group Inc. (acq 11-6-97; grpsl). Network: NBC. Washington Atty: Arter & Hadden.
Key Personnel:
John Hoffmann . . . VP, gen mgr & progmg dir
Debra Palmer. . . . sls dir, gen sls mgr & adv mgr
Sarah Snow . . . prom mgr
Jeff Hadley . . . chief of engrg

Kansas City, MO (DMA 31)

***KCPT**—Analog channel: 19. Digital channel: 19. On air date: Mar 29, 1961. 125 E. 31st St., Kansas City, MO 64108. Phone: (816) 756-3580. Fax: (816) 931-2500. E-mail: kcpt@kcpt.org. Web Site: www.kcpt.org. Licensee: Public TV 19 Inc. (acq 1-1-72; $22,226; 2-14-72). Network: PBS. Washington Atty: Arter & Hadden.
Key Personnel:
William Reed . . . CEO & pres
William T. Reed . . . gen mgr
Bonnie Rabicoff . . . adv mgr

KCTV—Analog channel: 5. On air date: Sept 27, 1953. Box 5555, Kansas City, MO 64109-0155. 4500 Shawnee Mission Pkwy., Fairway, KS 66205. Phone: (913) 677-5555. Fax: (913) 677-7284. E-mail: kctv5@kctv5.com. Web Site: www.kctv5.com. Licensee: Meredith Corp. Group owner: Meredith Broadcasting Group, Meredith Corp., see Cross-Ownership (acq 10-1-53; $2 million; 11-23-53). Network: CBS. Rep: TeleRep. Lathrop & Gage, L.C. Washington Atty: Haley, Bader & Potts.
Key Personnel:
Kirk Black . . . gen mgr
Susan Brier . . . gen sls mgr
Ken Bauer . . . prom dir, adv mgr & news dir
Beth Green. . . . progmg dir
Dan Somes . . . engrg dir & chief of engrg

KCWE—Analog channel: 29. On air date: September 1996. 1049 Central, Kansas City, MO 64105. Phone: (816) 221-2900. Phone: (816) 760-9129. Fax: (816) 760-9149. Web Site: www.thekansascitychannel.com. Licensee: KCWE-TV Inc.. Ownership: Sonia G. Salzman. (acq 11-4-99; $558,000 for 60% of stock). Network: UPN. Rep: MMT.
Key Personnel:
Robert Liepold . . . pres
Wayne Godsey . . . gen mgr
Shannon Hart . . . gen sls mgr
Susie Kirkpatrick . . . natl sls mgr
Chad Leabo . . . prom mgr
Karen King . . . progmg mgr
Olivia Dorsey . . . pub affrs dir
Jerry Agresti . . . engrg dir

KMBC-TV—Analog channel: 9. On air date: Aug 1, 1952. 1049 Central, Kansas City, MO 64105. Phone: (816) 221-9999. Fax: (816) 760-9245. Web Site: www.thekansascitychannel.com. Licensee: KMBC Hearst-Argyle Television Inc. Group owner: Hearst-Argyle Television Inc. (acq 7-16-97; grpsl). Network: ABC. Rep: Eagle Television Sales. Washington Atty: Brooks, Pierce, McLendon, Humphrey & Leonard. News staff: 55; News: 28 hrs wkly.
Key Personnel:
David Barrett . . . CEO
Wayne Godsey . . . pres, VP & gen mgr
Peggy Madigan . . . gen sls mgr
Kim Sitta . . . natl sls mgr
Denise Dailey . . . rgnl sls mgr
Blake Hodges. . . . mktg dir
Bob Lorenzen . . . prom mgr
Karen King. . . . progmg dir
Michael Sipes. . . . news dir
Olivia Dorsey . . . pub affrs dir
Jerry Agresti . . . engrg dir & chief of engrg

KMCI—Analog channel: 38. Digital channel: 36. On air date: February 1988. 4720 Oak St., Kansas City, MO 64112. Phone: (816) 753-4141. Fax: (816) 932-4122. E-mail: comments@kmci.com. Web Site: www.kmci.com. Licensee: Scripps Howard Broadcasting Co. Group owner: (group owner; (acq 2-3-2000). Rep: Harrington, Righter & Parsons. Washington Atty: Baker & Hostetler.
Key Personnel:
Jim Swineheart. . . . VP & gen mgr
Craig Allison . . . stn mgr
Jim Neal . . . opns mgr
Berry Pinney . . . chief of engrg

***KMOS-TV**—Analog channel: 6. On air date: Dec 22, 1979. Central Missouri State Univ., Wood 11, Warrensburg, MO 64093. Phone: (660) 543-4155. Fax: (660) 543-8863. Web Site: www.kmos.cmsu.edu. Licensee: Central Missouri State University. (acq 6-6-78; $1,000). Network: PBS. Washington Atty: Shaw Pittman.
Key Personnel:
Donald W. Peterson . . . gen mgr
Fred Hunt. . . . opns mgr
Mark Pearce. . . . dev dir
Michael O'Keefe . . . prom mgr, progmg mgr & film buyer
Dorothy McGrath . . . pub affrs dir
Dan L. Davis. . . . chief of engrg
John Long. . . . chief of engrg

KPXE—Analog channel: 50. On air date: Dec 1, 1978. 4720 Oak St., Kansas City, MO 64112. Phone: (816) 924-5050. Fax: (816) 931-1818. Web Site: www.pax.tv/kpxe. Licensee: Paxson Kansas City License Inc. Group owner: Paxson Communications Corp. (acq 3-3-97; $16.4 million).. Network: PAX TV. Washington Atty: Wiley, Rein & Fielding.
Key Personnel:
Frank Barajas. . . . gen mgr
Alan Fuchsman . . . adv dir
Dave Campbell . . . chief of engrg

KSHB-TV—Analog channel: 41. Digital channel: 42. On air date: Sept 28, 1970. 4720 Oak St., Kansas City, MO 64112. Phone: (816) 753-4141. Fax: (816) 932-4122. Web Site: www.nbcactionnews.com. Licensee: Scripps Howard Broadcasting Co. Group owner: (group owner; (acq 10-28-77; FTR: 10-3-77). Network: NBC. Rep: Harrington, Righter & Parsons. Washington Atty: Baker & Hostetler. News staff: 75; News: 32 hrs wkly.
Key Personnel:
Craig Allison . . . stn mgr
Jim Neal . . . opns mgr & gen sls mgr
Jim Swinehart . . . VP, gen mgr & prom dir
Berry Pinney. . . . chief of engrg

KSMO-TV—Analog channel: 62. Digital channel: 47. On air date: Dec 7, 1983. 10 E. Cambridge Cir. Dr., Suite 300, Kansas City, KS 66103. Phone: (913) 621-6262. Fax: (913) 621-4703. Licensee: KSMO Licensee Inc. Group owner: Sinclair Broadcast Group Inc. (acq 1996; $9 million). Network: WB. Rep: Millennium Sales & Marketing.
Key Personnel:
Mark Martin . . . gen mgr
Jim Brown . . . gen sls mgr
Mitchell Hershey . . . natl sls mgr
Judy Crawford . . . rgnl sls mgr
Shanika Strings . . . mktg dir
Jeff Clement . . . prom dir
R.J. Morris. . . . progmg dir & pub affrs dir
Bob Schneider . . . chief of engrg

WDAF-TV—Analog channel: 4. On air date: Oct 16, 1949. 3030 Summit, Kansas City, MO 64108. Phone: (816) 753-4567. Fax: (816) 931-3984. E-mail: wdaftv4@wdaftv4.com. Web Site: www.wdaftv4.com.. Stn video via satellite: Fox Network Licensee: WDAF License Inc. Group owner: Fox Television Stations Inc. (acq 1-23-97; grpsl). Network: Fox. Rep: Fox Stations Sales. News staff: 115; News: 49 hrs wkly.
Key Personnel:
Cheryl McDonald . . . VP & gen mgr
Kelly Satalowich . . . sls VP

Kirksville

see Ottumwa, IA-Kirksville, MO market

Poplar Bluff

see Paducah, KY-Cape Girardeau, MO-Harrisburg-Mount Vernon, IL market

Springfield, MO (DMA 78)

KOLR-TV—Analog channel: 10. On air date: Mar 14, 1953. 2650 E. Division, Springfield, MO 65803. Phone: (417) 862-1010. Fax: (417) 862-6439. Web Site: www.kolr10.com. Licensee: Mission Broadcasting Inc. Group owner: (group owner; acq 12-17-03). Network: CBS. Rep: Katz Radio. News staff: 30; News: 22 hrs wkly.
Key Personnel:
Dean Wasson . . . gen mgr & progmg mgr
Dave Thomason . . . gen sls mgr & prom mgr
Molly MacGowan . . . natl sls mgr
Polly Van Doran. . . . news dir
David Smith. . . . pub affrs dir, engrg dir & chief of engrg

***KOZK**—Analog channel: 21. On air date: Jan 21, 1975. 901 S. National, Springfield, MO 65804. Phone: (417) 836-3500. Fax: (417) 863-3569. E-mail: opt@smsu.edu. Web Site: www.opt.org. Licensee: Board of Governors of Southwest Missouri State University. (acq

4-25-01; $1.3 million. assumption of debt with KOZJ(TV) Joplin). Network: PBS. Washington Atty: Dow, Lohnes & Albertson.

KSFX-TV—Analog channel: 27. Digital channel: 28. On air date: Sept 22, 1968. 2650 E. Division St., Springfield, MO 65803. Phone: (417) 862-2727. Fax: (417) 831-4209. Fax: (417) 862-4535. Web Site: www.fox27.com. Licensee: Nexstar Finance Inc. Group owner: Nexstar Broadcasting Group Inc. (acq 12-31-2003; grpsl). Network: Fox. Washington Atty: Arter & Hadden.
Key Personnel:
Dave Thomason . . . . VP & gen sls mgr
Mark Gordon . . . . gen mgr
Dave Bowen . . . . adv mgr
Nancy Bingaman . . . . progmg dir
Randy Selvidge . . . . chief of engrg

KSPR—Analog channel: 33. On air date: Mar 17, 1983. Box 6030, Springfield, MO 65801-6030. 1359 St. Louis St., Springfield, MO 65802. Phone: (417) 831-1333. Fax: (417) 831-4125. Web Site: www.springfield33.com. Licensee: Piedmont Television of Springfield License LLC. Group owner: Piedmont Television Holdings LLC (acq 10-1-97; grpsl). Network: ABC. Washington Atty: Cohn & Marks. News staff: 21; News: 9 hrs wkly.
Key Personnel:
Paul Brissette . . . . CEO
Dave Tillery . . . . VP & gen mgr
Lee Redick . . . . gen sls mgr
Dax Bedell . . . . mktg mgr & prom mgr
James Trussell . . . . progmg mgr
Erik Schrader . . . . news dir
Neal Evans . . . . chief of engrg

KWBM—Analog channel: 31. On air date: 2002. 1200 E. Woodhurst Dr., Suite S400, Springfield, MO 65804-3785. Phone: (417) 877-9231. Fax: (417) 877-9015. Web Site: www.wb31.com. Licensee: EBC Harrison Inc. (acq 9-21-2004; $8,666,670).. Network: WB.
Key Personnel:
Debbie James . . . . pres & gen mgr
Charley James . . . . gen sls mgr

KWFT—Analog channel: 34. On air date: 2000. 1 Shackleford Dr., Suite 400, Little Rock, AR 72211. Phone: (501) 219-2400. Fax: (501) 221-7908. Licensee: TV 34 Inc. Group owner: Equity Broadcasting Corp. (acq 8-23-99).
Key Personnel:
Greg Fess . . . . pres
Glenn Charlesworth . . . . CFO
Max Hooper . . . . exec VP
James Hearnsberger . . . . VP
Debbie James . . . . gen sls mgr
Terrill Weiss . . . . stn mgr & gen sls mgr
Frank White . . . . prom dir
Nathan Stamp . . . . progmg dir
Doug Krile . . . . news dir
Sheryl Lackey . . . . pub affrs dir
Paul Brandenburg . . . . engrg dir
Don Jones . . . . engrg mgr

KYTV—Analog channel: 3. On air date: Oct 1, 1953. Box 3500, Springfield, MO 65808. 999 W. Sunshine, Springfield, MO 65807. Phone: (417) 268-3000. Fax: (417) 268-3100. E-mail: ky3@ky3.com. Web Site: www.ky3.com. Licensee: KY-3 Inc. Group owner: Schurz Communications Inc. (acq 2-19-87; $50.8 million; 1-19-87). Network: NBC. Washington Atty: Hogan & Hartson. News staff: 40; News: 40 hrs wkly.
Key Personnel:
Mike Scott . . . . gen mgr
Denny Van Valkenburgh . . . . gen sls mgr
Denny Van Valkenburg . . . . mktg dir & mktg mgr
Trenna Underhill . . . . progmg dir & progmg mgr
Tom McKleroy . . . . chief of engrg

St. Joseph, MO
(DMA 201)

KQTV—Analog channel: 2. Digital channel: 53. On air date: Sept 27, 1953. Box 8369, 40th & Faraon Sts., Saint Joseph, MO 64508. Phone: (816) 364-2222. Fax: (816) 364-3787. Fax: TWX: 910-777-7872. E-mail: kq2@kq2.com. Web Site: www.kq2.com. Licensee: Nexstar Broadcasting Inc. Group owner: Nexstar Broadcasting Group Inc. (acq 2-14-97; with WTWO(TV) Terre Haute, IN). Network: ABC. Washington Atty: Drinker, Biddle & Reath. News staff: 18; News: 16 hrs wkly.
Key Personnel:
Heather Shearin . . . . VP & gen mgr
Steve Cline . . . . opns mgr

KTAJ-TV—Analog channel: 16. On air date: Oct 6, 1986. 4402 A S. 40th St., Saint Joseph, MO 64503. Phone: (816) 364-1616. Fax: (816) 364-6729. E-mail: ktaj@tbn.org. Web Site: www.tbn.org. Licensee: Trinity Christian Center of Santa Ana Inc. dba Trinity Broadcasting Network. Group owner: Trinity Broadcasting Network (acq 5-8-00; grpsl).
Key Personnel:
Paul Crouch . . . . pres
Jan Crouch . . . . VP
Julie A. Cluck. stn mgr, mktg mgr, prom mgr, adv mgr & progmg mgr
Andrae Hannon . . . . pub affrs dir
Jeff Landers . . . . engrg dir & chief of engrg

St. Louis, MO
(DMA 21)

KDNL-TV—Analog channel: 30. Digital channel: 31. On air date: June 8, 1969. 1215 Cole St., Saint Louis, MO 63106. Phone: (314) 436-3030. Fax: (314) 259-5504. Licensee: KDNL Licensee L.L.C. Group owner: Sinclair Broadcast Group Inc. (acq 5-30-96). Network: ABC. Washington Atty: Shaw, Pittman.
Key Personnel:
Tom Tipton . . . . gen mgr
Jim Wright . . . . opns dir & engrg dir
John Strassner . . . . gen sls mgr
Andrea Schaffer . . . . natl sls mgr
Sandra Habeck . . . . progmg mgr
Liz Crider . . . . news dir & pub affrs dir
Val Taylor . . . . prom

***KETC**—Analog channel: 9. Digital channel: 39. On air date: Sept 20, 1954. 3655 Olive St., Saint Louis, MO 63108. Phone: (314) 512-9000. Fax: (314) 512-9005. Web Site: www.ketc.org. Licensee: St. Louis Regional Educational and Public Television Commission. Network: PBS. Washington Atty: Dow, Lohnes & Albertson.
Key Personnel:
James Baum . . . . CEO & pres
Richard Skalski . . . . CFO
Dean Orton . . . . sr VP, gen mgr, sls VP & mktg VP
Chrys Marlow . . . . opns dir, engrg dir & chief of engrg
Jennifer Ehlon . . . . dev dir
Matt Andrew . . . . sls dir & mktg dir
Terri Gales . . . . prom mgr
Patti Kistler . . . . adv dir & progmg dir
Patrick Murphy . . . . pub affrs dir

KMOV—Analog channel: 4. Digital channel: 56. On air date: July 8, 1954. One Memorial Dr., Saint Louis, MO 63102. Phone: (314) 621-4444. Fax: (314) 444-3367. Fax: (314) 444-3368. E-mail: channel4@kmov.com. Web Site: www.kmov.com. Licensee: KMOV-TV Inc. Group owner: Belo Corp., Broadcast Division (acq 6-02-97; grpsl). Network: CBS. Rep: TeleRep. Washington Atty: Wiley, Rein & Fielding. News staff: 70; News: 29 hrs wkly.
Key Personnel:
Allan Cohen . . . . pres & gen mgr
Peggy Milner . . . . CFO
Jim Rothschild . . . . opns dir & prom mgr
Robert Totsch . . . . gen sls mgr
Paul Conaty . . . . natl sls mgr
Debbie Milligan . . . . mktg dir
Liz Mullen . . . . progmg mgr
Marty Van Housen . . . . news dir
Walt Nichol . . . . engrg dir & chief of engrg

KNLC—Analog channel: 24. On air date: Sept 12, 1982. Box 924, Saint Louis, MO 63188. 1411 Locust, Saint Louis, MO 63188. Phone: (314) 436-2424. Fax: (314) 436-2434. E-mail: victor@knlc.tv. Web Site: www.knlc.tv. Licensee: New Life Evangelistic Center Inc. Washington Atty: Midlen & Guillot.
Key Personnel:
Larry Rice . . . . pres & gen mgr
Rax Redlich . . . . VP
Jim Barnes . . . . stn mgr
Judy Redlich . . . . sls dir
Victor Anderson . . . . progmg dir
Bob Dimmler . . . . chief of engrg

KPLR-TV—Analog channel: 11. Digital channel: 11. On air date: Apr 28, 1959. 2250 Ball Dr., Saint Louis, MO 63146. Phone: (314) 447-1111. Fax: (314) 447-6404. E-mail: administration4@tribune.com. Web Site: www.wb11tv.com. Licensee: KPLR Inc. Group owner: Tribune Broadcasting Co. (acq 3-21-2003; $275 million. with KWBP(TV) Salem, OR). Network: WB. Rep: MMT. News: 4 hrs wkly.
Key Personnel:
Bill Lanesey . . . . sr VP, VP & gen mgr
Glen P. Callanan . . . . gen sls mgr

KSDK—Analog channel: 5. Digital channel: 35. On air date: Feb 8, 1947. 1000 Market St., Saint Louis, MO 63101. Phone: (314) 421-5055. Fax: (314) 444-5164. Web Site: www.ksdk.com. Licensee: Multimedia KSDK Inc. Group owner: Gannett Broadcasting (acq 11-30-95; grpsl). Network: NBC. Rep: Petry Television Inc.. Washington Atty: Dow, Lohnes & Albertson.
Key Personnel:
Lynn Beall . . . . gen mgr
Mike Meara . . . . gen sls mgr
Andrea Allman . . . . mktg dir & mktg mgr
Michelle Shcoley . . . . adv mgr & news dir
Rebecca Rahm . . . . progmg dir & progmg mgr
Mike Tamme . . . . chief of engrg

KTVI—Analog channel: 2. Digital channel: 43. On air date: Aug 10, 1953. 5915 Berthold Ave., Saint Louis, MO 63110. Phone: (314) 647-2222. Fax: (314) 644-7419. E-mail: info@fox2ktvi.com. Web Site: www.fox2ktvi.com. Licensee: KTVI License Inc. Group owner: Fox Television Stations Inc. (acq 11-96; grpsl). Network: Fox. Washington Atty: Pepper & Corazzini. News: 18 hrs wkly.
Key Personnel:
Craig Ghiotti . . . . CFO
Spencer Koch . . . . VP & gen mgr
Kurt Krueger . . . . gen sls mgr
Cindy Rosen . . . . natl sls mgr
Steve Mills . . . . rgnl sls mgr
Kathryn Hansen . . . . prom dir
Elaine Claspill . . . . progmg dir
Brad Remington . . . . news dir
Jay Gill . . . . engrg dir
Ernie Dachel . . . . chief of engrg

WRBU—Analog channel: 46. On air date: September 1989. 1408 N. Kingshighway Blvd., Suite 300, St. Louis, MO 63113. Phone: (314) 256-4600. Fax: (314) 256-4655. Licensee: Roberts Broadcasting Co. Group owner: (group owner). Network: UPN. Rep: Harrington, Righter & Parsons. Washington Atty: Dow, Lohnes & Albertson. News staff: 4.
Key Personnel:
Michael V. Roberts . . . . CEO
Steven C. Roberts . . . . COO
Gregg Filandrinos . . . . exec VP & gen mgr
Bonni Burns . . . . sls dir & gen sls mgr
Dan Cohan . . . . natl sls mgr
Sam Lawson . . . . prom dir
Stan Marinorr . . . . progmg dir
Jammie Holland . . . . pub affrs dir
Chris Meisch . . . . chief of engrg

Montana

Billings, MT
(DMA 170)

KHMT—Analog channel: 4. On air date: Aug 16, 1995. 445 S. 24th St. W., Suite 404, Billings, MT 59102. Phone: (406) 652-7366. Fax: (406) 652-6963. Web Site: www.abc6.fox4.tv. Licensee: Mission Broadcasting Inc. Group owner: (group owner; acq 12-30-2003). Network: Fox. Washington Atty: Cohn & Marks.
Key Personnel:
Scott Bruce . . . . gen mgr & opns mgr
John Pulasky . . . . gen sls mgr & natl sls mgr
Kria Afchim . . . . prom dir & prom mgr
Patricia King . . . . progmg dir
Todd Reno . . . . news dir
Ron Walden . . . . chief of engrg

KSVI—Analog channel: 6. On air date: 1993. 445 S. 24th St. W., Billings, MT 59102. Phone: (406) 652-4743. Fax: (406) 652-6963. Web Site: www.abc6fox4.tv. Licensee: Nexstar Finance Inc. Group owner: Nexstar Broadcasting Group Inc. (acq 12-31-03; grpsl). Network: ABC. Washington Atty: Arter & Hadden.
Key Personnel:
Scott H. Bruce . . . . gen mgr
John Pulasky . . . . gen sls mgr
Kris Aschim . . . . prom dir & prom mgr
Patricia King . . . . progmg dir
Ron Walden . . . . chief of engrg

KTVQ—Analog channel: 2. Digital channel: 10. On air date: Nov 9, 1953. Box 2557, Billings, MT 59103. 3203 3rd Ave. N., Billings, MT 59101. Phone: (406) 252-5611. Fax: (406) 252-9938. E-mail: q2news@ktvq.com. Web Site: www.ktvq.com. Licensee: Evening Post Publishing Co. Group owner: Cordillera Communications Inc. (acq 1994; $8.5 million). Network: CBS. Rep: Harrington, Righter & Parsons. Washington Atty: Dow, Lohnes & Albertson. News staff: 21; News: 17 hrs wkly.
Key Personnel:
Monty Wallis . . . . pres & gen mgr
Pam Hofferber . . . . opns mgr & progmg dir

KULR-TV—Analog channel: 8. Digital channel: 11. On air date: Mar 15, 1958. Box 80810, Billings, MT 59108-0810. 2045 Overland Ave., Billings, MT 59102. Phone: (406) 656-8000. Fax: (406) 652-8207. E-mail: generalmanager@kulr.com. Web Site: www.kulr8.com. Licensee: MMM License II LLC. Group owner: MAX Media L.L.C. (acq 6-9-2004; $11 million).. Network: NBC. Rep: Katz Radio. News staff: 24; News: 17 hrs wkly.
Key Personnel:
John A. Trinder . . . pres
Bruce Cummings . . . gen mgr

KYUS-TV—Analog channel: 3.Not on air, target date: unknown:. Stn currently dark c/o KXGN-TV, 210 S. Douglas, Glendive, MT 59330. Phone: (406) 377-3377. Fax: (406) 365-2181. E-mail: kxgnkdzn@midrivers.com. Web Site: www.glendivebroadcasting.com. Licensee: KYUS-TV Broadcasting Corp. Network: NBC. Rep: Adam Young.
Key Personnel:
Stephen A. Marks . . . pres
Paul Sturlaugson . . . gen mgr
Dan Frenzel . . . progmg dir

Bozeman

see Butte-Bozeman, MT market

Butte-Bozeman, MT (DMA 193)

KBTZ—Analog channel: 24. On air date: Aug 1, 2002. Equity Broadcasting Corp., 1 Shackleford Dr., Suite 400, Little Rock, AR 72211. 5115 US Hwy. 93 S., Missoula, MT 59804. Phone: (406) 542-8900. Fax: (501) 604-8004. Licensee: Montana License Sub, Inc. Group owner: Equity Broadcasting Corp. Network: Network: Network: Fox, PAX TV, UPN.

KBZK—Analog channel: 7. On air date: September 1987. Box 6040, Bozeman, MT 59715. 1128 E. Main, Bozeman, MT 59715. Phone: (406) 586-3280. Fax: (406) 586-4135. Web Site: kbzk.com. Licensee: KCTZ Communications Inc. Group owner: Cordillera Communications Inc. (acq 12-93). Network: CBS. Washington Atty: Dow, Lohnes & Albertson.
Key Personnel:
Terry Hurley . . . pres
Pat Cooney . . . gen mgr
Tim Gazy . . . stn mgr, gen sls mgr & mktg mgr
Phil Konecny . . . news dir
Andy Suk . . . engrg dir
Ron Schlosser . . . chief of engrg

KTVM—Analog channel: 6. On air date: May 12, 1970. 201 S. Wallace, Suite A5, Bozeman, MT 59715. Phone: (406) 586-0296. Fax: (406) 586-0554. E-mail: news@ktvm.com. Web Site: www.ktvm.com. Licensee: BlueStone License Holdings Inc. Group owner: Lamco Communications Inc. (acq 1998; grpsl). Network: NBC. Rep: Katz Radio. Washington Atty: Koteen & Naftalin.
Key Personnel:
Keith Sommer . . . gen mgr
Steve Fetvit . . . gen mgr
Jean Zosel . . . prom dir & progmg dir
Charlie Cannaliato . . . chief of engrg

***KUSM**—Analog channel: 9. On air date: Oct 1, 1984. Box 173340, Bozeman, MT 59717-3340. Phone: (406) 994-3437. Fax: (406) 994-6545. E-mail: kusm@montanapbs.org. Web Site: www.montanapbs.org. Licensee: Montana State University. Network: PBS.
Key Personnel:
Jack Hyyppa . . . gen mgr
George Cole . . . dev dir
Bill Bilverstone . . . prom dir
Aaron Pruitt . . . progmg dir
Gene Brodeur . . . pub affrs dir
Dean Lawver . . . engrg dir & chief of engrg

KWYB—Analog channel: 18. On air date: September 1996. 505 W. Park, Butte, MT 59701. 2200 Stephens Ave., Missoula, MT 59801. Phone: (406) 782-7185; (406) 542-8900. Fax: (406) 723-9269; (406) 728-4800. Web Site: www.kwyb.com. Licensee: MMM License LLC. Group owner: MAX Media LLC (acq 2-5-01; grpsl). Network: ABC. Washington Atty: Reddy, Begley & McCormick.
Key Personnel:
Linda Baumann. pres, gen mgr, natl sls mgr, natl sls mgr & mktg mgr
Linda Julius . . . prom VP & progmg mgr
Linda Tracy . . . prom mgr
Jim Kozora . . . chief of engrg
Mike Warner . . . engrg dir & chief of engrg

KXLF-TV—Analog channel: 4. On air date: Aug 14, 1953. 1003 S. Montana, Butte, MT 59701. Phone: (406) 496-8400. Fax: (406) 782-8906. E-mail: kxlf@kxlf.com. Web Site: www.kxlf.com. Licensee: KXLF Communications Inc. Group owner: Cordillera Communications Inc. (acq 12-15-86; grpsl; 9-29-86). Network: CBS. Rep: Harrington, Righter & Parsons. Washington Atty: Dow, Lohnes & Albertson. News staff: 9; News: 9 hrs wkly.
Key Personnel:
Pat Cooney . . . gen mgr, stn mgr & gen sls mgr
Pat Chittenden . . . prom dir & prom mgr
Lynn Hopewell . . . progmg dir
William Jarrett . . . news dir
Ron Schlosser . . . chief of engrg

Glendive, MT (DMA 210)

KXGN-TV—Analog channel: 5. On air date: Nov 1, 1957. 210 S. Douglas, Glendive, MT 59330. Phone: (406) 377-3377. Fax: (406) 365-2181. E-mail: kxgnkdzn@midrivers.com. Web Site: www.glendivebroadcasting.com. Licensee: Glendive Broadcasting Corp.. Ownership: Stephen A. Marks. Group owner: Glendive Broadcasting Corp. Network: Network: CBS, NBC. Rep: Hooper Jones.
Key Personnel:
Stephen A. Marks . . . pres
Paul Sturlaugson . . . gen mgr, gen sls mgr, adv mgr & news dir
Lauri Harbig . . . progmg dir
Mike Huseby . . . chief of engrg

Great Falls, MT (DMA 188)

KBAO—Analog channel: 13. On air date: Dec 5, 2001. c/o KTVH, 100 W. Lyndale, Helena, MT 59601. Phone: (406) 457-1212. Fax: (406) 442-5106. Web Site: www.ktvh.com. Licensee: Beartooth Communications Co. Group owner: (group owner). Network: NBC.
Key Personnel:
Kathy Ernest . . . gen mgr, gen sls mgr, mktg mgr & adv mgr
Greg Pace . . . prom mgr
Mike Anderson . . . chief of engrg

KBBJ—Analog channel: 9. On air date: Dec 5, 2001. c/o KTVH, 100 W. Lyndale, Helena, MT 59601. Phone: (406) 457-1212. Fax: (406) 442-5106. Web Site: www.ktvh.com. Licensee: Beartooth Communications Co. Group owner: (group owner).
Key Personnel:
Kathy Ernst . . . gen mgr & gen sls mgr
Greg Pace . . . prom dir
Mike Anderson . . . chief of engrg

KFBB-TV—Analog channel: 5. On air date: Mar 21, 1954. Box 1139, Great Falls, MT 59403-1139. 3200 Old Havre Hwy., Black Eagle, MT 59414. Phone: (406) 453-4377. Fax: (406) 727-9703. Fax: (406) 453-3226. E-mail: kfbb@kfbb.com. Web Site: www.kfbb.com. Licensee: KFBB L.L.C. Group owner: Dix Communications (acq 7-1-82; $5.2 million;. FTR: 5-17-82). Network: ABC. Rep: Katz Radio. Washington Atty: Baker & Hostetler. News staff: 6; News: 6 hrs wkly.
Key Personnel:
Susan Johnson. gen mgr, gen sls mgr, prom mgr, adv mgr & progmg dir
John Brady . . . chief of engrg

KLMN—Analog channel: 26. On air date: 2003. 5115 US Hwy. 93 S., Missoula, MT 59804. Phone: (406) 542-8900. Fax: (501) 604-8004. Licensee: Montana License Sub, Inc. Group owner: Equity Broadcasting Corp.

KRTV—Analog channel: 3. Digital channel: 7. On air date: Oct 5, 1958. Box 2989, Great Falls, MT 59403. 3300 Old Havre Hwy., Black Eagle, MT 59414. Phone: (406) 791-5400. Fax: (406) 791-5479. E-mail: krtv@krtv.com. Web Site: www.krtv.com. Licensee: KRTV Communications Inc. Group owner: Cordillera Communications Inc. June, 1986 Network: CBS. Rep: Harrington, Righter & Parsons. Washington Atty: Dow, Lohnes & Albertson. News staff: 15; News: 15 hrs wkly.

KTGF—Analog channel: 16. Digital channel: 45. On air date: Sept 21, 1986. 118 6th St. S., Great Falls, MT 59405. Phone: (406) 761-8816. Fax: (406) 454-3484. E-mail: ktgf@ktgf.com. Web Site: www.ktgf.com. Licensee: Destiny Licenses LLC.. Ownership: Destiny Communications LLC, 100% Group owner: MAX Media LLC (acq 11-24-2004; $3 million. with translator K47DP Lewistown). Network: Network: Fox, UPN. Washington Atty: Garvey, Schubert & Barer.
Key Personnel:
Darnell Washington . . . pres
Jack May. gen mgr, gen sls mgr, natl sls mgr, mktg mgr, prom dir & adv mgr
Linda Julius . . . progmg dir
Martin Hastings . . . chief of engrg

Helena, MT (DMA 206)

KMTF—Analog channel: 10. Digital channel: 29. On air date: 1998. 100 W. Lindale Ave., Helena, MT 59601. Phone: (406) 457-1010. Fax: (406) 442-5106. Licensee: Rocky Mountain Broadcasting Co. Network: WB.
Key Personnel:
Suzanne Rogers . . . gen mgr
Paul Albertson . . . stn mgr & gen sls mgr

KTVH—Analog channel: 12. On air date: Jan 1, 1958. Box 6125, Helena, MT 59604. 100 W. Lyndale, Helena, MT 59601. Phone: (406) 457-1212. Fax: (406) 442-5106. Web Site: www.ktvh.com. Licensee: Beartooth Communications Co. Group owner: Sunbelt Communications Co. (acq 7-9-97). Network: NBC. Washington Atty: Gerald S. Rourke. News staff: 8; News: 7 hrs wkly.
Key Personnel:
Kathy Ernest. gen mgr, gen sls mgr, mktg mgr, adv mgr & progmg dir
Greg Pace . . . prom dir & prom mgr
Mike Anderson . . . chief of engrg

Missoula, MT (DMA 169)

KCFW-TV—Analog channel: 9. On air date: June 10, 1968. Box 857, Kalispell, MT 59901. 401 First Ave. E., Kalispell, MT 59901. Phone: (406) 755-5239. Fax: (406) 752-8002. E-mail: news@kcfw.com. Web Site: www.nbcmontana.com. Licensee: BlueStone License Holdings Inc. Group owner: Lamco Communications Inc. (acq 1998; grpsl). Network: NBC. Rep: Katz Radio. Washington Atty: Cohn & Marks. News staff: 5; News: 6 hrs wkly.
Key Personnel:
Keith Sommer . . . VP & gen mgr
Sheila Winchel . . . stn mgr
Terri Anderson . . . gen sls mgr
Janice Miller . . . news dir
Chris Neuhausen . . . chief of engrg

KECI-TV—Analog channel: 13. On air date: July 1, 1954. 340 W. Main, Missoula, MT 59802. Box 5268, Missoula, MT 59802. Phone: (406) 721-2063. Fax: (406) 721-2083/(406) 549-6507. Web Site: www.nbcmontana.com. Licensee: BlueStone License Holdings Inc. Group owner: Lamco Communications Inc. (acq 5-15-98; grpsl). Network: NBC. Rep: Katz Radio. Washington Atty: Koteen & Naftalin.
Key Personnel:
Andy Stabler . . . CEO
Keith Sommer . . . gen mgr & natl sls mgr
Steve Fetveit . . . rgnl sls mgr
Jean Zosel . . . mktg dir, prom dir & progmg dir
Jim Harmon . . . news dir
Charlie Cannaliato . . . chief of engrg

KMMF—Analog channel: 17. On air date: May 1, 2001. 5115 US Hwy. 93, Missoula, MT 59804. Phone: (406) 542-8900. Licensee: Montana License Sub, Inc. Group owner: Equity Broadcasting Corp. Network: Fox. Washington Atty: Irwin, Caampbell & Tannenwald.

KPAX-TV—Analog channel: 8. On air date: June 5, 1970. Box 4827, Missoula, MT 59806. 1049 W. Central, Missoula, MT 59801. Phone: (406) 542-4400. Fax: (406) 543-7111. E-mail: office@kpax.com. Web Site: www.kpax.com. Licensee: KPAX-TV Communications Inc. Group owner: Cordillera Communications Inc. Network: CBS. Washington Atty: Dow, Lohnes & Albertson. News: 15 hrs wkly.
Key Personnel:
Bob Hermes . . . pres, gen mgr, opns mgr & mktg mgr
Jim McLean . . . sls dir, gen sls mgr & adv mgr
Tammy Engle . . . progmg dir
Greg Schieferstein . . . news dir
Larry Arbaugh . . . chief of engrg

KTMF—Analog channel: 23. On air date: Nov 16, 1990. 2200 Stephens Ave., Missoula, MT 59801. Phone: (406) 542-8900. Fax: (406) 728-4800. E-mail: ktmf@ktmf.com. Web Site: www.ktmf.com. Licensee: MMM License LLC. Group owner: MAX Media LLC (acq 2-5-01; grpsl). Network: ABC. Washington Atty: Reddy, Begley & McCormick.
Key Personnel:
Linda Gray . . . pres

Linda Baumann . . . . gen mgr
Linda Bawmann . . . . gen sls mgr & natl sls mgr
Melissa Mooney . . . . natl sls mgr
Linda Tracy . . . . mktg mgr, adv mgr, progmg VP & pub affrs dir
Linda . Tracy . . . . prom VP
Linda Julius . . . . progmg dir & progmg mgr
Anna Cloer . . . . news dir
Jim Kazora . . . . engrg dir & chief of engrg
Mike Warner . . . . opns dir, chief of opns & engrg dir

***KUFM-TV**—Analog channel: 11. On air date: Jan 18, 1997. Broadcast Media, PARTV 180, Missoula, MT 59812. Phone: (406) 243-4101. Fax: (406) 243-3299. Web Site: www.montanapbs.org. Licensee: The University of Montana. Network: PBS.
Key Personnel:
William Marcus . . . . gen mgr
Daniel Daugerive . . . . opns dir

Nebraska

Alliance

see Rapid City, SD market

Hastings

see Lincoln & Hastings-Kearney, NE market

Kearney

see Lincoln & Hastings-Kearney, NE market

Lincoln & Hastings-Kearney, NE (DMA 103)

KGIN—Analog channel: 11. Digital channel: 32. On air date: Oct 1, 1961. Box 1069, Grand Island, NE 68801. Phone: (308) 382-6100. Fax: (308) 382-3216. E-mail: kgin1011@hotmail.com. Web Site: www.kolnkgin.com. Licensee: WEAU Licensee Corp. Group owner: Gray Television Inc. (acq 7-30-98; grpsl). Network: CBS. Rep: Continental Television Sales. Washington Atty: Pepper & Corazzini.

KHAS-TV—Analog channel: 5. On air date: Jan 1, 1956. 6475 Osborne Dr. W., Hastings, NE 68901. 6475 Osborne Dr. W., Overton, NE 68901. Phone: (402) 463-1321. Fax: (402) 463-6551. E-mail: khas@khastv.com. Web Site: www.khas.msnbc.com. Licensee: Greater Nebraska Television Inc. Group owner: (group owner; acq 8-27-97; $4.5 million).. Network: NBC. Washington Atty: Fletcher, Heald & Hildreth.
Key Personnel:
Ulysses Carlini . . . . gen mgr
Connie Caldwell . . . . gen sls mgr
Jackie Ackerman . . . . prom mgr
Jackie Arkerman. . . . . progmg dir
Jeff Marouser . . . . chief of engrg

KHGI-TV—Analog channel: 13. On air date: Dec 24, 1953. Box 220, Kearney, NE 68848-0220. 1078 25th Rd., Axtell, NE 68924. Phone: (308) 743-2494. Fax: (308) 743-2644. Web Site: nebraska.tv. Licensee: Pappas Telecasting of Central Nebraska L.P. (DE limited partnership). Group owner: Pappas Telecasting Companies (acq 7-1-96; grpsl). Network: ABC. Rep: Harrington, Righter & Parsons. News staff: 26; News: 17.5 hrs wkly.
Key Personnel:
Harry J. Pappas . . . . CEO & pres
Dennis Davis . . . . exec VP
Stephen Morris. . . . . VP & gen mgr

***KHNE-TV**—Analog channel: 29. On air date: Nov 17, 1968. Box 83111, Lincoln, NE 68501. 1800 N. 33rd St., Lincoln, NE 68503. Phone: (402) 472-3611. Fax: (402) 471-8089. Web Site: www.mynptv.org. Licensee: Nebraska Educational Telecommunications Commission. Network: PBS. Washington Atty: Dow, Lohnes & Albertson.
Key Personnel:
Rod Bates . . . . gen mgr
Michael Beach . . . . mktg dir & engrg dir
Paul Sautter . . . . chief of engrg

KLKE—Analog channel: 24. On air date: March 30, 1996. c/o KLKN(TV), 3240 S. 10th St., Lincoln, NE 68502. Phone: (402) 434-8000. Fax: (914) 793-3400. Web Site: www.klkntv.com. Licensee: Citadel Communications Co. L.L.C. Group owner: (group owner) Network: ABC. Washington Atty: Latham & Watkins.
Key Personnel:
Roger Moody . . . . gen mgr
Dan Ackerman . . . . chief of engrg

KLKN—Analog channel: 8. On air date: Dec 3, 1964. 3240 S. 10th St., Lincoln, NE 68502. Phone: (402) 434-8000. Fax: (402) 436-2236. E-mail: 8@klkntv.com. Web Site: www.klkntv.com. Licensee: Citadel Communications Co. L.L.C. Group owner: Citadel Communications Co. Ltd. (acq 11-15-86; 7-28-86). Network: ABC. Rep: Millennium Sales & Marketing. Washington Atty: Latham & Watkins. News staff: 21; News: 22 hrs wkly.
Key Personnel:
Philip Lombardo . . . . pres
Colleen Roach-Gally . . . . CFO
Raymond Cole . . . . exec VP
Roger Moody . . . . gen mgr
Jeff Swanson . . . . opns dir
Ken Maddox. . . . . rgnl sls mgr

***KLNE-TV**—Analog channel: 3. Digital channel: 26. On air date: Sept 6, 1965. Box 83111, Lincoln, NE 68501. 1800 N. 33rd St., Lincoln, NE 68503. Phone: (402) 472-3611. Fax: (402) 472-1785. E-mail: net1@unl.edu. Web Site: www.netnebraska.org. Licensee: Nebraska Educational Telecommunications Commission. Network: PBS. Washington Atty: Dow, Lohnes & Albertson.
Key Personnel:
Rod Bates . . . . gen mgr
Michael Beach . . . . news dir & engrg dir
Paul Sautter . . . . chief of engrg

***KMNE-TV**—Analog channel: 7. On air date: Sept 1, 1967. Box 83111, Lincoln, NE 68501. 1800 N. 33rd St., Lincoln, NE 68503. Phone: (402) 472-3611. Fax: (402) 471-8089. Web Site: www.mynptv.org. Licensee: Nebraska Educational Telecommunications Commission. Network: PBS. Washington Atty: Dow, Lohnes & Albertson.
Key Personnel:
Rod Bates . . . . gen mgr
Michael Beach . . . . mktg dir & engrg dir
Paul Sautter . . . . chief of engrg

KOLN—Analog channel: 10. Digital channel: 25. On air date: Feb 18, 1953. Box 30350, Lincoln, NE 68503. 40th & W Sts., Lincoln, NE 68503. Phone: (402) 467-4321. Fax: (402) 467-9210. E-mail: info@kolnkgin.com. Web Site: www.kolnkgin.com. Licensee: Gray Television Licensee Inc. Group owner: Gray Television Inc. (acq 7-30-98; grpsl). Network: CBS. Rep: Continental Television Sales. Washington Atty: Venable, Baetijer, Howard & Civiletti.
Key Personnel:
Frank Jonas . . . . pres
Lisa Guill . . . . gen mgr & opns mgr
Kris Ryan . . . . gen sls mgr
Marty Winters . . . . natl sls mgr
Troy Frankforter . . . . prom mgr & progmg mgr
Randy Lube . . . . news dir
Mindy Burback. . . . . pub affrs dir
Brent Haun . . . . chief of engrg

KOWH—Analog channel: 51.Not on air, target date: unknown: Lincoln Broadcasting LLC, World-Herald Sq., Omaha, NE 68102-1138. Phone: (402) 444-1172. Permittee: Lincoln Broadcasting LLC.. Ownership: World Investments Inc. Washington Atty: Hogan & Hartson.

KSNB-TV—Analog channel: 4. On air date: Oct 1, 1965. Box 220, Kearney, NE 68848-0220. R.R. 1, Harde, NE 68848-0220. Phone: (308) 743-2494. Phone: (402) 226-2011. Fax: (308) 743-2644. Licensee: Colins Broadcasting Co. (acq 2-17-99; $333,333). Network: Fox. Rep: Harrington, Righter & Parsons. News: 13 hrs wkly.

KTVG—Analog channel: 17. On air date: December 1992. Box 220, Kearney, NE 68848. 1078 25th Rd., Axtell, NE 68848. Phone: (308) 734-2794. Fax: (308) 743-2644. Licensee: Hill Broadcasting Inc. Network: Fox. Rep: Harrington, Righter & Parsons.

***KUON-TV**—Analog channel: 12. Digital channel: 40. On air date: Nov 1, 1954. Box 83111, Lincoln, NE 68501. 1800 N. 33rd St., Lincoln, NE 68503. Phone: (402) 472-3611. Fax: (402) 472-1785. E-mail: net1@unl.edu. Web Site: www.netnebraska.org. Licensee: University of Nebraska. (acq 7-28-54; 8-2-54). Network: PBS. Washington Atty: Dow, Lohnes & Albertson.

KWNB-TV—Analog channel: 6. On air date: Feb 9, 1956. Box 220, Kearney, NE 68848. R2, Hayes Center, NE 69032. Phone: (308) 743-2494. Phone: (308) 286-3300. Fax: (308) 743-2644. Web Site: nebraska.tv. Licensee: Pappas Telecasting of Central Nebraska L.P. (DE limited partnership). Group owner: Pappas Telecasting Companies (acq 7-1-96; grpsl). Network: ABC. Rep: Harrington, Righter & Parsons. News staff: 26; News: 17.5 hrs wkly.
Key Personnel:
Harry J. Pappas . . . . CEO & pres
Dennis Davis . . . . CFO
Stephen Morris. . . . . VP & gen mgr
Ron Barbarita . . . . gen sls mgr
Scott Swensen . . . . progmg dir
Mark Baumert . . . . news dir
Jerry Fuehrer. . . . . chief of engrg

McCook

see Wichita-Hutchinson Plus, KS market

Merriman

see Sioux Falls (Mitchell), SD market

Norfolk

see Sioux City, IA market

North Platte, NE (DMA 209)

KNOP-TV—Analog channel: 2. On air date: Dec 2, 1958. Box 749, North Platte, NE 69103. N. Hwy. 83, North Platte, NE 69101. Phone: (308) 532-2222. Fax: (308) 532-9579. E-mail: lewysknop@knoptv.com. Web Site: www.knop.msnbc.com. Licensee: Greater Nebraska Television Inc. Group owner: (group owner; acq 10-28-70; FTR: 11-16-70). Network: NBC. Rep: Blair Television. Washington Atty: Fletcher, Heald & Hildreth. News staff: 10; News: 15 hrs wkly.
Key Personnel:
Ulysses Carlini Sr. . . . . exec VP
Lewys Carlini . . . . gen mgr & mktg dir
Darlene Lyman. . . . . gen sls mgr
Gregg Hoover . . . . prom dir & pub affrs dir
Mike McNeil . . . . chief of engrg

***KPNE-TV**—Analog channel: 9. Digital channel: 16. On air date: Sept 12, 1966. Box 83111, Lincoln, NE 68501. 1800 N. 33rd St., Lincoln, NE 68503. Phone: (402) 472-3611. Fax: (402) 472-1785. E-mail: net1@unl.edu. Web Site: www.netnebraska.org. Licensee: Nebraska Educational Telecommunications Commission. Network: PBS. Washington Atty: Dow, Lohnes & Albertson.
Key Personnel:
Rod Bates . . . . gen mgr
Michael Beach . . . . mktg dir & engrg dir
Paul Sautter . . . . chief of engrg

Omaha, NE (DMA 76)

***KBIN**—Analog channel: 32. Digital channel: 33. On air date: Sept 7, 1975. Box 6450, 6450 Corporate Dr., c/o Iowa Public TV, Johnston, IA 50131. Phone: (515) 242-3100. Fax: (515) 242-4151. E-mail: public_information@iptv.org. Web Site: www.iptv.org. Licensee: Iowa Public Broadcasting Board. Network: PBS. Washington Atty: Dow, Lohnes & Albertson.

KETV—Analog channel: 7. Digital channel: 20. On air date: Sept 17, 1957. 2665 Douglas St., Omaha, NE 68131-2699. Phone: (402) 345-7777. Fax: (402) 978-8922 (sales). Fax: (402) 522-7755. Web Site: www.theomahachannel.com. Licensee: KETV Hearst-Argyle Television Inc. Group owner: Hearst-Argyle Television Inc. (acq 3-18-99; grpsl). Network: ABC. Rep: Eagle Television Sales. News: 37 hrs wkly.
Key Personnel:
Joel Vilmenay. . . . . pres & gen mgr
Brian Sather. . . . . gen sls mgr
Rose Ann Shannon . . . . news dir
Warren Behrens . . . . chief of engrg

***KHIN**—Analog channel: 36. Digital channel: 35. On air date: Sept 7, 1975. Box 6450, 6450 Corporate Dr., c/o Iowa Public TV, Johnston, IA 50131-6450. Phone: (515) 242-3100. Fax: (515) 242-4151. E-mail: public_information@iptv.org. Web Site: www.iptv.org. Licensee: Iowa Public Broadcasting Board. Network: PBS. Washington Atty: Dow, Lohnes & Albertson.

KMTV—Analog channel: 3. Digital channel: 45. On air date: Sept 1, 1949. 10714 Mockingbird Dr., Omaha, NE 68127. Phone: (402) 592-3333. Fax: (402) 597-7698. Web Site: www.km3news.com. Licensee: Emmis Television License LLC. Group owner: Emmis Communications Corp. (acq 10-1-2000; grpsl). Network: CBS. News: 23 hrs wkly.

KPTM—Analog channel: 42. Digital channel: 43. On air date: Apr 6, 1986. 4625 Farnam St., Omaha, NE 68132. Phone: (402) 558-4200. Fax: (402) 554-4290. Web Site: www.kptm.com. Licensee: KPTM (TV) License LLC. Group owner: Pappas Telecasting Companies (acq 3-14-86). Network: Fox. Rep: TeleRep. Washington Atty: Paul, Hastings, Janofsky & Walker. News staff: 20; News: 7 hrs wkly.
Key Personnel:
Howard Shrier . . . . . COO & exec VP
Harry J. Pappas . . . . . pres
Dale R. Oswald . . . . . gen mgr
Darrin McDonald . . . . . stn mgr & gen sls mgr
Chris McDade . . . . . opns mgr
Shane Beardslee . . . . . gen sls mgr & natl sls mgr
Ed Zachary . . . . . rgnl sls mgr
Donna Ridgley . . . . . prom mgr
Darlene Goldsberry . . . . . progmg mgr
Dale Scherbring . . . . . engrg VP
Rick Graham . . . . . chief of engrg

KXVO—Analog channel: 15. On air date: June 10, 1995. 4625 Farnam, Omaha, NE 68132. Phone: (402) 554-1500. Fax: (402) 554-4290. Web Site: www.kxvo.com. Licensee: Mitts Telecasting Co. (acq 6-13-00; $972,000). Rep: TeleRep. Washington Atty: Bryan Cave.
Key Personnel:
Dale R. Oswald . . . . . gen mgr
Darrin McDonald . . . . . stn mgr

***KYNE-TV**—Analog channel: 26. On air date: Oct 19, 1965. Box 83111, Lincoln, NE 68501. 1800 N. 33rd St., Lincoln, NE 68503. Phone: (402) 472-3611. Fax: (402) 471-8089. Web Site: www.mynptv.org. Licensee: Nebraska Educational Telecommunications Commission. Network: PBS. Washington Atty: Dow, Lohnes & Albertson.
Key Personnel:
Rod Bates . . . . . gen mgr
Michael Beach . . . . . engrg dir
Paul Sautter . . . . . chief of engrg

WOWT—Analog channel: 6. Digital channel: 22. On air date: Aug 29, 1949. 3501 Farnam St., Omaha, NE 68131-3356. Phone: (402) 346-6666. Fax: (402) 233-7880. E-mail: sixonline@wowt.com. Web Site: wowt.com. Licensee: Gary Television Licensee Inc. Group owner: Gray Television Inc. (acq 10-02; grpsl). Network: NBC. Rep: Continental Television Sales. Washington Atty: Fletcher, Heald & Hildreth. News staff: 52; News: 37 hrs wkly.

Scottsbluff

see Cheyenne, WY-Scottsbluff, NE market

Nevada

Elko

see Salt Lake City, UT market

Ely

see Salt Lake City, UT market

Las Vegas, NV (DMA 51)

KBLR—Analog channel: 39. Digital channel: 40. On air date: Apr 20, 1989. 73 Spectrum Blvd., Las Vegas, NV 89101. Phone: (702) 258-0039. Fax: (702) 258-0556. Web Site: www.kblr39.com. Licensee: Summit Media Limited Partnership.. Ownership: Scott Gentry, Bruce F. Becker, William O'Connell, et al. (acq 1993; $1.5 million; 9-20-93). Network: Telemundo (Spanish). Washington Atty: KMZ Rosenman. News staff: 8; News: 2 hrs wkly.
Key Personnel:
Carlos Sanchez . . . . . VP & gen mgr
Ellen Walker . . . . . gen sls mgr
Bill George . . . . . natl sls mgr
Mariana Laas . . . . . news dir

KFBT—Analog channel: 33. On air date: Aug 1, 1989. 3830 S. Jones Blvd., Las Vegas, NV 89103. Phone: (702) 952-4600. Fax: (702) 873-1233. Web Site: www.wblasvegas.com. Licensee: Channel 33 Inc. Group owner: Sinclair Broadcast Group Inc. (acq 2-23-00; $33 million for stock). Rep: Adam Young. Washington Atty: Fletcher, Heald & Hildreth.
Key Personnel:
Rob Weisbord . . . . . gen mgr
Chris Cohen . . . . . gen sls mgr
Pio Rongavilla . . . . . adv mgr
Tina Miller . . . . . progmg dir
Steve Galvin . . . . . chief of engrg

KINC—Analog channel: 15. On air date: October 1995. 500 Pilot Rd., Suite D, Las Vegas, NV 89119. Phone: (702) 434-0015. Fax: (702) 434-0527. Web Site: www.kinc.entravision.com. Licensee: Entravision Holdings L.L.C. Group owner: Entravision Communications Co. L.L.C. Network: Univision (Spanish). Washington Atty: Thompson Hine L.L.P.. News: 5 hrs wkly.
Key Personnel:
Chris Roman . . . . . gen mgr
Bob Rodriquez . . . . . gen sls mgr
Salvador Carrera . . . . . natl sls mgr
Karina Barcena . . . . . prom dir & prom mgr
Juan Aviles . . . . . news dir
John Garcia . . . . . chief of engrg

KLAS-TV—Analog channel: 8. Digital channel: 7. On air date: July 22, 1953. Box 15047, Las Vegas, NV 89114. 3228 Channel 8 Dr., Saint Petersburg, NV 89109. Phone: (702) 792-8888. Fax: (702) 734-7437. Web Site: www.klastv.com. Licensee: KLAS Inc., a Nevada Corp. Group owner: Landmark Communications Inc. (acq 7-1-78; $8 million). Network: CBS. Washington Atty: Hogan & Hartson.
Key Personnel:
Emily Neilson . . . . . pres & gen mgr
Linda Bonnici . . . . . sls VP
Michael Watkins . . . . . gen sls mgr
Tamara Chase . . . . . natl sls mgr
Lee Minard . . . . . mktg dir
Kathy Kramer . . . . . progmg dir
Melissa Cipriano . . . . . pub affrs dir
Doug Kramer . . . . . chief of engrg

***KLVX**—Analog channel: 10. On air date: Mar 25, 1968. 4210 Channel 10 Dr., Las Vegas, NV 89119. Phone: (702) 799-1010. Fax: (702) 799-5586. Web Site: www.klvx.org. Licensee: Clark County School District Board of Trustees. Network: PBS. Washington Atty: Wiley, Rein & Fielding.

KMCC—Analog channel: 34. Digital channel: 32. On air date: 2005. 3100 S. Needles Hwy., Suite 1700, Las Vegas, NV 89029. Phone: (702) 298-2222. Fax: (702) 298-3495. Licensee: Mojave Broadcasting Co.. Ownership: Suzanne E. Rogers, 48% of votes; Perry C. Rogers, 28% of votes; and Kimberly Rogers Cell, 24% of votes. Rep: Blair Television. Washington Atty: Wiley, Rein & Fielding.
Key Personnel:
Suzanne E. Rogers . . . . . pres
Brian Plant . . . . . exec VP
Perry C. Rogers . . . . . VP
Bruce Clark . . . . . gen mgr & chief of engrg

KTNV—Analog channel: 13. Digital channel: 12. On air date: May 4, 1956. 3355 S. Valley View Blvd., Las Vegas, NV 89102. Phone: (702) 876-1313. Fax: (702) 871-1961. E-mail: ktnv13@ktnv.com. Web Site: www.ktnv.com. Licensee: Journal Broadcast Corp. Permittee: KTNV-TV/Channel 13 Group owner: Journal Broadcast Group Inc. (acq 6-29-79). Network: ABC. Rep: Petry Television Inc.. Washington Atty: Crowell & Moring. News staff: 60; News: 22 hrs wkly.
Key Personnel:
Steve Smith . . . . . CEO & chmn
Doug Kiel . . . . . pres
Paul Bonaiuto . . . . . CFO & exec VP
Jim Prather . . . . . VP, gen mgr & stn mgr
Ron Adair . . . . . opns dir, opns mgr & chief of opns

KVBC—Analog channel: 3. Digital channel: 2. On air date: Oct 1, 1979. 1500 Foremaster Ln., Las Vegas, NV 89101. Phone: (702) 642-3333. Fax: (702) 657-3152 (news). E-mail: news3@kvbc.com. Web Site: www.kvbc.com. Licensee: Valley Broadcasting Co.. Ownership: James Rogers, 49.97%; Louis Wiener Jr. Estate, 30%; Janet Rogers, 12.53%. Network: NBC. Washington Atty: Dow, Lohnes & Albertson. News staff: 55; News: 29 hrs wkly.
Key Personnel:
James E. Rogers . . . . . CEO
Ralph Toddre . . . . . pres
Gene Greenberg . . . . . exec VP & gen mgr
Mark Nutini . . . . . opns mgr
Joanne Nasby . . . . . natl sls mgr
Leslie Fox-Priest . . . . . rgnl sls mgr
Kathy Minicozzi . . . . . mktg dir
Dale Wyman . . . . . prom dir
Judy Reich . . . . . progmg dir & pub affrs dir
Jamie Ioos . . . . . news dir
Mark Guranik . . . . . engrg dir & chief of engrg

KVVU-TV—(Henderson).Analog channel: 5. On air date: October 1967. 25 TV-5 Dr., Henderson, NV 89014. Phone: (702) 435-5555. Fax: (702) 451-4220. Web Site: www.kvvu.com. Licensee: KVVU Broadcasting Corp. Group owner: Meredith Broadcasting Group, Meredith Corp., see Cross-Ownership (acq 5-85; $36 million). Network: Fox. Rep: TeleRep. Washington Atty: Haley, Bader & Potts.
Key Personnel:
Kevin O'Brien . . . . . pres
Susan Lucas . . . . . VP & gen mgr
Jill Saarela . . . . . gen sls mgr
Henry Krajewski . . . . . natl sls mgr
Lisa Amerson . . . . . rgnl sls mgr
Todd Brown . . . . . rgnl sls mgr
Troy Carlson . . . . . rgnl sls mgr
Terri Peck . . . . . mktg mgr & prom dir
Leilani Molinaro . . . . . progmg mgr
Mark Neerman . . . . . news dir
Jack Smith . . . . . engrg dir & chief of engrg

KVWB—Analog channel: 21. On air date: July 31, 1984. 3830 S. Jones Blvd., Las Vegas, NV 89103. Phone: (702) 382-2121. Fax: (702) 382-1351. Web Site: www.wblasvegas.com. Licensee: KUPN Licensee L.L.C. Group owner: Sinclair Broadcast Group Inc. (acq 5-30-97; $87 million). Network: WB. Washington Atty: Dow, Lohnes & Albertson.
Key Personnel:
David Smith . . . . . CEO, pres & opns mgr
David Amy . . . . . CFO
Rob Weisbord . . . . . gen mgr
Sonia Maxwell . . . . . stn mgr, sls dir & gen sls mgr
Chris Cohen . . . . . gen sls mgr & natl sls mgr
Eric Dahl . . . . . prom dir
Tina Miller . . . . . progmg dir & pub affrs dir

Reno, NV (DMA 114)

KAME-TV—Analog channel: 21. On air date: Oct 1, 1983. 4920 Brookside Way, Reno, NV 89502. Phone: (775) 856-2121. Fax: (775) 856-2100. Licensee: Broadcast Development Corp. (acq 2-28-94). Rep: TeleRep. Washington Atty: Bryan Cave.
Key Personnel:
Martin Ozer . . . . . VP & gen mgr
Ray Stofer . . . . . chief of opns & chief of engrg

KEGS—Analog channel: 7. On air date: 2002. Equity Broadcasting Corp., 1 Shackleford Dr., Suite 400, Little Rock, AR 72211. Phone: (501) 219-2400. Fax: (501) 604-8004. Licensee: Nevada Channel 3 Inc.

***KNPB**—Analog channel: 5. On air date: October 1983. 1670 N. Virginia St., Reno, NV 89503. Phone: (775) 784-4555. Fax: (775) 784-1438. E-mail: info@knpb.org. Web Site: www.knpb.org. Licensee: Channel 5 Public Broadcasting Inc. Network: PBS. Washington Atty: Schwartz, Woods & Miller.
Key Personnel:
Ron Smith . . . . . gen mgr, gen sls mgr & mktg mgr
Jacquline Cashmere . . . . . adv mgr
Barbara Harmon . . . . . progmg dir
Tim Stoffel . . . . . chief of engrg

KOLO-TV—Analog channel: 8. On air date: Sept 27, 1953. 4850 Ampere Dr., Reno, NV 89502. Phone: (775) 858-8888. Fax: (775) 858-8855. Web Site: www.kolotv.com. Licensee: Gray Television Licensee Corp. Group owner: Gray Television Inc. (acq 12-10-2002; $41.5 million. with K12IX Austin, K58AO Crystal Bay, K03DN Ely/McGill and K49CK Stead/Lawton, all NV). Network: ABC. Rep: Millennium Sales & Marketing. Washington Atty: Haley, Bader & Potts. News: 22 hrs wkly.

KREN-TV—Analog channel: 27. On air date: Nov 1, 1985. 940 Matley Ln., Suite 15, Reno, NV 89502. Phone: (775) 333-2727. Fax: (775) 327-6827. Licensee: Reno License LLC. Group owner: Pappas Telecasting Companies (acq 2-10-95; $3 million;. FTR: 5-8-95). Network: WB. Rep: Harrington, Righter & Parsons. Washington Atty: Fletcher, Heald & Hildreth.
Key Personnel:
Harry Pappas . . . . . CEO
Leopoldo L. Ramos . . . . . gen mgr
Maria Jimenez . . . . . stn mgr & opns dir
Barry Poles . . . . . rgnl sls mgr
Brian Bird . . . . . prom dir & pub affrs dir

Broadcasting & Cable Yearbook 2006

B-61

Directory of Television

Debbie Sweeney . . . . progmg VP
James Ocon . . . . chief of engrg

KRNV—Analog channel: 4. On air date: Sept 30, 1962. Box 7160, Reno, NV 89510. 1790 Vassar St., Reno, NV 89502. Phone: (775) 322-4444. Fax: (775) 785-1200. Fax: (775) 785-1206. Web Site: www.krnv.com. Licensee: Sierra Broadcasting Co.. Ownership: James E. Rogers. Group owner: Sunbelt Communications Co. (acq 9-13-89). Network: NBC. Washington Atty: Gerald S. Rourke. News staff: 26; News: 14 hrs wkly.
Key Personnel:
Carrie Walker . . . . gen mgr
Mike West . . . . gen sls mgr & mktg mgr
Barbara Monroy . . . . progmg dir
John Finkbohner . . . . chief of engrg

KRXI-TV—Analog channel: 11. On air date: Dec 3, 1995. 4920 Brookside Way, Reno, NV 89502. Phone: (775) 856-1100. Fax: (775) 856-1101. Web Site: foxreno.com. Licensee: KTVU Partnership. Network: Fox. Rep: TeleRep. Washington Atty: Dow, Lohnes & Albertson.

KTVN—Analog channel: 2. Digital channel: 13. On air date: June 4, 1967. Box 7220, Reno, NV 89510. 4925 Energy Way, Reno, NV 89502. Phone: (775) 858-2222. Fax: (775) 861-4298. E-mail: ktvn@ktvn.com. Web Site: www.ktvn.com. Licensee: Sarkes Tarzian Inc. Group owner: (group owner; acq 8-13-80; $12.5 million). Network: CBS. Rep: Katz Radio. Washington Atty: Leventhal, Senter & Lerman. News staff: 33; News: 19.5 hrs wkly.
Key Personnel:
Tom Tarzian . . . . chmn
Tom Tolar . . . . pres
Bob Davis . . . . CFO
Lawson Fox . . . . gen mgr
John Richardson . . . . gen sls mgr
Sharon Facque . . . . natl sls mgr
Michelle Loftin . . . . prom mgr & pub affrs dir
Pat Hall . . . . progmg dir
Gina Martini . . . . news dir
Al Richards . . . . engrg dir
Jack Antonio . . . . chief of engrg

KWNV—Analog channel: 7. On air date: 1998. c/o KRNV, 1790 Vassar St., Reno, NV 89502. Phone: (775) 322-4444. Fax: (775) 785-1200. Licensee: Sierra Broadcasting Co. Network: NBC.
Key Personnel:
Mary Beth Farrell . . . . stn mgr & gen sls mgr
John Finkbohner . . . . opns dir & engrg dir
Pam Zunini . . . . mktg dir
Doug Tepe . . . . prom dir
Ralph Toddre . . . . COO, pres, gen mgr & progmg dir
Barbara Monroy . . . . progmg mgr
Jon Killoran . . . . news dir

New Hampshire

Concord
see Boston (Manchester, NH) market

Derry
see Boston (Manchester, NH) market

Durham
see Boston (Manchester, NH) market

Keene
see Boston (Manchester, NH) market

Littleton
see Portland-Auburn, ME market

Manchester
see Boston (Manchester, NH) market

Merrimack
see Boston (Manchester, NH) market

New Jersey

Atlantic City
see Philadelphia market

Burlington
see Philadelphia market

Camden
see Philadelphia market

Linden
see New York market

Montclair
see New York market

New Brunswick
see New York market

Newark
see New York market

Newton
see New York market

Paterson
see New York market

Secaucus
see New York market

Trenton
see Philadelphia market

Vineland
see Philadelphia market

West Milford
see New York market

Wildwood
see Philadelphia market

New Mexico

Albuquerque-Santa Fe, NM (DMA 47)

KASA-TV—Analog channel: 2. Digital channel: 27. On air date: May 8, 1981. 1377 University Blvd. N.E., Albuquerque, NM 87102. Phone: (505) 246-2222. Fax: (505) 766-7705. E-mail: kasa@kasa.com. Web Site: www.kasa.com. Licensee: Raycom National License Subsidiary LLC. Group owner: Raycom Media Inc. (acq 9-2-99; grpsl). Network: Fox. Rep: TeleRep. Washington Atty: Wiley, Rein & Fielding.
Key Personnel:
Erick B. Steffens . . . . pres & gen mgr
Brian Anderson . . . . rgnl sls mgr, mktg mgr & prom mgr
Marsha Pollaro . . . . progmg dir & progmg mgr
Rosalie Drake . . gen sls mgr, natl sls mgr, adv mgr & pub affrs dir
Dudley Bullock . . . . chief of engrg

KASY-TV—Analog channel: 50. On air date: Oct 6, 1995. 8341 Washington N.E., Albuquerque, NM 87113. Phone: (505) 797-1919. Fax: (505) 938-4401. E-mail: reception@kwbq.com. Web Site: www.upn50tv.com. Licensee: Acme Television Licenses of New Mexico L.L.C. Group owner: Acme Communications Inc. (acq 6-18-99; $25.4 million). Network: UPN. Washington Atty: Leventhal, Senter & Lerman.
Key Personnel:
John Greenwood . . . . gen mgr
Kevin Tucker . . . . gen sls mgr
Jamie McDowell . . . . prom mgr & adv mgr
Judie Baldwin . . . . progmg dir
Tony Liperato . . . . chief of engrg

*****KAZQ**—Analog channel: 32. On air date: Oct 12, 1987. 4501 Montgomery Blvd. N.E., Albuquerque, NM 87109. Phone: (505) 884-8355. Fax: (505) 883-1229. E-mail: kazq32@kazq32.org. Web Site: www.kazq32.org.. Stn video via satellite: Echostar Satellite 148 Channel 8817 Licensee: Alpha-Omega Broadcasting of Albuquerque Inc. Washington Atty: Midlen Law Center.
Key Personnel:
Brenton Franks . . . . gen mgr
Jeffrey Helmers . . . . dev dir & mktg mgr
Howard Holley . . . . progmg dir
Robert Ramseyer . . . . chief of engrg

KBIM-TV—Analog channel: 10. Digital channel: 41. On air date: Feb 26, 1966. Box 910, Roswell, NM 88201. 214 N. Main St., Roswell, NM 88201. Phone: (505) 622-2120. Fax: (505) 623-6606. Web Site: www.kbimtv.com. Licensee: Emmis Television License LLC. Group owner: Emmis Communications Corp. (acq 9-25-2000; grpsl). Network: CBS. Rep: Katz Radio. Washington Atty: Reed, Smith, Shaw & McClay. News staff: 11; News: 6 hrs wkly.
Key Personnel:
Richard Gotlieb . . . . pres
Gene Munsey . . . . VP, gen mgr, gen sls mgr & adv mgr
Kevin Harris . . . . opns mgr
Marcus Damberger . . . . chief of engrg

KCHF—Analog channel: 11. On air date: Jan 21, 1984. Box 4338, Albuquerque, NM 87196. 216-TV E. Frontage Rd., Santa Fe, NM 87505. Phone: (505) 345-1991 (radio). Phone: (505) 473-1111. Fax: (505) 345-5669. Web Site: www.kchf.com. Licensee: Son Broadcasting Inc. Washington Atty: Gammon & Grange.
Key Personnel:
Belarmino R. Gonzalez . . . . CEO & chmn
Belarmino R. Gonzales . . . . pres
Vickie Archiveque . . . . CFO
Annette Garcia . . . . VP & stn mgr
Blackie Gonzales . . . . gen mgr
Leo Lesaca . . . . sls dir & gen sls mgr
Mary Kay Gonzales . . . . prom mgr & progmg dir
Rob Ramseyer . . . . chief of engrg

KHFT—Analog channel: 29. On air date: 1989. Box 3757, Lubbock, TX 79452. 9800 University Ave., Lubbock, TX 77551-5556. Phone: (806) 745-3434. Fax: (806) 748-1949. Licensee: Ramar Communications II Ltd. Group owner: (group owner; acq 6-4-97; $200,000).. Washington Atty: Leventhal, Senter & Lerman.
Key Personnel:
Brad Moran . . . . pres
Chuck Hinez . . . . gen mgr
Scott Cawthron . . . . opns mgr
Terri Holt . . . . progmg dir

KLUZ-TV—Analog channel: 41. On air date: September 1987. 2725 F Broadbent Pkwy. N.E., Albuquerque, NM 87107. Phone: (505) 342-4141. Phone: (505) 344-5589. Fax: (505) 344-8714. Web Site: www.univision.com. Licensee: Entravision Holdings L.L.C. Group owner: Entravision

Communications Co. L.L.C. (acq 3-21-99). Network: Univision (Spanish). News staff: 10; News: 1/2 hr wkly.

Key Personnel:
Walter Ulloa . . . . . CEO
Phillip Wilkinson . . . . . pres
John DiLorenzo . . . . . CFO
Margarita Wilder . . . . . gen mgr & gen sls mgr
Gretchen Young . . . . . mktg mgr & pub affrs dir
Theresa Broderick . . . . . mktg mgr
Adriana Gautreau . . . . . progmg dir
Kambiz Victory . . . . . chief of engrg

KNAT—Analog channel: 23. On air date: Oct 17, 1975. 1510 Coors Rd. N.W., Albuquerque, NM 87121. Phone: (505) 836-6585. Fax: (505) 831-8725. E-mail: cmansfield@tbn.org. Web Site: www.tbn.org. Licensee: Trinity Broadcasting Network. Group owner: (group owner; acq 5-8-00; grpsl). Network: NBC. Washington Atty: Joseph E. Dunne III.

Key Personnel:
Terry Hickey . . . . . CEO
Cynthia Mansfield . . . . . gen mgr & dev dir

***KNMD-TV**—Analog channel: 9.Not on air, target date: unknown: 1130 University Blvd. N.E., Albuquerque, NM 87102. Phone: (505) 277-2121. Fax: (505) 277-2191. E-mail: viewer@knme.org. Web Site: www.knmetv.org. Permittee: The Regents of the University of New Mexico. Network: PBS. Washington Atty: Dow, Lohnes & Albertson, LLC.

Key Personnel:
Ted A. Garcia . . . . . CEO & gen mgr
Skitch Ferguson . . . . . mktg mgr
Shirley Casados . . . . . progmg dir
Jim Gale . . . . . chief of engrg

***KNME-TV**—Analog channel: 5. On air date: May 5, 1958. 1130 University Blvd. N.E., Albuquerque, NM 87102. Phone: (505) 277-2121. Fax: (505) 277-2191. Web Site: www.knmetv.org. Licensee: Regents of University of New Mexico and Board of Education, Albuquerque. Network: PBS. Washington Atty: Dow, Lohnes & Albertson. News staff: 4; News: one hr wkly.

Key Personnel:
Ted A. Garcia . . . . . CEO & gen mgr
Jim Gale . . . . . opns dir
Joanne Bacamann . . . . . dev dir

KOAT-TV—Analog channel: 7. Digital channel: 21. On air date: Sept 28, 1953. Box 25982, Albuquerque, NM 87125. 3801 Carlisle N.E., Albuquerque, NM 87107. Phone: (505) 884-7777. Fax: (505) 884-6282. E-mail: koatdesk@hearst.com. Web Site: www.thenewmexicochannel.com. Licensee: KOAT Hearst-Argyle Television Inc. Group owner: Hearst-Argyle Television Inc. (acq 3-18-99; grpsl). Network: ABC. Rep: Katz Radio. Washington Atty: Brooks, Pierce, McLendon, Humphrey & Leonard.

Key Personnel:
Mary Lynn Roper . . . . . pres & gen mgr
Brian Bouloy . . . . . opns dir
Teri Hernandez . . . . . opns mgr

KOBF—Analog channel: 12. On air date: 1972. Box 1620, Farmington, NM 87499. 825 W. Broadway, Farmington, NM 87499. Phone: (505) 326-1141. Fax: (505) 327-5196. Web Site: www.kobftv.com. Licensee: KOB-TV L.L.C. Group owner: Hubbard Broadcasting Inc. (acq 9-19-83; $2.35 million; 8-15-83). Network: NBC. Washington Atty: Fletcher, Heald & Hildreth. News staff: 6; News: 4 hrs wkly.

Key Personnel:
Steve Henderson . . . . . gen mgr
Scott Michlan . . . . . news dir
Dan Harlin . . . . . chief of engrg

KOBG-TV—Analog channel: 6. On air date: 2001. Box 1351, Albuquerque, NM 87103. Phone: (505) 243-4411. Fax: (505) 764-2522. Licensee: KOB-TV LLC. Network: NBC.

KOBR—Analog channel: 8. On air date: June 24, 1953. 124 E. 4th St., Roswell, NM 88201. Phone: (505) 625-8888. Fax: (505) 625-8866. E-mail: lcook@kobtv.com. Web Site: kobrtv.com. Licensee: Stanley S. Hubbard Revocable Trust. Group owner: Hubbard Broadcasting Inc. (acq 8-10-01). Network: NBC. Washington Atty: Fletcher, Heald & Hildreth. News staff: 4.

Key Personnel:
Stanley S. Hubbard . . . . . pres
Lee Cook . . . . . gen mgr
Jason Jensen . . . . . prom mgr
Scott Michlin . . . . . news dir
Wayne Koontz . . . . . chief of engrg

KOB-TV—Analog channel: 4. On air date: Nov 29, 1948. Box 1351, Albuquerque, NM 87103. 4 Broadcast Plaza S.W., Albuquerque, NM 87104. Phone: (505) 243-4411. Fax: (505) 764-2522. Web Site: www.kobtv.com. Licensee: KOB-TV L.L.C. Group owner: Hubbard Broadcasting Inc. (acq 3-15-57; grpsl; 3-18-57). Network: NBC. Washington Atty: Fletcher, Heald & Hildreth. News: 12 hrs wkly.

Key Personnel:
Mike Burgess . . . . . VP & gen mgr
Susan Connor . . . . . stn mgr & opns mgr
Barbara Wagoner . . . . . gen sls mgr
Jeff Finkel . . . . . natl sls mgr
Gerard Demarest . . . . . prom dir
Juanita Garay . . . . . progmg mgr
Brian Rackham . . . . . news dir
Susan Bradley . . . . . pub affrs dir
Sean Anker . . . . . engrg dir & chief of engrg

KOCT—Analog channel: 6. On air date: August 1959. Box 25982, Albuquerque, NM 87125. 3801 Carlisle N.E., Albuquerque, NM 87125. Phone: (505) 884-7777. Fax: (505) 884-6282. Web Site: www.thenewmexicochannel.com. Licensee: KOAT Hearst-Argyle Television Inc. Group owner: Hearst-Argyle Television Inc. (acq 3-18-99; grpsl). Network: ABC. Washington Atty: Verner, Liipfert, Bernhard, McPherson & Hand.

Key Personnel:
Mary Lynn Roper . . . . . gen mgr
Barbara Burzillo . . . . . gen sls mgr, adv mgr & pub affrs dir
Jennifer Crisco . . . . . natl sls mgr & prom mgr
John Trambley . . . . . progmg dir
Sue Stephens . . . . . news dir
Dan Brown . . . . . chief of engrg

KOFT—Analog channel: 3.Not on air, target date: unknown: Box 25982, Albuquerque, NM 87125. 3801 Carlisle N.E., Albuquerque, NM 87125. Phone: (505) 884-7777. Fax: (505) 884-6282. Web Site: www.thenewmexicochannel.com. Permittee: KOAT Hearst-Argyle Television Inc. Network: ABC. Washington Atty: Verner, Liipfert, Bernhard, McPherson & Hand.

Key Personnel:
Mary Lynn Roper . . . . . pres & gen mgr
Barbara Burzillo . . . . . gen sls mgr & adv mgr
Jennifer Crisco . . . . . prom mgr
John Trambley . . . . . progmg dir
Bruce Bennett . . . . . pub affrs dir
Dan Brown . . . . . chief of engrg

KOVT—Analog channel: 10. On air date: Sept 9, 1987. Box 25982, c/o KOAT-TV, Albuquerque, NM 87125. 3801 Carlisle N.E., Albuquerque, NM 87125. Phone: (505) 884-7777. Fax: (505) 884-6282. Web Site: www.thenewmexicochannel.com. Licensee: KOAT Hearst-Argyle Television Inc. Group owner: Hearst-Argyle Television Inc. (acq 3-18-99; grpsl). Network: ABC. Washington Atty: Verner, Liipfert, Bernhard, McPherson & Hand.

Key Personnel:
Mary Lynn Roper . . . . . pres & gen mgr
Barbara Burzillo . . . . . gen sls mgr & adv mgr
Jennifer Crisco . . . . . prom mgr
John Trumbley . . . . . progmg dir
Paul Shipley . . . . . news dir
Daan Brown . . . . . chief of engrg

KREZ-TV—Analog channel: 6. Digital channel: 15. On air date: Sept 4, 1965. Box 2508, Durango, CO 81302. 158 Bodo Dr., Durango, CO 81302. Phone: (970) 259-6666. Fax: (970) 247-8472. Licensee: Emmis Television License LLC. Group owner: Emmis Communications Corp. (acq 9-25-2000; grpsl). Network: Network: CBS, NBC. Rep: Katz Radio.

***KRMU**—Analog channel: 20.Not on air, target date: unknown: 1089 Bannock St., Denver, CO 80204. Phone: (303) 892-6666. Fax: (303) 620-5600. Web Site: www.rmpbs.org. Permittee: Rocky Mountain Public Broadcasting Network Inc.

Key Personnel:
James N. Morgese . . . . . pres & gen mgr
Charlie Goldsmith . . . . . dev dir
Karen Hill . . . . . dev dir
Donna Sandford . . . . . progmg dir
James Schoedler . . . . . engrg dir

KRPV—Analog channel: 27. On air date: Sept 15, 1986. Box 61000, Midland, TX 79711. Box 967, 2606 S. Main, Roswell, NM 88203-0967. Phone: (432) 563-0420. Fax: (432) 563-1736. E-mail: info@ptcbglc.com. Web Site: www.godslearningchannel.com. Licensee: Prime Time Christian Broadcasting.

Key Personnel:
Al Cooper . . . . . CEO, pres & gen mgr
Tommy Cooper . . . . . VP
Jeff Tveit . . . . . stn mgr & gen sls mgr

KRQE—Analog channel: 13. Digital channel: 16. On air date: Oct 3, 1953. 13 Broadcast Plaza S.W., Albuquerque, NM 87104. Phone: (505) 243-2285. Fax: (505) 248-1464. Web Site: www.krqe.com. Licensee: Emmis Television License LLC. Group owner: Emmis Communications Corp. (acq 9-25-2000; grpsl). Network: CBS. Rep: Harrington, Righter & Parsons. Washington Atty: Reed, Smith, Shaw & McClay. News staff: 65; News: 24 hrs wkly.

Key Personnel:
Bill Anderson . . . . . gen mgr
Fred Woskoff . . . . . opns dir, progmg dir & progmg mgr
Arnie Ronston . . . . . sls dir & gen sls mgr
Mary Lou Davis . . . . . natl sls mgr
Kim Smith . . . . . rgnl sls mgr
Parker Harms . . . . . mktg dir & prom mgr
Michelle Donaldson . . . . . news dir
Marilyn Painter . . . . . pub affrs dir
Frank Lilley . . . . . engrg dir

KRWB-TV—Analog channel: 21. On air date: 2004. 8341 Washington N.E., Albuquerque, NM 87113. Phone: (505) 797-1919. Fax: (505) 938-4401. Permittee: Acme Television Licenses of New Mexico LLC. Group owner: ACME Communications Inc. (acq 1-7-2004).

KTEL-TV—Analog channel: 25. On air date: 2001. Box 30068, Albuquerque, NM 87190. 2400 Monroe St. N. E., Albuquerque, NM 87110. Phone: (505) 884-5353. Fax: (505) 889-8390. E-mail: gzavala@kteltv.com. Licensee: Ramar Communications II Ltd. Group owner: (group owner; (acq 8-10-99; $10,000)..

Key Personnel:
Ray Moran . . . . . CEO
Brad Moran . . . . . pres
Gabriel Zavala . . . . . gen mgr

KTFQ-TV—Analog channel: 14. On air date: Apr 28, 1999. 211 Montano Rd. N.W., Suite A, Albuquerque, NM 87107. Phone: (505) 345-0014. Fax: (505) 345-4217. Web Site: www.paxalbuquerque.tv. Licensee: TeleFutura Albuquerque LLC. Group owner: Univision Communications Inc. (acq 5-30-03; $20 million). Network: TeleFutura (Spanish).

Key Personnel:
John Welch . . . . . gen mgr
Barb Wagoner . . . . . gen sls mgr
Kathy Salazar . . . . . rgnl sls mgr
Steve Vinke . . . . . chief of engrg

KTLL-TV—Analog channel: 33. On air date: 2002. Box 3757, Ramar Communications, Lubbock, TX 79452. Phone: (806) 745-3434. Fax: (806) 748-1949. Licensee: Ramar Communications II Ltd. Group owner: (group owner; (acq 1-24-2001). Network: Telemundo (Spanish).

Key Personnel:
Brad Moran . . . . . pres & gen mgr
Gabriel Zavala . . . . . gen mgr

KWBQ—Analog channel: 19. On air date: December 1998. 8341 Washington St. N.E., Albuquerque, NM 87113. Phone: (505) 797-1919. Fax: (505) 344-1145. E-mail: promotions@wb19tv.com. Web Site: www.wb19tv.com. Licensee: Acme TV Licenses of New Mexico L.L.C. Group owner: ACME Communications Inc. Network: WB.

Key Personnel:
John Greenwood . . . . . gen mgr
Kevin Tucker . . . . . gen sls mgr
Jamie McDowell . . . . . prom mgr & adv mgr
Julie Baldwin . . . . . progmg dir
Tony Liperato . . . . . chief of engrg

Clovis

see Amarillo, TX market

Las Cruces

see El Paso, TX market

Portales

see Amarillo, TX market

Santa Fe

see Albuquerque-Santa Fe, NM market

New York

Albany-Schenectady-Troy, NY (DMA 55)

WCDC—Analog channel: 19. On air date: Feb 5, 1954. 341 Northern Blvd., Albany, NY 12204. Phone: (518) 436-4822. Fax: (518) 462-6065. E-mail: news@news10.com. Web Site: www.wten.com. Licensee: Young Broadcasting of Albany Inc. Group owner: Young Broadcasting Inc. (acq 10-11-89; grpsl; 9-11-89). Network: ABC. Washington Atty: Wiley, Rein & Fielding. News staff: 37; News: 15 hrs wkly.

WEWB—Analog channel: 45. On air date: Sept 27, 1993. 14 Corporate Woods Blvd., Albany, NY 12211. Phone: (518) 431-3150. Fax: (518) 431-3155. E-mail: questions@wb45.com. Web Site: www.wb45.com. Licensee: WEWB L.L.C. Group owner: Tribune Broadcasting Co. (acq 9-8-99; $18.5 million).. Network: WB.
Key Personnel:
Diane Howard . . . VP & gen mgr
Daniel Houtz . . . mktg dir
Lisa Henderson . . . pub affrs dir
Franco LaPietra. . . . chief of engrg

***WMHT**—Analog channel: 17. On air date: May 2, 1962. Box 17, Schenectady, NY 12301. 17 Fern Ave., Schenectady, NY 12306. Phone: (518) 357-1700. Fax: (518) 357-1709. Web Site: www.wmht.org. Licensee: WMHT Educational Telecommunications. Network: PBS. Washington Atty: Schwartz, Woods & Miller.

WNYA—Analog channel: 51.Not on air, target date: unknown: Venture Technologies Group LLC, 5670 Wilshire Blvd., Suite 1300, Los Angeles, CA 90036. Phone: (323) 965-5400. Permittee: Venture Technologies Group LLC.. Ownership: Lawrence H. Rogow (acq 7-30-2003).

WNYT—Analog channel: 13. On air date: June 15, 1956. Box 4035, 715 N. Pearl St., Albany, NY 12204. Phone: (518) 436-4791. Fax: (518) 436-8524. Web Site: www.wnyt.com. Licensee: WNYT-TV LLC. Group owner: Hubbard Broadcasting Inc. (acq 9-19-96). Network: NBC.

WRGB—(Schenectady).Analog channel: 6. On air date: Jan 13, 1928. 1400 Balltown Rd., Schenectady, NY 12309. Phone: (518) 346-6666. Fax: (518) 381-3721 (sls). Fax: (518) 381-3707 (progm). Web Site: www.wrgb.com. Licensee: Freedom Broadcasting of New York Licensee L.L.C. Group owner: Freedom Communications Inc. (acq 3-4-86; FTR: 11-25-85). Network: CBS. Rep: TeleRep. Washington Atty: Latham & Watkins. News: 25 hrs wkly.
Key Personnel:
Alan Bell . . . CEO
Doreen Wade . . . pres
Matt Sames . . . gen sls mgr
Robert Hewitt . . . natl sls mgr
Lisa Jackson . . . prom mgr & pub affrs dir
Robert J. Furlong . . . VP, gen mgr & progmg mgr
Beau Duffy. . . . news dir
Fred Lass . . . engrg dir & chief of engrg

WTEN—Analog channel: 10. On air date: Oct 14, 1953. 341 Northern Blvd., Albany, NY 12204. Phone: (518) 436-4822. Fax: (518) 462-6065. E-mail: news@news10.com. Web Site: www.wten.com. Licensee: Young Broadcasting of Albany Inc. Group owner: Young Broadcasting Inc. (acq 10-11-89; grpsl). Network: ABC. Washington Atty: Wiley, Rein & Fielding. News staff: 50; News: 22 hrs wkly.
Key Personnel:
Rene Laspina. . . . pres & gen mgr
Vera Hope . . . gen sls mgr
Terry Kowalski . . . natl sls mgr, mktg mgr & adv mgr
Renee Laspina . . . progmg dir & news dir
Herald Lansing . . . . chief of engrg

WXXA-TV—Analog channel: 23. On air date: July 30, 1982. 28 Corporate Cir., Albany, NY 12203. Phone: (518) 862-2323. Phone: (518) 862-0995. Fax: (518) 862-0865. Fax: (518) 862-0930. Web Site: www.fox23news.com. Licensee: Clear Channel Broadcasting Inc. Group owner: Clear Channel Communications Inc. (acq 12-1-94; $25.5 million). Network: Fox. Rep: Millennium Sales & Marketing. News staff: 45; News: 10 hrs wkly.
Key Personnel:
Lowry Mays . . . CEO
Bill Moll . . . pres & exec VP
Steve Kimctian . . . exec VP
Jeffrey Whitson . . . gen mgr
Chuck Hunt . . . sls dir
Ardelle Hirsch . . . natl sls mgr & mktg
Paul Pelliccia . . . progmg dir
Gene Ross. . . . news dir
Sargent Cathrall . . . chief of engrg

WYPX—Analog channel: 55. On air date: Dec 14, 1987. 1 Charles Blvd, Albany, NY 12284. Phone: (518) 464-0143. Fax: (518) 464-0633. Web Site: www.pax.tv. Licensee: Channel 55 of Albany Inc. Group owner: Paxson Communications Corp. (acq 6-1-96; $2.5 million). Rep: NBC TV Stations Sales. News: 5 hrs wkly.
Key Personnel:
Dean Goodman . . . CEO
Lowell "Bud" Paxson . . . chmn
Steve Baboulis . . . stn mgr
Laura Dubossarsky . . . opns mgr
Tony McManus. . . . gen sls mgr
Charmaine Ushkow . . . natl sls mgr & rgnl sls mgr
Alana Feldman. . . . prom mgr
Claude Pine . . . pub affrs dir & chief of engrg

Binghamton, NY (DMA 154)

WBNG-TV—Analog channel: 12. Digital channel: 21. On air date: Dec 1, 1949. 560 Columbia Dr., Johnson City, NY 13790. Phone: (607) 729-8812. Fax: (607) 797-6211. E-mail: wbng@wbngtv.com. Web Site: www.wbng.com. Licensee: Television Station Group License Subsidiary LLC. Group owner: Television Station Group LLC (acq 10-27-2000; grpsl). Network: CBS. Rep: TeleRep. Washington Atty: Bryan Cave. News: 17 hrs wkly.
Key Personnel:
Joseph McNamara. . . . gen mgr
Bob Krummunecker . . . gen sls mgr
Kate Garger . . . progmg dir
Greg Catlin. . . . news dir
Mike Calkins . . . chief of engrg

WICZ-TV—Analog channel: 40. Digital channel: 8. On air date: Nov 1, 1957. 4600 Vestal Pkwy. E., Vestal, NY 13850. Phone: (607) 770-4040. Fax: (607) 798-7950. E-mail: fox40@wicz.com. Web Site: www.wicz.com. Licensee: Stainless Broadcasting L.P. Group owner: Northwest Broadcasting Inc. (acq 7-15-97; $16 million cash-out merger with KTVZ(TV) Bend, OR). Network: Fox. Washington Atty: Leventhal, Senter & Lerman. News staff: 13; News: 2 hrs wkly.
Key Personnel:
Brian Brady . . . CEO
Bill Quarles . . . CFO
John Leet . . . gen mgr

WIVT—Analog channel: 34. On air date: Nov 25, 1962. 203 Ingraham Hill Rd., Binghamton, NY 13903. Phone: (607) 771-3434. Fax: (607) 723-1034. Web Site: www.NewsChannel34.com. Licensee: Central NY News Inc. Group owner: Clear Channel Communications Inc. (acq 6-14-02; grpsl). Network: ABC. Rep: Blair Television.
Key Personnel:
Steve Kimatian. . . . pres
John Birchall . . . VP, gen mgr & gen sls mgr
John King . . . opns VP, engrg VP & chief of engrg
Abiodun Sadik . . . chief of opns
Maura Burtis. . . . natl sls mgr & rgnl sls mgr
Jim La Vasser . . . prom mgr
Dan Stein . . . progmg dir
Lisa Lovell Ayers . . . news dir

***WSKG-TV**—Analog channel: 46. On air date: May 12, 1968. Box 3000, Binghamton, NY 13902. 601 Gates Rd., Vestal, NY 13850. Phone: (607) 729-0100. Fax: (607) 729-7328. Fax: (607) 231-0996. E-mail: wskg_mail@pbs.org. Web Site: www.wskg.com. Licensee: WSKG Public Telecommunications Council. Network: PBS. Washington Atty: Dow, Lohnes & Albertson.
Key Personnel:
Gary Reinbolt . . . CEO & pres
Nancy Christensen. . . . opns dir & gen sls mgr

Buffalo, NY (DMA 46)

WGRZ-TV—Analog channel: 2. On air date: Aug 14, 1954. 259 Delaware Ave., Buffalo, NY 14202. Phone: (716) 849-2222. Fax: (716) 849-7602. Web Site: www.wgrz.com. Licensee: Multimedia Entertainment Inc. Group owner: Gannett Broadcasting (acq 1-27-97; grpsl). Network: NBC.
Key Personnel:
Jim Toellner . . . pres & gen mgr
Boomer Connell . . . opns dir & engrg dir
Bill Shepard . . . gen sls mgr
David Luka . . . natl sls mgr
Allise Sikes . . . mktg dir & prom dir
Paulette Harris. . . . progmg mgr
Ellen Crooke . . . news dir

WIVB-TV—Analog channel: 4. On air date: May 14, 1948. 2077 Elmwood Ave., Buffalo, NY 14207. Phone: (716) 874-4410. Fax: (716) 879-4896. Web Site: www.wivb.com. Licensee: WIVB Broadcasting L.L.C. Group owner: LIN Television Corporation (acq 12-16-97). Network: CBS. Washington Atty: Covington & Burling.
Key Personnel:
Dan Meyers . . . gen mgr, mktg mgr & adv mgr
Diane Breen . . . progmg dir
John Merrill . . . chief of engrg

WKBW-TV—Analog channel: 7. On air date: Nov 30, 1958. 7 Broadcast Plaza, Buffalo, NY 14202. Phone: (716) 845-6100. Fax: (716) 842-1855. Fax: TWX: 710-522-1846. Web Site: www.wkbw.com. Licensee: Granite Broadcasting Corp. Group owner: (group owner; acq 1995; $13.42 million). Network: ABC. Rep: TeleRep. Washington Atty: Akin, Gump, Strauss, Haver & Feld.
Key Personnel:
William Ransom. . . . gen mgr
Harry Norton . . . chief of engrg

***WNED-TV**—Analog channel: 17. On air date: Mar 30, 1959. Box 1263, Buffalo, NY 14240. Horizons Plaza, 140 Lower Terr., Buffalo, NY 14202. Phone: (716) 845-7000. Fax: (716) 845-7036. Web Site: www.wned.org. Licensee: Western New York Public Broadcasting Association. Network: PBS. Washington Atty: Schwartz, Woods & Miller.
Key Personnel:
Donald Boswell . . . CEO & pres
Michael Trapper . . . CFO, gen sls mgr, mktg mgr & adv mgr
Richard Daly . . . sr VP & film buyer
Ron Santora . . . progmg dir
John Herrington. . . . chief of engrg

WNGS—Analog channel: 67. On air date: 1997. 9279 Dutch Hill Rd., West Valley, NY 14171. Phone: (716) 942-3000. Fax: (716) 942-3010. Web Site: www.wngstv.com. Licensee: EBC Buffalo Inc. Group owner: Equity Broadcasting Corp. (acq 6-25-2004; $5 million).. Network: UPN.
Key Personnel:
Caroline Powley. . . . gen mgr
Martin Bininsz . . . rgnl sls mgr
Bill Smith . . . progmg VP

WNLO—Analog channel: 23. On air date: May 13, 1987. 2077 Elmwood Ave., Buffalo, NY 14207. Phone: (716) 874-4410. Fax: (716) 879-4896. Web Site: www.wivb.com. Licensee: WIVB Broadcasting L.L.C. Group owner: LIN Television Corporation (acq 6-6-2001; $26.2 million).. Network: CBS. Washington Atty: Covington & Burling.
Key Personnel:
Dan Meyers . . . mktg mgr & adv mgr
Diane Breen . . . progmg dir
John Merrill . . . chief of engrg

WNYB—Analog channel: 26. On air date: Sept 24, 1988. 5775 Big Tree Rd., Orchard Park, NY 14127. Phone: (716) 662-2659. Fax: (716) 667-2499. E-mail: wnyb@tct-net.org. Web Site: www.tct.tv. Licensee: Faith Broadcasting Network Inc. Group owner: Tri-State Christian Television (acq 5-7-02).

WNYO-TV—Analog channel: 49. On air date: Sept 2, 1987. 699 Hertel Ave., Suite 100, Buffalo, NY 14207. Phone: (716) 875-4949. Fax: (716) 875-4919. Web Site: www.wb49.net. Licensee: New York Television Inc. Group owner: Sinclair Broadcast Group Inc. (acq 12-10-01; $51.5 million. for stock).

WPXJ-TV—Analog channel: 51. On air date: 2000. 601 Clearwater Park Rd., West Palm Beach, FL 33401. 259 Delaware Ave., Buffalo, NY 14202. Phone: (716) 852-1818. Fax: (716) 852-8288. Web Site: www.pax.tv. Permittee: Paxson Communications Corp. (acq 7-15-97; $3 million). Network: PAX TV.
Key Personnel:
Lou Friefeld. . . . VP
Ken Beedle . . . gen mgr
Barb Lipka . . . opns mgr

WUTV—Analog channel: 29. On air date: Dec 21, 1970. 951 Whitehaven Rd., Grand Island, NY 14072. Phone: (716) 773-7531. Fax: (716) 773-5753. Licensee: WUTV Licensee LLC. Group owner: Sinclair Broadcast Group Inc. (acq 12-10-01; grpsl). Network: Fox. Rep: Katz Radio, Harrington, Righter & Parsons. Washington Atty: Arter & Hadden.

Key Personnel:
Donald Moran . . . . . gen mgr
Rick Chiaino. . . . . gen sls mgr
Andrea Glinski. . . . . rgnl sls mgr & mktg mgr
Jon May . . . . . progmg dir, progmg mgr & pub affrs dir
Michael Anger . . . . . chief of engrg

Elmira, NY (DMA 173)

WENY-TV—Analog channel: 36. On air date: Nov 19, 1969. 474 Old Ithaca Rd., Horseheads, NY 14845. Phone: (607) 739-3636. Fax: (607) 739-1418. E-mail: info@weny.com. Web Site: www.weny.com. Licensee: Lilly Broadcasting L.L.C. (acq 10-17-99; $4.8 million).. Network: ABC. Washington Atty: Cordon & Kelly. News: 10 hrs wkly.
Key Personnel:
Kevin Lilly . . . . . CEO & pres
Brian Lilly. . . . . exec VP & VP
Nick White . . . . . VP
Jason Arnold . . . . . gen mgr, stn mgr & opns mgr

WETM-TV—Analog channel: 18. On air date: Sept 10, 1956. Box 1207, Elmira, NY 14901. 101 E. Water St., Elmira, NY 14901. Phone: (607) 733-5518. Fax: (607) 734-1176. E-mail: info@wetmtv.com. Web Site: www.wetmtv.com. Licensee: Central NY News Inc. Group owner: Smith Broadcasting Group Inc. (acq 10-1-2004; $13 million).. Network: NBC. Rep: Katz Radio. Washington Atty: Hogan & Hartson. News staff: 21; News: 14 hrs wkly.
Key Personnel:
Randy Reid. . . . . gen mgr & progmg dir
Bob Cibulsky . . . . . gen sls mgr & rgnl sls mgr
Steve Lucarelli . . . . . natl sls mgr
Nicola Pytell . . . . . prom dir
Scott Nichols . . . . . news dir
Chris Zell . . . . . chief of engrg

***WSKA**—Analog channel: 30.Not on air, target date: unknown: Box 3000, Binghamton, NY 13902-3000. Phone: (607) 729-0100. Fax: (607) 729-7328. Web Site: www.wskg.com. Permittee: WSKG Public Telecommunications Council. Network: PBS.
Key Personnel:
Gary Reinbolt. . . . . gen mgr
Linda Cohen. . . . . gen sls mgr
Suzanne Miller-Cormier . . . . . mktg mgr
Shannon Murdie. . . . . adv mgr
Michael Pufky . . . . . chief of engrg

WYDC—Analog channel: 48. On air date: September 1994. 33 E. Market St., Corning, NY 14830. Phone: (607) 937-5000. Fax: (607) 937-4019. E-mail: jmattison@wydctv.com. Web Site: www.wydctv.com. Licensee: WYDC Inc.. Ownership: Bill Christian, CEO (acq 11-19-97; $1.75 million).. Network: Fox. Washington Atty: Drinker Biddle & Reath LLP.

New York (DMA 1)

WABC-TV—Analog channel: 7. Digital channel: 45. On air date: Aug 10, 1948. 7 Lincoln Sq., New York, NY 10023. Phone: (212) 456-7777. Fax: (212) 456-2290. Web Site: www.7online.com. Licensee: ABC Inc. Group owner: (group owner). Network: ABC.
Key Personnel:
Dave Davis . . . . . pres & gen mgr
Evelyn del Cerro . . . . . opns mgr
Scott Simensky. . . . . sls VP & gen sls mgr
Debra O'Connell . . . . . mktg dir & mktg mgr
Art Moore . . . . . progmg VP & progmg dir
Kenny Plotnik. . . . . news dir
Saundra Thomas. . . . . pub affrs dir
Bill Beam . . . . . engrg VP & engrg dir
Kurt Hanson . . . . . chief of engrg

WCBS-TV—Analog channel: 2. Digital channel: 56. On air date: July 1, 1941. 524 W. 57 St., New York, NY 10019. Phone: (212) 975-4321. Fax: (212) 975-9387. E-mail: cbsnewyork@cbs.com. Web Site: www.cbs2ny.com. Licensee: CBS Broadcasting Inc. Group owner: Viacom Television Stations Group. Network: CBS. Rep: CBS Spot Sales.

***WEDW**—Analog channel: 49. Digital channel: 52. On air date: Dec 17, 1967. 1049 Asylum Ave., Hartford, CT 06105. Phone: (860) 278-5310. Fax: (860) 275-7403. Web Site: www.cptv.org. Licensee: Connecticut Public Broadcasting. Network: PBS.
Key Personnel:
Jerry Franklin . . . . . pres, gen mgr & engrg VP
Meg Sakellarides. . . . . CFO
Larry Rifkin. . . . . exec VP
Haig Papasian . . . . . opns VP
Joseph Zareski . . . . . opns dir & chief of engrg
Christopher Flynn. . . . . dev VP & news dir

***WFME-TV**—Analog channel: 66. Digital channel: 29. On air date: 1997. 289 Mt. Pleasant Ave., West Orange, NJ 07052. Phone: (973) 736-3600. Fax: (973) 736-4832. Fax: (510) 562-1023. E-mail: wfme@wfme.net. Web Site: www.familyradio.com. Licensee: Family Stations Inc. Group owner: (group owner).
Key Personnel:
Harold Camping. . . . . pres & gen mgr
Charles Menut. . . . . stn mgr
Charles H. Menut. . . . . opns mgr & chief of engrg

WFTY-TV—Analog channel: 67. On air date: November 1973. 3200 Expressway Dr. S., Islandia, NY 11749. Phone: (631) 582-6700. Fax: (631) 582-8337. Web Site: www.univision.com. Licensee: Univision New York LLC. Group owner: Univision Communications Inc. (acq 5-21-01; grpsl). Washington Atty: Wiley, Rein & Fielding. News: 4 hrs wkly.
Key Personnel:
Cristina Schwarz . . . . . VP & gen mgr
David Marinace. . . . . chief of engrg

WFUT-TV—Analog channel: 68. On air date: Sept 29, 1974. Univison 41, 500 Frank W. Burr Blvd., 6th Fl/, Teaneck, NJ 07666. Phone: (201) 287-4141. Fax: (201) 287-9422. Licensee: Univision Partnership of New Jersey. Group owner: Univision Communications Inc. (acq 5-21-01; grpsl). Washington Atty: Shaw, Pittman.
Key Personnel:
Cristina Schwarz . . . . . gen mgr
Michelle Liebowitz . . . . . gen sls mgr
Mark Duval. . . . . mktg dir
Maria Lopez . . . . . progmg dir
David Barth . . . . . chief of engrg

***WLIW**—Analog channel: 21. Digital channel: 22. On air date: Jan 6, 1969. Box 21, Channel 21 Dr., Plainview, NY 11803. Phone: (516) 367-2100. Fax: (516) 349-0760. Web Site: www.wliw.org. Licensee: Educational Broadcasting Corp. (acq 1-31-03). Network: Network: CBS, PBS. Washington Atty: Schwartz, Woods & Miller.

WLNY—Analog channel: 55. On air date: Apr 28, 1985. 270 S. Service Rd., Suite 55, Melville, NY 11747. Phone: (631) 777-8855. Fax: (631) 777-8180. E-mail: ny55@aol.com. Web Site: www.wlnytv.com. Licensee: WLNY-TV Inc. Washington Atty: Cohn & Marks. News: 2 hrs wkly.
Key Personnel:
Marvin R. Chauvin . . . . . CEO
David Feinblatt . . . . . pres & gen mgr
Gerald Diorio . . . . . opns VP
Elliot Simmons . . . . . sls VP & rgnl sls mgr
Andy Starr . . . . . natl sls mgr
Richard Rose. . . . . news dir
Richard Mulliner . . . . . engrg mgr

WMBC-TV—Analog channel: 63. Digital channel: 18. On air date: Apr 26, 1993. 99 Clinton Rd., West Caldwell, NJ 07006. Phone: (973) 852-0300. Fax: (973) 808-5516. E-mail: info@wmbctv.com. Web Site: www.wmbctv.com. Licensee: Mountain Broadcasting Corp.. Ownership: Sun Young Joo, 92%. Washington Atty: Fleischman & Walsh. News staff: 8; News: 5 hrs wkly.
Key Personnel:
Sun Young Joo . . . . . chmn & pres
Victor C. Joo . . . . . gen mgr

WNBC—Analog channel: 4. Digital channel: 28. On air date: July 1, 1941. 30 Rockefeller Plaza, New York, NY 10112. Phone: (212) 664-4444. Fax: (212) 664-2994 (news). Licensee: NBC Telemundo License Co. Group owner: NBC TV Station Division (acq 6-5-86; grpsl). Network: NBC.
Key Personnel:
Frank Comerford . . . . . pres & gen mgr
Jennifer Sobel . . . . . CFO
Dan Forman . . . . . sr VP, stn mgr & news dir
Mathew Braatz . . . . . opns dir
Mark Lund. . . . . sls VP
Kathryn Scheets . . . . . mktg VP
David Hyman. . . . . prom VP
Vicki McDonald . . . . . prom dir
Adele Rifkin . . . . . progmg dir

***WNET**—(Newark).NJ Analog channel: 13. On air date: Jan 2, 1948. 450 W. 33rd St., New York, NY 10001-2605. Phone: (212) 560-1313. Fax: (212) 560-1314. Web Site: www.thirteen.org. Licensee: Educational Broadcasting Corp. (acq 1970). Network: PBS. Washington Atty: Leventhal, Senter & Lerman. News: 5 hrs wkly.

***WNJB**—Analog channel: 58. Digital channel: 8. On air date: June 5, 1973. Box 777, Trenton, NJ 08625-0777. 25 S. Stockton St., Trenton, NJ 08608-1832. Phone: (609) 777-5000. Fax: (609) 777-5400. Web Site: www.njn.net. Licensee: New Jersey Public Broadcasting Authority. Network: PBS. Washington Atty: Schwartz, Woods & Miller. News: 2 hrs wkly.
Key Personnel:
Elizabeth Christopherson . . . . . pres, gen mgr & engrg dir
Joseph Montuoro . . . . . chmn & progmg dir

***WNJN**—Analog channel: 50. Digital channel: 51. On air date: June 5, 1973. Box 777, Trenton, NJ 08625-0777. 25 S. Stockton St., Trenton, NJ 08608-1832. Phone: (609) 777-5000. Fax: (609) 633-2917. Web Site: www.njn.net. Licensee: New Jersey Public Broadcasting Authority. Network: PBS. Washington Atty: Schwartz, Woods & Miller. News: 3 hrs wkly.
Key Personnel:
Elizabeth G. Christopherson . . . . . gen mgr
Joann Ruscio . . . . . mktg mgr
William Schnorbus . . . . . chief of engrg

WNJU—(Linden).NJ Analog channel: 47. On air date: May 16, 1965. 2200 Fletcher Ave., 6th Floor, Fort Lee, NJ 07024. Phone: (201) 969-4247. Fax: (201) 969-4120. Web Site: www.noticiero47.com. Licensee: NBC Telemundo License Co. Group owner: Telemundo Group Inc. (acq 4-12-02; grpsl). Network: Telemundo (Spanish). Washington Atty: Hogan & Hartson.

***WNYE-TV**—Analog channel: 25. Digital channel: 24. On air date: Apr 3, 1967. 112 Tillary St., Brooklyn, NY 11201. Phone: (718) 250-5800. Fax: (718) 855-8863. E-mail: wnyemail@wnye.org. Web Site: www.wnye.org. Licensee: New York City Dept. of Info Technology & Telecommunications. Washington Atty: Arnold & Porter.
Key Personnel:
Terence M. O'Driscoll. . . . . gen mgr
Chang Kim . . . . . chief of opns & chief of engrg
Lilach Dekel. . . . . progmg mgr

WNYW—Analog channel: 5. Digital channel: 44. On air date: May 2, 1944. 205 E. 67th St., New York, NY 10021. Phone: (212) 452-5555. Fax: (212) 249-1182. Web Site: fox5ny.com. Licensee: Fox Television Stations Inc. Group owner: (group owner; acq 11-14-86; grpsl). Network: Fox.
Key Personnel:
James Clayton. . . . . VP & gen mgr
Al Shjarback . . . . . opns VP & engrg VP
Scott Mathews . . . . . news dir
Ira Sierra . . . . . pub affrs dir
Edward Harris . . . . . engrg dir

WPIX—Analog channel: 11. On air date: June 15, 1948. 220 E. 42nd St., New York, NY 10017. Phone: (212) 949-1100. Fax: (212) 210-2591. Web Site: www.wb11.com. Licensee: WPIX Inc. Group owner: Tribune Broadcasting Co. Network: WB. Rep: TeleRep. Washington Atty: Sidley & Austin. News: 19.5 hrs wkly.
Key Personnel:
Betty Ellen Berlamino . . . . . VP & gen mgr
Bob Marra . . . . . gen sls mgr
Laurel Light . . . . . opns dir & prom dir
Karen Scott . . . . . news dir

WPXN-TV—Analog channel: 31. On air date: Nov 1, 1962. 30 Rockefeller Plaza, 6th Fl., New York, NY 10112. Phone: (212) 664-4444. Fax: (212) 664-4799. Web Site: www.pax.tv. Licensee: Paxson Communications License Co. L.L.C. Group owner: Paxson Communications Corp. (acq 3-4-98; $257.5 million). Network: PAX TV.
Key Personnel:
Frank Camerford . . . . . gen mgr
Shakira Jones . . . . . opns mgr
Lew Leone . . . . . gen sls mgr
Ken Gelb . . . . . natl sls mgr
Allison Cahill . . . . . progmg dir
Jack Davidson . . . . . chief of engrg

WRNN-TV—Analog channel: 62. On air date: Dec 15, 1985. 721 Broadway, Kingston, NY 12401-3449. Phone: (845) 339-6200. Fax: (845) 339-6264. Fax: (845) 339-6210(news). E-mail: comments@rnntv.com. Web Site: www.rnntv.com. Licensee: WRNN License Co. LLC. (acq 7-31-01). Washington Atty: Baker & Hostetler. News staff: 9; News: 82 hrs wkly.
Key Personnel:
Richard French . . . . . gen mgr
Josh Golden. . . . . engrg VP

WSAH—Analog channel: 43. On air date: Sept 28, 1987. 7 Wakely St., Seymour, CT 06483. Phone: (203) 881-1153. Fax: (203) 881-1302. Licensee: WSAH License Inc. Group owner: Scripps Howard Broadcasting Co. (acq 2-27-2004; grpsl). Washington Atty: Crowell & Moring.

WTBY-TV—Analog channel: 54. On air date: Apr 19, 1981. Box 534, 11 Merrit Blvd., Fishkill, NY 12524. Phone: (845) 896-4610. Fax: (845) 896-4614. E-mail: wtby@tbn.org. Web Site: www.tbn.org. Licensee: Trinity Broadcasting of N.Y. Inc. Group owner: Trinity Broadcasting Network (acq 7-13-82; $2.97 million;. FTR: 6-21-82). Washington Atty: Joseph E. Dunne III.

Key Personnel:
Paul Crouch . . . . pres
Grace Cephas . . . . gen mgr
Paula Mitchell . . . . pub affrs dir
Paul Swartzendruber. . . . . chief of engrg

WWOR-TV—(Secaucus).NJ Analog channel: 9. Digital channel: 38. On air date: Oct 11, 1949. 9 Broadcast Plaza, Secaucus, NJ 07096. Phone: (201) 348-0009. Web Site: www.upn9.com. Licensee: Fox Television Stations Inc. Group owner: (group owner; acq 7-31-01; grpsl). News staff: 70; News: 7 hrs wkly.

Key Personnel:
James Clayton . . . . gen mgr
Al Shjarback . . . . opns VP & prom mgr

WXTV—Analog channel: 41. Digital channel: 40. On air date: Aug 4, 1968. 500 Frank W. Burr Blvd., 6th Fl., Teaneck, NJ 07666-6802. Phone: (201) 287-4141. Fax: (201) 287-9423. Fax: (201) 287-9427 (news). Licensee: WXTV License Partnership G.P. Group owner: Univision Communications Inc. (acq 1986; grpsl). Network: Univision (Spanish). Washington Atty: Shaw, Pittman. News: 17 hrs wkly.

Key Personnel:
Cristina Schwarz . . . . gen mgr
Michelle Liebowitz. . . . . sls VP & gen sls mgr
Mark Duval . . . . mktg mgr, prom dir & prom mgr
Maria D. Lopez . . . . progmg dir
David Barth . . . . chief of engrg

North Pole

see Burlington, VT-Plattsburgh, NY market

Plattsburgh

see Burlington, VT-Plattsburgh, NY market

Rochester, NY (DMA 75)

WHAM-TV—Analog channel: 13. Digital channel: 59. On air date: Sept 15, 1962. Box 20555, Rochester, NY 14602-0555. 4225 West Henrietta Rd., Rochester, NY 14623. Phone: (585) 334-8700. Fax: (585) 359-1570. Web Site: 13wham.com. Licensee: Central NY News Inc. Group owner: Clear Channel Communications Inc. (acq 6-14-2002; grpsl). Network: ABC. Rep: Millennium Sales & Marketing. Washington Atty: Wiley, Rein & Fielding. News staff: 58; News: 24 hrs wkly.

Key Personnel:
Kent Beckwith . . . . VP & gen mgr
Earol Nolan . . . . gen sls mgr
Mark Zeqer . . . . natl sls mgr
David DiProsa . . . . rgnl sls mgr
Steve Dave . . . . prom dir
Chuck Samuels . . . . news dir
Stan Manson . . . . engrg mgr
Ted McWharf . . . . engrg mgr

WHEC-TV—Analog channel: 10. Digital channel: 58. On air date: Nov 1, 1953. 191 East Ave., Rochester, NY 14604. Phone: (585) 546-5670. Fax: (585) 454-7433. Fax: (585) 546-5688. Web Site: www.10nbc.com. Licensee: WHEC-TV LLC. Group owner: Hubbard Broadcasting Inc. (acq 9-19-96). Network: NBC. Rep: Petry Television Inc.. Washington Atty: Arent, Fox, Kintner, Plotkin & Kahn. News: 22 hrs wkly.

Key Personnel:
Arnold Klinsky . . . . gen mgr
Sherron Sheridan. . . . . opns mgr

WROC-TV—Analog channel: 8. On air date: June 14, 1949. 201 Humboldt St., Rochester, NY 14610-1093. Phone: (585) 288-8400. Fax: (585) 288-7679. Web Site: www.wroctv.com. Licensee: Nexstar Finance Inc. Group owner: Nexstar Broadcasting Group Inc. (acq 12-9-99; $46 million).. Network: CBS. News staff: 40; News: 14 hrs wkly.

Key Personnel:
Tim Busch . . . . sr VP
Marc Jaromin . . . . VP & gen mgr
Don Loy . . . . stn mgr, opns mgr & progmg mgr
John Martin . . . . natl sls mgr
Sue Dobmeier . . . . prom mgr
Bob Kirk. . . . . news dir
Eric McLenbacker. . . . . chief of engrg

WUHF—Analog channel: 31. Digital channel: 28. On air date: January 1980. 360 East Ave., Rochester, NY 14604. Phone: (585) 232-3700. Fax: (585) 546-4774. Web Site: foxrochester.com. Licensee: WUHF Licensee LLC. Group owner: Sinclair Broadcast Group Inc. (acq 4-12-02; for assumption liabilities). Network: Fox. Washington Atty: Arter & Hadden. News staff: 15; News: 7 hrs wkly.

Key Personnel:
Matt Kreiner. . . . . VP & gen mgr
Don Roberts . . . . chief of opns

***WXXI-TV**—Analog channel: 21. Digital channel: 16. On air date: September 1966. Box 30021, Rochester, NY 14603-3021. 280 State St., Rochester, NY 14614. Phone: (585) 325-7500. Fax: (585) 258-0338. Web Site: www.wxxi.org. Licensee: WXXI Public Broadcasting Council. Network: PBS. Washington Atty: Schwartz, Woods & Miller. News staff: 4; News: 2 hrs wkly.

Schenectady

see Albany-Schenectady-Troy, NY market

Syracuse, NY (DMA 77)

***WCNY-TV**—Analog channel: 24. On air date: Dec 20, 1965. Box 2400, Syracuse, NY 13220-2400. 506 Old Liverpool Rd., Liverpool, NY 13088. Phone: (315) 453-2424. Fax: (315) 451-8824. E-mail: wcny-online@wcny.org. Web Site: www.wcny.org. Licensee: Public Broadcasting Council of Central New York. Network: PBS. Washington Atty: Dow, Lohnes & Albertson.

Key Personnel:
Michael A. Fields. . . . . CEO & pres
Colleen Edwards . . . . CFO
Paul Dunn . . . . stn mgr
Peter Hirsch . . . . mktg dir
David Valesky. . . . . prom dir
John Duffy. . . . . engrg VP & chief of engrg

WNYI—Analog channel: 52. On air date: 2004. 9279 Dutch Hill Rd., West Valley, NY 14171. Phone: (716) 942-3000. Fax: (716) 942-3010. Licensee: EBC Syracuse Inc. Group owner: Equity Broadcasting Corp. (acq 8-6-2004;. $5 million. with KWWF(TV) Waterloo, IA).

Key Personnel:
William M. Smith. . . . . VP
Caroline Powley. . . . . gen mgr

WNYS-TV—Analog channel: 43. On air date: Oct 7, 1989. 1000 James St., Syracuse, NY 13203. Phone: (315) 471-4343. Fax: (315) 471-8889. Web Site: www.wb43.com. Licensee: RKM Media Inc.. Ownership: Ron Philips. (acq 7-2-96). Washington Atty: Fletcher, Heald & Hildreth.

Key Personnel:
Aaron Olander . . . . gen mgr
Peter Spartano . . . . opns dir
Donald O'Connor. . . . . gen sls mgr
Krystern Bellwen . . . . natl sls mgr
Ed Kampf. . . . . rgnl sls mgr
Ed Sautter . . . . prom mgr
Megan Edwards . . . . progmg mgr
Roy Taylor. . . . . engrg dir & chief of engrg

WSPX-TV—Analog channel: 56. On air date: Nov 24, 1998. 1030 James St., Syracuse, NY 13203. Phone: (315) 477-9400. Fax: (315) 474-5082. Web Site: www.pax.tv. Licensee: Paxson Syracuse License Inc.. Ownership: Paxson Communications of Syracuse-56 Inc., 100% (acq 4-29-99).

Key Personnel:
Jim Lutton . . . . gen mgr
Chris Geiger . . . . stn mgr
Margo McCaffery . . . . opns mgr
Dave Rhea . . . . gen sls mgr & natl sls mgr
Bill Barber. . . . . chief of engrg

WSTM-TV—Analog channel: 3. On air date: Feb 15, 1950. 1030 James St., Syracuse, NY 13203. Phone: (315) 477-9400. Fax: (315) 474-5082. Web Site: www.wstm.com. Licensee: WSTM License Subisdiary Inc. Group owner: Raycom Media (acq 4-97). Network: NBC. Rep: TeleRep. Washington Atty: Covington & Burling.

Key Personnel:
Jim Lutton . . . . VP & gen mgr
Chris Geiger. . . . . gen sls mgr
Dave Rhea . . . . rgnl sls mgr

WSYR-TV—Analog channel: 9. Digital channel: 17. On air date: Sept 9, 1962. Box 699, 5904 Bridge St., East Syracuse, NY 13057. Phone: (315) 446-9999. Fax: (315) 446-9283. E-mail: newschannel9@wixt.com. Web Site: www.wixt.com. Licensee: Central NY News Inc. Group owner: Clear Channel Communications Inc. (acq 6-30-2002; grpsl). Network: ABC. Rep: Blair Television. News staff: 40; News: 19 hrs wkly.

Key Personnel:
Stephen Kimatian. . . . . pres
Theresa E. Underwood . . . . VP, gen mgr & stn mgr
John King . . . . opns dir, engrg VP & engrg dir
Sally Stamp . . . . gen sls mgr
Bill Evans . . . . natl sls mgr
Todd Guard . . . . rgnl sls mgr
Brian Damm . . . . prom dir
Vince Spicola . . . . progmg dir
Jim Tortora. . . . . news dir
Francis Fasuyi. . . . . engrg mgr
Craig Riker . . . . chief of engrg
Dick Albro . . . . chief of engrg

WSYT—Analog channel: 68. On air date: Feb 15, 1986. 1000 James St., Syracuse, NY 13203. Phone: (315) 472-6800. Fax: (315) 471-8889. Web Site: www.wsyt68.com. Licensee: WSYT Licensee L.P. Group owner: Sinclair Broadcast Group Inc. (acq 7-7-98; grpsl). Network: Fox. News: 3.5 hrs wkly.

Key Personnel:
Aaron Olander . . . . gen mgr
Peter Spartano . . . . opns dir
Donald O'Connor. . . . . gen sls mgr
Krystern Bellen. . . . . natl sls mgr
Ed Kampf. . . . . rgnl sls mgr
Jim Kirwan . . . . prom mgr
Megan Edwards. . . . . progmg dir
Robert Pritchard . . . . engrg dir

WTVH—Analog channel: 5. On air date: Dec 1, 1948. 980 James St., Syracuse, NY 13203. Phone: (315) 425-5555. Fax: (315) 425-5513. E-mail: wtvh@wtvh.com. Web Site: www.wtvh.com. Licensee: WTVH License Inc. Group owner: Granite Broadcasting Corp. Network: CBS. Rep: Harrington, Righter & Parsons. Washington Atty: Akin, Gump, Strauss, Hauer & Feld. News staff: 42; News: 24 hrs wkly.

Key Personnel:
Les Vann . . . . pres & gen mgr
Mark Manders . . . . gen sls mgr
Bill Dingman. . . . . natl sls mgr
Matt Rosenfeld. . . . . rgnl sls mgr
Molly Herwood. . . . . progmg mgr
Loren Tobia . . . . news dir & pub affrs dir
Terry Beacham . . . . chief of engrg

Troy

see Albany-Schenectady-Troy, NY market

Utica, NY (DMA 166)

WFXV—Analog channel: 33. On air date: Dec 9, 1986. 5956 Smith Hill Rd., Utica, NY 13503. Phone: (315) 337-3300. Fax: (315) 797-5409. Web Site: www.utica.tv. Licensee: Nexstar Finance Inc. Group owner: Nexstar Broadcasting Group Inc. (acq 12-31-03; grpsl). Network: Fox. Washington Atty: Arter & Hadden.

WKTV—Analog channel: 2. On air date: Dec 1, 1949. Box 2, Utica, NY 13503. 5936 Smith Hill Rd., Utica, NY 13503. Phone: (315) 733-0404. Fax: (315) 793-3498. Web Site: www.wktv.com. Licensee: Smith Media License Holdings LLC. Group owner: Smith Broadcasting Group Inc. (acq 11-8-2004; grpsl). Network: NBC. Rep: Continental Television Sales. Washington Atty: Hogan & Hartson.

Key Personnel:
Stephen Merren. . . . . exec VP
Vic Vetters . . . . gen mgr
Frank Abbadessa. . . . . rgnl sls mgr
Tom Erskine. . . . . prom mgr
Tom Coyne . . . . progmg mgr
Jerry Walsh . . . . news dir
Tom McNicholl . . . . chief of engrg

WUTR—Analog channel: 20. On air date: Feb 28, 1970. 5956 Smith Hill Rd., Utica, NY 13503. Phone: (315) 797-5220. Fax: (315) 797-5409. Web Site: www.wutr.com. Licensee: Mission Broadcasting Inc. Group owner: (group owner; acq 3-5-2004; $3.725 million).. Network: ABC.

Key Personnel:
Diane Siembab . . . . stn mgr
Jim Castellano. . . . . opns mgr & rgnl sls mgr
Steve Gienett. . . . . sls dir & gen sls mgr
Allen Williams . . . . prom mgr
Kay Howland . . . . progmg dir & news dir
Bob Hajec. chief of engrg

Watertown, NY
(DMA 175)

***WNPI-TV**—Analog channel: 18. On air date: Aug 30, 1971. 1056 Arsenal St., Watertown, NY 13601. Phone: (315) 782-3142. Fax: (315) 782-2491. Web Site: www.wpbstv.org. Licensee: St. Lawrence Valley ETV Council. Network: PBS. Washington Atty: Schwartz, Woods & Miller.
Key Personnel:
Thomas F. Hanley . . . . pres & gen mgr
Lynn Brown . . . . dev dir & progmg dir
Timothy O'Connor . . . . sls dir
Joline Furgison . . . . mktg dir & progmg mgr

***WPBS-TV**—Analog channel: 16. On air date: Aug 5, 1971. 1056 Arsenal St., Watertown, NY 13601. Phone: (315) 782-3142. Fax: (315) 782-2491. Web Site: www.wpbstv.org. Licensee: St. Lawrence Valley ETV Council. Network: PBS. Washington Atty: Schwartz, Woods & Miller.
Key Personnel:
Thomas F. Hanley . . . . pres & gen mgr
Lynn Brown . . . . dev dir & progmg dir
Timothy O'Connor . . . . sls dir

WWNY-TV—(Carthage).Analog channel: 7. On air date: Oct 22, 1954. 120 Arcade St., Watertown, NY 13601. Phone: (315) 788-3800. Fax: (315) 782-7468. Fax: (315) 788-3787. E-mail: wwny@wwnytv.net. Web Site: wwnytv.net. Licensee: United Communications Corp. Group owner: (group owner; acq 12-5-81; $8.1 million;. FTR: 6-1-81). Network: CBS. Rep: Katz Radio. Washington Atty: Wood, Maines & Brown, Chartered. News staff: 16; News: 19 hrs wkly.
Key Personnel:
Cathy Pircsuk. gen mgr
Patrick Powers . . . . gen sls mgr
Kelley Shepard . . . . mktg mgr & prom dir
Jim Corbin . . . . progmg dir
David Monroe . . . . chief of engrg

WWTI—Analog channel: 50. On air date: January 1988. Box 6250, Watertown, NY 13601. Phone: (315) 785-8850. Fax: (315) 785-0127. Web Site: newswatch50.com. Licensee: Central NY News Inc. Group owner: Clear Channel Communications Inc. (acq 6-14-02; grpsl). Network: Network: ABC, Fox. News staff: 11; News: 5 hrs wkly.
Key Personnel:
David Males . . . . gen mgr, gen sls mgr & natl sls mgr
John Moore . . . . news dir
Keith Rudes . . . . chief of engrg

North Carolina

Asheville

see Greenville-Spartanburg, SC-Asheville, NC-Anderson, SC market

Charlotte, NC
(DMA 28)

WAXN-TV—Analog channel: 64. Digital channel: 50. On air date: Oct 15, 1994. 1901 North Tryon St., Charlotte, NC 28206. Phone: (704) 338-9999. Fax: (704) 371-3131. Web Site: www.action64.com. Licensee: WSOC-TV Holdings Inc. Group owner: Cox Communications Inc. (acq 1-31-00). Rep: TeleRep. Washington Atty: Dow, Lohnes & Albertson.
Key Personnel:
Lee Armstrong . . . . pres & gen mgr
Annette Parks Taylor . . . . opns mgr
Shawn Bartelt . . . . sls dir
Cil Frazier . . . . mktg dir
Bobby Collins. . . . . prom dir
Kay Hall . . . . progmg dir
Robin Whitmeyer . . . . news dir
Jerry Black . . . . engrg dir

WBTV—Analog channel: 3. Digital channel: 23. On air date: July 15, 1949. One Julian Price Pl., Charlotte, NC 28208. Phone: (704) 374-3500. Fax: (704) 374-3614. Web Site: www.wbtv.com. Licensee: Jefferson Pilot. Group owner: Jefferson-Pilot Communications Co. Network: CBS. Washington Atty: Wiley, Rein & Fielding.
Key Personnel:
Mary Macmillan . . . . gen mgr
Don Shaw . . . . opns dir
Ron Yoslov . . . . chief of opns

WCCB—Analog channel: 18. Digital channel: 27. On air date: Dec 7, 1953. One Television Pl., Charlotte, NC 28205. Phone: (704) 372-1800. Fax: (704) 376-3415. Fax: (704) 332-7941. E-mail: wccb@fox18wccb.com. Web Site: www.fox18wccb.com. Licensee: North Carolina Broadcasting Partners. Group owner: Bahakel Communications Network: Fox. Rep: Katz Radio. News staff: one.
Key Personnel:
Jeff Arrowood. . . . . prom dir
Kimberly Seegais . . . . progmg dir
Rick Aydlett . . . . chief of engrg

WCNC-TV—Analog channel: 36. Digital channel: 22. On air date: July 9, 1967. 1001 Wood Ridge Center Dr., Charlotte, NC 28217-1901. Phone: (704) 329-3636. Fax: (704) 357-4980. Web Site: www.nbc6.com. Licensee: WCNC-TV Inc. Group owner: Belo Corp., Broadcast Division (acq 1997; grpsl). Network: NBC. Rep: Harrington, Righter & Parsons. Washington Atty: Wiley, Rein & Fielding.
Key Personnel:
Stuart B. Powell . . . . pres, VP & gen mgr
John Dolive. . . . . opns dir

WHKY-TV—Analog channel: 14. Digital channel: 40. On air date: Feb 14, 1968. Box 1059, Hickory, NC 28603. 526 Main Ave. S.E., Hickory, NC 28603. Phone: (828) 322-5115. Fax: (828) 322-8256. E-mail: whky@whky.com. Web Site: www.whky.com. Licensee: Long Communications LLC.. Ownership: Thomas E. Long, 49%; Roberta S. Long, 41%; Jeffrey Long, 10% (acq 12-31-2001; with WHKY(AM) Hickory). Washington Atty: Hardy & Carey. News staff: 4; News: 5 hrs wkly.
Key Personnel:
Thomas Long. . . . . gen mgr
Jeff Long . . . . stn mgr, natl sls mgr & prom mgr

WJZY—Analog channel: 46. On air date: Mar 9, 1987. 3501 Performance Rd., Charlotte, NC 28214. Phone: (704) 398-0046. Fax: (704) 393-8407. E-mail: info@upn46.com. Web Site: www.upn46.com. Licensee: WJZY-TV Inc. Group owner: Capitol Broadcasting Co. Inc. (acq 11-87; $1.581 million). Network: UPN. Washington Atty: Fletcher, Heald & Hildreth.
Key Personnel:
James Goodmon . . . . pres
Will Davis. VP & gen mgr
Shawn Harris . . . . sls dir
Matt Livoti . . . . gen sls mgr & rgnl sls mgr
Brian Corrigan . . . . natl sls mgr
Andre Boyd . . . . prom mgr
Joe Heaton . . . . progmg dir & pub affrs dir
John Bishop . . . . chief of engrg

***WNSC-TV**—Analog channel: 30. On air date: Jan 3, 1978. Box 11766, Rock Hill, SC 29731. 454 S. Anderson Rd., Rock Hill, SC 29731. Phone: (803) 324-3184. Fax: (803) 324-0580. Web Site: www.muetv.org. Licensee: S.C. Educ TV Commission. Network: PBS.
Key Personnel:
Maurice Bresnahan . . . . pres
John Bullington. . . . . stn mgr & progmg dir
Bruce Bauman . . . . sls dir
David Taylor . . . . chief of engrg

WSOC-TV—Analog channel: 9. Digital channel: 34. On air date: Apr 28, 1957. Box 34665, Charlotte, NC 28234. 1901 N. Tryon St., Charlotte, NC 28206. Phone: (704) 338-9999. Web Site: www.wsoctv.com. Licensee: WSOC-TV Holdings Inc. Group owner: Cox Broadcasting Inc. (acq 4-13-59; grpsl; 4-13-59). Network: ABC. Rep: TeleRep. Washington Atty: Dow, Lohnes & Albertson.
Key Personnel:
Lee Armstrong . . . . VP & gen mgr
Dave Siegler. . . . . opns mgr

***WTVI**—Analog channel: 42. On air date: Aug 27, 1965. 3242 Commonwealth Ave., Charlotte, NC 28205. Phone: (704) 372-2442. Fax: (704) 335-1358. Web Site: www.wtvi.org. Licensee: Charlotte-Mecklenburg Public Broadcasting Authority. Network: PBS. Washington Atty: Schwartz, Woods & Miller.
Key Personnel:
Elsie Garner . . . . CEO & gen mgr
Gary DeSantis. . . . . dev VP
Regina Berry . . . . progmg dir

***WUNE-TV**—Analog channel: 17. Digital channel: 54. On air date: Sept 11, 1967. Bryan Ctr., 10 T.W. Alexander Dr., Research Triangle Park, NC 27709. Phone: (919) 549-7000. Fax: (919) 549-7201. E-mail: mwhitson@unctv.org. Web Site: www.unctv.org. Licensee: University of North Carolina. Network: PBS. Washington Atty: Schwartz, Woods & Miller.
Key Personnel:
Margaret Harrison Suppler . . . . chmn & gen mgr
Tom Howe . . . . gen mgr
Bob Royster . . . . opns dir
Delores James . . . . dev dir

***WUNG-TV**—Analog channel: 58. Digital channel: 44. On air date: Sept 11, 1967. Box 14900, Bryan Ctr., 10 T.W. Alexander Dr., Research Triangle Park, NC 27709-4900. Phone: (919) 549-7000. Fax: (919) 549-7201. Web Site: www.unctv.org. Licensee: University of North Carolina. Network: PBS. Washington Atty: Schwartz, Woods & Miller.
Key Personnel:
Tom Howe . . . . gen mgr
Diane Lucas . . . . progmg dir
Steve Volstad . . . . mktg

WWWB—Analog channel: 55. On air date: October 1994. 3501 Performance Rd., Charlotte, NC 28214. Phone: (704) 398-0046. Fax: (704) 393-8407. E-mail: info@charlotteswb.com. Web Site: www.charlotteswb.com. Licensee: WWWB-TV Inc. Group owner: Capitol Broadcasting Co. Inc. (acq 2—00; $4.5 million).. Network: WB.
Key Personnel:
Jim Goodmon . . . . pres
Will Davis. VP & gen mgr
Shawn Harris. . . . . sls dir
Brian Corrigan . . . . natl sls mgr
Gary Shields. . . . . rgnl sls mgr
Robin Symes . . . . mktg dir
Andre Boyd . . . . prom mgr
Joe Heaton . . . . progmg dir & pub affrs dir
John Bishop . . . . chief of engrg

Durham

see Raleigh-Durham (Fayetteville), NC market

Fayetteville

see Raleigh-Durham (Fayetteville), NC market

Greensboro-High Point-Winston Salem, NC
(DMA 48)

WFMY-TV—Analog channel: 2. On air date: Sept 22, 1949. Box TV2, Greensboro, NC 27420. 1615 Phillips Ave., Greensboro, NC 27405. Phone: (336) 379-9369. Fax: (336) 273-3444. E-mail: news2@wfmy.com. Web Site: www.wfmynews2.com. Licensee: WFMY Television Corp. Group owner: Gannett Broadcasting (division of Gannett Co. Inc.) (acq 2-1-88). Network: CBS. News: 32 hrs wkly.
Key Personnel:
Deborah Hooper. . . . . pres, gen mgr & progmg dir
Andy Hitchcock . . . . opns dir
Bill Lancaster . . . . gen sls mgr
Ken Crandall . . . . rgnl sls mgr
Cecilia Adams. . . . . mktg mgr & prom mgr
David Briscse . . . . progmg mgr
Darren Richards. news dir
Shirley Frye . . . . pub affrs dir
Jim Walton . . . . chief of engrg

WGHP—Analog channel: 8. Digital channel: 35. On air date: Oct 14, 1963. HP-8, High Point, NC 27261. 2005 Francis St., High Point, NC 27263. Phone: (336) 841-8888. Fax: (336) 841-8051. Licensee: Fox Television Stations Inc. Group owner: (group owner; acq 1-96; $135 million with WBRC-TV Birmingham, AL). Network: Fox. Washington Atty: Koteen & Naftalin. News staff: 75; News: 32 hrs wkly.

WGPX—Analog channel: 16. Digital channel: 14. On air date: Aug 7, 1984. 1114 N. O'Henry Blvd., Greensboro, NC 27405. Phone: (336) 703-6135. Fax: (336) 703-6138. Web Site: www.pax.tv. Licensee: Paxson Greensboro License Inc. Group owner: Paxson Communications Corp. (acq 1996; $5.5 million). Network: PAX TV. Rep: Roslin. Washington Atty: Baraff, Koerner, Olender & Hochberg.
Key Personnel:
Denise Sappington . . . . rgnl sls mgr
Bruce Hart. chief of engrg

Broadcasting & Cable Yearbook 2006

B-67

WLXI-TV—Analog channel: 61. Digital channel: 43. On air date: Mar 1, 1984. 2109 Patterson St., Greensboro, NC 27407. Phone: (336) 855-5610. Fax: (336) 855-3645. Licensee: Radiant Life Ministries Inc. Group owner: Tri-State Christian Television (acq 10-7-91; $1.9 million; 10-28-91). Washington Atty: Joseph E. Dunne III.

WTWB-TV—Analog channel: 20. On air date: Oct 30, 1985. 622-G Guilford College Rd., Greensboro, NC 27409. Phone: (336) 510-2020. Fax: (336) 517-2020. Web Site: wtwb.com. Licensee: WTWB of the Triad LLC. Group owner: Pappas Telecasting Companies (acq 1995; $4 million).. Rep: TeleRep. Washington Atty: Paul, Hastings, Janofsky & Walker LLP.
Key Personnel:
Kathi Lester . . . gen mgr
Michelle Harper . . . gen sls mgr
Mindy Bloom . . . sls dir & natl sls mgr
David Edrington . . . progmg mgr
Don Moore . . . chief of engrg

***WUNL-TV**—Analog channel: 26. Digital channel: 32. On air date: Feb 22, 1973. Box 14900, Research Triangle Park, NC 27709-4900. Bryan Ctr., 10 T.W. Alexander Dr., Research Triangle Park, NC 27709-4900. Phone: (919) 549-7000. Fax: (919) 549-7201. E-mail: mwhitson@unctv.org. Web Site: www.unctv.org. Licensee: University of North Carolina. Network: PBS. Washington Atty: Schwartz, Woods & Miller.
Key Personnel:
Margaret Harrison Suppler . . . chmn & gen mgr
Tom Howe . . . gen mgr
Bob Royster . . . opns dir
Delores James . . . dev dir

WUPN-TV—Analog channel: 48. On air date: May 9, 1981. 3500 Myer Lee Dr., Winston Salem, NC 27101. Phone: (336) 274-4848. Fax: (336) 723-8217. Web Site: www.upn48.com. Licensee: WUPN Licensee LLC. Group owner: Sinclair Broadcast Group Inc. (acq 12-10-01; $50,000. and cancellation of debt). Network: UPN. Rep: Millennium Sales & Marketing. Washington Atty: Arter & Hadden. News: 7 hrs wkly.

WXII-TV—Analog channel: 12. On air date: Sept 30, 1953. 700 Coliseum Dr., Winston-Salem, NC 27116. Phone: (336) 721-9944. Fax: (336) 721-0856. Web Site: www.wxii12.com. Licensee: WXII Hearst-Argyle Television Inc. Group owner: Hearst-Argyle Television Inc. (acq 3-18-99; grpsl). Network: NBC. Washington Atty: Brooks, Pierce, McLendon, Humphrey & Leonard.
Key Personnel:
David Barrett . . . CEO, pres & sr VP
Harry Hawks . . . CFO
Terry Mackin . . . exec VP
Henry E. Price . . . gen mgr
Michael Pulitzer . . . stn mgr

WXLV-TV—Analog channel: 45. On air date: Sept 24, 1979. 3500 Myer-Lee Dr., Winston-Salem, NC 27101. Phone: (336) 722-4545. Fax: (336) 723-8217. Web Site: www.abc45.com. Licensee: WXLV Licensee LLC. Group owner: Sinclair Broadcast Group Inc. (acq 12-10-01; grpsl). Network: ABC. Washington Atty: Arter & Hadden. News: 2.5 hrs wkly.

Greenville-New Bern-Washington, NC (DMA 105)

WCTI—(New Bern).Analog channel: 12. On air date: Sept 1, 1963. Box 12325, 225 Glenburnie Dr., New Bern, NC 28561. Phone: (252) 638-1212. Fax: (252) 637-4141. Fax: (252) 636-6855. Web Site: www.thenewsleader.com. Licensee: Newport License Holdings Inc.. Ownership: Newport Broadcasting Inc., 100% (acq 4-29-2004; $4 million).. Network: ABC. Rep: Continental Television Sales. Washington Atty: Koteen & Naftalin.
Key Personnel:
Sandy DiPasquale . . . pres
Clay Milstead . . . VP & gen mgr

WEPX—Analog channel: 38. On air date: Dec 9, 1998. 3398 S. Memorial Dr., Suite E, Greenville, NC 27834. Phone: (252) 756-0814. Fax: (252) 756-9250. Licensee: Paxson Greenville License Inc. Group owner: Paxson Communications Corp. (acq 4-13-99; $3.55 million).

WFXI—Analog channel: 8. On air date: Nov 1, 1989. Box 2069, 5441 Hwy. 70E., Morehead City, NC 28557. Phone: (252) 240-0888. Fax: (252) 240-2028. Web Site: www.fox8fox14.com. Licensee: Piedmont Television of Eastern Carolina License LLC. Group owner: Piedmont Television Holdings LLC (acq 1995; $4.644 million. for stn assets and $56,000 for CP). Network: Fox. Washington Atty: Cohn & Marks. News: 4 hrs wkly.
Key Personnel:
Paul Brissette . . . CEO, chmn & pres
Bill Fielder . . . exec VP
Don Fisher . . . VP, gen mgr & natl sls mgr
Scott Foley . . . opns dir
Lisa Leonard . . . gen sls mgr & rgnl sls mgr
Billy Poplin . . . rgnl sls mgr
Nicole Flowers . . . prom mgr
Linda Murphy . . . progmg dir
Andrea Griffith . . . news dir
Ed Schmidt . . . chief of engrg

WITN-TV—(Washington).Analog channel: 7. Digital channel: 32. On air date: Sept 28, 1955. Box 468, Hwy. 17 S., Washington, NC 27889. Phone: (252) 946-3131. Fax: (252) 946-0550. E-mail: witn@witntv.com. Web Site: www.witntv.com. Licensee: Gray Television Licensee Inc. Group owner: Gray Television Inc. (acq 8-1-97; $39.4 million).. Network: NBC.
Key Personnel:
Michael D. Weeks . . . VP & gen mgr
Michael Riddle . . . opns mgr

WNCT-TV—Analog channel: 9. On air date: Dec 22, 1953. Box 898, Greenville, NC 27835-0898. 3221 South Evans St., Greenville, NC 27834. Phone: (252) 355-8500. Fax: (252) 355-8568. Web Site: www.wnct.com. Licensee: Media General Broadcasting Inc. Group owner: Media General Broadcast Group (acq 3-21-97; grpsl). Network: CBS. Rep: MMT. Washington Atty: Dow, Lohnes & Albertson.
Key Personnel:
Vickie E. Storm . . . gen mgr
Nancy Davis . . . gen sls mgr
Melissa Pleas . . . news dir
Bertie Cartwright . . . chief of engrg

WPXU-TV—Analog channel: 35.Not on air, target date: unknown: c/o WEPX, 3398 S. Memorial Dr., Suite E, Greenville, NC 27834. Phone: (252) 439-0538. Fax: (252) 439-0638. Permittee: Paxson Jacksonville License Inc. Group owner: Paxson Communications Corp. (acq 10-1-99; $200,000)..
Key Personnel:
John O. Lewis . . . gen mgr & sls dir
Bob Young . . . stn mgr & natl sls mgr
Sean Springman . . . gen sls mgr
Sean Springman . . . rgnl sls mgr
Dave Hutchings . . . engrg dir

***WUND-TV**—Analog channel: 2. Digital channel: 20. On air date: Sept 10, 1965. Box 14900, Research Triangle Park, NC 27709-4900. Bryan Ctr., 10 T.W. Alexander Dr., Research Triangle Park, NC 27709. Phone: (919) 549-7000. Fax: (919) 549-7201. E-mail: mwhitson@unctv.org. Web Site: www.unctv.org. Licensee: University of North Carolina. Network: PBS.
Key Personnel:
Margaret Harrison Suppler . . . chmn
Tom Howe . . . gen mgr
Bob Royster . . . opns dir
Delores James . . . dev dir

***WUNK-TV**—Analog channel: 25. On air date: 1972. Box 14900, Research Triangle Park, NC 27709-4900. Bryan Ctr., 10 T.W. Alexander Dr., Research Triangle Park, NC 27709. Phone: (919) 549-7000. Fax: (919) 549-7201. E-mail: mwhitson@unctv.org. Web Site: www.unctv.org. Licensee: University of North Carolina. Network: PBS. Washington Atty: Schwartz, Woods & Miller. News staff: 15; News: 3 hrs wkly.
Key Personnel:
Margaret Harrison Suppler . . . chmn & gen mgr
Tom Howe . . . gen mgr
Bob Royster . . . opns dir
Delores James . . . dev dir

***WUNM-TV**—Analog channel: 19. On air date: March 1982. Box 14900, Bryan Ctr., 10 T.W. Alexander Dr., Research Triangle Park, NC 27709-4900. Phone: (919) 549-7000. Fax: (919) 549-7201. Web Site: www.unctv.org. Licensee: University of North Carolina. Network: PBS. Washington Atty: Schwartz, Woods & Miller.
Key Personnel:
Tom Howe . . . gen mgr
Steve Volstad . . . mktg dir
Diane Lucas . . . progmg dir

WYDO—Analog channel: 14. On air date: June 30, 1992. 3398 S. Memorial Dr., Suite E, Greenville, NC 27834. Phone: (252) 756-0814. Fax: (252) 756-9250. Licensee: Piedmont Television of Eastern Carolina License LLC. Group owner: GOCOM Communications Network: Fox. Washington Atty: Wilkinson, Barker, Knauer & Quinn.

High Point

see Greensboro-High Point-Winston Salem, NC market

Lumberton

see Florence-Myrtle Beach, SC market

Manteo

see Norfolk-Portsmouth-Newport News, VA market

New Bern

see Greenville-New Bern-Washington, NC market

Raleigh-Durham (Fayetteville), NC (DMA 29)

WFPX—Analog channel: 62. Digital channel: 36. On air date: Mar 14, 1985. Drawer 62, Lumber Bridge, NC 28357. 19734 NC 71 Hwy N., Lumber Bridge, NC 28357. Phone: (910) 843-3884. Phone: (910) 843-3885. Fax: (910) 843-2873. E-mail: robbierocket@pax.net. Web Site: www.pax.tv. Licensee: Paxson Communications License Co. L.L.C. Group owner: Paxson Communications Corp. (acq 10-20-97; $4.5 million). Network: PAX TV. Rep: Adam Young. Washington Atty: Baraff, Koerner, Olender & Hochberg.
Key Personnel:
Claudia Henry . . . rgnl sls mgr
Tim Walkenhorst . . . rgnl sls mgr
Robbie Brock . . . progmg dir, pub affrs dir & chief of engrg
Allen McCarty . . . engrg dir

WLFL—Analog channel: 22. Digital channel: 57. On air date: Dec 18, 1981. 3012 Highwoods Blvd., Suite 101, Raleigh, NC 27604. Phone: (919) 872-9535. Fax: (919) 878-3877. Web Site: www.wb22tv.com. Licensee: WLFL Licensee L.L.C. Group owner: Sinclair Broadcast Group Inc. Network: WB. Rep: Millennium Sales & Marketing. Washington Atty: Shaw, Pittman. News staff: 36; News: 7 hrs wkly.

WNCN—Analog channel: 17. Digital channel: 55. On air date: Apr 11, 1988. 1205 Front St., Raleigh, NC 27609. Phone: (919) 836-1717. Fax: (919) 836-1747. Web Site: www.nbc17.com. Licensee: NBC Telemundo License Co. Group owner: NBC TV Stations Division. Network: NBC. News: 30 hrs wkly.
Key Personnel:
Michael Ward . . . pres & gen mgr
John Shannon . . . sls VP
Tawnya Richardson . . . natl sls mgr
Karen Klein . . . rgnl sls mgr
Mary Ann Balbo . . . mktg mgr
Geri Howard . . . prom dir
Larry Wall . . . progmg dir & pub affrs dir
Nannette Wilson . . . news dir
Chris Stout . . . engrg mgr
Russell Mizelle . . . chief of engrg

WRAL-TV—Analog channel: 5. Digital channel: 53. On air date: Dec 15, 1956. Box 12000, Raleigh, NC 27605. 2619 Western Blvd., Raleigh, NC 27606. Phone: (919) 821-8555. Fax: (919) 821-8566. Fax: TWX: 510-928-1833. Web Site: www.wral.com. Licensee: Capitol Broadcasting Co. Inc. Group owner: (group owner) Network: CBS. Rep: TeleRep. Washington Atty: Fletcher, Heald & Hildreth. News staff: 100; News: 29.5 hrs wkly.
Key Personnel:
Jim Goodmon . . . CEO & pres
Jim Hefner . . . gen mgr
James Farmer . . . opns mgr
Quinn Koontz . . . gen sls mgr
Cindy Sink . . . prom mgr
Jimmy Goodmon . . . progmg mgr
John Harris . . . news dir
Pete Sockett . . . chief of engrg

WRAY-TV—Analog channel: 30. Digital channel: 42. On air date: 1995. 4909 Suite E. Expressway Dr., Wilson, NC 27895-3583. Phone: (252) 243-0584. Fax: (252) 237-6290. Licensee: WRAY Inc. Group owner: Scripps Howard Broadcasting Co. (acq 2-27-2004; grpsl).

WRAZ—Analog channel: 50. On air date: 1995. Box 30050, Durham, NC 27702. 512 S. Mangum St., Durham, NC 27701. Phone: (919)

595-5050. Fax: (919) 595-5028. Web Site: www.fox50.com. Licensee: WRAZ-TV Inc. Group owner: Capitol Broadcasting Co. Inc. (acq 2000; $1 million).. Network: Fox. Rep: TeleRep. Washington Atty: Holland & Knight.
Key Personnel:
James F. Goodmon . . . . CEO, pres & CFO
Thomas Schenck . . . . gen mgr
Chris Downey . . . . opns mgr
Jim Gamble. . . . . chief of opns & chief of engrg
Evelyn Booker . . . . gen sls mgr
Matthew P. Donegan . . . . natl sls mgr
Niel Sollod . . . . rgnl sls mgr
Kevin Kolbe . . . . mktg dir & prom dir
Joanne Stanley . . . . progmg mgr
John Harris . . . . news dir

WRDC—Analog channel: 28. Digital channel: 27. On air date: Nov 4, 1968. 3012 Highwoods Blvd., Raleigh, NC 27604. Phone: (919) 872-2854. Fax: (919) 878-3758. Web Site: www.wrdc28.com. Licensee: Raleigh (WRDC-TV) Licensee Inc. Group owner: Sinclair Broadcast Group Inc. (acq 11-15-01; $2.3 million. in stock). Network: UPN. Rep: Millennium Sales & Marketing. Washington Atty: Fisher, Wayland, Cooper, Leader & Zaragoza.
Key Personnel:
Neal Davis. . . . . gen mgr, sls dir & gen sls mgr
Tim Prichard. . . . . natl sls mgr
Heather Kuh. . . . . mktg mgr
Kim Rivenbark. . . . . prom mgr
Gary Todd. . . . . engrg dir
Rome Thibeaut. . . . . chief of engrg

WRPX—Analog channel: 47. Digital channel: 15. On air date: Aug 31, 1987. 1205 Front St., Suite 160, Raleigh, NC 27609. Phone: (919) 836-1717. Fax: (919) 836-1546. Web Site: www.pax.tv. Licensee: Paxson Raleigh License Inc. Group owner: Paxson Communications Corp. (acq 4-5-00; grpsl). Rep: Roslin. Washington Atty: Mitchell, Fielstra & Assoc.
Key Personnel:
John Shannon. VP, gen mgr, opns dir, sls dir, gen sls mgr & progmg mgr
Sam Garfield. . . . . chief of engrg

WTVD—Analog channel: 11. Digital channel: 52. On air date: Sept 2, 1954. 411 Liberty, Durham, NC 27701. Phone: (919) 683-1111. Fax: (919) 682-7476 (sales). Fax: (919) 682-7225. Web Site: www.abc11tv.com. Licensee: WTVD Television LLC. Group owner: (group owner; acq 5-24-57; $1,417,800; 5-3-57). Network: ABC. Washington Atty: Wilmer, Cutler & Pickering.

***WUNC-TV**—Analog channel: 4. Digital channel: 59. On air date: Jan 8, 1955. Box 14900, Research Triangle Park, NC 27709-4900. Bryan Ctr., 10 T.W. Alexander Dr., Research Triangle Park, NC 27709. Phone: (919) 549-7000. Fax: (919) 549-7201. E-mail: mwhitson@unctv.org. Web Site: www.unctv.org. Licensee: University of North Carolina. Network: PBS. Washington Atty: Schwartz, Woods & Miller.
Key Personnel:
Margaret Harrison Suppler. . . . . chmn
Tom Howe . . . . gen mgr
Bob Royster . . . . opns dir
Delores James. . . . . dev dir

***WUNP-TV**—Analog channel: 36. Digital channel: 39. On air date: 1985. Box 14900, Research Triangle Park, NC 27709-4900. Bryan Ctr., 10 T. W. Alexander Dr., Research Triangle Park, NC 27709. Phone: (919) 549-7000. Fax: (919) 549-7201. Web Site: www.unctv.org. Licensee: University of North Carolina. Network: PBS. Washington Atty: Schwartz, Woods & Miller.
Key Personnel:
Margaret Harrison Suppler . . . . chmn & gen mgr
Tom Howe. . . . . gen mgr
Bob Royster . . . . opns dir
Delores James. . . . . dev dir

WUVC-TV—Analog channel: 40. Digital channel: 38. On air date: June 1, 1981. 230 Donaldson St., 3dr Fl., ., Fayetteville, NC 28301. Lake Plaza East, 900 Ridgefield Dr., Ste. 100, Raleigh, NC 27609. Phone: (910) 323-4040. Fax: (910) 323-3924. Web Site: www.univision.com. Licensee: Capital Broadcasting Partners. Group owner: Univisiion Communications Inc. (acq 3-31-03). Network: Univision (Spanish). Washington Atty: Brooks, Pierce, McLendon, Humphrey & Leonard.
Key Personnel:
A. Jerrold Perrenchio. . . . . CEO & chmn
Michael Wortsman . . . . pres
George Blank . . . . CFO & exec VP
Maria Montano . . . . gen mgr & gen sls mgr
Todd Schlachter . . . . natl sls mgr
Lizette Cruz-Watko . . . . pub affrs dir
William Acevedo . . . . chief of engrg

Washington

see Greenville-New Bern-Washington, NC market

Wilmington, NC (DMA 140)

WECT—Analog channel: 6. On air date: Apr 9, 1954. 322 Shipyard Blvd., Wilmington, NC 28412. Phone: (910) 791-8070. Fax: (910) 392-1509. E-mail: wect@wect.com. Web Site: www.wect.com. Licensee: Raycom America License Subsidiary LLC. Group owner: Raycom Media Inc. (acq 9-12-96; grpsl). Network: NBC. Rep: Harrington, Righter & Parsons. Covington & Burling
Key Personnel:
Paul McTear. . . . . CEO & pres
John Shine . . . . gen mgr & progmg mgr
Karl Davis. . . . . gen sls mgr & natl sls mgr
Beth Young . . . . rgnl sls mgr
Herschel Howie . . . . prom mgr
Clara Ditmer . . . . film buyer & pub affrs dir
Raeford Brown . . . . news dir
Martin Layne. . . . . chief of engrg

WSFX-TV—Analog channel: 26. On air date: Sept 24, 1984. 322 Shipyard Blvd., Wilmington, NC 28412. Box 2626, Wilmington, NC 28402. Phone: (910) 343-8826. Fax: (910) 202-0493. E-mail: go'halloran@wsfx.com. Web Site: www.wfsx.com. Licensee: Southeastern Media Holdings Inc. (acq 8-5-03; $14 million).. Network: Network: Fox, UPN. Rep: MMT. Washington Atty: Baraff, Koerner, Olender & Hochberg. News staff: 6; News: news progmg2.5 hrs wkly.
Key Personnel:
Michael E. Reed . . . . CEO
Gary O'Halloran. . . . . VP, gen mgr, gen sls mgr & natl sls mgr
David Milligan . . . . opns mgr
Herschel Howie . . . . prom mgr
Mary Southerland. . . . . progmg mgr
Raeford Brown . . . . news dir
Dan Ullner. . . . . chief of engrg

***WUNJ-TV**—Analog channel: 39. On air date: 1971. Box 14900, Research Triangle Park, NC 27709-4900. Bryan Ctr., 10 T.W. Alexander Dr., Research Triangle Park, NC 27709-4900. Phone: (919) 549-7000. Fax: (919) 549-7201. Web Site: www.unctv.org. Licensee: University of North Carolina. Network: PBS. Washington Atty: Schwartz, Woods & Miller.
Key Personnel:
Tom Howe . . . . gen mgr
Steve Volstad . . . . mktg dir
Diane Lucas . . . . progmg dir

WWAY—Analog channel: 3. On air date: Oct 1, 1964. Box 2068, 615 N. Front St., Wilmington, NC 28402. Phone: (910) 762-8581. Fax: (910) 762-8367. Fax: (910) 341-7926. E-mail: jsmith@wwaytv3.com. Web Site: www.wwaytv3.com. Licensee: Libco Inc. Group owner: Liberty Corp. (acq 6-24-99; $35 million).. Network: ABC. Rep: Katz Radio.

North Dakota

Bismarck

see Minot-Bismarck-Dickinson, ND market

Dickinson

see Minot-Bismarck-Dickinson, ND market

Fargo-Valley City, ND (DMA 118)

KBRR—Analog channel: 10. On air date: July 1985. Box 9115, Fargo, ND 58106. Phone: (701) 277-1515. Fax: (701) 277-1830. Licensee: Red River Broadcast Co. L.L.C. Group owner: (group owner) Network: Fox. Washington Atty: Crowell & Moring.
Key Personnel:
Kathy Lau . . . . VP, gen mgr & progmg dir
Todd Anderson . . . CEO, pres, gen sls mgr, mktg mgr & adv mgr
Chuck Knudson. . . . . chief of engrg

***KCGE-DT**—Analog channel: 0. Digital channel: 16. On air date: October 2003. Box 3240, Fargo, ND 58108. Phone: (701) 241-6900. Fax: (701) 239-7650. E-mail: info@prairiepublic.org. Web Site: www.prairiepublic.org. Licensee: Prairie Public Broadcasting Inc. Network: PBS.

KCPM—Analog channel: 27. On air date: Jan 1, 2003. Box 9292, Fargo, ND 58106. Phone: (605) 335-3393. Fax: (605) 334-5575. Licensee: G.I.G. of North Dakota LLC. (acq 8-7-01).

***KFME**—Analog channel: 13. On air date: Jan 19, 1964. Box 3240, Fargo, ND 58108-3240. 207 N. 5th St., Fargo, ND 58102. Phone: (701) 241-6900. Fax: (701) 239-7650. E-mail: info@prairiepublic.org. Web Site: www.prairiepublic.org. Licensee: Prairie Public Broadcasting Inc. Network: PBS. Washington Atty: Dow, Lohnes & Albertson.
Key Personnel:
John E. Harris III. . . . . CEO & pres
Don Berg. . . . . VP
Nancy L. Wood. . . . . dev dir

***KGFE**—Analog channel: 2. On air date: Sept 9, 1974. Box 3240, Fargo, ND 58108-3240. 207 N. 5th St., Fargo, ND 58102. Phone: (701) 241-6900. Fax: (701) 239-7650. E-mail: info@prairiepublic.org. Web Site: www.prairiepublic.org. Licensee: Prairie Public Broadcasting Inc. Network: PBS. Washington Atty: Dow, Lohnes & Albertson.

***KJRE**—Analog channel: 19. On air date: May 12, 1992. Box 3240, Fargo, ND 58108-3240. 207 N. 5th St., Fargo, ND 58102. Phone: (701) 241-6900. Fax: (701) 239-7650. E-mail: info@prairiepublic.org. Web Site: www.prairiepublic.org. Licensee: Prairie Public Broadcasting Inc. Network: PBS. Washington Atty: Dow, Lohnes & Albertson.

KJRR—Analog channel: 7. On air date: Sept 1, 1988. Box 9115, Fargo, ND 58106. Phone: (701) 277-1515. Fax: (701) 277-1830. Licensee: Red River Broadcast Co. L.L.C. Group owner: (group owner). Network: Fox. Washington Atty: Crowell & Moring.
Key Personnel:
Myron Kunin. . . . . CEO
Ro Grignon . . . . pres
Kathy Lau. . . . . VP & gen mgr

KNRR—Analog channel: 12. On air date: 1985. Box 9115, Fargo, ND 58106. Phone: (701) 277-1515. Fax: (701) 277-1830. Licensee: Red River Broadcast Co. L.L.C. Group owner: (group owner) Network: Fox. Washington Atty: Crowell & Moring.
Key Personnel:
Menou Kunia . . . . CEO
Ro Grignon . . . . pres
Kathy Lau. . . . . VP & gen mgr

KVLY-TV—Analog channel: 11. Digital channel: 44. On air date: Oct 11, 1959. Box 1878, Fargo, ND 58107. 1350 21st Ave. S., Fargo, ND 58103. Phone: (701) 237-5211. Fax: (701) 232-0493. Fax: (701) 237-5396. E-mail: mail@kvlytv11.com. Web Site: www.kvlytv11.com. Licensee: North Dakota Television License Sub, L.L.C. Group owner: Wicks Television L.L.C. (acq 11-22-2002; grpsl). Network: NBC. Rep: Blair Television. Washington Atty: Wyrick, Robbins, Yates & Pontin. News staff: 36; News: 16 hrs wkly.
Key Personnel:
Robert D. Gluck . . . . CEO
Charley Johnson . . . . gen mgr
Jeff Petrik. . . . . opns mgr

KVRR—Analog channel: 15. On air date: Feb 14, 1983. Box 9115, Fargo, ND 58106. Phone: (701) 277-1515. Fax: (701) 277-1830. Licensee: Red River Broadcast Co L.L.C. Group owner: (group owner) Network: Fox. Washington Atty: Crowell & Moring.
Key Personnel:
Myron Kunin . . . . chmn
Ro Grignon . . . . pres
Kathy Lau. . . . . VP & gen mgr

KXJB-TV—(Valley City).Analog channel: 4. Digital channel: 38. On air date: Sept 11, 1954. 1350 21st Ave. S., Fargo, ND 58103-3313. Phone: (701) 282-0444. Fax: (701) 232-0497. E-mail: news@kvoytv11.com. Web Site: www.kx4.com. Licensee: Catamount Broadcasting of Fargo L.L.C. Group owner: Catamount Broadcast Group (acq 11-2-99). Network: CBS. Rep: Continental Television Sales. Washington Atty: Cohn & Marks. News staff: 20; News: 10 hrs wkly.

WDAY-TV—Analog channel: 6. On air date: June 1, 1953. Box 2466, Fargo, ND 58108. 301 S. 8th St., Fargo, ND 58103. Phone: (701) 237-6500. Fax: (701) 241-5368. Web Site: www.new.in-forum.com.

Licensee: Forum Communications Co. Group owner: (group owner; acq 7-20-60; $900,000; 7-25-60). Network: ABC. Rep: Katz Radio.
Key Personnel:
Lloyd Case . . . COO
William Marcil . . . CEO & pres
Mark Prather . . . gen mgr
Susan Eider . . . opns mgr
Carol Ann Horn . . . gen sls mgr
Jennifer Folden . . . progmg mgr
Tom Thompson . . . chief of engrg

WDAZ-TV—Analog channel: 8. On air date: Jan 29, 1967. Box 12639, Grand Forks, ND 58208. 2220 S. Washington, Grand Forks, ND 58208. Phone: (701) 775-2511. Fax: (701) 746-8565. E-mail: bkerr@wdaz.com. Web Site: www.wdaz.com. Licensee: Forum Communications Co. Group owner: (group owner) Network: ABC. Rep: Katz Radio. Washington Atty: Holland & Knight.
Key Personnel:
Robert Kerr . . . gen mgr
Rob Horken . . . gen sls mgr & adv dir
Mike Brue . . . news dir
Jeff Awes . . . engrg dir & chief of engrg

Minot-Bismarck-Dickinson, ND (DMA 157)

***KBME-TV**—Analog channel: 3. Digital channel: 22. On air date: June 18, 1979. Box 3240, Fargo, ND 58108-3240. 207 N. 5th St., Fargo, ND 58102. Phone: (701) 241-6900. Fax: (701) 239-7650. E-mail: info@prariepublic.org. Web Site: www.prairiepublic.org. Licensee: Prairie Public Broadcasting Inc. Network: PBS. Washington Atty: Dow, Lohnes & Albertson.
Key Personnel:
John E. Harris III . . . CEO
John Harris III . . . pres
Don Berg . . . VP
Nancy L. Wood . . . dev dir

KBMY—Analog channel: 17. On air date: Mar 31, 1985. Box 7277, Bismarck, ND 58507. 3128 E. Broadway, Bismarck, ND 58507. Phone: (701) 223-1700. Fax: (701) 258-0886. Licensee: KBMY-KMCY LLC. Group owner: Forum Communications Co. Network: ABC. Rep: Katz Radio. Washington Atty: Marmet & McCombs.

***KDSE**—Analog channel: 9. Digital channel: 20. On air date: Aug 4, 1982. Box 3240, 207 N. 5th St., Fargo, ND 58108-3240. Phone: (701) 241-6900. Fax: (701) 239-7650. E-mail: info@prairiepublic.org. Web Site: www.prairiepublic.com. Licensee: Prairie Public Broadcasting Inc. Network: PBS. Washington Atty: Dow, Lohnes & Albertson.

KFYR-TV—Analog channel: 5. On air date: Dec 19, 1953. Box 1738, Bismarck, ND 58502. 200 N. 4th St., Bismarck, ND 58502. Phone: (701) 255-5757. Fax: (701) 255-8220. Web Site: www.kfyr.com. Licensee: North Dakota Television License Sub, L.L.C. Group owner: Wicks Television L.L.C. (acq 11-22-02; grpsl). Network: NBC. Washington Atty: Hogan & Hartson. News staff: 29; News: 24 hrs wkly.
Key Personnel:
Bob Denver . . . opns dir & mktg mgr
Terry Fleck . . . sls dir & natl sls mgr
Syd Steward . . . rgnl sls mgr
Bob Hughes . . . progmg dir

KMCY—Analog channel: 14. On air date: June 22, 1985. 3128 E. Broadway, Bismarck, NC 58507. First Ave. Bldg., 131 First Ave. S.W., Minot, ND 58702. Phone: (701) 223-1700. Fax: (701) 258-0886. Licensee: KBMY-KMCY LLC. Group owner: Forum Communications Co. Network: ABC. Rep: Katz Radio. Washington Atty: Marmet & McCombs.
Key Personnel:
Kent Lein . . . gen mgr
Calvin Aberley . . . chief of engrg

KMOT—Analog channel: 10. On air date: Jan 21, 1958. Box 1120, Minot, ND 58702. 1800 S.W. 16th, Minot, ND 58702. Phone: (701) 852-4101. Fax: (701) 838-8195. Web Site: www.kmot.com. Licensee: North Dakota Television License Sub, L.L.C. Group owner: Wicks Television L.L.C. (acq 11-22-02; grpsl). Network: NBC. Washington Atty: Hogan & Hartson.

KNDX—Analog channel: 26.Not on air, target date: Nov 1999: PO Box 4026, Bismarck, ND 58502. Phone: (701) 355-0026. Fax: (701) 250-7244. Permittee: Prime Cities Broadcasting Inc. Network: Fox.

***KPSD-TV**—Analog channel: 13. Digital channel: 25. On air date: September 1973. Box 5000, Vermillion, SD 57069-5000. 555 N. Dakota St., Vermillion, SD 57069. Phone: (605) 677-5861. Phone: (800) 456-0766. Fax: (605) 677-5010. E-mail: programming@sdpb.org. Web Site: www.sdpd.org. Licensee: South Dakota Board of Directors for Educational Telecommunications. Network: PBS.
Key Personnel:
Julie Andersen . . . pres
Terry Spencer . . . dev dir & dev mgr
Bob Bosse . . . progmg dir

KQCD-TV—Analog channel: 7. On air date: July 28, 1980. Box 1577, 373 21st St. E., Dickinson, ND 58501. Phone: (701) 483-7777. Fax: (701) 483-8231. Licensee: North Dakota Television License Sub, L.L.C. Group owner: Wicks Television L.L.C. (acq 11-22-02; grpsl). Network: NBC. Washington Atty: Hogan & Hartson.
Key Personnel:
Holly Stewart . . . gen mgr
Rich Beierle . . . chief of engrg

***KQSD-TV**—Analog channel: 11. On air date: Jan 1, 1976. Box 5000, Vermillion, SD 57069-5000. 555 N. Dakota St., Vermillion, SD 57069. Phone: (605) 677-5861. Phone: (800) 456-0766. Fax: (605) 677-5010. E-mail: programming@sdpb.org. Web Site: www.sdpd.org. Licensee: South Dakota Board of Directors for Educational Telecommunications. Network: PBS.
Key Personnel:
Julie Andersen . . . pres
Craig Jensen . . . opns mgr
Terry Spencer . . . dev dir
Bob Bosse . . . progmg dir & progmg mgr

***KSRE**—Analog channel: 6. Digital channel: 57. On air date: January 1980. Box 3240, 207 N. 5th St., Fargo, ND 58108-3240. Phone: (701) 241-6900. Fax: (701) 239-7650. Web Site: www.prairiepublic.com. Licensee: Prairie Public Broadcasting. Network: PBS. Washington Atty: Dow, Lohnes & Albertson.

KUMV-TV—Analog channel: 8. On air date: Feb 11, 1957. Box 1287, Kansas City, ND 58802-1287. Phone: (701) 572-4676. Fax: (701) 572-0118. E-mail: kumvtv@nccray.com. Licensee: North Dakota Television License Sub, L.L.C. Group owner: Wicks Television L.L.C. (acq 11-22-02; grpsl). Network: NBC. News staff: 2; News: 6 hrs wkly.

***KWSE**—Analog channel: 4. Digital channel: 51. On air date: March 1983. Box 3240, 207 N. 5th St., Fargo, ND 58108-3240. Phone: (701) 241-6900. Fax: (701) 239-7650. E-mail: info@prairiepublic.org. Web Site: www.prairiepublic.org. Licensee: Prairie Public Broadcasting Inc. Network: PBS. Washington Atty: Dow, Lohnes & Albertson.

KXMA-TV—Analog channel: 2. On air date: October 1956. Drawer B, Dickinson, ND 58602. 1625 W. Villard, Dickinson, ND 58601. Phone: (701) 483-1400. Fax: (701) 483-1401. E-mail: webmasterb@kxnet.com. Web Site: www.kxma.com. Licensee: Reiten Television Inc. Group owner: (group owner; acq 12-4-84; $362,500).. Network: CBS. Washington Atty: Fisher, Wayland, Cooper, Leader & Zaragoza.
Key Personnel:
Tim Reiten . . . gen mgr
Julie Bernhardt . . . natl sls mgr
Darren Lenertz . . . rgnl sls mgr
Jeff Nelson . . . news dir
Bill Kohler . . . chief of engrg

KXMB-TV—Analog channel: 12. On air date: Nov 19, 1955. 1811 N. 15th St., Bismarck, ND 58501. Phone: (701) 223-9197. Fax: (701) 223-3320. Web Site: www.kxmb.com. Licensee: Reiten Television Inc. Group owner: (group owner; acq 1-27-71; $1.2 million;. FTR: 2-8-71). Network: CBS. Rep: Katz Radio. Washington Atty: Fisher, Wayland, Cooper, Leader & Zaragoza. News staff: 11; News: 9 hrs wkly.
Key Personnel:
Tim Reiten . . . gen mgr
Julie Bernhardt . . . natl sls mgr
Darren Lenertz . . . rgnl sls mgr
Jeff Nelson . . . news dir
Rocky Hefry . . . chief of engrg

KXMC-TV—Analog channel: 13. On air date: Apr 1, 1953. Box 1686, Minot, ND 58722. 3425 S. Broadway, Minot, ND 58701. Phone: (701) 852-2104. Fax: (701) 838-9360. Web Site: www.kxmc.com. Licensee: Reiten Television Inc. Group owner: (group owner; acq 7-31-74; FTR: 8-19-74). Network: CBS. Rep: Continental Television Sales. Washington Atty: Fisher, Wayland, Cooper, Leader & Zaragoza. News staff: 10; News: 9 hrs wkly.
Key Personnel:
David Reiten . chmn, gen mgr, opns mgr, progmg VP & film buyer
Tim Reiten . . . pres
Darren Lenertz . . . gen sls mgr, prom dir & prom mgr
Julie Bernhardt . . . natl sls mgr & rgnl sls mgr
Linda Sand . . . progmg mgr
Jim Olson . . . news dir
Carla Burbidge . . . pub affrs dir
Robert Turneau . . . chief of engrg

KXMD-TV—Analog channel: 11. On air date: Oct 25, 1969. Box 790, Williston, ND 58801. 1802 13th Ave. W., Williston, NC 58801. Phone: (701) 572-2345. Fax: (701) 572-0658. Licensee: Reiten Television Inc. Group owner: (group owner). Network: CBS. Rep: Katz Radio. Washington Atty: Fisher, Wayland, Cooper, Leader & Zaragoza.

KXND—Analog channel: 24. On air date: 2001. Prime Cities Broadcasting Inc., 112 High Ridge Ave., Ridgefield, CT 06877-4422. Phone: (203) 431-3366. Phone: (701) 355-0026. Fax: (203) 431-3864. Licensee: Prime Cities Broadcasting Inc. Network: Fox.

Valley City

see Fargo-Valley City, ND market

Ohio

Athens

see Charleston-Huntington, WV market

Cambridge

see Wheeling, WV-Steubenville, OH market

Cincinnati, OH (DMA 33)

***WCET**—Analog channel: 48. Digital channel: 34. On air date: July 26, 1954. 1223 Central Pkwy., Cincinnati, OH 45214-2890. Phone: (513) 381-4033. Fax: (513) 381-7520. E-mail: comments@cetconnect.org. Web Site: www.cerconnect.org. Licensee: Greater Cincinnati TV Educational Foundation. Network: PBS. Washington Atty: Dow, Lohnes & Albertson.
Key Personnel:
Jack Dominic . . . COO
Susan Howarth . . . CEO, pres & gen mgr

WCPO-TV—Analog channel: 9. Digital channel: 10. On air date: July 26, 1949. 1720 Gilbert Ave., Cincinnati, OH 45202. Phone: (513) 721-9900. Fax: (513) 721-7717. E-mail: bfee@wcpo.com. Web Site: www.wcpo.com. Licensee: Scripps Howard Broadcasting Co. Group owner: (group owner) Network: ABC. Washington Atty: Baker & Hostetler. News staff: 70; News: 24 hrs wkly.

***WCVN**—Analog channel: 54. Digital channel: 24. On air date: Sept 9, 1969. 600 Cooper Dr., Lexington, KY 40502. Phone: (859) 258-7000. Fax: (859) 258-7399. Web Site: www.ket.org. Licensee: Kentucky Authority for Educational TV. Network: PBS.
Key Personnel:
Malcolm Wall . . . CEO & stn mgr
Sally Hamilton . . . CFO
Craig Cornwell . . . opns mgr
Ron Griffin . . . sls dir & rgnl sls mgr
Mary Campbell . . . prom dir
Tona Barklely . . . prom mgr
Dick Hoffman . . . progmg dir
Bill Goodman . . . pub affrs dir
Robert Ball . . . engrg dir

***WKON**—Analog channel: 52. Digital channel: 44. On air date: Sept 23, 1968. c/o WKLE, 600 Cooper Dr., Lexington, KY 40502. Phone: (859) 258-7000. Fax: (859) 258-7390. Web Site: www.ket.org. Licensee: Kentucky Authority for Educational TV. Network: PBS.
Key Personnel:
Malcolm Wall . . . CEO & gen mgr
Sally Hamilton . . . CFO
Craig Cornwell . . . opns mgr
Michele Ripley . . . dev dir
Ron Griffin . . . sls dir
Mary Campbell . . . prom dir
Tona Barkley . . . prom mgr
Dick Hoffman . . . progmg dir
Bill Goodman . . . pub affrs dir
Robert Ball . . . engrg dir

WKRC-TV—Analog channel: 12. On air date: April 1949. 1906 Highland Ave., Cincinnati, OH 45219. Phone: (513) 763-5500. Fax: (513) 651-0704. Web Site: www.wkrc.com. Licensee: Citicasters Licenses Inc. (NEW). Group owner: Clear Channel Communications Inc. (acq 1999; grpsl). Network: CBS. Rep: TeleRep. Washington Atty: Hogan & Hartson.

WLWT—Analog channel: 5. Digital channel: 35. On air date: Feb 9, 1948. 1700 Young St., Cincinnati, OH 45202. Phone: (513) 412-5000. Fax: (513) 412-6121. E-mail: newsdesk@channelcincinnati.com. Web Site: www.channelcincinnati.com. Licensee: Hearst-Argyle Stations Inc. Group owner: Hearst-Argyle Television Inc. (acq 7-16-97; grpsl). Network: NBC. Rep: Eagle Television Sales. Washington Atty: Brooks, Pierce, McLendon, Humphrey & Leonard.

***WPTO**—Analog channel: 14. On air date: Oct 14, 1959. 110 S. Jefferson St., Dayton, OH 45402. Phone: (937) 220-1600. Fax: (937) 220-1642. Web Site: www.thinktv.org. Licensee: Greater Dayton Public Television Inc. 1975 Network: PBS. Washington Atty: Dow, Lohnes & Albertson. News staff: one; News: one hr wkly.

Key Personnel:

David Fogarty . . . pres & gen mgr
Suzanne O'Brien . . . CFO
Kay High . . . dev dir
Kitty Lensman . . . mktg dir
Sue Brinson . . . prom mgr
Gloria Skurski . . . progmg dir
Jim Wiener . . . progmg mgr
H. Fred Stone . . . engrg dir
George Hopstetter . . . engrg mgr & chief of engrg

WSTR-TV—Analog channel: 64. Digital channel: 33. On air date: January 1980. 5177 Fishwick Dr., Cincinnati, OH 45216. Phone: (513) 641-4400. Fax: (513) 242-2633. Web Site: www.wb64.net. Licensee: Sinclair Communications Group. Group owner: Sinclair Broadcast Group Inc. (acq 1996; $11 million). Network: WB. Washington Atty: Cole, Raywid & Braverman.

Key Personnel:

Merry Ewing . . . gen mgr
Jeff Fosco . . . natl sls mgr
Pete Ferrar . . . prom mgr
Rick White . . . progmg dir
William Butler . . . film buyer
Terry Roberts . . . engrg mgr

WXIX-TV—(Newport).KY Analog channel: 19. Digital channel: 29. On air date: Aug 1, 1968. 19 Broadcast Plaza, 635 W. 7th St., Cincinnati, OH 45203. Phone: (513) 421-1919. Fax: (513) 421-3022. Web Site: www.fox19.com. Licensee: Raycom National License Subsidiary LLC. Group owner: Raycom Media Inc. (acq 1998; $45 million;. grpsl). Network: Fox. Washington Atty: Kaye, Scholer, Fierman, Hays & Handler. News staff: 57; News: 23 hrs wkly.

Key Personnel:

Milton Maltz . . . CEO
John Chaffee . . . pres
John Long . . . gen mgr
Rick Oliver . . . opns mgr & progmg dir
Alison Frommeyer . . . natl sls mgr & rgnl sls mgr
Ron Stricker . . . natl sls mgr & rgnl sls mgr

Cleveland, OH (DMA 16)

WBNX-TV—(Akron).Analog channel: 55. Digital channel: 30. On air date: Dec 1, 1985. Box 91660, Cleveland, OH 44101. 2690 State Rd., Cuyahoga Falls, OH 44223. Phone: (440) 843-5555. Fax: (440) 843-7070 (sales). Fax: (440) 842-5597 (main stn). E-mail: clevelandswb@wbnx.com. Web Site: www.wbnx.com. Licensee: Winston Broadcasting Network Inc. (acq 5-20-87; 1-19-87). Network: WB. Rep: Adam Young.

Key Personnel:

Annie Keith . . . exec VP & stn mgr
Lou Spangler . . . pres & gen mgr
Colleen Metheney . . . opns mgr
Eddie Brown . . . gen sls mgr
Debbie Stone . . . prom dir

WDLI-TV—Analog channel: 17. Digital channel: 39. On air date: Jan 3, 1967. 6600 Atlantic Blvd., Louisville, OH 44641. Phone: (330) 875-5542. Fax: (330) 875-9986. Licensee: Trinity Broadcasting Network. Group owner: (group owner; acq 4-15-86; $4.5 million;. FTR: 9-23-85). Washington Atty: Joseph E. Dunne III.

***WEAO**—Analog channel: 49. On air date: September 1975. Box 5191, 1750 Campus Center Dr., Kent, OH 44240-5191. Phone: (330) 677-4549. Fax: (330) 678-0688. E-mail: hr@wneo.pbs.org. Web Site: www.pbs4549.org. Licensee: Northeastern Educational TV of Ohio Inc. Network: PBS. Washington Atty: Dow, Lohnes & Albertson. News: one hr wkly.

Key Personnel:

Trina Cutter . . . pres
Trinia Cutter . . . gen mgr
Don Freeman . . . opns dir & dev dir
Bob Tullis . . . opns mgr
Lisa Martinez . . . dev VP

WEWS—Analog channel: 5. Digital channel: 15. On air date: Dec 17, 1947. 3001 Euclid Ave., Cleveland, OH 44115. Phone: (216) 431-5555. Fax: (216) 431-3666. Web Site: www.newsnet5.com. Licensee: Scripps Howard Broadcasting Co. Group owner: (group owner, see Cross-Ownership) Network: ABC. Rep: Katz Radio. Washington Atty: Baker & Hostetler. News: 22 hrs wkly.

WGGN-TV—Analog channel: 52. On air date: Dec 5, 1982. Box 247, 3809 Maple Ave., Castalia, OH 44824. Phone: (419) 684-5311. Fax: (419) 684-5378. E-mail: wggn@lrbcg.com. Web Site: www.cfbroadcast.com. Licensee: Christian Faith Broadcasting Inc. Group owner: (group owner) Washington Atty: Joseph E. Dunne III.

Key Personnel:

Shelby Gillam . . . pres
Rusty Yost . . . gen mgr & chief of engrg

WJW—Analog channel: 8. Digital channel: 31. On air date: Dec 19, 1949. 5800 S. Marginal Rd., Cleveland, OH 44103. Phone: (216) 431-8888. Fax: (216) 432-4282. Web Site: www.fox8cleveland.com. Licensee: WJW License Inc. Group owner: Fox Television Stations Inc. (acq 11-96; grpsl). Network: Fox.

Key Personnel:

Scott Andreani . . . VP
Michael Renda . . . gen mgr
Paul Perizini . . . gen sls mgr
Paul Bodamer . . . natl sls mgr
Barb Toth . . . rgnl sls mgr
Kevin Salyer . . . prom VP & progmg VP
Greg Easterly . . . news dir
Tom Cretter . . . engrg dir

WKYC-TV—Analog channel: 3. Digital channel: 2. On air date: October 1948. 1333 Lakeside Ave., Cleveland, OH 44114. Phone: (216) 344-3333. Fax: (216) 344-3326. E-mail: news@wkyc.com. Web Site: www.wkyc.com. Licensee: WKYC-TV Inc. Group owner: Gannett Broadcasting (acq 12-4-95; grpsl). Network: NBC.

WMFD-TV—Analog channel: 68. Digital channel: 12. On air date: Mar 3, 1988. 2900 Park Ave. W., Mansfield, OH 44906. Phone: (419) 529-5900. Fax: (419) 529-2319. E-mail: comments@wmfd.com. Web Site: wmfd.com. Licensee: Mid-State Television Inc. (acq 5-31-92; 6-15-92). Washington Atty: Fletcher, Heald & Hildreth. News staff: 12; News: 36 hrs wkly.

Key Personnel:

Gunther Meisse . . . pres & gen mgr
Robert Meisse . . . opns mgr

WOAC—Analog channel: 67. On air date: March 1982. 4385 Sherman Rd., Kent, OH 44240. Phone: (330) 677-6760. Licensee: WRAY Inc. Group owner: Scripps Howard Broadcasting Co. (acq 2-27-2004; grpsl). Washington Atty: Wiley, Rein & Fielding LLP.

WOIO—Analog channel: 19. Digital channel: 10. On air date: May 19, 1985. 1717 E. 12th St., Cleveland, OH 44114. Phone: (216) 771-1943. Fax: (216) 515-7152. Web Site: www.woio.com. Licensee: Raycom National Inc. Group owner: Raycom Media Inc. (acq 8-13-98). Network: CBS. Rep: TeleRep. Washington Atty: Covington & Burling.

Key Personnel:

Bill Applegate . . . gen mgr
Lisa McManus . . . stn mgr & progmg mgr
Jim Stunek . . . opns mgr & engrg dir
Lynda Nicholls . . . gen sls mgr
Rob Boenau . . . mktg dir & prom dir
Steve Doerr . . . news dir
Emily Davis . . . pub affrs dir

WQHS-TV—Analog channel: 61. On air date: Mar 3, 1981. 2861 W. Ridgewood Dr., Parma, OH 44134. Phone: (440) 888-0061. Fax: (440) 888-7023. Licensee: Univision Partnership of Ohio. Group owner: Univision Communications Inc. (acq 5-21-01; grpsl). Network: Univision (Spanish). Washington Atty: Wiley, Rein & Fielding.

Key Personnel:

Rolo Daurtes . . . gen mgr
Sharon Roman . . . gen sls mgr
Dave Smith . . . chief of engrg

WUAB—Analog channel: 43. Digital channel: 28. On air date: Sept 15, 1968. 1717 E. 12th St., Cleveland, OH 44114. Phone: (216) 771-1943. Fax: (216) 515-7170. Web Site: www.wuab.com. Licensee: Raycom National Inc. Group owner: Raycom Media Inc. (acq 3-2-00). Network: UPN. Washington Atty: Covington & Burling.

Key Personnel:

Bill Applegate . . . gen mgr
Jim Stunek . . . opns dir & chief of engrg
Lynda Nicholls . . . gen sls mgr
Rob Boenau . . . mktg mgr & prom mgr
Lisa McManus . . . progmg mgr
Steve Doerr . . . news dir
Emily Davis . . . pub affrs dir
Todd Galloway . . . chief of engrg

***WVIZ-TV**—Analog channel: 25. On air date: Feb 7, 1965. 4300 Brookpark Rd., Cleveland, OH 44134-1191. Phone: (216) 398-2800. Fax: (216) 749-2560. Web Site: www.wviz.org. Licensee: Ideastream. (acq 2-27-01). Network: PBS.

Key Personnel:

Jerry Wareham . . . CEO & pres
Kit Jensen . . . COO
Tony Smith . . . CFO
Mark Smukler . . . gen mgr & stn mgr
Kent A. Geist . . . dev dir
Bob Stern . . . gen sls mgr
Maureen Paschke . . . mktg dir
Gene Sasso . . . prom dir & adv dir
Gary Bluhm . . . chief of engrg

WVPX—Analog channel: 23. On air date: July 19, 1953. 1 S. Main St., Akron, OH 44308-1803. 1333 Lakeside Ave., Cleveland, OH 44114. Phone: (216) 344-3333. Fax: (216) 344-3326. E-mail: 23news@wkyc.com. Web Site: www.akron23.tv. Licensee: Paxson Akron License Inc. Group owner: Paxson Communications Corp. (acq 2-29-96; $40 million; with WBPT(TV) Bridgeport, CT). Washington Atty: Dow, Lohnes & Albertson.

Key Personnel:

Laura Hausman . . . gen mgr
Moff Bresnahan . . . gen mgr
Laura Griggy . . . opns mgr & pub affrs dir
Rich Karolczak . . . gen sls mgr
Dave Mac Kenzie . . . chief of engrg

Columbus, OH (DMA 34)

WBNS-TV—Analog channel: 10. On air date: Oct 5, 1949. Box 1010, Columbus, OH 43216. 770 Twin Rivers Dr., Columbus, OH 43215. Phone: (614) 460-3700. Fax: (614) 460-3890. Web Site: www.10tv.com. Licensee: WBNS TV Inc. Group owner: Dispatch Broadcast Group Network: CBS. Washington Atty: Sidley & Austin. News staff: 80; News: 31 hrs wkly.

Key Personnel:

Tom Griesdorn . . . gen mgr
Frank Wilson . . . opns dir, mktg dir & progmg dir
Mike Berry . . . opns mgr
Susan McEldoon . . . sls dir
Pat Wise . . . natl sls mgr
Doug Jones . . . prom mgr
John Cardenas . . . news dir
Chuck White . . . pub affrs dir
John Owen . . . engrg dir

WCMH-TV—Analog channel: 4. On air date: Apr 3, 1949. 3165 Olentangy River Rd., Columbus, OH 43202. Box 4, Columbus, OH 43216. Phone: (614) 263-4444. Fax: (614) 447-9107. E-mail: nbc4columbus@abc.com. Web Site: www.nbc4columbus.com. Licensee: NBC Telemundo License Co. Group owner: NBC TV Stations Division (acq 2-2-96; grpsl). Network: NBC. News staff: 60; News: 31.5 hrs wkly.

Key Personnel:

Craig Robinson . . . pres & gen mgr
Debra Grivois . . . opns dir & chief of engrg
Mike Cash . . . sls VP
Juilee Clark . . . natl sls mgr
Ken Lubker . . . rgnl sls mgr
Dana Pearson . . . mktg mgr
Janna Buckey . . . prom VP & adv VP
Jean Nemeti . . . progmg dir & pub affrs dir
Stan Sanders . . . news dir

***WOSU-TV**—Analog channel: 34. On air date: Feb 20, 1956. 2400 Olentangy River Rd., Columbus, OH 43210. Phone: (614) 292-9678. Fax: (614) 688-3399. Web Site: wosu.org. Licensee: Ohio State University. Network: PBS. Washington Atty: Dow, Lohnes & Albertson.

Key Personnel:

Thomas Rieland . . . gen mgr
Edwin Clay . . . stn mgr
John Prosek . . . opns mgr
Mary Verina . . . dev dir

Directory of Television Ohio

Don Scott . . . mktg mgr
Theresa Ravencraft . . . progmg dir
Cindy Gaillard . . . pub affrs dir
Tom Lahr . . . chief of engrg

WSFJ—Analog channel: 51. On air date: Mar 9, 1980. 3948 Townsfair Way, Suite 220, Columbus, OH 43219. Phone: (614) 416-6080. Fax: (614) 416-6345. E-mail: comments@pax51.com. Web Site: www.wsfj.com. Licensee: Guardian Vision International Inc. Network: PAX TV. Washington Atty: Koerner & Olender P.C.. News staff: one.

WSYX—Analog channel: 6. Digital channel: 13. On air date: Aug 30, 1949. 1261 Dublin Rd., Columbus, OH 43215. Phone: (614) 481-6666. Fax: (614) 481-6828. Web Site: www.wsyx6.com. Licensee: WSYX Licensee Inc. Group owner: Sinclair Broadcast Group Inc. (acq 1998; $228 million). Network: ABC. Rep: Millennium Sales & Marketing.

Key Personnel:
John Quigley . . . gen mgr
Tony D'Angelo . . . sls dir
Lorie Luthman . . . gen sls mgr
Mike Hansen . . . mktg dir
Rick White . . . progmg dir
David Silverstein . . . news dir
Dan Carpenter . . . chief of engrg

WTTE—Analog channel: 28. Digital channel: 36. On air date: June 1, 1984. 1261 Dublin Rd., Cols, OH 43215. Phone: (614) 481-6666. Fax: (614) 485-1458. Web Site: www.wtte28.com. Licensee: Columbus (WTTE-TV) Licensee Inc. Group owner: Cunningham Broadcasting Corporation (acq 1-9-2002). Network: Fox. Rep: Millennium Sales & Marketing.

Key Personnel:
John Quigley . . . gen mgr
Tony D'Angelo . . . sls dir
Mike Hansen . . . mktg dir
Rick White . . . progmg dir & progmg mgr
David Silverstein . . . news dir
Eric Clarke . . . pub affrs dir
Dan Carpenter . . . chief of engrg

WWHO—Analog channel: 53. Digital channel: 46. On air date: Aug 31, 1987. 1160 Dublin Rd., Columbus, OH 43215. Phone: (614) 485-5300. Fax: (614) 485-5339. E-mail: upn53@wwhotv.com. Web Site: www.upn53.com. Licensee: UPN Stations Group Inc. Group owner: Viacom Television Stations Group. Network: Network: UPN, WB. Washington Atty: Wiley, Rein & Fielding.

Key Personnel:
Jeff Cash . . . pres
Shaun McDonald . . . VP & gen mgr
Lisa Barhorst . . . gen sls mgr
Joe Mulligan . . . natl sls mgr
Ellen Daly . . . rgnl sls mgr
Marcia Miano . . . mktg mgr
Rob Wamsley . . . prom mgr
Lance Carwile . . . progmg mgr
Diana Schildmeyer . . . pub affrs dir
Mark Seekins . . . engrg mgr & chief of engrg

Dayton, OH (DMA 56)

WBDT—Analog channel: 26. Digital channel: 18. On air date: September 1980. 2589 Corporate Pl., Miamisburg, OH 45342. Phone: (937) 384-9226. Fax: (937) 384-7392. Web Site: www.wb26tv.com. Licensee: Acme Television Licenses of Ohio L.L.C. Group owner: Acme Communications Inc. (acq 6-14-99; grpsl).

Key Personnel:
Stan Gill . . . VP & gen mgr
Gregg Abbott . . . opns mgr & progmg mgr
John Hannon . . . gen sls mgr
Melanie Simon . . . natl sls mgr
Dan Marchese . . . rgnl sls mgr
Brian Mercer . . . mktg dir
Chris Iller . . . prom dir
Al Schmidt . . . chief of engrg

WDTN—Analog channel: 2. On air date: Mar 15, 1949. 4595 S. Dixie Ave., Dayton, OH 45439. Box 741, Dayton, OH 45401. Phone: (937) 293-2101. Fax: (937) 294-6542. Web Site: www.wdtn.com. Licensee: WDTN Broadcasting LLC. Group owner: LIN Television Corporation (acq 11-8-2002; grpsl). Network: NBC. Rep: Blair Television.

Key Personnel:
Greg Bendin . . . gen mgr & progmg VP
Jim Atkinson . . . chief of opns & chief of engrg
Julie Zoumbaris . . . sls VP
Mo Dillon . . . gen sls mgr
Jodie Hursh . . . natl sls mgr
Jason Doyle . . . prom VP
Jason Heath . . . news dir
Sharon Howard . . . pub affrs dir

WHIO-TV—Analog channel: 7. On air date: Feb 26, 1949. 1414 Wilmington Ave., Dayton, OH 45420. Box 1206, Dayton, OH 45420. Phone: (937) 259-2111. Fax: (937) 259-2005. E-mail: fonline@whiotv.com. Licensee: WHIO-TV Holdings Inc. Group owner: Cox Broadcasting Network: CBS. Rep: TeleRep. Washington Atty: Dow, Lohnes & Albertson.

Key Personnel:
Lee Armstrong . . . VP
Harry Delaney . . . gen mgr
Don Kemper . . . stn mgr, progmg dir & film buyer
Chuck Eastman . . . opns dir, engrg dir & chief of engrg
John Hayes . . . gen sls mgr
Steve Niswonger . . . prom dir
Julie Weindel . . . news dir

WKEF—Analog channel: 22. On air date: Sept 27, 1964. 1731 Soldiers Home Rd., Dayton, OH 45418. Phone: (937) 263-2662. Fax: (937) 268-2332. Web Site: www.nbc22.com. Licensee: Max Television of Dayton L.P. Group owner: Sinclair Broadcast Group Inc. (acq 7-7-98; grpsl). Network: ABC. Washington Atty: Wiley, Rein & Fielding. News staff: 27; News: 7 hrs wkly.

Key Personnel:
Bill Ross . . . gen mgr
Roland Martel . . . opns mgr

WKOI-TV—Analog channel: 43. Digital channel: 39. On air date: May 11, 1982. Box 1057, Richmond, IN 47375. 1702 S. 9th St., Richmond, IN 47375. Phone: (765) 935-2390. Web Site: www.tbn.org. Licensee: Trinity Broadcasting of Indiana. Group owner: Trinity Broadcasting Network (acq 9-81). Washington Atty: Gammon & Grange.

Key Personnel:
Paul Crouch . . . pres
Mary Laird . . . gen mgr & opns mgr

***WPTD**—Analog channel: 16. On air date: Mar 20, 1967. 110 S. Jefferson St., Dayton, OH 45402-2415. Phone: (937) 220-1600. Fax: (937) 220-1642. Web Site: www.thinktv.org. Licensee: Greater Dayton Public TV Inc. Network: PBS. Washington Atty: Dow, Lohnes & Albertson. News staff: one; News: one hr wkly.

Key Personnel:
David Fogarty . . . pres & gen mgr
Suzanne O'Brien . . . CFO
George Hopstetter . . . opns mgr & engrg mgr
Kay High . . . dev dir & dev mgr
Kitty Lensman . . . mktg dir
Sue Brinson . . . prom mgr
Gloria Skurski . . . progmg dir
Jim Wiener . . . progmg mgr
H. Fred Stone . . . engrg dir

WRGT-TV—Analog channel: 45. On air date: Sept 23, 1984. 45 Broadcast Plaza, Dayton, OH 45408. Phone: (937) 263-4500. Fax: (937) 268-5265. Web Site: www.wrgtfox45.com. Licensee: WRGT Licensee LLC. Group owner: Cunningham Broadcasting Corporation (acq 11-15-2001; grpsl). Network: Fox. Washington Atty: Arter & Hadden.

Key Personnel:
Bill Ross . . . gen mgr
Joe Marino . . . gen sls mgr

Lima, OH (DMA 194)

WLIO—Analog channel: 35. On air date: March 1953. Box 1689, Lima, OH 45802. 1424 Rice Ave., Lima, OH 45802. Phone: (419) 228-8835. Fax: (419) 229-7091. Fax: (419) 225-6109. Web Site: www.wlio.com. Licensee: Lima Communications Corp. Group owner: BlockCommunications Inc. (acq 2-1-72; $1.5 million).. Network: NBC. Rep: Katz Radio. Washington Atty: Dow, Lohnes & Albertson. News staff: 17; News: 24 hrs wkly.

Key Personnel:
Bruce A. Opperman . . . pres & gen mgr
Dave Plaugher . . . CFO
Dave Plauqher . . . stn mgr
Kevin Creamer . . . sls VP
Vickie Shurelds . . . prom mgr, progmg dir & film buyer
Lon Tegels . . . news dir
Tom Hendrixson . . . pub affrs dir
Fred Vobbe . . . engrg VP & chief of engrg

WTLW—Analog channel: 44. On air date: June 13, 1982. 1844 Baty Rd., Lima, OH 45807. Phone: (419) 339-4444. Fax: (419) 339-1736. E-mail: kbowers@wtlw.com. Web Site: www.wtlw.com. Licensee: American Christian Television Services Inc. Washington Atty: Wiley, Rein & Fielding.

Portsmouth

see Charleston-Huntington, WV market

Steubenville

see Wheeling, WV-Steubenville, OH market

Toledo, OH (DMA 70)

***WBGU-TV**—Analog channel: 27. On air date: Feb 10, 1964. 245 Troup St., Bowling Green, OH 43403. Phone: (419) 372-2700. Fax: (419) 372-7048. E-mail: www@wbgc.bqsu.edu. Web Site: www.wbgu.org. Licensee: Bowling Green State University. (acq 11-17-76; 12-13-76). Network: PBS. Washington Atty: Cohn & Marks.

Key Personnel:
Patrick Fitzgerald . . . gen mgr
Ron Gargasz . . . stn mgr
Neil McCabe . . . dev dir
Cindy Fisher . . . dev mgr
Deb Boyce . . . prom dir
Mike Fitzpatrick . . . progmg dir
Al Bowe . . . chief of engrg

***WGTE-TV**—Analog channel: 30. On air date: Oct 10, 1960. 1270 S. Detroit Ave., Toledo, OH 43614. Box 30, Toledo, OH 43614. Phone: (419) 380-4600. Fax: (419) 380-4710. Web Site: www.wgte.org. Licensee: Public Broadcasting Foundation of N.W. Ohio. Network: PBS. Washington Atty: Schwartz, Woods & Miller.

Key Personnel:
Marlon P. Kiser . . . CEO, pres & gen mgr
George Jones . . . chmn
Marlon Kiser . . . CFO
Barbara Heslop . . . opns mgr
Ross Pfeiffer . . . dev dir
Karen Szymaniski . . . sls dir
Becky Harris . . . mktg dir
Darren LaShelle . . . progmg dir & progmg mgr
Dan Niedzwiecki . . . engrg dir

WLMB—Analog channel: 40. On air date: Oct 19, 1998. Box 908, Dominion Broadcasting Inc., 26693 Eckel Rd., Perrysburg, OH 43552. Phone: (419) 874-8862. Fax: (419) 874-8867. E-mail: info@wimb.com. Web Site: wlmb.com. Licensee: Dominion Broadcasting Inc.. Ownership: Larry Whatley, 33.3%; Ron Mighell, 33.3%; Jamey Schmitz, 33.3%. Washington Atty: Wiley, Rein & Fielding.

WNWO-TV—Analog channel: 24. Digital channel: 49. On air date: May 3, 1966. 300 S. Byrne Rd., Toledo, OH 43615. Phone: (419) 535-0024. Fax: (419) 535-0202. Web Site: www.nbc24.com. Licensee: Raycom National Inc. Group owner: Raycom Media Inc. (acq 1996). Network: NBC. Rep: TeleRep. News: 22 hrs wkly.

WTOL—Analog channel: 11. On air date: Dec 5, 1958. 730 N. Summit St., Toledo, OH 43699-1111. Phone: (419) 248-1111. Fax: (419) 244-7104. E-mail: news@wtol.com. Web Site: www.wtol.com. Licensee: Libco Inc. Group owner: Liberty Corp. (acq 4-15-65; grpsl; FTR: 3-15-65). Network: CBS. Rep: Harrington, Righter & Parsons. Washington Atty: Dow, Lohnes & Albertson. News staff: 50; News: 25 hrs wkly.

Key Personnel:
Bob Chirdon . . . gen mgr
Linda Blackburn . . . gen sls mgr
Nancy Bright . . . natl sls mgr
Steve Israel . . . progmg dir
Rick Williams . . . news dir & pub affrs dir
Eric Bergman . . . chief of engrg

WTVG—Analog channel: 13. On air date: July 21, 1948. 4247 Dorr St., Toledo, OH 43607. Phone: (419) 531-1313. Fax: (419) 531-1399. Web Site: www.13abc.com. Licensee: WTVG Inc. Group owner: Capital Cities/ABC Video Enterprises International (acq 1995; $155 million with WJRT-TV Flint, MI). Network: ABC. Rep: Katz Radio. Washington Atty: Koteen & Naftalin. News staff: 30; News: 10 hrs wkly.

Key Personnel:
David Zamichow . . . pres & gen mgr
Matt Black . . . opns mgr
Mary Gerken . . . sls dir
Christine Isaacson . . . prom dir
Tamara Rost . . . progmg dir
Brian Trauring . . . news dir
Ernestine Weathers . . . pub affrs dir
Barry Gries . . . engrg dir

WUPW—Analog channel: 36. On air date: Sept 22, 1985. Four SeaGate, Toledo, OH 43604. Phone: (419) 244-3600. Fax: (419)

244-8842. E-mail: wupw@wupw.com. Web Site: foxtoledo.com. Licensee: WUPW Broadcasting LLC. Group owner: LIN Television Corporation (acq 11-8-2002; grpsl). Network: Fox. Rep: Blair Television. Washington Atty: Shrinsky, Weitzman & Eisen. News staff: 5; News: 5 hrs wkly.
Key Personnel:
Ray Maselli . . . . . gen mgr
Gary Yoder . . . . . gen sls mgr & natl sls mgr
Brian Lorenzen. . . . . rgnl sls mgr
John Colling. . . . . mktg dir & prom dir
Cathy Stoner . . . . . progmg dir
Jose Svasez . . . . . news dir
Steve Crum . . . . . engrg dir

Youngstown, OH (DMA 102)

WFMJ-TV—Analog channel: 21. On air date: Mar 8, 1953. 21 WFMJ, 101 W. Boardman St., Youngstown, OH 44503. Phone: (330) 744-8611. Fax: (330) 744-3402. E-mail: information@wfmj.com. Web Site: www.wfmj.com. Licensee: WFMJ Television Inc.. Ownership: Mark A. Brown and Betty H. Brown Jagnow. (acq 7-14-93; 8-2-93). Network: NBC. Washington Atty: Fisher, Wayland, Cooper, Leader & Zaragoza. News staff: 20; News: 10 hrs wkly.
Key Personnel:
John Grdic. . . . . gen mgr & rgnl sls mgr
Kathie Brickman . . . . . natl sls mgr
Jack Stevenson . . . . . mktg dir
Joe Romano . . . . . prom dir
Mona Alexander. . . . . news dir
Carl Bryant . . . . . pub affrs dir
Bob Flis. . . . . chief of engrg

WKBN-TV—Analog channel: 27. Digital channel: 41. On air date: Jan 6, 1953. 3930 Sunset Blvd., Youngstown, OH 44512. Phone: (330) 782-1144. Fax: (330) 782-3504. Fax: (330) 783-1834. Web Site: www.wkbn.com. Licensee: Piedmont Television of Youngstown License LLC. Group owner: Piedmont Television Holdings LLC (acq 10-29-99). Network: CBS. Rep: Continental Television Sales. Washington Atty: Bryan Cave. News staff: 50; News: 25 hrs wkly.
Key Personnel:
Paul Brissette . . . . . CEO & pres
William Fielder. . . . . CFO
David Coy . . . . . gen mgr
John Amann . . . . . opns mgr & prom mgr
Jill Duffy . . . . . natl sls mgr
Nikki Manuel. . . . . rgnl sls mgr
Phyllis Rappach. . . . . progmg dir
Gary Coursen. . . . . news dir
Thomas Zocolo . . . . . chief of engrg

***WNEO**—Analog channel: 45. On air date: May 1973. Box 5191, 1750 Campus Center Dr., Kent, OH 44240-5191. Phone: (330) 677-4549. Fax: (330) 678-0688. E-mail: hr@wneo.pbs.org. Web Site: www.pbs4549.org. Licensee: Northeastern Educational TV of Ohio Inc. Network: PBS. Washington Atty: Dow, Lohnes & Albertson. News: one hr wkly.
Key Personnel:
Trina Cutter . . . . . pres & gen mgr
Don Freeman. . . . . opns dir
Bob Tullis. . . . . opns mgr
Lisa Martinez . . . . . dev VP

WYTV—Analog channel: 33. On air date: Oct 30, 1957. 3800 Shady Run Rd., Youngstown, OH 44502. Phone: (330) 783-2930. Fax: (330) 782-8154. Web Site: www.wytv.com. Licensee: Chelsey Broadcasting Co. of Youngstown LLC. Group owner: Chelsey Broadcasting Co. (acq 8-29-02; grpsl). Network: ABC. Washington Atty: Covington & Burling. News staff: 19; News: 15 hrs wkly.
Key Personnel:
Dave Trabert . . . . . gen mgr
Dan Messersmith. . . . . gen sls mgr
Ross Lytle . . . . . prom mgr
Cathy Lake . . . . . progmg mgr
Pat Livingston . . . . . news dir
Bill Lough . . . . . chief of engrg

Zanesville, OH (DMA 202)

WHIZ-TV—Analog channel: 18. On air date: May 23, 1953. 629 Downard Rd., Zanesville, OH 43701. Phone: (740) 452-5431. Fax: (740) 452-6553. Web Site: www.whizamfmtv.com. Licensee: Southeastern Ohio TV System.. Ownership: Norma Littick Revocable Trust. Network: NBC. Rep: Katz Radio. Washington Atty: Leventhal, Senter & Lerman. News staff: 14; News: 10 hrs wkly.
Key Personnel:
N.J. Littick . . . . . chmn
H.C. Littick . . . . . pres
Van Vannelli . . . . . VP
Doug Pickrell . . . . . sls dir
Barbara Mitter . . . . . progmg VP
George Hiotis. . . . . news dir
Ken Cash . . . . . chief of engrg

Oklahoma

Ada

see Sherman, TX-Ada, OK market

Lawton

see Wichita Falls, TX & Lawton, OK market

Oklahoma City, OK (DMA 45)

KAUT-TV—Analog channel: 43. On air date: Nov 3, 1980. 11901 N. Eastern Ave., Oklahoma City, OK 73131. Phone: (405) 516-4300. Fax: (405) 516-4329. Web Site: www.upn43.com. Licensee: Viacom Stations Group of OKC LLC. Group owner: Viacom Television Stations Group (acq 7-15-98). Network: UPN.
Key Personnel:
Bill Maples . . . . . VP & gen mgr
Nick Nicoll. . . . . dev mgr & prom mgr
J.C. Lowe. . . . . gen sls mgr
Tina Dawson. . . . . natl sls mgr
Tim Murphy . . . . . rgnl sls mgr
Jamie Bolton . . . . . progmg dir
William Nichols . . . . . chief of engrg

***KETA**—Analog channel: 13. On air date: Apr 13, 1956. Box 14190, 7403 N. Kelley, Oklahoma City, OK 73113. Phone: (405) 848-8501. Fax: (405) 841-9216. Licensee: Oklahoma Educational TV Authority. Network: PBS. Washington Atty: Cohn & Marks. News staff: 8; News: 3 hrs wkly.
Key Personnel:
John McCarroll . . . . . gen mgr
Bill Thrash. . . . . stn mgr & progmg dir
Mike Palmer . . . . . opns dir
Susie Dowdy . . . . . prom mgr
Dick Pryor . . . . . news dir
Earle Conners . . . . . engrg dir

KEYU—Analog channel: 31.Not on air, target date: unknown: Equity Broadcasting Corp., 1 Shackleford Dr., Suite 400, Little Rock, AR 72211. Phone: (501) 219-2400. Fax: (501) 716-3502. Permittee: Borger Broadcasting Inc. Group owner: Equity Broadcasting Corp.

KFOR-TV—Analog channel: 4. Digital channel: 27. On air date: June 6, 1949. 444 E. Britton Rd., Oklahoma City, OK 73113. Phone: (405) 424-4444. Fax: (405) 478-6206. E-mail: news@kfor.com. Web Site: www.kfor.com. Licensee: New York Times Management Services. Group owner: The New York Times Co. (acq 1996; $155 million).. Network: NBC. Rep: Katz Radio. Washington Atty: Koteen & Naftalin. News staff: 73; News: 29 hrs wkly.

KOCB—Analog channel: 34. On air date: Oct 28, 1979. 1228 .E. Wilshire Blvd., Oklahoma City, OK 73111. Phone: (405) 478-3434. Fax: (405) 478-1027. Licensee: KOCB Licensee L.L.C. Group owner: Sinclair Broadcast Group Inc. (acq 1996; $63 million with WDKY-TV Danville, KY). Rep: Harrington, Righter & Parsons.
Key Personnel:
Randy Pratt . . . . . gen mgr
Don Shafer . . . . . opns mgr

KOCM—Analog channel: 46.Not on air, target date: unknown: Daystar Television Network, Box 612066, Dallas, TX 75261-2066. Phone: (817) 571-1229. Fax: (817) 571-7458. E-mail: cpmments@daystar.com. Web Site: www.daystartv.net. Permittee: Word of God Fellowship Inc.. Ownership: Marcus D. Lamb, 25%; Jimmie F. Lamb, 25%; Joni T. Lamb, 25%; John T. Calender, 25% (acq 8-19-02; $3.6 million)..

KOCO-TV—Analog channel: 5. Digital channel: 5. On air date: July 15, 1954. 1300 E. Britton Rd., Oklahoma City, OK 73131. Phone: (405) 478-3000. Fax: (405) 475-5242. Web Site: www.channeloklahoma.com. Licensee: Hearst-Argyle Stations Inc. Group owner: Hearst-Argyle Television Inc. (acq 7-16-97; grpsl). Network: ABC.
Key Personnel:
Brent Hensley . . . . . pres & gen mgr
Greg Turner . . . . . opns dir
Tom Comerford. . . . . gen sls mgr
Sherrie Brown . . . . . news dir
David Evans . . . . . engrg dir & chief of engrg

KOKH-TV—Analog channel: 25. On air date: Jan 26, 1979. 1228 E. Wilshire Blvd., Oklahoma City, OK 73111. Box 14925, Oklahoma City, OK 73111. Phone: (405) 843-2525. Fax: (405) 478-4343. Licensee: Sullivan Broadcasting Co. IV Inc. Group owner: Sinclair Broadcast Group Inc. (acq 1998; grpsl). Network: Fox. Rep: Harrington, Righter & Parsons.

KOPX—Analog channel: 62. Digital channel: 50. On air date: February 1997. 444 E. Britton Rd., Oklahoma City, OK 73114. Phone: (405) 478-9562. Fax: (405) 478-1789. Web Site: www.pax.tv. Licensee: Paxson Oklahoma City License Inc. Group owner: Paxson Communications Corp. (acq 9-27-96; $6.395 million). Network: NBC. Washington Atty: Dow, Lohnes and Albertson PLLC.
Key Personnel:
Jeff Sagansky . . . . . CEO & pres
Lowell "Bud" Paxson . . . . . chmn
Carol Wright-Holzhaver . . . . . VP
Tim Morrissey. . . . . gen mgr
Dian Johnson . . . . . opns mgr
Dean M. Woodman . . . . . chief of opns
Seth A. Grossman . . . . . dev VP
Steve Appel . . . . . gen sls mgr & natl sls mgr
Wes Milbourn . . . . . gen sls mgr
Marsha Davis . . . . . rgnl sls mgr
David A. Glenn. . . . . engrg VP
Robert Ablah. . . . . chief of engrg

KSBI—Analog channel: 52. Digital channel: 51. On air date: Sept 19, 1988. 1350 S.E. 82nd St., Oklahoma City, OK 73149. Phone: (405) 631-7335. Fax: (405) 631-7367. E-mail: info@kbitv.com. Web Site: www.ksbitv.com. Licensee: Family Broadcasting Group Inc.. Ownership: Angela Brus, 38.4%; Brady M. Brus, 22.8%; Brenda Deimund, 22.8%; and Seekfirst Media Partners LLC, 16%. Washington Atty: Booth, Freret, Imlay & Tepper. News staff: 40.
Key Personnel:
Brady Brus . . . . . CEO, pres & gen mgr
Brenda Bennett . . . . . VP
Greg Kuhn . . . . . opns mgr
Tommy Muffitt . . . . . gen sls mgr
Jack Mills . . . . . chief of engrg

KTBO-TV—Analog channel: 14. Digital channel: 15. On air date: Mar 6, 1981. 1600 E. Heffner Rd., Oklahoma City, OK 73131. Phone: (405) 848-1414. E-mail: comments@tbn.org. Web Site: www.tbn.org. Licensee: Trinity Broadcasting of Oklahoma City Inc. Group owner: Trinity Broadcasting Network. Washington Atty: Joseph E. Dunne III.
Key Personnel:
Paul Crouch . . . . . pres
Liuda Cooke . . . . . gen mgr
Jan Crouch . . . . . prom dir & pub affrs dir

KTUZ-TV—Analog channel: 30. Digital channel: 29. On air date: 2000. 5101 S. Shields Blvd., Oklahoma City, OK 73129. Phone: (405) 616-9900. Fax: (405) 616-0328. Licensee: Oklahoma Land Company LLC. Group owner: Tyler Media Broadcasting Corp. (acq 9-30-2004; $12,375,000). Network: Telemundo (Spanish).

KUOK—Analog channel: 35.Not on air, target date: unknown: Equity Broadcasting Corp., 1 Shackleford Dr., Suite 400, Little Rock, AR 72211. Phone: (501) 219-2400. Fax: (501) 716-3502. Permittee: Woodward Broadcasting Inc. Group owner: Equity Broadcasting Corp.
Key Personnel:
Larry Morton. . . . . pres
Gordon Hodges . . . . . gen mgr

***KWET**—Analog channel: 12. Digital channel: 8. On air date: Aug 6, 1978. Box 14190, 7403 N. Kelley Ave., Oklahoma City, OK 73113. Phone: (405) 848-8501. Fax: (405) 841-9216. Web Site: www.oeta.onenet.net. Licensee: Oklahoma Educational TV Authority. Network: PBS. Washington Atty: Cohn & Marks. News staff: 20; News: 4 hrs wkly.
Key Personnel:
John McCarroll . . . . . gen mgr
Bill Thrash . . . . . stn mgr
Mike Palmer. . . . . opns mgr
Dick Pryor . . . . . prom mgr, news dir & pub affrs dir
Earle Connors . . . . . engrg dir

KWTV—Analog channel: 9. On air date: Dec 20, 1953. 7401 N. Kelley Ave., Oklahoma City, OK 73113. Phone: (405) 843-6641. Fax: (405) 841-9135. Web Site: www.kwtv.com. Licensee: Kelley International Licensing L.L.C. (Nevada). Network: CBS. Rep: TeleRep. Washington

Atty: Holland & Knight.
Key Personnel:
Kelly Dyer . . . gen mgr
Alan Hicks . . . mktg dir
Elizabeth Taylor . . . prom dir
Julia Cameron . . . engrg dir & chief of engrg

Tulsa, OK
(DMA 60)

KDOR-TV—Analog channel: 17. Digital channel: 15. On air date: Jan 11, 1987. 2120 N. Yellowood, Broken Arrow, OK 74012. Phone: (918) 250-0777. Fax: (918) 461-8817. E-mail: kdor@tbn.org. Web Site: www.tbn.org. Licensee: Trinity Broadcasting Network. Group owner: (group owner; acq 5-8-00; grpsl).
Key Personnel:
Paul Crouch Sr. . . . CEO & pres
Bob Higley . . . VP
Craig Nelson . . . gen mgr

KGEB—Analog channel: 53. On air date: Jan 24, 1996. 7777 S. Lewis Ave., Tulsa, OK 74171. Phone: (918) 488-5300. Fax: (918) 495-7388. E-mail: kgeb@oru.edu. Web Site: www.kgeb.net. Licensee: University Broadcasting Inc.
Key Personnel:
Walter Richardson . . . gen mgr
Christi Vanover. . . . progmg mgr
William P. Lee . . . chief of engrg

KJRH—Analog channel: 2. On air date: Dec 5, 1954. 3701 S. Peoria Ave., Tulsa, OK 74105-3269. Phone: (918) 743-2222. Fax: (918) 748-1460. E-mail: news@kjrh.com. Web Site: www.teamtulsa.com. Licensee: Scripps Howard Broadcasting Co. Group owner: Scripps Howard Stations, see Cross-Ownership (acq 1-1-71; $7.8 million). Network: NBC. Washington Atty: Baker & Hostetler. News staff: 50; News: 19 hrs wkly.
Key Personnel:
Ken Lowe. . . . CEO
Michael Kronley . . . gen mgr
Bill Sevenoaks . . . gen sls mgr
Angie Burkett . . . prom mgr
Bill Seitzler. . . . news dir
Samantha Knowlton. . . . pub affrs dir
Dale Vennes . . . chief of engrg

***KOED-TV**—Analog channel: 11. On air date: Jan 12, 1959. 811 N. Sheridan, Tulsa, OK 74115. Phone: (918) 838-7611/7614. Fax: (918) 838-1807. Licensee: Oklahoma Educational TV Authority. Network: PBS. Washington Atty: Cohn & Marks.
Key Personnel:
Robert L. Allen . . . exec VP
Royal Aills. . . . gen mgr, stn mgr & news dir
Richard Ladd. . . . chief of engrg

***KOET**—Analog channel: 3. On air date: Aug 22, 1978. Box 14190, 7403 N. Kelley Ave., Oklahoma City, OK 73113. Phone: (405) 848-8501. Fax: (405) 841-9216. Licensee: Oklahoma Educational Television Authority. Network: PBS. Washington Atty: Cohn & Marks.
Key Personnel:
John McCarroll . . . gen mgr
Bill Thrash. . . . stn mgr & progmg dir
Mike Palmer . . . opns dir
Susie Dowdy . . . prom mgr
Dick Pryor . . . news dir
Earle Connors . . . engrg dir

KOKI-TV—Analog channel: 23. On air date: Oct 26, 1980. 2625 S. Memorial Dr., Tulsa, OK 74129. Phone: (918) 491-0023. Fax: (918) 491-6650. Web Site: www.fox23.com. Licensee: Clear Channel Broadcasting Licenses Inc. Group owner: Clear Channel Communications Inc. (acq 8-5-92). Network: Fox. Washington Atty: Cohn & Marks. News staff: 38; News: 7 hrs wkly.
Key Personnel:
Bill Moll. . . . pres
Craig Millar . . . VP & gen mgr
Don Perry . . . VP
David Brace. . . . dev dir & natl sls mgr
Holly Allen . . . sls dir
Matt Kidwell. . . . natl sls mgr
Stephanie Spry. . . . rgnl sls mgr
Deedra Determan . . . mktg mgr & prom mgr
Chooi Ning. . . . progmg dir
Sean McLaughlin . . . news dir
Brian Egan . . . chief of engrg

KOTV—Analog channel: 6. On air date: Nov 30, 1949. Box 6, Tulsa, OK 74101. 302 S. Frankfort, Tulsa, OK 74101. Phone: (918) 732-6000. Fax: (918) 732-6016. Licensee: Griffin Licensing L.L.C.. Ownership: David F. Griffin, 65.2% member. (acq 12-6-00; $82 million). Network: CBS. Rep: TeleRep. Washington Atty: Dow, Lohnes & Albertson. News staff: 40.
Key Personnel:
Bud Brown . . . pres, VP & stn mgr
Lisa Colvacs. . . . CFO
Regina Moon . . . gen mgr
John Quesnel . . . opns mgr
Ron Harig . . . news dir
Don Dobbs . . . chief of engrg

***KRSC-TV**—Analog channel: 35. On air date: July 1, 1987. 1701 W. Will Rogers Blvd., Claremore, OK 74017-3252. Phone: (918) 343-7772, stn. Fax: (918) 343-7952. Web Site: www.rsu.edu. Licensee: Board of Regents of Oklahoma Colleges. Washington Atty: Schwartz, Woods & Miller.
Key Personnel:
Virgle Smith . . . gen mgr
Rick Gray . . . opns VP & progmg dir
Melissa Clary . . . opns dir
Ruth Anne Thomas . . . opns mgr
Vivian Roberts . . . progmg dir
Dave McFadden . . . chief of engrg
Jim Plaster . . . chief of engrg

KTFO—Analog channel: 41. On air date: May 17, 1981. 2625 S. Memorial Dr., Tulsa, OK 74129-2600. Phone: (918) 888-5100. Fax: (918) 493-5739. Web Site: www.upn41.com. Licensee: Clear Channel Broadcasting Licenses Inc. Group owner: Clear Channel Communications Inc. (acq 5-1-00; grpsl). Network: UPN. Rep: Millennium Sales & Marketing. Washington Atty: Ward & Mendelsohn.
Key Personnel:
Bill Moll. . . . pres
Craig Millar . . . VP & gen mgr
David Brace . . . gen sls mgr
Matt Kidwell . . . natl sls mgr
Stephanie Spry. . . . rgnl sls mgr
Deedra Determan . . . mktg dir & mktg mgr
Chooi Ning. . . . progmg dir
Sean McLaughlin . . . news dir
Brian Egan . . . engrg mgr

KTPX—Analog channel: 44. Digital channel: 28. On air date: July 1997. 3701 S. Peoria, Suite 101, Tulsa, OK 74105. 5800 E. Skelly Dr.(Master Control), Tulsa, OK 74135. Phone: (918) 748-1570. Fax: (918) 748-1575. Web Site: www.pax.tv. Licensee: Paxson Tulsa License Inc. Group owner: Paxson Communications Corp. (acq 8-21-98; $404,000 for 51% of stock). Network: PAX TV.
Key Personnel:
Bill Sevenoaks . . . gen sls mgr
Peter A. De Les Dernier . . . stn mgr & pub affrs dir

KTUL—Analog channel: 8. On air date: Sept 18, 1954. Box 8, Tulsa, OK 74101-0008. 3333 S. 29th W Ave., Tulsa, OK 74063. Phone: (918) 445-8888. Fax: (918) 445-9316. Web Site: www.ktul.com. Licensee: KTUL L.L.C. Group owner: Allbritton Communications Co. (acq 4-83; grpsl). Network: ABC. Washington Atty: Hogan & Hartson. News staff: 50; News: 17 hrs wkly.
Key Personnel:
Pat Baldwin . . . pres & gen mgr
Garry Porterfield . . . gen sls mgr
Carol Jones . . . natl sls mgr
Marcia Baker . . . rgnl sls mgr
Deborah Kurin . . . mktg dir
Larry Nitz . . . prom mgr
Amy Miller . . . progmg mgr
Lee Williams . . . news dir
Randi Carson . . . pub affrs dir
David Shaffer . . . engrg mgr
Roger Herring. . . . opns dir & chief of engrg

KWBT—Analog channel: 19. On air date: Sept 12, 1999. 233 South Detroit Ave., Suite 100, Tulsa, OK 74120. Phone: (918) 270-1919. Fax: (918) 280-0019. Web Site: www.wb19.com. Licensee: Tulsa Communications L.L.C. Group owner: Cascade Broadcasting Group L.L.C. (acq 12-20-01; grpsl).
Key Personnel:
Derek Criss . . . gen mgr & sls VP
Ken Kinder . . . prom mgr
Gary Mariow . . . chief of engrg

KWHB—Analog channel: 47. On air date: Apr 1, 1985. 8835 S. Memorial, Tulsa, OK 74133. Phone: (918) 254-4701. Fax: (918) 254-5614. Web Site: www.lesea.com. Licensee: LeSea Broadcasting. Group owner: (group owner; acq 5-14-86; $3.4 million; 4-14-86). Washington Atty: John Fiorini.
Key Personnel:
Peter Sumrall. . . . CEO & VP
Bill Paddock . . . gen mgr

Oregon

Bend, OR
(DMA 197)

***KOAB-TV**—Analog channel: 3. On air date: Feb 24, 1970. 7140 S.W. Macadam Ave., Portland, OR 97709. Phone: (503) 244-9900. Fax: (503) 293-1919. E-mail: audience-services@opb.org. Web Site: www.opb.org. Licensee: Oregon Public Broadcasting.. Ownership: Charles J. Swindells. (acq 9-20-93; grpsl; 10-11-93). Network: PBS. Washington Atty: Schwartz, Woods & Miller.
Key Personnel:
Jack Galmiche. . . . COO
Maynard E. Orme . . . CEO & pres
Dan Metziga. . . . dev dir

KTVZ—Analog channel: 21. On air date: Nov 6, 1977. 62990 O. B. Riley Rd., Bend, OR 97701. Phone: (541) 383-2121. Fax: (541) 382-1616. E-mail: ktvz@ktvz.com. Web Site: www.ktvz.com. Licensee: NPG of Oregon Inc. Group owner: News-Press & Gazette Co. (acq 4-17-02; $18.9 million).. Network: NBC. Rep: Petry Television Inc.. News staff: 12; News: 9 hrs wkly.

Eugene, OR
(DMA 120)

KCBY-TV—Analog channel: 11. On air date: Oct 1, 1960. 3451 Broadway, North Bend, OR 97459. Phone: (541) 269-1111. Fax: (541) 269-7464. E-mail: webmaster@kcby.com. Web Site: www.kcby.com. Licensee: Fisher Broadcasting - Oregon TV L.L.C. Group owner: Fisher Broadcasting Company (acq 12-4-01; grpsl). Network: CBS. Rep: Katz Radio. Washington Atty: Dow, Lohnes & Albertson. News staff: 4.
Key Personnel:
Dino Francois . . . prom dir & news dir
Joe Lowe . . . pub affrs dir & chief of engrg
Paul Greene . . . progmg dir & chief of engrg

***KEPB-TV**—Analog channel: 28. On air date: Sept 27, 1990. 7140 S.W. Macadam Ave., Portland, OR 97219. Phone: (503) 244-9900. Fax: (503) 293-1919. Web Site: www.opb.org. Licensee: Oregon Public Broadcasting.. Ownership: Board of directors. (acq 9-20-93; grpsl; 10-11-93). Network: PBS.
Key Personnel:
Maynard E. Orme . . . CEO & pres
Jack Galmiche . . . COO & sr VP
Tom Doggett . . . progmg VP & progmg dir
Morgan Holm . . . news dir & pub affrs dir
Michael Tondreau. . . . engrg VP

KEZI—Analog channel: 9. On air date: Dec 19, 1960. Box 7009, Eugene, OR 97401. 2975 Chad Dr., Eugene, OR 97401. Phone: (541) 485-5611. Fax: (541) 342-1568. E-mail: kezi@kezi.com. Web Site: kezi.com. Licensee: KEZI Inc. Group owner: Chambers Communications Corp. (acq 8-30-83; $18 million).. Network: ABC.
Key Personnel:
Carolyn S. Chambers . . . CEO & chmn
Scott Chambers. . . . pres & gen mgr

KLSR-TV—Analog channel: 34. On air date: Oct 31, 1991. 2940 Chad Dr., Eugene, OR 97408. Phone: (541) 683-2525. Fax: (541) 683-8016. Licensee: California Oregon Broadcasting Inc. Group owner: (group owner; acq 9-1-94; $2.65 million;. FTR: 9-19-94). Network: Fox. Washington Atty: Fletcher, Heald & Hildreth.
Key Personnel:
Patricia Smullin. . . . pres
Mark Metzger. . . . gen mgr & gen sls mgr
Johnathon Johnson . . . opns dir
Aleck Thompson . . . natl sls mgr & rgnl sls mgr
Bob Broderick . . . prom dir, news dir & pub affrs dir
Sandra Dornon-Belmont. . . . progmg dir
Tim Hershiser . . . engrg dir & chief of engrg

KMTR—Analog channel: 16. On air date: Oct 4, 1982. 3825 International Ct., Springfield, OR 97477. Phone: (541) 746-1600. Fax: (503) 747-0866. Web Site: www.kmtr.com. Licensee: Ackerley Media Group Inc. Group owner: Clear Channel Communications Inc. (acq 6-14-02; grpsl). Network: NBC. Blair. Washington Atty: Rubin, Winston, Diercks, Harris & Cooke. News staff: 22; News: 15 hrs wkly.
Key Personnel:
Cambra Ward. . . . VP, gen mgr & stn mgr
Kurt Thelen . . . opns mgr

KMTX-TV—Analog channel: 46. On air date: Apr 8, 1992. 3825 International Ct., Springfield, OR 97477-1090. Phone: (541) 746-1600. Fax: (541) 747-0866. Web Site: www.kmtr.com. Licensee: Ackerley Media Group Inc. Group owner: Clear Channel Communications Inc. (acq 6-14-02; grpsl). Network: NBC. Washington Atty: Rubin, Winston, Diercks, Harris & Cooke. News: 22 hrs wkly.
Key Personnel:
Cambra Ward . . . . VP, gen mgr, stn mgr & progmg dir
Kurt Thelen . . . . opns mgr & chief of engrg
Mike Chisholm . . . . gen sls mgr
Robert McMichaels . . . . news dir

KMTZ—Analog channel: 23. On air date: July 8, 1991. 3825 International Ct., Springfield, OR 97477. Phone: (541) 747-1600. Fax: (541) 747-0866. Web Site: www.kmtr.com. Licensee: AK Media Group Inc. Group owner: Clear Channel Communications Inc. (acq 6-14-02; grpsl). Network: NBC. Blair. News: 22 hrs wkly.
Key Personnel:
Cambra Ward . . . . VP
Cambra Ward. gen mgr
Kurt Thelen . . . . opns mgr

***KOAC-TV**—Analog channel: 7. On air date: Oct 7, 1957. 7140 S.W. Macadam Ave., Portland, OR 97219. Phone: (503) 244-9900. Fax: (503) 293-1919. Web Site: www.opb.org. Licensee: Oregon Public Broadcasting.. Ownership: Board of directors. (acq 1993; grpsl; 9-20-93). Network: PBS. Washington Atty: Schwartz, Woods & Miller.
Key Personnel:
Maynard E. Orme . . . . CEO & pres
Jack Galmiche . . . . COO & sr VP
Tom Doggett . . . . progmg VP & progmg dir
Morgan Holm . . . . news dir & pub affrs dir
Michael Tondreau. . . . . engrg VP & chief of engrg

KPIC—Analog channel: 4. On air date: Apr 1, 1956. Box 1345, 655 W. Umpqua, Roseburg, OR 97470. Phone: (541) 672-4481. Fax: (541) 672-4482. E-mail: sales@kpic.com. Web Site: www.kpic.com. Licensee: South West Oregon TV Broadcasting Corp. Group owner: Fisher Broadcasting Company (acq 1999; grpsl). Network: CBS. Rep: Katz Radio. Washington Atty: Dow, Lohnes & Albertson. News staff: 4; News: 14 hrs wkly.
Key Personnel:
Ben Tucker . . . . pres
Dave Weinkauf . . . . gen mgr
Don Clithero . . . . stn mgr & opns mgr
Greg Raschio . . . . . . gen sls mgr, natl sls mgr & rgnl sls mgr
Dino Francois . . . . prom mgr
Paul Greene . . . . progmg dir
Dan Bain . . . . news dir
Tegan Yarbrough . . . . pub affrs dir
Jim Bowen . . . . engrg dir
Mike Hill . . . . chief of engrg

KTVC—Analog channel: 36. On air date: 1988. Equity Broadcasting Corp., 1 Shackleford Dr., Suite 400, Little Rock, AR 72211. Phone: (501) 219-2400. Fax: (501) 221-1101. Licensee: Roseburg Broadcasting Inc. Group owner: Equity Broadcasting Corp. (acq 11-30-01; $800,000).. Network: UPN. Washington Atty: Irwin, Campbell & Tannenwald.
Key Personnel:
Greg Fess. . . . . CEO & gen mgr
Glenn Charlesworth . . . . CFO
Max Hooper . . . . exec VP
James Hearnsberger . . . . sr VP

KVAL-TV—Analog channel: 13. Digital channel: 25. On air date: Apr 16, 1954. Box 1313, Eugene, OR 97440. 4575 Blanton Rd., Eugene, OR 97405. Phone: (541) 342-4961. Fax: (541) 342-7252 (sales). Fax: (541) 342-2635 (admin). E-mail: kval@kval.com. Web Site: www.kval.com. Licensee: Fisher Broadcasting - Oregon TV L.L.C. Group owner: Fisher Broadcasting Company (acq 12-4-01; grpsl). Network: CBS. Rep: Continental Television Sales. Washington Atty: Shaw Pittman. News: 17 hrs wkly.
Key Personnel:
Ben Tucker . . . . pres
David Weinkauf . . . . VP & gen mgr
Paul Greene. opns mgr

Klamath Falls

see Medford-Klamath Falls, OR market

Medford-Klamath Falls, OR (DMA 141)

***KBDM**—Analog channel: 20.Not on air, target date: unknown: c/o KKVV Radio, 3185 S. Highland Dr., Suite 13, Las Vegas, NV 89109. Fax: (702) 731-5588. Permittee: Northern California Public TV.

KBLN—Analog channel: 30. On air date: 2002. Better Life Television, Box 766, Grants Pass, OR 97528. Phone: (877) 741-2588. Fax: (541) 474-9409. E-mail: bltv@budget.net. Web Site: www.budget.net/~bltv. Licensee: Better Life Television Inc. (acq 2-20-01).
Key Personnel:
Marta Davis. . . . . stn mgr
Ron Davis . . . . stn mgr

KDKF—Analog channel: 31. On air date: Oct 17, 1989. Box 4220, Klamath Falls, OR 97603. 231 E. Main St., Klamath Falls, OR 97603. Phone: (541) 773-1212. Fax: (541) 883-8931. Web Site: www.kdrv.com. Licensee: Soda Mountain Broadcasting Inc. Group owner: Chambers Communications Corp. (acq 12-5-01). Network: ABC. Rep: Katz Radio. Washington Atty: Fletcher, Heald & Hildreth. News staff: 20; News: 12 hrs wkly.

KDRV—Analog channel: 12. On air date: Feb 26, 1984. Box 4220, Medford, OR 97504. Phone: (541) 773-1212. Fax: (541) 779-9261. Web Site: www.kdrv.com. Licensee: Soda Mountain Broadcasting Inc. Group owner: Chambers Communications Corp. (acq 12-5-01). Network: ABC. Washington Atty: Fisher, Wayland, Cooper, Leader & Zaragoza.

***KFTS**—Analog channel: 22. On air date: March 1989. 34 S. Fir St., Medford, OR 97501. Phone: (541) 779-0808. Fax: (541) 779-2178. Web Site: www.soptv.org. Licensee: Southern Oregon Public Television Inc. Network: PBS.
Key Personnel:
Mark Stanislawski . . . . CEO, pres & gen mgr
Dotti Wilson . . . . dev dir
Tom Werner . . . . chief of engrg

KMVU—Analog channel: 26. Digital channel: 27. On air date: Aug 8, 1994. 820 Crater Lake Ave., Suite 105, Medford, OR 97504. Phone: (541) 772-2600. Fax: (541) 772-7364. Web Site: www.fox26medford.com. Licensee: Broadcasting Communications L.L.C. Group owner: Northwest Broadcasting Inc. Network: Fox. Rep: Continental Television Sales. Washington Atty: Leventhal, Senter & Lerman.
Key Personnel:
Brian Brady . . . . pres
Cary Jones. . . . . gen mgr

KOBI—Analog channel: 5. On air date: Aug 1, 1953. Box 1489, Medford, OR 97501. 125 S.Fir, Medford, OR 97501. Phone: (541) 779-5555. Fax: (541) 779-5564. E-mail: kobi@kobi5.com. Web Site: www.localnewscomesfirst.com. Licensee: California Oregon Broadcasting Inc. Group owner: (group owner). Network: NBC. Rep: Blair Television. Washington Atty: Wiley, Rein & Fielding.
Key Personnel:
Patricia C. Smullin . . . . pres
John Larkin . . . . gen mgr
Wally Babbridge . . . . gen sls mgr
Alan Plotkin . . . . natl sls mgr
Larry Black. . . . . prom dir
Donna Rodriguez . . . . progmg dir
Dan Acklen. . . . . news dir
Steve Aase . . . . chief of engrg

KOTI—Analog channel: 2. On air date: Aug 12, 1956. Box 2K, 222 S. 7th, Klamath Falls, OR 97601. Phone: (541) 882-2222. Fax: (541) 883-7664. Web Site: www.localnewscomesfirst.com. Licensee: California Oregon Broadcasting Inc. Group owner: (group owner). Network: NBC. Washington Atty: Wiley, Rein & Fielding.
Key Personnel:
Patricia Smallin. pres
John Larkin . . . . gen mgr
Wally Babbidge . . . . gen sls mgr
Alan Plotkin . . . . natl sls mgr
Larry Black. . . . . prom dir
Donna Rodriquez . . . . progmg dir
Dan Acklen. . . . . news dir
Steve Aase . . . . chief of engrg

***KSYS**—Analog channel: 8. On air date: Jan 17, 1977. 34 S. Fir St., Medford, OR 97501. Phone: (541) 779-0808. Fax: (541) 779-2178. Web Site: www.soptv.org. Licensee: Southern Oregon Public Television Inc. Network: PBS.
Key Personnel:
Mark Stanislawski . . . . CEO, pres & gen mgr
Dotti Wilson . . . . dev dir
Tom Werner . . . . chief of engrg

KTVL—Analog channel: 10. Digital channel: 35. On air date: Oct 3, 1961. Box 10, Medford, OR 97501. 1440 Rossanley Dr., Medford, OR 97501. Phone: (541) 773-7373. Fax: (541) 779-0451. E-mail: ktvl@ktvl.com. Web Site: www.ktvl.com. Licensee: Freedom Broadcasting of Oregon Licensee L.L.C. Group owner: Freedom Broadcasting Inc. (acq 8-28-81; $12.5 million).. Network: CBS. Rep: TeleRep. Washington Atty: Latham & Watkins. News: 16 hrs wkly.
Key Personnel:
Kingsley Kelley. . . . . VP & gen mgr
Jennifer Beres . . . . opns mgr
John White . . . . gen sls mgr
Lila Hampton . . . . natl sls mgr
Barry Tevis . . . . prom mgr
Sheila Giorgetti . . . . progmg dir
Gordon Godfrey. . . . . news dir
Carl Randall . . . . chief of engrg

Pendleton

see Yakima-Pasco-Richland-Kennewick, WA market

Portland, OR (DMA 24)

KATU—Analog channel: 2. Digital channel: 43. On air date: Mar 15, 1962. 2153 N.E. Sandy Blvd., Portland, OR 97232. Box 2, Portland, OR 97207. Phone: (503) 231-4222. Fax: (503) 231-4233. E-mail: thedesk@katu.com. Web Site: www.katu.com. Licensee: Fisher Broadcasting - Portland TV L.L.C. Group owner: Fisher Broadcasting Company (acq 12-4-01; grpsl). Network: ABC. Rep: TeleRep. Washington Atty: Fisher, Wayland, Cooper, Leader & Zaragoza. News: 24 hrs wkly.
Key Personnel:
Bill Krippaehne Jr. CEO
Ben Tucker . . . . pres
Warren Spector . . . . CFO
Dave Olmsted . . . . gen mgr
Stan Hubert. . . . . stn mgr & gen sls mgr
Darby Britto . . . . opns mgr
Diane Gervais . . . . natl sls mgr
Steve Denari. . . . . prom dir & pub affrs dir
Julie Mespelt . . . . progmg mgr
Mike Rausch . . . . news dir
Alan Batdorf . . . . chief of engrg

KGW—Analog channel: 8. Digital channel: 46. On air date: Dec 15, 1956. 1501 S.W. Jefferson St., Portland, OR 97201. Phone: (503) 226-5000. Fax: (503) 226-4448. Web Site: www.kgw.com. Licensee: KGW-TV Inc. Group owner: Belo Corp., Broadcast Division (acq 1997; grpsl). Network: NBC. Rep: Blair Television. Washington Atty: Wiley, Rein & Fielding. News: 35 hrs wkly.
Key Personnel:
Paul Fry. . . . . pres & gen mgr
Josy Ansley . . . . opns mgr
Dave Presner. . . . . sls dir
Susan Nguyen . . . . mktg dir
Brenda Buratti. . . . . prom dir & progmg dir
Rod Gramer . . . . news dir

***KNMT-TV**—Analog channel: 24. On air date: Nov 17, 1989. 432 N.E. 74th Ave., Portland, OR 97213. Phone: (503) 252-0792. Fax: (503) 256-4205. Web Site: www.nmtv.org. Licensee: National Minority TV Inc.. Ownership: Paul F. Crouch; Jane Duff; Jan Crouch.
Key Personnel:
Jane P. Duff. . . . . pres
Dr. Paul F. Crouch . . . . VP
Adolfo Carbajal . . . . stn mgr & progmg mgr
Bonnie Gaulding . . . . pub affrs dir
Steven Hendrix. . . . . chief of engrg

KOIN—Analog channel: 6. Digital channel: 40. On air date: Oct 15, 1953. 222 S.W. Columbia St., Portland, OR 97201. Phone: (503) 464-0600. Fax: (503) 464-0655. E-mail: koin@koin.com. Web Site: www.koin.com. Licensee: Emmis Television License LLC. Group owner: Emmis Communications Corp. (acq 10-1-2000; grpsl). Network: CBS. News: 27 hrs wkly.
Key Personnel:
David B. Lippoff . . . . gen mgr & progmg dir
John Tamerlano . . . . gen sls mgr
JoAnne James. . . . . natl sls mgr
Dan Salamone. . . . . mktg dir & news dir
Lee A. Wood. . . . . engrg dir

***KOPB-TV**—Analog channel: 10. On air date: Feb 6, 1961. 7140 S.W. Macadam Ave., Portland, OR 97219-3099. Phone: (503) 244-9900. Fax: (503) 293-1919. E-mail: audience-services@opb.org. Web Site: www.opb.org. Licensee: Oregon Public Broadcasting.. Ownership: Board of directors. (acq 9-20-93; grpsl; 10-11-93). Network: PBS. Washington Atty: Schwartz, Woods & Miller.
Key Personnel:
Jack Galmiche. . . . . COO
Maynard E. Orme . . . . CEO & pres
Dan Metziga. . . . . dev dir

KPDX—(Vancouver).WA Analog channel: 49. Digital channel: 48. On air date: October 1983. 14975 N.W. Greenbrier Pkwy., Beaverton, OR 97006-5731. Phone: (503) 906-1249. Fax: (503) 548-6220. E-mail: kptunews@kptu.com. Web Site: www.kpdx.com. Licensee: Meredith Corp. Group owner: Meredith Broadcasting Group, Meredith Corp. (acq 7-1-97; grpsl). Network: UPN. Rep: TeleRep.

KPOU—Analog channel: 16.Not on air, target date: unknown: Equity Broadcasting Corp., 1 Shackleford Dr., Suite 400, Little Rock, AR 72211. Phone: (501) 219-2400. Fax: (501) 716-3502. Permittee: La Grande Broadcasting Inc. Group owner: Equity Broadcasting Corp. (acq 10-20-00).

KPTV—Analog channel: 12. Digital channel: 30. On air date: Sept 20, 1952. 14975 N.W. Greenbrier Pkwy., Beaverton, OR 97006. Phone: (503) 906-1249. Fax: (503) 548-6910. E-mail: webstaff@kptv.com. Web Site: kptv.com. Licensee: Meredith Corp. Group owner: Meredith Broadcasting Group, Meredith Corp. (acq 5-13-02; swap). Network: Fox. Rep: TeleRep. News: 27 hrs wkly.

Key Personnel:
Teresa Burgess . . . . . VP & gen mgr
Michael Brostek . . . . . gen sls mgr
Matt Hyatt . . . . . prom mgr
Lee Petrik . . . . . progmg dir & progmg mgr

KPXG—Analog channel: 22. On air date: Nov 21, 1981. 1501 SW. Jefferson, Portland, OR 97201. Phone: (503) 222-2221. Fax: (503) 222-4613. Web Site: www.paxtv.com. Licensee: Paxson Portland License Inc. Group owner: Paxson Communications Corp. (acq 5-14-98; $30 million). Rep: NBC TV Stations Sales.

***KTVR**—Analog channel: 13. Digital channel: 5. On air date: Dec 6, 1964. 7140 S.W. Macadam Ave., Portland, OR 97219-3099. Phone: (503) 244-9900. Fax: (503) 293-1919. Web Site: www.opb.org. Licensee: Oregon Public Broadcasting.. Ownership: Board of directors. (acq 1993; grpsl; 9-20-93). Network: PBS. Washington Atty: Schwartz, Woods & Miller.

Key Personnel:
Maynard E. Orme . . . . . CEO & pres
Jack Galmiche . . . . . sr VP & chief of opns
Tom Doggett . . . . . progmg dir
Morgan Holm . . . . . news dir & pub affrs dir
Mike Tondreau . . . . . chief of engrg

KWBP—Analog channel: 32. Digital channel: 33. On air date: May 1989. 10255 S.W. Arctic Dr., Beaverton, OR 97005. Phone: (503) 644-3232. Fax: (503) 626-3576. E-mail: questions@wb32tv.com. Web Site: www.wb32tv.com. Licensee: Tribune Broadcast Holdings Inc. Group owner: Tribune Broadcasting Co. (acq 3-25-2003; $275 million. with KPLR-TV Saint Louis, MO). Network: WB. Rep: MMT. Washington Atty: Dickstein, Shapiro, Morin & Oshinsky.

Key Personnel:
Kieran Clarke . . . . . VP & gen mgr
Corina Klaas-Torseth . . . . . opns mgr & progmg mgr
John Manzi . . . . . gen sls mgr
Anne Van Gordon . . . . . natl sls mgr & rgnl sls mgr
John Clarke . . . . mktg mgr, prom mgr, adv mgr & pub affrs dir
Jamie McDowell . . . . . prom VP
Bob Shaw . . . . . film buyer
Pat Shearer . . . . . chief of engrg

Pennsylvania

Altoona

see Johnstown-Altoona, PA market

Erie, PA (DMA 142)

WFXP—Analog channel: 66. On air date: Sept 2, 1986. 8455 Peach St., Erie, PA 16509. Phone: (814) 864-2400. Fax: (814) 864-5393. Web Site: www.wfxptv.com. Licensee: Mission Broadcasting of Wichita Falls Inc. Group owner: Mission Broadcasting Inc. (acq 10-22-98). Network: Fox. Washington Atty: Arter & Hadden. News: 3 hrs wkly.

Key Personnel:
Beverly Joyce . . . . . stn mgr
Scott Osborne . . . . . gen sls mgr

WICU-TV—Analog channel: 12. Digital channel: 52. On air date: Mar 15, 1949. 3514 State St., Erie, PA 16508. Phone: (814) 454-5201. Fax: (814) 455-0703. E-mail: omfp@wicu12.com. Web Site: www.wicu12.com. Licensee: SJL of Pennsylvania License Subsidiary LLC. (acq 8-96; $11 million).. Network: NBC. Rep: Katz Radio. Washington Atty: Latham & Watkins. News staff: 20; News: 22 hrs wkly.

Key Personnel:
Sandy Benton . . . . . pres & gen mgr
Tim Dunst . . . . . sls dir & gen sls mgr
Coreen Scott . . . . . prom dir
Judy Shannon . . . . . progmg dir
Phil Hayes . . . . . news dir
John Wilkosz . . . . . engrg dir & chief of engrg

WJET-TV—Analog channel: 24. On air date: Apr 2, 1966. 8455 Peach St., Erie, PA 16509. Phone: (814) 864-2400. Fax: (814) 868-3041. Web Site: www.wjettv.com. Licensee: Nexstar Finance Inc. Group owner: Nexstar Broadcasting Group Inc. (acq 12-16-97; $18.5 million).. Network: ABC. Washington Atty: Drinker, Riddle & Reath. News staff: 29; News: 39 hrs wkly.

Key Personnel:
Louis Gattozzi . . . . . VP & gen mgr
Bob Bach . . . . . rgnl sls mgr
Steve Freifeld . . . . . mktg dir
Craig Schertzer . . . . . prom mgr
Mary Scheuer . . . . . progmg mgr & pub affrs dir
Louis A. Gattozzi . . . . . film buyer
Chris Huston . . . . . news dir
Lorne Earle . . . . . chief of engrg

***WQLN**—Analog channel: 54. On air date: Aug 13, 1967. 8425 Peach St., Erie, PA 16509. Phone: (814) 864-3001. Fax: (814) 864-4077. E-mail: wqln@wqln.org. Web Site: www.wqln.org. Licensee: Public Broadcasting of Northwest Pa. Inc. Network: PBS. Washington Atty: Dow, Lohnes & Albertson.

Key Personnel:
Dwight Miller . . . . . pres & gen mgr
Tracey B. Ferrier . . . . . VP
Ed Upton . . . . . engrg dir

WSEE—Analog channel: 35. Digital channel: 16. On air date: Apr 24, 1954. 1220 Peach St., Erie, PA 16501. Phone: (814) 455-7575. Fax: (814) 454-5541. E-mail: wsee@35wsee.com. Web Site: www.35wsee.com. Licensee: Lilly Broadcasting of Pennslvania License Subsidiary LLC.. Ownership: Kevin T. Lilly, 100% (acq 11-28-02;. $10 million).. Network: CBS. Washington Atty: Lathan & Watkins. News staff: 30; News: 10 hrs wkly.

Key Personnel:
Kevin T. Lilly . . . . . pres
Brian Lilly . . . . . gen mgr
Cheryl Beers . . . . . natl sls mgr
Doug Beers . . . . . rgnl sls mgr
Tracy Stufft . . . . . stn mgr & progmg dir
John Christenson . . . . . news dir

Harrisburg-Lancaster-Lebanon-York, PA (DMA 42)

WGAL—Analog channel: 8. On air date: Mar 18, 1949. Box 7127, Lancaster, PA 17604. 1300 Columbia Ave., Lancaster, PA 17603. Phone: (717) 393-5851. Fax: (717) 393-9484. Web Site: www.wgal.com. Licensee: WGAL Hearst-Argyle Television Inc. Group owner: Hearst-Argyle Television Inc. (acq 1999; grpsl). Network: NBC. Rep: Eagle Television Sales. Washington Atty: Brooks, Pierce. News staff: 53; News: 29 hrs wkly.

Key Personnel:
Paul Quinn . . . . . pres & gen mgr
Bob Good . . . . . opns mgr
Nancy Tulli . . . . . gen sls mgr
Andy Scheid . . . . . natl sls mgr
John Baldwin . . . . . mktg mgr, prom mgr & pub affrs dir
Carol Jacoby . . . . . progmg dir & progmg mgr
Dan O'Donnell . . . . . news dir
Robert Good . . . . . chief of engrg

WGCB-TV—Analog channel: 49. On air date: Apr 28, 1979. Box 88, Red Lion, PA 17356-0088. 2900 Windsor Rd., Kansas City, PA 17356. Phone: (717) 246-1681. Fax: (717) 244-9316. Web Site: www.wgcbtv.com. Licensee: Red Lion Broadcasting Co.. Ownership: John H. Norris 100%. Washington Atty: Booth, Freret, Imlay and Tepper.

Key Personnel:
John H. Norris . . . . . CEO
Clyde H. Campbell . . . . . CFO
John Norris . . . . . gen mgr
Anna L. Plourde-Norris . . . . . dev VP
Gordon Moul . . . . . natl sls mgr
Jerry Jacobs . . . . . mktg dir
Clyde Campbell . . . . . adv dir
John Peeling . . . . . progmg dir
Susan Brown . . . . . stn mgr, opns dir, prom dir & pub affrs dir
Donald Horst . . . . . chief of engrg

WHP-TV—Analog channel: 21. On air date: Apr 15, 1953. 3300 N. Sixth St., Harrisburg, PA 17110. Phone: (717) 238-2100. Fax: (717) 238-8744. Fax: (717) 236-0198. Web Site: www.whptv.com. Licensee: Clear Channel Broadcasting Licenses Inc. Group owner: Clear Channel Communications Inc. (acq 1995; $30 million).. Network: CBS. News staff: 23; News: 20 hrs wkly.

Key Personnel:
Matt Uhl . . . . . VP & gen mgr
Lou Castriota Sr. . . . . . opns dir & progmg dir
Stu Brenner . . . . . natl sls mgr
Sherry Taylor . . . . . prom dir
Greg Zoerb . . . . . news dir
Rob Hershey . . . . . engrg dir

WHTM-TV—Analog channel: 27. On air date: June 19, 1953. Box 5860, 3235 Hoffman St., Harrisburg, PA 17110-5860. Phone: (717) 236-2727. Fax: (717) 232-5272. Web Site: www.abc27.com. Licensee: Harrisburg Television Inc. Group owner: Allbritton Communication Co. (acq 1996; $113 million). Network: ABC. Washington Atty: Hogan & Hartson. News staff: 40; News: 20 hrs wkly.

Key Personnel:
Joe Lewin . . . . . pres & gen mgr
Rob Saylor . . . . . gen sls mgr
Paul Roda . . . . . natl sls mgr
Larry Maloney . . . . . rgnl sls mgr
Randy Whitaker . . . . . mktg dir
Betty Bryan Fish . . . . . prom dir
Tishia Kohr . . . . . progmg dir
Keith Blaisdell . . . . . news dir
Caroline Wilson . . . . . pub affrs dir
Don Landis . . . . . chief of engrg

***WITF-TV**—Analog channel: 33. Digital channel: 36. On air date: Nov 22, 1964. Box 2954, Harrisburg, PA 17105. 1982 Locust Ln., Harrisburg, PA 17109. Phone: (717) 236-6000. Fax: (717) 236-4628. E-mail: info@witf.org. Web Site: www.witf.org. Licensee: WITF Inc. Network: PBS. Washington Atty: Dow, Lohnes & Albertson.

Key Personnel:
Kathleen A. Pavelko . . . . . CEO & pres
Gregory Poland . . . . . CFO
Barry Stoner . . . . . sr VP
Michael Greenwald . . . . . dev VP
Charles Lichty . . . . . sls VP
Sue Baldwin-Way . . . . . prom dir
Craig Cohen . . . . . progmg dir
Ron Kain . . . . . engrg dir

WLYH-TV—Analog channel: 15. On air date: Oct 15, 1953. 3300 N. Sixth St., Harrisburg, PA 17011. Phone: (717) 238-2100. Fax: (717) 238-8744. Licensee: Television Station Group License Subsidiary LLC. Group owner: Television Station Group LLC (acq 10-27-2000; grpsl).

Key Personnel:
George Lilly . . . . . pres
Matthew T. Uhl . . . . . VP & gen mgr
Lou Castriota Sr. . . . . . opns dir & progmg dir
Stuart Brenner . . . . . natl sls mgr
Sherry Taylor . . . . . prom dir
Rob Hershey . . . . . chief of engrg

WPMT—Analog channel: 43. On air date: Dec 22, 1952. 2005 S. Queen St., York, PA 17403. Phone: (717) 843-0043. Fax: (717) 843-9741. E-mail: fox43@mail.fox43.com. Web Site: www.fox43.com. Licensee: Tribune Television Co. Group owner: Tribune Broadcasting Co. (acq 7-15-97; grpsl). Network: Fox. Rep: TeleRep.

Key Personnel:
Dennis FitzSimons . . . . . CEO
Pat Mullen . . . . . pres
John A. Riggle . . . . . VP & gen mgr
Keith McFarland . . . . . opns dir
Peter Rosella . . . . . gen sls mgr
Dave Farish . . . . . prom mgr
Sandy Hawk . . . . . progmg dir & progmg mgr
Jim DePury . . . . . news dir
Denise Durham . . . . . pub affrs dir
Jim Myers . . . . . engrg dir

Johnstown-Altoona, PA (DMA 97)

WATM-TV—Analog channel: 23. Digital channel: 24. On air date: November 1974. 1450 Scalp Ave., Johnstown, PA 15904. Phone: (814) 266-8088. Phone: (814) 949-8823. Fax: (814) 266-7749. Fax: (814) 949-4780. Web Site: www.abc23.com. Licensee: Palm Television L.P.. Ownership: Gregory P. Filandrinos. (acq 8-17-99; $12.5 million). Network: ABC. Rep: Katz Radio. Washington Atty: Hogan & Hartson. News staff: 10; News: 3 hrs wkly.

Key Personnel:

Frank Quitoni . . . . pres & gen mgr
Jim Penna . . . . news dir

WJAC-TV—Analog channel: 6. Digital channel: 34. On air date: Sept 15, 1949. 49 Old Hickory Ln., Johnstown, PA 15905. Phone: (814) 255-7600. Fax: (814) 255-7675. Web Site: www.wjactv.com. Licensee: WPXI-TV Holdings Inc. Group owner: Cox Broadcasting (acq 9-22-00). Network: NBC. Washington Atty: Dow, Lohnes & Albertson. News staff: 38; News: 25 hrs news wkly.
Key Personnel:
Richard D. Schrott . . . . VP
Richard B. Schrott . . . . gen mgr

WKBS-TV—Analog channel: 47. On air date: 1985. One Signal Hill Dr., Wall, PA 15148-1499. Phone: (877) 437-4446. Fax: (412) 824-5442. Web Site: www.ctvn.org. Licensee: Cornerstone Television Inc. Group owner: (group owner) Washington Atty: Gammon & Grange.

***WPSX-TV**—Analog channel: 3. On air date: Mar 1, 1965. 102 Wagner Buld., University Park, PA 16802-3899. Phone: (814) 865-3333. Fax: (814) 863-9786. E-mail: tzk1@psu.edu. Web Site: www.wpsx.psu.edu. Licensee: The Pennsylvania State University. Network: PBS. Washington Atty: Paul, Hastings, Janofsky & Walker.
Key Personnel:
Ted Krichels . . . . gen mgr
Kate Domico . . . . opns dir
Spencer Lewis . . . . dev dir
Carol Wonsavage . . . . mktg dir & prom mgr
Ashear Barr . . . . adv dir
Tracy Vosburgh . . . . stn mgr & progmg dir
Carl Fisher . . . . chief of engrg

WTAJ-TV—Analog channel: 10. On air date: Mar 1, 1953. 5000 6th Ave., Altoona, PA 16602. Phone: (814) 942-1010. Fax: (814) 946-8746. E-mail: smith@wtajtv.com. Web Site: www.wtajtv.com. Licensee: Television Station Group License Subsidiary LLC. Group owner: Television Station Group LLC (acq 10-27-2000; grpsl). Network: CBS. Rep: TeleRep. Washington Atty: Latham & Watkins. News staff: 39; News: 29 hrs wkly.

WWCP-TV—Analog channel: 8. On air date: Oct 13, 1986. 1450 Scalp Ave., Johnstown, PA 15904. Phone: (814) 266-8088. Fax: (814) 266-7749. Web Site: www.fox8tv.com. Licensee: Peak Media of Pennsylvania Licensee L.L.C.. Ownership: Peak Media of Pennsylvania LLC. Network: Network: Fox, ABC. Rep: Katz Radio. Washington Atty: Hogan & Hartson. News staff: 10; News: 5 hrs wkly.
Key Personnel:
Frank Quitoni . . . . pres & gen mgr
Jim Penna . . . . news dir

Lancaster

see Harrisburg-Lancaster-Lebanon-York, PA market

Lebanon

see Harrisburg-Lancaster-Lebanon-York, PA market

Philadelphia (DMA 4)

KYW-TV—Analog channel: 3. Digital channel: 26. On air date: Sept 3, 1941. 101 S. Independence Mall E., Philadelphia, PA 19106. Phone: (215) 238-4700. Fax: (215) 238-4783. Web Site: www.kyw.com. Licensee: CBS Broadcasting Inc. Group owner: Viacom Television Stations Group (acq 5-4-2000; grpsl). Network: CBS. Rep: CBS Spot Sales. Washington Atty: Wilkes, Artis, Hedrick & Lane.
Key Personnel:
Michael Colleran . . . . VP & gen mgr
Bob Fein . . . . stn mgr
Charlie Dunn . . . . sls dir
Roy Coddington . . . . natl sls mgr
Oscar Welch . . . . mktg dir
Perry Casciato . . . . progmg dir
Susan Schiller . . . . news dir
Mitch Poleski . . . . chief of engrg

WBPH-TV—Analog channel: 60. On air date: 1991. 813 N. Fenwick St., Allentown, PA 18109. Phone: (610) 433-4400. Fax: (610) 433-8251. E-mail: info@wbph.org. Web Site: www.wbph.org. Licensee: Sonshine Family TV Inc.. Ownership: Patricia Huber, 100%.

WCAU—Analog channel: 10. Digital channel: 67. On air date: Mar 15, 1948. 10 Monument Rd., Bala Cynwyd, PA 19004. Phone: (610) 668-5510. Fax: (610) 668-3700. E-mail: nbc10@nbc.com. Web Site: www.nbc10.com. Licensee: NBC Telemundo License Co. Group owner: NBC TV Stations Division (acq 9-10-95). Network: NBC. Rep: NBC TV Stations Sales. News staff: 110; News: 21 hrs wkly.
Key Personnel:
Dennis Bianchi . . . . pres & gen mgr
Joe Marsini . . . . CFO
Jim Barger . . . . opns dir & engrg dir
Joe Collins . . . . sls VP
Lauren Bacigalupi . . . . prom VP & adv VP
Lawana Scales . . . . progmg dir
Chris Blackman . . . . news dir
JoAnne Wilder . . . . pub affrs dir

WFMZ-TV—Analog channel: 69. Digital channel: 46. On air date: Nov 25, 1976. 300 E. Rock Rd., Allentown, PA 18103. Phone: (610) 797-4530. Fax: (610) 798-4089. Fax: (610) 791-2288 (sales). Web Site: www.WFMZ.com. Licensee: Maranatha Broadcasting Co.. Ownership: Richard C. Dean, 54%; others, 46%. Washington Atty: Bentley Law Offices. News staff: 65; News: 58 hrs wkly.
Key Personnel:
Barry Fisher . . . . pres & gen mgr
Mike Kulp . . . . CFO
Brad Rinehart . . . . news dir

WGTW-TV—Analog channel: 48. Digital channel: 27. On air date: August 1992. 3900 Main St., Philadelphia, PA 19127. Phone: (215) 930-0482. Fax: (215) 930-0496. Licensee: Trinity Christian Center of Santa Ana Inc. (acq 10-1-2004; $7 million. plus assumption of $41 million in debt).
Key Personnel:
Dorothy Brunson . . . . pres & gen mgr
Edward Brunson . . . . opns mgr
John Duffrn . . . . sls VP
Catherine Pugh . . . . mktg mgr
Kim Starisky . . . . prom mgr & pub affrs dir
Frank Voight . . . . progmg mgr
Kurtis Davis . . . . engrg dir
Al Box . . . . chief of engrg

***WHYY-TV**—Analog channel: 12. On air date: Sept 12, 1963. Independence Mall W., 150 N. 6th St., Philadelphia, PA 19106. 625 Orange St., Wilmington, DE 19106. Phone: (215) 351-1200. Phone: (302) 888-1200. Fax: (215) 351-0398. Web Site: www.whyy.org. Licensee: WHYY Inc.. Ownership: WHYY Inc. Network: PBS. Washington Atty: Schwartz, Woods & Miller. News staff: 10; News: 5 hrs wkly.
Key Personnel:
William J. Marrazzo . . . . CEO & pres
Bruce Flamm . . . . CFO
Paul Gluck . . . . VP & stn mgr
Deborah Hoxter . . . . sls dir
Nessa R. Forman . . . . prom VP
David Rubinsohn . . . . progmg dir
William J. Weber . . . . engrg VP

***WLVT-TV**—Analog channel: 39. On air date: September 1965. 123 Sesame St., Bethlehem, PA 18015. Phone: (610) 867-4677. Fax: (610) 867-3544. Web Site: www.wlvt.org. Licensee: Lehigh Valley Public Telecommunications Corp. Network: PBS. Washington Atty: Schwartz, Woods & Miller.
Key Personnel:
Patricia Simon . . . . CEO
Patricia Simons . . . . pres
Ron Heft . . . . opns dir
Rebecca Fromm . . . . progmg VP
Cal Hartley . . . . progmg dir & engrg dir

WMCN-TV—Analog channel: 53. Digital channel: 50. On air date: Oct 1, 1986. 1 S. New York Ave., Atlantic City, NJ 08401. Phone: (609) 441-1120. Fax: (609) 441-9559. E-mail: contact@wwac.tv. Web Site: www.wwac.tv. Licensee: Lenfest Broadcasting L.L.C.. Ownership: H. Chase Lenfest, member/owner (acq 7-19-00; $9 million).. Washington Atty: Schwartz, Woods & Miller.
Key Personnel:
H. Chase Lenfest . . . . pres & CEO
Robert M. Lund . . . . VP & gen mgr
Rachel van Hest . . . . mktg mgr
Mark Chesterton . . . . progmg mgr
Vojislav Radosavljevic . . . . chief of engrg

WMGM-TV—Analog channel: 40. On air date: Jan 25, 1966. 1601 New Rd., Linwood, NJ 08221. Phone: (609) 927-4440. Fax: (609) 926-8875. E-mail: nbc40wmgm@hotmail.com. Web Site: www.nbc40.net. Licensee: Access.1 New Jersey License Co. Group owner: Access.1 Communications Corp. (acq 2004; grpsl). Network: NBC. News: 8 hrs wkly.
Key Personnel:
Chesley Maddox-Dorsey . . . . pres
Arthur Benjamin . . . . CFO & VP
Ron Smith . . . . gen mgr

***WNJS**—Analog channel: 23. Digital channel: 22. On air date: Oct 23, 1972. Box 777, Trenton, NJ 08625-0777. 25 S. Stockton St., Trenton, NJ 08608-1832. Phone: (609) 777-5000. Fax: (609) 777-5400. Fax: (609) 633-2912. Web Site: www.njn.net. Licensee: New Jersey Public Broadcasting Authority. Network: PBS. Washington Atty: Schwartz, Woods & Miller. News: 2 hrs wkly.
Key Personnel:
Andre Butts . . . . progmg dir
William Schnorbus . . . . chief of engrg

***WNJT**—Analog channel: 52. Digital channel: 43. On air date: Apr 5, 1971. Box 777, Trenton, NJ 08625-0777. 25 S. Stockton St., Trenton, NJ 08608-1832. Phone: (609) 777-5000. Fax: (609) 633-2917. Web Site: www.njn.net. Licensee: New Jersey Public Broadcasting Authority. Network: PBS. Washington Atty: Schwartz, Woods & Miller. News: 2 hrs wkly.
Key Personnel:
Elizabeth G. Christopherson . . . . gen mgr
Joann Ruscio . . . . mktg mgr
Andre Butts . . . . progmg dir
William Schnorbus . . . . chief of engrg

WPHL-TV—Analog channel: 17. Digital channel: 54. On air date: Sept 17, 1965. 5001 Wynnefield Ave., Philadelphia, PA 19131. Phone: (215) 878-1700. Fax: (215) 879-3665. E-mail: wphltv@aol.com. Web Site: www.wb17.com. Licensee: Tribune Broadcasting Co. Group owner: (group owner, see Cross-Ownership; acq 4-17-92; $19 million; 5-18-92). Network: WB. Rep: TeleRep. Washington Atty: Koteen & Naftalin.
Key Personnel:
Vince Giannini . . . . VP & gen mgr
Patrick Loftus . . . . gen sls mgr
Sarit Rus . . . . prom dir
Chuck Carter . . . . news dir
Rachael Amara . . . . pub affrs dir

WPPX—Analog channel: 61. Digital channel: 31. On air date: July 9, 1986. 10 Monument Rd., Bala Cynwyd, PA 19004. Phone: (610) 949-7480. Fax: (610) 949-7494. Web Site: www.pax.tv. Licensee: Paxson Communications Corp. Group owner: (group owner; acq 1-20-95; $9.635 million; 3-20-95).
Key Personnel:
Robert Marc Backman . . . . gen mgr
Joe Collins . . . . gen sls mgr
Shawn Edwards . . . . rgnl sls mgr
Daniel Borowicz . . . . chief of engrg

WPSG—Analog channel: 57. Digital channel: 32. On air date: June 15, 1981. 101 S. Independence Mall E., Kansas City, PA 19106. Phone: (215) 574-5757. Fax: (215) 574-5786. E-mail: upn57@wpsg.com. Web Site: www.upn57.com. Licensee: Viacom Stations Group of Philadelphia Inc. Group owner: Viacom Television Stations Group (acq 1995). Network: UPN. Washington Atty: Fisher, Wayland, Cooper, Leader & Zaragoza.
Key Personnel:
Michael Colleran . . . . VP & gen mgr
Greg Benedeth . . . . gen mgr, rgnl sls mgr & mktg dir
Bob Fein . . . . stn mgr
Susan Schiller . . . . news dir

WPVI-TV—Analog channel: 6. Digital channel: 64. On air date: Sept 13, 1947. 4100 City Ave., Philadelphia, PA 19131. Phone: (215) 878-9700. Fax: (215) 581-4515. Fax: (215) 581-4530 (news). Web Site: www.wpvi.com. Licensee: ABC Inc. Group owner: (group owner; acq 4-27-71; grpsl). Network: ABC. Washington Atty: Wilmer, Cutler & Pickering.
Key Personnel:
Rebecca Campbell . . . . pres & gen mgr
James Aronow . . . . sls dir
Dirk Ohley . . . . natl sls mgr
Tim Giannetino . . . . natl sls mgr
Bob Liga . . . . rgnl sls mgr
Paula McDermott . . . . mktg mgr
Caroline Welch . . . . progmg dir
Carla Carpenter . . . . news dir
Linda Munich . . . . pub affrs dir
James Gilbert . . . . engrg dir

WTVE—Analog channel: 51. On air date: February 1980. 1729 N. 11th St., Reading, PA 19604. Phone: (610) 921-9181. Fax: (610) 921-9139. Web Site: wtve.com. Licensee: Reading Broadcasting Inc. Washington

Directory of Television Pennsylvania

Atty: Leventhal, Senter & Lerman.
Key Personnel:
Frank McCracken . . . pres, gen mgr, gen sls mgr & progmg mgr
Kimberley Bradley . . . . . . opns VP, opns mgr & pub affrs dir
Gibson White. . . . . chief of engrg

WTXF-TV—Analog channel: 29. Digital channel: 42. On air date: May 18, 1965. 330 Market St., Philadelphia, PA 19106. Phone: (215) 925-2929. Fax: (215) 925-2420. Web Site: www.foxphiladelphia.com. Licensee: Fox TV Stations of Philadelphia Inc. Group owner: Fox Television Stations Inc. (acq 1995; $200 million).. Network: Fox. News: 25 hrs wkly.
Key Personnel:
Bob Simone . . . . VP
Dave Huddleston . . . . gen mgr
George Cummings . . . . opns mgr
Ramona Alexander . . . . gen sls mgr
Joe Rooney . . . . natl sls mgr
Ted Kramer . . . . natl sls mgr
Lisa Oswald . . . . rgnl sls mgr
Larry Ferenchick. . . . . mktg dir
Audrey Fish . . . . prom VP
Holly Gauntt . . . . news dir
Jennifer Best . . . . pub affrs dir
Steve James . . . . engrg VP

WUVP-TV—Analog channel: 65. Digital channel: 66. On air date: July 13, 1981. 4449 N. Delsea Dr., Newfield, NJ 08344. Phone: (856) 691-6565. Fax: (856) 691-2483. E-mail: notibreve_65@univision.net. Web Site: www.univision.com. Licensee: Univision Partnership of Vineland. Group owner: Univision Communications Inc. (acq 5-21-01; grpsl). Network: Univision (Spanish).
Key Personnel:
Diana Bald . . . . gen mgr
Bob Webb . . . . gen sls mgr
Ken Nanus . . . . natl sls mgr
Eddie Petrosky. . . . . rgnl sls mgr
Josue Duarte . . . . prom mgr
Aida Rosario . . . . pub affrs dir
John Skelnik . . . . chief of engrg

WWSI—Analog channel: 62. Digital channel: 49. On air date: 1990. 1341 N. Delaware Ave., Suite 408, Philadelphia, PA 19125. One S. New York Ave., Atlantic City, NJ 08401. Phone: (215) 634-8862. Phone: (609) 449-0049. Fax: (215) 425-2683. Fax: (609) 441-9559. Web Site: www.wwsi-tv.com. Licensee: Hispanic Broadcasters of Philadelphia L.L.C.. Ownership: Council Tree Hispanic Broadcasters L.L.C. (acq 5-14-02). Network: Telemundo (Spanish). News staff: 4; News: 2.5 hrs wkly.
Key Personnel:
Jimmy Rivers . . . . gen mgr
Michael Brendzel. . . . . dev VP

***WYBE**—Analog channel: 35. On air date: June 10, 1990. 8200 Ridge Ave., Philadelphia, PA 19128-1604. Phone: (215) 483-3900. Fax: (215) 483-6908. Web Site: www.wybe.org. Licensee: Independence Public Media of Philadelphia Inc. Network: PBS. Washington Atty: Arter & Hadden. News staff: 1; News: 3 hrs wkly.
Key Personnel:
Norman Barnum . . . . CFO
Sherri Culver . . . . gen mgr
Stephanie Campbell. . . . . dev dir
Kim Brown . . . . sls dir
Shivani Jani . . . . mktg dir
Jessica Kegelman . . . . prom mgr
Joni Helton. progmg dir
April Polutan. . . . . pub affrs dir
Ed DiCesare. . . . . engrg VP

Pittsburgh, PA
(DMA 22)

KDKA-TV—Analog channel: 2. Digital channel: 25. On air date: January 1949. One Gateway Ctr., Pittsburgh, PA 15222. Phone: (412) 575-2200. Fax: (412) 575-3207. Licensee: CBS Broadcasting Inc. Group owner: Viacom Television Stations Group (acq 5-4-2000; grpsl). Network: CBS. Rep: CBS Spot Sales. Washington Atty: Wilkes, Artis, Hedrick & Lane.

WCWB—Analog channel: 22. Digital channel: 42. On air date: Sept 26, 1978. 750 Ivory Ave., Pittsburgh, PA 15214. Phone: (412) 931-5300. Fax: (412) 931-8029. Web Site: www.wcwb22.com. Licensee: WCWB Licensee LLC. Group owner: Sinclair Broadcast Group Inc. (acq 12-10-01; $17.808 million).. Network: WB. Rep: Millennium Sales & Marketing. Washington Atty: Shaw Pittman.
Key Personnel:
Alan Frank. . . . . gen mgr
Jim Lapiana . . . . sls dir
Kerry Check . . . . pub affrs dir & engrg dir

***WGPT**—Analog channel: 36. On air date: 1986. 11767 Owings Mills Blvd., Owings Mills, MD 21117-1499. Phone: (410) 356-5600. Fax: (410) 581-6579. E-mail: comments@mpt.org. Web Site: www.mpt.org. Licensee: Maryland Public Broadcasting Commission. Network: PBS. Washington Atty: Schwartz, Woods & Miller.
Key Personnel:
Robert Shuman . . . . CEO & pres
Larry Unger . . . . CFO
George Benaman . . . . opns VP

WNPA—Analog channel: 19. On air date: Oct 15, 1953. 1 Gateway Center, Pittsburgh, PA 15222. Phone: (412) 575-2200. Fax: (412) 575-2500. Licensee: Viacom Stations Group of Pittsburgh Inc. Group owner: Viacom Television Stations Group (acq 12-9-98; $39 million).. Network: UPN.

***WNPB-TV**—Analog channel: 24. Digital channel: 33. On air date: Feb 23, 1969. 191 Scott Ave., Morgantown, WV 26508. Phone: (304) 284-1440. Fax: (304) 284-1454. E-mail: audienceservices@wvpubcast.org. Web Site: www.wvpubcast.org. Licensee: West Virginia Educational Broadcasting Authority. (acq 7-1-83). Network: PBS. Washington Atty: Wilkinson, Barker, Knauer & Quinn. News staff: 2; News: one hr wkly.
Key Personnel:
Bill Acker . . . . gen mgr & dev dir
Jack Wells . . . . stn mgr

WPCB-TV—Analog channel: 40. On air date: Apr 15, 1979. Signal Hill Dr., Wall, PA 15148-1499. Phone: (412) 824-3930. Fax: (412) 824-5442. E-mail: drichert@ctvn.org. Web Site: www.ctvn.org. Licensee: Cornerstone Television Inc. (acq 7-78). Washington Atty: Shaw Pittman.
Key Personnel:
Ron Hembree . . . . pres
Chuck Alexander . . . . CFO
Kim Carter . . . . dev mgr
Alyson Hayes . . . . mktg dir & progmg VP
Dede Hayes . . . . progmg dir
Blake Richert . . . . engrg VP & engrg dir

WPGH-TV—Analog channel: 53. Digital channel: 43. On air date: July 14, 1953. 750 Ivory Ave., Pittsburgh, PA 15214. Phone: (412) 931-5300. Fax: (412) 931-8029. Web Site: www.wpgh53.com. Licensee: WPGH Licensee L.L.C. Group owner: Sinclair Broadcast Group Inc. (acq 8-30-91; $55 million;. FTR: 7-15-91). Network: Fox. Rep: Millennium Sales & Marketing. Washington Atty: Shaw Pitman. News staff: 33; News: 6 hrs wkly.
Key Personnel:
Alan Frank. . . . . gen mgr
Kerry Check . . . . opns dir
Jim Lapiana . . . . sls dir

WPXI—Analog channel: 11. Digital channel: 48. On air date: Sept 1, 1957. 11 Television Hill, Box 1100, Pittsburgh, PA 15214. Phone: (412) 237-1100. Fax: (412) 323-8097. Licensee: WPXI-TV Holdings Inc. Group owner: Cox Broadcasting (acq 1-1-65; $20.5 million; 11-30-64). Network: NBC. Rep: TeleRep. Washington Atty: Dow, Lohnes & Albertson.

***WQED**—Analog channel: 13. On air date: Apr 1, 1954. 4802 Fifth Ave., Pittsburgh, PA 15213. Phone: (412) 622-1300. Fax: (412) 622-6413. E-mail: viewers@wqed.org. Web Site: www.wqed.org. Licensee: WQED Multimedia. Network: PBS. Washington Atty: Schwartz, Woods & Miller.
Key Personnel:
George L. Miles Jr. . . . . CEO, pres & pres
Robert F. Petrilli . . . . COO
Herbert Bennett Conner. . . . . chmn
B.J. Leber . . . . sr VP & stn mgr
Deborah Acklin . . . . sr VP
Robert Petrulli. sr VP
Karen Farmer White . . . . VP
Lilli Mosco . . . . VP & dev VP
Rick Vaccarelli . . . . sls dir & adv dir
Gigi Saladna . . . . prom mgr
Chris Fennimore. . . . . progmg dir
Jocelyn Hough . . . . news dir
Michelle Pagano Heck. . . . . pub affrs dir
Paul Byers. . . . . engrg dir

WQEX—Analog channel: 16. On air date: Sept 14, 1959. 4802 Fifth Ave., Pittsburgh, PA 15213. Phone: (412) 622-1300. Fax: (412) 622-1488. E-mail: wqexviewers@wqed.org. Web Site: www.wqed.org/wqex. Licensee: WQED Multimedia. Washington Atty: Schwartz, Woods & Miller.
Key Personnel:
George Miles . . . . pres
Robert Petreilli . . . . sr VP
Keyola Panza . . . . stn mgr
Rick Vaccarelli . . . . sls dir
Gigi Saladna . . . . prom mgr
Paul Byers. . . . . engrg dir

WTAE-TV—Analog channel: 4. Digital channel: 51. On air date: Sept 14, 1958. 400 Ardmore Blvd., Pittsburgh, PA 15221. Phone: (412) 242-4300. Fax: (412) 244-4595. Web Site: www.thepittsburghchannel.com. Licensee: WTAE Hearst-Argyle Television Inc. Group owner: Hearst-Argyle Television Inc. (acq 7-16-97; grpsl). Network: ABC. Rep: Eagle Television Sales. Washington Atty: Brooks, Pierce, McLendon, Humphrey & Leonard. News staff: 70; News: 32 hrs wkly.
Key Personnel:
Rick Henry. . . . . pres & gen mgr
Dan Henninger. . . . . opns mgr
Bob Bee . . . . gen sls mgr & natl sls mgr
Leslie Wojdowski . . . . mktg mgr
Sherry Carpenter . . . . prom dir
Bob Longo . . . . news dir
Dave Kasperek . . . . engrg dir

Scranton

see Wilkes Barre-Scranton, PA market

Wilkes Barre-Scranton, PA
(DMA 53)

WBRE-TV—(Wilkes-Barre).Analog channel: 28. On air date: Jan 1, 1953. 62 S. Franklin St., Wilkes-Barre, PA 18701-1201. Phone: (570) 823-2828. Fax: (570) 823-4523. E-mail: 28news@nbga.net. Web Site: www.wbre.com. Licensee: Nexstar Finance Inc. Group owner: Nexstar Broadcasting Group Inc. (acq 11-14-97; $47 million).. Network: NBC. Washington Atty: Drinker, Biddle & Reath, LLP. News staff: 68; News: 24 hrs wkly.
Key Personnel:
John Dittmeier . . . . VP & gen mgr
Randy Williams. . . . . stn mgr & opns dir

WILF—Analog channel: 53. Digital channel: 29. On air date: Jan 22, 1993. 1181 Hwy. 315, Plains, PA 18702. Phone: (570) 970-5600. Fax: (570) 970-5604. E-mail: nepatoday@pgtv.com. Web Site: www.nepatoday.com. Licensee: Pegasus Broadcast Associates L.P., debtor-in-possession. Group owner: Pegasus Broadcast Television Inc. (acq 1993; FTR: 2-15-93). Network: Fox. Washington Atty: Shaw, Pittman.
Key Personnel:
Jim Bisagni . . . . gen mgr & gen sls mgr
Dan Mecca . . . . natl sls mgr
Ed Hart. . . . . rgnl sls mgr

WNEP-TV—Analog channel: 16. Digital channel: 49. On air date: Feb 9, 1954. 16 Montage Mountain Rd., Moosic, PA 18507. Phone: (570) 346-7474. Fax: (570) 347-0359. E-mail: email@wnep.com. Web Site: www.wnep.com. Licensee: New York Times Management Services. Group owner: The New York Times Co. (acq 12-30-85; $40 million;. FTR: 9-23-85). Network: ABC. Rep: Millennium Sales & Marketing. Washington Atty: Holland & Knight. News staff: 64; News: 23 hrs wkly.
Key Personnel:
Mrs. C. Lou Kirchen . . . . pres & gen mgr
David Lewandoski . . . . opns mgr
Lou Abitabilo. . . . . sls VP
Mike Last . . . . natl sls mgr
Chuck Morgan . . . . rgnl sls mgr
Diane Frain. . . . . mktg dir
Laurie LaMaster . . . . prom dir & prom mgr
Debbie Drechin . . . . progmg mgr
Dennis Fisher. news dir
Frank Gerardi . . . . pub affrs dir
Mike Morkavage . . . . chief of engrg

WOLF-TV—Analog channel: 56. Digital channel: 45. On air date: June 3, 1985. 1181 Hwy. 315, Plains, PA 18702. Phone: (570) 970-5600. Fax: (570) 970-5604. E-mail: fox56@pgtv.com. Web Site: www.nepatoday.com. Licensee: WOLF License Corp., debtor-in-possession. Group owner: Pegasus Broadcast Television Inc. Network: Fox. Petry Washington Atty: Shaw, Pittman. News: 3.5 hrs wkly.
Key Personnel:
Michael Yanuzzi . . . . VP & gen mgr
Jim Bisagni . . . . gen sls mgr
Dan Mecca . . . . natl sls mgr
Ed Hart. . . . . rgnl sls mgr

WQPX—Analog channel: 64. Digital channel: 32. On air date: 1999. 16 Montage Mountain Rd., Moosic, PA 18507. Phone: (570) 344-6400. Fax: (570) 344-3303. Web Site: www.paxtv.com. Licensee: Paxson Scranton License Inc. Group owner: Paxson Communications Corp. (acq 7-31-98; $6 million).. Washington Atty: Schwartz, Woods & Miller.

WSWB—Analog channel: 38. Digital channel: 31. On air date: Nov 26, 1998. 1181 Hwy. 315, Plains, PA 18702. Phone: (570) 970-5600. Fax: (570) 970-5601. Licensee: KB Prime Media L.L.C. Group owner: (group owner; acq 11-10-98; $500,000).. Network: WB. Washington Atty: Fisher, Wayland, Cooper, Leader & Zaragoza.
Key Personnel:
Guyon W. Turner . . . . . pres
Michael Yanuzzi . . . . . gen mgr & gen sls mgr
Aldo Cardoni . . . . . opns mgr
Ed Hart . . . . . natl sls mgr
Thom Welby . . . . . rgnl sls mgr
Doug Cook . . . . . mktg dir & prom dir
Erica Kumpas . . . . . progmg dir
Steve Phillips . . . . . pub affrs dir
Rich Chofey . . . . . chief of engrg

***WVIA-TV**—Analog channel: 44. On air date: Sept 26, 1966. 100 WVIA Way, Pittston, PA 18640-6197. Phone: (570) 826-6144. Phone: (570) 344-1244. Fax: (570) 655-1180. Licensee: Northeastern Pennsylvania Educational TV Association. Network: PBS. Washington Atty: Dow, Lohnes & Albertson.
Key Personnel:
A. William Kelly . . . . . CEO, pres & gen mgr
Bart Ecker . . . . . chmn
Ronald Stravirsky . . . . . CFO
Thomas P. Curra . . . . . stn mgr
Mollie Worrell . . . . . dev VP
Mike Burnside . . . . . pub affrs dir
Joseph Glynn . . . . . engrg VP

WYOU—Analog channel: 22. On air date: June 7, 1953. 409 Lackawanna Ave., Scranton, PA 18503. Phone: (570) 961-2222. Fax: (570) 344-4484. Web Site: www.wyou.com. Licensee: Mission Broadcasting Inc. Group owner: (group owner; acq 1-5-98; $21 million).. Network: CBS. Rep: Blair Television. Washington Atty: Drinker, Biddle & Reath LLP. News: 19.5 hrs wkly.
Key Personnel:
John Dittmeier . . . . . gen mgr
Randy Williams . . . . . opns dir & natl sls mgr
Steve Genett . . . . . natl sls mgr
Bob Spager . . . . . rgnl sls mgr
Susan Kalinowski . . . . . progmg dir & progmg mgr
Frank Andrews . . . . . news dir

York

see Harrisburg-Lancaster-Lebanon-York, PA market

Rhode Island

Providence, RI-New Bedford, MA (DMA 49)

WDPX—Analog channel: 58. On air date: July 19, 1985. 1120 Soldiers Field Rd., Boston, MA 02134. Phone: (617) 787-6868. Fax: (617) 787-4114. Web Site: www.paxtv.net. Licensee: Paxson Boston-68 License Inc. Group owner: Paxson Communications Corp. (acq 5-2-00; grpsl). Washington Atty: Arter & Hadden.

WJAR—Analog channel: 10. On air date: July 10, 1949. 23 Kenney Dr., Cranston, RI 02920. Phone: (401) 455-9100. Fax: (401) 455-9168. Fax: (401) 455-9140. Web Site: www.turnto10.com. Licensee: NBC Telemundo License Co. Group owner: NBC TV Stations Division (acq 1996; grpsl). Network: NBC. Rep: NBC TV Stations Sales.
Key Personnel:
Lisa Churchville . . . . . pres & gen mgr
Clark Smith . . . . . opns VP, opns dir & chief of engrg
Jeff Walkes . . . . . sls VP
Valerie McCain . . . . . natl sls mgr
Clare Eckert . . . . . prom VP & adv VP
Elaine Moy-Gederman . . . . . progmg VP
Betty Jo Cugini . . . . . news dir

WLNE—(New Bedford).MA Analog channel: 6. On air date: Jan 1, 1963. 10 Orms St., Providence, RI 02904. Phone: (401) 453-8000. Fax: (401) 331-4399. Web Site: www.abc6.com. Licensee: Freedom Broadcasting of Southern New England Licensee LLC. Group owner: Freedom Broadcasting Inc. (acq 12-14-82; $15.5 million).. Network: ABC. Rep: TeleRep. Washington Atty: Latham & Watkins.
Key Personnel:
Roland T. Adeszko . . . . . VP & gen mgr
Jim Brown . . . . . opns mgr, engrg dir & chief of engrg
Sue McCaugney . . . . . gen sls mgr
Joe Friedman . . . . . rgnl sls mgr
Judy Shoemaker . . . . . prom dir
Kathy Gazda . . . . . news dir

WLWC—(New Bedford).MA Analog channel: 28. Digital channel: 22. On air date: Apr 17, 1997. One State St., Providence, RI 02908. Phone: (401) 351-8828. Fax: (401) 351-0222. Web Site: www.upn28.com. Licensee: C-28 FCC Licensee Subsidiary Inc. Group owner: Viacom Television Stations Group (acq 10-15-2001). Network: Network: UPN, WB. Washington Atty: Keck, Mahin & Cate.
Key Personnel:
Julio Marenghi . . . . . pres & gen mgr
Al Turner . . . . . sls VP
Pam Bergeron . . . . . sls dir
Lisa Resanello . . . . . rgnl sls mgr
Lee Kinberg . . . . . progmg dir
Jack Barny . . . . . chief of engrg

WNAC-TV—Analog channel: 64. On air date: December 1981. 25 Catamore Blvd., East Providence, RI 02914. Phone: (401) 438-7200. Fax: (401) 434-3761. Web Site: www.fox64.com. Licensee: WNAC LLC.. Ownership: Super Towers Inc., 100% (acq 4-22-2002). Network: Fox. Rep: Blair Television.
Key Personnel:
Jay Howell . . . . . pres, VP & gen mgr
Gregg Monte . . . . . opns mgr
Ann McIntyre . . . . . gen sls mgr
Nancy Mayers . . . . . natl sls mgr
Josef Holloway . . . . . mktg VP
Susan Tracy-Durant . . . . . prom mgr
Pam Brennan . . . . . progmg mgr
Gary Brown . . . . . news dir
Glenn Laxton . . . . . pub affrs dir
William Hague . . . . . engrg dir & chief of engrg

WPRI-TV—Analog channel: 12. On air date: Mar 27, 1955. 25 Catamore Blvd., East Providence, RI 02914-1203. Phone: (401) 438-7200. Fax: (401) 434-3761. Web Site: www.wpri.com. Licensee: TVL Broadcasting of Rhode Island LLC. Group owner: LIN Television Corporation (acq 11-8-2002; grpsl). Network: CBS. Rep: Blair Television.
Key Personnel:
Jay Howell . . . . . pres, VP & gen mgr
Gregg Monte . . . . . opns mgr
Ann McIntyre . . . . . gen sls mgr
Patti St. Pierre . . . . . natl sls mgr
Patrick Wholey . . . . . rgnl sls mgr
Josef Holloway . . . . . mktg dir
Susan Tracy-Durant . . . . . prom mgr
Pam Brennan . . . . . progmg mgr
Gary Brown . . . . . news dir
Glenn Laxton . . . . . pub affrs dir
William Hague . . . . . chief of engrg

WPXQ—Analog channel: 69. On air date: Apr 2, 1992. 23 Kenney Dr., Cranston, RI 02920. Phone: (401) 455-9263. Fax: (401) 455-9156. E-mail: Robert.melfi@nbc.com. Web Site: www.pax.tv. Licensee: Ocean State Television L.L.C.. Ownership: A joint venture of Paxson Communications Corp. and Offshore Broadcasting Corp. (Raymond Yorke, 100%). Group owner: Paxson Communications Corp. (acq 8-2-96). Network: PAX TV. Washington Atty: Cohn & Marks. News: 5 hrs wkly.

***WSBE-TV**—Analog channel: 36. Digital channel: 21. On air date: June 5, 1967. 50 Park Ln., Providence, RI 02907. Phone: (401) 222-3636. Fax: (401) 222-3407. E-mail: info@rlpbs.org. Web Site: www.rlpbs.org. Licensee: Rhode Island Public Telecommunications Authority. Network: PBS. Washington Atty: Schwartz, Woods & Miller.
Key Personnel:
David Piccerelli . . . . . CFO
Dexter B. Merry . . . . . chief of opns
Sheila Springer . . . . . dev dir
Kathryn Larsen . . . . . progmg dir
Robert Knott . . . . . chief of engrg

South Carolina

Allendale

see Augusta, GA market

Anderson

see Greenville-Spartanburg, SC-Asheville, NC-Anderson, SC market

Beaufort

see Savannah, GA market

Charleston, SC (DMA 101)

WCBD-TV—Analog channel: 2. On air date: Sept 25, 1954. 210 W. Coleman Blvd., Mt. Pleasant, SC 29464. Phone: (843) 884-2222. Fax: (843) 881-3410. Web Site: www.wcbd.com. Licensee: Media General Broadcasting Inc. Group owner: Media General Broadcast Group (acq 3-1-83; $8 million; 1-24-83). Network: NBC. Rep: Harrington, Righter & Parsons. Washington Atty: Cohn & Marks. News staff: 29; News: 17 hrs wkly.
Key Personnel:
Patric J. Ryal . . . . . gen sls mgr & natl sls mgr
Mark Bradley . . . . . mktg mgr
Richard Fordham Jr. . . . . . gen mgr & progmg dir
Carl Parks . . . . . chief of engrg

WCIV—Analog channel: 4. On air date: Oct 23, 1962. Box 22165, Charleston, SC 29413-2165. 888 Allbritton Blvd., Mt. Pleasant, SC 29464. Phone: (843) 881-4444. Fax: (843) 849-2507 (admin). Fax: (843) 849-2515 (sales). Web Site: www.abcnews4.com. Licensee: WCIV L.L.C. Group owner: Allbritton Communications Co. (acq 1-26-76; grpsl). Network: ABC. Rep: Katz Radio. Washington Atty: Hogan & Hartson. News staff: 32; News: 12 hrs wkly.
Key Personnel:
Austin Walker . . . . . opns mgr & prom mgr
Suzanne Teagle . . . . . gen mgr & natl sls mgr
Chuck Groome . . . . . rgnl sls mgr
Deborah Jackson . . . . . progmg mgr
Perry Boxx . . . . . news dir
Lowell Beckner . . . . . chief of engrg

WCSC-TV—Analog channel: 5. On air date: June 19, 1953. 2126 Charlie Hall Blvd., Charleston, SC 29414. Box 160005, Charleston, SC 29416. Phone: (843) 402-5555. Fax: (843) 402-5793. Web Site: www.wcsc.com. Licensee: Jefferson-Pilot Communications Co.. Ownership: William E. Blackwell. (acq 9-3-93; $15.5 million; 9-27-93). Network: CBS. News staff: 44; News: 21 hrs wkly.
Key Personnel:
Rita O'Neill . . . . . gen mgr
Brian Stephenson . . . . . dev mgr
Amy Spencer . . . . . gen sls mgr
Amanda Childs . . . . . prom mgr
Riten O'Neil . . . . . progmg mgr
Don Pratt . . . . . news dir
Eldon Brown . . . . . engrg dir
Lowell Knoff . . . . . chief of engrg

***WITV**—Analog channel: 7. Digital channel: 49. On air date: Jan 19, 1964. 1101 George Rogers Blvd., Columbia, SC 29201. Phone: (803) 737-3545. Web Site: www.myetv.org. Licensee: South Carolina ETV Commission. Network: PBS. Washington Atty: Dow, Lohnes & Albertson.

WMMP—Analog channel: 36. On air date: November 1992. 4301 Arco Ln., Charleston, SC 29418. Phone: (843) 744-2424. Fax: (843) 554-9649. E-mail: comments@wmmp36.com. Web Site: www.wmmp36.com. Licensee: WMMP Licensee L.P. Group owner: Sinclair Broadcast Group Inc. (acq 1998; grpsl).
Key Personnel:
David Tynan . . . . . VP & gen mgr
Allison Aldridge . . . . . gen mgr & gen sls mgr
Jason Lewis . . . . . mktg mgr & prom mgr
Bill Littleton . . . . . progmg dir & progmg mgr

WTAT-TV—Analog channel: 24. On air date: Sept 7, 1985. 4301 Arco Ln., North Charleston, SC 29418. Phone: (843) 744-2424. Fax: (843) 554-9649. E-mail: comments@wmmp36.com. Web Site: www.wtat24.com. Licensee: WTAT Licensee LLC. Group owner: Cunningham Broadcasting Corporation (acq 11-15-2001; grpsl). Network: Fox. Washington Atty: Arter & Hadden. News: 3.5 hrs wkly.
Key Personnel:
David Tynan . . . . . gen mgr
Allison Aldridge . . . . . gen sls mgr
Jason Lewis . . . . . prom VP & prom mgr
Bill Littleton . . . . . progmg dir

Columbia, SC (DMA 83)

WACH—Analog channel: 57. On air date: Sept 1, 1981. 1400 Pickens St., Columbia, SC 29201. Phone: (803) 252-5757. Fax: (803) 212-7270. E-mail: webmaster@wach.com. Web Site: www.wach.com.

Licensee: Raycom America License Subsidiary LLC. Group owner: Raycom Media Inc. (acq 12-15-97; grpsl). Network: Fox. Rep: TeleRep. Washington Atty: Covington & Burling.

Key Personnel:
Scott McBride . . . VP & gen mgr
Dan Orta . . . opns mgr & chief of engrg
Cheri Spets . . . gen sls mgr
Barbara Bethea . . . rgnl sls mgr, mktg dir & prom dir
Lisa Cruz . . . progmg dir
Mike Woolfolk. . . . news dir
Reese Barkley . . . pub affrs dir

WBHQ—Analog channel: 63. On air date: 1997. 120 Pontiac Business Center D, Elgin, SC 29150. Phone: (803) 419-6363. Fax: (803) 419-6399. E-mail: mail@midlandswb4.com. Web Site: www.midlandswb4.com. Licensee: Columbia Broadcasting Inc.. Ownership: Dove Broadcasting Inc. (acq 11-99). Network: UPN.

WIS—Analog channel: 10. On air date: Nov 7, 1953. 1111 Bull St., Columbia, SC 29201. Box 367, Columbia, SC 29202. Phone: (803) 799-1010. Fax: (803) 758-1171. E-mail: wislistens@wis-tv.com. Web Site: www.wistv.com. Licensee: Libco Inc. Group owner: Liberty Corp. Network: NBC. Rep: Harrington, Righter & Parsons. Washington Atty: Dow, Lohnes & Albertson. News: 26.5 hrs wkly.

Key Personnel:
Melbourne Stebbins. . . . VP & gen mgr
Brent Lane . . . gen sls mgr
Quentin Kenney . . . gen sls mgr & rgnl sls mgr
Barry Ahrendt . . . mktg dir & progmg dir
Tina Lugue-Blacklocke . . . news dir
Ken Thayer . . . chief of engrg

WLTX—Analog channel: 19. On air date: Sept 1, 1953. 6027 Garners Ferry Rd., Columbia, SC 29209. Phone: (803) 776-3600. Fax: (803) 695-3714. Web Site: www.wltx.com. Licensee: Pacific and Southern Co. Inc. Group owner: Gannett Broadcasting (acq 4-29-98; $87.5 million). Network: CBS. Rep: Blair Television. News: 23 hrs wkly.

Key Personnel:
Rich O'Dell . . . gen mgr & progmg dir
Bob Heinzelmann. . . . gen sls mgr
Charles Alexander . . . rgnl sls mgr
Rob Thomas . . . mktg mgr & prom dir
Mike Garber . . . news dir
Dan Stalnaker . . . chief of engrg

WOLO-TV—Analog channel: 25. Digital channel: 8. On air date: Oct 1, 1961. Box 4217, Columbia, SC 29240. 5807 Shakespeare Rd., Columbia, SC 29240. Phone: (803) 754-7525. Fax: (803) 754-6147. Licensee: South Carolina Broadcasting Partners. (acq 7-20-92). Network: ABC. Rep: Katz Radio.

***WRJA-TV**—Analog channel: 27. On air date: Sept 7, 1975. 18 N. Harvin St., Sumter, SC 29150. Phone: (803) 773-5546. Fax: (803) 775-1059. E-mail: wrjatv@ftc-i.net. Web Site: www.wrja.org. Licensee: South Carolina ETV Commission. Network: PBS.

Key Personnel:
William Anderson . . . gen mgr
Kevin Jordan . . . engrg mgr

***WRLK-TV**—Analog channel: 35. On air date: Sept 5, 1966. Box 11000, Columbia, SC 29211. 1101 George Rogers Blvd., Columbia, SC 29211. Phone: (803) 737-3200. Fax: (803) 737-3417. E-mail: mail@myetv.org. Web Site: www.myetv.org. Licensee: South Carolina ETV Commission. Network: PBS. Washington Atty: Dow, Lohnes & Albertson.

Key Personnel:
Maurice "Moss" Bresnahan. . . . CEO & pres
L.W. Griffin Jr. . . . engrg VP & engrg dir

WZRB—Analog channel: 47.Not on air, target date: unknown: Roberts Broadcasting Co., 1408 N. Kingshighway Blvd. #300, St. Louis, MO 63113. Phone: (314) 367-0090. Fax: (314) 367-0174. Permittee: Roberts Broadcasting USA LLC. Group owner: Roberts Broadcasting Co. Washington Atty: Dow, Lohnes & Albertson.

Florence-Myrtle Beach, SC
(DMA 108)

WBTW—Analog channel: 13. On air date: Oct 18, 1954. 3430 N. TV Rd., Florence, SC 29501-0013. 101 McDonald Ct., Myrtle Beach, SC 29588. Phone: (843) 317-1313. Fax: (843) 317-1410. Web Site: www.wbtw.com. Licensee: Media General Communications Inc. Group owner: Media General Broadcast Group (acq 3-27-00; grpsl). Network: CBS. Rep: Harrington, Righter & Parsons. News staff: 38:; News: 78 hrs wkly.

Key Personnel:
Michael J. Pumo . . . VP, gen mgr & gen mgr
Michael Caplan. . . . gen sls mgr
Chuck Spruill . . . mktg mgr
Gina Katzmark . . . news dir
Scott Johnson . . . chief of engrg

WFXB—Analog channel: 43. Digital channel: 18. On air date: July 5, 1984. Box 8309, Myrtle Beach, SC 29578. 3364 Huger St., Myrtle Beach, SC 29577. Phone: (843) 828-4300. Fax: (843) 828-4343. E-mail: 43listens@wfxb.com. Web Site: www.wfxb.com. Licensee: GE Media Inc.. Ownership: James McGregor Everett. (acq 1996; $1,500,010).. Network: Fox. Rep: Millennium Sales & Marketing. Washington Atty: Fisher, Wayland, Cooper, Leader & Zaragoza. News staff: 50+; News: 2.5 hrs wkly.

Key Personnel:
James McGregor Everett. . . . pres
David Carfolite . . . VP & gen mgr
David Milligan. . . . chief of opns

***WHMC**—Analog channel: 23. On air date: Sept 2, 1980. 1101 George Rogers Blvd., Columbia, SC 29201. Phone: (803) 737-3545. Phone: (803) 737-9959. Fax: (803) 737-3495. E-mail: mail@myetv.org. Web Site: www.myetv.org. Licensee: South Carolina Educational TV Commission. Network: PBS.

Key Personnel:
Maurice "Moss" Bresnahan . . . CEO, pres & stn mgr
L.W. Griffin Jr. . . . engrg VP

***WJPM-TV**—Analog channel: 33. On air date: Sept 3, 1967. 1101 George Rogers Blvd., Columbia, SC 29201. Phone: (803) 737-3545. Phone: (803) 737-9959. Fax: (803) 737-3495. E-mail: mail@myetv.org. Web Site: www.myetv.org. Licensee: South Carolina ETV Commission. Network: PBS.

WPDE-TV—Analog channel: 15. On air date: Nov 22, 1980. 1194 Atlantic Ave., Conway, SC 29526. Phone: (843) 234-9733. Fax: (843) 234-9739. E-mail: feedback@wdpe.com. Web Site: www.wpdetv.com. Licensee: Grand Strand Communications. Group owner: Diversified Communications (acq 8-13-85; $14.5 million; 6-3-85). Network: ABC. Washington Atty: Irwin, Campbell & Tannenwald.

***WUNU**—Analog channel: 31. Digital channel: 25. On air date: Sept 23, 1996. Box 14900, Research Triangle Park, NC 27709-4900. Bryan Ctr., 10 T.W. Alexander Dr., Research Triangle Park, NC 27709. Phone: (919) 549-7000. Fax: (919) 549-7201. E-mail: mwhitson@unetv.org. Web Site: www.unctv.org. Licensee: University of North Carolina. Network: PBS. Washington Atty: Schwartz, Woods & Miller.

Key Personnel:
Margaret Harrison Suppler. . . . chmn
Tom Howe . . . chmn & gen mgr
Bob Royster . . . opns dir
Delores James. . . . dev dir

WWMB—Analog channel: 21. On air date: Nov 1, 1994. Box 51150, Myrtle Beach, SC 29579. Phone: (843) 234-9733. Fax: (843) 234-0116. Web Site: www.wpdetv.com. Licensee: Atlantic Media Group.. Ownership: Albert D. Ervin, C. Lenoir Sturkie and Jeffrey S. Salter (acq 7-30-93; FTR: 8-23-93).

Key Personnel:
Al Ervin. . . . CEO & gen mgr
Billy Huggins . . . stn mgr, chief of engrg & chief of engrg
Debbie Yost . . . opns dir
Sira Christensen . . . gen sls mgr
Lee Camp. . . . rgnl sls mgr
Michelle Camp. . . . prom mgr
Linda McCaskill . . . progmg mgr
Mike Gathrie . . . engrg mgr

Greenville-Spartanburg, SC-Asheville, NC-Anderson, SC
(DMA 35)

WASV-TV—Analog channel: 62. On air date: June 1986. Box 1717, Spartanburg, SC 29304. Phone: (864) 576-7777. Fax: (864) 595-4615. Web Site: www.wasv.com. Licensee: Media General Broadcasting of South Carolina Holdings Inc. Group owner: Media General Broadcast Group (acq 1-15-02; $4.5 million).. Network: UPN. Washington Atty: Dow, Lohnes & Albertson.

Key Personnel:
Jim Zimmerman . . . pres
Jim Conschafter. . . . sr VP
Phil Lane . . . gen mgr
Jimmy Lizer . . . opns mgr

WBSC-TV—Analog channel: 40. On air date: Dec 1, 1953. 100 Verdae Blvd., Suite 410, Greenville, SC 29607. Phone: (864) 297-1313. Fax: (864) 297-8085. Web Site: www.wb40.com. Licensee: Anderson (WFBC-TV) Licensee Inc. Group owner: Cunningham Broadcasting Corporation (acq 1-7-2002). Network: WB.

Key Personnel:
David D. Smith. . . . pres
J. Duncan Smith . . . exec VP
Frederick G. Smith. . . . VP
Steven M. Marks . . . chief of opns
Darren Shapiro. . . . sls VP
Gregg Sigel . . . natl sls mgr
Jeff Sleete . . . mktg VP & mktg dir
M. William Butler . . . progmg VP
Joe DeFeo . . . news dir & pub affrs dir

WGGS-TV—Analog channel: 16. On air date: October 1972. Box 1616, Greenville, SC 29602. 3409 Rutherford Rd., Taylors, SC 29687. Phone: (864) 244-1616. Fax: (864) 292-8481. E-mail: ccbtv16@aol.com. Web Site: www.dovebroadcasting.com. Licensee: Carolina Christian Broadcasting Inc.. Ownership: James H. Thompson, 92%. Washington Atty: Bechtel & Cole.

Key Personnel:
James W. Thompson. . . . pres & gen mgr
Joanne Thompson . . . VP
Billy Rainey . . . sls dir
Kathy Newell. . . . natl sls mgr
Gene Gibson. . . . chief of engrg
Kym MacKinnon . . . progmg

WHNS—Analog channel: 21. On air date: Apr 1, 1984. 21 Interstate Ct., Greenville, SC 29615. Phone: (864) 288-2100. Fax: (864) 297-0728. E-mail: whns@foxcarolina.com. Web Site: www.foxcarolina.com. Licensee: Meredith Corp. Group owner: Meredith Broadcasting Group, Meredith Corp. (acq 7-1-97; grpsl). Network: Fox. Rep: TeleRep. Washington Atty: Dow, Lohnes & Albertson. News staff: 24; News: 6 hrs wkly.

Key Personnel:
William Kerr . . . CEO & chmn
Kevin O'Brien . . . pres
Dalton Lee . . . CFO
Douglas Lowe . . . exec VP
Stan Crumley . . . VP, gen mgr, progmg dir & progmg mgr
Terry Conway . . . gen sls mgr
Alan DeFlorio . . . natl sls mgr
Ron Kelly . . . rgnl sls mgr
Jay Malpass. . . . mktg mgr
Dick Goggin. . . . prom mgr
Kyann Lewis . . . news dir
Jerry Garvin . . . chief of engrg

WLOS—(Asheville).NC Analog channel: 13. On air date: Sept 18, 1954. 110 Technology Dr., Asheville, NC 28803. Phone: (828) 684-1340. Fax: (828) 651-4618. E-mail: news@wlos.com. Web Site: www.wlos.com. Licensee: WLOS Licensee L.L.C. Group owner: Sinclair Broadcast Group Inc. (acq 6-96). Network: ABC. Rep: Harrington, Righter & Parsons. Washington Atty: Dow, Lohnes & Albertson. News staff: 57; News: 24 hrs wkly.

Key Personnel:
David Smith. . . . CEO
David Amy . . . CFO
Steve Marks . . . VP
Jack Conners. . . . gen mgr
Rollin Tompkins . . . opns mgr
Jim Carrier . . . chief of opns

WNEG-TV—Analog channel: 32. On air date: Sept 9, 1984. 100 Blvd., Toccoa, GA 30577. Phone: (706) 886-0032. Fax: (706) 886-7033. Web Site: www.wneg32.com. Licensee: Media General Communications Inc. Group owner: Media General Broadcast Group (acq 3-27-00; grpsl). Network: CBS. Washington Atty: Covington & Burling. News staff: 6; News: 13 hrs wkly.

Key Personnel:
Ben Daniels . . . gen mgr & stn mgr
Eric Brown . . . opns mgr
David Austin. . . . gen sls mgr
Tony Garrison . . . prom mgr
Stephanie Harrison . . . progmg mgr
J. Walker . . . chief of engrg

***WNEH**—Analog channel: 38. On air date: Sept 10, 1984. 1101 George Rogers Blvd., Columbia, SC 29201. Phone: (803) 737-3545. E-mail: mail@myetv.org. Web Site: www.myetv.org. Licensee: South Carolina Educational TV Commission. Network: PBS.

***WNTV**—Analog channel: 29. On air date: Sept 15, 1963. 1101 George Rogers Blvd., Columbia, SC 29201. Phone: (803) 737-3545. Phone: (803) 737-9959. Fax: (803) 737-3495. E-mail: mail@myetv.org. Web Site: www.myetv.org. Licensee: South Carolina ETV Commission. Network: PBS.

Key Personnel:
Maurice "Moss" Bresnahan . . . . CEO, pres & stn mgr
L.W. Griffin Jr. . . . . engrg VP

***WRET-TV**—Analog channel: 49. On air date: Sept 4, 1980. Box 4069, Media Bldg., 800 University Way, Spartanburg, SC 29305-4069. Phone: (864) 503-9371. Fax: (864) 503-3615. Web Site: www.wret.org. Licensee: South Carolina Educational TV Commission. Network: PBS. Washington Atty: Dow, Lohnes & Albertson.
Key Personnel:
William Richardson . . . . progmg mgr
Don Fortner . . . . chief of engrg

WSPA-TV—(Spartanburg).Analog channel: 7. On air date: Apr 29, 1956. Box 1717, Spartanburg, SC 29304. 250 International Dr., Spartanburg, SC 29303. Phone: (864) 576-7777. Fax: (864) 587-4480. Web Site: www.wspa.com. Licensee: Media General Broadcasting of So. Carolina Holding Inc. Group owner: Media General Broadcasting of So. Carolina Holding (acq 3-27-00; grpsl). Network: CBS. Washington Atty: Dow, Lohnes. News staff: 51; News: 26.5 hrs wkly.
Key Personnel:
Jim Zimmerman . . . . pres
Phil Lane . . . . VP & gen mgr
Jimmy Lizer . . . . opns mgr
Marilyn Hammoud . . . . gen sls mgr
Bill Shatten . . . . mktg dir

***WUNF-TV**—Analog channel: 33. On air date: Sept 11, 1967. Box 14900, Research Triangle Park, NC 27709-4900. Bryan Ctr., 10 T.W. Alexander Dr., Research Triangle Park, NC 27709. Phone: (919) 549-7000. Fax: (919) 549-7201. E-mail: mshitson@unctv.org. Web Site: www.unctv.org. Licensee: University of North Carolina. Network: PBS. Washington Atty: Schwartz, Woods & Miller.
Key Personnel:
Margaret Harrison Suppler . . . . chmn
Tom Howe . . . . gen mgr
Bob Royster . . . . opns dir
Delores James . . . . dev dir & engrg dir

WYFF—Analog channel: 4. On air date: Dec 31, 1953. Box 788, Greenville, SC 29602. 505 Rutherford St., Greenville, SC 29609. Phone: (864) 242-4404. Fax: (864) 240-5329. E-mail: news4@wyff.com. Web Site: www.thecarolinachannel.com. Licensee: WYFF Hearst-Argyle Television Inc. Group owner: Hearst-Argyle Television Inc. (acq 3-18-99; grpsl). Network: NBC. Rep: Eagle Television Sales. Washington Atty: Brooks, Pierce, McLendon, Humphrey & Leonard. News staff: 55; News: 28 hrs wkly.
Key Personnel:
Michael J. Hayes . . . . pres & gen mgr
Doug Durkee. . . . . opns dir, opns mgr & chief of engrg
Arika Zink. . . . . gen sls mgr
Jimmy Denton . . . . natl sls mgr
Mark McGeary . . . . rgnl sls mgr
Cathy Petropoulos . . . . mktg dir
Marsa Jarrett . . . . prom mgr & pub affrs dir
Stephanie Sloka . . . . progmg dir & film buyer
Andy Still . . . . news dir

Hardeeville

see Savannah, GA market

Myrtle Beach

see Florence-Myrtle Beach, SC market

Rock Hill

see Charlotte, NC market

Spartanburg

see Greenville-Spartanburg, SC-Asheville, NC-Anderson, SC market

South Dakota

Eagle Butte

see Minot-Bismarck-Dickinson, ND market

Lowry

see Minot-Bismarck-Dickinson, ND market

Mitchell

see Sioux Falls (Mitchell), SD market

Rapid City, SD (DMA 178)

***KBHE-TV**—Analog channel: 9. Digital channel: 26. On air date: July 1967. 3650 Skyline Dr., Rapid City, SD 57701. Phone: (605) 394-2551. Fax: (605) 394-6895. E-mail: admin@sdpb.org. Web Site: www.sdpb.org. Licensee: South Dakota Board of Directors for Educational Telecommunications. Network: PBS.
Key Personnel:
Julie Anderson . . . . exec VP
Terry Spencer . . . . dev dir

KCLO-TV—Analog channel: 15. On air date: November 1988. 501 S. Philips Ave., Sioux Falls, SD 57104. Phone: (605) 336-1100. Fax: (605) 334-3447. Web Site: www.keloland.com. Licensee: Young Broadcasting of Rapid City Inc. Group owner: (group owner; acq 1996; grpsl). Network: CBS.
Key Personnel:
Karen Floyd . . . . progmg dir
Mark Millage . . . . news dir
Paul Farmer . . . . . . opns mgr, mktg dir, prom dir & news dir
John Hertz. chief of engrg

KEVN-TV—Analog channel: 7. On air date: July 4, 1976. Box 677, Rapid City, SD 57709. 2000 Skyline Dr., Rapid City, SD 57701. Phone: (605) 394-7777. Fax: (605) 348-9128. Fax: (605) 394-3652. E-mail: kevn@kevn.com. Web Site: www.kevn.com. Licensee: KEVN Inc., debtor-in-possession. Group owner: Mission TV LLC (acq 2-26-2004; with KIVV-TV Lead). Network: Fox. Rep: Millennium Sales & Marketing. Washington Atty: Law Offices of Hogan & Hartson. News staff: 14; News: 9 hrs wkly.
Key Personnel:
Bob Slocum . . . . CFO
Cindy McNeil . . . . VP & gen mgr
Lindsay Bold. . . . . opns mgr
Jon Fisher . . . . gen sls mgr
Jack Caudill . . . . news dir

KHSD-TV—Analog channel: 11. On air date: Nov 2, 1966. Box 1760, Rapid City, SD 57709-1760. Phone: (605) 342-2000. Fax: (605) 342-7305. Web Site: www.kotatv.com. Licensee: Duhamel Broadcasting Enterprises. Group owner: (group owner) Network: ABC. Rep: Katz Radio. Washington Atty: Shaw Pittman.
Key Personnel:
William F. Duhamel . . . . pres & gen mgr
Monte Loss. . . . . opns dir
Steve Duffy . . . . gen sls mgr
Gerry Fenske . . . . rgnl sls mgr
Fred Whitley. . . . . prom mgr
Monte Loos . . . . progmg dir, film buyer & engrg dir
John Petersen . . . . news dir

KIVV-TV—Analog channel: 5. On air date: July 4, 1976. Box 677, Rapid City, SD 57709. 2000 Skyline Dr., Rapid City, SD 57709. Phone: (605) 394-7777. Fax: (605) 348-9128. E-mail: kevn@kevn.com. Web Site: www.kevn.com. Licensee: KEVN Inc., debtor-in-possession. Group owner: Mission TV LLC (acq 2-26-2004; with KEVN-TV Rapid City). Network: Fox. Rep: Millennium Sales & Marketing. Washington Atty: Law Offices of Hogan & Hartson. News staff: 14; News: 9 hrs wkly.
Key Personnel:
Bob Slocum . . . . CFO
Cindy McNeil . . . . VP & gen mgr
Lindsay Bold. . . . . opns mgr
Jon Fisher . . . . gen sls mgr
Jack Caudill . . . . news dir

KNBN—Analog channel: 21. On air date: May 14, 2000. Box 9549, Rapid City, SD 57709. 2424 S. Plaza Dr., Rapid City, SD 57709. Phone: (605) 355-0024. Fax: (605) 355-9274. E-mail: webmaster@newscenter1.com. Web Site: www.newscenter1.com. Licensee: Rapid Broadcasting Co. Group owner: (group owner). Network: NBC. News: 3 hrs wkly.
Key Personnel:
Jim Simpson. . . . . VP & gen mgr
Wes DesJardins . . . . opns mgr
Darren Koehne. . . . . gen sls mgr
Trent Taylor . . . . rgnl sls mgr

KOTA-TV—Analog channel: 3. On air date: July 1, 1955. Box 1760, Rapid City, SD 57709-1760. 518 St. Joseph St., Rapid City, SD 57709-1760. Phone: (605) 342-2000. Fax: (605) 342-7305. Web Site: www.kotatv.com. Licensee: Duhamel Broadcasting Enterprises. Group owner: (group owner) Network: ABC. Rep: Katz Radio. Washington Atty: Shaw Pittman. News: 9 hrs wkly.
Key Personnel:
William F. Duhamel . . . . pres & gen mgr
Monte Loos. opns mgr, progmg dir, film buyer, engrg mgr & chief of engrg
Steve Duffy . . . . natl sls mgr
Gerry Fenske . . . . rgnl sls mgr
Fred Whitley. . . . . prom mgr
John Peterson . . . . news dir

KSGW-TV—Analog channel: 12. On air date: Oct 28, 1977. Box 1760, Rapid City, SD 57709-1760. Phone: (605) 342-2000. Fax: (605) 342-7305. Web Site: www.kotatv.com. Licensee: Duhamel Broadcasting Enterprises. Group owner: (group owner) Network: ABC. Rep: Katz Radio. Washington Atty: Shaw Pittman. News: 8 hrs wkly.
Key Personnel:
William Duhamel . . . . pres & gen mgr
Steve Duffy . . . . gen sls mgr
Gerry Fenske . . . . rgnl sls mgr
Fred Whitley . . . . prom dir
Monte Loos . . . . progmg dir & film buyer
John Petersen . . . . news dir
Bud Mathison . . . . engrg mgr

KSWY—Analog channel: 7. On air date: 2002. Box 1540, Mills, WY 82664. Phone: (307) 577-0013. Fax: (307) 577-5251. Licensee: Sunbelt Communications Co. Group owner: (group owner). Network: NBC.
Key Personnel:
William Sullivan . . . . gen mgr
Joey Parker . . . . news dir

***KTNE-TV**—Analog channel: 13. Digital channel: 17. On air date: Sept 7, 1966. Box 83111, Lincoln, NE 68501. 1800 N. 33rd St., Lincoln, NE 68503. Phone: (402) 472-3611. Fax: (402) 472-1785. E-mail: net1@unl.edu. Web Site: www.netnebraska.org. Licensee: Nebraska Educational Telecommunications Commission. Network: PBS. Washington Atty: Dow, Lohnes & Albertson.

***KZSD-TV**—Analog channel: 8. Digital channel: 23. On air date: Feb 8, 1978. Box 5000, Vermillion, SD 57069-5000. 555 N. Dakota St., Vermillion, SD 57069-5000. Phone: (605) 677-5861. Fax: (605) 677-5010. E-mail: programming@sdpb.org. Web Site: www.sdpb.org. Licensee: South Dakota Board of Directors for Educational Telecommunications. Network: PBS.
Key Personnel:
Julie Andersen . . . . pres
Craig Jensen . . . . opns mgr
Terry Spencer . . . . dev dir
Carol Robertson. prom dir
Bob Bosse . . . . progmg dir
Stacey Decker. engrg mgr

Sioux Falls (Mitchell), SD (DMA 116)

KABY-TV—Analog channel: 9. On air date: Nov 28, 1958. 717 Hwy. 281 N., Aberdeen, SD 57401. Phone: (605) 225-9200. Phone: (605) 336-1300. Fax: (605) 225-9226. Licensee: South Dakota Television License Sub. L.L.C. Group owner: Wicks Television L.L.C. (acq 2-27-2004; grpsl). Network: ABC.
Key Personnel:
Jack Hansen . . . . gen mgr
Eugene Schultz. . . . . chief of engrg

***KCSD-TV**—Analog channel: 23. On air date: June 13, 1995. Box 5000, Vermillion, SD 57069-5000. 555 N. Dakota St., Vermillion, SD 57069-5000. Phone: (605) 677-5861. Fax: (605) 677-5010. E-mail: programming@sdpb.org. Web Site: www.sdpb.org. Licensee: South Dakota Board of Directors for Educational Telecommunications.
Key Personnel:
Julie Andersen . . . . pres
Craig Jensen . . . . opns mgr
Terry Spencer. . . . . dev mgr
Carol Robertson. prom dir
Bob Bosse. . . . . progmg dir & progmg mgr
Stacey Decker. engrg mgr

KDLO-TV—Analog channel: 3. On air date: September 1955. 501 S. Phillips, Sioux Falls, SD 57104. Phone: (605) 336-1100. Fax: (605) 334-3447. Web Site: www.kdlo-tv.com. Licensee: Young Broadcasting of Sioux Falls Inc. Group owner: Young Broadcasting Inc. (acq 6-1-96;

grpsl). Network: CBS. Rep: Adam Young. Washington Atty: Leventhal, Senter & Lerman.
Key Personnel:
Mark Antonitis . . . gen mgr
John Hertz . . . chief of engrg

KDLT-TV—Analog channel: 46. Digital channel: 47. On air date: November 1998. c/o KDLT(TV), 3600 S. Westport Ave., Sioux Falls, SD 57106-6325. Phone: (605) 361-5555. Fax: (605) 361-7017. Fax: (605) 361-3982. E-mail: info@kdlt.com. Web Site: www.kdlt.com. Licensee: Red River Broadcast Co. L.L.C. Group owner: (group owner) Network: NBC. Rep: Harrington, Righter & Parsons. Washington Atty: Holland and Knight. News staff: 25; News: 13 hrs wkly.
Key Personnel:
Myron Kunin . . . CEO
Ro Grignon . . . pres
Kathy Lau . . . VP
Gary Bolton . . . gen mgr
Susan Endres . . . opns mgr
Mari Ossenfort . . . sls dir & gen sls mgr
Bobbi Lower . . . news dir
Donald Sturzenbecher . . . chief of engrg

KDLV-TV—Analog channel: 5. On air date: June 12, 1960. 3600 S. Westport Ave., Sioux Falls, SD 57106-6325. Phone: (605) 361-5555. Fax: (605) 361-3982/(605) 361-7017. Web Site: www.kdlv.com. Licensee: Red River Broadcast Co. L.L.C. Group owner: (group owner; acq 8-26-94; $4 million; 9-12-94). Network: NBC. Washington Atty: Crowell & Moring. News staff: 20; News: 9 hrs wkly.
Key Personnel:
Ro Grignon . . . pres
Gary Bolton . . . gen mgr
Mari Ossenfort . . . gen sls mgr & adv mgr
Peter Chang . . . prom mgr & pub affrs dir
Susan Endres . . . opns mgr & progmg mgr
Joel Knip . . . news dir
Don Sturzenbecher . . . chief of engrg

***KDSD-TV**—Analog channel: 16. On air date: Jan 1, 1972. Box 5000, Vermillion, SD 57069-5000. 555 N. Dakota St., Vermillion, SD 57069-5000. Phone: (605) 677-5861. Fax: (605) 677-5010. E-mail: programming@sdpb.org. Web Site: www.sdpb.org. Licensee: South Dakota Board of Directors for Educational Telecommunications. Network: PBS.
Key Personnel:
Julie Andersen . . . pres
Bob Bosse . . . stn mgr & progmg dir
Craig Jensen . . . opns mgr
Terry Spencer . . . dev dir
Carol Robertson . . . prom dir
Stacey Decker . . . engrg mgr

KELO-TV—Analog channel: 11. On air date: May 1953. 501 S. Phillips, Sioux Falls, SD 57104. Phone: (605) 336-1100. Fax: (605) 334-3447. Fax: (605) 357-5530. Web Site: www.keloland.com. Licensee: Young Broadcasting of Sioux Falls Inc. Group owner: Young Broadcasting Inc. (acq 6-1-96; grpsl). Network: CBS. Rep: Adam Young. Washington Atty: Leventhal, Senter & Lerman.
Key Personnel:
Paul Farmer . . . mktg dir & prom dir
Karen Floyd . . . progmg dir
Mark Millage . . . news dir
John Hertz . . . chief of engrg

***KESD-TV**—Analog channel: 8. Digital channel: 18. On air date: Feb 6, 1968. 5000 Vermillion, Brookings, SD 57069. Phone: (605) 688-4191. E-mail: sdpr@sdpb.org. Web Site: www.sdpb.org. Licensee: South Dakota Board of Directors for Educational Telecommunications. Network: PBS. Washington Atty: Cohn & Marks.
Key Personnel:
Julie Anderson . . . exec VP
Terry Spencer . . . dev dir

KPLO-TV—Analog channel: 6. On air date: July 1957. 501 S. Phillips, Sioux Falls, SD 57104. Phone: (605) 336-1100. Fax: (605) 334-3447. E-mail: info@findithere.keloland.com. Web Site: www.keloland.com. Licensee: Young Broadcasting of Sioux Falls Inc. Group owner: Young Broadcasting Inc. (acq 6-1-96; grpsl). Network: CBS. Rep: Adam Young. Washington Atty: Leventhal, Senter & Lerman.
Key Personnel:
Mark Millage . . . gen mgr & news dir
Paul Farmer . . . mktg dir & prom dir
Karen Floyd . . . progmg dir
John Hertz . . . chief of engrg

KPRY-TV—Analog channel: 4. On air date: February 1976. 300 N. Dakota Ave., Sioux Falls, SD 57104. Phone: (605) 336-1300. Fax: (605) 336-7936. Licensee: South Dakota Television License Sub. L.L.C. Group owner: Wicks Television L.L.C. (acq 2-27-2004; grpsl). Network: ABC. Washington Atty: Arent, Fox, Kintner, Plotkin & Kahn. News staff: 45; News: 15 hrs wkly.
Key Personnel:
Jack Hanson . . . gen mgr
Eugene Schultz . . . chief of engrg

***KRNE-TV**—Analog channel: 12. On air date: Dec 9, 1968. Box 83111, Lincoln, NE 68501. 1800 N. 33rd St., Lincoln, NE 68503. Phone: (402) 472-3611. Fax: (402) 472-1785. E-mail: net1@unl.edu. Web Site: www.netnebraska.org. Licensee: Nebraska Educational Telecommunications Commission. Network: PBS. Washington Atty: Dow, Lohnes & Albertson.
Key Personnel:
Rod Bates . . . gen mgr
Michael Beach . . . engrg dir
Paul Sautter . . . chief of engrg

KSFY-TV—Analog channel: 13. On air date: July 31, 1960. 300 N. Dakota Ave., Suite 100, Sioux Falls, SD 57104. Phone: (605) 336-7936. Fax: (605) 336-3468. Web Site: www.ksfy.com. Licensee: South Dakota Television License Sub. L.L.C. Group owner: Wicks Television L.L.C. (acq 2-27-2004; grpsl). Network: ABC. Rep: TeleRep. News staff: 30; News: 15 hrs wkly.

***KSMN**—Analog channel: 20. On air date: 1997. 120 W. Schlieman, Appleton, MN 56208. Phone: (520) 320-2622. Fax: (320) 289-2634. E-mail: yourtv@pioneer.org. Web Site: www.pioneer.org. Licensee: West Central Minnesota Educational TV Co. Network: PBS.
Key Personnel:
Glen Cerny . . . pres & gen mgr
Kay Stenstuen . . . adv mgr
Shirley Schwarz . . . progmg dir
Jon Panzer . . . chief of engrg

***KTSD-TV**—Analog channel: 10. Digital channel: 21. On air date: Aug 1, 1970. Box 5000, Vermillion, SD 57069-5000. 555 N. Dakota St., Vermillion, SD 57069-5000. Phone: (605) 677-5861. Phone: (800) 456-0766. Fax: (605) 677-5010. E-mail: programming@sdpb.org. Web Site: www.sdpb.org. Licensee: South Dakota Board of Directors for Educational Telecommunications. Network: PBS.
Key Personnel:
Julie Andersen . . . pres
Craig Jensen . . . opns mgr
Terry Spencer . . . dev dir
Bob Bosse . . . progmg dir

KTTM—Analog channel: 12. Digital channel: 22. On air date: Sept 7, 1991. c/o KTTW, 2817 W. 11th St., Sioux Falls, SD 57104. Phone: (605) 338-0017. Fax: (605) 338-7173. E-mail: fox17@kttw.com. Web Site: www.kttw.com/home.htm. Licensee: Independent Communications Inc. Network: Fox.

KTTW—Analog channel: 17. Digital channel: 7. On air date: Nov 1, 1986. Box 5103, Sioux Falls, SD 57117-5103. 2817 W. 11th St., Sioux Falls, SD 57104. Phone: (605) 338-0017. Fax: (605) 338-7173. E-mail: fox17@kttw.com. Web Site: www.kttw.com/home.htm. Licensee: Independent Communications Inc. (acq 3-9-88). Network: Fox. Washington Atty: Reddy, Begley & McCormick.

***KUSD-TV**—Analog channel: 2. On air date: July 5, 1961. Box 5000, Vermillion, SD 57069. 555 N. Dakota St., Vermillion, SD 57069. Phone: (605) 677-5861. Fax: (605) 677-5010. E-mail: programming@sdpb.org. Web Site: www.sdpb.org. Licensee: South Dakota Board of Directors for Educational Telecommunications. Network: PBS. Washington Atty: Cohn & Marks.
Key Personnel:
Julie Andersen . . . pres
Craig Jensen . . . opns mgr
Terry Spencer . . . dev dir
Carol Robertson . . . prom dir
Bob Bosse . . . progmg dir
Stacey Decker . . . engrg mgr

KWSD—Analog channel: 36. On air date: 2001. Box 9549, Rapid City, SD 57709. Midwest Broadcasting Co., 2424 S. Plaza Dr., Rapid City, SD 57702. Phone: (605) 355-0024. Fax: (605) 355-9274. E-mail: jsimpson@newscenter1.com. Web Site: www.newscenter1.com. Licensee: Rapid Broadcasting Co. Group owner: (group owner; acq 1-5-01). Network: WB. News: 2 hrs wkly.
Key Personnel:
Jim Simpson . . . VP & gen mgr
Wes DesJardins . . . opns mgr
Darren Koehne . . . gen sls mgr
Trent Taylor . . . rgnl sls mgr

Tennessee

Chattanooga, TN (DMA 86)

***WCLP-TV**—Analog channel: 18. On air date: Feb 1, 1967. 2765 Ft. Mountain State Park Rd., Chatsworth, GA 30705. Phone: (706) 695-2422. Licensee: Georgia Public Telecommunications Commission. Network: PBS. Washington Atty: Arent, Fox, Kintner, Plotkin & Kahn.

WDEF-TV—Analog channel: 12. On air date: Apr 25, 1954. 3300 Broad St., Chattanooga, TN 37408. Phone: (423) 785-1200. Fax: (423) 785-1271. E-mail: news@wdef.com. Web Site: www.wdef.com. Licensee: Media General Broadcasting Inc. Group owner: Media General Broadcast Group (acq 3-21-97; grpsl). Network: CBS. Rep: Harrington, Righter & Parsons. Washington Atty: Wiley, Rein & Fielding. News staff: 32; News: 24.5 hrs wkly.

WDSI-TV—Analog channel: 61. Digital channel: 40. On air date: Jan 24, 1972. 1101 E. Main St., Chattanooga, TN 37408. Phone: (423) 265-0061. Fax: (423) 265-3636. E-mail: feedback@ourtennesseevalley.com. Web Site: www.ourtennesseevalley.com. Licensee: WDSI License Corp., debtor-in-possession. Group owner: Pegasus Broadcast Television Inc. (acq 2-18-93; $21 million. with WDBD(TV) Jackson, MS; FTR: 3-8-93). Network: Fox. Washington Atty: George H. Shapiro.
Key Personnel:
Mike Costa . . . gen mgr
Larry Pink . . . chief of opns & chief of engrg
Tracye McCarthy . . . gen sls mgr
Pete Remmert . . . natl sls mgr
Tripp Dudley . . . prom dir
Rick Lane . . . prom mgr
Yolanda Collins . . . progmg dir
Bill Dobilas . . . news dir

WELF-TV—Analog channel: 23. On air date: 1994. 384 S. Campus Rd., Lookout Mountain, GA 30750. Phone: (706) 820-1663. Fax: (706) 820-1735. Licensee: Trinity Broadcasting Network. Group owner: (group owner; acq 5-8-00; grpsl).

WFLI-TV—Analog channel: 53. On air date: May 25, 1987. 6024 Shallowford Rd., Suite 100, Chattanooga, TN 37421. Phone: (423) 893-9553. Fax: (423) 893-9853. Web Site: wflitv.net. Licensee: Meredith Corp. Group owner: Meredith Broadcasting Group, Meredith Corp. (acq 8-25-2004; $8.5 million).. Network: WB. Rep: MMT. Washington Atty: Dow, Lohnes & Albertson.
Key Personnel:
Deb Corson . . . exec VP, VP & gen mgr
Bill Chrisman . . . opns mgr
Kevin Mize . . . gen sls mgr
Brandon Strickland . . . prom mgr

WRCB-TV—Analog channel: 3. Digital channel: 13. On air date: May 6, 1956. 900 Whitehall Rd., Chattanooga, TN 37405. Phone: (423) 267-5412. Fax: (423) 267-6840. Fax: (423) 756-3148 (news). E-mail: ttolar@wrcbtv.com. Web Site: www.wrcbtv.com. Licensee: Sarkes Tarzian Inc. Group owner: (group owner; acq 10-82; $16 million; 10-18-82). Network: NBC. Rep: Continental Television Sales. Washington Atty: Leventhal, Senter & Lerman. News: 22 hrs wkly.
Key Personnel:
Tom Tarzian . . . chmn
Bob Davis . . . CFO
Tom Tolar . . . pres & gen mgr
Doug Loveridge . . . opns mgr
Doug Short . . . gen sls mgr
Duane Bryan . . . prom dir
Pam Teague . . . progmg dir
Bill Wallace . . . news dir
Ed Aslinger . . . chief of engrg

***WTCI**—Analog channel: 45. On air date: Mar 8, 1970. 4411 Amnicola Hwy., Chattanooga, TN 37406. Phone: (423) 629-0045. Fax: (423) 698-8557. Web Site: www.wtcitv45.com. Licensee: The Greater Chattanooga PTV Corp. (acq 7-84). Network: PBS. Washington Atty: Dow, Lohnes & Albertson.
Key Personnel:
Martha Umiker . . . CFO
Victor A. Hogstrom . . . pres & gen mgr
Kelly Williams . . . progmg VP & pub affrs dir
Kevin Lusk . . . pub affrs dir

WTVC—Analog channel: 9. On air date: Feb 11, 1958. Box 60028, Chattanooga, TN 37406-6028. 4279 Benton Dr., Chattanooga, TN 37406. Phone: (423) 756-5500. Fax: (423) 757-7400. Fax: (423)

757-7401. E-mail: news@newschannel9.com. Web Site: www.wtvc.com. Licensee: Freedom Broadcasting of Tennessee Licensee L.L.C. Group owner: Freedom Broadcasting Inc. (acq 12-13-83; grpsl; FTR: 1-2-84). Network: ABC. Rep: TeleRep. Washington Atty: Latham & Watkins. News staff: 55; News: 32 hrs wkly.
Key Personnel:
Dennis W. Brown . . . . . opns mgr
Michael Costa . . . . . VP, gen mgr & natl sls mgr

Jackson, TN (DMA 174)

WBBJ-TV—Analog channel: 7. On air date: Mar 5, 1955. 346 Muse St., Jackson, TN 38301. Phone: (731) 424-4515. Fax: (731) 424-9299. Web Site: www.wbbjtv.com. Licensee: Tennessee Broadcasting Partners. (acq 7-20-92). Network: ABC. Rep: Katz Radio.
Key Personnel:
Jerry Moore . . . . . gen mgr
Robert Fay . . . . . gen sls mgr
Anthony Matrisciano . . . . . progmg dir
Ken Galey . . . . . news dir
Randy McCaskill . . . . . chief of engrg

WJKT—Analog channel: 16. Digital channel: 39. On air date: Apr 16, 1985. 2701 Union Ext., Memphis, TN 38112. Phone: (901) 323-2430. Fax: (901) 323-9503. Web Site: www.wjkt24.com. Licensee: Clear Channel Broadcasting Licenses Inc. Group owner: Clear Channel Communications Inc. (acq 9-29-00). Network: UPN.

***WLJT-TV**—Analog channel: 11. On air date: Feb 1, 1968. Box 966, Martin, TN 38237-0966. Clement Hall, U.T.-Martin, Martin, TN 38238. Phone: (731) 881-7561. Fax: (731) 881-7566. E-mail: wljt@wljt.org. Web Site: www.wljt.org. Licensee: West Tennessee Public Television Council Inc. Network: PBS.
Key Personnel:
Dave Hinman . . . . . CEO & opns dir
Bud Grimes . . . . . pres
Monica Shumake . . . . . CFO
Emily Elliston . . . . . VP
Katrina Cobb . . . . . opns dir & prom dir
Shorri Puckett . . . . . dev dir
Robbie Green . . . . . mktg mgr

Knoxville, TN (DMA 59)

WAGV—Analog channel: 44.Not on air, target date: unknown: Box 151, Vansant, VA 24656. 8594 Hidden Valley Rd., Abingdon, VA 24210. Phone: (276) 676-3806. Fax: (276) 935-8857. Permittee: Living Faith Ministries Inc.
Key Personnel:
Fredia Lou Keene . . . . . CFO
Lisa C. Smith . . . . . sls dir
Michael D. Smith . . . . . CEO, pres, gen mgr, sls VP & mktg dir

WATE-TV—Analog channel: 6. On air date: Oct 1, 1953. Box 2349, Knoxville, TN 37901. 1306 N.E. Broadway, Knoxville, TN 37901. Phone: (865) 637-6666. Fax: (865) 525-4091. Web Site: www.wate.com. Licensee: WATE G.P. Group owner: Young Broadcasting Inc. (acq 11-14-94; grpsl; 9-12-94). Network: ABC. Rep: Adam Young. News staff: 35; News: 15 hrs wkly.
Key Personnel:
Jan Wade . . . . . gen mgr & progmg dir
Brian Mayfield . . . . . gen sls mgr
John Higdon . . . . . natl sls mgr
John Pennington . . . . . mktg dir
Aaron Ramey . . . . . news dir
Bill Evans . . . . . pub affrs dir
Bob Williams . . . . . chief of engrg

WBIR-TV—Analog channel: 10. On air date: Aug 13, 1956. 1513 Hutchison Ave., Knoxville, TN 37917. Phone: (865) 637-1010. Fax: (865) 637-6280. Fax: (865) 637-6380. E-mail: wbir@wbir.gannett.com. Web Site: www.wbir.com. Licensee: Gannett Pacific Corp. Group owner: Gannett Broadcasting (acq 12-4-95; grpsl). Network: NBC. Washington Atty: Wiley, Rein & Fielding. News staff: 50; News: 24 hrs wkly.
Key Personnel:
Jeff Lee . . . . . pres & gen mgr
Dean Littleton . . . . . gen sls mgr
David Cowen . . . . . progmg dir
Bill Shory . . . . . news dir
Steve Dean . . . . . prom dir & pub affrs dir
Gary Davis . . . . . chief of engrg

WBXX-TV—Analog channel: 20. On air date: Oct 4, 1997. 10427 Cogdill Rd., Suite 100, Knoxville, TN 37932. Phone: (865) 777-9220. Fax: (865) 777-9221. E-mail: promotions@wb20tv.com. Web Site: www.wb20tv.com. Licensee: Acme Television Licenses of Tennessee L.L.C. Group owner: Acme Communications Inc. (acq 8-28-97; $13.2 million). Network: WB. Rep: MMT. Washington Atty: Dickstein Shapiro Morin & Oshinsky L.L.P..
Key Personnel:
Dan Phillippi . . . . . VP & gen mgr
Joanne Marcenkus . . . . . gen sls mgr
Lisa Faulkner . . . . . progmg dir
Dean Davidson . . . . . chief of engrg
Anna Robins . . . . . prom

***WETP-TV**—Analog channel: 2. On air date: Mar 15, 1967. 1611 E. Magnolia Ave., Knoxville, TN 37917. Phone: (865) 595-0220. Fax: (865) 595-0300. E-mail: viewer_mail@wsjk.pbs.org. Web Site: www.wsjk-wkop.org. Licensee: East Tennessee Public Communications Corp. (acq 10-1-83). Network: PBS.
Key Personnel:
Jim Tindell . . . . . pres & gen mgr
Frank Miller . . . . . opns VP
Elaine Tomber . . . . . dev dir & mktg dir
Evelyn Clarke . . . . . prom mgr
Colvin Idol . . . . . progmg dir
Chris Smith . . . . . pub affrs dir
Mike Knight . . . . . chief of engrg

***WKOP-TV**—Analog channel: 15. On air date: Aug 15, 1990. 1611 E. Magnolia Ave., Knoxville, TN 37917. Phone: (865) 595-0220. Fax: (865) 595-0300. E-mail: viewer_mail@wskj.pbs.org. Web Site: www.wskj-wkop.org. Licensee: East Tennessee Public Communications Corp. Network: PBS.
Key Personnel:
Jim Tindell . . . . . pres & gen mgr
Frank Miller . . . . . opns VP
Elaine Tomber . . . . . dev dir & mktg dir
Evelyn Clarke . . . . . prom mgr
Colvin Idol . . . . . progmg dir
Chris Smith . . . . . pub affrs dir
Mike Knight . . . . . chief of engrg

WMAK— Digital channel: 7. On air date: July 31, 2004. 6215 Kingston Pike, Knoxville, TN 37919-4044. Phone: (865) 584-9094. Fax: (865) 584-9098. Licensee: Knoxville Channel 7 LLC. Group owner: (group owner). Washington Atty: Fletcher, Heald & Hildreth.

WPXK—Analog channel: 54. On air date: Mar 12, 1991. Bldg. D, 9000 Executive Park Dr., Suite 300, Knoxville, TN 37923. Phone: (865) 693-4343. Fax: (865) 251-4305. Web Site: www.pax.tv. Licensee: Paxson Knoxville Licensee Inc. Group owner: Paxson Communications Corp. (acq 9-23-98). Network: PAX TV.
Key Personnel:
Carol Wright-Holzhauer . . . . . VP
Angela Galyon . . . . . opns mgr

WTNZ—Analog channel: 43. Digital channel: 34. On air date: Dec 31, 1983. Bldg. D, 9000 Executive Park Dr., Suite 300, Knoxville, TN 37923. Phone: (865) 693-4343. Fax: (865) 691-6904. Fax: (865) 691-6770. Web Site: wtnzfox43.com. Licensee: Raycom America License Subsidiary LLC. Group owner: Raycom Media Inc. (acq 1996; grpsl). Network: Fox. Rep: TeleRep. Washington Atty: Covington & Burling. News staff: 6; News: 4 hrs wkly.
Key Personnel:
Paul McTear . . . . . CEO & CFO
John Hayes . . . . . gen mgr

WVLR—Analog channel: 48.Not on air, target date: unknown: 306 Kyker Ferry Rd., Koduk, FL 37764. Phone: (865) 932-4803. Fax: (865) 932-4102. Web Site: wvlrtv48.com. Permittee: Volunteer ChristianTelevision Inc. (acq 4-22-02).
Key Personnel:
Theron Woodward . . . . . gen mgr
Scott Dunkel . . . . . chief of engrg
Tom Evensen . . . . . chief of engrg

WVLT-TV—Analog channel: 8. On air date: Dec 8, 1988. Box 59088, Knoxville, TN 37950. 6450 Papermill Rd., Knoxville, TN 37919. Phone: (865) 450-8888. Fax: (865) 450-8869. Web Site: www.volunteertv.com. Licensee: Gray Television Licensee Inc. Group owner: Gray Television Inc. (acq 1996; $165 million. with WCTV(TV) Thomasville, GA). Network: CBS. Rep: Continental Television Sales. News staff: 40; News: 22 hrs wkly.
Key Personnel:
Chris Baker . . . . . CFO, exec VP & gen mgr
Steve Crabtree . . . . . opns VP, opns mgr & opns mgr

Memphis, TN (DMA 44)

WBUY-TV—Analog channel: 40. On air date: Sept 13, 1991. 3447 Cazassa Rd., Memphis, TN 38116-3609. Phone: (901) 396-9541. Fax: (901) 396-9585. E-mail: wbuy@tbn.org. Web Site: www.tbn.org. Licensee: Trinity Broadcasting Network. Group owner: (group owner; acq 5-8-00; grpsl).
Key Personnel:
Nina Gardner . . . . . stn mgr
Cliff Pickell . . . . . opns dir & progmg dir
Douglas Puryear . . . . . chief of engrg

WHBQ-TV—Analog channel: 13. On air date: Sept 27, 1953. 485 S. Highland St., Memphis, TN 38111. Phone: (901) 320-1313. Fax: (901) 323-0092. Fax: (901) 320-1366 (News). Web Site: www.foxmemphis.com. Licensee: Fox Television Stations Inc. Group owner: (group owner; acq 7-5-95; $80 million). Network: Fox. Rep: Fox Stations Sales. News staff: 55; News: 27 hrs wkly.
Key Personnel:
Rupert Murdoch . . . . . chmn
Lachlan Murdock . . . . . pres
Betsy Swanson . . . . . CFO
Tom Herwitz . . . . . exec VP
John Koski . . . . . gen mgr, progmg dir & pub affrs dir
Michael Lewis . . . . . gen sls mgr
Kim Moore . . . . . natl sls mgr
Paul Sloan . . . . . prom VP & prom dir
Ken Jobe . . . . . news dir
David Brant . . . . . chief of engrg

***WKNO-TV**—Analog channel: 10. On air date: June 25, 1956. Box 241880, Memphis, TN 38124-1880. 900 Getwell Rd., Memphis, TN 38111. Phone: (901) 458-2521. Fax: (901) 325-6505. E-mail: wknopi@wkno.org. Web Site: www.wkno.org. Licensee: Mid-South Public Communications Foundation. Network: PBS. Washington Atty: Schwartz, Woods & Miller.
Key Personnel:
Michael LaBonia . . . . . CEO & pres
Russ A. Abernathy . . . . . stn mgr
Charles McLarty . . . . . dev dir

WLMT—Analog channel: 30. On air date: April 1983. Clear Channel Television Ctr, 2701 Union Ext., Memphis, TN 38112. Phone: (901) 323-2430. Fax: (901) 323-9503. E-mail: eyewitnessnews @upn30memphis.com. Web Site: www.upn30memphis.com. Licensee: Clear Channel Broadcasting Licenses Inc. Group owner: Clear Channel Communications Inc. (acq 10-20-00). Washington Atty: McFadden, Evans & Sill.
Key Personnel:
Jim Doty . . . . . gen sls mgr
Robyn Callaway . . . . . opns dir & rgnl sls mgr
Jim Turpin . . . . . news dir

***WMAV-TV**—Analog channel: 18. Digital channel: 36. On air date: May 19, 1972. 3825 Ridgewood Rd., Jackson, MS 39211. Phone: (601) 432-6565. Fax: (601) 432-6654. Fax: (601) 432-6311. Web Site: www.mpbonline.org. Licensee: Mississippi Authority for Educational TV. News staff: 4.
Key Personnel:
Marie Antoon . . . . . exec VP & gen mgr
Gene Edwards . . . . . opns dir
Ty Warren . . . . . dev dir
Ron Evans . . . . . mktg mgr
Art Starkey . . . . . prom dir & progmg dir
Dick Rizzo . . . . . news dir & pub affrs dir
Keith Martin . . . . . engrg dir

WMC-TV—Analog channel: 5. On air date: Dec 11, 1948. 1960 Union Ave., Memphis, TN 38104. Phone: (901) 726-0555. Fax: (901) 278-7633. Web Site: www.wmctvstations.com. Licensee: Raycom America License Subsidiary LLC. Group owner: Raycom Media Inc. (acq 1997; grpsl). Network: NBC. Rep: TeleRep. Washington Atty: Goldberg, Godles, Wiener & Wright.
Key Personnel:
Howard Meagle . . . . . VP & gen mgr
Gary Macko . . . . . natl sls mgr
Jim Himes . . . . . rgnl sls mgr & mktg VP
Lori Beth Pickle . . . . . mktg dir
Richard Enderwood . . . . . prom dir
Peggy Phillip . . . . . news dir

WPTY-TV—Analog channel: 24. On air date: Sept 10, 1978. 2701 Union Ave. Ext., Memphis, TN 38112. Phone: (901) 323-2430. Fax: (901) 323-9503. Web Site: www.abc24.com. Licensee: Clear Channel Radio Licenses Inc. Group owner: Clear Channel Communications Inc. (acq 8-5-92; 4-13-92). Network: ABC. Washington Atty: Wiley, Rein & Fielding. News staff: 50; News: 7 hrs wkly.

Directory of Television Texas

WPXX-TV—Analog channel: 50. Digital channel: 51. On air date: October 1994. 1960 Union Ave., Memphis, TN 38115. Phone: (901) 729-3273. Fax: (901) 729-3274. Web Site: www.pax.tv. Licensee: Flinn Broadcasting Corp. (acq 8-27-90; $220,000;. FTR: 11-19-90). Network: PAX TV.

WREG-TV—Analog channel: 3. Digital channel: 28. On air date: Jan 1, 1956. 803 Channel 3 Dr., Memphis, TN 38103. Phone: (901) 543-2333. Fax: (901) 543-2198. Fax: (901) 543-2167 (news). Licensee: New York Times Management Services. Group owner: The New York Times Co. (acq 8-8-71; $10,966,410).. Network: CBS. Rep: Eagle Television Sales. Washington Atty: Koteen & Naftalin. News staff: 50.
Key Personnel:
Bob Eoff . . . . . pres & gen mgr
Ronald A. Walter . . . . . exec VP
Ronald Walter . . . . . stn mgr
Jim Anhalt . . . . . opns VP & engrg VP
Maureen O'Connor . . . . . sls VP
Maury Eikner-Tower . . . . . mktg dir & mktg mgr
Wes Pollard . . . . . prom VP & prom dir
Michele Gors . . . . . news dir

Nashville, TN
(DMA 30)

***WCTE**—Analog channel: 22. On air date: Aug 21, 1978. Box 2040, Cookeville, TN 38502. Stadium Dr., Cookeville, TN 38501. Phone: (931) 528-2222. Fax: (931) 372-6284. Web Site: www.wcte.org. Licensee: Upper Cumberland Broadcast Council. (acq 12-20-85; 11-18-85). Network: PBS.
Key Personnel:
Dr. Ken Garry . . . . . pres & gen mgr
Becky Magura . . . . . stn mgr & dev dir
Robert Huddleston . . . . . chief of engrg

WHTN—Analog channel: 39. On air date: Dec 30, 1983. 9582 Lebanon Rd., Mt. Juliet, TN 37122. Phone: (615) 754-0039. Fax: (615) 754-0047. E-mail: info@nashville39.com. Web Site: www.ctnonline.com. Licensee: Christian Television Network Inc.. Ownership: David C. Gibbs III, 20%; Jimmy Smith, 20%; Robert D'Andrea, 20%; Virginia Oliver, 20%; and Wayne Wetzel, 20%. Washington Atty: Gammon & Grange. News staff: one; News: 2 hrs wkly.

WJFB—Analog channel: 66. On air date: 1989. 200 E. Spring St., Lebanon, TN 37087. Phone: (615) 444-8206. Fax: (615) 444-7592. Licensee: Bryant Broadcasting Inc.. Ownership: Joe Bryant, 100%.

WKRN-TV—Analog channel: 2. Digital channel: 27. On air date: Nov 29, 1953. 441 Murfreesboro Rd., Nashville, TN 37210. Phone: (615) 259-2200. Fax: (615) 244-2117. Web Site: www.wkrn.com. Licensee: WKRN G.P. Group owner: Young Broadcasting Inc. (acq 4-17-89; $42 million; 5-8-89). Network: ABC. Rep: Adam Young. Washington Atty: Wiley, Rein & Fielding. News staff: 45; News: 25 hrs wkly.
Key Personnel:
Mike Sechrist . . . . . VP & gen mgr
Mike Tarrolley . . . . . mktg dir
Michele Dube . . . . . progmg dir
Steve Sabato . . . . . news dir
Gene Parker . . . . . chief of engrg

WNAB—Analog channel: 58. Digital channel: 23. On air date: Nov 29, 1995. 2994 Sidco Dr., Nashville, TN 37204. Phone: (615) 650-5858. Fax: (615) 650-5859. Fax: (615) 650-5843. Web Site: wnab.com. Licensee: Nashville License Holdings L.L.C.. Ownership: Michael Lambert, mgng member. (acq 10-14-98; $30 million). Network: WB.
Key Personnel:
Michael Lambert . . . . . pres
J.P. Hannan . . . . . CFO
Brian Hannan . . . . . opns VP
Sandra Lee . . . . . gen sls mgr
Gary Shipley . . . . . natl sls mgr & rgnl sls mgr
Lee Scott . . . . . prom mgr
Kent Bailey . . . . . progmg mgr
Dennis Breckey . . . . . chief of engrg

***WNPT**—Analog channel: 8. On air date: Sept 10, 1962. 161 Rains Ave., Nashville, TN 37203. Phone: (615) 259-9325. Fax: (615) 248-6120. E-mail: tv8@wnpt.net. Web Site: www.wnpt.net. Licensee: Nashville Public Television Inc. Network: PBS. Washington Atty: Schwartz, Woods & Miller.
Key Personnel:
Steven M. Bass . . . . . CEO & pres
Beth Curley . . . . . sr VP & chief of opns
Charles Brimbelow . . . . . VP
Harmon McBride . . . . . progmg dir

WNPX—Analog channel: 28. Digital channel: 36. On air date: Sept 3, 1993. 1281 N. Mt. Juliet Rd., Suite K, Mt. Juliet, TN 37122. Phone: (615) 773-6100. Fax: (615) 726-2854. Fax: (615) 773-6106. Web Site: www.pax.tv. Licensee: Paxson Communications License Co. L.L.C. Group owner: Paxson Communications Corp. (acq 9-4-97; $4.3 million). Network: PAX TV.
Key Personnel:
Lowell "Bud" Paxson . . . . . CEO
Dan Barber . . . . . gen sls mgr

WPGD-TV—Analog channel: 50. On air date: Sept 23, 1992. 36 Music Village Blvd., Hendersonville, TN 37075. Phone: (615) 822-1243. Fax: (615) 822-1642. Web Site: www.wpgd.org. Licensee: Trinity Broadcasting Network. Group owner: (group owner; acq 7-00; grpsl).
Key Personnel:
Renee Brewer . . . . . gen mgr
Steve Galiher . . . . . stn mgr
Harry Monroe . . . . . chief of engrg

WSMV-TV—Analog channel: 4. Digital channel: 10. On air date: Sept 30, 1950. 5700 Knob Rd., Nashville, TN 37209. Phone: (615) 353-4444. Fax: (615) 353-2375. Web Site: www.wsmv.com. Licensee: Meredith Corp. Group owner: Meredith Broadcasting Group, Meredith Corp. (acq 11-1-94; $159 million; 12-5-94). Network: NBC. Rep: TeleRep. Washington Atty: Wilmer, Cutler & Pickering.

WTVF—Analog channel: 5. On air date: Aug 6, 1954. 474 James Robertson Pkwy., Nashville, TN 37219. Phone: (615) 244-5000. Fax: (615) 248-5353. Fax: TWX: 810-371-1168. E-mail: news@newschannel5.com. Web Site: www.newschannel5.com. Licensee: NewsChannel 5 Network LP. Group owner: Landmark Communications Inc. (acq 9-12-91; $46 million; 9-30-91). Network: CBS. Rep: Katz Radio. Washington Atty: Hogan & Hartson. News: 24 hrs wkly.
Key Personnel:
Debbie Turner . . . . . gen mgr
Mark Binda . . . . . progmg dir
Mike Cutler . . . . . news dir

WUXP—Analog channel: 30. Digital channel: 21. On air date: Feb 18, 1984. 631 Mainstream Dr., Nashville, TN 37228. Phone: (615) 259-5630. Fax: (615) 259-3962. Web Site: www.upn30.com. Licensee: WUXP Licensee LLC. Group owner: Sinclair Broadcast Group Inc. (acq 12-10-01; $2.829 million).. Network: UPN. Washington Atty: Arter & Hadden.
Key Personnel:
Stephen A. Mann . . . . . gen mgr
Mark Dillon . . . . . stn mgr
Pam Combest . . . . . sls dir
Dejuan Buford . . . . . gen sls mgr
Dale Bukowski . . . . . natl sls mgr
Greg Carr . . . . . rgnl sls mgr
Lee R. Scott . . . . . mktg dir, prom dir, adv dir & progmg dir
Deborah Williams . . . . . prom mgr & adv mgr
Iman Tate . . . . . progmg mgr
Lee Peterson . . . . . pub affrs dir
Gibson Prichard . . . . . engrg mgr
David Birdsong . . . . . chief of engrg

WZTV—Analog channel: 17. Digital channel: 15. On air date: March 1976. 631 Mainstream Dr., Nashville, TN 37228. Phone: (615) 259-5617. Fax: (615) 259-3962. E-mail: comments@wztv.com. Web Site: www.wztv.com. Licensee: WZTV Licensee LLC. Group owner: Sinclair Broadcast Group Inc. (acq 12-10-01; grpsl). Network: Fox. Washington Atty: Arter & Hadden. News staff: 9; News: 7 hrs wkly.
Key Personnel:
Craig Millar . . . . . gen mgr
Steve Mann . . . . . stn mgr
Pamela Minnicks . . . . . gen sls mgr
Beckey Dan . . . . . prom dir
David Birdsong . . . . . chief of engrg

Tri-Cities, TN-VA
(DMA 89)

WCYB-TV—Analog channel: 5. On air date: Aug 13, 1956. 101 Lee St., Bristol, VA 24201. Phone: (276)-645-1555. Fax: (276) 645-1513. Web Site: www.wcyb.tv. Licensee: BlueStone License Holdings Inc. Group owner: Lamco Communications Inc. (acq 3-17-77; $8,618,636;. FTR: 3-28-77). Network: NBC. Washington Atty: Koteen & Naftalin.

WEMT—Analog channel: 39. Digital channel: 38. On air date: Nov 8, 1985. Box 3489 CRS, Johnson City, TN 37602-3489. 3206 Hanover Rd., Johnson City, TN 37602-3489. Phone: (423) 283-3900. Fax: (423) 283-4938. Web Site: www.wemt39.com. Licensee: WEMT Licensee L. P. Group owner: Sinclair Broadcast Group Inc. (acq 7-7-98; grpsl). Network: Fox. Washington Atty: Shaw, Pittman.
Key Personnel:
Leesa Wilcher . . . . . gen mgr & gen sls mgr
Amy McClary . . . . . rgnl sls mgr
Jim Hartline . . . . . chief of engrg

WJHL-TV—Analog channel: 11. On air date: Oct 26, 1953. Box 1130, Johnson City, TN 37605. 338 E. Main St., Johnson City, TN 37601. Phone: (423) 926-2151. Fax: (423) 434-4537. E-mail: jdempsey@wjhl.com. Web Site: www.wjhl.com. Licensee: Media General Broadcasting Inc. Group owner: Media General Broadcast Group (acq 3-21-97; grpsl). Network: CBS. Rep: Harrington, Righter & Parsons. Washington Atty: Dow, Lohnes and Albertson.
Key Personnel:
Jack Dempsey . . . . . gen mgr & film buyer
R. Lamar Reid . . . . . gen sls mgr
Rachel Maden . . . . . mktg dir
Christine Riser . . . . . news dir
Mike Moore . . . . . chief of engrg

WKPT-TV—Analog channel: 19. Digital channel: 27. On air date: Aug 20, 1969. Box 1971, Kingsport, TN 37662. 222 Commerce St., Kingsport, TN 37662. Phone: (423) 246-9578. Fax: (423) 246-6261/(423) 246-1863. E-mail: gdv@wkpttv.com. Web Site: www.wkpttv.com. Licensee: Holston Valley Broadcasting Corp.. Ownership: Glenwood Communications Corp, 100%. Group owner: Glenwood Communications Corp. Network: ABC. Rep: Harrington, Righter & Parsons. Washington Atty: Cordon & Kelly. News staff: 30; News: 12 hrs wkly.
Key Personnel:
Bette Lawson . . . . . CFO
George E. DeVault Jr. . . . . . pres & gen mgr
Bobby Flowers . . . . . opns mgr
Fred Falin . . . . . progmg VP & progmg dir

WLFG—Analog channel: 68. On air date: 1995. 8594 Hidden Valley Rd., Abingdon, VA 24210. Phone: (276) 676-3806. Fax: (276) 676-3572. E-mail: mike@livingfaithtelevision.com. Licensee: Tookland Pentecostal Church.
Key Personnel:
Michael D. Smith . . . . . CEO & chmn
Michael D. Smith . . . . . pres
Lisa Smith . . . . . VP & progmg VP
Michael D. Smith . . . . . gen mgr
Wade McGeorge . . . . . sls dir
Ray Dotson . . . . . engrg mgr

***WMSY-TV**—Analog channel: 52. Digital channel: 42. On air date: Aug 1, 1981. Box 13246, Roanoke, VA 24032. 1215 McNeil Dr., Roanoke, VA 24015. Phone: (540) 344-0991. Fax: (540) 344-2148. E-mail: brptv@wbra.org. Web Site: www.wbra.org. Licensee: Blue Ridge Public Television Inc. Network: PBS. Washington Atty: Cohn & Marks.
Key Personnel:
Edwin Whitmore . . . . . chmn
Anita Sims . . . . . CFO
Beverly Fitzpatrick Jr. . . . . . exec VP
Jack K. Neal . . . . . CEO, pres & gen mgr

***WSBN-TV**—Analog channel: 47. Digital channel: 32. On air date: Mar 29, 1971. Box 13246, Roanoke, VA 24032. 1215 McNeil Dr. S.W., Roanoke, VA 24032. Phone: (540) 344-0991. Fax: (540) 344-2148. E-mail: brptv@wbra.org. Web Site: www.wbra.org. Licensee: Blue Ridge Public Television Inc. Network: PBS. Washington Atty: Cohn & Marks.
Key Personnel:
Beverly Fitzpatrick . . . . . chmn & exec VP
Jack Neal . . . . . gen mgr
Barbara Spencer . . . . . pub affrs dir
Ron Smith . . . . . engrg VP & chief of engrg

Texas

Abilene-Sweetwater, TX
(DMA 163)

KPCB—Analog channel: 17. On air date: 1997. Box 61000, Midland, TX 79711-1000. 88 E. County Rd. 112, Snyder, TX 79549. Phone: (325) 573-9517. Fax: (325) 573-9417. E-mail: info@ptcbglc.com. Web Site: www.godslearningchannel.com. Licensee: Prime Time Christian Broadcasting Inc.

KRBC-TV—Analog channel: 9. On air date: Aug 31, 1953. Box 5309, Abilene, TX 79608. Phone: (325) 692-4242. Fax: (325) 695-9922. E-mail: ksbcnews@krbc.tv. Web Site: www.krbc.tv. Licensee: Mission Broadcasting Inc. Group owner: (group owner; acq 6-13-03; $10 million. with KSAN-TV San Angelo). Network: NBC. Washington Atty:

Hogan & Hartson.
Key Personnel:
David Smith. . . . . CEO & CFO
Dennis Thatcher. . . . . CEO & VP
Gayle Kiger . . . . . gen mgr
Justin Riggar . . . . . gen sls mgr
Tom Vodak. . . . . news dir

KTAB-TV—Analog channel: 32. On air date: Oct 6, 1979. Box 5309, Abilene, TX 79608. 4510 S. 14th St., Abilene, TX 79605. Phone: (915) 695-2777. Fax: (915) 695-9922. E-mail: news@ktabtv.com. Web Site: www.ktabtv.com. Licensee: Nexstar Finance Inc. Group owner: Nexstar Broadcasting Group Inc. (acq 8-15-99; $16.7 million).. Network: CBS. Rep: Katz Radio. News staff: 12; News: 8 hrs wkly.

KTXS-TV—(Sweetwater).Analog channel: 12. Digital channel: 20. On air date: Jan 30, 1956. Box 2997, Abilene, TX 79604. 4420 N. Clack, Abilene, TX 79604. Phone: (325) 677-2281. Fax: (325) 676-9231. E-mail: star12@ktxs.com. Web Site: www.ktxs.com. Licensee: BlueStone License Holdings Inc. Group owner: Lamco Communications Inc. Network: ABC. Washington Atty: Holland & Knight, LLP.
Key Personnel:
Jackie Rutledge . . . . . VP, gen mgr, gen sls mgr & film buyer
David Caldwell. . . . . prom mgr
Sylvia Holmes . . . . . progmg dir
Iain Munro . . . . . news dir
Leland Ohlhausen. . . . . chief of engrg

KXVA—Analog channel: 15. On air date: Jan 17, 2001. 500 Chestnut, Ste. 804, Abilene, TX 79602. Phone: (325) 672-5606. Fax: (325) 676-2437. Web Site: www.kxvafox.com. Licensee: Sage Broadcasting Corp. (acq 12-28-2004). Network: Fox. Rep: Millennium Sales & Marketing. Washington Atty: Fletcher, Heard and Hildreth0.
Key Personnel:
Bill Carter. . . . . pres
Michele Howse . . . . . gen mgr

Amarillo, TX
(DMA 130)

***KACV-TV**—Analog channel: 2. On air date: Aug 29, 1988. Box 447, Amarillo, TX 79178. 2408 S. Jackson, Amarillo, TX 79178. Phone: (806) 371-5222. Fax: (806) 371-5258. E-mail: kacvtv@actx.edu. Web Site: www.kacvtv.org. Licensee: Amarillo Junior College District. Network: PBS.
Key Personnel:
Joyce Herring. . . . . gen mgr
Hilda Patterson. . . . . dev dir
Joanna Latham . . . . . dev mgr
Ellen Robertson Neal . . . . . pub affrs dir
Larry Gregg . . . . . engrg dir
Donald H. Ford. . . . . chief of engrg

KAMR-TV—Analog channel: 4. On air date: Mar 18, 1953. Box 751, 1015 S. Fillmore St., Amarillo, TX 79101. Phone: (806) 383-3321. Fax: (806) 381-2943. E-mail: nbc4@kamr.com. Web Site: www.kamr.com. Licensee: Nexstar Finance Inc. Group owner: Nexstar Broadcasting Group Inc. (acq 12-31-03; grpsl). Network: NBC. Washington Atty: Arter & Hadden.
Key Personnel:
Mark McKay . . . . . gen mgr & progmg dir
Sherry Avara. . . . . gen sls mgr
Tim Sturgess. . . . . exec VP & natl sls mgr
Heather Brunson . . . . . rgnl sls mgr
David Toma . . . . . prom mgr
NyLynn Nichols . . . . . news dir
Ken High . . . . . chief of engrg

KCIT—Analog channel: 14. On air date: Oct 1, 1982. Box 1414, Amarillo, TX 79105. 1015 S. Fillmore, Amarillo, TX 79101. Phone: (806) 374-1414. Fax: (806) 371-0408. Fax: (806) 381-2943. Web Site: fox14.tv. Licensee: Mission Broadcasting Inc. Group owner: (group owner; acq 1999; $28.5 million. with KJTL(TV) Wichita Falls). Network: Fox. Rep: Blair Television.
Key Personnel:
Jim O'Malley . . . . . gen mgr & progmg dir
Sherry Avara. . . . . gen sls mgr
Tim Sturgess . . . . . natl sls mgr
David Toma. . . . . mktg dir
Wesley Willson . . . . . chief of engrg

***KENW**—Analog channel: 3. On air date: Sept 1, 1974. Eastern New Mexico Univ., 52 Broadcast Ctr., Portales, NM 88130. Phone: (505) 562-2112. Fax: (505) 562-2590. E-mail: kenwtv@enmu.edu. Web Site: www.kenw.org. Licensee: Regents of Eastern New Mexico University. Network: PBS. News staff: 2; News: 3 hrs wkly.
Key Personnel:
Steven Gamble. . . . . pres
K. Paul Jones. . . . . VP
Dwane Ryan . . . . . gen mgr
Rena Garret . . . . . mktg dir & mktg mgr
Linda Stefanovic. . . . . progmg dir
Don Criss. . . . . pub affrs dir
Jeff Burmeister . . . . . chief of engrg

KFDA-TV—Analog channel: 10. Digital channel: 9. On air date: Apr 4, 1953. Box 10, Amarillo, TX 79105-0010. 7900 Broadway, Amarillo, TX 79108. Phone: (806) 383-1010. Phone: (806) 383-6397. Fax: (806) 381-9859. Web Site: www.newschannel10.com. Licensee: Panhandle Telecasting Co. Group owner: R.H. Drewry Group (acq 10-4-76; $3 million;. FTR: 9-13-76). Network: CBS. Washington Atty: Shaw Pittman. News staff: 25; News: 13 hrs wkly.
Key Personnel:
Bill Drewry . . . . . pres
Robert Drewry . . . . . pres
Larry Patton . . . . . sr VP
Mike Lee. . . . . VP, gen mgr, adv mgr, progmg dir & film buyer
Tim Cato . . . . . opns mgr
Joyce Austin . . . . . gen sls mgr, natl sls mgr & rgnl sls mgr
Tonya Triveno . . . . . progmg mgr
Kari King . . . . . news dir
Walt Howard . . . . . mktg dir, prom mgr & pub affrs dir
Tim Winn . . . . . chief of engrg

KPTF—Analog channel: 18. On air date: 2002. Box 61000, Midland, TX 79711-1000. Phone: (432) 563-0420. Fax: (432) 563-1736. E-mail: studio@ptcbglc.com. Web Site: www.ptcbglc.com. Licensee: Prime Time Christian Broadcasting Inc. (acq 12-23-99).

KVIH-TV—Analog channel: 12. Digital channel: 20. On air date: December 1957. One Broadcast Ctr., Amarillo, TX 79101. Phone: (806) 373-1787. Fax: (806) 371-7329. Licensee: Barrington Broadcasting Texas Corp. Group owner: New Vision Group LLC (acq 6-15-2005; $22.5 million. with KVII-TV Amarillo, TX). Network: ABC. Rep: Katz Radio. Washington Atty: Wiley, Rein & Fielding.
Key Personnel:
K. James Yager . . . . . pres
Mac Douglas . . . . . VP
Lynn Fairbanks . . . . . gen mgr & gen sls mgr
Keith Workman. . . . . rgnl sls mgr
Curtis Weaver . . . . . prom mgr
Paula Harris . . . . . progmg dir
Bill Canady . . . . . chief of engrg

KVII-TV—Analog channel: 7. Digital channel: 23. On air date: Nov 1, 1957. One Broadcast Ctr., Amarillo, TX 79101. Phone: (806) 373-1787. Fax: (806) 371-7329. Web Site: www.kvii.com. Licensee: Barrington Broadcasting Texas Corp. Group owner: New Vision Group LLC (acq 6-15-2005; $22.5 million. with KVIH-TV Clovis, NM). Network: ABC. Rep: Katz Radio. Washington Atty: Wiley, Rein & Fielding. News: 36 hrs wkly.
Key Personnel:
K. James Yager . . . . . pres
Lyn Fairbanks. . . . . gen mgr
Dusty Green . . . . . opns dir, opns mgr & news dir
Connie Mosley. . . . . gen sls mgr & rgnl sls mgr
Bill Canady . . . . . chief of engrg

Austin, TX
(DMA 54)

KEYE-TV—Analog channel: 42. On air date: Dec 4, 1983. 10700 Metric Blvd., Austin, TX 78758. Phone: (512) 835-0042. Fax: (512) 837-6753. Web Site: www.keyetv.com. Licensee: CBS Stations Group of Texas L.P. Group owner: Viacom Television Stations Group acq 8-3-99; $160 million).. Network: CBS. Rep: TeleRep. Washington Atty: Akin, Gump, Strauss, Hauer & Feld. News staff: 50; News: 20 hrs wkly.
Key Personnel:
Gary Schneider . . . . . gen mgr
Dusty Granberry . . . . . opns mgr
Jeff Stern . . . . . sls dir
Fred Undstrom . . . . . natl sls mgr
Ira Poole . . . . . natl sls mgr & rgnl sls mgr
Lee Maaz. . . . . rgnl sls mgr
Steve Colkins . . . . . rgnl sls mgr
Stan Teater . . . . . prom mgr
Gary Vinson. . . . . progmg mgr
Tim Gardner . . . . . news dir
Art Smith . . . . . chief of engrg

***KLRU-TV**—Analog channel: 18. Digital channel: 22. On air date: May 4, 1979. 2504 Whitis St., Bldg. 5, Austin, TX 78712. Phone: (512) 471-4811. Fax: (512) 475-9090. Web Site: www.klru.org. Licensee: Capital of Texas Public Telecomm. Network: PBS. Washington Atty: Cohn & Marks.
Key Personnel:
Bill Stotesbery . . . . . CEO, CEO & pres
Pat Wertz. . . . . CFO
Dick Peterson. . . . . exec VP & opns VP
Karin Morrison . . . . . VP
Lori Holliday. . . . . dev VP
Ed Bailey . . . . . sls VP
Maury Sullivan . . . . . mktg VP & adv VP
Cheryl Sawyer . . . . . prom VP
Maria Rodriguez . . . . . progmg VP
David Kuipers . . . . . engrg VP

KNVA—Analog channel: 54. On air date: Aug 1, 1994. Box 684647, Austin, TX 78767. 908 W. Martin Luther King Blvd., Austin, TX 78768. Phone: (512) 478-5400. Fax: (512) 476-1520. Web Site: www.thewb54.com. Licensee: 54 Broadcasting Inc.. Ownership: Diane Levy, 25%; Frank Goldberg, 25%; Mark Goldberg, 25%; and Richard Goldberg, 25% (acq 6-10-2004).
Key Personnel:
Carlos Fernandez . . . . . gen mgr
Pat Niekamp. . . . . gen sls mgr
David Rash . . . . . natl sls mgr
Martha Goodwin . . . . . rgnl sls mgr
Jim Canning . . . . . prom dir
Regina Soto . . . . . progmg dir
Bruce Whitaker . . . . . news dir
Mark Dunham . . . . . engrg dir

KTBC—Analog channel: 7. On air date: Nov 27, 1952. 119 E. 10th St., Austin, TX 78701. Phone: (512) 476-7777. Fax: (512) 495-7001. E-mail: management@fox7.com. Web Site: www.fox7.com. Licensee: KTBC License Inc. Group owner: Fox Television Stations Inc. (acq 1-97). Network: Fox. News staff: 54; News: 24 hrs wkly.
Key Personnel:
Danny Baker . . . . . VP & gen mgr
Ken Smith. . . . . opns VP, engrg VP & chief of engrg
Mark Rodman . . . . . sls VP & gen sls mgr
Kathie Smith . . . . . mktg VP, prom VP & prom dir
Holly Morrison-Breaux . . . . . progmg dir
Pam Vaught . . . . . news dir
Rob Cunningham. . . . . pub affrs dir

KVUE-TV—Analog channel: 24. Digital channel: 33. On air date: Sept 12, 1971. Box 9927, Austin, TX 78766. 3201 Steck Ave., Austin, TX 78757. Phone: (512) 459-6521. Fax: (512) 533-2215. Fax: (512) 533-2233 (news). Web Site: www.kvue.com. Licensee: KVUE-TV Inc. Group owner: Belo Corp., Broadcast Division (acq 6-1-99; swap with KXTV(TV) Sacramento, CA). Network: ABC. Rep: Harrington, Righter & Parsons.

KXAM-TV—Analog channel: 14. On air date: Sept 6, 1991. Box 490, Austin, TX 78767. 908 W. Martin Luther King Jr. Blvd., Austin, TX 78701. Phone: (512) 476-3636. Fax: (512) 476-1520. Fax: (512) 469-0630. Licensee: KXAN Inc. Group owner: LIN Television Corp. Network: NBC.
Key Personnel:
Carlso S. Fernandez . . . . . gen mgr
James Holowaty. . . . . opns dir
Teansie Garfield . . . . . gen sls mgr
David Walker . . . . . natl sls mgr
Jim Canning . . . . . prom dir & pub affrs dir
Bruce Whitaker . . . . . news dir
Mark Dunham . . . . . engrg dir

KXAN-TV—Analog channel: 36. On air date: Feb 12, 1965. Box 490, Austin, TX 78767. 908 W. Martin Luther King Blvd., Austin, TX 78701. Phone: (512) 476-3636. Fax: (512) 476-1520. Fax: (512) 469-0630. Web Site: www.kxan.com. Licensee: KXAN Inc. Group owner: LIN Television Corporation (acq 11-14-94; FTR: 12-12-94). Network: NBC. Washington Atty: Covington & Burling. News staff: 60; News: 22 hrs wkly.
Key Personnel:
Carlos S. Fernandez . . . . . gen mgr
James Holowaty. . . . . opns dir
Teansie Garfield . . . . . gen sls mgr
David Walker . . . . . rgnl sls mgr
Jim Canning . . . . . prom dir
Bruce Whitaker . . . . . news dir
Mark Dunham . . . . . engrg dir

Beaumont-Port Arthur, TX
(DMA 138)

KBMT—Analog channel: 12. On air date: June 18, 1961. Box 1550, 525 I-10 S., Dover, TX 77704. Phone: (409) 838-1212. Phone: (409) 833-7512. Fax: (409) 835-1617. Licensee: Texas Telecasting Inc. Group owner: McKinnon Broadcasting Co. (acq 11-1-76; $2.4 million; 11-15-77). Network: ABC. Rep: Katz Radio. Washington Atty: Cohn & Marks. News staff: 26; News: 13 hrs wkly.

Key Personnel:
Michael McKinnon . . . . . . pres
Mark McKinnon . . . . . . VP & gen mgr
David King . . . . . . gen mgr, gen sls mgr & natl sls mgr
Don Williams . . . . . . opns dir
Elda Gaudet . . . . . . rgnl sls mgr
Don Haener . . . . . . prom mgr
Elizabeth West . . . . . . progmg dir
Miles Resnick . . . . . . news dir
Mark Cormier . . . . . . chief of engrg

KBTV-TV—(Port Arthur).Analog channel: 4. On air date: Oct 22, 1957. Box 3257, Port Arthur, TX 77643. 6155 Eastex Fwy., Ste. 300, Beaumont, TX 77706. Phone: (409) 985-5557. Phone: (409) 840-4444. Fax: (409) 985-4927. Fax: (409) 899-4639 (news). Web Site: www.kbtv4.tv. Licensee: Nexstar Finance Inc. Group owner: Nexstar Broadcasting Group Inc. (acq 11-6-97; grpsl). Network: NBC. Rep: Blair Television. Washington Atty: Drinker, Biddle & Roth.
Key Personnel:
Perry Sook . . . . . . CEO & pres
Duane Lammers . . . . . . COO
Shirley Green . . . . . . CFO
Van Greer . . . . . . VP & gen mgr
Kent Domingue . . . . . . chief of opns
Keith Smith . . . . . . gen sls mgr
Jon Black . . . . . . prom mgr
Karen Blum . . . . . . progmg mgr
Paul Bergen . . . . . . news dir
Jennifer Steen . . . . . . pub affrs dir
Charlie Ravell . . . . . . chief of engrg

KFDM-TV—Analog channel: 6. Digital channel: 21. On air date: Apr 24, 1955. Box 7128, 2955 I-10 E., Beaumont, TX 77726-7128. Phone: (409) 892-6622. Fax: (409) 892-6665. Web Site: www.kfdm.com. Licensee: Freedom Broadcasting of Texas Licensee L.L.C. Group owner: Freedom Broadcasting Inc. (acq 1-4-84; grpsl; FTR: 1-2-84). Network: CBS. Rep: TeleRep. Washington Atty: Latham & Watkins.

***KITU-TV**—Analog channel: 34. On air date: June 21, 1986. 11221 IH 10, Orange, TX 77630. Phone: (409) 745-3434. Fax: (409) 745-4752. Web Site: www.communityedtv.org. Licensee: Community Educational Television Inc.
Key Personnel:
Dr. Reginald Cherry . . . . . . pres
Wayne Ozio . . . . . . gen mgr & stn mgr

Brownsville

see Harlingen-Weslaco-Brownsville-McAllen, TX market

Bryan

see Waco-Temple-Bryan, TX market

Corpus Christi, TX (DMA 129)

***KEDT**—Analog channel: 16. On air date: Oct 15, 1972. 4455 S. Padre Island Dr., Suite 38, Corpus Christi, TX 78411. Phone: (361) 855-2213. Fax: (361) 855-3877. Web Site: www.kedt.org. Licensee: South Texas Public Broadcasting System. Network: PBS. Washington Atty: Schwartz, Woods & Miller.
Key Personnel:
Trey McCampbell . . . . . . chmn
Don Dunlap . . . . . . pres & gen mgr
Norma Camarillo . . . . . . CFO
Myra Lombardo . . . . . . VP
Cody Blount . . . . . . opns dir, engrg dir & chief of engrg
Molly Goodwin . . . . . . sls dir
Robert Chabot . . . . . . prom VP & mus dir
Sylvia Coronado . . . . . . progmg dir & progmg mgr
Johanna Zwernemann . . . . . . asst music dir

KIII—Analog channel: 3. On air date: May 4, 1964. 5002 S. Padre Island Dr., Corpus Christi, TX 78411. Box 6669, Corpus Christi, TX 78411. Phone: (361) 986-8300. Fax: (361) 986-8311. E-mail: kiiitv@kiiitv.com. Licensee: Channel 3 of Corpus Christi Inc. Group owner: McKinnon Broadcasting Co. (acq 7-79; $171,720). Network: ABC. Rep: Continental Television Sales. Washington Atty: Cohn & Marks. News staff: 30; News: 17.5 hrs wkly.
Key Personnel:
Michael D. McKinnon . . . . . . pres
Dick Drilling . . . . . . VP, gen mgr & progmg dir
Scott Jones . . . . . . opns dir
Bill Beck . . . . . . gen sls mgr
Larry Hogue . . . . . . natl sls mgr
Richard Longoria . . . . . . news dir
Ralph Quiroz . . . . . . chief of engrg

KORO—Analog channel: 28. On air date: Apr 15, 1977. Box 2667, Corpus Christi, TX 78403. 102 N. Mesquite, Corpus Christi, TX 78403. Phone: (361) 883-2823. Fax: (361) 883-2931. Licensee: Entravision Holdings L.L.C. Group owner: Entravision Communications Co. L.L.C. (acq 3-17-98; $1.336 million). Network: Univision (Spanish). Washington Atty: Mullin, Rhyne, Emmons & Topel. News staff: 5; News: 5 hrs wkly.

KRIS-TV—Analog channel: 6. On air date: May 22, 1956. Box 840, Corpus Christi, TX 78403. 409 S. Staples, Corpus Christi, TX 78403. Phone: (361) 886-6100. Fax: (361) 887-6666. Fax: TWX: 910-876-1442. Web Site: www.kristv.com. Licensee: KVOA Communications Inc. Group owner: Cordillera Communications Inc. Network: NBC. Washington Atty: Nixon, Hargrave, Devans & Doyle. News staff: 31; News: 14 hrs wkly.
Key Personnel:
Tim Noble . . . . . . pres, gen mgr & gen mgr
Bob Webb . . . . . . chief of opns
Don Grubaugh . . . . . . gen sls mgr & natl sls mgr
Roger Brandt . . . . . . gen sls mgr
Jay Sanchez . . . . . . prom mgr
James H. Smith . . . . . . progmg dir
Sandra Richards . . . . . . news dir
Steve West . . . . . . chief of engrg

KZTV—Analog channel: 10. On air date: Sept 30, 1956. Box TV-10, Corpus Christi, TX 78401. 301 Artesian St., Corpus Christi, TX 78401. Phone: (361) 883-7070. Fax: (361) 882-8553. Web Site: www.cbs10kztv.com. Licensee: Eagle Creek of Corpus Christi LLC. Group owner: Eagle Creek Broadcasting LLC (acq 6-13-02; grpsl). Network: CBS. News staff: 18.
Key Personnel:
Dale Remy . . . . . . gen mgr
Annette Dellano . . . . . . rgnl sls mgr
Sheri Randall . . . . . . progmg dir
Kent Harrell . . . . . . news dir
Bill Oglesby . . . . . . chief of engrg

Dallas-Ft. Worth (DMA 7)

KDAF—Analog channel: 33. Digital channel: 32. On air date: July 29, 1984. 8001 Carpenter Fwy., Dallas, TX 75247. Phone: (214) 252-9233. Fax: (214) 252-3379. E-mail: wb33news@tribune.com. Web Site: wb33.com. Licensee: Tribune Broadcasting Co. Group owner: (group owner; acq 7-15-97; grpsl). Network: WB. Rep: MMT.

KDFI—Analog channel: 27. Digital channel: 36. On air date: Jan 26, 1981. 400 N. Griffin St., Dallas, TX 75202. Phone: 214-720-4444. Fax: (214) 720-3207. E-mail: kdfi27@foxinc.com. Web Site: www.kdfitv.com. Licensee: New DMIC Inc. Group owner: Fox Television Stations Inc. (acq 2-18-00; $6.2 million). Rep: Fox Stations Sales.
Key Personnel:
Kathy Saunders . . . . . . VP
Mark LeValley . . . . . . engrg VP

KDFW—Analog channel: 4. Digital channel: 35. On air date: Dec 3, 1949. 400 N. Griffin St., Dallas, TX 75202. Phone: (214) 720-4444. Fax: (214) 720-3177 (gen.mgr.). Fax: (214) 720-3263 (news). E-mail: kdfw@foxtv.com. Web Site: www.kdfwfox4.com. Licensee: KDFW License Inc. Group owner: Fox Television Stations Inc. (acq 1-97; grpsl). Network: Fox. News: 50 hrs wkly.
Key Personnel:
Kathy Saunders . . . . . . VP & gen mgr
Dennis Welsh . . . . . . sls VP
Jeff Gurley . . . . . . gen sls mgr
Stephanie Holloway . . . . . . natl sls mgr
Zack Smith . . . . . . natl sls mgr
Don Adams . . . . . . rgnl sls mgr
John Kukla . . . . . . prom VP
Joe Kozlowski . . . . . . prom mgr
Andy Alexander . . . . . . progmg dir
Maria Barrs . . . . . . news dir
Rochelle Brown . . . . . . pub affrs dir
Mark LeValley . . . . . . engrg VP

***KDTN**—Analog channel: 2. On air date: Feb 2, 1988. Box 612066, Dallas, TX 75261. Phone: (817) 571-1229. Fax: (817) 571-7458. Web Site: www.daystar.com. Licensee: Community Television Educators of DFW Inc.. Ownership: Dr. Alan Bullock, 20%; Jack Howard, 20%; Joni Lamb, 20%; Kory Ford, 20%; and Marcus D. Lamb, 20% (acq 10-24-03; $20 million)..

***KDTX-TV**—Analog channel: 58. On air date: June 1986. 2823 W. Irving Blvd., Irving, TX 75061-4236. Phone: (972) 313-1333. Fax: (972) 790-5853. Web Site: www.tbn.org. Licensee: Trinity Broadcasting of Texas Inc. Group owner: Trinity Broadcasting Network (acq 7-86; $1.6 million; 5-6-86).
Key Personnel:
Paul F. Crouch . . . . . . pres
Steve Fjordbak . . . . . . gen mgr & progmg dir
Jennye Gardner . . . . . . pub affrs dir
Jim Forman . . . . . . chief of engrg

***KERA-TV**—Analog channel: 13. On air date: Sept 14, 1960. 3000 Harry Hines Blvd., Dallas, TX 75201. Phone: (214) 871-1390. Fax: (214) 754-0635. Web Site: www.kera.org. Licensee: North Texas Public Broadcasting Inc. Network: PBS. Washington Atty: Schwartz, Woods & Miller.

KFWD—Analog channel: 52. Digital channel: 51. On air date: Sept 1, 1988. 606 Young St., Dallas, TX 75202. Phone: (214) 977-6780. Fax: (214) 977-6544. Web Site: www.kfwd.tv.. Stn video via satellite: Direct/Dish Licensee: HIC Broadcast Inc. Washington Atty: Dow, Lohnes & Albertson.
Key Personnel:
Roland Hernandez . . . . . . CEO
Wayne Casa . . . . . . VP & gen mgr
Tony J. Montes . . . . . . stn mgr & progmg dir
Lisa Wegmann . . . . . . gen sls mgr
Landy Compton . . . . . . chief of engrg

KLDT—Analog channel: 55. On air date: 1999. 2450 Rockbrook, Louisville, TX 75067. Phone: (972) 316-2115. Fax: (972) 316-1112. Web Site: www.mastercontrol.com. Licensee: Johnson Broadcasting of Dallas Inc.

KMPX—Analog channel: 29. On air date: Sept 15, 1993. Box 612066, Dallas, TX 75261. 4201 Pool Rd., Colleyville, TX 75261. Phone: (817) 571-1229. Fax: (817) 571-7458. E-mail: comments@daystar.com. Web Site: www.daystar.tv. Licensee: Liberman Television of Dallas License Corp. Group owner: Liberman Broadcasting Inc. (acq 1-12-2004; $37 million)..

KPXD—Analog channel: 68. On air date: December 1996. 3900 Barnett St., Ft. Worth, TX 76103. Phone: (817) 654-6467. Web Site: www.pax.tv. Licensee: Paxson Dallas License Inc. Group owner: Paxson Communications Corp. (acq 4-4-97; $2.5 million for 51%).

KSTR-TV—Analog channel: 49. Digital channel: 48. On air date: Apr 17, 1984. 2323 Bryan St., Ste. 1900, Dallas, TX 75201. Phone: (214) 954-4900. Fax: (214) 954-4920. Licensee: Univision Partnership of Dallas. Group owner: Univision Communications Inc. (acq 6-6-01; grpsl). Network: TeleFutura (Spanish). Washington Atty: Wiley, Rein & Fielding.

KTAQ—Analog channel: 47. On air date: April 1, 1994. Box 8547, Greenville, TX 75404. 1058 Country Rd., Greenville, TX 75404. Phone: (903) 455-8847. Fax: (903) 455-8891. Licensee: Simons Broadcasting LP.. Ownership: Mike Simons, 99%; and Simons Asset Management L.L.C., 1% (acq 4-1-92; $50,000. for CP; FTR: 4-13-92).

KTVT—Analog channel: 11. Digital channel: 19. On air date: Sept 11, 1955. Box 2495, Fort Worth, TX 76113. 5233 Bridge St., Fort Worth, TX 76103. Phone: (817) 451-1111/654-1100. Fax: (817) 457-1897. E-mail: ktvt@ktvt.com. Web Site: www.cbs11tv.com. Licensee: CBS Stations Group of Texas L.P. Group owner: Viacom Television Stations Group (acq 8-3-99; $485 million. in stock). Network: CBS. Washington Atty: Leventhal, Senter & Lerman. News staff: 100; News: 27 hrs wkly.
Key Personnel:
Steve Mauldin . . . . . . pres & gen mgr
Gary Schneider . . . . . . sr VP, VP & stn mgr
Steve Williams . . . . . . opns mgr
Adam Levy . . . . . . sls dir
David Hershey . . . . . . mktg dir & prom dir
Ken Foote . . . . . . progmg dir
Tom Doerr . . . . . . news dir
Bill Schully . . . . . . engrg mgr

KTXA—(Arlington).Analog channel: 21. Digital channel: 18. On air date: Jan 4, 1981. 10111 N. Central Expwy., Dallas, TX 75231. 5233 Bridge St., Fort Worth, TX 76103. Phone: (214) 743-2100. Fax: (214) 743-2121. Fax: (214) 743-2150. E-mail: ktvt@ktvt.com. Web Site: www.upn21.com. Licensee: Viacom Television Stations Group of Dallas/Fort Worth L.P. Group owner: Viacom Television Stations Group (acq 2-28-91). Network: UPN. Washington Atty: Leventhal, Senter & Lerman.

Key Personnel:
Steve Mauldin . . . pres & gen mgr
Gary Schneider . . . sr VP & stn mgr
Steve Williams . . . opns mgr
Julia O'Hickey . . . sls dir
Kyle Brawner . . . natl sls mgr
David Hershey . . . mktg dir & prom dir
Ken Foote . . . progmg dir
Bill Schully . . . engrg mgr

KUVN-TV—(Garland).Analog channel: 23. On air date: Sept 25, 1986. 2323 Bryan St., Suite 1900, Dallas, TX 75201-2646. Phone: (214) 758-2300. Fax: (214) 758-2324. Web Site: www.univision.com. Licensee: KUVN License Partnership L.P. Group owner: Univision Communications Inc. (acq 5-88; $5.2 million). Network: Univision (Spanish). News staff: 22; News: 10 hrs wkly.

KXAS-TV—Analog channel: 5. Digital channel: 41. On air date: Sept 29, 1948. Box 1780, Fort Worth, TX 76101. 3900 Barnett, Fort Worth, TX 76103. Phone: (817) 429-5555. Phone: (214) 745-5555. Fax: (817) 654-6362. E-mail: nbc5i@nbc.com. Web Site: www.nbc5i.com. Licensee: Station Venture Operations L.P.. Ownership: NBC Telemundo License Co., 79.62% of the equity; Hicks Muse, 20.38% of the equity (acq 3-2-98). Network: NBC. Rep: NBC TV Stations Sales. News: 37 hrs wkly.
Key Personnel:
Thomas M. O'Brien . . . pres & gen mgr
Jim Borden . . . opns mgr

KXTX-TV—Analog channel: 39. Digital channel: 40. On air date: Feb 5, 1968. 3900 Harry Hines Blvd., Dallas, TX 75219. Phone: (214) 521-3900. Fax: (214) 523-5946. Web Site: www.telemundodallas.com. Licensee: NBC Telemundo License Co. Group owner: NBC TV Stations Division (acq 4-12-02; grpsl). Rep: Harrington, Righter & Parsons. Washington Atty: Fisher, Wayland, Cooper, Leader & Zaragoza.
Key Personnel:
Jose Valle . . . gen mgr
Brian McCall . . . opns mgr

WFAA-TV—Analog channel: 8. Digital channel: 9. On air date: Sept 17, 1949. Communications Ctr., 606 Young St., Dallas, TX 75202-4870. Phone: (214) 748-9631. Fax: (214) 977-6268. Fax: TWX: 910-861-4139. Web Site: wfaa.com. Licensee: WFAA-TV L.P. Group owner: Belo Corp., Broadcast Division (acq 2-50). Network: ABC. Rep: TeleRep. Washington Atty: Wiley, Rein & Fielding. News staff: 85; News: 28 hrs wkly.
Key Personnel:
Robert W. Iecherd . . . CEO
Kathy Clements . . . pres & gen mgr
Eric Nelson . . . natl sls mgr
Linda Ross . . . natl sls mgr
Nick Nicholson . . . mktg VP
Jim Glass . . . prom dir
Cathy Helean . . . prom mgr
David Walther . . . progmg dir
David Johnson . . . engrg dir

El Paso, TX
(DMA 100)

***KCOS**—Analog channel: 13. Digital channel: 30. On air date: Aug 18, 1978. 500 W. University Ave., El Paso, TX 79968-0650. Phone: (915) 747-6500. Fax: (915) 747-6605. E-mail: craig_brush@kcos.pbs.org. Web Site: www.kcostv.org. Licensee: El Paso Public Television Foundation. Network: PBS. Washington Atty: Cohn & Marks.
Key Personnel:
Craig Brush . . . CEO, pres & gen mgr
Robbie Paul . . . chmn
Barbara Hakim . . . CFO

KDBC-TV—Analog channel: 4. Digital channel: 32. On air date: Dec 14, 1952. Box 1799, El Paso, TX 79999. 2201 Wyoming Ave., El Paso, TX 79999. Phone: (915) 496-4444. Fax: (915) 496-4593 (new). Fax: (915) 496-4591 (sls). Web Site: www.kdbc.com. Licensee: KDBC License LLC. Group owner: Pappas Telecasting Companies (acq 3-29-2004; $20 million).. Network: CBS. News staff: 25; News: 15 hrs wkly.
Key Personnel:
Bram Watkins . . . gen mgr
Pat McGinnes . . . chief of opns
Debra Hastings . . . rgnl sls mgr
David Morgan . . . news dir
Pat McGinnis . . . chief of engrg

KFOX-TV—Analog channel: 4. Digital channel: 15. On air date: August 1979. 6004 N. Mesa, El Paso, TX 79912. Phone: (915) 833-8585. Fax: (915) 833-1358. Web Site: www.kfoxtv.com. Licensee: KTVU Partnership. Group owner: Cox Broadcasting (acq 1996; $20.855 million). Network: Fox. Rep: TeleRep. Washington Atty: Dow, Lohnes & Albertson. News staff: 23; News: 6 hrs wkly.

KINT-TV—Analog channel: 26. On air date: May 5, 1984. 5426 N. Mesa, El Paso, TX 79912. Phone: (915) 581-1126. Fax: (915) 581-1393. Licensee: Entravision Communications Co. L.L.C. Group owner: (group owner; acq 6-4-97; grpsl). Network: Univision (Spanish). Washington Atty: Thompson, Hine & Flory L. News staff: 14; News: 10 hrs wkly.
Key Personnel:
David Candelaria . . . gen mgr
Diana De Lara . . . gen sls mgr
Dan Kempner . . . natl sls mgr
Abel Rodriguez . . . prom dir & pub affrs dir
Sylvia Martinez . . . progmg dir
Gustavo Barraza . . . news dir
Alfredo Durand . . . chief of engrg

***KRWG-TV**—Analog channel: 22. On air date: June 29, 1973. Box 30001, MSC TV22, NMSU, Las Cruces, NM 88003. Rm. 100, Jordan St., NMSU, Las Cruces, NM 88003. Phone: (505) 646-2222. Fax: (505) 646-1924. Fax: (505) 646-2160. E-mail: krwgtv@nmsu.edu. Web Site: www.krwg-tv.org. Licensee: Regents of New Mexico State University. Network: PBS. Washington Atty: Dow, Lohnes & Albertson. News: 3 hrs wkly.
Key Personnel:
Colin Gromatzky . . . gen mgr
J.D. Jarvis . . . opns mgr
Anthony Casaus . . . dev dir
Gary Worth . . . news dir
William Saggerson . . . chief of engrg

***KSCE**—Analog channel: 38. Digital channel: 39. On air date: Apr 15, 1989. 6400 Escondido Dr., El Paso, TX 79912. Phone: (915) 585-8838. Fax: (915) 585-8841. E-mail: ksce@aol.com. Web Site: www.kscetv.com. Licensee: Channel 38 Christian Television. Washington Atty: James L. Oyster.
Key Personnel:
Andrew Paschall . . . chmn
Grace Rendall . . . VP, gen mgr & opns dir

KTDO—Analog channel: 48. Digital channel: 47. On air date: Nov 11, 1984. 10033 Carnegie, El Paso, TX 79925. Phone: (915) 591-9595. Fax: (915) 591-9896. Web Site: www.telemundo.com. Licensee: ZGS El Paso Televison L.P.. Ownership: ZGS Broadcast Holdings Inc., 100% (acq 9-13-2004; $11.8 million). Network: Telemundo (Spanish). Rep: Katz Radio. Washington Atty: Reed, Smith, Shaw & McClay.
Key Personnel:
Monica Diaz . . . gen sls mgr, mktg mgr & adv mgr
Michelle Lujan . . . progmg dir
Jaime Martinez . . . chief of engrg

KTFN—Analog channel: 65. On air date: 1991. 5426 N. Mesa, El Paso, TX 79912. Phone: (915) 581-1126. Fax: (915) 581-1393. Licensee: Entravision Holdings LLC. Group owner: Entravision Communications Corp. (acq 12-10-01; $18 million)..
Key Personnel:
Dan Kempner . . . pres & natl sls mgr
David Candelaria . . . gen mgr
Diana DeLara . . . gen sls mgr
Abel Rodriguez . . . prom dir
Alfredo Durand . . . progmg dir & chief of engrg

KTSM-TV—Analog channel: 9. On air date: Jan 4, 1953. 801 N. Oregon St., El Paso, TX 79902. Phone: (915) 532-5421. Fax: (915) 532-6793. E-mail: ktsmtv@whc.net. Web Site: www.ktsm.com. Licensee: ComCorp of El Paso License Corp. Group owner: Communications Corp. of America (acq 7-25-97; $30.5 million for stock with KTSM-AM-FM). Network: NBC. Rep: Millennium Sales & Marketing. Washington Atty: Fletcher, Heald & Hildreth. News staff: 33; News: 19.5 hrs wkly.
Key Personnel:
Larry Bracher . . . gen mgr
Danny Aguilar . . . sls VP & gen sls mgr
Jack Ballesteros . . . natl sls mgr
Victor Veuegus . . . news dir
Courtney Elam . . . pub affrs dir
Ernie Hartt . . . engrg dir

KVIA-TV—Analog channel: 7. On air date: Sept 1, 1956. 4140 Rio Bravo, El Paso, TX 79902. Phone: (915) 496-7777. Fax: (915) 532-0070. E-mail: kvia@kvia.com. Web Site: www.kvia.com. Licensee: NPG of Texas L.P. (acq 12-9-94; $19.9 million; 1-23-95). Network: ABC. Rep: Katz Radio. Washington Atty: Robert Thompson. News staff: 30; News: 31.5 hrs wkly.
Key Personnel:
David Bradley . . . CEO
John Kueneke . . . pres
Kevin Lovell . . . gen mgr
Chris Swann . . . opns mgr
Nathan Price . . . sls dir
Dan Overstreet . . . natl sls mgr
David Gonzalez . . . prom dir
Karla Huelga . . . progmg dir & pub affrs dir
Eric Huseby . . . news dir
Elias Ventanilla . . . chief of engrg

XHIJ—(Ciudad Juarez).MEX Analog channel: 44. On air date: Oct 16, 1980. 5925 Cromo Dr., El Paso, TX 79912. Phone: (915) 585-6344. Phone: (915) 577-0045. Fax: (915) 585-6333. Web Site: www.canal44.com. Licensee: Arnoldo Cabada De la O.. Ownership: Arnoldo Cabada De la O, 52%; Luis Cabada Alvidrez, Sergio Cabada Alvidrez & Jesus Cabada Alvidrez, each 16%. Network: Telemundo (Spanish). News staff: 20; News: 15 hrs wkly.

Ft. Worth

see Dallas-Ft. Worth market

Harlingen-Weslaco -Brownsville-McAllen, TX
(DMA 93)

KGBT-TV—Analog channel: 4. Digital channel: 31. On air date: October 1953. 9201 W. Expwy. 83, Harlingen, TX 78552. Phone: (956) 366-4444. Fax: (956) 366-4494. Web Site: www.kgbt4.com. Licensee: Libco Inc. Group owner: Liberty Corp. (acq 10-23-98; $42 million).. Network: CBS. Rep: Katz Radio. Washington Atty: Dow, Lohnes & Albertson. News staff: 33; News: 19 hrs wkly.
Key Personnel:
Jim Keebor . . . pres
Coby Cooper . . . gen mgr
Phil Rich . . . opns mgr
Randy Roberts . . . gen sls mgr
Beau Pillet . . . mktg dir & prom mgr
Henry Chu . . . news dir

***KLUJ-TV**—Analog channel: 44. On air date: June 25, 1984. Box 1647, 1920 Al Coneway Dr., Suite 117, Harlingen, TX 78551. Phone: (956) 425-4225. Fax: (956) 412-1740. E-mail: klujtv@xanadu2.net. Licensee: Community Educational TV Inc. (acq 4-84). Network: PBS. Washington Atty: Joseph E. Dunne III.

***KMBH**—Analog channel: 60. On air date: Oct 8, 1985. Box 2147, Harlingen, TX 78551. 1701 Tennessee St., Harlingen, TX 78551. Phone: (956) 421-4111. Fax: (956) 421-4150. E-mail: rgveduca@aol.com. Web Site: www.kmbh.org. Licensee: RGV Educational Broadcasting Inc. Network: PBS. Washington Atty: Ross & Hardies.
Key Personnel:
Father Pedro Briseno . . . CEO, pres & gen mgr
Gustavo Morales . . . opns mgr & progmg mgr
John Ross . . . chief of engrg

KNVO—Analog channel: 48. On air date: Oct 12, 1992. 801 N. Jackson Rd., Suite 850, McAllen, TX 78501. Phone: (956) 687-4848. Fax: (956) 687-7784. Licensee: Entravision Holdings L.L.C. Group owner: Entravision Communications Co. L.L.C (acq 4-25-97). Network: Univision (Spanish). Washington Atty: Schwartz, Woods & Miller.

KRGV-TV—Analog channel: 5. On air date: Apr 10, 1954. Box 5, Weslaco, TX 78599. 900 E. Expwy. 83, Weslaco, TX 78599. Phone: (956) 968-5555. Fax: (956) 973-5003. Web Site: www.newschannel5.tv. Licensee: Mobile Video Tapes Inc. Group owner: Manship Stns (acq 1-28-64; grpsl; 2-3-64). Network: ABC. Washington Atty: Cohn & Marks. News staff: 28; News: 12 hrs wkly.
Key Personnel:
Richard Manship . . . chmn & pres
Ray Alexander . . . gen mgr
Michelle Martone . . . opns mgr & progmg dir
John Kittleman . . . gen sls mgr
Robert Ledesma . . . sls dir & natl sls mgr
Jerry Berg . . . prom mgr
Jenny Martinez . . . news dir
Jerry Lee Berg . . . pub affrs dir
Chuck Salge . . . chief of engrg

***KTLM**—Analog channel: 40. Digital channel: 20. On air date: Oct 8, 1999. 7th Fl., 3900 N. 10th St., McAllen, TX 78501. Phone: (956) 686-0040. Fax: (956) 686-0770. Licensee: Sunbelt Multimedia Co. (acq 3-30-00; $600,000). Network: Telemundo (Spanish). News staff: 12; News: 8 hrs wkly.

Directory of Television Texas

KVEO—Analog channel: 23. On air date: Dec 19, 1981. 394 N. Expressway, Brownsville, TX 78521. Box 4314, Brownsville, TX 78521. Phone: (956) 544-2323. Fax: (956) 544-4636. Web Site: www.kveo.com. Licensee: Communications Corp. of America. Group owner: (group owner; acq 2-13-95; 5-8-95). Network: NBC. Washington Atty: Fletcher, Heald & Hildreth.
Key Personnel:
Tom Galloway . . . pres
Wayne Elmore . . . CFO
Clark White . . . VP
Amy Villarreal . . . gen mgr
Robert Gutierrez . . . gen sls mgr
Jackie Lynn . . . prom dir
Lisa Kidd-Hagle . . . progmg dir
Tommy Balli . . . engrg mgr

Houston (DMA 11)

KAZH—Analog channel: 57. Digital channel: 41. On air date: 1987. 2620 Fountain View, Ste.322, Houston, TX 77057. Phone: (713) 467-5757. Fax: (713) 783-4157. Licensee: KAZH License LLC. Group owner: Pappas Telecasting Companies (acq 7-7-99; $28 million). Network: Azteca America (Spanish).
Key Personnel:
Harry J. Pappas . . . CEO & pres
Emilio Nicolas Jr. . . . gen mgr

***KETH-TV**—Analog channel: 14. On air date: July 1987. 10902 S. Wilcrest Dr., Houston, TX 77099. Phone: (281) 561-5828. Fax: (281) 561-9793. Web Site: www.communityedtv.org/keth. Licensee: Community Educational Television Inc. News: 3 hrs wkly.
Key Personnel:
Laura Hanks . . . opns mgr
Rod Harty . . . chief of engrg

KFTH-TV—Analog channel: 67. Digital channel: 36. On air date: Jan 27, 1986. 9440 Kirby, Houston, TX 77054. Phone: (713) 662-4545. Fax: (713) 592-0148. Licensee: TeleFutura Houston LLC. Group owner: Univision Communications Inc. (acq 5-21-2001; grpsl). Network: TeleFutura (Spanish).
Key Personnel:
Jerold Perenchio . . . CEO
Mike Wortsman . . . pres
Thomas Arnost . . . pres
George Blank . . . CFO
Craig H. Bland . . . VP & gen mgr
Jose Oti . . . gen sls mgr
Chas Witson . . . natl sls mgr
Michael Thomas . . . rgnl sls mgr
Arlene Kelsch . . . mktg mgr
Charlie Lozano . . . prom VP
Sanjuio Salazar . . . progmg mgr
Grace Olivares-Hernandez . . . pub affrs dir
Tom Daniels . . . chief of engrg

KHOU-TV—Analog channel: 11. Digital channel: 31. On air date: Mar 22, 1953. 1945 Allen Pkwy., Houston, TX 77019. Phone: (713) 526-1111. Fax: (713) 521-4326. E-mail: 11listens@khou.com. Web Site: www.khou.com. Licensee: KHOU-TV L.P. Group owner: Belo Corp., Broadcast Division (acq 1984; grpsl; 11-17-83). Network: CBS. Rep: TeleRep.
Key Personnel:
Peter Diaz . . . pres & gen mgr
Susan McEldoon . . . sls dir
Keith Connors . . . news dir
Blane Huhn . . . engrg dir

KHWB—Analog channel: 39. Digital channel: 38. On air date: Jan 6, 1967. 7700 Westpark Dr., Houston, TX 77063. Phone: (713) 781-3939. Fax: (713) 435-2859. Web Site: huoustonswb.com. Licensee: KHWB Inc. Group owner: Tribune Broadcasting Co. (acq 1-17-96; $95 million. plus $6). Network: WB. Rep: Harrington, Righter & Parsons. Washington Atty: Sidley & Austin. News staff: 34; News: 4 hrs wkly.

***KLTJ**—Analog channel: 22. On air date: July 22, 1989. 1050 Gemini, Houston, TX 77058. Phone: (281) 212-1022. Fax: (281) 212-1031. E-mail: comments@daystar.com. Web Site: www.daystartv.net. Licensee: Word of God Fellowship Inc. aka Community TV Educators. (acq 10-18-99; $9.5 million)..

KNWS-TV—Analog channel: 51. Digital channel: 52. On air date: Nov 3, 1993. 8440 Westpark, Houston, TX 77063. Phone: (713) 974-5151. Fax: (713) 974-5188. Web Site: www.knws51.com. Licensee: Johnson Broadcasting Inc.. Ownership: Douglas R. Johnson, 100%. Washington Atty: Smithwick & Belendiuk.
Key Personnel:
Douglas R. Johnson . . . pres
Jack Dabbah . . . gen mgr & stn mgr
Chris Bourne . . . opns dir & chief of opns

KPRC-TV—Analog channel: 2. Digital channel: 35. On air date: Jan 1, 1949. Box 2222, Houston, TX 77252. 8181 Southwest Fwy., Houston, TX 77074. Phone: (713) 222-2222. Fax: (713) 270-9334. Web Site: www.click2houston.com. Licensee: Post-Newsweek Stations Inc. Group owner: (group owner; acq 4-22-94; 5-2-94). Network: NBC. Rep: MMT. Washington Atty: Covington & Burling. News staff: 80; News: 24 hrs wkly.
Key Personnel:
Steve Wasserman . . . VP & gen mgr
Tammy Dean . . . opns dir
Steve Danowski . . . gen sls mgr
Nancy Shafran . . . news dir
Dale Werner . . . chief of engrg

KPXB—Analog channel: 49. Digital channel: 5. On air date: June 16, 1989. 256 N. Sam Houston Pkwy. E., Suite 49, Houston, TX 77060. Phone: (281) 820-4900. Fax: (281) 820-3916. E-mail: kpxb@electrotex.com. Web Site: www.paxhouston.tv. Licensee: Paxson Houston License Inc. Group owner: Paxson Communications Corp. (acq 1995; $7.9 million). Network: PAX TV. Rep: Katz Radio. Washington Atty: Pepper & Corazzini.

KRIV—Analog channel: 26. Digital channel: 27. On air date: Aug 15, 1971. Box 22810, Houston, TX 77227. 4261 Southwest Fwy., Houston, TX 77027. Phone: (713) 479-2600. Fax: (713) 479-2604. Licensee: Fox Television Stations Inc. Group owner: (group owner) Network: Fox. Washington Atty: Molly Pauker.
Key Personnel:
D'Artagnan Bebel . . . gen mgr
Charles Hughes . . . opns VP & engrg VP
Sheila Birenbaun . . . opns dir
Du Juan McCoy . . . sls VP
Larry Parker . . . prom VP
Stan Wasilik . . . progmg dir
Kathy Williams . . . news dir
Lisa Whitlock . . . pub affrs dir

KTBU—Analog channel: 55. Digital channel: 42. On air date: July 15, 1998. 7026 Old Katy Rd., Suite 201, Houston, TX 77024. Phone: (713) 864-1999. Fax: (713) 864-1993. Web Site: www.thetube.net. Licensee: Humanity Interested Media L.P.. Ownership: Channel 55 Broadcasting LLC, gen ptnr, 0.1%; HIM Inc., limited ptnr, 99.9% (acq 9-29-2004; $6 million)..
Key Personnel:
Donald E. Iloff Jr. . . . gen mgr
Bruce Dinehart . . . stn mgr
Phil Lonsway . . . gen sls mgr
Lara Bell . . . pub affrs dir
Eric Peterson . . . chief of engrg

KTMD—Analog channel: 47. On air date: Dec 12, 1987. 1235 N. Loop W., Suite 125, Houston, TX 77008. Phone: (713) 974-4848. Fax: (713) 243-7850. Fax: (713) 782-5575. Web Site: www.ktmd.com. Licensee: NBC Telemundo License Co. Group owner: Telemundo Group Inc. (acq 4-12-02; grpsl). Network: Telemundo (Spanish). Washington Atty: Hogan & Hartson. News staff: 14; News: 7 hrs wkly.
Key Personnel:
Roel Medina . . . gen mgr
Dominic Fails . . . gen sls mgr
Gregorio Cervantes . . . natl sls mgr

KTRK-TV—Analog channel: 13. Digital channel: 32. On air date: Nov 20, 1954. Box 13, Houston, TX 77005. 3310 Bissonnet St., Houston, TX 77001. Phone: (713) 666-0713. Fax: (713) 663-4574. Web Site: www.ABC13.com. Licensee: ABC Inc. Group owner: (group owner; acq 7-17-67). Network: ABC.

KTXH—Analog channel: 20. On air date: Nov 7, 1982. 4261 Southwest Frwy., Houston, TX 77027. Phone: (713) 479-2600. Fax: (713) 479-2859. Licensee: Fox Television Stations Inc. Group owner: (group owner; acq 11-6-01; with WDCA(TV) Washington, DC in swap for KBHK-TV San Francisco, CA). Network: UPN.
Key Personnel:
D'Artagnan Bebel . . . gen mgr
Charles Hughes . . . opns VP

***KUHT**—Analog channel: 8. Digital channel: 9. On air date: May 12, 1953. 4343 Elgin St., Houston, TX 77204-0008. Phone: (713) 748-8888. Phone: (800) 364-8300. Fax: (713) 743-8867. Web Site: www.houstonpbs.org. Licensee: University of Houston System, Board of Regents. Network: PBS. Washington Atty: Dow, Lohnes & Albertson.
Key Personnel:
John Hesse . . . gen mgr & stn mgr
Steve Pyndus . . . opns dir

KXLN-TV—Analog channel: 45. On air date: Sept 18, 1987. 9440 Kirby Dr., Houston, TX 77054. Phone: (713) 662-4545. Fax: (713) 668-9054. Web Site: www.univision.com. Licensee: KXLN License Partnership G.P. Group owner: Univision Communications Inc. (acq 2-24-95; 5-22-95). Network: Univision (Spanish). Washington Atty: Fisher, Wayland, Cooper, Leader & Zaragoza. News staff: 23; News: 7 hrs wkly.
Key Personnel:
Craig Bland . . . VP, gen mgr & stn mgr
Jeff Hoffman . . . stn mgr
Jose Oti . . . gen sls mgr
Charles Wilson . . . natl sls mgr
Charlie Lozano . . . prom dir
Cindy Chisum . . . progmg dir
Juan Garcia . . . news dir
Grace C. Olivares . . . pub affrs dir
Chuck Promrose . . . chief of engrg

KZJL—Analog channel: 61. On air date: 1995. 11767 Katy Freeway, Houston, TX 77079. Phone: (281) 835-3181. Fax: (281) 835-3556. Licensee: KZJL License Corp. Group owner: Liberman Broadcasting Inc. (acq 1-10-01; $57 million).

Laredo, TX (DMA 190)

KGNS-TV—Analog channel: 8. Digital channel: 15. On air date: Jan 6, 1956. Box 2829, 120 W. Del Mar Blvd., Johnson City, TX 78045. Phone: (956) 727-8888. Fax: (956) 727-5336. E-mail: email8@pro8news.com. Web Site: pro8news.com. Licensee: SagamoreHill Broadcasting of Texas LLC.. Ownership: SagamoreHill Broadcasting LLC, 100% (acq 9-28-2004; $14.4 million).. Network: Network: NBC, ABC. Rep: Katz Radio. Washington Atty: Dow, Lohnes & Albertson.
Key Personnel:
Louis Wall . . . pres
Mary Nell Sanchez . . . gen mgr
Carlos Salinas . . . natl sls mgr & rgnl sls mgr
Ramiro Saucedo . . . prom mgr
Armando Gomez . . . adv mgr & pub affrs dir
Velia Herrera . . . progmg dir
Richard Rucha . . . news dir
David York . . . chief of engrg

KLDO-TV—Analog channel: 27. On air date: Dec 17, 1984. 222 Bob Bullock Loop, Perry, TX 78043. Phone: (956) 727-0027. Fax: (956) 727-2673. Licensee: Entravision Holdings L.L.C. Group owner: Entravision Communications Co. L.L.C. (acq 7-30-97; $6.2 million). Network: Univision (Spanish). Washington Atty: Martin E. Firestone.
Key Personnel:
Terry Elena Ordaz . . . gen mgr
Elia Solis . . . gen sls mgr & film buyer
Jose Gomez . . . rgnl sls mgr
Jose Salinas . . . prom mgr & progmg dir
Marisa Limon . . . news dir
Merlin Miller . . . chief of engrg

KVTV—Analog channel: 13. On air date: Dec 29, 1973. Box 2039, 2600 Shea & Ana St., Laredo, TX 78040. Phone: (956) 723-2923. Fax: (956) 723-0474. Web Site: www.kvtv.com. Licensee: Eagle Creek of Laredo LLC. Group owner: Eagle Creek Broadcasting LLC (acq 6-13-02; grpsl). Network: CBS.
Key Personnel:
Dale Remy . . . gen mgr & stn mgr
Joe Herrera . . . gen sls mgr
Carol Rostohar . . . prom dir & pub affrs dir
Kent Harrell . . . news dir
George Sanders . . . chief of engrg

Longview

see Tyler-Longview (Lufkin & Nacogdoches), TX market

Lubbock, TX (DMA 145)

KAMC—Analog channel: 28. On air date: Nov 12, 1968. 7403 S. University, Lubbock, TX 79423. Phone: (806) 745-2828. Fax: (806) 748-1080. E-mail: 28news@abc28.com. Web Site: www.abc28.net. Licensee: Mission Broadcasting Inc. Group owner: (group owner; acq 12-17-2003). Network: ABC. Washington Atty: Bryan Cave. News staff: 26; News: 39 hrs wkly.
Key Personnel:

David S. Smith . . . . . pres & gen mgr
John Dittmeier . . . . . exec VP
A.C. Wimberly . . . . . gen mgr, stn mgr & progmg dir
Chuck Spaugh . . . . . opns dir
Eric Thomas . . . . . gen sls mgr
Jeff Pitner . . . . . prom dir & pub affrs dir
Russ Protect . . . . . news dir
Monte Williams . . . . . engrg dir

KCBD—Analog channel: 11. On air date: May 10, 1953. 5600 Avenue A, Lubbock, TX 79404. Phone: (806) 744-1414. Fax: (806) 744-0449. E-mail: kcbd@kcbd.com. Web Site: www.kcbd.com. Licensee: Libco Inc. Group owner: Liberty Corp. (acq 2-17-2000; $59.8 million).. Network: NBC. Washington Atty: Dow, Lohnes & Albertson.

Key Personnel:
Dan Jackson . . . . . gen mgr & gen sls mgr
Brent McClure . . . . . opns mgr, mktg dir & prom mgr
Beverly McBeth . . . . . gen sls mgr
Peggy Sullivan . . . . . progmg mgr
Benji Snead . . . . . news dir
Ricky Price . . . . . chief of engrg

KJTV-TV—Analog channel: 34. On air date: Dec 10, 1981. Box 3757, Lubbock, TX 79452. 9800 University Ave., Lubbock, TX 79452. Phone: (806) 745-3434. Fax: (806) 748-1949. Web Site: www.fox34.com. Licensee: Ramar Communications II Ltd. Group owner: (group owner) Network: Fox. Rep: Millennium Sales & Marketing. Washington Atty: Leventhal, Senter & Lerman. News staff: 20; News: 7 hrs wkly.

Key Personnel:
Brad Moran . . . . . gen mgr
Scott Cawthron . . . . . opns mgr
Marc Gilmour . . . . . gen sls mgr
Jana Hill . . . . . prom mgr
Terri Holt . . . . . progmg mgr

KLBK-TV—Analog channel: 13. On air date: Nov 13, 1952. 7403 S. University Ave., Perry, TX 79407. Phone: (806) 745-2345. Fax: (806) 748-2250. Web Site: www.klbk.com. Licensee: Nexstar Finance Inc. Group owner: Nexstar Broadcasting Group Inc. (acq 12-31-03; grpsl). Network: CBS. Washington Atty: Arter & Hadden. News staff: 47; News: 27 hrs wkly.

Key Personnel:
Greg McAlister . . . . . gen mgr
Chuck Spaugn . . . . . opns mgr
A.C. Wimberly . . . . . progmg mgr
Russ Poteet . . . . . news dir
Mike Randolph . . . . . chief of engrg

KPTB—Analog channel: 16. On air date: 1999. Box 61000, Midland, TX 79711. 5604 Martin Luther King Blvd., Lubbock, TX 79404. Phone: (806) 747-4977. Fax: (806) 749-7732. E-mail: info@ptcbglc.com. Web Site: www.godslearningchannel.com. Licensee: Prime Time Christian Broadcasting Inc.

***KTXT-TV**—Analog channel: 5. Digital channel: 39. On air date: Oct 16, 1962. Box 42161, Lubbock, TX 79409-2161. 17th St. & Indiana Ave., Lubbock, TX 79409-2161. Phone: (806) 742-2209. Fax: (806) 742-1274. E-mail: pat.cates@ttu.edu. Web Site: www.ktxt.org. Licensee: Texas Tech University. Network: PBS. Washington Atty: Cohn & Marks.

Key Personnel:
Eric Voyles . . . . . CFO & prom dir
Pat Cates . . . . . gen mgr
Tim Chambers . . . . . dev dir
Michelle Dillard . . . . . progmg mgr & progmg
Martin Quintero . . . . . chief of engrg

KUPT—Analog channel: 22. On air date: 2002. 9800 University Ave., Lubbock, TX 79423. Phone: (806) 745-3434. Fax: (806) 798-9387. E-mail: bmoran@ramorcom.com. Licensee: Woods Communications Corp. Group owner: (group owner) Network: UPN.

Lufkin

see Tyler-Longview (Lufkin & Nacogdoches), TX market

McAllen

see Harlingen-Weslaco-Brownsville-McAllen, TX market

Midland

see Odessa-Midland, TX market

Nacogdoches

see Tyler-Longview (Lufkin & Nacogdoches), TX market

Odessa-Midland, TX (DMA 158)

KMID—Analog channel: 2. On air date: Dec 18, 1953. Box 60230, 3200 Laforce Blvd., Midland, TX 79711. Phone: (432) 563-2222. Fax: (432) 563-5819. E-mail: news@kmid.tv. Web Site: www.kmid.tv. Licensee: Nexstar Finance Inc. Group owner: Nexstar Broadcasting Group Inc. (acq 7-31-00; $10 million).. Network: ABC. Rep: Blair Television. Washington Atty: Cohn & Marks. News staff: 23; News: 17 hrs wkly.

KMLM—Analog channel: 42. On air date: Oct 18, 1988. Box 61000, Midland, TX 79711-1000. 3719 S. County Rd. 1305, Odessa, TX 79765. Phone: (915) 432-0420. Fax: (915) 432-1736. E-mail: info@ptcbglc.com. Web Site: www.godslearningchannel.com. Licensee: Prime Time Christian Broadcasting Inc.

Key Personnel:
Tommie Cooper . . . . . gen mgr & stn mgr
Matt Montgomery . . . . . chief of engrg

***KOCV-TV**—Analog channel: 36. On air date: Mar 24, 1986. Box 3912, Odessa, TX 79760. 302 East 29th St., Odessa, TX 79762. Phone: (432) 331-7814. Phone: (432) 580-0036. Fax: (432) 334-3756. E-mail: dudlneytl@ector-county.k12.tx.us. Web Site: www.kocv-tv.org. Licensee: Ector County Independent School District. (acq 1-14-2004; $1).. Network: PBS.

Key Personnel:
Wendell Sollis . . . . . CEO
Lynn Dudney . . . . . gen mgr
Amy Young . . . . . opns mgr

KOSA-TV—Analog channel: 7. On air date: Jan 1, 1956. Box 4186, Odessa, TX 79760. 4101 E. 42nd St., J-7, Odessa, TX 79762. Phone: (432) 580-5672. Fax: (432) 580-8010. E-mail: news@cbs7.com. Web Site: www.cbs7.com. Licensee: ICA Broadcasting I Ltd. (acq 3-10-00; $8 million).. Network: CBS. Rep: Continental Television Sales. Washington Atty: Richard Hayes. News staff: 22; News: 16 hrs wkly.

Key Personnel:
John Bushman . . . . . chmn
Barry Marks . . . . . pres & gen mgr
John Nichols . . . . . CFO
Dale Palmer . . . . . stn mgr
Rick McGee . . . . . opns mgr

KPEJ—Analog channel: 24. Digital channel: 23. On air date: June 16, 1986. Box 11009, 1550 W. I-20, Odessa, TX 79763. Phone: (432) 580-0024. Fax: (432) 337-3707. E-mail: jfaltus@kpejtv.com. Web Site: www.kpejtv.com. Licensee: Comcorp of Texas License Corp. Group owner: Communications Corp. of America (acq 10-31-90; grpsl; 11-19-90). Network: Fox. Washington Atty: Fletcher, Heald & Hildreth.

Key Personnel:
Dale Harris . . . . . gen mgr
Jayne Faltus . . . . . progmg mgr

KPXK—Analog channel: 30. On air date: 2001. Paxson Communications Corp., 601 Clearwater Park Rd., West Palm Beach, FL 33401. Phone: (432) 563-5795. Web Site: www.pax.tv. Licensee: WinStar Odessa Inc. Group owner: Paxson Communications Corp. (acq 9-4-98). Network: PAX TV.

KUPB—Analog channel: 18. On air date: 2001. Box 61907, Midland, TX 79711. 10313 West County Road 117, Midland, TX 79706. Phone: (432) 563-1826. Fax: (432) 563-0215. Web Site: www.entravision.com. Licensee: Entravision Holdings LLC. Group owner: Entravision Communications Corp. Network: Univision (Spanish). Washington Atty: Thompson, Hine & Flory L.

Key Personnel:
Walter Ulloa . . . . . CEO
Philip C. Wilkinson . . . . . pres
John DeLorenzo . . . . . CFO
Larry Safir . . . . . exec VP
Leticia Martinez . . . . . gen mgr

KWAB-TV—Analog channel: 4. On air date: Jan 15, 1956. Box 60150, Midland, TX 79711. Phone: (432) 263-4901. Fax: (432) 263-3630. Web Site: www.kwes.com. Licensee: Midessa Television Co.. Ownership: Midessa Television Co. (acq 9-9-91; $4.85 million. with KWES-TV Odessa; FTR: 9-23-91). Network: NBC.

KWES-TV—Analog channel: 9. Digital channel: 13. On air date: Dec 1, 1958. Box 60150, Midland, TX 79711-0150. 11320 County Rd. 127 W., Midland, TX 79711. Phone: (432) 567-9999. Fax: (432) 567-9992. Web Site: www.mywesttexas.com. Licensee: Midessa Television Co. Group owner: R.H. Drewry Group (acq 10-31-91; $4.85 million. with KWAB(TV) Big Spring; FTR: 9-23-91). Network: NBC.

Port Arthur

see Beaumont-Port Arthur, TX market

San Angelo, TX (DMA 196)

KIDY—Analog channel: 6. Digital channel: 19. On air date: May 12, 1984. 406 S. Irving, San Angelo, TX 76903. Phone: (325) 655-6006. Phone: (325) 673-2345 (sales). Fax: (325) 655-8461. Fax: (325) 672-4816 (sales). E-mail: kidy@foxsanangelo.com. Web Site: foxsanangelo.com. Licensee: Sage Broadcasting Corp. Network: Network: Fox, UPN. Rep: Millennium Sales & Marketing. Washington Atty: Fletcher, Heeald & Hildreth. News staff: 2.

Key Personnel:
Paris Schindler . . . . . CEO
Bill Carter . . . . . pres
Sherri Goode . . . . . stn mgr
Teddye Read . . . . . natl sls mgr
Pam Winn . . . . . rgnl sls mgr

KLST—Analog channel: 8. On air date: June 23, 1953. 2800 Armstrong St., San Angelo, TX 76903-2799. Phone: (325) 949-8800. Fax: (325) 658-4006. E-mail: klst@klst.net. Web Site: www.klst.tv. Licensee: Nexstar Broadcasting Inc. (acq 9-2-2004; $12 million).. Network: CBS. Rep: Katz Radio. Washington Atty: Skadden, Arps, Slate, Meagher & Flom. News staff: 12; News: 17 hrs wkly.

Key Personnel:
Perry Sook . . . . . pres
Joy Kimbell . . . . . exec VP
Tom Stovall . . . . . gen mgr
Mark McCain . . . . . opns mgr
Lanny Kiest . . . . . gen sls mgr
Don Plachno . . . . . prom mgr
Gordon Hay . . . . . progmg dir
Kathy Munoz . . . . . news dir
Roland Bigley . . . . . chief of engrg

KSAN-TV—Analog channel: 3. On air date: Feb 8, 1962. 2800 Armstrong St., San Angelo, TX 7690. Phone: (325) 949-8800. Fax: (325) 655-3040. E-mail: nbc3@wcc.com. Web Site: www.ksan.tv. Licensee: Mission Broadcasting Inc. Group owner: (group owner; acq 6-13-03; $10 million. with KRBC-TV Abilene). Network: NBC. Rep: Blair Television. Washington Atty: Kenkel, Barnard & Edmundson.

Key Personnel:
Sherri Scott . . . . . stn mgr
Albert Gutierrez . . . . . rgnl sls mgr
Kathy Munoz . . . . . news dir
Ed Huwa . . . . . chief of engrg

San Antonio, TX (DMA 37)

KABB—Analog channel: 29. On air date: Dec 17, 1987. 4335 N.W. Loop 410, San Antonio, TX 78229-5168. Phone: (210) 366-1129. Fax: (210) 377-4758. E-mail: kabbtv@kabb.com. Web Site: www.kabb.com. Licensee: KABB Licensee L.L.C. Group owner: Sinclair Broadcast Group Inc. Network: Fox. Rep: Millennium Sales & Marketing. Washington Atty: Shaw, Pittman. News staff: 35; News: 7 hrs wkly.

Key Personnel:
Dean Radla . . . . . sls dir
Robert Canales . . . . . natl sls mgr

KBEJ—Analog channel: 2. 5400 Fredericksburg Rd., San Antonio, TX 78229. Phone: (210) 366-5000. Fax: (210) 348-9142. Fax: (210) 377-8779. Web Site: www.mysanantonio.com. Licensee: Corridor Television L.L.P. Network: UPN.

Key Personnel:
Robert G. McGann . . . . . gen mgr
Boots Walker . . . . . sls dir
Frank Peterman . . . . . engrg dir

KENS-TV—Analog channel: 5. On air date: Feb 15, 1950. Box TV5, San Antonio, TX 78299. 5400 Fredericksburg Rd., San Antonio, TX 78229. Phone: (210) 366-5000. Fax: (210) 377-0740. Web Site: www.mysanantonio.com. Licensee: KENS-TV Inc. Group owner: Belo Corp., Broadcast Division (acq 1997; $75 million. with co-located AM

Directory of Television Texas

plus interest in Television Food Network) Network: CBS. Rep: TeleRep. Washington Atty: Wiley, Rein & Fielding. News staff: 55; News: 24 hrs wkly.
Key Personnel:
Bob McGann . . . gen mgr
Boots Walker . . . sls dir
Allen Lansing . . . prom dir
Kurt Davis . . . news dir
Frank Peterman . . . engrg dir

***KHCE-TV**—Analog channel: 23. On air date: July 1989. 15533 Capital Port Dr., San Antonio, TX 78249. Box 691246, San Antonio, TX 78249. Phone: (210) 479-0123. Fax: (210) 492-5679. Licensee: San Antonio Educational TV Inc.. Ownership: Dr. Reginald Cherry, 17%; Dr. Paul F. Crouch, 17%; Richard Clayton Trotter, 17%; Janice W. Crouch, 17%; Ruth Brown, 17%; Cynthia S. Diaz, 17% (acq 9-4-97; $3.125 million. gift).
Key Personnel:
Paul Crouch . . . pres
Dr. Cherry . . . VP
Laura Hanks . . . gen mgr
Dorcas Rogers . . . stn mgr
Jessica Mathews . . . progmg dir
Eddie Gonzoles . . . pub affrs dir
Mike Bundrant . . . engrg VP

***KLRN**—Analog channel: 9. On air date: Sept 10, 1962. 501 Broadway, San Antonio, TX 78215-1820. Phone: (210) 270-9000. Fax: (210) 270-9078. E-mail: info@klrn.org. Web Site: www.klrn.org. Licensee: Alamo Public Telecommunications Council. (acq 8-11-89). Network: PBS. Washington Atty: Cohn & Marks.
Key Personnel:
Mike Novak . . . chmn
Joanne Winik . . . pres & gen mgr
Charles Vaughn . . . sr VP
Patrick Lopez . . . sr VP
Cynthia Shields . . . dev VP

KPXL—Analog channel: 26. On air date: Feb 19, 1999. 6100 Bandera Rd., Suite 304, San Antonio, TX 78238. Phone: (210) 682-2626. Fax: (210) 682-3155. E-mail: bhogg@kmol.com. Web Site: www.pax.tv. Licensee: Paxson San Antonio License Inc. Group owner: Paxson Communications Corp. (acq 6-24-99; $5 million. for remaining 51%). Network: PAX TV.

KRRT—Analog channel: 35. On air date: Nov 6, 1985. 4335 N.W. Loop 410, San Antonio, TX 78229-5168. Phone: (210) 366-1129. Fax: (210) 377-4758. E-mail: krrt@krrt.com. Web Site: www.krrt.com. Licensee: San Antonio (KRRT-TV) Licensee Inc. Group owner: Sinclair Broadcast Group Inc. (acq 12-10-01; grpsl).. Network: WB. Washington Atty: Shaw, Pittman.
Key Personnel:
Dean Radla . . . sls dir
Robert Canales . . . natl sls mgr
Laurie Meyer . . . rgnl sls mgr
Hope Roth . . . prom dir

KSAT-TV—Analog channel: 12. On air date: Jan 21, 1957. 1408 N. St. Mary's St., San Antonio, TX 78215. Phone: (210) 351-1200. Fax: (210) 351-1310. Web Site: www.clickonsa.com. Licensee: Post-Newsweek Stations Inc. Group owner: (group owner; acq 2-28-94; 5-2-94). Network: ABC. Rep: MMT. Washington Atty: Covington & Burling. News: 21 hrs wkly.

KTRG—Analog channel: 10. On air date: September 1996. Box 530391, Harlingen, TX 78553. Phone: (956) 421-2635. Fax: (956) 428-7556. Licensee: Ortiz Broadcasting Corp.. Ownership: Aracelis Ortiz, executrix of the estate of Carlos Ortiz. (acq 7-24-97; $160,000)..

KVAW—Analog channel: 16. Digital channel: 18. On air date: 1991. 2524 Veterans Blvd., Eagle Pass, TX 78852. Phone: (830) 773-3668. Fax: (830) 773-3668. Licensee: Dr. Joseph A. Zavaletta.. Ownership: Dr. Joseph A. Zavaletta, 100% (acq 8-23-2004; $300,000)..

KVDA—Analog channel: 60. On air date: Sept 10, 1989. 6234 San Pedro, San Antonio, TX 78216. Phone: (210) 340-8860/8661. Fax: (210) 341-3962/(210)341-2051(news). Web Site: www.kvda.com. Licensee: NBC Telemundo License Co. Group owner: Telemundo Group Inc. (acq 4-12-02; grpsl). Network: Telemundo (Spanish). Washington Atty: Hogan & Hartson. News staff: 11; News: 10 hrs wkly.
Key Personnel:
Clara Rivas . . . VP & gen mgr
Lee Pitluk . . . gen sls mgr
Maricela Arce . . . prom dir
Kathleen Sachez . . . progmg mgr
Dan Garcia . . . news dir
Maricela Arce . . . pub affrs dir
Roger Topping . . . chief of engrg

KWEX-TV—Analog channel: 41. On air date: June 10, 1955. 411 E. Durango Blvd., San Antonio, TX 78204. Phone: (210) 227-4141/(210) 242-7451 (news). Fax: (210) 227-0469/(210) 226-0131 (news). Web Site: www.univision.com. Licensee: KWEX L.P., G.P. Group owner: Univision Communications Inc. (acq 7-86; grpsl). Network: Univision (Spanish). Washington Atty: Fisher, Wayland, Cooper, Leader & Zaragoza. News: 5 hrs wkly.

WOAI-TV—Analog channel: 4. Digital channel: 58. On air date: Dec 11, 1949. Box 2641, San Antonio, TX 78299. 1031 Navarro St., San Antonio, TX 78299-2641. Phone: (210) 226-4444. Fax: (210) 224-9898. Web Site: www.woai.com. Licensee: CCB Texas Licenses L.P. Group owner: Clear Channel Communications Inc. (acq 9-21-01; grpsl). Network: NBC. Washington Atty: Wilmer, Cutler & Pickering. News staff: 43; News: 11 hrs wkly.
Key Personnel:
Brooks Hogg . . . VP & gen mgr
Richard Quiroga . . . opns mgr
Greg Derkowski . . . prom mgr
Ginger Zumaeta . . . adv dir
Carolyn Mastin . . . progmg mgr
Mark Pipitone . . . news dir
Liz Quinones . . . pub affrs dir
Harold Friesenhahn . . . chief of engrg

Sherman, TX-Ada, OK (DMA 161)

KTEN—Analog channel: 10. Digital channel: 26. On air date: June 1, 1954. 10 High Point Cir., Denison, TX 75020. Phone: (903) 337-4000. Fax: (908) 465-1207. Fax: (903) 465-1368. E-mail: 10news@kten.com. Web Site: www.kten.com. Licensee: Channel 49 Acquisition Corp.. Ownership: Lockwood Corp. Network: NBC. Rep: Continental Television Sales. Washington Atty: Brooks, Pierce, McLendon, Humprey & Leonard. News staff: 25; News: 20 hrs wkly.
Key Personnel:
Asa Jessee . . . gen mgr
Ken Braswell . . . gen sls mgr
Steve Korioth . . . news dir
Kris Anderson . . . chief of engrg

KXII—Analog channel: 12. On air date: July 1956. Box 1175, 4201 Texoma Pkwy., Sherman, TX 75090. Phone: (903) 892-8123. Fax: (903) 893-7858. Web Site: www.kxii.com. Licensee: Gray Television Licensee Inc. Group owner: Gray Television Inc. (acq 6-29-99; $41.5 million).. Network: CBS. Rep: Millennium Sales & Marketing. Washington Atty: Cordon & Kelly. News: 30 hrs wkly.
Key Personnel:
Rick Dean . . . VP, gen mgr & progmg dir
Joel Scarbrough . . . opns mgr & prom dir
Todd Bates . . . sls dir, gen sls mgr & rgnl sls mgr
Matt Brown . . . news dir
Randy Wells . . . chief of engrg

Sweetwater

see Abilene-Sweetwater, TX market

Temple

see Waco-Temple-Bryan, TX market

Texarkana

see Shreveport, LA market

Tyler-Longview (Lufkin & Nacogdoches), TX (DMA 111)

KCEB—Analog channel: 54. On air date: July 20, 2003. 701 N. Access Rd., Longview, TX 75602. Phone: (903) 236-0051. Fax: (903) 753-6637. Licensee: Estes Broadcasting Inc.. Ownership: Dimension Enterprises Ltd. (acq 11-24-2003). Network: UPN. Washington Atty: Fletcher, Heald & Hildreth.
Key Personnel:
Tony Cruz . . . gen mgr
Tyrene Carl . . . gen sls mgr

KETK-TV—Analog channel: 56. Digital channel: 22. On air date: March 1987. 4300 Richmond Rd., Tyler, TX 75703. Phone: (903) 581-5656. Fax: (903) 561-1648. Web Site: www.nbc56.com. Licensee: Comcorp of Tyler License Corp. Group owner: Communications Corp. of America (acq 11-12-2004; $38 million).. Network: NBC. Washington Atty: Fletcher, Heald & Hildreth. News staff: 37; News: 19.5 hrs wkly.
Key Personnel:
John Gaston . . . gen mgr
David Lott . . . opns mgr
Tony Cruz . . . sls dir
Robert Dodd . . . prom dir
Yolanda Clater . . . progmg dir
Janet Gregg . . . news dir
Steve Magee . . . engrg dir

KFXK—Analog channel: 51. Digital channel: 31. On air date: Sept 9, 1984. 701 N. Access Rd., Longview, TX 75602. Phone: (903) 236-0051. Fax: (903) 753-6637. Web Site: www.fox51.com. Licensee: White Knight Broadcasting of Longview License Corp. Group owner: White Knight Holdings Inc. (acq 9-1-99; $11.5 million for stock plus 3 low-power stns). Network: Fox.
Key Personnel:
Sheldon Galloway . . . pres
John Gaston . . . gen mgr
Tony Cruz . . . sls dir & natl sls mgr
Robert Dodd . . . prom dir
Mike Stallcup . . . progmg mgr
Chuck McDonald . . . news dir

KLTV—Analog channel: 7. On air date: Oct 15, 1954. Box 957, 105 W. Ferguson, Tyler, TX 75702. Phone: (903) 597-5588. Fax: (903) 510-7847. Web Site: www.kltv.com. Licensee: Civco Inc. Group owner: Liberty Corp. (acq 9-25-00; grpsl). Network: ABC. Washington Atty: Dow, Lohnes & Albertson.
Key Personnel:
Brad Streit . . . gen mgr
Mary Ryan . . . opns dir & natl sls mgr
Pat Stacey . . . gen sls mgr
Mark Scirto . . . rgnl sls mgr
Debbie Sallec . . . prom mgr
Cathy Carmichael . . . progmg dir
Kenny Boles . . . news dir
Butch Adair . . . chief of engrg

KTRE—Analog channel: 9. On air date: Aug 31, 1955. Box 729, Lufkin, TX 75902. Phone: (936) 853-5873. Fax: (936) 853-3084. Web Site: www.ktre.com. Licensee: Civco Inc. Group owner: Liberty Corp. (acq 9-25-00; grpsl). Network: ABC. Rep: Katz Radio. Washington Atty: Dow, Lohnes & Albertson. News staff: 15; News: 20 hrs wkly.
Key Personnel:
Hayne Hipp . . . CEO
Howard Schrott . . . chmn & CFO
James Keelor . . . pres
Leon Long . . . exec VP
Artie Bedard . . . sr VP & VP

KYTX—Analog channel: 19. Digital channel: 18. On air date: Sept 1, 1991. 2211 ESE Loop 323, Tyler, TX 75701. 320 E. Methvin St., Longview, TX 75601. Phone: (903) 581-2211. Fax: (903) 581-5769. Web Site: www.cbs19.tv. Licensee: MMT License LLC. Group owner: MAX Media L.L.C. (acq 4-12-2004; $4 million).. Network: CBS. Rep: Blair Television. Washington Atty: William Mullen. News staff: 25; News: 13.5 hrs wkly.
Key Personnel:
Philip H. Hurley . . . gen mgr
John Gaston . . . gen sls mgr
Myra O'Neal . . . natl sls mgr
Brandon Baker . . . prom mgr
Margore Strout . . . progmg mgr
Bob Lenertz . . . news dir
Moe Strout . . . chief of engrg

Victoria, TX (DMA 205)

KAVU-TV—Analog channel: 25. On air date: July 4, 1982. 3808 N. Navarro, Victoria, TX 77901. Phone: (361) 575-2500. Fax: (361) 575-2255. Web Site: www.kavu-tv.com. Licensee: Saga Broadcasting LLC. Group owner: Saga Communications Inc. (acq 10-20-98; $11.875 million;. with KNAL(AM) Victoria). Network: ABC. Rep: Katz Radio. Washington Atty: Baraff, Koerner, Olender & Hochberg. News staff: 13; News: 8 hrs wkly.
Key Personnel:
Jeff Pryor . . . gen mgr
John Garcia . . . opns mgr
Darren Lehrmann . . . gen sls mgr
Kristin Thompson . . . prom mgr
Rebecca Sarlls . . . progmg dir
Doug Tisdale . . . news dir

Mandy Garcia . . . . . pub affrs dir
Brian Weber . . . . . engrg mgr

KVCT—Analog channel: 19. On air date: Nov 21, 1969. Box 4929, 3808 N. Navarro St., Victoria, TX 77901. Phone: (361) 575-2500. Fax: (361) 575-2255. Licensee: Surtsey Media LLC. Group owner: (group owner; acq 4-26-99). Network: Fox.

Key Personnel:
Jeff Pryor . . . . . gen mgr
John Garcia . . . . . opns mgr
Darren Lehrmann . . . . . gen sls mgr
Kristin Thompson . . . . . prom dir
Rebecca Sarlls . . . . . progmg dir
Doug Tisdale . . . . . news dir
Kathy Keith . . . . . pub affrs dir
Mandy Gracia . . . . . pub affrs dir
Brian Weber . . . . . chief of engrg

Waco-Temple-Bryan, TX (DMA 95)

KAKW-TV—Analog channel: 62. On air date: 1996. 2233 W. Northloop Blvd., Austin, TX 78731. Phone: (512) 453-8899. Fax: (512) 533-2874. Licensee: Univision Communications Inc. Group owner: (group owner; acq 12-10-01; $12 million). Network: Univision (Spanish).

***KAMU-TV**—Analog channel: 15. On air date: Feb 15, 1970. Texas A&M Univ., College Station, TX 77843-4244. Phone: (979) 845-5611. Fax: (979) 845-1643. Web Site: www.kamu.tamu.edu. Licensee: Texas A&M University. Network: PBS.

Key Personnel:
Rodney Zent . . . . . gen mgr
Jon Bennett . . . . . stn mgr & progmg dir
John Prihoda . . . . . opns mgr
Elaine Hoyak . . . . . dev dir
Wayne Pecena . . . . . engrg dir
Ken Nelson . . . . . chief of engrg

KBTX-TV—Analog channel: 3. Digital channel: 59. On air date: May 22, 1957. Drawer 3730, 4141 E. 29th St., Bryan, TX 77802. Phone: (979) 846-7777. Fax: (979) 846-1490 (sls). Fax: (979) 846-1888 (news). Web Site: www.kbtx.com. Licensee: Gray Television Licensee, Inc. Group owner: Gray Television Inc. (acq 6-29-99; $97.5 million. cash and shares with KWTX-TV Waco). Network: CBS. Rep: Millennium Sales & Marketing. News staff: 30; News: 19 hrs. wkly.

Key Personnel:
Jon Boaz . . . . . gen sls mgr
Mike Wright . . . . . VP, gen mgr & natl sls mgr
Mike Barger . . . . . news dir
Ayrrie Dixon . . . . . prom

KCEN-TV—Analog channel: 6. Digital channel: 9. On air date: Nov 1, 1953. 17 S. 3rd St., Temple, TX 76501. Phone: (254) 859-5481. Fax: (254) 859-4004. E-mail: news@kcentv.com. Web Site: www.kcentv.com. Licensee: Channel 6 Inc.. Ownership: Anyse Sue Mayborn, 100%. Network: NBC. Washington Atty: Baker & Hostetler. News staff: 33; News: 17 hrs wkly.

Key Personnel:
Anyse Sue Mayborn . . . . . pres
W. Randy Odil . . . . . VP & gen mgr

***KNCT**—Analog channel: 46. On air date: Nov 23, 1970. Box 1800, Killeen, TX 76540-9990. Telecommunications Bldg., 6200 W. Centex Expwy., Killeen, TX 76540-9990. Phone: (254) 526-1176. Fax: (254) 526-1850. E-mail: knct@knct.org. Web Site: www.knct.org. Licensee: Central Texas College. Network: PBS. News staff: one; News: one hr wkly.

Key Personnel:
Max Rudolph . . . . . gen mgr
Fred McNeilly . . . . . prom mgr
Ruth Wedergren . . . . . progmg dir & film buyer
Steve Sulzer . . . . . engrg mgr

***KWBU-TV**—Analog channel: 34. On air date: May 22, 1989. One Bear Pl., # 97296, Waco, TX 76798-7296. Phone: (254) 710-3472. Phone: (254) 710-7888. Fax: (254) 710-3874. E-mail: clare_paul@kwbu.pbs.org. Web Site: www.kwbu.org. Licensee: Brazos Valley Public Broadcasting Foundation.. Ownership: Baylor University. (acq 12-6-93; $80,000; 12-20-93). Network: PBS. Washington Atty: Cohn & Marks.

Key Personnel:
Kliff Kuehl . . . . . CEO & gen mgr
Larry Brumley . . . . . chmn & pres
Nab Holmes . . . . . dev dir
Clare Paul . . . . . prom mgr & progmg mgr
Michael Hagerty . . . . . news dir & pub affrs dir
Tony Poole . . . . . engrg dir & chief of engrg

KWKT—Analog channel: 44. Digital channel: 57. On air date: March 1988. Box 2544, Waco, TX 76702-2544. 8803 Woodway Dr., Waco, TX 76712. Phone: (254) 776-3844. Fax: (254) 776-8032. Web Site: kwkt.com. Licensee: Comcorp of Texas License Corp. Group owner: Communications Corp. of America (acq 10-31-90; grpsl; FTR: 11-19-90). Network: Network: WB, Fox. Rep: Katz Radio, Millennium Sales & Marketing. Washington Atty: Fletcher, Heald & Hildreth.

Key Personnel:
Duane Sartor . gen mgr, stn mgr, opns mgr, mktg mgr & progmg dir
Bill Knobler . . . . . gen sls mgr
Robin Rice . . . . . natl sls mgr
Amy Bishop . . . . . prom mgr & pub affrs dir
Lou Strowger . . . . . chief of engrg

KWTX-TV—Analog channel: 10. On air date: April 1955. Box 2636, Waco, TX 76702-2636. 6700 American Plaza, Waco, TX 76712. Phone: (254) 776-1330. Fax: (254) 751-1088 (sales). Fax: (254) 776-4010 (news). E-mail: mail@kwtx.com. Web Site: www.kwtx.com. Licensee: Gray Television Licensee Inc. Group owner: Gray Television Inc. (acq 6-29-99; $97.5 million. cash and shares with KBTX-TV Bryan). Network: CBS. Rep: Millennium Sales & Marketing. Washington Atty: Venable Attorneys at Law. News staff: 36; News: 20 hrs wkly.

Key Personnel:
Rich Adams . . . . . pres & gen mgr
Ken Musgrave . . . . . opns mgr

KXXV—Analog channel: 25. On air date: Jan 1, 1985. Box 2522, Waco, TX 76702. 1909 S. New Rd., Waco, TX 76702. Phone: (254) 754-2525. Fax: (254) 752-1002. E-mail: news25@kxxv.com. Web Site: www.kxxv.com. Licensee: Centex Television L.P. Group owner: R.H. Drewry Group (acq 1994). Network: ABC. News staff: 18; News: 14.5 hrs wkly.

Key Personnel:
Jerry Pursley . . . . . gen mgr & gen sls mgr
Larry Patton . . . . . sls VP
Darlene Mahler . . . . . natl sls mgr & rgnl sls mgr
Tami Kadlacek . . . . . progmg dir & progmg mgr
Dennis Kinney . . . . . news dir
Kris Swearingen . . . . . chief of engrg

KYLE—Analog channel: 28. On air date: Oct 31, 1994. 2402 Broadmoor Dr., Suite B-101, Bryan, TX 77805. Phone: (979) 774-1800. Fax: (979) 774-1901. Web Site: www.kyle28.com. Licensee: Comcorp of Bryan License Corp. Group owner: Communications Corp. of America (acq 1996; $1.1 million). Network: Fox. Washington Atty: Gardner, Carton & Douglas.

Key Personnel:
Duane Sartor . . . . . stn mgr & gen sls mgr
Doug Williams . . . . . gen sls mgr
Lou Strauger . . . . . chief of engrg

Weslaco

see Harlingen-Weslaco-Brownsville-McAllen, TX market

Wichita Falls, TX & Lawton, OK (DMA 144)

KAUZ-TV—Analog channel: 6. On air date: Mar 1, 1953. Box 2130, One Broadcast Ave., Wichita Falls, TX 76307. Phone: (940) 322-6957. Fax: (940) 761-3331. Fax: TWX: 910-890-5836. E-mail: email@kauz.com. Web Site: www.kauz.com. Licensee: Hoak Media of Wichita Falls L.P. Group owner: Hoak Media Corporation (acq 11-5-2003; $8.2 million).. Network: CBS. Rep: Harrington, Righter & Parsons. Washington Atty: Covington & Burling. News staff: 20; News: 15 hrs wkly.

Key Personnel:
Kyle Williams . . . . . gen mgr, natl sls mgr & progmg mgr
Gary Lucus . . . . . opns mgr
Mark Walker . . . . . rgnl sls mgr
Jackie McCartney . . . . . prom mgr
Drew Hadwall . . . . . news dir
Leon Heoffner . . . . . chief of engrg

KFDX-TV—Analog channel: 3. On air date: Apr 12, 1953. 4500 Seymour Hwy., Wichita Falls, TX 76309. Box 4888, Wichita Falls, TX 76309. Phone: (940) 691-0003. Fax: (940) 692-1441. E-mail: kfdx@kfdx.com. Web Site: www.kfdx.com. Licensee: Nexstar Finance Inc. Group owner: Nexstar Broadcasting Group Inc. (acq 11-6-97; grpsl). Network: NBC. Washington Atty: Arter & Hadden. News staff: 24; News: 17 hrs wkly.

Key Personnel:
Julie Pruett . . . . . gen mgr
Greg Collier . . . . . opns mgr
Stephanie Darland . . . . . rgnl sls mgr
Troy Short . . . . . VP & prom mgr
Terry Porter . . . . . chief of engrg

KJTL—Analog channel: 18. On air date: May 18, 1985. Box 4888, 4500 Seymour Hwy., Wichita Falls, TX 76309. Phone: (940) 691-1808. Fax: (940) 696-5766. E-mail: kjtl@fox18.com. Web Site: www.kjtlfox18.com. Licensee: Mission Broadcasting of Wichita Falls License Inc. Group owner: Mission Broadcasting Inc. (acq 1999; $28.5 million with KCIT(TV) Amarillo). Network: Fox. Washington Atty: Spector & Goldberg.

KSWO-TV—Analog channel: 7. On air date: Mar 8, 1953. Box 708, Hwy. 7, Lawton, OK 73502. Phone: (580) 355-7000. Fax: (580) 357-3811. Fax: TWX: 910-836-3600. Web Site: www.kswo.com. Licensee: KSWO TV Inc. Group owner: R.H. Drewry Group Network: ABC.

Key Personnel:
R.H. Drewry . . . . . pres
Larry Patton . . . . . gen mgr
Mike Taylor . . . . . chief of opns & progmg dir
Jennifer Tipton . . . . . gen sls mgr & mktg dir
Jan Stratton . . . . . news dir
Joe Bartnik . . . . . chief of engrg

Utah

Salt Lake City, UT (DMA 36)

KBCJ—Analog channel: 6.Not on air, target date: unknown: Equity Broadcasting Corp., 1 Shackleford Dr., Suite 400, Little Rock, AR 72211. Phone: (501) 219-2400. Fax: (501) 716-3502. Permittee: Vernal Broadcasting Inc. Group owner: Equity Broadcasting Corp. (acq 5-11-01).

KBEO—Analog channel: 11. On air date: 2002. KM Communications Inc., 3654 Jarvis Ave., Skokie, IL 60076. Phone: (847) 674-0864. Fax: (847) 674-9188. Web Site: www.kbeo.net. Licensee: Pocatello Channel 15 L.L.C.. Ownership: Myoung Hwa Bae, 100%.

Key Personnel:
Myoung Hwa Bae . . . . . pres
Brian Nugent . . . . . gen mgr, gen sls mgr & progmg dir
Biran Nugent . . . . . news dir

KBJN—Analog channel: 3. On air date: 2001. 417 W. Plumb Ln., Reno, NV 89509. Phone: (775) 786-7600. Fax: (775) 786-7764. Licensee: Valley Broadcasting Co. Group owner: Sunbelt Communications Co. (acq 12-15-03). Network: NBC.

***KBNY**—Analog channel: 6.Not on air, target date: unknown: Equity Broadcasting Corp., 1 Shackleford Dr., Suite 400, Little Rock, AR 72211. Phone: (501) 219-2400. Fax: (501) 604-8404. Permittee: Kaleidoscope Foundation Inc.

***KBYU-TV**—Analog channel: 11. On air date: Nov 15, 1965. 2000 Ironton Blvd., Provo, UT 84606. Phone: (801) 422-8450. Fax: (801) 422-8478. E-mail: kbyu@byu.edu. Web Site: www.kbyu.org. Licensee: Brigham Young University. Network: PBS. Washington Atty: Wilkinson, Barker, Knauer & Quinn. News staff: 3; News: 3 hrs wkly.

Key Personnel:
John Reim . . . . . CEO
Chris Twitty . . . . . opns dir
Derek Marquis . . . . . dev dir
Jim Bell . . . . . mktg mgr
Randy Rawe . . . . . prom mgr
Wendy Thomas . . . . . progmg mgr
Rebecca Cressman . . . . . news dir
Brian Leifson . . . . . chief of engrg

KCBU—Analog channel: 12. On air date: Dec. 1, 2001. Equity Broadcasting Corp., 1 Shackleford Dr., Suite 400, Little Rock, AR 72211. Phone: (501) 219-2400. Fax: (501) 716-3502. Licensee: Logan 12 Inc. Group owner: Equity Broadcasting Corp. (acq 2-1-2001; $4 million)..

KCSG—Analog channel: 4. Digital channel: 14. On air date: September 1985. 1067 E. Tabernacle, Suite 7B, St. George, UT 84770. Phone: (435) 986-9715. Fax: (435) 986-9716. Web Site: www.kcsg.com. Licensee: Daniel Matheson & Stephen Wade dba Broadcast West. (acq 6-3-02; $450,000).. Rep: Roslin.

Key Personnel:
Dan Matheson . . . . . gen mgr
Joshua Aikens . . . . . opns dir
Andi Jensen . . . . . news dir

KENV—Analog channel: 10. On air date: March 1997. 1025 Chilton Cir., Elko, NV 89801. Phone: (775) 777-8500. Fax: (775) 777-7758. E-mail: kenvtv@frontiernet.net. Licensee: Ruby Mountain Broadcasting Co. Group owner: Sunbelt Communications Co. (acq 11-8-96). Network: NBC.
Key Personnel:
Joe Keebler . . . gen mgr, adv mgr & progmg dir
Bryan Baker . . . chief of engrg

KGWR-TV—Analog channel: 13. On air date: Oct 21, 1977. 1856 Skyview Dr., Casper, WY 82601. Phone: (307) 234-1111. Fax: (307) 234-4005. Licensee: Chelsey Broadcasting Co. of Casper LLC. Group owner: Chelsey Broadcasting Co. (acq 10-21-02; grpsl). Network: CBS. Washington Atty: Covington & Burling.
Key Personnel:
Mark Nalbone . . . gen mgr
Terry Lane . . . opns mgr

KJWY—Analog channel: 2. On air date: 1991. Box 7454, 970 W. Broadway, Suite 217, Jackson, WY 83002. Phone: (307) 733-2066. Fax: (307) 733-4834. Licensee: Two Ocean Broadcasting Co. Group owner: Sunbelt Communications Co. (acq 11-95; grpsl). Network: NBC. News staff: one; News: 5 hrs wkly.
Key Personnel:
James Rogers . . . CEO
Ralph Toddre . . . exec VP
Christel Rahme . . stn mgr, sls dir, adv dir, progmg dir & news dir
Robin Estopinal . . . engrg dir

KJZZ-TV—Analog channel: 14. On air date: Feb 14, 1989. 5181 Amelia Earhart Dr., Salt Lake City, UT 84116. Box 22630, Salt Lake City, UT 84116. Phone: (801) 537-1414. Fax: (801) 238-6414. Web Site: kjzz.com. Licensee: Larry H. Miller Communications Corp.. Ownership: Larry H. Miller, 100%. (acq 2-12-93; 3-15-93). Washington Atty: Fleischman & Walsh. News staff: 10; News: 10 hrs wkly.
Key Personnel:
Randy Rigby . . . gen mgr
Mark Harris . . . opns dir
Lynn Lamb . . . sls VP & natl sls mgr
Chris Baum . . . gen sls mgr
Jon Crump . . . rgnl sls mgr
Norma Lloyd . . . mktg dir & prom mgr
Robert Quigley . . . progmg dir & pub affrs dir
Mike Grover . . . chief of engrg

KPNZ—Analog channel: 24. On air date: 1999. 150 N. Wright Brothers Dr., Suite 520, Salt Lake City, UT 84116. Phone: (801) 519-2424. Fax: (801) 359-1272. E-mail: info@z24tv.com. Web Site: www.z24tv.com. Licensee: Utah Communications LLC. Network: UPN.

KSL-TV—Analog channel: 5. Digital channel: 38. On air date: June 1, 1949. 55 N. Third W., Kansas City, UT 84110-1160. Phone: (801) 575-5555. Fax: (801) 575-5830 (sales). Fax: (801) 575-5560 (news). Web Site: www.ksl.com. Licensee: Bonneville International Corp. Group owner: (group owner) Network: NBC. Washington Atty: Wilkinson, Barker, Knauer & Quinn. News staff: 65; News: 21 hrs wkly.

KSTU—Analog channel: 13. On air date: Oct 9, 1978. 5020 W. Amelia Earhart Dr., Salt Lake City, UT 84116. Phone: (801) 532-1300. Fax: (801) 537-5335. E-mail: news@fox13.com. Web Site: www.fox13.com. Licensee: Fox Television Stations Inc. Group owner: (group owner; acq 2-26-90; $41 million). Network: Fox. News: 22 hrs wkly.
Key Personnel:
Tim Ermish . . . VP & gen mgr
Patti Penn . . . natl sls mgr
Bill Collins . . . rgnl sls mgr
Melanie Say . . . prom VP & progmg VP
Al Schultz . . . engrg VP

KTMW—Analog channel: 20. On air date: 2002. 314 S. Redwood Rd., Salt Lake City, UT 84104-3536. Phone: (801) 973-9838. Fax: (801) 973-7145. E-mail: ktmw20@aol.com. Web Site: www.tv20.org. Licensee: Alpha & Omega Communications LLC.. Ownership: Connie Whitney, 33.33%; Isaac Max Jaramillo, 33.33%; and Patricia Openshaw, 33.33% (acq 7-31-2003; $1.5 million).. Rep: Apex Media Sales Inc..
Key Personnel:
Max Jargmillo . . . pres
Dennis Ermel . . . gen mgr & progmg mgr
Curt Rhead . . . opns mgr
Mary Covington . . . prom mgr
Dennis Silver . . . chief of engrg

KTVX—Analog channel: 4. On air date: Apr 15, 1948. 2175 W. 1700 S., Salt Lake City, UT 84104. Phone: (801) 975-4444. Fax: (801) 975-4442. Web Site: www.abc4.tv. Licensee: Clear Channel Broadcasting Licenses Inc. Group owner: Clear Channel Communications Inc. (acq 9-21-2001; grpsl). Network: ABC. Washington Atty: Wilmer, Cutler & Pickering. News staff: 50; News: 14 hrs wkly.
Key Personnel:
Steve Spendlove . . . VP & gen mgr
Mike Spiecha . . . opns dir
Scott Terrill . . . prom dir
Karen Zabriskie . . . progmg mgr
David Bird . . . news dir & engrg dir
Bob Lyon . . . chief of engrg

***KUED**—Analog channel: 7. On air date: Jan 20, 1958. 101 S. Wasatch Dr., Room 215, Salt Lake City, UT 84112. Phone: (801) 581-7777. Fax: (801) 585-5096. Web Site: www.kued.org. Licensee: University of Utah. Network: PBS.

***KUEN**—Analog channel: 9. On air date: Dec 1, 1986. 101 Wasatch Dr., Suite 215, Salt Lake City, UT 84112. Phone: (801) 581-2999. Fax: (801) 585-6105. E-mail: resources@uen.org. Web Site: www.uen.org. Licensee: Utah State Board of Regents.

***KUES**—Analog channel: 19.Not on air, target date: 2001: 101 Wasatch Dr., Salt Lake City, UT 84112. Phone: (801) 581-2999. Fax: (801) 581-3576. Permittee: University of Utah.

***KUEW**—Analog channel: 18.Not on air, target date: unknown: 101 Wasatch Dr., Salt Lake City, UT 84112. Phone: (801) 581-2999. Fax: (801) 585-6105. Permittee: University of Utah.

KUPX—Analog channel: 16. Digital channel: 29. On air date: November 1997. 466 C Lawndale Dr., Salt Lake City, UT 84115. Phone: (801) 474-0016. Fax: (801) 463-9667. Web Site: www.pax.tv. Licensee: Paxson Salt Lake City License Inc. Group owner: Paxson Communications Corp. Network: PAX TV.

KUSG—Analog channel: 12. Digital channel: 9. On air date: Aug 12, 1999. 299 S. Main, Ste 156, Salt Lake City, UT 84111. Phone: (801) 973-3000. Fax: (801) 973-3002. Web Site: www.kutv.com. Licensee: KUTV Holdings Inc. Group owner: Viacom Television Stations Group. Network: CBS. Rep: CBS Spot Sales.
Key Personnel:
David W. Phillips . . . VP
David Phillips . . . gen mgr
Scott Jones . . . opns dir
Kipp Greene . . . engrg dir & chief of engrg

KUTF—Analog channel: 3. Digital channel: 3. On air date: 2003. Price Broadcasting Inc., 1 Shackleford Dr., Suite 400, Little Rock, AR 72211. Phone: (501) 219-2400. Fax: (501) 716-3502. Licensee: Price Broadcasting Inc. (acq 9-6-2002). Network: TeleFutura (Spanish).

KUTH—Analog channel: 32. On air date: 2003. 525 S. 300 W., Suite 1, Salt Lake City, UT 84101. Phone: (801) 519-9784. Fax: (801) 519-9785. Web Site: www.univision-utah.com. Licensee: Univision Television Group Inc. Group owner: Cocola Broadcasting Companies (acq 10-20-2004; $9.5 million). Network: Univision (Spanish).
Key Personnel:
Arlene Urias . . . gen mgr & gen sls mgr
Adrien Seixas . . . natl sls mgr
Karla Hernandez . . . rgnl sls mgr

KUTV—Analog channel: 2. On air date: Sept 26, 1954. 299 S. Main St., Suite 150, Salt Lake City, UT 84111. Phone: (801) 973-3000. Fax: (801) 973-3387. Web Site: www.kutv2.com. Licensee: KUTV Holdings Inc. Group owner: Viacom Television Stations Group (acq 9-10-95). Network: CBS. Rep: CBS Spot Sales. Washington Atty: CBS Inc.. News staff: 73; News: 34.5 hrs wkly.
Key Personnel:
Dave Phillips . . . gen mgr
Scott Jones . . . opns mgr

KUWB—Analog channel: 30. Digital channel: 17. On air date: October 1985. 6135 S. Stratler St., Murray, UT 84107. Phone: (801) 281-0330. Fax: (801) 281-4503. Web Site: www.utanswb.com. Licensee: Acme Television Licenses of Utah L.L.C. Group owner: Acme Communications Inc. (acq 3-30-99). Network: Network: WB, NBC. Rep: MMT.
Key Personnel:
Stan Gill . . . VP & gen mgr
Ron Fessenden . . . stn mgr
Paul Rossi . . . gen sls mgr

Vermont

Burlington, VT-Plattsburgh, NY (DMA 90)

WCAX-TV—Analog channel: 3. On air date: Sept 26, 1954. Box 608, Burlington, VT 05402. Phone: (802) 652-6300. Fax: (802) 652-6319. Web Site: www.wcax.com. Licensee: Mount Mansfield TV Inc.. Ownership: Peter R. Martin, James S. Martin, Marcia H. Martin Boyer and Donald P. Martin. (acq 8-20-98). Network: CBS. Rep: Harrington, Righter & Parsons. Metrospot. Washington Atty: Wilmer, Cutler & Pickering. News staff: 35; News: 15 hrs wkly.
Key Personnel:
Stuart T. Martin . . . pres
Peter Martin . . . exec VP, gen mgr & progmg dir
Phil Scharf . . . opns dir
Bruce Grindle . . . gen sls mgr & natl sls mgr
Jim Strader . . . prom dir & pub affrs dir
Marselis Parsons . . . news dir
Ted Teffner . . . engrg VP

***WCFE-TV**—Analog channel: 57. Digital channel: 38. On air date: Mar 6, 1977. One Sesame St., Plattsburgh, NY 12901. Phone: (518) 563-9770. Fax: (518) 561-1928. E-mail: mlpbs@mountain.pbs.org. Web Site: www.mountainlake.org. Licensee: Mountain Lake Public Telecommunications Council. Network: PBS. Washington Atty: Dow, Lohnes & Albertson.
Key Personnel:
Alice Recore . . . CEO, COO, pres & gen mgr
Sharlene Petro-Durgan . . . CFO
Charlie Zarbo . . . chief of opns & engrg dir
Kevi Prenoveau . . . dev mgr & rgnl sls mgr
Marie Mercier . . . prom dir & adv dir
Brian Garrand . . . progmg mgr

***WETK**—Analog channel: 33. On air date: Oct 16, 1967. 88 Ethan Allen Ave., Colchester, VT 05446-3129. Phone: (802) 655-4800. Fax: (802) 655-6593. E-mail: view@vpt.org. Web Site: www.vpt.org. Licensee: Vermont ETV Inc. (acq 11-6-89). Network: PBS. Washington Atty: Covington & Burling.
Key Personnel:
John King . . . CEO & pres
Dan Harvey . . . CFO, VP & gen mgr
Lee Ann Lee . . . dev VP & mktg VP

WFFF-TV—Analog channel: 44. On air date: 1997. 298 Mountain View Dr., Colchester, VT 05446. Phone: (802) 660-9333. Fax: (802) 660-8673. E-mail: comments@foxnews.com. Web Site: www.fox44.net. Licensee: Smith Media License Holdings LLC. (acq 11-15-2004; grpsl). Network: Fox.

WNNE-TV—Analog channel: 31. On air date: Sept 27, 1978. Box 1310, White River Junction, VT 05001. Phone: (802) 295-3100. Fax: (802) 295-9056. Fax: (802) 295-3983. Web Site: wnne.com. Licensee: Hearst-Argyle Stations Inc. Group owner: Hearst-Argyle Television Inc. Network: NBC.

WPTZ—(North Pole).NY Analog channel: 5. On air date: Dec 8, 1954. 5 Television Dr., Plattsburgh, NY 12901. 533 Roosevelt Highway, Colchester, VT 05446. Phone: (518) 561-5555. Fax: (518) 561-5940. Web Site: www.thechamplainchannel.com. Licensee: Hearst-Argyle Stations Inc. Group owner: Hearst-Argyle Television Inc. (acq 6-1-98). Network: NBC. News staff: 31; News: 14.5 hrs wkly.
Key Personnel:
Paul Sands . . . gen mgr
Bruce Lawson . . . sls dir
Chris Duley . . . natl sls mgr
Susan Acklen . . . prom mgr
Joe Krone . . . progmg dir
Andy Wormser . . . news dir
Andrew Lombard . . . chief of engrg

***WVER**—Analog channel: 28. On air date: Mar 18, 1968. 204 Ethan Allen Ave., Colchester, VT 05446. Phone: (802) 655-4800. Fax: (802) 655-6593. E-mail: veiw@vpt.org. Web Site: www.vpt.org. Licensee: Vermont ETV Inc. Network: PBS. Washington Atty: Covington & Burling.
Key Personnel:
John E. King . . . CEO & pres
John Marshall . . . chmn
Andrea Bergeon . . . CFO
Dan Harvey . . . gen mgr
Lee Ann Lee . . . dev VP
Peter Shea . . . sls dir
Jeff Vande Griek . . . prom dir
Kelly Luoma . . . progmg mgr & film buyer
Joe Merone . . . pub affrs dir
Rob Belle-Isle . . . engrg VP & engrg dir
Ronald Whitcomb . . . chief of engrg

WVNY—Analog channel: 22. On air date: Aug 19, 1968. 530 Shelburne Rd., Burlington, VT 05401. Phone: (802) 860-2222. Fax: (802) 865-9976. E-mail: abc22@abc22.com. Web Site: www.abc22.com. Licensee: Lambert Broadcasting of Burlington LLC.. Ownership: Michael Lambert, 100% (acq 5-21-2005; $10.2 million plus assumption of liabilities). Network: ABC. Rep: Katz Radio, Continental Television Sales. Washington Atty: Fisher, Wayland, Cooper, Leader & Zaragoza.

Virginia

Key Personnel:
Erik V. Storck	gen mgr, gen sls mgr & natl sls mgr
Ken Kaszubowski	opns dir & progmg dir
Linda Noyes	prom mgr
Matthew Servis	chief of engrg

*****WVTA**—Analog channel: 41. Digital channel: 24. On air date: Mar 18, 1968. 204 Ethan Allen Ave., Colchester, VT 05446. Phone: (802) 655-4800. Fax: (802) 655-6593. E-mail: view@vpt.org. Web Site: www.vpt.org. Licensee: Vermont ETV Inc. Network: PBS. Washington Atty: Covington & Burling.
Key Personnel:
John E. King	CEO & pres
Dan Harvey	VP, gen mgr & dev VP
Lee Ann Lee	dev VP
Peter Shea	sls dir
Jeff Vande Griek	prom dir
Kelly Luoma	progmg mgr & film buyer
Joseph Merone	pub affrs dir
Rob Belle-Isle	engrg VP & engrg dir
Ronald Whitcomb	chief of engrg

*****WVTB**—Analog channel: 20. Digital channel: 18. On air date: Feb 26, 1968. 204 Ethan Allen Ave., Colchester, VT 05446. Phone: (802) 655-4800. Fax: (802) 655-6593. E-mail: view@vpt.org. Web Site: www.vpt.org. Licensee: Vermont ETV Inc. Network: PBS.
Key Personnel:
John King	CEO & pres
Dan Harvey	VP, VP & gen mgr
Lee Ann Lee	dev VP

Virginia

Arlington

see Washington, DC (Hagerstown, MD) market

Bristol

see Tri-Cities, TN-VA market

Charlottesville, VA
(DMA 185)

WCAV—Analog channel: 19. On air date: Aug 15, 2004. 999 2nd St. S.E., Charlottesville, VA 22902. Phone: (434) 242-1919. Fax: (434) 220-0398. Web Site: www.wcav.tv. Licensee: Gray Television Licensee Inc. Group owner: Gray Television Inc. (acq 5-28-2004; $1 million. for CP). Network: CBS.
Key Personnel:
Roger Burchett	gen mgr
Jim McCabe	gen sls mgr
Rick Barrick	news dir

*****WHTJ**—Analog channel: 41. On air date: May 19, 1989. 1821 Avon St. Ext., Suite 100, Charlottesville, VA 22902. Phone: (434) 295-7671. Fax: (434) 295-2813. Web Site: www.ideastations.org. Licensee: Commonwealth Public Broadcsting Corp. Network: PBS. Washington Atty: Wiley, Rein & Fielding.
Key Personnel:
Conni Lombardo	VP & stn mgr
Westwood Smithers Jr.	exec VP, gen mgr & gen mgr
Lisa Tait	dev VP & dev dir
John Felton	progmg VP & progmg dir

WVIR-TV—Analog channel: 29. On air date: Mar 11, 1973. Box 769, 503 E. Market St., Charlottesville, VA 22902. Phone: (434) 220-2900. Fax: (434) 220-2904. Web Site: www.nbc29.com. Licensee: Virginia Broadcasting Corp. Group owner: Waterman Broadcasting Corp. Network: NBC. Rep: Continental Television Sales. Washington Atty: Cohn & Marks. News staff: 40; News: 32 hrs wkly.
Key Personnel:
Harold Wright	VP, gen mgr & mktg dir
Jim Fernald	gen sls mgr
Ralph Tobias	prom dir & progmg dir
Neal Bennett	news dir
Bob Jenkins	chief of engrg

Fairfax

see Washington, DC (Hagerstown, MD) market

Front Royal

see Washington, DC (Hagerstown, MD) market

Goldvein

see Washington, DC (Hagerstown, MD) market

Grundy

see Tri-Cities, TN-VA market

Harrisonburg, VA
(DMA 181)

WHSV-TV—Analog channel: 3. On air date: Oct 19, 1953. 50 N. Main St., Harrisonburg, VA 22802. Phone: (540) 433-9191. Fax: (540) 433-4028; (540)433-2700 (news). E-mail: whsv@whsv.com. Web Site: www.whsv.com. Licensee: WEAU Licensee Corp. Group owner: Gray Television Inc. (acq 8-29-02; grpsl). Network: ABC. Washington Atty: Covington & Burling. News staff: 15; News: 16 hrs wkly.
Key Personnel:
Tracey Jones	gen mgr & progmg mgr
Bob Gray	gen mgr
Tim Merritt	gen sls mgr
Tina Wood	natl sls mgr & rgnl sls mgr
Tracie Meadows	mktg mgr & prom mgr
Jeremy Harman	news dir
Ben Williams	chief of engrg

*****WVPT**—Analog channel: 51. On air date: Sept 9, 1968. 298 Port Republic Rd., Harrisonburg, VA 22801. Phone: (540) 434-5391. Fax: (540) 434-7084. Web Site: www.wvpt.net. Licensee: Shenandoah Valley ETV Corp. Network: PBS. Washington Atty: Covington & Burling.
Key Personnel:
Jeffrey G. Lenhart	chmn
Bert Schmidt	pres & gen mgr
Tony Mancari	opns VP

Lynchburg

see Roanoke-Lynchburg, VA market

Manassas

see Washington, DC (Hagerstown, MD) market

Marion

see Tri-Cities, TN-VA market

Newport News

see Norfolk-Portsmouth-Newport News, VA market

Norfolk-Portsmouth-Newport News, VA
(DMA 41)

WAVY-TV—(Portsmouth).Analog channel: 10. Digital channel: 31. On air date: Sept 1, 1957. 300 Wavy St., Portsmouth, VA 23704. Phone: (757) 393-1010. Fax: (757) 399-7628. Web Site: www.wavy.com. Licensee: WAVY Broadcasting L.L.C. Group owner: LIN Television Corporation (acq 12-16-97; grpsl). Network: NBC. Washington Atty: Covington & Burling. News staff: 80; News: 31 hrs wkly.
Key Personnel:
Doug Davis	pres & gen mgr
John Cochran	gen sls mgr
Judy Triska	prom dir
Joe Weller	progmg dir
Les Garrenton	engrg dir

WGNT—Analog channel: 27. On air date: Oct 1, 1961. 1318 Spratley St., Portsmouth, VA 23704-1829. Phone: (757) 393-2501. Fax: (757) 399-3303. E-mail: upn27@wgnttv.com. Web Site: www.upn27.com. Licensee: UPN Television Stations Inc. Group owner: Viacom Television Stations Group (acq 10-31-97; $42.5 million).. Network: UPN.
Key Personnel:
Steven Soldinger	VP & gen mgr
Jon Erkenbrack	stn mgr & gen sls mgr
Chuck Martin	natl sls mgr
Rich Davis	prom dir & progmg dir
Kafi Rouse	pub affrs dir
George Randell	chief of engrg
Bob Webb	sls
Lon Goldman	sls

WHRE—Analog channel: 21.Not on air, target date: unknown: 168 Business Park Dr., Suite 200, Virginia Beach, VA 23462. Phone: (757) 473-3702. Licensee: Copeland Channel 21 LLC.

*****WHRO-TV**—(Hampton-Norfolk).Analog channel: 15. Digital channel: 16. On air date: Oct 2, 1961. 5200 Hampton Blvd., Norfolk, VA 23508. Phone: (757) 889-9400. Fax: (757) 489-0007. E-mail: info@whro.org. Web Site: www.whro.org. Licensee: Hampton Roads Educ. Telecommunications Association Inc. Network: PBS. Washington Atty: Cohn & Marks. News staff: 2; News: 1 hrs wkly.
Key Personnel:
Joseph Widoff	CEO, pres & CFO
Carol Vollbrecht	CFO
John Heimerl	gen mgr
Virginia Thumm	sr VP & dev dir

WPXV—Analog channel: 49. Digital channel: 46. On air date: 1994. 300 Wavy St., Portsmouth, VA 23703. Phone: (757) 490-1249. Fax: (757) 499-1679. Web Site: www.paxnorfolk.tv. Licensee: Paxson Communications License Co. L.L.C. Group owner: Paxson Communications Corp. (acq 12-18-97; $14.75 million). Network: PAX TV.

WSKY-TV—Analog channel: 4. On air date: Oct 1, 2001. Box 269, Kitty Hawk, NC 27949. 258-B Foster Forbes Rd., Powells Point, NC 27966. Phone: (757) 382-0004. Fax: (757) 382-0365. E-mail: programming@wsky4.com. Web Site: www.wsky4.com. Licensee: Sky Television L.L.C.. Ownership: Danbeth Communications Inc., 51% (acq 8-19-02). Washington Atty: Leventhal, Senter and Lerman.
Key Personnel:
Glenn Holterhaus	CEO, pres & gen mgr
Jacquelyn Smullen	CFO & VP
Tom Powers	opns VP & opns dir
Ruthi Lee	gen sls mgr
Ed Marlowe	prom mgr & progmg mgr
Jamie Arbuckle	pub affrs dir

WTKR—Analog channel: 3. On air date: Apr 2, 1950. 720 Boush St., Norfolk, VA 23501-0300. Phone: (757) 446-1000. Fax: (757) 446-1376. Web Site: www.wtkr.com. Licensee: New York Times Management Services. Group owner: The New York Times Co. (acq 3-9-95; $76 million).. Network: CBS. Rep: Katz Radio. Washington Atty: Reed, Smith, Shaw & McClay.

WTVZ—Analog channel: 33. On air date: Sept 24, 1979. 900 Granby St., Norfolk, VA 23510. Phone: (757) 622-3333. Fax: (757) 623-1541. E-mail: comments@wtv233.com. Web Site: wtvz33.com. Licensee: WTVZ Licensee L.L.C. Group owner: Sinclair Broadcast Group Inc. (acq 2-9-95; $47 million; 5-8-95). Network: WB. Washington Atty: Gardner, Carton & Douglas.
Key Personnel:
Scott Sanders	gen mgr
Bill Barber	chief of engrg

WVBT—Analog channel: 43. Digital channel: 29. On air date: March 1993. 243 Wythe St., Portsmouth, VA 23704. Phone: (757) 393-4343. Fax: (757) 393-7615. Web Site: www.fox43tv.com. Licensee: WAVY Broadcasting LLC. Group owner: LIN Television Corporation (acq 1-9-2002; $4.25 million).. Network: Fox. Washington Atty: Covington & Burling.
Key Personnel:
Mark Gentner	stn mgr
Bert Contestabile	natl sls mgr
John Lipscomb	rgnl sls mgr

WVEC-TV—(Hampton).Analog channel: 13. Digital channel: 41. On air date: Sept 19, 1953. 613 Woodis Ave., Norfolk, VA 23510. Phone: (757) 625-1313. Fax: (757) 628-6220. Fax: (757) 628-5855 (news). Web Site: www.wvec.com. Licensee: WVEC Television Inc. Group owner: Belo Corp., Broadcast Division (acq 11-28-83; grpsl; 12-29-83). Network: ABC. Rep: TeleRep. News staff: 65; News: 24 hrs wkly.
Key Personnel:
Mario A. Hewitt	VP
Chris Klein	sls dir & adv dir
Eileen Baggett	natl sls mgr
Kari Armstrong	mktg dir
Deborah Shollenberger	progmg dir
Wendy Juren	pub affrs dir
Peter Dennant	engrg dir

Norton

see Tri-Cities, TN-VA market

Petersburg

see Richmond-Petersburg, VA market

Portsmouth

see Norfolk-Portsmouth-Newport News, VA market

Richmond-Petersburg, VA (DMA 61)

***WCVE-TV**—Analog channel: 23. On air date: Sept 14, 1964. 23 Sesame St., Richmond, VA 23235. Phone: (804) 320-1301. Fax: (804) 320-8729. Web Site: www.ideastations.org. Licensee: Commonwealth Public Broadcasting Corp. Network: PBS. Washington Atty: Wiley, Rein & Fielding.
Key Personnel:
Dr. Charles Sydnor . . . . . pres
Westwood Smithers Jr. . . . . . exec VP & gen mgr
Lisa Tait . . . . . dev VP
John Felton . . . . . progmg VP

***WCVW**—Analog channel: 57. Digital channel: 44. On air date: Dec 22, 1966. 23 Sesame St., Richmond, VA 23235. Phone: (804) 320-1301. Fax: (804) 320-8729. Web Site: www.ideastations.org. Licensee: Commonwealth Public Broadcasting Corporation. Network: PBS. Washington Atty: Wiley, Rein & Fielding.
Key Personnel:
Connie Lombargo. . . . . pres
Westwood Smithers Jr. . . . . . exec VP & gen mgr
Lisa Tait . . . . . dev VP
John Felton . . . . . progmg VP & progmg VP

WRIC-TV—(Petersburg).Analog channel: 8. On air date: Aug 15, 1955. 301 Arboretum Pl., Richmond, VA 23236-3464. Phone: (804) 330-8888. Fax: (804) 330-8881. E-mail: webmaster@wric.com. Web Site: www.wric.com. Licensee: Young Broadcasting Inc. Group owner: (group owner; acq 11-14-94; grpsl; 9-12-94). Network: ABC. Rep: Adam Young. Washington Atty: Wiley, Rein & Fielding.
Key Personnel:
Robert Peterson. . . . . gen mgr
Matthew Zelkird . . . . . stn mgr

WRLH-TV—Analog channel: 35. On air date: Feb 20, 1982. 1925 Westmoreland St., Richmond, VA 23230. Phone: (804) 358-3535. Phone: (804) 359-3510. Fax: (804) 358-1495. Web Site: www.fox35.com. Licensee: WRLH Licensee LLC. Group owner: Sinclair Broadcast Group Inc. (acq 12-10-01; grpsl). Network: Fox. Washington Atty: Arter & Hadden. News staff: 15; News: 3 hrs wkly.

WTVR-TV—Analog channel: 6. On air date: Apr 22, 1948. 3301 W. Broad St., Richmond, VA 23230. Phone: (804) 254-3600. Fax: (804) 254-3699. Web Site: www.wtvr.com. Licensee: Elcom of Virginia License Subsidiary LLC. Group owner: Raycom Media Inc. (acq 7-25-97; grpsl). Network: CBS. Rep: TeleRep. Washington Atty: Covington & Burling.
Key Personnel:
Peter Maroney . . . . . VP, gen mgr & sls dir
Don Cox. . . . . opns dir & chief of engrg
Tina Woody . . . . . opns mgr
Stephen Hayes. . . . . gen sls mgr
James Taguchi . . . . . natl sls mgr
Steve Young. . . . . rgnl sls mgr
Bill Anderson . . . . . mktg dir
Andy Schwabe. . . . . prom mgr
Kris Pyers . . . . . prom mgr & progmg mgr
Rick Howard . . . . . news dir

WUPV—Analog channel: 65. On air date: Mar 9, 1990. 3914 Wistar Rd., Richmond, VA 23228. Phone: (804) 672-6565. Fax: (804) 672-6571. Web Site: www.upnrichmond.com. Licensee: Bell Broadcasting L.L.C.. Ownership: TV 65 Broadcasting L.C. (acq 7-18-97). Network: UPN.

WWBT—Analog channel: 12. On air date: Apr 29, 1956. Box 12, Richmond, VA 23218. 5710 Midlothian Tpke., Richmond, VA 23225. Phone: (804) 230-1212. Fax: (804) 230-2500. Web Site: www.nbc12.com. Licensee: Jefferson-Pilot Broadcasting Co. of Virginia. Group owner: Jefferson-Pilot Communications Co. (acq 1968; $5 million). Network: Network: NBC, WB. Washington Atty: Wiley, Rein & Fielding.
Key Personnel:
Dennis Glass . . . . . CEO
John Shreves . . . . . pres
Donald S. Richards . . . . . gen mgr
Michael Park. . . . . opns mgr
Ellen Shuler . . . . . gen sls mgr
Nancy Kent . . . . . news dir

Roanoke-Lynchburg, VA (DMA 67)

***WBRA-TV**—Analog channel: 15. Digital channel: 3. On air date: Aug 1, 1967. Box 13246, Roanoke, VA 24032. 1215 McNeil Dr. S.W., Roanoke, VA 24015. Phone: (540) 344-0991. Fax: (540) 344-2148. E-mail: brptv@wbra.org. Web Site: www.wbra.org. Licensee: Blue Ridge Public Television Inc. Network: PBS. Washington Atty: Cohn & Marks.
Key Personnel:
Jack K. Neal . . . . . CEO, pres & gen mgr
Edwin Whitmore . . . . . chmn
Scott Davidson. . . . . CFO
Beverly Fitzpatrick Jr. . . . . . exec VP
Cynthia Gray. . . . . dev VP & dev mgr
Bob Ballou. . . . . sls dir
Sandy Broughton . . . . . prom dir
Sherry Spradlin . . . . . progmg dir
Ron Smith . . . . . engrg VP

WDBJ—Analog channel: 7. Digital channel: 18. On air date: Oct 3, 1955. Box 7, Roanoke, VA 24022-0007. 2807 Hershberger Rd, Roanoke, VA 24017-1941. Phone: (540) 344-7000. Fax: (540) 344-5097. E-mail: firstinitiallastname@wdbj7.com. Web Site: www.wdbj7.com. Licensee: WDBJ Television Inc. Group owner: Schurz Communications Inc. (acq 11-1-69; $8.2 million; 11-10-69). Network: CBS. Rep: Harrington, Righter & Parsons. Washington Atty: Fletcher, Heald & Hildreth. News staff: 54; News: 18 hrs wkly.
Key Personnel:
Robert G. Lee . . . . . pres & gen mgr
Edward W. Allen . . . . . CFO
Carl Guffey . . . . . opns dir, pub affrs dir & engrg dir
Ray Sullivan . . . . . gen sls mgr
Tom Fraticelli . . . . . natl sls mgr
Kelly Zuber . . . . . prom mgr
Mike Bell . . . . . progmg dir
Jim Kent. . . . . news dir

WDRL-TV—Analog channel: 24. On air date: August 1994. 5002 Airport Rd., Roanoke, VA 24012. Phone: (540) 366-2424. Fax: (540) 366-7530. E-mail: manager@wdrl-tv.com. Web Site: www.wdrl-tv.com. Licensee: Melvin N. Eleazer, debtor in possession.. Ownership: Melvin N. Eleazer, 100%. (acq 4-9-03). Network: UPN.
Key Personnel:
Mel Eleazer . . . . . gen mgr
Lon Mirolli. . . . . opns mgr
Dave Ross . . . . . rgnl sls mgr
Nel Kirt. . . . . pub affrs dir

WFXR-TV—Analog channel: 27. On air date: March 1986. Box 2127, Roanoke, VA 24009-2127. 2618 Colonial Ave. S.W., Roanoke, VA 24015. Phone: (540) 344-2127. Fax: (540) 345-1912. Fax: (540) 342-2753. Web Site: www.fox2127.com. Licensee: Grant Broadcasting System II Inc. Group owner: (group owner; acq 9-93; $5.5 million with WJPR(TV) Lynchburg; 6-14-93). Network: Fox. Washington Atty: Birch, Horton, Bittner & Cherot. News staff: 2; News: 2 hrs wkly.

WJPR—Analog channel: 21. On air date: February 1986. Box 2127, Roanoke, VA 24009-2127. 2618 Colonial Ave. S.W., Roanoke, VA 24015. Phone: (540) 344-2127. Fax: (540) 345-1912/(540) 342-2753. Web Site: www.fox2127.com. Licensee: Grant Broadcasting System II Inc. (acq 9-15-93; $5.5 million. with satellite stn WFXR-TV Roanoke; FTR: 6-14-93) Network: Fox. Washington Atty: Birch, Horton, Bittner & Cherot. News staff: 2; News: one hr wkly.

WPXR—Analog channel: 38. Digital channel: 36. On air date: Jan 3, 1986. 401 3rd St. S.W., Roanoke, VA 24011. Phone: (540) 857-0038. Fax: (540) 345-8568. Web Site: www.pax.tv. Licensee: Paxson Communications License Co. L.L.C. Group owner: Paxson Communications Corp. (acq 10-28-97). Network: PAX TV. News: one hr wkly.
Key Personnel:
Kathy Mohn . . . . . gen mgr
Candy Craigger . . . . . gen sls mgr
George Stein. . . . . chief of engrg

WSET-TV—Analog channel: 13. Digital channel: 34. On air date: Feb 8, 1953. Box 11588, Lynchburg, VA 24506-1588. 2320 Langhorne Rd., Lynchburg, VA 24501. Phone: (434) 528-1313. Fax: (434) 947-9212. Fax: (434) 847-0458. E-mail: wset@wset.com. Web Site: www.wset.com. Licensee: WSET Incorporated. Group owner: Allbritton Communications Co. (acq 10-76; grpsl). Network: ABC. Rep: Continental Television Sales. Washington Atty: Sidley, Austin, Brown & Wood LLP. News staff: 34; News: 9.5 hrs wkly.
Key Personnel:
Randall J. Smith . . . . . pres & gen mgr
Doug Daniel . . . . . opns dir
Sue Schamerhorn . . . . . sls dir
Bruce Kirk . . . . . news dir

WSLS-TV—Analog channel: 10. On air date: Dec 11, 1952. Box 10, Roanoke, VA 24022-0010. 401 3rd St. S.W., Roanoke, VA 24011. Phone: (540) 981-9110. Fax: (540) 343-3157/(540)343-2059. Web Site: www.wsls.com. Licensee: Media General Broadcasting Inc. Group owner: Media General Broadcast Group (acq 3-21-97; grpsl). Network: NBC. Washington Atty: Wiley, Rein & Fielding. News staff: 33; News: 15 hrs wkly.
Key Personnel:
Kathy Mohn . . . . . VP & gen mgr
Robert Kerry . . . . . opns VP
Candy Crigger . . . . . gen sls mgr
Scott Martin . . . . . natl sls mgr
Daniel Coyle . . . . . mktg VP

Tri-Cities

see Tri-Cities, TN-VA market

Washington

Kennewick

see Yakima-Pasco-Richland-Kennewick, WA market

Pasco

see Yakima-Pasco-Richland-Kennewick, WA market

Richland

see Yakima-Pasco-Richland-Kennewick, WA market

Seattle-Tacoma, WA (DMA 12)

KBCB—Analog channel: 24. Digital channel: 19. On air date: December 1994. 4164 Meridian St., Suite 102, Bellingham, WA 98226. 800 5th Ave., Suite 4100, Seattle, WA 98104. Phone: (360) 647-8842. Phone: (206) 447-1430. Fax: (360) 647-9204. Fax: (206) 447-1431. E-mail: kbcb@kbcbtv.com. Web Site: www.kbcbtv.com.. Stn video via satellite: Dish Channel 8621, DirectTV Channel 24 Licensee: World Television of Washington L.L.C.. Ownership: Venture Technologies Group LLC, 68.67%; and Frank Washington, 31.33%. Washington Atty: Wiley, Rein & Fielding. News: 4 hrs wkly.
Key Personnel:
Garry Spire . . . . . CEO
Larry Rogow . . . . . chmn
Paul Koplin . . . . . pres
Dewi Cashion . . . . . CFO & gen mgr
Brian Holton . . . . . VP
Shelli Jones. . . . . stn mgr
Karen Bean . . . . . opns mgr

***KBTC-TV**—Analog channel: 28. On air date: Sept 25, 1961. 2320 S. 19th St., Tacoma, WA 98405. Phone: (253) 680-7700. Fax: (253) 680-7725. Web Site: www.kbtc.org. Licensee: Bates Technical College. (acq 11-29-91; with KXOT(FM) Tacoma; FTR: 12-16-91). Network: PBS.
Key Personnel:
Debbie Emond . . . . . gen mgr
Paul Jackson . . . . . stn mgr & progmg dir
Darin Gerchak. . . . . chief of opns & chief of engrg
Sherri Stanton . . . . . dev dir
Mary Thompson. . . . . prom dir
Lamont Walton . . . . . news dir

***KCKA**—Analog channel: 15. On air date: October 1982. 2320 S. 19th St., Tacoma, WA 98405. Phone: (253) 680-7700. Fax: (253) 680-7725. Web Site: www.kbtc.org. Licensee: Bates Technical College. (acq 11-29-91; 12-16-91). Network: PBS. Washington Atty: Akin, Gump, Strauss, Hauer & Feld.

Key Personnel:
Debbie Emond . . . gen mgr
Paul Jackson . . . stn mgr & progmg dir
Sherri Stanton . . . dev dir
Mary Thompson . . . prom dir
Lamont Walton . . . news dir & pub affrs dir
Darin Gerchak . . . chief of engrg

KCPQ—(Tacoma).Analog channel: 13. Digital channel: 18. On air date: 1954. 1813 Westlake Ave. N., Seattle, WA 98109-2706. Phone: (206) 674-1313. Fax: (206) 674-1777. E-mail: askus@kcpq.com. Web Site: www.kcpq.com. Licensee: Tribune Television Northwest Inc. Group owner: Tribune Broadcasting Co. (acq 2-22-99; $370 million swap with WGNX(TV) Atlanta, GA). Network: Fox. Rep: Harrington, Righter & Parsons. Washington Atty: Sidley & Austin. News staff: 44; News: 21 hrs wkly.

Key Personnel:
Dennis Fitzsimons . . . CEO, chmn & pres
Pamela Pearson . . . gen mgr
Mark Boe . . . stn mgr
Paul Rennie . . . sls dir
Houman Aliabadi . . . natl sls mgr
Mark Fredo . . . prom dir
Janet Muniz . . . prom mgr
Natalie Grant . . . progmg dir
Bill Kaczaraba . . . news dir
Marty Gustafson . . . pub affrs dir
Michael Goodman . . . engrg dir

***KCTS-TV**—Analog channel: 9. Digital channel: 41. On air date: Dec 7, 1954. 401 Mercer, Seattle, WA 98109. Phone: (206) 728-6463. Fax: (206) 443-6691. E-mail: viewer@kcts.org. Web Site: www.kcts.org. Licensee: KCTS Television.. Ownership: KCTS Television board of directors (acq 7-15-87). Network: PBS. Washington Atty: Dow, Lohnes & Albertson.

Key Personnel:
William Mohler . . . CEO
Bob Flowers . . . chmn
Randy Brinson . . . gen mgr
Cliff Anderson . . . engrg dir & chief of engrg

KHCV—Analog channel: 45. On air date: 2001. 100 Fourth Ave. N., Suite 660, Seattle, WA 98109. Phone: (206) 404-1515. Fax: (206) 404-1525. E-mail: khcvtv@khcvtv.com. Web Site: www.khcvtv.com. Licensee: North Pacific International Television Inc. (acq 12-24-92; FTR: 11-23-92).

Key Personnel:
Dr. Kenneth Casey . . . pres
Charlene Casey . . . CFO
Tim Kammer . . . opns mgr
Stephanie Ogle . . . progmg dir
Chris Casey . . . engrg VP

KING-TV—Analog channel: 5. Digital channel: 48. On air date: Nov 25, 1948. 333 Dexter Ave. N., Seattle, WA 98124. Phone: (206) 448-5555. Fax: (206) 448-3936. Web Site: www.king5.com. Licensee: KING-TV Inc. Group owner: Belo Corp., Broadcast Division (acq 1997; grpsl). Network: NBC. Rep: TeleRep. Washington Atty: Fletcher, Heald & Hildreth.

KIRO-TV—Analog channel: 7. Digital channel: 39. On air date: Feb 8, 1958. 2807 3rd Ave., Seattle, WA 98121. Phone: (206) 728-7777. Fax: (206) 728-8230. Web Site: www.kirotv.com. Licensee: KIRO-TV Holdings Inc. Group owner: Cox Broadcasting (acq 4-16-97). Network: CBS. Rep: TeleRep. Washington Atty: Wilkinson, Barker, Knauer & Quinn. News staff: 115; News: 46 hrs wkly.

Key Personnel:
John Woodin . . . gen mgr
Holly Grombihler . . . dev mgr
Sandy Zogg . . . sls dir
Pat Norris . . . gen sls mgr & rgnl sls mgr
Dave Blakely . . . natl sls mgr
Romco Solomon . . . rgnl sls mgr
Scott Gee . . . prom mgr
Therese Weiler . . . progmg dir
Helen Swenson . . . news dir
Judy Sladky . . . pub affrs dir
John Walters . . . engrg dir
Paul Polzin . . . chief of engrg

KOMO-TV—Analog channel: 4. Digital channel: 38. On air date: Dec 10, 1953. 140 4th Ave. N., Seattle, WA 98109. Phone: (206) 404-4000. Fax: (206) 404-4034. Web Site: www.komotv.com. Licensee: Fisher Broadcasting - Seattle TV L.L.C. Group owner: Fisher Broadcasting Company (acq 12-4-01; grpsl). Network: ABC. Rep: Continental Television Sales. Washington Atty: Shaw Pittman.

Key Personnel:
Richard Warsinske . . . gen mgr
Sandy Montgomery . . . stn mgr
Steve Gahler . . . sls VP & natl sls mgr
Carlos Espinoza . . . mktg dir & prom mgr
Doreen Kaylor . . . progmg dir
Jim Tellus . . . news dir

KONG-TV—Analog channel: 16. On air date: 1997. 333 Dexter Ave. N., Seattle, WA 98109. Phone: (206) 448-3166. Fax: (206) 448-3167. Web Site: www.kongtv.com. Licensee: KONG-TV Inc. Group owner: Belo Corp., Broadcast Division (acq 2-18-00). Washington Atty: Thompson, Hine & Flory L.

KSTW—(Tacoma).Analog channel: 11. On air date: Mar 1, 1953. 602 Oakesdale Ave. S.W., Renton, WA 98055. Phone: (206) 441-1111. Fax: (206) 441-1116. Web Site: upn11.com. Licensee: UPN Television Stations Inc. Group owner: Viacom Television Stations Group (acq 4-16-97). Network: UPN. News: 7 hrs wkly.

Key Personnel:
Gary Wordlaw . . . VP, gen mgr & gen sls mgr
Mike Seifert . . . gen mgr & gen sls mgr
Rich Roberge . . . natl sls mgr
Jamie Cowan . . . mktg dir
Nate Newby . . . prom mgr
Phil Kane . . . progmg dir
Ron Diotte . . . engrg dir

KTBW-TV—Analog channel: 20. Digital channel: 14. On air date: Mar 30, 1984. 1909 S. 341st Pl., Federal Way, WA 98003. Phone: (253) 927-7720. Phone: (253) 874-7420. Fax: (253) 874-7432. E-mail: ktbw@tbn.org. Licensee: Trinity Broadcasting of Washington. Group owner: Trinity Broadcasting Network

Key Personnel:
Paul F. Crouch . . . pres
Mary Jane Allen . . . stn mgr

KTWB-TV—Analog channel: 22. On air date: June 22, 1985. 1813 Westlake Ave., Seattle, WA 98109. Phone: (206) 674-1313. Fax: (206) 674-1777. E-mail: askus@ktwbtv.com. Web Site: www.ktwbtv.com. Licensee: Tribune Television Holdings Inc. Group owner: Tribune Broadcasting Co. (acq 6-98). Network: WB. Rep: TeleRep. Washington Atty: Sidley & Austin.

Key Personnel:
Dennis Fitzsimons . . . CEO & pres
Pamela Pearson . . . gen mgr
Mark Boe . . . stn mgr
Paul Rennie . . . sls dir
Adam Bischoff . . . natl sls mgr
Mark Fredo . . . prom dir
Janet Muniz . . . prom mgr
Natalie Grant . . . progmg dir
Marty Gustafson . . . pub affrs dir
Michael Goodman . . . engrg dir & chief of engrg

KVOS-TV—Analog channel: 12. On air date: June 3, 1953. 1151 Ellis St., Bellingham, WA 98225. Phone: (360) 671-1212. Phone: (604) 681-1212 (sales). Fax: (360) 647-0824. Fax: (604) 736-4510. Web Site: www.kvos.com. Licensee: Ackerley Media Group Inc. Group owner: Clear Channel Communications Inc. (acq 6-14-02; grpsl). Rep: Airtime TV. Washington Atty: Rubin, Winston, Diercks, Harris & Cooke. News staff: 10; News: 3 hrs wkly.

***KWDK**—Analog channel: 56. On air date: 2000. 18014 72nd Ave. S., Kent, WA 98032. Phone: (425) 251-4313. Web Site: www.daystar.com. Licensee: Puget Sound Educational TV Inc.

KWOG—Analog channel: 51. Digital channel: 50.Not on air, target date: unknown: 18000 International Blvd., Suite 601, Seattle, WA 98188. Phone: (206) 248-6834. Fax: (206) 248-6818. Permittee: African-American Broadcasting Co. of Bellevue Inc. (acq 1996; $45,000 for CP).

KWPX—Analog channel: 33. Digital channel: 32. On air date: May 17, 1989. 333 Dexter Ave. N., Seattle, WA 98109. Phone: (206) 441-5780. Fax: (206) 441-5788. Web Site: www.pax.tv. Licensee: Paxson Communications License Co. L.L.C. Group owner: Paxson Communications Corp. (acq 2-2-98; $35 million). Network: PAX TV.

Spokane, WA (DMA 80)

KAYU-TV—Analog channel: 28. On air date: Oct 31, 1982. 4600 S. Regal St., Spokane, WA 99223. Phone: (509) 448-2828. Fax: (509) 448-0926. Web Site: www.kayutv.com. Licensee: Mountain Licenses L.P. Group owner: Northwest Broadcasting Inc. (acq 1996; $6.44 million).. Network: Fox. Rep: Millennium Sales & Marketing. Washington Atty: Leventhal, Senter and Lerman. News: 3 hrs wkly.

Key Personnel:
Brian Brady . . . CEO
Bill Quarles . . . CFO
Jon Rand . . . gen mgr
Rick Andrycha . . . opns mgr
David Lockhert . . . gen sls mgr

***KCDT**—Analog channel: 26. On air date: October 1991. c/o KAID, 1455 N. Orchard St., Boise, ID 83706. Box 443101, University of Idaho, Moscow, ID 83844-3101. Phone: (208) 885-1226. E-mail: idptv@idptv.pbs.org. Web Site: www.idahoptv.org. Licensee: State Board of Education, State of Idaho. Network: PBS. Washington Atty: Fletcher, Heald & Hildreth.

Key Personnel:
Peter Morrill . . . gen mgr
Kris Freeland . . . stn mgr
Kim Philipps . . . dev dir

KGPX—Analog channel: 34. 1201 W. Spregue Ave., Spokane, WA 99201. Phone: (509) 340-3400. Fax: (509) 340-3417. Web Site: www.paxspokane.tv. Permittee: Paxson Spokane License Inc.

Key Personnel:
Amber Morales . . . opns mgr
Bill Storms . . . gen sls mgr
Don Kukuk . . . chief of engrg

KHQ-TV—Analog channel: 6. Digital channel: 15. On air date: Dec 20, 1952. PO Box 600, Spokane, WA 99210-0600. 1201 W. Sprague Ave., Spokane, WA 99201-4102. Phone: (509) 448-6000. Fax: (509) 448-4694. E-mail: q6news@khq.com. Web Site: www.khq.com. Licensee: KHQ Inc. Group owner: (group owner) Network: NBC. Rep: Blair Television. Washington Atty: Skadden, Arps. News staff: 45; News: 26 hrs wkly.

Key Personnel:
Betsy Cowles . . . chmn
Lon C. Lee . . . pres
Doug Miles . . . opns dir
Bill Storms . . . gen sls mgr
Mike Jackson . . . prom mgr
Mike Dugger . . . progmg mgr
Patricia McRae . . . news dir

KLEW-TV—Analog channel: 3. Digital channel: 32. On air date: December 1955. PO Box 615, Lewiston, ID 83501. 2626 17th St., Lewiston, ID 83501. Phone: (208) 746-2636. Fax: (208) 746-4819. E-mail: info@klewtv.com. Web Site: www.klewtv.com. Licensee: Fisher Broadcasting - Washington TV L.L.C. Group owner: Fisher Broadcasting Company (acq 12-4-01; grpsl). Network: CBS. Rep: Katz Radio. Washington Atty: Shaw Pittman. News staff: 4; News: 12 hrs wkly.

Key Personnel:
Fred Fickenwirth . . . stn mgr & gen sls mgr
Greg Meyer . . . news dir
Margo Aragon . . . pub affrs dir
Marlin Jackson . . . chief of engrg

KQUP—Analog channel: 24. On air date: 2005. Equity Broadcasting Inc., 1Shackleford Dr., Suite 400, Little Rock, AR 72211. Phone: (501) 219-2400. Fax: (501) 604-8004. Permittee: Pullman Broadcasting Inc. Group owner: Equity Broadcasting Corp. (acq 8-23-99).

KREM-TV—Analog channel: 2. On air date: Oct 31, 1954. Box 8037, Spokane, WA 99203. 4103 S. Regal, Spokane, WA 99203. Phone: (509) 448-2000. Fax: (509) 448-6397 (news). Fax: (509) 448-2090 (sales). Web Site: www.krem.com. Licensee: KREM-TV Inc. Group owner: Belo Corp., Broadcast Division (acq 9-92; grpsl; 9-16-91). Network: CBS. Washington Atty: Covington & Burling. News staff: 36; News: 17 hrs wkly.

Key Personnel:
Robert Decherd . . . CEO
Jim Maroney . . . exec VP
Bud Brown . . . gen mgr
Amy Warren . . . gen sls mgr
Bruce Felt . . . prom dir
Christine Werfelmann . . . progmg dir
Rich Levenson . . . news dir
Boyd Lundberg . . . chief of engrg

KSKN—Analog channel: 22. On air date: Oct 1, 1983. 4103 S. Regal, Spokane, WA 99223-7377. Phone: (509) 448-2000. Fax: (509) 448-2090. Web Site: www.kskn22.com. Licensee: KSKN Television Inc. Group owner: Belo Corp., Broadcast Division (acq 8-24-01; $5 million).. News staff: 5; News: 14 hrs wkly.

Key Personnel:
Albert B. Brown . . . pres, sr VP, gen mgr & progmg dir
Dan Lamphere . . . opns dir & opns mgr

Amy Warren . . . . . gen sls mgr
R.J. Merritt . . . . . rgnl sls mgr
Cary Seward. . . . . prom dir & prom mgr
Rich Lebenson . . . . . news dir
John Souza . . . . . engrg dir
Boyd Lundberg . . . . . chief of engrg

***KSPS-TV**—Analog channel: 7. On air date: Apr 24, 1967. S. 3911 Regal St., Spokane, WA 99223. Phone: (509) 354-7800. Fax: (509) 354-7757. Web Site: www.ksps.org. Licensee: Spokane School District No. 81. Network: PBS. Washington Atty: Garvey, Schubert & Barer.
Key Personnel:
Claude Kistler. . . . . gen mgr
Patty Starkey . . . . . dev dir
Kerry Faggiano . . . . . prom mgr
Bill Stanley. . . . . progmg dir
Cary Balzer . . . . . progmg mgr

***KUID-TV**—Analog channel: 35. Digital channel: 12. On air date: July 1, 1965. c/o KAID, 1455 N. Orchard St., Boise, ID 83706. Box 443101, University of Idaho, Moscow, ID 83844-3101. Phone: (208) 885-1226. E-mail: idptv@idptv.pbs.org. Web Site: www.idahoptv.org. Licensee: State Board of Education, State of Idaho. Network: PBS. Washington Atty: Fletcher, Heald & Hildreth.
Key Personnel:
Peter Morrill . . . . . gen mgr
Kris Freeland . . . . . stn mgr
Kim Philipps . . . . . dev dir

***KWSU-TV**—Analog channel: 10. On air date: Sept 24, 1962. 382 Murrow Communications Ctr., Washington State Univ., Pullman, WA 99164-2530. Box 642530, Pullman, WA 99164-2530. Phone: (509) 335-6511. Fax: (509) 335-3772. E-mail: kwsu@wsu.edu. Web Site: www.kwsu.org. Licensee: Washington State University. Network: PBS. Washington Atty: Dow, Lohnes & Albertson.
Key Personnel:
Karen Olstad . . . . . COO
Dennis Haarsager . . . . . gen mgr
Tom Hungate. . . . . opns dir & opns mgr
Sarah McDaniel . . . . . dev dir
Kathy Dahmen . . . . . mktg dir
Warren Wright . . . . . stn mgr & progmg dir
Ralph Hogan . . . . . engrg mgr

KXLY-TV—Analog channel: 4. Digital channel: 13. On air date: Feb 22, 1953. 500 W. Boone Ave., Spokane, WA 99201. Phone: (509) 324-4000. Fax: (509) 328-5274. Licensee: Spokane TV Inc. Group owner: Evening Telegram Company—Morgan Murphy Stns (acq 1-17-63; grpsl; 1-63). Network: ABC. Rep: Harrington, Righter & Parsons. Washington Atty: Manatl, Phelps, Phillips. News: 19 hrs wkly.
Key Personnel:
Elizabeth M. Burns . . . . . pres
Steve Herling . . . . . gen mgr

Tacoma

see Seattle-Tacoma, WA market

Vancouver

see Portland, OR market

Yakima-Pasco-Richland-Kennewick, WA (DMA 126)

KAPP—Analog channel: 35. On air date: Sept 21, 1970. Box 10208, Yakima, WA 98909-1208. 1610 S. 24th Ave., Yakima, WA 98902. Phone: (509) 453-0351. Fax: (509) 453-3623. E-mail: comments@kapptv.com. Web Site: www.kapptv.com. Licensee: Apple Valley Broadcasting Inc. Group owner: Morgan Murphy Stations Network: ABC. Washington Atty: Manatt, Phelps & Phillips.
Key Personnel:
Elizabeth Burns. . . . . pres
Darrell Blue . . . . . VP & gen mgr
Brian Paul . . . . . stn mgr
Catherine Weitz . . . . . opns mgr & gen sls mgr
Mike Balmelli . . . . . news dir
James McCullaugh . . . . . chief of engrg

KAZW-TV—Analog channel: 9. On air date: 2002. 424 E. Yakima Ave., Yakima, WA 98901. Phone: (509) 575-0999. Fax: (509) 575-9562. Licensee: Casa of Washington LLC. Group owner: Pappas Telecasting Companies (acq 11-7-02; $3 million). Network: Azteca America (Spanish).
Key Personnel:
Efrain Flores. . . . . gen sls mgr
Ken Beedle . . . . . gen mgr & progmg dir
Jeffrey Brown . . . . . chief of engrg

KEPR-TV—Analog channel: 19. Digital channel: 14. On air date: Dec 28, 1954. Box 2648, Pasco, WA 99302. 2807 W. Lewis, Pasco, WA 99302. Phone: (509) 547-0547. Fax: (509) 547-2845. Web Site: www.keprtv.com. Licensee: Fisher Broadcasting - Washington TV L.L.C. Group owner: Fisher Broadcasting Company (acq 12-4-01; grpsl). Network: CBS. Rep: Katz Radio. Washington Atty: Wiley, Rein & Fielding. News staff: 12; News: 17 hrs wkly.
Key Personnel:
Ben Tucker . . . . . pres
Ken Messer . . . . . gen mgr
David Pray . . . . . stn mgr
Brad Gayken . . . . . opns mgr
Steve Crow . . . . . gen sls mgr & natl sls mgr
Randy Irwin . . . . . prom mgr
Stu Seibel . . . . . progmg dir
Cris Headley . . . . . pub affrs dir
John McDaniel . . . . . chief of engrg

KFFX-TV—Analog channel: 11. On air date: 1999. 2509 W. Falls Ave., Kennewick, WA 99336. 4600 S. Regal St., Spokane, WA 99223. Phone: (509) 735-1700. Fax: (509) 735-1004. Web Site: www.kffxtv.com. Licensee: Mountain Licenses L.P. Group owner: Northwest Broadcasting Inc. (acq 9-27-00; $239,659. for CP). Network: Fox. Rep: Millennium Sales & Marketing.
Key Personnel:
Brian Brady . . . . . CEO
Bill Quarles . . . . . CFO
Jon Rand . . . . . gen mgr
Kathy Balcom . . . . . stn mgr
Rick Andrycha . . . . . opns mgr
Lynn Creager . . . . . natl sls mgr
Lonnie Eaton . . . . . rgnl sls mgr
Chloe Houser . . . . . prom dir & pub affrs dir
Ron Sweatte . . . . . chief of engrg

KIMA-TV—Analog channel: 29. Digital channel: 33. On air date: July 19, 1953. Box 702, Yakima, WA 98907. 2801 Terrace Heights Dr., Yakima, WA 98901. Phone: (509) 575-0029. Fax: (509) 248-1218. E-mail: information@kimatv.com. Web Site: www.kimatv.com. Licensee: Fisher Communications, Inc. Group owner: Fisher Broadcasting Company (acq 12-4-01; grpsl). Network: Network: CBS, UPN. Rep: Katz Radio. Washington Atty: Shaw Pittman. News staff: 28; News: 17 hrs wkly.
Key Personnel:
Ben Tucker . . . . . CEO & pres
Mr. Phelps Fisher . . . . . chmn
Mr. Robert Bateman. . . . . CFO
Ken Messer . . . . . VP & gen mgr
Karla Griffin . . . . . opns mgr
Steve Crow . . . . . gen sls mgr & natl sls mgr
Harriet Pettie . . . . . rgnl sls mgr
Stu Siebel . . . . . progmg dir
Mike Conklin . . . . . news dir
Cliff Grady. . . . . chief of engrg

KNDO—Analog channel: 23. On air date: Oct 15, 1959. 1608 S. 24th Ave., Yakima, WA 98902. Phone: (509) 248-2300. Fax: (509) 225-2363. Web Site: www.kndo.com. Licensee: KHQ Inc. Group owner: (group owner; acq 6-17-99; $22.25 million with KNDU(TV) Richland). Network: NBC. Washington Atty: Hogan & Hartson. News staff: 9; News: 15 hrs wkly.
Key Personnel:
Lon Lee. . . . . pres
Paul Dughi . . . . . gen mgr
Bob Thomas . . . . . gen sls mgr
Raymond Ochs . . . . . mktg dir
Susan Martinez . . . . . progmg dir
Gary Darigold. . . . . news dir
Mark Kennedy . . . . . engrg dir & chief of engrg

KNDU—Analog channel: 25. On air date: July 1, 1961. 3312 W. Kennewick Ave., Kennewick, WA 99336. Phone: (509) 737-6700. Fax: (509) 737-6767. Web Site: www.kndu.com. Licensee: KHQ Inc. Group owner: (group owner; (acq 6-17-99; $22.25 million. with KNDO(TV) Yakima). Network: NBC. Washington Atty: Hogan & Hartson. News staff: 22; News: 22.5 hrs wkly.
Key Personnel:
Paul Dughi. . . . . gen mgr
Bob Thomas. . . . . gen sls mgr
Sheri Bissell . . . . . natl sls mgr
Randy Brown . . . . . rgnl sls mgr
Susan Martinez . . . . . progmg dir
Christine Brown . . . . . news dir

***KTNW**—Analog channel: 31. On air date: Oct 18, 1987. Box 642530, 382 Murrow Communications Ctr., Washington State Univ., Pullman, WA 99164-2530. Phone: (509) 335-6588. Fax: (509) 335-3772. E-mail: nwptv@wsu.edu. Web Site: www.kwsu.org. Licensee: Washington State University. Network: PBS. Washington Atty: Dow, Lohnes & Albertson.
Key Personnel:
Karen Olstad . . . . . COO
Dennis Haarsager. . . . . VP, gen mgr & gen mgr
Tom Hungate . . . . . opns dir
Sarah McDaniel . . . . . dev dir
Kathy Dahmen . . . . . mktg dir
Warren Wright . . . . . stn mgr & progmg dir
Linda Peppel . . . . . progmg mgr
Ralph Hogan . . . . . engrg dir & engrg mgr

KVEW—Analog channel: 42. On air date: Oct 30, 1970. 601 N. Edison, Kennewick, WA 99336. Phone: (509) 735-8369. Fax: (509) 735-1836 (news). Fax: (509) 735-7889. Licensee: Apple Valley Broadcasting Inc. Group owner: Morgan Murphy Stations Network: ABC.
Key Personnel:
Darrell Blue . . . . . VP & gen mgr
Brian Paul . . . . . stn mgr
Catherine Weitz . . . . . opns mgr & natl sls mgr
Chris Danielle. . . . . news dir
James McCullaugh . . . . . chief of engrg

***KYVE**—Analog channel: 47. Digital channel: 21. On air date: Nov 1, 1962. 1105 S. 15th Ave., Yakima, WA 98902. Phone: (509) 452-4700. Fax: (509) 452-4704. Web Site: www.kyve.org. Licensee: KCTS Television.. Ownership: KCTS Television board of directors (acq 8-1-94; FTR: 8-22-94). Network: PBS. Washington Atty: Schwartz, Woods & Miller.
Key Personnel:
Bill Mohler . . . . . CEO
Mark Leonard. . . . . gen mgr
Brenda Setterlund . . . dev mgr, mktg mgr, mktg mgr & prom mgr
Chris Splawn . . . . . progmg mgr
Rod Venable . . . . . stn mgr & chief of engrg

West Virginia

Beckley

see Bluefield-Beckley-Oak Hill, WV market

Bluefield-Beckley-Oak Hill, WV (DMA 148)

WLFB—Analog channel: 40.Not on air, target date: unknown: Box 151, Vansant, VA 24656. 8594 Hidden Valley Rd., Abingdon, VA 24210. Phone: (276) 676-3806. Fax: (276) 676-3572. Permittee: Living Faith Ministries Inc.
Key Personnel:
Micheal D. Smith . . . . . CEO
Michael D. Smith . . . . . pres & gen mgr
Fredia Keene . . . . . CFO

WOAY-TV—Analog channel: 4. On air date: Dec 14, 1954. Box 3001, Rte. 16 S., Oak Hill, WV 25901. Phone: (304) 469-3361. Fax: (304) 465-1420. E-mail: news@woay.com. Licensee: Thomas Broadcasting Co. Network: ABC. Rep: Katz Radio. Washington Atty: Fletcher, Heald & Hildreth.
Key Personnel:
Robert R. Thomas III . . . . . pres
Al Marra . . . . . gen mgr & progmg dir
Mike Wilson . . . . . gen sls mgr
Bert Haney. . . . . news dir
Jim Martin. . . . . chief of engrg

***WSWP-TV**—Analog channel: 9. On air date: Nov 1, 1970. PO Box 9004, Beckley, WV 25802. 124 Industrial Dr., Beaver, WV 25813. Phone: (304) 254-7840. Fax: (304) 254-7879. Web Site: www.wvpubcast.org. Licensee: West Virginia Educational Broadcasting Authority. Network: PBS. News: 5 hrs wkly.
Key Personnel:
Rita Ray . . . . . CEO
Mike Meador. . . . . gen mgr & stn mgr
Marilyn DeVita . . . . . dev dir

WVNS-TV—Analog channel: 59. Digital channel: 48. On air date: Jan 1, 1997. Box 509, Ghent, WV 25843. 141 Old Cline Rd., Ghent, WV 25843. Phone: (304) 787-5959. Fax: (304) 787-2440. E-mail: fbarnes@wvnstv.com. Web Site: www.cbs59.com. Licensee: West Virginia Media Holdings LLC. Group owner: (group owner; acq 1-9-03). Network: CBS. Rep: Petry Television Inc.. Washington Atty:

Borsari & Paxson.

Key Personnel:

Bray Cary . . . CEO & pres
Marstow W. Becker . . . chmn
Charlie Dusic . . . CFO
Chris Leister . . . sr VP
Frank Barnes . . . gen mgr
Sue Bosio . . . opns mgr
Gary Bowden . . . sls VP
Jack Scott . . . gen sls mgr
Robert McCallister . . . rgnl sls mgr
John Fawcett . . . prom dir
M.J. Coss . . . progmg dir
Gary Kirk . . . chief of engrg

WVVA—Analog channel: 6. Digital channel: 24. On air date: July 31, 1955. Box 1930, Rt. 460 Bypass, Bluefield, WV 24701. Phone: (304) 325-5487. Fax: (304) 327-5586. Web Site: www.wvva.com. Licensee: WVVA TV Inc. Group owner: Quincy Newspapers Inc., see Cross-Ownership (acq 5-1-79; $8 million; 4-23-79). Network: NBC. Rep: Blair Television. Washington Atty: Wilkinson, Barker, Knauer & Quinn. News staff: 20; News: 27 hrs wkly.

Key Personnel:

Thomas A. Oakley . . . CEO
Ralph M. Oakley . . . COO
Larry Roe . . . VP & gen mgr
Danny Via . . . opns dir & engrg dir
Jim Briggs . . . sls dir & mktg dir

Charleston-Huntington, WV (DMA 62)

WCHS-TV—Analog channel: 8. On air date: Aug 15, 1954. 1301 Piedmont Rd., Charleston, WV 25301. Phone: (304) 346-5358. Fax: (304) 346-4765. E-mail: info@wchstv.com. Web Site: www.wchstv.com. Licensee: WCHS Licensee L.L.C. Group owner: Sinclair Broadcast Group Inc. (acq 10-8-97). Network: ABC. Washington Atty: Fisher, Wayland, Cooper, Leader & Zaragoza.

Key Personnel:

Harold Cooper . . . gen mgr
Paul Fox . . . prom dir
Lori Marquette . . . progmg dir
Terry Cole . . . news dir
Raymon Beckner . . . chief of engrg

WHCP—Analog channel: 30. On air date: Oct 5, 1998. 800 Gallia, Suite 430, Portsmouth, OH 45662. Phone: (740) 353-3391. Fax: (740) 353-3372. E-mail: wb30@whcp-tv.com. Web Site: www.whcp-tv.com. Licensee: Television Properties Inc.. Ownership: Commonwealth Broadcasting Group Inc., 88%; Kenneth Russell, 12% (acq 7-11-02). Network: Network: WB, UPN.

Key Personnel:

Charles M. Harker . . . pres
Butch Wilkison . . . gen mgr, opns mgr, progmg dir & engrg VP
Chuck Jones . . . gen sls mgr

***WKAS**—Analog channel: 25. On air date: Sept 23, 1968. c/o WKLE, 600 Cooper Dr., Lexington, KY 40502. Phone: (859) 258-7000. Fax: (859) 258-7390. Web Site: www.ket.org. Licensee: Kentucky Authority for Educational TV. Network: PBS.

Key Personnel:

Malcolm Wall . . . CEO & gen mgr
Sally Hamilton . . . CFO
Craig Cornwell . . . opns mgr
Michele Ripley . . . dev dir
Ron Griffin . . . sls dir & rgnl sls mgr
Mary Campbell . . . prom dir
Tona Barkley . . . prom mgr
Dick Hoffman . . . progmg dir
Bill Goodman . . . pub affrs dir
Robert Hall . . . engrg dir

***WKPI**—Analog channel: 22. On air date: Apr 8, 1968. c/o WKLE, 600 Cooper Dr., Lexington, KY 40502. Phone: (859) 233-3000. Fax: (859) 258-7390. Web Site: www.ket.org. Licensee: Kentucky Authority for Educational TV. Network: PBS.

Key Personnel:

Malcolm Wall . . . CEO & gen mgr
Sally Hamilton . . . CFO
Craig Cornwell . . . opns mgr
Michele Ripley . . . dev dir
Ron Griffin . . . sls dir & rgnl sls mgr
Mary Campbell . . . prom dir
Tona Barkley . . . prom mgr
Dick Hoffman . . . progmg dir
Bill Goodman . . . pub affrs dir
Robert Ball . . . engrg dir

WLPX-TV—Analog channel: 29. Digital channel: 39. On air date: Aug 28, 1998. 600 C Prestige Dr., Hurricane, WV 25526. Phone: (304) 760-1029. Fax: (304) 760-1036. Web Site: www.paxcharleston.tv. Licensee: Paxson Charleston License Inc. Group owner: Paxson Communications Corp. (acq 10-28-98; $8.25 million).. Network: PAX TV. Rep: NBC TV Stations Sales. Washington Atty: Dan J. Alpert.

Key Personnel:

Bud Paxson . . . CEO
Doug Barker . . . pres
Stephen Appel . . . VP
Steven Stanley . . . stn mgr

***WOUB-TV**—Analog channel: 20. On air date: Jan 3, 1963. 9 S. College St., Athens, OH 45701. Phone: (740) 593-4555. Fax: (740) 593-0240. Licensee: Ohio University. Network: PBS. Washington Atty: Dow, Lohnes & Albertson. News staff: 3; News: 3 hrs wkly.

Key Personnel:

Carolyn Bailey-Lewis . . . gen mgr
David Wiseman . . . opns VP
Steve Skidmore . . . opns dir
Scott Martin . . . opns mgr
Doug Partusch . . . dev dir, gen sls mgr, mktg dir, prom dir & adv dir
Carol Layh . . . rgnl sls mgr
Loring Lovett . . . rgnl sls mgr
Olivea Oldham . . . prom mgr & adv mgr
Mark Brewer . . . progmg dir & film buyer
Joan Pittman . . . progmg mgr
Tim Sharp . . . news dir
Dave Wiseman . . . engrg VP
Dave Riley . . . engrg dir

WOWK-TV—Analog channel: 13. On air date: Oct 2, 1955. 555 Fifth Ave., Huntington, WV 25701. Phone: (304) 525-1313. Fax: (304) 529-4910. Web Site: wowktv.com. Licensee: West Virginia Media Holdings LLC. Group owner: (group owner; acq 4-8-02; $40.5 million).. Network: CBS. Rep: TeleRep. Washington Atty: Bryan Cave.

Key Personnel:

Harry Delaney . . . pres
Chris Leister . . . gen mgr
Brent Cowen . . . gen sls mgr
John Fawcett . . . mktg dir & prom dir
M.J. Coss . . . progmg dir
Rod Fowler . . . news dir
Warren Kunkle . . . chief of engrg

***WPBO-TV**—Analog channel: 42. On air date: October 1973. 2400 Olentangy River Rd., Columbus, OH 43210. Phone: (614) 292-9678. Fax: (614) 688-3343. E-mail: wosu@wosu.org. Web Site: www.wosu.org. Licensee: The Ohio State University. Network: PBS. Washington Atty: Dow, Lohnes & Albertson.

Key Personnel:

Thomas Rieland . . . gen mgr
Edwin Clay . . . stn mgr
John Prosek . . . opns mgr
Mary Yerina . . . dev dir
Don Scott . . . mktg dir & mktg mgr

***WPBY-TV**—Analog channel: 33. On air date: July 14, 1969. 600 Capitol St., Charleston, WV 25301. Phone: (304) 556-4900. Fax: (304) 556-4982. Licensee: West Virginia Educational Broadcasting Authority. Network: PBS.

Key Personnel:

Mike Meador . . . gen mgr
Marilyn DiVita . . . dev dir & dev mgr
Craig Lanham . . . progmg dir
Greg Collard . . . news dir & pub affrs dir

WSAZ-TV—Analog channel: 3. Digital channel: 23. On air date: Nov 15, 1949. Box 2115, 645 Fifth Ave., Huntington, WV 25721. Phone: (304) 697-4780. Fax: (304) 208-3066. E-mail: newschannel3@wsaz.com. Web Site: www.wsaz.com. Licensee: Emmis Television License LLC. Group owner: Emmis Communications Corp. (acq 9-25-2000; grpsl). Network: NBC. Rep: Katz Radio.

Key Personnel:

Don Ray . . . gen mgr
Aaron Withrow . . . opns dir

WTSF—Analog channel: 61. On air date: Apr 30, 1983. Box 2320, Ashland, KY 41105-2320. 3100 Bath Ave., Ashland, KY 41101. Phone: (606) 329-2700. Fax: (606) 324-9256. Web Site: www.wtsftv.com. Licensee: Word of God Fellowship Inc.. Ownership: Jimmie F. Lamb, 25%; John T. Calender, 25%; Joni T. Lamb, 25%; and Marcus D. Lamb, 25% (acq 4-18-03).

WVAH-TV—Analog channel: 11. On air date: Sept 19, 1982. 11 Broadcast Plaza, Hurricane, WV 25526. Phone: (304) 757-0011. Fax: (304) 757-7533. E-mail: info@wvah.com. Web Site: www.wvah.com. Licensee: WVAH Licensee LLC. Group owner: Cunningham Broadcasting Corporation (acq 11-15-2001; grpsl). Network: Fox. Washington Atty: Arter & Hadden. News staff: 38; News: 7 hrs wkly.

Key Personnel:

Harold Cooper . . . pres & gen mgr
Paul Fox . . . prom dir
Lori Marquette . . . news dir
Raymond Beckner . . . chief of engrg

Clarksburg

see Clarksburg-Weston, WV market

Huntington

see Charleston-Huntington, WV market

Martinsburg

see Washington, DC (Hagerstown, MD) market

Morgantown

see Pittsburgh, PA market

Oak Hill

see Bluefield-Beckley-Oak Hill, WV market

Parkersburg, WV (DMA 187)

WTAP-TV—Analog channel: 15. Digital channel: 49. On air date: Oct 8, 1953. One Television Plaza, Parkersburg, WV 26101. Phone: (304) 485-4588. Fax: (304) 422-3920. E-mail: gm@wtap.com. Web Site: www.wtap.com. Licensee: Gray Television Group, Inc. Group owner: Gray Television Inc. (acq 8-29-02; grpsl). Network: NBC. Rep: Continental Television Sales. Washington Atty: Covington & Burling. News staff: 17; News: 20 hrs wkly.

Key Personnel:

Roger Sheppard . . . VP & gen mgr
Dirk Kreiss . . . natl sls mgr
Joyce Ancrile . . . prom dir
Shane Vass . . . gen sls mgr & progmg dir
Bruce Layman . . . news dir
Joe Dumas . . . chief of engrg

Weston

see Clarksburg-Weston, WV market

Wheeling, WV-Steubenville, OH (DMA 152)

***WOUC-TV**—Analog channel: 44. Digital channel: 35. On air date: July 23, 1973. 9 S. College St., Athens, OH 45701. Phone: (740) 593-4555. Fax: (740) 593-0240. Licensee: Ohio University. (acq 12-10-75; 12-22-75). Network: PBS. Washington Atty: Cohn & Marks.

Key Personnel:

Carolyn Bailey-Lewis . . . gen mgr
David Wiseman . . . opns VP, engrg VP & engrg dir
Steve Skidmore . . . opns dir
Scott Martin . . . opns mgr
Doug Partusch . . . dev dir, gen sls mgr & adv dir
Carol Layh . . . rgnl sls mgr
Loring Lovett . . . rgnl sls mgr
Douglas Partusch . . . mktg dir
Olivea Oldham . . . prom mgr & adv mgr
Mark Brewer . . . progmg dir
Joan Pittman . . . progmg mgr
Dave Riley . . . engrg dir

WTOV-TV—Analog channel: 9. On air date: Dec 24, 1953. Box 9999, Steubenville, OH 43952. 9 Red Donnelly Plaza (also shipping), Mingo Junction, OH 43938. Phone: (740) 282-9999. Phone: (304) 232-6933. Fax: (740) 282-0439. Web Site: www.wtov9.com. Licensee: WTOV-TV Holdings Inc. Group owner: Cox Broadcasting (acq 9-22-00; $58 million).. Network: Network: NBC, ABC. Rep: TeleRep. Washington Atty: Dow,Lohnes & Albertson. News staff: 28; News: 12 hrs wkly.

Key Personnel:

Andrew Fisher . . . pres
Bruce Baker . . . exec VP
Tim McCoy . . . VP & gen mgr
Mike Seachman . . . opns mgr
Tom Pleva . . . gen sls mgr
Sherry Hansen . . . prom dir

Melissa Knollinger . . . . news dir
Leonard Smith . . . . chief of engrg

WTRF-TV—Analog channel: 7. On air date: Oct 23, 1953. 96 16th St., Wheeling, WV 26003. Phone: (304) 232-7777. Fax: (304) 232-4975. Web Site: www.wtrf.com. Licensee: West Virginia Media Holdings LLC. Group owner: (group owner; acq 3-12-02; grpsl). Network: CBS. Rep: Petry Television Inc.. Washington Atty: Edmundson & Edmundson. News staff: 28; News: 26 hrs wkly.
Key Personnel:
Roger Lyons . . . . gen mgr
Charlotte Cohen . . . . gen sls mgr
Jane DomBroski . . . . prom dir
M.J. Coss . . . . progmg dir
Brenda Davehart . . . . news dir
Brad Stanford . . . . chief of engrg

Wisconsin

Appleton

see Green Bay-Appleton, WI market

Eau Claire

see La Crosse-Eau Claire, WI market

Green Bay-Appleton, WI (DMA 69)

WACY—Analog channel: 32. On air date: Mar 7, 1984. 1391 North Rd., Green Bay, WI 54307-2328. Phone: (920) 733-3232. Fax: (920) 494-9550. Web Site: www.upn32.com. Licensee: Ace TV Inc.. Ownership: Shirley A. Martin (acq 5-25-00). Network: UPN. Washington Atty: Shaw Pittman.

WBAY-TV—Analog channel: 2. On air date: Mar 17, 1953. 115 S. Jefferson St., Green Bay, WI 54301. Phone: (920) 432-3331. Phone: (800) 242-8090. Fax: (920) 432-7808. Fax: (920) 432-1190 (news). Web Site: www.wbay.com. Licensee: Young Broadcasting of Green Bay Inc. Group owner: Young Broadcasting Inc. (acq 8-24-94; grpsl; 9-12-94). Network: ABC. Rep: Adam Young. Washington Atty: Brooks, Pierce, McClendon & Humphry. News staff: 100; News: 19 hrs wkly.
Key Personnel:
Don Carmichael . . . . gen mgr
Richard Millhiser . . . . opns dir

WFRV-TV—Analog channel: 5. On air date: May 21, 1955. 1181 E. Mason, Marinette, WI 54301. Phone: (920) 437-5411. Fax: (920) 437-4576. Web Site: www.wfrv.com. Licensee: CBS Broadcasting Inc. Group owner: Viacom Television Stations Group (acq 2-16-92; grpsl). Network: CBS.
Key Personnel:
Perry Kidder . . . . VP, VP & gen mgr
Jackie Stewart . . . . gen sls mgr
Monica Zegers . . . . mktg mgr
Lee Hitter . . . . news dir
Dale Mitchell . . . . chief of engrg

WFXS—Analog channel: 55. On air date: Dec 1, 1999. 1000 N. 3rd St., Wausau, WI 54403. Phone: (715) 847-1155. Fax: (715) 847-1156. E-mail: rraff@wfxs.com. Web Site: www.wfxs.com. Licensee: Davis Television Wausau L.L.C. Network: Fox. Rep: Millennium Sales & Marketing. Washington Atty: Leventhal, Senter & Lerhman. News: 3 hrs wkly.
Key Personnel:
Robert Raff . . . . gen mgr
Tim Brusky . . . . opns dir
Janel Daul . . . . gen sls mgr
Deb Steinfest . . . . prom dir
Randy Winter . . . . news dir

WGBA—Analog channel: 26. Digital channel: 41. On air date: Dec 31, 1980. 1391 North Rd., Green Bay, WI 54313. Phone: (920) 494-2626. Fax: (920) 494-9950. Web Site: www.nbc26.com. Licensee: Journal Broadcast Corp. (acq 10-7-2004; $43.25 million).. Network: NBC. Rep: Petry Television Inc.. Washington Atty: Shaw Pittman. News staff: 33; News: 16 hrs wkly.
Key Personnel:
James P. Prather . . . . CEO & pres
Guyanne Taylor . . . . stn mgr

WIWB—Analog channel: 14. On air date: Feb 22, 1984. 975 Parkview Rd., Suite 4, Green Bay, WI 54304. Phone: (920) 983-9014. Fax: (920) 983-9424. E-mail: promotions@wb14tv.com. Web Site: www.wb14tv.com. Licensee: Acme Television Licenses of Wisconsin L.L.C. Group owner: Acme Communications Inc. (acq 6-1-99; grpsl). Network: WB. Rep: MMT. Washington Atty: Dickstein, Shapiro, Morin & Oshinsky LLP.
Key Personnel:
Stephen M. Shanks . . . . gen mgr
Todd Zielgler . . . . gen sls mgr
Chris Sack . . . . natl sls mgr
Donnielle Carter . . . . mktg mgr & prom mgr
Tee Mathewson . . . . progmg mgr
Dale Juedes . . . . chief of engrg

WLUK-TV—Analog channel: 11. Digital channel: 51. On air date: Sept 11, 1954. Box 19011, 787 Lombardi Ave., Green Bay, WI 54307-9011. Phone: (920) 494-8711. Fax: (920) 494-9100 (sales). E-mail: info@wluk.com. Web Site: www.wluk.com. Licensee: Emmis Television License LLC. Group owner: Emmis Communications Corp. (acq 7-16-98; grpsl). Network: Fox. Rep: Katz Radio.

***WPNE**—Analog channel: 38. Digital channel: 42. On air date: Sept 12, 1972. 3319 W. Beltline Hwy., Madison, WI 53713. Phone: (608) 263-2121. Fax: (608) 263-9763. E-mail: comments@wpt.org. Web Site: www.wpt.org. Licensee: State of Wisconsin-Educational Communications Board. Network: PBS. Washington Atty: Dow, Lohnes & Albertson.
Key Personnel:
Malcolm Brett . . . . gen mgr & progmg mgr
Mike Edgette . . . . opns dir
Jon Miskowski . . . . dev dir

WWAZ-TV—Analog channel: 68. Digital channel: 44. On air date: Dec 1, 2000. 254 Winnebago Dr., Fond Du Lac, WI 54935. Phone: (920) 921-6368. Fax: (920) 907-8330. Licensee: WMMF License LLC. Group owner: Pappas Telecasting Companies (acq 3-10-2001). Washington Atty: Paul Hastings.
Key Personnel:
Harry J. Pappas . . . . CEO & pres
Dennis Davis . . . . COO
Richard Elmdorf . . . . CFO
LeBon G. Abercrombie . . . . exec VP
Dale Scherbring . . . . VP
La Fawn Vannest . . . . VP
Peter Pappas . . . . VP
Howard Shrier . . . . gen mgr
Mike Angelos . . . . dev VP

La Crosse-Eau Claire, WI (DMA 127)

WEAU-TV—Analog channel: 13. Digital channel: 39. On air date: Dec 17, 1953. Box 47, Eau Claire, WI 54702. 1907 S. Hastings Way, Eau Claire, WI 54701. Phone: (715) 835-1313. Fax: (715) 832-0246. E-mail: info@weau.com. Web Site: www.weau.com. Licensee: WEAU Licensee Corp. Group owner: Gray Television Inc. (acq 8-1-98; grpsl). Network: NBC. Rep: Continental Television Sales. Washington Atty: Pepper & Corazzini. News: 21 hrs wkly.
Key Personnel:
Jason Effinger . . . . gen mgr
Emily Edwards . . . . opns mgr
Mr. Terry McHugh . . . . gen sls mgr
Mr. John Hoffland . . . . news dir

WEUX—Analog channel: 48. On air date: February 1993. 1324 W. Clairemont Ave., Suite 3, Eau Claire, WI 54701. Phone: (715) 831-2548. Fax: (715) 831-2550. E-mail: info@fox25fox48.com. Web Site: www.fox25fox48.com. Licensee: Grant Media LLC. Group owner: (group owner; acq 1996; $6.25 million. with WLAX(TV) La Crosse). Network: Fox.
Key Personnel:
Jeff Armstrong . . . . gen mgr
Clay Koenig . . . . gen sls mgr
Barb Quillin . . . . prom dir
Pat Stiphout . . . . prom dir
Mark Burg . . . . chief of engrg

***WHLA-TV**—Analog channel: 31. Digital channel: 30. On air date: Dec 3, 1973. 3319 W. Beltline Hwy., Madison, WI 53713. Phone: (608) 264-9600. Fax: (608) 264-9664. Web Site: www.ecb.org. Licensee: State of Wisconsin-Educational Communications Board. Network: PBS. Washington Atty: Dow, Lohnes & Albertson.
Key Personnel:
Byron Knight . . . . gen mgr & stn mgr
Michael Bridgeman . . . . gen mgr, mktg dir & prom mgr
Mike Edgette . . . . opns dir
Jon Miskowski . . . . dev dir
Mary Clare Sorenson . . . . adv dir & progmg mgr
Kathy Bissen . . . . news dir
Dick Taugher . . . . chief of engrg

WKBT—Analog channel: 8. On air date: Aug 8, 1954. 141 S. 6th St., La Crosse, WI 54601. Phone: (608) 782-4678. Fax: (608) 782-4674. E-mail: schorski@wkbt.com. Web Site: www.wkbt.com. Licensee: QueenB Television L.L.C. Group owner: Morgan Murphy Stations (acq 3-31-2000; $22 million).. Network: CBS. Rep: Harrington, Righter & Parsons.
Key Personnel:
David Sanks . . . . exec VP
Scott Chorski . . . . gen mgr
Dick Konrad . . . . opns mgr & chief of engrg
Barb Pervisky . . . . gen sls mgr
Alex Knox . . . . prom mgr
Maria Roswall . . . . progmg dir & progmg mgr
Anne Paape . . . . news dir

WLAX—Analog channel: 25. On air date: Sept 28, 1986. Box 2529, La Crosse, WI 54602. 1305 Interchange Pl., La Crosse, WI 54603. Phone: (608) 781-0025. Fax: (608) 781-1456. E-mail: info@fox25fox48.com. Web Site: www.fox25fox48.com. Licensee: Grant Media LLC. Group owner: (group owner; acq 5-15-96; $6.25 million. with WEUX(TV) Chippewa Falls). Network: Fox. Rep: Petry Television Inc..
Key Personnel:
Milton Grant . . . . pres & gen mgr
Jeff Armstrong . . . . stn mgr

WQOW-TV—Analog channel: 18. Digital channel: 15. On air date: Sept 20, 1980. 5545 Hwy. 93 S., Eau Claire, WI 54701. Phone: (715) 835-1881. Fax: (715) 835-8009. E-mail: info@wqow.com. Web Site: www.wqow.com. Licensee: WXOW/WQOW Television Inc. Group owner: Quincy Newspapers Inc., see Cross-Ownership (acq 6-1-2001; grpsl). Network: ABC. Rep: Blair Television. Washington Atty: Wilkinson, Barker, Knauer LLP. News staff: 16; News: 18 hrs wkly.
Key Personnel:
Tom Oakley . . . . chmn
Ralph Oakley . . . . pres
Charles "Chuck" Roth . . . . gen mgr
John J. Ganahl . . . . stn mgr

WXOW-TV—Analog channel: 19. On air date: Mar 7, 1970. Box C-4019, La Crosse, WI 54602-4019. 3705 County Hwy. 25, La Crescent, MN 55947. Phone: (507) 895-9969. Fax: (507) 895-8124. Web Site: www.wxow.com. Licensee: WXOW-WQOW Television Inc. Group owner: Quincy Newspapers Inc., see Cross-Ownership (acq 6-1-01). Network: ABC. Rep: Blair Television. Washington Atty: Wilkinson, Barker & Knauer, L.L.P.. News staff: 24; News: 18 hrs wkly.
Key Personnel:
Chuck Roth . . . . VP & gen mgr
Dave Booth . . . . stn mgr
Jarrett Liddicoat . . . . chief of engrg

Madison, WI (DMA 85)

WBUW—Analog channel: 57. Digital channel: 32. On air date: June 28, 1999. 2814 Syene Rd., Madison, WI 53713. Phone: (608) 270-5700. Phone: (608) 270-5701. Fax: (608) 270-5717. E-mail: keith@wb57.com. Web Site: www.wb57.com. Licensee: Acme Television Licenses of Madison LLC. Group owner: Acme Communications Inc. (acq 1-1-2003). Network: WB. Rep: MMT. Washington Atty: Borsari & Paxson.
Key Personnel:
Jamie Kellner . . . . CEO & chmn
Doug Gealy . . . . COO & pres
Tom Allen . . . . CFO
Matt Phelps . . . . opns mgr & progmg mgr
Katherine Ramirez . . . . dev mgr & natl sls mgr
Sharon Weiler . . . . sls VP
Tom Keeler . . . . gen mgr, stn mgr & gen sls mgr
Kevin Orchard . . . . natl sls mgr
Karen Paschke . . . . mktg mgr & pub affrs dir
Jamie McDowell . . . . prom VP & adv VP
Matt Creamer . . . . prom mgr & adv mgr
Robert Shaw . . . . progmg VP
Colin Campbell . . . . film buyer
Erin Hunsader . . . . news dir & engrg dir
Brent Stephenson . . . . engrg VP
Jeff Juniet . . . . chief of engrg

***WHA-TV**—Analog channel: 21. On air date: May 3, 1954. 821 University Ave., Madison, WI 53706. Phone: (608) 263-2121. Fax: (608) 263-9763. Licensee: University of Wisconsin Board of Regents. Network: PBS. Washington Atty: Dow, Lohnes & Albertson.
Key Personnel:
Malcolm Brett . . . . gen mgr & stn mgr

Mike Edgette . . . . . opns mgr
Jon Miskowski . . . . . dev dir

WISC-TV—Analog channel: 3. On air date: June 24, 1956. Box 44965, Madison, WI 53744-4965. Phone: (608) 271-4321. Fax: (608) 278-5568. Web Site: www.channel3000.com. Licensee: TV Wisconsin Inc. Group owner: Morgan Murphy Stns. Network: CBS. Rep: Harrington, Righter & Parsons. Washington Atty: Manatt, Phelps & Phillips. News staff: 30; News: 30 hrs wkly.
Key Personnel:
Elizabeth Murphy Burns . . . . . pres
David Sanks . . . . . exec VP & gen mgr
Jill Sommers . . . . . opns dir, gen sls mgr & progmg dir

WKOW-TV—Analog channel: 27. Digital channel: 26. On air date: July 1953. 5727 Tokay Blvd., Madison, WI 53719. Phone: (608) 274-1234. Fax: (608) 274-9514. Web Site: www.wkowtv.com. Licensee: WKOW Television Inc. Group owner: Quincy Newspapers Inc., see Cross-Ownership (acq 5-22-01; grpsl). Network: ABC. Rep: Katz Radio. Washington Atty: Rosenman & Colin. News staff: 28; News: 22 hrs wkly.

WMSN-TV—Analog channel: 47. On air date: June 8, 1986. 7847 Big Sky Dr., Madison, WI 53719. Phone: (608) 833-0047. Fax: (608) 833-5055. Fax: (608) 833-0665 (Natl Sls). E-mail: comments@fox47.com. Web Site: www.fox47.com. Licensee: WMSN Licensee LLC. Group owner: Sinclair Broadcast Group Inc. (acq 12-10-01; grpsl). Network: Fox.
Key Personnel:
Marshall Porter . . . . . gen mgr
Joan Kellner . . . . . gen sls mgr
Audra Johnson . . . . . prom dir
Sarah Wand . . . . . progmg dir & progmg mgr
Al Zobel . . . . . news dir & engrg mgr
Kerry Makie . . . . . chief of engrg

WMTV—Analog channel: 15. Digital channel: 19. On air date: July 1953. 615 Forward Dr., Madison, WI 53711. Phone: (608) 274-1515/(608) 274-1500 (news). Fax: (608) 271-5193/(608) 271-5194 (news). E-mail: feedback@nbc15.com. Web Site: www.nbc15.com. Licensee: Gray Television Licensee Inc. Group owner: Gray Television Inc. (acq 8-29-2002; grpsl). Network: NBC. Washington Atty: Covington & Burling. News staff: 36; News: 19 hrs wkly.
Key Personnel:
J. Mack Robinson . . . . . pres
Jim Ryan . . . . . CFO
Robert Prather Jr. . . . . . exec VP
Bob Smith . . . . . gen mgr
Sara McCormack . . . . . gen sls mgr
Ellen Buss . . . . . progmg mgr
Rob Crain . . . . . news dir
Tom Weeden . . . . . chief of engrg

Menomonie

see Minneapolis-St. Paul, MN market

Milwaukee, WI (DMA 32)

WCGV-TV—Analog channel: 24. On air date: Mar 17, 1980. 4041 N. 35th St., Milwaukee, WI 53216. Phone: (414) 442-7050. Fax: (414) 874-1899. E-mail: comments@wcgv24.com. Web Site: www.upn24.net. Licensee: WCGV Licensee L.L.C. Group owner: Sinclair Broadcast Group Inc. (acq 5-23-94; grpsl; 11-19-90). Network: UPN. Rep: TeleRep.
Key Personnel:
David Ford . . . . . gen mgr
Milan Macksimovic . . . . . opns mgr
Paul Rudolph . . . . . chief of opns

WDJT-TV—Analog channel: 58. On air date: November 1988. 809 S. 60th St., Milwaukee, WI 53214. Phone: (414) 777-5800. Fax: (414) 777-5802. Web Site: www.feedbackcbs58.com. Licensee: WDJT-TV L.P. Group owner: Weigel Broadcasting Co. Network: CBS. Rep: Roslin. Washington Atty: Cohn & Marks.
Key Personnel:
Norman Shapiro . . . . . pres
Jim Hall . . . . . gen mgr & stn mgr
Deanna Monaghan . . . . . gen sls mgr
Grant Uitti . . . . . news dir

WISN-TV—Analog channel: 12. Digital channel: 34. On air date: Oct 27, 1954. Box 402, Milwaukee, WI 53201. Phone: (414) 342-8812. Fax: (414) 342-4486. Web Site: www.themilwaukeechannel.com. Licensee: WISN Hearst-Argyle Television Inc., a Californiaûcorp. Group owner: Hearst-Argyle Television Inc. (acq 7-16-97; grpsl). Network: ABC. Rep: Continental Television Sales. Washington Atty: Peper, Martin, Jensen, Maichel & Hetlage.
Key Personnel:
Frank Biancuzzo . . . . . gen mgr
Pete Monfre . . . . . gen sls mgr
Dean Maytag . . . . . progmg dir
Barb Maushard . . . . . news dir
Pablo Rios . . . . . chief of engrg

WITI—Analog channel: 6. Digital channel: 33. On air date: May 21, 1956. 9001 N. Green Bay Rd., Milwaukee, WI 53209. Phone: (414) 355-6666. Fax: (414) 586-2141. E-mail: fox6news@foxtv.com. Web Site: www.fox6milwaukee.com. Licensee: WITI License Inc. Group owner: Fox Television Stations Inc. (acq 11-96; grpsl). Network: Fox. Washington Atty: Pepper & Corazzini.
Key Personnel:
Parveen Hughes . . . . . CFO
Chuck Steinmetz . . . . . VP & gen mgr
Don Hain . . . . . opns VP & engrg VP
Mike Neale . . . . . sls VP
Bob O'Neil . . . . . natl sls mgr
Greg Sloan . . . . . rgnl sls mgr
Lori Wucherer . . . . . prom VP
Bob Clinkingbeard . . . . . news dir
Kelly Skindzelewski . . . . . pub affrs dir
Cori Ritter . . . . . progmg

WJJA—Analog channel: 49. On air date: Jan 27, 1990. 4311 E. Oakwood Rd., Oak Creek, WI 53154. Phone: (414) 764-4953. Fax: (414) 764-5190. Licensee: TV-49 Inc.. Ownership: Joel Kinlow, 99%; Arvis Kinlow, 1%.
Key Personnel:
Joe Kinlow. pres, gen mgr, stn mgr, dev mgr, gen sls mgr, progmg dir & news dir
Bruce Herzog . . . . . chief of engrg

***WMVS**—Analog channel: 10. Digital channel: 8. On air date: Oct 28, 1957. 1036 N. 8th St., Milwaukee, WI 53233. Phone: (414) 271-1036. Fax: (414) 297-7536. Web Site: www.mptv.org. Licensee: Milwaukee Area District Board of Vocational, Technical & Adult Education. Network: PBS. Washington Atty: Dow, Lohnes & Albertson.
Key Personnel:
Ellis Bromberg . . . . . gen mgr
Kate Tierney . . . . . opns mgr & prom dir
Tom Dvorak . . . . . progmg dir
Dan Jones . . . . . news dir
David Felland . . . . . chief of engrg

***WMVT**—Analog channel: 36. Digital channel: 35. On air date: Jan 23, 1963. 4th Fl., 1036 N. 8th St., Milwaukee, WI 53233. Phone: (414) 271-1036. Fax: (414) 297-7536. Web Site: www.mptv.org. Licensee: Milwaukee Area District Board of Vocational, Technical & Adult Education. Network: PBS. Washington Atty: Dow, Lohnes & Albertson.
Key Personnel:
Ellis Bromberg . . . . . gen mgr
Kate Tierney . . . . . opns VP & prom dir
Tom Dvorak . . . . . progmg dir
Dan Jones . . . . . news dir
David Felland . . . . . engrg dir & chief of engrg

WPXE—Analog channel: 55. On air date: June 1, 1988. 720 E. Capitol Dr., Milwaukee, WI 53212-1371. Phone: (414) 967-5592. Fax: (414) 967-5597. Web Site: www.pax.tv. Licensee: Paxson Milwaukee License Inc. Group owner: Paxson Communications Corp. (acq 2-18-00; grpsl). Network: PAX TV. Rep: NBC TV Stations Sales. Washington Atty: Gardner, Carton & Douglas. News: 3 hrs wkly.
Key Personnel:
Mark Le Grand . . . . . gen mgr & gen sls mgr
Lon Rudolph . . . . . natl sls mgr

WTMJ-TV—Analog channel: 4. On air date: December 1947. 720 E. Capitol Dr., Milwaukee, WI 53212. Phone: (414) 332-9611. Fax: (414) 967-5378. Web Site: www.touchtmj4.com. Licensee: Journal Broadcast Corp. Group owner: Journal Broadcast Group Inc. Network: NBC. Washington Atty: Hogan & Hartson.
Key Personnel:
Mark Strachota . . . . . gen mgr, gen sls mgr & natl sls mgr
Mar LeGrand . . . . . rgnl sls mgr
Betsy McCormack . . . . . progmg dir
Sean O'Flaherty . . . . . mktg mgr & news dir
Randy Price . . . . . chief of engrg

WVCY-TV—Analog channel: 30. Digital channel: 22. On air date: Jan 11, 1983. 3434 W. Kilbourn Ave., Milwaukee, WI 53208. Phone: (414) 935-3000. Fax: (414) 935-3015. E-mail: tv30@vcyamerica.org. Web Site: www.vcyamerica.org. Licensee: VCY/America Inc. Group owner: (group owner) Washington Atty: Wiley, Rein & Fielding.
Key Personnel:
Dr. Randall Melchert . . . . . pres
Vic Eliason . . . . . VP & gen mgr
Jim Cronin . . . . . opns mgr
Jim Schneider . . . . . progmg dir & pub affrs dir
Andy Eliason . . . . . chief of engrg

WVTV—Analog channel: 18. On air date: July 1, 1959. 4041 N. 35th St., Milwaukee, WI 53216. Phone: (414) 442-7050. Fax: (414) 874-1898. Fax: (414) 874-1899. Web Site: www.wb18.net. Licensee: WVTV Licensee Inc. Group owner: Glencairn Ltd. (acq 2-1-2002). Network: WB. Rep: TeleRep.
Key Personnel:
David Smith . . . . . CEO & pres
David Ford . . . . . gen mgr
Milan Macksimovic . . . . . opns mgr
Paul Rudulph . . . . . chief of opns

WWRS-TV—Analog channel: 52. On air date: 1997. N. 6707 Madison Rd., Ironridge, WI 53035. Phone: (920) 387-9052. Fax: (920) 387-9053. E-mail: business@wwrs-52.org. Web Site: www.nationalminoritytv.org. Licensee: National Minority T.V. Inc.. Ownership: not for profit Corp. (acq 2-16-99; $3,300,000).. Washington Atty: Shaw Pittman.

Rhinelander

see Wausau-Rhinelander, WI market

Superior

see Duluth, MN-Superior, WI market

Wausau-Rhinelander, WI (DMA 133)

WAOW-TV—Analog channel: 9. On air date: May 7, 1965. 1908 Grand Ave., Wausau, WI 54403. Phone: (715) 842-2251. Fax: (715) 848-0195. Fax: (715) 842-7808. E-mail: info@waow.com. Web Site: www.waow.com. Licensee: WAOW-WYOW Television Inc. Group owner: Quincy Newspapers Inc., see Cross Ownership (acq 5-22-2001; grpsl). Network: ABC. Rep: Blair Television. Washington Atty: Wilkinson, Baker & Knauer, LLP. News staff: 26; News: 15.5 hrs wkly.
Key Personnel:
Thomas A. Oakley . . . . . CEO
Ralph M. Oakley . . . . . COO
Laurin Jorstad . . . . . VP & gen mgr
Randy Winters . . . . . opns mgr
Carol Kellum . . . . . gen sls mgr
Tim Atterberg . . . . . gen sls mgr & rgnl sls mgr
Mark Oliver . . . . . mktg dir & prom dir
Tricia Atterberg . . . . . progmg dir
Randy Winter . . . . . news dir
Russ Crass . . . . . chief of engrg

WBIJ—Analog channel: 4. On air date: 2004. 4529 Hickory Heights Ave., Oshkosh, WI 54904. Phone: (920) 589-2511. Licensee: Selenka Communications L.L.C.

***WHRM-TV**—Analog channel: 20. Digital channel: 24. On air date: 1975. 3319 W. Beltline Hwy., Madison, WI 53713. Phone: (608) 264-9600. Fax: (608) 264-9664. Web Site: www.ecb.org. Licensee: Wisconsin Educational Communications Board. Network: PBS. Washington Atty: Dow, Lohnes & Albertson.
Key Personnel:
Bryon Knight . . . . . gen mgr
Mike Edgette . . . . . opns dir
Jon Miskowski . . . . . dev dir
Michael Bridgeman . . . . . mktg dir & prom mgr
Mary Clare Sorenson . . . . . adv dir
Kathy Bissen . . . . . progmg mgr & news dir
Dennis Behr . . . . . chief of engrg

WJFW-TV—Analog channel: 12. On air date: Oct 20, 1966. Box 858, 3217 County Trunk G, Rhinelander, WI 54501. Phone: (715) 365-8812. Fax: (715) 365-8810. E-mail: wjfwtv12@newnorth.net. Web Site: www.wjfw-nbc12.com. Licensee: Northland Television LLC. Group owner: Rockfleet Broadcasting Inc. Network: NBC. Rep: Blair Television. Washington Atty: Wiley, Rein & Fielding. News staff: 13; News: 13.5 hrs wkly.
Key Personnel:
Robert Krieghoff . . . . . gen mgr, prom mgr & progmg dir
Charlotte Berens . . . . . natl sls mgr
Robert Schmidtbauer . . . . . CFO & prom mgr
Heather Schellock . . . . . news dir
Brian Henning . . . . . chief of engrg

***WLEF-TV**—Analog channel: 36. Digital channel: 47. On air date: December 1977. 3319 W. Beltline Hwy., Madison, WI 53713. Phone: (608) 264-9600. Fax: (608) 264-9664. Web Site: www.wpt.org. Licensee: State of Wisconsin-Educational Communications Board. Network: PBS. Washington Atty: Dow, Lohnes & Albertson.
Key Personnel:
Byron Knight . . . gen mgr
Mike Edgette . . . opns dir
Jon Miskowski . . . dev dir
Michael Bridgeman . . . mktg dir & prom mgr
Mary Clare Sorenson . . . adv dir & progmg mgr
Kathy Bissen . . . news dir
Dick Taugher . . . chief of engrg

WSAW-TV—Analog channel: 7. Digital channel: 40. On air date: Oct 23, 1954. 1114 Grand Ave., Wausau, WI 54403. Phone: (715) 845-4211. Fax: (715) 845-2649. Web Site: www.wsaw.com. Licensee: WEAU Licensee Corp. Group owner: Gray Television Inc. (acq 8-29-02; grpsl). Network: CBS. Rep: Continental Television Sales. News staff: 21; News: 15 hrs wkly.
Key Personnel:
Al Lancaster . . . VP & gen mgr
Betsy Keefe . . . sls dir, gen sls mgr, natl sls mgr & rgnl sls mgr
Tom Stemmler . . . opns mgr & prom dir
Patti Watson . . . progmg mgr
Gil Buettner . . . news dir
Jane Ploeger . . . pub affrs dir
Phil Hejtmanek . . . chief of engrg

WTPX—Analog channel: 46.Not on air, target date: unknown: Paxson Communications Corp., 601 Clearwater Park Rd., West Palm Beach, FL 33401. Phone: (561) 659-4122. Permittee: Paxson Wausau License Inc. Group owner: Paxson Communications Corp. (acq 4-18-00; $887,500. for CP).

WYOW—Analog channel: 34. On air date: 1997. Box 2705, Eagle River, WI 54521. 528 W. Pine St., Suite B, Eagle River, WI 54521. Phone: (715) 477-2020. Fax: (715) 477-2438. E-mail: wyowtv34@newnorth.net. Licensee: WAOW-WYOW Television Inc. Group owner: Quincy Newspapers Inc., see Cross-Ownership (acq 5-22-2001; grpsl). Network: ABC. Rep: Blair Television. Washington Atty: Wilkinson, Barker & Knauer, LLP..
Key Personnel:
Thomas A. Oakley . . . CEO
Ralph Oakley . . . COO
Laurin Jorstad . . . gen mgr
Carol Kellum . . . gen sls mgr
Tim Atterberg . . . rgnl sls mgr
Mark Oliver . . . mktg dir & prom mgr
Tricia Atterberg . . . progmg dir
Randy Winter . . . news dir
Russ Crass . . . chief of engrg

Wyoming

Casper-Riverton, WY (DMA 198)

***KCWC-TV**—Analog channel: 4. Digital channel: 8. On air date: January 1983. Central Wyoming College, 2660 Peck Ave., Riverton, WY 82501. Phone: (307) 856-6944. Fax: (307) 856-3893. Web Site: wyoptv.org. Licensee: Central Wyoming College. Network: PBS. Washington Atty: Fletcher, Heald & Hildreth.
Key Personnel:
Dan Schiedel . . . gen mgr
J. Amend . . . prom VP
Rubydee Calvert . . . progmg dir
Bob Connelly . . . chief of engrg

KCWY—Analog channel: 13. On air date: 2002. Box 1540, Mills, WY 82644. 141 Progress Circle, Mills, WY 82644. Phone: (307) 577-0013. Fax: (307) 577-5251. E-mail: bsullivan@kcwy13.com. Web Site: kcwy13.com. Licensee: Sweetwater Broadcasting Co. Group owner: Sunbelt Communications Co. Network: NBC. Rep: Blair Television. News staff: 13; News: 20 hrs wkly.
Key Personnel:
Bill Sullivan . . . VP & gen mgr
Peggy Porter . . . rgnl sls mgr
Joey Parker . . . news dir
Lonn Peterson . . . chief of engrg

KFNB-TV—Analog channel: 20. On air date: Oct 31, 1984. 1856 Skyview Dr., Casper, WY 82601. Phone: (307) 577-5923. Phone: (307) 577-5924. Fax: (307) 577-5928. E-mail: klwy@coffey.com. Licensee: WyoMedia Corp. Network: Fox. Washington Atty: Irwin, Campbell & Tannenwald.
Key Personnel:
Mark Nalboe . . . gen mgr
Terry Lane . . . opns mgr & progmg dir
Tina Nalbone . . . gen sls mgr
Joe Lownden . . . prom mgr
Greg Flabager . . . news dir
Dave Ericson . . . chief of engrg

KFNE—Analog channel: 10. On air date: Dec 22, 1957. 1856 Skyview Dr., Suite One, Casper, WY 82601. Phone: (307) 577-5923/5924. Fax: (307) 577-5928. E-mail: klwy@coffey.com. Licensee: First National Broadcasting Corp. Network: ABC.
Key Personnel:
Mark Nalbone . . . gen mgr
Terry Lane . . . opns mgr & progmg dir
Tina Nalbone . . . gen sls mgr
Joe Lowndes . . . prom dir
Dave Ericson . . . chief of engrg

KGWC-TV—Analog channel: 14. On air date: Aug 12, 1981. 2923 E. Lincolnway, Cheyenne, WY 82001. Phone: (307) 634-7755. Fax: (307) 634-7511. Licensee: Chelsey Broadcasting Co. of Casper LLC. Group owner: Chelsey Broadcasting Co. (acq 10-21-02; grpsl). Network: Network: CBS, Fox. Washington Atty: Dow, Lohnes & Albertson.
Key Personnel:
Mark Nalbone . . . gen mgr
Terry Lane . . . opns mgr & progmg dir
Tina Nalbone . . . gen sls mgr
Joe Lownden . . . prom dir
Greg Flabager . . . news dir
Dave Ericson . . . chief of engrg

KGWL-TV—Analog channel: 5. On air date: Sept 10, 1982. 1856 Skyview Dr., Caasper, WY 82601. Phone: (307) 234-1111. Fax: (307) 234-4005. Licensee: Chelsey Broadcasting Co. of Casper LLC. Group owner: Chelsey Broadcasting Co. (acq 10-21-02; grpsl). Network: CBS. Washington Atty: Covington & Burling.
Key Personnel:
Mark Nalbone . . . gen mgr
Terry Lane . . . opns mgr

***KPTW**—Analog channel: 6.Not on air, target date: unknown: Central Wyoming College, 2660 Peck Ave., Riverton, WY 82501. Phone: (307) 856-6944. Fax: (307) 856-3893. Web Site: wyoptv.org. Permittee: Central Wyoming College.

KTWO-TV—Analog channel: 2. On air date: Mar 1, 1957. 1896 Skyview Drive, Casper, WY 82601-9638. Phone: (307) 237-3711. Fax: (307) 237-4458. E-mail: k2@k2tv.com. Web Site: www.k2tv.com. Licensee: Wyoming Channel 2 Inc. Group owner: Equity Broadcasting Corp. (acq 3-26-2001; $3.5 million with KDEV(TV) Cheyenne). Network: ABC. Rep: Millennium Sales & Marketing. News staff: 23; News: 15 hrs wkly.
Key Personnel:
Tom Grant . . . news dir
Phyl King . . . sls

Cheyenne, WY-Scottsbluff, NE (DMA 195)

KDEV—Analog channel: 33. On air date: Aug 28, 1987. 4200 E. 2nd St., Cheyenne, WY 82609. Phone: (307) 237-3711. Fax: (307) 234-9866. Web Site: www.katv.com. Licensee: Denver Broadcasting Inc. Group owner: Equity Broadcasting Corp. (acq 3-26-2001; $3.5 million with KTWO-TV Casper). Rep: Millennium Sales & Marketing. News staff: 17; News: 15 hrs wkly.
Key Personnel:
Lori Kemper . . . gen mgr
Jim Hawks . . . stn mgr, gen sls mgr & progmg dir
Ava Becks . . . news dir
Deo Carmichael . . . chief of engrg

KDUH-TV—Analog channel: 4. On air date: Mar 5, 1958. Box 1529, Scottsbluff, NE 69363-1529. 1523 1st Ave., Scottsbluff, NE 69361. Phone: (308) 632-3071. Fax: (308) 632-3596. Web Site: www.kduhtv.com. Licensee: Duhamel Broadcasting Enterprises. Group owner: (group owner) Network: ABC. Rep: Katz Radio. Washington Atty: Fisher, Wayland, Cooper, Leader & Zaragoza. News staff: 6; News: 2 hrs wkly.
Key Personnel:
William Duhamel . . . pres
Patrick Maag . . . stn mgr
Monte Loos . . . opns dir

KGWN-TV—Analog channel: 5. On air date: Mar 22, 1954. 2923 E. Lincolnway, Cheyenne, WY 82001. Phone: (307) 634-7755. Fax: (307) 637-8604. E-mail: news@kgwn.tv. Web Site: www.kgwn.tv. Licensee: SagamoreHill Broadcasting Co. of Wyoming/Northern Colorado LLC. Group owner: (group owner; acq 12-22-2003; $6.5 million. with KSTF(TV) Scottsbluff, NE). Network: CBS. Rep: Continental Television Sales. Washington Atty: Dow, Lohnes & Albertson. News staff: 16; News: 15 hrs wkly.
Key Personnel:
Louis Wall . . . pres
Joan Turner . . . gen mgr & natl sls mgr
Keith Lindstrom . . . rgnl sls mgr
Barbara Parenti . . . progmg dir
Krachel Whiting . . . news dir
Tony Schaefer . . . chief of engrg

KLWY—Analog channel: 27. On air date: 1992. 1856 Skyview Dr., Casper, WY 82601. Phone: (307) 577-5923. Fax: (307) 577-5928. E-mail: klwy@coffey.com. Licensee: Wyomedia Corp. (acq 12-4-91; $100,000; 1-6-92). Network: Fox.
Key Personnel:
Mark Nalbone . . . gen mgr
Terry Lane . . . opns mgr & progmg dir
Tina Nalbone . . . gen sls mgr & rgnl sls mgr
Joe Lowndes . . . prom dir
Greg Flabager . . . news dir
Dave Ericson . . . chief of engrg

KSTF—Analog channel: 10. On air date: Aug 7, 1955. 3385 N. 10th St., Gering, NE 69341. Phone: (308) 632-6107. Fax: (308) 632-3470. E-mail: kstf@prarieweb.com. Web Site: www.kgwn.tv. Licensee: SagamoreHill Broadcasting Co. of Wyoming/Northern Colorado LLC. Group owner: (group owner; acq 12-22-2003; $6.5 million. with KGWN-TV Cheyenne, WY). Network: Network: CBS, Fox. Rep: Katz Radio. Washington Atty: Dow, Lohnes & Albertson. News staff: 6; News: 8 hrs wkly.
Key Personnel:
Joan Turner . . . gen mgr
Jodi Lange . . . gen sls mgr & adv mgr
Keith Lynstrom . . . gen sls mgr
Barbara Parenti . . . mktg mgr, progmg dir & news dir
Tony Schaefer . . . chief of engrg

KTUW—Analog channel: 16.Not on air, target date: unknown: 1 Shackleford Dr., Suite 400, Little Rock, AR 72211. Phone: (501) 219-2400. Fax: (501) 221-1101. Permittee: EBC Scottsbluff Inc. Group owner: Equity Broadcasting Corp. Washington Atty: Irwin, Campbell & Tannenwald.

Clarksburg-Weston, WV (DMA 165)

WBOY-TV—Analog channel: 12. On air date: Nov 17, 1957. 904 W. Pike St., Clarksburg, WV 26301. 912 W. Pike St., Clarksburg, WV 26301. Phone: (304) 623-3311. Fax: (304) 624-6152. E-mail: wboy@wboy.com. Web Site: www.wboy.com. Licensee: West Virginia Media Holdings LLC. Group owner: (group owner; acq 10-25-01; $20 million).. Network: NBC. Washington Atty: Latham & Watkins. News staff: 16; News: 24 hrs wkly.
Key Personnel:
Bray Cary . . . CEO & pres
Marty Becker . . . chmn
Charlie Dusic . . . CFO
Gary McNair . . . VP, gen mgr & progmg dir
John Coley . . . opns mgr
Bob Calvert . . . gen sls mgr
Chris Leister . . . natl sls mgr
John Fawcett . . . mktg mgr & adv mgr
Kelli Robinson . . . prom mgr & adv mgr
Jim Platzer . . . news dir
Bob Hardman . . . chief of engrg

WDTV—Analog channel: 5. Digital channel: 6. On air date: June 1, 1960. Box 480, 5 Television Dr., Bridgeport, WV 26330. Phone: (304) 848-5000. Fax: (304) 842-7501. E-mail: timdefazio@wdtv.com. Web Site: www.wdtv.com. Licensee: W. Russell Withers Jr. Group owner: Withers Broadcasting Co. (acq 5-8-73; $600,000; 4-16-73). Network: CBS. Rep: Katz Radio. Washington Atty: Gardner, Carton & Douglas. News staff: 21; News: 18.5 hrs wkly.
Key Personnel:
W. Russell Withers Jr. . . . pres
Tim Defazio . . . gen mgr & dev dir
John Breen . . . opns dir

WVFX—Analog channel: 46. On air date: Feb 8, 1981. 775 W. Pike St., Clarksburg, WV 26301. Phone: (304) 622-9839. Fax: (304) 623-9021. E-mail: bstanton@wvfx.com. Web Site: www.wvfx.com.

American Samoa

Licensee: Davis Television Clarksburg L.L.C. (acq 1-26-99). Network: Fox. Washington Atty: Leventhal, Senter & Lerman.

Jackson

see Salt Lake City, UT market

Laramie

see Denver, CO market

Rawlins

see Denver, CO market

Riverton

see Casper-Riverton, WY market

Rock Springs

see Salt Lake City, UT market

Sheridan

see Rapid City, SD market

American Samoa

Pago Pago

*KVZK-2—Analog channel: 2. On air date: 1964. Box 2567, Pago Pago, AS 96799. Phone: (684) 633-4191. Fax: (684) 633-1044. E-mail: siviapaolo@yahoo.cm. Web Site: www.asg-gov.com/agencies/opi.asg.htm. Licensee: The Government of American Samoa. Network: PBS.

*KVZK-4—Analog channel: 4. Box 2567, Pago Pago, AS 96799. Phone: (684) 633-4191. Fax: (684) 633-1044. E-mail: siviapaolo@yahoo.com. Web Site: www.asg-gov.com/agencies/opi.asg.htm. Licensee: The Government of American Samoa. Network: Network: ABC, CBS.

*KVZK-5—Analog channel: 5. On air date: Oct 5, 1964. Box 2567, Pago Pago, AS 96799. Phone: (684) 633-4191. Fax: (684) 633-1044. E-mail: siviapaolo@yahoo.com. Web Site: www.asg-gov.com/agencies/opi.asg.htm. Licensee: The Government of American Samoa. Network: Network: ABC, CBS.

Guam

Hagatna

*KGTF—Analog channel: 12. On air date: Oct 30, 1970. Box 21449, GMF, GU 96921. 194 Sesame St., Washington Dr., Mangiloo, GU 96921. Phone: (671) 734-2207. Phone: (671) 734-3476. Fax: (671) 734-5483. E-mail: kgtf12@kgtf.org. Web Site: www.kgtf.org. Licensee: Guam Educational Telecommunications Corp. Network: PBS. Washington Atty: Cohn & Marks.

KUAM-TV—Analog channel: 8. On air date: Aug 5, 1956. Calvo Commercial Ctr., 600 Harmon Loop Rd., Dededo, GU 96912. Phone: (671) 637-5826. Fax: (671) 637-9865. Web Site: www.kuam.com. Licensee: Pacific Telestations Inc.. Ownership: Edward M. Calvo (acq 1988). Network: Network: NBC, CBS. Washington Atty: Haley, Bader & Potts. News staff: 20; News: 14 hrs wkly.
Key Personnel:
Joseph Calvo . . . . . . exec VP, gen mgr, sVP & gen sls mgr
Marie Calvo-Monge . . . . stn mgr
Christie San Agustin . . . . prom dir
Annie San Nicolas . . . . progmg mgr
Richard Garman . . . . engr mgr & chief of engrg
Sabrina Salas . . . . news dir & chief of engrg

Tamuning

KTGM—Analog channel: 14. On air date: Oct 19, 1988. 692 N. Marine Dr., Suite 308, Tamuning, GU 96913. Phone: (671) 649-8814. Fax: (671) 649-0371. E-mail: abc14@ite.net. Licensee: Island Broadcasting Inc.. Ownership: David M. Larson, 66%; Edmund Y. Lee, 17%. Network: ABC. Washington Atty: Davis Wright Tremaine.
Key Personnel:
David Larson . . . . pres & gen mgr
Marie Leon Guerrero . . . . stn mgr, gen sls mgr & progmg mgr

Puerto Rico

Aguada

WQHA—Analog channel: 50. On air date: 1995. Box 3869, Carolina, PR 00984-3869. Phone: (787) 750-4090. Fax: (787) 701-4245. Licensee: Concilio Mision Cristiana Fuente de Agua Viva.
Key Personnel:
Hector Perez . . . . gen mgr
Joel Velez . . . . gen sls mgr
Fabian Rivera . . . . progmg dir
Ramon Rivera . . . . chief of engrg

Aguadilla

*WELU—Analog channel: 32. On air date: 1987. Box 1093, Hormigueros, PR 00660. Phone: (787) 849-4020. Fax: (787) 849-2092. Licensee: Pabellon Educational Broadcasting Inc. (acq 4-28-00).
Key Personnel:
Hector Perez . . . . pres & gen mgr
Joel Velez . . . . gen sls mgr
Fabian Rivera . . . . progmg dir
Ramon Rivera . . . . chief of engrg

WOLE-TV—Analog channel: 12. On air date: May 13, 1960. Box 1200, Mayaguez, PR 00681-1200. Mckinley Edif. Westerbank Piso 7, Mayaguez, PR 00681-1200. Phone: (787) 833-1200. Phone: (787) 891-8100. Fax: (787) 831-6330. Fax: (787) 891-3380. Licensee: Western Broadcasting Corp. of Puerto Rico.. Ownership: Du Art Film Labs Inc., 61.2%; Jose Bechara, 30.6%; Alfonso Giminez-Aguayo, 8.2%.
Key Personnel:
Luis Morales . . . . gen mgr
Wilson Lugo . . . . gen sls mgr
Santiago Hernandez . . . . progmg dir
Doel Oriol . . . . chief of engrg

WVEO—Analog channel: 44. Digital channel: 17. On air date: October 1974. Southwestern B/C Inc., 1554 Bori St., Rio Piedras, PR 00927-6113. Phone: (787) 882-0422. Fax: (787) 281-9758. Licensee: International Broadcasting Corp. (acq 10-7-2004; $1,382,961. with WXRF(AM) Guayama).
Key Personnel:
Pedro Roman Collazo . . . . gen mgr
Margarita Nazario . . . . progmg dir

Arecibo

WCCV-TV—Analog channel: 54. On air date: Nov 15, 1981. Box 949, Bo. Membrillo, Carr. #2, Camuy, PR 00627. Phone: (787) 262-5400. Phone: (787) 898-5120. Fax: (787) 262-0541. Web Site: www.cdminternational.com. Licensee: Asociacion Evan. Cristo Viene Inc.. Ownership: Francisco Valazquez, 88%; Wilfredo Almodovar, 6%; Juana Roman, 5%; Patricio R. Fermaintt, 2%.

WMEI—Analog channel: 60.Not on air, target date: unknown: GPO 7017, Caguas, PR 00726. Permittee: Hector Negroni Cartagena.

Bayamon

WDWL—Analog channel: 36. On air date: 1991. Box 50615, Levittown Stn, PR 00950. Phone: (787) 795-8113. Fax: (787) 795-8140. E-mail: jesusjr@prtc.net. Web Site: www.teleadoracion.com. Licensee: Bayamon Christian Network.. Ownership: Felix Berrios, 20%; Simon Castillo, 20%; Wilfredo Diaz, 20%; David Perez, 20%; Luciano Rodriguez, 20%.
Key Personnel:
Jesus Velez . . . . pres

Zoraida Jostinano . . . . gen mgr
David Baez . . . . chief of engrg

Caguas

WLII—Analog channel: 11. Digital channel: 56. On air date: May 27, 1960. Box 10000, San Juan, PR 00908-1000. One 3rd St., San Juan, PR 00908. Phone: (787) 724-1111. Fax: (787) 722-3505. Fax: (787) 723-0094. Licensee: WLII/WSUR Inc. Group owner: Raycom Media Inc. (acq 5-23-2005; with WSUR-TV Ponce). Washington Atty: Kaye, Scholer, Fierman, Hays & Handler.
Key Personnel:
Larry Sands . . . . gen mgr
Carlos Pagan . . . . gen sls mgr
Jessica Rodriguez . . . . progmg dir & progmg mgr
Jose Morales . . . . news dir
Andres Diaz . . . . chief of engrg

*WUJA—Analog channel: 58. On air date: September 1985. Box 4039, Balle Arryba Heights Stn, Carolina, PR 00984. Phone: (787) 750-5858. Fax: (787) 757-1500. Licensee: Caguas Educational TV Inc.

Carolina

WRFB—Analog channel: 52. On air date: August 1998. Box 1833, Carolina, PR 00984-1833. Phone: (787) 762-5500. Fax: (787) 752-1825. Licensee: R.Y.F. Broadcasting Inc.. Ownership: Enrique A. (Rickin) Sanchez, 50%; Blanche Vidal de Sanchez, 50%. Washington Atty: John L. Tierney.

Fajardo

*WMTJ—Analog channel: 40. On air date: January 1985. Box 21345, San Juan, PR 00928-1345. Isadoro Color, Rd. 176, San Juan, PR 00928. Phone: (787) 766-2600. Fax: (787) 250-8546. Web Site: www.suagm.edu. Licensee: Ana G. Mendez Educational Foundation. Washington Atty: Dow, Lohnes & Albertson.

WPRV-TV—Analog channel: 13. On air date: 1991. Box 1967, San Juan, PR 00902-1967. Margary De Castro, Carolina, PR 00902-1967. Phone: (787) 276-1300. Fax: (787) 276-1307. Licensee: Catholic, Apostolic and Roman Church of Puerto Rico. Washington Atty: Mullin, Rhyne, Emmons & Topel.

WRUA—Analog channel: 34. On air date: 1997. Box 310, Bayamon, PR 00960. Phone: (787) 279-3434. Fax: (787) 279-5549. Licensee: Eastern Television Corp. (acq 2-4-00; $335,000)..

Guayama

WIDP—Analog channel: 46. On air date: 1999. Box 21065, San Juan, PR 00928. Phone: (787) 999-0360. E-mail: info@teletriunfo.com. Licensee: Ebenezer Broadcasting Group Inc. Washington Atty: Shaw Pittman LLP.
Key Personnel:
Moises Flores . . . . gen mgr
Carlos Vasquez . . . . opns dir

Mayaguez

*WIPM-TV—Analog channel: 3. On air date: Apr 28, 1961. Box 190909, Hato Rey, PR 00919. Phone: (787) 834-0164. Fax: (787) 832-9139. Licensee: Puerto Rico Public Broadcasting Corp. Network: PBS. Washington Atty: Steptoe & Johnson.
Key Personnel:
Eduardo Bado . . . . gen mgr
Reinaldo Perez . . . . opns dir
Diane Ramos . . . . gen sls mgr
Mirta Rodriguez . . . . progmg dir
Rebecca Torres . . . . news dir
Jorge Gonzalez . . . . chief of engrg

WNJX-TV—Analog channel: 22. On air date: Apr 27, 1986. c/o WAPA-TV, Apartado 362052, San Juan, PR 00936. Phone: (787) 792-4444. Fax: (787) 782-4420. Licensee: WNJX-TV Inc. Group owner: LIN Television Corporation (acq 3-1-2001; up to $1.075 million. for stock).
Key Personnel:
Joe Ramos . . . . gen mgr
Jonathan Garcia . . . . gen sls mgr

Margarita Millan . . . . progmg dir
Enrique Cruz . . . . news dir
Jose Guerra . . . . chief of engrg

WORA-TV—Analog channel: 5. On air date: Oct 1, 1955. Box 43, Mayaguez, PR 00681. Phone: (787) 831-5555/(787) 721-4054. Fax: (787) 833-0075/(787) 724-1554. E-mail: gatoro@woratv.com. Licensee: Telecinco Inc.. Ownership: Alfredo R. deArellano Jr. and family, 100%. Washington Atty: Bryan Cave.
Key Personnel:
Jose Toro . . . . gen mgr & gen sls mgr
Ramon Guzman . . . . progmg dir
Carlos Sepulveda . . . . news dir
Fred Toledo . . . . chief of engrg

WOST—Analog channel: 16.Not on air, target date: unknown: Box 1553, Quebradillas, PR 00678. Permittee: Signal Broadcasting.

Naranjito

WECN—Analog channel: 64. On air date: April 1986. Box 310, Bayamon, PR 00960. Hwy. 167, Naranjito, PR 00960. Phone: (787) 799-1480. E-mail: evn@centennialpr.net. Licensee: Encuentro Christian Network.. Ownership: Rafael Torres Ortega, 11.11%; Iris Padilla, 11.11%; Ramon Luis Acevedo, 11.11%; Jofre Ayala, 11.11%; Daramid Ayala, 11.11% (acq 9-87; $175,000;. FTR: 4-13-87). Washington Atty: Irwin, Campbell & Tannenwald.

Ponce

WKPV—Analog channel: 20. Digital channel: 19. On air date: Aug 6, 1985. Box 2050, Attn: Edwin Pujols, San Juan, PR 00936-2050. Phone: (787) 792-4760. Phone: (787) 705-4153. Fax: (787) 782-7825. E-mail: edwn.pujols@wapa-tv.com. Licensee: S & E Network Inc. Group owner: LIN Television Corporation (acq 8-2-2001; grpsl).

*WQTO—Analog channel: 26. On air date: November 1986. Box 21345, San Juan, PR 00928-1345. Isadoro Color, Rd. 176, San Juan, PR 00928. Phone: (787) 766-2600. Fax: (787) 250-8546. Web Site: www.suagm.edu. Licensee: Systema Universitario Ana G. Mendez Inc. Washington Atty: Dow, Lohnes & Albertson.

WSTE—Analog channel: 7. On air date: Feb 2, 1958. Call Box 15096, San Juan, PR 00902. Phone: (787) 724-7777. Fax: (787) 725-5870. Licensee: Siete Grand Television Inc.. Ownership: Jerry B.& Esther M. Hartman. (acq 8-1-91; $6 million; 8-26-91).
Key Personnel:
Maria Negron . . . . gen sls mgr
Wanda Costanzo . . . . gen mgr, gen sls mgr & progmg dir
Gilberto Vera . . . . chief of engrg

WSUR-TV—Analog channel: 9. Digital channel: 43. On air date: February 1958. Box 10000, San Juan, PR 00908-1000. One 3rd St., San Juan, PR 00908. Phone: (787) 724-1111. Fax: (787) 722-3505. Fax: (787) 723-0094. Licensee: WLII/WSUR Inc. Group owner: Raycom Media Inc. (acq 5-23-2005; with WLII(TV) Caguas). Network: Univision (Spanish). Washington Atty: Hamel & Park.
Key Personnel:
Larry Sands . . . . sr VP, VP & gen mgr
Carlos Pagan . . . . gen sls mgr & mktg dir
Manuel Santiago . . . . prom dir
Jessica Rodriguez . . . . progmg dir
Jose Morales . . . . news dir
Andres Diaz . . . . chief of engrg

WTIN—Analog channel: 14. On air date: 1998. Box 362050, San Juan, PR 00936-2050. Phone: (787) 792-4444. Fax: (787) 782-7825. Licensee: Televicentro of Puerto Rico LLC. Group owner: LIN Television Corporation (acq 5-6-2004; $5 million).. Washington Atty: Baraff, Koerner, Olender & Hochberg.
Key Personnel:
Margarita Millan . . . . progmg VP
Jose Guerra . . . . engrg VP

WVOZ-TV—Analog channel: 48. On air date: 1994. Bori 1554 St. Urb Point, San Juan, PR 00927. Phone: (787) 274-1800. Fax: (787) 281-9758. Licensee: International Broadcasting Corp. Group owner: (group owner; acq 10-9-01; grpsl).
Key Personnel:
Margarita Nazario . . . . gen mgr & gen sls mgr
Roman Callazo . . . . progmg dir
Rudi Rivas . . . . chief of engrg

San Juan

WAPA-TV—Analog channel: 4. On air date: April 1954. Apartado 362052, San Juan, PR 00936-2050. Phone: (787) 792-4444. Fax: (787) 782-4420. Web Site: www.televicentropr.com. Licensee: Televicentro of Puerto Rico L.L.C. Group owner: LIN Television Corporation (acq 7-12-2000; grpsl). Rep: Katz Radio. Washington Atty: Fletcher, Heald & Hildreth. News staff: 29; News: 8 hrs wkly.
Key Personnel:
Joe Ramos . . . . gen mgr
Jonathan Garcia . . . . gen sls mgr
Margarita Millan . . . . progmg dir
Enrique Cruz . . . . news dir
Jose Guerra . . . . chief of engrg

*WIPR-TV—Analog channel: 6. On air date: Jan 6, 1958. Box 190909, Hato Rey, PR 00919. Phone: (787) 766-0505. Fax: (787) 753-9846. Licensee: Puerto Rico Public Broadcasting Corp. Network: PBS. Washington Atty: Steven Huffines.
Key Personnel:
Yolanda Zabala . . . . gen mgr
Susanne Marte . . . . opns dir
Maria Reina de la Puebla . . . . progmg dir
Rebecca Torres . . . . news dir
Jorge Gonzalez . . . . chief of engrg

WJPX—Analog channel: 24. Digital channel: 21. On air date: Feb 15, 1987. Apartado 362050, Attn: Edwin Pujols, San Juan, PR 00936-2050. Phone: (787) 792-4444. Phone: (787) 706-4153. Fax: (787) 782-7825. E-mail: edwin.pujols@wapa-tv.com. Licensee: S&E Network Inc. Group owner: LIN Television Corporation (acq 8-2-2001; grpsl). Washington Atty: Dow, Lohnes & Albertson.
Key Personnel:
Joe Ramos . . . . gen mgr
Edwin Pujols . . . . stn mgr
Jonathan Garcia . . . . gen sls mgr
Margarita Millan . . . . progmg dir
Enrique Cruz . . . . news dir
Jose Guerra . . . . chief of engrg

WKAQ-TV—Analog channel: 2. On air date: Mar 28, 1954. Box 366222, San Juan, PR 00936-6222. 383 Roosevelt Ave., Hato Rey, PR 00919. Phone: (787) 758-2222. Phone: (787) 641-2222. Fax: (787) 641-2175. Fax: (787) 641-2184. Web Site: www.telemundopr.com. Licensee: NBC Telemundo License Co. Group owner: Telemundo Group Inc. (acq 4-10-2002; grpsl). Network: Telemundo (Spanish). Washington Atty: Hogan & Hartson. News staff: 40; News: 24 hrs wkly.
Key Personnel:
Luis Roldan . . . . gen mgr
Jose Medina . . . . opns mgr & chief of engrg
Paco Pregues . . . . sls dir
Iliana Santiago . . . . progmg dir
Ruban Roman . . . . news dir

WSJU-TV—Analog channel: 30. Digital channel: 31. On air date: 1985. 1508 Calle Bori, Urb. Antonsanti, San Juan, PR 00927. Phone: (787) 756-8700. Fax: (787) 765-2965. Web Site: www.canal30pr.com. Licensee: Aerco Broadcasting Corp.. Ownership: Angel O. Roman Lopez, 50%; Ruth E. Roman Lopez, 50% (acq 1-11-2005). Washington Atty: Borsari & Assoc..
Key Personnel:
Angel O. Roman Lopez . . . . pres & gen mgr
Sergio Ballesteros . . . . gen sls mgr
Rudi Rivas . . . . chief of engrg

WTCV—Analog channel: 18. On air date: Aug 19, 1984. Bori 1554, San Juan, PR 00927-6113. Phone: (787) 274-1800. Fax: (787) 281-9758. Licensee: International Broadcasting Corp. Group owner: (group owner; acq 10-9-01; grpsl). Washington Atty: Marmet & McCombs.
Key Personnel:
Pedro Roman . . . . pres, pres & gen mgr
Margarita Nazario . . . . gen sls mgr & prom dir

San Sebastian

WJWN-TV—Analog channel: 38. Digital channel: 39. Box 2050, Attn: Edwin Pujols, San Juan, PR 00936-2050. Phone: (787) 792-4760. Phone: (787) 706-4153. Fax: (787) 782-7825. E-mail: edwin.pujols@wapa-tv.com. Licensee: S&E Network Inc. Group owner: LIN Television Corporation (acq 8-2-2001; grpsl).

Yauco

WIRS—Analog channel: 42. On air date: Dec 1, 1991. Box 310, Bayamon, PR 00960-0310. Phone: (787) 799-1480. Licensee: Televicentro of Puerto Rico LLC. Group owner: LIN Television Corporation (acq 12-11-2003; $4.45 million)..

Virgin Islands

Charlotte Amalie

*WTJX-TV—Analog channel: 12. On air date: 1972. Box 7879, 158-158A Haypiece Hill, St. Thomas, VI 00801. Phone: (340) 774-6255. Fax: (340) 774-7092. Web Site: wtjx.org. Licensee: Virgin Islands Public Television System Board of Directors. Network: PBS. Washington Atty: Schwartz, Woods & Miller.
Key Personnel:
Sonia Kelly-Wiliams . . . . chmn
Michael Bornn . . . . gen mgr

WVXF—Analog channel: 17. On air date: 1999. Niski Ctr., Suite 714, St. Thomas, VI 00802. Phone: (340) 775-1297. Web Site: www.wvxf.com. Licensee: Storefront Television.. Ownership: LKK Group Corp., 50%; and Bluewater LLC, 50% (acq 9-27-2004; $600,000).. Network: CBS. Washington Atty: Dow, Lohnes & Albertson.

WZVI—Analog channel: 43.Not on air, target date: unknown: c/o Thomas J. Dougherty Jr., Kilpatrick, Stockton LLP, 607 14th St. N.W., Washington, DC 20005. Phone: (202) 508-5836. Fax: (202) 508-5858. Permittee: Marri Broadcasting LP.

Christiansted

WCVI-TV—Analog channel: 39. Digital channel: 23. On air date: Mar 1, 2000. Box 24027, Christiansted, VI 00824. Phone: (340) 713-9927. Fax: (340) 773-0712. E-mail: mbox@wcvi.tv. Web Site: www.wcvi.tv. Permittee: Virgin Blue Inc. Network: UPN.
Key Personnel:
Mary Adamshick . . . . progmg dir
Victor Gold . . . . gen mgr, gen sls mgr & chief of engrg

WSVI—Analog channel: 8. On air date: January 1966. Box 8ABC, Christiansted, St. Croix, VI 00823. Phone: (340) 778-5008; (803) 732-1757. Fax: (340) 778-5011. E-mail: wsvi-tv@worldnet.att.net. Licensee: ABC. Network: ABC. Rep: Roslin. Washington Atty: Marmet & McCombs.
Key Personnel:
David Lampel . . . . gen mgr
Kimberly Alexander . . . . gen mgr & stn mgr
Jackie Schrock . . . . sls dir
Denisha Brown . . . . news dir
Chester Benjamin . . . . chief of engrg

WVIF—Analog channel: 15. On air date: 2001. 5660 Southwick Blvd., Toledo, OH 43614. Phone: (419) 861-3815. Fax: (419) 861-3818. Licensee: CMCG St. Croix License LLC. Group owner: MAX Media L.L.C. (acq 2-7-2003; $10 million. with WPFO(TV) Waterville, ME).

Mexico

Ciudad Juarez

see El Paso, TX market

Tijuana

see San Diego, CA market

Directory of TV Stations in Canada

Alberta

Ashmont

CFRN-TV-4—Analog channel: 12. On air date: 1966. c/o CFRN-TV, 18520 Stony Plain Rd., Edmonton, AB T5S 1A8. Phone: (780) 483-3311. Fax: (780) 484-4426. E-mail: cfrn@ctv.ca. Web Site: www.cfrntv.ca. Licensee: CFRN-TV, a div. of CTV Television Inc.

Bonnyville

CBXFT-1—Analog channel: 6. Box 555, c/o CBXFT, Edmonton, AB T5J 2P4. c/o CBXFT, Edmonton City Centre, 10062-102 Ave., Suite 123, Edmonton, AB T5J 2Y8. Phone: (780) 468-7500. Fax: (780) 468-7792. Web Site: www.cbc.ca. Licensee: Canadian Broadcasting Corp. Network: Radio Canada.
Key Personnel:
Don Orchard . . . . CFO
Lionel Bonneville . . . . gen mgr

Calgary

CBRT—Analog channel: 9. On air date: Sept 1, 1975. 1724 Westmount Blvd. N.W., Calgary, AB T2P 2M7. Phone: (403) 521-6000. Fax: (403) 521-6007. E-mail: del_simon@cbc.ca. Web Site: cbc.ca. Licensee: CBC. Network: CBC.
Key Personnel:
Carole Taylor . . . . chmn
Robert Rabinovich . . . . pres
Harold Redekopp . . . . exec VP
Don Orchard . . . . gen mgr, opns dir & opns mgr
Wendy Ell . . . . sls dir
Pat Paproski . . . . rgnl sls mgr
Irene Karras . . . . mktg mgr
Del Simon . . . . prom mgr
Fred Youngs . . . . progmg dir
Nancy Rose . . . . progmg mgr
Laurie Long . . . . news dir
Lindsay Rutschke . . . . chief of engrg

CFCN-TV—Analog channel: 4. On air date: September 1960. Broadcast House, 80 Patina Rise S.W., Calgary, AB T3H 2W4. Phone: (403) 240-5600. Fax: (403) 240-5711. E-mail: cfcnnews@ctv.ca. Web Site: www.cfcnplus.ca. Licensee: CTV Television Inc. **Group owner:** (group owner) Network: CTV.

CIAN-TV—Analog channel: 13. On air date: 1989. 3720 76 Ave., Edmonton, AB T6B 2N9. Phone: (780) 440-7777. Fax: (780) 440-8899. Web Site: www.accesslearning.com/accesstv. Licensee: Learning and Skills Television of Alberta Ltd. Ownership: CHUM Ltd., 60%; Olympus Management, 20%; 1006228 Ontario Inc., 15.5%; and Jay Switzer, 4.5%. (acq 1995).
Key Personnel:
Ron Keast . . . . CEO
Moses Znaimer . . . . chmn
Dr. Ronald Keast . . . . pres
Peter Palframan . . . . CFO & VP
Richard Hiron . . . . adv dir

CICT-TV—Analog channel: 2. On air date: October 1954. 222 23rd St. N.E., Calgary, AB T2E 7N2. Phone: (403) 235-7777. Fax: (403) 248-0252. Web Site: www.canada.com. Licensee: Calgary TV.. Ownership: Westcom TV Group Ltd. News staff: 50; News: 13 hrs wkly.
Key Personnel:
C. McGinley . . . . VP & gen mgr
Norm Michaelis . . . . opns dir
Greg Campbell . . . . gen sls mgr
J. Eisler . . . . mktg dir
Lynda Ritz . . . . prom mgr
Dawna Docherty . . . . progmg dir
Dave Budge . . . . news dir
Jeff Eisler . . . . pub affrs dir
Dan Gold . . . . engrg VP

CKAL-TV—Analog channel: 5. On air date: Sept 20, 1997. 535 7th Ave. S.W., Calgary, AB T2P 0Y4. Phone: (403) 508-2222. Fax: (403) 508-2224. Web Site: www.a-channel.com. Licensee: Craig Media Inc. Group owner: (group owner). (acq 11-19-2004; grpsl).
Key Personnel:
Drew Craig . . . . CEO & pres
Andy Pernal . . . . CFO
Al Thorgeikson . . . . gen mgr
Mike Pietrus . . . . news dir

Coronation

CKRD-TV-1—Analog channel: 10. On air date: 1960. c/o RDTV, 2840 Bremner Ave., 2nd floor, Red Deer, AB T4R 1M9. Phone: (403) 346-2573. Fax: (403) 346-9980. E-mail: rdtv@globalyv.ca. Web Site: www.rdtv.com. Licensee: Global Communications Ltd. Group owner: CanWest Global Communications Corp. Network: CBC. News staff: 12; News: 5 hrs wkly.

Drumheller

CFCN-TV-1—Analog channel: 12. c/o CFCN-TV, 80 Patina Rise S.W., Calgary, AB T3H 2W4. Phone: (403) 240-5600. Fax: (403) 240-5773. E-mail: cfcnnews@ctv.ca. Web Site: www.cfcn.ca. Licensee: CTV Television Inc. Network: CTV.

Edmonton

CBXFT—Analog channel: 11. On air date: 1970. Box 555, Edmonton, AB T5J 2P4. Edmonton City Centre, 10062-102 Ave., Suite 123, Edmonton, AB T5J 2Y8. Phone: (780) 468-7500. Fax: (780) 468-7868. Web Site: www.cbc.ca. Licensee: CBC. Network: CBC. News staff: 15; News: 2 hrs wkly.
Key Personnel:
Don Orchard . . . . CFO & opns dir
Carol Nielsen . . . . chief of engrg

CBXT—Analog channel: 5. On air date: 1961. Box 555, Edmonton, AB T5J 2P4. Edmonton City Centre, 10062-102 Ave., Suite 123, Edmonton, AB T5J 2Y8. Phone: (780) 468-7500. Fax: (780) 468-7893. Web Site: www.cbc.ca. Licensee: CBC. Network: CBC.

CFRN-TV—Analog channel: 3. On air date: Oct 17, 1954. 18520 Stony Plain Rd., Edmonton, AB T5S 1A8. Phone: (780) 483-3311. Fax: (780) 484-4426. Web Site: www.cfrntv.ca. Licensee: CFRN TV, a div. of CTV Television Inc. Group owner: CTV Inc. (acq 1998). Network: CTV. News: 12 hrs wkly.
Key Personnel:
Fred Filthaut . . . . VP & gen mgr
David Fisher . . . . prom dir

CITV-TV—Analog channel: 13. On air date: 1974. 5325 Allard Way, Edmonton, AB T6H 5B8. Phone: (780) 436-1250. Fax: (780) 438-4613. E-mail: edmonton@globalyv.ca. Web Site: www.canada.com. Licensee: Global Television Network Inc. Group owner: Canwest Global (acq 2-6-91). News staff: 33; News: 11 hrs wkly.

*CJAL-TV—Analog channel: 9. On air date: Apr 1, 1991. 3720 76th Ave., Edmonton, AB T6B 2N9. Phone: (780) 440-7777. Fax: (780) 440-8899. E-mail: access@incentre.net. Web Site: www.accesslearning.com. Licensee: Learning and Skills Television of Alberta Ltd.. Ownership: CHUM Ltd., 60%; Olympus Management Ltd., 20%; 1006228 Ontario Ltd., 15.5%; Jay Switzer, 5.5%. Group owner: CHUM Ltd. (acq 9-1-95).
Key Personnel:
Dr. Ronald Keast . . . . CEO & pres
Ronald Keast . . . . CEO
Moses Znaimer . . . . chmn
Peter Palframan . . . . exec VP
Richard Hiron . . . . sls dir
Jill Bonenfant . . . . progmg dir
John Wood . . . . engrg dir

CKEM-TV—Analog channel: 51. On air date: Sept 18, 1997. 10212 Jasper Ave., Edmonton, AB T5J 5A3. Phone: (780) 424-2222. Fax: (780) 424-0357. E-mail: webmaster@appliedthemalsciences.com. Web Site: www.a-channel.com. Licensee: Craig Media Inc. Group owner: (group owner). (acq 11-19-2004; grpsl).
Key Personnel:
Jim Haskins . . . . gen mgr
John Cuccaro . . . . opns mgr
Art Eden . . . . rgnl sls mgr
Barry Close . . . . prom mgr

Chris Duncan . . . . news dir
Peter Nobel . . . . engrg mgr

Fort McMurray

CBXFT-6—Analog channel: 12. On air date: Mar 1, 1970. Box 555, Edmonton, AB T5J 2P4. c/o CBC, Edmonton City Centre, 10062-102 Ave., Suite 123, Edmonton, AB T5J 2Y8. Phone: (780) 468-7500. Fax: (780) 468-7792. Web Site: www.cbc.ca. Licensee: Canadian Broadcasting Corp. Network: Radio Canada.

Grande Prairie

CBXAT—Analog channel: 10. Box 555, c/o CBXT, Edmonton, AB T5J 2P4. Edmonton City Centre, 10062-102 Ave., Suite 123, Edmonton, AB T5J 2Y8. Phone: (780) 468-7500. Fax: (780) 468-7893. Web Site: www.cbc.ca. Licensee: CBC. Network: CBC.
Key Personnel:
Don Orchard . . . . CFO & opns dir
Carol Nielsen . . . . chief of engrg

CBXFT-8—Analog channel: 19. Box 555, Edmonton, AB T5J 2P4. Edmonton City Centre, 10062-102 Ave., Suite 123, Edmonton, AB T5J 2Y8. Phone: (780) 468-7500. Fax: (780) 468-7792. Web Site: www.cbc.ca. Licensee: CBC. Network: Radio Canada.
Key Personnel:
Don Orchard . . . . opns dir
Carol Nielsen . . . . chief of engrg

CFRN-TV-1—Analog channel: 13. c/o CFRN-TV, 18520 Stony Plain Rd., Edmonton, AB T5S 1A8. Phone: (780) 483-3311. Fax: (780) 484-4426. Web Site: www.cfrntv.ca. Licensee: CFRN-TV, a div. of CTV Television Inc. Network: CTV.

Grouard Mission-High Prairie

CFRN-TV-8—Analog channel: 18. On air date: November 1981. c/o CFRN-TV, 18520 Stony Plain Rd., Edmonton, AB T5S 1A8. Phone: (780) 483-3311. Fax: (780) 484-4426. E-mail: cfrn@ctv.ca. Web Site: www.cfrntv.ca. Licensee: CFRN TV, a div. of CTV Television Inc. Network: CTV.

High Prairie

CBXAT-2—Analog channel: 2. Box 555, Edmonton, AB T5J 2P4. c/o CBXT, Edmonton City Centre, 10062-102 Ave., Suite 123, Edmonton, AB T5J 2Y8. Phone: (780) 468-7500. Fax: (780) 468-7893. Web Site: www.cbc.ca. Licensee: CBC. Network: CBC.
Key Personnel:
Don Orchard . . . . exec VP & opns dir
Carol Nielsen . . . . chief of engrg

Lac La Biche

CFRN-TV-5—Analog channel: 2. c/o CFRN-TV, 18520 Stony Plain Rd., Edmonton, AB T5S 1A8. Phone: (780) 483-3311. Fax: (780) 484-4426. E-mail: cfrn@ctv.ca. Web Site: www.cfrntv.ca. Licensee: CFRN-TV, a div. of CTV Television Inc. Network: CTV.

Lethbridge

CFCN-TV-5—Analog channel: 13. c/o CFCN-TV, 80 Patina Rise S.W., Calgary, AB T3H 2W4. Phone: (403) 240-5600. Fax: (403) 240-5773. E-mail: cfcnnews@ctv.ca. Web Site: www.cfcnplus.ca. Licensee: CTV Television Inc. Group owner: (group owner) Network: CTV.

CISA-TV—Analog channel: 7. On air date: 1955. 1401-28 Street N., Lethbridge, AB T1H 6H9. Phone: (403) 327-1521. Fax: (403) 320-2620. E-mail: cisa@globaltv.ca. Web Site: www.canada.com/lethbridge. Licensee: Global Communications Ltd. Group owner: CanWest Global Communications Corp. (acq 9-1-2000; grpsl). News staff: 19; News: 12 hrs wkly.

Broadcasting & Cable Yearbook 2006

Directory of Television

CJIL-TV—Analog channel: 17. On air date: 1995. Box 1566, 450 31st St. N., Lethbridge, AB T1H 3Z3. Phone: (403) 380-3399. Fax: (403) 380-3322. Licensee: Miracle Channel.
Key Personnel:
Brad Lockhart . . . . gen mgr
Len Whyte . . . . chief of engrg

Lloydminster

CITL-TV—Analog channel: 4. On air date: July 28, 1976. 5026 50th St., Lloydminster, AB T9V 1P3. Phone: (780) 875-3321. Fax: (780) 875-4704. Web Site: www.ctv.ca. Licensee: NewCap Inc. Group owner: Midwest Broadcasting. (acq 12-22-2004; C$6,304,000. with CKSA-TV Lloydminster). Network: CTV.
Key Personnel:
R.G. Steele . . . . pres
Ken Ruptash . . . . gen mgr

CKSA-TV—Analog channel: 2. On air date: Sept 23, 1960. 5026 50th St., Lloydminster, AB T9V 1P3. Phone: (780) 875-3321. Fax: (780) 875-4704. Licensee: NewCap Inc. Group owner: Midwest Broadcasting. (acq 12-22-2004; C$6,304,000. with CITL-TV Lloydminster). Network: CBC.
Key Personnel:
R.G. Steele . . . . pres
Ken Ruptash . . . . gen mgr

Lougheed

CFRN-TV-7—Analog channel: 7. On air date: Sept 7, 1979. c/o CFRN-TV, 18520 Stony Plain Rd., Edmonton, AB T5S 1A8. Phone: (780) 483-3311. Fax: (780) 484-4426. E-mail: cfrn@ctv.ca. Web Site: www.cfrntv.ca. Licensee: CFRN TV, a div. of CTV Television Inc. Network: CTV.

Manning

CBXAT-3—Analog channel: 12. On air date: Oct 7, 1968. Box 555, Edmonton, AB T5J 2P4. c/o CBC, Edmonton City Centre, 10062-102 Ave., Suite 123, Edmonton, AB T5J 2Y8. Phone: (780) 468-7500. Fax: (780) 468-7779. Web Site: www.radio-canada.ca. Licensee: CBC. Network: CBC.
Key Personnel:
Don Orchard . . . . exec VP, opns dir & engrg mgr
Carol Nielsen . . . . chief of engrg

Meander River

CJTG-TV—Analog channel: 13. On air date: 1994. Box 60, High Level, AB T0H 0S0. Licensee: Tache Gondihe Society.

Medicine Hat

CFCN-TV-8—Analog channel: 8. c/o CFCN-TV, 60 Patina Rise S.W., Calgary, AB T3H 2W4. Phone: (403) 240-5600. Fax: (403) 240-5711. E-mail: cfcnnews@ctv.ca. Web Site: www.cfcn.ca. Licensee: CTV Television Inc. Network: CTV.

CHAT-TV—Analog channel: 6. On air date: 1957. Box 1270, Medicine Hat, AB T1A 7H5. 10 Boundary Rd., Red Cliff, AB T0J 2P0. Phone: (403) 529-1270. Fax: (403) 529-1292. Web Site: www.1270chat@monach.net. Licensee: Jim Pattison Broadcast Group Ltd. (the general partner) and Jim Pattison Industries Ltd. (the limited partner) carrying on business as Jim Pattison Broadcast Group L.P. Group owner: The Jim Pattison Broadcast Group (acq 12-21-2000; grpsl). Network: CBC. Rep: Airtime TV.
Key Personnel:
Dwaine Dietrich . . . . gen mgr
Joel Simmons . . . . chief of engrg

Peace River

CFRN-TV-2—Analog channel: 3. On air date: 1970. c/o CFRN-TV, 18520 Stony Plain Rd., Edmonton, AB T5S 1A8. Phone: (780) 483-3311. Fax: (780) 484-4426. E-mail: cfrn@ctv.ca. Web Site: www.cfrntv.ca. Licensee: CFRN-TV, a div. of CTV Television Inc. Network: CTV.

Pivot

CHAT-TV-1—Analog channel: 4. Box 1270, Medicine Hat, AB T1A 7H5. 10 Boundary Rd., Red Cliff, AB T0J 2P0.Canada Phone: (403) 529-1270. Fax: (403) 529-1292. E-mail: www.1270chat@monach.net. Licensee: Jim Pattison Broadcast Group Ltd. (the general partner) and Jim Pattison Industries Ltd. (the limited partner) carrying on business as Jim Pattison Broadcast Group L.P. Group owner: The Jim Pattison Broadcast Group (acq 12-21-2000; grpsl). Network: CBC.
Key Personnel:
Dwaine Dietrich . . . . gen mgr
Joel Simmons . . . . chief of engrg

Red Deer

CFRN-TV-6—Analog channel: 8. c/o CFRN-TV, 18520 Stony Plain Rd., Edmonton, AB T5S 1A8. Phone: (780) 483-3311. Fax: (780) 484-4426. E-mail: cfrn@ctv.ca. Web Site: www.cfrntv.ca. Licensee: CFRN-TV, a div. of CTV Television Inc. Network: CTV.

CKRD-TV—Analog channel: 6. On air date: 1956. 2840 Bremner Ave. 2nd Fl., Red Deer, AB T4R 1M9. Phone: (403) 346-2573. Fax: (403) 346-9980. E-mail: rdtv@globaltv.ca. Web Site: www.rdtv.com. Licensee: Global Communications Ltd. Group owner: CanWest Global Communications Corp. (acq 2000; grpsl). Network: CBC.

Slave Lake

CFRN-TV-9—Analog channel: 4. On air date: November 1981. c/o CFRN-TV, 18520 Stony Plain Rd., Edmonton, AB T5S 1A8. Phone: (780) 483-3311. Fax: (780) 484-4426. E-mail: cfrn@ctv.ca. Web Site: www.cfrntv.ca. Licensee: CFRN TV, a div. of CTV Television Inc.

Whitecourt

CFRN-TV-3—Analog channel: 12. c/o CFRN-TV, 18520 Stony Plain Rd., Edmonton, AB T5S 1A8. Phone: (780) 483-3311. Fax: (780) 484-4426. E-mail: cfrn@ctv.ca. Web Site: www.cfrntv.ca. Licensee: CFRN-TV, a div. of CTV Television Inc. Network: CTV.

British Columbia

Bowen Island

CHAN-TV-2—Analog channel: 3. Global BC, 7850 Enterprise St., Burnaby, BC V5A 1V7. Phone: (604) 420-2288. Fax: (604) 422-6651. Licensee: Global Communications Ltd. Group owner: Global BC. Network: Global.
Key Personnel:
Roy Gardner . . . . gen mgr
Bob Urban . . . . gen mgr
Brett Monlove . . . . gen sls mgr
Ruth Powell . . . . rgnl sls mgr
John Ridley . . . . prom dir
Ian Mayson . . . . news dir
John O'Connor . . . . engrg VP

Brackendale

CHAN-TV-5—Analog channel: 9. Global BC, 7850 Enterprise St., Burnaby, BC V5A 1V7. Phone: (604) 420-2288. Fax: (604) 421-9427. Licensee: Global Communications Ltd. Group owner: Global BC. Network: Global.

Campbell River

CHEK-TV-5—Analog channel: 13. c/o CHEK-TV, 780 King's Rd., Victoria, BC V8T 5A2. Phone: (250) 383-2435. Fax: (250) 384-7766. Web Site: www.canada.com/victoria/chtv. Licensee: Global Communications Ltd. Group owner: CanWest Global Communications Corp. Network: Global.

Canal Flats

CBUBT-1—Analog channel: 12. Box 4600, c/o CBUT, Vancouver, BC V6B 4A2. 700 Hamilton St., Vancouver, BC V6B 4A2. Phone: (604) 662-6000. Fax: (604) 662-6335. Web Site: www.cbc.ca. Licensee: CBC. Network: CBC.

Chilliwack

CHAN-TV-1—Analog channel: 11. 7850 Enterprise St., Burnaby, BC V5A 1V7. Canada. Phone: (604) 420-2288. Fax: (604) 421-9427. Licensee: Global Communications Ltd. Group owner: Global BC. Network: Global.

Cranbrook

CBUBT-7—Analog channel: 10. On air date: 1962. Box 4600, c/o CBUT-TV, Vancouver, BC V6B 4A2. 700 Hamilton St., Vancouver, BC V6B 4A2. Phone: (604) 662-6000. Fax: (604) 662-6335. Web Site: www.cbc.ca. Licensee: CBC. Network: CBC.

Dawson Creek

CJDC-TV—Analog channel: 5. On air date: 1958. NTV, Northern Television, 901 102nd Ave., Dawson Creek, BC V1G 2B6. Phone: (250) 782-3341. Fax: (250) 782-3154. Licensee: Standard Radio Inc. Group owner: Standard Broadcasting Corp. (acq 4-19-02; grpsl). Network: CBC. News staff: 4; News: 15 hrs wkly.

Fraser Valley

CHNU-TV—Analog channel: 66. On air date: Sept 15, 2001. Box 100, Surrey, BC V3T 4W4. Phone: (604) 576-6880. Fax: (604) 576-6895. E-mail: office@nowtv.ca. Web Site: www.nowtv.ca. Licensee: Rogers Broadcasting Ltd. (acq 5-20-2005; C$13 million with CIIT-TV Winnipeg, MB).
Key Personnel:
Rael Merson . . . . pres
Terry Mahoney . . . . gen mgr

Kamloops

CBUFT-2—Analog channel: 50. On air date: February 1979. 700 Hamilton St., Vancouver, BC V6B 4A2. Phone: (604) 662-6000. Fax: (604) 662-6161. Web Site: www.radio-canada.ca/c-b. Licensee: Societe Radio Canada. Network: Radio Canada.

CFJC-TV—Analog channel: 4. On air date: 1957. 460 Pemberton Terr., Kamloops, BC V2C 1T5. Phone: (250) 372-3322. Fax: (250) 374-0445. E-mail: info@cfjctv.com. Web Site: www.cfjctv.com. Licensee: Jim Pattison Broadcast Group Ltd. (the general partner) and Jim Pattison Industries Ltd. (the limited partner) carrying on business as Jim Pattison Broadcast Group L.P. Group owner: Group owner:The Jim Pattison Broadcast Group (acq 1987). Network: CBC. News staff: 8; News: 14 hrs wkly.
Key Personnel:
Richard W. Arnish . . . . pres & gen mgr
Dave Somerton . . . . opns mgr

Kelowna

CHBC-TV—Analog channel: 2. On air date: September 1957. 342 Leon Ave., Kelowna, BC V1Y 6J2. Phone: (250) 762-4535. Fax: (250) 860-2422. Fax: (250) 868-0662. E-mail: comments@chbc.com. Web Site: www.chbc.com. Licensee: Global Communications Ltd. Group owner: CanWest Global Communications Corp. News staff: 23; News: 16 hrs wkly.
Key Personnel:
Keith Williams . . . . gen mgr
Rob Weller . . . . opns mgr

Prince George

CKPG-TV—Analog channel: 2. On air date: 1961. 1810 Third Ave., 2nd Fl, Prince George, BC V2M 164. Canada. Phone: (250) 564-8861. Web Site: www.ckpgtv.com. Fax: (250) 562-8768. E-mail: ckpgmail@ckpg.bc.ca. Licensee: Jim Pattison Broadcast Group LP. (the general partner) and Jim Pattison Industries Ltd. (the limited

Manitoba — Stations in Canada

partner) carrying on business as Jim Pattison Broadcast Group L.P. Group owner: The Jim Pattison Broadcast Group (acq 12-21-2000); grpsl). Network: CBC. Rep: Airtime TV.

Pritchard

CHKM-TV-1—Analog channel: 9. Global BC, 7850 Enterprise St., Burnaby, BC V5A 1V7. Phone: (604) 420-2288. Fax: (604) 422-6698. Web Site: www.canada.com/vancouver/globaltv. Licensee: Global Communications Ltd. Group owner: Global BC. Network: Global.

Squamish

CHAN-TV-3—Analog channel: 7. Global BC, 7850 Enterprise St., Burnaby, BC V5A 1V7. Phone: (604) 420-2288. Fax: (604) 422-6651. Licensee: Global Communications Ltd. Group owner: Global BC. Network: Global.
Key Personnel:
Roy Gardner . . . . gen mgr
Bob Urban . . . . opns mgr
Brett Monlove . . . . gen sls mgr
Ruth Powell . . . . rgnl sls mgr
John Ridley . . . . prom dir
Ian Mayson . . . . news dir
John O'Connor . . . . engrg dir

Terrace

CBUFT-3—Analog channel: 11. On air date: Aug 27, 1979. 700 Hamilton St., Vancouver, BC V6B 4A2. Phone: (604) 662-6000. Fax: (604) 662-6161. Web Site: www.radio-canada.ca/c-b. Licensee: Societe Radio Canada. Network: Radio Canada.

CFTK-TV—Analog channel: 3. On air date: 1962. 4625 Lazelle Ave., Terrace, BC V8G 1S4. Phone: (250) 635-6316. Fax: (250) 638-6320. Licensee: Standard Radio Inc. Group owner: Standard Broadcasting Corp. (acq 4-19-02; grpsl). Network: CBC.
Key Personnel:
Doug Anderson . . . . gen mgr
Brian Faylinch . . . . chief of engrg

Valemount

CHVC-TV—Analog channel: 7. On air date: 1994. Box 922, Valemount, BC V0E 2Z0. Phone: (250) 566-8288. Fax: (250) 566-5655. Licensee: The Valemount Entertainment Society.

Vancouver

CBUFT—Analog channel: 26. On air date: Sept 27, 1976. 700 Hamilton St., Vancouver, BC V6B 4A2. Phone: (604) 662-6000. Fax: (604) 662-6161. Web Site: www.radio-canada.ca/c-b. Licensee: Societe Radio-Canada. Network: Radio Canada.
Key Personnel:
Lionel Bonneville . . . . gen mgr
Brigitte Tesniere . . . . prom dir
Michele Smolkin . . . . stn mgr & progmg dir

CBUT—Analog channel: 2. Digital channel: 58. On air date: Dec 16, 1953. Box 4600, 700 Hamilton St., Vancouver, BC V6B 4A2. Phone: (604) 662-6000. Fax: (604) 662-6414. Web Site: www.cbc.ca. Licensee: CBC. Network: CBC.

CHAN-TV—Analog channel: 8. Digital channel: 22. On air date: Oct 31, 1960. 7850 Enterprise St., Burnaby, BC V5A 1V7. Phone: (604) 420-2288. Fax: (604) 421-9257. Fax: (604) 444-9561. Licensee: Global Communications Ltd. Group owner: CanWest Global Communications Corp. Network: Global.

CHNM-TV—Analog channel: 42. On air date: June 27, 2003. Channel M, 88 E. Pender St., Vancouver, BC V6A 3X3. Phone: (604) 678-8000. Fax: (604) 678-3810. Web Site: www.channelm.ca. Licensee: The partners of Multivan Broadcast L.P. Rep: Airtime TV.
Key Personnel:
Art Reitmayer . . . . CEO & pres
Peter Gillespie . . . . opns VP & engrg VP
Bruce Hamlin . . . . sls dir
Johnny Michel . . . . prom VP & progmg VP
Teresa Wat . . . . news dir

CIVT-TV—Analog channel: 32. Digital channel: 33. On air date: Sept 22, 1997. 750 Burrard St., Suite 300, Vancouver, BC V6Z 1X5. Phone: (604) 608-2868. Fax: (604) 608-2698. E-mail: bccomments@ctv.ca. Web site: www.ctv.ca. Licensee: CTV Television Inc. Group owner: CTV Inc. Network: CTV.
Key Personnel:
Ivan Fecan . . . . CEO
Rick Brace . . . . pres
Robin Fillingham . . . . CFO
Jim Rusnak . . . . sr VP, VP & gen mgr
Jim Olsen . . . . opns mgr & prom mgr
Louise Clark . . . . dev dir
Lynne Forbes . . . . gen sls mgr & rgnl sls mgr
Doug Elphick . . . . natl sls dir
Brenda Vasas . . . . progmg dir & progmg dir
Tom Walters . . . . news dir
Vladimir Rybarczyk . . . . engrg mgr

CKVU-TV—Analog channel: 10. On air date: Sept 1, 1976. 180 W. Second Ave., Vancouver, BC V5Y 3T9. Phone: (604) 876-1344. Fax: (604) 876-3100. Web Site: www.citytv.com. Licensee: CHUM Television Vancouver Inc. Group owner: CHUM Ltd. (acq 10-15-01; C$130 million)..
Key Personnel:
Jay Switzer . . . . CEO
Stephen Tapp . . . . pres & exec VP
Brad Phillips . . . . VP & gen mgr
Ed Yiu . . . . opns dir, chief of opns & engrg dir
Neil Tegart . . . . opns mgr, engrg mgr & chief of engrg
David Kirkwood . . . . sls VP
John Voiles . . . . rgnl sls mgr
Steve Scarrow . . . . mktg VP & mktg dir
Tamara Poirier . . . . prom dir
Prem Gill . . . . progmg dir & pub affrs dir
Debbie Millette . . . . progmg dir
Bud Pierce . . . . news dir

Victoria

CHEK-TV—Analog channel: 6. On air date: 1956. 780 Kings Rd., Victoria, BC V8T 5A2. Phone: (250) 383-2435. Fax: (250) 384-7766. Licensee: Global Communications Ltd. Group owner: CanWest Global Communications Corp. Network: Global.

CIVI-TV—Analog channel: 53. On air date: Oct 4, 2001. 1420 Broad St., Victoria, BC V8W 2B1. Phone: (250) 381-2484. Fax: (250) 381-2485. E-mail: thenewvi@thenewvi.com. Web Site: www.achannel.ca/victoria. Licensee: CHUM Ltd. Group owner: (group owner).
Key Personnel:
Richard Gray . . . . stn mgr
John Voiles . . . . rgnl sls mgr
Debbie Millette . . . . progmg mgr
Hudson Mack . . . . news dir
Jen Wong . . . . prom
Brian Gatensby . . . . engr

Whistler

CHAN-TV-7—Analog channel: 9. Global BC, 7850 Enterprise St., Burnaby, BC V5A 1V7. Phone: (604) 420-2288. Fax: (604) 421-9427. Licensee: Global Communications Ltd. Group owner: Global BC. Network: Global.

Manitoba

Baldy Mountain

CBWST—Analog channel: 8. c/o CBWT, Winnipeg, MB R3C 2H1. 541 Portage Ave., Winnipeg, MB R3B 2G1. Phone: (204) 788-3222. Phone: (204) 788-3141. Fax: (204) 788-3639. Licensee: CBC. Network: CBC.
Key Personnel:
John Bertrand . . . . gen mgr
John Mang . . . . opns mgr

Brandon

CBWFT-10—Analog channel: 21. On air date: Feb 11, 1978. Box 160, Winnipeg, MB R3C 2H1. c/o CBC, 541 Portage Ave., Winnipeg, MB R3C 2H1. Phone: (204) 788-3222. Phone: (204) 788-3141. Fax: (204) 788-3639. Web Site: www.radio-canada.ca. Licensee: CBC. Network: CBC.
Key Personnel:
Lionel Bonneville . . . . gen mgr
Richard Augert . . . . stn mgr
Philippe Vrignon . . . . progmg mgr

CKX-TV—Analog channel: 5. On air date: 1955. 2940 Victoria Ave., Brandon, MB R7B 3Y3. Phone: (204) 728-1150. Fax: (204) 727-2505. E-mail: ckxtv@mb.sympatico.ca. Licensee: Craig Media Inc. Group owner: (group owner). (acq 11-19-2004; grpsl). Network: CBC. News staff: 20; News: 15 hrs wkly.
Key Personnel:
Alan Cruise . . . . gen mgr
Brian Atkinson . . . . stn mgr & news dir

CKYB-TV—Analog channel: 4. c/o CKY-TV, Polo Park, Winnipeg, MB R3G 0L7. Phone: (204) 788-3300. Fax: (204) 788-3399. Licensee: CTV Television Inc. Group owner: CTV Inc. (acq 8-2-01; grpsl). Network: CTV.

Fisher Branch

CBWGT—Analog channel: 10. Box 160, Winnipeg, MB R3C 2H1. c/o CBWT, 541 Portage Ave., Winnipeg, MB R3B 2G1. Phone: (204) 788-3222. Phone: (204) 788-3141. Fax: (204) 788-3639. Licensee: CBC. Network: CBC.
Key Personnel:
John Bertrand . . . . gen mgr
John Mang . . . . opns mgr

Flin Flon

CBWBT—Analog channel: 10. Box 160, c/o CBWT, Winnipeg, MB R3C 2H1. c/o CBWT, 541 Portage Ave., Winnipeg, MB R3B 2G1. Phone: (204) 788-3222. Phone: (204) 788-3141. Fax: (204) 788-3639. Licensee: CBC. Network: CBC.
Key Personnel:
John Bertrand . . . . opns dir
John Mang . . . . opns mgr

Foxwarren

CKX-TV-1—Analog channel: 11. c/o CKX-TV, 2940 Victoria Ave., Brandon, MB R7B 3Y3. Phone: (204) 728-1150. Fax: (204) 727-2505. Licensee: Craig Media Inc. Group owner: (group owner). (acq 11-19-2004; grpsl). Network: CBC.
Key Personnel:
Alan Cruise . . . . gen mgr
Glenn Edmonson . . . . gen sls mgr
Rich Chudley . . . . progmg dir
Paul Weger . . . . chief of engrg

Lac du Bonnet

CBWT-2—Analog channel: 4. Box 160, c/o CBWT, Winnipeg, MB R3C 2H1. c/o CBWT, 541 Portage Ave., Winnipeg, MB R3B 2G1. Phone: (204) 788-3222. Phone: (204) 788-3141. Fax: (204) 788-3639. Licensee: CBC. Network: CBC.
Key Personnel:
John Bertrand . . . . gen mgr
John Mang . . . . opns mgr

Mafeking

CBWYT—Analog channel: 2. On air date: July 14, 1978. Box 160, c/o CBWT, MB R3C 2H1. c/o CBC, 541 Portage Ave., Winnipeg, MB R3B 2G1. Phone: (204) 788-3222. Phone: (204) 788-3141. Fax: (204) 788-3639. Licensee: CBC. Network: CBC.

Ste-Rose-du-Lac

CBWFT-4—Analog channel: 3. On air date: May 15, 1976. Box 160, Winnipeg, MB R3C 2H1. c/o CBWFT, 541 Portage Ave., Winnipeg, MB R3C 2H1. Phone: (204) 788-3222. Phone: (204) 788-3141. Fax: (204) 788-3639. Licensee: CBC. Network: CBC.
Key Personnel:
Lionel Bonneville . . . . gen mgr
Richard Augert . . . . stn mgr
Wayne Yonka . . . . engrg dir & chief of engrg

Directory of Television

Winnipeg

CBWFT—Analog channel: 3. On air date: 1960. Box 160, Winnipeg, MB R3C 2H1. 541 Portage Ave., Winnipeg, MB R3C 2H1. Phone: (204) 788-3141. Fax: (204) 788-3639. Web Site: www.radio-canada.ca. Licensee: Societe Radio-Canada. Network: Radio Canada.
Key Personnel:
Lionel Bonneville .... gen mgr
Richard Augert .... stn mgr
Philippe Vrignon .... progmg dir

CBWT—Analog channel: 6. On air date: 1954. Box 160, Winnipeg, MB R3C 2H1. 541 Portage Ave., Winnipeg, MB R3B 2G1. Phone: (204) 788-3222. Fax: (204) 788-3167. E-mail: communications@winnipeg.cbc.ca. Web Site: www.cbc.ca/manitoba. Licensee: CBC. Network: CBC.
Key Personnel:
John Bertrand .... gen mgr & opns mgr
John Mang .... opns mgr

CHMI-TV—(Portage la Prairie).Analog channel: 13. On air date: Oct 17, 1986. #8 Forks Market Rd., Winnipeg, MB R3C 4Y3. Phone: (204) 947-9613. Fax: (204) 956-0811. E-mail: winnipegfeedback@a-channel.com. Web Site: www.a-channel.com. Licensee: Craig Media Inc. Group owner: (group owner). (acq 11-19-2004; grpsl). News staff: 35; News: 34 hrs wkly.
Key Personnel:
Cam Cowie .... VP & gen mgr
Christine Hamilton .... opns mgr
Glen Cassie .... news dir

CKND-TV—Analog channel: 9. On air date: Sept 1, 1975. 603 St. Mary's Rd., Winnipeg, MB R2M 3L8. Phone: (204) 233-3304. Fax: (204) 233-5615. Web Site: www.globaltv.com. Licensee: CanWest Television Inc. Group owner: CanWest Global Communications Corp. News staff: 19; News: 12 hrs wkly.

CKY-TV—Analog channel: 7. On air date: 1960. Polo Park, 1440 Rapelje Ave., Winnipeg, MB R3G 0L7. Phone: (204) 788-3300. Fax: (204) 788-3399. Web Site: www.cky.com. Licensee: CTV Television Inc. Group owner: CTV Inc. Network: CTV.
Key Personnel:
Diane Kashton .... pres & prom dir
Elaine Ali .... VP
Bill Hanson .... gen mgr
Kenneth Peron .... opns mgr
Wally Comrie .... gen sls mgr
Winnie Navarro .... progmg dir
Jeff Bollenbach .... news dir

New Brunswick

Bon Accord

CBAT-TV-1—Analog channel: 6. Box 2200, c/o CBAT, Fredericton, NB E3B 5G4. Phone: (506) 451-4000. Fax: (506) 451-4003. Web Site: www.cbc.ca. Licensee: CBC. (acq 4-29-94). Network: CBC.

Campbellton

CBAT-TV-4—Analog channel: 4. On air date: Nov 1, 1976. Box 2200, c/o CBAT, Fredericton, NB E3B 5G4. Phone: (506) 451-4000. Fax: (506) 451-4003. Web Site: www.cbc.ca. Licensee: CBC. (acq 4-29-94). Network: CBC.

CKCD-TV—Analog channel: 7. 191 Halifax St., Moncton, NB E1C 9R7. Phone: (506) 857-2600. Fax: (506) 857-2618. E-mail: ckcw@ctv.ca. Licensee: CTV Television Inc. Group owner: CTV Inc. (acq 11-1-97). Network: CTV.
Key Personnel:
Ivan Fecan .... CEO
Rick Brace .... pres
Robin Fillingham .... CFO
Elaine Ali .... exec VP
Mike Elgie .... VP & gen mgr
Brian Lewis .... stn mgr, gen sls mgr & adv mgr
John Silver .... opns mgr
Renee Fournier .... prom mgr
Jane Hefler .... progmg mgr
Jay Witherbee .... news dir & pub affrs dir
Carson McDavid .... engrg dir & chief of engrg

Fredericton-Saint John

CBAT—Analog channel: 4. On air date: 1954. Box 2200, Fredericton, NB E3B 5G4. Phone: (506) 451-4000. Fax: (506) 451-4003. Web Site: www.cbc.ca. Licensee: CBC. (acq 4-29-94). Network: CBC. Rep: Brydson.

Moncton

CBAFT—Analog channel: 11. On air date: 1959. Box 950, Moncton, NB E1C 8N8. 250 University Ave., Moncton, NB E1C 5K3. Phone: (506) 853-6666. Phone: (506) 853-6740 (Stn Dir). Fax: (506) 867-8031. Fax: (506) 853-6601 (news). Web Site: http://radiocanada.ca.atlantique. Licensee: Societe Radio-Canada. Network: Radio Canada.
Key Personnel:
Louise Imbeault .... gen mgr & progmg dir
Jacques Robichaud .... opns mgr
Michel Bertin .... gen sls mgr
Mrs. Johanna Huard .... mktg dir
Donald Langis .... news dir
William Mallis .... chief of engrg

CBAT-TV-2—Analog channel: 7. On air date: Sept 21, 1969. Box 950, Moncton, NB E1C 8N8. Phone: (506) 853-6666. Fax: (506) 867-8031. Fax: (506) 853-6601. Web Site: www.cbc.ca. Licensee: CBC. (acq 4-29-94). Network: CBC.

CKCW-TV—Analog channel: 2. On air date: 1954. 191 Halifax St., Moncton, NB E1C 9R7. Phone: (506) 857-2600. Fax: (506) 857-26187. E-mail: ckcw@ctv.ca. Web Site: www.ctv.ca. Licensee: CTV Television Inc. Group owner: CTV Inc. (acq 11-1-97). Network: CTV.
Key Personnel:
Ivan Fecan .... CEO
Rick Brace .... pres
Robin Fillingham .... CFO
Elaine Ali .... exec VP
Mike Elgie .... VP & gen mgr
Brian Lewis .... stn mgr, gen sls mgr & adv mgr
John Silver .... opns mgr
Renee Fournier .... prom mgr
Jane Hefler .... progmg mgr
Jay Witherbee .... news dir & pub affrs dir
Carson McDavid .... chief of engrg

Saint John

CKLT-TV—Analog channel: 9. 75 Prince William St., Suite 420, St. John, NB E2L 2B2. Phone: (506) 658-1010. Fax: (506) 658-1208. E-mail: cklt@ctv.ca. Web Site: www.ctv.ca. Licensee: CTV Television Inc. Group owner: CTV Inc. (acq 11-1-97). Network: CTV.
Key Personnel:
Ivan Fecan .... CEO
Rick Brace .... pres
Robin Fillingham .... CFO
Elaine Ali .... exec VP
Mike Elgie .... VP & gen mgr
Brian Lewis .... gen mgr, stn mgr, gen sls mgr & adv mgr
John Silver .... opns mgr
Renee Fournier .... prom mgr
Jane Hefler .... progmg mgr
Jay Witherbee .... news dir & pub affrs dir
Carson McDavid .... chief of engrg

Upsalquitch Lake

CKAM-TV—Analog channel: 12. On air date: unknown. c/o CKCW-TV, 191 Halifax St., Moncton, NB E1C 9R7. Phone: (506) 857-2600. Fax: (506) 857-2618. E-mail: ckcw@ctv.ca. Licensee: CTV Television Inc. Group owner: CTV Inc. (acq 11-1-97). Network: CTV.Ottawa Atty: . Ottawa atty: Alexander, Pearson & Dawson
Key Personnel:
Ivan Fecan .... CEO
Rick Brace .... pres
Robin Fillingham .... CFO
Elaine Ali .... exec VP
Mike Elgie .... VP & gen mgr
Brian Lewis .... stn mgr, gen sls mgr & adv mgr
John Silver .... opns mgr
Renee Fournier .... prom mgr
Jay Witherbee .... news dir & pub affrs dir
Carson McDavid .... engrg dir & chief of engrg

Newfoundland

Argentia

CJOM-TV—Analog channel: 3. On air date: September 1957. Box 2020, c/o CJON-TV, 446 Logy Bay Rd., St. John's, NF A1C 5S2. Phone: (709) 722-5015. Fax: (709) 726-5107. E-mail: ntv@ntv.ca. Web Site: www.ntv.ca. Licensee: Newfoundland Broadcasting Co. Ltd. Group owner: (group owner; acq 9-1-77). Network: CTV. News staff: 12; News: 11 hrs wkly.

Baie Verte

CBNAT-1—Analog channel: 3. On air date: Sept 15, 1968. 95 University Ave., St. John's, NF A1B 1Z4. Phone: (709) 576-5000. Fax: (709) 576-5155. Web Site: www.cbc.ca/nl. Licensee: CBC. Network: CBC.

Bonavista

CJWB-TV—Analog channel: 10. On air date: 1972. Box 2020, NTV Studio Bldg., 446 Logy Bay Rd., St. John's, NF A1C 5S2. Phone: (709) 722-5015. Fax: (709) 726-5107. E-mail: ntv@ntv.ca. Web Site: www.ntv.ca. Licensee: Newfoundland Broadcasting Co. Ltd. Group owner: (group owner) Network: CTV. News staff: 12; News: 11 hrs wkly.

Bonne Bay

CBYT-3—Analog channel: 2. On air date: Mar 12, 1971. 95 University Ave., St. John's, NF A1B 1Z4. Phone: (709) 576-5000. Fax: (709) 576-5155. Licensee: CBC. Network: Network: CBC, CBC Radio One.

Botwood

CBNAT—Analog channel: 11. On air date: Dec 21, 1967. 95 University Ave., St. John's, NF A1B 1Z4. Phone: (709) 576-5000. Fax: (709) 576-5155. Web Site: www.cbc.ca/nl. Licensee: CBC. Network: CBC. News staff: one.

Corner Brook

CJWN-TV—Analog channel: 10. On air date: December 1974. Box 2020, NTV Studio Bldg., 446 Logy Bay Rd., St. John's, NF A1C 5S2. Phone: (709) 722-5015. Fax: (709) 726-5107. Web Site: www.ntv.ca. Licensee: Newfoundland Broadcasting Co. Ltd. Group owner: (group owner) Network: CTV.

Grand Bank

CJOX-TV-1—Analog channel: 2. On air date: 1972. Box 2020, NTV Studio Bldg., 446 Logy Bay Rd., St. John's, NF A1C 5S2. Phone: (709) 722-5015. Fax: (709) 726-5107. E-mail: ntv@ntv.ca. Web Site: www.ntv.ca. Licensee: Newfoundland Broadcasting Co. Ltd. Group owner: (group owner) Network: CTV. News staff: 12; News: 11 hrs wkly.

Grand Falls

CJCN-TV—Analog channel: 4. On air date: 1963. Box 2020, NTV Studio Bldg., 446 Logy Bay Rd., St. John's, NF A1C 5S2. Phone: (709) 722-5015. Fax: (709) 726-5107. Web Site: www.nvt.ca. Licensee: Newfoundland Broadcasting Co. Ltd. Group owner: (group owner) Network: CTV. News staff: 12; News: 11 hrs wkly.
Key Personnel:
Scott Stirling .... pres
Jim Furlong .... news dir

Labrador City

*****CBNLT**—Analog channel: 13. On air date: Nov 7, 1973. 95 University Ave., St. John's, NF A1B 1Z4. Phone: (709) 576-5000. Fax: (709) 576-5155. Web Site: www.cbc.ca/nl. Licensee: CBC. Network: CBC. News staff: one.

Northwest Territories

Marystown

CBNT-3—Analog channel: 5. On air date: Nov 30, 1965. Box 12010, c/o CBNT, 95 University Ave., St. John's, NF A1B 3T8. Phone: (709) 576-5000. Fax: (709) 576-5099. Licensee: Canadian Broadcasting Corp. Network: CBC.
Key Personnel:
Diane Humber . . . . gen mgr
Keith Durnford . . . . engrg mgr & chief of engrg

Mount St. Margaret

CBNAT-9—Analog channel: 9. On air date: Nov 30, 1973. 95 University Ave., St. John's, NF A1B 1Z4. Phone: (709) 576-5000. Fax: (709) 576-5155. Web Site: www.cbc.ca/nl. Licensee: CBC. Network: CBC.

Placentia

CBNT-2—Analog channel: 12. On air date: Nov 27, 1965. Box 12010, c/o CBNT, 95 University Ave., St. John's, NF A1B 3T8. Phone: (709) 576-5000. Fax: (709) 576-5099. Licensee: Canadian Broadcasting Corp. Network: CBC.
Key Personnel:
Diane Humber . . . . gen mgr
Keith Durnford . . . . engrg mgr & chief of engrg

Port Rexton

CBNT-1—Analog channel: 13. On air date: October 1964. Box 12010, c/o CBNT, 95 University Ave., St. John's, NF A1B 3T8. Phone: (709) 576-5000. Fax: (709) 576-5099. Fax: (709) 576-5144. Licensee: Canadian Broadcasting Corp. Network: CBC.
Key Personnel:
Diane Humber . . . . gen mgr
Keith Durnford . . . . chief of engrg

Saint Anthony

CBNAT-4—Analog channel: 6. On air date: Oct 21, 1968. 95 University Ave., St. John's, NF A1B 1Z4. Phone: (709) 576-5000. Fax: (709) 576-5155. Web Site: www.cbc.ca/nl. Licensee: CBC. Network: CBC.

Saint John's

CBNT—Analog channel: 8. On air date: 1964. Box 12010, Stn A, Saint John's, NF A1B 3T8. 95 University Ave., Saint John's, NF A1B 1Z4. Phone: (709) 576-5000. Fax: (709) 576-5155. Web Site: www.cbc.ca/nl. Licensee: CBC. Network: CBC.

St John's

CJON-TV—Analog channel: 6. On air date: September 1955. Box 2020, 446 Logy Bay Rd., St John's, NF A1C 5S2. Phone: (709) 722-5015. Fax: (709) 576-5107. E-mail: ntv@ntv.ca. Web Site: www.ntv.ca. Licensee: Newfoundland Broadcasting Co. Ltd. Group owner: (group owner) Network: CTV.Ottawa Atty: . Ottawa atty: Johnston & Buchan News staff: 12; News: 11 hrs wkly.

Stephenville

CJSV-TV—Analog channel: 4. On air date: 1973. Box 2020, NTV Studio Bldg., 446 Logy Bay Rd., St. John's, NF A1C 5S2. Phone: (709) 722-5015. Fax: (709) 726-5107. Web Site: www.ntv.ca. Licensee: Newfoundland Broadcasting Co. Ltd. Group owner: (group owner) Network: CTV. News staff: 12; News: 11 hrs wkly.
Key Personnel:
Scott Stirling . . . . pres
Jim Furlong . . . . news dir

Northwest Territories

Inuvik

*CHAK-TV—Analog channel: 6. Bag Service No. 8, 155 Mackenzie Rd., Inuvik, NT X0E OTO. Phone: (867) 777-7600. Phone: (867) 920-5400. Fax: (867) 777-7640. Licensee: CBC. Network: CBC. News staff: 2.

Yellowknife

*CFYK-TV—Analog channel: 8. On air date: 1968. Box 160, Yellowknife, NT X1A2N2. Canada. 5002 Forest Dr., Yellowknife, NT X1A2N2.Canada Phone: (867) 920-5400. Fax: (867) 920-5489. E-mail: mike-linder@cbc.ca. Web Site: www.cbcnorth.ca. Licensee: CBC. Network: CBC.

Nova Scotia

Antigonish

CJCB-TV-2—Analog channel: 9. c/o CJCB-TV, 1283 George St., Sydney, NS B1P 1N7. Phone: (902) 562-5511. Fax: (902) 562-9714. E-mail: cjcb@ctv.ca. Web Site: www.ctv.ca. Licensee: ATV Cape Breton. Network: CTV.
Key Personnel:
Glenn McLanders . . . . gen mgr & stn mgr
Edgar Bennett . . . . engrg dir

Caledonia

CJCH-TV-6—Analog channel: 6. 2885 Robie St., Halifax, NS B3K 5Z4. 2885 Robie St., Halifax, NS B3J 2Z4. Phone: (902) 453-4000. Fax: (902) 454-3202. E-mail: cjch@ctv.ca. Web Site: www.ctv.ca. Licensee: CTV Television Inc. Group owner: Baton Broadcasting Inc. Network: CTV.

Canning

CJCH-TV-1—Analog channel: 10. 2885 Robie St., 2885 Robie St., Halifax, NS B3K 5Z4. Phone: (902) 453-4000. Fax: (902) 454-3302. E-mail: cjch@ctv.ca. Web Site: www.ctv.ca. Licensee: Atlantic Television System. Group owner: CTV Television Inc. Network: CTV.
Key Personnel:
Michael Elgie . . . . gen mgr
Ian MacArthur . . . . gen sls mgr
Jane Hefler . . . . progmg mgr
Jay Witherbee . . . . news dir
Gary Robertson . . . . chief of engrg

Cheticamp

CBHFT-4—Analog channel: 10. Box 950, c/o CBAFT, Moncton, NB E1C 8N8. Canada. Phone: (506) 853-6666. Fax: (506) 853-6729. Web Site: www.cbc.ca. Licensee: Societe Radio-Canada.. Ownership: Crown Corp. Network: Radio Canada.

CBIT-2—Analog channel: 2. c/o CBIT, 285 Alexandra St., Sydney, NS B1S 2E8. Phone: (902) 539-5050. Fax: (902) 539-1562. E-mail: frank_king@cbc.ca. Licensee: CBC. Network: CBC.

Halifax

CBHFT—Analog channel: 13. On air date: 1971. Box 950, c/o CBAFT, Moncton, NB E1C 8N8. Canada. Phone: (506) 853-6666. Fax: (506) 853-6739. Web Site: www.cbc.ca. Licensee: Societe Radio-Canada. Network: CBC.

CBHT—Analog channel: 3. On air date: 1954. Box 3000, 1840 Bell Rd., Halifax, NS B3J 3E9. Phone: (902) 420-8311. Fax: (902) 420-4010. Web Site: www.halofax.cbc.ca. Licensee: CBC. Network: CBC.
Key Personnel:

Ron Crocker . . . . gen mgr
Lenny Jackson . . . . opns mgr
Penny Longley . . . . dev mgr
John Channing . . . . rgnl sls mgr

CIHF-TV—Analog channel: 8. On air date: Sept 5, 1988. 14 Akerley Blvd., Dartmouth, NS B3B 1J3. A-500, One Brunswick Sq., Saint John, NB E2L 4B1.Canada Phone: (902) 481-7400. Phone: (506) 632-3400. Fax: (902) 468-2154. Web Site: www.canada.com. Licensee: Global Communications Ltd. Group owner: CanWest Global System (acq 8-29-94; $11 million). News staff: 40; News: 17 hrs wkly.
Key Personnel:
Rick Camilleri . . . . CEO
Leonard Asper . . . . chmn
John Burgis . . . . CFO
Barry Saunders . . . . gen mgr

CJCH-TV—Analog channel: 9. On air date: Jan 1, 1961. Box 1653, Halifax, NS B3J 2Z4. 2885 Robie St., Halifax, NS B3J 2Z4. Phone: (902) 453-4000. Fax: (902) 454-3302. Fax: (902) 454-3202. Web Site: www.ctv.ca. Licensee: CTV Television Inc. Group owner: CTV Inc. Network: CTV.
Key Personnel:
Michael Elgie . . . . VP & gen mgr
Ian MacArthur . . . . gen sls mgr
Renee Fournier . . . . mktg mgr
Jane Hefler . . . . progmg mgr
Jay Witherbee . . . . news dir
Gary Robertson . . . . chief of engrg

Inverness

CJCB-TV-1—Analog channel: 6. c/o CJCB-TV, 1283 George St., Sydney, NS B1P 1N7. Phone: (902) 562-5511. Fax: (902) 562-9714. E-mail: cjcb@ctv.ca. Web Site: www.ctv.ca. Licensee: ATV Cape Breton. Network: CTV.

Isle Madame

CIMC-TV—Analog channel: 10. On air date: June 2003. Box 87, Arichat, NS B0E 1A0. 705 Lower Rd., Arichat, NS B0E 1A0. Phone: (902) 226-1928. Fax: (902) 226-1331. E-mail: telile@ns.sympatico.ca. Web Site: www.telile.tv. Licensee: Telile:Isle Madame Community Television Association/Association Television Communautaire de l'Ile Madame.

Mulgrave

CBHFT-2—Analog channel: 7. Box 590, c/o CBAFT, Moncton, NB E1C 8N8. Canada. Phone: (506) 853-6666. Fax: (506) 867-8031. Web Site: www.cbc.ca. Licensee: CBC. Network: CBC.

CBHT-11—Analog channel: 12. Box 3000, c/o CBHT, 5600 Sackville St., Halifax, NS B3J 3E9. 1840 Bell Rd., Halifax, NS B3H 2Z5. Phone: (902) 420-8311. Fax: (902) 420-4010. Licensee: CBC. Network: CBC.
Key Personnel:
Penny Longley . . . . dev mgr
John Channing . . . . rgnl sls mgr
Ron Crocker . . . . gen mgr & engrg mgr

Sheet Harbour

CBHT-4—Analog channel: 11. Box 3000, c/o CBHT, 5600 Sackville St., Halifax, NS B3J 3E9. 1840 Bell Rd., Halifax, NS B3H 2Z5.Canada Phone: (902) 420-8311. Fax: (902) 420-4137. E-mail: canadanowns @halifax.cbc.cca. Web Site: www.halifax.cbc.ca. Licensee: CBC. Network: CBC.

Sydney

CBHFT-3—Analog channel: 13. Box 950, c/o CBAFT, Moncton, NB E1C 8N8. Canada. Phone: (506) 853-6666. Fax: (506) 867-8031. Web Site: www.cbc.ca. Licensee: CBC. Network: CBC.

CBIT—Analog channel: 5. On air date: 1972. 285 Alexandra St., Sydney, NS B1S 2E8. Phone: (902) 539-5050. Fax: (902) 539-1562. E-mail: frank_king@cbc.ca. Licensee: CBC. Network: CBC.

CJCB-TV—Analog channel: 4. On air date: 1954. 1283 George St., Sydney, NS B1P 1N7. Phone: (902) 562-5511. Fax: (902) 562-9714.

Directory of Television

Ontario

E-mail: cjcb@ctv.ca. Web Site: www.ctv.ca. Licensee: ATV Cape Breton. Group owner: CTV Inc. Network: CTV.
Key Personnel:
Glenn McLanders . . . . gen mgr & gen sls mgr
Gary Robinson . . . . opns dir
Renee Fournier . . . . mktg mgr & prom mgr
Jane Hefler . . . . progmg mgr
Jay Witherbee . . . . news dir
Edgar Bennett . . . . chief of engrg

Yarmouth

CBHFT-1—Analog channel: 3. Box 950, c/o CBAFT, Moncton, NB E1C 8N8. Canada. Phone: (506) 853-6666. Fax: (506) 867-8031. Web Site: www.cbc.ca. Licensee: CBC. Network: Radio Canada.

CBHT-3—Analog channel: 11. Box 3000, c/o CBHT, 5600 Sackville St., Halifax, NS B3J 3E9. Phone: (902) 420-8311. Fax: (902) 420-4010. Web Site: www.halifax.cbc.ca. Licensee: CBC. Network: CBC.
Key Personnel:
Ron Crocker . . . . gen mgr
Lenny Jackson . . . . chief of opns
Penny Longley . . . . dev mgr
John Channing . . . . rgnl sls mgr

Ontario

Bancroft

CIII-TV-2—Analog channel: 2. On air date: January 1974. 81 Barber Greene Rd., Toronto, ON M3C 2A2. Phone: (416) 446-5311. Fax: (416) 446-5447. E-mail: newstips@globaltv.com. Web Site: www.canada.ca. Licensee: Global Communications Ltd., div. of CanWest Global Systems. Group owner: Global Television Network. Network: Global.
Key Personnel:
Bill Hunt . . . . gen mgr
Ed Holmes . . . . opns dir

Barrie

CKVR-TV—Analog channel: 3. On air date: Sept 28, 1955. Box 519, Barrie, ON L4M 4T9. 33 Beacon St., Barrie, ON L4M 4S7. Phone: (705) 734-3300. Fax: (705) 733-0302. Fax: (705) 734-2061. E-mail: thenewvr@thenewvr.com. Web Site: www.achannel.ca. Licensee: CKVR Ch 3, division of CHUM Ltd. Group owner: CHUM Ltd. News staff: 30; News: 14 hrs wkly.
Key Personnel:
Allan Waters . . . . pres
Doug Garraway . . . . VP & gen mgr
Bob McLaughlin . . . . opns mgr & news dir
Allan Schwebel . . . . sls VP & mktg VP
Paul Woodhouse . . . . sls dir
Dan Hamilton . . . . gen sls mgr
Hugh Black . . . . mktg dir, prom dir & prom mgr
Quincy Raby . . . . mktg mgr
Peggy Hebden . . . . progmg dir & film buyer
Brian Cathline . . . . chief of engrg

Chatham

***CICO-TV-59**—Analog channel: 59. On air date: June 1976. Box 200 Stn Q, c/o TV Ontario, Toronto, ON M4T 2T1. 2180 Yonge St., Toronto, ON M4S 2B9. Phone: (416) 484-2600. Fax: (416) 484-6285. E-mail: asktvo@tvo.org. Web Site: www.tvo.org. Licensee: Ontario Educational Communications Authority.
Key Personnel:
Lee Robock . . . . COO & gen mgr
Isabel Bassett . . . . pres
Ray Newell . . . . opns dir
Anne Cochran . . . . mktg dir

Cornwall

CJOH-TV-8—Analog channel: 8. On air date: 1958. 1500 Merivale Rd., Ottawa, ON K2E 6Z5. Phone: (613) 224-1313. Fax: (613) 274-4215. E-mail: cjoh@ctv.com. Web Site: www.cjoh.ca. Licensee: CTV Television Inc. Group owner: (group owner) Network: CTV.
Key Personnel:
Louis Douville . . . . VP & gen mgr
Art Clarke . . . . opns mgr
Brent Corbeil . . . . sls dir & prom mgr

Dan Champagne . . . . gen sls mgr
Scott Hannant . . . . news dir

Deseronto

CJOH-TV-6—Analog channel: 6. On air date: September 1972. Box 5813, Merivale Depot, Ottawa, ON K2C 3G6. Phone: (613) 224-1313. Fax: (613) 274-4215. E-mail: cjoh@ctv.ca. Web Site: www.cjoh.com. Licensee: CTV Television Inc. Group owner: CTV Inc. Network: CTV.
Key Personnel:
Louis Douville . . . . VP & gen mgr
Art Clarke . . . . opns mgr
Delma Devoe . . . . dev mgr
Dan Champagne . . . . gen sls mgr
Brent Corbeil . . . . prom mgr
Scott Honnant . . . . news dir

Dryden

CBWDT—Analog channel: 9. Box 500, Stn A, Toronto, ON M5W 1E6. Phone: (416) 205-3311. Web Site: www.cbc.ca. Licensee: CBC. Network: CBC.

Elliot Lake

CBLFT-6—Analog channel: 12. Box 3220, Stn C, Ottawa, ON K1Y 1E4. Phone: (613) 288-6000. Fax: (416) 205-3628. Web Site: www.cbc.ca. Licensee: Canadian Broadcasting Corp. Network: CBC.

CICI-TV-1—Analog channel: 5. On air date: 1958. c/o MC-TV, 699 Frood Rd., Sudbury, ON P3C 5A3. Phone: (705) 674-8301. Fax: (705) 674-2789. Web Site: www.ctv.ca. Licensee: CTV Television Inc. Group owner: Baton Broadcasting Inc. Network: CTV. News staff: 15; News: 10 hrs wkly.
Key Personnel:
Scott Lund . . . . VP & gen mgr
John Eddy . . . . opns mgr
Wendy Watson . . . . gen sls mgr
Don Chapman . . . . news dir
John Ledingham . . . . engrg mgr

Geraldton

CBLAT—Analog channel: 13. Box 500, Stn A, c/o CBLT, Toronto, ON M5W 1E6. Phone: (416) 205-3311. Web Site: www.cbc.ca. Licensee: CBC. Network: CBC.

Hamilton

CHCH-TV—Analog channel: 11. Digital channel: 18. On air date: June 4, 1954. Box 2230, Stn. A, 163 Jackson St. W., Hamilton, ON L8N 3A6. Phone: (905) 522-1101. Fax: (905) 523-8778. E-mail: news@chtv.ca. Web Site: www.chtv.com. Licensee: Global Communications Ltd. Group owner: CanWest Global Communications Corp. (acq 7-6-00). Network: Global.

CITS-TV—Analog channel: 36. Digital channel: 35. On air date: Sept 30, 1998. 1295 N. Service Rd., Burlington, ON L7R 4X5. Phone: (905) 331-7333. Fax: (905) 332-6005. E-mail: cts@ctstv.com. Web Site: www.ctstv.com. Licensee: Crossroads Television System.
Key Personnel:
Fred Vanstone . . . . chmn
Dick Gray . . . . pres
Terry Maskel . . . . opns mgr
Glenn Stewart . . . . gen sls mgr
Michelle Gillies . . . . prom mgr
Rob Sheppard . . . . progmg mgr

Hearst

CBLFT-5—Analog channel: 7. Box 3220, Stn C, Ottawa, ON K1Y 1E4. Phone: (613) 288-6000. Fax: (416) 205-3628. Web Site: www.cbc.ca. Licensee: Canadian Broadcasting Corp. Network: Radio Canada.

Kapuskasing

CBLFT-4—Analog channel: 12. Box 3220, Stn C, Ottawa, ON K1Y 1E4. Phone: (613) 288-6000. Fax: (416) 205-3628. Web Site: www.cbc.ca. Licensee: Canadian Broadcasting Corp.

Kearns

CITO-TV-2—Analog channel: 11. Box 620, c/o MCTV-CTV, 681 Pine St. N., Timmins, ON P4N 7G3. Phone: (705) 264-4211. Fax: (705) 264-3266. Licensee: CTV Television Inc. Group owner: CTV Inc. Network: CTV.
Key Personnel:
Scott Lund . . . . gen mgr & stn mgr
Jason Laneville . . . . sls dir

Kenora

CBWAT—Analog channel: 8. c/o CBC, 541 Portage Ave, Winnipeg, MB R3B 2G1. Canada. Phone: (204) 788-3222. Fax: (204) 788-3643. Web Site: www.winnipeg.cbc.ca. Licensee: CBC. Network: CBC.

CJBN-TV—Analog channel: 13. On air date: April 1983. 102 Tenth St., Keewatin, ON P0X 1C0. 104 Tenth St., Keewatin, ON P9N 3X8. Phone: (807) 547-2852. Fax: (807) 547-2348. E-mail: darrylm@norcomcable.ca. Web Site: www.norcomcable.ca. Licensee: Norcom Telecommunications Ltd. Network: CTV. Rep: Brydson. News staff: 2; News: one hr wkly.
Key Personnel:
Warren Ritchie . . . . gen mgr
Darryl Michaluk . . . natl sls mgr, mktg dir, prom dir & progmg dir

Kingston

CKWS-TV—Analog channel: 11. On air date: 1954. 170 Queen St., Kingston, ON K7K 1B2. Phone: (613) 544-2340. Fax: (613) 544-5508. E-mail: news@ckwstv.com. Web Site: www.ckwstv.com. Licensee: 591987 B.C. Ltd. Group owner: Corus Entertainment Inc. (acq 3-24-00; grpsl). Network: CBC. News: 12 hrs wkly.
Key Personnel:
Tom Brennan . . . . gen mgr & stn mgr
John Tucker . . . . sls VP & sls dir
Michael Lavelle . . . . gen sls mgr
Tracy Baker . . . . prom dir
Kelly Wiley . . . . prom mgr
Rob McDonald . . . . news dir
Larry Cameron . . . . engrg VP

Kitchener

***CICO-TV-28**—Analog channel: 28. On air date: January 1976. Box 200 c/o TV Ontario, Toronto, ON M4T 2T1. 2180 Yonge St., Toronto, ON M4S 2P9. Phone: (416) 484-2600. Fax: (416) 484-6285. E-mail: asktvo@tvo.org. Web Site: www.tvo.org. Licensee: Ontario Educational Communications Authority.

CKCO-TV—Analog channel: 13. On air date: Mar 1, 1954. Box 91026, 864 King St. W., Kitchener, ON N2G 4E9. Phone: (519) 578-1313. Fax: (519) 743-0730 (news). Licensee: CKCO-TV Division of CTV Inc. Group owner: CTV Inc. (acq 8-31-97). Network: CTV.
Key Personnel:
Ivan Fecan . . . . CEO
Robin Fillingham . . . . CFO
Dennis Watson . . . . VP & gen mgr
Dave MacNeill . . . . opns dir
Cameron Crassweller . . . . rgnl sls mgr
Janet Taylor . . . . prom mgr, adv mgr, progmg mgr & pub affrs dir
Larry Rose . . . . news dir
Dave Melse . . . . chief of engrg

London

CFPL-TV—Analog channel: 10. On air date: Nov 28, 1953. Box 5810, London, ON N6A 6E9. 1 Communications Road, London, ON N6A 6E9. Phone: (519) 686-8810. Fax: (519) 668-3288. E-mail: newsnow@thenewpl.com. Web Site: www.achannel.ca. Licensee: CHUM Television. Group owner: CHUM Ltd. (acq 1997).

***CICO-TV-18**—Analog channel: 18. On air date: April 1976. Box 200 Stn Q, c/o TV Ontario, Toronto, ON M4T 2T1. 2180 Yonge St., Toronto, ON M4S 2B9. Phone: (416) 484-2600. Fax: (416) 484-6285. E-mail: asktvo@tvo.org. Web Site: www.tvo.org. Licensee: Ontario Educational Communications Authority.
Key Personnel:
Isabel Bassett . . . . pres
Lee Robock . . . . gen mgr
Ray Newell . . . . opns dir
Anne Cochran . . . . mktg dir

Broadcasting & Cable Yearbook 2006

Manitouwadge

CBLAT-1—Analog channel: 8. Box 500, Stn A, c/o CBLT, Toronto, ON M5W 1E6. Phone: (416) 205-3311. Fax: (416) 205-7166. Web Site: www.cbc.ca. Licensee: Canadian Broadcasting Corp. Network: CBC.

Marathon

CBLAT-4—Analog channel: 11. On air date: May 16, 1968. Box 500, Stn A, c/o CBLT, Toronto, ON M5W 1E6. Phone: (416) 205-3311. Fax: (416) 205-2552. Web Site: www.cbc.ca. Licensee: Canadian Broadcasting Corp. Network: CBC.

Midland

CIII-TV-7—Analog channel: 7. On air date: Nov 24, 1987. 81 Barber Greene Rd., Toronto, ON M3C 2A2. Phone: (416) 446-5477. Fax: (416) 446-5502. E-mail: newstips@globaltv.com. Web Site: www.canada.com. Licensee: Global Communications Ltd., div. of CanWest Global System. Group owner: Global Television Network
Key Personnel:
Bill Hunt . . . . gen mgr
Ed Holmes . . . . opns dir

North Bay

CKNY-TV—Analog channel: 10. On air date: October 1981. 245 Oak St. E., North Bay, ON P1B 8P8. Phone: (705) 476-3111. Fax: (705) 495-4474. Fax: (705) 495-0922 (news). E-mail: northbaynews@ctv.ca. Web Site: www.ctv.ca. Licensee: CTV Television Inc. Group owner: CTV Inc. (acq 1991). Network: CTV. News: 10 hrs wkly.
Key Personnel:
Scott Lund . . . . pres & gen mgr
Ron Driscoll . . . . gen sls mgr

Oil Springs

CIII-TV-29—Analog channel: 29. On air date: Jan 6, 1974. 81 Barber Greene Rd., Toronto, ON M3C 2A2. Phone: (416) 446-5311. Fax: (416) 446-5447. E-mail: newstips@globaltv.com. Web Site: www.canada.com. Licensee: Global Communications, div. of CanWest Global Systems. Group owner: Global Television Network
Key Personnel:
Bill Hunt . . . . gen mgr
Ed Holmes . . . . opns dir
Mark Walewski . . . . chief of engrg

Oshawa

CHEX-TV-2—Analog channel: 22. On air date: 1993. 743 Monaghan Rd., Peterborough, ON K9J 5K2. Phone: (705) 742-0451. Fax: (705) 742-7274. Licensee: 591987 B.C. Ltd. Group owner: Corus Entertainment Inc. (acq 3-24-00; grpsl). Network: CBC.

Ottawa

CBOFT—Analog channel: 9. Box 3220, Stn C, Ottawa, ON K1Y 1E4. Ottawa Broadcast Centre, 181 Queen St., Ottawa, ON K1P 1K9. Phone: (613) 288-6000. Phone: (613) 288-6750. Fax: (613) 288-6770. E-mail: tjottawa-gatincau@radio-canada.ca. Web Site: www/radio-canada.ca. Licensee: CBC. Network: Radio Canada.

CBOT—Analog channel: 4. On air date: 1953. Box 3220, Stn C, Ottawa, ON K1Y 1E4. Ottawa Broadcast Centre, 181 Queen St., Ottawa, ON K1P 1K9. Phone: (613) 288-6000. Phone: (613) 288-6445. Fax: (613) 288-6423. E-mail: canadanow@attawa.cbc.ca. Web Site: www.cbc.ca. Licensee: CBC. Network: CBC.

*CICO-TV-24—Analog channel: 24. On air date: Oct 17, 1975. Box 200, c/o TV Ontario, Toronto, ON M4T 2T1. 2180 Yonge St., Toronto, ON M4S 2B9. Phone: (416) 484-2600. Fax: (416) 484-6285. E-mail: asktvo@tvo.org. Web Site: www.tvo.org. Licensee: Ontario Educational Communications Authority.

CIII-TV-6—Analog channel: 6. On air date: Jan 6, 1974. 81 Barber Greene Rd., Toronto, ON M3C 2A2. Phone: (416) 446-5311. Fax: (416)446-5447. E-mail: newstips@globaltv.com. Web Site: www.canada.com. Licensee: Global Communications Ltd., div. of CanWest Global System. Group owner: Global Television Network (acq 3-22-77).
Key Personnel:
Bill Hunt . . . . gen mgr & engrg dir
Ed Holmes . . . . opns dir
Mark Walewski . . . . chief of engrg

CJOH-TV—Analog channel: 13. On air date: March 1961. Box 5813, Merivale Depot, Ottawa, ON K2C 3G6. 1500 Merivale Rd., Nepean, ON K2E 6Z5. Phone: (613) 224-1313. Fax: (613) 274-4215. E-mail: cjoh@ctv.ca. Web Site: www.cjoh.ca. Licensee: CTV Television Inc. Group owner: (group owner) Network: CTV. Rep: Canadian Broadcast Sales.
Key Personnel:
Louis Douville . . . . VP & gen mgr
Art Clarke . . . . opns mgr
Dan Champagne . . . . sls VP & gen sls mgr
Brent Corbeil . . . . prom mgr
Scott Hannant . . . . news dir

Owen Sound

CIII-TV-4—Analog channel: 4. On air date: June 27, 1988. 81 Barber Greene Rd., Toronto, ON M3C 2A2. Phone: (416) 446-5311. Fax: (416) 446-5447. E-mail: newstips@globaltv.com. Web Site: www.canada.com. Licensee: Global Communications, div. of CanWest Global System. Group owner: Global Television Network
Key Personnel:
Bill Hunt . . . . gen mgr
Ed Holmes . . . . opns dir

Pembroke

CHRO-TV—Analog channel: 5. On air date: 1961. Box 1010, Pembroke, ON K8A 6Y6. 87 George St., Ottawa, ON K1N 9H7. Phone: (613) 789-0606. Phone: (613) 735-1036. Fax: (613) 789-6590. E-mail: comments@thenewro.com. Web Site: www.thenewro.com. Licensee: CHUM Ltd. Group owner: (group owner; acq 1997). Rep: Integrated Media Sales. News: 30 hrs wkly.
Key Personnel:
Nigel Fuller . . . . VP & gen mgr
Greg Orr . . . . gen sls mgr
Elizabeth Davis . . . . news dir
Robert Edgley . . . . chief of engrg

Peterborough

CHEX-TV—Analog channel: 12. On air date: 1955. 743 Monaghan Rd., Peterborough, ON K9J 5K2. Phone: (705) 742-0451. Fax: (705) 742-7274. Licensee: 5191987 B.C. Ltd. Group owner: Corus Entertainment Inc. (acq 3-24-00; grpsl). Network: CBC. Rep: TeleRep.
Key Personnel:
John Cassaday . . . . CEO
Ron Johnston . . . . gen mgr & stn mgr
Paul Burke . . . . opns mgr

CIII-TV-27—Analog channel: 27. On air date: Oct 5, 1988. 81 Barber Greene Rd., Toronto, ON M3C 2A2. Phone: (416) 446-5311. Fax: (416) 446-5431. Web Site: www.globaltv.com. Licensee: Global Communications, div of CanWest Global System. Group owner: Global Television Network.

Sarnia

CKCO-TV-3—Analog channel: 42. On air date: November 1975. Box 91026, c/o CKCO-TV, 864 King St. W., Kitchener, ON N2G 4E9. Phone: (519) 578-1313. Fax: (519) 743-0730. Licensee: CKCO-TV Division of CTV Inc. Group owner: CTV Inc. (acq 8-31-97).
Key Personnel:
Ivan Fecan . . . . CEO
Dennis A. Watson . . . . VP
Dennis Watson . . . . gen mgr
Dave MacNeill . . . . opns dir
Cameron Crassweller . . . . rgnl sls mgr
Janet Taylor . . . . prom mgr, adv mgr, progmg mgr & pub affrs dir
Larry Rose . . . . news dir
Dave Melse . . . . chief of engrg

Sault Ste. Marie

CHBX-TV—Analog channel: 2. On air date: September 1978. 119 East St., Sault Ste. Marie, ON P6A 3C7. Phone: (705) 759-8232. Fax: (705) 759-7783. E-mail: saultnews@ctv.ca. Web Site: www.ctv.ca. Licensee: CTV Television Inc. Group owner: (group owner) Network: CTV. Rep: Canadian Broadcast Sales.

*CICO-TV-20—Analog channel: 20. On air date: October 1978. Box 200, c/o TV Ontario, Toronto, ON M4T 2T1. 2180 Yonge St., Toronto, ON M4S 2B9. Phone: (416) 484-2600. Fax: (416) 484-6285. E-mail: asktvo@tvo.org. Web Site: www.tvo.org. Licensee: Ontario Educational Communications Authority. Group owner: Baton Broadcasting Inc.

Stevenson

CIII-TV-22—Analog channel: 22. On air date: 1974. 81 Barber Greene Rd., Toronto, ON M3C 2A2. Phone: (416) 446-5311. Fax: (416) 446-5447. E-mail: newstips@globaltv.com. Web Site: www.canada.com/toronto/globaltv. Licensee: Global Communications Ltd. Group owner: Global Television Network. Network: Global. Rep: CanWest Media Sales Inc..
Key Personnel:
Bill Hunt . . . . gen mgr
Ed Holmes . . . . opns dir

Sturgeon Falls

CBLFT-1—Analog channel: 7. Box 3220, Stn C, Ottawa, ON K1Y 1E4. Phone: (613) 288-6000. Fax: (416) 205-3628. Web Site: www.cbc.ca. Licensee: Canadian Broadcasting Corp. Network: Radio Canada.

Sudbury

CBLFT-2—Analog channel: 13. Box 3220, Stn C, Ottawa, ON K1Y 1E4. Phone: (613) 288-6000. Fax: (416) 205-3628. Web Site: www.cbc.ca. Licensee: Canadian Broadcasting Corp. Network: Radio Canada.

CICI-TV—Analog channel: 5. On air date: Oct 25, 1953. 699 Frood Rd., Sudbury, ON P3C 5A3. Phone: (705) 674-8301. Fax: (705) 674-2706. Web Site: www.ctv.ca. Licensee: CTV Television Inc. Group owner: (group owner; (acq 4-1-80). Network: CTV. News staff: 15; News: 10 hrs wkly.
Key Personnel:
Scott Lund . . . . VP & gen mgr
John Eddy . . . . opns mgr

*CICO-TV-19—Analog channel: 19. On air date: June 30, 1978. Box 200 Stn Q, c/o TV Ontario, Toronto, ON M4T 2T1. 2180 Yonge St., Toronto, ON M4S 2B9. Phone: (416) 484-2600. Fax: (416) 484-6285. E-mail: asktvo@tvo.org. Web Site: www.tvo.org. Licensee: Ontario Educational Communications Authority.
Key Personnel:
Isabel Bassett . . . . pres
Lee Robock . . . . gen mgr
Ray Newell . . . . opns dir

Thunder Bay

CHFD-TV—Analog channel: 4. On air date: 1972. 87 N. Hill St., Thunder Bay, ON P7A 5V6. Phone: (807) 346-2600. Fax: (807) 345-9923. E-mail: tbtv@tbtv.com. Web Site: tbtv.com. Licensee: Thunder Bay Electronics Ltd.. Ownership: H.F. Dougall, Esq., 100%. Network: CTV.
Key Personnel:
H.F. Dougall . . . . pres
Don Caron . . . . CFO
Ann Snell . . . . opns dir
Miller Labelle . . . . progmg dir

*CICO-TV-9—Analog channel: 9. On air date: June 1978. Box 200 Stn Q, c/o TV Ontario, Toronto, ON M4TT 2T1. 2180 Yonge St., Toronto, ON M4S 2B9. Phone: (416) 484-2600. Phone: (416) 484-2654. Fax: (416) 484-6285. E-mail: asktvo@tvo.org. Web Site: www.tvo.org. Licensee: Ontario Educational Communications Authority.
Key Personnel:
Lee Robock . . . . COO
Isabel Bassett . . . . pres
Lee Rogock . . . . gen mgr
Ray Newell . . . . opns dir
Anne Cochran . . . . mktg dir

CKPR-TV—Analog channel: 2. On air date: 1954. 87 N. Hill St., Thunder Bay, ON P7A 5V6. Phone: (807) 346-2600. Fax: (807) 345-9923. E-mail: tbt@tbtv.com. Web Site: www.tbtv.com. Licensee: Thunder Bay Electronics Ltd.. Ownership: H.F. Dougall, Esq., 100%. Network: CBC. News: 11 hrs wkly.
Key Personnel:
H.F. Dougall . . . . pres

Ann Snell . . . . . opns dir & news dir
M.E. LaBelle . . . . . progmg dir

Timmins

CBLFT-3—Analog channel: 9. Box 3220, Stn C, Ottawa, ON K1Y 1E4. Phone: (613) 288-6000. Fax: (416) 205-3628. Web Site: www.cbc.ca. Licensee: CBC.

CITO-TV—Analog channel: 3. Box 620, 681 Pine St. N., Timmins, ON P4N 7G3. Phone: (705) 264-4211. Fax: (705) 264-3266. E-mail: newsroom@ctv.ca. Web Site: www.ctv.ca. Licensee: CTV Television Inc. Group owner: CTV Inc. Network: CTV.

Toronto

CBLFT—Analog channel: 25. Digital channel: 24. On air date: Mar 23, 1973. Box 3220, Stn C, Ottawa, ON K1Y 1E4. Phone: (613) 288-6000. Fax: (416) 205-3628. Web Site: www.cbc.ca. Licensee: CBC. Network: Radio Canada.

CBLT—Analog channel: 5. Digital channel: 20. On air date: Sept 8, 1952. Box 500, Stn A, Toronto, ON M5W 1E6. 205 Wellington St. W., Somerset, ON M5V 367. Phone: (416) 205-3311. Fax: (416) 205-7166. Web Site: www.cbc.ca. Licensee: CBC. Network: CBC. News staff: 45; News: 10 hrs wkly.

CFMT-TV—Analog channel: 47. On air date: Sept 3, 1979. 545 Lakeshore Blvd. W., Toronto, ON M5V 1A3. Phone: (416) 260-0047. Fax: (416) 260-3621. E-mail: cfmt@rci.rogers.com. Web Site: www.omnitv.ca. Licensee: Rogers Broadcasting Ltd.

CFTO-TV—Analog channel: 9. Digital channel: 40. On air date: Jan 1, 1961. 9 Channel 9 Ct., Scarborough, ON M1S 4B5. Phone: (416) 332-5000. Fax: (416) 332-5022. E-mail: cftonews@ctv,ca. Web Site: www.ctv.ca. Licensee: CTV Television Inc. Group owner: (group owner) Network: CTV.

***CICA-TV**—Analog channel: 19. On air date: Sept 27, 1970. Box 200, Stn Q, c/o TV Ontario, Toronto, ON M4T 2T1. 2180 Yonge St., Toronto, ON M4S 2B9. Phone: (416) 484-2600. Fax: (416) 484-6285. E-mail: asktvo@tvo.org. Web Site: www.tvo.org. Licensee: Ontario Educational Communications Authority.
Key Personnel:
Lee Robock . . . . . COO & gen mgr
Isabel Bassett . . . . . pres
Ray Newell . . . . . opns dir
Anne Cochran . . . . . mktg dir

CIII-TV—(Paris).Analog channel: 6. On air date: Jan 6, 1974. 81 Barber Greene Rd., Toronto, ON M3C 2A2. Phone: (416) 446-5311. Fax: (416) 446-5447. E-mail: newstips@globaltv.com. Web Site: www.canada.com. Licensee: Global Communications Ltd., div. of CanWest Global System. Group owner: Global Television Network (acq 3-22-77). Network: Global.
Key Personnel:
Bill Hunt . . . . . gen mgr
Ed Holmes . . . . . opns dir
Mark Walewski . . . . . chief of engrg

CIII-TV-41—Analog channel: 41. Digital channel: 65. On air date: Oct 22, 1987. 81 Barber Greene Rd., Toronto, ON M3C 2A2. Phone: (416) 446-5311. Fax: (416) 446-5447. E-mail: newstips@globaltv.com. Web Site: www.canada.com. Licensee: Global Communications Ltd. Group owner: Global Television Network
Key Personnel:
Bill Hunt . . . . . gen mgr
Ed Holmes . . . . . opns dir
Mark Walewski . . . . . engr

CITY-TV—Analog channel: 57. Digital channel: 53. On air date: Sept 28, 1972. 299 Queen St. W., Toronto, ON M5V 2Z5. Phone: (416) 591-5757. Fax: (416) 340-7005. Web Site: www.citytv.com. Licensee: CITY-TV, div. of Chum Ltd. Group owner: CHUM Ltd. (acq 1976). News: 25 hrs wkly.
Key Personnel:
Maria Hale . . . . . pres & VP
John Morrison . . . . . opns mgr & gen sls mgr
Dan Hamilton . . . . . sls VP & prom dir
Susan Arthur . . . . . mktg dir
Bev Nenson . . . . . prom dir & prom mgr
Jenny Norush . . . . . adv dir
Ellen Baine . . . . . progmg VP, progmg dir & film buyer
Stephen Hurlbut . . . . . news dir
Sarah Cranford . . . . . pub affrs dir
Bruce Conan . . . . . engrg dir

CJMT-TV—Analog channel: 69. Digital channel: 66. On air date: Sept 16, 2002. 545 Lake Shore Blvd. W., Toronto, ON M5V 1A3. Phone: (416) 260-0060. Fax: (416) 260-3621. E-mail: info@omni2.ca. Web Site: www.omnitv.ca/OMNI2. Licensee: Rogers Broadcasting Ltd. Group owner: (group owner).

CKXT-TV—Analog channel: 52. Digital channel: 66. On air date: Sept 19, 2003. Toronto 1, Craig Media Inc., 25 Ontario St., 2nd Fl., Toronto, ON M5A 4L6. Phone: (416) 601-0010. Fax: (416) 601-0004. E-mail: claudia.dambrough@craigmedia.ca. Web Site: www.toronto1.ca. Licensee: Craig Media Inc. Group owner: (group owner).

Wawa

CBLAT-3—Analog channel: 9. Box 500, c/o CBLT, Stn A, Toronto, ON M5W 1E6. Phone: (416) 205-3311. Web Site: www.cbc.ca. Licensee: Canadian Broadcasting Corp. Network: CBC.

Wiarton

CKCO-TV-2—Analog channel: 2. On air date: June 1, 1971. Box 91026, c/o CKCO-TV, 864 King St. W., Kitchener, ON N2G 4E9. Phone: (519) 578-1313. Fax: (519) 743-0730. Licensee: CKCO-TV Div. of CTV. Group owner: CTV Inc. (acq 8-31-97).
Key Personnel:
Ivan Fecan . . . . . CEO
Dennis Watson . . . . . VP & gen mgr
Dave MacNeill . . . . . opns dir
Cameron Crassweller . . . . . rgnl sls mgr
Janet Taylor . . . prom mgr, adv mgr, progmg mgr & pub affrs dir
Larry Rose . . . . . news dir
Dave Melse . . . . . chief of engrg

Windsor

***CBEFT**—Analog channel: 54. On air date: July 16, 1976. 825 Riverside W., Windsor, ON N9A 5K9. Phone: (519) 255-3411. Fax: (519) 255-3412. Licensee: Societe Radio Canada. Network: Radio Canada.

CBET—Analog channel: 9. On air date: Sept 16, 1954. 825 Riverside Dr. W., Windsor, ON N9A 5K9. Phone: (519) 255-3411. Fax: (519) 255-3412. Licensee: Canadian Broadcasting Corp. (acq 7-23-75). Network: CBC. Rep: Canadian Broadcast Sales. News staff: 18; News: 3 hrs wkly.
Key Personnel:
Janice Stein . . . . . gen mgr & stn mgr
Joanne Hoppe . . . . . opns mgr

CHWI-TV—Analog channel: 16. On air date: Oct 18, 1993. 300 Oullette Ave., Suite 200, Windsor, ON N9A 7B4. Phone: (519) 977-7432. Fax: (519) 977-0564. E-mail: newsnow@thenewwi.com. Web Site: www.achannel.ca. Licensee: CHUM Television. Group owner: CHUM Ltd. (acq 1997).
Key Personnel:
Greg Mudry . . . . . gen mgr
Jim Kippen . . . . . opns mgr

***CICO-TV-32**—Analog channel: 32. On air date: July 1976. Box 200, Stn Q, Toronto, ON M4T 2T1. 2180 Yonge St., Toronto, ON M4S 2B9. Phone: (416) 484-2600. Fax: (416) 484-6285. E-mail: asktvo@tvo.org. Web Site: www.tvo.org. Licensee: Ontario Educational Communication Authority.
Key Personnel:
Isabel Bassett . . . . . pres
Lee Robock . . . . . gen mgr
Ray Newell . . . . . opns dir
Anne Cochran . . . . . mktg dir

Wingham

CKNX-TV—Analog channel: 8. On air date: 1955. 215 Carling Terr., Wingham, ON N0G 2W0. Phone: (519) 357-4438. Fax: (519) 357-4398. E-mail: newsnow@thenewnx.com. Web Site: www.achannel.ca. Licensee: CHUM Television. Group owner: CHUM Ltd. (acq 1997).
Key Personnel:
Greg Mudry . . . . . gen mgr
Jim Kippen . . . . . opns mgr
Tom Fitz-Gerald . . . . . gen sls mgr
Don Mumford . . . . . progmg mgr
Cal Johnstone . . . . . news dir

Prince Edward Island

Charlottetown

CBCT—Analog channel: 13. On air date: 1968. Box 2230, Charlottetown, PE C1A 8B9. 430 University Ave., Charlottetown, PE C1A 8B9. Phone: (902) 629-6400. Fax: (902) 629-6518. Licensee: CBC.. Ownership: CBC (Crown Corp). Network: CBC.
Key Personnel:
Linda Callagham . . . . . gen mgr
Craig Mackie . . . . . stn mgr

CKCW-TV-1—Analog channel: 8. 191 Halifax St., Moncton, NB E1C 9R7. Canada. Phone: (506) 857-2600. Fax: (506) 857-2617. E-mail: ckcw@ctv.ca. Web Site: www.ctv.ca. Licensee: CTV Television Inc. Group owner: CTV Inc. (acq 11-1-97). Network: CTV.
Key Personnel:
Ivan Fecan . . . . . CEO
Rick Brace . . . . . pres
Robin Fillingham . . . . . CFO
Elaine Ali . . . . . exec VP
Mike Elgie . . . . . VP & gen mgr
Brian Lewis . . . . . stn mgr, gen sls mgr & adv mgr
John Silver . . . . . opns mgr
Renee Fournier . . . . . prom dir & prom mgr
Jane Hefler . . . . . progmg dir
Jay Witherbee . . . . . news dir & pub affrs dir
Carson McDavid . . . . . chief of engrg

Saint Edward

CKCW-TV-2—Analog channel: 5. On air date: November 1982. 191 Halifax St., Moncton, NB E1C 9R7. Canada. Phone: (506) 857-2600. Fax: (506) 857-2617. E-mail: ckcw@ctv.ca. Web Site: www.ctv.ca.. Stn video via satellite: Bell Expressir Licensee: CTV Television Inc. Group owner: CTV Inc. (acq 11-1-97). Network: CTV.
Key Personnel:
Ivan Fecan . . . . . CEO
Rick Brace . . . . . pres
Robin Fillingham . . . . . CFO
Elaine Ali . . . . . exec VP
Mike Elgie . . . . . VP & gen mgr
Brian Lewis . . . . . stn mgr, gen sls mgr & adv mgr
John Silver . . . . . opns dir & opns mgr
Renee Fournier . . . . . prom dir & prom mgr
Jay Witherbee . . . . . news dir & pub affrs dir
Carson McDavid . . . . . chief of engrg

Quebec

Baie-Trinite

***CIVF-TV**—Analog channel: 12. On air date: Nov 15, 1982. 1000 Fullum, Montreal, PQ H2K 3L7. Phone: (514) 521-2424. Fax: (514) 873-2601. Fax: (514) 873-4413. E-mail: info@telequebec.qc.ca. Web Site: www.telequebec.tv. Licensee: Societe de telediffusion du Quebec. Group owner: Tele-Quebec.
Key Personnel:
Paule Beaugrand-Champagne . . . . . pres
Pierre De Lorme . . . . . gen mgr

Bearn-Fabre

CKRN-TV-3—Analog channel: 3. 171 Jean Proulx St., Gatineau, PQ J8Z 1W5. Phone: (819) 770-1040. Fax: (819) 770-0272. Web Site: www.radionord.com. Licensee: Radio Nord Communications Inc. Group owner: (group owner). Network: Radio Canada.
Key Personnel:
Pierre R. Brosseau . . . . . pres
Michael Noiseux . . . . . gen mgr

Carleton

CHAU-TV—Analog channel: 5. On air date: Oct 17, 1959. 349 Blvd. Peron, Carleton, PQ G0C 1J0. Phone: (418) 364-3344. Fax: (418)

Quebec

364-7168. Licensee: CHAU-TV Communications Ltee. Group owner: Tele Inter-Rives Ltee. (acq 1-5-01). Network: TVA.

Chapeau

*CIVP-TV—Analog channel: 23. 1000 Fullum, Montreal, PQ H2K 3L7. Phone: (514) 521-2424. Fax: (514) 873-2601. Fax: (514) 864-4222. E-mail: info@telequebec.tv. Web Site: www.telequebec.tv. Licensee: Societe de telediffusion du Quebec. Group owner: Tele-Quebec.
Key Personnel:
Paule Beaugrand-Champagne . . . . pres
Pierre De Lorme . . . . gen mgr

Chicoutimi

CBJET—Analog channel: 58. PO Box 6000, 1400 boul. Rene Levesque E., Montreal, PQ H3C 3A8. Phone: (514) 597-6000. Phone: (514) 597-6000. Fax: (514) 597-4537. Web Site: www.cbc.ca. Licensee: CBC. Network: CBC.

*CIVV-TV—Analog channel: 8. On air date: November 1982. 1000 Fullum, Montreal, PQ H2K 3L7. Phone: (514) 521-2424. Fax: (514) 873-2601. Fax: (514) 864-4222. E-mail: info@telequebec.qc.ca. Web Site: www.telequebec.tv. Licensee: Societe de telediffusion du Quebec. Group owner: Tele-Quebec. Network: TeleFutura (Spanish).
Key Personnel:
Paule Beaugrand-Champagne . . . . pres
Pierre De Lorme . . . . gen mgr

CJPM-TV—Analog channel: 6. On air date: Apr 14, 1963. Box 600, One Mont Ste-Claire St., Saguenay, PQ G7H 5G3. Phone: (418) 549-2576. Fax: (418) 549-1130. E-mail: cjpm@saglac.qc.ca. Web Site: www.reseau.tva.ca. Licensee: Groupe TVA Inc. Group owner: (group owner). Network: TVA. Rep: Brydson. News: 6 hrs wkly.
Key Personnel:
Raynald Briere . . . . pres
Roger Jobin . . . . gen mgr, sls dir, prom dir & progmg dir
Myriam Donaldson . . . . news dir

Gatineau

CFGS-TV—Analog channel: 34. On air date: Sept 7, 1986. 171 Jean-Proulx St., Gatineau, PQ J8Z 1W5. Phone: (819) 770-1040. Fax: (819) 770-0272. E-mail: tqs@radionord.com. Web Site: www.radionord.com. Licensee: Radio Nord Communications Inc. Group owner: (group owner). Network: Quatre Saisons. Rep: Canadian Broadcast Sales.
Key Personnel:
Pierre R. Brosseau . . . . CEO & pres
Robert H. Parent . . . . gen mgr
Michel Noiseux . . . . opns dir

CHOT-TV—Analog channel: 40. On air date: Oct 30, 1978. 171 Jean-Proulx St., Gatineau, PQ J8Z 1W5. Phone: (819) 770-1040. Fax: (819) 770-1490 (news). E-mail: chot@radionord.com. Web Site: www.radionord.com. Licensee: Radio Nord Communications Inc. Group owner: (group owner). Network: TVA.
Key Personnel:
Pierre R. Brosseau . . . . CEO & pres
Robert H. Parent . . . . gen mgr
Michel Noiseux . . . . opns dir
Benoit Pilote . . . . sls dir
Eric Brousseau . . . . prom mgr
Daniele Young . . . . news dir

*CIVO-TV—Analog channel: 30. On air date: Aug 14, 1977. 1000 Fullum, Montreal, PQ H2K 3L7. Phone: (514) 521-2424. Fax: (514) 873-2601. Fax: (514) 873-7464. Licensee: Societe de telediffusion du Quebec. Group owner: Tele-Quebec.

Iles-de-la-Madeleine

CBIMT—Analog channel: 12. On air date: Nov 9, 1964. PO Box 6000, 1400 boul. Rene Levesque E., Montreal, PQ H3C 3A8. Phone: (514) 597-6000. Fax: (514) 597-4537. Web Site: www.cbc.ca. Licensee: CBC. Network: Radio Canada.

Jonquiere

CFRS-TV—Analog channel: 4. On air date: Sept 7, 1986. 2303 rue Sir Wilfred Laurier, Jonquiere, PQ G7X 5Z2. Phone: (418) 542-4551. Fax: (418) 542-7217. Fax: (418) 542-8319. Web Site: www.cgotv.ca.

Licensee: Cogeco Radio-Television Inc. (acq 11-24-98; C$5,754,626 with CKTV-TV Jonquiere). Network: Quatre Saisons.
Key Personnel:
Martin Gagnon . . . . gen mgr
Michel Goulet . . . . opns dir
Andre Houle . . . . sls dir
Annie Tremblay . . . . mktg dir

La Tuque

CBVT-2—Analog channel: 3. PO Box 6000, 1400 boul. Rene Levesque E., Montreal, PQ H3C 3A8. Phone: (514) 597-6000. Fax: (514) 597-6510. Web Site: www.cbc.ca. Licensee: CBC. Network: Radio Canada.

Malartic

CBVD-TV—Analog channel: 5. CBC Television, 1400 Rene Levesque E., Montreal, PQ H2L 2M2. Phone: (514) 597-6000. Phone: (514) 597-4537. Web Site: montreal.cbc.ca. Licensee: CBC. Network: CBC.

Mont-Laurier

CBFT-2—Analog channel: 3. On air date: Dec 3, 1962. Box 6000, Montreal, PQ H3C 3A8. Phone: (514) 597-6000. Fax: (514) 597-6354. Web Site: www.cbc.ca. Licensee: Societe Radio Canada. Network: Radio Canada.

Montreal

CBFT—Analog channel: 2. Digital channel: 19. On air date: 1952. PO Box 6000, 1400 boul. Rene Levesque E., Montreal, PQ H3C 3A8. Phone: (514) 597-6000. Phone: (514) 597-4282. Fax: (514) 597-4316. E-mail: auditoire@radio-canada.ca. Web Site: radio-canada.ca. Licensee: CBC.. Ownership: CBC. Network: Radio Canada.
Key Personnel:
Daniel Gourd . . . . VP
Richard Portelance . . . . sls dir & gen sls mgr
Loren Thibeault . . . . natl sls mgr
Alain Messier . . . . mktg dir
Danielle Rivard . . . . mktg mgr
Andre Beau det . . . . adv dir
Mario Clement . . . . progmg dir

CBMT—Analog channel: 6. Digital channel: 20. On air date: 1954. PO Box 6000, 1400 boul. Rene Levesque E., Montreal, PQ H3C 3A8. Phone: (514) 597-6000. Fax: (514) 597-5280. Licensee: CBC. Network: CBC.

CFCF-TV—Analog channel: 12. On air date: Jan 20, 1961. CTV Television Inc., 1205 Papineau Ave., Montreal, PQ H2K 4R2. Phone: (514) 273-6311. Fax: (514) 276-9399. E-mail: cfcfpromo@ctv.ca. Web Site: www.cfcf.ca. Licensee: CTV Television Inc. Group owner: (group owner; acq 9-21-01; C$141.5 million).. Network: CTV.

CFJP-TV—Analog channel: 35. Digital channel: 42. On air date: Sept 7, 1986. 612 Rue St-Jacques Bur 100, Montreal, PQ H3C 5R1. Phone: (514) 390-6035. Fax: (514) 390-0773. E-mail: tvpublic@tqs.ca. Web Site: www.tqs.ca. Licensee: TQS Inc.. Ownership: Quebecor Inc., 85.99%. (acq 1997). News staff: 51; News: 12 hrs wkly.
Key Personnel:
Michael J. Carter . . . . pres
Luc Doyon . . . . VP & gen mgr
Sophie Ferron . . . . opns dir
Robert PeRusse . . . . dev dir

CFTM-TV—Analog channel: 10. Box 170, Stn C, Montreal, PQ H2L 4P6. Phone: (514) 790-0461. Phone: (514) 526-9251. Fax: (514) 598-6082. Web Site: www.tva.canoe.com. Licensee: TVA Group Inc. Network: TVA.

*CFTU-TV—Analog channel: 29. On air date: Aug 20, 1985. 4750 Ave. Henri-Julien, Bureau 100, local 0058, Montreal, PQ H2T 3E4. Phone: (514) 841-2626. Fax: (514) 284-9363. E-mail: info@canal.qc.ca. Web Site: www.canal.qc.ca. Licensee: Corp. pour l'Avancement de Nouvelles Applications des Langages. (acq 5-86).
Key Personnel:
Michel Umbriaco . . . . pres
Guy Massicotte . . . . VP
Sylvie Godbout . . . . chmn & gen mgr

*CIVM-TV—Analog channel: 17. Digital channel: 27. On air date: Jan 19, 1975. 1000 Fullum, Montreal, PQ H2K 3L7. Phone: (514) 521-2424. Fax: (514) 873-2601. E-mail: info@telequebec.qc.ca. Web Site: www.telequebec.tv.. Ownership: Public television. News staff: 25; News: 5 hrs wkly.

CJNT-TV—Analog channel: 62. On air date: 1997. 1600 Blvd., De Maisonneuve E., 9th Fl., Montreal, PQ H2L 4P2. Phone: (514) 522-4150. Fax: (514) 522-9579. Web Site: www.canada.com. Licensee: 3649091 Canada Ltd. Group owner: CanWest Global Communications Corp. (acq 11-29-00).

Quebec City

CBVT—Analog channel: 11. Digital channel: 12. On air date: 1964. 888 Saint-Jean St., Quebec, PQ G1R 5H6. Phone: (418) 654-1341. Fax: (418) 656-8567. Web Site: www.cbc.ca. Licensee: CBC. Network: Radio Canada.

CFAP-TV—Analog channel: 2. On air date: Sept 4, 1989. 330 St.-Vallier St. East, Quebec City, PQ G1K 9C5. Phone: (418) 624-2222. Fax: (418) 624-3099. Fax: (418) 624-0162. E-mail: www@tqs.ca. Licensee: TQS Inc. Group owner: Cogeco Radio-Television Inc. (acq 2-15-02; grpsl). Network: Quatre Saisons. News staff: 29; News: 10 hrs wkly.
Key Personnel:
Rene Guimond . . . . pres
Renaud Francoeur . . . . gen mgr, progmg dir & news dir
Jean Simard . . . . opns dir, chief of opns & engrg dir
Joel Godin . . . . sls dir & mktg dir
Pierre Martineau . . . . pub affrs dir
Denise Delisle . . . . engrg mgr

CFCM-TV—Analog channel: 4. On air date: July 17, 1954. 1000 Ave. Myrand, Sainte-Foy, PQ G1V 2W3. Phone: (418) 688-9330. Fax: (418) 681-4239. Web Site: www.tva.ca. Licensee: Tele-Metropole Inc. Group owner: Groupe TVA Inc.

*CIVQ-TV—Analog channel: 15. On air date: Jan 19, 1975. 1000 Fullum, Montreal, PQ H2K 3L7. Phone: (514) 521-2424. Fax: (514) 873-2601. Fax: (514) 873-4413. E-mail: info@telequebec.qc.ca. Web Site: www.telequebec.tv. Licensee: Societe de telediffusion du Quebec. Group owner: Tele-Quebec.
Key Personnel:
Paule Beaugrand-Champagne . . . . pres
Pierre De Lorme . . . . gen mgr

CKMI-TV—Analog channel: 20. On air date: 1957. 1000 Myrand Ave., Ste.-Foy, PQ G1V 2W3. 1600 Boul.de Maisonneuve East, Montreal, PQ G1V 2W3. Phone: (418) 682-2020. Phone: (514) 521-4323. Fax: (418) 682-2620. Fax: (514) 521-2829. E-mail: globalnews.quf@globaltv.ca. Web Site: www.globaltv.ca. Licensee: Global Television Network. (acq 1997).
Key Personnel:
Marven Rogers . . . . gen mgr
Karen Macdonald . . . . stn mgr
Michel Yeos . . . . opns dir & opns mgr
Suzanne Lapalme . . . . sls dir
Masikc Vergcilles . . . . prom mgr
Karen McDonald . . . . progmg mgr
Waren Smith . . . . news dir
Michel Paquet . . . . engrg mgr

Rimouski

CFER-TV—Analog channel: 11. On air date: June 4, 1978. 465 boul. Ste.-Anne, Pointe-au-Pere, PQ G5M 1G1. Phone: (418) 722-6011. Fax: (418) 724-7810. Fax: (418) 723-0857. Web Site: www.tva.canoe.com. Licensee: Tele-Metropole Inc. Group owner: Groupe TVA Inc. Network: TVA.

*CIVB-TV—Analog channel: 22. On air date: Oct 15, 1981. 1000 Fullum, Montreal, PQ H2K 3L7. Phone: (514) 521-2424. Fax: (514) 873-2601. Fax: (514) 873-4413. E-mail: info@telequebec.qc.ca. Web Site: www.telequebec.tv. Licensee: Societe de telediffusion du Quebec. Group owner: Tele-Quebec.
Key Personnel:
Paule Beaugrand-Champagne . . . . pres
Pierre De Lorme . . . . gen mgr

Directory of Television

CJBR-TV—Analog channel: 2. On air date: November 1954. 273 St. Jeans Baptiste W., Rimouski, PQ G5L 4J8. Phone: (418) 723-2217. Phone: (418) 723-4730. Fax: (418) 743-6126. Licensee: CBC. Network: CBC.

Riviere-du-Loup

CFTF-TV—Analog channel: 29. On air date: 1988. 103 des Equipements Parc Industriel, Rivieres-du-Loup, PQ G5R 5W7. 298 Boulevard Armand-Theriault, Bureau 100, Riviere-du-Loup, PQ G5R 4C2. Phone: (418) 862-2909. Fax: (418) 862-8147. E-mail: cftf@qc.aira.com. Licensee: Television MBS Inc. Group owner: Tele Inter-Rives Ltee.
Key Personnel:
Marc Simard . . . . pres
Catherine Simard . . . . gen mgr, dev VP & mktg VP
Michel Belanger . . . . opns VP & progmg VP
Ginette Dumant . . . . sls VP & rgnl sls mgr
Yves Belanger . . . . sls dir
Nancy Fortin . . . . prom VP
Germain Gelinas . . . . engrg VP

CIMT-TV—Analog channel: 9. On air date: Sept 18, 1978. 15 Rue de la Chute, Riviere-du-Loup, PQ G5R 5B7. Phone: (418) 867-1341. Fax: (418) 867-4710. Licensee: Tele Inter-Rives Ltee. Group owner: (group owner). Network: TVA.

CKRT-TV—Analog channel: 7. On air date: 1961. 15 Rue de la Chute, Riviere-du-Loup, PQ G5R 5B7. Phone: (418) 867-1341. Fax: (418) 867-4710. Licensee: CKRT-TV Ltee. Group owner: Tele Inter-Rives Ltee. Network: CBC.

Rouyn

***CIVA-TV**—Analog channel: 8. On air date: Jan 18, 1980. 1000 Fullum, Montreal, PQ H2K 3L7. Phone: (514) 521-2424. Fax: (514) 873-2601. Fax: (514) 864-4222. E-mail: info@telequebec.qc.ca. Web Site: www.telequebec.tv. Licensee: Societe de telediffusion du Quebec. Group owner: Tele-Quebec.
Key Personnel:
Paule Beaugrand-Champagne . . . . pres
Pierre De Lorme . . . . gen mgr

Rouyn-Noranda

CKRN-TV—Analog channel: 4. On air date: 1957. 380 Murdoch, Rouyn-Noranda, PQ J9X 1G5. Phone: (819) 762-0741. Fax: (819) 762-6331. Web Site: www.radionord.com. Licensee: Radio Nord Communications Inc. Group owner: (group owner). Network: Radio Canada.
Key Personnel:
Pierre R. Brosseau . . . . pres
Ghislain Beaulieu . . . . gen mgr
Michel Plante . . . . opns dir & progmg mgr
Frantz Boivin . . . . sls dir
Philippe Chatillon . . . . news dir
Gerald Landry . . . . chief of engrg

Sept-Iles

CFER-TV-2—Analog channel: 5. On air date: Nov 13, 1981. c/o CFER-TV, 465 boul. Ste. Anne, Pointe-au-Pere, PQ G5M 1G1. Phone: (418) 722-6011. Fax: (418) 724-7810. Fax: (418) 723-0854 (news). Web Site: www.tva.canoe.com. Licensee: Groupe TVA Inc. Group owner: (group owner). Network: TVA.

***CIVG-TV**—Analog channel: 9. On air date: Nov 5, 1982. c/o Tele-Quebec, 1000 Fullum, Montreal, PQ H2K 3L7. Phone: (514) 521-2424. Fax: (514) 873-2601. Fax: (514) 873-7464. Web Site: www.telequebec.tv. Licensee: Societe de telediffusion du Quebec. Group owner: Tele-Quebec.

Sherbrooke

CFKS-TV—Analog channel: 30. On air date: September 1986. 2830 Boul. St-Martin Est, Suite 200, Laval, PQ H7E 5A1. Phone: (819) 565-9999. Fax: (819) 822-4205. Web Site: www.cogeco.com. Licensee: Cogeco Radio-Television Inc. Group owner: Cogeco Inc. Network: Quatre Saisons.

CHLT-TV—Analog channel: 7. On air date: Aug 12, 1956. 3330 Ouest Rue King, Sherbrooke, PQ J1L 1C9. Phone: (819) 565-7777. Fax:

(819) 565-4650. Fax: (819) 563-0141. Licensee: Tele-Metropole Inc. Group owner: Groupe TVA Inc. (acq 7-9-90). Network: TVA.

***CIVS-TV**—Analog channel: 24. On air date: Feb 26, 1982. 1000 Fullum, Montreal, PQ H2K 3L7. Phone: (514) 521-2424. Fax: (514) 873-2601. Fax: (514) 864-4222. E-mail: info@telequebec.qc.ca. Web Site: www.telequebec.tv. Licensee: Societe de telediffusion du Quebec. Group owner: Tele-Quebec.
Key Personnel:
Paule Beaugrand-Champagne . . . . pres
Pierre De Lorme . . . . gen mgr

CKSH-TV—Analog channel: 9. On air date: Sept 1, 1974. 2830 boul. St-Martin Est, Suite 200, Laval, PQ H7E 5A1. Phone: (819) 565-9999. Fax: (819) 822-4205. Web Site: www.cogeco.com. Licensee: Cogeco Radio-Television Inc. Group owner: Cogeco Inc. Network: CBC.

Temiscaning

CBFST-2—Analog channel: 12. PO Box 6000, 1400 boul. Rene Levesque E., Montreal, PQ H3C 3A8. Phone: (514) 597-6000. Fax: (514) 597-4537. Web Site: www.cbc.ca. Licensee: CBC. Network: Radio Canada.

Trois-Rivieres

CFKM-TV—Analog channel: 16. On air date: Sept 7, 1986. Box 277, Trois-Rivieres, PQ G9A 5G3. Phone: (819) 377-6053. Fax: (819) 377-5442. Licensee: Cogeco Radio-Television Inc. Group owner: Cogeco Inc. Network: Quatre Saisons.

CHEM-TV—Analog channel: 8. On air date: Aug 29, 1976. 3625 boul. Chanoine-Moreau, Trois-Rivieres, PQ G8Y 5N6. Phone: (819) 376-8880. Fax: (819) 376-2906. Licensee: Tele-Metropole Inc. Group owner: Groupe TVA Inc. (acq 7-9-90). Network: TVA.
Key Personnel:
Richard Renault . . . . gen mgr & stn mgr
Gerald Trives . . . . chief of engrg

***CIVC-TV**—Analog channel: 45. On air date: Oct 7, 1981. c/o Tele-Quebec, 1000 Fullum, Montreal, PQ H2K 3L7. Phone: (514) 521-2424. Fax: (514) 873-2601. Fax: (514) 864-4222. E-mail: info@telequebec.qc.ca. Web Site: www.telequebec.tv. Licensee: Societe de telediffusion du Quebec. Group owner: Tele-Quebec.
Key Personnel:
Paule Beaugrand-Champagne . . . . pres
Pierre De Lonrme . . . . pres & gen mgr

CKTM-TV—Analog channel: 13. On air date: Apr 15, 1958. Box 277, Trois-Rivieres, PQ G9A 5G3. Phone: (819) 377-6053. Fax: (819) 377-5442. E-mail: s.guilbeault@cgotv.ca. Web Site: www.cgotv.ca. Licensee: Cogeco Radio-Television Inc. Group owner: Cogeco Inc. Network: CBC.

Val d'Or

CFVS-TV—Analog channel: 25. On air date: Jan 19, 1987. 1729 3ieme Ave., Val d'Or, PQ J9P 1W3. Phone: (819) 825-0010. Fax: (819) 825-7313. Web Site: www.radionord.net. Licensee: Radio Nord Communications Inc. Group owner: (group owner) Network: Quatre Saisons.
Key Personnel:
Pierre R. Brosseau . . . . pres
Ghislain Beaulieu . . . . gen mgr & gen sls mgr
Frantz Boivin . . . . stn mgr & gen sls mgr
Michael Plante . . . . opns mgr, prom dir & progmg dir
Philippe Chatillon . . . . news dir
Gerald Landry . . . . chief of engrg

Saskatchewan

Bellegarde

CBKFT-9—Analog channel: 26. On air date: Mar 15, 1980. Box 540, Regina, SK S4P 4A1. Phone: (306) 347-9540. Fax: (306) 347-9493. Licensee: Societe Radio Canada. Network: Radio Canada.
Key Personnel:
David Kyle . . . . gen mgr & opns dir
Steve Tomchuck . . . . chief of engrg

Saskatchewan

Colgate

CKCK-TV-1—Analog channel: 12. On air date: Dec 15, 1962. c/o CKCK-TV, Box 2000, One Hwy. 1 East, Regina, SK S4P 3E5. Phone: (306) 569-2000. Fax: (306) 522-0090. E-mail: ckck@ctv.ca. Web Site: www.ctv.ca. Licensee: CTV Television Inc. Group owner: (group owner) Network: CTV.

Cypress Hills

CBCP-TV-2—Analog channel: 2. On air date: Oct 1, 1979. c/o CBKT, 2440 Broad St., Regina, SK S4P 4A1. Phone: (306) 347-9540. Fax: (306) 347-9748. Licensee: CBC. Network: CBC.
Key Personnel:
Derek Dalton . . . . VP
David Kyle . . . . opns mgr

Debden

CBKFT-3—Analog channel: 22. On air date: Dec 2, 1979. Box 540, 2440 Broad St., Regina, SK S4P 4A1. Phone: (306) 347-9540. Fax: (306) 347-9635. Web Site: radio-canada.ca. Licensee: Societe Radio Canada. Network: Radio Canada.
Key Personnel:
Lionel Bonneville . . . . gen mgr
David Kyle . . . . opns dir
Steve Tomchuck . . . . chief of engrg

Golden Prairie

CKMC-TV-1—Analog channel: 10. On air date: Dec 15, 1988. c/o CKCK-TV, Box 2000, One Hwy. 1 East, Regina, SK S4P 3E5. Phone: (306) 569-2000. Fax: (306) 522-0090. Web Site: www.ctv.ca. Licensee: CTV Television Inc. Group owner: (group owner) Network: CTV.
Key Personnel:
Dennis Dunlop . . . . gen mgr
Les Sampson . . . . chief of engrg

Gravelbourg

CBKFT-6—Analog channel: 39. On air date: Mar 13, 1980. Box 540, 2440 Broad St., Regina, SK S4P 4A1. Phone: (306) 347-9540. Fax: (306) 347-9493. Licensee: Societe Radio Canada. Network: Radio Canada.
Key Personnel:
Lionel Bonneville . . . . gen mgr
David Kyle . . . . opns dir
Steve Tomchuck . . . . chief of engrg

Melfort

CKBQ-TV—Analog channel: 2. On air date: 1973. Box 540, Reginia, SK S4P 4A1. Phone: (306) 347-9540. Phone: (306) 956-7400. Fax: (306) 347-9635. Web Site: www.saskcbc.ca. Licensee: CTV Television Inc. Group owner: CTV Inc. Network: CBC.
Key Personnel:
Lionel Bonneville . . . . gen mgr
David Kyle . . . . opns dir

North Battleford

CFQC-TV-2—Analog channel: 6. On air date: 1972. c/o CFQC-TV, 216 First Ave. N., Saskatoon, SK S7K 3W3. Phone: (306) 665-8600. Fax: (306) 665-0450. E-mail: cfqcnews@ctv.ca. Web Site: www.ctv.ca. Licensee: TV West Inc. Network: CTV.
Key Personnel:
Dennis Dunlop . . . . gen mgr
Denis Gilbertson . . . . opns mgr
Barry Berglund . . . . gen sls mgr
Merin Coutts . . . . mktg dir
Geoff Bradley . . . . prom mgr
Bonnie MacKenzie . . . . progmg mgr
Les Sampson . . . . engrg mgr

Ponteix

CBCP-TV-3—Analog channel: 3. On air date: November 1979. Box 540, c/o CBKT, 2440 Broad St., Regina, SK S4P 4A1. Phone: (306) 347-9540. Fax: (306) 347-9758 (French). Licensee: CBC. Network: CBC.
Key Personnel:

Broadcasting & Cable Yearbook 2006

Yukon Territory

Lionel Bonneville . . . . gen mgr
David Kyle . . . . opns dir
Steve Tomchuck . . . . chief of engrg

Prince Albert

CIPA-TV—Analog channel: 9. On air date: Jan 12, 1987. 22 10th St. W., Prince Albert, SK S6V 3A5. Phone: (306) 922-6066. Fax: (306) 763-3041. E-mail: cipa@ctv.ca. Web Site: www.ctv.ca. Licensee: CTV Television Inc. Group owner: CTV Inc. (acq 8-1-86). Network: CTV. News staff: 5.

Regina

CBKFT—Analog channel: 13. On air date: Sept 27, 1976. Box 540, 2440 Broad St., Regina, SK S4P 4A1. Phone: (306) 347-9540. Fax: (306) 347-9635. Web Site: www.radio-canada.ca/regions/saskatchewan/index.shtml. Licensee: Societe Radio Canada. Network: Radio Canada.

CBKT—Analog channel: 9. On air date: 1969. Box 540, Regina, SK S4P 4A1. Phone: (306) 347-9540. Fax: (306) 347-9616. Web Site: www.sask.cbc.ca. Licensee: CBC. Network: CBC.
Key Personnel:
David Kyle . . . . opns mgr & progmg mgr
Carley Wawryk . . . . gen sls mgr
Scott Hollowell . . . . news dir
Rikki Bote . . . . mktg

CFRE-TV—Analog channel: 11. On air date: Sept 6, 1987. 370 Hoffer Dr., Regina, SK S4N 7A4. Phone: (306) 775-4000. Fax: (306) 721-4817. Web Site: www.canada.com. Licensee: Global Communications Ltd. Group owner: CanWest Global Communications Corp.
Key Personnel:
Paul Godfrey . . . . opns mgr
Stan Schmidt . . . . gen mgr & gen sls mgr
Bill Wright . . . . prom mgr
Doug Hoover . . . . film buyer
Les Staff . . . . news dir
Len Virog . . . . chief of engrg

CKCK-TV—Analog channel: 2. On air date: July 28, 1954. Box 2000, Regina, SK S4P 3E5. One Hwy. 1 East, Regina, SK S4P 3E5. Phone: (306) 569-2000. Fax: (306) 522-0090. E-mail: ckck@ctv.ca. Web Site: www.ctv.ca. Licensee: CTV Television Inc. Group owner: (group owner) Network: CTV. News: 15.5 hrs local news wkly.

Saint Brieux

CBKFT-4—Analog channel: 7. On air date: Dec 17, 1979. Box 540, 2440 Broad St., Regina, SK S4P 4A1. Phone: (306) 347-9540. Fax: (306) 347-9635. Web Site: radio-canada.ca/regions/saskatchewan/index.shtml. Licensee: Societe Radio Canada. Network: Radio Canada.

Saskatoon

CBKST—Analog channel: 11. On air date: Oct 17, 1971. 144 Second Ave. South, Saskatoon, SK S7K 1K5. Phone: (306) 956-7400. Fax: (306) 347-9650 (admin). Web Site: www.cbc.ca/sask. Licensee: CBC. Network: CBC.

CFQC-TV—Analog channel: 8. On air date: 1954. 216 First Ave. N., Saskatoon, SK S7K 3W3. Phone: (306) 665-8600. Fax: (306) 665-0450. E-mail: cfqcnews@ctv.ca. Web Site: www.ctv.ca. Licensee: CFQC Broadcasting Ltd. Group owner: CTV Inc. (acq 1972). Network: CTV.
Key Personnel:
Dennis Dunlop . . . . gen mgr
Denis Gibertson . . . . opns VP & opns mgr
Barry Berglund . . . . gen sls mgr
Merin Coutts . . . . mktg dir & mktg mgr
Geoff Bradley . . . . prom mgr
Bonnie Mackenzie . . . . progmg mgr
Dale Neufeld . . . . news dir
Les Sampson . . . . chief of engrg

CFSK-TV—Analog channel: 4. On air date: Sept 6, 1987. 218 Robin Crescent, Saskatoon, SK S7L 7C3. Phone: (306) 665-6969. Fax: (306) 665-6069. Licensee: CanWest Television Inc.. Ownership: CanWest Broadcasting Ltd., 100%. Network: Global. News staff: 17; News: 10 hrs wkly.

Shaunavon

CBCP-TV-1—Analog channel: 7. c/o CBKT, Box 540, Regina, SK S4P 4A1. Phone: (306) 347-9540. Fax: (306) 347-9616. Web Site: www.sask.cbc.ca. Licensee: CBC. Network: CBC.

Stranraer

CBKST-1—Analog channel: 9. 144 Second Ave. South, Saskatoon, SK S7K 1K5. Phone: (306) 956-7400. Fax: (306) 347-9616 (admin). Fax: (306) 956-9417 (news). Web Site: www.cbc.ca. Licensee: CBC. Network: CBC.

Swift Current

CKMC-TV—Analog channel: 12. On air date: Oct 20, 1976. c/o CKCK-TV, Box 2000, Regina, SK S4P 3E5. c/o CKCK-TV, One Hwy. 1 East, Regina, SK S4P 3E5. Phone: (306) 569-2000. Fax: (306) 522-0090. E-mail: ckck@ctv.ca. Web Site: www.ctv.ca. Licensee: CTV Television Inc. Group owner: (group owner) Network: CTV.

Warmley

CIEW-TV—Analog channel: 7. c/o CICC-TV, 95 E. Broadway St., Yorkton, SK S3N 0L1. Phone: (306) 783-3685. Fax: (306) 782-7212.
Web Site: www.ctv.ca. Licensee: CTV Television Inc. Group owner: Baton Broadcasting Inc. Network: CTV.

Willow Bunch

CBKT-2—Analog channel: 10. CBC TV, Box 540, 2440 Broad St., Regina, SK S4P 4A1. Phone: (306) 347-9666. Fax: (306) 347-9635. Web Site: www.sask.cbc.ca. Licensee: CBC. Network: CBC.
Key Personnel:
David Kyle . . . . gen mgr
Nigel Sims . . . . progmg dir
Jonaathan Shanks . . . . news dir
Jeff Nenson . . . . chief of engrg

CKCK-TV-2—Analog channel: 6. On air date: May 29, 1963. c/o CKCK-TV, Box 2000, One Hwy. 1 East, Regina, SK S4P 3E5. Phone: (306) 569-2000. Fax: (306) 522-0090. E-mail: ckck@ctv.ca. Web Site: www.ctv.ca. Licensee: CTV Television Inc. Group owner: (group owner) Network: CTV.

Xenon Park

CBKFT-5—Analog channel: 21. On air date: Feb 19, 1979. Box 540, c/o CBKFT, 2440 Broad St., Regina, SK S4P 4A1. Phone: (306) 347-9540. Fax: (306) 347-9493. Fax: (306) 347-9635. Licensee: CBC. Network: CBC.
Key Personnel:
David Kyle . . . . gen mgr & progmg dir
Debbie Carpentier . . . . opns mgr
Carly Caverly . . . . gen sls mgr
Jonathan Shanks . . . . progmg dir
Steve Tomchuk . . . . chief of engrg

Yorkton

CICC-TV—Analog channel: 10. On air date: 1974. 95 E. Broadway, Yorkton, SK S3N 0N1. Phone: (306) 786-8400. Fax: (306) 782-7212. E-mail: cicc@ctv.ca. Web Site: www.ctv.ca. Licensee: CTV Television Inc. Group owner: (group owner) Network: CTV.
Key Personnel:
Dennis Dunlop . . . . gen mgr
Bob Maloney . . . . opns mgr, progmg dir & news dir
Wade Moffatt . . . . gen sls mgr
Peter Whitehead . . . . chief of engrg

Yukon Territory

White Horse

CFWH-TV—Analog channel: 6. 3103 3rd Ave., White Horse, YT Y1A 1E5. Phone: (867) 668-8400. Fax: (867) 668-8408. Web Site: www.north.cbc.ca. Licensee: CBC. Network: CBC.
Key Personnel:
Frank Fry . . . . . . gen mgr, opns mgr, opns mgr & progmg dir
James Miller . . . . news dir

U.S. Television Stations by Call Letters

*KAAH-TV Honolulu, HI
KAAL Rochester, MN-Mason City, IA-Austin, MN
KAAS-TV Wichita-Hutchinson Plus, KS
KABB San Antonio, TX
KABC-TV Los Angeles
KABY-TV Sioux Falls (Mitchell), SD
KACB-TV Lafayette, LA
*KACV-TV Amarillo, TX
KADN Lafayette, LA
KAEF Eureka, CA
*KAET Phoenix, AZ
*KAFT Ft. Smith-Fayetteville-Springdale-Rogers, AR
*KAID Boise, ID
KAII-TV Wailuku HI
KAIL Fresno-Visalia, CA
KAIT Jonesboro, AR
KAJB Yuma, AZ-El Centro, CA
KAKE-TV Wichita-Hutchinson Plus, KS
*KAKM Anchorage, AK
KAKW-TV Waco-Temple-Bryan, TX
KALB-TV Alexandria, LA
*KALO Honolulu, HI
KAMC Lubbock, TX
KAME-TV Reno, NV
KAMR-TV Amarillo, TX
*KAMU-TV Waco-Temple-Bryan, TX
KAPP Yakima-Pasco-Richland-Kennewick, WA
KAQY Monroe, LA-El Dorado, AR
KARD Monroe, LA-El Dorado, AR
KARE Minneapolis-St. Paul, MN
KARK-TV Little Rock-Pine Bluff, AR
KASA-TV Albuquerque-Santa Fe, NM
KASN Little Rock-Pine Bluff, AR
KASW Phoenix, AZ
KASY-TV Albuquerque-Santa Fe, NM
KATC Lafayette, LA
KATN Fairbanks, AK
KATU Portland, OR
KATV Little Rock-Pine Bluff, AR
KAUT-TV Oklahoma City, OK
KAUZ-TV Wichita Falls, TX & Lawton, OK
KAVU-TV Victoria, TX
*KAWB Minneapolis-St. Paul, MN
*KAWE Minneapolis-St. Paul, MN
KAYU-TV Spokane, WA
KAZA-TV Los Angeles
KAZH Houston
*KAZQ Albuquerque-Santa Fe, NM
KAZT-TV Phoenix, AZ
KAZW-TV Yakima-Pasco-Richland-Kennewick, WA
KBAK-TV Bakersfield, CA
KBAO Great Falls, MT
KBBJ Great Falls, MT
KBCA Alexandria, LA
KBCB Seattle-Tacoma, WA
KBCI-TV Boise, ID
KBCJ Salt Lake City, UT
*KBDI-TV Denver, CO
KBDK Wichita-Hutchinson Plus, KS
*KBDM Medford-Klamath Falls, OR
KBEH Santa Barbara-Santa Maria-San Luis Obispo, CA
KBEJ San Antonio, TX
KBEO Salt Lake City, UT
KBFD Honolulu, HI
*KBGH Twin Falls, ID
*KBHE-TV Rapid City, SD
KBHK-TV San Francisco-Oakland-San Jose
KBIM-TV Albuquerque-Santa Fe, NM
*KBIN Omaha, NE
KBJN Salt Lake City, UT
KBJR-TV Duluth, MN-Superior, WI
KBLN Medford-Klamath Falls, OR
KBLR Las Vegas, NV
*KBME-TV Minot-Bismarck-Dickinson, ND

KBMT Beaumont-Port Arthur, TX
KBMY Minot-Bismarck-Dickinson, ND
*KBNY Salt Lake City, UT
KBRR Fargo-Valley City, ND
KBSD-TV Wichita-Hutchinson Plus, KS
KBSH-TV Wichita-Hutchinson Plus, KS
KBSI Paducah, KY-Cape Girardeau, MO-Harrisburg-Mount Vernon, IL
KBSL-TV Wichita-Hutchinson Plus, KS
*KBSV Sacramento-Stockton-Modesto, CA
*KBTC-TV Seattle-Tacoma, WA
KBTV-TV Beaumont-Port Arthur, TX
KBTX-TV Waco-Temple-Bryan, TX
KBTZ Butte-Bozeman, MT
KBVU Eureka, CA
KBWB San Francisco-Oakland-San Jose
*KBYU-TV Salt Lake City, UT
KBZK Butte-Bozeman, MT
*KCAH Monterey-Salinas, CA
KCAL Los Angeles
KCAU-TV Sioux City, IA
KCBA Monterey-Salinas, CA
KCBD Lubbock, TX
KCBS-TV Los Angeles
KCBU Salt Lake City, UT
KCBY-TV Eugene, OR
KCCI Des Moines-Ames, IA
KCCO-TV Minneapolis-St. Paul, MN
KCCW-TV Minneapolis-St. Paul, MN
*KCDT Spokane, WA
KCEB Tyler-Longview (Lufkin & Nacogdoches), TX
KCEC Denver, CO
KCEN-TV Waco-Temple-Bryan, TX
*KCET Los Angeles
KCFG Phoenix, AZ
KCFW-TV Missoula, MT
*KCGE-DT Fargo-Valley City, ND
KCHF Albuquerque-Santa Fe, NM
KCIT Amarillo, TX
*KCKA Seattle-Tacoma, WA
KCLO-TV Rapid City, SD
KCNC-TV Denver, CO
KCNS San Francisco-Oakland-San Jose
KCOP Los Angeles
*KCOS El Paso, TX
KCOY-TV Santa Barbara-Santa Maria-San Luis Obispo, CA
KCPM Fargo-Valley City, ND
KCPQ Seattle-Tacoma, WA
*KCPT Kansas City, MO
KCRA-TV Sacramento-Stockton-Modesto, CA
KCRG-TV Cedar Rapids-Waterloo & Dubuque, IA
*KCSD-TV Sioux Falls (Mitchell), SD
KCSG Salt Lake City, UT
*KCSM-TV San Francisco-Oakland-San Jose
KCTS-TV Seattle-Tacoma, WA
KCTV Kansas City, MO
KCVU Chico-Redding, CA
*KCWC-TV Casper-Riverton, WY
KCWE Kansas City, MO
KCWY Casper-Riverton, WY
KDAF Dallas-Ft. Worth
KDBC-TV El Paso, TX
*KDCK Wichita-Hutchinson Plus, KS
KDEN Denver, CO
KDEV Cheyenne, WY-Scottsbluff, NE
KDFI Dallas-Ft. Worth
KDFW Dallas-Ft. Worth
*KDIN-TV Des Moines-Ames, IA
KDKA-TV Pittsburgh, PA
KDKF Medford-Klamath Falls, OR
KDLH Duluth, MN-Superior, WI
KDLO-TV Sioux Falls (Mitchell), SD
KDLT-TV Sioux Falls (Mitchell), SD
KDLV-TV Sioux Falls (Mitchell), SD

KDMD Anchorage, AK
KDMI Des Moines-Ames, IA
KDNL-TV St. Louis, MO
KDOC-TV Los Angeles
KDOR-TV Tulsa, OK
KDRV Medford-Klamath Falls, OR
*KDSD-TV Sioux Falls (Mitchell), SD
*KDSE Minot-Bismarck-Dickinson, ND
KDSM-TV Des Moines-Ames, IA
*KDTN Dallas-Ft. Worth
*KDTP Phoenix, AZ
KDTV San Francisco-Oakland-San Jose
*KDTX-TV Dallas-Ft. Worth
KDUH-TV Cheyenne, WY-Scottsbluff, NE
KDVR Denver, CO
KECI-TV Missoula, MT
KECY-TV Yuma, AZ-El Centro, CA
*KEDT Corpus Christi, TX
*KEET Eureka, CA
KEGS Reno, NV
KEJB Monroe, LA-El Dorado, AR
KELO-TV Sioux Falls (Mitchell), SD
*KEMV Little Rock-Pine Bluff, AR
KENS-TV San Antonio, TX
KENV Salt Lake City, UT
KENW Amarillo, TX
*KEPB-TV Eugene, OR
KEPR-TV Yakima-Pasco-Richland-Kennewick, WA
*KERA-TV Dallas-Ft. Worth
KERO-TV Bakersfield, CA
*KESD-TV Sioux Falls (Mitchell), SD
KESQ-TV Palm Springs, CA
*KETA Oklahoma City, OK
*KETC St. Louis, MO
*KETG Little Rock-Pine Bluff, AR
*KETH-TV Houston
KETK-TV Tyler-Longview (Lufkin & Nacogdoches), TX
*KETS Little Rock-Pine Bluff, AR
KETV Omaha, NE
*KETZ Monroe, LA-El Dorado, AR
KEVN-TV Rapid City, SD
KEYC-TV Mankato, MN
KEYE-TV Austin, TX
KEYT-TV Santa Barbara-Santa Maria-San Luis Obispo, CA
KEYU Oklahoma City, OK
KEZI Eugene, OR
KFBB-TV Great Falls, MT
KFBT Las Vegas, NV
KFCT Denver, CO
KFDA-TV Amarillo, TX
KFDM-TV Beaumont-Port Arthur, TX
KFDX-TV Wichita Falls, TX & Lawton, OK
KFFX-TV Yakima-Pasco-Richland-Kennewick, WA
KFJX Joplin, MO-Pittsburg, KS
KFMB-TV San Diego, CA
*KFME Fargo-Valley City, ND
KFNB-TV Casper-Riverton, WY
KFNE Casper-Riverton, WY
KFNR Denver, CO
KFOR-TV Oklahoma City, OK
KFOX-TV El Paso, TX
KFPH-TV Phoenix, AZ
KFPX Des Moines-Ames, IA
KFQX Grand Junction-Montrose, CO
KFRE-TV Fresno-Visalia, CA
KFSF-TV San Francisco-Oakland-San Jose
KFSM-TV Ft. Smith-Fayetteville-Springdale-Rogers, AR
KFSN-TV Fresno-Visalia, CA
KFTA Ft. Smith-Fayetteville-Springdale-Rogers, AR
KFTC Minneapolis-St. Paul, MN
KFTH-TV Houston
KFTR-TV Los Angeles

*KFTS Medford-Klamath Falls, OR
KFTU-TV Tucson (Sierra Vista), AZ
KFTV Fresno-Visalia, CA
KFTY San Francisco-Oakland-San Jose
KFVE Honolulu, HI
KFVS-TV Paducah, KY-Cape Girardeau, MO-Harrisburg-Mount Vernon, IL
KFWD Dallas-Ft. Worth
KFXA Cedar Rapids-Waterloo & Dubuque, IA
KFXB Cedar Rapids-Waterloo & Dubuque, IA
KFXF Fairbanks, AK
KFXK Tyler-Longview (Lufkin & Nacogdoches), TX
KFXP Idaho Falls-Pocatello, ID
KFYR-TV Minot-Bismarck-Dickinson, ND
KGAN Cedar Rapids-Waterloo & Dubuque, IA
KGBT-TV Harlingen-Weslaco-Brownsville-McAllen, TX
KGEB Tulsa, OK
KGET-TV Bakersfield, CA
*KGFE Fargo-Valley City, ND
KGIN Lincoln & Hastings-Kearney, NE
KGMB Honolulu, HI
KGMC Fresno-Visalia, CA
KGMD-TV Hilo HI
KGMV Wailuku HI
KGNS-TV Laredo, TX
KGO-TV San Francisco-Oakland-San Jose
KGPE Fresno-Visalia, CA
KGPX Spokane, WA
*KGTF Hagatna GU
KGTV San Diego, CA
KGUN Tucson (Sierra Vista), AZ
KGW Portland, OR
KGWB-TV Davenport, IA-Rock Island-Moline, IL
KGWC-TV Casper-Riverton, WY
KGWL-TV Casper-Riverton, WY
KGWN-TV Cheyenne, WY-Scottsbluff, NE
KGWR-TV Salt Lake City, UT
KHAS Lincoln & Hastings-Kearney, NE
KHAW-TV Hilo HI
KHBC-TV Hilo HI
KHBS Ft. Smith-Fayetteville-Springdale-Rogers, AR
*KHCE-TV San Antonio, TX
KHCV Seattle-Tacoma, WA
*KHET Honolulu, HI
KHFT Albuquerque-Santa Fe, NM
KHGI-TV Lincoln & Hastings-Kearney, NE
*KHIN Omaha, NE
KHIZ Los Angeles
KHMT Billings, MT
*KHNE-TV Lincoln & Hastings-Kearney, NE
KHNL Honolulu, HI
KHOG-TV Ft. Smith-Fayetteville-Springdale-Rogers, AR
KHON-TV Honolulu, HI
KHOU-TV Houston
KHQA-TV Quincy, IL-Hannibal, MO-Keokuk, IA
KHQ-TV Spokane, WA
KHRR Tucson (Sierra Vista), AZ
KHSD-TV Rapid City, SD
KHSL-TV Chico-Redding, CA
KHVO Hilo HI
KHWB Houston
KICU-TV San Francisco-Oakland-San Jose
KIDA Twin Falls, ID
KIDK Idaho Falls-Pocatello, ID
KIDY San Angelo, TX

KIEM-TV Eureka, CA
KIFI-TV Idaho Falls-Pocatello, ID
KIII Corpus Christi, TX
*KIIN Cedar Rapids-Waterloo & Dubuque, IA
KIKU Honolulu, HI
KIMA-TV Yakima-Pasco-Richland-Kennewick, WA
KIMO Anchorage, AK
KIMT Rochester, MN-Mason City, IA-Austin, MN
KINC Las Vegas, NV
KING-TV Seattle-Tacoma, WA
KINT-TV El Paso, TX
KION-TV Monterey-Salinas, CA
*KIPT Twin Falls, ID
KIRO-TV Seattle-Tacoma, WA
*KISU-TV Idaho Falls-Pocatello, ID
*KITU-TV Beaumont-Port Arthur, TX
KITV Honolulu, HI
KIVI Boise, ID
KIVV-TV Rapid City, SD
*KIXE-TV Chico-Redding, CA
KJCT Grand Junction-Montrose, CO
KJLA Los Angeles
KJNP-TV Fairbanks, AK
*KJRE Fargo-Valley City, ND
KJRH Tulsa, OK
KJRR Fargo-Valley City, ND
KJTL Wichita Falls, TX & Lawton, OK
KJTV-TV Lubbock, TX
KJUD Juneau, AK
KJWY Salt Lake City, UT
KJZZ-TV Salt Lake City, UT
KKAI Honolulu, HI
*KKAP Little Rock-Pine Bluff, AR
KKCO Grand Junction-Montrose, CO
KKJB Boise, ID
KKPX San Francisco-Oakland-San Jose
KKTV Colorado Springs-Pueblo, CO
KLAS-TV Las Vegas, NV
KLAX-TV Alexandria, LA
KLBK-TV Lubbock, TX
KLBY Wichita-Hutchinson Plus, KS
*KLCS Los Angeles
KLDO-TV Laredo, TX
KLDT Dallas-Ft. Worth
KLEI Kailua-Kona HI
*KLEP Little Rock-Pine Bluff, AR
KLEW-TV Spokane, WA
KLFY-TV Lafayette, LA
KLJB-TV Davenport, IA-Rock Island-Moline, IL
KLKE Lincoln & Hastings-Kearney, NE
KLKN Lincoln & Hastings-Kearney, NE
KLMN Great Falls, MT
*KLNE-TV Lincoln & Hastings-Kearney, NE
*KLPA-TV Alexandria, LA
*KLPB-TV Lafayette, LA
*KLRN San Antonio, TX
KLRT Little Rock-Pine Bluff, AR
*KLRU-TV Austin, TX
KLSR-TV Eugene, OR
KLST San Angelo, TX
*KLTJ Houston
*KLTL-TV Lake Charles, LA
*KLTM-TV Monroe, LA-El Dorado, AR
*KLTS-TV Shreveport, LA
KLTV Tyler-Longview (Lufkin & Nacogdoches), TX
*KLUJ-TV Harlingen-Weslaco-Brownsville-McAllen, TX
KLUZ-TV Albuquerque-Santa Fe, NM
*KLVX Las Vegas, NV
KLWY Cheyenne, WY-Scottsbluff, NE
KMAS-TV Denver, CO
KMAU Wailuku HI
KMAX-TV Sacramento-Stockton-Modesto, CA
KMBC-TV Kansas City, MO

U.S. Television Stations by Call Letters

*KMBH Harlingen-Weslaco-Brownsville-McAllen, TX
KMCC Las Vegas, NV
KMCI Kansas City, MO
KMCT-TV Monroe, LA-El Dorado, AR
KMCY Minot-Bismarck-Dickinson, ND
*KMEB Wailuku HI
KMEG Sioux City, IA
KMEX-TV Los Angeles
KMGH-TV Denver, CO
KMGT Honolulu, HI
KMID Odessa-Midland, TX
KMIR-TV Palm Springs, CA
KMIZ Columbia-Jefferson City, MO
KMLM Odessa-Midland, TX
KMMF Missoula, MT
*KMNE-TV Lincoln & Hastings-Kearney, NE
KMOH-TV Phoenix, AZ
*KMOS-TV Kansas City, MO
KMOT Minot-Bismarck-Dickinson, ND
KMOV St. Louis, MO
KMPH Fresno-Visalia, CA
KMPX Dallas-Ft. Worth
KMSB-TV Tucson (Sierra Vista), AZ
KMSP-TV Minneapolis-St. Paul, MN
KMSS-TV Shreveport, LA
KMTF Helena, MT
*KMTP-TV San Francisco-Oakland-San Jose
KMTR Eugene, OR
KMTV Omaha, NE
KMTX-TV Eugene, OR
KMTZ Eugene, OR
KMVT Twin Falls, ID
KMVU Medford-Klamath Falls, OR
KMWB Minneapolis-St. Paul, MN
KNAT Albuquerque-Santa Fe, NM
KNAZ-TV Phoenix, AZ
KNBC Los Angeles
KNBN Rapid City, SD
*KNCT Waco-Temple-Bryan, TX
KNDO Yakima-Pasco-Richland-Kennewick, WA
KNDU Yakima-Pasco-Richland-Kennewick, WA
KNDX Minot-Bismarck-Dickinson, ND
KNIN-TV Boise, ID
KNLC St. Louis, MO
KNLJ Columbia-Jefferson City, MO
*KNMD-TV Albuquerque-Santa Fe, NM
*KNME-TV Albuquerque-Santa Fe, NM
*KNMT-TV Portland, OR
KNOE-TV Monroe, LA-El Dorado, AR
KNOP-TV North Platte, NE
*KNPB Reno, NV
KNRR Fargo-Valley City, ND
KNSD San Diego, CA
KNSO Fresno-Visalia, CA
KNTV San Francisco-Oakland-San Jose
KNVA Austin, TX
KNVN Chico-Redding, CA
KNVO Harlingen-Weslaco-Brownsville-McAllen, TX
KNWA-TV Ft. Smith-Fayetteville-Springdale-Rogers, AR
KNWS-TV Houston
*KNXT Fresno-Visalia, CA
KNXV-TV Phoenix, AZ
KOAA-TV Colorado Springs-Pueblo, CO
*KOAB-TV Bend, OR
*KOAC-TV Eugene, OR
KOAM-TV Joplin, MO-Pittsburg, KS
KOAT-TV Albuquerque-Santa Fe, NM
KOBF Albuquerque-Santa Fe, NM
KOBG-TV Albuquerque-Santa Fe, NM
KOBI Medford-Klamath Falls, OR
KOBR Albuquerque-Santa Fe, NM
KOB-TV Albuquerque-Santa Fe, NM
KOCB Oklahoma City, OK
*KOCE-TV Los Angeles
*KOCM Oklahoma City, OK
KOCO-TV Oklahoma City, OK
KOCT Albuquerque-Santa Fe, NM
*KOCV-TV Odessa-Midland, TX
KODE-TV Joplin, MO-Pittsburg, KS

*KOED-TV Tulsa, OK
*KOET Tulsa, OK
KOFT Albuquerque-Santa Fe, NM
KOGG Wailuku HI
KOIN Portland, OR
KOKH-TV Oklahoma City, OK
KOKI-TV Tulsa, OK
KOLD-TV Tucson (Sierra Vista), AZ
KOLN Lincoln & Hastings-Kearney, NE
KOLO-TV Reno, NV
KOLR-TV Springfield, MO
KOMO-TV Seattle-Tacoma, WA
KOMU-TV Columbia-Jefferson City, MO
KONG-TV Seattle-Tacoma, WA
*KOOD Wichita-Hutchinson Plus, KS
*KOPB-TV Portland, OR
KOPX Oklahoma City, OK
KORO Corpus Christi, TX
KOSA-TV Odessa-Midland, TX
KOTA-TV Rapid City, SD
KOTI Medford-Klamath Falls, OR
KOTV Tulsa, OK
KOVR Sacramento-Stockton-Modesto, CA
KOVT Albuquerque-Santa Fe, NM
KOWH Lincoln & Hastings-Kearney, NE
*KOZJ Joplin, MO-Pittsburg, KS
*KOZK Springfield, MO
KPAX-TV Missoula, MT
*KPAZ-TV Phoenix, AZ
*KPBS San Diego, CA
KPCB Abilene-Sweetwater, TX
KPDX Portland, OR
KPEJ Odessa-Midland, TX
KPHO-TV Phoenix, AZ
KPHZ Phoenix, AZ
KPIC Eugene, OR
KPIF Idaho Falls-Pocatello, ID
KPIX-TV San Francisco-Oakland-San Jose
KPLC Lake Charles, LA
KPLO-TV Sioux Falls (Mitchell), SD
KPLR-TV St. Louis, MO
KPMR Santa Barbara-Santa Maria-San Luis Obispo, CA
*KPNE-TV North Platte, NE
KPNX Phoenix, AZ
KPNZ Salt Lake City, UT
KPOB-TV Paducah, KY-Cape Girardeau, MO-Harrisburg-Mount Vernon, IL
KPOU Portland, OR
KPPX Phoenix, AZ
KPRC-TV Houston
KPRY-TV Sioux Falls (Mitchell), SD
*KPSD-TV Minot-Bismarck-Dickinson, ND
KPTB Lubbock, TX
KPTF Amarillo, TX
KPTH Sioux City, IA
KPTM Omaha, NE
*KPTS Wichita-Hutchinson Plus, KS
KPTV Portland, OR
*KPTW Casper-Riverton, WY
KPVI Idaho Falls-Pocatello, ID
KPWB-TV Des Moines-Ames, IA
KPXB Houston
KPXC-TV Denver, CO
KPXD Dallas-Ft. Worth
KPXE Kansas City, MO
KPXG Portland, OR
KPXJ Shreveport, LA
KPXK Odessa-Midland, TX
KPXL San Antonio, TX
KPXM Minneapolis-St. Paul, MN
KPXN Los Angeles
KPXO Kaneohe HI
KPXR Cedar Rapids-Waterloo & Dubuque, IA
KQCA Sacramento-Stockton-Modesto, CA
KQCD-TV Minot-Bismarck-Dickinson, ND
*KQCT Davenport, IA-Rock Island-Moline, IL
KQDS-TV Duluth, MN-Superior, WI

*KQED San Francisco-Oakland-San Jose
*KQSD-TV Minot-Bismarck-Dickinson, ND
KQTV St. Joseph, MO
KQUP Spokane, WA
KRBC-TV Abilene-Sweetwater, TX
KRCA Los Angeles
*KRCB San Francisco-Oakland-San Jose
KRCG Columbia-Jefferson City, MO
KRCR-TV Chico-Redding, CA
KRDO-TV Colorado Springs-Pueblo, CO
KREG-TV Denver, CO
KREM-TV Spokane, WA
KREN-TV Reno, NV
KREX-TV Grand Junction-Montrose, CO
KREY-TV Grand Junction-Montrose, CO
KREZ-TV Albuquerque-Santa Fe, NM
KRGV-TV Harlingen-Weslaco-Brownsville-McAllen, TX
KRII Duluth, MN-Superior, WI
*KRIN Cedar Rapids-Waterloo & Dubuque, IA
KRIS-TV Corpus Christi, TX
KRIV Houston
*KRMA-TV Denver, CO
*KRMJ Grand Junction-Montrose, CO
*KRMT Denver, CO
*KRMU Albuquerque-Santa Fe, NM
*KRNE-TV Sioux Falls (Mitchell), SD
KRNV Reno, NV
KRON-TV San Francisco-Oakland-San Jose
KRPV Albuquerque-Santa Fe, NM
KRQE Albuquerque-Santa Fe, NM
KRRT San Antonio, TX
*KRSC-TV Tulsa, OK
KRTV Great Falls, MT
KRWB-TV Albuquerque-Santa Fe, NM
KRWF Minneapolis-St. Paul, MN
*KRWG-TV El Paso, TX
KRXI-TV Reno, NV
KSAN-TV San Angelo, TX
KSAS-TV Wichita-Hutchinson Plus, KS
KSAT-TV San Antonio, TX
KSAX Minneapolis-St. Paul, MN
KSAZ-TV Phoenix, AZ
KSBI Oklahoma City, OK
KSBN-TV Ft. Smith-Fayetteville-Springdale-Rogers, AR
KSBW Monterey-Salinas, CA
KSBY Santa Barbara-Santa Maria-San Luis Obispo, CA
KSCC Wichita-Hutchinson Plus, KS
KSCE El Paso, TX
KSCI Los Angeles
KSDK St. Louis, MO
KSEE Fresno-Visalia, CA
KSFX-TV Springfield, MO
KSFY-TV Sioux Falls (Mitchell), SD
KSGW Rapid City, SD
KSHB-TV Kansas City, MO
KSHV Shreveport, LA
*KSIN Sioux City, IA
KSKN Spokane, WA
KSLA-TV Shreveport, LA
KSL-TV Salt Lake City, UT
*KSMN Sioux Falls (Mitchell), SD
KSMO-TV Kansas City, MO
*KSMQ-TV Rochester, MN-Mason City, IA-Austin, MN
KSMS-TV Monterey-Salinas, CA
KSNB-TV Lincoln & Hastings-Kearney, NE
KSNC Wichita-Hutchinson Plus, KS
KSNF Joplin, MO-Pittsburg, KS
KSNG Wichita-Hutchinson Plus, KS
KSNK Wichita-Hutchinson Plus, KS
KSNT Topeka, KS
KSNW Wichita-Hutchinson Plus, KS
KSPR Springfield, MO
*KSPS-TV Spokane, WA
KSPX Sacramento-Stockton-Modesto, CA

*KSRE Minot-Bismarck-Dickinson, ND
KSTC-TV Minneapolis-St. Paul, MN
KSTF Cheyenne, WY-Scottsbluff, NE
KSTP-TV Minneapolis-St. Paul, MN
KSTR-TV Dallas-Ft. Worth
KSTS San Francisco-Oakland-San Jose
KSTU Salt Lake City, UT
KSTW Seattle-Tacoma, WA
KSVI Billings, MT
KSWB-TV San Diego, CA
*KSWK Wichita-Hutchinson Plus, KS
KSWO-TV Wichita Falls, TX & Lawton, OK
KSWT Yuma, AZ-El Centro, CA
KSWY Rapid City, SD
*KSYS Medford-Klamath Falls, OR
KTAB-TV Abilene-Sweetwater, TX
KTAJ-TV St. Joseph, MO
KTAL-TV Shreveport, LA
KTAQ Dallas-Ft. Worth
KTAS Santa Barbara-Santa Maria-San Luis Obispo, CA
KTBC Austin, TX
KTBN-TV Los Angeles
KTBO-TV Oklahoma City, OK
KTBS-TV Shreveport, LA
KTBU Houston
KTBW-TV Seattle-Tacoma, WA
KTBY Anchorage, AK
*KTCA-TV Minneapolis-St. Paul, MN
*KTCI-TV Minneapolis-St. Paul, MN
KTDO El Paso, TX
*KTEH San Francisco-Oakland-San Jose
*KTEJ Jonesboro, AR
KTEL-TV Albuquerque-Santa Fe, NM
KTEN Sherman, TX-Ada, OK
KTFD-TV Denver, CO
KTFF-TV Fresno-Visalia, CA
KTFK-TV Sacramento-Stockton-Modesto, CA
KTFL Phoenix, AZ
KTFN El Paso, TX
KTFO Tulsa, OK
KTFQ-TV Albuquerque-Santa Fe, NM
KTGF Great Falls, MT
KTGM Tamuning GU
KTHV Little Rock-Pine Bluff, AR
*KTIN Des Moines-Ames, IA
KTIV Sioux City, IA
KTKA-TV Topeka, KS
KTLA Los Angeles
KTLL-TV Albuquerque-Santa Fe, NM
*KTLM Harlingen-Weslaco-Brownsville-McAllen, TX
KTLN-TV San Francisco-Oakland-San Jose
KTMD Houston
KTMF Missoula, MT
KTMW Salt Lake City, UT
KTNC-TV San Francisco-Oakland-San Jose
*KTNE-TV Rapid City, SD
KTNL Juneau, AK
KTNV Las Vegas, NV
*KTNW Yakima-Pasco-Richland-Kennewick, WA
*KTOO-TV Juneau, AK
KTPX Tulsa, OK
KTRE Tyler-Longview (Lufkin & Nacogdoches), TX
KTRG San Antonio, TX
KTRK-TV Houston
KTRV Boise, ID
*KTSC Colorado Springs-Pueblo, CO
*KTSD-TV Sioux Falls (Mitchell), SD
KTSF San Francisco-Oakland-San Jose
KTSM-TV El Paso, TX
KTTC Rochester, MN-Mason City, IA-Austin, MN
KTTM Sioux Falls (Mitchell), SD
KTTU-TV Tucson (Sierra Vista), AZ
KTTV Los Angeles
KTTW Sioux Falls (Mitchell), SD
KTUL Tulsa, OK
KTUU-TV Anchorage, AK

KTUW Cheyenne, WY-Scottsbluff, NE
KTUZ-TV Oklahoma City, OK
KTVA Anchorage, AK
KTVB Boise, ID
KTVC Eugene, OR
KTVD Denver, CO
KTVE Monroe, LA-El Dorado, AR
KTVF Fairbanks, AK
KTVG Lincoln & Hastings-Kearney, NE
KTVH Helena, MT
KTVI St. Louis, MO
KTVK Phoenix, AZ
KTVL Medford-Klamath Falls, OR
KTVM Butte-Bozeman, MT
KTVN Reno, NV
KTVO Ottumwa, IA-Kirksville, MO
KTVQ Billings, MT
*KTVR Portland, OR
KTVT Dallas-Ft. Worth
KTVU San Francisco-Oakland-San Jose
KTVW-TV Phoenix, AZ
KTVX Salt Lake City, UT
KTVZ Bend, OR
KTWB-TV Seattle-Tacoma, WA
KTWO-TV Casper-Riverton, WY
*KTWU Topeka, KS
KTXA Dallas-Ft. Worth
KTXH Houston
KTXL Sacramento-Stockton-Modesto, CA
KTXS-TV Abilene-Sweetwater, TX
*KTXT-TV Lubbock, TX
*KUAC-TV Fairbanks, AK
KUAM-TV Hagatna GU
*KUAS-TV Tucson (Sierra Vista), AZ
*KUAT-TV Tucson (Sierra Vista), AZ
KUBD Ketchikan AK
*KUED Salt Lake City, UT
*KUEN Salt Lake City, UT
*KUES Salt Lake City, UT
*KUEW Salt Lake City, UT
*KUFM-TV Missoula, MT
*KUHT Houston
*KUID-TV Spokane, WA
KULR-TV Billings, MT
KUMV-TV Minot-Bismarck-Dickinson, ND
KUNO-TV San Francisco-Oakland-San Jose
KUOK Oklahoma City, OK
*KUON-TV Lincoln & Hastings-Kearney, NE
KUPB Odessa-Midland, TX
KUPK-TV Wichita-Hutchinson Plus, KS
KUPN Denver, CO
KUPT Lubbock, TX
KUPX Salt Lake City, UT
KUSA-TV Denver, CO
*KUSD-TV Sioux Falls (Mitchell), SD
KUSG Salt Lake City, UT
KUSI-TV San Diego, CA
*KUSM Butte-Bozeman, MT
KUTF Salt Lake City, UT
KUTH Salt Lake City, UT
KUTP Phoenix, AZ
KUTV Salt Lake City, UT
KUVE-TV Tucson (Sierra Vista), AZ
KUVI-TV Bakersfield, CA
KUVN-TV Dallas-Ft. Worth
KUVS-TV Sacramento-Stockton-Modesto, CA
KUWB Salt Lake City, UT
KVAL-TV Eugene, OR
KVAW San Antonio, TX
KVBC Las Vegas, NV
*KVCR-TV Los Angeles
KVCT Victoria, TX
KVDA San Antonio, TX
KVEA Los Angeles
KVEO Harlingen-Weslaco-Brownsville-McAllen, TX
KVEW Yakima-Pasco-Richland-Kennewick, WA
KVHP Lake Charles, LA
KVIA-TV El Paso, TX
*KVIE Sacramento-Stockton-Modesto, CA

Broadcasting & Cable Yearbook 2006

B-115

U.S. Television Stations by Call Letters

KVIH-TV Amarillo, TX
KVII-TV Amarillo, TX
KVIQ Eureka, CA
KVLY-TV Fargo-Valley City, ND
KVMD Los Angeles
KVOA Tucson (Sierra Vista), AZ
KVOS-TV Seattle-Tacoma, WA
*KVPT Fresno-Visalia, CA
KVRR Fargo-Valley City, ND
KVTH Little Rock-Pine Bluff, AR
KVTJ Jonesboro, AR
KVTN Little Rock-Pine Bluff, AR
KVTV Laredo, TX
KVUE-TV Austin, TX
KVVU-TV Las Vegas, NV
KVWB Las Vegas, NV
KVYE Yuma, AZ-El Centro, CA
*KVZK-2 Pago Pago AS
*KVZK-4 Pago Pago AS
*KVZK-5 Pago Pago AS
KWAB-TV Odessa-Midland, TX
KWBA Tucson (Sierra Vista), AZ
KWBF Little Rock-Pine Bluff, AR
KWBM Springfield, MO
*KWBN Honolulu, HI
KWBP Portland, OR
KWBQ Albuquerque-Santa Fe, NM
KWBT Tulsa, OK
*KWBU-TV Waco-Temple-Bryan, TX
KWCH-TV Wichita-Hutchinson Plus, KS
*KWCM-TV Minneapolis-St. Paul, MN
KWCV Wichita-Hutchinson Plus, KS
*KWDK Seattle-Tacoma, WA
KWES-TV Odessa-Midland, TX
*KWET Oklahoma City, OK
KWEX-TV San Antonio, TX
KWFT Springfield, MO
KWGN-TV Denver, CO
KWHB Tulsa, OK
KWHD Denver, CO
KWHE Honolulu, HI
KWHH Hilo HI
KWHM Wailuku HI
KWHY-TV Los Angeles
KWKB Cedar Rapids-Waterloo & Dubuque, IA
KWKT Waco-Temple-Bryan, TX
KWNB-TV Lincoln & Hastings-Kearney, NE
KWNV Reno, NV
KWOG Seattle-Tacoma, WA
KWPX Seattle-Tacoma, WA
KWQC-TV Davenport, IA-Rock Island-Moline, IL
KWSD Sioux Falls (Mitchell), SD
*KWSE Minot-Bismarck-Dickinson, ND
*KWSU-TV Spokane, WA
KWTV Oklahoma City, OK
KWTX-TV Waco-Temple-Bryan, TX
KWWF Cedar Rapids-Waterloo & Dubuque, IA
KWWL Cedar Rapids-Waterloo & Dubuque, IA
KWYB Butte-Bozeman, MT
*KWYP-TV Denver, CO
KXAM-TV Austin, TX
KXAN-TV Austin, TX
KXAS-TV Dallas-Ft. Worth
KXGN-TV Glendive, MT
KXII Sherman, TX-Ada, OK
KXJB-TV Fargo-Valley City, ND
KXLA Los Angeles
KXLF-TV Butte-Bozeman, MT
KXLN-TV Houston
KXLT-TV Rochester, MN-Mason City, IA-Austin, MN
KXLY-TV Spokane, WA
KXMA-TV Minot-Bismarck-Dickinson, ND
KXMB-TV Minot-Bismarck-Dickinson, ND
KXMC-TV Minot-Bismarck-Dickinson, ND
KXMD-TV Minot-Bismarck-Dickinson, ND
KXND Minot-Bismarck-Dickinson, ND
*KXNE-TV Sioux City, IA

KXRM-TV Colorado Springs-Pueblo, CO
KXTF Twin Falls, ID
KXTV Sacramento-Stockton-Modesto, CA
KXTX-TV Dallas-Ft. Worth
KXVA Abilene-Sweetwater, TX
KXVO Omaha, NE
KXXV Waco-Temple-Bryan, TX
KYES Anchorage, AK
*KYIN Rochester, MN-Mason City, IA-Austin, MN
KYLE Waco-Temple-Bryan, TX
KYMA Yuma, AZ-El Centro, CA
*KYNE-TV Omaha, NE
KYOU-TV Ottumwa, IA-Kirksville, MO
KYPX Little Rock-Pine Bluff, AR
KYTV Springfield, MO
KYTX Tyler-Longview (Lufkin & Nacogdoches), TX
*KYUK-TV Bethel AK
KYUS-TV Billings, MT
*KYVE Yakima-Pasco-Richland-Kennewick, WA
KYW-TV Philadelphia
KZJL Houston
*KZSD-TV Rapid City, SD
KZTV Corpus Christi, TX
WAAY-TV Huntsville-Decatur (Florence), AL
WABC-TV New York
WABG-TV Greenwood-Greenville, MS
WABI-TV Bangor, ME
WABM Birmingham (Anniston, Tuscaloosa), AL
*WABW-TV Albany, GA
WACH Columbia, SC
*WACS-TV Albany, GA
WACX Orlando-Daytona Beach-Melbourne, FL
WACY Green Bay-Appleton, WI
WADL Detroit
WAFB Baton Rouge, LA
WAFF Huntsville-Decatur (Florence), AL
WAGA Atlanta
WAGM-TV Presque Isle, ME
WAGT Augusta, GA
WAGV Knoxville, TN
*WAIQ Montgomery (Selma), AL
WAKA Montgomery (Selma), AL
WALA-TV Mobile, AL-Pensacola (Ft. Walton Beach), FL
WALB Albany, GA
WAMI-TV Miami-Ft. Lauderdale, FL
WAND Champaign & Springfield-Decatur, IL
WANE-TV Ft. Wayne, IN
WAOE Peoria-Bloomington, IL
WAOW-TV Wausau-Rhinelander, WI
WAPA-TV San Juan PR
WAPT Jackson, MS
WAQP Flint-Saginaw-Bay City, MI
WASV-TV Greenville-Spartanburg, SC-Asheville, NC-Anderson, SC
*WATC Atlanta
WATE-TV Knoxville, TN
WATL Atlanta
WATM-TV Johnstown-Altoona, PA
WAVE Louisville, KY
WAVY-TV Norfolk-Portsmouth-Newport News, VA
WAWD Mobile, AL-Pensacola (Ft. Walton Beach), FL
WAWS Jacksonville, FL
WAXN-TV Charlotte, NC
WAZE-TV Evansville, IN
WBAL-TV Baltimore, MD
WBAY-TV Green Bay-Appleton, WI
WBBH-TV Ft. Myers-Naples, FL
WBBJ-TV Jackson, TN
WBBM-TV Chicago
*WBCC Orlando-Daytona Beach-Melbourne, FL
WBDC-TV Washington, DC (Hagerstown, MD)
WBDT Dayton, OH
WBFF Baltimore, MD
WBFS-TV Miami-Ft. Lauderdale, FL

*WBGU-TV Toledo, OH
WBHQ Columbia, SC
WBIF Panama City, FL
WBIH Montgomery (Selma), AL
WBIJ Wausau-Rhinelander, WI
*WBIQ Birmingham (Anniston, Tuscaloosa), AL
WBIR-TV Knoxville, TN
WBKB-TV Alpena, MI
WBKI-TV Louisville, KY
WBKO Bowling Green, KY
WBKP Marquette, MI
WBMM Montgomery (Selma), AL
WBNA Louisville, KY
WBNG-TV Binghamton, NY
WBNS-TV Columbus, OH
WBNX-TV Cleveland, OH
WBOC-TV Salisbury, MD
WBOY-TV Clarksburg-Weston, WV
WBPG Mobile, AL-Pensacola (Ft. Walton Beach), FL
WBPH-TV Philadelphia
WBPX Boston (Manchester), NH
*WBRA-TV Roanoke-Lynchburg, VA
WBRC Birmingham (Anniston, Tuscaloosa), AL
WBRE-TV Wilkes Barre-Scranton, PA
WBRZ Baton Rouge, LA
WBSC-TV Greenville-Spartanburg, SC-Asheville, NC-Anderson, SC
WBSF Flint-Saginaw-Bay City, MI
WBTV Charlotte, NC
WBTW Florence-Myrtle Beach, SC
WBUI Champaign & Springfield-Decatur, IL
WBUP Marquette, MI
WBUW Madison, WI
WBUY-TV Memphis, TN
WBXX-TV Knoxville, TN
WBZL Miami-Ft. Lauderdale, FL
WBZ-TV Boston (Manchester), NH
WCAU Philadelphia
WCAV Charlottesville, VA
WCAX-TV Burlington, VT-Plattsburgh, NY
*WCBB Portland-Auburn, ME
WCBD-TV Charleston, SC
WCBI-TV Columbus-Tupelo-West Point, MS
WCBS-TV New York
WCCB Charlotte, NC
WCCO-TV Minneapolis-St. Paul, MN
WCCU Champaign & Springfield-Decatur, IL
WCCV-TV Arecibo PR
WCDC Albany-Schenectady-Troy, NY
*WCES-TV Augusta, GA
*WCET Cincinnati, OH
*WCEU Orlando-Daytona Beach-Melbourne, FL
*WCFE-TV Burlington, VT-Plattsburgh, NY
WCFN Champaign & Springfield-Decatur, IL
WCFT-TV Birmingham (Anniston, Tuscaloosa), AL
WCGV-TV Milwaukee, WI
WCHS-TV Charleston-Huntington, WV
WCIA Champaign & Springfield-Decatur, IL
*WCIQ Birmingham (Anniston, Tuscaloosa), AL
WCIU-TV Chicago
WCIV Charleston, SC
WCJB Gainesville, FL
WCLF Tampa-St. Petersburg (Sarasota), FL
WCLJ-TV Indianapolis, IN
*WCLP-TV Chattanooga, TN
WCMH-TV Columbus, OH
*WCML-TV Alpena, MI
*WCMU-TV Flint-Saginaw-Bay City, MI
*WCMV Traverse City-Cadillac, MI
*WCMW Traverse City-Cadillac, MI
WCNC-TV Charlotte, NC
WCNY-TV Syracuse, NY
WCOV-TV Montgomery (Selma), AL
WCPB Salisbury, MD

WCPO-TV Cincinnati, OH
WCPX Chicago
WCSC-TV Charleston, SC
WCSH Portland-Auburn, ME
*WCTE Nashville, TN
WCTI Greenville-New Bern-Washington, NC
WCTV Tallahassee, FL-Thomasville, GA
WCTX Hartford & New Haven, CT
WCVB-TV Boston (Manchester), NH
*WCVE-TV Richmond-Petersburg, VA
WCVI-TV Christiansted VI
*WCVN Cincinnati, OH
*WCVW Richmond-Petersburg, VA
WCWB Pittsburgh, PA
WCYB-TV Tri-Cities, TN-VA
WDAF-TV Kansas City, MO
WDAM-TV Hattiesburg-Laurel, MS
WDAY-TV Fargo-Valley City, ND
WDAZ-TV Fargo-Valley City, ND
WDBB Birmingham (Anniston, Tuscaloosa), AL
WDBD Jackson, MS
WDBJ Roanoke-Lynchburg, VA
WDCA Washington, DC (Hagerstown, MD)
*WDCO-TV Macon, GA
*WDCP-TV Flint-Saginaw-Bay City, MI
*WDCQ-TV Flint-Saginaw-Bay City, MI
WDEF-TV Chattanooga, TN
WDFX-TV Dothan, AL
WDHN Dothan, AL
WDHS Marquette, MI
WDIO-TV Duluth, MN-Superior, WI
*WDIQ Montgomery (Selma), AL
WDIV Detroit
WDJT-TV Milwaukee, WI
WDKA Paducah, KY-Cape Girardeau, MO-Harrisburg-Mount Vernon, IL
WDKY-TV Lexington, KY
WDLI-TV Cleveland, OH
WDLP-TV Miami-Ft. Lauderdale, FL
*WDPB Salisbury, MD
WDPX Providence, RI-New Bedford, MA
WDRB Louisville, KY
WDRL-TV Roanoke-Lynchburg, VA
*WDSE-TV Duluth, MN-Superior, WI
WDSI-TV Chattanooga, TN
WDSU New Orleans, LA
*WDTI Indianapolis, IN
WDTN Dayton, OH
WDTV Clarksburg-Weston, WV
WDWB Detroit
WDWL Bayamon PR
*WEAO Cleveland, OH
WEAR-TV Mobile, AL-Pensacola (Ft. Walton Beach), FL
WEAU-TV La Crosse-Eau Claire, WI
*WEBA-TV Augusta, GA
WECN Naranjito PR
WECT Wilmington, NC
*WEDH Hartford & New Haven, CT
*WEDN Hartford & New Haven, CT
*WEDU Tampa-St. Petersburg (Sarasota), FL
*WEDW New York
*WEDY Hartford & New Haven, CT
WEEK-TV Peoria-Bloomington, IL
WEHT Evansville, IN
*WEIQ Mobile, AL-Pensacola (Ft. Walton Beach), FL
*WEIU-TV Champaign & Springfield-Decatur, IL
*WEKW-TV Boston (Manchester), NH
WELF-TV Chattanooga, TN
*WELU Aguadilla PR
WEMT Tri-Cities, TN-VA
*WENH Boston (Manchester), NH
WENY-TV Elmira, NY
WEPX Greenville-New Bern-Washington, NC
WESH Orlando-Daytona Beach-Melbourne, FL
*WETA-TV Washington, DC (Hagerstown, MD)
*WETK Burlington, VT-Plattsburgh, NY

WETM-TV Elmira, NY
*WETP-TV Knoxville, TN
WEUX La Crosse-Eau Claire, WI
WEVV Evansville, IN
WEWB Albany-Schenectady-Troy, NY
WEWS Cleveland, OH
WEYI-TV Flint-Saginaw-Bay City, MI
WFAA-TV Dallas-Ft. Worth
WFBD Mobile, AL-Pensacola (Ft. Walton Beach), FL
WFDC-TV Washington, DC (Hagerstown, MD)
WFFF-TV Burlington, VT-Plattsburgh, NY
WFFT-TV Ft. Wayne, IN
WFGC West Palm Beach-Ft. Pierce, FL
WFGX Mobile, AL-Pensacola (Ft. Walton Beach), FL
WFIE Evansville, IN
*WFIQ Huntsville-Decatur (Florence), AL
WFLA-TV Tampa-St. Petersburg (Sarasota), FL
WFLD Chicago
WFLI-TV Chattanooga, TN
WFLX West Palm Beach-Ft. Pierce, FL
WFME-TV New York
WFMJ-TV Youngstown, OH
WFMY-TV Greensboro-High Point-Winston Salem, NC
WFMZ-TV Philadelphia
WFOR-TV Miami-Ft. Lauderdale, FL
*WFPT Washington, DC (Hagerstown, MD)
WFPX Raleigh-Durham (Fayetteville), NC
WFQX-TV Traverse City-Cadillac, MI
WFRV-TV Green Bay-Appleton, WI
WFSB Hartford & New Haven, CT
*WFSG Panama City, FL
*WFSU-TV Tallahassee, FL-Thomasville, GA
WFTC Minneapolis-St. Paul, MN
WFTE Louisville, KY
WFTS Tampa-St. Petersburg (Sarasota), FL
WFTT-TV Tampa-St. Petersburg (Sarasota), FL
WFTV Orlando-Daytona Beach-Melbourne, FL
WFTX Ft. Myers-Naples, FL
WFTY-TV New York
*WFUM Flint-Saginaw-Bay City, MI
WFUP Traverse City-Cadillac, MI
WFUT-TV New York
*WFWA Ft. Wayne, IN
WFXB Florence-Myrtle Beach, SC
WFXG Augusta, GA
WFXI Greenville-New Bern-Washington, NC
WFXL Albany, GA
WFXP Erie, PA
WFXR-TV Roanoke-Lynchburg, VA
WFXS Green Bay-Appleton, WI
WFXT Boston (Manchester), NH
WFXU Tallahassee, FL-Thomasville, GA
WFXV Utica, NY
WFXW Terre Haute, IN
*WFYI Indianapolis, IN
WGAL Harrisburg-Lancaster-Lebanon-York, PA
WGBA Green Bay-Appleton, WI
*WGBC Meridian, MS
*WGBH-TV Boston (Manchester), NH
WGBO-TV Chicago
*WGBX-TV Boston (Manchester), NH
*WGBY-TV Springfield-Holyoke, MA
WGCB-TV Harrisburg-Lancaster-Lebanon-York, PA
WGCL-TV Atlanta
*WGCU Ft. Myers-Naples, FL
WGEM-TV Quincy, IL-Hannibal, MO-Keokuk, IA
WGEN-TV Miami-Ft. Lauderdale, FL
WGFL Gainesville, FL
WGGB-TV Springfield-Holyoke, MA
WGGN-TV Cleveland, OH

U.S. Television Stations by Call Letters

WGGS-TV Greenville-Spartanburg, SC-Asheville, NC-Anderson, SC
WGHP Greensboro-High Point-Winston Salem, NC
*WGIQ Columbus, GA
WGMB Baton Rouge, LA
WGME-TV Portland-Auburn, ME
WGNM Macon, GA
WGNO New Orleans, LA
WGNT Norfolk-Portsmouth-Newport News, VA
WGN-TV Chicago
*WGPT Pittsburgh, PA
WGPX Greensboro-High Point-Winston Salem, NC
WGRZ-TV Buffalo, NY
WGSA Savannah, GA
*WGTE-TV Toledo, OH
WGTQ Traverse City-Cadillac, MI
WGTU Traverse City-Cadillac, MI
*WGTV Atlanta
WGTW-TV Philadelphia
*WGVK Grand Rapids-Kalamazoo-Battle Creek, MI
*WGVU-TV Grand Rapids-Kalamazoo-Battle Creek, MI
WGXA Macon, GA
WHAG-TV Washington, DC (Hagerstown, MD)
WHAM-TV Rochester, NY
WHAS-TV Louisville, KY
*WHA-TV Madison, WI
WHBF-TV Davenport, IA-Rock Island-Moline, IL
WHBQ-TV Memphis, TN
WHBR Mobile, AL-Pensacola (Ft. Walton Beach), FL
WHCP Charleston-Huntington, WV
WHDF Huntsville-Decatur (Florence), AL
WHDH-TV Boston (Manchester, NH)
WHEC-TV Rochester, NY
*WHFT-TV Miami-Ft. Lauderdale, FL
WHIO-TV Dayton, OH
*WHIQ Huntsville-Decatur (Florence), AL
WHIZ-TV Zanesville, OH
WHKY-TV Charlotte, NC
*WHLA-TV La Crosse-Eau Claire, WI
WHLT Hattiesburg-Laurel, MS
WHMB-TV Indianapolis, IN
*WHMC Florence-Myrtle Beach, SC
WHME-TV South Bend-Elkhart, IN
WHNO New Orleans, LA
WHNS Greenville-Spartanburg, SC-Asheville, NC-Anderson, SC
WHNT-TV Huntsville-Decatur (Florence), AL
WHOI Peoria-Bloomington, IL
WHO-TV Des Moines-Ames, IA
WHP-TV Harrisburg-Lancaster-Lebanon-York, PA
WHPX Hartford & New Haven, CT
WHRE Norfolk-Portsmouth-Newport News, VA
*WHRM-TV Wausau-Rhinelander, WI
*WHRO-TV Norfolk-Portsmouth-Newport News, VA
*WHSG-TV Atlanta
WHSV-TV Harrisonburg, VA
*WHTJ Charlottesville, VA
WHTM-TV Harrisburg-Lancaster-Lebanon-York, PA
WHTN Nashville, TN
WHTV Lansing, MI
*WHUT-TV Washington, DC (Hagerstown, MD)
*WHWC-TV Minneapolis-St. Paul, MN
*WHYY-TV Philadelphia
WIAT Birmingham (Anniston, Tuscaloosa), AL
WIBW-TV Topeka, KS
WICD Champaign & Springfield-Decatur, IL
WICS Champaign & Springfield-Decatur, IL
WICU-TV Erie, PA
WICZ-TV Binghamton, NY

WIDP Guayama PR
WIFR Rockford, IL
*WIIQ Montgomery (Selma), AL
WILF Wilkes Barre-Scranton, PA
*WILL-TV Champaign & Springfield-Decatur, IL
WILX-TV Lansing, MI
WINK-TV Ft. Myers-Naples, FL
WINM Ft. Wayne, IN
*WIPB Indianapolis, IN
*WIPM-TV Mayaguez PR
*WIPR-TV San Juan PR
WIPX Indianapolis, IN
WIRS Yauco PR
WIRT Duluth, MN-Superior, WI
WIS Columbia, SC
WISC-TV Madison, WI
WISE-TV Ft. Wayne, IN
WISH-TV Indianapolis, IN
WISN-TV Milwaukee, WI
*WITF-TV Harrisburg-Lancaster-Lebanon-York, PA
WITI Milwaukee, WI
WITN-TV Greenville-New Bern-Washington, NC
*WITV Charleston, SC
WIVB-TV Buffalo, NY
WIVT Binghamton, NY
WIWB Green Bay-Appleton, WI
WJAC-TV Johnstown-Altoona, PA
WJAL Washington, DC (Hagerstown, MD)
WJAR Providence, RI-New Bedford, MA
WJBF Augusta, GA
WJBK Detroit
WJCL Savannah, GA
*WJCT Jacksonville, FL
*WJEB-TV Jacksonville, FL
WJET-TV Erie, PA
WJFB Nashville, TN
WJFW-TV Wausau-Rhinelander, WI
WJHG-TV Panama City, FL
WJHL-TV Tri-Cities, TN-VA
WJJA Milwaukee, WI
WJKT Jackson, TN
WJLA-TV Washington, DC (Hagerstown, MD)
WJMN-TV Marquette, MI
*WJPM-TV Florence-Myrtle Beach, SC
WJPR Roanoke-Lynchburg, VA
WJPX San Juan PR
WJRT-TV Flint-Saginaw-Bay City, MI
*WJSP-TV Columbus, GA
WJSU-TV Birmingham (Anniston, Tuscaloosa), AL
WJTC Mobile, AL-Pensacola (Ft. Walton Beach), FL
WJTV Jackson, MS
WJW Cleveland, OH
WJWB Jacksonville, FL
*WJWJ-TV Savannah, GA
WJWN-TV San Sebastian PR
WJXT Jacksonville, FL
WJXX Jacksonville, FL
WJYS Chicago
WJZ-TV Baltimore, MD
WJZY Charlotte, NC
WKAQ-TV San Juan PR
*WKAR-TV Lansing, MI
*WKAS Charleston-Huntington, WV
WKBD Detroit
WKBN-TV Youngstown, OH
WKBS-TV Johnstown-Altoona, PA
WKBT La Crosse-Eau Claire, WI
WKBW-TV Buffalo, NY
WKCF Orlando-Daytona Beach-Melbourne, FL
WKDH Columbus-Tupelo-West Point, MS
WKEF Dayton, OH
*WKGB-TV Bowling Green, KY
*WKHA Lexington, KY
*WKLE Lexington, KY
*WKMA Evansville, IN
WKMG-TV Orlando-Daytona Beach-Melbourne, FL
WKMJ Louisville, KY

*WKMR Lexington, KY
*WKMU Paducah, KY-Cape Girardeau, MO-Harrisburg-Mount Vernon, IL
*WKNO-TV Memphis, TN
*WKOH Evansville, IN
WKOI-TV Dayton, OH
*WKON Cincinnati, OH
*WKOP-TV Knoxville, TN
WKOW-TV Madison, WI
*WKPC-TV Louisville, KY
*WKPD Paducah, KY-Cape Girardeau, MO-Harrisburg-Mount Vernon, IL
*WKPI Charleston-Huntington, WV
WKPT-TV Tri-Cities, TN-VA
*WKPV Ponce PR
WKRC-TV Cincinnati, OH
WKRG-TV Mobile, AL-Pensacola (Ft. Walton Beach), FL
WKRN-TV Nashville, TN
*WKSO-TV Lexington, KY
WKTV Utica, NY
WKYC-TV Cleveland, OH
*WKYT-TV Lexington, KY
*WKYU-TV Bowling Green, KY
*WKZT-TV Louisville, KY
*WLAE-TV New Orleans, LA
WLAJ Lansing, MI
WLAX La Crosse-Eau Claire, WI
WLBT Jackson, MS
WLBZ Bangor, ME
WLCB-TV Orlando-Daytona Beach-Melbourne, FL
WLDM Birmingham (Anniston, Tuscaloosa), AL
*WLED-TV Portland-Auburn, ME
*WLEF-TV Wausau-Rhinelander, WI
WLEX-TV Lexington, KY
WLFB Bluefield-Beckley-Oak Hill, WV
WLFG Tri-Cities, TN-VA
WLFI-TV Lafayette, IN
WLFL Raleigh-Durham (Fayetteville), NC
WLGA Columbus, GA
WLII Caguas PR
WLIO Lima, OH
*WLIW New York
WLJC-TV Lexington, KY
*WLJT-TV Jackson, TN
WLKY-TV Louisville, KY
WLLA Grand Rapids-Kalamazoo-Battle Creek, MI
WLMB Toledo, OH
WLMT Memphis, TN
WLNE Providence, RI-New Bedford, MA
WLNS-TV Lansing, MI
WLNY New York
WLOS Greenville-Spartanburg, SC-Asheville, NC-Anderson, SC
WLOV-TV Columbus-Tupelo-West Point, MS
WLOX Biloxi-Gulfport, MS
*WLPB-TV Baton Rouge, LA
WLPX-TV Charleston-Huntington, WV
*WLRN-TV Miami-Ft. Lauderdale, FL
WLS-TV Chicago
WLTV Miami-Ft. Lauderdale, FL
WLTX Columbia, SC
WLTZ Columbus, GA
WLUC-TV Marquette, MI
WLUK-TV Green Bay-Appleton, WI
WLVI-TV Boston (Manchester, NH)
*WLVT-TV Philadelphia
WLWC Providence, RI-New Bedford, MA
WLWT Cincinnati, OH
WLXI-TV Greensboro-High Point-Winston Salem, NC
WLYH-TV Harrisburg-Lancaster-Lebanon-York, PA
*WMAA Columbus-Tupelo-West Point, MS
*WMAB-TV Columbus-Tupelo-West Point, MS
*WMAE-TV Columbus-Tupelo-West Point, MS
*WMAH-TV Biloxi-Gulfport, MS
*WMAI Greenwood-Greenville, MS
WMAK Knoxville, TN

*WMAO-TV Greenwood-Greenville, MS
WMAQ-TV Chicago
WMAR-TV Baltimore, MD
*WMAU-TV Jackson, MS
*WMAV-TV Memphis, TN
*WMAW-TV Meridian, MS
WMAZ-TV Macon, GA
WMBB Panama City, FL
WMBC-TV New York
WMBD-TV Peoria-Bloomington, IL
WMCF-TV Montgomery (Selma), AL
WMCN-TV Philadelphia
WMC-TV Memphis, TN
WMDN Meridian, MS
WMDT Salisbury, MD
*WMEA-TV Portland-Auburn, ME
*WMEB-TV Bangor, ME
WMEC Quincy, IL-Hannibal, MO-Keokuk, IA
*WMED-TV Bangor, ME
WMEI Arecibo PR
*WMEM-TV Presque Isle, ME
WMFD-TV Cleveland, OH
*WMFE-TV Orlando-Daytona Beach-Melbourne, FL
WMFP Boston (Manchester, NH)
WMGM-TV Philadelphia
WMGT-TV Macon, GA
*WMHT Albany-Schenectady-Troy, NY
WMMP Charleston, SC
WMOR-TV Tampa-St. Petersburg (Sarasota), FL
*WMPB Baltimore, MD
*WMPN-TV Jackson, MS
*WMPT Baltimore, MD
WMPV-TV Mobile, AL-Pensacola (Ft. Walton Beach), FL
WMQF Marquette, MI
WMSN-TV Madison, WI
WMSY-TV Tri-Cities, TN-VA
*WMTJ Fajardo PR
WMTV Madison, WI
WMTW-TV Portland-Auburn, ME
WMUR-TV Boston (Manchester, NH)
*WMVS Milwaukee, WI
*WMVT Milwaukee, WI
*WMYC Jackson, MS
WNAB Nashville, TN
WNAC-TV Providence, RI-New Bedford, MA
WNBC New York
WNCF Montgomery (Selma), AL
WNCN Raleigh-Durham (Fayetteville), NC
WNCT-TV Greenville-New Bern-Washington, NC
WNDS Boston (Manchester, NH)
WNDU-TV South Bend-Elkhart, IN
WNDY-TV Indianapolis, IN
*WNED-TV Buffalo, NY
WNEG-TV Greenville-Spartanburg, SC-Asheville, NC-Anderson, SC
*WNEH Greenville-Spartanburg, SC-Asheville, NC-Anderson, SC
WNEM-TV Flint-Saginaw-Bay City, MI
*WNEO Youngstown, OH
WNEP-TV Wilkes Barre-Scranton, PA
*WNET New York
WNEU Boston (Manchester, NH)
WNGS Buffalo, NY
*WNIN Evansville, IN
*WNIT-TV South Bend-Elkhart, IN
*WNJB New York
*WNJN New York
*WNJS Philadelphia
*WNJT Philadelphia
WNJU New York
WNJX-TV Mayaguez PR
WNKY Bowling Green, KY
WNLO Buffalo, NY
*WNMU-TV Marquette, MI
WNNE Burlington, VT-Plattsburgh, NY
WNOL-TV New Orleans, LA
WNPA Pittsburgh, PA
*WNPB-TV Pittsburgh, PA
*WNPI-TV Watertown, NY
*WNPT Nashville, TN

WNPX Nashville, TN
*WNSC-TV Charlotte, NC
*WNTV Greenville-Spartanburg, SC-Asheville, NC-Anderson, SC
WNTZ Jackson, MS
WNUV Baltimore, MD
*WNVC Washington, DC (Hagerstown, MD)
*WNVT Washington, DC (Hagerstown, MD)
WNWO-TV Toledo, OH
*WNYA Albany-Schenectady-Troy, NY
WNYB Buffalo, NY
*WNYE-TV New York
WNYI Syracuse, NY
*WNYO-TV Buffalo, NY
*WNYS-TV Syracuse, NY
WNYT Albany-Schenectady-Troy, NY
WNYW New York
WOAC Cleveland, OH
WOAI-TV San Antonio, TX
WOAY-TV Bluefield-Beckley-Oak Hill, WV
WOFL Orlando-Daytona Beach-Melbourne, FL
WOGX Gainesville, FL
WOIO Cleveland, OH
WOI-TV Des Moines-Ames, IA
WOLE-TV Aguadilla PR
WOLF-TV Wilkes Barre-Scranton, PA
WOLO-TV Columbia, SC
WOOD-TV Grand Rapids-Kalamazoo-Battle Creek, MI
WOPX Orlando-Daytona Beach-Melbourne, FL
WORA-TV Mayaguez PR
WOST Mayaguez PR
*WOSU-TV Columbus, OH
WOTF-TV Orlando-Daytona Beach-Melbourne, FL
WOTV Grand Rapids-Kalamazoo-Battle Creek, MI
*WOUB-TV Charleston-Huntington, WV
*WOUC-TV Wheeling, WV-Steubenville, OH
WOWK-TV Charleston-Huntington, WV
WOWT Omaha, NE
WPAN Mobile, AL-Pensacola (Ft. Walton Beach), FL
*WPBA Atlanta
WPBF West Palm Beach-Ft. Pierce, FL
WPBN-TV Traverse City-Cadillac, MI
*WPBO-TV Charleston-Huntington, WV
*WPBS-TV Watertown, NY
*WPBT Miami-Ft. Lauderdale, FL
*WPBY-TV Charleston-Huntington, WV
WPCB-TV Pittsburgh, PA
WPCT Panama City, FL
WPDE-TV Florence-Myrtle Beach, SC
WPEC West Palm Beach-Ft. Pierce, FL
WPFO Portland-Auburn, ME
WPGA-TV Macon, GA
WPGD-TV Nashville, TN
WPGH-TV Pittsburgh, PA
WPGX Panama City, FL
WPHL-TV Philadelphia
WPIX New York
WPLG Miami-Ft. Lauderdale, FL
WPME Portland-Auburn, ME
WPMI-TV Mobile, AL-Pensacola (Ft. Walton Beach), FL
WPMT Harrisburg-Lancaster-Lebanon-York, PA
*WPNE Green Bay-Appleton, WI
*WPPB-TV West Palm Beach-Ft. Pierce, FL
WPPX Philadelphia
WPRI-TV Providence, RI-New Bedford, MA
WPRV-TV Fajardo PR
WPSD-TV Paducah, KY-Cape Girardeau, MO-Harrisburg-Mount Vernon, IL
WPSG Philadelphia
*WPSX-TV Johnstown-Altoona, PA
WPTA Ft. Wayne, IN
*WPTD Dayton, OH

U.S. Television Stations by Call Letters

*WPTO Cincinnati, OH
WPTV West Palm Beach-Ft. Pierce, FL
WPTY-TV Memphis, TN
WPTZ Burlington, VT-Plattsburgh, NY
WPVI-TV Philadelphia
WPWR-TV Gary IN
WPXA Atlanta
WPXC-TV Jacksonville, FL
WPXD Detroit
WPXE Milwaukee, WI
WPXG Boston (Manchester, NH)
WPXH Birmingham (Anniston, Tuscaloosa), AL
WPXI Pittsburgh, PA
WPXJ-TV Buffalo, NY
WPXK Knoxville, TN
WPXL New Orleans, LA
WPXM Miami-Ft. Lauderdale, FL
WPXN-TV New York
WPXP West Palm Beach-Ft. Pierce, FL
WPXQ Providence, RI-New Bedford, MA
WPXR Roanoke-Lynchburg, VA
WPXS Paducah, KY-Cape Girardeau, MO-Harrisburg-Mount Vernon, IL
WPXT Portland-Auburn, ME
WPXU-TV Greenville-New Bern-Washington, NC
WPXV Norfolk-Portsmouth-Newport News, VA
WPXW Washington, DC (Hagerstown, MD)
WPXX-TV Memphis, TN
WQAD-TV Davenport, IA-Rock Island-Moline, IL
*WQEC Quincy, IL-Hannibal, MO-Keokuk, IA
*WQED Pittsburgh, PA
WQEX Pittsburgh, PA
WQHA Aguada PR
WQHS-TV Cleveland, OH
*WQLN Erie, PA
WQOW-TV La Crosse-Eau Claire, WI
*WQPT Davenport, IA-Rock Island-Moline, IL
WQPX Wilkes Barre-Scranton, PA
WQRF-TV Rockford, IL
*WQTO Ponce PR
WRAL-TV Raleigh-Durham (Fayetteville), NC
WRAY-TV Raleigh-Durham (Fayetteville), NC
WRAZ Raleigh-Durham (Fayetteville), NC
WRBJ Jackson, MS
WRBL Columbus, GA
WRBU St. Louis, MO
WRBW Orlando-Daytona Beach-Melbourne, FL
WRCB-TV Chattanooga, TN
WRC-TV Washington, DC (Hagerstown, MD)
WRDC Raleigh-Durham (Fayetteville), NC
WRDQ Orlando-Daytona Beach-Melbourne, FL
WRDW-TV Augusta, GA
WREG-TV Memphis, TN
*WRET-TV Greenville-Spartanburg, SC-Asheville, NC-Anderson, SC
WREX-TV Rockford, IL
WRFB Carolina PR
WRGB Albany-Schenectady-Troy, NY
WRGT-TV Dayton, OH
WRIC-TV Richmond-Petersburg, VA
*WRJA-TV Columbia, SC
WRJM-TV Montgomery (Selma), AL
WRLH-TV Richmond-Petersburg, VA
*WRLK-TV Columbia, SC
WRNN-TV New York
WROC-TV Rochester, NY

WRPX Raleigh-Durham (Fayetteville), NC
WRSP-TV Champaign & Springfield-Decatur, IL
WRTV Indianapolis, IN
WRUA Fajardo PR
WRXY-TV Ft. Myers-Naples, FL
WSAH New York
WSAV-TV Savannah, GA
WSAW-TV Wausau-Rhinelander, WI
WSAZ-TV Charleston-Huntington, WV
*WSBE-TV Providence, RI-New Bedford, MA
WSBK-TV Boston (Manchester, NH)
*WSBN-TV Tri-Cities, TN-VA
WSBT-TV South Bend-Elkhart, IN
WSB-TV Atlanta
WSCV Miami-Ft. Lauderdale, FL
*WSEC Champaign & Springfield-Decatur, IL
WSEE Erie, PA
WSET-TV Roanoke-Lynchburg, VA
WSFA Montgomery (Selma), AL
WSFJ Columbus, OH
WSFX-TV Wilmington, NC
WSIL-TV Paducah, KY-Cape Girardeau, MO-Harrisburg-Mount Vernon, IL
*WSIU-TV Paducah, KY-Cape Girardeau, MO-Harrisburg-Mount Vernon, IL
WSJU-TV San Juan PR
WSJV South Bend-Elkhart, IN
*WSKA Elmira, NY
*WSKG-TV Binghamton, NY
WSKY-TV Norfolk-Portsmouth-Newport News, VA
WSLS-TV Roanoke-Lynchburg, VA
WSMH Flint-Saginaw-Bay City, MI
WSMV-TV Nashville, TN
WSNS Chicago
WSOC-TV Charlotte, NC
WSPA-TV Greenville-Spartanburg, SC-Asheville, NC-Anderson, SC
WSPX-TV Syracuse, NY
*WSRE Mobile, AL-Pensacola (Ft. Walton Beach), FL
WSST-TV Albany, GA
WSTE Ponce PR
WSTM-TV Syracuse, NY
WSTR-TV Cincinnati, OH
WSUR-TV Ponce PR
WSVI Christiansted VI
WSVN Miami-Ft. Lauderdale, FL
WSWB Wilkes Barre-Scranton, PA
*WSWP-TV Bluefield-Beckley-Oak Hill, WV
WSYM-TV Lansing, MI
WSYR-TV Syracuse, NY
WSYT Syracuse, NY
WSYX Columbus, OH
WTAE-TV Pittsburgh, PA
WTAJ-TV Johnstown-Altoona, PA
WTAP-TV Parkersburg, WV
WTAT-TV Charleston, SC
WTBS Atlanta
WTBY-TV New York
*WTCE-TV West Palm Beach-Ft. Pierce, FL
*WTCI Chattanooga, TN
WTCT Paducah, KY-Cape Girardeau, MO-Harrisburg-Mount Vernon, IL
WTCV San Juan PR
WTEN Albany-Schenectady-Troy, NY
WTEV-TV Jacksonville, FL
WTGL-TV Orlando-Daytona Beach-Melbourne, FL
WTGS Savannah, GA
WTHI-TV Terre Haute, IN
WTHR Indianapolis, IN
WTIC-TV Hartford & New Haven, CT
WTIN Ponce PR
*WTIU Indianapolis, IN

WTJP-TV Birmingham (Anniston, Tuscaloosa), AL
WTJR Quincy, IL-Hannibal, MO-Keokuk, IA
*WTJX-TV Charlotte Amalie VI
WTKR Norfolk-Portsmouth-Newport News, VA
WTLF Tallahassee, FL-Thomasville, GA
WTLH Tallahassee, FL-Thomasville, GA
WTLJ Grand Rapids-Kalamazoo-Battle Creek, MI
WTLV Jacksonville, FL
WTLW Lima, OH
WTMJ-TV Milwaukee, WI
WTNH-TV Hartford & New Haven, CT
WTNZ Knoxville, TN
WTOC-TV Savannah, GA
WTOG Tampa-St. Petersburg (Sarasota), FL
WTOK-TV Meridian, MS
WTOL Toledo, OH
WTOM-TV Traverse City-Cadillac, MI
WTOV-TV Wheeling, WV-Steubenville, OH
WTPX Wausau-Rhinelander, WI
WTRF-TV Wheeling, WV-Steubenville, OH
WTSF Charleston-Huntington, WV
WTSP Tampa-St. Petersburg (Sarasota), FL
WTTA Tampa-St. Petersburg (Sarasota), FL
WTTE Columbus, OH
WTTG Washington, DC (Hagerstown, MD)
WTTK Indianapolis, IN
WTTO Birmingham (Anniston, Tuscaloosa), AL
*WTTW Chicago
WTVA Columbus-Tupelo-West Point, MS
WTVC Chattanooga, TN
WTVD Raleigh-Durham (Fayetteville), NC
WTVE Philadelphia
WTVF Nashville, TN
WTVG Toledo, OH
WTVH Syracuse, NY
*WTVI Charlotte, NC
WTVJ Miami-Ft. Lauderdale, FL
WTVK Ft. Myers-Naples, FL
WTVM Columbus, GA
WTVO Rockford, IL
*WTVP Peoria-Bloomington, IL
WTVQ-TV Lexington, KY
WTVR-TV Richmond-Petersburg, VA
*WTVS Detroit
WTVT Tampa-St. Petersburg (Sarasota), FL
WTVW Evansville, IN
WTVX West Palm Beach-Ft. Pierce, FL
WTVY Dothan, AL
WTVZ Norfolk-Portsmouth-Newport News, VA
WTWB-TV Greensboro-High Point-Winston Salem, NC
WTWC-TV Tallahassee, FL-Thomasville, GA
WTWO Terre Haute, IN
WTXF-TV Philadelphia
WTXL-TV Tallahassee, FL-Thomasville, GA
WTXX Hartford & New Haven, CT
WUAB Cleveland, OH
*WUFT Gainesville, FL
WUFX Jackson, MS
WUHF Rochester, NY
*WUJA Caguas PR
*WUNC-TV Raleigh-Durham (Fayetteville), NC

*WUND-TV Greenville-New Bern-Washington, NC
*WUNE-TV Charlotte, NC
*WUNF-TV Greenville-Spartanburg, SC-Asheville, NC-Anderson, SC
*WUNG-TV Charlotte, NC
WUNI Boston (Manchester, NH)
*WUNJ-TV Wilmington, NC
*WUNK-TV Greenville-New Bern-Washington, NC
*WUNL-TV Greensboro-High Point-Winston Salem, NC
*WUNM-TV Greenville-New Bern-Washington, NC
*WUNP-TV Raleigh-Durham (Fayetteville), NC
*WUNU Florence-Myrtle Beach, SC
WUPA Atlanta
WUPL New Orleans, LA
WUPN-TV Greensboro-High Point-Winston Salem, NC
WUPV Richmond-Petersburg, VA
WUPW Toledo, OH
WUPX-TV Lexington, KY
WUSA Washington, DC (Hagerstown, MD)
*WUSF-TV Tampa-St. Petersburg (Sarasota), FL
*WUSI-TV Terre Haute, IN
WUTB Baltimore, MD
WUTF-TV Boston (Manchester, NH)
WUTR Utica, NY
WUTV Buffalo, NY
WUVC-TV Raleigh-Durham (Fayetteville), NC
WUVG-TV Atlanta
WUVN Hartford & New Haven, CT
WUVP-TV Philadelphia
WUXP Nashville, TN
WVAG Tallahassee, FL-Thomasville, GA
WVAH-TV Charleston-Huntington, WV
*WVAN-TV Savannah, GA
WVBT Norfolk-Portsmouth-Newport News, VA
WVCY-TV Milwaukee, WI
WVEA-TV Tampa-St. Petersburg (Sarasota), FL
WVEC-TV Norfolk-Portsmouth-Newport News, VA
WVEN-TV Orlando-Daytona Beach-Melbourne, FL
WVEO Aguadilla PR
*WVER Burlington, VT-Plattsburgh, NY
WVFX Clarksburg-Weston, WV
*WVIA-TV Wilkes Barre-Scranton, PA
WVIF Christiansted VI
WVII-TV Bangor, ME
WVIR-TV Charlottesville, VA
WVIT Hartford & New Haven, CT
*WVIZ-TV Cleveland, OH
WVLA Baton Rouge, LA
WVLR Knoxville, TN
WVLT-TV Knoxville, TN
WVNS-TV Bluefield-Beckley-Oak Hill, WV
WVNY Burlington, VT-Plattsburgh, NY
WVOZ-TV Ponce PR
*WVPT Harrisonburg, VA
WVPX Cleveland, OH
*WVPY Washington, DC (Hagerstown, MD)
*WVTA Burlington, VT-Plattsburgh, NY
*WVTB Burlington, VT-Plattsburgh, NY
WVTM-TV Birmingham (Anniston, Tuscaloosa), AL
WVTV Milwaukee, WI
WVUE New Orleans, LA
*WVUT Terre Haute, IN
WVVA Bluefield-Beckley-Oak Hill, WV
WVXF Charlotte Amalie VI
WWAY Wilmington, NC
WWAZ-TV Green Bay-Appleton, WI

WWBT Richmond-Petersburg, VA
WWCP-TV Johnstown-Altoona, PA
WWDP Boston (Manchester, NH)
WWHO Columbus, OH
WWJ-TV Detroit
WWLP Springfield-Holyoke, MA
WWL-TV New Orleans, LA
WWMB Florence-Myrtle Beach, SC
WWMT Grand Rapids-Kalamazoo-Battle Creek, MI
WWNY-TV Watertown, NY
WWOR-TV New York
*WWPB Washington, DC (Hagerstown, MD)
WWPX Washington, DC (Hagerstown, MD)
WWRS-TV Milwaukee, WI
WWSB Tampa-St. Petersburg (Sarasota), FL
WWSI Philadelphia
WWTI Watertown, NY
WWTO-TV Chicago
WWTV Traverse City-Cadillac, MI
WWUP-TV Traverse City-Cadillac, MI
WWWB Charlotte, NC
*WXEL-TV West Palm Beach-Ft. Pierce, FL
WXFT-TV Chicago
*WXGA-TV Jacksonville, FL
WXIA-TV Atlanta
WXII-TV Greensboro-High Point-Winston Salem, NC
WXIN Indianapolis, IN
WXIX-TV Cincinnati, OH
WXLV-TV Greensboro-High Point-Winston Salem, NC
WXMI Grand Rapids-Kalamazoo-Battle Creek, MI
WXOW-TV La Crosse-Eau Claire, WI
WXPX Tampa-St. Petersburg (Sarasota), FL
WXTV New York
WXTX Columbus, GA
WXVT Greenwood-Greenville, MS
WXXA-TV Albany-Schenectady-Troy, NY
*WXXI-TV Rochester, NY
WXXV-TV Biloxi-Gulfport, MS
WXYZ-TV Detroit
*WYBE Philadelphia
*WYCC Chicago
WYDC Elmira, NY
*WYDN Boston (Manchester, NH)
WYDO Greenville-New Bern-Washington, NC
*WYES-TV New Orleans, LA
WYFF Greenville-Spartanburg, SC-Asheville, NC-Anderson, SC
*WYIN Chicago
WYLE Huntsville-Decatur (Florence), AL
WYMT-TV Lexington, KY
WYOU Wilkes Barre-Scranton, PA
WYOW Wausau-Rhinelander, WI
WYPX Albany-Schenectady-Troy, NY
WYTV Youngstown, OH
WYZZ-TV Peoria-Bloomington, IL
WZDX Huntsville-Decatur (Florence), AL
WZPX Grand Rapids-Kalamazoo-Battle Creek, MI
WZRB Columbia, SC
WZTV Nashville, TN
WZVI Charlotte Amalie VI
WZVN-TV Ft. Myers-Naples, FL
WZZM-TV Grand Rapids-Kalamazoo-Battle Creek, MI
XETV San Diego, CA
XEWT-TV San Diego, CA
XHIJ El Paso, TX

Canadian Television Stations by Call Letters

CBAFT Moncton, NB
CBAT Fredericton-Saint John, NB
CBAT-TV-1 Bon Accord, NB
CBAT-TV-2 Moncton, NB
CBAT-TV-4 Campbellton, NB
CBCP-TV-1 Shaunavon, SK
CBCP-TV-2 Cypress Hills, SK
CBCP-TV-3 Ponteix, SK
CBCT Charlottetown, PE
*CBEFT Windsor, ON
CBFST-2 Temiscaning, PQ
CBFT Montreal, PQ
CBFT-2 Mont-Laurier, PQ
CBHFT Halifax, NS
CBHFT-1 Yarmouth, NS
CBHFT-2 Mulgrave, NS
CBHFT-3 Sydney, NS
CBHFT-4 Cheticamp, NS
CBHT Halifax, NS
CBHT-11 Mulgrave, NS
CBHT-3 Yarmouth, NS
CBHT-4 Sheet Harbour, NS
CBIMT Iles-de-la-Madeleine, PQ
CBIT Sydney, NS
CBIT-2 Cheticamp, NS
CBJET Chicoutimi, PQ
CBKFT Regina, SK
CBKFT-3 Debden, SK
CBKFT-4 Saint Brieux, SK
CBKFT-5 Xenon Park, SK
CBKFT-6 Gravelbourg, SK
CBKFT-9 Bellegarde, SK
CBKST Saskatoon, SK
CBKST-1 Stranraer, SK
CBKT Regina, SK
CBKT-2 Willow Bunch, SK
CBLAT Geraldton, ON
CBLAT-1 Manitouwadge, ON
CBLAT-3 Wawa, ON
CBLAT-4 Marathon, ON
CBLFT Toronto, ON
CBLFT-1 Sturgeon Falls, ON
CBLFT-2 Sudbury, ON
CBLFT-3 Timmins, ON
CBLFT-4 Kapuskasing, ON
CBLFT-5 Hearst, ON
CBLFT-6 Elliot Lake, ON
CBLT Toronto, ON
CBMT Montreal, PQ
CBNAT Botwood, NF
CBNAT-1 Baie Verte, NF
CBNAT-4 Saint Anthony, NF
CBNAT-9 Mount St. Margaret, NF
*CBNLT Labrador City, NF

CBNT Saint John's, NF
CBNT-1 Port Rexton, NF
CBNT-2 Placentia, NF
CBNT-3 Marystown, NF
CBOFT Ottawa, ON
CBOT Ottawa, ON
CBRT Calgary, AB
CBUBT-1 Canal Flats, BC
CBUBT-7 Cranbrook, BC
CBUFT Vancouver, BC
CBUFT-2 Kamloops, BC
CBUFT-3 Terrace, BC
CBUT Vancouver, BC
CBVD-TV Malartic, PQ
CBVT Quebec City, PQ
CBVT-2 La Tuque, PQ
CBWAT Kenora, ON
CBWBT Flin Flon, MB
CBWDT Dryden, ON
CBWFT Winnipeg, MB
CBWFT-10 Brandon, MB
CBWFT-4 Ste-Rose-du-Lac, MB
CBWGT Fisher Branch, MB
CBWST Baldy Mountain, MB
CBWT Winnipeg, MB
CBWT-2 Lac du Bonnet, MB
CBWYT Mafeking, MB
CBXAT Grande Prairie, AB
CBXAT-2 High Prairie, AB
CBXAT-3 Manning, AB
CBXFT Edmonton, AB
CBXFT-1 Bonnyville, AB
CBXFT-6 Fort McMurray, AB
CBXFT-8 Grande Prairie, AB
CBXT Edmonton, AB
CBYT-3 Bonne Bay, NF
CFAP-TV Quebec City, PQ
CFCF-TV Montreal, PQ
CFCM-TV Quebec City, PQ
CFCN-TV Calgary, AB
CFCN-TV-1 Drumheller, AB
CFCN-TV-5 Lethbridge, AB
CFCN-TV-8 Medicine Hat, AB
CFER-TV Rimouski, PQ
CFER-TV-2 Sept-Iles, PQ
CFGS-TV Gatineau, PQ
CFJC-TV Kamloops, BC
CFJP-TV Montreal, PQ
CFKM-TV Trois-Rivieres, PQ
CFKS-TV Sherbrooke, PQ
CFMT-TV Toronto, ON
CFPL-TV London, ON
CFQC-TV Saskatoon, SK
CFQC-TV-2 North Battleford, SK

CFRE-TV Regina, SK
CFRN-TV Edmonton, AB
CFRN-TV-1 Grande Prairie, AB
CFRN-TV-2 Peace River, AB
CFRN-TV-3 Whitecourt, AB
CFRN-TV-4 Ashmont, AB
CFRN-TV-5 Lac La Biche, AB
CFRN-TV-6 Red Deer, AB
CFRN-TV-7 Lougheed, AB
CFRN-TV-8 Grouard Mission-High Prairie, AB
CFRN-TV-9 Slave Lake, AB
CFRS-TV Jonquiere, PQ
CFSK-TV Saskatoon, SK
CFTF-TV Riviere-du-Loup, PQ
CFTK-TV Terrace, BC
CFTM-TV Montreal, PQ
CFTO-TV Toronto, ON
*CFTU-TV Montreal, PQ
CFVS-TV Val d'Or, PQ
CFWH-TV White Horse, YT
*CFYK-TV Yellowknife, NT
*CHAK-TV Inuvik, NT
CHAN-TV Vancouver, BC
CHAN-TV-1 Chilliwack, BC
CHAN-TV-2 Bowen Island, BC
CHAN-TV-3 Squamish, BC
CHAN-TV-5 Brackendale, BC
CHAN-TV-7 Whistler, BC
CHAT-TV Medicine Hat, AB
CHAT-TV-1 Pivot, AB
CHAU-TV Carleton, PQ
CHBC-TV Kelowna, BC
CHBX-TV Sault Ste. Marie, ON
CHCH-TV Hamilton, ON
CHEK-TV Victoria, BC
CHEK-TV-5 Campbell River, BC
CHEM-TV Trois-Rivieres, PQ
CHEX-TV Peterborough, ON
CHEX-TV-2 Oshawa, ON
CHFD-TV Thunder Bay, ON
CHKM-TV-1 Pritchard, BC
CHLT-TV Sherbrooke, PQ
CHMI-TV Portage la Prairie, MB
CHNM-TV Vancouver, BC
CHNU-TV Fraser Valley, BC
CHOT-TV Gatineau, PQ
CHRO-TV Pembroke, ON
CHVC-TV Valemount, BC
CHWI-TV Windsor, ON
CIAN-TV Calgary, AB
*CICA-TV Toronto, ON
CICC-TV Yorkton, SK
CICI-TV Sudbury, ON
CICI-TV-1 Elliot Lake, ON

*CICO-TV-18 London, ON
*CICO-TV-19 Sudbury, ON
*CICO-TV-20 Sault Ste. Marie, ON
*CICO-TV-24 Ottawa, ON
*CICO-TV-28 Kitchener, ON
*CICO-TV-32 Windsor, ON
*CICO-TV-59 Chatham, ON
*CICO-TV-9 Thunder Bay, ON
CICT-TV Calgary, AB
CIEW-TV Warmley, SK
CIHF-TV Halifax, NS
CIII-TV Paris, ON
CIII-TV-2 Bancroft, ON
CIII-TV-22 Stevenson, ON
CIII-TV-27 Peterborough, ON
CIII-TV-29 Oil Springs, ON
CIII-TV-4 Owen Sound, ON
CIII-TV-41 Toronto, ON
CIII-TV-6 Ottawa, ON
CIII-TV-7 Midland, ON
CIMC-TV Isle Madame, NS
CIMT-TV Riviere-du-Loup, PQ
CIPA-TV Prince Albert, SK
CISA-TV Lethbridge, AB
CITL-TV Lloydminster, AB
CITO-TV Timmins, ON
CITO-TV-2 Kearns, ON
CITS-TV Hamilton, ON
CITV-TV Edmonton, AB
CITY-DT Toronto, ON
CITY-TV Toronto, ON
*CIVA-TV Rouyn, PQ
*CIVB-TV Rimouski, PQ
*CIVC-TV Trois-Rivieres, PQ
*CIVF-TV Baie-Trinite, PQ
*CIVG-TV Sept-Iles, PQ
CIVI-TV Victoria, BC
*CIVM-TV Montreal, PQ
*CIVO-TV Gatineau, PQ
*CIVP-TV Chapeau, PQ
*CIVQ-TV Quebec City, PQ
*CIVS-TV Sherbrooke, PQ
CIVT-TV Vancouver, BC
*CIVV-TV Chicoutimi, PQ
*CJAL-TV Edmonton, AB
CJBN-TV Kenora, ON
CJBR-TV Rimouski, PQ
CJCB-TV Sydney, NS
CJCB-TV-1 Inverness, NS
CJCB-TV-2 Antigonish, NS
CJCH-TV Halifax, NS
CJCH-TV-1 Canning, NS
CJCH-TV-6 Caledonia, NS
CJCN-TV Grand Falls, NF

CJDC-TV Dawson Creek, BC
CJIL-TV Lethbridge, AB
CJMT-TV Toronto, ON
CJNT-TV Montreal, PQ
CJOH-TV Ottawa, ON
CJOH-TV-6 Deseronto, ON
CJOH-TV-8 Cornwall, ON
CJOM-TV Argentia, NF
CJON-TV St John's, NF
CJOX-TV-1 Grand Bank, NF
CJPM-TV Chicoutimi, PQ
CJSV-TV Stephenville, NF
CJTG-TV Meander River, AB
CJWB-TV Bonavista, NF
CJWN-TV Corner Brook, NF
CKAL-TV Calgary, AB
CKAM-TV Upsalquitch Lake, NB
CKBQ-TV Melfort, SK
CKCD-TV Campbellton, NB
CKCK-TV Regina, SK
CKCK-TV-1 Colgate, SK
CKCK-TV-2 Willow Bunch, SK
CKCO-TV Kitchener, ON
CKCO-TV-2 Wiarton, ON
CKCO-TV-3 Sarnia, ON
CKCW-TV Moncton, NB
CKCW-TV-1 Charlottetown, PE
CKCW-TV-2 Saint Edward, PE
CKEM-TV Edmonton, AB
CKLT-TV Saint John, NB
CKMC-TV Swift Current, SK
CKMC-TV-1 Golden Prairie, SK
CKMI-TV Quebec City, PQ
CKND-TV Winnipeg, MB
CKNX-TV Wingham, ON
CKNY-TV North Bay, ON
CKPG-TV Prince George, BC
CKPR-TV Thunder Bay, ON
CKRD-TV Red Deer, AB
CKRD-TV-1 Coronation, AB
CKRN-TV Rouyn-Noranda, PQ
CKRN-TV-3 Bearn-Fabre, PQ
CKRT-TV Riviere-du-Loup, PQ
CKSA-TV Lloydminster, AB
CKSH-TV Sherbrooke, PQ
CKTM-TV Trois-Rivieres, PQ
CKVR-TV Barrie, ON
CKVU-TV Vancouver, BC
CKWS-TV Kingston, ON
CKXT-TV Toronto, ON
CKX-TV Brandon, MB
CKX-TV-1 Foxwarren, MB
CKYB-TV Brandon, MB
CKY-TV Winnipeg, MB

U.S. Television Stations by Analog Channel

Channel 2
KTUU-TV Anchorage, AK
KATN Fairbanks, AK
*WDIQ Dozier, AL
*KETS Little Rock, AR
*KVZK-2 Pago Pago, AS
KNAZ-TV Flagstaff, AZ
KCBS-TV Los Angeles, CA
KTVU Oakland, CA
KWGN-TV Denver, CO
WESH Daytona Beach, FL
*WPBT Miami, FL
WSB-TV Atlanta, GA
KHBC-TV Hilo, HI
KHON-TV Honolulu, HI
KGAN Cedar Rapids, IA
KBCI-TV Boise, ID
WBBM-TV Chicago, IL
WTWO Terre Haute, IN
KSNC Great Bend, KS
WBRZ Baton Rouge, LA
*WGBH-TV Boston, MA
WMAR-TV Baltimore, MD
WLBZ Bangor, ME
WJBK Detroit, MI
*KTCA-TV Saint Paul, MN
KQTV Saint Joseph, MO
KTVI Saint Louis, MO
*WMAB-TV Mississippi State, MS
KTVQ Billings, MT
*WUND-TV Columbia, NC
WFMY-TV Greensboro, NC
KXMA-TV Dickinson, ND
*KGFE Grand Forks, ND
KNOP-TV North Platte, NE
KASA-TV Santa Fe, NM
KTVN Reno, NV
WGRZ-TV Buffalo, NY
WCBS-TV New York, NY
WKTV Utica, NY
WDTN Dayton, OH
KJRH Tulsa, OK
KOTI Klamath Falls, OR
KATU Portland, OR
KDKA-TV Pittsburgh, PA
WKAQ-TV San Juan, PR
WCBD-TV Charleston, SC
*KUSD-TV Vermillion, SD
WKRN-TV Nashville, TN
*WETP-TV Sneedville, TN
*KACV-TV Amarillo, TX
*KDTN Denton, TX
KBEJ Fredericksburg, TX
KPRC-TV Houston, TX
KMID Midland, TX
KUTV Salt Lake City, UT
KREM-TV Spokane, WA
WBAY-TV Green Bay, WI
KTWO-TV Casper, WY
KJWY Jackson, WY

Channel 3
*KTOO-TV Juneau, AK
KFTU-TV Douglas, AZ
KTVK Phoenix, AZ
KIEM-TV Eureka, CA
KCRA-TV Sacramento, CA
KEYT-TV Santa Barbara, CA
KREG-TV Glenwood Springs, CO
KUPN Sterling, CO
WFSB Hartford, CT
WEAR-TV Pensacola, FL
*WEDU Tampa, FL
WRBL Columbus, GA
WSAV-TV Savannah, GA
KGMV Wailuku, HI
KIMT Mason City, IA
KIDK Idaho Falls, ID
KLEW-TV Lewiston, ID
WCIA Champaign, IL
WSIL-TV Harrisburg, IL
*KSWK Lakin, KS

KSNW Wichita, KS
WAVE Louisville, KY
KATC Lafayette, LA
KTBS-TV Shreveport, LA
WJMN-TV Escanaba, MI
WWMT Kalamazoo, MI
KDLH Duluth, MN
KTVO Kirksville, MO
KYTV Springfield, MO
WLBT Jackson, MS
KRTV Great Falls, MT
KYUS-TV Miles City, MT
WBTV Charlotte, NC
WWAY Wilmington, NC
*KBME-TV Bismarck, ND
*KLNE-TV Lexington, NE
KMTV Omaha, NE
KOFT Farmington, NM
*KENW Portales, NM
KBJN Ely, NV
KVBC Las Vegas, NV
WSTM-TV Syracuse, NY
WKYC-TV Cleveland, OH
*KOET Eufaula, OK
*KOAB-TV Bend, OR
*WPSX-TV Clearfield, PA
KYW-TV Philadelphia, PA
*WIPM-TV Mayaguez, PR
KDLO-TV Florence, SD
KOTA-TV Rapid City, SD
WRCB-TV Chattanooga, TN
WREG-TV Memphis, TN
KBTX-TV Bryan, TX
KIII Corpus Christi, TX
KSAN-TV San Angelo, TX
KFDX-TV Wichita Falls, TX
KCBU Price, UT
WHSV-TV Harrisonburg, VA
WTKR Norfolk, VA
WCAX-TV Burlington, VT
WISC-TV Madison, WI
WSAZ-TV Huntington, WV

Channel 4
KTBY Anchorage, AK
*KYUK-TV Bethel, AK
KUBD Ketchikan, AK
KJNP-TV North Pole, AK
WTVY Dothan, AL
KARK-TV Little Rock, AR
*KVZK-4 Pago Pago, AS
KTFL Flagstaff, AZ
KVOA Tucson, AZ
KNBC Los Angeles, CA
KRON-TV San Francisco, CA
KCNC-TV Denver, CO
KFQX Grand Junction, CO
WRC-TV Washington, DC
WJXT Jacksonville, FL
WFOR-TV Miami, FL
KITV Honolulu, HI
KTIV Sioux City, IA
*KAID Boise, ID
WHBF-TV Rock Island, IL
WTTV Bloomington, IN
KLBY Colby, KS
WWL-TV New Orleans, LA
WBZ-TV Boston, MA
WTOM-TV Cheboygan, MI
WDIV Detroit, MI
WCCO-TV Minneapolis, MN
WDAF-TV Kansas City, MO
KMOV Saint Louis, MO
WCBI-TV Columbus, MS
KXLF-TV Butte, MT
KHMT Hardin, MT
*WUNC-TV Chapel Hill, NC
WSKY-TV Manteo, NC
KXJB-TV Valley City, ND
*KWSE Williston, ND
KDUH-TV Scottsbluff, NE
KSNB-TV Superior, NE

KOB-TV Albuquerque, NM
KRNV Reno, NV
WIVB-TV Buffalo, NY
WNBC New York, NY
WCMH-TV Columbus, OH
KFOR-TV Oklahoma City, OK
KPIC Roseburg, OR
WTAE-TV Pittsburgh, PA
WAPA-TV San Juan, PR
WCIV Charleston, SC
WYFF Greenville, SC
KPRY-TV Pierre, SD
WSMV-TV Nashville, TN
KAMR-TV Amarillo, TX
KWAB-TV Big Spring, TX
KDFW Dallas, TX
KDBC-TV El Paso, TX
KFOX-TV El Paso, TX
KGBT-TV Harlingen, TX
KBTV-TV Port Arthur, TX
WOAI-TV San Antonio, TX
KCSG Cedar City, UT
KTVX Salt Lake City, UT
KOMO-TV Seattle, WA
KXLY-TV Spokane, WA
WBIJ Crandon, WI
WTMJ-TV Milwaukee, WI
WOAY-TV Oak Hill, WV
*KCWC-TV Lander, WY

Channel 5
KYES Anchorage, AK
WKRG-TV Mobile, AL
KFSM-TV Fort Smith, AR
*KVZK-5 Pago Pago, AS
KPHO-TV Phoenix, AZ
KTLA Los Angeles, CA
KPIX-TV San Francisco, CA
KREX-TV Grand Junction, CO
KOAA-TV Pueblo, CO
WTTG Washington, DC
*WUFT Gainesville, FL
WPTV West Palm Beach, FL
WAGA Atlanta, GA
KFVE Honolulu, HI
WOI-TV Ames, IA
KIDA Sun Valley, ID
WMAQ-TV Chicago, IL
KALB-TV Alexandria, LA
WCVB-TV Boston, MA
WABI-TV Bangor, ME
WNEM-TV Bay City, MI
WBKP Calumet, MI
KSTP-TV Saint Paul, MN
KCTV Kansas City, MO
KSDK Saint Louis, MO
KXGN-TV Glendive, MT
KFBB-TV Great Falls, MT
WRAL-TV Raleigh, NC
KFYR-TV Bismarck, ND
KHAS-TV Hastings, NE
*KNME-TV Albuquerque, NM
KVVU-TV Henderson, NV
*KNPB Reno, NV
WNYW New York, NY
WPTZ North Pole, NY
WTVH Syracuse, NY
WLWT Cincinnati, OH
WEWS Cleveland, OH
KOCO-TV Oklahoma City, OK
KOBI Medford, OR
WORA-TV Mayaguez, PR
WCSC-TV Charleston, SC
KIVV-TV Lead, SD
KDLV-TV Mitchell, SD
WMC-TV Memphis, TN
WTVF Nashville, TN
KXAS-TV Fort Worth, TX
*KTXT-TV Lubbock, TX
KENS-TV San Antonio, TX
KRGV-TV Weslaco, TX
KSL-TV Salt Lake City, UT

WCYB-TV Bristol, VA
KING-TV Seattle, WA
WFRV-TV Green Bay, WI
WDTV Weston, WV
KGWN-TV Cheyenne, WY
KGWL-TV Lander, WY

Channel 6
WBRC Birmingham, AL
*KEMV Mountain View, AR
KMOH-TV Kingman, AZ
*KUAT-TV Tucson, AZ
KVIQ Eureka, CA
KSBY San Luis Obispo, CA
*KVIE Sacramento, CA
*KRMA-TV Denver, CO
KREZ-TV Durango, CO
WTVJ Miami, FL
WKMG-TV Orlando, FL
WJBF Augusta, GA
WCTV Thomasville, GA
KLEI Kailua-Kona, HI
KWQC-TV Davenport, IA
KIVI Nampa, ID
KPVI Pocatello, ID
WRTV Indianapolis, IN
KBSD-TV Ensign, KS
WPSD-TV Paducah, KY
WDSU New Orleans, LA
WLNE New Bedford, MA
WCSH Portland, ME
XETV Tijuana, MEX
*WCML-TV Alpena, MI
WLNS-TV Lansing, MI
WLUC-TV Marquette, MI
KAAL Austin, MN
*KMOS-TV Sedalia, MO
WABG-TV Greenwood, MS
KSVI Billings, MT
KTVM Butte, MT
WECT Wilmington, NC
WDAY-TV Fargo, ND
*KSRE Minot, ND
KWNB-TV Hayes Center, NE
WOWT Omaha, NE
KOCT Carlsbad, NM
KOBG-TV Silver City, NM
*KBNY Ely, NV
WRGB Schenectady, NY
WSYX Columbus, OH
KOTV Tulsa, OK
KOIN Portland, OR
WJAC-TV Johnstown, PA
WPVI-TV Philadelphia, PA
*WIPR-TV San Juan, PR
KPLO-TV Reliance, SD
WATE-TV Knoxville, TN
KFDM-TV Beaumont, TX
KRIS-TV Corpus Christi, TX
KIDY San Angelo, TX
KCEN-TV Temple, TX
KTAL-TV Texarkana, TX
KAUZ-TV Wichita Falls, TX
KBCJ Vernal, UT
WTVR-TV Richmond, VA
KHQ-TV Spokane, WA
WITI Milwaukee, WI
KBJR-TV Superior, WI
WVVA Bluefield, WV
*KPTW Casper, WY

Channel 7
*KAKM Anchorage, AK
KFXF Fairbanks, AK
*WCIQ Mount Cheaha, AL
KATV Little Rock, AR
KAZT-TV Prescott, AZ
KVYE El Centro, CA
KABC-TV Los Angeles, CA
KRCR-TV Redding, CA
KGO-TV San Francisco, CA
KMGH-TV Denver, CO

WJLA-TV Washington, DC
*WJCT Jacksonville, FL
WSVN Miami, FL
WJHG-TV Panama City, FL
KAII-TV Wailuku, HI
KWWL Waterloo, IA
KTVB Boise, ID
WLS-TV Chicago, IL
WTVW Evansville, IN
KBSH-TV Hays, KS
KOAM-TV Pittsburg, KS
KPLC Lake Charles, LA
WHDH-TV Boston, MA
WVII-TV Bangor, ME
WXYZ-TV Detroit, MI
WPBN-TV Traverse City, MI
KCCO-TV Alexandria, MN
KHQA-TV Hannibal, MO
WDAM-TV Laurel, MS
KBZK Bozeman, MT
WITN-TV Washington, NC
KQCD-TV Dickinson, ND
KJRR Jamestown, ND
*KMNE-TV Bassett, NE
KETV Omaha, NE
KOAT-TV Albuquerque, NM
KEGS Goldfield, NV
KWNV Winnemucca, NV
WKBW-TV Buffalo, NY
WWNY-TV Carthage, NY
WABC-TV New York, NY
WHIO-TV Dayton, OH
KSWO-TV Lawton, OK
*KOAC-TV Corvallis, OR
WSTE Ponce, PR
*WITV Charleston, SC
WSPA-TV Spartanburg, SC
KEVN-TV Rapid City, SD
WBBJ-TV Jackson, TN
KVII-TV Amarillo, TX
KTBC Austin, TX
KVIA-TV El Paso, TX
KOSA-TV Odessa, TX
KLTV Tyler, TX
*KUED Salt Lake City, UT
WDBJ Roanoke, VA
KIRO-TV Seattle, WA
*KSPS-TV Spokane, WA
WSAW-TV Wausau, WI
WTRF-TV Wheeling, WV
KSWY Sheridan, WY

Channel 8
KJUD Juneau, AK
WAKA Selma, AL
KAIT Jonesboro, AR
*KAET Phoenix, AZ
KUNO-TV Fort Bragg, CA
KSBW Salinas, CA
KFMB-TV San Diego, CA
KJCT Grand Junction, CO
*KTSC Pueblo, CO
WTNH-TV New Haven, CT
WGEN-TV Key West, FL
WFLA-TV Tampa, FL
*WGTV Athens, GA
*WXGA-TV Waycross, GA
KUAM-TV Hagatna, GU
KCCI Des Moines, IA
KIFI-TV Idaho Falls, ID
*WSIU-TV Carbondale, IL
WQAD-TV Moline, IL
WISH-TV Indianapolis, IN
*KPTS Hutchinson, KS
KNOE-TV Monroe, LA
WVUE New Orleans, LA
WMTW-TV Poland Spring, ME
WAGM-TV Presque Isle, ME
WOOD-TV Grand Rapids, MI
WDHS Iron Mountain, MI
WGTQ Sault Ste. Marie, MI
*WDSE-TV Duluth, MN

Broadcasting & Cable Yearbook 2006

B-120

U.S. Television Stations by Analog Channel

KOMU-TV Columbia, MO
KULR-TV Billings, MT
KPAX-TV Missoula, MT
WGHP High Point, NC
WFXI Morehead City, NC
WDAZ-TV Devils Lake, ND
KUMV-TV Williston, ND
KLKN Lincoln, NE
KSNK McCook, NE
KOBR Roswell, NM
KLAS-TV Las Vegas, NV
KOLO-TV Reno, NV
WROC-TV Rochester, NY
WJW Cleveland, OH
KTUL Tulsa, OK
*KSYS Medford, OR
KGW Portland, OR
WWCP-TV Johnstown, PA
WGAL Lancaster, PA
*KESD-TV Brookings, SD
*KZSD-TV Martin, SD
WVLT-TV Knoxville, TN
*WNPT Nashville, TN
WFAA-TV Dallas, TX
*KUHT Houston, TX
KGNS-TV Laredo, TX
KLST San Angelo, TX
WRIC-TV Petersburg, VA
WSVI Christiansted, VI
WKBT La Crosse, WI
WCHS-TV Charleston, WV
*KWYP-TV Laramie, WY

Channel 9

*KUAC-TV Fairbanks, AK
*KETG Arkadelphia, AR
KCFG Flagstaff, AZ
KGUN Tucson, AZ
KECY-TV El Centro, CA
KCAL Los Angeles, CA
*KIXE-TV Redding, CA
*KQED San Francisco, CA
KUSA-TV Denver, CO
WUSA Washington, DC
WFTV Orlando, FL
WTVM Columbus, GA
*WVAN-TV Savannah, GA
KGMD-TV Hilo, HI
KGMB Honolulu, HI
KCRG-TV Cedar Rapids, IA
KCAU-TV Sioux City, IA
KNIN-TV Caldwell, ID
WGN-TV Chicago, IL
*WNIN Evansville, IN
*KOOD Hays, KS
WAFB Baton Rouge, LA
WWTV Cadillac, MI
*KAWE Bemidji, MN
KMSP-TV Minneapolis, MN
KMBC-TV Kansas City, MO
*KETC Saint Louis, MO
WTVA Tupelo, MS
*KUSM Bozeman, MT
KBBJ Havre, MT
KCFW-TV Kalispell, MT
WSOC-TV Charlotte, NC
WNCT-TV Greenville, NC
*KDSE Dickinson, ND
*KPNE-TV North Platte, NE
WMUR-TV Manchester, NH
WWOR-TV Secaucus, NJ
*KNMD-TV Santa Fe, NM
WSYR-TV Syracuse, NY
WCPO-TV Cincinnati, OH
WTOV-TV Steubenville, OH
KWTV Oklahoma City, OK
KEZI Eugene, OR
WSUR-TV Ponce, PR
KABY-TV Aberdeen, SD
*KBHE-TV Rapid City, SD
WTVC Chattanooga, TN
KRBC-TV Abilene, TX
KTSM-TV El Paso, TX
KTRE Lufkin, TX
KWES-TV Odessa, TX
*KLRN San Antonio, TX
*KUEN Ogden, UT

*KCTS-TV Seattle, WA
KAZW-TV Walla Walla, WA
WAOW-TV Wausau, WI
*WSWP-TV Grandview, WV

Channel 10

*WBIQ Birmingham, AL
WALA-TV Mobile, AL
KTVE El Dorado, AR
KSAZ-TV Phoenix, AZ
KXTV Sacramento, CA
KGTV San Diego, CA
KREY-TV Montrose, CO
WPLG Miami, FL
WTSP Saint Petersburg, FL
WALB Albany, GA
*KMEB Wailuku, HI
*KISU-TV Pocatello, ID
WGEM-TV Quincy, IL
WTHI-TV Terre Haute, IN
KBSL-TV Goodland, KS
KAKE-TV Wichita, KS
KLFY-TV Lafayette, LA
*WCBB Augusta, ME
*WMEM-TV Presque Isle, ME
WBUP Ishpeming, MI
WILX-TV Onondaga, MI
WWUP-TV Sault Ste. Marie, MI
*KWCM-TV Appleton, MN
WDIO-TV Duluth, MN
KTTC Rochester, MN
KBRR Thief River Falls, MN
KOLR-TV Springfield, MO
KMTF Helena, MT
KMOT Minot, ND
KOLN Lincoln, NE
KSTF Scottsbluff, NE
KBIM-TV Roswell, NM
KOVT Silver City, NM
KENV Elko, NV
*KLVX Las Vegas, NV
WTEN Albany, NY
WHEC-TV Rochester, NY
WBNS-TV Columbus, OH
KTEN Ada, OK
KTVL Medford, OR
*KOPB-TV Portland, OR
WTAJ-TV Altoona, PA
WCAU Philadelphia, PA
WJAR Providence, RI
WIS Columbia, SC
*KTSD-TV Pierre, SD
WBIR-TV Knoxville, TN
*WKNO-TV Memphis, TN
KFDA-TV Amarillo, TX
KZTV Corpus Christi, TX
KTRG Del Rio, TX
KWTX-TV Waco, TX
WAVY-TV Portsmouth, VA
WSLS-TV Roanoke, VA
*KWSU-TV Pullman, WA
*WMVS Milwaukee, WI
KFNE Riverton, WY

Channel 11

KTVA Anchorage, AK
KTVF Fairbanks, AK
KTHV Little Rock, AR
KPHZ Holbrook, AZ
KMSB-TV Tucson, AZ
KYMA Yuma, AZ
KTTV Los Angeles, CA
KNTV San Jose, CA
KKTV Colorado Springs, CO
KKCO Grand Junction, CO
WINK-TV Fort Myers, FL
*WFSU-TV Tallahassee, FL
WXIA-TV Atlanta, GA
WTOC-TV Savannah, GA
KHAW-TV Hilo, HI
*KHET Honolulu, HI
*KDIN-TV Des Moines, IA
KMVT Twin Falls, ID
*WTTW Chicago, IL
KSNG Garden City, KS
*KTWU Topeka, KS
WHAS-TV Louisville, KY
KAQY Columbia, LA

WBAL-TV Baltimore, MD
WBKB-TV Alpena, MI
KRII Chisholm, MN
KARE Minneapolis, MN
KPLR-TV Saint Louis, MO
WTOK-TV Meridian, MS
*KUFM-TV Missoula, MT
WTVD Durham, NC
KVLY-TV Fargo, ND
KXMD-TV Williston, ND
KGIN Grand Island, NE
*WENH-TV Durham, NH
KCHF Santa Fe, NM
KRXI-TV Reno, NV
WPIX New York, NY
WTOL Toledo, OH
*KOED-TV Tulsa, OK
KCBY-TV Coos Bay, OR
KFFX-TV Pendleton, OR
WPXI Pittsburgh, PA
WLII Caguas, PR
KHSD-TV Lead, SD
*KQSD-TV Lowry, SD
KELO-TV Sioux Falls, SD
WJHL-TV Johnson City, TN
*WLJT-TV Lexington, TN
KTVT Fort Worth, TX
KHOU-TV Houston, TX
KCBD Lubbock, TX
*KBYU-TV Provo, UT
KSTW Tacoma, WA
WLUK-TV Green Bay, WI
WVAH-TV Charleston, WV
KBEO Jackson, WY
KFNR Rawlins, WY

Channel 12

WSFA Montgomery, AL
KPNX Mesa, AZ
KHSL-TV Chico, CA
KCOY-TV Santa Maria, CA
*KBDI-TV Broomfield, CO
*WHYY-TV Wilmington, DE
WTLV Jacksonville, FL
WPEC West Palm Beach, FL
WRDW-TV Augusta, GA
*KGTF Hagatna, GU
KMAU Wailuku, HI
*KIIN-TV Iowa City, IA
KTRV Nampa, ID
*WILL-TV Urbana, IL
KWCH-TV Hutchinson, KS
*WYES-TV New Orleans, LA
KSLA-TV Shreveport, LA
*WMEB-TV Orono, ME
XEWT-TV Tijuana, MEX
WJRT-TV Flint, MI
KEYC-TV Mankato, MN
KCCW-TV Walker, MN
KFVS-TV Cape Girardeau, MO
KODE-TV Joplin, MO
*WMAE-TV Booneville, MS
WJTV Jackson, MS
KTVH Helena, MT
WCTI New Bern, NC
WXII-TV Winston-Salem, NC
KXMB-TV Bismarck, ND
KNRR Pembina, ND
*KUON-TV Lincoln, NE
*KRNE-TV Merriman, NE
KVIH-TV Clovis, NM
KOBF Farmington, NM
WBNG-TV Binghamton, NY
WKRC-TV Cincinnati, OH
*KWET Cheyenne, OK
KDRV Medford, OR
KPTV Portland, OR
WICU-TV Erie, PA
WOLE-TV Aguadilla, PR
WPRI-TV Providence, RI
KTTM Huron, SD
WDEF-TV Chattanooga, TN
KBMT Beaumont, TX
KSAT-TV San Antonio, TX
KXII Sherman, TX
KTXS-TV Sweetwater, TX
KUTF Logan, UT

KUSG Saint George, UT
WWBT Richmond, VA
*WTJX-TV Charlotte Amalie, VI
KVOS-TV Bellingham, WA
WISN-TV Milwaukee, WI
WJFW-TV Rhinelander, WI
WBOY-TV Clarksburg, WV
KSGW-TV Sheridan, WY

Channel 13

KIMO Anchorage, AK
KTNL Sitka, AK
WVTM-TV Birmingham, AL
*KAFT Fayetteville, AR
KFPH-TV Flagstaff, AZ
KOLD-TV Tucson, AZ
KSWT Yuma, AZ
*KEET Eureka, CA
KCOP Los Angeles, CA
KOVR Stockton, CA
KRDO-TV Colorado Springs, CO
WMBB Panama City, FL
WTVT Tampa, FL
WMAZ-TV Macon, GA
KHVO Hilo, HI
KHNL Honolulu, HI
WHO-TV Des Moines, IA
*KIPT Twin Falls, ID
WPXS Mount Vernon, IL
WREX-TV Rockford, IL
WTHR Indianapolis, IN
KUPK-TV Garden City, KS
WIBW-TV Topeka, KS
WBKO Bowling Green, KY
*KLTM-TV Monroe, LA
WJZ-TV Baltimore, MD
*WMED-TV Calais, ME
WGME-TV Portland, ME
WZZM-TV Grand Rapids, MI
*WNMU-TV Marquette, MI
WIRT Hibbing, MN
KRCG Jefferson City, MO
WLOX Biloxi, MS
KBAO Lewistown, MT
KECI-TV Missoula, MT
WLOS Asheville, NC
*KFME Fargo, ND
KXMC-TV Minot, ND
*KTNE-TV Alliance, NE
KHGI-TV Kearney, NE
*WNET Newark, NJ
KRQE Albuquerque, NM
KTNV Las Vegas, NV
WNYT Albany, NY
WHAM-TV Rochester, NY
WTVG Toledo, OH
*KETA Oklahoma City, OK
KVAL-TV Eugene, OR
*KTVR La Grande, OR
WQED Pittsburgh, PA
WPRV-TV Fajardo, PR
WBTW Florence, SC
*KPSD-TV Eagle Butte, SD
KSFY-TV Sioux Falls, SD
WHBQ-TV Memphis, TN
*KERA-TV Dallas, TX
*KCOS El Paso, TX
KTRK-TV Houston, TX
KVTV Laredo, TX
KLBK-TV Lubbock, TX
KSTU Salt Lake City, UT
WVEC-TV Hampton, VA
WSET-TV Lynchburg, VA
KCPQ Tacoma, WA
WEAU-TV Eau Claire, WI
WOWK-TV Huntington, WV
KCWY Casper, WY
KGWR-TV Rock Springs, WY

Channel 14

KDTV San Francisco, CA
KTFD-TV Boulder, CO
*WABW-TV Pelham, GA
WPXA Rome, GA
KTGM Tamuning, GU
KWHH Hilo, HI
KWHE Honolulu, HI
KMEG Sioux City, IA

*WSEC Jacksonville, IL
WFIE Evansville, IN
KBDK Hoisington, KS
KFJX Pittsburg, KS
KARD West Monroe, LA
*WCMU-TV Mount Pleasant, MI
*WMAW-TV Meridian, MS
WYDO Greenville, NC
WHKY-TV Hickory, NC
KMCY Minot, ND
KTFQ-TV Albuquerque, NM
*WPTO Oxford, OH
KTBO-TV Oklahoma City, OK
WTIN Ponce, PR
*WEBA-TV Allendale, SC
KCIT Amarillo, TX
*KETH-TV Houston, TX
KXAM-TV Llano, TX
KJZZ-TV Salt Lake City, UT
WFDC-TV Arlington, VA
WIWB Suring, WI
KGWC-TV Casper, WY

Channel 15

WHDF Florence, AL
WPMI-TV Mobile, AL
KNXV-TV Phoenix, AZ
*KPBS San Diego, CA
*WCEU New Smyrna Beach, FL
KOGG Wailuku, HI
KYOU-TV Ottumwa, IA
KPIF Pocatello, ID
WICD Champaign, IL
WANE-TV Fort Wayne, IN
*WKPC-TV Louisville, KY
KADN Lafayette, LA
*KSMQ-TV Austin, MN
KPOB-TV Poplar Bluff, MO
WXVT Greenville, MS
KVRR Fargo, ND
KXVO Omaha, NE
KINC Las Vegas, NV
WLYH-TV Lancaster, PA
WPDE-TV Florence, SC
KCLO-TV Rapid City, SD
*WKOP-TV Knoxville, TN
KXVA Abilene, TX
*KAMU-TV College Station, TX
WHRO-TV Hampton-Norfolk, VA
*WBRA-TV Roanoke, VA
WVIF Christiansted, VI
*KCKA Centralia, WA
WMTV Madison, WI
WTAP-TV Parkersburg, WV

Channel 16

KLRT Little Rock, AR
*WUSF-TV Tampa, FL
*WUSI-TV Olney, IL
WTJR Quincy, IL
WNDU-TV South Bend, IN
WBOC-TV Salisbury, MD
KSNF Joplin, MO
KTAJ-TV Saint Joseph, MO
WAPT Jackson, MS
KTGF Great Falls, MT
WGPX Burlington, NC
KTUW Scottsbluff, NE
*WPBS-TV Watertown, NY
*WPTD Dayton, OH
KMTR Eugene, OR
KPOU La Grande, OR
WQEX Pittsburgh, PA
WNEP-TV Scranton, PA
WOST Mayaguez, PR
*WJWJ-TV Beaufort, SC
WGGS-TV Greenville, SC
*KDSD-TV Aberdeen, SD
WJKT Jackson, TN
*KEDT Corpus Christi, TX
KVAW Eagle Pass, TX
KPTB Lubbock, TX
KUPX Provo, UT
KONG-TV Everett, WA

U.S. Television Stations by Analog Channel

Channel 17
WDBB Bessemer, AL
*KLEP Newark, AR
KGET-TV Bakersfield, CA
WJWB Jacksonville, FL
*WLRN-TV Miami, FL
WTBS Atlanta, GA
KDSM-TV Des Moines, IA
WAND Decatur, IL
WTVO Rockford, IL
WXMI Grand Rapids, MI
*KTCI-TV Saint Paul, MN
KMIZ Columbia, MO
*WMAU-TV Bude, MS
KMMF Missoula, MT
WNCN Goldsboro, NC
*WUNE-TV Linville, NC
KBMY Bismarck, ND
KTVG Grand Island, NE
*WNED-TV Buffalo, NY
*WMHT Schenectady, NY
WDLI-TV Canton, OH
KDOR-TV Bartlesville, OK
WPHL-TV Philadelphia, PA
KTTW Sioux Falls, SD
WZTV Nashville, TN
KPCB Snyder, TX
WVXF Charlotte Amalie, VI

Channel 18
WDHN Dothan, AL
KTTU-TV Tucson, AZ
*KVPT Fresno, CA
KSCI Long Beach, CA
*KRMJ Grand Junction, CO
WUVN Hartford, CT
WKCF Clermont, FL
*WCLP-TV Chatsworth, GA
KLJB-TV Davenport, IA
WLFI-TV Lafayette, IN
KAAS-TV Salina, KS
WLEX-TV Lexington, KY
*KLTL-TV Lake Charles, LA
WHTV Jackson, MI
*WMAV-TV Oxford, MS
KWYB Butte, MT
WCCB Charlotte, NC
WETM-TV Elmira, NY
*WNPI-TV Norwood, NY
WHIZ-TV Zanesville, OH
WTCV San Juan, PR
*KLRU-TV Austin, TX
KPTF Farwell, TX
KUPB Midland, TX
KJTL Wichita Falls, TX
*KUEW Saint George, UT
WQOW-TV Eau Claire, WI
WVTV Milwaukee, WI

Channel 19
WHNT-TV Huntsville, AL
*KTEJ Jonesboro, AR
KUVS-TV Modesto, CA
*KBGH Filer, ID
WHOI Peoria, IL
WAZE-TV Madisonville, KY
WXIX-TV Newport, KY
WCDC Adams, MA
WMQF Marquette, MI
*WDCP-TV University Center, MI
*KCPT Kansas City, MO
*WMAH-TV Biloxi, MS
*WUNM-TV Jacksonville, NC
*KJRE Ellendale, ND
*KXNE-TV Norfolk, NE
KWBQ Santa Fe, NM
WOIO Shaker Heights, OH
KWBT Muskogee, OK
WNPA Jeannette, PA
WLTX Columbia, SC
WKPT-TV Kingsport, TN
KYTX Nacogdoches, TX
KVCT Victoria, TX
*KUES Richfield, UT
WCAV Charlottesville, VA
KEPR-TV Pasco, WA
WXOW-TV La Crosse, WI

Channel 20
WCOV-TV Montgomery, AL
KBWB San Francisco, CA
*KBDM Yreka City, CA
KTVD Denver, CO
*KRMU Durango, CO
WTXX Waterbury, CT
WDCA Washington, DC
WBBH-TV Fort Myers, FL
WCJB Gainesville, FL
*WCES-TV Wrens, GA
KIKU Honolulu, HI
KWKB Iowa City, IA
*WYCC Chicago, IL
WICS Springfield, IL
*WFYI Indianapolis, IN
WHNO New Orleans, LA
WDWB Detroit, MI
*KSMN Worthington, MN
WTWB-TV Lexington, NC
WUTR Utica, NY
*WOUB-TV Athens, OH
WKPV Ponce, PR
WBXX-TV Crossville, TN
KTXH Houston, TX
KTMW Salt Lake City, UT
*WVTB Saint Johnsbury, VT
KTBW-TV Tacoma, WA
*WHRM-TV Wausau, WI
KFNB-TV Casper, WY

Channel 21
WTTO Birmingham, AL
WMPV-TV Mobile, AL
*KPAZ-TV Phoenix, AZ
KFTV Hanford, CA
KXRM-TV Colorado Springs, CO
*WTCE-TV Fort Pierce, FL
WPXC-TV Brunswick, GA
KWHM Wailuku, HI
*KTIN Fort Dodge, IA
WPTA Fort Wayne, IN
*KDCK Dodge City, KS
WBNA Louisville, KY
*WKMU Murray, KY
KPXJ Minden, LA
*WCMW Manistee, MI
KQDS-TV Duluth, MN
*KOZK Springfield, MO
WPXG Concord, NH
KRWB-TV Roswell, NM
KVWB Las Vegas, NV
KAME-TV Reno, NV
*WLIW Garden City, NY
*WXXI-TV Rochester, NY
WFMJ-TV Youngstown, OH
KTVZ Bend, OR
WHP-TV Harrisburg, PA
WWMB Florence, SC
WHNS Greenville, SC
KNBN Rapid City, SD
KTXA Arlington, TX
WJPR Lynchburg, VA
WHRE Virginia Beach, VA
*WHA-TV Madison, WI

Channel 22
WBMM Tuskegee, AL
*KRCB Cotati, CA
KWHY-TV Los Angeles, CA
KFCT Fort Collins, CO
WCLF Clearwater, FL
WDLP-TV Key West, FL
WJCL Savannah, GA
KWWF Waterloo, IA
*WMEC Macomb, IL
WSBT-TV South Bend, IN
*WVUT Vincennes, IN
*WKPI Pikeville, KY
WWLP Springfield, MA
*WMPT Annapolis, MD
*KAWB Brainerd, MN
WHLT Hattiesburg, MS
WLFL Raleigh, NC
*KRWG Las Cruces, NM
WKEF Dayton, OH
*KFTS Klamath Falls, OR

Channel 23
WLDM Tuscaloosa, AL
KAEF Arcata, CA
KERO-TV Bakersfield, CA
*KBSV Ceres, CA
WLTV Miami, FL
*WSRE Pensacola, FL
WELF-TV Dalton, GA
KPWB-TV Ames, IA
WBUI Decatur, IL
WIFR Freeport, IL
WNDY-TV Marion, IN
*WKZT-TV Elizabethtown, KY
WPFO Waterville, ME
*WKAR-TV East Lansing, MI
KMWB Minneapolis, MN
KBSI Cape Girardeau, MO
*WMAO-TV Greenwood, MS
KTMF Missoula, MT
*WNJS Camden, NJ
KNAT Albuquerque, NM
WXXA-TV Albany, NY
WNLO Buffalo, NY
WVPX Akron, OH
KOKI-TV Tulsa, OK
KMTZ Coos Bay, OR
WATM-TV Altoona, PA
*WHMC Conway, SC
*KCSD-TV Sioux Falls, SD
KVEO Brownsville, TX
KUVN-TV Garland, TX
KHCE-TV San Antonio, TX
*WCVE-TV Richmond, VA
KNDO Yakima, WA

Channel 24
KFTA-TV Fort Smith, AR
KNVN Chico, CA
KSEE Fresno, CA
*KVCR-TV San Bernardino, CA
KMAS-TV Steamboat Springs, CO
*WEDH Hartford, CT
*WMFE-TV Orlando, FL
WTLF Tallahassee, FL
WGXA Macon, GA
*KYIN Mason City, IA
*WQPT-TV Moline, IL
KSAS-TV Wichita, KS
*WKYU-TV Bowling Green, KY
*KLPB-TV Lafayette, LA
*KLTS-TV Shreveport, LA
WUTB Baltimore, MD
KNLC Saint Louis, MO
WMDN Meridian, MS
KBTZ Butte, MT
KXND Minot, ND
KLKE Albion, NE
*WCNY-TV Syracuse, NY
WNWO-TV Toledo, OH
*KNMT-TV Portland, OR
WJET-TV Erie, PA
WJPX San Juan, PR
WTAT-TV Charleston, SC
WPTY-TV Memphis, TN
KVUE-TV Austin, TX
KPEJ Odessa, TX
KPNZ Ogden, UT
WDRL-TV Danville, VA
KBCB Bellingham, WA
KQUP Pullman, WA
WCGV-TV Milwaukee, WI
*WNPB-TV Morgantown, WV

Channel 25
*WHIQ Huntsville, AL
KVTN Pine Bluff, AR
*KCAH Watsonville, CA

Channel 26
WYLE Florence, AL
*WAIQ Montgomery, AL
KVTH Hot Springs, AR
KTSF San Francisco, CA
KMPH Visalia, CA
WHPX New London, CT
*WETA-TV Washington, DC
WVEN-TV Daytona Beach, FL
WZVN-TV Naples, FL
WAGT Augusta, GA
*KAAH-TV Honolulu, HI
KGWB-TV Burlington, IA
*KCDT Coeur d'Alene, ID
WCIU-TV Chicago, IL
WGNO New Orleans, LA
*WMEA-TV Biddeford, ME
KFTC Bemidji, MN
*KOZJ Joplin, MO
KLMN Great Falls, MT
WSFX-TV Wilmington, NC
*WUNL-TV Winston-Salem, NC
KNDX Bismarck, ND
*KYNE-TV Omaha, NE
WNYB Jamestown, NY
WBDT Springfield, OH
KMVU Medford, OR
*WQTO Ponce, PR
KINT-TV El Paso, TX
KRIV Houston, TX
KPXL Uvalde, TX
WGBA Green Bay, WI

Channel 27
*KUAS-TV Tucson, AZ
WRDQ Orlando, FL
WTXL-TV Tallahassee, FL
*KSIN Sioux City, IA
WTCT Marion, IL
*WQEC Quincy, IL
WCCU Urbana, IL
KSNT Topeka, KS
WKYT-TV Lexington, KY
*WLPB-TV Baton Rouge, LA
WUNI Worcester, MA
*WCMV Cadillac, MI
KSFX-TV Springfield, MO
WLOV-TV West Point, MS
KCPM Grand Forks, ND
KRPV Roswell, NM
KREN-TV Reno, NV
*WBGU-TV Bowling Green, OH
WKBN-TV Youngstown, OH
WHTM-TV Harrisburg, PA
*WRJA-TV Sumter, SC
KDFI Dallas, TX
KLDO-TV Laredo, TX
WGNT Portsmouth, VA
WFXR-TV Roanoke, VA
WKOW-TV Madison, WI
KLWY Cheyenne, WY

Channel 28
*KCET Los Angeles, CA
WPGX Panama City, FL
WFTS Tampa, FL
*WJSP-TV Columbus, GA
KFXA Cedar Rapids, IA
WSJV Elkhart, IN
WLWC New Bedford, MA
*WCPB Salisbury, MD
*WFUM Flint, MI
WRDC Durham, NC
WTTE Columbus, OH
*KEPB-TV Eugene, OR
WBRE-TV Wilkes-Barre, PA
WTGS Hardeeville, SC
WNPX Cookeville, TN
KYLE Bryan, TX
KORO Corpus Christi, TX
KAMC Lubbock, TX
*WVER Rutland, VT
KAYU-TV Spokane, WA
*KBTC-TV Tacoma, WA
*WHWC-TV Menomonie, WI

Channel 29
WBIH Selma, AL
KHOG-TV Fayetteville, AR
KBAK-TV Bakersfield, CA
KBVU Eureka, CA
KSPX Sacramento, CA
WFLX West Palm Beach, FL
*WDCO-TV Cochran, GA
WTTK Kokomo, IN
*WKPD Paducah, KY
*WKSO-TV Somerset, KY
KVHP Lake Charles, LA
WGTU Traverse City, MI
WFTC Minneapolis, MN
KCWE Kansas City, MO
*WMPN-TV Jackson, MS
*KHNE-TV Hastings, NE
KHFT Hobbs, NM
WUTV Buffalo, NY
WTXF-TV Philadelphia, PA
*WNTV Greenville, SC
KMPX Decatur, TX
KABB San Antonio, TX
WVIR-TV Charlottesville, VA
KIMA-TV Yakima, WA
WLPX-TV Charleston, WV

Channel 30
*KETZ El Dorado, AR
KFSN-TV Fresno, CA
KCVU Paradise, CA
KPXN San Bernardino, CA
WVIT New Britain, CT
*WGCU Fort Myers, FL
WAWS Jacksonville, FL
*WPBA Atlanta, GA
*WTIU Bloomington, IN
KDNL-TV Saint Louis, MO
*WGBC Meridian, MS
WRAY-TV Wilson, NC
*WSKA Corning, NY
WHCP Portsmouth, OH
*WGTE-TV Toledo, OH
KTUZ-TV Shawnee, OK
KBLN Grants Pass, OR
WSJU-TV San Juan, PR
*WNSC-TV Rock Hill, SC
WLMT Memphis, TN
WUXP Nashville, TN
KPXK Odessa, TX
KUWB Ogden, UT
WVCY-TV Milwaukee, WI

Channel 31
WAAY-TV Huntsville, AL
KWBM Harrison, AR
KMAX-TV Sacramento, CA
KVMD Twentynine Palms, CA
KDVR Denver, CO
WFXL Albany, GA
KFXP Pocatello, ID
WMBD-TV Peoria, IL
*WKOH Owensboro, KY
KLAX-TV Alexandria, LA

U.S. Television Stations by Analog Channel

*WWPB Hagerstown, MD
WPXD Ann Arbor, MI
*WMAI Cleveland, MS
*WUNU Lumberton, NC
WPXN-TV New York, NY
WUHF Rochester, NY
KEYU Elk City, OK
KDKF Klamath Falls, OR
WNNE-TV Hartford, VT
*KTNW Richland, WA
*WHLA-TV La Crosse, WI

Channel 32

WNCF Montgomery, AL
*KMTP-TV San Francisco, CA
*WHUT-TV Washington, DC
WMOR-TV Lakeland, FL
WNEG-TV Toccoa, GA
KBFD Honolulu, HI
*KBIN Council Bluffs, IA
*KRIN Waterloo, IA
WFLD Chicago, IL
WLKY-TV Louisville, KY
*WLAE-TV New Orleans, LA
*WMYC Yazoo City, MS
*KAZQ Albuquerque, NM
KWBP Salem, OR
*WELU Aguadilla, PR
KTAB-TV Abilene, TX
KUTH Provo, UT
WACY Appleton, WI

Channel 33

KDMD Anchorage, AK
WCFT-TV Tuscaloosa, AL
KTVW-TV Phoenix, AZ
KTAS San Luis Obispo, CA
KTLL-TV Durango, CO
WBFS-TV Miami, FL
WHBR Pensacola, FL
WISE-TV Fort Wayne, IN
KWCV Wichita, KS
WVLA Baton Rouge, LA
KMSS-TV Shreveport, LA
WFQX-TV Cadillac, MI
KSPR Springfield, MO
*WUNF-TV Asheville, NC
KFBT Las Vegas, NV
WFXV Utica, NY
WYTV Youngstown, OH
*WITF-TV Harrisburg, PA
*WJPM-TV Florence, SC
KDAF Dallas, TX
WTVZ Norfolk, VA
*WETK Burlington, VT
KWPX Bellevue, WA
*WPBY-TV Huntington, WV
KDEV Cheyenne, WY

Channel 34

WDFX-TV Ozark, AL
KWFT Eureka Springs, AR
KMEX-TV Los Angeles, CA
WTVX Fort Pierce, FL
WUVG-TV Athens, GA
WGSA Baxley, GA
*WNIT-TV South Bend, IN
WBKI-TV Campbellsville, KY
WRBJ Magee, MS
KMCC Laughlin, NV
WIVT Binghamton, NY
*WOSU-TV Columbus, OH
KOCB Oklahoma City, OK
KLSR-TV Eugene, OR
WRUA Fajardo, PR
*KITU-TV Beaumont, TX
KJTV-TV Lubbock, TX
*KWBU-TV Waco, TX
KGPX Spokane, WA
WYOW Eagle River, WI

Channel 35

KCBA Salinas, CA
WFGX Fort Walton Beach, FL
WPXM Miami, FL
WOFL Orlando, FL
*KUID-TV Moscow, ID
KXTF Twin Falls, ID

*WWTO-TV LaSalle, IL
*WKHA Hazard, KY
*WKMA Madisonville, KY
WPME Lewiston, ME
*WDCQ-TV Bad Axe, MI
*WGVU-TV Grand Rapids, MI
WUFX Vicksburg, MS
WPXU-TV Jacksonville, NC
WLIO Lima, OH
*KRSC-TV Claremore, OK
KUOK Woodward, OK
WSEE Erie, PA
*WYBE Philadelphia, PA
*WRLK-TV Columbia, SC
KRRT Kerrville, TX
WRLH-TV Richmond, VA
KAPP Yakima, WA

Channel 36

*WFIQ Florence, AL
*KKAP Little Rock, AR
KMIR-TV Palm Springs, CA
KICU-TV San Jose, CA
WFTX Cape Coral, FL
WATL Atlanta, GA
*KQCT Davenport, IA
*KHIN Red Oak, IA
KSCC Hutchinson, KS
WTVQ-TV Lexington, KY
*WGPT Oakland, MD
WCNC-TV Charlotte, NC
*WUNP-TV Roanoke Rapids, NC
WENY-TV Elmira, NY
WUPW Toledo, OH
KTVC Roseburg, OR
WDWL Bayamon, PR
*WSBE-TV Providence, RI
WMMP Charleston, SC
KWSD Sioux Falls, SD
KXAN-TV Austin, TX
*KOCV-TV Odessa, TX
*WMVT Milwaukee, WI
*WLEF Park Falls, WI

Channel 38

KASN Pine Bluff, AR
KCNS San Francisco, CA
KPMR Santa Barbara, CA
WTTA Saint Petersburg, FL
WLTZ Columbus, GA
*KALO Honolulu, HI
WCPX Chicago, IL
WFXW Terre Haute, IN
KMCI Lawrence, KS
*WKMR Morehead, KY
WNOL-TV New Orleans, LA
WSBK-TV Boston, MA
WADL Mount Clemens, MI
WEPX Greenville, NC
WSWB Scranton, PA
WJWN-TV San Sebastian, PR
*WNEH Greenwood, SC
*KSCE El Paso, TX
WPXR Roanoke, VA
*WPNE Green Bay, WI

Channel 39

*KDTP Phoenix, AZ
KNSD San Diego, CA
WBZL Miami, FL
KFPX Newton, IA
KKJB Boise, ID
WQRF-TV Rockford, IL
*WFWA Fort Wayne, IN
KMCT-TV West Monroe, LA
*WUNJ-TV Wilmington, NC
KBLR Paradise, NV
*WLVT-TV Allentown, PA
WEMT Greeneville, TN
WHTN Murfreesboro, TN
KXTX-TV Dallas, TX
KHWB Houston, TX
WCVI-TV Christiansted, VI

Channel 40

WJSU-TV Anniston, AL
KHBS Fort Smith, AR
KHRR Tucson, AZ

KTXL Sacramento, CA
KTBN-TV Santa Ana, CA
WWSB Sarasota, FL
WTWC-TV Tallahassee, FL
KFXB Dubuque, IA
WHMB-TV Indianapolis, IN
WNKY Bowling Green, KY
WGGB-TV Springfield, MA
WBUY-TV Holly Springs, MS
WDBD Jackson, MS
WUVC-TV Fayetteville, NC
WMGM-TV Wildwood, NJ
WICZ-TV Binghamton, NY
WLMB Toledo, OH
WPCB-TV Greensburg, PA
*WMTJ Fajardo, PR
WBSC-TV Anderson, SC
*KTLM Rio Grande City, TX
WLFB Bluefield, WV

Channel 41

*WIIQ Demopolis, AL
*KRMT Denver, CO
WMGT-TV Macon, GA
WDRB Louisville, KY
KBCA Alexandria, LA
WOTV Battle Creek, MI
KPXM Saint Cloud, MN
KSHB-TV Kansas City, MO
WXTV Paterson, NJ
KLUZ-TV Albuquerque, NM
KTFO Tulsa, OK
KWEX-TV San Antonio, TX
*WHTJ Charlottesville, VA
*WVTA Windsor, VT

Channel 42

WIAT Birmingham, AL
*WEIQ Mobile, AL
KWBF Little Rock, AR
KTNC-TV Concord, CA
KESQ-TV Palm Springs, CA
*WXEL-TV West Palm Beach, FL
WCLJ-TV Bloomington, IN
KSAX Alexandria, MN
*WTVI Charlotte, NC
KPTM Omaha, NE
*WPBO-TV Portsmouth, OH
WIRS Yauco, PR
KEYE-TV Austin, TX
KMLM Odessa, TX
*WVPY Front Royal, VA
KVEW Kennewick, WA

Channel 43

*WGIQ Louisville, AL
KEJB El Dorado, AR
KGMC Clovis, CA
*KCSM-TV San Mateo, CA
WSAH Bridgeport, CT
WOTF-TV Melbourne, FL
WYZZ-TV Bloomington, IL
WKOI-TV Richmond, IN
WZPX Battle Creek, MI
KRWF Redwood Falls, MN
*WMAA Columbus, MS
WNYS-TV Syracuse, NY
WUAB Lorain, OH
KAUT-TV Oklahoma City, OK
WPMT York, PA
WFXB Myrtle Beach, SC
WTNZ Knoxville, TN
WVBT Virginia Beach, VA
WZVI Charlotte Amalie, VI

Channel 44

WPXH Gadsden, AL
KXLA Rancho Palos Verdes, CA
KBHK-TV San Francisco, CA
WJTC Pensacola, FL
WTOG Saint Petersburg, FL
WVAG Valdosta, GA
*KWBN Honolulu, HI
KPTH Sioux City, IA
WSNS Chicago, IL
WEVV Evansville, IN
WAGV Harlan, KY
WGMB Baton Rouge, LA

*WGBX-TV Boston, MA
XHIJ Ciudad Juarez, MEX
*WOUC-TV Cambridge, OH
WTLW Lima, OH
KTPX Okmulgee, OK
*WVIA-TV Scranton, PA
WVEO Aguadilla, PR
*KLUJ-TV Harlingen, TX
KWKT Waco, TX
WFFF-TV Burlington, VT

Channel 45

WMCF-TV Montgomery, AL
KUTP Phoenix, AZ
KUVI-TV Bakersfield, CA
WLCB-TV Leesburg, FL
*WHFT-TV Miami, FL
KSHV Shreveport, LA
WBFF Baltimore, MD
WFUP Vanderbilt, MI
KSTC-TV Minneapolis, MN
WKDH Houston, MS
WXLV-TV Winston-Salem, NC
WEWB Schenectady, NY
*WNEO Alliance, OH
WRGT-TV Dayton, OH
*WTCI Chattanooga, TN
KXLN-TV Rosenberg, TX
KHCV Seattle, WA

Channel 46

KUVE-TV Green Valley, AZ
KION-TV Monterey, CA
KFTR-TV Ontario, CA
WTVK Naples, FL
WPCT Panama City Beach, FL
WGCL-TV Atlanta, GA
WRBU East St. Louis, IL
WHME-TV South Bend, IN
*WKLE Lexington, KY
WWDP Norwell, MA
WBSF Bay City, MI
WJZY Belmont, NC
*WSKG-TV Binghamton, NY
KOCM Norman, OK
KMTX-TV Roseburg, OR
WIDP Guayama, PR
KDLT-TV Sioux Falls, SD
*KNCT Belton, TX
WTPX Antigo, WI
WVFX Clarksburg, WV

Channel 47

KGPE Fresno, CA
WTEV-TV Jacksonville, FL
*WTVP Peoria, IL
WMDT Salisbury, MD
WSYM-TV Lansing, MI
KXLT-TV Rochester, MN
WRPX Rocky Mount, NC
WNJU Linden, NJ
KWHB Tulsa, OK
WKBS-TV Altoona, PA
WZRB Columbia, SC
KTMD Galveston, TX
KTAQ Greenville, TX
*WSBN-TV Norton, VA
*KYVE Yakima, WA
WMSN-TV Madison, WI

Channel 48

WAFF Huntsville, AL
KVTJ Jonesboro, AR
KSTS San Jose, CA
WFBD Destin, FL
KPXR Cedar Rapids, IA
*WYDN Worcester, MA
WNTZ Natchez, MS
WUPN-TV Greensboro, NC
WGTW-TV Burlington, NJ
KTDO Las Cruces, NM
WYDC Corning, NY
*WCET Cincinnati, OH
WVOZ-TV Ponce, PR
WVLR Tazewell, TN
KNVO McAllen, TX
WEUX Chippewa Falls, WI

Channel 49

KYPX Camden, AR
*KNXT Visalia, CA
*WEDW Bridgeport, CT
WRXY-TV Tice, FL
WTLH Bainbridge, GA
WCFN Springfield, IL
*WIPB Muncie, IN
KTKA-TV Topeka, KS
WDKA Paducah, KY
WPXL New Orleans, LA
WAQP Saginaw, MI
*WLED-TV Littleton, NH
WNYO-TV Buffalo, NY
*WEAO Akron, OH
WGCB-TV Red Lion, PA
*WRET-TV Spartanburg, SC
KPXB Conroe, TX
KSTR-TV Irving, TX
WPXV Norfolk, VA
KPDX Vancouver, WA
WJJA Racine, WI

Channel 50

*KOCE-TV Huntington Beach, CA
KFTY Santa Rosa, CA
KCEC Denver, CO
WBDC-TV Washington, DC
WFTT-TV Tampa, FL
KKAI Kailua, HI
WPWR-TV Gary, IN
KACB-TV New Iberia, LA
WKBD Detroit, MI
KPXE Kansas City, MO
WRAZ Raleigh, NC
WNDS Derry, NH
*WNJN Montclair, NJ
KASY-TV Albuquerque, NM
WWTI Watertown, NY
WQHA Aguada, PR
WPGD-TV Hendersonville, TN
WPXX-TV Memphis, TN

Channel 51

KNWA-TV Rogers, AR
KPPX Tolleson, AZ
KNSO Merced, CA
KUSI-TV San Diego, CA
WSCV Fort Lauderdale, FL
WBIF Marianna, FL
WOGX Ocala, FL
*WEIU-TV Charleston, IL
WNYA Pittsfield, MA
WPXT Portland, ME
KOWH Lincoln, NE
WPXJ-TV Batavia, NY
WSFJ Newark, OH
WTVE Reading, PA
KNWS-TV Katy, TX
KFXK Longview, TX
*WVPT Staunton, VA
KWOG Bellevue, WA

Channel 52

KVEA Corona, CA
WTGL-TV Cocoa, FL
*WKON Owenton, KY
*WGVK Kalamazoo, MI
*WEKW-TV Keene, NH
*WNJT Trenton, NJ
WNYI Ithaca, NY
WGGN-TV Sandusky, OH
KSBI Oklahoma City, OK
WRFB Carolina, PR
KFWD Fort Worth, TX
*WMSY-TV Marion, VA
WWRS-TV Mayville, WI

Channel 53

KAIL Fresno, CA
KWHD Castle Rock, CO
*WEDN Norwich, CT
WPAN Fort Walton Beach, FL
WGFL High Springs, FL
*WKGB-TV Bowling Green, KY
WLAJ Lansing, MI
WMCN-TV Atlantic City, NJ
WWHO Chillicothe, OH

Broadcasting & Cable Yearbook 2006

B-123

U.S. Television Stations by Analog Channel

KGEB Tulsa, OK
WPGH-TV Pittsburgh, PA
WILF Williamsport, PA
WFLI-TV Cleveland, TN
*WNVT Goldvein, VA

Channel 54

WZDX Huntsville, AL
KAZA-TV Avalon, CA
KAJB Calipatria, CA
*KTEH San Jose, CA
WFXG Augusta, GA
WXTX Columbus, GA
*WCVN Covington, KY
WUPL Slidell, LA
WNUV Baltimore, MD
WTLJ Muskegon, MI
WTBY-TV Poughkeepsie, NY
*WQLN Erie, PA
WCCV-TV Arecibo, PR
WPXK Jellico, TN
KNVA Austin, TX
KCEB Longview, TX

Channel 55

WBPG Gulf Shores, AL
WACX Leesburg, FL
WSST-TV Cordele, GA
WRSP-TV Springfield, IL
WFFT-TV Fort Wayne, IN
WYPX Amsterdam, NY
WLNY Riverhead, NY
WBNX-TV Akron, OH
WWWB Rock Hill, SC
KTBU Conroe, TX
KLDT Lake Dallas, TX
WPXE Kenosha, WI
WFXS Wittenberg, WI

Channel 56

KDOC-TV Anaheim, CA
WOPX Melbourne, FL
*WFSG Panama City, FL
KMGT Waimanalo, HI
KDMI Des Moines, IA
*WYIN Gary, IN
WDKY-TV Danville, KY
WLVI-TV Cambridge, MA
*WTVS Detroit, MI
WSPX-TV Syracuse, NY
WOLF-TV Hazleton, PA
KETK-TV Jacksonville, TX
*WNVC Fairfax, VA
*KWDK Tacoma, WA

Channel 57

KSBN-TV Springdale, AR
KJLA Ventura, CA
WFXU Live Oak, FL
*WATC Atlanta, GA
WYMT-TV Hazard, KY
*WGBY-TV Springfield, MA
*WCFE-TV Plattsburgh, NY
WPSG Philadelphia, PA
WACH Columbia, SC
KAZH Baytown, TX
*WCVW Richmond, VA
WBUW Janesville, WI

Channel 58

KWBA Sierra Vista, AZ
*KLCS Los Angeles, CA
KQCA Stockton, CA
WAWD Fort Walton Beach, FL
WPGA-TV Perry, GA
WFTE Salem, IN
WDPX Vineyard Haven, MA
*WUNG-TV Concord, NC
*WNJB New Brunswick, NJ
*WUJA Caguas, PR

WNAB Nashville, TN
*KDTX-TV Dallas, TX
WDJT-TV Milwaukee, WI

Channel 59

KFRE-TV Sanger, CA
KPXC-TV Denver, CO
WCTX New Haven, CT
*WJEB-TV Jacksonville, FL
WAOE Peoria, IL
WXIN Indianapolis, IN
WVNS-TV Lewisburg, WV

Channel 60

WTJP-TV Gadsden, AL
WXFT-TV Aurora, IL
WNEU Merrimack, NH
WBPH-TV Bethlehem, PA
WMEI Arecibo, PR
*KMBH Harlingen, TX
KVDA San Antonio, TX
WWPX Martinsburg, WV

Channel 61

KASW Phoenix, AZ
KTFF-TV Porterville, CA
WTIC-TV Hartford, CT
WPPX Wilmington, DE
WFGC Palm Beach, FL
WTSF Ashland, KY
WLXI-TV Greensboro, NC
WQHS-TV Cleveland, OH
WDSI-TV Chattanooga, TN
KZJL Houston, TX

Channel 62

KRCA Riverside, CA
WVEA-TV Venice, FL
WJYS Hammond, IN
WMFP Lawrence, MA
*WFPT Frederick, MD
WWJ-TV Detroit, MI

KSMO-TV Kansas City, MO
WASV-TV Asheville, NC
WFPX Fayetteville, NC
WWSI Atlantic City, NJ
WRNN-TV Kingston, NY
KOPX Oklahoma City, OK
KAKW-TV Killeen, TX

Channel 63

KBEH Oxnard, CA
*WPPB-TV Boca Raton, FL
*WHSG-TV Monroe, GA
WINM Angola, IN
WIPX Bloomington, IN
WMBC-TV Newton, NJ
WBHQ Sumter, SC

Channel 64

KHIZ Barstow, CA
KTFK-TV Stockton, CA
*WDPB Seaford, DE
WGNM Macon, GA
WLLA Kalamazoo, MI
WAXN-TV Kannapolis, NC
WSTR-TV Cincinnati, OH
WQPX Scranton, PA
WECN Naranjito, PR
WNAC-TV Providence, RI

Channel 65

KKPX San Jose, CA
*WEDY New Haven, CT
WRBW Orlando, FL
WLJC-TV Beattyville, KY
WUVP-TV Vineland, NJ
KTFN El Paso, TX
WUPV Ashland, VA

Channel 66

WLGA Opelika, AL
KFSF-TV Vallejo, CA
WXPX Bradenton, FL

KPXO Kaneohe, HI
WGBO-TV Joliet, IL
WUTF-TV Marlborough, MA
WSMH Flint, MI
*WFME-TV West Milford, NJ
WFXP Erie, PA
WJFB Lebanon, TN
WPXW Manassas, VA

Channel 67

WRJM-TV Troy, AL
KSMS-TV Monterey, CA
WPXP Lake Worth, FL
WUPX-TV Morehead, KY
*WMPB Baltimore, MD
WFTY-TV Smithtown, NY
WNGS Springville, NY
WOAC Canton, OH
KFTH-TV Alvin, TX

Channel 68

WABM Birmingham, AL
KTLN-TV Novato, CA
*WBCC Cocoa, FL
WKMJ Louisville, KY
WBPX Boston, MA
WJAL Hagerstown, MD
WFUT-TV Newark, NJ
WSYT Syracuse, NY
WMFD-TV Mansfield, OH
KPXD Arlington, TX
WLFG Grundy, VA
WWAZ-TV Fond du Lac, WI

Channel 69

KSWB-TV San Diego, CA
WAMI-TV Hollywood, FL
WUPA Atlanta, GA
*WDTI Indianapolis, IN
WFMZ-TV Allentown, PA
WPXQ Block Island, RI

Canadian Television Stations by Channel

Channel 2
CICT-TV Calgary AB
CBXAT-2 High Prairie AB
CFRN-TV-5 Lac La Biche AB
CKSA-TV Lloydminster AB
CHBC-TV Kelowna BC
CKPG-TV Prince George BC
CBUT Vancouver BC
CBWYT Mafeking MB
CKCW-TV Moncton NB
CBYT-3 Bonne Bay NF
CJOX-TV-1 Grand Bank NF
CBIT-2 Cheticamp NS
CIII-TV-2 Bancroft ON
CHBX-TV Sault Ste. Marie ON
CKPR-TV Thunder Bay ON
CKCO-TV-2 Wiarton ON
CBFT Montreal PQ
CFAP-TV Quebec City PQ
CJBR-TV Rimouski PQ
CBCP-TV-2 Cypress Hills SK
CKBQ-TV Melfort SK
CKCK-TV Regina SK

Channel 3
CFRN-TV Edmonton AB
CFRN-TV-2 Peace River AB
CHAN-TV-2 Bowen Island BC
CFTK-TV Terrace BC
CBWFT-4 Ste-Rose-du-Lac MB
CBWFT Winnipeg MB
CJOM-TV Argentia NF
CBNAT-1 Baie Verte NF
CBHT Halifax NS
CBHFT-1 Yarmouth NS
CKVR-TV Barrie ON
CITO-TV Timmins ON
CKRN-TV-3 Bearn-Fabre PQ
CBVT-2 La Tuque PQ
CBFT-2 Mont-Laurier PQ
CBCP-3 Ponteix SK

Channel 4
CFCN-TV Calgary AB
CITL-TV Lloydminster AB
CHAT-TV-1 Pivot AB
CFRN-TV-9 Slave Lake AB
CFJC-TV Kamloops BC
CKYB-TV Brandon MB
CBWT-2 Lac du Bonnet MB
CBAT-TV-4 Campbellton NB
CBAT Fredericton-Saint John NB
CJCN-TV Grand Falls NF
CJSV-TV Stephenville NF
CJCB-TV Sydney NS
CBOT Ottawa ON
CIII-TV-4 Owen Sound ON
CHFD-TV Thunder Bay ON
CFRS-TV Jonquiere PQ
CFCM-TV Quebec City PQ
CKRN-TV Rouyn-Noranda PQ
CFSK-TV Saskatoon SK

Channel 5
CKAL-TV Calgary AB
CBXT Edmonton AB
CJDC-TV Dawson Creek BC
CKX-TV Brandon MB
CBNT-3 Marystown NF
CBIT Sydney NS
CICI-TV-1 Elliot Lake ON
CHRO-TV Pembroke ON

Channel 6
CICI-TV Sudbury ON
CBLT Toronto ON
CKCW-TV-2 Saint Edward PE
CHAU-TV Carleton PQ
CBVD-TV Malartic PQ
CFER-TV-2 Sept-Iles PQ

Channel 6
CBXFT-1 Bonnyville AB
CHAT-TV Medicine Hat AB
CKRD-TV Red Deer AB
CHEK-TV Victoria BC
CBWT Winnipeg MB
CBAT-TV-1 Bon Accord NB
CBNAT-4 Saint Anthony NF
CJON-TV St John's NF
CJCH-TV-6 Caledonia NS
CJCB-TV-1 Inverness NS
*CHAK-TV Inuvik NT
CJOH-TV-6 Deseronto ON
CIII-TV-6 Ottawa ON
CIII-TV Paris ON
CJPM-TV Chicoutimi PQ
CBMT Montreal PQ
CFQC-TV-2 North Battleford SK
CKCK-TV-2 Willow Bunch SK
CFWH-TV White Horse YT

Channel 7
CISA-TV Lethbridge AB
CFRN-TV-7 Lougheed AB
CHAN-TV-3 Squamish BC
CHVC-TV Valemount BC
CKY-TV Winnipeg MB
CKCD-TV Campbellton NB
CBAT-TV-2 Moncton NB
CBHFT-2 Mulgrave NS
CBLFT-5 Hearst ON
CIII-TV-7 Midland ON
CBLFT-1 Sturgeon Falls ON
CKRT-TV Riviere-du-Loup PQ
CHLT-TV Sherbrooke PQ
CBKFT-4 Saint Brieux SK
CBCP-TV-1 Shaunavon SK
CIEW-TV Warmley SK

Channel 8
CFCN-TV-8 Medicine Hat AB
CFRN-TV-6 Red Deer AB
CHAN-TV Vancouver BC
CBWST Baldy Mountain MB
CBNT Saint John's NF
CIHF-TV Halifax NS
*CFYK-TV Yellowknife NT
CJOH-TV-8 Cornwall ON
CBWAT Kenora ON
CBLAT-1 Manitouwadge ON
CKNX-TV Wingham ON
CKCW-TV-1 Charlottetown PE
*CIVV-TV Chicoutimi PQ
*CIVA-TV Rouyn PQ
CHEM-TV Trois-Rivieres PQ
CFQC-TV Saskatoon SK

Channel 9
CBRT Calgary AB
*CJAL-TV Edmonton AB
CHAN-TV-5 Brackendale BC
CHKM-TV-1 Pritchard BC
CHAN-TV-7 Whistler BC
CKND-TV Winnipeg MB
CKLT-TV Saint John NB

CBNAT-9 Mount St. Margaret NF
CJCB-TV-2 Antigonish NS
CJCH-TV Halifax NS
CBWDT Dryden ON
CBOFT Ottawa ON
*CICO-TV-9 Thunder Bay ON
CBLFT-3 Timmins ON
CFTO-TV Toronto ON
CBLAT-3 Wawa ON
CBET Windsor ON
CIMT-TV Riviere-du-Loup PQ
*CIVG-TV Sept-Iles PQ
CKSH-TV Sherbrooke PQ
CIPA-TV Prince Albert SK
CBKT Regina SK
CBKST-1 Stranraer SK

Channel 10
CKRD-TV-1 Coronation AB
CBXAT Grande Prairie AB
CBUBT-7 Cranbrook BC
CKVU-TV Vancouver BC
CBWGT Fisher Branch MB
CBWBT Flin Flon MB
CJWB-TV Bonavista NF
CJWN-TV Corner Brook NF
CJCH-TV-1 Canning NS
CBHFT-4 Cheticamp NS
CIMC-TV Isle Madame NS
CFPL-TV London ON
CKNY-TV North Bay ON
CFTM-TV Montreal PQ
CKMC-TV-1 Golden Prairie SK
CBKT-2 Willow Bunch SK
CICC-TV Yorkton SK

Channel 11
CBXFT Edmonton AB
CHAN-TV-1 Chilliwack BC
CBUFT-3 Terrace BC
CKX-TV-1 Foxwarren MB
CBAFT Moncton NB
CBNAT Botwood NF
CBHT-4 Sheet Harbour NS
CBHT-3 Yarmouth NS
CHCH-TV Hamilton ON
CITO-TV-2 Kearns ON
CKWS-TV Kingston ON
CBLAT-4 Marathon ON
CBVT Quebec City PQ
CFER-TV Rimouski PQ
CFRE-TV Regina SK
CBKST Saskatoon SK

Channel 12
CFRN-TV-4 Ashmont AB
CFCN-TV-1 Drumheller AB
CBXFT-6 Fort McMurray AB
CBXAT-3 Manning AB
CFRN-TV-3 Whitecourt AB
CBUBT-1 Canal Flats BC
CKAM-TV Upsalquitch Lake NB
CBNT-2 Placentia NF
CBHT-11 Mulgrave NS
CBLFT-6 Elliot Lake ON
CBLFT-4 Kapuskasing ON
CHEX-TV Peterborough ON
*CIVF-TV Baie-Trinite PQ
CBIMT Iles-de-la-Madeleine PQ
CFCF-TV Montreal PQ
CBFST-2 Temiscaning PQ
CKCK-TV-1 Colgate SK

CKMC-TV Swift Current SK

Channel 13
CIAN-TV Calgary AB
CITV-TV Edmonton AB
CFRN-TV-1 Grande Prairie AB
CFCN-TV-5 Lethbridge AB
CJTG-TV Meander River AB
CHEK-TV-5 Campbell River BC
CHMI-TV Portage la Prairie MB
*CBNLT Labrador City NF
CBNT-1 Port Rexton NF
CBHFT Halifax NS
CBHFT-3 Sydney NS
CBLAT Geraldton ON
CJBN-TV Kenora ON
CKCO-TV Kitchener ON
CJOH-TV Ottawa ON
CBLFT-2 Sudbury ON
CBCT Charlottetown PE
CKTM-TV Trois-Rivieres PQ
CBKFT Regina SK

Channel 15
*CIVQ-TV Quebec City PQ

Channel 16
CHWI-TV Windsor ON
CFKM-TV Trois-Rivieres PQ

Channel 17
CJIL-TV Lethbridge AB
*CIVM-TV Montreal PQ

Channel 18
CFRN-TV-8 Grouard Mission-High Prairie AB
*CICO-TV-18 London ON

Channel 19
CBXFT-8 Grande Prairie AB
*CICO-TV-19 Sudbury ON
*CICA-TV Toronto ON

Channel 20
*CICO-TV-20 Sault Ste. Marie ON
CKMI-TV Quebec City PQ

Channel 21
CBWFT-10 Brandon MB
CBKFT-5 Xenon Park SK

Channel 22
CHEX-TV-2 Oshawa ON
CIII-TV-22 Stevenson ON
*CIVB-TV Rimouski PQ
CBKFT-3 Debden SK

Channel 23
*CIVP-TV Chapeau PQ

Channel 24
*CICO-TV-24 Ottawa ON
*CIVS-TV Sherbrooke PQ

Channel 25
CBLFT Toronto ON
CFVS-TV Val d'Or PQ

Channel 26
CBUFT Vancouver BC
CBKFT-9 Bellegarde SK

Channel 27
CIII-TV-27 Peterborough ON

Channel 28
*CICO-TV-28 Kitchener ON

Channel 29
CIII-TV-29 Oil Springs ON
*CFTU-TV Montreal PQ
CFTF-TV Riviere-du-Loup PQ

Channel 30
*CIVO-TV Gatineau PQ
CFKS-TV Sherbrooke PQ

Channel 32
CIVT-TV Vancouver BC
*CICO-TV-32 Windsor ON

Channel 34
CFGS-TV Gatineau PQ

Channel 35
CFJP-TV Montreal PQ

Channel 36
CITS-TV Hamilton ON

Channel 39
CBKFT-6 Gravelbourg SK

Channel 40
CHOT-TV Gatineau PQ

Channel 41
CIII-TV-41 Toronto ON

Channel 42
CHNM-TV Vancouver BC
CKCO-TV-3 Sarnia ON

Channel 45
*CIVC-TV Trois-Rivieres PQ

Channel 47
CFMT-TV Toronto ON

Channel 50
CBUFT-2 Kamloops BC

Channel 51
CKEM-TV Edmonton AB

Channel 52
CKXT-TV Toronto ON

Channel 53
CIVI-TV Victoria BC

Channel 54
*CBEFT Windsor ON

Channel 57
CITY-TV Toronto ON

Channel 58
CBJET Chicoutimi PQ

Channel 59
*CICO-TV-59 Chatham ON

Channel 62
CJNT-TV Montreal PQ

Channel 66
CHNU-TV Fraser Valley BC

Channel 69
CJMT-TV Toronto ON

U.S. Television Stations by Digital Channel

Channel 2
KREX-TV Grand Junction, CO
WWMT Kalamazoo, MI
KVBC Las Vegas, NV
WKYC-TV Cleveland, OH

Channel 3
WDLP-TV Key West, FL
WBBM-TV Chicago, IL
KCBU Price, UT
*WBRA-TV Roanoke, VA

Channel 4
WMAZ-TV Macon, GA
WDKY-TV Danville, KY
WPXT Portland, ME

Channel 5
*KETS Little Rock, AR
KNSO Merced, CA
KOCO-TV Oklahoma City, OK
*KTVR La Grande, OR
KPXB Conroe, TX

Channel 6
*KTOO-TV Juneau, AK
WDTV Weston, WV

Channel 7
KAIL Fresno, CA
WFLA-TV Tampa, FL
WLJC-TV Beattyville, KY
WOOD-TV Grand Rapids, MI
KRTV Great Falls, MT
KLAS-TV Las Vegas, NV
KTTW Sioux Falls, SD
WMAK Knoxville, TN

Channel 8
WSVN Miami, FL
KGMD-TV Hilo, HI
KHON-TV Honolulu, HI
WBNA Louisville, KY
*WNJB New Brunswick, NJ
WICZ-TV Binghamton, NY
*KWET Cheyenne, OK
WOLO-TV Columbia, SC
*WMVS Milwaukee, WI
*KCWC-TV Lander, WY

Channel 9
WJSU-TV Anniston, AL
WALA-TV Mobile, AL
KFSN-TV Fresno, CA
WPLG Miami, FL
KIFI-TV Idaho Falls, ID
WISH-TV Indianapolis, IN
KFDA-TV Amarillo, TX
WFAA-TV Dallas, TX
*KUHT Houston, TX
KCEN-TV Temple, TX
KUSG Saint George, UT

Channel 10
WTNH-TV New Haven, CT
WXIA-TV Atlanta, GA
KNIN-TV Caldwell, ID
KTVQ Billings, MT
WCPO-TV Cincinnati, OH
WOIO Shaker Heights, OH
WSMV-TV Nashville, TN

Channel 11
*WDIQ Dozier, AL
*KEET Eureka, CA
WESH Daytona Beach, FL
WLFI-TV Lafayette, IN
*WGVU-TV Grand Rapids, MI
KPLR-TV Saint Louis, MO
KULR-TV Billings, MT

Channel 12
KNTV San Jose, CA
KKCO Grand Junction, CO
WTXX Waterbury, CT
WGEN-TV Key West, FL
WTVT Tampa, FL
WFXL Albany, GA
*KUID-TV Moscow, ID
*WNIN Evansville, IN
WYMT-TV Hazard, KY
*WMEM-TV Presque Isle, ME
KRCG Jefferson City, MO
KSNK McCook, NE
KTNV Las Vegas, NV
WMFD-TV Mansfield, OH
WWPX Martinsburg, WV

Channel 13
WPEC West Palm Beach, FL
KTRV Nampa, ID
KOAM-TV Pittsburg, KS
KTVN Reno, NV
WSYX Columbus, OH
WRCB-TV Chattanooga, TN
KWES-TV Odessa, TX
KXLY-TV Spokane, WA

Channel 14
WRDQ Orlando, FL
KYOU-TV Ottumwa, IA
*WKSO-TV Somerset, KY
WKBD Detroit, MI
WGPX Burlington, NC
KCSG Cedar City, UT
KEPR-TV Pasco, WA
KTBW-TV Tacoma, WA

Channel 15
KUNO-TV Fort Bragg, CA
KSBY San Luis Obispo, CA
KREZ-TV Durango, CO
KFQX Grand Junction, CO
WBBH-TV Fort Myers, FL
WGNO New Orleans, LA
WRPX Rocky Mount, NC
WEWS Cleveland, OH
KDOR-TV Bartlesville, OK
KTBO-TV Oklahoma City, OK
WZTV Nashville, TN
KFOX-TV El Paso, TX
KGNS-TV Laredo, TX
WFDC-TV Arlington, VA
KHQ-TV Spokane, WA
WQOW-TV Eau Claire, WI

Channel 16
KSWT Yuma, AZ
KUSA-TV Denver, CO
WELF-TV Dalton, GA
KDSM-TV Des Moines, IA
WTVO Rockford, IL
KSNG Garden City, KS
*WKHA Hazard, KY
KADN Lafayette, LA
WJAL Hagerstown, MD
*KCGE-DT Crookston, MN
*KTCI-TV Saint Paul, MN
*WMAH-TV Biloxi, MS
*KXNE-TV Norfolk, NE
*KPNE-TV North Platte, NE
KRQE Albuquerque, NM
*WXXI-TV Rochester, NY
WSEE Erie, PA
*WHRO-TV Hampton-Norfolk, VA

Channel 17
KPHO-TV Phoenix, AZ
KVIQ Eureka, CA
*KRMJ Grand Junction, CO
WKCF Clermont, FL
WTCT Marion, IL
KLBY Colby, KS
*WKPC-TV Louisville, KY

Channel 18
KFSM-TV Fort Smith, AR
KUVS-TV Modesto, CA
KUSI-TV San Diego, CA
*KRMA-TV Denver, CO
KHVO Hilo, HI
WAND Decatur, IL
KUPK-TV Garden City, KS
*WKYU-TV Bowling Green, KY
*WMAU-TV Bude, MS
WMBC-TV Newton, NJ
WBDT Springfield, OH
WFXB Myrtle Beach, SC
*KESD-TV Brookings, SD
KEVN-TV Rapid City, SD
KTXA Arlington, TX
KVAW Eagle Pass, TX
KYTX Nacogdoches, TX
WDBJ Roanoke, VA
*WVTB Saint Johnsbury, VT
KCPQ Tacoma, WA

Channel 19
*WIIQ Demopolis, AL
KSWB-TV San Diego, CA
KBWB San Francisco, CA
KTVD Denver, CO
WBZL Miami, FL
WGCL-TV Atlanta, GA
KIKU Honolulu, HI
*WUSI-TV Olney, IL
WISE-TV Fort Wayne, IN
KWCH-TV Hutchinson, KS
*WGBH-TV Boston, MA
WXMI Grand Rapids, MI
*KCPT Kansas City, MO
WSYT Syracuse, NY
WKPV Ponce, PR
KTVT Fort Worth, TX
KIDY San Angelo, TX
KBCB Bellingham, WA
WMTV Madison, WI

Channel 20
KJNP-TV North Pole, AK
*KPAZ-TV Phoenix, AZ
KFTV Hanford, CA
KCVU Paradise, CA
*KRMU Durango, CO
*WLRN-TV Miami, FL
*KLTL-TV Lake Charles, LA
WCVB-TV Boston, MA
*KSMQ-TV Austin, MN
KCCW-TV Walker, MN
*WUND-TV Columbia, NC
*KDSE Dickinson, ND
KETV Omaha, NE
KVIH-TV Clovis, NM
*KTLM Rio Grande City, TX
KTXS-TV Sweetwater, TX
KREM-TV Spokane, WA

Channel 21
KMAX-TV Sacramento, CA
KHAW-TV Hilo, HI
WPXS Mount Vernon, IL
KAKE-TV Wichita, KS
WUPX-TV Morehead, KY
WBOC-TV Salisbury, MD
WDWB Detroit, MI
WFTC Minneapolis, MN
KOAT-TV Albuquerque, NM
WBNG-TV Binghamton, NY
WJPX San Juan, PR

Channel 22
*WFIQ Florence, AL
WFOR-TV Miami, FL
WOFL Orlando, FL
WTXL-TV Tallahassee, FL
KGMB Honolulu, HI
KSNC Great Bend, KS
WLWC New Bedford, MA
KMWB Minneapolis, MN
WCNC-TV Charlotte, NC
*KBME-TV Bismarck, ND
WOWT Omaha, NE
*WNJS Camden, NJ
*WLIW Garden City, NY
KTTM Huron, SD
*KLRU-TV Austin, TX
KETK-TV Jacksonville, TX
WVCY-TV Milwaukee, WI

Channel 23
KVOA Tucson, AZ
KVMD Twentynine Palms, CA
KREG-TV Glenwood Springs, CO
*WMFE-TV Orlando, FL
WJCL Savannah, GA
*WQPT-TV Moline, IL
WUTF-TV Marlborough, MA
WBTV Charlotte, NC
*KZSD-TV Martin, SD
WNAB Nashville, TN
KVII-TV Amarillo, TX
KPEJ Odessa, TX
WCVI-TV Christiansted, VI
WSAZ-TV Huntington, WV

Channel 24
*KUAC-TV Fairbanks, AK
*WHIQ Huntsville, AL
KBEH Oxnard, CA
KGO-TV San Francisco, CA
WTSP Saint Petersburg, FL
KGMV Wailuku, HI
WPTA Fort Wayne, IN
WTHI-TV Terre Haute, IN
*WCVN Covington, KY
WTLJ Muskegon, MI
KCCO-TV Alexandria, MN
*WMAB-TV Mississippi State, MS
*WNYE-TV New York, NY
WATM-TV Altoona, PA
KVEO Brownsville, TX
*WVTA Windsor, VT
*WHRM-TV Wausau, WI
WVVA Bluefield, WV

Channel 25
KMSB-TV Tucson, AZ
KGTV San Diego, CA
KOVR Stockton, CA
WFGX Fort Walton Beach, FL
WVEA-TV Venice, FL
WATL Atlanta, GA
WRTV Indianapolis, IN
*WMAO-TV Greenwood, MS
*WUNU Lumberton, NC
KOLN Lincoln, NE
KVAL-TV Eugene, OR
KDKA-TV Pittsburgh, PA
WTVE Reading, PA
*KPSD-TV Eagle Butte, SD
WPTY-TV Memphis, TN

Channel 26
KTVF Fairbanks, AK
WTJP-TV Gadsden, AL
KUTP Phoenix, AZ

Channel 27
WKRG-TV Mobile, AL
*WAIQ Montgomery, AL
KFTA-TV Fort Smith, AR
KTSF San Francisco, CA
*WETA-TV Washington, DC
*WXEL-TV West Palm Beach, FL
WAGA Atlanta, GA
KFXA Cedar Rapids, IA
WTVA Tupelo, MS
WCCB Charlotte, NC
WRDC Durham, NC
WGTW-TV Burlington, NJ
KASA-TV Santa Fe, NM
KFOR-TV Oklahoma City, OK
KMVU Medford, OR
WKPT-TV Kingsport, TN
WKRN-TV Nashville, TN
KRIV Houston, TX
*WHWC-TV Menomonie, WI

Channel 28
WGFL High Springs, FL
WFLX West Palm Beach, FL
*KSIN Sioux City, IA
KBCI-TV Boise, ID
KTVB Boise, ID
*WFPT Frederick, MD
KSFX-TV Springfield, MO
WNBC New York, NY
WUHF Rochester, NY
WUAB Lorain, OH
KTPX Okmulgee, OK
WREG-TV Memphis, TN

Channel 29
*KAET Phoenix, AZ
KPIX-TV San Francisco, CA
WFTS Tampa, FL
KMAU Wailuku, HI
WXIX-TV Newport, KY
WVUE New Orleans, LA
WUNI Worcester, MA
*WMPB Baltimore, MD
KMTF Helena, MT
*WFME-TV West Milford, NJ
KTUZ-TV Shawnee, OK
WILF Williamsport, PA
KIVV-TV Lead, SD
KUPX Provo, UT
WVBT Virginia Beach, VA

Channel 30
*KPBS San Diego, CA
*KQED San Francisco, CA
*WKOH Owensboro, KY
KVHP Lake Charles, LA
WBNX-TV Akron, OH
KPTV Portland, OR
*KCOS El Paso, TX
*WNVT Goldvein, VA
*WHLA-TV La Crosse, WI

Channel 31
WLGA Opelika, AL
KSAZ-TV Phoenix, AZ
KTLA Los Angeles, CA
WPPX Wilmington, DE
*WSRE Pensacola, FL
WRDW-TV Augusta, GA
KCCI Des Moines, IA
WFLD Chicago, IL

U.S. Television Stations by Digital Channel

KWCV Wichita, KS
WFXT Boston, MA
WGTU Traverse City, MI
KDNL-TV Saint Louis, MO
WJW Cleveland, OH
WSWB Scranton, PA
WSJU-TV San Juan, PR
KGBT-TV Harlingen, TX
KHOU-TV Houston, TX
KFXK Longview, TX
WAVY-TV Portsmouth, VA

Channel 32
KARK-TV Little Rock, AR
KDOC-TV Anaheim, CA
KDVR Denver, CO
WBFS-TV Miami, FL
KLEW-TV Lewiston, ID
WPSD-TV Paducah, KY
KLAX-TV Alexandria, LA
WCCO-TV Minneapolis, MN
WITN-TV Washington, NC
*WUNL-TV Winston-Salem, NC
KGIN Grand Island, NE
KMCC Laughlin, NV
WPSG Philadelphia, PA
WQPX Scranton, PA
KDAF Dallas, TX
KDBC-TV El Paso, TX
KTRK-TV Houston, TX
*WSBN-TV Norton, VA
KWPX Bellevue, WA
WBUW Janesville, WI

Channel 33
KBAK-TV Bakersfield, CA
WFSB Hartford, CT
*WCEU New Smyrna Beach, FL
*KBIN Council Bluffs, IA
WBKO Bowling Green, KY
KDLH Duluth, MN
WGRZ-TV Buffalo, NY
WSTR-TV Cincinnati, OH
KWBP Salem, OR
KVUE-TV Austin, TX
KIMA-TV Yakima, WA
WITI Milwaukee, WI
*WNPB-TV Morgantown, WV

Channel 34
KGPE Fresno, CA
KRCR-TV Redding, CA
KTAS San Luis Obispo, CA
KFSF-TV Vallejo, CA
KWGN-TV Denver, CO
WHPX New London, CT
WUSA Washington, DC
WVLA Baton Rouge, LA
*KTCA-TV Saint Paul, MN
WSOC-TV Charlotte, NC
*WCET Cincinnati, OH
WJAC-TV Johnstown, PA
WTNZ Knoxville, TN
WSET-TV Lynchburg, VA
WISN-TV Milwaukee, WI

Channel 35
KGUN Tucson, AZ
KMEX-TV Los Angeles, CA
KCRA-TV Sacramento, CA
KCNC-TV Denver, CO
WFTX Cape Coral, FL
WLTZ Columbus, GA
*KHIN Red Oak, IA
KALB-TV Alexandria, LA
KARE Minneapolis, MN
KSDK Saint Louis, MO
WGHP High Point, NC
*WOUC-TV Cambridge, OH
WLWT Cincinnati, OH
KTVL Medford, OR
KDFW Dallas, TX
KPRC-TV Houston, TX
*WMVT Milwaukee, WI

Channel 36
WTVY Dothan, AL
KPNX Mesa, AZ
KNBC Los Angeles, CA
WTTG Washington, DC
KAII-TV Wailuku, HI
WJYS Hammond, IN
KMCI Lawrence, KS
*WKMU Murray, KY
WJRT-TV Flint, MI
*WMAV-TV Oxford, MS
WFPX Fayetteville, NC
WTTE Columbus, OH
*WITF-TV Harrisburg, PA
WNPX Cookeville, TN
KFTH-TV Alvin, TX
KDFI Dallas, TX
WPXR Roanoke, VA
KSTW Tacoma, WA

Channel 38
KSEE Fresno, CA
*WFSG Panama City, FL
WKMJ Louisville, KY
*WKMR Morehead, KY
WJZ-TV Baltimore, MD
WUVC-TV Fayetteville, NC
KXJB-TV Valley City, ND
WWOR-TV Secaucus, NJ
*WCFE-TV Plattsburgh, NY
WEMT Greeneville, TN
KHWB Houston, TX
KSL-TV Salt Lake City, UT
KOMO-TV Seattle, WA

Channel 39
WJLA-TV Washington, DC
WFTV Orlando, FL
WSAV-TV Savannah, GA
WKOI-TV Richmond, IN
WFXW Terre Haute, IN
WSBK-TV Boston, MA
WZZM-TV Grand Rapids, MI
WADL Mount Clemens, MI
*KETC Saint Louis, MO
*WUNP-TV Roanoke Rapids, NC
WDLI-TV Canton, OH
KWTV Oklahoma City, OK
WJWN-TV San Sebastian, PR
WJKT Jackson, TN
*KSCE El Paso, TX
*KTXT-TV Lubbock, TX
KIRO-TV Seattle, WA
WEAU-TV Eau Claire, WI
WLPX-TV Charleston, WV

Channel 40
KNSD San Diego, CA
*KRMT Denver, CO
WACX Leesburg, FL
KITV Honolulu, HI
*WSIU-TV Carbondale, IL
*WFWA Fort Wayne, IN
WTVQ-TV Lexington, KY
WWTV Cadillac, MI
KPXM Saint Cloud, MN
WHKY-TV Hickory, NC
*KUON-TV Lincoln, NE
WXTV Paterson, NJ
KBLR Paradise, NV
KOIN Portland, OR
WDSI-TV Chattanooga, TN
KXTX-TV Dallas, TX
WTKR Norfolk, VA
WSAW-TV Wausau, WI

Channel 41
*WEIQ Mobile, AL
WZVN-TV Naples, FL
WRBW Orlando, FL
WICD Champaign, IL
*WKPD Paducah, KY
WLVI-TV Cambridge, MA
WUTB Baltimore, MD
WXYZ-TV Detroit, MI
WDBD Jackson, MS
KBIM-TV Roswell, NM

WKBN-TV Youngstown, OH
KAZH Baytown, TX
KXAS-TV Fort Worth, TX
WVEC-TV Hampton, VA
*KCTS-TV Seattle, WA
WGBA Green Bay, WI
WCHS-TV Charleston, WV

Channel 42
KHRR Tucson, AZ
KWHY-TV Los Angeles, CA
WXPX Bradenton, FL
WJBF Augusta, GA
WICS Springfield, IL
WNDU-TV South Bend, IN
*WKLE Lexington, KY
WHDH-TV Boston, MA
*WMPT Annapolis, MD
KSHB-TV Kansas City, MO
WRAY-TV Wilson, NC
WTXF-TV Philadelphia, PA
WCWB Pittsburgh, PA
KTBU Conroe, TX
*WMSY-TV Marion, VA
*WCVE-TV Richmond, VA
*KWDK Tacoma, WA
*WPNE Green Bay, WI

Channel 43
KCAL Los Angeles, CA
WUPA Atlanta, GA
WVAG Valdosta, GA
KFXB Dubuque, IA
WCPX Chicago, IL
*WKZT-TV Elizabethtown, KY
*WGBX-TV Boston, MA
*WTVS Detroit, MI
KTVI Saint Louis, MO
WLXI-TV Greensboro, NC
KPTM Omaha, NE
*WNJT Trenton, NJ
WEWB Schenectady, NY
KATU Portland, OR
WPGH-TV Pittsburgh, PA
WSUR-TV Ponce, PR
*WRET-TV Spartanburg, SC
WPXW Manassas, VA

Channel 44
*WGIQ Louisville, AL
KWBA Sierra Vista, AZ
KHIZ Barstow, CA
KGMC Clovis, CA
WDPB Seaford, DE
WRSP-TV Springfield, IL
*WDTI Indianapolis, IN
*WKON Owenton, KY
*WWPB Hagerstown, MD
WCSH Portland, ME
WZPX Battle Creek, MI
WWJ-TV Detroit, MI
KSTC-TV Minneapolis, MN
*WMAW-TV Meridian, MS
*WUNG-TV Concord, NC
KVLY-TV Fargo, ND
WNYW New York, NY
*WCVW Richmond, VA
WWAZ-TV Fond du Lac, WI

Channel 45
WPXH Gadsden, AL
KBHK-TV San Francisco, CA
*WEDN Norwich, CT
WJTC Pensacola, FL
WGNM Macon, GA
WXIN Indianapolis, IN
KSNW Wichita, KS
WDIV Detroit, MI
KTGF Great Falls, MT
KMTV Omaha, NE
WABC-TV New York, NY
WOLF-TV Hazleton, PA
*WJPM-TV Florence, SC

Channel 46
KQCA Stockton, CA
KWHD Castle Rock, CO
*WTVP Peoria, IL
WFIE Evansville, IN
WTHR Indianapolis, IN
WMTW-TV Poland Spring, ME
WWHO Chillicothe, OH
KGW Portland, OR
WFMZ-TV Allentown, PA
WPXV Norfolk, VA

Channel 47
WPMI-TV Mobile, AL
WAMI-TV Hollywood, FL
WFTT-TV Tampa, FL
*WTTW Chicago, IL
*WYDN Worcester, MA
KSMO-TV Kansas City, MO
KTDO Las Cruces, NM
KDLT-TV Sioux Falls, SD
*WLEF-TV Park Falls, WI

Channel 48
WRJM-TV Troy, AL
*KOCE-TV Huntington Beach, CA
KTFF-TV Porterville, CA
KSPX Sacramento, CA
WRC-TV Washington, DC
WFBD Destin, FL
WFXU Live Oak, FL
WOPX Melbourne, FL
WTTV Bloomington, IN
KTKA-TV Topeka, KS
*WKGB-TV Bowling Green, KY
WXXV-TV Gulfport, MS
KWHB Tulsa, OK
WPXI Pittsburgh, PA
KSTR-TV Irving, TX
KING-TV Seattle, WA
KPDX Vancouver, WA
WVNS-TV Lewisburg, WV

Channel 49
WAFF Huntsville, AL
KYPX Camden, AR
KSTS San Jose, CA
KJLA Ventura, CA
WAWD Fort Walton Beach, FL
WDRB Louisville, KY
WWUP-TV Sault Ste. Marie, MI
WWSI Atlantic City, NJ
WNWO-TV Toledo, OH
WNEP-TV Scranton, PA
*WITV Charleston, SC
WTAP-TV Parkersburg, WV

Channel 50
KNWA-TV Rogers, AR
*KTEH San Jose, CA
*KNXT Visalia, CA
WTVX Fort Pierce, FL
WTLH Bainbridge, GA
*KDIN-TV Des Moines, IA
KSTP-TV Saint Paul, MN
WAXN-TV Kannapolis, NC
WMCN-TV Atlantic City, NJ
KOPX Oklahoma City, OK
KWOG Bellevue, WA

Channel 51
WNCF Montgomery, AL
KXLA Rancho Palos Verdes, CA
WBDC-TV Washington, DC
WFMY-TV Greensboro, NC
*KWSE Williston, ND
*WNJN Montclair, NJ
KSBI Oklahoma City, OK
WTAE-TV Pittsburgh, PA
WPXX-TV Memphis, TN
KFWD Fort Worth, TX
WLUK-TV Green Bay, WI

Channel 52
KESQ-TV Palm Springs, CA
*WEDW Bridgeport, CT
WWSB Sarasota, FL

WLS-TV Chicago, IL
WWDP Norwell, MA
WMAR-TV Baltimore, MD
WTVD Durham, NC
WICU-TV Erie, PA
KNWS-TV Katy, TX

Channel 53
*WBIQ Birmingham, AL
KABC-TV Los Angeles, CA
*KVIE Sacramento, CA
KQTV Saint Joseph, MO
WRAL-TV Raleigh, NC

Channel 54
WGEM-TV Quincy, IL
WREX-TV Rockford, IL
*WUNE-TV Linville, NC
WPHL-TV Philadelphia, PA
WWBT Richmond, VA

Channel 55
KFMB-TV San Diego, CA
WHAS-TV Louisville, KY
*WMAE-TV Booneville, MS
WNCN Goldsboro, NC
KOTV Tulsa, OK

Channel 56
*WCIQ Mount Cheaha, AL
KNXV-TV Phoenix, AZ
KTVU Oakland, CA
KWQC-TV Davenport, IA
WCLJ-TV Bloomington, IN
KLFY-TV Lafayette, LA
*WCPB Salisbury, MD
KMOV Saint Louis, MO
WCBS-TV New York, NY
KJRH Tulsa, OK
WLII Caguas, PR

Channel 57
KRON-TV San Francisco, CA
WILX-TV Onondaga, MI
WLFL Raleigh, NC
*KSRE Minot, ND
*WENH-TV Durham, NH
KWKT Waco, TX

Channel 58
WJBK Detroit, MI
WHEC-TV Rochester, NY
WOAI-TV San Antonio, TX

Channel 59
*KCET Los Angeles, CA
WKYT-TV Lexington, KY
WBAL-TV Baltimore, MD
*WUNC-TV Chapel Hill, NC
WMUR-TV Manchester, NH
WHAM-TV Rochester, NY
WYFF Greenville, SC
KBTX-TV Bryan, TX

Channel 60
KCBS-TV Los Angeles, CA

Channel 61
KSCI Long Beach, CA
KXTV Sacramento, CA

Channel 63
KTNC-TV Concord, CA

Channel 64
WPVI-TV Philadelphia, PA

Channel 65
KTTV Los Angeles, CA

Channel 66
KCOP Los Angeles, CA
WUVP-TV Vineland, NJ

Channel 67
WCAU Philadelphia, PA

Channel 68
KRCA Riverside, CA

Broadcasting & Cable Yearbook 2006

Spanish-Language Television Stations

The following Spanish-language television stations operate within the United States or near the U.S. border. Stations are listed by Designated Market Area (DMA), city of license, call letters and channel. Stations in U.S. territories do not fall within any Desigianted Market Areas. For further information on individual stations, see Directory of Television Stations in the U.S. beginning on page B-14.

Arizona

Phoenix, AZ
  *KPHZ Holbrook (ch 11)
Phoenix, AZ
  *KMOH-TV Kingman (ch 6)
Phoenix, AZ
  *KTVW-TV Phoenix (ch 33)
Tucson (Sierra Vista), AZ
  *KFTU-TV Douglas (ch 3)
Tucson (Sierra Vista), AZ
  *KHRR Tucson (ch 40)

California

Fresno-Visalia, CA
  *KFTV Hanford (ch 21)
Fresno-Visalia, CA
  *KNSO Merced (ch 51)
Los Angeles
  *KAZA-TV Avalon (ch 54)
Los Angeles
  *KVEA Corona (ch 52)
Los Angeles
  *KMEX-TV Los Angeles (ch 34)
Los Angeles
  *KTLA Los Angeles (ch 5)
Los Angeles
  *KWHY-TV Los Angeles (ch 22)
Los Angeles
  *KFTR-TV Ontario (ch 46)
Los Angeles
  *KRCA Riverside (ch 62)
Los Angeles
  *KJLA Ventura (ch 57)
Monterey-Salinas, CA
  *KSMS-TV Monterey (ch 67)
Sacramento-Stockton-Modesto, CA
  *KUVS-TV Modesto (ch 19)
Sacramento-Stockton-Modesto, CA
  *KTFK-TV Stockton (ch 64)
San Francisco-Oakland-San Jose
  *KTNC-TV Concord (ch 42)
San Francisco-Oakland-San Jose
  *KDTV San Francisco (ch 14)
San Francisco-Oakland-San Jose
  *KSTS San Jose (ch 48)
San Francisco-Oakland-San Jose
  *KFSF-TV Vallejo (ch 66)
Santa Barbara-Santa Maria-San Luis Obispo, CA
  *KTAS San Luis Obispo (ch 33)
Santa Barbara-Santa Maria-San Luis Obispo, CA
  *KPMR Santa Barbara (ch 38)
Yuma, AZ-El Centro, CA
  *KAJB Calipatria (ch 54)
Yuma, AZ-El Centro, CA
  *KVYE El Centro (ch 7)

Colorado

Denver, CO
  *KCEC Denver (ch 50)
Denver, CO
  *KMAS-TV Steamboat Springs (ch 24)

Florida

Miami-Ft. Lauderdale, FL
  *WSCV Fort Lauderdale (ch 51)
Miami-Ft. Lauderdale, FL
  *WDLP-TV Key West (ch 22)
Miami-Ft. Lauderdale, FL
  *WLTV Miami (ch 23)
Orlando-Daytona Beach-Melbourne, FL
  *WVEN-TV Daytona Beach (ch 26)
Orlando-Daytona Beach-Melbourne, FL
  *WOTF-TV Melbourne (ch 43)
Tampa-St. Petersburg (Sarasota), FL
  *WFTT-TV Tampa (ch 50)
Tampa-St. Petersburg (Sarasota), FL
  *WVEA-TV Venice (ch 62)

Georgia

Atlanta
  *WUVG-TV Athens (ch 34)

Illinois

Chicago
  *WSNS Chicago (ch 44)
Chicago
  *WGBO-TV Joliet (ch 66)

Massachusetts

Boston (Manchester, NH)
  *WUTF-TV Marlborough (ch 66)
Boston (Manchester, NH)
  *WUNI Worcester (ch 27)

Nevada

Las Vegas, NV
  *KINC Las Vegas (ch 15)
Las Vegas, NV
  *KBLR Paradise (ch 39)

New Hampshire

Boston (Manchester, NH)
  *WNEU Merrimack (ch 60)

New Jersey

New York
  *WNJU Linden (ch 47)
New York
  *WFUT-TV Newark (ch 68)
New York
  *WXTV Paterson (ch 41)
Philadelphia
  *WWSI Atlantic City (ch 62)
Philadelphia
  *WUVP-TV Vineland (ch 65)

New Mexico

Albuquerque-Santa Fe, NM
  *KLUZ-TV Albuquerque (ch 41)
Albuquerque-Santa Fe, NM
  *KTFQ-TV Albuquerque (ch 14)

El Paso, TX
  *KTDO Las Cruces (ch 48)

North Carolina

Raleigh-Durham (Fayetteville), NC
  *WUVC-TV Fayetteville (ch 40)

Ohio

Cleveland, OH
  *WQHS-TV Cleveland (ch 61)

Oklahoma

Oklahoma City, OK
  *KTUZ-TV Shawnee (ch 30)

Texas

Corpus Christi, TX
  *KORO Corpus Christi (ch 28)
Dallas-Ft. Worth
  *KXTX-TV Dallas (ch 39)
Dallas-Ft. Worth
  *KUVN-TV Garland (ch 23)
El Paso, TX
  *KINT-TV El Paso (ch 26)
El Paso, TX
  *KSCE El Paso (ch 38)
El Paso, TX
  *KTFN El Paso (ch 65)
Harlingen-Weslaco-Brownsville-McAllen, TX
  *KNVO McAllen (ch 48)
Harlingen-Weslaco-Brownsville-McAllen, TX
  *KTLM Rio Grande City (ch 40)
Houston
  *KFTH-TV Alvin (ch 67)
Houston
  *KAZH Baytown (ch 57)
Houston
  *KTMD Galveston (ch 47)
Houston
  *KXLN-TV Rosenberg (ch 45)
Laredo, TX
  *KLDO-TV Laredo (ch 27)
Odessa-Midland, TX
  *KUPB Midland (ch 18)
San Antonio, TX
  *KTRG Del Rio (ch 10)
San Antonio, TX
  *KVDA San Antonio (ch 60)
San Antonio, TX
  *KWEX-TV San Antonio (ch 41)
Waco-Temple-Bryan, TX
  *KAKW-TV Killeen (ch 62)

Utah

Salt Lake City, UT
  *KUTH Provo (ch 32)

Virginia

Washington, DC (Hagerstown, MD)
  *WFDC-TV Arlington (ch 14)

Washington

Yakima-Pasco-Richland-Kennewick, WA
  *KAZW-TV Walla Walla (ch 9)

Mexico

El Paso, TX
  *XHIJ Ciudad Juarez (ch 44)
San Diego, CA
  *XEWT-TV Tijuana (ch 12)

U.S. TV Stations Providing News Programming

Abilene-Sweetwater, TX
KTAB-TV, 8 hrs weekly

Albany, GA
WALB, 15 hrs weekly
WFXL, 2.5 hrs weekly

Albany-Schenectady-Troy, NY
WCDC, 15 hrs weekly
WRGB, 25 hrs weekly
WTEN, 22 hrs weekly
WXXA-TV, 10 hrs weekly
WYPX, 5 hrs weekly

Albuquerque-Santa Fe, NM
KBIM-TV, 6 hrs weekly
KLUZ-TV, .5 hr weekly
KNME-TV, 1 hr weekly
KOBF, 4 hrs weekly
KOB-TV, 12 hrs weekly
KRQE, 24 hrs weekly

Alexandria, LA
KLAX-TV, 4 hrs weekly

Alpena, MI
WBKB-TV, 5.5 hrs weekly

Amarillo, TX
KENW, 3 hrs weekly
KFDA-DT, 2.5 hrs weekly
KFDA-TV, 13 hrs weekly
KVII-TV, 36 hrs weekly

Anchorage, AK
KTUU-TV, 12 hrs weekly
KTVA, 7 hrs weekly
KYES, 1 hr weekly

Atlanta
WAGA, 38 hrs weekly
WGCL-DT, 29 hrs weekly
WGCL-TV, 29 hrs weekly
WPBA, 1.5 hrs weekly

Augusta, GA
WAGT, 8 hrs weekly
WJBF, 22 hrs weekly
WRDW-TV, 20 hrs weekly

Austin, TX
KEYE-TV, 20 hrs weekly
KTBC, 24 hrs weekly
KXAN-TV, 22 hrs weekly

Bakersfield, CA
KBAK-TV, 27 hrs weekly
KGET-TV, 27 hrs weekly

Baltimore, MD
WBAL-TV, 24 hrs weekly

Bangor, ME
WABI-TV, 25 hrs weekly
WLBZ, 33 hrs weekly
WVII-TV, 6 hrs weekly

Baton Rouge, LA
WBRZ, 22 hrs weekly
WLPB-TV, 1 hr weekly
WVLA, 6 hrs weekly

Beaumont-Port Arthur, TX
KBMT, 13 hrs weekly

Bend, OR
KTVZ, 9 hrs weekly

Billings, MT
KTVQ, 17 hrs weekly
KULR-TV, 17 hrs weekly

Biloxi-Gulfport, MS
WLOX, 18 hrs weekly

Binghamton, NY
WBNG-TV, 17 hrs weekly
WICZ-TV, 2 hrs weekly

Birmingham (Anniston, Tuscaloosa), AL
WBRC, 21 hrs weekly
WDBB, 15 hrs weekly
WIAT, 6 hrs weekly
WJSU-TV, 9 hrs weekly
WPXH, 8 hrs weekly
WVTM-TV, 24 hrs weekly

Bluefield-Beckley-Oak Hill, WV
WSWP-TV, 5 hrs weekly
WVVA, 27 hrs weekly

Boise, ID
KAID, 3 hrs weekly
KBCI-TV, 15.5 hrs weekly
KIVI, 16 hrs weekly
KTRV, 3 hrs weekly
KTVB, 27 hrs weekly

Boston (Manchester, NH)
WBPX, 20 hrs weekly
WBZ-TV, 20 hrs weekly
WCVB-DT, 25 hrs weekly
WCVB-TV, 26 hrs weekly
WENH-TV, 2 hrs weekly
WFXT, 7 hrs weekly
WLVI-TV, 7 hrs weekly
WNDS, 5 hrs weekly
WSBK-TV, 4 hrs weekly
WUNI, 3 hrs weekly

Bowling Green, KY
WBKO, 17 hrs weekly
WKYU-TV, 1 hr weekly

Burlington, VT-Plattsburgh, NY
WCAX-TV, 15 hrs weekly
WPTZ, 14.5 hrs weekly

Butte-Bozeman, MT
KXLF-TV, 9 hrs weekly

Casper-Riverton, WY
KCWY, 20 hrs weekly
KTWO-TV, 15 hrs weekly

Cedar Rapids-Waterloo & Dubuque, IA
KFXA, 4 hrs weekly
KFXB, 5 hrs weekly
KGAN, 12 hrs weekly
KWWL, 22 hrs weekly

Champaign & Springfield-Decatur, IL
WEIU-TV, 3 hrs weekly
WICD, 17 hrs weekly
WICS, 22 hrs weekly

Charleston, SC
WCBD-TV, 17 hrs weekly
WCIV, 12 hrs weekly
WCSC-TV, 21 hrs weekly
WTAT-TV, 3.5 hrs weekly

Charleston-Huntington, WV
WOUB-TV, 3 hrs weekly
WVAH-TV, 7 hrs weekly

Charlotte, NC
WHKY-TV, 5 hrs weekly

Charlottesville, VA
WVIR-TV, 32 hrs weekly

Chattanooga, TN
WDEF-TV, 24.5 hrs weekly
WRCB-TV, 22 hrs weekly
WTVC, 32 hrs weekly

Cheyenne, WY-Scottsbluff, NE
KDEV, 15 hrs weekly
KDUH-TV, 2 hrs weekly
KGWN-TV, 15 hrs weekly
KSTF, 8 hrs weekly

Chicago
WGN-TV, 32 hrs weekly
WLS-TV, 8 hrs weekly
WSNS, 5 hrs weekly
WTTW, 5 hrs weekly

Chico-Redding, CA
KCVU, 2.5 hrs weekly
KHSL-TV, 20 hrs weekly
KRCR-TV, 16 hrs weekly

Cincinnati, OH
WCPO-TV, 24 hrs weekly
WPTO, 1 hr weekly
WXIX-TV, 23 hrs weekly

Clarksburg-Weston, WV
WBOY-TV, 24 hrs weekly
WDTV, 18.5 hrs weekly

Cleveland, OH
WEAO, 1 hr weekly
WEWS, 22 hrs weekly
WMFD-TV, 36 hrs weekly

Colorado Springs-Pueblo, CO
KKTV, 27 hrs weekly
KOAA-TV, 7 hrs weekly
KXRM-TV, 3.5 hrs weekly

Columbia, SC
WIS, 26.5 hrs weekly
WLTX, 23 hrs weekly

Columbia-Jefferson City, MO
KMIZ, 19 hrs weekly
KOMU-TV, 20 hrs weekly
KRCG, 14 hrs weekly

Columbus, OH
WBNS-TV, 31 hrs weekly
WCMH-TV, 31.5 hrs weekly

Columbus-Tupelo-West Point, MS
WLOV-TV, 2.5 hrs weekly
WTVA, 21 hrs weekly

Corpus Christi, TX
KIII, 17.5 hrs weekly
KORO, 5 hrs weekly
KRIS-TV, 14 hrs weekly

Dallas-Ft. Worth
KDFW, 50 hrs weekly
KTVT, 27 hrs weekly
KUVN-TV, 10 hrs weekly
KXAS-DT, 30 hrs weekly
KXAS-TV, 37 hrs weekly
WFAA-TV, 28 hrs weekly

Davenport, IA-Rock Island-Moline, IL
KLJB-TV, 3 hrs weekly
WHBF-TV, 7 hrs weekly
WQAD-TV, 22.5 hrs weekly

Dayton, OH
WKEF, 7 hrs weekly
WPTD, 1 hr weekly

Denver, CO
KMAS-TV, 1 hr weekly
KPXC-TV, 24 hrs weekly
KRMA-TV, 1 hr weekly
KUPN, 17 hrs weekly
KWGN-TV, 25 hrs weekly

Des Moines-Ames, IA
KCCI, 17 hrs weekly
KDSM-TV, 4 hrs weekly
KFPX, 2.5 hrs weekly
WHO-TV, 29 hrs weekly
WOI-TV, 15 hrs weekly

Detroit
WJBK, 36 hrs weekly

Dothan, AL
WDHN, 7 hrs weekly
WTVY, 16 hrs weekly

Duluth, MN-Superior, WI
KBJR-TV, 10 hrs weekly
KDLH, 12 hrs weekly
WDIO-TV, 9 hrs weekly

El Paso, TX
KDBC-TV, 15 hrs weekly
KFOX-TV, 6 hrs weekly
KINT-TV, 10 hrs weekly
KRWG-TV, 3 hrs weekly
KTSM-TV, 19.5 hrs weekly
KVIA-TV, 31.5 hrs weekly
XHIJ, 15 hrs weekly

Elmira, NY
WENY-TV, 10 hrs weekly
WETM-TV, 14 hrs weekly

Erie, PA
WFXP, 3 hrs weekly
WICU-TV, 22 hrs weekly
WJET-TV, 39 hrs weekly
WSEE, 10 hrs weekly

Eugene, OR
KMTR, 15 hrs weekly
KMTX-TV, 22 hrs weekly
KMTZ, 22 hrs weekly
KPIC, 14 hrs weekly
KVAL-TV, 17 hrs weekly

Eureka, CA
KAEF, 2 hrs weekly

Evansville, IN
WEVV, 9 hrs weekly
WTVW, 22.5 hrs weekly

Fairbanks, AK
KATN, 6 -11 hrs weekly
KFXF, 10 hrs weekly
KTVF, 5 hrs weekly

Fargo-Valley City, ND
KVLY-TV, 16 hrs weekly
KXJB-TV, 10 hrs weekly

Flint-Saginaw-Bay City, MI
WEYI-TV, 8 hrs weekly
WJRT-TV, 27 hrs weekly

Florence-Myrtle Beach, SC
WBTW, 78 hrs weekly
WFXB, 2.5 hrs weekly

Fresno-Visalia, CA
KAIL, 3 hrs weekly
KFRE-TV, 2 hrs weekly
KFSN-TV, 30 hrs weekly
KFTV, 8 hrs weekly
KGPE, 28 hrs weekly
KMPH, 7 hrs weekly

Ft. Myers-Naples, FL
WBBH-TV, 32 hrs weekly
WINK-TV, 29 hrs weekly
WZVN-DT, 19.5 hrs weekly
WZVN-TV, 19.5 hrs weekly

Ft. Smith-Fayetteville-Springdale-Rogers, AR
KFSM-TV, 28 hrs weekly
KFTA-TV, 20.5 hrs weekly
KHBS, 15 hrs weekly
KNWA-TV, 17 hrs weekly

Ft. Wayne, IN
WANE-TV, 22 hrs weekly
WFWA, 2 hrs weekly
WISE-TV, 14 hrs weekly
WPTA, 31 hrs weekly

Gainesville, FL
WCJB, 17 hrs weekly
WOGX, 7 hrs weekly
WUFT, 3 hrs weekly

Grand Junction-Montrose, CO
KKCO, 28 hrs weekly
KREX-TV, 30 hrs weekly

Grand Rapids-Kalamazoo-Battle Creek, MI
WGVK, 1 hr weekly
WOTV, 13 hrs weekly
WWMT, 25 hrs weekly
WWMT-DT, 24.5 hrs weekly
WXMI, 4 hrs weekly
WZZM-TV, 22 hrs weekly

Great Falls, MT
KFBB-TV, 6 hrs weekly
KRTV, 15 hrs weekly

Green Bay-Appleton, WI
WBAY-TV, 19 hrs weekly
WFXS, 3 hrs weekly
WGBA, 16 hrs weekly

U.S. TV Stations Providing News Programming

Greensboro-High Point-Winston Salem, NC
WFMY-TV, 32 hrs weekly
WGHP, 32 hrs weekly
WUPN-TV, 7 hrs weekly
WXLV-TV, 2.5 hrs weekly

Greenville-New Bern-Washington, NC
WFXI, 4 hrs weekly
WUNK-TV, 3 hrs weekly

Greenville-Spartanburg, SC-Asheville, NC-Anderson, SC
WHNS, 6 hrs weekly
WLOS, 24 hrs weekly
WNEG-TV, 13 hrs weekly
WSPA-TV, 26.5 hrs weekly
WYFF, 28 hrs weekly

Greenwood-Greenville, MS
WABG-TV, 13 hrs weekly

Harlingen-Weslaco-Brownsville-McAllen, TX
KGBT-TV, 19 hrs weekly
KRGV-TV, 12 hrs weekly
KTLM, 8 hrs weekly

Harrisburg-Lancaster-Lebanon-York, PA
WGAL, 29 hrs weekly
WHP-TV, 20 hrs weekly
WHTM-TV, 20 hrs weekly

Harrisonburg, VA
WHSV-TV, 16 hrs weekly

Hartford & New Haven, CT
WCTX, 4 hrs weekly
WFSB, 36 hrs weekly
WTIC-TV, 6 hrs weekly
WTNH-TV, 32 hrs weekly

Hattiesburg-Laurel, MS
WDAM-TV, 20 hrs weekly

Helena, MT
KTVH, 7 hrs weekly

Honolulu, HI
KBFD, 6 hrs weekly
KFVE, 3 hrs weekly
KHNL, 168 hrs weekly
KHON-TV, 25 hrs weekly
KITV, 20 hrs weekly

Houston
KETH-TV, 3 hrs weekly
KHWB, 4 hrs weekly
KHWB-DT, 4 hrs weekly
KPRC-TV, 24 hrs weekly
KTMD, 7 hrs weekly
KXLN-TV, 7 hrs weekly

Huntsville-Decatur (Florence), AL
WAFF, 26 hrs weekly
WYLE, 15 hrs weekly

Idaho Falls-Pocatello, ID
KIDK, 15 hrs weekly
KIFI-TV, 30 hrs weekly
KPVI, 17 hrs weekly

Indianapolis, IN
WHMB-TV, 1 hr weekly
WRTV-DT, 20 hrs weekly
WTIU, 3 hrs weekly
WXIN, 19 hrs weekly

Jackson, MS
WAPT, 14 hrs weekly
WJTV, 21 hrs weekly

Jacksonville, FL
WJXT, 51 hrs weekly
WTEV-TV, 22 hrs weekly
WTLV, 17 hrs weekly

Johnstown-Altoona, PA
WATM-TV, 3 hrs weekly
WJAC-TV, 25 hrs weekly
WTAJ-TV, 29 hrs weekly
WWCP-TV, 5 hrs weekly

Jonesboro, AR
KAIT, 17 hrs weekly

Joplin, MO-Pittsburg, KS
KFJX, 3 hrs weekly
KOAM-TV, 19 hrs weekly
KODE-TV, 16 hrs weekly

Juneau, AK
KJUD, 5 hrs weekly
KTOO-TV, 1 hr weekly

Kansas City, MO
KMBC-TV, 28 hrs weekly
KSHB-TV, 32 hrs weekly
WDAF-TV, 49 hrs weekly

Knoxville, TN
WATE-TV, 15 hrs weekly
WBIR-TV, 24 hrs weekly
WTNZ, 4 hrs weekly
WVLT-TV, 22 hrs weekly

La Crosse-Eau Claire, WI
WEAU-TV, 21 hrs weekly
WQOW-TV, 18 hrs weekly
WXOW-TV, 18 hrs weekly

Lafayette, IN
WLFI-TV, 22 hrs weekly

Lafayette, LA
KATC, 19.5 hrs weekly
KLFY-TV, 14 hrs weekly

Lake Charles, LA
KVHP, 9 hrs weekly

Lansing, MI
WLAJ, 5 hrs weekly
WSYM-TV, 8.5 hrs weekly

Las Vegas, NV
KBLR, 2 hrs weekly
KBLR-DT, 2 hrs weekly
KINC, 5 hrs weekly
KTNV, 22 hrs weekly
KVBC, 29 hrs weekly

Lexington, KY
WDKY-TV, 4 hrs weekly
WKYT-TV, 43 hrs weekly
WTVQ-DT, 22 hrs weekly
WTVQ-TV, 22 hrs weekly

Lima, OH
WLIO, 24 hrs weekly

Lincoln & Hastings-Kearney, NE
KHGI-TV, 17.5 hrs weekly
KLKN, 22 hrs weekly
KSNB-TV, 13 hrs weekly
KWNB-TV, 17.5 hrs weekly

Little Rock-Pine Bluff, AR
KARK-TV, 22 hrs weekly
KTHV, 20 hrs weekly

Los Angeles
KCBS-TV, 26 hrs weekly
KHIZ, 5 hrs weekly
KLCS, 5 hrs weekly
KMEX-TV, 17 hrs weekly
KOCE-TV, 3 hrs weekly
KSCI, 12 hrs weekly
KTLA, 22 hrs weekly
KTLA-DT, 22 hrs weekly
KTTV, 25 hrs weekly
KWHY-TV, 12 hrs weekly

Louisville, KY
WDRB, 33.5 hrs weekly
WLKY-TV, 37.5 hrs weekly

Lubbock, TX
KAMC, 39 hrs weekly
KJTV-TV, 7 hrs weekly
KLBK-TV, 27 hrs weekly

Macon, GA
WMAZ-TV, 27 hrs weekly
WPGA-TV, 3 hrs weekly

Madison, WI
WISC-TV, 30 hrs weekly
WKOW-TV, 22 hrs weekly
WMTV, 19 hrs weekly

Mankato, MN
KEYC-TV, 10 hrs weekly

Marquette, MI
WBKP, 10 hrs weekly
WLUC-TV, 15 hrs weekly
WNMU-TV, 1 hr weekly

Medford-Klamath Falls, OR
KDKF, 12 hrs weekly
KTVL, 16 hrs weekly

Memphis, TN
WHBQ-TV, 27 hrs weekly
WPTY-TV, 7 hrs weekly

Meridian, MS
WMDN, 7.5 hrs weekly
WTOK-TV, 15 hrs weekly

Miami-Ft. Lauderdale, FL
WAMI-TV, 3 hrs weekly
WBZL, 3.5 hrs weekly
WBZL-DT, 3.5 hrs weekly
WFOR-TV, 30 hrs weekly
WSCV, 3 hrs weekly

Milwaukee, WI
WPXE, 3 hrs weekly

Minneapolis-St. Paul, MN
KAWB, 2.5 hrs weekly
KAWE, 2.5 hrs weekly
KMSP-TV, 19.5 hrs weekly
KSTP-TV, 27.5 hrs weekly
WCCO-TV, 23 hrs weekly
WFTC, 3.5 hrs weekly

Minot-Bismarck-Dickinson, ND
KFYR-TV, 24 hrs weekly
KUMV-TV, 6 hrs weekly
KXMB-TV, 9 hrs weekly
KXMC-TV, 9 hrs weekly

Missoula, MT
KCFW-TV, 6 hrs weekly
KPAX-TV, 15 hrs weekly

Mobile, AL-Pensacola (Ft. Walton Beach), FL
WALA-TV, 23 hrs weekly
WEAR-TV, 14 hrs weekly
WPMI-TV, 5 hrs weekly

Monroe, LA-El Dorado, AR
KMCT-TV, 6 hrs weekly
KNOE-TV, 22 hrs weekly
KTVE, 13 hrs weekly

Monterey-Salinas, CA
KCBA, 10 hrs weekly
KION-TV, 8 hrs weekly
KSBW, 26 hrs weekly

Montgomery (Selma), AL
WAKA, 9 hrs weekly
WNCF, 1 hr weekly

Nashville, TN
WHTN, 2 hrs weekly
WKRN-TV, 25 hrs weekly
WTVF, 24 hrs weekly
WZTV, 7 hrs weekly

New Orleans, LA
WDSU, 18 hrs weekly
WHNO, 10 hrs weekly

New York
WFTY-TV, 4 hrs weekly
WLNY, 2 hrs weekly
WMBC-DT, 5 hrs weekly
WMBC-TV, 5 hrs weekly
WNET, 5 hrs weekly
WNJB, 2 hrs weekly
WNJN, 3 hrs weekly
WNJN-DT, 3 hrs weekly
WPIX, 19.5 hrs weekly
WRNN-TV, 82 hrs weekly
WWOR-TV, 7 hrs weekly
WXTV, 17 hrs weekly

Norfolk-Portsmouth-Newport News, VA
WAVY-TV, 31 hrs weekly
WHRO-TV, 1 hr weekly
WVEC-TV, 24 hrs weekly

North Platte, NE
KNOP-TV, 15 hrs weekly

Odessa-Midland, TX
KMID, 17 hrs weekly
KOSA-TV, 16 hrs weekly

Oklahoma City, OK
KETA, 3 hrs weekly
KFOR-TV, 29 hrs weekly
KWET, 4 hrs weekly

Omaha, NE
KETV, 37 hrs weekly
KMTV, 23 hrs weekly
KPTM, 7 hrs weekly
WOWT, 37 hrs weekly

Orlando-Daytona Beach-Melbourne, FL
WFTV, 25 hrs weekly
WKCF, 3 hrs weekly
WKMG-TV, 24 hrs weekly

Ottumwa, IA-Kirksville, MO
KTVO, 14 hrs weekly

Paducah, KY-Cape Girardeau, MO-Harrisburg-Mount Vernon, IL
KBSI, 2 hrs weekly
KFVS-TV, 28 hrs weekly

WPSD-DT, 23 hrs weekly
WPSD-TV, 23 hrs weekly
WSIU-TV, 2 hrs weekly

Palm Springs, CA
KESQ-TV, 17 hrs weekly
KMIR-TV, 8 hrs weekly

Panama City, FL
WMBB, 143 hrs weekly

Parkersburg, WV
WTAP-TV, 20 hrs weekly

Peoria-Bloomington, IL
WEEK-TV, 16 hrs weekly
WHOI, 7 hrs weekly

Philadelphia
WCAU, 21 hrs weekly
WCAU-DT, 21 hrs weekly
WFMZ-DT, 37 hrs weekly
WFMZ-TV, 58 hrs weekly
WHYY-TV, 5 hrs weekly
WMGM-TV, 8 hrs weekly
WNJS, 2 hrs weekly
WNJS-DT, 2 hrs weekly
WNJT, 2 hrs weekly
WTXF-TV, 25 hrs weekly
WWSI, 2.5 hrs weekly
WYBE, 3 hrs weekly

Phoenix, AZ
KAET, 3 hrs weekly
KPHO-DT, 22 hrs weekly
KPHO-TV, 11 hrs weekly
KSAZ-TV, 38 hrs weekly

Pittsburgh, PA
WNPB-TV, 1 hr weekly
WPGH-DT, 6 hrs weekly
WPGH-TV, 6 hrs weekly
WTAE-TV, 32 hrs weekly

Portland, OR
KATU, 24 hrs weekly
KGW, 35 hrs weekly
KGW-DT, 35 hrs weekly
KOIN, 27 hrs weekly
KPTV, 27 hrs weekly
KPTV-DT, 27 hrs weekly

Portland-Auburn, ME
WGME-TV, 25 hrs weekly
WMTW-TV, 13.5 hrs weekly
WPME, 3.5 hrs weekly
WPXT, 3.5 hrs weekly

Presque Isle, ME
WAGM-TV, 14 hrs weekly

Providence, RI-New Bedford, MA
WPXQ, 5 hrs weekly

Quincy, IL-Hannibal, MO-Keokuk, IA
KHQA-TV, 13 hrs weekly
WGEM-TV, 25 hrs weekly

Raleigh-Durham (Fayetteville), NC
WLFL, 7 hrs weekly
WNCN, 30 hrs weekly
WNCN-DT, 30 hrs weekly
WRAL-TV, 29.5 hrs weekly

Rapid City, SD
KEVN-TV, 9 hrs weekly
KIVV-TV, 9 hrs weekly
KNBN, 9 hrs weekly
KOTA-TV, 9 hrs weekly
KSGW-TV, 8 hrs weekly

U.S. TV Stations Providing News Programming

Reno, NV
KOLO-TV, 22 hrs weekly
KRNV, 14 hrs weekly
KTVN, 19.5 hrs weekly

Richmond-Petersburg, VA
WRLH-TV, 3 hrs weekly

Roanoke-Lynchburg, VA
WDBJ, 18 hrs weekly
WFXR-TV, 2 hrs weekly
WJPR, 1 hr weekly
WPXR, 1 hr weekly
WSET-TV, 9.5 hrs weekly
WSLS-TV, 15 hrs weekly

Rochester, MN-Mason City, IA-Austin, MN
KAAL, 11 hrs weekly
KIMT, 19 hrs weekly
KTTC, 11 hrs weekly
KXLT-TV, 7 hrs weekly

Rochester, NY
WHAM-TV, 24 hrs weekly
WHEC-TV, 22 hrs weekly
WROC-TV, 14 hrs weekly
WUHF, 7 hrs weekly
WXXI-DT, 1 hr weekly
WXXI-TV, 2 hrs weekly

Rockford, IL
WIFR, 19 hrs weekly
WTVO, 7 hrs weekly

Sacramento-Stockton-Modesto, CA
KCRA-TV, 55 hrs weekly
KOVR, 22 hrs weekly
KSPX, 7 hrs weekly
KTXL, 7 hrs weekly
KUVS-TV, 12 hrs weekly

Salisbury, MD
WBOC-TV, 31 hrs weekly
WDPB, 3 hrs weekly
WMDT, 12 hrs weekly

Salt Lake City, UT
KBYU-TV, 3 hrs weekly
KJWY, 5 hrs weekly
KJZZ-TV, 10 hrs weekly
KSL-TV, 21 hrs weekly
KSTU, 22 hrs weekly
KTVX, 14 hrs weekly
KUTV, 34.5 hrs weekly

San Angelo, TX
KLST, 17 hrs weekly

San Antonio, TX
KABB, 7 hrs weekly
KENS-TV, 24 hrs weekly
KSAT-TV, 21 hrs weekly
KVDA, 10 hrs weekly
KWEX-TV, 5 hrs weekly
WOAI-TV, 11 hrs weekly

San Diego, CA
KSWB-TV, 3 hrs weekly
KUSI-TV, 25 hrs weekly
XETV, 20 hrs weekly
XEWT-TV, 11 hrs weekly

San Francisco-Oakland-San Jose
KDTV, 5 hrs weekly
KFTY, 7 hrs weekly
KICU-TV, .5 hr weekly
KNTV, 20 hrs weekly
KPIX-TV, 20 hrs weekly
KQED, .5 hr weekly
KRCB, 1 hr weekly
KRON-TV, 42 hrs weekly
KSTS, 3 hrs weekly
KTSF, 15 hrs weekly
KTSF-DT, 15 hrs weekly

Santa Barbara-Santa Maria-San Luis Obispo, CA
KBEH, 3 hrs weekly
KCOY-TV, 28 hrs weekly
KEYT-TV, 21 hrs weekly
KTAS, 3 hrs weekly

Savannah, GA
WJCL, 5 hrs weekly
WJWJ-TV, 2.5 hrs weekly
WTGS, 5 hrs weekly

Seattle-Tacoma, WA
KBCB, 4 hrs weekly
KCPQ, 21 hrs weekly
KIRO-TV, 46 hrs weekly
KSTW, 7 hrs weekly
KVOS-TV, 3 hrs weekly

Sherman, TX-Ada, OK
KTEN, 20 hrs weekly
KXII, 30 hrs weekly

Sioux City, IA
KTIV, 19 hrs weekly

Sioux Falls (Mitchell), SD
KDLT-TV, 13 hrs weekly
KDLV-TV, 9 hrs weekly
KPRY-TV, 15 hrs weekly
KSFY-TV, 15 hrs weekly

KWSD, 2 hrs weekly

South Bend-Elkhart, IN
WSBT-TV, 22 hrs weekly
WSJV, 16 hrs weekly

Spokane, WA
KAYU-TV, 3 hrs weekly
KHQ-TV, 26 hrs weekly
KLEW-TV, 12 hrs weekly
KREM-TV, 17 hrs weekly
KSKN, 14 hrs weekly
KXLY-TV, 19 hrs weekly

Springfield, MO
KOLR-TV, 22 hrs weekly
KSPR, 9 hrs weekly
KYTV, 40 hrs weekly

St. Joseph, MO
KQTV, 16 hrs weekly

St. Louis, MO
KMOV, 29 hrs weekly
KMOV-DT, 29 hrs weekly
KPLR-TV, 4 hrs weekly
KTVI, 18 hrs weekly
KTVI-DT, 7 hrs weekly

Syracuse, NY
WSYR-TV, 19 hrs weekly
WSYT, 3.5 hrs weekly
WTVH, 24 hrs weekly

Tallahassee, FL-Thomasville, GA
WTWC-TV, 14 hrs weekly
WTXL-TV, 24 hrs weekly

Tampa-St. Petersburg (Sarasota), FL
WTOG, 5 hrs weekly
WTVT, 46 hrs weekly
WVEA-TV, 2.5 hrs weekly
WWSB, 21 hrs weekly

Terre Haute, IN
WFXW, 2 hrs weekly
WTWO, 20 hrs weekly
WVUT, 5 hrs weekly

Toledo, OH
WNWO-TV, 22 hrs weekly
WTOL, 25 hrs weekly
WTVG, 10 hrs weekly
WUPW, 5 hrs weekly

Topeka, KS
KSNT, 17 hrs weekly
KTKA-TV, 15 hrs weekly
WIBW-TV, 22.5 hrs weekly

Traverse City-Cadillac, MI
WFQX-TV, 3 hrs weekly
WFUP, 3 hrs weekly

Tri-Cities, TN-VA
WKPT-TV, 12 hrs weekly

Tucson (Sierra Vista), AZ
KGUN, 22 hrs weekly
KHRR, 5 hrs weekly
KOLD-TV, 27 hrs weekly
KVOA, 22 hrs weekly

Tulsa, OK
KJRH, 19 hrs weekly
KOKI-TV, 7 hrs weekly
KTPX-DT, 2.5 hrs weekly
KTUL, 17 hrs weekly

Twin Falls, ID
KMVT, 10 hrs weekly
KXTF, 2 hrs weekly

Tyler-Longview (Lufkin & Nacogdoches), TX
KETK-TV, 19.5 hrs weekly
KTRE, 20 hrs weekly
KYTX, 13.5 hrs weekly

Victoria, TX
KAVU-TV, 8 hrs weekly

Waco-Temple-Bryan, TX
KBTX-TV, 19 . hrs weekly
KCEN-TV, 17 hrs weekly
KNCT, 1 hr weekly
KWTX-TV, 20 hrs weekly
KXXV, 14.5 hrs weekly

Washington, DC (Hagerstown, MD)
WHAG-TV, 20 hrs weekly
WJAL, 5 hrs weekly
WJLA-TV, 24 hrs weekly
WNVC, 1 hr weekly
WTTG-DT, 30 hrs weekly
WUSA, 39 hrs weekly

Watertown, NY
WWNY-TV, 19 hrs weekly
WWTI, 5 hrs weekly

Wausau-Rhinelander, WI
WAOW-TV, 15.5 hrs weekly
WJFW-TV, 13.5 hrs weekly
WSAW-TV, 15 hrs weekly

West Palm Beach-Ft. Pierce, FL
WPBF, 20 hrs weekly
WPEC, 24 hrs weekly
WPTV, 27 hrs weekly

Wheeling, WV-Steubenville, OH
WTOV-TV, 12 hrs weekly
WTRF-TV, 26 hrs weekly

Wichita Falls, TX & Lawton, OK
KAUZ-TV, 15 hrs weekly
KFDX-TV, 17 hrs weekly

Wichita-Hutchinson Plus, KS
KAKE-TV, 16 hrs weekly
KBSH-TV, 24 hrs weekly
KUPK-DT, 7 hrs weekly
KUPK-TV, 7 hrs weekly
KWCH-TV, 24 hrs weekly

Wilkes Barre-Scranton, PA
WBRE-TV, 24 hrs weekly
WNEP-TV, 23 hrs weekly
WOLF-DT, 3.5 hrs weekly
WOLF-TV, 3.5 hrs weekly
WYOU, 19.5 hrs weekly

Wilmington, NC
WSFX-TV, 2.5 hrs weekly

Yakima-Pasco-Richland-Kennewick, WA
KEPR-TV, 17 hrs weekly
KIMA-TV, 17 hrs weekly
KNDO, 15 hrs weekly
KNDU, 22.5 hrs weekly

Youngstown, OH
WFMJ-TV, 10 hrs weekly
WKBN-TV, 25 hrs weekly
WNEO, 1 hr weekly
WYTV, 15 hrs weekly

Yuma, AZ-El Centro, CA
KSWT, 5 hrs weekly
KVYE, 5 hrs weekly
KYMA, 12 hrs weekly

Zanesville, OH
WHIZ-TV, 10 hrs weekly

Nielsen DMA Market Atlas

The Designated Market Area (DMA) is a geographic market design that defines each television market exclusive of others, based on measured viewing patterns. Each market's DMA consists of all the counties in which the home market stations receive a preponderance of viewing, and every county is allocated exclusively to one DMA—there is no overlap. The total of all DMAs represents the total television households in the United States.

The DMA is a standard market definition. As a television buying tool, it is a geographical and demographic means for maximum efficiency. As a station tool, it has applications for sales, programming, and promotion planning.

Following, in alphabetical order, are Nielsen's 210 markets for 2005 with coverage maps for each, with county by county breakouts of TV households. Other data includes the markets' stations, their cities of license, channel numbers, and network affiliations.

Coverage maps show total survey areas in light shading, the DMAs themselves in dark shading and white, with Nielsen Metro ratings in white. The survey areas consist of all counties in which the home market stations are viewed to a significant extent including via cable. The Metro Areas usually conform to U.S. Census Standard Metropolitan statistical areas.

Non-DMA markets do not meet Nielsen's criteria for having a DMA of their own. They are listed with the DMA of which they are a part.

A cross-reference list of cities in multi-city DMAs appears on page B-216.

All maps © 2005 Nielsen Media Research.

Abilene-Sweetwater, TX (163)

DMA TV Households: 112,950
%of U.S. TV Households: .103

KRBC-TV Abilene, TX, ch. 9, NBC
KTXS-TV Sweetwater, TX, ch. 12, ABC
KXVA Abilene, TX, ch. 15, Fox
KPCB Snyder, TX, ch. 17, IND
KTAB-TV Abilene, TX, ch. 32, CBS

DMA Counties	State	TV Households
Brown	TX	14,610
Callahan	TX	5,100
Coleman	TX	3,520
Eastland	TX	7,260
Fisher	TX	1,790
Haskell	TX	2,350
Jones	TX	5,740
Knox	TX	1,540
Mitchell	TX	2,750
Nolan	TX	6,040
Runnels	TX	4,180
Scurry	TX	5,700
Shackelford	TX	1,280
Stephens	TX	3,550
Stonewall	TX	590
Taylor	TX	46,950

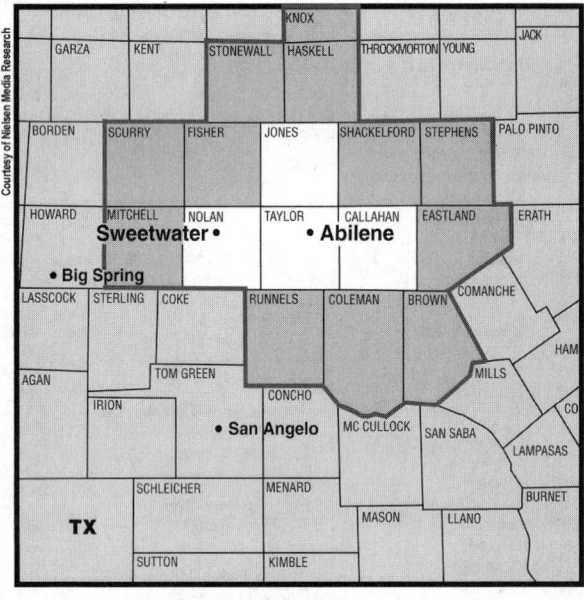

Albany, GA (147)

DMA TV Households: 151,970
% of U.S. TV Households: .139

WALB Albany, GA, ch. 10, NBC
*****WABW-TV** Pelham, GA, ch. 14, ETV
*****WACS-TV** Dawson, GA, ch. 25, ETV
WFXL Albany, GA, ch. 31, Fox
WSST-TV Cordele, GA, ch. 55, IND

DMA Counties	State	TV Households	DMA Counties	State	TV Households
Atkinson	GA	2,800	Dougherty	GA	36,080
Baker	GA	1,660	Irwin	GA	3,760
BenHill	GA	6,430	Lee	GA	9,800
Berrien	GA	6,400	Mitchell	GA	8,260
Calhoun	GA	1,840	Terrell	GA	4,040
Coffee	GA	14,010	Tift	GA	14,690
Colquitt	GA	16,160	Turner	GA	3,440
Cook	GA	6,020	Worth	GA	8,240
Crisp	GA	8,340			

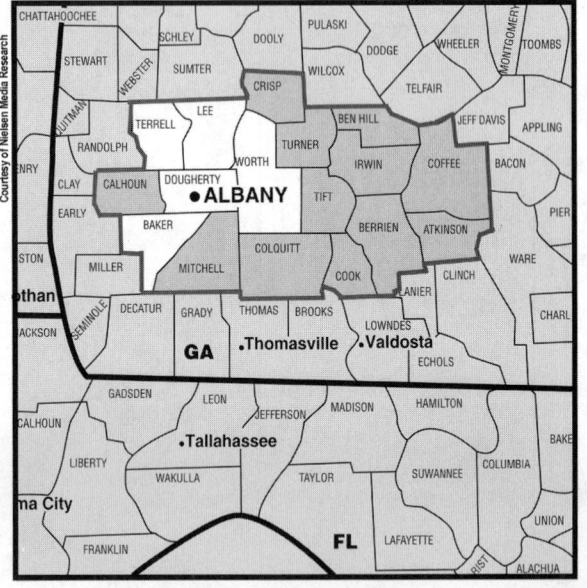

Nielsen DMA Market Atlas

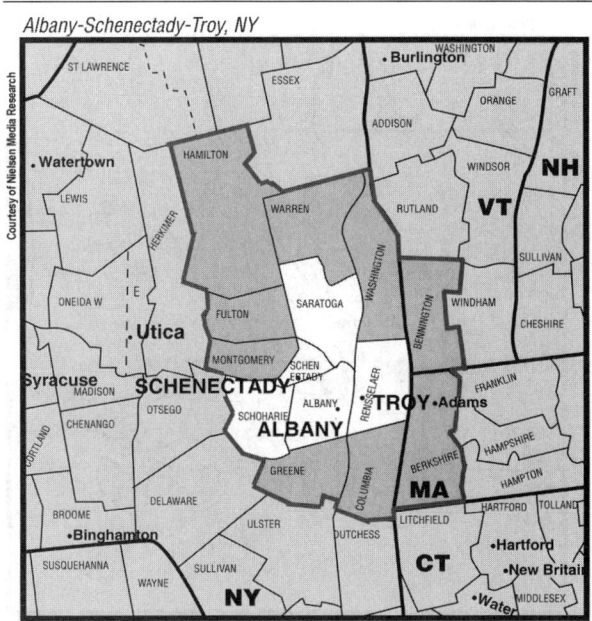

Albany-Schenectady-Troy, NY

Albany-Schenectady-Troy, NY (55)

DMA TV Households: 555,640
% of U.S. TV Households: .507

WRGB Schenectady, NY, ch. 6, CBS
WTEN Albany, NY, ch. 10, ABC
WNYT Albany, NY, ch. 13, NBC
***WMHT** Schenectady, NY, ch. 17, ETV
WCDC Adams, MA, ch. 19, satellite to WTEN
WXXA-TV Albany, NY, ch. 23, Fox
WEWB Schenectady, NY, ch. 45, WB
WYPX Amsterdam, NY, ch. 55, IND

DMA Counties	State	TV Households	DMA Counties	State	TV Households
Berkshire	MA	56,120	Rensselaer	NY	61,990
Albany	NY	123,540	Saratoga	NY	85,810
Columbia	NY	25,500	Schenectady	NY	60,850
Fulton	NY	22,380	Schoharie	NY	12,180
Greene	NY	18,800	Warren	NY	27,300
Hamilton	NY	2,380	Washington	NY	23,770
Montgomery	NY	20,230	Bennington	VT	14,790

Albuquerque-Santa Fe (47)

DMA TV Households: 649,680
% of U.S. TV Households: .593

KASA-TV Santa Fe, NM, ch. 2, Fox
KOFT Farmington, NM, ch. 3, ABC
KOB-TV Albuqerque, NM, ch. 4, NBC
***KNME-TV** Albuquerque, NM, ch. 5, ETV
KREZ-TV Durango, CO, ch. 6, satellite to KREX-TV
KOCT Carlsbad, NM, ch. 6, satellite to KOAT-TV
KOBG-TV Silver City, NM, ch. 6, satellite to KOB-TV
KOAT-TV Albuquerque, NM, ch. 7, ABC
KOBR Roswell, NM, ch. 8, NBC
KNMD-TV Santa Fe, NM, ch. 9, ETV
KBIM-TV Roswell, NM, ch. 10, CBS
KOVT Silver City, NM, ch. 10, ABC
KCHF Santa Fe, NM, ch. 11, IND
KOBF Farmington, NM, ch. 12, NBC
KRQE Albuquerque, NM, ch. 13, CBS
KTFQ-TV Albuquerque, NM, ch. 14, TeleFutura
KWBQ Santa Fe, NM, ch. 19, WB
***KRMU** Durango, CO, ch. 20, ETV
KRWB-TV Roswell, NM, ch. 21, IND
KNAT Albuquerque, NM, ch. 23, IND
KTEL-TV Carlsbad, NM, ch. 25, IND
KRPV Roswell, NM, ch. 27, IND
KHFT Hobbs, NM, ch. 29, IND
***KAZQ** Albuquerque, NM, ch. 32, ETV
KTLL-TV Durango, CO, ch. 33, IND
KLUZ-TV Albuquerque, NM, ch. 41, IND
KASY-TV Albuquerque, NM, ch. 50, UPN

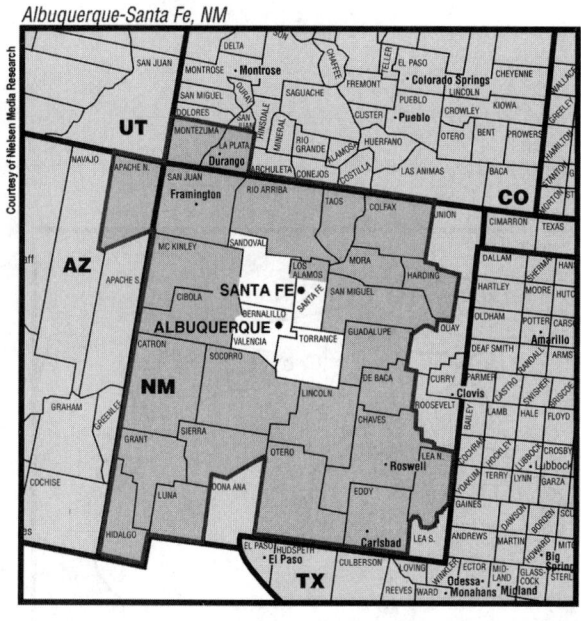

Albuquerque-Santa Fe, NM

DMA Counties	State	TV Households	DMA Counties	State	TV Households
Apache North	AZ	13,410	Lincoln	NM	8,780
La Plata	CO	17,490	Los Almos	NM	7,940
Montezuma	CO	9,420	Luna	NM	9,640
Bernalillo	NM	235,050	McKinley	NM	19,470
Catron	NM	1,140	Mora	NM	2,000
Chaves	NM	22,190	Otero	NM	23,250
Cibola	NM	8,630	Rio Arriba	NM	14,910
Colfax	NM	5,700	San Juan	NM	41,490
DeBaca	NM	710	San Miguel	NM	10,490
Eddy	NM	19,610	Santa Fe	NM	55,110
Grant	NM	11,780	Sierra	NM	5,690
Guadalupe	NM	1,620	Socorro	NM	6,510
Harding	NM	300	Taos	NM	12,040
Hidalgo	NM	1,820	Torrance	NM	5,860
Lea North	NM	18,100	Valencia	NM	23,250

Broadcasting & Cable Yearbook 2006

Nielsen DMA Market Atlas

Alexandria, LA (176)

DMA TV Households: 94,350
% of U.S. TV Households: .086

KALB-TV Alexandria, LA, ch. 5, NBC
*KLPA-TV Alexandria, LA, ch. 25, ETV
KLAX-TV Alexandria, LA, ch. 31, ABC
KBCA Alexandria, LA, ch. 41, IND

DMA Counties	State	TV Households
Avoyelles	LA	15,270
Grant	LA	7,370
La Salle	LA	5,230
Rapides	LA	49,040
Vernon	LA	17,440

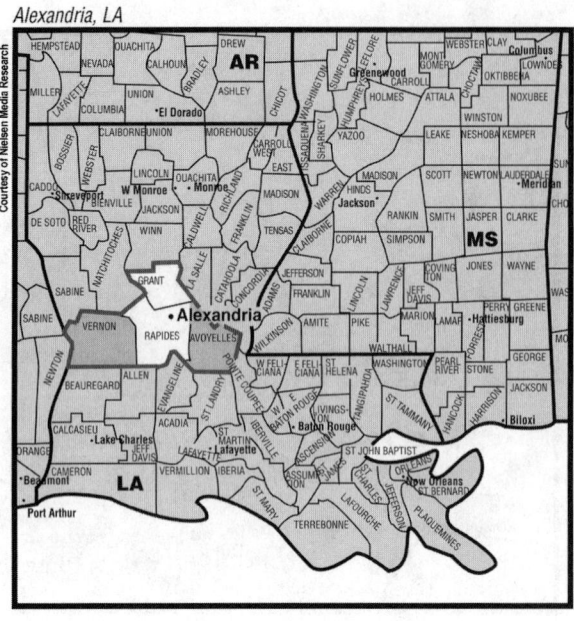

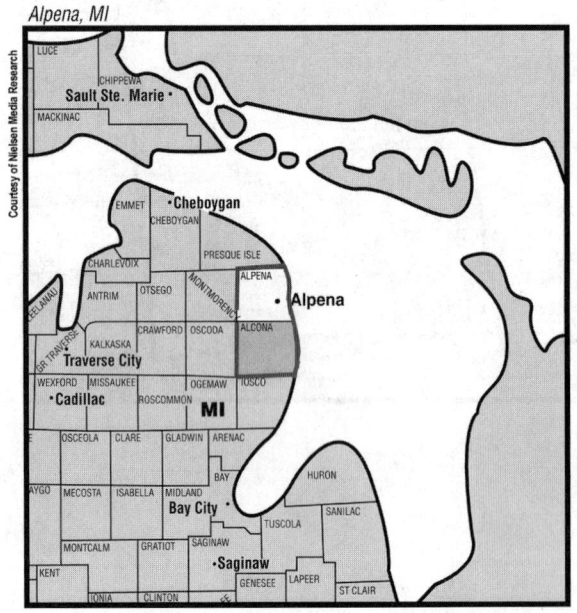

Alpena, MI (208)

DMA TV Households: 17,930
% of U.S. TV Households: .016

*WCML-TV Alpena, MI, ch. 6, ETV
WBKB-TV Alpena, MI, ch. 11, CBS

DMA Counties	State	TV Households
Alcona	MI	5,100
Alpena	MI	12,830

Broadcasting & Cable Yearbook 2006

Nielsen DMA Market Atlas

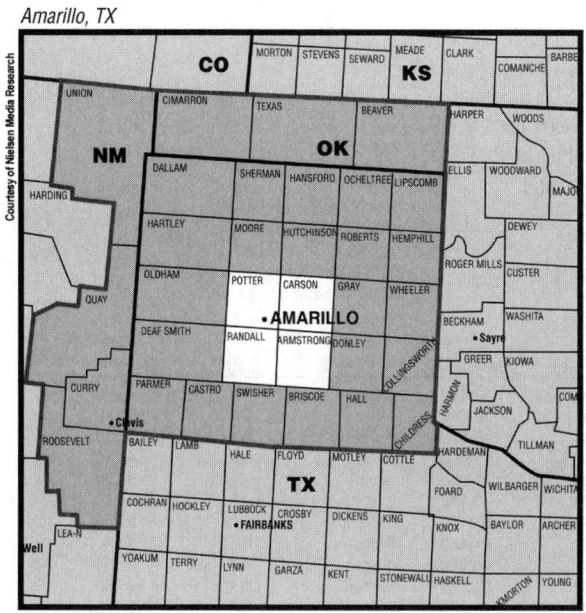

Amarillo, TX

Amarillo, TX (130)

DMA TV Households: 190,120
% of U.S. TV Households: .173

*KACV-TV Amarillo, TX, ch. 2, ETV
*KENW Portales, NM, ch. 3, ETV
KAMR-TV Amarillo, TX, ch. 4, NBC
KVII-TV Amarillo, TX, ch. 7, ABC
KFDA-TV Amarillo, TX, ch. 10, CBS
KVIH-TV Clovis, NM, ch. 12, satellite to KVII-TV
KCIT Amarillo, TX, ch. 14, Fox
KBGD Farwell, TX, ch. 18, IND

DMA Counties	State	TV Households	DMA Counties	State	TV Households
Curry	NM	17,300	Gray	TX	8,410
Quay	NM	4,040	Hall	TX	1,480
Roosevelt	NM	6,580	Hansford	TX	1,960
Union	NM	1,490	Hartley	TX	1,490
Beaver	OK	2,040	Hemphill	TX	1,380
Cimarron	OK	1,180	Hutchinson	TX	8,930
Texas	OK	6,640	Lipscomb	TX	1,170
Armstrong	TX	780	Moore	TX	6,670
Briscoe	TX	680	Ochiltree	TX	3,150
Carson	TX	2,480	Oldham	TX	780
Castro	TX	2,580	Parmer	TX	3,260
Childress	TX	2,330	Potter	TX	41,600
Collingsworth	TX	1,250	Randall	TX	44,020
Cottle	TX	780	Roberts	TX	300
Dallam	TX	2,120	Sherman	TX	1,030
DeafSmith	TX	6,110	Swisher	TX	2,660
Donley	TX	1,570	Wheeler	TX	1,880

Anchorage, AK (155)

DMA TV Households: 139,960
% of U.S. TV Households: .128

KTUU-TV Anchorage, ch. 2, NBC
KTBY Anchorage, ch. 4, Fox
KYES Anchorage, ch. 5, IND
*KAKM Anchorage, ch. 7, ETV
KTVA Anchorage, ch. 11, CBS
KIMO Anchorage, ch. 13, ABC

DMA Counties	State	TV Households
Anchorage	AK	98,460
Kenai-Pensla	AK	18,150
Matanka-Sustn	AK	23,350

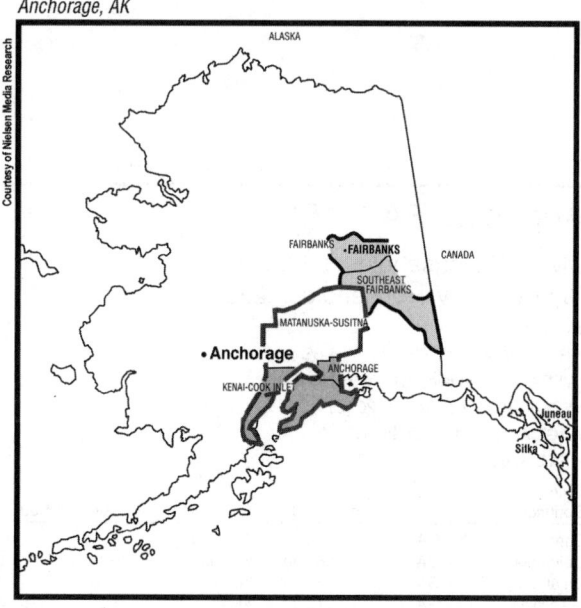

Anchorage, AK

Broadcasting & Cable Yearbook 2006

Nielsen DMA Market Atlas

Atlanta, GA

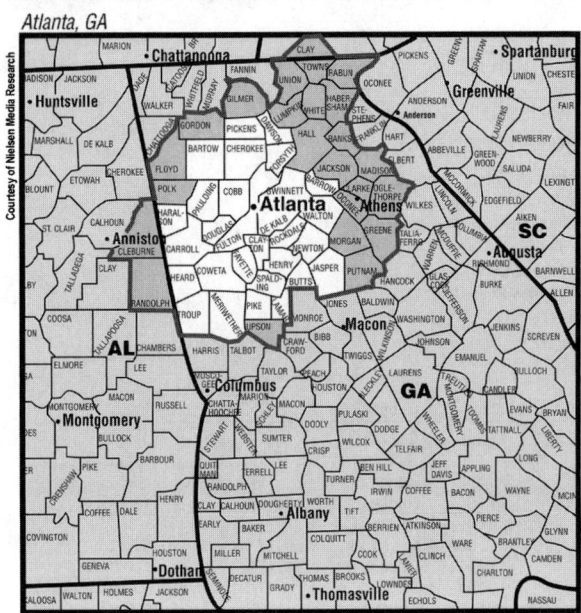

Atlanta (9)

DMA TV Households: 2,092,000
% of U.S. TV Households: 1.879

WSB-TV Atlanta, ch. 2, ABC
WAGA Atlanta, ch. 5, Fox
*****WGTV** Athens, GA, ch. 8, ETV
WXIA-TV Atlanta, ch. 11, NBC
WPXA Rome, GA, ch. 14, IND
WTBS Atlanta, ch. 17, IND
*****WPBA** Atlanta, ch. 30, ETV
WUVG-TV Athens, GA, ch. 34, Univision
WATL Atlanta, ch. 36, WB
WGCL-TV Atlanta, ch. 46, CBS
*****WATC** Atlanta, ch. 57, ETV
WHSG-TV Monroe, GA, ch. 63, IND
WUPA Atlanta, ch. 69, UPN

DMA Counties	State	TV Households	DMA Counties	State	TV Households
Cleburne	AL	6,000	Heard	GA	3,980
Randolph	AL	8,600	Henry	GA	56,440
Banks	GA	5,870	Jackson	GA	17,390
Barrow	GA	19,960	Jasper	GA	4,710
Bartow	GA	31,280	Lamar	GA	5,870
Butts	GA	7,910	Lumpkin	GA	8,380
Carroll	GA	37,430	Madison	GA	10,540
Cherokee	GA	61,160	Meriwether	GA	8,560
Clarke	GA	40,040	Morgan	GA	6,130
Clayton	GA	91,520	Newton	GA	29,080
Cobb	GA	244,980	Oconee	GA	9,730
Coweta	GA	37,390	Oglethorpe	GA	5,190
Dawson	GA	7,710	Paulding	GA	36,630
DeKalb	GA	247,470	Pickens	GA	11,120
Douglas	GA	38,260	Pike	GA	5,400
Fannin	GA	9,150	Polk	GA	14,820
Fayette	GA	35,500	Putnam	GA	7,960
Floyd	GA	35,100	Rabun	GA	6,510
Forsyth	GA	45,970	Rockdale	GA	26,550
Fulton	GA	316,260	Spalding	GA	22,690
Gilmer	GA	10,240	Towns	GA	4,450
Gordon	GA	17,960	Troup	GA	22,630
Greene	GA	6,210	Union	GA	8,530
Gwinnett	GA	235,820	Upson	GA	11,020
Habersham	GA	14,470	Walton	GA	25,430
Hall	GA	52,990	White	GA	9,360
Haralson	GA	10,820	Clay	NC	4,280

Augusta, GA (115)

DMA TV Households: 246,620
% of U.S. TV Households: .225

WJBF Augusta, GA, ch. 6, ABC
WRDW-TV Augusta, GA, ch. 12, CBS
*****WEBA-TV** Allendale, SC, ch. 14, ETV
*****WCES-TV** Wrens, GA, ch. 20, ETV
WAGT Augusta, GA, ch. 26, NBC
WFXG Augusta, GA, ch. 54, Fox

DMA Counties	State	TV Households	DMA Counties	State	TV Households
Burke	GA	8,300	Taliaferro	GA	860
Columbia	GA	35,930	Warren	GA	2,450
Emanuel	GA	8,150	Wilkes	GA	4,380
Glascock	GA	1,090	Aiken	SC	59,210
Jefferson	GA	6,110	Allendale	SC	3,890
Jenkins	GA	3,340	Bamberg	SC	6,060
Lincoln	GA	3,390	Barnwell	SC	9,340
McDuffie	GA	8,180	Edgefield	SC	8,510
Richmond	GA	73,380	McCormick	SC	4,100

Augusta, GA

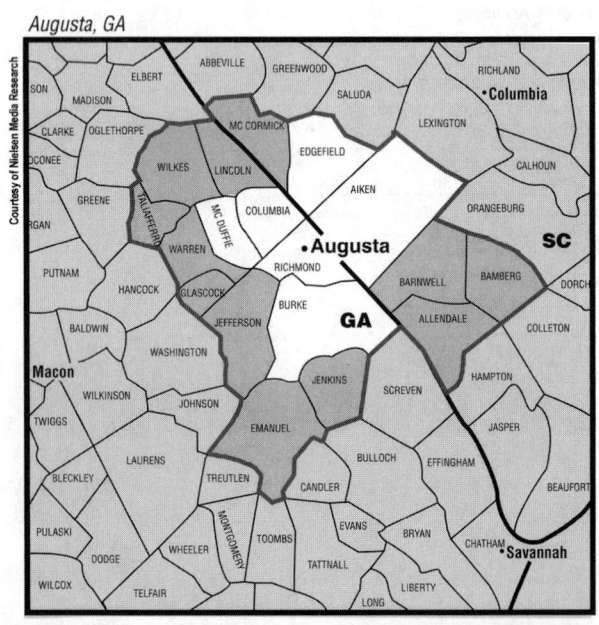

Nielsen DMA Market Atlas

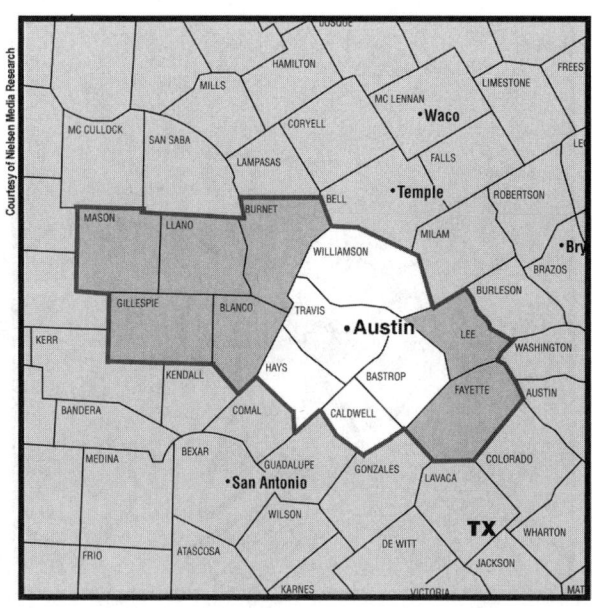

Austin, TX (54)

DMA TV Households: 567,870
% of U.S. TV Households: .518

KTBC Austin, TX, ch. 7, Fox
KXAM-TV Llano, TX, ch. 14, satellite to KXAN-TV
*KLRU-TV Austin, TX, ch. 18, ETV
KVUE-TV Austin, TX, ch. 24, ABC
KXAN-TV Austin, TX, ch. 36, NBC
KEYE-TV Austin, TX, ch. 42, CBS
KNVA Austin, TX, ch. 54, IND

DMA Counties	State	TV Households
Bastrop	TX	23,670
Blanco	TX	3,510
Burnet	TX	14,820
Caldwell	TX	12,220
Fayette	TX	8,790
Gillespie	TX	9,190
Hays	TX	41,190
Lee	TX	5,890
Llano	TX	8,510
Mason	TX	1,640
Travis	TX	328,670
Williamson	TX	109,650

Bakersfield, CA (128)

DMA TV Households: 194,180
% of U.S. TV Households: .177

KGET-TV Bakersfield, CA, ch.17, NBC
KERO-TV Bakersfield, CA, ch. 23, ABC
KBAK-TV Bakersfield, CA, ch. 29, CBS
KUVI-TV Bakersfield, CA, ch. 45, IND

DMA Counties	State	TV Households
Kern West	CA	194,180

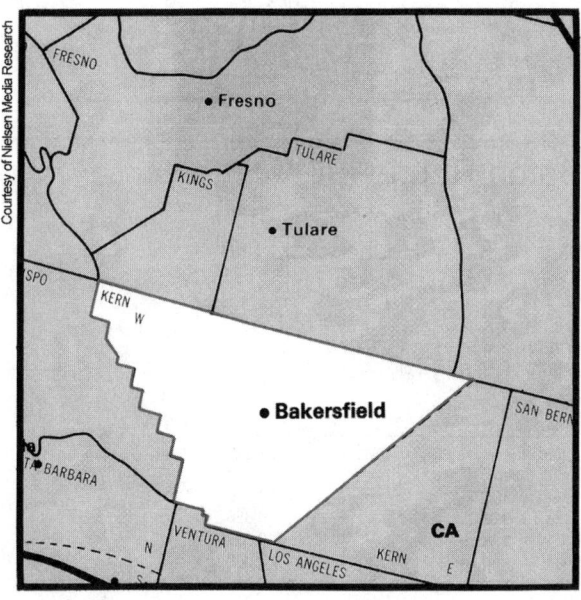

Broadcasting & Cable Yearbook 2006

Nielsen DMA Market Atlas

Baltimore (23)

DMA TV Households: 1,087,730
% of U.S. TV Households: .993

WMAR-TV Baltimore, ch. 2, ABC
WBAL-TV Baltimore, ch. 11, NBC
WJZ-TV Baltimore, ch. 13, CBS
*WMPT Annapolis, MD, ch. 22, ETV
WUTB Baltimore, ch. 24, UPN
WBFF Baltimore, ch. 45, Fox
WNUV Baltimore, ch. 54, WB
*WMPB Baltimore, ch. 67, ETV

DMA Counties	State	TV Households	DMA Counties	State	TV Households
Anne Arundel	MD	190,510	Harford	MD	88,560
Baltimore	MD	315,170	Howard	MD	97,880
BaltimoreCity	MD	249,650	Kent	MD	8,030
Caroline	MD	11,660	Queen Annes	MD	17,450
Carroll	MD	58,820	Talbot	MD	14,840
Cecil	MD	35,160			

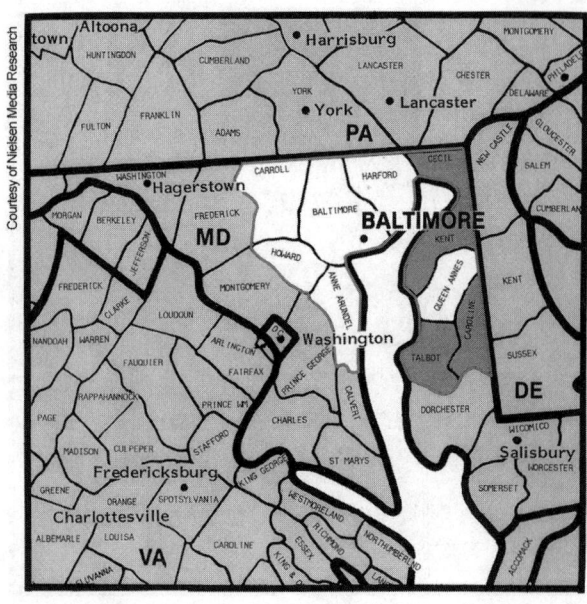

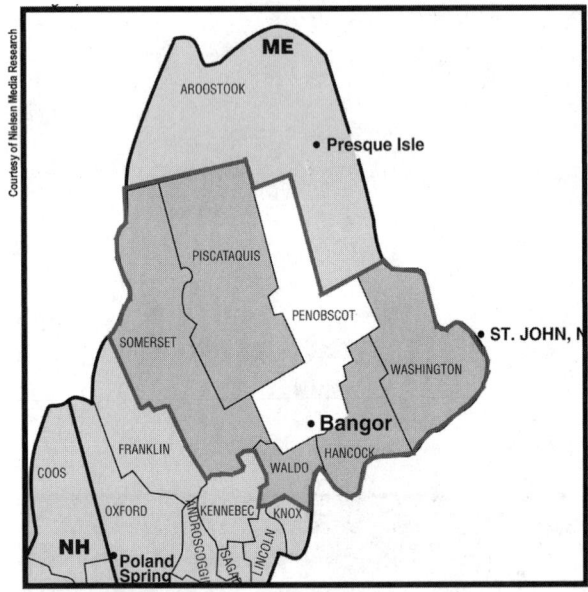

Bangor, ME (151)

DMA TV Households: 144,740
% of U.S. TV Households: .132

WLBZ Bangor, ME, ch. 2, NBC
WABI-TV Bangor, ME, ch. 5, CBS
WVII-TV Bangor, ME, ch. 7, ABC
*WMEB-TV Orono, ME, ch. 12, ETV
*WMED-TV Calais, ME, ch. 13, ETV

DMA Counties	State	TV Households
Hancock	ME	23,050
Penobscot	ME	61,600
Piscataquis	ME	7,790
Somerset	ME	21,390
Waldo	ME	16,420
Washington	ME	14,490

Baton Rouge (96)

DMA TV Households: 306,910
% of U.S. TV Households: .280

WBRZ Baton Rouge, ch. 2, ABC
WAFB Baton Rouge, ch. 9, CBS
*WLPB-TV Baton Rouge, ch. 27, ETV
WVLA Baton Rouge, ch. 33, NBC
WGMB Baton Rouge, ch. 44, Fox

DMA Counties	State	TV Households
Ascension	LA	31,310
Assumption	LA	8,660
East Baton Rouge	LA	158,510
East Feliciana	LA	6,850
Iberville	LA	10,580
Livingston	LA	38,580
Pointe Coupee	LA	8,540
St. Helena	LA	3,930
St. Mary	LA	19,410
West Baton Rouge	LA	7,910
West Feliciana	LA	3,680
Amite	MS	5,360
Wilkinson	MS	3,590

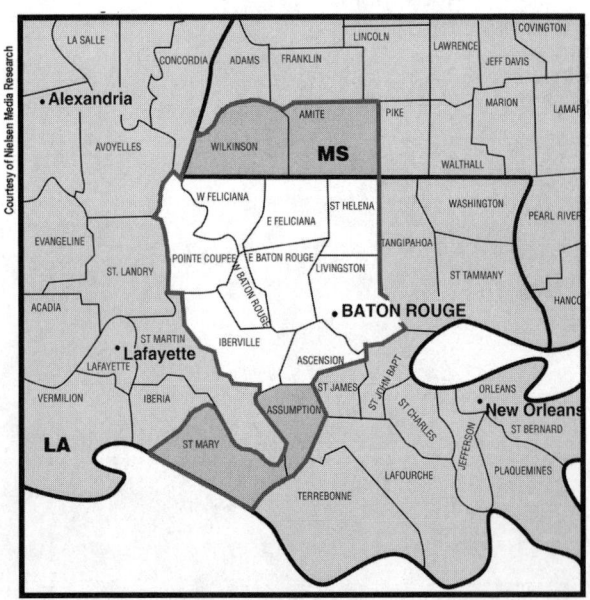

Broadcasting & Cable Yearbook 2006

Nielsen DMA Market Atlas

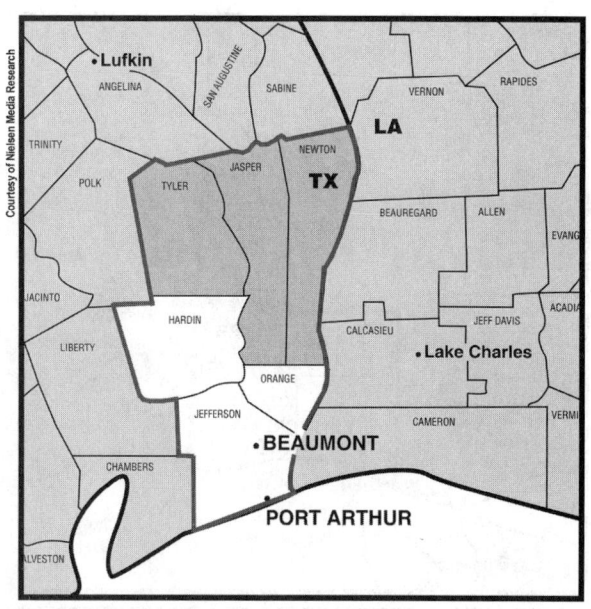

Beaumont-Port Arthur, TX (138)

DMA TV Households: 168,740
% of U.S. TV Households: .154

KBTV-TV Port Arthur, TX, ch. 4, NBC
KFDM-TV Beaumont, TX, ch. 6, CBS
KBMT Beaumont, TX, ch. 12, ABC
***KITU-TV** Beaumont, TX, ch. 34, ETV

DMA Counties	State	TV Households
Hardin	TX	18,470
Jasper	TX	13,590
Jefferson	TX	91,420
Newton	TX	5,560
Orange	TX	32,080
Tyler	TX	7,620

Bend, OR (197)

DMA TV Households: 52,550
% of U.S. TV Households: .048

***KOAB-TV** Bend, OR, ch. 3, ETV
KTVZ Bend, OR, ch. 21, NBC

DMA Counties	State	TV Households
Deschutes	OR	52,550

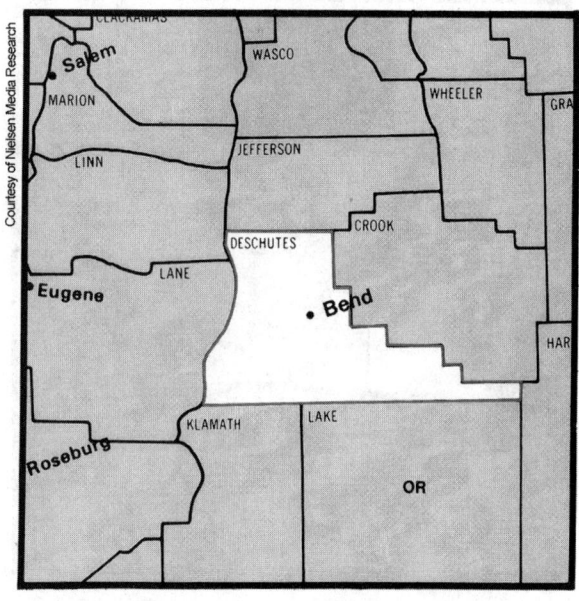

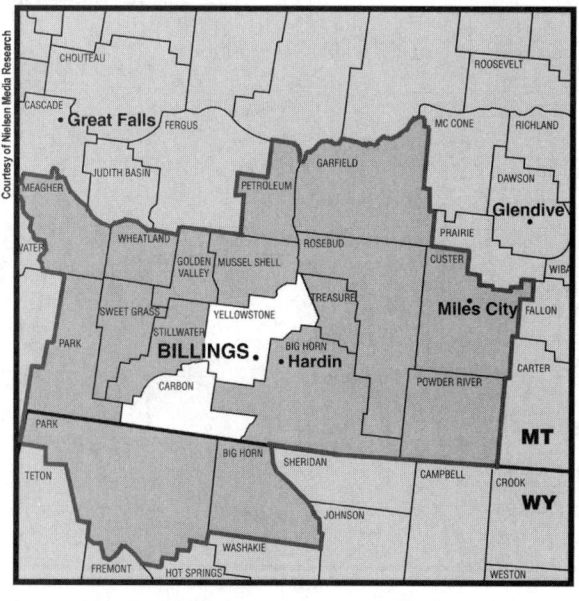

Billings, MT (170)

DMA TV Households: 102,370
% of U.S. TV Households: .093

KTVQ Billings, MT, ch. 2, CBS
KYUS-TV Miles City, MT, ch. 3, satellite to KULR-TV
KHMT Hardin, MT, ch. 4, Fox
KSVI Billings, MT, ch. 6, ABC
KULR-TV Billings, MT, ch. 8, NBC

DMA Counties	State	TV Households	DMA Counties	State	TV Households
Big Horn	MT	3,980	Powder River	MT	680
Carbon	MT	4,140	Rosebud	MT	3,240
Custer	MT	4,600	Stillwater	MT	3,300
Garfield	MT	580	Sweet Grass	MT	1,380
Golden Valley	MT	380	Treasure	MT	290
Meagher	MT	760	Wheatland	MT	780
Musselshell	MT	1,820	Yellowstone	MT	54,670
Park	MT	6,690	Big Horn	WY	4,060
Petroleum	MT	190	Park	WY	10,830

Broadcasting & Cable Yearbook 2006

Nielsen DMA Market Atlas

Biloxi-Gulfport, MS (156)

DMA TV Households: 137,590
% of U.S. TV Households: .126

WLOX Biloxi, MS, ch. 13, ABC
***WMAH** Biloxi, MS, ch. 19, ETV
WXXV-TV Gulfport, MS, ch. 25, IND

DMA Counties	State	TV Households
George	MS	7,280
Greene	MS	4,220
Harrison	MS	71,660
Jackson	MS	49,480
Stone	MS	4,950

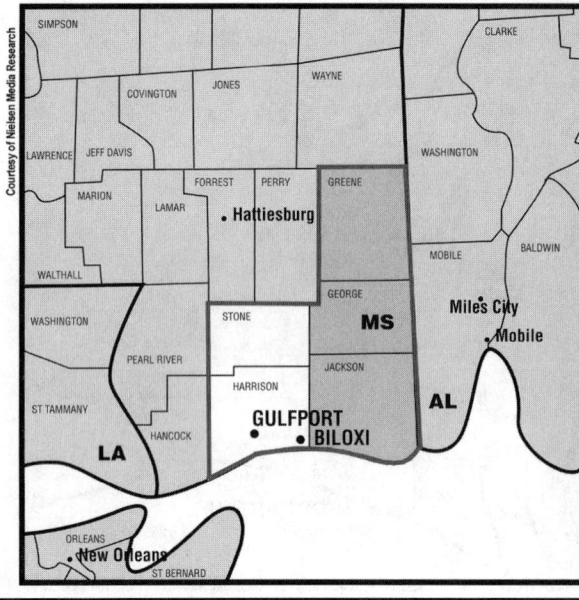

Binghamton, NY (154)

DMA TV Households: 141,350
% of U.S. TV Households: .129

WBNG-TV Binghamton, NY, ch. 12, CBS
WIVT Binghamton, NY, ch. 34, ABC
WICZ-TV Binghamton, NY, ch. 40, Fox
***WSKG** Binghamton, NY, ch. 46, ETV

DMA Counties	State	TV Households
Broome	NY	81,530
Chenango	NY	20,480
Delaware	NY	19,070
Tioga	NY	20,270

Birmingham (Anniston and Tuscaloosa), AL (40)

DMA TV Households: 717,300
% of U.S. TV Households: .655

WBRC Birmingham, AL, ch. 6, Fox
***WCIQ** Mt. Cheaha, AL, ch. 7, ETV
***WBIQ** Birmingham, AL, ch. 10, ETV
WVTM-TV Birmingham, AL, ch. 13, NBC
WDBB Bessemer, AL, ch. 17, Fox
WTTO Birmingham, AL, ch. 21, WB
WLDM Tuscaloosa, AL, ch. 23, IND
WCFT-TV Tuscaloosa, AL, ch. 33, ABC
WJSU-TV Anniston, AL, ch. 40, ABC
WIAT Birmingham, AL, ch. 42, CBS
WPXH Gadsden, AL, ch. 44, PAX TV
WTJP-TV Gadsden, AL, ch. 60, IND
WABM Birmingham, AL, ch. 68, UPN

DMA Counties	State	TV Households	DMA Counties	State	TV Households
Bibb	AL	7,880	Hale	AL	6,910
Blount	AL	20,810	Jefferson	AL	263,170
Calhoun	AL	46,860	Marion	AL	12,440
Cherokee	AL	10,290	Pickens	AL	7,890
Chilton	AL	16,060	St. Clair	AL	26,900
Clay	AL	5,890	Shelby	AL	65,000
Cullman	AL	31,810	Talladega	AL	31,490
Etowah	AL	42,230	Tuscaloosa	AL	66,650
Fayette	AL	7,600	Walker	AL	28,800
Greene	AL	4,050	Winston	AL	10,160

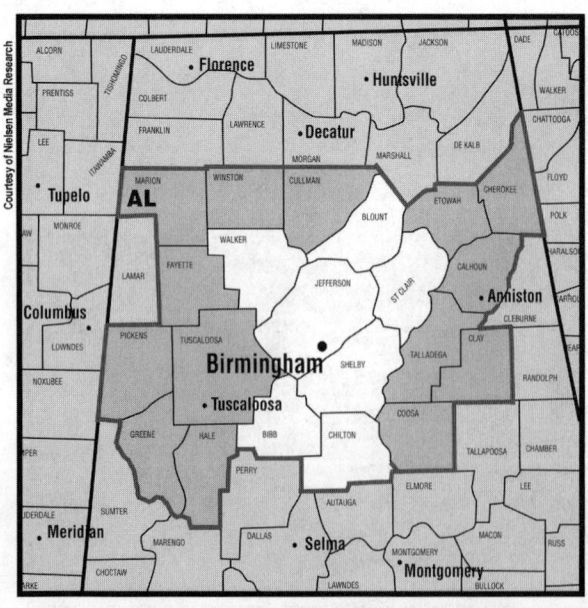

Broadcasting & Cable Yearbook 2006

Nielsen DMA Market Atlas

Bluefield-Beckley-Oak Hill, WV

Bluefield-Beckley-Oak Hill, WV (148)

DMA TV Households: 148,760
% of U.S. TV Households: .136

WOAY-TV Oak Hill, WV, ch. 4, ABC
WVVA Bluefield, WV, ch. 6, NBC
***WSWP-TV** Grandview, WV, ch. 9, ETV
WLFB Bluefield, WV, ch. 40, IND
WVNS-TV Lewisburg, WV, ch. 59, CBS

DMA Counties	State	TV Households
Tazewell	VA	18,810
Fayette	WV	19,280
Greenbrier	WV	15,020
McDowell	WV	10,590
Mercer	WV	26,910
Monroe	WV	5,180
Pocahontas	WV	3,530
Raleigh	WV	32,840
Summers	WV	5,910
Wyoming	WV	10,690

Boise, ID (122)

DMA TV Households: 223,890
% of U.S. TV Households: .204

KBCI-TV Boise, ID, ch. 2, CBS
***KAID** Boise, ID, ch. 4, ETV
KIVI Nampa, ID, ch. 6, ABC
KTVB Boise, ID, ch. 7, NBC
KNIN-TV Caldwell, ID, ch. 9, UPN
KTRV Nampa, ID, ch. 12, Fox

DMA Counties	State	TV Households
Ada	ID	123,640
Adams	ID	1,440
Boise	ID	2,770
Camas	ID	380
Canyon	ID	53,310
Elmore	ID	8,730
Gem	ID	5,670
Owyhee	ID	3,810
Payette	ID	7,440
Valley	ID	3,200
Washington	ID	3,660
Grant	OR	3,670
Malheur	OR	98,030

Boise, ID

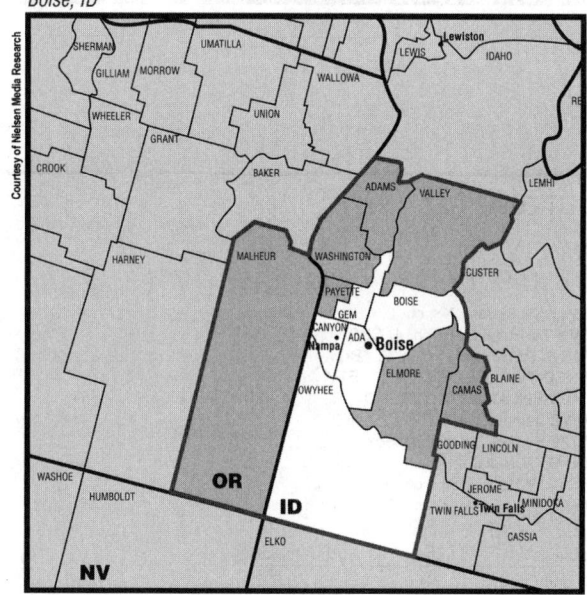

Boston, MA (Manchester, NH)

Boston (Manchester, NH) (5)

DMA TV Households: 2,391,840
% of U.S. TV Households: 2.183

***WGBH-TV** Boston, ch. 2, ETV
WBZ-TV Boston, ch. 4, CBS
WCVB-TV Boston, ch. 5, ABC
WHDH-TV Boston, ch. 7, NBC
WMUR-TV Manchester, NH, ch. 9, ABC
***WENH-TV** Durham, NH, ch. 11, ETV
WPXG Concord, NH, ch. 21, satellite to WBPX
WFXT Boston, ch. 25, Fox
WUNI Worcester, MA, ch. 27, Univision
WSBK-TV Boston, ch. 38, UPN
***WGBX-TV** Boston, ch. 44, ETV
WWDP Norwell, MA, ch. 46, IND
***YDN** Worcester, MA, ch. 48, ETV
WNDS Derry, NH, ch. 50, IND
***WEKW-TV** Keene, NH, ch. 52, ETV
***WLVI-TV** Cambridge, MA, ch. 56, WB
WNEU Merrimack, NH, ch. 60, Telemundo
WMFP Lawrence, MA, ch. 62, IND
WUTF-TV Marlborough, MA, ch. 66, TeleFutura
WBPX Boston, ch. 68, PAX TV

DMA Counties	State	TV Households	DMA Counties	State	TV Households
Barnstable	MA	99,040	Worcester	MA	300,060
Dukes	MA	6,730	Belknap	NH	24,970
Essex	MA	281,790	Cheshire	NH	29,450
Middlesex	MA	564,310	Hillsborough	NH	152,150
Nantucket	MA	4,170	Merrimack	NH	56,090
Norfolk	MA	253,390	Rockingham	NH	112,220
Plymouth	MA	178,160	Strafford	NH	46,250
Suffolk	MA	265,590	Windham	VT	17,470

Broadcasting & Cable Yearbook 2006

Nielsen DMA Market Atlas

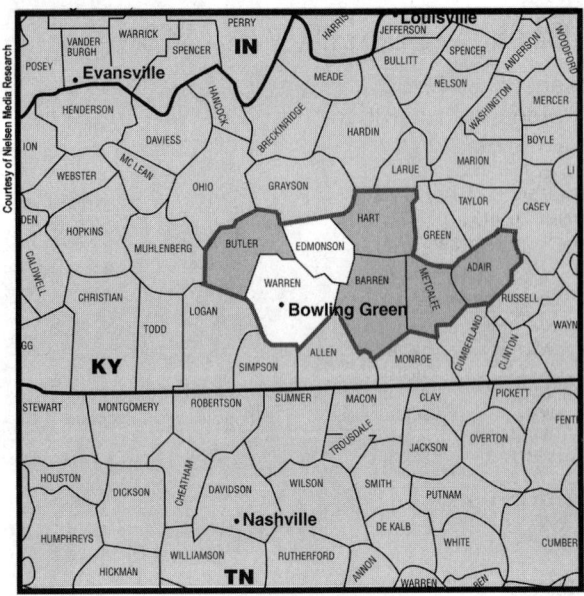

Bowling Green, KY (182)

DMA TV Households: 81,470
% of U.S. TV Households: .074

WBKO Bowling Green, KY, ch. 13, ABC
***WKYU-TV** Bowling Green, KY, ch. 24, ETV
WKNT Bowling Green, KY, ch. 40, NBC
***WKGB-TV** Bowling Green, KY, ch. 53, ETV

DMA Counties	State	TV Households
Adair	KY	6,870
Barren	KY	16,220
Butler	KY	5,230
Edmonson	KY	4,870
Hart	KY	6,880
Metcalfe	KY	4,030
Warren	KY	37,370

Buffalo, NY (46)

DMA TV Households: 651,970
% of U.S. TV Households: .595

WGRZ-TV Buffalo, NY, ch. 2, NBC
WIVB-TV Buffalo, NY, ch. 4, CBS
WKBW-TV Buffalo, NY, ch. 7, ABC
***WNED-TV** Buffalo, NY, ch. 17, ETV
WNLO Buffalo, NY, ch. 23, IND
WNYB Jamestown, NY, ch. 26, IND
WUTV Buffalo, NY, ch. 29, Fox
WNYO-TV Buffalo, NY, ch. 49, IND
WPXJ-TV Batavia, NY, ch. 51, IND
WNGS Springville, NY, ch. 67, IND

DMA Counties	State	TV Households
Allegany	NY	18,530
Cattaraugus	NY	32,210
Chautauqua	NY	53,640
Erie	NY	380,710
Genesee	NY	23,220
Niagara	NY	88,730
Wyoming	NY	15,120
McKean	PA	17,820
Potter	PA	6,720

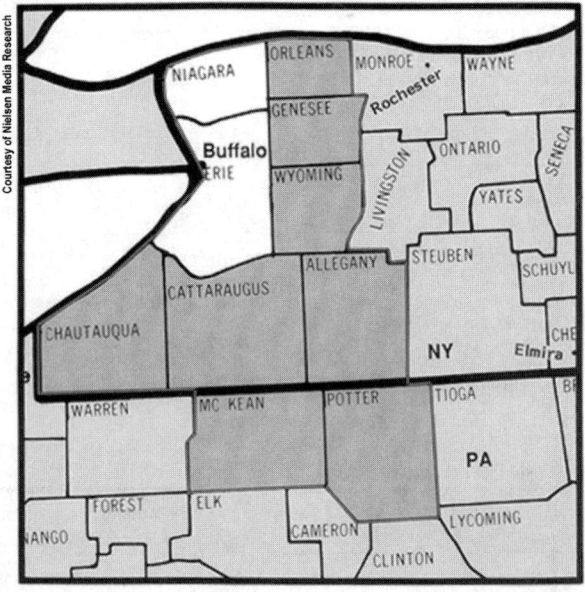

Nielsen DMA Market Atlas

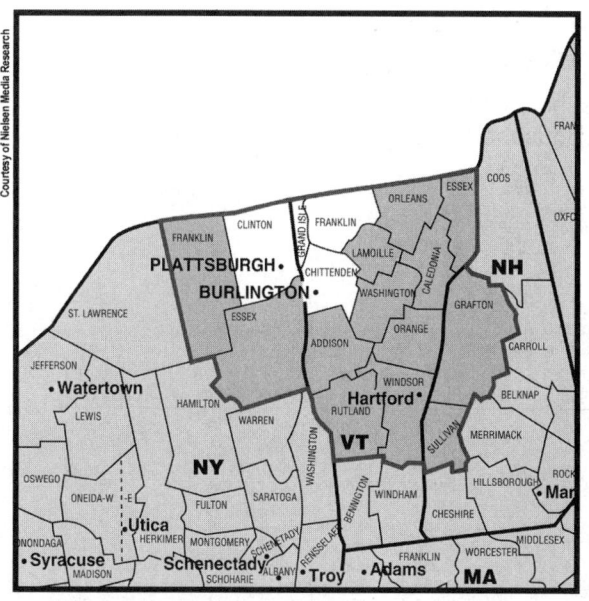

Burlington, VT-Plattsburgh, NY (90)

DMA TV Households: 329,200
% of U.S. TV Households: .300

WCAX-TV Burlington, VT, ch. 3, CBS
WPTZ North Pole (Plattsburgh), NY, ch. 5, NBC
***WVTB** St. Johnsbury, VT, ch. 20, satellite to WETK
WVNY Burlington, VT, ch. 22, ABC
***WVER** Rutland, VT, ch. 28, satellite to WETK
WNNE Hartford, VT, ch. 31, NBC
***WETK** Burlington, VT, ch. 33, ETV
***WVTA** Windsor, VT, ch. 41, satellite to WETK
WFFF-TV Burlington, VT, ch. 44, Fox
***WLED-TV** Littleton, NH, ch. 49, ETV
***WCFE-TV** Plattsburgh, NY, ch. 57, ETV

DMA Counties	State	TV Households	DMA Counties	State	TV Households
Grafton	NH	32,580	Franklin	VT	17,440
Sullivan	NH	17,730	Grand Isle	VT	3,190
Clinton	NY	31,450	Lamoille	VT	9,820
Essex	NY	15,460	Orange	VT	11,620
Franklin	NY	17,980	Orleans	VT	11,390
Addison	VT	13,640	Rutland	VT	25,810
Caledonia	VT	11,760	Washington	VT	24,310
Chittenden	VT	57,900	Windsor	VT	24,060
Essex	VT	2,720			

Butte-Bozeman (193)

DMA TV Households: 57,680
% of U.S. TV Households: .053

KXLF-TV Butte, MT, ch. 4, CBS
KTVM Butte, MT, ch. 6, satellite to KECI-TV
KBZK Bozeman, MT, ch. 7, Fox
***KUSM** Bozeman, MT, ch. 9, ETV
KWYB Butte, MT, ch. 18, ABC
KBTZ Butte, MT, ch. 24, Fox, PAX TV, UPN

DMA Counties	State	TV Households
Beaverhead	MT	3,040
Deer Lodge	MT	3,720
Gallatin	MT	28,110
Jefferson	MT	3,870
Madison	MT	2,990
Powell	MT	2,270
Silver Bow	MT	13,680

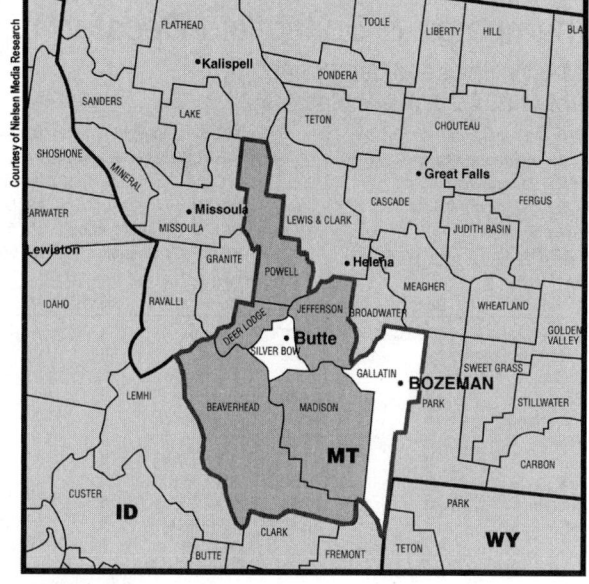

Casper-Riverton, WY (198)

DMA TV Households: 51,850
% of U.S. TV Households: .047

KTWO-TV Casper, WY, ch. 2, ABC
***KCWC-TV** Lander, WY, ch. 4, ETV
KGWL-TV Lander, WY, ch. 5, CBS
***KPTW** Casper, WY, ch. 6, ETV
KFNE Riverton, WY, ch. 10, satellite to KFNB
KCWY Casper, WY, ch. 13, NBC
KGWC-TV Casper, WY, ch. 14, CBS
KFNB Casper, WY, ch. 20, Fox

DMA Counties	State	TV Households
Converse	WY	4,940
Fremont	WY	13,690
Hot Springs	WY	2,000
Natrona	WY	28,200
Washakie	WY	3,020

Broadcasting & Cable Yearbook 2006

Nielsen DMA Market Atlas

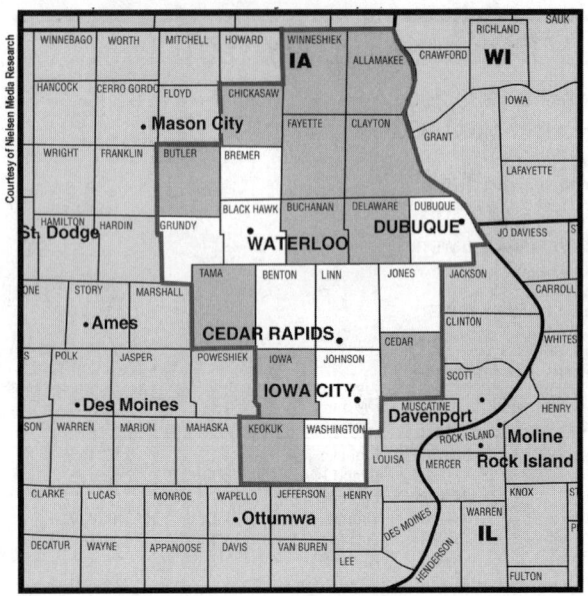

Cedar Rapids-Waterloo-Iowa City & Dubuque, IA (88)

DMA TV Households: 331,610
% of U.S. TV Households: .303

KGAN Cedar Rapids, IA, ch. 2, CBS
KWWL Waterloo, IA, ch. 7, NBC
KCRG-TV Cedar Rapids, IA, ch. 9, ABC
***KIIN-TV** Iowa City, IA, ch. 12, ETV
KWKB Iowa City, IA, ch. 20, IND
KWWF Waterloo, IA, ch. 22, UPN
KFXA Cedar Rapids, IA, ch. 28, IND
***KRIN** Waterloo, IA, ch. 32, ETV
KFXB Dubuque, IA, ch. 40, ABC
KPXR Cedar Rapids, IA, ch. 48, IND

DMA Counties	State	TV Households	DMA Counties	State	TV Households
Allamakee	IA	5,720	Fayette	IA	8,540
Benton	IA	10,240	Grundy	IA	4,950
Black Hawk	IA	49,240	Iowa	IA	6,250
Bremer	IA	9,060	Johnson	IA	46,260
Buchanan	IA	7,940	Jones	IA	7,770
Butler	IA	6,150	Keokuk	IA	4,500
Cedar	IA	7,260	Linn	IA	80,330
Chickasaw	IA	5,000	Tama	IA	6,850
Clayton	IA	7,350	Washington	IA	8,120
Delaware	IA	6,860	Winneshiek	IA	7,830
Dubuque	IA	35,390			

Champaign & Springfield-Decatur, IL (82)

DMA TV Households: 382,460
% of U.S. TV Households: .349

WCIA Champaign, IL, ch. 3, CBS
***WILL-TV** Urbana, IL, ch. 12, ETV
***WSEC** Jacksonville, IL, ch. 14, ETV
WICD Champaign, IL, ch. 15, satellite to WICS
WAND Decatur, IL, ch. 17, ABC
WICS Springfield, IL, ch. 20, NBC
WBUI Decatur, IL, ch. 23, WB
WCCU Urbana, IL, ch. 27, satellite to WRSP-TV
WCFN Springfield, IL, ch. 49, UPN
***WEIU-TV** Charleston, IL, ch. 51, ETV
WRSP-TV Springfield, IL, ch. 55, Fox

DMA Counties	State	TV Households	DMA Counties	State	TV Households
Cass	IL	5,460	Iroquois	IL	11,910
Champaign	IL	74,920	Logan	IL	10,940
Christian	IL	13,970	Macon	IL	45,170
Coles	IL	20,700	Menard	IL	4,950
Cumberland	IL	4,350	Morgan	IL	13,740
DeWitt	IL	6,750	Moultrie	IL	5,570
Douglas	IL	7,550	Piatt	IL	6,640
Edgar	IL	7,710	Sangamon	IL	81,110
Effingham	IL	13,460	Shelby	IL	8,940
Ford	IL	5,540	Vermilion	IL	33,080

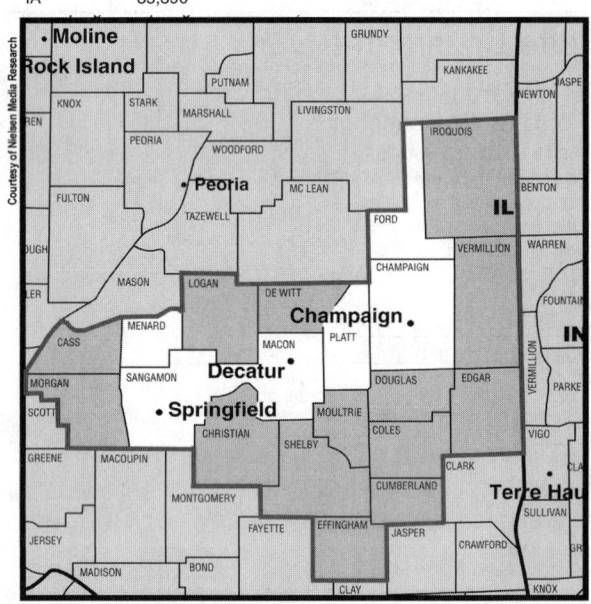

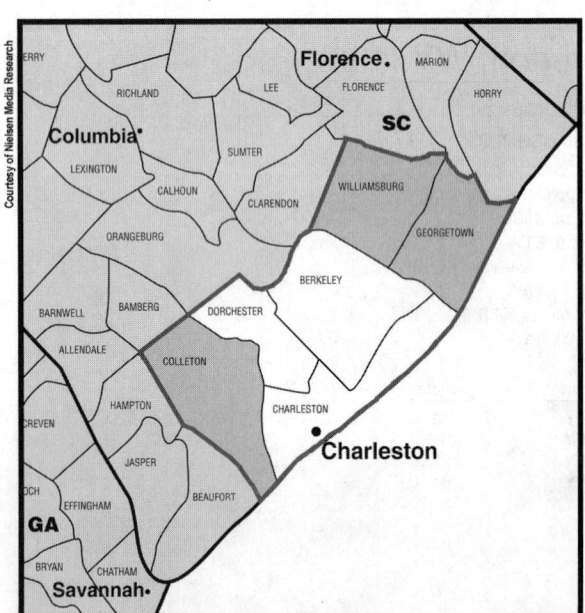

Charleston, SC (101)

DMA TV Households: 282,740
% of U.S. TV Households: .258

WCBD-TV Charleston, SC, ch. 2, IND
WCIV Charleston, SC, ch. 4, ABC
WCSC-TV Charleston, SC, ch. 5, CBS
***WITV** Charleston, SC, ch. 7, ETV
WTAT-TV Charleston, SC, ch. 24, Fox
WMMP Charleston, SC, ch. 36, IND

DMA Counties	State	TV Households
Berkeley	SC	55,200
Charleston	SC	136,600
Colleton	SC	15,800
Dorchester	SC	40,400
Georgetown	SC	25,100
Williamsburg	SC	14,200

Broadcasting & Cable Yearbook 2006

Nielsen DMA Market Atlas

Charleston-Huntington, WV

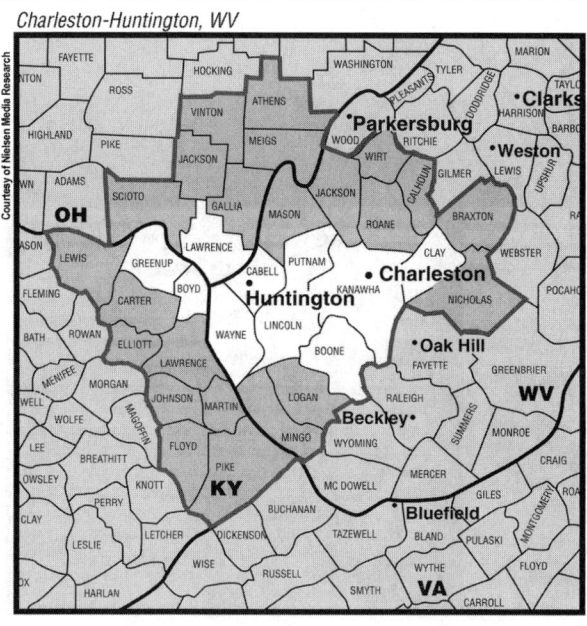

Charleston-Huntington, WV (62)

DMA TV Households: 508,750
% of U.S. TV Households: .464

WSAZ-TV Huntington, WV, ch. 3, NBC
WCHS-TV Charleston, WV, ch. 8, ABC
WVAH-TV Charleston, WV, ch. 11, Fox
WOWK-TV Huntington, WV, ch. 13, CBS
***WOUB-TV** Athens, OH, ch. 20, ETV
***WKPI** Pikeville, KY, ch. 22, ETV
***WKAS** Ashland, KY, ch. 25, ETV
WLPX-TV Charleston, WV, ch. 29, PAX TV
WHCP Portsmouth, OH, ch. 30, UPN, WB
***WPBY-TV** Huntington, WV, ch. 33, ETV
***WPBO-TV** Portsmouth, OH, ch. 42, ETV
WTSF Ashland, KY, ch. 61, IND

DMA Counties	State	TV Households	DMA Counties	State	TV Households
Boyd	KY	20,370	Boone	WV	10,260
Carter	KY	10,940	Braxton	WV	5,750
Elliott	KY	2,850	Cabell	WV	40,820
Floyd	KY	17,850	Calhoun	WV	2,840
Greenup	KY	15,190	Clay	WV	4,100
Johnson	KY	9,580	Jackson	WV	11,600
Lawrence	KY	6,270	Kanawha	WV	85,580
Lewis	KY	5,390	Lincoln	WV	8,930
Martin	KY	5,010	Logan	WV	15,240
Pike	KY	28,650	Mason	WV	10,970
Athens	OH	23,650	Mingo	WV	11,710
Gallia	OH	12,520	Nicholas	WV	10,830
Jackson	OH	12,940	Putnam	WV	21,330
Lawrence	OH	25,930	Roane	WV	6,100
Meigs	OH	9,590	Wayne	WV	17,550
Scioto	OH	30,400	Wirt	WV	2,240
Vinton	OH	5,180			

Charlotte, NC (28)

DMA TV Households: 1,004,440
% of U.S. TV Households: .917

WBTV Charlotte, NC, ch. 3, CBS
WSOC-TV Charlotte, NC, ch. 9, ABC
WHKY-TV Hickory, NC, ch. 14, IND
***WUNE-TV** Linville, NC, ch. 17, ETV
WCCB Charlotte, NC, ch. 18, Fox
***WNSC-TV** Rock Hill, SC, ch. 30, ETV
WCNC-TV Charlotte, NC, ch. 36, NBC
***WTVI** Charlotte, NC, ch. 42, ETV
WJZY Belmont, NC, ch. 46, UPN
WWWB Rock Hill, SC, ch. 55, WB
***WUNG-TV** Concord, NC, ch. 58, ETV
WAXN-TV Kannapolis, NC, ch. 64, IND

Charlotte, NC

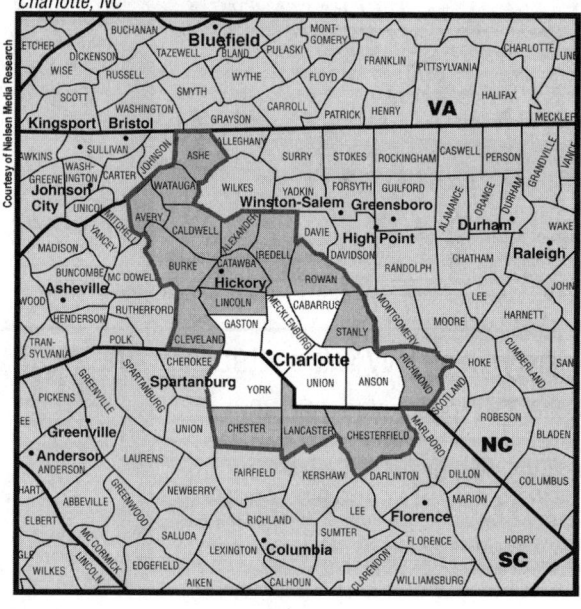

DMA Counties	State	TV Households	DMA Counties	State	TV Households
Alexander	NC	14,060	Lincoln	NC	26,080
Anson	NC	9,330	Mecklenburg	NC	303,400
Ashe	NC	10,810	Richmond	NC	18,000
Avery	NC	6,730	Rowan	NC	51,060
Burke	NC	34,760	Stanly	NC	22,560
Cabarrus	NC	55,310	Union	NC	54,100
Caldwell	NC	31,700	Watauga	NC	16,160
Catawba	NC	57,990	Chester	SC	13,130
Cleveland	NC	38,410	Chesterfield	SC	17,370
Gaston	NC	76,490	Lancaster	SC	24,700
Iredell	NC	53,030	York	SC	69,260

Broadcasting & Cable Yearbook 2006

Nielsen DMA Market Atlas

Charlottesville, VA (185)

DMA TV Households: 69,930
% of U.S. TV Households: .064

WCAV Charlottesville, VA, ch. 19, CBS
WVIR-TV Charlottesville, VA, ch. 29, NBC
***WHTJ** Charlottesville, VA, ch. 41, ETV

DMA Counties	State	TV Households
Albemarle	VA	49,320
Fluvanna	VA	9,440
Greene	VA	6,190
Madison	VA	4,980

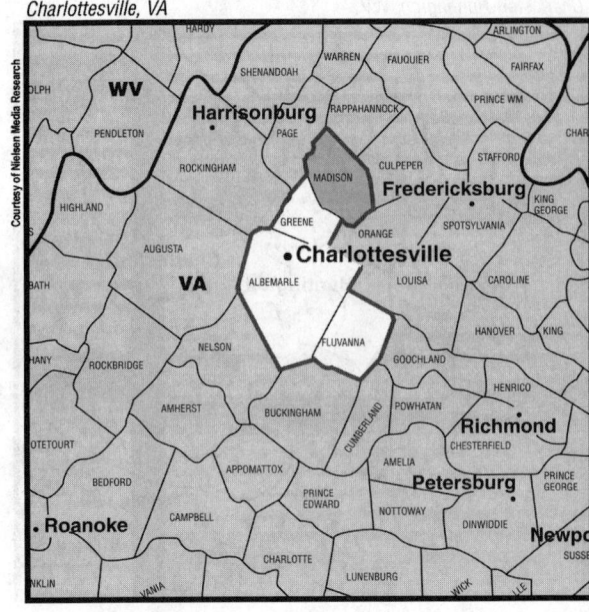

Charlottesville, VA

Chattanooga, TN (86)

DMA TV Households: 353,210
% of U.S. TV Households: .322

WRCB-TV Chattanooga, ch. 3, NBC
WTVC Chattanooga, ch. 9, ABC
WDEF-TV Chattanooga, ch. 12, CBS
***WCLP-TV** Chatsworth, GA, ch. 18, ETV
WELF Dalton, GA, ch. 23, IND
***WTCI** Chattanooga, ch. 45, ETV
WFLI-TV Cleveland, TN, ch. 53, WB
WDSI-TV Chattanooga, ch. 61, Fox

DMA Counties	State	TV Households	DMA Counties	State	TV Households
Catoosa	GA	23,440	Grundy	TN	5,780
Chattooga	GA	10,270	Hamilton	TN	126,000
Dade	GA	6,140	Marion	TN	11,360
Murray	GA	14,840	McMinn	TN	21,030
Walker	GA	24,810	Meigs	TN	4,550
Whitfield	GA	30,300	Polk	TN	6,820
Cherokee	NC	10,980	Rhea	TN	11,780
Bledsoe	TN	4,430	Sequatchie	TN	4,890
Bradley	TN	35,790			

Chattanooga, TN

Cheyenne, WY-Scottsbluff, NE (195)

DMA TV Households: 53,920
% of U.S. TV Households: .049

KDUH-TV Scottsbluff, NE, ch. 4, satellite to KOTA-TV
KGWN-TV Cheyenne, WY, ch. 5, CBS (ABC-NBC)
KSTF Scottsbluff, NE, ch. 10, satellite to KGWN-TV
KTUW Scottsbluff, NE, ch. 16, IND
KLWY Cheyenne, WY, ch. 27, IND
KKTU Cheyenne, WY, ch. 33, satellite to KTWO-TV

DMA Counties	State	TV Households
Scottsbluff	NE	15,060
Goshen	WY	5,010
Laramie	WY	33,850

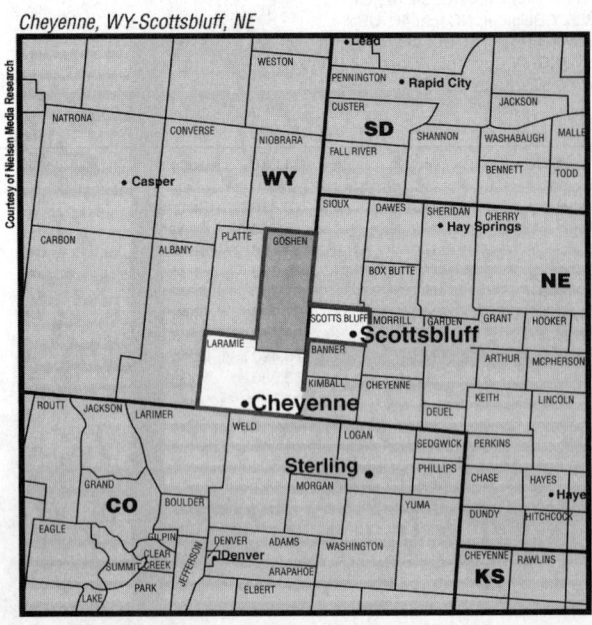

Cheyenne, WY-Scottsbluff, NE

Broadcasting & Cable Yearbook 2006

Nielsen DMA Market Atlas

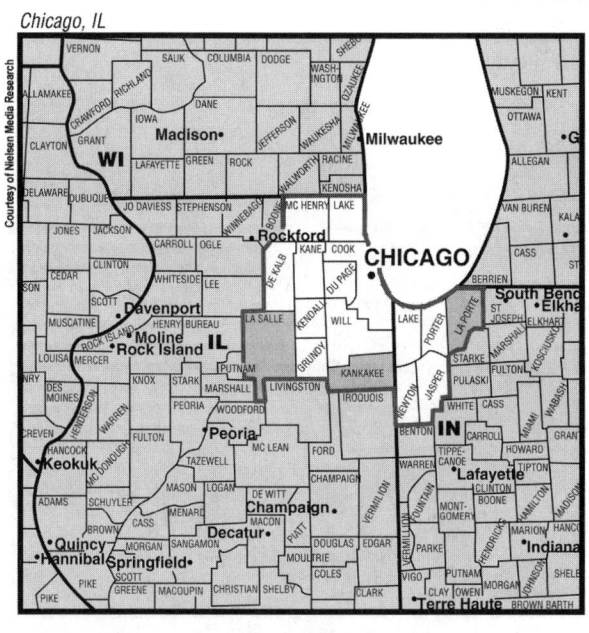
Chicago, IL

Chicago (3)

DMA TV Households: 3,417,330
% of U.S. TV Households: 3.118

WBBM-TV Chicago, ch. 2, CBS
WMAQ-TV Chicago, ch. 5, NBC
WLS-TV Chicago, ch. 7, ABC
WGN-TV Chicago, ch. 9, WB
*WTTW Chicago, ch. 11, ETV
*WYCC Chicago, ch. 20, ETV
WCIU-TV Chicago, ch. 26, IND
WFLD Chicago, ch. 32, Fox
WWTO-TV LaSalle, IL, ch. 35, IND
WCPX Chicago, ch. 38, IND
WSNS Chicago, ch. 44, Telemundo
WPWR-TV Gary, IN, ch. 50, UPN
*WYIN Gary, IN, ch. 56, ETV
WXFT-TV Aurora, IL, ch. 60, TeleFutura
WJYS Hammond, IN, ch. 62, IND
WGBO-TV Joliet, IL, ch. 66, Univision

DMA Counties	State	TV Households	DMA Counties	State	TV Households
Cook	IL	1,921,580	Lake	IL	232,740
DeKalb	IL	34,180	McHenry	IL	101,000
DuPage	IL	335,930	Will	IL	208,830
Grundy	IL	15,420	Jasper	IN	11,380
Kane	IL	155,320	La Porte	IN	41,710
Kankakee	IL	39,260	Lake	IN	186,060
Kendall	IL	25,340	Newton	IN	5,350
LaSalle	IL	43,680	Porter	IN	59,550

Chico-Redding, CA (131)

DMA TV Households: 189,310
% of U.S. TV Households: .173

KRCR-TV Redding, CA, ch. 7, ABC
*KIXE Redding, CA, ch. 9, ETV
KHSL-TV Chico, CA, ch. 12, CBS
KNVN Chico, CA, ch. 24, NBC
KCVU Paradise, CA, ch. 30, Fox

DMA Counties	State	TV Households
Butte	CA	80,640
Glenn	CA	9,120
Modoc	CA	3,590
Shasta	CA	68,880
Tehama	CA	21,610
Trinity	CA	5,470

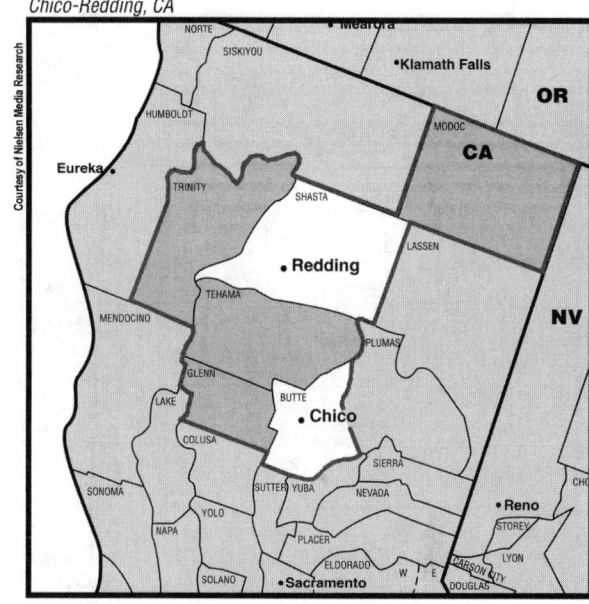
Chico-Redding, CA

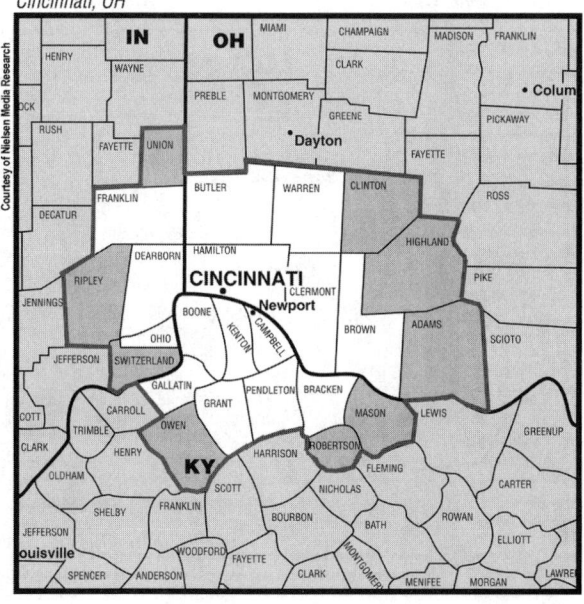
Cincinnati, OH

Cincinnati (33)

DMA TV Households: 883,230
% of U.S. TV Households: .806

WLWT Cincinnati, ch. 5, NBC
WCPO-TV Cincinnati, ch. 9, ABC
WKRC-TV Cincinnati, ch. 12, CBS
*WPTO Oxford, OH, ch. 14, ETV
WXIX-TV Newport, KY, ch. 19, Fox
*WCET Cincinnati, ch. 48, ETV
*WKON Owenton, KY, ch. 52, ETV
*WCVN Covington, KY, ch. 54, ETV
WSTR-TV Cincinnati, ch. 64, WB

DMA Counties	State	TV Households	DMA Counties	State	TV Households
Dearborn	IN	17,950	Mason	KY	7,040
Franklin	IN	8,180	Owen	KY	4,080
Ohio	IN	2,270	Pendleton	KY	5,560
Ripley	IN	10,380	Robertson	KY	890
Switzerland	IN	3,680	Adams	OH	10,790
Union	IN	2,740	Brown	OH	16,500
Boone	KY	37,790	Butler	OH	129,750
Bracken	KY	3,370	Clermont	OH	71,920
Campbell	KY	35,490	Clinton	OH	16,380
Gallatin	KY	2,970	Hamilton	OH	339,710
Grant	KY	8,950	Highland	OH	16,030
Kenton	KY	61,570	Warren	OH	69,040

Broadcasting & Cable Yearbook 2006

Nielsen DMA Market Atlas

Clarksburg-Weston, WV (165)

DMA TV Households: 109,480
% of U.S. TV Households: .100

WDTV Weston, WV, ch. 5, CBS (ABC)
WBOY-TV Clarksburg, WV, ch. 12, NBC (ABC)
WVFX Clarksburg, WV, ch. 46, IND

DMA Counties	State	TV Households
Barbour	WV	6,220
Doddridge	WV	2,890
Gilmer	WV	2,650
Harrison	WV	27,980
Lewis	WV	7,230
Marion	WV	24,150
Randolph	WV	11,060
Ritchie	WV	4,270
Taylor	WV	6,450
Tucker	WV	3,060
Upshur	WV	9,200
Webster	WV	4,320

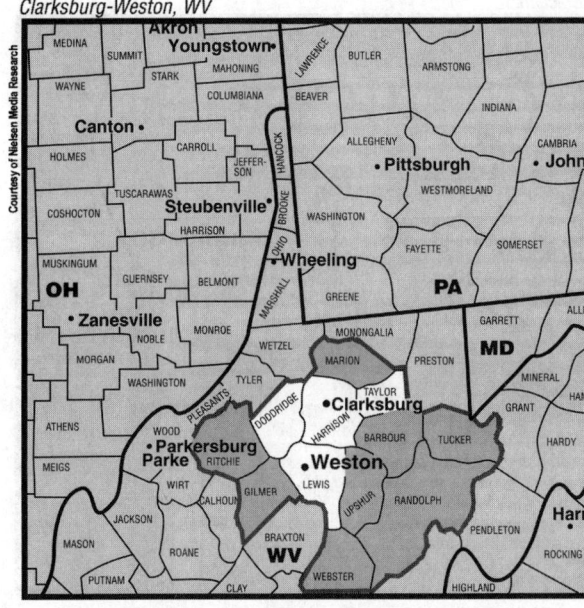
Clarksburg-Weston, WV

Cleveland-Akron (Canton), OH

Cleveland-Akron (Canton), OH (16)

DMA TV Households: 1,556,670
% of U.S. TV Households: 1.420

WKYC-TV Cleveland, ch. 3, NBC
WEWS Cleveland, ch. 5, ABC
WJW Cleveland, ch. 8, Fox
WDLI-TV Canton, OH, ch. 17, IND
WOIO Shaker Heights, OH, ch. 19, CBS
WVPX Akron, OH, ch. 23, IND
*WVIZ-TV Cleveland, ch. 25, ETV
WUAB Lorain, OH, ch. 43, UPN
*WEAO Akron, OH, ch. 49, ETV
WGGN-TV Sandusky, OH, ch. 52, IND
WBNX-TV Akron, OH, ch. 55, WB
WQHS-TV Cleveland, ch. 61, Univision
WOAC Canton, OH, ch. 67, IND
WMFD-TV Mansfield, OH, ch. 68, IND

DMA Counties	State	TV Households	DMA Counties	State	TV Households
Ashland	OH	20,490	Lorain	OH	112,960
Ashtabula	OH	39,980	Medina	OH	62,030
Carroll	OH	11,830	Portage	OH	59,910
Cuyahoga	OH	558,380	Richland	OH	49,760
Erie	OH	32,420	Stark	OH	149,500
Geauga	OH	33,480	Summit	OH	222,940
Holmes	OH	9,630	Tuscarawas	OH	35,710
Huron	OH	23,230	Wayne	OH	41,160
Lake	OH	93,260			

Colorado Springs-Pueblo, CO (92)

DMA TV Households: 313,170
% of U.S. TV Households: .286

KOAA-TV Pueblo, CO, ch. 5, NBC
*KTSC Pueblo, CO, ch. 8, ETV
KKTV Colorado Springs, ch. 11, CBS
KRDO-TV Colorado Springs, ch. 13, ABC
KXRM-TV Colorado Springs, ch. 21, Fox

DMA Counties	State	TV Households
Baca	CO	1,640
Bent	CO	1,840
Crowley	CO	1,370
El Paso	CO	204,750
Fremont	CO	15,650
Huerfano	CO	3,140
Kiowa	CO	580
Las Animas	CO	6,170
Otero	CO	7,520
Pueblo	CO	57,920
Teller	CO	8,670

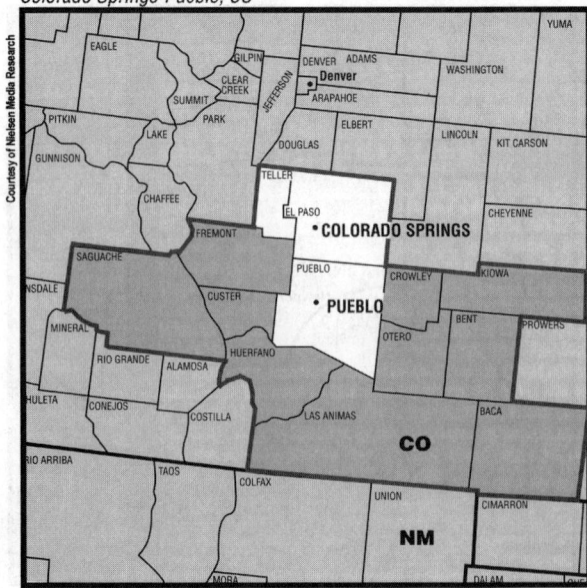
Colorado Springs-Pueblo, CO

Columbia-Jefferson City, MO (139)

DMA TV Households: 167,390
% of U.S. TV Households: .153

KOMU-TV Columbia, MO, ch. 8, NBC
KRCG Jefferson City, MO, ch. 13, CBS
KMIZ Columbia, MO, ch. 17, ABC
KNLJ Jefferson City, MO, ch. 25, IND

DMA Counties	State	TV Households
Audrain	MO	9,770
Boone	MO	55,880
Callaway	MO	14,950
Chariton	MO	3,450
Cole	MO	28,040
Cooper	MO	6,000
Howard	MO	3,660
Maries	MO	3,530
Miller	MO	9,680
Moniteau	MO	5,200
Montgomery	MO	4,710
Morgan	MO	7,880
Osage	MO	5,170
Randolph	MO	9,470

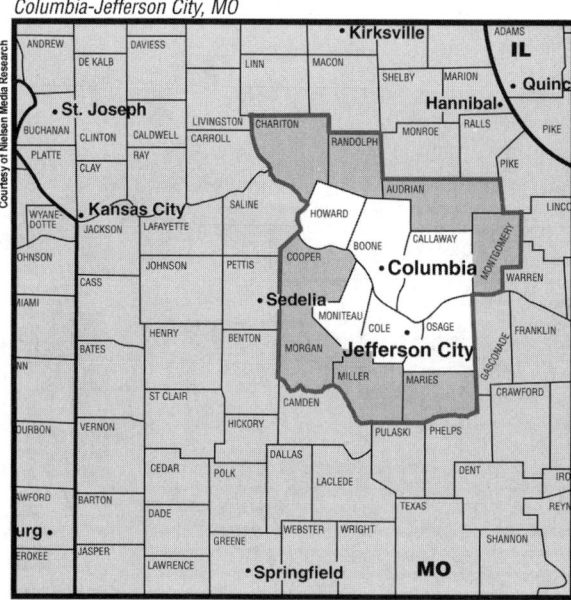

Columbia, SC (83)

DMA TV Households: 374,680
% of U.S. TV Households: .342

WIS Columbia, SC, ch. 10, NBC
WLTX Columbia, SC, ch. 19, CBS
WOLO-TV Columbia, SC, ch. 25, ABC
***WRJA-TV** Sumter, SC, ch. 27, ETV
***WRLK-TV** Columbia, SC, ch. 35, ETV
WZRB Columbia, SC, ch. 47, IND
WACH Columbia, SC, ch. 57, IND
WBHQ Sumter, SC, ch. 63, UPN

DMA Counties	State	TV Households
Calhoun	SC	6,430
Clarendon	SC	12,720
Fairfield	SC	9,440
Kershaw	SC	21,690
Lee	SC	7,400
Lexington	SC	91,590
Newberry	SC	14,740
Orangeburg	SC	34,940
Richland	SC	128,440
Saluda	SC	7,200
Sumter	SC	40,090

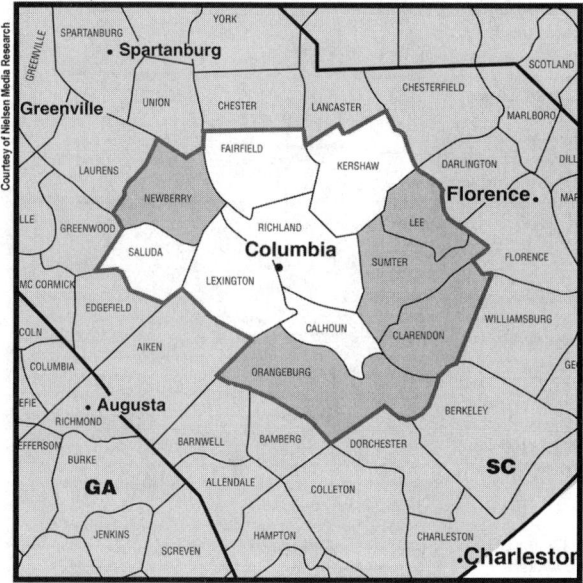

Columbus, GA (125)

DMA TV Households: 208,860
% of U.S. TV Households: .191

WRBL Columbus, GA, ch. 3, CBS
WTVM Columbus, GA, ch. 9, ABC
***WJSP-TV** Columbus, GA, ch. 28, ETV
WLTZ Columbus, GA, ch. 38, NBC
***WGIQ** Louisville, AL, ch. 43, ETV
WXTX Columbus, GA, ch. 54, Fox
WSWS-TV Opelika, AL, ch. 66, IND

DMA Counties	State	TV Households	DMA Counties	State	TV Households
Barbour	AL	10,450	Quitman	GA	980
Chambers	AL	14,470	Randolph	GA	2,760
Lee	AL	48,570	Schley	GA	1,570
Russell	AL	19,750	Stewart	GA	1,950
Chattahoochee	GA	4,890	Sumter	GA	12,190
Clay	GA	1,370	Talbot	GA	2,650
Harris	GA	9,980	Taylor	GA	3,410
Marion	GA	2,730	Webster	GA	880
Muscogee	GA	70,260			

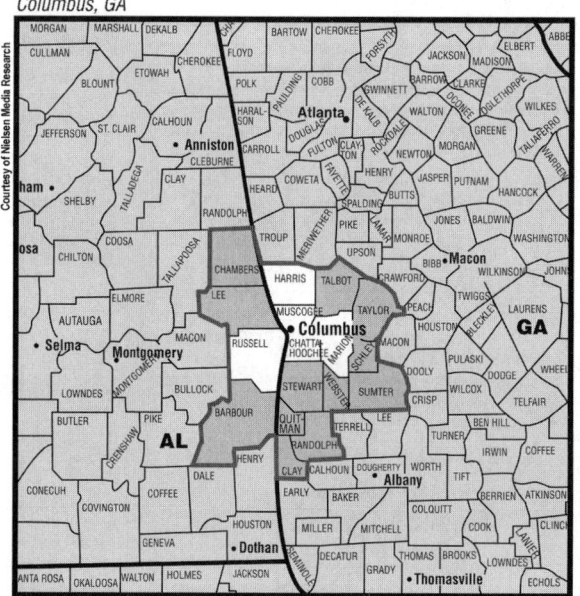

Nielsen DMA Market Atlas

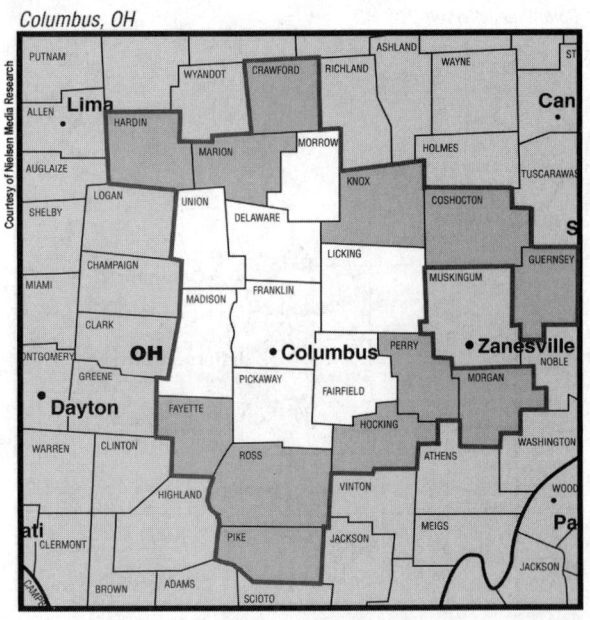

Columbus, OH (34)

DMA TV Households: 854,040
% of U.S. TV Households: .788

WCMH-TV Columbus, OH, ch. 4, NBC
WSYX Columbus, OH, ch. 6, ABC
WBNS-TV Columbus, OH, ch. 10, CBS
WTTE Columbus, OH, ch. 28, Fox
*WOSU-TV Columbus, OH, ch. 34, ETV
WSFJ Newark, OH, ch. 51, PAX TV
WWHO Chillicothe, OH, ch. 53, UPN, WB

DMA Counties	State	TV Households	DMA Counties	State	TV Households
Coshocton	OH	14,410	Licking	OH	58,930
Crawford	OH	18,730	Madison	OH	13,820
Delaware	OH	46,720	Marion	OH	24,440
Fairfield	OH	47,890	Morgan	OH	6,210
Fayette	OH	11,060	Morrow	OH	11,830
Franklin	OH	456,550	Perry	OH	12,480
Guernsey	OH	15,640	Pickaway	OH	18,040
Hardin	OH	11,820	Pike	OH	10,790
Hocking	OH	10,940	Ross	OH	27,340
Knox	OH	20,760	Union	OH	15,320

Columbus-Tupelo-West Point, MS (132)

DMA TV Households: 187,650
% of U.S. TV Households: .171

*WMAB-TV Mississippi State, MS, ch. 2, ETV
WCBI-TV Columbus, MS, ch. 4, CBS
WTVA Tupelo, MS, ch. 9, NBC
*WMAE-TV Boonevile, MS, ch. 12, ETV
WLOV-TV West Point, MS, ch. 27, Fox
*WMAA Columbus, MS, ch. 43, ETV
WKDH Houston, MS, ch. 45, ABC

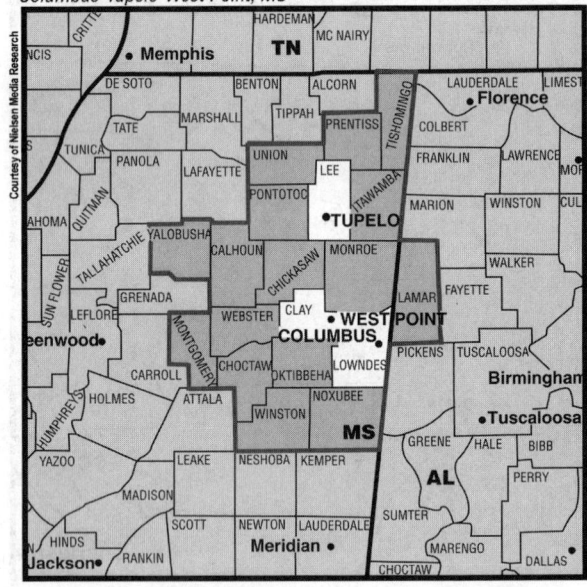

DMA Counties	State	TV Households	DMA Counties	State	TV Households
Lamar	AL	6,180	Noxubee	MS	4,000
Calhoun	MS	5,990	Oktibbeha	MS	16,170
Chickasaw	MS	7,140	Pontotoc	MS	10,410
Choctaw	MS	3,680	Prentiss	MS	9,960
Clay	MS	8,140	Tishomingo	MS	7,820
Itawamba	MS	8,870	Union	MS	10,160
Lee	MS	30,760	Webster	MS	3,740
Lowndes	MS	22,330	Winston	MS	7,600
Monroe	MS	14,760	Yalobusha	MS	5,460
Montgomery	MS	4,480			

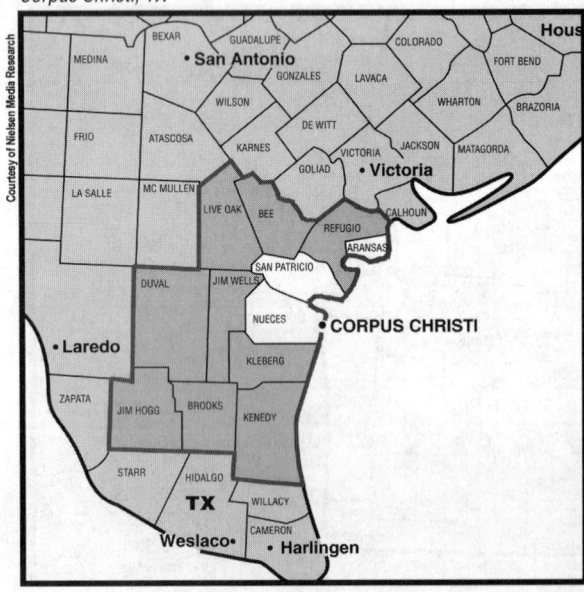

Corpus Christi, TX (129)

DMA TV Households: 193,290
% of U.S. TV Households: .176

KIII Corpus Christi, TX, ch. 3, ABC
KRIS-TV Corpus Christi, TX, ch. 6, NBC
KZTV Corpus Christi, TX, ch. 10, CBS
*KEDT Corpus Christi, TX, ch. 16, ETV
KORO Corpus Christi, TX, ch. 28, Univision

DMA Counties	State	TV Households
Aransas	TX	9,860
Bee	TX	9,190
Brooks	TX	2,620
Duval	TX	4,240
Jim Hogg	TX	1,740
Jim Wells	TX	13,450
Kenedy	TX	100
Kleberg	TX	10,770
Live Oak	TX	4,120
Nueces	TX	111,600
Refugio	TX	2,870
San Patricio	TX	22,730

Broadcasting & Cable Yearbook 2006

Nielsen DMA Market Atlas

Dallas-Ft. Worth, TX

Dallas-Fort Worth, TX (7)

DMA TV Households: 2,292,760
% of U.S. TV Households: 2.092

*KDTN Denton, TX, ch. 2, ETV
KDFW Dallas, ch. 4, Fox
KXAS-TV Fort Worth, ch. 5, NBC
WFAA-TV Dallas, ch. 8, ABC
KTVT Fort Worth, ch. 11, CBS
*KERA-TV Dallas, ch. 13, ETV
KTXA Fort Worth, ch. 21, UPN
KUVN-TV Garland, TX, ch. 23, Univision
KDFI Dallas, ch. 27, IND
KMPX Decatur, TX, ch. 29, IND
KDAF Dallas, ch. 33, WB
KXTX-TV Dallas, ch. 39, Telemundo
KTAQ Greenville, TX, ch. 47, IND
KSTR-TV Irving, TX, ch. 49, TeleFutura
KFWD Fort Worth, ch. 52, IND
KLDT Lake Dallas, TX, ch. 55, IND
KDTX-TV Dallas, ch. 58, IND
KPXD Arlington, TX, ch. 68, IND

DMA Counties	State	TV Households	DMA Counties	State	TV Households
Anderson	TX	15,620	Hopkins	TX	12,710
Bosque	TX	6,940	Hunt	TX	30,810
Collin	TX	236,630	Jack	TX	2,990
Comanche	TX	5,190	Johnson	TX	49,460
Cooke	TX	14,280	Kaufman	TX	29,040
Dallas	TX	815,340	Lamar	TX	18,650
Delta	TX	2,050	Navarro	TX	17,270
Denton	TX	196,140	Palo Pinto	TX	10,700
Ellis	TX	42,830	Parker	TX	36,270
Erath	TX	12,130	Rains	TX	4,410
Fannin	TX	11,540	Red River	TX	5,640
Freestone	TX	7,040	Rockwall	TX	19,750
Hamilton	TX	3,240	Somervell	TX	2,750
Henderson	TX	30,420	Tarrant	TX	582,680
Hill	TX	13,160	Van Zandt	TX	19,160
Hood	TX	18,540	Wise	TX	19,380

Davenport, IA-Rock Island-Moline, IL (94)

DMA TV Households: 309,900
% of U.S. TV Households: .283

WHBF-TV Rock Island, IL, ch. 4, CBS
KWQC-TV Davenport, IA, ch. 6, NBC
WQAD-TV Moline, IL, ch. 8, ABC
KLJB-TV Davenport, IA, ch. 18, Fox
*WQPT-TV Moline, IL, ch. 24, ETV
KGWB-TV Burlington, IA, ch. 26, IND
*KQCT Davenport, IA, ch. 36, satellite to *WQPT-TV

DMA Counties	State	TV Households	DMA Counties	State	TV Households
Bureau	IL	14,180	Whiteside	IL	23,620
Carroll	IL	6,620	Clinton	IA	20,310
Henderson	IL	3,300	Des Moines	IA	16,740
Henry	IL	20,220	Henry	IA	7,390
Jo Daviess	IL	9,680	Jackson	IA	8,240
Knox	IL	21,490	Louisa	IA	4,440
Mercer	IL	6,750	Muscatine	IA	16,210
Rock Island	IL	60,250	Scott	IA	63,510
Warren	IL	6,950			

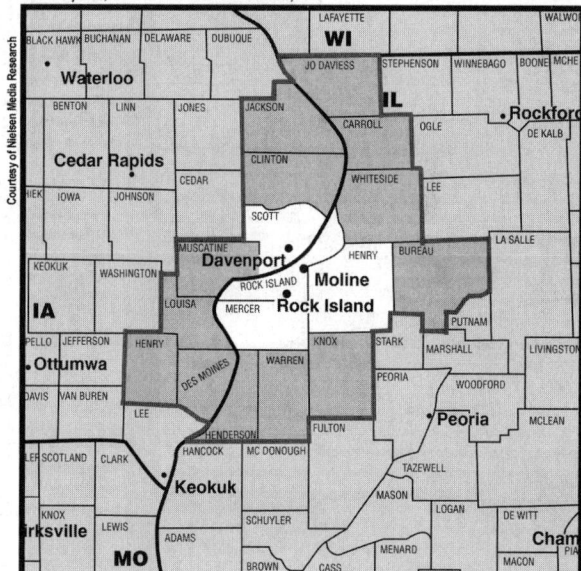
Davenport, IA-Rock Island-Moline, IL

Broadcasting & Cable Yearbook 2006

Nielsen DMA Market Atlas

Dayton, OH (56)

DMA TV Households: 537,710
% of U.S. TV Households: .491

WDTN Dayton, OH, ch. 2, NBC
WHIO-TV Dayton, OH, ch. 7, CBS
***WPTD** Kettering, OH, ch. 16, ETV
WKEF Dayton, OH, ch. 22, ABC
WBDT Springfield, OH, ch. 26, IND
WKOI-TV Richmond, IN, ch. 43, IND
WRGT-TV Dayton, OH, ch. 45, Fox

DMA Counties	State	TV Households
Wayne	IN	28,170
Auglaize	OH	17,890
Champaign	OH	15,600
Clark	OH	57,090
Darke	OH	20,540
Greene	OH	59,150
Logan	OH	18,380
Mercer	OH	15,290
Miami	OH	40,200
Montgomery	OH	230,610
Preble	OH	16,290
Shelby	OH	18,500

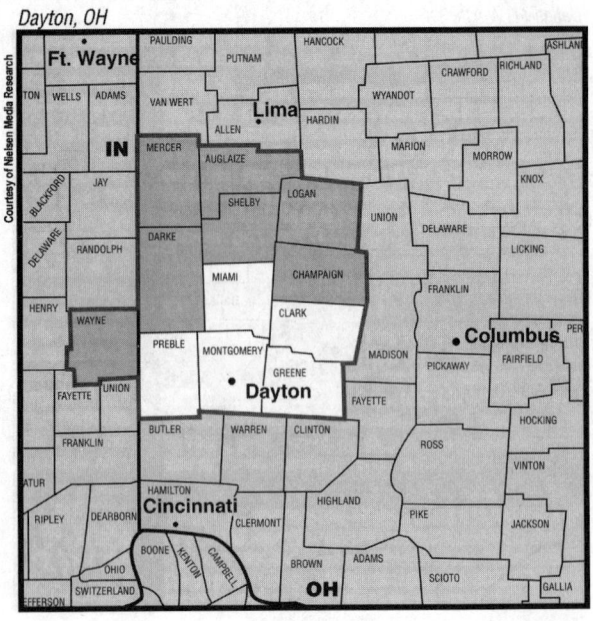

Denver (18)

DMA TV Households: 1,401,760
% of U.S. TV Households: 1.279

KWGN-TV Denver, ch. 2, WB
KREG-TV Glenwood Springs, CO, ch. 3, CBS
KUPN Sterling, CO, ch. 3, satellite to KTVD
KCNC-TV Denver, ch. 4, CBS
***KRMA-TV** Denver, ch. 6, ETV
KMGH-TV Denver, ch. 7, ABC
***KWYP-TV** Laramie, WY, ch. 8, ETV
KUSA-TV Denver, ch. 9, NBC
KFNR Rawlins, WY, ch. 11, Fox
***KBDI-TV** Broomfield, CO, ch. 12, ETV
KTFD-TV Boulder, CO, ch. 14, TeleFutura
KTVD Denver, ch. 20, UPN
KFCT Fort Collins, CO, ch. 22, satellite to KDVR
KMAS-TV Steamboat Springs, CO, ch. 24, Telemundo
KDEN Longmont, CO, ch. 25, IND
KDVR Denver, ch. 31, Fox
***KRMT** Denver, ch. 41, ETV
KCEC Denver, ch. 50, Univision
KWHD Castle Rock, CO, ch. 53, IND
KPXC-TV Denver, ch. 59, IND

DMA Counties	State	TV Households	DMA Counties	State	TV Households
Adams	CO	135,570	Ouray	CO	1,620
Alamosa	CO	5,420	Park	CO	6,720
Arapahoe	CO	203,900	Phillips	CO	1,780
Archuleta	CO	4,200	Pitkin	CO	5,970
Boulder	CO	102,860	Prowers	CO	4,890
Chaffee	CO	6,910	Rio Blanco	CO	2,320
Cheyenne	CO	740	Rio Grande	CO	4,730
Clear Creek	CO	4,110	Routt	CO	8,340
Conejos	CO	2,860	Saguache	CO	2,410
Costilla	CO	1,510	San Juan	CO	280
Delta	CO	11,620	San Miguel	CO	3,070
Denver	CO	227,620	Sedgwick	CO	1,090
Dolores	CO	620	Summit	CO	9,880
Douglas	CO	83,880	Washington	CO	1,910
Eagle	CO	16,080	Weld	CO	75,540
Elbert	CO	7,540	Yuma	CO	3,760
Garfield	CO	17,610	Box Butte	NE	4,680
Gilpin	CO	1,980	Cheyenne	NE	4,170
Grand	CO	5,490	Dawes	NE	3,550
Gunnison	CO	5,480	Deuel	NE	890
Hinsdale	CO	400	Garden	NE	980
Jackson	CO	690	Grant	NE	290
Jefferson	CO	206,490	Hooker	NE	290
Lake	CO	2,560	Keith	NE	3,460
Kit Carson	CO	2,960	Kimball	NE	1,590
Larimer	CO	102,370	Sheridan	NE	2,340
Lincoln	CO	1,960	Todd	SD	2,620
Logan	CO	7,720	Campbell	WY	13,900
Morgan	CO	9,540	Carbon	WY	5,940
Moffat	CO	5,050	Johnson	WY	3,350
Niobrara	WY	860	Platte	WY	3,560

Broadcasting & Cable Yearbook 2006

Nielsen DMA Market Atlas

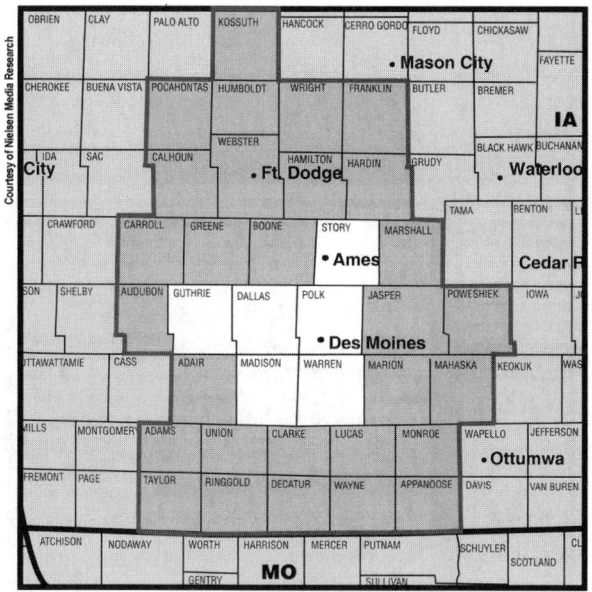

Des Moines-Ames, IA (73)

DMA TV Households: 412,230
% of U.S. TV Households: .376

WOI-TV Ames, IA, ch. 5, ABC
KCCI Des Moines, IA, ch. 8, CBS
***KDIN-TV** Des Moines, IA, ch. 11, ETV
WHO-TV Des Moines, IA, ch. 13, NBC
KDSM-TV Des Moines, IA, ch. 17, Fox
***KTIN** Fort Dodge, IA, ch. 21, ETV
KPWB-TV Ames, IA, ch. 23, WB
KFPX Newton, IA, ch. 39, PAX TV
KDMI Des Moines, IA, ch. 56, IND

DMA Counties	State	TV Households	DMA Counties	State	TV Households
Adair	IA	3,190	Lucas	IA	3,760
Adams	IA	1,790	Madison	IA	5,550
Appanoose	IA	5,770	Mahaska	IA	8,850
Audubon	IA	2,550	Marion	IA	12,180
Boone	IA	10,470	Marshall	IA	15,100
Calhoun	IA	4,300	Monroe	IA	3,120
Carroll	IA	8,630	Pocahontas	IA	3,370
Clarke	IA	3,560	Polk	IA	156,620
Dallas	IA	18,540	Poweshiek	IA	7,700
Decatur	IA	3,300	Ringgold	IA	2,150
Franklin	IA	4,380	Story	IA	31,270
Greene	IA	3,980	Taylor	IA	2,640
Guthrie	IA	4,760	Union	IA	5,050
Hamilton	IA	6,660	Warren	IA	15,740
Hardin	IA	7,340	Wayne	IA	2,760
Humboldt	IA	4,130	Webster	IA	15,590
Jasper	IA	15,210	Wright	IA	5,500
Kossuth	IA	6,720			

Detroit (10)

DMA TV Households: 1,943,930
% of U.S. TV Households: 1.774

WJBK Detroit, ch. 2, Fox
WDIV Detroit, ch. 4, NBC
WXYZ-TV Detroit, ch. 7, ABC
CBET Windsor, ON, ch. 9, CBC
WDWB Detroit, ch. 20, WB
WPXD Ann Arbor, MI, ch. 31, IND
WADL Mount Clemens, MI, ch. 38, IND
WKBD Detroit, ch. 50, UPN
***WTVS** Detroit, ch. 56, ETV
WWJ-TV Detroit, ch. 62, CBS

DMA Counties	State	TV Households
Lapeer	MI	33,390
Livingston	MI	64,640
Macomb	MI	335,590
Monroe	MI	58,080
Oakland	MI	487,520
Sanilac	MI	16,940
St. Clair	MI	66,050
Washtenaw	MI	133,950
Wayne	MI	747,770

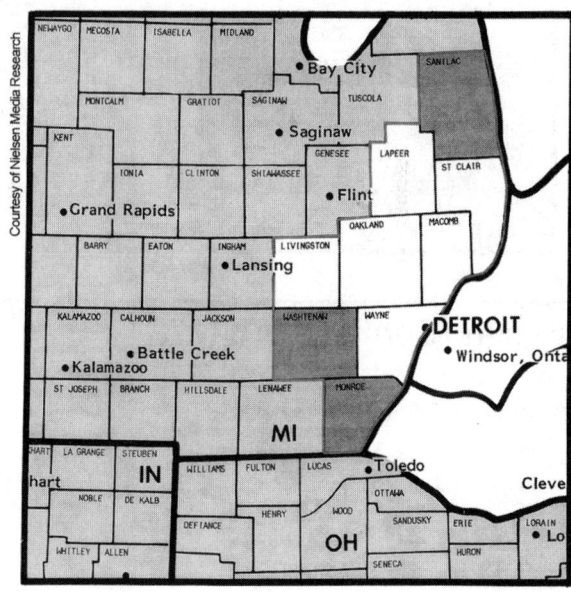

Broadcasting & Cable Yearbook 2006

Dothan, AL (172)

DMA TV Households: 98,850
% of U.S. TV Households: .090

WTVY Dothan, AL, ch. 4, CBS
WDHN Dothan, AL, ch. 18, ABC
WDFX-TV Ozark, AL, ch. 34, Fox

DMA Counties	State	TV Households
Coffee	AL	18,480
Dale	AL	19,560
Geneva	AL	10,520
Henry	AL	6,810
Houston	AL	38,750
Early	GA	4,730

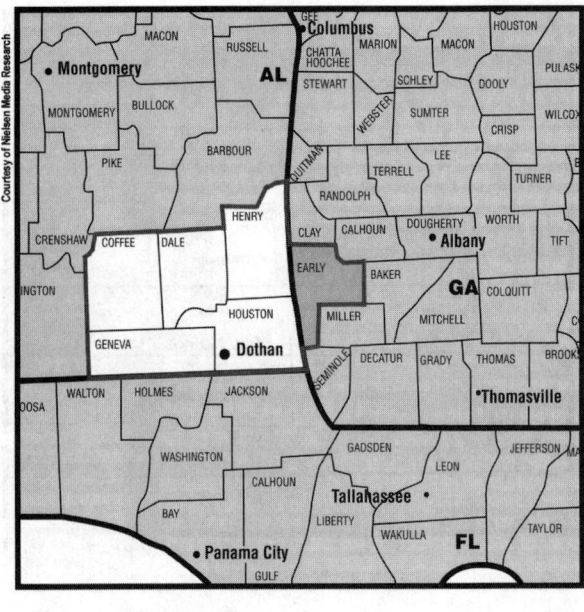

Duluth, MN-Superior, WI (136)

DMA TV Households: 175,030
% of U.S. TV Households: .160

KDLH Duluth, MN, ch. 3, CBS
KBJR-TV Superior, WI, ch. 6, NBC
*WDSE-TV Duluth, MN, ch. 8, ETV
WDIO-TV Duluth, MN, ch. 10, ABC
KRII Chisholm, MN, ch. 11, satellite to KBJR-TV
WIRT Hibbing, MN, ch. 13, satellite to WDIO-TV
KQDS-TV Duluth, MN, ch. 21, Fox

DMA Counties	State	TV Households
Gogebic	MI	7,320
Carlton	MN	13,130
Cook	MN	2,320
Itasca	MN	18,320
Koochiching	MN	5,970
Lake	MN	4,750
St. Louis	MN	82,020
Ashland	WI	6,540
Bayfield	WI	6,200
Douglas	WI	18,420
Iron	WI	3,180
Sawyer	WI	6,860

Elmira (Corning), NY (173)

DMA TV Households: 98,270
% of U.S. TV Households: .090

WETM-TV Elmira, NY, ch. 18, NBC
*WSKA Corning, NY, ch. 30, ETV
WENY-TV Elmira, NY, ch. 36, ABC
WYDC Corning, NY, ch. 48, Fox

DMA Counties	State	TV Households
Chemung	NY	35,450
Schuyler	NY	7,660
Steuben	NY	39,270
Tioga	PA	15,890

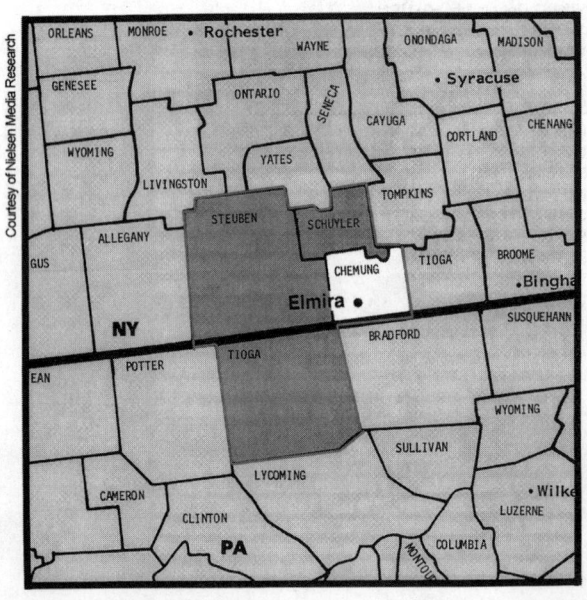

Nielsen DMA Market Atlas

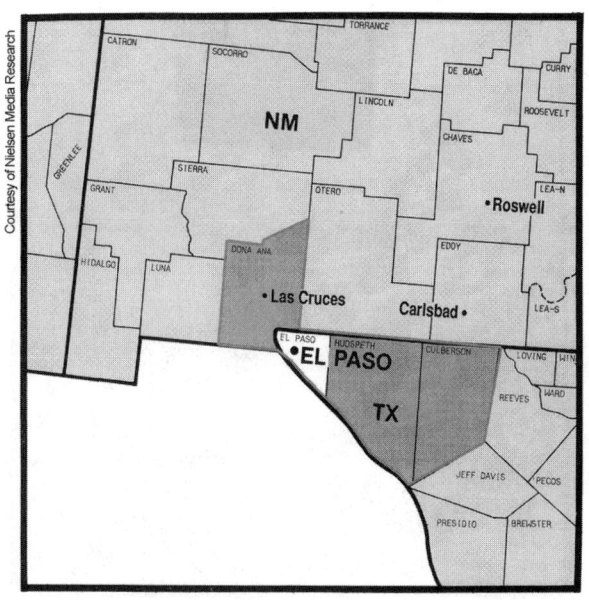

El Paso (Las Cruces, NM) (100)

DMA TV Households: 283,440
% of U.S. TV Households: .263

KDBC-TV El Paso, ch. 4, CBS
KVIA-TV El Paso, ch. 7, ABC
KTSM-TV El Paso, ch. 9, NBC
***KCOS** El Paso, ch. 13, ETV
KFOX-TV El Paso, ch. 14, Fox
***KRWG-TV** Las Cruces, NM, ch. 22, ETV
KINT-TV El Paso, ch. 26, Univision
***KSCE** El Paso, ch. 38, ETV
KTDO Las Cruces, NM, ch. 48, Telemundo
KTFN El Paso, ch. 65, IND

DMA Counties	State	TV Households
Dona Ana	NM	62,840
Culberson	TX	980
El Paso	TX	223,550
Hudspeth	TX	1,070

Erie, PA (142)

DMA TV Households: 158,910
% of U.S. TV Households: .145

WICU-TV Erie, PA, ch. 12, NBC
WJET-TV Erie, PA, ch. 24, ABC
WSEE Erie, PA, ch. 35, CBS
***WQLN** Erie, PA, ch. 54, ETV
WFXP Erie, PA, ch. 66, Fox

DMA Counties	State	TV Households
Crawford	PA	34,350
Erie	PA	107,350
Warren	PA	17,210

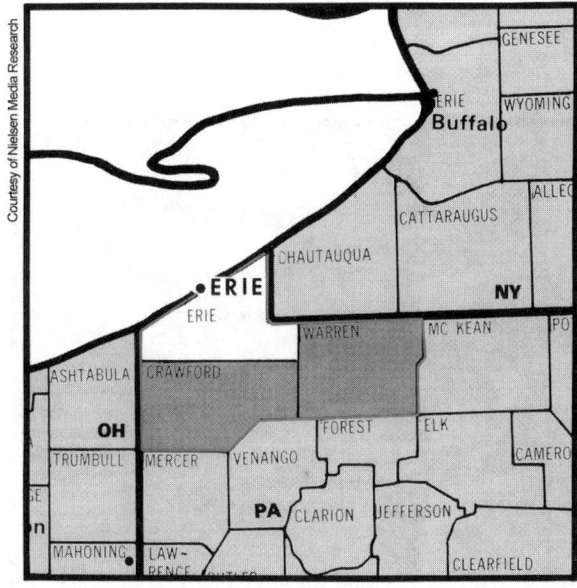

Eugene, OR (120)

DMA TV Households: 229,360
% of U.S. TV Households: .209

KPIC Roseburg, OR, ch. 4, satellite to KVAL-TV
***KOAC-TV** Corvallis, OR, ch. 7, ETV
KEZI Eugene, OR, ch. 9, ABC
KCBY-TV Coos Bay, OR, ch. 11, satellite to KVAL-TV
KVAL-TV Eugene, OR, ch. 13, CBS
KMTR Eugene, OR, ch. 16, NBC
KMTZ Coos Bay, OR, ch. 23, satellite to KMTR
***KEPB-TV** Eugene, OR, ch. 28, ETV
KLSR-TV Eugene, OR, ch. 34, Fox
KTVC Roseburg, OR, ch. 36, UPN
KMTX-TV Roseburg, OR, ch. 46, satellite to KMTR

DMA Counties	State	TV Households
Benton	OR	29,690
Coos	OR	26,200
Douglas	OR	41,190
Lane	OR	132,280

Broadcasting & Cable Yearbook 2006

Nielsen DMA Market Atlas

Eureka, CA (192)

DMA TV Households: 58,380
% of U.S. TV Households: .053

KIEM-TV Eureka, CA, ch. 3, NBC
KVIQ Eureka, CA, ch. 6, CBS
*KEET Eureka, CA, ch. 13, ETV
KAEF Arcata, CA, ch. 23, Fox
KBVU Eureka, CA, ch. 29, IND

DMA Counties	State	TV Households
Del Norte	CA	8,720
Humboldt	CA	49,660

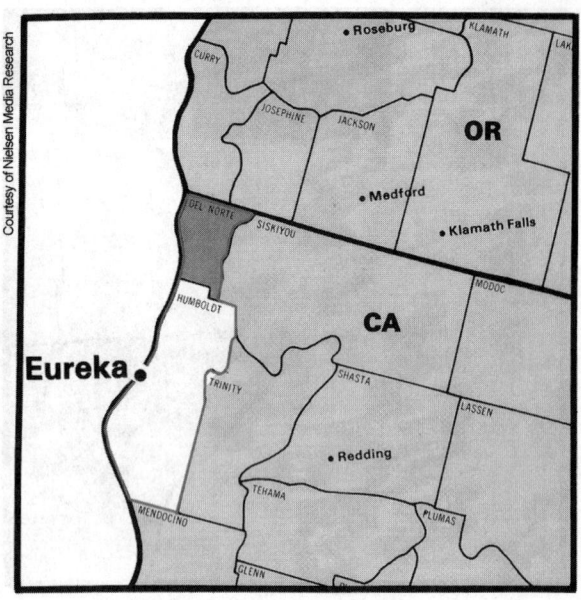

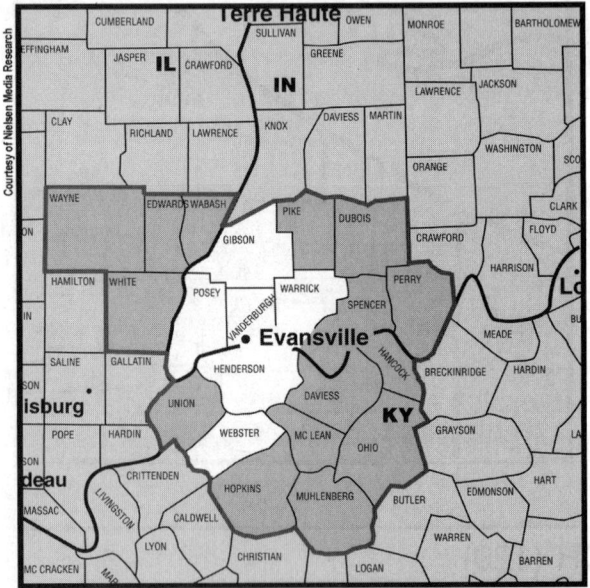

Evansville, IN (99)

DMA TV Households: 289,840
% of U.S. TV Households: .264

WTVW Evansville, IN, ch. 7, Fox
*WNIN Evansville, IN, ch. 9, ETV
WFIE Evansville, IN, ch. 14, NBC
WAZE-TV Madisonville, KY, ch. 19, IND
WEHT Evansville, IN, ch. 25, ABC
*WKOH Owensboro, KY, ch. 31, ETV
*WKMA Madisonville, KY, ch. 35, ETV
WEVV Evansville, IN, ch. 44, CBS

DMA Counties	State	TV Households	DMA Counties	State	TV Households
Edwards	IL	2,890	Warrick	IN	21,360
Wabash	IL	5,140	Daviess	KY	37,590
Wayne	IL	7,100	Hancock	KY	3,330
White	IL	6,430	Henderson	KY	18,740
Dubois	IN	15,490	Hopkins	KY	19,510
Gibson	IN	13,300	McLean	KY	4,050
Perry	IN	7,430	Muhlenberg	KY	12,430
Pike	IN	5,110	Ohio	KY	9,170
Posey	IN	10,220	Union	KY	5,960
Spencer	IN	7,620	Webster	KY	5,470
Vanderburgh	IN	71,500			

Broadcasting & Cable Yearbook 2006

Nielsen DMA Market Atlas

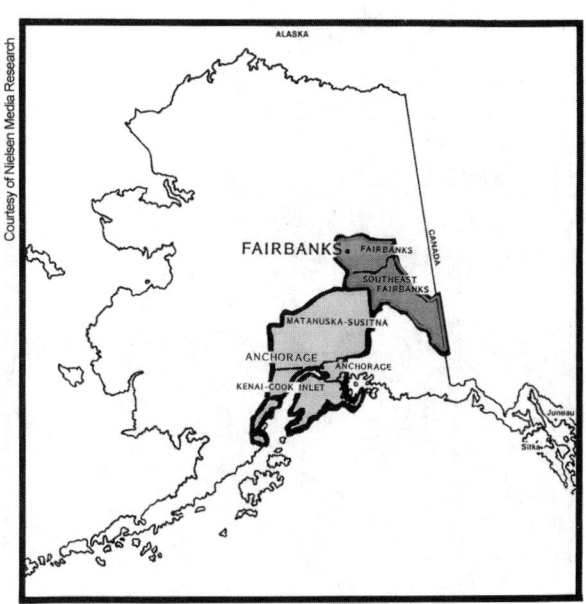

Fairbanks, AK (204)

DMA TV Households: 31,640
% of U.S. TV Households: .029

KATN Fairbanks, AK, ch. 2, ABC
KJNP-TV North Pole, AK, ch. 4, IND
KFXF Fairbanks, AK, ch. 7, Fox
*KUAC-TV Fairbanks, AK, ch. 9, ETV
KTVF Fairbanks, AK, ch. 11, NBC

DMA Counties	State	TV Households
Fairbanks-Plus	AK	31,640

Fargo-Valley City, ND (118)

DMA TV Households: 235,490
% of U.S. TV Households: .215

*KGFE Grand Forks, ND, ch. 2, ETV
KXJB-TV Valley City, ND, ch. 4, CBS
WDAY-TV Fargo, ND, ch. 6, ABC
KJRR Jamestown, ND, ch. 7, satellite to KVRR
WDAZ-TV Devils Lake, ND, ch. 8, satellite to WDAY-TV
KBRR Thief River Falls, MN, ch. 10, satellite to KVRR
KVLY-TV Fargo, ND, ch. 11, NBC
KNRR Pembina, ND, ch. 12, IND
*KFME Fargo, ND, ch. 13, ETV
KVRR Fargo, ND, ch. 15, Fox
*KJRE Ellendale, ND, ch. 19, satellite to KFME
KCPM Grand Forks, ND, ch. 27, IND

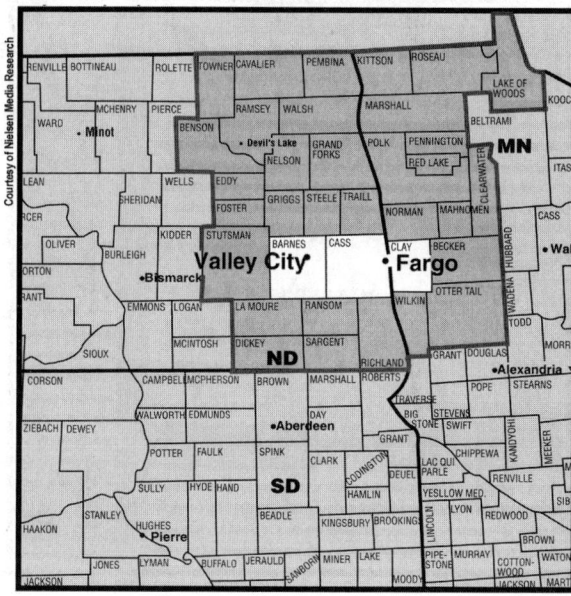

DMA Counties	State	TV Households	DMA Counties	State	TV Households
Becker	MN	12,430	Cavalier	ND	1,890
Clay	MN	19,510	Dickey	ND	2,180
Clearwater	MN	3,250	Eddy	ND	1,080
Kittson	MN	1,980	Foster	ND	1,390
Lake of the Woods	MN	1,820	Grand Forks	ND	25,260
Mahnomen	MN	1,980	Griggs	ND	1,090
Marshall	MN	4,050	La Moure	ND	1,890
Norman	MN	2,860	Nelson	ND	1,490
OtterTail	MN	22,990	Pembina	ND	3,370
Pennington	MN	5,620	Ramsey	ND	4,750
Polk	MN	12,060	Ransom	ND	2,370
RedLake	MN	1,750	Richland	ND	6,820
Roseau	MN	6,170	Sargent	ND	1,770
Wilkin	MN	2,700	Steele	ND	790
Barnes	ND	4,550	Stutsman	ND	8,820
Benson	ND	2,280	Towner	ND	1,090
Cass	ND	55,000	Traill	ND	3,260
Walsh	ND	4,760			

Broadcasting & Cable Yearbook 2006

Nielsen DMA Market Atlas

Flint-Saginaw-Bay City, MI (65)

DMA TV Households: 479,520
% of U.S. TV Households: .438

WNEM-TV Bay City, MI, ch. 5, CBS
WJRT-TV Flint, MI, ch. 12, ABC
***WCMU-TV** Mt. Pleasant, MI, ch. 14, ETV
***WDCP-TV** University Center, MI, ch. 19, ETV
WEYI-TV Saginaw, MI, ch. 25, NBC
***WFUM** Flint, MI, ch. 28, ETV
***WDCQ-TV** Bad Axe, MI, ch. 35, ETV
WBSF Bay City, MI, ch. 46, IND
WAQP Saginaw, MI, ch. 49, IND
WSMH Flint, MI, ch. 66, Fox

DMA Counties	State	TV Households
Arenac	MI	6,860
Bay	MI	44,870
Genesee	MI	176,460
Gladwin	MI	11,390
Gratiot	MI	14,680
Huron	MI	14,580
Iosco	MI	12,080
Isabella	MI	23,740
Midland	MI	33,340
Ogemaw	MI	9,240
Saginaw	MI	82,050
Shiawassee	MI	28,110
Tuscola	MI	22,120

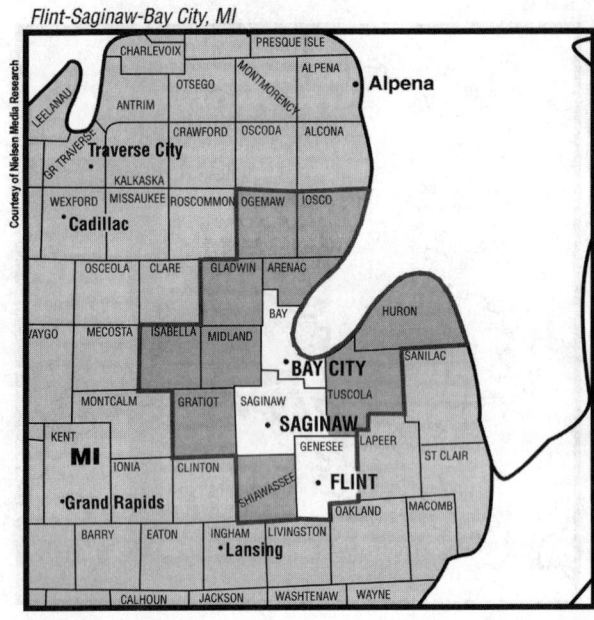

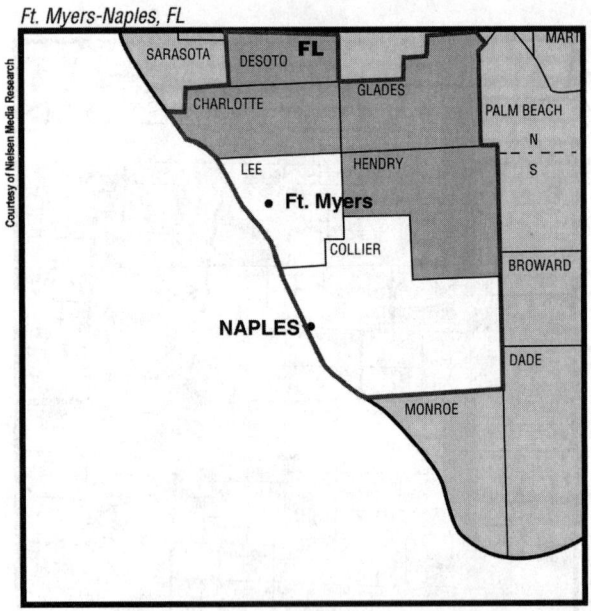

Ft. Myers-Naples, FL (68)

DMA TV Households: 444,130
% of U.S. TV Households: .405

WINK-TV Fort Myers, FL, ch. 11, CBS
WBBH-TV Fort Myers, FL, ch. 20, NBC
WZVN-TV Naples, FL, ch. 26, ABC
***WGCU** Fort Myers, FL, ch. 30, ETV
WFTX Cape Coral, FL, ch. 36, Fox
WTVK Naples, FL, ch. 46, IND
WRXY-TV Tice, FL, ch. 49, IND

DMA Counties	State	TV Households
Charlotte	FL	71,730
Collier	FL	124,020
De Soto	FL	11,180
Glades	FL	3,950
Hendry	FL	10,760
Lee	FL	222,490

Nielsen DMA Market Atlas

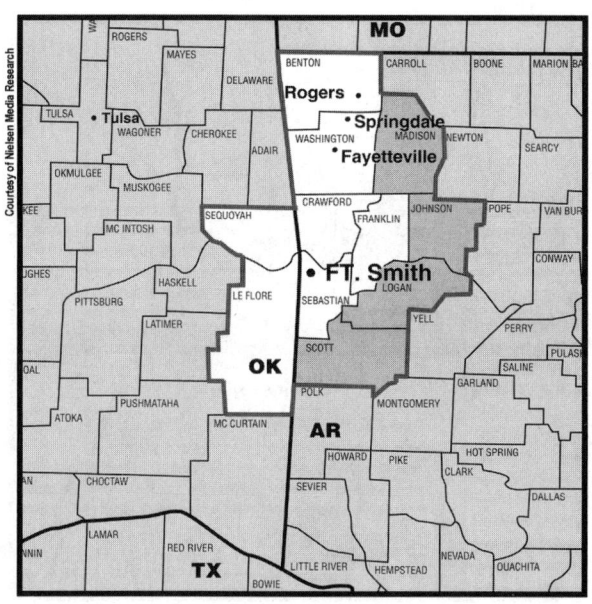

Ft. Smith-Fayetteville-Springdale-Rogers, AR (107)

DMA TV Households: 267,03
% of U.S. TV Households: .244

KFSM-TV Fort Smith, AR, ch. 5, CBS
*KAFT Fayetteville, AR, ch. 13, ETV
KFTA-TV Fort Smith, AR, ch. 24, NBC
KHOG-TV Fayetteville, AR, ch. 29, satellite to KHBS
KHBS Fort Smith, AR, ch. 40, ABC
KNWA-TV Rogers, AR, ch. 51, NBC
KSBN-TV Springdale, AR, ch. 57, IND

DMA Counties	State	TV Households
Benton	AR	66,810
Crawford	AR	20,920
Franklin	AR	6,980
Johnson	AR	8,940
Logan	AR	8,960
Madison	AR	5,360
Scott	AR	4,230
Sebastian	AR	45,900
Washington	AR	65,970
LeFlore	OK	18,070
Sequoyah	OK	14,890

Ft. Wayne, IN (104)

DMA TV Households: 271,890
% of U.S. TV Households: .248

WANE-TV Fort Wayne, IN, ch. 15, CBS
WPTA Fort Wayne, IN, ch. 21, ABC
WISE-TV Fort Wayne, IN, ch. 33, NBC
*WFWA Fort Wayne, IN, ch. 39, ETV
WFFT-TV Fort Wayne, IN, ch. 55, Fox
WINM Angola, IN, ch. 63, IND

DMA Counties	State	TV Households
Adams	IN	11,880
Allen	IN	135,440
De Kalb	IN	15,980
Huntington	IN	14,530
Jay	IN	8,390
Noble	IN	17,070
Steuben	IN	13,080
Wabash	IN	13,070
Wells	IN	10,500
Whitley	IN	12,510
Paulding	OH	7,690
Van Wert	OH	11,750

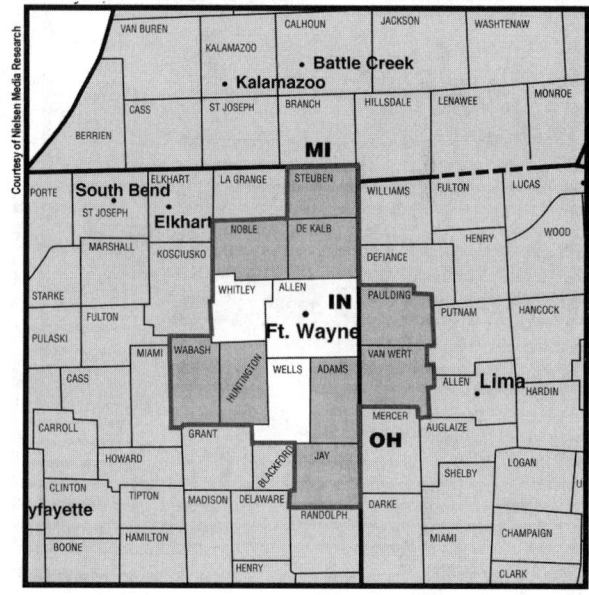

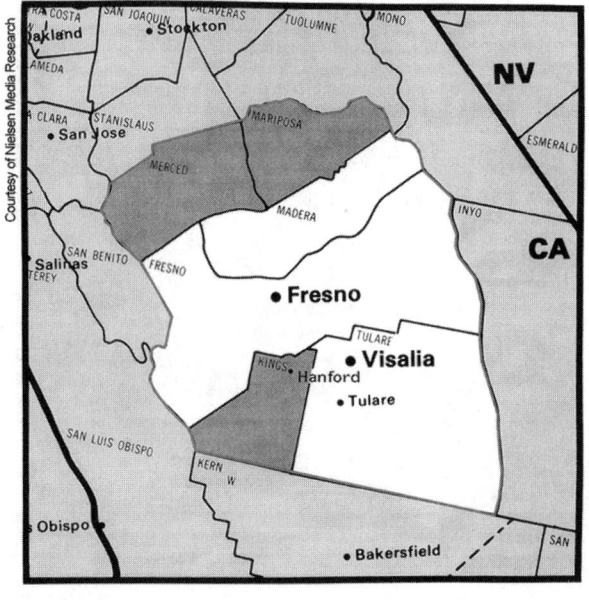

Fresno-Visalia, CA (58)

DMA TV Households: 527,770
% of U.S. TV Households: .482

*KVPT Fresno, CA, ch. 18, ETV
KFTV Hanford, CA, ch. 21, Univision
KSEE Fresno, CA, ch. 24, NBC
KMPH Visalia, CA, ch. 26, Fox
KFSN-TV Fresno, CA, ch. 30, ABC
KGMC Clovis, CA, ch. 43, IND
KGPE Fresno, CA, ch. 47, CBS
*KNXT Visalia, CA, ch. 49, ETV
KNSO Merced, CA, ch. 51, Telemundo
KAIL Fresno, CA, ch. 53, UPN
KFRE-TV Sanger, CA, ch. 59, WB
KTFF-TV Porterville, CA, ch. 61, TeleFutura

DMA Counties	State	TV Households
Fresno	CA	262,520
Kings	CA	36,690
Madera	CA	38,730
Mariposa	CA	6,700
Merced	CA	69,100
Tulare	CA	114,030

Broadcasting & Cable Yearbook 2006

Nielsen DMA Market Atlas

Gainesville, FL (162)

DMA TV Households: 116,670
% of U.S. TV Households: .106

*WUFT Gainesville, FL, ch. 5, ETV
WCJB Gainesville, FL, ch. 20, ABC
WOGX Ocala, FL, ch. 51, IND
WGFL High Springs, FL, ch. 53, CBS

DMA Counties	State	TV Households
Alachua	FL	90,970
Dixie	FL	5,390
Gilchrist	FL	5,530
Levy	FL	14,780

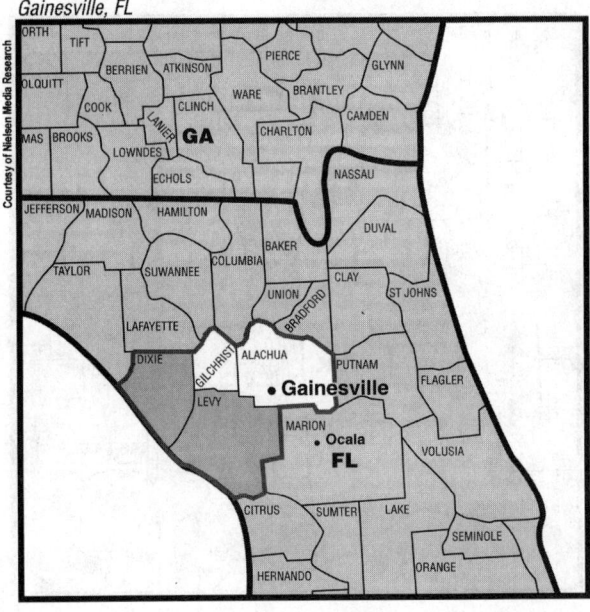

Glendive, MT (210)

DMA TV Households: 5,150
% of U.S. TV Households: .005

KXGN-TV Glendive, MT, ch. 5, CBS (NBC)

DMA Counties	State	TV Households
Dawson	MT	3,510
Fallon	MT	1,150
Prairie	MT	490

Grand Junction-Montrose, CO (189)

DMA TV Households: 63,650
% of U.S. TV Households: .058

KFQX Grand Junction, CO, ch. 4, Fox
KREX-TV Grand Junction, CO, ch. 5, CBS
KJCT Grand Junction, CO, ch. 8, ABC
KREY-TV Montrose, CO, ch. 10, satellite to KREX-TV
KKCO Grand Junction, CO, ch. 11, NBC
*KRMJ Grand Junction, CO, ch. 18, ETV

DMA Counties	State	TV Households
Mesa	CO	49,540
Montrose	CO	14,110

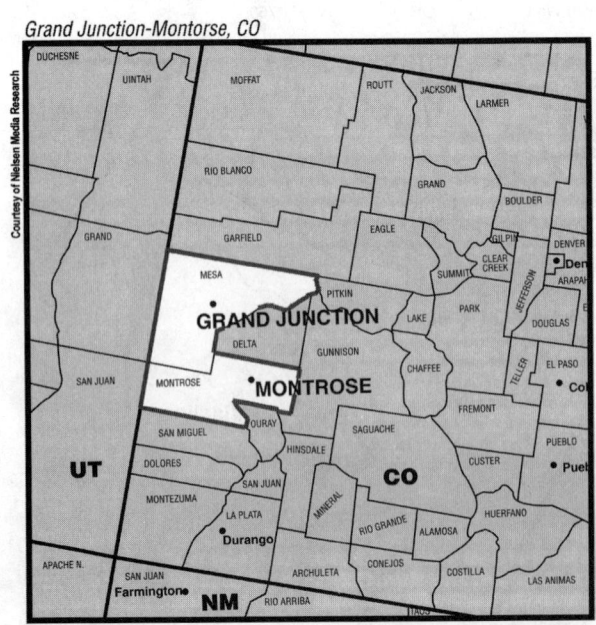

Nielsen DMA Market Atlas

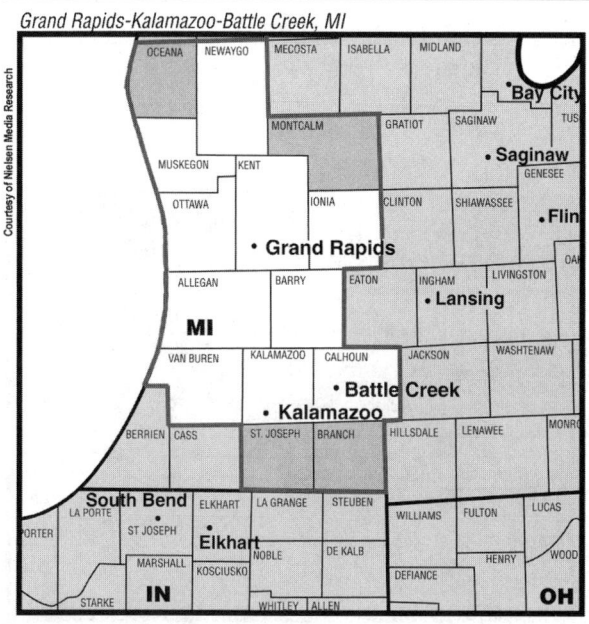
Grand Rapids-Kalamazoo-Battle Creek, MI

Grand Rapids-Kalamazoo-Battle Creek, MI (38)

DMA TV Households: 732,600
% of U.S. TV Households: .668

WWMT Kalamazoo, MI, ch. 3, CBS
WOOD-TV Grand Rapids, MI, ch. 8, NBC
WZZM-TV Grand Rapids, MI, ch. 13, ABC
WXMI Grand Rapids, MI, ch. 17, Fox
*WGVU-TV Grand Rapids, MI, ch. 35, ETV
WOTV Battle Creek, MI, ch. 41, ABC
WZPX Battle Creek, MI, ch. 43, PAX TV
*WGVK Kalamazoo, MI, ch. 52, ETV
WTLJ Muskegon, MI, ch. 54, IND
WLLA Kalamazoo, MI, ch. 64, IND

DMA Counties	State	TV Households	DMA Counties	State	TV Households
Allegan	MI	40,980	Montcalm	MI	23,120
Barry	MI	22,440	Muskegon	MI	65,420
Branch	MI	16,460	Newaygo	MI	18,230
Calhoun	MI	55,060	Oceana	MI	10,360
Ionia	MI	21,930	Ottawa	MI	87,820
Kalamazoo	MI	97,170	St. Joseph	MI	23,580
Kent	MI	220,730	Van Buren	MI	29,300

Great Falls, MT (188)

DMA TV Households: 64,650
% of U.S. TV Households: .059

KRTV Great Falls, MT, ch. 3, CBS
KFBB-TV Great Falls, MT, ch. 5, ABC
KBBJ Havre, MT, ch. 9, IND
KBAO Lewistown, MT, ch. 13, IND
KTGF Great Falls, MT, ch. 16, NBC
KLMN Great Falls, MT, ch. 26, Fox, PAX TV, UPN

DMA Counties	State	TV Households
Blaine	MT	2,300
Cascade	MT	31,540
Chouteau	MT	1,970
Fergus	MT	4,710
Glacier	MT	4,200
Hill	MT	6,210
Judith Basin	MT	850
Liberty	MT	780
Phillips	MT	1,630
Pondera	MT	2,230
Teton	MT	2,380
Toole	MT	1,910
Valley	MT	2,940

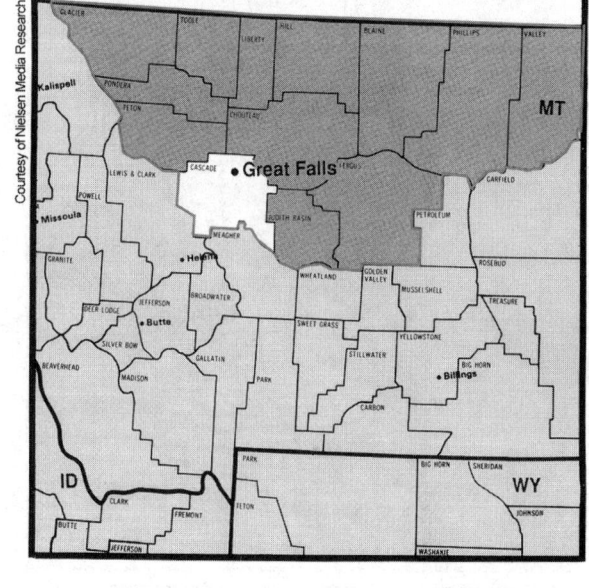

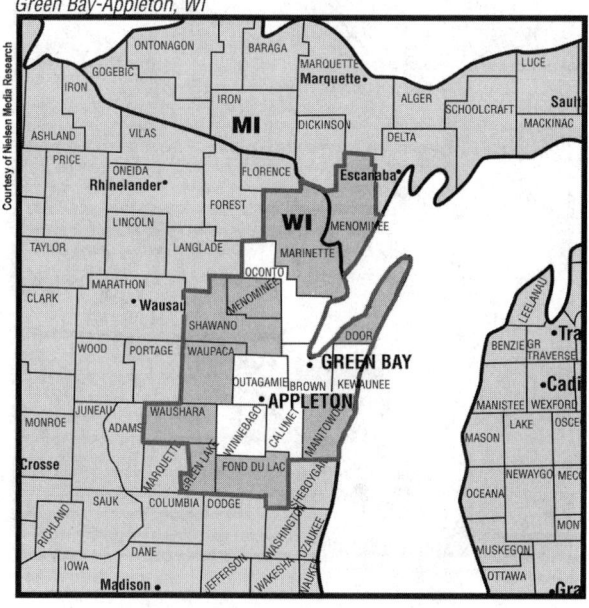
Green Bay-Appleton, WI

Green Bay-Appleton, WI (69)

DMA TV Households: 433,640
% of U.S. TV Households: .396

WBAY-TV Green Bay, WI, ch. 2, ABC
WFRV-TV Green Bay, WI, ch. 5, CBS
WLUK-TV Green Bay, WI, ch. 11, Fox
WIWB Suring, WI, ch. 14, IND
WGBA Green Bay, WI, ch. 26, NBC
WACY Appleton, WI, ch. 32, IND
*WPNE Green Bay, WI, ch. 38, ETV
WFXS Wittenberg, WI, ch. 55, Fox
WWAZ-TV Fond du Lac, WI, ch. 68, IND

DMA Counties	State	TV Households	DMA Counties	State	TV Households
Menominee	MI	10,700	Marinette	WI	18,330
Brown	WI	93,660	Menominee	WI	1,400
Calumet	WI	17,090	Oconto	WI	15,210
Door	WI	12,680	Outagamie	WI	65,680
Fond du Lac	WI	38,670	Shawano	WI	16,390
Green Lake	WI	7,870	Waupaca	WI	20,740
Kewaunee	WI	8,060	Waushara	WI	9,950
Manitowoc	WI	33,610	Winnebago	WI	63,600

Broadcasting & Cable Yearbook 2006

Nielsen DMA Market Atlas

Greensboro-High Point-Winston Salem, NC (48)

DMA TV Households: 648,860
% of U.S. TV Households: .592

WFMY-TV Greensboro, NC, ch. 2, CBS
WGHP High Point, NC, ch. 8, Fox
WXII-TV Winston-Salem, NC, ch. 12, NBC
WGPX Burlington, NC, ch. 16, PAX TV
WTWB-TV Lexington, NC, ch. 20, WB
*****WUNL-TV** Winston-Salem, NC, ch. 26, ETV
WXLV-TV Winston-Salem, NC, ch. 45, ABC
WUPN-TV Greensboro, NC, ch. 48, IND
WLXI-TV Greensboro, NC, ch. 61, IND

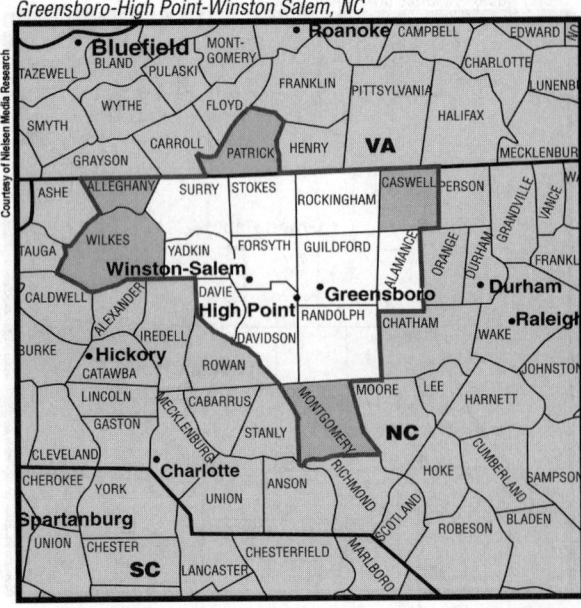

Greensboro-High Point-Winston Salem, NC

DMA Counties	State	TV Households	DMA Counties	State	TV Households
Alamance	NC	54,570	Randolph	NC	52,970
Alleghany	NC	4,850	Rockingham	NC	37,880
Caswell	NC	8,880	Stokes	NC	18,150
Davidson	NC	61,080	Surry	NC	29,140
Davie	NC	14,890	Wilkes	NC	27,890
Forsyth	NC	129,830	Yadkin	NC	15,050
Guilford	NC	175,3500	Patrick	VA	8,170
Montgomery	NC	10,160			

Greenville-New Bern-Washington, NC

Greenville-New Bern-Washington, NC (105)

DMA TV Households: 270,200
% of U.S. TV Households: .247

*****WUND-TV** Columbia, NC, ch. 2, ETV
WITN-TV Washington, NC, ch. 7, NBC
WFXI Morehead City, NC, ch. 8, Fox
WNCT-TV Greenville, NC, ch. 9, CBS
WCTI New Bern, NC, ch. 12, ABC
WYDO Greenville, NC, ch. 14, Fox
*****WUNM-TV** Jacksonville, NC, ch. 19, ETV
*****WUNK-TV** Greenville, NC, ch. 25, ETV
WPXU-TV Jacksonville, NC, ch. 35, IND
WEPX Greenville, NC, ch. 38, IND

DMA Counties	State	TV Households	DMA Counties	State	TV Households
Beaufort	NC	19,170	Lenoir	NC	23,630
Bertie	NC	7,760	Martin	NC	10,000
Carteret	NC	26,490	Onslow	NC	46,660
Craven	NC	35,640	Pamlico	NC	5,130
Duplin	NC	19,230	Pitt	NC	56,230
Greene	NC	7,330	Tyrrell	NC	1,540
Hyde	NC	1,950	Washington	NC	5,410
Jones	NC	4,030			

Greenville-Spartanburg, SC-Asheville, NC-Anderson, SC (35)

DMA TV Households: 813,210
% of U.S. TV Households: .742

WYFF Greenville, SC, ch. 4, NBC
WSPA-TV Spartanburg, SC, ch. 7, CBS
WLOS Asheville, NC, ch. 13, ABC
WGGS-TV Greenville, SC, ch. 16, IND
WHNS Greenville, SC, ch. 21, Fox
*****WNTV** Greenville, SC, ch. 29, ETV
WNEG-TV Toccoa, GA, ch. 32, IND
*****WUNF-TV** Asheville, NC, ch. 33, ETV
*****WNEH** Greenwood, SC, ch. 38, ETV
WBSC-TV Anderson, SC, ch. 40, WB
*****WRET-TV** Spartanburg, SC, ch. 49, ETV
WASV-TV Asheville, NC, ch. 62, UPN

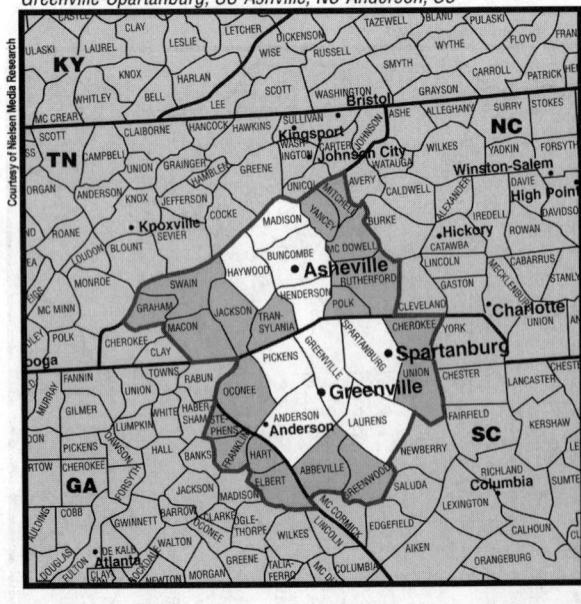

Greenville-Spartanburg, SC-Ashville, NC-Anderson, SC

DMA Counties	State	TV Households	DMA Counties	State	TV Households
Elbert	GA	8,240	Rutherford	NC	25,830
Franklin	GA	8,380	Swain	NC	5,280
Hart	GA	9,640	Transylvania	NC	12,720
Stephens	GA	9,900	Yancey	NC	7,050
Buncombe	NC	88,360	Abbeville	SC	10,220
Graham	NC	3,480	Anderson	SC	70,450
Haywood	NC	24,200	Cherokee	SC	21,620
Henderson	NC	40,180	Greenville	SC	159,320
Jackson	NC	13,860	Greenwood	SC	26,720
Macon	NC	13,420	Laurens	SC	27,380
Madison	NC	8,130	Oconee	SC	29,380
McDowell	NC	16,940	Pickens	SC	42,740
Mitchell	NC	6,660	Spartanburg	SC	103,100
Polk	NC	8,110	Union	SC	12,180

Broadcasting & Cable Yearbook 2006

Nielsen DMA Market Atlas

Greenwood-Greenville, MS (183)

DMA TV Households: 78,160
% of U.S. TV Households: .071

WABG-TV Greenwood, MS, ch. 6, ABC
WXVT Greenville, MS, ch. 15, CBS
***WMAO-TV** Greenwood, MS, ch. 23, ETV
***WMAI** Cleveland, MS, ch. 31, ETV

DMA Counties	State	TV Households
Chicot	AR	4,930
Bolivar	MS	13,280
Carroll	MS	4,000
Grenada	MS	8,700
Leflore	MS	12,220
Sunflower	MS	8,940
Tallahatchie	MS	5,010
Washington	MS	21,080

Harlingen-Weslaco-Brownsville-McAllen, TX (93)

DMA TV Households: 312,300
% of U.S. TV Households: .285

KGBT-TV Harlingen, TX, ch. 4, CBS
KRGV-TV Weslaco, TX, ch. 5, ABC
KVEO Brownsville, TX, ch. 23, NBC
KTLM Rio Grande City, TX, ch. 40, Telemundo
***KLUJ-TV** Harlingen, TX, ch. 44, ETV
KNVO McAllen, TX, ch. 48, Univision
***KMBH** Harlingen, TX, ch. 60, ETV

DMA Counties	State	TV Households
Cameron	TX	108,910
Hidalgo	TX	182,130
Starr	TX	15,700
Willacy	TX	5,560

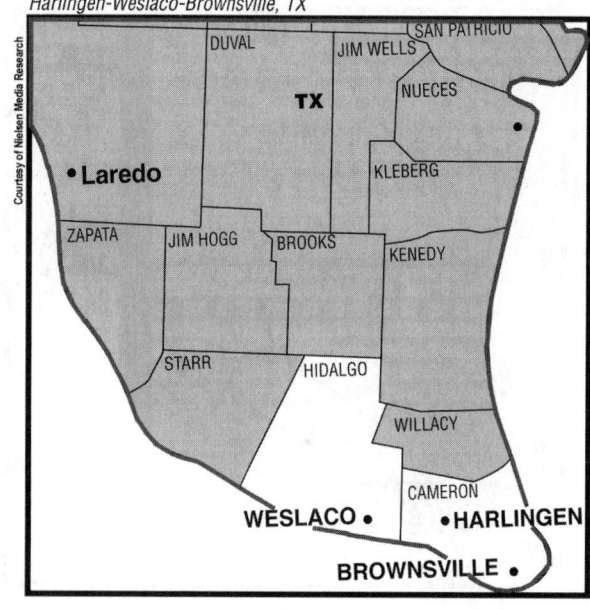

Harrisburg-Lancaster-Lebanon-York, PA (42)

DMA TV Households: 702,590
% of U.S. TV Households: .641

WGAL Lancaster, PA, ch. 8, NBC
WLYH-TV Lancaster, PA, ch. 15, IND
WHP-TV Harrisburg, PA, ch. 21, CBS
WHTM-TV Harrisburg, PA, ch. 27, ABC
***WITF-TV** Harrisburg, PA, ch. 33, ETV
WPMT York, PA, ch. 43, Fox
WGCB-TV Red Lion, PA, ch. 49, IND

DMA Counties	State	TV Households
Adams	PA	36,860
Cumberland	PA	87,800
Dauphin	PA	104,100
Juniata	PA	8,700
Lancaster	PA	173,290
Lebanon	PA	47,480
Mifflin	PA	17,830
Perry	PA	17,220
York	PA	157,270

Broadcasting & Cable Yearbook 2006

Nielsen DMA Market Atlas

Harrisonburg, VA (181)

DMA TV Households: 85,550
% of U.S. TV Households: .078

WHSV-TV Harrisonburg, VA, ch. 3, ABC
*****WVPT** Staunton, VA, ch. 51, ETV

DMA Counties	State	TV Households
Augusta	VA	43,940
Rockingham	VA	38,570
Pendleton	WV	3,040

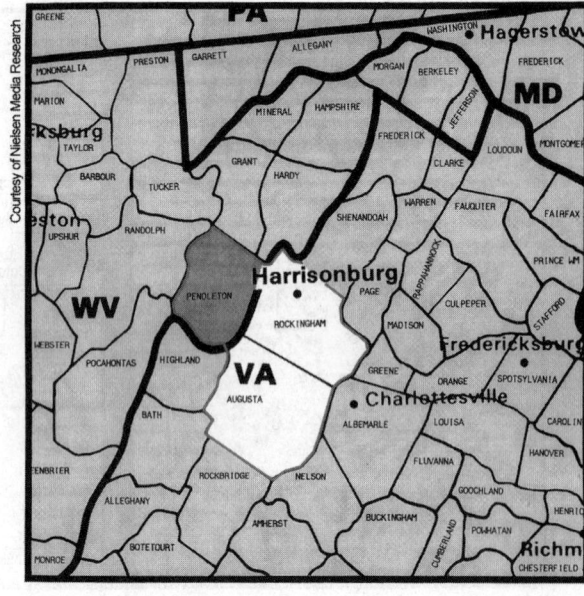

Hartford & New Haven, CT (27)

DMA TV Households: 1,017,530
% of U.S. TV Households: .928

WFSB Hartford, CT, ch. 3, CBS
WTNH-TV New Haven, CT, ch. 8, ABC
WUVN Hartford, CT, ch. 18, Univision
WTXX Waterbury, CT, ch. 20, WB
*****WEDH** Hartford, CT, ch. 24, ETV
WHPX New London, CT, ch. 26, PAX TV
WVIT New Britain, CT, ch. 30, NBC
*****WEDN** Norwich, CT, ch. 53, ETV
WCTX New Haven, CT, ch. 59, UPN
WTIC-TV Hartford, CT, ch. 61, Fox
*****WEDY** New Haven, CT, ch. 65, ETV

DMA Counties	State	TV Households
Hartford	CT	345,560
Litchfield	CT	74,760
Middlesex	CT	65,580
New Haven	CT	329,620
New London	CT	103,090
Tolland	CT	55,350
Windham	CT	43,570

Hattiesburg-Laurel, MS (168)

DMA TV Households: 104,800
% of U.S. TV Households: .094

WDAM-TV Laurel, MS, ch. 7, NBC
WHLT Hattiesburg, MS, ch. 22, CBS

DMA Counties	State	TV Households
Covington	MS	7,660
Forrest	MS	23,310
Jasper	MS	6,890
Jones	MS	24,620
Lamar	MS	15,810
Marion	MS	9,060
Perry	MS	4,510
Wayne	MS	7,940

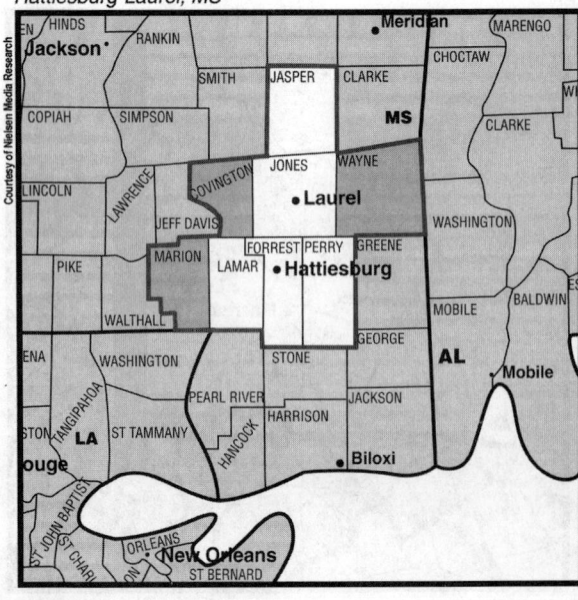

Broadcasting & Cable Yearbook 2006

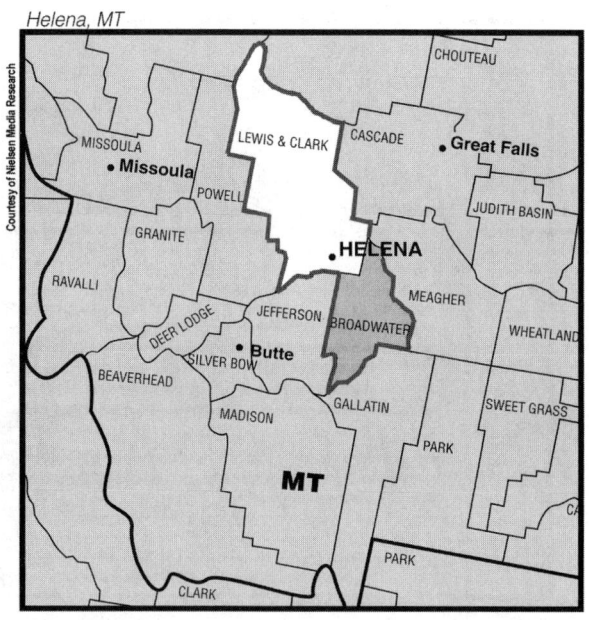

Helena (206)

DMA TV Households: 25,360
% of U.S. TV Households: .023

KMTF Helena, MT, ch. 10, PAX TV
KTVH Helena, MT, ch. 12, NBC

DMA Counties	State	TV Households
Broadwater	MT	1,710
Lewis and Clark	MT	23,650

Honolulu, HI (71)

DMA TV Households: 417,120
% of U.S. TV Households: .381

KHON-TV Honolulu, ch. 2, Fox
KITV Honolulu, ch. 4, ABC
KFVE Honolulu, ch. 5, WB
KGMB Honolulu, ch. 9, CBS
***KHET** Honolulu, ch. 11, ETV
KHNL Honolulu, ch. 13, NBC
KWHE Honolulu, ch. 14, IND
KIKU Honolulu, ch. 20, UPN
KAAH-TV Honolulu, ch. 26, IND
KBFD Honolulu, ch. 32, IND
***KALO** Honolulu, ch. 38, ETV
***KWBN** Honolulu, ch. 44, ETV
KKAI Kailua, HI, ch. 50, IND
KMGT Waimanalo, HI, ch. 56, IND

DMA Counties	State	TV Households
Hawaii	HI	55,610
Honolulu	HI	295,870
Kauai	HI	21,450
Maui	HI	44,190

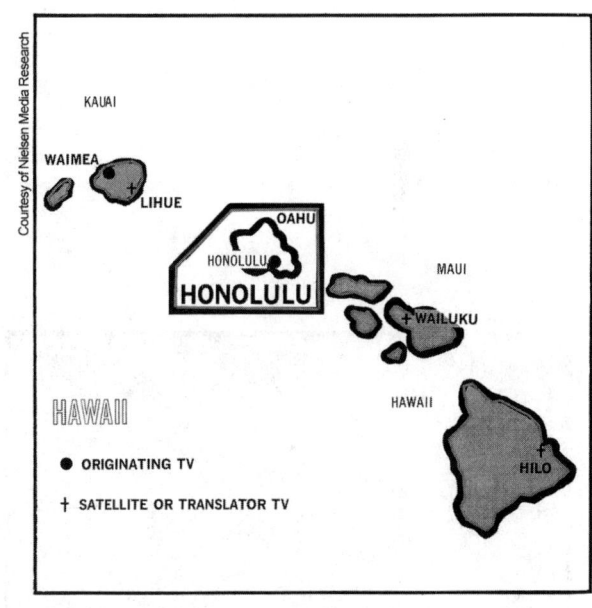

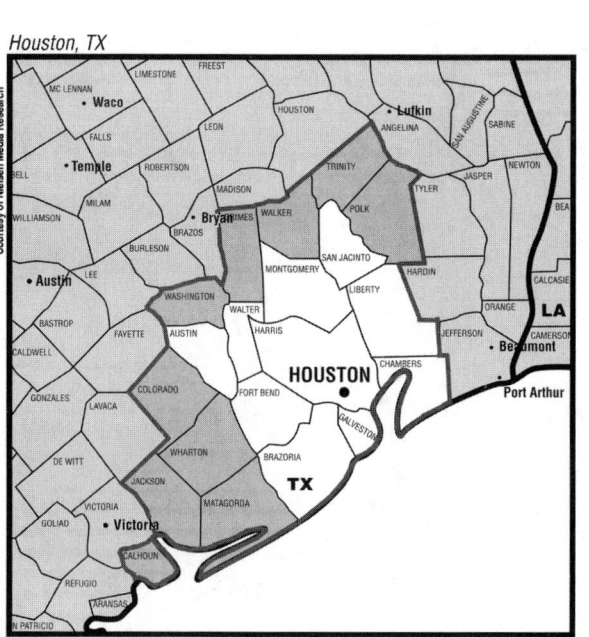

Houston (11)

DMA TV Households: 1,902,810
% of U.S. TV Households: 1.736

KPRC-TV Houston, ch. 2, NBC
***KUHT** Houston, ch. 8, ETV
KHOU-TV Houston, ch. 11, CBS
KTRK-TV Houston, ch. 13, ABC
***KETH-TV** Houston, ch. 14, ETV
KTXH Houston, ch. 20, IND
***KLTJ** Galveston, TX, ch. 22, ETV
KRIV-TV Houston, ch. 26, Fox
KHWB Houston, ch. 39, WB
KXLN-TV Rosenberg, TX, ch. 45, Univision
KTMD Galveston, TX, ch. 47, Telemundo
KPXB Conroe, TX, ch. 49, IND
KNWS-TV Katy, TX, ch. 51, IND
KTBU Conroe, TX, ch. 55, IND
KAZH Baytown, TX, ch. 57, Azteca America
KZJL Houston, ch. 61, IND
KFTH-TV Alvin, TX, ch. 67, TeleFutura

DMA Counties	State	TV Households	DMA Counties	State	TV Households
Austin	TX	9,500	Liberty	TX	25,160
Brazoria	TX	92,680	Matagorda	TX	13,900
Calhoun	TX	7,360	Montgomery	TX	126,450
Chambers	TX	10,440	Polk	TX	16,630
Colorado	TX	7,830	San Jacinto	TX	8,850
Fort Bend	TX	138,840	Walker	TX	18,730
Galveston	TX	103,310	Waller	TX	11,620
Grimes	TX	8,370	Washington	TX	11,400
Harris	TX	1,265,920	Wharton	TX	14,980
Jackson	TX	5,080			

Nielsen DMA Market Atlas

Huntsville-Decatur (Florence), AL (84)

DMA TV Households: 370,160
% of U.S. TV Households: .338

WHDF Florence, AL, ch. 15, NBC
WHNT-TV Huntsville, AL, ch. 19, CBS
***WHIQ** Huntsville, AL, ch. 25, ETV
WYLE Florence, AL, ch. 26, IND
WAAY-TV Huntsville, AL, ch. 31, ABC
***WFIQ** Florence, AL, ch. 36, ETV
WAFF Huntsville, AL, ch. 48, NBC
WZDX Huntsville, AL, ch. 54, IND

DMA Counties	State	TV Households
Colbert	AL	22,710
De Kalb	AL	26,060
Franklin	AL	11,960
Jackson	AL	22,030
Lauderdale	AL	36,350
Lawrence	AL	13,790
Limestone	AL	26,420
Madison	AL	119,620
Marshall	AL	33,370
Morgan	AL	45,040
Lincoln	TN	12,810

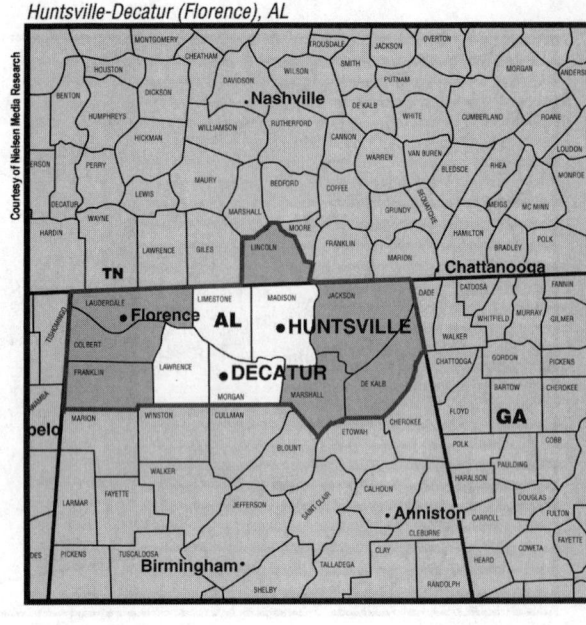

Huntsville-Decatur (Florence), AL

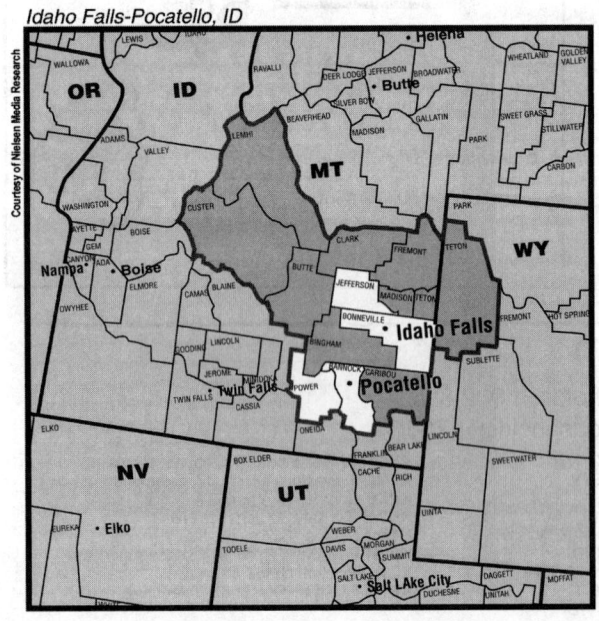

Idaho Falls-Pocatello, ID

Idaho Falls-Pocatello, ID (164)

DMA TV Households: 112,700
% of U.S. TV Households: .103

KIDK Idaho Falls, ID, ch. 3, CBS
KPVI Pocatello, ID, ch. 6, ABC
KIFI-TV Idaho Falls, ID, ch. 8, NBC
***KISU-TV** Pocatello, ID, ch. 10, ETV
KPIF Pocatello, ID, ch. 15, IND
KFXP Pocatello, ID, ch. 31, Fox

DMA Counties	State	TV Households
Bannock	ID	27,290
Bingham	ID	14,100
Bonneville	ID	31,400
Butte	ID	1,070
Caribou	ID	2,550
Clark	ID	290
Custer	ID	1,550
Fremont	ID	4,040
Jefferson	ID	6,500
Lemhi	ID	3,090
Madison	ID	8,240
Power	ID	2,440
Teton	ID	2,630
Teton	WY	7,510

Broadcasting & Cable Yearbook 2006

Nielsen DMA Market Atlas

Indianapolis, IN

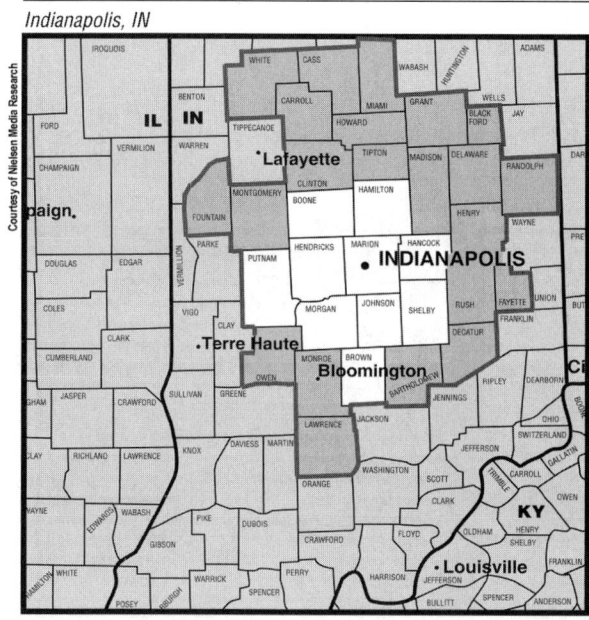

Indianapolis (25)

DMA TV Households: 1,053,020
% of U.S. TV Households: .961

WTTV Bloomington, IN, ch. 4, WB
WRTV Indianapolis, ch. 6, ABC
WISH-TV Indianapolis, ch. 8, CBS
WTHR Indianapolis, ch. 13, NBC
***WFYI** Indianapolis, ch. 20, ETV
WNDY-TV Marion, IN, ch. 23, UPN
WTTK Kokomo, IN, ch. 29, satellite to WTTV
***WTIU** Bloomington, IN, ch. 30, ETV
WHMB-TV Indianapolis, ch. 40, IND
WCLJ-TV Bloomington, IN, ch. 42, IND
***WIPB** Muncie, IN, ch. 49, ETV
WXIN Indianapolis, ch. 59, Fox
WIPX Bloomington, IN, ch. 63, IND
***WDTI** Indianapolis, ch. 69, ETV

DMA Counties	State	TV Households	DMA Counties	State	TV Households
Bartholomew	IN	28,590	Howard	IN	35,610
Blackford	IN	5,690	Johnson	IN	47,130
Boone	IN	18,870	Lawrence	IN	19,130
Brown	IN	5,990	Madison	IN	52,780
Carroll	IN	7,740	Marion	IN	355,540
Cass	IN	15,350	Miami	IN	14,050
Clinton	IN	12,450	Monroe	IN	48,050
Decatur	IN	9,580	Montgomery	IN	14,630
Delaware	IN	46,490	Morgan	IN	25,880
Fayette	IN	10,090	Owen	IN	8,910
Fountain	IN	6,930	Putnam	IN	12,710
Grant	IN	27,770	Randolph	IN	10,650
Hamilton	IN	84,040	Rush	IN	6,920
Hancock	IN	23,690	Shelby	IN	16,890
Hendricks	IN	45,810	Tipton	IN	6,460
Henry	IN	19,210	White	IN	9,390

Jackson, MS (91)

DMA TV Households: 327,670
% of U.S. TV Households: .299

WLBT Jackson, MS, ch. 3, NBC
WJTV Jackson, MS, ch. 12, CBS
WAPT Jackson, MS, ch. 16, ABC
***WMAU-TV** Bude, MS, ch. 17, ETV
***WMPN-TV** Jackson, MS, ch. 29, ETV
***WMYC** Yazoo City, MS, ch. 32, ETV
WRBJ Magee, MS, ch. 34, IND
WUFX Vicksburg, MS, ch. 35, IND
WDBD Jackson, MS, ch. 40, Fox
WNTZ Natchez, MS, ch. 48, Fox

DMA Counties	State	TV Households	DMA Counties	State	TV Households
Adams	MS	13,250	Leake	MS	7,940
Attala	MS	7,580	Lincoln	MS	12,650
Claiborne	MS	3,360	Madison	MS	29,900
Copiah	MS	10,250	Pike	MS	14,850
Franklin	MS	3,100	Rankin	MS	48,650
Hinds	MS	89,800	Scott	MS	9,990
Holmes	MS	7,040	Sharkey	MS	2,150
Humphreys	MS	3,520	Simpson	MS	10,210
Issaquena	MS	590	Smith	MS	5,930
Jeff Davis	MS	5,150	Walthall	MS	5,560
Jefferson	MS	3,320	Warren	MS	18,530
Lawrence	MS	5,180	Yazoo	MS	9,170

Jackson, MS

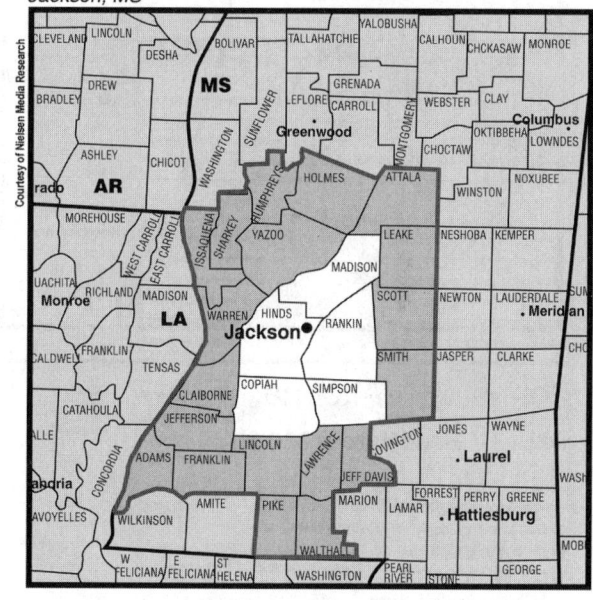

Broadcasting & Cable Yearbook 2006

Nielsen DMA Market Atlas

Jackson, TN (174)

DMA TV Households: 94,770
% of U.S. TV Households: .086

WBBJ-TV Jackson, TN, ch. 7, ABC
*WLJT-TV Lexington, TN, ch. 11, ETV
WJKT Jackson, TN, ch. 16, satellite to WLMT

DMA Counties	State	TV Households
Carroll	TN	11,670
Chester	TN	5,720
Hardin	TN	10,720
Henderson	TN	10,530
Madison	TN	36,600

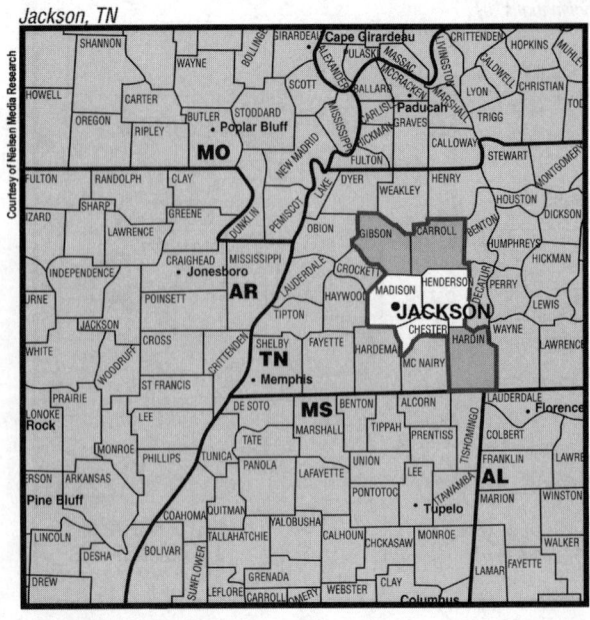

Jacksonville, FL (52)

DMA TV Households: 613,000
% of U.S. TV Households: .559

WJXT Jacksonville, FL, ch. 4, IND
*WJCT Jacksonville, FL, ch. 7, ETV
*WXGA-TV Waycross, GA, ch. 8, ETV
WTLV Jacksonville, FL, ch. 12, NBC
WJWB Jacksonville, FL, ch. 17, WB
WPXC-TV Brunswick, GA, ch. 21, PAX TV
WJXX Orange Park, FL, ch. 25, ABC
WAWS Jacksonville, FL, ch. 30, Fox
WTEV-TV Jacksonville, FL, ch. 47, CBS
*WJEB-TV Jacksonville, FL, ch. 59, ETV

DMA Counties	State	TV Households	DMA Counties	State	TV Households
Baker	FL	7,730	Union	FL	3,500
Bradford	FL	9,050	Brantley	GA	6,020
Clay	FL	59,130	Camden	GA	15,400
Columbia	FL	22,940	Charlton	GA	3,650
Duval	FL	323,870	Glynn	GA	29,090
Nassau	FL	24,580	Pierce	GA	6,440
Putnam	FL	28,560	Ware	GA	13,670
St. Johns	FL	59,370			

Johnstown-Altoona, PA (97)

DMA TV Households: 300,850
% of U.S. TV Households: .275

*WPSX-TV Clearfield, PA, ch. 3, ETV
WJAC-TV Johnstown, PA, ch. 6, NBC
WWCP-TV Johnstown, PA, ch. 8, Fox
WTAJ-TV Altoona, PA, ch. 10, CBS
WATM-TV Altoona, PA, ch. 23, ABC
WKBS-TV Altoona, PA, ch. 47, IND

DMA Counties	State	TV Households
Bedford	PA	19,820
Blair	PA	51,230
Cambria	PA	60,470
Cameron	PA	2,380
Centre	PA	52,230
Clearfield	PA	33,200
Elk	PA	14,150
Huntingdon	PA	16,930
Jefferson	PA	18,740
Somerset	PA	31,700

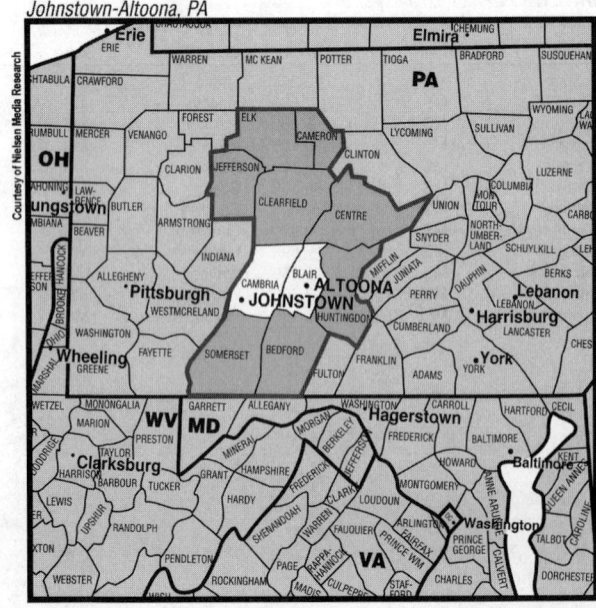

Broadcasting & Cable Yearbook 2006

Nielsen DMA Market Atlas

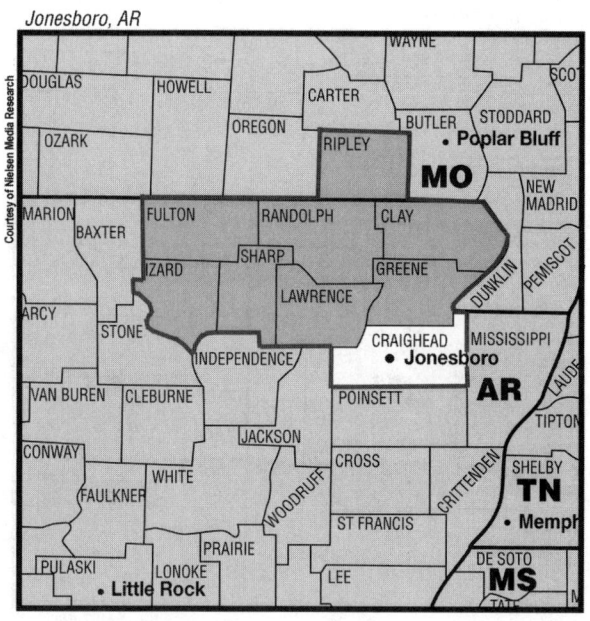

Jonesboro, AR (179)

DMA TV Households: 93,100
% of U.S. TV Households: .085

KAIT Jonesboro, AR, ch. 8, ABC
***KTEJ** Jonesboro, AR, ch. 19, ETV
KVTJ Jonesboro, AR, ch. 48, IND

DMA Counties	State	TV Households
Clay	AR	7,010
Craighead	AR	33,820
Greene	AR	15,370
Izard	AR	5,380
Lawrence	AR	6,890
Randolph	AR	7,280
Sharp	AR	7,230
Ripley	MO	5,420

Joplin, MO-Pittsburg, KS (146)

% of U.S. TV Households: .139
DMA TV Households: 152,310

KOAM-TV Pittsburg, KS, ch. 7, CBS
KODE-TV Joplin, MO, ch. 12, ABC
KFJX Pittsburg, KS, ch. 14, Fox
KSNF Joplin, MO, ch. 16, NBC
***KOZJ** Joplin, MO, ch. 26, ETV

DMA Counties	State	TV Households
Allen	KS	5,530
Bourbon	KS	5,830
Cherokee	KS	8,310
Crawford	KS	15,410
Labette	KS	8,860
Neosho	KS	6,440
Wilson	KS	3,860
Woodson	KS	1,510
Barton	MO	4,980
Jasper	MO	42,700
McDonald	MO	8,030
Newton	MO	20,820
Vernon	MO	7,720
Ottawa	OK	12,310

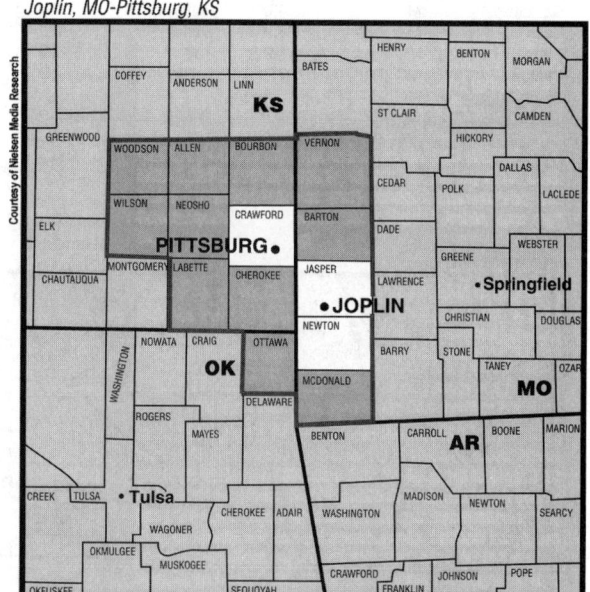

Juneau, AK (207)

DMA TV Households: 25,070
of U.S. TV Households: .023

***KTOO-TV** Juneau, AK, ch. 3, ETV
KUBD Ketchikan, AK, ch. 4, IND
KJUD Juneau, AK, ch. 8, ABC
KTNL Sitka, AK, ch. 13, CBS

DMA Counties	State	TV Households
Juneau	AK	25,070

Broadcasting & Cable Yearbook 2006

Nielsen DMA Market Atlas

Kansas City, MO (31)

DMA TV Households: 894,580
% of U.S. TV Households: .816

WDAF-TV Kansas City, MO, ch. 4, Fox
KCTV Kansas City, MO, ch. 5, CBS
***KMOS-TV** Sedalia, MO, ch. 6, ETV
KMBC-TV Kansas City, MO, ch. 9, ABC
***KCPT** Kansas City, MO, ch. 19, ETV
KCWE Kansas City, MO, ch. 29, UPN
KMCI Lawrence, KS, ch. 38, IND
KSHB-TV Kansas City, MO, ch. 41, NBC
KPXE Kansas City, MO, ch. 50, PAX TV
KSMO-TV Kansas City, MO, ch. 62, WB

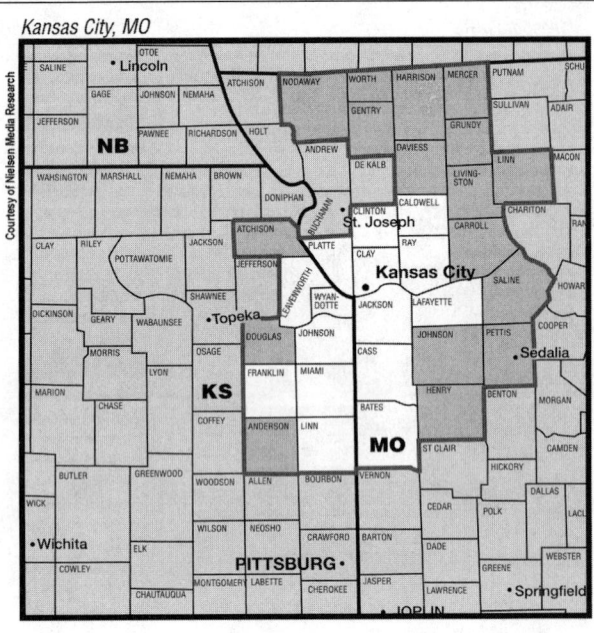

DMA Counties	State	TV Households	DMA Counties	State	TV Households
Anderson	KS	3,240	Daviess	MO	3,090
Atchison	KS	6,250	Gentry	MO	2,480
Douglas	KS	39,790	Grundy	MO	4,320
Franklin	KS	9,740	Harrison	MO	3,500
Johnson	KS	194,720	Henry	MO	9,310
Leavenworth	KS	24,820	Jackson	MO	267,970
Linn	KS	3,850	Johnson	MO	18,210
Miami	KS	10,630	Lafayette	MO	12,480
Wyandotte	KS	58,360	Linn	MO	5,360
Bates	MO	6,480	Livingston	MO	5,630
Caldwell	MO	3,670	Mercer	MO	1,480
Carroll	MO	4,030	Pettis	MO	15,220
Cass	MO	33,940	Platte	MO	32,790
Clay	MO	78,970	Ray	MO	9,130
Clinton	MO	7,790	Saline	MO	8,410
Worth	MO	890			

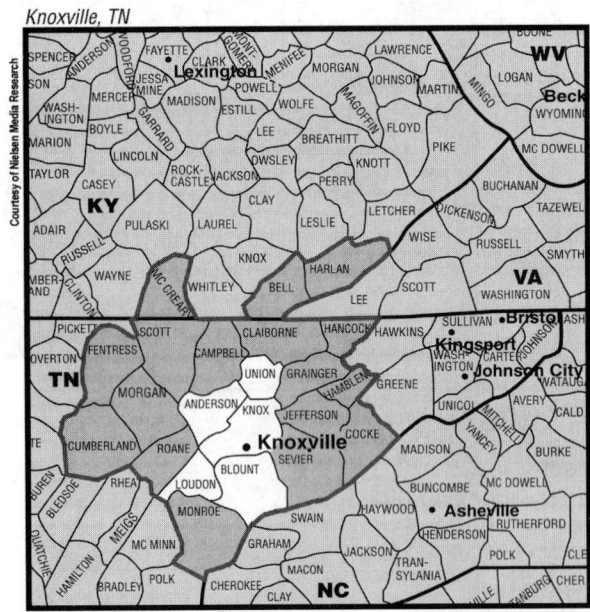

Knoxville, TN (59)

DMA TV Households: 513,630
% of U.S. TV Households: .469

***WETP-TV** Sneedville, TN, ch. 2, ETV
WATE-TV Knoxville, TN, ch. 6, ABC
WMAK Knoxville, TN, ch. 7, IND
WVLT-TV Knoxville, TN, ch. 8, CBS
WBIR-TV Knoxville, TN, ch. 10, NBC
***WKOP-TV** Knoxville, TN, ch. 15, ETV
WBXX-TV Crossville, TN, ch. 20, WB
WTNZ Knoxville, TN, ch. 43, Fox
WAGV Harlan, KY, ch. 44, IND
WVLR Tazewell, TN, ch. 48, IND
WPXK Jellico, TN, ch. 54, PAX TV

DMA Counties	State	TV Households
Bell	KY	12,500
Harlan	KY	13,340
McCreary	KY	6,780
Anderson	TN	30,610
Blount	TN	46,400
Campbell	TN	16,810
Claiborne	TN	12,440
Cocke	TN	14,640
Cumberland	TN	21,590
Fentress	TN	6,990
Grainger	TN	8,870
Hamblen	TN	23,830
Hancock	TN	2,850
Jefferson	TN	18,670
Knox	TN	166,080
Loudon	TN	17,830
Monroe	TN	16,850
Morgan	TN	7,120
Roane	TN	21,940
Scott	TN	8,820
Sevier	TN	31,260
Union	TN	7,410

Broadcasting & Cable Yearbook 2006

La Crosse-Eau Claire, WI (127)

DMA TV Households: 206,490
% of U.S. TV Households: .188

WKBT La Crosse, WI, ch. 8, CBS
WEAU-TV Eau Claire, WI, ch. 13, NBC
WQOW-TV Eau Claire, WI, ch. 18, ABC
WXOW-TV La Crosse, WI, ch. 19, ABC
WLAX La Crosse, WI, ch. 25, Fox
***WHLA-TV** La Crosse, WI, ch. 31, ETV
WEUX Chippewa Falls, WI, ch. 48, IND

DMA Counties	State	TV Households
Houston	MN	7,910
Winona	MN	18,630
Buffalo	WI	5,600
Chippewa	WI	23,050
Clark	WI	12,010
Crawford	WI	6,770
Eau Claire	WI	37,630
Jackson	WI	7,430
La Crosse	WI	43,020
Monroe	WI	16,110
Rusk	WI	6,120
Trempealeau	WI	11,290
Vernon	WI	10,920

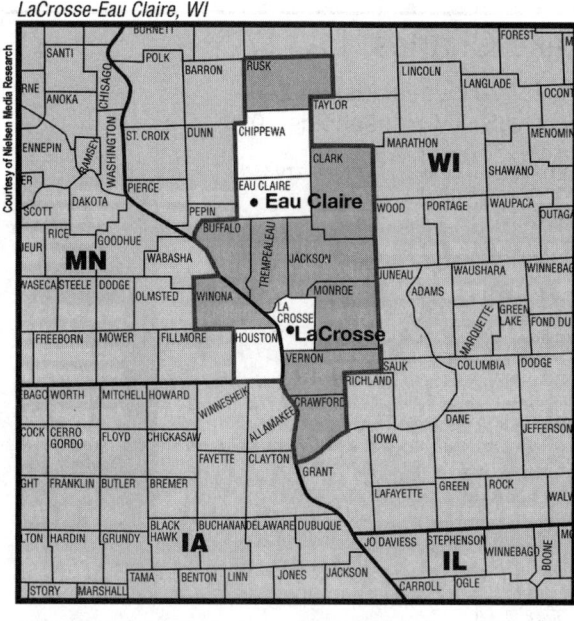

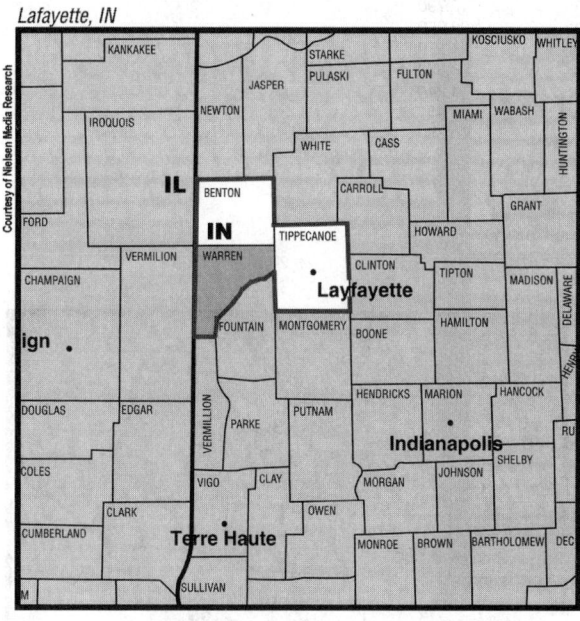

Lafayette, IN (186)

DMA TV Households: 65,060
% of U.S. TV Households: .059

WLFI-TV Lafayette, IN, ch. 18, CBS

DMA Counties	State	TV Households
Benton	IN	3,450
Tippecanoe	IN	58,260
Warren	IN	3,350

Nielsen DMA Market Atlas

Lake Charles, LA (177)

DMA TV Households: 94,240
% of U.S. TV Households: .086

KPLC Lake Charles, LA, ch. 7, NBC
***KLTL-TV** Lake Charles, LA, ch. 18, ETV
KVHP Lake Charles, LA, ch. 29, Fox

DMA Counties	State	TV Households
Allen	LA	8,180
Beauregard	LA	12,410
Calcasieu	LA	70,090
Cameron	LA	3,560

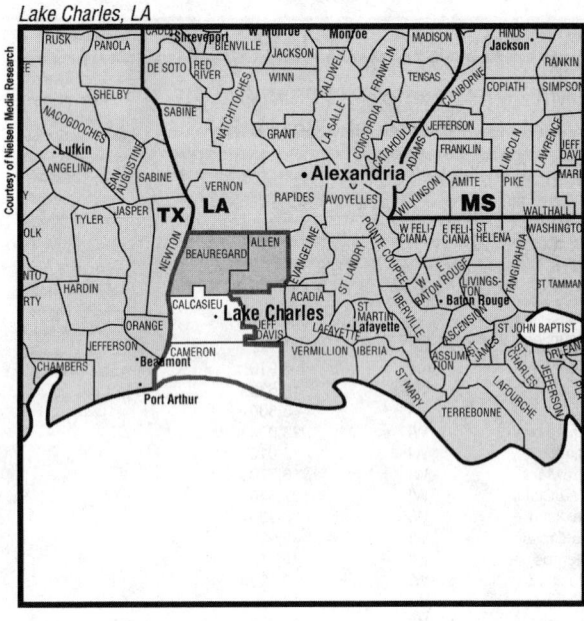

Lafayette, LA (123)

DMA TV Households: 220,740
% of U.S. TV Households: .201

KATC Lafayette, LA, ch. 3, ABC
KLFY-TV Lafayette, LA, ch. 10, CBS
KADN Lafayette, LA, ch. 15, Fox
***KLPB-TV** Lafayette, LA, ch. 24, ETV
KACB-TV New Iberia, LA, ch. 50, IND

DMA Counties	State	TV Households
Acadia	LA	21,730
Evangeline	LA	12,790
Iberia	LA	26,250
Jefferson Davis	LA	11,570
Lafayette	LA	75,320
St. Landry	LA	34,240
St. Martin	LA	18,460
Vermilion	LA	20,380

Lansing, MI (110)

DMA TV Households: 259,240
% of U.S. TV Households: .237

WLNS-TV Lansing, MI, ch. 6, CBS
WILX-TV Onondaga, MI, ch. 10, NBC
WHTV Jackson, MI, ch. 18, IND
***WKAR-TV** East Lansing, MI, ch. 23, ETV
WSYM-TV Lansing, MI, ch. 47, Fox
WLAJ Lansing, MI, ch. 53, ABC

DMA Counties	State	TV Households
Clinton	MI	25,690
Eaton	MI	42,810
Hillsdale	MI	17,700
Ingham	MI	112,150
Jackson	MI	60,890

Broadcasting & Cable Yearbook 2006

Laredo, TX (190)

DMA TV Households: 62,720
% of U.S. TV Households: .057

KGNS-TV Laredo, TX, ch. 8, NBC
KVTV Laredo, TX, ch. 13, CBS
KLDO-TV Laredo, TX, ch. 27, Univision

DMA Counties	State	TV Households
Webb	TX	58,400
Zapata	TX	4,320

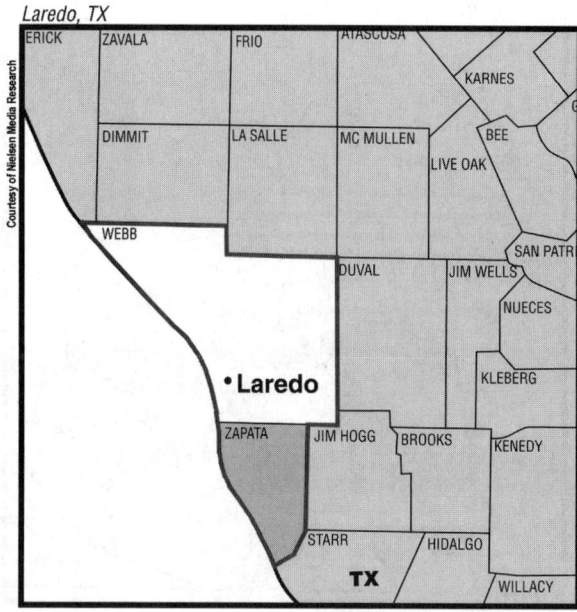

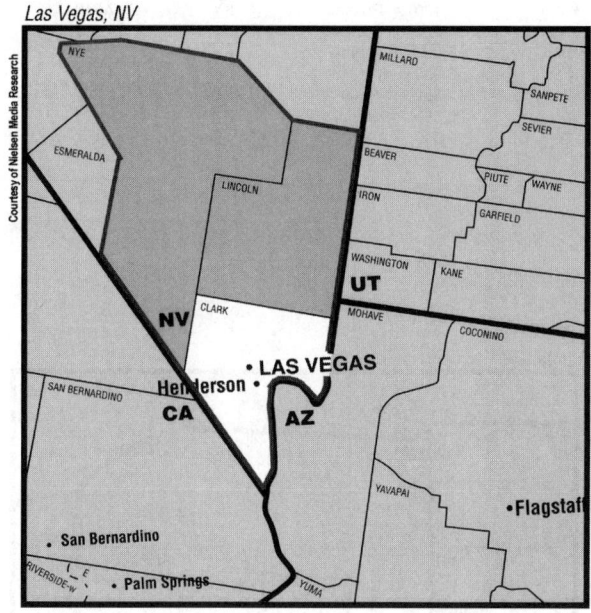

Las Vegas (51)

DMA TV Households: 614,150
% of U.S. TV Households: .560

KVBC Las Vegas, ch. 3, NBC
KVVU-TV Henderson, NV, ch. 5, Fox
KLAS-TV Las Vegas, ch. 8, CBS
*****KLVX** Las Vegas, ch. 10, ETV
KTNV Las Vegas, ch. 13, ABC
KINC Las Vegas, ch. 15, Univision
KVWB Las Vegas, ch. 21, WB
KFBT Las Vegas, ch. 33, IND
KMCC Laughlin, NV, ch. 34, IND
KBLR Paradise, NV, ch. 39, Telemundo

DMA Counties	State	TV Households
Clark	NV	597,580
Lincoln	NV	1,620
Nye	NV	14,950

Nielsen DMA Market Atlas

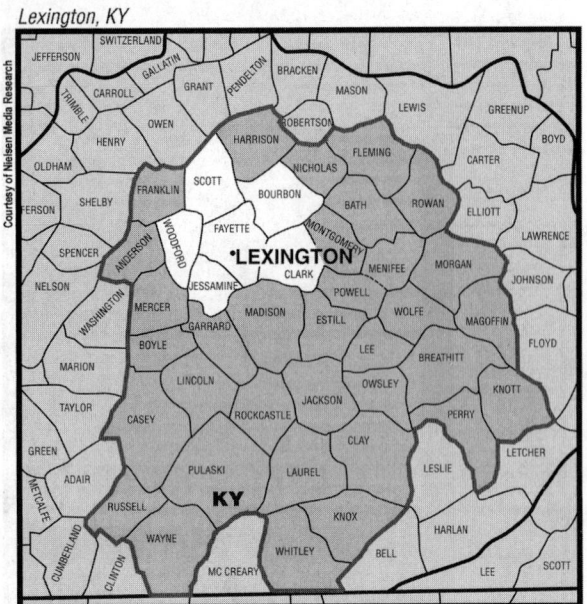

Lexington, KY

Lexington, KY (64)

DMA TV Households: 481,120
% of U.S. TV Households: .439

WLEX-TV Lexington, KY, ch. 18, NBC
WKYT-TV Lexington, KY, ch. 27, CBS
***WKSO-TV** Somerset, KY, ch. 29, ETV
***WKHA** Hazard, KY, ch. 35, ETV
WTVQ-TV Lexington, KY, ch. 36, ABC
***WKMR** Morehead, KY, ch. 38, ETV
***WKLE** Lexington, KY, ch. 46, ETV
WDKY-TV Danville, KY, ch. 56, Fox
WYMT-TV Hazard, KY, ch. 57, CBS
WLJC-TV Beattyville, KY, ch. 65, IND
WUPX-TV Morehead, KY, ch. 67, IND

DMA Counties	State	TV Households	DMA Counties	State	TV Households
Anderson	KY	7,750	Lincoln	KY	9,920
Bath	KY	4,730	Madison	KY	30,130
Bourbon	KY	8,010	Menifee	KY	2,640
Boyle	KY	10,830	Mercer	KY	9,000
Breathitt	KY	5,840	Montgomery	KY	9,640
Casey	KY	6,520	Morgan	KY	5,020
Clark	KY	13,880	Nicholas	KY	2,750
Clay	KY	8,610	Owsley	KY	1,780
Estill	KY	6,110	Perry	KY	12,130
Fayette	KY	114,340	Powell	KY	5,190
Fleming	KY	5,700	Pulaski	KY	24,070
Franklin	KY	20,610	Rockcastle	KY	6,580
Garrard	KY	6,320	Rowan	KY	8,100
Harrison	KY	7,190	Russell	KY	7,210
Jackson	KY	5,320	Scott	KY	14,260
Jessamine	KY	15,320	Wayne	KY	8,150
Knott	KY	6,930	Whitley	KY	14,640
Knox	KY	12,860	Wolfe	KY	2,800
Laurel	KY	22,550	Woodford	KY	9,400
Lee	KY	3,010			

Lima, OH (194)

DMA TV Households: 54,200
% of U.S. TV Households: .049

WLIO Lima, OH, ch. 35, NBC (ABC)
WTLW Lima, OH, ch. 44, IND

DMA Counties	State	TV Households
Allen	OH	41,510
Putnam	OH	12,690

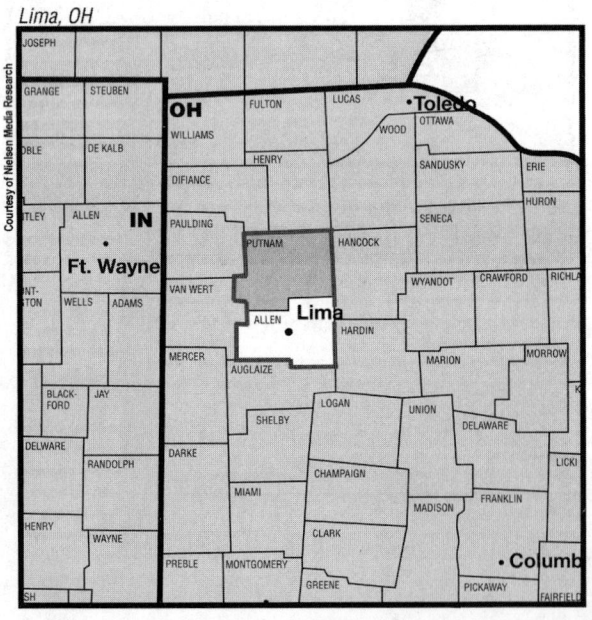

Lima, OH

Broadcasting & Cable Yearbook 2006

Lincoln & Hastings-Kearney, NE (103)

DMA TV Households: 275,230
% of U.S. TV Households: .251

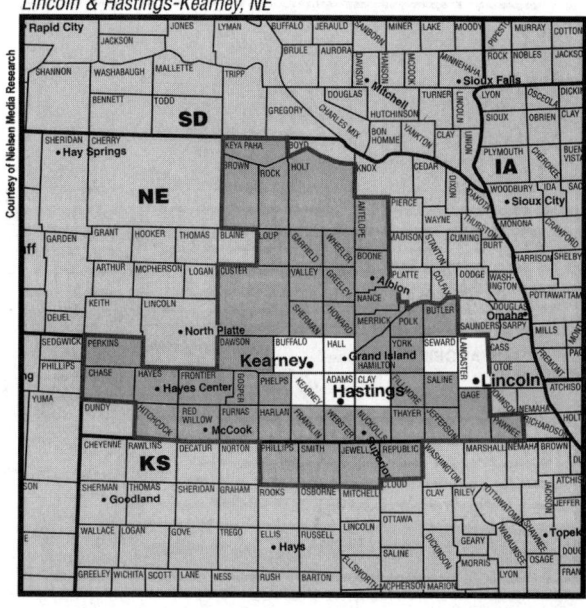

*KLNE-TV Lexington, NE, ch. 3, ETV
KSNB-TV Superior, NE, ch. 4, satellite to KTVG
KHAS-TV Hastings, NE, ch. 5, NBC
KWNB-TV Hayes Center, NE, ch. 6, satellite to KHGI-TV
*KMNE-TV Bassett, NE, ch. 7, ETV
KLKN Lincoln, NE, ch. 8, ABC
KOLN Lincoln, NE, ch. 10, CBS
KGIN Grand Island, NE, ch. 11, satellite to KOLN
*KUON-TV Lincoln, NE, ch. 12, ETV
KHGI-TV Kearney, NE, ch. 13, ABC
KTVG Grand Island, NE, ch. 17, Fox
KLKE Albion, NE, ch. 24, satellite to KLKN
*KHNE-TV Hastings, NE, ch. 29, ETV
KOWH Lincoln, NE, ch. 51, IND

DMA Counties	State	TV Households	DMA Counties	State	TV Households
Jewell	KS	1,490	Hitchcock	NE	1,290
Phillips	KS	2,280	Holt	NE	4,430
Republic	KS	2,180	Howard	NE	2,570
Smith	KS	1,690	Jefferson	NE	3,370
Adams	NE	11,840	Kearney	NE	2,680
Antelope	NE	2,860	Keya Paha	NE	390
Boone	NE	2,270	Lancaster	NE	105,990
Brown	NE	1,540	Loup	NE	300
Buffalo	NE	16,520	Merrick	NE	3,170
Butler	NE	3,440	Nance	NE	1,390
Chase	NE	1,690	Nuckolls	NE	2,170
Clay	NE	2,690	Pawnee	NE	1,170
Custer	NE	4,630	Perkins	NE	1,190
Dawson	NE	8,500	Phelps	NE	3,780
Fillmore	NE	2,570	Polk	NE	2,190
Franklin	NE	1,390	Red Willow	NE	4,610
Frontier	NE	1,090	Rock	NE	700
Furnas	NE	2,180	Saline	NE	5,260
Gage	NE	9,630	Seward	NE	6,200
Garfield	NE	800	Sherman	NE	1,390
Gosper	NE	790	Thayer	NE	2,390
Greeley	NE	990	Valley	NE	1,880
Hall	NE	20,570	Webster	NE	1,570
Hamilton	NE	3,560	Wheeler	NE	300
Harlan	NE	1,490	York	NE	5,670
Hayes	NE	500			

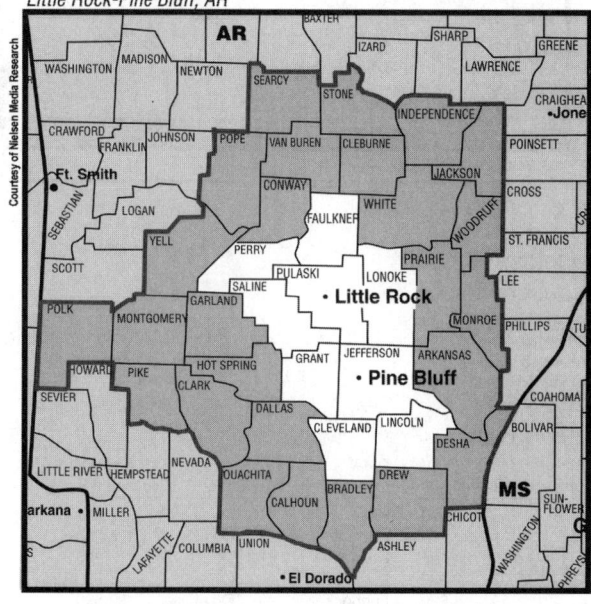

Little Rock-Pine Bluff, AR (57)

DMA TV Households: 531,770
% of U.S. TV Households: .485

*KETS Little Rock, AR, ch. 2, ETV
KARK-TV Little Rock, AR, ch. 4, NBC
*KEMV Mountain View, AR, ch. 6, ETV
KATV Little Rock, AR, ch. 7, ABC
*KETG Arkadelphia, AR, ch. 9, ETV
KTHV Little Rock, AR, ch. 11, CBS
KLRT Little Rock, AR, ch. 16, Fox
*KLEP Newark, AR, ch. 17, ETV
KVTN Pine Bluff, AR, ch. 25, IND
KVTH Hot Springs, AR, ch. 26, IND
*KKAP Little Rock, AR, ch. 36, ETV
KASN Pine Bluff, AR, ch. 38, IND
KWBF Little Rock, AR, ch. 42, IND
KYPX Camden, AR, ch. 49, IND

DMA Counties	State	TV Households	DMA Counties	State	TV Households
Arkansas	AR	8,100	Lonoke	AR	21,490
Bradley	AR	4,700	Monroe	AR	3,750
Calhoun	AR	2,310	Montgomery	AR	3,690
Clark	AR	8,860	Ouachita	AR	11,220
Cleburne	AR	10,560	Perry	AR	4,150
Cleveland	AR	3,250	Pike	AR	4,450
Conway	AR	8,200	Polk	AR	7,800
Dallas	AR	3,280	Pope	AR	20,830
Desha	AR	5,620	Prairie	AR	3,840
Drew	AR	7,330	Pulaski	AR	152,950
Faulkner	AR	35,550	Saline	AR	35,170
Garland	AR	39,370	Searcy	AR	3,350
Grant	AR	6,560	Stone	AR	4,780
Hot Spring	AR	12,200	Van Buren	AR	6,970
Independence	AR	13,640	White	AR	26,810
Jackson	AR	6,500	Woodruff	AR	3,220
Jefferson	AR	30,090	Yell	AR	7,880
Lincoln	AR	4,200			

Nielsen DMA Market Atlas

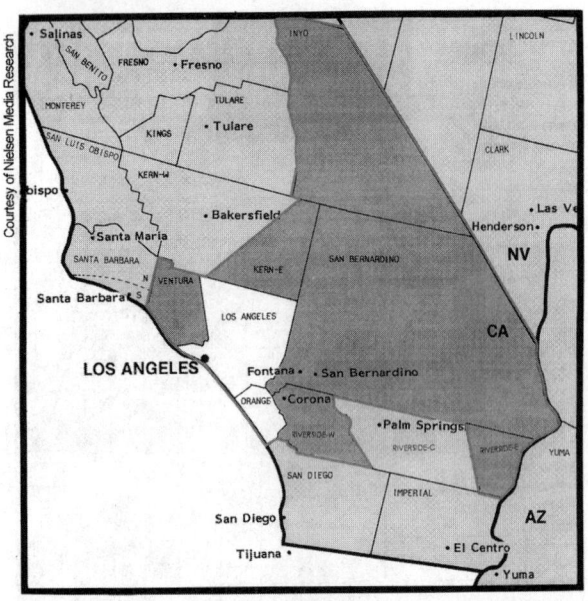

Los Angeles, CA (2)

DMA TV Households: 5,431,140
% of U.S. TV Households: 4.956

KCBS-TV Los Angeles, ch. 2, CBS
KNBC Los Angeles, ch. 4, NBC
KTLA Los Angeles, ch. 5, WB
KABC-TV Los Angeles, ch. 7, ABC
KCAL Los Angeles, ch. 9, IND
KTTV Los Angeles, ch. 11, Fox
KCOP Los Angeles, ch. 13, UPN
KSCI Long Beach, CA, ch. 18, IND
KWHY-TV Los Angeles, ch. 22, IND
*KVCR-TV San Bernardino, CA, ch. 24, ETV
*KCET Los Angeles, ch. 28, ETV
KPXN San Bernardino, CA, ch. 30, IND
KVMD Twentynine Palms, CA, ch. 31, IND
KMEX-TV Los Angeles, ch. 34, Univision
KTBN-TV Santa Ana, CA, ch. 40, IND
KXLA Rancho Palos Verdes, CA, ch. 44, IND
KFTR-TV Ontario, CA, ch. 46, TeleFutura
*KOCE-TV Huntington Beach, CA, ch. 50, ETV
KVEA Corona, CA, ch. 52, Telemundo
KAZA-TV Avalon, CA, ch. 54, Azteca America
KDOC-TV Anaheim, CA, ch. 56, IND
KJLA Ventura, CA, ch. 57, IND
*KLCS Los Angeles, ch. 58, ETV
KRCA Riverside, CA, ch. 62, IND
KHIZ Barstow, CA, ch. 64, IND

DMA Counties	State	TV Households	DMA Counties	State	TV Households
Inyo	CA	7,590	Riverside East	CA	6,120
Kern East	CA	26,320	Riverside West	CA	434,330
Los Angeles	CA	3,192,450	San Bernardino	CA	559,350
Orange	CA	950,650	Ventura	CA	254,330

Louisville, KY (50)

DMA TV Households: 637,680
% of U.S. TV Households: .582

WAVE Louisville, KY, ch. 3, NBC
WHAS-TV Louisville, KY, ch. 11, ABC
*WKPC-TV Louisville, KY, ch. 15, ETV
WBNA Louisville, KY, ch. 21, PAX TV
*WKZT-TV Elizabethtown, KY, ch. 23, ETV
WLKY-TV Louisville, KY, ch. 32, CBS
WBKI-TV Campbellsville, KY, ch. 34, WB
WDRB Louisville, KY, ch. 41, Fox
WFTE Salem, IN, ch. 58, UPN
*WKMJ Louisville, KY, ch. 68, ETV

DMA Counties	State	TV Households	DMA Counties	State	TV Households
Clark	IN	41,610	Green	KY	4,930
Crawford	IN	4,380	Hardin	KY	36,610
Floyd	IN	27,990	Henry	KY	6,060
Harrison	IN	14,080	Jefferson	KY	295,790
Jackson	IN	16,390	Larue	KY	5,300
Jefferson	IN	12,630	Marion	KY	7,010
Jennings	IN	10,520	Meade	KY	10,500
Orange	IN	7,980	Nelson	KY	15,420
Scott	IN	9,350	Oldham	KY	17,190
Washington	IN	10,560	Shelby	KY	13,470
Breckinridge	KY	7,670	Spencer	KY	5,550
Bullitt	KY	25,020	Taylor	KY	9,560
Carroll	KY	4,040	Trimble	KY	3,560
Grayson	KY	10,130	Washington	KY	4,380

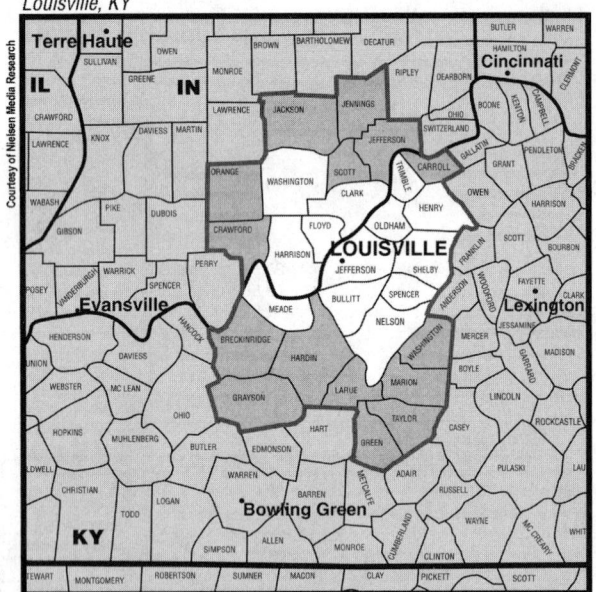

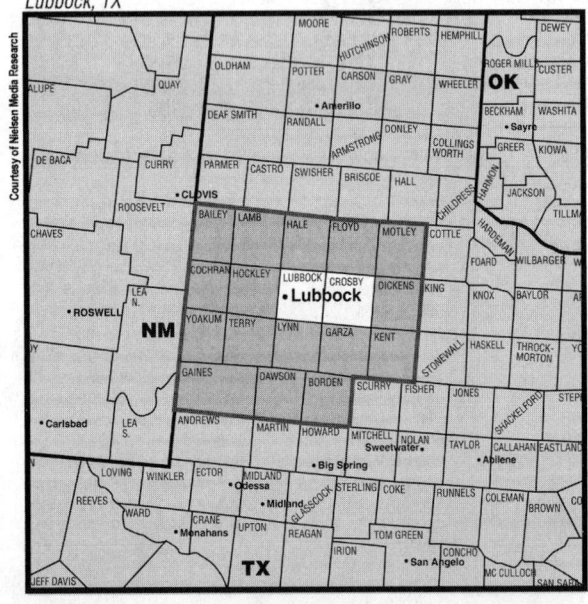

Lubbock, TX (145)

DMA TV Households: 152,620
% of U.S. TV Households: .139

*KTXT-TV Lubbock, TX, ch. 5, ETV
KCBD Lubbock, TX, ch. 11, NBC
KLBK-TV Lubbock, TX, ch. 13, CBS
KPTB Lubbock, TX, ch. 16, IND
KUPT Wolfforth, TX, ch. 22, UPN
KAMC Lubbock, TX, ch. 28, ABC
KJTV-TV Lubbock, TX, ch. 34, Fox

DMA Counties	State	TV Households	DMA Counties	State	TV Households
Bailey	TX	2,190	Hale	TX	11,610
Borden	TX	270	Hockley	TX	8,210
Cochran	TX	1,190	Kent	TX	290
Crosby	TX	2,380	Lamb	TX	5,350
Dawson	TX	4,320	Lubbock	TX	97,590
Dickens	TX	930	Lynn	TX	2,180
Floyd	TX	2,550	Motley	TX	580
Gaines	TX	4,490	Terry	TX	4,160
Garza	TX	1,870	Yoakum	TX	2,460

Broadcasting & Cable Yearbook 2006

Macon, GA (119)

DMA TV Households: 230,000
% of U.S. TV Households: .210

WMAZ-TV Macon, GA, ch. 13, CBS
WGXA Macon, GA, ch. 24, Fox
*WDCO-TV Cochran, GA, ch. 29, ETV
WMGT-TV Macon, GA, ch. 41, NBC
WPGA-TV Perry, GA, ch. 58, IND
WGNM Macon, GA, ch. 64, IND

DMA Counties	State	TV Households	DMA Counties	State	TV Households
Baldwin	GA	15,180	Macon	GA	4,690
Bibb	GA	60,180	Monroe	GA	8,600
Bleckley	GA	4,560	Peach	GA	8,880
Crawford	GA	4,500	Pulaski	GA	3,560
Dodge	GA	7,330	Telfair	GA	4,060
Dooly	GA	3,910	Treutlen	GA	2,630
Hancock	GA	3,320	Twiggs	GA	3,830
Houston	GA	46,640	Washington	GA	7,390
Johnson	GA	3,730	Wheeler	GA	2,250
Jones	GA	9,840	Wilcox	GA	2,970
Laurens	GA	18,030	Wilkinson	GA	3,920

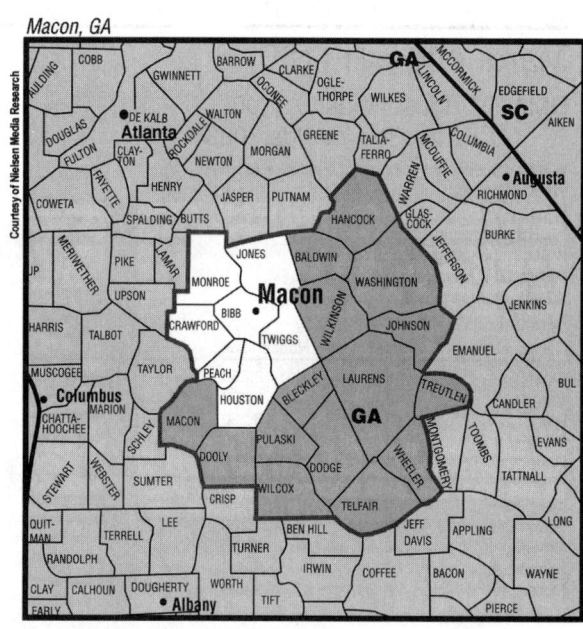

Madison, WI (85)

DMA TV Households: 364,000
% of U.S. TV Households: .332

WISC-TV Madison, WI, ch. 3, CBS
WMTV Madison, WI, ch. 15, NBC
*WHA-TV Madison, WI, ch. 21, ETV
WKOW-TV Madison, WI, ch. 27, ABC
WMSN-TV Madison, WI, ch. 47, Fox
WBUW Janesville, WI, ch. 57, IND

DMA Counties	State	TV Households
Columbia	WI	21,440
Dane	WI	187,370
Grant	WI	19,140
Green	WI	13,850
Iowa	WI	9,210
Juneau	WI	10,280
Lafayette	WI	6,460
Marquette	WI	5,720
Richland	WI	7,190
Rock	WI	60,440
Sauk	WI	22,900

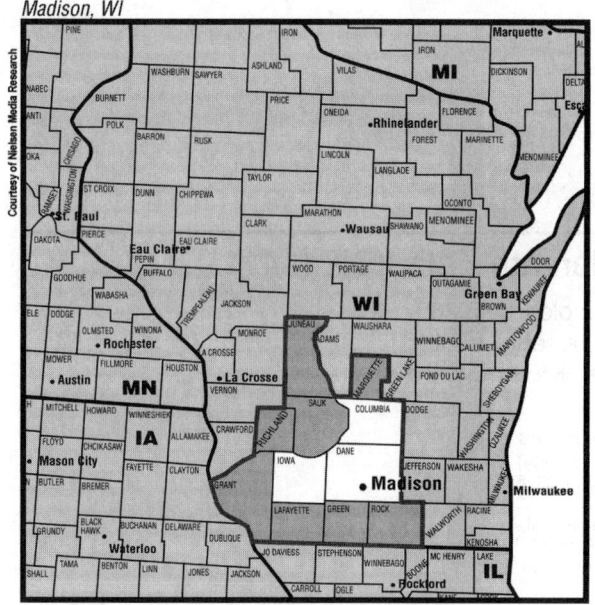

Mankato, MN (199)

DMA TV Households: 51,390
% of U.S. TV Households: .047

KEYC-TV Mankato, MN, ch. 12, CBS

DMA Counties	State	TV Households
Blue Earth-Nicollet South	MN	27,570
Brown	MN	10,500
Martin	MN	8,840
Watonwan	MN	4,480

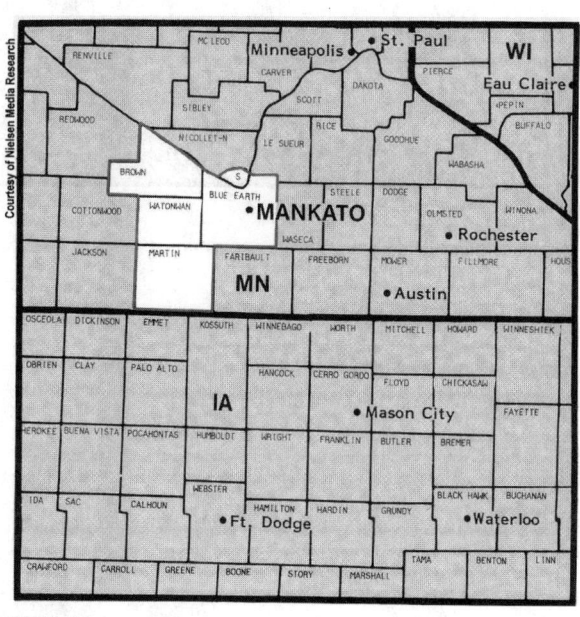

Broadcasting & Cable Yearbook 2006

Nielsen DMA Market Atlas

Marquette, MI (180)

DMA TV Households: 91,100
% of U.S. TV Households: .083

WJMN-TV Escanaba, MI, ch. 3, satellite to WFRV-TV
WBKP Calumet, MI, ch. 5, ABC
WLUC-TV Marquette, MI, ch. 6, NBC
WDHS Iron Mountain, MI, ch. 8, IND
WBUP Ishpeming, MI, ch. 10, ABC
***WNMU-TV** Marquette, MI, ch. 13, ETV
WMQF Marquette, MI, ch. 19, Fox

DMA Counties	State	TV Households
Alger	MI	3,850
Baraga	MI	3,400
Delta	MI	16,230
Dickinson	MI	11,470
Houghton	MI	13,150
Iron	MI	5,550
Keweenaw	MI	970
Marquette	MI	27,120
Ontonagon	MI	3,430
Schoolcraft	MI	3,640
Florence	WI	2,290

Marquette, MI

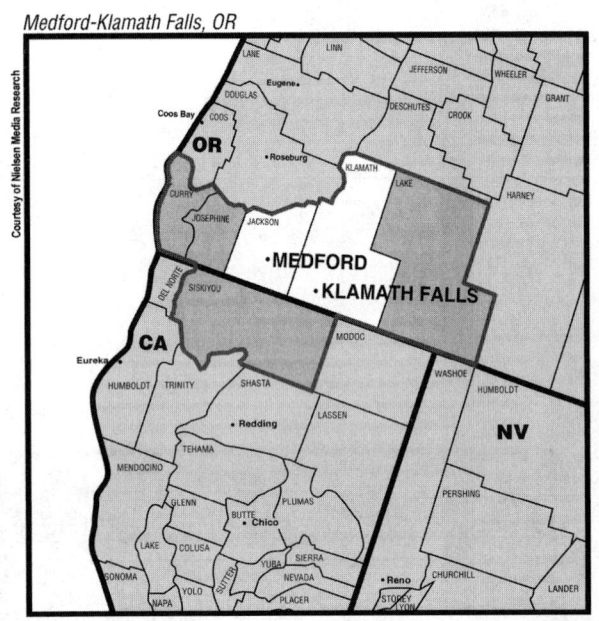

Medford-Klamath Falls, OR

Medford-Klamath Falls, OR (141)

DMA TV Households: 162,260
% of U.S. TV Households: .148

KOTI Klamath Falls, OR, ch. 2, satellite to KOBI
KOBI Medford, OR, ch. 5, NBC
***KSYS** Medford, OR, ch. 8, ETV
KTVL Medford, OR, ch. 10, CBS
KDRV Medford, OR, ch. 12, ABC
***KBDM** Yreka City, CA, ch. 20, ETV
***KFTS** Klamath Falls, OR, ch. 22, satellite to *KSYS
KMVU Medford, OR, ch. 26, IND
KBLN Grants Pass, OR, ch. 30, IND
KDKF Klamath Falls, OR, ch. 31, ABC

DMA Counties	State	TV Households
Siskiyou	CA	17,800
Curry	OR	9,610
Jackson	OR	74,600
Josephine	OR	31,570
Klamath	OR	25,600
Lake	OR	3,080

Broadcasting & Cable Yearbook 2006

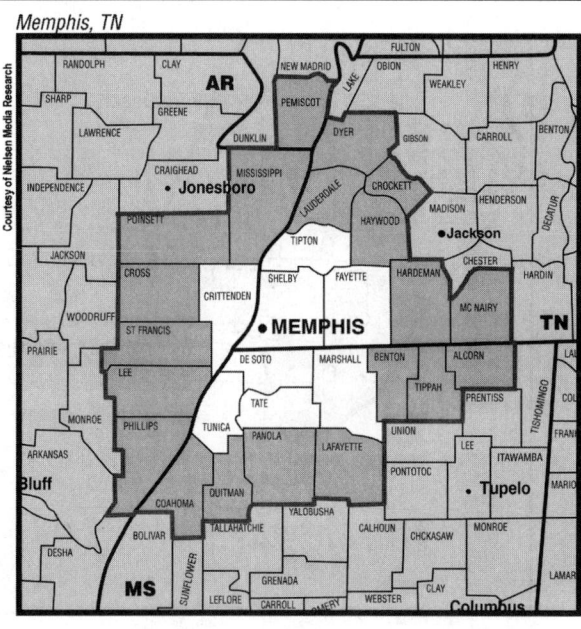
Memphis, TN

Memphis (44)

DMA TV Households: 658,250
% of U.S. TV Households: .601

WREG-TV Memphis, ch. 3, CBS
WMC-TV Memphis, ch. 5, NBC
*****WKNO-TV** Memphis, ch. 10, ETV
WHBQ-TV Memphis, ch. 13, Fox
*****WMAV-TV** Oxford, MS, ch. 18, ETV
WPTY-TV Memphis, ch. 24, ABC
WLMT Memphis, ch. 30, IND
WBUY-TV Holly Springs, MS, ch. 40, IND
WPXX-TV Memphis, ch. 50, PAX TV

DMA Counties	State	TV Households	DMA Counties	State	TV Households
Crittenden	AR	18,970	Tate	MS	9,380
Cross	AR	7,490	Tippah	MS	8,270
Lee	AR	4,760	Tunica	MS	3,900
Mississippi	AR	17,910	Pemiscot	MO	7,680
Phillips	AR	8,710	Crockett	TN	5,550
St. Francis	AR	9,790	Dyer	TN	14,610
Poinsett	AR	9,940	Fayette	TN	12,760
Alcorn	MS	14,680	Gibson	TN	19,280
Benton	MS	2,970	Hardeman	TN	9,540
Coahoma	MS	9,860	Haywood	TN	7,660
DeSoto	MS	48,840	Lauderdale	TN	9,650
Lafayette	MS	15,500	McNairy	TN	10,090
Marshall	MS	12,660	Shelby	TN	342,140
Panola	MS	12,920	Tipton	TN	19,630
Quitman	MS	3,390			

Meridian, MS (184)

DMA TV Households: 72,280
% of U.S. TV Households: .066

WTOK-TV Meridian, MS, ch. 11, ABC
*****WMAW-TV** Meridian, MS, ch. 14, ETV
WMDN Meridian, MS, ch. 24, CBS
WGBC Meridian, MS, ch. 30, NBC

DMA Counties	State	TV Households
Choctaw	AL	6,290
Sumter	AL	5,580
Clarke	MS	6,990
Kemper	MS	3,840
Lauderdale	MS	30,060
Neshoba	MS	11,080
Newton	MS	8,440

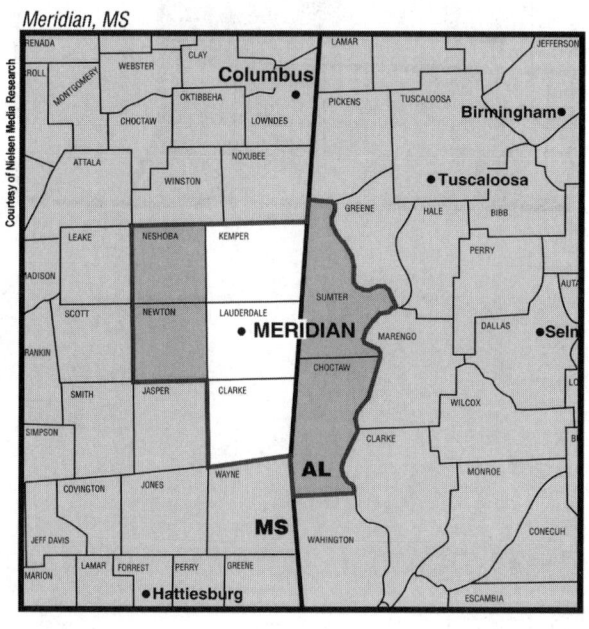
Meridian, MS

Broadcasting & Cable Yearbook 2006

Nielsen DMA Market Atlas

Miami-Ft. Lauderdale, FL (17)

DMA TV Households: 1,496,810
% of U.S. TV Households: 1.394

*WPBT Miami, ch. 2, ETV
WFOR-TV Miami, ch. 4, CBS
WTVJ Miami, ch. 6, NBC
WSVN Miami, ch. 7, Fox
WGEN-TV Key West, FL, ch. 8, IND
WPLG Miami, ch. 10, ABC
*WLRN-TV Miami, ch. 17, ETV
WDLP-TV Key West, FL, ch. 22, IND
WLTV Miami, ch. 23, Univision
WBFS-TV Miami, ch. 33, UPN
WPXM Miami, ch. 35, IND
WBZL Miami, ch. 39, WB
WHFT-TV Miami, ch. 45, IND
WSCV Fort Lauderdale, FL, ch. 51, Telemundo
WAMI-TV Hollywood, FL, ch. 69, TeleFutura

DMA Counties	State	TV Households
Broward	FL	680,040
Miami-Dade	FL	783,610
Monroe	FL	33,160

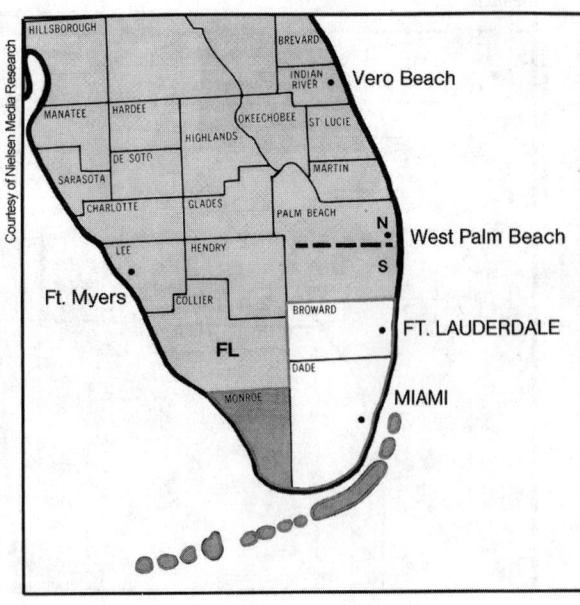

Milwaukee, WI (32)

DMA TV Households: 886,770
% of U.S. TV Households: .809

WTMJ-TV Milwaukee, ch. 4, NBC
WITI Milwaukee, ch. 6, Fox
*WMVS Milwaukee, ch. 10, ETV
WISN-TV Milwaukee, ch. 12, ABC
WVTV Milwaukee, ch. 18, WB
WCGV-TV Milwaukee, ch. 24, UPN
WVCY-TV Milwaukee, ch. 30, IND
*WMVT Milwaukee, ch. 36, ETV
WJJA Racine, WI, ch. 49, IND
WWRS-TV Mayville, WI, ch. 52, IND
WPXE Kenosha, WI, ch. 55, PAX TV
WDJT-TV Milwaukee, ch. 58, CBS

DMA Counties	State	TV Households
Dodge	WI	33,120
Jefferson	WI	30,080
Kenosha	WI	59,690
Milwaukee	WI	378,700
Ozaukee	WI	33,370
Racine	WI	73,760
Sheboygan	WI	45,320
Walworth	WI	36,520
Washington	WI	48,030
Waukesha	WI	148,180

Nielsen DMA Market Atlas

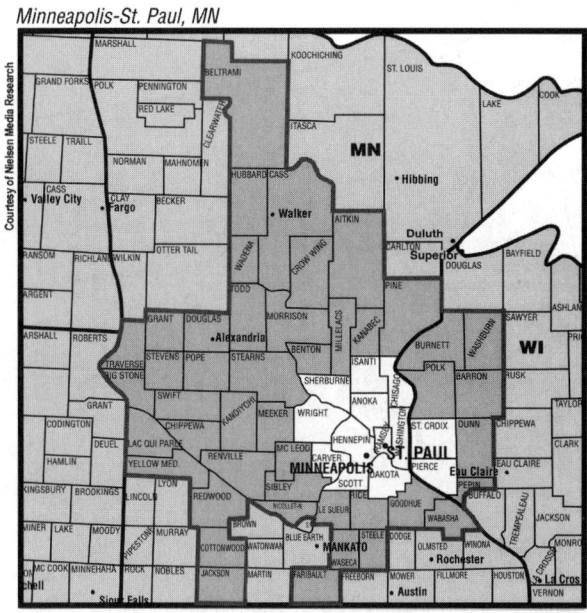
Minneapolis-St. Paul, MN

Minneapolis-St. Paul, MN (14)

DMA TV Households: 1,665,540
% of U.S. TV Households: 1.520

*KTCA-TV St. Paul, ch. 2, ETV
WCCO-TV Minneapolis, ch. 4, CBS
KSTP-TV St. Paul, ch. 5, ABC
KCCO-TV Alexandria, MN, ch. 7, CBS
*KAWE Bemidji, MN, ch. 9, ETV
KMSP-TV Minneapolis, ch. 9, Fox
*KWCM-TV Appleton, MN, ch. 10, ETV
KARE Minneapolis, ch. 11, NBC
KCCW-TV Walker, MN, ch. 12, satellite to KCCO-TV

*KTCI-TV St. Paul, ch. 17, ETV
*KAWB Brainerd, MN, ch. 22, ETV
KMWB Minneapolis, ch. 23, IND
KFTC Bemidji, MN, ch. 26, IND
*WHWC-TV Menomonie, WI, ch. 28, ETV
WFTC Minneapolis, ch. 29, Fox
KPXM St. Cloud, MN, ch. 41, IND
KSAX Alexandria, MN, ch. 42, ABC
KRWF Redwood Falls, MN, ch. 43, ABC
KSTC-TV Minneapolis, ch. 45, IND

DMA Counties	State	TV Households	DMA Counties	State	TV Households
Aitkin	MN	6,760	Pepin	MN	2,950
Anoka	MN	117,090	Pine	MN	10,520
Beltrami	MN	15,500	Pope	MN	4,570
Benton	MN	15,110	Ramsey	MN	198,130
Big Stone	MN	2,290	Redwood	MN	6,380
Carver	MN	28,380	Renville	MN	6,620
Cass	MN	11,380	Rice	MN	20,270
Chippewa	MN	5,260	Scott	MN	39,220
Chisago	MN	17,160	Sherburne	MN	26,810
Cottonwood	MN	4,720	Sibley	MN	5,750
Crow Wing	MN	23,890	Stearns	MN	51,160
Dakota	MN	142,680	Steele	MN	13,490
Douglas	MN	14,210	Stevens	MN	3,750
Faribault	MN	6,460	Swift	MN	4,040
Goodhue	MN	17,670	Todd	MN	9,290
Grant	MN	2,490	Traverse	MN	1,590
Hennepin	MN	457,000	Wabasha	MN	8,560
Hubbard	MN	7,570	Wadena	MN	5,290
Isanti	MN	13,530	Waseca	MN	6,990
Jackson	MN	4,560	Washington	MN	80,110
Kanabec	MN	6,240	Wright	MN	38,320
Kandiyohi	MN	15,940	Yellow Medicine	MN	4,150
Lacqui Parle	MN	3,270	Barron	WI	18,350
Le Sueur	MN	10,380	Burnett	WI	6,920
Lyon	MN	9,470	Dunn	WI	15,220
McLeod	MN	14,190	Pierce	WI	13,860
Meeker	MN	8,820	Polk	WI	17,690
Mille Lacs	MN	9,740	St. Croix	WI	28,510
Morrison	MN	12,460	Washburn	WI	6,880
Nicollet-North	MN	5,930			

Minot-Bismarck-Dickinson, ND (157)

DMA TV Households: 135,760
% of U.S. TV Households: .124

KXMA-TV Dickinson, ND, ch. 2, satellite to KXMC-TV
*KBME-TV Bismarck, ND, ch. 3, ETV
*KWSE Williston, ND, ch. 4, ETV
KFYR-TV Bismarck, ND, ch. 5, NBC
*KSRE Minot, ND, ch. 6, ETV
KQCD-TV Dickinson, ND, ch. 7, NBC
KUMV-TV Williston, ND, ch. 8, satellite to KFYR-TV
*KDSE Dickinson, ND, ch. 9, ETV
KMOT Minot, ND, ch. 10, satellite to KFYR-TV

KXMD-TV Williston, ND, ch. 11, satellite to KXMC-TV
*KQSD-TV Lowry, SD, ch. 11, ETV
KXMC-TV Minot, ND, ch. 13, CBS
KXMB-TV Bismarck, ND, ch. 12, satellite to KXMC-TV
*KPSD-TV Eagle Butte, SD, ch. 13, ETV
KMCY Minot, ND, ch. 14, ABC
KBMY Bismarck, ND, ch. 17, ABC
KXND Minot, ND, ch. 24, Fox
KNDX Bismarck, ND, ch. 26, IND

Minot-Bismarck-Dickinson (Williston), ND

DMA Counties	State	TV Households	DMA Counties	State	TV Households
Daniels	MT	890	McHenry	ND	2,460
McCone	MT	780	McIntosh	ND	1,380
Richland	MT	3,760	McKenzie	ND	2,080
Roosevelt	MT	3,420	McLean	ND	3,770
Sheridan	MT	1,430	Mercer	ND	3,300
Wibaux	MT	380	Morton	ND	10,080
Adams	ND	1,080	Mountrail	ND	2,570
Billings	ND	400	Oliver	ND	790
Bottineau	ND	2,890	Pierce	ND	1,880
Bowman	ND	1,290	Renville	ND	1,100
Burke	ND	990	Rolette	ND	4,540
Burleigh	ND	29,960	Sheridan	ND	680
Divide	ND	980	Sioux	ND	1,070
Dunn	ND	1,360	Slope	ND	290
Emmons	ND	1,690	Stark	ND	9,040
Golden Valley	ND	700	Ward	ND	22,430
Grant	ND	1,170	Wells	ND	1,970
Hettinger	ND	1,090	Williams	ND	8,130
Kidder	ND	1,100	Campbell	ND	680
Logan	ND	890	Corson	SD	1,270

Broadcasting & Cable Yearbook 2006

Nielsen DMA Market Atlas

Missoula, MT (169)

DMA TV Households: 103,810
% of U.S. TV Households: .095

KPAX-TV Missoula, MT, ch. 8, satellite to KXLF-TV
KCFW-TV Kalispell, MT, ch. 9, NBC
*KUFM-TV Missoula, MT, ch. 11, ETV
KECI-TV Missoula, MT, ch. 13, NBC (ABC)
KMMF Missoula, MT, ch. 17, Fox
KTMF Missoula, MT, ch. 23, IND

DMA Counties	State	TV Households
Flathead	MT	31,790
Granite	MT	1,270
Lake	MT	10,500
Mineral	MT	1,630
Missoula	MT	38,710
Ravalli	MT	15,460
Sanders	MT	4,450

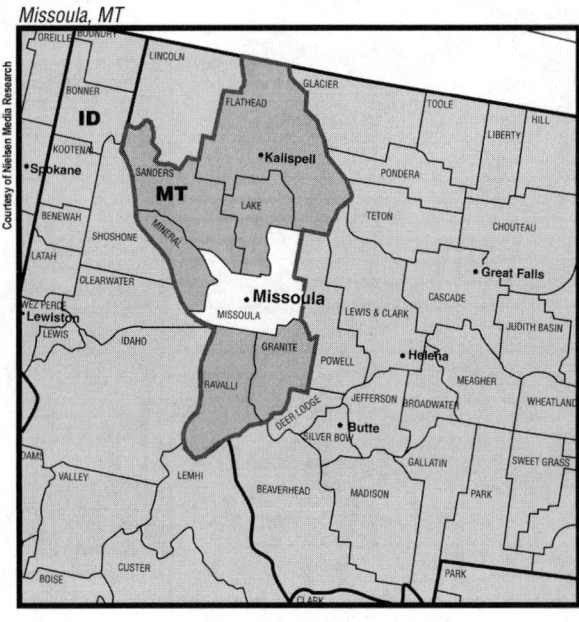

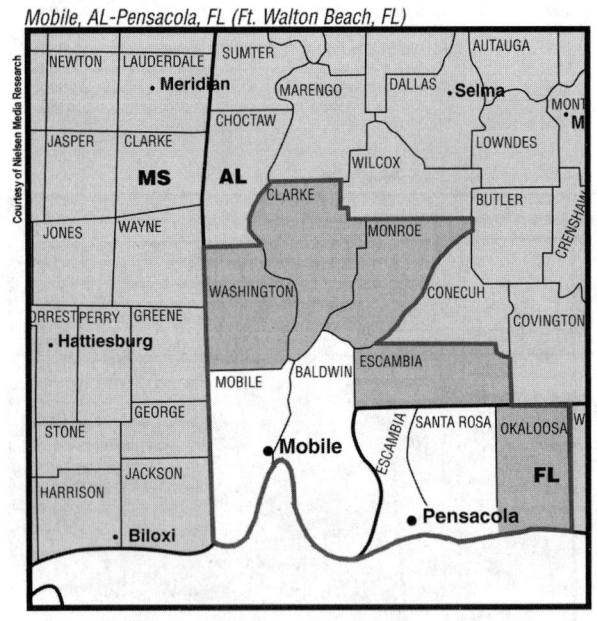

Mobile, AL-Pensacola (Ft. Walton Beach), FL (63)

DMA TV Households: 492,070
% of U.S. TV Households: .449

WEAR-TV Pensacola, FL, ch. 3, ABC
WKRG-TV Mobile, AL, ch. 5, CBS
WALA-TV Mobile, AL, ch. 10, Fox
WPMI-TV Mobile, AL, ch. 15, NBC
WMPV-TV Mobile, AL, ch. 21, IND
*WSRE Pensacola, FL, ch. 23, ETV
WHBR Pensacola, FL, ch. 33, IND
WFGX Fort Walton Beach, FL, ch. 35, IND
*WEIQ Mobile, AL, ch. 42, ETV
WFBD Pensacola, FL, ch. 44, UPN
WJTC Destin, FL, ch. 48, IND
WPAN Fort Walton Beach, FL, ch. 53, IND
WBPG Gulf Shores, AL, ch. 55, WB
WAWD Fort Walton Beach, FL, ch. 58, IND

DMA Counties	State	TV Households
Baldwin	AL	62,980
Clarke	AL	10,830
Escambia	AL	14,300
Mobile	AL	151,830
Monroe	AL	9,530
Washington	AL	6,830
Escambia	FL	112,610
Okaloosa	FL	72,820
Santa Rosa	FL	50,700

Broadcasting & Cable Yearbook 2006

Nielsen DMA Market Atlas

Monroe, LA-El Dorado, AR (135)

DMA TV Households: 176,380
% of U.S. TV Households: .161

KNOE-TV Monroe, LA, ch. 8, CBS
KTVE El Dorado, AR, ch. 10, NBC
KAQY Columbia, LA, ch. 11, ABC
***KLTM-TV** Monroe, LA, ch. 13, ETV
KARD West Monroe, LA, ch. 14, Fox
***KETZ** El Dorado, AR, ch. 30, ETV
KMCT-TV West Monroe, LA, ch. 39, IND
KEJB El Dorado, AR, ch. 43, UPN

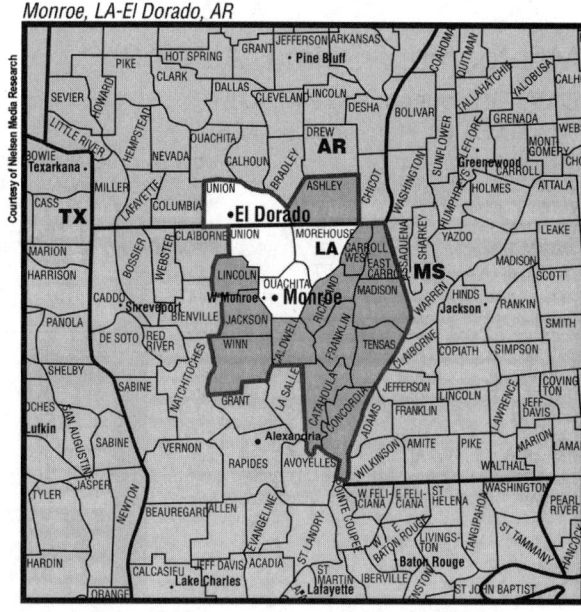

DMA Counties	State	TV Households	DMA Counties	State	TV Households
Ashley	AR	9,290	Madison	LA	4,210
Union	AR	17,730	Morehouse	LA	11,650
Caldwell	LA	3,960	Ouachita	LA	56,830
Catahoula	LA	3,970	Richland	LA	7,510
Concordia	LA	7,420	Tensas	LA	2,250
East Carroll	LA	2,770	Union	LA	9,310
Franklin	LA	7,660	West Carroll	LA	4,500
Jackson	LA	6,180	Winn	LA	5,700
Lincoln	LA	15,440			

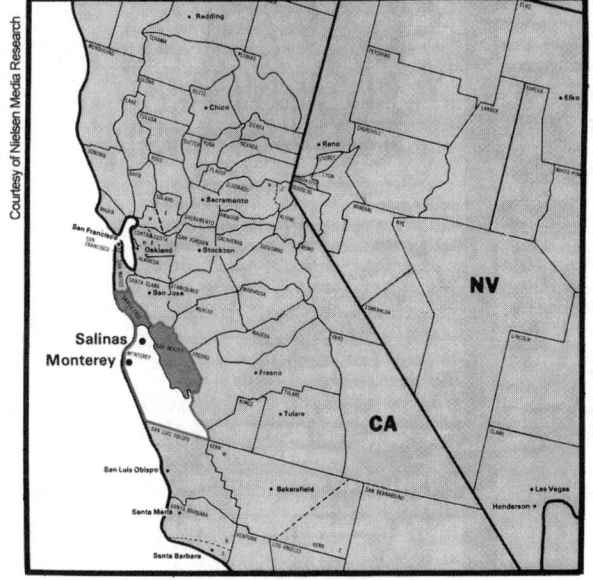

Monterey-Salinas, CA (124)

DMA TV Households: 218,450
% of U.S. TV Households: .199

KSBW Salinas, CA, ch. 8, NBC
***KCAH** Watsonville, CA, ch. 25, ETV
KCBA Salinas, CA, ch. 35, Fox
KION-TV Monterey, CA, ch. 46, CBS
KSMS-TV Monterey, CA, ch. 67, Univision

DMA Counties	State	TV Households
Monterey	CA	118,570
San Benito	CA	16,160
Santa Cruz	CA	83,720

Broadcasting & Cable Yearbook 2006

Nielsen DMA Market Atlas

Montgomery-Selma, AL (113)

DMA TV Households: 247,800
% of U.S. TV Households: .226

*WDIQ Dozier, AL, ch. 2, ETV
WAKA Selma, AL, ch. 8, CBS
WSFA Montgomery, AL, ch. 12, NBC
WCOV-TV Montgomery, AL, ch. 20, Fox
WBMM Tuskegee, AL, ch. 22, IND
*WAIQ Montgomery, AL, ch. 26, ETV
WBIH Selma, AL, ch. 29, IND
WNCF Montgomery, AL, ch. 32, ABC
*WIIQ Demopolis, AL, ch. 41, ETV
WMCF-TV Montgomery, AL, ch. 45, IND
WRJM-TV Troy, AL, ch. 67, IND

DMA Counties	State	TV Households
Autauga	AL	18,020
Bullock	AL	3,850
Butler	AL	8,340
Conecuh	AL	5,660
Covington	AL	15,540
Crenshaw	AL	5,570
Dallas	AL	17,590
Elmore	AL	25,620
Lowndes	AL	5,130
Macon	AL	8,800
Marengo	AL	8,900
Montgomery	AL	87,220
Perry	AL	4,330
Pike	AL	11,860
Tallapoosa	AL	16,480
Wilcox	AL	4,890

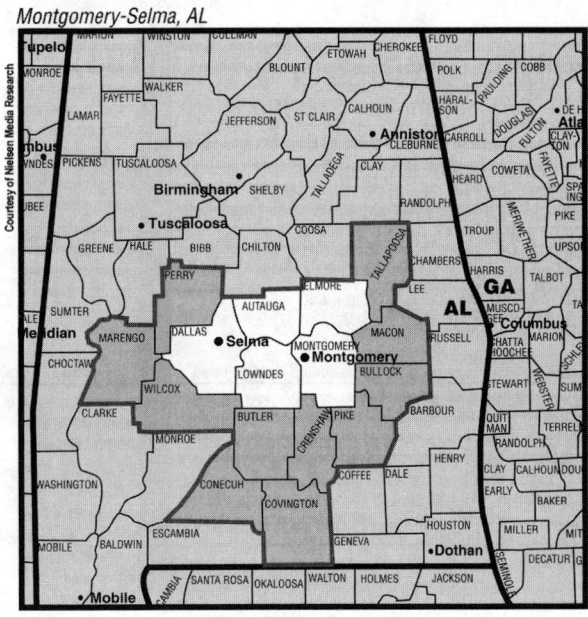

Montgomery-Selma, AL

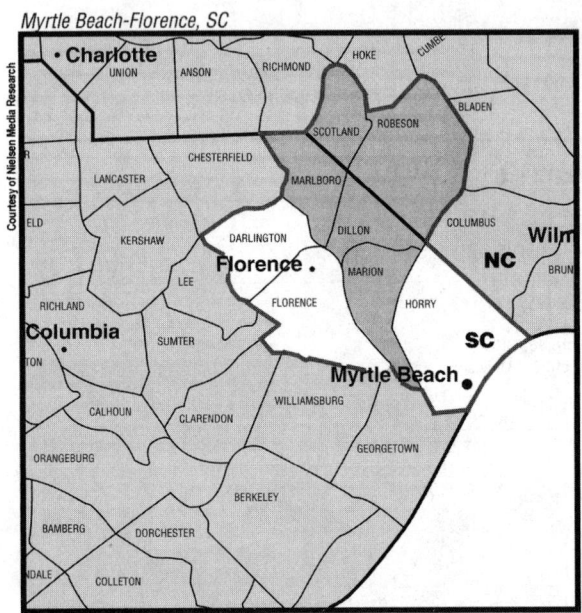

Myrtle Beach-Florence, SC

Myrtle Beach-Florence, SC (108)

DMA TV Households: 265,370
% of U.S. TV Households: .242

WBTW Florence, SC, ch. 13, CBS
WPDE-TV Florence, SC, ch. 15, ABC
WWMB Florence, SC, ch. 21, IND
*WHMC Conway, SC, ch. 23, ETV
*WUNU Lumberton, NC, ch. 31, ETV
*WJMP-TV Florence, SC, ch. 33, ETV
WFXB Myrtle Beach, SC, ch. 43, Fox

DMA Counties	State	TV Households
Robeson	NC	45,390
Scotland	NC	13,620
Darlington	SC	26,960
Dillon	SC	11,730
Florence	SC	50,600
Horry	SC	92,790
Marion	SC	13,600
Marlboro	SC	10,680

Broadcasting & Cable Yearbook 2006

Nielsen DMA Market Atlas

Nashville (30)

DMA TV Households: 916,170
% of U.S. TV Households: .836

WKRN-TV Nashville, ch. 2, ABC
WSMV Nashville, ch. 4, NBC
WTVF Nashville, ch. 5, CBS
***WNPT** Nashville, ch. 8, ETV
WZTV Nashville, ch. 17, Fox
***WCTE** Cookeville, TN, ch. 22, ETV
WNPX Cookeville, TN, ch. 28, IND
WUXP Nashville, ch. 30, UPN
WHTN Murfreesboro, TN, ch. 39, IND
WPGD-TV Hendersonville, TN, ch. 50, IND
WNAB Nashville, ch. 58, WB
WJFB Lebanon, TN, ch. 66, IND

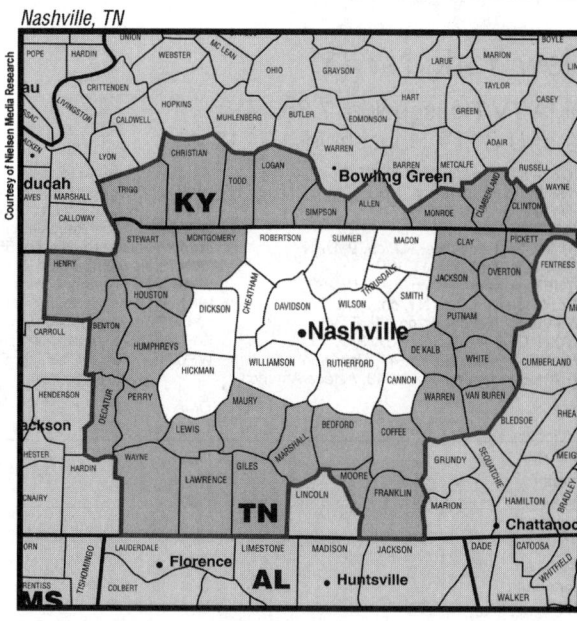

Nashville, TN

DMA Counties	State	TV Households	DMA Counties	State	TV Households
Allen	KY	7,220	Jackson	TN	4,580
Christian	KY	23,440	Lawrence	TN	15,380
Clinton	KY	4,160	Lewis	TN	4,510
Cumberland	KY	2,940	Macon	TN	8,380
Logan	KY	10,340	Marshall	TN	10,550
Monroe	KY	4,720	Maury	TN	28,530
Simpson	KY	6,610	Montgomery	TN	51,550
Todd	KY	4,350	Moore	TN	2,370
Trigg	KY	5,430	Overton	TN	8,150
Bedford	TN	15,000	Perry	TN	3,050
Benton	TN	6,840	Pickett	TN	2,160
Cannon	TN	5,190	Putnam	TN	25,930
Cheatham	TN	13,610	Robertson	TN	21,940
Clay	TN	3,440	Rutherford	TN	77,000
Coffee	TN	19,960	Smith	TN	7,110
Davidson	TN	236,660	Stewart	TN	5,120
Decatur	TN	4,650	Sumner	TN	54,510
DeKalb	TN	7,300	Trousdale	TN	2,870
Dickson	TN	17,400	Van Buren	TN	2,260
Franklin	TN	15,970	Warren	TN	15,810
Giles	TN	11,760	Wayne	TN	5,900
Henry	TN	13,030	White	TN	9,420
Hickman	TN	8,580	Williamson	TN	52,560
Houston	TN	3,200	Wilson	TN	36,780
Humphreys	TN	7,510			

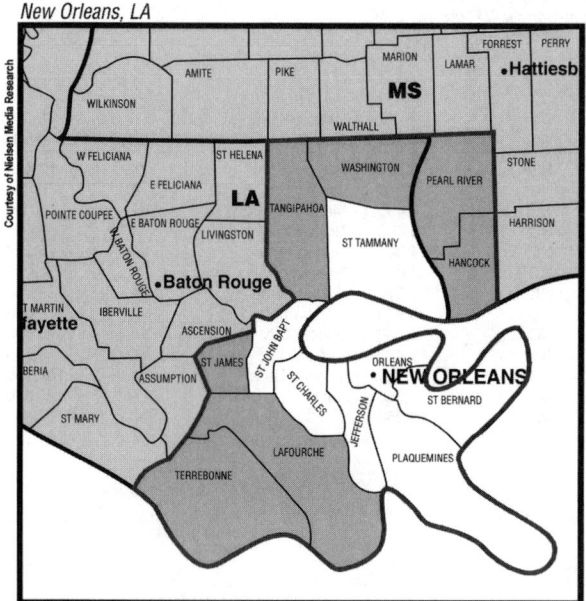

New Orleans, LA

New Orleans (43)

DMA TV Households: 675,760
% of U.S. TV Households: .617

WWL-TV New Orleans, ch. 4, CBS
WDSU-TV New Orleans, ch. 6, NBC
WVUE New Orleans, ch. 8, Fox
***WYES-TV** New Orleans, ch. 12, ETV
WHNO New Orleans, ch. 20, IND
WGNO New Orleans, ch. 26, ABC
***WLAE-TV** New Orleans, ch. 32, ETV
WNOL-TV New Orleans, ch. 38, IND
WPXL New Orleans, ch. 49, IND
WUPL Slidell, LA, ch. 54, UPN

DMA Counties	State	TV Households	DMA Counties	State	TV Households
Jefferson	LA	178,390	St. John the Baptist	LA	15,490
Lafourche	LA	33,820	St. Tammany	LA	79,260
Orleans	LA	178,880	Tangipahoa	LA	38,410
Plaquemines	LA	9,900	Terrebonne	LA	37,810
St. Bernard	LA	25,660	Washington	LA	16,240
St. Charles	LA	17,020	Hancock	MS	18,310
St. James	LA	7,210	Pearl River	MS	19,360

Broadcasting & Cable Yearbook 2006

Nielsen DMA Market Atlas

New York, NY (1)

DMA TV Households: 7,355,710
% of U.S. TV Households: 6.712

WCBS-TV New York, ch. 2, CBS
WNBC New York, ch. 4, NBC
WNYW New York, ch. 5, Fox
WABC-TV New York, ch. 7, ABC
WWOR-TV Secaucus, NJ, ch. 9, UPN
WPIX New York, ch. 11, WB
*WNET Newark, NJ, ch. 13, ETV
*WLIW Garden City, NY, ch. 21, ETV
*WNYE-TV New York, ch. 25, ETV
WPXN-TV New York, ch. 31, PAX TV
WXTV Paterson, NJ, ch. 41, Univision
WSAH Bridgeport, CT, ch. 43, Azteca America
WNJU Linden, NJ, ch. 47, Telemundo
*WEDW Bridgeport, CT, ch. 49, ETV
*WNJN Montclair, NJ, ch. 50, ETV
WTBY-TV Poughkeepsie, NY, ch. 54, IND
WLNY Riverhead, NY, ch. 55, IND
*WNJB New Brunswick, NJ, ch. 58, ETV
WMBC-TV Newton, NJ, ch. 63, IND
WRNN-TV Kingston, NY, ch. 63, IND
*WFME-TV West Milford, NJ, ch. 66, ETV
WFTY-TV Smithtown, NY, ch. 67, IND
WFUT-TV Newark, NJ, ch. 68, TeleFutura

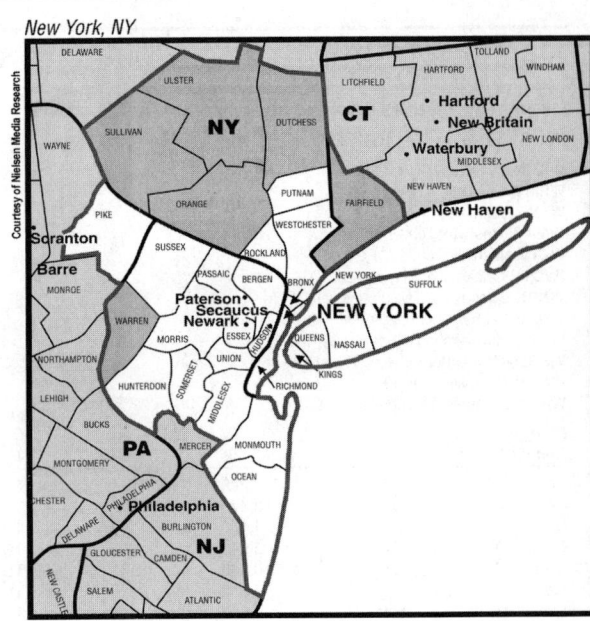

DMA Counties	State	TV Households
Fairfield	CT	327,580
Bergen	NJ	335,860
Essex	NJ	279,350
Hudson	NJ	225,390
Hunterdon	NJ	47,090
Middlesex	NJ	277,510
Monmouth	NJ	234,220
Morris	NJ	178,820
Ocean	NJ	218,400
Passaic	NJ	161,620
Somerset	NJ	114,780
Sussex	NJ	55,160
Union	NJ	184,870
Warren	NJ	42,210
Bronx	NY	464,770
Dutchess	NY	104,600
Kings	NY	831,910
Nassau	NY	445,760
New York	NY	713,080
Orange	NY	123,690
Putnam	NY	34,900
Queens	NY	742,720
Richmond	NY	164,810
Rockland	NY	92,490
Suffolk	NY	496,400
Sullivan	NY	27,520
Ulster	NY	68,580
Westchester	NY	340,040
Pike	PA	20,580

Norfolk-Portsmouth-Newport News, VA (41)

DMA TV Households: 707,750
% of U.S. TV Households: .646

WTKR Norfolk, VA, ch. 3, CBS
WSKY-TV Manteo, NC, ch. 4, IND
WAVY-TV Portsmouth, VA, ch. 10, NBC
WVEC-TV Hampton, VA, ch. 13, ABC
*WHRO-TV Hampton-Norfolk, VA, ch. 15, ETV
WGNT Portsmouth, VA, ch. 27, IND
WTVZ Norfolk, VA, ch. 33, Fox
WVBT Virginia Beach, VA, ch. 43, IND
WPXV Norfolk, VA, ch. 49, IND

DMA Counties	State	TV Households
Camden	NC	3,270
Chowan	NC	5,610
Currituck	NC	8,490
Dare	NC	14,490
Gates	NC	4,040
Hertford	NC	9,020
Northamton	NC	8,810
Pasquotank	NC	13,840
Perquimans	NC	4,930
Accomack	VA	15,430
ChesapeakeCity	VA	75,510
Gloucester	VA	13,950
Hampton City	VA	54,260
Isle of Wight	VA	12,480
James City	VA	26,280
Mathews	VA	4,000
Norfolk City	VA	89,130
Northampton	VA	5,290
Newport News City	VA	71,280
Portsmouth City	VA	37,630
Southampton	VA	9,900
Suffolk City	VA	28,440
Surry	VA	2,660
Virginia Beach	VA	162,140
York	VA	26,870

Broadcasting & Cable Yearbook 2006

North Platte, NE (209)

DMA TV Households: 15,590
% of U.S. TV Households: .014

KNOP-TV North Platte, NE, ch. 2, NBC
***KPNE-TV** North Platte, NE, ch. 9, ETV

DMA Counties	State	TV Households
Arthur	NE	200
Blaine	NE	200
Lincoln	NE	14,420
Logan	NE	290
McPherson	NE	190
Thomas	NE	290

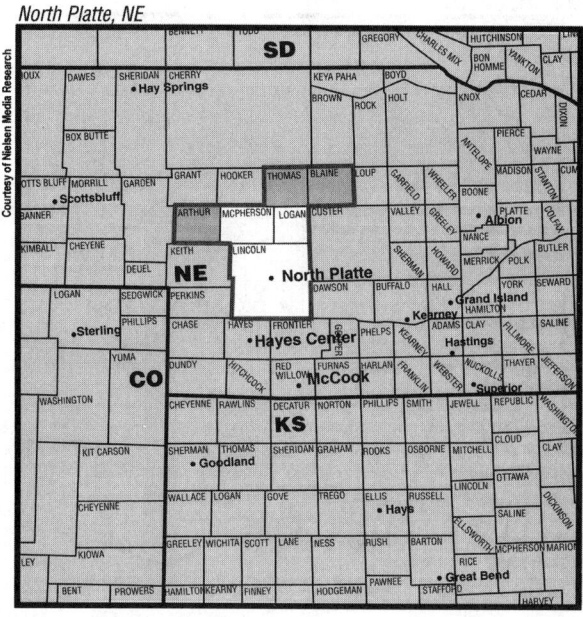

Odessa-Midland, TX (158)

DMA TV Households: 135,450
% of U.S. TV Households: .124

KMID Midland, TX, ch. 2, ABC
KWAB-TV Big Spring, TX, ch. 4, satellite to KTPX
KOSA-TV Odessa, TX, ch. 7, CBS
KWES-TV Odessa, TX, ch. 9, NBC
KUPB Midland, TX, ch. 18, Univision
KPEJ Odessa, TX, ch. 24, IND
KPXK Odessa, TX, ch. 30, PAX TV
***KOCV-TV** Odessa, TX, ch. 36, ETV
KMLM Odessa, TX, ch. 42, IND

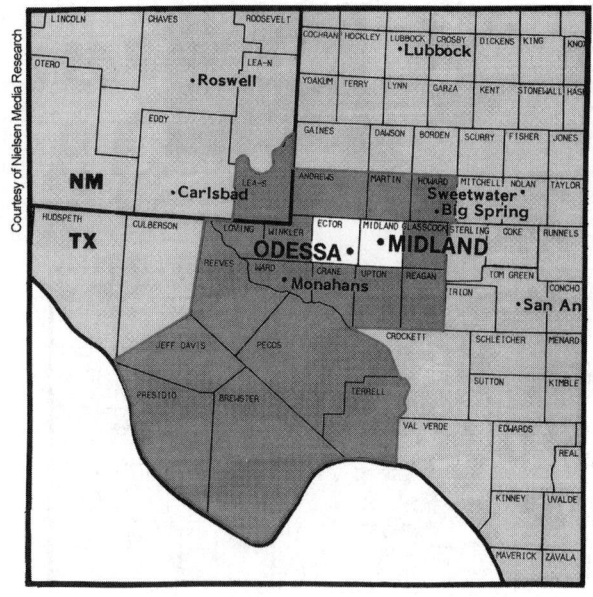

DMA Counties	State	TV Households	DMA Counties	State	TV Households
Lea South	NM	1,880	Midland	TX	44,030
Andrews	TX	4,780	Pecos	TX	4,870
Brewster	TX	3,240	Presidio	TX	2,660
Crane	TX	1,280	Reagan	TX	1,090
Ector	TX	45,380	Reeves	TX	3,840
Glasscock	TX	500	Terrell	TX	360
Howard	TX	11,390	Upton	TX	1,250
Jeff Davis	TX	830	Ward	TX	3,940
Loving	TX	100	Winkler	TX	2,440
Martin	TX	1,590			

Nielsen DMA Market Atlas

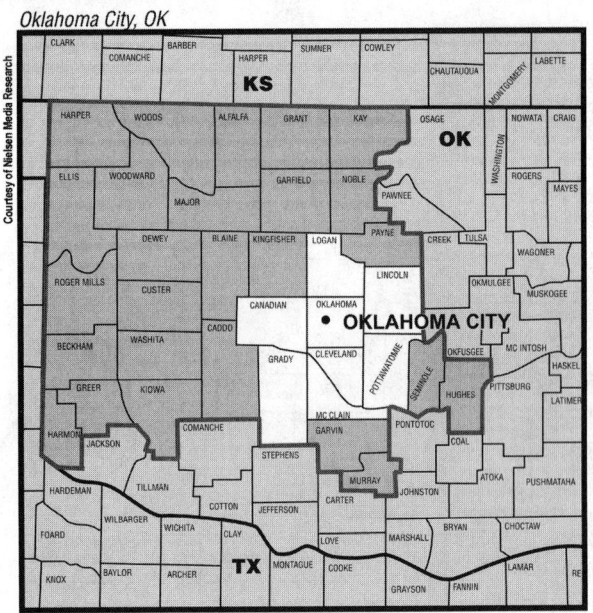

Oklahoma City, OK

Oklahoma City (45)

DMA TV Households: 655,250
% of U.S. TV Households: .598

KFOR-TV Oklahoma City, ch. 4, NBC
KOCO-TV Oklahoma City, ch. 5, ABC
KWTV Oklahoma City, ch. 9, CBS
*****KWET** Cheyenne, OK, ch. 12, ETV
*****KETA** Oklahoma City, ch. 13, ETV
KTBO-TV Oklahoma City, ch. 14, IND
KOKH-TV Oklahoma City, ch. 25, Fox
KTUZ-TV Shawnee, OK, ch. 30, Telemundo
KEYU Elk City, OK, ch. 31, IND
KOCB Oklahoma City, ch. 34, IND
KUOK Woodward, OK, ch. 35, IND
KAUT-TV Oklahoma City, ch. 43, IND
KOCM Norman, OK, ch. 46, IND
KSBI Oklahoma City, ch. 52, IND
KOPX Oklahoma City, ch. 62, IND

DMA Counties	State	TV Households	DMA Counties	State	TV Households
Alfalfa	OK	2,040	Kay	OK	18,410
Beckham	OK	7,362	Kingfisher	OK	5,330
Blaine	OK	3,930	Kiowa	OK	4,130
Caddo	OK	10,820	Lincoln	OK	12,150
Canadian	OK	34,720	Logan	OK	13,210
Cleveland	OK	87,250	Major	OK	2,860
Custer	OK	9,540	McClain	OK	10,740
Dewey	OK	1,840	Murray	OK	5,050
Ellis	OK	1,730	Noble	OK	4,420
Garfield	OK	22,760	Oklahoma	OK	276,850
Garvin	OK	10,720	Payne	OK	28,090
Grady	OK	18,570	Pottawatomie	OK	25,610
Grant	OK	1,970	Roger Mills	OK	1,330
Greer	OK	2,080	Seminole	OK	9,280
Harmon	OK	1,060	Washita	OK	4,260
Harper	OK	1,380	Woods	OK	3,470
Hughes	OK	5,190	Woodward	OK	7,190

Omaha (76)

DMA TV Households: 396,450
%of U.S. TV Households: .362

KMTV Omaha, ch. 3, CBS
WOWT Omaha, ch. 6, NBC
KETV Omaha, ch. 7, ABC
KXVO Omaha, ch. 15, IND
*****KYNE-TV** Omaha, ch. 26, ETV
*****KBIN** Council Bluffs, IA, ch. 32, ETV
*****KHIN** Red Oak, IA, ch. 36, ETV

DMA Counties	State	TV Households	DMA Counties	State	TV Households
Cass	IA	5,960	Colfax	NE	3,450
Crawford	IA	6,370	Cuming	NE	3,770
Fremont	IA	3,160	Dodge	NE	14,400
Harrison	IA	6,150	Douglas	NE	189,820
Mills	IA	5,570	Johnson	NE	1,880
Montgomery	IA	4,570	Nemaha	NE	2,760
Page	IA	6,420	Otoe	NE	6,060
Pottawattamie	IA	34,500	Platte	NE	12,02
Shelby	IA	4,9700	Richardson	NE	3,640
Atchison	MO	2,670	Sarpy	NE	50,340
Burt	NE	2,990	Saunders	NE	7,660
Cass	NE	9,860	Washington	NE	7,470

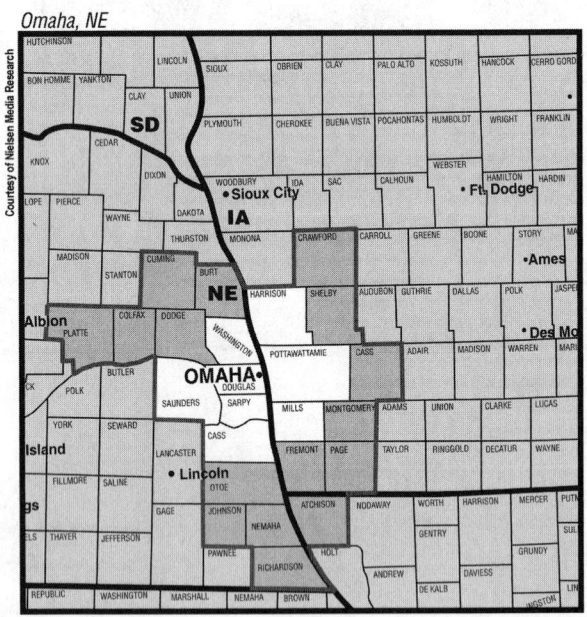

Omaha, NE

Broadcasting & Cable Yearbook 2006

Nielsen DMA Market Atlas

Orlando-Daytona Beach-Melbourne, FL (20)

DMA TV Households: 1,303,150
% of U.S. TV Households: 1.189

WESH Daytona Beach, FL, ch. 2, NBC
WKMG-TV Orlando, FL, ch. 6, CBS
WFTV Orlando, FL, ch. 9, ABC
*****WCEU** New Smyrna Beach, FL, ch. 15, ETV
WKCF Clermont, FL, ch. 18, WB
*****WMFE-TV** Orlando, FL, ch. 24, ETV
WVEN-TV Daytona Beach, FL, ch. 26, Univision
WRDQ Orlando, FL, ch. 27, IND
WOFL Orlando, FL, ch. 35, Fox
WOTF-TV Melbourne, FL, ch. 43, TeleFutura
WLCB-TV Leesburg, FL, ch. 45, IND
WTGL-TV Cocoa, FL, ch. 52, IND
WACX Leesburg, FL, ch. 55, IND
WOPX Melbourne, FL, ch. 56, PAX TV
WRBW Orlando, FL, ch. 65, UPN
*****WBCC** Cocoa, FL, ch. 68, ETV

DMA Counties	State	TV Households
Brevard	FL	217,990
Flagler	FL	29,120
Lake	FL	107,680
Marion	FL	121,230
Orange	FL	368,860
Osceola	FL	77,640
Seminole	FL	154,330
Sumter	FL	26,550
Volusia	FL	199,750

Ottumwa, Iowa-Kirksville, MO (200)

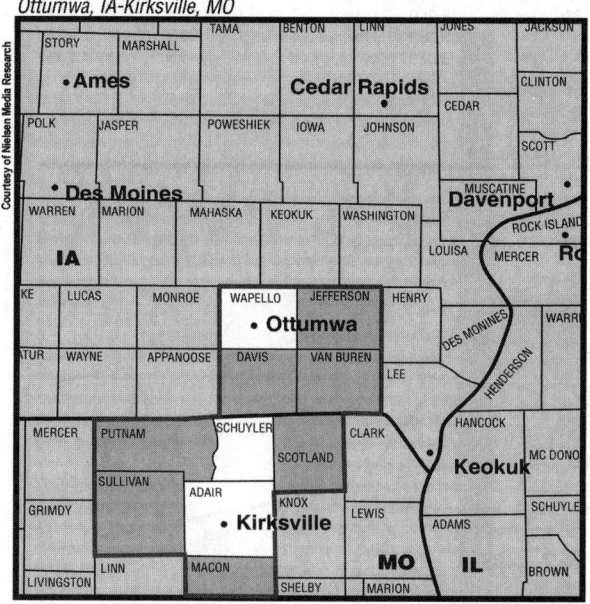

DMA TV Households: 51,190
% of U.S. TV Households: .047

KTVO Kirksville, MO, ch. 3, ABC
KYOU-TV Ottumwa, IA, ch. 15, IND

DMA Counties	State	TV Households
Davis	IA	3,110
Jefferson	IA	6,400
Van Buren	IA	3,180
Wapello	IA	14,580
Adair	MO	9,290
Macon	MO	6,300
Putnam	MO	2,160
Schuyler	MO	1,780
Scotland	MO	1,730
Sullivan	MO	2,660

Broadcasting & Cable Yearbook 2006

Nielsen DMA Market Atlas

Paducah, KY-Cape Girardeau, MO-Harrisburg-Mt. Vernon, IL

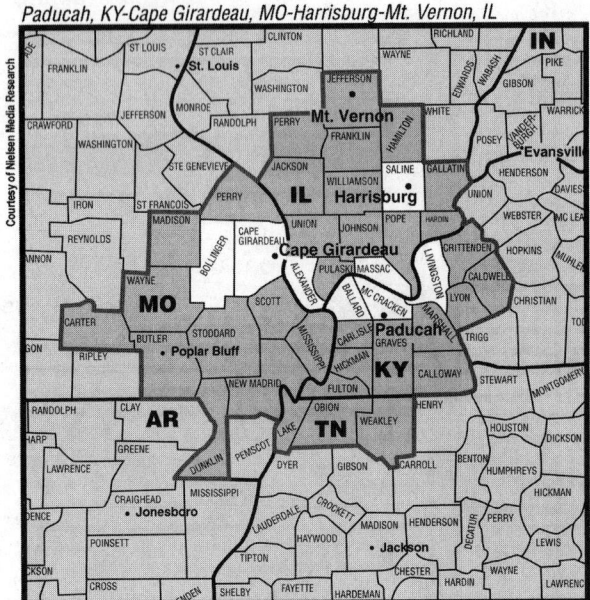

Paducah, KY-Cape Girardeau, MO-Harrisburg, IL (79)

DMA TV Households: 384,860
% of U.S. TV Households: .351

WSIL-TV Harrisburg, IL, ch. 3, ABC
WPSD-TV Paducah, KY, ch. 6, NBC
*WSIU-TV Carbondale, IL, ch. 8, ETV
KFVS-TV Cape Girardeau, MO, ch. 12, CBS
WPXS Mount Vernon, IL, ch. 13, IND
KPOB-TV Poplar Bluff, MO, ch. 15, satellite to WSIL-TV
*WKMU Murray, KY, ch. 21, ETV
KBSI Cape Girardeau, MO, ch. 23, Fox
WTCT Marion, IL, ch. 27, IND
*WKPD Paducah, KY, ch. 29, ETV
WDKA Paducah, KY, ch. 49, IND

DMA Counties	State	TV Households	DMA Counties	State	TV Households
Alexander	IL	3,640	Graves	KY	14,870
Franklin	IL	16,540	Hickman	KY	2,180
Gallatin	IL	2,680	Livingston	KY	3,940
Hamilton	IL	3,250	Lyon	KY	2,860
Hardin	IL	1,980	Marshall	KY	13,010
Jackson	IL	23,930	McCracken	KY	27,840
Jefferson	IL	15,660	Bollinger	MO	4,730
Johnson	IL	4,210	Butler	MO	16,860
Massac	IL	6,310	Cape Girardeau	MO	27,760
Perry	IL	8,400	Carter	MO	2,330
Pope	IL	1,680	Dunklin	MO	12,940
Pulaski	IL	2,760	Madison	MO	4,720
Saline	IL	10,640	Mississippi	MO	6,250
Union	IL	7,220	New Madrid	MO	7,510
Williamson	IL	26,340	Perry	MO	7,040
Ballard	KY	3,380	Scott	MO	16,070
Caldwell	KY	5,430	Stoddard	MO	12,050
Calloway	KY	14,380	Wayne	MO	5,490
Carlisle	KY	2,280	Lake	TN	2,270
Crittenden	KY	3,680	Obion	TN	13,340
Fulton	KY	3,060	Weakley	TN	13,350

Palm Springs, CA (159)

DMA TV Households: 135,190
% of U.S. TV Households: .123

KMIR-TV Palm Springs, CA, ch. 36, NBC
KESQ-TV Palm Springs, CA, ch. 42, ABC

DMA Counties	State	TV Households
Riverside Central	CA	135,190

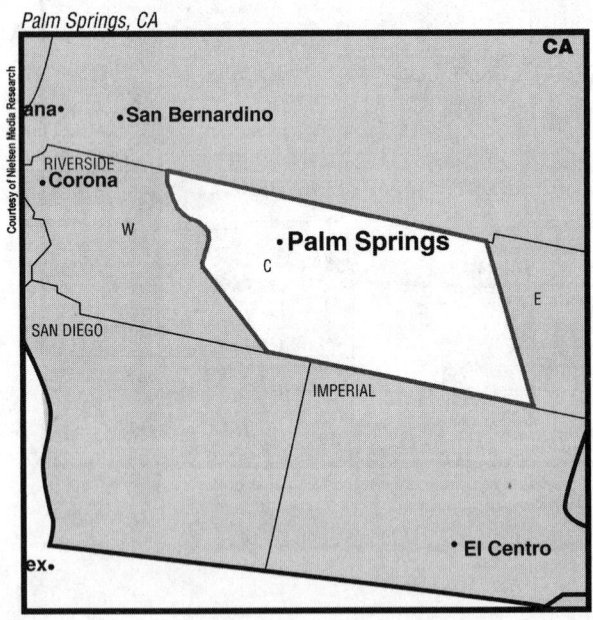

Palm Springs, CA

Nielsen DMA Market Atlas

Panama City, FL (160)

DMA TV Households: 134,770
% of U.S. TV Households: .123

WJHG-TV Panama City, FL, ch. 7, NBC
WMBB Panama City, FL, ch. 13, ABC
WPGX Panama City, FL, ch. 28, IND
WPCT Panama City Beach, FL, ch. 46, IND
WBIF Marianna, FL, ch. 51, IND
*WFSG Panama City, FL, ch. 56, ETV

DMA Counties	State	TV Households
Bay	FL	64,430
Calhoun	FL	4,560
Franklin	FL	3,790
Gulf	FL	6,100
Holmes	FL	7,330
Jackson	FL	17,380
Liberty	FL	2,410
Walton	FL	20,330
Washington	FL	8,470

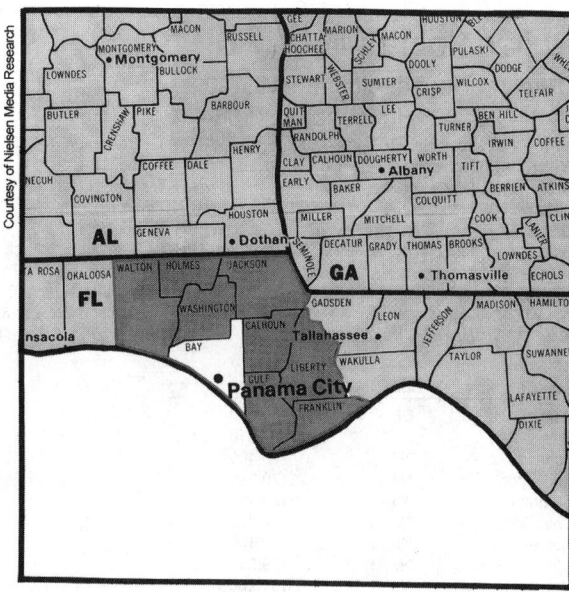

Parkersburg, WV (187)

DMA TV Households: 64,790
% of U.S. TV Households: .059

WTAP-TV Parkersburg, WV, ch. 15, NBC

DMA Counties	State	TV Households
Washington	OH	25,220
Pleasants	WV	2,870
Wood	WV	36,700

Peoria-Bloomington, IL (117)

DMA TV Households: 242,020
% of U.S. TV Households: .221

WHOI Peoria, IL, ch. 19, ABC
WEEK-TV Peoria, IL, ch. 25, NBC
WMBD-TV Peoria, IL, ch. 31, CBS
WYZZ-TV Bloomington, IL, ch. 43, Fox
*WTVP Peoria, IL, ch. 47, ETV
WAOE Peoria, IL, ch. 59, IND

DMA Counties	State	TV Households
Fulton	IL	14,700
Livingston	IL	13,720
Marshall	IL	5,240
Mason	IL	6,350
McLean	IL	60,660
Peoria	IL	72,600
Putnam	IL	2,480
Stark	IL	2,470
Tazewell	IL	50,880
Woodford	IL	12,920

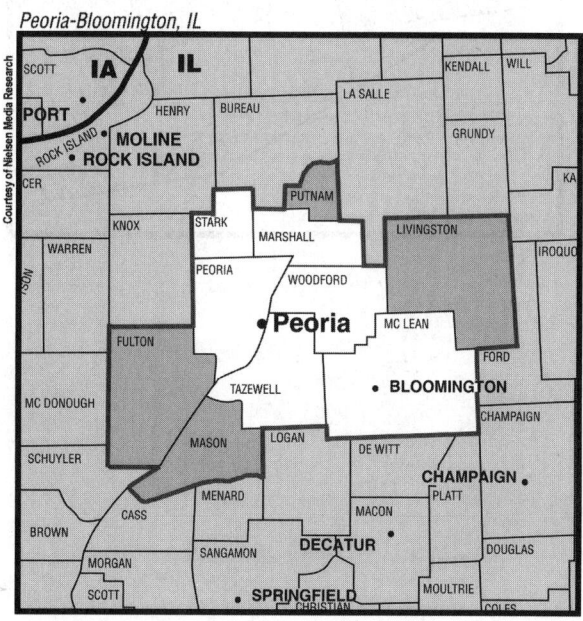

Broadcasting & Cable Yearbook 2006

Nielsen DMA Market Atlas

Philadelphia (4)

DMA TV Households: 2,919,410
% of U.S. TV Households: 2.664

KYW-TV Philadelphia, ch. 3, CBS
WPVI-TV Philadelphia, ch. 6, ABC
WCAU Philadelphia, ch. 10, NBC
WHYY-TV Wilmington, DE, ch. 12, ETV
WPHL-TV Philadelphia, ch. 17, WB
*****WNJS** Camden, NJ, ch. 23, ETV
WTXF-TV Philadelphia, ch. 29, Fox
*****WYBE** Philadelphia, ch. 35, ETV
*****WLVT-TV** Allentown, PA, ch. 39, ETV
WMGM-TV Wildwood, NJ, ch. 40, NBC
WGTW-TV Burlington, NJ, ch. 48, IND
WTVE Reading, PA, ch. 51, IND
*****WNJT** Trenton, NJ, ch. 52, ETV
WMCN-TV Atlantic City, NJ, ch. 53, IND
WPSG Philadelphia, ch. 57, UPN
WBPH-TV Bethlehem, PA, ch. 60, IND
WPPX Wilmington, DE, ch. 61, IND
WWSI Atlantic City, NJ, ch. 62, Telemundo
WUVP-TV Vineland, NJ, ch. 65, Univision
WFMZ-TV Allentown, PA, ch. 69, IND

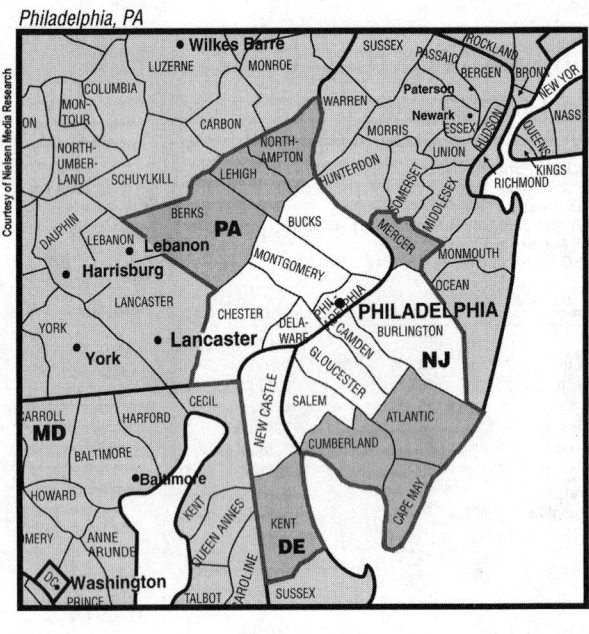

DMA Counties	State	TV Households
Kent	DE	52,190
New Castle	DE	197,210
Atlantic	NJ	99,460
Burlington	NJ	170,390
Camden	NJ	190,490
Cape May	NJ	42,110
Cumberland	NJ	51,130
Gloucester	NJ	99,590
Mercer	NJ	131,280
Salem	NJ	24,910
Berks	PA	145,570
Bucks	PA	230,190
Chester	PA	172,430
Delaware	PA	209,120
Lehigh	PA	126,690
Montgomery	PA	299,390
Northampton	PA	109,500
Philadelphia	PA	567,760

Phoenix (Prescott), AZ (15)

DMA TV Households: 1,596,950
% of U.S. TV Households: 1.457

KNAZ-TV Flagstaff, AZ, ch. 2, NBC
KTVK Phoenix, ch. 3, IND
KTFL Flagstaff, AZ, ch. 4, IND
KPHO-TV Phoenix, ch. 5, CBS
KMOH-TV Kingman, AZ, ch. 6, satellite to KBEH
KAZT-TV Prescott, AZ, ch. 7, IND
*****KAET** Phoenix, ch. 8, ETV
KCFG Flagstaff, AZ, ch. 9, IND
KSAZ-TV Phoenix, ch. 10, Fox
KPHZ Holbrook, AZ, ch. 11, IND
KPNX Mesa, AZ, ch. 12, NBC
KFPH-TV Flagstaff, AZ, ch. 13, IND
KNXV-TV Phoenix, ch. 15, ABC
KPAZ-TV Phoenix, ch. 21, IND
KTVW-TV Phoenix, ch. 33, Univision
KDTP Phoenix, ch. 39, IND
KUTP Phoenix, ch. 45, IND
KPPX Tolleson, AZ, ch. 51, IND
KASW Phoenix, ch. 61, IND

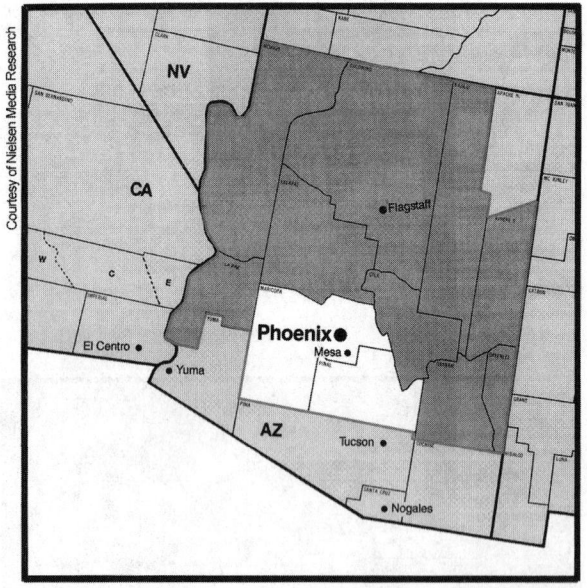

DMA Counties	State	TV Households
Apache S.	AZ	4,520
Coconino	AZ	43,220
Gila	AZ	20,230
Graham	AZ	9,880
Greenlee	AZ	2,840
La Paz	AZ	8,730
Maricopa	AZ	1,254,030
Mohave	AZ	70,570
Navajo	AZ	31,210
Pinal	AZ	73,730
Yavapai	AZ	77,990

Broadcasting & Cable Yearbook 2006

Nielsen DMA Market Atlas

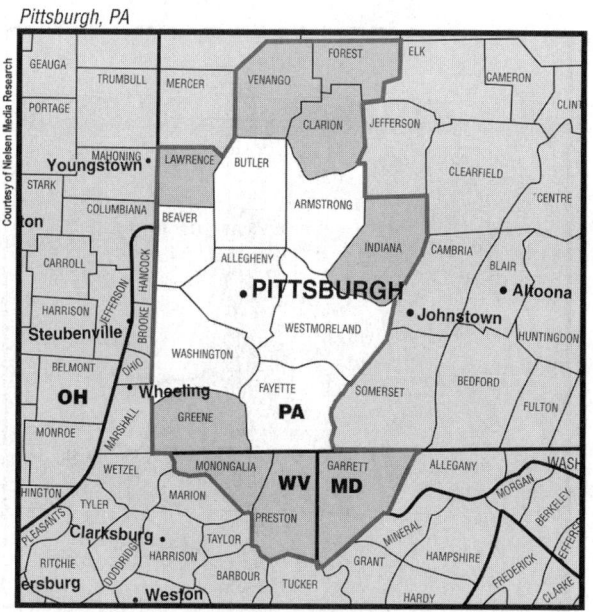

Pittsburgh (22)

DMA TV Households: 1,186,010
% of U.S. TV Households: 1.082

KDKA-TV Pittsburgh, ch. 2, CBS
WTAE-TV Pittsburgh, ch. 4, ABC
WPXI Pittsburgh, ch. 11, NBC
*****WQED** Pittsburgh, ch. 13, ETV
WQEX Pittsburgh, ch. 16, IND
WNPA Jeannette, PA, ch. 19, UPN
WCWB Pittsburgh, ch. 22, WB
*****WNPB-TV** Morgantown, WV, ch. 24, ETV
*****WGPT** Oakland, MD, ch. 36, ETV
WPCB-TV Greensburg, PA, ch. 40, IND
WPGH-TV Pittsburgh, ch. 53, Fox

DMA Counties	State	TV Households	DMA Counties	State	TV Households
Garrett	MD	11,520	Greene	PA	15,260
Allegheny	PA	532,430	Indiana	PA	34,820
Armstrong	PA	29,200	Lawrence	PA	36,890
Beaver	PA	72,480	Venango	PA	22,370
Butler	PA	70,570	Washington	PA	83,460
Clarion	PA	15,910	Westmoreland	PA	151,970
Fayette	PA	59,750	Monongalia	WV	35,360
Forest	PA	1,980	Preston	WV	12,040

Portland-Auburn, ME (74)

DMA TV Households: 409,060
% of U.S. TV Households: .373

WCSH Portland, ME, ch. 6, NBC
WMTW-TV Poland Spring, ME, ch. 8, ABC
*****WCBB** Augusta, ME, ch. 10, ETV
WGME-TV Portland, ME, ch. 13, CBS
WPFO Waterville, ME, ch. 23, Fox
*****WMEA-TV** Biddeford, ME, ch. 26, ETV
WPME Lewiston, ME, ch. 35, IND
WPXT Portland, ME, ch. 51, IND

DMA Counties	State	TV Households
Androscoggin	ME	45,050
Cumberland	ME	112,470
Franklin	ME	12,320
Kennebec	ME	50,940
Knox	ME	17,130
Lincoln	ME	15,280
Oxford	ME	23,650
Sagadahoc	ME	15,190
York	ME	83,280
Carroll	NH	19,610
Coos	NH	14,140

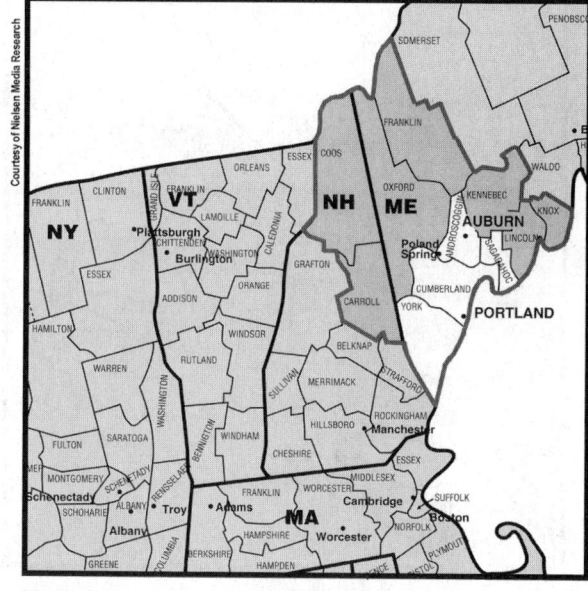

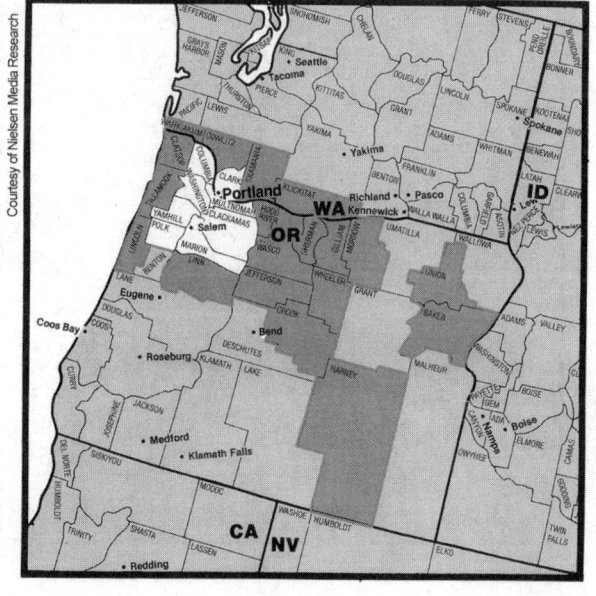

Portland, OR (24)

DMA TV Households: 1,086,900
% of U.S. TV Households: .992

KATU Portland, OR, ch. 2, ABC
KOIN Portland, OR, ch. 6, CBS
KGW-TV Portland, OR, ch. 8, NBC
*****KOPB-TV** Portland, OR, ch. 10, ETV
KPTV Portland, OR, ch. 12, Fox
*****KTVR** La Grande, OR, ch. 13, ETV
KPOU La Grande, OR, ch. 16, IND
KPXG Salem, OR, ch. 22, IND
KNMT Portland, OR, ch. 24, IND
KWBP Salem, OR, ch. 32, WB
KPDX Vancouver, WA, ch. 49, UPN

DMA Counties	State	TV Households	DMA Counties	State	TV Households
Baker	OR	6,750	Polk	OR	24,320
Clackamas	OR	136,500	Sherman	OR	650
Clatsop	OR	14,270	Tillamook	OR	10,040
Columbia	OR	17,380	Union	OR	9,280
Crook	OR	7,890	Wasco	OR	9,030
Gilliam	OR	770	Washington	OR	182,330
Harney	OR	2,810	Wheeler	OR	680
Hood River	OR	6,700	Yamhill	OR	30,130
Jefferson	OR	6,890	Clark	WA	138,500
Lincoln	OR	19,270	Cowlitz	WA	35,810
Linn	OR	39,640	Klickitat	WA	7,080
Marion	OR	103,430	Skamania	WA	3,710
Multnomah	OR	288,930	Wahkiakum	WA	1,350

Broadcasting & Cable Yearbook 2006

Nielsen DMA Market Atlas

Presque Isle, ME (203)

DMA TV Households: 31,840
% of U.S. TV Households: .029

WAGM-TV Presque Isle, ME, ch. 8, CBS (ABC, NBC)
*WMEM-TV Presque Isle, ME, ch. 10, ETV

DMA Counties	State	TV Households
Aroostook	ME	31,840

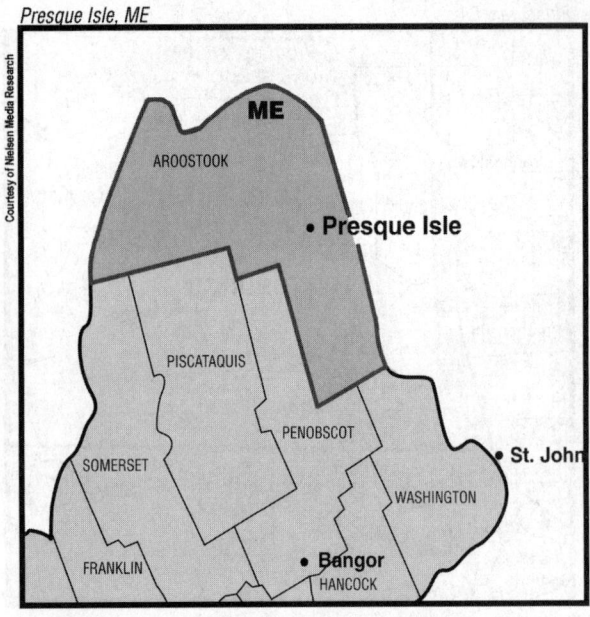

Providence, RI-New Bedford, MA (49)

DMA TV Households: 644,980
% of U.S. TV Households: .589

WLNE New Bedford, MA, ch. 6, ABC
WJAR Providence, RI, ch. 10, NBC
WPRI-TV Providence, RI, ch. 12, CBS
WLWC New Bedford, MA, ch. 28, UPN, WB
*WSBE-TV Providence, RI, ch. 36, ETV
WDPX Vineyard Haven, MA, ch. 58, satellite to WBPX
WNAC-TV Providence, RI, ch. 64, Fox
WPXQ Block Island, RI, ch. 69, PAX TV

DMA Counties	State	TV Households
Bristol	MA	216,080
Bristol	RI	19,650
Kent	RI	71,510
Newport	RI	36,820
Providence	RI	250,440
Washington	RI	50,480

Quincy, IL-Hannibal, MO-Keokuk, IA (167)

DMA TV Households: 105,070
% of U.S. TV Households: .096

KHQA-TV Hannibal, MO, ch. 7, CBS
WGEM-TV Quincy, IL, ch. 10, NBC
WTJR Quincy, IL, ch. 16, IND
*WMEC Macomb, IL, ch. 22, ETV
*WQEC Quincy, IL, ch. 27, ETV

DMA Counties	State	TV Households	DMA Counties	State	TV Households
Adams	IL	26,610	Clark	MO	3,070
Brown	IL	2,060	Knox	MO	1,720
Hancock	IL	7,640	Lewis	MO	3,750
McDonough	IL	12,370	Marion	MO	11,210
Pike	IL	6,640	Monroe	MO	3,750
Schuyler	IL	2,970	Ralls	MO	3,770
Scott	IL	2,280	Shelby	MO	2,650
Lee	IA	14,580			

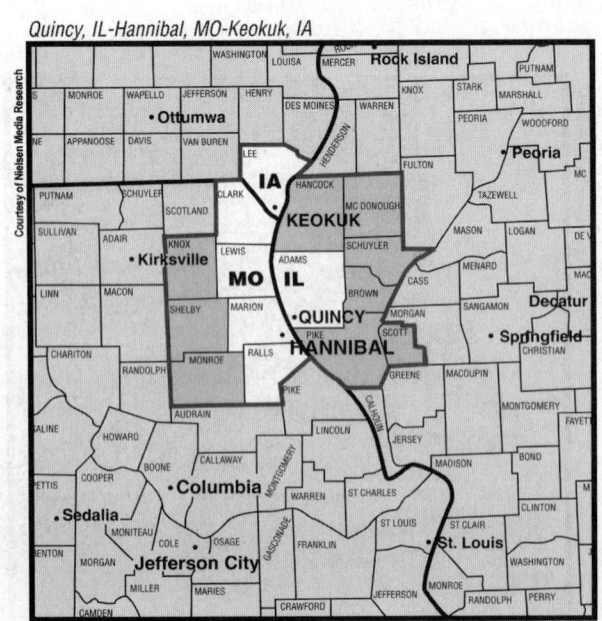

Raleigh-Durham (Fayetteville), NC (29)

DMA TV Households: 966,720
% of U.S. TV Households: .882

*WUNC-TV Chapel Hill, NC, ch. 4, ETV
WRAL-TV Raleigh, NC, ch. 5, CBS
WTVD Durham, NC, ch. 11, ABC
WNCN Goldsboro, NC, ch. 17, NBC
WLFL Raleigh, NC, ch. 22, WB
WRDC Durham, NC, ch. 28, UPN
WRAY-TV Wilson, NC, ch. 30, IND
*WUNP-TV Roanoke Rapids, NC, ch. 36, ETV
WUVC-TV Fayetteville, NC, ch. 40, Univision
WRPX Rocky Mount, NC, ch. 47, IND
WRAZ Raleigh, NC, ch. 50, Fox
WFPX Fayetteville, NC, ch. 62, IND

DMA Counties	State	TV Households	DMA Counties	State	TV Households
Chatham	NC	23,110	Moore	NC	33,390
Cumberland	NC	109,190	Nash	NC	35,010
Durham	NC	94,360	Orange	NC	44,390
Edgecombe	NC	20,110	Person	NC	14,970
Franklin	NC	20,410	Sampson	NC	23,280
Granville	NC	18,640	Vance	NC	16,680
Halifax	NC	22,130	Wake	NC	273,880
Harnett	NC	37,870	Warren	NC	7,920
Hoke	NC	13,390	Wayne	NC	42,960
Johnston	NC	53,830	Wilson	NC	29,640
Lee	NC	18,250	Mecklenburg	VA	13,310

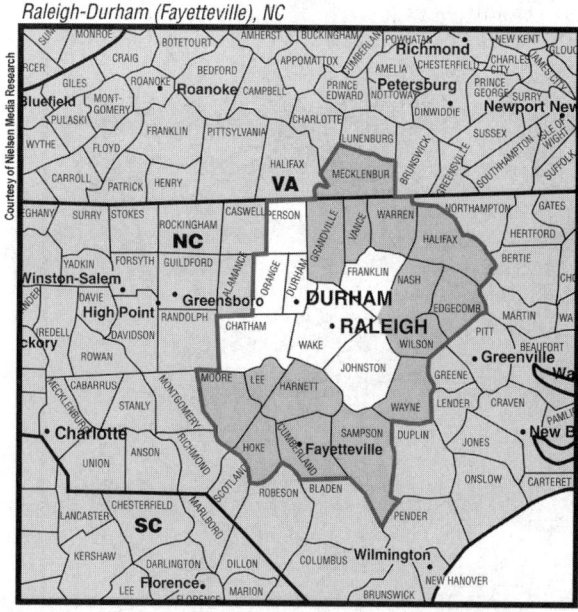

Rapid City, SD (178)

DMA TV Households: 93,220
% of U.S. TV Households: .085

KOTA-TV Rapid City, SD, ch. 3, ABC
KIVV-TV Lead, SD, ch. 5, satellite to KEVN-TV
KEVN-TV Rapid City, SD, ch. 7, Fox
KSWY Sheridan, WY, ch. 7, NBC
*KZSD-TV Martin, SD, ch. 8, ETV
*KBHE-TV Rapid City, SD, ch. 9, ETV
KHSD-TV Lead, SD, ch. 11, satellite to KOTA-TV
KSGW-TV Sheridan, WY, ch. 12, satellite to KOTA-TV
*KTNE-TV Alliance, NE, ch. 13, ETV
KCLO-TV Rapid City, SD, ch. 15, IND
KNBN Rapid City, SD, ch. 21, NBC

DMA Counties	State	TV Households	DMA Counties	State	TV Households
Carter	MT	470	Jackson	SD	880
Banner	NE	290	Lawrence	SD	9,220
Morrill	NE	2,080	Meade	SD	9,480
Sheridan	NE	2,460	Pennington	SD	37,220
Sioux	NE	590	Perkins	SD	1,380
Bennett	SD	1,070	Shannon	SD	2,970
Butte	SD	3,490	Ziebach	SD	760
Custer	SD	3,200	Crook	WY	2,390
Fall River	SD	2,970	Sheridan	WY	11,430
Haakon	SD	780	Weston	WY	2,690
Harding	SD	440			

Reno (114)

DMA TV Households: 246,700
% of U.S. TV Households: .225

KTVN Reno, ch. 2, CBS
KRNV Reno, ch. 4, NBC
*KNPB Reno, ch. 5, ETV
KEGS Goldfield, NV, ch. 7, IND
KWNV Winnemucca, NV, ch. 7, satellite to KRNV
KOLO-TV Reno, ch. 8, ABC
KRXI-TV Reno, ch. 11, Fox
KAME-TV Reno, ch. 21, IND
KREN-TV Reno, ch. 27, IND

DMA Counties	State	TV Households	DMA Counties	State	TV Households
Alpine	CA	470	Humboldt	NV	4,910
El Dorado East	CA	13,250	Lander	NV	1,510
Lassen	CA	9,570	Lyon	NV	15,700
Mono	CA	4,550	Mineral	NV	2,090
Carson City	NV	20,910	Pershing	NV	1,770
Churchill	NV	9,080	Storey	NV	1,500
Douglas	NV	18,220	Washoe	NV	142,790
Esmeralda	NV	380			

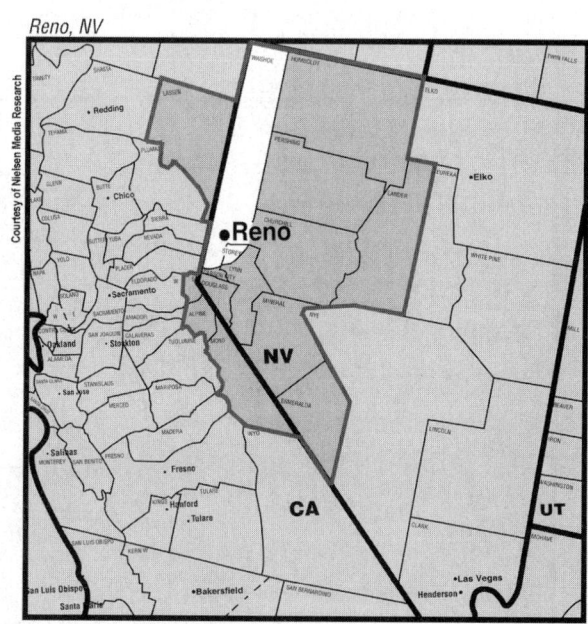

Nielsen DMA Market Atlas

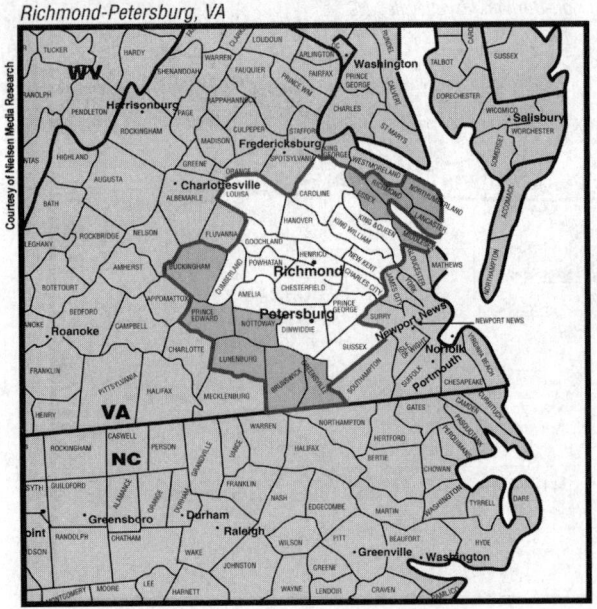

Richmond-Petersburg, VA (61)

DMA TV Households: 509,860
% of U.S. TV Households: .465

WTVR-TV Richmond, VA, ch. 6, CBS
WRIC-TV Petersburg, VA, ch. 8, ABC
WWBT Richmond, VA, ch. 12, NBC
*****WCVE-TV** Richmond, VA, ch. 23, ETV
WRLH-TV Richmond, VA, ch. 35, Fox
*****WCVW** Richmond, VA, ch. 57, ETV
WUPV Ashland, VA, ch. 65, UPN

DMA Counties	State	TV Households	DMA Counties	State	TV Households
Amelia	VA	4,630	King William	VA	5,360
Brunswick	VA	6,410	Lancaster	VA	5,210
Buckingham	VA	5,690	Louisa	VA	11,330
Caroline	VA	8,760	Lunenburg	VA	5,120
Charles City	VA	2,930	Middlesex	VA	4,430
Chesterfield	VA	111,540	New Kent	VA	5,720
Cumberland	VA	3,790	Northumberland	VA	5,690
Dinwiddie	VA	22,820	Nottoway	VA	5,710
Essex	VA	4,230	Powhatan	VA	8,570
Goochland	VA	7,150	Prince Edward	VA	6,990
Greensville	VA	5,990	Prince George	VA	20,740
Hanover	VA	34,710	Richmond	VA	3,250
Henrico	VA	113,820	Richmond City	VA	82,370
King and Queen	VA	2,840	Sussex	VA	4,060

Roanoke-Lynchburg, VA (67)

DMA TV Households: 455,670
% of U.S. TV Households: .407

WDBJ Roanoke, VA, ch. 7, CBS
WSLS-TV Roanoke, VA, ch. 10, NBC
WSET-TV Lynchburg, VA, ch. 13, ABC
*****WBRA-TV** Roanoke, VA, ch. 15, ETV
WJPR Lynchburg, VA, ch. 21, Fox
WDRL-TV Danville, VA, ch. 24, UPN
WFXR-TV Roanoke, VA, ch. 27, satellite to WJPR
WPXR Roanoke, VA, ch. 38, PAX TV

DMA Counties	State	TV Households	DMA Counties	State	TV Households
Alleghany	VA	9,490	Giles	VA	7,090
Amherst	VA	12,100	Grayson	VA	6,770
Appomattox	VA	5,450	Halifax	VA	14,980
Bath	VA	2,070	Henry	VA	30,340
Bedford	VA	27,590	Highland	VA	1,060
Bland	VA	2,760	Montgomery	VA	37,200
Botetourt	VA	12,360	Nelson	VA	6,080
Campbell	VA	47,270	Pittsylvania	VA	45,460
Carroll	VA	15,510	Pulaski	VA	14,860
Charlotte	VA	5,200	Roanoke	VA	88,110
Craig	VA	2,140	Rockbridge	VA	13,480
Floyd	VA	6,120	Wythe	VA	12,070
Franklin	VA	20,110			

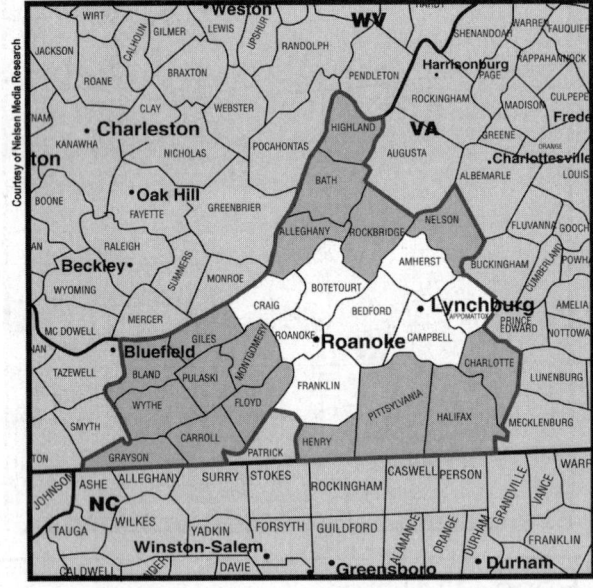

Rochester, MN-Mason City, IA-Austin, MN (153)

DMA TV Households: 142,300
% of U.S. TV Households: .130

KIMT Mason City, IA, ch. 3, CBS
KAAL Austin, MN, ch. 6, ABC
KTTC Rochester, MN, ch. 10, NBC
*****KSMQ-TV** Austin, MN, ch. 15, ETV
*****KYIN** Mason City, IA, ch. 24, ETV
KXLT-TV Rochester, MN, ch. 47, Fox

DMA Counties	State	TV Households
Cerro Gordo	IA	18,800
Floyd	IA	6,750
Hancock	IA	4,710
Howard	IA	3,870
Mitchell	IA	4,350
Winnebago	IA	4,670
Worth	IA	3,180
Dodge	MN	7,150
Fillmore	MN	8,440
Freeborn	MN	13,150
Mower	MN	15,750
Olmsted	MN	51,750

Broadcasting & Cable Yearbook 2006

Rochester, NY (75)

DMA TV Households: 396,880
% of U.S. TV Households: .362

WROC-TV Rochester, NY, ch. 8, CBS
WHEC-TV Rochester, NY, ch. 10, NBC
WHAM-TV Rochester, NY, ch. 13, ABC
***WXXI-TV** Rochester, NY, ch. 21, ETV
WUHF Rochester, NY, ch. 31, Fox

DMA Counties	State	TV Households
Livingston	NY	22,380
Monroe	NY	196,360
Ontario	NY	40,230
Rochester City	NY	93,240
Wayne	NY	35,620
Yates	NY	9,050

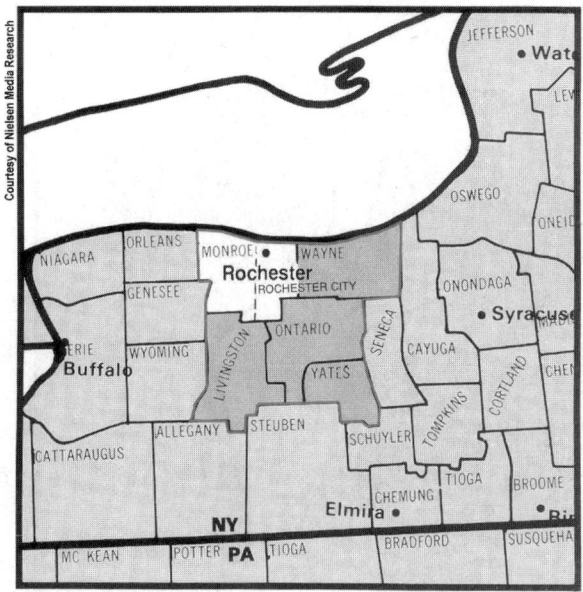

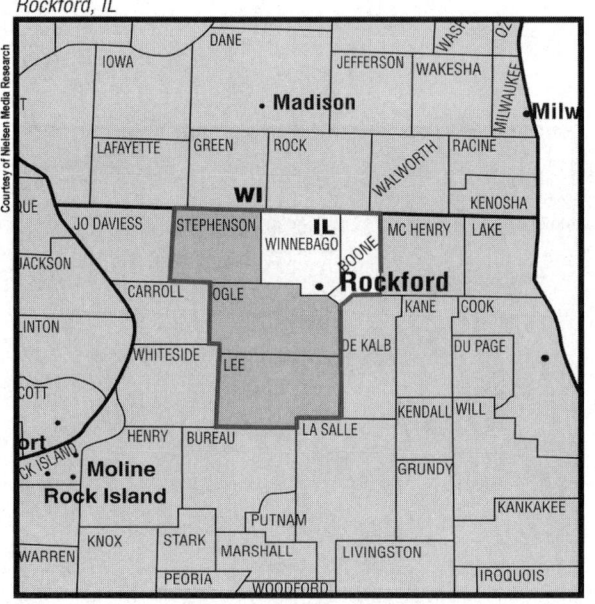

Rockford, IL

Rockford, IL (134)

DMA TV Households: 181,180
% of U.S. TV Households: .165

WREX-TV Rockford, IL, ch. 13, ABC
WTVO Rockford, IL, ch. 17, NBC
WIFR Rockford, IL, ch. 23, CBS
WQRF-TV Rockford, IL, ch. 39, Fox

DMA Counties	State	TV Households
Boone	IL	16,630
Lee	IL	13,020
Ogle	IL	20,320
Stephenson	IL	19,590
Winnebago	IL	111,620

Sacramento-Stockton-Modesto, CA (19)

DMA TV Households: 1,315,030
% of U.S. TV Households: 1.20

KCRA-TV Sacramento, CA, ch. 3, NBC
***KVIE** Sacramento, CA, ch. 6, ETV
KXTV Sacramento, CA, ch. 10, ABC
KOVR Stockton, CA, ch. 13, CBS
KUVS-TV Modesto, CA, ch. 19, Univision
***KBSV** Ceres, CA, ch. 23, ETV
KSPX Sacramento, CA, ch. 29, IND
KMAX-TV Sacramento, CA, ch. 31, IND
KTXL Sacramento, CA, ch. 40, Fox
KQCA Stockton, CA, ch. 58, IND
KTFK Stockton, CA, ch. 64, TeleFutura

DMA Counties	State	TV Households	DMA Counties	State	TV Households
Amador	CA	13,140	San Joaquin	CA	203,720
Calaveras	CA	17,680	Sierra	CA	1,470
Colusa	CA	6,160	Solano East	CA	83,700
El Dorado West	CA	49,660	Stanislaus	CA	156,660
Nevada	CA	37,510	Sutter	CA	28,340
Placer	CA	111,500	Tuolumne	CA	22,300
Plumas	CA	8,560	Yolo	CA	63,550
Sacramento	CA	489,760	Yuba	CA	21,320

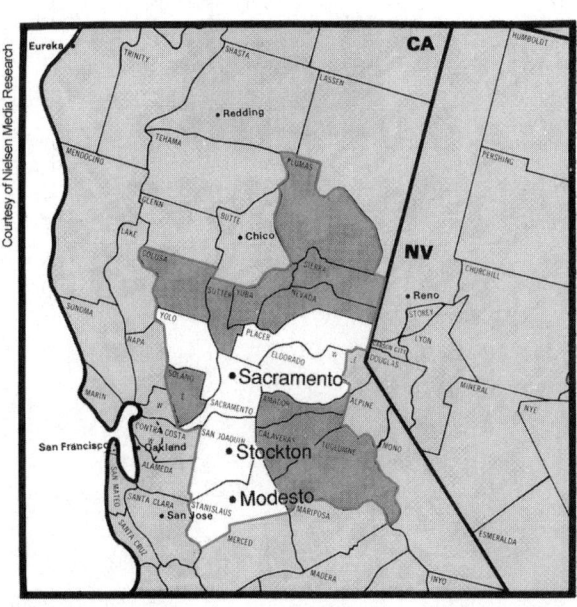

Broadcasting & Cable Yearbook 2006

Nielsen DMA Market Atlas

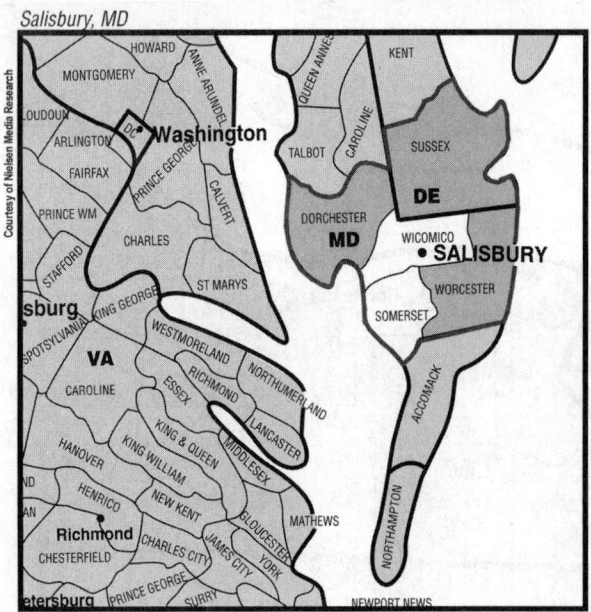

Salisbury, MD

Salisbury, MD (150)

DMA TV Households: 146,510
% of U.S. TV Households: .134

WBOC-TV Salisbury, MD, ch. 16, CBS (NBC)
***WCPB** Salisbury, MD, ch. 28, ETV
WMDT Salisbury, MD, ch. 47, ABC (NBC)
***WDPB** Seaford, DE, ch. 64, ETV

DMA Counties	State	TV Households
Sussex	DE	69,610
Dorchester	MD	12,750
Somerset	MD	8,760
Wicomico	MD	33,830
Worcester	MD	21,560

Salt Lake City, UT (36)

DMA TV Households: 800,000
% of U.S. TV Households: .730

KUTV Salt Lake City, ch. 2, CBS
KJWY Jackson, WY, ch. 2, NBC
KBJN Ely, NV, ch. 3, NBC
KUTF Price, UT, ch. 3, TeleFutura
KCSG Cedar City, UT, ch. 4, IND
KTVX Salt Lake City, ch. 4, ABC
KSL-TV Salt Lake City, ch. 5, NBC
***KBNY** Ely, NV, ch. 6, ETV
KBCJ Vernal, UT, ch. 6, IND
***KUED** Salt Lake City, ch. 7, ET
***KUEN** Ogden, UT, ch. 9, ETV
KENV Elko, NV, ch. 10, NBC
***KBYU-TV** Provo, UT, ch. 11, ETV
KBEO Jackson, WY, ch. 11, IND
KCBU Logan, UT, ch. 12, IND
KUSG St. George, UT, ch. 12, IND
KSTU Salt Lake City, ch. 13, Fox
KGWR-TV Rock Springs, WY, ch. 13, CBS
KJZZ-TV Salt Lake City, ch. 14, IND
KUPX Provo, UT, ch. 16, IND
***KUEW** St. George, UT, ch. 18, ETV
***KUES** Richfield, UT, ch. 19, ETV
KTMW Salt Lake City, ch. 20, IND V
KPNZ Ogden, UT, ch. 24, UPN
KUWB Ogden, UT, ch. 30, WB
KUTH Provo, UT, ch. 32, Univision

DMA Counties	State	TV Households	DMA Counties	State	TV Households
Bear Lake	ID	2,170	Morgan	UT	2,170
Franklin	ID	3,660	Piute	UT	490
Oneida	ID	1,410	Rich	UT	670
Elko	NV	14,050	Salt Lake	UT	302,680
Eureka	NV	570	San Juan	UT	3,5670
White Pine	NV	2,940	Sanpete	UT	6,630
Beaver	UT	2,030	Sevier	UT	6,230
Box Elder	UT	13,720	Summit	UT	12,020
Cache	UT	28,970	Tooele	UT	15,570
Carbon	UT	7,120	Uintah	UT	8,950
Daggett	UT	290	Utah	UT	110,570
Davis	UT	79,430	Wasatch	UT	5,590
Duchesne	UT	4,890	Washington	UT	36,670
Emery	UT	3,450	Wayne	UT	880
Garfield	UT	1,360	Weber	UT	68,680
Grand	UT	2,920	Lincoln	WY	5,870
Iron	UT	11,540	Sublette	WY	2,5520
Juab	UT	2,570	Sweetwater	WY	14,090
Kane	UT	2,030	Uinta	WY	7,140
Millard	UT	3,870			

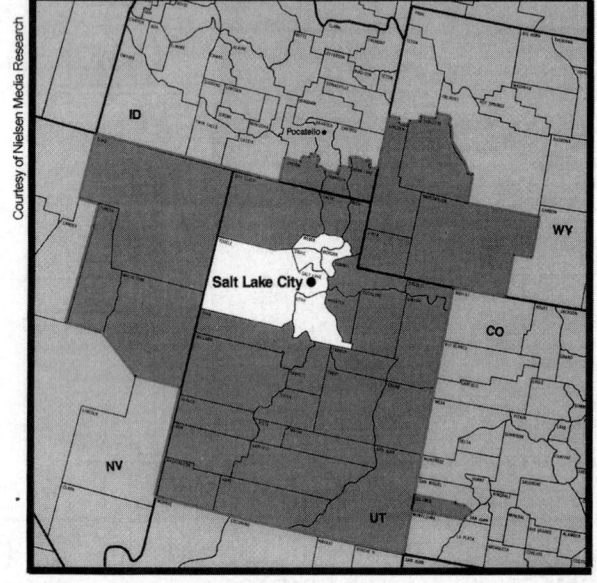

Broadcasting & Cable Yearbook 2006

Nielsen DMA Market Atlas

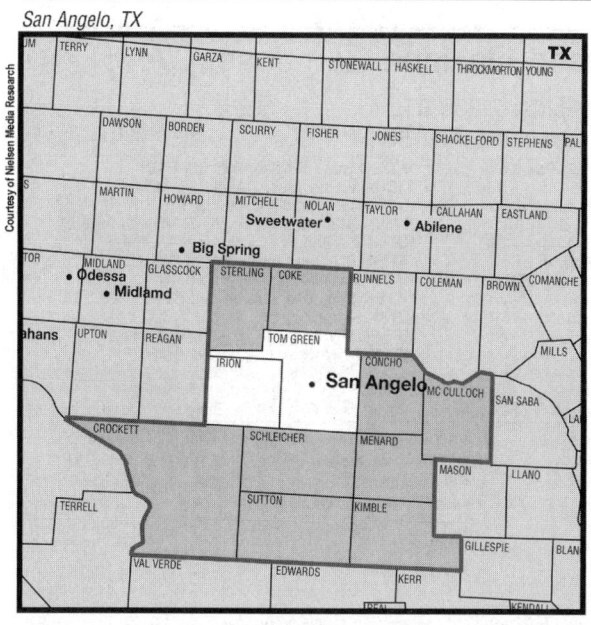

San Angelo, TX (196)

DMA TV Households: 53,530
% of U.S. TV Households: .049

KSAN-TV San Angelo, TX, ch. 3, satellite to KRBC-TV
KIDY San Angelo, TX, ch. 6, Fox
KLST San Angelo, TX, ch. 8, CBS

DMA Counties	State	TV Households
Coke	TX	1,570
Concho	TX	980
Crockett	TX	1,460
Irion	TX	680
Kimble	TX	1,900
McCulloch	TX	3,170
Menard	TX	950
Schleicher	TX	1,080
Sterling	TX	490
Sutton	TX	1,530
Tom Green	TX	39,720

San Antonio, TX (37)

DMA TV Households: 748.950
% of U.S. TV Households: .683

KBEJ Fredericksburg, TX, ch. 2, UPN
WOAI-TV San Antonio, TX, ch. 4, NBC
KENS-TV San Antonio, TX, ch. 5, CBS
***KLRN** San Antonio, TX, ch. 9, ETV
KTRG Del Rio, TX, ch. 10, IND
KSAT-TV San Antonio, TX, ch. 12, ABC
KVAW Eagle Pass, TX, ch. 16, IND
KHCE-TV San Antonio, TX, ch. 23, ETV
KPXL Uvalde, TX, ch. 26, PAX TV
KABB San Antonio, TX, ch. 29, Fox
KRRT Kerrville, TX, ch. 35, WB
KWEX-TV San Antonio, TX, ch. 41, Univision
KVDA San Antonio, TX, ch. 60, Telemundo

DMA Counties	State	TV Households	DMA Counties	State	TV Households
Atascosa	TX	13,900	Kerr	TX	18,410
Bandera	TX	7,740	Kinney	TX	1,220
Bexar	TX	521,850	LaSalle	TX	1,840
Comal	TX	33,620	Lavaca	TX	7,540
DeWitt	TX	7,140	Maverick	TX	13,520
Dimmit	TX	3,260	McMullen	TX	390
Edwards	TX	780	Medina	TX	13,770
Frio	TX	4,900	Real	TX	1,180
Goliad	TX	2,720	Uvalde	TX	8,490
Gonzales	TX	7,000	Val Verde	TX	14,800
Guadalupe	TX	34,560	Wilson	TX	12,730
Karnes	TX	4,490	Zavala	TX	3,370
Kendall	TX	9,730			

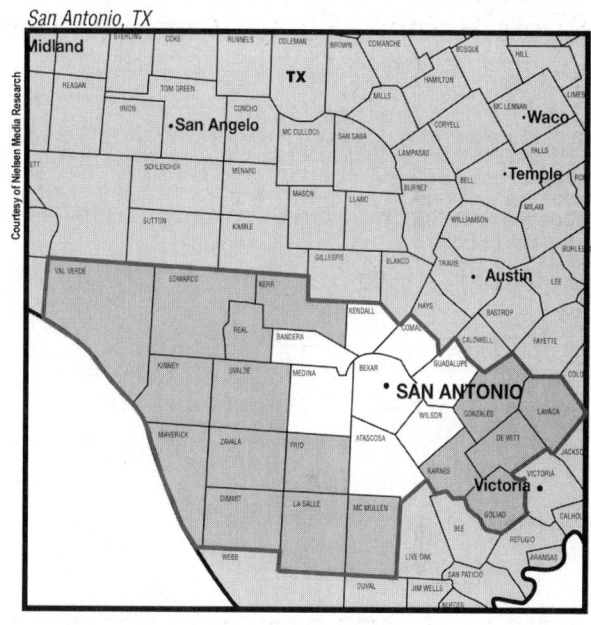

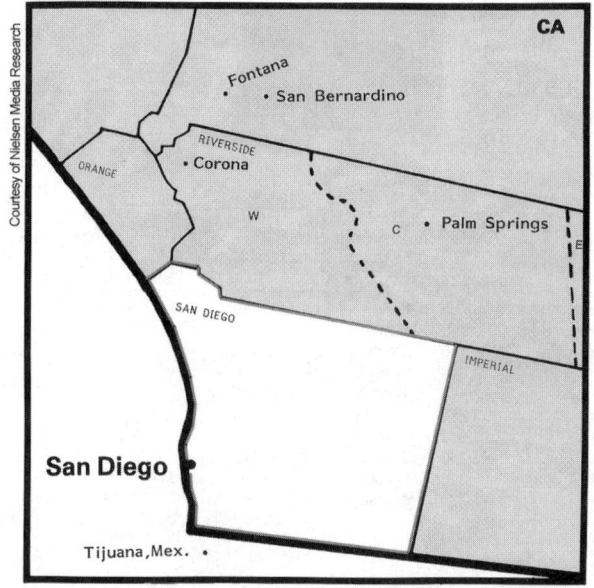

San Diego (26)

DMA TV Households: 1,025,730
% of U.S. TV Households: .936

XETV Tijuana, Mexico, ch. 6, Fox
KFMB-TV San Diego, ch. 8, CBS
KGTV San Diego, ch. 10, ABC
***KPBS** San Diego, ch. 15, ETV
KNSD San Diego, ch. 39, NBC
KUSI-TV San Diego, ch. 51, IND
KSWB-TV San Diego, ch. 69, WB

DMA Counties	State	TV Households
San Diego	CA	1,025,730

Broadcasting & Cable Yearbook 2006

Nielsen DMA Market Atlas

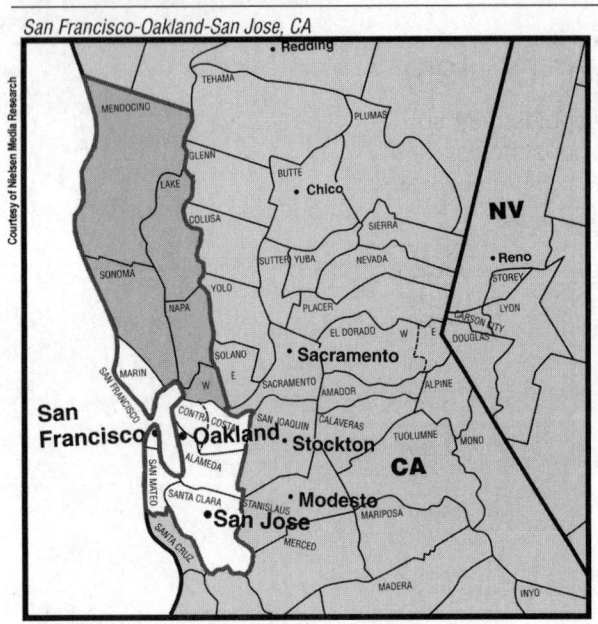

San Francisco-Oakland-San Jose, CA (6)

DMA TV Households: 2,359,870
% of U.S. TV Households: 2.153

KTVU Oakland, CA, ch. 2, Fox
KRON-TV San Francisco, ch. 4, IND
KPIX-TV San Francisco, ch. 5, CBS
KGO-TV San Francisco, ch. 7, ABC
KUNO-TV Fort Bragg, CA, ch. 8, IND
*KQED San Francisco, ch. 9, ETV
KNTV San Jose, CA, ch. 11, NBC
KDTV San Francisco, ch. 14, Univision
KBWB San Francisco, ch. 20, WB
*KRCB Cotati, CA, ch. 22, ETV
KTSF San Francisco, ch. 26, IND
*KQEC San Francisco, ch. 32, ETV
KICU-TV San Jose, CA, ch. 36, IND
KCNS San Francisco, ch. 38, IND
KTNC-TV Concord, CA, ch. 42, Azteca America
KBHK-TV San Francisco, ch. 44, UPN
*KCSM-TV San Mateo, CA, ch. 43, ETV
KFTY Santa Rosa, CA, ch. 50, IND
*KTEH San Jose, CA, ch. 54, ETV
KKPX San Jose, CA, ch. 65, IND
KFSF-TV Vallejo, CA, ch. 66, TeleFutura
KTLN-TV Novato, CA, ch. 68, IND

DMA Counties	State	TV Households	DMA Counties	State	TV Households
Alameda	CA	504,600	San Francisco	CA	300,390
Contra Costa	CA	355,070	San Mateo	CA	239,000
Lake	CA	24,680	Santa Clara	CA	545,950
Marin	CA	94,670	Solano West	CA	50,950
Mendocino	CA	31,140	Sonoma	CA	166,980
Napa	CA	46,440			

Santa Barbara-Santa Maria-San Luis Obispo, CA (121)

DMA TV Households: 224,710
% of U.S. TV Households: .205

KEYT-TV Santa Barbara, CA, ch. 3, ABC
KSBY San Luis Obispo, CA, ch. 6, NBC
KCOY-TV Santa Maria, CA, ch. 12, CBS
KTAS San Luis Obispo, CA, ch. 33, Telemundo
KPMR Santa Barbara, CA, ch. 38, Univision
KBEH Oxnard, CA, ch. 63, IND

DMA Counties	State	TV Households
San Luis Obispo	CA	93,220
Santa Barbara N.	CA	61,500
Santa Barbara S.	CA	69,990

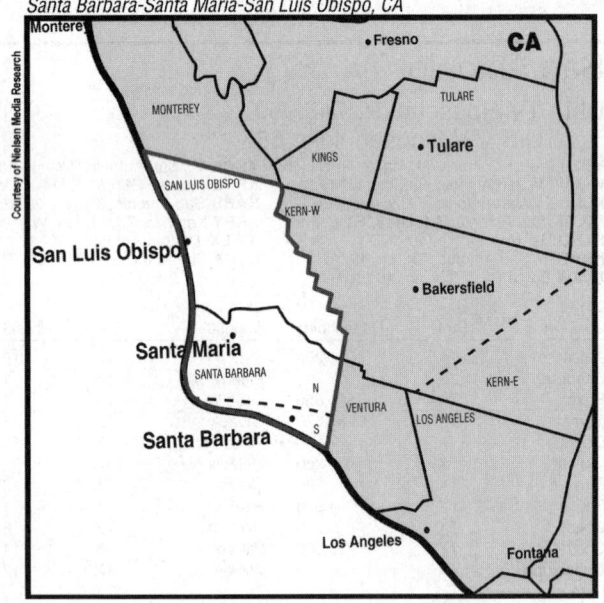

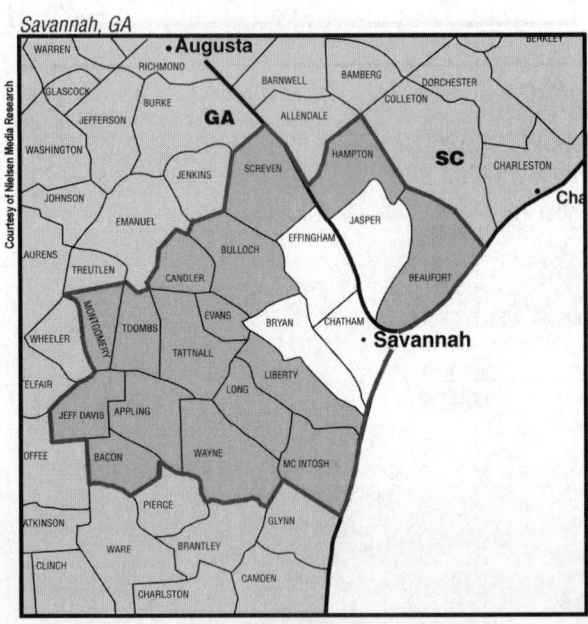

Savannah, GA (98)

DMA TV Households: 293,170
% of U.S. TV Households: .268

WSAV-TV Savannah, GA, ch. 3, NBC
*WVAN-TV Savannah, GA, ch. 9, ETV
WTOC-TV Savannah, GA, ch. 11, CBS
*WJWJ-TV Beaufort, SC, ch. 16, ETV
WJCL Savannah, GA, ch. 22, ABC
WTGS Hardeeville, SC, ch. 28, Fox
WGSA Baxley, GA, ch. 34, IND

DMA Counties	State	TV Households	DMA Counties	State	TV Households
Appling	GA	6,720	Long	GA	3,630
Bacon	GA	3,910	McIntosh	GA	4,300
Bryan	GA	9,790	Montgomery	GA	3,070
Bulloch	GA	22,350	Screven	GA	5,890
Candler	GA	3,540	Tattnall	GA	6,990
Chatham	GA	92,250	Toombs	GA	10,120
Effingham	GA	15,840	Wayne	GA	10,080
Evans	GA	4,250	Beaufort	SC	52,700
Jeff Davis	GA	5,000	Hampton	SC	7,750
Liberty	GA	17,770	Jasper	SC	7,220

Broadcasting & Cable Yearbook 2006

Nielsen DMA Market Atlas

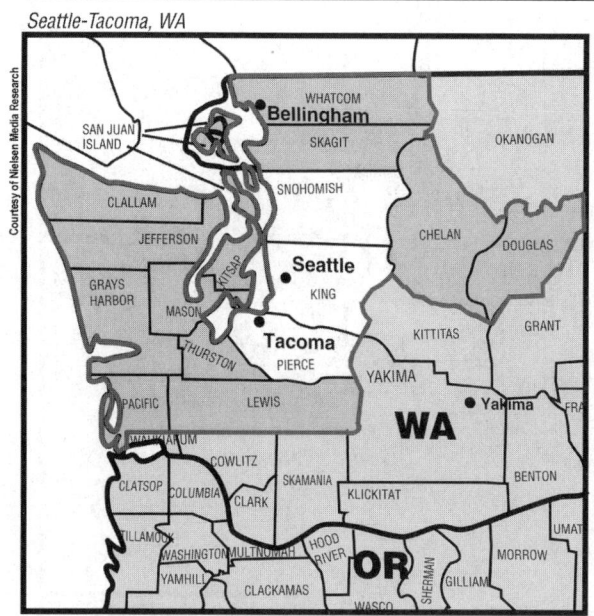

Seattle-Tacoma, WA (12)

DMA TV Households: 1,690,640
% of U.S. TV Households: 1.543

KOMO-TV Seattle, ch. 4, ABC
KING-TV Seattle, ch. 5, NBC
KIRO-TV Seattle, ch. 7, CBS
***KCTS-TV** Seattle, ch. 9, ETV
KSTW Tacoma, WA, ch. 11, IND
KVOS-TV Bellingham, WA, ch. 12, IND
KCPQ Tacoma, WA, ch. 13, Fox
***KCKA** Centralia, WA, ch. 15, ETV
KONG-TV Everett, WA, ch. 16, IND

KTBW-TV Tacoma, WA, ch. 20, IND
KTWB-TV Seattle, ch. 22, IND
KBCB Bellingham, WA, ch. 24, IND
***KBTC-TV** Tacoma, WA, ch. 28, ETV
KWPX Bellevue, WA, ch. 33, IND
KHCV Seattle, ch. 45, IND
KWOG Bellevue, WA, ch. 51, IND
***KWDK** Tacoma, WA, ch. 56, ETV

DMA Counties	State	TV Households	DMA Counties	State	TV Households
Chelan	WA	23,850	Mason	WA	19,180
Clallam	WA	27,550	Pacific	WA	8,980
Douglas	WA	11,800	Pierce	WA	275,740
Grays Harbor	WA	27,040	San Juan	WA	6,580
Island	WA	29,440	Skagit	WA	39,520
Jefferson	WA	12,190	Snohomish	WA	236,650
King	WA	704,720	Thurston	WA	86,230
Kitsap	WA	89,340	Whatcom	WA	65,310
Lewis	WA	26,520			

Sherman, TX-Ada, OK (161)

DMA TV Households: 123,540
% of U.S. TV Households: .113

KTEN Ada, OK, ch. 10, NBC
KXII Sherman, TX, ch. 12, CBS

DMA Counties	State	TV Households
Atoka	OK	5,230
Bryan	OK	14,700
Carter	OK	18,410
Choctaw	OK	6,260
Coal	OK	2,270
Johnston	OK	4,050
Love	OK	3,410
Marshall	OK	5,480
Pontotoc	OK	13,970
Pushmataha	OK	4,630
Grayson	TX	45,130

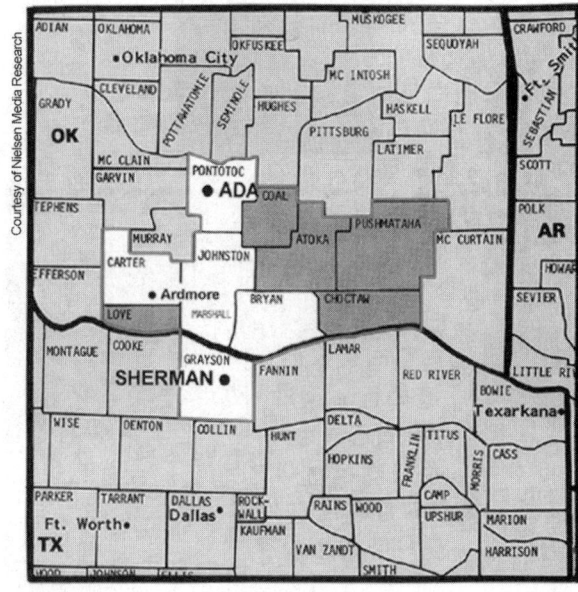

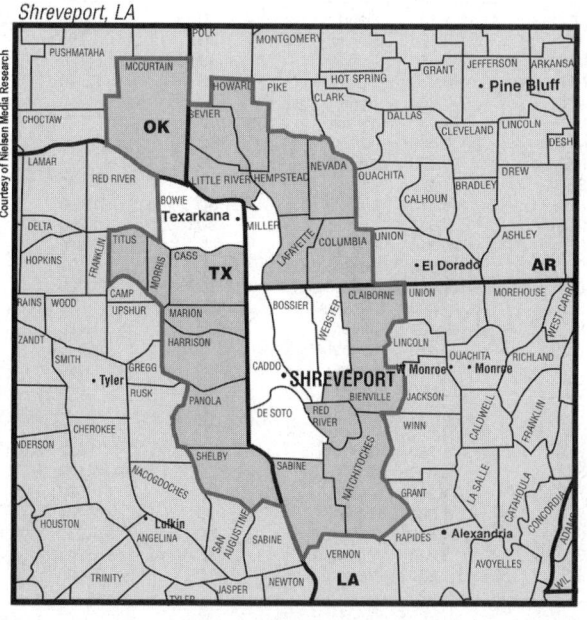

Shreveport, LA (81)

DMA TV Households: 382,700
% of U.S. TV Households: .349

KTBS-TV Shreveport, LA, ch. 3, ABC
KTAL-TV Texarkana, TX, ch. 6, NBC
KSLA-TV Shreveport, LA, ch. 12, CBS
KPXJ Minden, LA, ch. 21, PAX TV, UPN
***KLTS-TV** Shreveport, LA, ch. 24, ETV
KMSS-TV Shreveport, LA, ch. 33, Fox
KSHV Shreveport, LA, ch. 45, IND

DMA Counties	State	TV Households	DMA Counties	State	TV Households
Columbia	AR	9,700	Natchitoches	LA	14,430
Hempstead	AR	8,620	Red River	LA	3,330
Howard	AR	5,560	Sabine	LA	9,180
Lafayette	AR	3,420	Webster	LA	16,640
Little River	AR	5,370	McCurtain	OK	12,810
Miller	AR	16,480	Bowie	TX	34,150
Nevada	AR	3,700	Cass	TX	12,320
Sevier	AR	5,560	Harrison	TX	23,580
Bienville	LA	6,010	Marion	TX	4,550
Bossier	LA	39,310	Morris	TX	5,310
Caddo	LA	98,270	Panola	TX	8,830
Claiborne	LA	6,200	Shelby	TX	9,730
DeSoto	LA	10,170	Titus	TX	9,470

Broadcasting & Cable Yearbook 2006

Nielsen DMA Market Atlas

Sioux City, IA (143)

DMA TV Households: 157,340
% of U.S. TV Households: .144

*KUSD-TV Vermillion, SD, ch. 2, ETV
KTIV Sioux City, IA, ch. 4, NBC
KCAU-TV Sioux City, IA, ch. 9, ABC
KMEG Sioux City, IA, ch. 14, CBS
*KXNE-TV Norfolk, NE, ch. 19, ETV
*KSIN Sioux City, IA, ch. 27, ETV
KPTH Sioux City, IA, ch. 44, Fox

DMA Counties	State	TV Households	DMA Counties	State	TV Households
Buena Vista	IA	7,260	Woodbury	IA	38,580
Cherokee	IA	5,180	Cedar	NE	3,480
Clay	IA	7,270	Dakota	NE	7,070
Dickinson	IA	7,160	Dixon	NE	2,290
Emmet	IA	4,460	Knox	NE	3,600
Ida	IA	3,080	Madison	NE	13,670
Monona	IA	4,080	Pierce	NE	2,870
O'Brien	IA	5,770	Stanton	NE	2,380
Palo Alto	IA	3,850	Thurston	NE	2,190
Plymouth	IA	9,450	Wayne	NE	3,170
Sac	IA	4,380	Union	SD	5,230
Sioux	IA	10,870			

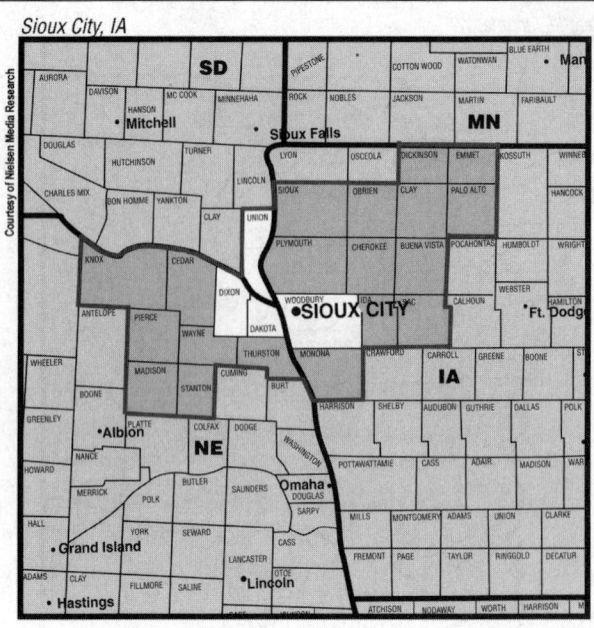

Sioux City, IA

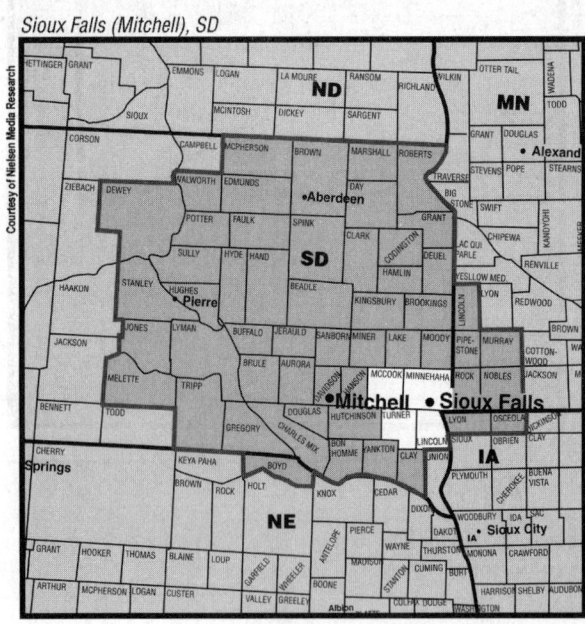

Sioux Falls (Mitchell), SD

Sioux Falls (Mitchell), SD (116)

DMA TV Households: 242,930
% of U.S. TV Households: .222

KDLO-TV Florence, SD, ch. 3, satellite to KELO-TV
KPRY-TV Pierre, SD, ch. 4, satellite to KSFY-TV
KDLV-TV Mitchell, SD, ch. 5, NBC
KPLO-TV Reliance, SD, ch. 6, satellite to KELO-TV
*KESD-TV Brookings, SD, ch. 8, ETV
KABY-TV Aberdeen, SD, ch. 9, satellite to KSFY-TV
*KTSD-TV Pierre, SD, ch. 10, ETV
KELO-TV Sioux Falls, SD, ch. 11, CBS
*KRNE-TV Merriman, NE, ch. 12, ETV
KTTM Huron, SD, ch. 12, Fox
KSFY-TV Sioux Falls, SD, ch. 13, ABC
*KDSD-TV Aberdeen, SD, ch. 16, ETV
KTTW Sioux Falls, SD, ch. 17, Fox
*KSMN Worthington, MN, ch. 20, ETV
*KCSD-TV Sioux Falls, SD, ch. 23, ETV
KWSD Sioux Falls, SD, ch. 36, WB
KDLT-TV Sioux Falls, SD, ch. 46, IND

DMA Counties	State	TV Households	DMA Counties	State	TV Households
Lyon	IA	4,290	Hand	SD	1,490
Osceola	IA	2,660	Hanson	SD	1,260
Lincoln	MN	2,580	Hughes	SD	6,720
Murray	MN	3,670	Hutchinson	SD	2,940
Nobles	MN	7,600	Hyde	SD	600
Pipestone	MN	4,030	Jerauld	SD	970
Rock	MN	3,830	Jones	SD	460
Boyd	NE	970	Kingsbury	SD	2,270
Aurora	SD	1,080	Lake	SD	4,260
Beadle	SD	6,770	Lincoln	SD	11,490
Homme	SD	2,580	Lyman	SD	1,380
Brookings	SD	10,710	Marshall	SD	1,680
Brown	SD	14,510	McCook	SD	2,190
Brule	SD	1,980	McPherson	SD	1,080
Buffalo	SD	480	Mellette	SD	680
Charles Mix	SD	3,260	Miner	SD	1,080
Clark	SD	1,470	Minnehaha	SD	61,640
Clay	SD	4,650	Moody	SD	2,490
Codington	SD	10,520	Potter	SD	1,090
Davison	SD	7,590	Roberts	SD	3,730
Day	SD	2,370	Sanborn	SD	1,040
Deuel	SD	1,760	Spink	SD	2,530
Dewey	SD	1,890	Stanley	SD	1,180
Douglas	SD	1,250	Sully	SD	590
Edmunds	SD	1,580	Tripp	SD	2,480
Faulk	SD	890	Turner	SD	3,360
Grant	SD	3,050	Walworth	SD	2,240
Gregory	SD	1,880	Yankton	SD	8,090
Hamlin	SD	2,020			

Broadcasting & Cable Yearbook 2006

Nielsen DMA Market Atlas

South Bend-Elkhart, IN

South Bend-Elkhart, IN (87)

DMA TV Households: 332,860
% of U.S. TV Households: .304

WNDU-TV South Bend, IN, ch. 16, NBC
WSBT-TV South Bend, IN, ch. 22, CBS
WSJV Elkhart, IN, ch. 28, Fox
***WNIT-TV** South Bend, IN, ch. 34, ETV
WHME-TV South Bend, IN, ch. 46, IND

DMA Counties	State	TV Households
Elkhart	IN	67,800
Fulton	IN	8,060
Kosciusko	IN	28,020
Lagrange	IN	11,220
Marshall	IN	17,130
Pulaski	IN	5,250
St. Joseph	IN	101,620
Starke	IN	8,720
Berrien	MI	64,680
Cass	MI	20,360

Spokane, WA (80)

DMA TV Households: 384,060
% of U.S. TV Households: .350

KREM-TV Spokane, WA, ch. 2, CBS
KLEW-TV Lewiston, ID, ch. 3, satellite to KIMA-TV
KXLY-TV Spokane, WA, ch. 4, ABC
KHQ-TV Spokane, WA, ch. 6, NBC
***KSPS-TV** Spokane, WA, ch. 7, ETV
***KWSU-TV** Pullman, WA, ch. 10, ETV
KSKN Spokane, WA, ch. 22, IND
KQUP Pullman, WA, ch. 24, IND
***KCDT** Coeur d'Alene, ID, ch. 26, ETV
KAYU-TV Spokane, WA, ch. 28, Fox
KGPX Spokane, WA, ch. 34, IND
***KUID-TV** Moscow, ID, ch. 35, ETV

DMA Counties	State	TV Households	DMA Counties	State	TV Households
Benewah	ID	3,420	Adams	WA	5,030
Bonner	ID	15,190	Asotin	WA	8,410
Boundary	ID	3,550	Columbia	WA	1,570
Clearwater	ID	3,070	Ferry	WA	2,910
Idaho	ID	5,780	Garfield	WA	970
Kootenai	ID	44,980	Grant	WA	24,960
Latah	ID	12,180	Lincoln	WA	4,090
Lewis	ID	1,490	Okanogan	WA	14,040
Nez Perce	ID	15,350	Pend Oreille	WA	4,720
Shoshone	ID	5,430	Spokane	WA	167,420
Lincoln	MT	7,580	Stevens	WA	14,770
Wallowa	OR	2,910	Whitman	WA	14,240

Spokane, WA

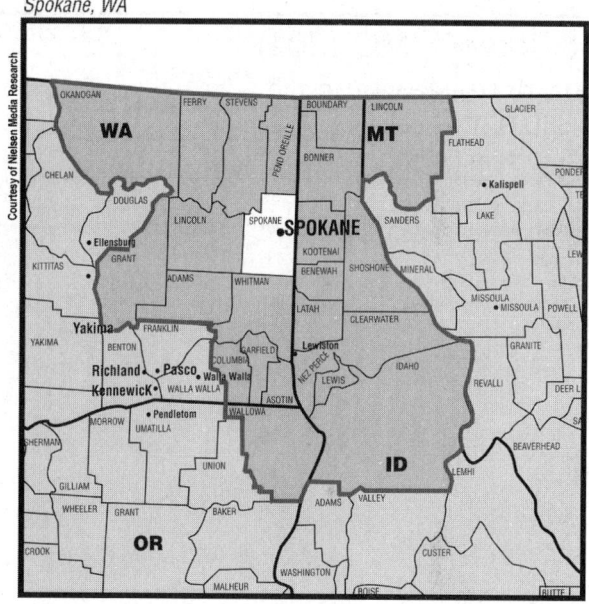

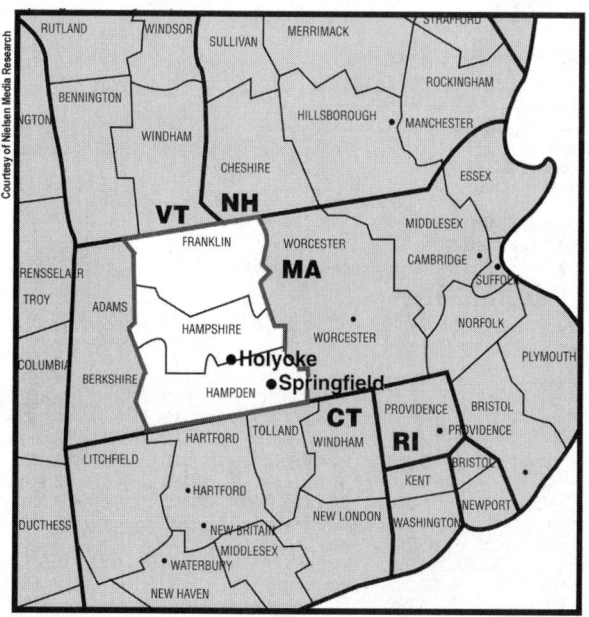

Springfield-Holyoke, MA (106)

DMA TV Households: 267,500
% of U.S. TV Households: .244

WWLP Springfield, MA, ch. 22, NBC
WGGB-TV Springfield, MA, ch. 40, ABC
***WGBY-TV** Springfield, MA, ch. 57, ETV

DMA Counties	State	TV Households
Franklin	MA	29,480
Hampden	MA	179,780
Hampshire	MA	58,240

Broadcasting & Cable Yearbook 2006

Nielsen DMA Market Atlas

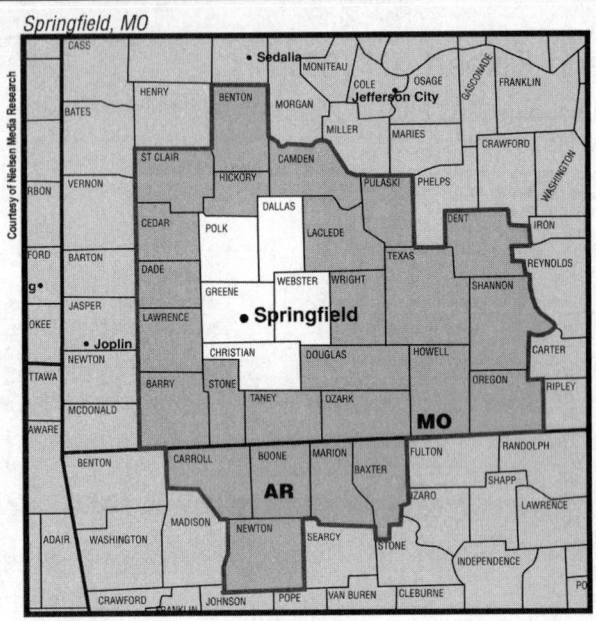

Springfield, MO (78)

DMA TV Households: 388,530
% of U.S. TV Households: .355

KYTV Springfield, MO, ch. 3, NBC
KOLR Springfield, MO, ch. 10, CBS
*****KOZK** Springfield, MO, ch. 21, ETV
KSFX-TV Springfield, MO, ch. 27, Fox
KWBM Harrison, AR, ch. 31, WB
KSPR Springfield, MO, ch. 33, ABC
KWFT Eureka Springs, AR, ch. 34, IND

DMA Counties	State	TV Households	DMA Counties	State	TV Households
Baxter	AR	17,300	Hickory	MO	3,960
Boone	AR	14,270	Howell	MO	14,480
Carroll	AR	10,330	Laclede	MO	13,200
Marion	AR	6,710	Lawrence	MO	13,960
Newton	AR	3,540	Oregon	MO	4,150
Barry	MO	13,600	Ozark	MO	3,900
Benton	MO	8,080	Polk	MO	10,250
Camden	MO	16,590	Pulaski	MO	15,900
Cedar	MO	5,550	Shannon	MO	3,320
Christian	MO	24,560	St. Clair	MO	4,010
Dade	MO	3,060	Stone	MO	12,470
Dallas	MO	6,160	Taney	MO	16,870
Dent	MO	5,970	Texas	MO	9,860
Douglas	MO	5,270	Webster	MO	11,920
Greene	MO	102,120	Wright	MO	7,170

St. Joseph, MO (201)

DMA TV Households: 48,740
% of U.S. TV Households: .044

KQTV St. Joseph, MO, ch. 2, ABC
KTAJ-TV St. Joseph, MO, ch. 16, IND

DMA Counties	State	TV Households
Doniphan	KS	3,190
Andrew	MO	6,450
Buchanan	MO	32,870
De Kalb	MO	4,070
Holt	MO	2,160

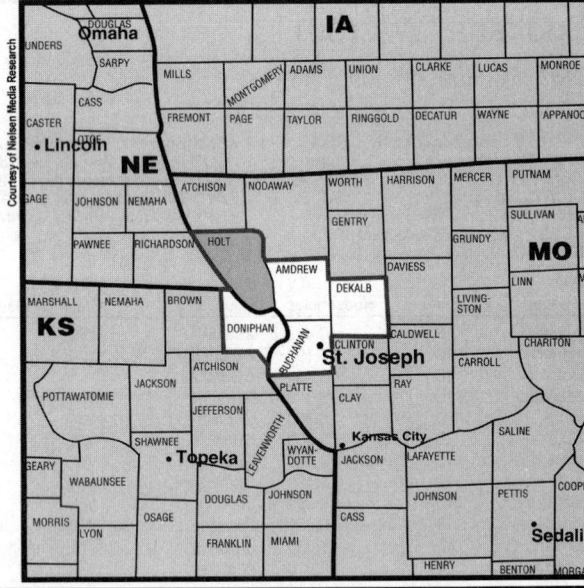

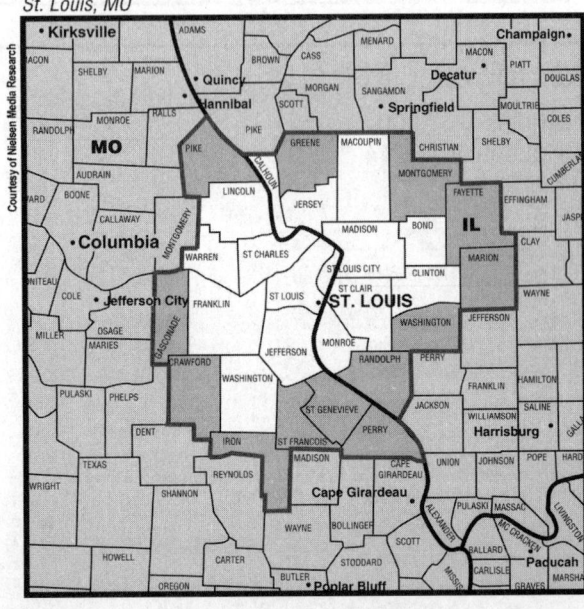

St. Louis (21)

DMA TV Households: 1,216,700
% of U.S. TV Households: 1.110

KTVI St. Louis, ch. 2, Fox
KMOV St. Louis, ch. 4, CBS
KSDK St. Louis, ch. 5, NBC
*****KETC** St. Louis, ch. 9, ETV
KPLR-TV St. Louis, ch. 11, WB
KNLC St. Louis, ch. 24, IND
KDNL-TV St. Louis, ch. 30, ABC
WRBU East St. Louis, IL, ch. 46, UPN

DMA Counties	State	TV Households	DMA Counties	State	TV Households
Bond	IL	6,340	Crawford	MO	9,240
Calhoun	IL	2,070	Franklin	MO	37,090
Clay	IL	5,670	Gasconade	MO	6,350
Clinton	IL	13,520	Iron	MO	4,050
Fayette	IL	8,060	Jefferson	MO	77,420
Greene	IL	5,700	Lincoln	MO	16,350
Jersey	IL	8,550	Pike	MO	6,490
Macoupin	IL	19,610	St. Charles	MO	117,350
Madison	IL	105,120	St. Francois	MO	22,410
Marion	IL	16,030	St. Louis	MO	407,370
Monroe	IL	11,510	St. Louis-Ind	MO	135,760
Montgomery	IL	11,260	Ste. Genevieve	MO	6,860
Randolph	IL	11,920	Warren	MO	10,610
St. Clair	IL	99,960	Washington	MO	8,960
Washington	IL	5,830			

Broadcasting & Cable Yearbook 2006

Nielsen DMA Market Atlas

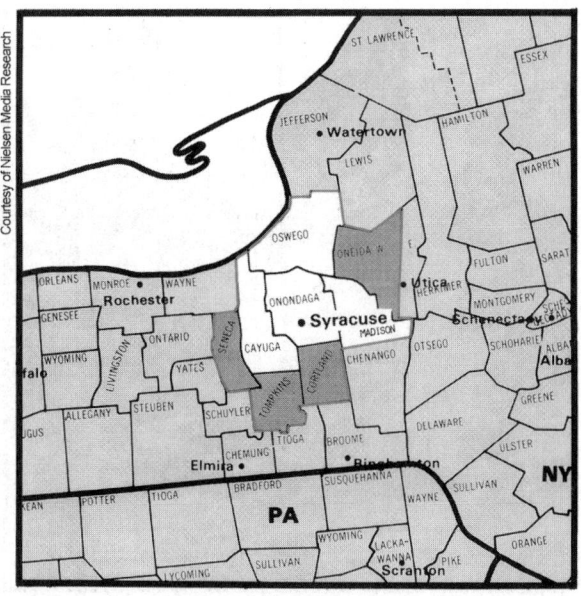

Syracuse, NY (77)

DMA TV Households: 395,400
% of U.S. TV Households: .361

WSTM-TV Syracuse, NY, ch. 3, NBC
WTVH Syracuse, NY, ch. 5, CBS
WIXT Syracuse, NY, ch. 9, ABC
*WCNY-TV Syracuse, NY, ch. 24, ETV
WNYS-TV Syracuse, NY, ch. 43, IND
WNYI Ithaca, NY, ch. 52, IND
WSPX-TV Syracuse, NY, ch. 56, IND
WSYT Syracuse, NY, ch. 68, Fox

DMA Counties	State	TV Households
Cayuga	NY	31,340
Cortland	NY	18,770
Madison	NY	26,320
Oneida West	NY	34,760
Onondaga	NY	185,080
Oswego	NY	47,620
Seneca	NY	13,810
Tompkins	NY	37,700

Tallahassee, FL-Thomasville, GA (109)

DMA TV Households: 259,720
% of U.S. TV Households: .237

WCTV Thomasville, GA, ch. 6, CBS
*WFSU-TV Tallahassee, FL, ch. 11, ETV
WTLF Tallahassee, FL, ch. 24, UPN
WTXL-TV Tallahassee, FL, ch. 27, ABC
WTWC-TV Tallahassee, FL, ch. 40, NBC
WVAG Valdosta, GA, ch. 44, UPN
WTLH Bainbridge, GA, ch. 49, Fox
WFXU Live Oak, FL, ch. 57, UPN

DMA Counties	State	TV Households	DMA Counties	State	TV Households
Gadsden	FL	16,710	Brooks	GA	6,230
Hamilton	FL	4,420	Decatur	GA	10,490
Jefferson	FL	5,430	Echols	GA	1,360
Lafayette	FL	2,200	Grady	GA	9,090
Leon	FL	102,380	Lanier	GA	2,750
Madison	FL	6,850	Lowndes	GA	34,420
Suwannee	FL	13,820	Miller	GA	2,450
Taylor	FL	7,690	Seminole	GA	3,550
Wakulla	FL	10,000	Thomas	GA	17,220

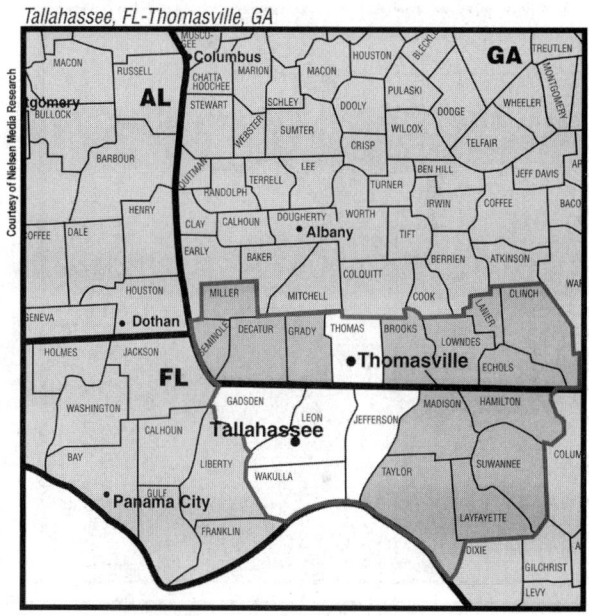

Tampa-St. Petersburg (Sarasota), FL (13)

DMA TV Households: 1,671,040
% of U.S. TV Households: 1.525

*WEDU Tampa, FL, ch. 3, ETV
WFLA-TV Tampa, FL, ch. 8, NBC
WTSP St. Petersburg, FL, ch. 10, CBS
WTVT Tampa, FL, ch. 13, Fox
*WUSF-TV Tampa, FL, ch. 16, ETV
WCLF Clearwater, FL, ch. 22, IND
WFTS Tampa, FL, ch. 28, ABC
WMOR-TV Lakeland, FL, ch. 32, IND
WTTA St. Petersburg, FL, ch. 38, WB
WWSB Sarasota, FL, ch. 40, ABC
WTOG St. Petersburg, FL, ch. 44, UPN
WFTT-TV Tampa, FL, ch. 50, TeleFutura
WVEA-TV Venice, FL, ch. 62, Univision
WXPX Bradenton, FL, ch. 66, PAX TV

DMA Counties	State	TV Households
Citrus	FL	57,990
Hardee	FL	8,090
Hernando	FL	62,500
Highlands	FL	38,830
Hillsborough	FL	428,080
Manatee	FL	125,110
Pasco	FL	167,520
Pinellas	FL	418,210
Polk	FL	200,380
Sarasota	FL	164,330

Broadcasting & Cable Yearbook 2006

Nielsen DMA Market Atlas

Terre Haute, IN (149)

DMA TV Households: 146,860
% of U.S. TV Households: .134

WTWO Terre Haute, IN, ch. 2, NBC
WTHI-TV Terre Haute, IN, ch. 10, CBS
***WUSI-TV** Olney, IL, ch. 16, ETV
***WVUT** Vincennes, IN, ch. 22, ETV
WBAK-TV Terre Haute, IN, ch. 38, Fox

DMA Counties	State	TV Households	DMA Counties	State	TV Households
Clark	IL	7,060	Greene	IN	13,440
Crawford	IL	7,560	Knox	IN	15,350
Jasper	IL	3,840	Martin	IN	4,140
Lawrence	IL	6,300	Parke	IN	6,530
Richland	IL	6,590	Sullivan	IN	7,940
Clay	IN	10,370	Vermillion	IN	6,640
Daviess	IN	10,510	Vigo	IN	40,590

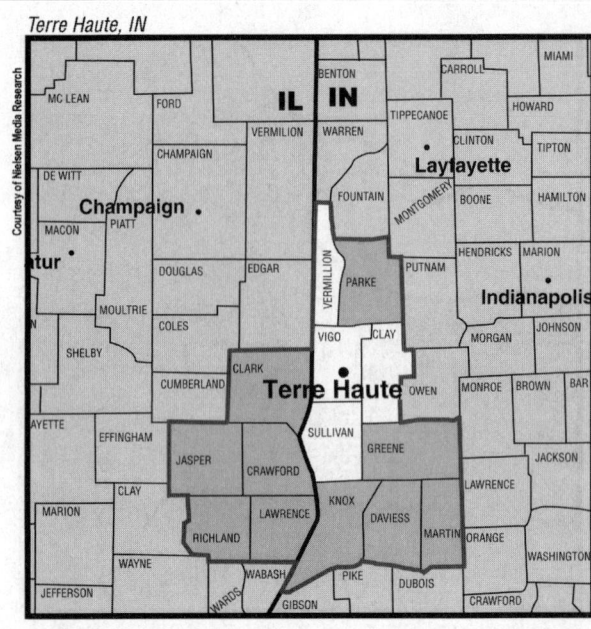

Toledo, OH (70)

DMA TV Households: 432,430
% of U.S. TV Households: .395

WTOL Toledo, OH, ch. 11, CBS
WTVG Toledo, OH, ch. 13, ABC
WNWO-TV Toledo, OH, ch. 24, NBC
***WBGU-TV** Bowling Green, OH, ch. 27, ETV
***WGTE-TV** Toledo, OH, ch. 30, ETV
WUPW Toledo, OH, ch. 36, Fox
WLMB Toledo, OH, ch. 40, IND

DMA Counties	State	TV Households
Lenawee	MI	37,940
Defiance	OH	15,320
Fulton	OH	16,050
Hancock	OH	29,450
Henry	OH	11,240
Lucas	OH	186,660
Ottawa	OH	17,190
Sandusky	OH	24,490
Seneca	OH	22,420
Williams	OH	15,030
Wood	OH	47,500
Wyandot	OH	9,140

Topeka, KS (137)

DMA TV Households: 171,470
% of U.S. TV Households: .156

***KTWU** Topeka, KS, ch. 11, ETV
WIBW-TV Topeka, KS, ch. 13, CBS
KSNT Topeka, KS, ch. 27, NBC
KTKA-TV Topeka, KS, ch. 49, ABC

DMA Counties	State	TV Households
Brown	KS	4,130
Clay	KS	3,450
Cloud	KS	3,870
Coffey	KS	3,410
Geary	KS	9,570
Jackson	KS	4,960
Jefferson	KS	7,010
Lyon	KS	13,330
Marshall	KS	4,270
Morris	KS	2,470
Nemaha	KS	3,720
Osage	KS	6,540
Pottawatomie	KS	6,990
Riley	KS	22,610
Shawnee	KS	70,140
Wabaunsee	KS	2,560
Washington	KS	2,440

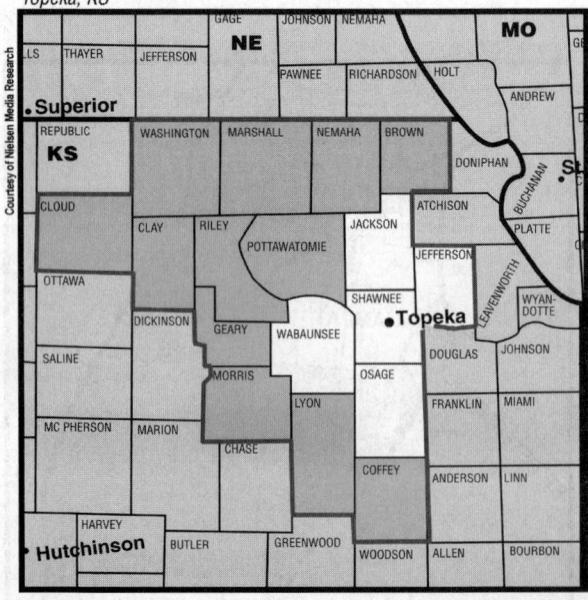

Nielsen DMA Market Atlas

Traverse City-Cadillac, MI (112)

DMA TV Households: 249,450
% of U.S. TV Households: .228

WTOM-TV Cheboygan, MI, ch. 4, satellite to WPBN-TV
WPBN-TV Traverse City, MI, ch. 7, NBC
WGTQ Sault Ste. Marie, MI, ch. 8, satellite to WGTU
WWTV Cadillac, MI, ch. 9, CBS
WWUP-TV Sault Ste. Marie, MI, ch. 10, satellite to WWTV
***WCMW** Manistee, MI, ch. 21, ETV
***WCMV** Cadillac, MI, ch. 27, ETV
WGTU Traverse City, MI, ch. 29, ABC
WFQX-TV Cadillac, MI, ch. 33, Fox
WFUP Vanderbilt, MI, ch. 45, IND

Traverse City-Cadillac, MI

DMA Counties	State	TV Households	DMA Counties	State	TV Households
Antrim	MI	9,760	Mackinac	MI	4,890
Benzie	MI	7,120	Manistee	MI	10,380
Charlevoix	MI	10,880	Mason	MI	11,650
Cheboygan	MI	11,710	Mecosta	MI	15,980
Chippewa	MI	13,740	Missaukee	MI	5,960
Clare	MI	13,040	Montmorency	MI	4,660
Crawford	MI	6,120	Osceola	MI	9,150
Emmet	MI	13,470	Oscoda	MI	3,820
Grand Traverse	MI	33,460	Otsego	MI	9,720
Kalkaska	MI	6,810	Presque Isle	MI	6,250
Lake	MI	4,990	Roscommon	MI	11,860
Leelanau	MI	9,090	Wexford	MI	12,490
Luce	MI	2,450			

Tri-Cities, TN-VA (89)

DMA TV Households: 329,910
% of U.S. TV Households: .301

WCYB-TV Bristol, VA, ch. 5, NBC
WJHL-TV Johnson City, TN, ch. 11, CBS
WKPT-TV Kingsport, TN, ch. 19, ABC
WEMT Greeneville, TN, ch. 39, Fox
***WSBN-TV** Norton, VA, ch. 47, ETV
***WMSY-TV** Marion, VA, ch. 52, ETV
WLFG Grundy, VA, ch. 68, IND

DMA Counties	State	TV Households	DMA Counties	State	TV Households
Leslie	KY	5,020	Buchanan	VA	10,300
Letcher	KY	10,410	Dickenson	VA	6,940
Carter	TN	25,360	Lee	VA	10,570
Greene	TN	27,130	Russell	VA	11,560
Hawkins	TN	23,190	Scott	VA	10,020
Johnson	TN	7,180	Smyth	VA	13,690
Sullivan	TN	65,390	Washington	VA	29,500
Unicoi	TN	7,790	Wise	VA	19,150
Washington	TN	46,710			

Broadcasting & Cable Yearbook 2006

Nielsen DMA Market Atlas

Tucson (Sierra Vista), AZ (72)

DMA TV Households: 417,070

% of U.S. TV Households: .381

KFTU-TV Douglas, AZ, ch. 3, TeleFutura
KVOA Tucson, AZ, ch. 4, NBC
*KUAT-TV Tucson, AZ, ch. 6, ETV
KGUN Tucson, AZ, ch. 9, ABC
KMSB-TV Tucson, AZ, ch. 11, Fox
KOLD-TV Tucson, AZ, ch. 13, CBS
KTTU-TV Tucson, AZ, ch. 18, UPN
*KUAS-TV Tucson, AZ, ch. 27, ETV
KHRR Tucson, AZ, ch. 40, Telemundo
KUVE-TV Green Valley, AZ, ch. 46, Univision
KWBA Sierra Vista, AZ, ch. 58, WB

DMA Counties	State	TV Households
Cochise	AZ	47,640
Pima	AZ	356,940
Santa Cruz	AZ	12,490

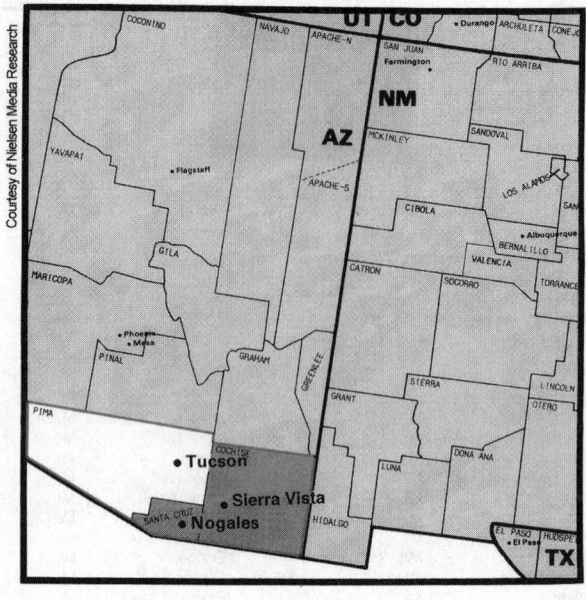

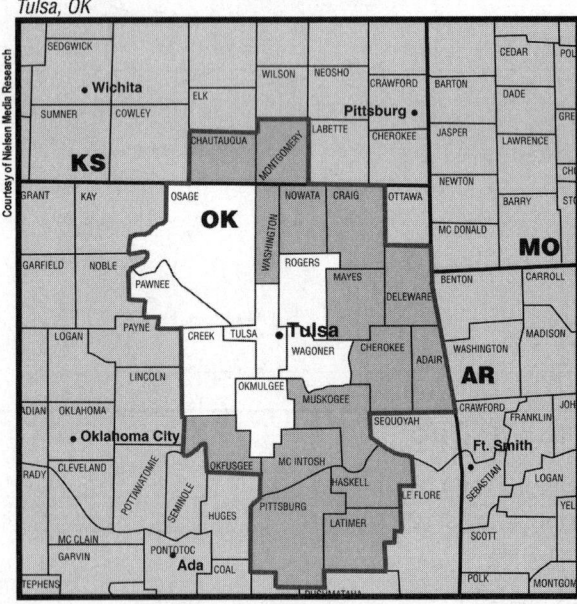

Tulsa, OK (60)

DMA TV Households: 510,960

% of U.S. TV Households: .466

KJRH Tulsa, OK, ch. 2, NBC
*KOET Eufaula, OK, ch. 3, ETV
KOTV Tulsa, OK, ch. 6, CBS
KTUL Tulsa, OK, ch. 8, ABC
*KOED-TV Tulsa, OK, ch. 11, ETV
KDOR-TV Bartlesville, OK, ch. 17, IND
KWBT Muskogee, OK, ch. 19, WB
KOKI-TV Tulsa, OK, ch. 23, Fox
*KRSC-TV Claremore, OK, ch. 35, ETV
KTFO Tulsa, OK, ch. 41, UPN
KTPX Okmulgee, OK, ch. 44, IND
KWHB Tulsa, OK, ch. 47, IND
KGEB Tulsa, OK, ch. 53, IND

DMA Counties	State	TV Households
Chautauqua	KS	1,660
Montgomery	KS	14,010
Adair	OK	7,650
Cherokee	OK	16,910
Craig	OK	5,460
Creek	OK	25,920
Delaware	OK	15,700
Haskell	OK	4,740
Latimer	OK	3,890
Mayes	OK	14,860
McIntosh	OK	8,310
Muskogee	OK	27,140
Nowata	OK	4,240
Okfuskee	OK	4,050
Okmulgee	OK	15,040
Osage	OK	16,980
Pawnee	OK	6,350
Pittsburg	OK	17,180
Rogers	OK	29,050
Tulsa	OK	227,890
Wagoner	OK	23,500
Washington	OK	20,430

Nielsen DMA Market Atlas

Twin Falls, ID (191)

DMA TV Households: 59,940
% of U.S. TV Households: .055

KIDA Sun Valley, ID, ch. 5, IND
KMVT Twin Falls, ID, ch. 11, CBS
***KIPT** Twin Falls, ID, ch. 13, satellite to *KAID
***KBGH** Filer, ID, ch. 19, ETV
KXTF Twin Falls, ID, ch. 35, IND

DMA Counties	State	TV Households
Blaine	ID	8,450
Cassia	ID	7,040
Gooding	ID	4,920
Jerome	ID	6,390
Lincoln	ID	1,570
Minidoka	ID	6,610
Twin Falls	ID	24,960

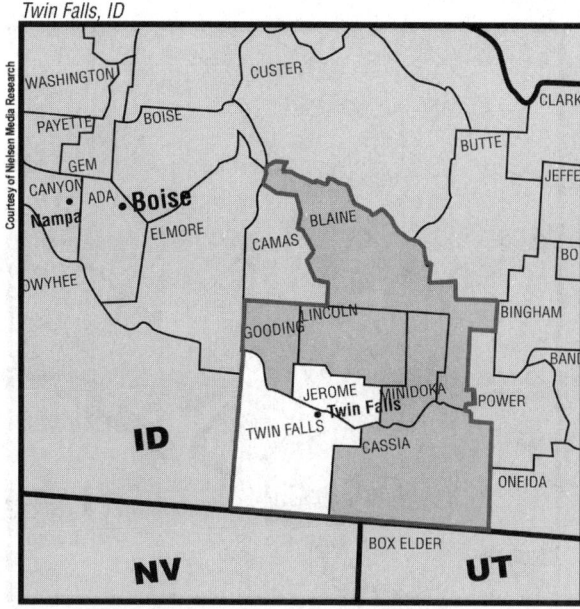

Tyler-Longview (Lufkin & Nacogdoches), TX (111)

DMA TV Households: 254,170
% of U.S. TV Households: .232

KLTV Tyler, TX, ch. 7, ABC
KTRE Lufkin, TX, ch. 9, satellite to KLTV
KYTX Nacogdoches, TX, ch. 19, CBS
KFXK Longview, TX, ch. 51, Fox
KCEB Longview, TX, ch. 54, UPN
KETK-TV Jacksonville, TX, ch. 56, NBC

DMA Counties	State	TV Households
Angelina	TX	29,010
Camp	TX	4,510
Cherokee	TX	16,920
Franklin	TX	3,710
Gregg	TX	43,820
Houston	TX	8,080
Nacogdoches	TX	22,260
Rusk	TX	17,540
Sabine	TX	4,330
San Augustine	TX	3,710
Smith	TX	70,310
Upshur	TX	13,960
Wood	TX	16,010

Utica, NY (166)

DMA TV Households: 106,690
% of U.S. TV Households: .097

WKTV Utica, NY, ch. 2, NBC
WUTR Utica, NY, ch. 20, ABC
WFXV Utica, NY, ch. 33, Fox

DMA Counties	State	TV Households
Herkimer	NY	25,960
Oneida East	NY	56,910
Otsego	NY	23,820

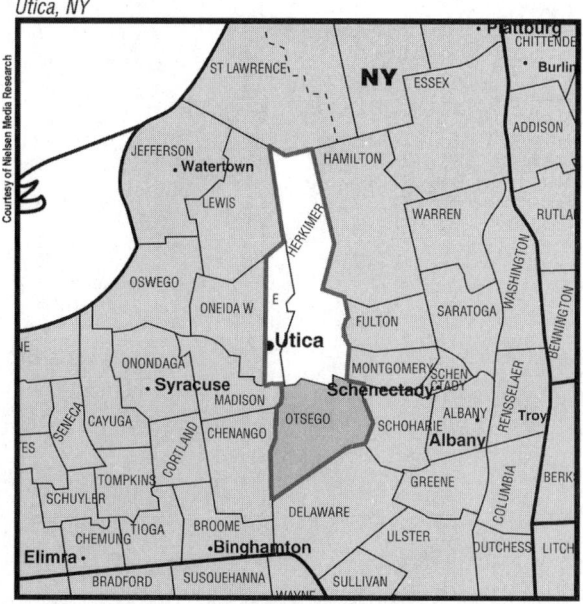

Broadcasting & Cable Yearbook 2006

Nielsen DMA Market Atlas

Victoria, TX (205)

DMA TV Households: 30,180
% of U.S. TV Households: .028

KVCT Victoria, TX, ch. 19, Fox
KAVU-TV Victoria, TX, ch. 25, ABC

DMA Counties	State	TV Households
Victoria	TX	30,180

Waco-Temple-Bryan, TX (95)

DMA TV Households: 308,970
% of U.S. TV Households: .282

KBTX-TV Bryan, TX, ch. 3, satellite to KWTX-TV
KCEN-TV Temple, TX, ch. 6, ABC
KWTX-TV Waco, TX, ch. 10, CBS
*__KAMU-TV__ College Station, TX, ch. 15, ETV
KXXV Waco, TX, ch. 25, NBC
KYLE Bryan, TX, ch. 28, satellite to KWKT
*__KWBU-TV__ Waco, TX, ch. 34, ETV
KWKT Waco, TX, ch. 44, Fox
*__KNCT__ Belton, TX, ch. 46, ETV
KAKW-TV Killeen, TX, ch. 62, Univision

DMA Counties	State	TV Households
Bell	TX	90,970
Brazos	TX	59,360
Burleson	TX	6,620
Coryell	TX	19,720
Falls	TX	6,140
Lampasas	TX	7,250
Leon	TX	6,440
Limestone	TX	8,100
Madison	TX	3,700
McLennan	TX	81,000
Milam	TX	9,440
Mills	TX	1,850
Robertson	TX	6,220
San Saba	TX	2,160

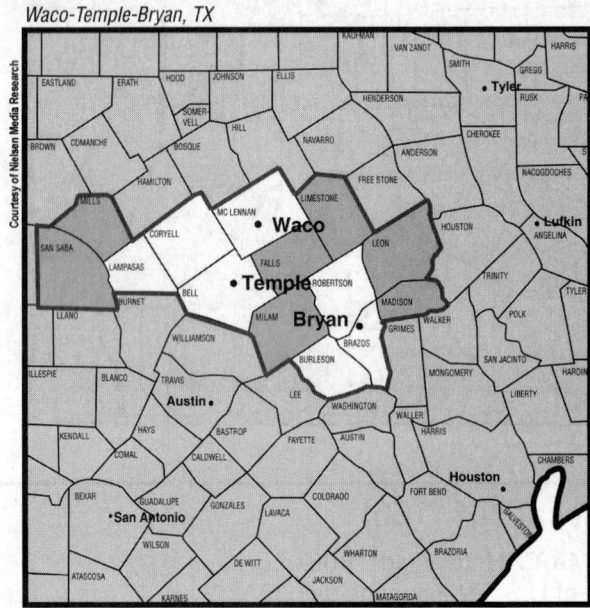

Nielsen DMA Market Atlas

Washington, DC (Hagerstown, MD) (8)

DMA TV Households: 2,241,610
% of U.S. TV Households: 2.045

WRC-TV Washington, ch. 4, NBC
WTTG Washington, ch. 5, Fox
WJLA-TV Washington, ch. 7, ABC
WUSA Washington, ch. 9, CBS
WFDC-TV Arlington, VA, ch. 14, TeleFutura
WDCA Washington, ch. 20, UPN
WHAG-TV Hagerstown, MD, ch. 25, NBC
***WETA-TV** Washington, ch. 26, ETV
***WWPB** Hagerstown, MD, ch. 31, ETV
***WHUT-TV** Washington, ch. 32, ETV
***WVPY** Front Royal, VA, ch. 42, ETV
WBDC-TV Washington, ch. 50, WB
***WNVT** Goldvein, VA, ch. 53, ETV
***WNVC** Fairfax, VA, ch. 56, ETV
WWPX Martinsburg, WV, ch. 60, PAX TV
***WFPT** Frederick, MD, ch. 62, ETV
WPXW Manassas, VA, ch. 66, PAX TV
WJAL Hagerstown, MD, ch. 68, IND

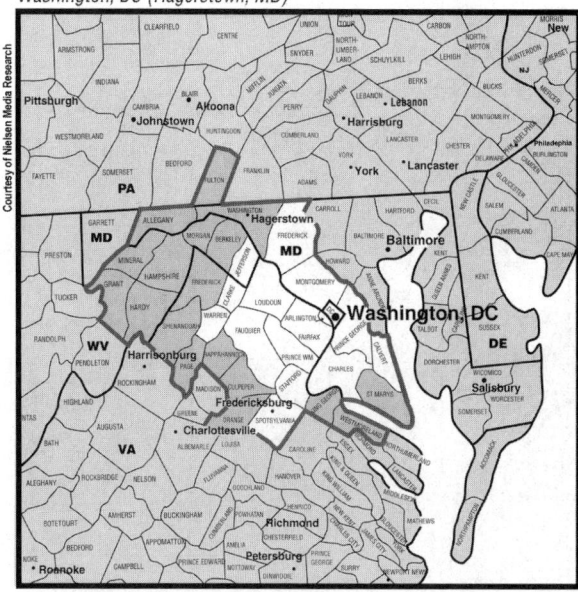

Washington, DC (Hagerstown, MD)

DMA Counties	State	TV Households
Dist. of Columbia	DC	239,850
Allegany	MD	28,400
Calvert	MD	30,380
Charles	MD	48,850
Frederick	MD	79,730
Montgomery	MD	343,490
Prince George	MD	304,400
St. Marys	MD	34,640
Washington	MD	52,720
Fulton	PA	5,980
Arlington	VA	148,130
Clarke	VA	5,670
Culpeper	VA	14,180
Fairfax	VA	380,750
Fauquier	VA	22,820
Frederick	VA	35,990
King George	VA	6,970
Loudoun	VA	86,370
Orange	VA	11,660
Page	VA	9,750
Prince William	VA	135,170
Rappahannock	VA	2,670
Shenandoah	VA	15,600
Spotsylvania	VA	50,160
Stafford	VA	38,680
Warren	VA	12,930
Westmoreland	VA	7,000
Berkeley	WV	35,040
Grant	WV	4,430
Hampshire	WV	7,970
Hardy	WV	5,280
Jefferson	WV	18,750
Mineral	WV	10,790
Morgan	WV	6,410

Watertown, NY (175)

DMA TV Households: 94,390
% of U.S. TV Households: .086

WWNY-TV Carthage, NY, ch. 7, CBS (ABC, NBC)
***WPBS-TV** Watertown, NY, ch. 16, ETV
***WNPI-TV** Norwood, NY, ch. 18, ETV
WWTI Watertown, NY, ch. 50, IND

DMA Counties	State	TV Households
Jefferson	NY	42,770
Lewis	NY	10,260
St. Lawrence	NY	41,360

Broadcasting & Cable Yearbook 2006

Nielsen DMA Market Atlas

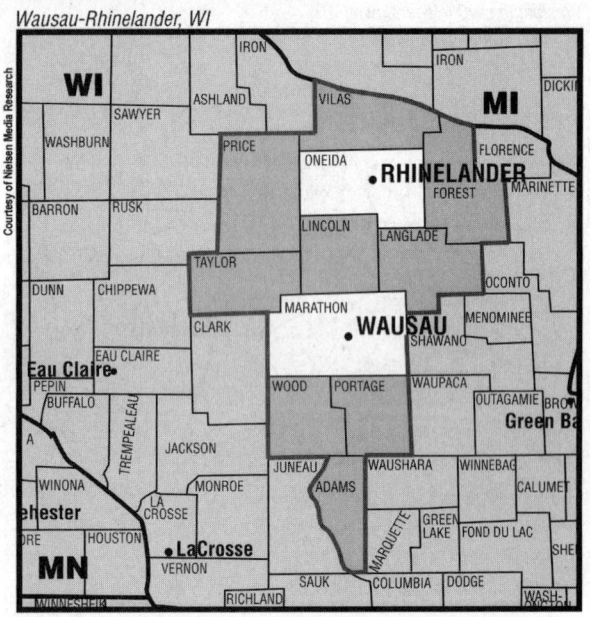
Wausau-Rhinelander, WI

Wausau-Rhinelander, WI (133)

DMA TV Households: 181,780
% of U.S. TV Households: .166

WBIJ Crandon, WI, ch. 4, IND
WSAW-TV Wausau, WI, ch. 7, CBS
WAOW-TV Wausau, WI, ch. 9, ABC
WJFW-TV Rhinelander, WI, ch. 12, NBC
***WHRM-TV** Wausau, WI, ch. 20, ETV
WYOW Eagle River, WI, ch. 34, ABC
***WLEF-TV** Park Falls, WI, ch. 36, ETV
WTPX Antigo, WI, ch. 46, IND

DMA Counties	State	TV Households
Adams	WI	8,980
Forest	WI	4,180
Langlade	WI	8,630
Lincoln	WI	12,190
Marathon	WI	50,290
Oneida	WI	15,790
Portage	WI	26,370
Price	WI	6,570
Taylor	WI	7,790
Vilas	WI	9,720
Wood	WI	31,270

West Palm Beach-Ft. Pierce, FL (39)

DMA TV Households: 729,010
% of U.S. TV Households: .665

WPTV West Palm Beach, FL, ch. 5, NBC
WPEC West Palm Beach, FL, ch. 12, CBS
***WTCE-TV** Fort Pierce, FL, ch. 21, ETV
WPBF Tequesta, FL, ch. 25, ABC
WFLX West Palm Beach, FL, ch. 29, Fox
WTVX Ft. Pierce, FL, ch. 34, UPN, WB
***WXEL-TV** West Palm Beach, FL, ch. 42, ETV
WFGC Palm Beach, FL, ch. 61, IND
***WPPB-TV** Boca Raton, FL, ch. 63, ETV
WPXP Lake Worth, FL, ch. 67, IND

DMA Counties	State	TV Households
Indian River	FL	54,560
Martin	FL	60,140
Okeechobee	FL	13,200
Palm Beach North	FL	301,810
Palm Beach South	FL	210,230
St. Lucie	FL	89,070

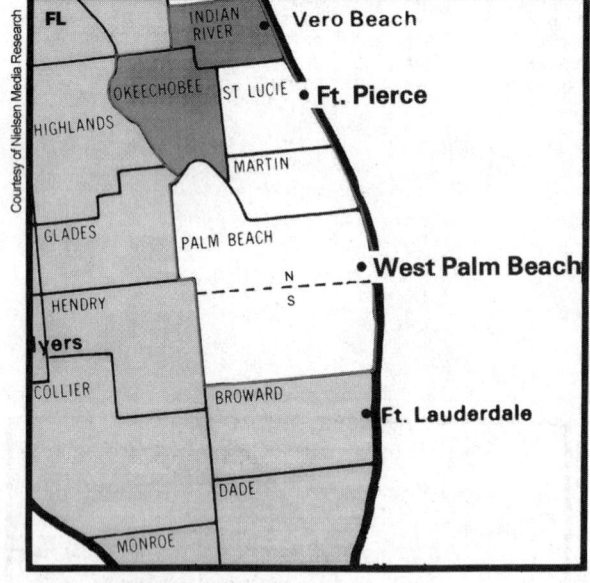

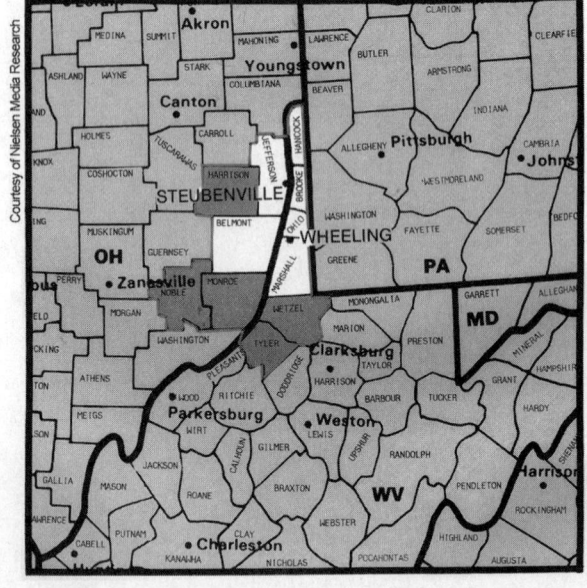

Wheeling, WV-Steubenville, OH (152)

DMA TV Households: 144,330
% of U.S. TV Households: .132

WTRF-TV Wheeling, WV, ch. 7, CBS (ABC)
WTOV-TV Steubenville, OH, ch. 9, NBC (ABC)
***WOUC-TV** Cambridge, OH, ch. 44, ETV

DMA Counties	State	TV Households
Belmont	OH	28,720
Harrison	OH	6,650
Jefferson	OH	30,130
Monroe	OH	5,900
Noble	OH	4,600
Brooke	WV	10,540
Hancock	WV	13,600
Marshall	WV	14,290
Ohio	WV	18,950
Tyler	WV	3,850
Wetzel	WV	7,100

Broadcasting & Cable Yearbook 2006

Nielsen DMA Market Atlas

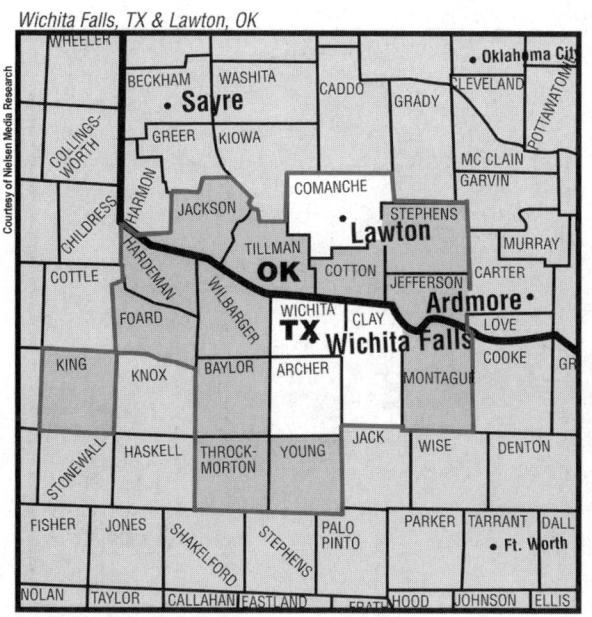

Wichita Falls, TX & Lawton, OK (144)

DMA TV Households: 156,300
% of U.S. TV Households: .143

KFDX-TV Wichita Falls, TX, ch. 3, NBC
KAUZ-TV Wichita Falls, TX, ch. 6, CBS
KSWO-TV Lawton, OK, ch. 7, ABC
KJTL Wichita Falls, TX, ch. 18, Fox

DMA Counties	State	TV Households	DMA Counties	State	TV Households
Comanche	OK	39,670	Foard	TX	600
Cotton	OK	2,580	Hardeman	TX	1,770
Jackson	OK	9,920	King	TX	90
Jefferson	OK	2,560	Montague	TX	7,840
Stephens	OK	17,100	Throckmorton	TX	590
Tillman	OK	3,350	Wichita	TX	48,230
Archer	TX	3,470	Wilbarger	TX	5,150
Baylor	TX	1,660	Young	TX	7,140
Clay	TX	4,580			

Wichita-Hutchinson Plus, KS (66)

DMA TV Households: 445,690
% of U.S. TV Households: .407

KSNC Great Bend, KS, ch. 2, satellite to KSNW
KSNW Wichita, KS, ch. 3, NBC
*KSWK Lakin, KS, ch. 3, ETV
KLBY Colby, KS, ch. 4, ABC
KSWT Liberal, KS, ch. 5, IND
KBSD-TV Ensign, KS, ch. 6, satellite to KWCH-TV
KBSH-TV Hays, KS, ch. 7, satellite to KWCH-TV
KSNK McCook, NE, ch. 8, satellite to KSNW
*KOOD Hays, KS, ch. 9, ETV
KAKE-TV Wichita, KS, ch. 10, ABC
KBSL-TV Goodland, KS, ch. 10, satellite to KBSH-TV
KSNG Garden City, KS, ch. 11, satellite to KSNW
KWCH-TV Hutchinson, KS, ch. 12, CBS
KUPK-TV Garden City, KS, ch. 13, ABC
KBDK Hoisington, KS, ch. 14, satellite to KSAS-TV
KAAS-TV Salina, KS, ch. 18, satellite to KSAS-TV
*KDCK Dodge City, KS, ch. 21, ETV
KSAS-TV Wichita, KS, ch. 24, Fox
KWCV Wichita, KS, ch. 33, WB
KSCC Hutchinson, KS, ch. 36, UPN

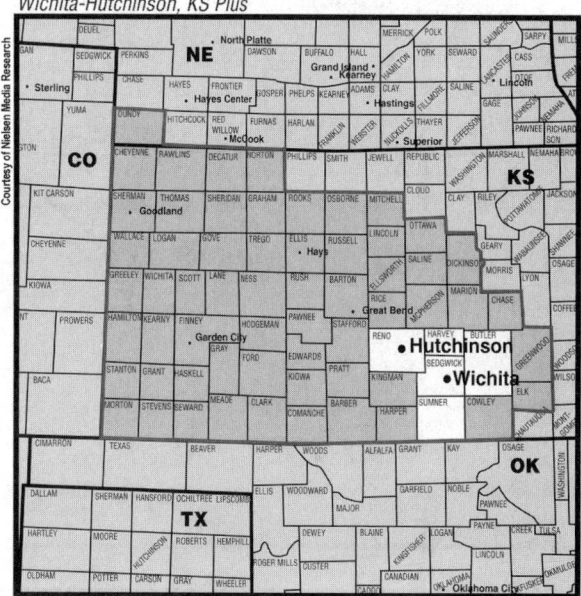

DMA Counties	State	TV Households	DMA Counties	State	TV Households
Barber	KS	2,070	Marion	KS	4,900
Barton	KS	11,140	McPherson	KS	10,490
Butler	KS	22,160	Meade	KS	1,690
Chase	KS	1,240	Mitchell	KS	2,720
Cheyenne	KS	1,190	Morton	KS	1,180
Clark	KS	890	Ness	KS	1,390
Comanche	KS	880	Norton	KS	2,200
Cowley	KS	13,560	Osborne	KS	1,770
Decatur	KS	1,390	Ottawa	KS	2,370
Dickinson	KS	7,910	Pawnee	KS	2,480
Edwards	KS	1,270	Pratt	KS	3,870
Elk	KS	1,290	Rawlins	KS	1,290
Ellis	KS	11,310	Reno	KS	24,570
Ellsworth	KS	2,380	Rice	KS	3,790
Finney	KS	11,900	Rooks	KS	2,190
Ford	KS	10,560	Rush	KS	1,490
Gove	KS	1,130	Russell	KS	2,980
Graham	KS	1,190	Saline	KS	21,180
Grant	KS	2,600	Scott	KS	1,850
Gray	KS	2,000	Sedgwick	KS	180,110
Greeley	KS	580	Seward	KS	7,310
Greenwood	KS	3,020	Sheridan	KS	1,090
Hamilton	KS	990	Sherman	KS	2,480
Harper	KS	2,530	Stafford	KS	1,880
Harvey	KS	12,800	Stanton	KS	890
Haskell	KS	1,380	Stevens	KS	1,860
Hodgeman	KS	790	Sumner	KS	9,450
Kearny	KS	1,560	Thomas	KS	3,180
Kingman	KS	3,170	Trego	KS	1,280
Kiowa	KS	1,220	Wallace	KS	570
Lane	KS	800	Wichita	KS	870
Lincoln	KS	1,480	Dundy	NE	860
Logan	KS	1,080			

Broadcasting & Cable Yearbook 2006

Nielsen DMA Market Atlas

Wilkes Barre-Scranton, PA (53)

DMA TV Households: 592,560
% of U.S. TV Households: .541

WNEP-TV Scranton, PA, ch. 16, ABC
WYOU Scranton, PA, ch. 22, CBS
WBRE-TV Wilkes-Barre, PA, ch. 28, NBC
WSWB Scranton, PA, ch. 38, WB
*****WVIA-TV** Scranton, PA, ch. 44, ETV
WILF Williamsport, PA, ch. 53, Fox
WOLF-TV Hazleton, PA, ch. 56, Fox
WQPX Scranton, PA, ch. 64, IND

DMA Counties	State	TV Households	DMA Counties	State	TV Households
Bradford	PA	25,010	Northumberland	PA	38,470
Carbon	PA	25,020	Schuylkill	PA	59,670
Clinton	PA	14,570	Snyder	PA	13,770
Columbia	PA	25,640	Sullivan	PA	2,540
Lackawanna	PA	86,490	Susquehanna	PA	16,480
Luzerne	PA	131,110	Union	PA	13,370
Lycoming	PA	46,890	Wayne	PA	19,180
Monroe	PA	56,460	Wyoming	PA	11,100
Montour	PA	6,790			

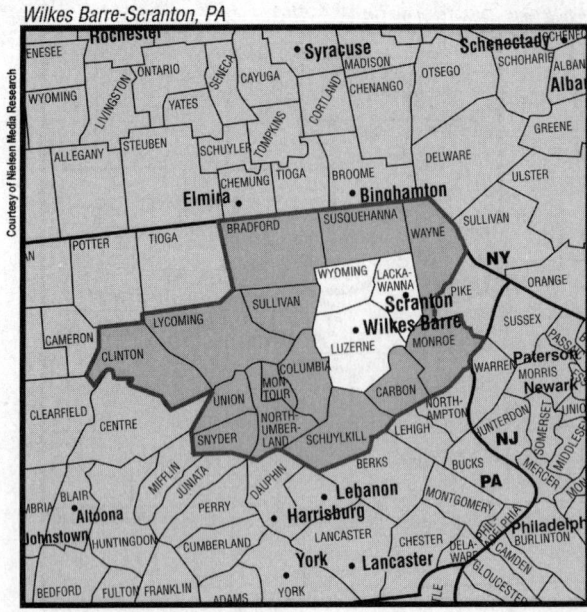

Wilmington, NC (140)

DMA TV Households: 163,560
% of U.S. TV Households: .149

WWAY Wilmington, NC, ch. 3, ABC
WECT Wilmington, NC, ch. 6, NBC
WSFX-TV Wilmington, NC, ch. 26, Fox
*****WUNJ-TV** Wilmington, NC, ch. 39, ETV

DMA Counties	State	TV Households
Bladen	NC	13,570
Brunswick	NC	36,180
Columbus	NC	21,520
New Hanover	NC	74,880
Pender	NC	17,410

Yakima-Pasco-Richland-Kennewick, WA (126)

DMA TV Households: 207,180
% of U.S. TV Households: .189

KAZW-TV Walla Walla, WA, ch. 9, Azteca America
KFFX-TV Pendleton, OR, ch. 11, Fox
KEPR-TV Pasco, WA, ch. 19, satellite to KIMA-TV
KNDO Yakima, WA, ch. 23, NBC
KNDU Richland, WA, ch. 25, satellite to KNDO
KIMA-TV Yakima, WA, ch. 29, CBS
*****KTNW** Richland, WA, ch. 31, ETV
KAPP Yakima, WA, ch. 35, ABC
KVEW Kennewick, WA, ch. 42, satellite to KAPP
*****KYVE** Yakima, WA, ch. 47, ETV

DMA Counties	State	TV Households
Morrow	OR	3,850
Umatilla	OR	24,700
Benton	WA	57,340
Franklin	WA	16,110
Kittitas	WA	13,020
Walla Walla	WA	19,600
Yakima	WA	72,560

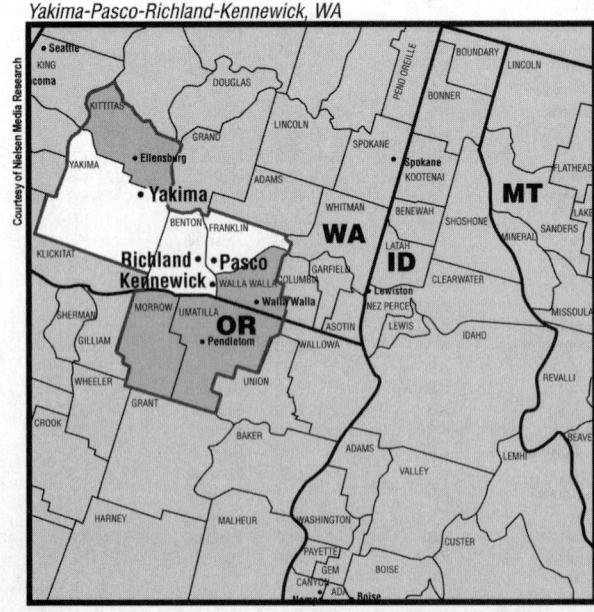

Nielsen DMA Market Atlas

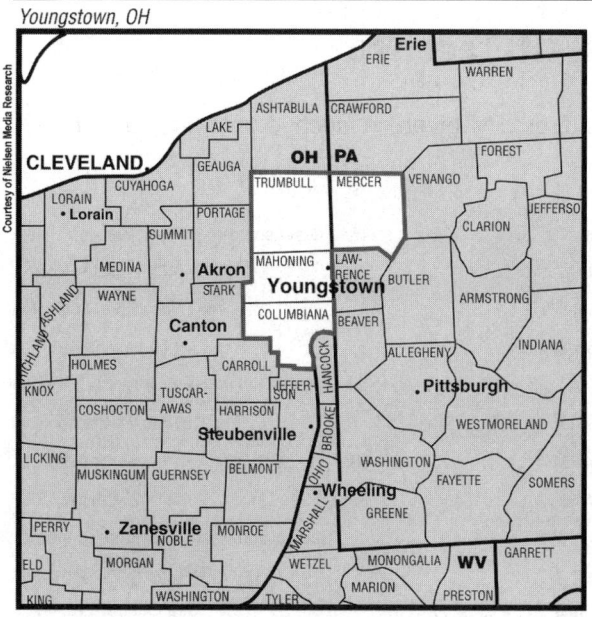
Youngstown, OH

Youngstown, OH (102)

DMA TV Households: 281,340
% of U.S. TV Households: .257

WFMJ-TV Youngstown, OH, ch. 21, NBC
WKBN-TV Youngstown, OH, ch. 27, CBS
WYTV Youngstown, OH, ch. 33, ABC
*****WNEO** Alliance, OH, ch. 45, ETV

DMA Counties	State	TV Households
Columbiana	OH	42,980
Mahoning	OH	102,130
Trumbull	OH	89,270
Mercer	PA	46,960

Yuma, AZ-El Centro, CA (171)

DMA TV Households: 99,490
% of U.S. TV Households: .091

KVYE El Centro, CA, ch. 7, Univision
KECY-TV El Centro, CA, ch. 9, Fox
KYMA Yuma, AZ, ch. 11, NBC
KSWT Yuma, AZ, ch. 13, CBS, Telemundo
KAJB Calipatria, CA, ch. 54, TeleFutura

DMA Counties	State	TV Households
Yuma	AZ	58,390
Imperial	CA	41,100

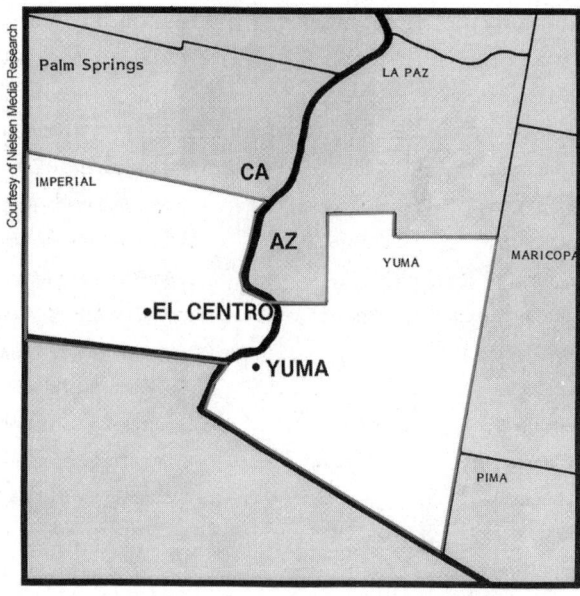

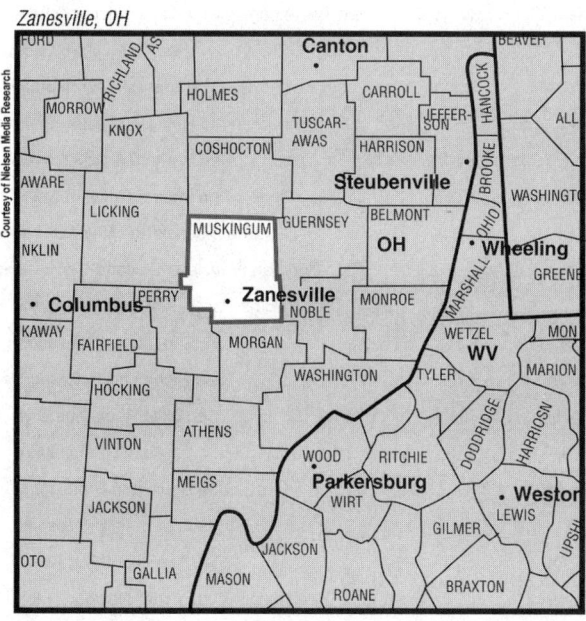
Zanesville, OH

Zanesville, OH (202)

DMA TV Households: 33,240
% of U.S. TV Households: .030

WHIZ-TV Zanesville, OH, ch. 18, NBC

DMA County	State	TV Households
Muskingum	OH	33,240

Broadcasting & Cable Yearbook 2006

Multi-City DMA Cross-Reference

The following cities are in hyphenated markets, but are not the first city given in such a market; i.e., Troy in Albany-Schenectady-Troy, NY. They are listed alphabetically.

Ada, OK	See Sherman-Ada
Akron, OH	See Cleveland-Akron (Canton)
Altoona, PA	See Johnstown-Altoona
Ames, IA	See Des Moines-Ames
Anderson, SC	See Greenville-Spartanburg-Asheville-Anderson
Anniston, AL	See Birmingham (Anniston, Tuscaloosa)
Appleton, WI	See Green Bay-Appleton
Asheville, NC	See Greenville-Spartanburg-Asheville-Anderson
Auburn, ME	See Portland-Auburn
Austin, MN	See Rochester-Mason City-Austin
Battle Creek, MI	See Grand Rapids-Kalamazoo-Battle Creek
Bay City, MI	See Flint-Saginaw-Bay City
Beckley, WV	See Bluefield-Beckley-Oak Hill
Bismarck, ND	See Minot-Bismarck-Dickinson
Bloomington, IL	See Peoria-Bloomington
Bozeman, MT	See Butte-Bozeman
Brownsville, TX	See Harlingen-Weslaco-Brownsville-McAllen
Bryan, TX	See Waco-Temple-Bryan
Cadillac, MI	See Traverse City-Cadillac
Canton, OH	See Cleveland-Akron (Canton)
Cape Girardeau, MO	See Paducah-Cape Girardeau-Harrisburg-Mount Vernon
Daytona Beach, FL	See Orlando-Daytona Beach-Melbourne
Decatur, AL	See Huntsville-Decatur-Florence
Decatur, IL	See Champaign & Springfield-Decatur
Dickinson, ND	See Minot-Bismarck-Dickinson
Dubuque, IA	See Cedar Rapids-Waterloo-Iowa City & Dubuque
Durham, NC	See Raleigh-Durham
Eau Claire, WI	See La Crosse-Eau Claire
El Centro, CA	See Yuma-El Centro
El Dorado, AR	See Monroe-El Dorado
Elkhart, IN	See South Bend-Elkhart
Fayetteville, AR	See Ft. Smith-Fayetteville-Springdale-Rogers
Fayetteville, NC	See Raleigh-Durham (Fayetteville)
Florence, AL	See Huntsville-Decatur-Florence
Florence, SC	See Myrtle Beach-Florence
Ft. Lauderdale, FL	See Miami-Ft. Lauderdale
Ft. Pierce, FL	See West Palm Beach-Ft. Pierce
Ft. Walton Beach, FL	See Mobile-Pensacola (Ft. Walton Beach)
Ft. Worth, TX	See Dallas-Ft. Worth
Greenville, MS	See Greenwood-Greenville
Gulfport, MS	See Biloxi-Gulfport
Hagerstown, MD	See Washington, DC (Hagerstown)
Hannibal, MO	See Quincy-Hannibal-Keokuk
Harrisburg, IL	See Paducah-Cape Girardeau-Harrisburg-Mount Vernon
Hastings, NE	See Lincoln & Hastings-Kearney Plus
High Point, NC	See Greensboro-High Point-Winston Salem
Holyoke, MA	See Springfield-Holyoke
Huntington, WV	See Charleston-Huntington
Hutchinson, KS	See Wichita-Hutchinson Plus
Iowa City, IA	See Cedar Rapids-Waterloo-Iowa City & Dubuque
Jefferson City, MO	See Columbia-Jefferson City
Kalamazoo, MI	See Grand Rapids-Kalamazoo-Battle Creek
Kearney, NE	See Lincoln & Hastings-Kearney Plus
Kennewick, WA	See Yakima-Pasco-Richland-Kennewick
Keokuk, IA	See Quincy-Hannibal-Keokuk
Kirksville, MO	See Ottumwa-Kirksville
Klamath Falls, OR	See Medford-Klamath Falls
Lancaster, PA	See Harrisburg-Lancaster-Lebanon-York
Laurel, MS	See Hattiesburg-Laurel
Lawton, OK	See Wichita Falls & Lawton
Lebanon, PA	See Harrisburg-Lancaster-Lebanon-York
Longview, TX	See Tyler-Longview (Lufkin & Nacogdoches)
Lufkin, TX	See Tyler-Longview (Lufkin & Nacogdoches)
Lynchburg, VA	See Roanoke-Lynchburg
Manchester, NH	See Boston (Manchester)
Mason City, IA	See Rochester-Mason City-Austin
McAllen, TX	See Harlingen-Weslaco-Brownsville-McAllen
Melbourne, FL	See Orlando-Daytona Beach-Melbourne
Midland, TX	See Odessa-Midland
Mitchell, SD	See Sioux Falls (Mitchell)
Modesto, CA	See Sacramento-Stockton-Modesto
Moline, IL	See Davenport-Rock Island-Moline
Montrose, CO	See Grand Junction-Montrose
Nacogdoches, TX	See Tyler-Longview (Lufkin & Nacogdoches)
Naples, FL	See Ft. Myers-Naples
New Bedford, MA	See Providence-New Bedford
New Bern, NC	See Greenville-New Bern-Washington
New Haven, CT	See Hartford & New Haven
Newport News, VA	See Norfolk-Portsmouth-Newport News
Oak Hill, WV	See Bluefield-Beckley-Oak Hill
Oakland, CA	See San Francisco-Oakland-San Jose
Pasco, WA	See Yakima-Pasco-Richland-Kennewick
Pensacola, FL	See Mobile-Pensacola
Petersburg, VA	See Richmond-Petersburg
Pine Bluff, AR	See Little Rock-Pine Bluff
Pittsburg, KS	See Joplin-Pittsburg
Plattsburgh, NY	See Burlington-Plattsburgh
Pocatello, ID	See Idaho Falls-Pocatello
Port Arthur, TX	See Beaumont-Port Arthur
Portsmouth, VA	See Norfolk-Portsmouth-Newport News

Broadcasting & Cable Yearbook 2006

Multi-City DMA Cross-Reference

Pueblo, CO . . . . See Colorado Springs-Pueblo
Redding, CA . . . . .See Chico-Redding
Rhinelander, WI . . . . .See Wausau-Rhinelander
Richland, WA. .See Yakima-Pasco-Richland-Kennewick
Riverton, WY . . . . .See Casper-Riverton
Rock Island, IL. .See Davenport-Rock Island-Moline
Rogers, AR . . . . .See Ft. Smith-Fayetteville-Springdale-Rogers
Saginaw, MI . . . . .See Flint-Saginaw-Bay City
St. Paul, MN . . . . .See Minneapolis-St. Paul
St. Petersburg, FL. . . . . .See Tampa-St. Petersburg-Sarasota
Salinas, CA . . . . .See Monterey-Salinas
San Jose, CA . . . . .See San Francisco-Oakland-San Jose
San Luis Obispo, CA . . . . .See Santa Barbara-Santa Maria-San Luis Obispo
Santa Fe, NM . . . . .See Albuquerque-Santa Fe
Santa Maria, CA . . . . .See Santa Barbara-Santa Maria-San Luis Obispo
Sarasota, FL. . . . . .See Tampa-St. Petersburg-Sarasota
Schenectady, NY . . . . .See Albany-Schenectady-Troy
Scottsbluff, NE. . . . . .See Cheyenne-Scottsbluff
Scranton, PA. . . . . .See Wilkes Barre-Scranton
Selma, AL. . . . . .See Montgomery (Selma)
Sierra Vista, AZ. . . . . .See Tucson (Sierra Vista)
Spartanburg, SC. . . . . .See Greenville-Spartanburg-Asheville-Anderson
Springdale, AR . . . . .See Ft. Smith-Fayetteville-Springdale-Rogers
Springfield, IL. . . . . .See Champaign & Springfield-Decatur
Steubenville, OH . . . . .See Wheeling-Steubenville
Stockton, CA. . . . . .See Sacramento-Stockton-Modesto
Superior, WI . . . . .See Duluth-Superior
Sweetwater, TX. . . . . .See Abilene-Sweetwater
Tacoma, WA . . . . .See Seattle-Tacoma
Temple, TX . . . . .See Waco-Temple-Bryan
Thomasville, GA .See Tallahassee-Thomasville
Troy, NY . . . . .See Albany-Schenectady-Troy
Tupelo, MS . . . . .See Columbus-Tupelo-West Point
Tuscaloosa, AL . . . . .See Birmingham (Anniston, Tuscaloosa)
Valley City, ND. . . . . .See Fargo-Valley City
Visalia, CA. . . . . .See Fresno-Visalia
Washington, NC . . . . .See Greenville-New Bern-Washington
Waterloo, IA . . . . .See Cedar Rapids-Waterloo-Iowa City & Dubuque
Weslaco, TX. . . . . .See See Harlingen-Weslaco-Brownsville-McAllen
Weston, WV . . . . .See Clarksburg-Weston
West Point, MS. .See Columbus-Tupelo-West Point
Winston Salem, NC . . . . .See Greensboro-High Point-Winston Salem
York, PA . . . . .See Harrisburg-Lancaster-Lebanon-York

Section C
Cable

Top 25 Cable/Satellite Operators	C-2
The Top 25 Cable/Satellite TV Operators	C-3
Top 100 Cable Clusters/Systems	C-4
Top 100 Cable Clusters/Systems, by Owner	C-6
Cable Penetration by DMA	C-7
Top 50 DMA by Cable Penetration	C-11
Bottom 50 DMA by Cable Penetration	C-13
Top 50 DMA by Cable Households	C-15

Databooks, Industry Reports, Executive Summits, Expert Intelligence Newsletters, Valuation Appraisals, Consulting

kagan® Research

No Matter How Things Change...
we've been studying the state of and the future of the broadcast and cable businesses for 35 years...and still Kagan Research is the only expert intelligence firm industry executives consistently rely on to tell them what to focus on in the next 10 years.

Exclusive Forecasts Appraisals Benchmarks Insights & Data.

Call 1-800-307-2529 or visit kagan.com | For inquiries please call 1-831-624-1536 or email to info@kagan.com

Top 25 Cable/Satellite Operators

Ranked by Basic Subscribers*

Rank	Company	Subscribers
1	Comcast Cable Comm.	21,448,000
2	DIRECTV	14,670,000
3	EchoStar	11,455,000
4	Time Warner Cable	10,905,000
5	Cox Communications	6,283,100
6	Charter Communications	5,943,100
7	Adelphia Comm. (1)	5,130,900
8	Cablevision Systems	3,005,600
9	Bright House Networks (e)	2,180,000
10	Mediacom LLC	1,446,000
11	Insight Communications	1,257,200
12	CableOne	702,800
13	Cebridge Connection (e)	449,200
14	RCN Corp.	371,000
15	Bresnan (e)	300,100
16	WideOpenWest (e)	292,500
17	Service Electric (e)	285,000
18	Atlantic Broadband	249,200
19	Armstrong Group of Cos.	227,300
20	Susquehanna Cable	226,100
21	Midcontinent Communications	195,000
22	Pencor Services (e)	181,900
23	Knology Holdings	179,800
24	Northland Communications	160,100
25	Millennium Digital Media (e)	156,300

* As of June 30, 2005.
(e) Estimate.
(1) Includes Non-Filing Entities and Rigas Entities, including customers in Brazil and Puerto Rico.
© 2005 Kagan Research, LLC. Reprinted with permission.

The Top 25 Cable/Satellite TV Operators

Ranked by Basic Cable Subscribers

1 Comcast Cable

1500 Market St., East Tower, Philadelphia, PA 19102
Phone: (215) 665-1700; Fax: (215) 981-7790; Web: http://www.comcast.com
Steve Burke, president, Comcast Cable Communications/COO, Comcast Corp.
NASDAQ Symbols: CMCSA, CMCSK
Basic Subs: 21,448,000

2 DirecTV

2230 Imperial Highway, El Segundo, CA 90245
Phone: (310) 535-5000; Fax: (310) 535-5225; Web: http://www.directv.com
Roxanne Austin, president
NYSE Symbol: DTV (Fox Entertainment Group, a publicly traded 82/% owned subsidiary of News Corp, owns 34/%)
Basic Subs: 14,670,000

3 Echostar

9631 South Meridian Blvd., Englewood, CO 80112
Web: http://www.dishnetwork.com Charles Ergen, chairman/CEO
NASDAQ Symbol: (DISH)
Basic Subs: 11,455,000

4 Time Warner Cable

290 Harbor Dr., Stamford, CT, 06902
Phone: (203) 328-0600; Fax: (203) 328-0690; Web: http://www.aoltimewarner.com
Richard D. Parsons, chairman/CEO
NYSE Symbol: TWX
Basic Subs: 10,905,000

5 Cox

1400 Lake Hearn Dr., Atlanta, GA 30319
Phone: (404) 843-5000; Fax: (404) 847-6336; Web: http://www.cox.com
James O. Robbins, president/CEO
NYSE Symbol: COX (Cox Enterprises owns approximately 63/%)
Basic Subs: 6,283,100

6 Charter

12405 Powerscourt Dr., St. Louis, MO 63131
Phone: (314) 965-0555; Fax: (314) 965-8793; Web: http://www.charter.com
Carl Vogel, president/CEO
NASDAQ Symbol: CHTR
Basic Subs: 5,943,100

7 Adelphia

5619 DTC Pkwy., Greenwood Village, CO 80111
Phone: (303) 268-6300; Fax: (303) 268-6495; http://www.adelphia.com
William Schleyer, chairman/CEO
Ownership: In Chapter 11 bankruptcy-protection proceedings
Basic Subs: 5,130,900

8 Cablevision Systems

1111 Stewart Ave., Bethpage, NY 11714
Phone: (516) 803-2300; Web: http://www.cablevision.com
James Dolan, president/CEO
NYSE Symbol: CVC
Basic Subs: 3,005,600

9 Bright House Network

5000 Campuswood Dr., East Syracuse, NY 13057
Phone: (315) 438-4100; Fax: (315) 438-4643
Robert Miron, chairman/CEO
Ownership: Private (Advance/Newhouse Communications and Time Warner Entertainment)
Basic Subs: 2,180,000

10 Mediacom

100 Crystal Run Rd., Middletown, NY 10941
Phone: (845) 695-2600; Fax: (845) 695-2639; Web: http://www.knology.com
Rocco B. Commisso, chairman/CEO
NASDAQ Symbol: MCCC
Basic Subs: 1,446,000

11 Insight Communications

810 Seventh Ave., New York, NY 10019
Phone: (917) 286-2300; Fax: (917) 286-2301; Web: http://www.insight-com.com
Michael Willner, president/CEO
NASDAQ Symbol: ICCI (Comcast owns 50/%)
Basic Subs: 1,257,200

12 Cable One

1314 N. Third St., 3rd Fl., Phoenix, AZ 85004
Phone: (602) 364-6000; Fax: (602) 364-6010; Web: http://www.cableone.net
Thomas O. Might, president/CEO
NYSE Symbol: WPO (The Washington Post Co.)
Basic Subs: 702,800

13 Cebridge Connections

12444 Powerscourt Dr., Ste. 450, St. Louis, MO 63131
Phone: (314) 965-2020; Fax: (314) 965-0500; Web: http://www.cebridge.net
Bill Shreffler, president/COO
Ownership: Private
Basic Subs: 449,200

14 RCN

105 Carnegie Center, Princeton, NJ 08540
Phone: (609) 734-3700; Fax: (609) 951-8632; Web: http://www.rcn.com
Dave C. McCort, chairman/CEO
Ownership: In Chapter 11 bankruptcy-protection proceedings
Basic Subs: 371,000

15 Bresnan

777 Westchester Ave., White Plains, NY 10604
Phone: (914) 641-3300; Fax: (914) 641-3424; Web: http://www.bresnan.com
William Bresnan, president/CEO
Ownership: Private (William Bresnan and other investors, including Comcast)
Basic Subs: 300,100

16 WideOpenWest

900 W. Castleton Rd., Castle Rock, CO 80104
Phone: (800) 257-0925; Web: http://www.wideopenwest.com
Colleen Abdoulah, president
Ownership: Private
Basic Subs: 292,500*

17 Service Electric

2260 Ave. A, Bethlehem, PA 18017
Phone: (610) 865-9100; Fax: (610) 865-5031; Web: http://www.sectv.com
John E. Walson, president/CEO
Ownership: Private (Walson family)
Basic Subs/Penetration: 285,000/70/%

18 Atlantic Broadband

1 Batterymarch Park, Suite 405, Quincy, MA 02169
Phone: (617) 786-8800; Fax: (671) 786-8803; Web: http://www.atlanticbb.com David Keefe, CEO
Ownership: Private
Basic Subs: 249,200

19 Armstrong Group of Cos.

One Armstrong Place, Butler, PA 16001
Phone: (724) 283-0925; Fax: (724) 283-9655; Web: http://www.armstrongonewire.com
Dru Sedwick, president
Ownership: Private (Armstrong Holdings)
Basic Subs: 227,300

20 Susquehanna

Susquehanna Commerce Center West, 140 E. Market St., York, PA 17401
Phone: (717) 852-2395; Fax: (717) 771-1439; Web: http://www.suscom.net
James Munchel, president/COO
Ownership: Private (Susquehanna Media)
Basic Subs: 226,100

21 Midcontinent Communications

5001 W. 41st St., Sioux Falls, SD 57106
Phone: (605) 357-5491; Fax: (605) 339-4419; Web: http://www.midcocomm.com
Mark Niblick, president/CEO
Ownership: Private (Midcontinent Media and Comcast Corp.)
Basic Subs: 195,000

22 Pencor Services

613 Third St., PO Box 215, Palmerton, PA 18071
Phone: (610) 826-2551; Fax: (610) 826-7626; Web: http://www.brctv.com
Fred Reinhard, president
Ownership: Private (Pencor Services)
Basic Subs: 181,900

23 Knology Holdings

1241 O.G. Skinner Dr., West Point, GA 31833
Phone: (706) 645-3000; Fax: (706) 645-0148; Web: http://www.knology.com
Rodger L. Johnson, president/CEO
NASDAQ Symbol: KNOL
Basic Subs: 179,800

24 Northland

1201 Third Ave., Ste. 3600, Seattle, WA 98101
Phone: (206) 621-1351; Fax: (206) 623-9015; Web: http://www.northlandcabletv.com
John Whetzell, president/COO
Ownership: Private
Basic Subs: 160,100

25 Millennium Digital Media

120 South Central Ave., Suite 150, Saint Louis, MO 63105
Phone: (314) 802-2222; Fax: (314) 802-2300; Web: http://www.mdm.net
Kelvin R. Westbrook, president
Basic Subs: 156,300

Broadcasting & Cable Yearbook 2006

Top 100 Cable Clusters/Systems

Ranked by Basic Subscribers*

Rank	System	Subscribers
1	Cablevision Systems Corp., Greater New York Area, NY	2,963,001
2	Comcast, Boston, MA	1,937,608
3	Time Warner Cable, Los Angeles, CA	1,918,746
4	Comcast, Philadelphia, PA	1,906,925
5	Comcast, Chicago, IL	1,760,735
6	Comcast, San Francisco Bay Area, CA	1,608,716
7	Time Warner Cable, New York, NY	1,379,086
8	Comcast, Seattle, WA	1,030,982
9	Bright House Networks, Tampa Bay, FL	1,011,169
10	Comcast, Detroit, MI	981,693
11	Comcast, Washington, DC	959,979
12	Time Warner Cable, Cleveland-Akron (Canton), OH	854,077
13	Cox Comm., Middle America Cox	777,629
14	Bright House Networks, Central FL	776,651
15	Cox Comm., AZ	774,216
16	Comcast, Atlanta, GA	769,072
17	Time Warner Cable, Houston, TX	753,857
18	Mediacom, South Central Region	746,000
19	Comcast, Miami, FL	739,534
20	Comcast, New York, NY	720,139
21	Mediacom, North Central Region	712,000
22	Comcast, Denver, CO	665,945
23	Comcast, Baltimore, MD	649,301
24	Comcast, Pittsburgh, PA	606,967
25	Comcast, Hartford & New Haven, CT	546,759
26	Cox Comm., San Diego, CA	542,222
27	Comcast, St. Paul & Minneapolis, MN	539,088
28	Comcast, Sacramento, CA	535,240
29	Cox Comm., OK	501,020
30	Time Warner Cable, Raleigh-Durham, NC	471,280
31	Cox Comm., New England	456,647
32	Charter Comm., St. Louis Metro, MO	447,400
33	Time Warner Cable, Charlotte, NC	426,081
34	Cox Comm., Hampton Roads, VA	420,805
35	Time Warner Cable, Milwaukee, WI	416,684
36	Comcast, Portland, OR	407,139
37	Cox Comm., Las Vegas, NV	403,259
38	Time Warner Cable, HI	397,253
39	Time Warner Cable, Cincinnati, OH	388,981
40	Time Warner Cable, San Antonio, TX	384,016
41	Time Warner Cable, Albany, NY	380,700
42	Comcast, Harrisburg-Lancaster-Lebanon-York, PA	377,823
43	Comcast, Grand Rapids-Kalamazoo-Battle Creek, MI	369,623
44	Comcast, West Palm Beach-Ft. Pierce, FL	368,374
45	Time Warner Cable, Columbus, OH	364,973
46	Charter Comm., New England	358,700
47	Comcast, Jacksonville & Brunswick, FL	357,671
48	Charter Comm., AL	354,800
49	Time Warner Cable, Greensboro, NC	351,808
50	Comcast, Nashville, TN	334,612

Broadcasting & Cable Yearbook 2006

Top 100 Cable Clusters/Systems

Rank	System	Subscribers
51	Time Warner Cable, Austin, TX	316,594
52	Cox Comm., KS	309,425
53	Charter Comm., SC	305,100
54	Charter Comm., GA	304,800
55	Time Warner Cable, Kansas City, MO	303,350
56	Time Warner Cable, San Diego, CA	301,355
57	Charter Comm., Los Angeles Metro, CA	297,300
58	Charter Comm., Northwest Region	293,400
59	Time Warner Cable, Syracuse, NY	280,128
60	Charter Comm., Southern MN	279,300
61	Comcast, Richmond-Petersburg, VA	278,389
62	Charter Comm., East TN/KY	276,000
63	Cox Comm., Orange County, CA	273,541
64	Insight Comm., Louisville, KY	271,700
65	Comcast, Indianapolis, IN	270,728
66	Cox Comm., New Orleans, LA	270,171
67	Charter Comm., WV	267,900
68	Time Warner Cable, Rochester, NY	264,868
69	Comcast, Ft. Myers-Naples, FL	259,726
70	Cox Comm., Northern VA	257,425
71	Time Warner Cable, Portland-Auburn, ME	255,182
72	Charter Comm., NC/VA	245,800
73	Comcast, Salt Lake City, UT	244,436
74	Cox Comm., West TX	229,423
75	Charter Comm., Southern WI	226,500
76	Charter Comm., West TN/KY	222,700
77	Charter Comm., Mid-America	215,000
78	Comcast, Fresno-Visalia, CA	208,365
79	Comcast, Tampa/Sarasota, FL	203,743
80	Comcast, Wheeling-Steubenville, WV	201,694
81	Comcast, Memphis, TN	201,000
82	Charter Comm., Eastern MI	198,800
83	Charter Comm., Northern MI	197,200
84	Charter Comm., Central CA	197,000
85	Charter Comm., Western MI	194,800
86	Charter Comm., Eastern WI	190,800
87	Cox Comm., Omaha, NE	190,382
88	Comcast, Albuquerque-Santa Fe, NM	186,514
89	Cox Comm., Baton Rouge, LA	179,011
90	Charter Comm., LA/MS	178,200
91	Cox Comm., Gulf Coast/FL	167,955
92	Charter Comm., Ft. Worth, TX	167,300
93	Comcast, Eugene, OR	164,600
94	Time Warner Cable, Columbia, SC	163,619
95	Comcast, Salisbury, MD	162,441
96	Charter Comm., MN/WI	162,000
97	Comcast, Knoxville, TN	160,911
98	Time Warner Cable, Green Bay, WI	147,981
99	Charter Comm., NV	146,500
100	Charter Comm., Inland Empire	137,800

* As of December 2004.
© 2005 Kagan Research, LLC. Reprinted with permission.

Top 100 Cable Clusters/Systems, by Owner

System rankings are given in parentheses.

BRIGHT HOUSE NETWORKS
Central Florida (14)
Tampa Bay (9)

CABLEVISION
Greater New York (1)

CHARTER
AL (48)
Central CA (84)
East TN/KY (62)
Eastern MI (82)
Eastern WI (86)
Ft. Worth TX (92)
GA (54)
Inland Empire (100)
LA/MS (90)
Los Angeles Metro (57)
Mid-America (77)
MN/WI (96)
NC/VA (72)
New England (46)
Northern MI (83)
Northwest Region (58)
NV (99)
SC (53)
Southern MN (60)
Southern WI (75)
St. Louis Metro (32)
West TN/KY (76)
Western MI (85)
WV (67)

COMCAST
Albuquerque-Santa Fe NM (88)
Atlanta GA (16)
Baltimore MD (23)
Boston MA (2)
Chicago IL (5)
Denver CO (22)
Detroit MI (10)
Eugene OR (93)
Fresno-Visalia CA (78)
Ft. Meyers-Naples FL (69)
Grand Rapids-Kalamazoo-Battle Creek MI (43)
Harrisburg-Lancaster-Lebanon-York PA (42)
Hartford & New Haven CT (25)
Indianapolis IN (65)
Jacksonville & Brunswick FL (47)
Knoxville (97)
Memphis TN (81)
Miami (19)
Nashville TN (50)
New York NY (20)
Philadelphia PA (4)
Pittsburgh PA (24)
Portland OR (36)
Richmond-Petersburg VA (61)

Sacramento CA (28)
Salisbury MD (95)
Salt Lake City UT (73)
San Francisco Bay Area CA (6)
Seattle WA (8)
St. Paul & Minneapolis MN (27)
Tampa/Sarasota FL (79)
Washington DC (11)
West Palm Beach-Ft. Pierce FL (44)
Wheeling-Steubenville WV (80)

COX
AZ (15)
Baton Rouge LA (89)
Gulf Coast/FL (91)
Hampton Roads VA (34)
KS (52)
Las Vegas NV (37)
Middle America (13)
New England (31)
New Orleans LA (66)
Northern VA (70)
OK (29)
Omaha NE (87)
Orange County CA (63)
San Diego CA (26)
West TX (74)

INSIGHT
Louisville (64)

MEDIACOM
North Central Region (21)
South Central Region (18)

TIME WARNER
Albany NY (41)
Austin TX (51)
Charlotte NC (33)
Cincinnati OH (39)
Cleveland-Akron (Canton) OH (12)
Columbia SC (94)
Columbus OH (45)
Green Bay WI (98)
Greensboro NC (49)
HI (38)
Houston TX (17)
Kansas City MO (55)
Los Angeles CA (3)
Milwaukee WI (35)
New York (7)
Portland-Auburn ME (71)
Raleigh-Durham NC (30)
Rochester NY (68)
San Antonio TX (40)
San Diego CA (56)
Syracuse (59)

© 2005 Kagan Research, LLC. Reprinted with permission. Research

Cable Penetration by DMA

Listed below are the Neilsen Media Research Designated Market Areas (DMAs) with the number of cable homes and the percentage of penetration.

Designated Market Area	Cable Households	Cable Penetration (%)
Abilene-Sweetwater	66,060	58
Albany, GA	101,640	67
Albany-Schenectady-Troy	438,410	79
Albuquerque-Santa Fe	335,500	52
Alexandria, LA	63,920	68
Alpena	11,620	65
Amarillo	117,970	62
Anchorage	87,010	62
Atlanta	1,425,580	69
Augusta	170,530	69
Austin	378,670	67
Bakersfield	129,390	67
Baltimore	799,000	73
Bangor	67,540	47
Baton Rouge	232,100	76
Beaumont-Port Arthur	119,260	71
Bend, OR	32,010	61
Billings	55,190	54
Biloxi-Gulfport	98,300	71
Binghamton	107,770	76
Birmingham (Anniston, Tuscaloosa)	457,450	64
Bluefield-Beckley-Oak Hill	110,770	74
Boise	87,590	39
Boston (Manchester)	2,043,550	85
Bowling Green	49,490	61
Buffalo	475,280	73
Burlington-Plattsburgh	186,400	57
Butte-Bozeman	29,000	50
Casper-Riverton	34,310	66
Cedar Rapids-Waterloo & Dubuque	213,920	65
Champaign & Springfield-Decatur	262,850	69
Charleston, SC	193,530	68
Charleston-Huntington	363,770	72
Charlotte	670,130	67
Charlottesville	44,960	64
Chattanooga	239,330	68
Cheyenne-Scottsbluff	39,550	73
Chicago	2,423,160	71
Chico-Redding	92,760	49
Cincinnati	571,620	65
Clarksburg-Weston	72,050	66
Cleveland-Akron (Canton)	1,109,490	71
Colorado Springs-Pueblo	183,120	58
Columbia, SC	217,110	58
Columbia-Jefferson City	84,090	50
Columbus, GA	159,800	77
Columbus, OH	618,300	71
Columbus-Tupelo-West Point	99,320	53
Corpus Christi	145,300	75
Dallas-Fort Worth	1,066,450	47
Davenport-Rock Island-Moline	194,870	63
Dayton	384,720	72
Denver	800,360	57
Des Moines-Ames	223,680	54
Detroit	1,389,840	71

Broadcasting & Cable Yearbook 2006

Cable Penetration by DMA

Designated Market Area	Cable Households	Cable Penetration (%)
Dothan	70,580	71
Duluth-Superior	82,980	47
El Paso (Las Cruces)	164,350	57
Elmira	72,310	74
Erie	105,620	66
Eugene	138,140	60
Eureka	40,300	69
Evansville	175,760	61
Fairbanks	12,530	40
Fargo-Valley City	148,540	63
Flint-Saginaw-Bay City	321,080	67
Myrtle Beach-Florence	185,540	70
Fort Myers-Naples	330,820	74
Fort Smith-Fayetteville-Springdale-Rogers	160,430	60
Fort Wayne	144,500	53
Fresno-Visalia	256,290	49
Gainesville	79,130	68
Glendive	3,560	69
Grand Junction-Montrose	35,620	56
Grand Rapids-Kalamazoo-Battle Creek	438,930	60
Great Falls	36,600	57
Green Bay-Appleton	248,720	57
Greensboro-High Point-Winston Salem	441,080	68
Greenville-New Bern-Washington	169,820	63
Greenville-Spartanburg-Asheville-Anderson	469,410	58
Greenwood-Greenville	54,860	70
Harlingen-Weslaco-Brownsville-McAllen	142,650	46
Harrisburg-Lancaster-Lebanon-York	572,480	81
Harrisonburg	54,900	64
Hartford & New Haven	890,100	87
Hattiesburg-Laurel	57,710	55
Helena	14,390	57
Honolulu	374,620	90
Houston	1,063,300	56
Huntsville-Decatur, Florence	249,990	68
Idaho Falls-Pocatello	50,140	44
Indianapolis	665,480	63
Jackson, MS	181,130	55
Jackson, TN	58,410	62
Jacksonville, Brunswick	419,520	68
Johnstown-Altoona	233,060	77
Jonesboro	55,880	60
Joplin-Pittsburg	75,470	50
Juneau	17,830	71
Kansas City	571,750	64
Knoxville	340,300	66
La Crosse-Eau Claire	120,340	58
Lafayette, IN	47,330	73
Lafayette, LA	156,350	71
Lake Charles	64,750	69
Lansing	171,410	66
Laredo	42,640	68
Las Vegas	452,510	74
Lexington	307,870	64
Lima	39,340	73
Lincoln & Hastings-Kearney	182,100	66
Little Rock-Pine Bluff	301,790	57
Los Angeles	3,214,160	59
Louisville	405,940	64

Cable Penetration by DMA

Designated Market Area	Cable Households	Cable Penetration (%)
Lubbock	86,510	57
Macon	154,580	67
Madison	220,510	61
Mankato	36,710	71
Marquette	65,420	72
Medford-Klamath Falls	98,150	60
Memphis	383,240	58
Meridian	35,430	49
Miami-Fort Lauderdale	1,091,250	73
Milwaukee	568,450	64
Minneapolis-St. Paul	934,580	56
Minot-Bismarck-Dickinson	80,310	59
Missoula	47,120	45
Mobile-Pensacola (Fort Walton Beach)	358,890	73
Monroe-El Dorado	107,890	61
Monterey-Salinas	143,310	66
Montgomery (Selma)	179,150	72
Nashville	554,900	61
New Orleans	529,420	78
New York	5,978,720	81
Norfolk-Portsmouth-Newport News	537,880	76
North Platte	9,810	63
Odessa-Midland	101,840	75
Oklahoma City	408,220	62
Omaha	294,130	74
Orlando-Daytona Beach-Melbourne	954,390	73
Ottumwa-Kirksville	27,810	54
Paducah-Cape Girardeau-Harrisburg-Mt. Vernon	189,920	49
Palm Springs	114,320	85
Panama City	87,960	65
Parkersburg	49,550	76
Peoria-Bloomington	166,470	69
Philadelphia	2,410,920	83
Phoenix (Prescott)	951,370	60
Pittsburgh	934,690	79
Portland, OR	636,950	59
Portland-Auburn	308,640	75
Presque Isle	19,100	60
Providence-New Bedford	528,590	82
Quincy-Hannibal-Keokuk	55,420	53
Raleigh-Durham (Fayetteville)	597,350	62
Rapid City	60,970	65
Reno	154,490	63
Richmond-Petersburg	313,810	62
Roanoke-Lynchburg	262,920	59
Rochester, NY	286,840	72
Rochester-Mason City-Austin	93,340	65
Rockford	118,130	65
Sacramento-Stockton-Modesto	735,510	56
Salisbury	111,710	76
Salt Lake City	350,850	44
San Angelo	39,350	74
San Antonio	485,140	65
San Diego	862,030	84
San Francisco-Oakland-San Jose	1,805,920	77
Santa Barbara-Santa Maria-San Luis Obispo	167,450	75
Savannah	209,480	71
Seattle-Tacoma	1,221,300	72
Sherman, TX-Ada, OK	64,210	52

Cable Penetration by DMA

Designated Market Area	Cable Households	Cable Penetration (%)
Shreveport	206,020	54
Sioux City	93,520	59
Sioux Falls (Mitchell)	151,370	62
South Bend-Elkhart	167,160	50
Spokane	212,170	55
Springfield, MO	166,390	43
Springfield-Holyoke	230,280	86
St. Joseph	31,100	64
St. Louis	632,540	52
Syracuse	305,370	77
Tallahassee-Thomasville	177,480	68
Tampa-St. Petersburg, Sarasota	1,255,590	75
Terre Haute	82,480	56
Toledo	296,610	69
Topeka	115,000	67
Traverse City-Cadillac	130,070	52
Tri-Cities, TN-VA	239,750	73
Tucson (Sierra Vista)	245,240	59
Tulsa	296,750	58
Twin Falls	25,630	43
Tyler-Longview (Lufkin & Nacogdoches)	147,770	58
Utica	79,930	75
Victoria	21,740	72
Waco-Temple-Bryan	206,800	67
Washington, DC (Hagerstown)	1,620,340	72
Watertown	66,010	70
Wausau-Rhinelander	90,840	50
West Palm Beach-Fort Pierce	586,860	81
Wheeling-Steubenville	109,060	76
Wichita Falls & Lawton	100,370	64
Wichita-Hutchinson Plus	302,370	68
Wilkes Barre-Scranton	453,640	77
Wilmington	118,010	72
Yakima-Pasco-Richland-Kennewick	144,550	55
Youngstown	205,190	73
Yuma-El Centro	52,410	53
Zanesville	25,760	77

© 2004 Nielsen Media Research. Reprinted with permission.

Top 50 DMA by Cable Penetration

Listed below are the Nielsen Media Research Designated Market Areas (DMAs) ranked by percentage of cable penetration.

Rank	Designated Market Area	Cable Penetration (%)
1	Honolulu	90
2	Hartford & New Haven	87
3	Springfield-Holyoke	86
4	Boston (Manchester)	85
4	Palm Springs	85
6	San Diego	84
7	Philadelphia	83
8	Providence-New Bedford	82
9	Harrisburg-Lancaster-Lebanon-York	81
9	New York	81
9	West Palm Beach-Fort Pierce	81
12	Albany-Schenectady-Troy	79
12	Pittsburgh	79
14	New Orleans	78
15	Columbus, GA	77
15	Johnstown-Altoona	77
15	San Francisco-Oakland-San Jose	77
15	Syracuse	77
15	Wilkes Barre-Scranton	77
15	Zanesville	77
21	Baton Rouge	76
21	Binghamton	76
21	Norfolk-Portsmouth-Newport News	76
21	Parkersburg	76
21	Salisbury	76
21	Wheeling-Steubenville	76
27	Corpus Christi	75
27	Odessa-Midland	75
27	Portland-Auburn	75
27	Santa Barbara-Santa Maria-San Luis Obispo	75
27	Tampa-St. Petersburg, Sarasota	75
27	Utica	75
33	Bluefield-Beckley-Oak Hill	74
33	Elmira	74
33	Fort Myers-Naples	74
33	Las Vegas	74
33	Omaha	74
33	San Angelo	74
39	Baltimore	73
39	Buffalo	73
39	Cheyenne-Scottsbluff	73
39	Lafayette, IN	73
39	Lima	73
39	Miami-Fort Lauderdale	73
39	Mobile-Pensacola (Fort Walton Beach)	73
39	Orlando-Daytona Beach-Melbourne	73
39	Tri-Cities, TN-VA	73
39	Youngstown	73
49	Charleston-Huntington	72

Broadcasting & Cable Yearbook 2006

Top 50 DMA by Cable Penetration

Rank	Designated Market Area	Cable Penetration (%)
49	Dayton	72
49	Marquette	72
49	Montgomery (Selma)	72
49	Rochester, NY	72
49	Seattle-Tacoma	72
49	Victoria	72
49	Washington, DC (Hagerstown)	72
49	Wilmington	72

© 2004 Nielsen Media Research. Reprinted with permission.

Bottom 50 DMA by Cable Penetration

Listed below are the Nielsen Media Research Designated Market Areas (DMAs) ranked by percentage of cable penetration. Boise and Fairbanks have the lowest percentage.

Rank	Designated Market Area	Cable Penetration (%)
1	Boise	39
2	Fairbanks	40
3	Springfield, MO	43
3	Twin Falls	43
5	Idaho Falls-Pocatello	44
5	Salt Lake City	44
7	Missoula	45
8	Harlingen-Weslaco-Brownsville-McAllen	46
9	Bangor	47
9	Dallas-Fort Worth	47
9	Duluth-Superior	47
12	Chico-Redding	49
12	Fresno-Visalia	49
12	Meridian	49
12	Paducah-Cape Girardeau-Harrisburg-Mt. Vernon	49
16	Butte-Bozeman	50
16	Columbia-Jefferson City	50
16	Joplin-Pittsburg	50
16	South Bend-Elkhart	50
16	Wausau-Rhinelander	50
21	Albuquerque-Santa Fe	52
21	Sherman, TX-Ada, OK	52
21	St. Louis	52
21	Traverse City-Cadillac	52
25	Columbus-Tupelo-West Point	53
25	Fort Wayne	53
25	Quincy-Hannibal-Keokuk	53
25	Yuma-El Centro	53
29	Billings	54
29	Des Moines-Ames	54
29	Ottumwa-Kirksville	54
29	Shreveport	54
33	Hattiesburg-Laurel	55
33	Jackson, MS	55
33	Spokane	55
33	Yakima-Pasco-Richland-Kennewick	55
37	Grand Junction-Montrose	56
37	Houston	56
37	Minneapolis-St. Paul	56
37	Sacramento-Stockton-Modesto	56
37	Terre Haute	56
42	Burlington-Plattsburgh	57
42	Denver	57
42	El Paso (Las Cruces)	57
42	Great Falls	57

Broadcasting & Cable Yearbook 2006

Bottom 50 DMA by Cable Penetration

Rank	Designated Market Area	Cable Penetration (%)
42	Green Bay-Appleton	57
42	Helena	57
42	Little Rock-Pine Bluff	57
42	Lubbock	57
50	Abilene-Sweetwater	58
50	Colorado Springs-Pueblo	58
50	Columbia, SC	58
50	Greenville-Spartanburg-Asheville-Anderson	58
50	La Crosse-Eau Claire	58
50	Memphis	58
50	Tulsa	58
50	Tyler-Longview (Lufkin & Nacogdoches)	58

© 2004 Nielsen Media Research. Reprinted with permission.

Top 50 DMA by Cable Households

Listed below are the Nielsen Media Research Designated Market Areas (DMAs) ranked by cable television households.

Rank	Designated Market Area	Cable Penetration (%)	Cable Households
1	New York	81	5,978,720
2	Los Angeles	59	3,214,160
3	Chicago	71	2,423,160
4	Philadelphia	83	2,410,920
5	Boston (Manchester)	85	2,043,550
6	San Francisco-Oakland-San Jose	77	1,805,920
7	Washington, DC (Hagerstown)	72	1,620,340
8	Atlanta	69	1,425,580
9	Detroit	71	1,389,840
10	Tampa-St. Petersburg, Sarasota	75	1,255,590
11	Seattle-Tacoma	72	1,221,300
12	Cleveland-Akron (Canton)	71	1,109,490
13	Miami-Fort Lauderdale	73	1,091,250
14	Dallas-Fort Worth	47	1,066,450
15	Houston	56	1,063,300
16	Orlando-Daytona Beach-Melbourne	73	954,390
17	Phoenix (Prescott)	60	951,370
18	Pittsburgh	79	934,690
19	Minneapolis-St. Paul	56	934,580
20	Hartford & New Haven	87	890,100
21	San Diego	84	862,030
22	Denver	57	800,360
23	Baltimore	73	799,000
24	Sacramento-Stockton-Modesto	56	735,510
25	Charlotte	67	670,130
26	Indianapolis	63	665,480
27	Portland, OR	59	636,950
28	St. Louis	52	632,540
29	Columbus, OH	71	618,300
30	Raleigh-Durham (Fayetteville)	62	597,350
31	West Palm Beach-Fort Pierce	81	586,860
32	Harrisburg-Lancaster-Lebanon-York	81	572,480
33	Kansas City	64	571,750
34	Cincinnati	65	571,620
35	Milwaukee	64	568,450
36	Nashville	61	554,900
37	Norfolk-Portsmouth-Newport News	76	537,880
38	New Orleans	78	529,420
39	Providence-New Bedford	82	528,590
40	San Antonio	65	485,140
41	Buffalo	73	475,280
42	Greenville-Spartanburg-Asheville-Anderson	58	469,410
43	Birmingham (Anniston, Tuscaloosa)	64	457,450
44	Wilkes Barre-Scranton	77	453,640
45	Las Vegas	74	452,510
46	Greensboro-High Point-Winston Salem	68	441,080
47	Grand Rapids-Kalamazoo-Battle Creek	60	438,930
48	Albany-Schenectady-Troy	79	438,410
49	Jacksonville, Brunswick	68	419,520
50	Oklahoma City	62	408,220

© 2004 Nielsen Media Research. Reprinted with permission.

Section D
Radio

Radio Group Ownership D-2
Radio Listings
- Key to Radio Listings D-32
- Directory of Radio Stations in the U.S. D-33
- Directory of Radio Stations in Canada D-574
- Miscellaneous Radio Services D-605
- Satellite Services D-607
- U.S. AM Stations by Call Letters D-608
- U.S. FM Stations by Call Letters D-620
- Canadian AM Stations by Call Letters D-642
- Canadian FM Stations by Call Letters D-643
- U.S. AM Stations by Frequency D-645
- U.S. FM Stations by Frequency D-657
- Canadian AM Stations by Frequency D-679
- Canadian FM Stations by Frequency D-680

US and Canada Radio Formats
- Radio Formats Defined D-682
- U.S. and Canada Radio Programming Formats D-684

Programming on Radio Stations in the US and Canada
- Programming on U.S. Radio Stations D-686
- Programming on Canadian Radio Stations D-729
- Special Programming on U.S. Radio Stations D-733
- Special Programming on Canadian Radio Stations D-751

Radio Markets
- U.S. Radio Markets D-753
- U.S. Radio Markets: Arbitron Metro Survey Area Ranking D-764

Broadcasting & Cable Yearbook 2006

Radio Group Ownership

A

ABC Inc. 77 W. 66th St., New York, NY 10023-6298. Phone: (212) 456-7777. Web Site: www.abc.com. Ownership: ABC Enterprises Inc., 100%. Note: ABC Enterprises Inc. is 100% owned by Disney Enterprises Inc. Disney Enterprises Inc. is 100% owned by The Walt Disney Co.

Stns. 50 AM. 15 FM. KDIS-FM Little Rock, AR; KMIK Tempe, AZ; KLOS-FM Los Angeles, CA; KABC Los Angeles, CA; KSPN(AM) Los Angeles, CA; KMKY Oakland, CA; KDIS(AM) Pasadena, CA; KIID(AM) Sacramento, CA; KGO San Francisco, CA; KDDZ Arvada, CO; WDZK Bloomfield, CT; WMAL Washington, DC; WBWL Jacksonville, FL; WMYM(AM) Miami, FL; WDYZ(AM) Orlando, FL; WMNE(AM) Riviera Beach, FL; WWMI Saint Petersburg, FL; WDWD Atlanta, GA; WYAY-FM Gainesville, GA; WSDZ Belleville, IL; WZZN(FM) Chicago, IL; WMVP Chicago, IL; WLS Chicago, IL; WRDZ La Grange, IL; WPJX(AM) Zion, IL; WRDZ-FM Plainfield, IN; KQAM Wichita, KS; WDRD(AM) Newburg, KY; WBYU New Orleans, LA; WMKI(AM) Boston, MA; WDRQ-FM Detroit, MI; WJR Detroit, MI; WFDF Flint, MI; WGVY(FM) Cambridge, MN; WGVZ(FM) Eden Prairie, MN; KQRS-FM Golden Valley, MN; WGVX(FM) Lakeville, MN; KXXR-FM Minneapolis, MN; KPHN Kansas City, MO; WGFY Charlotte, NC; WWJZ Mount Holly, NJ; KALY Los Ranchos de Albuquerque, NM; WDDY(AM) Albany, NY; WEPN(AM) New York, NY; WABC(AM) New York, NY; WPLJ(FM) New York, NY; WWMK Cleveland, OH; KMUS(AM) Sperry, OK; KDZR(AM) Lake Oswego, OR; KKSL(AM) Lake Oswego, OR; WEAE Pittsburgh, PA; WDDZ(AM) Pawtucket, RI; KESN(FM) Allen, TX; KTYS(FM) Flower Mound, TX; WBAP Fort Worth, TX; KMIC(AM) Houston, TX; KMKI Plano, TX; KRDY(AM) San Antonio, TX; KWDZ(AM) Salt Lake City, UT; WDZY Colonial Heights, VA; WHKT Portsmouth, VA; WRJR(AM) Portsmouth, VA; WJZW-FM Woodbridge, VA; KKDZ Seattle, WA; WKSH(AM) Sussex, WI

Stns. 10 TV. WLS, Chicago; WJRT-TV, Flint-Saginaw-Bay City, MI; KFSN-TV, Fresno-Visalia, CA; KTRK, Houston; KABC, Los Angeles; WABC-TV, New York; WPVI, Philadelphia; WTVD, Raleigh-Durham (Fayetteville), NC; KGO, San Francisco-Oakland-San Jose; WTVG, Toledo, OH

Robert A. Iger, pres; Phillip J. Meek, pres; Lawrence J. Pollock, chmn owned TV stns.

ARKLATEX Radio Inc. 111 Westwood Dr., De Queen, AR 71832. Phone: (870) 642-2446. Fax: (870) 642-2442. Ownership: Jay Wallace Bunyard and Teresa Sharon Bunyard Living Revocable Trust, Jay and Teresa Bunyard sole voting trustees, 100%.

Stns. 1 AM. 2 FM. KMTB-FM Murfreesboro, AR; KNAS-FM Nashville, AR; KBHC Nashville, AR

Jay Bunyard, pres; Bonita Smith, CFO.

AVC Communications Inc. Box 338, Cambridge, OH 43725. Phone: (740) 432-5605. Fax: (740) 432-1991. Web Site: www.yourradioplace.com. Ownership: W. Grant Hafley, 100%.

Stns. 1 AM. 1 FM. WILE-FM Byesville, OH; WILE Cambridge, OH

Grant Hafley, pres.

Aberdeen Radio Ranch Inc. 701 N. 4th St., Aberdeen, SD 57401. Phone: (701) 219-0355. Fax: (605) 229-4849. Ownership: James D. Ingstad, 33.3%; Robert J. Ingstad, 33.3%; and Todd Ingstad, 33.3%.

Stns. 2 AM. 4 FM. KBFO(FM) Aberdeen, SD; KGIM Aberdeen, SD; KSDN Aberdeen, SD; KSDN-FM Aberdeen, SD; KGIM-FM Redfield, SD; KNBZ-FM Redfield, SD

Acadia Broadcasting Ltd. Box 2000, Saint John, NB E2L 3T4. Canada. Phone: (506) 633-3323. Fax: (506) 644-3485. Ownership: Brunswick News Inc., 100%.

Stns. 6 FM. CHSJ-FM Saint John, NB; CHWV-FM Saint John, NB; CHTD-FM Saint Stephen, NB; CKBW-FM Bridgewater, NS; CKBW-FM-1 Liverpool, NS; CKBW-FM-2 Shelburne, NS

Access.1 Communications Corp. 11 Penn Plaza, 16th Fl., New York, NY 10001. Phone: (212) 714-1000. Fax: (212) 714-1563. Ownership: Sydney L. Small, 54.12%; Black Enterprise/Greenwich Street Capital Partners, 19.47%; MESBIC Ventures Inc., 5.54%; Chesley Maddox-Dorsey, 2.84%; and Adriane Gaines, 1.85%.

Stns. 7 AM. 11 FM. KSYR(FM) Benton, LA; KDKS-FM Blanchard, LA; KBTT(FM) Haughton, LA; KLKL(FM) Minden, LA; KOKA Shreveport, LA; WMGM-FM Atlantic City, NJ; WGYM(AM) Hammonton, NJ; WTKU-FM Ocean City, NJ; WOND Pleasantville, NJ; WUSS(AM) Pleasantville, NJ; WWRL New York, NY; KOYE(FM) Frankston, TX; KOOI-FM Jacksonville, TX; KFRO Longview, TX; KYKX-FM Longview, TX; KCUL Marshall, TX; KTAL-FM Texarkana, TX; KKUS(FM) Tyler, TX

Stns. 1 TV. WMGM, Philadelphia

Chesley Maddox-Dorsey, pres/COO; Sydney L. Small, chmn/CEO.

Ad Astra Per Aspera Broadcasting Inc. 106 N. Main St., Hutchinson, KS 67501-5219. Phone: (620) 665-5758. Fax: (620) 665-6655. E-mail: ksku@ourtownusa.ngt. Ownership: Cliff C. Shank, 71%; Michael G. Hill, 14%.

Stns. 3 FM. KSKU-FM Hutchinson, KS; KXKU(FM) Lyons, KS; KGGG-FM Sterling, KS

Cliff C. Shank, gen mgr; Michael G. Hill, VP.

Adelman Broadcasting Inc. 731 N. Balsam, Ridgecrest, CA 93555. Phone: (760) 371-1700. Fax: (760) 371-1824. Web Site: adelmanbroadcasting.com. Ownership: Robert Adelman, 100%.

Stns. 1 AM. 3 FM. KEDD-FM Johannesburg, CA; KRAJ-FM Johannesburg, CA; KLOA Ridgecrest, CA; KLOA-FM Ridgecrest, CA

Adonai Radio Group 2448 E. 81st St., Suite 5500, Tulsa, OK 74137. Phone: (918) 492-2660. Fax: (918) 492-8840. E-mail: mail@kxoj.com. Web Site: www.kxoj.com.

Stns. 2 AM. 6 FM. KEOJ-FM Caney, KS; KTFR-FM Chelsea, OK; KEMX-FM Locust Grove, OK; KBIX Muskogee, OK; KMMY-FM Muskogee, OK; KYAL(AM) Sapulpa, OK; KXOJ-FM Sapulpa, OK; KCXR(FM) Taft, OK

Michael P. Stephens, pres.

Air South Radio Inc. Box 2116, Tupelo, MS 38803. Phone: (662) 842-9595. Fax: (662) 842-9568. Ownership: Olvie E. Sisk; Kathern Sisk.

Stns. 3 FM. WLZA(FM) Eupora, MS; WFTA-FM Fulton, MS; WCNA-FM Potts Camp, MS

Olive E. Sisk, pres; Kathern Sisk, sec/treas.

Aisling Broadcasting of Banner Elk LLC 353 Midland Dr., Asheville, NC 28804. Phone: (828) 254-3384. Ownership: Jonathan Hoffman, 50%; Donna Hoffman, 50%.

Stns. 3 AM. 3 FM. WZJS-FM Banner Elk, NC; WECR-FM Beech Mountain, NC; WXIT Blowing Rock, NC; WATA Boone, NC; WMMY(FM) Jefferson, NC; WECR Newland, NC

Alaska Broadcast Communications Inc. 3161 Channel Dr., Suite 2, Juneau, AK 99801. Phone: (907) 586-3630. Fax: (907) 463-3685. Web Site: www.kjno.com.

Stns. 3 AM. KJNO Juneau, AK; KTKN Ketchikan, AK; KIFW Sitka, AK

Steve Rhyner, gen mgr; Shelly Kinkaid, progmg VP.

Alexandra Communications Inc. 1600 Gray Lynn Dr., Walla Walla, WA 99362. Phone: (509) 527-1000. Fax: (509) 529-5534. Ownership: Thomas D. Hodgins, 50%; and Cheryl Hodgins, 50%.

Stns. 1 AM. 2 FM. KIXT(FM) Bay City, OR; KLKY(FM) Stanfield, OR; KUJ Walla Walla, WA

Allegheny Mountain Network Stations Box 247, Tyrone, PA 16686. Phone: (814) 684-3200. Fax: (814) 684-1220. Web Site: amnet@aol.com. Ownership: Cary H. Simpson.

Stns. 5 AM. 3 FM. WFRM Coudersport, PA; WNBQ-FM Mansfield, PA; WEEO-FM McConnellsburg, PA; WKMC Roaring Spring, PA; WKBI Saint Marys, PA; WQRM-FM Smethport, PA; WTRN Tyrone, PA; WNBT Wellsboro, PA

Cary Simpson, pres; John F. Simpson, VP.

Amaturo Groups 3101 N. Federal Hwy., Suite 601, Fort Lauderdale, FL 33306-1042. Phone: (954) 565-1411. Fax: (954) 565-1311. E-mail: jca@amaturogroups.com. Ownership: Amaturo Group of L.A. Inc. (Joseph C. Amaturo, gen ptnr): KLIT(FM), KELT(FM) and KMLT(FM).

Stns. 3 FM. KLIT(FM) Fountain Valley, CA; KELT-FM Riverside, CA; KMLT-FM Thousand Oaks, CA

Joseph C. Amaturo, pres.

American Family Radio Box 3206, Tupelo, MS 38803. Phone: (662) 844-8888. Fax: (662) 842-6791. E-mail: comments@afr.net. Web Site: www.afr.net. Ownership: American Family Association, a nonprofit organization.

Stns. 146 FM. WALN-FM Carrollton, AL; WAQG-FM Ozark, AL; WAQU-FM Selma, AL; WAKD-FM Sheffield, AL; WAXU-FM Troy, AL; KAPG(FM) Bentonville, AR; KOUX(FM) Blytheville, AR; KBCM(FM) Blytheville, AR; KBDO(FM) Des Arc, AR; KBNV(FM) Fayetteville, AR; KARH(FM) Forrest City, AR; KAOW(FM) Fort Smith, AR; KBPW(FM) Hampton, AR; KBMJ(FM) Heber Springs, AR; KAOG(FM) Jonesboro, AR; KANX(FM) Sheridan, AR; KBMH(FM) Holbrook, AZ; WFFL(FM) Panama City, FL; WBJY-FM Americus, GA; WAEF-FM Cordele, GA; WAWH-FM Dublin, GA; WBKG-FM Macon, GA; WASW-FM Waycross, GA; KAYP(FM) Burlington, IA; KIAD(FM) Dubuque, IA; KBDC(FM) Mason City, IA; KWVI(FM) Waverly, IA; WBEL-FM Cairo, IL; WBMF-FM Crete, IL; WAXR-FM Geneseo, IL; WAWF-FM Kankakee, IL; WAWJ(FM) Marion, IL; WAPO-FM Mount Vernon, IL; WWGN-FM Ottawa, IL; WZRS(FM) Pana, IL; WSLE(FM) Salem, IL; WQSG(FM) Lafayette, IN; KXJH(FM) Linton, IN; WWMU(FM) Muncie, IN; WRXH(FM) Plymouth, IN; WHNI(FM) Rochester, IN; WATI-FM Vincennes, IN; KAXR(FM) Arkansas City, KS; KBJQ(FM) Bronson, KS; KBMP(FM) Enterprise, KS; KBDA(FM) Great Bend, KS; KARF(FM) Independence, KS; KBQC(FM) Independence, KS; KRBW-FM Ottawa, KS; KAKA(FM) Salina, KS; KBUZ(FM) Topeka, KS; KCFN(FM) Wichita, KS; WAPD-FM Campbellsville, KY; WBMK-FM Morehead, KY; WAXG-FM Mt. Sterling, KY; WGCF(FM) Paducah, KY; KAPM(FM) Alexandria, LA; KAXV(FM) Bastrop, LA; KBAN(FM) De Ridder, LA; KYLC(FM) Lake Charles, LA; KAVK(FM) Many, LA; KPAQ(FM) Plaquemine, LA; KSUL(FM) Port Sulphur, LA; KAPI(FM) Ruston, LA; KSJY(FM) Saint Martinville, LA; WMCQ(FM) Muskegon, MI; KBPG(FM) Montevideo, MN; KQRB(FM) Windom, MN; KBOJ(FM) Worthington, MN; KAUF(FM) Kennett, MO; KBGM(FM) Park Hills, MO; WPRG(FM) Columbia, MS; WCSO(FM) Columbus, MS; WAUM-FM Duck Hill, MS; WQVI(FM) Forest, MS; WQST-FM Forest, MS; WAOY-FM Gulfport, MS; WAII-FM Hattiesburg, MS; WYTF(FM) Indianola, MS; WATP-FM Laurel, MS; WAQL-FM McComb, MS; WASM-FM Natchez, MS; WAVI-FM Oxford, MS; WPAS(FM) Pascagoula, MS; WATU-FM Port Gibson, MS; WJZB(FM) Starkville, MS; WAQB-FM Tupelo, MS; WAJS-FM Tupelo, MS; WZKM(FM) Waynesboro, MS; WYAZ(FM) Yazoo City, MS; KGFA(FM) Great Falls, MT; KAFH(FM) Great Falls, MT; WBKU-FM Ahoskie, NC; WXBE(FM) Beaufort, NC; WJKA(FM) Jacksonville, NC; WAAE-FM New Bern, NC; WBFY-FM Pinehurst, NC; WRAE(FM) Raeford, NC; KNFA(FM) Grand Island, NE; KNHA(FM) Hastings, NE; KAYA(FM) Hubbard, NE; KAQF(FM) Clovis, NM; WJJE(FM) Delaware, OH; WVSO(FM) South Vienna, OH; WBJV-FM Steubenville, OH; KQPD(FM) Ardmore, OK; KAYC(FM) Durant, OK; KXRT(FM) Idabel, OK; KVRS-FM Lawton, OK; KARG(FM) Poteau, OK; KAYM(FM) Weatherford, OK; KANL(FM) Baker City, OR; KAPK(FM) Grants Pass, OR; WAWN-FM Franklin, PA; WLGY(FM) Nanty Glo, PA; KASD(FM) Rapid City, SD; KSFS(FM) Sioux Falls, SD; WAUO-FM Hohenwald, TN; WAMP-FM Jackson, TN; WAWI-FM Lawrenceburg, TN; WIGH-FM Lexington, TN; WAUV-FM Ripley, TN; WAZD-FM Savannah, TN; WBIA-FM Shelbyville, TN; WAUT-FM Tullahoma, TN; KAQD(FM) Abilene, TX; KAVW(FM) Amarillo, TX; KBCX(FM) Big Spring, TX; KAXH(FM) Borger, TX; KAFR(FM) Conroe, TX; KCKT(FM) Crockett, TX; KZFT(FM) Fannett, TX; KTXG(FM) Greenville, TX; KSUR(FM) Mart, TX; KMEO(FM) Mertzon, TX; KBMM(FM) Odessa, TX; KAVO(FM) Pampa, TX; KBAH(FM) Plainview, TX; KBDE(FM) Temple, TX; KAYK(FM) Victoria, TX; WAUQ-FM Charles City, VA; WARN-FM Culpeper, VA; KAYB(FM) Sunnyside, WA; WBHZ-FM Elkins, WV; WPWV(FM) Princeton, WV; KWYH(FM) Cheyenne, WY

Tim Wildmon, pres/CEO.

American General Media Box 2700, Bakersfield, CA 93303. Phone: (661) 328-0118. Fax: (661) 328-1648. Ownership: Anthony S. Brandon, Lawrence Brandon, L. Rogers Brandon.

Stns. 8 AM. 13 FM. KIQO-FM Atascadero, CA; KISV-FM Bakersfield, CA; KBID Bakersfield, CA; KERN Bakersfield, CA; KGEO Bakersfield, CA; KBOX(FM) Lompoc, CA; KRQK-FM Lompoc, CA; KPAT-FM Orcutt, CA; KKAL(FM) Paso Robles, CA; KKJG-FM San Luis Obispo, CA; KLRM(FM) San Luis Obispo, CA; KZOZ-FM San Luis Obispo, CA; KKXX-FM Shafter, CA; KERI(AM) Wasco-Greenacres, CA; KKIM Albuquerque, NM; KLVO-FM Belen, NM; KARS Belen, NM; KZNM(FM) Los Alamos, NM; KAGM(FM) Los Lunas, NM; KVSF(AM) Santa Fe, NM; KTRC(AM) Santa Fe, NM

L. Rogers Brandon, VP.

American Radio Brokers Inc./SFO 1255 Post St., Suite 1023, San Francisco, CA 94109. Phone: (415) 441-3377.

Broadcasting & Cable Yearbook 2006

Radio Group Ownership

Fax: (415) 674-1480. Ownership: Chester Coleman, 100%.
Anchorage, AK 99507. American Radio Brokers Inc., 2509 Eide St., Suite 6. Phone: (907) 277-5652. Fax: (907) 344-5728.

Stns: 2 AM. 1 FM. KAXX Eagle River, AK; KADX(FM) Houston, AK; KABN(AM) Concord, CA

Chester Coleman, pres/CEO.

Americom 11400 W. Olympic Blvd, Suite 780, Los Angeles, CA 90064. Phone: (310) 481-0440. Fax: (310) 481-0445.

Stns: 2 AM. 3 FM. KLCA-FM Tahoe City, CA; KZTQ(FM) Carson City, NV; KRNO(FM) Incline Village, NV; KJFK(AM) Reno, NV; KBZZ(AM) Sparks, NV

Tom Quinn, pres/CEO.

Amistad Communications Inc. 7480 Greenwood Rd., Shreveport, LA 71119. Phone: (318) 938-1885. Fax: (318) 425-7507.

Stns: 2 AM. 1 FM. KBEF(FM) Gibsland, LA; KASO Minden, LA; KSYB(AM) Shreveport, LA

Anaheim Broadcasting Corp. Box 2668, Del Mar, CA 92014-5668. Phone: (858) 794-1626. Fax: (858) 794-4068. Ownership: Tim Sullivan.

Stns: 2 FM. KCAL-FM Redlands, CA; KOLA(FM) San Bernardino, CA

Tim Sullivan, pres; Doug Lida, CFO.

Anastos Media Group Inc. 21 Malta Commons, 100 Saratoga Village Blvd, Malta, NY 12020. Phone: (518) 899-3000. Fax: (518) 899-3057. E-mail: star1013fm@aol.com. Web Site: www.star1013.com.

Stns: 4 AM. 1 FM. WPEP Taunton, MA; WABY(AM) Mechanicville, NY; WUAM(AM) Saratoga Springs, NY; WVKZ Schenectady, NY; WQAR-FM Stillwater, NY

Scott Collins, pres.

Anderson Radio Broadcasting Inc. 581 N. Reservoir Rd., Polson, MT 59860. Phone: (406) 883-5255. Ownership: Dennis L. Anderson, 50%; and Nila Y. Anderson, 50%.

Stns: 1 AM. 2 FM. KIBG(FM) Wallace, ID; KERR Polson, MT; KQRK-FM Ronan, MT

Apex Broadcasting Inc. 1964 Ashley River Rd., Charleston, SC 29407. Phone: (843) 852-9003. Fax: (843) 852-9041.

Stns: 1 AM. 6 FM. KTSR(FM) De Quincy, LA; KJEF(AM) Jennings, LA; KJMH(FM) Lake Arthur, LA; KBXG(FM) Lake Charles, LA; WAVF-FM Hanahan, SC; WXST(FM) Hollywood, SC; WCSQ(FM) Manning, SC

Houston L. Pearce, chmn; G. Dean Pearce, pres.

Archway Broadcasting Group 1513 E. Cleveland Ave., Bldg. 100B, Suite 250, East Point, GA 30344. Phone: (404) 762-9942. Fax: (404) 209-8134. Web Site: www.archwaybroadcasting.com.

Stns: 1 AM. 10 FM. WRLD-FM Valley, AL; KHTE-FM England, AR; KOLL-FM Lonoke, AR; WRCG Columbus, GA; WCGQ-FM Columbus, GA; WKCN-FM Lumpkin, GA; WWNK(FM) Farmville, NC; WRHT-FM Morehead City, NC; WWHA(FM) Oriental, NC; WLGT(FM) Washington, NC; WRHD(FM) Williamston, NC

Al Vicente, pres/CEO; Chris Fleming, exec VP; Pat Sullivan, CFO; Brian Krysz, VP.

Arkansas County Broadcasters Inc. Box 789, Wynne, AR 72396-0789. Phone: (870) 238-8141. Fax: (870) 238-5997. Ownership: Bobby Caldwell, 50%; C.B. Moery Jr., 50%. Note: Bobby Caldwell owns 100% of East Arkansas Broadcasters Inc. (see listing) and 50% of Combined Media Group Inc. (see listing).

Stns: 1 AM. 2 FM. KDEW-FM De Witt, AR; KAFN(FM) Gould, AR; KWAK Stuttgart, AR

Arklatex LLC 615 W. Olive, Texarkana, TX 75501. Phone: (903) 793-4671. Fax: (903) 792-4261. E-mail: alex@101jams.com.

Stns: 2 AM. 3 FM. KBYB(FM) Hope, AR; KTOY(FM) Texarkana, AR; KFYX(FM) Texarkana, AR; KCMC Texarkana, TX; KTFS(AM) Texarkana, TX

Mike Simpson, gen mgr; Alex Rain, opns mgr.

Artistic Media Partners Inc. 5520 E. 75th St., Indianapolis, IN 46250. Phone: (317) 594-0600. Fax: (317) 594-9567. E-mail: artradio@aol.com. Web Site: www.artisticradio.com. Ownership: Arthur A. Angotti.

Stns: 2 AM. 9 FM. WSHP(FM) Attica, IN; WBWB-FM Bloomington, IN; WLFF(FM) Brookston, IN; WDDB(FM) Columbia City, IN; WHCC(FM) Ellettsville, IN; WZOW-FM Goshen, IN; WLAS(AM) Lafayette, IN; WAZY-FM Lafayette, IN; WOZW(FM) New Carlisle, IN; WNDV South Bend, IN; WNDV-FM South Bend, IN

Arthur A. Angotti, pres/CEO; Arthur A. Angotti III, sr VP.

Asterisk Inc. 2848 E. Oakland Park Blvd., Fort Lauderdale, FL 33306. Phone: (954) 566-7559. Fax: (954) 564-6753. Ownership: Richard S. Ingham, 100%.

Stns: 3 FM. WXJZ(FM) Gainesville, FL; WYGC(FM) High Springs, FL; WMFQ-FM Ocala, FL

Frederick H. Ingham, pres.

Astor Broadcast Group 1835 Aston Ave., Carlsbad, CA 92008. Phone: (760) 729-1000. Fax: (760) 476-9604.

Stns: 3 AM. KFSD(AM) Escondido, CA; KSPA(AM) Ontario, CA; KCEO Vista, CA

Peri Corso, gen mgr.

Astral Media Inc. 2100 rue Sainte-Catherine Ouest, Bureau 1000, Montreal, PQ H3H 2T3. Canada. Phone: (514) 939-5000. Fax: (514) 939-1515. Web Site: www.astralmedia.com. Ownership: Abgreen Holdings Ltd., 55.71% vote; 654625 Ontario Inc., 13.63% vote.

Stns: 2 AM. 26 FM. CKBC-FM Bathurst, NB; CIBX-FM Fredericton, NB; CKHJ(AM) Fredericton, NB; CIKX-FM Grand Falls, NB; CJCJ-FM Woodstock, NB; CKTY-FM Truro, NS; CKTO-FM Truro, NS; CFVM-FM Amqui, PQ; CJDM-FM Drummondville, PQ; CHRD-FM Drummondville, PQ; CIMF-FM Gatineau, PQ; CKTF-FM Gatineau, PQ; CIMO-FM Magog, PQ; CITE-FM Montreal, PQ; CKMF-FM Montreal, PQ; CITF-FM Quebec, PQ; CHIK-FM Quebec, PQ; CIKI-FM Rimouski, PQ; CJOI-FM Rimouski, PQ; CJMM-FM Rouyn-Noranda, PQ; CJAB-FM Saguenay, PQ; CFEI-FM Saint Hyacinthe, PQ; CFZZ-FM Saint Jean-Iberville, PQ; CKSM Shawinigan, PQ; CITE-FM-1 Sherbrooke, PQ; CHEY-FM Trois Rivieres, PQ; CIGB-FM Trois Rivieres, PQ; CJMV-FM Val d'Or, PQ

Ian Greenberg, pres/CEO.

Astro Tele-Communications Corp. Rhode Island Box 920365, Needham, MA 02492. Phone: (781) 444-4754. Fax: (781) 444-8630. E-mail: addelco@gis.net. Web Site: www.wadk.com. Ownership: Maurice B. Polayes, 100%.

Stns: 1 AM. 1 FM. WJZS(FM) Block Island, RI; WADK Newport, RI

Maurice B. Polayes, pres.

Atlantic Coast Radio L.L.C. 779 Warren Avenue, Portland, ME 04103. Phone: (207) 773-9695. Fax: (207) 761-4406. Web Site: www.redhot95.com.

Stns: 3 AM. 3 FM. WJJB(AM) Brunswick, ME; WLOB Portland, ME; WLOB-FM Rumford, ME; WRED-FM Saco, ME; WJJB-FM Topsham, ME; WJAE Westbrook, ME

J.J. Jeffrey, pres.

Azteca Broadcasting Corp. 323 E. San Joaquin St., Tulare, CA 93274. Phone: (559) 686-1370. Fax: (559) 685-1394. E-mail: wwwkgen@sbcglobal.net.

Stns: 3 AM. 1 FM. KGEN-FM Hanford, CA; KGEN Tulare, CA; KXEQ Reno, NV; KSVN Ogden, UT

Margarita Hernandez, gen mgr.

B

Back Bay Broadcasters Inc. 1110 Central Ave., Pawtucket, RI 02861-2262. Phone: (401) 724-7600. Fax: (401) 728-1865. Ownership: Peter H. Ottmar, 40.1%; David J. Ottmar, 26.1%; John Maguire, 19.0%; and Barbara Ottmar, 7.2%.

Stns: 17 FM. WRPW(FM) Colfax, IL; WYST(FM) Fairbury, IL; WWCT(FM) Farmington, IL; WDQZ(FM) Lexington, IL; WGKC-FM Mahomet, IL; WDQX(FM) Morton, IL; WIHN-FM Normal, IL; WXCL(FM) Pekin, IL; WXMP(FM) Peoria, IL; WZPW(FM) Peoria, IL; WQQB(FM) Rantoul, IL; WEVX(FM) Rantoul, IL; WEBX-FM Tuscola, IL; WBAZ(FM) Bridgehampton, NY; WHBE(FM) East Hampton, NY; WEHM(FM) Southampton, NY; WBEA(FM) Southold, NY

Peter H. Ottmar, chmn; John Maguire, CEO.

Backyard Broadcasting LLC 1685 Four Mile Dr. Reisterstown Rd., Suite 208, Baltimore, MD 21208. Phone: (410) 580-5888. Fax: (410) 602-9066. Web Site: www.bybradio.com. Ownership: Boston Ventures Limited Partnership VI; PCG Media Investment Partners LLC; Barry Drake.

Stns: 8 AM. 19 FM. WHTI-FM Alexandria, IN; WHBU Anderson, IN; WURK-FM Elwood, IN; WHTY-FM Hartford City, IN; WLBC-FM Muncie, IN; WERK-FM Muncie, IN; WXFN Muncie, IN; WWJK(FM) Jackson, MS; WRXW(FM) Pearl, MS; WNKI-FM Corning, NY; WWLZ Horseheads, NY; WPGI-FM Horseheads, NY; WNGZ-FM Montour Falls, NY; WPIG-FM Olean, NY; WHDL Olean, NY; WTYX(AM) Watkins Glen, NY; WCXR-FM Lewisburg, PA; WBZD-FM Muncy, PA; WZXR-FM South Williamsport, PA; WWPA Williamsport, PA; WRVH(FM) Williamsport, PA; WILQ-FM Williamsport, PA; KELO(AM) Sioux Falls, SD; KELO-FM Sioux Falls, SD; KRRO(FM) Sioux Falls, SD; KTWB(FM) Sioux Falls, SD; KWSN(AM) Sioux Falls, SD

Barry Drake, pres; Robin A. Smith, VP/CFO; Tom Atkins, VP & dir engrg.

Badger Communications L.L.C. N. 2880 Roosevelt Rd., Marinette, WI 54143. Phone: (715) 735-6631. Fax: (715) 732-0125. Web Site: www.badgertheareradio.com.

Stns: 5 AM. 1 FM. WJMS Ironwood, MI; WAGN Menominee, MI; WMAM Marinette, WI; WJMT Merrill, WI; WSFQ-FM Peshtigo, WI; WXCO Wausau, WI

David Winters, pres/CEO; Jim Medley, opns mgr.

Bahakel Communications Box 32488, Charlotte, NC 28232. Phone: (704) 372-4434. Fax: (704) 335-9904. Ownership: The Cy N. Bahakel Trust Dated January 12, 2005, 100%.

Stns: 4 AM. 5 FM. KILO-FM Colorado Springs, CO; KYZX(FM) Pueblo West, CO; KOKZ-FM Waterloo, IA; KWLO Waterloo, IA; KXEL Waterloo, IA; KFMW-FM Waterloo, IA; WABG(AM) Greenwood, MS; WDEF-FM Chattanooga, TN; WDOD Chattanooga, TN

Stns: 5 TV. WCCU, Champaign & Springfield-Decatur, IL; WRSP-TV, Champaign & Springfield-Decatur, IL; WCCB, Charlotte, NC; WABG, Greenwood-Greenville, MS; WAKA, Montgomery (Selma), AL

Cy N. Bahakel, pres; Beverly Poston, exec VP/COO; Stephen Bahakel, Sr VP radio div; Russell Schwartz, Sr VP business affrs/gen counsel; Ed Conrad, Sr VP finance; Bill Napier, VP eng/tech; Anna Rufty, VP Hum Res..

Baker Family Stations (Positive Radio Group). Box 889, Blacksburg, VA 24063. Phone: (540) 552-4252. Fax: (540) 951-5282. Ownership: Principal owners: Vernon H. Baker, Edward A. Baker, Virginia L. Baker.

Stns: 12 AM. 17 FM. WOKT Cannonsburg, KY; WTJY-FM Asheboro, NC; WPIR-FM Hickory, NC; WXRI-FM Winston-Salem, NC; WLGN Logan, OH; WLGN-FM Logan, OH; WMPO Middleport-Pomeroy, OH; WTGR-FM Union City, OH; WCQR-FM Kingsport, TN; WKEX Blacksburg, VA; WFIC(AM) Collinsville, VA; WPER-FM Culpeper, VA; WOKD-FM Danville, VA; WBNN-FM Dillwyn, VA; WPIN-FM Dublin, VA; WKTR Earlysville, VA; WKNV Fairlawn, VA; WODY Fieldale, VA; WOKG(FM) Galax, VA; WPIM-FM Martinsville, VA; WRXT-FM Roanoke, VA; WPAR-FM Salem, VA; WKGM Smithfield, VA; WPIB-FM Bluefield, WV; WAMN Green Valley, WV; WOKU Hurricane, WV; WBGS Point Pleasant, WV; WPCN-FM Point Pleasant, WV; WCEF-FM Ripley, WV

Vernon H. Baker, CEO; Edward A. Baker, pres; Virginia L. Baker, treas.

Baldridge-Dumas Communications Inc. 605 San Antonio Ave., Many, LA 71449. Phone: (318) 256-5924. Fax: (318) 256-0950. Ownership: Tedd W. Dumas, 50%; Patricia M. Baldridge Declaration of Trust, 50%.

Stns: 1 AM. 4 FM. KWLA Many, LA; KZBL-FM Natchitoches, LA; KDBH(FM) Natchitoches, LA; KTHP(FM) Hemphill, TX; KTEZ(FM) Mount Enterprise, TX

Tedd Dumas, pres; Rhonda Benson, gen mgr.

Vernon R Baldwin Inc. 8686 Michael Ln., Fairfield, OH 45014. Phone: (513) 829-7700. Ownership: Vernon R. Baldwin, VP. Note: John Logan owns 49% of WWLT(FM) Manchester, KY.

Stns: 3 AM. 4 FM. WHIR-FM Danville, KY; WWLT-FM Manchester, KY; WVRB-FM Wilmore, KY; WCNW Fairfield, OH; WMOH Hamilton, OH; WNLT-FM Harrison, OH; WKFI Wilmington, OH

Vernon R. Baldwin, pres.

Barnstable Broadcasting Inc. 2 Newton Executive Park, Newton, MA 02462-1434. Phone: (617) 527-0062. Fax: (617) 630-0960. Ownership: Albert J. Kaneb; Michael A. Kaneb.

Stns: 1 AM. 7 FM. WTPT-FM Forest City, NC; WBZO-FM Bay Shore, NY; WLVG-FM Center Moriches, NY; WHLI Hempstead, NY; WRCN-FM Riverhead, NY; WMJC(FM) Smithtown, NY; WROQ-FM Anderson, SC; WGVC(FM) Simpsonville, SC

Albert J. Kaneb, chmn/CEO; Michael A. Kaneb, pres/COO; James L. Paglia, VP/CFO.

Bayshore Broadcasting Corp. Box 280, Owen Sound, ON N4K 5P5. Canada. Phone: (519) 376-2030. Fax: (519) 371-4242. E-mail: bayshore@radioowensound.com. Web Site: www.radioowensound.com. Ownership: Controlled by Douglas C. Caldwell.

Stns: 1 AM. 2 FM. CFOS(AM) Owen Sound, ON; CIXK-FM Owen Sound, ON; CKYC-FM Owen Sound, ON

Beasley Broadcast Group Inc. 3033 Riviera Dr., Suite 200, Naples, FL 34103. Phone: (239) 263-5000. Fax: (239) 263-8191. E-mail: email@bbgi.com. Web Site: www.bbgi.com. Ownership: George G. Beasley.

Stns: 16 AM. 26 FM. WSBR Boca Raton, FL; WKIS-FM

Radio Group Ownership

Boca Raton, FL; WRXK-FM Bonita Springs, FL; WXKB-FM Cape Coral, FL; WJBX-FM Fort Myers Beach, FL; WJPT(FM) Fort Myers Villas, FL; WQAM Miami, FL; WPOW-FM Miami, FL; WWCN North Fort Myers, FL; WWNN Pompano Beach, FL; WHSR Pompano Beach, FL; WAEC Atlanta, GA; WRDW(AM) Augusta, GA; WGAC Augusta, GA; WGUS(AM) Augusta, GA; WWWE(AM) Hapeville, GA; WCHZ-FM Harlem, GA; WKDG(FM) Martinez, GA; WGAC-FM Warrenton, GA; WRCA Waltham, MA; WAZZ Fayetteville, NC; WNCT Greenville, NC; WNCT-FM Greenville, NC; WXNR-FM Grifton, NC; WFLB-FM Laurinburg, NC; WKML-FM Lumberton, NC; WIKS-FM New Bern, NC; WSFL-FM New Bern, NC; WMGV-FM Newport, NC; WTEL(AM) Red Springs, NC; WUKS-FM Saint Pauls, NC; WZFX-FM Whiteville, NC; WTMR Camden, NJ; KSTJ-FM Boulder City, NV; KKLZ-FM Las Vegas, NV; KJUL-FM Knob Las Vegas, NV; WXTU-FM Philadelphia, PA; WWDB(AM) Philadelphia, PA; WRDW-FM Philadelphia, PA; WKXC-FM Aiken, SC; WSLT-FM Clearwater, SC; WGOR(FM) New Ellenton, SC

George G. Beasley, chmn/CEO; Bruce G. Beasley, pres/COO; Caroline Beasley, VP/CFO; Brian Beasley, VP opns.

Bee Broadcasting Inc. Box 5409, Kalispell, MT 59903. Phone: (406) 755-8700. Fax: (406) 755-8770. Web Site: www.kbbz.com.
Stns: 1 AM. 3 FM. KKMT-FM Columbia Falls, MT; KBBZ(FM) Kalispell, MT; KDBR(FM) Kalispell, MT; KJJR Whitefish, MT
Benny Bee, pres.

Benton-Weatherford Broadcasting Inc. of Tennessee 110 India Rd., Paris, TN 38242. Phone: (731) 644-9455. Fax: (731) 644-9970. E-mail: wmuf@bellsouth.net. Ownership: Gary Benton, Len Watson.
Stns: 2 AM. 2 FM. WMUF-FM Henry, TN; WHDM McKenzie, TN; WLZK-FM Paris, TN; WMUF Paris, TN
Gary Benton, pres.

Berkshire Broadcasting Corp. c/o WLAD(AM) and WDAQ(FM), 198 Main St., Danbury, CT 06810. Phone: (203) 744-4800. Fax: (203) 778-4655. Web Site: www.98q.com.
Stns: 2 AM. WLAD Danbury, CT; WREF Ridgefield, CT
Irv Goldstein, VP/gen mgr.

Best Broadcast Group 107 S. Main St., Brookfield, MO 64628. Phone: (660) 258-3383. Fax: (660) 258-7307. E-mail: corporate@bestbroadcastgroup.com. Web Site: www.bestbroadcastgroup.com. Ownership: Phil Chirillo; Dale Palmer
Stns: 2 AM. 2 FM. KFMZ(AM) Brookfield, MO; KZBK(FM) Brookfield, MO; KLTI Macon, MO; KZZT-FM Moberly, MO
Dale Palmer, VP/gen mgr; Phil Chirillo, pres.

Bethesda Christian Broadcasting Box 168, Rapid City, SD 57709. Phone: (719) 481-0100. Fax: (719) 481-4649. E-mail: bcbpres@aol.com. Web Site: www.klmp.com. Ownership: Nonprofit bd of directors.
Stns: 1 FM. KLMP-FM Rapid City, SD
Mark Plummer, pres.

Bible Broadcasting Network 11530 Carmel Commons Blvd., Charlotte, NC 28226. Phone: (704) 523-5555. Fax: (704) 522-1967. Web Site: www.bbnradio.org. Ownership: Nonprofit, non-stock corporation.
Stns: 3 AM. 24 FM. WYFD-FM Decatur, AL; WYFB-FM Gainesville, FL; WYFO-FM Lakeland, FL; WYFE-FM Tarpon Springs, FL; WYFK-FM Columbus, GA; WYFS-FM Savannah, GA; WYFW-FM Waynesboro, GA; WYFB-FM Winder, GA; KYFW-FM Wichita, KS; KYFL-FM Monroe, LA; WYFP-FM Harpswell, ME; WYFQ(AM) Charlotte, NC; WYFL-FM Henderson, NC; WYFQ-FM Wadesboro, NC; WYFY Rome, NY; WYFU-FM Masontown, PA; WYFV-FM Cayce, SC; WYFG-FM Gaffney, SC; WYFH-FM North Charleston, SC; WYFC-FM Clinton, TN; WYFN Nashville, TN; KYFP-FM Palestine, TX; KYFS-FM San Antonio, TX; KYFO-FM Ogden, UT; WYFJ-FM Ashland, VA; WYFT-FM Luray, VA; WYFI-FM Norfolk, VA

Lowell Davey, pres; Leo Galletta, opns mgr.

Bick Broadcasting Co. Box 711, 119 N. Third St., Hannibal, MO 63401. Phone: (573) 221-3450. Fax: (573) 221-5331. E-mail: kickfm@bickbroadcasting.com. Web Site: www.979kickfm.com. Ownership: Frank C. Bick, 46%; James P. Bick, 46%; James E. Janes, 8%.
Stns: 3 AM. 4 FM. KPCR(AM) Quincy, IL; KRRY(FM) Canton, MO; KHMO Hannibal, MO; KXKX-FM Knob Noster, MO; KICK-FM Palmyra, MO; KSDL-FM Sedalia, MO; KSIS(AM) Sedalia, MO
James E. Janes, pres.

Bicoastal Media L.L.C. 140 N. Main St., Lake Port, CA 94953. Phone: (707) 263-6113. Fax: (707) 263-0939.
Stns: 8 AM. 12 FM. KATA Arcata, CA; KPOD Crescent City, CA; KPOD-FM Crescent City, CA; KFMI-FM Eureka, CA; KGOE Eureka, CA; KKHB-FM Eureka, CA; KNTI-FM Lakeport, CA; KXBX Lakeport, CA; KQPM-FM Ukiah, CA; KBDN(FM) Bandon, OR; KWRO Coquille, OR; KOOS-FM North Bend, OR; KACW(FM) North Bend, OR; KBBR(AM) North Bend, OR; KJNI(FM) Rainier, OR; KJMX(FM) Reedsport, OR; KRQT-FM Castle Rock, WA; KLYK(FM) Kelso, WA; KEDO Longview, WA; KBAM Longview, WA

Ken Dennis, CEO; Mike Wilson, pres.

Big League Broadcasting LLC 3350 Peachtree Rd., Suite 1610, Atlanta, GA 30326-1040. Phone: (404) 467-1877. Fax: (404) 231-5923. Ownership: Andrew Philip Saltzman, 20.435% of votes, 24.375% of equity; Stephen Shapiro, 20.435% of votes, 24.375% of equity; Jeffrey Bloomberg, 16.61% of votes, 16.75% of equity; and others.
Stns: 2 AM. 1 FM. KFNS(AM) Wood River, IL; KRFT(AM) De Soto, MO; KFNS-FM Troy, MO

Big River Broadcasting Corp. 624 Sam Phillips St., Florence, AL 35630. Phone: (256) 764-8121. Fax: (256) 764-8169. E-mail: nmartin@bigriverbroadcasting.com. Web Site: www.wqlt.com.
Stns: 2 FM. WXFL(FM) Florence, AL; WQLT(FM) Florence, AL

Birach Broadcasting Corp. 21700 Northwestern Hwy., Suite 1190, Southfield, MI 48075. Phone: (248) 557-3500. Fax: (248) 557-3241. E-mail: sima@birach.com. Web Site: www.birach.com. Ownership: Sima Birach, 100%.
Stns: 12 AM. WNWI Oak Lawn, IL; WNZK Dearborn Heights, MI; WCXI(AM) Fenton, MI; WMJH Rockford, MI; WSDS(AM) Salem Township, MI; WPON Walled Lake, MI; WMFN Zeeland, MI; WEW Saint Louis, MO; WTOR Youngstown, NY; WWCS Canonsburg, PA; WGOP(AM) Pocomoke City, MD; WDMV(AM) Poolesville, MD
Sima Birach, pres.

Birch Broadcasting Corp. 11971 Glenmore Dr., Coral Springs, FL 33071-7806. Phone: (954) 323-8531. Ownership: Thomas C. Birch, 51%; and Aurora D.P. Birch, 49%.
Stns: 1 AM. 2 FM. WLUS-FM Clarksville, VA; WSHV(AM) South Hill, VA; WKSK-FM South Hill, VA

Bob Bittner Broadcasting Inc. 443 Concord Ave, Cambridge, MA 02138. Phone: (617) 868-7400. Web Site: www.wjib740.com. Ownership: Robert Miles Bittner, 100%.
Stns: 2 AM. WJIB Cambridge, MA; WJTO Bath, ME
Robert Miles Bittner, pres/CEO.

Black Crow Media Group LLC 126 W. International Speedway Blvd., Daytona Beach, FL 32114. Phone: (386) 255-9300. Web Site: www.4icrow.com. Ownership: J. Michael Linn, 100%.
Stns: 8 AM. 20 FM. WAHR-FM Huntsville, AL; WLOR Huntsville, AL; WRTT-FM Huntsville, AL; WNDB Daytona Beach, FL; WNDA(AM) De Land, FL; WKRO-FM Edgewater, FL; WCJX-FM Five Points, FL; WVYB-FM Holly Hill, FL; WQHL(AM) Live Oak, FL; WQHL-FM Live Oak, FL; WXHT(FM) Madison, FL; WHOG-FM Ormond-by-the-Sea, FL; WDMG Douglas, GA; WBHB Fitzgerald, GA; WRDO-FM Fitzgerald, GA; WVGA(FM) Lakeland, GA; WDMG-FM Ocilla, GA; WSTI-FM Quitman, GA; WKZZ-FM Tifton, GA; WQPW-FM Valdosta, GA; WVLD Valdosta, GA; WWRQ-FM Valdosta, GA; WKAA(FM) Willacoochee, GA; WFKX(FM) Henderson, TN; WHHM-FM Henderson, TN; WZDQ(FM) Humboldt, TN; WJAK Jackson, TN; WWYN(FM) McKenzie, TN

Mike Linn, pres/CEO.

Black Media Works Inc. 1150 W. King St., Cocoa, FL 32922. Phone: (321) 632-1000. Fax: (321) 636-0000.
Stns: 3 FM. WJCB(FM) Clewiston, FL; WJFP-FM Fort Pierce, FL; KAYT(FM) Jena, LA
Kimberly Holman Kassis, pres.

Blackburn Group Inc. 140 Fullerton, Suite 1905, London, ON N6A 5P2. Canada. Phone: (519) 679-8680. Fax: (519) 679-5321. Ownership: Kilbyrne Investments Corp., 100%.
Stns: 2 AM. 4 FM. CHYR-FM Leamington, ON; CFGX-FM Sarnia, ON; CHOK Sarnia, ON; CHKS-FM Sarnia, ON; CKNX Wingham, ON; CKNX-FM Wingham, ON
Sandy Green, pres.

Blakeney Communications Inc. Box 6408, Laurel, MS 39441. Phone: (601) 649-0095. Fax: (601) 649-8199. E-mail: b95@b95country.com. Web Site: www.b95country.com.
Stns: 4 FM. WKZW-FM Bay Springs, MS; WXRR-FM Hattiesburg, MS; WXHB(FM) Richton, MS; WBBN(FM) Taylorsville, MS
Larry Blakeney, pres/CEO.

Bliss Communications Inc. Box 5001, One S. Parker Dr., Janesville, WI 53547-5001. Phone: (608) 754-3311. Fax: (608) 754-8038. E-mail: sbliss@gazetteextra.com.
Stns: 3 AM. 1 FM. WCLO Janesville, WI; WRJN Racine, WI; WBKV West Bend, WI; WBWI-FM West Bend, WI

Bliss Communications Inc. publishes *Ironwood* (MI) *Daily Globe*, *The Delavan* (WI) *Enterprise*, *The Week* (Delavan, II), *MidWeek* (Delavan, WI), *The Jotter* (Janesville, WI), the *Janesville* (WI) *Gazette*, the *Eagle Herald* (Marinette, WI), & the *Monroe* (WI) *Times*.
Sidney H. Bliss, pres/CEO.

Blount Communications Group 8 Lawrence Rd., Derry, NH 03038. Phone: (603) 437-9337. Fax: (603) 434-1035. E-mail: warv@aol.com. Web Site: www.lifechangingradio.com. Ownership: William A. Blount, Deborah C. Blount.
Stns: 5 AM. 1 FM. WFIF Milford, CT; WVNE(AM) Leicester, MA; WNEB Worcester, MA; WBCI-FM Bath, ME; WDER Derry, NH; WARV Warwick, RI
William A. Blount, pres; Deborah C. Blount, exec VP; David O. Young, VP.

Blue Ridge Radio Inc. 312 Robin Rd., Mount Airy, NC 27030. Phone: (336) 786-4498. Fax: (336) 789-7792.
Stns: 3 AM. 1 FM. WSYD Mount Airy, NC; WPAQ Mount Airy, NC; WBRF-FM Galax, VA; WWWJ Galax, VA
Earlene Epperson, pres; Ralph Epperson, VP; John Mullins, chief engr.

Bluewater Broadcasting Co. LLC 6300 N.E. 1st Ave., Suite 202, Fort Lauderdale, FL 33334-1901. Phone: (954) 434-5508. Ownership: Alta Bluewater Holdings Inc., 85.5% equity interest; Jeffrey Scott Bouchard, 8.82% equity interest; Richard H. Pestrichelli, 2.84% equity interest; and Scott McQueen, 2.84% equity interest.
Stns: 1 AM. 3 FM. WQKS-FM Montgomery, AL; WACV Montgomery, AL; WBAM-FM Montgomery, AL; WJWZ-FM Wetumpka, AL

Bold Gold Media Group L.P. c/o Vince Benedetto, HC6 Box 6229, Hawley, PA 18428. Phone: (570) 226-7466. Fax: (570) 253-6297. Web Site: www.infocow.net. Ownership: Vince Benedetto, 100%
Stns: 1 AM. 3 FM. WDNB(FM) Jeffersonville, NY; WYCY-FM Hawley, PA; WPSN(AM) Honesdale, PA; WDNH-FM Honesdale, PA

Bonneville International Corporation Broadcast House, Box 1160, Salt Lake City, UT 84110-1160. Phone: (801) 575-7500. Fax: (801) 575-7521. Web Site: www.bonnint.com. Ownership: Deseret Management Corp. Deseret Management Corp. owns *The Deseret Morning News*, a Salt Lake City, UT, daily.
Stns: 14 AM. 24 FM. KPKX(FM) Phoenix, AZ; KMVP Phoenix, AZ; KTAR(AM) Phoenix, AZ; KZBR(FM) San Francisco, CA; KOIT San Francisco, CA; KOIT-FM San Francisco, CA; KDFC-FM San Francisco, CA; WTOP Washington, DC; WGMS-FM Washington, DC; KBLI Blackfoot, ID; KCVI(FM) Blackfoot, ID; KLCE-FM Blackfoot, ID; KSLJ(AM) Blackfoot, ID; KFTZ-FM Idaho Falls, ID; KSSL(AM) Idaho Falls, ID; KTHK(FM) Idaho Falls, ID; WDRV(FM) Chicago, IL; WILV(FM) Chicago, IL; WVRV-FM East St. Louis, IL; WARH(FM) Granite City, IL; WTMX-FM Skokie, IL; WWDV(FM) Zion, IL; WIL(AM) Saint Louis, MO; WIL-FM Saint Louis, MO; KREC(FM) Brian Head, UT; KQMB(FM) Midvale, UT; KSNN-FM Saint George, UT; KDXU Saint George, UT; KRSP-FM Salt Lake City, UT; KSFI-FM Salt Lake City, UT; KSL Salt Lake City, UT; KUTR(AM) Taylorsville, UT; KUNF(AM) Washington, UT; WTOP-FM Warrenton, VA; WWVZ-FM Braddock Heights, MD; WXTR Frederick, MD; WFED(AM) Silver Spring, MD; WWZZ(FM) Waldorf, MD

Stns: 1 TV. KSL, Salt Lake City, UT
Bruce T. Reese, pres/CEO; Robert A. Johnson, exec VP & COO.

Border Media Partners LLC 201 Main St., Suite 2001, Fort Worth, TX 76102. Phone: (817) 335-5999. Fax: (817) 335-1197. Web Site: www.bmpradio.com. Ownership: The Goldman Sachs Group Inc., 48.85%; RGG Radio LLC, 16.29%; DBVA BMP Holdings LLC, 9.32%.
Stns: 12 AM. 11 FM. KJAV-FM Alamo, TX; KFON Austin, TX; KJON(AM) Carrollton, TX; KWOW-FM Clifton, TX; KXXS-FM Dripping Springs, TX; KURV Edinburg, TX; KTFM(FM) Floresville, TX; KFJZ Fort Worth, TX; KXEB(AM) Frisco, TX; KLEY-FM Jourdanton, TX; KLNT Laredo, TX; KNEX-FM Laredo, TX; KELG(AM) Manor, TX; KBDR(FM) Mirando City, TX; KRIO-FM Pearsall, TX; KOKE Pflugerville, TX; KFNI Pleasanton, TX; KBUC(FM) Raymondville, TX; KSOX Raymondville, TX; KZSP-FM South Padre Island,

Radio Group Ownership

TX; KESO-FM South Padre Island, TX; KSAH(AM) Universal City, TX; KTXZ West Lake Hills, TX

Bott Radio Network 10550 Barkley, Overland Park, KS 66212. Phone: (913) 642-7770. Fax: (913) 642-1319. Web Site: www.bottradionetwork.com. Ownership: Richard P. Bott Sr.

Stns: 8 AM. 14 FM. KCIV(FM) Mount Bullion, CA; WFCV Fort Wayne, IN; KCVW(FM) Kingman, KS; KCCV-FM Olathe, KS; KCCV Overland Park, KS; KKCV(FM) Rozel, KS; KCVT(FM) Silver Lake, KS; KSIV(AM) Clayton, MO; KJCV(FM) Country Club, MO; KMCV(FM) High Point, MO; KBCV(AM) Hollister, MO; KLTE-FM Kirksville, MO; KLEX Lexington, MO; KAYX(FM) Richmond, MO; KSIV-FM Saint Louis, MO; KSCV(FM) Springfield, MO; KCRL(FM) Sunrise Beach, MO; KAMI Cozad, NE; KCVN(FM) Cozad, NE; KQCV Oklahoma City, OK; KQCV-FM Shawnee, OK; WCRV Collierville, TN

Rich Bott II, exec VP; Richard Bott Sr., pres/CEO.

Brewer Broadcasting Corp. 1305 Carter St., Chattanooga, TN 37402. Phone: (423) 265-9494. Fax: (423) 266-2335. E-mail: jlb@brewerradio.com. Web Site: www.brewerradio.com. Ownership: Estate of James R. Brewer, James L. Brewer, Maytha N. Brewer.

Stns: 4 AM. 1 FM. WHON Centerville, IN; WBAC(AM) Cleveland, TN; WDNT(AM) Dayton, TN; WDNT-FM Dayton, TN; WXQK(AM) Spring City, TN

James L. Brewer Sr., pres.

Bristol Broadcasting Co. Inc. Box 1389, Bristol, VA 24203. Phone: (276) 669-8112. Fax: (276) 669-0541. Ownership: W.L. Nininger.

Stns: 7 AM. 9 FM. WLIE-FM Golconda, IL; WLLE(FM) Clinton, KY; WNGO(AM) Mayfield, KY; WKYQ-FM Paducah, KY; WKYX Paducah, KY; WDDJ(FM) Paducah, KY; WDXR Paducah, KY; WPAD Paducah, KY; WXBQ-FM Bristol, TN; WTZR(FM) Elizabethton, TN; WAEZ(FM) Greeneville, TN; WFHG-FM Abingdon, VA; WFHG(AM) Bristol, VA; WVTS(AM) Charleston, WV; WBES(AM) Dunbar, WV; WZJO(FM) Dunbar, WV

W.L. Nininger, pres & gen mgr.

Broadcast Communications Inc. Box 990, Greensburg, PA 15601. Phone: (724) 853-7000.

Stns: 4 AM. 2 FM. WKHB(AM) Irwin, PA; WKFB(AM) Jeannette, PA; WXXP(AM) Waynesburg, PA; WANB-FM Waynesburg, PA; WROG-FM Cumberland, MD; WCMD(AM) Cumberland, MD

Robert M. Stevens, pres; Ashley R. Stevens, VP.

Broadcast Entertainment Corp. 1000 Sycamore, Clovis, NM 88101. Phone: (505) 762-6200. Fax: (505) 762-8800. E-mail: kkyckica@plateautel.net. Ownership: Thomas Crane, Ron Pierson, Rick Keefer.

Stns: 2 AM. 3 FM. KICA Clovis, NM; KKYC-FM Clovis, NM; KMUL(AM) Farwell, TX; KICA-FM Farwell, TX; KMUL-FM Muleshoe, TX

Ron Pierson, pres; Rick Keefer, CEO.

Brooke Communications Inc. 1445 W. Harvard Ave., Roseburg, OR 97470. Phone: (541) 672-6641. Fax: (541) 673-7598. Ownership: William E. Markham Trust, Patrick A. Markham.

Stns: 2 AM. 3 FM. KQEN(AM) Roseburg, OR; KRNR Roseburg, OR; KRSB-FM Roseburg, OR; KAVJ(FM) Sutherlin, OR; KKMX(FM) Tri City, OR

David Hansen, gen sls mgr; Mike Carter, opns mgr; Patrick A. Markham, pres & gen mgr.

Brothers Broadcasting Corp. Box D, Rensselaer, IN 47978. Phone: (219) 866-4104. Fax: (219) 866-5106. E-mail: wirn@ffni.com. Ownership: John Balvich, 100%.

Stns: 1 FM. WIBN-FM Earl Park, IN

John Balvich, pres & gen mgr.

Bryan Broadcasting Corp. Box 3248, Bryan, TX 77805-3248. Phone: (979) 846-1150. Fax: (979) 846-1521. Ownership: William R. Hicks, 89%; and Ben D. Downs, 11%.

Stns: 2 AM. KZNE(AM) College Station, TX; WTAW(AM) College Station, TX

Buckley Broadcasting Corp. 166 West Putnam Ave., Greenwich, CT 06830. Phone: (203) 661-4307. Fax: (203) 622-7341. E-mail: rbuckley@buckleyradio.com. Web Site: www.buckleyradio.com. Ownership: Steven Buckley; Dana Buckley; Richard Buckley; Martha Fahnoe

Stns: 4 AM. 9 FM. KKBB-FM Bakersfield, CA; KNZR Bakersfield, CA; KUBB-FM Mariposa, CA; KWAV-FM Monterey, CA; KLLY-FM Oildale, CA; KHTN(FM) Planada, CA; KIOO-FM Porterville, CA; KSMJ(FM) Shafter, CA; KSEQ-FM Visalia, CA; WDRC(AM) Hartford, CT; WDRC-FM Hartford, CT; WMMW Meriden, CT; WSNG Torrington, CT; WWCO(AM) Waterbury, CT; WSEN(AM) Baldwinsville, NY; WOR New York, NY; WFBL(AM) Syracuse, NY

Richard Buckley, pres; Joseph Bilotta, COO.

Burbach Broadcasting Group 100 Ryan Ct.,, Suite 98, Pittsburgh, PA 15205. Phone: (412) 489-1001. Fax: (412) 278-1002. Ownership: Estate of John L. Laubach Jr., Nicholas A. Galli, chmn/pres.

Stns: 4 AM. 7 FM. WGIE(FM) Clarksburg, WV; WOBG Clarksburg, WV; WXKX(AM) Clarksburg, WV; WRZZ-FM Elizabeth, WV; WGYE(FM) Mannington, WV; WXIL-FM Parkersburg, WV; WGGE(FM) Parkersburg, WV; WADC Parkersburg, WV; WHBR-FM Parkersburg, WV; WVNT(AM) Parkersburg, WV; WOBG-FM Salem, WV

Nicholas A. Galli, pres & gen mgr; Thomas Bayer, VP finance.

Burt Broadcasting Inc. Box 1848, Alamogordo, NM 88311. Phone: (505) 434-1414. Fax: (505) 434-2213. E-mail: burtbroadcasting@charter.net. Ownership: William F. Burt, 50%; Donnie L. Burt, 50%.

Stns: 1 AM. 2 FM. KINN Alamogordo, NM; KYEE-FM Alamogordo, NM; KKBO(FM) Alamogordo, NM

Bill Burt, gen mgr.

Bustos Media LLC 3100 Fite Cir., Suite 101, Sacramento, CA 95827. Phone: (916) 368-6300. Fax: (916) 368-6334. E-mail: abustos@bustosmedia.com. Web Site: www.bustosmedia.com.

Stns: 11 AM. 11 FM. KTTA-FM Esparto, CA; KKFS(FM) Lincoln, CA; KBBU(FM) Modesto, CA; KZSJ(AM) San Martin, CA; KMUZ Gresham, OR; KZNY(AM) Milwaukie, OR; KGDD(AM) Oregon City, OR; KXMG(AM) Portland, OR; KMMG(FM) Weston, OR; KREH Pecan Grove, TX; KRRD(AM) Centerville, UT; KDUT(FM) Randolph, UT; KWMG(AM) Auburn-Federal Way, WA; KZTB(FM) Benton City, WA; KDDS-FM Elma, WA; KULE Ephrata, WA; KULE-FM Ephrata, WA; KZTA-FM Naches, WA; KZML(FM) Quincy, WA; KZTS(AM) Sunnyside, WA; KYXE(AM) Union Gap, WA; KBMG(FM) Evanston, WY

Amador S. Bustos, pres.

Butler County Radio Network Inc. 112 Hollywood Dr., Suite 203, Butler, PA 16001. Phone: (724) 287-5778. Fax: (724) 282-9188. Web Site: www.wbut.com. Ownership: Daniel R. Vernon, 25%; Linda D. Harvey, 25%; Scott W. Briggs, 25%; and Victoria A. Hinterberger, 25%.

Stns: 2 AM. 1 FM. WBUT Butler, PA; WISR Butler, PA; WLER-FM Butler, PA

Vicki Hinterberger, gen mgr.

C

CHUM Ltd. 1331 Yonge St., Toronto, ON M4T 1Y1. Canada. Phone: (416) 925-6666. Fax: (416) 926-1380. Web Site: www.chumlimited.com. Ownership: Alan Waters, controlling shareholder.

Stns: 12 AM. 8 FM. CHBN-FM Edmonton, AB; CHQM-FM Vancouver, BC; CKST Vancouver, BC; CHBE-FM Victoria, BC; CFAX Victoria, BC; CFWM-FM Winnipeg, MB; CFRW(AM) Winnipeg, MB; CJCH Halifax, NS; CJPT-FM Brockville, ON; CFJR-FM Brockville, ON; CKKW Kitchener, ON; CKLY-FM Lindsay (city of Kawartha Lakes), ON; CHST-FM London, ON; CFGO Ottawa, ON; CFRA Ottawa, ON; CKPT Peterborough, ON; CHUM Toronto, ON; CKLW Windsor, ON; CKWW Windsor, ON; CKGM Montreal, PQ

Stns: 13 TV. CKVR, Barrie, ON; CKX, Brandon, MB; CKAL, Calgary, AB; CKEM, Edmonton, AB; CJAL, Edmonton, AB; CKX-1, Foxwarren, MB; CFPL-TV, London, ON; CHMI, Portage la Prairie, MB; CITY-TV, Toronto, ON; CKVU, Vancouver, BC; CIVI-TV, Victoria, BC; CHWI-TV, Windsor, ON; CKNX, Wingham, ON

Stephen Tapp, exec VP; Paul Ski, exec VP; Jay Switzer, pres/CEO; Peter Miller, VP; David Kirkwood, exec VP; Sarah Crawford, VP; Mary Powers, VP; Denise Cooper, VP; Alan Mayne, CFO.

CRISTA Broadcasting 19303 Fremont Ave. N., Seattle, WA 98133. Phone: (206) 546-7350. Fax: (206) 546-7372. E-mail: comments@spirit1053.com. Web Site: www.spirit1053.com.

Stns: 1 AM. 2 FM. KCIS(AM) Edmonds, WA; KCMS(FM) Edmonds, WA; KWPZ(FM) Lynden, WA

Tony Bollen, VP; Jim Gwinn, pres; Tim Beltz, exec VP.

CSN International 3232 W. MacArthur Blvd., Santa Ana, CA 92704. Phone: (714) 825-9663. Fax: (714) 825-9660. Web Site: www.csnradio.com.

Stns: 1 AM. 72 FM. KVJC(FM) Globe, AZ; KJCU(FM) Laytonville, CA; KJCQ(FM) Quincy, CA; KOGR(FM) Rosedale, CA; WYJC(FM) Greenville, FL; WUJC(FM) Saint Marks, FL; KHJC(FM) Lihue, HI; KIHS(FM) Adel, IA; KZJB(FM) Pocatello, ID; KWJT(FM) Rathdrum, ID; KEFX-FM Twin Falls, ID; KTWD(FM) Wallace, ID; WJCZ(FM) Milford, IL; WPJC(FM) Pontiac, IL; WJCY(FM) Cicero, IN; WOJC(FM) Crothersville, IN; WHLP(FM) Hanna, IN; WQKO-FM Howe, IN; WJCJ(FM) Ladoga, IN; WWTS(FM) Logansport, IN; WTMK(FM) Lowell, IN; WJCO(FM) Montpelier, IN; WCJL(FM) Morgantown, IN; WFGL Fitchburg, MA; WJWT(FM) Gardner, MA; WSMA(FM) Scituate, MA; WJCX-FM Pittsfield, ME; WCVM-FM Bronson, MI; WJCE(FM) Elkton, MI; KGSF(FM) Anderson, MO; WKTBJ(FM) Festus, MO; KRSS(FM) Tarkio, MO; WWUN-FM Clarksdale, MS; WGTC(FM) Hickory, MS; KJFT(FM) Arlee, MT; KYWH(FM) Lockwood, MT; WGPS(FM) Elizabeth City, NC; WJIJ(FM) Norlina, NC; WPGT(FM) Roanoke Rapids, NC; WAJC(FM) Wilson, NC; KCJL(FM) Lincoln, ND; KOSJ(FM) Mitchell, NE; WWFP(FM) Brigantine, NJ; KKCJ(FM) Cannon AFB, NM; KPKJ(FM) Mentmore, NM; KNMA(FM) Socorro, NM; WJCA(FM) Albion, NY; WIFF(FM) Binghamton, NY; KJCC(FM) Carnegie, OK; KDJC(FM) Baker City, OR; KJCH(FM) Coos Bay, OR; KPIJ(FM) Junction City, OR; KEFS(FM) North Powder, OR; KKJA(FM) Redmond, OR; KAJC(FM) Salem, OR; WREQ-FM Ridgebury, PA; WWHW(FM) Dillon, SC; KWRC(FM) Rapid City, SD; KYJC(FM) Commerce, TX; KDKR(FM) Decatur, TX; KSGR(FM) Portland, TX; WJYA-FM Emporia, VA; WJYJ-FM Fredericksburg, VA; WJCN(FM) Nassawadox, VA; WPVA-FM Waynesboro, VA; KKRS(FM) Davenport, WA; KTJC(FM) Kelso, WA; KBLD(FM) Kennewick, WA; WJWD(FM) Marshall, WI; KLWD(FM) Gillette, WY; KWYC(FM) Orchard Valley, WY; KWCF(FM) Sheridan, WY; KRWT(FM) West Laramie, WY

Charles W. Smith, pres; Mike Stocklin, dir opns.

CTC Media Group Inc. Box 353, Royal Oak, MD 21662. Phone: (410) 964-5700. E-mail: ctcmedia@coastalnet.com.

Stns: 4 AM. WSME(AM) Camp Lejeune, NC; WNOS New Bern, NC; WWNB New Bern, NC; WECU(AM) Winterville, NC

Edwin Lee Afflerbach, pres/CEO.

Calvary Evangelistic Mission Inc. Box 367000, San Juan, PR 00936-7000. Phone: (787) 724-1190. Fax: (787) 722-5395. E-mail: radio@therockradio.org. Web Site: www.therockradio.org. Ownership: Dr. James Christensen, 11.1% of votes; Clair D. Miller, 11.1% of votes; James A. Looman, 11.1% of votes; Pablo E. Fernandez, 11.1% of votes; Raul Zevallos, 11.1% of votes; Vernon Green, 11.1% of votes; Wallace B. Bishop Jr., 11.1% of votes; Gwendolyn Santiago, 11.1% of votes; and Ruth Luttrell, 11.1% of votes.

Stns: 3 AM. WCGB Juana Diaz, PR; WBMJ San Juan, PR; WIVV Vieques, PR

Ruth Lutterall, pres; Janet Luttrell, gen mgr; Nila Luttrell, CFO.

Cameron Broadcasting Inc. 1615 Orange Tree Ln., Suite 102, Redlands, CA 92374. Phone: (909) 793-2233. Fax: (909) 798-6984.

Stns: 3 AM. 2 FM. KZZZ(AM) Bullhead City, AZ; KFLG(AM) Bullhead City, AZ; KAAA Kingman, AZ; KLUK(FM) Needles, CA; KNKK(FM) Needles, CA

William Jaeger, pres/CEO; Chris Sutherland, mktg dir.

CanWest Global Communications Corp. 201 Portage Ave., 31st Fl., Winnipeg, MB R3B 3L7. Canada. Phone: (204) 956-2025. Fax: (204) 947-9841. E-mail: bleslie@canwest.com. Web Site: www.canwestglobal.com. Ownership: Asper Family 85% voting shares, 45% of equity.

Stns: 3 FM. CJZZ-FM Winnipeg, MB; CHAL-FM Halifax, NS; CKBT-FM Kitchener-Waterloo, ON

Stns: 13 TV. CHEK-5, Campbell River, BC; CKRD-1, Coronation, AB; CITV, Edmonton, AB; CIHF, Halifax, NS; CHCH, Hamilton, ON; CHBC, Kelowna, BC; CISA-TV, Lethbridge, AB; CJNT, Montreal, PQ; CKRD, Red Deer, AB; CFRE, Regina, SK; CHAN, Vancouver, BC; CHEK, Victoria, BC; CKND-TV, Winnipeg, MB

Leonard Asper, pres/CEO.

Capital Media Corp. 30 Park Ave., Cohoes, NY 12047-3330. Phone: (518) 237-1330. Fax: (518) 235-4468. E-mail: info@whaz.com. Web Site: www.whaz.com.

Stns: 1 AM. 4 FM. WZEC(FM) Hoosick Falls, NY; WBAR-FM Lake Luzerne, NY; WMYY-FM Schoharie, NY; WHAZ Troy, NY; WMNV-FM Rupert, VT

Paul F. Lotters, pres & gen mgr; Steve Klob, opns dir.

Capitol Broadcasting Co. Inc. Box 12000, Raleigh, NC 27605. Phone: (919) 821-8555. Fax: (919) 821-8733. Ownership: Capitol Holding Co. Inc.

Stns: 2 FM. WRAL(FM) Raleigh, NC; WFXQ-FM Chase City, VA

Stns: 4 TV. WWWB, Charlotte, NC; WJZY, Charlotte, NC; WRAL-TV, Raleigh-Durham (Fayetteville), NC; WRAZ, Raleigh-Durham (Fayetteville), NC

James F. Goodmon, pres/CEO.

Capps Broadcast Group 2003 N.W. 56th Dr., Pendleton, OR 97801. Phone: (541) 276-1511. Fax: (541) 276-1480.
Stns: 3 AM. 2 FM. KCMB(FM) Baker City, OR; KWRL-FM La Grande, OR; KTIX Pendleton, OR; KUMA Pendleton, OR; KTEL Walla Walla, WA

Randy McKone, pres & gen mgr.

Cariboo Central Interior Radio Inc. 1940 Third Ave., Prince George, BC V2M 1G7. Canada. Phone: (250) 564-2524. Fax: (250) 562-6611. Ownership: R.A. East, 30%; S.W. Davis, 30%. Note: Group also owns CFFM-FM-2 Quesnel and CIRX-FM-1 Vanderhoof, both BC (both originating stns).
Stns: 5 AM. 3 FM. CKBX 100 Mile House, BC; CFLD Burns Lake, BC; CIRX-FM Prince George, BC; CJCI-FM Prince George, BC; CKCQ-FM Quesnel, BC; CFBV Smithers, BC; CIVH Vanderhoof, BC; CKWL Williams Lake, BC

Terry Shepherd, pres.

Carlson Communications International 3606 S. 500 W., Salt Lake City, UT 84115. Phone: (801) 262-5624. Fax: (801) 266-1510. Ownership: Ralph J. Carlson, only stockholder with 10% or more.
Stns: 2 AM. 2 FM. KRJC-FM Elko, NV; KTSN Elko, NV; KCYN(FM) Moab, UT; KDYL(AM) South Salt Lake, UT

Carroll Broadcasting Co. 1119 E. Plaza Dr., Carroll, IA 51401. Phone: (712) 792-4321. Fax: (712) 792-6667. Web Site: www.carrollbroadcasting.com.
Stns: 1 AM. 1 FM. KCIM Carroll, IA; KIKD-FM Lake City, IA

Mary Collison, pres.

Carroll Enterprises Inc. Box 549, Tawas City, MI 48764. Phone: (989) 362-3417. Fax: (989) 362-4544. E-mail: wkjc@wkjc.com. Web Site: www.wkjc.com.
Stns: 1 AM. 1 FM. WKJZ-FM Hillman, MI; WIOS Tawas City, MI

John Carroll Jr., pres & gen mgr.

Jimmy Ray Carroll Stns Box 271, Kemmerer, WY 83101. Phone: (307) 877-0000. Fax: (307) 877-5524.
Stns: 5 AM. 4 FM. KGLM-FM Anaconda, MT; KANA(AM) Anaconda, MT; KBCK(AM) Deer Lodge, MT; KWUD(AM) Woodville, TX; KEVA Evanston, WY; KWYW(FM) Lost Cabin, WY; KTRZ-FM Riverton, WY; KDNO(FM) Thermopolis, WY; KTHE Thermopolis, WY

Jimmy Ray Carroll, owner.

Carter Broadcast Group Inc. 11131 Colorado Ave., Kansas City, MO 64137. Phone: (816) 763-2040. Fax: (816) 966-1055. Ownership: Michael Carter
Stns: 1 AM. 1 FM. KSJM(FM) Winfield, KS; KPRT Kansas City, MO

Michael Carter, pres.

Casey Network LLC 908 Opelika Rd., Auburn, AL 36830. Phone: (334) 821-0744. Fax: (334) 821-4031.
Stns: 2 AM. WTRP La Grange, GA; WRLA(AM) West Point, GA

James Jarrell, pres/CEO.

Centennial Broadcasting LLC 3443 Robinhood Rd., Suite H, Winston-Salem, NC 27106. Phone: (336) 794-7971. Ownership: G Force LLC, 73.75%; Centennial Management Inc., 25%; Allen B. Shaw, 0.71%; Steven H. Watts, 0.36%; and Christopher Jarrell, 0.18%.
Stns: 4 FM. WBWR(FM) Bedford, VA; WZZU(FM) Lynchburg, VA; WLNI-FM Lynchburg, VA; WZZI-FM Vinton, VA

Center Broadcasting Co. Inc. 307 San Augustine St., Center, TX 75935. Phone: (936) 598-3304. Fax: (936) 598-9537.
Stns: 1 AM. 1 FM. KDET Center, TX; KQSI(FM) San Augustine, TX

Tracy Broadway, gen mgr.

Central Wisconsin Broadcasting Inc. Box 387, 1201 E. Division St., Neillsville, WI 54456. Phone: (715) 743-3333. Fax: (715) 743-2288. E-mail: 1075therock@tds.net. Web Site: 1075therock.com. Ownership: J. Kevin and Margaret L. Grap, 100%.
Stns: 1 AM. 1 FM. WCCN Neillsville, WI; WPKG(FM) Neillsville, WI

J. Kevin Grap, gen mgr.

Cessna Communications Inc. Box 1, Bedford, PA 15522. Phone: (814) 623-1000. Fax: (814) 623-9692. E-mail: cesscomm@earthlink.net. Ownership: Jay B. Cessna; John H. Cessna.
Stns: 1 AM. 2 FM. WBVE(FM) Bedford, PA; WBFD(AM) Bedford, PA; WAYC-FM Bedford, PA

Jay Cessna, pres.

Chaparral Communications Box 100, Jackson, WY 83001. Phone: (307) 733-2120. Fax: (307) 733-4760. E-mail: jacksonholeradio@onewest.net. Web Site: www.jacksonholeradio.com. Ownership: Jerrold Lundquist.
Stns: 2 AM. 7 FM. KWYS-FM Island Park, ID; KSKI-FM Sun Valley, ID; KYZK(FM) Sun Valley, ID; KECH-FM Sun Valley, ID; KEZQ-FM West Yellowstone, MT; KJAX(FM) Jackson, WY; KSGT Jackson, WY; KZJH-FM Jackson, WY; KPOW Powell, WY

Scott Anderson, gen mgr.

Cherry Creek Radio LLC 501 S. Cherry St., Suite 480, Denver, CO 80246. Phone: (303) 468-6500. Fax: (303) 468-6555. E-mail: jschwartz@cherrycreekradio.com. Ownership: Arlington Capital Partners L.P., 97.716% of votes, 80.131% of total assets; ACP/CCR Holdings LLC, 17.585% of total assets.
Stns: 13 AM. 19 FM. KWCD-FM Bisbee, AZ; KTAN(AM) Sierra Vista, AZ; KZMK-FM Sierra Vista, AZ; KSIQ-FM Brawley, CA; KROP(AM) Brawley, CA; KRLT-FM South Lake Tahoe, CA; KOWL(AM) South Lake Tahoe, CA; KTHN(FM) La Junta, CO; KBLJ(AM) La Junta, CO; KLMR-FM Lamar, CO; KLMR Lamar, CO; KKXK-FM Montrose, CO; KUBC(AM) Montrose, CO; KBNG(FM) Ridgway, CO; KVVR(FM) Dutton, MT; KHKR-FM East Helena, MT; KMON Great Falls, MT; KMON-FM Great Falls, MT; KLFM-FM Great Falls, MT; KCAP Helena, MT; KBLL Helena, MT; KBLL-FM Helena, MT; KZMT-FM Helena, MT; KTHC-FM Sidney, MT; KEYZ Williston, ND; KCOM Comanche, TX; KYOX(FM) Comanche, TX; KSTV-FM Dublin, TX; KSTV Stephenville, TX; KZHR-FM Dayton, WA; KONA Kennewick, WA; KONA-FM Kennewick, WA

Joe Schwartz, pres/CEO; Dan Gittings, exec VP/dir sls; Dennis Goodman, exec VP/dir opns.

The Chickasaw Nation Box 609, Ada, OK 74821-0609. Phone: (580) 332-1212. Fax: (580) 332-0128. Web Site: www.chickasaw.net. Ownership: The Chickasaw Nation, an Indian tribal government, is governed by a legislature.
Stns: 1 AM. 2 FM. KADA Ada, OK; KADA-FM Ada, OK; KYKC-FM Byng, OK

Christian Broadcasting System Ltd. 29200 Vassar Dr. Ste.150, Livonia, MI 48152. Phone: (248) 477-4600. Fax: (248) 477-6911.
Stns: 4 AM. 1 FM. WLYV Fort Wayne, IN; WLCM Charlotte, MI; WLQV Detroit, MI; WSNL(AM) Flint, MI; WJIV-FM Cherry Valley, NY

Jon R. Yinger, pres/CEO; Ralph Van Luven, VP; Sally Van Luven, sec; Vicky Yinger, treas.

Christian Faith Broadcasting Inc. 3809 Maple Ave., Castalia, OH 44824. Phone: (419) 684-5311. Fax: (419) 684-5378. E-mail: wggn@lrbcg.com.
Stns: 3 FM. WJKW-FM Athens, OH; WGGN-FM Castalia, OH; WLRD(FM) Willard, OH
Stns: 2 TV. WGGN, Cleveland, OH; WLLA, Grand Rapids-Kalamazoo-Battle Creek, MI

Shelby Gillam, pres; Rusty Yost, VP.

Churchill Communications LLC 871 Country Club Rd., Eugene, OR 97401. Phone: (541) 344-5500. Fax: (541) 485-2550. Ownership: Suzanne Arlie, 100%.
Stns: 3 AM. KOPT(AM) Eugene, OR; KLZS(AM) Eugene, OR; KXOR(AM) Junction City, OR

Citadel Broadcasting Corp. 7201 W. Lake Mead Blvd., Suite 400, Las Vegas, NV 89128. Phone: (702) 804-5200. Fax: (702) 804-5936. Web Site: www.citadelbroadcasting.com. Ownership: Forstmann Little Funds, 58%; and public shareholders, 42%.
Stns: 57 AM. 140 FM. WZRR-FM Birmingham, AL; WAPI Birmingham, AL; WJOX Birmingham, AL; WYSF-FM Birmingham, AL; WUHT(FM) Birmingham, AL; WFFN-FM Cordova, AL; WDGM(FM) Greensboro, AL; WRAX(FM) Helena, AL; WBEI(FM) Reform, AL; WJRD(AM) Tuscaloosa, AL; WTUG-FM Tuscaloosa, AL; WTSK Tuscaloosa, AL; KPZK-FM Cabot, AR; KVLO(FM) Humnoke, AR; KPZK(AM) Little Rock, AR; KURB-FM Little Rock, AR; KAAY Little Rock, AR; KARN Little Rock, AR; KIPR-FM Pine Bluff, AR; KARN-FM Sheridan, AR; KOKY-FM Sherwood, AR; KLAL-FM Wrightsville, AR; KSZR(FM) Oro Valley, AZ; KIIM-FM Tucson, AZ; KTUC Tucson, AZ; KCUB Tucson, AZ; KHYT-FM Tucson, AZ; KWIN-FM Lodi, CA; KDJK(FM) Mariposa, CA; KHKK-FM Modesto, CA; KESP(AM) Modesto, CA; KATM(FM) Modesto, CA; KHOP-FM Oakdale, CA; KWYL(FM) South Lake Tahoe, CA; KJOY-FM Stockton, CA; KWNN-FM Turlock, CA; KKML(AM) Colorado Springs, CO; KVOR Colorado Springs, CO; KKFM-FM Colorado Springs, CO; KKMG-FM Pueblo, CO; WSUB Groton, CT; WXLM(FM) Stonington, CT; KWQW(FM) Boone, IA; KGGO-FM Des Moines, IA; KBGG(AM) Des Moines, IA; KHKI-FM Des Moines, IA; KJJY(FM) West Des Moines, IA; KIZN-FM Boise, ID; KQFC-FM Boise, ID; KBOI Boise, ID; KKGL-FM Nampa, ID; KTIK Nampa, ID; KZMG(FM) New Plymouth, ID; WWKI-FM Kokomo, IN; WMDH New Castle, IN; WMDH-FM New Castle, IN; WXOK Baton Rouge, LA; WIBR Baton Rouge, LA; KMEZ-FM Belle Chasse, LA; WCDV(FM) Hammond, LA; WEMX-FM Kentwood, LA; WDVW(FM) La Place, LA; KRRQ-FM Lafayette, LA; KSMB-FM Lafayette, LA; KLRZ-FM Larose, LA; KRDJ(FM) New Iberia, LA; KXKC(FM) New Iberia, LA; KQXL-FM New Roads, LA; KKND-FM Port Sulphur, LA; KNEK Washington, LA; WFHN-FM Fairhaven, MA; WXLO-FM Fitchburg, MA; WBSM New Bedford, MA; WWFX(FM) Southbridge, MA; WMAS Springfield, MA; WORC-FM Webster, MA; WMME-FM Augusta, ME; WJZN(AM) Augusta, ME; WCYY-FM Biddeford, ME; WCLZ(FM) Brunswick, ME; WSHK(FM) Kittery, ME; WCYI(FM) Lewiston, ME; WBLM-FM Portland, ME; WJBQ-FM Portland, ME; WBPW(FM) Presque Isle, ME; WQHR-FM Presque Isle, ME; WOZI(FM) Presque Isle, ME; WTVL(AM) Waterville, ME; WEBB-FM Waterville, ME; WIOG(FM) Bay City, MI; WHNN-FM Bay City, MI; WFMK(FM) East Lansing, MI; WVFN(AM) East Lansing, MI; WTRX Flint, MI; WFBE-FM Flint, MI; WLAV-FM Grand Rapids, MI; WKLQ(FM) Greenville, MI; WTNR(FM) Holland, MI; WJIM(AM) Lansing, MI; WITL-FM Lansing, MI; WKQZ-FM Midland, MI; WKOQ(FM) Newaygo, MI; WYLZ-FM Pinconning, MI; WILZ-FM Saginaw, MI; WRBO(FM) Como, MS; WKSY-FM Picayune, MS; WOKQ-FM Dover, NH; WSAK(FM) Hampton, NH; WHOM-FM Mt. Washington, NH; WPKQ(FM) North Conway, NH; KBZU(FM) Albuquerque, NM; KNML(AM) Albuquerque, NM; KDRF(FM) Albuquerque, NM; KRST-FM Albuquerque, NM; KKOB Albuquerque, NM; KKOB-FM Albuquerque, NM; KTBL(AM) Los Ranchos de Albuquerque, NM; KBUL-FM Carson City, NV; KNEV-FM Reno, NV; KKOH Reno, NV; WYOS(AM) Binghamton, NY; WNBF Binghamton, NY; WBBF(AM) Buffalo, NY; WHTT-FM Buffalo, NY; WGRF-FM Buffalo, NY; WEDG-FM Buffalo, NY; WWYL(FM) Chenango Bridge, NY; WKRT Cortland, NY; WAQX-FM Manlius, NY; WMOS(FM) Montauk, NY; WHLD Niagara Falls, NY; WLTI(FM) Syracuse, NY; WNTQ(FM) Syracuse, NY; WWLS-FM Bethany, OK; KKWD(FM) Edmond, OK; KINB(FM) Kingfisher, OK; WWLS Moore, OK; WKY Oklahoma City, OK; KYIS-FM Oklahoma City, OK; KATT-FM Oklahoma City, OK; WLEV-FM Allentown, PA; WCAT-FM Carlisle, PA; WSJR(FM) Dallas, PA; WCTO-FM Easton, PA; WXTA-FM Edinboro, PA; WIOV-FM Ephrata, PA; WQHZ(FM) Erie, PA; WRIE Erie, PA; WBSX(FM) Hazleton, PA; WMHX(FM) Hershey, PA; WBHT-FM Mountain Top, PA; WBHD(FM) Olyphant, PA; WIOV Reading, PA; WARM Scranton, PA; WMGS-FM Wilkes-Barre, PA; WQXA York, PA; WPRO Providence, RI; WSKO Providence, RI; WSKO-FM Wakefield-Peacedale, RI; WWKX-FM Woonsocket, RI; WXTC Charleston, SC; WSSX-FM Charleston, SC; WSUY-FM Charleston, SC; WTMA Charleston, SC; WISW Columbia, SC; WLXC-FM Lexington, SC; WTCB-FM Orangeburg, SC; WMGL-FM Ravenel, SC; WNKT-FM Saint George, SC; WWWZ-FM Summerville, SC; WGOC Blountville, TN; WGOW Chattanooga, TN; WOGT-FM East Ridge, TN; WGFX-FM Gallatin, TN; WNRX(FM) Jefferson City, TN; WJCW Johnson City, TN; WKIN Kingsport, TN; WNML(AM) Knoxville, TN; WIVK-FM Knoxville, TN; WNML-FM Loudon, TN; WGKX-FM Memphis, TN; WXMX(FM) Millington, TN; WMPW(FM) Munford, TN; WKDF-FM Nashville, TN; WOKI(FM) Oliver Springs, TN; WGOW-FM Soddy-Daisy, TN; KJQS(AM) Murray, UT; KPQP(FM) Ogden, UT; KBER(FM) Ogden, UT; KENZ-FM Orem, UT; KKAT(AM) Salt Lake City, UT; KBEE(FM) Salt Lake City, UT; KEYF-FM Cheney, WA; KEYF(AM) Dishman, WA; KGA Spokane, WA; KJRB Spokane, WA; KBBD(FM) Spokane, WA

Farid Suleman, chmn/CEO; Judy Ellis, COO.

Clancy-Mance Communications 199 Wealtha Ave., Watertown, NY 13601. Phone: (315) 782-1240. Fax: (315) 782-0312. Ownership: Jack Clancy, David Mance.
Stns: 3 AM. 4 FM. WBDR(FM) Cape Vincent, NY; WTOJ(FM) Carthage, NY; WBDI(FM) Copenhagen, NY; WGIX-FM Gouverneur, NY; WSLB Ogdensburg, NY; WCDO Sidney, NY; WATN Watertown, NY

David Mance, pres/gen mgr; John Clancy, sec/treas.

Clarion County Broadcasting Corp. 1168 Greenville Pike, Clarion, PA 16214-0688. Phone: (814) 226-4500. Fax: (814) 226-5898. Web Site: www.insideclarioncounty.com. Ownership: William S. Hearst, 100%.
Stns: 2 AM. 2 FM. WWCH Clarion, PA; WCCR-FM Clarion, PA; WKQW Oil City, PA; WKQW-FM Oil City, PA

Clark County Broadcasting Inc. Box 40, Arkadelphia, AR 71923. Phone: (870) 246-9272. Ownership: Jay Wallace Bunyard and Teresa Sharon Bunyard Living Revocable

Broadcasting & Cable Yearbook 2006

D-6

Radio Group Ownership

Trust, Jan and Teresa Bunyard sole voting trustees, 100%.
Stns: 1 AM. 1 FM. KVRC Arkadelphia, AR; KYXK(FM) Gurdon, AR

Jay Bunyard, pres/CEO.

Clarke Broadcasting Corp. 1175 Fairview Dr., Suite N, Carson City, NV 89701. Phone: (775) 887-0588. Fax: (775) 887-1752.
Stns: 1 AM. KVML(AM) Sonora, CA

H. Randolph Holder, pres; Larry England, gen mgr.

Classic Communications Inc. Box 1600, Woodward, OK 73802-1600. Phone: (580) 256-1450. Fax: (580) 254-9102. Ownership: Sherre D. House, 50%; Blake Brewer, 25%; and Bret Brewer, 25%.
Stns: 1 AM. 2 FM. KSIW Woodward, OK; KWDQ-FM Woodward, OK; KWFX-FM Woodward, OK

Clear Channel Communications Inc. 200 E. Basse Rd., San Antonio, TX 78209. Phone: (210) 822-2828. Fax: (210) 822-2299. E-mail: markpmays@clearchannel.com. Web Site: www.clearchannel.com. Ownership: Thomas O. Hicks, 6.5%; L. Lowry Mays, 5.2%. Publicly traded company with the majority of its shares owned by the investing public.
Stns: 339 AM. 688 FM. KASH-FM Anchorage, AK; KBFX(FM) Anchorage, AK; KENI Anchorage, AK; KGOT-FM Anchorage, AK; KTZN Anchorage, AK; KYMG-FM Anchorage, AK; KFBX(AM) Fairbanks, AK; KIAK-FM Fairbanks, AK; KKED-FM Fairbanks, AK; KAKQ-FM Fairbanks, AK; WSTH-FM Alexander City, AL; WMJJ-FM Birmingham, AL; WRTR(FM) Brookwood, AL; WZBQ-FM Carrollton, AL; WDRM-FM Decatur, AL; WHOS Decatur, AL; WTXT-FM Fayette, AL; WAGH-FM Fort Mitchell, AL; WAAX Gadsden, AL; WQEN(FM) Gadsden, AL; WGMZ-FM Glencoe, AL; WTAK-FM Hartselle, AL; WENN(FM) Hoover, AL; WBHP Huntsville, AL; WDXB(FM) Jasper, AL; WHLW(FM) Luverne, AL; WXQW-FM Meridianville, AL; WWMG(FM) Millbrook, AL; WPMI(AM) Mobile, AL; WKSJ-FM Mobile, AL; WRKH-FM Mobile, AL; WHAL(AM) Phenix City, AL; WGSY-FM Phenix City, AL; WBFA-FM Smiths, AL; WWXQ-FM Trinity, AL; WZHT-FM Troy, AL; WACT Tuscaloosa, AL; WLAY-FM Tuscumbia, AL; KMJI(FM) Ashdown, AR; KHKN(FM) Benton, AR; KMJX-FM Conway, AR; KKIX-FM Fayetteville, AR; KEZA-FM Fayetteville, AR; KMAG-FM Fort Smith, AR; KWHN(AM) Fort Smith, AR; KWHF(FM) Harrisburg, AR; KDJE(FM) Jacksonville, AR; KIYS(FM) Jonesboro, AR; KNEA(AM) Jonesboro, AR; KFIN(FM) Jonesboro, AR; KSSN-FM Little Rock, AR; KMXF-FM Lowell, AR; KMSX(FM) Maumelle, AR; KOSY(AM) Texarkana, AR; KYGL-FM Texarkana, AR; KFXR-FM Chinle, AZ; KTZR-FM Green Valley, AZ; KOHT-FM Marana, AZ; KZZP-FM Mesa, AZ; KYOT-FM Phoenix, AZ; KOY Phoenix, AZ; KNIX-FM Phoenix, AZ; KMXP-FM Phoenix, AZ; KGME(AM) Phoenix, AZ; KESZ-FM Phoenix, AZ; KXEW South Tucson, AZ; KNST Tucson, AZ; KRQQ-FM Tucson, AZ; KWFM(AM) Tucson, AZ; KWMT-FM Tucson, AZ; KTTI-FM Yuma, AZ; KQSR(FM) Yuma, AZ; KZXY-FM Apple Valley, CA; KIXW Apple Valley, CA; KHYL-FM Auburn, CA; KDFO(AM) Bakersfield, CA; KGET(AM) Bakersfield, CA; KUSS(FM) Carlsbad, CA; KSBL-FM Carpinteria, CA; KDFO-FM Delano, CA; KRDU Dinuba, CA; KHTS-FM El Cajon, CA; KSPE-FM Ellwood, CA; KEZL-FM Fowler, CA; KCBL Fresno, CA; KALZ(FM) Fresno, CA; KATJ-FM George, CA; KURQ(FM) Grover Beach, CA; KRZR-FM Hanford, CA; KAVL Lancaster, CA; KSMY(FM) Lompoc, CA; KBIG-FM Los Angeles, CA; KFI Los Angeles, CA; KOST-FM Los Angeles, CA; KIIS-FM Los Angeles, CA; KHHT(FM) Los Angeles, CA; KLAC Los Angeles, CA; KYSR-FM Los Angeles, CA; KTLK(AM) Los Angeles, CA; KSTT-FM Los Osos-Baywood Park, CA; KIXA-FM Lucerne Valley, CA; KMRQ(FM) Manteca, CA; KTOM-FM Marina, CA; KJSN-FM Modesto, CA; KFIV Modesto, CA; KTPI(AM) Mojave, CA; KVVS(FM) Mojave, CA; KQKE(AM) Oakland, CA; KNEW Oakland, CA; KOCN-FM Pacific Grove, CA; KOSO-FM Patterson, CA; KSTE Rancho Cordova, CA; KGGI-FM Riverside, CA; KDIF Riverside, CA; KOSS-FM Rosamond, CA; KGBY-FM Sacramento, CA; KFBK Sacramento, CA; KDON-FM Salinas, CA; KZFX(AM) Salinas, CA; KPRC-FM Salinas, CA; KABL(AM) Salinas, CA; KKDD San Bernardino, CA; KTDD(AM) San Bernardino, CA; KGB-FM San Diego, CA; KMYI(FM) San Diego, CA; KIOZ-FM San Diego, CA; KOGO(AM) San Diego, CA; KLSD(AM) San Diego, CA; KIOI-FM San Francisco, CA; KISQ-FM San Francisco, CA; KMEL-FM San Francisco, CA; KKSF-FM San Francisco, CA; KYLD-FM San Francisco, CA; KUFX-FM San Jose, CA; KSJO-FM San Jose, CA; KSLY-FM San Luis Obispo, CA; KVEC San Luis Obispo, CA; KTYD-FM Santa Barbara, CA; KIST-FM Santa Barbara, CA; KBKO Santa Barbara, CA; KIST(AM) Santa Barbara, CA; KUYL(AM) Stockton, CA; KQOD-FM Stockton, CA; KCNL(FM) Sunnyvale, CA; KTPI-FM Tehachapi, CA; KMYT(FM) Temecula, CA; KTMQ(FM) Temecula, CA; KBOS-FM Tulare, CA; KFSO-FM Visalia, CA; KVBL Visalia, CA; KRSX-FM Yermo, CA; KBCO-FM Boulder, CO; KBPI(FM) Denver, CO; KRFX-FM Denver, CO; KOA Denver, CO; KHOW Denver, CO; KMGG(FM) Denver, CO; KTCL-FM Fort Collins, CO; KIIX(AM) Fort Collins, CO; KIBT(FM) Fountain, CO; KSME(FM) Greeley, CO; KVUU-FM Pueblo, CO; KCCY(FM) Pueblo, CO; KDZA-FM Pueblo, CO; KCSJ Pueblo, CO; KGHF Pueblo, CO; KPHT(FM) Rocky Ford, CO; KKZN(AM) Thornton, CO; KCOL(AM) Wellington, CO; KKLI-FM Widefield, CO; WPKX-FM Enfield, CT; WHCN-FM Hartford, CT; WKSS-FM Hartford, CT; WAVZ New Haven, CT; WELI New Haven, CT; WWYZ-FM Waterbury, CT; WPHH(FM) Waterbury, CT; WMZQ-FM Washington, DC; WWDC-FM Washington, DC; WBIG-FM Washington, DC; WASH-FM Washington, DC; WIHT(FM) Washington, DC; WWRC(AM) Washington, DC; WTEM Washington, DC; WFUS(FM) Bradenton, FL; WPLA-FM Callahan, FL; WBTP(FM) Clearwater, FL; WXTB-FM Clearwater, FL; WMMV Cocoa, FL; WJRR-FM Cocoa Beach, FL; WTKS-FM Cocoa Beach, FL; WSRZ-FM Coral Cove, FL; WTZB(FM) Englewood, FL; WHYI-FM Fort Lauderdale, FL; WBGG-FM Fort Lauderdale, FL; WMIB(FM) Fort Lauderdale, FL; WOLZ-FM Fort Myers, FL; WKGR-FM Fort Pierce, FL; WLDI-FM Fort Pierce, FL; WSYR-FM Gifford, FL; WJBT-FM Green Cove Springs, FL; WOLL-FM Hobe Sound, FL; WFXJ(AM) Jacksonville, FL; WROO-FM Jacksonville, FL; WQIK-FM Jacksonville, FL; WKEY-FM Key West, FL; WEOW-FM Key West, FL; WAIL-FM Key West, FL; WZJZ(FM) Lehigh Acres, FL; WMMB Melbourne, FL; WPBH(FM) Mexico Beach, FL; WINZ(AM) Miami, FL; WIOD Miami, FL; WLVE-FM Miami Beach, FL; WMGE(FM) Miami Beach, FL; WBWT(FM) Midway, FL; WMGF-FM Mount Dora, FL; WBTT(FM) Naples Park, FL; WFKS(FM) Neptune Beach, FL; WQTM(AM) Orlando, FL; WRUM(FM) Orlando, FL; WPAP-FM Panama City, FL; WDIZ Panama City, FL; WFBX(FM) Parker, FL; WTKX-FM Pensacola, FL; WYCL-FM Pensacola, FL; WFLF(AM) Pine Hills, FL; WCTH-FM Plantation Key, FL; WFKZ-FM Plantation Key, FL; WCKT(FM) Port Charlotte, FL; WEBZ-FM Port St. Joe, FL; WCCF(AM) Punta Gorda, FL; WXSR-FM Quincy, FL; WZZR(FM) Riviera Beach, FL; WSRQ(AM) Sarasota, FL; WCVU(FM) Solana, FL; WAVW(FM) Stuart, FL; WTNT-FM Tallahassee, FL; WHNZ(AM) Tampa, FL; WFLA(AM) Tampa, FL; WXXL-FM Tavares, FL; WKEZ-FM Tavenier, FL; WLTQ-FM Venice, FL; WDDV(AM) Venice, FL; WZTA(AM) Vero Beach, FL; WCZR(FM) Vero Beach, FL; WQOL-FM Vero Beach, FL; WRLX-FM West Palm Beach, FL; WJNO(AM) West Palm Beach, FL; WBZT(AM) West Palm Beach, FL; WJYZ Albany, GA; WKLS(FM) Atlanta, GA; WGST Atlanta, GA; WBBQ-FM Augusta, GA; WIBL(FM) Augusta, GA; WRAK-FM Bainbridge, GA; WBZY(FM) Bowdon, GA; WSOL-FM Brunswick, GA; WWVA-FM Canton, GA; WQMT-FM Chatsworth, GA; WDAK Columbus, GA; WSHE(AM) Columbus, GA; WVRK-FM Columbus, GA; WDAL Dalton, GA; WBLJ(AM) Dalton, GA; WMWR(AM) Dry Branch, GA; WQBZ-FM Fort Valley, GA; WIBB-FM Fort Valley, GA; WYNF(FM) Gray, GA; WMGP(FM) Hogansville, GA; WLCG Macon, GA; WCOH Newnan, GA; WVWA(FM) Peachtree City, GA; WTUN(FM) Ringgold, GA; WUUS(AM) Rossville, GA; WRXR-FM Rossville, GA; WTKS(AM) Savannah, GA; WAEV-FM Savannah, GA; WSOK Savannah, GA; WTLY(FM) Thomasville, GA; WOBB-FM Tifton, GA; WRBV-FM Warner Robins, GA; WEBL(FM) Warner Robins, GA; KDNN(FM) Honolulu, HI; KHBZ(AM) Honolulu, HI; KHVH Honolulu, HI; KSSK(AM) Honolulu, HI; KUCD(FM) Pearl City, HI; KSSK-FM Waipahu, HI; KASI Ames, IA; KCCQ(FM) Ames, IA; KDRB(FM) Ankeny, IA; KBUR Burlington, IA; KGRS-FM Burlington, IA; KMJM(AM) Cedar Rapids, IA; WMT Cedar Rapids, IA; WMT-FM Cedar Rapids, IA; KCHA Charles City, IA; KCHA-FM Charles City, IA; KLKK-FM Clear Lake, IA; KMXG(FM) Clinton, IA; KCQQ(FM) Davenport, IA; WOC Davenport, IA; WLLR-FM Davenport, IA; WHO(AM) Des Moines, IA; KXNO(AM) Des Moines, IA; KKDM-FM Des Moines, IA; KKEZ-FM Fort Dodge, IA; KWMT Fort Dodge, IA; KBKB Fort Madison, IA; KBKB-FM Fort Madison, IA; KXKT(FM) Glenwood, IA; KXIC Iowa City, IA; KKRQ-FM Iowa City, IA; KGLO(AM) Mason City, IA; KIAI(FM) Mason City, IA; KCZE(FM) New Hampton, IA; KSMA-FM Osage, IA; KSEZ-FM Sioux City, IA; KMNS Sioux City, IA; KGLI-FM Sioux City, IA; KWSL Sioux City, IA; KFXD(AM) Boise, ID; KSAS-FM Caldwell, ID; KLLP-FM Chubbuck, ID; KXLT-FM Eagle, ID; KCIX(FM) Garden City, ID; KID Idaho Falls, ID; KID-FM Idaho Falls, ID; KIDO(AM) Nampa, ID; KWIK Pocatello, ID; KCDA(FM) Post Falls, ID; KEZJ-FM Twin Falls, ID; KLIX Twin Falls, ID; KATZ-FM Alton, IL; WKSC-FM Chicago, IL; WGRB(AM) Chicago, IL; WGCI-FM Chicago, IL; WLIT-FM Chicago, IL; WNUA-FM Chicago, IL; KMJM-FM Columbia, IL; KUUL(FM) East Moline, IL; WVZA-FM Herrin, IL; WXAJ(FM) Hillsboro, IL; WRLL(AM) Johnston City, IL; WDDD Johnston City, IL; WDDD-FM Marion, IL; WFXN(AM) Moline, IL; WTAO-FM Murphysboro, IL; WVAZ-FM Oak Park, IL; WFMB(AM) Springfield, IL; WCVS-FM Virden, IL; WFRX West Frankfort, IL; WQUL-FM West Frankfort, IL; WTFX-FM Clarksville, IN; WRZX-FM Indianapolis, IN; WFBQ-FM Indianapolis, IN; WNDE Indianapolis, IN; WQMF-FM Jeffersonville, IN; WZKF(FM) Salem, IN; KZCH(FM) Derby, KS; KZSN-FM Hutchinson, KS; KRBB-FM Wichita, KS; KTHR(FM) Wichita, KS; WSFE(AM) Burnside, KY; WSEK(FM) Burnside, KY; WKED-FM Frankfort, KY; WFKY Frankfort, KY; WXRA(AM) Georgetown, KY; WBUL-FM Lexington, KY; WMXL-FM Lexington, KY; WLKT-FM Lexington-Fayette, KY; WKRD(AM) Louisville, KY; WKJK Louisville, KY; WLUE(FM) Louisville, KY; WMKJ(FM) Mt. Sterling, KY; WUBT(FM) Russellville, KY; WCND Shelbyville, KY; WJZO(FM) Shelbyville, KY; WKEQ-FM Somerset, KY; WSFC Somerset, KY; WLLK-FM Somerset, KY; WKQQ-FM Winchester, KY; KZMZ-FM Alexandria, LA; KDBS Alexandria, LA; WJBO Baton Rouge, LA; WPYR(AM) Baton Rouge, LA; WYNK-FM Baton Rouge, LA; KRVE-FM Brusly, LA; WSKR Denham Springs, LA; KHEV(FM) Houma, LA; WRNO-FM New Orleans, LA; WODT New Orleans, LA; WYLD New Orleans, LA; WNOE-FM New Orleans, LA; KKST-FM Oakdale, LA; KVKI-FM Shreveport, LA; KWKH(AM) Shreveport, LA; KEEL(AM) Shreveport, LA; WJMN-FM Boston, MA; WXKS Everett, MA; WKOX Framingham, MA; WHYN Springfield, MA; WSNE-FM Taunton, MA; WNNZ Westfield, MA; WTAG Worcester, MA; WKCG-FM Augusta, ME; WABI Bangor, ME; WLKE-FM Bar Harbor, ME; WBFB-FM Belfast, ME; WCME-FM Boothbay Harbor, ME; WQSS-FM Camden, ME; WGUY(FM) Dexter, ME; WKSQ-FM Ellsworth, ME; WFAU Gardiner, ME; WVOM-FM Howland, ME; WIGY-FM Madison, ME; WRKD Rockland, ME; WFZX(FM) Searsport, ME; WTOS-FM Skowhegan, ME; WUBB-FM York Center, ME; WTKA Ann Arbor, MI; WWWW(FM) Ann Arbor, MI; WBCK Battle Creek, MI; WRCC Battle Creek, MI; WNIC-FM Dearborn, MI; WDTW(AM) Dearborn, MI; WDTW-FM Detroit, MI; WMXD-FM Detroit, MI; WDFN Detroit, MI; WJLB-FM Detroit, MI; WKQI-FM Detroit, MI; WBCT-FM Grand Rapids, MI; WTKG Grand Rapids, MI; WOOD Grand Rapids, MI; WVTI-FM Holland, MI; WWKN-FM Marshall, MI; WKBZ(AM) Muskegon, MI; WMUS(FM) Muskegon, MI; WSNX-FM Muskegon, MI; WSHZ(FM) Muskegon, MI; WMRR-FM Muskegon Heights, MI; WLBY(AM) Saline, MI; KQQL-FM Anoka, MN; KNFX Austin, MN; KQHT-FM Crookston, MN; KRVI(FM) Detroit Lakes, MN; KLDJ-FM Duluth, MN; WEBC Duluth, MN; KMFX-FM Lake City, MN; KYSM Mankato, MN; KTCZ-FM Minneapolis, MN; KFXN Minneapolis, MN; KFAN Minneapolis, MN; KJZI(FM) Minneapolis, MN; KVOX Moorhead, MN; KXLP(FM) New Ulm, MN; KBMX(FM) Proctor, MN; KDWB-FM Richfield, MN; KWEB(AM) Rochester, MN; KRCH(FM) Rochester, MN; KEEY-FM Saint Paul, MN; KSNR-FM Thief River Falls, MN; KMFX Wabasha, MN; KSWF(FM) Aurora, MO; KTOZ-FM Pleasant Hope, MO; KSLZ-FM Saint Louis, MO; KSD-FM Saint Louis, MO; KLOU-FM Saint Louis, MO; KATZ Saint Louis, MO; KIGL(FM) Seligman, MO; KGMY Springfield, MO; KXUS-FM Springfield, MO; WESE-FM Baldwyn, MS; WMJY-FM Biloxi, MS; WBVV(FM) Booneville, MS; WWKZ(FM) Columbus, MS; WJKX-FM Ellisville, MS; WFOR Hattiesburg, MS; WUSW-FM Hattiesburg, MS; WHER-FM Heidelberg, MS; WHAL-FM Horn Lake, MS; WJDX Jackson, MS; WHLH(FM) Jackson, MS; WMSI-FM Jackson, MS; WZRX Jackson, MS; WQJQ-FM Kosciusko, MS; WNSL-FM Laurel, MS; WEEZ Laurel, MS; WYYW-FM Marion, MS; WJDQ-FM Meridian, MS; WFFX Meridian, MS; WBUV(FM) Moss Point, MS; WWZD-FM New Albany, MS; WMSO(FM) Newton, MS; WQYZ-FM Ocean Springs, MS; WKNN-FM Pascagoula, MS; WZLD(FM) Petal, MS; WKMQ(AM) Tupelo, MS; WTUP Tupelo, MS; WZKS-FM Union, MS; WSTZ-FM Vicksburg, MS; KISN(FM) Belgrade, MT; KKBR-FM Billings, MT; KBBB(FM) Billings, MT; KBUL Billings, MT; KCTR-FM Billings, MT; KMMS Bozeman, MT; KMMS-FM Bozeman, MT; KZMY(FM) Bozeman, MT; KLCY East Missoula, MT; KLYQ Hamilton, MT; KBAZ(FM) Hamilton, MT; KMHK-FM Hardin, MT; KPRK Livingston, MT; KXLB(FM) Livingston, MT; KYSS-FM Missoula, MT; KGVO Missoula, MT; KSEN Shelby, MT; KZIN-FM Shelby, MT; KLTC-FM Superior, MT; WWNC Asheville, NC; WRSN-FM Burlington, NC; WDCG-FM Durham, NC; WGBT(FM) Eden, NC; WPEK(AM) Fairview, NC; WQNQ(FM) Fletcher, NC; WMYI(FM) Hendersonville, NC; WLYT-FM Hickory, NC; WMAG(FM) High Point, NC; WVBZ(FM) High Point, NC; WRFX-FM Kannapolis, NC; WCDG(FM) Moyock, NC; WRVA-FM Rocky Mount, NC; WEND-FM Salisbury, NC; WIBT(FM) Shelby, NC; WKKT-FM Statesville, NC; WSIC Statesville, NC; WMXF(AM) Waynesville, NC; WRDU-FM Wilson, NC; WTQR-FM Winston-Salem, NC; KBMR Bismarck, ND; KFYR Bismarck, ND; KQDY(FM) Bismarck, ND; KSSS-FM Bismarck, ND; KXMR Bismarck, ND; KZRX-FM Dickinson, ND; KCAD(FM) Dickinson, ND; KFGO Fargo, ND; WDAY-FM Fargo, ND; KJKJ-FM Grand Forks, ND; KKXL Grand Forks, ND; KDAM(FM) Hope, ND; KFAB-FM Kindred, ND; KMXA-FM Minot, ND; KRRZ Minot, ND; KIZZ-FM Minot, ND; KCJB Minot, ND; KTGL-FM Beatrice,

NE; KHUS(FM) Bennington, NE; KIBZ(FM) Crete, NE; KLMY(FM) Lincoln, NE; KMCX-FM Ogallala, NE; KOGA Ogallala, NE; KOGA-FM Ogallala, NE; KGOR-FM Omaha, NE; KEFM-FM Omaha, NE; KFAB Omaha, NE; KZKX-FM Seward, NE; KSFT-FM South Sioux City, NE; WERZ-FM Exeter, NH; WGIP Exeter, NH; WGXL-FM Hanover, NH; WTSL Hanover, NH; WXXK-FM Lebanon, NH; WGIR Manchester, NH; WGIR-FM Manchester, NH; WVRR-FM Newport, NH; WHEB-FM Portsmouth, NH; WQSO-FM Rochester, NH; WHCY-FM Blairstown, NJ; WSUS-FM Franklin, NJ; WHTZ-FM Newark, NJ; WNNJ Newton, NJ; KZRR-FM Albuquerque, NM; KABQ Albuquerque, NM; KBQI(FM) Albuquerque, NM; KPEK-FM Albuquerque, NM; KCQL Aztec, NM; KKFG-FM Bloomfield, NM; KTEG(FM) Bosque Farms, NM; KSYU-FM Corrales, NM; KTRA-FM Farmington, NM; KDAG(FM) Farmington, NM; KFMQ-FM Gallup, NM; KGLX(FM) Gallup, NM; KAZX(FM) Kirtland, NM; KBAC(FM) Las Vegas, NM; KABQ-FM Santa Fe, NM; KXTC-FM Thoreau, NM; KSFQ-FM White Rock, NM; KWNR-FM Henderson, NV; KQOL-FM Las Vegas, NV; KSNE-FM Las Vegas, NV; KWID(FM) Las Vegas, NV; WPYX-FM Albany, NY; WHRL-FM Albany, NY; WPHR(FM) Auburn, NY; WKKF(FM) Ballston Spa, NY; WINR Binghamton, NY; WISY-FM Canandaigua, NY; WCTW-FM Catskill, NY; WWDG(FM) DeRuyter, NY; WALK(AM) East Patchogue, NY; WRWD(AM) Ellenville, NY; WFKP(FM) Ellenville, NY; WENE(AM) Endicott, NY; WBBI(FM) Endwell, NY; WCPV-FM Essex, NY; WBBS-FM Fulton, NY; WRWD-FM Highland, NY; WFXF(FM) Honeoye Falls, NY; WHUC Hudson, NY; WZCR(FM) Hudson, NY; WKGS-FM Irondequoit, NY; WGHQ Kingston, NY; WKTU(FM) Lake Success, NY; WIXT(AM) Little Falls, NY; WSKU(FM) Little Falls, NY; WBWZ-FM New Paltz, NY; WAXQ-FM New York, NY; WLTW-FM New York, NY; WWPR-FM New York, NY; WEAV Plattsburgh, NY; WVTK(FM) Port Henry, NY; WKIP Poughkeepsie, NY; WPKF(FM) Poughkeepsie, NY; WRNQ-FM Poughkeepsie, NY; WOKR(FM) Remsen, NY; WADR Remsen, NY; WHTK Rochester, NY; WHAM Rochester, NY; WRNY Rome, NY; WTRY-FM Rotterdam, NY; WBPM(FM) Saugerties, NY; WGY Schenectady, NY; WNVE(FM) South Bristol Township, NY; WYYY-FM Syracuse, NY; WHEN Syracuse, NY; WSYR Syracuse, NY; WOFX(AM) Troy, NY; WUTQ Utica, NY; WMXW-FM Vestal, NY; WSKS(FM) Whitesboro, NY; WXZO(FM) Willsboro, NY; WHLO Akron, OH; WARF(AM) Akron, OH; WNCO Ashland, OH; WYBL(FM) Ashtabula, OH; WFUN Ashtabula, OH; WXEG-FM Beavercreek, OH; WNUS-FM Belpre, OH; WKDD(FM) Canton, OH; WLZT(FM) Chillicothe, OH; WCHI Chillicothe, OH; WBEX Chillicothe, OH; WSAI(AM) Cincinnati, OH; WKRC Cincinnati, OH; WLW Cincinnati, OH; WVMX-FM Cincinnati, OH; WCKY(AM) Cincinnati, OH; WTAM Cleveland, OH; WMMS-FM Cleveland, OH; WMJI-FM Cleveland, OH; WGAR-FM Cleveland, OH; WMJK(FM) Clyde, OH; WBVB-FM Coal Grove, OH; WCOL-FM Columbus, OH; WNCI-FM Columbus, OH; WTVN(AM) Columbus, OH; WLWD(FM) Columbus Grove, OH; WMMX-FM Dayton, OH; WTUE-FM Dayton, OH; WONE Dayton, OH; WONW Defiance, OH; WZOM-FM Defiance, OH; WDFM-FM Defiance, OH; WJER-FM Dover, OH; WZOO-FM Edgewood, OH; WDKF(FM) Englewood, OH; WZRX-FM Fort Shawnee, OH; WXXR(FM) Fredericktown, OH; WFXN-FM Galion, OH; WDSJ(FM) Greenville, OH; WFJX(FM) Hilliard, OH; WSRW Hillsboro, OH; WSRW-FM Hillsboro, OH; WBKS(FM) Ironton, OH; WIRO Ironton, OH; WLQT-FM Kettering, OH; WIMA Lima, OH; WXXF(FM) Loudonville, OH; WMAN Mansfield, OH; WLTP(AM) Marietta, OH; WRVB-FM Marietta, OH; WMRN Marion, OH; WDIF-FM Marion, OH; WKFS-FM Milford, OH; WMVO(AM) Mount Vernon, OH; WQIO-FM Mount Vernon, OH; WNDH-FM Napoleon, OH; WBBG(FM) Niles, OH; WPFX-FM North Baltimore, OH; WFXJ-FM North Kingsville, OH; WBUK(FM) Ottawa, OH; WMLX-FM Saint Mary's, OH; WCPZ(FM) Sandusky, OH; WVKF(FM) Shadyside, OH; WIZE Springfield, OH; WTTF Tiffin, OH; WVKS-FM Toledo, OH; WSPD Toledo, OH; WRVF(FM) Toledo, OH; WIOT(FM) Toledo, OH; WCWA Toledo, OH; WYNT-FM Upper Sandusky, OH; WCHO(AM) Washington Court House, OH; WKBN Youngstown, OH; WNIO(AM) Youngstown, OH; KIZS(FM) Broken Arrow, OK; KTBT(FM) Collinsville, OK; KLAW(FM) Lawton, OK; KVRW-FM Lawton, OK; KZCD(FM) Lawton, OK; KXXY-FM Oklahoma City, OK; KTST-FM Oklahoma City, OK; KTOK(AM) Oklahoma City, OK; KHBZ-FM Oklahoma City, OK; KQLL-FM Owasso, OK; KZBB-FM Poteau, OK; KKBD(FM) Sallisaw, OK; KMOD-FM Tulsa, OK; KTBZ(AM) Tulsa, OK; KAKC(AM) Tulsa, OK; KTHH(AM) Albany, OR; KRKT-FM Albany, OR; KIFS(FM) Ashland, OR; KKCW-FM Beaverton, OR; KLOO Corvallis, OR; KEJO Corvallis, OR; KZZE-FM Eagle Point, OR; KPNW Eugene, OR; KDUK-FM Florence, OR; KRWQ-FM Gold Hill, OR; KMED Medford, OR; KLDZ(FM) Medford, OR; KPOJ(AM) Portland, OR; KEX Portland, OR; WAEB Allentown, PA; WKAP Allentown, PA; WZZO-FM Bethlehem, PA; WTKT(AM) Harrisburg, PA; WKBO Harrisburg, PA; WHP Harrisburg, PA; WRBT-FM Harrisburg, PA; WRKK Hughesville, PA; WLAN Lancaster, PA; WVRT(FM) Mill Hall, PA; WSNI(FM) Philadelphia, PA; WIOQ-FM Philadelphia, PA; WJJZ-FM Philadelphia, PA; WDAS Philadelphia, PA; WUSL-FM Philadelphia, PA; WKST-FM Pittsburgh, PA; WDVE-FM Pittsburgh, PA; WPGB(FM) Pittsburgh, PA; WXDX-FM Pittsburgh, PA; WBGG(AM) Pittsburgh, PA; WRAW Reading, PA; WBYL(FM) Salladasburg, PA; WBLJ-FM Shamokin, PA; WAKZ(FM) Sharpsville, PA; WKGB-FM Susquehanna, PA; WRAK Williamsport, PA; WHJJ Providence, RI; WHJY-FM Providence, RI; WWBB-FM Providence, RI; WKSP(FM) Aiken, SC; WYKZ(FM) Beaufort, SC; WLTY-FM Cayce, SC; WEZL-FM Charleston, SC; WALC-FM Charleston, SC; WLTQ(AM) Charleston, SC; WVOC Columbia, SC; WCOS Columbia, SC; WNOK(FM) Columbia, SC; WSCC-FM Goose Creek, SC; WLFJ(AM) Greenville, SC; WESC-FM Greenville, SC; WGVL Greenville, SC; WLVH-FM Hardeeville, SC; WBZT-FM Mauldin, SC; WRFQ-FM Mt. Pleasant, SC; WPCH(AM) North Augusta, SC; WXLY-FM North Charleston, SC; WXBT(FM) West Columbia, SC; WUSY-FM Cleveland, TN; WPTN Cookeville, TN; WHUB Cookeville, TN; WTJS Jackson, TN; WRVW-FM Lebanon, TN; WBMC McMinnville, TN; WAKI McMinnville, TN; WDIA Memphis, TN; WEGR(FM) Memphis, TN; WREC(AM) Memphis, TN; KJMS-FM Memphis, TN; WYNU-FM Milan, TN; WLAC Nashville, TN; WSIX-FM Nashville, TN; WKXJ(FM) Signal Mountain, TN; WMAX-FM South Pittsburg, TN; WTZX Sparta, TN; WSMT Sparta, TN; WKZP(FM) Spencer, TN; KYYW(AM) Abilene, TX; KEYJ-FM Abilene, TX; KSLI(AM) Abilene, TX; KFGL(FM) Abilene, TX; KULL-FM Abilene, TX; KIXZ Amarillo, TX; KMML-FM Amarillo, TX; KMXJ-FM Amarillo, TX; KATP(FM) Amarillo, TX; KASE-FM Austin, TX; KVET-FM Austin, TX; KPEZ-FM Austin, TX; KLVI Beaumont, TX; KYKR-FM Beaumont, TX; KLUB-FM Bloomington, TX; KVNS(AM) Brownsville, TX; KTEX-FM Brownsville, TX; KKYS-FM Bryan, TX; KNFX-FM Bryan, TX; KTUX-FM Carthage, TX; KUNO Corpus Christi, TX; KRYS-FM Corpus Christi, TX; KMXR-FM Corpus Christi, TX; KFXR(AM) Dallas, TX; KDMX(FM) Dallas, TX; KZPS-FM Dallas, TX; KHKS-FM Denton, TX; KRPT(FM) Devine, TX; KAFX-FM Diboll, TX; KBFM(FM) Edinburg, TX; KHEY(AM) El Paso, TX; KPRR-FM El Paso, TX; KTSM(AM) El Paso, TX; KDGE(FM) Fort Worth, TX; KEGL-FM Fort Worth, TX; KHFI-FM Georgetown, TX; KCOL-FM Groves, TX; KBRQ(FM) Hillsboro, TX; KPWW-FM Hooks, TX; KPRC Houston, TX; KODA-FM Houston, TX; KTRH Houston, TX; KHMX-FM Houston, TX; KTBZ-FM Houston, TX; KKRW-FM Houston, TX; KBME Houston, TX; KBGE(AM) Kilgore, TX; KKTX-FM Kilgore, TX; KIIZ-FM Killeen, TX; KKCL-FM Lorenzo, TX; KKAM Lubbock, TX; KQBR(FM) Lubbock, TX; KFYO Lubbock, TX; KYKS-FM Lufkin, TX; KAGG(FM) Madisonville, TX; KHKZ(FM) Mercedes, TX; KCRS(AM) Midland, TX; KCHX(FM) Midland, TX; KQXX-FM Mission, TX; KFZX-FM Monahans, TX; KSFA Nacogdoches, TX; KLFX-FM Nolanville, TX; KMRK-FM Odessa, TX; KKMY-FM Orange, TX; KIOC-FM Orange, TX; KSAB-FM Robstown, TX; KFMK-FM Round Rock, TX; WOAI San Antonio, TX; KQXT-FM San Antonio, TX; KTKR San Antonio, TX; KXXM-FM San Antonio, TX; KNCN-FM Sinton, TX; KKYR-FM Texarkana, TX; KTYL-FM Tyler, TX; KNUE(FM) Tyler, TX; KQVT(FM) Victoria, TX; KIXS-FM Victoria, TX; KBGO(FM) Waco, TX; KWTX Waco, TX; KWTX-FM Waco, TX; WACO-FM Waco, TX; KISX-FM Whitehouse, TX; KNIN-FM Wichita Falls, TX; KWFS Wichita Falls, TX; KBZS(FM) Wichita Falls, TX; KJMY(FM) Bountiful, UT; KXRV(FM) Centerville, UT; KALL(AM) North Salt Lake City, UT; KNRS Salt Lake City, UT; KODJ-FM Salt Lake City, UT; KZHT(FM) Salt Lake City, UT; KOSY-FM Spanish Fork, UT; WYYD-FM Amherst, VA; WSNZ(FM) Appomattox, VA; WCHV Charlottesville, VA; WKAV Charlottesville, VA; WCJZ(FM) Charlottesville, VA; WSUH(FM) Crozet, VA; WACL-FM Elkton, VA; WFQX-FM Front Royal, VA; WKCY Harrisonburg, VA; WVGM Lynchburg, VA; WROV-FM Martinsville, VA; WOWI-FM Norfolk, VA; WKUS(FM) Norfolk, VA; WRVQ-FM Richmond, VA; WRVA Richmond, VA; WRNL Richmond, VA; WBTJ(FM) Richmond, VA; WTVR-FM Richmond, VA; WZBL(FM) Roanoke, VA; WGMN Roanoke, VA; WHTE-FM Ruckersville, VA; WSNV(FM) Salem, VA; WKDW Staunton, VA; WCYK-FM Staunton, VA; WKSI-FM Stephens City, VA; WJJS-FM Vinton, VA; WKCI(AM) Waynesboro, VA; WTFX(AM) Winchester, VA; WJCD(FM) Windsor, VA; WAZR-FM Woodstock, VA; WEZF-FM Burlington, VT; WCVR-FM Randolph, VT; WWWT Randolph, VT; WSYB Rutland, VT; WTSM(FM) Springfield, VT; WMXR-FM Woodstock, VT; KNBQ(FM) Centralia, WA; KELA Centralia-Chehalis, WA; KMNT(FM) Chehalis, WA; KFNK(FM) Eatonville, WA; KQSN(FM) Naches, WA; KIXZ-FM Opportunity, WA; KOLW(FM) Othello, WA; KEYW-FM Pasco, WA; KFLD Pasco, WA; KJR Seattle, WA; KUBE-FM Seattle, WA; KPTQ(AM) Spokane, WA; KKZX-FM Spokane, WA; KQNT(AM) Spokane, WA; KHHO Tacoma, WA; KDBL(FM) Toppenish, WA; KRVO(FM) Vancouver, WA; KXRX-FM Walla Walla, WA; KUTI(AM) Yakima, WA; KIT Yakima, WA; WISM-FM Altoona, WI; WQRB-FM Bloomer, WI; WATQ(FM) Chetek, WI; WBIZ Eau Claire, WI; WIBA Madison, WI; WTSO Madison, WI; WMEQ(AM) Menomonie, WI; WQBW(FM) Milwaukee, WI; WISN Milwaukee, WI; WRIT-FM Milwaukee, WI; WOKY Milwaukee, WI; WKKV-FM Racine, WI; WMAD(FM) Sauk City, WI; WXXM(FM) Sun Prairie, WI; WMIL-FM Waukesha, WI; WMRE Charles Town, WV; WVHU(AM) Huntington, WV; WTCR-FM Huntington, WV; WTCR Kenova, WV; WAMX-FM Milton, WV; WZZW Milton, WV; WHNK(AM) Parkersburg, WV; WDMX-FM Vienna, WV; WEGW-FM Wheeling, WV; WBBD Wheeling, WV; WWVA(AM) Wheeling, WV; KIGN(FM) Burns, WY; KKTL Casper, WY; KTWO Casper, WY; KTRS-FM Casper, WY; KWYY-FM Casper, WY; KLEN-FM Cheyenne, WY; KQLF(FM) Cheyenne, WY; KOWB Laramie, WY; KCGY(FM) Laramie, WY; KRVK(FM) Midwest, WY; KGAB Orchard Valley, WY; WSMJ(FM) Baltimore, MD; WPOC-FM Baltimore, MD; WCAO Baltimore, MD; WTNT(AM) Bethesda, MD; WFMD(AM) Frederick, MD; WFRE(FM) Frederick, MD; WWFG-FM Ocean City, MD; WDKZ(FM) Salisbury, MD; WTGM Salisbury, MD; WSBY-FM Salisbury, MD; WOSC-FM Bethany Beach, DE; WDOV Dover, DE; WLBW-FM Fenwick Island, DE; WDSD-FM Smyrna, DE; WILM Wilmington, DE; WWTX(AM) Wilmington, DE; XETRA Tijuana, MEX

Stns: 35 TV. WXXA-TV, Albany-Schenectady-Troy, NY; KGET-TV, Bakersfield, CA; WIVT, Binghamton, NY; WKRC, Cincinnati, OH; WETM, Elmira, NY; KMTR, Eugene, OR; KMTX, Eugene, OR; KMTZ, Eugene, OR; KVIQ, Eureka, CA; KTVF, Fairbanks, AK; KGPE, Fresno-Visalia, CA; WHP-TV, Harrisburg-Lancaster-Lebanon-York, PA; WJKT, Jackson, TN; WTEV-TV, Jacksonville, FL; WAWS, Jacksonville, FL; KLRT, Little Rock-Pine Bluff, AR; KASN, Little Rock-Pine Bluff, AR; WPTY, Memphis, TN; WLMT, Memphis, TN; WPMI-TV, Mobile, AL-Pensacola (Ft. Walton Beach), FL; WJTC, Mobile, AL-Pensacola (Ft. Walton Beach), FL; KION-TV, Monterey-Salinas, CA; WHAM-TV, Rochester, NY; KTVX, Salt Lake City, UT; WOAI-TV, San Antonio, TX; KFTY, San Francisco-Oakland-San Jose; KCOY, Santa Barbara-Santa Maria-San Luis Obispo, CA; KVOS, Seattle-Tacoma, WA; WSYR-TV, Syracuse, NY; KTFO, Tulsa, OK; KOKI, Tulsa, OK; WWTI, Watertown, NY; KSAS-TV, Wichita-Hutchinson Plus, KS; KAAS, Wichita-Hutchinson Plus, KS; KBDK, Wichita-Hutchinson Plus, KS

L. Lowry Mays, chmn; Mark P. Mays, pres/CEO; Randall T. Mays, exec VP; Kenneth E. Wyker, sr VP; Herbert W. Hill Sr., sr VP; Don Perry, exec VP.

Coast Radio Company Inc. 600 E. Main St., Vacaville, CA 95688. Phone: (707) 446-0200. Fax: (707) 446-0122. Ownership: James E. Levitt, 35.3% voting interest; John F. Levitt, 35.3% voting interest; Lauren Leigh Levitt 1996 Trust, James E. Levitt, trustee, 7.35% voting interest; Joseph Curtis Levitt 1996 Trust, James E. Levitt, trustee, 7.35% voting interest; Jessica Nicole Sanders 1996 Trust, John F. Levitt, trustee, 7.35% voting interest; and John Patrick Levitt 1996 Trust, John F. Levitt, trustee, 7.35% voting interest.

Stns: 3 FM. KKIQ-FM Livermore, CA; KUIC-FM Vacaville, CA; KKDV(FM) Walnut Creek, CA

Cogeco Radio-Television Inc. 612 St. Jacques, Suite 100, Montreal, PQ H3C 5R1. Canada. Phone: (514) 390-6035. Fax: (514) 390-6070. Ownership: Cogeco Inc., 100%.

Stns: 4 FM. CJMF-FM Quebec, PQ; CJEC-FM Quebec, PQ; CFGE-FM Sherbrooke, PQ; CJEB-FM Trois Rivieres, PQ

Stns: 1 TV. CFAP, Quebec City, PQ

Rene Guimond, pres/CEO; Luc Doyon, VP; Therese David, VP; Guy Meunier, sls VP; Jacques Boiteau, gen mgr; Geoffrey O. Brow, gen mgr.

Cohan Radio Group Inc. 3750 US 27N, Suite 1, Sebring, FL 33870. Phone: (863) 382-9999. Fax: (863) 382-1982. E-mail: cohanradiogroup@htn.net. Web Site: www.cohanradiogroup.com.

Stns: 3 AM. 2 FM. WWOJ(FM) Avon Park, FL; WWTK(AM) Lake Placid, FL; WWLL(FM) Sebring, FL; WITS(AM) Sebring, FL; WJCM(AM) Sebring, FL

Peter L. Coughlin, pres.

Columbia Gorge Broadcasters Inc. Box 360, Hood River, OR 97031. Phone: (541) 386-1511. Fax: (541) 386-7155. Web Site: www.kihrk105.com. E-mail: gary@gorgeradio.com.

Stns: 2 AM. KIHR Hood River, OR; KACI The Dalles, OR

Greg Walden, pres; Mylene Walden, VP; Gary Grossman, gen mgr.

Combined Communications Box 5037, Bend, OR 97708. Phone: (541) 382-5263. Fax: (541) 388-0456. E-mail: mcheney@bendradio.com. Web Site: www.klrr.com.

Broadcasting & Cable Yearbook 2006

D-8

Stns: 1 AM. 2 FM. KBND Bend, OR; KTWS(FM) Bend, OR; KMTK(FM) Bend, OR

Chuck Chackel, pres.

Combined Media Group Inc. Box 789, Wynne, AR 72396. Phone: (870) 238-8141. Fax: (870) 238-5997. Ownership: Bobby Caldwell, 45%; Timothy B. Scott, 45%; and Scott Siler, 10%. Note: Bobby Caldwell owns 50% of Arkansas County Broadcasters Inc. (see listing) and 100% of East Arkansas Broadcasters Inc. (see listing).

Stns: 2 AM. KPOC(AM) Pocahontas, AR; KRLW Walnut Ridge, AR

Tim Scott, gen mgr.

Commonwealth Broadcasting Corp. 113 W. Public Sq., Suite 400, Glasgow, KY 42141. Phone: (270) 659-2002. Fax: (270) 651-1771. Ownership: Steven W. Newberry, Vickie V. Newberry.

Stns: 9 AM. 14 FM. WBRT Bardstown, KY; WTCO Campbellsville, KY; WCKQ-FM Campbellsville, KY; WPTQ(FM) Cave City, KY; WIEL Elizabethtown, KY; WTSZ(AM) Eminence, KY; WTSZ-FM Eminence, KY; WOVO(FM) Glasgow, KY; WCDS(AM) Glasgow, KY; WGRK-FM Greensburg, KY; WAKY Greensburg, KY; WKMO-FM Hodgenville, KY; WHHT(FM) Horse Cave, KY; WLBN Lebanon, KY; WLSK-FM Lebanon, KY; WTHX(FM) Lebanon Junction, KY; WTTL Madisonville, KY; WYMV(FM) Madisonville, KY; WAVJ-FM Princeton, KY; WPKY Princeton, KY; WWKY(FM) Providence, KY; WAKY-FM Springfield, KY; WRZI-FM Vine Grove, KY

Steven W. Newberry, pres/CEO; W. Dale Thornhill, exec VP.

Communications Capital Managers LLC 1111 Michigan Ave., Suite 301, East Lansing, MI 48823-1096. Phone: (517) 351-3333. Fax: (517) 351-4481.

Stns: 5 AM. 4 FM. WMCD(FM) Claxton, GA; WDXQ(AM) Cochran, GA; WDXQ-FM Cochran, GA; WPTB(AM) Statesboro, GA; WWNS Statesboro, GA; WSYL Sylvania, GA; KPCH-FM Dubach, LA; KRUS Ruston, LA; KNBB-FM Ruston, LA

Michael Oesterle, CEO; Deb Grugen, CFO.

Community Radio Network Inc. Box 446, Monticello, AR 71657. Phone: (870) 367-6854. Fax: (870) 367-9564. E-mail: crn@ccc-cable.net.

Stns: 1 AM. 1 FM. KXSA-FM Dermott, AR; KHBM Monticello, AR

P.Q. Gardner, pres; Brooke Lathan, stn mgr.

Connoisseur Media LLC 136 Main St., Suite 202, Westport, CT 06880-3304. Phone: (203) 227-1978. Ownership: CM Broadcast Management LLC, mgng member, 100% votes.

Stns: 3 FM. WVWN(FM) Heyworth, IL; WVMG(FM) Normal, IL; WDNQ(FM) Kenova, WV

Contemporary Communications 9408 Grand Gate St., Las Vegas, NV 89143. Phone: (702) 898-4669. Fax: (208) 567-6865. E-mail: contemporary@cox.net. Ownership: Larry G. Fuss, 100%.

Stns: 1 AM. 2 FM. KKHJ(FM) Pago Pago, AS; WKXY(FM) Clarksdale, MS; WROX Clarksdale, MS

Larry Fuss, pres.

Convergent Broadcasting LLC 1766 Washington Ave., Portland, ME 04103-1624. Phone: (207) 878-0095. Ownership: Housatonic Micro Fund SBIC LP, 58.27%; Housatonic Equity Investors SBIC LP, 36.79%; Daniel Duman, 1.975%; George Silverman, 1.975%; and Bruce A. Biette, .99%.

Stns: 7 FM. WYND-FM Hatteras, NC; WFMZ(FM) Hertford, NC; WVOD(FM) Manteo, NC; WZPR(FM) Nags Head, NC; KPUS(FM) Gregory, TX; KJKE(FM) Ingleside, TX; KKPN(FM) Rockport, TX

Corus Entertainment Inc. 630 3rd Ave. S.W., Suite 105, Calgary, AB T2P 4L4. Canada. Phone: (403) 444-4244. Fax: (403) 444-4242. Web Site: www.corusent.com. Ownership: J.R. Shaw controls an aggregate of 80% of the voting rights.

Stns: 20 AM. 20 FM. CFGQ-FM Calgary, AB; CKRY-FM Calgary, AB; CKNG-FM Edmonton, AB; CISN-FM Edmonton, AB; CHED Edmonton, AB; CKNW New Westminster, BC; CHMJ(AM) Vancouver, BC; CJOB Winnipeg, MB; CIQB-FM Barrie, ON; CHAY-FM Barrie, ON; CFNY-FM Brampton, ON; CJXY-FM Burlington, ON; CJDV-FM Cambridge, ON; CKCB-FM Collingwood, ON; CJSS-FM Cornwall, ON; CFLG-FM Cornwall, ON; CJUL(AM) Cornwall, ON; CJOY Guelph, ON; CHML Hamilton, ON; CFMK-FM Kingston, ON; CFFX(AM) Kingston, ON; CFPL London, ON; CILQ-FM North York, ON; CKRU Peterborough, ON; CFHK-FM St. Thomas, ON; CFMJ(AM) Toronto, ON; CKDK-FM Woodstock, ON; CJRC(AM) Gatineau, PQ; CFOM-FM Levis, PQ; CHMP-FM Longueuil, PQ; CFEL-FM Montmagny, PQ; CINW(AM) Montreal, PQ; CKAC Montreal, PQ; CHRC Quebec, PQ; CKRS(AM) Saguenay, PQ; CIME-FM Saint Jerome, PQ; CHLT Sherbrooke, PQ; CKTS Sherbrooke, PQ; CHLN Trois Rivieres, PQ; CINF(AM) Verdun, PQ

Stns: 3 TV. CKWS, Kingston, ON; CHEX-TV-2, Oshawa, ON; CHEX, Peterborough, ON

John M. Cassaday, pres.

Coshocton Broadcasting Co. 114 N. Sixth St., Coshocton, OH 43812. Phone: (740) 622-1560. Fax: (740) 622-7940. Ownership: Bruce Wallace, 100%.

Stns: 1 AM. 1 FM. WTNS Coshocton, OH; WKLM-FM Millersburg, OH

Bruce Wallace, pres & gen mgr.

Costa-Eagle Radio Ventures L.P. 462 Merrimack St., Methuen, MA 01844. Phone: (978) 686-9966. Fax: (978) 687-1180. Web Site: www.ceradio.com. E-mail: pcosta@ceradio.com. Ownership: Costa Communications, 51%; and Cambridge Acquisitions, 49%.

Stns: 3 AM. WCCM(AM) Haverhill, MA; WNNW(AM) Lawrence, MA; WCEC(AM) Salem, NH

Cox Enterprises Inc. 6205 Peachtree Dunwoody Rd., Atlanta, GA 30328. Phone: (678) 645-0000. Web Site: www.coxenterprises.com. Ownership: Dayton Cox Trust-A, Barbara Cox Anthony, Anne Cox Chambers and Richard L. Braunstein, trustees, 41.06368% votes; Anne Cox Chambers Atlanta Trust, Barbara Cox Anthony, trustee, 28.94032% votes; and Barbara Cox Anthony Atlanta Trust, Anne Cox Chambers, trustee, 28.94032% votes.

Stns: 13 AM. 64 FM. WZZK-FM Birmingham, AL; WBPT(FM) Birmingham, AL; WAGG(AM) Birmingham, AL; WZZK(AM) Birmingham, AL; WNCB(FM) Homewood, AL; WBHJ-FM Tuscaloosa, AL; WBHK-FM Warrior, AL; WEZN-FM Bridgeport, CT; WPLR-FM New Haven, CT; WNLK(AM) Norwalk, CT; WEFX-FM Norwalk, CT; WKHL-FM Stamford, CT; WFYV-FM Atlantic Beach, FL; WHQT-FM Coral Gables, FL; WCFB-FM Daytona Beach, FL; WSUN-FM Holiday, FL; WMXQ-FM Jacksonville, FL; WOKV Jacksonville, FL; WAPE-FM Jacksonville, FL; WJGL(FM) Jacksonville, FL; WPYO(FM) Maitland, FL; WHDR(FM) Miami, FL; WFLC-FM Miami, FL; WEDR-FM Miami, FL; WDUV-FM New Port Richey, FL; WDBO Orlando, FL; WHTQ-FM Orlando, FL; WMMO-FM Orlando, FL; WXGL(FM) Saint Petersburg, FL; WPOI(FM) Saint Petersburg, FL; WHPT(FM) Sarasota, FL; WWRM(FM) Tampa, FL; WSB Atlanta, GA; WSB-FM Atlanta, GA; WBTS(FM) Doraville, GA; WFOX(FM) Gainesville, GA; WALR-FM La Grange, GA; KCCN-FM Honolulu, HI; KRTR(AM) Honolulu, HI; KINE-FM Honolulu, HI; KRTR-FM Kailua, HI; KPHW(FM) Kaneohe, HI; KKNE(AM) Waipahu, HI; WSFR-FM Corydon, IN; WVEZ(FM) Louisville, KY; WPTI(FM) Louisville, KY; WRKA-FM Saint Matthews, KY; WBAB(FM) Babylon, NY; WGBB Freeport, NY; WBLI-FM Patchogue, NY; WHFM-FM Southampton, NY; WHIO Dayton, OH; WHKO-FM Dayton, OH; WDPT(FM) Piqua, OH; WZLR(FM) Xenia, OH; KRTQ-FM Sand Springs, OK; KRAV-FM Tulsa, OK; KRMG Tulsa, OK; KJSR-FM Tulsa, OK; KWEN-FM Tulsa, OK; WJMZ-FM Anderson, SC; WHZT(FM) Seneca, SC; KTHT(FM) Cleveland, TX; KHPT(FM) Conroe, TX; KONO-FM Helotes, TX; KLDE(FM) Lake Jackson, TX; KKBQ-FM Pasadena, TX; KKYX San Antonio, TX; KONO San Antonio, TX; KISS-FM San Antonio, TX; KCYY(FM) San Antonio, TX; KSMG(FM) Seguin, TX; KELZ-FM Terrell Hills, TX; WDYL-FM Chester, VA; WKHK-FM Colonial Heights, VA; WKLR-FM Fort Lee, VA; WMXB-FM Richmond, VA

Stns: 13 TV. WSB, Atlanta; WSOC-TV, Charlotte, NC; WAXN-TV, Charlotte, NC; WHIO, Dayton, OH; KFOX, El Paso, TX; WJAC, Johnstown-Altoona, PA; WRDQ, Orlando-Daytona Beach-Melbourne, FL; WFTV, Orlando-Daytona Beach-Melbourne, FL; WPXI, Pittsburgh, PA; KTVU, San Francisco-Oakland-San Jose; KICU, San Francisco-Oakland-San Jose; KIRO, Seattle-Tacoma, WA; WTOV-TV, Wheeling, WV-Steubenville, OH

Cox Enterprises Inc. owns the following daily newspapers: The (Grand Junction, CO) *Daily Sentinel; Palm Beach* (FL) *Daily News* and *The Palm Beach* (FL) *Post; The Atlanta* (GA) *Journal & Constitution; The Daily Advance* (Elizabeth City), *The* (Greenville) *Daily Reflector* and the *Rocky Mount Telegram*, all NC; *Dayton Daily News* and the *Springfield News-Sun*, both OH; *Austin American-Statesman, Longview News-Journal, The Lufkin Daily News, News Messenger* (Marshall), *The* (Nacogdoches) *Daily Sentinel* and the *Waco Tribune-Herald*, all TX. Cox also owns weekly newspapers and shoppers in CO, FL, NC, OH, and TX.

James C. Kennedy, chmn/CEO; Dennis Berry, pres; Andrew S. Fisher, pres & Cox Television; Robert F. Neil, pres/CEO & Cox Radio Inc..

Crain Media Group LLC 200 S. Commerce, Suite 702, Little Rock, AR 72201. Phone: (501) 537-0720. Fax: (501) 537-0722. Ownership: Crain Investments, 100%.

Stns: 3 AM. 4 FM. KAPZ Bald Knob, AR; KCNY(FM) Bald Knob, AR; KAWW(AM) Heber Springs, AR; KAWW-FM Heber Springs, AR; KSMD(FM) Pangburn, AR; KWCK Searcy, AR; KWCK-FM Searcy, AR

Crain publishes 22 trade magazines including *Advertising Age*.

Paul Coates, gen mgr; Phil Weaver, gen mgr.

Crawford Broadcasting Co. Box 3003, Blue Bell, PA 19422. Phone: (215) 628-3500. Fax: (215) 628-0818. Web Site: www.crawfordbroadcasting.com. Ownership: Donald B. Crawford is sole owner of all the stns except WMUZ(FM), WRDT(AM), WEXL(AM), KJSL(AM) and KSTL(AM). WMUZ(FM), WRDT(AM), WEXL(AM), KJSL(AM) and KSTL(AM) are owned by Donald B. Crawford and Dean A. Crawford.

Stns: 17 AM. 11 FM. WYDE(AM) Birmingham, AL; WDJC-FM Birmingham, AL; WXJC(AM) Birmingham, AL; WXJC-FM Cordova, AL; WYDE-FM Cullman, AL; KBRT Avalon, CA; KLDC Brighton, CO; KCMN Colorado Springs, CO; KLTT Commerce City, CO; KLZ Denver, CO; KLVZ(AM) Denver, CO; KCBR Monument, CO; WYCA(FM) Crete, IL; WYRB(FM) Genoa, IL; WSRB(FM) Lansing, IL; WPWX(FM) Hammond, IN; WMUZ-FM Detroit, MI; WRDT(AM) Monroe, MI; WEXL Royal Oak, MI; KJSL Saint Louis, MO; KSTL Saint Louis, MO; WDCD(AM) Albany, NY; WDCX-FM Buffalo, NY; WPTR(FM) Clifton Park, NY; WLGZ(AM) Rochester, NY; WRCI(FM) Webster, NY; KKPZ(AM) Portland, OR; KAAM(AM) Garland, TX

Donald B. Crawford, pres/CEO.

Criswell Communications Box 619000, Dallas, TX 75261-9000. Phone: (817) 792-3800. Fax: (817) 277-9929. E-mail: kcbi@kcbi.org. Web Site: www.kcbi.org.

Stns: 1 AM. 3 FM. KSYE-FM Frederick, OK; KCBI(FM) Dallas, TX; KCRN San Angelo, TX; KCRN-FM San Angelo, TX

Ronald L. Harris, exec VP; Dr. Jerry Johnson, pres.

The Cromwell Group Inc. Cromwell Radio Group and Affiliates. Box 150846, Nashville, TN 37215. Phone: (615) 361-7560. Fax: (615) 366-4313. Ownership: Bayard H. Walters, 100%.

Stns: 6 AM. 12 FM. WCBH-FM Casey, IL; WWGO-FM Charleston, IL; WCRA Effingham, IL; WZUS(FM) Macon, IL; WMCI-FM Mattoon, IL; WHQQ(FM) Neoga, IL; WEJT-FM Shelbyville, IL; WZNX(FM) Sullivan, IL; WPMB Vandalia, IL; WKRV-FM Vandalia, IL; WLME(FM) Cannelton, IN; WTCJ Tell City, IN; WKCM Hawesville, KY; WVJS(AM) Owensboro, KY; WBIO(FM) Philpot, KY; WCTZ Clarksville, TN; WQZQ-FM Dickson, TN; WBUZ(FM) La Vergne, TN

Bayard H. Walters, pres; Thomas Crocker, CFO.

Crossroads Communications Inc. 1301 Ohio St., Terre Haute, IN 47807. Phone: (812) 234-9770. Fax: (812) 238-1576. E-mail: wsdm@wsdm.com. Ownership: Michael A. Petersen, 53%; Dan T. Lacy, 47%.

Stns: 2 AM. 2 FM. WSDX(AM) Brazil, IN; WSDM-FM Brazil, IN; WAXI-FM Rockville, IN; WBOW(AM) Terre Haute, IN

Michael A. Petersen, pres/gen mgr; Dan Lacy, CFO.

Cumulus Media Inc. 3535 Piedmont Rd., Atlanta, GA 30305. Phone: (404) 949-0700. Fax: (404) 949-0740. E-mail: bill@cumulusb.com. Web Site: www.cumulus.com.

Chicago, IL 60601. Cumulus Broadcasting Inc., 875 N. Michigan Ave., Suite 3650. Phone: (312) 867-0091. Fax: (312) 867-0098.

Stns: 77 AM. 178 FM. WVNN Athens, AL; WYOK-FM Atmore, AL; WDLT-FM Chickasaw, AL; WDLT Fairhope, AL; WUMP Madison, AL; WGOK Mobile, AL; WBLX-FM Mobile, AL; WHHY-FM Montgomery, AL; WMSP Montgomery, AL; WNZZ Montgomery, AL; WXFX-FM Prattville, AL; KQSM-FM Bentonville, AR; KFAY Farmington, AR; KKEG-FM Fayetteville, AR; KBBQ-FM Fort Smith, AR; KYNF(FM) Prairie Grove, AR; KAMO-FM Rogers, AR; KMCK-FM Siloam Springs, AR; KZRA Springdale, AR; KLSZ-FM Van Buren, AR; KMGQ(FM) Goleta, CA; KRUZ(FM) Santa Barbara, CA; KVYB(FM) Santa Barbara, CA; KVEN Ventura, CA; KHAY-FM Ventura, CA; KBBY-FM Ventura, CA; KKNN-FM Delta, CO; KEKB-FM Fruita, CO; KEXO Grand Junction, CO; KBKL(FM) Grand Junction, CO; KMXY-FM Grand Junction, CO; WICC Bridgeport, CT; WINE Brookfield, CT; WEBE-FM Westport, CT; WFTW Fort Walton Beach, FL; WZNS-FM Fort Walton Beach, FL; WYZB-FM Mary Esther, FL; WINT(AM) Melbourne, FL; WNCV-FM Niceville, FL; WCOA Pensacola, FL; WHKR-FM Rockledge, FL; WSJZ-FM Sebastian, FL; WGLF(FM) Tallahassee, FL; WHBT(AM) Tallahassee, FL; WHBX(FM) Tallahassee, FL; WGPC Albany, GA; WALG Albany, GA; WWLD(FM) Cairo, GA; WQVE-FM Camilla, GA; WPEZ(FM) Jeffersonville, GA; WJAD-FM Leesburg, GA; WMAC Macon, GA; WLZN(FM) Macon, GA; WDEN-FM Macon, GA; WAYS(AM) Macon, GA; WIFN(FM) Macon, GA; WDDO Macon, GA; WPRW-FM

Martinez, GA; WMGB(FM) Montezuma, GA; WEGC-FM Sasser, GA; WEAS-FM Savannah, GA; WBMQ Savannah, GA; WZAT-FM Savannah, GA; WJCL-FM Savannah, GA; WJLG Savannah, GA; WIXV-FM Savannah, GA; WTYB(FM) Springfield, GA; WZBN(FM) Sylvester, GA; WJOD-FM Asbury, IA; KQCS(FM) Bettendorf, IA; KOEL-FM Cedar Falls, IA; KHAK-FM Cedar Rapids, IA; KDAT(FM) Cedar Rapids, IA; KJOC Davenport, IA; KLYV-FM Dubuque, IA; WDBQ Dubuque, IA; KXGE-FM Dubuque, IA; KCRR(FM) Grundy Center, IA; KRNA-FM Iowa City, IA; KBEA-FM Muscatine, IA; KOEL(AM) Oelwein, IA; KKHQ-FM Oelwein, IA; WXXQ-FM Freeport, IL; WDBQ-FM Galena, IL; KBOB-FM Geneseo, IL; WKGL-FM Loves Park, IL; WXLP-FM Moline, IL; WZOK-FM Rockford, IL; WROK Rockford, IL; KCHZ(FM) Ottawa, KS; KQTP-FM Saint Marys, KS; KMAJ Topeka, KS; KTOP Topeka, KS; KWIC-FM Topeka, KS; WCYN-FM Cynthiana, KY; WXZZ-FM Georgetown, KY; WVLK Lexington, KY; WLTO-FM Nicholasville, KY; WLRO-FM Richmond, KY; KQLK(FM) De Ridder, LA; KYKZ-FM Lake Charles, LA; KAOK Lake Charles, LA; KBIU(FM) Lake Charles, LA; KQHN(FM) Oil City, LA; KRMD-FM Shreveport, LA; KMJJ-FM Shreveport, LA; KVMA-FM Shreveport, LA; KKGB-FM Sulphur, LA; WEZQ-FM Bangor, ME; WQCB-FM Brewer, ME; WDEA Ellsworth, ME; WBZN-FM Old Town, ME; WKFR-FM Battle Creek, MI; WWCK Flint, MI; WDZZ-FM Flint, MI; WKMI Kalamazoo, MI; WTWR-FM Monroe, MI; WMHG(AM) Muskegon, MI; WRSR-FM Owosso, MI; WRKR-FM Portage, MI; KDHL Faribault, MN; KRFO Owatonna, MN; KFIL Preston, MN; KOLM(AM) Rochester, MN; KROC(AM) Rochester, MN; KLCX-FM Saint Charles, MN; KVGO-FM Spring Valley, MN; KYBA-FM Stewartville, MN; KOQL-FM Ashland, MO; KPLA(FM) Columbia, MO; KFRU Columbia, MO; KBXR(FM) Columbia, MO; KBBM(FM) Jefferson City, MO; KLIK(AM) Jefferson City, MO; KJMO(FM) Jefferson City, MO; KMJK(FM) Lexington, MO; KRWP(FM) Stockton, MO; WSMS(FM) Artesia, MS; WKOR-FM Columbus, MS; WJWF(AM) Columbus, MS; WKOR(AM) Starkville, MS; WSSO(AM) Starkville, MS; WRCQ-FM Dunn, NC; WFNC Fayetteville, NC; WAAV Leland, NC; WFNC-FM Lumberton, NC; WKQB-FM Southern Pines, NC; WMNX-FM Wilmington, NC; WWQQ-FM Wilmington, NC; WGNI-FM Wilmington, NC; KKCT-FM Bismarck, ND; KACL(FM) Bismarck, ND; KLXX Bismarck-Mandan, ND; WRRB(FM) Arlington, NY; WCZX-FM Hyde Park, NY; WPDA-FM Jeffersonville, NY; WKNY Kingston, NY; WKXP(FM) Kingston, NY; WALL Middletown, NY; WFAF(FM) Mount Kisco, NY; WDBY(FM) Patterson, NY; WEOK Poughkeepsie, NY; WFAS(AM) White Plains, NY; WZAD-FM Wurtsboro, NY; WRQN-FM Bowling Green, OH; WRQK-FM Canton, OH; WRWK(FM) Delta, OH; WXKR-FM Port Clinton, OH; WSOM Salem, OH; WWWM-FM Sylvania, OH; WTOD Toledo, OH; WLQR Toledo, OH; WBBW Youngstown, OH; KOMS-FM Poteau, OK; KEHK-FM Brownsville, OR; KUJZ(FM) Creswell, OR; KSCR(AM) Eugene, OR; KZEL-FM Eugene, OR; KUGN Eugene, OR; WTCY Harrisburg, PA; WTPA-FM Mechanicsburg, PA; WWIZ-FM Mercer, PA; WLLF-FM Mercer, PA; WWKL(FM) Palmyra, PA; WPIC Sharon, PA; WSEA(FM) Atlantic Beach, SC; WIQB(AM) Conway, SC; WYNN Florence, SC; WXJY-FM Georgetown, SC; WSYN-FM Georgetown, SC; WHSC Hartsville, SC; WWFN-FM Lake City, SC; WCMG-FM Latta, SC; WYMB Manning, SC; WHLZ(FM) Marion, SC; WMXT-FM Pamplico, SC; WDAI-FM Pawley's Island, SC; WYAK-FM Surfside Beach, SC; KYBB(FM) Canton, SD; KIKN-FM Salem, SD; KXRB(AM) Sioux Falls, SD; KSOO(AM) Sioux Falls, SD; WNFN(FM) Belle Meade, TN; WRQQ(FM) Goodlettsville, TN; WQQK-FM Hendersonville, TN; WWTN-FM Manchester, TN; WSM-FM Nashville, TN; WHRP(FM) Tullahoma, TN; KQIZ-FM Amarillo, TX; KPUR Amarillo, TX; KTLT(FM) Anson, TX; KIKR Beaumont, TX; KQXY-FM Beaumont, TX; KTCX-FM Beaumont, TX; KFNC(FM) Beaumont, TX; KOOC(FM) Belton, TX; KYYI-FM Burkburnett, TX; KZRK-FM Canyon, TX; KPUR-FM Canyon, TX; KARX(FM) Claude, TX; KSSM(FM) Copperas Cove, TX; KSTB-FM Crystal Beach, TX; KOLI-FM Electra, TX; KCDD(FM) Hamlin, TX; KUSJ(FM) Harker Heights, TX; KHXS-FM Merkel, TX; KMND Midland, TX; KBAT(FM) Midland, TX; KGEE-FM Monahans, TX; KBED(AM) Nederland, TX; KRIL Odessa, TX; KODM-FM Odessa, TX; KKLY(FM) Pecos, TX; KAYD-FM Silsbee, TX; KTEM Temple, TX; KLTD-FM Temple, TX; KBCY(FM) Tye, TX; KLUR-FM Wichita Falls, TX; KQXC-FM Wichita Falls, TX; KIOL(FM) Willis, TX; WBRW-FM Blacksburg, VA; WFNR Blacksburg, VA; WFNR-FM Christiansburg, VA; WPSK-FM Pulaski, VA; WRAD Radford, VA; WJLW-FM Allouez, WI; WDUZ-FM Brillion, WI; WPCK(FM) Denmark, WI; WQLH-FM Green Bay, WI; WDUZ(AM) Green Bay, WI; WOGB-FM Kaukauna, WI; WNAM Neenah-Menasha, WI; WPKR-FM Omro, WI; WOSH Oshkosh, WI; WWWX-FM Oshkosh, WI

Richard W. Denning, chmn; Lewis W. Dickey Jr., VP.

The Curators of the University of Missouri (Business Services Division). University of Missouri, 316 University Hall, Columbia, MO 65211. Phone: (573) 882-2388. Fax: (573) 882-0010. Web Site: www.umsystem.edu. Ownership: (Business Services Division).

Stns: 5 FM. KBIA(FM) Columbia, MO; KCUR-FM Kansas City, MO; KMNR-FM Rolla, MO; KUMR-FM Rolla, MO; KWMU-FM Saint Louis, MO

Stns: 1 TV. KOMU, Columbia-Jefferson City, MO

Michael Dunn, gen mgr; Martin Siddall, gen mgr.

Curtis Media Group 3012 Highwoods Blvd., Raleigh, NC 27604. Phone: (919) 876-0674. Fax: (919) 790-8369. Web Site: www.curtismedia.com. Ownership: Donald W. Curtis.

Stns: 7 AM. 4 FM. WPCM Burlington, NC; WDNC(AM) Durham, NC; WKIX(FM) Goldsboro, NC; WFMC Goldsboro, NC; WGBR Goldsboro, NC; WWNF(FM) Kinston, NC; WYRN(AM) Louisburg, NC; WWMY(FM) Raleigh, NC; WDNZ(AM) Raleigh, NC; WBBB-FM Raleigh, NC; WCLY Raleigh, NC

Donald W. Curtis, pres/CEO.

D

DCBroadcasting Inc. Box 1009, Jasper, IN 47547-1009. Phone: (812) 634-9232. Fax: (812) 482-3696. E-mail: pknies@psci.net. Web Site: www.dcbroadcasting.com.

Stns: 1 AM. 4 FM. WBDC(FM) Huntingburg, IN; WRZR-FM Loogootee, IN; WORX-FM Madison, IN; WXGO Madison, IN; WAXL-FM Santa Claus, IN

Paul Knies, pres; Caroline Knies, VP; Giesla Knies Schepers, sec.

DFWU Inc. 1101 N. 81 Hwy., Marlow, OK 73055. Phone: (580) 658-9292. Fax: (580) 658-2561. E-mail: kfxi@texhoma.net. Web Site: www.kfxi.com.

Stns: 1 AM. 2 FM. KFXI-FM Marlow, OK; KVLH Pauls Valley, OK; KIXO-FM Sulphur, OK

K.D. Austin, pres & gen mgr.

DMC Broadcasting Inc. Box 1914, Taos, NM 87571. Phone: (505) 758-4491. Fax: (505) 758-4452. Ownership: Darren Cordova, 100%.

Stns: 3 FM. KKIT-FM Angel Fire, NM; KKTC(FM) Taos, NM; KXMT(FM) Taos, NM

Dailey Corp. Box 10, New Martinsviille, WV 26155. Phone: (304) 455-1111. Fax: (304) 455-1170. Web Site: www.powercountry104.com. Ownership: Calvin E. Dailey Jr., 100%.

Stns: 1 AM. 1 FM. WETZ New Martinsville, WV; WYMJ(FM) New Martinsville, WV

Calvin Dailey Jr., pres.

Dakota Communications Ltd. Box 364, Pierre, SD 57501. Phone: (605) 224-5434. Ownership: Duane D. Butt, 50%; and Barbara G. Butt, 50%.

Stns: 4 AM. KIUL Garden City, KS; KFLA Scott City, KS; KIJV Huron, SD; KOKK Huron, SD

Davidson Media Group LLC 1812 Davie Ave., Statesville, NC 28677. Phone: (704) 873-4802. Fax: (704) 873-4803. Ownership: CapStreet II L.P., 38.51% of votes, 38.6% of total assets; Citicorp North America Inc., 32.74% of votes, 32.81% of total assets; Black Enterprise/Greenwich Street Corporate Growth Partners L.P., 10.91% of votes, 10.94% of total assets.

Stns: 18 AM. 4 FM. KAKS(FM) Huntsville, AR; WXCT(AM) Southington, CT; KCZZ(AM) Mission, KS; WSPR Springfield, MA; WACM West Springfield, MA; WMKM Inkster, MI; KLBP(AM) Brooklyn Park, MN; KLBB Saint Paul, MN; WCXN Claremont, NC; WTIK Durham, NC; WSTS-FM Fairmont, NC; WWBG Greensboro, NC; WSGH Lewisville, NC; WNOW Mint Hill, NC; WTOB Winston-Salem, NC; WKKB(FM) Middletown, RI; WAKX-FM Narragansett Pier, RI; WBZK York, SC; WNSG Nashville, TN; WMDB Nashville, TN; WTOX(AM) Glen Allen, VA; WVXX(AM) Norfolk, VA

Davis Broadcasting Inc. 2203 Wynnton Rd., Columbus, GA 31906. Phone: (706) 576-3565. Fax: (706) 576-3683. Web Site: www.foxie105.com. Ownership: Gregory A. Davis, 76%.

Stns: 2 AM. 4 FM. WKZJ(FM) Eufaula, AL; WEAM-FM Buena Vista, GA; WLKQ-FM Buford, GA; WOKS Columbus, GA; WEAM Columbus, GA; WIOL(FM) Greenville, GA

Gregory A. Davis, pres/CEO.

Deer Creek Broadcasting LLC 2225 First Ave., Napa, CA 94558. Phone: (707) 226-2309. Ownership: Elliot B. Evers, 43.75% of votes, 12.08% of total assets; Duff Ackerman & Goodrich QP Fund II L.P., 26.89% of votes, 7.43% of total assets; John McSorley, 12.49% of votes, 3.45% of total assets; Greg D. Widroe, 12.49% of votes, 3.45% of total assets; Duff Ackerman & Goodrich II L.P., 2.55% of votes, 0.70% of total assets; DAG GP Fund II LLC, 1.53% of votes, 0.42% of total assets; and DAG II Partners Fund LLC, 0.30% of votes, 0.08% of total assets.

Stns: 1 AM. 4 FM. KMXI-FM Chico, CA; KPAY Chico, CA; KHHZ(FM) Oroville, CA; KHSL-FM Paradise, CA; WIZN-FM Vergennes, VT

Delmarva Broadcasting Co. Box 7492, 2727 Shipley Rd., Wilmington, DE 19803. Phone: (302) 478-2700. Fax: (302) 478-0100. E-mail: business@dbc1.com. Web Site: www.delmarvabroadcasting.com. Ownership: Steinman

Stns: 2 AM. 7 FM. WXCY(FM) Havre de Grace, MD; WQJZ-FM Ocean Pines, MD; WXMD(FM) Pocomoke City, MD; WICO(AM) Salisbury, MD; WXJN-FM Lewes, DE; WNCL(FM) Milford, DE; WAFL-FM Milford, DE; WDEL Wilmington, DE; WSTW-FM Wilmington, DE

Lancaster Inteligencer-Journal & *New Era*, Lancaster, PA, have the same ownership (Steinman) as Delmarva Broadcasting Co.

Stations (operated independently).

Julian H. Booker, pres/CEO.

Dickey Broadcasting Co. 3535 Piedmont Rd., Bldg. 14, Suite 1200, Atlanta, GA 30305. Phone: (404) 688-0068. Fax: (404) 995-4045. Web Site: www.680thefan.com.

Stns: 3 AM. WALR Atlanta, GA; WFOM Marietta, GA; WCNN North Atlanta, GA

David W. Dickey, pres/CEO.

Dierking Communications Inc. 1212 Eleventh Rd., Marysville, KS 66508. Phone: (785) 562-2361. Fax: (785) 562-2188. E-mail: kndy@diodecom.net.

Stns: 2 AM. KNDY Marysville, KS; KQNK Norton, KS

Bruce Dierking, gen mgr & pres.

Dispatch Broadcast Group 770 Twin Rivers Dr., Columbus, OH 43215. Phone: (614) 460-3700. Fax: (614) 460-2809. Web Site: www.10tv.com. Ownership: Dispatch Printing Company

Stns: 1 AM. 1 FM. WBNS Columbus, OH; WBNS-FM Columbus, OH

Stns: 2 TV. WBNS, Columbus, OH; WTHR, Indianapolis, IN

Owns *The Columbus* (OH) *Dispatch, This Week* & *Ohio Magazine.*

Tamara J. Clapsaddle, controller; Michael J. Fiorile, pres.

Dockins Communications Inc. 540 Maple Valley Dr., Farmington, MO 63640. Phone: (573) 701-9590. Fax: (573) 701-9696. Ownership: Fred Dockins Sr., 100%. Note: Fred Dockins Sr. also owns 100% of KPWB-AM-FM Piedmont, MO.

Stns: 1 AM. 2 FM. KTNX(FM) Arcadia, MO; KYLS Fredericktown, MO; KYLS-FM Ironton, MO

Dos Costas Communications Corp. 1818 S. Australian Ave., Suite 102, West Palm Beach, FL 33409. Phone: (561) 655-6615. Ownership: Roland A. Ulloa, 100%.

Stns: 3 FM. KDUC-FM Barstow, CA; KXXZ-FM Barstow, CA; KDUQ-FM Ludlow, CA

Roland A. Ulloa, pres; Jime Garza, VP/gen mgr.

Double O Radio Corp. 625 Madison Ave., 3rd Fl., New York, NY 10022. Phone: (212) 486-4446. Ownership: Double O Corp., 100%.

Stns: 2 AM. 12 FM. WAKT-FM Callaway, FL; WPFM-FM Panama City, FL; WASJ(FM) Panama City Beach, FL; WRBA(FM) Springfield, FL; WDHI-FM Delhi, NY; WIYN-FM Deposit, NY; WBKT-FM Norwich, NY; WCHN Norwich, NY; WKXZ-FM Norwich, NY; WZOZ-FM Oneonta, NY; WDLA Walton, NY; WDLA-FM Walton, NY; WWNQ(FM) Forest Acres, SC; WWNU(FM) Irmo, SC

DreamCatcher Communications Inc. 114 S. Manchester Ave., West Union, OH 45693. Phone: (937) 544-9722. Fax: (937) 544-5523. E-mail: c103@lycos.com. Ownership: Donald Bowles, 50%; Venita Bowles, 50%.

Stns: 1 AM. 1 FM. WFLE Flemingsburg, KY; WRAC-FM West Union, OH

Don Bowles, pres/CEO; Ted Foster, stn mgr.

Duhamel Broadcasting Enterprises Box 1760, Rapid City, SD 57709. Phone: (605) 342-2000. Fax: (605) 342-7305. Web Site: www.kotatv.com. Ownership: William F. Duhamel, 63%; Peter A. and Lois G. Duhamel, 37%.

Stns: 1 AM. 1 FM. KOTA Rapid City, SD; KDDX(FM) Spearfish, SD

Stns: 4 TV. KDUH, Cheyenne, WY-Scottsbluff, NE; KHSD-TV, Rapid City, SD; KOTA-TV, Rapid City, SD; KSGW-TV, Rapid City, SD

William F. Duhamel, pres.

Durham Radio Inc. 1200 Airport Blvd., Suite 207, Oshawa, ON L1J 8P5. Canada. Phone: (905) 428-9600. Fax: (905) 571-1150. Ownership: Douglas E. Kirk; 80%, Mary Kirk 15%.

Stns: 1 AM. 2 FM. CJKX-FM Ajax, ON; CIWV-FM Hamilton, ON; CKDO Oshawa, ON

Douglas E. Kirk, chmn/pres; Steve Kassay, VP opns; Steve Macaulay, VP sls; Lill Bolton, admin dir.

E

EMF Broadcasting 5700 West Oaks Blvd., Rocklin, CA 95765. Phone: (916) 251-1600. Fax: (916) 251-1650. Web Site: www.emfbroadcasting.com. Ownership: Educational Media Foundation, 100%. Educational Media Foundation is a nonprofit, nonstock corporation, governed by a seven-member board of directors.

Stns: 4 AM. 154 FM. KAKL(FM) Anchorage, AK; KBGR(FM) Beebe, AR; KLMZ(FM) Fouke, AR; KLRO(FM) Hot Springs, AR; KJLV(FM) Hoxie, AR; KJBR-FM Marked Tree, AR; KKLT(FM) Texarkana, AR; KKLV(FM) Turrell, AR; KLFS(FM) Van Buren, AR; KLVA(FM) Casa Grande, AZ; KLVK(FM) Fountain Hills, AZ; KAIH(FM) Lake Havasu City, AZ; KAIC(FM) Tucson, AZ; KVID(FM) Barstow, CA; KBNF(FM) Chester, CA; KARQ(FM) East Sonora, CA; KLVY-FM Fairmead, CA; KLVG(FM) Garberville, CA; KLVS(FM) Grass Valley, CA; KHRI(FM) Hollister, CA; KLVJ-FM Julian, CA; KDRH(FM) King City, CA; KHKL(FM) Laytonville, CA; KLVN(FM) Livingston, CA; KLVC-FM Magalia, CA; KMJC-FM Mount Shasta, CA; KPCO Quincy, CA; KGBM(FM) Randsburg, CA; KLVB(FM) Red Bluff, CA; KKRO(FM) Redding, CA; KAIS(FM) Redwood Valley, CA; KLVH(FM) San Luis Obispo, CA; KSRI(FM) Santa Cruz, CA; KLVR-FM Santa Rosa, CA; KQKL(FM) Selma, CA; KGLV(FM) Shafter, CA; KYLU(FM) Tehachapi, CA; KYKL(FM) Tracy, CA; KULV(FM) Ukiah, CA; KXRD-FM Victorville, CA; KARA(FM) Williams, CA; KLRD-FM Yucaipa, CA; KLCQ(FM) Eaton, CO; KLHV(FM) Fort Collins, CO; KLXV(FM) Glenwood Springs, CO; KLFV(FM) Grand Junction, CO; KLRY(FM) Gypsum, CO; KHCO(FM) Hayden, CO; KFDN(FM) Lakewood, CO; KLDV(FM) Morrison, CO; KLBV(FM) Steamboat Springs, CO; KLZV(FM) Sterling, CO; WKVH(FM) Monticello, FL; WVRI(FM) Pavo, GA; KILV(FM) Castana, IA; KLRX(FM) Wapello, IA; KAIO(FM) Idaho Falls, ID; KARJ(FM) Kuna, ID; KLRI(FM) Rigby, ID; WCLR(FM) Arlington Heights, IL; WSRI(FM) Sugar Grove, IL; WSOH(FM) New Washington, IN; WJLR-FM Seymour, IN; KAIG(FM) Dodge City, KS; KTLI-FM El Dorado, KS; KWBI(FM) Great Bend, KS; WRVG(FM) Georgetown, KY; WKVY(FM) Somerset, KY; WXKY-FM Stanford, KY; KLXA-FM Alexandria, LA; KWDF Ball, LA; WQCK-FM Clinton, LA; KIKL(FM) Lafayette, LA; WKMY(FM) Winchendon, MA; WAKL(FM) Flint, MI; WWZP(FM) Freeland, MI; KMKL(FM) North Branch, MN; KKLW(FM) Willmar, MN; KLRQ(FM) Clinton, MO; WKVF(FM) Byhalia, MS; WKNZ-FM Collins, MS; KQLU(FM) Belgrade, MT; KLRV(FM) Billings, MT; KRFR(FM) Bozeman, MT; KHLV(FM) Helena, MT; KLKM(FM) Kalispell, MT; KBIL(FM) Park City, MT; WZRI(FM) Spring Lake, NC; KNRI(FM) Bismarck, ND; KDJZ(FM) Harwood, ND; KLJA(FM) Jamestown, ND; KVLQ(FM) Lincoln, ND; KLNB(FM) Grand Island, NE; KMLV(FM) Ralston, NE; KLJV(FM) Scottsbluff, NE; KFLV(FM) Wilber, NE; KVLK(FM) Belen, NM; KQLV(FM) Bosque Farms, NM; KLLU(FM) Gallup, NM; KLGQ(FM) Grants, NM; KRLU(FM) Roswell, NM; KQRI(FM) Socorro, NM; KAIZ(FM) Mesquite, NV; KLRH(FM) Sparks, NV; WKVU(FM) Utica, NY; WLKP(FM) Belpre, OH; WYKL(FM) Crestline, OH; WJYC(FM) Delhi Hills, OH; WOKL(FM) Troy, OH; KKVO-FM Altus, OK; KWRI(FM) Bartlesville, OK; KARU(FM) Cache, OK; KKRD(FM) Enid, OK; KWKL(FM) Grandfield, OK; KYLV-FM Oklahoma City, OK; KKRI(FM) Pocola, OK; KTKL(FM) Stigler, OK; KLOY(FM) Astoria, OR; KVLB(FM) Bend, OR; KLVP-FM Cherryville, OR; KIDH(FM) Jordan Valley, OR; KKLJ(FM) Klamath Falls, OR; KKLP(FM) La Pine, OR; KGRI(FM) Lebanon, OR; KLON(FM) Rockaway Beach, OR; KJKL(FM) Selma, OR; KLVU-FM Sweet Home, OR; KLVP(AM) Tigard, OR; KAIK(FM) Tillamook, OR; KZRI(FM) Welches, OR; KLOV(FM) Winchester, OR; WKVC(FM) North Myrtle Beach, SC; KLRJ(FM) Aberdeen, SD; WPLX(AM) Germantown, TN; WKVZ(FM) Ripley, TN; KXLV(FM) Amarillo, TX; KXRI(FM) Amarillo, TX; KLRW(FM) Byrne, TX; KKLM(FM) Corpus Christi, TX; KLOW(FM) Dripping Springs, TX; KXCR-FM El Paso, TX; KVLZ(FM) Gatesville, TX; KKLU(FM) Lubbock, TX; KZLV(FM) Lytle, TX; KPOS(FM) Post, TX; KFRI(FM) Stanton, TX; KLVW(FM) West Odessa, TX; KNKL(FM) North Ogden, UT; KAER(FM) Saint George, UT; KSBC(FM) Nile, WA; KLOP(FM) Ocean Park, WA; KRKL(FM) Walla Walla, WA; WDKL(FM) Grafton, WV; WKVW(FM) Marmet, WV; WLKV(FM) Ripley, WV; KLWC(FM) Casper, WY; KLWV(FM) Chugwater, WY; KAIW(FM) Laramie, WY

Richard Jenkins, pres; Lloyd Parker, gen mgr; Mike Novak, VP progmg.

Eagle Bluff Enterprises 932 County Rd. 448, Poplar Bluff, MO 63901. Phone: (573) 686-3700.

Stns: 2 AM. 2 FM. KACE(AM) Birch Tree, MO; KFEB(FM) Campbell, MO; KOEA-FM Doniphan, MO; KDFN Doniphan, MO

Steven C. Fuch, pres.

Eagle Communications Group 2703 Hall St., Suite 15, Hays, KS 67601. Phone: (785) 625-4000. Fax: (785) 625-8030. Web Site: www.eaglecom.net. Ownership: Eagle Communications Inc. Employee Stock Ownership Trust. Cable TV.

Stns: 6 AM. 12 FM. KVGB Great Bend, KS; KVGB-FM Great Bend, KS; KHAZ-FM Hays, KS; KJLS-FM Hays, KS; KKQY-FM Hill City, KS; KHOK-FM Hoisington, KS; KHUT-FM Hutchinson, KS; KWBW Hutchinson, KS; KHMY(FM) Pratt, KS; KSKG-FM Salina, KS; KFEQ(AM) Saint Joseph, MO; KSFT Saint Joseph, MO; KSJQ(FM) Savannah, MO; KAAQ(FM) Alliance, NE; KCOW Alliance, NE; KQSK(FM) Chadron, NE; KELN-FM North Platte, NE; KOOQ North Platte, NE

Eagle's Nest Inc. Box 710, Roanoke, AL 36274. Phone: (334) 863-4139. Fax: (334) 863-2540. Web Site: www.eagle1023.com. Ownership: Jim Vice, 51%; Kay Vice, 49%.

Stns: 2 AM. WELR Roanoke, AL; WLAG La Grange, GA

Jim Vice, pres.

Earls Broadcasting Co. 202 Courtney St., Branson, MO 65616. Phone: (417) 334-6003. Fax: (417) 334-7141. Web Site: www.komc.com.

Stns: 1 AM. 1 FM. KOMC Branson, MO; KOMC-FM Kimberling City, MO

Charles C. Earls, CEO; Scottie Earls, gen mgr; Scott Earls, pres.

East Carolina Radio Group 2422 S. Wrightsville Ave., Nags Head, NC 27959. Phone: (252) 449-8331. Fax: (252) 449-8354. Web Site: www.ecri.net.

Stns: 3 AM. 3 FM. WRSF(FM) Columbia, NC; WERX-FM Columbia, NC; WZBO(AM) Edenton, NC; WCNC(AM) Elizabeth City, NC; WKJX(FM) Elizabeth City, NC; WOBX(AM) Wanchese, NC

Rick Loesch, pres.

East Kentucky Broadcasting Corp. Box 2200, Pikeville, KY 41502. Phone: (606) 437-4051. Fax: (606) 432-2809. E-mail: wpke@wpke.com. Web Site: www.wdhr.com. Ownership: Walter E. May; Pamela May; Keith Casebolt

Stns: 3 AM. 3 FM. WPKE-FM Coal Run, KY; WEKB(AM) Elkhorn City, KY; WDHR-FM Pikeville, KY; WLSI Pikeville, KY; WPKE Pikeville, KY; WZLK-FM Virgie, KY

Walter E. May, pres; Keith Casebolt, gen mgr.

East Kentucky Radio Network Inc. Box 2200, Pikeville, KY 41502. Phone: (606) 437-4051. Fax: (606) 432-2809. Ownership: Walter E. May; Pamela May; Keith Casebolt.

Stns: 2 AM. WPRT Prestonsburg, KY; WBTH Williamson, WV

Walter E. May, pres; Keith Casebolt, VP; Pamela May, sec/treas.

East Texas Broadcasting Inc. Box 990, Mount Pleasant, TX 75456. Phone: (903) 572-8726. Fax: (903) 572-7232. Ownership: John Mitchell; Bud Kitchens.

Stns: 2 AM. 5 FM. KIMP(AM) Mount Pleasant, TX; KOYN-FM Paris, TX; KPLT Paris, TX; KBUS(FM) Paris, TX; KSCN(FM) Pittsburg, TX; KSCH-FM Sulphur Springs, TX; KALK(FM) Winfield, TX

John Mitchell, chmn; Bud Kitchens, pres; Bob Gibson, VP.

Eastern Broadcasting Group Inc. 92 Middlesex Ct., Slingerlands, NY 12159. Phone: (518) 439-3982. Fax: (518) 439-2866. E-mail: quickmickg@aol.com. Ownership: Michael J. Sbuttoni, 100%.

Stns: 3 AM. WNRR(AM) Augusta, GA; WYSR(AM) High Point, NC; WCEO(AM) Columbia, SC

Michael J. Sbuttoni, pres.

Edwards Communications L.C. 125 Eagles Nest Dr., Seneca, SC 29678. Phone: (864) 882-3272. Fax: (864) 882-3718. Ownership: Steve Edwards, 50%; Jerry Edwards, 50%

Stns: 3 AM. 5 FM. WHSB-FM Alpena, MI; WIDL-FM Caro, MI; WKYO Caro, MI; WWTH(FM) Oscoda, MI; WHAK Rogers City, MI; WHAK-FM Rogers City, MI; KTAK-FM Riverton, WY; KVOW Riverton, WY

Jerry Edwards, pres; Steve Edwards Jr., VP.

Elyria-Lorain Broadcasting Co. Box 4006, Elyria, OH 44036. Phone: (440) 322-3761. Fax: (440) 284-3189. Ownership: Lorain County Printing & Publishing Co., 100%.

Stns: 2 AM. 1 FM. WEOL Elyria, OH; WKFM-FM Huron, OH; WLKR(AM) Norwalk, OH

Lorain County Printing & Publishing Co. publishes *Chronicle-Telegram* (Elyria) and *Medina Gazette* (Medina), both OH.

Gary L. Kneisley, pres.

Emmis Communications Corp. 3500 W. Olive Ave.,, Suite 1450, Burbank, CA 91436. Phone: (818) 238-9154. Fax: (818) 238-9158. Web Site: www.emmis.com. Ownership: Jeffrey H. Smulyan, approximately 61% votes.

Stns: 2 AM. 21 FM. KKFR-FM Glendale, AZ; KPWR-FM Los Angeles, CA; KZLA-FM Los Angeles, CA; WKQX-FM Chicago, IL; WLUP-FM Chicago, IL; WRDA(FM) Jerseyville, IL; WYXB(FM) Indianapolis, IN; WIBC(AM) Indianapolis, IN; WLHK(FM) Shelbyville, IN; WTHI-FM Terre Haute, IN; WWVR-FM West Terre Haute, IN; KSHE(FM) Crestwood, MO; KFTK(FM) Florissant, MO; KIHT-FM Saint Louis, MO; KPNT-FM Sainte Genevieve, MO; WRKS(FM) New York, NY; WQHT-FM New York, NY; WQCD(FM) New York, NY; KLBJ Austin, TX; KGSR-FM Bastrop, TX; KROX-FM Buda, TX; KDHT(FM) Cedar Park, TX; KBPA(FM) San Marcos, TX

Stns: 25 TV. KBIM, Albuquerque-Santa Fe, NM; KREZ, Albuquerque-Santa Fe, NM; KRQE, Albuquerque-Santa Fe, NM; WSAZ-TV, Charleston-Huntington, WV; WFTX, Ft. Myers-Naples, FL; WLUK-TV, Green Bay-Appleton, WI; KGMD, Hilo, HI; KHAW, Hilo, HI; KHON-TV, Honolulu, HI; KGMB, Honolulu, HI; WALA-TV, Mobile, AL-Pensacola (Ft. Walton Beach), FL; WBPG, Mobile, AL-Pensacola (Ft. Walton Beach), FL; WVUE, New Orleans, LA; KMTV, Omaha, NE; WKCF, Orlando-Daytona Beach-Melbourne, FL; KOIN, Portland, OR; WTHI, Terre Haute, IN; KSNT, Topeka, KS; KGUN, Tucson (Sierra Vista), AZ; KAII, Wailuku, HI; KGMV, Wailuku, HI; KSNW, Wichita-Hutchinson Plus, KS; KSNC, Wichita-Hutchinson Plus, KS; KSNG, Wichita-Hutchinson Plus, KS; KSNK, Wichita-Hutchinson Plus, KS

The publishing unit of Emmis Communications publishes seven magazines: *Allanta Magazine, Cincinnati Magazine, Los Angeles Magazine, Wildlife Journal, Indianapolis Monthly* and *Texas Monthly*.

Rick Cummings, pres; Randy Bongarten, pres.

Empire Broadcasting Corp. Box 995, San Jose, CA 95108. Phone: (408) 293-8030. Fax: (408) 293-6124. Web Site: www.kliv.com. Ownership: Robert Kieve, Vincent Lopopolo, Myron S. Lewis.

Stns: 1 AM. 1 FM. KRTY-FM Los Gatos, CA; KLIV San Jose, CA

Robert Kieve, pres; John McLeod, progmg VP.

Emporia's Radio Stations Inc. Box 968, Emporia, KS 66801. Phone: (620) 342-1400. Fax: (620) 342-0804. Ownership: Steve Sauder, 100%.

Stns: 1 AM. 1 FM. KVOE Emporia, KS; KVOE-FM Emporia, KS

Lea Firestone, pres; Lee Schroeder, gen mgr.

Encore Broadcasting L.L.C. 3303 N. Midkiff, Suite 115, Midland, TX 79705. Phone: (432) 520-9912. Fax: (432) 520-0112. Ownership: Tommy R. Vascocu, 52.16%; C.R. Bailey, 9.33%; Wagner Family Partnership VI, 9.3%; Larry Daniels, 8.18%; MKO Enterprises, 7.83%; R.F. Bailey, 4.4%; Eastern Exploration, 4.4%; and James J. Woodcock, 4.4%.

Stns: 1 AM. 7 FM. KKCN(FM) Ballinger, TX; KQRX-FM Midland, TX; KHKX(FM) Odessa, TX; KMCM-FM Odessa, TX; KELI-FM San Angelo, TX; KGKL San Angelo, TX; KGKL-FM San Angelo, TX; KNRX(FM) Sterling City, TX

Entercom Communications Corp. 401 City Ave.,, Suite 809, Bala-Cynwyd, PA 19004. Phone: (610) 660-5610. Fax: (610) 660-5620. Web Site: www.entercom.com. Ownership: Joseph M. Field.

Stns: 31 AM. 62 FM. KSSJ-FM Fair Oaks, CA; KRXQ-FM Sacramento, CA; KSEG-FM Sacramento, CA; KWOD-FM Sacramento, CA; KCTC Sacramento, CA; KDND(FM) Sacramento, CA; KEZW Aurora, CO; KQMT(FM) Denver, CO; KOSI-FM Denver, CO; KALC(FM) Denver, CO; WKTK-FM Crystal River, FL; WSKY-FM Micanopy, FL; WTPI-FM Indianapolis, IN; KDGS(FM) Andover, KS; KFH-FM Clearwater, KS; KFBZ(FM) Haysville, KS; KUDL-FM Kansas City, KS; KXTR(AM) Kansas City, KS; KKHK(AM) Kansas City, KS; KQRC-FM Leavenworth, KS; KFH(AM) Wichita, KS; KNSS(AM) Wichita, KS; KEYN-FM Wichita, KS; WKBU(FM) Kenner, LA; WEZB-FM New Orleans, LA; WTKL-FM New Orleans, LA; WSMB New Orleans, LA; WWL(AM) New Orleans, LA; WRKO Boston, MA; WEEI Boston, MA; WQSX(FM) Lawrence, MA; WVEI(AM) Worcester, MA;

KMBZ Kansas City, MO; KCSP(AM) Kansas City, MO; KRBZ(FM) Kansas City, MO; KYYS-FM Kansas City, MO; WDAF-FM Liberty, MO; WQMG-FM Greensboro, NC; WPET Greensboro, NC; WSMW(FM) Greensboro, NC; WJMH-FM Reidsville, NC; WMQX-FM Winston-Salem, NC; WWKB Buffalo, NY; WWWS Buffalo, NY; WGR Buffalo, NY; WBEN Buffalo, NY; WFKL(FM) Fairport, NY; WKSE-FM Niagara Falls, NY; WBZA(FM) Rochester, NY; WBEE-FM Rochester, NY; WLKK(FM) Wethersfield Township, NY; KRSK(FM) Molalla, OR; KFXX(AM) Portland, OR; KYCH-FM Portland, OR; KGON-FM Portland, OR; KSLM Salem, OR; WFEZ(FM) Avoca, PA; WGGI-FM Benton, PA; WDMT(FM) Pittston, PA; WGGY-FM Scranton, PA; WBZU(AM) Scranton, PA; WKRF(FM) Tobyhanna, PA; WKZN(AM) West Hazleton, PA; WKRZ-FM Wilkes-Barre, PA; WILK Wilkes-Barre, PA; WEEI-FM Westerly, RI; WOLI-FM Easley, SC; WYRD Greenville, SC; WOLT-FM Greer, SC; WSPA(AM) Spartanburg, SC; WORD(AM) Spartanburg, SC; WMBZ(FM) Germantown, TN; WRVR-FM Memphis, TN; WWTQ(AM) Memphis, TN; WWDE-FM Hampton, VA; WNVZ-FM Norfolk, VA; WVKL-FM Norfolk, VA; WPTE-FM Virginia Beach, VA; KNRK-FM Camas, WA; KIRO Seattle, WA; KISW-FM Seattle, WA; KQBZ-FM Seattle, WA; KTTH(AM) Seattle, WA; KNDD-FM Seattle, WA; KMTT-FM Tacoma, WA; KBSG-FM Tacoma, WA; KKSN(AM) Vancouver, WA; WOLX-FM Baraboo, WI; WMYX-FM Milwaukee, WI; WSSP(AM) Milwaukee, WI; WMMM-FM Verona, WI; WCHY(FM) Waunakee, WI; WXSS-FM Wauwatosa, WI

Joseph M. Field, chmn/CEO; David J. Field, pres/COO; John C. Donlevle, exec VP; Steve Fisher, sr VP; Eugene D. Levin, treas; Martin Hadfield, VP engrg; Deborah Kane, VP sls.

Entravision Communications Corp. 2425 Olympic Blvd., Suite 6000W, Santa Monica, CA 90404. Phone: (310) 447-3872. Fax: (310) 447-3899. E-mail: kthompson@entravision.com. Web Site: www.entravision.com. Ownership: Walter F. Ulloa, Philip W. Wilkinson, Paul Zevnik.

Stns: 13 AM. 41 FM. KVVA-FM Apache Junction, AZ; KMIA(AM) Black Canyon City, AZ; KDVA(FM) Buckeye, AZ; KLNZ-FM Glendale, AZ; KZLZ-FM Kearny, AZ; KRRN(FM) Kingman, AZ; KSSE(FM) Arcadia, CA; KSEH(FM) Brawley, CA; KCVR-FM Columbia, CA; KXSE(FM) Davis, CA; KWST(AM) El Centro, CA; KSSD(FM) Fallbrook, CA; KLOK-FM Greenfield, CA; KMXX-FM Imperial, CA; KCVR Lodi, CA; KRCX-FM Marysville, CA; KDLE(FM) Newport Beach, CA; KTSE-FM Patterson, CA; KLYY(FM) Riverside, CA; KBMB(FM) Sacramento, CA; KBRG(FM) San Jose, CA; KLOK San Jose, CA; KDLD(FM) Santa Monica, CA; KSES-FM Seaside, CA; KCCL-FM Shingle Springs, CA; KMBX(AM) Soledad, CA; KLOB-FM Thousand Palms, CA; KMIX-FM Tracy, CA; KSSC(FM) Ventura, CA; KPVW(FM) Aspen, CO; KMXA Aurora, CO; KJMN-FM Castle Rock, CO; KXPK-FM Evergreen, CO; WLQY Hollywood, FL; KRZY Albuquerque, NM; KRZY-FM Santa Fe, NM; KQRT(FM) Las Vegas, NV; KRNV-FM Reno, NV; KTCY(FM) Azle, TX; KKPS-FM Brownsville, TX; KVLY-FM Edinburg, TX; KINT-FM El Paso, TX; KHRO(AM) El Paso, TX; KYSE(FM) El Paso, TX; KOFX-FM El Paso, TX; KFRQ-FM Harlingen, TX; KGOL Humble, TX; KBZO Lubbock, TX; KZZA(FM) Muenster, TX; KZMP-FM Pilot Point, TX; KNVO-FM Port Isabel, TX; KZMP(AM) University Park, TX; KAIQ(FM) Wolfforth, TX; WACA Wheaton, MD

Stns: 17 TV. KLUZ, Albuquerque-Santa Fe, NM; WUNI, Boston (Manchester, NH); KORO, Corpus Christi, TX; KCEC, Denver, CO; KINT, El Paso, TX; KTFN, El Paso, TX; KNVO, Harlingen-Weslaco-Brownsville-McAllen, TX; WUVN, Hartford & New Haven, CT; KLDO, Laredo, TX; KINC, Las Vegas, NV; KSMS, Monterey-Salinas, CA; KUPB, Odessa-Midland, TX; WVEN-TV, Orlando-Daytona Beach-Melbourne, FL; KPMR, Santa Barbara-Santa Maria-San Luis Obispo, CA; WVEA-TV, Tampa-St. Petersburg (Sarasota), FL; WJAL, Washington, DC (Hagerstown, MD); KVYE, Yuma, AZ-El Centro, CA

Walter F. Ulloa, chmn/CEO; Philip Wilkinson, pres/COO; Larry Safir, exec VP.

Equicom Inc. 1240 E. Villa Maria, Bryan, TX 77802. Phone: (979) 776-1240. Fax: (979) 776-4700.

Stns: 1 AM. 2 FM. KTAM Bryan, TX; KXCS(FM) Cameron, TX; KZTR-FM Franklin, TX

Dan Ginzel, gen mgr.

Equity Communications LP 8025 Black Horse Pike, Bayport One, Suite 100-102, West Atlantic City, NJ 08232. Phone: (609) 484-8444. Fax: (609) 646-6331. E-mail: gfequity@aol.com. Web Site: 951wayv.com.

Stns: 2 AM. 7 FM. WAYV(FM) Atlantic City, NJ; WMID(AM) Atlantic City, NJ; WAIV(FM) Cape May, NJ; WGBZ(FM) Cape May Court House, NJ; WTTH(FM) Margate City, NJ; WZBZ(FM) Pleasantville, NJ; WZXL(FM) Wildwood, NJ; WCMC(AM) Wildwood, NJ; WDTH(FM) Wildwood Crest, NJ

Gary S. Fisher, pres.

Eureka Broadcasting Co. 1101 Marsh Rd., Eureka, CA 95501. Phone: (707) 442-5744. Ownership: Barbara Papstein, 50%; Hugo Papstein, 28%; and Brian Papstein, 22%.

Stns: 3 AM. 2 FM. KEKA-FM Eureka, CA; KINS Eureka, CA; KWSW Eureka, CA; KURY Brookings, OR; KURY-FM Brookings, OR

Hugo Papstein, gen mgr.

Evangel Ministries Inc. 1909 W. 2nd, Appleton, WI 54914. Phone: (920) 749-9456. Fax: (920) 749-0474. Web Site: www.christianfamilyradio.net.

Stns: 1 FM. WEMY-FM Green Bay, WI

Evanov Radio Group 5302 Dundas St. W., Toronto, ON M9B 1B2. Canada. Phone: (416) 213-1035. Fax: (416) 233-8617. Ownership: William Evanov, 83.9%; and Paul Evanov, 16.1%.

Stns: 1 AM. 3 FM. CKHZ-FM Halifax, NS; CIAO Brampton, ON; CKDX-FM Newmarket, ON; CIDC-FM Orangeville, ON

Bill Evanov, pres.

F

Fairfield Media Group Inc. 57 S. Court St., Fairfield, IA 52556. Phone: (641) 472-4191. Fax: (641) 472-2071. Web Site: www.radiovillage.com.

Stns: 2 AM. KMCD Fairfield, IA; KBIZ Ottumwa, IA

Jay Mitchell, pres.

Family Life Communications Inc. Box 35300, Tucson, AZ 85740. Phone: (520) 742-6976. Fax: (520) 742-6979. Web Site: www.flc.org. Ownership: All stns are owned by Family Life Communications Inc. A nonprofit, noncommercial Christian organization. No individual stockholders.

Stns: 4 AM. 9 FM. KFLR-FM Phoenix, AZ; KFLT Tucson, AZ; KFLT-FM Tucson, AZ; WUFN(FM) Albion, MI; WUNN(AM) Mason, MI; WUGN-FM Midland, MI; WUFL Sterling Heights, MI; KFLQ(FM) Albuquerque, NM; KWFL-FM Roswell, NM; KRGN-FM Amarillo, TX; KAMY(FM) Lubbock, TX; KFLB(AM) Odessa, TX; KFLB-FM Odessa, TX

Randy L. Carlson, pres; Michael Brinks, VP.

Family Life Network Box 506, Bath, NY 14810. Phone: (607) 776-4151. Fax: (607) 776-6929. E-mail: mail@fln.org. Web Site: www.fln.org. Ownership: Not-for-profit corporation.

Stns: 12 FM. WCOF(FM) Arcade, NY; WCIK-FM Bath, NY; WCIY-FM Canandaigua, NY; WCOV-FM Clyde, NY; WCIH-FM Elmira, NY; WCID-FM Friendship, NY; WCOT-FM Jamestown, NY; WCII-FM Spencer, NY; WCOU-FM Warsaw, NY; WCIG(FM) Carbondale, PA; WCOG-FM Galeton, PA; WCIT(FM) Trout Run, PA

Rick Snavely, pres/CEO.

Family Radio Network Inc. Box 957, Wilmington, NC 28402. Phone: (910) 763-2452. Fax: (910) 763-6578. E-mail: familyradio@familyradio.to. Web Site: www.familyradio.to.

Stns: 3 AM. 1 FM. WMYT Carolina Beach, NC; WWIL Wilmington, NC; WLSG(AM) Wilmington, NC; WDVV-FM Wilmington, NC

Family Stations Inc. 290 Hegenberger Rd., Oakland, CA 94621. Phone: (510) 568-6200. Fax: (510) 568-6190. Ownership: Nonprofit corporation.

Stns: 12 AM. 49 FM. WBFR-FM Birmingham, AL; KPHF-FM Phoenix, AZ; KFRB-FM Bakersfield, CA; KHAP(FM) Chico, CA; KFRJ(FM) China Lake, CA; KFRP(FM) Coalinga, CA; KECR El Cajon, CA; KFNO-FM Fresno, CA; KEFR-FM Le Grand, CA; KFRN Long Beach, CA; KEBR Rocklin, CA; KEDR-FM Sacramento, CA; KFRC San Francisco, CA; KHFR(FM) Santa Maria, CA; KFRS-FM Soledad, CA; KPRA-FM Ukiah, CA; KFRY(FM) Pueblo, CO; WCTF Vernon, CT; WMFL-FM Florida City, FL; WFTI-FM Saint Petersburg, FL; WWFR(FM) Stuart, FL; WFRC-FM Columbus, GA; KDFR(FM) Des Moines, IA; KEGR(FM) Fort Dodge, IA; KYFR Shenandoah, IA; WJCH-FM Joliet, IL; WQLZ(FM) Taylorville, IL; KPOR-FM Emporia, KS; WOFR(FM) Schoolcraft, MI; KFRD(FM) Butte, MT; KFRW(FM) Great Falls, MT; KBFR(FM) Bismarck, ND; WKDN-FM Camden, NJ; WFME-FM Newark, NJ; WFBF-FM Buffalo, NY; WFRH-FM Kingston, NY; WFRS-FM Smithtown, NY; WFRW-FM Webster, NY; WCUE Cuyahoga Falls, OH; WOTL-FM Toledo, OH; WYTN-FM Youngstown, OH; KYOR(FM) Newport, OR; KPFR(FM) Pine Grove, OR; KQFE-FM Springfield, OR; WUFR(FM) Bedford, PA; WEFR-FM Erie, PA; WFRJ-FM Johnstown, PA; WFCH-FM Charleston, SC; KKAA Aberdeen, SD; KQFR(FM) Rapid City, SD; KQKD Redfield, SD; KFRT(FM) Bay City, TX; KTXB-FM Beaumont, TX; KUFR-FM Salt Lake City, UT; KARR Kirkland, WA; KJVH-FM Longview, WA; WMWK-FM Milwaukee, WI; WJJO-FM Watertown, WI; WFSI-FM Annapolis, MD; WBGR Baltimore, MD; WBMD Baltimore, MD

Stns: 1 TV. WFME, New York

Harold Camping, pres.

Family Worship Center Church Inc. Box 262550, Baton Rouge, LA 70826. Phone: (225) 768-3224. Web Site: www.jsm.org. Ownership: Jimmy Swaggart, 8.33% vote; Frances Swaggart, 8.33% vote; Donnie Swaggart, 8.33% vote; Harold Lee, 8.33% vote; Peggy Lee, 8.33% vote; Clyde Fuller, 8.33% vote; Elizabeth Fuller, 8.33% vote; Roy Chacon, 8.33% vote; Beulah Chacon, 8.33% vote; Jack Daugherty, 8.33% vote; Barbara Studley, 8.33% vote; and Debbie Swaggart, 8.33% vote.

Stns: 5 AM. 10 FM. WQUA-FM Citronelle, AL; KNHD Camden, AR; KUUZ-FM Lake Village, AR; KPSH(FM) Coachella, CA; KBDD(FM) Winfield, KS; WJFM-FM Baton Rouge, LA; KTOC-FM Jonesboro, LA; WTGY-FM Charleston, MS; WJNS-FM Yazoo City, MS; WJYM Bowling Green, OH; KMFS(AM) Guthrie, OK; WAYB-FM Graysville, TN; WSTN Somerville, TN; KNRB(FM) Atlanta, TX; KALT(AM) Atlanta, TX

Jimmy Swaggart, pres; David Whitelaw, opns dir.

Fawcett Broadcasting Ltd. Box 777, Fort Frances, ON P9A 3N1. Canada. Phone: (807) 274-7580. Fax: (807) 274-8746. Ownership: Howard G. Fawcett, 100%.

Stns: 3 AM. 2 FM. CKDR-6 Atikokan, ON; CKDR Dryden, ON; CFOB-FM Fort Frances, ON; CJRL-FM Kenora, ON; CKDR-5 Red Lake, ON

E. P. Fawcett, chmn; H. G. Fawcett, pres.

Federated Media Box 2500, Elkhart, IN 46515. Phone: (574) 295-2500. Fax: (574) 294-4014.

Stns: 4 AM. 7 FM. WQHK-FM Decatur, IN; WBYT-FM Elkhart, IN; WTRC Elkhart, IN; WMEE-FM Fort Wayne, IN; WFWI-FM Fort Wayne, IN; WKJG(AM) Fort Wayne, IN; WOWO Fort Wayne, IN; WLEG(FM) Ligonier, IN; WAOR-FM Niles, MI; WNIL Niles, MI; WBYR-FM Van Wert, OH

Federated Media publishes *The* (Elkhart, IN) *Truth*.

John F. Dille III, pres.

Feller Broadcasting 3910 S. Southeastern Ave., Townhouse B, Sioux Falls, SD 57103. Phone: (605) 376-5844. Ownership: Nicholas J. Feller, 51%; and Robbie J. Feller, 49%.

Stns: 1 AM. 2 FM. KSQB-FM Dell Rapids, SD; KWSF(FM) Flandreau, SD; KSQB(AM) Sioux Falls, SD

The Findlay Publishing Co. 701 W. Sandusky St., Findlay, OH 45840. Phone: (419) 422-5151. Fax: (419) 422-2937. E-mail: daveglass@findlayoh.com.

Stns: 2 AM. 4 FM. WRBI-FM Batesville, IN; WCSI(AM) Columbus, IN; WINN(FM) Columbus, IN; WWWY(FM) North Vernon, IN; WKXA-FM Findlay, OH; WFIN Findlay, OH

The Findlay Publishing Co. publishes the *Findlay* (OH) *Courier*.

Karl Heminger, pres.

Finger Lakes Radio Group 3568 Lenox Rd., Geneva, NY 14456. Phone: (315) 781-7000. Fax: (315) 781-7700. Web Site: www.fingerlakes1.com.

Stns: 3 AM. WAUB Auburn, NY; WFLR Dundee, NY; WSFW Seneca Falls, NY

George Kimble, pres; Alan Bishop, VP/gen mgr.

First Broadcasting Investment Partners LLC c/o First Broadcasting LLC, 750 N. St. Paul, 10th Fl., Dallas, TX 75201. Phone: (214) 855-0002. Fax: (214) 855-5145. E-mail: info@firstbroadcasting.com. Web Site: www.firstbroadcasting.com. Ownership: Ronald Unkefer, Gary Lawrence, Alta Communications.

Stns: 8 AM. 7 FM. KXCL(FM) Placerville, CA; WAAM Ann Arbor, MI; WVIM-FM Coldwater, MS; WAXZ-FM Georgetown, OH; WOXY-FM Oxford, OH; WAOL-FM Ripley, OH; KEOR Atoka, OK; KCLE(AM) Cleburne, TX; KMGS(AM) Highland Park, TX; KJSA Mineral Wells, TX; KREL(AM) Quanah, TX; KAZZ(FM) Deer Park, WA; KBDB-FM Forks, WA; KBIS(AM) Forks, WA; WAMD Aberdeen, MD

Ronald Unkefer, chmn/CEO; Gary Lawrence, vice chmn & pres; Tom McMillin, CFO.

First Media Radio LLC 306 Port St., Easton, MD 21601. Phone: (410) 822-3301. Fax: (410) 822-0576.

Stns: 7 AM. 12 FM. WTRG(FM) Gaston, NC; WWDR(AM) Murfreesboro, NC; WZAX-FM Nashville, NC; WPWZ(FM) Pinetops, NC; WCBT Roanoke Rapids, NC; WPTM-FM Roanoke Rapids, NC; WRMT(AM) Rocky Mount, NC; WSMY Weldon, NC; WZWW-FM Bellefonte, PA; WOWQ(FM) DuBois, PA; WLAK-FM Huntingdon, PA; WMRF-FM

Broadcasting & Cable Yearbook 2006

D-12

Radio Group Ownership

Lewistown, PA; WIEZ Lewistown, PA; WWDW(FM) Alberta, VA; WWZW(FM) Buena Vista, VA; WYTT(FM) Emporia, VA; WREL Lexington, VA; WJLS-FM Beckley, WV; WEMD(AM) Easton, MD

Alex Kolobielski, pres/CEO.

First Natchez Radio Group Box 768, Natchez, MS 39121. Phone: (601) 442-4895. Fax: (601) 446-8260.
Stns: 1 AM. 3 FM. KTGV(FM) Jonesville, LA; WNAT Natchez, MS; WKSO(FM) Natchez, MS; WQNZ-FM Natchez, MS

Marie Perkins, pres; Stephen Perkins, VP; Margaret Perkins, gen mgr.

Fisher Broadcasting Company 100 4th Ave. N., Suite 440, Suite 1525, Seattle, WA 98109. Phone: (206) 404-7000. Fax: (206) 404-7050. Web Site: www.fisherbroadcasting.com. Ownership: Fisher Commmunications Inc., 100%.
Stns: 8 AM. 19 FM. KRQS(FM) Alberton, MT; KYYA-FM Billings, MT; KBLG Billings, MT; KRZN(FM) Billings, MT; KRKX(FM) Billings, MT; KXTL Butte, MT; KAAR(FM) Butte, MT; KMBR-FM Butte, MT; KIKF(FM) Cascade, MT; KINX(FM) Great Falls, MT; KXGF Great Falls, MT; KAAK(FM) Great Falls, MT; KQDI Great Falls, MT; KQDI-FM Great Falls, MT; KXDR-FM Hamilton, MT; KYLT Missoula, MT; KGGL-FM Missoula, MT; KGRZ Missoula, MT; KZOQ-FM Missoula, MT; KBQQ(FM) Pinesdale, MT; KZPH-FM Cashmere, WA; KYSN-FM East Wenatchee, WA; KWWW-FM Quincy, WA; KAAP(FM) Rock Island, WA; KOMO Seattle, WA; KPLZ-FM Seattle, WA; KWWX Wenatchee, WA
Stns: 10 TV. KBCI-TV, Boise, ID; KCBY, Eugene, OR; KPIC, Eugene, OR; KVAL, Eugene, OR; KIDK, Idaho Falls-Pocatello, ID; KATU, Portland, OR; KOMO, Seattle-Tacoma, WA; KLEW-TV, Spokane, WA; KIMA-TV, Yakima-Pasco-Richland-Kennewick, WA; KEPR, Yakima-Pasco-Richland-Kennewick, WA

Benjamin Tucker, pres.

Foothills Radio Group LLC Box 1678, Lenoir, NC 28645. Phone: (828) 758-1033. Fax: (828) 757-3300. Ownership: Donald W. Curtis, 50%; William M. McClatchey Jr., 50%.
Stns: 2 AM. 1 FM. WJRI Lenoir, NC; WKGX Lenoir, NC; WKVS-FM Lenoir, NC

William M. McClatchey Jr., pres.

Ford Broadcasting Inc. Box 8146, 910 Fairview St., Kannapolis, NC 28083. Phone: (704) 857-1101. Fax: (704) 857-0680. E-mail: info@fordbroadcasting.com. Web Site: www.fordbroadcasting.com.
Stns: 2 AM. WRNA China Grove, NC; WRKB Kannapolis, NC

Carl Ford, pres/CEO.

Forever Broadcasting One Forever Dr., Hollidaysburg, PA 16648. Phone: (814) 941-9800. Fax: (814) 943-2754. Web Site: www.foreverradio.com. Ownership: Kerby Confer, Donald Alt, Carol Logan, Lynn Deppen.
Stns: 13 AM. 18 FM. WVAM Altoona, PA; WWOT(FM) Altoona, PA; WFBG Altoona, PA; WALY-FM Bellwood, PA; WXXO(FM) Cambridge Springs, PA; WUUZ(FM) Cooperstown, PA; WYOT(FM) Ebensburg, PA; WFRA Franklin, PA; WWGY(FM) Grove City, PA; WRKY-FM Hollidaysburg, PA; WHUN Huntingdon, PA; WWLY(FM) Huntingdon, PA; WFGI(FM) Johnstown, PA; WNTJ(AM) Johnstown, PA; WRKW(FM) Johnstown, PA; WPRR(AM) Johnstown, PA; WKYE(FM) Johnstown, PA; WMGW Meadville, PA; WXOT(FM) Mount Union, PA; WKST(AM) New Castle, PA; WJST(AM) New Castle, PA; WOYL Oil City, PA; WQWK(FM) Pleasant Gap, PA; WLKJ(FM) Portage, PA; WHUZ(FM) Saegertown, PA; WLKH(FM) Somerset, PA; WNTW(AM) Somerset, PA; WLTS(FM) State College, PA; WJHT(FM) State College, PA; WMAJ State College, PA; WTIV Titusville, PA

Carol Logan, pres.

Forever Communications Inc. 2465 Russellville Rd., Bowling Green, KY 42101. Phone: (270) 843-3333. Fax: (270) 843-0454. Web Site: www.beaverfm.com. Ownership: Kerby E. Confer Grantor Retained Annuity Trust, Kerby E. Confer, trustee, 35%; Donald J. Alt Grantor Retained Annuity Trust, Donald J. Alt, trustee, 30.2%; William K. McGinnis, 30%.
Stns: 3 AM. 3 FM. WBVR-FM Auburn, KY; WBGN(AM) Bowling Green, KY; WLYE-FM Glasgow, KY; WNBS Murray, KY; WRKY(AM) Murray, KY; WUHU(FM) Smiths Grove, KY

Brad Hogan, gen mgr; Christine Hillard, pres.

Fort Bend Broadcasting Co. 1110 W. William Cannon Dr., Suite 402, Austin, TX 78745-5460. Phone: (512) 383-1112. Ownership: Roy E. Henderson, owner. Note: Roy E. Henderson also owns WTCU(FM) Fife Lake, MI; and KNUZ(AM) Bellville, TX.

Stns: 2 AM. 12 FM. WCUZ(FM) Bear Lake, MI; WOUF(FM) Beulah, MI; WBNZ(FM) Frankfort, MI; WLDR(AM) Kingsley, MI; WLDR-FM Traverse City, MI; KULF-FM Brenham, TX; KULM-FM Columbus, TX; KGUL-FM Edna, TX; KZAM-FM Ganado, TX; KHLT Hallettsville, TX; KHTZ(FM) Navasota, TX; KROY(FM) Palacios, TX; KAJI(FM) Point Comfort, TX; KYKM-FM Yoakum, TX

Roy E. Henderson, pres.

Fort Myers Broadcasting Co. 2824 Palm Beach Blvd., Fort Myers, FL 33916. Phone: (239) 334-1111. Fax: (239) 334-0744. Ownership: Brian A. McBride.
Stns: 2 AM. 2 FM. WINK(AM) Fort Myers, FL; WINK-FM Fort Myers, FL; WPTK(AM) Pine Island Center, FL; WTLQ-FM Punta Rassa, FL
Stns: 1 TV. WINK-TV, Ft. Myers-Naples, FL

Forum Communications Co. Box 2020, Fargo, ND 58107. Phone: (701) 235-7311. Fax: (701) 241-5406. Web Site: www.in-forum.com.
Stns: 1 AM. 1 FM. WZUU-FM Allegan, MI; WDAY Fargo, ND
Stns: 4 TV. WDAY, Fargo-Valley City, ND; WDAZ, Fargo-Valley City, ND; KBMY, Minot-Bismarck-Dickinson, ND; KMCY, Minot-Bismarck-Dickinson, ND

Forum Communications Co. owns the *Alexandria* (MN) *Echo Press; The Pioneer,* Bemidji, MN; *Detroit Lakes* (MN) *Tribune; The Becker County Record,* Detroit Lakes, MN; *Park Rapids* (MN) *Enterprise; The Wadena* (MN) *Pioneer Journal; West Central Daily Tribune,* Willmar, MN; *The Daily Globe;* Worthington, MN; *The Daily Republic,* Mitchell SD; *The Dickinson Press,* Dickinson, ND & *The* (ND) *Forum.*

William C. Marcil, pres.

Foster Communications Co. Inc. Box 2191, San Angelo, TX 76902-2191. Phone: (325) 949-2112. Fax: (325) 944-0851. Ownership: Fred M. Key, 100% of votes, 95% of total assets.
Stns: 1 AM. 3 FM. KIXY-FM San Angelo, TX; KKSA San Angelo, TX; KWFR-FM San Angelo, TX; KCLL(FM) San Angelo, TX

Fred M. Key, pres; J. Randall Phair, gen sls mgr; Jay Michaels, chief of opns; Shannon J. Roach, CFO.

Four Corners Broadcasting L.L.C. Drawer P, Durango, CO 81302. Phone: (970) 259-4444. Fax: (970) 247-1005. E-mail: fcb@frontier.net. Web Site: www.radiodurango.com. Ownership: Four Corners Communications L.L.C., Fordstone, IN.
Stns: 1 AM. 2 FM. KKDC(FM) Dolores, CO; KIQX-FM Durango, CO; KIUP Durango, CO

Allen Brill, CEO; Ward S. Holmes, gen mgr.

4-K Radio Inc. Box 936, Lewiston, ID 83501. Phone: (208) 743-2502. Fax: (208) 743-1995. E-mail: radiorip@aol.com. Web Site: www.koze.com. Ownership: Eugene Hamblin Trust; Michael R. Ripley.
Stns: 2 AM. 2 FM. KORT Grangeville, ID; KORT-FM Grangeville, ID; KOZE Lewiston, ID; KOZE-FM Lewiston, ID

Michael R. Ripley, pres.

4M Communications Inc. 308 West Broad St., Richmond, VA 23220. Phone: (804) 643-0990. Fax: (804) 643-4990. Web Site: www.radiorichmond.com. Ownership: Charles, Milkis, 25%; Michael Mazursky, 25%; Gary Milkis, 25%; Steven Milkis, 25%.
Stns: 2 AM. WLEE(AM) Richmond, VA; WVNZ(AM) Richmond, VA

Charles R. Milkis, owner; Michael O. Mazursky, owner.

Four Rivers Broadcasting Inc. Box 1729, Yreka, CA 96097. Phone: (530) 842-4158. Fax: (530) 842-7635. Web Site: www.mtshastalive.com. Ownership: Alta California Broadcasting Inc., 100%.
Stns: 4 FM. KTDE(FM) Gualala, CA; KMFB-FM Mendocino, CA; KNTK(FM) Weed, CA; KSYC-FM Yreka, CA

John Anthony, gen mgr.

The Free Lance-Star Publishing Co. 616 Amelia St., Fredericksburg, VA 22401. Phone: (540) 373-1500. Fax: (540) 374-5525.
Stns: 1 AM. 2 FM. WWUZ-FM Bowling Green, VA; WYSK Fredericksburg, VA; WYSK-FM Spotsylvania, VA

The Free Lance-Star Publishing Co., publishes the *Fredericksburg* (VA) *Free Lance-Star.*

Josiah P. Rowe III, ; Florence C. Barnick, assoc publisher; Nicholas J. Cadwallender, assoc publisher; John Moen, gen mgr radio stns.

Freedom Communications of Connecticut Inc. 330 Main St., Hartford, CT 06106. Phone: (860) 524-0001. Fax: (860) 548-1922. Ownership: Richard Weaver-Bey,

50% of votes; and Stephen Brisker, 50% of votes.
Stns: 3 AM. WKND(AM) Manchester, CT; WLAT(AM) New Britain, CT; WNEZ(AM) Windsor, CT

Stephen Brisker, pres/CEO & chmn.

Friends Communications Inc. 121 W. Maumee St., Adrian, MI 49221-2019. Phone: (517) 265-1500. Fax: (517) 263-4525. E-mail: friends@tc3net.com. Ownership: Bob Elliot, 100%.
Stns: 1 AM. 1 FM. WABJ Adrian, MI; WBZV(FM) Hudson, MI

Bob Elliot, pres; Moneca Morton, gen sls mgr.

Fritz Communications Inc. 1355 N. Dutton Ave. #225, Santa Rosa, CA 95401-7107. Phone: (707) 546-9185. Fax: (707) 546-9188. Ownership: KLRS(FM), KKCY(FM), KCEZ(FM), KMJE(FM), KTHU(FM), KRQR(FM), KBHX(FM) and KAWX(FM) are licensed to Results Radio Licensee L.L.C. KRPQ(FM) and KMHX(FM) are licensed to Results Radio of Sonoma L.P. (Fritz Communications Inc., corporate gen ptnr). KSRT(FM) is licensed to Results Radio of the North State LLC.
Stns: 14 FM. KEWB-FM Anderson, CA; KLRS-FM Chico, CA; KSRT(FM) Cloverdale, CA; KKCY-FM Colusa, CA; KTHU(FM) Corning, CA; KMJE-FM Gridley, CA; KCEZ(FM) Los Molinos, CA; KRQR-FM Orland, CA; KNCQ-FM Redding, CA; KRPQ-FM Rohnert Park, CA; KESR(FM) Shasta Lake City, CA; KKXS(FM) Shingletown, CA; KHRD(FM) Weaverville, CA; KMHX-FM Windsor, CA

Jack Fritz, pres/CEO.

J. & J. Fritz Media Ltd. Box 311, Fredericksburg, TX 78624. Phone: (830) 997-2197. Fax: (830) 997-2198.
Stns: 1 AM. 3 FM. KEEP-FM Bandera, TX; KNAF Fredericksburg, TX; KNAF-FM Fredericksburg, TX; KFAN-FM Johnson City, TX

Jayson Fritz, gen mgr; Jan Fritz, gen sls mgr.

G

GCC Bend LLC 969 S. W. Colorado, Bend, OR 97702. Phone: (541) 388-3300. Fax: (541) 389-7885. Web Site: www.ksjj.com. Ownership: Gross Holdings L.P., 100%.
Stns: 1 AM. 3 FM. KMGX(FM) Bend, OR; KXIX-FM Bend, OR; KICE(AM) Bend, OR; KSJJ-FM Redmond, OR

Dana Horner, COO.

GHB Radio Group 1776 Briarcliff Rd. N.E., Suite A, Atlanta, GA 30306-2106. Phone: (404) 875-1110. Fax: (404) 875-1186. Ownership: George H. Buck Jr.
Stns: 13 AM. 2 FM. WMGY Montgomery, AL; WYZE Atlanta, GA; WTIX New Orleans, LA; WCGC Belmont, NC; WHVN Charlotte, NC; WEGO Concord, NC; WAME(AM) Statesville, NC; WIST(FM) Thomasville, NC; WBLO(AM) Thomasville, NC; WSVM(AM) Valdese, NC; WNMX-FM Waxhaw, NC; WNAP Norristown, PA; WOLS Florence, SC; WHYM(AM) Lake City, SC; WAVO Rock Hill, SC

Jacob E. Bogan, COO; George H. Buck Jr., pres.

Galaxy Communications L.P. 235 Walton St., Syracuse, NY 13202. Phone: (315) 472-9111. Fax: (315) 472-1888. Web Site: www.galaxycommunications.com.
Stns: 4 AM. 7 FM. WTKW-FM Bridgeport, NY; WKLL-FM Frankfort, NY; WTLA North Syracuse, NY; WSGO Oswego, NY; WZUN(FM) Phoenix, NY; WSCP-FM Pulaski, NY; WRCZ(FM) Ravena, NY; WSCP Sandy Creek-Pulaski, NY; WEGQ(FM) Scotia, NY; WRCK-FM Utica, NY; WTLB Utica, NY

Ed Levine, pres; Mimi Griswold, VP progmg.

Galesburg Broadcasting Co. 154 E. Simmons St., Galesburg, IL 61401. Phone: (309) 342-5131. Fax: (309) 342-0840. E-mail: results@galesburgradio.com. Web Site: www.galesburgradio.com. Ownership: John Pritchard, pres, 100%.
Stns: 1 AM. 3 FM. WAAG-FM Galesburg, IL; WGIL Galesburg, IL; WLSR-FM Galesburg, IL; WKAY(FM) Knoxville, IL

John T. Pritchard, pres.

Gateway Radio Works Inc. Box 1010, Owingsville, KY 40360. Phone: (606) 674-2266. Fax: (606) 674-6700. Ownership: Hays McMakin, 100%.
Stns: 1 AM. 2 FM. WIVY(FM) Morehead, KY; WMST(AM) Mt. Sterling, KY; WKCA(FM) Owingsville, KY

Hays McMakin, pres; Jeff Ray, VP/gen mgr.

Genesis Communications Inc. 2110 Powers Ferry Rd., Suite 198, Atlanta, GA 30339. Phone: (678) 324-0170. Fax: (678) 324-0174. E-mail: ceo@radiogenesis.com. Ownership: Bruce C. Maduri, J. Donald Childress.
Stns: 5 AM. WLVU(AM) Dunedin, FL; WHOO(AM)

Broadcasting & Cable Yearbook 2006

D-13

Radio Group Ownership

Kissimmee, FL; WAMT(AM) Pine Castle-Sky Lake, FL; WWBA Pinellas Park, FL; WIXC(AM) Titusville, FL

J. Donald Childress, VP.

Georgia-Carolina Radiocasting Companies Drawer E, Toccoa, GA 30577. Phone: (864) 297-7264. Fax: (864) 297-7266. E-mail: sutton@gacaradio.com. Web Site: www.gacaradio.com. Ownership: Douglas M. Sutton Jr., 100% of all stns except WSNW(AM) and WWOF(AM)-WGOG(FM). M. Terry Carter owns 50% and Douglas M. Sutton Jr. owns 50% of WSNW(AM) and WWOF(AM)-WGOG(FM).

Stns: 8 AM. 5 FM. WRBN-FM Clayton, GA; WGHC(AM) Clayton, GA; WLVX(FM) Elberton, GA; WSGC(AM) Elberton, GA; WSGC-FM Elberton, GA; WNEG Toccoa, GA; WNCC-FM Franklin, NC; WFSC Franklin, NC; WRGC Sylva, NC; WSNW(AM) Seneca, SC; WBCU Union, SC; WWOF(AM) Walhalla, SC; WGOG(FM) Walhalla, SC

M. Terry Carter, VP; Douglas M. Sutton, Jr, pres/CEO; Tom Stanwood, VP & COO.

Gestion Appalaches inc. C.P. 69, Thetford Mines, PQ G6G 5S3. Canada. Phone: (418) 335-7533. Phone: (819) 752-2785. Fax: (418) 335-9009. Fax: (819) 752-3182. Ownership: Francois Labbe, 99.9%; Fiducie familiale F. Labbe, .07%; and Annie Labbie, .03%.

Stns: 3 FM. CFJO-FM Thetford Mines, PQ; CKLD-FM Thetford Mines, PQ; CFDA-FM Victoriaville, PQ

Annie Labbe, gen mgr.

Gleason Radio Group 555 Center St., Auburn, ME 04210. Phone: (207) 748-5868. Fax: (207) 784-4700. E-mail: dick@gleasonmedia.com. Web Site: www.gleasonmedia.com. Ownership: Richard D. Gleason, 100%.

Stns: 3 AM. 2 FM. WCNM(AM) Lewiston, ME; WTBM(FM) Mexico, ME; WOXO-FM Norway, ME; WTME(AM) Rumford, ME; WKTQ South Paris, ME

Richard Gleason, pres.

Gleiser Communications LLC 1001 E. Southeast Loop 323,, Suite 455, Tyler, TX 75701. Phone: (903) 593-2519. Fax: (903) 597-4141. E-mail: info@ktbb.com. Web Site: www.gleisercom.com. Ownership: Broadcasting partnors holdings, LP, Paul L. Gleiser.

Stns: 3 AM. 1 FM. KEES Gladewater, TX; KTBB Tyler, TX; KYZS Tyler, TX; KDOK-FM Tyler, TX

Paul Gleiser, pres/CEO.

Glenwood Communications Corp. 222 Commerce St., Kingsport, TN 37660. Phone: (423) 246-9578. Fax: (423) 246-6261. E-mail: golz@wkpttv.com. Web Site: www.wkpttv.com. Ownership: William M. Boyd; Hugh N. Boyd Trust.

Stns: 4 AM. WOPI Bristol, TN; WKTP Jonesborough, TN; WKPT Kingsport, TN; WMEV Marion, VA

Stns: 1 TV. WKPT-TV, Tri-Cities, TN-VA

George E. DeVault Jr., pres.

Glory Communications Inc. Box 2355, West Columbia, SC 29171. Phone: (803) 939-9530. Fax: (803) 939-9469. Ownership: Alex Snipe, 100%.

Stns: 1 AM. 5 FM. WSPX-FM Bowman, SC; WGCV(AM) Cayce, SC; WPDT-FM Johnsonville, SC; WTUA-FM Saint Stephen, SC; WFMV(FM) South Congaree, SC; WLJI-FM Summerton, SC

Alex Snipe, pres/CEO.

Goforth Media Inc. Box 1328, Mobile, AL 36633. Phone: (251) 473-8488. Fax: (251) 473-8854. E-mail: wgoforth@goforth.org. Web Site: www.goforth.org. Ownership: No stock. Nonprofit.

Stns: 1 FM. WBHY-FM Mobile, AL

Wilbur Goforth, pres; Steve Riggs, VP; Stephen Goforth, VP.

Gold Coast Broadcasting LLC 2284 S. Victoria, Suite 2M, Ventura, CA 93003. Phone: (805) 289-1400. Phone: (805) 339-0773. Fax: (805) 644-4251. Ownership: Point Broadcasting Company 88.51%, Jeri Lynn Broadcasting 6.32%, August G Inc. 5.17%.

Stns: 3 AM. 3 FM. KOCP-FM Camarillo, CA; KFYV(FM) Ojai, CA; KCAQ(FM) Oxnard, CA; KVTA Port Hueneme, CA; KUNX(AM) Santa Paula, CA; KKZZ(AM) Ventura, CA

John Q. Hearne, chmn; Miles Sexton, pres.

Golden West Broadcasting Ltd. Box 950, Altona, MB R0G 0B0. Canada. Phone: (204) 324-6464. Fax: (204) 324-8918. E-mail: info@cfamradio.com. Web Site: www.goldenwestradio.ca. Ownership: Elmer Hildebrand Ltd., 38.73%; Elmer Hildebrand Investments Inc., 19.23%; Elmer Hildebrand, 10.04%; and others, 32%.

Stns: 13 AM. 6 FM. CHRB High River, AB; CFAM Altona, MB; CJRB Boissevain, MB; CFRY Portage la Prairie, MB; CJPG-FM Portage la Prairie, MB; CHSM Steinbach, MB; CJEL-FM Winkler, MB; CKMW Winkler-Morden, MB; CHVN-FM Winnipeg, MB; CJSL Estevan, SK; CFYM Kindersley, SK; CKVX-FM Kindersley, SK; CHAB Moose Jaw, SK; CJYM Rosetown, SK; CJSN Shaunavon, SK; CIMG-FM Swift Current, SK; CKFI-FM Swift Current, SK; CKSW Swift Current, SK; CFSL Weyburn, SK

Elmer Hildebrand, pres/CEO; Menno Friesen, VP; Lyndon Friesen, VP.

Good Karma Broadcasting L.L.C. Box 902, Beaver Dam, WI 53916. Phone: (920) 885-4442. Fax: (920) 885-2152.

Stns: 4 AM. 1 FM. WTJK South Beloit, IL; WBEV Beaver Dam, WI; WTLX-FM Columbus, WI; WTTN Watertown, WI; WAUK Waukesha, WI

Rick Armon, opns dir.

Good News Communications Inc. 3222 S. Richey Ave., Tucson, AZ 85713. Phone: (520) 790-2440. Fax: (520) 790-2937.

Stns: 5 AM. KAPR Douglas, AZ; KJAA Globe, AZ; KNXN Sierra Vista, AZ; KVOI Tucson, AZ; KGMS(AM) Tucson, AZ

Douglas E. Martin, pres; Mary R. Martin, sec.

Good News Media Inc. Box 1400, Traverse City, MI 49685-1400. Phone: (231) 946-1400. Fax: (231) 946-3959. Web Site: www.wljn.com.

Stns: 2 AM. 1 FM. WLJW(AM) Cadillac, MI; WLJN Elmwood Township, MI; WLJN-FM Traverse City, MI

Doug Knorr, pres.

Good News Network 2278 Wortham Lane, Grovetown, GA 30813-5103. Phone: (706) 309-9610. Phone: (800) 926-4669. Fax: (706) 309-9669. E-mail: ctbarinowski@comcast.net. Web Site: www.gnnradio.org.

Stns: 3 AM. 5 FM. WQRX Valley Head, AL; WPMA(FM) Buckhead, GA; WWGF-FM Donalsonville, GA; WLPF-FM Ocilla, GA; WZIQ-FM Smithville, GA; WKTM-FM Soperton, GA; WZQZ(AM) Trion, GA; WBLR Batesburg, SC

Clarence Barinowski, pres/CEO.

Gore-Overgaard Broadcasting Inc. 11310 E. Arabian Park Dr., Scottsdale, AZ 85259. Phone: (480) 314-0144. Fax: (480) 314-4942. Ownership: Cordell Overgaard, Harold Gore.

Stns: 2 AM. KBIF Fresno, CA; WROD Daytona Beach, FL

Harold W. Gore, pres.

Grace Broadcasting Services Inc. 25 Stonebrook Pl., Suite G, #322, Jackson, TN 38305. Phone: (731) 663-3931. Fax: (731) 663-9804. Web Site: www.gracebroadcasting.com. Ownership: Charles Ennis, 55.8%; Lacy Ennis, 31.1%; Ray Smith, 7.5%; Dr. Buck Morton, 1.9%; and Phillip Chambers, 0.2%. Note: Group also owns 50% of WTRB(AM) Ripley, TN.

Stns: 2 AM. 5 FM. WWGM(FM) Alamo, TN; WTKB-FM Atwood, TN; WFGZ-FM Lobelville, TN; WSIB-FM Selmer, TN; WDTM Selmer, TN; WTNE Trenton, TN; WTNE-FM Trenton, TN

Graham Newspapers Inc. 620 Oak St., Graham, TX 76450. Phone: (940) 549-1330. Fax: (940) 549-8628.

Stns: 2 AM. KROO Breckenridge, TX; KSWA Graham, TX

Bruce McGrew, gen mgr.

Great Lakes Radio Inc. 2025 US 41 W., Marquette, MI 49855. Phone: (906) 227-7777. Phone: (906) 228-6800. Fax: (906) 475-8888. Fax: (906) 228-8128. E-mail: todd@greatlakesradio.org. Web Site: www.greatlakesradio.org.

Stns: 1 AM. 4 FM. WPIQ(M) Manistique, MI; WFXD-FM Marquette, MI; WRUP-FM Munising, MI; WQXO Munising, MI; WKQS-FM Negaunee, MI

Todd S. Noordyk, pres.

Great Scott Broadcasting 224 Maugers Mill Rd., Pottstown, PA 19464. Phone: (610) 326-4000. Fax: (610) 326-7984. E-mail: mike.licata@1370wpaz.com. Web Site: www.1370wpaz.com. Ownership: Faye Scott, special trustee, Charles Mott & James Worthington, co-trustees, Family Trust U/D/T dated 11/6/81, 86.72% of total assets; Faye Scott Annuity Trust U/D/T dated 3/6/02, Charles Mott & James Worthington, co-trustees, 6.64% of total assets; Faye Scott & James Worthington, co-trustees, Marital Trust U/D/T dated 11/6/81, 100% of votes, 0.98% of total assets.

Stns: 2 AM. 7 FM. WPAZ Pottstown, PA; WOCQ-FM Berlin, MD; WKHI(FM) Fruitland, MD; WKHW-FM Pocomoke City, MD; WJKI(FM) Bethany Beach, DE; WJWL Georgetown, DE; WKDB(FM) Laurel, DE; WZEB(FM) Ocean View, DE; WGBG-FM Seaford, DE

Faye Scott, CEO; Mike Licata, gen mgr/controller.

Great South RFDC L.L.C. 415 College St., Greenville, AL 36037. Phone: (334) 875-9315. Ownership: Paul Scott Alexander, 50%; Paul Reynolds, 50%.

Stns: 5 FM. WEZZ-FM Clanton, AL; WKGA(FM) Dadeville, AL; WFNU(FM) Repton, AL; WZLM(FM) Talladega, AL; WSMO(FM) Thomaston, AL

Greater Media Inc. 35 Braintree Hill Office Park, Suite 300, Braintree, MA 02184. Phone: (781) 348-8600. Fax: (781) 348-8680. Web Site: www.greatermedia.com. Ownership: Bordes family, 100%.

Stns: 4 AM. 14 FM. WTKK(FM) Boston, MA; WMJX-FM Boston, MA; WBOS-FM Brookline, MA; WROR-FM Framingham, MA; WKLB-FM Lowell, MA; WCSX-FM Birmingham, MI; WMGC-FM Detroit, MI; WRIF(FM) Detroit, MI; WWTR(AM) Bridgewater, NJ; WDHA-FM Dover, NJ; WJRZ-FM Manahawkin, NJ; WMTR Morristown, NJ; WMGQ(FM) New Brunswick, NJ; WCTC(AM) New Brunswick, NJ; WRAT-FM Point Pleasant, NJ; WPEN Philadelphia, PA; WBEN-FM Philadelphia, PA; WMMR-FM Philadelphia, PA

Greater Media, Inc. owns 100% of The Sentinel Publishing Co., publisher of twelve weekly newspapers: the *Sentinel* of East Brunswick, the *Edison/Metuchen Sentinel*, the *Woodbridge Sentinel*, the *North/South Brunswick Sentinel*, the *Atlanticville* of Long Branch, the *Bulletin* of Brick Township, the *Examiner* of Allentown, the *Hub* of Red Bank, the *Independent* of Middletown, the *News Transcript* of Freehold, the *Suburban* of Sayreville, and the *Tri-Town News* of Howell, Lakewood, Jackson and Plumsted, all NJ.

Peter H. Smyth, pres/CEO.

Group Radio Antenne 6 Inc. 568 boul. St. Joseph, Roberval, PQ G8H 2K6. Canada. Phone: (418) 275-1831. Fax: (418) 275-2475. Ownership: Gestion Malev Inc., 50%; Gestion Tremblay & Leclerc Inc., 50%.

Stns: 3 AM. 1 FM. CFGT Alma, PQ; CFED Chapais, PQ; CJMD Chibougamau, PQ; CHRL-FM Roberval, PQ

Marc-Andre Levesque, pres; Rosaire Leclerc, pres.

Guaranty Broadcasting Co. Box 2231, Baton Rouge, LA 70821. Phone: (225) 388-9898. Fax: (225) 344-3077.

Stns: 5 FM. WTGE(FM) Baker, LA; WYPY(FM) Baton Rouge, LA; WDGL-FM Baton Rouge, LA; KNXX(FM) Donaldsonville, LA; WNXX(FM) Jackson, LA

Guyann Corp. Box 1930, Flagstaff, AZ 86002. Phone: (928) 774-5231. Fax: (928) 779-2988. Web Site: www.kaff.com. Ownership: Guy Christian, 100%.

Stns: 2 AM. 3 FM. KAFF Flagstaff, AZ; KAFF-FM Flagstaff, AZ; KMGN-FM Flagstaff, AZ; KNOT(AM) Prescott, AZ; KTMG(FM) Prescott, AZ

Guy Christian, pres.

H

Haliburton Broadcasting Group Inc. 57 Elm Ave., Toronto, ON M4W 1N6. Canada. Phone: (416) 925-0488. Fax: (416) 925-6256. Web Site: www.hbgradio.com. Ownership: Standard Broadcasting Corp.

Stns: 11 FM. CHMS-FM Bancroft, ON; CFBG-FM Bracebridge, ON; CHPB-FM Cochrane, ON; CKNR-FM Elliot Lake, ON; CHOH-FM Hearst, ON; CJWL-FM Iroquois Falls, ON; CKAP-FM Kapuskasing, ON; CKLP-FM Parry Sound, ON; CHYC-FM Sudbury, ON; CHMT-FM Timmins, ON; CHYK-FM Timmins, ON

Christopher Grossman, pres; Kim Ward, VP opns mgr.

Hall Communications Inc. Box 2038,, 404 W. Lime St., Lakeland, FL 33806. Phone: (863) 682-8184. Fax: (863) 683-2409. Web Site: www.hallradio.com.

Stns: 8 AM. 11 FM. WNLC-FM East Lyme, CT; WKNL(FM) New London, CT; WCTY-FM Norwich, CT; WICH Norwich, CT; WILI-FM Willimantic, CT; WILI(AM) Willimantic, CT; WWRZ-FM Fort Meade, FL; WONN Lakeland, FL; WLKF Lakeland, FL; WPCV-FM Winter Haven, FL; WCTK-FM New Bedford, MA; WNBH New Bedford, MA; WKOL-FM Plattsburgh, NY; WLPA Lancaster, PA; WROZ-FM Lancaster, PA; WSJW(FM) Starview, PA; WLKW(AM) West Warwick, RI; WOKO-FM Burlington, VT; WJOY Burlington, VT

Arthur J. Rowbotham, pres.

Haugo Broadcasting Inc. Box 1680, Rapid City, SD 57709. Phone: (605) 343-0888. Fax: (605) 342-3075.

Stns: 1 AM. 1 FM. KSQY-FM Deadwood, SD; KTOQ Rapid City, SD

Chris Haugo, pres.

Heartland Christian Broadcasters Inc. Box 433, International Falls, MN 56649. Phone: (218) 285-7398. Fax: (218) 285-7419. Ownership: Chuck Scherer, 20%; Dan Griffith,

Radio Group Ownership

20%; Jim Hummel, 20%; Mike Worth, 20%; and Tom Wherley, 20%.

Stns: 3 FM. KADU(FM) Hibbing, MN; KBHW(FM) International Falls, MN; KXBR(FM) International Falls, MN

Heartland Communications Group LLC 4650 W. Spencer St., Appleton, WI 54914. Phone: (920) 882-4750. Fax: (920) 882-4751. Web Site: www.heartlandcomm.com. Ownership: Granite Equity L.P., 50.24% equity; The Thomas L. Bookey Family L.P., 42.3% equity; and James L. Gregori, 7.46% equity. Note: Group is managed by a five-member board of governors.

Stns: 5 AM. 8 FM. WOLV-FM Houghton, MI; WCCY Houghton, MI; WHKB(FM) Houghton, MI; WIKB Iron River, MI; WIKB-FM Iron River, MI; WJJH-FM Ashland, WI; WATW Ashland, WI; WBSZ(FM) Ashland, WI; WRJO-FM Eagle River, WI; WERL Eagle River, WI; WNXR(FM) Iron River, WI; WCQM-FM Park Falls, WI; WNBI Park Falls, WI

Tom Bookey, CEO; James Gregori, pres.

He's Alive Inc. Box 540, Grantsville, MD 21536. Phone: (301) 895-3292. Fax: (301) 895-3293. E-mail: hesalive@hesalive.net. Web Site: www.hesalive.net. Ownership: Non-stock, nonprofit organization.

Stns: 4 FM. WRIJ(FM) Masontown, PA; WPCL(FM) Northern Cambria, PA; WLIC-FM Frostburg, MD; WAIJ-FM Grantsville, MD

Dewayne Johnson, pres.

Bennie E. Hewett Stns Box 907670, Gainesville, GA 30501-0911. Phone: (770) 536-3890. Fax: (770) 536-4103. Ownership: Bennie Hewett.

Stns: 1 AM. 2 FM. WBMH(FM) Grove Hill, AL; WRJX(AM) Jackson, AL; WHOD(FM) Jackson, AL

Bennie E. Hewett, pres.

Hi-Favor Broadcasting LLC 136 S. Oak Knoll Ave., Pasadena, CA 91101. Phone: (626) 356-4230. Fax: (626) 795-9185. Ownership: Daisy Publishing Co. Inc., Pasadena, CA, 100%.

Stns: 3 AM. KLTX Long Beach, CA; KEZY(AM) San Bernardino, CA; KSDO San Diego, CA

High Desert Broadcasting LLC 570 East Ave. Q9, Palmdale, CA 93550. Phone: (661) 947-3107. Fax: (661) 272-5688. Ownership: John Hearne.

Stns: 2 AM. 3 FM. KGMX-FM Lancaster, CA; KWJL(AM) Lancaster, CA; KUTY Palmdale, CA; KLKX-FM Rosamond, CA; KKZQ-FM Tehachapi, CA

Miles Sexton, pres.

Hill Country Broadcasting Corp. 2125 Sidney Baker North, Kerrville, TX 78028. Phone: (325) 446-3371. Phone: (830) 896-1230. Fax: (830) 792-4142. Ownership: Kent Foster.

Stns: 2 AM. 3 FM. KMBL Junction, TX; KOOK-FM Junction, TX; KERV Kerrville, TX; KYXX(FM) Ozona, TX; KHOS-FM Sonora, TX

Ken Foster, pres.

Hoeflicker Stns Box 88, Glen Elder, KS 67446. Phone: (785) 545-3220. Web Site: www.kdnskzdy@nckcn.com. Ownership: Herbert R. Hoeflicker, 50%; Ruby J. Hoeflicker, 50%.

Stns: 1 FM. KZDY-FM Cawker City, KS

Herbert R. Hoeflicker, pres & gen mgr; Ruby J. Hoeflicker, VP/sec treas.

Holladay Broadcasting of Louisiana LLC Box 4808, Monroe, LA 71211. Phone: (318) 398-1618. Ownership: Robert H. Holladay, 100%.

Stns: 2 AM. 4 FM. KJMG-FM Bastrop, LA; KRVV-FM Bastrop, LA; KLIP-FM Monroe, LA; KMLB Monroe, LA; KRJO(AM) Monroe, LA; WBBV-FM Vicksburg, MS

Holy Family Communications 6325 Sheridan Dr., Williamsville, NY 14221. Phone: (716) 839-6117. Fax: (716) 839-0400. Web Site: www.wlof.net. Ownership: James N. Wright, 33.33%; Joanne Wright, 33.33%; and Mary Ellen Capece, 33.33%.

Stns: 3 AM. 1 FM. WLOF(FM) Attica, NY; WHIC(AM) Rochester, NY; WLOA(AM) Farrell, PA; WQOR(AM) Olyphant, PA

James N. Wright, pres.

Horizon Broadcasting Group L.L.C. 854 N.E. 4th St., Bend, OR 97701. Phone: (541) 383-3825. Fax: (541) 383-3403.

Stns: 1 AM. 3 FM. KQAK-FM Bend, OR; KRCO Prineville, OR; KLTW-FM Prineville, OR; KWLZ-FM Warm Springs, OR

Keith Shipman, pres.

Horne Radio Group Box 24250, Knoxville, TN 37933-2250. Phone: (865) 675-4105. Fax: (865) 675-4859. E-mail: knoxvilletalk@aol.com. Web Site: www.wkvl.com.

Stns: 7 AM. 2 FM. WMTY(AM) Farragut, TN; WKVL(AM) Knoxville, TN; WLOD Loudon, TN; WKVL-FM Loudon, TN; WGAP Maryville, TN; WMTN Morristown, TN; WDMXK-FM Morristown, TN; WATO Oak Ridge, TN; WDEH Sweetwater, TN

Douglas A. Horne, pres.

Houston Christian Broadcasters Inc. KHCB Radio Network, c/o KHCB-AM-FM, 2424 South Blvd., Houston, TX 77098-5196. Phone: (713) 520-5200. Web Site: www.khcb.org.

Stns: 2 AM. 10 FM. KHCL(FM) Arcadia, LA; KHIB(FM) Bastrop, TX; KHVT(FM) Bloomington, TX; KHCB Galveston, TX; KANJ(FM) Giddings, TX; KHCH(AM) Huntsville, TX; KHCJ(FM) Jefferson, TX; KHKV(FM) Kerrville, TX; KKER(FM) Kerrville, TX; KHML(FM) Madisonville, TX; KHCP(FM) Paris, TX; KHTA(FM) Wake Village, TX

Bruce E. Munsterman, pres & gen mgr; Bonnie C. BeMent, asst gen mgr.

Hubbard Broadcasting Inc. 3415 University Ave., St. Paul, MN 55114. Phone: (651) 646-5555. Fax: (651) 642-4103. E-mail: jmahoney@hbi.com.

Stns: 2 AM. 2 FM. WFMP(FM) Coon Rapids, MN; KSTP Saint Paul, MN; KSTP-FM Saint Paul, MN; WIXK(AM) New Richmond, WI

Stns: 13 TV. WNYT, Albany-Schenectady-Troy, NY; KOBG-TV, Albuquerque-Santa Fe, NM; KOB, Albuquerque-Santa Fe, NM; KOBF, Albuquerque-Santa Fe, NM; KOBR, Albuquerque-Santa Fe, NM; WDIO, Duluth, MN-Superior, WI; WIRT, Duluth, MN-Superior, WI; KRWF, Minneapolis-St. Paul, MN; KSAX, Minneapolis-St. Paul, MN; KSTP, Minneapolis-St. Paul, MN; KSTC-TV, Minneapolis-St. Paul, MN; KAAL, Rochester, MN-Mason City, IA-Austin, MN; WHEC, Rochester, NY

Stanley S. Hubbard, chmn/pres/CEO; Stanley E. Hubbard II, VP; Virginia H. Morris, VP; Robert W. Hubbard, VP; Julia D. Coyte, VP; Gerald D. Deeney, sr VP/treas/CFO; Harold C. Crump, VP; C. Thomas Newberry, VP; Linda S. Tremere, VP; Sue J. Cook, VP; Edward J. Aiken, VP; Kari Rominski, sec; Gary R. Macomber, asst sec.

Huth Broadcasting Box 669, Marysville, CA 95901. Phone: (530) 742-5555. Fax: (530) 741-3758. Ownership: Tom F. Huth, 100%. Note: Tom F. Huth owns 49.9% of the stock of Sierra Radio Inc., licensee of KTOR(AM) Westwood, CA.

Stns: 3 AM. KMYC(AM) Marysville, CA; KBLF Red Bluff, CA; KOBO Yuba City, CA

I

IHR Educational Broadcasting Box 180, Tahoma, CA 96142. Phone: (530) 584-5700. Fax: (530) 584-5705. E-mail: info@ihradio.org. Web Site: www.ihradio.org.

Stns: 7 AM. 2 FM. KAHI Auburn, CA; KCIK(AM) Blue Lake, CA; KJPG(AM) Frazier Park, CA; KPJP(FM) Greenville, CA; KJOP Lemoore, CA; KWG(AM) Stockton, CA; KSMH(AM) West Sacramento, CA; KXXQ(FM) Milan, NM; KIHM(AM) Reno, NV

Icicle Broadcasting Inc. 7475 KOHO Pl., Leavenworth, WA 98826. Phone: (509) 548-1011. Fax: (509) 548-3222. Web Site: www.kohoradio.com.

Stns: 1 AM. 1 FM. KOZI Chelan, WA; KOHO-FM Leavenworth, WA

Gary Mathews, gen mgr.

Idaho Wireless Corp. Box 97, Pocatello, ID 83204. Phone: (208) 234-1290. Fax: (208) 234-9451.

Stns: 1 AM. 1 FM. KORR-FM American Falls, ID; KOUU Pocatello, ID

Paul Anderson, gen mgr.

IdaVend Broadcasting Inc. 805 Stewart Ave., Lewiston, ID 83501. Phone: (208) 743-1551. Fax: (208) 743-4440. E-mail: rprasil@idavend.com. Ownership: Robert Prasil, Gary Prasil, Dorothy Prasil.

Stns: 1 AM. 2 FM. KMOK(FM) Lewiston, ID; KRLC Lewiston, ID; KVTY-FM Lewiston, ID

Robert Prasil, gen mgr.

Illinois Bible Institute Inc. Box 140, Carlinville, IL 62626. Phone: (217) 854-4600. Fax: (217) 854-4610. E-mail: rwhitworth@idcag.org. Web Site: www.wibi.org.

Stns: 6 FM. WTSG-FM Carlinville, IL; WIBI-FM Carlinville, IL; WBGL-FM Champaign, IL; WBMV-FM Mount Vernon, IL; WCIC-FM Pekin, IL; WPRC(FM) Princeton, IL

Richard C. Whitworth, dir.

Impact Radio LLC 59750 Constantine Rd., Three Rivers, MI 49093-9303. Phone: (269) 278-1815. Fax: (269) 273-7975. E-mail: drumsey@wlkm.com. Ownership: Dennis W. Rumsey.

Stns: 2 AM. 2 FM. WLKM Three Rivers, MI; WLKM-FM Three Rivers, MI; WQCT Bryan, OH; WBNO-FM Bryan, OH

Dennis W. Rumsey, pres.

Infinity Broadcasting Corp. 1515 Broadway, 46th Fl., New York, NY 10036. Phone: (212) 846-3939. Web Site: www.infinityradio.com. Ownership: Viacom Inc., 100%. Note: Viacom Inc. also owns the Viacom Television Stations Group (see listing under TV Group Ownership, Section B).

Stns: 42 AM. 124 FM. KMLE-FM Chandler, AZ; KOOL-FM Phoenix, AZ; KZON(FM) Phoenix, AZ; KFPT(AM) Clovis, CA; KOQO-FM Fresno, CA; KMJ Fresno, CA; KKDG(FM) Fresno, CA; KSKS-FM Fresno, CA; KWYE(FM) Fresno, CA; KMGV-FM Fresno, CA; KRAK(AM) Hesperia, CA; KTWV-FM Los Angeles, CA; KNX Los Angeles, CA; KRTH-FM Los Angeles, CA; KLSX-FM Los Angeles, CA; KFWB Los Angeles, CA; KEZN-FM Palm Desert, CA; KROQ-FM Pasadena, CA; KHWD(FM) Roseville, CA; KYMX-FM Sacramento, CA; KZZO-FM Sacramento, CA; KNCI-FM Sacramento, CA; KHTK Sacramento, CA; KFRG-FM San Bernardino, CA; KYXY-FM San Diego, CA; KPLN-FM San Diego, CA; KYCY-FM San Francisco, CA; KFRC-FM San Francisco, CA; KEAR-FM San Francisco, CA; KCBS San Francisco, CA; KITS-FM San Francisco, CA; KLLC-FM San Francisco, CA; KXFG-FM Sun City, CA; KVFG(FM) Victorville, CA; KSFM-FM Woodland, CA; KDJM(FM) Broomfield, CO; KIMN-FM Denver, CO; KXKL-FM Denver, CO; WZMX-FM Hartford, CT; WTIC Hartford, CT; WRCH-FM New Britain, CT; WJHM-FM Daytona Beach, FL; WOCL-FM De Land, FL; WLLD-FM Holmes Beach, FL; WPBZ-FM Indiantown, FL; WMBX-FM Jensen Beach, FL; WJBW-FM Jupiter, FL; WSJT-FM Lakeland, FL; WOMX-FM Orlando, FL; WYUU(FM) Safety Harbor, FL; WQYK-FM Saint Petersburg, FL; WBZZ(AM) Seffner, FL; WRBQ-FM Tampa, FL; WIRK-FM West Palm Beach, FL; WEAT-FM West Palm Beach, FL; WAOK Atlanta, GA; WZGC-FM Atlanta, GA; WSCR(AM) Chicago, IL; WJMK-FM Chicago, IL; WXRT-FM Chicago, IL; WUSN-FM Chicago, IL; WBBM Chicago, IL; WCKG-FM Elmwood Park, IL; KFKF-FM Kansas City, KS; WAQZ(FM) Fort Thomas, KY; WZLX-FM Boston, MA; WODS-FM Boston, MA; WBCN-FM Boston, MA; WBMX-FM Boston, MA; WBZ Boston, MA; WOMC-FM Detroit, MI; WWJ Detroit, MI; WVMV-FM Detroit, MI; WYCD-FM Detroit, MI; WXYT Detroit, MI; WCCO Minneapolis, MN; KZJK(FM) Saint Louis Park, MN; KMXV-FM Kansas City, MO; KSRC-FM Kansas City, MO; KBEQ-FM Kansas City, MO; KEZK-FM Saint Louis, MO; KMOX Saint Louis, MO; KYKY-FM Saint Louis, MO; WFNA(AM) Charlotte, NC; WKQC(FM) Charlotte, NC; WSOC-FM Charlotte, NC; WFNZ Charlotte, NC; WPEG-FM Concord, NC; WBAV-FM Gastonia, NC; WSML Graham, NC; WMFR High Point, NC; WSJS Winston-Salem, NC; KMXB-FM Henderson, NV; KKJJ(FM) Henderson, NV; KLUC-FM Las Vegas, NV; KXNT North Las Vegas, NV; KXTE-FM Pahrump, NV; WZNE-FM Brighton, NY; WYRK-FM Buffalo, NY; WJYE-FM Buffalo, NY; WBUF(FM) Buffalo, NY; WECK Cheektowaga, NY; WBLK-FM Depew, NY; WFAN New York, NY; WCBS New York, NY; WINS New York, NY; WNEW-FM New York, NY; WXRK-FM New York, NY; WRMM-FM Rochester, NY; WPXY-FM Rochester, NY; WCMF-FM Rochester, NY; WUBE-FM Cincinnati, OH; WKRQ-FM Cincinnati, OH; WAZU-FM Circleville, OH; WDOK-FM Cleveland, OH; WNCX(FM) Cleveland, OH; WQAL-FM Cleveland, OH; WXTM(FM) Cleveland Heights, OH; WLVQ-FM Columbus, OH; WGRR-FM Hamilton, OH; WHOK-FM Lancaster, OH; KVMX(FM) Banks, OR; KLTH(FM) Lake Oswego, OR; KINK(FM) Portland, OR; KUFO-FM Portland, OR; KCMD(AM) Portland, OR; KUPL-FM Portland, OR; WZPT-FM New Kensington, PA; WIP Philadelphia, PA; WPHT Philadelphia, PA; KYW Philadelphia, PA; WDSY-FM Pittsburgh, PA; WRKZ(FM) Pittsburgh, PA; KDKA Pittsburgh, PA; WMFS(FM) Bartlett, TN; WMC(AM) Memphis, TN; WMC-FM Memphis, TN; KKMJ-FM Austin, TX; KLUV-FM Dallas, TX; KLLI(FM) Dallas, TX; KJKK(FM) Dallas, TX; KRLD Dallas, TX; KOAI-FM Fort Worth, TX; KVIL-FM Highland Park-Dallas, TX; KHJZ-FM Houston, TX; KILT Houston, TX; KAMX(FM) Luling, TX; KIKK Pasadena, TX; KJCE Rollingwood, TX; KSRX(FM) San Antonio, TX; KTSA San Antonio, TX; KXBT(FM) Taylor, TX; WJFK-FM Manassas, VA; KPTK(AM) Seattle, WA; KMPS-FM Seattle, WA; KJAQ(FM) Seattle, WA; KZOK-FM Seattle, WA; KBKS-FM Tacoma, WA; WLZL(FM) Annapolis, MD; WJFK Baltimore, MD; WQSR-FM Baltimore, MD; WWMX-FM Baltimore, MD; WARW-FM Bethesda, MD; WHFS(FM) Catonsville, MD; WPGC Morningside, MD; WPGC-FM Morningside, MD

Joel Hollander, chmn/CEO; Ken O'Keefe, exec VP; Brian Ongaro, sr VP; Clancy Woods, sr VP.

Radio Group Ownership

Ingstad Brothers Broadcasting LLC Box 1248, Minnetonka, MN 55345. Phone: (952) 938-0575. Fax: (952) 938-2295. Ownership: Thomas E. Ingstad, 49%; Tor Ingstad, 49%; and Randy K. Holland, 2%.
Stns: 3 AM. 1 FM. KCHK New Prague, MN; KNUJ(AM) New Ulm, MN; KYMN Northfield, MN; KNUJ-FM Sleepy Eye, MN

Robert Ingstad Broadcast Properties Box 994, Valley City, ND 58072. Phone: (701) 845-1490. Fax: (701) 845-1245. Ownership: Robert E. Ingstad, Janice M. Ingstad, Robert J. Ingstad and Todd M. Ingstad.
Stns: 10 AM. 10 FM. KSKZ(FM) Copeland, KS; KBUF(AM) Holcomb, KS; KFXX-FM Hugoton, KS; KSSA-FM Ingalls, KS; KWKR(FM) Leoti, KS; KSKL-FM Scott City, KS; KULY Ulysses, KS; KDIO Ortonville, MN; KDAK Carrington, ND; KYNU-FM Carrington, ND; KQDJ Jamestown, ND; KDDR Oakes, ND; KOVC Valley City, ND; KRVX(FM) Wimbledon, ND; KMLO-FM Lowry, SD; KMSD Milbank, SD; KOLY Mobridge, SD; KGFX Pierre, SD; KPLO-FM Reliance, SD; KBWS-FM Sisseton, SD
Robert E. Ingstad, pres.

Tom Ingstad Broadcasting Group Box 1248, Minnetonka, MN 55345. Phone: (952) 938-0575. Fax: (952) 938-2295.
Stns: 4 AM. 3 FM. KARP-FM Dassel, MN; KKRC-FM Granite Falls, MN; KDUZ Hutchinson, MN; KDMA Montevideo, MN; KMRS Morris, MN; KRVY-FM Starbuck, MN; KKAQ Thief River Falls, MN
Tom Ingstad, pres/CEO.

Inland Northwest Broadcasting LLC 805 Stewart Ave., Lewiston, ID 83501. Phone: (208) 791-2605. Ownership: Robert Prasil, 50%; and Melva Prasil, 50%.
Stns: 2 AM. 2 FM. KCLX Colfax, WA; KMAX Colfax, WA; KRAO-FM Colfax, WA; KZZL-FM Pullman, WA

Inner City Broadcasting 3 Park Ave., 41st Fl., New York, NY 10016. Phone: (212) 447-1000. Fax: (212) 447-5197. E-mail: info@wbls.com. Web Site: www.wbls.com.
Stns: 9 AM. 10 FM. KBLX-FM Berkeley, CA; KVTO Berkeley, CA; KVVN Santa Clara, CA; WSRF Fort Lauderdale, FL; WJMI-FM Jackson, MS; WKXI Jackson, MS; WOAD Jackson, MS; WKXI-FM Magee, MS; WOAD-FM Pickens, MS; WLIB New York, NY; WBLS-FM New York, NY; WURP(AM) Braddock, PA; WHAT Philadelphia, PA; WZMJ-FM Batesburg, SC; WOIC(AM) Columbia, SC; WARQ(FM) Columbia, SC; WHXT-FM Orangeburg, SC; WMFX(FM) Saint Andrews, SC; WWDM(FM) Sumter, SC
Pierre Sutton, chmn/CEO.

Inter-Island Communications Inc. 1868 Halsey Dr., Piti, GU 96915. Phone: (671) 477-7108. Fax: (671) 477-6411. Ownership: Edward H. Poppe Jr., Frances W. Poppe.
Stns: 2 AM. 4 FM. KSTO(FM) Hagatna, GU; KTWG(AM) Hagatna, GU; KISH(FM) Hagatna, GU; KZMI(FM) Garapan-Saipan, NP; KCNM-FM Garapan-Saipan, NP; KCNM(AM) Garapan-Saipan, NP
Edward H. Poppe Jr., pres.

International Broadcasting Corp. 1554 Bori St., San Juan, PR 00927-6113. Phone: (787) 274-1800. Fax: (787) 281-9758. Ownership: Pedro Roman Collazo, 100%. Note: Pedro Roman Collazo, as an individual, owns WVOZ(AM) San Juan, PR.
Stns: 7 AM. 1 FM. WRSJ(AM) Bayamon, PR; WGIT(AM) Canovanas, PR; WVOZ-FM Carolina, PR; WIBS Guayama, PR; WXRF Guayama, PR; WTIL Mayaguez, PR; WEKO(AM) Morovis, PR; WCHQ(AM) Quebradillas, PR
Stns: 3 TV. WVEO, Aguadilla, PR; WVOZ, Ponce, PR; WTCV, San Juan, PR
Pedro Roman Callazo, pres; Margarita Nazario, gen mgr.

J

J&V Communications Inc. 222 Hazard St., Orlando, FL 32804. Phone: (407) 841-8282. Fax: (407) 841-8250. Ownership: Jesus Torrado, Virgen Torrado.
Stns: 2 AM. WOTS Kissimmee, FL; WPRD Winter Park, FL
John Torrado, pres; Frank F. Vaught, opns mgr.

JNE Investments Box 60991, Palo Alto, CA 94306. Ownership: Value Investment Trust, 100%.
Stns: 3 AM. KSDG Julian, CA; WMII(AM) Manistique, MI; KTXV(AM) Frankston, TX

JWC Broadcasting 259 S. Willow Ave., Cookeville, TN 38501. Phone: (931) 528-6064. Fax: (931) 520-1590. Ownership: Joe W. Wilmoth, 99%; and Reba Wilmoth, 1%.
Stns: 1 AM. 3 FM. WATX Algood, TN; WBXE-FM Baxter, TN; WLQK(FM) Livingston, TN; WKXD-FM Monterey, TN
Joel Wilmoth, pres.

Jabar Communications Inc. 5081 Rivers Ave., North Charleston, SC 29406. Phone: (843) 554-1063. Fax: (843) 554-1088. E-mail: traffic@jabarcommunications.com. Web Site: jabarcommunications.com.
Stns: 1 AM. 2 FM. WJNI(FM) Ladson, SC; WAZS-FM McClellanville, SC; WAZS(AM) Summerville, SC
Thomas Daniel, pres.

Jablamo LLC 9D Johnson Rd., Latham, NY 12110. Phone: (518) 330-8910. Ownership: Amber L. Morrell, 25%; James M. Morrell, 25%; Joseph B. Morrell, 25%; and Michael P. Morrell, 25%.
Stns: 4 AM. 3 FM. WYNY(AM) Cross City, FL; WKZY-FM Cross City, FL; WDVH(AM) Gainesville, FL; WTMN(AM) Gainesville, FL; WRZN Hernando, FL; WHHZ(FM) Newberry, FL; WTMG-FM Williston, FL

Jackson County Broadcasting Inc. Box 667, 295 E. Main St., Jackson, OH 45640. Phone: (740) 286-3023. Fax: (740) 286-6679. E-mail: jmossbarger@jbiradio.com. Ownership: Alan Stockmeister
Stns: 1 AM. 1 FM. WCJO-FM Jackson, OH; WYPC Wellston, OH
Jerry Mossbarger, gen mgr.

Jackson Radio Works Inc. 1700 Glenshire Dr., Jackson, MI 49201. Phone: (517) 787-9546. Fax: (517) 787-7517. E-mail: bgoldsen@wkhm.com. Web Site: www.wkhm.com. Ownership: Bruce & Susan Goldsen, 100%
Stns: 2 AM. 1 FM. WKHM-FM Brooklyn, MI; WIBM Jackson, MI; WKHM(AM) Jackson, MI

Jacobs Media Corp. Box 10, Gainesville, GA 30503. Phone: (770) 532-9921. Fax: (770) 532-0506. E-mail: jayjacobs@wdun.com. Web Site: www.wdun.com. Ownership: Elizabeth Jacobs Carswell.
Stns: 2 AM. 1 FM. WMJE-FM Clarkesville, GA; WDUN Gainesville, GA; WGGA Gainesville, GA
John W. Jacobs III, pres/CEO; Jay Andrews, VP bcstg.

James Crystal Inc. 6600 N. Andrews Ave., Suite 160, Fort Lauderdale, FL 33309. Phone: (954) 315-1515. Fax: (954) 315-1555. Web Site: www.jamescrystal.net. Ownership: James W. Hilliard, Crystal H. Armstrong.
Stns: 10 AM. KXEG(AM) Phoenix, AZ; KXXT(AM) Tolleson, AZ; WORL Altamonte Springs, FL; WLVJ(AM) Boynton Beach, FL; WDJA(AM) Delray Beach, FL; WFLL(AM) Fort Lauderdale, FL; WJBW(AM) Jupiter, FL; WJNA(AM) Royal Palm Beach, FL; WFTL(AM) West Palm Beach, FL; KINF(AM) Roswell, NM
James C. Hilliard, pres.

Jefferson-Pilot Communications Co. 3350 Peachtree Rd., Penthouse Suite, Atlanta, GA 30326. Phone: (404) 261-2970. Fax: (404) 365-9020. Web Site: www.jpcc.com. Ownership: Jefferson-Pilot Corp., 100%.
Stns: 5 AM. 9 FM. KSOQ-FM Escondido, CA; KIFM-FM San Diego, CA; KBZT(FM) San Diego, CA; KSON-FM San Diego, CA; KKFN Denver, CO; KCKK Lakewood, CO; KJCD(FM) Longmont, CO; WLYF(FM) Miami, FL; WMXJ-FM Pompano Beach, FL; WAXY South Miami, FL; WQXI Atlanta, GA; WSTR-FM Smyrna, GA; WBT Charlotte, NC; WBT-FM Chester, SC
Stns: 2 TV. WBTV, Charlotte, NC; WWBT, Richmond-Petersburg, VA
Clark Brown, pres.

Jodesha Broadcasting Inc. Box 1198, Aberdeen, WA 98520. Phone: (360) 533-3000. Fax: (360) 532-1456. E-mail: bossbill@jodesha.com. Web Site: www.jodesha.com. Ownership: William J and Susan Wolfenbarger.
Stns: 1 AM. 2 FM. KBKW Aberdeen, WA; KSWW(FM) Montesano, WA; KJET-FM South Bend, WA
William J. Wolfenbarger, pres; Susan Wolfenbarger, sec/treas.

Johnson Enterprises Inc. 338 S. KLEY Dr., Wellington, KS 67152. Phone: (620) 326-3341. Fax: (620) 326-8512. E-mail: kley@sutv.com. Web Site: www.kleyam.com. Ownership: E. Gordon Johnson, Susan G. Johnson.
Stns: 2 AM. 1 FM. KLEY(AM) Wellington, KS; KWME-FM Wellington, KS; KKLE(AM) Winfield, KS
E. Gordon Johnson, pres.

Journal Communications Inc. 333 W. State St., Milwaukee, WI 53203. Phone: (414) 224-2616. Fax: (414) 224-2469. Web Site: www.jc.com. Ownership: Journal Communications Inc., 100%.
Stns: 10 AM. 20 FM. KGMG-FM Oracle, AZ; KMXZ-FM Tucson, AZ; KZPT-FM Tucson, AZ; KGEM Boise, ID; KCID Caldwell, ID; KRVB(FM) Nampa, ID; KQXR-FM Payette, ID; KYQQ-FM Arkansas City, KS; KFXJ(FM) Augusta, KS; KMXW(FM) Newton, KS; KFTI(AM) Wichita, KS; KICT-FM Wichita, KS; KSGF-FM Ash Grove, MO; KZRQ-FM Mount Vernon, MO; KSPW(FM) Sparta, MO; KSGF(AM) Springfield, MO; KBBX-FM Nebraska City, NE; KOMJ(AM) Omaha, NE; KKCD-FM Omaha, NE; KEZO-FM Omaha, NE; KXSP(AM) Omaha, NE; KQCH(FM) Omaha, NE; KHLP-FM Omaha, NE; KXBL(FM) Henryetta, OK; KFAQ(AM) Tulsa, OK; WMYU(FM) Karns, TN; WKHT(FM) Knoxville, TN; WQBB Powell, TN; WWST(FM) Sevierville, TN; WTMJ Milwaukee, WI
Stns: 6 TV. KIVI, Boise, ID; WGBA, Green Bay-Appleton, WI; WSYM, Lansing, MI; KTNV, Las Vegas, NV; WTMJ, Milwaukee, WI; KMIR-TV, Palm Springs, CA
Journal Communications Inc., publisher of the morning *Milwaukee (WI) Journal Sentinel*, owns 100% of Journal Broadcast Corp.
Douglas G. Kiel, pres.

Joy Christian Communications Inc. Box 602, Centre, AL 35960. Phone: (256) 927-4027. Fax: (256) 927-4028. Web Site: www.joychristian.com. Ownership: Andrew L. Smith, 25%; Ed L. Smith, 25%; Marie P. Smith, 25%; and Melissa McGrew Smith, 25%.
Stns: 3 AM. WRFS(AM) Alexander City, AL; WZTQ(AM) Centre, AL; WLYJ(AM) Jasper, AL

J-Systems Franchising Corp. Hotel Traylor, 1444 Hamilton St., Allentown, PA 18102. Phone: (610) 435-5913. Fax: (610) 435-8918. E-mail: wmgh@ptdpro606.net. Web Site: www.wmgh.com. Ownership: Harold G. Fulmer III, 100%.
Stns: 1 AM. 1 FM. WLSH Lansford, PA; WMGH-FM Tamaqua, PA
Harold G. Fulmer III, pres.

K

KCD Enterprises Inc. Box 1100, Bartlesville, OK 74005. Phone: (918) 336-1001. Fax: (918) 336-3939. E-mail: radio@ibartlesvilleradio.net. Web Site: www.bartlesvilleradio.com. Ownership: Kevin Potter, 50%; Dorea Potter, 50%.
Stns: 1 AM. 1 FM. KWON Bartlesville, OK; KRIG-FM Nowata, OK
Kevin Potter, pres & gen mgr.

KEA Radio Inc. Box 966, Scottsboro, AL 35768. Phone: (256) 259-2341. Fax: (256) 574-2156. Web Site: www.wkeafm.com. Ownership: Ronald H. Livengood; Gene Sisk; Ivous Sisk; Diane Livengood.
Stns: 2 FM. WKEA-FM Scottsboro, AL; WMXN-FM Stevenson, AL
Ronald H. Livengood, pres; Gene Sisk, VP; Diane Livengood, sec; Ivous Sisk, treas.

KERM Inc. 201 W. 2nd, Russellville, AR 72801. Phone: (479) 968-1184. Fax: (479) 967-5278. E-mail: karv610@cei.net.
Stns: 3 AM. 1 FM. KARV-FM Ola, AR; KURM Rogers, AR; KARV Russellville, AR; KLTK South West City, MO
Chris Womack, gen mgr; James K. Womack, pres.

KHWY Inc. 12381 Wilshire Blvd. #105, Los Angeles, CA 90025. Phone: (310) 820-4628. Fax: (310) 826-7866. E-mail: khwyha@earthlink.com. Web Site: www.thehighwaystations.com. Ownership: Howard B. Anderson; Kirk M. Anderson.
Stns: 8 FM. KIXF-FM Baker, CA; KHRQ(FM) Baker, CA; KHWY-FM Essex, CA; KIXW-FM Lenwood, CA; KHDR(FM) Lenwood, CA; KHWZ-FM Ludlow, CA; KHYZ-FM Mountain Pass, CA; KRXV-FM Yermo, CA
Howard B. Anderson, pres/CEO; Kirk M. Anderson, exec VP; Jean Sheranian, sec.

KM Communications Inc. 3654 Jarvis Ave., Skokie, IL 60076. Phone: (847) 674-0864. Fax: (847) 674-9188. Web Site: www.kmcommunications.com.
Stns: 1 AM. 5 FM. WPNG(FM) Pearson, GA; KTKB(FM) Hagatna, GU; KQMG Independence, IA; KQMG-FM Independence, IA; WLCN(FM) Atlanta, IL; WMKB(FM) Earlville, IL
Stns: 2 TV. KWKB, Cedar Rapids-Waterloo & Dubuque, IA; KEJB, Monroe, LA-El Dorado, AR
Myoung Hwa Bae, pres; Kevin J. Bae, VP/gen mgr.

KNZA Inc. Box 104, Hiawatha, KS 66434-0104. Phone: (785) 547-3461. Fax: (785) 547-9900. Ownership: Greg Buser, 51%; Robert Hilton, 45%.
Stns: 3 FM. KNZA-FM Hiawatha, KS; KMZA-FM Seneca, KS; KLZA-FM Falls City, NE
Greg Buser, pres; Robert Hilton, sec/treas.

Radio Group Ownership

K95.5 Inc. 3405 E. Louisville, Broken Arrow, OK 74014. Phone: (918) 230-2165. Fax: (918) 838-0546. E-mail: Paynewh@aol.com. Web Site: www.k955.com. Ownership: William H. Payne 100% stockholder.
Stns: 1 AM. 3 FM. KTNT-FM Eufaula, OK; KITX-FM Hugo, OK; KTFX Sand Springs, OK; KTFX-FM Warner, OK
William H. Payne, pres.

KOOR Communications Inc. Box 2295, New London, NH 03257. Phone: (603) 448-0500. Fax: (603) 448-6601. E-mail: bob@wntk.com. Web Site: www.wntk.com.
Stns: 4 AM. 1 FM. WQTH Hanover, NH; WUVR(AM) Lebanon, NH; WNTK-FM New London, NH; WNTK Newport, NH; WNBX Springfield, VT
Robert L. Vinikoor, pres; Sheila E. Vinikoor, VP; Robert L. Vinikoor, gen mgr.

KSPD Inc. (Inspired Family Radio). 1440 S. Weideman Ave., Boise, ID 83709. Phone: (208) 377-3790. Fax: (208) 377-3792. E-mail: info@myfamilyradio.com. Web Site: www.myfamilyradio.com. Ownership: Lee Schafer, 50%; Beth A. Schafer, 50%.
Stns: 1 AM. 2 FM. KSPD Boise, ID; KBXL(FM) Caldwell, ID; KDZY-FM McCall, ID
Lee Schafer, gen mgr; David Schafer, asst mgr.

KSRM Inc. 40960 K. Beach Rd., Kenai, AK 99611. Phone: (907) 283-5811. Fax: (907) 283-9177. E-mail: info@radiokenai.com. Web Site: www.radiokenai.com.
Stns: 1 AM. 2 FM. KWHQ-FM Kenai, AK; KKIS-FM Soldotna, AK; KSRM Soldotna, AK
John Davis, pres; Cherie Curry, gen mgr.

KTLO L.L.C. Box 2010, Mountain Home, AR 72654. Phone: (870) 425-3101. Fax: (870) 424-4314. E-mail: sales@ktlo.com. Web Site: www.ktlo.com. Ownership: Mountain Lakes Broadcasting Corp., 91.89%.
Stns: 1 AM. 2 FM. KTLO Mountain Home, AR; KTLO-FM Mountain Home, AR; KCTT-FM Yellville, AR

Kaspar Broadcasting Group 1401 W. Barner St., Frankfort, IN 46041. Phone: (765) 659-3338. Fax: (765) 659-3338. Web Site: www.kasparradio.com.
Stns: 2 AM. 1 FM. WSHW-FM Frankfort, IN; WILO Frankfort, IN; KWRE Warrenton, MO
Vern Kaspar, pres/CEO; Russ Kaspar, VP.

Kemp Communications Inc. 3800 Howard Hughes Pkwy., Wells Fargo Tower, 17th Fl., Las Vegas, NV 89109. Phone: (702) 385-6000. Ownership: Will Kemp, 100%.
Stns: 1 AM. 2 FM. KSXX(FM) Payson, AZ; KBTB(AM) Las Vegas, NV; KVEG(FM) Mesquite, NV

Key Broadcasting Inc. Box 1227, Corbin, KY 40702. Phone: (606) 528-8787. Fax: (606) 528-9928. Ownership: Terry E. Forcht.
Stns: 8 AM. 7 FM. WIKK-FM Newton, IL; WVLN Olney, IL; WSEI-FM Olney, IL; WPRS Paris, IL; WACF-FM Paris, IL; WCDQ(FM) Crawfordsville, IN; WIMC(FM) Crawfordsville, IN; WCVL Crawfordsville, IN; WAIN Columbia, KY; WAIN-FM Columbia, KY; WHOP(AM) Hopkinsville, KY; WHOP-FM Hopkinsville, KY; WFTG London, KY; WSIP Paintsville, KY; WTCW Whitesburg, KY
Terry E. Forcht, pres/CEO

Keymarket Communications LLC 100 Ryan Ct., Suite 98, Pittsburgh, PA 15205. Phone: (412) 489-1001. Fax: (412) 279-5500. Web Site: www.froggyland.com.
Stns: 6 AM. 6 FM. WOMP Bellaire, OH; WOMP-FM Bellaire, OH; WOHI East Liverpool, OH; WOGF(FM) East Liverpool, OH; WSTV Steubenville, OH; WASP Brownsville, PA; WFGI(AM) Charleroi, PA; WPNT(AM) Connellsville, PA; WKPL(FM) Ellwood City, PA; WOGG(FM) Oliver, PA; WPKL(FM) Uniontown, PA; WUKL(FM) Bethlehem, WV
Gerald Getz, pres/CEO.

Kindred Communications Inc. 401 11th St., Suite 200, Huntington, WV 25701. Phone: (304) 523-8401. Fax: (304) 523-4848. Web Site: www.kindredcom.net.
Stns: 2 AM. 2 FM. WCMI Ashland, KY; WDGG-FM Ashland, KY; WRVC-FM Catlettsburg, KY; WRVC Huntington, WV
Mike Kirtner, pres & gen mgr.

Kirkman Broadcasting Inc. Indigo Executive Park, 60 Markfield Dr., Suite 4, Charleston, SC 29407. Phone: (843) 763-6631. Web Site: www.kirkmanbroadcasting.com.
Stns: 4 AM. WQNT(AM) Charleston, SC; WQSC Charleston, SC; WTMZ Dorchester Terrace-Brentwood, SC; WQTK(AM) Moncks Corner, SC
Gil Kirkman, pres/CEO.

Knight Quality Stations Box 8209, St. Thomas, VI 00801. Phone: (340) 776-4585. Fax: (340) 774-4455. E-mail: contact@kqsvi.net. Ownership: Randolph H. Knight; N. Scott Knight; Robert A. Knight; Gordon P. Ackley.
Stns: 1 AM. 2 FM. WVWI Charlotte Amalie, VI; WVJZ-FM Charlotte Amalie, VI; WWKS-FM Cruz Bay, VI
Randolph H. Knight, pres; Mark Bastin, gen mgr & gen sls mgr.

Kona Coast Radio LLC 6807 Foxglove Dr., Cheyenne, WY 82009. Phone: (307) 778-9318. Fax: (307) 632-9349. Ownership: Victor A. Michael Jr.
Stns: 1 AM. 6 FM. KRKY(AM) Granby, CO; KKHI(FM) Kremmling, CO; KVUW(FM) Wendover, NV; KFMH(FM) Belle Fourche, SD; KRQU(FM) Laramie, WY; KHIH(FM) Laramie, WY; KVAN(FM) Rock River, WY
Victor A. Michael Jr., owner.

Koser Radio Group P.O. Box 352, Rice Lake, WI 54868. Phone: (715) 234-2131. Fax: (715) 234-6942.
Stns: 2 AM. WAQE Rice Lake, WI; WJMC Rice Lake, WI
Thomas A. Koser, pres.

Kovas Communications of Indiana Inc. 2212 Inverness Lakes Crossing, Fort Wayne, IN 46804. Phone: (260) 432-0408. Ownership: Joseph W. Walburn, 100%.
Stns: 4 AM. WKKD Aurora, IL; WCGO Chicago Heights, IL; WMCW(AM) Harvard, IL; WLVA Lynchburg, VA

Kuiper Stns Box 1808, Grand Rapids, MI 49501. Phone: (616) 451-9387. Fax: (616) 451-8460. Ownership: William E. Kuiper Sr.
Stns: 2 AM. WFUR Grand Rapids, MI; WKPR Kalamazoo, MI
William E. Kuiper Sr., gen mgr & pres.

L

LKCM Radio Group L.P. 301 Commerce St., Fort Worth, TX 76102. Phone: (817) 332-3235. Ownership: LKCM Capital Group Inc., gen ptnr, 100% of votes.
Stns: 4 FM. KYBE-FM Frederick, OK; KRVA-FM Campbell, TX; KRVF(FM) Kerens, TX; KFWR(FM) Mineral Wells, TX

L M Communications Inc. 401 W. Main St.,, Suite 301, Lexington, KY 40507. Phone: (859) 233-1515. Fax: (859) 233-1517. E-mail: jmac@lmcomm.com. Web Site: www.lmcomm.com.
Stns: 4 AM. 5 FM. WBVX(FM) Carlisle, KY; WLXG Lexington, KY; WBTF-FM Midway, KY; WCDA-FM Versailles, KY; WYBB-FM Folly Beach, SC; WCOO(FM) Kiawah Island, SC; WMON Montgomery, WV; WJYP(AM) Saint Albans, WV; WSCW South Charleston, WV
Lynn Martin, pres; James E. MacFarlane, gen mgr.

La Crosse Radio Group Box 2017, La Crosse, WI 54602. Phone: (608) 782-8335. Fax: (608) 782-8340. Web Site: www.lacrosseradiogroup.com. Ownership: All stns except WFBZ(FM): Howard G. Bill, 45%; TCOM Inc., 45%; and Patrick H. Smith, 10%. WFBZ(FM): Mike Schmitz, 50%; and Ed Sullivan, 50%.
Stns: 1 AM. 4 FM. KQEG-FM La Crescent, MN; WQCC-FM La Crosse, WI; WLFN La Crosse, WI; WFBZ-FM Trempealeau, WI; WKBH-FM West Salem, WI
Patrick H. Smith, gen mgr.

La Favorita Inc. Box 746, Austell, GA 30106. Phone: (770) 944-0900. Fax: (770) 944-9794. Web Site: www.radiolafavorita.com. Ownership: Samuel Zamarron, pres; Graciela Zamarron, VP.
Stns: 3 AM. WAOS(AM) Austell, GA; WXEM Buford, GA; WLBA Gainesville, GA
Samuel Zamarron, pres/CEO; Graciela Zamarron, VP.

La Promesa Foundation 1406 E. Garden Ln., Midland, TX 79702. Phone: (432) 682-1485. Fax: (432) 682-5230. Web Site: www.lapromesa.org. Ownership: La Promesa Foundation is a non-stock, non-profit corporation.
Stns: 1 AM. 2 FM. KBKN(FM) Lamesa, TX; KBMD(FM) Marble Falls, TX; KJBC(AM) Midland, TX

La Salle County Broadcasting Corp. 1 Broadcast Lane, Oglesby, IL 61348. Phone: (815) 223-3100. Fax: (815) 223-3095. E-mail: wajk@ivynet.com. Web Site: www.wlpo.net. Ownership: Peter Miller.
Stns: 1 AM. 2 FM. WAJK-FM La Salle, IL; WLPO La Salle, IL; WKOT-FM Marseilles, IL
Peter Miller, pres, owns 95% of Daily News-Tribune Inc., which publishes the *News Tribune*.
Peter Miller, pres; Joyce McCullough, VP; John Spencer, progmg dir.

Lake Cities Broadcasting Corp. Box 999, Angola, IN 46703. Phone: (260) 665-9554. Fax: (260) 665-9064. E-mail: wrki@wrki.com. Web Site: www.wlki.com. Ownership: Thomas R. Andrews, William Kerner Jr., David Czurak.
Stns: 1 AM. WMSH Sturgis, MI
Thomas R. Andrews, pres; William Kerner Jr., VP.

Lake Michigan Broadcasting Inc. 5941 W. U.S. 10, Ludington, MI 49431. Phone: (231) 843-3438. Fax: (231) 843-1886. Web Site: www.wkla.com. Ownership: Lynn S. Baerwolf, Personal Representative of the Estate of Roger K. Baerwolf, Deceased, 65%; Scott J. Seeburger, 19%; John J. Hausbeck, 16%.
Stns: 2 AM. 3 FM. WKLA Ludington, MI; WKLA-FM Ludington, MI; WMTE-FM Manistee, MI; WMTE Manistee, MI; WKZC-FM Scottville, MI

Lake Region Radio Works Box 882, Devils Lake, ND 58301. Phone: (701) 662-7563. Fax: (701) 662-2222. E-mail: kzzyfm@gondtc.com. Web Site: www.lrradioworks.com.
Stns: 1 AM. 3 FM. KDLR Devils Lake, ND; KDVL-FM Devils Lake, ND; KQZZ-FM Devils Lake, ND; KZZY(FM) Devils Lake, ND
Curtis D. Teigen, opns mgr.

Lakes Radio Inc. 524 Ludington, Suite 300, Escanaba, MI 49829. Phone: (906) 789-9700. Fax: (906) 789-9700. Web Site: www.radioresultsnetwork.com.
Stns: 2 AM. 2 FM. WCHT Escanaba, MI; WGKL-FM Gladstone, MI; WCMM-FM Gulliver, MI; WTIQ Manistique, MI
Rick Duerson, pres.

Lakeshore Media L.L.C. 980 N. Michigan Ave., Suite 1880, Chicago, IL 60611. Phone: (312) 204-9900. Fax: (312) 587-9520. Ownership: Bruce Buzil, 50% votes; and Christopher F. Devine, 50% votes.
Stns: 1 AM. 2 FM. KHIL Willcox, AZ; KWCX-FM Willcox, AZ; KMXQ-FM Socorro, NM

Langer Broadcasting Group L.L.C. Box 380699, Murdock, FL 33938-0699. Phone: (508) 820-2430. Ownership: Alexander G. Langer, 100%.
Boston, MA 02114. Langer Broadcasting Corp., 164 Canal St., Suite 450. Phone: (617) 859-9639.
Stns: 3 AM. WSRO(AM) Ashland, MA; WFYL(AM) McConnellsburg, PA; WPYT(AM) Wilkinsburg, PA

Latin Entertainment Network Inc. 4630 S. Kirkman Rd. #153, Orlando, FL 32811-2802. Phone: (407) 903-1061. Web Site: www.lenmedia.com. Ownership: Anthony M. Hernandez, 25.054%; Scott E. Wood, 25.054%; Antonio M. Hernandez, 12.527%; and Migdalia Hernandez, 12.527%.
Stns: 2 AM. 4 FM. KHDV(FM) King City, CA; KEXA(FM) Salinas, CA; KRAY-FM Salinas, CA; KTGE Salinas, CA; KMJV(FM) Soledad, CA; WKTF(AM) Vienna, GA

Latino Communications LLC 600 Grant St., Suite 600, Denver, CO 80203. Phone: (303) 733-5266. Fax: (303) 733-5242. E-mail: kbno@kbno.net. Web Site: www.kbno.net. Ownership: Alex Cranberg, 49%; Zee Ferrufino, 26%; and Frank Ponce, 25%.
Stns: 3 AM. KBNO(AM) Denver, CO; KXRE Manitou Springs, CO; KAVA Pueblo, CO
Zee Ferrufino, pres/CEO.

Lew Latto Group of Northland Radio Stations 5732 Eagle View Dr., Duluth, MN 55803-9498. Phone: (218) 729-9888. Fax: (218) 729-9888. E-mail: LewLatto@aol.com. Ownership: Lew Latto, 100%.
Stns: 1 AM. 2 FM. KGPZ-FM Coleraine, MN; KRBT Eveleth, MN; WEVE-FM Eveleth, MN
Lew Latto, pres.

Lazer Broadcasting Corp. 200 S. A St., 4th Fl., Oxnard, CA 93030. Phone: (805) 240-2060. Ownership: Alfredo Plascencia, 100%.
Stns: 4 AM. 8 FM. KXSB-FM Big Bear Lake, CA; KXZM(FM) Felton, CA; KXRS-FM Hemet, CA; KXSM(FM) Hollister, CA; KSRN(FM) Kings Beach, CA; KBTW(FM) Lenwood, CA; KLMM(FM) Morro Bay, CA; KOXR Oxnard, CA; KLUN(FM) Paso Robles, CA; KCAL Redlands, CA; KZER(AM) Santa Barbara, CA; KSBQ Santa Maria, CA
Alfredo Plascencia, CEO; Terry Janisch, gen mgr.

Le Sea Broadcasting Box 12, South Bend, IN 46624. Phone: (574) 291-8200. Fax: (574) 291-9043. E-mail: leseabroadcasting@lesea.com. Web Site: www.lesea.com.
Stns: 1 AM. 3 FM. WHPZ-FM Bremen, IN; WHME-FM South Bend, IN; WDOW-FM Dowagiac, MI; WDOW Dowagiac, MI
Stns: 8 TV. KWHD, Denver, CO; KWHH, Hilo, HI; KWHE, Honolulu, HI; WHMB-TV, Indianapolis, IN; WHNO,

Radio Group Ownership

New Orleans, LA; WHME, South Bend-Elkhart, IN; KWHB, Tulsa, OK; KWHM, Wailuku, HI

Peter Sumrall, pres/CEO.

Legacy Communications Corp. Box 1450, St. George 84771-1450. Phone: (435) 628-1000. Fax: (435) 628-6636. E-mail: legacy1@infowest.com. Web Site: www.legacy.cc. Ownership: Randall Family Trust; Bear River Trust; Bate Family Trust; Diamond Media, LLC; American Media Corporation.

Stns: 5 AM. 1 FM. KPTO(AM) Pocatello, ID; KITT(FM) Soda Springs, ID; KBET(AM) Winchester, NV; KYFO(AM) Ogden, UT; KENT(AM) Parowan, UT; KNFL(AM) Tremonton, UT

E. Morgan Skinner Jr., pres; R. Michael Bull, controller; Lavon Randall, chmn.

Legacy Communications LLC 2729 Brentwood Blvd., Grand Island, NE 68801. Phone: (308) 381-0206. Ownership: Jay Vavricek, mng member, 100%.

Stns: 3 AM. 2 FM. KRGY(FM) Aurora, NE; KMMJ Grand Island, NE; KRGI Grand Island, NE; KRGI-FM Grand Island, NE; KIMB Kimball, NE

Legend Communications L.L.C. 5074 Dorsey Hall Dr., Suite 205, Ellicott City, MD 21042. Phone: (410) 740-0250. Fax: (410) 740-7222. E-mail: larry@patcomm.com. Ownership: Larry Patrick, Susan Patrick.

Stns: 4 AM. 6 FM. KDKD Clinton, MO; KDKD-FM Clinton, MO; WLWF(FM) Ravenswood, WV; KBBS Buffalo, WY; KLGT-FM Buffalo, WY; KODI Cody, WY; KGWY-FM Gillette, WY; KZMQ Greybull, WY; KCGL(FM) Powell, WY; KZZS(FM) Story, WY

Larry Patrick, pres; Susan Patrick, exec VP.

Leighton Enterprises Inc. Box 1458, St. Cloud, MN 56302. Phone: (320) 251-1450. Fax: (320) 251-8952. Web Site: www.1047kcld.com. Ownership: Al Leighton.

Stns: 4 AM. 4 FM. KYCK-FM Crookston, MN; KDLM Detroit Lakes, MN; KCNN East Grand Forks, MN; KZPK-FM Paynesville, MN; KBOQ(FM) Pelican Rapids, MN; KNSI Saint Cloud, MN; KCML(FM) Saint Joseph, MN; KNOX Grand Forks, ND

Al Leighton, chmn/CEO; John Sowada, pres; Dennis Niess, VP.

Liberman Broadcasting Inc. 1845 Empire Ave., Burbank, CA 91504. Phone: (818) 729-5300. Fax: (818) 729-5678. E-mail: LBlmedia@aol.com. Ownership: Lenard D. Liberman, 47.5-49% votes, 40-42.5% equity; Jose Liberman 2003 Annuity Trust, 23.75-24.5% votes, 20-21.25% equity; Esther Liberman 2003 Annuity Trust, 23.75-24.5% votes, 20-21.25% equity; public shareholders of Liberman Broadcasting Inc., 2-5% votes, 15-20% equity.

Stns: 5 AM. 10 FM. KEBN(FM) Garden Grove, CA; KBUE(AM) Long Beach, CA; KHJ(AM) Los Angeles, CA; KBUA(FM) San Fernando, CA; KWIZ-FM Santa Ana, CA; KXGJ-FM Bay City, TX; KQQK(FM) Beaumont, TX; KJOJ Conroe, TX; KIOX-FM El Campo, TX; KJOJ-FM Freeport, TX; KQUE Houston, TX; KEYH Houston, TX; KNOR(FM) Krum, TX; KTJM-FM Port Arthur, TX; KSEV Tomball, TX

Stns: 3 TV. KMPX, Dallas-Ft. Worth; KZJL, Houston; KRCA, Los Angeles

Lenard Liberman, pres; Brett Zane, CEO.

Liggett Communications L.L.C. 808 Huron Ave., Port Huron, MI 48060. Phone: (810) 982-9000. Fax: (810) 987-9380.

Stns: 2 AM. WHLX(AM) Marine City, MI; WPHM Port Huron, MI

Larry Smith, VP/gen mgr; Robert Liggett, pres.

Linder Broadcasting Group Box 1420, Mankato, MN 56002. Phone: (507) 345-4537. Fax: (507) 345-5364. Web Site: www.katoinfo.com. Ownership: Donald Linder, John Linder.

Stns: 3 AM. 7 FM. KOWZ-FM Blooming Prairie, MN; KTOE(AM) Mankato, MN; KARZ(FM) Marshall, MN; KMHL Marshall, MN; KOLV-FM Olivia, MN; KXAC-FM Saint James, MN; KRRW-FM Saint James, MN; KNSG-FM Springfield, MN; KARL(FM) Tracy, MN; KOWZ(FM) Waseca, MN

John Linder, pres.

Little Falls Radio Corp. 25801 Nacre St. N.W., St. Francis, MN 55070. Phone: (763) 862-9909. E-mail: rod.grams@att.net. Web Site: www.fallsradio.com. Ownership: Rod Grams, 50%; and Chrstina Rae Grams, 50%.

Stns: 1 AM. 1 FM. WYRQ-FM Little Falls, MN; KLTF Little Falls, MN

J.R. Livesay Group Box 322, Mattoon, IL 61938-0322. Phone: (217) 234-6464. Fax: (217) 234-6019. E-mail: wlbh@wlbh.com. Ownership: J.R. Livesay II owns 50% of WLBH-AM-FM. Shirley L. Herrington owns 35% of WLBH-AM-FM.

Stns: 1 AM. WLBH Mattoon, IL

J.R. Livesay II, chmn; Shirley L. Herrington, CFO.

Locally Owned Radio LLC 21361 Hwy. 30, Twin Falls, ID 83301. Phone: (208) 735-8300. Fax: (208) 733-4196. Ownership: Porter Hogan Charitable Trust, Jennifer Meeks, trustee; Wendell M. Starke, Lawrence C. Johnson, Stephanie S. Johnson.

Stns: 2 AM. 3 FM. KISY(FM) Gooding, ID; KIKX-FM Ketchum, ID; KMHI Mountain Home, ID; KTPZ(FM) Mountain Home, ID; KTFI Twin Falls, ID

Larry Johnson, pres; Jerry Fender, opns mgr.

Lotus Communications Corp. 3301 Barham Blvd., Suite 200, Los Angeles, CA 90068. Phone: (323) 512-2225. Fax: (323) 512-2224. E-mail: hq@lotuscorp.com. Web Site: www.lotuscorp.com.

Stns: 12 AM. 13 FM. KFMA-FM Green Valley, AZ; KCMT(FM) Oro Valley, AZ; KLPX-FM Tucson, AZ; KTKT Tucson, AZ; KLBN-FM Auberry, CA; KPSL-FM Bakersfield, CA; KWAC Bakersfield, CA; KCHJ Delano, CA; KGST Fresno, CA; KWKW Los Angeles, CA; KMMM(FM) Madera, CA; KIWI(FM) McFarland, CA; KWKU(AM) Pomona, CA; KIRN(AM) Simi Valley, CA; KOMP-FM Las Vegas, NV; KBAD Las Vegas, NV; KENO Las Vegas, NV; KXPT-FM Las Vegas, NV; KWWN(AM) Las Vegas, NV; KDOT-FM Reno, NV; KHIT Reno, NV; KOZZ-FM Reno, NV; KPLY(AM) Reno, NV; KUUB(FM) Sun Valley, NV; KZEP-FM San Antonio, TX

Howard A. Kalmenson, pres; Jerry Roy, sr VP; Bill Shriftman, sr VP; Lindy Williams, sr VP.

Lovcom Inc. Box 5086, Sheridan, WY 82801. Phone: (307) 672-7421. Fax: (307) 672-2933. E-mail: kimlove@wavecom.net. Web Site: www.sheridanmedia.com. Ownership: W.K. Love and family.

Stns: 2 AM. 1 FM. KROE(AM) Sheridan, WY; KWYO Sheridan, WY; KYTI-FM Sheridan, WY

W. K. Love, gen mgr.

M

MAX Media L.L.C. 900 Laskin Rd., Virginia Beach, VA 23451. Phone: (757) 437-9800. Fax: (757) 437-0034. Web Site: www.maxmedia.com. Ownership: MBG-GG LLC, 34.90%; MBG Quad-C Investors I Inc., 34.39%; Aardvarks Also LLC, 10.77%; Colonnade Max Investors Inc., 9.71%; Quad-C Max Investors Inc., 9.34%; MBG Quad-Investors II Inc., 0.52%; and Quad-C Max Investors II Inc., 0.37%.

Stns: 11 AM. 23 FM. KVLD(FM) Atkins, AR; KCAB Dardanelle, AR; KVOM Morrilton, AR; KVOM-FM Morrilton, AR; KWKK-FM Russellville, AR; WCIL Carbondale, IL; WUEZ(FM) Carterville, IL; WXLT(FM) Christopher, IL; WOOZ-FM Harrisburg, IL; WJPF Herrin, IL; KEZS-FM Cape Girardeau, MO; KGIR Cape Girardeau, MO; KCGQ-FM Gordonville, MO; KLSC(FM) Malden, MO; KMAL(AM) Malden, MO; KWOC Poplar Bluff, MO; KJEZ-FM Poplar Bluff, MO; KKLR-FM Poplar Bluff, MO; KGKS-FM Scott City, MO; KSIM Sikeston, MO; WQDK-FM Ahoskie, NC; WGAI(AM) Elizabeth City, NC; WWNC(FM) Hatteras, NC; WCXL(FM) Kill Devil Hills, NC; WFYY(FM) Bloomsburg, PA; WYGL-FM Elizabethville, PA; WWBE-FM Mifflinburg, PA; WLGL-FM Riverside, PA; WYGL Selinsgrove, PA; WCMS(AM) Newport News, VA; WGH-FM Newport News, VA; WXMM(FM) Norfolk, VA; WFOG(FM) Suffolk, VA; WXEZ-FM Yorktown, VA

Stns: 9 TV. KULR-TV, Billings, MT; WNKY, Bowling Green, KY; KWYB, Butte-Bozeman, MT; WVIF, Christiansted, VI; KTMF, Missoula, MT; WPFO, Portland-Auburn, ME; WGTQ, Traverse City-Cadillac, MI; WGTU, Traverse City-Cadillac, MI; KYTX, Tyler-Longview (Lufkin & Nacogdoches), TX

John A. Trinder, pres.

M&M Broadcasters Ltd. Box 1629, c/o KTFW(FM), Cleburne, TX 76033. Phone: (817) 572-4400. Fax: (817) 572-1915. Web Site: www.countrygoldradio.com. Ownership: Gary Moss, 80%; George Mazti, 20%.

Stns: 2 AM. 1 FM. KTON Belton, TX; KTFW(AM) Burleson, TX; KTFW-FM Glen Rose, TX

Gary Moss, pres.

MBC Grand Broadcasting Inc. 1360 E. Sherwood Dr., Grand Junction, CO 81501. Phone: (970) 254-2100. Fax: (970) 245-7551. Web Site: www.gjradio.com. Ownership: Richard C. Dean.

Stns: 1 AM. 2 FM. KNZZ(AM) Grand Junction, CO; KMGJ(FM) Grand Junction, CO; KMOZ-FM Grand Junction, CO

Richard C. Dean, pres.

MB Media Group Inc. 251 W. Hilton Dr., St. George, UT 84770. Phone: (435) 586-5900. Fax: (435) 586-0437.

Stns: 2 AM. 1 FM. KMXM(FM) Colorado City, AZ; KSUB Cedar City, UT; KNNZ(AM) Cedar City, UT

Wally Brazzeal, pres.

MCL/MCM-Inc. 103 Springer Bldg., 3411 Silverside Rd., Wilmington, DE 19810. Phone: (302) 478-6160. Ownership: Solway Inc., 100%. Note: Solway Inc. is 100% owned by Sheridan Broadcasting Corp., Pittsburgh, PA.

Stns: 2 AM. 2 FM. WATV Birmingham, AL; WAMO-FM Beaver Falls, PA; WJJJ(FM) Greensburg, PA; WPGR(AM) Monroeville, PA

M.R.S. Ventures Inc. 100 E. Ferguson, Suite 614, Tyler, TX 75702. Phone: (903) 595-4795. Fax: (903) 593-2666. E-mail: jdonrussell@aol.com. Ownership: Jerry D. Russell, 100%.

Stns: 2 AM. 6 FM. KRKD(FM) Dermott, AR; KZYQ-FM Lake Village, AR; KCLA Pine Bluff, AR; KOTN Pine Bluff, AR; KPBQ-FM Pine Bluff, AR; WDTL-FM Cleveland, MS; WRKG(FM) Drew, MS; WZYQ-FM Mound Bayou, MS

MTD Inc. Box 2010, Ruidoso Downs, NM 88346. Phone: (505) 258-9922. Fax: (505) 258-2363. E-mail: kruikwmw@trailnet.com. Web Site: www.ruidoso.net/krui. Ownership: R.D. Hubbard, 75%; Mike Warren, 25%.

Stns: 1 AM. 4 FM. KNMB(FM) Cloudcroft, NM; KWMW-FM Maljamar, NM; KIDX(FM) Ruidoso, NM; KRUI Ruidoso Downs, NM; KTUM(FM) Tatum, NM

Bruce Rimbo, pres; Timothy Keithley, gen mgr.

MTS Broadcasting Box 237, Cambridge, MD 21613. Phone: (410) 228-4800. Fax: (410) 228-0130. E-mail: theheat@intercom.net. Web Site: www.mtslive.com.

Stns: 1 AM. 2 FM. WCEM Cambridge, MD; WTDK-FM Federalsburg, MD; WAAI(FM) Hurlock, MD

Thomas C. Mulitz, pres/CEO.

MacDonald Broadcasting Co. Box 1776, Saginaw, MI 48605. Phone: (989) 752-8161. Fax: (989) 752-8102. E-mail: wkcq@chartermi.net. Web Site: www.98fmkcq.com. Ownership: Ken MacDonald Jr. Note: Group also owns and operates a Muzak franchise in a six-county area in mid-Michigan.

Stns: 2 AM. 4 FM. WMJO(FM) Essexville, MI; WHZZ-FM Lansing, MI; WILS Lansing, MI; WSAG(FM) Pinconning, MI; WSAM Saginaw, MI; WKCQ-FM Saginaw, MI

Kenneth MacDonald Jr., CEO; Duane Alverson, pres.

MacDonald Garber Broadcasting Co. 2095 U.S. 131 S., Petoskey, MI 49770. Phone: (231) 347-8713. Fax: (231) 347-8782. Web Site: www.lite96.com.

Stns: 2 AM. 1 FM. WATT Cadillac, MI; WKHQ-FM Charlevoix, MI; WMBN(AM) Petoskey, MI

Trish MacDonald Garber, pres.

Magnum Broadcasting Inc. Box 426, Warren, PA 16866. Phone: (814) 726-1090. Ownership: Michael M. Stapleford, 100%.

Stns: 2 AM. 2 FM. WBLF Bellefonte, PA; WUBZ-FM Philipsburg, PA; WPHB Philipsburg, PA; WZYY-FM Renovo, PA

Magnum Radio Inc. 1021 N. Superior Ave., Suite 5, Tomah, WI 54660. Phone: (608) 372-9600. Fax: (608) 372-7566. E-mail: magnumradio@charter.net. Ownership: David R. Magnum, 87.91%. Note: Sister corporation Magnum Communications Inc. owns WBKY(FM) Portage and WDLS(AM)-WNNO-FM Wisconsin Dells, both WI. Sister corporation Magnum Broadcasting Inc. owns WAUN-FM Kewaunee and WSRG(FM) Sturgeon Bay, both WI.

Stns: 1 AM. 2 FM. WXYM(FM) Tomah, WI; WBOG(AM) Tomah, WI; WTMB(FM) Tomah, WI

Dave Magnum, pres.

Mahaffey Enterprises Inc. Box 4584, Springfield, MO 65808. Phone: (417) 883-9180. Fax: (417) 883-9096. Ownership: John B. Mahaffey, Fredna B. Mahaffey, Robert B. Mahaffey.

Stns: 3 AM. 8 FM. KGGF Coffeyville, KS; KKRK(FM) Coffeyville, KS; KUSN(FM) Dearing, KS; KGGF-FM Fredonia, KS; KDAA(FM) Rolla, MO; KTTR Rolla, MO; KZNN-FM Rolla, MO; KTTR-FM Saint James, MO; KSPI Stillwater, OK; KGFY-FM Stillwater, OK; KTTR-FM Stillwater, OK

John B. Mahaffey, chmn; Robert B. Mahaffey, pres/CEO.

Main Line Broadcasting LLC 829 Colony Ct., Bryn Mawr, PA 19010. Phone: (610) 527-3307. Ownership: Arlington Capital Partners II L.P., 100%.

Stns: 2 AM. 3 FM. WCHA Chambersburg, PA; WIKZ-FM

Radio Group Ownership

Chambersburg, PA; WQCM(FM) Greencastle, PA; WHAG Halfway, MD; WDLD(FM) Halfway, MD

The MainQuad Group 10228 Governor Dr., Chapel Hill, NC 27514. Phone: (252) 544-3882.
Stns: 1 AM. 3 FM. WHAP Hopewell, VA; WCUL(FM) Orange, VA; WARV-FM Petersburg, VA; WBBT-FM Powhatan, VA
Dan Berman, pres.

Malkan Broadcast Associates Box 9757, Corpus Christi, TX 78469. Phone: (361) 883-3516. Fax: (361) 882-9767. E-mail: kzfm@aol.com. Ownership: Malkan Broadcasting Management L.L.C, gen ptnr; Matthew Malkan, Executor of the Estate of Audrey Malkan; Malkan Family Trust; Matthew Malkan; and Hope Malkan.
Stns: 1 AM. 3 FM. WMSR-FM Collinwood, TN; KZFM(FM) Corpus Christi, TX; KXDF Corpus Christi, TX; KKBA(FM) Kingsville, TX

Mapleton Communications LLC 10900 Wilshire Blvd., Suite 1500, Los Angeles, CA 90024. Phone: (310) 209-7221. Fax: (310) 209-7239.
Stns: 8 AM. 16 FM. KBRE(FM) Atwater, CA; KPYG(FM) Cambria, CA; KBOQ(FM) Carmel, CA; KCDU(FM) Carmel, CA; KBLO(FM) Corcoran, CA; KPIG-FM Freedom, CA; KHIP(FM) Gonzales, CA; KFYE(FM) Kingsburg, CA; KTME Lompoc, CA; KWSZ(FM) Lompoc, CA; KTIQ(AM) Merced, CA; KHPO(FM) Merced, CA; KYOS Merced, CA; KPIG(AM) Piedmont, CA; KXTZ-FM Pismo Beach, CA; KYNS(AM) San Luis Obispo, CA; KUHL Santa Maria, CA; KMBY-FM Seaside, CA; KXDZ(FM) Templeton, CA; KLOQ-FM Winton, CA; KTMT Ashland, OR; KBOY-FM Medford, OR; KAKT(FM) Phoenix, OR; KCMX Phoenix, OR
Adam Nathanson, pres; Raul Salvador, VP finance; Mike Anthony, progmg VP; Dale Hendry, VP opns.

Maritime Broadcasting 226 Union St., Saint John, NB E2L 1B1. Canada. Phone: (506) 658-2330. Fax: (506) 658-5116. E-mail: mlee@nb.aibn.com. Web Site: www.mbsradio.com.
Stns: 2 AM. CKDY Digby, NS; CKAD Middleton, NS
Dave Clarkson, gen sls mgr; Robert Pace, CEO.

Mars Hill Network 4044 Makyes Rd., Syracuse, NY 13215. Phone: (315) 469-5051. Web Site: www.marshillnetwork.org. Ownership: Not-for-profit corporation. Note: Group also has a radio net, 16 translators.
Stns: 3 FM. WMHI-FM Cape Vincent, NY; WMHR-FM Syracuse, NY; WMHN-FM Webster, NY
Clayton Roberts, pres; Michael Gettman, VP; Wayne Taylor, gen mgr.

Martin Broadcasting Inc. 4638 Decker Dr., Baytown, TX 77520. Phone: (210) 333-0050. Fax: (210) 333-0081. E-mail: kchl1480@yahoo.com.
Stns: 7 AM. 6 FM. WLVV Mobile, AL; KRMY Killeen, TX; KCHL San Antonio, TX; CFAN-FM Miramichi City, NB; CHOY-FM Moncton, NB; CFBC Saint John, NB; CIOK-FM Saint John, NB; CJCW Sussex, NB; CKEN-FM Kentville, NS; CKWM-FM Kentville, NS; CHER Sydney, NS; CFAB Windsor, NS; CJRW-FM Summerside, PE
Darrell E. Martin, pres.

Martz Communications Group 955 S. Virginia St., Reno, NV 89502. Phone: (415) 359-1030. Fax: (415) 359-1050. Ownership: Timothy D. Martz, 100%.
Stns: 2 AM. 7 FM. WNCQ-FM Canton, NY; WRCD-FM Canton, NY; WYUL-FM Chateaugay, NY; WVNV-FM Malone, NY; WICY Malone, NY; WMSA Massena, NY; WYSX(FM) Morrisonville, NY; WVLF(FM) Norwood, NY; WPAC(FM) Ogdensburg, NY
Timothy D. Martz, pres/CEO.

Maverick Media LLC 136 Main St., Suite 202, Westport, CT 06880. Phone: (203) 227-2800. Fax: (203) 227-4819.
Stns: 6 AM. 14 FM. KVRV(FM) Monte Rio, CA; KSRO Santa Rosa, CA; KXFX-FM Santa Rosa, CA; WXRX-FM Belvidere, IL; WFPS-FM Freeport, IL; WFRL Freeport, IL; WNTA Rockford, IL; WGFB(FM) Rockton, IL; WYHY(FM) Winnebago, IL; WDOH-FM Delphos, OH; WUZZ-FM Lima, OH; WLJM Lima, OH; WFGF(FM) Lima, OH; WZOQ(FM) Wapakoneta, OH; WEAQ Chippewa Falls, WI; WDRK(FM) Cornell, WI; WIAL-FM Eau Claire, WI; WAXX-FM Eau Claire, WI; WAYY(AM) Eau Claire, WI; WECL-FM Elk Mound, WI
Gary S. Rozynek, pres/CEO.

McCook Radio Group L.L.C. Box 333, McCook, NE 69001. Phone: (308) 345-5400. Fax: (308) 345-4720. Web Site: www.kicx.net. Ownership: Connie M.Stout, 50%; and David M. Stout, 50%.
Stns: 2 AM. 2 FM. KFNF-FM Oberlin, KS; KRKU(FM) McCook, NE; KNAX(AM) McCook, NE; KBRL McCook, NE
Dave Stout, pres & gen mgr.

McGraw/Elliott Group Stations 228 Randolph Ave., Elkins, WV 26241. Phone: (304) 636-8800. Fax: (304) 636-8801. E-mail: rmegfrontoffice@verizon.net. Ownership: Richard H. McGraw, 50%; Karen G. McGraw, 50%. Cable TV.
Stns: 1 AM. 3 FM. WBVQ(FM) Barrackville, WV; WBTQ-FM Buckhannon, WV; WBUC Buckhannon, WV; WELK-FM Elkins, WV
Richard H. McGraw, CEO.

McKenzie River Broadcasting Company, Inc. 925 Country Club Rd., Suite 200, Eugene, OR 97401. Phone: (541) 484-9400. Fax: (541) 344-9424. Ownership: Renate R. Tilson, 49.21%; John Q. Tilson III, 47.8%; and Anne G. Oxarart Trust, 2.99%.
Stns: 3 FM. KMGE-FM Eugene, OR; KKNU(FM) Springfield-Eugene, OR; KEUG(FM) Veneta, OR
John Q. Tilson, pres.

McMurray Communications Inc. 3335 W. 8th St., Safford, AZ 85546. Phone: (928) 428-1230. Fax: (928) 428-1311. E-mail: traffic@eaznet.com. Web Site: www.mysouthernaz.com.
Stns: 1 AM. 1 FM. KWRQ-FM Clifton, AZ; KATO Safford, AZ
Harry S. McMurray, pres/CEO; David Nathan, gen mgr.

McNaughton-Jakle Stations 14 Douglas Avenue, Elgin, IL 60120. Phone: (847) 741-7700. Fax: (847) 468-0000. E-mail: mail@wrmn.com. Web Site: www.wrmn1410.com. Ownership: Bradley L. Beesley, K. Richard Jakle.
Stns: 3 AM. 1 FM. WBIG Aurora, IL; WJKL-FM Elgin, IL; WRMN Elgin, IL; KSHP North Las Vegas, NV
(Joseph E. McNaughton & family) identified with *The Davis Enterprise, Fairfield Republic* & the *Placerville Mountain Democrat,* all CA.
K. Richard Jakle, chmn/pres.

Media Logic LLC Box 430, Fort Morgan, CO 80701-0430. Phone: (970) 867-5674. Fax: (970) 542-1023. Ownership: Wayne Johnson, 90%; and Richard Lindsey, 10%.
Stns: 2 AM. 1 FM. KFTM Fort Morgan, CO; KATR-FM Otis, CO; KRDZ Wray, CO
Wayne Johnson, gen mgr.

Media One Group 147 Bell St., Suite 200, Chagrin Falls, OH 44022. Phone: (440) 893-8114.
Stns: 2 AM. 3 FM. WWSE-FM Jamestown, NY; WHUG(FM) Jamestown, NY; WJTN Jamestown, NY; WKSN Jamestown, NY; WQFX-FM Russell, PA

Media Power Group Inc. 100 Gran Bulevar Paseos, Suite 403A, San Juan, PR 00926. Phone: (787) 292-1700. Fax: (787) 292-1717. E-mail: wskn1320@yahoo.com. Ownership: PR Grupo Radio Nacional Inc., 25%; Jose Enrique Fernandez, 25%; Arturo Diaz Jr., 25%; and Empresas Bechara Inc., 25%.
Stns: 4 AM. WLEY Cayey, PR; WDEP(AM) Ponce, PR; WSKN(AM) San Juan, PR; WKFE Yauco, PR
Eduardo Albino Rivero, pres; Joe Pagan, VP.

Mega Communications Inc. 255 Executive Dr. #409, Plainview, NY 11803. Phone: (516) 349-4900. Fax: (516) 349-4931. E-mail: eran@megastations.net. Web Site: megastations.net.
Stns: 4 AM. 3 FM. WLCC Brandon, FL; WMGG(AM) Largo, FL; WNUE-FM Titusville, FL; WEMG(AM) Camden, NJ; WKDL(AM) Alexandria, VA; WBPS-FM Warrenton, VA; WBZS-FM Prince Frederick, MD
Eran Schreiber, CFO.

Melia Communications Inc. Box 569, Goodland, KS 67735. Phone: (785) 899-2309. Fax: (785) 899-3062. E-mail: kloe@eaglecom.net. Web Site: www.kloe.com. Ownership: Martin K. Melia, 50%; Kathleen J. Melia, 50%.
Stns: 1 AM. 1 FM. KWGB-FM Colby, KS; KLOE Goodland, KS
Kathleen J. Melia, VP; Martin K. Melia, gen mgr & pres.

Mentor Partners Inc. 18720 16 Mile Rd., Big Rapids, MI 49307. Phone: (231) 796-7000. Fax: (231) 796-7951. Ownership: Jeffrey Scarpelli, 100%.
Stns: 1 AM. 2 FM. WYBR-FM Big Rapids, MI; WBRN Big Rapids, MI; WWBR(FM) Big Rapids, MI

Mercury Broadcasting Co. Inc. 115 E. Travis, Suite 533, San Antonio, TX 78205. Phone: (210) 222-0973. Fax: (210) 222-0975. Ownership: Van H. Archer III.
Stns: 1 AM. 1 FM. WKBF Rock Island, IL; WFMX-FM Statesville, NC
Stns: 1 TV. KSCC, Wichita-Hutchinson Plus, KS
Van H. Archer III, pres/CEO.

Meredith Broadcasting Group, Meredith Corp. 1716 Locust St., Des Moines, IA 50309-3023. Phone: (515) 284-2159. Fax: (515) 284-2514. Web Site: www.meredith.com. Ownership: Meredith Broadcasting is an operating group of Meredith Corp., Des Moines, IA.
Stns: 1 AM. WNEM(AM) Bridgeport, MI
Stns: 11 TV. WGCL-TV, Atlanta; WFLI, Chattanooga, TN; WNEM-TV, Flint-Saginaw-Bay City, MI; WHNS, Greenville-Spartanburg, SC-Asheville, NC-Anderson, SC; WFSB, Hartford & New Haven, CT; KCTV, Kansas City, MO; KVVU, Las Vegas, NV; WSMV, Nashville, TN; KPHO, Phoenix, AZ; KPTV, Portland, OR; KPDX, Portland, OR
The publishing group includes:
Magazines: *American Baby, American Patchwork & Quilting, Better Homes & Gardens, Country Home, Country Home Country Gardens, Creative Home, Decorating, Do It Yourself, Garden, Deck, and Landscape, Garden Shed, Ladies' Home Journal, Midwest Living, MORE, Renovation Style, Successful Farming, Traditional Home,* and *Wood,* along with more than 170 special interest titles.
Paul Karpowic, pres; Douglas Lowe, exec VP.

Meridian Broadcasting Inc. 2824 Palm Beach Blvd., Fort Myers, FL 33916. Phone: (239) 337-2346. Fax: (239) 332-0767. Ownership: Joseph C. Schwartzel.
Stns: 1 AM. 2 FM. WRQC(FM) Estero, FL; WTLT-FM Naples, FL; WNOG Naples, FL
Joseph C. Schwartzel, pres.

Metropolitan Radio Group Inc. 318 E. Pershing St., Springfield, MO 65806. Phone: (417) 862-0852. Fax: (417) 862-9079. Ownership: Gary L. Acker.
Stns: 7 AM. 5 FM. KGHT Sheridan, AR; KNKN-FM Pueblo, CO; KRMX Pueblo, CO; WBRD Palmetto, FL; WRXB Saint Petersburg Beach, FL; WTMY Sarasota, FL; KORI-FM Mansfield, LA; KJVC-FM Mansfield, LA; KIOU Shreveport, LA; KTKC-FM Springhill, LA; KUNQ-FM Houston, MO; KIJN Farwell, TX
Mark L. Acker, pres.

Meyer Communications Inc. Box 3676, Springfield, MO 65808. Phone: (417) 862-3990. Fax: (417) 869-7675. Web Site: www.ktxrfm.com. E-mail: manager@radiospringfield.com. Ownership: Kenneth E. Meyer, 100%.
Stns: 1 AM. 3 FM. KBFL(FM) Buffalo, MO; KTXR-FM Springfield, MO; KWTO Springfield, MO; KWTO-FM Springfield, MO
Kenneth E. Meyer, pres.

Michael Radio Group 6807 Foxglove Dr., Cheyenne, WY 82009. Phone: (307) 778-9318.
Stns: 4 FM. KKTN(FM) Victor, ID; KMQS(FM) Victor, ID; KGRK(FM) Glenrock, WY; KRKI(FM) Newcastle, WY

Mid Atlantic Network Box 3300, Winchester, VA 22604. Phone: (540) 667-2224. Fax: (540) 722-3295. Ownership: John P. Lewis, David P. Lewis, Howard P. Lewis.
Stns: 2 AM. 2 FM. WWRE(FM) Berryville, VA; WFVA(AM) Fredericksburg, VA; WWRT(FM) Strasburg, VA; WINC Winchester, VA
John P. Lewis, pres.

Mid-America Radio Group Inc. Box 1970, Martinsville, IN 46151. Phone: (765) 349-1485. Fax: (765) 342-3569. E-mail: mid-americaradio@scican.net. Ownership: David Keister, principal owner.
Stns: 5 AM. 7 FM. WIOU Kokomo, IN; WBAT Marion, IN; WGOM Marion, IN; WMCB Martinsville, IN; WVNI-FM Nashville, IN; WARU Peru, IN; WMYK(FM) Peru, IN; WARU-FM Roann, IN; WHZR-FM Royal Center, IN; WSKT-FM Spencer, IN; WCJC-FM Van Buren, IN; WJOT-FM Wabash, IN
David C. Keister, pres.

Midwest Communications Inc. Box 23333, Green Bay, WI 54305. Phone: (414) 435-3771. Fax: (414) 455-1155. Ownership: D.E. Wright, 100%.
Stns: 13 AM. 13 FM. WTVB(AM) Coldwater, MI; WNWN-FM Coldwater, MI; WHTC(AM) Holland, MI; WNWN Portage, MI; WYVN(FM) Saugatuck, MI; KDAL Duluth, MN; KTCO-FM Duluth, MN; WMFG Hibbing, MN; WNMT Nashwauk, MN; KMFG(FM) Nashwauk, MN; WUSZ-FM Virginia, MN; WTAQ(AM) Green Bay, WI; WNFL Green Bay, WI; WOFM-FM Mosinee, WI; WROE-FM Neenah-Menasha, WI; WNCY-FM Neenah-Menasha, WI; WOZZ-FM New London, WI; WIZD-FM Rudolph, WI; WRIG Schofield, WI; WHBL(AM) Sheboygan, WI; WHBZ(FM) Sheboygan Falls, WI; WLYD(FM) Sturgeon Bay, WI; WGEE(AM) Superior, WI; WDSM Superior, WI; WDEZ-FM Wausau, WI; WSAU Wausau, WI
D.E. Wright, pres.

The Mid-West Family Broadcast Group Box 253, Madison, WI 53701. Phone: (608) 273-1000. Fax: (608) 273-3588. E-mail: tom.walker@mwfbg.net. Web Site: www.madisonsource.com. Ownership: The Estate of William R. Walker, Philip Fisher, Thomas M. Kushak.

Stns: 8 AM. 14 FM. WYVR(FM) Petersburg, IL; WMAY(AM) Springfield, IL; WCNF-FM Benton Harbor, MI; WYTZ-FM Bridgman, MI; WSPZ-FM Hartford, MI; WSJM Saint Joseph, MI; WCSY-FM South Haven, MI; WSPZ(AM) South Haven, MI; KCLH(FM) Caledonia, MN; KQYB-FM Spring Grove, MN; KQRA(FM) Brookline, MO; KKLH(FM) Marshfield, MO; KOMG(FM) Ozark, MO; KOSP(FM) Willard, MO; WHIT-FM De Forest, WI; WIZM La Crosse, WI; WIZM-FM La Crosse, WI; WKTY La Crosse, WI; WTUX(AM) Madison, WI; WLMV(AM) Madison, WI; WTDY Madison, WI; WWQM-FM Middleton, WI

Thomas A. Walker, pres; Richard T. Record, dir.

Midwestern Broadcasting Co. 314 E. Front St., Traverse City, MI 49684. Phone: (231) 947-7675. Fax: (231) 929-3988. Web Site: www.wtcmi.com. Ownership: Ross Biederman, 52.5%; William Kiker Estate, 16.25%; William McClay, 15%.

Stns: 3 AM. 3 FM. WATZ Alpena, MI; WBCM(FM) Boyne City, MI; WJZQ(FM) Cadillac, MI; WCZW(FM) Charlevoix, MI; WCCW(AM) Traverse City, MI; WTCM(AM) Traverse City, MI

Ross Biederman, pres.

Millcreek Broadcasting L.L.C. 980 N. Michigan Ave.,, Suite 1880, Chicago, IL 60611. Phone: (312) 204-9900. Fax: (312) 587-9520. Ownership: Alta Communications VII LP, 79% (percentage of total assets).

Stns: 4 FM. KNJQ(FM) Manti, UT; KUDE(FM) Nephi, UT; KUDD(FM) Roy, UT; KUUU(FM) South Jordan, UT

Christopher Devine, pres; Bruce Buzil, exec VP.

Millennium Radio Group LLC 220 Northpointe Pkwy., Suite D, Amherst, NY 14228. Phone: (716) 639-9300. Fax: (719) 639-8782. Ownership: UBS Capital Americas; Alta Communications; Mercy Capital Partners LP.

Stns: 4 AM. 8 FM. WADB Asbury Park, NJ; WJLK-FM Asbury Park, NJ; WPUR-FM Atlantic City, NJ; WKXW(AM) Atlantic City, NJ; WFPG-FM Atlantic City, NJ; WSJO(FM) Egg Harbor City, NJ; WOBM Lakewood, NJ; WCHR-FM Manahawkin, NJ; WIXM(FM) Millville, NJ; WOBM-FM Toms River, NJ; WBUD Trenton, NJ; WKXW-FM Trenton, NJ

Charles W. Banta, chmn; James Donahoe, pres/CEO.

Miller Communications Inc. Box 1269, Sumter, SC 29151. Phone: (803) 775-2321. Fax: (803) 773-4856. Web Site: www.miller.fm. Ownership: Frank H. Avent, 31.33%; William Duncan, 24.37%; Harold T. Miller Jr., 20.89%; Theresa Miller, 20.89%; and David Baker, 2.5%.

Stns: 2 AM. 8 FM. WWBD-FM Bamberg, SC; WSIM(FM) Bishopville, SC; WGFG-FM Branchville, SC; WWKT-FM Kingstree, SC; WDKD Kingstree, SC; WQKI-FM Orangeburg, SC; WIGL(FM) Saint Matthews, SC; WDXY Sumter, SC; WICI(FM) Sumter, SC; WIBZ-FM Wedgefield, SC

Harold T. Miller Jr., pres/CEO; Dave Baker, VP; Theresa Miller, VP/gen mgr.

Miller Media Group Box 169, 918 East Park, Taylorville, IL 62568-0169. Phone: (217) 824-3395. Fax: (217) 824-3301. Web Site: www.randyradio.com. Ownership: Randal J. Miller owns 100% of WKEI(AM)-WJRE(FM), 70% of WMKR(FM) and WTIM-FM, and 100% of WRAN(FM). Lawrence Travis owns 30% of WMKR(FM) and WTIM-FM. Note: Group also owns the Hometown Illinois Radio Network, an ad-hoc network of 50 radio stns that broadcasts state boys basketball tournaments, and reports from the Illinois State Fair and Illinois Farm Bureau annual meeting.

Stns: 1 AM. 4 FM. WJRE(FM) Galva, IL; WKEI(AM) Kewanee, IL; WMKR(FM) Pana, IL; WTIM-FM Taylorville, IL; WRAN(FM) Tower Hill, IL

Randal J. Miller, pres; Cathaleen R. Miller, sec/treas.

Milwaukee Radio Alliance L.L.C. 2979 N. Mayfair Rd., Milwaukee, WI 53222. Phone: (414) 771-1021. Fax: (414) 771-3036. E-mail: hurwitz@milwaukeeradio.com. Web Site: www.milwaukeeradio.com. Ownership: All Pro Broadcasting, 50%; Shamrock Communications, 50%.

Stns: 1 AM. 1 FM. WMCS Greenfield, WI; WJZI-FM Milwaukee, WI

Willie Davis, chmn; William Lynette, pres.

Minn-Iowa Christian Broadcasting Inc. Box 72, Blue Earth, MN 56013. Phone: (507) 526-3233. Fax: (507) 526-3235. E-mail: kjly@kjly.com. Web Site: www.kjly.com.

Stns: 4 FM. KJYL-FM Eagle Grove, IA; KJCY(FM) Saint Ansgar, IA; KJIA(FM) Spirit Lake, IA; KJLY-FM Blue Earth, MN

Matt Dorfner, exec dir.

Mississippi Broadcasters L.L.C. Box 1699, Meridian, MS 39302. Phone: (601) 693-2661. Fax: (601) 483-0826. Ownership: Clay Holladay, 100%.

Stns: 4 FM. WMLV(FM) Butler, AL; WJXM(FM) De Kalb, MS; WMMZ-FM Meridian, MS; WKZB(FM) Stonewall, MS

Clay E. Holladay, pres & gen mgr.

Monarch Broadcasting Inc. 212 W. Cypress St., Altus, OK 73521. Phone: (580) 482-1450. Fax: (580) 482-3420. Web Site: www.kwhw.com. Ownership: Matthew L. Ward and Kristin Ward, 51%; and Deborah Ward-Ingstad, 49%. Note: Matthew L. Ward is sole officer, dir and shareholder of KIMM Radio Inc., licensee of KIMM(AM) Rapid City, SD.

Stns: 1 AM. 1 FM. KWHW Altus, OK; KQTZ-FM Hobart, OK

Matthew L. Ward, pres.

Montrose Broadcasting Corp. Box 248, 9 Locust St., Montrose, PA 18801. Phone: (570) 278-2811. Fax: (570) 278-1442. E-mail: mail@wpel.org. Web Site: www.wpel.org. Ownership: Non Profit Non Stock Corporation.

Stns: 2 AM. 1 FM. WPGM Danville, PA; WPEL Montrose, PA; WBGM-FM New Berlin, PA

Larry Souder, pres.

The Moody Bible Institute of Chicago 820 N. LaSalle Blvd., Chicago, IL 60610. Phone: (312) 329-4301. Fax: (312) 329-8980. Web Site: www.moody.edu.

Stns: 3 AM. 25 FM. WMBV-FM Dixons Mills, AL; WMFT(FM) Tuscaloosa, AL; WRMB-FM Boynton Beach, FL; WHGN(FM) Crystal River, FL; WKES-FM Lakeland, FL; WKZM-FM Sarasota, FL; KMDY-FM Keokuk, IA; WMBI(AM) Chicago, IL; WMBI-FM Chicago, IL; WDLM East Moline, IL; WJCG-FM Monee, IL; WGNR-FM Anderson, IN; WIWC-FM Kokomo, IN; WMBL(FM) Mitchell, IN; WHPL-FM West Lafayette, IN; WJSO-FM Pikeville, KY; WGNB-FM Zeeland, MI; WMBU-FM Forest, MS; KSPL-FM Kalispell, MT; KMBN(FM) Las Cruces, NM; WCRF-FM Cleveland, OH; WVML(FM) Millersburg, OH; WVME(FM) Meadville, PA; WVMN-FM New Castle, PA; WMBW-FM Chattanooga, TN; WFCM Smyrna, TN; KMLW-FM Moses Lake, WA; KMBI-FM Spokane, WA

Joseph Stowell, pres; Robert Neff, VP bcstg.

Moon Broadcasting 1200 W. Venice Blvd., Los Angeles, CA 90006. Phone: (213) 745-6224. Fax: (213) 745-7577. Web Site: www.moonbroadcasting.com. Ownership: Abel DeLuna, 100%.

Stns: 8 AM. 8 FM. KIQQ Barstow, CA; KAEH(FM) Beaumont, CA; KMQA-FM East Porterville, CA; KDAC Fort Bragg, CA; KMEN(FM) Mendota, CA; KIQQ-FM Newberry Springs, CA; KAAT(FM) Oakhurst, CA; KTNS Oakhurst, CA; KTOB(AM) Petaluma, CA; KRRS Santa Rosa, CA; KUKI Ukiah, CA; KUKI-FM Ukiah, CA; KLLK Willits, CA; KLES-FM Mabton, WA; KZXR Prosser, WA; KMNA(FM) Prosser, WA

Abel DeLuna, pres.

The Morey Organization Inc. 1103 Stewart Ave., Garden City, NY 11530. Phone: (516) 228-6570. Web Site: www.moreyorg.com.

Stns: 3 FM. WDRE(FM) Calverton-Roanoke, NY; WLIR-FM Hampton Bays, NY; WBON-FM Westhampton, NY

Jed Morey, COO; John Caracciolo, pres.

Morgan County Industries Inc. 129 College St., West Liberty, KY 41472. Phone: (606) 743-3145. Fax: (606) 743-9557.

Stns: 2 AM. 1 FM. WCBJ-FM Campton, KY; WMOR Morehead, KY; WLKS West Liberty, KY

Paul Lyons, COO.

Morris Radio LLC 725 Broad St., Augusta, GA 30903-0936. Phone: (706) 823-3331. Fax: (706) 823-3212. Web Site: www.morris.com. Ownership: Owned by Morris Communications Company LLC. Group also owns the Kansas Agriculture Network, Topeka, KS; Kansas Information Network, Topeka, KS; and the Wildcat Sports Network, Topeka, KS.

Stns: 15 AM. 11 FM. KBRJ(FM) Anchorage, AK; KEAG-FM Anchorage, AK; KFQD Anchorage, AK; KHAR Anchorage, AK; KMXS-FM Anchorage, AK; KWHL-FM Anchorage, AK; KNWZ(AM) Coachella, CA; KKUU(FM) Indio, CA; KNWQ(AM) Palm Springs, CA; KXPS(AM) Thousand Palms, CA; KNWT(AM) Thousand Palms, CA; KNWH(AM) Twentynine Palms, CA; KDGL(FM) Yucca Valley, CA; KABI Abilene, KS; KBLS(FM) North Fort Riley, KS; KSAL Salina, KS; KSAL-FM Salina, KS; KYEZ-FM Salina, KS; WIBW Topeka, KS; KGNC Amarillo, TX; KXRO Aberdeen, WA; KWOK(AM) Hoquiam, WA; KXXK(FM) Hoquiam-Aberdeen, WA; KWIQ(AM) Moses Lake North, WA; KKRT Wenatchee, WA; KWLN(FM) Wilson Creek, WA

Morris Publishing Group owns the following daily newspapers: *Amarillo* (Texas) *Globe-News*, *Athens* (GA) *Banner-Herald, The Augusta* (GA) *Chronicle, Brainerd* (MN) *Dispatch, The Daily Ardmoreite*, Ardmore, OK, *Dodge City* (Kan.) *Daily Globe, The Examiner,* Independence, MO, *The Florida Times-Union,* Jacksonville, *The Grand Island* (NE) *Independent, Hannibal* (MO) *Courier-Post, Hillsdale* (MI) *Daily News, The Holland* (MI) *Sentinel, Juneau* (AK) *Empire, Log Cabin Democrat,* Conway, AK, *Lubbock* (Texas) *Avalanche-Journal, The Morning Sun,* Pittsburg, KS, *News Chief,* Winter Haven, FL, *The Newton* (KS) *Kansan, The Oak Ridger,* Oak Ridge, TN, *Peninsula Clarion,* Kenai, AK, *The St. Augustine* (FL) *Record, Savannah* (GA) *Morning News, The Shawnee* (OK) *News-Star, The Topeka* (KS) *Capital-Journal, Yankton* (SD) *Daily Press & Dakotan, York* (NE) *News-Times. Magazines include: Athens Magazine, Augusta Magazine, Coastal Antiques and Art, Coastal Senior, Eco Latino* (Athens), *Eco Latino* (St. Augustine), *Gainesville Life, Her Voice, Hers Kansas, LOUNGE, Savannah Coastal Parent, Savannah Magazine, Senior Living, She's OK!, Skirt!, Water's Edge, West Michigan Senior Times. Other publications include 37 non-daily newspapers and shoppers.*

Michael D. Osterhout, COO.

Mortenson Broadcasting Co. 3270 Blazer Pkwy. #101, Lexington, KY 40509-1847. Phone: (859) 245-1000. Fax: (859) 245-1600. Ownership: Jack Mortenson, 100%.

Stns: 11 AM. 2 FM. WJMM-FM Keene, KY; WLLV Louisville, KY; WLOU Louisville, KY; WWFT(AM) Nicholasville, KY; WCGW Nicholasville, KY; KGGN Gladstone, MO; KRVA Cockrell Hill, TX; KGGR Dallas, TX; KHVN Fort Worth, TX; KKGM(AM) Fort Worth, TX; KTNO(AM) University Park, TX; WEMM-FM Huntington, WV; WEMM(AM) Huntington, WV

Jack Mortenson, pres.

Mt. Rushmore Broadcasting Inc. 218 N. Wolcott, Casper, WY 82602. Phone: (307) 265-1984. Fax: (307) 266-3295. E-mail: mtrushmore@wyoming.com. Web Site: www.wyomingradio.com.

Stns: 5 AM. 9 FM. KRMQ-FM Clovis, NM; KAWK(FM) Custer, SD; KFCR Custer, SD; KZMX Hot Springs, SD; KZMX-FM Hot Springs, SD; KASS(FM) Casper, WY; KVOC Casper, WY; KHOC-FM Casper, WY; KMLD(FM) Casper, WY; KQLT-FM Casper, WY; KRAL Rawlins, WY; KIQZ(FM) Rawlins, WY; KGOS Torrington, WY; KERM-FM Torrington, WY

Jan Charles Gray, pres/CEO.

Mountain Communications Box 211, Saranac Lake, NY 12983-0211. Phone: (518) 891-1544. Fax: (518) 891-1545. Ownership: Prescott House LLC owns 100% of WIRD(AM)-WLPW(FM) and WRGR(FM). Edward S. Morgan, the sole member of Prescott House LLC, is also the controlling stockholder of WNBZ(AM)-WYZY(FM).

Stns: 2 AM. 3 FM. WIRD Lake Placid, NY; WLPW-FM Lake Placid, NY; WNBZ Saranac Lake, NY; WYZY(FM) Saranac Lake, NY; WRGR-FM Tupper Lake, NY

Ted Morgan, owner.

Mountain Dog Media 254 Winnebago Dr., Fond du Lac, WI 54935. Phone: (920) 921-1071. Fax: (920) 921-0757.

Stns: 2 AM. 2 FM. KFIZ Fond du Lac, WI; WFON(FM) Fond du Lac, WI; WXER(FM) Plymouth, WI; WCLB(AM) Sheboygan, WI

Randy Hopper, pres.

Mountain Wireless Inc. Box 159, Skowhegan, ME 04976. Phone: (207) 474-5171. Fax: (207) 474-3299.

Stns: 1 AM. 2 FM. WCTB-FM Fairfield, ME; WHQO-FM Skowhegan, ME; WSKW Skowhegan, ME

Alan W. Anderson, pres.

Mt. Washington Radio & Gramophone L.L.C. Box 2008, Conway, NH 03818. Phone: (603) 356-8870. Fax: (603) 356-8875. E-mail: office@wmwv.com. Web Site: www.wmwv.com. Ownership: Ronald Frizzell, 51%; Greg Frizzell, 25%; Arnold Lerner, 24%.

Stns: 2 FM. WVMJ(FM) Conway, NH; WMWV-FM Conway, NH

Ron Frizzell, pres.

Muirfield Broadcasting Inc. 200 Short Rd., Southern Pines, NC 28387. Phone: (910) 692-2107. Fax: (910) 692-6849. Web Site: www.star1025fm.com. Ownership: Walker Morris.

Stns: 1 AM. 1 FM. WIOZ Pinehurst, NC; WIOZ-FM Southern Pines, NC

Walker Morris, pres.

Multicultural Radio Broadcasting Inc. 449 Broadway, New York, NY 10013. Phone: (212) 966-1059. Fax: (212) 966-9580. Web Site: www.mrbi.net. Ownership: Arthur S. Liu, 51%; and Yvonne S. Liu, 49%.

Stns: 36 AM. KIDR Phoenix, AZ; KQTL Sahuarita, AZ;

Radio Group Ownership

KWRU(AM) Fresno, CA; KYPA Los Angeles, CA; KAZN Pasadena, CA; KATD Pittsburg, CA; KAHZ(AM) Pomona, CA; KSON San Diego, CA; KEST San Francisco, CA; KIQI San Francisco, CA; KSJX(AM) San Jose, CA; KBLA Santa Monica, CA; KALI West Covina, CA; WJCC(AM) Miami Springs, FL; WNMA Miami Springs, FL; WEXY Wilton Manors, FL; WGFS Covington, GA; WNTD Chicago, IL; WLYN Lynn, MA; WAZN(AM) Watertown, MA; WJDM Elizabeth, NJ; WWRU(AM) Jersey City, NJ; WNSW Newark, NJ; WPAT Paterson, NJ; WTTM Princeton, NJ; WHWH Princeton, NJ; WNYG Babylon, NY; WZRC New York, NY; WKDM(AM) New York, NY; KXYZ Houston, TX; KMNY(AM) Hurst, TX; KVJY Pharr, TX; KZDC San Antonio, TX; WZHF Arlington, VA; KXPA Bellevue, WA; WLXE(AM) Rockville, MD

Arthur S. Liu, pres/CEO.

Munbilla Broadcasting Properties Ltd. 5526 Hwy. 281 N., Marble Falls, TX 78654. Phone: (830) 693-5551. Fax: (830) 693-5107. Ownership: B. Shane Fox, 100%.

Stns: 1 AM. 3 FM. KBEY(FM) Burnet, TX; KRHC(AM) Burnet, TX; KHLB(FM) Burnet, TX; KHLE(FM) Mason, TX

Duane Fox, gen mgr; Sabrina Preiss, traf mgr; Bill Woleben, chief engr & opns mgr.

Morgan Murphy Stations (Evening Telegram Co) Box 44965, Madison, WI 53744-4965. Phone: (608) 271-4321. Fax: (608) 271-6111. E-mail: talkback@wisctv.com. Web Site: www.channel3000.com. Ownership: Evening Telegram Co. owns 100% of KVEW(TV), KXLY-AM-FM-TV, KXLY-DT and KAPP(TV). Evening Telegram Co. owns 84.4% of Television Wisconsin Inc., with an additional 15.2% of the stn held by Evening Telegram stockholders.

Stns: 4 AM. 3 FM. KXLX(AM) Airway Heights, WA; KXLY Spokane, WA; KZZU-FM Spokane, WA; KEZE-FM Spokane, WA; WGLR Lancaster, WI; WPVL Platteville, WI; WPVL-FM Platteville, WI

Stns: 5 TV. WKBT, La Crosse-Eau Claire, WI; WISC, Madison, WI; KXLY, Spokane, WA; KAPP, Yakima-Pasco-Richland-Kennewick, WA; KVEW, Yakima-Pasco-Richland-Kennewick, WA

The Evening Telegram principals own *Madison Magazine*, Madison, WI.

Elizabeth Murphy Burns, pres; George Nelson, exec VP; David Sanks, exec VP; Steve Herling, exec VP; Darrell Blue, VP/gen mgr; Scott Chorski, VP/gen mgr.

Muzzy Broadcasting L.L.C. 500 Division St., Stevens Point, WI 54481. Phone: (715) 341-9800. Fax: (715) 341-0000. Web Site: www.979wspt.com. Ownership: Richard L. Muzzy.

Stns: 1 AM. 1 FM. WKQH-FM Marathon, WI; WSPT Stevens Point, WI

Richard L. Muzzy, pres.

N

NRC Broadcasting Inc. 1201 Eighteenth St., Suite 250, Denver, CO 80202. Phone: (303) 675-4698. Fax: (303) 296-7030. Web Site: www.nrcbroadcasting.com. Ownership: Anschutz Co., 60.9%; Tim Brown, 33.5%; Ray Skibitsky, 2.8%; and Dave Rogers, 2.8%.

Stns: 1 AM. 10 FM. KSPN-FM Aspen, CO; KNFO-FM Basalt, CO; KSMT-FM Breckenridge, CO; KTUN-FM Eagle, CO; KKCH-FM Glenwood Springs, CO; KRMR(FM) Hayden, CO; KIDN-FM Hayden, CO; KCUV(AM) Littleton, CO; KFMU-FM Oak Creek, CO; KJAC(FM) Timnath, CO; KSKE-FM Vail, CO

Tim Brown, chmn/CEO; Ray Skibitsky, pres/COO; Dave Rogers, CFO.

Nassau Broadcasting Partners L.P. 619 Alexander Rd., 3rd Fl., Princeton, NJ 08540. Phone: (609) 452-9696. Fax: 609) 419-0143. Web Site: www.nassaubroadcasting.com.

Stns: 15 AM. 31 FM. WTHT(FM) Auburn, ME; WBQI(FM) Bar Harbor, ME; WLVP(AM) Gorham, ME; WBYA(FM) Islesboro, ME; WBQQ-FM Kennebunk, ME; WHXQ(FM) Kennebunkport, ME; WFNK(FM) Lewiston, ME; WLAM(AM) Lewiston, ME; WHXR(FM) North Windham, ME; WBQW-FM Scarborough, ME; WBQX-FM Thomaston, ME; WNHW(FM) Belmont, NH; WHDQ-FM Claremont, NH; WTSV Claremont, NH; WJYY-FM Concord, NH; WNNH-FM Henniker, NH; WLNH-FM Laconia, NH; WEMJ Laconia, NH; WWHQ(FM) Meredith, NH; WFNQ(FM) Nashua, NH; WCFR-FM Walpole, NH; WLKZ-FM Wolfeboro, NH; WWYY-FM Belvidere, NJ; WCHR(AM) Flemington, NJ; WPHY(AM) Trenton, NJ; WTHK(FM) Trenton, NJ; WPST(FM) Trenton, NJ; WTKZ Allentown, PA; WEEX Easton, PA; WYNS Lehighton, PA; WPLY(AM) Mount Pocono, PA; WVPO Stroudsburg, PA; WORK-FM Barre, VT; WSNO Barre, VT; WZLF(FM) Bellows Falls, VT; WWFY(FM) Berlin, VT; WEXP(FM) Brandon, VT; WMOO-FM Derby Center, VT; WWOD(FM) Hartford, VT; WIKE Newport, VT; WXLF(FM) White River Junction, VT; WNHV White River Junction, VT; WVAY(FM) Wilmington, VT; WARK Hagerstown, MD; WWEG(FM) Hagerstown, MD; WAFY-FM Middletown, MD

Louis F. Mercatani, pres.

Nebraska Rural Radio Association Box 880, Lexington, NE 68850. Phone: (308) 324-2371. Fax: (308) 324-5786. E-mail: krvnam@krvn.com. Web Site: www.krvn.com. Ownership: Rural Radio Network, 100%.

Stns: 3 AM. 2 FM. KRVN Lexington, NE; KNEB Scottsbluff, NE; KNEB-FM Scottsbluff, NE; KTIC West Point, NE; KWPN-FM West Point, NE

Eric Brown, sec/treas; Dale Hanson, pres; Larry Huokins, VP.

Neely Enterprises Box 861, Rock Hill, SC 29731. Phone: (803) 329-2664. Phone: (803) 329-2760. Fax: (803) 329-3317. Fax: (803) 329-8652.

Stns: 2 AM. 1 FM. WLTC Gastonia, NC; WGCD Chester, SC; WAAW-FM Williston, SC

Frank Neely, pres.

Neuhoff Family L.P. 1501 N. Washington, Danville, IL 61832. Phone: (217) 442-1700. Phone: (217) 787-9200. Fax: (217) 431-1489. Web Site: www.wdnlfm.com. Ownership: Neuhoff Corp., North Palm Beach, FL, 100% of votes.

Stns: 1 AM. 1 FM. WRHK-FM Danville, IL; WDAN(AM) Danville, IL

Stns: 1 TV. KMVT, Twin Falls, ID

Mike Hulvey, gen mgr; Geoff Neuhoff, pres.

Nevada County Broadcasters Inc. 1255 E. Main St., Suite A, Grass Valley, CA 95945. Phone: (530) 272-3424. Fax: (530) 272-2872. E-mail: knco@nccn.com. Web Site: www.knco.com.

Stns: 2 AM. 1 FM. KNCO Grass Valley, CA; KNCO-FM Grass Valley, CA; KUBA Yuba City, CA

Bob Breck, CEO.

New Media Broadcasters Inc. 2210 31st St. N., Havre, MT 59501-8003. Phone: (406) 265-7841. Fax: (406) 265-8855. E-mail: nmb@nmbi.com. Web Site: www.nmbi.com. Ownership: C. David Leeds, 100%.

Stns: 1 AM. 2 FM. KRYK-FM Chinook, MT; KOJM Havre, MT; KPQX-FM Havre, MT

C. David Leeds, pres.

New Northwest Broadcasters LLC 15405 S.E. 37th St., Suite 130, Bellevue, WA 98006. Phone: (425) 653-2310. Fax: (425) 653-2454. Web Site: www.nnbradio.com. Ownership: E. Perot Bissell, 50%; and Bradford N. Creswell, 50%.

Stns: 11 AM. 20 FM. KFAT(FM) Anchorage, AK; KDBZ(FM) Anchorage, AK; KUWL-FM College, AK; KWLF-FM Fairbanks, AK; KXLR-FM Fairbanks, AK; KCBF Fairbanks, AK; KFAR Fairbanks, AK; KQEZ-FM Houston, AK; KRPM(FM) Houston, AK; KZRV(FM) Billings, MT; KQBL(FM) Billings, MT; KGHL Billings, MT; GHL-FM Billings, MT; KRSQ-FM Laurel, MT; KKEE(AM) Astoria, OR; KAST Astoria, OR; KYSF-FM Bonanza, OR; KAGO Klamath Falls, OR; KKJX(AM) Klamath Falls, OR; KCRX-FM Seaside, OR; KARY-FM Grandview, WA; KVAS(FM) Ilwaco, WA; KTCR Kennewick, WA; KAQX(FM) Long Beach, WA; KIOK-FM Richland, WA; KALE Richland, WA; KBBO(AM) Selah, WA; KNLT-FM Walla Walla, WA; KUJ-FM Walla Walla, WA; KHHK-FM Yakima, WA; KJOX(AM) Yakima, WA

Pete Benedetti, CEO.

New South Communications Inc. Box 5797, Meridian, MS 39302. Phone: (601) 693-2661. Fax: (601) 483-0826. Ownership: F.E. Holladay, 100%.

Stns: 2 AM. 4 FM. KJLO-FM Monroe, LA; WYOY-FM Gluckstadt, MS; WUSJ(FM) Jackson, MS; WALT Meridian, MS; WIIN Ridgeland, MS; WJKK-FM Vicksburg, MS

F.E. Holladay, pres.

New West Broadcasting Corp. 1145 Kilauea Ave., Hilo, HI 96720. Phone: (808) 935-5461. Fax: (808) 935-7761. Ownership: NWB Holdings Inc., 80% stockholder; and Christopher S. Leonard, 20% stockholder.

Stns: 1 AM. 2 FM. KNWB-FM Hilo, HI; KPUA Hilo, HI; KAOY(FM) Kealakekua, HI

The New York Times Co. 229 W. 43rd St., New York, NY 10036. Phone: (212) 556-1234. Web Site: www.nytco.com. Ownership: (See also Cross-Ownership, Sect. A.)

Stns: 1 AM. WQXR-FM New York, NY

Stns: 8 TV. WQAD, Davenport, IA-Rock Island-Moline, IL; WHO-TV, Des Moines-Ames, IA; KFSM-TV, Ft. Smith-Fayetteville-Springdale-Rogers, AR; WHNT, Huntsville-Decatur (Florence), AL; WREG, Memphis, TN; WTKR, Norfolk-Portsmouth-Newport News, VA; KFOR, Oklahoma City, OK; WNEP, Wilkes Barre-Scranton, PA

The New York Times Co. publishes *The New York Times, The Boston* (MA) *Globe* and the *Worcester Telegram & Gazette,* Worcester, MA, and fifteen regional newspapers located throughout the southeast and in California.

Cynthia Augustine, pres.

NewCap Inc. 745 Windmill Rd., Dartmouth, NS B3B1C2. Canada. Phone: (902) 468-7557. Fax: (902) 468-7558. Web Site: www.ncc.ca. Ownership: H.R. Steele, Blavin & Company.

Stns: 25 AM. 22 FM. CKBA Athabasca, AB; CJPR-FM Blairmore, AB; CIBQ Brooks, AB; CIQX-FM Calgary, AB; CFCW Camrose, AB; CKDQ Drumheller, AB; CKRA-FM Edmonton, AB; CIRK-FM Edmonton, AB; CJYR(AM) Edson, AB; CJXK-FM Grand Centre (Cold Lake), AB; CKVH High Prairie, AB; CIYR-FM Hinton, AB; CKSA-FM Lloydminster, AB; CKGY-FM Red Deer, AB; CIZZ-FM Red Deer, AB; CHLW Saint Paul, AB; CKWA Slave Lake, AB; CKSQ Stettler, AB; CKKY Wainwright, AB; CKWY-FM Wainwright, AB; CFOK(AM) Westlock, AB; CKJR Wetaskiwin, AB; CFRK-FM Fredericton, NB; CKIM Baie Verte, NF; CHVO Carbonear, NF; CFLC-FM Churchill Falls, NF; CKVO Clarenville, NF; CKXX-FM Corner Brook, NF; CFCB Corner Brook, NF; CKGA Gander, NF; CKXD-FM Gander, NF; CFLN Goose Bay, NF; CKCM Grand Falls, NF; CKXG-FM Grand Falls-Windsor, NF; CHCM Marystown, NF; CFNW Port au Choix, NF; CFCV-FM Saint Andrews, NF; CKIX-FM Saint John's, NF; VOCM(AM) Saint John's, NF; CFSX Stephenville, NF; CFLW Wabush, NF; CKUL-FM Halifax, NS; CIHT-FM Ottawa, ON; CHNO-FM Sudbury, ON; CJUK-FM Thunder Bay, ON; CKTG-FM Thunder Bay, ON; CHTN Charlottetown, PE

Stns: 2 TV. CITL, Lloydminster, AB; CKSA, Lloydminster, AB

H.R. Steele, chmn; Scott Weatherby, CEO; R.G. Steele, pres/CEO.

Newfoundland Broadcasting Co. (NTV & OZ Networks). Box 2020, St. John's, NF A1C 5S2. Canada. Phone: (709) 722-5015. Fax: (709) 726-5107. E-mail: ozfm@ozfm.com. Web Site: www.ntv.ca. Ownership: Geoffrey W. Stirling, 89.95%; G. Scott Stirling, 10%; and others, 0.05%.

Stns: 8 FM. CJOZ-FM Bonavista Bay, NF; CJKK-FM Clarenville, NF; CKOZ-FM Corner Brook, NF; CIOZ-FM Marystown, NF; CHOS-FM Rattling Brook, NF; CKSS-FM Red Rocks, NF; CHOZ-FM Saint John's, NF; CIOS-FM Stephenville, NF

Stns: 6 TV. CJOM, Argentia, NF; CJWB, Bonavista, NF; CJWN, Corner Brook, NF; CJOX-1, Grand Bank, NF; CJCN, Grand Falls, NF; CJSV, Stephenville, NF

Scott G. Stirling, pres/CEO; Doug Neal, engrg dir.

NewRadio Group LLC 2875 Mount Vernon Rd. S.E., Cedar Rapids, IA 52403. Phone: (319) 862-0300. Fax: (319) 286-9383. E-mail: sjones@newradiogroup.com. Ownership: Quass Communications L.L.C., 100% of votes. Percentage of total assets: Alta NRG Holdings Inc., 61.91%; Quass Communications L.L.C., 1.81%; and insulated members, 36.28%.

Stns: 9 AM. 7 FM. WIXN Dixon, IL; WSEY(FM) Oregon, IL; WRKX(FM) Ottawa, IL; WCMY(AM) Ottawa, IL; WJBD Salem, IL; WFAW Fort Atkinson, WI; WDLB Marshfield, WI; WLKD Minocqua, WI; WBDL-FM Reedsburg, WI; WRDB Reedsburg, WI; WOBT Rhinelander, WI; WHDG-FM Rhinelander, WI; WOSQ-FM Spencer, WI; WKCH-FM Whitewater, WI; WYTE-FM Whiting, WI; WFHR Wisconsin Rapids, WI

Mary Quass, pres/CEO.

News-Press & Gazette Co. Box 29, St. Joseph, MO 64502. Phone: (816) 271-8500. Fax: (816) 271-8695. Ownership: David R. Bradley Jr., Henry H. Bradley, Lyle E. Leimkuhler. Cable TV: NPG Cable of Arizona.

Stns: 1 AM. 1 FM. KESQ Indio, CA; KUNA-FM La Quinta, CA

Stns: 4 TV. KTVZ, Bend, OR; KVIA-TV, El Paso, TX; KIFI, Idaho Falls-Pocatello, ID; KESQ-TV, Palm Springs, CA

News-Press & Gazette Co. publishes the *St. Joseph News-Press,* St. Joseph, MO.

John Kueneke, pres.

Newsweb Corp. 1645 W. Fullerton Ave., Chicago, IL 60614. Phone: (773) 975-0401. Fax: (773) 975-1301. Ownership: Fred Eychaner, 100%.

Stns: 5 AM. 4 FM. WKIE-FM Arlington Heights, IL; WAIT(AM) Chicago, IL; WSBC(AM) Chicago, IL; WCFJ Chicago Heights, IL; WCPT(AM) Crystal Lake, IL; WDEK-FM De Kalb, IL; WKIF-FM Kankakee, IL; WRZA(FM) Park Forest, IL; WNDZ Portage, IN

Stns: 2 TV. KTVD, Denver, CO; KUPN, Denver, CO

Fred Eychaner, CEO; Charley Gross, COO.

Radio Group Ownership

NextMedia Group Inc. 6312 S. Fiddler's Green Cir., Suite 360E, Englewood, CO 80111. Phone: (303) 694-9118. Fax: (303) 694-4940. Web Site: www.nextmediagroup.net.

Stns: 12 AM. 45 FM. WERV-FM Aurora, IL; WRXQ(FM) Coal City, IL; WSOY-FM Decatur, IL; WDZ(AM) Decatur, IL; WDZQ(FM) Decatur, IL; WWYW(FM) Dundee, IL; WJOL Joliet, IL; WCZQ-FM Monticello, IL; WKRS Waukegan, IL; WXLC-FM Waukegan, IL; WZSR-FM Woodstock, IL; WXQL(FM) Carrollton, MI; WCEN-FM Hemlock, MI; WSGW Saginaw, MI; WTLZ-FM Saginaw, MI; WQZL(FM) Belhaven, NC; WKXB-FM Burgaw, NC; WANG Havelock, NC; WSSM(FM) Havelock, NC; WXQR-FM Jacksonville, NC; WQSL-FM Jacksonville, NC; WILT(FM) Jacksonville, NC; WRNS-FM Kinston, NC; WSFM(FM) Oak Island, NC; WAZO(FM) Southport, NC; WERO(FM) Washington, NC; WMFD Wilmington, NC; WRQR-FM Wilmington, NC; KTHX-FM Dayton, NV; KURK(FM) Reno, NV; KRZQ-FM Sparks, NV; KJZS(FM) Sparks, NV; WHBC Canton, OH; KVSO(AM) Ardmore, OK; KKAJ-FM Ardmore, OK; KTRX(FM) Dickson, OK; KLAK(FM) Durant, OK; KYNZ(FM) Lone Grove, OK; WRTS-FM Erie, PA; WJET(AM) Erie, PA; WFGO-FM Erie, PA; WFNN(AM) Erie, PA; WUSE(FM) Fairview, PA; WRKT-FM North East, PA; WYAV(FM) Myrtle Beach, SC; WMYB(FM) Myrtle Beach, SC; WQJM(FM) Myrtle Beach, SC; WKZQ-FM Myrtle Beach, SC; WRNN(FM) Socastee, SC; WKMT-FM Bells, TX; KONE(FM) Lubbock, TX; KLLL-FM Lubbock, TX; KMMX(FM) Tahoka, TX; KMAD-FM Whitesboro, TX; WLIP Kenosha, WI; WEXT-FM Sturtevant, WI; WJBR-FM Wilmington, DE

Steven Dinetz, CEO; Skip Weller, pres.

Nicolet Broadcasting Inc. 3030 Park Drive, Suite 3, Sturgeon Bay, WI 54235. Phone: (920) 746-9430. Fax: (920) 746-9433. E-mail: wbbk@doorcountydailynews.com. Web Site: www.doorcountydailynews.com. Ownership: Roger Utnehmer.

Stns: 3 FM. WRLU-FM Algoma, WI; WBDK-FM Algoma, WI; WRKU-FM Forestville, WI

Roger Utnehmer, pres & gen mgr.

Noalmark Broadcasting Corp. 202 W. 19th St., El Dorado, AR 71730. Phone: (870) 862-7777. Fax: (870) 862-0203. Ownership: William C. Nolan Jr., 65%; Edwin B. Alderson Jr., 35%.

Stns: 6 AM. 10 FM. KMRX(FM) El Dorado, AR; KELD El Dorado, AR; KMLK(FM) El Dorado, AR; KAGL(FM) El Dorado, AR; KELD-FM Hampton, AR; KLAZ-FM Hot Springs, AR; KPZA(AM) Hot Springs, AR; KBHS(AM) Hot Springs, AR; KVMA Magnolia, AR; KBOK(AM) Malvern, AR; KLEZ(FM) Malvern, AR; KWDO(FM) Waldo, AR; KYKK(AM) Hobbs, NM; KIXN(FM) Hobbs, NM; KPER(FM) Hobbs, NM; KPZA-FM Jal, NM

William C. Nolan Jr., pres; Edwin B. Alderson Jr., exec VP; Paul Starr, VP; Anna Canterbury, sec/treas.

Norsan Consulting and Management Inc. Box 2148, Tucker, GA 30085. Phone: (770) 414-5026. Ownership: Norberto Sanchez, 100%.

Stns: 4 AM. WVOJ(AM) Fernandina Beach, FL; WNNR(AM) Jacksonville, FL; WGSP Charlotte, NC; WXNC(AM) Monroe, NC

North American Broadcasting Co. Inc. 1458 Dublin Rd., Columbus, OH 43215. Phone: (614) 481-7800. Fax: (614) 481-8070. Web Site: www.nabco-inc.com. Ownership: Norma Mnich; Matthew Mnich.

Stns: 1 AM. 2 FM. WBZX-FM Columbus, OH; WMNI Columbus, OH; WTDA(FM) Westerville, OH

Norma Mnich, chmn; Matthew Mnich, pres/CEO; Mark Jividen, VP.

North Cascades Broadcasting Inc. Box 151, Omak, WA 98841. Phone: (509) 826-0100. Fax: (509) 826-3929. Web Site: www.komw.net.

Stns: 1 AM. 1 FM. KOMW Omak, WA; KZBE-FM Omak, WA

John Andrist, pres.

Northeast Broadcasting Company Inc. 288 S. River Rd., Bedford, NH 03110. Phone: (603) 668-9999. Fax: (603) 668-6470. Ownership: Steven A. Silberberg, Ed Flanagan.

Stns: 9 AM. 15 FM. WNYN-FM Athol, MA; WGAW Gardner, MA; WXRV-FM Haverhill, MA; WJOE-FM Orange-Athol, MA; WKBR Manchester, NH; WTWK(AM) Plattsburgh, NY; WXAL-FM Addison, VT; WDOT(FM) Danville, VT; WFAD Middlebury, VT; WNCS-FM Montpelier, VT; WSKI Montpelier, VT; WRJT-FM Royalton, VT; WRSA(FM) Saint Albans, VT; WWMP(FM) Waterbury, VT; KSHF(FM) Cheyenne, WY; KRAE Cheyenne, WY; KCUG(FM) Chugwater, WY; KTED(FM) Douglas, WY; KBOG(FM) Douglas, WY; KANT(FM) Guernsey, WY; KIMX(FM) Laramie, WY; KHAT(AM) Laramie, WY; KROW(FM) Lovell, WY; KHAD(FM) Mills, WY

Steven Silberberg, CEO; Edward Flanagan, VP.

Northeast Colorado Broadcasting LLC 220 State St., Suite 106, Fort Morgan, CO 80701. Phone: (970) 867-7271. Fax: (970) 867-2676. Ownership: Alexander L. Creighton, 66.67%; Ross O. Miller, 33.33%.

Stns: 1 AM. 2 FM. KPRB-FM Brush, CO; KSIR Brush, CO; KPMX(FM) Sterling, CO

Alec L. Creighton, gen mgr.

Northeast Communications Corp. 110 Babbit Rd., Franklin, NH 03235. Phone: (603) 934-2500. Fax: (603) 934-2933. E-mail: onair@mix941fm.com. Web Site: www.mix941fm.com. Ownership: Jeff Fisher, 44.5%; Chris Fisher, 17.5%; and Phil Fisher, 16.5%.

Stns: 2 AM. 1 FM. WFTN Franklin, NH; WSCY-FM Moultonborough, NH; WPNH Plymouth, NH

Jeff Fisher, pres; Fred Caruso, progmg dir; Rick Ganley, progmg dir; Cathy Keyser, opns mgr.

Northern Christian Radio Inc. Box 695, Gaylord, MI 49734-0695. Phone: (800) 545-8857. Phone: (989) 732-6274. E-mail: ncr@ncradio.org. Web Site: www.ncradio.org.

Stns: 3 FM. WOLW-FM Cadillac, MI; WTHN(FM) Sault Ste. Marie, MI; WHST-FM Tawas City, MI

Northern Star Broadcasting L.L.C. 1356 Mackinaw Ave., Cheboygan, MI 49721. Phone: (231) 627-2341. Fax: (231) 627-7000. E-mail: cmonk@nsbroadcasting.com.

Stns: 4 AM. 12 FM. WCKC-FM Cadillac, MI; WCBY Cheboygan, MI; WGFM(FM) Cheboygan, MI; WGFN(FM) Glen Arbor, MI; WJZJ(FM) Glen Arbor, MI; WIMK-FM Iron Mountain, MI; WIAN Ishpeming, MI; WLJZ(FM) Mackinaw City, MI; WDMJ Marquette, MI; WUPK-FM Marquette, MI; WAVC-FM Mio, MI; WNGE-FM Negaunee, MI; WIHC-FM Newberry, MI; WZNL-FM Norway, MI; WIDG Saint Ignace, MI; WYSS-FM Sault Ste. Marie, MI

Chris Monk, VP; Palmer Pyle, pres.

Northwestern College & Radio 3003 Snelling Ave. N., St. Paul, MN 55113-1598. Phone: (651) 631-5000. Fax: (651) 631-5086. E-mail: phvirts@nwc.edu. Web Site: www.nwc.edu. Ownership: Non-profit organization. Northwestern College, St. Paul, is the owner and operator of the 15 radio licenses.

Stns: 5 AM. 8 FM. WSMR-FM Sarasota, FL; KNWM(FM) Madrid, IA; KNWI(FM) Osceola, IA; KNWS Waterloo, IA; KDNI(FM) Duluth, MN; KDNW(FM) Duluth, MN; KTIS Minneapolis, MN; KTIS-FM Minneapolis, MN; KFNW-FM Fargo, ND; KFNW(AM) West Fargo, ND; KNWC(AM) Sioux Falls, SD; WNWC-FM Madison, WI; WNWC(AM) Sun Prairie, WI

Dr. Paul Virts, sr VP; Dr. Alan Cureton, pres.

O

Omni Broadcasting Co. Box 1656, Bemidji, MN 56619-1656. Phone: (218) 444-1500. Fax: (218) 759-0345. Ownership: Louis H. Buron Jr., Mary Campbell, Mike Boen.

Stns: 5 AM. 10 FM. KULO(FM) Alexandria, MN; KBHP(FM) Bemidji, MN; KBUN Bemidji, MN; KKZY-FM Bemidji, MN; KLIZ Brainerd, MN; KLIZ-FM Brainerd, MN; KUAL-FM Brainerd, MN; KVBR Brainerd, MN; WJJY-FM Brainerd, MN; KBLB(FM) Nisswa, MN; KIKV-FM Sauk Centre, MN; KNSP Staples, MN; KWAD Wadena, MN; KKWS-FM Wadena, MN; KLLZ-FM Walker, MN

Louis H. Buron Jr., pres/CEO; Mary Campbell, VP.

On Top Communications Inc. 4601 Presidents Dr., Suite 134, Lanham, MD 20706. Phone: (301) 731-3000. Fax: (301) 731-0021. Ownership: OCP IV On Top Inc., 38.7% of votes, 20.2% of total assets; MMG Ventures LP, 30.6% of votes, 16% of total assets; The Bon Secours Community Investment Fund LP, 17.4% of votes, 9.1% of total assets; Opportunity Capital Corp., 5.3% of votes, 2.8% of total assets.

Stns: 5 FM. WFFM(FM) Ashburn, GA; WRXZ(FM) Sylvester, GA; KNOU(FM) Empire, LA; WRJH-FM Brandon, MS; WWHV(FM) Virginia Beach, VA

Steve Hegwood, pres.

One Ten Broadcast Group Inc. 2 E. Main St., Shawnee, OK 74801-6906. Phone: (405) 878-1803. E-mail: kirc1059@aol.com. Ownership: Linda D. Jones, executrix of estate of Herman L. Jones, 100%.

Stns: 1 AM. 1 FM. KIRC(FM) Seminole, OK; KWSH Wewoka, OK

Linda Jones, pres.

The O'Neal Broadcasting Corp. Box 2016, Monticello, MS 39654. Phone: (601) 587-9363. Fax: (601) 587-9401. Ownership: Marcus Rusty O'Neal, 100%.

Stns: 1 AM. 1 FM. WOEG Hazlehurst, MS; WRQO-FM Monticello, MS

Marcus Rusty O'Neal, pres.

Opus Broadcasting Systems Inc. 511 Rossanley Dr., Medford, OR 97501. Phone: (541) 772-0322. Fax: (541) 772-4233. Ownership: Henry Flock, 70%; Dean Flock, 20%; Alan Benz, 5%; and John Lavoie, 5%.

Stns: 2 AM. 2 FM. KCNA(FM) Cave Junction, OR; KROG-FM Grants Pass, OR; KRTA Medford, OR; KEZX(AM) Medford, OR

Dean Flock, gen mgr.

Opus Media Holdings LLC 900 Third Ave., 26th Fl., New York, NY 10022. Phone: (212) 634-3376. Ownership: Opus Capital LLC, 100% of votes.

Stns: 11 FM. WHTF-FM Havana, FL; WEGT(FM) Lafayette, FL; WUTL(FM) Tallahassee, FL; WAIB-FM Tallahassee, FL; KBKK(FM) Ball, LA; KEZP-FM Bunkie, LA; KQLQ(FM) Columbia, LA; KXRR(FM) Monroe, LA; KMYY(FM) Rayville, LA; KLAA(FM) Tioga, LA; KZRZ(FM) West Monroe, LA

Richard Linhart, chmn; James Shea, pres/CEO.

The Original Company Inc. Box 242, Vincennes, IN 47591. Phone: (812) 882-6060. Fax: (812) 885-2604. E-mail: info@originalcompany.com. Web Site: www.originalcompany.com. Ownership: Mark R. Lange, 50%; Saundra K. Lange, 50%.

Stns: 3 AM. 7 FM. WUZR-FM Bicknell, IN; WREB-FM Greencastle, IN; WQTY-FM Linton, IN; WBTO Linton, IN; WRCY(AM) Mount Vernon, IN; WYFX(FM) Mount Vernon, IN; WBTO-FM Petersburg, IN; WZDM-FM Vincennes, IN; WAOV Vincennes, IN; WWBL-FM Washington, IN

Mark R. Lange, pres.

Ouachita Broadcasting Inc. Box 1450, Mena, AR 71953. Phone: (479) 394-1450. Ownership: Jay Bunyard, 50%; and Bobby Caldwell, 50%.

Stns: 1 AM. 3 FM. KILX(FM) Hatfield, AR; KQOR(FM) Mena, AR; KENA(AM) Mena, AR; KENA-FM Mena, AR

Our Three Sons Broadcasting L.L.P. Box 307, Rock Hill, SC 29731. Phone: (803) 324-1340. Fax: (803) 324-2860. Web Site: www.wrhi.com. Ownership: Allan M. Miller, mngg ptnr; Manning Kimmel, ptnr.

Stns: 1 AM. 1 FM. WVSZ-FM Chesterfield, SC; WRHI Rock Hill, SC

Allan M. Miller, pres.

Buck Owens Productions Inc. 3223 Sillect, Bakersfield, CA 93308. Phone: (661) 326-1011. Fax: (661) 328-7503.

Stns: 1 AM. KUZZ Bakersfield, CA

Alvis E. Owens Jr., pres.

P

Pacific Empire Radio Corp. 228 1st St., Idaho Falls, ID 83401. Phone: (208) 528-6813. Fax: (208) 529-6927. E-mail: kclkam@aol.com. Web Site: www.hot106.fm.com. Ownership: Mark L. Bolland and Mary Bolland, JTWROS, 34.3%; John Taylor and Connie Taylor, JTWROS, 30.7%; AIA Services Corp. 401K & Profit Sharing Plan, FBO John Taylor, 13.6%; Hillcrest Aircraft Co., 6.84%; and Randolph Lamberjack, 6%.

Stns: 4 AM. 7 FM. KATW(FM) Lewiston, ID; KSEI Pocatello, ID; KGTM(FM) Rexburg, ID; KRXK(AM) Rexburg, ID; KBJX(FM) Shelley, ID; KQZB(FM) Troy, ID; KBKR Baker City, OR; KRJT(FM) Elgin, OR; KLBM La Grande, OR; KVAB-FM Clarkston, WA; KCLK-FM Clarkston, WA

Mark Bolland, pres/CEO.

Pacific Radio Group Inc. 311 Ano St., Kahului, HI 96732. Phone: (808) 877-5566. Fax: (808) 871-0666. E-mail: bergson@pacificradiogroup.com. Web Site: www.kpoa.com. Ownership: Ed Johnson, Robert Van Dine, Chuck Bergson.

Stns: 4 AM. 10 FM. KHLO Hilo, HI; KAPA(FM) Hilo, HI; KKBG-FM Hilo, HI; KPVS-FM Hilo, HI; KLEO(FM) Kahaluu, HI; KNUI Kahului, HI; KJKS(FM) Kahului, HI; KLUA(FM) Kailua-Kona, HI; KKON(AM) Kealakekua, HI; KLHI-FM Lahaina, HI; KPOA-FM Lahaina, HI; KJMD(FM) Pukalani, HI; KMVI Wailuku, HI; KAGB(FM) Waimea, HI

Chuck Bergson, CEO; Robert Van Dine, dir.

Pacific West Broadcasting Inc. Box 1430, Newport, OR 97365. Phone: (541) 265-2266. Fax: (541) 265-6397. E-mail: info@ybcradio.com. Web Site: ybcradio.com. Ownership: David J. & Linda R. Miller, 100%.

Stns: 1 AM. 2 FM. KBCH Lincoln City, OR; KCRF-FM

Radio Group Ownership

Lincoln City, OR; KNCU(FM) Newport, OR

David Miller, pres.

Pacifica Foundation Inc. (dba Pacific Radio). 1925 Martin Luther King Jr. Way, Berkeley, CA 94704. Phone: (510) 849-2590. Web Site: www.pacifica.org. Ownership: (dba Pacific Radio).

Stns: 5 FM. KPFA-FM Berkeley, CA; KPFK-FM Los Angeles, CA; WPFW-FM Washington, DC; WBAI-FM New York, NY; KPFT-FM Houston, TX

Dan Coughlin, exec dir.

Pamal Broadcasting Ltd. 6 Johnson Rd., Latham, NY 12110. Phone: (518) 786-6600. Fax: (518) 786-6610. Web Site: www.pamal.com. Ownership: James Morrell, owner.

Stns: 7 AM. 19 FM. WRGO-FM Cedar Key, FL; WXBM-FM Milton, FL; WMEZ-FM Pensacola, FL; WDVH-FM Trenton, FL; WPNI(AM) Amherst, MA; WRNX-FM Amherst, MA; WBEC-FM Pittsfield, MA; WROW Albany, NY; WKLI-FM Albany, NY; WZMR-FM Altamont, NY; WBNR-FM Beacon, NY; WXPK(FM) Briarcliff Manor, NY; WFFG-FM Corinth, NY; WMML Glens Falls, NY; WENU-FM Hudson Falls, NY; WIZR Johnstown, NY; WLNA(AM) Peekskill, NY; WSPK-FM Poughkeepsie, NY; WENU(AM) South Glens Falls, NY; WFLY-FM Troy, NY; WAJZ-FM Voorheesville, NY; WKBE-FM Warrensburg, NY; WEBK-FM Killington, VT; WJEN-FM Rutland, VT; WJJR-FM Rutland, VT; WJAN-FM Sunderland, VT

Pamplin Broadcasting 888 S.W. Fifth Ave., Suite 790, Portland, OR 97204. Phone: (503) 223-4321. Fax: (503) 222-2850. E-mail: kpam@kpam.com.

Stns: 3 AM. 1 FM. KDUN(AM) Reedsport, OR; KPAM Troutdale, OR; KTSL-FM Medical Lake, WA; KKAD(AM) Vancouver, WA

Andrea Marek, pres; Paul Clithero, gen mgr.

Pappas Telecasting Companies 500 S. Chinowth Rd., Visalia, CA 93277. Phone: (559) 733-7800. Fax: (559) 733-7878. Ownership: Harry J. Pappas.

Stns: 2 AM. 1 FM. KVBE(FM) Hanford, CA; KTRB Modesto, CA; KPMP(AM) Modesto, CA

Stns: 18 TV. WLGA, Columbus, GA; KPWB, Des Moines-Ames, IA; KDBC, El Paso, TX; KMPH, Fresno-Visalia, CA; KFRE-TV, Fresno-Visalia, CA; WWAZ-TV, Green Bay-Appleton, WI; WTWB-TV, Greensboro-High Point-Winston Salem, NC; KAZH, Houston; KWNB, Lincoln & Hastings-Kearney, NE; KHGI, Lincoln & Hastings-Kearney, NE; KAZA-TV, Los Angeles; KPTM, Omaha, NE; KREN, Reno, NV; KTNC, San Francisco-Oakland-San Jose; KUNO-TV, San Francisco-Oakland-San Jose; KPTH, Sioux City, IA; KAZW-TV, Yakima-Pasco-Richland-Kennewick, WA; KSWT, Yuma, AZ-El Centro, CA

Harry J. Pappas, pres/CEO.

Paradis Broadcasting of Alexandria Inc. 1312 Broadway, Alexandria, MN 56308. Phone: (320) 763-3131. Fax: (320) 763-5641. E-mail: thefolks@kxra.com. Web Site: www.kxra.com. Ownership: Mel Paradis, 60%; Brett Paradis, 40%.

Stns: 1 AM. 1 FM. KXRZ(FM) Alexandria, MN; KXRA Alexandria, MN

Mel Paradis, CEO; Brett Paradis, pres & gen mgr; Bill Franzen, VP.

Paragon Communications Inc. Box 945, Elk City, OK 73648. Phone: (580) 225-9696. Fax: (580) 225-9699. E-mail: keco@io2online.com. Web Site: www.kecofm.com.

Stns: 1 AM. 2 FM. KADS Elk City, OK; KECO(FM) Elk City, OK; KXOO(FM) Elk City, OK

Blake Brewer, pres & gen mgr.

The Jim Pattison Broadcast Group 460 Pemberton Terrace, Kamloops, BC V2C 1T5. Canada. Phone: (250) 372-3322. Fax: (250) 374-0445. Web Site: www.jpbroadcast.com. Ownership: Jim Pattison Group.

Stns: 3 AM. 17 FM. CIBW-FM Drayton Valley, AB; CJXX-FM Grande Prairie, AB; CHLB-FM Lethbridge, AB; CFMY-FM Medicine Hat, AB; CHAT Medicine Hat, AB; CHUB-FM Red Deer, AB; CFDV-FM Red Deer, AB; CHBW-FM Rocky Mountain House, AB; CJBZ-FM Taber, AB; CHBZ-FM Cranbrook, BC; CHDR-FM Cranbrook, BC; CJDR-FM Fernie, BC; CKBZ-FM Kamloops, BC; CKOV Kelowna, BC; CKLZ-FM Kelowna, BC; CKOV Kelowna, BC; CKDV-FM Prince George, BC; CKKN-FM Prince George, BC; CJJR-FM Vancouver, BC; CKBD Vancouver, BC

Stns: 4 TV. CFJC-TV, Kamloops, BC; CHAT, Medicine Hat, AB; CHAT-1, Pivot, AB; CKPG, Prince George, BC

Rick Arnish, pres.

Pearson Broadcasting 9530 Miolothian Pike, Richmond, VA 23235. Phone: (804) 521-0603. Fax: (804) 674-8938. Ownership: Max H. Pearson, 100%.

Stns: 4 FM. KBCN-FM Marshall, AR; KTTG-FM Mena, AR; KERX(FM) Paris, AR; KMAC-FM Gainesville, MO

Max H. Pearson, pres; Bruce W. Hale, VP.

Peg Broadcasting Crossville LLC 961 Miller Ave., Crossville, TN 38555. Phone: (931) 707-1102. Fax: (931) 707-1220. Ownership: Jeffrey H. Shaw, 50%; and John T. Crunk Jr., 50%.

Stns: 2 AM. 2 FM. WPBX(FM) Crossville, TN; WOWF-FM Crossville, TN; WAEW Crossville, TN; WCSV Crossville, TN

Peggy Sue Broadcasting Corp. Box 838, Richlands, VA 24641. Phone: (276) 964-4066. Fax: (276) 963-4927. Ownership: Henry Beam, 50%; Dirk Hall, 49%; and Peggy Beam, 1%.

Stns: 1 AM. 1 FM. WNRG Grundy, VA; WRIC-FM Richlands, VA

Pembrook Pines Media Group 1705 Lake St., Elmira, NY 14901. Phone: (607) 733-5626. Fax: (607) 733-5627. E-mail: ppinesmedia1@stny.rr.com. Web Site: www.wlvy94rock.com. Ownership: Robert J. Pfuntner, 100%. Company also owns Pembrook Pines Media agency.

Stns: 5 AM. 3 FM. WZKZ-FM Alfred, NY; WABH Bath, NY; WELM Elmira, NY; WEHH Elmira Heights-Horseheads, NY; WOEN(AM) Olean, NY; WMXO-FM Olean, NY; WOKN-FM Southport, NY; WPIE Trumansburg, NY

Robert J. Pfuntner, pres/CEO.

Peninsula Communications Inc. Box 109, Homer, AK 99603. Phone: (907) 235-6000. Fax: (907) 235-6683. E-mail: kwavefm@xyz.net. Ownership: David F. Becker, 50%; Eileen L. Becker, 50%.

Stns: 3 AM. 3 FM. KGTL Homer, AK; KWVV-FM Homer, AK; KXBA(FM) Nikiski, AK; KPEN-FM Soldotna, AK

Tim White, opns mgr; Dave Webb, production mgr; David Becker, gen mgr.

Perception Media Group Inc. 1848 Clay St. S.E., Roanoke, VA 24013. Phone: (540) 343-7109. Fax: (540) 343-2306. E-mail: 3wr@3wradio.com. Web Site: www.3wrradio.com.

Stns: 3 AM. WCQV(AM) Moneta, VA; WNRV(AM) Narrows-Pearisburg, VA; WWWR Roanoke, VA

Ben Peyton, pres/CEO; Barbara Evans, gen mgr.

Perry Publishing & Broadcasting Co. c/o KVSP(AM), 1528 N.E. 23rd St., Oklahoma City, OK 73111. Phone: (405) 425-4100. Fax: (405) 424-8811. Web Site: www.kvsp.com.

Stns: 3 AM. 5 FM. KVSP(FM) Anadarko, OK; KJMM-FM Bixby, OK; KDDQ(FM) Comanche, OK; KPNS(AM) Duncan, OK; KKRX Lawton, OK; KXCA(FM) Lawton, OK; KRMP(AM) Oklahoma City, OK; KGTO Tulsa, OK

Russell Perry, pres/CEO.

Petracom Media L.L.C. 1527 N. Dale Mabry, Suite 105, Lutz, FL 33548. Phone: (813) 948-2554. Fax: (813) 948-2557. Web Site: www.petracommedia.com. Ownership: Henry Ash.

Stns: 2 AM. 2 FM. KDJI Holbrook, AZ; KZUA-FM Holbrook, AZ; KSNX-FM Show Low, AZ; KVWM(AM) Show Low, AZ

Henry A. Ash, pres/CEO; Joseph M. Fry, CFO; F. Lewis Robertson, COO.

Pharis Broadcasting Inc. Box 908, Fort Smith, AR 72902. Phone: (479) 288-1047. Fax: (479) 288-0942. E-mail: ssrg@sbcglobal.net. Web Site: www.fortsmithradiogroup.com. Ownership: William L. Pharis, 51%; Karen Ann Pharis, 49%.

Stns: 2 AM. 3 FM. KOLX-FM Barling, AR; KRBK(FM) Booneville, AR; KFPW Fort Smith, AR; KHGG(AM) Van Buren, AR; KRWA-FM Waldron, AR

William L. Pharis, pres/CEO; Karen A. Pharis, gen mgr & sec.

Phillips Broadcasting Inc. 100 Fisher Dr., Trinidad, CO 81082. Phone: (719) 846-3355. Fax: (719) 846-4711. E-mail: kcrt@adelphia.net.

Stns: 1 AM. 1 FM. KCRT Trinidad, CO; KBKZ(FM) Raton, NM

David Phillips, pres.

Phoenix Media Communications Group 126 Brookline Ave., Boston, MA 02215. Phone: (617) 536-5390. Fax: (617) 859-8201. Web Site: www.thephoenix.com.

Stns: 1 AM. 2 FM. WFNX(FM) Lynn, MA; WPHX(AM) Sanford, ME; WFEX(FM) Peterborough, NH

Barry Morris, pres; Stephen Mindich, CEO.

Piedmont Communications Inc. Box 271, Orange, VA 22960. Phone: (540) 672-1000. Fax: (540) 672-0282. Ownership: Thomas B. Dond, 22.6%; A. Pierce Stone & Pamela H. Stone, 11%; The Cook Family Trust, Mrs. Toy E. Cook, trustee, Richard S. Cook, atty in fact, 9.8%; Lloyd M. Garnett & Barbara G. Garnett, 8.6%; Robert F. Gillespie Jr., 8.6%; and Harry B. Sedwick Jr., 8.6%.

Stns: 2 AM. 1 FM. WCVA Culpeper, VA; WOJL(FM) Louisa, VA; WVCV Orange, VA

Pikes Peak Broadcasting Co. Box 1457, Colorado Springs, CO 80901. Phone: (719) 632-1515. Fax: (719) 475-0815. Web Site: www.krdotv.com. Ownership: The Harry Hoth family.

Stns: 1 AM. KRDO(AM) Colorado Springs, CO

Stns: 2 TV. KRDO-TV, Colorado Springs-Pueblo, CO; KJCT, Grand Junction-Montrose, CO

Patti L. Hoth, pres; Neil D. Klockziem, gen mgr.

Pilgrim Communications Inc. 54 Monument Cir., Suite 250, Indianapolis, IN 46204. Phone: (317) 655-9999.

Stns: 1 AM. KVLE(AM) Vail, CO

Pillar of Fire Inc. Box 9058, Weston Canal Rd., Zarepath, NJ 08890. Phone: (732) 469-0991. Fax: (732) 469-2115. E-mail: info@star991fm.com. Web Site: www.star991fm.com. Ownership: No stockholders; non-profit corporation.

Stns: 1 AM. 2 FM. KPOF Denver, CO; WAWZ(FM) Zarepath, NJ; WAKW-FM Cincinnati, OH

Pillar of Fire Inc. publishes one religious periodical, a semi-monthly for the family *Pillar of Fire*.

Allen Davis, dir opns; Robert B. Dallenbach, pres; Scott Taylor, stn mgr.

Pittman Broadcasting Services LLC 307 S. Jefferson Ave., Covington, LA 70433. Phone: (985) 892-3661. Web Site: www.pittmanbroadcasting.com. Ownership: Marcus Pittman, 50%; and Janet Pittman, 50%.

Stns: 4 AM. 3 FM. WOMN(AM) Franklinton, LA; WUUU(FM) Franklinton, LA; KFXZ(AM) Lafayette, LA; KVOL Lafayette, LA; KKSJ(FM) Maurice, LA; KTSJ(FM) Opelousas, LA; WMYQ Newton, MS

Marcus Pittman, pres.

Platinum Broadcasting Co. Box 789, Junction City, KS 66441. Phone: (785) 762-5525. Fax: (785) 762-5387. E-mail: platinum@kjck.com. Web Site: www.kjck.com.

Stns: 1 AM. 1 FM. KJCK Junction City, KS; KQLA-FM Ogden, KS

Mark Ediger, pres.

Plessinger Radio Group (R.L. Plessinger Holding Co.). 8354 Fryer Rd., Georgetown, OH 45121. Phone: (937) 378-6151. Fax: (937) 378-4143. E-mail: rick@waxz.com. Web Site: www.977waxz.com. Ownership: (R.L. Plessinger Holding Co.)

Stns: 1 AM. 2 FM. WOYS-FM Apalachicola, FL; WOCY-FM Carrabelle, FL; WCVG Covington, KY

Richard Plessinger, pres/CEO.

Point Broadcasting Company 715 Broadway, Suite 320, Santa Monica, CA 90401. Phone: (310) 451-4430. Fax: (310) 451-1423. Ownership: John Hearne Revocable Trust. Note: Owns stns through subsidiaries: Gold Coast Broadcasting LLC (see listing) and High Desert Broadcasting LLC (see listing). Also owns 50% of KHRN(FM) Huron, CA and 31.8% of KHRQ(FM) Baker and KHDR(FM) Lenwood, both CA.

Stns: 1 FM. KCEL(FM) California City, CA

John Hearne, chmn/pres.

Pollack Broadcasting Co. 6699 Wild Berry Lane, Memphis, TN 38119. Phone: (901) 753-0768. Fax: (901) 753-0868. Ownership: William H. Pollack, 33 I/3%; Martin S. Belz, 33 I/3%; David L. Pollack, 33 I/3%.

Stns: 3 AM. 3 FM. KBOA-FM Piggott, AR; KCRV Caruthersville, MO; KCRV-FM Caruthersville, MO; KBOA Kennett, MO; KTMO(FM) New Madrid, MO; KMIS Portageville, MO

Stns: 2 TV. KLAX, Alexandria, LA; KIEM, Eureka, CA

William H. Pollack, pres.

Polnet Communications Ltd. 3656 W. Belmont Ave., Chicago, IL 60618. Phone: (773) 588-6300. Fax: (773) 588-0834.

Stns: 5 AM. WKTA Evanston, IL; WEEF Highland Park, IL; WNVR Vernon Hills, IL; WRKL New City, NY; WLIM Patchogue, NY

Walter Kotaby, pres; Kent D. Gustafson, VP & CEO.

Porter County Broadcasting Corp. 2755 Sager Rd., Valparaiso, IN 46383. Phone: (219) 462-8125. Ownership: Leonard J. Ellis Trust, 27.10%; Bernice A. Ellis Trust, 27.10%; Leigh Ellis, 15.25%; Neehah Ellis, 15.25%; and Marissa Wilson, 15.25%.

Stns: 1 AM. 3 FM. WXRD-FM Crown Point, IN; WZVN-FM Lowell, IN; WAKE Valparaiso, IN; WLJE-FM Valparaiso, IN

Radio Group Ownership

Premier Broadcasters 1133 Kresky, Centralia, WA 98531. Phone: (360) 736-1355. Fax: (360) 736-4761. Web Site: www.live95.com. Ownership: Rod Etherton.
Stns: 1 AM. 2 FM. KITI Chehalis-Centralia, WA; KRXY-FM Shelton, WA; KITI-FM Winlock, WA
Rod Etherton, pres.

Press Communications L.L.C. 1350 Campus Pkwy., Suite 106, Neptune, NJ 07753. Phone: (732) 751-1119. Fax: (732) 751-1726. Ownership: Mark D. Lass, 16.5%; Alfred D. Colantoni, 16.5%; Jules L. Plangere III, 16.5%; Jules Plangere Jr., 16.5%; Robert E. McAllan, 16.5%; Richard T. Morena, 10.5%; and E. Donald Lass, 7%.
Stns: 1 AM. 5 FM. WHTG Eatontown, NJ; WHTG-FM Eatontown, NJ; WWZY-FM Long Branch, NJ; WBBO-FM Ocean Acres, NJ; WKOE-FM Ocean City, NJ; WBHX-FM Tuckerton, NJ

Prettyman Broadcasting Co. 1606 W. King St., Martinsburg, WV 25401. Phone: (304) 263-8868. Fax: (304) 263-8906. Web Site: www.wepm.com.
Stns: 1 AM. 2 FM. WEPM Martinsburg, WV; WLTF(FM) Martinsburg, WV; WICL(FM) Williamsport, MD
William E. Prettyman, pres/CEO; Yogi Yoder, gen mgr.

Daniel F. Priestley Stns 131 Silver Rd., Bangor, ME 04401. Phone: (207) 947-9697. Fax: (207) 989-5251. Ownership: Daniel F. Priestley, Jacelynn L. Priestley.
Stns: 3 AM. WNZT(AM) Hermon, ME; WWNZ(AM) Veazie, ME; WNZS(AM) Veazie, ME

Priority Communications 51 W. Long Ave., DuBois, PA 15801. Phone: (814) 375-5260. Fax: (814) 375-5262.
Stns: 2 AM. 1 FM. WCDK-FM Cadiz, OH; WCED DuBois, PA; WEIR Weirton, WV
Jay M. Philippone, pres.

Priority Radio Inc. Box 7679, Newark, DE 19719-7679. Phone: (302) 731-7270. Fax: (302) 738-3090. Web Site: www.wxhl.com. Ownership: Jennifer Hare, 33.3%; Rev. Steve Hare, 33.3%.
Stns: 1 AM. 2 FM. WVBH(FM) Beach Haven West, NJ; WSRY(AM) Elkton, MD; WXHL-FM Christiana, DE

Programmers Broadcasting Inc. Box 28, Bottineau, ND 58318-0028. Phone: (701) 228-5151. Fax: (701) 228-2483. Ownership: John Kircher, 50%; and Jean Kircher, 50%.
Stns: 3 FM. KBTO(FM) Bottineau, ND; KWGO(FM) Burlington, ND; KTZU(FM) Velva, ND

Progressive Broadcasting System Inc. Box 307, Elkhart, IN 46515. Phone: (574) 875-5166. Fax: (574) 875-6662. Web Site: www.wfrn.com.
Stns: 2 FM. WFRN-FM Elkhart, IN; WFRI-FM Winamac, IN
Edwin Moore, pres.

Progressive United Communications Inc. 316 N. River St., Claxton, GA 30417. Phone: (912) 739-3035. Fax: (912) 739-0050. Ownership: Frank C. Cummings, 33%; Martha C. Cummings, 33%; and Paschell C. Mix, 33%.
Stns: 3 AM. WACQ(AM) Carrville, AL; WDLK Dadeville, AL; WCLA Claxton, GA
Paschell C. Mix, pres; Frank C. Cummings, VP; Martha C. Cummings, sec/treas.

Q

Qantum Communications Corp. 3 Stamford Landing,, Suite 210, Stamford, CT 06902. Phone: (203) 388-0048. Ownership: Frank D. Osborn, 61.74% of votes; Frank Washington, 19.03% of votes; Osborn Family Partners L.P., 15.23% of votes; Michael F. Mangan, 3.85% of votes; William Nelson III and Frank D. Osborn, as trustees of the Osborn 2002 Family Trust, a trust in favor of the children of Frank D. Osborn, 0.15% of votes.
Stns: 7 AM. 21 FM. WKKR-FM Auburn, AL; WMXA-FM Opelika, AL; WTLM Opelika, AL; WZMG Pepperell, AL; WMXZ-FM De Funiak Springs, FL; WWAV-FM Santa Rosa Beach, FL; WMOG Brunswick, GA; WGIG(AM) Brunswick, GA; WHFX(FM) Darien, GA; WBGA(FM) Saint Simons Island, GA; WWSN-FM Waycross, GA; WYNR(FM) Waycross, GA; WCJM-FM West Point, GA; WPLV West Point, GA; WCIB-FM Falmouth, MA; WCOD-FM Hyannis, MA; WRZE-FM Nantucket, MA; WXTK-FM West Yarmouth, MA; WLQB(FM) Ocean Isle Beach, NC; WQSD(FM) Briarcliff Acres, SC; WGTR-FM Bucksport, SC; WJMX-FM Cheraw, SC; WDAR-FM Darlington, SC; WDSC Dillon, SC; WJMX Florence, SC; WWXM(FM) Garden City, SC; WGSS-FM Kingstree, SC; WWRK(FM) Scranton, SC
Frank Osborn, pres.

Quarnstrom Media Group LLC 1104 Cloquet Ave., Cloquet, MN 55720. Phone: (218) 879-4534. Fax: (218) 879-1962. Ownership: Alan & Linda Quarnstrom, 100%.
Stns: 3 AM. 5 FM. KKIN Aitkin, MN; KKIN-FM Aitkin, MN; KFGI(FM) Crosby, MN; KGHS International Falls, MN; WCMP Pine City, MN; WCMP-FM Pine City, MN; WLMX-FM Balsam Lake, WI; WXCX(FM) Siren, WI
Aian Quarnstrom, pres; Don Welch, VP.

Quincy Newspapers Inc. 130 S. Fifth St., Quincy, IL 62301. Phone: (217) 223-5100. Fax: (217) 223-5019. Web Site: www.qni.biz.
Stns: 1 AM. 1 FM. WGEM Quincy, IL; WGEM-FM Quincy, IL
Stns: 11 TV. WVVA, Bluefield-Beckley-Oak Hill, WV; WXOW, La Crosse-Eau Claire, WI; WQOW, La Crosse-Eau Claire, WI; WKOW, Madison, WI; WGEM-TV, Quincy, IL-Hannibal, MO-Keokuk, IA; KTTC, Rochester, MN-Mason City, IA-Austin, MN; WREX-TV, Rockford, IL; KTIV, Sioux City, IA; WSJV, South Bend-Elkhart, IN; WYOW, Wausau-Rhinelander, WI; WAOW, Wausau-Rhinelander, WI
Quincy Newspapers Inc. owns the *Quincy* (IL) *Herald-Whig*, and the *New Jersey Herald*, Newton, NJ.
Thomas A. Oakley, pres.

Quinte Broadcasting Ltd. Box 488, Belleville, ON K8N 5B2. Canada. Phone: (613) 969-5555. Fax: (613) 969-8122. Ownership: Herbert M. Morton, 66.67%; and Joyce Mulock, 33.33%.
Stns: 1 AM. 2 FM. CIGL-FM Belleville, ON; CJBQ Belleville, ON; CJTN-FM Quinte West, ON

Quorum Radio Partners Inc. 8512 Beech Ln., McKinney, TX 75070. Phone: (972) 529-1192. Fax: (972) 540-2454.
Stns: 1 AM. 2 FM. KOZX-FM Cabool, MO; KELE Mountain Grove, MO; KELE-FM Mountain Grove, MO
Todd W. Fowler, pres/CEO.

Quorum Radio Partners of Virginia Inc. 8512 Beech Ln., McKinney, TX 75070. Phone: (972) 529-1192. Fax: (972) 540-2454. Ownership: Todd W. Fowler, 31.25%; Michael A. Stone, 31.25%; Jevin S. Jensen, 20%; Robert Barnett, 10%; and Kevin T. Lilly, 5%.
Stns: 2 AM. 2 FM. WIQO-FM Covington, VA; WKEY Covington, VA; WKCJ-FM Lewisburg, WV; WSLW White Sulphur Springs, WV
Todd W. Fowler, pres/CEO.

R

The RAFTT Corp. 3633 Farm to Market Rd. 437, Rogers, TX 76569. Phone: (281) 565-7064. Ownership: Herford Agri-Fuel Inc., 100%.
Stns: 3 AM. KYRO Potosi, MO; KILE Bellaire, TX; KWBC Navasota, TX

RR Broadcasting 2100 E. Tahquitz Canyon Way, Palm Springs, CA 92262. Phone: (760) 325-2582. Fax: (760) 322-3562. Ownership: Rozene R. Supple, 100%.
Stns: 2 AM. KGAM Palm Springs, CA; KPSI Palm Springs, CA
Mike Keane, gen mgr.

Radio America Ltd. 10602 Outpost Dr., North Potomac, MD 20878. Phone: (301) 251-5131. Ownership: NoEl Media Holdings LLC, 75%; and Media Networks America LLC, 25%.
Stns: 1 AM. 2 FM. KSNO-FM Snowmass Village, CO; KBCR Steamboat Springs, CO; KBCR-FM Steamboat Springs, CO

Radio Cleveland Inc. Drawer 780, Cleveland, MS 38732. Phone: (662) 843-4091. Fax: (662) 843-9805. E-mail: wcld@tecinfo.com. Web Site: www.radiomiss.com. Ownership: Homer Sledge Jr., pres, 37.1/5%; Kevin W. Cox, treas, 37.1/2%; Clint L. Webster, gen mgr, 37.1/2%.
Stns: 1 AM. 2 FM. WAID-FM Clarksdale, MS; WCLD Cleveland, MS; WMJW-FM Cleveland, MS
Clint L. Webster, gen mgr.

Radio Dubuque Inc. Box 659, Dubuque, IA 52004. Phone: (563) 690-0800. Fax: (563) 588-5688. Ownership: Donald L. Rabbitt, 70%; Thomas Parsley, 25%; and Paul Hemmer, 5%.
Stns: 1 AM. 2 FM. KDTH Dubuque, IA; KGRR-FM Epworth, IA; WVRE(FM) Dickeyville, WI
Thomas Parsley, gen mgr.

Radio Greeneville Inc. Box 278, Greeneville, TN 37744. Phone: (423) 638-4147. Fax: (423) 638-1979. E-mail: wgrv@greeneville.com. Web Site: www.greeneville.com/wgrv. Ownership: Ronald & Nellie R.Metcalfe; Paul O. Metcalfe.
Stns: 1 AM. 1 FM. WSMG Greeneville, TN; WIKQ(FM) Tusculum, TN
Ronald Metcalfe, pres.

The Radio Group Box 1319, Columbia, LA 71418. Phone: (318) 649-7959. Fax: (318) 649-5874. Ownership: Tom D. Gay, 100%.
Stns: 3 FM. KFNV-FM Ferriday, LA; KAPB-FM Marksville, LA; KMAR-FM Winnsboro, LA
Tom D. Gay, gen mgr.

Radio Maria Inc. 601 Washington St., Alexandria, LA 71301. Phone: (318) 561-6145. Fax: (318) 449-9954. Web Site: www.radiomaria.us. Ownership: Radio Maria is a not-for-profit corporation run by a board of directors.
Stns: 3 AM. 2 FM. KJMJ(AM) Alexandria, LA; KOJO-FM Lake Charles, LA; KBIO(FM) Natchitoches, LA; KNIR New Iberia, LA; KDEI(AM) Port Arthur, TX

Radio Nord Communications Inc. 380 Murdoch, Rowyn-Norando, PQ J9X 1G5. Canada. Phone: (514) 866-8686. Fax: (514) 866-8056. Web Site: www.radionord.com.
Stns: 8 FM. CHPR-FM Hawkesbury, ON; CFIX-FM Chicoutimi, PQ; CHVD-FM Dolbeau-Mistassini, PQ; CHLX-FM Gatineau, PQ; CJLA-FM Lachute, PQ; CKLX-FM Montreal, PQ; CHOA-FM Rouyn-Noranda, PQ; CHGO-FM Val d'Or, PQ
Stns: 5 TV. CKRN-3, Bearn-Fabre, PQ; CFGS-TV, Gatineau, PQ; CHOT-TV, Gatineau, PQ; CKRN-TV, Rouyn-Noranda, PQ; CFVS, Val d'Or, PQ
Pierre R. Brosseau, pres.

Radio One Inc. 5900 Princess Garden Pkwy., Lanham, MD 20706. Phone: (301) 306-1111. Fax: (301) 306-9426. Web Site: www.radio-one.com. Ownership: Alfred C. Liggins, 39.4% of voting shares; Catherine L. Hughes, 16.7% of voting shares.
Stns: 10 AM. 55 FM. KKBT(FM) Los Angeles, CA; WYCB Washington, DC; WKYS-FM Washington, DC; WVCG Coral Gables, FL; WFXA-FM Augusta, GA; WAEG-FM Evans, GA; WPZE(FM) Fayetteville, GA; WHTA(FM) Hampton, GA; WAMJ(FM) Mableton, GA; WJZZ-FM Roswell, GA; WTHB-FM Waynesboro, GA; WAKB-FM Wrens, GA; WFUN-FM Bethalto, IL; WEGK(FM) Charlestown, IN; WTLC-FM Greenwood, IN; WTLC Indianapolis, IN; WHHH-FM Indianapolis, IN; WGZB-FM Lanesville, IN; WYJZ(FM) Lebanon, IN; WIZF-FM Erlanger, KY; WMJM-FM Jeffersontown, KY; WXMA(FM) Louisville, KY; WDJX-FM Louisville, KY; WLRS(FM) Shepherdsville, KY; WILD Boston, MA; WBOT(FM) Brockton, MA; WDMK-FM Detroit, MI; WHTD(FM) Mount Clemens, MI; WCHB Taylor, MI; KTTB(FM) Glencoe, MN; WPZS(FM) Albemarle, NC; WFXC-FM Durham, NC; WNNL-FM Fuquay-Varina, NC; WQNC(FM) Harrisburg, NC; WFXK-FM Tarboro, NC; WRNB(FM) Pennsauken, NJ; WZAK-FM Cleveland, OH; WENZ-FM Cleveland, OH; WERE Cleveland, OH; WJMO Cleveland Heights, OH; WCKX-FM Columbus, OH; WING Dayton, OH; WGTZ-FM Eaton, OH; WJYD(FM) London, OH; WDHT-FM Springfield, OH; WXMG-FM Upper Arlington, OH; WKSW-FM Urbana, OH; WROU-FM West Carrollton, OH; WPPZ-FM Jenkintown, PA; WPHI-FM Media, PA; KBFB(FM) Dallas, TX; KSOC(FM) Gainesville, TX; KMJQ-FM Houston, TX; KBXX(FM) Houston, TX; KROI(FM) Seabrook, TX; WPZZ(FM) Crewe, VA; WCDX-FM Mechanicsville, VA; WKJM(FM) Petersburg, VA; WROU(AM) Petersburg, VA; WKJS(FM) Richmond, VA; WQOK-FM South Boston, VA; WWIN Baltimore, MD; WERQ-FM Baltimore, MD; WMMJ-FM Bethesda, MD; WWIN-FM Glen Burnie, MD
Catherine Hughes, chairperson; Alfred Liggins, pres/CEO; Mary Catherine Sneed, COO; Scott Royster, CFO; Darrell Huckaby, VP progmg; Tony Washington, VP sls; Charles Kinney, engrg dir.

Radio Palouse Inc. Box 1, Pullman, WA 99163. Phone: (509) 332-6551. Fax: (509) 332-5151. E-mail: khtr@aol.com. Web Site: www.border104.com.
Stns: 2 AM. KQQQ Pullman, WA; KUUX(AM) Pullman, WA
Bill Weed, gen mgr.

Radio Vermont Group Inc. Box 550, Waterbury, VT 05676. Phone: (802) 244-7321. Fax: (802) 244-1771.
Stns: 2 AM. 3 FM. WVAA(AM) Burlington, VT; WLVB-FM Morrisville, VT; WCVT-FM Stowe, VT; WDEV-FM Warren, VT; WDEV Waterbury, VT
Ken Squier, pres; Eric Michaels, VP.

Radio Works Inc. 111 Westwood Dr., De Queen, AR 71832. Phone: (870) 642-3637. Ownership: Jay Wallace Bunyard and Teresa Sharon Bunyard Living Revocable Trust, Jay and Teresa Bunyard, sole voting trustees, 100%.

Broadcasting & Cable Yearbook 2006

Radio Group Ownership

Stns: 3 FM. KAMD-FM Camden, AR; KMGC-FM Camden, AR; KCXY(FM) East Camden, AR

RadioJones LLC Box 5356, Atlanta, GA 31107-5356. Phone: (404) 432-1450. Ownership: Dennis Jones, 100%.
Stns: 2 AM. 2 FM. WELT(FM) East Dublin, GA; WJAT Swainsboro, GA; WXRS Swainsboro, GA; WXRS-FM Swainsboro, GA

RadioWorks Inc. 2830 Sandy Hollow Rd., Rockford, IL 61109. Phone: (815) 874-7861. Fax: (815) 874-2202.
Stns: 2 FM. WXXB(FM) Delphi, IN; WKHY(FM) Lafayette, IN

Robert E. Rhea Jr., pres; David W. McAley, exec VP.

Rama Communications Inc. 3765 N. John Young Pkwy., Orlando, FL 32804. Phone: (407) 523-2770. Fax: (407) 523-2888. Web Site: www.gospelrama.com.
Stns: 7 AM. WNTF Bithlo, FL; WTIR(AM) Cocoa Beach, FL; WKIQ Eustis, FL; WQBQ Leesburg, FL; WOKB Winter Garden, FL; WLAA(AM) Winter Garden, FL; WFVR Valdosta, GA

Sabita Persaud, pres.

Ramar Communications II Ltd. Box 3757, Lubbock, TX 79452. Phone: (806) 745-3434. Fax: (806) 748-1949. Web Site: www.ramarcom.com. E-mail: bmoran@ramarcom.com. Ownership: Ray Moran, 51%; Brad Moran, 49%.

Lubbock, TX 79423, 9800 University Ave.
Stns: 1 AM. 3 FM. KLZK(FM) Brownfield, TX; KJTV(AM) Lubbock, TX; KXTQ-FM Lubbock, TX; KSTQ-FM Plainview, TX
Stns: 4 TV. KTLL-TV, Albuquerque-Santa Fe, NM; KHFT, Albuquerque-Santa Fe, NM; KTEL-TV, Albuquerque-Santa Fe, NM; KJTV-TV, Lubbock, TX

Ray Moran, chmn; Brad Moran, pres.

Rawlco Radio Ltd. 715 Saskatchewan Crescent West, Saskatoon, SK S7M 5V7. Canada. Phone: (306) 934-2222. Fax: (306) 933-3300. Ownership: Rawlco Inc., 100%.
Stns: 5 AM. 4 FM. CJNS Meadow Lake, SK; CJNS-FM Meadow Lake, SK; CJNB North Battleford, SK; CKBI Prince Albert, SK; CHQX-FM Prince Albert, SK; CKCK-FM Regina, SK; CJME(AM) Regina, SK; CJDJ-FM Saskatoon, SK; CKOM(AM) Saskatoon, SK

Pam Leyland, pres; Gordon Rawlinson, CEO.

Red Rock Radio Corp. 501 Lake Ave. S., Duluth, MN 55802. Phone: (218) 728-9500. Fax: (218) 723-1499.
Stns: 6 FM. KAOD(FM) Babbitt, MN; KBAJ(FM) Deer River, MN; KQDS-FM Duluth, MN; WXXZ-FM Grand Marais, MN; WWAX-FM Hermantown, MN; KZIO-FM Two Harbors, MN

Ro Grignon, pres.

Regent Communications Inc. 100 E. River Center Blvd., 9th Fl., Covington, KY 41011. Phone: (859) 292-0030. Fax: (859) 814-0136. E-mail: wstakelin@regentcomm.com.
Stns: 18 AM. 44 FM. KRRX-FM Burney, CA; KFMF-FM Chico, CA; KQPT(FM) Colusa, CA; KZAP-FM Paradise, CA; KALF(FM) Red Bluff, CA; KNRO(AM) Redding, CA; KQMS Redding, CA; KSHA-FM Redding, CA; KNNN(FM) Shasta Lake City, CA; KRDG-FM Shingletown, CA; KTRR-FM Loveland, CO; KKQZ(FM) Wellington, CO; KUAD-FM Windsor, CO; WIXO(FM) Bartonville, IL; WJBC Bloomington, IL; WJEZ(FM) Dwight, IL; WFYR-FM Elmwood, IL; WPIA(FM) Eureka, IL; WVEL-FM Glasford, IL; WBWN-FM Le Roy, IL; WYNG(FM) Mount Carmel, IL; WVEL Pekin, IL; WGLO-FM Pekin, IL; WTRX-FM Pontiac, IL; WGBF Evansville, IN; WJLT(FM) Evansville, IN; WDKS-FM Newburgh, IN; WGBF-FM Henderson, KY; WKDQ-FM Henderson, KY; WOMI(AM) Owensboro, KY; KROF Abbeville, LA; KFTE-FM Breaux Bridge, LA; KRKA(FM) Erath, LA; KMDL-FM Kaplan, LA; KPEL Lafayette, LA; WFNT Flint, MI; WRCL(FM) Frankenmuth, MI; WNWZ Grand Rapids, MI; WGRD-FM Grand Rapids, MI; WFGR-FM Grand Rapids, MI; WLSP Lapeer, MI; WWBN-FM Tuscola, MI; WTRV-FM Walker, MI; KMXK-FM Cold Spring, MN; WJON Saint Cloud, MN; KKSR(FM) Sartell, MN; KLZZ-FM Waite Park, MN; KXSS(AM) Waite Park, MN; WGNA-FM Albany, NY; WQBJ-FM Cobleskill, NY; WABT-FM Mechanicville, NY; WTMM Rensselaer, NY; WODZ-FM Rome, NY; WFRG-FM Utica, NY; WIBX Utica, NY; WTNY Watertown, NY; WNER(AM) Watertown, NY; WSWR-FM Shelby, OH; KSII-FM El Paso, TX; KROD El Paso, TX; KKPL(FM) Cheyenne, WY; KARS-FM Laramie, WY

Terry S. Jacobs, chmn/CEO; William L. Stakelin, pres/COO; Anthony Vasconcellos, sr VP & CFO.

Reier Broadcasting Co. Inc. Box 20, Bozeman, MT 59718. Phone: (406) 587-9999. Fax: (406) 587-5855. Ownership: William R. Reier Sr., 100%.
Stns: 2 AM. 2 FM. KBOZ Bozeman, MT; KOBB Bozeman, MT; KBOZ-FM Bozeman, MT; KOZB(FM) Livingston, MT

Relevant Radio 3200 Riverside Dr., Green Bay, WI 54307. Phone: (800) 342-0306. Fax: (920) 469-3023. E-mail: info@relevantradio.com. Web Site: www.relevantradio.com. Ownership: Mark C. Follett, 33.33% of votes; John Cavil, 33.3% of votes; and Robert Atwell, 33.33% of votes.
Stns: 13 AM. 4 FM. WMYR Fort Myers, FL; WCNZ(AM) Marco Island, FL; WVOI(AM) Marco Island, FL; WAUR Sandwich, IL; WWCA Gary, IN; WADW(FM) Pickford, MI; WLOL(AM) Minneapolis, MN; KSMM Shakopee, MN; WZUM Carnegie, PA; WYNW(FM) Birnamwood, WI; WDVM(AM) Eau Claire, WI; WKBH Holmen, WI; WJOK Kaukauna, WI; WZRK(AM) Lake Geneva, WI; WMMA(FM) Nekoosa, WI; WPJP(FM) Port Washington, WI; WHFA(AM) Poynette, WI

Mark Follett, chmn/CEO.

Renda Broadcasting Corp. (Renda Radio Inc.). 900 Parish Street, 4th Fl, Pittsburgh, PA 15220. Phone: (412) 875-1800. Fax: (412) 875-1801. Ownership: S.F. Renda, 100%.
Stns: 5 AM. 16 FM. WWGR-FM Fort Myers, FL; WEJZ-FM Jacksonville, FL; WGUF-FM Marco, FL; WSGL-FM Naples, FL; WGNE-FM Palatka, FL; WSOS-FM Saint Augustine, FL; WJGO(FM) Tice, FL; WKQL(FM) Brunswick, GA; KHTT-FM Muskogee, OK; KMGL-FM Oklahoma City, OK; KOKC(AM) Oklahoma City, OK; KOMA(FM) Oklahoma City, OK; KRXO-FM Oklahoma City, OK; KBEZ(FM) Tulsa, OK; WLCY-FM Blairsville, PA; WYTR(FM) Brookville, PA; WCCS Homer City, PA; WDAD Indiana, PA; WQMU-FM Indiana, PA; WJAS Pittsburgh, PA; WECZ Punxsutawney, PA

Anthony F. Renda, pres; Maryann Kelly, VP/controller; Alan Serena, VP opns; Judy Reich, VP sls.

The Result Radio Group Box 767, Winona, MN 55987-0767. Phone: (507) 452-4000. Fax: (507) 452-9494. E-mail: jpapenfuss@winonaradio.com. Ownership: Jerry Papenfuss.
Stns: 5 AM. 3 FM. KBEW Blue Earth, MN; KBRF Fergus Falls, MN; KJJK Fergus Falls, MN; KPRW-FM Perham, MN; KWNO-FM Rushford, MN; KAGE Winona, MN; KWNO Winona, MN; KHME(FM) Winona, MN

Jerry Papenfuss, owner.

Results Broadcasting 1456 E. Green Bay St., Shawano, WI 54166. Phone: (715) 524-2194. Fax: (715) 524-9980. Ownership: Bruce D. Grassman, 100%.
Stns: 3 AM. 7 FM. WOBE-FM Crystal Falls, MI; WJNR-FM Iron Mountain, MI; WHTO(FM) Iron Mountain, MI; WACD-FM Antigo, WI; WATK Antigo, WI; WFCL Clintonville, WI; WJMQ(FM) Clintonville, WI; WTCH Shawano, WI; WOWN-FM Shawano, WI; WLSL(FM) Three Lakes, WI

Bruce Grassman, pres.

Reynolds Radio Inc. Box 11196, College Station, TX 77842. Phone: (979) 696-1196. E-mail: rusty@reynoldsradio.com. Web Site: www.theblaze.cc.
Stns: 3 FM. KAZE(FM) Ore City, TX; KLBL(FM) White Oak, TX; KBLZ(FM) Winona, TX

Kenneth R. Reynolds, pres.

Rhattigan Broadcasting (Texas) LP 185 E. 85th St., Suite 21L, New York, NY 10028. Phone: (347) 236-6995. Ownership: Rhattigan Broadcasting LLC, 99%; and Rhattigan Broadcasting (Texas) Inc., 1%.
Stns: 5 AM. 4 FM. KBST Big Spring, TX; KBST-FM Big Spring, TX; KBTS(FM) Big Spring, TX; KEPS Eagle Pass, TX; KVOP(AM) Plainview, TX; KREW(FM) Plainview, TX; KVOU Uvalde, TX; KVOU-FM Uvalde, TX; KUVA-FM Uvalde, TX

The River Group Box 1816, Greenville, MS 38702-1816. Phone: (662) 378-2617. Fax: (662) 378-8341. Ownership: George E. Pine III and James P. Karr Jr.
Stns: 1 AM. 2 FM. WBAQ-FM Greenville, MS; WNIX(AM) Greenville, MS; WIQQ-FM Leland, MS

George E. Pine III, pres; James P. Karr Jr., VP.

F W Robbert Broadcasting Co. Inc. 2730 Loumor Ave., Metairie, LA 70001. Phone: (504) 831-6941. Web Site: www.wwcr.com. Ownership: Fred P. Westenberger, 51%; Chris P. Westenberger, 9.75%; Fritz N. Westenberger, 9.75%; Lisa M. Westenberger, 9.75%; Eric M. Westenberger, 9.75%; George McClintock, 10%.
Stns: 3 AM. WVOG New Orleans, LA; WMQM(AM) Lakeland, TN; WNQM Nashville, TN

Fred P. Westenberger, pres; Eric M. Westenberger, gen mgr.

Roberts Communications Inc. 6174 Hwy. 57, Macon, GA 31277. Phone: (478) 745-3301. Fax: (478) 742-2293. Web Site: www.foxie107.com.
Stns: 2 AM. 1 FM. WQMJ(FM) Forsyth, GA; WXKO Fort Valley, GA; WXJO(AM) Gordon, GA

Michael A. Roberts, pres/CEO.

Robinson Corporation E7601A County Rd. SS, Viroqua, WI 54665. Phone: (608) 637-7200. Fax: (608) 637-7299. Ownership: David Robinson, Jane Robinson.
Stns: 2 AM. 1 FM. WPRE Prairie du Chien, WI; WVRQ(AM) Viroqua, WI; WVRQ-FM Viroqua, WI

David Robinson, pres; Jeff Robinson, opns mgr; James Graham, gen sls mgr.

Rodgers Broadcasting Corp. Box 1646, Richmond, IN 47374. Phone: (765) 962-6533. Fax: (765) 966-1499. Ownership: David Rodgers, 100%.
Stns: 3 AM. 3 FM. WBML Macon, GA; WCNB(AM) Connersville, IN; WIFE-FM Connersville, IN; WKBV(AM) Richmond, IN; WFMG-FM Richmond, IN; WZZY-FM Winchester, IN

David Rodgers, pres.

Estuardo Valdemar Rodriguez and Leonor Rodriguez Stns 1010 Vermont Ave. N.W., Suite 100, Washington, DC 20005. Phone: (202) 638-1959. Fax: (202) 393-7464. Ownership: Estuardo Valdemar Rodriguez, 50%; Leonor Rodriguez, 50%. Note: Estuardo Valdemar Rodriguez also is the licensee of WLLN(AM) Lillington, NC.
Stns: 6 AM. WLLQ(AM) Chapel Hill, NC; WRTG Garner, NC; WLNR Kinston, NC; WGSB Mebane, NC; WREV Reidsville, NC; WLLY Wilson, NC

Rogers Broadcasting Ltd. 777 Jarvis St., Toronto, ON M4Y 3B7. Canada. Phone: (416) 935-8200. Web Site: www.rogers.com. Ownership: Rogers Media Inc., 100%. Note: Rogers Media Inc. is 100% owned by Rogers Communications Inc.
Stns: 5 AM. 28 FM. CFFR Calgary, AB; CHMN-FM Canmore, AB; CFRV-FM Lethbridge, AB; CJRX-FM Lethbridge, AB; CKQC-FM Abbotsford, BC; CKGO-FM-1 Boston Bar, BC; CKCL-FM Chilliwack, BC; CKSR-FM Chilliwack, BC; CFSR-FM Hope, BC; CISP-FM Pemberton, BC; CKKS-FM Sechelt, BC; CKWX-FM Vancouver, BC; CKIZ-FM Vernon, BC; CHTT-FM Victoria, BC; CIOC-FM Victoria, BC; CISW-FM Whistler, BC; CITI-FM Winnipeg, MB; CKY-FM Winnipeg, MB; CKNI-FM Moncton, NB; CHNI-FM Saint John, NB; CJNI-FM Halifax, NS; CKAT North Bay, ON; CHUR-FM North Bay, ON; CICX-FM Orillia, ON; CHAS-FM Sault Ste. Marie, ON; CJQM-FM Sault Ste. Marie, ON; CKBY-FM Smiths Falls, ON; CIGM Sudbury, ON; CJMX-FM Sudbury, ON; CJQQ-FM Timmins, ON; CKGB-FM Timmins, ON; CJCL Toronto, ON; CJAQ-FM Toronto, ON
Stns: 2 TV. CHNU-TV, Fraser Valley, BC; CJMT-TV, Toronto, ON

Rael Merson, pres.

Rooney Moon Broadcasting Inc. 208 E. Grand Ave., Clovis, NM 88101. Phone: (505) 763-4649. Fax: (505) 763-1693. E-mail: info.rmb@yucca.net. Web Site: www.bettermix.com.
Stns: 1 AM. KSEL Portales, NM

Steve Rooney, pres.

Rose City Radio Corp. 0234 Southwest Bancroft St., Portland, OR 97239. Phone: (503) 243-7595. Fax: (503) 417-7662. Web Site: www.kxlradio.com.
Stns: 4 AM. KMPC(AM) Los Angeles, CA; WWZN(AM) Boston, MA; WSNR(AM) Jersey City, NJ; KXL Portland, OR

Tim McNamara, VP/gen mgr.

Roswell Radio Inc./Quay Broadcasters Inc. Box 670, Roswell, NM 88202. Phone: (505) 622-6450. Fax: (505) 622-9041. Ownership: John M. Dunn, 100%.
Stns: 2 AM. 3 FM. KBCQ(FM) Roswell, NM; KMOU-FM Roswell, NM; KPSA(AM) Roswell, NM; KSFX-FM Roswell, NM; KTNM Tucumcari, NM

John M. Dunn, pres.

Route 81 Radio LLC 127 Willowbrook Ln., 2nd Fl., West Chester, PA 19382. Phone: (610) 696-8181. Fax: (610) 696-5072. E-mail: lloyd@route81radio.com. Web Site: route81radio.com. Ownership: WallerSutton 2000 L.P., 40%; Avalon Equity Fund LP, 40%; and Meetinghouse Media Inc., 20%.
Stns: 8 AM. 4 FM. WENI-FM Big Flats, NY; WCBA Corning, NY; WGMM(FM) Corning, NY; WENI(AM) Corning, NY; WENY Elmira, NY; WENY-FM Elmira, NY; WNAK-FM Carbondale, PA; WCDL(AM) Carbondale, PA; WHYL Carlisle, PA; WCOJ(AM) Coatesville, PA; WAZL Hazleton, PA; WNAK Nanticoke, PA

Lloyd B. Roach, CEO; Ken Karaszkiewicz, CFO.

Rubber City Radio Group Inc. 1795 W. Market St., Akron, OH 44313. Phone: (330) 869-9800. Fax: (330) 864-6799. E-mail: mail@wakr.net. Web Site: www.wqmx.com.

Ownership: Thomas Mandel.

Stns: 1 AM. 5 FM. WQTX(FM) Charlotte, MI; WVIC(FM) Jackson, MI; WJXQ-FM Jackson, MI; WTXQ(FM) Saint Johns, MI; WAKR Akron, OH; WQMX-FM Medina, OH

Thomas Mandel, pres; Mark Biviano, VP; Nick Anthony, VP.

Ruby Radio Corp. 1250 Lamoille Hwy., Suite 944, Elko, NV 89801. Phone: (775) 777-1196. Fax: (775) 777-9587. Ownership: Ken Sutherland, 50%; and Mary A. Sutherland, 50%.

Stns: 1 AM. 1 FM. KHIX-FM Carlin, NV; KELY Ely, NV

Runnels Broadcasting System L.L.C. Box 2710, Alamogordo, NM 88311-2710. Phone: (505) 437-1505. Fax: (505) 437-5566. E-mail: phil@snmradio.com. Web Site: www.snmradio.com.

Stns: 2 AM. 5 FM. KNMZ-FM Alamogordo, NM; KRSY(AM) Alamogordo, NM; KNFT Bayard, NM; KNFT-FM Bayard, NM; KPZE-FM Carlsbad, NM; KRSY-FM La Luz, NM; KPSA-FM Lordsburg, NM

Phillip Runnels, gen mgr.

S

SIGA Broadcasting Corp. 1302 N. Shepherd Dr., Houston, TX 77008. Phone: (713) 868-5559. Fax: (713) 868-9631. Ownership: Gabriel Arango, 50%; and Silvia Arango 50%.

Stns: 4 AM. KTMR Edna, TX; KGBC Galveston, TX; KAML Kenedy-Karnes City, TX; KLVL Pasadena, TX

STARadio Corp. 329 Main St., Quincy, IL 62301. Phone: (217) 224-4102. Fax: (217) 224-4133. E-mail: reception@staradio.com. Ownership: Howard A. Doss, Derek Parrish and Jack Whitley.

Stns: 1 AM. 4 FM. WTAD Quincy, IL; WQCY(FM) Quincy, IL; WYKT-FM Wilmington, IL; KGRC-FM Hannibal, MO; KZZK-FM New London, MO

Mike Moyers, gen mgr.

Saga Communications Inc. 73 Kercheval Ave.,, Suite 201, Grosse Pointe Farms, MI 48236. Phone: (313) 886-7070. Fax: (313) 886-7150. E-mail: chapsburg@sagacom.com. Web Site: www.sagacommunications.com. Ownership: Edward K. Christian, 56.5% of the voting stock. Other Interests: Illinois Radio Network, Michigan Radio Network, Michigan Farm Radio Network.

Stns: 25 AM. 50 FM. KDEZ(FM) Jonesboro, AR; KDXY-FM Lake City, AR; KJBX(FM) Trumann, AR; KLTI-FM Ames, IA; KSTZ(FM) Des Moines, IA; KIOA(FM) Des Moines, IA; KAZR(FM) Pella, IA; KICD Spencer, IA; KICD-FM Spencer, IA; KLLT(FM) Spencer, IA; WIXY-FM Champaign, IL; WLRW-FM Champaign, IL; WXTT(FM) Danville, IL; WYMG(FM) Jacksonville, IL; WABZ(FM) Sherman, IL; WTAX(AM) Springfield, IL; WQQL(FM) Springfield, IL; WDBR(FM) Springfield, IL; WCFF(FM) Urbana, IL; WCVQ-FM Fort Campbell, KY; WJQI(AM) Fort Campbell, KY; WVVR(FM) Hopkinsville, KY; WZZP(FM) Hopkinsville, KY; WEGI(FM) Oak Grove, KY; WHNP(AM) East Longmeadow, MA; WPVQ(FM) Greenfield, MA; WHMQ(AM) Greenfield, MA; WHMP Northampton, MA; WLZX(FM) Northampton, MA; WAQY-FM Springfield, MA; WRSI(FM) Turners Falls, MA; WOQL(FM) Winchendon, MA; WVAE(AM) Biddeford, ME; WBAE Portland, ME; WGAN(AM) Portland, ME; WPOR(FM) Portland, ME; WZAN Portland, ME; WMGX(FM) Portland, ME; WYNZ-FM Westbrook, ME; WOXL-FM Biltmore Forest, NC; WLZR(AM) Canton, NC; WMLL(FM) Bedford, NH; WKBK(AM) Keene, NH; WKNE(FM) Keene, NH; WZBK(AM) Keene, NH; WFEA Manchester, NH; WZID(FM) Manchester, NH; WINQ(FM) Winchester, NH; WYXL-FM Ithaca, NY; WNYY(AM) Ithaca, NY; WQNY-FM Ithaca, NY; WHCU Ithaca, NY; WBCO Bucyrus, OH; WSNY-FM Columbus, OH; WODB(FM) Delaware, OH; WJZA-FM Lancaster, OH; WJZK(FM) Richwood, OH; KMIT-FM Mitchell, SD; KUQL(FM) Wessington Springs, SD; WKFN(AM) Clarksville, TN; WINA Charlottesville, VA; WQMZ(FM) Charlottesville, VA; WWWV-FM Charlottesville, VA; WJOI Norfolk, VA; WAFX-FM Suffolk, VA; WKVT Brattleboro, VT; WRSY(FM) Marlboro, VT; KGMI Bellingham, WA; KBAI(AM) Bellingham, WA; KPUG Bellingham, WA; WFMR(FM) Brookfield, WI; WJMR-FM Menomonee Falls, WI; WKLH-FM Milwaukee, WI; WJYI Milwaukee, WI; WHQG(FM) Milwaukee, WI

Stns: 3 TV. WXVT, Greenwood-Greenville, MS; KOAM, Joplin, MO-Pittsburg, KS; KAVU, Victoria, TX

Edward K. Christian, pres/CEO; Marcia Lobaito, VP business affrs; Sam Bush, CFO; Warren Lada Sr., VP opns.

Salem Communications Corp. 4880 Santa Rosa Rd., Suite 100, Camarillo, CA 93012. Phone: (805) 987-0400. Fax: (805) 384-4511. Web Site: www.salem.cc.

Stns: 70 AM. 33 FM. KPXQ(AM) Glendale, AZ; KKNT(AM) Phoenix, AZ; KFSH-FM Anaheim, CA; KXMX(AM) Anaheim, CA; KFIA Carmichael, CA; KVMG(FM) Dunnigan, CA; KRLA(AM) Glendale, CA; KCEE(FM) Grass Valley, CA; KLMG(FM) Jackson, CA; KKLA-FM Los Angeles, CA; KDAR(FM) Oxnard, CA; KNTS(AM) Palo Alto, CA; KTKZ Sacramento, CA; KTIE(AM) San Bernardino, CA; KCBQ San Diego, CA; KFAX San Francisco, CA; KPRZ San Marcos-Poway, CA; KIIS(AM) Thousand Oaks, CA; KRKS-FM Boulder, CO; KZNT(AM) Colorado Springs, CO; KBJD Denver, CO; KRKS(AM) Denver, CO; KNUS Denver, CO; KBIQ(FM) Manitou Springs, CO; KGFT-FM Pueblo, CO; WNTR(AM) Dunedin, FL; WZNZ Jacksonville, FL; WZAZ Jacksonville, FL; WJGR Jacksonville, FL; WKAT North Miami, FL; WTBN(AM) Pinellas Park, FL; WTWD(AM) Plant City, FL; WBGB-FM Ponte Vedra Beach, FL; WLSS(AM) Sarasota, FL; WLTA Alpharetta, GA; WFSH-FM Athens, GA; WGKA(AM) Atlanta, GA; WAFS(AM) Atlanta, GA; WNIV Atlanta, GA; KGMZ-FM Aiea, HI; KGU Honolulu, HI; KHNR(AM) Honolulu, HI; KAIM-FM Honolulu, HI; KHCM(AM) Honolulu, HI; KHUI(FM) Honolulu, HI; KHNR-FM Honolulu, HI; WYLL(AM) Chicago, IL; WIND Chicago, IL; WFIA-FM New Albany, IN; WBOB Florence, KY; WFIA Louisville, KY; WGTK(AM) Louisville, KY; WRVI-FM Valley Station, KY; WROL Boston, MA; WTTT(AM) Boston, MA; WEZE Boston, MA; WDTK(AM) Detroit, MI; KYCR Golden Valley, MN; WWTC Minneapolis, MN; KKMS Richfield, MN; KGBI-FM Omaha, NE; KCRO Omaha, NE; WWDJ Hackensack, NJ; WMCA New York, NY; WTSJ Cincinnati, OH; WKNR(AM) Cleveland, OH; WHKW(AM) Cleveland, OH; WFHM-FM Cleveland, OH; WHK(AM) Cleveland, OH; WRFD(AM) Columbus-Worthington, OH; WHKZ(AM) Warren, OH; KAST-FM Astoria, OR; KPDQ-FM Portland, OR; KFIS(FM) Scappoose, OR; WFIL(AM) Philadelphia, PA; WNTP(AM) Philadelphia, PA; WORD-FM Pittsburgh, PA; WFFI(FM) Kingston Springs, TN; WFFH(FM) Smyrna, TN; WVRY-FM Waverly, TN; WBOZ-FM Woodbury, TN; KTEK Alvin, TX; KLTY(FM) Arlington, TX; KSKY(AM) Balch Springs, TX; KNIT(AM) Dallas, TX; KWRD-FM Highland Village, TX; KNTH(AM) Houston, TX; KPXI-FM Overton, TX; KSLR San Antonio, TX; KLUP(AM) Terrell Hills, TX; KKHT-FM Winnie, TX; WAVA(FM) Arlington, VA; WABS Arlington, VA; WBTK(AM) Richmond, VA; KGNW Burien-Seattle, WA; KIKN Port Angeles, WA; KTFH(AM) Seattle, WA; KKOL Seattle, WA; KLFE Seattle, WA; KKMO Tacoma, WA; WRRD(AM) Jackson, WI; WFZH(FM) Mukwonago, WI; WITH(AM) Baltimore, MD

Edward G. Atsinger III, pres/CEO; Stuart W. Epperson, chmn; Eric H. Halvorson, VP/COO.

Sand Hill Media Corp. Box 570, Logan, UT 84323. Phone: (435) 752-1390. Ownership: Sand Hill Media 2001, 100%.

Stns: 1 AM. 3 FM. KUPI(AM) Ammon, ID; KUPI-FM Idaho Falls, ID; KQEO(FM) Idaho Falls, ID; KADQ-FM Rexburg, ID

Sandab Communications L.P. II 2201 Old Court Rd., Baltimore, MD 21208. Phone: (508) 771-1224. Web Site: www.wqrc.com.

Stns: 2 FM. WQRC(FM) Barnstable, MA; WOCN-FM South Yarmouth, MA

Stephen Seymour, pres; Scott Frothinghan, VP; Gregory Bone, gen mgr.

Sandusky Radio 515 Park Ave., Apt. 4A, New York, NY 10022. Phone: (212) 355-3074. Fax: (212) 355-3075. Ownership: Alice S. White trust. All 100% owned by the White and Rau families.

Stns: 3 AM. 4 FM. KDKB(FM) Mesa, AZ; KAZG(AM) Scottsdale, AZ; KDUS Tempe, AZ; KLSY-FM Bellevue, WA; KRWM-FM Bremerton, WA; KIXI Mercer Island-Seattle, WA; KWJZ(FM) Seattle, WA

Sandusky Newspapers Inc. publishes the *Sandusky Register, Norwalk Reflector* (OH) *Kingsport Times-News*(TN) *Grand Haven Tribune*(MI) *Ogden Standard-Examiner*(UT) *Johnson City Press, Lebanon Democrat* (TN) and five weekly newspapers, *Erwin Record, Jonesborough Herald & Tribune, Mountain City Tomahawk, Hartsville Vidette* and the *Mt. Juliet News*.

David A. Rau, chmn/CEO; Norman Rau, pres; Peter W. Vogt, CFO.

Schurz Communications Inc. 225 W. Colfax Ave., South Bend, IN 46626. Phone: (219) 287-1001. Fax: (219) 287-2257. E-mail: mburdick@schurz.com. Ownership: Franklin D. Schurz Jr., James M. Schurz, Scott C. Schurz and Mary Schurz, trustees.

Stns: 2 AM. 3 FM. WASK-FM Battle Ground, IN; WKOA-FM Lafayette, IN; WASK Lafayette, IN; WSBT South Bend, IN; WNSN-FM South Bend, IN

Stns: 4 TV. WAGT, Augusta, GA; WDBJ, Roanoke-Lynchburg, VA; WSBT, South Bend-Elkhart, IN; KYTV, Springfield, MO

Schurz Communications publishes the following nwsprs: *Imperial Valley Press, Southside Times-Beech, Times; Bedford Times-Mail, Bloomington Herald-Times* , & *South Bend Tribune, Martinsville Reporter, Danville Advocate-Messenger, The Herald Mail Co.; Daily American*, Somerset, PA.

Marcia K. Burdick, sr VP bcstg; Franklin D. Schurz Jr., pres.

Sea-Comm Inc. 122 Cinema Dr., Wilmington, NC 28403. Phone: (910) 772-6300. Fax: (910) 772-6310. Web Site: www.sea-comm.com. Ownership: N. Eric Jorgensen, 100%.

Stns: 4 FM. WLTT(FM) Shallotte, NC; WBNU(FM) Shallotte, NC; WWTB(FM) Topsail Beach, NC; WBNE(FM) Wrightsville Beach, NC

Paul Knight, gen mgr; Rick Jorgenson, pres/CEO.

Searcy Broadcasting Inc. 121 Radio Heights Dr., Searcy, AR 72143. Phone: (501) 305-0977. Fax: (501) 305-2977.

Stns: 1 AM. 1 FM. KABK-FM Augusta, AR; KZTD(AM) Cabot, AR

Ken Madden, pres.

Seaton Stations Manhattan Broadcasting Inc., 2414 Casement Rd., Manhattan, KS 66502. Phone: (785) 776-1350. Fax: (785) 539-1000.

Stns: 1 AM. 2 FM. KMAN Manhattan, KS; KXBZ-FM Manhattan, KS; KACZ(FM) Riley, KS

Seaton Goup of newspapers includes the *Manhattan Mercury* & *Winfield Courier*, both KS; *Alliance Times-Herald* & *Hastings Tribune*, both NE; *The Black Hills Pioneer*, Spearfish, SD; *Sheridan* (WY) *Press*.

Richard Wartell, gen mgr.

Seattle Streaming Radio LLC Box 348, Sedalia, CO 80135. Phone: (303) 688-5162. Fax: (303) 660-4930. Ownership: David M. Drucker, 80%; and Penny Drucker, 20%.

Stns: 3 AM. WKIZ Key West, FL; KBRO Bremerton, WA; KNTB Lakewood, WA

Seward County Broadcasting Co. 1410 N. Western, Liberal, KS 67901. Phone: (620) 624-3891. Fax: (620) 624-7885. E-mail: sales@kscb.net. Web Site: www.kscb.net. Ownership: Jack Landon, Robert Larrabee, Stuart Melchert.

Stns: 1 FM. KLDG-FM Liberal, KS

Stuart Melchert, gen mgr.

Shamrock Communications Inc. 149 Penn Ave., Scranton, PA 18503. Phone: (570) 348-9108. Fax: (570) 348-9109. Web Site: www.nepanews.com. Ownership: Principal owners: William R. Lynett, James J. Haggerty, Edward J. Lynett, George V. Lynett. Shamrock Communications owns 50% of the Milwaukee Radio Alliance LLC (see listing).

Stns: 2 AM. 7 FM. KTSO(FM) Glenpool, OK; KMYZ-FM Pryor, OK; WQFN(FM) Forest City, PA; WQFM-FM Nanticoke, PA; WPZX(FM) Pocono Pines, PA; WEJL Scranton, PA; WEZX-FM Scranton, PA; WBAX Wilkes-Barre, PA; WZBA(FM) Westminster, MD

Publications include *Orlando Weekly*, Orlando, FL; *City Paper*, Baltimore, MD; *Metro Times* (Detroit), Detroit, MI; *Owego Pennysaver*, Owego, NY; *Pocono Shopper* (Monroe County Edition), East Stroudsburg, *Susquehanna County Independent, Susquehanna County Weekender*, Montrose, *Pottsville Republican and Evening Herald*, Pottsville, *ADI, Electric City, Good Times, Northeast Pennsylvania Business Journal, Scranton Times-Tribune, Suburban Weekly, Tri-Boro Banner, Valley Advantage*, all Scranton, *News Item, Shamokin, Daily Review, The Bradford Sullivan Pennysaver, The Farmer's Friend*, Towanda, *Troy Pennysaver*, Troy, *New Age-Examiner, Wyoming County Advance*, Tunkhannock, *The Citizen Standard, Valley View, Citizens Voice*, Wilkes-Barre, all PA; *San Antonio Current*, San Antonio, TX.

William R. Lynett, pres; Jim Loftus, COO.

Shepherd Group Box 430, Moberly, MO 65270. Phone: (660) 263-5800. Fax: (660) 263-2300. E-mail: daves@regionalradio.com.

Stns: 7 AM. 6 FM. KAAN Bethany, MO; KMRN Cameron, MO; KKWK(FM) Cameron, MO; KREI Farmington, MO; KTJJ-FM Farmington, MO; KJFF(AM) Festus, MO; KBNN Lebanon, MO; KJEL-FM Lebanon, MO; KIRK-FM Macon, MO; KRES-FM Moberly, MO; KWIX Moberly, MO; KJPW Waynesville, MO; KJPW-FM Waynesville, MO

David Shepherd, pres.

Sierra Broadcasting Corp. 3015 Johnstonville Rd., Susanville, CA 96130. Phone: (530) 257-2121. Fax: (530) 257-6955. E-mail: info@theradionetwork.com. Web Site: www.theradionetwork.com.

Stns: 1 AM. 1 FM. KHJQ-FM Susanville, CA; KSUE Susanville, CA

Rod Chambers, gen mgr; George Carl, VP.

Radio Group Ownership

Simmons Broadcasting Inc. 1403 Third St., Langdon, ND 58249. Phone: (701) 256-1080. Fax: (701) 256-1081. E-mail: kndkkicksbs@utma.com. Ownership: Robert N. Simmons, 50%; and Diane R. Simmons, 50%. Note: Pursuant to a loc mktg agreement, group provides substantially all of the progmg for KXPO(AM)-KAUJ(FM) Grafton, ND.

Stns: 1 AM. 3 FM. KAOC(FM) Cavalier, ND; KNDK Langdon, ND; KNDK-FM Langdon, ND; KYTZ(FM) Walhalla, ND

Simmons Media Group 515 South 700 East, Salt Lake City, UT 84102. Phone: (801) 524-2600. Fax: (801) 524-6002. Web Site: www.simmonsmedia.com. Ownership: The David E. Simmons 201 Trust, The Matthew R. Simmons 201 Trust, The Laurence E. Simmons 201 Trust, The Julia S. Watkins 201 Trust, The Elizabeth S. Hoke 201 Trust and The Harris H. Simmons 201 Trust.

Stns: 13 AM. 9 FM. KSUD West Memphis, AR; WESL East St. Louis, IL; KSLG(AM) Saint Louis, MO; KKNS(AM) Corrales, NM; KZNX(AM) Creedmoor, TX; KLRK(FM) Marlin, TX; KRQX Mexia, TX; KYCX-FM Mexia, TX; KWNX(AM) Taylor, TX; KQRL(AM) Waco, TX; KRZI(AM) Waco, TX; KRAR-FM Brigham City, UT; KXOL Brigham City, UT; KEGH(FM) Brigham City, UT; KJQN(FM) Coalville, UT; KEGA(FM) Oakley, UT; KXRK-FM Provo, UT; KOVO Provo, UT; KZNS(AM) Salt Lake City, UT; KDWY(FM) Diamondville, WY; KAOX(FM) Kemmerer, WY; KMER Kemmerer, WY

David Simmons, chmn; Craig Hanson, pres; Bruce W. Thomas, CFO; Bret Leifson, controller; Alan Hague, opns VP.

Sinclair Communications Inc. 999 Waterside Dr., Norfolk, VA 23510. Phone: (317) 838-7130. Fax: (317) 838-7225. Web Site: www.sinclairstations.com. Ownership: John L. Sinclair, chmn; Robert Sinclair, J. David Sinclair, Ann Adams.

Stns: 2 AM. 6 FM. KXTS(FM) Calistoga, CA; KRSH(FM) Healdsburg, CA; KSXY(FM) Middletown, CA; WPYA(FM) Chesapeake, VA; WROX-FM Exmore, VA; WTAR(AM) Norfolk, VA; WNIS Norfolk, VA; WZNR(FM) Poquoson, VA

John L. Sinclair, chmn; J. David Sinclair, pres.

629112 Saskatchewan LTD. 345 4th Ave. S., Saskatoon, SK S7K 5S5. Canada. Phone: (306) 244-1975. Fax: (306) 665-8484.

Stns: 1 AM. 1 FM. CJWW Saskatoon, SK; CJMK-FM Saskatoon, SK

Elmer Hildebrand, CEO; Vic Dubois, gen mgr.

Somar Communications Inc. 28095 Three Notch Rd., Suite 2-B, Mechanicsville, MD 20659. Phone: (301) 870-5550. Fax: (301) 884-0280.

Stns: 2 AM. 3 FM. WKIK-FM California, MD; WKIK La Plata, MD; WPTX(AM) Lexington Park, MD; WMDM-FM Lexington Park, MD; WSMD-FM Mechanicsville, MD

Roy Robertson, pres/CEO.

Sorensen Pacific Broadcasting Inc. 111 W. Chanlan Santo Papa, Suite 800, Hagatna, GU 96910. Phone: (671) 477-5700. Fax: (671) 477-3982. E-mail: comments@radiopacific.com. Web Site: www.radiopacific.com. Ownership: Rex W. Sorensen, 97.6%.

Stns: 1 AM. 3 FM. KGUM-FM Dededo, GU; KGUM(AM) Hagatna, GU; KPXP(FM) Garapan-Saipan, NP; KRSI-FM Garapan-Saipan, NP

Rex Sorensen, chmn/CEO; Jon Anderson, pres.

Sorenson Broadcasting Corp. 2804 S. Ridgeview Way, Sioux Falls, SD 57105. Phone: (605) 334-1117. Fax: (605) 338-0326. E-mail: sorenson@sbcradio.com. Web Site: www.sbcradio.com. Ownership: Dean P. Sorenson, 100%.

Stns: 6 AM. 9 FM. KUQQ-FM Milford, IA; KIHK-FM Rock Valley, IA; KSOU Sioux Center, IA; KSOU-FM Sioux Center, IA; KUOO-FM Spirit Lake, IA; KAYL Storm Lake, IA; KAYL-FM Storm Lake, IA; KCUE Red Wing, MN; KWNG-FM Red Wing, MN; KORN Mitchell, SD; KQRN-FM Mitchell, SD; KLXS-FM Pierre, SD; KCCR Pierre, SD; KKYA-FM Yankton, SD; KYNT Yankton, SD

Dean Sorenson, pres.

South Central Communications Corp. Box 3848, Evansville, IN 47736. Phone: (812) 424-8284. Fax: (812) 426-7925. Web Site: www.wiky.com. Ownership: John D. Engelbrecht, 80%, J.P. Engelbrecht, 20%.

Stns: 1 AM. 10 FM. WYXY(FM) Boonville, IN; WLFW(FM) Chandler, IN; WEOA Evansville, IN; WABX-FM Evansville, IN; WSTO-FM Owensboro, KY; WIMZ-FM Knoxville, TN; WJXB-FM Knoxville, TN; WTXM-FM Maryville, TN; WCJK(FM) Murfreesboro, TN; WJXA-FM Nashville, TN; WRMX-FM Norris, TN

Stns: 2 TV. WAZE-TV, Evansville, IN; WMAK, Knoxville, TN

John D. Engelbrecht, pres; J.P. Engelbrecht, VP.

Southeast Kansas Broadcasting Co. 250 N. Water, Suite 300, Wichita, KS 67202. Phone: (620) 431-3700. Fax: (620) 431-4643. E-mail: kkoy@kkoy.com. Web Site: www.kkoy.com. Ownership: Murfin Inc.

Stns: 1 AM. 1 FM. KSNP(FM) Burlington, KS; KKOY Chanute, KS

Phil McComb, gen mgr.

Southeastern Oklahoma Radio LLC Box 1011, Hartshorne, OK 74547. Phone: (918) 297-2501. Ownership: Bob and Sheila Turnbow (jointly), 33.33%; Lee Anderson, 33.33%; and Richard C. Lerblance, 33.33%. Note: Richard C. Lerblance also owns 33.33% of KESC(FM) Wilburton, OK.

Stns: 2 AM. 2 FM. KMCO-FM McAlester, OK; KNED McAlester, OK; KTMC McAlester, OK; KTMC-FM McAlester, OK

Southern Broadcasting Companies Inc. 1010 Tower Pl., Bogart, GA 30622. Phone: (706) 369-7301. Fax: (706) 353-1967. Web Site: www.magic1021.com. Ownership: Paul C. Stone.

Stns: 4 AM. 6 FM. WRFC Athens, GA; WGAU Athens, GA; WSRM(FM) Coosa, GA; WGMG-FM Crawford, GA; WMGZ(FM) Eatonton, GA; WKGQ Milledgeville, GA; WRGA Rome, GA; WPUP-FM Royston, GA; WNGC(FM) Toccoa, GA; WXKT-FM Washington, GA

Paul Stone, pres; Traci Long, gen mgr.

Southern Communications Corp. 306 S. Kanawaha St., Beckley, WV 25801. Phone: (304) 253-7000. Fax: (304) 255-1044. Web Site: www.103cir.com. Ownership: R. Shane Southern, 50.4%; Karen L. Martin, 24.8%; and Kristin E. Wallace, 24.8%.

Stns: 3 AM. 4 FM. WCIR-FM Beckley, WV; WIWS Beckley, WV; WWNR Beckley, WV; WMTD Hinton, WV; WMTD-FM Hinton, WV; WTNJ-FM Mount Hope, WV; WAXS-FM Oak Hill, WV

Jay Quesenberry, gen mgr; R. Shane Southern, pres.

Southern Media Group Inc. Box 810, Crossville, TN 38557-0810. Phone: (931) 484-1057. Fax: (931) 707-0580. E-mail: info@southernmediagroup.net. Web Site: www.southernmediagroup.net. Ownership: Kirk Tollett, 80%; and Jennifer Tollett, 20%.

Stns: 1 AM. 1 FM. WBZH(FM) Harriman, TN; WOFE(AM) Rockwood, TN

Kirk Tollett, pres.

Southern Wabash Communications Corp. 435 37th Ave. N., Nashville, TN 37209. Phone: (615) 844-1039. Fax: (615) 777-2284. Web Site: www.wnsr.com.

Stns: 2 AM. 2 FM. WSJD-FM Princeton, IN; WNTC-FM Drakesboro, KY; WNSR Brentwood, TN; WMGC Murfreesboro, TN

Randy Bell, pres; Ted Johnson, gen mgr.

Southwest Broadcasting Inc. 206 N. Front, McComb, MS 39648. Phone: (601) 684-4116. Fax: (601) 684-4654. E-mail: spots@k106.net. Ownership: C. Wayne Dowdy, 100%.

Stns: 2 AM. 6 FM. WTGG-FM Amite, LA; WJSH(FM) Folsom, LA; WZFL-FM Centreville, MS; WAZA-FM Liberty, MS; WAKH-FM McComb, MS; WAPF(AM) McComb, MS; WAKK(AM) McComb, MS; WFCG(FM) Tylertown, MS

C. Wayne Dowdy, pres.

Spanish Broadcasting System Inc. 2601 South Bayshore Dr.,, PH 2, Coconut Grove, FL 33133. Phone: (305) 441-6901. Fax: (305) 446-5148. Web Site: www.spanishbroadcasting.com. Ownership: Raul Alarcon Sr., Raul Alarcon Jr., Jose Grimalt.

Stns: 20 FM. KLAX-FM East Los Angeles, CA; KXOL Los Angeles, CA; KRZZ(FM) San Francisco, CA; WRMA-FM Fort Lauderdale, FL; WCMQ-FM Hialeah, FL; WXDJ-FM North Miami Beach, FL; WLEY-FM Aurora, IL; WPAT-FM Paterson, NJ; WSKQ-FM New York, NY; WODA(FM) Bayamon, PR; WCMA-FM Fajardo, PR; WMEG-FM Guayama, PR; WZET(FM) Hormigueros, PR; WNOD(FM) Mayaguez, PR; WIOB-FM Mayaguez, PR; WIOC-FM Ponce, PR; WZMT-FM Ponce, PR; WEGM(FM) San German, PR; WZNT-FM San Juan, PR; WIOA(FM) San Juan, PR

Raul Alarcon Sr., chmn; Raul Alarcon Jr., pres/CEO; Jose Grimalt, exec VP.

Spanish Peaks Broadcasting Inc. 3046 E. Dimple Dell Cir., Sandy, UT 84092. Phone: (801) 560-9595. Ownership: Kevin Terry, 100%.

Stns: 3 FM. KDTR(FM) Florence, MT; KKNS-FM Missoula, MT; KKVU(FM) Stevensville, MT

Spotlight Broadcasting LLC Box 8888, Metairie, LA 70011. Phone: (504) 309-7260. Fax: (504) 309-7262. E-mail: kmrc@kmrc1430.com. Web Site: www.kmrc1430.com.

Stns: 3 AM. WABL Amite, LA; KMRC Morgan City, LA; KAGY Port Sulphur, LA

Patrick Andras, pres.

Standard Broadcasting Corp. 2 St. Clair Ave. W., Suite 1100, Toronto, ON M4V 1L6. Canada. Phone: (416) 960-9911. Fax: (416) 323-6828. Ownership: Slaight Communications Inc., 100%.

Stns: 22 AM. 20 FM. CKMX Calgary, AB; CIBK-FM Calgary, AB; CFRN Edmonton, AB; CFMG-FM Saint Albert, AB; CFKC Creston, BC; CJDC Dawson Creek, BC; CKRX-FM Fort Nelson, BC; CHRX-FM Fort St. John, BC; CKNL-FM Fort St. John, BC; CKGR Golden, BC; CKIR Invermere, BC; CKFR(AM) Kelowna, BC; CKTK-FM Kitimat, BC; CKKC Nelson, BC; CKZX-FM New Denver, BC; CJOR Osoyoos, BC; CKOR Penticton, BC; CHTK Prince Rupert, BC; CKCR Revelstoke, BC; CISL Richmond, BC; CKXR Salmon Arm, BC; CFTK Terrace, BC; CJAT-FM Trail, BC; CKZZ-FM Vancouver, BC; CICF-FM Vernon, BC; CKXA-FM Brandon, MB; CKX-FM Brandon, MB; CFQX-FM Selkirk, MB; CKMM-FM Winnipeg, MB; CKOC Hamilton, ON; CHAM Hamilton, ON; CJBK(AM) London, ON; CJBX-FM London, ON; CKSL London, ON; CIQM-FM London, ON; CHVR-FM Pembroke, ON; CHRE-FM Saint Catharines, ON; CKTB Saint Catharines, ON; CFRB Toronto, ON; CJEZ-FM Toronto, ON; CJAD Montreal, PQ; CHOM-FM Montreal, PQ

Stns: 2 TV. CJDC, Dawson Creek, BC; CFTK, Terrace, BC

Gary Slaight, pres/CEO.

Stanford Communications Inc. Box 458, Amory, MS 38821. Phone: (662) 256-9726. Fax: (662) 256-9725. E-mail: wamywafm@traceroad.net. Web Site: www.fm95radio.com.

Stns: 2 AM. WWZQ Aberdeen, MS; WAMY Amory, MS

Ed Stanford, pres; Teresa Stanford, sec/treas.

Starcast Systems Inc. Box F, Keyser, WV 26726. Phone: (301) 786-4661. Fax: (304) 788-1662. E-mail: wqzk@wqzk.com. Web Site: www.wqzk.com. Ownership: Jack Mullen II, William P. Kelly, Curtis Durst.

Stns: 2 AM. 1 FM. WBHN Bryson City, NC; WKLP Keyser, WV; WQZK-FM Keyser, WV

Jack I. Mullen II, pres.

Starlight Broadcasting Co. Box 106, 314 Main, Hartford, KY 42347. Phone: (270) 298-3268. Fax: (270) 298-9326. Web Site: www.wxmz.com.

Stns: 1 AM. 1 FM. WAIA(AM) Beaver Dam, KY; WKYA-FM Greenville, KY

Andy Anderson, pres/CEO.

Staton Broadcasting Inc. 6316 Peake Rd., Macon, GA 31210. Phone: (478) 301-2117. Ownership: Cecil P. Staton, 100%.

Stns: 2 AM. 4 FM. WQXZ(FM) Cordele, GA; WQSY(AM) Cordele, GA; WMRZ(FM) Dawson, GA; WCEH Hawkinsville, GA; WHKN-FM Millen, GA; WPMX-FM Statesboro, GA

Studstill Broadcasting 3905 Progress Blvd., Peru, IL 61354. Phone: (815) 224-2100. Phone: (815) 224-2100 (Corp). Fax: (815) 224-2066. Ownership: Owen L. Studstill; Lamar Studstill; Cole C. Studstill.

Stns: 1 AM. 5 FM. WGLC-FM Mendota, IL; WALS-FM Oglesby, IL; WBZG(FM) Peru, IL; WIVQ(FM) Spring Valley, IL; WYYS(FM) Streator, IL; WSPL(AM) Streator, IL

Owen L. Studstill, pres; Lamar Studstill, chmn; Cole C. Studstill, opns off.

Styles Media Group LLC Box 28346, Panama City Beach, FL 32411. Phone: (850) 234-8388. Fax: (850) 230-6988. Web Site: www.stylesmedia.com. Ownership: Styles Management Co. LLC, mngg member; Donald G. McCoy, 29.57%; Stephen A. Bodzin, trustee of Anne S. Reich 1984 Revocable Trust, 21.13%; Kim Styles DiBacco, 7.75%; Thomas A. DiBacco, 7.75%.

Stns: 4 AM. 9 FM. WTVY-FM Dothan, AL; WKMX-FM Enterprise, AL; WLDA(FM) Fort Rucker, AL; WQLS Ozark, AL; KDAI(FM) Ontario, CA; KDAY(FM) Redondo Beach, CA; WYYX-FM Bonifay, FL; WILN-FM Panama City, FL; WPCF(AM) Panama City Beach, FL; WVVE(FM) Panama City Beach, FL; WYOO-FM Springfield, FL; WBBK Blakely, GA; WSEM Donalsonville, GA

Kim Styles, gen mgr; Thomas DiBacco, ptnr.

Sudbury Services Inc. Box 989, Blytheville, AR 72316. Phone: (870) 762-2093. Fax: (870) 763-8459. Web Site: www.thundercountry963.com. Ownership: Harold L. Sudbury Jr., Lydia Sudbury Langston, LaNeal Sudbury Salter. Cable TV: Blytheville TV Cable Co., Blytheville, AR.

Stns: 3 AM. 3 FM. KLCN Blytheville, AR; KAMJ-FM Gosnell, AR; KHPA-FM Hope, AR; KSSW(FM) Nashville,

Radio Group Ownership

AR; KNBY Newport, AR; KTPA Prescott, AR

Harold Sudbury Jr., pres.

Summit City Radio Group 2000 Lower Huntington Rd., Fort Wayne, IN 46819. Phone: (260) 747-1511. Fax: (260) 747-3999. Web Site: www.summitcityradio.com.

Stns: 1 AM. 5 FM. WXTW(FM) Auburn, IN; WNHT(FM) Churubusco, IN; WYLT(FM) Fort Wayne, IN; WGL Fort Wayne, IN; WXKE(FM) Huntington, IN; WCKZ(FM) Roanoke, IN

Kristine Foate, CEO.

Sumter Broadcasting Co. Inc. Box 727, Americus, GA 31709. Phone: (229) 924-1390. Fax: (229) 928-2337. Web Site: www.americusradio.com.

Stns: 1 AM. 1 FM. WDEC-FM Americus, GA; WISK Americus, GA

Steve Lashley, pres.

Sun Mountain Inc. 9045 Hobble Creek, Billings, MT 59101. Phone: (406) 665-2828. Fax: (406) 665-2131. Web Site: www.bigskyradio.net. Ownership: Richard Solberg, 100%.

Stns: 3 AM. KHDN Hardin, MT; KBSR Laurel, MT; KYLW(AM) Lockwood, MT

Sun Valley Radio Inc. 810 W. 200 North, Logan, UT 84321. Phone: (435) 752-1390. Fax: (435) 752-1392. Ownership: M. Kent Frandsen, owner.

Stns: 2 AM. 4 FM. KKEX-FM Preston, ID; KLZX(FM) Weston, ID; KLGN Logan, UT; KVNU Logan, UT; KZHK-FM Saint George, UT; KGNT(FM) Smithfield, UT

M. Kent Frandsen, pres.

Sunbelt Broadcasting Corp. Box 351, Columbia, MS 39429. Phone: (601) 731-2298. E-mail: wjdr@zzip.com.

Stns: 2 FM. WCJU-FM Prentiss, MS; WJDR-FM Prentiss, MS

Thomas F. McDaniel, pres.

Sunbury Broadcasting Corp. Box 1070, Sunbury, PA 17801. Phone: (570) 286-5838. Fax: (570) 743-7837. Ownership: Lois W. Haddon, 90.7%; Dr. Harry H. Haddon Jr., 8%; and Roger S. Haddon Jr., 1.3%.

Stns: 1 AM. 2 FM. WEGH-FM Northumberland, PA; WKOK Sunbury, PA; WQKX-FM Sunbury, PA

Sunrise Broadcasting Corp. Box 2307, Newburgh, NY 12550. Phone: (845) 561-2131. Fax: (845) 561-2138. Web Site: www.wgnyfm.com. Ownership: CVC Capital Corp.

Stns: 2 AM. WJGK(AM) Kingston, NY; WGNY Newburgh, NY

J. Klebe, pres.

Superior Broadcasting of Denver LLC 8975 E. Kenyon Ave., Denver, CO 80237. Phone: (720) 529-1431. Fax: (720) 529-1418. Ownership: Alta-Superior Holdings Inc., class B preferred unit holder; New Bedford Trust, Christopher F. Devine & Bruce Buzil, co-trustees; and others.

Stns: 3 FM. KKCS-FM Colorado Springs, CO; KXDC(FM) Estes Park, CO; KFVR-FM La Junta, CO

Susquehanna Radio Corp. Box 1432, York, PA 17405. Phone: (717) 852-2132. Fax: (717) 771-1436. Web Site: www.susquehannaradio.com. Ownership: A subsidiary of Susquehanna Pfaltzgraff Co. Cable TV.

Stns: 11 AM. 22 FM. KFFG-FM Los Altos, CA; KFOG-FM San Francisco, CA; KNBR San Francisco, CA; KSAN-FM San Mateo, CA; KTCT San Mateo, CA; WNNX-FM Atlanta, GA; WWWQ(FM) College Park, GA; WISG(FM) Fishers, IN; WFMS-FM Indianapolis, IN; WAVG(AM) Jeffersonville, IN; WJJK(FM) Noblesville, IN; WZZB Seymour, IN; WQKC-FM Seymour, IN; KCJK(FM) Garden City, MO; KCFX(FM) Harrisonville, MO; KCMO Kansas City, MO; KCMO-FM Kansas City, MO; WRRM-FM Cincinnati, OH; WMOJ-FM Fairfield, OH; WYGY(FM) Lebanon, OH; WGLD(AM) Red Lion, PA; WSOX-FM Red Lion, PA; WSBA York, PA; WARM-FM York, PA; KTCK Dallas, TX; KLIF(AM) Dallas, TX; KYNG(AM) Denison-Sherman, TX; KPLX(FM) Fort Worth, TX; KIKT-FM Greenville, TX; KDBN(FM) Haltom City, TX; KRBE(FM) Houston, TX; KTDK(FM) Sanger, TX; KKLF(AM) Sherman, TX

Louis J. Appell Jr., chmn.

T

Talking Stick Communications LLC 421 S. Second St., Elkhart, IN 46514. Phone: (574) 258-5483. Ownership: Alec C. Dille, 60%; John F. Dille IV, 20%; and Sarah D. Erlacher, 20%.

Stns: 1 AM. 2 FM. WYPW(FM) Nappanee, IN; WRSW Warsaw, IN; WRSW-FM Warsaw, IN

Alec C. Dille, pres.

Talley Radio Stations Box 10, Litchfield, IL 62056. Phone: (217) 324-5921. Fax: (217) 532-2431. E-mail: wsmi@wsmiradio.com. Web Site: wsmiradio.com. Ownership: Hayward L. Talley.

Stns: 1 AM. 2 FM. WSMI Litchfield, IL; WSMI-FM Litchfield, IL; WAOX-FM Staunton, IL

Hayward L. Talley, pres; Brian Talley, sr VP.

Tama Broadcasting Inc. 5207 Washington Blvd., Tampa, FL 33619. Phone: (813) 620-1300. Fax: (813) 628-0713. Web Site: www.wtmp.com. Ownership: Black Enterprise/Greenwich Street Corporate Growth Partners L.P., 49%; Glenn W. Cherry, 41%; and Charles W. Cherry, 10%.

Stns: 1 AM. 8 FM. WHJX(FM) Baldwin, FL; WTMP-FM Dade City, FL; WTMP Egypt Lake, FL; WJSJ(FM) Fernandina Beach, FL; WSJF(FM) Saint Augustine Beach, FL; WFJO(FM) Folkston, GA; WSGA(FM) Hinesville, GA; WSSJ(FM) Hinesville, GA; WMZD(FM) Statesboro, GA

Glenn W. Cherry, CEO.

Sarkes Tarzian Inc. Box 62, Bloomington, IN 47402. Phone: (812) 332-7251. Fax: (812) 331-4575. Ownership: Tom Tarzian; Mary Tarzian estate.

Stns: 1 AM. 3 FM. WTTS-FM Bloomington, IN; WGCL Bloomington, IN; WLDE-FM Fort Wayne, IN; WAJI(FM) Fort Wayne, IN

Stns: 2 TV. WRCB-TV, Chattanooga, TN; KTVN, Reno, NV

Tom Tarzian, chmn.

Team Radio LLC Box 2509, Ponca City, OK 74602. Phone: (580) 765-2485. Fax: (580) 767-1103. Web Site: www.eteamradio.com. Ownership: William L. Coleman, 100%.

Stns: 2 AM. 2 FM. KOKB Blackwell, OK; KOKP Perry, OK; KPNC-FM Ponca City, OK; KLOR-FM Ponca City, OK

Bill Coleman, gen mgr.

Tejas Broadcasting Ltd. LLP 5201 N. O'Connor Blvd., Suite 500, Irving, TX 75039. Phone: (972) 692-3310. Ownership: Ultimately controlled by James L. Anderson.

Stns: 1 AM. 7 FM. KBZD(FM) Amarillo, TX; KTNZ Amarillo, TX; KQFX-FM Borger, TX; KLTG-FM Corpus Christi, TX; KGRW-FM Friona, TX; KLHB(FM) Odem, TX; KMJR(FM) Portland, TX; KOUL-FM Sinton, TX

Jim Anderson, CEO.

TeleSouth Communications Inc. 6311 Ridgewood Rd., Jackson, MS 39211. Phone: (601) 957-1700. Fax: (601) 957-2389. Web Site: www.supertalkms.com. Ownership: Steve Davenport

Stns: 3 AM. 5 FM. WKCU Corinth, MS; WFMN-FM Flora, MS; WKXG Greenwood, MS; WTCD(FM) Indianola, MS; WQLJ-FM Oxford, MS; WFMM-FM Sumrall, MS; WTNM(FM) Water Valley, MS; WROB(AM) West Point, MS

Stephen C. Davenport, pres/CEO.

Textron Financial Corp. 40 Westminster St., Providence, RI 02903. Phone: (401) 621-4200. Web Site: www.textronfinancial.com. Ownership: Textron Inc., 100%.

Stns: 5 AM. 8 FM. KPGG(FM) Ashdown, AR; KRFM-FM Show Low, AZ; KVSL Show Low, AZ; KMOQ-FM Baxter Springs, KS; KJML-FM Columbus, KS; KCAR-FM Galena, KS; KQYX(AM) Joplin, MO; KBTN Neosho, MO; KBTN-FM Neosho, MO; KCAR Clarksville, TX; KGAP-FM Clarksville, TX; KEWL-FM New Boston, TX; KEWL(AM) Texarkana, TX

Three Eagles Communications 19340 Furrow Rd., Monument, CO 80132. Phone: (719) 481-9378. Fax: (719) 481-8793. E-mail: rjohnson@threeeagle.com. Ownership: Rolland C. Johnson.

Stns: 15 AM. 15 FM. KIAQ-FM Clarion, IA; KVFD(AM) Fort Dodge, IA; KRIB(AM) Mason City, IA; KYTC-FM Northwood, IA; KTLB-FM Twin Lakes, IA; WCCQ-FM Crest Hill, IL; KATE Albert Lea, MN; KCPI(FM) Albert Lea, MN; KAUS Austin, MN; KQAD(AM) Luverne, MN; KEEZ-FM Mankato, MN; KLGR Redwood Falls, MN; KRBI(AM) Saint Peter, MN; KITN-FM Worthington, MN; KWOA Worthington, MN; KWOA-FM Worthington, MN; KZEN-FM Central City, NE; KTTT Columbus, NE; KLIR-FM Columbus, NE; KJSK Columbus, NE; KFRX(FM) Lincoln, NE; KRKR(FM) Lincoln, NE; KBRK Brookings, SD; KDBX(FM) Clear Lake, SD; KJAM(AM) Madison, SD; KKSD-FM Milbank, SD; KJJQ Volga, SD; KDLO-FM Watertown, SD; KSDR Watertown, SD; KWAT Watertown, SD

Rolland C. Johnson, chmn/CEO; Gary Buchanan, pres/COO.

3 Point Media 980 N. Michigan Ave., Suite 1880, Chicago, IL 60611. Phone: (312) 204-9900. Fax: (312) 587-9520.

Stns: 1 AM. 7 FM. KKLD(FM) Prescott Valley, AZ; WSOS(AM) Saint Augustine Beach, FL; KFMS(FM) Franklin, ID; KBZB(FM) Pioche, NV; KMGR(FM) Delta, UT; KCUA(FM) Naples, UT; KHTB(FM) Provo, UT; KYLZ(FM) Tremonton, UT

Three Trees Communications Inc. 113 E. College Ave., Ashburn, GA 31714. Phone: (229) 567-9038. Ownership: James Andrew Howard, 33.33%; James Thomas Overton, 33.33%; and Andrew H. Reeves, 33.33%.

Stns: 1 AM. 2 FM. WJYF-FM Nashville, GA; WTIF-FM Omega, GA; WTIF Tifton, GA

Thunderbolt Broadcasting Co. Box 318, 1410 N. Lindell St., Martin, TN 38237. Phone: (731) 587-9526. Fax: (731) 587-5079. Ownership: Paul Freeman Tinkle, trustee of the Paul Freeman Tinkle Revocable Trust, 40.42%; Jimmy C. Smith, 23.75%; Thomas L. Moore Jr., 19.16%; and Fred C. Stoker, 16.67%.

Stns: 1 AM. 2 FM. WCDZ(FM) Dresden, TN; WCMT(AM) Martin, TN; WCMT-FM South Fulton, TN

Paul Freeman Tinkle, pres.

Track 1 Media of Sterling LLC Box 830, Sterling, CO 80751. Phone: (970) 522-1607. Fax: (970) 522-1322. E-mail: knng@rodinetechnology.com. Ownership: Larry Levy, 89.5%; and Ellen Levy, 10.5%.

Stns: 1 AM. 1 FM. KSTC Sterling, CO; KNEC-FM Yuma, CO

Larry Levy, owner; Betty Carlson, gen mgr.

Tracy Broadcasting Corp. Box 532, Scottsbluff, NE 69363-0532. Phone: (308) 635-1320. Fax: (308) 635-1905. Web Site: www.tracybroadcasting.com. Ownership: Michael Tracy.

Stns: 2 AM. 4 FM. KOLT-FM Bridgeport, NE; KOZY-FM Gering, NE; KBFZ(FM) Kimball, NE; KMOR(FM) Scottsbluff, NE; KOLT Scottsbluff, NE; KOAQ Terrytown, NE

Larry Swikard, gen mgr; Michael Tracy, pres.

Tri-Market Radio Broadcasters Inc. & Eagle Rock Broadcasting Inc. 300 W. 120 South, Rupert, ID 83350. Phone: (208) 436-4757. Phone: (208) 678-2244. Fax: (208) 436-3050. Fax: (208) 678-2246.

Stns: 2 AM. 2 FM. KBAR Burley, ID; KZDX-FM Burley, ID; KFTA(AM) Rupert, ID; KKMV-FM Rupert, ID

Kim Lee, gen mgr.

Triad Broadcasting Co. L.L.C. 2511 Garden Rd., Bldg. A, Suite 104, Monterey, CA 93940. Phone: (831) 655-6350. Fax: (831) 655-6355. E-mail: jpeterson@triadbroadcasting.com. Web Site: www.triadbroadcasting.com. Ownership: Northwest Equity Partners, Shamrock Capital Advisors, Bank of America Capital Investors.

Stns: 15 AM. 20 FM. WGCO(FM) Midway, GA; WIRL(AM) Peoria, IL; WMBD Peoria, IL; WSWT-FM Peoria, IL; WPBG-FM Peoria, IL; KLTA(FM) Breckenridge, MN; KBMW Breckenridge, MN; KQWB-FM Moorhead, MN; KVOX-FM Moorhead, MN; WTNI(AM) Biloxi, MS; WXBD Biloxi, MS; WCPR-FM D'Iberville, MS; WUJM(FM) Gulfport, MS; WXYK-FM Gulfport, MS; WXRG-FM Pascagoula, MS; KPFX-FM Fargo, ND; KQWB(AM) West Fargo, ND; KWBE Beatrice, NE; KKUL-FM Lincoln, NE; KLIN Lincoln, NE; KFGE-FM Milford, NE; WGZR(FM) Bluffton, SC; WFXH(AM) Hilton Head Island, SC; WLOW(FM) Port Royal, SC; WWVV(FM) Ridgeland, SC; KFXS-FM Rapid City, SD; KKLS Rapid City, SD; KOUT-FM Rapid City, SD; KBHB Sturgis, SD; WBDY Bluefield, VA; WHQX-FM Cedar Bluff, VA; WTZE Tazewell, VA; WKEZ Bluefield, WV; WHIS Bluefield, WV; WKOY-FM Princeton, WV

Judy Peterson, VP; Thomas Douglas, CFO.

Tribune Broadcasting Co. 435 N. Michigan Ave., Suite 1800, Chicago, IL 60611. Phone: (312) 222-3333. Fax: (312) 329-0611. Web Site: www.tribune.com. Ownership: Robert R. McCormick Tribune Foundation, 13.3%; The Chandler Trusts, 11.6%; Vanguard Fiduciary Trust Co., 6.9%.

Stns: 1 AM. WGN(AM) Chicago, IL

Stns: 27 TV. WEWB, Albany-Schenectady-Troy, NY; WATL, Atlanta; WLVI, Boston (Manchester, NH); WGN, Chicago; KDAF, Dallas-Ft. Worth; KWGN, Denver, CO; WXMI, Grand Rapids-Kalamazoo-Battle Creek, MI; WPMT, Harrisburg-Lancaster-Lebanon-York, PA; WTIC, Hartford & New Haven, CT; WTXX, Hartford & New Haven, CT; KHWB, Houston; WXIN, Indianapolis, IN; WTTK, Indianapolis, IN; WTTV, Indianapolis, IN; KTLA, Los Angeles; WBZL, Miami-Ft. Lauderdale, FL; WGNO, New Orleans, LA; WNOL, New Orleans, LA; WPIX, New York; WPHL, Philadelphia; KWBP, Portland, OR; KTXL, Sacramento

Broadcasting & Cable Yearbook 2006

Radio Group Ownership

-Stockton-Modesto, CA; KSWB, San Diego, CA; KCPQ, Seattle-Tacoma, WA; KTWB, Seattle-Tacoma, WA; KPLR, St. Louis, MO; WBDC, Washington, DC (Hagerstown, MD)

Patrick J. Mullen, pres.

Tri-County Broadcasting Inc. Box 366, Sauk Rapids, MN 56379. Phone: (320) 252-6200. Fax: (320) 252-9367. Ownership: Herbert M. Hoppe, 51% of votes; Valeria Hoppe, 49% of votes.

Stns: 2 AM. 1 FM. WVAL Sauk Rapids, MN; WBHR Sauk Rapids, MN; WHMH-FM Sauk Rapids, MN

Truth Broadcasting Corp. 4405 Providence Ln., Suite D, Winston-Salem, NC 27106. Phone: (336) 759-0363. Fax: (336) 759-0366. E-mail: tbooth@830wtru.com. Web Site: www.830wtru.com. Ownership: Stuart W. Epperson Jr., 100%.

Stns: 6 AM. WZRH(AM) Dallas, NC; WCOG Greensboro, NC; WKEW Greensboro, NC; WTRU(AM) Kernersville, NC; WDRU(AM) Wake Forest, NC; WPOL Winston-Salem, NC

Stuart Epperson, pres.

Tschudy Broadcast Group 15 Campbell St., Luray, VA 22835. Phone: (540) 743-3000. Fax: (540) 743-3002.

Stns: 1 AM. 1 FM. WPDX(AM) Clarksburg, WV; WZST-FM Westover, WV

Earl Judy Jr., pres; Richard Yoder, gen mgr.

2510 Licenses LLC 100 Ryan Ct., Suite 98, Pittsburgh, PA 15205. Phone: (412) 489-1001. Fax: (412) 489-1002. Ownership: Nicholas A. Galli, 100%.

Stns: 2 AM. 4 FM. WBUS(FM) Boalsburg, PA; WCCL(FM) Central City, PA; WKVB(FM) Port Matilda, PA; WBHV(AM) Somerset, PA; WRSC State College, PA; WOWY(FM) University Park, PA

Twenty-One Sound Communications Inc. 3418 Douglas Rd., Florissant, MO 63034. Phone: (314) 921-9330. Fax: (314) 830-4141. Ownership: Randy Wachter, 100%. Note: Randy Wachter also owns 50% of KLPW(AM) Union, MO. Group is a party to a time brokerage agreement for KLPW-FM Union, MO.

Stns: 3 FM. KESY(FM) Cuba, MO; KNSX-FM Steelville, MO; KKAC(FM) Vandalia, MO

Tyler Media Broadcasting Corp. 5101 S. Shields Blvd., Oklahoma City, OK 73129. Phone: (405) 616-5500. Fax: (405) 616-5505. Web Site: www.kkng.com. Ownership: Ty A. Tyler, Tony J. Tyler and Tony J. Tyler 2000 Irrevocable Trust, Tony J. Tyler, trustee.

Stns: 2 AM. 2 FM. KOCY(AM) Del City, OK; KKNG-FM Newcastle, OK; KTUZ-FM Okarche, OK; KTLR(AM) Oklahoma City, OK

Stns: 1 TV. KTUZ-TV, Oklahoma City, OK

Skip Stow, market mgr; Robert De Negri, CFO.

U

US Stations LLC 125 Corporate Terr., Hot Springs, AR 71913. Phone: (501) 525-9700. Fax: (501) 525-9739. Web Site: www.usstations.com. Ownership: Charles Shinn, 52%; JADE Communications Inc., 20%; Gary Terrell, 20%; and Y95 Radio Inc., 8%.

Stns: 2 AM. 4 FM. KWXE-FM Glenwood, AR; KWXI Glenwood, AR; KYDL(FM) Hot Springs, AR; KQUS-FM Hot Springs, AR; KZNG Hot Springs, AR; KLXQ(FM) Mountain Pine, AR

United Ministries 300 E. Rock Rd., Allentown, PA 18103. Phone: (970) 254-5565. Fax: (970) 254-5550. Ownership: Non-stock, not-for-profit corporation.

Stns: 2 AM. 1 FM. KDTA Delta, CO; KJOL(AM) Grand Junction, CO; WBMR-FM Telford, PA

Unity Broadcasting Inc. 517 No. Beebe, Fremont, MI 49412-1909. Phone: (231) 924-4700. Fax: (231) 924-9746. Web Site: www.kickingcountry975.com. Ownership: Donald James Noordyk, 100%.

Stns: 2 AM. 3 FM. WSHN Fremont, MI; WVIB(FM) Holton, MI; WLCS-FM North Muskegon, MI; WODJ(AM) Whitehall, MI; WEFG-FM Whitehall, MI

Don Noordyk, gen mgr.

Universal Broadcasting of New York Inc. Corporate Offices, 1086 Teaneck Rd., Teaneck, NJ 07666. Phone: (201) 837-0400. Fax: (201) 837-9664. E-mail: wvnj1160am@aol.com. Web Site: www.wvnj.com. Ownership: Howard Warshaw and Miriam Warshaw.

Stns: 2 AM. WVNJ Oakland, NJ; WTHE Mineola, NY

Miriam Warshaw, pres; Howard Warshaw, VP.

Univision Radio 3102 Oak Lawn, Suite 215, Dallas, TX 75219. Phone: (214) 525-7700. Fax: (214) 525-7750. Web Site: www.hispanicbroadcasting.com. Ownership: Univision Communications Inc., 100% (see listing under TV Group Ownership, Section B).

Stns: 16 AM. 51 FM. KKMR(FM) Arizona City, AZ; KMRR(FM) Globe, AZ; KHOT-FM Paradise Valley, AZ; KOMR(FM) Sun City, AZ; KHOV-FM Wickenburg, AZ; KOND(FM) Clovis, CA; KSCA-FM Glendale, CA; KRCD(FM) Inglewood, CA; KTNQ Los Angeles, CA; KLVE-FM Los Angeles, CA; KLLE(FM) North Fork, CA; KLNV-FM San Diego, CA; KLQV-FM San Diego, CA; KSOL(FM) San Francisco, CA; KVVZ(FM) San Rafael, CA; KVVF(FM) Santa Clara, CA; KSQL(FM) Santa Cruz, CA; KRCV(FM) West Covina, CA; WRTO-FM Goulds, FL; WQBA Miami, FL; WAMR-FM Miami, FL; WAQI Miami, FL; WRTO(AM) Chicago, IL; WPPN(FM) Des Plaines, IL; WOJO-FM Evanston, IL; WVIV-FM Highland Park, IL; WVIX(FM) Joliet, IL; WCAA-FM Newark, NJ; KJFA(FM) Albuquerque, NM; KIOT-FM Los Lunas, NM; KAJZ(FM) Rio Rancho, NM; KKSS-FM Santa Fe, NM; KKRG(FM) Santa Fe, NM; KRGT(FM) Indian Springs, NV; KISF-FM Las Vegas, NV; KLSQ(AM) Whitney, NV; WZAA(FM) Garden City, NY; WADO New York, NY; WUKQ-FM Mayaguez, PR; WUKQ(AM) Ponce, PR; WKAQ San Juan, PR; KDXX(FM) Benbrook, TX; KCOR-FM Comfort, TX; KPTI(FM) Crystal Beach, TX; KFZO(FM) Denton, TX; KAMA El Paso, TX; KBNA(AM) El Paso, TX; KBNA-FM El Paso, TX; KLNO(FM) Fort Worth, TX; KFLC(AM) Fort Worth, TX; KOVE-FM Galveston, TX; KINV(FM) Georgetown, TX; KGBT Harlingen, TX; KLAT Houston, TX; KLTN-FM Houston, TX; KESS-FM Lewisville, TX; KQBT(FM) Llano, TX; KGBT-FM McAllen, TX; KLTO-FM McQueeney, TX; KPTY(FM) Missouri City, TX; KQBU-FM Port Arthur, TX; KHCK-FM Robinson, TX; KRTX Rosenberg-Richmond, TX; KAHL(AM) San Antonio, TX; KXTN-FM San Antonio, TX; KCOR(AM) San Antonio, TX; KBBT(FM) Schertz, TX

McHenry T. Tichenor Jr., pres/CEO.

Uno Radio Group Box 363222, San Juan, PR 00936-3222. Phone: (787) 758-1300. Fax: (787) 756-8545. E-mail: isoto@unoradio.com. Web Site: www.unoradio.com. Ownership: Jesus M. Soto.

Stns: 6 AM. 5 FM. WFDT(FM) Aguada, PR; WIVA-FM Aguadilla, PR; WCMN Arecibo, PR; WNEL Caguas, PR; WORA Mayaguez, PR; WPRP Ponce, PR; WLEO(AM) Ponce, PR; WRIO-FM Ponce, PR; WFID-FM Rio Piedras, PR; WPRM-FM San Juan, PR; WUNO(AM) San Juan, PR

Jesus M. Soto, CEO; Luis A. Soto, pres; Anthony Soto, exec VP progmg; Raymond Totti, sls VP; Luis Gonzalez, VP finance; Pedro J. Gonzalez, VP progmg; Alberte Pereira, VP engrg.

Urban Radio Licenses LLC 273 Azalea Rd., Suite 1-308, Mobile, AL 36609. Phone: (251) 343-4900. Ownership: Urban Radio Communications LLC, 100%. Note: Urban Radio Communications LLC also owns KMXH(FM) Alexandria and KBCE(FM) Boyce, both LA.

Stns: 2 AM. 8 FM. WLAY Muscle Shoals, AL; WVNA-FM Muscle Shoals, AL; WMXV(FM) Russellville, AL; WVNA Tuscumbia, AL; WACR-FM Aberdeen, MS; WAJV-FM Brooksville, MS; WMSU(FM) Starkville, MS; WIMX-FM Gibsonburg, OH; WJZE-FM Oak Harbor, OH; WJOR-FM Saint Joseph, TN

V

VCY America Inc. 3434 W. Kilbourn Ave., Milwaukee, WI 53208. Phone: (414) 935-3000. Fax: (414) 935-3015. E-mail: vcy@vcyamerica.org. Web Site: www.vcyamerica.org.

Stns: 1 AM. 14 FM. KVCY-FM Fort Scott, KS; KCVS(FM) Salina, KS; WVCN(FM) Baraga, MI; WVCM(FM) Iron Mountain, MI; WJIC-FM Zanesville, OH; KVCF(FM) Freeman, SD; KVCX-FM Gregory, SD; KVFL(FM) Pierre, SD; WVCF-FM Eau Claire, WI; WVFL(FM) Fond du Lac, WI; WVCY-FM Milwaukee, WI; WVCY Oshkosh, WI; WVCX(FM) Tomah, WI; WEGZ(FM) Washburn, WI; WVRN(FM) Wittenberg, WI

Stns: 1 TV. WVCY, Milwaukee, WI

Vic Eliason, VP/gen mgr.

Vernal Enterprises Inc. Box 1032, Indiana, PA 15701-1032. Phone: (724) 543-1380. Fax: (724) 543-1140. Ownership: Larry L. Schrecongost, 51%; Nancy W. Schrecongost, 49%.

Stns: 3 AM. 1 FM. WRDD Ebensburg, PA; WTYM Kittanning, PA; WHPA(FM) Northern Cambria, PA; WNCC(AM) Northern Cambria, PA

Vero Beach Broadcasters LLC 1235 16th St., Vero Beach, FL 32960. Phone: (772) 567-0937. Fax: (772) 562-4747. Web Site: wosnfm.com. Ownership: Mitchell Rubenstein, Laurie Silvers and Robert McAllan.

Stns: 1 AM. 3 FM. WOSN-FM Indian River Shores, FL; WGYL-FM Vero Beach, FL; WTTB Vero Beach, FL; WGNX(FM) Vero Beach, FL

Jim Davis, gen mgr.

VerStandig Broadcasting 4850 Connecticut Ave. N.W., Suite 103, Washington, DC 20008. Phone: (202) 244-1422. Fax: (202) 362-4149. Ownership: John VerStandig, 1996 VerStandig Children's Trust, M. Belmont VerStandig Trust.

Stns: 4 AM. 6 FM. WHGT(AM) Chambersburg, PA; WPPT(FM) Mercersburg, PA; WFYN(FM) Waynesboro, PA; WCBG(AM) Waynesboro, PA; WBHB-FM Bridgewater, VA; WJDV(FM) Broadway, VA; WHBG Harrisonburg, VA; WQPO-FM Harrisonburg, VA; WSVA Harrisonburg, VA; WAYZ(FM) Hagerstown, MD

John VerStandig, CEO.

Victoria RadioWorks Ltd. 8023 Vantage Dr., Suite 840, San Antonio, TX 78230. Phone: (210) 340-7080. Fax: (210) 341-1777. Ownership: John W. Barger, pres of gen ptnr.

Stns: 2 AM. 3 FM. KITE(FM) Port Lavaca, TX; KVIC(FM) Victoria, TX; KNAL(AM) Victoria, TX; KVNN(AM) Victoria, TX; KEPG-FM Victoria, TX

John Barger, pres.

Vidalia Communications Corp. Box 900, Vidalia, GA 30475. Phone: (912) 537-9202. Fax: (912) 537-4477. E-mail: wtcq@vidaliacommunications.com. Web Site: www.vidaliacommunications.com.

Stns: 1 AM. 1 FM. WYUM-FM Mount Vernon, GA; WVOP Vidalia, GA

Advance-Progress Newspaper Inc., publisher of the weekly Advance, is part of the partnership of Vidalia Communications Corp.

John Ladson III, pres; Zack Fowler, gen mgr.

Viper Communications Broadcast Group Box 225, Osage Beach, MO 65065. Phone: (573) 348-2772. Fax: (573) 348-2779. Web Site: www.krmsradio.com.

Stns: 3 AM. 2 FM. WENG Englewood, FL; KRMS Osage Beach, MO; KRMS-FM Osage Beach, MO; KFBD-FM Waynesville, MO; KOZQ Waynesville, MO

Dennis Klautzer, VP/gen mgr.

Visionary Related Entertainment L.L.C. P. O. Box 38, Kahului, HI 96733. Phone: (808) 244-9145. Fax: (808) 244-8247. E-mail: kaoi@kaoi.net. Web Site: www.kaoi.net. Ownership: Visionary Related Entertainment Inc., 50.1% of votes, 40.58% of total assets; Frontier Radio Investors L.L.C., 49.9% of votes, 59.42% of total assets.

Stns: 3 AM. 10 FM. KUAI Eleele, HI; KUMU-FM Honolulu, HI; KPOI-FM Honolulu, HI; KQMQ-FM Honolulu, HI; KSHK-FM Kekaha, HI; KAOI(AM) Kihei, HI; KTBH-FM Kurtistown, HI; KQNG Lihue, HI; KDLX(FM) Makawao, HI; KNUQ-FM Paauilo, HI; KSRF-FM Poipu, HI; KAOI-FM Wailuku, HI; KDDB(FM) Waipahu, HI

John Detz, pres.

Vox Radio Group L.P. Box 1230, Claremont, NH 03743. Phone: (603) 542-7735. Fax: (603) 542-3780. Web Site: www.voxradio.com. Ownership: Bruce Danziger, Jeffery Shapiro, Ken Barlow.

Stns: 4 AM. 9 FM. WWUS-FM Big Pine Key, FL; WCNK-FM Key West, FL; WAVK(FM) Marathon, FL; WSBS Great Barrington, MA; WMNB-FM North Adams, MA; WNAW North Adams, MA; WBEC Pittsfield, MA; WUPE-FM Pittsfield, MA; WUHN Pittsfield, MA; WWHK(FM) Concord, NH; WNYQ-FM Queensbury, NY; WZXI-FM Buffalo Gap, VA; WSIG(FM) Mount Jackson, VA

Bruce G. Danziger, principal; Jeffrey Shapiro, principal; Ken Barlow, principal.

W

WAMC/Northeast Public Radio 318 Central Ave., Albany, NY 12206. Phone: (518) 465-5233. Fax: (518) 432-6974. E-mail: mail@wamc.org. Web Site: www.wamc.org. Ownership: Non-stock educ corporation.

Stns: 2 AM. 7 FM. WAMQ-FM Great Barrington, MA; WAMC(AM) Albany, NY; WAMC-FM Albany, NY; WCAN-FM Canajoharie, NY; WAMK-FM Kingston, NY; WOSR-FM Middletown, NY; WCEL-FM Plattsburgh, NY; WANC-FM Ticonderoga, NY; WRUN Utica, NY

Alan Chartock, pres/CEO; David Galletly, VP.

WAY-FM Media Group Inc. 1012 McEwen Dr., Franklin, TN 37067. Phone: (615) 261-9293. Fax: (615) 261-3967. Web Site: www.wayfm.com.

Stns: 14 FM. WAYH(FM) Harvest, AL; KBWA(FM) Brush, CO; KXWA(FM) Loveland, CO; KXWY(FM) Rye,

Radio Group Ownership

CO; WAYJ-FM Fort Myers, FL; WAYF(FM) West Palm Beach, FL; WAYT(FM) Thomasville, GA; KYWA(FM) Wichita, KS; WAYD(FM) Auburn, KY; KWYA(FM) Astoria, OR; WAYQ(FM) Clarksville, TN; WAYM(FM) Columbia, TN; WAYW(FM) New Johnsonville, TN; KWYQ(FM) Longview, WA

Bob Augsburg, pres/CEO; Dusty Rhodes, sr VP; Lloyd Parker, COO.

WENK Broadcast Group Inc. 1729 Nailling Dr., Union City, TN 38261. Phone: (731) 885-1240. Fax: (731) 885-3405. E-mail: wenk@charter.net. Ownership: Bill Latimer; Robert Kirkland; Robert Terrell Jr.

Stns: 2 AM. 2 FM. WWKF-FM Fulton, KY; WTPR-FM McKinnon, TN; WTPR Paris, TN; WENK Union City, TN

Terry Hailey, pres; Bill Latimer, chmn.

WOLF Radio Inc. 401 W. Kirkpatrick St., Syracuse, NY 13204. Phone: (315) 472-0222. Fax: (315) 478-7745. Ownership: Craig L. Fox, 51%; George W. Kimble, 49%.

Stns: 2 AM. 2 FM. WWLF(AM) Auburn, NY; WOLF-FM Oswego, NY; WBGJ-FM Sylvan Beach, NY; WOLF Syracuse, NY

Craig Fox, pres.

WPAY/WPFB Inc. 4505 Central Ave., Middletown, OH 45044. Phone: (513) 422-3625. Fax: (513) 424-9732. Web Site: www.rebel1059.com. Ownership: Ruth M. Braden & Douglas L. Braden, 100%.

Stns: 2 AM. 1 FM. WPFB Middletown, OH; WPFB-FM Middletown, OH; WPAY Portsmouth, OH

Douglas L. Branden, pres.

WPW Broadcasting Inc. c/o WLRB(AM)-WKAI(FM)-WLMD(FM), 119 W. Carroll, Macomb, IL 61455. Phone: (309) 833-5561. Fax: (309) 833-3460. Web Site: www.radiomacomb.com.

Stns: 7 AM. 10 FM. KCLN Clinton, IA; KZEG(FM) Clinton, IA; KWCC-FM Muscatine, IA; KWPC Muscatine, IA; WLMD-FM Bushnell, IL; WCDD(FM) Canton, IL; WBYS Canton, IL; WLBK De Kalb, IL; WAIK Galesburg, IL; WLRB Macomb, IL; WKAI-FM Macomb, IL; WMOI-FM Monmouth, IL; WRAM Monmouth, IL; WPWQ(FM) Mount Sterling, IL; WKXQ-FM Rushville, IL; KWBZ(FM) Monroe City, MO; WSLD-FM Whitewater, WI

David Madison, pres/CEO.

WRD Entertainment Inc. Box 2077, Batesville, AR 72503. Phone: (870) 793-4196. Fax: (870) 793-5222. E-mail: rob@maxfm.com. Web Site: maxfm.com.

Stns: 2 AM. 3 FM. KAAB Batesville, AR; KBTA Batesville, AR; KBTA-FM Batesville, AR; KKIK(FM) Horseshoe Bend, AR; KWOZ-FM Mountain View, AR

John R. Grace, pres; Gary Bridgman, gen mgr.

WZOE Inc. Box 69, Princeton, IL 61356. Phone: (815) 875-8014. Ownership: Steve Samet, 100%.

Stns: 1 AM. 1 FM. WRVY-FM Henry, IL; WZOE Princeton, IL

Steve Samet, pres/gen mgr.

Wagenvoord Advertising Group Inc. 2360 N.E. Coachman Rd., Clearwater, FL 33765. Phone: (727) 726-8247. Fax: (727) 799-8866. Web Site: www.tantalk1340.com. Ownership: Dave Wagenvoord, 50%; Lola Wagenvoord, 50%.

Stns: 3 AM. WTAN Clearwater, FL; WDCF Dade City, FL; WZHR(AM) Zephyrhills, FL

Lola Wagenvoord, gen mgr.

Wagonwheel Communications Corp. 40 Shoshone Ave., Green River, WY 82935. Phone: (307) 875-6666. Fax: (303) 875-5847. Ownership: Alan W. Harris, 100%. Note: Alan W. Harris also owns 49% of KYCS(FM) Rock Springs, WY.

Stns: 1 AM. 2 FM. KFRZ-FM Green River, WY; KUGR Green River, WY; KZWB(FM) Green River, WY

Waitt Broadcasting Inc. 1125 S. 103rd Rd., Suite 200, Omaha, NE 68124-1071. Phone: (402) 330-2520. Fax: (402) 330-2445. Web Site: www.waittmedia.com.

Stns: 8 AM. 9 FM. KLGA Algona, IA; KLGA-FM Algona, IA; KWBG Boone, IA; KQWC Webster City, IA; KQWC-FM Webster City, IA; KKYY(FM) Whiting, IA; KQLS-FM Colby, KS; KXXX Colby, KS; KZRD(FM) Dodge City, KS; KGNO Dodge City, KS; KZLS-FM Great Bend, KS; KGTR-FM Larned, KS; KNNS Larned, KS; KSLS-FM Liberal, KS; KYUU Liberal, KS; KILS-FM Minneapolis, KS; KWLS Pratt, KS

Stns: 1 TV. KMEG, Sioux City, IA

Norman Waitt Jr., CEO.

Waitt Radio Inc. 1125 S. 103rd St., Suite 200, Omaha, NE 68124. Phone: (402) 330-2520. Ownership: Norman W. Waitt Jr., chmn, 100% of votes. Note: Waitt Media Inc. owns 100% of total assets.

Stns: 9 AM. 11 FM. KQKQ-FM Council Bluffs, IA; KHBT-FM Humboldt, IA; KSSH(FM) Ingalls, KS; KLCH(FM) Lake City, MN; KOZN(AM) Bellevue, NE; KYDZ(AM) Bellevue, NE; KBLR-FM Blair, NE; KHUB Fremont, NE; KFMT-FM Fremont, NE; KLIQ(FM) Hastings, NE; KUVR Holdrege, NE; KRNY(FM) Kearney, NE; KGFW Kearney, NE; KLTQ(FM) Lincoln, NE; KODY North Platte, NE; KXNP-FM North Platte, NE; KKAR Omaha, NE; KOIL(AM) Plattsmouth, NE; KCTY-FM Plattsmouth, NE; KTCH Wayne, NE

Waller Broadcasting Box 1648, Jacksonville, TX 75766. Phone: (903) 586-2527. Fax: (903) 586-1394. E-mail: jacksonville@wallerbroadcasting.com. Web Site: www.wallerbroadcasting.com. Ownership: Dudley Waller, owner.

Stns: 1 AM. 4 FM. KFRO-FM Gilmer, TX; KLJT-FM Jacksonville, TX; KEBE Jacksonville, TX; KDVE(FM) Pittsburg, TX; KXAL-FM Tatum, TX

Dudley Waller, pres/CEO.

Wallingford Broadcasting Co. 128 Big Hill Ave., Richmond, KY 40475. Phone: (859) 623-1340. Fax: (859) 623-1341. E-mail: coyote@chpl.net. Web Site: www.wcyo.com.

Stns: 2 AM. 1 FM. WKXO Berea, KY; WLFX(FM) Berea, KY; WEKY Richmond, KY

Kelly Wallingford, pres/CEO; Kendra Steele, opns mgr.

Walton Stns Box 776, Kermit, TX 79745. Phone: (432) 586-3366. Fax: (432) 586-3958. Ownership: John B. Walton, 100%.

Stns: 1 AM. KBUY Ruidoso, NM

John Walton, pres; Harold Oakes, gen mgr.

Woodrow Michael Warren Stns Box 106, Alturas, CA 96101. Phone: (530) 233-4842. Fax: (530) 233-4173.

Stns: 3 FM. KALT-FM Alturas, CA; KLCR-FM Lakeview, OR; KWTR-FM Big Lake, TX

Woodrow Michael Warren, pres; Matt Warren, opns mgr.

Watts Communications Inc. Box 100, Brownwood, TX 76804. Phone: (325) 646-3536. Fax: (325) 646-5347. Web Site: www.wattsradio.net. Ownership: Phil Watts 100%

Stns: 1 AM. 1 FM. KXYL-FM Brownwood, TX; KSTA Coleman, TX

Phil Watts, pres; Cathie Marie Hail, mgr.

Wayne County Broadcasting Co. Box 310, Fairfield, IL 62837. Phone: (618) 842-2159. Fax: (618) 847-5907. Ownership: Thomas S. Land; David H. Land; Judith L. Moore; Cynthia L. Cummins.

Stns: 1 AM. 2 FM. WOKZ(FM) Fairfield, IL; WFIW(AM) Fairfield, IL; WFIW-FM Fairfield, IL

Thomas S. Land, chmn.

West Virginia Radio Corp. 1251 Earl L. Core Rd., Morgantown, WV 26505. Phone: (304) 296-0029. Fax: (304) 296-3876. Ownership: John R. Raese, David A. Raese.

Stns: 2 AM. 3 FM. WSWW Charleston, WV; WDNE Elkins, WV; WKAZ-FM Miami, WV; WRVZ-FM Pocatalico, WV; WFBY(FM) Weston, WV

Morgantown (WV) *Dominion-Post* is affiliated with Metronews Radio Network and West Virginia Radio Corp.

Dale B. Miller, pres/CEO; Harvey Kercheval, opns VP; Joe Parsons, sls VP.

Western Slope Communications LLC 751 Horizon Court, Suite 225, Grand Junction, CO 81506. Phone: (970) 241-6460. Fax: (970) 241-6452. E-mail: kiss@kissradio.com. Web Site: www.kissradio.com.

Stns: 2 AM. 2 FM. KAVP(AM) Colona, CO; KRVG(FM) Glenwood Springs, CO; KAYW(FM) Meeker, CO; KRGS(AM) Rifle, CO

Steve Wennerstrom, pres; John Monroe, gen mgr.

Wheeler Broadcasting Inc. Drawer K, Grand Coulee, WA 99133. Phone: (509) 633-2020. Fax: (509) 633-1014. E-mail: keygfm@bigdam.net. Ownership: Deanna D. Wheeler, 30%; Verl D. Wheeler, 30%; Mark Wheeler and Nilufer Wheeler, 23%; Tonya D. Baker and Scott B. Baker, 10%.

Stns: 1 AM. 1 FM. KXAA(FM) Cle Elum, WA; KEYG Grand Coulee, WA

Verl D. Wheeler, pres/CEO; Mark Wheeler, VP/gen mgr.

Mel Wheeler Inc. 5009 S. Hulen, Suite 101, Fort Worth, TX 76132-1989. Phone: (817) 294-7644. Fax: (817) 294-8519. Ownership: Estate of Mel Wheeler, 68%; Clark Wheeler, 10.2%; Leonard Wheeler, 11.1%; Steve Wheeler, 10.6%.

Stns: 2 AM. 3 FM. WVBE-FM Lynchburg, VA; WXLK-FM Roanoke, VA; WVBE(AM) Roanoke, VA; WSLQ-FM Roanoke, VA; WFIR(AM) Roanoke, VA

Stns: 2 TV. KPOB, Paducah, KY-Cape Girardeau, MO-Harrisburg-Mount Vernon, IL; WSIL-TV, Paducah, KY-Cape Girardeau, MO-Harrisburg-Mount Vernon, IL

Leonard Wheeler, pres; Clark Wheeler, VP.

Whitley Broadcasting Co. Inc. 522 Main St., Williamsburg, KY 40769. Phone: (606) 549-2285. Phone: (606) 549-5565. Ownership: David Paul Estes, 100%.

Stns: 1 AM. 1 FM. WEZJ Williamsburg, KY; WEKX-FM Jellico, TN

David Paul Estes, pres.

Wilkins Communications Network Inc. Box 444, Spartanburg, SC 29304. Phone: (864) 585-1885. Fax: (864) 597-0687. E-mail: info@wilkinsradio.com. Web Site: www.wilkinsradio.com.

Stns: 10 AM. WBXR Hazel Green, AL; WFAM(AM) Augusta, GA; KLNG(AM) Council Bluffs, IA; WBRI Indianapolis, IN; KCNW(AM) Fairway, KS; WSKY(AM) Asheville, NC; KXKS Albuquerque, NM; WWNL(AM) Pittsburgh, PA; WELP(AM) Easley, SC; WLMR(AM) Chattanooga, TN

Robert Wilkins, pres; Mitchell Mathis, VP; LuAnn Wilkins, exec VP.

Wilks Broadcast Group LLC 3775 Mansell Rd., Alpharetta, GA 30022. Phone: (770) 772-4077. Ownership: Wilks Broadcast Group Holdings LLC, 100%. Note: Wilks Broadcast Group LLC is an affiliate of The Wicks Group of Companies L.L.C. (www.wicksgroup.com), a New York based private equity firm.

Stns: 3 FM. KJFX-FM Fresno, CA; KUUS(FM) San Joaquin, CA; KFRR-FM Woodlake, CA

Williams Communications Inc. 801 Noble St,, 8th Fl., Suite 30, Anniston, AL 36201. Phone: (256) 236-1880. Fax: (256) 236-4480. Ownership: Walton E. Williams Jr., 51%; and Melinda Williams, 49%.

Stns: 6 AM. 7 FM. WHMA Anniston, AL; WHMA-FM Ashland, AL; WRHY(FM) Centre, AL; WFMH(AM) Cullman, AL; WMCJ(AM) Cullman, AL; WFMH-FM Holly Pond, AL; WZZX Lineville, AL; WTRB-FM Sylacauga, AL; WFCT(FM) Apalachicola, FL; WLTG Panama City, FL; WKHC-FM Dahlonega, GA; WCLE-FM Calhoun, TN; WCLE Cleveland, TN

Walton E. Williams Jr., pres.

Willis Broadcasting Corp. 645 Church St., Suite 400, Norfolk, VA 23510. Phone: (757) 622-4600. Fax: (757) 624-6515.

Stns: 14 AM. 3 FM. WAYE Birmingham, AL; WRAG Carrollton, AL; WTJH East Point, GA; KDLA De Ridder, LA; KLPL Lake Providence, LA; WBOK New Orleans, LA; WGRM Greenwood, MS; WGRM-FM Greenwood, MS; WSRC Durham, NC; WBXB(FM) Edenton, NC; WGTM Wilson, NC; WBTE Windsor, NC; WSDT Soddy-Daisy, TN; WCPK Chesapeake, VA; WHFD-FM Lawrenceville, VA; WGPL Portsmouth, VA; WPCE Portsmouth, VA

Levi Willis, pres.

Wilson Broadcasting Inc. 805 N. Lena St., Suite 13, Dothan, AL 36303. Phone: (334) 671-1753. Fax: (334) 677-6923. Web Site: www.wjjn.greatnow.com.

Stns: 1 AM. 2 FM. WJJN-FM Columbia, AL; WAGF Dothan, AL; WAGF-FM Dothan, AL

James R. Wilson III, gen mgr.

Winton Road Broadcasting Co. LLC Box 2700, Bakersfield, CA 93303. Phone: (661) 328-0118. Fax: (661) 328-1648. Ownership: Anthony S. Brandon, 66%; L. Rogers Brandon, 33%.

Stns: 3 AM. 2 FM. KISZ-FM Cortez, CO; KVFC Cortez, CO; KPTE-FM Durango, CO; KDGO Durango, CO; KENN Farmington, NM

Rogers Brandon, pres.

The Wireless Group Inc. Box 198, Brownsville, TN 38012. Phone: (731) 772-3700. Ownership: Carlton Veirs, pres, 50%; Lyle Reid, 50%. (See also Cross-Ownership, Sect. A.)

Stns: 1 AM. 1 FM. WNWS Brownsville, TN; WNWS-FM Jackson, TN

The Wireless Group Inc., publishes the weekly magazine *Hunting & Fishing News*.

Carlton Veirs, pres.

Withers Broadcasting Co. Box 1508, Mount Vernon, IL 62864. Phone: (618) 242-3500. Fax: (618) 242-4444. Ownership: W. Russell Withers Jr., 100%.

Stns: 9 AM. 7 FM. KOKX Keokuk, IA; WKIB(FM) Anna, IL; WILY Centralia, IL; WEBQ-FM Eldorado, IL; WISH-FM Galatia, IL; WEBQ Harrisburg, IL; WMOK Metropolis, IL; WZZT-FM Morrison, IL; WMIX Mount Vernon, IL; WMIX-FM

Radio Group Ownership

Mount Vernon, IL; WSSQ-FM Sterling, IL; WSDR Sterling, IL; WZZL-FM Reidland, KY; KAPE Cape Girardeau, MO; KUGT Jackson, MO; KRHW Sikeston, MO

Stns: 2 TV. WDTV, Clarksburg-Weston, WV; WDHS, Marquette, MI

W. Russell Withers Jr., pres.

Woodward Communications Inc. Box 688, Dubuque, IA 52004-0688. Phone: (563) 588-5687. Fax: (563) 588-5739. Web Site: www.wcinet.com. Ownership: M. Jeanne Woodward, F. Robert Woodward.

Stns: 2 AM. 4 FM. WSCO(AM) Appleton, WI; WAPL-FM Appleton, WI; WKSZ(FM) De Pere, WI; WHBY(AM) Kimberly, WI; WZOR(FM) Mishicot, WI; WECB-FM Seymour, WI

Woodward Communications Inc. publishes the *Telegraph Herald* and weekly newspapers and shoppers in Dyersville and Cascade, Iowa; Oregon, Fitchburg, Platteville, Prairie du Chien, Richland Center, Verona, Stoughton, Wisconsin.

Tom Yunt, pres.

Wooster Republican Printing Co. (dba Dix Communications). 212 E. Liberty St., Wooster, OH 44691. Phone: (330) 264-3511. Fax: (330) 263-5013. Web Site: www.dixcom.com. Ownership: (dba Dix Communications).

Stns: 3 AM. 6 FM. WNDT(FM) Alachua, FL; WOGK(FM) Ocala, FL; WNDD-FM Silver Springs, FL; WKVX Wooster, OH; WQKT(FM) Wooster, OH; WTBO Cumberland, MD; WKGO-FM Cumberland, MD; WFRB Frostburg, MD; WFRB-FM Frostburg, MD

Stns: 1 TV. KFBB, Great Falls, MT

Wooster Republican Printing Co. publishes *The Daily Record*, Wooster, OH.

Robert C. Dix, TV div chmn; G. Charles Dix, VP; Dale E. Gerber, CFO.

Word Broadcasting Network Inc. Box 19229, Louisville, KY 40259. Phone: (502) 964-3304. Fax: (502) 966-9692. Web Site: www.wbna21.com. Ownership: Robert W. Rodgers, 20%; Gregory A. Holt, 20%; Melissa Fraser, 20%; Cleddie Kieth, 20%; and Margaret A. Rodgers, 20%.

Stns: 3 AM. WYMM(AM) Jacksonville, FL; WVHI Evansville, IN; WYRM(AM) Norfolk, VA

Stns: 1 TV. WBNA, Louisville, KY

Bob Rogers, pres; Greg Holt, VP.

World Radio Network Inc. Box 3765, McAllen, TX 78502-3765. Phone: (956) 787-9788. Fax: (956) 787-9783. E-mail: wrn@hcjb.org. Web Site: www.wrn-rcm.org. Ownership: Non-profit corporation. Note: World Radio Network Inc. is affiliated with World Radio Missionary Fellowship Inc., which operates international sw missionary stn HCJB in Quito, Ecuador.

Stns: 8 FM. KRMB-FM Bisbee, AZ; KYRM(FM) Yuma, AZ; KRUC-FM Las Cruces, NM; KORM(FM) Astoria, OR; KBNJ(FM) Corpus Christi, TX; KVER-FM El Paso, TX; KBNL(FM) Laredo, TX; KVMV-FM McAllen, TX

Dr. Ted Haney, pres; Glenn Lafitte, dir.

Wright Broadcasting Systems Box 587, Weatherford, OK 73096. Phone: (580) 772-5939. Fax: (580) 772-1590. E-mail: traffic@wrightradio.com. Web Site: www.wrightwradio.com. Ownership: G. Harold Wright, 100%.

Stns: 1 AM. 2 FM. KCLI Clinton, OK; KQMX-FM Clinton, OK; KCDL(FM) Cordell, OK

G. Harold Wright, pres.

Wynne Enterprises LLC 1338 Oregon Ave., Klamath Falls, OR 97601. Phone: (541) 882-4656. Fax: (541) 884-2845. E-mail: kflskkrb@aol.com. Web Site: www.klamathradio.com. Ownership: Robert Wynne, Floyd Wynne, Barbara Wynne.

Stns: 1 AM. 1 FM. KFLS-FM Tulelake, CA; KFLS Klamath Falls, OR

Robert Wynne, pres/CEO; Floyd Wynne, VP.

Y

Yavapai Broadcasting Corp. 3405 E. Hwy. 89-A, Suite A, Cottonwood, AZ 86326. Phone: (928) 634-2286. Fax: (928) 634-2295. Web Site: www.myradioplace.com. Ownership: W. Grant Hafley.

Stns: 2 AM. 4 FM. KVRD-FM Cottonwood, AZ; KYBC(AM) Cottonwood, AZ; KZGL(FM) Cottonwood, AZ; KVNA-FM Flagstaff, AZ; KVNA(AM) Flagstaff, AZ; KQST-FM Sedona, AZ

Grant Hafley, pres; David J. Kessel, gen mgr.

Z

Zimmer Radio Group 2702 E. 32nd St., Joplin, MO 64804. Phone: (417) 624-1025. Fax: (417) 781-6842. Web Site: www.joplinradio.com. Ownership: Zimco Inc.

Stns: 3 AM. 7 FM. KLWN(AM) Lawrence, KS; KATI(FM) California, MO; KFAL Fulton, MO; KKCA-FM Fulton, MO; KWOS(AM) Jefferson City, MO; KTXY-FM Jefferson City, MO; KSYN-FM Joplin, MO; KIXQ(FM) Joplin, MO; KJMK-FM Webb City, MO; KXDG-FM Webb City, MO

Zoe Communications Inc. Box 190, Shell Lake, WI 54871. Phone: (715) 468-9500. Fax: (715) 468-9505. Web Site: www.zoestations.com.

Stns: 2 AM. 2 FM. WDMO(FM) Durand, WI; WPDR Portage, WI; WCSW Shell Lake, WI; WPLT(FM) Spooner, WI

Wendy Oberg, gen mgr.

The Zone Corp. Box 1929, Bangor, ME 04402. Phone: (207) 990-2800. Fax: (207) 990-2444. Web Site: www.zoneradio.com. Ownership: Stephen King is the sole stockholder.

Stns: 1 AM. 2 FM. WZON Bangor, ME; WKIT-FM Brewer, ME; WDME-FM Dover Foxcroft, ME

Stephen King, pres; Tabitha King, VP; Arthur B. Greene, sec/treas; Bobby Russell, gen mgr.

Key to Radio Listings

(1) WOF(AM)—**(2)** Oct 8, 1946: **(3)** 1000 khz. **(3a)** Stereo. **(3b)** Hrs opn: 24. **(4)** Box 1000 (99999). (909) 555-1000. FAX: (909) 999-9999. **(5)** Licensee: General Broadcasting Corp. (group owner; acq 7-20-69; $255,000 with co-located FM; **(5a)** FTR 2-12-83). **(6)** Net: ABC/E, AP; Mountain State Network. Rep: Jones & Company, Penn State. Format: MOR, C&W. Spec prog: Sp 3 hrs wkly. **(7)** John Jones, gen mgr; David Smith, chief engr. **(8)** Rates: $14; 13.50; 14; 12.50.

(1a) WOF-FM—**(2)** October 1959: **(9)** 101.1 mhz; 3 kw. Ant 300 ft. **(3a)** Stereo. **(10)** Dups AM 50%. Format: C&W. **(11)** WOF-TV affil. **(8)** Rates: $8.50; 7; 8.50; na.

(1) Station call letters as assigned by the Federal Communications Commission (FCC) or Canadian Radio-television and Telecommunications Commission (CRTC).

(1a) Station call letters for co-owned FM station. WOF-FM has the same ownership as WOF(AM), and the FM listing contains only information different from the AM. Co-owned AM and FM stations are often listed together, even when they have dissimilar call letters. In some instances FM may be listed first.

(2) Date station first went on air (regardless of subsequent ownership changes).

(3) Frequency in kilohertz.

(3a) WOF broadcasts in stereo.

(3b) WOF broadcasts 24 hours daily.

(4) Address and zip code, telephone and FAX. Teletype Writer Exchange number may also be included.

(5) Licensee name and date of acquisition (if not original owner). If the licensee is a group owner—a company with several broadcast properties—it is so identified, as a group owner of which the licensee is a subsidiary. Details on group owners are listed in Section A. If the station has been sold and the sale information is available, it is recorded after the acquisition date, ie. acq. date; purchase price; FTR date.

(5a) FTR date. FTR refers to *Broadcasting & Cable* magazine's weekly For the Record column that appeared in the magazine until June 8, 1998, where station sales were recorded as received from the FCC.

(6) Network, representative and programming. WOF national affiliates are ABC Entertainment Network and AP Network. The regional affiliate is Mountain State. The WOF national sales representative is Jones & Company and their regional sales representative is Penn State. The WOF program format is part middle-of-the-road, part country and western, with three hours weekly of special programming in Spanish.

(7) Key personnel.

(8) Advertising rates. This data indicates the prices the station charges for a one-minute spot, run 12-times-a-week during the following time slots: 6 a.m.-10 a.m.; 10 a.m.-3 p.m.; 3 p.m.-7 p.m.; 7 p.m.-midnight, respectively. If a time slot is not applicable, na replaces the rate.

(9) Frequency for WOF-FM is 101.1 megahertz, with 3 kilowatts of effective radiated power and an antenna height of 300 feet above average terrain. WOF-FM broadcasts in stereo (see **(3a)**).

(10) Programming. WOF-FM duplicates WOF(AM) programs 50% of the time and has a country and western format.

(11) Co-owned TV. WOF-TV has the same licensee as WOF-AM-FM.

Note: Listings for independent AM & FM stations follow the sample shown for WOF(AM).

An asterisk (*) preceding station call letters indicates noncommercial stations.

Directory of Radio Stations in the United States

Alabama

Abbeville

WIZB(FM)— Feb 2, 1968: 94.3 mhz; 25 kw. 285 ft. TL: N31 35 17 W85 16 51. (CP: Ant 458 ft.). Stereo. Box 8097, Dothan 36304-8097. Secondary address: 2563 Montgomery Hwy., Dothan 36303. Phone: (334) 699-5672. Fax: (334) 699-5034. E-mail: lprescott@hisradio943.com. Web Site: www.hisradio943.com. Licensee: Celebration Communications Co. Inc. (acq 7-98; $550,000). Network: Salem Radio Network. Gammon & Grange, P.C. Format: Contemp Christian. News: 3 hrs wkly. Target aud: 25-49; women. ♦Jim Campbell, CEO; Linda Prescott, gen mgr, gen sls mgr & gen sls mgr; Sonya Sallas, prom dir; Richard Posey, progmg dir; Ricky Carter, chief of engrg & engr.

Addison

WQAH-FM— 1996: 105.7 mhz; 6 kw. 328 ft. TL: N34 18 19 W87 04 24. Box 1048, Hartselle 35640. Phone: (256) 773-2563. Fax: (256) 773-6915. E-mail: radio@hiwaay.net. Licensee: Abercrombie Broadcasting FM Inc. (acq 2-7-2000). Format: Classic country. ♦Alvin Abercrombie, pres; Carol Lynn, gen mgr & progmg dir; Keith Abercrombie, engrg dir.

Alabaster

WQCR(AM)— Sept 28, 1981: 1500 khz; 2.3 kw-D (1.2 kw-CH). TL: N33 12 27 W86 45 34. Box 584 35007-2045. Phone: (205) 621-1617. E-mail: wgtt@earthlink.net. Licensee: WGTT Inc. (acq 4-21-92; $17,500;. FTR: 5-11-92). Format: Sp. ♦David Robinson, VP.

Albertville

WAVU(AM)— 1947: 630 khz; 1 kw-D, 28 w-N. TL: N34 14 28 W86 09 41. Box 190 35950. Secondary address: 3770 US Hwy. 431 35951. Phone: (256) 878-8575. Fax: (256) 878-1051. E-mail: tommylee@wqsb.com. Licensee: Sand Mountain Broadcasting Service Inc. Network: AP Radio. Fletcher, Heald & Hildreth. Format: Southern gospel, Christian. News staff: one. Target aud: 35 plus. ♦Pat M. Courington Jr., pres; Tommy Lee, gen mgr; Ted McCreless, gen sls mgr.

WQSB(FM)—Co-owned with WAVU(AM). 1948: 105.1 mhz; 2.7 kw. Ant 1,000 ft. TL: N34 09 27 W86 02 44. Stereo. E-mail: wqsb@aol.com. Web Site: www.wqsb.com. Format: Country. News staff: one. Target aud: 25-54. ♦Ted McCreless, dev VP & sls dir; Dale Stallings, mus dir; Linda Conner, pub affrs dir.

WWGC(AM)— April 1982: 1090 khz; 500 w-D. TL: N34 18 02 W86 16 01. Box 418 35950. Phone: (256) 894-6294. Fax: (256) 894-6294. Licensee: MVB Inc. (acq 4-13-2001). Format: Sp. ♦Shannon King, pres; Juan Vargas, gen mgr.

Alexander City

WRFS(AM)— May 31, 1947: 1050 khz; 1 kw-D; 48 w-N. TL: N32 56 51 W85 59 17. 1739 Radio Rd. 35010. Phone: (334) 821-0744. Fax: (256) 234-0721. E-mail: wrfs@webshoppee.net. Licensee: Joy Christian Communications Inc. (group owner; (acq 8-26-2004; $175,000). Network: ABC. Haley, Bader & Potts. Format: Adult Standards. Target aud: 25-54; adults. ♦Jimmy Jerrell, pres & CFO; Greg Holtan, gen mgr.

WSTH-FM— Sept 30, 1949: 106.1 mhz; 100 kw. 981 ft. TL: N32 45 33 W85 28 04. (CP: 85.8 kw, ant 1,047 ft.). Stereo. Box 687, Columbus, GA 31902. Secondary address: 1501 13th Ave., Columbus, GA 31901. Phone: (706) 576-3000. Fax: (706) 576-3010. Web Site: www.rooster106online.com. Licensee: Clear Channel Broadcasting Licenses Inc. Group owner: Clear Channel Communications Inc. (acq 5-9-03; $2.73 million. with WDAK(AM) Columbus, GA). Network: ABC. Format: Country. News staff: one. Target aud: General. ♦Jim Martin, gen mgr; Brian Waters, opns dir; Kevin Anderson, progmg dir; Frank McLemore, chief of engrg.

Aliceville

WZBQ(FM)—See Carrollton

Andalusia

WAAO-FM— Aug 24, 1987: 103.7 mhz; 3 kw. Ant 328 ft. TL: N31 20 27 W86 28 02. Stereo. Box 987, MLK Expressway 36420. Phone: (334) 222-1166. Fax: (334) 222-1167. E-mail: waao@waao.com. Web Site: www.waao.com. Licensee: Companion Broadcasting Service Inc. Format: Country. Target aud: General. ♦Lee Williams, pres & gen mgr.

***WSTF(FM)—** March 1996: 91.5 mhz; 5 kw. 361 ft. TL: N31 26 20 W86 30 48. Box 210789, Montgomery 36121-0789. Phone: (334) 271-8900. Fax: (334) 260-8962. E-mail: mail@faithradio.org. Web Site: www.faithradio.org. Licensee: Faith Broadcasting Inc. Format: Educ, relg, MOR. ♦Mark Williams, pres; Russell Dean, gen mgr; Gary Hundley, dev dir.

Anniston

WANA(AM)— August 1954: 1490 khz; 1 kw-U. TL: N33 41 15 W85 49 49. 115 W. 33rd St. 36201. Phone: (256) 237-1627. Fax: (256) 237-1628. E-mail: am1490wana@cableone.net. Licensee: Anniston Radio Co. (acq 6-87; $115,000; 8-24-87). Format: Gospel, black, urban. Target aud: 18-70; relg people who like southern & Black gospel. Spec prog: Black 12 hrs, farm one hr wkly. ♦Dewey Lankford, pres & gen mgr.

WDNG(AM)— July 1, 1957: 1450 khz; 1 kw-U. TL: N33 40 01 W85 50 56. 1115 Leighton Ave. 36207. Phone: (256) 236-8291. Fax: (256) 236-8292. Web Site: www.wdng.net. Licensee: WDNG Inc. (acq 6-30-87; $500,000; 7-6-87). Network: Network: CBS, ABC News/Talk. Format: News/talk. Target aud: General. ♦J.J. Dark, pres & gen mgr.

***WGRW(FM)—** July 1999: 90.7 mhz; 3 kw vert. 328 ft. TL: N33 29 19 W86 47 58. Word Works Inc., Box 2555 36202. Secondary address: 4265 Hill St. 36206. Phone: (256) 238-9990. Fax: (256) 237-1102. E-mail: jon@graceradio.com. Web Site: www.graceradio.com. Licensee: Word Works Inc. Network: Moody. Format: Christian. ♦Aaron Acker, pres; Jon Holder, gen mgr.

WHMA(AM)— 1938: 1390 khz; 5 kw-D, 1 kw-N, DA-N. TL: N33 42 31 W85 51 14. 801 Noble St. 36201. Phone: (256) 237-8741. Fax: (256) 231-9414. Licensee: Williams Communications Inc. (group owner; acq 8-12-03; $275,000). Format: Talk. News staff: one; News: 12 hrs wkly. Target aud: 25-54; those with upscale, mobile, discretionary incomes. ♦Walt Williams, gen mgr.

WZLM(FM)—See Talladega

Arab

WAFN-FM— Nov 5, 1979: 92.7 mhz; 6 kw. Ant 623 ft. TL: N34 21 04 W86 26 27. Stereo. Box 4184, Huntsville 35815. Secondary address: 981 N. Brindele Mt. Pkwy. 35815. Phone: (256) 586-9300. Fax: (256) 586-9301. E-mail: funradio@hiwaay.net. Web Site: www.fun927.com. Licensee: Fun Media Group Inc. (acq 7-31-97; $492,500). Network: CNN Radio. Format: Oldies. News staff: one; News: 3 hrs wkly. Target aud: 18-54. ♦Susan E. McKenney, pres; Michael St. John, CFO & gen mgr.

WRAB(AM)— Oct 25, 1961: 1380 khz; 1 kw-D. TL: N34 20 06 W86 28 07. Box 625 35016. Secondary address: 619 S. Brindlee Mountain Pkwy. 35016. Phone: (256) 586-4123. Fax: (256) 586-4124. Licensee: Reed Broadcasting LLC (acq 6-22-01; $163,000). Network: ABC Daytime Direction. Format: Country, relg, gospel. ♦Ed Reed, pres; Joey Yarbrough, exec VP; Archie Anderson, gen mgr.

Ashland

WHMA-FM— Oct 4, 1984: 95.5 mhz; 1.7 kw. Ant 617 ft. TL: N33 18 30 W85 50 58. (CP: Hobson City. 530 w, ant 1,089 ft. N33 37 38 W85 53 25). Stereo. 801 Noble St., Suite 30, Anniston 36201. Phone: (256) 236-1880. Fax: (256) 236-4480. Licensee: Williams Communications Inc. (group owner; (acq 8-2-2002; $2.88 million. with WZZX(AM) Lineville). Format: Country. Target aud: 18-54. Spec prog: Black 6 hrs wkly. ♦Walt Williams Jr., pres.

Athens

WKAC(AM)— September 1964: 1080 khz; 5 kw-D. TL: N34 50 13 W86 58 28. Box 1083 35612. Secondary address: 19245 Hwy. 127 35614. Phone: (256) 232-6827. Fax: (256) 232-6828. E-mail: wkac@companet.net. Web Site: www.wkac1080.com. Licensee: Limestone Broadcasting Co. Network: CNN Radio. Rgnl Reps. Format: Oldies. News: 6 hrs wkly. Target aud: 25-54; adults mid/upper income, blue/white collar. Spec prog: Farm 5 hrs, country 13 hrs wkly. ♦Kenneth A. Casey, pres; Keith Casey, gen mgr; Kirk Harvey, progmg dir.

WVNN(AM)— Nov 8, 1948: 770 khz; 10 kw-D, 250 w-N, DA-N. TL: N34 50 21 W86 55 44. Stereo. 1717 Hwy. 72 E. 35611. Phone: (256) 830-8300. Fax: (256) 232-6842. Web Site: www.wvnn.com. Licensee: Cumulus Licensing LLC. Group owner: Cumulus Media Inc. (acq 7-21-2003; grpsl). Network: Network: ABC Daytime Direction, ABC News/Talk. Rep: Christal. Format: News/talk. News staff: 3; News: 60 hrs wkly. Target aud: 25-64. Spec prog: Farm 2 hrs, gospel 3 hrs wkly. ♦Bill G. West, VP & gen mgr; John Mountz, opns mgr & progmg dir; Brian Pitts, sls dir & gen sls mgr; Wendy Black, prom dir; Marty Broman, news dir; Bill Schrode, chief of engrg.

WZYP(FM)—Co-owned with WVNN(AM). Oct 1, 1958: 104.3 mhz; 100 kw. 1,115 ft. TL: N34 49 05 W86 44 16. Stereo. Web Site: www.wzyp.net. Format: Top-40. News staff: 3; News: 3 hrs wkly. Target aud: 18-49. ♦John Holland, gen sls mgr & progmg dir.

Atmore

WASG(AM)— Nov 12, 1981: 550 khz; 10 kw-D, 143 w-N. TL: N30 34 45 W87 17 13. Stereo. 2070 N. Palafax, Pensacola, FL 32501. Phone: (850) 434-1230. Fax: (850) 469-9698. E-mail: mglin@aol.com. Licensee: 550 AM, Inc. Network: ABC Information & Entertainment. Format: Christian, talk. News staff: one; News: 9 hrs wkly. Target aud: 18-54. ♦Dara Glinter, exec VP; Michael B. Glinter, pres & gen mgr.

WNSI-FM— June 28, 1991: 105.9 mhz; 3.7 kw. 446 ft. TL: N31 00 26 W87 32 15. Stereo. 1318 S. Main St. 36502. Phone: (251) 368-2511. Fax: (251) 368-4227. E-mail: bosscountry@frontiernet.net. Licensee: Southern Media Communications Inc. (acq 3-4-98). Network: ABC Information & Entertainment. Format: Classic American country. News: 18 hrs wkly. Spec prog: American Indian one hr, Black one hr, farm 5 hrs, gospel 12 hrs wkly. ♦Walter Bowen, gen mgr.

WYOK(FM)— May 19, 1966: 104.1 mhz; 100 kw. 1,555 ft. TL: N30 37 35 W87 38 50. Stereo. 2800 Dauphin St., #104, Mobile 36606-2400. Phone: (251) 652-2000. Fax: (251) 652-2001. E-mail: mobile.prog@cumulus.com. Web Site: www.cumulus.com. Licensee: Cumulus Licensing Corp. Group owner: Cumulus Media Inc. (acq 10-18-99; grpsl). Cohn & Marks. Format: Hot adult contemp. News staff: one; News: 5 hrs wkly. Target aud: 25-40. ♦Gary Pizzati, gen mgr; Steve Crumbely, opns VP & opns mgr.

Attalla

WKXX(FM)—Licensed to Attalla. See Gadsden

Auburn

WANI(AM)—See Opelika

WAUD(AM)— Dec 22, 1947: 1230 khz; 1 kw-U. TL: N32 37 47 W85 28 08. 2514 S. College St., Suite 104 36830. Phone: (334) 887-3401. Fax: (334) 826-9599. Licensee: Tiger Communications Inc. (acq 2-26-98). Network: ABC Information & Entertainment. Rep: Rgnl Reps. Format: Sports, big band, jazz. News staff: one; News: 7 hrs wkly. Target aud: 25 plus. Spec prog: Gospel 2 hrs wkly. ♦Tom Hayley, pres; Chris Bailey, gen mgr.

***WEGL(FM)—** Apr 25, 1971: 91.1 mhz; 3 kw. 190 ft. TL: N32 36 11 W85 29 12. (CP: Ant 214 ft.). Stereo. Auburn Univ., 116 Foy Union 36849-5231. Phone: (334) 844-4114. Fax: (334) 844-4118. E-mail: wegl@auburn.edu. Web Site: www.wegl.auburn.edu. Licensee: Board of Trustees Auburn University. Format: College alternative. News staff: one; News: 6 hrs wkly. Target aud: College students. Spec prog:

Various specialty shows. ♦Saleem Walton, gen mgr; Lisa Kent, stn mgr & pub affrs dir; Avery Schroyer, opns dir.

WKKR(FM)— July 8, 1968: 97.7 mhz; 3.1 kw. 453 ft. TL: N32 33 54 W85 22 13. Stereo. Box 2329, Opelika 36803. Secondary address: 915 Veterans Pkwy., Opelika 36801. Phone: (334) 745-4657. Fax: (334) 749-1520. E-mail: genmorj@charter.net. Web Site: www.wkkr.com. Licensee: Qantum of Auburn License Co. LLC. Group owner: Qantum Communications Corp. (acq 7-2-03; grpsl). Gardner, Carton & Douglas. Format: Country. News staff: 2; News: 7 hrs wkly. Target aud: 25-54. ♦Frank Osborn, pres; Sandy Mathews, sls dir & gen sls mgr; Jim Powell, mktg mgr.

WTLM(AM)—See Opelika

Bay Minette

WBCA(AM)— 1958: 1110 khz; 10 kw-D. TL: N30 52 10 W87 46 09. 99 W. 4th St. 36507. Phone: (251) 937-5596. Phone: (251) 937-5260. Fax: (251) 937-5260. Licensee: Great American Radio Network Inc. (acq 6-1-98; $91,200). Network: ABC Information & Entertainment. Format: Southern gospel. Target aud: 18-64. ♦Jim Lee, pres.

WNSP(FM)— Oct 1, 1964: 105.5 mhz; 5.3 kw. 348 ft. TL: N30 49 34 W87 51 52. (CP: 1.9 kw, ant 410 ft.). Stereo. 1100-E Dauphin St., # E, Mobile 36604-2512. Phone: (251) 438-5460. Fax: (251) 438-5462. Web Site: www.wnsp.com. Licensee: Com+ L.L.C. (acq 7-6-98; $1.05 million). Format: Sports. Target aud: 18-49. ♦Ken Johnson, pres & gen mgr; Clint Crouch, opns mgr.

Bessemer

WZGX(AM)— June 1, 1950: 1450 khz; 1 kw-U. TL: N33 25 23 W86 57 17. 3300 Jaybird Rd. 35020. Phone: (205) 428-0146. Fax: (205) 426-3178. Licensee: Bessemer Radio Inc. (acq 9-1-88). Format: Rgnl Mexican. ♦Raul Ortal, gen mgr.

Birmingham

WAGG(AM)— 1927: 610 khz; 5 kw-D, 1 kw-N. TL: N33 29 40 W86 52 30. 950 22nd St., N., Suite 1000 35203. Phone: (205) 322-2987. Fax: (205) 322-2667. E-mail: wagg610@cox.com. Web Site: www.wagg610.com. Licensee: CXR Holdings L.L.C. Group owner: Cox Broadcasting (acq 9-9-97). Network: ABC. Rep: Christal. Dow, Lohnes & Albertson. Format: Gospel. News staff: 2; News: 5 hrs wkly. Target aud: 45 plus. ♦David Dubose, gen mgr.

WAPI(AM)— 1922: 1070 khz; 50 kw-D, 5 kw-N, DA-N. TL: N33 33 07 W86 54 40. 244 Goodwin Crest Dr., Suite 300 35209. Phone: (205) 942-1004. Fax: (205) 917-1906. Web Site: www.wapi1070.com. Licensee: Citadel Broadcasting Co. Group owner: Citadel Broadcasting Corp. (acq 4-26-2001; grpsl). Rep: Christal. Format: News/talk. Target aud: 35 plus. ♦Dale Daniels, gen mgr.

WYSF(FM)—Co-owned with WAPI(AM). 1947: 94.5 mhz; 100 kw. 1,214 ft. TL: N33 29 26 W86 47 48. Stereo. Web Site: www.wapi1070.com. Format: Hot adult contemp, soft rock. Target aud: 25-54; general.

WATV(AM)— May 20, 1946: 900 khz; 1 kw-U. TL: N33 32 14 W86 50 16. Stereo. Box 39054, 3025 Ensley Ave. 35208. Phone: (205) 780-2014. Fax: (205) 780-4034. E-mail: jlockkklin@watv900.com. Licensee: MCL/MCM-Inc. (group owner; acq 5-4-2004; $1.5 million). Network: ABC. Rep: Interep. Format: Black, oldies, relg. Target aud: 18 plus. Spec prog: Sports 10 hrs wkly. ♦Ron Davenport, pres.

WAYE(AM)— Aug 1, 1972: 1220 khz; 1 kw-D, 75 w-N. TL: N33 28 39 W86 50 57. (CP: TL: N33 28 41 W86 50 55). 836 Lomb Ave. S.W. 35211. Secondary address: 645 Church St., Suite 400, Norfolk, VA 35211. Phone: (205) 786-9293. Fax: (205) 786-9296. Licensee: Birmingham Christian Radio Inc. Group owner: Willis Broadcasting Corp. (acq 8-20-87; $225,000; 9-7-87). Format: Gospel. Target aud: 19 plus; loyal, mature & financially stable. ♦Bishop L. E. Willis, pres; Mary Agee, gen mgr.

***WBFR(FM)**— 1988: 89.5 mhz; 100 w. 672 ft. TL: N33 29 02 W86 48 35. 244 Goodwin Crest Dr., Suite 118 35209. Phone: (205) 942-3530. Phone: (510) 568-6200. Fax: (510) 568-6190. E-mail: info@familyradio.com. Web Site: www.familyradio.com. Licensee: Family Stations Inc. (group owner) Format: Relg, evangelical. ♦Stanley Jackson, gen mgr.

***WBHM(FM)**— December 1976: 90.3 mhz; 32 kw. 1,214 ft. TL: N33 29 19 W86 47 58. Stereo. Rebroadcasts WSGN(FM) Gadsden 100% 650 11th St. S. 35233-1221. Phone: (205) 934-2606. Fax: (205) 934-5075. Web Site: www.wbhm.org. Licensee: Board of Trustees, University of Alabama. Network: Network: NPR, PRI. Format: Class, news. Target aud: General. Spec prog: New age 8 hrs wkly. ♦Mike Morgan, gen mgr; Patrick Dorriety, opns mgr; Mary Hendley, dev dir.

WBPT(FM)— June 1959: 106.9 mhz; 100 kw. 1,150 ft. TL: N33 29 19 W86 47 58. Stereo. 301 Beacon Pkwy. W., Suite 200 35209. Phone: (205) 916-1100. Fax: (205) 916-1152. Web Site: www.birminghampoint.com. Licensee: CXR Holdings L.L.C. Group owner: Cox Broadcasting (acq 3-28-97; grpsl). Rep: Katz Radio. Format: Music of the 80s. News staff: one; News: 15 hrs wkly. Target aud: 25-54; affluent baby boomers. Spec prog: Best of the 80's and more. ♦Ray Nelson, gen mgr; Hurricane Shane, opns mgr, natl sls mgr & progmg dir; David Walls, gen sls mgr; Tom Scott, chief of engrg.

WDJC-FM— Apr 22, 1968: 93.7 mhz; 100 kw. 1,007 ft. TL: N33 26 36 W86 52 50. Stereo. 2727 19th Place S. 35209. Phone: (205) 879-3324. Fax: (205) 802-4555. Web Site: www.93.7wdjc.com. Licensee: Kimtron Inc. Group owner: Crawford Broadcasting Co. Format: Contemp Christian music. Target aud: 25-60; conservative middle income. ♦Donald B. Crawford, CEO, chmn & pres; Nathan Park, gen mgr.

WERC(AM)—Listing follows WMJJ(FM).

***WGIB(FM)**— 1983: 91.9 mhz; 600 w. 679 ft. TL: N33 29 02 W86 48 35. 1137 10th Pl. S. 35205. Phone: (205) 323-1516. Fax: (205) 323-2747. E-mail: nmills@gleniris.net. Web Site: www.glenirisbaptist.org. Licensee: Glen Iris Baptist School (acq 1-31-02). Format: Christian. ♦Chris Lamb, chmn & gen mgr; Nathan Mills, stn mgr, stn mgr & opns mgr; Rodney Reymond, progmg dir; Ron Haas, chief of engrg.

WJLD(AM)—(Fairfield). 1942: 1400 khz; 1 kw-U. TL: N33 28 36 W86 53 01. Box 19123 35219-9123. Secondary address: 1449 Spaulding Ishkooda Rd. 35211-5059. Phone: (205) 942-1776. Fax: (205) 942-4814. E-mail: wjld@juno.com. Web Site: www.wjld1400.com. Licensee: Richardson Broadcasting Corp. (acq 10-87). Network: Network: American Urban, ABC. Format: Black gospel, adult urban contemp, political talk. Target aud: 25-54; majority Black, adult, blue and white collar working class. ♦Gary R. Richardson, pres & gen mgr; Bob Friedman, opns VP & opns mgr.

WJOX(AM)— Oct 15, 1947: 690 khz; 50 kw-D, 30 w-N. TL: N33 26 56 W86 55 18. (CP: 500 w-N, DA-N). 244 Goodwin Crest Dr., Suite 300 35209-3714. Phone: (205) 945-4646. Fax: (205) 945-3999. Web Site: www.wjox690.com. Licensee: Citadel Broadcasting Co. Group owner: Citadel Broadcasting Corp. (acq 4-26-01; grpsl). Format: Sports. Target aud: 25-54. Spec prog: Gospel 5 hrs wkly. ♦Dale Daniels, gen mgr; Kerry Lambert, opns VP; Lenny Frisaro, sls dir; Steve Harrison, natl sls mgr; Jennifer Dixon, prom dir; Lisa Holifield, news dir; Will Berry, pub affrs dir; Frank Giardina, chief of engrg.

WZRR(FM)—Co-owned with WJOX(AM). December 1975: 99.5 mhz; 100 kw. 870 ft. TL: N33 26 28 W86 53 00. (CP: Ant 1,000 ft.). Fax: (205) 942-3175. Web Site: www.wzrr.com. Rep: Christal. Format: Classic rock. ♦Allen Dick, pres; Dave Henderlite, CFO; Davis Hawkins, opns VP; Kerry Lambert, opns mgr.

***WJSR(FM)**— Aug 11, 1977: 91.1 mhz; 100 w. 195 ft. TL: N33 39 07 W86 42 20. Stereo. 2601 Carson Rd. 35215. Phone: (205) 856-6095. Fax: (205) 856-7702. Licensee: Jefferson State Community College. Format: Classic rock. News: 4 hrs wkly. Target aud: 24-49; college population. ♦Ray Edwards, gen mgr.

***WLJR(FM)**— 1998: 88.5 mhz; 200 w. 623 ft. TL: N33 23 35 W86 39 48. Stereo. Briarwood Presbyterian Church, 2200 Briarwood Way 35243. Phone: (205) 978-2200. Fax: (205) 824-8419. Web Site: www.wljr.org. Licensee: Briarwood Presbyterian Church. Network: Moody. Southmayd & Miller. Format: Div, educ, relg. News: 10 hrs wkly. Target aud: General; upper middle class. ♦James Hulgan, gen mgr.

WLPH(AM)—See Irondale

WMJJ(FM)— June 1, 1961: 96.5 mhz; 100 kw. 1,027 ft. TL: N33 26 38 W86 42 10. Stereo. 530 Beacon Pkwy. W., Suite 600 35209. Phone: (205) 439-9600. Fax: (205) 439-8390. Fax: (205) 439-8391. Web Site: www.magic96fm.com. Licensee: Capstar TX L.P. Group owner: Clear Channel Communications Inc. (acq 8-30-00; grpsl). Reed, Smith, Shaw & McClay. Format: Adult contemp. Target aud: 25-54. ♦L. Lowry Mays, CEO; Jimmy Vineyard, opns mgr; Terry Barber, opns mgr & sls dir; Doug McAllister, rgnl sls mgr; Bill Barron, mktg dir & prom dir; Cindee Standridge, mktg dir; Tom Hanrahan, progmg dir; Brandy Srader, news dir; Bob Newberry, chief of engrg.

WERC(AM)—Co-owned with WMJJ(FM). May 25, 1925: 960 khz; 5 kw-U, DA-N. TL: N33 32 02 W86 51 07. Web Site: www.werctalk.com. Network: ABC Information & Entertainment. Format: News/talk. Target aud: adults. ♦Randy Jinks, gen sls mgr; Kyle Anderson, progmg dir.

WUHT(FM)— Sept 15, 1969: 107.7 mhz; 100 kw. Ant 1,237 ft. TL: N33 43 52 W86 37 57. 244 Goodwin Crest Dr., Suite 300 35209. Phone: (205) 945-4646. Phone: (205) 741-1077. Fax: (205) 942-3175. Web Site: www.hot1077radio.com. Licensee: Citadel Broadcasting Co. Group owner: Citadel Broadcasting Corp. (acq 4-26-2001; grpsl). Format: Alternative rock. Target aud: 18-34. ♦Dale Daniels, gen mgr; Kerry Lambert, opns mgr; Lenny Frisaro, sls dir & gen sls mgr; Dave Hennesy, prom mgr; Susan Groves, progmg dir; Mark Lindsey, mus dir; Lisa Holifield, news dir; Frank Giardina, engrg dir.

***WVSU-FM**— Apr 6, 1967: 91.1 mhz; 500 w vert. Ant 413 ft. TL: N33 27 47 W86 46 08. Stereo. Samford Univ., 800 Lakeshore Dr. 35229. Phone: (205) 726-2877. Fax: (205) 726-4032. E-mail: wvsu@samford.edu. Web Site: www.samford.edu/wvsu. Licensee: Samford University. Format: Smooth jazz. News: one hr wkly. Target aud: General. Spec prog: Samford Univ. athletics. ♦Andy Parrish, gen mgr.

WXJC(AM)— Apr 1, 1953: 850 khz; 50 kw-D, 1 kw-N, DA-2. TL: N33 37 25 W86 44 45. 244 Goodwin Crest Dr., Suite 126 35209. Phone: (205) 942-9033. Fax: (205) 942-1087. E-mail: wydeinfo@crawfordbroadcasting.com. Web Site: www.crawfordbroadcasting.com. Licensee: Kimtron Inc. Group owner: Crawford Broadcasting Co. (acq 11-12-99). Network: USA. Format: Southern gospel. Target aud: Under 12. ♦Steve Armstrong, gen mgr.

WYDE(AM)— Mar 25, 1953: 1260 khz; 5 kw-D, 44 w-N. TL: N33 31 29 W86 47 10. (CP: COL: Homewood, 1 kw-N, DA-N). 244 Goodwin Crest Dr. 35209. Phone: (205) 942-9033. Fax: (205) 942-1087. E-mail: wlgsinfo@crawfordbroadcasting.com. Web Site: www.crawfordbroadcasting.com. Licensee: Kimtron Inc. Group owner: Crawford Broadcasting Co. (acq 1994). Rep: McGavren Guild. Format: Talk. Target aud: 25-54; affluent professionals. ♦Steve Armstrong, gen mgr.

WZGX(AM)—See Bessemer

WZZK(AM)— 1950: 1320 khz; 5 kw-D, 111 w-N. TL: N33 33 41 W86 51 37. 301 Beacon Pkwy., Suite 200 35209. Phone: (205) 916-1100. Fax: (205) 916-1151. E-mail: wzzk@cox.com. Web Site: www.wzzk.com. Licensee: CXR Holdings L.L.C. Group owner: Cox Communications Inc. (acq 3-28-97; grpsl). Network: ABC. Rep: Christal. Dow, Lohnes & Albertson. Format: Country. News staff: 2; News: 2 hrs wkly. Target aud: 25-54. ♦Ray Nelson, gen mgr.

WZZK-FM— 1948: 104.7 mhz; 100 kw. 1,300 ft. TL: N33 29 02 W86 48 21. Stereo. 301 Beacon Pkwy. W., Suite 200 35209. Phone: (205) 916-1100. Fax: (205) 916-1151. E-mail: wzzk@cox.com. Web Site: www.wzzk.com. Licensee: CXR Holdings L.L.C. Group owner: Cox Broadcasting (acq 3-28-97; grpsl). Dow, Lohnes and Albertson. Format: Country. News staff: 2; News: 10 hrs wkly. Target aud: 25-54. ♦Ray Nelson, pres & gen mgr.

Boaz

WBSA(AM)— Oct 1, 1959: 1300 khz; 1 kw-D. TL: N34 12 50 W86 09 10. 1525 Wills Rd. 35957. Phone: (256) 593-4264. Fax: (256) 593-4265. Licensee: Watkins Broadcasting Inc. (acq 10-4-94; $100,000; 10-17-94). Format: Southern gospel. Target aud: General. ♦Chris Watkins, VP & stn mgr; Roger Watkins, pres & gen mgr.

Brantley

WAOQ(FM)— June 3, 1999: 100.3 mhz; 6 kw. 328 ft. TL: N31 42 26 W86 13 12. Box 83, Clanton 35045. Phone: (334) 335-2877. Fax: (205) 755- 3329. E-mail: waoq@waoq.com. Web Site: www.waoq.com. Licensee: Alatron Corp. Inc. Format: Country. Spec prog: Gospel 14 hrs wkly. ♦Robert E. Williams, pres; Christopher W. Johnson, gen mgr & progmg dir; Ken Lyons, stn mgr & gen sls mgr.

Stations in the U.S. — Alabama

Brewton

WEBJ(AM)— Aug 1, 1947: 1240 khz; 1 kw-U. TL: N31 06 35 W87 03 36. 301 Downing St. 36427-0736. Phone: (251) 867-5717. Fax: (251) 867-5718. Licensee: Candy Cashman Smith, individual. (acq 10-2-97). Gardner, Carton & Douglas. Format: Oldies of the 60s & 70s, talk. News staff: one; News: 20 hrs wkly. Target aud: 21 plus; 60% female, 40% male. Spec prog: Rush Limbaugh 15 hrs, community news 8 hrs, gospel 3 hrs wkly. ♦ Candy Cashman Smith, pres.

*WELJ(FM)— 1998: 90.9 mhz; 45 kw. Ant 502 ft. TL: N31 18 13 W87 02 50. Stereo. Box 347 36427. Secondary address: 42676 Hwy. 31 36427. Phone: (251) 809-1915. Fax: (251) 809-1916. Licensee: Gateway Public Radio (acq 10-12-00; $3,500). Format: Southern gospel, Christian. ♦ Earl Thompson, pres; Debra Johnson, gen mgr & stn mgr.

WKNU(FM)— Aug 19, 1974: 106.3 mhz; 3 kw. 300 ft. TL: N31 06 45 W87 01 19. Stereo. Box 468 36427. Secondary address: 2832 Ridge Rd. 36426. Phone: (251) 867-4824. Fax: (251) 867-7003. E-mail: wknu@bellsouth.net. Licensee: Ellington Radio Inc. (acq 12-28-78). Network: ABC Information & Entertainment. Format: C&W. News: 8 hrs wkly. Target aud: General. Spec prog: Gospel 2 hrs, relg 2 hrs wkly. ♦ Carol Ellington, pres, gen mgr & opns mgr; Hugh L. Ellington, exec VP & gen mgr.

Bridgeport

WYMR(AM)— Sept 19, 1961: 1480 khz; 1 kw-D. TL: N34 56 34 W85 42 26. Box 829, Trenton, GA 30752. Phone: (256) 495-3400. Fax: (256) 495-2500. Licensee: Dade County Broadcasting Inc. (acq 1-31-2002; $36,000). Format: Country. ♦ Evan Stone, pres.

Brookwood

WRTR(FM)—Licensed to Brookwood. See Tuscaloosa

Brundidge

WTBF-FM— Oct 1, 1997: 94.7 mhz; 14.5 kw. 433 ft. TL: N31 40 38 W85 56 43. Stereo. 67 Court Sq., Troy 36081. Phone: (334) 566-0300. Fax: (334) 566-5689. E-mail: wtbf@p-c-net.net. Web Site: www.wtbf947.com. Licensee: Troy Broadcasting Corp. Network: Network: Moody, ABC Information & Entertainment. Gardner, Carton & Douglas. Format: Oldies. News: 20 hrs wkly. Target aud: 28-60; 50s, 60s & 70s music listeners. ♦ Jim Roling, gen mgr; Doc Kirby, opns mgr.

Butler

WMLV(FM)— Nov 20, 1978: 93.5 mhz; 32 kw. Ant 610 ft. TL: N32 09 26 W88 29 17. Stereo. 3436 Hwy. 45 N., Meridian, MS 39301. Phone: (601) 693-2661. Fax: (601) 483-0826. E-mail: 935thebuzz@935thebuzz.com. Web Site: www.935thebuzz.com. Licensee: Mississippi Broadcasters L.L.C. (group owner), (acq 10-30-2002; $771,500). Format: Rock. ♦ Clay Holladay, stn mgr; Scott Stevens, opns mgr.

WPRN(AM)— July 11, 1959: . Stn currently dark 1330 khz; 5 kw-D. TL: N32 06 02 W88 14 07. 909 W. Pushmataha St. 36904-2441. Phone: (205) 459-3222. Fax: (251) 459-4140. Licensee: Butler Broadcasting Corp. (acq 1-75). Format: Country. ♦ Daryl Jackson, gen mgr.

Calera

WBYE(AM)— Jan 12, 1958: 1370 khz; 1 kw-D. TL: N33 05 26 W86 46 37. Box 1727 35040. Phone: (205) 668-1370. Licensee: WBYE Broadcasting Co. Inc. (acq 4-14-89; $100,754; 4-24-89). Format: Gospel. News: 15 hrs wkly. Target aud: 25-65. Spec prog: Farm 2 hrs, Sp one hr, gospel 11 hrs wkly. ♦ Frank Cumming, pres & chief of engrg; James Pouer, stn mgr.

Carrollton

*WALN(FM)— 1997: 89.3 mhz; 9.5 kw vert. 699 ft. TL: N33 13 06 W88 05 46. American Family Radio, Box 3206, Tupelo, MS 38803. Phone: (662) 844-8888. Fax: (662) 842-6791. Web Site: www.afr.net. Licensee: American Family Association. Group owner: American Family Radio Format: Inspirational Christian. ♦ Tim Waldmon, pres; Marvin Sanders, gen mgr; John Riley, progmg dir; Fred Jackson, news dir; Joey Moody, engrg dir.

WRAG(AM)— 1951: . Stn currently dark 590 khz; 1 kw-D. TL: N33 13 04 W88 05 48. Willis Broadcasting Corp., 646 Church St., Suite 400, Norfolk, VA 23510. Phone: (757) 622-4600. Licensee: Birmingham Christian Radio. Group owner: Willis Broadcasting Corp. (acq 10-16-97; $130,000. with WSPZ(AM) Tuscaloosa). Gammon & Grange.

WZBQ(FM)— February 1970: 94.1 mhz; 98 kw. Ant 1,007 ft. TL: N33 13 07 W88 05 47. Stereo. 3900 11th Ave., Tuscaloosa 35402. Phone: (205) 344-4589. Fax: (205) 366-9774. Web Site: www.941zbq.com. Licensee: Capstar TX L.P. Group owner: Clear Channel Communications Inc. (acq 8-30-00; grpsl). Format: CHR. Target aud: 18-49. ♦ Lori Moore, gen mgr; Russ Williams, opns mgr.

Carrville

WACQ(AM)—Licensed to Carrville. See Tallassee

Centre

WEIS(AM)— Sept 30, 1961: 990 khz; 1 kw-D, 30 w-N. TL: N34 09 10 W85 40 44. Box 297, 477 S. Pratt St. 35960. Phone: (256) 927-5152. Phone: (256) 927-4232. Fax: (256) 927-6503. E-mail: weis@powernet.org. Web Site: www.weis990am.com. Licensee: Baker Enterprises Inc. (acq 9-8-83; $157,675; 9-26-83). Timothy K. Brady. Format: Country, southern gospel. News staff: one; News: 10 hrs wkly. Target aud: General. ♦ Jerry Baker, pres & gen mgr.

WRHY(FM)— Oct 10, 1992: 105.9 mhz; 6 kw. 150 ft. TL: N34 12 51 W85 46 20. Box 215 35983. Phone: (256) 523-1059. Fax: (256) 523-9749. Web Site: www.y-106.com. Licensee: Williams Communications Inc. (group owner; acq 6-99; $380,000). Network: Network: Motor Racing Net, PRI. Format: Hot country. News: one hr wkly. Target aud: 25-54. ♦ Walt Williams, gen mgr; Bill Page, news dir.

WZTQ(AM)— Nov 9, 1962: 1560 khz; 1 kw-D. TL: N34 07 41 W85 38 27. Box 602, 3005 U.S. Hwy. 411 N. 35960. Phone: (256) 927-4027. Fax: (256) 927-4028. E-mail: wztq@joychristian.com. Web Site: www.joychristian.com. Licensee: Joy Christian Communications Inc. (acq 12-1-2003). Format: Southern gospel. News staff: one; News: 7 hrs wkly. Target aud: 25-55; working middle class, rural. Spec prog: Farm one hr wkly. ♦ Ed Smith, pres & gen mgr; Marie Smith, sr VP.

Centreville

WBIB(AM)— Dec 14, 1964: 1110 khz; 1 kw-D. TL: N32 58 01 W87 09 01. 2871 Main St., Brent 35034. Phone: (205) 926-9100. Fax: (205) 926-7400. Licensee: Bibb Broadcasting Corp. (acq 2002; $146,397). Rep: Keystone (unwired net). Format: Gospel, country. Target aud: Adults. ♦ Dennis Littleton, pres; Horrace Cruchfield, gen mgr.

Chickasaw

WDLT-FM—Licensed to Chickasaw. See Mobile

Citronelle

WQUA(FM)— June 25, 1989: 102.1 mhz; 15 kw. Ant 426 ft. TL: N31 05 04 W88 23 51. Stereo. 19000 3rd St., Citronell 36522. Secondary address: 11300 4th St., Suite 143, Saint Petersburg 33716. Phone: (251) 866-0600. Fax: (251) 661-7067 phone/fax. Licensee: Family Worship Center Church Inc. Group owner: ABC Inc. (acq 8-17-2005; $1.25 million). Network: ABC. Format: Children's radio. Spec prog: Black 18 hrs, gospel 6 hrs wkly. ♦ Larry Sutton, gen mgr & stn mgr.

WTLM(AM)—See Opelika

Clanton

WEZZ(FM)— May 15, 1953: 97.7 mhz; 3 kw. Ant 245 ft. TL: N32 50 08 W86 40 49. Box 1820 35046. Secondary address: 20747 Alabama Hwy. 22 35045. Phone: (205) 755-0980. Fax: (205) 280-0980. Licensee: Great South RFDC L.L.C. (group owner; acq 11-28-2003). Format: Country. ♦ Shelia Hayes, gen mgr.

Columbia

WJJN(FM)— September 1992: 92.1 mhz; 2.55 kw. 499 ft. TL: N31 10 56 W85 10 59. 805 N. Lena, Suite 13, Dothan 36303. Phone: (334) 671-1753. Fax: (334) 677-6923. Web Site: www.wjjn.com. Licensee: Wilson Broadcasting Inc. (group owner) Format: Urban contemp. ♦ James R. Wilson III, gen mgr.

Columbiana

WQEM(FM)— 2000: 101.5 mhz; 1.4 kw. Ant 640 ft. TL: N33 14 52 W86 42 36. 1137 Tenth Pl. S., Birmingham 35205. Phone: (205) 323-2747. Fax: (205) 323-2747 (Phone/Fax). Web Site: www.glenirisbaptist.org. Licensee: Glen Iris Baptist School (acq 12-24-02). Format: Teaching, gospel. ♦ Chris Lamb, chmn & gen mgr; Nathan Mills, opns mgr.

Cordova

WFFN(FM)— June 22, 1987: . Stn currently dark 95.3 mhz; 5 kw. Ant 354 ft. TL: N33 46 11 W87 12 06. (CP: COL Coaling. 17.5 kw, ant 840 ft. TL: N33 03 15 W87 32 57). Stereo. 142 Skyland Blvd., Tuscaloosa 35405. Phone: (205) 750-0929. Fax: (205) 349-1715. Licensee: Citadel Broadcasting Co. (acq 7-12-2005; grpsl). ♦ Farid Suleman, chmn.

WXJC-FM— 1997: 92.5 mhz; 2.2 kw. Ant 548 ft. TL: N33 38 55 W87 09 19. 244 Goodwin Crest Dr., Suite 126, Birmingham 35209. Phone: (205) 942-9033. Fax: (205) 942-1087. Web Site: www.crawfordbroadcasting.com. Licensee: Kimtron Inc. Group owner: Crawford Broadcasting Co. (acq 7-15-2004; $1.15 million). Format: Southern gospel. ♦ Steve Armstrong, gen mgr.

Cullman

WFMH(AM)— October 1946: 1340 khz; 670 w-U. TL: N34 10 49 W86 51 59. 1707 Warnke Rd, N.W. 35055. Phone: (256) 734-3271. Fax: (256) 734-3622. E-mail: wfmh@adelphia.net. Licensee: Williams Communications Inc. Group owner: Williams Communications Inc. (acq 7-20-2004; $2.45 million. with WFMH-FM Holly Pond). Rep: Keystone (unwired net). Format: Sports; Talk; News. News: 18 hrs wkly. Target aud: 25-54; middle & upper income adults. Spec prog: Farm 2 hrs wkly. ♦ Walt Williams, gen mgr.

WKUL(FM)— September 1967: 92.1 mhz; 6 kw. 328 ft. TL: N34 11 41 W86 43 52. Stereo. Box 803, 214 1st Ave. S.E. 35056. Phone: (256) 734-0183. Fax: (256) 739-2999. Web Site: www.wkul.com. Licensee: Jonathan Christian Corp. (acq 3-1-77). Network: ABC Information & Entertainment. Format: Country, sports, talk. News staff: one; News: 20 hrs wkly. Target aud: 25-54. Spec prog: Farm 15 hrs wkly. ♦ Don Mosley, pres; Ron Mosley, gen mgr; Rick Nix, opns mgr.

WMCJ(AM)— Mar 25, 1950: 1460 khz; 5 kw-D, 500 w-N, DA-N. TL: N34 10 44 W86 51 58. 20 Mill Creek Rd., Ste. A, Warrior 35180. Phone: (904) 241-3311. Fax: (904) 241-1402. Licensee: Williams Communications Inc. (acq 6-20-2005; $75,000). Format: Relg. ♦ Tom Moran, gen mgr.

WYDE-FM— Aug 6, 1949: 101.1 mhz; 100 kw. Ant 1,345 ft. TL: N34 04 56 W86 54 15. 244 Goodwin Crest Dr., Suite G 126, Birmingham 35209. Phone: (205) 942-9033. Fax: (205) 942-1087. Web Site: www.101thesource.com. Licensee: Kimtron Inc. Group owner: Crawford Broadcasting Co. (acq 6-14-02; $8.5 million). Rep: Allied Radio

Alabama

Partners. Format: Conservative talk, news. Target aud: Adults 25-44; primarily young professional females. ♦ Donald Crawford, pres; Steve Armstrong, gen mgr & stn mgr; Dave McDermott, opns mgr & progmg mgr; Shelby WAlker, news dir.

Dadeville

WDLK(AM)— Aug 11, 1980: 1450 khz; 1 kw-U. TL: N32 50 56 W85 46 10. 101 Broadnet St. 36853. Phone: (256) 825-2007. Fax: (256) 825-2199. Licensee: Progressive United Communications Inc. (group owner; acq 11-6-2000; $45,000). Format: Gospel, blues. ♦ Thomas Franklin, gen mgr.

*WELL-FM— Mar 1, 1990: 88.7 mhz; 100 kw. 328 ft. TL: N32 51 20 W85 46 31. (CP: Ant 305 ft.). Stereo. Box 284, 658 Horseshoe Bend Rd. 36853. Phone: (256) 825-6456. Fax: (256) 825-6426. E-mail: cassiekeyes@hotmail.com. Licensee: Tiger Communications Educational Foundation Inc. (acq 8-9-01; $325,000). Network: USA. Format: Christian. News staff: one. Target aud: 24 plus. ♦ Cassie Keyes, gen mgr.

WKGA(FM)— July 23, 1989: 100.3 mhz; 2.2 kw. Ant 546 ft. TL: N32 52 58 W85 49 16. Stereo. Box 253, Jacksons Gap 36861. Secondary address: 13263 Hwy. 280, Jacksons Gap 36861. Phone: (256) 825-4221. E-mail: www.wzlm@charter.net. Licensee: Great South RFDC LLC (group owner; acq 6-4-2003; $1.3 million). Network: ABC Daytime Direction. Format: Adult contemp. Target aud: 18-55. Spec prog: Gospel 3 hrs wkly. ♦ Tracy Blank, gen mgr.

Daleville

WCMA(AM)— Oct 25, 1983: . Stn currently dark 1560 khz; 5 kw-D, 2.5 kw-CH. TL: N31 16 35 W85 45 54. 2519 Country Rd. 24 36322. Phone: (334) 598-9856. Fax: (334) 598-1799. Licensee: Beebe Communications LLC (acq 4-21-2004; $135,000). Format: Southern gospel. Target aud: 25 plus. ♦ Joey Beebe, gen mgr; Joe Adams, sls dir.

Daphne

WAVH(FM)— May 15, 1993: 106.5 mhz; 50 kw. 449 ft. TL: N30 44 44 W88 05 40. Stereo. 2800 Dauphin St., Mobile 36606-2400. Phone: (251) 652-2000. Fax: (251) 652-2001. E-mail: mobile.prog@cumulus.com. Web Site: www.cumulus.com. Licensee: Baldwin Broadcasting Co., Debtor in Possession (acq 12-12-00). Rep: McGavren Guild. Wood, Maines & Brown. Format: Oldies. Target aud: 25-64; general. ♦ Gary Pizzati, gen mgr; Steve Crumbely, opns mgr.

Decatur

WAJF(AM)— Oct 3, 1953: 1490 khz; 1 kw-U. TL: N34 35 14 W86 59 13. Box 1501 35602. Phone: (256) 340-1490. Fax: (256) 350-2025. Web Site: www.wajf.net. Licensee: WAJF Inc. (acq 12-12-02; $150,000). Format: Talk. ♦ Troy Bryant, gen mgr.

WDRM(FM)—Listing follows WHOS(AM).

WHOS(AM)— October 1948: 800 khz; 1 kw-D, 215 w-N. TL: N34 35 55 W87 00 24. Box 21008, Huntsville 35824. Secondary address: 26869 Peoples Rd., Madison 35756. Phone: (256) 353-1750. Fax: (256) 350-2653. Licensee: Capstar TX L.P. Group owner: Clear Channel Communications Inc. (acq 7-18-00; grpsl). Format: 24 hr. News staff: 3. Target aud: 25-54. ♦ Rick Brown, gen mgr.

WDRM(FM)— Co-owned with WHOS(AM). September 1951: 102.1 mhz; 100 kw. 981 ft. TL: N34 49 08 W86 44 19. Stereo. Phone: (205) 353-1750. Web Site: www.wdrm.com. Format: Country.

WRSA-FM— Nov 23, 1965: 96.9 mhz; 100 kw. 1,010 ft. TL: N34 29 19 W86 37 08. Stereo. 8402 Memorial Pkwy S., Box 4144, Huntsville 35802. Phone: (256) 885-9797. Fax: (256) 885-9796. E-mail: wrsa@wrsa.com. Web site: www.lite969.com. Licensee: NCA Inc. (acq 3-18-02). Network: CBS. Format: Adult contemp. News staff: one; News: 20 hrs wkly. Target aud: 35 plus. ♦ Penny Nielson, CEO & pres; Nate Adams, opns mgr; Tom Panucci, gen mgr & gen sls mgr; John Malone, progmg dir; Don Rhoden, chief of engrg.

WWTM(AM)— May 1935: 1400 khz; 1 kw-U. TL: N34 36 44 W86 59 28. 1209 Danville Rd. S.W., Ste. N 35601. Phone: (256) 353-0361. Fax: (256) 353-0363. Web site: www.espn1400.info. Licensee: R&B Communications Inc. (acq 3-18-97). Network: ESPN Radio. Rep: Riley. Format: ESPN sports. Target aud: 25-54. ♦ Brian Black, pres, gen mgr & opns mgr.

*WYFD(FM)— May 7, 1975: 91.7 mhz; 3 kw. 787 ft. TL: N34 47 53 W86 38 24. Stereo. 8415-A S. Whitesburg Dr., Huntsville 35802. Phone: (256) 353-7951. Phone: (256) 650-0917. Fax: (256) 650-0917. Licensee: Bible Broadcasting Network. (group owner; acq 10-19-90; $75,000; 11-12-90). Format: Relg, educ. ♦ Lowell Davey, pres; Dave Phillips, stn mgr.

Demopolis

WXAL(AM)— Nov 9, 1947: 1400 khz; 1 kw-U. TL: N32 30 08 W87 00 24. (CP: 790 w). 1028 Hwy. 80 E. 36732. Phone: (334) 289-9811. Fax: (334) 289-2156. E-mail: win985@westal.net. Licensee: Ross Communications Inc. (acq 8-18-98; $456,300 with co-located FM). Network: Network: Westwood One, USA. Format: News/talk, Black gospel. Target aud: 25-54. ♦ Amy Douglas, CEO; Randall Douglas, chmn; Amy Ross, gen mgr.

WZNJ(FM)— Co-owned with WXAL(AM). 1975: 106.5 mhz; 25 kw. 492 ft. TL: N32 20 40 W87 37 43. Stereo. Network: Network: Westwood One, USA. Format: Oldies, sports. Target aud: 18-49.

Dixons Mills

*WMBV(FM)— Aug 15, 1988: 91.9 mhz; 62 kw. 613 ft. TL: N32 07 45 W87 44 16. Stereo. Box 91.9 FM, Marengo Co. Rd. 30 36736-0091. Secondary address: 10564 Marengo Community Rd. 30 36736. Phone: (334) 992-2425. Phone: (334) 992-2105. Fax: (334) 992-2637. E-mail: wmbv@moody.edu. Web Site: www.wmbv.org. Licensee: Moody Bible Institute. Group owner: The Moody Bible Institute of Chicago (acq 3-31-88). Network: Moody. Southmayd & Miller. Format: Relg. News: 10 hrs wkly. Target aud: 35-55; general. Spec prog: Financial 3 hrs, children 3 hrs, sports one hr wkly. ♦ Michael Easley, pres; Bob Neff, VP; Rob Moore, gen mgr.

Dora

WCOC(AM)— Apr 1, 1982: 1010 khz; 5 kw-D. TL: N33 48 04 W87 06 42. 6475 Hwy. 78, Cordova 35550. Phone: (205) 648-6926. Licensee: Azteca Communications of Alabama Inc. (acq 2-12-02; $190,000). Format: Sp. ♦ Brunie Hernandez, gen mgr.

Dothan

WAGF(AM)— Sept 29, 1932: 1320 khz; 1 kw-U, DA-N. TL: N31 14 56 W85 23 20. 805 N. Lena St., Suite 13 36303. Phone: (334) 671-1753. Fax: (334) 677-6923. Licensee: Wilson Broadcasting Inc. (group owner; acq 8-13-92; $60,000; 8-31-92). Format: Gospel. ♦ James Wilson III, gen mgr.

WAGF-FM— 1991: 101.3 mhz; 3 kw. 328 ft. TL: N31 12 02 W85 20 12. (CP: 820 w, ant 640 ft.). 805 N. Lena St., Suite 13 36303. Phone: (334) 677-7654. Fax: (334) 677-6923. E-mail: wtraffic@aol.com. Licensee: Wilson Broadcasting Inc. (group owner) Network: Jones Radio Networks. Rep: Rgnl Reps. Arter & Hadden. Format: Soft hits, lite adult contemp. Target aud: 25-54; female. ♦ James R. Wilson III, CEO, pres, gen mgr & opns VP.

*WDYF(FM)— 2004: 90.3 mhz; 9.2 kw. Ant 535 ft. TL: N31 19 31 W85 36 02. Box 210789, Montgomery 36121. Phone: (334) 271-8900. Fax: (334) 260-8962. E-mail: mail@faithradio.org. Web Site: www.faithradio.org. Licensee: Faith Broadcasting Inc. Format: Educ, relg, MOR. ♦ Mark Williams, pres; Bob Crittenden, exec VP; Russell Dean, gen mgr; Andrew Leuthold, opns mgr; Gary Hundley, dev dir.

WESP(FM)— Sept 1, 1989: 102.5 mhz; 10 kw. 462 ft. TL: N31 13 41 W85 21 06. Stereo. 3245 Montgomery Hwy., Suite 1 36303-2150. Phone: (334) 671-1025. Phone: (334) 712-9233. Fax: (334) 712-0374. E-mail: rock1025@rock1025.com. Web site: www.rock1025.com. Licensee: Gulf South Communications Inc. (acq 1999; $1.4 million). Rep: McGavren Guild. Format: Rock. Target aud: 25-54; men. ♦ Clay Holladay, pres; Ron Eubanks, gen mgr & stn mgr; Jerry Broadway, opns dir; Brian Lane, progmg dir & mus dir; Kevin Presley, news dir.

*WGTF(FM)— September 1988: 89.5 mhz; 19 kw. 213 ft. TL: N31 14 02 W85 26 02. 107 Wanda Ct. 36303. Licensee: Dothan Community Educational Radio Inc. Network: Bible Bcstg Net. Format: Traditional Christian. ♦ James W. Holloway, VP; Raymond Brown, pres & gen mgr.

WGZS(AM)— July 3, 1995: 700 khz; 1.6 kw-D. TL: N31 26 19 W85 17 22. 2070 N. Palafox St., Pensacola, FL 32501. Phone: (850) 434-1230. Fax: (850) 469-9698. Licensee: Good Samaritan Communications of Pioche Inc. (acq 10-7-03; $165,000). Haley, Bader & Potts. Format: Contemp Christian. News: 3 hrs wkly. ♦ Michael Glinter, gen mgr.

WOOF-FM— Sept 18, 1964: 99.7 mhz; 100 kw. 1,021 ft. TL: N31 15 07 W85 17 12. Stereo. Box 1427 36302. Secondary address: 2518 Columbia Hwy. 36303. Phone: (334) 792-1149. Fax: (334) 677-4612. E-mail: woof@ala.net. Web Site: www.997wooffm.com. Licensee: WOOF Inc. Rep: Christal. Shaw Pittman. Format: Adult contemp. News staff: 2; News: 3 hrs wkly. Target aud: 25-54; women 18-49 dominant. ♦ Rick Patrick, pres; Leigh Simpson, gen mgr, opns mgr, progmg dir & news dir; Hal Edwards, gen sls mgr; John Daniel, news dir.

WOOF(AM)— Feb 17, 1947: 560 khz; 5 kw-D, 117 w-N. TL: N31 13 05 W85 21 10. Stereo. Format: Sports, talk. Spec prog: Black gospel 17 hrs wkly.

*WRWA(FM)— December 1985: 88.7 mhz; 50 kw. 500 ft. TL: N31 12 30 W85 36 51. Stereo. Wallace Hall, Troy Univ., Troy 36082. Phone: (334) 670-3268. Fax: (334) 670-3934. E-mail: wtsu@troy.edu. Web Site: wtsu.troy.edu. Licensee: Troy State University. Network: Network: NPR, PRI. Format: Class, news. News: 25 hrs wkly. Target aud: General. Spec prog: Children one hr wkly. ♦ James Clower, gen mgr; Judy Davis, opns mgr.

WTVY-FM— Sept 20, 1968: 95.5 mhz; 100 kw. Ant 1,078 ft. TL: N31 15 16 W85 15 39. Stereo. Box 889 36302-2088. Secondary address: 285 N. Foster, 8th Fl. 36303. Phone: (334) 792-0047. Fax: (334) 712-9346. E-mail: sue@stylesmedia.com. Web Site: www.955wtvy.com. Licensee: Styles Media Group LLC (group owner; acq 7-27-2001). Network: ABC Daytime Direction. Rep: Christal. Kenkel & Associates. Format: Country. News staff: one; News: 5 hrs wkly. Target aud: 25-54. Spec prog: Farm 5 hrs, gospel 4 hrs, religion 3 hrs wkly. ♦ Tom Dibacco, CEO; Sue Hughes, gen mgr; Richard Reinhardt, opns mgr.

*WVOB(FM)— Dec 8, 1988: 91.3 mhz; 2.5 kw. 328 ft. TL: N31 10 57 W85 24 21. Box 1944 36302. Secondary address: 2573 Hodgesville Rd. 36301. Phone: (334) 671-9862. Fax: (334) 793-4344. E-mail: wvob913fm@bethanybc.edu. Web site: www.bethanyradionetwork.com. Licensee: Bethany Divinity College & Seminary Inc. Network: USA. Format: Educ, relg. News staff: one; News: 6 hrs wkly. Target aud: General; college students & relg community. ♦ Dr. H.D. Shuemake, CEO & gen mgr; Dr. Steve A. Shuemake, pres & stn mgr.

WWNT(AM)— Apr 30, 1947: 1450 khz; 1 kw-U. TL: N31 13 10 W85 22 14. 1733 Columbia Hwy. 36303. Phone: (334) 671-0075. Fax: (334) 671-0091. E-mail: larrymckee@aol.com. Web site: www.wwnt1450.com. Licensee: WWNT LLC (acq 6-10-83; $115,000;. FTR: 7-4-83). Network: USA. Format: Talk/news. News staff: 2. Target aud: 25-54 men; 25-54 males. ♦ Larry Williams, gen mgr; Debbie Murphy, stn mgr.

Elba

WELB(AM)— Nov 16, 1958: 1350 khz; 1 kw-D. TL: N31 27 10 W86 04 00. 20334 Hwy 87 36323. Phone: (334) 897-2216. Phone: (334) 897-2217. Fax: (334) 897-3694. E-mail: wztz@alaweb.com. Licensee: Elba Radio Co. (acq 3-4-76). Format: Classic country. News: 6 hrs wkly. Target aud: General. Spec prog: Gospel 12 hrs wkly. ♦ Doug Holderfield, gen mgr.

WZTZ(FM)— Co-owned with WELB(AM). Oct 1, 1986: 101.1 mhz; 640 w. 682 ft. TL: N31 24 41 W85 57 32. Stereo. Format: Modern country.

Enterprise

WDJR(FM)— July 1, 1968: 96.9 mhz; 100 kw. 1,515 ft. TL: N30 55 11 W85 44 30. Stereo. 3245 Montgomery Hwy, Dothan 36303. Phone: (334) 712-9233. Fax: (334) 712-0374. E-mail: ron@wdjr.com. Web Site: www.wdjr.com. Licensee: Gulf South Communications Inc. (acq 7-9-92; $700,000; 7-27-92). Format: Country. ♦ Ron Eubanks, gen mgr; Jerry Broadway, opns mgr.

WKMX(FM)— Nov 27, 1974: 106.7 mhz; 100 kw. 1,068 ft. TL: N31 24 41 W85 57 32. Stereo. 100 N. Main St. 36330. Phone: (334) 347-2278. Fax: (334) 393-2141. Web Site: www.wkmx.com. Licensee: Styles Media Group LLC (group owner; acq 8-4-2004; $4.5 million). Format: Adult contemp. News staff: one; News: 2 hrs wkly. Target aud: 25-49; rgnl radio for southeast AL, north FL & southwest GA. Spec prog: Farm 2 hrs, relg 8 hrs wkly. ♦ Doug Wynn, gen mgr.

Stations in the U.S. — Alabama

Developers & Brokers of Radio Properties
contact American Media Services at our suite:
Philadelphia Marriott Downtown
215-625-2900
843-972-2200
americanmediaservices.com
Charleston, SC
Dallas, TX • Chicago, Il • Austin, TX
American Media Services, LLC

Eufaula

WKZJ(FM)— 1969: 92.7 mhz; 39 kw. Ant 551 ft. TL: N32 07 58 W85 04 13. Stereo. Box 1358 36072-0531. Secondary address: 1347 S. Eufaula Ave. 36072-0531. Phone: (334) 687-2066. Fax: (334) 687-2067. E-mail: riversales@kenology.net. Web Site: www.theriverrocks.com. Licensee: Davis Broadcasting Inc. (group owner; (acq 7-20-2004; $2.7 million). Leventhal, Senter & Lerman. Format: Adult contemp, CHR. News staff: 2; News: 6 hrs wkly. ♦Gregory A. Davis, pres; Janet Armstead, gen mgr; Bernie Corcoran, opns mgr; Cheryl Davis, opns mgr; Angela Verdejo, gen sls mgr; Carl Conner, progmg VP.

WRVX(FM)— Mar 16, 1992: 97.9 mhz; 6 kw. Ant 328 ft. TL: N31 56 04 W85 12 27. Stereo. Box 1419 36072-1419. Secondary address: 1084 S. Eufaula Ave. 36027. Phone: (334) 616-0097. Fax: (334) 687-3600. E-mail: wrvxfm@eufaula.rr.com. Licensee: River Valley Media L.L.C. (acq 2-28-98; $200,000). Network: Jones Radio Networks. Format: Var. Target aud: 24 plus. ♦John Burns, pres & gen mgr.

WULA(AM)— 1948: 1240 khz; 1 kw-U. TL: N31 54 30 W85 09 51. Box 1419 36027-0531. Phone: (334) 616-0097. Fax: (334) 687-3600. Licensee: River Valley Media LLC (acq 5-21-2004; $95,000). Format: Sports, Talk, News. Target aud: 25-54; adults. Spec prog: Farm 2 hrs, Black 3 hrs wkly. ♦John Burns, pres.

Eutaw

WQZZ(FM)— August 1990: 104.3 mhz; 2.3 kw. 370 ft. TL: N32 54 16 W87 50 09. Box 70427, Tuscaloosa 35407. Secondary address: 601 Greensboro Ave., Suite 507, Tuscaloosa 35401. Phone: (205) 345-4787. Fax: (205) 345-4790. E-mail: jwlawson@bellsouth.net. Licensee: Jim Lawson Communications Inc. (acq 3-27-93). Format: Rhythm & blues, urban. ♦Jim Lawson, gen mgr & opns mgr.

Eva

WRJL-FM— 1996: 99.9 mhz; 6 kw. 328 ft. TL: N34 18 43 W86 43 54. 5610 Hwy. 55 E. 35621. Phone: (256) 796-8000. Fax: (256) 796-8515. Licensee: Rojo Inc. Format: Southern gospel. ♦Jo French, pres, gen mgr & gen mgr; Amy Holland, progmg dir; Greg French, chief of engrg.

Evergreen

WIJK(AM)— July 1, 1957: 1470 khz; 1 kw-D. TL: N31 26 29 W86 56 08. Box 705 36401. Secondary address: Hwy. 31 N 36401. Phone: (251) 578-2780. Fax: (251) 578-5399. Web Site: www.powerpig.com. Licensee: Star Broadcasting Inc. (acq 4-13-2004; $2.75 million. with co-located FM). Putbrese, Hunsaker & Trent P. Format: Sports, talk. News staff: 3; News: 20 hrs wkly. Target aud: 34-64. Spec prog: Religion 6 hrs wkly. ♦Luther Upton, gen mgr.

WPGG(AM)— Co-owned with WIJK(AM). Oct 25, 1982: 93.3 mhz; 100 kw. 417 ft. TL: N31 26 04 W86 56 07. Box 705, HC 35, Box 2-8 36401. Phone: (334) 578-2780. Fax: (334) 578-5399. E-mail: powerpig@wpgg.com. Web Site: www.powerpig.com. Putbrese, Hunsaker & Trent. Format: Country. Target aud: 25-54.

Fairfield

WJLD(AM)—Licensed to Fairfield. See Birmingham

Fairhope

WABF(AM)— Aug 12, 1961: 1220 khz; 1 kw-D, 64 w-N, DA-D. TL: N30 30 38 W87 54 13. Box 1220 36533. Secondary address: 460 S. Section St. 36533. Phone: (251) 928-2384. Fax: (251) 928-9229. Licensee: Gulf Coast Broadcasting Co. Inc. (acq 5-24-99). Putbrese, Hunsaker & Trent P. Format: Talk. News: 15 hrs wkly. Target aud: 45 plus; upscale. Spec prog: Farm one hr, Swap Shop 6 hrs, relg 6 hrs wkly. ♦R. Hagan, pres; Lori Dubois, gen mgr.

WDLT(AM)—Licensed to Fairhope. See Mobile

WZEW(FM)— Aug 28, 1966: 92.1 mhz; 13.5 kw. 449 ft. TL: N30 41 33 W88 02 29. Stereo. 1100 Dauphin St., Mobile 36608. Phone: (251) 433-9236. Phone: (251) 438-5460. Fax: (251) 438-5462. E-mail: 92zew@92zew.net. Web Site: www.92zew.net. Licensee: Baldwin Broadcasting Co. (acq 10-1-98; $1.425 million). Rep: Allied Radio Partners. Format: Adult alt. News staff: one; News: 6 hrs wkly. Target aud: 25-44. Spec prog: Jazz 6 hrs wkly. ♦Ken Johnson, gen mgr.

Fayette

WLDX(AM)— Sept 3, 1949: 990 khz; 1 kw-D, 42 w-N. TL: N33 41 06 W87 49 16. Box 189, 733 Columbus St. E. 35555. Phone: (205) 932-3318. Fax: (205) 932-3318. E-mail: wldx@wldx.com. Web Site: www.wldx.com. Licensee: Dean Broadcasting Inc. (acq 6-1-2005; $450,000). Network: ABC Information & Entertainment. Fletcher, Heald & Hildreth. Format: Country. Target aud: 25-55; middle-income adults. ♦Wailey Dean, pres.

WTXT(FM)— Jan 29, 1977: 98.1 mhz; 100 kw. 984 ft. TL: N33 34 31 W87 59 27. (CP: TL: N33 31 17 W87 51 38). Stereo. 2121 9th St., Suite B, Tuscalossa 35401. Phone: (205) 344-4589. Phone: (205) 349-3200. Fax: (205) 366-9774. E-mail: ddhamric@clearchannel.com. Web Site: www.98txt.com. Licensee: Clear Channel Communications Group owner: Clear Channel Communications Inc. (acq 8-30-00; grpsl). Network: ABC. Rep: Christal. Format: Contemp country. News staff: one. Target aud: 25-54. ♦Lori Moore, gen mgr; Russ Williams, opns mgr.

Florala

WKWL(AM)— Nov 3, 1979: 1230 khz; 1 kw-U. TL: N31 00 20 W86 19 53. Box 159 36442-0159. Phone: (334) 858-6162. Fax: (334) 858-6162. E-mail: wkwl@cyou.com. Licensee: Florala Broadcasting Co. Inc. Network: USA. Format: Southern gospel, Christian country. News staff: one; News: 15 hrs wkly. Target aud: 5 plus; general. Spec prog: Farm one hr, relg 12 hrs wkly. ♦Robert Williamson, pres & gen mgr.

Florence

WBCF(AM)— 1946: 1240 khz; 1 kw-U. TL: N34 47 02 W87 42 16. Stereo. Box 1316 35631. Secondary address: 525 E. Tennessee St. 35630. Phone: (256) 764-8170. E-mail: sales@wbcf.com. Web Site: www.wbcf.com. Licensee: BCB Inc. (acq 8-11-77). Network: Network: UPI, Westwood One. Format: News/talk. News staff: 2; News: 5 hrs wkly. Target aud: 25-54; adult, mature, affluent, educated, family, business. Spec prog: Music of your life 12 hrs, local news/weather 5 hrs wkly. hrs wkly. hrs wkly. ♦Benji Carle, pres, gen mgr & news dir; Pat Costa, CFO; Jim Carle, exec VP; Patricia Carle, VP; Melody Mills, gen sls mgr. Co-owned TV: WBCF-LP, WXFL-LP

*WFIX(FM)— Mar 20, 1988: 91.3 mhz; 30 kw. 600 ft. TL: N34 40 24 W87 42 56. Stereo. 113 N. Seminary St. 35630. Phone: (256) 764-9964. E-mail: wfix@wfix.net. Licensee: Tri-State Inspirational Broadcasting Inc. (acq 10-20-98; $100,000 for stock). Network: USA. Format: Adult contemp, Christian. News: 2 hrs wkly. Target aud: 25-54; upscale family oriented women & men. Spec prog: Sports, jazz, gospel 6 hrs wkly. ♦Mark Allen, gen mgr & opns mgr.

WQLT(FM)— May 29, 1967: 107.3 mhz; 100 kw. 1,000 ft. TL: N34 40 24 W87 42 56. Stereo. Box 932, 624 Sam Phillips St. 35631. Secondary address: 2046 Beltline Rd., S.W., Suite 4, Decatur 35601. Phone: (256) 764-8121. Fax: (256) 764-8169. Web Site: www.wqlt.com. Licensee: Big River Broadcasting Corp. (group owner) Network: ABC FM Connection. Format: Adult contemp. Target aud: 25-54. ♦Nick Martin, gen mgr; Rocky Reich, sls dir; Sharon Brook, gen sls mgr; Jimmy Oliver, prom mgr; Charlie Ross, progmg mgr; Greg Pace, chief of engrg.

WXFL(FM)— February 1992: 96.1 mhz; 20.5 kw. Ant 781 ft. TL: N34 40 24 W87 42 56. Stereo. 624 Sam Phillips St. 35630. Secondary address: 2046 Beltline Rd. SW, Suite 4, Decatur 35601. Phone: (256) 764-8121. Fax: (256) 764-8169. Web Site: www.wxfl.com. Licensee: Big River Broadcasting Corp. (group owner) Network: ABC. Format:

New country. News staff: one; News: 6 hrs wkly. Target aud: 18-49; general. ♦Knox Phillips, pres; Jerry Phillips, VP; Nick Martin, gen mgr.

Foley

WHEP(AM)— May 31, 1953: 1310 khz; 1 kw-D. TL: N30 26 06 W87 41 00. Box 1747 36536. Secondary address: 20109 Hadley Rd. 36535. Phone: (251) 943-7131. Fax: (251) 943-7031. Licensee: Stewart Broadcasting Co. Inc. (acq 5-1-61). Format: News/Talk/Sports/Mor. Target aud: 25 plus. Spec prog: Farm 2 hrs wkly. ♦Clark J. Stewart, pres & gen mgr.

Fort Mitchell

WAGH(FM)— 1988: 98.3 mhz; 6 kw. 328 ft. TL: N32 21 48 W85 03 06. Box 687, Columbus 31902. Secondary address: 1501 13th Ave., Columbus 31901. Phone: (706) 576-3000. Fax: (706) 576-3010. E-mail: rasheedaali@clearchannel.com. Web Site: www.magic98online.com. Licensee: Clear Channel Broadcasting Licenses Inc. Group owner: Clear Channel Communications Inc. (acq 2-21-02; grpsl). Format: Urban adult contemp. Target aud: 25-54; working Black adults. Spec prog: Relg 6 hrs wkly. ♦James R. Martin, gen mgr.

Fort Payne

WFPA(AM)— December 1949: 1400 khz; 1 kw-U. TL: N34 26 21 W85 42 09. Stereo. 1210 Johnson St. E. 35967. Phone: (256) 845-7721. Fax: (256) 845-6828. Web Site: www.wfpa.net. Licensee: Dobson Communications (acq 12-31-01; $120,000). Format: Oldies. News staff: one; News: 15 hrs wkly. Target aud: 18-49. ♦Tim Dobson, stn mgr.

WZOB(AM)— July 2, 1950: 1250 khz; 5 kw-U. TL: N34 26 23 W85 45 12. Box 680748 35968. Secondary address: Hwy. 35 W., Radio Dr. 35968. Phone: (256) 845-2810. Fax: (256) 845-7521. Licensee: Central Broadcasting Co. Inc. (acq 8-12-03). Dora-Clayton. Format: C&W. News staff: one. Spec prog: Farm 2 hrs, gospel 5 hrs, relg 5 hrs wkly. ♦Mike Kirby, pres; Doris Hobbs, stn mgr.

Fort Rucker

WLDA(FM)— 1991: 100.5 mhz; 6 kw. Ant 476 ft. TL: N31 19 38 W85 35 35. 285 N. Foster St., Dothan 36303. Phone: (334) 598-3374. Phone: (334) 712-9346. Fax: (334) 598-2362. Licensee: Styles Media Group LLC. (group owner; (acq 10-1-2003; $750,000). Network: ABC Information & Entertainment. Format: CHR. Target aud: 25-54; upscale baby boomers, acitive duty & retired military. Spec prog: Relg 5 hrs, Sp 4 hrs, blue 5 hrs wkly. ♦Cheri Clark, gen mgr; Richard Reinhardt, opns mgr; Amy Pollard, sls dir & gen sls mgr; Craig Cooper, progmg dir; Sue Hughes, gen mgr & chief of engrg.

Fruithurst

WCKS-FM— May 9, 1994: 102.7 mhz; 1.6 kw. 630 ft. TL: N33 37 24 W85 20 14. 102 Parkwood Cir., Carrollton, GA 30117. Phone: (770) 834-5477. Fax: (770) 830-1027. Web Site: www.wcks.com. Licensee: WCKS Inc. Format: Adult contemp. Target aud: 25-44. ♦Steve L. Gradick, pres & gen mgr; Sandy Kennedy, opns mgr.

Gadsden

WAAX(AM)— Oct 18, 1947: 570 khz; 5 kw-D, 500 w-N, DA-N. TL: N33 58 45 W86 05 15. 304 S. 4th St. 35902. Phone: (256) 543-9229. Fax: (256) 543-8777. Web Site: www.waax570.com. Licensee: Capstar TX L.P. Group owner: Clear Channel Communications Inc. (acq 8-30-2000; grpsl). Network: ABC Information & Entertainment. Format: News/talk. Target aud: 25-54. ♦Kathy Boggs, gen mgr; Pam Denham, stn mgr; Bill Seckbach, progmg dir; Carl Brady, news dir.

WQEN(FM)— Co-owned with WAAX(AM). Oct 7, 1966: 103.7 mhz; 77 kw. Ant 1,105 ft. TL: N33 49 33 W86 26 46. (CP: COL Trussville. 100 kw, ant 935 ft. TL: N33 26 38 W86 52 47). Stereo. 630 Beacon Pkwy. W., Suite 600, Birmingham 35209. Phone: (205) 439-9600. Fax: (205) 439-8390. Web Site: www.1037theq.com. Format: CHR, Top-40.

Alabama

♦ Jimmy Vineyard, gen mgr; Doug McCallister, stn mgr & sls dir; Doug Hamand, opns VP; Cindee Standridge, mktg dir; Daniel Wyatt, prom dir; Tommy Chuck, progmg dir; Madison Reeves, mus dir; Bob Newberry, engrg dir.

WGAD(AM)— May 26, 1947: 1350 khz; 5 kw-D, 1 kw-N, DA-N. TL: N34 01 03 W86 05 15. Box 1350, 750 Walnut St. 35902. Phone: (256) 546-1611. Phone: (256) 547-9061. Fax: (256) 547-9062. E-mail: dhedrick@wgad.com. Web Site: www.wgad.com. Licensee: The DR Group LLC (acq 10-20-2004; $250,000). Network: ABC. Format: Oldies. News: 16 hrs wkly. Target aud: 25 plus; general. Spec prog: Gospel 5 hrs wkly. ♦ Dave Hadrick, gen mgr.

WGMZ(FM)—(Glencoe). Oct 11, 1993: 93.1 mhz; 6 kw. 620 ft. TL: N33 57 16 W85 51 40. Stereo. Box 517 35902. Secondary address: 304 S. 4th St. 35901. Phone: (256) 549-0931. Fax: (256) 543-8777. E-mail: z931@clearchannel.com. Web Site: www.wgmz.com. Licensee: Capstar TX L.P. Group owner: Clear Channel Communications Inc. (acq 8-30-00; grpsl). Format: Classic hits of the 60s, 70s & 80s. News staff: one. Target aud: 35 plus. ♦ Mark Mayes, pres; Kathy Boggs, gen mgr.

WJBY(AM)—(Rainbow City). 1926: 930 khz; 5 kw-D, 500 w-N, DA-2. TL: N33 59 09 W86 02 15. Box 930 35902. Secondary address: 2725 Rainbow Dr., Rainbow City 35906. Phone: (256) 442-1222/442-5369. Fax: (256) 442-1229. E-mail: feedback@wjby.com. Web Site: www.wjby.com. Licensee: Gadsden Broadcasting Co. Inc. (acq 3-78). Network: USA. Format: Christian. News: 15 hrs wkly. Target aud: 25-54. ♦ Chris Stevens, gen mgr; Jim Tolbert, opns mgr; Mike Hooks, progmg dir.

WKXX(FM)—(Attalla). Aug 31, 1991: 102.9 mhz; 1.1 kw. 702 ft. TL: N33 58 28 W86 12 24. Stereo. 100 Spurlock St., Rainbow City 35906. Secondary address: Box 8405 35902. Phone: (256) 442-3944. Fax: (256) 442-7287. Web Site: www.wkxx.com. Licensee: Broadcast Media L.L.C. (acq 1-16-98; $650,000). Format: Hot adult contemp. News staff: one; News: 2 hrs wkly. Target aud: 18-49. ♦ Pat Courington Jr., CEO; Tommy Lee, gen mgr.

WMGJ(AM)— Sept 11, 1985: 1240 khz; 1 kw-U. TL: N34 00 04 W86 01 48. 815 Tuscaloosa Ave. 35901. Phone: (256) 546-4434. Fax: (256) 546-9645. Web site: www.wmgj.com. Licensee: Floyd L. Donald Broadcasting Co. Inc. Rep: Roslin. Format: Black, urban contemp. ♦ Floyd L. Donald, gen mgr.

*WSGN(FM)— Feb 11, 1975: 91.5 mhz; 6.3 kw. 520 ft. TL: N34 04 29 W86 01 11. Stereo. Box 227 35902-0227. Secondary address: 1001 George Wallace Dr. 35903. Phone: (256) 549-8439. Fax: (256) 549-8404. E-mail: nmullin@gadsdenstate.edu. Web Site: www.gadsdenstate.edu. Licensee: Gadsden State Community College. Gardner, Carton & Douglas. Format: Class, news. News: 34 hrs wkly. Target aud: General. Spec prog: Folk 2 hrs, new age 10 hrs wkly. ♦ Dr. Renee Culverhouse, pres; Neil D. Mullin, gen mgr.

*WTBB(FM)— July 20, 1999: 89.9 mhz; 4.8 kw. Ant 515 ft. TL: N34 06 03 W85 59 37. Stereo. Trinity Christian Academy, 1500 Airport Rd., Oxford 36203. Phone: (256) 831-3333. Fax: (256) 831-5895. E-mail: wtbb@trinityoxford.org. Web Site: www.trinityoxford.org. Licensee: Trinity Christian Academy. Fletcher, Heald & Hildreth. Format: Christian, relg. Spec prog: Sp one hr wkly. ♦ Dr. C.O. Grinstead, gen mgr.

Geneva

WGEA(AM)— Mar 17, 1953: 1150 khz; 1 kw-D, 35 w-N. TL: N31 01 21 W85 52 16. Box 339 36340. Secondary address: 420 Riverside Ave. 36340. Phone: (334) 684-7079. Fax: (334) 684-0329. Licensee: Shelley Broadcasting Co. (acq 10-26-87). Format: Country, gospel, news/talk. Target aud: 30 plus. ♦ Jack Mizell, pres; Doc Parker, gen mgr.

WRJM-FM— Sept 12, 1969: 93.7 mhz; 100 kw. 853 ft. TL: N31 02 42 W85 57 33. 285 E. Broad St., Ozark 36360. Phone: (334) 774-7673. Fax: (334) 774-6450. E-mail: hjmizell@wrjm.com. Web Site: www.wrjm.com. Licensee: Stage Door Development Inc. Network: Network: ABC, Westwood One. Rep: Rgnl Reps. John Borsari. Format: News/talk. Target aud: 30 plus. ♦ Jack Mizell, pres & gen mgr; Susannah Hodges, stn mgr, opns mgr & gen sls mgr; Boyd Mizell, engrg mgr & engr.

Georgiana

WFXX(FM)— 1999: 107.7 mhz; 42 kw. 535 ft. TL: N31 27 08 W86 37 07. 1352 River Falls St., Andalusia 36420. Phone: (334) 222-2222. Fax: (334) 427-8888. E-mail: wfxx@alaweb.com. Web Site: fox107.com. Licensee: Star Broadcasting Inc. (acq 3-29-2004; $975,000). Format: Adult Contemp. ♦ Jeffrey K. Haynes, pres; Kelly Haynes, gen mgr.

Glencoe

WGMZ(FM)—Licensed to Glencoe. See Gadsden

Greensboro

WDGM(FM)— 03/03/2002: 99.1 mhz; 25 kw. Ant 328 ft. TL: N32 49 46 W87 40 19. Box 70937, Tuscaloosa 35407. Phone: (205) 342-9948. Fax: (205) 366-9480. Licensee: Citadel Broadcasting Co. (acq 7-12-2005; grpsl). Network: ABC. Rep: Roslin. Gardner, Carton & Douglas. Target aud: 25+; male/female 25+.

Greenville

WGYV(AM)— Aug 18, 1948: 1380 khz; 1 kw-D. TL: N31 50 01 W85 52 16. Box 585, 1604 E. Commerce St. 36037. Phone: (334) 382-5444. Fax: (334) 382-5444. E-mail: wgyv@alaweb.com. Licensee: Robert John Williamson (acq 11-29-02). Format: News/talk, oldies. Target aud: 25-54; general. Spec prog: Black 6 hrs wkly. ♦ Terry Golden, gen mgr; Paulette Golden, pub affrs dir; Bob Luman, chief of engrg.

WKXN(FM)— July 18, 1977: 95.9 mhz; 4 kw. 225 ft. TL: N31 50 43 W86 38 56. (CP: 2.1 kw, ant 564 ft. TL: N31 56 52 W86 42 09). Box 369 36037. Secondary address: 563 Manningham Rd. 36037. Phone: (334) 382-6555. Fax: (334) 382-7770. E-mail: wkxn@wkxn.com. Web Site: www.wkxn.com. Licensee: Autaugaville Radio Inc. (acq 11-22-94; $287,500; 1-2-95). Format: Urban contemp, blues. ♦ Roscoe Miller, gen mgr & stn mgr.

WQZX(FM)— Aug 19, 1985: 94.3 mhz; 3.9 kw. 410 ft. TL: N31 54 40 W86 36 19. Stereo. 205 W. Commerce 36037. Phone: (334) 382-6633. Fax: (334) 382-6634. E-mail: q94@q94.net. Web Site: www.q94.net. Licensee: Haynes Broadcasting Inc. Network: ABC. Format: Modern country. ♦ Kyle Haynes, pres & gen mgr.

Grove Hill

WBMH(FM)— May 1999: 106.1 mhz; 12 kw. 472 ft. TL: N31 43 30 W87 54 58. Box 518, c/o The Radio Center, Jackson 36545. Phone: (251) 246-4431. Fax: (251) 246-1980. E-mail: bama1061@yahoo.com. Licensee: Capital Assets Inc. Group owner: Bennie E. Hewett Stns. Format: Classic country. ♦ Shirley Chandler, gen mgr.

Gulf Shores

WCSN-FM—(Orange Beach). July 2, 1996: 105.7 mhz; 5 kw. 246 ft. TL: N30 17 45 W87 33 42. Stereo. Box 1919 36547. Secondary address: 2421 E. Second St. 36542. Phone: (251) 967-1057. Fax: (251) 967-1050. E-mail: sunny105@gulftel.com. Web Site: www.sunny105.com. Licensee: Gulf Coast Broadcasting Co. Inc. (acq 10-31-97). Putbrese, Hunsaker & Trent. Format: Adult contemp. Target aud: 25-54; upscale. ♦ R. Lee Hagan, pres; Bryant Ellis, gen mgr & pub affrs dir; Charles Redden, gen mgr; Ron Wainscott, progmg dir.

Guntersville

WGSV(AM)— Apr 16, 1950: 1270 khz; 1 kw-D. TL: N34 18 31 W86 17 44. Box 220 35976. Phone: (256) 582-8131. Fax: (256) 582-4347. E-mail: wtwx@wtwx.com. Web Site: www.wgsv.com. Licensee: Guntersville Broadcasting Co. Inc. Format: News/talk. ♦ Lavell Jackson, pres; Kerry Jackson, gen mgr & opns mgr.

WTWX-FM—Co-owned with WGSV(AM). Aug 1, 1969: 95.9 mhz; 10.7 kw. 596 ft. TL: N34 20 14 W86 16 46. Phone: (256) 582-4946. Web Site: www.wtwx.com. Network: ABC FM Connection. Format: C&W.

*WJIA(FM)— September 1995: 88.5 mhz; 2.2 kw. 426 ft. TL: N34 25 33 W86 18 25. 5025 Spring Creek Dr. 35976. Phone: (256) 505-0885. Fax: (256) 505-0886. E-mail: jfm@wjia.org. Web Site: www.wjia.org. Licensee: Lake City Educational Broadcasting Inc. Format: Christian. ♦ Kevin Guffey, gen mgr.

Haleyville

WJBB(AM)— Apr 1, 1949: 1230 khz; 1 kw-U. TL: N34 14 00 W87 37 32. Drawer 370, 807 Hwy. 13 N. 35565. Phone: (205) 486-2277.

Directory of Radio

Phone: (205) 486-2278. Fax: (205) 486-3905. E-mail: wjbb@sonet.com. Licensee: Haleyville Broadcasting Co. Inc. (acq 1951). Rep: Rgnl Reps. Gardner, Carton & Douglas. Format: Southern gospel, loc news. News staff: one; News: 36 hrs wkly. Target aud: 25-55; professionals. Spec prog: Farm 3 hrs wkly. ♦ John L. Slatton, pres; Terry L. Slatton, gen mgr & opns VP; Debby Aderholt, dev dir & prom dir; Aubrey Haynes, sls VP & adv mgr; Robert Wakefield, progmg dir; Larry Gardner, mus dir & pub affrs dir; Sherron Hayes, news dir; Chester Barber, chief of engrg.

WJBB-FM— July 14, 1979: 92.7 mhz; 3.9 kw. 240 ft. TL: N34 14 00 W87 37 32. (CP: Ant 328 ft.). Stereo. E-mail: wjbb@southnet.net. Format: Country. Target aud: 24-55. ♦ John Slatton, CEO & chmn; Terry Slatton, exec VP; Andy Marbutt, opns mgr; Aubrey Haynes, sls dir.

Hamilton

WERH(AM)— Aug 24, 1950: 970 khz; 5 kw-D. TL: N34 07 01 W87 59 29. Box 1119 35570. Phone: (205) 921-3195. Fax: (205) 921-7187. E-mail: werh@sonet.net. Licensee: Kate F. Fite. (acq 4-1-58). Format: Country, gospel. Target aud: General. Spec prog: Farm. ♦ James B. Fowler, gen mgr; Geraldine Miller, adv mgr; Bryan Williams, mus dir; Bill Moates, chief of engrg.

WERH-FM— Apr 1, 1968: 92.1 mhz; 3 kw. 120 ft. TL: N34 07 01 W87 59 29. Stereo. 1597 Military St. S. 35570. Phone: (205) 921-3481. Format: Classic Rock. ♦ Mark Burleson, news dir.

Hanceville

WXRP(AM)— April 1986: 1170 khz; 460 w-D. TL: N34 04 28 W86 46 44. Maplewood Properties LLC, 4 Office Park Cir., Suite 101, Birmingham 35223. Phone: (205) 871-0323. Licensee: WJR Broadcasting LLC (acq 1999; $175,000). Format: Alternative rock. ♦ Ralph Jolly, gen mgr.

Hartselle

WTAK-FM— August 1992: 106.1 mhz; 5.4 kw. 725 ft. TL: N34 27 54 W86 38 36. Box 21008, Huntsville 25824. Secondary address: 26869 Peoples Rd., Madison 35756. Phone: (256) 353-1750. Fax: (256) 350-2653. Web Site: www.wtak.com. Licensee: Clear Channel Communications Group owner: Clear Channel Communications Inc. (acq 8-30-00; grpsl). Format: Classic rock. ♦ Rick Brown, gen mgr; Todd Berry, opns mgr; Carmellita Palmer, gen sls mgr; Jerry James, progmg dir; Carl Ampieri, chief of engrg.

WYAM(AM)— Oct 1, 1956: 890 khz; 2.5 kw-D. TL: N34 34 00 W86 54 46. Stereo. 1301 Central Pkwy. S.W., Decatur 35601. Phone: (256) 355-4567. Fax: (256) 351-1234. E-mail: wileywg@acninc.net. Licensee: Decatur Communications Properties LLC (acq 8-12-2003). Format: Rgnl Mexican. News staff: 2; News: 6 hrs wkly. Target aud: 18-60; General. ♦ Susan Wiley, exec VP; William Wiley, pres, gen mgr & opns VP.

Harvest

*WAYH(FM)— 2003: 88.1 mhz; 3.5 kw. Ant 669 ft. TL: N34 49 08 W86 44 19. 9582 Madison Blvd., Suite 8, Madison 35758. Phone: (256) 837-9293. Fax: (256) 772-6731. E-mail: contact@wayfm.com. Web Site: www.wayfm.com. Licensee: WAY-FM Media Group Inc. (group owner). Format: Contemp Christian. Target aud: 18-34; youth & young adults. ♦ Dusty Rhodes, COO; Bob Augsburg, pres; Thom Ewing, stn mgr; Ken Sinclair, progmg dir.

Hazel Green

WBXR(AM)— Dec 11, 1970: 1140 khz; 15 kw-D, DA. TL: N34 57 18 W86 38 32. 2926-D Huntsville Hwy., Fayetteville, TN 37334. Phone: (931) 433-7017. Fax: (931) 433-8282. E-mail: wbxr@wilkinsradio.com. Web Site: wilkinsradio.com. Licensee: New England Communications Inc. (acq 9-16-97; $150,000). Network: Salem Radio Network. Format: Relg, christian. Target aud: 35 plus. ♦ Robert L. Wilkins, pres; Mitchell Mathis, VP; Carla Payne, gen mgr & chief of opns; Greg Garrett, opns mgr.

Headland

WDBT(FM)— September 1992: 105.3 mhz; 11.5 kw. 485 ft. TL: N31 15 48 W85 18 24. 3245 Montgomery Hwy., Dothan 36303. Phone: (334) 712-9233. Fax: (334) 712-0374. E-mail: ron@wdjr.com. Web

Stations in the U.S.

Alabama

Developers & Brokers of Radio Properties
contact American Media Services at our suite:
Philadelphia Marriott Downtown
215-625-2900
843-972-2200
americanmediaservices.com
Charleston, SC
Dallas, TX • Chicago, IL • Austin, TX
American Media Services, LLC

Site: www.1053thebeat.com. Licensee: Gulf South Communications Inc. (acq 1-27-97; $745,000). Format: Rhythm and blues. ♦Ron Eubanks, gen mgr; Jerry Broadway, opns mgr.

Heflin

*WKNG-FM— May 2005: 89.1 mhz; 250 w. Ant 718 ft. TL: N33 33 18 W85 27 25. 102 Parkwood Cir., Carrollton, GA 30117. Phone: (770) 834-5477. Fax: (770) 830-1027. Licensee: Covenant Communications Inc. Format: Southern gospel. ♦Steven L. Gradick, gen mgr.

*WPIL(FM)— 2003: 91.7 mhz; 370 w. Ant 34 ft. TL: N33 39 07 W85 31 13. 908 Opelika Rd., Auburn 36830. Phone: (334) 821-0744. Fax: (334) 821-4031. Web Site: www.wpilfm.com. Licensee: Jimmy Jarrell Communications Foundation Inc. (acq 12-31-02). Format: Country/bluegrass. ♦Jimmy Jarrell, pres & gen mgr; Jack Curtis, stn mgr & progmg dir.

Helena

WRAX(FM)— July 15, 1991: 100.5 mhz; 93 kw. Ant 1,014 ft. TL: N33 05 42 W87 15 16. 244 Goodwin Crest Dr., Suite 300, Birmingham 35209. Phone: (205) 945-4646. Phone: (205) 741-1005. Fax: (205) 945-3994. Web Site: www.wrax.com. Licensee: Citadel Broadcasting Co. (group owner; acq 7-12-2005); grpsl). Format: Alternative. ♦Dale Daniels, gen mgr; Frank Giardina, opns mgr.

Hobson City

WHOG(AM)— Apr 15, 1991: 1120 khz; 500 w-D. TL: N33 36 50 W85 51 19. Radio Bldg., 1330 Noble St., Suite 25, Anniston 36201. Phone: (256) 236-6484. Fax: (256) 236-6484. E-mail: hog1120@aol.com. Licensee: Hobson City Broadcasting Co. Rep: Dora-Clayton. Format: Black, urban contemp. Target aud: General. Spec prog: Gospel 7 hrs wkly. ♦Mark Hogan, gen mgr & gen sls mgr; Jason Hogan, opns mgr; Paulette Miller, news dir.

Holly Pond

WFMH-FM— 1996: 95.5 mhz; 6 kw. 328 ft. TL: N34 06 16 W86 41 47. Stereo. 1707 Warnke Rd. N.W., Cullman 35055. Phone: (256) 734-3271. Fax: (256) 734-3622. E-mail: wfmhradio@aol.com. Licensee: Williams Communications. Group owner: Williams Communications Inc. (acq 7-20-2004; $2.45 million. with WFMH(AM) Cullman). Format: Country. News: 15 hrs wkly. Target aud: 35-64. ♦Mary Evelyn Jones, gen mgr; John Nichols, stn mgr & progmg dir.

Homewood

WNCB(FM)— 1998: 97.3 mhz; 2.6 kw. Ant 492 ft. TL: N33 27 37 W86 51 07. 301 Beacon Pkwy. W., Suite 200, Birmingham 35209. Phone: (205) 916-1100. Fax: (205) 916-1152. E-mail: wodl@cox.com. Web Site: www.wodl.com. Licensee: CXR Holdings L.L.C. Group owner: Cox Broadcasting (acq 6-8-99). Network: ABC. Rep: Katz Radio. Dow, Lohnes and Albertson. Format: New country. News staff: one; News: at 2 hrs wkly. ♦Justin Case, opns mgr & progmg dir; David Walls, gen sls mgr; Tom Scott, chief of engrg.

Hoover

WENN(FM)— September 1993: 105.5 mhz; 29.5 kw. Ant 623 ft. TL: N33 29 04 W86 48 25. 600 Beacon Pkwy. W., Suite 400, Birmingham 35209. Phone: (205) 439-9600. Fax: (205) 439-8390. Web Site: www.hallelujah1055.com. Licensee: Capstar TX L.P. Group owner: Clear Channel Communications Inc. (acq 8-30-2000; grpsl). Network: ABC Music Radio. Format: Gospel. News staff: one. Target aud: 25-54. ♦Jimmy Vineyard, gen mgr; Willis Pride, stn mgr.

Huntsville

WAHR(FM)— July 28, 1959: 99.1 mhz; 100 kw. 984 ft. TL: N34 47 53 W86 38 24. Stereo. 1900 Memorial Pkwy SW 35801-5002. Phone: (256) 536-1568. Fax: (256) 536-4416. Web Site: www.star99.fm.

Licensee: BCA Radio LLC. Group owner: Black Crow Media Group LLC (acq 11-15-2001; grpsl). Format: Adult contemp. Target aud: 25-55. ♦Bill Thomas, gen mgr.

WBHP(AM)— May 23, 1937: 1230 khz; 1 kw-U. TL: N34 43 09 W86 35 42. 401 14th St., Decatur 35601. Secondary address: Box 789, Decatur 35601. Phone: (256) 534-3521. E-mail: rbrown@wbhp.com. Licensee: Capstar TX L.P. Group owner: Clear Channel Communications Inc. (acq 8-30-00; grpsl). Network: ABC Information & Entertainment. Format: Country. Target aud: General. Spec prog: Farm 6 hrs wkly. ♦Rick Brown, gen mgr.

WDJL(AM)— Oct 1, 1968: 1000 khz; 10 kw-D, DA. TL: N34 46 47 W86 39 16. 2025 Sparkman Dr. 35810. Phone: (256) 852-1223. Fax: (256) 852-1900. Licensee: James K. Sharp dba 5th Avenue Broadcasting. (acq 8-95; $300,000). Network: Westwood One. Jack Pennington & Associates. Format: Gospel. Target aud: 35-65; upscale decision makers that enjoy hits of the 40s, 50s & 60s. Spec prog: Gospel comedy 6 hrs wkly. ♦Walter Peavy, pres & gen mgr.

WEUP(AM)— Mar 20, 1958: 1600 khz; 5 kw-D, 500 w-N, DA-D. TL: N34 45 32 W86 38 35. Stereo. 2609 Jordan Ln. N.W. 35816. Phone: (256) 837-9387. Fax: (256) 837-9404. Web Site: www.weupam.com. Licensee: Hundley Batts. Network: American Urban. Format: Gospel. Target aud: 25-54; adults. Spec prog: Jazz 2 hrs, community affrs one hr wkly. ♦Hundley Batts Sr., pres; Hundley Batts, gen mgr.

WEUV(AM)— 2001: 1700 khz; 10 kw-D, 1 kw-N. TL: N34 45 32 W86 38 35. 2609 Jordan Ln. N.W. 35816. Phone: (256) 837-9387. Fax: (256) 837-9404. Web Site: www.weupam.com. Licensee: Hundley Batts Sr. & Virginia Caples. Format: Gospel. ♦Hundley Batts, gen mgr.

*WJAB(FM)— May 9, 1991: 90.9 mhz; 100 kw. 334 ft. TL: N34 47 09 W86 34 00. Stereo. Alabama A&M University, Telecommunications Center, Box1687, Normal 35762. Secondary address: 3409 Meridian St. 35811. Phone: (256) 372-5795. Phone: (256) 372-5861 (request line). Fax: (256) 372-5907. Web Site: www.aamu.edu/wjab. Licensee: Board of Trustees Alabama A&M University. Network: NPR. Format: Jazz, blues, gospel. News: 5 hrs wkly. Spec prog: Black 3 hrs, oldies 3 hrs, reggae 4 hrs, Latin 2 hrs, gospel 5 hrs wkly. ♦Elizabeth Sloan-Ragland, gen mgr; Michael Burns, opns mgr.

WLOR(AM)— June 1948: 1550 khz; 50 kw-D, 500 w-N, DA-2. TL: N34 44 36 W86 35 39. 1900 Memorial Pkwy. S. 35801. Phone: (256) 536-1568. Fax: (256) 536-4416. E-mail: ed@jammin1550.am. Web Site: www.jammin1550.am. Licensee: BCA Radio LLC. Group owner: Black Crow Media Group LLC (acq 11-15-2001; grpsl). Network: ABC. Format: Black, gospel, urban contemp. News staff: one; News: 1 hr wkly. Target aud: General. ♦Bill Thomas, gen mgr.

*WLRH(FM)— Oct 13, 1976: 89.3 mhz; 100 kw. 810 ft. TL: N34 37 41 W86 30 59. Stereo. UAH Campus, John Wright Dr. 35899. Phone: (256) 895-9574. Fax: (256) 830-4577. Web Site: www.wlrh.org. Licensee: Alabama ETV Commission. (acq 12-14-77). Network: Network: PRI, NPR. Format: Class, news, variety. News staff: one; News: 40 hrs wkly. Target aud: General. ♦George Dickerson, gen mgr & stn mgr; Jennifer Jaudon-Johnston, dev dir.

*WOCG(FM)— Dec 1978: 90.1 mhz; 25 kw. 230 ft. TL: N34 45 28 W86 39 44. Stereo. Oakwood College, 7000 Adventist Blvd., N.W. 35896. Phone: (256) 726-7418. Fax: (256) 726-7417. E-mail: wocg@wocg.org. Web Site: www.wocg.org. Licensee: Oakwood College. Network: USA. Donald E. Martin. Format: Inspirational, Christian, light urban gospel. News: 14 hrs wkly. Target aud: 34-55; Families with interest in rel & educ progmg. ♦Delbert Baker, pres; Bruce Peifer, VP; Victoria L. Miller, gen mgr & opns mgr; Jody Stennis, progmg dir.

WRSA-FM—See Decatur

WRTT-FM— Oct 6, 1960: 95.1 mhz; 50 kw. 110 ft. TL: N34 42 56 W86 35 55. Stereo. 1900 S. Memorial Pkwy. 35801. Phone: (256) 536-1568. Fax: (256) 536-4416. Web Site: www.rocket951.fm. Licensee: BCA Radio LLC. Group owner: Black Crow Media Group LLC (acq 11-15-2001; grpsl). Format: Mainstream Rock. News staff: one; News: 22 hrs wkly. Target aud: 24-54; young adults, families. Spec prog: Relg. ♦Bill Thomas, gen mgr.

WTKI(AM)— November 1946: 1450 khz; 1 kw-U. TL: N34 43 30 W86 36 15. 2305 Holmes Ave. 35816. Phone: (256) 533-1450. Fax: (256) 536-4349. E-mail: ron@espn1450.com / mike@espn1450.com. Web Site: www.espn1450.com. Licensee: Mountain Mist Media LLC (acq 3-95). Network: Network: Network: ABC, ESPN Radio, Westwood One. Format: Sports. News: 2 hrs wkly. Target aud: 35 plus; sports-minded men and women, heavy local. Spec prog: Relg 4 hrs wkly. ♦David Barnhart, pres.

WUMP(AM)—See Madison

WZYP(FM)—See Athens

Irondale

WLPH(AM)— Dec 5, 1960: 1480 khz; 5 kw-D. TL: N33 32 54 W86 39 56. Box 100067, Birmingham 35210. Secondary address: 5200 Atlanta Hwy, E. 35210. Phone: (205) 956-5470. Fax: (205) 956-5471. Licensee: Birmingham Christian Radio Inc. (acq 5-13-97). Format: Gospel music. News staff: 3. Target aud: 13 plus; young teenagers to adults. ♦Debra Calhoun-George, gen mgr; Sylvia White, gen mgr & stn mgr.

Jackson

WHOD(FM)—Listing follows WRJX(AM).

WRJX(AM)— June 1, 1950: 1230 khz; 1 kw-U. TL: N31 32 38 W87 52 30. (CP: 1190 khz, 10 kw-D, 300 w-N). Box 518, Hwy. 43 N. 36545. Secondary address: 4428 College Ave. 36545. Phone: (251) 246-4431. Phone: (251) 246-5581. Fax: (251) 246-1980. E-mail: radiocenter@starband.com. Licensee: Capital Assets Inc. Group owner: Bennie E. Hewett Stations Network: ABC Information & Entertainment. Format: Black gospel. News staff: one. Target aud: 25-54; business minded, baby-boomers. ♦Faye Braswell, gen mgr; Shirley Chandler, sls VP.

WHOD(FM)—Co-owned with WRJX(AM). Aug 1, 1964: 94.5 mhz; 30 kw. 640 ft. TL: N31 28 59 W87 42 27. Network: ABC. Format: Hot adult contemp. News staff: one; News: 2 hrs wkly.

Jacksonville

WCKS(AM)— January 1986: 810 khz; 50 kw-D, 500 w-N, DA-2. TL: N33 50 58 W85 45 46. Box 8, Anniston 36202. Phone: (256) 237-0810. Fax: (256) 782-2489. E-mail: alabama810@bellsouth.net. Licensee: Alabama 810 LLC (acq 11-26-03). Format: Country. News staff: 2; News: 15 hrs wkly. Target aud: 35 plus; adults. Spec prog: Gospel 2 hrs wkly. ♦L. E. Gradick, exec VP & gen mgr; Teresa Goodman, gen mgr & stn mgr.

*WLJS-FM— Sept 29, 1975: 91.9 mhz; 3 kw. 246 ft. TL: N33 49 29 W85 45 49. Stereo. Box 3009, Self Hall @ Jacksonville State Univ. 36265. Phone: (256) 782-5300. Phone: (256) 782-5572. Fax: (256) 782-5645. Web Site: www.jsu.edu/92j. Licensee: Board of Trustees-Jacksonville State University. Network: NPR. Gardner, Carton & Douglas. Format: Var/div, class. Target aud: 18-34; college, young adult. Spec prog: Relg 3 hrs wkly. ♦Mike Stedham, gen mgr.

Jasper

WDXB(FM)— Mar 28, 1962: 102.5 mhz; 79 kw. 2,096 ft. TL: N33 28 51 W87 24 03. Stereo. 600 Beacon Pkwy. W., Suite 400, Birmingham 35209. Phone: (205) 439-9600. Fax: (205) 439-8390. Web Site: www.1025thebull.com. Licensee: Capstar TX L.P. Group owner: Clear Channel Communications Inc. (acq 8-30-00; grpsl). Format: Hit country. ♦Jimmy Vineyard, gen mgr; Doug Hamand, opns VP.

Broadcasting & Cable Yearbook 2006

Alabama | Directory of Radio

WIXI(AM)— Nov 2, 1946: 1360 khz; 1 kw-D, 42 w-N. TL: N33 49 12 W87 16 26. Stereo. Box 622, 409 9th Ave. 35501. Phone: (205) 384-3461. Phone: (205) 384-3221. E-mail: joy1360@wzpq.com. Licensee: James T. Lee (acq 9-1-99). Network: ABC Information & Entertainment. Rep: Allied Radio Partners. Fletcher, Heald & Hildreth. Format: Christian, Southern gospel. News: 4 hrs wkly. Target aud: General. Spec prog: Gospel 6 hrs wkly. ◆ Ed Smith, gen mgr; Joe Cook, stn mgr.

WLYJ(AM)— Mar 1, 1957: 1240 khz; 1 kw-U. TL: N33 48 54 W87 16 19. 1499 Airport Rd. N. 35504. Phone: (205) 221-2222. Phone: (256) 927-4027. Fax: (256) 927-4028. Licensee: Joy Christian Communications Inc. (acq 7-9-2004; $200,000). Format: Christian progmg. ◆ Ed Smith, pres & gen mgr; Roy Pounds, stn mgr.

Level Plains

WIRB(AM)—Not on air, target date: unknown: 1490 khz; 430 w-U. TL: N31 17 51 W85 47 33. 422 County Rd. 551, New Brockton 36351. Phone: (334) 894-5047. Fax: (334) 894-6684. Licensee: Virgle Leon Strictland, individually. ◆ Virgle Leon Strictland, gen mgr.

Lexington

WJHX(AM)— Feb 20, 1981: 620 khz; 5 kw-D, 99 w-N. TL: N34 58 37 W87 22 10. 1426 5th Ave. S.E., Decatur 35601. Licensee: Manuel Huerta (acq 5-30-2002; $100,000). ◆ Manuel Huerta, pres; Marcos Huerta, gen mgr.

Linden

WINL(FM)— April 1991: 98.5 mhz; 100 kw. 817 ft. TL: N32 07 34 W87 44 02. Stereo. Box 938, Demopolis 36732. Phone: (334) 289-9850. Fax: (334) 289-9811. E-mail: win985@westal.net. Web Site: www.bestcountryaround.com. Licensee: West Alabama Communications Inc. (acq 2-12-01; $1.28 million). Network: ABC. Rep: Dora-Clayton. Format: Country. Target aud: 25-54. Spec prog: Gospel 5 hrs, farm 10 hrs wkly. ◆ Amy Douglas, gen mgr & opns mgr.

WNPT-FM— Dec 19, 1990: 102.9 mhz; 40 kw. Ant 551 ft. TL: N32 27 40 W87 34 50. Stereo. Box 2000, Tuscaloosa 35403. Phone: (205) 758-5523. Fax: (205) 752-9696. E-mail: wtbc@dbtech.net. Licensee: John Sisty Enterprises Inc. (acq 11-28-2003; $450,000). Format: Classic country. ◆ John Sisty, pres; Ronnie Quarles, gen mgr.

Lineville

WZZX(AM)— 1967: 780 khz; 5 kw-D. TL: N33 17 04 W85 47 24. Box 26, Ashland 36251. Phone: (256) 354-4600. Fax: (256) 354-7224. E-mail: wasz@acs-isp.com. Licensee: Williams Communications Inc. (acq 7-25-2002; $2.88 million). Format: Country. ◆ Walt Williams Jr., CEO, chmn & pres; Walt Williams III, exec VP; Al Haynes, gen mgr & progmg dir; Al Hayes, stn mgr.

Lisman

WPRN-FM— 1997: 107.7 mhz; 6 kw. Ant 328 ft. TL: N32 05 27 W88 13 57. 909 W. Pushmataha, Butler 36904. Phone: (205) 459-3222. Fax: (205) 459-4140. Licensee: Butler Broadcasting Corp. (acq 11-5-99). Format: Country. ◆ Daryl Jackson, gen mgr.

Livingston

WSLY(FM)—See York

WYLS(AM)—See York

Luverne

WHLW(FM)— 1997: 104.3 mhz; 13.5 kw. Ant 1,830 ft. TL: N31 58 28 W86 09 44. Box 4420, Montgomery 36103. Secondary address: 203 Gunn Rd., Montgomery 36117. Phone: (334) 274-6464. Fax: (334) 274-6465. Licensee: Capstar TX L.P. Group owner: Clear Channel Communications Inc. (acq 8-30-2000; grpsl). Format: Classic hits. ◆ Arnessa Leverett, gen mgr.

Madison

WUMP(AM)— Mar 29, 1983: 730 khz; 1 kw-D, 123 w-N. TL: N34 41 46 W86 44 19. 1717 Hwy. 72 E., ., Athens 35611. Phone: (256) 830-8300. Web Site: www.730ump.com. Licensee: Cumulus Licensing LLC. Group owner: Cumulus Media Inc. (acq 7-21-2003; grpsl). Rep: McGavren Guild. Format: Sports. News staff: 2; News: 3 hrs wkly. Target aud: 18-54; males. Spec prog: Univ. of Alabama Sports. ◆ Bill West, gen mgr; Blair Trosper, gen sls mgr & progmg dir; Brian Pitts, gen sls mgr.

Marion

WJUS(AM)— Dec 8, 1951: 1310 khz; 5 kw-D. TL: N32 38 04 W87 17 48. Hwy. 5 36756. Phone: (334) 683-2043. Fax: (334) 872-2329. Licensee: Marion Radio Inc. (acq 6-86; $115,000; 6-30-86). Format: Urban contemp. ◆ Rev. Glenn King, gen mgr.

Meridianville

WXQW(FM)— June 8, 1995: 94.1 mhz; 3 kw. 328 ft. TL: N34 48 30 W86 34 27. Box 789, Decatur 35602. Secondary address: 200 Lime Quarry Rd., Madison 35758. Phone: (256) 837-1021. Fax: (256) 350-2653. E-mail: comments@wxqw.com. Web Site: www.wxq.com. Licensee: Capstar TX L.P. Group owner: Clear Channel Communications Inc. (acq 8-30-00; grpsl). Format: Oldies. ◆ Rick Brown, gen mgr; Todd Berry, opns mgr; Carmelita Palmer, gen sls mgr; Bruce Reynolds, progmg dir; Carl Sampieri, chief of engrg.

Millbrook

WWMG(FM)— Aug 1, 1993: 97.1 mhz; 3 kw. 328 ft. TL: N32 25 58 W86 20 07. Box 4420, Montgomery 36103. Secondary address: 203 Gunn Rd., Montgomery 36117. Phone: (334) 274-6464. Fax: (334) 274-6465. Web Site: www.mymagic97.com. Licensee: Capstar TX L.P. Group owner: Clear Channel Communications Inc. (acq 8-30-2000; grpsl). Network: Network: American Urban, Westwood One. Format: Adult contemp. ◆ Arnessa Leverett, gen mgr & stn mgr; Michael Long, opns mgr; Alberta Eaton, gen sls mgr; Darryl Elliott, progmg dir.

Mobile

WABB-FM— Feb 5, 1973: 97.5 mhz; 100 kw. Ant 1,551 ft. TL: N30 41 20 W87 49 49. Stereo. 1551 Springhill Ave. 36604. Phone: (251) 432-5572. Fax: (251) 438-4044. E-mail: b.dittman@wabb.com. Web Site: www.wabb.com. Licensee: WABB-FM Inc. (acq 8-30-2000; grpsl). Network: ABC FM Connection. Format: Top-40. ◆ Bernard Dittman, pres & gen mgr.

WABB(AM)— November 1948: 1480 khz; 5 kw-U, DA-N. TL: N30 43 11 W88 04 16. Box 2148 36652. Secondary address: 1551 Springhill Ave. 36604. Web Site: www.wabb.com. Group owner: Dittman Group Inc. Rep: Christal. Format: News/talk. Target aud: 18-49.

WAVH(FM)—See Daphne

***WBHY-FM**— Mar 20, 1992: 88.5 mhz; 50 kw. 624 ft. TL: N30 40 56 W87 49 41. Stereo. Box 1328 36633-1328. Secondary address: 2621-B Ralston Rd. 36606. Phone: (251) 473-8488. E-mail: power88@goforth.org. Web Site: www.goforth.org. Licensee: Goforth Media Inc. (group owner; acq 6-27-90; 7-30-90). Fletcher, Heald & Hildreth. Format: Contemp Christian mus. News: 7 hrs wkly. Target aud: 18-34. ◆ Robert Barber, CEO & opns mgr; Charles Smith, pres & gen sls mgr; Wilbur Goforth, gen mgr & opns mgr; Steve Riggs, chief of engrg.

WBHY(AM)— Dec 9, 1943: 840 khz; 10 kw-D. TL: N30 45 50 W88 06 36. Web Site: www.goforth.org. (Acq 4-11-86). Network: UPI. Format: Christian. Target aud: 34-64; Christians.

WBLX-FM—Listing follows WDLT(AM).

WDLT(AM)—(Fairhope). Apr 22, 1965: 660 khz; 10 kw-D, 850 w-N, DA-N. TL: N30 42 27 W88 03 55. 2800 BauPhin St. 36606. Phone: (251) 652-2000. Fax: (251) 652-2007. Licensee: Cumulus Licensing Corp. Group owner: Cumulus Media Inc. (acq 10-18-99; grpsl). Format: News radio. News staff: one. Target aud: 25 plus; Black adults. ◆ Gary Pizzati, gen mgr.

WBLX-FM—Co-owned with WDLT(AM). April 1976: 92.9 mhz; 98 kw. 1,555 ft. TL: N30 37 35 W87 38 50. Stereo. Network: ABC. Format: Urban contemp. Target aud: 12 plus; primarily Black women, 18-34.

WDLT-FM—(Chickasaw). 1980: 98.3 mhz; 40 kw. 548 ft. TL: N30 35 05 W88 15 57. Stereo. 2800 Dauphin St., Suite 104 36606. Phone: (251) 652-2000. Fax: (251) 652-2007. E-mail: mobile.prog@cumulus.com. Web Site: www.smooth98.com. Licensee: April Broadcasting Inc. Group owner: Cumulus Media Inc. (acq 10-18-99; grpsl). Format: Adult Contemp. News staff: one; News: 5 hrs wkly. Target aud: 25-54. Spec prog: Jazz 5 hrs, blues 18 hrs, pub affrs 4 hrs wkly. ◆ Gary Pizzati, gen mgr; Steve Crumbely, opns mgr.

WGOK(AM)— Nov 21, 1958: 900 khz; 1 kw-D, 381 w-N, DA-2. TL: N30 42 27 W88 03 55. Stereo. 2800 Dauphin St., Suite 104 36606. Phone: (251) 652-2000. Fax: (251) 652-2001. Web Site: www.cumulus.com. Licensee: Cumulus Licensing Corp. Group owner: Cumulus Media Inc. (acq 10-18-99; $6 million with WYOK(FM) Atmore). Rep: Roslin. Format: Gospel. Target aud: 18-54; Black adults. ◆ Dickie Roberds, pres; Kevin Wagner, stn mgr & gen sls mgr; Danny Wright, prom dir.

***WHIL-FM**— Aug 29, 1974: 91.3 mhz; 100 kw. 1,066 ft. TL: N30 41 20 W87 49 49. Stereo. Box 8509 36689-0509. Secondary address: 4000 Dauphin St. 36608. Phone: (251) 380-4685. Fax: (251) 460-2189. E-mail: whil@whil.org. Web Site: www.whil.org. Licensee: Spring Hill College. Network: Network: PRI, NPR. Dow, Lohnes & Albertson. Format: Class. News: 10 hrs wkly. Target aud: 35 plus. ◆ Jeffrey R. Stoll, gen mgr; Ben Harper, opns dir; Dennis Brown, dev dir; JoAnn Breland, progmg dir; Kurt Garrett, opns.

WIJD(AM)—See Prichard

WKSJ-FM— Apr 12, 1971: 94.9 mhz; 100 kw. 410 ft. TL: N30 35 36 W87 39 40. (CP: Ant 1,554 ft. TL: N30 37 35 W87 38 50). Stereo. 555 Broadcast Dr., 3rd Fl. 36606. Phone: (251) 450-0100. Fax: (251) 479-3418. Web Site: www.95ksj.com. Licensee: Clear Channel Radio Licenses Inc. Group owner: Clear Channel Communications Inc. (acq 11-21-97; grpsl). Network: ABC Information & Entertainment. David Coppock Format: Contemp country. News staff: 2; News: 25 hrs wkly. Target aud: 25-54; mid level to high class country music listeners. ◆ David Coppock, VP & gen mgr; Jeanie Hufford, stn mgr.

WLPR(AM)—(Prichard). Dec 31, 1986: 960 khz; 5 kw-U, DA-N. TL: N30 41 20 W87 49 49. Stereo. Box 1328 36633-1328. Phone: (251) 473-8488. E-mail: power88@goforth.org. Web Site: www.goforth.org. Licensee: Goforth Media Inc. (acq 1994). Network: Salem Radio Network. Rep: Salem. Fletcher, Heald & Hildreth. Format: Southern gospel. News: 6 hrs wkly. Target aud: 35 plus. ◆ Wilbur Goforth, gen mgr; Robert Barber, opns dir & engrg VP; Charlie Smith, gen sls mgr; Kenny Fowler, mus dir; Steve Riggs, chief of engrg.

WLVV(AM)— Feb 7, 1930: 1410 khz; 5 kw-U, DA-N. TL: N30 40 52 W88 00 02. (CP: 3.9 kw-U, DA-1. TL: N30 45 40 W88 08 05). 1263 Battleship Pkwy., Spanish Fort 36527. Phone: (251) 626-1090. Fax: (251) 626-1099. E-mail: wlvv@bellsouth.net. Web Site: www.wlvv.com. Licensee: WLVV Inc. (acq 4-14-99; $263,750). Group owner: Martin Broadcasting Inc. (acq 4-14-99; $263,750). Network: American Urban. Rep: Katz Radio. Format: Gospel, MOR. Target aud: 18-44; Black. ◆ Tom Alexander, gen mgr, gen sls mgr & progmg dir.

WMOB(AM)— Jan 25, 1961: 1360 khz; 5 kw-D, 212 w-N, DA-2. TL: N30 41 26 W88 01 33. Box 63 36601. Secondary address: 200 Addsco Rd. Causeway 36601. Phone: (251) 432-1360. Fax: (251) 432-1396. Licensee: Buddy Tucker Enterprises. (acq 4-84; $395,000; 4-9-84). Format: Relg. ◆ Theodore Tucker, pres; LeVaughn Tucker, VP; Buddy Tucker, gen mgr; Don Tucker, opns mgr.

WMXC(FM)—Listing follows WPMI(AM).

WPMI(AM)— 1946: 710 khz; 1 kw-D, 500 w-N. TL: N30 43 13 W88 03 34. Box 161489 36616. Secondary address: 555 Broadcast Dr. 36606. Phone: (251) 450-0100. Fax: (251) 479-3418. Licensee: Clear Channel Broadcasting Licenses Inc. Group owner: Clear Channel Communications Inc. (acq 11-21-97; grpsl). Network: Network: CBS, ABC News/Talk. Leventhal, Senter & Lerman. Format: News/talk, sports. Target aud: 25 plus. ◆ Dave Cappock, pres; Ron Cole, gen mgr & progmg dir; Bill King, news dir.

WMXC(FM)—Co-owned with WPMI(AM). Oct 16, 1947: 99.9 mhz; 100 kw. Ant 1,755 ft. TL: N30 41 20 W87 49 49. Stereo. Format: Adult contemp. Target aud: 25-54. ◆ Dan Mason, progmg dir.

WRKH(FM)— Dec 5, 1964: 96.1 mhz; 100 kw. 1,342 ft. TL: N30 41 20 W87 49 49. Stereo. 3rd Fl., 555 Broadcast Dr. 36606. Phone: (251) 450-0100. Fax: (251) 479-3418. Web Site: www.961therocket.com. Licensee: Clear Channel Radio Licenses Inc. Group owner: Clear Channel Communications Inc. (acq 11-21-97; grpsl). Rep: D & R

Broadcasting & Cable Yearbook 2006

D-40

Stations in the U.S. — Alabama

Developers & Brokers of Radio Properties — contact American Media Services at our suite: Philadelphia Marriott Downtown 215-625-2900. 843-972-2200. americanmediaservices.com. Charleston, SC. Dallas, TX · Chicago, IL · Austin, TX. American Media Services, LLC.

Radio. Format: Classic rock hits. News staff: 2; News: 2 hrs wkly. Target aud: 25-49; front edge baby boomers. ◆ David Coppock, VP & gen mgr; Jeanie Hufford, stn mgr.

*WTOH(FM)— September 1974: 105.9 mhz; 10 w. 290 ft. TL: N30 41 48 W88 08 15. (CP: Ant 327 ft.). 4000 Dauphin St. 36608. Phone: (334) 380-3840. Phone: (334) 380-3843. Fax: (334) 460-2185. Licensee: Spring Hill College. Format: Progsv. ◆ Varnell Lee, stn mgr.

Monroeville

WMFC(AM)— April 1952: 1360 khz; 780 w-D. TL: N31 30 51 W87 17 55. Box 645 36461. Secondary address: 961 Pineville Rd. 36460. Phone: (251) 575-3281. Phone: (251) 575-4061. Fax: (251) 575-3280. Licensee: Monroe Broadcasting Co. Inc. Format: Black gospel. Target aud: 25-54. ◆ Carolyn Stewart, chmn; David Stewart, pres, stn mgr & gen sls mgr; Howard Macht, chief of engrg.

WMFC-FM— December 1965: 99.3 mhz; 30 kw. Ant 308 ft. TL: N31 30 51 W87 17 55. Stereo. Network: Network: ABC Information & Entertainment, Jones Radio Networks. Format: Good time oldies. Target aud: General. ◆ Carol Casey, progmg dir.

WYNI(AM)— Dec 6, 1982: 930 khz; 5 kw-D, 48 w-N. TL: N31 29 40 W87 21 29. 873 S. Alabama Ave. 36460. Phone: (251) 575-7601. Fax: (251)-575-7703. Licensee: Southern Media Communications of Monroeville Inc. (acq 10-22-99). Format: Soft rock. ◆ Wendy Smith, gen mgr.

Montgomery

WACV(AM)— Jan 16, 1939: 1170 khz; 10 kw-D, 1 kw-N, DA-2. TL: N32 27 16 W86 17 21. Box 210723, 4101-A Wall St. 36121. Phone: (334) 244-1170. Fax: (334) 279-9563. Web Site: www.wacv1170am.com. Licensee: Bluewater Broadcasting Co. LLC (group owner; acq 4-21-2004; grpsl). Network: CBS. Format: News/talk, sports. News staff: one. Target aud: 25 plus. Spec prog: Farm 5 hrs wkly. ◆ Terry Barber, gen mgr; Don Markwell, prom dir & progmg dir.

WBAM-FM— Jan 1, 1961: 98.9 mhz; 100 kw. 1095 ft. TL: N32 24 11 W86 11 48. Stereo. 4101-A Wall St. 36106. Phone: (334) 244-0961. Fax: (334) 279-9563. Web Site: www.bamacountry989.com. Licensee: Bluewater Broadcasting Co. LLC (group owner; acq 4-19-2004). Rep: Christal. Format: Country. News staff: one; News: one hr wkly. Target aud: 12-54. ◆ Terry Barber, gen mgr.

WHHY-FM— Jan 9, 1962: 101.9 mhz; 100 kw. 1,200 ft. TL: N32 29 33 W86 08 50. (CP: TL: N32 24 11 W86 11 48). Stereo. One Commerce St., Suite 300 36104. Phone: (334) 240-9274. Fax: (334) 240-9219. Web Site: www.y102montgomery.com. Licensee: Cumulus Licensing Corp. Group owner: Cumulus Media Inc. (acq 3-12-01; grpsl). Rep: McGavren Guild. Format: CHR. News: one hr wkly. Target aud: 18-40. ◆ Lew Dickey, pres; Bernie Barker, gen mgr & natl sls mgr; Bill Jones, opns mgr; Don Parden, sls dir; Donna Headley, gen sls mgr; Joy Melton, gen sls mgr & news dir; Heather Williams, prom dir & prom mgr; Karen Rite, progmg dir; Larry Wilkins, chief of engrg.

WLWI(AM)—Co-owned with WHHY-FM. Apr 30, 1930: 1440 khz; 5 kw-D, 1 kw-N, DA-N. TL: N32 18 24 W86 13 40. (CP: TL: N32 24 11 W86 11 48). Fax: (334) 240-9211. Web Site: www.cumulus.com. Network: CNN Radio. Format: News/talk. News staff: one. Target aud: 18 plus. ◆ Bill Jones, opns dir; Bernie Barker, mktg dir; Richard Matthews, progmg dir.

*WLBF(FM)— Apr 4, 1984: 89.1 mhz; 100 kw. 537 ft. TL: N32 24 13 W86 11 50. Stereo. Box 210789 36121-0789. Phone: (334) 271-8900. Fax: (334) 260-8192. E-mail: mail@faithradio.org. Web Site: www.faithradio.org. Licensee: Faith Broadcasting Inc. Network: Network: Moody, USA. Southmayd & Miller. Format: Educ, relg, MOR. News: 14 hrs wkly. Target aud: General. ◆ Russell Dean, gen mgr; Donna Spears, opns mgr; Gary Hundley, dev dir.

WLWI-FM— Listing follows WMSP(AM).

WMGY(AM)— June 1, 1946: 800 khz; 1 kw-D, 193 w-N. TL: N32 24 48 W86 17 25. 2305 Upper Wetumpka Rd. 36107-1345. Phone: (334) 834-3710. Fax: (334) 834-3711. E-mail: davewmgy@aol.com. Licensee: WMGY Radio Inc. Group owner: GHB Radio Group (acq 7-75). Network: USA. Format: Southern gospel. News: 7 hrs wkly. Target aud: 35 plus. Spec prog: Black 15 hrs, sports 6 hrs wkly. ◆ Dane Harris, gen mgr.

WMSP(AM)— 1953: 740 khz; 50 kw-D, 73 w-N, DA-2. TL: N32 18 39 W86 17 25. One Commerce St., Suite 300 36104. Phone: (334) 240-9274. Fax: (334) 240-9219. Web Site: www.sportsradio740.com. Licensee: Cumulus Licensing Corp. Group owner: Cumulus Media Inc. (acq 12-12-98; grpsl). Network: ESPN Radio. Gardner, Carton & Douglas. Format: Sports. Target aud: Adults 18 plus. ◆ Lew Dickey, pres; Bernie Barker, gen mgr, natl sls mgr & mktg mgr; Bill Jones, opns mgr & progmg dir; Donna Hadley, gen sls mgr; Joy Melton, gen sls mgr; Heather Williams, prom dir; Richard Matthews, progmg mgr; Larry Wilkins, chief of engrg.

WLWI-FM—Co-owned with WMSP(AM). July 15, 1969: 92.3 mhz; 100 kw. 1,095 ft. TL: N32 24 13 W86 11 50. (CP: TL: N32 24 11 W86 11 48). Stereo. Web Site: www.wlwi.com. Network: CNN Radio. Format: Country. News staff: one. Target aud: 25-54. Spec prog: Gospel 4 hrs wkly. ◆ Darlene Dixon, mus dir; Marcus Hyles, news dir.

WMXS(FM)—Listing follows WNZZ(AM).

WNZZ(AM)— May 8, 1953: 950 khz; 1 kw-U, DA-N. TL: N32 26 23 W86 15 49. One Commerce St., Suite 300 36104. Phone: (334) 240-9274. Fax: (334) 240-9219. Web Site: www.cumulus.com. Licensee: Cumulus Licensing Corp. Group owner: Cumulus Media Inc. (acq 12-12-98; grpsl). Rep: Allied Radio Partners. Gardner, Carton & Douglas. Format: American standards, news. News staff: one. ◆ Lew Dickey, pres; Bernie Barker, gen mgr & mktg mgr; Bill Jones, opns dir & progmg dir; Donna Headley, gen sls mgr; Joy Melton, gen sls mgr; Heather Williams, prom dir; Richard Matthews, progmg mgr; Larry Wilkins, chief of engrg.

WMXS(FM)—Co-owned with WNZZ(AM). July 9, 1961: 103.3 mhz; 100 kw. 1,007 ft. TL: N32 24 48 W86 17 25. (CP: TL: N32 24 11 W86 11 48). Stereo. Web Site: www.mix103.com. Network: CNN Radio. Format: Adult contemp. Target aud: 25-54. ◆ Mike Alan, progmg dir; Marcus Hyles, news dir.

WQKS-FM— Dec 1, 1990: 96.1 mhz; 4.5 kw. 820 ft. TL: N32 21 32 W86 19 57. (CP: 900 w, ant 820 ft. TL: N32 22 03 W86 15 42). Stereo. 4101 A-Wall St. 36106. Phone: (334) 244-0961. Fax: (334) 279-9563. Web Site: www.alice961.net. Licensee: Bluewater Broadcasting Co. LLC (group owner; acq 4-21-2004; grpsl). Network: ABC. Format: Rockin Hits of the 70s 80s & 90s. News: one hr wkly. Target aud: 25-54. ◆ Terry Barber, gen mgr.

*WVAS(FM)— June 15, 1984: 90.7 mhz; 80 kw. 347 ft. TL: N32 21 58 W86 17 40. Stereo. Alabama State Univ., 915 S. Jackson St. 36101-0271. Phone: (334) 229-4287/229-4708. Fax: (334) 269-4995. Web Site: www.alasu.edu/wvas. Licensee: Alabama State University. (acq 6-83). Network: ABC FM Connection. Wilkes, Artis, Hedrick & Lane. Format: Smooth jazz, mellow vocals. News staff: 2; News: 5 hrs wkly. Target aud: General; African-American community. Spec prog: Black 5 hrs, gospel 5 hrs, blues 6 hrs, news/talk 4 hrs wkly. ◆ Dr. David Okeowo, gen mgr; Rick Hall, stn mgr.

WXVI(AM)— May 1947: 1600 khz; 5 kw-D, 1 kw-N, DA-2. TL: N32 23 40 W86 17 21. 912 South Perry St. 36104. Phone: (334) 263-4141. Fax: (334) 263-9191. Licensee: Sunshine 16 Radio Network Inc. (acq 11-3-94; $225,000;. FTR: 12-5-94). Network: American Urban. Rep: Roslin. Format: Christian. Target aud: 35 plus; urban. ◆ Ricardo Hall, stn mgr; Sharon Dunn, progmg mgr.

Moody

WURL(AM)— October 1984: 760 khz; 1 kw-D. TL: N33 35 13 W86 28 18. 2999 Radio Park Dr. 35004. Phone: (205) 699-9875. Fax: (205) 640-4379. E-mail: wurlradio@aol.com. Web Site: www.wurlradio.com. Licensee: Bill Davison Evangelistic Assn. (acq 9-89; $175,000; 10-2-89). Network: USA. Format: Gospel. Target aud: General. ◆ William J. Davison Sr., pres, gen mgr & gen sls mgr.

Moulton

WEUP-FM— Sept 1, 1991: 103.1 mhz; 6 kw. 328 ft. TL: N34 32 07 W87 13 31. Stereo. 2609 Jordon Ln. N.W., Huntsville 35816. Phone: (256) 837-9387. Web Site: 103weup.com. Licensee: Hundley Batts Sr. and Virginia Caples (acq 6-7-99; $775,000. with co-located AM). Network: USA. Rep: Rgnl Reps. Format: Urban, Hip-Hop. News staff: one. Target aud: 21-55. Spec prog: Relg one hr wkly. ◆ Hundley Batts Sr., gen mgr; Huntley Batts, gen sls mgr; Big Ant, progmg dir; Tony Jordan, news dir; John Haines, chief of engrg.

WHIY(FM)—Co-owned with WEUP-FM. Dec 11, 1963: 1190 khz; 2.5 kw-D. TL: N34 28 55 W87 18 04. Box 37, 13471 Court St. 35650. Phone: (256) 974-0681. Phone: (256) 897-0682. Format: Soul gospel. Target aud: General. ◆ Nancy Moore, gen mgr & dev dir; Ricky Sykes, progmg dir.

Muscle Shoals

WBCF(AM)—See Florence

WLAY(AM)— Jan 15, 1933: 1450 khz; 1 kw-U. TL: N34 45 29 W87 40 08. Stereo. 509 N. Main St., Tusumbia 35674. Phone: (256) 383-2525. Fax: (256) 389-1912. E-mail: donnajohnson@clearchannel.com. Licensee: Urban Radio Licenses LLC. Group owner: Clear Channel Communications Inc. (acq 5-13-2005; grpsl). M. Scott Johnson. Format: Sports. Target aud: 18-54. ◆ Michael Meeks, gen mgr.

WVNA-FM—Co-owned with WLAY(AM). Oct 28, 1964: 105.5 mhz; 1.05 w. 741 ft. TL: N34 40 24 W87 42 56. Stereo. Format: Classic rock. ◆ Steve Alston, prom mgr.

*WQPR(FM)— November 1987: 88.7 mhz; 20 kw. Ant 430 ft. TL: N34 34 41 W87 47 02. (CP: Ant 429 ft). Stereo. Phifer Annex, Suite 166, Tuscaloosa 35487. Phone: (205) 348-6644. Fax: (205) 348-6648. Web Site: www.apr.org. Licensee: Board of Trustees University of Alabama. Network: Network: PRI, NPR. Arter & Hadden. Format: Class, jazz, news & info. News staff: one; News: 5 hrs wkly. Spec prog: Bluegrass, blues, folk 5 hrs, new age 19 hrs wkly. ◆ Roger Duvall, stn mgr.

WSBM(AM)—See Florence

WXFL(FM)—See Florence

Northport

*WSJL(FM)—Not on air, target date: unknown: 88.1 mhz; 10 w horiz 20 kw vert. Ant 492 ft. TL: N33 28 51 W87 24 03. 1115 Honeysuckle Dr., Keene, TX 76059. Phone: (817) 641-3495. Licensee: Mary V. Harris Foundation. ◆ Linda De Romanett, pres & gen mgr.

Oneonta

WCRL(AM)— July 29, 1952: 1570 khz; 2.5 kw-D. TL: N33 57 16 W87 28 20. Box 490 35121. Secondary address: 908 2nd Ave. E. 35121. Phone: (205) 625-3333. Fax: (205) 625-5433. Web Site: www.wkld.com. Licensee: Blount County Broadcasting Service Inc. (acq 9-19-02). Network: Jones Radio Networks. Format: Hispanic 60s. ◆ L.D. Bentley, pres; Danny Bently, gen mgr.

WKLD(FM)—Co-owned with WCRL(AM). July 12, 1968: 97.7 mhz; 3.2 kw. Ant 367 ft. TL: N33 56 48 W86 29 06. Web Site: www.wkld.com. Format: Country. Spec prog: Atlanta Braves baseball.

Opelika

WANI(AM)— June 3, 1940: 1400 khz; 1 kw-U. TL: N32 38 13 W85 24 23. Box 950, Auburn 36831-0950. Secondary address: 197 E. University Dr., Auburn 36830. Phone: (334) 826-2929. Fax: (334) 826-9151. Web Site: www.wani1400.com. Licensee: Auburn Network

Alabama

Inc. (acq 11-7-97; $135,000). Format: News/talk. News staff: one. ♦ Mike Hubbard, pres; Andy Burcham, gen mgr.

WKKR(FM)—See Auburn

WMXA(FM)—Listing follows WTLM(AM).

WTLM(AM)— Aug 12, 1968: 1520 khz; 1 kw-D. TL: N32 39 13 W85 25 25. Box 2329 36803-2329. Secondary address: 915 Veterans Pkwy. 36801. Phone: (334) 745-4656. Fax: (334) 749-1520. Licensee: Qantum of Auburn License Co. LLC. Group owner: Qantum Communications Corp. (acq 7-2-03; grpsl). Gardner, Carton & Douglas. Format: MOR. News staff: one. Target aud: 50 plus. ♦ Jim Powell, gen mgr & mktg mgr; Sandy Matthews, sls dir; Woody Russ, progmg dir.

WMXA(FM)— Co-owned with WTLM(AM). July 1, 1991: 96.7 mhz; 3.5 w. 430 ft. TL: N32 33 54 W85 22 13. E-mail: wmxa@mindspring.com. Format: Adult contemp. News staff: one; News: 2 hrs wkly. Target aud: 18-49.

WZMG(AM)— (Pepperell). Oct 1, 1979: 910 khz; 650 w-D, 56 w-N, DA-1. TL: N32 56 30 W85 24 50. Box 2329, Qantum Communications 36803. Secondary address: 915 Veterns Pkwy. 36803. Phone: (334) 745-4656. Fax: (334) 745-2067. Licensee: Qantum of Auburn License Co. LLC. Group owner: Qantum Communications Corp. (acq 7-2-03; grpsl). Network: ABC. Format: Urban. Target aud: 25-54; African Americans. ♦ Jim Powell, mktg mgr & news dir.

Opp

WAMI(AM)— Dec 12, 1952: 860 khz; 1 kw-D, 47 w-N. TL: N31 18 54 W86 15 45. Stereo. Box 40 36467. Phone: (334) 493-3588. Fax: (334) 493-4182. E-mail: wami@alaweb.com. Web Site: www.wami.com. Licensee: Opp Broadcasting Co. Inc. Network: ABC. Format: Country classic. Target aud: 25-45; agricultural & garment industry workers. Spec prog: Gospel 15 hrs wkly. ♦ Harry Phillips, gen mgr.

WAMI-FM— Nov 9, 1973: 102.3 mhz; 3.4 kw. 230 ft. TL: N31 18 54 W86 15 45. Stereo.

***WJIF(FM)**— 1986: 91.9 mhz; 380 w. 164 ft. TL: N31 15 50 W86 13 26. 700 Hwy. 52 36467. Phone: (334) 493-4947. Fax: (334) 493-4947. Licensee: Opp Educational Broadcasting Foundation. Format: Southern gospel. ♦ Haywood Nawlin, gen mgr; Tammy Taylor, mus dir.

WOPP(AM)— Sept 19, 1980: 1290 khz; 2.5 kw-D, 500 w-N, DA-2. TL: N31 17 27 W86 13 51. Stereo. 1101 Cameron Rd. 36467-2407. Phone: (334) 493-4545. Fax: (334) 493-1035. Fax: (334) 493-4546. E-mail: wopp@wopp.com. Web Site: www.wopp.com. Licensee: E & R Broadcasting Inc. (acq 8-87). Rgnl Reps. Roy F. Perkins. Format: Progsv C&W, oldies mix. News staff: one; News: 16 hrs wkly. Target aud: 19-58; progsv & highly loc. Spec prog: Farm 2 hrs, Black 4 hrs, gospel 19 hrs wkly. ♦ Robert Boothe, gen mgr.

Orange Beach

WCSN-FM—Licensed to Orange Beach. See Gulf Shores

Orrville

WJAM-FM— August 1994: 107.9 mhz; 3.7 kw. Ant 410 ft. TL: N32 21 38 W87 09 12. 273 Persimmon Tree Rd., Selma 36701. Phone: (334) 875-9360. Fax: (334) 875-1340. E-mail: walx@charterinternet.com. Licensee: Scott Communications Inc. (acq 10-13-94). Format: Adult urban contemp. ♦ Scott Alexander, gen mgr.

Oxford

***WTBJ(FM)**— May 29, 1994: 91.3 mhz; 170 w. Ant 1,578 ft. TL: N33 29 07 W85 48 33. Stereo. c/o Trinity Christian Academy, 1500 Airport Rd. 36203. Phone: (256) 831-3333. Fax: (256) 831-5895. E-mail: truth@trinityoxford.org. Web Site: www.trinityoxford.org. Licensee: Trinity Christian Academy. Fletcher, Heald & Hildreth. Format: Educ, relg. Target aud: General. Spec prog: Sp one hr wkly. ♦ Dr. C.O. Grinstead, gen mgr.

WVOK(AM)— April 1956: 1580 khz; 2.5 kw-D, 22 w-N. TL: N33 26 55 W86 03 54. Box 3770 36203. Secondary address: 1215 Church St. 36203. Phone: (256) 835-1580. Fax: (256) 831-1500. Licensee: Woodard Broadcasting Co. (acq 5-62). Network: ABC. Format: Oldies. Target aud: 25-54. ♦ George Salmon, gen mgr; Jenni Light, rgnl sls mgr; Robert Ray, progmg dir.

WVOK-FM— Feb 19, 1990: 97.9 mhz; 280 kw. 1,082 ft. TL: N33 37 21 W85 52 22. Stereo. Web Site: www.k98.fm. Format: Hot adult contemp. ♦ Chuck Woodward, gen sls mgr; Chris Wright, progmg dir.

Ozark

***WAQG(FM)**— June 1998: 91.7 mhz; 3 kw. 321 ft. TL: N31 26 25 W85 33 49. Box 3206, American Family Radio, Tupelo, MS 38803. Phone: (601) 844-8888. Fax: (601) 842-6791. Web Site: www.afr.net. Licensee: American Family Radio. (group owner) Format: Inspirational Christian. ♦ Marvin Sanders, gen mgr; John Riley, progmg dir; Joe Moody, engrg dir.

WJRL-FM—Listing follows WQLS(AM).

WOAB(FM)—Listing follows WOZK(AM).

WOZK(AM)— May 3, 1953: 900 khz; 1 kw-D, 78 w-N. TL: N31 27 19 W85 40 58. Box 1109 36361. Phone: (334) 774-5600. Fax: (334) 774-1148. E-mail: wozk@alaweb.com. Licensee: Ozark Broadcasting Corp. Format: Adult standard. ♦ John Stein, gen mgr.

WOAB(FM)— Co-owned with WOZK(AM). July 9, 1967: 104.9 mhz; 6.0 kw. 275 ft. TL: N31 27 19 W85 40 53. Format: Country.

WQLS(AM)— April 1968: 1200 khz; 10 kw-D, 2.5 kw-CH. TL: N31 28 40 W85 41 07. 285 N. Foster St., Dothan 36302. Phone: (334) 792-0047. Fax: (334) 712-9346. E-mail: tom@wqls.com. Licensee: Styles Media Group LLC (group owner; acq 8-1-2002; $750,000. with co-located FM). Format: News/talk. Target aud: 25-64. Spec prog: Gospel 12 hrs wkly. ♦ Tom Love, gen mgr; Carl Blackburn, natl sls mgr.

WJRL-FM—Co-owned with WQLS(AM). Oct 5, 1968: 103.9 mhz; 25 kw. Ant 292 ft. TL: N31 26 25 W85 33 49. Stereo. Network: Moody. Format: Classic country. News staff: one; News: 15 hrs wkly. Spec prog: Gospel 8 hrs, jazz 4 hrs, oldies 6 hrs wkly.

Pell City

WFHK(AM)— Jan 7, 1956: 1430 khz; 5 kw-D. TL: N33 35 10 W86 19 35. 22 Cogswell Ave. 35125. Phone: (205) 338-1430. Fax: (205) 814-1430. Licensee: Stocks Broadcasting Inc. (acq 2-27-01; $275,000). Network: ABC Daytime Direction. Format: Country. ♦ John Simpson, gen mgr.

Pepperell

WZMG(AM)—Licensed to Pepperell. See Opelika

Phenix City

WDAK(AM)—See Columbus, GA

WGSY(FM)—Licensed to Phenix City. See Columbus GA

WHAL(AM)—Licensed to Phenix City. See Columbus GA

Piedmont

***WJCK(FM)**— April 1994: 88.3 mhz; 6 kw. 328 ft. TL: N34 04 11 W85 14 48. Box 111 36272. Phone: (256) 447-6008. Fax: (256) 447-0160. E-mail: wjck@wjck.org. Web Site: www.wjck.org. Licensee: Immanuel Broadcasting Network. Format: Relg. ♦ Ed Tuten, pres; Jane Tuten, VP & mus dir; Neil Hopper, gen mgr, opns mgr & progmg dir; Judy Williams, stn mgr; Phillip Baker, chief of engrg.

WPID(AM)— June 1953: 1280 khz; 1 kw-D, 84 w-N. TL: N33 55 50 W85 35 00. 412 Cedartown Hwy. 36272. Phone: (256) 447-9096. Fax: (256) 447-6669. Licensee: Piedmont Radio Co. (acq 6-15-84; $125,000). Format: Adult contemp, oldies. News: 2 hrs wkly. Target aud: 25-55. ♦ Jimmy Kennedy, gen mgr; Andy Kennedy, opns mgr.

Pine Hill

WKXK(FM)— 2000: 96.7 mhz; 9 kw. 544 ft. TL: N32 04 24 W87 35 27. Box 369, Greenville 36037. Secondary address: 563 Manningham Rd., Greenville 36037. Phone: (334) 382-6555. Fax: (334) 382-7770. E-mail: wkxn@alaweb.com. Web Site: www.wkxn.com. Licensee: Autaugaville Radio Inc. Format: Urban contemp, blues, gospel. ♦ Roscoe Miller, gen mgr & stn mgr.

Prattville

WIQR(AM)— March 1969: 1410 khz; 5 kw-D, 1 kw-N, DA-2. TL: N32 25 23 W86 26 21. 800 E. County Rd. 4 E., Prattville 36067. Phone: (334) 491-9477. E-mail: wiqr@hotmail.com. Licensee: Star Power Communications Corp. (acq 2-1-2001; $167,000). Alabama Net. Format: Local sports. Target aud: General. ♦ Greg Meadows, gen mgr.

WXFX(FM)— August 1977: 95.1 mhz; 50 kw. 492 ft. TL: N32 28 01 W86 24 15. Stereo. 1 Commerce St., Suite 300, Montgomery 36104. Phone: (334) 240-9274. Fax: (334) 240-9219. Web Site: www.wxfx.com. Licensee: Cumulus Licensing Corp. Group owner: Cumulus Media Inc. (acq 3-12-01; grpsl). Network: CNN Radio, Motor Racing Net. Rep: McGavren Guild. Format: Classic rock. News staff: one. Target aud: 25-54; upscale adults, two paycheck households. ♦ Bernie Barker, gen mgr; Bill Jones, opns mgr; Donna Headley, gen sls mgr; Rick Hendricks, progmg dir; Larry Wilkins, chief of engrg.

Priceville

WQAH(AM)— August 1986: 1310 khz; 1 kw-D. TL: N34 32 32 W86 54 14. Box 1048, Hartselle 35640. Secondary address: 219 Chestnut St., Hartselle 35640. Phone: (256) 353-4060. Fax: (256) 773-6915. Licensee: Abercrombie Broadcasting AM Inc. (acq 8-86). Format: Southern gospel. Target aud: 25-65. ♦ Keith Abercrombie, gen mgr.

Prichard

WIJD(AM)— June 13, 1966: 1270 khz; 5 kw-D, 103 w-N. TL: N30 44 44 W88 05 40. 555 Broadcast Dr., 3rd Flr., Mobile 36606. Phone: (251) 471-1208. Fax: (251) 471-1244. E-mail: mglin@aol.com. Web Site: www.wijd.us. Licensee: 1270 AM Inc. (acq 5-16-03; $100,000). Network: ABC Information & Entertainment. Format: Christian. Target aud: 35 plus. ♦ David Coppock, gen mgr.

WKSJ-FM—See Mobile

WLPR(AM)—Licensed to Prichard. See Mobile

Rainbow City

WJBY(AM)—Licensed to Rainbow City. See Gadsden

Rainsville

WVSM(AM)— May 16, 1967: 1500 khz; 1 kw-D. TL: N34 29 56 W85 50 34. Box 339, 368 McCurdy Ave. N. 35986. Phone: (256) 638-2137. E-mail: wvsm@hiwaay.net. Web Site: www.wvsm.net. Licensee: Sand Mountain Advertising Co. Inc. Format: Southern gospel. News staff: 4; News: 9 hrs wkly. Target aud: General. ♦ Karyon Guffey, VP & VP; Annie Ruth Huber, gen sls mgr; Mark Huber, pres, gen mgr & progmg dir.

Red Bay

WRMG(AM)— June 29, 1968: 1430 khz; 1 kw-D. TL: N34 24 51 W88 08 11. (CP: 3 kw-D). Box 656 35582. Secondary address: 202 7th Ave N. Phone: (256) 356-4458. Licensee: Jack W. Ivy Sr. (acq 12-18-01; $42,300). Format: Country, Southern gospel, Bluegrass. ♦ Jack W. Ivy Sr., pres & progmg dir; Jimmy R. Pyle, gen mgr.

Reform

WBEI(FM)— May 7, 1991: 101.7 mhz; 22.5 kw. Ant 725 ft. TL: N33 13 48 W87 50 50. 142 Skyland Blvd., Tuscaloosa 35405. Phone: (205) 345-7200. Fax: (205) 349-1715. Licensee: Citadel Broadcasting Co. (group owner; (acq 7-12-2005; grpsl). Format: Adult contemp. Target aud: 18-34. ♦ Brenda Bebout, gen mgr.

Repton

WFNU(FM)— Oct 1, 2002: 101.1 mhz; 3.1 kw. Ant 459 ft. TL: N31 26 45 W87 16 59. 873 S. Alabama Ave., Monroeville 36461. Phone: (251) 575-7601. Fax: (251) 575-7703. E-mail: fun101@frontiernet.net. Licensee: Great South RFDC L.L.C. (group owner; (acq 11-28-2003; $1.5 million). Format: Lite rock. ♦Wendy Smith, gen mgr, opns mgr & progmg dir; Robert Williams, chief of engrg.

Roanoke

WELR(AM)— April 1954: 1360 khz; 1 kw-D. TL: N33 09 45 W85 22 30. Box 710, 6855 Hwy. 431 36274. Phone: (334) 863-4139. Fax: (334) 863-2540. Licensee: Eagle's Nest Inc. (group owner; acq 10-15-88). Network: ABC Information & Entertainment. Gardner, Carton & Douglas. Format: Sports. ♦Jim Vice, pres & gen mgr; Coleman Vice, gen sls mgr; Kay Vice, opns mgr & prom mgr.

WELR-FM— Feb 14, 1969: 102.3 mhz; 3 kw horiz, 1.25 kw vert. 436 ft. TL: N33 13 14 W85 24 37. (CP: 9 kw, ant 544 ft.). Stereo. Secondary address: 304 Broome St., LaGrange 30240. Web Site: www.eagle1023.com. Network: ABC Information & Entertainment. Format: Country.

Robertsdale

WNSI(AM)— Mar 1, 1985: 1000 khz; 1 kw-D. TL: N30 32 10 W87 42 55. Box 1919, Gulf Shores 36542. Secondary address: Box 578, 18674 Berner Rd. 36542. Phone: (251) 947-2346. Fax: (251) 947-2347. Web Site: www.wnsiradio.com. Licensee: Great American Radio Network Inc. (acq 3-16-01; $180,000). Format: Sports, talk. News staff: one; News: 2 hrs wkly. Target aud: 45 plus; upscale. Spec prog: Religion 6 hrs wkly. ♦Mike Grace, gen mgr.

Rogersville

WYTK(FM)— January 1994: 93.9 mhz; 2.25 kw. 531 ft. TL: N34 51 52 W87 23 43. Box 397, Florence 35631. Phone: (256) 764-9390. Fax: (256) 764-7760. E-mail: the score@bellsouth.net. Web Site: www.939thescore.com. Licensee: Valley Broadcasting Inc. (acq 9-18-02; $900,000). Format: Sports. Target aud: 25-54; male. ♦Greg Thornton, pres & gen mgr; Al Mann, opns mgr.

Russellville

WGOL(AM)— May 29, 1949: 920 khz; 1 kw-D, 43 w-N. TL: N34 30 50 W87 42 55. 113 N. Washington Ave. 35653. Phone: (256) 332-0214. Fax: (256) 332-6104. Licensee: McCurry Broadcasting Co. Inc. (acq 7-29-98; $75,000). Format: Golden oldies. News: 9 hrs wkly. Target aud: 25-60. Spec prog: Black gospel 4 hrs, relg 10 hrs wkly. ♦Ron Underwood, stn mgr.

WKAX(AM)— Apr 3, 1974: 1500 khz; 1 kw-D. TL: N34 31 42 W87 42 41. 113 Washington Ave. N.W. 35653. Phone: (256) 332-6104. Phone: (256) 332-6103. Fax: (256) 332-7430. Licensee: Jamar Communications Inc. (acq 1999; $65,000). Format: Southern gospel, Sp. Target aud: 21-54. Spec prog: Black 4 hrs wkly. ♦Marshall R. Moore, pres & gen mgr.

WMXV(FM)— Sept 12, 1986: 103.5 mhz; 3.5 kw. Ant 430 ft. TL: N34 35 44 W87 40 47. Stereo. Phone: (256) 383-2525. Fax: (256) 389-1912. Web Site: www.mix1035.com. Licensee: Urban Radio Licenses LLC. Group owner: Clear Channel Communications Inc. (acq 5-13-2005; grpsl). Fletcher, Heald & Hildreth. Format: Oldies. News staff: one. Target aud: 18-49. ♦Todd Mannesses, opns mgr; Laura Crosby, news dir & pub affrs dir; Rob Green, chief of engrg.

Saraland

WKTT(AM)—Not on air, target date: unknown; 1160 khz; 15 kw-D, 250 w-N, DA-N. TL: N30 50 19 W88 05 32. 415 N. College St., Greenville 36037. Phone: (334) 382-8048. Licensee: Brantley Broadcast Associates. ♦Joan Reynolds, gen mgr.

Scottsboro

WKEA-FM— Nov 3, 1965: 98.3 mhz; 6 kw. 531 ft. TL: N34 34 50 W85 47 30. Stereo. 19784 John T. Reid Pkwy. 35768. Phone: (256) 259-2341. Fax: (256) 574-2156. E-mail: ron@wkeafm.com. Web site: www.wkeafm.com. Licensee: KEA Radio Inc. (group owner) Network: ABC Information & Entertainment. Format: Country. News staff: one; News: 2 hrs wkly. Target aud: 25-54. Spec prog: Farm one hr, relg 4 hrs wkly. ♦Gene Sisk, VP; Ronald H. Livengood, CEO, pres & gen mgr; Campbell Smith, opns mgr.

WWIC(AM)— June 13, 1950: 1050 khz; 1 kw-D, 101 w-N. TL: N34 40 23 W86 03 11. Box 759, 815 W. Willow St. 35768. Phone: (256) 259-1050. Fax: (256) 575-2411. E-mail: wwic@scottsboro.org. Web Site: www.wwicradio.com. Licensee: Scottsboro Broadcasting Co. Inc. (acq 1-14-2005; $88,306. for 50%). Format: C&W. News staff: one. ♦Greg Bell, pres & gen mgr.

WZCT(AM)— June 11, 1952: 1330 khz; 5 kw-D, 38 w-N. TL: N34 42 07 W86 00 15. Drawer A, 2002 E. Willow St. 35768. Phone: (256) 574-1330. Fax: (256) 218-3013. Licensee: Bonner and Carlile Enterprises. (acq 2-28-90). Network: Network: Reach Satellite, USA. Format: Southern gospel. News: 14 hrs wkly. Target aud: 25 plus. Spec prog: Sports 19 hrs wkly. ♦Rob Carlile, gen mgr, stn mgr, opns mgr & gen sls mgr; Mickey Bell, prom dir.

Selma

WALX(FM)—Listing follows WMRK(AM).

***WAPR(FM)**— May 5, 1996: 88.3 mhz; 1.85 kw horiz, 53 kw vert. 1,401 ft. TL: N32 08 30 W86 44 43. Phifer Hall Annex, Suite 166, Tuscaloosa 35487. Phone: (205) 348-6644. Fax: (205) 348-6648. Web Site: www.apr.org. Licensee: Ua-Asu-Tsu Educational Radio Corp. Network: Network: NPR, PRI. Format: Class, jazz, news. ♦Roger Duvall, pres & stn mgr.

***WAQU(FM)**— March 1998: 91.1 mhz; 21.5 kw. Ant 335 ft. TL: N32 24 17 W87 25 32. Box 3206, American Family Radio, Tupelo, MS 38803. Phone: (662) 844-8888. Fax: (662) 842-6791. Web site: www.afr.net. Licensee: American Family Association. Group owner: American Family Radio Format: Inspirational Christian. ♦Don Wildmon, CEO; Tim Wildmon, exec VP; Marvin Sanders, gen mgr; John Riley, progmg dir; Fred Jackson, news dir; Shan Easterling, chief of engrg.

WBFZ(FM)— 2001: 105.3 mhz; 50 kw. Ant 492 ft. TL: N32 16 18 W87 15 28. 1501 Jeff Davis Ave. 36703. Phone: (334) 872-2177. Fax: (334) 872-5577. Licensee: Inami Communications Corp. Inc. Format: Urban contemp. ♦Henry Sanders, pres; Charles Jones, gen mgr.

WDXX(FM)—Listing follows WHBB(AM).

WHBB(AM)— Nov 11, 1935: 1490 khz; 1 kw-U. TL: N32 26 02 W87 00 40. Box 1055 36702. Secondary address: 505 Lauderdale St. 36701. Phone: (334) 875-3350. Fax: (334) 874-6959. Web Site: www.wdxx.com. Licensee: Broadsouth Communications Inc. (acq 7-24-92; $400,000 with co-located FM; 8-17-92). Network: ABC Information & Entertainment. Rep: Rgnl Reps. Format: News/talk. News staff: one; News: 13 hrs wkly. Target aud: 25-54. Spec prog: Black 18 hrs, farm 10 hrs wkly. ♦Mike Reynolds, gen mgr.

WDXX(FM)— Co-owned with WHBB(AM). September 1965: 100.1 mhz; 50 kw. 288 ft. TL: N32 26 02 W87 00 40. Stereo. Format: Country. News staff: 2; News: 5 hrs wkly.

WMRK(AM)— Dec 19, 1946: 1340 khz; 1 kw-U. TL: N32 25 31 W86 59 47. 273 Persimmon Tree Rd. 36701. Phone: (334) 875-9360. Fax: (334) 875-1340. E-mail: walt@bellsouth.net. Licensee: Alexander Broadcasting Co. Inc. (acq 4-20-2005; with co-located FM). Format: Oldies. Target aud: 25-49. ♦Betty Alexander, mus dir; Scott Alexander, pres, gen mgr, progmg dir & chief of engrg.

WALX(FM)—Co-owned with WMRK(AM). Dec 12, 1973: 100.9 mhz; 50 kw. Ant 492 ft. TL: N32 21 40 W86 52 28. Stereo. Format: Hot adult contemp. Target aud: 18-40.

***WRNF(FM)**—Not on air, target date: unknown: 89.5 mhz; 6 kw vert. Ant 328 ft. TL: N32 32 50 W86 55 33. The Moody Bible Institute of Chicago, 820 N. LaSalle St., Chicago, IL 60610-3214. Phone: (312) 329-4301. Fax: (312) 329-8980. Licensee: The Moody Bible Institute of Chicago. ♦Robert C. Neff, VP & gen mgr.

Sheffield

***WAKD(FM)**— 1996: 89.9 mhz; 1 kw. 125 ft. TL: N34 44 25 W87 42 58. Box 3206, Tupelo, MS 38803. Phone: (662) 844-8888. Fax: (662) 842-6791. Web Site: www.afr.net. Licensee: American Family Association. Group owner: American Family Radio Format: Inspirational Christian. ♦Marvin Sanders, gen mgr; John Riley, progmg dir; Joey Moody, chief of engrg.

WBTG(AM)— Nov 6, 1963: 1290 khz; 1 kw-D, 79 w-N. TL: N34 46 27 W87 40 14. Box 518 35660. Secondary address: 1605 Gospel Rd. 35660. Phone: (256) 381-6800. Fax: (256) 381-6801. E-mail: announcements@wbtgradio.com. Web Site: www.wbtgradio.com. Licensee: Slatton & Associates. (acq 12-17-87). Network: Salem Radio Network. Format: Christian, talk, relg. Target aud: 25 up; conservative, mainstream family audience. ♦Paul Slatton, pres & gen mgr; Scott Carrier, prom dir; Dan Michaels, progmg dir; Orvil Nichols, mus dir.

WBTG-FM— July 2, 1969: 106.3 mhz; 6 kw. 682 ft. TL: N34 41 34 W87 47 49. Stereo. Phone: (205) 381-6800. Web Site: www.wbtgradio.com. (Acq 1-17-78). Format: Southern gospel. News: 12 hrs wkly. ♦Joyce Slatton, VP & mktg dir; Chuck Bradford, prom dir; Jerry Eagil, mus dir; Keith Balch, pub affrs dir.

Smiths

WBFA(FM)— 1998: 101.3 mhz; 6 kw. 328 ft. TL: N32 25 35 W85 08 20. Box 687, Columbus, GA 31902. Secondary address: 1501 13th Ave., Columbus, GA 31901. Phone: (706) 576-3000. Fax: (706) 576-3005. Web Site: b101online.com. Licensee: Clear Channel Broadcasting Licenses Inc. Group owner: Clear Channel Communications Inc. (acq 2-21-02; grpsl). Format: CHR. ♦Jim Martin, gen mgr & stn mgr.

Stevenson

WMXN-FM— June 13, 1977: 101.7 mhz; 2.3 kw. Ant 541 ft. TL: N34 41 02 W85 48 04. Stereo. Box 966, 19784 John T. Reid Pkwy., Scottsboro 35768. Phone: (256) 259-2341. Fax: (256) 574-2156. E-mail: ron@wkeafm.com. Web site: www.wkeafm.com. Licensee: KEA Radio Inc. (group owner; acq 1996). Fletcher, Heald & Hildreth. Format: Classic rock. ♦Gene Sisk, VP; Ron Livengood, pres & gen mgr; Campbell Smith, opns dir.

Sulligent

WVSA(AM)—See Vernon

Sumiton

WRSM(AM)— June 27, 1978: . Stn currently dark 1540 khz; 1 kw-D. TL: N33 45 50 W87 03 47. Box 100 35148. Licensee: Sumiton Broadcasting Co. Inc. ♦T. Herb Steadman, gen mgr.

Sylacauga

WFEB(AM)— March 1945: 1340 khz; 1 kw-U. TL: N33 10 16 W86 13 57. Box 358, 1209 Millerville Hwy. 35150. Phone: (256) 245-3281. Fax: (256) 245-3050. Licensee: Alabama Broadcasting Co Inc. Keystone (unwired net). Gardner, Carton & Douglas. Format: News/talk, sports. News staff: 3; News: 17 hrs wkly. Target aud: 25-54. Spec prog: Gospel 6 hrs wkly. ♦Bruce C. Carr, pres, gen mgr & gen sls mgr.

WTRB-FM— Dec 20, 1959: 98.3 mhz; 5 kw. 502 ft. TL: N33 12 23 W86 13 54. Stereo. Box 26, Ashland 36251. Phone: (256) 354-4600. Fax: (256) 354-7224. E-mail: b98@b98.biz. Web Site: www.b98.biz. Licensee: Williams Communications Inc. (group owner; acq 8-16-01). Network: ABC. Format: Adult contemp. News staff: one. Target aud: 25-54; mainly women. Spec prog: Black gospel 6 hrs wkly. ♦Cindy Stewart, VP & chief of opns; Walt Williams, gen mgr.

WYEA(AM)— May 16, 1948: 1290 khz; 1 kw-D, 50 w-N. TL: N33 11 15 W86 14 06. Box 629, One Motes Rd. 35150. Phone: (256) 249-4263. Fax: (256) 245-4355. E-mail: wyea@rocketmail.com. Web Site: wyearadio.com. Licensee: Spirit Broadcasting Co. Inc. (acq 4-13-2001). IRN Format: Christian country. News: 7 hrs wkly. Target aud: General. ♦John Vogel, pres & gen mgr; Brandon Baird, opns dir.

Talladega

WNUZ(AM)— 1945: 1230 khz; 1 kw-U. TL: N33 25 16 W86 07 13. 1301 Fort Lashley Ave. 35160. Phone: (256) 480-6040. Fax: (256) 480-6050. Licensee: Birmingham Christian Radio Inc. (acq 5-13-97; $30,000). Format: Full gospel. News staff: one. Target aud: 25-70; middle/upper middle, blue & white collar. Spec prog: Talk 5 hrs, Gospel 7 hrs, bluegrass 6 hrs wkly. ♦L.E. Willis Sr., pres; Jonnie Luster, gen mgr.

WTDR(FM)— Nov 10, 1972: 92.7 mhz; 250 w. 870 ft. TL: N33 24 42 W86 12 20. (CP: 400 w). Stereo. Drawer 329 35161. Secondary address: 34915 Alabama Hwy. 21 35160. Phone: (256) 741-6000. Fax: (256) 741-6080. Web Site: www.thunder927.com. Licensee: Jacobs Broadcast Group Inc. (acq 9-16-92; $570,000; 10-19-92). Format: Modern country. ♦James H. Jacobs, pres & gen mgr; Grady Sapp, opns mgr; Gloria Goode, gen sls mgr; Bill Moats, chief of engrg.

WZLM(FM)— Apr 4, 1990: 97.5 mhz; 2 kw. Ant 574 ft. TL: N33 25 00 W86 05 04. (CP: COL Goodwater. 5.1 kw, ant 354 ft. TL: N33 01 42 W85 59 23). Stereo. 702 E Battle St., Suite A 35160. Fax: (256) 761-9700. E-mail: star975@aol.com. Licensee: Great South RFDC LLC (group owner; acq 3-24-2003; $1.25 million). Network: CBS. Format: Oldies. News staff: one; News: 40 hrs wkly. Target aud: 25-54. ♦Paul Reynolds, pres.

Tallassee

WACQ(AM)—(Carrville). June 30, 1979: 1130 khz; 1 kw-D. TL: N32 33 22 W85 52 17. 320 Barnett Blvd. 36078. Phone: (334) 283-6888. Fax: (334) 283-6358. E-mail: WACQradio@elmore.rr.com. Licensee: Progressive United Communications Inc. (group owner; (acq 2-3-2000; $165,000). Network: ABC. Richard J. Hayes, Jr. Format: Oldies. News staff: one; News: 7 hrs wkly. Target aud: 25-54; baby boomers. Spec prog: Farm one hr, gospel 5 hrs wkly. ♦Randall Hughey, gen mgr.

WQNR(FM)— Oct 29, 1992: 99.9 mhz; 3.1 kw. 452 ft. TL: N32 34 37 W85 51 43. 2514 S. College St., Suite 104, Auburn 36832. Phone: (334) 887-9999. Fax: (334) 826-9599. Web Site: www.wqnr.com. Licensee: Tiger Communications Inc. (acq 1999; $686,000. plus $200 per game of Auburn University Women's Basketball season) Network: ABC. Gardner, Carton & Douglas. Format: AOR. Target aud: 25-54; adults. ♦Tom Hayley, pres & gen mgr; Kevin Jackson, opns dir.

WTLS(AM)— June 1, 1954: 1300 khz; 1.2 kw-D, 18 w-N. TL: N32 30 39 W85 53 33. Box 780146 36078. Secondary address: 2045 Hwy 229 36078. Phone: (334) 283-8200. Fax: (334) 283-8622. Web Site: www.1300wtls.com. Licensee: Michael Butler Broadcasting LLC (acq 8-24-99). Format: Full service. Spec prog: Farm 6 hrs wkly. ♦Michael Butler, pres & gen mgr; Leigh Anne Butler, gen sls mgr; Steve Butler, progmg VP.

Thomaston

WSMO(FM)— 2001: . Stn currently dark 97.7 mhz; 500 w. Ant 46 ft. TL: N32 16 49 W87 38 06. (CP: 3.7 kw, ant 423 ft. TL: N32 26 33 W87 46 04). 415 College St., Greenville 36037. Phone: (334) 382-8048. Phone: (334) 382-3239. Licensee: Great South RFDC L.L.C. (group owner; acq 11-28-2003; $375,000).

Thomasville

WJDB(AM)— July 16, 1956: 630 khz; 1 kw. TL: N31 52 58 W87 44 42. Box 219, 2211 Hwy. 43 S. 36784. Phone: (334) 636-4438. Fax: (334) 636-4439. E-mail: wjdb@dixienet1.com. Licensee: Griffin Broadcasting Corp. (acq 1-4-91; $375,000 with co-located FM; 1-28-91). Network: CBS. Format: Grooving oldies. News staff: one; News: 10 hrs wkly. Target aud: General. ♦Ivy Griffin, gen mgr, gen sls mgr & gen sls mgr.

WJDB-FM— Nov 2, 1972: 95.5 mhz; 9.6 kw. 525 ft. TL: N31 52 58 W87 44 42. Stereo. E-mail: wjdb@dixienet1.com. Format: Top 40 country. News: 10 hrs wkly. Target aud: General.

Trinity

WWXQ(FM)— Oct 4, 1992: 92.5 mhz; 3.1 kw. 423 ft. TL: N34 42 36 W87 04 54. Stereo. Box 789, Decatur 35758. Secondary address: 200 Lime Quarry Rd., Madison 35758. Phone: (256) 837-1021. Fax: (256) 350-2653. Web Site: www.wxqw.com. Licensee: Capstar TX L.P. Group owner: Clear Channel Communications Inc. (acq 8-30-00; grpsl). Format: Oldies. News: 6 hrs wkly. Target aud: 25-44; general. ♦Rick Brown, gen mgr; Todd Berry, opns mgr; Carmelita Palmer, gen sls mgr; Bruce Reynolds, progmg dir; Carl Ampieri, chief of engrg.

Troy

***WAXU(FM)**— 2001: 91.1 mhz; 1.089 kw. Ant 246 ft. TL: N31 47 22 W85 58 58. Drawer 3206, American Family Radio, Tupelo, MS 38803. Phone: (662) 844-8888. Fax: (662) 842-6791. Web Site: www.afr.net. Licensee: American Family Association. Group owner: American Family Radio Format: Inspirational Christian. ♦Marvin Sanders, gen mgr; John Riley, progmg dir.

WTBF(AM)— Feb 25, 1947: 970 khz; 5 kw-D, 500 w-N, DA-N. TL: N31 50 04 W85 56 00. 67 Court Sq. 36081. Phone: (334) 566-0300. Fax: (334) 566-5689. Web Site: www.wtbf.com. Licensee: Troy Broadcasting Corp. Format: Talk, community intensive progmg. News: 20 hrs wkly. Target aud: 35 plus; general. Spec prog: Farm 17 hrs wkly. ♦Jim Roling, VP & gen mgr; Dave Kirby, opns mgr & progmg dir; Joe Gilchrist, pres, chief of opns & chief of engrg.

***WTSU(FM)**— Mar 1, 1977: 89.9 mhz; 100 kw. 560 ft. TL: N32 03 33 W86 01 22. Stereo. Wallace Hall, Troy State Univ. 36082. Phone: (334) 670-3268. Fax: (334) 670-3934. E-mail: wtsu@troyst.edu. Web Site: wtsu.troyst.edu. Licensee: Troy State University. Network: Network: NPR, PRI. Format: News. Classical. News: 25 hrs wkly. Target aud: General. Spec prog: Children one hr wkly. ♦James Clower, gen mgr; Judy Davis, opns mgr; Fred Azbell, progmg dir & progmg mgr.

WZHT(FM)— Feb 28, 1973: 105.7 mhz; 100 kw. Ant 1,830 ft. TL: N31 58 28 W86 09 44. Stereo. Box 4420, Montgomery 36103. Secondary address: 203 Gunn Rd., Montgomery 36117. Phone: (334) 274-6464. Fax: (334) 274-6465. Web Site: www.myhot105.com. Licensee: Capstar TX L.P. Group owner: Clear Channel Communications Inc. (acq 8-30-00; grpsl). Network: Network: ABC, Westwood One. Rep: McGavren Guild. Latham & Watkins. Format: Urban. Target aud: 18-49. ♦Arnessa Leverett, gen mgr.

Tuscaloosa

WACT(AM)— September 1958: 1420 khz; 5 kw-D, 108 w-N. TL: N33 10 30 W87 33 18. Box 20126 35402-0126. Secondary address: 2121 9th St., Suite B 35401. Phone: (205) 344-4589. Fax: (205) 366-9774. E-mail: chrischampion@clearchannel.com. Licensee: Capstar TX L.P. Group owner: Clear Channel Communications Inc. (acq 8-30-2000; grpsl). Format: Sports. Target aud: 35 plus. ♦Lori Moore, gen mgr; Will Johnson, progmg dir; Missy Elmore, pub affrs dir; Lete Connelly, engrg dir & chief of engrg.

WRTR(FM)—Co-owned with WACT(AM). June 1, 1966: 105.9 mhz; 25 kw. Ant 269 ft. TL: N33 14 17 W87 29 06. Stereo. Network: USA. Format: Rock. Target aud: 25 plus.

WBHJ(FM)— 1952: 95.7 mhz; 100 kw. 981 ft. TL: N33 05 38 W87 15 15. Stereo. 950 22nd St. N., Suite 1000, Birmingham 35203. Phone: (205) 322-2987. Fax: (205) 322-2667. Web Site: www.957.jamz.com. Licensee: CXR Holdings L.L.C. Group owner: Cox Broadcasting (acq 10-6-98; $17 million. with WBHK(FM) Warrior). Network: Westwood One. Rep: Christal. Dow, Lohnes & Albertson. Format: CHR. News staff: one; News: one hr wkly. Target aud: 18-34; upscale baby boomers. Spec prog: Relg 5 hrs wkly. ♦Bob Neil, CEO; Neil Johnson, CFO; David DuBose, VP & gen mgr.

WJRD(AM)— Oct 10, 1936: 1150 khz; 5 kw-D, 1 kw-N, DA-N. TL: N33 15 02 W87 36 35. 142 Skyland Blvd. 35405. Phone: (205) 345-7200. Licensee: Citadel Broadcasting Co. (group owner; (acq 7-12-2005; grpsl). Network: ABC. Format: Btfl mus. Target aud: 35 plus; persons. ♦Davis Hawkins, gen mgr & gen sls mgr; Brenda BeBout, sls dir; Greg Thomas, stn mgr & progmg mgr.

***WMFT(FM)**— 2005: . Stn currently dark 88.9 mhz; 100 kw vert. Ant 522 ft. TL: N33 20 21 W87 21 31. The Moody Bible Institute of Chicago, 820 N. LaSalle Blvd., Chicago, IL 60610. Phone: (312) 329-4438. Licensee: The Moody Bible Institute of Chicago (group owner).

WTBC(AM)— Dec 23, 1946: 1230 khz; 1 kw-U. TL: N33 12 05 W87 32 00. Box 2000 35403. Secondary address: 2110 McFarland Blvd. E., Suite C 35404. Phone: (205) 758-5523. Fax: (205) 752-9696. E-mail: wtbc@dbtech.net. Web Site: www.wtbc1230.com. Licensee: John Sisty Enterprises Inc. (acq 2-14-02). Network: ABC. Alabama Net. Tim K. Brady. Format: News/talk, sports. News: 3 hrs wkly. Target aud: 25-54; upscale, affluent. Spec prog: Relg 3 hrs wkly. ♦John Sisty, CEO & pres; Dave McDaniel, opns mgr; Ronnie Quarles, COO, gen mgr & sls dir.

WTSK(AM)— February 1958: 790 khz; 5 kw-D, 36 w-N. TL: N33 11 17 W87 35 23. 142 Skyland Blvd. 35405. Phone: (205) 345-7200. Fax: (205) 349-1715. Web Site: www.wtug.com. Licensee: Citadel Broadcasting Co. (group owner; (acq 7-12-2005; grpsl). Rep: McGavren Guild. Format: Gospel. Target aud: 35 plus. ♦Voncile R. Pearce, gen mgr; Charles Anthony, opns mgr; Todd Livingston, gen sls mgr; Raven Guy, news dir; Olen Booth, chief of engrg.

WTUG(FM)—Co-owned with WTSK(AM). March 1979: 92.9 mhz; 100 kw. 981 ft. TL: N33 05 40 W87 29 58. Stereo. 142 Skyland Blvd. 35405. Phone: (205) 345-7200. Fax: (205) 349-1715. Format: Adult contemp. Target aud: 25-54. ♦Charles Anthony, progmg dir.

***WUAL-FM**— Jan 4, 1982: 91.5 mhz; 100 kw. 523 ft. TL: N33 05 40 W87 24 47. Stereo. Phifer Annex, Suite 166 35487. Phone: (205) 348-6644. Fax: (205) 348-6648. Licensee: Board of Trustees of the University of Alabama. Network: Network: PRI, NPR. Alabama Net. Arter & Hadden. Format: Class, jazz, news/talk. News staff: 3; News: 5 hrs wkly. Target aud: 35 plus. Spec prog: Bluegrass, blues, folk 5 hrs, new age 20 hrs wkly. ♦Roger Duvall, gen mgr & stn mgr.

***WVUA-FM**— Sept 7, 1972: 90.7 mhz; 160 w. 142 ft. TL: N33 12 33 W87 32 57. Stereo. Box 870152 35487-0152. Phone: (205) 348-6461. Fax: (205) 348-0375. E-mail: wvua@sa.ua.edu. Web Site: www.newrock907.com. Licensee: Board of Trustees University of Alabama. Format: Alternative. Target aud: 18-25; high school & college students. Spec prog: Christian 3 hrs, hardcore 3 hrs, blues 3 hrs, heavy metal 4 hrs, reggae 3 hrs wkly. ♦Loy Singleton, gen mgr; Graham Flaugan, stn mgr.

WWPG(AM)— Dec 10, 1951: 1280 khz; 5 kw-D, 500 w-N, DA-N. TL: N33 13 07 W87 34 05. 601 Greensboro Ave., Suite 507 35401. Phone: (205) 345-4787. Fax: (205) 345-4790. Licensee: Lawson of Tuscaloosa Inc. (acq 3-17-93; $160,000; 4-5-93). Network: Westwood One. Taylor, Smith & Parker. Format: Gospel. Target aud: 24-54; mature business audience. Spec prog: Jazz 2 hrs wkly. ♦Jim Lawson, pres & gen mgr; Mildred Porter, opns mgr.

Tuscumbia

WLAY-FM— May 2, 1962: 100.3 mhz; 100 kw. Ant 245 ft. TL: N34 45 24 W87 41 10. (CP: TL: N34 40 24 W87 42 56). Stereo. 509 N. Main St. 35674. Phone: (256) 383-2525. Fax: (256) 389-1912. Web Site: www.wlayfm.com. Licensee: Clear Channel Broadcasting Licenses Inc. (acq 12-19-2000; grpsl). Format: Country. News staff: 2; News: 60 hrs wkly. Target aud: 18-34. ♦Kevin Wagner, gen mgr; Jim Jackson, progmg dir.

WVNA(AM)— Apr 5, 1955: 1590 khz; 5 kw-D, 1 kw-N, DA-N. TL: N34 45 24 W87 36 35. 509 N. Main St. 35674. Phone: (256) 383-2525. Fax: (256) 389-1912. E-mail: donnajohnson@clearchannel.com. Licensee: Urban Radio Licenses LLC. Group owner: Clear Channel Communications Inc. (acq 5-13-2005; grpsl). Network: Network: CBS, ABC News/Talk. Format: News/talk, sports. News staff: 3; News: 60 hrs wkly. Target aud: 25-64. Spec prog: Atlanta Braves Network, loc talk shows & sport shows. ♦Kevin Wagner, gen mgr.

WZZA(AM)— Apr 17, 1960: 1410 khz; 500 w-D, 51 w-N. TL: N34 42 29 W87 41 35. 1570 Woodmont Dr. 35674. Phone: (256) 381-1862. Phone: (256) 383-5810. Fax: (256) 381-6006. E-mail: wzzaradio@aol.com. Licensee: Muscle Shoals Broadcasting. (acq 12-1-77). Network: American Urban. Format: Black, relg, urban contemp. News: 15 hrs wkly. Target aud: Black. ♦Jurado Bailey, pres & CFO; Tori Bailey, CEO, gen mgr & gen mgr; Dwight Winston, opns dir.

Stations in the U.S. — Alaska

Tuskegee

WBIL(AM)— July 1, 1952: 580 khz; 500 w-D, 139 w-N. TL: N32 22 36 W85 39 28. 118 S. Main St. 36083. Phone: (334) 727-2100. Fax: (334) 724-9169. Licensee: H&H Communications L.L.C. Group owner: Willis Broadcasting Corp. (acq 2-23-2005; $210,000). Format: Gospel. ♦Bernita Luke, gen mgr; Terry Harper, chief of engrg.

WTGZ(FM)— July 12, 1975: 95.9 mhz; 4.3 kw. 377 ft. TL: N32 28 17 W85 34 28. Stereo. 2514 S. College St., Suite 104, Auburn 36830. Phone: (334) 887-9999. Fax: (334) 826-9599. E-mail: info@thetiger.fm. Web Site: www.wtgz.com. Licensee: Tiger Communications Inc. (acq 2-26-98; $450,000). Format: Modern rock. Target aud: 18-34. ♦Tom Hayley, pres; Chris Bailey, gen mgr; Kevin Jackson, opns dir.

Union Springs

WQSI(FM)— Oct 15, 1975: 93.9 mhz; 12.5 kw. Ant 469 ft. TL: N32 19 04 W85 40 16. Stereo. 320 Barnett Blvd., Tallassee 36078. Phone: (334) 283-6888. Fax: (334) 283-6358. E-mail: wacqradio@elmore.rr.com. Licensee: H&H Communications L.L.C. (acq 5-20-2003; $450,000). Network: ABC. Richard J. Hayes Jr. Format: Classic country. News: 15 wkly. Target aud: 25-54; 40+ boomers, active, affluent southerners. ♦Randall Hughey, CEO; Fred Randall Hughey, gen mgr.

Valley

*WEBT(FM)— Jan 17, 1986: 91.5 mhz; 380 w. 85 ft. TL: N32 48 15 W85 10 43. 2615 64th Blvd. 36854. Phone: (334) 756-6923. Fax: (334) 756-8430. Licensee: Langdale Educational Broadcasting Foundation. Format: Southern gospel. Target aud: General. Spec prog: Southern gospel. ♦Tim Foster, stn mgr.

WRLD-FM— May 17, 1993: 95.3 mhz; 25 kw. Ant 328 ft. TL: N32 44 03 W85 07 53. 1353 13th Ave., Columbus, GA 31901. Phone: (706) 327-1217. Fax: (706) 596-4600. Web Site: www.boomer.fm. Licensee: ABG Georgia LLC. Group owner: Archway Broadcasting Group (acq 4-25-03; grpsl); Holland & Knight. Format: Oldies. Target aud: 35 plus. ♦Chuck Thompson, gen mgr.

Valley Head

WQRX(AM)— Feb 10, 1986: 870 kpz; 10 kw-D. TL: N34 33 20 W85 37 12. 2278 Wortham Ln., Grovetown, GA 30813. Phone: (706) 309-9610. Fax: (706) 309-9669. E-mail: cbarinowski@comcast.net. Web Site: www.gnnradio.org. Licensee: Barinowski Investment Co. Group owner: Good News Network (acq 10-13-99). Format: Sp. All Sp. Spec prog: Alabama Crimson Tide football & basketball games, Sp wkly. ♦Clarence Barinowski, pres, gen mgr, gen mgr & progmg dir; Nancy Fauekner, gen sls mgr & progmg dir.

Vernon

WJEC(FM)—Listing follows WVSA(AM).

WVSA(AM)— July 4, 1966: 1380 khz; 5 kw-D, 39 w-N. TL: N33 47 45 W88 07 03. Box 630 35592. Phone: (205) 695-9191. Fax: (205) 695-9131. E-mail: wjec1065@yahoo.com. Licensee: Lamar County Broadcasting Co. Inc. Format: Sports, talk. ♦Patricia Davis, gen mgr.

WJEC(FM)—Co-owned with WVSA(AM). Apr 1, 1991: 106.5 mhz; 6 kw. 328 ft. TL: N33 51 15 W88 01 55. Format: Southern gospel. ♦R. William Davis, CEO; Randy Wright, prom mgr; Curt Smith, progmg mgr.

Warrior

WBHK(FM)— Apr 22, 1992: 98.7 mhz; 14 kw. 945 ft. TL: N33 27 45 W86 50 59. 950 22nd St., Suite 1000, Birmingham 35203. Phone: (205) 322-2987. Fax: (205) 741-0987. E-mail: (205) 322-2390. E-mail: kissrequests@cox.com. Web Site: www.987kiss.com.Yes Licensee: CXR Holdings L.L.C. Group owner: Cox Broadcasting (acq 10-6-98; $17 million. with WBHJ(FM) Tuscaloosa). Network: ABC Information & Entertainment. Rep: Christal. Dow, Lohnes & Albertson. Format: Urban adult contemp. News staff: 2; News: 5 hrs wkly. Target aud: 25-54; general. ♦Bob Neil, pres; David DuBose, VP & gen mgr.

Wetumpka

WAPZ(AM)— Oct 2, 1954: 1250 khz; 5 kw-D, 80 w-N. TL: N32 29 06 W86 12 25. 2821 U.S. Hwy. 231 36092. Phone: (334) 567-2251. Fax: (334) 567-7971. Web Site: www.1250wapz.com. Licensee: J&W L.L.C. (acq 9-1-84; $235,000; 7-23-84). Format: Relg, Black, blues, news/talk, sports. Target aud: 12-100. ♦Johnny Roland, pres; Robert Henderson, gen mgr & gen sls mgr.

WJWZ(FM)— 1998: 97.9 mhz; 3 kw. 328 ft. TL: N32 27 08 W86 12 35. 4101-A Wall St., Montgomery 36106. Phone: (334) 244-0961. Fax: (334) 279-9563. Web Site: www.979-jamz.com. Licensee: Bluewater Broadcasting Co. LLC (group owner; acq 4-21-2004; grpsl). Format: Urban. ♦Terry Barber, gen mgr.

Winfield

WKXM(AM)— Aug 23, 1965: 1300 khz; 5 kw-D, 30 w-N, DA-D. TL: N33 55 52 W87 48 36. Box 608 35594. Secondary address: 655 Fairview Rd. 35594. Phone: (205) 487-3261. Fax: (205) 487-6991. E-mail: wkxm@dlis.net. Licensee: Ad-Media Management Corp. (acq 12-30-91; $365,000 with co-located FM; 1-27-92). Network: Network: Westwood One, CNN Radio. Format: Country, relg. Target aud: General. Spec prog: Sports 3 hrs wkly. ♦Maxine Harper, pres, gen mgr & gen sls mgr; Teresa Benton, opns mgr & mus dir; Doug Threadgill, news dir; Olen Booth, engrg mgr.

WKXM-FM— 1991: 97.7 mhz; 3.9 kw. Ant 403 ft. TL: N34 01 53 W87 48 06. Network: ABC. Format: Oldies. Target aud: General.

York

WSLY(FM)—Listing follows WYLS(AM).

WYLS(AM)— November 1970: 670 khz; 4.8 kw-D. TL: N32 31 24 W88 15 28. 11474 U.S. Hwy. 11 36925. Phone: (205) 392-5234. Fax: (205) 392-5536. Licensee: Grantell Broadcasting Co. (acq 11-21-03; with co-located FM). Format: Classic country. News staff: one; News: 15 hrs wkly. Target aud: 35 plus. ♦Tim Craddock, stn mgr, opns mgr, sls dir, progmg dir & news dir.

WSLY(FM)—Co-owned with WYLS(AM). September 1976: 104.9 mhz; 50 kw. 492 ft. TL: N32 16 54 W88 15 28. Stereo. Format: Urban contemp. News staff: one; News: 10 hrs wkly. Target aud: 18-54; Black. ♦Larry Carr, progmg dir; Gus Weiss, mus dir; Tim Craddock, adv mgr & pub affrs dir.

Alaska

Anchorage

KADX(FM)—(Houston). Apr 1, 1998: 94.7 mhz; 50 kw. Ant 371 ft. TL: N61 29 03 W149 45 52. Stereo. C/O American Radio Brokers, 1255 Post St., Suite 1011, San Francisco, CA 94109. Phone: (907) 277-5652. Phone: (415) 441-3377. Fax: (907) 344-5728. Fax: (415) 674-1480. Licensee: Chester Coleman. Group owner: American Radio Brokers Inc./SFO. Format: Hot talk. Target aud: 25-44; general. ♦Chester P. Coleman, CEO; Susan Richards, opns dir.

KAFC(FM)— Apr 4, 1999: 93.7 mhz; 27 kw. 663 ft. TL: N61 04 02 W149 44 36. Box 210389 99521. Secondary address: 6401 E. Northern Lights Blvd. 99504. Phone: (907) 333-5282. Fax: (907) 333-9851. Web Site: www.kafc.org. Licensee: Christian Broadcasting Inc. Format: Christian contemp music. ♦Tom Steigleman, gen mgr & opns mgr.

*KAKL(FM)— 2004: 88.5 mhz; 11 kw. Ant -82 ft. TL: N61 07 14 W149 53 42. Stereo. 5700 W. Oaks Blvd., Rocklin, CA 95765. Phone: (916) 251-1600. Fax: (916) 251-1650. E-mail: klove@klove.com. Web Site: www.klove.com. Licensee: Educational Media Foundation. Group owner: EMF Broadcasting. Network: K-Love. Shaw Pittman. Format: Contemp Christian. News staff: 3. Target aud: 25-44; Judeo Chrisitan, female. ♦Richard Jenkins, pres; Mike Novak, VP.

KASH-FM— Dec 1, 1985: 107.5 mhz; 100 kw. 1,014 ft. TL: N61 09 53 W149 41 05. Stereo. 800 E. Dimond Blvd., Suite 3-370 99515-2043. Phone: (907) 522-1515. Fax: (907) 743-5184. Web Site: www.kash1075.com. Licensee: Clear Channel Radio Licenses Inc. Group owner: Clear Channel Communications Inc. (acq 8-30-00; grpsl). Format: Country. Target aud: 25-54. ♦Gary Donovan, VP; Andy Lohman, gen mgr; Mark Murphy, opns mgr; Lori Sweet, gen sls mgr; Jim O'Brien, progmg dir; Dan Graft, chief of engrg.

*KATB(FM)— June 1985: 89.3 mhz; 4.9 kw. 572 ft. TL: N61 04 02 W149 44 04. (CP: Ant 344 ft. TL: N61 07 32 W149 42 46). Stereo. Box 210389 99521. Secondary address: 6401 E. Northern Lights Blvd. 99504. Phone: (907) 333-5282. Fax: (907) 333-9851. Web Site: www.katb.org. Licensee: Christian Broadcasting Inc. Network: Moody. Format: Relg. News: 5 hrs wkly. Target aud: 25-49; women. ♦Tom Steigleman, exec VP & gen mgr.

KAXX(AM)—(Eagle River). Dec 25, 1986: . Stn currently dark 1020 khz; 10 kw-U, DA-N. TL: N61 29 03 W149 45 52. 1255 Post St., Suite 1010, San Francisco, CA 94109-6705. Licensee: Chester P. Coleman. Group owner: American Radio Brokers Inc./SFO (acq 2-4-97; $150,000). Network: Network: CBS Radio, Westwood One. News staff: . ♦Chester Coleman, CEO, pres & gen mgr. Co-owned TV: KYES(TV) affil

KBFX(FM)— Oct 1, 1978: 100.5 mhz; 25 kw. 178 ft. TL: N61 11 52 W149 52 31. Stereo. 800 E. Dimond Blvd., Suite 3-370 99515-2043. Phone: (907) 522-1515. Fax: (907) 743-5186. Web Site: www.1005thefox.com. Licensee: Capstar TX L.P. Group owner: Clear Channel Communications Inc. (acq 8-7-00; grpsl). Format: Classic rock. ♦Andy Lohman, gen mgr.

KBRJ(FM)—Listing follows KHAR(AM).

KBYR(AM)— 1948: 700 khz; 10 kw-U. TL: N61 12 25 W149 55 20. 1399 W. 34th Ave., Suite 202 99503. Phone: (907) 278-5297. Fax: (907) 272-5297. E-mail: ttierney@kbyr.com. Web Site: www.wbyr.com. Licensee: Cobb Communications Inc. (acq 5-02.). Network: ABC. Rep: Allied Radio Partners. Format: News/talk. News staff: one. Target aud: 25-54. ♦Tom Tierney, CEO, pres & gen mgr; Justin McDonald, opns dir.

KDBZ(FM)— Feb 1, 1973: 102.1 mhz; 25 kw. 174 ft. TL: N61 20 10 W149 30 46. (CP: 23 kw, ant 82 ft.). Stereo. 11259 Tower Rd. 99515. Phone: (907) 344-4045. Fax: (907) 522-6053. E-mail: anc_dubs@newnw.com. Web Site: www.thebuzzfm.com. Licensee: New Northwest Broadcasters LLC (group owner; acq 8-12-99; $1.3 million). Format: Modern adult contemp. ♦Pete Benedetti, CEO; Trila Bumstead, CFO; Jim Richmond, gen mgr, sls VP & gen sls mgr; Ray Edwards, opns mgr & progmg dir.

KEAG(FM)— 1987: 97.3 mhz; 100 kw. 593 ft. TL: N61 25 22 W149 52 20. 301 Arctic Slope Ave. 99518. Phone: (907) 344-9622. Fax: (907) 349-7326. Web Site: www.kool973.com. Licensee: Morris Communications Corp. Group owner: Morris Communications Inc. (acq 10-15-98; grpsl). Format: Oldies. News staff: one; News: 3 hrs wkly. Target aud: 35-49. ♦Scott Smith, gen mgr.

KENI(AM)— July 15, 1967: 650 khz; 50 kw-U. TL: N61 09 58 W149 49 34. Stereo. 800 E. Dimond Blvd., Suite 3-370 99515. Phone: (907) 522-1515. Fax: (907) 743-5186. Web Site: www.keni650.com. Licensee: Capstar TX L.P. Group owner: Clear Channel Communications Inc. (acq 8-30-00; grpsl). Rep: Christal. Format: Talk. News staff: one; News: 5 hrs wkly. Target aud: 25-64. ♦Andy Lowman, gen mgr.

KGOT(FM)—Co-owned with KENI(AM). Sept 15, 1975: 101.3 mhz; 26 kw. -66 ft. TL: N61 09 58 W149 49 34. Stereo. Fax: (907) 522-0672.

Alaska

Web Site: www.kgot.com. Format: CHR, btfl music. News: 2 hrs wkly. Target aud: 12-44. ♦ Mark Murphy, opns mgr.

KFAT(FM)— Apr 1, 1997: 92.9 mhz; 100 kw. 1,269 ft. TL: N61 21 05 W149 29 10. Stereo. 11259 Tower Rd. 99515. Phone: (907) 344-4045. Fax: (907) 522-6053. E-mail: bpenny@newnw.com. Web Site: www.kfatfm.com. Licensee: New Northwest Broadcasters LLC (group owner; acq 7-30-99; $1.25 million. with KADX(FM) Houston). Network: ABC. Format: Top-40. Target aud: 18-54; men. ♦ Pete Benedetti, CEO; Trila Bumstead, CFO; Jim Richmond, gen mgr & sls VP; Ray Edwards, opns mgr & progmg dir. Co-owned TV: KYES(TV) affil.

KFQD(AM)— 1924: 750 khz; 50 kw-U. TL: N61 08 13 W149 50 06. Stereo. 301 Artic Slope Ave., Suite 200 99518. Phone: (907) 344-9622. Fax: (907) 349-7326. Web Site: www.kfqd.com. Licensee: Morris Communications Corp. Group owner: Morris Communications Inc. (acq 12-1-98; grpsl). Network: ABC Information & Entertainment. Rep: McGavren Guild. Format: News/talk. Target aud: 35 plus; higher income, upper demo. ♦ Dennis Bookey, gen mgr; Lindsey Silver, prom dir & prom mgr; Sharon Leighow, news dir; Paul Jewusiak, chief of engrg.

KWHL(FM)—Co-owned with KFQD(AM). Sept 18, 1982: 106.5 mhz; 100 kw. -89 ft. TL: N61 08 13 W149 50 06. Stereo. Web Site: www.kwhl.com. Format: Rock/AOR. Target aud: 18-44; medium income adults, mostly men. ♦ Larry Snider, progmg dir.

KHAR(AM)— Jan 7, 1961: 590 khz; 5 kw-U. TL: N61 07 12 W149 53 43. Stereo. 301 Artic Slope Ave., Suite 200 99518. Phone: (907) 344-9622. Fax: (907) 349-7326. Web Site: www.todayinak.com. Licensee: MCC Radio LLC. Group owner: Morris Communications Inc. (acq 12-1-98; grpsl). Rep: McGavren Guild. Format: Easy lstng. News: 3 hrs wkly. Target aud: 35 plus; white collar, professional, upper-income demographics. ♦ Dennis Bookey, gen mgr; Ron Clement, gen sls mgr; Paul Jewusiak, chief of engrg.

KLEF(FM)— Sept 16, 1988: 98.1 mhz; 25 kw. Ant -85 ft. TL: N61 11 17 W149 52 57. Stereo. 3601 C St., Suite 290 99503. Phone: (907) 561-5556. Fax: (907) 562-4219. E-mail: klef@klef.com. Licensee: Chinook Concert Broadcasters Inc. (acq 6-87; FTR: 6-8-87). Tacher. Format: Classical. Target aud: 25-64; highly educated, affluent adults. Spec prog: Children one hr wkly. ♦ Rich McClear, pres, progmg dir & news dir; Rick Goodfellow, gen mgr & stn mgr; Ron Zastron, chief of engrg.

KUDO(AM)—Co-owned with KLEF(FM). May 10, 1975: 1080 khz; 10 kw-U. TL: N61 07 12 W149 53 43. (Acq 10-14-97; $135,000). Rep: Allied Radio Partners. Format: News/talk. Target aud: 25 plus.

KMXS(FM)— Sept 1, 1987: 103.1 mhz; 100 kw. Ant 105 ft. TL: N61 11 33 W149 54 01. Stereo. 301 Artic Slope Ave. 99518. Phone: (907) 344-9622. Fax: (907) 349-7326. Web Site: www.kmxs.com. Licensee: Morris Communications Corp. Group owner: Morris Communications Inc. (acq 10-15-98; grpsl). Rep: McGavren Guild. Format: Hot adult contemp. News staff: one; News: 5 hrs wkly. Target aud: 25-44; female listeners. ♦ Scott Smith, gen mgr.

***KNBA(FM)**— September 1996: 90.3 mhz; 100 kw. 640 ft. TL: N61 25 22 W149 52 20. Stereo. 818 E. 9th Ave. 99501-3826. Phone: (907) 258-8880. Fax: (907) 258-8803. Web Site: www.knba.org. Licensee: Koahnic Broadcast Corp. Format: var/div. News staff: 3; News: 8 hrs wkly. Target aud: 20-50; well off, public radio listeners. ♦ Jaclyn Sallee, pres; Bruce Hilton, CFO; Liz Fullerton, opns mgr & dev mgr.

KNIK-FM— Sept 15, 1960: 105.7 mhz; 51 kw. Ant 1,069 ft. TL: N61 20 11 W149 30 48. Stereo. 6436 Homer Dr., Suite C 99518. Phone: (907) 562-8119. Fax: (907) 562-8117. Web Site: www.knik.com. Licensee: Ubik Corp. Rep: Interep. Format: Smooth jazz. News staff: one; News: 9 hrs wkly. Target aud: 25-54 plus. ♦ Mike Robbins, gen mgr & stn mgr.

***KRUA(FM)**— Feb 14, 1992: 88.1 mhz; 155 w. 292 ft. TL: N61 07 32 W149 42 46. 3211 Providence Dr. 99508. Phone: (907) 786-6500. Fax: (907) 786-6806. E-mail: aykrua1@uaa.alaska.edu. Web Site: www.krua.org. Licensee: University of Alaska-Anchorage. Wilkinson Barker Knauer. Format: Progvs, alt. News staff: 4; News: 10 hrs wkly. Target aud: General; college community/div. Spec prog: Var/div music 20 hrs, American Indian 3 hrs, sports one hr wkly. Var/div music 20 hrs, American Indian 3 hrs, sports one hr wkly ♦ Zac Clark, stn mgr.

***KSKA(FM)**— Aug 15, 1978: 91.1 mhz; 36 kw. 190 ft. TL: N61 11 25 W149 48 16. (CP: 100 kw, ant 617 ft.). Stereo. 3877 University Dr. 99508. Phone: (907) 561-1161. Fax: (907) 273-9435. Fax: (907) 273-9192. Web Site: www.kska.org. Licensee: Alaska Public Telecommunications Inc. (acq 1994). Network: Network: NPR, PRI. Format: In-depth news, jazz, div. News staff: 2; News: 70 hrs wkly. Target aud: 24 plus; professionals. Spec prog: Folk 4 hrs, Black 8 hrs, jazz 5 hrs, Sp 8 hrs wkly. ♦ Paul Stankavich, pres & gen mgr; Bede Trantina, stn mgr.

KTZN(AM)— May 2, 1948: 550 khz; 5 kw-U. TL: N61 12 25 W149 55 20. 800 E. Dimond Blvd., Suite 3-370 99515. Phone: (907) 522-1515. Fax: (907) 743-5184. Web Site: www.550thezone.com. Licensee: Capstar TX L.P. Group owner: Clear Channel Communications Inc. (acq 8-30-00; grpsl). Network: Network: ABC Information & Entertainment, ABC News/Talk. Rep: D & R Radio. Haley, Bader & Potts. Format: Sports. Target aud: 25-54. ♦ Andy Lohman, gen mgr.

KYMG(FM)— Jan 1, 1989: 98.9 mhz; 100 kw. 499 ft. TL: N61 25 22 W149 52 20. Stereo. 800 E. Diamond Blvd., Suite 3-370 99515. Phone: (907) 522-1515. Fax: (907) 349-6801. Web Site: www.magic989fm.com. Licensee: Clear Channel Radio Licenses Inc. Group owner: Clear Channel Communications Inc. (acq 8-30-00; grpsl). Becker & Finerfrock. Format: Adult contemp. News staff: one; News: 4 hrs wkly. Target aud: 25-49; mostly women. Spec prog: Relg one hr wkly. ♦ Gary Donovan, pres; Andy Lohman, gen mgr; Dave Flavin, stn mgr & progmg dir; Lori Sweet, gen sls mgr; Kurt Haider, news dir & chief of engrg.

Barrow

***KBRW(AM)**— Dec 22, 1975: 680 khz; 10 kw-U. TL: N71 15 24 W156 31 32. Box 109, 1695 Okpik St. 99723. Phone: (907) 852-6811. Fax: (907) 852-2274. Web Site: www.kbrw.org. Licensee: Silakkuagvik Communications Inc. Network: Network: PRI, NPR. Schwartz, Woods & Miller. Format: Var/div. News staff: one; News: 24 hrs wkly. Target aud: General. Spec prog: Class 2 hrs, jazz 6 hrs, relg one hr, Filipino 2 hrs, country 7 hrs wkly. ♦ Jim Vorderstrasse, pres; Robert C. Sommer, VP, gen mgr & stn mgr; Isaac Tuckfield, opns dir; Amber Jusefowytsch, dev dir, mktg dir & prom dir; Danny Sparrell, progmg dir & news dir; Charles M. Laykatis, chief of engrg.

KBRW-FM— Sept 1, 1996: 91.9 mhz; 890 w. 72 ft. TL: N71 17 20 W156 45 31. Network: Network: NPR, PRI. Format: Adult contemp, big band, class. News staff: one; News: 80 hrs wkly. Target aud: General.

Bethel

KYKD(FM)— November 1994: 100.1 mhz; 7.7 kw. 72 ft. TL: N60 48 20 W161 47 14. Stereo. Box 2428 99559. Secondary address: 406 Ptarmigan Rd. 99559. Phone: (907) 543-5953. Fax: (907) 543-5952. E-mail: kykdfm@unicom-alaska.com. Web Site: www.vfcm.org. Licensee: Voice For Christ Ministries Inc. Network: USA. Format: Christian music & info. News: 12 hrs wkly. Target aud: Alaskan bush/rural. ♦ Robert Eldridge, CEO; Ron Haggy, chmn; Jon Skillman, stn mgr.

***KYUK(AM)**— May 13, 1971: 640 khz; 10 kw-U. TL: N60 46 57 W161 53 00. Box 468, 640 Radio St. 99559. Phone: (907) 543-3131. Fax: (907) 543-3130. Web Site: www.kyuk.org. Licensee: Bethel Broadcasting Inc. Network: Network: PRI, NPR. Format: Bilingual talk & div mus, public info. Target aud: General. Spec prog: Class 4 hrs, country 4 hrs wkly. ♦ Fred Phillips, pres; Ronald Daugherty, gen mgr. Co-owned TV: *KYUK-TV affil

Big Lake

KAGV(AM)— Nov. 1, 2005: 1110 khz; 10 kw-U. TL: N61 38 03 W149 47 36. Box 474, Nenana 99760. Phone: (907) 832-5426. Web Site: www.vfcm.org/kagv.htm. Licensee: Voice for Christ Ministries Inc. Format: News/talk, music, Christian. ♦ Robert C. Eldridge, gen mgr; David Horning, progmg dir.

Chevak

***KCUK(FM)**— 1990: 88.1 mhz; 150 w. 75 ft. TL: N61 31 46 W165 35 20. (CP: 6 kw, ant 78 ft.). 985 KSD Way 99563. Phone: (907) 858-7015. Fax: (907) 858-7279. E-mail: ptuluk@vak.gcisa.net. Licensee: Kashunamiut School District. Format: Country, rock and roll, variety. ♦ Peter Tuluk, gen mgr.

College

KUWL(FM)— Sept 6, 1984: 103.9 mhz; 3 kw. 120 ft. TL: N64 51 32 W147 49 41. (CP: Ant -82 ft.). Stereo. 1060 Aspen Way, Fairbanks 99709. Phone: (907) 451-5910. Fax: (907) 451-5999. E-mail: kuwl@akradio.com. Web Site: www.akradio.com. Licensee: New Northwest Broadcasters LLC (group owner; acq 10-26-99; grpsl). Rep: Tacher. Format: Alternative rock. Target aud: 18-34. ♦ Pete Benedetti, CEO; Tryla Hooston, CFO; Perry Walley, gen mgr; Glenn Anderson, opns mgr.

Cordova

KCDV(FM)—Listing follows KLAM(AM).

KLAM(AM)— May 1953: 1450 khz; 250 w-U. TL: N60 32 20 W145 45 35. Box 60, One Forrestry Way 99574. Phone: (907) 424-3796. Fax: (907) 424-3737. E-mail: bayside@ctc.net. Web Site: bayview@ctcak.net. Licensee: Bayview Communications Inc. Network: ABC. Haley, Bader & Potts. Format: Country, classic rock, news & info. Target aud: General. ♦ J.R. Lewis, gen mgr.

Deadhorse

***KCDS(FM)**— 2000: 88.1 mhz; 90 w. Ant 105 ft. TL: N70 12 00 W148 28 02. Box 109, Barrow 99723. Phone: (907) 852-6811. Fax: (907) 852-2274. Web Site: www.kbrw.org. Licensee: Silakkuagvik Communications Inc. Format: Classic rock, new rock, adult contemp. Spec prog: Country. ♦ Robert C. Sommer, VP & gen mgr; Isaac Tuckfield, progmg dir.

Dillingham

***KDLG(AM)**— July 22, 1975: 670 khz; 10 kw-U. TL: N59 02 43 W158 27 07. Box 670 99576. Phone: (907) 842-5281. Fax: (907) 842-5645. Licensee: Dillingham City School District. Network: NPR. Format: Adult contemp, country, rock. News staff: one; News: 20 hrs wkly. Spec prog: Yupik one hr wkly. ♦ Judy Nelson, pres; Rob Carpenter, gen mgr.

KRUP(FM)— August 1995: 99.1 mhz; 6 kw. Ant 128 ft. TL: N59 02 31 W158 31 19. Box 157 99576. Secondary address: 301 Airport Rd. 99576. Phone: (907) 842-2333. Fax: (907) 842-5518. Licensee: McCormick Broadcasting. Format: Talk. ♦ Jackson McCormick, pres & gen mgr.

Eagle River

KAXX(AM)—Licensed to Eagle River. See Anchorage

Fairbanks

KAKQ-FM— Apr 4, 1981: 101.1 mhz; 25 kw. 131 ft. TL: N64 54 53 W147 38 54. Stereo. 546 9th Ave. 99701. Phone: (907) 450-1000. Fax: (907) 457-2128. Web Site: www.101magic.com. Licensee: Capstar TX L.P. Group owner: Clear Channel Communications Inc. (acq 8-30-00; grpsl). Network: Westwood One. Rep: Christal. Format: Adult contemp. News staff: 2; News: one hr wkly. Target aud: 25-44; working families & adults. Spec prog: Jazz 3 hrs wkly. ♦ Gary Donovan, sr VP; Pete Hutton, gen mgr.

KCBF(AM)— 1948: 820 khz; 10 kw-U. TL: N64 51 49 W147 45 06. 1060 Aspen St. 99709. Phone: (907) 451-5910. Fax: (907) 451-5999. Licensee: New Northwest Broadcasters LLC (group owner; acq 8-12-99; grpsl). Network: Network: CBS, Westwood One. Format: Sports. News staff: one; News: 4 hrs wkly. Target aud: 35-54. ♦ Perry Walley, gen mgr & stn mgr; Tracy Walton, progmg dir; Harvey Twite, news dir; Paige Smith, chief of engrg.

KXLR(FM)—Co-owned with KCBF(AM). July 1989: 95.9 mhz; 25 kw. 7 ft. TL: N64 51 49 W147 45 06. Stereo. Format: Classic rock. Target aud: 25-49. ♦ Crys Castle, progmg mgr. Co-owned TV: KTVF(TV) affil

KFAR(AM)— 1939: 660 khz; 10 kw-U. TL: N64 52 09 W147 49 20. 1060 Aspen St. 99709. Phone: (907) 451-5910. Fax: (907) 451-5999. Web Site: www.akradio.com. Licensee: New Northwest Broadcasters LLC (group owner; acq 9-8-81; $675,000;. FTR: 9-28-81). Network: ABC News/Talk. Fisher, Wayland, Cooper, Leader & Zaragoza L.L.P. Format: News/talk. Target aud: 25 plus. Spec prog: Gospel 2 hrs wkly. ♦ Perry Walley, gen mgr & gen sls mgr.

KWLF(FM)—Co-owned with KFAR(AM). Oct 31, 1987: 98.1 mhz; 25 kw. -7 ft. TL: N64 52 38 W147 48 46. (CP: 28 kw). Stereo. Web Site: www.akradio.com. Format: CHR. Target aud: 18 plus; general.

Stations in the U.S. — Alaska

KFBX(AM)— Sept 18, 1972: 970 khz; 10 kw-U. TL: N64 52 48 W147 40 29. 546 9th Ave. 99701. Phone: (907) 450-1000. Fax: (907) 457-2128. Licensee: Capstar TX L.P. Group owner: Clear Channel Communications Inc. (acq 8-30-2000; grpsl). Rep: Christal. Format: News, talk. News staff: one; News: 30 hrs wkly. Target aud: 35 plus; males. ♦ Pete Hutton, gen mgr; Cheys Castle, prom dir & prom mgr; Charlie O'Toole, progmg dir.

KIAK-FM—Co-owned with KFBX(AM). Sept 21, 1983: 102.5 mhz; 55 kw. 1,620 ft. TL: N64 52 45 W148 03 14. Stereo. Format: Country. Target aud: 18 plus; general. ♦ Pete Van Nort, progmg dir.

KKED(FM)— Sept 20, 1962: 104.7 mhz; 10.5 kw. 440 ft. TL: N64 54 42 W147 46 38. Stereo. 546 9th Ave. 99701. Phone: (907) 450-1000. Fax: (907) 457-2128. Web site: www.1047theedge.com. Licensee: Capstar TX L.P. Group owner: Clear Channel Communications Inc. (acq 8-30-00; grpsl). Format: Active rock. ♦ Pete Hutton, gen mgr.

*KSUA(FM)— Oct 10, 1985: 91.5 mhz; 3 kw. -16 ft. TL: N64 51 32 W147 49 41. Stereo. Box 750113, Univ. of Alaska, 307 Constitution Hall 99775. Phone: (907) 474-7054. Phone: (907) 474-5782. Fax: (907) 474-6314. E-mail: fyksua@uaf.edu. Web Site: www.uaf.edu/ksua. Licensee: The University of Alaska Board of Regents. Format: Progsv. Target aud: 14-35. Spec prog: Black 8 hrs, Sp 3 hrs, var/div music 19 hrs wkly. ♦ H.B. Telling, gen mgr; Chip Brookes, progmg dir; Greg Berry, chief of engrg.

*KUAC(FM)— 1962: 89.9 mhz; 38 kw. 1,660 ft. TL: N64 52 49 W148 03 08. Stereo. Box 755620, Univ. of Alaska-Fairbanks 99775-5620. Phone: (907) 474-7491. Fax: (907) 474-5064. Web Site: www.kuac.org. Licensee: University of Alaska. Network: Network: NPR, PRI. Format: Div, class, news/talk. News staff: 3; News: 32 hrs wkly. Target aud: General. Spec prog: Jazz 15 hrs, folk 10 hrs, blues 4 hrs, new age 3 hrs wkly. ♦ Greg Petrowich, CEO & gen mgr; Scott Diseth, stn mgr; Gretchen Gordon, dev dir. Co-owned TV: *KUAC-TV affil.

KUWL(FM)—See College

KYSC(FM)— 2001: 96.9 mhz; 920 w. Ant 1,607 ft. TL: N64 52 45 W148 03 14. 3098 Airport Way 99709. Phone: (907) 455-9690. Fax: (907) 455-4369. E-mail: kysc@gci.net. Licensee: Northern Radio Inc. (acq 5-20-2004; with KPFN(FM) Seward). Network: ABC. Format: Adult contemp. ♦ Fred Dunham, CEO; Don Cary, stn mgr.

Fort Yukon

KZPA(AM)— Sept 30, 1993: 900 khz; 5 kw-U. TL: N66 33 24 W145 12 04. Box 50, E. 3rd Ave. 99740. Phone: (907) 662-8255. Fax: (907) 662-2915. E-mail: kzparadio@hotmail.com. Licensee: Gwandak Public Broadcasting Inc. Format: Var/div. News: 6 hrs wkly. Target aud: All ages. ♦ Vickie Thomas, pres; Robert Thomas, gen mgr; Michael Vaughn, chief of engrg.

Galena

*KIYU(AM)— July 4, 1986: 910 khz; 5 kw-U. TL: N64 41 18 W156 43 29. Box 165 99741. Phone: (907) 656-1488. Fax: (907) 656-1734. E-mail: raven@kiyu.com. Web Site: www.kiyu.com. Licensee: Big River Public Broadcasting Corp. Network: NPR. Format: Country, oldies, rock. News staff: one; News: 35 hrs wkly. Target aud: General. Spec prog: Jazz 4 hrs, Alaska native 2 hrs wkly. ♦ Susie Sam, pres; Shadow Steele, gen mgr; Tim Bodony, stn mgr & opns dir.

Girdwood

*KEUL(FM)— September 1998: 88.9 mhz; 1.4 kw horiz. Ant 636 ft. TL: N60 57 44 W149 04 38. Stereo. Box 29, Glacier City Radio 99587. Phone: (907) 754-2489. E-mail: radio@glaciercity.us. Web Site: http://www.glaciercity.us. Licensee: Girdwood Community Club Inc. Format: Free form, free speech, electic. Target aud: Sole service provider. ♦ Lewis Leonard, VP & gen mgr.

Glennallen

KCAM(AM)— Apr 16, 1964: 790 khz; 5 kw-U. TL: N62 06 52 W145 32 07. Box 249, Mile 187 Glenn Hwy. 99588. Phone: (907) 822-5226. Fax: (907) 822-3761. E-mail: kcam@kcam.org. Web Site: www.kcam.org. Licensee: Northern Light Network. (acq 2-25-92). Network: Network: Moody, USA. Format: Diversified. News: 28 hrs wkly. Target aud: General. Spec prog: American Indian one hr, class 10 hrs, contemp Christian 8 hrs wkly. ♦ Andrew Mazzella, pres; Scott Yahr, stn mgr.

*KXGA(FM)— October 1994: 90.5 mhz; 3.2 kw. 219 ft. TL: N62 06 31 W146 10 25. (CP: Ant 750 ft.). c/o KCHU(AM), Box 467, Valdez 99686. Secondary address: c/o KCHU(AM), 128 Pioneer Dr., Valdez 99686. Phone: (907) 835-4665. Fax: (907) 835-2847. E-mail: kchu@cvinternet.net. Web Site: www.kchu.org. Licensee: Terminal Radio Inc. Format: Div, public radio. ♦ John Anderson, gen mgr & opns mgr; Lisa West, gen mgr.

Haines

*KHNS(FM)— Oct 4, 1980: 102.3 mhz; 3 kw. -1,220 ft. TL: N59 13 06 W135 25 29. Stereo. Box 1109, One Theater Ln. 99827. Phone: (907) 766-2020. Fax: (907) 766-2022. E-mail: khns@khns.org. Web Site: www.khns.org. Licensee: Lynn Canal Broadcasting. Network: NPR. Arter & Hadden. Format: Div, adult contemp, CHR. News staff: 2; News: 21 hrs wkly. Target aud: General. Spec prog: Black 4 hrs, class 14 hrs, C&W 17 hrs, folk 6 hrs, gospel 3 hrs, jazz 5 hrs wkly. ♦ Cherri Rakers, chmn & pres; John Hedrick, gen mgr.

Homer

*KBBI(AM)— Aug 4, 1979: 890 khz; 10 kw-U. TL: N59 40 14 W151 26 38. 3913 Kachemak Way 99603. Phone: (907) 235-7721. Fax: (907) 235-2357. E-mail: gm@kbbi.org. Web Site: www.kbbi.org. Licensee: Kachemak Bay Broadcasting Inc. Network: Network: PRI, NPR. Format: Public radio, eclectic music. News staff: one; News: 64 hrs wkly. Target aud: General. Spec prog: Reggae 3 hrs, jazz 5 hrs wkly. ♦ David S. Anderson, gen mgr; Jonathon Coke, dev dir; Sonja Lee, progmg dir; Paulette Wellington, mus dir; Mike Mason, news dir.

KGTL(AM)— Feb 11, 1981: 620 khz; 5 kw. TL: N59 41 03 W151 37 51. Box 109, 66060 Diamond Ridge Rd. 99603-0109. Phone: (907) 235-6000. Fax: (907) 235-6683. E-mail: kwavefm@xyz.net.Satcom C-5 Tr. 3 Licensee: Peninsula Communications Inc. (group owner) Network: USA. Southmayd & Miller. Format: Adult standards. News: 20 hrs wkly. Target aud: 35 plus; professionals. ♦ David F. Becker, pres & gen mgr.

KWVV-FM—Co-owned with KGTL(AM). Sept 22, 1979: 103.5 mhz; 100 kw. Ant 1,150 ft. TL: N59 41 03 W151 37 51. Stereo. Phone: (907) 235-6000. E-mail: kwavefm@xyz.net.Satcom C-5, transponder 3 Southmayd & Miller. Format: Adult contemp. News: 14 hrs wkly. Target aud: 18-49.

*KMJG(FM)— 2000: 88.9 mhz; 250 w. 666 ft. TL: N59 40 19 W151 30 30. Box 1121, Kasilof 99610. Phone: (907) 260-7702. Fax: (907) 262-1069. E-mail: KWJG915@gci.net. Web Site: www.KWJG.org. Licensee: Kasilof Public Broadcasting Inc. Format: Div, oldies. ♦ William Glynn, pres & gen mgr.

Houston

KADX(FM)—Licensed to Houston. See Anchorage

*KJHA(FM)— July 8, 1998: 88.7 mhz; 285 w. -161 ft. TL: N61 37 50 W149 48 49. Box 56359, North Pole 99705. Phone: (907) 488-2216. Fax: (907) 488-5246. Web Site: www.mosquitonet.com/~kjnp. Licensee: Evangelistic Alaska Missionary Fellowship Inc. Format: C&W, relg. Spec prog: Athabaskan Indian 2 hrs, Eskimo one hr wkly. ♦ Genevieve Nelson, CEO; Yvonne Carriker, pres; Richard Olson, VP; Roger Skold, gen mgr.

KQEZ(FM)— 1997: 92.1 mhz; 10 kw. 810 ft. TL: N61 20 10 W149 30 47. 11259 Tower Rd., Anchorage 99515. Phone: (907) 344-4045. Fax: (907) 522-6053. Web Site: www.kqezfm.com. Licensee: New Northwest Broadcasters LLC (group owner; acq 8-12-99; $1.1 million). Format: Adult contemp. ♦ Pete Benedetti, CEO; Trila Bumstead, CFO; Jim Richmond, gen mgr & sls VP; Ray Edwards, opns dir, opns mgr & progmg dir.

KRPM(FM)— 2000: 96.3 mhz; 6 kw. Ant 262 ft. TL: N61 33 58 W149 42 52. 11259 Tower Rd., Anchorage 99515. Phone: (907) 344-4045. Fax: (907) 522-6053. E-mail: jbanx@newnw.com. Web Site: www.krpmfm.com. Licensee: New Northwest Broadcasters LLC (group owner; acq 7-30-99). Format: Classic rock. Target aud: General. ♦ Pete Benedetti, CEO; Trila Bumstead, CFO; Jim Richmond, gen mgr & sls VP; Ray Edwards, opns mgr & progmg dir.

Juneau

KFMG(FM)— October 1999: 100.7 mhz; 6 kw. Ant -417 ft. TL: N58 17 09 W134 25 40. Stereo. 1000 Harbor Way, Suite 204 99801. Phone: (907) 586-2007. Fax: (907) 586-3802. E-mail: whiteoakbroadcasting@gci.net. Web Site: www.todaysbesthits.com. Licensee: White Oak Broadcasting of Alaska Inc. Format: Hot adult contemp. ♦ Jerome Dobson, chmn; Carolyn Goss, exec VP; Luann Dahl, sr VP; Neil Rones, CEO, pres & gen mgr; Cassy Blackwell, stn mgr.

KINY(AM)— May 28, 1935: 800 khz; 10 kw-D, 8 kw-N. TL: N58 18 05 W134 26 26. Stereo. 1107 W. 8th St., Suite 2 99801. Phone: (907) 586-1800. Fax: (907) 586-3266. E-mail: kiny@ptialaska.net. Web Site: www.kinyradio.com. Licensee: Alaska-Juneau Communications Inc. Network: ABC Information & Entertainment. Format: Adult contemp. News staff: 2; News: 4 hrs wkly. Target aud: General. ♦ Dennis W. Egan, pres & gen mgr; Kelly Peres, opns mgr; Tim Armstrong, gen sls mgr; Jim Morgan, prom dir; Charlie Gray, engrg dir.

KSUP(FM)—Co-owned with KINY(AM). Dec 1, 1984: 106.3 mhz; 10 kw. -1,007 ft. TL: N58 18 05 W134 26 26. Stereo. Phone: (907) 586-1063. E-mail: ksup@ptialaska.net. Web Site: www.ksupradio.com. Format: Classic, contemp rock. ♦ Kelly Peres, progmg dir.

KJNO(AM)— Oct 19, 1952: 630 khz; 5 kw-D, 1 kw-N. TL: N58 19 47 W134 28 17. 3161 Channel Dr., Suite 2 99801. Phone: (907) 586-3630. Fax: (907) 463-3685. Web Site: www.kjno.com. Licensee: Alaska Broadcast Communications Inc. (group owner; acq 1972; with co-located FM). Tacher Haley, Bader & Potts. Format: Talk. Target aud: 25-54. ♦ Roy Paschal, pres; Steve Rhyner, gen mgr; Justin McDonald, progmg dir.

KTKU(FM)—Co-owned with KJNO(AM). July 9, 1984: 105.1 mhz; 3.84 kw. -1,057 ft. TL: N58 19 47 W134 28 17. Stereo. Web Site: www.kjno.com. Network: ABC FM Connection. Format: Hot country.

KSRJ(FM)— 1999: 102.7 mhz; 6 kw. Ant -417 ft. TL: N58 17 09 W134 25 40. 1000 Harbor Way, Suite 204 99801. Phone: (907) 586-2007. Fax: (907) 586-3802. E-mail: whiteoakbroadcasting@gci.net. Licensee: White Oak Broadcasting of Alaska Inc. Format: Soft A/C. ♦ Jerome Dobson, chmn; Neil Rones, CEO, pres & gen mgr; Cassy Blackwell, stn mgr.

*KTOO(FM)— Jan 27, 1974: 104.3 mhz; 1.4 kw. -1,016 ft. TL: N58 18 04 W134 25 21. Stereo. 360 Egan Dr. 99801-1748. Phone: (907) 586-1670. Fax: (907) 586-3612. Fax: (907) 586-2561 (NEWS). E-mail: info@ktoo.org. Web Site: www.ktoo.org. Licensee: Capital Community Broadcasting Inc. Network: NPR, PRI. Schwartz, Woods & Miller. Format: Diversified, news. News staff: 14; News: 48 hrs wkly. Target aud: General. Spec prog: Children one hrs, folk 8 hrs, Sp 2 hsr, French 2 hrs, jazz 14 hrs, Alaska native one hr wkly. ♦ Bill Legere, pres & gen mgr; Jim Mahan, VP; James Mahan, stn mgr; Susan Fitzgerald, opns mgr; Cheryl Levitt, dev dir. Co-owned TV: *KTOO-TV affil.

Kasilof

*KWJG(FM)— July 29, 1998: 91.5 mhz; 1 kw. 262 ft. TL: N60 22 44 W151 11 30. Stereo. Box 1121, AR 99610. Phone: (907) 260-7702.

Broadcasting & Cable Yearbook 2006

Alaska

Fax: (907) 262-1069. Licensee: Kasilof Public Broadcasting Inc. Bechtel & Cole. Format: Oldies, variety/diverse. ♦William J. Glynn Jr., pres & gen mgr.

*KWMD(FM)—Not on air, target date: unknown:. Stn currently dark 90.5 mhz; 500 w horiz. Ant 197 ft. TL: N60 22 44 W151 11 30. 907 W. Dowling Rd., Suite 24, Anchorage 99518. Licensee: Alaska Educational Radio System Inc.

*KWVK(FM)—Not on air, target date: unknown:. Stn currently dark 89.5 mhz; 500 w horiz. Ant 197 ft. TL: N60 22 44 W151 11 30. 907 E. Dowling Rd., Suite 24, Anchorage 99518. Licensee: Alaska Educational Radio System Inc.

Kenai

*KDLL(FM)— 1981: 91.9 mhz; 4.9 kw. 72 ft. TL: N60 34 03 W151 07 25. Box 2111 99611. Phone: (907) 283-8433. Fax: (907) 283-6701. E-mail: kdlldev@alaska.net. Licensee: Pickle Hill Public Broadcasting Inc. Network: Network: NPR, PRI. Format: Var/div, news. News staff: one; News: 60 hrs wkly. Target aud: Affluent. Spec prog: American idian 10 hrs wkly. ♦Dave Anderson, gen mgr; Allen Auxier, stn mgr, dev dir, mktg dir, prom dir & adv dir; Sonja Lee, progmg dir; Ashley Gross, news dir.

KPEN-FM—See Soldotna

KSRM(AM)—See Soldotna

KWHQ-FM— Nov 18, 1976: 100.1 mhz; 3 kw. 260 ft. TL: N60 30 49 W151 11 19. Stereo. 40960 K-Beach Rd. 99611. Phone: (907) 283-9430. Fax: (907) 283-8700. Fax: (907) 283-9177. E-mail: radiokenai@gci.net. Web Site: www.radiokenai.com. Licensee: KSRM Inc. (group owner). 1972 Network: ABC Information & Entertainment. Pepper & Corazzini. Format: Modern country. News staff: 2; News: 12 hrs wkly. Target aud: 18-49. ♦John C. Davis, pres; Cherie Curry, gen mgr & stn mgr; Steve Holloway, opns mgr.

Ketchikan

KFMJ(FM)— Sept 23, 1996: 99.9 mhz; 115 w. Ant 2,234 ft. TL: N55 21 40 W131 47 43. Stereo. 516 Stedman St. 99901. Phone: (907) 247-3699. Fax: (907) 247-5365. E-mail: kfmj@alaska.fm. Web Site: www.kfmj.com. Licensee: TLP Communications Inc. Network: Network: ABC, USA. Format: Oldies. News: 18.5 hrs wkly. Target aud: 30 plus. ♦Robert J. Kern, chmn & pres; Jeannette Rosier, CFO; Jacque Meck, VP; Bob Kern, gen mgr.

KGTW(FM)—Listing follows KTKN(AM).

*KRBD(FM)— May 1976: 105.9 mhz; 15 kw. -105 ft. TL: N55 20 20 W131 37 21. Stereo. 123 Stedman 99901. Phone: (907) 225-9655. Fax: (907) 247-0808. Web Site: www.krbd.org. Licensee: Rainbird Community Broadcasting Corp. Network: Network: NPR, PRI. Format: Div. Target aud: General. Spec prog: Class 11 hrs, C&W 14 hrs, folk 10 hrs, jazz 10 hrs, tribal topics 5 hrs wkly. ♦Jeff Siefert, gen mgr; Maria Dudzak, opns mgr; Lilah Walker, dev dir.

KTKN(AM)— 1942: 930 khz; 5 kw-D, 1 kw-N. TL: N55 20 22 W131 38 12. 526 Stedman St. 99901. Phone: (907) 225-2193. Fax: (907) 225-0444. Licensee: Alaska Broadcast Communications Inc. (group owner). Network: ABC Information & Entertainment. Tacher. Haley, Bader & Potts. Format: Adult contemp, news/talk. News staff: 5; News: 20 hrs wkly. Target aud: 25 plus. ♦Blake Messer, gen mgr.

KGTW(FM)—Co-owned with KTKN(AM). November 1987: 106.7 mhz; 4 kw. -308 ft. TL: N55 20 22 W131 38 12. Stereo. Web Site: gateway1067.com. Network: ABC Daytime Direction. Format: Country. Target aud: 18 plus. ♦John Hunt, progmg dir.

Kodiak

*KMXT(FM)— June 1, 1976: 100.1 mhz; 3 kw. 3 ft. TL: N57 47 41 W152 23 28. Stereo. 620 Egan Way 99615. Phone: (907) 486-3181. Fax: (907) 486-2733. E-mail: kmxt@kmxt.org. Web Site: www.kmxt.org. Licensee: Kodiak Public Broadcasting Corp. (acq 10-2-75). Network: Network: NPR, PRI. Format: Div, news. News staff: 2; News: 5 hrs wkly. Target aud: General. Spec prog: Filipino 2 hrs, children one hr, Native American one hr, Sp one hr wkly. ♦Mike Wall, gen mgr; Fred Hawley, dev dir.

KRXX(FM)—Listing follows KVOK(AM).

KVOK(AM)— Nov 7, 1974: 560 khz; 1 kw-U. TL: N57 48 36 W152 20 54. Box 708 99615. Secondary address: 1315 Mill Bay Rd. 99615. Phone: (907) 486-5159. Fax: (907) 486-3044. Licensee: Kodiak Island Broadcasting Co. Inc. (acq 4-3-00; $500,000. with co-located FM). Network: ABC. Format: Country, talk. Target aud: 25-56. ♦Matt Wilson, gen mgr.

KRXX(FM)— Co-owned with KVOK(AM). 1987: 101.1 mhz; 3.1 kw. 46 ft. TL: N57 48 36 W152 20 54. Format: Classic rock, hot adult contemp. Target aud: 18-56.

Kotzebue

*KOTZ(AM)— March 1973: 720 khz; 10 kw-U. TL: N66 50 22 W162 34 05. Box 78 99752. Phone: (907) 442-3434. Fax: (907) 442-2292. Licensee: Kotzebue Broadcasting Inc. Format: Div. Target aud: General; 90% rural Eskimo, 10% white-collar caucasian. Spec prog: Class 4 hrs wkly. ♦Chester Ballot, pres; David Fogelman, gen mgr.

McCarthy

*KXKM(FM)— October 1994: 89.7 mhz; 102 w. -169 ft. TL: N61 24 58 W143 01 19. c/o KCHU(AM), Box 467, Valdez 99686. Secondary address: c/o KCHU(AM), 128 Pioneer Dr., Valdez 99686. Phone: (907) 835-4665. Fax: (907) 835-2847. E-mail: kchu@cvinternet.net. Web Site: www.kchu.org. Licensee: Terminal Radio Inc. Network: Network: NPR, PRI. Format: Div, educ, news/talk, public radio. News staff: one; News: 10 hrs wkly. Target aud: General. ♦Lisa West, gen mgr; John Anderson, opns mgr.

Naknek

KAKN(FM)— May 1987: 100.9 mhz; 3 kw. 338 ft. TL: N58 44 33 W156 58 39. Stereo. Box 0214 99633. Secondary address: Mile 2 AK Peninsula Hwy. 99633. Phone: (907) 246-7492. Fax: (907) 246-7462. E-mail: studio@victorynetwork.com. Web Site: www.victoryradionetwork.com. Licensee: Bay Broadcasting Co. Network: USA. Format: Light adult contemp Christian, southern gospel, news. News: 15 hrs wkly. Target aud: General; mobile town/village population & coml fishermen. Spec prog: Children 3 hrs wkly. ♦Rev. Thomas C. Olson, pres; Michael Johnson, VP; Chris Danielson, gen mgr; Roberta Foster, stn mgr; Tony Larson, progmg dir.

Nenana

KIAM(AM)— June 28, 1985: 630 khz; 10 kw-D, 3.1 kw-N. TL: N64 28 43 W149 05 10. Box 474 99760. Phone: (907) 832-5426. Fax: (907) 832-5450. E-mail: Alaskaradio@vfcm.org. Web Site: www.vfcm.org. Licensee: Voice for Christ Ministries. Network: USA. Format: Relg. News: 14 hrs news progm wkly. Target aud: General. Spec prog: American Indian 3 hrs, class one hr wkly. ♦Bob Eldridge, exec VP; Brian Blair, stn mgr; David Horning, gen mgr & mus dir.

Nikiski

KXBA(FM)— March 4, 2000: 93.3 mhz; 50 kw. Ant 243 ft. TL: N60 30 39 W151 16 12. Stereo. Box 109, Homer 99603-0109. Phone: (907) 262-6000. Fax: (907) 283-8461. Licensee: Peninsula Communications Inc. (group owner) Southmayd & Miller. Format: Oldies. News: 8 hrs wkly. Target aud: 25-54. ♦David F. Becker, pres & gen mgr; Tim White, opns mgr.

Nome

KICY(AM)— Apr 17, 1960: 850 khz; 50 kw-U, DA. TL: N64 29 15 W165 18 53. Box 820 99762. Secondary address: 408 W. D St. 99762. Phone: (907) 443-2213. Fax: (907) 443-2344. E-mail: office@kicy.org. Web Site: www.kicy.org. Licensee: Arctic Broadcasting Association (group owner). Network: Network: Network: ABC, Moody, Salem Radio Network. Alaska Broadcast Media Wombel, Carlyle, Sandridge & Rice. Format: Southern gospel, Russian. Target aud: 25-64. ♦Ted Haney, pres; Dennis Weidler, gen mgr & gen sls mgr.

KICY-FM— Sept 11, 1977: 100.3 mhz; 84 w. 40 ft. TL: N64 30 04 W165 24 39. Stereo. Web Site: www.kicy.org. Format: Christian. Target aud: 18-35. ♦Mark Hill, progmg dir; Patty Burchell, mus dir.

*KNOM(AM)— July 14, 1971: 780 khz; 25 kw-D, 14 kw-N. TL: N64 29 16 W165 17 58. 107 W. 3rd Ave. 99762. Phone: (907) 443-5221. Fax:

(907) 443-5757. E-mail: info@knom.org. Web Site: www.knom.org. Licensee: Catholic Bishop of Northern Alaska. Wilkinson, Barker & Knauer. Format: Div, relg, news/talk. News staff: 2; News: 30 hrs wkly. Target aud: General. Spec prog: Eskimo 6 hrs, CHR 12 hrs, relg 20 hrs, class 5 hrs, weather 14 hrs wkly. ♦Kelly Brabec, pres & progmg dir; Thomas Busch, CFO & gen mgr; Ric Schmidt, gen mgr & progmg dir; Thomas A. Busch, dev dir; Paul Korchin, news dir & chief of engrg.

KNOM-FM— May 17, 1993: 96.1 mhz; 88 w. -138 ft. TL: N64 29 56 W165 23 56. Stereo. Network: AP Radio. Wilkinson, Barker & Knauer. News staff: 2; News: 30 hrs wkly.

North Pole

*KJNP(AM)— Oct 11, 1967: 1170 khz; 50 kw-D, 21 kw-N. TL: N64 45 34 W147 19 26. Box 56359 99705. Phone: (907) 488-2216. Fax: (907) 488-5246. Licensee: Evangelistic Alaska Missionary Fellowship. Format: C&W, relg. Spec prog: Russian 11 hrs, Athabaskan Indian 2 hrs, Eskimo one hr wkly. ♦Yuonne Carriker, pres; Richard T. Olson, VP; Roger Skold, gen mgr.

KJNP-FM— Oct 11, 1977: 100.3 mhz; 25 kw. 1,570 ft. TL: N64 52 44 W148 03 10. Stereo. Format: Conservative btfl mus, relg.. Co-owned TV: *KJNP-TV affil.

Palmer

*KJLP(FM)— August 2005: 88.9 mhz; 250 w. Ant -210 ft. TL: N61 37 18 W149 01 16. Box 210389, Anchorage 99521. Secondary address: 6401 E. Northern Lights, Anchorage 99521. Fax: (907) 333-5282. Licensee: Christian Broadcasting Inc. Format: Christian. ♦Tom Steigleman, gen mgr.

Petersburg

*KFSK(FM)— September 1977: 100.9 mhz; 2 kw. -482 ft. TL: N56 48 55 W132 57 12. Stereo. Box 149 99833. Phone: (907) 772-3808. Fax: (907) 772-9296. E-mail: kfsk@alaska.net. Web Site: www.kfsk.org. Licensee: Narrows Broadcasting Corp. Network: Network: PRI, NPR, AP Network News. Format: News, pub affrs. ♦Rodney Anderson, pres; Tom Abbott, gen mgr; Suzanne Fuqua, dev dir.

KRSA(AM)— Sept 24, 1982: 580 khz; 5 kw-U, DA-1. TL: N56 40 23 W132 55 00. Box 650 99833. Phone: (907) 772-3891. Fax: (907) 772-4538. E-mail: krsa@alaska.net. Web Site: www.krsa.net. Licensee: Northern Light Network. (acq 2-20-92). Format: Relg, country. News: 20 hrs wkly. Target aud: General. Spec prog: Class 5 hrs, children, oldies 5 hrs wkly. ♦Andrew Mazzella, pres, gen mgr & stn mgr.

Saint Paul

*KUHB-FM— July 4, 1984: 91.9 mhz; 3 kw. 56 ft. TL: N57 07 14 W170 16 45. Stereo. Box 905, Pribilof School District 99660. Phone: (907) 546-2254. Fax: (907) 546-2367. E-mail: kuhb@yahoo.com. Licensee: Pribilof School District. Network: NPR. Format: Country, Oldies, Rock/AOR " A little bit of everything". ♦Malcolm Fleming, gen mgr; K. C. Jackson, stn mgr & chief of engrg.

Sand Point

*KSDP(AM)— Mar 2, 1983: 830 khz; 1 kw-U. TL: N55 21 06 W160 28 02. Box 328, City Bldg, 328 Main St. 99661. Phone: (907) 383-5737. Phone: (888) 260-5737 (ALASKA ONLY). Fax: (907) 383-5737. E-mail: ksdp@ksdpradio.com. Web Site: www.ksdpradio.com. Licensee: Aleutian Peninsula Broadcasting Inc. Network: Network: NPR, PRI. Format: Div. Target aud: General. Spec prog: Gospel. ♦Brian E. Koral, gen mgr.

Seward

KPFN(FM)— 1998: 105.9 mhz; 3 kw. -1,312 ft. TL: N60 05 27 W149 20 20. 3098 Airport Way, Fairbanks 99709. Phone: (907) 455-9690. Fax: (907) 455-4369. E-mail: kysc@gci.net. Licensee: Northern Radio Inc. (acq 5-20-2004; with KYSC(FM) Fairbanks). Format: Adult contemp. ♦Fred Dunham, CEO; Don Cary, gen mgr.

KSWD(AM)— November 1948: . Stn currently dark 950 khz; 1 kw-U. TL: N60 06 51 W149 26 44. 3098 Airport Way, Fairbanks 99709. Phone: (907) 455-9690. Licensee: Northern Radio Inc. (acq 12-20-2002; with KPFN(FM) Seward). ♦Don Cary, gen mgr.

Sitka

*KCAW(FM)— Feb 19, 1982: 104.7 mhz; 5 kw. -612 ft. TL: N57 03 13 W135 21 07. Stereo. 2 Lincoln St., Suite B 99835. Phone: (907) 747-5877. Phone: (907) 747-5879. Fax: (907) 747-5977. Web Site: www.ravenradio.org. Licensee: Raven Radio Foundation. Network: Network: NPR, PRI. Format: Div, news. Target aud: General. Spec prog: Class 15 hrs, Indian 3 hrs wkly. ♦Ken Fate, CEO; Kari Lundgren, chmn & pres; Amy Kramer Johnson, dev dir.

KIFW(AM)— September 1949: 1230 khz; 1 kw-U. TL: N57 03 27 W135 20 02. 611 Lake St. 99835. Phone: (907) 747-6626. Phone: (907) 747-5439. Fax: (907) 747-8455. E-mail: kifw@ptialaska.net. Licensee: Alaska Broadcast Communications Inc. (group owner; acq 12-21-00; grpsl). Network: ABC Information & Entertainment. Rep: Tacher. Haley, Bader & Potts. Format: MOR, oldies, news/talk. News: 60 hrs wkly. Target aud: 18-49; all demographics. ♦Steve Rhyner, pres; Blake Messer, stn mgr; Bobbie Rusk, gen sls mgr; Clint Daniels, news dir; Chris Kobger, chief of engrg.

KSBZ(FM)— Co-owned with KIFW(AM). Oct 18, 1990: 103.1 mhz; 3 kw. 144 ft. TL: N57 03 27 W135 20 02. Stereo. Phone: (907) 747-6627. Format: Country. Target aud: 18-34. ♦Amy Denny, pub affrs dir.

Soldotna

KKIS-FM— Mar 2, 1994: 96.5 mhz; 10 kw. 259 ft. TL: N60 31 26 W151 03 23. Stereo. 40960 K-Beach Rd., Kenai 99611. Phone: (907) 283-5821. Fax: (907) 283-9177. E-mail: info@radiokenai.com. Web Site: www.radiokenai.com. Licensee: KSRM Inc. (group owner; acq 12-7-01; $350,000. with co-located AM). Network: ABC. Pepper & Corazzini LLP. Format: Adult contemp, CHR. News staff: one; News: 2 hrs wkly. Target aud: 18-49. ♦Cherie Curry, gen mgr.

KSLD(AM)— Co-owned with KKIS-FM. Apr 6, 1985: 1140 khz; 10 kw-U. TL: N60 31 26 W151 03 23. Phone: (907) 283-8700. E-mail: ksld@radiokenai.com. Web Site: www.radiokenai.com. Network: Westwood One. Pepper and Corazzini. Format: Classic rock. Target aud: 25-59.

KPEN-FM— Dec 1, 1984: 101.7 mhz; 25 kw. 240 ft. TL: N60 30 40 W151 16 12. Stereo. Box 109, Homer 99603. Phone: (907) 262-6000. Phone: (907) 283-7451. Fax: (907) 235-6683. E-mail: kwavefm@xyz.net. Licensee: Peninsula Communications Inc. (group owner) Network: USA. Southmayd & Miller. Format: Country. Target aud: 25-54. ♦David F. Becker, pres & gen mgr; Tim White, opns mgr.

KSRM(AM)— Sept 27, 1967: 920 khz; 5 kw-U. TL: N60 30 49 W151 11 19. 40960 K-Beach Rd., Kenai 99611. Phone: (907) 283-5959. Fax: (907) 283-5811. E-mail: info@radiokenai.com. Web Site: www.radiokenai.com. Licensee: KSRM Inc. (group owner; acq 4-72). Network: ABC Information & Entertainment. Pepper & Corazzini. Format: News/talk. News staff: one; News: 105 hrs wkly. Target aud: 25-54. ♦John C. Davis, pres; Cherie Curry, gen mgr; Steve Holloway, opns mgr; J.R. Kitchens, progmg dir.

Sterling

*KRAW(FM)—Not on air, target date: unknown: 90.1 mhz; 1.2 kw horiz. Ant 20 ft. TL: N60 29 16 W150 47 38. 907 E. Dowling Rd., Suite 24, Anchorage 99518. Licensee: Alaska Educational Radio System Inc.

Talkeetna

*KTNA(FM)— February 1993: 88.5 mhz; 1.9 kw. 62 ft. TL: N62 19 05 W150 17 52. Stereo. Box 300, 2nd Ave. 99676. Phone: (907) 733-1700. Fax: (907) 733-1781. E-mail: info@ktna.org. Web Site: www.ktna.org. Licensee: Talkeetna Community Radio Inc. Network: Network: NPR, PRI. Format: Eclectic, news/talk. News staff: one; News: 15 hrs wkly. Target aud: General; rural Alaskans. Spec prog: Blues 5 hrs, light rock 5 hrs wkly. ♦Robert Ambrose, gen mgr & stn mgr; Mike Lindren, dev dir.

Tok

*KUDU(FM)— Mar 3, 1998: 91.9 mhz; 200 w. -121 ft. TL: N63 19 53 W143 07 02. Box 719 99780. Phone: (907) 883-4397. Phone: (907) 883-5855. Fax: (907) 883-5245. E-mail: office@lifetalk.net. Web Site: www.lifetalk.net. Licensee: Lifetalk Broadcasting Association. Format: Relg, inspirational music, talk. ♦Phil Follet, COO & pres; Steven Gallimore, pres; Jeremy Woodruff, progmg dir.

Unalakleet

KNSA(AM)— 1998: 930 khz; 2.5 kw-U. TL: N63 53 17 W160 41 29. Box 178 99684. Phone: (907) 624-3100. Phone: (907) 624-3101. Fax: (907) 624-3130. Licensee: Unalakleet Broadcasting Inc. Format: Rock. ♦Henry Ivanoff, stn mgr.

Unalaska

KIAL(AM)— Sept 1, 1978: 1450 khz; 50 w-U, DA-1. Box 181 99685-9999. Phone: (907) 581-1888. Fax: (907) 581-1634. E-mail: ucb@arctic.net. Licensee: Unalaska Community Broadcasting. Network: NPR. Format: Public radio. News staff: one; News: 4 hrs wkly. Spec prog: News 14 hrs, rock 8 hrs, relg 4 hrs, country 4 hrs, Black 4 hrs, gospel 2 hrs wkly. ♦Brian Stafford, pres.

Valdez

*KCHU(FM)— Aug 3, 1986: 770 khz; 9.7 kw-U. TL: N61 06 40 W146 15 39. Box 467, 128 Pioneer Dr. 99686. Phone: (907) 835-4665. Fax: (907) 835-2847. E-mail: kchu@cvinternet.net. Web Site: www.kchu.org. Licensee: Terminal Radio Inc. (acq 10-84; $250,000; 10-8-84). Network: Network: NPR, PRI. Format: Div. News staff: 2; News: 40 hrs wkly. Target aud: General. ♦Lisa West, gen mgr; John Anderson, opns dir.

KVAK(AM)— January 1983: 1230 khz; 1 kw-U. TL: N61 07 16 W146 15 25. Box 367 99686. Phone: (907) 835-5825. Fax: (907) 835-5158. Licensee: North Wave Communications Inc. (acq 1996). Network: ABC Information & Entertainment. Format: Country, talk. News: one hr wkly. Target aud: General. ♦Laurie Prax, pres.

KVAK-FM— May 28, 1999: 93.3 mhz; 6 kw. -1,958 ft. TL: N61 07 16 W146 15 25. Box 367, 501 E. Bremner St., Suite 2 99686. Format: Hot adult contemp.

Wasilla

KMBQ(FM)— Mar 15, 1985: 99.7 mhz; 51 kw. -187 ft. TL: N61 38 03 W149 26 25. Stereo. 2200 E. Parks Hwy. 99654. Phone: (907) 373-0222. Fax: (907) 376-1575. E-mail: john@kmbq. Web Site: www.kmbq.com. Licensee: KMBQ Corp. Network: CNN Radio. Garvey, Schukert & Barer. Format: Adult contemp. News staff: 2; News: 13 wkly. Target aud: 25-54; mid-upper class suburbanites & farm community. ♦John Klapperich, CEO, VP & gen mgr; Dean Mitchell, progmg dir; Danny Preston, progmg mgr, mus dir & chief of engrg.

Wrangell

*KSTK(FM)— July 2, 1977: 101.7 mhz; 3 kw. -294 ft. TL: N56 27 14 W132 22 54. Stereo. Box 1141, 202 St. Michael's 99929. Phone: (907) 874-2345. Fax: (907) 874-3293. E-mail: kstkfm@aptalaska.net. Licensee: Wrangell Radio Group Inc. Network: Network: NPR, PRI. Format: Diverse. News staff: 2; News: 20 hrs wkly. Target aud: General. Spec prog: Class 4 hrs, country 16 hrs, jazz 8 hrs wkly. ♦Diane O'Brien, pres; Peter Helgesen, gen mgr; Cindy Sweat, dev dir.

Arizona

Apache Junction

KVVA-FM— July 1, 1973: 107.1 mhz; 25 kw. 312 ft. TL: N33 26 48 W111 37 32. Stereo. 1641 E. Osborn Rd., Suite 8, Phoenix 85016. Phone: (602) 266-2005. Fax: (602) 279-2921. Licensee: Entravision Holdings LLC. Group owner: Entravision Communications Corp. (acq 7-28-00; grpsl). Cohn & Marks. Format: Adult contemp, Sp, Latin contemp. Target aud: 18-49; Hispanic. ♦Tom Duran, gen mgr.

Arizona City

KKMR(FM)— Apr 13, 1985: 106.5 mhz; 6 kw. Ant 292 ft. TL: N32 50 04 W111 38 15. 4745 N. 7th St., Suite 140, Phoenix 85014. Phone: (602) 308-7900. Fax: (602) 308-7979. Web Site: www.univision.com. Licensee: HBC License Corp. Group owner: Univision Radio (acq 9-22-2003; grpsl). Format: Sp contemp. Target aud: 25-54. ♦Mary McEvilly-Hernandez, gen mgr.

Bagdad

KFTT(FM)— 2002: 103.1 mhz; 4.9 kw. Ant 741 ft. TL: N34 32 56 W113 14 05. 10 Media Center Dr., Lake Havasu City 86403. Phone: (928) 855-1051. Fax: (928) 855-7996. E-mail: epress@maddog.net. Web Site: www.maddog.net. Licensee: Smoke and Mirrors LLC (acq 4-18-2001). Format: Adult standards. ♦Chris Rolando, gen mgr.

Benson

KAVV(FM)— April 1983: 97.7 mhz; 6 kw. 590 ft. TL: N31 54 24 W110 27 08. Stereo. Box 18899, Tucson 85731-8899. Secondary address: 156 W. 5th City 85602. Phone: (520) 586-9797. E-mail: cave@wvcnet.com. Licensee: Stereo 97 Inc. Format: C&W. Target aud: 25-49. Spec prog: Relg 3 hrs wkly. ♦Jack Lotsof, pres; Paul Lotsof, gen mgr, stn mgr, progmg dir & chief of engrg.

Bisbee

*KRMB(FM)— 1997: 90.1 mhz; 47 w. 2,247 ft. TL: N31 28 52 W109 57 30. Box 2520, Douglas 85603. Phone: (520) 364-5392. Fax: (520) 364-5392. Licensee: World Radio Network Inc. (group owner) Format: Relg, Sp.

KWCD(FM)— Oct 12, 1979: 92.3 mhz; 51 w. 2,217 ft. TL: N31 28 52 W109 57 30. Stereo. Box 2770, 2300 Busby Dr., Sierra Vista 85636-2770. Phone: (520) 458-4313. Fax: (520) 458-4317. E-mail: kwcd@c2i2.com. Licensee: CCR-Sierra Vista IV LLC. Group owner: Cherry Creek Radio LLC (acq 12-19-2003; grpsl). Network: Jones Radio Networks. Format: Country. News staff: one; News: one hr wkly. Target aud: 25-54; financially secure adults & military personnel. ♦Paul Orlando, gen mgr; Sean Lisle, opns mgr.

*KWRB(FM)— December 1996: 90.9 mhz; 58 w. 2,217 ft. TL: N31 28 52 W109 57 30. 96-C S. Carmichael, Sierra Vista 85635. Phone: (520) 452-8022. Fax: (520) 452-0927. E-mail: kwrb@hcjb.org. Web Site: www.kwrb.org. Licensee: World Radio Network Inc. Format: Christian, educ, inspirational. ♦Jerry Wagner, gen mgr; Mark Loving, opns dir.

Black Canyon City

KMIA(AM)— Sept 1, 1981: 710 khz; 22 kw-D, 3.9 kw-N, DA-2. TL: N34 04 48 W112 09 15. c/o KVVA-FM, 1641 E. Osborn Rd., Suite 8, Phoenix 85016. Phone: (602) 266-2005. Fax: (602) 279-2921. Licensee: Entravision Holdings LLC. Group owner: Entravision Communications Corp. (acq 7-28-00; grpsl). Format: Sp. Target aud: 18-54. ♦Tom Duran, gen mgr.

Buckeye

KDVA(FM)— 1993: 106.9 mhz; 6 kw. 305 ft. TL: N33 27 01 W112 35 58. 1641 E. Osborn Rd., Suite 8, Phoenix 85016. Phone: (602)

Arizona

266-2005. Fax: (602) 279-2921. Licensee: Entravision Holdings LLC. Group owner: Entravision Communications Corp. (acq 5-31-01; $10 million). Format: Latin Contempory, "Radio Romantica". Spec prog: Black 6 hrs, gospel 7 hrs wkly. ♦Tom Duran, gen mgr.

Bullhead City

KFLG(AM)— Oct 1, 1978: 1000 khz; 1 kw-D. TL: N35 10 10 W114 38 02. 1531 Jill Way, Suite 7 86442. Phone: (928) 763-5586. Fax: (928) 763-3775. Licensee: Cameron Broadcasting Inc. (group owner; acq 11-24-99). Network: CNN Radio. Format: Btfl mus, big band, MOR. Target aud: 24 plus; upper demographics. ♦Billy Williams, CEO & pres; Don Jaeger, VP; Bob Athey, opns mgr.

KZZZ(AM)— Nov 15, 1981: 1490 khz; 1 kw-U. TL: N35 05 10 W112 07 40. 1531 Jill Way, Suite 7 86442. Phone: (928) 763-5586. Fax: (928) 763-3775. Web Site: www.talkatoz.com. Licensee: Cameron Broadcasting Inc. (group owner; acq 7-91; $1.28 million. with KNKK(FM) Needles, CA; FTR: 7-29-91). Format: Talk. Target aud: 45 plus. ♦Don Jaeger, VP & gen mgr.

Casa Grande

*****KLVA(FM)**— Apr 8, 1976: 105.5 mhz; 50 kw. Ant 492 ft. TL: N33 00 14 W111 58 53. Stereo. K-Love Radio Network, 5700 W. Oaks Blvd., Rocklin, CA 95765. Phone: (916) 251-1600. Fax: (916) 251-1650-. E-mail: klove@klove.com. Web Site: www.klove.com.Yes Licensee: Educational Media Foundation. Group owner: EMF Broadcasting (acq 7-19-99). Network: K-Love. Shaw, Pittman. Format: Contemp Christian. Target aud: 25-44; Judeo-Christian, female. Spec prog: Sports 7 hrs wkly. ♦Richard Jenkins, pres.

Cave Creek

KFNX(AM)— June 27, 1997: 1100 khz; 50 kw-D, 1 kw-N, DA-2. TL: N33 47 52 W111 59 30. Stereo. 2001 N. 3rd St., Suite 102, Phoenix 85014. Phone: (602) 277-1100. Fax: (602) 248-1478. Licensee: North American Broadcasting Co. Inc., debtor in possession (acq 8-13-02). Format: Talk. News staff: 2. Target aud: 35 plus; Upscale. ♦Francis Battaglia, CEO.

Chandler

KMLE(FM)—Licensed to Chandler. See Phoenix

Chinle

KFXR-FM— August 1995: 107.3 mhz; 3.6 kw. 1,630 ft. TL: N36 21 07 W109 49 54. 1632 S. Second St., Gallup, NM 87301. Phone: (505) 863-9391. Fax: (505) 863-9393. Licensee: Clear Channel Broadcasting Licenses Inc. Group owner: Clear Channel Communications Inc. (acq 8-18-00). Format: Country. ♦Maryann Armijo, gen mgr.

Chino Valley

KFPB(FM)— 1999: 94.3 mhz; 4.1 kw. Ant 810 ft. TL: N34 49 32 W112 34 09. 8581 E. Florentine, Unit C, Prescott Valley 86314. Phone: (928) 775-2530. Fax: (928) 775-2532. Web Site: http://www.kfpbradio.com. Licensee: Prescott Radio Partners (acq 12-10-99; $250,000). Format: Country. ♦James Primm, gen mgr.

Claypool

KIKO-FM—Licensed to Claypool. See Miami

Clifton

KCUZ(AM)—Licensed to Clifton. See Safford

KWRQ(FM)—Licensed to Clifton. See Safford

Colorado City

KMXM(FM)— 1993: 107.3 mhz; 35 kw. Ant 1,138 ft. TL: N37 05 41 W113 11 06. 251 W. Hilton Dr., St. George, UT 84770. Phone: (435) 628-0484. Fax: (435) 673-8228. Web Site: www.mbmediagroup.com. Licensee: MB Media Group Inc. (group owner; acq 7-6-01). Format: Adult contemp. ♦Jerold Johnson, gen mgr.

Coolidge

KCKY(AM)— Nov 19, 1964: 1150 khz; 5 kw-D, 1 kw-N, DA-2. TL: N33 00 27 W111 32 54. 1445 W. Base Line Road, Phoenix 85041. Phone: (602) 426-1150. Phone: (602) 426-9606. Fax: (602) 276-8119. Licensee: Cortaro Broadcasting Corp. (acq 6-13-2003; exchange agreement with KEVT(AM) Cortaro). Format: Sp, Christian contemp. News staff: one. Target aud: General. ♦Moises Herrera, pres & stn mgr.

*****KCOO(FM)**— 2004: 89.9 mhz; 75 w horiz, 16 kw vert. Ant 3,474 ft. TL: N33 16 56 W110 49 12. 125 S. Main St., Bishop, CA 93515. Phone: (760) 872-4225. Licensee: Living Proof Inc. ♦Daniel McClenaghan, pres.

Cortaro

KEVT(AM)— 1994: 1030 khz; 10 kw-D, 1 kw-N, DA-2. TL: N32 20 51 W111 04 19. 2919 E. Broadway Blvd., Suite 230, Tucson 85716. Phone: (520) 889-8904. Fax: (520) 889-8573. Web Site: www.kevtradio.com. Licensee: One Mart Corp. (acq 6-13-2003; exchange agreement with KCKY(AM) Coolidge). Format: Sp, rgnl Mexican. Target aud: 24-54. ♦Armando Zamora, gen mgr; Araceli Espinoza, opns dir; Steve Nunez, gen sls mgr; Frank Luna, engrg dir.

Cottonwood

KVRD-FM—Listing follows KYBC(AM).

KYBC(AM)— Dec 20, 1964: 1600 khz; 1 kw-D, 46 w-N. TL: N34 43 15 W109 31 45. Box 187 86326. Phone: (928) 634-2286. Fax: (928) 634-2295. E-mail: kybc@myradioplace.com. Web Site: www.myradioplace.com. Licensee: Yavapai Broadcasting Corp. (group owner; acq 1-96; $750,000. with co-located FM). Network: Westwood One. Format: Adult standards, MOR. News staff: 2. Target aud: 18-plus. ♦W. Grant Hafley, pres; David J. Kessel, gen mgr; Jackie Bessler, sls dir; Paul Siabe, progmg dir; Paul David, news dir.

KVRD-FM—Co-owned with KYBC(AM). July 1991: 105.7 mhz; 380 w. 2,555 ft. TL: N34 41 15 W112 07 02. (CP: 300 w, ant 2,545 ft.). Stereo. Fax: (928) 634-2295. Web Site: www.myradioplace.com. Format: Country. News: 2 hrs wkly. Target aud: General. ♦Mark Bachman, progmg dir.

KZGL(FM)— August 1983: 95.9 mhz; 9 kw. 2,493 ft. TL: N34 41 14 W112 07 00. Stereo. Box 187 86326. Phone: (928) 634-2286. Fax: (928) 634-2295. E-mail: kzgl@myradioplace.com. Web Site: www.myradioplace.com. Licensee: Yavapai Broadcasting Corp. (acq; 10-1-2000; grpsl). Format: Rock/AOR. News: 7 hrs wkly. Target aud: 18-49. ♦W. Grant Hafley, pres; David J. Kessel, gen mgr; Rick Malone, opns mgr.

Dolan Springs

KOAS(FM)— Jan 7, 1976: 105.7 mhz; 100 kw horiz. Ant 1,761 ft. TL: N35 50 11 W114 19 08. Stereo. 2725 E. Desert Inn Rd., Suite 180, Las Vegas, NV 89121. Phone: (702) 784-4000. Fax: (702) 784-4040. Web Site: 1057theoasis.com. Licensee: Desert Sky Media LLC (acq 3-19-01). Format: Smooth jazz. ♦Frank Woodbeck, VP & gen mgr.

Douglas

KAPR(AM)— Mar 8, 1958: 930 khz; 2.5 kw-D. TL: N31 22 08 W109 31 45. 3222 S. Richey Ave., Tucson 85713. Phone: (520) 790-2440. Fax: (520) 790-2937. Web Site: www.kvoi.com. Licensee: Good Music Inc. Group owner: Good News Communications Inc. (acq 6-8-01; $187,500). Network: CNN Radio. Art Goodkind. Format: Christian ministry. News: 2 hrs wkly. Target aud: General; Sp speaking. ♦Doug Martin, CEO & gen mgr; Rhonda Curtis, CFO; Mary Martin, gen sls mgr & mktg VP.

KCDQ(FM)— Mar 15, 1979: 95.3 mhz; 3 kw. 210 ft. TL: N31 22 08 W109 31 45. Stereo. 500 E. Fry Blvd., Suite L-10, Sierra Vista 85635. Phone: (520) 459-8201. Fax: (520) 458-7104. Licensee: Cochise Broadcasting LLC (acq 6-8-01; $137,500). Network: Westwood One. Format: Contemporary hit. News: 11 hrs wkly. Target aud: 29-49. ♦Ted Tucker, gen mgr.

KDAP(AM)— 1946: 1450 khz; 1 kw-U. TL: N31 21 18 W109 31 45. Box 1179 85608. Secondary address: 2031 N. Sulphur Springs St. 85607. Phone: (520) 364-3486. Phone: (520) 364-3484. Fax: (520) 364-3483. Licensee: Howard N. Henderson (group owner; (acq 2-3-2005; $165,800. with co-located FM). Format: Sp. Target aud: General; loc Hispanic & Mexican residents. ♦Howard Henderson, gen mgr, gen sls mgr & progmg dir.

KDAP-FM— Nov 15, 1990: 96.5 mhz; 3 kw. Ant 30 ft. TL: N31 21 18 W109 33 06. Stereo. Phone: (520) 364-3484. Format: Country. News staff: one. Target aud: General.

*****KRMC(FM)**— 1996: 91.7 mhz; 3 kw. 236 ft. TL: N31 20 52 W109 28 42. Box 2520 85608. Phone: (520) 364-5392. Fax: (520) 364-5392. Licensee: World Radio Network Inc. Format: Christian, Sp, educ. Spec prog: Sp 24 hrs wkly. ♦David Johnson, pres; Glen Lafitte, gen mgr; James V. Heck, engrg dir; Warren Griffin, engrg mgr.

Drake

*****KJZA(FM)**—Not on air, target date: unknown: 89.5 mhz; 250 w. 1,702 ft. 642 E. Rt. 66, Williams 86046. Phone: (928) 541-1008. E-mail: kjzafm@yahoo.com. Licensee: St. Paul Bible College. Format: Christian. ♦Tom Ericson, gen mgr.

Duncan

KJIK(FM)— 2003: 100.7 mhz; 9.8 kw. Ant 2,348 ft. TL: N32 53 21 W109 19 20. 1850 W. Thatcher Blvd., Safford 85546-3306. Phone: (928) 428-4100. Fax: (928) 348-9581. Licensee: William S. Konopnicki. Format: Adult contemp. ♦Dan Curtis, gen mgr & opns mgr.

Eagar

KTHQ(FM)— 1996: 92.5 mhz; 100 kw. 984 ft. TL: N34 05 47 W109 27 52. Box 2020, Show Low 85902. Phone: (928) 532-1010. Fax: (928) 532-0101. E-mail: kthq@whitemtns.com. Licensee: William S. Konopnicki. Format: Country. ♦Camden Smith, gen mgr & gen sls mgr.

Flagstaff

KAFF(AM)— Oct 15, 1963: 930 khz; 5 kw-D, 50 w-N. TL: N35 11 26 W111 40 37. Box 1930 86002. Secondary address: 1117 W. Hwy. 66 86001. Phone: (928) 774-5231. Phone: (520) 774-5233. Fax: (928) 779-2988. Licensee: Guyann Inc. Group owner: Guyann Corp. (acq 9-1-88). Network: ABC Information & Entertainment. Format: Country. News staff: 2. Target aud: 25-54. ♦Guy Christian, CEO, pres & gen mgr; Jane Richardson, stn mgr, sls dir & gen sls mgr; Val Barret, prom dir & prom mgr; Chris Halstead, progmg dir; Hugh Morris, mus dir; George Davis, news dir; Jon Swett, chief of engrg.

KAFF-FM— October 1968: 92.9 mhz; 100 kw. 1,512 ft. TL: N34 58 07 W111 30 24. Stereo. E-mail: production@kaff.com. Web Site: www.kaff.com. Network: ABC. News staff: 2; News: 4 hrs wkly.

KFLX(FM)—(Kachina Village). February 1995: 105.1 mhz; 1 kw. 1,968 ft. TL: N35 14 26 W111 35 48. Stereo. 112 E. Rt. 66, Suite 105 86001. Phone: (928) 779-1177. Fax: (928) 774-5179. E-mail: eagle@redrockradio.com. Web Site: www.kflx.com. Licensee: Red Rock Communications Ltd. (acq 4-95). Arent, Fox, Kintner, Plotkin & Kahn. Format: Adult contemp, classic rock, new age. News staff: one; News: 4 hrs wkly. Target aud: 28-54; males. ♦Tom Rockler, pres; Jim Perrine, gen mgr; Dylan Fletcher, opns dir; Bobby Delrio, prom VP; Samantha Ward, pub affrs dir.

*****KJTA(FM)**— Dec 19, 2001: 89.9 mhz; 10 kw. 1,502 ft. TL: N34 58 06 W111 30 28. 1700 N. 2nd St. 86004. Phone: (928) 774-9514. Fax: (928) 774-9515. E-mail: kjta@kjta.org. Web Site: www.kjta.org. Licensee: Joy Public Broadcasting Corp. Format: Relg educ. ♦Dan Van der Zwaag, gen mgr, gen mgr & stn mgr.

KMGN(FM)— 1975: 93.9 mhz; 100 kw. 1,509 ft. TL: N34 58 08 W111 30 28. Stereo. Box 1930 86002. Secondary address: 1117 W Rt. 66 86001. Phone: (928) 774-5231. Fax: (928) 779-2988. Licensee: Guyann Inc. Group owner; acq 12-20-94; $925,000; 2-13-95). Network: ABC. Format: Classic rock. News staff: 2; News: 4 hrs wkly. Target aud: 25-54; upscale, educated, rgnl audience. ♦Guy Christian, pres & gen mgr; Janie Richardson, gen sls mgr; Rob Dowers, progmg dir.

*****KNAU(FM)**— Nov 24, 1970: 88.7 mhz; 100 kw. 1,549 ft. TL: N34 57 40 W111 31 00. Stereo. Box 5764, Northern Arizona Univ. 86011-5764. Phone: (928) 523-5628. Fax: (928) 523-7647. E-mail: knau@nau.edu. Web Site: www.knau.org. Licensee: Arizona Board of Regents for and

Stations in the U.S. Arizona

on behalf of Northern Arizona University. Network: Network: NPR, PRI. Arter & Hadden. Format: News & info, class. News staff: 3; News: 50 hrs wkly. Target aud: 25-54; educated, socially conscious achievers. Spec prog: Car talk. ◆John Stark, gen mgr; Dave Riek, opns mgr; Alice Ferris, dev dir; Jeff Norcross, mus dir; Mitch Teich, progmg mgr & news dir.

*KPUB(FM)— October 1995: 91.7 mhz; 500 w. 1,837 ft. TL: N35 14 34 W111 36 40. Box 5764, Northern Arizona Univ. 86011-5764. Phone: (928) 523-5628. Fax: (928) 523-7647. E-mail: knau@nau.edu. Web Site: www.knau.org. Licensee: Northern Arizona University. Network: Network: NPR, PRI. Format: News & info. News: 50 hrs wkly. Target aud: 25-54; educated, socially conscious achievers. ◆John Stark, gen mgr; Dave Riek, opns mgr; Alice Ferris, dev dir; Jeff Norcross, mus dir; Mitch Teich, news dir.

KRZS(FM)— Jan 15, 1988: . Stn currently dark 97.5 mhz; 100 kw. Ant 1,509 ft. TL: N34 58 06 W111 30 28. (CP: COL Dewey-Humboldt. 42 kw, ant 2,785 ft. TL: N34 14 05 W112 22 02). Stereo. Trumper Communications, 900 Oakmont Ln., Suite 210, Westmont, IL 60559. Phone: (630) 789-0090. Licensee: Trumper Communications III License LLC (acq 5-27-2005; $22.6 million). ◆Todd Plunkett, CFO.

KVNA(AM)— Aug 8, 1950: 600 khz; 5 kw-D, 500 w-N, DA-N. TL: N35 11 47 W111 40 28. 1800 S. Milton road 86001. Phone: (928) 526-2700. Fax: (928) 774-5852. E-mail: am600@radioflagstaff.com. Web Site: www.radioflagstaff.com. Licensee: Yavapai Broadcasting Corp. (acq 9-30-2000; grpsl). Network: Network: Westwood One, AP Network News, Jones Radio Networks. Format: Sports, news/talk. News staff: one; News: 25 hrs wkly. Target aud: General. Spec prog: Sp 3 hrs wkly, folk music 4hrs wkly. ◆W. Grant Hafley, pres; David J. Kessel, gen mgr; Mike Dougal, opns mgr & progmg dir; Mike Dougall, news dir.

KVNA-FM— 1999: 100.1 mhz; 5.2 kw. Ant 1,433 ft. TL: N34 58 05 W111 30 29. 1800 S. Milton Rd., Suite 105 86001. Phone: (928) 526-2700. Fax: (928) 774-5852. Licensee: Yavapai Broadcasting Corp. (acq 5-2-2005; $1.5 million). Format: Adult contemp. ◆Dave Kessel, gen mgr.

Florence

KCDX(FM)— 1999: 103.1 mhz; 2.7 kw. Ant 3,057 ft. TL: N33 17 55 W110 50 28. Box 36717, Tucson 85740. Phone: (520) 459-8201. Fax: (520) 458-7104. Licensee: Desert West Air Ranchers Corp. Format: Classic rock. ◆Ted Tucker, gen mgr.

Fountain Hills

*KLVK(FM)— May 2000: 89.1 mhz; 1.4 kw. Ant 935 ft. TL: N33 29 33 W111 38 23. (CP: 2.5 kw vert). 5700 West Oaks Blvd., Rocklin, CA 95765. Phone: (916) 251-1600. Fax: (916) 251-1650. E-mail: klove@klove.com. Web Site: www.klove.com. Licensee: Educational Media Foundation. Group owner: EMF Broadcasting (acq 3-11-03; grpsl). Network: K-Love. Shaw Pittman. Format: Contemp Christian. News staff: 3. Target aud: 25-33; Judeo Christian, female. ◆Richard Jenkins, pres; Mike Novak, VP; Keith Whipple, dev dir; Chris Joyce, prom dir; David Pierce, progmg mgr; Ed Lenane, mus dir.

Gilbert

KEDJ(FM)— Feb 25, 1981: 103.9 mhz; 99.59 kw. Ant 620 ft. TL: N33 14 50 W111 31 49. Stereo. 7434 E. Stetson Dr., Suite 265, Scottsdale 85251. Phone: (480) 423-9255. Fax: (480) 423-9382. E-mail: scott@theedge1039.com. Web Site: www.theedge1039.com. Licensee: NPR Phoenix L.L.C. (acq 9-96; $7.35 million). Rep: Roslin. Format: Alternative. News: 2 hrs wkly. Target aud: 18-34. ◆Scott Fey, CEO, pres & gen mgr; Jim Ryan, gen sls mgr.

Glendale

KKFR(FM)—Licensed to Glendale. See Phoenix

KLNZ(FM)—Licensed to Glendale. See Tempe

KPXQ(AM)—Licensed to Glendale. See Phoenix

Globe

KIKO(AM)—See Miami

KJAA(AM)— 1971: 1240 khz; 1 kw-U. TL: N33 22 51 W110 45 25. 3222 S. Richey Ave., Tucson 85713. Phone: (520) 790-2440. Fax: (520) 790-2937. E-mail: doug@kvoi.com. Web Site: kgms.com. Licensee: Good Music Inc. Group owner: Good News Communications Inc. (acq 4-30-01; $212,400). Format: Christian ministry. ◆Doug Martin, gen mgr.

*KLKA(FM)—Not on air, target date: unknown: 88.5 mhz; 24 w vert. Ant 3,385 ft. TL: N33 17 37 W110 50 09. 3185 S. Highland Dr., Suite 13, Las Vegas, NV 89109. Phone: (702) 731-5588. Licensee: American Educational Broadcasting Inc. ◆Carl J. Auel, pres.

KMRR(FM)— Sept 25, 1980: 100.3 mhz; 90 kw. 2,047 ft. TL: N33 17 23 W110 51 53. Stereo. 4745 N. Seventh St., Suite 140, Phoenix 85014. Phone: (602) 308-7900. Fax: (602) 308-7979. Web Site: www.netmio.com/radio/kmrr. Licensee: HBC License Corp. Group owner: Univision Radio (acq 9-22-2003; grpsl). Format: Adult contemp. Target aud: 18-49; upscale, well-educated, affluent adults. ◆Chris Morris, pres; Mary McEvilly-Hernandez, gen mgr; Shawna McCoy, gen sls mgr; Robbie Ramirez, progmg dir.

KRDE(FM)— October 1995: 94.1 mhz; 640w. 3,408 ft. TL: N33 17 37 W110 50 09. Box 1660 85502. Phone: (928) 402-9222. Fax: (928) 425-5063. E-mail: krxs@cableone.net. Licensee: Linda C. Corso. Format: Country, oldies. News staff: one; News: 6 hrs wkly. Target aud: 25-54; active, family building. Spec prog: American Indian 6 hrs, Americana 6 hrs wkly. ◆Linda Corso, CFO; Richard Potyka, pres & gen mgr; Mindy Chansley, opns mgr.

*KVJC(FM)— 2003: 91.9 mhz; 660 w. Ant 3,395 ft. TL: N33 17 37 W110 50 09. 1403 E. Ash St. 85502. Phone: (208) 402-9222. Phone: (208) 734-6633. E-mail: kvjc@csnradio.com. Web Site: www.csnradio.com. Licensee: CSN International (group owner). Format: Christian. ◆Jeffrey W. Smith, VP; Mike Stocklin, gen mgr; Don Mills, progmg dir & mus dir; Kelly Carlson, chief of engrg.

Grand Canyon

*KNAG(FM)—Not on air, target date: unknown: 90.3 mhz; 3 kw. 295 ft. TL: N35 56 44 W112 10 16. Box 5764, Flagstaff 86011. Phone: (928) 523-5628. Fax: (928) 523-6202. Web Site: www.knau.org. Licensee: Arizona Board of Regents/Northern Arizona University. Format: Class. ◆John Stark, gen mgr; Dave Riek, opns mgr; Alice Ferris, dev dir.

Green Valley

KFMA(FM)— Feb 20, 1983: 92.1 mhz; 50 kw. 492 ft. TL: N32 00 11 W110 47 49. Stereo. 3871 N. Commerce Dr., Tucson 85745. Phone: (520) 407-4500. Fax: (520) 407-4600. Web Site: www.kfma.com. Licensee: Arizona Lotus Corp. Group owner: Lotus Communications Corp. (acq 5-10-93; $1.26 million; 5-31-93). Rep: Christal. Format: Alternative. Target aud: 18-34. ◆Steve Groesbeck, gen mgr; Hans Rhey, prom mgr; Libby Carstenson, progmg mgr.

KGVY(AM)—Licensed to Green Valley. See Tucson

KTZR-FM—Licensed to Green Valley. See Tucson

Holbrook

*KBMH(FM)— 2002: 90.3 mhz; 250 w. Ant 141 ft. TL: N34 55 05 W110 08 25. Drawer 2440, Tupelo, MS 38803. Phone: (601) 844-8888. Fax: (662) 842-6791. Licensee: American Family Association. Group owner: American Family Radio Format: Christian. ◆Marvin Sanders, gen mgr; John Riley, progmg dir; Joey Moody, chief of engrg.

KDJI(AM)—Listing follows KZUA(FM).

KZUA(FM)— Dec 6, 1993: 92.1 mhz; 100 kw. 328 ft. TL: N34 52 25 W110 09 56. Stereo. 3051 S. White Mountain Rd., Suite D, Show Low 85901. Phone: (928) 532-3232. Fax: (928) 537-3991. E-mail: production @whitemountainradio.com. Licensee: Petracom of Holbrook L.L.C. (acq 2-26-2002; $650,000. with co-located AM). Network: Network: Westwood One, CNN Radio. Format: Contemp country. Target aud: 18-54; 57% female, 43% male. ◆Steve Johnson, gen mgr, progmg dir & chief of engrg.

KDJI(AM)—Co-owned with KZUA(FM). October 1955: 1270 khz; 5 kw-D, 130 w-N. TL: N34 53 55 W110 11 30. Network: Network: ABC, Westwood One. Format: News/Talk. Target aud: 35-65; 46% female, 54% male. Spec prog: Sports 10 hrs, farm 8 hrs wkly.

Hotevilla

*KUYI(FM)— Dec 20, 2000: 88.1 mhz; 69 kw. Ant 407 ft. TL: N35 48 29 W110 16 23. Box 1500, Kearns Canyon 86034. Phone: (928) 738-5505. Fax: (928) 738-5501. E-mail: kuyi@direcway.com. Web Site: www.kuyi.net. Licensee: Hopi Foundation. Format: Tribal radio, loc news, cultural events. News staff: 2; News: 6 hrs wkly. Target aud: 30+. ◆Loris Ann Taylor, gen mgr; Alicia Youvella, stn mgr; Abel Nash, opns mgr; Dan Kracer, news dir.

Kachina Village

KFLX(FM)—Licensed to Kachina Village. See Flagstaff

Kearny

KZLZ(FM)—Licensed to Kearny. See Tucson

Kingman

KAAA(AM)— Oct 7, 1949: 1230 khz; 1 kw-U. TL: N35 11 48 W114 01 18. 2534 Hualapai Mountain Rd. 86401-5300. Phone: (928) 753-2537. Fax: (928) 753-1551. Licensee: Cameron Broadcasting Inc. (group owner; acq 11-24-99; grpsl). Network: ABC Information & Entertainment. Cohn & Marks. Format: News/talk. Target aud: 25 plus. Spec prog: Sports. ◆Don Jaeger, gen mgr; Jeff Allen, progmg dir.

KFLG-FM—Co-owned with KAAA(AM). Dec 6, 1974: 94.7 mhz; 43 kw. Ant 2,591 ft. TL: N35 06 41 W113 53 08. Stereo. 1531 Jill Way, Suite 5, Bullhead City 86426. Phone: (520) 763-2100. Fax: (520) 763-3957. Format: Country. Target aud: 25-54; professionals.

KGMN(FM)— Feb 14, 1984: 100.1 mhz; 360 w. 761 ft. TL: N35 11 43 W114 06 51. (CP: 930 w, ant 2,896 ft. TL: N35 06 37 W133 52 55). Stereo. 812 E. Beale St. 86401. Phone: (928) 753-9100. Fax: (928) 753-1978. Web Site: www.kgmn.net. Licensee: New West Broadcasting Systems Inc. Network: Network: AP Radio, Jones Radio Networks. Format: Country. ◆Joe Hart, CEO; Rhonda Hart, VP & gen mgr; Kathy Krick, opns mgr; Steve Levin, progmg dir.

KRRN(FM)— November 1990: 92.7 mhz; 17 kw. Ant 1,889 ft. TL: N35 01 58 W114 21 57. (CP: COL Dolan Springs. 100 kw, ant 1,774 ft. TL: N35 39 07 W114 18 42). 1955 Casino Dr., Suite 101, Laughlin, NV 89029-1505. Phone: (928) 855-1051. Fax: (928) 855-7996. Licensee: Entravision Holdings LLC. Group owner: Entravision Communications Corp. (acq 8-29-02; $12.43 million). Network: ABC. Format: Oldies. ◆Rick Murphy, VP; Chris Sarros, gen mgr; Chris Rolando, stn mgr; Brian Calkins, news dir.

Lake Havasu City

*KAIH(FM)—Not on air, target date: unknown: 89.3 mhz; 440 w. Ant -512 ft. TL: N34 27 27 W114 20 07. 5700 West Oaks Blvd., Rocklin, CA 95765. Phone: (916) 251-1600. Fax: (916) 251-1650. Licensee: Educational Media Foundation. Group owner: EMF Broadcasting

Broadcasting & Cable Yearbook 2006

D-51

Arizona

KJJJ(FM)— May 24, 1994: 102.3 mhz; 1.05 kw. Ant 2,670 ft. TL: N34 33 06 W114 11 37. 1845 McCulloch Blvd., Suite A 86403. Phone: (928) 855-9336. Fax: (928) 855-9333. E-mail: radio@kjjjfm.com. Web Site: www.kjjjfm.com. Licensee: Steven M. Greeley. Format: Country. ♦ Steve Greeley, gen mgr.

*KNLB(FM)— July 1983: 91.1 mhz; 8 kw. Ant 453 ft. TL: N34 29 10 W114 13 06. Stereo. 510 N. Acoma Blvd. 86403. Phone: (928) 855-9110. Fax: (928) 453-2588. E-mail: info@knlb.com. Web Site: www.knlb.com. Licensee: Advance Ministries. Network: USA. Arent, Fox, Kintner, Plotkin & Kahn. Format: Relg, Christian. News: 8 hrs wkly. Target aud: General. ♦ Richard D. Tatham, pres; Faron Eckelbarger, stn mgr, progmg dir & chief of engrg.

KNTR(AM)— Sept 23, 1970: 980 khz; 1 kw-D, 49 w-N. TL: N34 30 12 W114 21 28. 1845 McCulloch Blvd., Suite A 86403. Phone: (928) 855-9336. Fax: (928) 855-9333. E-mail: speakout@kntram.com. Web Site: www.kntram.com. Licensee: Steven M. Greeley. (acq 12-8-99; $608,000). Network: PRI. Arent, Fox, Kintner, Plotkin & Kahn. Format: News and talk. News staff: one; News: 12 hrs wkly. Target aud: 35-64. ♦ Steve Greeley, gen mgr.

KRCY-FM— 1999: 96.7 mhz; 1.05 kw. 2,706 ft. TL: N34 33 06 W114 11 37. 10 Media Center Dr. 86403. Phone: (928) 855-1051. Fax: (928) 855-7996. Web Site: www.maddoq.net. Licensee: Rick L. Murphy. Format: Oldies. ♦ Rick L. Murphy, pres & gen mgr.

KRRK(FM)— Sept 9, 1974: 101.1 mhz; 20 kw. Ant 2,696 ft. TL: N34 33 06 W114 11 37. Stereo. 10 Media Center Dr. 86403. Phone: (928) 855-4560. Phone: (928) 855-1051. Fax: (928) 855-7996. Web Site: www.maddog.net. Licensee: Smoke and Mirrors LLC. (acq 11-29-99). Format: Classic rock. News staff: one; News: 5 hrs wkly. Target aud: 18-34. ♦ Chris Rolando, gen mgr.

KZUL-FM— 1986: 104.5 mhz; 1.05 kw. Ant 2,670 ft. TL: N34 33 06 W114 11 37. Stereo. Box 1866 86405. Phone: (928) 855-4560. Fax: (928) 855-7996. E-mail: epress@maddog.net. Web Site: www.maddog.net. Licensee: Mad Dog Wireless Inc. Network: ABC. Format: Adult contemp. Target aud: 25-54. ♦ Rick Murphy, pres; Chris Rolando, VP, gen mgr & progmg dir; Ron Nickle, gen sls mgr; Faron Eckleburger, chief of engrg.

Mammoth

*KLTU(FM)—Not on air, target date: unknown: 88.1 mhz; 160 w. Ant 3,552 ft. TL: N32 24 54 W110 42 56. 3222 S. Richey Ave., Tucson 85713. Phone: (520) 790-2440. Fax: (520) 790-2937. Licensee: Good News Radio Broadcasting Inc. (acq 6-8-2005). ♦ Doug Martin, gen mgr.

Marana

KOHT(FM)— Oct 1, 1984: 98.3 mhz; 6 kw. 200 ft. TL: N32 27 09 W111 05 09. Stereo. 3202 N. Oracle, Tucson 85705. Phone: (520) 618-2100. Fax: (520) 618-2165. E-mail: hot983comments@yahoo.com. Web Site: www.hot98.com. Licensee: Clear Channel Broadcasting Licenses Inc. Group owner: Clear Channel Communications Inc. (acq 6-22-01; grpsl). Format: CHR, rhythm & blues, hip hop. News staff: 2; News: 4 hrs wkly. Target aud: 18-49; Sp, contemp, white collar adults. ♦ Debbie Wagner, gen mgr; Tim Richards, opns mgr; Steve Clement, gen sls mgr; R. Dub, progmg dir; Mike Irby, chief of engrg.

KSAZ(AM)—Licensed to Marana. See Tucson

Mesa

KDKB(FM)— Apr 20, 1968: 93.3 mhz; 100 kw. 1,538 ft. TL: N33 20 04 W112 03 36. Stereo. 1167 W. Javelina 85210. Phone: (480) 897-9300. Fax: (480) rock@kdjb.com. Web Site: www.kdkb.com. Licensee: Mesa Radio Inc. Group owner: Sandusky Radio (acq 1977). Rep: Christal. Format: AOR. ♦ Norman Rau, pres; Chuck Artigue, gen mgr; Bob Weaver, gen sls mgr; Joe Bonadonna, prom mgr & progmg dir; Ray Thompson, chief of engrg.

KFNN(AM)—Licensed to Mesa. See Phoenix

*KJZZ(FM)—(Phoenix). 1951: 91.5 mhz; 96 kw. 1,607 ft. TL: N33 19 58 W112 03 53. Stereo. 1435 S. Dobson Rd. 85202. Phone: (480) 834-5627. Fax: (480) 835-5925. Web Site: www.kjzz.org. Licensee: Maricopa County Community College District. Network: Network: NPR, PRI. Format: Acoustic jazz, news. News staff: 5; News: 50 hrs wkly. Target aud: 25-54. ♦ Carl Matthusen, gen mgr; Bill Shedd, opns mgr; Bob Glazar, dev dir; Scott Williams, prom dir; Mark Moran, news dir; Dennis Gilliam, chief of engrg.

KXAM(AM)— 1946: 1310 khz; 5 kw-D, 500 w-N, DA-N. TL: N33 26 23 W111 50 09. 4725 N. Scottsdale Rd., Suite 234, Scottsdale 85251. Phone: (480) 423-1310. Fax: (480) 423-3867. E-mail: kxamradio@aol.com. Web Site: www.kxam.com. Licensee: Embee Broadcasting Inc. (acq 9-25-90). Network: Network: UPI, Westwood One, ABC. Hogan & Hartson. Format: Talk. News: 14 hrs wkly. Target aud: 35-64. ♦ Byron Gerson, pres & gen mgr; Don Sandler, stn mgr.

KZZP(FM)— 1967: 104.7 mhz; 100 kw. 1,550 ft. TL: N33 20 04 W112 03 35. Stereo. 645 E. Missouri Ave., Suite 360, Phoenix 85012. Phone: (602) 279-5577. Fax: (602) 230-2781. Web Site: www.1047kissfm.com. Licensee: Citicasters Licenses L.P. Group owner Clear Channel Communications Inc. (acq 6-99; grpsl). Format: CHR. News staff: one; News: 7 hrs wkly. Target aud: 18-34; women. ♦ Lowry Mays, CEO; Randy Michaels, chmn; John Hogan, pres; Susan Karis-Madigan, gen mgr; Alan Sledge, opns dir; Cathy Burau, gen sls mgr.

Miami

KIKO(AM)— June 13, 1958: 1340 khz; 1 kw-U. TL: N33 24 41 W110 50 17. 4501 Broadway 85539. Secondary address: 4501 Broadway, Claypool 85532. Phone: (928) 425-4471. Fax: (928) 425-9393. E-mail: radiokiko@gila.net.Westwood One 6 pm-6 am Licensee: Shoecraft Broadcasting Inc. (acq 5-31-01; with KIKO-FM Claypool). Network: Network: Westwood One, ABC Information & Entertainment. Shaw Pittman. Format: Sports, oldies, contemp hits. News staff: one; News: 8 hrs wkly. Target aud: 21-70; industrial/blue collar workers in loc copper mines, highest hourly wage earners. ♦ Ruth Shoecraft Wallace, CEO; Lucy Rodriguez, gen mgr.

KIKO-FM— Aug 1, 1991: 106.1 mhz; 6 kw. 297 ft. TL: N33 24 23 W110 48 18. Stereo. Phone: (928) 425-4472.Westwood One 24 hrs Network: Westwood One. Shaw Pittman. Format: Soft adult contemp. News staff: one; News: 6 hrs wkly. Target aud: 21-55; blue collar, housewives, white collar.

KQSS(FM)— Mar 30, 1987: 98.3 mhz; 6 kw. Ant -279 ft. TL: N33 24 30 W110 48 14. Stereo. Box 292 85539. Secondary address: 5734 McKinney, Globe 85501. Phone: (928) 425-7186. Fax: (928) 425-7982. Licensee: William D. Taylor. Format: Country. News staff: one; News: 5 hrs wkly. Target aud: 25-54. ♦ Bill Taylor, gen mgr & sls dir.

Morenci

KCUZ(AM)—See Safford

Nogales

*KNOG(FM)— Dec 16, 1995: 91.1 mhz; 3 kw. 154 ft. TL: N31 21 33 W110 53 54. Box 1614 85628. Secondary address: 150 W. First St. 85628. Phone: (520) 287-5206. Fax: (520) 287-3606. E-mail: knog91fm@theriver.com. Licensee: World Radio Network Inc. Network: Moody. Format: Sp contemp Christian, educ. News: 3 hrs wkly. Target aud: 18-49; Hispanics. Spec prog: Btfl music 5 hrs wkly. ♦ Marcos Romero, stn mgr; Mariana Romero, progmg dir & pub affrs dir.

KOFH(FM)— Apr 1, 1999: 99.1 mhz; 6 kw. 328 ft. TL: N31 20 46 W110 53 34. 934N Bjarano St., Suite 2 85621-1385. Phone: (520) 287-6885. Fax: (520) 287-8290. Licensee: Felix Corp. Format: Top-40, Sp & English. ♦ Oscar Felix Sr.; Carlos Campa, stn mgr, progmg dir & news dir.

KRDX(FM)— June 1978: 98.3 mhz; 215 w. Ant 228 ft. TL: N31 23 17 W110 55 38. Stereo. 67 E. Baffert Dr., Suite One 85621. Phone: (877) 335-5239. Fax: (520) 761-4957. Licensee: Desert West Air Ranchers Corp. (acq 6-24-99). ♦ Sonia Tabanico, gen mgr.

Oracle

KGMG(FM)— December 1984: 106.3 mhz; 430 w vert, 440 w horiz. 4,172 ft. TL: N32 26 26 W110 47 12. Stereo. 3438 N. Country Club Rd., Tucson 85716. Phone: (520) 795-1490. Fax: (520) 618-3161. Licensee: Journal Broadcast Corp. Group owner: Journal Broadcast Group Inc. (acq 4-15-98; $5.8 million). Rep: Christal. Format: Oldies. News: 2 hrs wkly. Target aud: 25-54; Hispanic and Anglo adults. ♦ Carl Gardner, pres; Terry Daniels, mktg mgr; Bobby Rich, progmg dir.

Oro Valley

KCMT(FM)— 2003: 102.1 mhz; 100 kw. Ant 66 ft. TL: N32 17 23 W111 01 06. (CP: Ant 266 ft). 3871 N. Commerce Dr., Tucson 85705. Phone: (520) 407-4500. Fax: (520) 407-4600. Licensee: Arizona Lotus Corp. Group owner: Lotus Communications Corp. Format: Rgnl Sp. ♦ Steve Groesbeck, gen mgr; Tara Hungate, rgnl sls mgr.

KSZR(FM)— Apr 28, 1992: 97.5 mhz; 3 kw. 299 ft. TL: N32 23 28 W111 01 48. (CP: 6 kw, ant 328 ft.). 575 W. Roger Rd., Tuscon 85705. Phone: (520) 887-1000. Fax: (520) 887-6397. Web Site: www.star975.com. Licensee: Citadel Broadcasting Co. Group owner: Citadel Broadcasting Corp. (acq 4-26-01; grpsl). Format: Adult Contemp, 70s & 80s. News staff: 2; News: 60 hrs wkly. Target aud: 25-54. ♦ Farid Suleman, CEO; Todd Lawley, gen mgr & stn mgr; Herb Crowe, opns dir; Ken Kowalcek, sls dir.

Page

*KNAD(FM)— 1998: 91.7 mhz; 500 w. 1,509 ft. TL: N36 41 51 W111 37 57. Box 5764, Flagstaff 86011-5764. Phone: (928) 523-5628. Fax: (928) 523-7647. Web Site: www.knau.org. Licensee: Arizona Board of Regents on behalf of Northern Arizona University. Format: News & info, class. ♦ John Stark, gen mgr; Dave Riek, opns mgr; Jeff Norcross, mus dir; Mitch Teich, news dir.

KPGE(AM)— May 15, 1971: 1340 khz; 1 kw-U. TL: N36 45 23 W111 27 32. Box 1030, 91 7th Ave. 86040. Phone: (928) 645-8181. Fax: (928) 645-3347. Web Site: kpge.com. Licensee: Lake Powell Communications Inc. (acq 7-1-91; with co-located FM; 6-17-91). Network: ABC. Format: Country. News staff: one; News: 15 hrs wkly. Target aud: 25-54. ♦ Dan Brown, gen mgr; Janet Brown, gen sls mgr; Deborah Phillips, news dir; Mark Jones, chief of engrg.

KXAZ(FM)—Co-owned with KPGE(AM). Sept 22, 1980: 93.3 mhz; 12.5 kw. 921 ft. TL: N36 46 42 W111 25 46. Stereo. Web Site: kxaz.com. Format: Adult contemp.

Paradise Valley

KHOT-FM— 1996: 105.9 mhz; 36 kw. Ant 577 ft. TL: N33 35 16 W111 45 38. 4745 N. 7th St., Suite 140-C, Phoenix 85014. Phone: (602) 308-7900. Fax: (602) 308-7979. Licensee: Univision Radio License Corp. Group owner: Univision Radio (acq 9-22-2003; grpsl). Format: Rgnl Mexican. ♦ Mary McEvilly-Hernandez, gen mgr; Fernando Gomez, mktg dir & prom mgr; Elvis Valle, progmg dir.

Parker

KLPZ(AM)— Sept 7, 1974: 1380 khz; 2.5 kw-D, 58 w-N. TL: N34 09 14 W114 17 15. 816 6th St. 85344. Phone: (928) 669-9274. Phone: (928) 669-9275. Fax: (928) 669-9300. Licensee: Keith Douglas Learn (acq 4-1-00). Network: Network: ABC Information & Entertainment, Jones Radio Networks. Format: Country, news/talk. News staff: 2; News: 2 hrs wkly. Target aud: 25-55. Spec prog: Farm one hr wkly. ♦ Keith Douglas Learn, pres.

KRIT(FM)— 2003: 93.9 mhz; 7.6 kw. Ant -154 ft. TL: N34 08 30 W114 17 50. Box 62, Keene, CA 93531. Phone: (661) 823-6201. Phone: (661) 837-0745. Web Site: www.campesina.com. Licensee: Farmworker Educational Radio Network Inc. Format: Rgnl, Sp. ♦ Anthony Chavez, exec VP; Jeff Russinsky, natl sls mgr; Paco Jacobo, progmg dir; Dave Whitehead, chief of engrg.

*KWFH(FM)— November 1984: 90.1 mhz; 460 w. -184 ft. TL: N34 08 53 W114 16 44. Stereo. 401 15th St. 85344. Phone: (520) 669-5683. Fax: (520) 669-5683. Licensee: Desert View Baptist Church. Network: Moody. Format: Relg. Target aud: General. ♦ Gary Covert, stn mgr & opns mgr; Louie Marsh, progmg dir; Keith Moses, mus dir.

Payson

KAJM(FM)— July 4, 1984: 104.3 mhz; 100 kw. 1,023 ft. TL: N34 25 48 W111 30 16. (CP: Ant 1,164 ft.). Stereo. 7434 E. Stetson Dr., Suite 255, Scottsdale 85251. Phone: (480) 994-9100. Phone: (800) 254-7510. Fax: (480) 423-8770. E-mail: operations@sierrah.com. Web Site: www.mega1043.com. Licensee: Sierra H. Broadcasting Inc. Network: Network: Westwood One, CNN Radio. Rep: Roslin. Format: Old school/rhythm & blues. Target aud: 25-54; general. ♦ Michael Mallace, gen mgr; Jack Preda, sls dir; Angela Manuel, prom dir; Alex Santa Maria, progmg dir; Steven Szalay, opns mgr & pub affrs dir; Richard White, engrg dir & engrg mgr; Michael Day, chief of engrg.

Stations in the U.S. — Arizona

Developers & Brokers of Radio Properties — contact American Media Services at our suite: Philadelphia Marriott Downtown, 215-625-2900, 843-972-2200, americanmediaservices.com, Charleston, SC. Dallas, TX · Chicago, IL · Austin, TX. American Media Services, LLC

KMOG(AM)— Nov 1, 1983: 1420 khz; 2.5 kw-D, 500 w-N, DA-N. TL: N34 16 00 W111 18 54. 500 E. Tyler Pkwy. 85541. Phone: (928) 474-5214. Fax: (928) 474-0236. E-mail: kmog@cybertrails.com. Licensee: Farrell Enterprises L.L.C. (acq 3-6-97). Network: ABC Information & Entertainment. Format: Country. News staff: one; News: 2 hrs wkly. Target aud: 25-54; working adults. ♦ Mike Farrell, pres; Blaine Kimball, gen mgr.

KNRJ(FM)— 2000: 101.1 mhz; 88 kw. 1,033 ft. TL: N34 25 51 W111 30 12. 7434 E. Stetson Dr., Suite 255, Scottsdale 85251. Phone: (480) 994-9100. Phone: (800) 254-7510. Fax: (480) 423-8770. E-mail: operations@sierrah.com. Web Site: www.energyarizonafm.com. Licensee: Sierra H. Broadcasting Inc. Network: Westwood One, CNN Radio. Format: Disco. Target aud: 18-35; upscale. ♦ Michael Mallace, gen mgr; Rod Carrillo, progmg dir; Steve Szalay, pub affrs dir.

KSXX(FM)—Not on air, target date: unknown: 99.3 mhz; 17.2 kw. Ant 403 ft. TL: N34 11 04 W111 20 16. 3800 Howard Hughes Pkwy., Wells Fargo Tower, 17th Fl., Las Vegas, NV 89109. Phone: (702) 385-6000. Licensee: Kemp Communications Inc. ♦ Will Kemp, pres & gen mgr.

Phoenix

KASA(AM)— Jan 6, 1967: 1540 khz; 10 kw-D, DA. TL: N33 22 36 W112 05 25. 1445 W. Baseline Rd. 85041. Phone: (602) 276-4241. Phone: (602) 276-5272. Fax: (602) 276-8119. Licensee: KASA Radio Hogar Inc. (group owner; (acq 8-26-92; $475,000;. FTR: 9-14-92). Cohn & Marks. Format: Relg. Target aud: General. ♦ Moses Herrera, pres, gen mgr & opns mgr.

KAZG(AM)—(Scottsdale). 1956: 1440 khz; 5 kw-D, 52 w-N. TL: N33 28 43 W111 56 24. 4343 E. Camelback Rd., Suite 200 85018. Phone: (480) 941-1007. Fax: (602) 260-5759. Licensee: Cactus Radio Inc. Group owner: Sandusky Radio (acq 6-5-98; with co-located FM). Format: Oldies. ♦ Chuck Artigue, gen mgr; Dean Mooney, gen sls mgr; Michael Bradford, prom dir & prom mgr; Dave Cooper, progmg dir.

KSLX-FM—Co-owned with KAZG(AM). Aug 1, 1969: 100.7 mhz; 100 kw. 1,847 ft. TL: N33 19 53 W112 03 47. Stereo. Web Site: www.kslx.com. Format: Classic rock.

*KBAQ-FM— Apr 26, 1993: 89.5 mhz; 91 w. 1,463 ft. TL: N33 19 58 W112 03 53. (CP: 12.5 kw, ant 2,316 ft. TL: N33 35 33 W112 34 49). Maircopa County Community Colleges, 1435 S. Dobson Rd., Mesa 85202. Phone: (480) 834-5627. Fax: (480) 835-5925. Licensee: College District. Network: NPR. Format: Class mus, news. ♦ Carl Matthusen, gen mgr; Lou Stanley, dev dir; Bob Glazar, sls dir; Scott Williams, progmg dir; Sterling Beeaff, mus dir; Dennis Gilliam, chief of engrg.

KESZ(FM)— July 1982: 99.9 mhz; 100 kw. 1,702 ft. TL: N33 20 01 W112 03 44. Stereo. 600 E. Gilbert Dr., Tempe 85281. Phone: (480) 966-6236. Fax: (480) 921-6365. Web Site: www.kez999.com. Licensee: Clear Channel Broadcasting Licenses Inc. Group owner: Clear Channel Communications Inc. (acq 5-14-99; $58 million). Network: AP Radio. Rep: Katz Radio. Format: Adult contemp. Target aud: General. ♦ Susan Karis-Madigan, gen mgr; Linda Little, rgnl sls mgr; Mary Evanson, prom dir.

*KFLR-FM— December 1985: 90.3 mhz; 2.2 kw. 354 ft. TL: N33 26 09 W112 06 35. (CP: 28.31 kw, ant 1,555 ft. TL: N33 20 02 W112 02 04). Stereo. 702 E. Thunderbird Rd. 85022-5310. Phone: (602) 978-0903. Fax: (602) 548-8089. E-mail: kflr@flc.org. Web Site: www.flc.org. Licensee: Family Life Broadcasting Inc. Group owner: Family Life Communications Inc. (acq 7-30-78). Format: Christian, inspirational. ♦ Randy Carlson, pres; Alan Cook, gen mgr & progmg dir; Fred Morse, opns mgr; Bruce Thurman, prom dir; Walter Ellis, engrg mgr & chief of engrg.

KFNN(AM)—(Mesa). November 1962: 1510 khz; 22 kw-D, 100 w-N. TL: N33 23 30 W111 50 16. 4800 N. Central Ave. 85012. Phone: (602) 241-1510. Fax: (602) 241-1540. E-mail: questions@kfnn.com. Web Site: www.kfnn.com. Licensee: CRC Broadcasting Co. Inc. (acq 1988). Network: Network: ABC News/Talk, CNN Radio. Akin, Gump, Strauss, Houer & Feld. Format: News/talk, business news, investment advice.

News staff: 3; News: 84 hrs wkly. Target aud: 30 plus; upscale, investment-oriented professionals & entrepreneurs; decision makers. ♦ Ronald E. Cohen, pres & gen mgr; Brian DuBose, opns mgr & progmg dir.

KFYI(AM)—Listing follows KYOT-FM.

KGME(AM)— 1940: 910 khz; 5 kw-U, DA-N. TL: N33 32 00 W112 07 18. 645 E. Missouri, Suite 119 85012. Phone: (602) 798-9322. Fax: (602) 650-5280. Web Site: www.xtra910.com. Licensee: AMFM Radio Licenses L.L.C. Group owner: Clear Channel Communications Inc. (acq 8-30-00; grpsl). Network: Network: CBS, Westwood One. Format: Sports/talk. News staff: 7. Target aud: General. ♦ Brad Gould, gen mgr & sls VP.

KIDR(AM)— Feb 1, 1958: 740 khz; 1 kw-D, 292 w-N, DA-2. TL: N33 21 55 W112 06 30. Stereo. 3030 N. Central Ave., Suite 220 85012-2784. Phone: (602) 234-8998. Fax: (602) 234-8998. Licensee: Multicultural Radio Broadcasting Licensee LLC. Group owner: Multicultural Radio Broadcasting Inc. (acq 2-4-2004; grpsl). Format: Sp news, talk, sports. News staff: 2; News: 10 hrs wkly. Target aud: 18-64; Hispanic. ♦ Dave Sweeney, CFO; Arturo Galvez, gen mgr & news dir.

KJZZ(FM)—Licensed to Phoenix. See Mesa

KKFR(FM)—(Glendale). Dec 19, 1979: 92.3 mhz; 98 kw. Ant 1,788 ft. TL: N33 19 58 W112 03 48. Stereo. 5300 N. Central Ave. 85012. Phone: (602) 274-6200. Web Site: www.power923.fm. Licensee: Emmis Radio License LLC. Group owner: Emmis Communications Corp. (acq 2000; $108 million. with KXPK(FM) Evergreen, CO). Format: Rhythm & blues, urban contemp. Target aud: 18-49. ♦ Mark Waters, gen mgr & stn mgr; Bruce St. James, progmg dir.

KKNT(AM)— June 1947: 960 khz; 5 kw-U, DA-N. TL: N33 39 12 W111 55 39. (CP: TL: N33 41 34 W112 00 09). 2425 E. Camelback Rd., Suite 570 85016. Phone: (602) 955-9600. Fax: (602) 955-7860. E-mail: jtimm@kknt960.com. Web Site: www.kknt960.com. Licensee: Common Ground Broadcasting Inc. Group owner: Salem Communications Corp. (acq 1996; $6.5 million). Network: Salem Radio Network. Format: News/talk. Target aud: 25-54; upscale adults. Spec prog: U of A football, basketball. ♦ Edward Atsinger III, CEO & news dir; Stuart Epperson, chmn; Joe D. Davis, exec VP & progmg mgr; Ken Gaines, VP; John Timm, gen mgr; Jim Seemiller, gen sls mgr.

KMIK(AM)—(Tempe). June 23, 1960: 1580 khz; 50 kw-U, DA-N. TL: N33 27 22 W111 50 01. Stereo. 2231 E. Camelback, Suite 102 85016. Phone: (602) 381-1580. Fax: (602) 840-1488. E-mail: marni.gerber@abc.com. Web Site: www.radiodisney.com. Licensee: Radio Disney Group LLC. Group owner: ABC Inc. (acq 9-10-98; $5.85 million). Network: ABC. Format: Radio Disney, children's Pop Top 40. ♦ Marni Gerber, gen mgr & stn mgr; Carl Jimenez, mktg dir & prom dir.

KMLE(FM)—(Chandler). Apr 18, 1980: 107.9 mhz; 100 kw. 1,735 ft. TL: N33 20 03 W112 03 43. Stereo. 840 N. Central 85004. Phone: (602) 452-1000. Fax: (602) 440-6530. Web Site: www.kmle108.com. Licensee: Infinity Radio Inc. Group owner: Infinity Broadcasting Corp. (acq 8-7-00; grpsl). Format: Country. News staff: 2. Target aud: 25-54. Spec prog: Camel Views one hr wkly. ♦ Mark Steinmetz, sr VP & gen mgr; Todd Wallace, opns dir; Jose Rodiles, gen sls mgr; Jay McCarthy, progmg dir; Doc Holiday, mus dir.

KMRR(FM)—See Globe

KMVP(AM)— Nov 23, 1949: 860 khz; 1 kw-D, DA-N. TL: N33 24 16 W112 07 24. 5300 N. Central Ave. 85012-1410. Phone: (602) 274-6200. Fax: (602) 241-6810. Web Site: www.espnradio860.com. Licensee: Bonneville Holding Co. Group owner: Emmis Communications Corp. (acq 1-14-2005; grpsl). Network: ESPN Radio. Format: Sports talk. Target aud: 25-54; sports enthusiast. ♦ Bruce T. Reese, CEO & pres; Mark Waters, sls dir; John Spilman, gen sls mgr; Dawn Suber-Paugh, natl sls mgr; Randy Eccles, prom mgr & progmg mgr; Tisa Vrable, progmg dir; Clayton Creekmore, engrg dir.

KMXP(FM)— October 1964: 96.9 mhz; 100 kw. 1,560 ft. TL: N33 20 03 W112 03 36. Stereo. 645 E. Missouri Ave., #360 85012. Phone: (602) 279-5577. Fax: (602) 230-2781. Web Site: www.mix969.com. Licensee: Citicasters Licenses L.P. Group owner: Clear Channel Communications Inc. (acq 5-4-99; grpsl). Format: Adult contemp. News staff: one. ♦ Lowry Mays, CEO; Randy Michaels, chmn; John Hogan, pres; Susan Karis-Madigan, gen mgr; Alan Sledge, opns dir; Shanna McCoy, sls dir.

KNAI(FM)—Licensed to Phoenix. See Keene CA

KNIX-FM— Sept 1, 1969: 102.5 mhz; 98 kw. 1,620 ft. TL: N33 19 58 W112 03 53. Stereo. 600 E. Gilbert Dr., Tempe 85281. Phone: (480) 966-6236. Fax: (480) 966-7435. Web Site: www.knixcountry.com. Licensee: Clear Channel Broadcasting Licenses Inc. Group owner: Clear Channel Communications Inc. (acq 6-1-99; $84 million). Format: Country. News staff: 3; News: one hr wkly. Target aud: 25-54. ♦ Susan Karis-Madigan, gen mgr; Shaun Holly, stn mgr & progmg dir; Art Morales, gen sls mgr; Becky Lynn, news dir.

KNUV(AM)—See Tolleson

KOMR(FM)—See Sun City

KOOL-FM— May 1956: 94.5 mhz; 100 kw. 1,655 ft. TL: N33 20 02 W112 03 42. Stereo. 4745 N. 7th St., Suite 210 85014. Phone: (602) 956-9696. Fax: (602) 285-1450. Web Site: www.koolradio.com. Licensee: Infinity Radio Inc. Group owner: Infinity Broadcasting Corp. (acq 8-7-00; grpsl). Rep: Christal. Format: Oldies. Target aud: 25-54. ♦ Todd Wallace, progmg dir.

KOY(AM)— May 1949: 1230 khz; 1 kw-U. TL: N33 26 09 W112 06 35. 600 E. Gilbert, Tempe 85281. Phone: (480) 966-6236. Fax: (480) 377-2477. Web Site: www.am1230koy.com. Licensee: AMFM Radio Licenses LLC. Group owner: Clear Channel Communications Inc. (acq 8-30-00; grpsl). Format: Oldies. ♦ Susan Karis-Madigan, gen mgr.

*KPHF(FM)— December 1991: 88.3 mhz; 22.5 kw. 997 ft. TL: N33 45 37 W112 05 29. c/o 290 Hegenberger Rd., Oakland, CA 94621. Phone: (602) 272-7220. Phone: (800) 835-4810. Fax: (510) 568-6190. Licensee: Family Stations Inc. (group owner; acq 12-91). Format: Relg. ♦ Harold Camping, pres & gen mgr; Charles Conn, opns mgr.

KPHX(AM)— June 10, 1958: 1480 khz; 1 kw-D, 500 w-N, DA-2. TL: N33 24 02 W112 06 28. (CP: 5 kw-D). 824 E. Washington St. 85034. Phone: (602) 257-1351. Fax: (602) 256-0741. Licensee: Continental Broadcasting Corp. (acq 2-80; $650,000; 2-18-80). Format: Comedy. ♦ Kent Ennoms, CEO; John Molina, gen mgr; Cam Maxwell, stn mgr & opns mgr; Jonathan Molina, opns VP.

KPKX(FM)—Listing follows KTAR(AM).

KPXQ(AM)—(Glendale). 1946: 1360 khz; 50 kw-D, 1 kw-N, DA-N. TL: N33 30 28 W112 13 01. 2425 E. Camelback Rd., Suite 570 85016. Phone: (602) 955-9600. Fax: (602) 955-7860. E-mail: info@kpxq1360.com. Web Site: www.kpxq1360.com. Licensee: Common Ground Broadcasting Inc. Group owner: Salem Communications Corp. (acq 6-23-99; $5 million). Network: ABC. Dow, Lohnes & Albertson. Format: Relg talk. News: 6 hrs wkly. Target aud: 25-54; adults. ♦ Edward Atsinger III, CEO; Stuart Epperson, pres; Joe D. Davis, exec VP; Ken Gaines, VP; John Timm, gen mgr; Pat Porter, opns mgr & progmg dir; Elkie Wills, prom dir; John Bortowski, chief of engrg.

KSUN(AM)— Aug 27, 1954: 1400 khz; 1 kw-U. TL: N33 23 23 W111 59 52. Stereo. 714 N. 3rd St. 85004. Phone: (602) 252-0030. Fax: (602) 252-4211. Licensee: Fiesta Radio Inc. (acq 10-86; $600,000; 12-8-86). Rep: Caballero. Format: Adult contemp, Sp. Target aud: 19-45. ♦ Pedro Marquez, pres; Peter Marques, gen mgr.

KTAR(AM)— June 21, 1922: 620 khz; 5 kw-U, DA-N. TL: N33 28 44 W112 00 06. 5300 N. Central Ave. 85012-1410. Phone: (602) 274-6200. Fax: (602) 266-3858. Fax: (602) 265-9941. Web Site: www.620ktar.com. Licensee: Bonneville Holding Co. Group owner: Emmis Communications Corp. (acq 1-14-2005; grpsl). Network: ABC

Arizona

Information & Entertainment. Rep: Interep, D & R Radio. Format: News/talk, sports. News staff: 16; News: 50 hrs wkly. Target aud: 35-54; listeners who want information. ♦Dawn Paugh, natl sls mgr; Tisa Vrable, progmg dir; Brian Barks, news dir; John Shade, chief of engrg.

KPKX(FM)—Co-owned with KTAR(AM). July 1, 1960: 98.7 mhz; 100 kw. 1,680 ft. TL: N33 20 00 W112 03 48. Stereo. Fax: (602) 266-3858. Fax: (602) 274-4477. Web Site: www.987thepeak.com. Format: Adult contemp. News staff: one; News: 2 hrs wkly. Target aud: Adults 25-54; lite rock. ♦Doug Brannan, prom dir; Joel Grey, progmg dir; Clayton Creekmore, engrg dir.

KXAM(AM)—See Mesa

KXEG(AM)— 1956: 1280 khz; 2.5 kw-D, 230 w-N. TL: N33 29 32 W112 08 28. 2800 N. 44th St., Suite 100 85012. Phone: (602) 296-3600. Fax: (602) 515-0111. E-mail: jess@kxeg1280.com. Web Site: www.kxeg1280.com. Licensee: JCE Licenses L.L.C. Group owner: James Crystal Inc. (acq 11-27-01; $2.3 million). Rep: Salem, Commercial Media Sales. Wilkinson, Barker, Knauer & Quinn. Format: Christian. Target aud: 25 plus; educated adults with disposable income. Spec prog: Sp 5 hrs wkly. ♦Jess Spurgin, gen mgr.

KXXT(AM)—See Tolleson

KYOT-FM— Oct 31, 1963: 95.5 mhz; 96 kw. 1,570 ft. TL: N33 20 06 W112 03 39. Stereo. 600 E. Gilbert Dr., Tempe 85281. Phone: (480) 966-6236. Fax: (480) 921-6365. Web Site: www.kyot.com. Licensee: AMFM Radio Licenses LLC. Group owner: Clear Channel Communications Inc. (acq 8-30-00; grpsl). Dow, Lohnes & Albertson. Format: Smoth jazz. News staff: one. Target aud: 25-54. ♦Susan Karis-Madigan, gen mgr; Kurt Viken, rgnl sls mgr; Mary Evanson, prom dir; Shaun Holly, progmg dir; Angie Handa, mus dir; John Baker, chief of engrg.

KFYI(AM)—Co-owned with KYOT-FM. October 1921: 550 khz; 5 kw-D, 1 kw-N. TL: N33 23 17 W112 00 22. 645 E. Missouri Ave., Suite 119 84012. Phone: (602) 798-9340. Fax: (602) 798-9364. Web Site: www.kfyi.com. Licensee: Westwood One. Rep: Christal. Format: News/talk. Target aud: 50 plus. Spec prog: Relg 2 hrs wkly. ♦Brad Gould, gen mgr, opns mgr & rgnl sls mgr; Maureen Miller, gen sls mgr; Laurie Canfillo, progmg dir; Michael Anthony, news dir.

KZON(FM)— July 5, 1964: 101.5 mhz; 100 kw. 1,740 ft. TL: N33 19 52 W112 03 46. 840 N. Central Ave. 85004. Secondary address: Box 353 85004. Phone: (602) 452-1000. Fax: (602) 420-9916. Fax: (602) 440-6530. Web Site: www.kzon.com. Licensee: Infinity Radio Inc. Group owner: Infinity Broadcasting Corp. (acq 12-20-99; grpsl). Leventhal, Senter & Lerman. Format: Alternative. News staff: one. Target aud: 25-44; female based. ♦Mark Steinmetz, VP & gen mgr; Todd Wallace, opns dir & sls dir; Nat Galvin, gen sls mgr & prom mgr; Chris Patyk, progmg dir.

KZZP(FM)—See Mesa

Prescott

KAHM(FM)— Sept 9, 1981: 102.1 mhz; 58 kw. 2,526 ft. TL: N34 41 14 W112 07 01. Stereo. Box 2529 86302. Secondary address: 510 Henry St. 86301. Phone: (928) 445-7800. Licensee: Southwest FM Broadcasting Co. Cohn & Marks. Format: Easy lstng. News staff: 3; News: 7 hrs wkly. Target aud: 35-64; mature, affluent. ♦Lou Silverstein, gen mgr & opns dir; Nancy Silverstein, progmg dir; Al Hartsell, engrg dir.

KYCA(AM)—Co-owned with KAHM(FM). August 1940: 1490 khz; 1 kw-U. TL: N34 33 03 W112 27 45. Box 1631 86302. Secondary address: 500 Henry St. 86302. Phone: (602) 445-1700. Licensee: Southwest Broadcasting Co. (acq 9-25-70). Network: Network: CBS, Westwood One. Cohn & Marks. Format: News/talk. News staff: 4; News: 20 hrs wkly. Target aud: 35-64; mature adults. ♦Lou Silverstein, pres; Bruce Taylor, gen mgr & news dir; Jason Zinzulletta, stn mgr & opns dir; John Rust, news dir.

*KGCB(FM)— Dec 5, 1994: 90.9 mhz; 58 kw. 2,532 ft. TL: N34 41 15 W112 07 02. Stereo. 5025 N. Hwy. 89 86301. Phone: (928) 776-0909. Fax: (928) 776-1736. Web Site: www.kgcb.org. Licensee: Grand Canyon Broadcasters Inc. Wilkinson, Barker, Knauer, LLP. Format: Contemp Christian, adult contemp, relg. Target aud: 25-54; adult, family audience. ♦Carole Stensrud, gen mgr & stn mgr; Mike Medlin, opns dir & progmg dir; Sue Scott, dev dir; Owen Wildman, pub affrs dir.

*KNAQ(FM)— September 1997: 89.3 mhz; 100 w. 1,584 ft. TL: N34 29 24 W112 31 59. Box 5764, Flagstaff 86011-5764. Phone: (928) 523-5628. Fax: (928) 523-6202. Web Site: www.knau.org. Licensee: Northern Arizona University. Format: NPR news, classical. ♦John Stark, gen mgr; Dave Riek, opns mgr & progmg mgr; Mitch Teich, news dir.

KNOT(AM)— June 22, 1957: 1450 khz; 1 kw-U. TL: N34 32 42 W112 26 46. Box 151 86302. Secondary address: 116 S. Alto 86303. Phone: (928) 445-6880. Fax: (928) 445-6852. E-mail: knot@knotradio.com. Web Site: www.knotradio.com. Licensee: Guyann Corp. (acq 2-4-2005; $1.7 million. with co-located FM). Network: ABC Music Radio. Format: MOR, adult contemp. News staff: one. Target aud: 35 plus. Spec prog: Jazz 2 hrs, sports 8 hrs wkly. ♦Guy Christian, pres; C. Pastore, gen mgr, stn mgr & opns mgr; P. Ezell, sls dir; Paul Hurt, progmg dir & progmg mgr; Doreen Conti, news dir; Mark Hill, chief of engrg.

KTMG(FM)—Co-owned with KNOT(AM). Nov 11, 1977: 99.1 mhz; 6 kw. 200 ft. TL: N34 34 29 W112 28 45. Stereo. Network: ABC. Format: Country. News staff: one. Target aud: 35 plus. ♦C. Pastore, stn mgr; Paul Hurt, mus dir.

KPPV(FM)—See Prescott Valley

Prescott Valley

KKLD(FM)— May 24, 1996: 98.3 mhz; 875 w. 2,526 ft. TL: N34 41 11 W112 06 58. Stereo. Box 187, Cottonwood 86326. Phone: (928) 634-5553. Fax: (928) 634-2295. E-mail: kkld@myradioplace.com. Web Site: www.myradioplace.com. Licensee: 3 Point Media - Prescott Valley LLC. (acq 5-2-2005; $8 million). Network: ABC. Format: Oldies. Target aud: 25-45. ♦David J. Kessel, stn mgr; Jackie Bessler, gen sls mgr; Juli Page, progmg dir; Paul David, news dir.

KPPV(FM)—Listing follows KQNA(AM).

KQNA(AM)— June 28, 1986: 1130 khz; 1 kw-D. TL: N34 37 46 W112 18 56. Box 26523 86312. Secondary address: 3755 Karicio Ln., Suite 2-C, Prescott 86303. Phone: (928) 445-8289. Phone: (800) 264-5449. Fax: (928) 442-0448. E-mail: info@kppv.com. Web Site: www.kqna.com. Licensee: Prescott Valley Broadcasting Co. (group owner; (acq 12-27-93; $75,000;. FTR: 1-10-94). Network: CNN Radio. David Tillotson, pres. Format: News/talk, sports. News staff: 3; News: 84 hrs wkly. Target aud: 35-64; middle - upper income, professionals & new consumers. ♦Sanford B. Cohen, pres & gen mgr; Terry P. Cohen, exec VP; Allison Flannery, natl sls mgr; Bill Monroe, news dir; Ken Byers, pub affrs dir; Mark Hills, engrg mgr.

KPPV(FM)—Co-owned with KQNA(AM). Sept 1, 1985: 106.7 mhz; 3.7 kw. 1,627 ft. TL: N34 29 25 W112 32 00. Stereo. Web Site: www.kppv.com. Network: Network: Jones Radio Networks, AP Radio. Format: Adult contemp. News staff: 2; News: 6 hrs wkly. Target aud: 25-54; middle to upper income professionals with families and disposable income.

Quartzsite

KBUX(FM)— November 1988: 94.3 mhz; 205 w. -161 ft. TL: N33 40 58 W114 13 59. Stereo. Box 40 85346. Phone: (928) 927-5111. Licensee: Buck Burdette. Format: Btfl music, country, oldies. Target aud: General; retired motor home & trailer owners wintering in warmer climate. ♦Maude J. Burdette, gen mgr; Maude Burdette, stn mgr; Marvin Vosper, progmg dir.

Red Mesa

*KRMH(FM)— 1998: 89.7 mhz; 4.5 kw. 134 ft. TL: N36 57 48 W109 22 39. HC 61 Box 40, Teec Nos Pos 86514. Phone: (928) 656-4100. Fax: (928) 656-4106. Web Site: www.redmesa.k12.az.us. Licensee: Red Mesa Unified School District No. 27. Format: Native American, var.

Safford

KATO(AM)— May 5, 1961: 1230 khz; 1 kw-U. TL: N32 49 30 W109 45 30. Drawer L 85548. Secondary address: 3335 W. 8th St., Thatcher 85552. Phone: (928) 428-1230. Fax: (928) 428-1311. Web Site: www.eaznet.com/~kato. Licensee: McMurray Communications Inc. (group owner; acq 12-17-92; $10,000. with co-located FM; FTR: 2-1-93). Network: ABC. Format: News/talk, sports. News staff: 7;

News: 25 hrs wkly. Target aud: 25-54; upscale, intelligent. ♦Bud McMurray, pres; Davis Nathan, gen mgr & sls dir; Reed Richins, opns mgr, progmg dir & chief of engrg.

KXKQ(FM)—Co-owned with KATO(AM). Aug 11, 1979: 94.1 mhz; 1 kw. Ant 4,287 ft. TL: N32 39 01 W109 50 53. Stereo. Web Site: www.katkountry94.com. Format: Country. News: one hr wkly. Target aud: 25-54. ♦Reed Richins, engrg dir.

KCUZ(AM)— (Clifton). July 31, 1969: 1490 khz; 1 kw-U. TL: N33 02 30 W109 17 40. Box 1330 85548-1330. Secondary address: 301B Hwy. 70E 85546. Phone: (928) 428-0916. Fax: (928) 428-7797. E-mail: kfmm@eaznet.com. Web Site: www.kfmmradio.com. Licensee: Wick Communications Co. (acq 6-8-01; with KFMM(FM) Thatcher). Format: Country. News staff: one; News: 7 hrs wkly. Target aud: 25-54. Spec prog: Relg 2 hrs, loc talk 8 hrs wkly. ♦Bob Wick, pres; Mike Hallford, gen mgr & prom dir; Dave Etter, opns mgr; Steve Reno, sls dir, news dir & pub affrs dir; Reed Richins, chief of engrg.

KFMM(FM)—Co-owned with KCUZ(AM). Dec 7, 1981: 99.1 mhz; 50 kw. 2,280 ft. TL: N32 53 22 W109 19 23. Stereo. Web Site: www.kfmmradio.com. News staff: one; News: 7 hrs wkly. Spec prog: Children 2 hrs wkly.

KWRQ(FM)—(Clifton). Oct 1, 1986: 102.3 mhz; 2.8 kw. 2,211 ft. TL: N32 53 23 W109 19 26. Stereo. Drawer L 85548-0886. Secondary address: 3335 West 8th St. 85546. Phone: (928) 428-1020. Fax: (928) 428-6818. Fax: (928) 428-1311. Licensee: McMurray Communications Inc. (group owner; acq 11-97; $350,000). Network: Jones Radio Networks. Format: Adult contemp. Target aud: 20-35; working females. ♦Bud McMurray, pres; Davis Nathan, gen mgr; Reed Richins, opns mgr.

Sahuarita

KQTL(AM)— Oct 12, 1985: 1210 khz; 10 kw-D, 1 kw-N, DA-N. TL: N32 02 04 W110 56 45. 2955 E. Broadway Blvd., Tucson 85716. Phone: (520) 628-1200. Fax: (520) 326-4927. Web Site: www.radiounica.com. Licensee: Multicultural Radio Broadcasting Licensee LLC. Group owner: Multicultural Radio Broadcasting Inc. (acq 2-4-2004; grpsl). Rep: Caballero. Format: News/talk, Christian. Target aud: General. ♦Francisco Zazueta, gen mgr.

Saint Johns

KWKM(FM)— 2001: 95.7 mhz; 100 kw. Ant 1,197 ft. TL: N34 14 59 W109 35 08. 1520 Commerce Dr., Show Low 85901. Phone: (928) 532-2949. Fax: (928) 532-3176. Web Site: www.kwkm.com. Licensee: KM Radio of St. Johns L.L.C. (acq 5-3-99). Network: ABC. Format: Adult contemp, classic rock. News: 1 hr wkly. Target aud: 18-44. Spec prog: News/talk 2 hrs, blues 2 hrs, alternative rock 2 hrs wkly. ♦John Banker, gen mgr.

Scottsdale

KAZG(AM)—Licensed to Scottsdale. See Phoenix

KSLX-FM—Licensed to Scottsdale. See Phoenix

Sedona

KAZM(AM)— Nov 1, 1974: 780 khz; 5 kw-D, 250 w-N, DA-N. TL: N34 51 38 W111 49 10. Stereo. Box 1525, 3400 W. Hwy. 89A 86339. Phone: (928) 282-4154. Fax: (928) 282-2230. E-mail: info@kazmradio.com. Web Site: www.kazmradio.com. Licensee: Tabback Broadcasting Co. Network: Westwood One. Brooks, Pierce, McLendon, Humphrey & Leonard. Format: New/talk, sports, music. News staff: 4; News: 16 hrs wkly. Target aud: 25 plus; baby boomers, professions, tourists. ♦Tom N. Tabback, exec VP, gen mgr & opns dir.

KQST(FM)— May 1, 1984: 102.9 mhz; 90 kw. 1,433 ft. TL: N34 58 05 W111 30 29. Stereo. 3405 E. Hwy. 89-A, Cottonwood 86326. Phone: (928) 634-2959. Fax: (928) 634-2295. Web Site: www.myradioplace.com. Licensee: Yavapai Broadcasting Corp. (acq 12-1-2004; $3 million). John A. Borsari. Format: Adult contemp, top-40. Target aud: 24-59. Spec prog: Univ. of Arizona Football, jazz 15 hrs, new age 10 hrs, relg 5 hrs, big band 4 hrs wkly. ♦W. Grant Hafley, pres; Dave Kessel, gen mgr; Jackie Bessler, gen sls mgr & prom dir; John Herring, progmg dir.

KSED(FM)— August 1994: 107.5 mhz; 98.4 kw. 1,463 ft. TL: N34 58 07 W111 30 22. Stereo. 112 E. Rt. 66, Suite 105, Flagstaff 86001. Phone: (928) 779-1177. Fax: (928) 774-5179. Licensee: Red Rock

Stations in the U.S. — Arizona

Communications Ltd. (acq 3-18-93; $100,000; 4-12-93). Network: NBC. Format: Special blend, country. News staff: one. ♦Tom Rockler, pres; Jim Perrine, gen mgr & sls dir; Dylan Fletcher, opns dir; Bobby Delrio, prom dir.

Seligman

KZKE(FM)— 1995: 103.3 mhz; 1.75 kw. 423 ft. TL: N35 19 26 W112 45 55. 812 E. Beale St., Kingman 86401. Phone: (928) 753-9100. Fax: (928) 753-1978. Licensee: Route 66 Broadcasting L.L.C. (acq 9-1-98). Format: Good time oldies. ♦Rhonda Hart, VP & gen mgr; JoAnn Oxsen, adv dir; Steve Levin, progmg dir.

Sells

*****KOHN(FM)**— 2004: 91.9 mhz; 10 kw. Ant 1,656 ft. TL: N32 07 59 W112 09 31. Box 835, Main St., Bldg. 49 85634. Phone: (520) 361-5011. Fax: (520) 361-3931. E-mail: sial.thonolig@tonation-rsr.gov. Licensee: Tohono O'Odham Nation. Format: Eclectic music, Native American. ♦Sial Thonolig, gen mgr.

Show Low

*****KNAA(FM)**— October 1997: 90.7 mhz; 100 w. 850 ft. TL: N34 12 17 W109 56 22. Box 5764, Flagstaff 86011-5764. Phone: (928) 717-1670. Web Site: www.knau.org. Licensee: Arizona Board of Regents. Network: NPR. Format: Class, news. ♦John Stark, gen mgr; Dave Riek, opns dir.

KRFM(FM)—Listing follows KVSL(AM).

KSNX(FM)—Listing follows KVWM(AM).

KVSL(AM)— July 6, 1968: 1450 khz; 1 kw-U. TL: N34 16 00 W110 20 10. 3051 S. White Mountain RD., Suite D 85901. Phone: (928) 532-3232. Fax: (928) 537-3991. E-mail: production@whitemountainradio.com. Licensee: FFD Holdings I Inc. (acq 12-20-2004; grpsl). Network: ABC. Format: Nostalgia oldies. Target aud: 45-65; 46% female, 54% male. Spec prog: Farm 2 hrs wkly. ♦Steve Johnson, gen mgr, gen sls mgr & progmg dir.

KRFM(FM)— Co-owned with KVSL(AM). July 1, 1983: 96.5 mhz; 100 kw. 994 ft. TL: N34 12 20 W109 56 26. Stereo. Web Site: www.ksnx.com. Network: Jones Radio Networks. Format: Hot adult contemp. Target aud: 18-34; 65% female & 35% male.

KVWM(AM)— May 17, 1957: 970 khz; 5 kw-D, 114 w-N. TL: N34 13 14 W110 01 49. 3051 S. White Mountain Rd., Suite D 85901. Phone: (928) 532-3232. Fax: (928) 537-3991. E-mail: production@whitemountainradio.com. Licensee: FFD Holdings I Inc. (acq 12-20-2004; grpsl). Network: Network: ABC, Westwood One. Format: News/talk. Target aud: 35-65; 46% female & 54% male. ♦Steve Johnson, gen mgr, gen sls mgr & progmg dir.

KSNX(FM)— Co-owned with KVWM(AM). Sept 13, 1964: 93.5 mhz; 25 kw. 150 ft. TL: N34 13 14 W110 01 49. Web Site: www.ksnx.com. Format: Good-time oldies. Target aud: 25-54; 50% female & 50% male.

Sierra Vista

KKYZ(FM)— Jan 1, 1995: 101.7 mhz; 3 kw. 328 ft. TL: N31 33 59 W110 13 57. Stereo. 500 E. Fry Blvd., Suite L-10 85635. Phone: (520) 459-8201. Fax: (520) 458-7104. E-mail: info@kkyz.com. Web Site: www.kkyz.com. Licensee: Cochise Broadcasting L.L.C. (acq 1-12-01). Format: Oldies. Target aud: 25-54. ♦Ted Tucker, gen mgr; Eileen Kuns, stn mgr, opns dir & opns mgr.

KNXN(AM)— June 20, 1980: 1470 khz; 2.5 kw-D, 39 w-N. TL: N31 32 53 W110 14 54. 680 Avenida del Sol 85635. Phone: (520) 459-1470. Fax: (520) 459-5418. Web Site: www.kgms.com. Licensee: Good Music Inc. Group owner: Good News Communications Inc. (acq 4-16-01; $300,000). Format: Inspirational talk, Christian. News staff: one; News: 5 hrs wkly. ♦Doug Martin, pres; Jeff Davenport, gen mgr.

KTAN(AM)— March 1957: 1420 khz; 1.5 kw-D, 500 w-N, DA-N. TL: N31 32 47 W110 16 29. Box 2770 85636. Secondary address: 2300 Busby Dr. 85636. Phone: (520) 458-4313. Fax: (520) 458-4317. Licensee: CCR-Sierra Vista IV LLC. Group owner: Cherry Creek Radio LLC (acq 12-19-2003; grpsl). Network: CBS. Baraff, Koerner & Olender. Format: News/talk, sports. News staff: one; News: 20 hrs wkly. Target aud: 25-54. ♦Paul Orlando, gen mgr; Rudy Sueskind, gen sls mgr & rgnl sls mgr; Debbie Simmons, mus dir.

KZMK(FM)—Co-owned with KTAN(AM). September 1973: 100.9 mhz; 3 kw. -46 ft. TL: N31 32 47 W110 16 29. Stereo. E-mail: k101@c2i2.com. Network: Westwood One. Format: Adult contemp. News staff: one; News: one hr wkly. Target aud: 18-49.

KWCD(FM)—See Bisbee

South Tucson

KJLL(AM)—Licensed to South Tucson. See Tucson

KXEW(AM)—Licensed to South Tucson. See Tucson

Springerville-Eagar

KQAZ(FM)— July 15, 1984: 101.7 mhz; 3 kw. -97 ft. TL: N34 08 17 W109 16 10. (CP: 1.1 kw). Stereo. Box 2020, Show Low 85902. Secondary address: 691 E. Deuce of Clubs, Show Low 85901. Phone: (928) 532-1010. Fax: (928) 532-0101. Web Site: www.majik101.com. Licensee: William Konopnicki. (acq 7-30-99; $175,000 with KRVZ(AM) Springerville-Eagar). Network: AP Radio. Format: Adult Alternative. ♦Camden Smith, gen mgr & progmg dir.

KRVZ(AM)— June 11, 1982: 1400 khz; 1 kw-U. TL: N34 08 17 W109 16 10. Box 1069, 1367 E. Main St. 85938. Secondary address: 1367 E. Main St. 85938. Phone: (928) 333-2080. Fax: (928) 333-2081. E-mail: krvz@frontiernet.net. Licensee: William Konopnicki. (acq 7-30-99; $175,000 with KQAZ(FM) Springerville). Network: Jones Radio Networks. Format: Oldies. ♦William Konopnicki, pres; Camden Smith, gen mgr; Dan Curtis, opns dir.

Sun City

KOMR(FM)— Mar 7, 1975: 106.3 mhz; 2.5 kw. 325 ft. TL: N33 36 05 W112 17 31. (CP: 23 kw, ant 725 ft.). Stereo. 4745 N. 7th St., Suite 140, Phoenix 85014. Phone: (602) 308-7900. Licensee: HBC License Corp. Group owner: Univision Radio (acq 9-22-2003; grpsl). Rep: Allied Radio Partners. Dow, Lohnes & Albertson. Format: Adult Contemp. Target aud: 35-54. ♦Mary McEvilly-Hernandez, gen mgr; Chris Morris, gen sls mgr; Fernando Gomez, prom dir; Robbie Ramirez, progmg dir.

Sun City West

KVIB(FM)— 2003: . Stn currently dark 95.1 mhz; 36 kw. Ant 2,598 ft. TL: N34 13 48 W112 21 02. Great Hill Equity Partners L.P., One Liberty Sq., Boston, MA 02109. Phone: (713) 963-0888. Licensee: Sun City License LLC (acq 3-10-2005; $18.7 million). ♦Stephen F. Gormley, gen mgr; Michael Cutchall, stn mgr.

Tempe

KDUS(AM)— Apr 16, 1960: 1060 khz; 5 kw-D, 500 w-N, DA-N. TL: N33 21 43 W111 58 03. 1900 W. Carmen 85283. Phone: (480) 838-0400. Fax: (480) 820-8469. Web Site: www.kdus.com. Licensee: Tempe Radio Inc. Group owner: Sandusky Radio (acq 1994; $20 million with co-located station). Format: Sports. News staff: one. Target aud: 18-34 males. ♦Chuck Artigue, gen mgr.

KUPD-FM—Co-owned with KDUS(AM). April 1960: 97.9 mhz; 100 kw. 1,620 ft. TL: N33 19 57 W112 03 53. Stereo. Web Site: www.98kupd.com. Wiley, Rein & Fielding. Format: AOR. ♦J.J. Jeffries, progmg dir.

KLNZ(FM)—(Glendale). Sept 1, 1997: 103.5 mhz; 62 kw. 2,428 ft. TL: N33 35 33 W112 34 49. Stereo. 501 N. 44th St., Suite 425, Phoenix 85008. Phone: (602) 266-2005. Fax: (602) 279-2921. Licensee: Entravision Holdings LLC. Group owner: Entravision Communications Corp. (acq 7-28-00; grpsl). Bechtel & Cole. Format: Sp, rgnl Mexican. Target aud: General. ♦Tom Duran, gen mgr; Chris Moncayo, gen sls mgr; Terry Strait, progmg dir; Ryan Oller, chief of engrg.

KMIK(AM)—Licensed to Tempe. See Phoenix

KNIX-FM—See Phoenix

Thatcher

KFMM(FM)—Licensed to Thatcher. See Safford

Tolleson

KNUV(AM)— Jan 23, 1961: 1190 khz; 5 kw-D, 250 w-N, DA-2. TL: N33 26 42 W112 15 54. New Radio Venture Inc., 140 E. Market St., York, PA 17401. Phone: (717) 852-2317. E-mail: edjackson@suspfz.com. Licensee: New Radio Venture LLC (acq 5-26-2005; $3.75 million). Cohn & Marks. ♦Maria Elena Llansa, gen mgr.

KXXT(AM)— Dec 12, 1962: 1010 khz; 15 kw-D, 250 w-N, DA-D. TL: N33 26 43 W112 12 23. 4000 N. Central Ave., Suite 720, Phoenix 85012. Phone: (602) 254-5001. Fax: (623) 245-1010. E-mail: jess@kxeg1280.com. Web Site: www.newstalk1010.net. Licensee: JCE Licenses L.L.C. Group owner: James Crystal Inc. (acq 8-8-2000; $4.5 million). Network: AP Network News. Format: News/talk. News staff: one. ♦Jess Spurgin, gen mgr & rgnl sls mgr; Phillip W. French, natl sls mgr; Bob Christy, progmg dir; Willis Girdner, chief of engrg.

Tuba City

*****KGHR(FM)**— Nov 27, 1991: 91.5 mhz; 100 w. Ant -26 ft. TL: N36 08 00 W111 13 23. (CP: 91.3 mhz; 50 kw, ant 1,053 ft. N36 21 27 W111 12 12). Stereo. Box 160 86045. Phone: (928) 283-5555. Fax: (928) 283-5557. Licensee: Tuba City High School Board Inc. Format: Country, native American, AAA. News: 20 hrs wkly. Target aud: General; Native American/Navajo. Spec prog: Pub affrs 5 hrs wkly. ♦John Bittner, stn mgr.

KTBA(AM)— 1980: 1050 khz; 5 kw-D, 5.2 w-N. TL: N36 07 54 W111 14 59. Box 9090, Window Rock 86515. Licensee: Western Indian Ministries Inc. (group owner; (acq 1980). Format: Adult Contemporary. ♦Lenora A. Brown, gen mgr; Jareleen Mitchell, progmg VP; Bill Vadasy, mus dir.

Tucson

*****KAIC(FM)**—Not on air, target date: unknown: 88.9 mhz; 1.8 kw vert. Ant 26 ft. TL: N32 36 56 W110 38 39. 5700 West Oaks Blvd., Rocklin, CA 95765. Phone: (916) 251-1600. Fax: (916) 251-1650. Licensee: Educational Media Foundation.

KCUB(AM)— August 1929: 1290 khz; 1 kw-U. TL: N32 16 37 W110 58 50. 575 W. Roger Rd. 85705. Phone: (520) 887-1000. Fax: (520) 887-6397. Licensee: Citadel Broadcasting Co. Group owner: Citadel Broadcasting Corp. (acq 4-26-2001; grpsl). Format: Sports. News staff: one. Target aud: 25-54. ♦Todd Lawley, gen mgr; Herb Crowe, opns VP; Ken Kowalcek, sls VP.

KIIM-FM—Co-owned with KCUB(AM). March 1954: 99.5 mhz; 90 kw. 2,037 ft. TL: N32 14 56 W111 06 59. Stereo. Format: Hot country.

KFFN(AM)—Listing follows KMXZ-FM.

Arizona Directory of Radio

***KFLT(AM)**— October 1977: 830 khz; 50 kw-D, 1 kw-N, DA-N. TL: N32 26 39 W111 05 27. Box 36868 85740. Secondary address: 7355 N. Oracle Rd., Suite 102 85704. Phone: (520) 797-3700. Fax: (520) 797-3375. E-mail: kflt@flc.org. Web Site: www.kflt.org. Licensee: Family Life Broadcasting System Inc. Group owner: Family Life Communications Inc. (acq 10-86; $125,000;. FTR: 4-14-86). Network: Moody. Format: Christian, inspirational. News staff: one; News: 15 hrs wkly. Target aud: 25-45; Christian families. ♦Randy Carlson, pres; Lee Escobedo, gen mgr; Dave Ficere, opns dir, dev dir & progmg dir; Joe Neubaum, mus dir; Carl Jackson, pub affrs dir; Randy Howard, chief of engrg.

KFLT-FM—Not on air, target date: unknown: 88.5 mhz; 1.5 kw vert. Ant 410 ft. TL: N32 00 11 W110 47 49. Licensee: Family Life Broadcasting Inc.

KGMS(AM)— Aug 10, 1963: 940 khz; 5 kw-D, 1 kw-N, DA-2. TL: N32 12 04 W111 01 02. 3222 S. Richey Ave. 85713. Phone: (520) 790-2440. Fax: (520) 790-2937. E-mail: info@kgms.com. Web Site: kgms.com. Licensee: Good Music Inc. Group owner: Good News Communications Inc. (acq 11-27-00; swap with KCEE(FM) Green Valley). Format: Christian ministry. Target aud: 35 plus. ♦Doug Martin, CEO, pres & gen mgr; Matt Manis, opns mgr.

KGVY(AM)—(Green Valley). Sept 23, 1981: 1080 khz; 1 kw-D. TL: N31 55 34 W110 59 45. Box 767, Green Valley 85622. Secondary address: 1510 W. Camino Antigua, Sahuarita 85629. Phone: (520) 399-1000. Fax: (520) 399-9300. E-mail: kgvyam@quest.net. Licensee: Green Valley Broadcasters Inc. (acq 7-23-98; $375,000). Network: ABC. Format: Oldies, CHR, MOR. News staff: 2; News: 13 hrs wkly. Target aud: 50 plus; mature, well educated, higher income, retired. Spec prog: Jazz, news. ♦Marshall Darris, gen mgr.

KHYT(FM)— August 1993: 107.5 mhz; 14.5 kw. 3,526 ft. TL: N32 24 54 W110 42 56. (CP: 82 kw, ant 2,027 ft.). 575 W. Roger 85705. Phone: (520) 887-1000. Fax: (520) 887-6397. Web Site: www.rock1075.com. Licensee: Citadel Broadcasting Co. Group owner: Citadel Broadcasting Corp. (acq 4-26-01; grpsl). Format: Classic rock. ♦Farid Suleman, CEO; Todd Lawley, gen mgr; Herb Crowe, opns dir; Ken Kowalcek, sls dir.

KJLL(AM)—(South Tucson). 1957: 1330 khz; 2 kw-D, 5 kw-N, DA-N. TL: N32 18 51 W110 50 17. 4320 N. Campbell, Suite 238 85718. Phone: (520) 529-5865. Fax: (520) 529-9324. Licensee: Hudson Communications Inc. (acq 1996; $36,000). Format: News/talk. ♦Jerry Misner, gen mgr.

KLPX(FM)—Listing follows KTKT(AM).

KMXZ-FM— Apr 11, 1973: 94.9 mhz; 97 kw. 1,952 ft. TL: N32 14 56 W111 06 59. Stereo. 3438 N. Country Club 85716. Phone: (520) 795-1490. Fax: (520) 327-2260. E-mail: mixfm@mixfm.com. Web Site: www.mixfm.com. Licensee: Journal Broadcast Corp. Group owner: Journal Broadcast Group Inc. (acq 1996; grpsl). Network: ABC. Crowell & Moring. Format: Adult contemp/soft rock. News staff: 2; News: 3 hrs wkly. Target aud: 25-54. ♦Carl Gardner, stn mgr; Jennifer Nunn, gen sls mgr; Bobby Rich, progmg VP; Greg Dunkin, news dir.

KFFN(AM)—Co-owned with KMXZ-FM. January 1957: 1490 khz; 1 kw-U. TL: N32 14 56 W110 55 29. Stereo. Format: Sports. News: 2 hrs wkly. Target aud: 18-49. ♦Rob Cook, progmg dir.

KNST(AM)— Oct 1, 1958: 790 khz; 5 kw-D, 500 w-N. TL: N32 14 54 W111 00 30. 3202 N. Oracle Rd. 85705. Phone: (520) 618-2100. Fax: (520) 618-2170. Licensee: Capstar TX L.P. Group owner: Clear Channel Communications Inc. (acq 8-30-00; grpsl). Network: Network: Network: Moody, ABC Information & Entertainment, ABC News/Talk. Rep: McGavren Guild. Format: News/talk, sports. News staff: 3. Target aud: 25-54. ♦Debbie Wagner, gen mgr.

KRQQ(FM)—Co-owned with KNST(AM). Feb 1, 1971: 93.7 mhz; 91 kw. 2,030 ft. TL: N32 14 56 W111 06 57. Stereo. Web Site: www.krq.com. Format: CHR, Top-40. News staff: one. Target aud: 18-54. ♦Mike Madigan, stn mgr.

KOHT(FM)—See Marana

KSAZ(AM)—(Marana). 1990: 580 khz; 5 kw-D, 390 w-N, DA-N. TL: N32 27 11 W111 17 04. 1011 N. Craycroft, Suite 302 85711. Phone: (520) 298-6880. Fax: (520) 298-6077. Licensee: Owl Broadcasting & Development Inc. (acq 4-89; $1.05 million;. 5-1-89). Network: ABC. Hogan & Hartson. Format: Timeless classics. Target aud: 35 plus. Spec prog: International 2 hrs wkly. ♦Phyllis Ehlinger, pres & gen mgr; William Ehlinger, exec VP.

KTKT(AM)— December 1949: 990 khz; 10 kw-D, 1 kw-N, DA-2. TL: N32 15 19 W111 00 32. 3871 N. Commerce 85705. Phone: (520) 407-4500. Fax: (520) 407-4600. Web Site: www.ktkt.com. Licensee: Arizona Lotus Corp. Group owner: Lotus Communications Corp. (acq 1973). Network: AP Radio. Rep: Lotus Entravision Reps LLC. Bryan Cave. Format: Sp oldies. Target aud: 25-54. Spec prog: Black one hr, relg 2 hrs wkly. ♦Steve Groesbeck, gen mgr.

KLPX(FM)—Co-owned with KTKT(AM). June 1, 1967: 96.1 mhz; 82 kw. 1,952 ft. TL: N32 14 56 W111 06 59. Stereo. Web Site: www.klpx.com. (Acq 6-79). Rep: D & R Radio. Bryan Cave. Format: Classic rock. Target aud: 25-54.

KTUC(AM)— July 10, 1926: 1400 khz; 1 kw-U. TL: N32 08 43 W110 53 38. (CP: TL: N32 14 56 W110 55 29). 575 W. Roger. 85705. Phone: (520) 887-1000. Fax: (520) 887-6397. Licensee: Citadel Broadcasting Co. Group owner: Citadel Broadcasting Corp. (acq 4-26-01; grpsl). Network: CBS. Rep: Katz Radio. Format: News/talk, sports. Target aud: General; college educated, upper income, politically active adults. ♦T. Lawley, gen mgr.

KTZR-FM—(Green Valley). Oct 21, 1990: 97.1 mhz; 1.75 kw. Ant 613 ft. TL: N31 58 37 W111 06 04. Stereo. 3202 N. Oracle Rd. 85705. Phone: (520) 618-2100. Fax: (520) 618-2165. Web Site: www.kwfmtucson.com. Licensee: Capstar TX L.P. Group owner: Clear Channel Communications Inc. Format: Latin pop. News staff: 2; News: 2 hrs wkly. Target aud: 18-35. ♦Debbie Wagner, gen mgr; Jerry Fernandez, progmg.

KUAT-FM—Listing follows KUAZ-FM.

***KUAZ(AM)**— Oct 7, 1968: 1550 khz; 50 kw-D. TL: N32 22 21 W111 05 52. Box 210067, Univ. of Arizona. 85721-0067. Phone: (520) 621-7548. Fax: (520) 621-3360. E-mail: kuat@arizona.edu. Web Site: www.kuat.org. Licensee: Arizona Board of Regents. Network: Network: NPR, PRI. Dow, Lohnes & Albertson. Format: News, jazz. Spec prog: Sp 3 hrs, Native American one hr wkly. ♦Jack Parris, gen mgr & stn mgr.

KUAT-FM—Co-owned with KUAZ-FM. May 19, 1975: 90.5 mhz; 12.5 kw. 3,580 ft. TL: N32 24 55 W110 42 54. Stereo. University of Arizona, Box 210067 85721-0067. Phone: (520) 621-5828. Fax: (520) 621-3360. E-mail: radio@kuat.arizona. Web Site: www.kuat.org. Format: Class. News: 7 hrs wkly. Target aud: 35 plus. Co-owned TV: *KUAT-TV affil.

***KUAZ-FM**— Apr 27, 1992: 89.1 mhz; 3 kw. 10 ft. TL: N32 22 21 W111 05 52. Box 210067, KUAT Communications Group/KUAZ, Univ. of Arizona 85721-0067. Phone: (520) 621-5828. Fax: (520) 621-3360. Web Site: www.kuaz.org. Licensee: Arizona Board of Regents for Benefit of the University of Arizona. (acq 4-92). Network: Network: NPR, PRI. Dow, Lohnes & Albertson. Format: NPR (news, info), jazz. News staff: 4; News: 38 hrs wkly. Target aud: General. Spec prog: Sp 3 hrs wkly. ♦Jack Parris, gen mgr; John Kelley, stn mgr; Colleen Greer, prom dir; Lyle Kesterson, progmg dir.

KVOI(AM)— Sept 23, 1953: 690 khz; 250 w-D, DA. TL: N32 15 11 W110 57 44. 3222 S. Richey Blvd. 85713-5453. Phone: (520) 790-2440. Fax: (520) 790-2937. E-mail: doug@kvoi.com. Web Site: www.kvoi.com. Licensee: Good News Broadcasting Inc. Group owner: Good News Communications Inc. (acq 9-53). Koteen & Naftalin. Format: News, talk. News staff: one; News: 10 hrs wkly. ♦Doug Martin, pres & gen mgr; Mary Martin, sls dir & gen sls mgr; Matt Manis, opns mgr & progmg dir; Larry Massey, chief of engrg.

KWFM(AM)— Feb 27, 1947: 1450 khz; 1 kw-U. TL: N32 12 04 W110 56 48. Stereo. 3202 N. Oracle Rd. 85705. Phone: (520) 618-2100. Fax: (520) 618-2200. Web Site: www.cool1450am.com. Licensee: Clear Channel Broadcasting Licenses Inc. Group owner: Clear Channel Communications Inc. (acq 6-28-01; grpsl). Format: Oldies. ♦Debbie Wagner, gen mgr; Deeanne Thomas, gen sls mgr; Alan Cook, progmg dir; Mike Irby, chief of engrg.

KWMT-FM— May 18, 1970: 92.9 mhz; 90 kw. 2,037 ft. TL: N32 14 56 W111 06 59. Stereo. 3202 N. Oracle Rd. 85705. Phone: (520) 618-2100. Fax: (520) 618-2165. Web Site: www.929themountain.com. Licensee: Capstar TX L.P. Group owner: Clear Channel Communications Inc. Format: Adult alternative. News staff: 2; News: 21 hrs wkly. ♦Debbie Wagner, gen mgr; Deanne Thomas, gen sls mgr; Tim Richards, opns mgr & progmg dir; Chris O'Gorman, news dir.

***KXCI(FM)**— Dec 17, 1983: 91.3 mhz; 340 w. 3,641 ft. TL: N32 24 54 W110 42 56. Stereo. 220 S. 4th Ave. 85701. Phone: (520) 623-1000, EXT. 13. Phone: (520) 622-5924. Fax: (520) 623-0758. Web Site: www.kxci.org. Licensee: Foundation for Creative Broadcasting Inc. (acq 2-17-2004). Format: Eclectic, progsv. News: 4 hrs wkly. Target aud: 18-49. Spec prog: American Indian 2 hrs, Black 4 hrs, folk 2 hrs, gospel 2 hrs, jazz 2 hrs, Sp 4 hrs wkly. ♦Larry Bruce, gen mgr; Michael Hyatt, sls dir; Roger Greer, progmg dir; Jim Blackwood, pub affrs dir.

KXEW(AM)—(South Tucson). May 10, 1963: 1600 khz; 1 kw-U, DA-N. TL: N32 11 48 W110 59 01. (CP: 2.5 kw-D). 3202 N. Oracle Rd. 85705. Phone: (520) 618-2100. Fax: (520) 618-2122. Web Site: www.tejano1600.com. Licensee: Clear Channel Broadcasting Licenses Inc. Group owner: Clear Channel Communications Inc. (acq 9-25-03). Cohn & Marks. Format: Sp, Tejano. Target aud: 25-54; blue collar Hispanics. ♦Debbie Wagner, gen mgr; Bob Feinman, opns mgr; Patti Ruiz, gen sls mgr; Andy Bonillas, progmg dir.

KZLZ(FM)—(Kearny). Aug 31, 1991: 105.3 mhz; 50 kw. 492 ft. TL: N32 49 38 W110 34 12. Stereo. 2959 E. Grant Rd. 85716. Phone: (520) 325-3054. Fax: (520) 325-3495. Licensee: Entravision Holdings LLC. Group owner: Entravision Communications Corp. (acq 7-28-00; grpsl). Arent, Fox, Kintner, Plotkin & Kahn. Format: Sp. Target aud: General. ♦Haz Montana, VP & progmg dir; Sonya Tabanico, gen mgr.

KZPT(FM)— May 4, 1994: 104.1 mhz; 3 kw. Ant 328 ft. TL: N32 17 23 W111 01 06. 3438 N. Country Club 85716. Phone: (520) 795-1490. Fax: (520) 327-2260. Web Site: www.1041thepoint.net. Licensee: Journal Broadcast Corp. Group owner: Journal Broadcast Group Inc. Format: CHR, adult contemp. Target aud: 25-54; males, persons. ♦Diana Frisch, gen mgr; Greg Dinkin, opns mgr; Jennifer Nunn, gen sls mgr.

Tusayan

KSGC(FM)— July 1, 1991: 92.1 mhz; 4.1 kw. Ant 335 ft. TL: N35 58 14 W112 07 53. Stereo. Box 3346, Grand Canyon 86023-3346. Secondary address: c/o We Cook Pizza & Pasta, Hwy. 64 86023. Phone: (928) 638-9552. Fax: (928) 638-9553. Licensee: Tusayan Broadcasting Co. Network: ABC. Format: Adult contemp. Target aud: 18-54; Grand Canyon visitors with disposable vacation income. ♦Brian Ciesielski, gen mgr; Wes Yellowstone, progmg dir.

Wellton

KCEC-FM— Oct 1, 2000: 104.5 mhz; 6.1 kw. 1,348 ft. TL: N32 40 22 W114 20 14. 670 East 32 St., Suite 12 A, Yuma 85364-3800. Phone: (661) 837-0745. Phone: (928) 782-5995. Fax: (661) 837-1612. Web Site: www.campesina.com. Licensee: Farmworker Educational Radio Network Inc. Borsari & Paxson. Format: Mexican rgnl. Target aud: 25-54; Hispanic market. ♦Anthony Chavez, exec VP; Rosella Lopez, gen mgr; Jeff Russinsky, gen sls mgr; Juan Rocha, progmg dir; Isabel Eggert, news dir; Dave Whitehead, chief of engrg.

Whiteriver

***KNNB(FM)**— Sept 11, 1982: 88.1 mhz; 630 w. 600 ft. TL: N33 45 47 W109 57 39. (CP: 1.25 kw, ant 640 ft.). Stereo. Box 310, Hwy. 73, Skill Ctr. Rd. 85941. Secondary address: Box 700 85941. Phone: (928) 338-5229. Phone: (928) 338-5211. Fax: (928) 338-1744. Licensee: Apache Radio Broadcasting Corp. Format: Div, educ. News staff: one; News: 3 hrs wkly. Target aud: 15-60. Spec prog: Apache 8 hrs wkly. ♦Kim Harvey, gen mgr & stn mgr; Maybelline Burnett, progmg dir; Udell Opah, chief of engrg.

Wickenburg

KBSZ(AM)— Jan 27, 1960: 1250 khz; 350 w-D, 202 w-N. TL: N33 55 32 W112 47 38. 340 W. Wickenburg Way, Ste. B 85390. Phone: (928) 668-1250. Fax: (928) 668-1251. E-mail: kbszz@cableaz.com. Web Site: www.kbsz-am.com. Licensee: Richard A. & Joann R. Peterson, joint tenants (acq 7-9-01). Format: Musical mix. ♦Pete Peterson, gen mgr & opns mgr.

KHOV-FM— Dec 2, 1983: 105.3 mhz; 6 kw. -1,364 ft. TL: N34 11 32 W112 45 13. Stereo. 4745 N. 7th St., Suite 140, Phoenix 85021. Phone: (602) 308-7900. Fax: (602) 308-7979. Web Site: www.univisionradio.com. Licensee: HBC License Corp. Group owner: Univision Radio (acq 9-22-2003; grpsl). Network: Jones Radio Networks. Wiley, Rein & Fielding. Format: Sp. News: 4 hrs wkly. Target aud: 35

Stations in the U.S.

Arkansas

plus; modern mature market. Spec prog: Jazz 2 hrs, relg one hr wkly. ♦ Mary McEvilly-Hernandez, gen mgr & stn mgr; Elvis Balle, progmg dir.

KSWG(FM)— January 1993: 96.3 mhz; 6.4 kw. 646 ft. 801 W. Wickenburg Way 85390. Phone: (928) 684-7804. Fax: (928) 684-7805. E-mail: kswg@directpc.com. Licensee: Circle S. Broadcasting Co. Inc. (acq 1990). Format: Country. ♦ Harold Shumway, pres; Mike Shumway, gen mgr & sls dir; Richard Lee, progmg dir.

Willcox

KHIL(AM)— Dec 2, 1959: 1250 khz; 5 kw-D, 196 w-N. TL: N32 16 00 W109 49 58. Box 1250 85644. Secondary address: 900 West Patte Rd. 85643. Phone: (520) 384-4626. Fax: (520) 384-4627. Licensee: Lakeshore Media L.L.C. (acq 12-18-2001; $1.1 million. with co-located FM). Network: USA. Format: C&W. ♦ Dan Curtis, gen mgr.

KWCX(FM)— July 8, 1976: 104.9 mhz; 730 w. Ant 3,175 ft. TL: N32 13 01 W109 36 26. Stereo. Box 1250 85644. Phone: (520) 384-4626. Fax: (520) 384-4627. Licensee: Lakeshore Media L.L.C. Group owner: Clear Channel Communications Inc. (acq 12-18-2001; $1.1 million with KHIL(AM) Willcox). Format: Classic country. ♦ Dan Curtis, gen mgr & sls.

Williams

KWMX(FM)— 1998: 96.7 mhz; 1 kw. 804 ft. TL: N35 14 36 W112 09 55. 112 E. Rt. 66, Suite 105, Flagstaff 86001. Phone: (928) 779-1177. Fax: (928) 774-5179. Licensee: Red Rock Communications II Ltd. (acq 1-8-98; $421,400). Format: Oldies. ♦ Thomas S. Rockler, pres; Jim Perrine, gen mgr & sls dir; Dylan Fletcher, opns dir; Bobby Delrio, prom dir.

KYET(AM)— Aug 17, 1992: 1180 khz; 10 kw-U. TL: N35 15 38 W112 10 55. 812 E. Beale St., Kingman 86401. Phone: (928) 753-9100. Fax: (928) 753-1978. Licensee: Grand Canyon Gateway Broadcasting L.L.C. (acq 9-19-97; $290,000). Network: ABC. Format: News/talk. News staff: 2; News: 16 hrs wkly. Target aud: 45-60; upper middle class conservatives. ♦ Rhonda Hart, pres; Joe Hart, gen mgr; Deana Campbell, sls VP & progmg VP; Steve Levin, prom VP; Dave Hawkins, news dir; Matt Krick, engrg VP.

Window Rock

KTNN(AM)— Feb 26, 1986: 660 khz; 50 kw-U, DA-N. TL: N35 53 41 W109 08 29. Box 2569 86515. Phone: (928) 871-2582. Fax: (928) 871-3479. E-mail: ktnn@cia-g.com. Web Site: www.navajoland.com/ktnn. Licensee: The Navajo Tribe. (acq 1-86). Format: Country. Navajo Tribe of Indians. Spec prog: American Indian. ♦ Chester Francis, gen mgr; Marilynn Van Wagner, gen sls mgr & prom mgr; Bill Riddle, asst music dir; Bernadette Chato, news dir; Ernie Manuelito, chief of engrg.

KWRK(FM)— Co-owned with KTNN(AM). October 1996: 96.1 mhz; 94 kw. 328 ft. TL: N35 33 36 W109 06 30. Format: Jazz.

KWIM(FM)— Sept 21, 1995: 104.9 mhz; 30 kw. Ant 298 ft. TL: N35 39 19 W109 01 59. Stereo. Box 9090, Western Indian Ministries 86515. Phone: (505) 371-5587. Fax: (505) 371-5588. E-mail: kwimkhac@cia-d.com. Web Site: www.westernindian.org. Licensee: Western Indian Ministries Inc. Format: Adult contemp, Christian, relg. ♦ Brenda Gable, gen mgr; Lenora A. Brown, gen mgr & stn mgr; Torres Oliver, gen sls mgr.

Winslow

KINO(AM)— Dec 18, 1962: 1230 khz; 1 kw-U. TL: N35 02 15 W110 43 00. Drawer K, East End of Easy St. 86047. Phone: (928) 289-3364. Fax: (928) 289-3366. E-mail: kinoradio@cox.net. Licensee: Sunflower Communications. (acq 1-15-77). Network: CBS. Format: Country. Target aud: General. Spec prog: Sp 3 hrs wkly. ♦ Loy Engelhardt, gen mgr.

Yuma

*KAWC(AM)— July 11, 1970: 1320 khz; 1 kw-D, 147 w-N. TL: N32 41 10 W114 29 38. Box 929 85366. Secondary address: 9500 S. Ave., #8E 85366. Phone: (928) 344-7690. Phone: (928) 344-4210. Fax: (928) 344-7740. Web Site: kawcradio.org. Licensee: Arizona Western College. Network: NPR. Format: Var, country, rock. News staff: one. Target aud: General. Spec prog: Sp 15 hrs wkly. ♦ Frank Preciado, gen mgr.

KAWC-FM— Mar 27, 1992: 88.9 mhz; 3 kw. 75 ft. TL: N32 41 10 W114 29 38. Stereo. Web Site: kawcradio.org. Format: Class, jazz, news. News staff: one.

KBLU(AM)—Listing follows KTTI(FM).

*KCFY(FM)— March 1992: 88.1 mhz; 3 kw. 239 ft. TL: N32 38 31 W114 33 34. Stereo. Box 1669 85366. Phone: (928) 341-9730. Fax: (928) 341-9099. E-mail: kcfy@kcfyfm.com. Web Site: www.kcfyfm.com. Licensee: Relevant Media Inc. (acq 3-7-2005; $636,000). Network: Salem Radio Network. Miller & Neely. Format: Christian. News: 4 hrs wkly. Target aud: 25-45; young to middle aged families. ♦ Greg S. Myers, gen mgr; Mike Bondora, prom dir.

KJOK(AM)— Dec 11, 1950: 1400 khz; 1 kw. TL: N32 39 06 W114 39 00. 949 S. Avenue B 85364. Phone: (928) 782-4321. Fax: (928) 343-1710. E-mail: oldiesradio@kjokyuma.com. Web Site: www.kjokyuma.com. Licensee: MonsterMedia L.L.C. (acq 1997; with co-located FM). Network: Jones Radio Network. Rep: McGavren Guild. Booth, Freret, Imlay & Tepper. Format: News/talk, sports, oldies. News staff: one; News: 30 hrs wkly. Target aud: 35 plus. Spec prog: Farm News 2 hrs wkly. ♦ Keith Lewis, CEO, gen mgr & gen sls mgr; John Schofield, progmg dir; Kim Johnson, news dir.

KQSR(FM)— Sept 5, 1986: 100.9 mhz; 3 kw. 274 ft. TL: N32 38 31 W114 33 34. (CP: Ant 1,075 ft.). Stereo. 755 W. 28th St. 85364. Phone: (928) 344-4980. Phone: (928) 726-9101. Fax: (928) 344-4983. Web Site: www.kyjtfm.com. Licensee: Capstar TX L.P. Group owner: Clear Channel Communications Inc. (acq 8-30-2000; grpsl). Format: Classic rock. Target aud: 25-54. ♦ Jeff Harris, gen mgr & sls dir; Cindy Landin, mktg mgr; Susan Nickell, progmg dir.

KTTI(FM)— Nov 6, 1970: 95.1 mhz; 25 kw. 97 ft. TL: N32 42 42 W114 38 58. (CP: 100 kw, ant 1,256 ft. TL: N32 40 25 W114 20 12). Stereo. 755 W. 28th St. 85364-7136. Phone: (928) 344-4980. Fax: (928) 344-4983. Licensee: Capstar TX L.P. Group owner: Clear Channel Communications Inc. (acq 8-30-00; grpsl). Rep: Allied Radio Partners. Format: Country. Target aud: 25-54. ♦ Jeff Harris, gen mgr; Cindy Landin, gen sls mgr; Susan Nickell, progmg dir & news dir; Shannon Pearson, chief of engrg.

KBLU(AM)—Co-owned with KTTI(FM). March 1940: 560 khz; 1 kw-U, DA-N. TL: N32 43 25 W114 38 39. Network: Westwood One. Format: News/talk. ♦ Tiffany Fair, progmg dir.

*KYRM(FM)— April 2000: 91.9 mhz; 6.3 kw. 407 ft. TL: N33 03 18 W114 49 37. Stereo. Box 5965 85366-5965. Secondary address: 2690 S. 3rd Ave. 85366. Phone: (928) 341-0919. Fax: (928) 314-4141. E-mail: kyrm@hcjb.org. Web Site: www.radiokyrm.org. Licensee: World Radio Network. Group owner: World Radio Network Inc. Format: Sp, Christian, relg. News: 6 hrs wkly. Hispanic population. Spec prog: Children 6 hrs. ♦ Douglas Swanson, stn mgr & engrg mgr; Rachel Swanson, progmg dir.

Arkansas

Arkadelphia

KDEL-FM—Listing follows KVRC(AM).

*KSWH(FM)— Sept 25, 1969: 99.9 mhz; 10 w. 70 ft. TL: N34 07 32 W93 03 48. Stereo. HSU Box 7872, Henderson State Univ. 71999-0001. Phone: (870) 230-5185. Fax: (870) 230-5144. E-mail: kswh@hsu.edu. Web Site: www.kswh.org. Licensee: Henderson State University. News staff: 2; News: 2 hrs wkly. Target aud: 18-36; activity-orienated youthful females. Spec prog: Alternative 15 hrs, contemp Christian 2 hrs, rap 15 hrs wkly. ♦ Randy A. Seale, gen mgr; Chris Owen, opns VP & opns dir; Don C. Jackson, dev dir.

KVRC(AM)— Sept 25, 1947: 1240 khz; 1 kw-U. TL: N34 06 39 W93 03 01. Box 40 71923. Secondary address: 3210 W. Pine 71923. Phone: (870) 246-9272. Fax: (870) 246-5878. Licensee: Clark County Broadcasting Inc. (group owner; (acq 8-1-2002; $400,000. with co-located FM). Format: Nostalgia. ♦ Kendra Harper, gen mgr.

KDEL-FM—Co-owned with KVRC(AM). June 12, 1977: 100.9 mhz; 3 kw. Ant 95 ft. TL: N34 06 39 W93 03 01. Stereo. Format: Adult contemp.

KYXK(FM)—See Gurdon

Ashdown

KMJI(FM)— May 25, 1985: 93.3 mhz; 7.4 kw. 597 ft. TL: N33 30 24 W94 12 25. Stereo. 2324 Arkansas Blvd., Texarkana 71854. Phone: (870) 772-3771. Fax: (870) 772-0364. Web Site: www.magic033.com. Licensee: Clear Channel Broadcasting Licenses Inc. Group owner: Clear Channel Communications Inc. (acq 6-11-02; $1.5 million). Format: Adult contemp. News staff: one; News: 7 hrs wkly. Target aud: General. Spec prog: Relg 4 hrs wkly. ♦ Ron Bird, gen mgr.

KPGG(FM)— May 19, 1972: 103.9 mhz; 5.1 kw. Ant 354 ft. TL: N33 36 06 W94 04 38. Stereo. 1323 College Dr., Texarkana, TX 75501. Phone: (903) 793-1109. Fax: (903) 794-4717. Licensee: FFD Holdings I Inc. Group owner: Petracom Media LLC (acq 12-20-2004; grpsl). Format: Country. News staff: one. ♦ Mike Basso, gen mgr.

Atkins

KVLD(FM)— October 1999: 99.3 mhz; 6 kw. 328 ft. TL: N35 13 10 W92 51 05. Box 10310, Russellville 72810. Phone: (479) 968-6816. Fax: (479) 968-2946. Web Site: www.rivervalleyradio.com. Licensee: MMA License LLC. Group owner: MAX Media L.L.C. (acq 4-21-03; grpsl). Format: Oldies.

Augusta

KABK-FM—Licensed to Augusta. See Mayflower

Bald Knob

KABK-FM—See Mayflower

KAPZ(AM)— Aug 18, 1980: 710 khz; 250 w-D, DA. TL: N35 16 32 W91 33 39. Box 1300, Searcy 72145. Secondary address: 111 N. Spring St., Searcy 72143. Phone: (501) 268-5072. Fax: (501) 279-2900. Licensee: Crain Media Group LLC (group owner; (acq 8-7-2002; grpsl). Format: News/talk. Spec prog: Farm 3 hrs wkly. ♦ Bill Weaver, gen mgr.

KCNY(FM)—Co-owned with KAPZ(AM). Oct 15, 1984: 107.1 mhz; 19 kw. Ant 305 ft. TL: N35 17 29 W91 40 24. (CP: COL Greenbrier. 12.5 kw, ant 466 ft. TL: N35 17 47 W92 19 11). Format: Adult contemp.

Barling

KOLX(FM)— Sept 1, 1987: 94.5 mhz; 18.5 kw. Ant 269 ft. TL: N35 15 54 W94 21 52. Stereo. Box 908, Fort Smith 72902. Phone: (479) 288-1047. Fax: (479) 288-0942. Licensee: Pharis Broadcasting Inc. (group owner; (acq 3-14-2002;. $350,000. with KFPW(AM) Fort Smith). Network: USA. Format: Talk, country. News: 5 hrs wkly. Target aud: 25-54; general. ♦ William Pharis, pres; Karen Pharis, gen mgr & stn mgr; Ernie Witt Jr., opns VP.

Arkansas

Batesville

KAAB(AM)— August 1980: 1130 khz; 1 kw-D, DA. TL: N35 16 32 W91 38 21. (CP: 20 w-N). 920 Harrison St. 72501. Secondary address: Box 2077 72503. Phone: (870) 793-4196. Fax: (870) 793-5222. E-mail: arweekly@cei.net. Licensee: WRD Entertainment Inc. (group owner). Format: Mexicana. Target aud: 18-44. Spec prog: Farm 5 hrs wkly. ◆John R. Grace, pres; Gary Bridgman, gen mgr.

KBTA(AM)— June 30, 1950: 1340 khz; 1 kw-U. TL: N35 44 39 W91 38 21. Box 2077, 920 Harrison, Suite C 72503. Phone: (870) 793-4196. Fax: (870) 793-5222. Web Site: maxfm.com. Licensee: W.R.D. Entertainment Inc. (group owner; acq 12-15-95). Format: Sports. News staff: 2; News: 22 hrs wkly. Target aud: 18 plus. ◆Rob Grace, pres; Gary Bridgman, gen mgr; Ben Johnson, progmg dir; Dale Johnson, chief of engrg.

KZLE(FM)—Co-owned with KBTA(AM). Mar 3, 1982: 93.1 mhz; 100 kw. 984 ft. TL: N35 53 27 W91 44 01. Stereo. E-mail: rob@maxfm.com. Web Site: maxfm.com. Format: Rock. Target aud: 24 plus. ◆Rob Grace, progmg dir & mus dir; Dale Johnson, engrg dir.

KBTA-FM— 1999: 99.5 mhz; 3.4 kw. Ant 426 ft. TL: N35 52 07 W91 35 14. 920 Harrison St. 72503. Phone: (870) 793-4196. Fax: (870) 793-5222. E-mail: garyb@swbell.net. Licensee: W.R.D. Entertainment Inc. (group owner). Format: Adult contemp. ◆Rob Grace, pres; Gary Bridgman, gen mgr; Matt Anderson, gen sls mgr; Ben Johnson, progmg dir; Dale Johnson, chief of engrg.

Beebe

KBGR(FM)— June 22, 1991: 101.5 mhz; 6 kw. Ant 328 ft. TL: N35 11 26 W91 54 45. 5700 West Oaks Blvd., Rocklin, CA 95765. Phone: (916) 251-1600. Fax: (916) 251-1650. Web Site: www.air1.com. Licensee: Educational Media Foundation. (group owner; (acq 6-9-2005; $525,000). Network: Air 1. Format: Christian hit music. ◆Richard Jenkins, pres.

Bella Vista

KBVA(FM)— November 1991: 106.5 mhz; 37 kw. 567 ft. TL: N36 18 21 W94 27 29. 1655 Hwy. 72 S.E., Gravette 72736. Phone: (479) 787-6411. Fax: (479) 787-6116. Licensee: Gayla Joy McKenzie. Format: Var. ◆Gayla Joy McKenzie, pres & gen mgr.

KREB(AM)—See Bentonville-Bella Vista

Bellefonte

KNWA(AM)— 1986: 1600 khz; 5 kw-D, 50 w-N. TL: N36 14 49 W93 05 06. Box 850, Harrison 72602. Secondary address: 600 S. Pine, Harrison 72601. Phone: (870) 741-1402. Fax: (870) 741-9702. Licensee: Harrison Radio Stations Inc. Format: Southern Gospel. ◆Tom Arnold, gen mgr, sls dir & mktg dir; Phillip Cary, progmg dir.

Benton

KEWI(AM)— June 26, 1953: 690 khz; 250 w-D, 73 w-N. TL: N34 31 57 W92 34 16. 115 S. Main St. 72015. Phone: (501) 778-6677. Phone: (501) 315-5394. Fax: (501) 778-7717. E-mail: kewi2@up-link.net. Web Site: www.kewi690.com. Licensee: Landers Broadcasting Co. Inc. (acq 5-95). Network: USA. Format: Loc news, oldies, sports, country, talk. News staff: one; News: 10 hrs wkly. Target aud: 25-65; all income levels. Spec prog: Farm 4 hrs, gospel 10 hrs, relg 5 hrs wkly. ◆Doris L. Landers, exec VP; Jim Landers, CEO, gen mgr & opns mgr.

KHKN(FM)— Jan 1, 1979: 106.7 mhz; 16 kw. 866 ft. TL: N34 47 56 W92 29 53. Stereo. 10800 Colonel Glenn, Little Rock 72204. Phone: (501) 433-1067. Fax: (501) 228-9547. Fax: (501) 227-5776. Licensee: Clear Channel Broadcasting Licenses Inc. Group owner: Clear Channel Communications Inc. (acq 9-12-97; grpsl). Bryan Cave. Format: Country. Target aud: 18-34. ◆Don Pollnow, gen mgr & progmg dir.

Bentonville

KAMO-FM—See Rogers

***KAPG(FM)**—Not on air, target date: unknown: 88.1 mhz; 1 kw. Ant 233 ft. TL: N36 23 37 W94 10 57. Drawer 2440, Tupelo, MS 38803. Phone: (662) 844-8888. Fax: (662) 842-6791. Licensee: American Family Association. Group owner: American Family Radio. Format: Christian. ◆Marvin Sanders, gen mgr; John Riley, progmg dir; Fred Jackson, news dir; Joey Moody, chief of engrg.

KFFK(AM)—See Rogers

KIGL(FM)—See Seligman, MO

KQSM-FM— Nov 7, 1983: 98.3 mhz; 100 kw. 617 ft. TL: N36 07 38 W93 59 23. Stereo. 24 East Meadow St., Suite 1, Fayetteville 72701. Phone: (479) 521-5566. Fax: (479) 521-0751. Web Site: www.sam98.com. Licensee: Cumulus Licensing Corp. Group owner: Cumulus Media Inc. (acq 2-1-99; grpsl). Format: Country. Target aud: 25-54. Spec prog: Class 2 hrs wkly. ◆Joe Conway, gen mgr.

KSEC(FM)—Not on air, target date: unknown: 95.7 mhz; 6 kw. Ant 328 ft. TL: N36 17 13 W94 12 32. 401 N. 2nd St., Rogers 72756. Phone: (479) 631-0202. Fax: (479) 631-6732. Licensee: Lazeta 957 Co. (acq 6-1-2005; $1.99 million). Format: Oldies. ◆Norman D. McChristian, gen mgr; Ken Couch, opns mgr.

Bentonville-Bella Vista

KREB(AM)— Feb 5, 1979: 1190 khz; 2.5 kw-D. TL: N36 23 17 W94 11 42. 1780 Holly St., Fayetteville 72703. Phone: (479) 582-3776. Fax: (479) 571-0995. Licensee: Butler Broadcasting Co. LLC (acq 10-13-99; $100,000). Network: USA. Format: Sports, talk. Target aud: 35 plus. ◆Peter Davidson, pres; Steve Butler, gen mgr.

Berryville

KTHS(AM)— February 1958: 1480 khz; 5 kw-D, 64 w-N. TL: N36 21 42 W93 33 40. Box 191, One Radio Dr. 72616. Phone: (870) 423-2147. Fax: (870) 423-2146. E-mail: studio@kthsradio.com. Licensee: KTHS/KSCC Inc. (acq 7-2-82). Network: ABC Information & Entertainment. Format: Modern country. News staff: one; News: 21.5 hrs. Target aud: General. Spec prog: Farm 15 hrs wkly. ◆James T. Earls, pres & gen mgr; William C. Autry, gen sls mgr; Linda Boyer, mus dir & news dir; Zeb Huffmaster, chief of engrg.

KTHS-FM— Dec 19, 1974: 107.1 mhz; 3.6 kw. 627 ft. TL: N36 20 45 W93 29 17. Stereo. News staff: one; News: 21.5 hrs wkly. Target aud: General.

Blytheville

***KBCM(FM)**— 2000: 88.3 mhz; 500 w. Ant 190 ft. TL: N35 54 45 W89 53 28. Drawer 2440, Tupelo, MS 38803. Phone: (662) 844-8888. Fax: (662) 844-9090. Licensee: American Family Association. Group owner: American Family Radio Format: Christian. ◆Marvin Sanders, gen mgr; John Riley, progmg dir.

KHLS(FM)— Listing follows KLCN(AM).

KLCN(AM)— 1922: 910 khz; 5 kw-D, 85 w-N. TL: N35 55 27 W89 52 18. Box 989 72316. Phone: (870) 762-2093. Fax: (870) 763-8459. Licensee: Sudbury Services Inc. Group owner: Sudbury Services Inc. & Newport Broadcasting Co. Format: Classic rock. ◆Ed White, gen mgr & news dir.

KHLS(FM)—Co-owned with KLCN(AM). 1948: 96.3 mhz; 100 kw. 450 ft. TL: N35 55 27 W89 52 18. (CP: Ant 351 ft. TL: N35 38 27 W89 56 54). Stereo. Format: C&W.

***KOUX(FM)**—Not on air, target date: unknown: 91.5 mhz; 1 kw. Ant 190 ft. TL: N35 54 45 W89 53 28. Drawer 2440, Tupelo, MS 38803. Phone: (662) 844-8888. Fax: (662) 842-6791. Licensee: American Family Association. Group owner: American Family Radio. ◆Marvin Sanders, gen mgr; John Riley, progmg dir; Fred Jackson, news dir; Joey Moody, chief of engrg.

Booneville

***KBHN(FM)**— 2005: 89.7 mhz; 59 kw. Ant 302 ft. TL: N35 08 25 W94 03 43. Box 6210, Fort Smith 72906. Phone: (479) 646-6700. Fax: (479) 646-1373. Web Site: www.kzfm.com. Licensee: Vision Ministries Inc. Format: Christian. ◆Marilyn K. Lynch, pres; Gary Brown, gen mgr & progmg dir.

KRBK(FM)—Licensed to Booneville. See Fort Smith

Brinkley

KBRI(AM)— Oct 25, 1959: 1570 khz; 250 w-D, 44 w-N. TL: N34 52 02 W91 12 04. Box 111, Hwy. 70 W. 72021. Phone: (870) 734-1570. Fax: (870) 734-1571. Licensee: East Arkansas Broadcasting Inc. Format: Gospel. News staff: one. Target aud: General. ◆Joey Rodgers, stn mgr; Stan Corneau, progmg dir; Sue Tate, chief of engrg.

KTRQ(FM)—Co-owned with KBRI(AM). October 1969: 102.3 mhz; 40 kw. Ant 548 ft. TL: N35 03 16 W90 44 36. Stereo. Format: Oldies.

Bryant

KKZR(FM)—Licensed to Bryant. See Malvern

Cabot

KPZK-FM— May 1993: 102.5 mhz; 3 kw. 328 ft. TL: N34 55 22 W92 00 32. Stereo. 700 Wellington Hills Rd., Little Rock 72211. Phone: (501) 401-0200. Fax: (501) 401-0367. Licensee: Citadel Broadcasting Co. Group owner: Citadel Broadcasting Corp. (acq 8-27-97; grpsl). Network: ABC. Rep: McGavren Guild. Eckert, Seamans, Cherin & Mellot. Format: Gospel. News staff: 4. Target aud: 25-49. ◆Jim Beard, gen mgr.

KZTD(AM)— Nov 16, 1980: 1350 khz; 2.5 kw-D, 73 w-N. TL: N34 59 59 W92 01 41. Box 94426, North Little Rock 72190. Phone: (501) 378-0104. Fax: (501) 305-2977. E-mail: kztd1350@hotmail.com. Web Site: www.lamexicana.com. Licensee: Searcy Broadcasting Inc. (group owner; acq 11-20-03). Format: Sp. Target aud: 18-49. ◆Ken Madden, pres; Phil Hall, gen mgr; Robert Tindle, opns dir; Christy Flynn, sls VP.

Calico Rock

KEZG(FM)—Not on air, target date: unknown: 97.1 mhz; 4.4 kw. Ant 781 ft. TL: N36 06 24 W92 18 53. 620 E. 13th St., Suite A, Texarkana 71854. Phone: (501) 454-7675. Licensee: Malvern Entertainment Corp. ◆Scott A. Gray, pres.

Camden

KAMD-FM— Dec 1, 1968: 97.1 mhz; 50 kw. Ant 456 ft. TL: N33 30 14 W92 48 38. Stereo. 133 Washington St. 71701. Phone: (870) 836-9567. Fax: (870) 836-9500. Web Site: www.camdenfm.com. Licensee: Radio Works Inc. (acq 12-13-2004; grpsl). Format: Adult contemp. ◆Donna Steward, stn mgr & sls dir; Greg Arnold, opns dir.

***KCAC(FM)**— June 11, 1990: 89.5 mhz; 250 w. 161 ft. TL: N33 34 31 W92 49 55. Stereo. 327 Stewart St. 71701. Phone: (870) 836-5289. Fax: (870) 836-9369. E-mail: kcacradio@hotmail.com. Web Site: http://www.kc89.com. Licensee: Southern Arkansas University Tech (acq 8-2-2005). Network: ABC. Cohn & Marks. Format: Alternative. Target aud: 18-35. ◆Steve Taylor, gen mgr; Payten Rayford, opns mgr.

KMGC(FM)— Nov 18, 1994: 104.5 mhz; 3 kw. 328 ft. TL: N33 30 14 W92 48 38. 133 Washington St. 71701. Phone: (870) 836-0104. Fax: (870) 836-9500. Web Site: www.camdenfm.com. Licensee: Radio Works Inc. (acq 12-13-2004; grpsl). Format: Urban contemp. ◆Donna Stewart, stn mgr; Greg Arnold, opns dir & mus dir.

KNHD(AM)— Aug 8, 1963: 1450 khz; 1 kw-U. TL: N33 33 49 W92 50 37. Box 262550, Baton Rouge, LA 70826. Phone: (225) 768-3224. Licensee: Family Worship Center Church Inc. (group owner; (acq 3-7-2002; grpsl). Format: Southern gospel mus. News staff: one. Target aud: 35 plus.

Cave City

***KZIG(FM)**— Jan 1, 1981: 89.9 mhz; 3.3 kw. Ant 351 ft. TL: N35 57 07 W91 32 58. Stereo. Box 190, 711 N. Main St. 72521. Phone: (870) 283-5331. Fax: (870) 283-3255. E-mail: bsisk@cavecity.ncsc.k12.ar.us. Licensee: Cave City Schools. Network: USA. Format: Relg, educ, div. Target aud: General. ◆Becky Sisk, gen mgr.

Cherokee Village

KFCM(FM)— May 18, 1981: 98.3 mhz; 3 kw. 298 ft. TL: N36 16 29 W91 30 18. Stereo. Box 909 72525. Phone: (870) 856-3249. Fax: (870) 895-4088. E-mail: hometownradio@centurytel.net. Licensee:

Stations in the U.S. — Arkansas

Developers & Brokers of Radio Properties — contact American Media Services at our suite: Philadelphia Marriott Downtown 215-625-2900 / 843-972-2200 / americanmediaservices.com / Charleston, SC / Dallas, TX · Chicago, Il · Austin, TX / American Media Services, LLC

KFCM Inc. (acq 11-29-89; $174,500; 12-18-89). Format: Oldies. News staff: 3; News: 25 hrs wkly. Target aud: 25-54. ♦James Bragg, pres & gen mgr.

Clarksville

KLYR(AM)— Mar 18, 1957: 1360 khz; 500 w-D, 98 w-N. TL: N35 28 21 W93 29 28. Box 188, Hwy. 64 W. 72830. Phone: (479) 754-3092. Fax: (479) 754-7227. Licensee: Randall P. Forrester. (acq 11-81; $31,816; 11-9-81). Format: C&W. News: 12 hrs wkly. Target aud: General. Spec prog: Relg 8 hrs wkly. ♦Randy Forrester, gen mgr.

KLYR-FM— 1974: 92.7 mhz; 3 kw. 292 ft. TL: N35 29 38 W93 32 21. Format: Country & Western.

KXIO(FM)— April 1991: 106.9 mhz; 5.9 kw. 112 ft. TL: N35 33 07 W93 24 33. 901 S. Rogers St. 72830. Phone: (479) 705-1069. Fax: (479) 754-5518. Web Site: www.kxio-radio.net. Licensee: Barnett Broadcasting Inc. (acq 10-17-01; $400,000). Format: Hot country. ♦Gary Barnett, gen mgr; Grant Merrill, progmg dir & news dir.

Clinton

KGFL(AM)— Oct 1, 1977: 1110 khz; 5 kw-D. TL: N35 33 30 W92 27 32. Box 1349 72031. Secondary address: Corner of Main & Griggs 24018. Phone: (501) 745-4474. Fax: (501) 745-4084. Licensee: King-Sulivan Radio (acq 4-3-01; $75,000. for 26% with co-located FM). Format: Oldies. Target aud: 35 plus. ♦Sid King, gen mgr.

KHPQ(FM)— Co-owned with KGFL(AM). Dec 23, 1982: 92.1 mhz; 10 kw. 571 ft. TL: N35 40 44 W92 30 30. Stereo. Network: Jones Radio Networks. Format: Country. Target aud: 25 plus. ♦Dixie Carter, pub affrs dir; Dave Britton, chief of engrg.

Colt

KTRQ(FM)—Licensed to Colt. See Brinkley

Conway

KASR(FM)—Listing follows KXXA(AM).

KCON(AM)— Nov 13, 1950: 1230 khz; 1 kw-U. TL: N35 04 23 W92 27 36. Box 4-5144, Student Center, 201 Donaghey Ave. 72035. Phone: (501) 450-3326. Fax: (501) 450-5874. E-mail: Montyr@uca.edu. Licensee: University of Central Arkansas Board of Trustees. (acq 11-20-98). Format: Adult Contemp. ♦Monty Rowell, gen mgr.

*KHDX(FM)— May 1973: 93.1 mhz; 8 w. 59 ft. TL: N35 06 01 W92 26 29. Stereo. Hendrix College, 1600 Washington Ave. 72032. Phone: (501) 450-1339. Phone: (501) 329-6811 (college #). Fax: (501) 450-1200. Web Site: www.hendrix.edu. Licensee: Hendrix College. Format: Full service. ♦Julie Marvin, gen mgr.

KMJX(FM)— June 1, 1967: 105.1 mhz; 79 kw. 1,053 ft. TL: N34 47 53 W92 29 33. Stereo. 10800 Colonel Glenn Rd., Little Rock 72204. Phone: (501) 217-5000. Fax: (501) 228-9547. E-mail: magic105fm@magic105fm.com. Web site: www.magic105fm.com. Licensee: Clear Channel Radio Licenses Inc. Group owner: Clear Channel Communications Inc. (acq 5-5-96; grpsl). Rep: Clear Channel. Wiley, Rein & Fielding. Format: Classic rock. News staff: one; News: 3 hrs wkly. Target aud: 18-49. ♦Llowrey Mays, chmn; Mark Mays, pres; Randall Mays, CFO; Bruce Demps, sr VP; Don Pollnow, gen mgr; Jeff Peterson, opns mgr & gen sls mgr; Casey Wagner, gen sls mgr & mus dir; Tom Wood, progmg.

*KUCA(FM)— Oct 10, 1966: 91.3 mhz; 5 kw. 154 ft. TL: N35 02 55 W92 27 49. Stereo. Box U-5144, Univ of Central Arkansas 72035. Secondary address: 201 Donaghey Ave. 72035. Phone: (501) 450-3326. Fax: (501) 450-5874. E-mail: Montyr@uca.edu. Licensee: University of Central Arkansas. Format: News, adult contemp. News: 10 hrs wkly. Target aud: 18-54; educated adults. ♦Monty Rowell, gen mgr; Jarrett Goldman, stn mgr.

KXXA(AM)— May 26, 1961: 1330 khz; 500 w-D, 64 w-N. TL: N35 06 00 W92 26 41. Box 1266 72033-1266. Phone: (501) 327-6611. Fax: (501) 327-7920. Licensee: Creative Media Inc. (acq 10-1-2004; with co-located FM). Format: All sports. Spec prog: Farm 6 hrs wkly. ♦Elaine Harrison, prom mgr; Michael D. Harrison, pres, gen mgr, sls dir & progmg dir.

KASR(FM)—Co-owned with KXXA(AM). April 1984: 92.7 mhz; 3 kw. 282 ft. TL: N35 06 46 W92 24 42. Box 1266, 117 Oak St., Suite 300 72032.

Corning

KBKG(FM)—Listing follows KCCB(AM).

KCCB(AM)— Feb 19, 1959: 1260 khz; 1 kw-D. TL: N36 24 00 W90 35 05. Box 398, 501 Bryan 72422. Phone: (870) 857-6646. Fax: (870) 857-6795. Licensee: Shields-Adkins Broadcasting Inc. Rep: Keystone (unwired net). Format: Lite. Target aud: General. ♦Jim Adkins, pres & gen mgr; Tina Privett, gen mgr.

KBKG(FM)—Co-owned with KCCB(AM). Sept 15, 1983: 93.5 mhz; 3 kw. 138 ft. TL: N36 24 00 W90 35 05. Stereo. Network: ABC. Format: Adult contemp, oldies. ♦Jim Adkins, CEO.

Cotton Plant

KAPW(FM)—Not on air, target date: unknown: 99.3 mhz; 6 kw. Ant 328 ft. TL: N34 58 07 W90 59 48. 1515 14th Ave., Suite 303, Oakland, CA 94606. Phone: (415) 373-2531. Licensee: Bradford Caldwell. ♦Bradford Caldwell, gen mgr.

Crossett

KAGH(AM)— January 1951: 800 khz; 240 w-D, 43 w-N. TL: N33 08 05 W91 56 49. Stereo. Box 697, 117 E. Wellfield Rd. 71635. Phone: (870) 364-2181. Phone: (870) 364-2182. Fax: (501) 364-2183. E-mail: kagh@cei.net. Licensee: Ashley County Broadcasters Inc. (acq 8-1-69). Network: Westwood One. Format: Country. ♦Russ Miller, progmg dir; Jerry Whitten, news dir; W. Barry Medlin, pres, gen mgr & chief of engrg.

KAGH-FM— Mar 16, 1967: 104.9 mhz; 6 kw. 300 ft. TL: N33 08 05 W91 56 49. Format: Country.

Danville

KYEL(FM)—Not on air, target date: unknown: 105.5 mhz; 6 kw. Ant 328 ft. TL: N35 07 16 W93 19 34. 3004 Kay Ln., Springdale 72762. Phone: (479) 890-7207. Fax: (479) 967-5278. Licensee: Danville FM Inc. Format: Country. ♦Diane Womack, gen mgr & sls; Chris Womack, stn mgr; Wayne Van de Pol, chief of engrg.

Dardanelle

KCAB(AM)— Mar 24, 1964: 980 khz; 5 kw-D. TL: N35 13 02 W93 10 08. Box 10310, Russellville 72812. Secondary address: 2705 E. Pkwy., Russellville 72802. Phone: (479) 968-6816. Fax: (479) 968-2946. Web Site: www.rivertalk980.com. Licensee: MMA License LLC. Group owner: MAX Media L.L.C. (acq 4-21-03; grpsl). Format: Sports/new. Target aud: 25-54; adults. ♦Jim Kelly, stn mgr; Tom Kamerling, news dir; Jim Alexander, chief of engrg.

KCJC(FM)—Co-owned with KCAB(AM). Jan 26, 1966: 102.3 mhz; 200 w. 1,227 ft. TL: N35 13 41 W93 15 20. (CP: 1.43 kw, ant 1,322 ft.). Web Site: www.rivertalk980.com. Network: ABC. Format: Country.

KWXT(AM)— October 1987: 1490 khz; 1 kw-U. TL: N35 13 08 W93 07 38. 701 E. Main, Suite 4, Russellville 72801. Phone: (479) 968-1337. Fax: (479) 968-1337. Licensee: George V. Domerese/Sherwood Broadcasting Co. (acq 9-2-92; $60,000; 9-21-92). Format: Christian country, gospel. ♦Tim Domerese, gen mgr; Jim Alexander, chief of engrg.

De Queen

*KBPU(FM)— 2002: 88.7 mhz; 250 w. Ant 122 ft. TL: N34 02 38 W94 17 41. Box 180, Tahoma, CA 96142. Phone: (530) 584-5700. Fax: (530) 584-5705. Web Site: www.ihradio.org. Licensee: Radio Assist Ministry Inc. (group owner; (acq 9-13-2004); grpsl). Format: Christian. ♦Clark Parrish, pres.

KDQN(AM)— Aug 1, 1956: 1390 khz; 500 w-D. TL: N34 01 57 W94 19 43. Box 311 71832. Secondary address: 921 W Collin Raye Dr. 71832. Phone: (870) 642-2446. Fax: (870) 642-2442. E-mail: numberonecountry@yahoo.com. Web Site: www.kdqn.net. Licensee: Jay W. Bunyard & Anne W. Bunyard. (acq 6-15-83; $475,000 with co-located FM; 7-4-83). Format: Sp. ♦Jay Bunyard, pres; Jon Bunyard, gen mgr; Victor Rojas, gen sls mgr.

KDQN-FM— Oct 6, 1978: 92.1 mhz; 50 kw. Ant 492 ft. TL: N34 13 35 W94 17 35. Stereo. Box 311 71832. Phone: (870) 642-2446. Fax: (870) 642-2442. Web Site: www.kdqn.net. Licensee: Jay W. Bunyard & Anne W. Bunyard. Format: Country. ♦Jon Bunyard, gen mgr & opns mgr.

De Witt

KDEW-FM— Sept 1, 1970: 97.3 mhz; 50 kw. 272 ft. TL: N34 16 09 W91 21 02. c/o KWAK-AM-FM, 1818 S. Buerkle, Stuttgart 72160. Phone: (870) 673-1595. E-mail: kwak@futura.com. Licensee: Arkansas County Broadcasters Inc. (group owner; acq 3-5-97; $150,000). Format: Country. ♦Scott Siler, gen mgr & mktg dir; Keith Hill, progmg dir; Jonathan Reaves, news dir; Jim Alexander, engrg dir.

Dermott

KRKD(FM)— Apr 1, 2000: 105.7 mhz; 3 kw. 328 ft. TL: N33 32 25 W91 22 39. Stereo. Box 5395, Greenville, MS 38704. Secondary address: 1024 N. Washington, Suite 206, Greenville, MS 38704. Phone: (662) 378-4103. Phone: (662) 846-0929. Fax: (662) 332-3103. E-mail: rock1057@deltaradio.net. Web Site: www.deltaradio.net.Jones Radio Net. Licensee: M.R.S. Ventures Inc. (group owner; acq 11-1-2003; grpsl). Wood, Maines & Brown, Chartered. Format: Classic rock. News staff: one. Target aud: General. ♦James H. Boggs, VP; Howard Johnson, gen mgr; Cindy Clancy, stn mgr.

KXSA-FM— Aug 24, 1924: 103.1 mhz; 5.5 kw. 328 ft. TL: N33 31 56 W91 34 28. 279 Midway, Monticello 71657. Phone: (870) 367-8528. Fax: (870) 367-9564. E-mail: crn@ccc-cable.net. Licensee: Community Radio Network Inc. (group owner; acq 5-19-99; grpsl). Format: Classic country. ♦P.Q. Gardner, pres; Ellen Gardner, opns VP; Chad Lovitz, progmg dir; Larry Criple, news dir.

Des Arc

*KBDO(FM)— 1999: 91.7 mhz; 56 kw vert. Ant 682 ft. TL: N35 00 08 W91 44 41. Box 3206, American Family Radio, Tupelo, MS 38803. Phone: (662) 844-8888, EXT. 204. Fax: (662) 842-6791. Licensee: American Family Association. Group owner: American Family Radio Format: Relg. ♦Marvin Sanders, gen mgr; Gary Vaile, stn mgr; John Riley, progmg dir; Joey Moody, chief of engrg.

KFLI(FM)— 2003: 104.7 mhz; 25 kw. Ant 328 ft. TL: N35 00 23 W91 40 20. 121 Radio Heights Dr., Searcy 72143. Phone: (501) 268-1047. Fax: (501) 305-2977. Web Site: www.oldiesradioonline.com. Licensee: George S. Flinn Jr. Format: Oldies. ♦Ken Madden, gen mgr.

Dumas

KXFE(FM)— Sept 1, 1980: . Stn currently dark 106.9 mhz; 25 kw. Ant 269 ft. TL: N33 58 11 W91 32 58. Stereo. Box 789, Wynne 72396.

Arkansas

Phone: (870) 238-8141. Fax: (870) 238-5997. Licensee: Arkansas County Broadcasters Inc. (acq 8-31-2004; $130,000). Format: Country. ♦ Bobby Caldwell, pres.

Earle

KCJF(FM)— 2004: 103.9 mhz; 12.5 kw. Ant 469 ft. TL: N35 27 01 W90 42 11. Box 789, Wynne 72396. Phone: (870) 238-5253. Fax: (870) 238-5997. Licensee: Catherine Joanna Flinn. Format: Classic rock. ♦ Bobby Caldwell, gen mgr.

East Camden

KCXY(FM)— Sept 28, 1987: 95.3 mhz; 100 kw. Ant 456 ft. TL: N33 30 14 W92 48 38. Stereo. Box 957, Camden 71701. Secondary address: 133 Washington St. S.W., Camden 71701. Phone: (870) 836-9567. Fax: (870) 836-9500. E-mail: y95@cablelinks.net. Web Site: www.camdenfm.net. Licensee: Radio Works Inc. (acq 12-13-2004; grpsl). Network: ABC Daytime Direction. Format: C&W. News staff: one; News: 15 hrs wkly. Target aud: 25-54. ♦ Jay Bunyard, pres; Donna Stewart, gen mgr & gen sls mgr; Greg Arnold, opns mgr & progmg dir.

El Dorado

KAGL(FM)— Sept 29, 1993: 93.3 mhz; 18 kw. Ant 354 ft. TL: N33 16 16 W92 39 17. Stereo. 2525 Northwest Ave. 71730. Phone: (870) 863-6126. Fax: (870) 863-4555. Web Site: www.totalradio.com. Licensee: Noalmark Broadcasting Corp. (group owner; acq 1-8-93; $10,000; 3-29-93). Rep: Target Broadcast Sales. Format: Classic rock. News staff: one; News: 15 hrs wkly. Target aud: 25-54; general. ♦ William C. Nolan, pres; Edwin Alderson, exec VP; Sandy Sanford, gen mgr.

*KBSA(FM)— December 1987: 90.9 mhz; 3 kw. Ant 581 ft. TL: N33 16 19 W92 42 12. Box 5250, Shreveport, LA 71135. Phone: (800) 552-8502. Phone: (318) 797-5150. Fax: (318) 797-5153. E-mail: listenermail@redriverradio.org. Web Site: www.redriverradio.org. Licensee: Board of Supervisors of Louisiana State University & A&M College. Network: Network: NPR, PRI. Format: Class, jazz, news. Target aud: 25+. ♦ Roy Gerritsen, gen mgr; Greg Hill, opns dir.

KDMS(AM)— May 8, 1950: 1290 khz; 5 kw-D, 106 w-N. TL: N33 12 27 W92 41 10. 1904 W. Hillsboro Road. Phone: (870) 863-5121. Fax: (870) 863-6221. Web Site: www.klbq99.com. Licensee: El Dorado Broadcasting Co. (acq 7-8-87; $950,000 with co-located FM; 4-6-87). Format: Adult contemp. ♦ Brett Miller, opns mgr & progmg dir; Rosh Partridge, pres, gen mgr & gen sls mgr; Norm Mason, chief of engrg.

KLBQ(FM)—Co-owned with KDMS(AM). Dec 23, 1963: 98.7 mhz; 14 kw. 298 ft. TL: N33 12 30 W92 41 16. Stereo. Format: Top-40, adult contemp.

KELD(AM)— Oct 17, 1935: 1400 khz; 1 kw-U. TL: N33 12 43 W92 39 48. (CP: TL: N33 14 14 W92 39 54). Stereo. 2525 Northwest Ave. 71730. Phone: (870) 863-6126. Phone: (870) 862-1400. Fax: (870) 863-4555. Web Site: www.totalradio.com. Licensee: Noalmark Broadcasting Corp. (group owner; acq 7-73). Rep: Target Broadcast Sales. Format: News/talk. News staff: one; News: 20 hrs wkly. Target aud: General. ♦ William C. Nolan Jr., pres; Edwin Alderson, exec VP; Sandy Sanford, gen mgr & sls dir; J. B. Billingly, opns dir.

KIXB(FM)—Co-owned with KELD(AM). Dec 9, 1963: 103.3 mhz; 100 kw. 571 ft. TL: N33 13 20 W92 55 28. Stereo. Phone: (870) 864-0103. E-mail: kix103@noalmark.com. Web Site: www.totalradio.com. Format: Country. News: 15 hrs wkly. Target aud: 18-54. ♦ William Nolan, CEO; J.B. Billingly, mus dir; Julie Nolan, pub affrs dir.

*KKDU(FM)—Not on air, target date: unknown: 88.9 mhz; 26 kw vert. Ant 121 ft. TL: N33 12 32 W92 42 10. Broadcasting for the Challenged Inc., 188 S. Bellevue, Suite 222, Memphis, TN 38104. Phone: (901) 375-9324. Phone: (870) 875-1108. Licensee: Broadcasting for the Challenged Inc. Format: Div. ♦ Rosh Partridge, stn mgr & opns mgr.

KMLK(FM)— 2000: 101.5 mhz; 6 kw. 328 ft. TL: N33 09 32 W92 37 47. 2525 N. West Ave. 71730. Phone: (870) 875-1015. Fax: (870) 863-4555. Licensee: Noalmark Broadcasting Corp. (group owner; acq 6-14-01). Format: Urban adult contemp. ♦ Sandy Sanford, gen mgr.

KMRX(FM)— May 12, 1984: 96.1 mhz; 100 kw. Ant 288 ft. TL: N33 16 21 W92 39 25. Stereo. 2525 Northwest Ave. 71730. Phone: (870) 863-6126. Fax: (870) 863-4555. Web Site: www.totalradio.com. Licensee: Noalmark Broadcasting Corp. (group owner; acq 7-31-97). Format: Adult contemp, contemp hit. News staff: one; News: 2 hrs wkly. Target aud: 18-34. ♦ Sandy Sanford, gen mgr; Chase Roberts, opns mgr & progmg dir; Jim Harris, news dir.

England

KHTE-FM— Sept 26, 1988: 96.5 mhz; 3 kw. 148 ft. TL: N34 32 45 W91 59 04. (CP: 25 kw). Stereo. 400 Hardin Rd., Suite 150, Little Rock 72211. Phone: (501) 219-1919. Fax: (501) 225-4610. Web Site: www.lick1063.com. Licensee: ABG Arkansas LLC. Group owner: Archway Broadcasting Group (acq 1-22-2003; $8 million. with KOLL-FM Lonoke). Format: Contemporary hit. ♦ Brad Hutchesonn, gen mgr; Bryan Stewart, stn mgr; Joe Ratliff, stn mgr & progmg dir.

KVDW(AM)— Aug 31, 1979: 1530 khz; 250 w-D. TL: N34 32 45 W91 59 04. (CP: COL: Scott, 500 w-D). 1005 Clearlake Rd. 72046. Phone: (501) 842-9308. Fax: (501) 842-9308. Licensee: Wells Broadcasting Inc. (acq 8-13-02; $35,000). Putbrese, Hunsaker & Trent, P. Format: Alternative rock. Target aud: 18-54; professionals, farmers, college educated. Spec prog: Farm 5 hrs, talk 10 hrs wkly. ♦ Vernon Wells, gen mgr.

Eudora

KAVH(FM)— 2001: 101.5 mhz; 6 kw. Ant 328 ft. TL: N33 11 58 W91 15 39. c/o WJJA(TV), 4311 E. Oakwood Rd., Oak Creek, WI 53154. Phone: (414) 764-4953. Licensee: Joel J. Kinlow. Group owner: Joel J. Kinlow Stns. Format: Var. ♦ Bruce Herz, opns dir; Joel Kinlow, gen mgr & progmg dir.

Eureka Springs

KTCN(FM)— May 13, 1985: 100.9 mhz; 1.1 kw. 531 ft. TL: N36 22 49 W93 44 53. Stereo. 114 Hwy. 23 S. 72632. Phone: (479) 253-9079. Fax: (479) 253-7308. Web Site: www.hereshelpnet.org. Licensee: New Life Evangelistic Center Inc. (acq 11-23-92; $90,000; 12-14-92). Network: ABC Daytime Direction. Format: Relg. News staff: one; News: 20 hrs wkly. Target aud: 35 plus; upper income & retired. Spec prog: Class 10 hrs, 50s & 60s mus 2 hrs wkly. ♦ Larry Rice, CEO & pres; Jim Barnes, gen mgr & opns mgr; Thomas Hoffman Jr., chief of opns.

Fairfield Bay

KFFB(FM)— Dec 31, 1981: 106.1 mhz; 50 kw. 500 ft. TL: N35 45 22 W92 14 49. Stereo. Box 1050 72088. Phone: (501) 884-6812. Fax: (501) 723-4861. E-mail: kffb@kffb.com. Web Site: www.kffb.com. Licensee: Freedom Broadcasting Inc. Network: ABC. Smithwick & Belendiuk. Format: MOR. News staff: one; News: 8 hrs wkly. Target aud: 35 plus; middle & upper income. ♦ Bob Connell, pres; Pam Connell, exec VP; Chad Whiteaker, stn mgr.

Farmington

KFAY(AM)— Dec 15, 1946: 1030 khz; 10 kw-D, 1 kw-N, DA-2. TL: N36 06 34 W94 10 59. Stereo. 24 E. Meadow St., Suite 1, Fayetteville 72701. Phone: (479) 521-5566. Fax: (479) 521-4968. Web Site: www.kfayam.com. Licensee: Cumulus Licensing Corp. Group owner: Cumulus Media Inc. (acq 2-1-99; grpsl). Format: News/talk. News staff: 6; News: 20 hrs wkly. Target aud: 25-64; general. ♦ Joe Conway, gen mgr.

Fayetteville

*KAYH(FM)— June 26, 2000: 89.3 mhz; 6 kw. Ant 380 ft. TL: N36 01 48 W94 05 10. Box 550, Family FM 89.3 72702. Phone: (479) 750-7707. Fax: (479) 750-7767. E-mail: familyfm89.3@sbc.net. Licensee: Family Vision Ministries Inc. (acq 12-19-01; $119,000). Format: Southern gospel. ♦ Robert Johnson, gen mgr.

*KBNV(FM)— 2000: 90.1 mhz; 7.1 kw horiz, 16 kw vert. Ant 466 ft. TL: N36 07 38 W93 59 23. Drawer 2440, Tupelo, MS 38803. Phone: (662) 844-8888. Fax: (662) 844-9090. Licensee: American Family Association. Group owner: American Family Radio Format: Christian. ♦ John Riley, progmg dir.

KEZA(FM)— Sept 6, 1983: 107.9 mhz; 99 kw. 1,259 ft. TL: N35 51 12 W94 01 33. Stereo. 4209 Frontage Rd. 72703. Phone: (479) 582-1079. Fax: (479) 582-5302. Web Site: www.magic1079.com. Licensee: Capstar TX L.P. Group owner: Clear Channel Communications Inc. (acq 8-30-00; grpsl). Format: Adult contemp. Target aud: 25-54. Spec prog: Jazz, oldies. ♦ Tony Beringer, gen mgr.

KKEG(FM)— Oct 16, 1964: 92.1 mhz; 1.15 kw. 459 ft. TL: N36 03 55 W94 12 24. (CP: 20.5 kw, ant 328 ft.). Stereo. 1780 Holly St. 72703. Phone: (479) 521-5566. Fax: (479) 521-0751. Web Site: www.921thekeg.com. Licensee: Cumulus Licensing Corp. Group owner: Cumulus Media Inc. (acq 2-1-99; grpsl). Rep: Roslin. Format: AOR, classic rock. News staff: one. Target aud: 18-49. ♦ Joe Conway, gen mgr.

KKIX(FM)— Oct 1, 1966: 103.9 mhz; 100 kw. 510 ft. TL: N36 01 17 W94 13 04. Stereo. Box 8190 72703. Phone: (479) 521-0104. Fax: (479) 444-8600. Web Site: www.kix104.com. Licensee: Capstar TX L.P. Group owner: Clear Channel Communications Inc. (acq 8-30-00; grpsl). Wiley, Rein & Fielding. Format: Country. News staff: one; News: 2 hrs wkly. Target aud: 25-54. ♦ Tony Beringer, gen mgr.

KMXF(FM)—See Lowell

KOFC(AM)— June 10, 1957: 1250 khz; 920 w-D, 45 w-N. TL: N36 04 29 W94 11 00. Box 550 72702-0550. Phone: (479) 750-7707. Fax: (479) 750-7767. E-mail: kofc@ipa.net. Licensee: William B. Disney. (acq 12-11-87; $95,000; 6-22-87). Network: USA. Format: Christian talk, teaching. News: 8 hrs wkly. Target aud: 35 plus; traditional Christian families. ♦ William B. Disney, pres; Robert Johnson, gen mgr & opns mgr.

*KUAF(FM)— Jan 15, 1973: 91.3 mhz; 60 kw. 1,105 ft. TL: N35 51 12 W94 01 33. Stereo. 747 W. Dickson St., Suite 2 72701-5023. Phone: (479) 575-2556. Fax: (479) 575-8440. Web Site: www.kuaf.com. Licensee: Board of Trustees University of Arkansas. Network: NPR. Format: News, class, jazz. News staff: 3; News: 45 hrs wkly. Target aud: 25-65. Spec prog: Folk 5 hrs, Black 5 hrs wkly. ♦ Rick Stockdell, gen mgr.

*KXUA(FM)— April 4, 2000: 88.3 mhz; 470 w vert. 262 ft. TL: N36 03 56 W94 10 30. Stereo. University of Arkansas, 406 Administration Bldg. 72701. Phone: (479) 575-4273. Licensee: Board of Trustees of University of Arkansas. Format: Alternative. Target aud: 12-24; high school and colege students. ♦ Rick Stockdell, gen mgr.

Fordyce

KBJT(AM)— Aug 1, 1959: 1570 khz; 810 w-D, 8 w-N. TL: N33 48 10 W92 26 10. (CP: 1590 khz; 4.7 kw-D, 35 w-N). 303 Spring St 71742. Phone: (870) 352-7137. Fax: (870) 352-7139. E-mail: kbjt@alltel.net. Web Site: kbjtkq.com. Licensee: KBJT Inc. (acq 9-1-77). Format: News/talk. Target aud: General. Spec prog: Gospel 11 hrs wkly. ♦ Gary Coates, pres & gen mgr; Saxon Coates, news dir; Carna Coates, pub affrs dir.

KQEW(FM)—Co-owned with KBJT(AM). Feb 23, 1982: 102.3 mhz; 25 kw. 328 ft. TL: N33 48 10 W92 26 10. Stereo. Licensee: Dallas Properties Inc. Format: C&W. Target aud: General. ♦ Randall Harvill, mus dir.

Forrest City

*KARH(FM)— 2000: 88.1 mhz; 3.7 kw. Ant 544 ft. TL: N35 12 11 W90 33 57. Drawer 3206, American Family Radio, Tupelo, MS 38803. Phone: (662) 844-8888. Fax: (662) 842-6791. Web Site: www.afr.net. Licensee: American Family Association. Group owner: American Family Radio Format: Relg. ♦ Marvin Sanders, gen mgr; John Riley, progmg dir; Joey Moody, chief of engrg.

KBFC(FM)—Listing follows KXJK(AM).

KXJK(AM)— Apr 29, 1949: 950 khz; 5 kw-D, 500 w-N. TL: N34 58 53 W90 51 27. Stereo. Box 707, 501 E. Broadway 72336. Phone: (870) 633-1252. Fax: (870) 633-1259. E-mail: radio@arkansas.net. Web Site: www.kxjk.com. Licensee: Forrest City Broadcasting Co. Inc. Network: ABC Daytime Direction. Midsouth Gene Smith. Format: Classic rock, news/talk. News staff: 2; News: 24 hrs wkly. Target aud: General. Spec prog: Farm 16 hrs wkly. ♦ William Fogg, gen mgr, mus dir & chief of engrg.

KBFC(FM)—Co-owned with KXJK(AM). Sept 22, 1960: 93.5 mhz; 25 kw. 340 ft. TL: N34 51 17 W90 55 02. Stereo. Web Site: www.kbfc.com. Format: Modern country. News: 4 hrs wkly. ♦ William Fogg, progmg dir.

Stations in the U.S.   Arkansas

Fort Smith

*KAOW(FM)— 1999: 88.9 mhz; 1 kw. 482 ft. TL: N35 26 50 W94 21 54. Box 2440, American Family Radio, Tupelo, MS 38803. Phone: (662) 844-8888. Fax: (662) 842-6791. Web Site: www.afr.net. Licensee: American Family Association. Group owner: American Family Radio Format: Relg. ♦ Marvin Sanders, gen mgr; John Riley, progmg dir; Joey Moody, chief of engrg.

KBBQ-FM— July 27, 1978: 100.7 mhz; 50 kw. Ant 459 ft. TL: N35 13 32 W94 20 29. Stereo. 3104 S. 70th St. 72903. Phone: (479) 452-0681. Fax: (479) 452-0873. Licensee: Cumulus Licensing Corp. Group owner: Cumulus Media Inc. (acq 5-1-99; $1 million). Format: Golden oldies. News: 7 hrs wkly. Target aud: 25-64. ♦ Smitty O'Loughlin, gen mgr.

KFPW(AM)— July 27, 1930: 1230 khz; 1 kw-U, DA-1. TL: N35 23 11 W94 21 44. Stereo. Box 908 72902. Secondary address: 323 N. Greenwood 72902. Phone: (501) 783-5379. Phone: (501) 288-1047. Fax: (501) 785-2638. Licensee: Pharis Broadcasting Inc. (group owner; (acq 3-14-2002; $850,000. with KOLX(FM) Barling). Network: ABC. Rep: Major Market Broadcasters Ltd. Riley Campbell & Tannenwald. Format: Big band, oldies. News staff: 2; News: 13 hrs wkly. Target aud: 35 plus; affluent. Spec prog: Sp 6 hrs wkly. ♦ Bill Pharis, chmn & pres; Karen Pharis, VP, gen mgr, gen sls mgr, prom mgr & news dir; Tommy Craft, sls dir; Ernie Witt, progmg dir; Mack Remington, pub affrs dir; Jim Barnes, engrg VP.

KFSA(AM)— Feb 13, 1947: 950 khz; 1 kw-D, 500 w-N, DA-2. TL: N35 25 58 W94 28 13. Stereo. Box 488 72901. Secondary address: 601 N. Greenwood 72902. Phone: (479) 782-9125. Fax: (479) 782-9127. Licensee: Fred H. Baker Sr. (acq 11-5-81; $297,000; 11-30-81). Network: ABC Information & Entertainment. Format: Southern gospel. Target aud: General. ♦ Fred H. Baker Sr., pres; Gary Keifer, gen mgr; Jerry Lynch, gen sls mgr & natl sls mgr; David J. Burdue, progmg dir; Dale L. Davenport, chief of engrg.

KISR(FM)— Co-owned with KFSA(AM). Aug 13, 1971: 93.7 mhz; 100 kw. 1,250 ft. TL: N35 31 22 W94 23 32. Stereo. Phone: (501) 785-2526. Web Site: www.kisr.net. Licensee: Stereo 93 Inc. Network: ABC FM Connection. Format: CHR. News staff: one. Target aud: 18-39. ♦ Fred Baker Jr., gen mgr & progmg dir; Gary Keifer, stn mgr; Carol Patterson, adv mgr; Rick Hayes, prom mgr & mus mgr; Dale L. Davenport, engrg dir.

KHGG(AM)—See Van Buren

KLSZ-FM—See Van Buren

KMAG(FM)— Dec 31, 1964: 99.1 mhz; 100 kw. 1,968 ft. TL: N35 09 56 W93 40 35. Stereo. 311 Lexington Ave. 72901. Phone: (479) 782-8888. Fax: (497) 785-5946. E-mail: info@kmag991.com. Web Site: www.kmag991.com. Licensee: Capstar TX L.P. Group owner: Clear Channel Communications Inc. (acq 8-30-00; grpsl). Format: Country. News staff: 2. Target aud: 25-54; females. ♦ Paul Swint, gen mgr; Lee Matthews, opns mgr & progmg dir; Tony Montgomery, sls dir & gen sls mgr; Daren Bobb, news dir; Allan Riley, chief of engrg.

KYHN(AM)—Co-owned with KMAG(FM). Nov 22, 1947: 1320 khz; 5 kw-U, DA-2. TL: N35 24 36 W94 21 30. Format: News/talk. News staff: 6; News: 40 hrs wkly. Target aud: 25-54.

KOMS(FM)—See Poteau, OK

KRBK(FM)—(Booneville). Nov 1, 1981: 104.7 mhz; 50 kw. 492 ft. TL: N35 11 01 W94 07 44. Stereo. Box 908 72902. Phone: (479) 288-1047. Fax: (479) 288-0942. Web Site: www.fox94.com. Licensee: Pharis Broadcasting Inc. (group owner; acq 11-20-97; $800,000). Rep: Commercial Media Sales. BRI Irwin, Campbell & Tannenwald. Format: Oldies. News staff: one; News: 10 hrs wkly. Target aud: 18-54. Spec prog: Leeza Gibbons Top-25 4 hrs, Paul Harvey 5 hrs wkly. ♦ Bill Pharis, pres; Karen Pharis, gen mgr; Ernie Witt, opns mgr.

KTCS-FM— Aug 15, 1964: 99.9 mhz; 100 kw. 1,919 ft. TL: N35 04 20 W94 40 50. Stereo. Box 180188 72918-0188. Secondary address: 5304 Hwy. 45 E. 72916. Phone: (479) 646-6151. Fax: (479) 646-3509. E-mail: ktcs@ktcs.com. Web Site: www.ktcs.com. Licensee: Big Chief Broadcasting Co. Format: Country. ♦ Lee Young, gen mgr, stn mgr & gen sls mgr; Melissa Harper, opns mgr; Darren Minor, progmg dir; Mary Livingston, news dir; Scott Reeves, chief of engrg.

KTCS(AM)— March 1956: 1410 khz; 1 kw-D. TL: N35 16 40 W94 22 35. Web Site: www.ktcs.com. (Acq 1961). Network: UPI. Format: Southern Gospel.

KWHN(AM)— 2001: 1650 khz; 10 kw-D, 1 kw-N. TL: N35 24 36 W94 21 30. 311 Lexington Ave. 72901. Phone: (479) 782-8888. Fax: (479) 782-0366. E-mail: info@kwhn.com. Web Site: www.kwhn.com. Licensee: Capstar TX L.P. Group owner: Clear Channel Communications Inc. Format: News/talk. ♦ Paul Swint, gen mgr; Tony Montgomery, sls dir; Darin Bobb, prom dir.

KZBB(FM)—See Poteau, OK

Fouke

*KLMZ(FM)— 2001: 104.3 mhz; 5 kw. Ant 361 ft. TL: N33 21 05 W93 50 41. EMF Broadcasting, 5700 West Oaks Blvd., Rocklin, CA 95765. Phone: (916) 251-1600. Fax: (916) 251-1650. E-mail: klove@klove.com. Web Site: www.klove.com. Licensee: Educational Media Foundation. Group owner: EMF Broadcasting (acq 12-18-03; $500,000). Format: K-Love. Shaw Pittman. Format: Contemp Christian. News staff: 3. Target aud: 25-44; Judeo Christian, female. ♦ Richard Jenkins, pres; Mike Novak, VP.

Glenwood

KWXE(FM)—Listing follows KWXI(AM).

KWXI(AM)— May 12, 1980: 670 khz; 5 kw-D. TL: N34 19 32 W93 33 27. Box 740, 180 Hwy. 70 E., Suite 11 71943. Phone: (870) 356-2151. Phone: (870) 356-2181. Fax: (870) 356-4684. E-mail: kwxe@ipa.net. Licensee: US Stations LLC (acq 2-9-2005; $530,000. with co-located FM). Network: CBS. Format: Country. Target aud: 34-54; affluent professionals. ♦ Kendra Harper, gen mgr & gen sls mgr; Doug Dumont, progmg dir & news dir; Danie Appleoff, chief of engrg.

KWXE(FM)—Co-owned with KWXI(AM). Nov 18, 1991: 104.5 mhz; 3 kw. 328 ft. TL: N34 18 38 W93 32 04. Stereo. News staff: one. Target aud: 25-50; general. ♦ Melinda Frizzell See, opns dir.

Gosnell

KAMJ(FM)— February 1999: 93.9 mhz; 2 kw. 328 ft. TL: N35 53 56 W89 52 48. Box 989, Blytheville 72315-0989. Phone: (870) 762-2093. Fax: (870) 763-8459. Licensee: Phoenix Broadcasting Group Inc. Group owner: Sudbury Services Inc. & Newport Broadcasting Co. Format: Urban contemp. ♦ Rob Hill, gen mgr.

Gould

KAFN(FM)— Apr 15, 1999: 102.5 mhz; 6 kw. Ant 328 ft. TL: N33 55 34 W91 28 54. 700 Wellington Hills Rd., Little Rock 72211. Phone: (501) 401-0200. Fax: (501) 401-0367. Web Site: www.karrnewsradio.com. Licensee: Arkansas County Broadcasters Inc. (group owner; acq 12-30-2003; $90,000). Format: News radio. ♦ Jim Beard, gen mgr.

Greenwood

KZKZ-FM— December 1981: 106.3 mhz; 1.7 kw. 433 ft. TL: N35 13 43 W94 15 45. (CP: 15 kw, ant 397 ft.). Stereo. 6420 S. Zero St., Fort Smith 72903. Phone: (479) 646-6700. Fax: (479) 646-1373. E-mail: kzkzfm@kzkzfm.com. Web Site: www.kzkzfm.com. Licensee: Family Communications Inc. (acq 5-11-93; 6-7-93). Format: Contemp Christian. ♦ Jerry Lynch, gen mgr; Jay Lynch, stn mgr.

Gurdon

KYXK(FM)— December 1984: 106.9 mhz; 17.5 kw. 298 ft. TL: N33 56 42 W93 10 43. Stereo. Box 40, Arkadelphia 71923. Secondary address: 601 S. 7th St., Arkadelphia 71923. Phone: (870) 246-9272. Fax: (870) 246-5878. Licensee: Clark County Broadcasting Inc. (group owner; acq 8-1-02). Booth, Freret, Imlay & Tepper. Format: Country. Target aud: 25-54; adults. ♦ Jay Bunyard, pres.

Hamburg

KHMB(FM)— 1996: 99.5 mhz; 3.2 kw. Ant 312 ft. TL: N33 17 19 W91 52 45. 203 Fairview Rd., Crossett 71635. Phone: (870) 364-4700. Fax: (870) 364-4770. Web Site: www.QLiteradio.com. Licensee: Kenneth Wayne Diebel. Format: Adult contemp. ♦ Dennis Maxwell, gen mgr.

Hampton

*KBPW(FM)— 2001: 88.1 mhz; 250 w. Ant 259 ft. TL: N33 32 11 W92 28 07. Box 2440, American Family Radio, Tupelo, MS 38803. Phone: (662) 844-8888. Fax: (662) 842-6791. Licensee: American Family Association Inc. Group owner: American Family Radio (acq 4-19-01). Format: Christian. ♦ Marvin Sanders, gen mgr; John Riley, progmg dir; Joey Moody, chief of engrg.

KELD-FM— Nov 26, 1984: 106.5 mhz; 17.5 kw. Ant 302 ft. TL: N33 32 23 W92 34 59. 100 E. Peach St., Suite 270, El Dorado 71730. Phone: (870) 863-5565. Fax: (870) 863-5567. Licensee: Noalmark Broadcasting Corp. (group owner; acq 2-21-03; $250,000). Format: News/talk. ♦ Sandy Sanford, gen mgr & opns dir.

Hardy

KOOU(FM)— Oct 4, 1993: 104.7 mhz; 6 kw. Ant 199 ft. TL: N36 18 17 W91 24 38. Stereo. Box 760 72542. Secondary address: 4000 Hwy. 62-412 72542. Phone: (870) 856-3249. Fax: (870) 856-4008. E-mail: magic1047fm@yahoo.com. Licensee: KOOU Inc. (acq 12-10-03). Network: ABC Daytime Direction. Format: Adult contemp. News staff: one; News: 4 hrs wkly. Target aud: 25-60; female/professional. ♦ Chris Atkins, gen mgr.

Harrisburg

KWHF(FM)— May 15, 1999: 95.9 mhz; 34 kw. Ant 489 ft. TL: N35 47 42 W90 47 35. Box 1737, Jonesboro 72403-1737. Secondary address: 407 W. Parker Rd., Jonesboro 72404. Phone: (870) 932-8400. Fax: (870) 932-3814. E-mail: larryjames@959thebuzz.com. Web Site: www.959thebuzz.com. Licensee: Clear Channel Broadcasting Licenses Inc. Group owner: Clear Channel Communications Inc. (acq 6-13-2002; $2.05 million. with KNEA(AM) Jonesboro). Dan Alpert. Format: Classic country. News staff: 2; News: 3 hrs wkly. Target aud: 28-65; Affluent baby boomers who have spendable income. ♦ Larry James, gen mgr.

Harrison

*KBPB(FM)— 2001: 91.9 mhz; 5.5 kw. Ant 341 ft. TL: N36 22 12 W93 13 23. 10795 Hwy. 65 N., Omaha 72662. Phone: (870) 426-1324. Licensee: New Life Evangelistic Center Inc. Format: Contemp Christian, Southern gospel. ♦ Larry Rice, gen mgr; Carl Swift, stn mgr; David Tiller, chief of opns.

KCWD(FM)— 1982: 96.1 mhz; 3 kw. 295 ft. TL: N36 16 36 W93 05 27. (CP: 8 kw, ant 1,191 ft.). Stereo. Box 850 72601. Secondary address: 600 S. Pine 72601. Phone: (870) 741-1402. Fax: (870) 741-9702. Web Site: www.kcwd.com. Licensee: Harrison Radio Station Inc. Network: ABC Information & Entertainment. Format: Classic rock. ♦ Tom Arnold, gen mgr & chief of opns.

KHOZ(AM)— Sept 28, 1946: 900 khz; 1 kw-D. TL: N36 14 35 W93 06 43. 1111 Radio Ave. 72601. Phone: (870) 741-2302. Fax: (870) 741-3299. E-mail: khoz@alltel.com. Web Site: www.khoz.com. Licensee: KHOZ LLC (acq 2005; $3.7 million. with co-located FM). Network:

Arkansas

CBS. Format: Talk, soft adult contemp. News staff: 2; News: 15 hrs wkly. Target aud: General. Spec prog: Gospel 10 hrs wkly. ◆Charles Earls, CEO; Scott Earls, pres; Scottie Earls, gen mgr.

KHOZ-FM— Mar 25, 1963: 102.9 mhz; 100 kw. 981 ft. TL: N36 26 11 W93 14 43. Stereo. Phone: (870) 741-2301. E-mail: scottieearls@krzk.com. Web Site: www.khoz.com. Network: CBS Radio. Format: Country. News staff: 2; News: 15 hrs wkly. Target aud: 25-54. ◆Bob Mitchell, prom dir & progmg dir; Jerry Bowman, mus dir; LaRay Shower, mus dir; Bill Wilcox, pub affrs dir.

Hatfield

KILX(FM)— 2001: 104.1 mhz; 28.5 kw. Ant 469 ft. TL: N34 32 42 W94 18 21. 1600 S. Reine St., Mena 71953. Phone: (479) 394-1450. Licensee: Ouachita Broadcasting Inc. (acq 3-8-99). Network: ABC Music Radio. Format: Hot adult contemp. ◆Dwight Douglas, gen mgr & opns mgr.

Heber Springs

KAWW(AM)— July 15, 1967: 1370 khz; 1 kw-D. TL: N35 29 10 W92 02 05. 111 North Spring St., Searcy 72143. Phone: (501) 268-7123. Fax: (501) 279-2900. Licensee: Crain Media Group LLC (group owner; acq 8-7-02; grpsl). Format: News/talk. News staff: one; News: one hr wkly. Target aud: 25-65. ◆Larry Crain, CEO; Phil Weaver, pres.

KAWW-FM— Sept 1, 1972: 100.7 mhz; 50 kw. Ant 328 ft. TL: N35 27 26 W92 02 11. Stereo. Box 1300, Searcy 72145. Phone: (501) 268-7123. Fax: (501) 279-2900. Licensee: Crain Media Group LLC (group owner; acq 8-7-02; grpsl). Format: Main stream adult contemp. Target aud: 25-54. ◆Larry Crain, CEO; Phil Weaver, exec VP.

***KBMJ(FM)**— 2002: 89.5 mhz; 50 kw vert. Ant 735 ft. TL: N35 44 00 W92 15 37. Drawer 2440, Tupelo, MS 38803. Phone: (662) 844-8888. Licensee: American Family Association. Group owner: American Family Radio Format: Christian. ◆Marvin Sanders, gen mgr; John Riley, progmg dir; Fred Jackson, news dir.

Helena

KFFA(AM)— Nov 19, 1941: 1360 khz; 1 kw-D, 90 w-N. TL: N34 31 39 W90 37 48. Box 430, 1360 Radio Dr. 72342. Phone: (870) 338-8361. Phone: (870) 338-8331. Fax: (870) 338-8332. E-mail: kffa@arkansas.net. Licensee: Delta Broadcasting Inc. (acq 3-80; $445,000; 3-10-80). Donald E. Martin. Format: Country. News: 25 hrs wkly. Target aud: 18-54. Spec prog: Farm 16 hrs, blues 8 hrs, Black 10 hrs, sports 15 hrs, gospel 4 hrs wkly. ◆Jim Howe, pres, mktg dir, adv VP & pub affrs dir; Rob Johnson, opns mgr, gen sls mgr, prom mgr & progmg mgr; Louis Smith, mus dir; Matt Motett, news dir; Jerry Campbell, engrg mgr.

KFFA-FM— 1972: 103.1 mhz; 13 kw. 318 ft. TL: N34 31 39 W90 37 46. Stereo. (Acq 5-84; grpsl; 5-7-84). Format: Adult contemp. News: 4 hrs wkly. ◆Jim Howe, CEO; Rob Johnson, progmg dir.

KJIW-FM— Jan 5, 1989: 94.5 mhz; 16 kw. 341 ft. TL: N34 31 28 W90 35 47. 204 Moore St. 72342. Phone: (870) 338-2700. Fax: (870) 338-3166. E-mail: kjiwfm@ipa.net. Licensee: Elijah Mondy Jr. (acq 1988). Rep: BRI. Format: Christian gospel. ◆Elijah Mondy Jr., pres & gen mgr; Belinda Mondy, opns VP; April Mondy, progmg dir & mus dir.

Hope

KBYB(FM)— Dec 31, 1984: 101.7 mhz; 50 kw. Ant 492 ft. TL: N33 41 20 W93 35 55. Stereo. 615 W. Olive, Texarkana, TX 75501. Phone: (903) 793-4671. Fax: (903) 792-4261. Licensee: Arklatex LLC. (group owner; (acq 1-4-2002); grpsl). Format: Jammin' oldies. Target aud: 25-54; females. ◆Harold Sudbury, gen mgr; Alex Rain, stn mgr & progmg mgr; Jayna Thomas, sls dir; Jay Calhoun, chief of engrg.

KHPA(FM)— Apr 21, 1977: 104.9 mhz; 3 kw. 298 ft. TL: N33 43 10 W93 29 07. (CP: 6 kw, ant 328 ft. TL: N33 43 12 W93 29 11). Stereo. Box 424 71802. Secondary address: 1600 S. Elm 71801. Phone: (870) 777-8868. Fax: (870) 777-8869. E-mail: supercountry105@yahoo.com. Licensee: Newport Broadcasting Co. Group owner: Sudbury Svcs Inc. & Newport Broadcasting Co. Format: Country. ◆Robert Hill, gen mgr; Rob Hill, stn mgr; Sonya Odom, sls dir; John McCoy, progmg dir & news dir; Kevin McKinnon, chief of engrg.

KXAR(AM)—Co-owned with KHPA(FM). Dec 12, 1947: 1490 khz; 690 w-U. TL: N33 41 20 W93 35 55. (Acq 8-26-99; $51,000). Network: ABC Daytime Direction. Format: Talk. Target aud: General; double income, stable, adult households. ◆Pamela Chism, chief of engrg.

Horseshoe Bend

KKIK(FM)— 2004: 106.5 mhz; 12 kw. Ant 476 ft. TL: N36 15 22 W91 55 23. 920 Harrison St., Batesville 72503. Phone: (870) 793-4196. Fax: (870) 793-5222. Licensee: WRD Entertainment Inc. (group owner). Format: Oldies. ◆Preston Grace, gen mgr.

Hot Springs

***KALR(FM)**— May 1989: 91.5 mhz; 3 kw. 485 ft. TL: N34 37 31 W93 00 37. Box 8500, 205 Radio Dr. 71910-8500. Phone: (501) 623-2300. Fax: (501) 623-8683. Licensee: Applied Life Ministries Inc. Format: Adult contemp Christian, praise. Target aud: 18-45. ◆Gabriel Allen, gen mgr.

KBHS(AM)— Oct 6, 1966: 1420 khz; 5 kw-D, 87 w-N. TL: N34 27 19 W93 03 26. Box 21430 71903. Secondary address: 208 Buena Vista Rd. 71902. Phone: (501) 525-1301. Fax: (501) 525-4344. E-mail: klaz@klaz.com. Web Site: www.klaz.com. Licensee: Noalmark Broadcasting Corp. (group owner; Rep: Target Broadcast Sales. Format: Adult contemp. Target aud: 35 plus; upscale, high-income residents & business people. ◆Eddie Tarpley, gen mgr.

KLAZ(FM)—Co-owned with KBHS(AM). October 1971: 105.9 mhz; 95 kw. 994 ft. TL: N34 30 19 W93 05 06. Stereo. Format: Adult contemp. Target aud: 18-49.

***KLRO(FM)**— Mar 20, 1984: 90.1 mhz; 38 kw. Ant 971 ft. TL: N34 30 18 W93 04 42. Stereo. 5700 West Oaks Blvd., Rocklin, CA 95765. Phone: (916) 251-1600. Fax: (916) 251-1650. Web Site: www.klove.com. Licensee: Educational Media Foundation. (acq 9-24-2004; $1.2 million). Network: K-Love. Format: Christian contemp, relg. ◆Richard Jenkins, gen mgr.

KPZA(AM)— Mar 10, 1953: 590 khz; 5 kw-D, 67 w-N. TL: N34 29 55 W92 58 45. Stereo. Box 21430 71903. Phone: (501) 525-4600. Fax: (501) 525-4344. Web Site: www.hsnp.com. Licensee: Noalmark Broadcasting Corp. (acq 12-13-2004; $140,000). Network: USA. Format: Sp. ◆Eddie Tarpley, gen mgr.

KQUS-FM—Listing follows KZNG(AM).

KYDL(FM)— June 18, 1965: 96.7 mhz; 2.6 kw. 320 ft. TL: N34 32 01 W93 03 24. (CP: 940 kw, ant 807 ft.). Stereo. 125 Corporate Terr. 71913-7248. Phone: (501) 525-9700. Fax: (501) 525-9739. Web Site: www.dl96.net. Licensee: US Stations LLC. Group owner: Powell Broadcasting (acq 2-1-2005; grpsl). Network: Westwood One. Format: Adult contemp. Target aud: 18 plus. ◆Gary Terrell, gen mgr.

KYXK(FM)—See Gurdon

KZNG(AM)— Jan 1, 1953: 1340 khz; 1 kw-U. TL: N34 29 43 W93 01 27. 125 Corporate Terr. 71913-7248. Phone: (501) 525-9700. Fax: (501) 525-9739. Web Site: www.kzng.net. Licensee: US Stations LLC. Group owner: Powell Broadcasting (acq 2-1-2005; grpsl). Network: ABC. Format: News/talk. News staff: one; News: 10 hrs wkly. Target aud: 18 plus. ◆Ted Mahn, gen mgr; Larry LeBlanc, opns dir & opns mgr; Rick Austin, gen sls mgr; Tom Duke, chief of engrg.

KQUS-FM—Co-owned with KZNG(AM). Feb 7, 1969: 97.5 mhz; 100 kw. 860 ft. TL: N34 24 11 W93 07 13. Stereo. Web Site: www.kqus.net. Network: ABC Information & Entertainment. Format: C&W. ◆Larry LeBlanc, progmg dir.

Hot Springs Village

KVRE(FM)— February 1994: 92.9 mhz; 25 kw. Ant 328 ft. TL: N34 38 34 W93 04 08. 122 DeSoto Center Dr. 71909. Phone: (501) 922-5678. Phone: (501) 922-5880. Fax: (501) 922-6626. E-mail: kvre@cox-internet.com. Licensee: Caddo Broadcasting Co. Format: Adult Standards (Music of Your Life). Target aud: 35 plus; general. ◆Polly Nichols, gen mgr; Wilma Eldredge, opns dir & opns mgr.

Hoxie

KJLV(FM)— Jan 20, 1988: 105.3 mhz; 25 kw. 328 ft. TL: N36 02 24 W90 59 11. 5700 W. Oaks Blvd., Rocklin, CA 95765. Phone: (707) 528-9236. Fax: (707) 528-9246. Phone: (916) 251-1650. Web Site: www.klove.com. Licensee: Educational Media Foundation. Group owner: EMF Broadcasting (acq 11-1-01; $1.3 million. with KJBR(FM) Marked Tree). Format: Contemp Christian. ◆Dick Jenkins, pres & gen mgr; Joe Miller, CFO; Mike Novak, sr VP; David Pierce, progmg dir; Sam Wallington, engrg dir.

Humnoke

KVLO(FM)— 1996: 101.7 mhz; 6 kw. 100 ft. TL: N34 32 58 W91 45 26. 700 Wellington Hill Rd., Little Rock 72211. Phone: (501) 401-0200. Fax: (501) 401-0365. Licensee: Citadel Broadcasting Co. Group owner: Citadel Broadcasting Corp. (acq 8-27-97; grpsl). Format: Gospel. ◆Jim Beard, VP & gen mgr.

Huntsville

KAKS(FM)— 1955: 99.5 mhz; 13.5 kw. Ant 443 ft. TL: N36 07 37 W93 51 57. 1780 Holly St., Fayetteville 72701. Phone: (479) 582-3776. Fax: (479) 571-0995. Licensee: Davidson Media Station KREB-FM Licensee LLC. (acq 2-10-2005; $3.9 million. with KCZZ(AM) Mission, KS). Network: ABC. Format: Sp. Target aud: 25-54; general. ◆Peter W. Davidson, pres & engrg mgr; Steve Butler, gen mgr.

Jacksonville

KDJE(FM)— Sept 29, 1969: 100.3 mhz; 82.9 kw. 1,054 ft. TL: N34 47 53 W92 29 33. Stereo. 10800 Colonel Glenn Rd., Little Rock 72204. Phone: (501) 217-5000. Fax: (501) 228-9547. E-mail: q100@q100fm.com. Web Site: www.q100fm.com. Licensee: Clear Channel Broadcasting Licenses Inc. Group owner: Clear Channel Communications Inc. (acq 5-15-96; grpsl). Rep: Clear Channel. Arent, Fox, Kintner, Plotkin & Kahn. Format: Alternative rock. News staff: one; News: 3 hrs wkly. Target aud: 18-49. ◆Don Pollnow, gen mgr; Casey Wagner, gen sls mgr; Jeff Peterson, opns dir & progmg dir.

Jonesboro

***KAOG(FM)**— 1999: 90.5 mhz; 1 kw. 243 ft. TL: N35 53 06 W90 42 38. Box 2440, American Family Radio, Tupelo, MS 38803. Phone: (662) 844-8888. Fax: (662) 842-6791. Web Site: www.afr.net. Licensee: American Family Association. Group owner: American Family Radio Format: Relg. ◆Marvin Sanders, gen mgr; John Riley, progmg dir; Joey Moody, chief of engrg.

***KASU(FM)**— May 17, 1957: 91.9 mhz; 100 kw. 689 ft. TL: N35 53 27 W90 40 26. Stereo. Box 2160, Arkansas State Univ., 104 Cooley, State University 72467. Phone: (870) 972-2200. Phone: (870) 972-3070. Fax: (870) 972-2997. E-mail: kasu@astate.edu. Web Site: www.kasu.org. Licensee: Arkansas State University. Network: PRI, NPR. Format: News, class, jazz. News staff: one; News: 45 hrs wkly. Target aud: General. Spec prog: New age, blues, folk 4 hrs, big band 2 hrs wkly. ◆Robert Franklin, stn mgr; June Taylor, opns mgr; Todd Rutledge, dev dir; Amy Davis, prom mgr; Marty Scarbrough, progmg dir; Greg Chance, news dir; Jimmie Rushing, chief of engrg.

KBTM(AM)—Listing follows KIYS(FM).

KDEZ(FM)— Nov 21, 1986: 100.5 mhz; 38 kw. Ant 558 ft. TL: N35 56 59 W90 39 58. Stereo. 314 Union Ave. 72401. Phone: (870) 933-8800. Fax: (870) 933-0403. E-mail: trey@triplefm.com. Web Site: www.z100rocks.com. Licensee: Saga Communications of Arkansas LLC. Group owner: Saga Communications Inc. (acq 11-8-02; grpsl). Format: Classic rock. News staff: one; News: one hr wkly. Target aud: 18-49. ◆Bill Pressly, pres & stn mgr; Trey Stafford, CEO, CFO, VP & gen mgr; Kevin Neathery, sls dir; Al Simpson, chief of engrg.

KFIN(FM)— Mar 4, 1974: 107.9 mhz; 100 kw. Ant 600 ft. TL: N35 47 56 W90 44 31. Stereo. Box 1737 72403-1737. Secondary address: 407 W. Parker Rd. 72404. Phone: (870) 932-8000. Fax: (870) 932-3814. Web Site: www.kfin.com. Licensee: Capstar TX L.P. Group owner: Clear Channel Communications Inc. (acq 1-18-01; grpsl). Fisher, Wayland, Cooper, Leader & Zaragoza. Format: Country. News staff: one; News: 9 hrs wkly. Target aud: 25-54; broad demographics. Spec prog: Farm 13 hrs wkly. ◆Larry James, gen mgr.

KIYS(FM)— 1947: 101.9 mhz; 100 kw. 1,059 ft. TL: N35 57 14 W90 41 41. Stereo. Box 1737 72403-1737. Secondary address: 407 W.

Parker Rd 72404. Phone: (870) 935-5598. Fax: (870) 932-3814. Web Site: www.1019kiysfm.com. Licensee: Capstar TX L.P. Group owner: Clear Channel Communications Inc. (acq 1-18-01; grpsl). Fisher, Wayland, Cooper, Leader & Zaragoza. Format: CHR. Target aud: 18-49; middle to upper middle income. ◆Larry James, CEO & gen mgr; Katy Wiliamson, VP & sls dir; Duce Foreman, mktg dir & prom dir; Kevin Box, progmg dir; Troy Owens, engrg VP & chief of engrg.

KBTM(AM)—Co-owned with KIYS(FM). Mar 15, 1930: 1230 khz; 1 kw-U. TL: N35 50 27 W90 39 44. Box 1737, 405 W. Parker Rd. 72403. Phone: (501) 932-8400. Format: News/talk. News staff: 2; News: 14 hrs wkly. Target aud: 45 plus; upscale adults. ◆Kevin Box, stn mgr & prom mgr.

KJBX(FM)—(Trumann). February 1991: 106.7 mhz; 6 kw. 328 ft. TL: N35 44 51 W90 37 49. Stereo. 314 Union Ave. 72401. Phone: (870) 933-8800. Fax: (870) 933-0403. E-mail: trey@triplefm.com. Web Site: www.themix1067.com. Licensee: Saga Communications of Arkansas LLC. Group owner: Saga Communications Inc. (acq 11-8-02; grpsl). Format: Adult contemp. News: 2 hrs wkly. Target aud: 25-54; women. ◆Bill Pressly, pres & stn mgr; Trey Stafford, CFO, VP & gen mgr; Kevin Neathery, sls VP & sls dir; Al Simpson, chief of engrg.

KNEA(AM)— Sept 20, 1950: 970 khz; 1 kw-D, 41 w-N. TL: N35 51 17 W90 43 40. Box 1737 72403. Phone: (870) 932-8400. Fax: (870) 932-3814. Licensee: Clear Channel Broadcasting Licenses Inc. Group owner: Clear Channel Communications Inc. (acq 6-13-2002; $2.05 million. with KWHF(FM) Harrisburg). Format: Sports, talk. News staff: 5. Target aud: General. Spec prog: Farm 6 hrs wkly. ◆Larry James, gen mgr; Katie Williamson, sls dir & gen sls mgr.

Lake City

KDXY(FM)—Licensed to Lake City. See Paragould

Lake Village

KUUZ(FM)— July 30, 1977: 95.9 mhz; 20 kw. Ant 302 ft. TL: N33 20 07 W91 07 33. Stereo. Family Worship Center Church Inc., 8919 World Ministry Ave., Baton Rouge, LA 70810. Phone: (225) 768-3688. Web Site: www.jsm.org/html/radio.htm. Licensee: Family Worship Center Church Inc. (group owner; acq 6-12-02; $500,000). Format: Relg. ◆Jimmy Swaggart, pres; John Santiago, gen mgr; David Whitelaw, opns mgr.

KZYQ(FM)— Dec 24, 1995: 103.5 mhz; 25 kw. 328 ft. TL: N33 17 04 W91 13 03. Stereo. Box 5395, Greenville, MS 38704. Secondary address: 1024 Washington, Suite 212, Greenville, MS 38704. Phone: (662) 846-0929. Fax: (662) 843-1410. E-mail: star103@deltaradio.net. Web Site: www.deltaradio.net.Jones Radio Net. Licensee: M.R.S. Ventures Inc. (group owner; acq 11-1-2003; grpsl). Network: Jones Radio Networks. Wood, Maines & Brown. Format: Oldies. Target aud: 25-54; adults. ◆James H. Boggs, VP; Howard Johnson, gen mgr; Cindy Clancy, stn mgr; Wendy Hodges, gen sls mgr & progmg dir; Kirk Harnack, engrg VP.

Lakeview

KKTZ(FM)— May 1, 1999: 93.5 mhz; 25 kw. 328 ft. TL: N36 31 22 W92 40 08. 2352 Hwy. 62 E., Mountain Home 72653. Phone: (870) 492-6022. Fax: (870) 492-2137. E-mail: radio@mountainhome.com. Web Site: ozarksradio.com. Licensee: John M. Dowdy. Format: Adult contemp. ◆Morgan Dowdy, CEO, pres & gen mgr; Stewart Brunner, VP; Roger Lowery, stn mgr; Josh Hall, opns mgr.

Little Rock

KAAY(AM)— Dec 20, 1924: 1090 khz; 50 kw-U, DA-N. TL: N34 46 20 W92 13 30. 700 Wellington Hills Rd. 72211. Phone: (501) 401-0200. Fax: (501) 401-0387. Licensee: Citadel Broadcasting Corp. Group owner: Citadel Broadcasting Corp. (acq 9-30-98; $5 million). Network: USA. Latham & Watkins. Format: Relg, southern gospel. Spec prog: Sp 2 hrs wkly. ◆Jim Beard, gen mgr; Barry McCorkindale, stn mgr & progmg dir; Bill Bromley, gen sls mgr.

***KABF(FM)**— Sept 31, 1984: 88.3 mhz; 91 kw. 777 ft. TL: N34 47 31 W92 28 38. Stereo. 2101 S. Main St. 72206. Phone: (501) 372-6119. Fax: (501) 376-3952. E-mail: kabf@acorn.org. Licensee: Arkansas Broadcasting Foundation. Format: Black, jazz, gospel, diversified. News staff: one; News: 12 hrs wkly. Target aud: General; low-moderate income & politically disenfranchised. Spec prog: Sp 10 hrs, folk 10 hrs, American Indian 3 hrs, bluegrass 6 hrs, Caribbean 4 hrs, talk 10 hrs wkly. ◆John Cain, stn mgr.

KABZ(FM)— 1967: 103.7 mhz; 100 kw. 1,510 ft. TL: N34 47 55 W92 29 58. Stereo. 2400 Cottondale Ln. 72202. Phone: (501) 661-1037. Fax: (501) 664-5871. Web Site: www.1037thebuzz.com. Licensee: Signal Media of Arkansas Inc. (acq 12-20-93; $2 million; 1-10-94). Rep: D & R Radio. Arter & Hadden. Format: Talk. News staff: one; News: 10 hrs wkly. Target aud: 18-49. ◆Philip Jonsson, pres & gen mgr.

KARN(AM)— 1928: 920 khz; 5 kw-U, DA-N. TL: N34 46 20 W92 09 30. 700 Wellington Hills Rd. 72211. Phone: (501) 401-0200. Fax: (501) 401-0387. E-mail: neal.gladner@citcomm.com. Web Site: www.karnnewsradio.com. Licensee: Citadel Broadcasting Co. Group owner: Citadel Broadcasting Corp. (acq 8-27-97; grpsl). Network: CBS. Format: News/talk. News staff: 10; News: 28 hrs wkly. Target aud: 35-64. ◆Jim Beard, gen mgr.

KDIS-FM— Aug 14, 1992: 99.5 mhz; 3 kw. Ant 312 ft. TL: N34 45 58 W92 17 38. (CP: 6 kw). 415 N. McKinley, Suite 610 72205. Phone: (501) 663-3300. Fax: (501) 663-3723. Web Site: www.radiodisney.com. Licensee: Radio Disney Group LLC. Group owner: ABC Inc. (acq 5-30-03; $2.56 million). Format: Children. ◆Lynda Goodbar, gen mgr.

KDJE(AM)—See Jacksonville

KGHT(AM)—(Sheridan). March 1982: 880 khz; 50 kw-D, 220 w-N. TL: N34 41 36 W92 18 21 (D), N34 18 21 W92 23 06 (N). 10000 Warden Rd., North Little Rock 72120. Phone: (501) 985-0880. Fax: (501) 985-0260. Fax: www.safehaven880.com. E-mail: safehavenradio@aol.com. Licensee: Metropolitan Radio Group Inc. (group owner; acq 1-97). Spec prog: Relg 5 hrs, gospel 16 hrs wkly. ◆Jim Schmidt, gen mgr & chief of opns.

KIPR(FM)—See Pine Bluff

KITA(AM)— October 1956: 1440 khz; 5 kw-D, 240 w-N. TL: N34 42 46 W92 16 48. 723 W. Daisy Bates Dr. 72202. Phone: (501) 375-1440. Fax: (501) 244-9842. E-mail: kita1440@earthlink.net. Licensee: Kita Inc. (acq 6-28-84; $675,000; 4-30-84). Edmundson & Edmundson. Format: Gospel. Target aud: 25-54; primarily women. Spec prog: Black 19 hrs wkly. ◆Kaysie Rusk, gen mgr; Tom Rusk, pres & gen sls mgr.

KJBN(AM)— 1946: 1050 khz; 1 kw-D, 19 w-N. TL: N34 45 57 W92 17 39. 1800 Maple St., Suite 300, North Little Rock 72114. Phone: (501) 791-1000. Fax: (501) 791-7121. Licensee: Joshua Ministries and Community Development Corp. (acq 8-26-92; $250,000; 9-21-92). Format: Contemp gospel music, teaching. Target aud: Career-oriented people. Spec prog: News/sports. ◆James Smith, gen mgr & gen sls mgr; Talisa Austin, prom mgr.

KKPT(FM)— Oct 26, 1960: 94.1 mhz; 100 kw. 1,601 ft. TL: N34 47 56 W92 29 41. Stereo. 2400 Cottondale Ln. 72202. Phone: (501) 664-9410. Fax: (501) 664-5871. Web Site: www.kkpt.com. Licensee: Signal Media of Arkansas. (acq 4-30-85; $2.75 million; 3-11-85). Format: Classic rock, Hits of the 60s, 70s, 80s & 90s. News staff: one; News: one hr wkly. Target aud: 25-54; adults. ◆Philip Jonsson, pres; Ron Collar, gen mgr.

***KLRE-FM**— February 1973: 90.5 mhz; 40 kw. 265 ft. TL: N34 40 29 W92 19 04. Stereo. 2801 S. University 72204. Phone: (501) 569-8485. Fax: (501) 569-8488. Web Site: www.klre.org. Licensee: University of Arkansas. (acq 7-95). Network: Network: PRI, NPR. Cohn & Marks. Format: Class. Target aud: 35-54. ◆Ben Fry, gen mgr & stn mgr; Mary Waldo, dev dir.

KMJX(FM)—See Conway

KPZK(AM)— 1929: 1250 khz; 2.5 kw-D, 1.2 kw-N, DA-2. TL: N34 42 05 W92 13 02. 700 Wellington Hills Rd. 72211. Phone: (501) 401-0200. Fax: (501) 401-0366. Licensee: Citadel Broadcasting Co. Group owner: Citadel Broadcasting Corp. (acq 9-19-97; grpsl). Rep: D & R Radio. Format: Gospel. News staff: one. Target aud: 50 plus. ◆Jim Beard, gen mgr.

KSSN(FM)— 1966: 95.7 mhz; 92 kw. 1,663 ft. TL: N34 47 57 W92 29 29. Stereo. 10800 Colonel Glenn Rd. 72204. Phone: (501) 217-5000. Fax: (501) 228-9547. E-mail: kssn@cei.net. Web Site: www.kssn.com. Licensee: Clear Channel Radio Licenses Inc. Clear Channel Communications Inc. (acq 9-12-97; grpsl). Rep: Clear Channel. Format: Contemp country. News staff: one; News: 2 hrs wkly. Target aud: 25-54. ◆Don Pollnow, gen mgr; Chad Heritage, opns dir & progmg dir; Casey Wagner, gen sls mgr.

***KUAR(FM)**— Sept 16, 1986: 89.1 mhz; 100 kw. 882 ft. TL: N34 47 50 W92 29 26. Stereo. 2801 S. University 72204. Phone: (501) 569-8485. Fax: (501) 569-8488. Web Site: www.kuar.org. Licensee: Board of Trustees of the University of Arkansas. Network: Network: NPR, PRI. Cohn & Marks. Format: News/talk, jazz. News staff: one; News: 86 hrs wkly. Target aud: 35-54. Spec prog: Folk 3 hrs wkly. ◆Ben Fry, gen mgr & stn mgr; Mary Waldo, dev dir.

KURB(FM)— July 7, 1972: 98.5 mhz; 99 kw. 1,286 ft. TL: N34 47 56 W92 29 44. Stereo. 700 Wellington Hills Rd. 72211. Phone: (501) 401-0200. Fax: (501) 401-0349. Web Site: www.b98.com. Licensee: Citadel Broadcasting Co. Group owner: Citadel Broadcasting Corp. Format: Hot adult contemp. ◆Jim Beard, gen mgr & gen sls mgr.

Lonoke

KOLL-FM— June 1982: 106.3 mhz; 50 kw. Ant 492 ft. TL: N34 46 30 W91 53 33. 400 Hardin Rd., Suite 150, Little Rock 72211. Phone: (501) 219-1919. Fax: (501) 225-4610. Web Site: www.koll1063.com. Licensee: ABG Arkansas LLC. Group owner: Archway Broadcasting Group (acq 1-22-2003; $8 million. with KHTE-FM England). Format: Oldies. ◆Brad Hutcheson, gen mgr.

Lowell

KMXF(FM)— June 30, 1992: 101.9 mhz; 50 kw. 708 ft. TL: N36 26 28 W93 58 22. Stereo. Box 8190, Fayetteville 72703. Phone: (479) 442-0102. Fax: (479) 587-8255. Web Site: www.hotmix1019.com. Licensee: Capstar TX L.P. Group owner: Clear Channel Communications Inc. (acq 8-30-00; grpsl). Dow, Lohnes & Albertson. Format: CHR. News staff: one; News: one hr wkly. Target aud: 25-44. ◆Tony Beringer, gen mgr.

Magnolia

KVMA(AM)— April 1948: 630 khz; 1 kw-D. TL: N33 17 59 W93 13 57. Box 430 71754. Secondary address: 131 S. Jackson 71753. Phone: (870) 234-5862. Fax: (870) 234-5865. E-mail: kvma@arkansas.net. Licensee: Noalmark Broadcasting Corp. (acq 8-1-2005; $165,000). Network: ABC Daytime Direction. Borsari & Paxson. Format: C&W. Target aud: General. Spec prog: Farm 2 hrs wkly. ◆William C. Nolan Jr., pres; Dan Gregory, VP & opns dir; Ken W. Sibley, gen mgr.

KZHE(FM)—See Stamps

Malvern

KBOK(AM)— August 1951: 1310 khz; 1 kw-D. TL: N34 22 25 W92 49 52. 302 S. Main St. 72104. Phone: (501) 332-6981. Phone: (501) 332-6982. Fax: (501) 332-6984. Web Site: www.hsnp.com. Licensee: Noalmark Broadcasting Corp. (group owner; acq 4-1-03; $62,500). Rep: BRI. Format: News, traditional country. News: 20 hrs wkly. Target aud: General. Spec prog: Talk 6 hrs, gospel 8 hrs wkly. ◆Eddie Tarpey, gen mgr.

KKZR(FM)—(Bryant). April 1989: 93.3 mhz; 5.6 kw. Ant 699 ft. TL: N34 47 31 W92 28 38. Stereo. 400 Hardin Rd., Suite 150, Little Rock 72211. Phone: (501) 219-1919. Fax: (501) 225-4610. Web Site:

Arkansas

www.933therazor.com. Licensee: ABG Arkansas LLC (acq 4-10-03; $3.6 million). Format: Active rock. Target aud: 18-45. ♦ Brad Hutcheson, gen mgr.

KLEZ(FM)— Apr 1, 1991: 101.5 mhz; 6 kw. Ant 322 ft. TL: N34 28 24 W92 55 51. Stereo. 208 Buena Vista Rd., Hot Springs 71913. Phone: (501) 525-4600. Fax: (501) 525-4344. E-mail: pob@klaz.com. Web Site: www.hsnp.com. Licensee: Noalmark Broadcasting Corp. (group owner; (acq 1-21-2003; $437,500). Miller & Miller, P.C. Format: Easy lstng. News: 3 hrs wkly. Target aud: 35-60. ♦ William C. Nolan Jr., pres; Eddie Tarpley, stn mgr.

Mammoth Spring

KALM(AM)—See Thayer, MO

KAMS(FM)— Jan 1, 1956: 95.1 mhz; 100 kw. 650 ft. TL: N36 32 58 W91 33 05. Stereo. Box 193 72554. Secondary address: N. Hwy. 63, Thayer, MO 65791. Phone: (417) 264-7211. Fax: (417) 264-7212. E-mail: kkountry@kkountry.com. Web Site: www.kkountry.com. Licensee: Ozark Radio Network Inc. Network: ABC Daytime Direction. Rep: Keystone (unwired net). Richard Hayes. Format: Classic country. News staff: one; News: 11 hrs wkly. Target aud: General. ♦ Shawn Neathery Marhefka, pres; Robert Eckman, gen mgr & opns VP; Mike Crase, opns mgr.

Marianna

KAKJ(FM)— 1994: 105.3 mhz; 6 kw. Ant 328 ft. TL: N34 47 14 W90 46 03. Stereo. Box 2870, 700 Martin Luther King Dr., Suite 2, West Helena 72390. Phone: (870) 633-9000. Fax: (870) 572-1845. E-mail: force2@sbcglobal.net. Web Site: www.force2radio.com. Licensee: Raymond & L.T. Simes II. Network: ABC. Format: Black, urban contemp. News staff: one. Target aud: All ages. ♦ Raymond Sims, CEO; Raymond Simes, pres, gen mgr & gen sls mgr; L.T. Simes II, VP; Elaine Simes, stn mgr & mktg dir; Larry Evans, opns mgr; Peter Turner, prom dir & progmg dir.

Marion

KXHT(FM)— February 1986: 107.1 mhz; 3 kw. 328 ft. TL: N35 09 23 W90 05 46. (CP: 2.75 kw, ant 479 ft.). 6080 Mt. Mariah Rd. Ext., Memphis, TN 38115. Phone: (901) 375-9324. Fax: (901) 375-9331. E-mail: mail@1071.com. Web Site: www.1701.com. Licensee: Flinn Broadcasting Corp. Format: Rap, hip hop. ♦ Lloyd Hetzer, gen mgr; Duane Hargrove, stn mgr.

Marked Tree

KJBR(FM)— 1993: 93.7 mhz; 3 kw. 288 ft. TL: N35 32 22 W90 26 35. 5700 W. Oaks Blvd., Rocklin, CA 95765. Phone: (916) 251-1600. Fax: (916) 251-1650. Web Site: www.klove.com. Licensee: Educational Media Foundation. Group owner: EMF Broadcasting (acq 11-1-01; $1.3 million. with KJLV(FM) Hoxie). Network: Air 1. Format: Contemp Christian. ♦ Richard Jenkins, pres; Mike Novak, VP; Lloyd Parker, gen mgr.

Marshall

KBCN-FM— Apr 25, 1983: 104.3 mhz; 100 kw. 820 ft. TL: N35 52 17 W92 39 10. (CP: Ant 1,016 ft.). Stereo. 100 Blue Bird St., Harrison 72601. Phone: (870) 743-1157. Fax: (870) 743-1168. E-mail: kbcnradio@hotmail.com. Licensee: Pearson Broadcasting of Marshall Inc. Group owner: Pearson Broadcasting (acq 4-30-93; $450,000; 5-24-93). Format: C&W. ♦ David R. Fransen, gen mgr.

KCGS(AM)— May 24, 1975: 960 khz; 5 kw-D. TL: N35 54 56 W92 38 20. Box 1044 72650. Secondary address: 260 Battle St. 72650. Phone: (870) 448-5567. Fax: (870) 448-5384. E-mail: kcgs@ozarkisp.net. Web Site: www.kcgs.com. Licensee: Southland Broadcasting Corp. (acq 8-20-2003). Network: USA. Format: Christian. News staff: 2; News: 10 hrs wkly. Target aud: General. Spec prog: Bible answers live 7 hrs wkly. ♦ Karl Leukert, gen mgr & opns VP; Ronald Woolsey, pres, dev VP & sls VP.

Marvell

***KVRN(FM)**— 1999: 90.7 mhz; 50 kw. 495 ft. TL: N34 36 29 W90 58 47. Stereo. Box 2292, West Helena 72390. Phone: (870) 572-1234. Fax: (870) 572-5515. Licensee: East Arkansas Educational Foundation. Format: Inspirational christian, CHR. ♦ Patrick Roberson, pres; Patrick Roberson IV, gen mgr; Alan Crisp, opns dir; Patrick Roberson III, opns mgr; Patrick Robertson, pub affrs dir; Jerry Campbell, chief of engrg.

Maumelle

KMSX(FM)— 1971: 94.9 mhz; 96 kw. 1,843 ft. TL: N34 26 31 W92 13 03. Stereo. 10800 Colonel Glenn Rd., Little Rock 72204. Phone: (501) 217-5000. Fax: (501) 228-9547. E-mail: cool95@cei.net. Web Site: www.cool 95.com. Licensee: Clear Channel Broadcasting Licenses Inc. Group owner: Clear Channel Communications Inc. (acq 9-12-97; grpsl). Rep: D & R Radio. Format: Adult contemp. News staff: one; News: 5 hrs wkly. Target aud: 25-54; baby boomers. ♦ Don Pollnow, gen mgr; Jeff Peterson, opns dir; Casey Wagner, gen sls mgr; Sonny Victory, progmg dir.

KWLR(FM)— 1998: 96.9 mhz; 4.6 kw. 377 ft. TL: N34 53 33 W92 24 50. Box 13197 72113. Secondary address: 10301 Maumelle Blvd., North Little Rock 72113. Phone: (501) 812-9700. Fax: (501) 812-9690. E-mail: kwlrword97@aol.com. Web Site: www.kwlr. Licensee: Flinn Broadcasting Corp. Format: Relg. ♦ Jerry White, gen mgr.

Mayflower

KABK-FM—(Augusta). Aug 27, 1979: 97.7 mhz; 28 kw. 649 ft. TL: N35 22 53 W91 31 30. Stereo. Box 262550, Baton Rouge, LA 70826. Phone: (225) 768-7000. E-mail: info@jsh.org. Web Site: www.jsm.org. Licensee: Searcy Broadcasting Inc. (group owner; acq 6-13-01). Format: Christian. Target aud: 25 plus. ♦ Ken Madden, pres & gen mgr.

McGehee

KVSA(AM)— June 29, 1953: 1220 khz; 1 kw-D, 40 w-N. TL: N33 33 39 W91 23 06. Box 110, Hwy. 65 71654. Phone: (870) 222-4200. Phone: (870) 538-5200. Fax: (870) 538-3389. E-mail: kvsa1220@yahoo.com. Licensee: Southeast Arkansas Broadcasters Inc. Rep: Keystone (unwired net). Format: Div. Spec prog: Farm 5 hrs wkly. ♦ Joyce Kinney, pres & gen mgr; Linda Stevens, progmg dir; Norm Mason, chief of engrg.

Melbourne

***KAEN(FM)**—Not on air, target date: unknown: 90.3 mhz; 1 kw. Ant 735 ft. TL: N36 04 42 W92 01 23. 88 Casey Jones Blvd., Jackson, TN 38305. Phone: (901) 664-3882. Licensee: Abundant Life Broadcasting. ♦ Tamara Durham, VP & gen mgr.

Mena

KENA(AM)— July 1950: 1450 khz; 1 kw-U. TL: N34 34 23 W94 14 55. Box 1450 71953. Secondary address: 1600 S. Reine St. 71953. Phone: (479) 394-1450. Licensee: Ouachita Broadcasting Inc. (acq 1-14-99; $750,000. with co-located FM). Format: Gospel. News staff: one; News: 10 hrs wkly. Target aud: 18 plus; industrial & agricultural workers, retirees, tourists & professionals. ♦ Dwight Douglas, gen mgr, stn mgr & mktg dir; Sue Canner, prom dir & mus dir; Matt Stone, news dir.

KENA-FM— 1969: 102.1 mhz; 12.5 kw. Ant 469 ft. TL: N34 32 42 W94 18 21. Network: ABC. Format: Country. News staff: one; News: 6 hrs wkly. ♦ Dwight Douglas, stn mgr, opns mgr & progmg mgr.

KQOR(FM)— 2001: 105.3 mhz; 8.1 kw. 564 ft. TL: N34 36 31 W94 14 19. Box 1450 71953. Phone: (479) 394-1450. Licensee: Ouachita Broadcasting Inc. (acq 3-8-99). Network: ABC Music Radio. Format: Oldies. ♦ Dwight Douglas, gen mgr & opns mgr.

KTTG(FM)— December 1994: 96.3 mhz; 100 kw. 1,314 ft. TL: N34 36 40 W94 16 20. Stereo. 2937 Hwy. 71 N. 71953. Phone: (479) 394-6198. Fax: (479) 784-7290. Licensee: Pearson Broadcasting of Mena Inc. Group owner: Pearson Broadcasting (acq 1995; $175,000). Rep: ABC Radio Sales. Format: ESPN sports/talk. News staff: one. Target aud: 18-49. ♦ Max Pearson, CEO & chmn; Bruce Hale, CFO; Tommy Craft, gen mgr; Jason Wade, progmg dir.

Monticello

KGPQ(FM)— May 1, 1997: 99.9 mhz; 25 kw. 328 ft. TL: N33 43 25 W91 48 28. 279 Midway Rt. 71657. Phone: (870) 367-8525. Fax: (870) 367-9564. E-mail: crn@ccc-cable.net. Licensee: Community Radio Network Inc. (acq 6-5-97). Format: CHR. ♦ P. Q. Gardner, gen mgr.

KHBM(AM)— April 1955: 1430 khz; 1 kw-D, 30 w-N. TL: N33 36 18 W91 47 14. 279 Midway Rt. 71657. Phone: (870) 367-6854. Fax: (870) 367-9564. E-mail: crn@ccc-cable.net. Licensee: Community Radio Network Inc. (group owner; acq 5-19-99; grpsl). Network: ABC Daytime Direction. Format: Music of Your Life. News staff: one; News: 10 hrs wkly. Target aud: General. ♦ P.Q. Gardner, pres & gen mgr.

KHBM-FM— Sept 1, 1967: 93.7 mhz; 6 kw. 341 ft. TL: N33 36 18 W91 47 14. (CP: 93.7 mhz, 25 kw). Stereo. 279 Midway Rt. 71655. Phone: (870) 367-6854. Fax: (870) 367-9564. E-mail: crn@ccc-cable.net. Licensee: Community Radio Network Inc. Network: ABC Daytime Direction. Format: Classic Hits. News staff: one; News: 8 hrs wkly. ♦ P. Q. Gardner, gen mgr.

KXSA-FM—See Dermott

Morrilton

KVOM(AM)— Dec 25, 1952: 800 khz; 250 w-D, 42 w-N. TL: N35 09 32 W92 46 13. Box 541, 1835 Hwy. 113 W. 72110. Phone: (501) 354-2484. Fax: (501) 354-5629. E-mail: kvom@kvom.com. Web Site: www.kvom.com. Licensee: MMA License LLC. Group owner: MAX Media L.L.C. (acq 4-21-03; grpsl). Network: AP Radio. Rep: Christal. Format: News/talk, sports. News staff: news progmg 70 hrs wkly News: 2;. Target aud: General. ♦ Rich Moellers, gen mgr.

KVOM-FM— 1981: 101.7 mhz; 6 kw. 226 ft. TL: N35 09 32 W92 46 13. Stereo. Web Site: www.kvom.com. Rep: Christal. Format: Country. News staff: news progmg 5 hrs wkly News: 2;. Target aud: General.

Mountain Home

***KCMH(FM)**— June 28, 1988: 91.5 mhz; 26 kw. Ant 472 ft. TL: N36 16 17 W92 25 20. Stereo. 126 S. Church St. 72653. Phone: (870) 425-2525. Fax: (870) 424-2626. E-mail: lorra@kcmhradio.com. Web Site: www.kcmhradio.com. Licensee: Christian Broadcasting Group of Mountain Home Inc. Network: Network: Moody, USA. Format: Educ, relg. News: 9 hrs wkly. Target aud: General. ♦ Carl Albright, pres; Lorra Queen, stn mgr & progmg dir; Michael Coolidge, VP & opns VP.

KOMT(FM)— Oct 25, 1985: 107.5 mhz; 100 kw. Ant 1,017 ft. TL: N36 29 13 W92 29 39. 2352 Hwy. 62 E. 72653. Phone: (870) 492-6022. Fax: (870) 492-2137. E-mail: radio@mountainhome.com. Web Site: www.ozarksradio.com. Licensee: MAC Partners. Network: ABC. Format: Big band, adult pop standard. Target aud: 25-54; females. ♦ Morgan Dowdy, CEO & pres; Stewart Brunner, VP & gen mgr; Roger Lowery, stn mgr & news dir; Josh Hall, opns mgr.

KPFM(FM)— June 6, 1984: 105.5 mhz; 33 kw. 590 ft. TL: N36 20 55 W92 24 01. Stereo. 2352 Hwy. 62 E. 72653. Phone: (870) 492-6022. Fax: (870) 492-2137. E-mail: radio@mountainhome.com. Web Site: ozarksradio.com. Licensee: Mountain Home Radio Station Inc. Network: ABC. Format: Country. News staff: one; News: 15 hrs wkly. Target aud: 24-64; females with families. ♦ Morgan Dowdy, CEO; Stewart Brunner, VP, VP & gen mgr; Roger Lowery, stn mgr; Josh Hall, opns mgr.

KTLO(AM)— May 30, 1953: 1240 khz; 1 kw-U. TL: N36 20 43 W92 23 40. Box 2010 72654. Secondary address: 620 Hwy 5 N. 72654. Phone: (870) 425-3101. Fax: (870) 424-4314. Web Site: www.ktlo.com. Licensee: KTLO L.L.C. (group owner; (acq 5-1-91). Network: ABC Information & Entertainment. Format: Country. News staff: 3; News: 11 hrs wkly. Target aud: 18-55; general. ♦ Bob Knight, gen mgr.

KTLO-FM— Jan 11, 1971: 97.9 mhz; 30 kw. Ant 636 ft. TL: N36 20 55 W92 23 59. Stereo. Network: ABC Information & Entertainment. Format: Easy lstng, MOR. Target aud: 40 plus.

Mountain Pine

KLXQ(FM)— 1996: 101.9 mhz; 6 kw. 328 ft. Stereo. 125 Corporate Terr., Hot Springs 71913. Phone: (501) 525-9700. Fax: (501) 525-9739. Web Site: www.klxq.net. Licensee: US Stations LLC. Group owner: Powell Broadcasting (acq 2-1-2005; grpsl). Format: Classic rock. ♦ Gary Terrell, gen mgr.

Stations in the U.S. — Arkansas

Developers & Brokers of Radio Properties
contact American Media Services at our suite:
Philadelphia Marriott Downtown
215-625-2900
843-972-2200
americanmediaservices.com
Charleston, SC
Dallas, TX · Chicago, Il · Austin, TX
American Media Services, LLC

Mountain View

KWOZ(FM)— Dec 1, 1981: 103.3 mhz; 100 kw. 987 ft. TL: N35 47 06 W91 57 44. Stereo. 920 Harrison St., Batesville 72503. Phone: (870) 793-4196. Fax: (870) 793-5222. E-mail: arkansas103@hotmail.com. Web Site: www.arkansas103.com. Licensee: WRD Entertainment Inc. (group owner). Network: ABC. Letcher, Heald, & Hildreth, P.L.C. Format: C&W. News staff: 2; News: 3 hrs wkly. Target aud: 18-54. ♦ Don Johnson, gen mgr & stn mgr; Matt Johnson, sls dir.

Murfreesboro

KMTB(FM)— May 18, 1983: 99.5 mhz; 20.5 kw. 358 ft. TL: N34 05 44 W93 41 31. Stereo. 1513 S. 4th, Nashville 71852. Phone: (870) 845-3601. Fax: (870) 845-3680. Licensee: ARKLATEX Radio Inc. (group owner; acq 8-28-2001; grpsl). Format: Country. ♦ Brent Pinkerton, gen mgr; Scott Dunson, opns dir.

Nashville

KBHC(AM)— May 1959: 1260 khz; 500 w-D. TL: N33 55 45 W93 51 01. 1513 S. 4th St. 71852. Phone: (870) 845-3601. Fax: (870) 845-3680. Licensee: ARKLATEX Radio Inc. (group owner; (acq 8-23-2001; grpsl). Rep: Keystone (unwired net). Format: MOR. ♦ Brent Pickerton, gen mgr; Kendra Harper, mus dir; Mandy McLaughlin, news dir.

KNAS(FM)—Co-owned with KBHC(AM). Feb 14, 1977: 105.5 mhz; 3 kw. 85 ft. TL: N33 55 45 W93 51 01. Stereo. Format: Oldies.

KSSW(FM)— 2003: 96.9 mhz; 6 kw. Ant 328 ft. TL: N34 00 41 W93 52 03. 1513 S. 4th St. 71852. Phone: (870) 845-3601. Fax: (870) 845-3680. Licensee: Don Campbell Group owner: Sudbury Services Inc. (acq 10-18-2002). Format: Adult contemp. ♦ Brent Pinkerton, gen mgr.

Newark

***KLLN(FM)**— Jan 1, 1985: 90.9 mhz; 4 kw. 456 ft. TL: N35 43 25 W91 26 40. 1502 N. Hill St. 72562. Phone: (870) 799-8969. Phone: (870) 799-8691. Fax: (870) 799-8647. E-mail: kllnfm@yahoo.com. Web Site: www.klln.fm. Licensee: Newark Public School. Format: Southern gospel. ♦ Fred Ahlborn, gen mgr.

Newport

KNBY(AM)— Oct 12, 1949: 1280 khz; 1 kw-D, 87 w-N. TL: N35 36 38 W91 15 02. Box 768 72112. Secondary address: 2025 McCarty Dr. 72112. Phone: (870) 523-5891. Fax: (870) 523-2967. E-mail: legends@rivercountry967.com. Licensee: Newport Broadcasting Co. Group owner: Sudbury Svcs. Inc. & Newport Broadcasting Co. Format: News/talk info. ♦ Harold Sudbury, pres; Dale Turner, gen mgr & news dir; Doug Holt, progmg dir & progmg mgr.

KOKR(FM)—Co-owned with KNBY(AM). Sept 1, 1966: 96.7 mhz; 35 kw. 548 ft. TL: N35 29 16 W91 26 13. Stereo. Format: Country.

North Crossett

KWLT(FM)— May 1, 1995: 102.7 mhz; 25 kw. Ant 328 ft. TL: N33 12 58 W91 55 42. Stereo. Box 697, 117 E. Wellfield Rd., Crosset 71635. Phone: (870) 364-2181. Phone: (870) 364-2182. Fax: (870) 364-2183. E-mail: kagh@alltel.net. Web Site: www.crossettradio.com. Licensee: South Ark Broadcasting Inc. Network: ABC. Format: Oldies. News: 2 hrs wkly. Target aud: General. ♦ Kevin Medlin, pres & gen mgr; Barry Medlin, gen sls mgr; Russell Miller, progmg dir.

North Little Rock

KDXE(AM)— May 9, 1957: 1380 khz; 5 kw-D, 2.5 kw-N, DA-2. TL: N34 52 49 W92 14 01. 2902 E. Kiehl Ave., Suite 1D, Sherwood 72120. Phone: (501) 221-1380. Fax: (501) 217-0016. E-mail: horn@totalsports1380.com. Web Site: www.totalsports1380.com. Licensee: AM1380 LLC (acq 6-1-99; $500,000). Network: Network: Sporting News Radio Network, ESPN Radio. Cohn & Marks. Format: Sports. Target aud: 25-54; men. ♦ Albert Phipps, pres; Arlen Horn, VP & gen mgr; Lee Malcolm, opns VP; Mark Hill, engrg VP.

KWBF-FM— 1995: 101.1 mhz; 6 kw. Ant 328 ft. TL: N34 49 52 W92 19 18. Stereo. 1 Shackleford Dr., Suite 400, Little Rock 72211. Phone: (501) 219-2400. Fax: (501) 604-8004. Licensee: Flinn Broadcasting Corp. Format: AOR. News staff: one; News: 15 hrs wkly. Target aud: 35-54. Spec prog: News 15 hrs wkly.

Ola

KARV-FM— Jan 1, 1998: 101.3 mhz; 850 w. 856 ft. TL: N34 59 46 W93 13 22. 201 W. 2nd, Russellville 72801. Phone: (479) 968-1184. Fax: (479) 967-5278. Licensee: KERM Inc. (group owner) Format: Country. News staff: 2; News: 20 hrs wkly. ♦ Kermit Womack, pres; Chris Womack, gen mgr.

Osceola

KOSE(AM)—(Wilson). Oct 11, 1949: 860 khz; 1 kw-D, 21 w-N. TL: N35 41 03 W89 58 57. Box 989, Blytheville 72316. Phone: (870) 762-2093. Fax: (870) 763-8459. Licensee: Newport Broadcasting Co. (acq 1996). Network: ABC Daytime Direction. Rep: Roslin. Format: Southern gospel. Target aud: 24-55; middle-class, blue/white collar workers. Spec prog: Black 6 hrs wkly, farm 5 hrs wkly. ♦ Ed White, gen mgr & opns mgr; Fred Chambers, gen sls mgr; Keith Cole, progmg dir; Tom Hill, chief of engrg.

KQDD(FM)—Co-owned with KOSE(AM). Sept 1, 1996: 107.3 mhz; 3 kw. 223 ft. Format: Classic hits.

Ozark

KDYN(AM)— Feb 5, 1969: 1540 khz; 500 w-D. TL: N35 29 16 W93 48 43. Box 1086, Puddin Ridge Rd. 72949. Phone: (479) 667-4567. Fax: (479) 667-5214. E-mail: kdyn@ozip.net. Web Site: www.realcountryonline.com. Licensee: Ozark Communications Inc. (acq 9-15-85). Network: ABC Information & Entertainment. Format: Country. News staff: one; News: 20 hrs wkly. Target aud: General. ♦ Marc Dietz, pres, gen mgr, sls dir, mktg mgr & progmg dir.

KDYN-FM— Oct 2, 1980: 96.7 mhz; 1.6 kw. 400 ft. TL: N35 29 10 W93 53 29. Stereo.

Pangburn

KSMD(FM)— Nov 2, 2003: 99.1 mhz; 25 kw. Ant 328 ft. TL: N35 23 43 W91 44 17. 111 N. Spring St., Searcy 72143. Phone: (501) 268-7123. Fax: (501) 279-2900. E-mail: production@heartarkansas.com. Licensee: Crain Media Group LLC (group owner; acq 10-15-02; $180,000. for CP). Format: News/talk. ♦ Phil Weaver, gen mgr; J.R. Runyon, opns dir & progmg dir; Dave Clark, chief of engrg.

Paragould

KDRS(AM)— Jan 1, 1947: 1490 khz; 1 kw-U. TL: N36 02 56 W90 27 44. 400 Tower Dr. 72450. Phone: (870) 236-7627. Fax: (870) 239-4583. E-mail: dina@kdrs.com. Web Site: www.kdrs.com. Licensee: MOR Media Inc. (acq 7-2-2002; $500,000. with co-located FM). Fletcher, Heald & Hildreth. Format: Southern gospel. News: 7 hrs wkly. ♦ Dina Mason, pres & gen mgr; Brian Osborn, opns mgr.

KDRS-FM— Mar 5, 1983: 107.1 mhz; 1.9 kw. 410 ft. TL: N36 01 48 W90 35 49. Stereo. Web Site: www.kdrs.com. Fletcher, Heald & Hildreth. Format: Adult contemp. Target aud: 18-44.

KDXY(FM)—(Lake City). Oct 4, 1971: 104.9 mhz; 25 kw. 480 ft. TL: N35 49 29 W90 33 54. Stereo. 314 Union Ave., Jonesboro 72401. Phone: (870) 933-8800. Fax: (870) 933-0403. E-mail: trey@triplefm.com. Web Site: www.thefox1049.com. Licensee: Saga Communications of Arkansas LLC. Group owner: Saga Communications Inc. (acq 11-8-02; grpsl). Format: Country. News staff: one; News: 6 hrs wkly. Target aud: 25-49. ♦ Bill Pressly, pres & stn mgr; Trey Stafford, CEO, CFO, VP & gen mgr; Kevin Neathery, sls VP & sls dir; Al Simpson, chief of engrg.

Paris

KERX(FM)— May 1981: 95.3 mhz; 50 kw. Ant 459 ft. TL: N35 17 13 W94 02 51. 1912 Church St., Fort Smith 72923-2305. Phone: (479) 484-7285. Fax: (479) 784-7390. E-mail: kconroy@x953rocks.com. Web Site: www.x953rocks.com. Licensee: Pearson Broadcasting of Paris Inc. Group owner: Pearson Broadcasting (acq 10-18-93; $42,000;. FTR: 11-8-93). Format: AOR. Target aud: 18-44; men & women. Spec prog: Blues 3 hrs wkly. ♦ Bruce Hale, CFO; Tommy Craft, gen mgr; Jason Wade, opns dir & progmg dir.

Piggott

KBOA-FM— Oct 15, 1983: 105.5 mhz; 6 kw. Ant 298 ft. TL: N36 19 50 W90 07 24. Stereo. Box 509, 1303 Southwest Dr., Kennett, MO 63857. Phone: (573) 888-4616. Fax: (573) 888-4890. E-mail: ktmo@i1.net. Licensee: Pollack Broadcasting Co. (group owner; acq 9-25-98; $450,000 with KBOA(AM) Kennett, MO). Format: Adult standards. News staff: one; News: 5 hrs wkly. Target aud: 18-55; young adults, young professionals, farmers. Spec prog: Farm 5 hrs wkly. ♦ William H. Pollack, pres; Perry Jones, gen mgr.

Pine Bluff

***KCAT(AM)**— April 1963: 1340 khz; 1 kw-U. TL: N34 12 47 W92 01 53. 1207 W. 6th 71601-3993. Phone: (870) 534-5001. Licensee: Mondy Burke Smith Broadcasting Network (acq 7-15-2004; $150,000). Format: Gospel. Target aud: 18-55. ♦ Elijah Mondy, gen mgr & progmg dir; Darren Smith, gen sls mgr; Belinda Mondy, mktg dir & chief of engrg; Kirkland Burke, mktg dir; Robert Holmes, mus dir.

KCLA(AM)— Jan 16, 1947: 1400 khz; 1 kw-U. TL: N34 11 33 W92 02 42. 920 Commerce Rd. 71601-7605. Phone: (870) 534-8978. Fax: (870) 534-8984. Licensee: M.R.S. Ventures Inc. (group owner; acq 4-29-2003; grpsl). Format: News/talk. News staff: 2. Target aud: 35 plus; lower to middle income. ♦ J. Don Russell, pres; Dawn Deane, gen mgr; Craig Eastham, sls VP & news dir; Floyd Donald, mus dir.

KZYP(FM)—Co-owned with KCLA(AM). Nov 1, 1984: 99.3 mhz; 3 kw. 200 ft. TL: N34 11 33 W92 02 42. Stereo. Format: Urban contemp. Target aud: 25-45; middle to upper income.

KIPR(FM)— 1963: 92.3 mhz; 100 kw. 938 ft. TL: N34 22 12 W92 10 07. Stereo. 700 Wellington Hills Rd., Little Rock 72211. Phone: (501) 401-0200. Fax: (501) 401-0366. Web Site: www.power923.com. Licensee: Citadel Broadcasting Co. Group owner: Citadel Broadcasting Corp. (acq 7-29-97; grpsl). Format: Urban contemp. Target aud: 18-44. ♦ Jim Beard, gen mgr.

KOTN(AM)— Mar 12, 1934: 1490 khz; 1 kw-U. TL: N34 13 15 W91 58 20. 920 Commerce Rd. 71601. Phone: (870) 534-8911. Fax: (870) 534-8984. Licensee: M.R.S. Ventures Inc. (group owner; acq 4-29-2003; $350,000). Network: Westwood One. Format: Adult contemp, news/talk, sports. News staff: one; News: 7 hrs wkly. Target aud: 25-54. ♦ Andy Hodges, gen mgr & mktg VP.

KPBQ-FM— Dec 23, 1991: 101.3 mhz; 25 kw. Ant 328 ft. TL: N34 15 13 W92 03 58. Stereo. 920 Commerce Rd. 71601. Phone: (870) 534-8911. Fax: (870) 534-8984. E-mail: delta4radio@netscape.net. Licensee: M.R.S. Ventures Inc. (group owner; acq 4-29-2003; grpsl). Network: ABC. Format: Country. Target aud: 12-60. Spec prog: Farm 2 hrs wkly. ♦ Andy Hodges, gen mgr.

***KUAP(FM)**— 1995: 89.7 mhz; 6 kw. 285 ft. TL: N34 14 33 W92 01 02. Theatre Masscom, 1200 N. University Dr., Suite 4964 71601. Phone: (870) 575-8951. Phone: (870) 543-8949. Fax: (870) 543-8968. Web Site: www.uapb.edu. Licensee: Board of Trustees of Univ. of Arkansas. Format: Urban contemp. ♦ Bionne Hill, stn mgr & mus dir; Sid Weatherford, chief of engrg.

Arkansas

Pocahontas

KPOC(AM)— Nov 15, 1950: 1420 khz; 1 kw-D. TL: N36 16 36 W90 57 18. Box 508 72455. Secondary address: One Radio Dr. 72455. Phone: (870) 892-5234. Fax: (870) 892-5235. Licensee: Combined Media Group Inc. (group owner; (acq 12-20-2001; $410,000. with co-located FM). Network: ABC Daytime Direction. Format: Light adult contemp. News staff: one. Target aud: 25-54; general. Spec prog: Farm 10 hrs wkly. ◆ Jamie Ward, gen sls mgr; Timothy Scott, pres, gen mgr & progmg dir; Larry Caldwell, chief of engrg.

KPOC-FM— Apr 25, 1969: 104.1 mhz; 6 kw. Ant 144 ft. TL: N36 16 38 W90 57 16. One Radio Dr. 72455.

Prairie Grove

KYNF(FM)— November 1999: 94.9 mhz; 21 kw. 761 ft. TL: N35 51 00 W94 23 00. Stereo. 24 E. Meadow, Suite 1, Fayetteville 72701. Phone: (479) 521-5566. Fax: (479) 521-0751. Web Site: www.y949.com. Licensee: Cumulus Licensing Corp. Group owner: Cumulus Media Inc. (acq 3-12-01; $2 million). Network: USA. Format: Adult contemp. News: 2 hrs wkly. Target aud: 30 plus; listeners who like positive, inspirational progmg. ◆ Joe Conway, gen mgr.

Prescott

KHPA(FM)—See Hope

KTPA(AM)— Dec 1, 1959: 1370 khz; 1 kw-D, 49 w-N. TL: N36 20 04 W94 10 41. Box 424, Hope 71802. Phone: (870) 777-8868. Phone: (870) 777-8869. Fax: (870) 777-8888. Licensee: Newport Broadcasting Co. Group owner: Sudbury Services Inc. & Newport Broadcasting Co. (acq 5-14-66). Network: UPI. Format: Gospel. ◆ Robert Hill, gen mgr; Sonya Odom, stn mgr & sls dir; John McCoy, progmg dir.

Rogers

KAMO-FM— 1971: 94.3 mhz; 5.2 kw. 709 ft. TL: N36 26 30 W93 58 26. Stereo. 24 E. Meadow St., Suite 1, Fayetteville 72701. Phone: (479) 521-5566. Fax: (479) 521 4968. Web Site: www.us94.com. Licensee: Cumulus Licensing Corp. Group owner: Cumulus Media Inc. (acq 12-10-98; grpsl). Format: Oldies. ◆ Joe Conway, gen mgr.

KFFK(AM)— Sept 16, 1954: 1390 khz; 1 kw-D. TL: N36 20 04 W94 10 41. Butler Broadcasting LLC, 1780 Holly St., Fayetteville 72701. Phone: (479) 582-3776. Fax: (479) 571-0995. Licensee: Butler Broadcasting Co. LLC (acq 10-13-99; grpsl). Network: ABC. Format: Sp. Target aud: 25-54. ◆ Steve Butler, pres; Steve Bulter, gen mgr; Katrice Summerland, gen sls mgr; Dave Jackson, progmg dir.

KURM(AM)— Nov 9, 1979: 790 khz; 5 kw-D, 500 w-N, DA-N. TL: N36 18 10 W94 06 47. 113 E. New Hope Rd. 72758. Phone: (479) 633-0790. Fax: (479) 631-9711. Licensee: KERM Inc. (group owner) Network: CBS. Format: Var/div. Spec prog: Farm 10 hrs wkly. ◆ Kermit Womack, pres & gen mgr; Diane Womack, sls VP & chief of engrg.

Russellville

KARV(AM)— Feb 25, 1947: 610 khz; 1 kw-D, 500 w-N, DA-2. TL: N35 17 56 W93 09 09. 201 W. 2nd 72801. Phone: (479) 968-6100. Fax: (479) 967-5278. Licensee: KERM Inc. (group owner; acq 10-22-92; $250,000;. FTR: 11-23-92). Network: CBS. Format: New/talk, sports. News staff: 4; News: 38 hrs wkly. Target aud: 35 plus; affluent adults. Spec prog: Farm 5 hrs wkly. ◆ Chris Womack, gen mgr.

***KMTC(FM)—** June 1987: 91.1 mhz; 360 w. 62 ft. TL: N35 18 11 W93 08 42. Box 570 72811-0570. Secondary address: 305 Lake Front Dr. 72802. Phone: (479) 967-7400. Fax: (479) 967-7894. Licensee: Russellville Educational Broadcasting Foundation. Network: USA. Format: Christian contemp. News: one hr wkly. Target aud: 18-55; Christian. ◆ Tom Underhill, CEO; Debbie Bewley, gen mgr; Melissa Krueger, stn mgr & progmg dir.

KWKK(FM)— Sept 29, 1985: 100.9 mhz; 6 kw. 295 ft. TL: N35 17 37 W93 10 39. Stereo. Box 10310 72812. Phone: (479) 968-6816. Fax: (479) 968-2946. Web Site: www.rivervalleyradio.com. Licensee: MMA License LLC. Group owner: MAX Media L.L.C. (acq 4-21-03; grpsl). Format: Adult contemp. News staff: one; News: 10 hrs wkly. Target aud: 18-49; young adults. ◆ Fran Harp, pres.

***KXRJ(FM)—** Apr 3, 1989: 91.9 mhz; 100 w. -92 ft. TL: N35 17 47 W93 08 18. Arkansas Tech Univ., Hwy. 7 N. 72801. Phone: (479) 964-0806. Phone: (479) 964-3282. Fax: (479) 498-6024. Web Site: www.broadcast.atu.edu. Licensee: Arkansas Tech University. Format: Div, class, progsv. News: 10 hrs wkly. Target aud: General. Spec prog: Educ, jazz 15 hrs wkly.

Salem

KCAB(AM)—See Dardanelle

KHOM(FM)— September 1977: 100.9 mhz; 50 kw. Ant 492 ft. TL: N36 35 38 W91 40 03. Stereo. Box 107, West Plains, MO 65775. Phone: (417) 255-0427. Fax: (417) 255-2907. E-mail: khom@khom.net. Web Site: www.khom.net. Licensee: Mountain Lakes Broadcasting Corp. (acq 12-14-99). Network: ABC. Format: Traditional country. News staff: one. Target aud: 35-54; adults. ◆ Bob Knight, gen mgr; John Thomason, gen mgr & stn mgr.

KSAR(FM)—See Thayer, MO

Searcy

KAPZ(AM)—See Bald Knob

KCNY(FM)—See Bald Knob

KWCK(AM)— Aug 25, 1951: 1300 khz; 5 kw-D, 30 w-N. TL: N35 15 27 W91 43 49. Box 1300 72145. Secondary address: 111 N. Spring St. 72143. Phone: (501) 268-7123. Fax: (501) 279-2900. Licensee: Crain Media Group LLC. (group owner; (acq 10-21-2002; grpsl). Format: Talk. Target aud: 25-64. Spec prog: Farm 10 hrs wkly. ◆ Bill Weaver, gen mgr.

KWCK-FM— October 1973: 99.9 mhz; 50 kw. 492 ft. TL: N35 26 50 W91 56 52. Stereo. Rep: BRI. Format: Country. News staff: one; News: 3 hrs wkly. Target aud: 18-49.

Sheridan

***KANX(FM)—** 1999: 91.1 mhz; 16.5 kw. 522 ft. TL: N34 17 26 W92 29 36. (CP: 40 kw). Box 2440, American Family Radio, Tupelo, MS 38803. Phone: (662) 844-8888. Fax: (662) 842-6791. Web Site: www.afr.net. Licensee: American Family Association. Group owner: American Family Radio Format: Relg. ◆ Marvin Sanders, gen mgr; John Riley, progmg dir.

KARN-FM— Nov 1, 1984: 102.9 mhz; 50 kw. 488 ft. TL: N34 25 08 W92 22 17. Stereo. 700 Wellington Hills Rd., Little Rock 72211. Phone: (501) 401-0200. Fax: (501) 401-0349. Web Site: www.karnnewsradio.com. Licensee: Citadel Broadcasting Co. Group owner: Citadel Broadcasting Corp. (acq 9-19-97; grpsl). Format: News, talk. News staff: one; News: 2 hrs wkly. Target aud: 35-64. ◆ Jim Beard, gen mgr; Bill Bromley, gen sls mgr; Bud Ford, progmg dir; Brian Butler, engrg mgr; Dan Case, chief of engrg.

KGHT(AM)—Licensed to Sheridan. See Little Rock

Sherwood

KMTL(AM)— Oct 31, 1983: 760 khz; 10 kw-D. TL: N34 49 34 W92 12 19. 2902 E. Kiehl Ave., Suite 3 72120. Secondary address: Box 6460, No. Little Rock 72124. Phone: (501) 835-1554. Licensee: George V. Domerese. Format: Relg. ◆ Tim Domerese, gen mgr & progmg dir; Tom Rusk, chief of engrg.

KOKY(FM)— 1994: 102.1 mhz; 4.1 kw. 387 ft. TL: N34 44 38 W92 16 32. 700 Wellington Hills Rd., Little Rock 72211. Phone: (501) 401-0200. Fax: (501) 401-0367. Web Site: www.koky.com. Licensee: Citadel Broadcasting Co. Group owner: Citadel Broadcasting Corp. (acq 10-23-97; grpsl). Cohn & Marks. Format: Adult contemp. ◆ Jim Beard, gen mgr.

Siloam Springs

***KLRC(FM)—** Oct 1, 1981: 101.1 mhz; 3.1 kw. 459 ft. TL: N36 11 25 W94 33 55. Stereo. John Brown Univ., 2000 W. University 72761. Phone: (479) 524-7101. Phone: (877) KLRC-101. Fax: (479) 524-7451. E-mail: klrc@klrc.edu. Web Site: www.klrc.com.klrc.com. Licensee: John Brown University. Network: USA. Format: Christian, relg. News: 2 hrs wkly. Target aud: 25-49. ◆ Charles W. Pollard, pres & chief of engrg; Sean Sawatzky, gen mgr.

KMCK(FM)— 1947: 105.7 mhz; 100 kw. 476 ft. TL: N36 11 07 W94 17 49. Stereo. 24 E. Meadow St., Suite 1, Fayetteville 72701. Phone: (479) 521-5566. Fax: (479) 521-0751. Web Site: www.power1057.com. Licensee: Cumulus Licensing Corp. Group owner: Cumulus Media Inc. (acq 12-10-98; grpsl). Rep: Christal. Richard Hayes. Format: CHR. Target aud: 18-49; contemp adults. ◆ Joe Conway, gen mgr.

KUOA(AM)— Apr 12, 1923: 1290 khz; 5 kw-D. TL: N36 11 25 W94 33 55. Box 870 72761. Secondary address: 206 N. Anderson Ave. 72761. Phone: (479) 524-7360. Fax: (479) 524-7451. Web Site: www.kuoa.com. Licensee: Cherokee Broadcasting Co. (acq 2-2-2005; $150,000). Network: Network: CBS Radio, AP Radio. Fletcher, Heald & Hildreth. Format: Var. News: 12 hrs wkly. Target aud: 25-60. ◆ Mitchell Johnson, pres, gen mgr & gen sls mgr; Dewey Johnson, VP & gen mgr; Pete Fretwell, news dir.

Springdale

KXNA(FM)— Sept 19, 1968: 104.9 mhz; 1 kw. 479 ft. TL: N36 10 48 W94 05 07. (CP: 2.75 kw). Stereo. Bulter Broadcasting LLC, 1780 Holly St., Fayetteville 72703. Phone: (479) 582-3776. Fax: (479) 571-0995. Licensee: Bulter Broadcasting LLC. (acq 10-13-99; grpsl). Rep: Christal. Format: Alternative. ◆ Steve Butler, gen mgr & mus dir.

KZRA(AM)— July 15, 1966: 1590 khz; 2.5 kw-D, 58 w-N. TL: N36 12 21 W94 07 11. 24 E. Meadow St., Suite 1, Fayetteville 72701. Phone: (479) 521-5566. Fax: (479) 521-0751. Licensee: Cumulus Licensing Corp. Group owner: Cumulus Media Inc. (acq 12-10-98; grpsl). Rep: Caballero. Richard Hayes. Format: Sp. Target aud: 18-54. ◆ Joe Conway, gen mgr.

Stamps

KZHE(FM)— October 1980: 100.5 mhz; 50 kw. 500 ft. TL: N33 26 01 W93 27 49. Stereo. 406 W. Union St., Magnolia 71753-3708. Phone: (870) 234-7790. Fax: (870) 234-7791. E-mail: kzhe@swbglobal.net. Web Site: www.kzhe.com. Licensee: A-1 Communications Inc. (acq 5-20-92; $85,000; 6-8-92). Format: Classic country. Target aud: 25-54. Spec prog: Gospel 8 hrs wkly. ◆ Troy Alphin, pres; Sharon Alphin, VP; Dave Sehon, gen mgr, stn mgr & opns mgr.

Stuttgart

KWAK(AM)— May 15, 1948: 1240 khz; 1 kw-U. TL: N34 29 27 W91 33 45. Box 910, 1818 S. Buerkle 72160. Phone: (870) 673-1595. Fax: (870) 673-8445. E-mail: kwik@futura.net. Licensee: Arkansas County Broadcasters Inc. (group owner). Network: ABC Daytime Direction. Format: Country, talk, info. Target aud: General. Spec prog: Farm 6 hrs wkly. ◆ Bobby Caldwell, pres; Scott Siler, stn mgr, gen sls mgr & progmg dir; Sandi Levi, mus dir; Johnathan Reaves, news dir.

KWAK-FM— Dec 15, 1987: 105.5 mhz; 3 kw. 325 ft. TL: N34 25 52 W91 26 08. Stereo. Format: Oldies.

Texarkana

KCMC(AM)—See Texarkana, TX

KFYX(FM)— June 11, 1968: 107.1 mhz; 2.9 kw. 479 ft. TL: N33 25 45 W94 07 11. Stereo. 615 Olive St., TX 75501. Phone: (903) 793-4671. Fax: (903) 792-4261. Licensee: ArkLaTex LLC (group owner; acq 1-4-02; grpsl). Network: ABC. Format: Traditional Country. News staff: one; News: 3 hrs wkly. Spec prog: Farm 2 hrs, gospel 2 hrs wkly. ◆ Harold Sudbury, gen mgr.

KHTA(FM)—See Wake Village TX

***KKLT(FM)—** 2004: 89.3 mhz; 1 w horiz, 5.7 kw vert. Ant 505 ft. TL: N33 23 36 W93 51 34. 5700 West Oaks Blvd., Rocklin, CA 95765. Phone: (916) 251-1600. Fax: (916) 251-1650. Web Site: www.klove.com. Licensee: Educational Media Foundation. (acq 1-11-2005; $125,000. for CP). Network: K-Love. Format: Christian. ◆ Richard Jenkins, pres.

KKYR-FM—See Texarkana, TX

KOSY(AM)— Nov 15, 1951: 790 khz; 1 kw-D, 500 w-N, DA-N. TL: N33 22 30 W94 01 00. 2324 Arkansas Blvd. 71854. Phone: (870)

Stations in the U.S.   California

Developers & Brokers of Radio Properties
contact American Media Services at our suite:
Philadelphia Marriott Downtown
215-625-2900
843-972-2200
americanmediaservices.com
Charleston, SC
Dallas, TX • Chicago, Il • Austin, TX
American Media Services, LLC

772-3771. Fax: (870) 772-0364. Web Site: www.kkyr.com. Licensee: Capstar TX L.P. Group owner: Clear Channel Communications Inc. (acq 8-30-00; grpsl). Format: Modern country. News staff: one. Target aud: General. ♦ Ron Bird, gen mgr.

KYGL(FM)—Co-owned with KOSY(AM). 1995: 106.3 mhz; 3 kw. 328 ft. TL: N33 22 39 W93 56 38. Format: Classic rock.

KTFS(AM)—See Texarkana, TX

KTOY(FM)— 1993: 104.7 mhz; 3 kw. Ant 390 ft. TL: N33 27 25 W94 10 59. 2409 College Dr., TX 75501. Phone: (903) 794-5869. Fax: (903) 793-1577. E-mail: ktoy1047@aol.com. Web Site: www.hitsandoldies.com. Licensee: Jo-Al Broadcasting Inc. (acq 4-11-2005; $1.5 million). Format: Urban. ♦ Al Davis, gen mgr; Emmie Gamble, stn mgr; Vincent Gamble, chief of engrg; Rodney Davis, sls.

Trumann

KJBX(FM)—Licensed to Trumann. See Jonesboro

Turrell

KKLV(FM)— Sept 1, 1999: 94.7 mhz; 6 kw. 328 ft. TL: N35 18 04 W90 19 34. 5700 W. Oaks Blvd., Rockin, CA 95765. Phone: (916) 251-1600. Fax: (916) 251-1650. Web Site: www.klove.com. Licensee: Educational Media Foundation. Group owner: EMF Broadcasting (acq 10-20-00; grpsl). Network: K-Love. Format: Contemp Christian. ♦ Lloyd Parker, gen mgr.

Van Buren

KAYR(AM)— Sept 6, 1979: 1060 khz; 500 w-D, DA. TL: N35 25 36 W94 18 11. 3104 S. 70th St., Fort Smith 72903. Phone: (479) 452-0681. Fax: (479) 452-0873. Web Site: www.fortsmithradio.com. Licensee: Cumulus Licensing Corp. Format: Sp. ♦ Smitty O'Loughlin, gen mgr.

KHGG(AM)— Nov 24, 1958: 1580 khz; 1 kw-D, 45 w-N. TL: N35 25 58 W94 19 47. Box 908, Fort Smith 72902. Phone: (479) 288-1047. Fax: (479) 288-0942. E-mail: koolproduction@sbcglobal.net. Web Site: www.fortsmithradiogroup.com. Licensee: Pharis Broadcasting Inc. (group owner; acq 9-20-93; $110,000;. FTR: 10-11-93). Format: News, sports. Target aud: General. Spec prog: Univ of Ark Football, mens/womens basketball, baseball, Van Buren high school football, basketball. ♦ William Pharis, CEO & pres; Karen Pharis, exec VP & gen mgr; Craig Smith, gen sls mgr; Ernie Witt, progmg dir.

*KLFS(FM)— 2004: 90.3 mhz; 2.4 kw vert. Ant 256 ft. TL: N35 23 37 W94 33 07. Stereo. 5700 W. Oaks Blvd., Rocklin, CA 95765. Phone: (916) 251-1600. Fax: (916) 251-1650. E-mail: klove@klove.com. Web Site: www.klove.com. Licensee: Educational Media Foundation. Group owner: EMF Broadcasting. Network: K-Love. Shaw Pittman. Format: Chrisitan. News staff: 3. Target aud: 25-44; Judeo Chrisitan, female. ♦ Richard Jenkins, pres; Mike Novak, VP.

KLSZ-FM— May 22, 1983: 102.7 mhz; 17 kw. Ant 574 ft. TL: N35 26 51 W94 21 54. Stereo. 3104 S. 70th St., Fort Smith 72903. Phone: (479) 452-0681. Fax: (479) 452-0873. Licensee: Cumulus Licensing Corp. Group owner: Cumulus Media Inc. (acq 8-99; $1.15 million). Format: Rock. ♦ Smitty O'Loughlin, gen mgr.

Waldo

KWDO(FM)—Not on air, target date: unknown: 99.1 mhz; 6 kw. Ant 328 ft. TL: N33 24 17 W93 12 07. Stereo. 131 S. Jackson & Magnolia, Memphis, TN 71757. Phone: (870) 234-5862. Fax: (870) 234-5865. E-mail: kvma@arkansas.net. Web Site: kvma.com. Licensee: Noalmark Broadcasting Corp. (acq 6-22-2005; $430,000). Borari & Paxsom. Format: Adult contemp. ♦ Ken Sibley, gen mgr.

Waldron

KRWA-FM— May 18, 1982: 103.1 mhz; 6.1 kw. Ant 1,351 ft. TL: N34 58 44 W93 56 42. Stereo. Box 908, Fort Smith 72902. Phone: (479) 288-1047. Fax: (479) 288-0942. Web Site: www.kzkzfm.com. Licensee: Pharis Broadcasting Inc. (group owner; acq 6-1-2003; $360,000). Rep: Commercial Media Sales. BRI Irwin, Campbell & Tannenwald. Format: Sports. News staff: one; News: 10 hrs wkly. Target aud: 25-54. ♦ William Pharis, pres; Karen Pharis, gen mgr & stn mgr; Ernie Witt Jr., opns dir.

Walnut Ridge

KRLW(AM)— June 29, 1951: 1320 khz; 1 kw-D. TL: N36 03 58 W90 56 24. 1 Radio Dr., Pocohantas 72455. Phone: (870) 886-6666. Fax: (870) 886-5719. E-mail: krlw@nex.net. Licensee: Combined Media Group Inc. (group owner; acq 7-25-01; with co-located FM). Network: CBS. Format: Oldies. ♦ Tim Scott, pres & gen mgr.

KRLW-FM— Mar 27, 1977: 106.3 mhz; 3 kw. 328 ft. TL: N36 03 58 W90 56 24. Stereo. Network: CBS. Format: Country. News staff: .

Warren

KWRF(AM)— August 1953: 860 khz; 250 w-D, 55 w-N. TL: N33 37 59 W92 03 51. 1255 N. Myrtle 71671. Phone: (870) 226-2653. Phone: (870) 226-2654. Fax: (870) 226-3039. Licensee: Jimmy L. Sledge & Gwen Sledge. (acq 4-12-91; $125,000 with co-located FM; 5-6-91). Format: C&W. News staff: one; News: 10 hrs wkly. Target aud: General. Spec prog: Gospel 8 hrs wkly. ♦ Gwen Sledge, opns VP; Jimmy Sledge, pres, gen mgr, gen sls mgr, mus dir, news dir & chief of engrg.

KWRF-FM— June 21, 1976: 105.5 mhz; 3 kw. Ant 250 ft. TL: N33 37 59 W92 03 51. ♦ Gwen Sledge, exec VP.

West Helena

KCLT(FM)— Dec 17, 1984: 104.9 mhz; 3 kw. 328 ft. TL: N34 30 56 W90 40 13. Stereo. Box 2870 72390. Secondary address: 700 Dr. Martin Luther King Dr., Suite 2 72390. Phone: (870) 572-9506. Fax: (870) 572-1845. E-mail: force2@sbcglobal.net. Web Site: www.force2radio.com. Licensee: West Helena Broadcasters Inc. (acq 8-8-84). Format: Black, blues, oldies. News staff: one; News: one hr wkly. Target aud: 25-54; general, mainly African-Americans. Spec prog: Gospel 15 hrs wkly. ♦ Raymond Simes, pres, VP & gen mgr; Elaine Sims, stn mgr; Larry Evans, opns mgr.

KFFA-FM—See Helena

West Memphis

KSUD(AM)— Dec 1, 1961: 730 khz; 250 w-U, DA-N. TL: N35 08 31 W90 08 05. 791 Walnut Knoll Ln. 3E., Cordova, TN 38018. Phone: (901) 751-1550. Fax: (901) 751-1654. E-mail: ffhammond@klove.com. Web Site: www.ksudradio.com. Licensee: Simmons-Austin, LS, LLC. Group owner: K-Love Radio Network (acq 6-13-2005; $2 million). Format: Contemp Christian music. Target aud: 25-54; family types. ♦ G. Craig Hanson, pres; Keith Whipple, VP & gen mgr; Lloyd Parker, gen sls mgr; Eric Allen, natl sls mgr & prom dir; Frank Hammond, rgnl sls mgr; Sam Wallington, chief of engrg.

White Hall

KTRN(FM)— November 1997: 104.5 mhz; 3 kw. 289 ft. TL: N34 13 13 W92 04 37. 2215 E. Harding, Suite 7, Pine Bluff 71601. Phone: (870) 536-5876 (on air). Phone: (870) 536 3282 (office). Fax: (870) 536-3475. Licensee: Bayou Broadcasting Inc. Format: Soft rock. Target aud: Women; 20 & up. ♦ Vickie Hooker, gen mgr & opns mgr.

Wilson

KOSE(AM)—Licensed to Wilson. See Osceola

Wrightsville

KLAL(FM)— March 1992: 107.7 mhz; 100 kw. Ant 741 ft. TL: N34 36 34 W92 14 14. 700 Wellington Hills Rd., Suite 920, Little Rock 72211. Phone: (501) 401-0200. Fax: (501) 401-0374. Web site: www.alice1077.com. Licensee: Citadel Broadcasting Co. Group owner: Citadel Broadcasting Corp. (acq 9-4-97). Format: Hot adult contemp. ♦ Jim Beard, gen mgr.

Wynne

KWYN(AM)— Sept 28, 1956: 1400 khz; 1 kw-U. TL: N35 15 21 W90 47 49. Box 789, 2758 Hwy. 64 72396. Phone: (870) 238-8141. Phone: (870) 238-8142. Fax: (870) 238-5997. E-mail: kwyn@ipa.net. Licensee: East Arkansas Broadcasters Inc. Network: CBS. Format: Talk, C&W, info. Target aud: General. Spec prog: Farm 6 hrs wkly. ♦ Bobby Caldwell, CEO & gen mgr; Lance Daniels, sls dir; Lindell Staggs, news dir; Jim Alexander, chief of engrg.

KWYN-FM— May 15, 1969: 92.5 mhz; 35 kw. 328 ft. TL: N35 11 59 W90 43 23. Stereo. Format: Country.

Yellville

KCTT-FM— 1986: 101.7 mhz; 2.45 kw. 331 ft. TL: N36 15 39 W92 41 42. Stereo. Box 2010, 620 Hwy. 5 N., Mountain Home 72654. Phone: (870) 449-4001. Phone: (870) 425-3101. Fax: (870) 424-4314. Web Site: www.ktlo.com. Licensee: KTLO L.L.C. (group owner; (acq 5-29-98; $215,000). Format: Oldies. Spec prog: Folk 10 hrs wkly. ♦ Bob Knight, CEO & gen mgr; Scottie Earls, chmn; Danny Ward, pres & stn mgr; Brad Haworth, opns VP.

California

Alameda

KNGY(FM)—Licensed to Alameda. See San Francisco

Alisal

KPRC-FM—See Salinas

Alturas

KALT-FM— July 2002: 106.5 mhz; 51 kw. Ant 508 ft. TL: N41 50 03 W120 21 03. 215 W. 2nd St. 96101. Phone: (530) 233-4842. Fax: (530) 233-4842. E-mail: kkalt@hdo.net. Licensee: Woodrow Michael Warren. Group owner: Woodrow Michael Warren Stns. Format: Classic rock. ♦ Mike Warren, gen mgr.

KCFJ(AM)— June 4, 1951: 570 khz; 5 kw-D, 200 w-N. TL: N41 30 07 W120 30 01. (CP: 5 kw-U, DA-N). Box 580 96101. Phone: (530) 233-3570. Fax: (530) 233-5570. Licensee: EDI Media Inc. (acq 6-5-02; with co-located FM). Network: Network: USA, ABC Information & Entertainment. Cohn & Marks. Format: News/talk. News staff: one; News: 3 hrs wkly. Target aud: General. Spec prog: Farm one hr wkly. ♦ R.L. Hansen, pres; W.H. Hansen, gen mgr; Carol Irwin, opns mgr, gen sls mgr, prom mgr & progmg dir; Dan Frey, news dir & chief of engrg.

KCNO(FM)—Co-owned with KCFJ(AM). Dec 4, 1990: 94.5 mhz; 100 kw. 106 ft. TL: N41 33 50 W120 24 55. (CP: 52 kw., ant -78 ft.). Format: #1 country. News: 17 hrs wkly. Target aud: General. ♦ Bill Hansen, sls dir & gen sls mgr.

Anaheim

KFSH-FM—Listing follows KXMX(AM).

KXMX(AM)— May 18, 1959: 1190 khz; 10 kw-D, 1.3 kw-N, DA-2. TL: N33 56 42 W117 51 44. (CP: 20 kw-D). Box 29023, Glendale 91209.

Broadcasting & Cable Yearbook 2006

D-67

California

Phone: (818) 956-5552. Fax: (818) 551-1110. E-mail: info@kkla.com. Licensee: Chase Radio Properties L.L.C. Group owner: Salem Communications Corp. (acq 8-24-00; grpsl). Format: Talk, Korean, Arabic. Target aud: Specialized ethnic groups. Spec prog: Gospel, relg, Pol, Sp, Vietnamese 2 hrs wkly. ♦Dave Armstrong, VP & gen mgr; Dawn McKahan, gen sls mgr; Kim Kelley, prom mgr; Chuck Tylor, progmg dir; Mark Pollock, chief of engrg.

KFSH-FM—Co-owned with KXMX(AM). Apr 16, 1961: 95.9 mhz; 6 kw. 328 ft. TL: N33 49 50 W117 48 39. Stereo. Box 29023, Glendale 91209. Web Site: www.thefish959.com. Wiley, Rein & Fielding. Format: Contemp Christian music. Target aud: 18-49.

Anderson

KEWB(FM)— Mar 20, 1983: 94.7 mhz; 4.2 kw. 1,565 ft. TL: N40 39 06 W122 31 32. Stereo. 1588 Charles Dr., Redding 96003. Phone: (530) 244-9700. Fax: (530) 244-9707. Web Site: www.power94booty.com. Licensee: Results Radio of Redding Licensee LLC. Group owner: Fritz Communications Inc. (acq 6-28-2000; grpsl). Arent, Fox, Kintner, Plotkin & Kahn. Format: CHR. Target aud: 18-49. ♦Beth Tappan, gen mgr; Laurie Curto, gen sls mgr.

Angwin

*****KNDL(FM)**— May 20, 1961: 89.9 mhz; 794 w. Ant 3,010 ft. TL: N38 40 09 W122 37 53. Stereo. 95 La Jota Dr. 94508. Phone: (707) 965-4155. Fax: (707) 965-4161. E-mail: kndl@thecandle.com. Web Site: www.thecandle.com. Licensee: Howell Mountain Broadcasting Co. Inc. Format: Relg. Target aud: 35-49; general. ♦Jim Chase, chmn; Tim Mitchell, pres; David Shantz, gen mgr.

Apple Valley

KIXW(AM)— June 5, 1954: 960 khz; 5 kw-D, 400 w-N, DA-2. TL: N34 31 00 W117 13 35. Box 1778, Victorville 92393. Secondary address: 12370 Hesperia Rd., Suite 17, Victorville 92393. Phone: (760) 241-1313. Fax: (760) 241-0205. Licensee: Regent Licensee of Victorville Inc. Group owner: Clear Channel Communications Inc. (acq 2000; grpsl). Format: Talk. Target aud: 18-54. ♦Paul Mitchell, gen mgr & news dir.

KZXY-FM—Co-owned with KIXW(AM). May 17, 1968: 102.3 mhz; 6 kw. 328 ft. TL: N34 24 40 W117 11 09. Stereo. Format: Adult contemp. Target aud: 25-54.

KWRN(AM)— Jan 26, 1991: 1550 khz; 5 kw-D, 500 w-N, DA-N. TL: N34 32 12 W117 09 22. Box 1283, Victorville 92393. Secondary address: 15165 7th St., Ste D, Victorville 92392. Phone: (760) 955-8722. Fax: (760) 955-5751. Web Site: www.wkrn1550.com. Licensee: Major Market Stations Inc. Network: ABC. Format: Sp Top-40 hits. Target aud: 34-54; adults with a stable job and disposable income. ♦William S. Roberts, chmn & pres; John Lindvall, CFO; Marilynn Kramar, VP & gen mgr; Steve Cruz, stn mgr; Alexa Corcuera, opns dir; Esther Garzon, dev dir; William Sullivan, engrg dir; Dick Vosper, chief of engrg.

Arcadia

KSSE(FM)— Dec 3, 1960: 107.1 mhz; 3 kw. 240 ft. TL: N34 10 51 W118 01 38. (CP: 6 kw, ant -43 ft.). 5700 Wilshire Blvd., Suite 250, Los Angeles 90036. Phone: (323) 900-6100. Fax: (323) 900-6200. Web Site: www.viva1071.com. Licensee: Entravision Holdings LLC. Group owner: Entravision Communications Corp. (acq 4-1-03; grpsl). Latham & Watkins. Format: Sp. Target aud: 24-39; general. ♦Karl Meyer, gen mgr; Tom Bell, gen sls mgr; Nestor Rocha, progmg dir & engrg dir.

Arcata

KATA(AM)— Nov 15, 1957: 1340 khz; 1 kw-U. TL: N40 51 12 W124 05 00. 5640 S. Broadway St., Eureka 95503-6905. Phone: (707) 442-2000. Fax: (707) 443-6848. Web Site: www.kata1340.com. Licensee: Bicoastal Media LLC. (group owner; acq 7-28-99; grpsl). Network: ABC. Rep: Allied Radio Partners. Format: Sports. Target aud: 25-54; upscale adults. ♦Mike Wilson, pres; Laurie Tate, VP, gen mgr, opns dir & opns mgr.

*****KHSU-FM**— October 1960: 90.5 mhz; 8.8 kw. 1,506 ft. TL: N40 43 36 W123 58 19. Stereo. Humboldt State Univ. 95521. Phone: (707) 826-4807. Fax: (707) 826-6082. E-mail: khsu@humboldt.edu. Web Site: www.khsu.org. Licensee: Humboldt State University. Network:

Network: NPR, PRI. Format: Var, news. News: 28 hrs wkly. Spec prog: World 14 hrs, jazz 10 hrs wkly. ♦Elizabeth Hans-McCrone, gen mgr; Charles Horn, dev dir; Katie Whiteside, opns mgr & progmg dir.

KXGO(FM)—Licensed to Arcata. See Eureka

Arnold

KBYN(FM)— Sept 1, 1995: 95.9 mhz; 860 w. Ant 863 ft. TL: N38 22 40 W120 11 33. Stereo. Box 1039, Hughson 95326. Secondary address: 4043 Geer Rd., Hughson 95326. Phone: (209) 883-8760. Fax: (209) 883-8769. E-mail: ngomez@lafavorita.net. Web Site: www.lafavorita.net. Licensee: KBYN Inc. (acq 3-28-01). Network: CBS. Shaw Pittman. Format: Sp, country. News staff: one; News: 3 hrs wkly. Target aud: 25-54; general. ♦Nelson Gomez, gen mgr.

*****KCFA(FM)**— Oct 2, 1995: 106.1 mhz; 3.8 kw. 840 ft. TL: N38 22 42 W120 11 36. 4043 Geer Rd., Box 1039, Hughson 95326. Phone: (209) 883-8760. Fax: (209) 883-8769. Web Site: www.lafavorita.net. Licensee: KCFA Inc. (acq 3-21-02). Format: Sp-Ethnic. News staff: one; News: 5 hrs wkly. Target aud: 30-50; Families. ♦Nelson Gomez, gen mgr & gen sls mgr; Ricardo Torres, progmg dir; Freddy Lopez, news dir; Chuck Hughes, chief of engrg.

Arroyo Grande

KLFF(AM)— Sept 1, 2002: 890 khz; 5 kw-U, DA-N. TL: N35 08 44 W120 31 15. Box 1561, San Luis Obispo 93406. Phone: (805) 541-4343. Fax: (805) 541-9101. E-mail: mail@890online.com. Web Site: www.890online.com. Licensee: Jerry J. Collins. Format: Relg. ♦Jerry J. Collins, pres; Joel Riley, gen mgr.

KXTK(AM)—Licensed to Arroyo Grande. See San Luis Obispo

Arvin

KMYX-FM— June 30, 1999: 92.5 mhz; 1.15 kw. 751 ft. TL: N35 11 45 W118 42 30. 6313 Schirra Ct., Bakersfield 93313. Phone: (661) 837-0745. Fax: (661) 837-1612. Web Site: www.campesina.com. Licensee: Farmworker Educ. Radio Network Inc. Borsari & Paxson. Format: Sp, rgnl Mexican. Target aud: 25-54; Hispanic market. ♦Anthony Chavez, pres, gen mgr & opns mgr; Arnulfo Rivas, stn mgr; Modesta Gonzalez, gen sls mgr; Humberto Salinas, natl sls mgr; Jesse Portillo, progmg dir & progmg mgr.

Atascadero

KIQO(FM)— May 19, 1979: 104.5 mhz; 5.6 kw. 1,410 ft. TL: N35 21 38 W120 39 21. Stereo. 3620 Sacramento Dr., Suite 204, San Luis Obispo 93401. Phone: (805) 781-2750. Fax: (805) 781-2758. Licensee: AGM California. Group owner: American General Media (acq 2-10-99; $1.5 million). Network: ABC. Rep: Allied Radio Partners. Format: Oldies. Target aud: 25-55. ♦Kathy Signorelli, gen mgr; Mark Wilson, gen sls mgr & chief of engrg.

Atherton

*****KCEA(FM)**— June 2, 1979: 89.1 mhz; 100 w. -216 ft. TL: N37 27 41 W122 10 30. (CP: Ant 5 ft.). Stereo. 555 Middle Field Rd. 94027. Phone: (650) 306-8823. Phone: (650) 306-8822. Fax: (650) 328-8706. Web Site: www.kcea.org. Licensee: Sequoia Union High School District. Format: Big band, Nostalgia, adult standards. Target aud: General. ♦Michael Isaacs, gen mgr; Trish Millet, pub affrs dir.

Atwater

KBRE(FM)— Oct 1, 1995: 92.5 mhz; 6 kw. 328 ft. TL: N37 16 42 W120 37 33. Stereo. 1020 W. Main St., Merced 95340-4521. Phone: (209) 723-2191. Fax: (209) 383-2950. Web Site: www.925thebear.com. Licensee: Mapleton Communications LLC (group owner; acq 6-1-2002; grpsl). Leventhal, Senter & Lerman. Format: Active rock. News staff: one; News: 3 hrs wkly. Men 25-49. ♦Andrew Adams, gen mgr, gen sls mgr & pub affrs dir; Jason LaChance, progmg dir; Michael Martinez, progmg dir.

Auberry

KLBN(FM)— July 12, 1992: 105.1 mhz; 590 w. 1,902 ft. TL: N37 04 25 W119 25 52. (CP: 600 w, ant 1,870 ft.). Stereo. 1110 E. Olive Ave., Fresno 93728. Phone: (559) 497-1100. Fax: (559) 497-1125. Web Site: www.labuena105.com. Licensee: Lotus Communications Corp.

Directory of Radio

(group owner) Format: Sp. Target aud: 18-34; .Young people of Mexican heritage who love to dance ♦Howard Kalmenson, pres; Daniel Crotty, gen mgr; Steve Wrath, sls dir; Denise Coronado, prom dir; Pepe DeMarco, progmg dir; Eduardo Leon, mus dir.

Auburn

KAHI(AM)— Nov 13, 1957: 950 khz; 5 kw-D, 4.2 kw-N, DA-2. TL: N38 51 28 W121 01 39. 985 Lincoln Way, Suite 103 95603. Phone: (530) 885-5636. Fax: (530) 885-0166. E-mail: KAHI@KAHI.com. Web Site: www.kahi.com. Licensee: IHR Educational Broadcasting (group owner; acq 4-28-99; $475,000. with KSMH(AM) West Sacramento). Fletcher, Heald & Hildreth. Format: Var. Target aud: 25-54; Community focused. ♦Jerry Henry, CEO, pres & gen mgr; Dave Rosenthal, opns mgr.

KHYL(FM)— Dec 21, 1961: 101.1 mhz; 36.3 kw. 577 ft. TL: N38 51 28 W121 01 39. Stereo. 1440 Ethan Way, Suite 200, Sacramento 95825. Phone: (916) 929-5325. Fax: (916) 925-0128. Web Site: www.v101fm.com. Licensee: AMFM Broadcasting Licenses LLC. Group owner: Clear Channel Communications Inc. (acq 8-30-2000; grpsl). Format: Oldies, urban adult contemp. News: 1 hr a wk. Target aud: 25-54. ♦Jeff Holden, gen mgr & sls dir.

Avalon

KBRT(AM)— June 1, 1952: 740 khz; 10 kw-D, DA. TL: N33 21 36 W118 22 18. Stereo. 3183 D Airway Ave., Costa Mesa 92626. Phone: (714) 754-4450. Fax: (714) 754-0735. E-mail: kbrtinfo@crawfordbroadcasting.com. Licensee: Kierton Inc. Group owner: Crawford Broadcasting Co. (acq 5-21-80). Format: Relg, talk. Target aud: Christian adult. ♦Donald Crawford Sr., pres; Don Crawford Jr., gen mgr & stn mgr; Todd Stickler, opns mgr.

*****KISL(FM)**— 2000: 88.7 mhz; 200 w. Ant 20 ft. TL: N33 20 32 W118 19 11. Box 1980 90704. Phone: (310) 510-7469. Fax: (310) 510-2272. E-mail: arts@cipas.org. Web Site: www.kisl.org. Licensee: Catalina Island Performing Arts Foundation (acq 3-15-00). Format: Var. ♦Aaron Pitts, stn mgr.

Avenal

*****KAAX(FM)**—Not on air, target date: unknown:. Stn currently dark 95.1 mhz; 920 w. Ant 656 ft. TL: N36 00 40 W120 04 26. 12550 Brookhurst St., Suite A, Garden Grove 92840. Licensee: Avenal Educational Services Inc.

Baker

KHRQ(FM)— 2002: 94.9 mhz; 1.4 kw. Ant 1,288 ft. TL: N35 26 09 W115 55 22. 1611 E. Main St., Barstow 92311. Phone: (760) 256-0326. Fax: (760) 256-9507. E-mail: tim@highwayradio.com. Licensee: The Drive LLC. Group owner: KHWY Inc. (acq 5-31-2003). Network: ABC. Hogan & Hartson. Format: Classic rock. ♦Howard Anderson, CEO & pres; Kirk Anderson, exec VP; Timothy Anderson, VP & gen mgr; Judy Robinson, sls VP; John Gregg, prom dir; Lance Todd, progmg dir; Keith Hayes, news dir; Thomas J. McNeill, engrg mgr.

KIXF(FM)— Mar 1, 1994: 101.5 mhz; 4.3 kw. Ant 1,322 ft. TL: N35 26 00 W115 55 25. Stereo. 1611 E. Main St., Barstow 92311. Phone: (760) 256-0326. Fax: (760) 256-9507. E-mail: time@highwayradio.com. Web Site: www.thehighwaystations.com. Licensee: KHWY Inc. (group owner; (acq 2-18-98; $1,741,444. with KIXW-FM Lenwood). Network: Network: Westwood One, CNN Radio. Hogan & Hartson. Format: Country. News staff: one. Target aud: 25-54; interstate travelers to Las Vegas & Laughlin, NV. Spec prog: Hourly traf report to service interstate travelers. ♦Howard B. Anderson, CEO & pres; Kirk Anderson, exec VP; Timothy B. Anderson, VP & gen mgr; Judy Robinson, sls VP; John Gregg, prom dir; Lance Todd, progmg dir; Keith Hayes, news dir; Thomas J. McNeill, engrg mgr.

Bakersfield

KAFY(AM)— 2000: 1100 khz; 4.2 kw-D, 800 w-N, DA-N. TL: N35 27 00 W118 56 48. Box 1039, Hughson 95326. Phone: (209) 883-8760. Fax: (209) 883-8769. Web Site: www.lafavorita.net. Licensee: KAFY Inc. (acq 3-28-01). Format: Sp talk. ♦Troy Polton, gen mgr; Richard Torres, opns mgr.

KBID(AM)— February 1958: 1350 khz; 1 kw-D, 33 w-N. TL: N35 21 00 W119 58 58. 1400 Easton Dr., Suite 144 93309. Phone: (661) 328-1410. Fax: (661) 328-0873. Web Site: www.liveradio.com. Licensee: AGM California. Group owner: American General Media (acq 7-25-97;

Stations in the U.S.   California

Developers & Brokers of Radio Properties
contact American Media Services at our suite:
Philadelphia Marriott Downtown
215-625-2900
843-972-2200
americanmediaservices.com
Charleston, SC
Dallas, TX · Chicago, Il · Austin, TX
American Media Services, LLC

$1.5 million. with KKXX-FM Shafter). Network: Westwood One. Format: Oldies. Target aud: 35-64. ♦ Roger Fessler, gen mgr; Chris Edwards, opns mgr & progmg dir; Toni Snyder, sls VP; Dave McElwain, sls dir; Tracy Peoples, prom dir; Rusty Burchfield, engrg dir.

KBKO-FM—Listing follows KDFO(AM).

KCWR(FM)— Mar 21, 1990: 107.1 mhz; 6 kw. 164 ft. TL: N35 22 08 W119 00 14. 3223 Sillect Ave. 93308. Phone: (661) 326-1011. Fax: (661) 328-7503. Fax: (661) 328-7537. Licensee: Buck Owens Production Co. Inc. (acq 7-27-93). Format: Country. ♦ Buck Owens, pres; Mel Owens Jr., CEO, gen mgr, opns mgr & dev mgr; Julie Randolph, gen sls mgr & mktg mgr.

KDFO(AM)— 1959: 800 khz; 1 kw-D, 440 w-N, DA-2. TL: N35 20 44 W118 59 33. 1100 Mohawk St., Suite 280 93309. Phone: (661) 322-9929. Fax: (661) 322-9239. Web Site: www.foxsportsradio800.com. Licensee: Clear Channel Broadcasting Licenses Inc. Group owner: Clear Channel Communications Inc. (acq 10-11-2000; grpsl). Format: Sports. Target aud: 25-54; adults. ♦ Jim Bell, VP; Tony Manes, progmg dir; Steve Mull, chief of engrg.

KBKO-FM—Co-owned with KDFO(AM). Aug 24, 1963: 96.5 mhz; 50 kw. 550 ft. TL: N35 29 08 W118 53 19. Stereo. Web Site: www.965kissfm.com. Rep: McGavren Guild. Arter & Hadden. Format: CHR. Target aud: 18-44.

KERN(AM)— Jan 3, 1932: 1410 khz; 1 kw-U. TL: N35 21 07 W118 56 48. 1400 Easton Dr., Suite 144 93309. Secondary address: Box 2700 93309. Phone: (661) 328-1410. Phone: (661) 326-1410. Fax: (661) 328-0873. Licensee: AGM California. Group owner: American General Media (acq 5-1-75). Network: Network: Westwood One, ABC Information & Entertainment. Rep: Christal. Format: News/talk. News staff: 3; News: 30 hrs wkly. Target aud: 25-54. Spec prog: Farm one hr, relg one hr wkly. ♦ Roger Fessler, exec VP & gen mgr.

KISV(FM)—Co-owned with KERN(AM). 1948: 94.1 mhz; 4.5 kw. 1,312 ft. TL: N35 26 20 W118 44 23. Stereo. Format: CHR rhythmic. Spec prog: Farm one hr, relg one hr wkly.

***KFRB(FM)**— August 1996: 91.3 mhz; 115 w. 1,368 ft. TL: N35 26 17 W118 44 22. c/o Family Stations, 290 Hegenberger Rd., Oakland 94621. Phone: (209) 389-4659. Web Site: www.familyradio.com. Licensee: Family Stations Inc. (group owner) Format: Relg. ♦ Harold Camping, pres & gen mgr.

KGEO(AM)— Jan 1, 1946: 1230 khz; 1 kw-U. TL: N35 20 53 W119 00 33. Stereo. 1400 Easton Dr., Suite 144 93309. Phone: (661) 631-1230. Phone: (661) 328-1410. Fax: (661) 328-0873. Licensee: AGM California. Group owner: American General Media (acq 12-9-92; $1.75 million. with co-located FM; FTR: 1-4-93). Network: Network: Network: CBS, Westwood One, ABC. Rep: McGavren Guild. Cohn & Marks. Format: Sports, talk. ♦ Roger Fessler, gen mgr.

KGFM(FM)—Co-owned with KGEO(AM). October 1964: 101.5 mhz; 4.8 kw. 1,280 ft. TL: N35 26 20 W118 44 23. (CP: 6.7 kw, ant 1,299 ft.). Stereo. Format: Easy lstng.

KGET(AM)— October 1946: 970 khz; 1 kw-D, 5 kw-N, DA-2. TL: N35 27 00 W118 56 48. 1100 Mohawk St., Ste 280 93309. Phone: (661) 322-9929. Fax: (661) 283-2963. Fax: (661) 283-2963. Web Site: www.newsradio970kget.com. Licensee: AMFM Radio Licenses LLC. Group owner: Clear Channel Communications Inc. (acq 12-22-2000; $1.4 million). Network: Network: UPI, CBS. Rep: Caballero. Format: News/talk. Target aud: 18-54. ♦ Jim Bell, VP.

KIWI(FM)—Listing follows KWAC(AM).

KKBB(FM)— November 1991: 99.3 mhz; 1.2 kw. 1,345 ft. TL: N35 26 17 W118 44 22. Stereo. Box 80658 93380. Secondary address: 3651 Pegasus Dr., Suite 107 93380. Phone: (661) 393-1900. Fax: (661) 393-1915. E-mail: jlove@kkbb.com. Web Site: www.grove993.com. Licensee: Buckley Communications Inc. Group owner: Buckley Broadcasting

Corp. (acq 10-3-94; $1 million; 10-17-94). Rep: D & R Radio. Format: Rhythmic Oldies. Target aud: 25-54; adults. ♦ Steve Darnell, gen mgr; Chris Townsend, opns mgr; Otis Warren, gen sls mgr; J. Love, progmg dir; Kathy King, news dir; Bob Turner, chief of engrg.

KKDJ(FM)—See Delano

KNZR(AM)— 1933: 1560 khz; 25 kw-D, 10 kw-N, DA-N. TL: N35 18 30 W119 02 09. Box 80658 93308. Secondary address: 3651 Pegasus Dr., Suite 107 93308. Phone: (661) 393-1900. Fax: (661) 393-1915. Web Site: www.knzr.com. Licensee: Buckley Broadcasting of California LLC. Group owner: Buckley Broadcasting Corp. (acq 1-25-90; $1 million;. FTR: 2-19-90). Network: CBS. Rep: D & R Radio. Shaw Pittman. Format: News/talk. News staff: 4; News: 40 hrs wkly. Target aud: 25-54. Spec prog: L.A. Dodgers. ♦ Steve Darnell, gen mgr; Chris Townsend, opns mgr.

***KPRX(FM)**— Feb 28, 1987: 89.1 mhz; 12 kw. 500 ft. TL: N35 29 10 W118 53 20. 3437 W. Shaw Ave., Suite 101, Fresno 93711. Phone: (559) 275-0764. Fax: (559) 275-2202. E-mail: kvpr@kvpr.org. Web Site: www.kvpr.org. Licensee: White Ash Broadcasting Inc. Network: NPR. Format: Class, news & info. ♦ Mariam Stepanian, pres & gen mgr; Jim Meyers, stn mgr & progmg dir; Patrice Loretta, opns mgr & dev dir; Steve Mull, chief of engrg.

KPSL-FM— Dec 15, 1985: 92.1 mhz; 2 kw. Ant 567 ft. TL: N35 29 11 W118 53 21. Stereo. 5200 Standard St. 93308. Phone: (661) 327-9711. Fax: (661) 327-0797. Licensee: Illinois Lotus Corp. Group owner: Lotus Communications Corp. (acq 8-24-99; grpsl). Format: Sp pop. ♦ Mike Allen, gen mgr; Isidro Roman, progmg dir.

KRAB(FM)—(Green Acres). Oct 1, 1991: 106.1 mhz; 25 kw. 410 ft. TL: N35 28 17 W119 01 38. 1100 Mohawk St., Suite 280 93309. Phone: (661) 322-9929. Fax: (661) 322-9239. Web Site: www.krab.com. Licensee: Clear Channel Communications Inc. Rep: McGavren Guild. Arter & Hadden. Format: AOR. Target aud: 18-49; predominantely male. ♦ Jim Bell, VP & gen mgr; Chris Nelson, gen sls mgr; Danny Spanks, progmg dir; Steve Mull, chief of engrg.

KSMJ(FM)—(Shafter). Mar 3, 1978: 97.7 mhz; 4.1 kw. Ant 397 ft. TL: N35 27 33 W119 01 13. Stereo. 3651 Pegasus Dr., Suite 107 93308. Phone: (661) 393-1900. Fax: (661) 393-1915. Web Site: www.977thebreeze.com. Licensee: Buckley Broadcasting of California LLC. Group owner: Buckley Broadcasting Corp. (acq 2-1-01; $2 million). Format: Jazz. Target aud: 18-49. ♦ Steve Darnell, gen mgr; Chris Townshend, opns dir & opns mgr.

***KTQX(FM)**— Apr 14, 1989: 90.1 mhz; 590 w. 3,572 ft. TL: N35 27 05 W118 35 10. 5005 E. Belmont Ave., Fresno 93727. Phone: (559) 455-5777. Fax: (559) 455-5778. Web Site: www.radiobilingue.org. Licensee: Radio Bilingue Inc. Format: Ethnic, multilingual, Sp. News staff: 5; News: 3 hrs wkly. Target aud: 16-60; Latino. ♦ Hugo Morales, CEO; Lisa Lim, dev VP; Maria Esana, gen mgr, opns mgr & gen sls mgr.

KUZZ(AM)— October 1946: 550 khz; 5 kw-D, DA-N. TL: N35 20 25 W118 56 14. Stereo. 3223 Sillect Ave. 93308. Phone: (661) 326-1011. Fax: (661) 328-7503. Licensee: Buck Owens Productions Inc. (group owner; acq 1986). Format: Country. Target aud: 25-54. ♦ Mel Owens Jr., CEO & gen mgr; Buck Owens, pres; Julie Randolph, gen sls mgr; Harvey Campbell, natl sls mgr; Jerry Hufford, prom dir; Evan Bridwell, progmg dir & mus dir; Mark Howell, news dir; Sylvia Cariker, pub affrs dir; Terry Gaiser, chief of engrg.

KUZZ-FM— 1968: 107.9 mhz; 6 kw. 1,364 ft. TL: N35 26 20 W118 44 24. Stereo. Web Site: www.kuzz.com.

KWAC(AM)— 1954: 1490 khz; 1 kw-U. TL: N35 24 07 W119 02 45. Stereo. 5200 Standard St. 93308. Phone: (661) 327-9711. Fax: (661) 327-0797. E-mail: info@thespanishradio.com. Web Site: kwac.com. Licensee: Illinois Lotus Corp. Group owner: Lotus Communications Corp. (acq 8-24-99; grpsl). Rep: Lotus Entravision Reps LLC. Format: Sp. News: 9 hrs wkly. Target aud: General. ♦ Howard Kalmenson, pres; Mike Allen, gen mgr; Juan M. Martinez, progmg dir & news dir; Anna Gallegos, pub affrs dir; Lloyd Moss, chief of engrg.

KIWI(FM)—Co-owned with KWAC(AM). July 11, 1989: 102.9 mhz; 25 kw. Ant 321 ft. TL: N35 19 16 W119 42 26. Stereo. E-mail: napo@radiolobo.com. Web Site: radiolobo.com. (Acq 12-18-00; $2.5 million. including a $10,000 three-year noncompete agreement). Rep: Lotus Entravision Reps LLC. Format: Mexican regional. Target aud: General. ♦ Eddie Leon, progmg dir; Juan Sanchez, mus dir.

Banning

KMET(AM)— 1948: 1490 khz; 1 kw-U. TL: N33 55 49 W116 55 20. 700 E. Redlands Blvd., Suite U, PMB 323, Redlands 92373. Secondary address: 572 Omar 92220. Phone: (951) 849-4644. Phone: (949) 261-6117. Fax: (951) 849-3114. E-mail: general@kmetam.com. Web Site: www.kmetam.com. Licensee: Sunset Broadcasting Inc. (acq 3-31-2003). Format: Smooth jazz, sports. News staff: one; News: 3 hrs wkly. Target aud: General; 35-64. Spec prog: Relg 4 hrs, women's sports 3 hrs wkly. ♦ Richard Nuthmann, pres; Adrian P. Madden, gen mgr & stn mgr; Mitch McClellan, opns mgr.

Barstow

KDUC(FM)— June 4, 1986: 94.3 mhz; 4.6 kw. 783 ft. TL: N34 58 15 W117 02 22. Stereo. 29000 Radio Road 92311. Phone: (760) 256-2121. Fax: (760) 256-5090. E-mail: doscostascommunications@yahoo.com. Licensee: Dos Costas Communications Corp. (group owner; acq 6-18-03; grpsl). Format: CHR. Target aud: 12-44. ♦ Troy Polton, gen mgr & mus dir.

KIQQ(AM)— Sept 29, 1960: 1310 khz; 5 kw-D, 118 w-N, DA-1. TL: N34 54 51 W117 00 59. 710 W. Old Hwy. 58 92311. Phone: (760) 255-2636. Fax: (760) 255-3236. E-mail: jramirez@lamaquinaamusical.net. Web Site: moonbroadcasting.com. Licensee: MBR Licensee LLC. Group owner: Moon Broadcasting (acq 8-7-2000). Network: Westwood One. Arent, Fox, Kintner, Plotkin & Kahn. Format: Sp, regnl Mexican. Target aud: 45 plus. ♦ Abel A. De Luna, chmn & pres; Irene Escalante, VP; Brad Sabel, opns VP; Isela Morelos, gen mgr & dev dir.

KRXV(FM)—See Yermo

KSZL(AM)— June 25, 1986: 1230 khz; 1 kw-U. TL: N34 54 44 W117 01 39. Stereo. 29000 Radio Rd. 92311. Phone: (760) 256-2121. Phone: (760) 256-5382. Fax: (760) 256-5090. E-mail: am1230kszl@yahoo.com.ABC/SMN Stardust Licensee: Dos Costas Communications Corp. (group owner; acq 6-18-03; grpsl). Network: Network: Westwood One, ABC Daytime Direction. Rep: Western Regional Broadcast Sales. Fleischman & Walsh, L.L.P. Format: News. News staff: 2; News: 12 hrs wkly. Target aud: 25 plus; Adults 35 years +. ♦ Jaime Garza, gen mgr & gen sls mgr; Michael Garcia, opns mgr, progmg dir & news dir; Brad Sobel, chief of engrg.

***KVID(FM)**—Not on air, target date: unknown: 89.1 mhz; 260 w. Ant 725 ft. TL: N34 58 17 W117 02 22. 5700 West Oaks Blvd., Rocklin 95765-3719. Phone: (916) 251-1600. Fax: (916) 251-1650. Licensee: Educational Media Foundation. ♦ Lloyd Parker, gen mgr.

***KWTH(FM)**—Not on air, target date: unknown: 91.3 mhz; 1.5 kw. Ant 233 ft. TL: N34 38 39 W116 37 38. Stereo. Box 637, Bishop 93515. Phone: (760) 872-4225. Fax: (760) 872-4155. E-mail: friar@schat.com. Licensee: Living Proof Inc. Format: Relg-Christian. ♦ Daniel McClenaghan, pres & gen mgr.

KXXZ(FM)— 1989: 95.9 mhz; 8.9 kw. Ant 485 ft. TL: N34 51 22 W117 03 00. Stereo. 29000 Radio Rd. 92311. Phone: (760) 256-2121. Fax: (760) 256-5090. E-mail: doscostas@yahoo.com. Licensee: Dos Costas Communications Corp. (group owner; acq 6-18-03; grpsl). Format: Sp contemp rhythmic. ♦ Roland Ulloa, gen mgr; Troy Polton, gen sls mgr; Mike Garcia, progmg dir.

Bayside

***KNHM(FM)**— Apr 15, 1992: 91.5 mhz; 550 w. Ant 508 ft. TL: N40 47 49 W124 02 47. Jefferson Public Radio, 1250 Siskiyou Blvd., Ashland, OR 97520. Phone: (707) 444-8727. Fax: (541) 552-8565. Web Site:

Broadcasting & Cable Yearbook 2006

California

www.jeffnet.org. Licensee: JPR Foundation Inc. (acq 3-24-2004; $130,000). ♦ Ronald Kramer, gen mgr & stn mgr; Paul Westhelle, dev mgr & mus dir.

Beaumont

KAEH(FM)— 1996: 100.9 mhz; 1.5 kw. Ant 479 ft. TL: N33 54 29 W116 59 45. Moon Broadcasting Riverside LLC, 1200 W. Venice Blvd., Los Angeles 90006. Phone: (909) 381-0969. Fax: (909) 381-0943. E-mail: postmaster@manbroadcasting.com. Web Site: www.moonbroadcasting.com/kaeh. Licensee: MBR Licensee LLC. Group owner: Moon Broadcasting (acq 2-13-2002; $1.7 million). Format: Rgnl Mexican. ♦ Abel A. DeLuna, pres.

Berkeley

*KALX(FM)— October 1967: 90.7 mhz; 500 w. Ant 778 ft. TL: N37 52 40 W122 14 44. Stereo. 26 Barrows #5650 94720-5650. Phone: (510) 642-1111. Web Site: kalx.berkeley.edu. Licensee: The Regents of the University of California. Format: Educ, div. News: 4 hrs wkly. ♦ Sandra Wasson, gen mgr; Shawn Reynaldo, opns mgr; John Romero, news dir; Bill Jones, engrg mgr & chief of engrg.

KBLX-FM—Listing follows KVTO(AM).

*KPFA(FM)— April 1949: 94.1 mhz; 59 kw. 1,330 ft. TL: N37 51 55 W122 13 12. Stereo. 1929 Martin Luther King Jr. Way 94704. Phone: (510) 848-6767. Fax: (510) 848-3812. E-mail: postmaster@kpfa.org. Web Site: www.kpfa.org. Licensee: Pacifica Foundation. Group owner: Pacifica Foundations Inc. dba Pacifica Radio Haley, Bader & Potts. Format: Div mus, pub affrs. News staff: 4; News: 11 hrs wkly. Target aud: 25-50. Spec prog: C&W 18 hrs, Black 18 hrs, jazz 15 hrs, folk 10 hrs, women 10 hrs, world 18 hrs wkly. ♦ Gus Newport, gen mgr; Luis Medina, mus dir; Mark Meriole, news dir; Jim Bennett, chief of engrg.

KVTO(AM)— May 22, 1922: 1400 khz; 1 kw-U. TL: N37 50 58 W122 17 44. 55 Hawthorne St., Suite 900, San Francisco 94105. Phone: (415) 284-1029. Fax: (415) 764-4959. Licensee: Urban Radio III L.L.C. Group owner: Inner City Broadcasting (acq 1979). Rep: D & R Radio. Format: Asian. Target aud: 25-54. ♦ Harvey Stone, pres & gen mgr; Barry Rose, gen sls mgr; Rhonda Amiz, natl mgr; Jamie Arbona, progmg dir; Paul Marks, chief of engrg.

KBLX-FM—Co-owned with KVTO(AM). Apr 29, 1949: 102.9 mhz; 50 kw. 1,290 ft. TL: N37 41 20 W122 26 07. Stereo. E-mail: info@kblx.com. Web Site: www.kblx.com. Format: Adult contemp, news. News staff: one; News: 20 hrs wkly. Target aud: 25-54; adults. ♦ George Dabis, opns mgr; Barry Rose, sls VP; Sandie Dibble, natl sls mgr & mktg mgr; Tara Cortez, prom mgr; Kevin Brown, progmg dir; Larry Elliott, mus dir; Brenda Ross, news dir; Susie Lee, pub affrs dir.

Beverly Hills

KKGO(AM)— October 1947: 1260 khz; 5 kw-U, DA-2. TL: N34 14 58 W118 27 15. 1500 Cotner Ave., Los Angeles 90025. Phone: (310) 478-5540. Fax: (310) 445-1439. Web Site: www.ksurf.com. Licensee: Mount Wilson FM Broadcasters Inc. (acq 11-20-92; $2.5 million;. FTR: 12-14-92). Rep: D & R Radio. Fisher, Wayland, Cooper, Leader & Zaragoza L.L.P. Format: Adult standards. News staff: 6; News: 22 hrs wkly. Target aud: 35 plus. ♦ Saul Levine, pres & gen mgr; Mike Johnson, opns dir.

Big Bear City

KBHR(FM)— Dec 17, 1995: 93.3 mhz; 1.5 kw. 663 ft. TL: N34 16 41 W116 47 31. Stereo. Box 2979, 501 W. Valley Blvd., Suite C-3 92314. Phone: (909) 584-5247. Fax: (909) 584-5347. E-mail: info@kbhr933.com. Web Site: www.kbhr933.com. Licensee: Parallel Broadcasting Inc. (acq 1-17-95; 3-13-95). Network: CNN Radio. Format: Triple A. News staff: one; News: 11 hrs wkly. Target aud: 25-54; upscale second home owners, resort visitors. Spec prog: CNN news 8 hrs, ski report one hr, fish report one hr wkly. ♦ Cathy Herrick, VP & opns dir; Jay Tunnell, sls dir; Rick Herrick, pres, gen mgr & progmg dir.

Big Bear Lake

KXSB(FM)— May 1, 1975: 101.7 mhz; 90 w. 1,500 ft. TL: N34 12 47 W116 51 59. (CP: 300 w). Stereo. Box 6940, 200 S. A St., Oxnard 93030. Secondary address: 1950 S. Sunwest Ln., #302, San Bernarino 92408. Phone: (909) 825-5020. Fax: (909) 884-5844. Fax: (909) 890-3849. E-mail: edith@radiolazer.com. Web Site: www.radiolazer.com. Licensee: Lazer Broadcasting Corp. (group owner; acq 1995; $750,000).

Rep: Lotus Entravision Reps LLC. Fletcher, Heald & Hildreth. Format: CHR, Sp. News staff: one; News: 2 hrs wkly. Target aud: 25-54; adults, serious minded. ♦ Alfredo Plascencia, CEO & pres; Vicki Bails, VP; Gerardo Palafox, prom dir; Salvador Prieto, progmg dir; Juan Carlos Hidalgo, progmg mgr.

Big Pine

KRHV(FM)— 1999: 93.3 mhz; 850 w. Ant 2,926 ft. TL: N36 58 33 W118 07 05. Box 1284, Mammoth Lakes 93546. Secondary address: 94 Laurel Mountain Rd., Mammoth Lakes 93546. Phone: (760) 934-8888. Fax: (760) 934-2429. E-mail: kmmtradioworks@yahoo.com. Licensee: David & Mary Digerness. Format: Classic rock. ♦ David A. Digerness, pres & chief of engrg; Shellie Woods, gen mgr, gen sls mgr, mktg dir & adv dir; Maryanne Digerness, stn mgr, gen sls mgr, mktg dir & adv dir; Spencer Myers, progmg dir.

Bishop

KBOV(AM)— Apr 1, 1953: 1230 khz; 1 kw-U. TL: N37 20 44 W118 23 43. Box 757 93515. Secondary address: S. Hwy. 395 93514. Phone: (760) 873-6324. Phone: (760) 873-5427. Fax: (760) 872-2639. E-mail: kibskbov@gnet.com. Web Site: www.395.com. Licensee: Great Country Broadcasting Inc. (acq 7-6-2004; $965,000. with co-located FM). Network: ABC Information & Entertainment. Rep: Western Regional Broadcast Sales. Format: Oldies. News staff: one; News: 8 hrs wkly. Target aud: General. ♦ John Dailey, gen mgr.

KIBS(FM)—Co-owned with KBOV(AM). Nov 1, 1974: 100.7 mhz; 1 kw. 2,960 ft. TL: N37 25 00 W118 11 00. Stereo. Format: Country. News staff: one; News: 8 hrs wkly.

*KWTW(FM)— 2002: 88.5 mhz; 900 w. Ant 2,916 ft. TL: N37 24 48 W118 11 08. Stereo. Box 637 93515. Secondary address: 125 S. Main St. 93514. Phone: (760) 872-4225. Fax: (760) 872-4155. E-mail: friar@schat.com. Web Site: www.kwtw.org. Licensee: Living Proof Inc. Format: Christian, relg. Target aud: General; all who want to hear the gospel. ♦ Daniel McClenaghan, pres & gen mgr.

Blue Lake

KCIK(AM)—Not on air, target date: unknown: 1450 khz; 250 w-U. TL: N40 52 52 W123 59 58. Box 180, Tahoma 96142. Phone: (530) 584-5700. Fax: (530) 584-5705. Web Site: www.ihradio.org. Licensee: IHR Educational Broadcasting (group owner; acq 3-28-03). Format: Relg-Catholic. ♦ Douglas M. Sherman, pres & gen mgr.

Blythe

KJMB(FM)— April 1975: 100.3 mhz; 36.4 kw. 174 ft. TL: N33 37 16 W114 35 28. Stereo. 681 N. 4th St. 92225. Phone: (760) 922-7143. Fax: (760) 922-2844. Licensee: Blythe Radio Inc. Network: USA. Format: Adult contemp. News staff: one; News: 10 hrs wkly. Target aud: 18-40; adults. Spec prog: Farm 5 hrs wkly. ♦ Jim Mayson, pres; James M. Morris, gen mgr.

Brawley

KROP(AM)—Licensed to Brawley. See El Centro

KSEH(FM)— April 4, 1988: 94.5 mhz; 50 kw. Ant 302 ft. TL: N32 54 40 W115 31 40. Stereo. 1803 N. Imperial Ave., El Centro 92243. Phone: (760) 482-7777. Fax: (760) 482-0099. Licensee: Entravision Holdings LLC. Group owner: Entravision Communications Corp. Network: ABC. Format: Latin pop. Target aud: 25-54. ♦ Eric Chavez, gen mgr.

KSIQ(FM)—Licensed to Brawley. See El Centro

Buena Park

*KBPK(FM)— July 6, 1970: 90.1 mhz; 20 w. 130 ft. TL: N33 51 35 W118 00 53. 321 E. Chapman Ave., Fullerton 92832. Phone: (714) 992-7419. E-mail: info@kbpk-fm.com. Web Site: www.kbpk-fm.com. Licensee: Buena Park School District. Booth, Freret, Imlay & Tepper. Format: Adult contemp. Target aud: 25-54. ♦ Edward Ford, opns dir; Peg Stewart, news dir; Jack Townsend, chief of engrg.

Directory of Radio

Burney

*KIBC(FM)— Nov 15, 1985: 90.5 mhz; 3 kw. 1,456 ft. TL: N40 52 29 W121 46 13. Box 1717, 20410 Marquette St. 96013. Phone: (530) 335-5422. E-mail: pastorbud@kibcfm.org. Web Site: www.kibcfm.org. Licensee: Burney Educational Broadcasting Foundation. Format: Educ, relg mus. Target aud: General. ♦ Wayne Hennessey, gen mgr; Jack Drake, chief of engrg.

*KNCA(FM)— July 1992: 89.7 mhz; 2.28 kw. 1,465 ft. TL: N40 52 30 W121 46 14. Stereo. Southern Oregon State College, 1250 Siskiyou Blvd., Ashland, OR 97520. Phone: (541) 552-6301. Web Site: www.jeffnet.org. Licensee: The State of Oregon, acting by and through the State Board of Higher Education. Network: Network: NPR, PRI. Ernest Sanchez. Format: Jazz, AAA, news. News staff: one; News: 45 hrs wkly. Target aud: General. Spec prog: Blues 6 hrs, folk 3 hrs, pub affrs 7 hrs wkly. ♦ Mitchell Christian, CFO; Ronald Kramer, CEO & gen mgr; Bryon Lambert, opns dir; Paul Westhelle, dev dir.

KRRX(FM)—Licensed to Burney. See Redding

Calexico

KICO(AM)— Apr 6, 1946: 1490 khz; 1 kw-U. TL: N32 41 58 W115 30 10. Box 232, 695 Hwy. 111 92231. Phone: (760) 357-5055. Fax: (760) 357-4168. Licensee: Hanson Broadcasting Co. of California (acq 10-22-2003). Rep: Caballero. Format: Sp. Target aud: 18-49; Hispanic. ♦ Douglas Hanson, gen mgr; Paul Raine, gen sls mgr; Noe Diaz, progmg mgr.

KQVO(FM)—Co-owned with KICO(AM). March 1984: 97.7 mhz; 6 kw. Ant 305 ft. TL: N32 40 48 W115 25 36. Stereo. c/o KPBS-FM, 5200 Campanile Dr., San Diego 92182-5400. Phone: (619) 594-1515. Fax: (619) 594-3812. Web Site: www.kpbs.org. Network: NPR. Format: News/talk, classical. ♦ Doug Myrland, gen mgr.

*KUBO(FM)— 1989: 88.7 mhz; 3 kw. 272 ft. TL: N32 47 57 W115 30 12. 531 Main St., #2, El Centro 92243. Phone: (760) 337-8051. Phone: (760) 337-8053. Fax: (760) 337-8519. E-mail: carlosleon @radiobilingue.com. Web Site: www.radiobilingue.com. Licensee: Radio Bilingue Inc. Format: Multilingual, Ethnic, Sp. News staff: 5; News: 3 hrs wkly. Target aud: 16-60; Latino. ♦ Hugo Morales, CEO; Maria Erana, opns dir; Maria Esana, progmg dir.

California City

KCEL(FM)— May 22, 1999: 106.9 mhz; 2.35 kw. Ant 522 ft. TL: N35 12 44 W117 45 11. Aloha Plaza, 8401 Calif. City Blvd., # 9 93505. Phone: (760) 373-1069. Fax: (760) 373-8808. E-mail: kcel@kcel.com. Web Site: www.kcel.com. Licensee: Point Broadcasting Co. Group owner: Point Broadcasting Company (acq 12-29-2003; $500,000). Network: ABC. Format: Rgnl Sp. News staff: one. Target aud: General. Spec prog: Gospel 3 hrs wkly.

Calipatria

KSSB(FM)— Feb 8, 1997: 100.9 mhz; 3 kw. Ant 148 ft. TL: N33 07 12 W115 30 47. Box 1708 92233. Phone: (760) 348-7908. Phone: (760) 344-5757. Fax: (760) 348-7908. Licensee: Phillip J. Plank. (acq 3-21-94; 6-20-94). News staff: one; News: 6 hrs wkly. Target aud: 25 plus; female/male. Spec prog: Religious 6 hrs wkly. ♦ Philip Plank, CEO & progmg dir; Theresa Plank, gen mgr; Dan Roman, opns mgr; Gene Carl, sls dir; Jennifer Plank, prom VP.

Calistoga

KXTS(FM)— 1996: 100.9 mhz; 64 w. 2,945 ft. TL: N38 40 10 W122 37 52. 2046 W. F St., Napa 94558. Phone: (707) 253-0665. Fax: (707) 258-8714. Licensee: Sinclair Telecable Inc. Group owner: Sinclair Communications Inc. (acq 8-3-2001; $3.5 million). Format: Spanish. Target aud: 25-52; upscale - 60% female. ♦ Bob Sinclair, pres; Debbie Morton, gen mgr & sls VP; George Carl, stn mgr; Krista Bowker, opns VP; Stacey Boyer, prom VP.

Camarillo

*KMRO(FM)— Jan 19, 1987: 90.3 mhz; 4.43 kw. Ant 1,250 ft. TL: N34 24 47 W119 11 10. Stereo. 2310 Ponderosa Dr., Suite 28 93010. Phone: (805) 482-4797. Fax: (805) 388-5202. E-mail: info@nuevavida.com. Web Site: www.nuevavida.com. Licensee: The Association for Community Education Inc. Miller & Neely. Format: Relg, Sp. Target aud: General; Hispanics. ♦ Phil Guthrie, pres; Mary Guthrie, gen mgr.

Stations in the U.S. California

KOCP(FM)— Aug 15, 1972: 95.9 mhz; 5 kw. 813 ft. TL: N34 06 47 W119 03 34. (CP: 1.25 kw, ant 1,440 ft. TL: 34 20 55 W119 20 13). Stereo. 2284 S. Victoria, Suite 2-G, Ventura 93003. Phone: (805) 289-1400. Fax: (805) 644-7906. E-mail: perryinthemorning@yahoo.com. Web Site: www.theoctopus959.com. Licensee: Gold Coast Broadcasting LLC (group owner; acq 1995; $1.2 million. with KMXO(AM) Santa Paula). Rep: Katz Radio. Format: Classic rock. Target aud: 25-54.

Cambria

KPYG(FM)— Oct 1, 1984: 94.9 mhz; 25 kw. 328 ft. TL: N35 31 26 W121 03 40. Stereo. 396 Buckley Rd., Suite 2, San Luis Obispo 93401. Phone: (805) 786-2580. Fax: (805) 547-9860. Web Site: www.kpyg.com. Licensee: Mapleton Communications LLC (group owner; acq 5-23-02; grpsl). Rep: Allied Radio Partners. Haley, Bader & Potts. Format: AAA. Target aud: 25-54. ♦Nancy Leichter, gen mgr.

KTEA(FM)— Nov 9, 2003: 103.5 mhz; 1.46 kw. Ant 679 ft. TL: N35 34 25.6 W121 04 36.7. 2976 Burton Dr. 93428. Phone: (805) 927-7079. E-mail: jim@ktea-pm.com. Web Site: www.kteafm.com. Licensee: James Robert Kampschroer. Format: Big band. ♦James Robert Kampschroer, pres & gen mgr; Rose Mary Kampschroer, progmg dir.

Camino

*KYCJ(FM)— 2005: 88.3 mhz; 50 w vert. Ant 508 ft. TL: N38 44 18 W120 42 10. 9019 N. West Ln., Stockton 95210-1401. Phone: (209) 477-3690. Fax: (209) 477-2762. E-mail: kycc@kycc.org. Web Site: www.kycc.org. Licensee: Your Christian Companion Network Inc. Format: Gospel, inspirational, adult contemp. ♦Shirley Garner, gen mgr.

Canyon Country

KHTS(AM)— June 1989: 1220 khz; 1 kw-D, 500 w-N, DA-2. TL: N34 27 55 W118 24 08. Stereo. 27225 Camp Plenty Rd., Suite 8, Santa Clarita 91351. Phone: (661) 298-1220. Fax: (661) 298-2020. Web Site: www.hometownstation.com. Licensee: Jeri Lyn Broadcasting Inc. (acq 10-24-2003; $900,000). Format: Full svc. ♦Carl Goldman, gen mgr.

Carlsbad

KUSS(FM)— Aug 22, 1965: 95.7 mhz; 29 kw. 639 ft. TL: N32 50 24 W117 14 52. Stereo. 9660 Granite Ridge Rd., San Diego 92123. Phone: (858) 292-2000. Fax: (858) 278-7957. Web Site: www.us957.com. Licensee: Citicasters Licenses L.P. Group owner: Clear Channel Communications Inc. (acq 5-4-99; grpsl). Hogan and Hartson. Format: Sixties and Seventies. Target aud: 25-54; general. ♦John Hogan, pres; Mike Glickenhaus, gen mgr; Jim Richards, opns VP; Cory Cuddeback, sls dir.

Carmel

KBOQ(FM)—Licensed to Carmel. See Monterey

KCDU(FM)— Apr 29, 1971: 101.7 mhz; 800 w. 590 ft. TL: N36 33 12 W121 47 05. Stereo. 60 Garden Ct., Suite 300, Monterey 93940-5341. Phone: (831) 658-5200. Fax: (831) 658-5299. Web Site: www.1017thebeach.com. Licensee: Mapleton Communications L.L.C. (group owner; acq 1-17-02; grpsl). Rep: McGavren Guild. Leventhal, Senter & Lerman. Format: Adult contemp 80s & 90s. Target aud: 25-54; upscale, educated, above average income. ♦Adam Nathanson, pres; Raul Salvador, CFO; Dale Hendry, gen mgr; Mike Anthony, opns VP; Ed Monroe, sls dir, gen sls mgr & natl sls mgr.

KRML(AM)— Dec 25, 1957: 1410 khz; 500 w-D, 16 w-N, 2.5 kw-U. TL: N36 32 06 W121 53 34. Stereo. Box 7300, The Eastwood Bldg., Carmel-By-The-Sea 93921. Phone: (831) 624-6431. Fax: (831) 624-6432. Secondary address: 236 Crossroads Blvd. 93923. Phone: (831) 625-5598. E-mail: info@thejazzandbluescompany.com. Web Site: www.thejazzandbluescompany.com. Licensee: Wisdom Broadcasting Co. Inc. (acq 4-23-2004; $725,000). Rep: A/D. McGavern Guild Putbrese, Hunsaker & Trent, P. Format: Blues, jazz. Target aud: 20 plus. Spec prog: Gospel 6 hrs wkly. ♦David Kimball, CFO.

Carmel Valley

KRXA(AM)— July 10, 1989: 540 khz; 10 kw-D, 500 w-N, DA-2. TL: N36 39 38 W121 32 29. Stereo. 495 Elder Ave., Suite 7, Sand City 93955. Phone: (831) 394-5792. Fax: (831) 899-7600. Web Site: www.krxa540.com. Licensee: KRFA-AM LLC (group owner; (acq 7-8-2005; $800,000). Format: Talk. ♦Hal Ginsberg, gen mgr; Matt Renner, opns dir; Peter B. Collins, progmg mgr.

Carmichael

KFIA(AM)— Jan 11, 1979: 710 khz; 25 kw-D, 1 kw-N, DA-2. TL: N38 49 58 W121 19 03. 1425 River Park Dr., Suite 520, Sacramento 95815. Phone: (916) 924-0710. Fax: (916) 924-1587. Licensee: Vista Broadcasting Inc. Group owner: Salem Communications Corp. (acq 2-15-95; FTR: 5-8-95). Format: Relg. Target aud: 35 plus; general. ♦Edward Atsinger III, pres; Robert B. Fox, gen mgr; Steve Gasser, opns mgr.

Carnelian Bay

KODS(FM)—Licensed to Carnelian Bay. See Reno NV

Carpinteria

KSBL(FM)— June 1, 1981: 101.7 mhz; 310 w. 810 ft. TL: N34 27 55 W119 40 37. Stereo. 414 E. Cota St., Santa Barbara 93101. Phone: (805) 879-8300. Fax: (805) 879-8430. Web Site: www.ksbl.com. Licensee: Citicasters Licenses L.P. Group owner: Clear Channel Communications Inc. (acq 5-4-99; grpsl). Network: Network: ABC, AP Radio. Format: Adult contemp. Target aud: 25-54; women. ♦Keith Royer, opns VP; Vince Hollian, gen sls mgr; Lin Aubuchon, prom dir.

Cartago

KWTY(FM)— November 1989: 102.9 mhz; 2 kw. -1,787 ft. TL: N36 19 16 W118 01 22. Stereo. Box 91, Olancha 93549. Phone: (760) 764-1111. Fax: (760) 764-1111. E-mail: gm@kwty.com. Licensee: Mark A. Miller (acq 7-25-2005). Format: Classic rock, rock. News: 7 hrs wkly. Target aud: General; 15-55 years (M-F), recreation/resort commuters. ♦Dan Owen, sls dir; Mark Miller, gen mgr, stn mgr & chief of engrg.

Cathedral City

KWXY(AM)—Licensed to Cathedral City. See Palm Springs

KWXY-FM—Licensed to Cathedral City. See Palm Springs

Ceres

*KBES(FM)— Sept 1, 1979: 89.5 mhz; 150 w horiz. 131 ft. TL: N37 35 21 W120 57 23. Box 4116, Modesto 95352. Phone: (209) 538-4130. Fax: (209) 538-2795. Web Site: www.betnahrain.org. Licensee: Bet Nahrain Inc. Format: Syrian. ♦Dr. Sargon Dadesho, gen mgr; Seimon Mamio, chief of engrg.

KVIN(AM)— Sept 15, 1963: 920 khz; 2.5 kw-U, DA-2. TL: N37 35 49 W121 04 15. 961 N. Emerald Ave., Ste A, Modesto 95351. Phone: (209) 544-1055. Fax: (209) 544-1055. E-mail: theriver@krvr.com. Web Site: www.krvr.com. Licensee: Threshold Communications (acq 9-5-01; $400,000). Format: Smooth jazz. ♦Jim Bryan, gen mgr.

Chester

KWLU(FM)— Apr 6, 1989: 98.9 mhz; 25 kw. Ant 2,463 ft. TL: N40 14 00 W120 01 11. Stereo. 5700 West Oaks Blvd., Rocklin 95765. Phone: (916) 251-1600. Fax: (916) 251-1650. Licensee: Educational Media Foundation. (acq 6-30-2005; $900,000 with KPCO(AM) Quincy). Format: Christian. ♦Lloyd Parker, gen mgr.

Chico

*KCHO(FM)— Apr 22, 1969: 91.7 mhz; 7.71 kw. 1,219 ft. TL: N39 57 30 W121 42 48. Stereo. California State Univ. 95929-0500. Phone: (530) 898-5896. Fax: (530) 898-4348. Web Site: www.kcho.org. Licensee: California State University, Chico Research Foundation. Network: Network: PRI, NPR. Cohn & Marks. Format: Class, jazz, news & info. News staff: one; News: 37 hrs wkly. Target aud: General. ♦Jack Brown, gen mgr; Beth Heberle, mktg dir; Steve McAleer, mktg mgr.

KFMF(FM)— Feb 1, 1974: 93.9 mhz; 2 kw. 1,128 ft. TL: N39 56 46 W121 43 17. Stereo. 1459 Humboldt Rd., Suite D 95928. Phone: (530) 899-3600. Fax: (530) 343-0243. Web Site: www.kfm.com. Licensee: Regent Broadcasting West Coast Inc. Group owner: Regent Communications Inc. (acq 8-21-97; grpsl). Rep: Christal. Format: Active rock. News staff: one; News: one hr wkly. Target aud: 18-44. ♦Dick Stein, gen mgr; Bill Wellington, opns mgr & news dir; Brian Fox, prom dir; Marty Griffin, progmg dir.

*KHAP(FM)— 1999: 89.1 mhz; 12 kw. 285 ft. TL: N39 43 37 W121 40 45. Box 7573 95927-7573. Phone: (530) 877-5650. Fax: (916) 641-8238. E-mail: kebr@jps.net. Web Site: www.familyradio.com.yes Licensee: Family Stations Inc. (group owner) Format: Relg, educ. ♦Harold Camping, pres; Thad McKinney, gen mgr.

KHSL-FM—See Paradise

KKXX(AM)—See Paradise

KLRS(FM)— June 1993: 92.7 mhz; 1.5 kw. 643 ft. TL: N39 48 25 W121 37 35. 856 Manzanita Ct. 95926. Phone: (530) 342-2200. Fax: (530) 342-2260. Web Site: www.colorsradio.com. Licensee: Results Radio Licensee L.L.C. Group owner: Fritz Communications Inc. (acq 6-11-99; grpsl). Format: Top 40. ♦Bob Cross, gen mgr; John Graham, gen sls mgr; Eric Brown, progmg dir.

KMXI(FM)—Listing follows KPAY(AM).

KPAY(AM)— Apr 17, 1935: 1290 khz; 5 kw-U, DA-N. TL: N39 44 00 W121 44 10. Stereo. 2654 Cramer Ln. 95928. Phone: (530) 345-0021. Fax: (530) 893-2121. Web Site: www.kpay.com. Licensee: Deer Creek Broadcasting LLC. (group owner; (acq 9-8-2004; grpsl). Format: News/talk. Target aud: 25 plus. ♦Dino Corbin, gen mgr & progmg mgr; Lisa Fitzgerald, mktg dir & prom dir; Larry Scott, progmg dir; Veronica Carter, mus dir.

KMXI(FM)—Co-owned with KPAY(AM). Nov 16, 1972: 95.1 mhz; 8.7 kw. 1,171 ft. TL: N39 56 46 W121 43 17. Stereo. Web Site: (530) 893-2121. Format: Adult contemp.

KQPT(FM)—(Colusa). September 1986: 107.5 mhz; 28 kw. 600 ft. TL: N39 17 17 W122 20 02. Stereo. 1459 Humboldt Rd., Suite D 95928-9100. Phone: (530) 899-3600. Fax: (530) 343-0243. Web Site: www.107thepoint.com. Licensee: Regent Broadcasting West Coast Inc. Group owner: Regent Communications Inc. (acq 8-21-97; grpsl). Rep: Christal. Format: Modern adult contemp. Target aud: 24-48. ♦Dick Stein, VP & gen mgr; Marty Griffin, progmg dir.

KZAP(FM)—See Paradise

*KZFR(FM)— July 6, 1990: 90.1 mhz; 6.3 kw. 587 ft. TL: N39 48 25 W121 37 35. Stereo. Box 3173 95927. Secondary address: 341 Broadway, Suite 411 95928. Phone: (530) 895-0706/895-0788. Fax: (530) 895-0775. Web Site: www.kzfr.org. Licensee: Golden Valley Community Broadcasters. Format: Div, news/talk. News: 8 hrs wkly. Spec prog: American Indian 2 hrs, Sp 6 hrs wkly. ♦Jill L. Paydon, gen mgr.

China Lake

*KFRJ(FM)— 2005: 91.1 mhz; 3 kw. Ant 1,282 ft. TL: N35 28 41 W117 41 58. Family Stations Inc., 4135 Northgate Blvd., Suite 1, Sacramento

California

95834. Phone: (510) 568-6200. Fax: (510) 568-6190. Web Site: familyradio.com. Licensee: Family Stations Inc. (group owner). Format: Relg. ♦Harold Camping, gen mgr.

KSSI(FM)— 1995: 102.7 mhz; 3 kw. -22 ft. TL: N35 39 06 W117 40 58. 701 Inyokern Rd., Suite C, Ridgecrest 93555. Phone: (760) 446-5774. Fax: (760) 446-5774. E-mail: kssirock@iwvisp.com. Web Site: www.kssifm.com. Licensee: Sound Enterprises. Format: AOR. Target aud: 25-54; general. ♦John Perrige, gen mgr.

Chowchilla

KNTO(FM)— Aug 1, 1992: 93.3 mhz; 2.95 kw. 335 ft. TL: N37 13 01 W120 11 57. Box 1039, 4043 Geer Rd., Hughson 95326. Phone: (209) 883-8760. Fax: (209) 883-8769. Web Site: www.lafavorita.net. Licensee: KSKD Inc. (acq 4-17-01; $450,000). Format: Sp, Mexican music. Target aud: 18-35; teens, young adults. ♦Nelson Gomez, pres & gen mgr; Ricardo Torres, progmg dir; Freddy Lopez, news dir.

Chualar

KHDC(FM)—Licensed to Chualar. See Salinas

Claremont

***KSPC(FM)**— February 1956: 88.7 mhz; 3 kw. -265 ft. TL: N34 05 38 W117 42 35. Stereo. Pomona College, 340 N. College Ave. 91711-6340. Phone: (909) 621-8157. Fax: (909) 607-1259. E-mail: director@kspc.org. Web Site: www.kspc.org. Licensee: Pomona College. Format: Alternative rock, div, jazz. Target aud: General. Spec prog: Pol 3 hrs, reggae 8 hrs, blues 4 hrs, pub affrs 3 hrs, hip hop/rap 6 hrs wkly.

KWKU(AM)—See Pomona

Cloverdale

KSRT(FM)— 2002: 107.1 mhz; 3.5 kw. Ant 430 ft. TL: N38 48 34 W123 02 56. 6640 Redwood Dr., Suite 202, Robert Park 94928. Phone: (707) 584-1058. Fax: (707) 584-7944. E-mail: jfritz@sonic.net. Web Site: www.jammin1071.com. Licensee: Results Radio of Sonoma Licensee LLC. (acq 11-5-2004; $2.9 million). Format: Urban top-40. ♦Neysa Hinton, gen mgr & gen sls mgr; Lauren Michaels, progmg dir; Ron Castro, chief of engrg.

Clovis

KFPT(AM)— May 2, 1977: 790 khz; 5 kw-D, 2.5 kw-N, DA-2. TL: N36 50 39 W119 41 13. 1071 W. Shaw Ave., Fresno 93711. Phone: (559) 490-1019. Fax: (559) 490-5889. Licensee: Infinity Radio Inc. Group owner: Infinity Broadcasting Corp. (acq 4-4-97; $6 million. with KOQO-FM Fresno). Rep: Katz Hispanic. Leventhal, Senter & Lerman. Format: Sp oldies. Target aud: 35 plus; Hispanic adults. ♦John Sykes, CEO; Jacques Tortoroli, CFO; Lisa Decker, VP; Chris Pancheo, gen mgr.

KOND(FM)—Licensed to Clovis. See Madera

Coachella

***KBXO(FM)**—Not on air, target date: unknown: 90.3 mhz; 340 w. Ant 574 ft. TL: N33 48 08 W116 13 30. Box 1924, Tulsa, OK 74101. Phone: (918) 455-5693. Web Site: www.oasisnetwork.org. Licensee: Creative Educational Media Corp. Inc. Format: Relg. ♦David Ingles, pres & gen mgr; David Warren, stn mgr & progmg dir.

KCLB-FM—Listing follows KNWZ(AM).

KNWZ(AM)— 1954: 970 khz; 5 kw-D, 1 kw-N, DA-2. TL: N33 41 12 W116 09 34. 1321 North Gene Autry Trail, Palm Springs 92262. Phone: (760) 322-7890. Fax: (760) 322-5493. Licensee: Morris Communications Corp. Group owner: Morris Communications Inc. (acq 1998; $7 million with co-located FM). Network: UPI. Format: Talk. Target aud: 18-49. ♦William S. Morris IV, chmn; William S. Morris III, pres; Darrel Fry, CFO; Michael Osterhaut, VP; Keith Martin, gen mgr; Gary Demardney, opns dir; David Nola, sls dir; Pete Fox, prom dir; Brian Long, progmg dir.

KCLB-FM—Co-owned with KNWZ(AM). Sept 1, 1960: 93.7 mhz; 26.5 kw. 640 ft. TL: N33 44 07 W116 13 27. Stereo. Format: Rock (AOR). Target aud: 18-54. ♦Dave Sparks, progmg dir.

***KPSH(FM)**—Not on air, target date: unknown: 90.9 mhz; 230 w. Ant 623 ft. TL: N33 52 03 W116 25 58. Family Worship Center Church Inc., 8919 World Ministry Ave., Baton Rouge, LA 70810. Phone: (225) 768-3374. Web Site: www.jsm.org. Licensee: Family Worship Center Church Inc. (group owner; acq 2-18-2004; $750,000. for CP). ♦Jimmy Swaggart, pres; David Whitelow, stn mgr; John Santiago, progmg dir.

Coalinga

***KDKL(FM)**— 1999: 88.3 mhz; 1.45 kw vert. 2,329 ft. TL: N36 22 11 W120 38 37. 5700 W. Oaks Blvd., Rocklin 95765. Phone: (800) 372-0888. Fax: (916) 251-1650. Web Site: www.klove.com. Licensee: Educational Media Foundation (acq 10-20-00; $80,000. for CP). Format: Contemp Christian. ♦Lloyd Parker, gen mgr.

***KFRP(FM)**—Not on air, target date: unknown: 90.7 mhz; 2.5 kw vert. Ant 1,197 ft. TL: N35 55 39 W120 22 46. Family Stations Inc., 4135 Northgate Blvd., Suite 1, Sacramento 95834. Phone: (510) 568-6200. Fax: (510) 568-6190. Licensee: Family Stations Inc. (group owner). Format: Relg.

KNGS(FM)—Not on air, target date: unknown: 100.1 mhz; 19 kw. Ant 794 ft. TL: N36 00 40 W120 04 26. c/o William L. Zawilla, 12550 Brookhurst, Garden Grove 92640. Phone: (714) 636-5040. Licensee: William L. Zawila. ♦William Zawila, gen mgr.

Columbia

KCVR-FM— August 1995: 98.9 mhz; 300 w. 1,443 ft. TL: N38 01 51 W120 21 03. (CP: 6 kw, ant 328 ft.). 6820 Pacific Ave., Suite A, Stockton 95207. Secondary address: 1620 N. Carpenter Rd., Bldg. D, Modesto 95351. Phone: (209) 474-0154. Fax: (209) 529-1528. Web Site: www.entravision.com. Licensee: Entravision Holdings LLC. Group owner: Entravision Communications Corp. (acq 7-28-00; grpsl). Format: Sp, btfl mus. ♦Lisa Sunday, gen mgr; Edgar Pineda, progmg dir.

Colusa

KKCY(FM)— May 1990: 103.1 mhz; 135 w. 1,964 ft. TL: N39 12 21 W121 49 11. Stereo. 861 Gray Ave, Suite K, Yuba City 95991. Phone: (530) 673-2200. Fax: (530) 673-3010. E-mail: resultsradio@syix.com. Web Site: www.kkcy.com. Licensee: Results Radio Licensee L.L.C. Group owner: Fritz Communications Inc. (acq 6-11-99; grpsl). Network: ABC Daytime Direction. Rep: Katz Radio. Kaye, Scholer, Fierman, Hays & Handler. Format: Country. News staff: one; News: 7 hrs wkly. Target aud: 18-64. Spec prog: Sp one hr wkly. ♦Jack Fritz, pres; Bob Cross, stn mgr; Michael Berry, sls dir & gen sls mgr; Dave Logasa, progmg dir.

KQPT(FM)—Licensed to Colusa. See Chico

Compton

KJLH-FM— April 1965: 102.3 mhz; 5.6 kw. Ant 338 ft. TL: N33 59 52 W118 21 32. Stereo. 161 N. La Brea Ave., Inglewood 90301. Phone: (310) 330-2200. Fax: (310) 330-5555. Fax: (310) 330-2244. E-mail: sales@kjlradio.com. Web Site: www.kjlhradio.com. Licensee: TAXI Productions Inc. (acq 6-79). Network: American Urban, ABC. Rep: McGavren Guild. Irwin, Campbell & Tannenwald. Format: Urban contemp, rhythm and blues. News staff: 2; News: 8.5 hrs wkly. Target aud: 25-49; African-American audience. Spec prog: Relg 7 hrs, gospel 6 hrs, talk 8.5 hrs, Christian 6 hrs wkly. ♦Stevland Morris, CEO; Karen Slade, gen mgr; Lawrence Williams, opns dir; Aundrae Russell, progmg dir; Jacquie Stephens, news dir; Barry Clark, chief of engrg.

Concord

KABN(AM)— June 1963: 1480 khz; 500 w-D, 5 kw-N, DA-1. TL: N38 00 59 W122 00 17. Stereo. 1255 Post St., Ste 1023, San Francisco 94109. Phone: (415) 441-3377. Fax: (415) 674-1480. Licensee: Concord Area Broadcasting Corp. Group owner: American Radio Brokers Inc./SFO (acq 3-1-86; $714,000;. FTR: 1-13-86). Format: Weather. Target aud: General. ♦Chester P. Coleman, chmn & gen mgr; Joseph Buerry, pres; J.J. Jeffries, progmg VP; Dan Tucker, progmg dir; Al Nino, progmg mgr; Merrie Melodies, mus dir; Remington Noble, news dir; Anita Martini, pub affrs dir; Phil Shea, engrg VP; Mike Dorrough, engrg dir; Richard "Julio" Haskey, chief of engrg.

***KVHS(FM)**— May 16, 1969: 90.5 mhz; 410 w. 450 ft. TL: N39 01 49 W122 00 04. Stereo. 1101 Alberta Way, Rm. S-2 94521. Phone: (925) 682-5847. Fax: (925) 609-5847. E-mail: kvhsgm@mail.com. Web Site: www.kvhs.com. Licensee: Clayton Valley High School. Format: Active/new rock, educ, alternative. Target aud: 18-34. ♦Melissa Foster-Wilson, gen mgr.

Copperopolis

KRVR(FM)— Jan 1, 1995: 105.5 mhz; 1 kw. 781 ft. TL: N37 56 55 W120 42 16. Stereo. 961 N. Emerald Ave., Suite A, Modesto 95351. Phone: (209) 544-1055. Fax: (209) 544-8105. E-mail: TheRiver@krvr.com. Web Site: krvr.com. Licensee: Threshold Communications. Rep: McGavren Guild, Interep. Donald E. Martin. Format: Smooth Jazz. Target aud: 35-64. ♦James Arata, pres; Jim Bryan, gen mgr; Doug Wulff, stn mgr & opns mgr.

Corcoran

KBLO(FM)— 1999: 102.3 mhz; 19.5 kw. Ant 380 ft. TL: N36 11 04 W119 24 01. 139 W. Olive Ave., Fresno 93728. Phone: (559) 233-8803. Fax: (559) 233-8871. Web Site: www.radiocanon.com. Licensee: Mapleton Communications LLC. (acq 6-1-2005; $2.1 million). Format: Sp. ♦Al Perez, gen mgr; Brenda Campa, gen sls mgr; Jorge Guillen, progmg dir; David Whitehead, chief of engrg.

Corning

KTHU(FM)— Apr 8, 1988: 100.7 mhz; 50 kw. 272 ft. TL: N39 53 17 W122 37 30. (CP: 20.5 kw, ant 1,742 ft.). Stereo. 856 Manzanita Ct., Chico 95926. Phone: (530) 342-2200. Fax: (530) 342-2260. E-mail: info@chicothunderheads.com. Web Site: www.chicothunderheads.com. Licensee: Results Radio Licensee L.L.C. Group owner: Fritz Communications Inc. (acq 6-11-99; grpsl). Kaye, Scholer, Fierman, Hays & Handler. Format: Classic rock. News staff: one. Target aud: 25-54. Spec prog: Sp one hr wkly. ♦Jack Fritz, pres; Bob Cross, gen mgr; John Graham, gen sls mgr; J. D. Davis, engrg VP.

Corona

KWRM(AM)— 1948: 1370 khz; 5 kw-D, 2.5 kw-N, DA-2. TL: N33 52 52 W117 32 33. Box 100 92878. Phone: (951) 737-1370. Fax: (951) 735-9572. E-mail: info@majormarket.com. Web Site: kwrm1370am.com. Licensee: Major Market Stations Inc. (acq 1968). Hardy & Carey. Format: Multilingual, sports, var/div. News staff: 2; News: 20 hrs wkly. Target aud: 18-49; young Hispanic adults. ♦John Lindvall, CFO; Marilynn Kramar, VP; Marilyn Kramer, gen mgr; William J. Roberts, CEO, chmn, pres & gen mgr; Damian Vasquez, opns dir; Esther Garzon, dev dir.

Crescent City

KCRE-FM— Mar 21, 1980: 94.3 mhz; 25 kw. Ant -305 ft. TL: N41 45 35 W124 09 49. Stereo. Box 1089 95531. Secondary address: 1345 Northcrest Dr. 95531. Phone: (707) 464-9561. Fax: (707) 464-4303. E-mail: kcre@charter.net. Licensee: KPOD L.L.C. (acq 7-30-02; $692,000). Format: Adult contemp. ♦Kelly Schellong, gen sls mgr; Renee Shanle-Hutzell, gen mgr & progmg dir; Kevin Sanders, chief of engrg.

KFVR(AM)— July 1950: 1310 khz; 1 kw-D. TL: N41 45 35 W124 09 49. 3560 Hillras Way, Fortuna 95540. Phone: (707) 725-9363. Fax: (707) 726-9446. Web Site: www.lanueva1090.com. Licensee: Del Rosario Talpa Inc. (acq 5-29-2003; $54,000). Format: Rgn Mexican. ♦Mario Meza, gen mgr.

***KHSR(FM)**— July 1999: 91.9 mhz; 800 w. 226 ft. TL: N41 50 36 W124 07 55. Stereo. Humboldt State University, 1 Harpst St., Arcata 95521. Phone: (707) 826-4807. Fax: (707) 826-6082. E-mail: khsu@humboldt.edu. Web Site: www.khsu.org. Licensee: Humboldt State University. Network: Network: NPR, PRI. Format: Class, news. Spec prog: World 14 hrs, jazz 10 hrs wkly. ♦Elizabeth Hans-McCrone, gen mgr; Charles Horn, dev dir; Katie Whiteside, progmg dir; Kevin Sanders, chief of engrg.

KPOD(AM)— Dec 5, 1959: 1240 khz; 778 w-U. TL: N41 45 35 W124 11 28. Box 1089, 1345 N. Crest Dr. 95531. Phone: (707) 464-3183. Fax: (707) 465-6703. E-mail: kpod@link.cc.com. Web Site: www.kpod.com. Licensee: KPOD LLC. Group owner: Bicoastal Media LLC (acq 3-31-00; $850,000. with co-located FM). Network: ABC. Format: Adult contemp. ♦Mike Wilson, pres & gen mgr; Renee Shaulehutzell, gen mgr & progmg dir.

Stations in the U.S. California

Developers & Brokers of Radio Properties
contact American Media Services at our suite:
Philadelphia Marriott Downtown
215-625-2900
843-972-2200
americanmediaservices.com
Charleston, SC
Dallas, TX • Chicago, Il • Austin, TX
American Media Services, LLC

KPOD-FM— January 1989: 97.9 mhz; 6 kw. Ant -128 ft. TL: N41 45 35 W124 11 28. Phone: (707) 464-1000. Web Site: www.kpod.com. Network: ABC. Cohn & Marks. Format: Hot country. ♦Michelle Smith, pub affrs dir.

Culver City

KIEV(AM)—Licensed to Culver City. See Los Angeles

Cupertino

*KKUP(FM)— May 15, 1972: 91.5 mhz; 200 w. 2,294 ft. TL: N37 06 40 W121 50 36. Stereo. Box 820 95015. Phone: (408) 260-2999. Phone: (408) 260-2997. Web Site: www.kkup.org. Licensee: Assurance Sciences Foundation Inc. Format: Eclectic, alternative, blues. Target aud: General. Spec prog: Brazilian 2 hrs, African 6 hrs, Indian 3 hrs, Sp 3 hrs, Latin American 8 hrs wkly. ♦Jim Thomas, chmn; Louise Steck, gen mgr; Steve Hathaway, progmg dir; Dave Barnett, chief of engrg.

Davis

*KDVS(FM)— Jan 1, 1968: 90.3 mhz; 9.2 kw. 105 ft. TL: N38 32 29 W121 45 03. Stereo. c/o KDVS-FM, Univ. of California, 14 Lower Freeborn Hall 95616. Phone: (530) 752-0728. Fax: (530) 752-8548. E-mail: gm@kdvs.org. Web Site: www.kdvs.org. Licensee: Regents of the University of California. Format: Eclectic rock, var. News: 13 hrs wkly. Target aud: General; loc community. ♦Steven Valentino, gen mgr; Heather Klinger, dev dir & sls dir; Paul Wilbur, prom dir; Brendon Boyle, progmg dir; Scenery Tirdner, progmg dir; Marcus Ulrich, news dir.

KXSE(FM)— February 1979: 104.3 mhz; 3.4 kw. Ant 436 ft. TL: N38 39 26 W121 43 12. 1436 Auburn Blvd., Sacramento 95815. Phone: (916) 646-4000. Fax: (916) 646-1958. E-mail: jverdier@entravision.com. Web Site: www.entravision.com. Licensee: Entravision Holdings LLC. Group owner: Entravision Communications Corp. (acq 7-28-2000; grpsl). Network: Network: Network: ABC, Westwood One, CBS. Mullin, Rhyne, Emmons & Topel. Format: Sp adult contemp. Target aud: 25-54. ♦Larry Lamanski, gen mgr; Joni Verdier, gen sls mgr; Salvador Lopez, prom dir & prom mgr; Nestor Rocha, progmg VP & progmg dir; Paul Waegele, chief of engrg.

Delano

KCHJ(AM)— Dec 1, 1951: 1010 khz; 5 kw-D, 1 kw-N, DA-2. TL: N35 48 40 W119 19 18. 5200 Standard St., Bakersfield 93308. Phone: (661) 327-9711. Fax: (661) 327-0797. E-mail: info@thespanishradio.com. Web Site: www.thespanishradio.com. Licensee: Illinois Lotus Corp. Group owner: Lotus Communications Corp. (acq 8-24-99; grpsl). Borsari & Paxson. Format: Sp. News staff: 2; News: 5 hrs wkly. Target aud: 18 plus; Sp speaking adults. Spec prog: Filipino 3 hrs wkly. ♦Howard Kalmenson, pres; Mike Allen, gen mgr; Bruce Thompson, stn mgr; Vicente Arias, stn mgr.

KDFO-FM— November 1968: 98.5 mhz; 50 kw. 499 ft. TL: N35 42 46 W118 47 22. 1100 Mohawk St., Suite 280, Bakersfield 93309. Phone: (661) 322-9929. Fax: (661) 283-2963. Web Site: www.985thefox.com. Licensee: Clear Channel Broadcasting Licenses Inc. Group owner: Clear Channel Communications Inc. (acq 10-16-00; grpsl). Format: Classic Rock. ♦Jim Bell, VP, gen mgr & gen mgr; Steve King, stn mgr & progmg dir; Chris Nelson, gen sls mgr; Steve Mull, chief of engrg.

KKDJ(FM)— Oct 2, 1986: 105.3 mhz; 50 kw. 547 ft. TL: N35 30 53 W119 03 41. Stereo. 1100 Mohawk St., Suite 280, Bakersfield 93309. Phone: (661) 322-9929. Fax: (661) 283-2963. Web Site: www.klite1053.com. Licensee: Clear Channel Communications Inc. (acq 4-94). Rep: McGavren Guild. Arter & Hadden. Format: Adult contemp. Target aud: 18-44. ♦Jim Bell, VP & gen mgr; Jim Bell, gen mgr; Steve King, stn mgr & progmg dir; Chris Nelson, gen sls mgr; Steve Mull, chief of engrg.

Dinuba

KRDU(AM)— Dec 26, 1946: 1130 khz; 5 kw-D, 6.2 kw-N, DA-2. TL: N36 29 03 W119 15 57. 597 N. Alta Ave. 93618. Secondary address: 83 East Shaw, Fresno 93727. Phone: (559) 591-1130. Fax: (559) 591-4822. Licensee: Capstar TX L.P. Group owner: Clear Channel Communications Inc. (acq 8-30-00; grpsl). Fletcher, Heald & Hildreth. Format: Relg. News staff: one; News: 7 hrs wkly. Target aud: 18-65. ♦Jim Tuck, gen mgr; Doug Diedrich, progmg dir; Mike Hauber, chief of engrg & chief of engrg.

KSOF(FM)—Co-owned with KRDU(AM). June 5, 1975: 98.9 mhz; 19 kw. 820 ft. TL: N36 38 15 W118 56 35. Stereo. 4991 E. McKinley, Suite 124, Fresno 93727. Phone: (559) 243-4300. Format: Soft rock. News: 2 hrs wkly. Target aud: 25-54; women. ♦Darrel Goodin, gen mgr; May Lou Goodin, opns VP; Dave Butler, gen sls mgr; Scott Keith, progmg dir; Dave Case, chief of engrg.

Dunnigan

KVMG(FM)— Sept 1, 1983: 105.5 mhz; 5.4 kw. Ant 140 ft. TL: N38 55 34 W121 54 10. Stereo. 1425 River Park Dr., Suite 520, Sacramento 95815. Phone: (916) 924-0710. Fax: (916) 924-1587. E-mail: info@1055thefish.net. Web Site: www.1055thefish.net. Licensee: Caron Broadcasting Inc. Group owner: Salem Communications Corp. (acq 1-11-2002; $8 million). Format: Christian. ♦Robert Fox, gen mgr; Steve Brock, gen sls mgr; Greg Lawson, prom dir; Mark Standriff, progmg dir; Dave Forten Berry, engrg dir.

Dunsmuir

KZRO(FM)— Dec 8, 1992: 100.1 mhz; 12.5 kw. 213 ft. TL: N41 17 20 W122 14 25. Stereo. Box 1234, Mt. Shasta 96067. Secondary address: 113 E. Alma St., Mt. Shasta 96067. Phone: (530) 926-1332. Fax: (530) 926-0737. E-mail: zmail@channelradio.com. Web Site: www.100fm.net. Licensee: Dennis Michael Crepps dba Big Tree Communications (acq 6-24-97). Network: Westwood One. Format: Classic rock, oldies. News staff: one. Target aud: 18-55; general. Spec prog: Children 2 hrs wkly. ♦Dennis Michaels, gen mgr, gen sls mgr, mktg dir, adv dir & progmg dir; Rob Hanson, chief of engrg.

Earlimart

KNAC(FM)—Not on air, target date: unknown: 93.5 mhz; 6 kw. Ant 177 ft. TL: N35 57 30 W119 15 00. 12550 Brookhurst St., Suite A, Garden Grove 92640. Phone: (714) 636-5040. Licensee: Earlimart Educational Foundation Inc. ♦William Zawila, gen mgr.

East Los Angeles

KLAX-FM— Apr 22, 1949: 97.9 mhz; 50 kw. 390 ft. TL: N34 00 24 W118 21 52. Stereo. 10281 W. Pico Blvd., Los Angeles 90064. Phone: (310) 203-0900. Fax: (310) 843-4961. Web Site: www.979laraza.com. Licensee: KLAX Licensing Inc. Group owner: Spanish Broadcasting System Inc. (acq 2-87). Rep: Caballero. Format: Sp, Rgnl Mexican. Target aud: 18-34. ♦Raul Alarcon Jr., CEO & pres; William B. Tanner, exec VP; David Haymore, gen mgr; Maria Elena Nava, opns dir & dev dir.

East Porterville

KMQA(FM)— Dec 1, 1989: 100.5 mhz; 1.5 kw. 465 ft. TL: N36 02 37 W118 56 08. (CP: 2.1 kw, ant 1,109 ft.). 1450 E. Bardsley Ave., Tulare 93274. Phone: (559) 687-3170. Fax: (559) 687-3175. E-mail: traffic@moonbroadcasting.com. Web Site: www.lamaquinamusical.net. Licensee: MBP Licensee LLC. Group owner: Moon Broadcasting (acq 12-29-98). Network: CNN Radio. Format: Mexican rgnl. Target aud: 25-40. ♦Irene Cruz, gen mgr; George Rayo, opns mgr & gen sls mgr; Pilar Reyes, gen sls mgr; Rey Ponce, prom dir.

East Sonora

*KARQ(FM)— 2005: 89.5 mhz; 1.3 kw vert. Ant 1,661 ft. TL: N38 03 46 W120 14 45. 5700 W. Oaks Blvd., Rocklin 95765. Phone: (916) 251-1600. Fax: (916) 251-1650. Web Site: www.air1.com. Licensee: Educational Media Foundation. Group owner: EMF Broadcasting. Network: Air 1. Shaw Pittman. Format: Christian. News staff: 3. Target aud: 25-44; Judeo Christian, female. ♦Richard Jenkins, pres; Mike Novak, VP; Lloyd Parker, gen mgr; Ed Lenane, opns dir; Keith Whipple, dev dir; Eric Allen, natl sls mgr; Chris Joyce, prom dir.

El Cajon

*KECR(AM)— 1955: 910 khz; 5 kw-U, DA-2. TL: N32 53 38 W116 55 35. 11865 Moreno Ave., Lakeside 92040. Phone: (619) 390-3481. Fax: (619) 443-7693. E-mail: kecr@nethere.com. Web Site: www.familyradio.com. Licensee: Family Stations Inc. (group owner: Family Stations Inc. acq 6-9-63). Format: Relg. Target aud: All ages; families. ♦Bill Babcock, gen mgr.

KHTS-FM—Licensed to El Cajon. See San Diego

El Centro

KGBA-FM—See Holtville

KICO(AM)—See Calexico

KROP(AM)—(Brawley). November 1946: 1300 khz; 1 kw-D, 500 w-N. TL: N33 00 40 W115 31 16. Box 238, 120 S. Plaza, Brawley 92227. Phone: (760) 344-1300. Fax: (760) 344-1763. Web Site: www.q96ksiq.com. Licensee: CCR-Brawley IV LLC. Group owner: Cherry Creek Radio LLC acq 6-99; $2 million. with co-located FM). Rep: Allied Radio Partners. Miller & Miller. Format: Country. Target aud: 25-54; male. ♦Tony Driskill, gen mgr; Carlos Cisneros, gen sls mgr.

KSIQ(FM)—Co-owned with KROP(AM). Sept 10, 1981: 96.1 mhz; 50 kw. 340 ft. TL: N32 57 12 W115 30 05. Stereo. Web Site: www.q96ksiq.com. Format: Mainstream top-40. News: one hr wkly. Target aud: 25-49; female. ♦Stephen Stodelle, mktg mgr & adv mgr; Tony Driskill, prom mgr & progmg mgr; Clif Glasgow, engrg dir.

KWST(AM)— June 21, 1958: 1430 khz; 1 kw-U. TL: N32 48 27 W115 32 18. Stereo. 1803 N. Imperial Ave. 92243. Phone: (760) 482-7777. Fax: (760) 482-0099. Web Site: www.univision.com. Licensee: Entravision Holding L.L.C. Group owner: Entravision Communications Co. L.L.C. (acq 1998; $4.8 million). Format: Adult contemp, oldies. Target aud: 25-49. ♦Albert Valdez, pres & opns mgr; Eric Chavez, gen mgr.

KXO(AM)— January 1927: 1230 khz; 1 kw-U. TL: N32 46 34 W115 32 58. Box 140 92244. Phone: (760) 352-1230. Web Site: www.kxoradio.com. Licensee: KXO Inc. (acq 1961). Network: CBS. Rep: McGavren Guild. Format: Oldies. Target aud: 18-49. Spec prog: Farm 7 hrs wkly. ♦Caroll Buckley, VP, gen sls mgr, prom mgr & progmg dir; Gene Brister, pres & gen mgr; Doug Melanson, chief of engrg.

KXOJ-FM—Co-owned with KYAL(AM). Feb 22, 1977: 100.9 mhz; 5 kw. 360 ft. TL: N36 03 38 W96 06 03. Stereo. E-mail: mail@kxoj.com. Web Site: www.kxoj.com. Format: Contemp Christian mus. ♦Mike Stephens, CEO; David Stephens, stn mgr, opns dir, dev dir & adv dir.

KXOX-FM— Apr 7, 1976: 96.7 mhz; 2.9 kw. 154 ft. TL: N32 29 16 W100 23 31. Stereo. News staff: one.

KXO-FM— Aug 2, 1976: 107.5 mhz; 25.5 kw. 155 ft. TL: N32 46 35 W115 32 58. Stereo. (Acq 1976.). Format: Adult contemp. Target aud: 25-49.

KXOQ(FM)—Co-owned with KOTC(AM). Dec 13, 1995: 104.3 mhz; 6 kw. 328 ft. TL: N36 21 01 W90 02 43. Phone: (573) 888-9878. Format: Oldies.

El Cerrito

*KECG(FM)— September 1978: 88.1 mhz; 17 w. Ant -66 ft. TL: N37 54 30 W122 17 39. Stereo. 540 Ashbury Ave. 94530. Phone: (510) 525-4472. Phone: (510) 525-0103. Fax: (510) 525-0554. E-mail:

California

kecg88@aol.com. Web Site: www.kecg.org. Licensee: West Contra Costa Unified School District. Network: USA. Format: Div, educ, jazz. News: 5 hrs wkly. Target aud: General. Spec prog: Gospel 5 hrs, Sp 3 hrs, Filipino 2 hrs wkly. ♦Philip H. Morgan Jr., stn mgr.

El Rio

KMLA(FM)— October 1996: 103.7 mhz; 480 w. 807 ft. TL: N34 18 10 W119 13 41. 355 S. A St., Suite 103, Oxnard 93030. Phone: (805) 385-5656. Fax: (805) 385-5690. E-mail: info@lam1037.com. Web Site: www.lam1037.com. Licensee: Gold Coast Radio L.L.C. (acq 12-6-96; $550,000). Format: Rgnl Mexican. ♦Guillermo Gonzalez, gen mgr & gen sls mgr; Trinidad Bejar, stn mgr; Rosa Rodriguez, prom dir.

Ellwood

KSPE-FM—Licensed to Ellwood. See Santa Barbara

Encinitas

KPRI(FM)— Jan 20, 1962: 102.1 mhz; 14.5 kw. Ant 817 ft. TL: N33 06 40 W117 12 05. Stereo. 5015 Shoreham Pl., Suite 102, San Diego 92122. Phone: (858) 678-0102. Fax: (858) 320-7024. E-mail: ilisten@authenticrock.com. Web Site: www.authenticrock.com. Licensee: Compass Radio of San Diego Inc. (acq 1996). Rep: Katz Radio. Shaw Pittman. Format: Triple A. News staff: one; News: 2 hrs wkly. Target aud: 18-34; upscale, well educated, young adult contemp mus fans. ♦Jonathan D. Schwartz, CFO & sr VP; Bob Hughes, gen mgr & opns mgr; Patrick Osburn, sls dir; Keith Miller, prom dir; Dona Shaieb, progmg dir.

Escondido

KFSD(AM)— June 1958: 1450 khz; 1 kw-U. TL: N33 07 11 W117 07 07. 1835 Aston Ave., Carlsbad 92008. Phone: (760) 729-1000. Fax: (760) 476-9604. Web Site: www.wcbr.classic.com. Licensee: North County Broadcasting Corp. Group owner: Astor Broadcast Group (acq 9-15-87; $3 million. with co-located FM; FTR: 6-29-87). Format: Class. News: 2 hrs wkly. Target aud: 35-64. ♦Arthur Astor, CEO & pres; Peri Corso, gen mgr; Rick Roome, opns mgr.

KSOQ-FM— July 1966: 92.1 mhz; 580 w. Ant 1,024 ft. TL: N33 06 39 W117 09 13. Stereo. Box 889004, San Diego 92168-9004. Secondary address: 1615 Murray Canyon Rd., Suite 710, San Diego 92108-4321. Phone: (619) 291-9797. Phone: (619) 297-3698. Fax: (619) 543-1353. Web Site: www.kson.com. Licensee: Jefferson-Pilot Communications Co. of California. Group owner: Jefferson-Pilot Communications Co. (acq 4-1-2004; $18 million). Format: Country. ♦Darrel Goodin, gen mgr; Dave Saunders, gen sls mgr; John Marks, progmg dir; Eric Schecter, chief of engrg.

Esparto

KTTA(FM)— 1996: 97.9 mhz; 6 kw. Ant 328 ft. TL: N38 45 33 W121 52 33. 1401 El Camino Ave., Suite 330, Sacramento 95815. Phone: (916) 443-1049. Fax: (916) 441-6480. E-mail: azteca16@aol.com. Web Site: www.lakebuena.com. Licensee: Bustos Media of California License LLC. (acq 12-15-2004; $21.7 million. with KBBU(FM) Modesto). Format: Rgnl Mexican. ♦Angie Balderas, gen mgr; Juan Gonzalez, progmg dir; Mark Sedaka, chief of engrg.

Essex

KHWY(FM)— May 1, 1991: 98.9 mhz; 10 kw. Ant 1,073 ft. TL: N34 52 50 W115 04 05. Box 1668, 1611 E. Main St., Barstow 92312. Phone: (760) 256-0326. Fax: (760) 256-9507. E-mail: tim@highwayradio.com. Web Site: www.thehighwaystations.com. Licensee: KHWY Inc. Network: AP Radio. Hogan & Hartson. Format: Adult contemp. News staff: one; News: 28 hrs wkly. Target aud: 35 plus; travelers on I-40 & I-15 & Mojave Desert residents. ♦Howard B. Anderson, CEO & pres; Kirk M. Anderson, exec VP; Timothy B. Anderson, VP & gen mgr; Judy Robinson, sls VP; John Gregg, prom dir & prom mgr; Lance Todd, progmg dir; Keith Hayes, news dir; Thomas J. McNeill, engrg mgr.

Eureka

KATA(AM)—See Arcata

KEKA-FM— Nov 1, 1983: 101.5 mhz; 100 kw. 3,200 ft. TL: N40 25 12 W124 05 00. Stereo. 1101 Marsh Rd. 95501. Phone: (707) 442-5744.

1-7-91). Network: ABC. Rep: Katz Radio. Format: Modern country. Target aud: 25-54. ♦Hugo Papstein, gen mgr.

KFMI(FM)— 1973: 96.3 mhz; 30 kw. 1,580 ft. TL: N40 43 36 W123 58 18. (CP: 100 kw). Stereo. 5460 S. Broadway 95503. Phone: (707) 442-2000. Fax: (707) 443-6848. E-mail: power963@hotmail.com. Web Site: www.power963.com. Licensee: Bicoastal Media LLC. (group owner; acq 7-28-99; grpsl). Network: Jones Radio Networks. Rep: Allied Radio Partners. Format: Hot adult contemp, CHR. Target aud: 18-36; upscale adults. ♦Ken Dennis, CEO; Mike Wilson, pres; Tom Huckabay, VP & gen mgr; Laurie Tate, opns dir.

KGOE(AM)— May 12, 1933: 1480 khz; 5 kw-D, 1 kw-N. TL: N40 44 28 W124 12 05. 5640 S. Broadway 95503. Phone: (707) 443-1621. Fax: (707) 443-6848. Licensee: Bicoastal Media LLC. (group owner; acq 7-28-99; grpsl). Network: Jones Radio Networks. Format: News/talk. Target aud: 25-54. ♦Tom Huckabay, gen mgr & gen sls mgr; Rollin Treehearn, prom dir; Tom Sebourn, progmg dir; Kevin Sanders, chief of engrg.

KRED-FM— Co-owned with KGOE(AM). Dec 17, 1979: 92.3 mhz; 25 kw. 1,544 ft. TL: N40 43 37 W123 58 25. Stereo. Format: Contemp country.

KINS(AM)— January 1946: 980 khz; 5 kw-D, 500 w-N, DA-N. TL: N40 48 05 W124 07 31. 1101 Marsh Rd. 95501. Phone: (707) 442-5744. Licensee: Eureka Broadcasting Co. (acq 3-1-58). Network: Network: CBS, Wall Street. Format: News/talk. News staff: 2. Target aud: 35 plus; upscale, educated. ♦Hugo Papstein, pres, gen mgr, gen sls mgr & progmg dir; Mark Householter, chief of engrg.

KKHB(FM)— 1994: 105.5 mhz; 28 kw. 1,588 ft. TL: N40 43 52 W123 57 06. 5640 S. Broadway 95503. Phone: (707) 442-2000. Fax: (707) 443-6848. Web Site: www.cool1055.com. Licensee: Bicoastal Media L.L.C. (group owner; acq 11-9-98; grpsl). Format: Oldies. ♦Tom Huckabay, gen mgr; Laurie Tate, opns dir; Victoria Bennington, gen sls mgr; Tom Sebourn, progmg dir.

***KMUE(FM)**— Aug 9, 1996: 88.3 mhz; 1.25 kw. 1,446 ft. TL: N40 43 52 W123 57 06. Box 135, Redway 95560-0135. Secondary address: 1144 Redway Dr., Redway 95560. Phone: (707) 923-2513. Fax: (707) 923-2501. E-mail: kmud@kmud.org. Web Site: www.kmud.org. Licensee: Redwood Community Radio Inc. Format: Talk, div, educ. ♦Dave Myers, opns mgr; David Lippe, dev dir & adv mgr; Michael Jacinto, progmg dir.

KNCR(AM)—See Fortuna

KWSW(AM)— Dec 20, 1979: 790 khz; 5 kw-D, 112 w-N. TL: N40 48 09 W124 08 20. 1101 Marsh Rd. 95501. Phone: (707) 442-5744. Licensee: Eureka Broadcasting Co. Inc. (acq 11-30-92; $105,000;. FTR: 12-21-92). Format: Talk. Target aud: 35 plus; baby boomers with discretionary income. ♦Hugo Papstein, pres, gen mgr & progmg dir; Brian Papstein, gen sls mgr; Mark Householter, chief of engrg.

KXGO(FM)— (Arcata). 1970: 93.1 mhz; 50 kw. Ant 1,666 ft. TL: N40 43 38 W123 58 22. Stereo. 603 F St. 95501. Phone: (707) 445-8104. Fax: (707) 445-3906. E-mail: operations@kxgo.com. Web Site: theclassicrockexperience.com. Licensee: Miller Broadcasting Co. (acq 11-1-97). By: Christal. Format: Classic rock. Target aud: 25-54; upscale adults. ♦Pattison Christensen, pres, stn mgr & natl sls mgr; Becky Reed, opns mgr; Randy Flevares, rgnl sls mgr, prom dir & progmg mgr.

Fair Oaks

KSSJ(FM)— Nov 25, 1970: 94.7 mhz; 86.6 kw. 2,072 ft. TL: N39 15 30 W119 42 36. Stereo. 5345 Madison Ave., Sacramento 95841-3141. Phone: (916) 334-7777. Fax: (916) 339-4281. E-mail: comments@kssj.com. Web Site: www.kssj.com. Licensee: Entercom Sacramento License L.L.C. Group owner: Entercom Communications Corp. (acq 11-4-97; $15.9 million). Format: Smooth jazz. ♦David Lichtman, gen mgr; Lee Hansen, stn mgr; Fred Hormell, gen sls mgr; Michelle Bouve, prom dir.

Fairfield

***KASK(FM)**—Not on air, target date: unknown: 91.5 mhz; 75 w. 649 ft. TL: N38 19 09 W121 59 30. 4738 Allendale Rd., Vacaville 95688. Phone: (707) 446-0900. Fax: (707) 447-0680. E-mail: manager@kask.org. Web Site: www.kask.org. Licensee: Maranatha Broadcasting. Format: Relg. ♦Glenn D. Toppenberg, pres & gen mgr; Mike Robertson, news dir.

Directory of Radio

KUIC(FM)—See Vacaville

Fairmead

***KLVY(FM)**— 1998: 91.1 mhz; 3.4 kw. 256 ft. TL: N37 13 01 W120 11 57. Stereo. 5700 W. Oaks Blvd., Rocklin 95765. Phone: (916) 251-1600. Fax: (916) 251-1650. E-mail: klove@klove.com. Web Site: www.klove.com. Licensee: Educational Media Foundation Inc. Group owner: EMF Broadcasting. Network: K-Love. Shaw Pittman. Format: Contemp Christian music. News staff: 3. Target aud: 25-44; Judeo-Christian, female. ♦Richard Jenkins, pres; Mike Novak, VP & progmg dir; Lloyd Parker, gen mgr; Ed Lenane, opns dir; Keith Whipple, dev dir; Chris Joyce, prom dir & prom mgr.

Fallbrook

KSSD(FM)— Nov 22, 1977: 107.1 mhz; 3 kw. 300 ft. TL: N33 23 01 W117 11 20. Stereo. 5700 Wilshire Blvd., Suite 250, Los Angeles 90036. Phone: (323) 900-6100. Fax: (323) 900-6127. Web Site: www.superestrella.com. Licensee: Entravision Holdings LLC. Group owner: Entravision Communications Corp. (acq 4-1-03; grpsl). Rep: Lotus Entravision Reps LLC. Cohn & Marks. Format: Sp, CHR. Target aud: 18-34. ♦Jeff Liberman, VP & gen mgr; Karl Meyer, gen mgr; Robert I. Mendoza, opns mgr; Tom Bell, gen sls mgr; Armando Guerrero, mktg dir & prom; Eugene McAffe, chief of engrg & engr.

Felton

KXZM(FM)— 1999: 93.7 mhz; 28 w. Ant 1,260 ft. TL: N37 03 43 W122 07 14. 200 South A St., Suite 400, Oxnard 93030. Phone: (805) 240-2070. Fax: (805) 240-5960. Licensee: Lazer Broadcasting Corp. (group owner; (acq 7-25-2005; $2.88 million. with KXSM(FM) Hollister). Format: Rgnl Mexican. ♦Alfredo Plascencia, pres; Daniel Osuna, gen mgr.

Ferndale

KAJK-FM— Apr 1, 1993: 99.1 mhz; 6 kw. 1,715 ft. TL: N40 30 03 W124 17 08. Stereo. 603 F St., Eureka 95501. Phone: (707) 445-3699. Fax: (707) 445-3906. E-mail: operations@ckxgo.com. Web Site: www.todaysbesthito.com. Licensee: Redwood Broadcasting Co. Inc. (acq 1999). Rep: Allied Radio Partners. Rosenman & Colin. Format: Hot adult contemp. News staff: one; News: 3 hrs wkly. Target aud: 25-54; upscale adults. ♦Pattison Christensen, pres & stn mgr; Randy Flevares, progmg dir.

Firebaugh

***KAJP(FM)**—Not on air, target date: unknown: 94.7 mhz; 900 w. Ant 66 ft. TL: N36 51 37 W120 27 19. 12550 Brookhurst St. #A, Garden Grove 92840-4834. Phone: (714) 636-5040. Licensee: Central Valley Educational Services Inc. ♦William Zawila, gen mgr.

Ford City

KZPE(FM)—Not on air, target date: unknown: 102.1 mhz; 6 kw. Ant 128 ft. TL: N35 00 02 W119 22 29. c/o Katten Muchin Zavis Rosenman, 1025 Thomas Jefferson St., Suite 700 East Lobby, Washington, DC 20007-5201. Phone: (714) 636-5040. Fax: (202) 298-7570. Licensee: Estate of H.L. Charles, Robert Willing, executor (acq 6-4-2004). ♦Shelley Sadowsky, gen mgr.

Fort Bragg

KDAC(AM)— June 1948: 1230 khz; 1 kw-U. TL: N39 26 35 W123 46 48. 1400 Kuki Ln., Ukiah 95482. Phone: (707) 466-5868. Phone: (707) 969-5868. Fax: (707) 466-5852. Fax: (707) 969-5852. Web Site: www.lamaquinamusical.net. Licensee: MBU Licensee LLC. Group owner: Moon Broadcasting (acq 9-15-2003; grpsl). Network: Network: ABC, CBS. Format: Sp. News staff: one; News: 24 hrs wkly. Target aud: 35 plus. ♦Tove Sorensen, gen mgr & opns mgr.

KOZT(FM)— Dec 5, 1981: 95.3 mhz; 35 kw. Ant 515 ft. TL: N39 24 24 W123 44 04. Stereo. 110 S. Franklin 95437. Phone: (707) 964-7277. Fax: (707) 964-9536. E-mail: thecoast@kozt.com. Web Site: www.kozt.com. Licensee: California Radio Partners Inc. (acq 12-1-90; FTR: 12-17-90). Miller & Neely P.C. Format: AAA. News staff: one; News: one hr wkly. Target aud: 25-49; affluent, educated consumers. ♦Tom Yates, CEO, gen mgr & opns dir; Vicky Watts, chmn & CFO.

KPMO(AM)—See Mendocino

Stations in the U.S. — California

Developers & Brokers of Radio Properties
contact American Media Services at our suite: Philadelphia Marriott Downtown
215-625-2900
843-972-2200
americanmediaservices.com
Charleston, SC
Dallas, TX • Chicago, Il • Austin, TX
American Media Services, LLC

KSAY(FM)— November 1988: 98.5 mhz; 3500 w. 453 ft. TL: N39 26 08 W123 48 15. Stereo. Box 2269, 684 C S. Main St. 95437. Phone: (707) 964-5729. Phone: (707) 964-5623. Fax: (707) 964-2722. E-mail: traffic@ksay.com. Web Site: www.ksay.com. Licensee: Axell Broadcasting. Network: Jones Radio Networks. Format: Adult contemp. News staff: one; News: 9 hrs wkly. Target aud: 18-49; primarily women. ♦ Wade Axell, gen mgr.

Fortuna

KNCR(AM)— Oct 31, 1966: 1090 khz; 10 kw-D. TL: N40 33 30 W124 07 24. 3560 Hillars Way 95540. Phone: (707) 725-9363. Fax: (707) 726-9446. E-mail: mario@lanueva1090.com. Web Site: www.lanueva1090.com. Licensee: Del Rosario Talpa Inc. (acq 5-17-2004; $37,500). Rosenman & Colin L.L.P. Format: Rgnl Mexican. News: 2 hrs wkly. Target aud: 25-54. ♦ Mario Meza, gen mgr & progmg dir; Sylvia Meza, gen sls mgr; Susana Romero, prom dir; Lee Olson, chief of engrg.

KWPT(FM)— May 15, 1992: 100.3 mhz; 2.95 kw. 1,807 ft. TL: N40 25 23 W124 06 21. 1713 Main St. 95540. Phone: (707) 725-3408. Fax: (707) 725-3423. E-mail: dave@kupt.com. Web Site: www.kuptfm.com. Licensee: S.T.E.G. Broadcasting LLC (acq 9-14-00; $555,000). Cohn & Marks. Format: Classic Hits. Target aud: 30-54; affluent, college educated. ♦ John Butler, gen mgr, gen sls mgr & adv dir; Dave Roble, gen sls mgr, prom dir, progmg dir & mus dir; Mark Dare, chief of engrg.

Fountain Valley

KLIT(FM)— 1993: 92.7 mhz; 690 w. Ant 961 ft. TL: N33 36 20 W117 48 35. 99 Long Ct., Suite 200, Thousand Oaks 91360. Phone: (805) 497-8511. Fax: (805) 497-8514. E-mail: info@927.com. Web Site: www.lite927.com. Licensee: Amaturo Group of L.A. Ltd. Group owner: Amaturo Groups (acq 1996; $5.5 million). Network: ABC. Format: Adult contemp. Target aud: 25-54. ♦ Joseph Amaturo, CEO & VP; Catherine Moreau, gen mgr & gen sls mgr; Dave Burns, opns dir.

Fowler

KEZL(FM)— Nov 7, 1980: 96.7 mhz; 22 kw. 348 ft. TL: N36 41 39 W119 43 57. Stereo. 83 E. Shaw Ave., Suite 150, Fresno 93710-7616. Phone: (559) 230-4300. Fax: (559) 243-4301. Web Site: www.smoothjazz967.com. Licensee: Clear Channel Radio Licenses Inc. Group owner: Clear Channel Communications Inc. (acq 8-30-00; grpsl). Format: Smooth jazz. Target aud: 25-54. ♦ Jeff Megrete, gen mgr; Dave Butler, gen sls mgr; Chris Miller, prom dir; Jay Weidenheimer, progmg dir; Dave Case, chief of engrg.

KQEQ(AM)— July 1, 1962: 1210 khz; 370 w-U. TL: N36 39 37 W119 41 01. 139 W. Olive Ave., Fresno 93728. Phone: (559) 233-8803. Fax: (559) 233-8871. E-mail: rak@computermail.net. Web Site: www.radiocanon.com. Licensee: RAK Communications Inc. (acq 9-30-94; FTR: 7-4-94). Network: American Urban. Rep: Katz Radio. Format: C&W, Sp, Hmong. Target aud: 18-49; adult urban listener who is Caucasian, African-American or Hispanic. ♦ Al Perez, gen mgr.

Frazier Park

KJPG(AM)— 1994: 1050 khz; 10 kw-D, 7 w-N, DA-D. TL: N35 01 28 W118 55 05 (D), N35 24 07 W119 02 47 (N). Box 180, Tahoma 96142. Phone: (530) 584-5700. Fax: (530) 584-5705. Web Site: www.ihradio.org. Licensee: IHR Educational Broadcasting. (group owner; acq 11-15-2003; $700,000). Format: Catholic. ♦ Douglas M. Sherman, pres & VP.

Freedom

KPIG-FM— Dec 1, 1987: 107.5 mhz; 5.4 kw. Ant 338 ft. TL: N36 50 06 W121 42 22. Stereo. 1110 Main St., Suite 16, Watsonville 95076. Phone: (831) 722-9000. Fax: (831) 722-7548. E-mail: sty@kpig.com. Web Site: www.kpig.com. Licensee: Mapleton Communications L.L.C. (group owner; acq 11-16-2001; grpsl). Format: AAA. Target aud: 25-54. ♦ Dale Hendry, gen mgr; Frank Caprista, opns mgr; Ed Monroe, gen sls mgr; Laura Hopper, progmg dir; Velden Levirich, chief of engrg.

Fremont

*KOHL(FM)— Sept 23, 1974: 89.3 mhz; 145 w. 407 ft. TL: N37 32 00 W121 54 35. Stereo. 43600 Mission Blvd. 94539. Phone: (510) 659-6221. Fax: (510) 659-6001. Web Site: www.kohlradio.com. Licensee: Fremont-Newark Community College Dist. Format: Contemp hit/Top 40. News: one hr wkly. Target aud: 18-34. ♦ Robert Dochterman, gen mgr; Tom Gomez, progmg dir; Matthew Graf, news dir & pub affrs dir.

Fresno

KALZ(FM)— Jan 6, 1962: 102.7 mhz; 50 kw. 500 ft. TL: N36 49 07 W119 30 33. Stereo. 83 E. Shaw Ave., Suite 150 93710. Phone: (559) 230-4300. Fax: (559) 243-4301. Web Site: www.myalice1027.com. Licensee: Capstar TX L.P. Group owner: Clear Channel Communications Inc. (acq 8-30-00; grpsl). Rep: Clear Channel. Format: Adult contemp. News staff: one; News: 20 hrs wkly. Target aud: 25-54; women. ♦ Jeff Negrete, VP & gen mgr; Robert "Bobby" Martin, opns mgr; Gary Clifford, gen sls mgr; Lance Minnite, natl sls mgr; Susie Hamlett, rgnl sls mgr; Chris Miller, prom dir.

KAVT(AM)— Not on air, target date: unknown: 1680 khz; 10 kw-D, 1 kw-N. TL: N36 46 14 W119 55 20. 139 W. Olive Ave. 93728. Phone: (559) 233-8803. Fax: (559) 233-8871. E-mail: rak@computermail.net. Web Site: www.radiocanon.net. Licensee: RAK Communications Inc. Format: Children. ♦ Albert R. Perez, gen mgr.

KBIF(AM)— Nov 17, 1947: 900 khz; 1 kw-D, 500 w-N, DA-N. TL: N36 41 30 W119 40 46. 3401 W. Holland Ave. 93722. Phone: (559) 222-0900. Fax: (559) 222-1573. E-mail: kbifkirv@aol.com. Web Site: www.kbif900am.com. Licensee: Gore-Overgaard Broadcasting Inc. (group owner) Network: USA. Format: Relg, foreign language, Asian. Spec prog: Sp 6 hrs, Punjabi 16 hrs wkly. ♦ Dana Kennon, gen mgr; Tony Donato, opns mgr & gen sls mgr.

KBOS-FM— (Tulare). 1965: 94.9 mhz; 16.4 kw. 847 ft. TL: N36 38 15 W118 56 35. Stereo. 83 East Shaw Ave., Ste. 150 93710. Phone: (559) 230-4300. Fax: (559) 243-4301. Web Site: www.b95forlife.com. Licensee: Capstar TX L.P. Group owner: Clear Channel Communications Inc. (acq 8-30-00; grpsl). Network: CBS Radio. Format: Rhythmic CHR. Target aud: 12-34. ♦ Jeff Negrete, VP & gen mgr; E. Curtis Johnson, opns dir & opns mgr; Joni Norvell, gen sls mgr; Maya Kiss, mktg mgr; Greg Hoffman, progmg dir; Dave Case, chief of engrg.

KCBL(AM)— June 26, 1953: 1340 khz; 1 kw-U. TL: N36 45 51 W119 47 08. 83 E. Shaw Ave., Suite 150 93710. Phone: (559) 243-4300. Fax: (559) 243-4301. Web Site: www.foxsportsradio1340.com. Licensee: Capstar TX L.P. Group owner: Clear Channel Communications Inc. (acq 8-30-00; grpsl). Network: CBS. Rep: CBS Radio. Format: All sports. Target aud: 18-49. ♦ Jeff Negrete, VP; Tony Rainaldi, stn mgr.

KCIV(FM)— See Mount Bullion

*KEYQ(AM)— Oct 14, 1957: 980 khz; 500 w-D, 48 w-N. TL: N36 44 28 W119 51 12. 2310 Ponderosa Dr., Suite 28, Camarillo 93010. Phone: (805) 482-4797. Phone: (559) 486-2981. Fax: (805) 388-5202. E-mail: info@nuevavida.com. Web Site: www.nuevavida.com. Licensee: The Association for Community Education Inc. Miller & Neely. Format: Relg, Sp. Target aud: General; Sp-speaking. ♦ Phil Guthrie, pres; Mary Guthrie, gen mgr.

*KFCF(FM)— June 9, 1975: 88.1 mhz; 2.4 kw. Ant 1,899 ft. TL: N37 04 23 W119 25 51. Stereo. Box 4364 93744. Secondary address: 1449 N. Wishon Ave. 93728. Phone: (559) 233-2221. Fax: (559) 233-5776. E-mail: kfcf@kfcf.org. Web Site: www.kfcf.org. Licensee: Fresno Free College Foundation. Arent, Fox, Kintner, Plotkin & Kahn. Format: Var. News: 12 hrs wkly. Target aud: General; intelligent, discerning, questioning. Spec prog: Southeast Asian languages one hr, American Indian 2 hrs, Sp 5 hrs wkly. ♦ Vic Bedoian, gen mgr; Rych Withers, opns VP, prom dir, mus dir & pub affrs dir; R.L. Stover, progmg dir & chief of engrg.

KFIG(AM)— January 1938: 1430 khz; 5 kw-U, DA-1. TL: N36 50 49 W119 40 46. 351 W. Cromwell, Suite 108 93711. Phone: (559) 447-3570. Fax: (559) 447-3579. E-mail: postmaster@espn1430.com. Web Site: www.espn1430.com. Licensee: Fat Dawgs 7 Broadcasting LLC (acq 6-16-2005; $2.5 million). Rep: Allied Radio Partners. Format: All sports. Target aud: 25 plus. ♦ Paul Swearengin, gen mgr; Jim Moore, opns mgr.

*KFNO(FM)— Feb 12, 1992: 90.3 mhz; 1.35 kw. 1,971 ft. TL: N37 04 26 W119 25 52. 706 W. Herndon Ave. 93650. Phone: (559) 435-4996. Fax: (916) 641-8238. Licensee: Family Stations Inc. (group owner) Format: Relg. ♦ Harold Camping, pres; Peggy Renschler, gen mgr.

KFPT(AM)—See Clovis

*KFSR(FM)— Oct 30, 1982: 90.7 mhz; 2.55 kw. 66 ft. TL: N36 48 42 W119 44 43. Stereo. California State Univ. of Fresno, 5201 N. Maple, MS SA#119 93740-8027. Phone: (559) 278-2598. Phone: (559) 278-4500. Fax: (559) 278-6985. E-mail: kfsrfresno@hotmail.com. Web Site: www.csufresno.edu/kfsr/. Licensee: California State University Fresno. Format: Jazz, alternative rock, div. News: 2 hrs wkly. Target aud: General. Spec prog: Blues 6 hrs, reggae 6 hrs, world 9 hrs, folk 3 hrs, western 1 hr wkly. ♦ Jim Wilson, gen mgr; Joe Moore, stn mgr; Frank Delgado, progmg dir & progmg mgr; Matthew Boan, pub affrs dir.

KGST(AM)— 1949: 1600 khz; 5 kw-U, DA-N. TL: N36 29 20 W119 19 33. 1110 E. Olive Ave. 93728. Phone: (559) 497-1100. Fax: (559) 497-1125. E-mail: jgonzalez@lotusfresno.com. Licensee: Lotus Communications Inc. (group owner; acq 8-1-85; $1.76 million; 4-22-85). Format: Sp. News staff: one; News: 2 hrs wkly. Target aud: 18 plus; Hispanic adults. ♦ Howard Kalmenson, pres; Daniel Crotty, gen mgr.

KIRV(AM)— Oct 1, 1962: 1510 khz; 10 kw-D. TL: N36 42 36 W119 50 06. 3401 W. Holland Ave. 93722. Phone: (559) 222-0900. Fax: (559) 222-1573. Web Site: www.kirv.com. Licensee: Gore-Overgaard Broadcasting Inc. (acq 4-24-99). Format: Christian, talk. Target aud: 25-54. ♦ Hal Gore, CEO; Cordel Overgaard, pres; Dana Kennon, gen mgr & stn mgr; Lisa Lupo, opns VP; Tony Donato, opns mgr & gen sls mgr.

KJFX(FM)— May 15, 1970: 95.7 mhz; 17.5 kw. 850 ft. TL: N36 56 55 W119 29 09. Stereo. 1066 E. Shaw Ave. 93710. Phone: (559) 255-1041. Fax: (559) 230-0177. Web Site: www.957thefox.com. Licensee: Wilks License Co.-Fresno LLC. (acq 6-1-2005; grpsl). Format: Classic rock. ♦ Steve Miller, gen mgr; Chris Squiers, progmg dir.

KJWL(FM)— Apr 29, 1994: 99.3 mhz; 5.03 kw. 349 ft. TL: N36 44 07 W119 47 10. 675 Santa Fe Ave. 93721. Phone: (559) 497-5118. Fax: (559) 497-9760. Web Site: www.kjwl.com. Licensee: John E. Ostlund. Network: CNN Radio. Format: Adult standards. Target aud: 35 plus; upscale. ♦ John E. Ostlund, pres & gen mgr; Dave Hull, opns mgr; Jennifer Books, dev mgr; Mike Kerr, gen sls mgr; Chris Nieto, prom dir; Jim Roberts, progmg dir.

KKDG(FM)— Dec 8, 1979: 105.9 mhz; 2.4 kw. Ant 1,960 ft. TL: N37 04 23 W119 25 51. Stereo. 1071 W. Shaw Ave. 93711. Phone: (559) 490-1019. Fax: (559) 490-5889. Licensee: Infinity Radio Inc. Group owner: Infinity Broadcasting Corp. (acq 11-13-98); grpsl). Rep: Katz Hispanic. Leventhal, Senter & Lerman. Format: Sp, adult contemp. Target aud: 25-49; Hispanic. ♦ Aaron Scoby, gen mgr; Danny Jackson, gen sls mgr; Bryan Plumlee, natl sls mgr.

KMGV(FM)— Mar 15, 1948: 97.9 mhz; 2.07 kw. 1,987 ft. TL: N36 44 09 W119 47 59. (CP: 10.5 kw, ant 1,076 ft.). Stereo. 1071 W. Shaw Ave. 93711. Phone: (559) 490-9800. Fax: (559) 490-4199. Licensee: Infinity Radio Inc. Group owner: Infinity Broadcasting Corp. (acq 11-13-98); grpsl). Format: Rhythm oldies. Target aud: 25-54. ♦ John Sykes, CEO; Joel Hollander, pres; Jacques Torton, CFO; Lisa Decker, sr VP; Al Smith, gen mgr.

KMJ(AM)— June 1925: 580 khz; 5 kw-U. TL: N36 41 37 W120 03 16. 1071 W. Shaw Ave. 93711. Phone: (559) 490-5800. Fax: (559) 490-5977. Web Site: www.kmj580.com. Licensee: Infinity Radio Inc. Group owner: Infinity Broadcasting Corp. (acq 11-13-98); grpsl).

Broadcasting & Cable Yearbook 2006

Network: ABC. Format: News/talk. News staff: 13; News: 44 hrs wkly. Target aud: 25-64. ♦Joe Mauk, CEO & chief of engrg; Al Smith, gen mgr; John Broeske, opns VP.

KSKS(FM)—Co-owned with KMJ(AM). 1946: 93.7 mhz; 68 kw. 1,912 ft. TL: N37 04 44 W119 25 47. Stereo. Fax: (559) 490-5944. Web Site: www.ksks.com. Format: Modern country. ♦Karen Franz, gen sls mgr.

KOQO-FM— Mar 15, 1948: 101.9 mhz; 2.25 w. 1,948 ft. TL: N37 04 25 W119 25 52. 1071 W. Shaw 93711. Phone: (559) 490-1019. Fax: (559) 490-5889. Licensee: Infinity Radio Inc. Group owner: Infinity Broadcasting Corp. (acq 11-13-98; grpsl). Rep: Katz Hispanic. Leventhal, Senter & Lerman. Format: Sp, Tejano. Target aud: 18-34; central CA Hispanics. ♦Chris Pachero, gen mgr; Lisa Decker, chief of opns; Aaron Scoby, gen sls mgr; Bryan Plumlee, natl sls mgr; Maria Ojeda, rgnl sls mgr.

KRZR(FM)—See Hanford

***KSJV(FM)**— July 4, 1980: 91.5 mhz; 16 kw. Ant 870 ft. TL: N35 38 15 W118 56 35. Stereo. 5005 E. Belmont Ave. 93727. Phone: (559) 455-5777. Fax: (559) 455-5778. Web Site: www.radiobilingue.org. Licensee: Radio Bilingue Inc. Format: Ethnic, Sp. News staff: 5; News: 3 hrs wkly. Target aud: 16-60; Latino. ♦Hugo Morales, CEO; Lisa Lim, dev dir; Maria Esana, gen mgr, opns dir, gen sls mgr & progmg dir.

KSOF(FM)—See Dinuba

***KVPR(FM)**— Oct 15, 1978: 89.3 mhz; 2.45 kw. 1,890 ft. TL: N37 04 25 W119 25 52. Stereo. 3437 W. Shaw Ave., Suite 101 93711. Phone: (559) 275-0764. Fax: (559) 275-2202. E-mail: kvpr@kvpr.org. Web Site: www.kvpr.org. Licensee: White Ash Broadcasting Inc. Network: NPR. Format: Class, news. News: 52 hrs wkly. ♦Mariam Stepanian, pres & gen mgr; Jim Meyers, stn mgr; Patrice Loretta, dev dir.

KWRU(AM)— 1937: 940 khz; 50 kw-U, DA-2. TL: N36 50 49 W119 39 46. 4910 E. Clinton Ave., Suite 107 93727. Phone: (559) 251-6128. Fax: (559) 452-0948. Web Site: www.radiovidaabundante.com. Licensee: Multicultural Radio Broadcasting Licensee LLC. Group owner: Multicultural Radio Broadcasting Inc. (acq 2-4-2004; grpsl). Network: ABC Information & Entertainment. Format: Sp, Christian. Target aud: 25-54. ♦Arthur S. Liu, pres; Alberto Felix, progmg dir.

KWYE(FM)— 1963: 101.1 mhz; 50 kw. 310 ft. TL: N36 44 10 W119 47 13. (CP: 10 kw, ant 1,076 ft.). Stereo. 1071 W. Shaw 93711. Phone: (559) 490-1011. Fax: (559) 490-5843. Web Site: www.y101hits.com. Licensee: Infinity Radio Inc. Group owner: Infinity Broadcasting Corp. (acq 11-13-98; grpsl). Rep: Katz Radio. Leventhal, Senter & Lerman,p. Format: Mainstream top 40. Target aud: 18-49; emphasis on women. ♦Joel Hollander, COO & pres; John Sykes, CEO & chmn; Jacques Tortoroli, CFO & exec VP; Chris Pacheco, VP & gen mgr.

KXEX(AM)— September 1962: 1550 khz; 5 kw-D, 2.5 kw-N, DA-2. TL: N36 46 14 W119 55 20. 139 W. Olive Ave. 93728. Phone: (559) 233-8803. Fax: (559) 233-8871. E-mail: rak@computermail.net. Licensee: RAK Communications Inc. (acq 8-10-94; $212,000; 8-22-94). Format: Sports. ♦Albert R. Perez, VP & gen mgr.

KYNO(AM)— October 1947: 1300 khz; 5 kw-D, 1 kw-N, DA-N. TL: N36 46 14 W119 45 00. 2125 N. Barton Ave. 93703. Phone: (559) 454-1300. Fax: (559) 453-2430. E-mail: rq1300@pacbel.net. Licensee: Spanish Catholic Radio of Fresno LLC (acq 10-7-99; $800,000). Format: Sp-relg Catholic. ♦Ray Carrasco, gen mgr.

Garberville

KHUM(FM)— 1996: 104.7 mhz; 50 kw. 2,650 ft. TL: N40 07 15 W123 41 27. Box 25, Ferndale 95536-0025. Secondary address: 1400 Main St., Suite 104, Ferndale 95536. Phone: (707) 786-5104. Fax: (707) 786-5100. E-mail: info@khum.com. Web Site: www.khum.com. Licensee: Lost Coast Communications Inc. (acq 11-5-01). Rep: McGavren Guild. Format: AAA, Broad based rock and roll. Target aud: 25-54; general. ♦Patrick Cleary, gen mgr; Cliff Berkowitz, opns VP, prom dir & progmg VP; Jennifer White, mktg dir; Mike Dronkers, mus dir; James Fulton, chief of engrg.

***KLVG(FM)**— 1999: 103.7 mhz; 11 kw. Ant 2,348 ft. TL: N40 20 05 W124 06 32. Stereo. 5700 W. Oak Blvd., Rocklin 95765. Phone: (916) 251-1600. Fax: (916) 251-1650. E-mail: klove@klove.com. Web Site: www.klove.com. Licensee: Educational Media Foundation. Group owner: EMF Broadcasting. Network: K-Love. Shaw Pittman. Format: Contemp Christian music. News staff: 3. Target aud: 25-44; female (Judeo-Christian). ♦Richard Jenkins, pres; Mike Novak, VP & progmg dir; Lloyd Parker, gen mgr; Ed Lenane, opns dir; Keith Whipple, dev dir; Chris Joyce, prom dir & prom mgr.

***KMUD(FM)**— May 28, 1987: 91.1 mhz; 180 w. 2,490 ft. TL: N40 07 13 W123 41 32. (CP: 5.5 kw, ant 2,601 ft). Box 135, 1144 Redway Dr., Redway 95560-0135. Phone: (707) 923-2513. Phone: (707) 923-3911 (STUDIO). Fax: (707) 923-2501. E-mail: kmud@kmud.org. Web Site: www.kmud.org. Licensee: Redwood Community Radio Inc. Michael Couzens. Format: Educ, div, talk. News staff: one; News: 6 hrs wkly. Target aud: General. Spec prog: Black 3 hrs, ethnic one hr, jazz 6 hrs, Sp 2 hrs, American Indian one hr wkly. ♦Dave Myers, opns mgr; David Lippe, dev dir; Michael Jacinto, progmg dir & progmg mgr; Estelle Fennell, news dir; Simon Frech, chief of engrg.

Garden Grove

KEBN(FM)— June 21, 1961: 94.3 mhz; 3 kw. Ant 246 ft. TL: N33 46 51 W117 53 33. Stereo. QueBuena, 1845 Empire Ave., Burbank 91504. Phone: (818) 729-5300. Fax: (818) 729-5683. E-mail: advertising@aquisuena.com. Web Site: www.aquisuena.com. Licensee: LBI Radio License Corp. Group owner: Liberman Broadcasting Inc. (acq 5-15-03; $35 million). Format: Sp. ♦Andrew Mars, gen mgr; Phillip Estevez, gen sls mgr; Edward Leon, progmg dir; Shannon Murdock, chief of engrg.

George

KATJ-FM— June 29, 1989: 100.7 mhz; 260 w. 1,548 ft. TL: N34 36 38 W117 17 18. Stereo. 12370 Hesperia Rd., Suite 16, Victorville 92392. Phone: (760) 241-1313. Fax: (760) 241-0205. E-mail: davekelli@clearchannel.com. Web Site: www.katcountry1007.com. Licensee: Clear Channel Broadcasting Licenses Inc. Group owner: Clear Channel Communications Inc. (acq 2000; grpsl). Network: CNN Radio. Rep: Katz Radio. Latham & Watkins. Format: Country. Target aud: 25-54; adults. ♦Larry Thornhill, gen mgr; Mark Mitchell, stn mgr; Chris Price, gen sls mgr; Dave Kelli, progmg dir.

Gilroy

KAZA(AM)— September 1957: 1290 khz; 5 kw-D, DA. TL: N37 09 48 W121 38 28. Box 1290, San Jose 95108. Phone: (408) 881-1290. Fax: (408) 881-1292. E-mail: sakes@kazaradio.com. Web Site: www.kazaradio.com. Licensee: Radio Fiesta Corp. (acq 5-14-73). Format: Oldies, Sp. ♦Soma Rodriguez, pres; Juan Sidhu, VP & opns mgr.

KBAY(FM)— Jan 1, 1970: 94.5 mhz; 1.23 kw. 2,535 ft. TL: N37 06 39 W121 50 37. 190 Park Center Plaza, Suite 200, San Jose 95113. Phone: (408) 287-5775. Fax: (408) 293-3341. E-mail: lkrysler@kbay.com. Web Site: www.kbay.com. Licensee: Elliot B. Evers as trustee under the San Jose Trust Group owner: Infinity Broadcasting Corp. (acq 7-29-2005; with KEZR(FM) San Jose). Rep: D & R Radio. Format: Soft Rock. News staff: one; News: 4 hrs wkly. Target aud: 35-54. ♦John Leathers, gen mgr; Michael Hobson, gen sls mgr; Jim Murphy, progmg dir; Lissa Kreisler, news dir; Michael Stockwell, chief of engrg.

Glendale

KRLA(AM)— 1928: 870 khz; 20 kw-D, 3 kw-N, DA-2. TL: N34 08 13 W118 13 34. Stereo. 701 N. Brand Blvd., Suite 550 91203. Phone: (818) 956-5552. Fax: (818) 551-1110. Web Site: www.krla870.com. Licensee: New Inspiration Broadcasting Co. Inc. Group owner: Salem Communications Corp. (acq 6-23-98; $33.4 million). Network: Salem Radio Network. Rep: Christal. SRR Haley, Bader & Potts. Format: News/talk. News: 35 hrs wkly. Target aud: 35 plus. ♦Michael Reichert, gen sls mgr & natl sls mgr; Chuck Tyler, progmg dir; Mark Pallock, chief of engrg.

KSCA(FM)— March 1951: 101.9 mhz; 2.4 kw. 2,848 ft. TL: N34 13 26 W118 03 45. (CP: 4.8 kw). Stereo. 655 N. Central Ave., Suite 2500 91203. Phone: (818) 500-4500. Fax: (818) 500-4580. Web Site: www.univision.com. Licensee: HBC License Corp. Group owner: Univision Radio (acq 9-22-2003; grpsl). Irving Gastfreund. Format: Sp, Mexican rgnl. Target aud: 25-54. ♦Michelle Hohman, VP, gen mgr & adv dir; Gary Stone, opns dir; Victor Camino, gen sls mgr; Veronica Nava, progmg dir; Tom Koza, chief of engrg.

Goleta

KMGQ(FM)— Jan 30, 1982: 106.3 mhz; 250 w. 827 ft. TL: N34 27 55 W119 40 38. Stereo. 3757 State St., Suite 206, Santa Barbara 93105. Phone: (805) 682-2895. Fax: (805) 682-5718. E-mail: pat.cantwell@cumulus.com. Web Site: www.kmgq1063.com. Licensee: Cumulus Licensing Corp. Group owner: Cumulus Media Inc. (acq 3-12-2001; grpsl). Rep: McGavren Guild. Fletcher, Heald & Hildreth. Format: Jazz, adult contemp. Target aud: 35-64; upscale, educated, professional, affluent. ♦Julee Shea, gen mgr.

Gonzales

KHIP(FM)— Oct 25, 1990: 104.3 mhz; 2.6 kw. 508 ft. TL: N36 40 06 W121 31 09. Stereo. 60 Garden Court, Suite 300, Monterey 93940. Phone: (831) 658-5200. Fax: (831) 658-5299. Web Site: www.thehippo.com. Licensee: Mapleton Communications L.L.C. (group owner; acq 11-16-01; grpsl). Rep: McGavren Guild. Leventhal, Senter & Lerman. Format: Classic rock. Target aud: 18-49; upscale, active young professionals. ♦Dale Hendry, gen mgr; Ed Monroe, gen sls mgr; Jessica Fox, prom dir; Kenny Allen, progmg dir.

KKMC(AM)— Sept 22, 1984: 880 khz; 10 kw-U, DA-2. TL: N36 33 46 W121 26 05. 30 E. San Joaquin St., Suite 501, Salinas 93901. Phone: (831) 424-5562. Fax: (831) 424-6437. E-mail: info@kkmc.com. Web Site: www.kkmc.com.Satcomlllr Licensee: Monterey County Broadcasters Inc. Network: USA. Format: Relg, Christian teaching and talk. News: 7 hrs wkly. Target aud: 25 plus; family oriented. Spec prog: Sp 5 hrs wkly. ♦Carl J. Auel, pres; John N. Dick, gen mgr; Lorraine Dick, gen sls mgr; John Dick, progmg dir; Carl Auel, news dir.

Grass Valley

KBAA(FM)— May 3, 2004: 103.3 mhz; 530 w. Ant 1,102 ft. TL: N39 14 45 W120 57 56. Stereo. 1425 River Park Dr., Suite 520, Sacramento 95815. Phone: (916) 924-0710. Fax: (916) 924-1587. Licensee: Caron Broadcasting Inc. Group owner: Salem Communications Corp. (acq 10-7-2003; $960,000). Format: Talk, oldies. News: Mews progmg 3 hrs wkly. Target aud: 25-54; adults. ♦Bob Fox, gen mgr; Steve Gasser, opns dir; Joey Mitchell, progmg dir; Bill Pranckitas, sls.

***KLVS(FM)**— September 1997: 99.3 mhz; 13 kw. Ant 466 ft. TL: N39 16 33 W120 53 49. (CP: 1 kw, ant 1,082 ft. TL: N39 14 45 W120 57 56). Stereo. 5700 W. Oaks Blvd., Rocklin 95765. Phone: (916) 251-1600. Fax: (916) 251-1650. E-mail: klove@klove.com. Web Site: www.klove.com. Licensee: Educational Media Foundation. Group owner: EMF Broadcasting (acq 9-12-96; $65,000). Network: K-Love. Shaw Pittman. Format: Contemp Christian. News staff: 3. Target aud: 25-44; Judeo-Christian, female. ♦Richard Jenkins, pres; Mike Novak, VP, progmg dir & chief of engrg; Lloyd Parker, gen mgr; Ed Lenane, opns dir; Keith Whipple, dev dir; Chris Joyce, prom dir & prom mgr.

KNCO(AM)— Oct 1, 1978: 830 khz; 5 kw-U. TL: N39 12 52 W121 00 55. 1255 E. Main St., Suite A 95945. Phone: (530) 272-3424. Fax: (530) 272-2872. E-mail: knco@nccn.com. Web Site: www.knco.com. Licensee: Nevada County Broadcasters Inc. (group owner). Network: Network: Network: ABC Information & Entertainment, AP Radio, CNN Radio. Fletcher, Heald & Hildreth. Format: News/talk. News staff: 4; News: 30 hrs wkly. Target aud: 35 plus; adults of western Nevada County. Spec prog: Christian 4 hrs wkly. ♦Bob Breck, CEO & gen mgr; Edward Sylvester, chmn; Scott Robertson, pres; Tom Fitzsimmons, progmg dir; Jim Kerr, news dir; Dale Harry, chief of engrg.

KNCO-FM— Sept 7, 1982: 94.1 mhz; 660 w. Ant 980 ft. TL: N39 14 44 W120 57 52. (CP: 94.1 mhz). Stereo. E-mail: star@knco.com. Web Site: www.mystarradio.com. Format: Adult contemp. News staff: one; News: 2 hrs wkly. Target aud: 25-44; residents of western Nevada County.

Green Acres

***KAXL(FM)**— May 4, 1994: 88.3 mhz; 360 w. 133 ft. TL: N35 23 02 W119 06 46. (CP: 21.14 kw, 328 ft.). 110 S. Montclair, Suite 205, Bakersfield 93309. Phone: (661) 832-2800. Fax: (661) 832-3164. E-mail: kaxl@kaxl.com. Web Site: www.kaxl.com. Licensee: Skyride Unlimted Inc. (acq 7-8-91; $4,000; 7-29-91). Leventhal, Senter & Lerman. Format: Contemp inspirational. News: 4 hrs wkly. Target aud: women 35 plus. ♦Doug Cowan, pres; Terri Blankenship, stn mgr; Dan Schaffer, opns mgr.

KRAB(FM)—Licensed to Green Acres. See Bakersfield

Greenfield

KLOK-FM— Aug 7, 1989: 99.5 mhz; 50 kw. 492 ft. TL: N36 27 51 W121 17 52. (CP: 30 kw, ant 640 ft.). 67 Garden Ct., Monterey 93940-5302. Phone: (831) 771-9950. Fax: (831) 373-6700. Licensee:

Stations in the U.S. — California

Entravision Holdings LLC. Group owner: Entravision Communications Corp. (acq 3-14-00; grpsl). Format: Rgnl Mexican. ♦Aaron Scoby, gen mgr.

KSEA(FM)— 1998: 107.9 mhz; 870 w. 1,637 ft. TL: N36 23 00 W121 25 40. 229 Pajaro St. 302 D., Salinas 93901. Phone: (831) 754-1469. Fax: (831) 754-1563. E-mail: kseaproduction@campesina.com. Web Site: www.campesina.com. Licensee: Farmworker Educational Radio Network Inc. (acq 3-13-97; $600,000). Borsari & Paxson. Format: Sp rgnl Mexican. Target aud: 18-54; Hispanic market. ♦Joel Mijares Jr, gen mgr.

Greenville

*KPJP(FM)— Sept 15, 2004: 89.3 mhz; 4.5 kw vert. Ant 2,348 ft. TL: N40 13 59 W121 01 08. Box 180, Tahoma 96142. Phone: (530) 584-5700. Fax: (530) 584-5705. E-mail: info@ihradio.org. Web Site: www.ihradio.org. Licensee: IHR Educational Broadcasting (group owner). Format: Relg Catholic. ♦Douglas M. Sherman, pres & gen mgr.

Gridley

KMJE(FM)— Oct 1, 1996: 101.5 mhz; 140 w. 1,975 ft. TL: N39 12 21 W121 49 11. 861 Gray Ave., Suite K, Yuba City 95991. Phone: (530) 673-2200. Fax: (530) 673-3010. E-mail: info@gosunny.com. Web Site: www.gosunny.com. Licensee: Results Radio Licensee L.L.C. Group owner: Fritz Communications Inc. (acq 6-11-99; grpsl). Format: Hot adult contemp. ♦Bob Cross, gen mgr; Michael Berry, sls dir & engrg VP; Sheri Holder, prom dir; Rex McNeill, progmg dir.

Groveland

*KXSR(FM)— May 8, 1992: 91.7 mhz; 4 kw. Ant 1,591 ft. TL: N38 03 46 W120 14 45. 7055 Folsom Blvd., Sacramento 95826. Phone: (916) 480-5900. Fax: (916) 487-3348. E-mail: npr@csus.edu. Web Site: www.capradio.org. Licensee: California State University Sacramento. Network: Network: NPR, PRI. Duane Morris LLP. Format: Class. Target aud: General; NPR listeners, eg. professionals, educators & administrators. ♦Michael Lazar, pres & gen mgr; Carl Watanabe, stn mgr, progmg dir & progmg mgr; John Brenneise, opns mgr; Beth Hassett, dev dir & mktg dir; Michael Frost, prom dir; Linda Onstad, adv dir; Joe Barr, news dir; Jeff Browne, engrg dir.

Grover Beach

KURQ(FM)— July 4, 1984: 107.3 mhz; 3.5 kw. Ant 1,650 ft. TL: N35 21 37 W120 39 18. Stereo. 51 Zaca Ln., Suite 100, San Luis Obispo 93401. Phone: (805) 545-0101. Fax: (805) 541-5303. Web Site: www.1073therock.com. Licensee: Clear Channel Broadcasting Licenses Inc. (acq 10-17-2000). Wiley, Rein & Fielding. Format: Active rock. News staff: one; News: 8 hrs wkly. Target aud: 18-44; emphasis on 25-34 year olds. ♦Rich Hawkins, gen mgr; Pattie Wagner, gen sls mgr; Adam Burns, progmg dir.

Guadalupe

KIDI(FM)— 1992: 105.5 mhz; 160 w. 1,342 ft. TL: N34 53 54 W120 35 28. 104 W. Chapel St., Santa Maria 93458. Phone: (805) 928-4334. Fax: (805) 349-2765. E-mail: kidiktap@aol.com. Licensee: Emerald Wave Media. (acq 5-1-97; $475,000 with KTAP(AM) Santa Maria). Format: Sp, Mexician rgnl. News staff: one; News: 5 hrs wkly. Target aud: 18-45; second generation bilingual Mexican Americans. ♦August Ruiz, gen mgr & gen sls mgr; Sofia Lariz, rgnl sls mgr.

Gualala

KTDE(FM)— August 1993: 100.5 mhz; 6 kw. 669 ft. TL: N38 49 33 W123 34 12. Box 1557 95445. Secondary address: 38958 Cypress Way 95445. Phone: (707) 884-1284. Fax: (707) 884-1229. E-mail: thetide@men.org. Web Site: www.ktde.com. Licensee: Four Rivers Broadcasting Inc. (group owner). (acq 7-21-2005; grpsl). Network: CBS. Cole, Raywid & Braverman. Format: Hot adult contemp, var/div.

Target aud: 30-55. Spec prog: Gospel one hr wkly. ♦John Power, CEO; John Anthony, gen mgr; Patricia Weber, opns mgr; Pam Knutson, rgnl sls mgr & prom dir.

Hamilton City

KRER(FM)— 2005: 101.7 mhz; 530 w. Ant 1,099 ft. TL: N39 56 46 W121 43 17. 601 Belvedere St., San Francisco 94117. Phone: (415) 391-2234. Licensee: Coloma Hamilton City LLC. ♦Scott Donohue, pres & gen mgr.

Hanford

KGEN-FM— Jan 1, 1997: 94.5 mhz; 3.3 kw. 443 ft. TL: N36 12 16 W119 33 52. Box 2040, Tulare 93275. Phone: (559) 685-1370. Fax: (559) 685-1394. E-mail: kgen@sbcglobal.net. Licensee: Azteca Broadcasting Corp. (group owner) Format: Sp, Rgnl Mexician. Target aud: 18 plus. ♦Margreta Hernandez, gen mgr; Isabel Duran, gen sls mgr; Ernesto Gaytan, progmg dir.

KIGS(AM)— Feb 1, 1948: 620 khz; 1 kw-U, DA-N. TL: N36 19 37 W119 33 58. 6165 E. Lacey Blvd. 93230. Phone: (559) 582-0361. Fax: (559) 582-3981. E-mail: info@kigs.com. Web Site: www.kigs.com. Licensee: Perreira Broadcasting (acq 7-15-90). Allan E. Aronowitz. Format: Foreign languages. News: 35 hrs wkly. Target aud: 18-49. ♦Tony Vieira, gen mgr.

KRZR(FM)— Dec 24, 1976: 103.7 mhz; 50 kw. 499 ft. TL: N36 33 36 W119 45 20. Stereo. 83 E. Shaw Ave., Suite 150, Fresno 93710. Phone: (559) 230-4300. Fax: (559) 243-4301. Web Site: www.krzr.com. Licensee: Capstar TX L.P. Group owner: Clear Channel Communications Inc. (acq 8-30-00; grpsl). Network: Network: ABC, AP Radio. Dow, Lohnes & Albertson. Format: AOR. News: one hr wkly. Target aud: 18-34; male. ♦Jeff Megrete, gen mgr; John Townsend, gen sls mgr; E. Curtis Johnson, progmg dir; Dave Case, chief of engrg.

KVBE(FM)— September 1976: 107.5 mhz; 20.3 kw. 784 ft. TL: N36 38 12 W118 56 34. Stereo. 5087 E. McKinley Ave., Fresno 93727. Phone: (559) 255-5600. Fax: (559) 252-4522. Web Site: www.kmphfm.com. Licensee: Pappas Radio of Fresno LLC. Group owner: Pappas Telecasting Companies (acq 7-5-2001). Network: Network: ABC, CNN Radio. Rep: Lotus Entravision Reps LLC. Fletcher, Heald & Hildreth. Format: Urban rhythm and blues. News staff: 10; News: 45 hrs wkly. Target aud: 35-54; high quality FM oriented news/talk listeners. ♦Harry J. Pappas, CEO; Charlie Pfaff, gen mgr; Jim P. Pappas, stn mgr; Marv Allen, opns dir; Jim Pappas, sls dir & gen sls mgr; Mark Thomas, progmg dir; Jim Moore, chief of engrg.

Hayward

*KCRH(FM)— Apr 10, 1981: 89.9 mhz; 18 w. Ant -134 ft. TL: N37 38 23 W122 06 16. 25555 Hesperian Blvd. 94545. Phone: (510) 723-6954. Fax: (510) 723-7155. E-mail: cglen@clpccd.cc.ca.us. Web Site: www.kcrhradio.com. Licensee: South County Community College District. Format: Var, urban contemp. News: 5 hrs wkly. Target aud: 17-35; general. Spec prog: Instructional one hr, pub affrs 5 hrs wkly. ♦Chad Mark Glen, prom dir, progmg dir & gen mgr.

Healdsburg

KFGY(FM)—Licensed to Healdsburg. See Santa Rosa

KNOB(FM)— 2002: 96.7 mhz; 2.4 kw. Ant 525 ft. TL: N38 44 08 W122 50 55. 3565 Standish Ave., Santa Rosa 95407. Phone: (707) 588-0707. Fax: (707) 588-0777. Licensee: JYH Broadcasting. Format: Eclectic. ♦Debbie Morton, gen mgr & gen sls mgr; Natalie Rowland, prom dir; Dan Ethan, chief of engrg.

KRSH(FM)— Feb 1, 1996: 95.9 mhz; 2.65 kw. Ant 502 ft. TL: N38 44 08 W122 50 55. 3565 Standish Ave., Santa Rosa 95407. Phone: (707) 588-0707. Fax: (707) 588-0777. E-mail: studio@krsh.com. Web Site: www.krsh.com. Licensee: Deas Communications Inc. Group owner: Sinclair Communications Inc. (acq 8-3-2001; $2.1 million). Format: AAA. Target aud: 25-49. ♦Debbie Morton, gen mgr & gen sls mgr;

Dean Kattari, stn mgr & progmg dir; Brad Kahn, rgnl sls mgr; Natalie Rowland, prom dir; Dan Ethen, chief of engrg.

Hemet

KSDT(AM)— Apr 10, 1959: 1320 khz; 500 w-D, 300 w-N, DA-2. TL: N33 44 59 W116 59 53. 1950 S. Sunwest Ln., San Bernadino 92408. Phone: (951) 925-1320. Fax: (951) 658-4843. Licensee: Rudex Broadcasting Ltd. (acq 9-30-2002; $250,000). Format: Mexican. ♦John Cooper, pres & gen mgr.

KXRS(FM)— Nov 9, 1963: 105.7 mhz; 170 w. Ant 1,023 ft. TL: N33 44 59 W116 59 53. Stereo. 1950 S. Sunwest Ln., Suite 302, San Bernardino 92408. Phone: (909) 825-5020. Fax: (909) 884-5844. E-mail: vb@radiolazer.com. Web Site: www.radiolazer.com. Licensee: Lazer Broadcasting Corp. (group owner; acq 2-94). Format: Rgnl Mexician. ♦Vicki Bails, gen mgr; Salvador Prieto, progmg dir.

Hesperia

KRAK(AM)— Feb 1, 1990: 910 khz; 700 w-D, 500 w-N, DA-2. TL: N34 23 19 W117 23 29. Stereo. 11920 Hesperia Rd. 92345. Phone: (760) 244-2000. Fax: (760) 244-1198. Web Site: stardust910.com. Licensee: Infinity Radio Inc. Group owner: Infinity Broadcasting Corp. (acq 7-19-00; $3,537,500. with KVFG(FM) Victorville). Network: ABC. Fleischman & Walsh L. Format: Nostalgic/adult standards. Target aud: 40 plus. ♦Tom Hoyt, gen mgr; John Covington, stn mgr.

Hollister

*KHRI(FM)— Dec 17, 2000: 90.7 mhz; 170 w. Ant -364 ft. TL: N36 52 02 W121 23 58. Stereo. 5700 W. Oaks Blvd., Rocklin 95765. Phone: (916) 251-1600. Fax: (916) 251-1650. E-mail: info@air1.com. Web Site: www.air1.com. Licensee: Educational Media Foundation. Group owner: EMF Broadcasting (acq 11-7-00; $30,000. for CP). Network: Air 1. Shaw Pittman. Format: Contemp Christian. News staff: 3. Target aud: 18-35; Judeo-Christian, female. ♦Richard Jenkins, pres; Mike Novak, VP; Lloyd Parker, gen mgr; Ed Lenane, opns dir; Keith Whopple, dev dir; Eric Allen, natl sls mgr; Chris Joyce, prom dir.

KMPG(AM)— 1966: 1520 khz; 5 kw-D, DA-2. TL: N36 50 16 W121 25 01. Box 369, 910 Monterey St. 95023. Phone: (831) 637-7994. Fax: (831) 637-4031. Web Site: www.kmpgradio@netzero.net. Licensee: Promo Radio Corp. (acq 12-19-2003). Format: Sp rgnl Mexican. Target aud: 18-49. ♦Rafael Meza, pres & gen mgr.

KXSM(FM)— 1979: 93.5 mhz; 110 w. Ant 2,296 ft. TL: N36 45 22 W121 30 06. Stereo. 200 South A St., Suite 400, Oxnard 93030. Phone: (805) 240-2070. Fax: (805) 240-5960. Licensee: Lazer Broadcasting Corp. (group owner; (acq 7-25-2005; $2.88 million. with KXZM(FM) Felton). Format: Rgnl Mexician. ♦Alfredo Plascencia, pres; Daniel Osuna, gen mgr.

Holtville

KGBA-FM— Aug 8, 1983: 100.1 mhz; 3 kw. 331 ft. TL: N32 48 10 W115 29 53. Stereo. Studio, 605 State St., El Centro 92243. Phone: (760) 352-9860. Fax: (760) 352-1883. E-mail: kgba@kgba.org. Web Site: www.kgba.org. Licensee: The Voice of International Christian Evangelism Inc. (acq 11-1-86; $350,000; 9-15-86). Miller & Miller. Format: Talk/other. News: 3 hrs wkly. Target aud: 25-55; adult family Christian conservatives. Spec prog: Chinese 14 hrs, children 4 hrs, gospel 7 hrs wkly. ♦Robert Sager, gen mgr; Mike Leonard, gen sls mgr; Sara Mae, progmg dir; Dean Imhof, chief of engrg.

Hoopa

*KIDE(FM)— December 1980: 91.3 mhz; 195 w. -1,560 ft. TL: N41 03 51 W123 41 05. (CP: 305 w). Stereo. Box 1220 95546. Phone: (530) 625-4245. Fax: (530) 625-4046. Web Site: www.kidefm.org. Licensee: Hoopa Valley Tribe. Format: Country. Spec prog: Hoopa Indian language, history & culture 20 hrs wkly. ♦Joseph Orozco, gen mgr & progmg dir.

California

Huron

KHRN(FM)— 2003: 98.3 mhz; 100 w. Ant 43 ft. TL: N36 12 05 W120 05 53. 504 E. Polk St., Coalinga 93210. Phone: (559) 935-4191. Fax: (559) 935-4191. Licensee: Huron Broadcasting LLC. Format: Oldies. ♦Rebecca Sexton, gen mgr.

Hydesville

KSLG-FM— Apr 13, 2001: 94.1 mhz; 17 kw. 1,860 ft. TL: N40 25 23 W124 06 21. Box 25, Ferndale 95536. Secondary address: 1400 Main St., Suite 104, Ferndale 95536. Phone: (707) 786-5104. Fax: (707) 786-5100. E-mail: info@khum.com. Web Site: www.kslg.com. Licensee: Lost Coast Communications Inc. (acq 11-5-01). Rep: McGavren Guild. Format: Modern rock. Target aud: 18-49. ♦Patrick Cleary, gen mgr; Cliff Berkowitz, opns VP & prom dir; Jennifer White, mktg dir & prom dir; Mike Dronkers, progmg dir.

Idyllwild

KATY-FM— Dec 1, 1989: 101.3 mhz; 1.55 kw. Ant 656 ft. TL: N33 43 31 W116 44 58. Stereo. 27450 Ynez Rd., Suite 316, Temecula 92591. Phone: (951) 506-1222. Fax: (951) 506-1213. E-mail: katytraffic@linkline.com. Web Site: www.katyfm.com. Licensee: All Pro Broadcasting Inc. (acq 3-21-01; $3.5 million. plus $100,000 for option to purchase for 51%). Leventhal, Senter & Lerman. Format: Adult contemp. News staff: one; News: 2 hrs wkly. Target aud: 25-49; affluent, upwardly mobile. ♦Duane Davis, exec VP & gen sls mgr; Bill McNulty, gen mgr; Kevin Watson, stn mgr & gen sls mgr; Willie D. Davis, CEO & opns mgr; Ginny Harman, progmg dir & news dir.

Imperial

KMXX(FM)— Sept 17, 1980: 99.3 mhz; 3 kw. 200 ft. TL: N32 51 44 W115 33 41. (CP 6 kw, ant 302 ft. TL: N32 54 W115 31 40). Stereo. 1803 N. Imperial Ave., El Centro 92243. Phone: (760) 352-2277. Fax: (760) 482-0099. Web Site: www.entravision.com. Licensee: Entravision Holdings LLC. Group owner: Entravision Communications Corp. (acq 7-31-00; grpsl). Rep: Katz Hispanic. Format: Rgnl Mexican. Target aud: 18-49. ♦Eric Chavez, gen mgr.

Independence

KSRW(FM)— Apr 12, 1996: 92.5 mhz; 870 w. 2,949 ft. TL: N36 58 38 W118 07 13. 1280 N. Main St., Suite J, Bishop 93514. Phone: (760) 873-5329. Fax: (760) 873-5328. E-mail: kday@schat.com. Licensee: Ms. Benett Kessler (acq 3-14-91; FTR: 4-1-91). Network: CNN Radio. Format: Adult contemp. News staff: one; News: 10 hrs wkly. Target aud: 30-65; professionals & retirees with average to above average buying power. ♦Benett Kessler, CEO & gen mgr.

Indio

KCLB-FM— See Coachella

*KCRI(FM)— 1995: 89.3 mhz; 3.3 kw. Ant 561 ft. TL: N33 48 07 W118 13 28. 1900 Pico Blvd., Santa Monica 90405. Phone: (310) 450-5183. Phone: (888) 600-kcrw. Fax: (310) 450-7172. Web Site: www.kcrw.com. Licensee: Santa Monica Community College. Network: NPR. Format: Eclectic, news. ♦Ruth Seymour, gen mgr; Jennifer Ferro, stn mgr; Mike Newport, opns mgr; Jacki Weber, dev dir.

KESQ(AM)— 1946: 1400 khz; 1 kw-U. TL: N33 43 37 W116 15 10. Stereo. 42650 Melanie Pl., Palm Desert 92211-5170. Phone: (760) 568-6830. Fax: (760) 568-3984. Licensee: Gulf-California Broadcast Co. Format: Regl, Sp. News staff: one; News: 7 hrs wkly. Target aud: General. ♦Martin Serna, gen mgr.

KJJZ(FM)— March 1993: 102.3 mhz; 600 w. 587 ft. TL: N33 48 07 W116 13 29. Box 1825, Palm Springs 92263. Phone: (760) 320-4550. Fax: (760) 320-3037. Web Site: www.102kjjz.com. Licensee: R.M. Broadcasting L.L.C. (acq 1-97; $1.231 million). Network: Westwood One. Rep: McGavren Guild. Fletcher, Heald & Hildreth. Format: Smooth jazz. News staff: one; News: 3 hrs wkly. Target aud: 25-49; Palm Springs baby boomers. ♦Todd Marker, VP & gen mgr; Cary James, prom dir; Jim Fitzgerald, progmg dir; Jeff Michaels, news dir; Ben Manierre, chief of engrg.

KKUU(FM)— Apr 13, 1984: 92.7 mhz; 4.2 kw. Ant 394 ft. TL: N33 52 15 W116 13 37. Stereo. 1321 N. Gene Autry Tr., Palm Springs 92262. Phone: (760) 322-7890. Fax: (760) 322-5493. E-mail: keith.martin@morris.com. Licensee: MCC Radio LLC. Group owner: Morris Radio LLC (acq 1998; $4.5 million). Rep: Christal. Format: Hip hop. News staff: one; News: 2 hrs wkly. Target aud: 25-54. ♦Michael Ostehaut, VP; Anthony Quiroz, gen mgr & opns dir; Keith Martin, gen mgr.

KNWZ(AM)— See Coachella

Inglewood

KRCD(FM)— 1959: 103.9 mhz; 4.1 kw. Ant 387 ft. TL: N34 00 26 W118 21 54. Stereo. 655 N Central Ave, Suite 2500, Glendale 91203-1422. Phone: (818) 500-4500. Fax: (818) 500-4560. Web Site: www.univision.com. Licensee: Univision Radio License Corp. Group owner: Univision Radio (acq 9-22-2003; grpsl). Network: CBC. Format: Adult contemp, Sp. Target aud: 25-44; women, 60% African-American, 30% Hispanic. ♦Darren Sarto, gen mgr; Roaldo Moran, gen sls mgr; Amalia Gonzalez, progmg dir; Tom Koza, chief of engrg.

KTYM(AM)— Feb 14, 1958: 1460 khz; 5 kw-D, 500 w-N, DA-2. TL: N34 00 24 W118 21 52. 6803 West Blvd. 90302. Phone: (310) 672-3700. Fax: (310) 673-2259. Web Site: www.ktym1460.com. Licensee: Trans America Broadcasting Corp. Miller & Miller, P.C. Format: Black, relg, var/div. News staff: 2; News: 2 hrs wkly. Target aud: 18-54. Spec prog: It 3 hrs, Armenian 2 hrs, Ger 2 hrs, Pol 2 hrs, Sp one hr wkly. ♦Gerardo Borrego, VP & gen mgr; Gary Reaers, gen sls mgr & progmg dir; Paul Wiren, chief of engrg. Co-owned TV: KAIL(TV) affil

Inyokern

*KZLU(FM)— Not on air, target date: unknown: 88.7 mhz; 180 w. Ant 1,309 ft. TL: N35 28 39 W117 41 58. Box 637, Bishop 93515. Phone: (714) 825-9673. Fax: (760) 872-4155. Web Site: www.livingproofinc.com. Licensee: Living Proof Inc. ♦Daniel McClenaghan, pres.

Irvine

*KUCI(FM)— Oct 1, 1969: 88.9 mhz; 200 w. -10 ft. TL: N33 38 41 W117 50 36. Stereo. Box 4362 92616-4362. Phone: (949) 824-6868. Fax: (949) 824-3741. E-mail: kuci@kuci.org. Web Site: www.kuci.org. Licensee: Regents of the University of California. Format: Div. ♦Arden Jermakian, gen mgr; Kevin Stockdale, dev dir; Darcy Staniforth, prom mgr; Herbert Carranza, progmg dir; Emilio Nunez, mus dir; Jarret Lovell, pub affrs dir; Mike Boyle, engrg mgr; Elaine Hawkes, chief of engrg.

Jackson

KLMG(FM)— Aug 16, 1973: . Stn currently dark 94.3 mhz; 4.3 kw. Ant 790 ft. TL: N38 24 10 W120 39 15. Stereo. 1401 El Camino Ave., Suite 330, Sacramento 95815. Phone: (916) 443-1049. Fax: (916) 441-6480. Licensee: Golden Gate Broadcasting Co. Inc. Group owner: Univision Radio (acq 12-23-2004). Format: Sp. ♦Amparo Perez-Cook, gen mgr.

Johannesburg

KEDD(FM)— March 1990: 103.9 mhz; 1.5 kw. 1,322 ft. TL: N35 28 39 W117 41 58. 731 N. Balsam St., Ridgecrest 93555. Phone: (760) 371-1700. Fax: (760) 371-1824. E-mail: adelman@iwvisp.com. Web Site: www.keppfm.com. Licensee: Adelman Broadcasting Inc. (group owner). Network: Network: ABC, Jones Radio Networks. Format: Sp. News staff: one; News: 7 hrs wkly. Target aud: 25-49. Spec prog: Classic rock 4 hrs wkly. ♦Robert Adelman, pres; Eric Kauffman, gen mgr & progmg dir; Kim Kauffman, sls dir; Kim Kaufman, prom dir.

KRAJ(FM)— October 1998: 100.9 mhz; 370 w. Ant 1,312 ft. TL: N35 28 41 W117 41 58. 731 N. Balsam, Ridgecrest 93555. Phone: (760) 371-1700. Fax: (760) 371-1824. E-mail: radio@iwvisp.com. Web Site: www.krajfm.com. Licensee: Adelman Broadcasting Inc. (group owner). acq 12-28-99; $45,000). Network: Jones Radio Networks. Format: Adult contemp. ♦Robert Adelman, pres; Eric Kauffman, gen mgr & progmg dir; Kim Kauffman, sls dir & prom dir.

Joshua Tree

KQCM(FM)— Nov 2, 1995: 92.1 mhz; 6 kw. Ant 230 ft. TL: N34 09 16 W116 12 04. Box 1437 92252. Phone: (760) 362-4264. E-mail: coppermountainbroadcasting@yahoo.com. Licensee: Copper Mountain Broadcasting Co. (acq 7-14-2004; $575,000. with KXCM(FM) Twentynine Palms). Network: Network: Westwood One, Jones Radio Networks. Leventhal, Senter, & Lerman, PLLC. Format: CHR. Target aud: 18-34. ♦Gary DeMaroney, gen mgr; Rebecca Westerman, pub affrs dir.

Julian

*KLVJ(FM)— Oct 23, 1991: 100.1 mhz; 110 w. Ant 2,286 ft. TL: N33 09 33 W116 36 53. Stereo. 5700 W. Oaks Blvd., Rocklin 95765. Phone: (916) 251-1600. Fax: (916) 251-1650. E-mail: klove@klove.com. Web Site: www.klove.com. Licensee: Educational Media Foundation. Group owner: EMF Broadcasting (acq 1-30-97; $34,168). Network: K-Love. Shaw Pittman. Format: Contemp Christian. News staff: 3. Target aud: 25-44; Judeo-Christian, female. ♦Richard Jenkins, pres; Mike Novak, VP & progmg dir; Lloyd Parker, gen mgr; Ed Lenane, opns dir; Keith Whipple, dev dir; Andy Ramirez, rgnl sls mgr.

KSDG(AM)— Not on air, target date: unknown: 890 khz; 3 kw-D, 330 w-N, DA-2. TL: N33 05 22 W116 34 49. Box 60991, Palo Alto 94306. Licensee: JNE Investments Inc. (acq 4-11-2001). ♦Jeffrey N. Eustis, pres.

June Lake

*KWTM(FM)— 2002: 90.9 mhz; 910 w. Ant 344 ft. TL: N38 05 14 W119 10 31. Box 637, Living Proof Inc., Bishop 93515. Secondary address: 125 S. Main St., Bishop 93514. Phone: (760) 872-4225. Fax: (760) 872-4155. E-mail: friar@cix.com. Web Site: www.kwtw.org. Licensee: Living Proof Inc. (acq 4-19-00; $250,000). Format: Christian. ♦Daniel McClenaghan, pres & gen mgr; Brian Law, opns mgr & progmg dir; Robert Branch, chief of engrg.

Keene

*KNAI(FM)— (Phoenix).AZ Oct 23, 1991: 88.3 mhz; 22.5 kw ST: ***WPHF-FM.** 997 ft. TL: N33 35 47 W112 05 29. Stereo. 3602 W. Thomas Rd., Suite 6, Phoenix, AZ 85019. Phone: (602) 269-3121. Fax: (602) 269-3020. Web Site: www.campesina.com. Licensee: National Farm Workers Service Center Inc. Vision Marketing Borsari & Paxson. Format: Sp, community pub affrs, mus. Target aud: 25-54; Hispanic market. ♦Paul Chavez, chmn; Anthony Chavez, gen mgr; Michael Nowakowski, opns dir; Jesse Portillo, progmg dir.

Kerman

KBHH(FM)— March 2001: 95.3 mhz; 6 kw. 328 ft. TL: N36 39 40 W120 09 59. 6313 Schirra Ct., Bakersfield 93313. Phone: (661) 837-0745. Fax: (661) 837-1612. Web Site: www.campesina.com. Licensee: Farmworker Educational Radio Network Inc. Borsari & Paxson. Format: Sp rgnl Mexican. Target aud: 25-54; Hispanic market. ♦Anthony Chavez, pres & gen mgr.

KOKO-FM— Apr 16, 1990: 94.3 mhz; 3 kw. 328 ft. TL: N36 44 29 W120 05 08. Stereo. 2775 E. Shaw Ave., Fresno 93710. Phone: (559) 292-9494. Fax: (559) 294-7041. E-mail: davidecaudillo@koko94.com. Web Site: www.kok94.com. Licensee: Big Broadcasting Inc. (acq 1999; $1.14 million). Rep: Caballero. Haley, Bader & Potts. Format: CHR, rhythm oldies. News staff: 4; News: 14 hrs wkly. Target aud: 18-54; Hispanic men & women. ♦Art Laboe, pres; David E. Caudillo, gen sls mgr.

Kernville

KCNQ(FM)— November 1985: 102.5 mhz; 130 w. 1,230 ft. TL: N35 37 21 W118 26 16. Stereo. Box 2008 93238-2008. Secondary address: 14 Sierra Dr. 93238. Phone: (760) 379-5636. Fax: (760) 376-3119. Licensee: Robert J. Bohn & Katherine M. Bohn. (acq 7-28-97). Network: ABC Information & Entertainment. Format: C&W. News staff: one; News: 18 hrs wkly. Target aud: General. Spec prog: Relg one hr wkly. ♦Anthony M. Bohn, CEO; Robert J. Bohn, pres; Stacy Bohn, gen mgr; Gary Huff, sls dir; Bob Jamison, progmg mgr & chief of engrg; Robert Pinney, news dir.

King City

*KDRH(FM)— 2001: 91.3 mhz; 300 w vert. Ant 75 ft. TL: N36 16 22 W121 05 02. 5700 W. Oaks Blvd., Rocklin 95765-3719. Phone: (916) 251-1600. Fax: (916) 251-1650. E-mail: info@air1.com. Web Site: www.air1.com. Licensee: Educational Media Foundation. Group owner: EMF Broadcasting (acq 11-7-00; $30,000. for CP). Network: Air 1. Shaw Pittman. Format: Contemp Christian. News: one hr wkly. Target aud: 18-25; teen, young adult. ♦Randy Cantrell, opns mgr; Brian O'Neal, progmg dir.

KHDV(FM)— 1981: 93.9 mhz; 5.4 kw. 719 ft. TL: N36 22 48 W121 12 57. Stereo. Box 1939, Salinas 93902. Secondary address: 548 Alisal St., Salinas 93905. Phone: (831) 757-1910. Fax: (831) 757-8015.

Stations in the U.S. California

E-mail: wolfhouseradio@yahoo.es. Licensee: Len Radio Broadcasting of California Licensee LLC. (group owner; (acq 2-16-2005); grpsl). Format: Sp, urban contemp, rgnl. Target aud: General. ♦ Ron Stevens, gen mgr.

KRKC(AM)— Sept 21, 1958: 1490 khz; 1 kw-U. TL: N36 13 34 W121 07 26. Box 628 93930. Secondary address: 1134 San Antonio Dr. 93930. Phone: (831) 385-5421. Phone: (831) 674-2278. Fax: (831) 385-0635. E-mail: bill@krkc.com. Web Site: www.krkc.com. Licensee: Radio Del Rey. (acq 9-2-82; $270,000; 9-13-82). Network: CBS. Rep: Farmakis, Katz Radio. Pepper & Corazzini. Format: Country. News staff: one. Target aud: 25-54. Spec prog: Farm 10 hrs, sports 9 hrs wkly. ♦ Bill Gittler, pres & gen mgr; Michael Davis, opns mgr.

KRKC-FM— Jan 30, 1989: 102.1 mhz; 2.6 kw. Ant 1,820 ft. TL: N35 57 06 W121 00 03. Stereo. 1134 San Antonio Dr. 93930. Phone: (831) 385-5421. Fax: (831) 385-0635. E-mail: krkc@dedot.com. Web Site: www.krkc.com. Licensee: King City Communications Corp. Network: AP Radio. Pepper & Corazzini. Format: Adult contemp. News staff: one; News: 1 hr wkly. Target aud: 18-49; men and women. ♦ Bill Gittler, pres & gen mgr; Michael Davis, opns dir & progmg dir; Dru Vincent, mus dir; Jeff Grice, news dir; Ron Warren, chief of engrg.

Kings Beach

KSRN(FM)— 1990: 107.7 mhz; 230 w. 2,883 ft. TL: N39 18 47 W119 53 00. Stereo. 1465 Terminal Way, Suite 3, Reno, NV 89502. Phone: (775) 324-4819. Fax: (775) 324-4832. Licensee: Lazer Broadcasting Corp. (group owner; acq 12-12-2003; $2.5 million). Network: ABC. Rep: Katz Radio. Format: Sp, rgnl Mexican. News: 5 hrs wkly. Target aud: 35-54; affluent, business professionals. Spec prog: Gospel one hr wkly. ♦ Jerry Juskiw, gen mgr; Don Parker, opns VP; Alicia Miranda, gen sls mgr; Salvador Prieto, progmg dir.

Kingsburg

*KFYE(FM)— 1992: 106.3 mhz; 16 kw. Ant 420 ft. TL: N36 26 50 W119 37 10. Stereo. 5700 W. Oaks Blvd., Rocklin 95765. Phone: (916) 251-1600. Fax: (916) 251-1650. E-mail: klove@klove.com. Web Site: www.klove.com. Licensee: Mapleton Communications LLC (group owner; acq 5-13-2004; $2 million). Network: K-Love. Shaw Pittman. Format: Contemp Christian. News staff: 3. Target aud: 25-44; Judeo-Christian, female. ♦ Adam Nathanson, pres; Lloyd Parker, gen mgr; Ed Lenane, opns dir; Keith Whipple, dev dir; Chris Joyce, prom dir & prom mgr; David Pierce, progmg mgr & mus dir.

La Jolla

KIFM(FM)—See San Diego

La Quinta

KUNA-FM— Aug 1, 1987: 96.7 mhz; 650 w. 578 ft. TL: N33 48 08 W116 13 30. Stereo. 42650 Melanie Pl., Palm Desert 92211-5170. Phone: (760) 568-6830. Fax: (760) 568-3984. Licensee: Gulf California Broadcasting Co. Group owner: News-Press & Gazette Co. Format: Rgnl Mexican. News staff: one; News: 25 hrs wkly. Target aud: 25-54. ♦ Martin Serna, gen mgr; Adolpho Iniguez, opns mgr.

La Selva Beach

KOMY(AM)— 1937: 1340 khz; 1 kw-D, 850 w-N. TL: N36 57 43 W121 58 51. c/o KSCO(AM), 2300 Portola Dr., Santa Cruz 95062. Phone: (831) 475-1080. Fax: (831) 475-2967. Web Site: www.ksco.com. Licensee: Zwerling Broadcasting System Ltd. (acq 6-5-97). Format: News/talk. News: 35 hrs wkly. Target aud: 25-64; people with an investment at risk in the community. ♦ Michael Zwerling, pres; Michael Olson, gen mgr; Jose Novo, stn mgr.

Lake Arrowhead

KCXX(FM)— June 1978: 103.9 mhz; 180 w. Ant 1,797 ft. TL: N34 14 03 W117 08 25. Stereo. 242 E. Airport Dr., Suite 106, San Bernardino 92408. Phone: (909) 384-1039. Phone: (909) 889-1039. Fax: (909) 888-7302. Web Site: www.x1039.com. Licensee: All-Pro Broadcasting Inc. (acq 9-10-92; $5 million. with KCKC(AM) San Bernardino; FTR: 9-28-92). Rep: McGavren Guild. Leventhal, Senter & Lerman. Format: Alternative rock. Target aud: 18-49. ♦ Willie Davis, CEO & pres; Bill McNulty, gen mgr & opns mgr; Kim Martinez, gen sls mgr; Mike Zara, prom mgr; Kelli Cluque, progmg dir.

Lake Isabella

KQAB(AM)— July 15, 1977: 1140 khz; 1 kw-D. TL: N35 38 20 W118 28 22. Box 2008, 14 Sierra Dr., Kernville 93238. Phone: (760) 379-5636. Fax: (760) 379-3119. E-mail: qab@care-ems.com. Web Site: www.qabmedia.com. Licensee: Robert J. and Katherine M. Bohn. (acq 7-24-97; $300,000 with co-located FM). Format: News/talk. News staff: one; News: 14 hrs wkly. Target aud: 50 plus; mature.

KVLI-FM—Co-owned with KQAB(AM). Oct 29, 1992: 104.5 mhz; 200 w. 1,260 ft. TL: N35 37 21 W118 26 16. Stereo. Web Site: www.qabmedia.com. Network: ABC. Format: Oldies. News staff: one; News: 12 hrs wkly. Target aud: 25-54.

Lakeport

KNTI(FM)— Oct 21, 1984: 99.5 mhz; 2.5 kw. 1,920 ft. TL: N39 07 50 W123 04 32. Stereo. 140 N. Main St. 95453. Phone: (707) 263-6113. Fax: (707) 263-0939. E-mail: mwilson@ncc.radio.com. Web Site: www.knti.com. Licensee: Bicoastal Media L.L.C. (group owner; acq 7-28-99; grpsl). Network: CNN Radio. Keck, Mahin & Cate. Format: Classic hits. News staff: one; News: 8 hrs wkly. Target aud: 25-54; family oriented, upscale, professional adults. Spec prog: Sp 3 hrs, new adult contemp 3 hrs wkly. ♦ Ken Dennis, CEO; Mike Wilson, pres; Tony Calumet, gen mgr; Eric Patrick, opns dir & progmg dir; George Feola, gen sls mgr; Paul Reading, news dir; Kevin Mostyn, pub affrs dir & chief of engrg.

KXBX(AM)— June 17, 1966: 1270 khz; 500 w-D, 97 w-N. TL: N39 00 50 W122 53 39. Box 759, 140 N. Main St. 95453. Phone: (707) 263-6113. Fax: (707) 263-0939. E-mail: mwilson@ncradio.com. Licensee: Bicoastal Media LLC. (group owner; acq 7-28-99; grpsl). Network: UPI, Westwood One. Format: MOR, nostalgia. News staff: one; News: 4 hrs wkly. Target aud: 40 plus; retirees. Spec prog: Sp 3 hrs, loc talk & info 5 hrs wkly. ♦ Mike Wilson, pres & gen mgr; Shalean Champlin, gen sls mgr; Paul Reading, news dir; Kevin Mostyn, engrg VP & chief of engrg.

KXBX-FM— Aug 31, 1984: 98.3 mhz; 3 kw. 300 ft. TL: N39 02 54 W122 45 59. Stereo. Format: Hot adult contemp.

Lancaster

KAVL(AM)— Sept 8, 1950: 610 khz; 4.9 kw-D, 4 kw-N, DA-2. TL: N34 42 22 W118 10 36. Stereo. 352 East Ave. K-4 93535. Phone: (661) 942-1121. Fax: (661) 723-5512. Web Site: www.foxsports610.com. Licensee: Citicasters Licenses L.P. Group owner: Clear Channel Communications Inc. (acq 5-4-99; grpsl). Network: USA. Pepper & Corazzini. Format: Sports. News staff: 2. Target aud: 25-44; predominantly male, commuters, sports fans. ♦ Larry Thornhill, gen mgr.

KGMX(FM)—Listing follows KWJL(AM).

*KTLW(FM)— July 3, 1997: 88.9 mhz; 5.8 kw. Ant 272 ft. TL: N34 51 03 W118 09 22. Stereo. Life On The Way Communications, 14820 Sherman Way, Van Nuys 91405. Phone: (818) 779-8444. Fax: (818) 779-8411. E-mail: ktlwinfo@ktlw.net. Web Site: www.ktlw.net. Licensee: Living Way Ministries Inc. Format: Inspirational, Christian music & teaching. Target aud: 25-54; 50% male, 50% female. ♦ Gary Curtis, exec VP & VP; Gary C. Curtis, gen mgr; Rita Medall, opns dir & opns mgr.

KUTY(AM)—See Palmdale

KWJL(AM)— August 1956: 1380 khz; 1 kw-D, DA. TL: N34 42 43 W118 10 34. Q-9, 570 East Ave., Palmdale 93550. Phone: (661) 947-3107. Fax: (661) 272-5688. Licensee: High Desert Broadcasting LLC. (group owner; (acq 1-21-97; with co-located FM). Format: Sp. News staff: 3; News: 25 hrs wkly. Target aud: 35 plus. ♦ Bruce Thompson, gen mgr; Gary Wilson, opns mgr; Amir Raheem, news dir; H. Scott Blake, chief of engrg.

KGMX(FM)—Co-owned with KWJL(AM). Oct 28, 1970: 106.3 mhz; 3 kw. 210 ft. TL: N34 44 41 W118 07 30. (CP: 3.66 kw, ant 256 ft.) Format: Hot adult contemp. Target aud: 24-54.

Laytonville

*KHKL(FM)— 2002: 91.9 mhz; 125 w. Ant 2,184 ft. TL: N39 41 41 W123 34 36. Stereo. 5700 W. Oaks Blvd., Rocklin 95765. Phone: (916) 251-1600. Fax: (916) 251-1650. E-mail: klove@klove.com. Web Site: www.klove.com. Licensee: Educational Media Foundation. Group owner: EMF Broadcasting. Network: K-Love. Shaw Pittman. Format: Contemp Christian. News staff: 3. Target aud: 25-44; Judeo Christian, female. ♦ Richard Jenkins, pres; Mike Novak, VP; Lloyd Parker, gen mgr; Ed Lenane, opns dir; Keith Whipple, dev dir; Chris Joyce, prom dir.

*KJCU(FM)— 2004: 89.9 mhz; 130 w. Ant 361 ft. TL: N39 26 35 W123 43 58. 468 S. Franklin St., Fort Bragg 95437. Secondary address: CSN International, 3000 W. Mac Arthur Blvd., Santa Ana 92704. Phone: (707) 964-2170. Licensee: CSN International (group owner). Format: Relg. ♦ Dan Gillman, gen mgr & progmg dir.

*KLAI(FM)—Not on air, target date: unknown: 90.3 mhz; 75 w. Ant 2,368 ft. TL: N39 41 38 W123 34 43. Box 135, Redway 95560-0135. Phone: (707) 923-2513. Fax: (707) 923-2501. Licensee: Redwood Community Radio Inc. Format: Div. ♦ Michael Jocinto, opns mgr; Simon Frech, chief of engrg.

*KVFR(FM)— 2005: 88.5 mhz; 1.2 kw vert. Ant 2,335 ft. TL: N39 41 38 W123 34 43. 5005 E. Belmont Ave., Fresno 93727. Phone: (559) 455-5777. Fax: (559) 455-5778. Web Site: www.radiobilingue.org. Licensee: Radio Bilingue Inc. (group owner). (acq 6-29-2005; $50,000 for CP). Format: Ethnic, multilingual, Sp.

Le Grand

*KEFR(FM)— Jan 11, 1985: 89.9 mhz; 1.8 kw. 2,142 ft. TL: N37 32 01 W120 01 50. Stereo. Box 52, 13306 Jefferson St. 95333. Phone: (209) 389-4659. Fax: (209) 389-0215. E-mail: kefr@k66.com. Web Site: www.familyradio.com. Licensee: Family Stations Inc. (group owner) Format: Educ, relg. Target aud: General. ♦ Harold Camping, pres; Craig Hulselas, progmg dir; Larry Milliken, stn mgr & chief of engrg.

Lemoore

KJOP(AM)— Dec 23, 1963: 1240 khz; 1 kw-U. TL: N36 18 47 W119 43 51. PO Box 180, Tahoma 96142. Phone: (530) 584-5700. Fax: (530) 584-5705. Web Site: www.ihradio.org. Licensee: IHR Educational Broadcasting (group owner; acq 12-22-2000; $125,000). Format: Catholic. ♦ Doug Sherman, pres; Joseph Nesta, stn mgr.

Lenwood

KBTW(FM)— April 2001: 104.5 mhz; 2.5 kw. 515 ft. TL: N34 51 20 W117 02 59. 1950 S. Sunwest Ln., Suite 300, San Bernadino 92408. Secondary address: 125 E. Fredericks St., Barstow 92311. Phone: (909) 825-5020. Phone: (760) 255-4246. Fax: (909) 884-5844. Fax: (760) 255-2406. Web Site: www.radiolazer.com. Licensee: Lazer Broadcasting Corp. (group owner; (acq 10-27-99; 450,000). Rep: Lotus Entravision Reps LLC. Fletcher, Heald & Hildreth. Format: Sp, rgnl Mexican. News: 2 hrs wkly. Target aud: 25-54; adult. ♦ Vicki Bails, gen mgr & gen sls mgr; Salvador Prieto, progmg dir.

KHDR(FM)— Dec 20, 2002: 96.9 mhz; 1 kw. Ant 797 ft. TL: N34 58 15 W117 02 22. Box 1668, Barstow 92312. Phone: (760) 256-0326. Fax: (760) 256-9507. E-mail: khwyha@earthlink.net. Web Site: www.thehighwaystations.com. Licensee: The Drive LLC. Group owner: KHWY Inc. (acq 2-25-2003). Network: AP Radio. Hogan & Hartson.

Broadcasting & Cable Yearbook 2006

California

Format: Classic rock, AOR. News staff: one. Target aud: General; travelers on I-15 and I-40. ♦ Howard B. Anderson, CEO & pres; Kirk M. Anderson, exec VP; Tim Anderson, stn mgr; Judy Robinson, gen sls mgr; Lance Todd, progmg dir.

KIXW-FM— November 1994: 107.3 mhz; 440 w. Ant 771 ft. TL: N34 58 13 W117 02 19. 1611 E. Main St., Barstow 92311. Phone: (760) 256-0326. Fax: (760) 256-9507. E-mail: tim@highwayradio.com. Web Site: www.thehighwaystations.com. Licensee: KHWY Inc. (group owner; acq 2-18-98; $1,741,444. with KIXF(FM) Baker). Network: CNN Radio, Westwood One. Hogan & Hartson. Format: Country. ♦ Howard Anderson, CEO & pres; Kirk Anderson, exec VP; Timothy Anderson, VP & gen mgr; Judy Robinson, sls VP; John Gregg, prom dir; Lance Todd, progmg dir; Keith Hayes, news dir; Thomas J. McNeill, engrg mgr.

Lincoln

KKFS(FM)— Nov 8, 1974: 103.9 mhz; 6 kw. Ant 328 ft. TL: N38 52 33 W121 07 30. Stereo. 1425 River Park Dr., Suite 520, Sacramento 95815. Phone: (916) 924-0710. Fax: (916) 924-1587. E-mail: info@1055thefish.net. Web Site: www.1055thefish.net. Licensee: Bustos Media of California License LLC. Group owner: First Broadcasting Investment Partners LLC (acq 7-28-2005; $23 million). Format: Contemp Christian. ♦ Robert Fox, gen mgr; Stu Roberts, gen sls mgr; Chirs Squires, progmg dir; Dave Fortenberry, engrg dir.

Lindsay

KZPO(FM)— 1999: 103.3 mhz; 280 w. Ant 2,624 ft. TL: N36 17 14 W118 50 17. Lindsay Broadcasting, 12550 Brookhurst St., Suite A, Garden Grove 92840. Phone: (714) 636-5040. E-mail: kingsradio@aol.com. Web Site: members.aol.com/kingradio. Licensee: Estate of Linda Ware, Cynthia Ramage, executor (acq 6-2-2004). Format: Nostalgia.

Livermore

KKIQ(FM)— May 1969: 101.7 mhz; 4.5 kw. 382 ft. TL: N37 35 42 W121 39 42. Stereo. 7901 Stoneridge Dr., Suite 525, Pleasanton 94588. Phone: (925) 455-4500. Fax: (925) 416-1211. Web Site: www.kkiq.com. Licensee: KKIQ Inc. (acq 6-19-98; $9 million). Network: AP Radio. Haley, Bader & Potts. Format: Adult contemp. News staff: one; News: 28 hrs wkly. Target aud: 25-54; high income & highly educated adults. ♦ John Levitt, gen mgr; Kristi Willard, gen sls mgr; Sylvia Manker, mktg mgr; Jim Hampton, progmg dir; John Higden, chief of engrg.

Livingston

*****KCJH(FM)**— 1997:: 89.1 mhz; 13.5 kw vert. Ant 305 ft. TL: N37 18 57 W120 43 20. 9019 N. West Ln., Stockton 95210. Phone: (209) 477-3690. Fax: (209) 477-2762. Licensee: Your Christian Companion Network Inc. (acq 7-20-98). Cohn & Marks. Format: Gospel, inspirational, adult contemp. Target aud: 35-55. ♦ Kenneth F. Haney, pres; Shirley Garner, VP & gen mgr; Adam Biddell, opns mgr & mus dir; Brent Regnart, progmg mgr; Brad Johnson, chief of engrg.

*****KLVN(FM)**— 1998: 88.3 mhz; 1.8 kw. 148 ft. TL: N37 18 57 W120 43 20. Stereo. 5700 W. Oaks Blvd., Rocklin 95765. Phone: (916) 251-1600. Fax: (916) 251-1650. E-mail: klove@klove.com. Web Site: www.klove.com. Licensee: Educational Media Foundation. Group owner: EMF Broadcasting. Network: K-Love. Shaw Pittman. Format: Contemp Christian music. News staff: 3. Target aud: 25-44; female (Judeo-Christian). ♦ Richard Jenkins, pres; Mike Novak, VP; Lloyd Parker, gen mgr; Ed Lenane, opns dir; Keith Whipple, dev dir; Chris Joyce, prom dir & prom mgr.

KSKD(FM)— Nov 1, 1984: 95.9 mhz; 3 kw. Ant 305 ft. TL: N37 18 57 W120 43 20. (CP: COL Dos Palos. 6 kw, ant 318 ft. TL: N36 55 35 W120 50 42). Stereo. Box 1039,, 4043 Greer Rd, Hughson 95326. Phone: (209) 883-8760. Fax: (209) 883-8769. Web Site: www.lafavorita.net. Licensee: All American Broadcasting Co. (acq 2-3-93; $198,000; 3-8-93). Rep: Lotus Entravision Reps LLC. Format: Sp, adult contemp. ♦ Nelson Gomez, pres & gen mgr; Richard Torez, progmg dir; Juan Carlos Ibarra, news dir; Chet Hughes, chief of engrg.

Lodi

KCVR(AM)— 1946: 1570 khz; 5 kw-D, 34 w-N, DA-2. TL: N34 09 18 W121 17 39. (CP: 500 w-N. TL: N38 05 10 W121 12 57). 6820 Pacific Ave., Suite 3, Stockton 95207. Secondary address: 1436 Auburn Blvd., Sacramento 95207. Phone: (209) 474-0154. Phone: (916) 646-4000. Fax: (323) 900-6127. Web Site: entravision.com. Licensee: Entravision Holdings LLC. Group owner: Entravision Communications Corp. (acq 7-28-00; grpsl). Format: Sp. ♦ Lisa Sunday, gen pmg & stn mgr.

KWIN(FM)— Dec 24, 1959: 97.7 mhz; 3 kw. 300 ft. TL: N38 03 05 W121 15 05. Stereo. 4643 Quail Lakes Dr., Suite 100, Stockton 95207. Secondary address: 1581 Cummins Dr., Suite 135, Modesto 95358. Phone: (209) 476-1230. Fax: (209) 522-2061. Web Site: www.kwin.com. Licensee: Citadel Broadcasting Co. Group owner: Citadel Broadcasting Corp. (acq 5-9-03; grpsl). Format: CHR. ♦ Joanne Matteri, CFO; Roy Williams, gen mgr; Kevin Proescher, gen sls mgr; Mark Sadacca, chief of engrg.

Loma Linda

KCAA(AM)— Nov 1, 1964: 1050 khz; 1.4 w-D, DA. TL: N33 59 22 W117 11 10. 19939 Gatling Ct., Katy, TX 77449. Secondary address: 254 Carousel Mall, San Bernardino 92401. Phone: (281) 599-9800. Fax: (909) 381-8935. E-mail: ceo@KCAAradio.com. Web Site: www.KCAAradio.com. Licensee: Broadcast Management Services Inc. (acq 2-97; $30,000). Fletcher Heald. Format: Country, talk/news. News staff: 3; News: 15 hrs wkly. Target aud: General. ♦ Fred Lundgren, CEO; Jim Hill, VP; Paren Lane, gen mgr; Ray Peyton, prom mgr; Lacey Kendall, progmg dir; S. Earl Statler, pub affrs dir; Dick Vosper, chief of engrg.

KSGN(FM)—See Riverside

Lompoc

KBOX(FM)—Licensed to Lompoc. See Santa Maria

*****KLWG(FM)**—Not on air, target date: unknown: 88.1 mhz; 20 w vert. Ant 1,128 ft. TL: N34 36 13 W120 29 17. Box 1241 93438. Phone: (805) 736-3741. Licensee: Calvary Chapel of Lompoc. ♦ Mark Galvan, gen mgr.

KRQK(FM)— Dec 18, 1979: 100.3 mhz; 3.65 kw. 863 ft. TL: N34 44 24 W120 26 42. Stereo. 2325 Skyway Dr., Suite J, Santa Maria 93455. Phone: (805) 922-1041. Fax: (805) 928-3069. Licensee: AGM-Santa Maria LP. Group owner: American General Media (acq 10-29-99; $1.3 million). Format: Rgnl Mexican. Target aud: 18-49. ♦ Rich Watson, gen mgr; Emily Stich, gen sls mgr & prom mgr; Wendy Snow, rgnl sls mgr; Carlos Cibrian, progmg dir.

*****KRQZ(FM)**— Sept 3, 2000: 91.5 mhz; 2 kw vert. Ant 1,050 ft. TL: N34 36 13 W120 29 17. Stereo. Trinity Church of the Nazarene, 500 E. North Ave. 93436. Phone: (805) 736-6415. Fax: (805) 736-2642. E-mail: krqz@trinaz.com. Web Site: www.radiou.com.Sky Angel Licensee: Trinity Church of the Nazarene. Gammon & Grange. Format: Christian rock. Target aud: 12-24 years. ♦ Mark Hostand, stn mgr.

KSMY(FM)— 1997: 106.7 mhz; 3.5 kw. Ant 879 ft. TL: N34 44 31 W120 26 46. 2215 Skyway Dr., Santa Maria 93455-1118. Phone: (805) 925-2582. Fax: (805) 928-1544. Licensee: Clear Channel Broadcasting Licenses Inc. Group owner: Clear Channel Communications Inc. (acq 10-11-00; grpsl). Format: Sp rgnl Mexician. ♦ Rich Hawkins, gen mgr; Patti Allen, gen sls mgr; Jennifer Grant, progmg dir; Zachery Ruckstela, chief of engrg.

KTME(AM)— May 25, 1963: 1410 khz; 500 w-D, 77 w-N, DA-2. TL: N34 39 47 W120 22 58. 716 E. Chapell, Santa Maria 93454. Phone: (805) 922-7727. Fax: (805) 349-0265. Licensee: Mapleton Broadcasting LLC (group owner; acq 4-21-2003; $1.3 million. with KUHL(AM) Santa Maria). Network: ABC. Format: News/talk. Target aud: 25-54. ♦ Adam Nathanson, pres; Nancy Leichter, gen mgr; John Barone, dev dir.

KWSZ(FM)— 1999: 105.1 mhz; 420 w. Ant 1,217 ft. TL: N34 41 28 W120 15 58. 716 E. Chapel St., Los Angeles 93454-4524. Phone: (805) 922-7727. Fax: (805) 349-0265. E-mail: oldies1051 @radiocentralcoast.com. Licensee: Mapleton Communications LLC (group owner; acq 5-5-2003; $1.05 million). Format: Oldies. ♦ Nancy Leichter, gen mgr & stn mgr.

Long Beach

KBUE(FM)— August 1961: 105.5 mhz; 3.0 kw. 403 ft. TL: N33 51 29 W118 13 22. Stereo. 1845 Empire Ave., Burbank 91504. Phone: (818) 729-5300. Fax: (818) 729-5678. E-mail: info@lbimedia.com. Web Site: www.aquisuena.com. Licensee: LBI Radio License Corp. Group owner: Liberman Broadcasting Inc. (acq 1995; $13 million). Format: Sp Mexican Rgnl. ♦ Andy Mars, gen mgr; Miguel Banojian, opns dir & opns mgr; Bill Estevez, gen sls mgr & engrg VP; Pepe Garza, progmg dir; Chris Buchanan, chief of engrg.

*****KFRN(AM)**— March 1924: 1280 khz; 1 kw-D, 690 w-N, DA-2. TL: N33 47 54 W118 14 47. Stereo. 3550 Longbeach Blvd., Suite D 4 90807. Phone: (562) 427-7773. Fax: (562) 427-7723. E-mail: kfmfnr@aol.com. Web Site: www.familyradio.com. Licensee: Family Stations Inc. (group owner; acq 9-19-77). Network: Family Radio. Format: Christian, edu, news. News: 70 hrs wkly. Target aud: Family spectrum. ♦ Harold Camping, pres & gen mgr; Ward Cayot, opns mgr; Suong Tran, pub affrs dir.

*****KKJZ(FM)**— Jan 3, 1950: 88.1 mhz; 30 kw. Ant 449 ft. TL: N33 47 58 W118 09 43. Stereo. 1288 N. Bellflower Blvd. 90815-4198. Phone: (562) 985-5566. Fax: (562) 985-2982. E-mail: info@kkjz.org. Web Site: www.jazzandblues.org.Telstar7, transponder 15, subcarriers 5.58 & 5.76 Licensee: California State University, Long Beach Foundation (acq 6-18-81; $15,000;. FTR: 4-27-81). Network: NPR. Fletcher, Heald & Hildreth. Format: Jazz, info. News staff: one; News: 5 hrs wkly. Target aud: 25-64; educated, opinion leaders, jazz & mus lovers. Spec prog: Blues 15 hrs wkly. ♦ Jeff Apler, chmn & news dir; Judy Jankowski, pres & gen mgr; Mark Roberts, VP & sls dir; Sean Heitkemper, stn mgr; Payal Kumar, opns mgr.

KLTX(AM)— 1926: 1390 khz; 5 kw-D, 3.6 w-N, DA-2. TL: N33 53 30 W118 11 03. 136 S. Oak Knoll Ave. #202, Pasadena 91101. Phone: (626) 356-4300. Fax: (626) 356-4230. Fax: (626) 817-9851. Web Site: www.nuevavida.com. Licensee: Hi-Favor Broadcasting LLC (group owner; acq 8-4-00; $30 million). Miller & Miller. Format: Relg, Sp. Target aud: 35 plus; mature audience. ♦ Roland Hinz, pres; Mary Guthrie, opns dir.

Los Altos

KFFG(FM)— Oct 17, 1960: 97.7 mhz; 1.65 kw. 433 ft. TL: N37 18 27 W122 05 36. (CP: 3.2 kw). Stereo. c/o KFOG, 55 Hawthorne St., San Francisco 94105. Phone: (415) 817-5364. Fax: (415) 995-7006. Web Site: www.kfog.com. Licensee: KFFG Lico Inc. Group owner: Susquehanna Radio Corp. (acq 1995; $8.25 million). Format: AOR. Target aud: 18-49. ♦ Valerie Blackburn, CFO; Dwight Walker, stn mgr; Dave Milner, sls dir; Jude Hellor, prom dir; Dave Benson, progmg dir; Haley Jones, mus dir.

*****KFJC(FM)**— Dec 4, 1959: 89.7 mhz; 250 w. 1,845 ft. TL: N37 19 14 W122 08 29. Stereo. 12345 El Monte Rd., Los Altos Hills 94022. Phone: (650) 949-7260. Fax: (650) 948-1085. E-mail: info@kfjc.org. Web Site: www.kfjc.org. Licensee: Foothill Community College Board of Trustees. Format: Free-form, eclectic. News: 9 hrs wkly. Target aud: 8-80; psychedelic speed freaks, radicals & other social outcasts. Spec prog: Country 8 hrs, bluegrass 8 hrs, jazz 7 hrs, progsv 4 hrs wkly. ♦ Eric Johnson, gen mgr; Al Zisch, sls dir & mus dir; Liz Clark, prom dir; Mark Loubauch, engrg mgr.

Los Angeles

KABC(AM)— Nov 15, 1929: 790 khz; 5 kw-U, DA-N. TL: N34 01 40 W118 22 20. 3321 S. La Cienega Blvd. 90016. Phone: (310) 840-4900. Fax: (310) 838-5222. Web Site: www.kabc.com. Licensee: KABC-AM Radio Inc. Group owner: ABC Inc. (acq 6-86; grpsl; FTR: 7-15-85). Network: ABC. Format: Talk. Target aud: 35 plus; upscale, affluent, college educated. ♦ John H. Davison, pres & gen mgr; Pete Dominguez, natl sls mgr; Shelley Wagner, mktg dir & prom dir; Roxane Requio, prom mgr; Erik Braverman, progmg dir; Eric Stanger, news dir; Nelkane Benton, pub affrs dir; Norm Avery, chief of engrg.

KLOS(FM)— Co-owned with KABC(AM). Dec 30, 1947: 95.5 mhz; 68 kw. 2,920 ft. TL: N34 13 37 W118 03 58. Stereo. Phone: (310) 840-4836. Phone: (310) 840-4800. Web Site: www.955klos.com. Network: ABC FM Connection. Format: Mainstream rock/AOR. ♦ Leonard Madrid, gen sls mgr; C.W. West, mktg dir & adv dir; Rita Wilde, progmg dir; Jim Villanueva, mus dir; Norm Avery, engrg dir.

KBIG-FM—Listing follows KLAC(AM).

KBLA(AM)—See Santa Monica

KBRT(AM)—See Avalon

KCBS-FM—Listing follows KNX(AM).

KDIS(AM)—See Pasadena

Developers & Brokers of Radio Properties
contact American Media Services
at our suite:
Philadelphia Marriott Downtown
215-625-2900
843-972-2200
americanmediaservices.com
Charleston, SC
Dallas, TX · Chicago, Il · Austin, TX
American Media Services, LLC

KFI(AM)— Apr 16, 1922: 640 khz; 50 kw-U. TL: N33 52 48 W118 00 48. 3400 W. Olive Ave., Suite 550, Burbank 91505. Phone: (818) 559-2252. Web Site: www.kfi640.com. Licensee: Capstar TX L.P. Group owner: Clear Channel Communications Inc. (acq 8-7-2000; grpsl). Rep: Christal. Format: Talk. Target aud: 25-54. ♦Greg Ashlock, gen mgr.

KOST(FM)—Co-owned with KFI(AM). Oct 9, 1957: 103.5 mhz; 12.5 kw. 3,100 ft. TL: N34 13 34 W118 03 55. 3400 W. Olive Ave., Suite 550, Burbank 91505. Phone: (818) 559-2252. Fax: (818) 637-2267. Web Site: www.kost1035.com. Licensee: AMFM Broadcasting Licenses LLC. Format: Adult contemp. ♦Craig Rossi, stn mgr; Stella Schwartz, progmg dir.

KFWB(AM)— Mar 25, 1925: 980 khz; 5 kw-U. TL: N34 04 11 W118 11 36. Stereo. 6230 Yucca St. 90028. Phone: (323) 871-4660. Fax: (323) 871-4681. Fax: (323) 871-4679. Web Site: www.kfwb.com. Licensee: Infinity Broadcasting East Inc. Group owner: Infinity Broadcasting Corp. (acq 11-13-98; grpsl). Network: CNN Radio. Rep: Infinity Radio Sales. Format: News. News staff: 60; News: 168 hrs wkly. Target aud: 25-54. ♦Pat Duffy, VP & gen mgr.

KHHT(FM)— Dec 29, 1948: 92.3 mhz; 43 kw. 2,910 ft. TL: N34 13 36 W118 03 57. Stereo. 3400 W. Olive Ave., Suite 550, Burbank 91505. Phone: (818) 559-2252. Fax: (818) 566-4517. E-mail: info@hot92jamz.com. Web Site: info@hot92jams.com. Licensee: AMFM Broadcasting Licenses LLC. Group owner: Clear Channel Communications Inc. (acq 8-30-2000; grpsl). Format: Urban contemp. Target aud: 18-49; females. ♦Greg Ashlock, gen mgr; Ron Vacchina, gen sls mgr; Mike Marino, progmg dir; Brian Clark, chief of engrg.

KHJ(AM)— Apr 13, 1922: 930 khz; 5 kw-U, DA-N. TL: N34 02 26 W118 22 14. Stereo. 1845 Empire Ave., Burbank 91504. Phone: (818) 729-5300. Fax: (818) 729-5678. E-mail: info@lbimedia.com. Licensee: LBI Radio License Corp. Group owner: Liberman Broadcasting Inc. (acq 3-27-90). Wiley, Rein & Fielding. Format: Sp. News staff: one. Target aud: 18-49. ♦Jose Liberman, pres; Andy Mars, gen mgr; Lenard Liberman, exec VP & gen mgr; Alfredo Rodriguez, progmg dir.

KIEV(AM)—(Culver City). January 1986: . Stn currently dark 1500 khz; 50 kw-D, 4.3 kw-N, DA-2. TL: N34 01 47 W118 05 58. Stereo. Royce International Broadcasting Co., 801 K St., 27th Fl., Sacramento 95814. Licensee: Royce International Broadcasting Co. (acq 1984). Rep: McGavren Guild. Verner, Liipfert, Bernhard, McPherson & Hand. ♦Edward R. Stolz II, pres & gen mgr.

KIIS-FM—Listing follows KTLK(AM).

KKBT(FM)— June 1, 1957: 100.3 mhz; 5.3 kw. Ant 3,005 ft. TL: N34 13 37 W118 03 58. Stereo. Box 1710, Hollywood 90078. Secondary address: 5900 Wilshire Blvd., Suite 1900 90036. Phone: (323) 634-1800. Fax: (323) 634-1888. Web Site: www.thebeatla.com. Licensee: Radio One Licenses LLC. Group owner: Radio One Inc. (acq 11-8-01; grpsl). Format: Urban contemp. Target aud: 25-54. ♦Sue Freund, gen mgr; Ron Turner, gen sls mgr; Leonard McGee, prom dir.

KKLA-FM— 1985: 99.5 mhz; 10.5 kw. 2,880 ft. TL: N34 13 26 W118 03 44. Stereo. Box 29023, Glendale 91209. Secondary address: 701 N. Brand Blvd., Suite 550, Glendale 91203. Phone: (818) 956-5552. Fax: (818) 551-1110. E-mail: info@kkla.com. Web Site: www.kkla.com. Licensee: New Inspiration Broadcasting Inc. Group owner: Salem Communications Corp. Network: Salem Radio Network. Rep: Salem. Format: Christian. Target aud: 25-55. ♦Terry Fahy, gen mgr; Jim Tinker, opns VP; Larry Marino, opns dir & chief of engrg; Bill Price, gen sls mgr & pub affrs dir; Chuck Tyler, progmg dir.

KLAC(AM)— 1924: 570 khz; 5 kw-U, DA-N. TL: N34 04 11 W118 11 36. Stereo. 3400 W. Olive Ave., Suite 550, Burbank 91505. Phone: (818) 559-2252. Web Site: www.xtrasportsradio.com. Licensee: AMFM Broadcasting Licenses LLC. Group owner: Clear Channel Communications Inc. (acq 8-30-2000; grpsl). Format: Sports. Target aud: 35-54. ♦Mark Austin Thomas, VP & opns VP; Ed Krampf, gen mgr; Jeff Thomas, gen sls mgr; V. Freeman, mktg VP; Bill Lewis, mktg dir; Andrea Garcia, prom dir; Robin Bertoluci, progmg VP; Chris Little, news dir; John Paoli, engrg dir.

KBIG-FM—Co-owned with KLAC(AM). Feb 15, 1959: 104.3 mhz; 65 kw. Ant 3,044 ft. TL: N34 13 36 W118 03 59. Stereo. Fax: (818) 637-2267. Fax: (818) 559-2252. Web Site: www.kbig.com. Network: UPI. Format: Adult contemp. Target aud: 25-54. ♦Bruce Reese, CEO.

KLSX(FM)— 1954: 97.1 mhz; 29.5 kw. Ant 2,998 ft. TL: N34 09 50 W118 11 46. Stereo. 5670 Wilshire Blvd.,, Suite 200 90036. Phone: (323) 971-9710. Fax: (323) 954-0971. Web Site: www.fmtalki.com. Licensee: Infinity Broadcasting East Inc. Group owner: Infinity Broadcasting Corp. (acq 7-23-97). Rep: CBS Radio. Format: Talk. Target aud: 25-54; adults. ♦Bob Moore, gen mgr; Ron Escarsega, opns mgr; David Severino, gen sls mgr; Bonnie Baker, natl sls mgr; George Flora, rgnl sls mgr.

KLVE(FM)—Listing follows KTNQ(AM).

KMPC(AM)— Sept 22, 1952: 1540 khz; 50 kw-D, 10 kw-N, DA-2. TL: N34 04 43 W118 11 05. Stereo. 2800 28th St., Suite 308, Santa Monica 90405. Phone: (310) 452-7100. Fax: (310) 452-8010. E-mail: jryan@kmpc1540.com. Web Site: www.1540theticket.com. Licensee: Rose City Radio Corp. (group owner; acq 3-23-01; grpsl). Format: Sports. ♦Roger Nadel, gen mgr.

KMRB(AM)—See San Gabriel

KMZT-FM— Feb 18, 1959: 105.1 mhz; 18 kw. 2,900 ft. TL: N34 13 45 W118 04 04. Stereo. Box 250028 90025. Phone: (310) 478-5540. Fax: (310) 445-1439. E-mail: webmaster@kmozart.com. Web Site: www.kmozart.com. Licensee: Mt. Wilson FM Broadcasters Inc. Network: AP Radio. Rep: CMBS. Cohn & Marks. Format: Class. ♦Saul Levine, pres & gen mgr; Linda Vali, sls dir; Michael Levine, mktg dir; Susan Foreman, prom dir; Dave Wagner, progmg VP.

KNX(AM)— Sept 10, 1920: 1070 khz; 50 kw-U. TL: N33 51 35 W118 20 56. Stereo. 6121 Sunset Blvd. 90028. Phone: (323) 460-3000. Fax: (323) 460-3114. Fax: (323) 460-3352. Web Site: www.knx1070.com. Licensee: Infinity Broadcasting East Inc. Group owner: Infinity Broadcasting Corp. (acq 9-36). Network: CBS. Rep: CBS Radio. Format: News. News staff: 40. Target aud: General. ♦Michael J. Masterson, gen sls mgr; Andrew Del Guercio, natl sls mgr; Howard Freshman, rgnl sls mgr, mktg dir, prom dir & adv dir; Pat Duffy, VP, gen mgr & mktg mgr; David G. Hall, progmg VP & progmg dir; Ed Pyle, news dir; David Ysais, pub affrs dir; Dave Conant, engrg mgr. Co-owned TV: KCBS-TV affil

KCBS-FM—Co-owned with KNX(AM). 1948: 93.1 mhz; 54 kw. 5,000 ft. TL: N34 13 57 W118 04 18. Stereo. Fax: (323) 463-9270. E-mail: arrow93@arrowfm.com. Web Site: www.arrowfm.com. Network: Westwood One. Rep: Interep. Format: Rock and roll classics, mus from the 70s. News staff: one; News: 3 hrs wkly. Target aud: 25-49.Mel Karmazin, CEO & chmn; Dan Mason, pres; Fario Suledian, CFO; Dave Van Dyke, VP & gen mgr; Jackie Herek, opns mgr; Brad West, gen sls mgr; Tim McClellan, natl sls mgr; Scott Springer, rgnl sls mgr; Tamara Goddard, mktg dir & adv dir; Jaime Korzenieski, prom mgr; Tommy Edwards, progmg dir; Clark Macy, mus dir; Lon Landis, news dir; Cynthia Eichler, pub affrs dir; Stephen Blodgett, engrg dir . Co-owned TV: KCBS-TV affil

***KPFK(FM)**— July 26, 1959: 90.7 mhz; 112 kw. 2,830 ft. TL: N34 13 45 W118 04 03. Stereo. 3729 Cahuenga Blvd. W., North Hollywood 91604. Phone: (818) 985-2711. Fax: (818) 763-7526. E-mail: gm@kpfk.org. Web Site: www.kpfk.org. Licensee: Pacifica Foundation. Group owner: Pacifica Foundation Inc. dba Pacifica Radio Haley, Bader & Potts. Format: Div, news/talk. News staff: 2; News: 11 hrs wkly. Target aud: General. Spec prog: Folk 5 hrs, jazz 14 hrs, gospel & Sp 2. ♦Eva Georgia, stn mgr; Nathan Scott, opns mgr; Archie Richardson, dev dir & dev mgr; Armando Gudino, progmg dir; M. T. Karthik, news dir.

KPWR(FM)— Dec 20, 1956: 105.9 mhz; 72 kw. 770 ft. TL: N34 09 50 W118 11 45. Stereo. 2600 W. Olive Ave., Suite 850, Burbank 91505. Phone: (818) 953-4200. Fax: (818) 848-0961. Web Site: www.power106.fm. Licensee: Emmis Radio License LLC. Group owner: Emmis Communications Corp. (acq 1-84; grpsl; FTR: 1-30-84). Rep: D & R Radio. Format: Rhythmic CHR. Target aud: 18-34. ♦Jeff Smulyan, CEO; Rick Cummings, pres; Val Maki, sr VP; Patrick Thomasson, gen sls mgr; Dianna Jason, mktg VP; Dennis Martin, chief of engrg.

KRCD(FM)—See Inglewood

KRLA(AM)—See Glendale

KRTH(FM)— 1941: 101.1 mhz; 51 kw. 3,130 ft. TL: N34 13 38 W118 04 00. (CP: 53.6 kw). Stereo. 5670 Wilshire, Suite 200 90036. Phone: (323) 936-5784. Fax: (323) 464-6101. Web Site: www.kearth101.com. Licensee: Infinity Broadcasting East Inc. Group owner: Infinity Broadcasting Corp. (acq 2-2-94; $116 million;. FTR: 4-18-94). Network: AP Network News. Rep: Infinity Radio Sales. Format: Oldies. Target aud: 25-64. ♦Maureen Lesourd, VP & gen mgr; Tracy Gilliam, sls VP & gen sls mgr; Lori Brasher, natl sls mgr; Diane Morales, prom dir & prom mgr; Jay Coffey, progmg dir. Co-owned TV: KCBS-TV affil

KSCA(FM)—See Glendale

KSPN(AM)— Feb 18, 1927:: 710 khz; 50 kw-D, 10 kw-N, DA-N. TL: N34 10 24 W118 24 24. 3321 S. La Cienega Blvd. 90016. Phone: (310) 840-2800. Fax: (310) 840-2848. Web Site: www.espnradio710.com. Licensee: KABC-AM Radio Inc. Group owner: ABC Inc. (acq 2-27-95; $17.5 million). Network: ABC. Format: Sports. News staff: 2. Target aud: General; famlies and moms. ♦John Davison, pres & gen mgr.

KTLK(AM)— 1927: 1150 khz; 50 kw-D, 44 kw-N, DA-2. TL: N34 02 00 W117 59 00. Stereo. 3400 W. Olive Ave., Suite 550, Burbank 91505. Phone: (818) 559-2252. Licensee: Citicasters Licenses L.P. Group owner: Clear Channel Communications Inc. (acq 5-4-99; grpsl). Format: Progressive talk. ♦Greg Ashlock, gen mgr; Don Martin, stn mgr.

KIIS-FM—Co-owned with KTLK(AM). 1948: 102.7 mhz; 8 kw. 2,960 ft. TL: N34 13 36 W118 03 57. Stereo. Fax: (818) 295-6466. Web Site: www.kiisfm.com. Format: CHR. Target aud: 18-34. ♦Roy Laughlin, gen mgr.

KTNQ(AM)— 1925: 1020 khz; 50 kw-U, DA-2. TL: N34 02 00 W117 59 00. Stereo. 655 N. Central Ave., Suite 2500, Glendale 91203. Phone: (818) 500-4500. Fax: (818) 500-4329. Web Site: www.ktnq.com. Licensee: KTNQ-AM License Corp. Group owner: Univision Radio (acq 9-22-2003; grpsl). Rep: Katz Hispanic. Format: Sp, news/talk. Target aud: 25-54. ♦Gary Stone, gen mgr.

KLVE(FM)—Co-owned with KTNQ(AM). May 2, 1959: 107.5 mhz; 29.5 kw. 3,100 ft. TL: N34 13 44 W118 04 02. Format: Adult contemp. Target aud: 18-49. ♦Veronica Herrador, prom dir; Santiago Nieto, progmg dir; Manuel Villasenor, pub affrs dir; Tom Koza, engrg dir.

KTWV(FM)— Mar 7, 1961: 94.7 mhz; 58 kw. 2,835 ft. TL: N34 13 29 W118 03 47. Stereo. 5670 Wilshire Blvd., Suite 200 90036. Phone: (323) 937-9283. E-mail: wave@ktwv.cbs.com. Web Site: www.947wave.com. Licensee: Infinity Broadcasting East Inc. Group owner: Infinity Broadcasting Corp. (acq 11-13-98; grpsl). Format: Smooth jazz. Target aud: 25-54. ♦Bob Moore, VP; Dan Weiner, gen mgr; Pat Amsbry, gen sls mgr; Paul Goldstein, progmg dir; Lynn Duke, engrg mgr & chief of engrg.

***KUSC(FM)**— 1946: 91.5 mhz; 39 kw. 2,922 ft. TL: N34 12 48 W118 03 41. Stereo. Box 77913 90007. Secondary address: 515 S. Figueroa St., Suite 2050 90071. Phone: (213) 225-7400. Fax: (213) 225-7410. E-mail: kusc@kusc.org. Web Site: www.kusc.org. Licensee: University of Southern California. Network: Network: PRI, NPR. Lawrence Bernstein. Format: Class. Target aud: 35 plus. ♦Brenda Barnes, pres; Eric DeWeese, gen mgr; Janet McIntyre, dev dir.

KWKW(AM)— Apr 14, 1931: 1330 khz; 5 kw-U, DA-N. TL: N34 01 10 W118 20 42. 3301 Barham Blvd., Suite 201 90068. Phone: (323) 851-5959. Fax: (323) 512-7460. E-mail: kwkw1330@aol.com. Web Site: www.kwkw1330.com. Licensee: Lotus Communications Corp. (group owner; (acq 1962). Format: Sp, news/talk, sports talk. News staff: 5; News: 20 hrs wkly. Target aud: 25 plus; Sp-speaking families. ♦Jim Kalmenson, pres & gen mgr.

Broadcasting & Cable Yearbook 2006

D-81

California

*KXLU(FM)— February 1957: 88.9 mhz; 3 kw. 12 ft. TL: N33 58 16 W118 24 56. Stereo. 1 LMU Drive 90045. Phone: (310) 338-2866. Phone: (310) 338-5958. Fax: (310) 338-5959. E-mail: kxlu889fm@hotmail.com. Web Site: www.kxlu.com. Licensee: Loyola Marymount University Board of Trustees. Format: Rock. News: 2 hrs wkly. Target aud: 16-30. Spec prog: Black 10 hrs, Children one hr, folk one hr wkly. ♦Brian Reyes, gen mgr.

KXOL-FM— 1949: 96.3 mhz; 7 kw. Ant 1,273 ft. TL: N34 11 46 W118 15 32. Stereo. 10281 W. Pico Blvd. 90064. Phone: (310) 203-0900. Fax: (310) 843-4961. Web Site: www.elsol963.com. Licensee: KXOL Licensing Inc. Group owner: Spanish Broadcasting System Inc. (acq 10-30-2003; $250 million). Format: Sp. Target aud: 18-54. ♦Raul Alcarcon Jr., CEO; Raul Alarcon Jr., pres; William Tanner, exec VP; David Haymore, gen mgr; Maria Elena Nava, opns mgr; Daniel Carrillo, gen sls mgr; Julietta Garcia, prom dir.

KYPA(AM)— 1926: 1230 khz; 1 kw-U. TL: N34 02 15 W118 16 35. 747 E. Green St., Suite 400, Pasadena 91101. Phone: (626) 844-8882. Fax: (626) 844-0156. Licensee: Multicultural Radio Broadcasting Licensee LLC. Group owner: Multicultural Radio Broadcasting Inc. (acq 2-20-98; grpsl). Network: ABC. Fleischman & Walsh L. Format: Korean. ♦David Sweeney, gen mgr & opns mgr.

KYSR(FM)— June 30, 1954: 98.7 mhz; 75 kw. 1,180 ft. TL: N34 07 08 W118 23 30. Stereo. 3400 W. Olive, Suite 550, Burbank 91505. Phone: (818) 559-2252. Fax: (818) 566-4517. E-mail: starprogramming @clearchannel.com. Web Site: www.star987.com. Licensee: AMFM Broadcasting Licenses LLC. Group owner: Clear Channel Communications Inc. (acq 8-30-2000; grpsl). Format: Hot adult contemp. Target aud: 25-54. Spec prog: Pub affrs 2 hrs wkly. ♦Brad Samuel, gen mgr; Keith Samuels, gen sls mgr; Angela Perelli, progmg dir; Chuck Ide, chief of engrg.

KZLA-FM— Aug 7, 1957: 93.9 mhz; 18.5 kw horiz, 16 kw vert. Ant 3,136 ft. TL: N34 13 57 W118 04 13. Stereo. 2600 W Olive Ave., 8th Fl., Burbank 91505. Phone: (818) 525-5000. Fax: (818) 525-5002. Web Site: www.kzla.com. Licensee: Emmis Radio License LLC. Group owner: Emmis Communicationsl Corp. (acq 9-26-2000; grpsl). Format: Country. Target aud: 25-54; women. ♦Jeff Smulyan, CEO & chmn; Rick Cummings, pres; Walter Berger, CFO; Val Maki, sr VP; R.J. Curtis, opns mgr; R. J. Curtis, progmg dir.

Los Banos

KLBS(AM)— May 1961: 1330 khz; 500 w-D, 5 kw-N, DA-N. TL: N37 05 51 W120 49 51. Stereo. 401 Pacheco Blvd. 93635. Phone: (209) 826-0578/826-4996. Fax: (209) 826-1906. E-mail: pr@klbs.com. Web Site: www.klbs.com. Licensee: Ethnic Radio Los Banos Inc. (acq 5-82). Format: Portuguese. Spec prog: Relg 8 hrs wkly. ♦Jose Encarnacao, gen mgr.

KQLB(FM)— November 1992: 106.9 mhz; 6 kw. 328 ft. TL: N36 55 35 W120 50 42. Stereo. 401 Pacheco Blvd. 93635. Phone: (209) 827-0101. Fax: (209) 826-1906. E-mail: pr@kqlb.com. Web Site: www.kqlb.com. Licensee: VLB Broadcasting Inc. (acq 12-26-91). Format: Spanish. ♦Batista Vieira, chmn; J.J. Encarnacao, gen mgr; Cidalia Sequeira, opns mgr; Saul Fiacco, progmg dir.

Los Gatos

KRTY(FM)— July 9, 1966: 95.3 mhz; 880 w. 860 ft. TL: N37 12 17 W121 56 56. Stereo. Box 995, San Jose 95108. Phone: (408) 293-8030. Fax: (408) 293-6124. Fax: (408) 995-0823. Web Site: www.krty.com. Licensee: KRTY Ltd. Group owner: Empire Broadcasting Corp. (acq 2-93; $3.31 million; 1-18-93). Rep: Major Market Broadcasters Ltd. Format: Country. News staff: one. Target aud: 25-54. ♦Bob Kieve, pres & gen mgr; Stuart Hinkle, natl sls mgr; Rich Menendez, rgnl sls mgr; Nate Deaton, mktg dir.

Los Molinos

KCEZ(FM)— 1999: 102.1 mhz; 25 kw. Ant 266 ft. TL: N39 53 16 W122 37 38. 856 Manzanita Ct., Chico 95926. Phone: (530) 342-2200. Fax: (530) 342-2260. Web Site: www.chicooldies.com. Licensee: Results Radio Licensee L.L.C. Group owner: Fritz Communications Inc. (acq 6-11-99; grpsl). Format: Oldies. ♦Bob Cross, gen mgr; John Graham, gen sls mgr; Steve Michaels, progmg dir; J.D. Davis, chief of engrg.

Los Osos-Baywood Park

KSTT-FM— 1987: 101.3 mhz; 4.86 kw. 1,506 ft. TL: N35 21 38 W120 39 21. (CP: 3.4 kw, ant 1,685 ft.). 51 Zaca Ln., Suite 100, San Luis Obispo 93401. Phone: (805) 545-0101. Fax: (805) 541-5303. Web Site: www.kstt.com. Licensee: Clear Channel Radio Licenses Inc. Group owner: Clear Channel Communications Inc. (acq 10-00; grpsl). Format: Soft adult contemp. News staff: one; News: 5 hrs wkly. Target aud: 25-54. ♦Rich Hawkins, gen mgr; Pattie Wagner, natl sls mgr; Greg Russo, mktg dir & prom dir.

Lucerne Valley

KIXA(FM)— November 1992: 106.5 mhz; 150 w. 1,066 ft. TL: N34 23 08 W117 03 25. 12370 Hesperia Rd., Suite 16, Victorville 92392. Phone: (760) 241-1313. Fax: (760) 241-0205. Web Site: www.thefox1065.com. Licensee: Clear Channel Broadcasting Licenses Inc. Group owner: Clear Channel Communications Inc. (acq 2000; grpsl). Format: Active rock. News: 18 hrs wkly. Target aud: 16-45. ♦Jason Houts, exec VP & engrg VP; Steve Sipe, sls dir; Chris Price, gen sls mgr; Coleen Quinn, progmg dir; Rowdy Walker, mus dir.

Ludlow

KDUQ(FM)— July 7, 1995: 102.5 mhz; 6 kw. Ant -164 ft. TL: N34 43 21 W116 10 04. Stereo. 29000 Radio Rd., Barstow 92311. Phone: (760) 256-2121. Fax: (760) 256-5090. E-mail: doscostas@yahoo.com.ABC/SMN Pine Gold Licensee: Dos Costas Communications Corp. (group owner; acq 6-18-03; grpsl). Network: Network: ABC, CBS. Rep: Western Regional Broadcast Sales. Fleischmann & Walsh. Format: CHR rhythmic. News staff: one; News: 7 hrs wkly. Target aud: 25-54:; adults. Spec prog: Relg one hr wkly. ♦Roland Ulloa, stn mgr; Troy Colton, opns mgr & gen sls mgr; Mike Garcia, progmg mgr; Brad Sobel, news dir & chief of engrg.

KHWZ(FM)— 1992: 100.1 mhz; 25 kw. Ant -216 ft. TL: N34 43 29 W116 09 24. Box 1668, Barstow 90025. Phone: (760) 256-0326. Fax: (760) 256-9507. E-mail: khwyha@earthlink.net. Web Site: www.thehighwaystations.com. Licensee: KHWY Inc. (group owner). Network: Network: CNN Radio, Westwood One. Format: AOR. News staff: one. Target aud: 35 plus; travelers on I-15 & I-40. ♦Howard B. Anderson, CEO & pres; Kirk M. Anderson, exec VP; Timothy B. Anderson, VP & gen mgr; Judy Robinson, gen sls mgr & rgnl sls mgr.

Madera

KHOT(AM)— Dec 31, 1956: 1250 khz; 1.5 kw-D, 1 kw-N, DA-2. TL: N36 57 58 W120 02 06. Box 180, Tahoma 96142. Phone: (530) 584-5700. Fax: (530) 584-5705. Web Site: www.ihradio.org. Licensee: Redwood Family Services Inc. Format: Relg-Catholic. News staff: one; News: 30 hrs wkly. Target aud: 25-54. ♦Doug Sherman, pres; Joseph Nesta, stn mgr.

KMMM(FM)— October 1992: 107.1 mhz; 9.9 kw. Ant 515 ft. TL: N37 07 40 W119 40 38. 1110 E. Olive Ave., Fresno 93728. Phone: (559) 497-1100. Fax: (559) 497-1125. E-mail: dcrotty@lotusfresno.com. Licensee: Illinois Lotus Corp. Group owner: Lotus Communications Corp. (acq 3-10-99). Leventhal, Senter & Lerman. Format: Sp. Target aud: 18-49. ♦Dan Crotty, gen mgr; Steve Wrath, gen sls mgr & prom mgr; Jose Berumen, progmg dir; Paul Klein Kramer, chief of engrg.

KOND(FM)—(Clovis). Sept 30, 1974: 92.1 mhz; 36.9 kw. Ant 567 ft. TL: N37 07 40 W119 40 38. Stereo. 1981 N. Gateway Blvd., Suite 101, Fresno 93727. Phone: (559) 456-4000. Fax: (559) 251-9555. Web Site: www.univisionradio.com. Licensee: Univision Radio License Corp. Group owner: Univision Radio (acq 2-18-2004; $8 million). Format: Sp adult contemp. ♦Robert Torres, VP & gen mgr.

Magalia

*KLVC(FM)— Jan 1, 1993: 88.3 mhz; 5.7 kw. 1,184 ft. TL: N39 57 45 W121 42 52. Stereo. 5700 W. Oaks Blvd., Rocklin 95765. Phone: (916) 251-1600. Fax: (916) 251-1650. E-mail: klove@klove.com. Web Site: www.klove.com. Licensee: Educational Media Foundation Inc. Group owner: EMF Broadcasting. Network: K-Love. Shaw Pittman. Format: Contemp Christian. News staff: 3. Target aud: 33—40; Judeo-Christian, female. ♦Richard Jenkins, pres; Mike Novak, VP & progmg dir; Lloyd Parker, gen mgr; Ed Lenane, opns dir; Keith Whipple, dev dir; Chris Joyce, prom dir & prom mgr.

Mammoth Lakes

KMMT(FM)— Apr 3, 1973: 106.5 mhz; 360 w. Ant 2,371 ft. TL: N37 37 42 W119 01 47. Stereo. Box 1284, 94 Laurel Mountain Rd. 93546. Phone: (760) 934-8888. Fax: (760) 934-2429. E-mail: kmmtradioworks@yahoo.com. Licensee: Mammoth Mountain F.M. Associates Inc. Format: Modern adult contemp. News staff: one; News: 2 hrs wkly. Target aud: 18-54; active, athletic, affluent adults. Spec prog: Jazz 2 hrs, classic rock 4 hrs wkly. ♦David A. Digerness, pres & chief of engrg; Shellie Woods, gen mgr & gen sls mgr; Maryanne Digerness, stn mgr & mktg dir; Spencer Myers, progmg dir.

Manteca

KMRQ(FM)— Jan 15, 1979: 96.7 mhz; 3 kw. 328 ft. TL: N37 43 45 W121 11 49. Stereo. 2121 Lancey Dr., Modesto 95355. Phone: (209) 551-1306. Fax: (209) 551-1359. Web Site: www.rock967.com. Licensee: Capstar TX L.P. Group owner: Clear Channel Communications Inc. (acq 8-30-00; grpsl). Mullin, Rhyne, Emmons & Topel. Format: Rock AOR. News staff: one. Target aud: 25-54. ♦Gary Halladay, VP & gen mgr; Greg Cobb, sls VP; Mike Hogan, gen sls mgr; Jack Paper, progmg VP & progmg dir.

Marina

KTOM-FM— Apr 6, 1982: 92.7 mhz; 6.9 kw. 567 ft. TL: N36 33 12 W121 47 05. Stereo. 903 N. Main St., Salinas 93906. Phone: (831) 755-8181. Fax: (831) 755-8193. Web Site: www.ktom.com. Licensee: Clear Channel Broadcasting Licenses Inc. Group owner: Clear Channel Communications Inc. (acq 9-22-97; grpsl). Rep: D & R Radio. Format: Country. News staff: one; News: 5 hrs wkly. Target aud: 25-54; men. ♦Kim Bryant, gen mgr; Rhonda McCormick, sls dir & gen sls mgr; Dennis Martin, progmg dir; Mike Blankbecler, chief of engrg.

Mariposa

KDJK(FM)— 1994: 103.9 mhz; 71 w. 2,047 ft. TL: N37 32 00 W120 01 29. Stereo. 1581 Cummins Dr., Suite 135, Modesto 95358-6402. Phone: (209) 572-0104. Fax: (209) 522-2061. Web Site: www.104thehawk.com. Licensee: Citadel Broadcasting Co. Group owner: Citadel Broadcasting Corp. (acq 7-30-93; $6 million;. FTR: 8-23-93). Rep: Christal. Format: Classic Rock. Target aud: 18-54. ♦Roy Williams, gen mgr; Richard Perry, opns dir & progmg dir; Jean Western, gen sls mgr; Gary Williams, engrg mgr & chief of engrg.

KUBB(FM)— July 4, 1977: 96.3 mhz; 1.9 kw. 2,112 ft. TL: N37 32 00 W120 01 29. Stereo. Box 429, 510 W. 19th St., Merced 95340. Phone: (209) 383-7900. Fax: (209) 723-8461. E-mail: mcadam@kubb.com. Web Site: www.kubb.com. Licensee: Buckley Broadcasting of Monterey. Group owner: Buckley Broadcasting Corp. (acq 7-1-85; $640,000; 5-20-85). Network: Westwood One. Rep: D & R Radio. Format: Country. News staff: one; News: 2 hrs wkly. Target aud: 25-54. Spec prog: Farm 2 hrs wkly. ♦Mike McAdam, gen mgr, gen sls mgr & rgnl sls mgr; Rene Roberts, opns dir & progmg dir; Sharon Cresswell, mktg dir; Drew Stone, prom dir.

Marysville

KKCY(FM)—See Colusa

KMYC(AM)— 1940: 1410 khz; 5 kw-D, 1 kw-N, DA-2. TL: N39 08 18 W121 33 15. Box 669 95901. Phone: (530) 742-5555. Fax: (530) 741-3758. E-mail: kmyc@xyix.com. Licensee: Thomas Huth. Group owner: Huth Broadcasting. . Format: Talk radio. News staff: one. Target aud: 18 plus; general. Spec prog: Indian/Punjabi 2 hrs wkly. ♦Thomas Huth, CEO, gen mgr & rgnl sls mgr; Jerry Snaper, engrg VP & chief of engrg.

KOBO(AM)—See Yuba City

KRCX-FM— Oct 12, 1994: 99.9 mhz; 1.74 kw. 2,181 ft. TL: N39 12 20 W121 49 10. Stereo. 1436 Auburn Blvd., Sacramento 95815. Phone: (916) 646-4000. Fax: (916) 646-1958. E-mail: jverdier@entravision.com. Web Site: www.entravision.com. Licensee: Entravision Holdings LLC. Group owner: Entravision Communications Corp. (acq 3-14-00; grpsl). Format: Mexican rgnl, Sp. News staff: 2. Target aud: 18-49. ♦Larry Lamanski, gen mgr; Joni Verdier, gen sls mgr; Salvador Lopez, prom dir; Nestor Rocha, progmg dir; Paul Waegele, chief of engrg.

KUBA(AM)—See Yuba City

Stations in the U.S. California

Developers & Brokers of Radio Properties

contact American Media Services at our suite:
Philadelphia Marriott Downtown
215-625-2900
843-972-2200
americanmediaservices.com
Charleston, SC
Dallas, TX · Chicago, Il · Austin, TX
American Media Services, LLC

McFarland

KIWI(FM)—Licensed to McFarland. See Bakersfield

Mecca

KRCK-FM— 2001: 97.7 mhz; 1.25 kw. Ant 718 ft. TL: N33 39 18 W115 59 16. 73-733 Fred Waring Dr., Suite 201, Palm Desert 92260. Phone: (760) 341-0123. Fax: (760) 341-7455. E-mail: sales@krck.com. Web Site: www.krck.com. Licensee: Playa Del Sol Broadcasters. Format: Rock of the 80s. ♦ Edward Stolz, gen mgr; Kevin Childs, stn mgr.

Mendocino

*****KAKX(FM)**— Jan 15, 1997: . Stn currently dark 89.3 mhz; 250 w. 7 ft. TL: N39 18 30 W123 48 02. Stereo. Box 1154 95460. E-mail: audio@mcn.org. Licensee: Mendocino Unified School District. Format: Educ, var, Rock.

KMFB(FM)— November 1966: 92.7 mhz; 3 kw. 165 ft. TL: N39 20 33 W123 46 51. Stereo. 101-E Boatyard Dr., Fort Bragg 95437. Secondary address: 14200 Prairie Way 95460. Phone: (707) 964-5307. Fax: (707) 964-3299. E-mail: tenniselbow53@email.com. Web Site: www.kmfb-fm.com. Licensee: Four Rivers Broadcasting Inc. (group owner; acq 7-21-2005; grpsl). Format: Vintage rock, professional sports. News staff: 4. Target aud: 35-54. ♦ Bob Woelfel, gen mgr, gen sls mgr, progmg dir, progmg mgr & mus dir; Liz Helenchild, mus dir; Ed Kowas, news dir.

*****KPMO(AM)**— Nov 16, 1966: 1300 khz; 5 kw-D, 77 w-N. TL: N39 20 33 W123 46 51. Jefferson Public Radio, 1250 Siskiyou Blvd., Ashland, OR 97520. Phone: (541) 552-6301. Fax: (541) 552-8565. Web Site: www.jeffnet.org. Licensee: JPR Foundation Inc. (acq 8-8-02). Network: Network: NPR, PRI. Ernest Sanchez. Format: News/talk. News staff: one. Target aud: General. ♦ Ronald Kramer, CEO; Ronald Kramer, gen mgr; Bryon Lambert, opns dir.

Mendota

KMEN(FM)—Not on air, target date: unknown: 100.5 mhz; 6 kw. Ant 144 ft. TL: N36 38 53 W120 20 56. Moon Broadcasting Porterville L.L.C., 1200 W. Venice Blvd., Los Angeles 90006. Phone: (213) 745-6224. Fax: (213) 745-7577. E-mail: postmaster @moonbroadcasting.com. Web Site: www.moonbroadcasting.com. Licensee: MBP Licensee LLC. Group owner: Moon Broadcasting (acq 3-30-2001; $350,000). Format: Rgnl Mexican. ♦ Abel A. de Luna, pres.

Merced

KABX-FM—Listing follows KYOS(AM).

*****KAMB(FM)**— Nov 6, 1967: 101.5 mhz; 1.85 kw. 2,093 ft. TL: N37 32 01 W120 01 46. Stereo. 90 E. 16th St. 95340-5099. Phone: (209) 723-1015. Fax: (209) 723-1945. E-mail: kamb@celebrationradio.com. Web site: www.celebrationradio.com. Licensee: Central Valley Broadcasting Co. Inc. Network: Network: Network: AP Radio, Moody, UPI. Fletcher, Heald & Hildreth. Format: Contemp Christian. News staff: one; News: 5 hrs wkly. Target aud: 29-54; Christian adults in central California. ♦ Dan Finn, pres; Tim Land, CEO & gen mgr; Mark Murdock, opns dir.

KBKY(FM)— January 2002: 94.1 mhz; 6 kw. 328 ft. TL: N37 27 59 W120 14 09. 450 Grogan Ave., Suite A 95340. Phone: (209) 385-9994. Fax: (209) 385-9982. E-mail: mmeroney941@mercednet.com. Web Site: www.foxsportsmerced.com. Licensee: KM Radio of Merced L.L.C. (acq 9-30-99). Format: Sports. ♦ Dave Putonen, gen sls mgr; Mike Meroney, gen mgr & prom mgr; Matthew Stone, progmg dir; Chuck Hughes, chief of engrg.

KHPO(FM)— May 14, 1992: 106.3 mhz; 4 kw. Ant 403 ft. TL: N37 25 35 W120 26 25. 1020 W. Main St. 95340-4521. Phone: (209) 723-2191. Fax: (209) 383-2950. Web Site: www.radiomerced.com. Licensee: Mapleton Communications LLC (group owner; acq 6-1-02; grpsl). Format: Classic hits. Target aud: 25-54; upscale professionals. ♦ Andrew Adams, gen mgr; Chad Gammage, gen sls mgr; Damian Galaarza, gen sls mgr; Chris Ashton, progmg dir; Rick McMillion, chief of engrg.

KTIQ(AM)— Nov 1, 1999: 1660 khz; 10 kw-D, 1 kw-N. TL: N37 16 41 W120 37 35. 1020 Main St. 95340. Phone: (209) 723-21911. Fax: (209) 383-2950. Licensee: Mapleton Communications LLC (group owner; acq 6-1-2002; grpsl). Format: News/talk, Sp. Target aud: 25-54. ♦ Andrew Adams, gen mgr & opns VP.

KUBB(FM)—See Mariposa

KYOS(AM)— October 1936: 1480 khz; 5 kw-U, DA-N. TL: N37 22 30 W120 27 37. 1020 W. Main 95340. Phone: (209) 723-2191. Fax: (209) 383-2950. Licensee: Mapleton Communications LLC (group owner; acq 6-5-2002; grpsl). Network: Network: CBS, ABC Information & Entertainment. Rep: Christal. Format: News/talk. News staff: 2; News: 20 hrs wkly. Target aud: 25-54. Spec prog: Farm 5 hrs, gospel one hr wkly. ♦ Edward G. Hoyt Jr., pres; Dale Hendrix, gen mgr; Andrew Adams, sls dir & progmg mgr.

KABX-FM—Co-owned with KYOS(AM). Dec 18, 1975: 97.5 mhz; 50 kw. 490 ft. TL: N37 22 31 W120 27 37. Stereo. Format: Oldies.

Middletown

KSXY(FM)— December 1993: 98.7 mhz; 340 w. 1,378 ft. TL: N38 45 55 W122 45 54. 3565 Standish Ave., Santa Rosa 95407. Phone: (707) 588-0707. Fax: (707) 588-0777. Web Site: www.hot987.fm. Licensee: Commonwealth Broadcasting LLC. Group owner: Sinclair Communications Inc. (acq 8-3-2001; $5.5 million). Format: Rhythmic CHR. ♦ Debbie Morton, gen mgr; Danny Wright, stn mgr; Crash Kelley, opns dir.

Mission Viejo

*****KSBR(FM)**— May 7, 1979: 88.5 mhz; 620 w. 600 ft. TL: N33 30 10 W117 36 06. Stereo. 28000 Marguerite Pkwy. 92692. Phone: (949) 582-5727. Fax: (949) 347-9693. Web Site: www.ksbr.net. Licensee: South Orange County Community College District. Format: Jazz. News staff: one. Target aud: 25-54. Spec prog: Latin 3 hrs, blues 3 hrs, reggae 3 hrs, electronic 4 hrs, ragtime 2 hrs, folk 2 hrs wkly. ♦ Terry Wedel, opns dir; Dawn Kamber, news dir; Mark Schiffelbein, engrg dir.

Modesto

*****KADV(FM)**— November 1988: 90.5 mhz; 1.5 kw. 200 ft. TL: N37 36 26 W120 57 26. Stereo. 2031 Academy Pl., Ceres 95307. Phone: (209) 537-1201. Fax: (209) 537-1945. E-mail: helpfs@kadv.org. Web Site: www.kadv.org. Licensee: Modesto Adventist Academy. Network: Moody. Format: Educ, relg. News: 14 hrs wkly. Target aud: 45 plus. Spec prog: Sp one hr wkly. ♦ Chris Nelson, chmn; Jerry Moore, gen mgr; Don Odell, prom dir; Steve White, stn mgr & progmg dir.

KATM(FM)—Listing follows KESP(AM).

KBBU(FM)— 1999: 93.9 mhz; 4 kw. Ant 403 ft. TL: N37 39 00 W121 01 24. 1401 El Camino Ave., Suite 330, Sacramento 95815. Phone: (916) 443-1049. Fax: (916) 441-6480. E-mail: abalderas@bustosmedia.com. Web Site: www.lakebuena.com. Licensee: Bustos Media of California License LLC. (acq 12-15-2004; $21.7 million. with KTTA(FM) Esparto). Format: Rgnl Mexican. ♦ Angie Balderas, gen mgr & stn mgr.

KCIV(FM)—See Mount Bullion

KESP(AM)— 1951: 970 khz; 1 kw-U, DA-2. TL: N37 41 28 W120 57 11. Stereo. 1581 Cummins Dr., Suite 135 95358. Phone: (209) 523-7756. Fax: (209) 522-2061. Web Site: www.espnradio970.com. Licensee: Citadel Broadcasting Co. Group owner: Citadel Broadcasting Corp. (acq 5-18-92; $12.5 million. grpsl, including co-located FM; FTR: 6-8-92). Network: Network: ABC, CBS. Rep: McGavren Guild. Format: MOR, sports. Target aud: 35 plus. ♦ Tommy Ehrman, gen mgr.

KATM(FM)—Co-owned with KESP(AM). 1948: 103.3 mhz; 50 kw. 500 ft. TL: N37 34 30 W121 21 13. Stereo. Web Site: www.espnradio970.com. Format: Country. Target aud: 25-64; mass appeal.

KFIV(AM)— 1950: 1360 khz; 4 kw-D, 950 w-N, DA-2. TL: N37 39 52 W120 57 00. 2121 Lancey Dr. 95355. Phone: (209) 551-1306. Fax: (209) 551-1359. Web site: www.kfiv1360.com. Licensee: Capstar TX L.P. Group owner: Clear Channel Communiications Inc. (acq 8-30-00; grpsl). Network: ABC. Format: News/talk. Target aud: 25-54. ♦ Gary Halladay, exec VP & gen mgr; Greg Edwards, opns dir; Greg Cobb, sls dir; Rick Myers, mktg dir; Jay Schell, prom dir; Tom Cody, progmg mgr; Tim St. Martin, news dir; Steve Minshall, chief of engrg.

KJSN(FM)—Co-owned with KFIV(AM). July 4, 1977: 102.3 mhz; 6 kw. 300 ft. TL: N37 40 47 W120 55 28. Stereo. Box 3408 95353. Web Site: www.sunny102fm.com. Format: Adult contemp. Target aud: 25-49. ♦ Max Miller, opns mgr; Rick Myers, sls VP; Rick Myers, gen sls mgr & rgnl sls mgr; Jay Schell, prom mgr; Gary Michaels, progmg dir; Tim St. Martin, pub affrs dir; Steve Minshall, engrg mgr.

KHKK(FM)— 1949: 104.1 mhz; 50 kw. 500 ft. TL: N37 39 10 W121 28 38. Stereo. 1581 Cummins Dr., Suite 135 95358-6402. Phone: (209) 572-0104. Fax: (209) 522-2061. Web site: www.104thehawk.com. Licensee: Citadel Broadcasting Co. Group owner: Citadel Broadcasting Corp. (acq 10-1-93). Rep: McGavren Guild. Format: Rock/AOR, classic rock. News staff: one; News: 5 hrs wkly. Target aud: 25-49; baby boomers who grew up with rock and roll. ♦ Roy Williams, VP & gen mgr; Richard Perry, progmg dir; Farid Suleman, engrg mgr & chief of engrg.

KHTN(FM)—See Planada

*****KMPO(FM)**— January 1984: 88.7 mhz; 2 kw. 1,500 ft. TL: N37 32 00 W120 01 29. Stereo. 5005 E. Belmont Ave., Fresno 93727. Phone: (559) 455-5777. Fax: (559) 455-5778. E-mail: mariax@radiobilingue.org. Web Site: www.radiobilingue.org. Licensee: Radio Bilingue Inc. Format: Ethnic. News staff: 5; News: 3 hrs wkly. Target aud: 16 plus; Latinos. Spec prog: Black 3 hrs, folk 4 hrs, Filipino one hr wkly. ♦ Hugo Morales, CEO; Maria Erana, gen mgr & opns dir.

KOSO(FM)—(Patterson). June 6, 1966: 93.1 mhz; 2.95 kw. 1,791 ft. TL: N37 30 14 W121 22 22. Stereo. 2121 Lancey Dr. 95355. Phone: (209) 551-1306. Fax: (209) 551-1359. Web Site: www.b931.com. Licensee: Capstar TX L.P. Group owner: Clear Channel Communications Inc. (acq 8-30-00; grpsl). Format: Adult contemp. News staff: one; News: 5 hrs wkly. Target aud: 25-54. ♦ Gary Granger, gen mgr.

KPMP(FM)—Not on air, target date: unknown: 840 khz; 4 kw-D, 10 kw-N, DA-2. TL: N37 36 11 W121 03 52 (D), N37 42 32 W120 43 27 (N). Pappas Telecasting Companies, 500 S. Chinowth Rd., Visalia 93277. Phone: (559) 733-7800. Fax: (559) 733-7878. Licensee: Pappas Radio of Modesto LLC Group owner: Pappas Telecasting Companies (acq 11-5-2003). ♦ Ron Abercrombie, exec VP; Harry J. Pappas, gen mgr.

KTRB(AM)— June 18, 1933: 860 khz; 50 kw-D, 10 kw-N, DA-2. TL: N37 42 32 W120 43 27. (CP: COL San Francisco. 50 kw-U, DA-2. TL: N38 09 30 W122 24 44 day, N37 35 28 W121 46 29 night). Stereo. 5087 E. McKinley Ave., Fresno 93727. Phone: (209) 526-8600. Phone: (209) 453-8879. Fax: (209) 578-3568. Fax: (209) 252-4522. Licensee: Pappas Radio of California, a California L.P. Group owner: Pappas Telecasting Companies (acq 3-30-2000). Network: AP Radio. Format: Talk. Target aud: 25-64; quality traditional news/talk listener. Spec prog: Pub affrs 2 hrs, legal affrs one hr wkly. ♦ Harry J. Pappas, CEO; Charlie Pfaff, gen mgr; Jim P. Pappas, stn mgr.

KVIN(AM)—See Ceres

Mojave

*****KCRY(FM)**— June 2000: 88.1 mhz; 10.5 kw. Ant -95 ft. TL: N35 07 20 W118 12 25. c/o KCRW(FM), 1900 Pico Blvd., Santa Monica 90405. Phone: (310) 450-5183. Fax: (310) 450-7171. Web Site: www.kcrw.com. Licensee: Santa Monica Community College District.

California

Network: NPR. Format: News, var. ◆ Ruth Seymour, gen mgr; Mike Newport, opns mgr; Jacki Weber, dev dir; Nic Harcourt, mus dir; Steve Herbert, chief of engrg.

KTPI(AM)— May 1, 1958: 1340 khz; 1 kw-U. TL: N35 02 23 W118 08 57. 348 E. Avenue K-4, Lancaster 93535. Phone: (661) 942-1121. Fax: (661) 723-5512. Licensee: Clear Channel Broadcasting Licenses Inc. Group owner: Clear Channel Communications Inc. (acq 11-21-03; grpsl). Network: ABC Information & Entertainment. Rep: Christal. Latham & Watkins. Target aud: 35 plus; Adult Christian community. ◆ Larry Thornhill, gen mgr.

KTPI-FM—See Tehachapi

KVVS(FM)— May 1966: 97.7 mhz; 3 kw. 145 ft. TL: N34 58 45 W118 10 02. (CP: Ant 300 ft.). Stereo. 348 East Ave. K4, Lancaster 93535. Phone: (818) 559-2252. Phone: (818) 295-6405. Fax: (818) 295-6466. E-mail: 977kilsfm@clearchannel.com. Web Site: www.977kilsfm.com. Licensee: Citicasters Licenses L.P. Group owner: Clear Channel Communications Inc. (acq 5-4-99; grpsl). Pepper & Corazzini. Format: Top 40s. News staff: one. Target aud: 18-49; active adults & young families. ◆ Larry Thornhill, gen mgr.

Monte Rio

KVRV(FM)—Licensed to Monte Rio. See Santa Rosa

Montecito

KJEE(FM)— March 1994: 92.9 mhz; 820 w. 886 ft. TL: N34 27 57 W119 40 37. 302 W. Carrillo St., 2nd Fl., Santa Barbara 93101. Phone: (805) 963-4676. Fax: (805) 963-8166. E-mail: sales@kjee.com. Web Site: www.kjee.com. Licensee: Montecito FM Inc. Format: Modern rock. Target aud: 18-34; general. ◆ Eddie Gutierrez, gen mgr; Steve Meade, rgnl sls mgr; Jeff Thiemer, prom VP.

Monterey

KBOQ(FM)—(Carmel). Dec 4, 1993: 95.5 mhz; 1.7 kw. 630 ft. TL: N36 33 09 W121 47 17. 2511 Garden Rd., Suite C-150 93940. Phone: (831) 656-9550. Fax: (831) 656-9551. E-mail: info@kbach.com. Web Site: www.kbach.com. Licensee: Mapleton Communications LLC. (acq 6-7-2005; $3.75 million). Rep: CMBS. Miller & Miller. Format: Class. News staff: one. Target aud: 35 plus. ◆ Adam Nathanson, pres; Ed Monroe, gen sls mgr; Sherrie McCullough, CFO, gen mgr & progmg mgr; Rick Meltzig, chief of engrg.

KIDD(AM)—Listing follows KWAV(FM).

KNRY(AM)— October 1935: 1240 khz; 1 kw-U. TL: N36 36 56 W121 53 53. 495 Elder Ave., San City 93955-3547. Phone: (831) 899-2600. Fax: (831) 899-5102. E-mail: ronstevens@kyaradio.com. Web Site: www.kyaradio.com. Licensee: People's Radio Inc. (group owner; acq 8-31-2000; $1.1 million. with KRXA(FM) Carmel Valley). Network: CBS. Haley, Bader & Potts. Format: News/talk. Target aud: 35 plus. ◆ Joe Rosa, pres & gen mgr.

KOCN(FM)—See Pacific Grove

KPRC-FM—See Salinas

KSES-FM—See Seaside

KTOM-FM—See Marina

KWAV(FM)— Oct 14, 1961: 96.9 mhz; 18 kw. 2,450 ft. TL: N36 32 05 W121 37 14. Stereo. Box 1391 93942. Phone: (831) 649-0969. Fax: (831) 649-3335. E-mail: kwav97fm@kwav.com. Web Site: www.kwav.com. Licensee: Buckley Broadcasting Corp. of Monterey. Group owner: Buckley Broadcasting Corp. (acq 5-1-80; $700,000; 3-17-80). Rep: D & R Radio. Format: Adult contemp. Target aud: 18-54; primarily women. ◆ Kathy Baker, gen mgr; Sue Clark, gen sls mgr; Bernie Moody, progmg dir; Karen Hamilton, news dir; Bob Turner, chief of engrg.

KIDD(AM)—Co-owned with KWAV(FM). 1955: 630 khz; 1 kw-U, DA-2. TL: N36 41 28 W121 48 00. E-mail: magic63am@magic63.com. Web Site: www.magic63.com. Licensee: Buckley Communications Inc. (acq 1995; $200,000). Format: Adult standards, big band, nostalgia. ◆ Jim Souza, sls dir; Kevin Kahl, progmg dir.

KZFX(AM)—See Salinas

Moraga

*****KSMC(FM)**— Sept 22, 1977: 89.5 mhz; 800 w. 95 ft. TL: N37 50 25 W122 06 36. Stereo. Box 3223, St. Mary's College 94575. Phone: (925) 631-4252. Phone: (925) 631-4772. Fax: (925) 376-5766. E-mail: ksmc@stmarys-ca.edu. Web Site: www.ksmc895.com. Licensee: Associated Students of St. Mary's College of California. Format: CHR, educ, country. Target aud: 15-30; young, urban & willing to experiment. Spec prog: Relg 2 hrs, class 4 hrs, Sp 3 hrs, jazz 5 hrs wkly. ◆ Noel Cilker, gen mgr; Jessica Fajardo, prom dir; Will McCoster, progmg dir; Nick McAlpine, mus dir; Ed Tywoniak, chief of engrg.

Moreno Valley

KHPI(AM)— 1991: . Stn currently dark 1530 khz; 10 kw-D, DA-3. TL: N34 00 42 W117 11 03. Box 909 92556. Secondary address: 24490 Sunnymead Blvd., #215 92553. Phone: (951) 247-5479. Fax: (951) 247-2790. Licensee: Dr. D.L. Van Voorhis. Fletcher, Heald & Hildreth. ◆ Dr. D.L. Van Voorhis, pres; Bill DeGeorge, gen mgr.

KHPY(AM)— Jan 16, 2003: 1670 khz; 10 kw-D, 9 kw-N. TL: N34 00 42 W117 11 03. Box 909 92556. Phone: (909) 247-5479. Fax: (909) 247-2790. Licensee: Delbert L. Van Voorhis. Format: Brokered time. ◆ Bill DeGeorge, gen mgr.

Morgan Hill

KSQQ(FM)— December 1990: 96.1 mhz; 530 w. 781 ft. TL: N37 10 03 W121 34 20. (CP: 1 kw). 1629-C Alum Rock Ave., San Jose 95116. Phone: (408) 258-9699. Fax: (408) 258-9770. E-mail: pr@ksqq.com. Web Site: www.ksqq.com. Licensee: Coyote Communications Inc. Format: Ethnic. ◆ Batista Vieira, pres & gen mgr; Peter Mieuli, VP; Aida Barbosa, sls dir.

Morro Bay

KLMM(FM)— September 1997: 94.1 mhz; 2.3 kw. 522 ft. TL: N35 22 48 W120 45 37. (CP: 630 w, ant 1,004 ft.). 200 E. Fester St., Suite 101, Santa Maria 93454-4467. Phone: (805) 928-9796. Fax: (805) 928-3367. E-mail: lazer94@acninc.net. Licensee: Lazer Broadcasting Corp. (group owner; acq 8-7-00; $1.115 million with KLUN(FM) Paso Robles). Booth, Freret, Imlay & Tepper. Format: Adult contemp, Sp. News: 6 hrs wkly. Target aud: 25-54; general. ◆ Alfredo Plasceneia, pres; Maricarmen Buch, gen mgr; Jose Llamas, chief of opns; Maricarmen Hernandez, gen sls mgr; Salvader Prieto, progmg dir.

KXTY(FM)— May 1, 1991: 99.7 mhz; 220 w horiz, 210 w vert. 1,633 ft. TL: N35 21 37 W120 39 18. 3620 Sacramento Dr., Suite 204, San Luis Obispo 93401. Phone: (805) 781-2750. Fax: (805) 781-2758. Licensee: Salisbury Broadcasting Corp. (acq 1994). Network: AP Network News. Rep: Allied Radio Partners. Format: News/talk, sports. News staff: 2. Target aud: 25-54. ◆ Charles Salisbury, CEO; Kathy Signorelli, gen mgr; Dick Mason, progmg dir; Bill Bordeaux, chief of engrg.

Moss Beach

*****KLSI(FM)**—Not on air, target date: unknown: 89.3 mhz; 1 w horiz, 8 w vert. Ant 1,663 ft. TL: N37 33 42 W122 28 37. California Hardrives Inc., 6910 N.W. 2nd Terr., Boca Raton, FL 33487-2325. Phone: (561) 912-9002. E-mail: bill@billlacey.com. Licensee: Educational Public Radio Inc. ◆ Bill Lacey, pres.

Mount Bullion

KCIV(FM)— Apr 24, 1989: 99.9 mhz; 1.85 kw. 2,099 ft. TL: N37 32 00 W120 01 29. 1031 15th St., Suite One, Modesto 95354. Phone: (209) 524-8999. Fax: (209) 524-9088. E-mail: kciv@bottradionetwork.com. Web Site: bottradionetwork.com. Licensee: Bott Communications Inc. Group owner: Bott Radio Network Format: Christian info. Target aud: 25-54; Christian family audience. ◆ Richard P. Bott, pres; Richard Bott II, VP; Kathleen Reynolds, stn mgr & opns mgr.

Mount Shasta

KMJC(AM)— June 12, 1947: 620 khz; 1 kw-D, 290 w-N. TL: N41 19 09 W122 18 35. Jefferson Public Radio, 1250 Siskiyou Blvd., Ashland, OR 97520. Phone: (541) 552-6301. Fax: (541) 552-8565. Web Site: www.jeffnet.org. Licensee: JPR Foundation Inc. (acq 8-8-02; $300,000.

Directory of Radio

with KSYC(AM) Yreka). Network: Network: NPR, PRI. Sanchez. Format: News/talk. News staff: one. Target aud: General. ◆ Ronald Kramer, gen mgr; Bryon Lambert, opns dir; Paul Westhelle, dev dir.

*****KMJC-FM**— Nov 26, 1977: 107.9 mhz; 3.5 kw. Ant -1,296 ft. TL: N41 19 09 W122 18 35. Educational Media Foundation, 5700 W. Oaks Blvd., Rocklin 95765. Phone: (916) 251-1600. Fax: (916) 251-1650. E-mail: klove@klove.com. Web Site: www.klove.com. Licensee: Educational Media Foundation Group owner: EMF Broadcasting (acq 11-13-02; $400,000). Network: CBS Radio. Shaw Pittman. Format: Contemp Christian. News staff: 3. Target aud: 25-44; Judeo Christian, female. ◆ Richard Jenkins, pres; Mike Novak, VP & progmg dir; Lloyd Parker, gen mgr; Ed Lenane, opns dir; Keith Whipple, dev dir; Chris Joyce, prom dir.

*****KNSQ(FM)**— 1994: 88.1 mhz; 2.28 kw. 2,385 ft. TL: N41 20 46 W122 11 42. (CP: 5 kw, ant 890 ft.). Stereo. Jefferson Public Radio, 1250 Siskiyou Blvd., Ashland, OR 97520. Phone: (541) 552-6301. Web Site: www.jeffnet.org. Licensee: The State of Oregon, acting by and through the State Board of Higher Education, for the benefit of Southern Oregon University. (acq 1991; 4-1-91). Network: Network: NPR, PRI. Ernest Sanchez. Format: Jazz, AAA, news. News staff: one; News: 45 hrs wkly. Target aud: General. Spec prog: Blues 6 hrs, folk 3 hrs, pub affrs 7 hrs wkly. ◆ Mitchell Christian, CFO; Ronald Kramer, CEO & gen mgr; Bryon Lambert, opns dir; Paul Westhelle, dev dir.

Mountain Pass

KHYZ(FM)— April 1980: 99.5 mhz; 10 kw. Ant 1,710 ft. TL: N35 29 27 W115 33 27. (CP: 8.4 kw, ant 1,807 ft.). Stereo. Box 1668, 1611 E. Main St., Barstow 92312. Phone: (760) 256-0326. Fax: (760) 256-9507. E-mail: tim@highwayradio.com. Web Site: www.thehighwaystations.com. Licensee: KHWY Inc. Network: AP Radio. Hogan & Hartson. Format: Adult contemp. News staff: one; News: 16 hrs wkly. Target aud: 35 plus; travelers & loc communities. ◆ Howard B. Anderson, CEO & pres; Kirk Anderson, exec VP; Timothy Anderson, VP & gen mgr; Judy Robinson, sls VP; John Gregg, prom dir; Lance Todd, progmg dir; Keith Hayes, news dir; Thomas J. McNeill, engrg mgr.

Mountain View

*****KSFH(FM)**— 1974: 87.9 mhz; 10 w. 100 ft. TL: N37 22 09 W122 05 00. (CP: 100 w, -246 ft.). 1885 Miramonte Ave. 94040. Phone: (650) 968-1213, EXT. 272. Fax: (650) 968-1706. Web Site: www.ksfh.com. Licensee: St. Francis High School of Mountain View California Inc. Format: Contemp hits, rock/AOR, urban contemp. News: 5 hrs wkly. Target aud: General; young adult, high school, college. ◆ Paul DeCunzo, CEO.

Napa

KVON(AM)— Dec 17, 1947: 1440 khz; 5 kw-D, 1 kw-N, DA-2. TL: N38 16 47 W122 18 06. 1124 Foster Rd. 94558. Phone: (707) 252-1440. Fax: (707) 226-7544. Web Site: www.kvon.com. Licensee: Wine Country Broadcasting Co. (acq 8-11-03; $3 million. with KVYN(FM) St. Helena). Network: Network: ABC Information & Entertainment, AP Radio. Rep: Christal. Format: News/talk. News staff: 3; News: 30 hrs wkly. Target aud: 35 plus. Spec prog: Sp 2 hrs. ◆ Jeff Schechtman, gen mgr & opns dir.

KVYN(FM)—See Saint Helena

Needles

KLUK(FM)— May 1984: 97.9 mhz; 2.8 kw. 1,571 ft. TL: N35 02 06 W114 22 09. (CP: 29.5 kw). Stereo. 1531 Jill Way, Suite 7, Bullhead City, AZ 86426-9341. Phone: (928) 763-5586. Fax: (928) 763-3775. E-mail: info@lucky98.com. Web Site: www.lucky98fm.com. Licensee: Cameron Broadcasting Inc. (group owner; acq 1-18-02; grpsl). Network: AP Radio. Format: Classic rock. Target aud: 25-54; adults. ◆ Don Jacobs, gen mgr.

KNKK(FM)—Not on air, target date: unknown: 107.1 mhz; 17 kw. Ant 1,909 ft. TL: N35 01 57 W114 21 57. 1615 Orange Tree Ln., Suite 102, Redlands 92374. Phone: (928) 763-5586. Fax: (928) 763-3775. E-mail: info@theknack107.com. Web Site: www.theknack107.com. Licensee: Cameron Broadcasting Inc. (group owner; acq 3-13-01). Format: Hits of the 80s & beyond. ◆ Don Jaeger, CEO & gen mgr; Mike Fletcher, gen sls mgr; Jared Balsely, progmg dir.

KTOX(AM)— October 1952: 1340 khz; 1 kw-U. TL: N34 51 10 W114 37 19. 100 Balboa Pl. 92363. Phone: (760) 326-4500. Fax: (760) 326-6849. E-mail: info@ktox1340am.com. Web Site: www.ktox1340am.com.

Stations in the U.S. California

Developers & Brokers of Radio Properties
contact American Media Services at our suite:
Philadelphia Marriott Downtown
215-625-2900
843-972-2200
americanmediaservices.com
Charleston, SC
Dallas, TX · Chicago, Il · Austin, TX
American Media Services, LLC

Licensee: Creative Broadcasting Services Inc. (acq 12-7-00; $200,000). Network: Jones Radio Networks. Womble, Carlyle, Sandridgee & Rice. Format: News/talk. News staff: one; News: 24 hrs wkly. Target aud: 18 plus. ♦ Robert T. Hayes, CEO; David T. Hayes, pres & gen mgr; Kelly Hayes, opns mgr.

Nevada City

*KVMR(FM)— July 17, 1978: 89.5 mhz; 1.96 kw. 980 ft. TL: N39 14 47 W120 57 48. Stereo. 401 Spring St. 95959. Phone: (530) 265-9073. Fax: (530) 265-9077. Web Site: www.kvmr.org. Licensee: Nevada City Community Broadcast Group. (acq 7-11-89; $32,000; 5-29-89). Format: Var. News: 2 hrs wkly. Spec prog: Country 7 hrs, Black 4 hrs, folk 13 hrs, blues 7 hrs, foreign/ethnic 20 hrs wkly. ♦ Jeffrey Brown, stn mgr & opns mgr.

Newberry Springs

KIQQ-FM— January 2001: 103.7 mhz; 6 kw. Ant 246 ft. TL: N34 53 19 W116 53 39. 710 W. Old Hwy. 58, Barstow 92311. Phone: (760) 255-2636. Fax: (760) 255-3236. Licensee: MBR Licensee LLC. Group owner: Moon Broadcasting (acq 11-5-99). Format: Rgnl Mexican. ♦ Alicia Avila, gen mgr.

Newport Beach

KDLE(FM)— Jan 31, 1964: 103.1 mhz; 300 w. Ant 964 ft. TL: N33 36 19 W117 48 38. Stereo. 5700 Wilshire Blvd., Suite 250, Los Angeles 90036. Phone: (323) 900-6100. Phone: (877) 452-1031. Fax: (323) 900-6200. E-mail: feedback@indie1031.fm. Web Site: www.indie1031.fm. Licensee: Entravision Holdings LLC. Group owner: Entravision Communications Corp. (acq 2000; grpsl). Latham & Watkins. Format: Alternative. News: one hr wkly. Target aud: 18-34; upscale youth in the Los Angeles Area. ♦ Karl Meyer, gen mgr; Dawn Duraco, gen sls mgr; Michael Steele, progmg dir; Rick Hunt, chief of engrg.

North Fork

KLLE(FM)— 1996: 107.9 mhz; 1.75 kw. Ant 1,227 ft. TL: N37 17 42 W119 33 51. 1981 N. Gateway, Suite 101, Fresno 93727. Phone: (559) 456-4000. Fax: (559) 251-9555. Web Site: www.univision.com. Licensee: Univision Radio License Corp. Group owner: Univision Radio (acq 9-22-2003; grpsl). Format: Rgnl Mexican. ♦ Robert Torres, gen mgr.

North Highlands

*KQEI-FM— Feb 21, 1992: 89.3 mhz; 3.1 kw vert. Ant 354 ft. TL: N38 42 38 W121 28 54. Stereo. 2601 Mariposa St., San Francisco 94110. Phone: (415) 553-2129. Fax: (415) 553-2241. Web Site: www.kqed.org. Licensee: KQED Inc. (acq 5-9-03; $3 million). Format: News/talk. ♦ Jo Anne Wallace, gen mgr.

Northridge

*KCSN(FM)— November 1963: 88.5 mhz; 320 w. 1,643 ft. TL: N34 19 11 W118 33 14. Stereo. 18111 Nordhoff St. 91330-8312. Phone: (818) 677-3090. Web Site: www.kcsn.org. Licensee: California State University Northridge. Network: Network: PRI, NPR. Arter & Hadden. Format: Class, var/div. News staff: one; News: 12 hrs wkly. Target aud: 35 plus; middle/upper middle-class, well educated. Spec prog: German 3 hrs, Jewish 3 hrs, bluegrass 5 hrs wkly. ♦ Fred Johnson, gen mgr; Les Perry, opns mgr; Laura Kelly, dev dir; Burton Cerlich, progmg dir; Michael Worrall, chief of engrg.

Oakdale

KHOP(FM)— Mar 11, 1985: 95.1 mhz; 29.5 kw. 633 ft. TL: N37 47 34 W120 31 08. (CP: 16 kw, ant 876 ft. TL: N37 49 39 W120 34 03). Stereo. 1581 Cummins Dr., Suite 135, Modesto 95358. Phone: (209) 766-5000. Fax: (209) 522-2061. Web Site: www.planet95.com. Licensee: Citadel Broadcasting Co. Group owner: Citadel Broadcasting Corp. (acq 1996; $5 million). Fletcher, Heald & Hildreth. Format: 80s & beyond. News staff: one; News: 3 hrs wkly. Target aud: 18-49. Spec prog: Jazz 2 hrs, blues 2 hrs wkly. ♦ Roy Williams, VP & gen mgr; Richard Perry, progmg dir.

Oakhurst

KAAT(FM)— Nov 1, 1982: 103.1 mhz; 25 kw. Ant 125 ft. TL: N37 25 08 W119 44 40. Stereo. Box 2020 93644. Secondary address: 40356 Oak Park Way, Suites E & F 93644. Phone: (559) 683-1031. Fax: (559) 683-5488. E-mail: mtkaat@sierratel.com. Web Site: www.kaat.com. Licensee: California Sierra Corp. (acq 3-3-2005; $4.75 million. with co-located AM). Format: Hispanic. Target aud: 25-54; general. Spec prog: Relg 2 hrs wkly. ♦ Abel DeLuna, pres & stn mgr.

KTNS(AM)—Co-owned with KAAT(FM). Nov 20, 1982: 1060 khz; 5 kw-D, 55 w-N. TL: N37 17 46 W119 36 23. Phone: (559) 683-1060. E-mail: tammy@kaat.com. Web Site: www.ktnsradio.com. Network: CNN Radio, Westwood One. Format: Adult contemp. News staff: 3. Target aud: 25-49.

Oakland

KISQ(FM)—See San Francisco

KMKY(AM)— July 1922: 1310 khz; 5 kw-U, DA-1. TL: N37 49 27 W122 19 10. 3rd. Fl., 900 Front St., San Francisco 94111. Phone: (415) 788-1310. Fax: (415) 788-1312. Web Site: www.disney.com. Licensee: KGO-AM Radio Inc. Group owner: ABC Inc. (acq 12-18-97; $6.25 million). Network: Radio Disney. Rep: Interep. Format: Children. Target aud: 2-14; kids, tweens & moms 25-54. ♦ Michael Luckoff, stn mgr; Martin Spisak, opns mgr.

KNEW(AM)— July 2, 1921:: 910 khz; 20 kw-D, 5 kw-N, DA-2. TL: N37 53 45 W122 19 25. 340 Townsend St., San Francisco 94107. Phone: (415) 538-1013. Fax: (415) 975-5573. E-mail: kencole@clearchannel.com. Web Site: www.910wnew.com. Licensee: AMFM Broadcasting Licenses LLC. Group owner: Clear Channel Communications Inc. (acq 8-30-2000; grpsl). Format: News/talk. News staff: 8; News: 65 hrs wkly. Target aud: 25-54. ♦ Edward Krampf, gen mgr; Scott Coan, gen sls mgr; Ken Cole, progmg dir.

KQKE(AM)— 1925: 960 khz; 5 kw-U, DA-1. TL: N37 49 40 W122 18 53. 340 Townsend St., Suite 4-960, San Francisco 94107-. Phone: (415) 977-0960. Fax: (415) 972-1107. E-mail: 960kabl@kabl.com. Web Site: www.960kabl.com. Licensee: AMFM Broadcasting Licenses LLC. Group owner: Clear Channel Communications Inc. (acq 8-30-2000; grpsl). Rep: Christal. Format: Talk. ♦ Ed Krampf, sr VP & gen mgr; Steve Watkins, gen mgr; Chris Edwards, stn mgr; Michael Martin, opns dir.

Oceanside

*KKSM(AM)— July 4, 1956: 1320 khz; 500 w-U, DA-1. TL: N33 12 08 W117 36 46. 1140 W. Mission Rd., San Marcos 92069. Phone: (760) 744-1150, EXT. 5576 and 3149. Fax: (760) 744-8123. Web Site: www.kksm.palomar.edu. Licensee: Palomar Community College District. (acq 4-1-96). Format: Eclectic, div. News staff: one; News: 10 hrs wkly. Target aud: 18-25; college age, mid-upper income, diverse ethnic. ♦ Meg Banta, gen mgr; Frank Rios, gen sls mgr; Abigail Palisoc, prom dir; Reb Navarro, progmg dir; David Quera, mus dir; Joan Rubin, mus dir; Ken Chapman, news dir; Kim Crittenden, pub affrs dir; Bob Royster, chief of engrg.

Oildale

KLLY(FM)— January 1985: 95.3 mhz; 12.5 kw. 394 ft. TL: N35 27 55 W119 01 04. Stereo. Box 80658, Bakersfield 93308. Secondary address: 3651 Pegasus, Suite 107, Bakersfield 93308. Phone: (661) 393-1900. Fax: (661) 393-1915. Web Site: www.klly.com. Licensee: Buckley Broadcasting of California LLC. Group owner: Buckley Broadcasting Corp. (acq 12-86; $1.3 million). FTR: 11-10-86). Rep: D & R Radio. Format: Modern. Target aud: 25-44; adults. ♦ Steve Darnell, gen mgr; Otis Warren, sls dir; Matt Antolik, rgnl sls mgr.

Ojai

KFYV(FM)— Jan 4, 1972: 105.5 mhz; 310 w. 1,437 ft. TL: N34 20 57 W119 20 07. Stereo. 2284 S. Victoria, Suite 2G, Ventura 93003. Phone: (805) 289-1400. Fax: (805) 644-7906. Web Site: www.live1055.fm. Licensee: Gold Coast Broadcasting LLC (group owner; acq 5-15-97; $2 million. with KKZZ(AM) Ventura). Network: AP Radio. Rep: Katz Radio. Format: Hot adult contemp. News staff: one; News: 3 hrs wkly. Target aud: 25-49; fun, upscale, classy adults.

*KLFH(FM)— 2003: 89.5 mhz; 97 w. Ant 1,322 ft. TL: N34 24 45 W119 11 16. Box 1561, San Luis Obispo 93406. Secondary address: 560 Higuera St., Suite G, San Luis Obispo 93401. Phone: (805) 541-4343. Fax: (805) 541-9101. E-mail: info@klife.org. Web Site: www.klife.org. Licensee: Shepherd Communications Inc. Format: CHR, Christian hits. ♦ Jim Fugler, gen mgr.

Ontario

KDAI(FM)— Jan 26, 1947: 93.5 mhz; 5 kw. Ant -131 ft. TL: N34 10 32 W117 34 26. Stereo. 5055 Wilshire Blvd., Suite 720, Los Angeles 90036. Phone: (323) 337-1600. Fax: (323) 337-1633. Web Site: www.935kday.com. Licensee: KDAI Licensing LLC. Group owner: Spanish Broadcasting System Inc. (acq 11-18-2004; $120 million. with KDAY(FM) Redondo Beach). Format: Hip-hop. ♦ Kimberly Fletcher, gen mgr.

KSPA(AM)— Jan 26, 1947: 1510 khz; 10 kw-D, 1 kw-N, DA-2. TL: N34 05 41 W117 36 46. 1045 S. East St., Anaheim 92805. Phone: (909) 483-1500. Fax: (909) 483-1515. E-mail: kspa1510@aol.com. Licensee: Ontario Broadcasting L.L.C. Group owner: Astor Broadcast Group. (acq 11-4-99). Format: Adult standards. News staff: one. Target aud: 18-49. ♦ Art Astor, pres & gen mgr; Joe Lyons, opns mgr.

Orange

KMXE(AM)— Jan 13, 1992: 830 khz; 50 kw-D, 20 kw-N, DA-N. TL: N33 55 43 W117 36 57. 15301 Ventura Blvd., Bldg. D, Suite 200, Sherman Oaks 91403. Phone: (818) 528-2050. Fax: (818) 784-8824. Licensee: Radiovisa Los Angeles LLC (acq 12-10-03; $37.5 million). Network: ABC. Format: Sp talk. News: 28 hrs wkly. Target aud: 25-54; male & female, high income, professionals. Spec prog: Sports. ♦ Zeke Chaidez, gen mgr & opns mgr.

Orange Cove

KMAK(FM)— Oct 27, 1990: 100.3 mhz; 72 w. 2,073 ft. TL: N36 44 45 W119 16 58. Stereo. 227 W. Teague Ave., Fresno 93711. Secondary address: 640 Park Blvd. 93662. Phone: (559) 217-3313. Fax: (559) 626-4381. Licensee: Richard B. Smith. Network: UPI. Arent, Fox, Kintner, Plotkin & Kahn. Format: Sp. News staff: one; News: 10 hrs wkly. Target aud: 18-54. ♦ Antonio Rabago, gen mgr, mktg dir & progmg dir; Angelica Martinez, progmg dir; Richard Smith, chief of engrg.

Orcutt

KGDP(AM)—Licensed to Orcutt. See Santa Maria

KPAT(FM)—Licensed to Orcutt. See Santa Maria

Orland

KRQR(FM)— January 1994: 106.7 mhz; 25 kw. 56 ft. TL: N39 53 17 W122 37 38. 856 Manzanita Court, Chico 95926. Phone: (530) 342-2200. Fax: (530) 342-2260. E-mail: info@zrockfm.com. Web Site: www.zrockfm.com. Licensee: Results Radio Licensee L.L.C. Group owner: Fritz Communications Inc. (acq 6-11-99; grpsl). Brown, Nietert & Kaufman. Format: Active rock/extreme alternative. ♦ Jack Fritz, pres; Bob Cross, gen mgr; Dain Sandoval, progmg dir; Ron Woodward, progmg mgr.

California | Directory of Radio

Oroville

KEWE(AM)—Listing follows KHHZ(FM).

KHHZ(FM)— July 6, 1979: 97.7 mhz; 1.5 kw. Ant 1,276 ft. TL: N39 30 18 W121 18 35. Stereo. 2654 Cramer Ln., Chico 95928. Phone: (530) 345-0021. Fax: (530) 893-2121. Licensee: Deer Creek Broadcasting LLC. (group owner; (acq 9-8-2004; grpsl). Format: Hispanic. Target aud: 18-49. ♦Dino Corbin, gen mgr; Bill Meyer, sls dir; Juan Villagrana, progmg dir; Veronica Carter, news dir; Dan Butner, chief of engrg.

KEWE(AM)— Co-owned with KHHZ(FM). Aug 4, 1962: 1340 khz; 1 kw-U. TL: N39 30 34 W121 35 55. Network: ESPN Radio. Format: Sports. ♦ Larry Scott, progmg dir.

Oxnard

KCAQ(FM)— Sept 27, 1958: 104.7 mhz; 5.1 kw. 1,580 ft. TL: N34 20 53 W119 20 07. 2284 S. Victoria, Suite 2G, Ventura 93003. Phone: (805) 289-1400. Fax: (805) 644-7906. Web Site: www.q1047.com. Licensee: Gold Coast Broadcasting LLC (group owner; acq 1996; $3.65 million. with KVTA(AM) Port Hueneme). Rep: Katz Radio. Format: CHR Rhythmic. Target aud: 18-44.

*****KCRU(FM)**— 1993: 89.1 mhz; 200 w. 853 ft. TL: N34 06 47 W119 03 34. 1900 Pico Blvd., Santa Monica 90405. Phone: (310) 450-5183. Fax: (310) 450-7172. Web Site: www.kcrw.com. Licensee: Santa Monica Community College District. Format: Var. ♦Ruth Seymour, gen mgr; Jennifer Ferro, stn mgr; Mike Newport, opns mgr; Jacki Weber, dev dir; Ariana Morgenstern, asst music dir; Steve Herbert, chief of engrg.

KDAR(FM)— Oct 28, 1974: 98.3 mhz; 1.5 kw. Ant 1,289 ft. TL: N34 20 55 W119 19 57. Stereo. Box 5626 93031. Secondary address: 500 Esplanade Dr., Suite 1500 93036. Phone: (805) 485-8881. Fax: (805) 656-5330. E-mail: radiomail@kdar.com. Web Site: www.kdar.com. Licensee: ATEP Radio Inc. Group owner: Salem Communications Corp. Format: Christian talk & mus. News: 2 hrs wkly. Target aud: 25-54; upscale adults with large families. ♦ Ed Atsinger, pres; Richard Trejo, gen mgr; Roy Bach, progmg dir.

KKZZ(AM)—See Ventura

KLJR-FM—See Santa Paula

KOCP(FM)—See Camarillo

KOXR(AM)— June 11, 1955: 910 khz; 5 kw-D, 1 kw-N, DA-2. TL: N34 16 58 W119 07 36. Box 6940 93031. Secondary address: 200 S. A St., Suite 400 93030. Phone: (805) 240-2070. Fax: (805) 240-5960. Licensee: Lazer Broadcasting Corp. (group owner; acq 1-11-99). Rep: Lotus Entravision Reps LLC. Fletcher, Heald & Hildredth. Format: Sp. Target aud: 25-54. ♦Alfredo Plascencia, CEO & pres; Jose Plascencia, gen mgr; Marco A. Del Castillo, stn mgr & opns dir; Salvador Prieto, progmg dir.

KUNX(AM)—See Santa Paula

KVEN(AM)—See Ventura

KXLM(FM)— 1991: 102.9 mhz; 5.5 kw. Ant 112 ft. TL: N34 14 12 W119 12 11. 200 S. A St., Suite 400 93030. Secondary address: Box 6940 93030. Phone: (805) 240-2070. Fax: (805) 240-5960. Web Site: radiolazer.com. Licensee: Kext Broadcasters Inc. Format: Sp, adult contemp. News staff: one; News: 2 hrs wkly. Target aud: 25-59. ♦Alfredo Plascencia, pres & gen mgr; Terry Janisch, gen sls mgr.

Pacific Grove

*****KAZU(FM)**— Oct 1, 1977: 90.3 mhz; 3.7 kw. Ant 522 ft. TL: N36 33 09 W121 47 17. Stereo. Box 210 93950. Secondary address: 167 Central Ave. 93950. Phone: (831) 375-7275. Fax: (831) 375-0235. E-mail: mail@kazu.org. Web Site: www.kazu.org. Licensee: Foundation of California State University Monterey Bay (acq 11-30-00; $150,000). Network: NPR. Garvey, Schubert & Barer. Format: News, info. News: 8 hrs wkly. Target aud: 25-65; general. Spec prog: Country 6 hrs, women's mus 6 hrs, gospel 4 hrs, folk 6 hrs, class 3 hrs, oldies 5 hrs wkly. ♦Garland Thompson, chief of opns; Douglas McKnight, dev dir; John McNally, gen mgr & progmg dir.

KOCN(FM)— Apr 10, 1977: 105.1 mhz; 1.8 kw. 600 ft. TL: N36 33 09 W121 47 17. (CP: 402 kw, ant 790 ft. TL: N36 30 38 W121 43 57). Stereo. 903 N. Main St., Salinas 93906. Phone: (831) 755-8181. Fax: (831) 755-8191. Licensee: Clear Channel Radio License Inc. Group owner: Clear Channel Communications Inc. (acq 9-22-97; grpsl). Network: Westwood One. Rep: Clear Channel. Format: Oldies. News staff: one. Target aud: 25-54; at work, double income households. ♦Rhonda McCormack, gen mgr & sls dir.

Palm Desert

KEZN(FM)— Nov 28, 1977: 103.1 mhz; 1.9 kw. 590 ft. TL: N33 51 58 W116 25 56. Stereo. 72-915 Parkview Dr. 92260. Secondary address: Box 291 92260. Phone: (760) 340-9383. Fax: (760) 340-5756. Web Site: www.ez103.com. Licensee: Infinity Radio Holdings Inc. Group owner: Infinity Broadcasting Corp. (acq 11-13-98; grpsl). Network: Westwood One. Rep: Allied Radio Partners. Leventhal, Senter & Lerman. Format: Adult contemp. News staff: one. Target aud: 25-64. ♦Tom Hoyt, gen mgr & prom dir.

*****KHCS(FM)**— January 1993: 91.7 mhz; 960 w. 574 ft. TL: N33 41 25 W116 17 14. Stereo. 2341 Duane Rd., Palm Springs 92262. Phone: (760) 341-1199. Fax: (760) 340-5869. E-mail: Khcs@juno.com. Web Site: www.joy92.org. Licensee: Prairie Avenue Gospel Center. Lauren A. Colby. Format: Inspirational, Christian. Target aud: 25-54. ♦Dan Pike, pres; Glen Kippel, gen mgr; R.F. Watts, chief of engrg.

Palm Springs

KDES-FM—Listing follows KPSI(AM).

KGAM(AM)— 1969: 1450 khz; 1 kw-U. TL: N33 48 02 W116 30 25. 2100 E. Tahquitz Canyon Way 92262. Phone: (760) 325-2582. Phone: (760) 320-8255. Fax: (760) 322-3562. Licensee: R & R Radio Corp. Group owner: RR Broadcasting (acq 4-8-2002; with co-located FM). Network: Network: ABC Information & Entertainment, ABC News/Talk. Rep: Christal. Cohn & Marks. Format: News/talk, talk. News staff: 2; News: 5 hrs wkly. Target aud: 25 plus; upscale, informed, involved adults. ♦ Rozene Supple, pres; Mike Keane, gen mgr; Mel Hill, rgnl sls mgr; Geoff Allan, prom dir; Steve Kelly, CFO, progmg dir & news dir; Barry O'Connor, chief of engrg.

KPSI-FM—Co-owned with KGAM(AM). June 1980: 100.5 mhz; 25 kw. Ant 121 ft. TL: N33 56 44 W116 24 34. Stereo. Phone: (760) 323-1005. Fax: (760) 320-4632. Web Site: www.mix1005.fm. Format: CHR, contemp hit.

KNWQ(AM)— Feb 12, 1946: 1140 khz; 10 kw-D, 2.5 kw-N, DA-2. TL: N33 51 39 W116 28 20. Stereo. 1321 N. Gene Autry Trail 92262. Phone: (760) 322-7890. Fax: (760) 322-5493. Web Site: www.desertfun.com. Licensee: Morris Communications Corp. Group owner: Morris Communications Inc. (acq 12-24-97; $4.5 million). Network: CBS. Rep: McGavren Guild. Format: News/talk. Target aud: 35-65. ♦William S. Morris IV, chmn; William S. Morris III, pres; Darrel Fry, CFO; Michael Osterhaut, VP; Keith Martin, gen mgr; Gary Demaroney, opns dir.

KPLM(FM)— Jan 24, 1983: 106.1 mhz; 50 kw. 391 ft. TL: N33 52 14 W116 13 39. Stereo. Box 1825 92263. Phone: (760) 320-4550. Fax: (760) 320-3037. E-mail: kplm@dc.rr.com. Web Site: thebig106.com. Licensee: RM Broadcasting L.L.C. (acq 9-10-98). Rep: Katz Radio. Koteen & Naftalin. Format: Country. News staff: one; News: 9 hrs wkly. Target aud: 25-54. ♦ Kory James, opns mgr; Todd Marker, gen mgr & sls dir; Hughes Hilles, gen sls mgr; Al Gordon, progmg dir.

*****KPSC(FM)**— April 1978: 88.5 mhz; 3 kw. 266 ft. TL: N33 52 14 W116 13 39. Stereo. Box 77913, Los Angeles 90007. Secondary address: 515 S. Figueroa St., Suite 2050, Los Angeles 90071. Phone: (213) 225-7400. Fax: (213) 225-7410. E-mail: kusc@kusc.org. Web Site: www.kusc.org. Licensee: University of Southern California. (acq 9-9-86). Network: PRI, NPR. Lawrence Bernstein. Format: Class. Target aud: 35 plus; general. ♦ Brenda Barnes, pres; Eric DeWeese, gen mgr; Janet McIntyre, dev VP & dev dir; Stephanie Ross, mktg dir.

KPSI(AM)— Oct 29, 1956: 920 khz; 5 kw-D, 1 kw-N, DA-2. TL: N33 51 29 W116 29 39. Stereo. 2100 E. Tahquitz Canyon Way 92262. Phone: (760) 325-2582. Fax: (760) 322-3562. Web Site: www.newstalk920.com. Licensee: R & R Radio Corp. Group owner: RR Broadcasting. Network: ABC Information & Entertainment. Rep: Christal. Format: News, talk. News staff: 4; News: 16 hrs wkly. Target aud: 25-54. Spec prog: American Indian 2 hrs wkly. ♦ Mike Keane, gen mgr; Steve Kelly, progmg dir.

KDES-FM—Co-owned with KPSI(AM). Feb 10, 1963: 104.7 mhz; 42 kw. 540 ft. TL: N33 51 56 W116 26 04. Stereo. E-mail: kdes@aol.com. Web Site: www.kdes.com. Cohn & Marks. Format: Oldies. ♦Greg Aratin, gen sls mgr; Kesha Duncan, prom mgr; Dave Wilson, progmg dir; Kacy Consiglio, progmg mgr; Steve Kelly, news dir.

KWXY-FM—(Cathedral City). Jan 19, 1969: 98.5 mhz; 50 kw. 499 ft. TL: N33 51 55 W116 26 10. Stereo. KWXY Broadcast Centre, Box 5470 92263. Phone: (760) 328-1104. Fax: (760) 328-7814. Web Site: www.kwxy.com. Licensee: Glen Barnett Inc. Garvey, Schubert & Barer. Format: Btfl mus. News staff: one; News: 16 hrs wkly. Target aud: 35 plus; affluent adults. Spec prog: Canadian news 2 hrs wkly. ♦Estelle Layton, exec VP; Glen Barnett, pres & gen mgr.

KWXY(AM)— Oct 4, 1964: 1340 khz; 1 kw-U. TL: N33 48 07 W116 27 44. Web Site: www.kwxy.com. News staff: one.

Palmdale

KUTY(AM)— August 1957: 1470 khz; 5 kw-U, DA-2. TL: N34 39 55 W118 00 40. Q-9, 570 East Ave. 93550. Phone: (661) 947-3107. Fax: (661) 272-5688. Licensee: High Desert Broadcasting LLC. (group owner; (acq 3-5-97). Format: News/talk. Target aud: 18-49; homeowners, married couples with discretionary income.

Palo Alto

KDFC-FM—See San Francisco

KNTS(AM)— 1947: 1220 khz; 5 kw-D, 147 w-N. TL: N37 29 04 W122 08 04. 39138 Fremont Blvd., 3rd Fl., Fremont 94538. Phone: (510) 713-1100. Fax: (510) 505-1448. Licensee: SCA-Palo Alto LLC. Group owner: Salem Communications Corp. (acq 6-28-2001; $9 million). Network: CBS. Rep: Salem. Format: News, talk, sports. News staff: 5; News: 70 hrs wkly. Target aud: 25-54; general. Spec prog: Technology news & interviews. ♦Ken Miller, gen mgr; Bobby Cole, opns dir; Darrell Howes, gen sls mgr; Amy Marsh, mktg dir & prom dir; Craig Roberts, chief of engrg.

KZSU(FM)—See Stanford

Paradise

KHSL-FM— Oct 15, 1983: 103.5 mhz; 1.6 kw. 1,250 ft. TL: N39 57 29 W121 42 50. Stereo. 2654 Cramer Ln., Chico 95928. Phone: (530) 345-0021. Fax: (530) 893-2121. Web Site: www.khsl.com. Licensee: Deer Creek Broadcasting LLC. (group owner; (acq 9-8-2004; grpsl). Rep: Katz Radio. Haley, Bader & Potts. Format: Country. News staff: one; News: 6 hrs wkly. Target aud: 25-54; active. ♦Dino Corbin, VP, gen mgr & mktg mgr; Bill Meyer, gen sls mgr; Rebecca Hoffer, prom dir; Lisa Fitzgerald, prom mgr.

KKXX(AM)— September 1960: 930 khz; 1 kw-D, 37 w-N. TL: N39 43 37 W121 40 45. (CP: 500 w-N). 1363 Longfellow, Chico 95926-7319. Phone: (530) 894-7325. Fax: (530) 894-2050. E-mail: randy@kkxx.net. Web Site: www.kkxx.net. Licensee: Butte Broadcasting Co. (acq 12-21-66). Format: News/talk, relg. ♦Carl J. Auel, pres; Matt McNeilly, gen mgr.

KZAP(FM)— June 4, 1977: 96.7 mhz; 1.5 kw. 1,289 ft. TL: N39 57 45 W121 42 40. Stereo. 1459 Humbolt Rd., Suite D, Chico 95928. Phone: (530) 899-3600. Fax: (530) 343-0243. E-mail: info@club967.com. Web Site: www.club967.com. Licensee: Regent Licensee of Chico Inc. Group owner: Regent Communications Inc. (acq 8-15-00; $233,333 for stock). Network: ABC. Format: Hip hop, rap. Target aud: 25-49. Spec prog: Blues 3 hrs wkly. ♦ Dick Stein, gen mgr.

Pasadena

KAZN(AM)— Sept 12, 1942: 1300 khz; 5 kw-D, 1 kw-N, DA-2. TL: N34 09 38 W118 04 46. Stereo. 747 E. Green, Suite 101 91101. Phone: (626) 568-1300. Fax: (626) 568-3666. Web Site: www.mrbi.net. Licensee: Multicultural Radio Broadcasting Licensee LLC. Group owner: Multicultural Radio Broadcasting Inc. (acq 5-11-98; $12 million). Format: Chinese. News: 90 hrs wkly. Target aud: Chinese. ♦ Arthur S. Liu, pres; Kevin Chu, gen mgr.

KDIS(AM)— Feb 7, 1942: 1110 khz; 50 kw-D, 20 kw-N, DA-2. TL: N34 06 50 W117 50 51. Stereo. 3321 S. La Cienega Blvd., Los Angeles 90016. Phone: (310) 840-2800. Web Site: www.radiodisney.com/kdisam1110. Licensee: KABC-AM Radio Inc. Group owner: ABC Inc. (acq 12-19-00; $65 million). Network: Radio Disney. Format: Children's progmg.

Broadcasting & Cable Yearbook 2006

D-86

Stations in the U.S. — California

Developers & Brokers of Radio Properties — contact American Media Services at our suite: Philadelphia Marriott Downtown 215-625-2900 / 843-972-2200 / americanmediaservices.com / Charleston, SC / Dallas, TX · Chicago, Il · Austin, TX — American Media Services, LLC

♦John Davison, pres & gen mgr; Bob Koontz, sls dir; Pete Dominguez, natl sls mgr; Nelkane Benton, pub affrs dir.

*KPCC(FM)— September 1957: 89.3 mhz; 680 w. 2,922 ft. TL: N34 13 35 W118 03 58. Stereo. 1570 E. Colorado Blvd. 91106. Phone: (626) 585-7000. Fax: (626) 585-7916. E-mail: mail@kpcc.org. Web Site: www.kpcc.org. Licensee: Pasadena Area Community College District Board of Trustees. Network: Network: Network: NPR, PRI, CBC Radio One. Format: New/talk/information. News: 6 hrs wkly. Target aud: 25-55. ♦Bill Davis, CEO & gen mgr; Doug Johnson, opns dir & opns mgr.

KROQ-FM— 1974: 106.7 mhz; 5.6 kw. 2,000 ft. TL: N34 11 47 W118 15 30. 5901 Venice Blvd., Los Angeles 90034. Phone: (323) 930-1067. Fax: (323) 931-1067. Web Site: www.kroq.com. Licensee: Infinity Broadcasting of Los Angeles Inc. Group owner: Infinity Broadcasting Corp. (acq 11-13-98; grpsl). Format: Alternative rock. Target aud: 18-34. ♦Trip Reeb, VP & gen mgr.

KSSE(FM)—See Arcadia

Paso Robles

KKAL(FM)— Nov 20, 1972: 92.5 mhz; 17 kw. 760 ft. TL: N35 38 45 W120 44 16. (CP: 4.8 kw, ant 1,428 ft.). Stereo. 3620 Sacramento Dr., Suite 204, San Luis Obispo 93401. Phone: (805) 781-2750. Fax: (805) 781-2758. Web Site: www.kkalonline.com. Licensee: AGM California. Group owner: American General Media (acq 1997; $675,000). Format: Classic country. News staff: one; News: 12 hrs wkly. Target aud: 18 plus. ♦Kathy Signorelli, gen mgr.

KLUN(FM)— August 1995: 103.1 mhz; 1.2 kw. 761 ft. TL: N35 38 45 W120 44 16. Stereo. 200 E. Fesler St., Suite 101, Santa Maria 93454. Phone: (805) 928-9796. Fax: (805) 928-3367. E-mail: mariet@radiolazer.com. Web Site: radiolazer.com. Licensee: Lazer Broadcasting Corp. (group owner; acq 8-7-00; $1.115 million with KLMM(FM) Morro Bay). Booth, Freret, Imlay & Tepper. Format: Adult contemp, Sp, news/talk. Target aud: 25-54; general. ♦Alfredo Placencia, pres; Maricarmen Buch, gen mgr; Jose Llas, progmg dir; Bill Bordoux, chief of engrg.

KPRL(AM)— Oct 1, 1946: 1230 khz; 1 kw-U. TL: N35 39 15 W120 40 52. Box 7 93447. Phone: (805) 238-1230. Fax: (805) 238-5332. E-mail: kprl@tcsn.net. Web Site: www.kprl.com. Licensee: North County Communications LLC (acq 5-1-2003; $900,000). Network: ABC Information & Entertainment. Rep: Western Regional Broadcast Sales. Garvey, Schubert & Barer. Format: News/talk, sports. News staff: one; News: one hr wkly. Target aud: 25 plus. ♦Kevin Will, CEO, pres & opns mgr.

Patterson

KOSO(FM)—Licensed to Patterson. See Modesto

KTSE-FM— 1996: 97.1 mhz; 3 kw. 328 ft. TL: N37 29 26 W121 13 16. Stereo. 6820 Pacific Ave., Suite 3A, Stockton 95207. Phone: (209) 474-0154. Fax: (209) 474-0316. Licensee: Entravision Holdings LLC. Group owner: Entravision Communications Corp. (acq 7-28-00; grpsl). Format: Sp. ♦Lisa Sunday, CFO, gen mgr, opns mgr & gen sls mgr; Jorge Moreno, prom dir; Homero Campos, progmg VP; Valentina Rupio, mus dir; Jeff Paz, news dir; Paul Shin, chief of engrg.

Pebble Beach

*KSPB(FM)— Sept 22, 1978: 91.9 mhz; 1 kw. 485 ft. TL: N36 35 11 W121 55 21. 3152 Forest Lake Rd. 93953. Phone: (831) 626-5300. Fax: (831) 625-5078. Fax: (831) 625-5208. E-mail: webmaster@kspb.org. Web Site: www.kspb.org. Licensee: Robert Louis Stevenson School. Format: Progsv. Spec prog: Black 18 hrs, oldies 4 hrs, reggae 2 hrs, hard rock 2 hrs wkly. ♦Hamish Tyler, gen mgr.

Pescadero

*KPDO(FM)—Not on air, target date: unknown: 89.3 mhz; 100 w. Ant -148 ft. TL: N37 15 23 W122 24 43. Box 25, Loma Mar 94021. Licensee: Pescadero Public Radio Service Inc.

Petaluma

KTOB(AM)— Jan 10, 1950: 1490 khz; 1 kw-U. TL: N35 39 15 W120 40 52. c/o Radio Station KRRS(AM), Box 2277, Santa Rosa 95405. Secondary address: c/o Radio Station KRRS(AM), 1410 Neotomas Ave., Suite 104, Santa Rosa 95405. Phone: (707) 545-1460. Fax: (707) 545-0112. E-mail: krrs@sonic.net. Web Site: www.moonradios.com. Licensee: Moon Broadcasting Licensee LLC. Group owner: Moon Broadcasting (acq 12-13-2001; $1.28 million). Rep: Caballero. Format: Spanish regional. Target aud: 25-54; contemporary Hispanic families. ♦Abel DeLuna Sr., CEO; Able DeLuna, pres; Arelia DeLuna, CFO; Maggie LeClerc, gen mgr & stn mgr; Benoit LeClerc, opns dir; Miriam Gomez, opns mgr.

Philo

*KZYX(FM)— October 1989: 90.7 mhz; 3.41 kw. 1,686 ft. TL: N39 01 22 W123 31 17. Box 1 95466. Phone: (707) 895-2324. Fax: (707) 895-2451. Web Site: www.kzyx.org. Licensee: Mendocino County Public Broadcasting. Network: NPR. Format: News, talk radio, div music. Target aud: General. Spec prog: Black 8 hrs, class 14 hrs, folk 8 hrs, gospel 2 hrs, jazz 11 hrs, blues 3 hrs. ♦Mitchell Holman, gen mgr; Burton Segall, opns dir.

Piedmont

KPIG(AM)— May 1947: 1510 khz; 8 kw-D, 230 w-N, DA-2. TL: N37 49 02 W122 17 10. 1110 Main St., Suite 16, Watsonville 95076. Phone: (831) 722-9000. Fax: (831) 722-7548. Web Site: www.kpig.com. Licensee: Mapleton Communications LLC. (acq 7-27-2005; $5.1 million). Format: AAA. ♦Dale Hendry, gen mgr; Frank Caprista, opns mgr.

Pismo Beach

KXTZ(FM)— Dec 7, 1974: 95.3 mhz; 4.2 kw. 390 ft. TL: N35 09 24 W120 38 11. Stereo. 396 Buckley Rd., Suite 2, San Luis Obispo 93401. Phone: (805) 786-2570. Fax: (805) 547-9860. Licensee: Mapleton Communications LLC (group owner; acq 5-23-02; grpsl). Rep: Allied Radio Partners. Haley, Bader & Potts. Format: Classic hits. News staff: one; News: one hr wkly. Target aud: 18-49. Spec prog: Talk one hr wkly. ♦Nancy Lechter, gen mgr & opns mgr.

Pittsburg

KATD(AM)— September 1949: 990 khz; 5 kw-U. TL: N38 04 49 W121 50 33. Stereo. 145 Natoma St., 4th Fl., San Francisco 94105. Phone: (415) 978-5378. Fax: (415) 978-5380. Licensee: Way Broadcasting Licensee LLC. Group owner: Multicultural Radio Broadcasting Inc. (acq 2-4-2004; grpsl). Keck, Mahin & Cate. Format: Sp. News: 50 hrs wkly. Target aud: 25-54; middle upper income. ♦Arthur Liu, pres; Judy Re, gen mgr; David Liu, opns dir & opns mgr.

Placerville

KXCL(FM)— Dec 9, 1982: 92.1 mhz; 2.95 kw. Ant 331 ft. TL: N38 45 31 W120 44 59. Stereo. 298 Commerce Cir., Sacramento 95815. Phone: (916) 576-7333. Fax: (916) 929-5330. Web Site: www.bob921.com. Licensee: First Broadcasting Sacramento Licensing LLC. Group owner: First Broadcasting Investment Partners LLC (acq 5-19-2003; $7.12 million). Format: Music mix. ♦Gary Lawrence, pres; Carew Berry, gen mgr.

Planada

KHTN(FM)— 1966: 104.7 mhz; 1.95 kw. Ant 2,080 ft. TL: N37 32 01 W120 01 46. Stereo. 510 W. 19th St., Merced 95340. Phone: (209) 383-7900. Fax: (209) 723-8461. Web Site: www.hot1047fm.com. Licensee: Buckley Communications Inc. Group owner: Buckley Broadcasting Corp. (acq 9-21-95; $500,000). Rep: D & R Radio. Format: Contemp hit. Target aud: 21-34; women. ♦Mike McAdam, VP & gen mgr; Rene Roberts, opns mgr.

Point Arena

KYOE(FM)— 2003: 102.3 mhz; 1.2 kw. Ant 1,417 ft. TL: N38 53 44 W123 32 34. Box 366 95468. Phone: (707) 882-2323. Fax: (707) 882-3258. Licensee: Del Mar Trust. Format: Country. ♦Karen J. Hay, gen mgr.

Point Reyes Station

*KWMR(FM)— May 2, 1999: 90.5 mhz; 18 w. Ant 1,066 ft. TL: N38 04 48 W122 51 57. Box 1262 94956. Secondary address: 11431 State Rte. One #8 Phone: (415) 663-8068. Fax: (415) 663-0746. E-mail: kay@kwmr.org. Web Site: www.kwmr.org. Licensee: West Marin Community Radio Inc. Format: Community radio. ♦Kay Clements, gen mgr; Adrienne Pfeiffer, dev dir.

Pollock Pines

*KPPN(FM)—Not on air, target date: unknown: 89.9 mhz; 100 w. Ant 482 ft. TL: N38 44 18 W120 42 10. 95 La Jota Dr., Angwin 94508. Phone: (707) 965-4155. Fax: (707) 965-4161. Web Site: www.thecandle.com. Licensee: Howell Mountain Broadcasting Co. ♦David Shantz, gen mgr.

Pomona

KAHZ(AM)— May 12, 1947: 1600 khz; 5 kw-U, DA-N. TL: N34 01 48 W117 43 35. 747 E. Green St., Floor 4, Pasadena 91101. Phone: (626) 844-8882. Fax: (626) 844-2928. Web Site: www.mrbi.net. Licensee: Multicultural Radio Broadcasting Licensee LLC. Group owner: Multicultural Radio Broadcasting Inc. (acq 11-17-98; $7.55 million). Format: Business news/talk, Chinese. Target aud: 30 plus; money oriented. ♦Arthur Liu, pres; Felix Guo, gen mgr; Jeremy Landau, opns dir & gen sls mgr; Rick Hunt, chief of engrg.

KWKU(AM)— Dec 23, 1960: 1220 khz; 250 w-U, DA-2. TL: N34 01 11 W117 43 03. (CP: 930 w-D). 363 S. Park Ave., Suite 105 91766. Phone: (909) 865-3323. Fax: (909) 865-0342. Web Site: www.kwkuradio.com. Licensee: Lotus Communications Corp. (group owner; acq 2-00; $750,000). Gammon & Grange. Format: Sp, news/talk, sports. News staff: one; News: 7 hrs wkly. Target aud: 24-64. Spec prog: Relg 15 hrs wkly. ♦Juan Rodriguez, gen mgr.

Port Hueneme

KCAQ(FM)—See Oxnard

KVTA(AM)— July 1958: 1520 khz; 10 kw-D, 1 kw-N, DA-2. TL: N34 10 02 W119 08 02. 2284 S. Victoria Ave., Suite 2 G, Ventura 93003. Phone: (805) 289-1400. Fax: (805) 644-7906. Web Site: www.kvtaam1520.com. Licensee: Gold Coast Broadcasting LLC (group owner; acq 1996; $3.65 million. with KCAQ(FM) Oxnard). Leibowitz & Spencer. Format: News/talk. Target aud: 25-54. ♦Chip Ehrhardt, gen mgr.

Porterville

KIOO(FM)— Aug 1, 1972: 99.7 mhz; 24 kw. 690 ft. TL: N36 06 26 W119 01 45. Stereo. 617 W. Tulare, Visalia 93277. Phone: (559) 627-9710. Fax: (559) 627-1590. E-mail: raym@q97.com. Web Site: www.997classicrock.com. Licensee: Buckley Broadcasting Corp. (group owner; acq 3-1-94; $360,000; 5-2-94). Rep: D & R Radio. Format: Adult classic rock. News staff: one. Target aud: 25-44. ♦Rick Buckley, pres; Ray McCarty, VP & gen mgr; Alexa Smith, opns mgr.

KTIP(AM)— 1947: 1450 khz; 1 kw-U. TL: N36 05 44 W119 03 10. 1660 N. Newcomb 93257. Phone: (559) 784-1450. Fax: (559)

California

784-2482. E-mail: live@ktip.com. Web Site: www.ktip.com. Licensee: Mayberry Broadcasting Co. Inc. (acq 9-14-00; $130,000. for 51%). Network: Network: ABC, Westwood One. Rgnl Reps. Dow, Lohnes & Albertson. Format: News/talk. News staff: 2; News: 23 hrs wkly. Target aud: 25 plus. Spec prog: Gospel 12 hrs, health show one hr, loc travel one hr wkly, national health 3hrs. ♦ Larry Stoneburner, pres; Larry & Mimi Stoneburner, gen mgr; Kent Hopper, chief of opns, progmg dir & news dir; Michael Partipilo, sls dir; Mimi Stoneburner, mktg dir; P.K. Whitmire, news dir; Ron Neil, chief of engrg.

Prunedale

*KLVM(FM)— Feb 28, 1986: 89.7 mhz; 210 w. Ant 2,053 ft. TL: N36 45 22 W121 30 05. Stereo. 8145 Prunedale N. Rd., Salinas 93907. Phone: (831) 663-6022. Fax: (831) 663-1663. E-mail: klove@klove.com. Web Site: www.klove.com. Licensee: Prunedale Educational Foundation. Network: K-Love. Format: Adult contemp, Christian. Target aud: 25-35; Judeo-Christian female. ♦ Dr. E.L. Moon, pres & gen mgr.

Quincy

KHGQ(FM)— 1997: 100.3 mhz; 900 w. -1,125 ft. TL: N39 56 14 W120 56 51. 250 W. Nopah Vista Ave., Parump, NV 89060. Phone: (775) 751-9709. Fax: (775) 751-3624. Licensee: Hilltop Church (acq 7-18-2005). Format: News/talk. ♦ Keily Miller, gen mgr & opns mgr; Chris Compton, stn mgr; Randy Creff, chief of engrg.

*KJCQ(FM)—Not on air, target date: unknown: 88.5 mhz; 790 w. Ant 2,194 ft. TL: N40 14 00 W121 01 11. CSN International, 3232 MacArthur Blvd., Santa Ana 92704. Phone: (714) 825-9663. Fax: (714) 825-9660. Licensee: CSN International (group owner). Format: Christian. ♦ Jeffrey W. Smith, pres.

KNLF(FM)— June 10, 1996: 95.9 mhz; 500 w. -499 ft. TL: N39 58 03 W120 53 34. Box 117, 440 Lawrence St. 95971. Phone: (530) 476-3306. Fax: (530) 283-5135. Web Site: www.knlfradio.com. Licensee: New Life Broadcasting. Network: USA. Format: Sports, talk, Christian, Contemp. News: 10 hrs wkly. Target aud: 18-54. ♦ Ron Trumbo, pres.

KPCO(AM)— Aug 16, 1963: 1370 khz; 5 kw-D, 500 w-N, DA-2. TL: N39 56 54 W120 53 54. Stereo. 395 Main St. 95971. Phone: (530) 283-1370. Fax: (530) 283-5117. Licensee: Educational Media Foundation. (acq 6-30-2005; $900,000 with KWLU(FM) Chester). Format: News/talk, hits from 40's, 50's, & 60's. ♦ Bob Fink, pres; Bob Darling, VP & gen mgr; Will Taylor, news dir.

*KQNC(FM)— 2005: 88.1 mhz; 500 w. Ant 1,135 ft. TL: N39 56 14 W120 56 51. Capital Public Radio Inc., 7055 Folsom Blvd., Sacramento 95826. Phone: (916) 480-5900. Fax: (916) 487-3348. E-mail: npr@csus.edu. Web Site: www.csus.edu/npr. Licensee: California State University, Sacramento. Network: NPR. Duane Morris LLP. Format: Jazz, news & info. ♦ Michael Lazar, pres & gen mgr; Carl Watanabe, stn mgr & prom mgr; John Brenneise, opns mgr; Beth Hassett, dev dir & mktg dir; Linda Onstad, sls dir & adv dir; Joe Barr, news dir; Jeff Browne, engrg dir.

Rancho Cordova

KSTE(AM)— Apr 19, 1990: 650 khz; 21.4 kw-D, 920 w-N, DA-2. TL: N38 28 47 W121 16 38. 1440 Ethan Way, # 200, Sacramento 95825. Phone: (916) 929-5325. Fax: (916) 929-2236. Web Site: www.talk650kste.com. Licensee: AMFM Broadcasting Licenses LLC. Group owner: Clear Channel Communications Inc. (acq 8-30-2000; grpsl). Network: Network: ABC, Westwood One. Format: Talk. News staff: 4; News: 15 hrs wkly. Target aud: 25-54. ♦ Jeff Holden, gen mgr; Ken Kohl, opns dir.

Rancho Mirage

KMRJ(FM)— July 17, 1998: 99.5 mhz; 3 kw. 328 ft. TL: N33 52 15 W116 13 37. Stereo. 1061 S. Palm Canyon Dr., Palm Springs 92264. Phone: (760) 778-6995. Fax: (760) 778-1249. E-mail: tom@m995.com. Web Site: www.m995.com. Licensee: Mitchell Media Inc. Rep: Katz Radio. Dickstein Shapiro Morin & Oshinsky. Format: The modern mix, alternative, new age, AOR. Target aud: 25-35; young families, working adults. ♦ Daniel P. Mitchell III, chmn & pres; Maurine B. Mitchell, CFO; Thomas Carr Mitchell, stn mgr; Dwight Arnold, dev VP & prom mgr; Mark Moceri, sls dir & engr.

Randsburg

*KGBM(FM)— December 2001: 89.7 mhz; 2 kw. Ant 1,269 ft. TL: N35 28 41 W117 41 58. 5700 W. Oaks Blvd., Rocklin 95765. Phone: (916) 251-1600. Fax: (916) 251-1650. E-mail: info@air1.com. Web Site: www.air1.com. Licensee: Educational Media Foundation. Group owner: EMF Broadcasting (acq 4-19-02). Network: Air 1. Shaw Pittman. Format: Contemp Christian. News staff: 3. Target aud: 18-35; Judeo-Christian female. ♦ Richard Jenkins, pres; Mike Novak, VP; Lloyd Parker, gen mgr; Keith Whipple, dev dir.

Red Bluff

KALF(FM)— 1978: 95.7 mhz; 7 kw. 1,265 ft. TL: N39 55 03 W122 40 12. Stereo. 1459 Humboldt Rd., Suite D, Chico 95928-9100. Phone: (530) 899-3600. Fax: (530) 343-0243. Web Site: www.kalf.com. Licensee: Regent Broadcasting West Coast Inc. Group owner: Regent Communications Inc. (acq 8-21-97; grpsl). Rep: Christal. Smithwick & Belendiuk. Format: Country. News staff: one; News: 10 hrs wkly. Target aud: 25-54. ♦ Dick Stein, gen mgr.

KBLF(AM)— 1946: 1490 khz; 1 kw-U. TL: N40 11 28 W122 12 54. Stereo. 756 Hickory St. 96080. Phone: (530) 527-1490. Fax: (530) 527-3525. E-mail: kblfam@yahoo.com. Web Site: www.kblf.com. Licensee: Tom Huth. Group owner: Huth Broadcasting (acq 8-11-98; $5,000). Network: Network: Westwood One, PRI. Format: Memories. Target aud: 35-64. Spec prog: Farm 5 hrs, Sp 4 hrs wkly. ♦ Cal Hunter, gen mgr.

*KLVB(FM)— November 1985: 102.7 mhz; 5.5 kw. Ant 1,414 ft. TL: N40 20 41 W121 56 48. Stereo. 5700 W. Oaks Blvd., Rocklin 95765. Phone: (916) 251-1600. Fax: (916) 251-1650. E-mail: klove@klove.com. Web Site: www.klove.com. Licensee: Educational Media Foundation. Group owner: EMF Broadcasting (acq 1-11-2001; $750,000). Network: K-Love. Rep: D & R Radio. Shaw Pittman. Format: Christian contemp. News staff: 3. Target aud: 25-44; Judeo Christian, female. ♦ Richard Jenkins, pres; Lloyd Parker, gen mgr; Ed Lenane, stn mgr & opns dir.

Redding

KEWB(FM)—See Anderson

*KFPR(FM)— Nov 17, 1994: 88.9 mhz; 750 w 3,578 ft. TL: N40 36 10 W122 38 58. Stereo. 603 N. Market 96003. Secondary address: Box 990061 95929. Phone: (530) 241-5246. Fax: (530) 241-5246. E-mail: npr@awwwsome.com. Web Site: www.wfpr.org. Licensee: California State University, Chico Research Foundation. Network: NPR, PRI. Cohn & Marks. Format: Var/div. Target aud: General. Spec prog: Sp 4 hrs wkly. ♦ Jack Brown, gen mgr; Mike Birdsill, opns dir.

*KKRO(FM)— Nov 15, 2002: 91.5 mhz; 290 w. Ant 1,033 ft. TL: N40 46 43 W121 50 00. Stereo. 5700 W. Oaks Blvd., Rocklin 95765. Phone: (916) 251-1600. Fax: (916) 251-1650. E-mail: info@air1.com. Web Site: www.air1.com. Licensee: Educational Media Foundation Inc. Group owner: EMF Broadcasting. Network: Air 1. Format: Contemp Christian. News staff: 3. Target aud: 27-33; Judeo-Christian female. ♦ Richard Jenkins, pres; Mike Novak, VP; Lloyd Parker, gen mgr.

KLXR(AM)— August 1956: 1230 khz; 1 kw-U. TL: N40 33 14 W122 22 53. 1326 Market St. 96001. Phone: (530) 244-5082. Fax: (530) 244-5698. E-mail: mike@am1230klxr.com. Licensee: Michael R. Quinn (acq 12-31-99; $125,000). Network: Westwood One. Pepper & Corazzini, LLP. Format: Adult standards, btfl music. Target aud: 35 plus. Spec prog: Jazz 2 hrs wkly. ♦ Bob Williams, gen mgr & progmg dir.

KNCQ(FM)— Oct 29, 1985: 97.3 mhz; 100 kw. 3,569 ft. TL: N40 36 10 W122 38 58. Stereo. 1588 Charles Dr. 96003-1459. Phone: (530) 244-9700. Fax: (530) 244-9707. Web Site: www.q97country.com. Licensee: Results Radio of Redding Licensee LLC. Group owner: Fritz Communications Inc. Rep: D & R Radio. Format: Country. Target aud: 25-54. ♦ Beth Tappan, gen mgr.

KNRO(AM)— 2001: 1670 khz; 10 kw-D, 1 kw-N. TL: N40 33 14 W122 22 53. 3360 Alta Mesa Dr. 96002-2831. Phone: (530) 226-9500. Fax: (530) 221-4940. Web Site: www.espn1670.com. Licensee: Regent Licensee of Redding Inc. Group owner: Regent Communications Inc. Format: Sports. ♦ Lisa Geraci, gen mgr.

Directory of Radio

KQMS(AM)— Sept 14, 1954: 1400 khz; 1 kw-U. TL: N40 33 33 W122 19 42. 3360 Alta Mesa Dr. 96002. Phone: (530) 226-9500. Fax: (530) 221-6653. E-mail: lisag@reddingradio.com. Licensee: Regent Broadcasting West Coast Inc. Group owner: Regent Communications Inc. (acq 8-21-97; grpsl). Rep: McGavren Guild. Format: News/talk. ♦ William Stakelin, pres; Lisa Geraci, gen mgr.

KSHA(FM)—Co-owned with KQMS(AM). Sept 1, 1981: 104.3 mhz; 100 kw. 1,560 ft. TL: N40 39 14 W122 31 12. Stereo. Format: Lite rock. ♦ Dennis Kennedy, progmg dir.

KRRX(FM)—(Burney). May 1985: 106.1 mhz; 100 kw. 2,000 ft. TL: N40 54 21 W121 49 38. Stereo. 3360 Alta Mesa Dr. 96002. Phone: (530) 226-9500. Fax: (530) 221-4940. E-mail: krrx@reddingradio.com. Web Site: 106x.com. Licensee: Regent Broadcasting of Redding. Group owner: Regent Communications Inc. (acq 5-29-98; grpsl). Grif Johnson. Format: Rock/AOR. News staff: 2. Target aud: 25-54; upscale. ♦ Lisa Geraci, gen mgr; Jim Davison, opns dir; Jordan Perry, sls dir; Chris Gonzalez, prom dir.

*KVIP(AM)— Jan 4, 1970: 540 khz; 2.5 kw-D, 17 w-N. TL: N40 37 25 W122 16 49. Box 492727 96049-2727. Secondary address: 1139 Hartnell Ave. 96002. Phone: (530) 222-4455. E-mail: info@kvip.org. Web Site: www.kvip.org. Licensee: Pacific Cascade Communications Corp. (acq 12-69). Network: Network: Moody, Salem Radio Network. Format: Inspirational, traditional Christian, talk. News staff: 2; News: 14 hrs wkly. Target aud: General. ♦ David L. Morrow, VP; Steve Hafen, gen mgr, news dir & pub affrs dir; Ted Hering, progmg dir; Larry Cardoza, engrg dir; Paul Brown, chief of engrg.

KVIP-FM— Oct 19, 1975: 98.1 mhz; 30 kw. 1,710 ft. TL: N40 36 10 W122 38 58. Stereo. Web Site: www.kvip.org.

Redlands

KCAL(AM)— April 1959: 1410 khz; 5 kw-D, 4 kw-N, DA-N. TL: N34 04 08 W117 12 06. 1950 S. Sunwest, San Bernardino 92408. Phone: (909) 825-5020. Fax: (909) 884-5844. E-mail: edith@radiolazer.com. Web Site: www.radiolazer.com. Licensee: Lazer Broadcasting Corp. (group owner; acq 8-7-01; $2.35 million). Format: Sp. News staff: 2. Target aud: 18-49, 25-64; Mexican origin, Latin American. ♦ Alfredo Placencia, CEO, chmn & exec VP; Vicki Bails-Leth, VP & gen mgr.

KCAL-FM— 1965: 96.7 mhz; 3 kw. 377 ft. TL: N34 11 51 W117 17 10. Stereo. 1940 Orange Tree Ln., Suite 200 92374. Phone: (909) 793-3554. Fax: (909) 798-6627. Web Site: www.kcalfm.com. Licensee: Anaheim Broadcasting Corp. (group owner) Rep: D & R Radio. Format: Adult rock. Target aud: 16-30. ♦ Jeff Parke, VP & gen mgr; Steve Hoffman, opns mgr.

Redondo Beach

KDAY(FM)— Aug 4, 1961: 93.5 mhz; 3.4 kw. Ant 433 ft. TL: N33 51 35 W118 20 56. Stereo. 5055 Wilshire Blvd., Suite 720, Los Angeles 90036. Phone: (323) 337-1600. Fax: (323) 337-1633. Web Site: www.935kday.com. Licensee: KDAY Licensing LLC. Group owner: Spanish Broadcasting System Inc. (acq 11-18-2004; $120 million. with KDAI(FM) Ontario). Format: Hip-hop. ♦ Kimberly Fletcher, gen mgr; Lisa Alta Moreno, gen sls mgr; Anthony Acampora, progmg dir; Larry Slover, chief of engrg.

Redwood Valley

*KAIS(FM)—Not on air, target date: unknown: 88.7 mhz; 15 w. Ant 1,935 ft. TL: N38 56 54 W123 13 04. 5700 West Oaks Blvd., Rocklin 95765. Phone: (916) 251-1600. Fax: (916) 251-1650. Licensee: Educational Media Foundation. ♦ Richard Jenkins, pres; Lloyd Parker, gen mgr.

Ridgecrest

KLOA(AM)— Dec 11, 1956: 1240 khz; 250 w-U. TL: N35 37 24 W117 41 10. 731 N. Balsam St. 93555. Phone: (760) 375-8888. Fax: (760) 371-1824. E-mail: radio@iwvisp.com. Web Site: www.kloaam.com. Licensee: Adelman Broadcasting Inc. (group owner). Format: Adult standards. ♦ Robert Adelman, pres; Eric Kauffman, progmg dir; James Rowles, chief of engrg.

KLOA-FM— 1979: 104.9 mhz; 750 w. 1 ft. TL: N35 37 24 W117 41 10. Stereo. Web Site: www.kloafm.com. Format: Country.

Stations in the U.S. — California

Developers & Brokers of Radio Properties

contact American Media Services at our suite: Philadelphia Marriott Downtown 215-625-2900
843-972-2200
americanmediaservices.com
Charleston, SC
Dallas, TX · Chicago, Il · Austin, TX
American Media Services, LLC

KWDJ(AM)— Apr 7, 1974: 1360 khz; 1 kw-D, 38 w-N. TL: N35 36 58 W117 38 35. 121 W. Ridgecrest Blvd. 93555-2606. Phone: (760) 384-4937. Fax: (760) 384-4978. Licensee: James & Donna Knudsen. (acq 9-30-91; $250,000 with co-located FM; 10-28-91). Network: ABC Information & Entertainment. Rep: Western Regional Broadcast Sales. Pepper & Corazzini. Format: Classical country. News staff: one; News: 11 hrs wkly. Target aud: 25-54; educated adults with high disposable income. ♦James L. Knudsen, pres & opns VP.

*KWTD(FM)— May 2005: . Stn currently dark 91.9 mhz; 7.5 kw. Ant 1,243 ft. TL: N35 28 39 W117 41 58. Stereo. Box 637, Bishop 93515. Phone: (760) 872-6215. Fax: (760) 872-4155. Licensee: Living Proof Inc. Format: Christian. ♦Daniel McClenaghan, CEO.

KZIQ-FM— Jan 1, 1978: 92.7 mhz; 1.5 kw. 1,296 ft. TL: N33 36 58 W117 38 35. Stereo. 121 W. Ridgecrest Blvd. 93555-2606. Phone: (760) 384-4937. Licensee: James & Donna Knudsen. Format: Lite adult contemp. News: 2 hrs wkly. ♦James Knudsen, stn mgr.

Rio Dell

*KNHT(FM)— 1999: 107.3 mhz; 3.3 kw. Ant 1,702 ft. TL: N40 30 03 W124 17 10. Jefferson Public Radio, 1250 Siskiyou Blvd., Ashland, OR 97520. Phone: (541) 552-6301. Fax: (541) 552-8565. Web Site: www.jeffnet.org. Licensee: The State of Oregon, acting by and through the State Board of Higher Education, for the benefit of Southern Oregon University. (acq 1-6-00). Network: Network: NPR, PRI. Ernest Sanchez. Format: Classical music, news. News staff: one; News: 35 hrs wkly. ♦Mitchell Christian, CFO; Ronald Kramer, CEO & gen mgr; Bryon Lambert, opns dir; Paul Westhelle, dev dir.

Rio Vista

*KRVH(FM)— Nov 7, 1972: 101.5 mhz; 10 w. 60 ft. TL: N38 09 17 W121 41 48. 410 S. 4th St. 94571. Phone: (707) 374-6336. Fax: (707) 374-6810. Licensee: River Delta Unified School District. Format: CHR. Target aud: 13-19; young adult. ♦William Fulk, gen mgr.

Riverbank

KCBC(AM)— Apr 5, 1987: 770 khz; 50 kw-D, 1 kw-N, DA-2. TL: N37 47 51 W120 53 01. Stereo. 10948 Cleveland Ave., Oakdale 95361. Phone: (209) 847-7700. Fax: (209) 847-1769. E-mail: kcbcradio@surfside.net. Licensee: Kiertron Inc. (acq 12-30-92; $1 million; 1-25-93). Format: Relg. News staff: one; News: 25 hrs wkly. Target aud: 25-49. ♦Don Crawford Sr., pres; Don Crawford Jr., gen mgr; Virginia Marsau, opns VP & opns mgr.

Riverside

KDIF(AM)— Nov 15, 1941: 1440 khz; 1 kw-U. TL: N34 01 37 W117 21 27. Stereo. 2030 Iowa Ave., Ste A 92507. Phone: (951) 784-4210. Fax: (951) 274-4971. Licensee: Citicasters Licenses L.P. Group owner: Clear Channel Communications Inc. (acq 5-4-99; grpsl). Verner, Liipfert, Bernhard, McPherson & Hand. Format: Sp. News staff: 2; News: 7 hrs wkly. Target aud: 25-54; Hispanic. Spec prog: Hablando Claro one hr wkly. ♦Bob Ridzak, pres, gen mgr & opns dir.

KELT(FM)— 1959: 92.7 mhz; 6 kw. 328 ft. TL: N34 11 51 W117 17 09. Stereo. 99 Long Ct., Suite 200, Tousand Oaks 91360. Phone: (951) 805) 497-8511. Fax: (951) 805-497-8514. Web Site: www.92.7fm.com. Licensee: Amaturo Group of L.A. Ltd. Group owner: Amaturo Group Ltd. (acq 1-6-93; $3.25 million; 2-1-93). Format: Soft adult contemp. Target aud: 25-54. ♦Catherine Moreau, gen mgr & sls dir.

KFRG(FM)—See San Bernardino

KGGI(FM)— Jan 23, 1965: 99.1 mhz; 2.55 kw. 1,843 ft. TL: N34 14 04 W117 08 24. Stereo. 2030 Iowa Ave., Suite A 92507. Phone: (951) 684-1991. Fax: (951) 274-4949. Web Site: www.991kggifm.com. Licensee: AMFM Broadcasting Licenses LLC. Group owner: Clear Channel Communications Inc. (acq 8-30-2000; grpsl). Rep: McGavren Guild. Format: CHR. Target aud: 18-49. ♦Bob Ridzak, gen mgr.

KLYY(FM)— Mar 17, 1959: 97.5 mhz; 72 kw. 1,571 ft. TL: N33 57 57 W117 17 21. (CP: Ant 1,827 ft.). Stereo. 5700 Wilshire Blvd., Suite 250, Los Angeles 90036. Phone: (323) 900-6100. Fax: (323) 900-6127. Web Site: www.oye975.com. Licensee: Entravision Holdings LLC. Group owner: Entravision Communications Corp. (acq 4-20-00; grpsl). Rep: Lotus Entravision Reps LLC. Format: Cumbia. Target aud: 18-49. ♦Jeff Liberman, VP; Karl Meyer, gen mgr; Robert I. Mendoza, opns mgr & gen sls mgr; Armando Guerrero, mktg dir, prom dir & prom; Nestor Rocha, progmg VP & progmg dir; Eugene McAfel, chief of engrg & engr.

KPRO(AM)— June 22, 1957: 1570 khz; 5 kw-D, 194 w-N, DA-2. TL: N33 55 54 W117 23 47. 7351 Lincoln Ave. 92504. Phone: (951) 688-1570. Fax: (951) 688-7009. E-mail: kproval@aol.com. Licensee: Impact Radio Inc. (acq 7-25-2005). Pepper & Corazzini. Format: Relg. Target aud: General. ♦Ronnie Olenick, pres; Valorie Stitely, gen mgr & stn mgr.

*KSGN(FM)— January 1970: 89.7 mhz; 3 kw. 300 ft. TL: N34 11 51 W117 17 10. Stereo. 11498 Pierce St. 92505. Phone: (909) 687-5746. Fax: (909) 785-2288. Licensee: Good News Radio. Network: USA. Format: Christian educ, relg. News: 12 hrs wkly. Target aud: General; Christians & church goers. ♦Dennis Johnson, chmn, pres & CFO; Dawn Hibbard, gen mgr; Bruce Potterton, stn mgr & engrg dir; Art Garza, dev dir & sls dir; Jackie Neff, mktg mgr, prom mgr & pub affrs dir; Dave Masters, progmg dir; Ernest Beck, asst music dir; Jon Foreman, chief of engrg.

*KUCR(FM)— October 1966: 88.3 mhz; 750 w. 291 ft. TL: N33 58 11 W117 17 50. (CP: 150 w, ant 1,620 ft.). Stereo. 691 Linden St. 92521. Phone: (951) 787-3737. Fax: (951) 787-3240. E-mail: kucr@citrus.ucr.edu. Web Site: www.kucr.org. Licensee: The Regents of the University of California. Format: Div, alternative rock. Spec prog: Black 18 hrs, class 14 hrs, jazz 6 hrs wkly. ♦Louis Van Den Berg, gen mgr; Dexter Thomas, asst music dir; Walter Douglas, prom dir, progmg dir & news dir; Jeff Armantrout, pub affrs dir; Bill Elledge, chief of engrg.

Rocklin

*KEBR(AM)— July 27, 1988: 1210 khz; 5 kw-D, 500 w-N, DA-D. TL: N38 27 46 W121 07 49. 4135 Northgate Blvd., Suite 1, Sacramento 95834-1226. Phone: (916) 641-8191. Fax: (916) 641-8238. Web Site: www.familyradio.com. Licensee: Family Stations Inc. (group owner) Format: Relg. Target aud: General. ♦Harold Camping, pres; Peggy Renschler, stn mgr & opns mgr.

Rohnert Park

KRPQ(FM)— Mar 4, 1986: 104.9 mhz; 2.25 kw. 548 ft. TL: N38 23 31 W122 40 40. Stereo. 6640 Redwood Dr., Suite 202 94928. Phone: (707) 584-1058. Fax: (707) 584-7944. Web Site: www.q105.com. Licensee: Results Radio of Sonoma Licensee LLC. Group owner: Fritz Communications Inc. (acq 8-31-94; $2.08 million;. FTR: 10-24-94). Covington & Burling. Format: Contemp country. Target aud: 25-54. ♦Neysa Hinton, gen mgr & opns mgr.

Rosamond

KLKX(FM)— Sept 1, 1993: 93.5 mhz; 3 kw. Ant 207 ft. TL: N34 51 03 W118 09 22. Q-9, 570 East Ave., Palmdale 93550. Phone: (661) 947-3107. Fax: (661) 272-5688. Web Site: www.935thequake.com. Licensee: High Desert Broadcasting LLC (group owner; acq 3-7-2002; grpsl). Network: Westwood One. Arent, Fox, Kintner, Plotkin & Kahn. Format: Classic rock, news, interviews. Target aud: 25-54. ♦Bruce Thomps, gen mgr; Gary Wilson, opns mgr.

KOSS(FM)— Mar 1, 1985: 105.5 mhz; 3 kw. 328 ft. TL: N34 51 03 W118 09 22. Stereo. 352 E. Ave. K-4, Lancaster 93535. Phone: (661) 942-1121. Fax: (661) 723-5512. Web Site: www.oasis1055.com. Licensee: Clear Channel Broadcasting Licenses Inc. Group owner: Clear Channel Communications Inc. (acq 11-21-03; grpsl). Format: Adult contemp. News: 4 hrs wkly. ♦Larry Thornhill, gen mgr; Mark Mitchell, opns mgr.

Rosedale

*KOGR(FM)—Not on air, target date: unknown: 88.9 mhz; 3.6 kw. Ant 1,653 ft. TL: N35 03 00 W120 02 23. CSN International, 3232 W. MacArthur Blvd., Santa Ana 92704. Phone: (714) 825-9663. Fax: (714) 825-9660. Licensee: CSN International. (group owner). ♦Jeffrey Smith, pres.

Roseville

KFSG(AM)— 2001: 1690 khz; 10 kw-D, 1 kw-N. TL: N38 44 22 W121 12 50. 3463 Ramona Ave., Suite 15, Sacramento 95826. Phone: (916) 456-3288. Fax: (916) 456-3324. E-mail: radiopoder@juno.com. Licensee: Way Broadcasting Licensee LLC (acq 6-13-00; grpsl). Format: Sp, Christian. ♦Rosa Garza, gen mgr.

KHWD(FM)—Licensed to Roseville. See Sacramento

KLIB(AM)— Apr 1, 1968: 1110 khz; 5 kw-D, 500 w-N, DA-2. TL: N38 44 22 W121 12 48. 3463 Romona Ave., Suite 15, Sacramento 95826. Phone: (916) 456-3288. Fax: (916) 456-3324. E-mail: radiopoder@juno.com. Licensee: Way Broadcasting Licensee LLC (acq 4-20-2000; grpsl). Rep: Caballero. Format: Ethnic. News staff: one. Target aud: 18 plus; Hispanic. Spec prog: Sacramento Knights indoor soccer, Sacramento Kings NBA basketball. ♦Rosa Garza, gen mgr.

Sacramento

KBMB(FM)— October 1996: 103.5 mhz; 6 kw. 312 ft. TL: N38 33 59 W121 28 47. (CP: Ant 308 ft). 1436 Auburn Blvd. 95815. Phone: (916) 646-4000. Fax: (916) 927-7376. Web Site: www.1035thebomb.com. Licensee: Entravision Holdings LLC. Group owner: Entravision Communications Corp. (acq 9-30-2004; $16.1 million). Format: Urban. Target aud: 18-49. ♦Larry LeManski, gen mgr; Alisha Harris, opns mgr & gen sls mgr; Tom DelRio, gen sls mgr & progmg dir.

KCBC(AM)—See Riverbank

KCTC(AM)— April 1945: 1320 khz; 5 kw-U, DA-2. TL: N38 42 42 W121 19 44. Stereo. 5345 Madison Ave. 95841. Phone: (916) 334-7777. Fax: (916) 339-4572. Web Site: kctc.com. Licensee: Entercom Sacramento License LLC. Group owner: Entercom Communications Corp. (acq 10-17-97). Network: Network: Westwood One, ABC. Format: Nostalgia. News: 5 hrs wkly. Target aud: 35 plus. ♦John Geary, VP; David Lichtman, gen mgr.

KDND(FM)— Aug 1, 1945: 107.9 mhz; 50 kw. 403 ft. TL: N38 42 38 W121 28 54. Stereo. 5345 Madison Ave. 95841. Phone: (916) 334-7777. Fax: (916) 334-1092. Web Site: www.endonline.com. Licensee: Entercom Sacramento License L.L.C. Group owner: Entercom Communications Corp. (acq 6-3-97; $27.5 million). Rep: D & R Radio. Format: CHR. News staff: one. Target aud: 25-44. ♦John Geary, pres; John Greary, gen mgr; Sara McLure, gen sls mgr; David Lichtman, mktg VP; Steve Weed, stn mgr & progmg dir; Mick Rush, engrg dir.

*KEDR(FM)— 1997: 88.1 mhz; 8.4 kw. 994 ft. TL: N38 14 50 W121 30 03. Stereo. 4135 Northgate Blvd., Suite One 95834-1226. Phone: (916) 641-8191. Fax: (916) 641-8238. Licensee: Family Stations Inc. (group owner) Format: Relg. ♦Harold Camping, pres; Peggy Renschler, gen mgr & opns mgr.

KFBK(AM)— 1922: 1530 khz; 50 kw-D, DA-2. TL: N38 50 54 W121 28 58. 1440 Ethan Way, Suite 200 95825. Phone: (916) 929-5325. Fax: (916) 925-6326. Web Site: www.kfbk.com. Licensee: AMFM Broadcasting Licenses LLC. Group owner: Clear Channel Communications Inc. (acq 8-30-2000; grpsl). Network: Network: ABC Information & Entertainment, ABC News/Talk. Format: News/talk. News staff: 8; News: 45 hrs wkly. ♦Jeff Marcus, pres; Jerry Del Core, gen mgr; Ken Kohl, opns mgr; Jeff Holden, sls VP & natl sls mgr; Sarah Simpson, gen sls mgr; Helen Dahdouh, natl sls mgr; Susan Wells, prom dir & prom mgr; Martin Doyal, news dir; Ross DuClair, chief of engrg.

KGBY(FM)— Co-owned with KFBK(AM). 1946: 92.5 mhz; 50 kw. 499 ft. TL: N38 42 26 W121 28 33. Stereo. Fax: (916) 925-9292. Web Site:

www.y92.com. Format: Lite rock. News: one hr wkly. ♦Amy Bingham, prom dir & prom mgr; Mike Berlak, progmg dir, mus dir & pub affrs dir.

KFIA(AM)—See Carmichael

KHTK(AM)— November 1926: 1140 khz; 50 kw-U, DA-2. TL: N38 23 34 W121 11 51. 5244 Madison Ave 95841. Phone: (916) 338-8700. Fax: (916) 338-9227. Web Site: www.khtkam.com. Licensee: Infinity Radio Holdings Inc. Group owner: Infinity Broadcasting Corp. (acq 11-13-98; grpsl). Format: Sports. News: 10 hrs wkly. Target aud: 25-44. Spec prog: Farm 4 hrs wkly. ♦Doug Harvill, VP & gen mgr; Michael Hernandez, stn mgr; Mike Remey, opns dir & progmg dir.

KNCI(FM)—Co-owned with KHTK(AM). Feb 21, 1960: 105.1 mhz; 50 kw. 500 ft. TL: N38 38 31 W121 05 25. Stereo. Phone: (916) 338-9200. Web Site: www.kncifm.com. Format: Country. ♦Steve Cottingim, stn mgr; Mark Evans, opns dir.

KHWD(FM)—(Roseville). June 1970: 93.7 mhz; 25 kw. 328 ft. TL: N38 44 22 W121 12 50. Stereo. 5244 Madison Ave. 95841. Phone: (916) 338-9200. Fax: (916) 338-9155. Web Site: www.howard937.com. Licensee: Infinity Radio Holdings Inc. Group owner: Infinity Broadcasting Corp. (acq 11-13-98; grpsl). Koteen & Naftalin. Format: Alternative rock. News staff: one; News: 2 hrs wkly. Target aud: 25-54. ♦Doug Harvill, gen mgr & mktg mgr; Jeff Keller, gen sls mgr; Dave Sozinho, progmg dir; Steve Cottingin, gen mgr & chief of engrg.

KIID(AM)— Aug 1, 1945: 1470 khz; 5 kw-D, 1 kw-N, DA-2. TL: N38 35 30 W121 27 47. 8842 Quail Ln., Granite Bay 95746. Phone: (916) 780-1470. Fax: (916) 780-1493. Web Site: www.radiodisney.com. Licensee: Radio Disney Group LLC. Group owner: ABC Inc. (acq 12-19-00; $3.31 million). Network: Radio Disney. Format: Children. ♦Judy Remy, stn mgr.

KJAY(AM)— May 23, 1963: 1430 khz; 500 w-D, DA. TL: N38 29 39 W121 32 47. 5030 S. River Rd., West Sacramento 95691. Phone: (916) 371-5101. Phone: (916) 371-5104. Fax: (916) 371-1459. Licensee: KJAY L.L.C. (acq 11-94). Network: USA. Fisher, Wayland, Cooper, Leader & Zaragoza L.L.P. Format: International. Target aud: 25-64. Spec prog: Hmong, Russian. ♦Trudi Powell, pres; Jerry Sieber, gen mgr.

KRXQ(FM)— Nov 1, 1959: 98.5 mhz; 50 kw. 500 ft. TL: N38 38 35 W121 05 51. Stereo. Box 60408, 5345 Madison Ave. 95841. Phone: (916) 334-7777. Fax: (916) 339-4559. Web Site: www.krxq.net. Licensee: Entercom Sacramento License L.L.C. Group owner: Entercom Communications Corp. (acq 7-28-98; grpsl). Rep: McGavren Guild. Fletcher, Heald & Hildreth. Format: Rock. News staff: one. Target aud: 25-40; males. Spec prog: Blues one hr wkly. ♦John Geary, pres & VP; David Lichtman, gen mgr.

KSAC(AM)— 1938: 1240 khz; 1 kw-U. TL: N38 35 17 W121 28 05. 1017 Front St., 2nd Fl. 95814. Phone: (916) 553-3000. Fax: (916) 553-3013. Web Site: www.1240talkcity.com. Licensee: Diamond Broadcasting Group owner: Moon Broadcasting (acq 11-19-2004; $3 million). Format: News/talk, sports. Target aud: 18 plus; Hispanics. ♦Paula Nelson, gen mgr; Mirinda Johnson, chief of opns.

KSEG(FM)— 1959: 96.9 mhz; 50 kw. 500 ft. TL: N38 38 54 W121 28 40. Stereo. 5345 Madison Ave. 95841-3141. Phone: (916) 334-7777. Fax: (916) 339-4280. Web Site: www.eagle969.com. Licensee: Entercom Sacramento License L.L.C. Group owner: Entercom Communications Corp. (acq 1-7-97; $45 million. with KRAK(FM) Roseville). Rep: D & R Radio. Format: Classic rock. Target aud: 18-49. ♦John Geary, pres & VP; David Lichtman, gen mgr.

KSFM(FM)—(Woodland). Feb 4, 1961: 102.5 mhz; 50 kw. 500 ft. TL: N38 35 20 W121 43 30. Stereo. 1750 Howe Ave., Suite 500 95825. Phone: (916) 920-1025. Fax: (916) 929-5341. Web Site: www.ksfm.com. Licensee: Infinity Radio of Sacramento Inc. Group owner: Infinity Broadcasting Corp. (acq 11-13-98; grpsl). Network: Westwood One. Leventhal, Senter & Lerman. Format: Rhythm and blues. Target aud: 12-44. ♦Doug Harvill, gen mgr.

KSMH(AM)—See West Sacramento

KTKZ(AM)— 1952: 1380 khz; 5 kw-U, DA-2. TL: N38 33 19 W121 10 51. 1425 River Park Dr., Suite 520 95815. Phone: (916) 924-0710. Fax: (916) 924-1587. Web Site: www.ktkz.com. Licensee: Vista Broadcasting Inc. Group owner: Salem Communications Corp. (acq 3-11-97; $1.5 million). Format: Talk. Target aud: 35 plus; general. ♦Robert B. Fox, gen mgr; Steve Gasser, opns mgr; Stu Roberts, gen sls mgr; Eric Hogue, progmg dir.

KWOD(FM)— Apr 1, 1957: 106.5 mhz; 50 kw. Ant 410 ft. TL: N38 38 30 W121 05 25. Stereo. 5345 Madison Ave. 95841. Phone: (916) 334-7777. Fax: (916) 339-5668. Web Site: www.kwod.net. Licensee: Entercom Sacramento License LLC. Group owner: Entercom Communications Corp. (acq 5-19-2003; $25 million). Format: Alternative. Target aud: 18-49; new rock, mass appeal. ♦John Geary, VP; David Lichtman, gen mgr; Curtiss Johnson, stn mgr.

KXCL(FM)—See Placerville

***KXHV(FM)**— January 1993: 89.7 mhz; 300 w. 85 ft. TL: N38 31 52 W121 22 54. c/o Sacramento High School, 2315 34th St. 95817. Phone: (916) 277-7062. Fax: (916) 277-6823. Licensee: Sacramento City Unified School District. Format: Div, rock and roll. Target aud: 13-19; high school students. ♦Shaun Carpenter, gen mgr.

***KXJZ(FM)**— July 1, 1991: 88.9 mhz; 50 kw. Ant 500 ft. TL: N38 16 25 W121 30 11. Stereo. 3416 American River Dr., Suite B 95864. Phone: (916) 480-5900. Fax: (916) 487-3348. E-mail: npr@csus.edu. Web Site: www.capradio.org. Licensee: California State University, Sacramento. Network: Network: NPR, PRI. Duane Morris LLP. Format: Jazz, news & info. News staff: 5; News: 90 hrs wkly. Target aud: General; NPR Listeners, eg. professionals, educators, administrators. Spec prog: World mus 2 hrs, blues 7 hrs wkly. ♦Michael Lazar, pres & gen mgr; Carl Watanabe, stn mgr, progmg dir & progmg mgr; John Brenneise, opns mgr; Beth Hassett, dev dir & mktg dir; Linda Onstad, gen sls mgr, rgnl sls mgr & adv dir; Michael Frost, prom dir; Gary Vercelli, mus dir; Joe Barr, news dir; Jeff Browne, engrg dir.

***KXPR(FM)**— October 1964: 90.9 mhz; 50 kw. 500 ft. TL: N38 42 38 W121 28 54. Stereo. 7055 Folsom Blvd. 95864. Phone: (916) 480-5900. Fax: (916) 487-3348. E-mail: npr@csus.edu. Web Site: www.capradio.org. Licensee: California State University, Sacramento. Network: Network: NPR, PRI. Duane Morris, LLP. Format: Class. Target aud: General; NPR listeners,ex. professionals, educators & administrators. ♦Michael Lazar, pres & gen mgr; Carl Watanabe, stn mgr, progmg dir & progmg mgr; John Brenneise, opns mgr; Beth Hassett, dev dir & mktg dir; Linda Onstad, adv dir; Cheryl Dring, mus dir; Joe Barr, news dir; Jeff Browne, engrg dir.

***KYDS(FM)**— Jan 24, 1979: 91.5 mhz; 410 w. 108 ft. TL: N38 36 33 W121 21 38. 4300 El Camino Ave. 95821. Phone: (916) 971-7453. Fax: (916) 971-4353. E-mail: esantillanes@sanjuan.ed. Licensee: San Juan Unified School District. Format: Var. ♦Ed Santillanes, gen mgr.

KYMX(FM)— 1947: 96.1 mhz; 50 kw. 476 ft. TL: N38 38 09 W121 33 11. Stereo. 280 Commerce Cir. 95815. Phone: (916) 923-6800. Fax: (916) 922-2830. Web Site: www.kymx.com. Licensee: Infinity Radio Inc. Group owner: Infinity Broadcasting Corp. (acq 11-13-98; grpsl). Format: Adult contemp. News staff: one; News: 3 hrs wkly. Target aud: 25-54; Women ages 25-54. ♦Joel Hollander, pres; Jaque Tortorolli, CFO; Lisa Decker, sr VP; Doug Harvill, gen mgr & mktg mgr; Michelle Magee, stn mgr; Steve Cottingim, sls dir; Michelle Magee, gen sls mgr; Bryan Jackson, progmg dir.

KZZO(FM)— October 1958: 100.5 mhz; 115 kw. 328 ft. TL: N38 38 30 W121 05 25. Stereo. 280 Commerce Cir. 95815. Phone: (916) 923-6800. Fax: (916) 922-2830. Web Site: www.radiozone.com. Licensee: Infinity Radio Inc. Group owner: Infinity Broadcasting Corp. (acq 11-13-98; grpsl). Rep: Christal. Format: Adult contemp. News staff: one; News: 3 hrs wkly. Target aud: 25-44. ♦Michelle Magee, stn mgr; Dell Goetz, sls dir & gen sls mgr; Steve Cottingim, gen mgr & sls dir; Doug Harvill, mktg mgr; Byran Kennedy, progmg dir.

Saint Helena

KVYN(FM)— November 1976: 99.3 mhz; 3 kw. 226 ft. TL: N38 25 34 W122 19 33. (CP: Ant 259 ft.). Stereo. 1124 Foster Rd., Napa 94558. Phone: (707) 252-1440. Phone: (707) 258-1111. Fax: (707) 226-7544. Web Site: www.kuyn.com. Licensee: Wine Country Broadcasting Co. (acq 8-11-03; $3 million. with KVON(AM) Napa). Network: ABC. Rep: Christal. Robinson Silverman Pearce Aronsohn & Berman. Format: Adult contemp. Target aud: 25-45. Spec prog: Folk 2 hrs wkly. ♦Roger O. Walther, pres; Jeff Schechtman, gen mgr.

Salinas

KABL(AM)— 1947: 1460 khz; 10 kw-U, DA-1. TL: N36 43 59 W121 35 32. 903 N. Main St. 93906. Phone: (831) 755-8181. Fax: (831) 755-8193. Licensee: Clear Channel Broadcasting Licenses Inc. Group owner: Clear Channel Communications Inc. Format: Standards. Target aud: 55+. ♦Jeff Wilson, VP & gen mgr.

KBOQ(FM)—See Monterey

KDBV(AM)— July 17, 1963: 980 khz; 10 kw-U, DA-2. TL: N36 43 58 W121 35 32. 548 Alisal St. 93905. Phone: (831) 757-1910. Fax: (831) 757-8015. Licensee: Centro Cristiano Vida Abundante Inc. (acq 5-21-2004; $850,000). Brown, Nietert & Kaufman. Format: Sp, Christian. Target aud: 18-49; Hispanics. ♦Ron Stevens, gen mgr.

KDON-FM— December 1959: 102.5 mhz; 15 kw. Ant 2,371 ft. TL: N36 45 23 W121 30 05. Stereo. 903 N. Main St. 93906. Phone: (831) 755-8181. Fax: (831) 755-8193. Web Site: www.kdon.com. Licensee: Clear Channel Radio License Inc. Group owner: Clear Channel Communications Inc. (acq 9-22-97; grpsl). Rep: Christal. Format: Hip hop. News staff: one. Target aud: 18-54. ♦Rhonda McCormick, gen mgr & gen sls mgr.

KEXA(FM)— Mar 10, 1997: 97.9 mhz; 2.9 kw. Ant 112 ft. TL: N36 36 32 W121 40 59. 548 E. Alisal St. 93905. Phone: (831) 757-1910. Fax: (831) 757-8015. Licensee: Len Radio Broadcasting of California Licensee LLC. (group owner; (acq 2-16-2005; grpsl). Format: Urban. ♦Ron Stevens, gen mgr.

***KHDC(FM)**—(Chualar). June 28, 1981: 90.9 mhz; 3 kw. 194 ft. TL: N36 32 54 W121 26 34. Stereo. 161 Main St. 93901. Phone: (831) 757-8039. Fax: (831) 757-9854. Web Site: www.radiobilingue.org. Licensee: Radio Bilingue Inc. (acq 11-86; $70,000; 5-12-86). Format: Multilingual, ethnic, Sp. ♦Hugo Morales, CEO & gen mgr; Delia Saldivar, gen mgr & progmg dir; Maria Esana, chief of engrg.

KNRY(AM)—See Monterey

KPRC-FM—Listing follows KZFX(AM).

KRAY-FM— Dec 5, 1977: 103.5 mhz; 6 kw. Ant 512 ft. TL: N36 42 32 W121 36 46. Stereo. Box 1939 93902. Secondary address: 548 Alisal St. 93905. Phone: (831) 757-1910. Fax: (831) 757-8015. Licensee: Len Radio Broadcasting of California Licensee LLC. (group owner; (acq 2-16-2005; grpsl). Format: LaBuena. ♦Ron Stevens, gen mgr & chief of engrg.

KTGE(AM)— July 4, 1963: 1570 khz; 500 w-D. TL: N36 41 49 W121 37 22. (CP: 5 kw-D, 500 w-N, DA-2. TL: N36 39 38 W121 32 29). Box 1939 93901. Secondary address: 548 Alisal St., Salinas 93905. Phone: (831) 757-5911. Fax: (831) 757-8015. E-mail: wolfhouseradio@yahoo.es. Licensee: Len Radio Broadcasting of California Licensee LLC. (group owner; (acq 2-16-2005; grpsl). Format: Sp, rgnl Mexican. Target aud: Adults 24-54. ♦Ron Stevens, gen mgr; Ramon Castro, gen sls mgr; Vicente Romero, progmg dir.

KWAV(FM)—See Monterey

KZFX(AM)— Sept 27, 1947: 1380 khz; 5 kw-U, DA-2. TL: N36 41 49 W121 37 22. 903 N. Main St. 93906. Phone: (831) 755-8181. Fax: (831) 755-8193. Licensee: Clear Channel Broadcasting Licenses Inc. Group owner: Clear Channel Communications Inc. (acq 9-22-97; grpsl). Network: ABC Information & Entertainment. Anderson, Kill, Olick & Oshinsky. Format: Sports. News staff: one; News: 11 hrs wkly. Target aud: 25-54. ♦Kim Bryant, gen mgr.

KPRC-FM—Co-owned with KZFX(AM). Sept 16, 1964: 100.7 mhz; 910 w. 2,575 ft. TL: N36 32 05 W121 37 14. (CP: 1.4 kw, ant 2,385 ft.). Stereo. Web Site: www.ktom.com. Format: Country. News staff: one.

San Ardo

***KBDH(FM)**— Jan 21, 2001: 91.7 mhz; 2.7 kw. Ant 1,781 ft. TL: N35 57 06 W121 00 03. Stereo. 203 8th Ave, Santa Cruz 95062. Phone: (831) 476-2800. Fax: (831) 476-2802. E-mail: kusp@kusp.org. Web Site: www.kusp.org. Licensee: Pataphysical Broadcasting Foundation. Network: NPR. Format: Div. News: 44 hrs wkly. ♦Terry Green, gen mgr & stn mgr; Paula Kenyon, dev dir.

San Bernardino

KEZY(AM)— August 1947: 1240 khz; 1 kw-U. TL: N34 04 55 W117 18 17. Box 500, Camarillo 93011. Phone: (805) 482-4797. Fax: (626)

817-9851. Licensee: Hi-Favor Broadcasting LLC (group owner; acq 8-27-01; $4 million). Network: USA. Miller & Miller. Format: Sp, relg. News: 2 hrs wkly. Target aud: 30 plus. ♦Roland Hinz, pres; Mary Guthrie, gen mgr & progmg dir; John Campa, stn mgr & gen sls mgr.

KFRG(FM)— August 1974: 95.1 mhz; 50 kw. 489 ft. TL: N34 11 51 W117 17 10. Stereo. 900 E. Washington St., Suite 315, Colton 92324. Phone: (909) 825-9525. Fax: (909) 825-0441. Web Site: www.kfrog.com. Licensee: Infinity Radio Inc. Group owner: Infinity Broadcasting Corp. (acq 11-13-98; grpsl). Rep: McGavren Guild. Format: Country. News staff: one; News: 3 hrs wkly. Target aud: 25-54; dual income families. ♦Tom Hoyt, VP & gen mgr; Lee Doughlas, opns mgr.

KKDD(AM)— 1947: 1290 khz; 5 kw-U, DA-2. TL: N34 07 27 W117 17 57. 2030 Iowa Ave., Suite A, Riverside 92507. Phone: (951) 684-1991. Fax: (951) 274-4911. Web Site: www.radiodisney.com. Licensee: AMFM Broadcasting Licenses LLC. Group owner: Clear Channel Communications Inc. (acq 8-30-2000; grpsl). Format: Radio Disney. News staff: one; News: 10 hrs wkly. ♦Bob Ridzak, gen mgr.

KLYY(FM)—See Riverside

KOLA(FM)— June 15, 1959: 99.9 mhz; 29.5 kw. 1,663 ft. TL: N33 57 55 W117 16 59. Stereo. 1940 Orange Tree Ln., Suite 200, Redlands 92374. Phone: (909) 793-3554. Fax: (909) 798-6627. Web Site: www.imakolanut.com. Licensee: Anaheim Broadcasting Corp. (group owner; acq 1995; $5 million). Format: Oldies. News: one hr wkly. Target aud: 25-54. ♦Jeff Parke, gen mgr & opns mgr.

KTDD(AM)— Oct 15, 1947: 1350 khz; 5 kw-D, 500 w-N, DA-2. TL: N34 05 37 W117 17 57. (CP: 600 w-N). 2030 Iowa Ave., Suite A, Riverside 92507. Phone: (951) 684-1991. Fax: (951) 274-4911. Web Site: www.thetoad1350.com. Licensee: Citicasters Licenses L.P. Group owner: Clear Channel Communications Inc. (acq 5-4-99; grpsl). Rep: McGavren Guild. Leventhal, Senter & Lerman. Format: Country. News: 15 hrs wkly. Target aud: 25-64. ♦Bob Ridzak, gen mgr.

KTIE(AM)— 1929: 590 khz; 1 kw-U, DA-2. TL: N34 04 18 W117 17 50. 992 Inland Ctr. Dr. 92408. Phone: (909) 885-6555 Ext. 101. Fax: (909) 383-8889. Web Site: www.ktie590.com. Licensee: Caron Broadcasting Inc. Group owner: Salem Communications Corp. (acq 8-29-2001; $7 million). Format: News/talk. Target aud: 35-54 Male / Female; Upscale, educated, home owners, Business decision makers. ♦Terry Fahy, gen mgr; Ron Stark, gen sls mgr.

*KVCR(FM)— December 1953: 91.9 mhz; 3.8 kw. 1,605 ft. TL: N33 57 57 W117 17 05. (CP:3.8. kw, ant 1,620 ft.). Stereo. 701 S. Mt. Vernon Ave. 92410. Phone: (909) 384-4444. Fax: (909) 885-2116. E-mail: hometeam@kvcr.pbs.org. Web Site: www.kvcr.org. Licensee: San Bernardino Community College Dist. Network: Network: NPR, PRI. Format: News, talk. News staff: 5; News: 50 hrs wkly. Target aud: General. ♦Larry Ciecalone, gen mgr; Steve Ward, opns mgr. Co-owned TV: *KVCR-TV affil

San Clemente

KWVE(FM)— Nov 16, 1971: 107.9 mhz; 530 w. Ant 3,792 ft. TL: N33 42 40 W117 31 55. Stereo. 3000 W. MacArthur Blvd., Suite 500, Santa Ana 92704. Phone: (714) 918-6207. Fax: (714) 918-6256. E-mail: kwve@kwve.com. Web Site: www.kwve.com. Licensee: Calvary Chapel of Costa Mesa Inc. (acq 4-15-85). Latham & Watkins. Format: Relg, Christian. News staff: one; News: 3-5 hrs wkly. Target aud: General. Spec prog: Children 3 hrs wkly. ♦Charles W. Smith, pres; Jeffrey Dorman, gen mgr, opns dir & opns mgr.

San Diego

KBZT(FM)— Mar 6, 1960: 94.9 mhz; 21.8 kw. 710 ft. TL: N32 50 21 W117 14 57. Stereo. 1615 Murray Canyon Rd., Suite 710 92108. Phone: (619) 297-3698. Fax: (619) 543-1353. Web Site: www.fm49sd.com. Licensee: Jefferson-Pilot Communications Co. (acq 9-13-96; $25 million for stock). Format: Alt. Target aud: 18-49. ♦Darrel Goodin, gen mgr & stn mgr.

KCBQ(AM)— 1946: 1170 khz; 50 kw-D, 4.5 kw-N, DA-2. TL: N32 54 29 W116 54 34. 9255 Towne Centre Dr., Suite 535 92121. Phone: (858) 535-1210. Fax: (858) 535-1212. E-mail: info@kcbq.com. Web Site: www.kcbq.com. Licensee: Radio 1210 Inc. Group owner: Salem Communications Corp. (acq 8-23-00; $5 million). Network: Network: AP Radio, ABC. News: 5 hrs wkly. Target aud: 35-64; baby boomers that grew up in the 50s & early 60s. ♦Judy Bowen, gen mgr; Heather Lloyd, opns mgr.

KECR(AM)—See El Cajon

KFMB(AM)— May 19, 1941: 760 khz; 50 kw-U, DA-N. TL: N32 50 32 W117 01 29. (CP: TL: N32 50 36 W117 01 28). Stereo. Box 85888 92186. Secondary address: 7677 Engineer Rd. 92186. Phone: (858) 292-7600. Fax: (858) 279-7676. Licensee: Midwest Television Inc. (group owner; acq 4-1-64). Network: CBS. Rep: McGavren Guild. Covington & Burling. Format: News/talk. News staff: 10. Target aud: 25-54. ♦August C. Meyer Jr., CEO; Ed Trimble, pres; Tracy D. Johnson, gen mgr & opns dir; Joe Hood, gen sls mgr; Dave Sniff, progmg dir; Fred D'Ambrosi, news dir; Dayna Monroe, pub affrs dir; Mike Sommerville, chief of engrg.

KFMB-FM— Sept 21, 1959: 100.7 mhz; 30 kw horiz, 26.5 kw vert. 620 ft. TL: N32 50 17 W117 14 56. (CP: 38.4 kw, ant 536 ft.). Stereo. Fax: (858) 279-3380. Format: Hot adult contemp. ♦Gina Landau, gen sls mgr; Kim Leeds, prom mgr; Scott Sands, progmg dir; Jen Sewell, mus dir. Co-owned TV: KFMB-TV affil.

KGB-FM—Listing follows KLSD(AM).

KHTS-FM—(El Cajon). 1961: 93.3 mhz; 1.8 kw. Ant 1,885 ft. TL: N32 41 48 W116 56 10. Stereo. 9660 Granite Ridge Dr. 92123. Phone: (858) 292-2000. Fax: (858) 522-5707. Web Site: www.channel933.com. Licensee: Citicasters Licenses L.P. Group owner: Clear Channel Communications Inc. (acq 5-4-99; grpsl). Hogan & Hartson. Format: CHR. Target aud: 18-34. ♦Bob Bolinger, gen mgr & sls dir; Jim Richards, opns VP; Bill Lennert, mktg dir; Geoff Alan, prom mgr; Jack Evans, progmg VP; Diana Laird, progmg mgr.

KIFM(FM)— Feb 4, 1960: 98.1 mhz; 28 kw. 640 ft. TL: N32 50 17 W117 14 56. Stereo. 1615 Murray Canyon Rd., Suite 710 92108-4321. Phone: (619) 297-3698. Fax: (619) 543-1353. Web Site: www.kifm.com. Licensee: Jefferson-Pilot Communications Co. of California. Group owner: Jefferson-Pilot Communications Co. (acq 8-1-96; $28.75 million). Rep: CBS Radio. Format: Smooth Jazz. News: 2 hrs wkly. Target aud: 25-54; upscale adults. ♦Darrel Goodin, gen mgr & stn mgr.

KIOZ(FM)— 1954: 105.3 mhz; 29 kw. 620 ft. TL: N32 50 17 W117 14 56. Stereo. 9660 Granite Ridge Dr. 92123. Phone: (858) 292-2000. Fax: (858) 715-3180. Web Site: www.rock1053.com. Licensee: Citicasters Licenses L.P. Group owner: Clear Channel Communications Inc. (acq 5-4-99; grpsl). Hagan and Hartson. Format: Rock. News staff: one; News: one hr wkly. Target aud: 18-49; upscale, well educated, young adult rock fans. ♦Bob Bolinger, gen mgr.

KLNV(FM)— June 26, 1960: 106.5 mhz; 50 kw. 440 ft. TL: N32 43 17 W117 04 11. Stereo. 600 W. Broadway, Suite 2150 92101. Phone: (619) 235-0600. Fax: (619) 744-4300. Web Site: www.lanueva1065.com. Licensee: HBC San Diego License Corp. Group owner: Univision Radio (acq 9-22-2003; grpsl). Format: Regional Mexican. Target aud: 18-49; young adult, contemp mus fans, upscale, well-educated. ♦Peter Moore, gen mgr.

KLQV(FM)— May 20, 1963: 102.9 mhz; 32 kw. 616 ft. TL: N32 41 48 W116 56 10. Stereo. 600 W. Broadway, Suite 2150 92101. Phone: (619) 235-0600. Fax: (619) 744-4300. Web Site: www.univison.com. Licensee: HBC San Diego License Corp. Group owner: Univision Radio (acq 9-22-2003; grpsl). Format: Sp. Target aud: 25-44. ♦Peter Moore, gen mgr.

KLSD(AM)— July 14, 1922: 1360 khz; 5 kw-D, 1 kw-N. TL: N32 43 49 W117 05 01. 9660 Granite Ridge Dr. 92123. Phone: (858) 292-2000. Fax: (858) 715-3372. Web Site: www.am1360klsd.com. Licensee: Citicasters Licenses L.P. Group owner: Clear Channel Communications Inc. (acq 1999; grpsl). Rep: CBS Radio. Format: Progressive talk. Target aud: 45-64; mature listeners with discretionary income. ♦Kelly Kibler, gen mgr; Cliff Albert, stn mgr; Bobby Salvato, sls dir; Rob Worden, gen sls mgr; Dan Charleston, natl sls mgr; Bill Lennert, mktg dir; Sherry Toennies, prom dir; Dave Mason, progmg dir; Jane Morton, news dir; Bill Thompson, chief of engrg.

KGB-FM—Co-owned with KLSD(AM). 1956: 101.5 mhz; 50 kw. 500 ft. TL: N32 43 49 W117 05 01. Stereo. Web Site: www.101kgb.com. Hogan & Hartson. Format: Classic rock. Target aud: 25-54.

KMYI(FM)— 1949: 94.1 mhz; 100 kw. 640 ft. TL: N33 50 21 W117 14 57. 9660 Granite Ridge Dr. 92123. Phone: (858) 292-2000. Fax: (858) 715-3336. Web Site: www.my941.com. Licensee: Citicasters Licenses L.P. Group owner: Clear Channel Communications Inc. (acq 5-4-99; grpsl). Hogan and Hartson. Format: Hot adult contemp. Target aud: 35-54; general, women. ♦Kelly Kilber, gen mgr; Jim Richards, opns VP; Tim McCarthy, gen sls mgr; Duncan Peyton, progmg dir.

KOGO(AM)— 1926: 600 khz; 5 kw-U, DA-1. TL: N32 43 17 W117 04 11. 9660 Granite Ridge Dr. 92123-2657. Phone: (858) 292-2000. Fax: (858) 715-3379. E-mail: kogo@clearchannel.com. Web Site: www.kogo.com. Licensee: Citicasters Licenses L.P. Group owner: Clear Channel Communications Inc. (acq 1999; grpsl). Network: ABC. Kaye, Scholer, Fierman, Hays & Handler. Format: News/talk. News staff: 10; News: 22 hrs wkly. Target aud: 25-54; issue oriented talk radio listeners. ♦Bob Bolinger, gen mgr.

*KPBS-FM— Sept 12, 1960: 89.5 mhz; 1.77 kw. Ant 1,902 ft. TL: N32 41 47 W116 56 07. (CP: 26 kw, ant 676 ft. TL: N32 50 24 W117 15 06). Stereo. 5200 Campanile Dr. 92182-5400. Phone: (619) 594-8100. Phone: (619) 594-1515. Fax: (619) 594-3812. E-mail: letters@kpbs.org. Web Site: www.kpbs.org. Licensee: San Diego State University. Network: Network: PRI, NPR. Dow, Lohnes & Albertson. Format: News/talk, class. News staff: 7; News: 11 hrs wkly. Target aud: 35-49; actualizers & fulfilled educ professionals. ♦Tom Karlo, CFO; Doug Myrland, gen mgr; John Decker, opns dir.

KPLN(FM)— 1965: 103.7 mhz; 36 kw. 580 ft. TL: N32 50 21 W117 14 57. Stereo. 8033 Linda Vista Rd. 92111-5108. Phone: (858) 560-1037. Fax: (858) 571-0326. Web Site: www.planetfm.com. Licensee: Infinity Radio Inc. Group owner: Infinity Broadcasting Corp. (acq 8-7-00; grpsl). Rep: Christal. Format: Classic rock hits. Target aud: 25-54; adults, men. ♦Bob Bolinger, VP & gen mgr; Charlie Quinn, opns mgr.

KPRI(FM)—See Encinitas

KSDO(AM)— October 1947: 1130 khz; 10 kw-U, DA-2. TL: N32 51 04 W117 57 51. 136 S. Oak Knoll Ave., Suite 302, Pasadena 91101. Phone: (626) 356-4230. Fax: (626) 795-9185. Web Site: www.ksdo.com. Licensee: Hi-Favor Broadcasting LLC (group owner; acq 4-1-03; $10 million). . Network: ABC. Format: Sp-relg. News staff: 10. Target aud: 25-54. ♦Mary Guthrie, gen mgr.

*KSDS(FM)— December 1951: 88.3 mhz; 3 kw. Ant 246 ft. TL: N32 48 19 W117 10 09. Stereo. 1313 Park Blvd. 92101. Phone: (619) 388-3037. Fax: (619) 388-3928. E-mail: markd@jazz88online.org. Web Site: www.ksds-fm.org. Licensee: San Diego Community College District. Network: NPR. James S. Bubar. Format: Jazz, blues. News staff: one; News: 7 hrs wkly. Target aud: 25-65 plus; affluent, professional adults. ♦Mark DeBoskey, stn mgr & sls mgr; Claudia Russell, prom dir; Joe Kocherhans, progmg dir; Bob Broms, mus dir & news dir; Larry Quick, chief of engrg.

KSON(AM)— 1946: 1240 khz; 1 kw-U. TL: N32 41 40 W117 07 17. Stereo. 1615 Murray Canyon Rd., Ste 710 92108-4321. Secondary address: Box 889004 92168-9004. Phone: (619) 570-1973. Phone: (619) 718-7103. Licensee: Multicultural Radio Broadcasting License LLC. Group owner: Jefferson-Pilot Communications Co. (acq 6-13-2005; $4.85 million). Format: Chinese. ♦David Sweeney, gen mgr.

KSON-FM— Jan 15, 1964: 97.3 mhz; 50 kw. Ant 440 ft. TL: N32 43 13 W117 04 14. Stereo. 1615 Murray Canyon Rd., Suite 710 92108. Phone: (619) 291-9797. Fax: (619) 543-1353. Web Site: www.kson.com. Licensee: Jefferson-Pilot Communications Co. of California. Group owner: Jefferson-Pilot Communications Co. (acq 2-7-85). Format: Country. ♦Darrel Goodin, gen mgr & opns dir.

KSSD(FM)—See Fallbrook

KURS(AM)— Nov 1, 1992: 1040 khz; 9.5 kw-D, 4.5 kw-N, DA-2. TL: N32 54 21 W116 55 40. 296 H St., Suite 300, Chula Vista 91910. Phone: (619) 426-5645. Fax: (619) 409-4182. E-mail: jc@psnradio.com. Web Site: www.psnradio.com. Licensee: Quetzal Bilingual Communications Inc. Format: Adult standards. ♦Jaime Bonilla, pres; Jacqueline Saenz, gen mgr.

KYXY(FM)— 1960: 96.5 mhz; 41 kw. Ant 540 ft. TL: N33 52 00 W116 25 29. Stereo. 8033 Linda Vista Rd. 92111-5108. Phone: (858) 571-7600. Fax: (858) 571-0326. Web Site: www.kyxy.com. Licensee: Infinity Radio Operations Inc. Group owner: Infinity Broadcasting Corp. (acq 8-7-00; grpsl). Rep: Christal. Format: Soft rock. Target aud: 25-54; adults, women. ♦Bob Bolinger, VP & gen mgr; Charlie Quinn, opns mgr.

XETRA(AM)—(Tijuana).MEX 1934: 690 khz; 77 kw-D, 50 kw-N. 3400 W. Olive Ave., Suite 550, Burbank 91505. Phone: (818) 559-2252. Licensee: Clear Channel Communications Inc. (group owner; (acq 1999; grpsl). Network: ABC. Format: Adult standards. Target aud: 25-54; men. ♦Kevin McCarthy, exec VP & gen mgr; Dan Weiner, sls dir.

XETRA-FM— 1978: 91.1 mhz; 100 kw. 1,000 ft. Stereo. Web Site: www.91x.com. Haley, Bader & Potts. Format: Alternative. News staff: one. Target aud: 18-49; very active, college educated, above market average income, single. ♦Mike Glickenhaus, exec VP; Bill Lipis, stn mgr & mktg dir; Tim Dukes, opns VP.

XHRM-FM—(Tijuana).MEX January 1981: 92.5 mhz; 100 kw. 548 ft. Stereo. 9660 Granite Ridge Dr. 92123. Phone: (858) 292-2000. Fax: 858) 522-5717. Web Site: www.magic925.com. Licensee: The Rivas Kaloyan Family. Format: Adult contemp, rhythmic oldies, today's rhythm and blues. Target aud: 18-49. ♦Kerry Kbvlee, gen mgr & stn mgr; Mike Glickenhouse, gen mgr.

San Fernando

KBUA(FM)— Nov 14, 1958: 94.3 mhz; 3 kw. 95 ft. TL: N34 17 03 W118 28 17. Stereo. 1845 Empire Ave., Burbank 91504. Phone: (818) 729-5300. Fax: (818) 729-5683. Web Site: www.aquisuena.com. Licensee: LBI Radio License Corp. Group owner: Liberman Broadcasting Inc. (acq 1997; $10.8 million). Format: Mexican rgnl. ♦Lenard Liberman, pres & VP; Pepe Garza, stn mgr & progmg dir; Philip Estevez, gen sls mgr; Chris Buchanan, chief of engrg.

San Francisco

***KALW(FM)**— Mar 20, 1941: 91.7 mhz; 1.9 kw. 920 ft. TL: N37 45 17 W122 26 44. Stereo. 500 Mansell 94134. Phone: (415) 841-4121. Fax: (415) 841-4125. E-mail: kalwradio@yahoo.com. Web Site: www.kalw.org. Licensee: San Francisco Unified School District. Network: Network: PRI, NPR. Format: NPR, BBC, Local. News: 68 hrs wkly. Target aud: General; news & info-oriented listeners. Spec prog: Diversified. ♦Nicole Sawaya, gen mgr; William Helgeson, opns mgr; Dianne Keogh, dev dir.

KCBC(AM)—See Riverbank

KCBS(AM)— April 1909: 740 khz; 50 kw, DA-2. TL: N38 08 23 W122 31 45. 865 Battery St., 3rd Fl. 94111. Phone: (415) 765-4000. Fax: (415) 765-4080. Web Site: www.kcbs.com. Licensee: Infinity Broadcasting East Inc. Group owner: Infinity Broadcasting Corp. (acq 1996). Network: CBS. Format: News. Target aud: 25-54. ♦Steve DiNardo, gen mgr; Patrick Corr, stn mgr; Karl Isotalo, natl sls mgr; Louis Kaplan, progmg dir.

KLLC(FM)—Co-owned with KCBS(AM). Feb 1, 1948: 97.3 mhz; 82 kw. 1,014 ft. TL: N37 50 57 W122 29 56. Stereo. Phone: (415) 765-4097. Fax: (415) 765-4084. E-mail: studio@radioalice.com. Web Site: www.radioalice.com. Rep: CBS Radio. Format: Modern adult contemp. Target aud: 18-54.

KCNL(FM)—See Sunnyvale

KDFC-FM— Sept 1, 1947: 102.1 mhz; 33 kw. 1,050 ft. TL: N37 50 57 W122 29 56. 201 Third St., Suite 1200, Suite 2300 94103. Phone: (415) 764-1021. Fax: (415) 777-2291. Web Site: www.kdfc.com. Licensee: Bonneville Holding Co. Group owner: Bonneville International Corp. (acq 7-2-97; $54.5 million). Rep: CBS Radio. Format: Class. Target aud: 25-54; educated, upscale. ♦Chuck Tweedle, gen mgr; Bill Lueth, opns mgr & progmg dir; John Leathers, gen sls mgr.

***KEAR(FM)**— 1958: 106.9 mhz; 80 kw. 1,120 ft. TL: N37 50 58 W122 29 56. Stereo. 290 Hegenberger Rd., Oakland 94621-1436. Phone: (510) 568-6200. Fax: (510) 568-6190. Web Site: www.familyradio.com. Licensee: Infinity Radio Inc. (group owner; (acq 7-28-2005; $95 million). Network: Family Radio. Format: Relg. Target aud: General. ♦Harold Camping, gen mgr.

KEST(AM)— 1926: 1450 khz; 1 kw-U. TL: N37 46 41 W122 23 16. (CP: TL: N37 45 37 W122 22 56). 145 Natoma St., Suite 400 94105. Phone: (415) 978-5378. Fax: (415) 978-5380. Web Site: www.kestradio.com. Licensee: Multicultural Radio Broadcasting Licensee LLC. Group owner: Multicultural Radio Broadcasting Inc. (acq 3-31-98; grpsl). Format: Personal growth talk, foreign language. News staff: one; News: 6 hrs wkly. Target aud: 25 plus. Spec prog: Chinese, Japanese, Indian, gospel, new age. ♦Arthur S. Liu, pres; Julie Re, gen mgr & opns mgr.

KFAX(AM)— 1925: 1100 khz; 50 kw-U, DA-1. TL: N37 37 56 W122 07 49. Box 8125, Fremont 94537. Phone: (510) 713-1100. Fax: (510) 505-1448. Web Site: www.kfax.com. Licensee: Golden Gate Broadcasting Co. Inc. Group owner: Salem Communications Corp. (acq 9-1-84). Network: Salem Radio Network. Rep: Salem. Format: Relg, talk. News: 4 hrs wkly. Target aud: 25-54; females, families, college educated. Spec prog: Contemp Christian music 5 hrs weekly, children one hr wkly. ♦Ken Miller, gen mgr; Bobby Cole, opns dir & opns mgr; Darnell Howes, gen sls mgr; Amy Marsh, mktg dir, prom dir & progmg dir; Craig Roberts, news dir & chief of engrg.

KFOG(FM)—Listing follows KNBR(AM).

KFRC(AM)— Sept 24, 1924: 610 khz; 5 kw-U. TL: N37 50 58 W122 17 44. Stereo. 500 Washington St., 2nd Fl. 94111. Phone: (415) 391-9970. Fax: (415) 951-2329. Web Site: www.kfrc.com. Licensee: Family Stations Inc. Group owner: CBS Radio (acq 4-21-2005; $35 million). Format: Oldies. Target aud: 25-54. ♦Earnest L. James, VP & gen mgr; Brian Thomas, opns mgr, gen sls mgr & progmg mgr; Melanie Sherman, prom dir & prom mgr; Phil Lerza, chief of engrg.

KFRC-FM— 1949: 99.7 mhz; 40 kw. Ant 1,299 ft. TL: N37 41 15 W122 26 04. Stereo. 500 Washington St., 2nd Fl. 94111. Phone: (415) 391-9970. Fax: (415) 951-2329. Web Site: www.kfrc.com. Licensee: Infinity KFRC-FM Inc. (acq 1-96; grpsl). Format: Oldies. ♦Earnest L. James, VP & gen mgr; Brian Thomas, opns dir & progmg dir; Scott Schuman, sls dir; Melanie Sherman, mktg dir; Phil Lerza, chief of engrg.

KGO(AM)— Jan 8, 1924: 810 khz; 50 kw-U, DA-1. TL: N37 31 39 W122 06 05. 900 Front St. 94111-1450. Phone: (415) 398-5600. Fax: (415) 391-2795. Web Site: www.kgo.com. Licensee: KGO-AM Radio Inc. Group owner: ABC Inc. (acq 1986). Network: ABC Information & Entertainment. Rep: ABC Radio Sales, Interep. Wilmer, Cutler & Pickering. Format: News/talk. Target aud: 25-54; general. ♦Michael Luckoff, pres & gen mgr; Jack Swanson, opns dir.

KIOI(FM)— Oct 27, 1957: 101.3 mhz; 125 kw. 1,160 ft. TL: N37 41 24 W122 26 13. (CP: TL: N37 41 15 W122 26 01). Stereo. 340 Townsend St., Suite 5-101 94107. Phone: (415) 538-1013. Fax: (415) 975-5573. Licensee: AMFM Broadcasting Licenses LLC. Group owner: Clear Channel Communications Inc. (acq 8-30-2000; grpsl). Rep: Christal. Latham & Watkins. Format: Adult contemp. News staff: one; News: one hr wkly. Target aud: 25-54. ♦Scott Bastable, gen mgr & opns mgr; Anna Eppinger, gen sls mgr & rgnl sls mgr; Casey Keating, progmg dir.

KIQI(AM)— 1957: 1010 khz; 10 kw-D, 500 w-N, DA-2. TL: N37 49 33 W122 18 39. (CP: COL: Sunnyvale, 15 kw-D, 1.5 kw-N). 145 Natoma St., 4th Fl. 94105. Phone: (415) 978-5378. Fax: (415) 978-5380. Licensee: Multicultural Radio Broadcasting Licensee LLC. Group owner: Multicultural Radio Broadcasting Inc. (acq 2-4-2004; grpsl). Format: Sp, talk/news. News staff: 3. Target aud: 24-54. ♦Arthur Liu, pres & prom mgr; David Lui, opns dir & mus dir; Judy Re, gen mgr & progmg dir.

KISQ(FM)— July 17, 1958: 98.1 mhz; 75 kw. Ant 1,015 ft. TL: N37 51 04 W122 29 50. Stereo. 340 Townsend St. 94107. Phone: (415) 975-5555. Fax: (877) 547-7329. Web Site: www.981kissfm.com. Licensee: AMFM Broadcasting Licenses LLC. Group owner: AMFM Inc. (acq 8-30-2000; grpsl). Rep: McGavren Guild. Format: Oldies. Target aud: 25-54; women. Spec prog: Gospel 3 hrs wkly. ♦Joe Cariffe, gen mgr; Wanda Cornelius, prom dir & prom mgr; Michael Erickson, progmg dir; David Williams, chief of engrg.

KITS(FM)— June 1, 1964: 105.3 mhz; 15 kw. 1,200 ft. TL: N37 41 20 W122 26 07. Stereo. 875 Battery St. 94111-1513. Phone: (415) 512-1053. Fax: (415) 777-0608. Web Site: www.live105.com. Licensee: Infinity Broadcasting East Inc. Group owner: Infinity Broadcasting Corp. (acq 5-7-97). Format: New rock alternative. ♦Steve DiNardo, gen mgr.

KKSF(FM)— Nov 3, 1947: 103.7 mhz; 7.2 kw. 1,470 ft. TL: N37 45 19 W122 27 05. Stereo. 4th Fl., 340 Townsend St. 94107. Phone: (415) 975-5555. Fax: (415) 975-5573. Web Site: www.kksf.com. Licensee: AMFM Broadcasting Licenses LLC. Group owner: Clear Channel Communications Inc. (acq 8-30-2000; grpsl). Format: Adult contemp, jazz/fusion, new age. News staff: one; News: 5 hrs wkly. Target aud: 25-49. ♦Ed Krampf, gen mgr; Ken Jones, opns mgr.

KLOK(AM)—See San Jose

KMEL(FM)— Nov 30, 1960: 106.1 mhz; 69 kw. 1,290 ft. TL: N37 41 24 W122 26 13. Stereo. 340 Townsend St. 94107. Phone: (415) 538-1061. Fax: (415) 975-5573. Licensee: AMFM Broadcasting Licenses LLC. Group owner: Clear Channel Communications Inc. (acq 8-30-2000; grpsl). Rep: Christal. Format: CHR. ♦Scott Bastable, gen mgr; Anna Eppinger, gen sls mgr; Casey Keating, progmg dir.

KMKY(AM)—See Oakland

KNBR(AM)— 1922: 680 khz; 50 kw-U. TL: N37 31 49 W122 16 29. 55 Hawthorne St., Suite 1100 94105. Phone: (415) 995-6800. Fax: (415) 995-6867. E-mail: sports@knbr.com. Web Site: www.knbr.com. Licensee: KNBR Lico Inc. Group owner: Susquehanna Radio Corp. (acq 5-24-89; $17.5 million; 6-12-89). Network: Network: ABC, Westwood One. Format: Sports talk, personality. Target aud: 18 plus; predominently men. Spec prog: Real estate, fishing, golf, San Francisco Giants, Golden State Warriors. ♦Tony Salvadore, VP & gen mgr; Bob Agnew, opns mgr.

KFOG(FM)—Co-owned with KNBR(AM). Mar 1, 1963: 104.5 mhz; 7.9 kw. 1,454 ft. TL: N37 45 20 W122 27 05. E-mail: kfog@kfog.com. Web Site: www.kfog.com. Licensee: KFFG Lico Inc. Format: Rock. News staff: one; News: 4 hrs wkly.

KNEW(AM)—See Oakland

KNGY(FM)—(Alameda). Aug 1, 1959: 92.7 mhz; 3.6 kw. Ant 420 ft. TL: N37 47 54 W122 24 59. Stereo. 1801 Harrison St., Oakland 94612. Phone: (510) 762-0927. Fax: (510) 465-4990. E-mail: sdillard@marathonmedia.com. Web Site: www.power927fm.com. Licensee: Flying Bear Licensing LLC (acq 12-23-2004; $33.64 million). Format: Urban contemp. ♦Skip Dillard, gen mgr & progmg dir; Trevor Simpson, prom dir & prom dir; Julia Westland, adv mgr; Eric "E-Rock" Nagrampa, mus dir; Paul Strater, chief of engrg.

KOHL(FM)—See Fremont

KOIT(AM)— 1926: 1260 khz; 5 kw-D, 1 kw-N. TL: N37 42 59 W122 23 38. 455 Market St., Suite 2300 94105. Phone: (415) 777-0965. Fax: (415) 896-0965. Licensee: Bonneville Holding Co. Group owner: Bonneville International Corp. Network: UPI. Format: Adult contemp. Target aud: 25-54; upscale adults who earn an average of $30,000. ♦Charles R. Tweedle, pres; Mavis Sin, opns VP; Sharon Warren, gen sls mgr; Maribeth Doran, natl sls mgr; Bill Conway, progmg dir; Julie Deppish, asst music dir; Sherry Brown, news dir; Debi Mechanic, engrg dir.

KOIT-FM— 1959: 96.5 mhz; 33 kw. 1,410 ft. TL: N37 45 20 W122 27 05. ♦Bill Conway, stn mgr.

***KPOO(FM)**— April 1971: 89.5 mhz; 270 w. 540 ft. TL: N37 47 33 W122 24 52. Stereo. Box 423030 94142. Secondary address: 1329 Divisadero St. 94142. Phone: (415) 346-5373. Fax: (415) 346-5173. E-mail: 895fm@kpoofmsf.com. Web Site: www.kpoofmsf.com. Licensee: Poor Peoples' Radio Inc. Format: Div. ♦Terry Collins, pres; Jerome Parsons, gen mgr & progmg dir; Harrison Chastang, news dir; Marilyn Fowler, pub affrs dir; Dave Billicci, chief of engrg.

***KQED-FM**— June 1969: 88.5 mhz; 110 w. Ant 1,270 ft. TL: N37 41 23 W177 26 12. Stereo. 2601 Mariposa St. 94110. Phone: (415)

553-2316. Fax: (415) 553-2241. Web Site: www.kqed.org. Licensee: KQED Inc. Network: Network: NPR, PRI. Format: News/talk. News staff: 9; News: 160 hrs wkly. Target aud: General. ◆Jack Clarke, chmn; Jo Anne Wallace, gen mgr; Monty Carlos, opns mgr. Co-owned TV: KQED(TV) affil.

KQKE(AM)—See Oakland

KRZZ(FM)— February 1959: 93.3 mhz; 50 kw horiz, 47 kw vert. Ant 492 ft. TL: N37 43 27 W122 07 07. Stereo. 455 Market St., Suite 2300 94105. Phone: (415) 391-9330. Fax: (415) 543-3753. Licensee: KRZZ Licensing LLC. Group owner: Infinity Broadcasting Corp. (acq 12-7-2004). Format: rgnl Mexican. Target aud: 25-54. ◆Peter C. Remington, VP & gen mgr; Lisa Kruglov, gen sls mgr; Jesse Portillo, progmg dir.

KSFO(AM)— Aug 1, 1925: 560 khz; 5 kw-U, DA-N. TL: N37 44 44 W122 22 40. 900 Front St. 94111. Phone: (415) 398-5600. Fax: (415) 658-5401. Web Site: www.ksfo560.com. Licensee: KGO-AM Radio Inc. (acq 10-91; $13 million with co-located FM; 11-4-91). Format: Talk/News. Target aud: 25-54. ◆Michael Luckoff, pres & gen mgr; Jack Swanson, opns mgr.

KSOL(FM)— Dec 10, 1959: 98.9 mhz; 6 kw. 1,143 ft. TL: N37 45 20 W122 27 05. Stereo. 750 Battery St. # 200 94111. Phone: (415) 989-5765. Fax: (415) 733-5766. Web Site: www.univision.com. Licensee: TMS License California Inc. Group owner: Univision Radio (acq 9-22-2003); grpsl). Format: Sp, Mexican rgnl. News staff: one. Target aud: 18-54. ◆Tony Perlongo, gen mgr.

*KUSF(FM)— April 1964: 90.3 mhz; 3 kw. 300 ft. TL: N37 46 34 W122 26 54. Stereo. 2130 Fulton St. 94117-1080. Phone: (415) 386-5873. Fax: (415) 386-6469. E-mail: kusf@usfca.edu. Web Site: www.kusf.org. Licensee: University of San Francisco. (acq 1973). Format: Alternative mus, div, educ. Target aud: College educated, affluent, multicultural. Spec prog: Chinese 9 hrs, class 6 hrs, relg 5 hrs, jazz 3 hrs, Fr 2 hrs, Turkish 2 hrs, It one hr, Pol one hr, Armenian one hr, Finnish one hr, Irish one hr wkly. ◆Steve Runyon, gen mgr.

KYCY(AM)— 1947: 1550 khz; 10 kw-U, DA-2. TL: N37 31 49 W122 16 29. Stereo. 865 Battery St., 2nd Fl., 4th floor 94111. Phone: (415) 391-9970. Fax: (415) 397-7655. Licensee: Infinity Broadcasting East Inc. Group owner: Infinity Broadcasting Corp. (acq 12-14-00); grpsl). Format: Talk. Target aud: 12 plus; affluent, home-owning, highly educated, business professionals. Spec prog: Jazz. ◆Joe Armao, VP; Doug Stern, gen mgr; Matthew Pierce, stn mgr.

KYLD(FM)— Mar 12, 1958: 94.9 mhz; 35 kw. 1,290 ft. TL: N37 41 22 W122 26 10. Stereo. 340 Townsend St. 94107. Phone: (415) 975-5555. Fax: (415) 975-5573. Web Site: www.wild949.com. Licensee: AMFM Broadcasting Licenses LLC. Group owner: Clear Channel Communications Inc. (acq 8-30-2000); grpsl). Format: Urban contemp, CHR. Target aud: 25-54. ◆Ed Krampt, gen mgr.

KZBR(FM)— 1959: 95.7 mhz; 6.9 kw. 1,500 ft. TL: N37 41 23 W122 26 12. Stereo. 201 3rd St. 94103. Phone: (415) 957-0957. Fax: (415) 356-8394. Web Site: www.957maxfm.com. Licensee: Bonneville Holding Co. Group owner: Bonneville International Corp. (acq 5-7-97). Format: 70s, 80s, & 90s music. News staff: one. Target aud: 18-49. ◆John Parish, gen sls mgr.

San Gabriel

KMRB(AM)— 1942: 1430 khz; 5 kw-U, DA-2. TL: N34 07 10 W118 04 57. 2nd Fl., 747 E. Green St., Pasadena 91101. Phone: (626) 844-8882. Fax: (626) 792-8890. Licensee: Polyethnic Broadcasting Licensee LLC (acq 1994). Format: Asian. Target aud: General. Spec prog: Thai 2 hrs, Ethiopian 2 hrs wkly. ◆Arthur Liu, pres; David Sweeney, exec VP & gen mgr; Kevin Chu, stn mgr; Katherine Lieu, gen sls mgr; Hon Vu, chief of engrg.

San Jacinto

KWIE(FM)— Sept 23, 1990: 96.1 mhz; 1.4 kw. Ant 686 ft. TL: N34 02 13 W116 58 07. Stereo. 1845 Business Ctr. Dr., Suite 106, San Bernardino 92408. Phone: (909) 663-1961. Fax: (909) 663-1996. E-mail: kwrp-fm@hotmail.com. Web Site: www.wild96.com. Licensee: KWIE Licensing LLC (acq 10-9-98). Network: USA. Format: Hip hop, rhythm and blues. News: 15 hrs wkly. Target aud: 35 plus. ◆Don McCoy, CEO; John Squyres, pres; Kimberly Fletcher, gen mgr; Joe Perez, opns mgr; Carlos Santos, gen sls mgr & prom mgr; Mikey Fuentes, progmg dir.

San Joaquin

KUUS(FM)— 1999: 105.5 mhz; 25 kw. Ant 328 ft. TL: N36 36 28 W119 59 49. 1066 E. Shaw Ave., Fresno 93710. Phone: (559) 230-0104. Fax: (559) 230-0177. Licensee: Wilks License Co.-Fresno LLC. Group owner: The Mondosphere Broadcasting Group. (acq 6-1-2005); grpsl). Format: Country. ◆Jody Rosen, gen mgr.

San Jose

KAZA(AM)—See Gilroy

KBRG(FM)— Mar 4, 1963: 100.3 mhz; 14.5 kw. 2,580 ft. TL: N37 06 40 W121 50 34. Stereo. 655 Campbell Technology Pkwy., Suite 225, Campbell 95008. Phone: (408) 540-5683. Fax: (408) 540-5678. Licensee: Entravision Holdings LLC. Group owner: Entravision Communications Corp. (acq 3-14-00); grpsl). Format: Sp. ◆Mike Murphy, gen mgr.

KEZR(FM)— July 3, 1967: 106.5 mhz; 50 kw. 430 ft. TL: N37 21 43 W121 45 23. Stereo. 190 Park Ctr. Plaza, Suite 200 95113-2223. Phone: (408) 287-5775. Fax: (408) 293-3341. Web Site: www.todaysbestmix.com. Licensee: Elliot B. Evers as trustee under the San Jose Trust Group owner: Infinity Broadcasting Corp. (acq 7-29-2005); with KBAY(FM) Gilroy). Rep: Christal. Format: Adult contemp. Target aud: 18-39. ◆Joe Armao, VP; John Leathers, gen mgr; Jim Murphy, opns mgr.

KFAX(AM)—See San Francisco

KFFG(FM)—See Los Altos

KKSF(FM)—See San Francisco

KLIV(AM)— 1946: 1590 khz; 5 kw-U, DA-N. TL: N37 19 45 W121 51 23. Box 995 95108. Secondary address: 750 Story Rd. 95122. Phone: (408) 293-8030. Fax: (408) 293-6124. Web Site: www.kliv.com. Licensee: Empire Broadcasting Corp. (group owner; acq 7-1-67). Network: CNN Radio. Rep: Christal. Format: News. News staff: 8. Target aud: General. Spec prog: San Jose soccer earthquakes. ◆Robert S. Kieve, pres & gen mgr; George Sampion, progmg dir & news dir; Tina Ferguson, gen sls mgr & chief of engrg.

KLOK(AM)— Oct 19, 1946: 1170 khz; 50 kw-D, 5 kw-N, DA-2. TL: N37 18 41 W121 48 58. 655 Campbell Technology Pkwy., Suite 225, Campbell 95008. Phone: (408) 540-5683. Fax: (408) 540-5678. Licensee: Entravision Holdings LLC. Group owner: Entravision Communications Corp. (acq 3-14-00); grpsl). Format: Cumbia. Target aud: 18-49. ◆Michael Murphy, gen mgr.

*KMTG(FM)— May 17, 1977: 89.3 mhz; 300 w. Ant -312 ft. TL: N37 12 06 W121 51 42. 6677 Camden Ave. 95120. Licensee: San Jose Unified School District.

KSJO(FM)— December 1946: 92.3 mhz; 50 kw. 464 ft. TL: N37 12 33 W121 46 30. Stereo. 1420 Koll Cir., Suite A 95112. Phone: (408) 453-5400. Fax: (408) 452-1330. Web Site: www.ksjo.com. Licensee: Citicasters Licenses L.P. Group owner: Clear Channel Communications Inc. (acq 5-4-99); grpsl). Rep: McGavren Guild. Format: Sp. Target aud: 18-49; active adults. ◆Kim Bryant, gen mgr.

*KSJS(FM)— Feb 22, 1963: 90.5 mhz; 235 w. 407 ft. TL: N37 12 33 W121 46 30. Stereo. San Jose State Univ., Theater Arts Dept., HGH 126 95192-0094. Phone: (408) 924-4549. Fax: (408) 924-4545. Fax: (408) 924-4558. E-mail: ksjs@ksjs.org. Web Site: www.ksjs.org. Licensee: San Jose State University. Format: Diversified. Target aud: 18-34; students & community members. ◆Nick Martinez, gen mgr.

KSJX(AM)— June 24, 1948: 1500 khz; 10 kw-D, 5 kw-N, DA-2. TL: N37 21 28 W121 52 17. 501 Wooster Ave. 95116. Phone: (408) 280-1515. Fax: (408) 280-1585. E-mail: ksjx1500@sbcglobal.net. Licensee: Multicultural Radio Broadcasting Licensee LLC. Group owner: Multicultural Radio Broadcasting Inc. (acq 2-20-98; grpsl). Format: Asian, Vietnamese. News staff: 2. Target aud: 25-54; managerial, professional, homeowners. Spec prog: Mandarin Chinese 10 hrs, Vietnamese. ◆Arthur Liu, pres; Andrea Yamazaki, gen mgr & stn mgr; Victor Nguyen, opns mgr.

KUFX(FM)— July 1, 1959: 98.5 mhz; 12.5 kw. 880 ft. TL: N37 12 17 W121 56 56. Stereo. 1420 Koll Cir., Suite A 95112. Phone: (408) 452-5400. Fax: (408) 452-1330. Web Site: www.kfox.com. Licensee: Citicasters Licenses L.P. Group owner: Clear Channel Communications Inc. (acq 5-4-99; grpsl). Rep: CBS Radio. Leventhal, Senter & Lerman. Format: Classic rock. Target aud: 18-49; general. ◆Kim Bryant, gen mgr.

KVVF(FM)—See Santa Clara

KVVN(AM)—(Santa Clara). Dec 18, 1964: 1430 khz; 1 kw-D, 2.5 kw-N, DA-2. TL: N37 19 47 W121 51 58. 1125 E. Santa Clara St., Suite 1 95116. Phone: (415) 648-7980. Fax: (415) 695-9055. E-mail: sales@inlanguageradio.com. Licensee: Urban Radio III L.L.C. Group owner: Inner City Broadcasting (acq 3-24-97; $2.2 million). Koteen & Naftalin. Format: Vietnamese. News staff: one; News: 14 hrs wkly. Target aud: 23-34; Hispanic. ◆Jaime Arbona, pres & gen mgr; Tri Dang, stn mgr; Phung Dang, opns dir.

KZSF(AM)— June 21, 1947: 1370 khz; 5 kw-U, DA-2. TL: N37 21 28 W121 52 17. Stereo. 3031 Tisch Way, Suite 3, Plaza W. 95128. Phone: (408) 247-0100. Fax: (408) 247-4353. E-mail: lakaliente1370am@mexico.com. Web Site: www.1370.com. Licensee: Carlos A. Duharte (acq 7-31-01; $5 million). Network: UPI. Rep: Allied Radio Partners. Interep Format: Sp; regional Mexican. Target aud: 18-49. ◆Carlos A. Duharte, CEO, chmn, pres, sr VP, gen mgr & stn mgr.

San Luis Obispo

*KCBX(FM)— July 25, 1975: 90.1 mhz; 5.3 kw. 1,420 ft. TL: N35 21 38 W120 39 21. Stereo. 4100 Vachell Ln. 93401. Phone: (805) 549-8855. Fax: (805) 781-3025. E-mail: kcbx@kcbx.org. Web Site: www.kcbx.org. Licensee: KCBX Inc. Network: NPR. Cohn & Marks. Format: Class, jazz, news. News: 32 hrs wkly. Target aud: General. Spec prog: Folk 15 hrs wkly. ◆Frank Lanzone, pres & gen mgr; Hank Hadley, opns mgr; Paul Severtson, dev dir.

*KCPR(FM)— 1968: 91.3 mhz; 2 kw. -350 ft. TL: N35 17 58 W120 40 26. Stereo. Graphic Arts, California Polytechnic State Univ. 93407. Phone: (805) 756-5277. Phone: (805) 756-2965. Web Site: www.kcpr.org. Licensee: California Polytechnic State University. Format: Div. News: 4 hrs wkly. Target aud: General; Cal Poly students, San Luis Obispo community. Spec prog: Sp 3 hrs, metal 3 hrs, blues 3 hrs,. ◆Tyler Johnson, gen mgr.

KIQO(FM)—See Atascadero

KJDJ(AM)— Feb 8, 1988: 1030 khz; 2.5 kw-D, 700 w-N. TL: N35 17 58 W120 40 24. 604 E. Chapel St., Santa Maria 93454. Phone: (805) 928-1030. Licensee: Padre Serra Communications Inc. (acq 4-94). Format: Contemp Sp. ◆Manuel Salvador, gen mgr & progmg dir.

KKJG(FM)— Jan 1, 1984: 98.1 mhz; 3.6 kw. 1,624 ft. TL: N35 21 37 W120 39 18. Stereo. 3620 Sacramento Dr., Suite 204 93401. Phone: (805) 781-2750. Fax: (805) 781-2758. Web Site: www.jugcountry.com. Licensee: AGM San Luis Obispo L.P. Group owner: American General Media (acq 7-1-97; $1.5 million). Rep: Allied Radio Partners. Format: Country. Target aud: 25-54. ◆Kathy Signorelli, gen mgr.

KKJL(AM)— Feb 6, 1960: 1400 khz; 1 kw-U. TL: N35 15 51 W120 39 56. Box 1400 93406. Secondary address: 50 Zaca Ln., Suite 90 93401. Phone: (805) 544-1400. Fax: (805) 543-0787. E-mail: kkjl1400@aol.com. Web Site: www.kkjl1400.com. Licensee: San Luis Obispo Broadcasting Inc. (acq 9-9-86). Network: CNN Radio. Leventhal, Senter & Lerman. Format: Adult standards, sports. Target aud: 35 plus; adults males & females. Spec prog: San Francisco 49'ers, Giants, Los Angeles Lakers. ♦Guy Hackman, pres & gen mgr; Kyle Ronemus, VP & stn mgr; Mary S. Brown, opns mgr.

***KLFF-FM**— Sept 26, 1995: 89.3 mhz; 4.4 kw. 1,430 ft. TL: N35 21 37 W120 39 17. Stereo. Box 1561 93406. Secondary address: 560 Higuera St., Suite G 93401. Phone: (805) 541-4343. Fax: (805) 541-9101. E-mail: info@klife.org. Web Site: www.klife.org. Licensee: Logos Broadcasting Corp. Network: Salem Radio Network. Joseph E. Dunne III. Format: Christian hit music. Target aud: 18-34; Christians. ♦Dan M. Lemburg, pres; Dr. Daniel Woods, CFO; Jon Fugler, gen mgr; Tanya Streder, opns mgr; Noonie Fugler, progmg dir.

KLRM(FM)— Dec 10, 1995: 97.1 mhz; 2.5 kw. 1,020 ft. TL: N35 15 11 W120 45 41. 2325 Skyway Dr., Suite J., Santa Maria 93455. Secondary address: Box 5579, Santa Maria 93454. Phone: (805) 922-1041. Fax: (805) 928-3069. Web Site: www.liveradio.com. Licensee: GTM San Louis Obispo American General Media Format: Sp. ♦Rich Watson, gen mgr.

***KLVH(FM)**— Mar 25, 1999: 88.5 mhz; 3 kw. Ant 1,401 ft. TL: N35 21 38 W120 39 21. 5700 W. Oak Blvd., Rocklin 95765. Phone: (916) 251-1600. Fax: (916) 251-1650. E-mail: klove@klove.com. Web Site: www.klove.com. Licensee: Educational Media Foundation. Group owner: EMF Broadcasting (acq 5-12-99). Network: K-Love. Shaw Pittman. Format: Contemp Christian music. News staff: 3. Target aud: 25-44; Judeo Christian, female. ♦Richard Jenkins, pres; Mike Novak, VP; Lloyd Parker, gen mgr; Ed Lenane, opns dir; Keith Whipple, dev dir.

KSLY-FM— December 1959: 96.1 mhz; 5.6 kw. 1,410 ft. TL: N35 21 38 W120 39 21. Stereo. 51 Zaca Ln., Suite 110 93401. Phone: (805) 545-0101. Fax: (805) 541-5303. Web Site: www.ksly.com. Licensee: Clear Channel Radio Licenses Inc. Group owner: Clear Channel Communications Inc. (acq 10-00; grpsl). Format: Top 40. ♦Rich Hawkins, gen mgr.

KURQ(FM)—See Grover Beach

KVEC(AM)— May 1937: 920 khz; 1 kw-D, 500 w-N. TL: N35 17 58 W120 40 24. 51 Zaca Ln., Suite 100 93401. Phone: (805) 545-0101. Fax: (805) 541-5303. Web Site: www.920kvec.com. Licensee: AMFM Radio Licenses LLC. Group owner: Clear Channel Communications Inc. (acq 12-12-2000; $950,000. including five-year noncompete agreement). Network: Network: CBS, ABC Information & Entertainment. Format: News/talk, sports, business. News staff: 4; News: 45 hrs wkly. Target aud: 35 plus; affluent decision & newsmakers, sports fans, business owners & retirees. Spec prog: Dodgers baseball, NFL/NCAA football, finance, senior focus, health, real estate. ♦Rich Hawkins, gen mgr.

KXTK(AM)—(Arroyo Grande). June 29, 1962: 1280 khz; 10 kw-D, 2.5 kw-N, DA-2. TL: N35 08 44 W120 31 15. Box 14910 93406. Phone: (805) 547-1280. Fax: (805) 543-1508. E-mail: sports@espnradio1280.com. Web Site: espnradio1280.com. Licensee: Pacific Coast Media LLC (acq 10-20-2004; $700,000). Network: Network: ESPN Radio, Westwood One. Format: Sports. Target aud: 25 plus. ♦Mike Chellsen, gen mgr, gen sls mgr & progmg dir; Bill Bordeaux, engr.

KYNS(AM)— Dec 13, 1949:: 1340 khz; 790 w-U. TL: N35 14 03 W120 40 33. 396 Buckley Rd., Suite 2 93401. Phone: (805) 786-2570. Fax: (805) 547-9860. Licensee: Mapleton Communications LLC (group owner; acq 3-19-03; $370,000). Format: Progressive news/talk. ♦Adam Nathanson, pres; Nancy Leichter, gen mgr.

KZOZ(FM)— 1962: 93.3 mhz; 29.5 kw. 1,470 ft. TL: N35 21 38 W120 39 21. Stereo. 3620 Sacramento Dr., Suite 204 93401. Phone: (805) 781-2750. Fax: (805) 781-2758. E-mail: sales@americangeneralmedia.com. Web Site: www.kzoz.com. Licensee: AGM California. Group owner: American General Media (acq 6-89; grpsl). Rep: Allied Radio Partners. Format: Classic rock, AOR. ♦Bill Heirendt, gen mgr, opns dir & gen sls mgr; Kathy Signorelli, gen mgr; David Atwood, progmg dir.

San Marcos-Poway

KPRZ(AM)— 1986: 1210 khz; 20 kw-D, 5 kw-N, DA-2. TL: N33 04 12 W117 11 35. 9255 Towne Centre Dr., Suite 535, San Diego 92121. Phone: (858) 535-1210. Fax: (858) 535-1212. E-mail: kprz@kprz.com. Web Site: www.kprz.com. Licensee: Radio 1210 Inc. Group owner: Salem Communications Corp. (Acq 1986). Network: Salem Radio Network. Format: Christian, talk. News: 15 hrs wkly. Target aud: 25-54; conservative, pro-family. Spec prog: Sp 22 hrs wkly. ♦Edward G. Astinger III, CEO & pres; David Evans, CFO; Judy Bowen, gen mgr; Heather Lloyd, opns mgr.

San Martin

KZSJ(AM)— November 1995: 1120 khz; 5 kw-D, 150 w-N. TL: N36 57 49 W121 29 22. 2670 S. White Rd., Suite 165, San Jose 95148. Phone: (408) 223-3130. Fax: (408) 223-3131. E-mail: qhxradio@aol.com. Web Site: www.quehuongmedia.com. Licensee: KZSJ Radio LLC. Group owner: Bustos Media Holdings (acq 2-26-99). Format: Vietnamese. Hispanic. ♦Amador Bustos, chmn; Raul Salvador, CFO; John Bustos, exec VP & opns mgr; Khoi Nguyen, gen mgr.

San Mateo

***KCSM(FM)**— October 1964: 91.1 mhz; 11.5 kw. 371 ft. TL: N37 32 12 W122 20 02. 1700 W. Hillsdale Blvd. 94402. Phone: (650) 574-9136. Phone: (650) 574-6586. Fax: (650) 524-6975. Web Site: www.kcsm.org. Licensee: San Mateo County Community College District. Network: PRI. Format: Jazz. Target aud: 40 plus; males. Spec prog: Blues 3 hrs wkly. ♦Marilyn Lawrence, gen mgr; Alisa Clancy, opns dir; Melanie Berson, progmg dir. Co-owned TV: *KCSM-TV affil.

KSAN(FM)— September 1963: 107.7 mhz; 8.9 kw. 1,162 ft. TL: N37 41 20 W122 26 07. Stereo. 55 Hawthorne, Suite1000, San Francisco 94105. Phone: (415) 981-5726. Fax: (415) 995-7061. Web Site: www.1077thebone.net. Licensee: Susquehanna Radio Corp. (group owner; acq 5-29-97; $44 million). Rep: McGavren Guild. Format: Classic rock. Target aud: 25-54. ♦Dwight Walker, VP & gen mgr; Dick Kelley, gen sls mgr; Larry Sharpe, progmg dir; Eric Steinberg, engrg dir & chief of engrg.

KTCT(AM)—Co-owned with KSAN(FM). 1948: 1050 khz; 50 kw-D, 10 kw-N, DA-2. TL: N37 39 02 W122 09 08. Stereo. Phone: (415) 864-1050. Fax: (415) 995-6867. Web Site: www.theticket1050.com. (Acq 7-21-97; $15 million). Network: Westwood One. Format: Sports. Target aud: 25-54. ♦Tony Salvadore, gen mgr; Lee Hammer, progmg mgr.

San Rafael

***KSRH(FM)**— May 1, 1980: 88.1 mhz; 10 w. 66 ft. TL: N37 58 16 W122 30 47. AR 101, 185 Mission Ave. 94901. Phone: (415) 457-5314. Licensee: San Rafael High School District. Format: Div, Black. News: 5 hrs wkly. Target aud: 12-29. Spec prog: Fr one hr wkly. ♦Chris Russo, gen mgr.

KVVZ(FM)— June 1, 1961:: 100.7 mhz; 910 w. Ant 810 ft. TL: N37 59 25 W122 29 58. Stereo. 750 Battery St., Suite 200, San Francisco 94111. Phone: (415) 733-5765. Fax: (415) 733-5766. Web Site: www.univision.com. Licensee: Univision Radio License Corp. Group owner: Salem Communications Corp. (acq 3-1-2005; exchange for KOSL(FM) Jackson). Format: Sp pop. ♦Tony Perlongo, gen mgr.

Santa Ana

KALI-FM— Feb 6, 1980: 106.3 mhz; 3 kw. 130 ft. TL: N33 45 21 W117 51 16. (CP: Ant 203 ft. TL: N33 45 21 W117 51 17). Stereo. 747 E. Green St., Suite 400, Pasadena 91101. Phone: (626) 844-8882. Fax: (626) 844-0156. Licensee: KALI-FM Licensee LLC. Format: Asian. Target aud: 18-44. ♦Arthur Liu, pres; David Sweeney, gen mgr.

KVNR(AM)—Listing follows KWIZ(FM).

KWIZ(FM)— 1947: 96.7 mhz; 3 kw. 206 ft. TL: N33 48 08 W117 47 43. Stereo. 3101 W. 5th St. 92703. Phone: (714) 554-5000. Fax: (714) 554-9362. Web Site: www.sonido967.com. Licensee: LBI Radio License Corp. Group owner: Liberman Broadcasting Inc. (acq 1997; $11.2 million). Format: Sp, Tropical. Target aud: 18 plus; Asian. ♦Winnie Coombs, stn mgr; Enrique Mayans, progmg mgr; Shannon Murdock, chief of engrg.

KVNR(AM)—Co-owned with KWIZ(FM). Nov 26, 1926: 1480 khz; 5 kw-U, DA-2. TL: N33 45 06 W117 54 36. 15781 Brookhurst St., Suite 101, Westminster 92683. Phone: (714) 918-4444. Fax: (714) 918-4445. E-mail: radio@littlesoigonradio.com. Web Site: www.littlesoiganradio.com. (Acq 1-88; $6.25 million with co-located FM; 1-4-88). Rep: Allied Radio Partners. Format: Vietnamese. Target aud: 18-49. ♦Ninh Vu, pres; Kathleen Bui, gen mgr; Joe Dinh, chief of engrg.

Santa Barbara

KBKO(AM)— April 1926: 1490 khz; 1 kw-U. TL: N34 24 57 W119 41 10. Stereo. 414 East Cota St. 93101. Phone: (805) 879-8300. Fax: (805) 879-8430. Licensee: Citicasters Licenses L.P. Group owner: Clear Channel Communications Inc. (acq 5-4-99; grpsl). Rep: Caballero. Farrand, Cooper & Bruiniers. Format: Mexican. News staff: one; News: 7 hrs wkly. Target aud: 16-65; Hispanic. ♦Richard C. Marsh, CEO; J.D. Freedman, gen mgr; Marlene Huddy, opns dir; Jose Fierroz, progmg VP & progmg dir; Ransom Bullard, chief of engrg.

KSPE-FM—Co-owned with KBKO(AM). Feb 6, 1989: 94.5 mhz; 81 kw. 2,949 ft. TL: N34 31 32 W119 57 28. Format: Sp oldies.

***KCSB-FM**— November 1964: 91.9 mhz; 620 w. 2,910 ft. TL: N34 31 31 W119 57 29. (CP: Ant 1,879 ft.). Stereo. Box 13401 93107. Phone: (805) 893-3757. Fax: (805) 893-7832. E-mail: info@kcsb.org. Web Site: www.kcsb.org. Licensee: Regents of the University of California. Format: Var. News: 9 hrs wkly. Spec prog: Sp 12 hrs, Japanese pop one hr, East Indian 2 hrs, reggae 6 hrs, American Indian 3 hrs wkly. ♦Elizabeth Robinson, gen mgr.

KDB(FM)— Feb 14, 1960: 93.7 mhz; 12.5 kw. 870 ft. TL: N34 27 58 W119 40 37. Stereo. Box 91660 93190. Phone: (805) 966-4131. Fax: (805) 966-4788. E-mail: kdb@kdb.com. Web Site: www.kdb.com. Licensee: Pacific Broadcasting Co. (acq 11-6-2003; transfer of stock). Rep: Clear Channel. Fletcher, Heald & Hildreth. Format: Class music. News: one hr wkly. Target aud: Adults; affluent, influential & educated. ♦Roby Scott, gen mgr; Richard Bickle, opns dir & progmg dir; Bob Scott, sls dir & progmg dir.

KIST(AM)— 1946: 1340 khz; 650 w-U. TL: N34 25 07 W119 41 10. Stereo. 414 E. Cotta St. 93101. Phone: (805) 879-8300. Fax: (805) 879-8430. Licensee: Citicasters Licenses L.P. Group owner: Clear Channel Communications Inc. (acq 5-4-99; grpsl). Network: ESPN Radio. Rep: Katz Radio. Format: Sports, talk. Target aud: 25-54. ♦J. D. Freeman, gen mgr; Keith Royer, opns dir; Terry King, gen sls mgr; Jeff Williams, progmg dir & news dir.

KIST-FM— 1998: 107.7 mhz; 710 w. 1,758 ft. TL: N34 30 10 W119 50 56. 414 E. Cota St. 93101. Phone: (805) 879-8300. Fax: (805) 879-8430. Web Site: www.fm1077fb.com. Licensee: Citicasters Licenses L.P. Group owner: Clear Channel Communications Inc. (acq 5-4-99; grpsl). Network: ABC. Rep: Katz Radio. Format: AOR. ♦Keith Royer, progmg dir & progmg mgr.

KMGQ(FM)—See Goleta

***KQSC(FM)**— July 1985: 88.7 mhz; 12 kw. 866 ft. TL: N34 27 55 W119 40 37. Stereo. 515 S. Figueroa St., Suite 2050 90071. Phone: (213) 225-7400. Fax: (213) 225-7410. E-mail: kusc@kusc.org. Web Site: www.kusc.org. Licensee: University of Southern California. Network: Network: PRI, NPR. Lawrence Bernstein. Format: Class. News: 3 hrs wkly. Target aud: 35 plus. ♦Brenda Barnes, pres; Eric DeWeese, gen mgr.

KRUZ(FM)— Sept 1, 1957: 97.5 mhz; 17.5 kw. 2,920 ft. TL: N34 31 31 W119 57 29. 3757 State St., Suite 206 93105. Phone: (805) 682-2895. Fax: (805) 682-5718. Web Site: www.cumulus.com. Licensee: Cumulus Licensing Corp. Group owner: Cumulus Media Inc. (acq 3-12-2001; grpsl). Rep: McGavren Guild. Format: Smooth Jazz. Target aud: 35-64; young, educated, upscale adults. ♦Julee Shea, gen mgr.

KSBL(FM)—See Carpinteria

***KSBX(FM)**— Apr 1, 2003: 89.5 mhz; 50 w. Ant 899 ft. TL: N34 27 57 W119 40 37. Stereo. KCBX Public Radio, 4100 Vachell Ln., San Luis Obispo 93401. Phone: (805) 549-8855. Phone: (805) 781-3025. E-mail: kcbx@kcbx.org. Web Site: www.kcbx.org. Licensee: KCBX Inc. Network: NPR. Margaret Merisante Format: Class, jazz. News: 30 hrs wkly. ♦Frank Lanzone, gen mgr; Hank Hadey, opns mgr; Paul Severtson, dev dir.

KTMS(AM)—Listing follows KTYD(FM).

KTYD(FM)— Aug 11, 1972: 99.9 mhz; 34 kw. 1,278 ft. TL: N34 28 15 W119 40 33. Stereo. 414 E. Cota St. 93101. Phone: (805) 879-8300. Fax: (805)879-8430. Web Site: www.ktyd.com. Licensee: Citicasters Licenses L.P. Group owner: Clear Channel Communications Inc. (acq

Stations in the U.S. — California

Developers & Brokers of Radio Properties
contact American Media Services at our suite: Philadelphia Marriott Downtown 215-625-2900
843-972-2200
americanmediaservices.com
Charleston, SC
Dallas, TX · Chicago, Il · Austin, TX
American Media Services, LLC

5-7-97; grpsl). Rep: Katz Radio. Wiley, Rein & Fielding. Format: AOR. News staff: one; News: 3 hrs wkly. Target aud: 18-49; upscale adults. Spec prog: Pub affrs one hr wkly. ♦ Keith Royer, VP & progmg dir; J.D. Freeman, gen mgr; Vince Hollian, gen sls mgr; Lin Aubuchon, mktg dir & prom dir; Ran Bullard, chief of engrg.

KTMS(AM)—Co-owned with KTYD(FM). Aug 11, 1962: 990 khz; 5 kw-D, 500 w-N, DA-2. TL: N34 28 15 W119 40 33. Stereo. Web Site: www.990am.com. Network: Network: ABC, CNN Radio. Format: Talk. News staff: 2; News: 4 hrs wkly. Target aud: 25 plus; upscale adults. ♦ Keith Royer, opns mgr; Jeff Williams, progmg dir.

KVYB(FM)— Aug 8, 1961: 103.3 mhz; 105 kw. 2,980 ft. TL: N34 31 30 W119 57 10. Stereo. 3757 State St., Suite 206 93105. Phone: (805) 682-2895. Fax: (805) 682-5718. E-mail: webmaster@kruz.com. Web Site: www.kruz.com. Licensee: Cumulus Licensing Corp. Group owner: Cumulus Media inc. (acq 4-2000). Rep: McGavren Guild. Format: Adult contemp. Target aud: 18-54; general. ♦ Jonathon Pinch, COO; Lewis W. Dickey Jr., pres; Martin Gausvik, CFO; John W. Dickey, exec VP; Richard Denning, VP; Pat Cantwell, gen mgr; Mark De Anda, opns dir; Julee Shea, sls dir; Adam Gilbert, natl sls dir; Kimberly Hasselbring, prom dir; Mandye Thomas, progmg dir; J.D. Strahler, chief of engrg.

KZER(AM)— Oct 31, 1937: 1250 khz; 2.5 kw-D, 1 kw-N, DA-2. TL: N34 25 06 W119 49 05. 1330 Cacique St. 93103. Phone: (805) 963-7824. Fax: (805) 240-5960. E-mail: jose@radio/azer.com. Web Site: www.radiolazer.com. Licensee: Lazer Broadcasting Corp. (group owner; acq 12-18-2003; $1.5 million). Hogan & Hartson. Format: Sp. News staff: 3; News: 140 hrs wkly. Target aud: 25 plus; upscale, educated listeners. ♦ Jose Plaascencia, gen mgr; Jose Plascencia, opns mgr; Salvador Prieto, progmg dir.

KZSB(AM)— March 1961: 1290 khz; 500 w-D, 122 w-N. TL: N34 25 07 W119 41 10. Stereo. 331 N. Milpas St., Suite F 93103. Phone: (805) 568-1444. Fax: (800) 365-6255. Licensee: Santa Barbara Broadcasting Inc. (acq 3-1-2005; $750,000). Network: Westwood One. Format: News/talk. Target aud: 18 plus; mature adults. ♦ Dennis M. Weibling, pres; Les Carroll, gen mgr & natl sls mgr; Betty Carroll, progmg mgr, mus dir & pub affrs dir.

Santa Clara

KLIV(AM)—See San Jose

*KSCU(FM)— July 1, 1978: 103.3 mhz; 30 w. 179 ft. TL: N37 20 53 W121 56 25. Stereo. Santa Clara Univ., 500 El Camino Real 3207 95053. Phone: (408) 554-4413. Fax: (408) 554-5738. Web Site: www.kscu.org. Licensee: President and Board of Trustees of Santa Clara University. Format: Modern alternative rock. News: one hr wkly. Target aud: 14-34; Young adult who like modern music. Spec prog: Hip-hop 15 hrs, Blues 3 hrs, loud rock 6 hrs, world one hr wkly. ♦ Dominic Guzzetti, gen mgr; Cameron Collins, prom dir & progmg dir; Ryan Schmidt, prom dir & progmg dir; Gordon Young, news dir; Victoria Duran, pub affrs dir; Bill Orr, engrg dir & chief of engrg.

KVVF(FM)— Sept 25, 1964: 105.7 mhz; 50 kw. Ant 500 ft. TL: N37 21 32 W121 45 22. Stereo. 750 Battery St., Suite 200, San Francisco 94111. Phone: (415) 733-5765. Fax: (415) 733-5766. Web Site: www.univision.com. Licensee: Univision Radio License Corp. Group owner: Univision Radio (acq 9-22-2003; grpsl). Rep: Katz Hispanic. Format: Sp pop. ♦ Tony Perlongo, gen mgr.

KVVN(AM)—Licensed to Santa Clara. See San Jose

Santa Cruz

KBOQ(FM)—See Monterey

*KFER(FM)— 1992: 89.9 mhz; 200 w. 26 ft. TL: N37 00 45 W121 58 25. Box 13 95063. Phone: (813) 464-8295. Fax: (831) 464-8427. Licensee: Santa Cruz Educational Broadcasting Foundation. Moody. Format: Var. News: 15 hrs wkly. Target aud: General. ♦ Mildred Holmes, pres; Dr. Stan Monteith, gen mgr.

KSCO(AM)— Sept 21, 1947: 1080 khz; 10 kw-D, 5 kw-N, DA-2. TL: N36 57 43 W121 58 51. 2300 Portola Dr. 95062. Phone: (831) 479-1080. Fax: (831) 475-2967. Web Site: www.ksco.com. Licensee: Zwerling Broadcasting System Ltd. (acq 1-31-91; $600,000; 12-31-90). Format: News/talk. News staff: 8; News: 35 hrs wkly. Target aud: 25 plus; well educated professionals, managers. ♦ Michael L. Zwerling, pres; Michael Olson, gen mgr.

KSQL(FM)— Sept 2, 1961: 99.1 mhz; 1.1 kw. 2,487 ft. TL: N37 06 40 W121 50 34. Stereo. 750 Battery St., Suite 200, San Francisco 94111-1412. Phone: (415) 989-5765. Fax: (415) 733-5766. Web site: www.univision.com. Licensee: TMS License California Inc. Group owner: Univision Radio (acq 9-22-2003; grpsl). Format: Sp, Mexican rgnl. News staff: one; News: 4 hrs wkly. Target aud: 25-54. ♦ Tony Perlongo, gen mgr.

*KSRI(FM)— Feb 28, 2001: 90.7 mhz; 316 w. Ant 364 ft. TL: N37 00 10 W122 03 05. Stereo. 5700 W. Oak Blvd., Rocklin 95765. Phone: (916) 251-1600. Fax: (916) 251-1650. E-mail: info@air1.com. Web Site: www.air1.com. Licensee: Educational Media Foundation. Group owner: EMF Broadcasting (acq 8-17-00; $295,000). Network: Air 1. Shaw Pittman. Format: Contemp Christian. News staff: 3. Target aud: 18-35; Judeo-Christian, female. ♦ Richard Jenkins, pres; Mike Novak, VP; Lloyd Parker, gen mgr; Keith Whipple, dev dir.

*KUSP(FM)— Apr 14, 1972: 88.9 mhz; 1.25 kw. 2,496 ft. TL: N36 32 05 W121 37 14. Stereo. 203 8th Ave. 95062. Phone: (831) 476-2800. Fax: (831) 476-2802. E-mail: kusp@kusp.org. Web Site: www.kusp.org. Licensee: Pataphysical Broadcasting Foundation Inc. Network: NPR. Format: Div. News: 44 hrs wkly. ♦ Terry Green, gen mgr & stn mgr; Paula Kenyon, dev dir & sls dir.

*KZSC(FM)— August 1974: 88.1 mhz; 1.36 kw. 350 ft. TL: N37 00 10 W122 03 05. Stereo. 1156 High St. 95064. Phone: (831) 459-2811. Fax: (831) 459-4734. Web Site: kzsc.kzsc.edu. Licensee: Regents of University of California. Format: Div. News: 40 hrs wkly. Target aud: 18-plus; college students up till late 30's. ♦ Michael Bryant, gen mgr.

Santa Margarita

KWWV(FM)— July 21, 1986: 106.1 mhz; 950 w. 1,467 ft. TL: N35 21 38 W120 39 21. Stereo. 3620 Sacramento Dr., Suite 204, San Luis Obispo 934201. Phone: (805) 781-2750. Fax: (805) 781-2758. Web Site: www.wild1061.com. Licensee: Salisbury Broadcasting Corp. (acq 4-1-99; $1 million). Rep: Allied Radio Partners. Format: Chr/top40. News staff: 2; News: 6 hrs wkly. Target aud: 18-34; upscale homeowners. ♦ Kathy Signorelli, gen mgr.

Santa Maria

KBOX(FM)—(Lompoc). Dec 24, 1968: 104.1 mhz; 5.7 kw. 710 ft. TL: N34 43 50 W120 26 01. Stereo. Box 5579 93456-5579. Secondary address: 2325-J Skyway Dr. 93455. Phone: (805) 922-1041. Fax: (805) 928-3069. Licensee: AGM-Santa Maria LP. Group owner: American General Media (acq 2-1-2000). Hogan & Hartson. Format: Adult contemp. News staff: one. Target aud: 25-54. ♦ Rich Watson, pres & gen mgr; Kurt Olson, opns mgr & progmg dir; Emily Stich, gen sls mgr & natl sls mgr; John Bartel, chief of engrg.

KGDP(AM)—(Orcutt). July 4, 1988: 660 khz; 10 kw-D, 1 kw-N, DA-2. TL: N34 57 04 W120 22 38. (CP: COL Oildale. 2.5 kw-U, DA-2. TL: N35 27 11 W118 56 35). 2225 Skyway Dr., Suite B 92455. Phone: (805) 928-7707. Fax: (805) 922-8582. E-mail: kgdp@kgdp660.com. Web Site: www.kgdp660.com. Licensee: Radio Representatives Inc. Group owner: Norwood J. Patterson Network: USA. Format: Christian, talk. Target aud: 35-65. ♦ Steve Cox, gen mgr.

*KGDP-FM—Not on air, target date: unknown: 90.7 mhz; 3 kw. Ant 731 ft. TL: N34 44 20 W120 26 41. 1416 Hollister Ln., Los Osos 93402. Phone: (805) 528-1996. Fax: (805) 922-8582. E-mail: kgdp@kgdp660.com. Web Site: kgdp660.com. Licensee: People of Action. Format: Sp/English, Christian, talk radio. ♦ Steve Cox, gen mgr.

*KHFR(FM)— 2005: 89.7 mhz; 2.45 kw vert. Ant 1,866 ft. TL: N34 54 37 W120 11 08. Family Stations Inc., 4135 Northgate Blvd., Suite 1, Sacramento 95834. Phone: (916) 641-8191. Fax: (916) 641-8238. Web Site: www.familyradio.com. Licensee: Family Stations Inc. (group owner). Format: Relg. ♦ Peggy Renschler, gen mgr.

KPAT(FM)—(Orcutt). 1993: 95.7 mhz; 3.3 kw. 735 ft. TL: N34 44 20 W120 26 41. 2325 Skyway Dr., Suite J 93455. Phone: (805) 922-1041. Fax: (805) 928-3069. Licensee: AGM-Santa Maria LP. Group owner: American General Media (acq 12-1-99; $900,000). Network: USA. Format: R&B Old School. ♦ Rich Watson, gen mgr & pub affrs dir; Emily Stich, gen sls mgr; Wendy Snow, rgnl sls mgr; Rosa Barreto, prom dir; Danny Garite, progmg dir.

KSBQ(AM)— Sept 1, 1961: 1480 khz; 1 kw-D, 61 w-N. TL: N34 57 02 W120 29 22. Box 6940, Oxnard 93030. Secondary address: 200 E. Fesler St., Suites 101 & 201 93454. Phone: (805) 240-2070. Phone: (805) 928-9796. Fax: (805) 240-5960. Fax: (805) 928-3367. Licensee: Lazer Broadcasting Corp. (group owner; acq 12-29-99; $225,000). Rep: Lotus Entravision Reps LLC. Fletcher Heald & Hildreth. Format: Christian. Target aud: 18-49; adults. ♦ Alfredo Plascencia, CEO & pres.

KSMA(AM)— 1946: 1240 khz; 1 kw-U. TL: N34 57 02 W120 29 27. 2215 Skyway Dr. 93456. Phone: (805) 925-2582. Fax: (805) 928-1544. Licensee: Bathysphere Broadcasting L.P. (acq 9-30-99; with co-located FM). Network: CBS. Rep: Allied Radio Partners. Format: News/talk. ♦ Rich Hawkins, stn mgr.

KSNI-FM—Co-owned with KSMA(AM). 1960: 102.5 mhz; 17.5 kw. 774 ft. TL: N34 50 08 W120 24 06. Stereo. Format: Contemp country.

KTAP(AM)— June 10, 1962: 1600 khz; 470 w-D. TL: N34 58 48 W120 27 12. 104 W. Chapel St. 93458. Phone: (805) 928-4334. Fax: (805) 349-2765. E-mail: kidiktap@aol.com. Licensee: Emerald Wave Media. (acq 3-6-97; $475,000 with KIDI(FM) Guadalupe). Mark Van Burgh. Format: Sp, Mexican. News staff: one; News: 4 hrs wkly. Target aud: General; first generation Mexicans. ♦ August Ruiz, gen mgr.

KUHL(AM)— April 1946: 1440 khz; 5 kw-D, 1 kw-N, DA-N. TL: N34 59 02 W120 27 10. 716 E. Chapel 93454. Phone: (805) 922-7727. Fax: (805) 349-0265. E-mail: kuhl@radiocontrolcoast.com. Licensee: Mapleton Communications LLC (group owner; acq 4-21-2003; $1.3 million. with KTME(AM) Lompoc). Network: Network: ABC Information & Entertainment, ABC News/Talk. Format: News/talk. Target aud: 35-64; upscale news & sports listeners. ♦ Adam Nathanson, pres; Nancy Leichter, gen mgr; John Barone, opns dir.

KURQ(FM)—See Grover Beach

KXFM(FM)— 1959: 99.1 mhz; 1.8 kw. 1,905 ft. TL: N34 54 37 W120 11 08. Stereo. 2215 Skyway Dr. 93454. Phone: (805) 925-2582. Fax: (805) 928-1544. Web Site: www.991thefox.com. Licensee: Clear Channel Communications Inc. (acq 2-29-96). Format: Classic rock. Target aud: 18-49; contemp, active adults. ♦ Rich Hawkins, gen mgr; Jennifer Grant, opns dir.

KXTK(AM)—See San Luis Obispo

KZOZ(FM)—See San Luis Obispo

Santa Monica

KBLA(AM)— 1947: 1580 khz; 50 kw-U, DA-2. TL: N34 05 08 W118 15 24. Stereo. 747 E. Green St., Suite 400, Pasadena 91101. Phone: (626) 844-8882. Fax: (626) 844-0156. Web Site: www.mrbi.net. Licensee: Multicultural Radio Broadcasting Licensee LLC. Group owner: Multicultural Radio Broadcasting Inc. (acq 2-4-2004; grpsl). Format: Spanish Christian. News staff: one. ♦ Jose Calles, stn mgr.

*KCRW(FM)— Jan 1, 1946: 89.9 mhz; 6.9 kw. 1,110 ft. TL: N34 07 08 W118 23 30. Stereo. 1900 Pico Blvd. 90405. Phone: (310) 450-5183. Fax: (310) 450-7172. E-mail: mail@kcrw.org. Web Site: www.kcrw.org. Licensee: Santa Monica College District. (acq 8-3-76). Network:

Network: NPR, PRI. Format: Div, news. News staff: 3; News: 14 hrs wkly. Target aud: General; 18-55 year old consumers. Spec prog: African, contemp, jazz, Latino, drama. ♦Ruth Seymour, gen mgr; Jennifer Ferro, stn mgr; Mike Newport, opns dir; Jacki Weber, dev dir.

KDLD(FM)— 1963: 103.1 mhz; 3.7 kw. Ant 269 ft. TL: N34 00 53 W118 22 50. Stereo. 570 Wilshire Blvd., Suite 250, Los Angeles 90036. Phone: (323) 900-6100. Fax: (323) 900-6200. Web Site: www.kdl.com. Licensee: Entravision Holdings LLC. Group owner: Entravision Communications Corp. (acq 2000). Format: Rhythmic CHR / dance, alternative. News: one hr wkly. Target aud: 25-54; upscale adults in Los Angeles' westside. ♦Karl Meyer, gen mgr; Nestor Rocha, progmg VP & mus dir; Robert Isaac, opns dir & engrg dir.

Santa Paula

KLJR-FM— Oct 4, 1976: 96.7 mhz; 87 w. 1,500 ft. TL: N34 19 33 W119 02 18. (CP: 278 w). Stereo. Box 6940, Oxnard 93030. Secondary address: 200 S. A St., Suite 400, Oxnard 93030. Phone: (805) 240-2070. Fax: (805) 240-5960. Licensee: Lazer Broadcasting Corp. (acq 3-31-98; $925,000;. FTR: 11-4-91). Rep: Lotus Entravision Reps LLC. Fletcher, Heald & Hildreth. Format: Sp, adult contemp, CHR. Target aud: 25-54; general. ♦Alfredo Plascencia, CEO & pres.

KUNX(AM)— 1948: 1400 khz; 1 kw-U. TL: N34 19 48 W119 05 31. Stereo. 2284 S. Victoria Ave., Suite 2 G, Ventura 93003. Phone: (805) 289-1400. Fax: (805) 644-7906. Licensee: Gold Coast Broadcasting LLC (group owner; acq 8-18-99; grpsl). Format: Sp. ♦Chip Ehrhardt, gen mgr.

Santa Rosa

***KBBF(FM)**— May 30, 1973: 89.1 mhz; 1 kw. 2,770 ft. TL: N38 39 23 W122 36 54. Box 7189 95407. Phone: (707) 545-8833. Fax: (707) 545-6244. E-mail: kbbfradio@aol.com. Licensee: Bilingual Broadcasting Foundation Inc. Format: Educ, Sp, bilingual. ♦Felipe Ramirez, gen mgr.

KFGY(FM)—Listing follows KSRO(AM).

***KLVR(FM)**— Oct 15, 1982: 91.9 mhz; 840 w. Ant 2,988 ft. TL: N38 40 09 W122 50 24. Stereo. 5700 W. Oaks Blvd., Rocklin 95765. Phone: (916) 251-1600. Fax: (916) 251-1650. E-mail: klove@klove.com. Web Site: www.klove.com. Licensee: Educational Media Foundation. Group owner: EMF Broadcasting (acq 1986). Network: K-Love. Shaw Pittman. Format: Contemp Christian. News staff: 3. Target aud: 25-44; Judeo-Christian females. ♦Richard Jenkins, pres; Mike Novak, VP; Lloyd Parker, gen mgr; Ed Lenane, opns dir; Keith Whipple, dev dir.

***KRCB-FM**— September 1993: 91.1 mhz; 120 w. 731 ft. TL: N38 44 25 W122 50 46. Stereo. 5850 Labath Ave., Rohnert Park 94928. Phone: (707) 585-8522. Fax: (707) 585-1363. Web Site: www.krcb.org. Licensee: Rural California Broadcasting Corp. Network: Network: NPR, PRI. Format: Class, progsv, news/talk. News staff: one; News: 15 hrs wkly. Target aud: General. Spec prog: Folk 6 hrs, jazz 6 hrs wkly. ♦Dan Lanahan, chmn; Nancy Dobbs, CEO & pres. Co-owned TV: *KRCB-TV affil.

KRRS(AM)— Apr 1, 1962: 1460 khz; 1 kw-D, 33 w-N, DA-2. TL: N38 22 13 W122 43 39. Stereo. Box 2277 95405. Phone: (707) 545-1460. Fax: (707) 545-0112. E-mail: krrs@sonic.net. Web Site: www.moonradios.com. Licensee: Moon Broadcasting Licensee LLC. Group owner: Moon Broadcasting (acq 1993; $400,000;. FTR: 9-6-93). Rep: Caballero. Format: Sp. Target aud: 25-54; contemporary Hispanic families. ♦Abel DeLuna Sr., CEO; Abel A. DeLuna, pres; Arelia DeLuna, CFO; Maggie LeClerc, gen mgr; Miriam Gomez, opns mgr.

KSRO(AM)— May 1937: 1350 khz; 5 kw-U, DA-N. TL: N38 26 22 W122 44 51. Box 2158 95405. Secondary address: 1410 Neotomas Ave. 95405. Phone: (707) 543-0100. Fax: (707) 571-1097. Web Site: www.ksro.com. Licensee: Maverick Media of Santa Rosa License LLC. Group owner: Maverick Media LLC (acq 12-16-02; grpsl). Format: News/talk. Target aud: 35-64. ♦Rick Eytcheson, gen mgr; Jill Lynch, gen sls mgr; Carol Batchelor, prom mgr; Brian Hudson, progmg dir.

KFGY(FM)—Co-owned with KSRO(AM). Dec 21, 1979: 92.9 mhz; 2.3 kw. 1,800 ft. TL: N38 45 45 W122 50 24. Stereo. Web Site: www.froggy929.com. Format: Country. Target aud: 18-44. Spec prog: Jazz 5 hrs wkly. ♦Sanai Lojko, gen sls mgr; Greg Kodiak, prom dir; Racquel Wooley, prom mgr.

KVRV(FM)—(Monte Rio). Nov 20, 1977: 97.7 mhz; 250 w. 1,122 ft. TL: N38 29 08 W123 02 05. Stereo. Box 2158 95405. Phone: (707) 543-0100. Fax: (707) 571-1097. Web Site: www.977theriver.com. Licensee: Maverick Media of Santa Rosa License LLC. Group owner: Maverick Media LLC (acq 12-16-02; grpsl). Format: Classic rock. Target aud: 25-54. ♦Diane Hubel, gen mgr.

KXFX(FM)— Dec 23, 1974: 101.7 mhz; 2.2 kw. 1,056 ft. TL: N38 30 31 W122 39 41. Stereo. Box 2158 95405. Secondary address: 1410 Neotomas Ave., Suite 200 95405. Phone: (707) 543-0100. Fax: (707) 571-1097. Web Site: www.kxfx.com. Licensee: Maverick Media of Santa Rosa License LLC. Group owner: Maverick Media LLC (acq 12-16-02; grpsl). Pepper & Corazzini. Format: AOR, classic rock. Target aud: General. ♦Lauren Marks, prom mgr.

KZST(FM)— Apr 18, 1971: 100.1 mhz; 6 kw. 240 ft. TL: N38 25 07 W122 40 33. Stereo. Box 100 95402. Secondary address: 3392 Mendocino Ave. 95402. Phone: (707) 528-4434. Fax: (707) 527-8216. Web Site: www.kzst.com. Licensee: Redwood Empire Stereocasters. Rep: McGavren Guild. Haley, Bader & Potts. Format: Adult contemp. News staff: 2. Target aud: 25-54. ♦Tom Skinner, gen mgr.

Santa Ynez

KRAZ(FM)— 2001: 105.9 mhz; 65 w. Ant 2,932 ft. TL: N34 31 32 W119 57 00. 1693 Mission Dr., Suite D202, Solvang 93463. Phone: (805) 688-8386. Fax: (805) 688-2271. Licensee: Knight Broadcasting Inc. (acq 4-30-01; $325,000. for CP). Network: ABC. Format: Country. ♦Shawn Knight, gen mgr.

Seaside

KMBY-FM— October 1996: 103.9 mhz; 1.4 kw. 604 ft. TL: N36 30 17 W121 54 21. Stereo. 60 Garden Court, Suite 300, Monterey 93940-5341. Phone: (831) 658-5200. Fax: (831) 658-5299. Web Site: www.x1039fm.com. Licensee: Mapleton Communications LLC (group owner; acq 1-24-02; $1.85 million). Rep: McGavren Guild. Format: Alt rock. News staff: one. Target aud: 18-54; working women & men. Spec prog: Urban oldies 4 hrs wkly. ♦Adam Nathanson, pres; Raul Salvador, CFO; Dale Hendry, gen mgr; Mike Anthony, opns VP; Kenny Allen, opns mgr.

KSES-FM— Nov 22, 1972: 107.1 mhz; 1.85 kw. 587 ft. TL: N36 33 12 W121 47 05. Stereo. 67 Garden Ct., Monterey 93940. Phone: (831) 333-9735. Fax: (831) 333-9750. Licensee: Entravision Holdings LLC. Group owner: Entravision Communications Corp. (acq 3-14-00; grpsl). Format: Contemp Sp hits. Target aud: 18-49. ♦Aaron Scoby, gen mgr.

Sebastopol

KJZY(FM)— Nov 5, 1995: 93.7 mhz; 6 kw. 216 ft. TL: N38 25 07 W122 40 33. Stereo. Box 100, Santa Rosa 95402. Phone: (707) 528-4434. Fax: (707) 527-8216. E-mail: gordon@kjzy.com. Web Site: www.kjzy.com. Licensee: Redwood Empire Sterocasters. Format: Smooth jazz. ♦Tom Skinner, gen mgr.

Selma

***KQKL(FM)**— Aug 6, 2003: 88.5 mhz; 17 kw. Ant 397 ft. TL: N36 26 50 W119 37 10. Stereo. 5700 W. Oaks Blvd., Rocklin 95765. Phone: (916) 251-1600. Fax: (916) 251-1650. E-mail: klove@klove.com. Web Site: www.klove.com. Licensee: Educational Media Foundation. Group owner: EMF Broadcasting. Network: K-Love. Shaw Pittman. Format: Contemp Christian. News staff: 3. Target aud: 25-44; Judeo Christian, female. ♦Richard Jenkins, pres; Mike Novak, VP; Lloyd Parker, gen mgr; Ed Lenane, opns dir; Keith Whipple, dev dir.

Shafter

***KGLV(FM)**—Not on air, target date: unknown: 89.5 mhz; 50 kw vert. Ant 482 ft. TL: N35 35 25 W119 30 17. 5700 W. Oaks Blvd., Rocklin 95765. Phone: (916) 251-1600. Fax: (916) 251-1650. Licensee: Educational Media Foundation. Group owner: EMF Broadcasting (acq 1-14-2005). ♦Richard Jenkins, pres; Lloyd Parker, gen mgr.

***KGZO(FM)**— June 6, 1996: 90.9 mhz; 1.9 kw. 2070 ft. TL: N35 16 51 W119 44 52. Stereo. 2310 Ponderosa Dr., Suite 28, Camarillo 93010. Phone: (805) 482-4797. Phone: (661) 792-9071. Fax: (805) 388-5202. E-mail: info@nuevavida.com. Web Site: www.nuevavida.com. Licensee: The Association for Community Education Inc. (acq 7-30-97;). Miller & Neely. Format: Relg, Sp. Target aud: General. ♦Phil Guthrie, pres; Mary Guthrie, gen mgr.

KKXX-FM— 1994: 93.1 mhz; 4 kw. 403 ft. TL: N35 28 21 W119 01 40. 1400 Easton Dr., Suite 144, Bakersfield 93309. Phone: (661) 328-1410. Fax: (661) 328-0873. Web Site: www.pirateradio931.com. Licensee: AGM California. Group owner: American General Media (acq 7-25-97; $1.5 million. with KBID(AM) Bakersfield). Format: Pirate radio. News staff: 4; News: 2 hrs wkly. Target aud: 18-49; men. ♦Roger Fessler, gen mgr.

KSMJ(FM)—Licensed to Shafter. See Bakersfield

Shasta

KCNR(AM)— Aug 13, 1967: 1460 khz; 750 w-U. TL: N40 33 14 W122 22 53. 1326 Market St., Redding 96001. Phone: (530) 244-5082. Fax: (530) 244-5698. Licensee: M C Allen Productions (acq 10-9-96; $35,000). Network: ABC Information & Entertainment. News staff: 8; News: 7 hrs wkly. Target aud: 24-55. ♦Mike Johnson, chief of engrg; Mike Quinn, gen mgr, progmg dir & chief of engrg.

Shasta Lake City

KESR(FM)— 1998: 107.1 mhz; 1.4 kw. 1,361 ft. TL: N40 39 06 W122 31 32. 1588 Charles Dr., Redding 96003. Phone: (530) 244-9700. Fax: (530) 244-9707. Licensee: Results Radio of Redding Licensee LLC. Group owner: Fritz Communications Inc. (acq 5-28-2000; grpsl). Format: Adult contemp. ♦Jack Fritz, pres & gen mgr; Beth Tappan, gen mgr; Carmy Ferrari, opns mgr; Laurie Curto, gen sls mgr; Rob Reid, progmg dir; Bryant Smith, chief of engrg.

KJPR(AM)— 2005: 1330 khz; 1 kw-U, DA-2. TL: N40 40 48 W122 16 01. Jefferson Public Radio, 1250 Siskiyou Blvd., Ashland, OR 97520. Phone: (541) 552-6301. Fax: (541) 552-8565. Web Site: www.jeffnet.org. Licensee: JPR Foundation Inc. (acq 2-9-2004). Format: News, information. ♦Ronald Kramer, gen mgr; Bryon Lambert, opns dir; Paul Westhelle, dev dir.

KNNN(FM)— Oct 26, 1989: 99.3 mhz; 1.6 kw. Ant 1,525 ft. TL: N40 39 15 W122 31 12. 3360 Alta Mesa Dr., Redding 96002. Phone: (530) 226-9500. Fax: (530) 221-4940. E-mail: knnn@reddingradio.com. Web Site: www.mix993fm.com. Licensee: Regent Acquisition Corp. Group owner: Regent Communications Inc. (acq 5-29-98; grpsl). Format: CHR. Target aud: 25-54. Spec prog: Jazz 3 hrs wkly. ♦Lisa Geraci, gen mgr.

Shingle Springs

KCCL-FM— May 1, 1989: 101.9 mhz; 47 kw. 505 ft. TL: N38 51 12 W120 56 23. Stereo. 1436 Auburn Blvd., Sacramento 95815. Phone: (916) 646-4000. Fax: (916) 646-3237. Web Site: www.kool1019.fm. Licensee: Entravision Holdings LLC. Group owner: Entravision Communications Corp. (acq 3-14-00; grpsl). Thompson, Hine & Flory L.L.P. Format: Oldies. Target aud: 25-54. ♦Larry Lemanski, gen mgr.

Shingletown

KKXS(FM)— January 2001: 96.1 mhz; 600 w. Ant 1,023 ft. TL: N40 29 54 W121 53 25. Fritz Communications Inc., 1355 N. Dutton Ave. #225, Santa Rosa 95401-7107. Phone: (530) 244-9700. Fax: (530) 244-9707. Web Site: www.kicks96radio.com. Licensee: Results Radio of Redding Licensee LLC. Group owner: Fritz Communications Inc. (acq 3-29-99; $125,000. for 50%). Format: Smooth jazz. ♦Beth Tappan, gen mgr; Bryant Smith, gen mgr & chief of engrg; Carmelo Ferrari, opns dir; Laurie Curto, gen sls mgr; Matt Reisz, progmg dir.

KRDG(FM)— Aug 1, 1995: 105.3 mhz; 10 kw. 1,056 ft. TL: N40 29 54 W121 53 25. Stereo. 3360 Alta Mesa Dr., Reading 96002. Phone: (530) 226-9500. Fax: (530) 221-4940. Web Site: www.readingradio.com. Licensee: Regent Acquisition Corp. Group owner: Regent Communications Inc. (acq 5-29-98; grpsl). Bechtel & Cole. Format: Good time oldies. Target aud: 25-54; active adults with families. ♦Lisa Geraci, gen mgr; Jordan Perry, gen sls mgr; Jim Bremer, chief of engrg.

Simi Valley

KIRN(AM)— Sept 21, 1984: 670 khz; 5 kw-D, 1 kw-N. TL: N34 19 10 W118 42 58. 3301 Barham Blvd. #300, Los Angeles 90068. Phone: (323) 851-5476. Fax: (323) 512-7452. E-mail: pomzaffari@670amkirn.com. Web Site: www.670amksrn.com. Licensee: Lotus Oxnard Corp. Group owner: Lotus Communications Corp. (acq 12-11-96; $4.2 million). Jerome Boros, Bryan Caves, Robinson Silverman. Format: Farsi, MOR, news/talk, sports. News staff: 3; News: 14 hrs wkly. Persian,

Irawian, Farsi. ♦ Howard Kalmenson, pres; John Paley, VP; Hossein Hedjazi, progmg VP; John Cooper, chief of engrg; Poopak Mozaffari, mktg.

Soledad

KFRS(FM)— 2002: 89.9 mhz; 250 w vert. Ant 305 ft. TL: N36 16 25 W121 16 12. 4135 Northgate Blvd., Suite 1, Sacramento 95834. Phone: (916) 641-8191. Fax: (916) 641-8238. Licensee: Family Stations Inc. (group owner) Format: Relg. ♦ Peggy Renschler, gen mgr.

KMBX(AM)— 1992: 700 khz; 2.5 kw-D, 700 w-N. TL: N36 27 51 W121 17 52. 67 Garden Ct., Monterey 93940. Phone: (831) 333-9735. Fax: (831) 333-9750. Licensee: Entravision Holdings LLC. Group owner: Entravision Communications Corp. (acq 3-14-00; grpsl). Rep: Caballero. Format: Contemp Sp mus. Target aud: 18-49. ♦ Andrew Lugo, gen mgr & gen sls mgr; Jeff Liberman, opns VP.

KMJV(FM)— Oct 1, 1991: 106.3 mhz; 6 kw, 1,720 ft. TL: N36 22 48 W121 12 57. Stereo. 548 E. Alisal St., Salinas 93905. Phone: (831) 757-1910. Fax: (831) 771-1685. Licensee: Len Radio Broadcasting of California Licensee LLC. (group owner; (acq 2-16-2005; grpsl). Format: Mexican rgnl. Target aud: 18-44. ♦ Joe Armao, gen mgr.

Solvang

KSYV(FM)— Sept 22, 1982: 96.7 mhz; 420 w. Ant 1,217 ft. TL: N34 41 28 W120 15 58. Stereo. 1693 Mission Dr., Suite D 202 93463. Phone: (805) 688-5798. Fax: (805) 688-2271. E-mail: radio@knightbroadcasting.com. Licensee: Knight Broadcasting Inc. (acq 11-2-01). Network: AP Network News. Format: Adult contemp, news. News: 126 hrs wkly. Target aud: 24-54; female 60%, male 40%. ♦ Shawn Knight, gen mgr & opns dir.

Sonoma

*KSVY(FM)— 2005: 91.3 mhz; 2.5 kw vert. Ant -305 ft. TL: N38 16 47 W122 26 47. 168 W. Napa St. 95476. Phone: (707) 933-0808. Fax: (707) 933-1573. E-mail: ksvy@ksvy.org. Web Site: www.ksvy.org. Licensee: Commonbond Foundation. Format: Community radio. ♦ Bill Hammett, pres & gen mgr.

Sonora

KVML(AM)— 1949: 1450 khz; 1 kw-U. TL: N38 00 30 W120 21 45. 342 S. Washington 95370. Phone: (209) 533-1450. Fax: (209) 533-9520. Licensee: Clarke Broadcasting Corp. (group owner; acq 12-86; with co-located FM; 10-6-86). Network: ABC. Leventhal, Senter & Lerman. Format: News/talk. News staff: 2; News 25 hrs wkly. Target aud: 25 plus; general. Spec prog: Relg 3 hrs, sports 15 hrs wkly. ♦ H. Randolph Holder Jr., pres; Larry England, gen mgr; Gary Granger, gen sls mgr; Kim Fischer, prom dir; Ed Haley, adv mgr; Mark Truppner, progmg dir; Joseph Kreiss, news dir; John Petter, chief of engrg.

KZSQ-FM—Co-owned with KVML(AM). Oct 3, 1973: 92.7 mhz; 380 w. 1,289 ft. TL: N38 00 30 W120 21 45. Stereo. Format: Adult contemp. News staff: 2; News: 4 hrs wkly. Target aud: 25-54. ♦ D.J. Riendeau, progmg dir; Justin Flores, progmg dir.

Soquel

KYAA(AM)— 2001: 1200 khz; 25 kw-D, 10 kw-N. TL: N36 39 38 W121 32 29. 495 Elder Ave., Sand City 93955. Phone: (831) 899-2600. Fax: (831) 899-5102. E-mail: kyaknry@aol.com. Licensee: People's Radio Inc. (group owner). Format: East Indian. ♦ Jim Vossen, chief of opns.

South Lake Tahoe

KOWL(AM)— November 1956: 1490 khz; 1 kw-U. TL: N38 56 34 W119 57 25. 2435 E. Venice Dr., Suite 120 96150. Phone: (530) 541-6681. Fax: (530) 541-4822. E-mail: kowl@krltfm.com. Web Site: www.krltfm.com. Licensee: CCR-Lake Tahoe IV LLC. Group owner: Cherry Creek Radio LLC (acq 12-19-2003; grpsl). Format: News/talk, sports. ♦ Betsy Miller, gen mgr.

KRLT(FM)— June 23, 1976: 93.9 mhz; 6 kw. -190 ft. TL: N38 57 38 W119 56 26. Stereo. 2435 E. Venice Dr., Suite 120 96150. Phone: (530) 541-6681. Fax: (530) 541-4822. E-mail: krlt@krltfm.com. Web Site: www.krltfm.com. Licensee: CCR-Lake Tahoe IV LLC. Group owner: Cherry Creek Radio LLC (acq 12-19-2003; grpsl). Format: 80s, 90s & today. News: 10 hrs wkly. Target aud: 25-54. ♦ Betsy Miller, gen mgr.

KTHO(AM)— Mar 17, 1963: 590 khz; 2.5 kw-D, 500 w-N, DA-N. TL: N38 55 00 W119 57 46. Box 5686, State Line, NV 89449. Secondary address: 2520 Lake Tahoe Blvd. 96150. Phone: (530) 543-0590. Fax: (530) 543-1101. E-mail: stan@590ktho.com. Licensee: Live Wire Media Partners LLC (acq 12-13-2004; $650,000). Format: News/talk, sports. News staff: one; News: 40 hrs wkly. Target aud: 25-54; locals & visitors, working population and retired. ♦ Stan Koplowitz, gen mgr.

KWYL(FM)— 1995: 102.9 mhz; 39 kw. Ant 2,926 ft. TL: N39 18 38 W119 53 01. Stereo. 595 E. Plumb Ln., Reno, NV 89502. Phone: (775) 789-6700. Fax: (775) 789-6767. Web Site: www.wild1029.com. Licensee: Citadel Broadcasting Co. Group owner: Citadel Broadcasting Corp. (acq 5-9-03; grpsl). Format: Urban, rap, hip hop. Target aud: 25-54. ♦ Dana Johnson, gen mgr; Martin Stabbert, opns mgr; Gregg Moore, gen sls mgr; Maurice Ayala, progmg dir.

South Oroville

KYIX(FM)— Feb 1, 1994: 104.9 mhz; 260 w. 1,548 ft. TL: N39 39 04 W121 27 43. 13 Jean Lane, Chico 95926. Phone: (530) 894-7325. Fax: (530) 894-2050. E-mail: randy@bigshow.net. Web Site: www.y105.net. Licensee: Butte Broadcasting Co. (acq 1994). Format: Christian. ♦ Randy Zachary, gen mgr.

Stanford

*KZSU(FM)— Oct 10, 1964: 90.1 mhz; 500 w. -10 ft. TL: N37 24 42 W122 10 41. Stereo. Box 20190 94309. Phone: (650) 725-4868. Phone: (650) 725-4868. Fax: (650) 725-5865. Licensee: Trustees of Leland Stanford Jr. University. Crowell & Moring. Format: Eclectic, educ. Target aud: 13-plus; independent-thinking individuals who value unique programming. ♦ Chaun-Mei Lee, gen mgr; Lois Kellerman, prom dir; Chris Constantino, adv dir; Jack Wang, progmg dir; Bill Cuevas, mus dir; Clint Taylor, news dir; Eli Lazarus, news dir; Lisa Dornell, pub affrs dir; Mark Lawrence, chief of engrg.

Stockton

KHKK(FM)—See Modesto

KJOY(FM)— June 15, 1968: 99.3 mhz; 2.35 kw. 330 ft. TL: N38 01 21 W121 16 03. Stereo. 4643 Quail Lake Dr., Suite 100 95207-1833. Phone: (209) 572-0104. Fax: (209) 522-2061. Web Site: www.993kjoy.com. Licensee: Citadel Broadcasting Co. Group owner: Citadel Broadcasting Corp. (acq 5-9-03; grpsl). Format: Adult contemp. Target aud: 25-54. ♦ Roy Williams, gen mgr.

KMIX(FM)—See Tracy

KQOD(FM)— Jan 24, 1980: 100.1 mhz; 6 kw. 285 ft. TL: N38 01 21 W121 16 03. Stereo. 2121 Lancey Dr., Modesto 95355. Phone: (209) 551-1306. Fax: (209) 551-1359. Web Site: www.mega100online.com. Licensee: Capstar TX L.P. Group owner: Clear Channel Communications Inc. (acq 11-18-99). Format: Oldies. Target aud: 25-54. ♦ Greg Granger, gen sls mgr.

KSTN(AM)— November 1949: 1420 khz; 5 kw-D, 1 kw-N, DA-2. TL: N37 55 32 W121 14 44. 2171 Ralph Ave. 95206. Phone: (209) 948-5786. Licensee: San Joaquin Broadcasting Co. Format: Oldies. News staff: one; News: 20 hrs wkly. Target aud: 18-40. Spec prog: Farm 3 hrs, relg 5 hrs wkly. ♦ Knox LaRue, pres, stn mgr & progmg dir; John Hampton, mus dir.

KSTN-FM— 1962: 107.3 mhz; 8.1 kw. 1,610 ft. TL: N37 49 17 W121 46 49. Format: Sp. Target aud: General. Spec prog: Sp, Por 4 hrs wkly. ♦ Julio Barrios, progmg dir; Paul Shinn, chief of engrg.

*KUOP(FM)— Sept 22, 1947: 91.3 mhz; 7 kw. 1,220 ft. TL: N37 28 48 W121 21 02. Stereo. 7055 Folsom Blvd., Sacramento 95826. Phone: (916) 480-5900. Fax: (916) 487-3348. E-mail: npr@csus.edu. Web Site: www.capradio.org. Licensee: University of the Pacific. Network: Network: NPR, PRI. Dow, Lohnes & Albertson. Format: News, info, class. News staff: one; News: 90 hrs wkly. Target aud: General; NPR listeners, eg. professionals, educators, administrators. ♦ Mike Lazer, pres & gen mgr; John Brenneise, opns dir; Beth Hassett, dev dir & mktg dir; Linda Onstad, adv dir; Cheryl Dring, progmg dir & mus dir; Joe Barr, news dir; Jeff Browne, chief of engrg.

KUYL(AM)— 1947: 1280 khz; 1 kw-U, DA-N. TL: N37 58 55 W121 13 44. Stereo. 2121 Lancey Dr., Modesto 95355. Phone: (209) 551-1306. Fax: (209) 551-1359. E-mail: lighthouseonline@hotmail.com. Web Site: www.lighthouse1280.com. Licensee: Capstar TX L.P. Group owner: Clear Channel Communications Inc. (acq 8-30-00; grpsl). Format: Christian. News staff: 3; News: 20 hrs wkly. Target aud: 25-64. ♦ Gary Granger, gen mgr.

*KWG(AM)— Nov 22, 1921: 1230 khz; 900 w-U. TL: N37 57 34 W121 15 28. PO Box 7635 95267. Phone: (209) 462-8307. Web Site: ihradio.org. Licensee: IHR Educational Broadcasting (group owner; acq 10-18-99; $441,227). Format: Catholic. Target aud: 25-54. ♦ Joseph Nesta, gen mgr & stn mgr; Dale Harry, chief of engrg.

KWIN(FM)—See Lodi

*KYCC(FM)— Feb 24, 1975: 90.1 mhz; 26 kw. Ant 230 ft. TL: N37 57 10 W121 17 11. Stereo. 9019 N. West Ln. 95210. Phone: (209) 477-3690. Fax: (209) 477-2762. E-mail: kycc@kycc.org. Web Site: www.kycc.org. Licensee: Your Christian Companion Network Inc. (acq 7-20-98). Network: USA. Cohn & Marks. Format: Gospel, inspirational, adult contemp. Target aud: 25-45. Spec prog: Black 6 hrs, health one hr wkly. ♦ Shirley Garner, exec VP & gen mgr; Adam Biddell, opns mgr.

Sun City

KXFG(FM)— March 1997: 92.9 mhz; 6 kw. 328 ft. TL: N33 35 36 W117 08 50. 900 E. Washington St., Suite 315, Colton 92324. Phone: (909) 825-9525. Fax: (909) 825-0441. Web Site: www.kfrog.com. Licensee: Infinity Radio Inc. Group owner: Infinity Broadcasting Corp. (acq 11-13-98; grpsl). Rep: Allied Radio Partners. Format: Country. ♦ Tom Hoyt, gen mgr; Lee Douglas, opns mgr.

Sunnyvale

KCNL(FM)— January 1961: 104.9 mhz; 6 kw. Ant -154 ft. TL: N37 19 23 W121 45 15. Stereo. 1420 Koll Cir., Suite A, San Jose 95112. Phone: (408) 453-5400. Fax: (408) 452-1330. E-mail: johnallers@channel1049.com. Web Site: www.channel1049.com. Licensee: Clear Channel Broadcasting Licenses Inc. Group owner: Clear Channel Communications Inc. (acq 2-2-2004; grpsl). Rep: Caballero. Format: Alternative. Target aud: 18-49. ♦ Kim Bryant, gen mgr.

Susanville

*KFLL(FM)—Not on air, target date: unknown: 88.1 mhz; 25 kw. Ant -456 ft. TL: N40 24 12 W120 34 25. Broadcasting for the Challenged Inc., 188 S. Bellevue, Suite 222, Memphis, TN 38104. Phone: (901) 375-9324. Licensee: Broadcasting for the Challenged Inc. ♦ Shea Flynn, gen mgr.

KHJQ(FM)— May 25, 1983: 92.3 mhz; 9.5 kw. Ant 1,102 ft. TL: N40 27 13 W120 34 14. Stereo. 3015 Johnstonville Rd. 96130. Phone: (530) 257-2121. Fax: (530) 257-6955. Licensee: Sierra Broadcasting Corp. (group owner; acq 1-7-97; $50,000). Format: Hot Adult contemp. Spec prog: Class 5 hrs wkly. ♦ Rodney Chambers, gen mgr.

KJDX(FM)—Listing follows KSUE(AM).

California

KLZN(FM)—Not on air, target date: unknown: 96.3 mhz; 2.4 kw. Ant 1,056 ft. TL: N40 27 14 W120 34 13. 448 Paseo Companeros, Chico 95928-8857. Licensee: Gary Katz. ♦ Gary Katz, gen mgr.

KSUE(AM)— Apr 22, 1948: 1240 khz; 1 kw-U. TL: N40 23 43 W120 37 32. 3015 Johnstonville Rd. 96130. Phone: (530) 257-2121. Fax: (530) 257-6955. Web Site: www.theradionetwork.com. Licensee: Sierra Broadcasting Corp. (group owner) Pepper & Corazzini. Format: News/talk. Target aud: 35-54. Spec prog: Relg 3 hrs wkly. ♦ Rod Chambers, pres & gen mgr; Sam Short, opns dir & progmg dir; Mike Smith, news dir; Brittany Chambers, pub affrs dir; Mike Martindale, chief of engrg.

KJDX(FM)—Co-owned with KSUE(AM). Aug 19, 1976: 93.3 mhz; 100 kw. 1,155 ft. TL: N40 27 13 W120 34 14. Stereo. Web Site: www.theradionetwork.com. Format: Hot country. Target aud: 25-64.

Sutter

*****KXJS(FM)**— 2004: 88.7 mhz; 550 w. Ant 1,978 ft. TL: N39 12 20 W121 49 10. Capital Public Radio Inc., 7055 Folsom Blvd., Sacramento 95826. Phone: (916) 480-5900. Fax: (916) 487-3348. E-mail: npr@csus.edu. Web Site: www.csus.edu/npr. Licensee: California State University, Sacramento. Duane Morris, LLP. Format: Jazz, news & info. ♦ Michael Lazar, pres & gen mgr; Carl Watanabe, stn mgr & progmg mgr; John Brenneise, opns mgr; Beth Hassett, dev dir & mktg dir; Linda Onstad, adv dir; Joe Barr, news dir; Jeff Browne, engrg dir.

Sutter Creek

KLMG(FM)—See Jackson

Taft

KBDS(FM)— June 1986: 103.9 mhz; 6 kw. Ant 328 ft. TL: N35 07 04 W119 27 33. Stereo. 6313 Schirra Ct., Bakersfield 93313. Phone: (661) 837-0745. Fax: (661) 837-1612. E-mail: network@campesina.com. Web Site: www.campesina.com. Licensee: Radio Campesina Bakersfield Inc. (acq 1994) $135,000 plus assumption of debt valued at $283,000. with co-located AM). Borsari & Paxson. Format: Mexican. Target aud: 25-54; Hispanic. ♦ Anthony Chavez, gen mgr.

Tahoe City

*****KKTO(FM)**— Oct 3, 1997: 90.5 mhz; 38 kw vert. 2,939 ft. TL: N39 18 38 W119 53 01. Stereo. 7055 Folsom Blvd., Sacramento 95826. Phone: (916) 480-5900. Fax: (916) 487-3348. E-mail: npr@csus.edu. Web Site: www.capradio.org. Licensee: California State University, Sacramento. Network: Network: NPR, PRI. Duane Morris LLP. Format: Class, info, news. News staff: 4; News: 90 hrs wkly. Target aud: General; NPR listeners, eg. professionals, educators, administrators. ♦ Michael Lazar, pres & gen mgr; Carl Watanabe, stn mgr, progmg dir & progmg mgr; John Brenneise, opns mgr; Beth Hassett, dev dir & mktg dir; Michael Frost, prom dir; Linda Onstad, adv dir; Cheryl Dring, mus dir; Joe Barr, news dir; Jeff Browne, engrg dir.

KLCA(FM)—Licensed to Tahoe City. See Reno NV

Tehachapi

KKZQ(FM)— 2001: 100.1 mhz; 340 w. Ant 620 ft. TL: N35 04 30 W118 22 07. 570 East Ave. Q-9, Palmdale 93550. Phone: (661) 947-3107. Fax: (661) 272-5688. Web Site: www.edge100.com. Licensee: High Desert Broadcasting LLC (group owner). Format: Alternative modern rock. Target aud: 18-49. ♦ Bruce Thompson, gen mgr; Gary Wilson, opns mgr.

KTPI-FM— Jan 8, 1982: 103.1 mhz; 1.9 kw. Ant 577 ft. TL: N35 04 30 W118 22 08. Stereo. 352 E. Ave k-4, Lancaster 93535. Phone: (661) 942-1121. Fax: (661) 723-5512. Web Site: www.ktpi.com. Licensee: Clear Channel Broadcasting Licenses Inc. Group owner: Clear Channel Communications Inc. (acq 11-21-2003; grpsl). Rep: Christal. Latham & Watkins. Format: Country. News staff: one; News: 2 hrs wkly. Target aud: 25-54. ♦ Larry Thornhill, gen mgr & sls dir.

*****KYLU(FM)**—Not on air, target date: unknown: 88.7 mhz; 140 w. Ant 3,693 ft. TL: N35 27 10 W118 35 25. 5700 West Oaks Blvd., Rocklin 95765. Phone: (916) 251-1600. Fax: (916) 251-1650. Licensee: Educational Media Foundation. ♦ Lloyd Parker, gen mgr.

Temecula

KMYT(FM)— 2000: 94.5 mhz; 320 w. 771 ft. TL: N33 28 51 W117 10 58. 27349 Jefferson Ave., Suite 116 92590. Phone: (951) 296-9050. Fax: (951) 296-9077. E-mail: josephraineri@clearchannel.com. Licensee: Clear Channel Broadcasting Licenses Inc. Group owner: Clear Channel Communications Inc. (acq 6-11-01; $4.5 million. including five-year noncompete agreement). Format: Smooth jazz. ♦ John Roberts, gen mgr & gen sls mgr; Bob Ridzak, stn mgr; Bill Georgi, progmg dir; Allen Keppler, mus dir; Rich Mena, chief of engrg.

*****KRTM(FM)**— Jan 1, 1989: 88.9 mhz; 3 kw. Ant -151 ft. TL: N33 30 35 W117 09 30. 39405 Murrieta Hot Springs Rd., Murrieta 92563. Phone: (909) 696-0774. Fax: (909) 461-0292. E-mail: krtm@csnradio.com. Web Site: www.calvarychapel.com/krtm. Licensee: Penfold Communications (acq 6-11-98; $234,788). Network: CSN. Format: Christian. Target aud: 25-45. ♦ Chuck Smith, pres; Bill Graves, gen mgr & progmg dir.

KTMQ(FM)— 2001: 103.3 mhz; 1.25 kw. Ant 715 ft. TL: N33 28 51 W117 10 58. 27349 Jefferson Ave., Suite 116 92590. Phone: (951) 256-9050. Licensee: Clear Channel Broadcasting Licenses Inc. Group owner: Clear Channel Communications Inc. (acq 5-24-01; $6.225 million). Hogan and Hartson. Format: Classic rock. ♦ Bob Ridzak, gen mgr.

Templeton

KXDZ(FM)— 2004: 100.5 mhz; 1.35 kw. Ant 361 ft. TL: N35 30 19 W120 37 18. 396 Buckley Rd., Suite 2, San Luis Obispo 93401. Phone: (805) 786-2570. Fax: (805) 547-9860. Licensee: Mapleton Communications LLC (group owner; (acq 5-23-2002;. grpsl). Format: Classic Hits. ♦ Nancy Leichter, gen mgr.

Thousand Oaks

*****KCLU(FM)**— Oct 20, 1994: 88.3 mhz; 3.2 kw. Ant 518 ft. TL: N34 13 05 W118 56 42. Stereo. 60 W. Olsen Rd., Suite 4400 91360. Phone: (805) 493-3900. Phone: (805) 493-9200. Fax: (805) 493-3982. Web Site: www.kclu.org. Licensee: California Lutheran University. Network: Network: NPR, PRI. Leventhal, Senter & Lerman. Format: Jazz, news/talk, educ. News staff: one; News: 36 hrs wkly. Target aud: General. Spec prog: Blues 5 hrs wkly. ♦ Mary Olson, stn mgr; Joanne Cunha, dev dir.

*****KDSC(FM)**— Dec 4, 1979: 91.1 mhz; 4.9 kw. 1,280 ft. TL: N34 24 47 W119 11 10. Stereo. Box 77913, Los Angeles 90007. Secondary address: 515 S. Figueroa St., Suite 2050, Los Angeles 90071. Phone: (213) 225-7400. Fax: (213) 225-7410. E-mail: kusc@usc.org. Web Site: www.kusc.org. Licensee: University of Southern California (acq 3-17-82). Network: Network: PRI, NPR. Format: Class. News: 3 hrs wkly. Target aud: 35 plus. ♦ Brenda Barnes, pres; Eric DeWeese, gen mgr; Janet McIntyre, dev dir.

KIIS(AM)— Sept 20, 1971: 850 khz; 500 w-D, 250 w-N, DA-2. TL: N34 12 07 W118 49 47. c/o Radio Station KRLA(AM), 701 N. Brand Blvd., Suite 550, Glendale 91203. Phone: (818) 956-5552. Fax: (818) 551-1110. Web Site: www.krla870.com. Licensee: New Inspiration Broadcasting Co. Inc. Group owner: Salem Communications Corp. (acq 8-16-2004; $800,000). Format: News/talk. ♦ Terry Fahy, gen mgr.

KMLT(FM)— Apr 1, 1963: 92.7 mhz; 3.1 kw. Ant 462 ft. TL: N34 12 21 W118 49 04. Stereo. 99 Long Court, Suite 200 91360. Phone: (805) 497-8511. Fax: (805) 497-8514. Web Site: www.927jillfm.com. Licensee: Amaturo Group of L.A. Ltd. Group owner: Amaturo Group Ltd. (acq 1996; $2 million). Pepper & Corazzini. Format: Adult contemp. News staff: one. Target aud: 25-54; employed professional adults, especially women. ♦ Catherine Moreau, VP & gen mgr; Joseph Amaturo, CEO & progmg dir.

Thousand Palms

KLOB(FM)— Apr 21, 1994: 94.7 mhz; 1.8 kw. Ant 606 ft. TL: N33 52 07 W116 25 58. 41601 Corporate Way, Palm Desert 92260-1986. Phone: (760) 341-5837. Fax: (760) 341-0951. E-mail: klobtraffic@entravision.com. Web Site: www.entravision.com. Licensee: Entravision Holdings LLC. Group owner: Entravision Communications Corp. (acq 2-27-97). Format: Adult latin contemporary. ♦ Philip Wilkinson, pres; Tony Billett, gen mgr.

KNWT(AM)— Dec 7, 1963: 1270 khz; 5 kw-D, 750 w-N, DA-2. TL: N33 51 04 W116 23 36. 1321 N. Gene Autry Trail, Palm Springs 92262. Phone: (760) 322-7890. Fax: (760) 322-5493. Web Site: www.desertfun.com. Licensee: MCC Radio LLC. Group owner: Morris Radio LLC (acq 12-24-97; $2.25 million. with KDGL(FM) Yucca Valley). Format: Talk. News staff: 3; News: 20 hrs wkly. Target aud: 25 plus. ♦ William S. Morris IV, chmn; William S. Morris III, pres; Darrell Fry, CFO; Michael Ostehaut, VP; Keith Martin, gen mgr; Larry Snider, opns dir.

KXPS(AM)— Nov 14, 1992: 1010 khz; 3.6 kw-D, 400 w-N, DA-2. TL: N33 50 35 W116 25 39. Stereo. 1321 N. Gene Autry Tr., Palm Springs 92262. Phone: (760) 322-7890. Fax: (760) 322-5493. Web Site: www.1010kxps.com. Licensee: Morris Communications Corp. Group owner: Morris Communications Inc. (acq 12-24-97; $2.25 million. with KDGL(FM) Yucca Valley). Rep: CMBS. Haley, Bader & Potts. Format: Talk, sports. Spec prog: Relg 17 hrs wkly. ♦ William Morris, CEO; Michael Ostehaut, VP; Keith Martin, gen mgr; Larry Snider, chief of opns & chief of engrg.

Tipton

KCRZ(FM)— 1997: 104.9 mhz; 2.3 kw. 528 ft. TL: N36 10 07 W119 15 04. Stereo. 1401 W. Caldwell, Visalia 93277. Phone: (559) 553-1500. Fax: (559) 627-1496. Web Site: www.z1049.com. Licensee: Lemoore Wireless Co. Inc. Network: ABC. Format: Hot adult contemp. Target aud: 25-64. ♦ Wayne B. Foster, gen mgr.

Torrance

KFOX(AM)— January 1998: 1650 khz; 10 kw-D, 490 w-N. TL: N33 53 30 W118 11 03 (D), N33 53 30 W118 11 03 (N). 4525 Wilshire Blvd., 3rd Fl., Los Angeles 90010. Phone: (323) 935-0606. Fax: (323) 935-8885. Web Site: www.koreatimes.com. Licensee: Chagal Communications Inc. (acq 5-25-00; $30 million). Format: Adult contemp, Korean. ♦ Grant Chang, gen mgr.

Tracy

KMIX(FM)— Dec 14, 1966: 100.9 mhz; 6 kw. 328 ft. TL: N37 37 32 W121 23 58. Stereo. 6820 Pacific Ave., Suite 3, Stockton 95207. Phone: (209) 474-0154. Fax: (209) 474-0316. Web Site: www.lavuena.com. Licensee: Entravision Holdings LLC. Group owner: Entravision Communications Corp. (acq 7-28-00; grpsl). Format: Sp. ♦ Lisa Sunday, gen mgr; Cesar Medina, stn mgr.

*****KYKL(FM)**— 2004: 90.7 mhz; 210 w. Ant 1,745 ft. TL: N37 33 37 W121 36 19. Stereo. 5700 W. Oaks Blvd., Rocklin 95765. Phone: (916) 251-1600. Fax: (916) 251-1650. E-mail: klove@klove.com. Web Site: www.klove.com. Licensee: Educational Media Foundation. Group owner: EMF Broadcasting. Network: K-Love. Shaw Pittman. Format: Contemp Christian. News staff: 3. Target aud: 25-44; Judeo Christian, female. ♦ Richard Jenkins, pres; Mike Novak, VP; Lloyd Parker, gen mgr; Ed Lenane, opns dir; Keith Whipple, dev dir.

Truckee

KTKE(FM)—Not on air, target date: unknown: 101.5 mhz; 140 w. Ant 1,988 ft. TL: N39 14 29 W120 08 20. Truckster Broadcasting Inc., 2307 Princess Anne St., Greensboro, NC 27408. Phone: (336) 286-2087. Phone: (530) 587-9330. Licensee: Truckster Broadcasting Inc. Format: Soft Adult Contemp. ♦ Hartley Lesser, gen mgr & progmg dir.

Tulare

KBOS-FM—Licensed to Tulare. See Fresno

KGEN(AM)— 1957: 1370 khz; 1 kw-D, 136 w-N. TL: N36 10 51 W119 19 44. Box 2040 93275. Secondary address: 323 E. San Joaquin Ave. 93274. Phone: (559) 685-1370. Fax: (559) 685-1394. Licensee: Azteca Broadcasting Corp. (group owner) Format: Sp, Mexican. Target aud: General. ♦ Margaretia Hernandez, gen mgr.

KJUG(AM)—Licensed to Tulare. See Visalia

KJUG-FM—Licensed to Tulare. See Visalia

Tulelake

KFLS-FM— July 23, 1993: 96.5 mhz; 20 kw. 2,155 ft. TL: N42 05 50 W121 37 59. Stereo. Box 1450, Klamath Falls, OR 97601. Secondary address: 1338 Oregon Ave., Klamath Falls, OR 97601. Phone: (541) 882-4656. Fax: (541) 884-2845. E-mail: traffic@klamathradio.com.

Stations in the U.S. — California

Developers & Brokers of Radio Properties — contact American Media Services at our suite: Philadelphia Marriott Downtown 215-625-2900 • 843-972-2200 • americanmediaservices.com • Charleston, SC • Dallas, TX · Chicago, Il · Austin, TX — American Media Services, LLC

Web Site: www.klamathradio.com. Licensee: Wynne Enterprises LLC (group owner). Tacher. Format: Country. Target aud: 18-49. ♦ Robert Wynne, CEO, chmn, pres & gen mgr; Leslie Hougan, gen sls mgr; Randy Adams, progmg dir; Lyle Ahrens, news dir; Russ Jump, chief of engrg.

Turlock

*KBDG(FM)— January 1977: 90.9 mhz; 150 w. 94 ft. TL: N37 29 59 W120 49 41. (CP: 780 w). Box 192 95381. Secondary address: 1600 E. Canal Dr. 95380. Phone: (209) 668-7176. Fax: (209) 668-2322. Licensee: Assyrian American Civic Club. (acq 1-7-94; $17,000; 1-31-94). ♦ William Julian, pres; Zaia Sargies, stn mgr.

*KCSS(FM)— Aug 13, 1975: 91.9 mhz; 400 w. 112 ft. TL: N37 31 35 W120 51 25. 801 W. Monte Vista Ave. 95382. Phone: (209) 667-3378 (office). Phone: (209) 667-3900 (stn). Fax: (209) 667-3901. Web Site: www.kcss.net. Licensee: California State University, Stanislaus. Format: Div, blues, modern rock. Target aud: 18-54. Spec prog: Class 9 hrs, jazz 4 hrs, Americana 10 hrs, wkly. ♦ Greg Jacquay, gen mgr; Melissa Garcia, dev VP & dev dir.

KLOC(AM)— October 1949: 1390 khz; 5 kw-U, DA-2. TL: N37 31 48 W120 41 37. Box 1039, Hughson 95326. Phone: (209) 883-8760. Fax: (209) 883-8769. E-mail: ngomez@lafavorita.net. Web Site: www.lafavorita.net. Licensee: La Favorita Broadcasting Inc. (acq 5-16-03; $500,000). Format: Sp. ♦ Nelson Gomez, gen mgr.

KWNN(FM)— Mar 3, 1978: 98.3 mhz; 1.6 kw. 390 ft. TL: N37 34 46 W120 50 48. (CP: 2 kw). Stereo. 1581 Cummins Dr., Suite 100, Modesto 95358. Phone: (209) 476-1230. Fax: (209) 957-1833. Licensee: Citadel Broadcasting Co. Group owner: Citadel Broadcasting Corp. (acq 12-12-03). Rep: Christal. Format: Contemp hit/Top-40. ♦ Roy Williams, gen mgr; Jean Western, sls VP & gen sls mgr.

Twain Harte

KKBN(FM)— Oct 19, 1985: 93.5 mhz; 400 w. Ant 1,262 ft. TL: N38 00 30 W120 21 45. Stereo. 342 S. Washington St., Sonora 95370. Phone: (209) 533-1450. Fax: (209) 533-9520. E-mail: lenglandcbc@mlode.com. Web Site: www.kkbnfm.com. Licensee: Clarke Broadcasting Corp. (group owner; acq 3-1-00; $2.2 million). Leventhal, Senter & Lerman. Format: Country. News staff: 2; News: 4 hrs wkly. Target aud: 25-54; general. ♦ H. Randolph Holder Jr., pres; Larry England, gen mgr.

Twentynine Palms

KCDZ(FM)— July 15, 1989: 107.7 mhz; 7 kw. 328 ft. TL: N34 09 15 W116 11 50. Stereo. 6448 Hallee, Suite 5, Joshua Tree 92252. Phone: (760) 366-8471. Fax: (760) 366-2976. E-mail: z107@cci-29palms.com. Web Site: www.kcdzfm.com. Licensee: Morongo Basin Broadcasting Corp. Network: ABC. Richard S. Becker & Associates. Format: Adult contemp / CHR. News staff: 2; News: 10 hrs wkly. Target aud: 25-54; baby boomers. ♦ Cynthia M. Daigneault, pres & gen mgr; Gary Daigneault, exec VP & VP.

KNWH(AM)— Apr 3, 1961: 1250 khz; 1 kw-D, 105 w-N. TL: N34 08 11 W116 10 07. 1321 N. Gene Autry Trail, Palm Springs 92262. Phone: (760) 322-7890. Fax: (760) 322-5493. Web Site: www.desertfun.com. Licensee: MCC Radio LLC. (acq 1-12-2005; $100,000). Format: News/talk. ♦ William S. Morris IV, pres.

KXCM(FM)— Apr 1, 1965: 96.3 mhz; 6 kw. Ant 243 ft. TL: N34 09 15 W116 11 50. Stereo. Box 1437, Joshua Tree 92252. Phone: (760) 362-4264. E-mail: coppermountainbroadcasting@yahoo.com. Licensee: Copper Mountain Broadcasting Co. (acq 7-14-2004; $575,000. with KQCM(FM) Joshua Tree). Format: Country. ♦ Gary DeMaroney, gen mgr.

Ukiah

*KPRA(FM)— 1988: 89.5 mhz; 710 w. 1,135 ft. TL: N39 07 01 W123 13 54. 4135 Northgate Blvd., Sacramento 95834. Phone: (707) 468-8802. Licensee: Family Stations Inc. (group owner; acq 2-3-86). Format: Relg. ♦ Jeffrey Brown, opns mgr; Tom Driggers, chief of engrg.

KQPM(FM)— February 1989: 105.9 mhz; 2.9 kw. 2,017 ft. TL: N39 09 00 W123 12 30. 140 N. Main St., Lakeport 95453. Phone: (707) 263-6113. Phone: (707) 468-5336. Fax: (707) 263-0939. Licensee: Bicoastal Media L.L.C. (group owner; acq 7-28-99; grpsl). Format: Country. ♦ Ken Dennis, CEO; Mike Wilson, pres & gen mgr; Eric Patrick, opns mgr.

KUKI(AM)— Oct 1, 1950: 1400 khz; 1 kw-U. TL: N39 10 03 W123 13 02. 1400 KUKI Ln. 95482. Phone: (707) 466-5868. Web Site: www.kukifm.com. Licensee: MBU Licensee LLC. Group owner: Moon Broadcasting (acq 9-15-2003; grpsl). Pepper & Corazzini. Format: Foreign/ethnic. News staff: 2; News: 25 hrs wkly. Target aud: 25 plus; upwardly mobile adults. ♦ Tove Sorensen, VP, stn mgr, opns dir & mus dir; Fran Thomas, news dir.

KUKI-FM— Oct 16, 1974: 103.3 mhz; 2.8 kw. Ant 1,791 ft. TL: N39 19 36 W123 16 12. Stereo. Phone: (707) 466-5868. Fax: (707) 466-5852. Web Site: www.kukifm.com. Network: ABC. Format: Country. News staff: one; News: 7 hrs wkly. Target aud: 25-54.

*KULV(FM)— Sept 22, 2003: 97.1 mhz; 130 w. Ant 1,978 ft. TL: N39 07 50 W123 04 32. Stereo. 5700 W. Oaks Blvd., Rocklin 95765. Phone: (916) 251-1600. Fax: (916) 251-1650. E-mail: klove@klove.com. Web Site: www.klove.com. Licensee: Educational Media Foundation. Group owner: EMF Broadcasting. Network: K-Love. Shaw Pittman. Format: Contemp Chrisitan. News staff: 3. Target aud: 25-44; Judeo Christian, female. ♦ Richard Jenkins, pres; Mike Novak, VP; Lloyd Parker, gen mgr; Ed Lenane, opns dir; Keith Whipple, dev dir.

KWNE(FM)— 1968: 94.5 mhz; 2.15 kw. 2,053 ft. TL: N39 07 50 W123 04 32. Stereo. Box 1056 95482. Secondary address: 1100 Hastings Rd., Suite B 95482. Phone: (707) 462-1451. Phone: (707) 462-0945. Fax: (707) 462-4670. E-mail: kwine@kwine.com. Web Site: www.kwine.com. Licensee: Broadcasting Corp of Mendocino County. (acq 10-1-78). Borsari & Paxson. Format: Hot adult contemp. News staff: one; News: 12 hrs wkly. Target aud: 18-54; young adult. Spec prog: Sp 4 hrs, farm one hr wkly. ♦ Guilford Dye, pres & gen mgr; Gudrun Dye, VP; Mike Spencer, stn mgr.

Vacaville

KUIC(FM)— Nov 1, 1968: 95.3 mhz; 4.3 kw. 280 ft. TL: N38 17 56 W121 59 54. (CP: 594 w, ant 1,948 ft. TL: N38 23 48 W122 06 03). Stereo. KUIC Plaza, 600 E. Main St. 95688. Phone: (707) 446-0200. Fax: (707) 446-0122. Web Site: www.kuic.com. Licensee: KUIC Inc. (acq 10-6-98). Garvey, Schubert & Barer. Format: Adult contemp. News staff: 3; News: one hr wkly. Target aud: General; middle class, professionals. ♦ Jim Levitt, CEO; John Levitt, pres, CFO & gen mgr.

Vallejo

KDIA(AM)— Mar 19, 1996: 1640 khz; 10 kw-D, 1 kw-N. TL: N38 07 04 W122 15 24. Stereo. 3260 Blume Dr., Richmond 95806. Phone: (510) 222-4242. Fax: (510) 262-9054. E-mail: andy.santamaria@kdia.com. Web Site: www.kdia.com. Licensee: Baybridge Communications L.L.C. Format: Teaching Ministries. News: 5 hrs wkly. Target aud: 25-54. Spec prog: Relg 5 hrs, Black 2 hrs, gospel 7 hrs wkly. ♦ Andy Santamaria, gen mgr.

KDYA(AM)— Aug 1, 1947: 1190 khz; 1 kw-D. TL: N38 07 04 W122 15 24. (Also 1640 khz; 10 kw-D, 1 kw-N). Stereo. 3260 Blume Dr. Richmond 95806. Phone: (510) 222-4242. Fax: (510) 262-9054. E-mail: andy.santamaria@gospel1190.net. Web Site: www.gospel1190.net. Licensee: Baybridge Communications L.L.C. (acq 1-29-99). Format: Gospel. News: 5 hrs wkly. Target aud: 25-54. Spec prog: Relg 5 hrs, Black 2 hrs, gospel 7 hrs wkly. ♦ Andy Santamaria, pres & gen mgr; Clifford Brown, opns mgr.

Ventura

KBBY-FM— Dec 27, 1962: 95.1 mhz; 10.8 kw. 925 ft. TL: N34 14 12 W119 12 11. 1376 Walters St. 93003. Phone: (805) 642-8595. Fax: (805) 656-5838. Web Site: www.cumulus.com. Licensee: Cumulus Licensing Corp. Group owner: Cumulus Media Inc. (acq 9-22-00; grpsl). Network: Westwood One. Format: Hot Adult Contemp. Target aud: 18-54. ♦ Gail Furillo, gen mgr; J.D. Strahler, opns mgr.

KCAQ(FM)—See Oxnard

KHAY(FM)—Listing follows KVEN(AM).

KKZZ(AM)— Oct 15, 1994: 1590 khz; 5 kw-U, DA-2. TL: N34 14 12 W119 12 11. 2284 S. Victoria, Suite 2G 93003. Phone: (805) 289-1400. Fax: (805) 644-7906. Web Site: www.1590kkzz.com. Licensee: Gold Coast Broadcasting LLC (group owner; acq 2-10-97; $2 million. with KFYV(FM) Ojai). Format: Adult standards. Target aud: 35 plus. ♦ Chip Ehrhardt, gen mgr.

KLJR-FM—See Santa Paula

KOCP(FM)—See Camarillo

KSSC(FM)— November 1989: 107.1 mhz; 280 w. 872 ft. TL: N34 18 10 W119 13 45. (CP: 420 w). Stereo. 5700 Wilshire Blvd., Suite 250, Los Angeles 90036. Phone: (805) 648-2807. Fax: (323) 900-6200. Web Site: www.1071superstriella.com. Licensee: Entravision Holdings LLC. Group owner: Entravision Communications Corp. (acq 4-1-03; grpsl). Format: Contemp Sp. ♦ Karl Meyer, gen mgr.

KUNX(AM)—See Santa Paula

KVEN(AM)— March 1948: 1450 khz; 1 kw-U. TL: N34 15 39 W119 14 28. 1376 Walter St. 93003. Phone: (805) 642-8595. Fax: (805) 656-5838. Web Site: www.kven.com. Licensee: Cumulus Licensing Corp. Group owner: Cumulus Media Inc. (acq 9-22-00; grpsl). Network: ABC Information & Entertainment. Erwin Krasnow. Format: Hits of the 50s & 60s. Target aud: 25 plus; affluent, educated, professional with above average income. ♦ Gail Fruillo, gen mgr & stn mgr; Ernie Bingham, gen sls mgr; James Wortman, prom mgr; Brian D. Wilson, news dir; J.D. Strahler, chief of engrg.

KHAY(FM)— Co-owned with KVEN(AM). Jan 1, 1962: 100.7 mhz; 39 kw. 1,210 ft. TL: N34 20 55 W119 19 57. Stereo. Phone: (805) 642-8595. Fax: (805) 656-5838. Web Site: www.khay.com. Format: Country. Target aud: 18-54. ♦ Mark Hill, progmg dir.

KVTA(AM)—See Port Hueneme

Victorville

KATJ-FM—See George

*KHMS(FM)— Jan 3, 1993: 88.5 mhz; 200 w. 1,512 ft. TL: N34 36 40 W117 17 20. c/o Faith Communications Corp., 2201 S. 6th St., Las Vegas, NV 89104. Phone: (702) 731-5452. Fax: (702) 731-1992. Web Site: www.sosradio.net. Licensee: Faith Communications Corp. (acq 4-5-91; 4-22-91). Cohn & Marks. Format: Adult contemp, Christian. Target aud: 25-44; young families. ♦ Brad Staley, gen mgr.

KIXW(AM)—See Apple Valley

KRSX(AM)— Sept 1, 1961: 1590 khz; 500 w-D, 135 w-N. TL: N34 32 15 W117 18 42. 15700 Village Dr., Suite A 92394. Phone: (760) 243-7903. Fax: (760) 243-7183. E-mail: quebuenavicyorville@yahoo.com. Licensee: Rudex Broadcasting Limited Corp. (acq 3-19-2004; $176,005). Format: Sp, Regional Mexican. Target aud: 18-34 & 14-57; Primary 18-34 Secondary 14-57. ♦ John Cooper, pres; Dino Mercado, gen sls mgr.

KVFG(FM)— Aug 18, 1980: 103.1 mhz; 95 w. 1,424 ft. TL: N34 36 45 W117 17 31. (CP: 310 w, ant 1,401 ft.). Stereo. 11920 Hesperia Rd.,

California

Hesperia 92345. Phone: (760) 244-2000. Fax: (760) 244-1198. Web Site: www.kfrog103.com. Licensee: Infinity Radio Inc. Group owner: Infinity Broadcasting Corp. (acq 7-19-00; $3,537,500. with KRAK(AM) Hesperia). Network: ABC. Fleischman & Walsh. Format: Country. Target aud: 25-54. ◆John Covington, stn mgr; Tom Hoyt, gen mgr & opns mgr.

*KXRD(FM)— Oct 18, 1994: 89.5 mhz; 1.25 kw. 1,410 ft. TL: N34 36 44 W117 17 27. Box 1000, 35225 Ave. A, Suite 105, Yucaipa 92399. Phone: (909) 790-1849. Phone: (888) 417-2014. Fax: (916) 251-1650. Web Site: www.airl.com. Licensee: Educational Media Foundation. Group owner: EMF Broadcasting (acq 1-22-99). Network: Air 1. Format: Contemp Christian. News: 7 hrs wkly. Target aud: 18-34. ◆Tim Bromleewe, gen mgr; Andy Ramirez, rgnl sls mgr.

KZXY-FM—See Apple Valley

Visalia

*KARM(FM)— 1990: 89.7 mhz; 1 kw. 810 ft. TL: N36 38 10 W118 56 32. 1300 S. Woodland Dr. 93277. Phone: (559) 627-5276. Fax: (559) 627-5288. E-mail: karm@karm.com. Web Site: www.karm.com. Licensee: Harvest Broadcasting Co. Network: ABC. Format: Inspirational, Christian. ◆Dr. Frank Baughman, chmn; Loren Olson, gen mgr.

*KDUV(FM)— Jan 1, 1992: 88.9 mhz; 1 kw. 2,647 ft. TL: N36 17 14 W118 50 17. 130 N. Kelsey, Suite H-1 93291. Phone: (559) 651-4111. Fax: (559) 651-4115. Web Site: www.kduvfm.com. Licensee: Community Educational Broadcasting Inc. Format: Christian hit radio. ◆Bob Croft, gen mgr.

KFSO-FM—Listing follows KVBL(AM).

KJUG(AM)— (Tulare). Aug 1, 1946: 1270 khz; 5 kw-D, 1 kw-N, DA-N. TL: N36 13 10 W119 18 51. 717 N. Mooney Blvd., Tulare 93274. Phone: (559) 686-2866. Fax: (559) 686-7265. Web Site: www.kjugfm.com. Licensee: Westcoast Broadcasting Inc. (acq 5-1-81). Network: ABC Information & Entertainment. Format: Classic country. News staff: one; News: 7 hrs wkly. Target aud: 25-49. Spec prog: Farm 5 hrs wkly. ◆Larry W. Woods, pres; Wayne B. Foster, gen mgr; Charlie Hoskins, gen sls mgr; Dave Daniels, prom dir & progmg dir; Paul Kleinkramer, chief of engrg.

KJUG-FM— May 6, 1965: 106.7 mhz; 1.2 kw. 6,100 ft. TL: N36 17 08 W118 50 17. Stereo. Web Site: www.kjugfm.com. Format: Today's country. Target aud: 18-54.

KSEQ(FM)— October 1984: 97.1 mhz; 17 kw. 777 ft. TL: N36 38 08 W118 56 32. Stereo. 617 W. Tulare Ave. 93277. Phone: (559) 627-9710. Fax: (559) 627-1590. Web Site: www.q97.com. Licensee: Buckley Broadcasting of Monterey. Group owner: Buckley Broadcasting Corp. (acq 12-87). Rep: D & R Radio. Format: CHR. Target aud: 18-49. ◆Rick Buckley, pres; Ray McCarty, VP & gen mgr; Alexa Smith, opns dir.

KSLK(FM)— Nov 22, 1994: 96.1 mhz; 4.8 kw. Ant 360 ft. TL: N36 21 59 W119 10 46. Stereo. 1450 E. Bardsley Ave., Tulare 93274. Phone: (559) 687-3170. Fax: (559) 687-3175. Web Site: www.moonbroadcasting.com. Licensee: New Visalia Broadcasting Inc. Format: Sp contemp. ◆Robert Eurich, pres; Irene Cruz, gen mgr.

KVBL(AM)— January 1948: 1400 khz; 1 kw-U. TL: N36 21 14 W119 17 02. 83 E. Shaw Ave, Suite 150, Fresno 93710-7616. Phone: (559) 230-4300. Fax: (209) 591-1130. Licensee: Capstar TX L.P. Group owner: Clear Channel Communications Inc. (acq 8-30-00; grpsl). Rep: McGavren Guild. Format: Sports. Target aud: 25-64; general.

KFSO-FM—Co-owned with KVBL(AM). Sept 1, 1951: 92.9 mhz; 18.5 kw horiz, 17 kw vert. 820 ft. TL: N36 38 10 W118 56 33. (CP: 17.5 kw, ant 853 ft. TL: N36 38 10 W118 56 34). Stereo. Web Site: www.kfso.com. Format: Oldies.

Vista

KCEO(AM)— Nov 3, 1967: 1000 khz; 2.5 kw-D, 250 w-N, DA-2. TL: N33 13 59 W117 16 09. 1835 Aston Ave., Carlsbad 92008. Phone: (760) 729-1000. Fax: (760) 476-9604. Web Site: www.kceoradio.com. Licensee: North County Broadcasting Corp. Group owner: Astor Broadcast Group (acq 4-30-97; $2.6 million). Network: Westwood One. Format: Talk. News: 20 hrs wkly. Target aud: 35 plus. ◆Arthur Astor, pres; Susan E. Burke, exec VP; Rick Rone, opns dir & opns mgr.

Walnut

*KSAK(FM)— Jan 10, 1974: 90.1 mhz; 3.5 w. 460 ft. TL: N34 02 53 W117 51 43. (CP: Ant 410 ft.). 1100 N. Grand Ave. 91789. Phone: (909) 594-5611, EXT. 4678. Web Site: www.ksak.com. Licensee: Mount San Antonio Community College District. Format: Christian, urban contemp, modern rock. Target aud: 18-25; students. ◆Cason Smith, gen mgr & opns mgr.

Walnut Creek

KKDV(FM)— Dec 10, 1959: 92.1 mhz; 3 kw. Ant 89 ft. TL: N37 53 59 W122 05 38. Stereo. 1660 Olympic Blvd., Suite 215 94596. Phone: (925) 825-9000. Fax: (925) 287-7801. Web Site: www.ksjo.com. Licensee: Contra Costa County Radio Inc. (acq 7-29-2005; $7 million). Rep: Caballero. Lotus. Format: Adult contemp. Target aud: 18-49. ◆Jack Chunn, gen mgr; Justin Wittmayer, gen sls mgr & natl sls mgr; Clark Reid, progmg dir.

Wasco

*KFHL(FM)—Not on air, target date: unknown:. Stn currently dark 91.7 mhz; 6 kw. Ant 289 ft. TL: N35 24 55 W119 14 01. Box 7346, Las Vegas, NV 89125. Phone: (909) 796-5717. Licensee: Mary V. Harris Foundation.

Wasco-Greenacres

KERI(AM)— May 17, 1950: 1180 khz; 50 kw-D, 10 kw-N, DA-2. TL: N35 34 17 W119 19 26. 1400 Easton Dr., Suite 144, Bakersfield 93309. Phone: (661) 328-1410. Fax: (661) 328-0873. E-mail: keri@keri.com. Web Site: www.keri.com. Licensee: AGM California. Group owner: American General Media (acq 9-27-2004; $1.83 million). Format: Family talk, relg. ◆Roger Fessler, gen mgr.

Weaverville

KHRD(FM)— 2000: 103.1 mhz; 600 w. Ant 3,592 ft. TL: N40 36 10 W122 38 58. 1588 Charles Dr., Redding 96003. Phone: (530) 244-9700. Fax: (530) 244-9707. Web Site: www.red1031.com. Licensee: Results Radio of Redding Licensee LLC. Group owner: Fritz Communications Inc. (acq 6-11-99; grpsl). Format: Classic rock. ◆Beth Tappan, gen mgr; Carmy Ferrari, opns mgr & progmg dir; Laurie Curto, gen sls mgr; Bryant Smith, chief of engrg.

KWCA(FM)—Not on air, target date: unknown: 101.1 mhz; 250 w. Ant 1,555 ft. TL: N40 41 05 W122 44 56. 203 Center St. Phone: (530) 623-2600. Fax: (530) 623-2600. Licensee: George S. Flinn Jr. Format: AAA. ◆George S. Flinn Jr., gen mgr.

Weed

KNTK(FM)— November 1983: 102.3 mhz; 5.5 kw. 1,437 ft. TL: N41 21 12 W122 15 35. Stereo. 1934 S. Mt. Shasta Blvd., Mount Shasta 96094. Phone: (530) 926-5946. Fax: (530) 926-0830. E-mail: kntk@sbcgobal.net. Licensee: Four Rivers Broadcasting Inc. (group owner; (acq 7-21-2005; grpsl). Network: ABC Information & Entertainment. Format: News/talk. News staff: one; News: 6 hrs wkly. Target aud: 25-54. Spec prog: Nostalgia 2 hrs wkly. ◆John Anthony, gen mgr.

West Covina

KALI(AM)— Sept 25, 1963: 900 khz; 500 w-D, DA. TL: N34 01 54 W117 56 06. 747 E. Green St., Suite 400, Pasadena 91101. Phone: (626) 844-8882. Fax: (626) 844-0156. Web Site: www.mrbi.net. Licensee: Multicultural Radio Broadcasting Licensee LLC. Group owner: Multicultural Radio Broadcasting Inc. (acq 10-5-98; $9 million). Format: Sp Christian. ◆Arthur S. Liu, pres; David Sweeney, VP, gen mgr, opns VP & opns VP.

KRCV(FM)— Nov 18, 1957: 98.3 mhz; 2.3 w. 328 ft. TL: N34 01 22 W117 56 15. (CP: 650 w, ant 971 ft.). Stereo. 655 N Central Ave, Suite 2500, Glendale 91203-1422. Phone: (818) 500-4500. Fax: (818) 500-4560. Licensee: HBC License Corp. Group owner: Univision Radio (acq 9-22-2003; grpsl). Rep: Caballero. Format: Sp oldies. News: 3 hrs wkly. Target aud: 18-49; Sp speaking Hispanics, primarily of Mexican origin. ◆Roaldo Moran, gen sls mgr; Amalia Gonzalez, progmg dir; Tom Koza, chief of engrg.

Directory of Radio

West Sacramento

KSMH(AM)— February 1999: 1620 khz; 10 kw-D, 1 kw-N. TL: N38 35 17 W121 28 05. Box 7635, Stockton 95267. Phone: (209) 462-8307. Web Site: www.ihradio.org. Licensee: IHR Educational Broadcasting. (group owner; (acq 4-28-99; $475,000. with KAHI(AM) Auburn). Format: Relg/Catholic. ◆Joseph Nesta, stn mgr.

Westwood

KTOR(FM)— 2003: 99.7 mhz; 90 w. Ant 2,483 ft. TL: N40 14 21 W121 01 52. Box 2371, Chico 95927. Phone: (530) 256-2400. Fax: (530) 256-3780. E-mail: ktor@frontiernet.net. Licensee: Sierra Radio Inc. (acq 9-4-2002; for 51% of CP). Format: Classic rock. ◆Eileen Majors, gen mgr; Justin Miller, opns mgr.

Williams

*KARA(FM)— Oct 28, 2003: 99.1 mhz; 900 w. Ant 108 ft. TL: N39 08 07 W122 07 58. Stereo. 5700 W. Oaks Blvd., Rocklin 95765. Phone: (916) 251-1600. Fax: (916) 251-1650. E-mail: klove@klove.com. Web Site: www.klove.com. Licensee: Educational Media Foundation. Group owner: EMF Broadcasting. Network: Air 1. Shaw Pittman. Format: Contemp Christian. News staff: 3. Target aud: 18-35; Judeo-Christian, female. ◆Richard Jenkins, pres; Mike Novak, VP; Lloyd Parker, gen mgr; Keith Whipple, dev dir.

Willits

KLLK(AM)— Aug 5, 1985: 1250 khz; 5.4 kw-D, 2.7 kw-N, DA-2. TL: N39 23 58 W123 19 20. 1400 Kuki Ln., Ukiah 95482. Phone: (707) 466-5868. Fax: (707) 466-5852. Web Site: www.lamaquinamusical.net. Licensee: MBU Licensee LLC. Group owner: Moon Broadcasting (acq 9-15-2003; grpsl). Haley, Bader & Potts. Format: Regional Mexican. News: 8 hrs wkly. Target aud: 18-49; adults who like a progsv mix of modern rock mus. ◆Tove Sorensen, VP, stn mgr & opns dir.

KMKX(FM)— Feb 19, 2000: 93.5 mhz; 890 w. Ant 2,873 ft. TL: N39 30 59 W123 05 21. Stereo. Box 1056, Ukiah 95482. Phone: (707) 462-1483. Fax: (707) 459-6629. Fax: (707) 462-4670. Web Site: www.maxrocks.com. Licensee: Radio Millennium L L C (acq 2-3-00). Network: Westwood One. Borsari & Paxson. Format: AOR. News staff: one; News: 1 hr wkly. Target aud: 18-60; adults. ◆Guilford Dye, pres & gen mgr; Gudrun Dye, VP; Mike Spencer, stn mgr.

*KZYZ(FM)— 1995: 91.5 mhz; 600 w. 1,820 ft. Stereo. Box 1, Philo 95466. Phone: (707) 895-2324. Fax: (707) 895-2451. E-mail: kzyx@pacific.net. Web Site: www.kzyx.org. Licensee: Mendocino County Public Broadcasting. Format: News, talk radio, div music. ◆Mitchell Holman, gen mgr; Burton Segall, opns dir; Mary Aigner, dev dir & sls dir.

Willows

KCHC(FM)—Not on air, target date: unknown: 106.3 mhz; 6 kw. Ant 328 ft. TL: N39 29 30 W121 56 51. Pacific Spanish Network Inc., 296 H St., 2nd Fl., Chula Vista 91910. Phone: (858) 279-9844. Licensee: Pacific Spanish Network Inc.

KIQS(AM)— Dec 29, 1961: 1560 khz; 250 w-D. TL: N39 31 44 W122 10 09. 1564 Arlington Ct., Turlock 95382. Phone: (209) 277-8433. Licensee: Radio Pan de Vida LLC Group owner: Huth Broadcasting (acq 1-14-2005; $400,000). Law office of Dennis J. Kelly. ◆Martin Alberto Godinez, gen mgr.

Windsor

KMHX(FM)— June 20, 1997: 104.1 mhz; 250 w. 1,105 ft. TL: N38 32 24 W122 57 39. Stereo. 6640 Redwood Dr. #202, Rohnert Park 94928. Phone: (707) 584-1058. Fax: (707) 584-7944. Web Site: www.mix1041.com. Licensee: Results Radio of Sonoma Licensee LLC. Group owner: Fritz Communications Inc. (acq 10-22-98; $1,331,930). Rep: Christal. Covington & Burling. Format: Hot adult contemp. Target aud: 25-54. ◆Neysa Hinton, gen mgr.

Winton

KLOQ-FM— 1994: 98.7 mhz; 6 kw. 246 ft. TL: N37 16 42 W120 37 33. (CP: Ant 298 ft. TL: N37 16 41 W120 37 35). 1020 W. Main St., Merced 95340. Phone: (209) 723-2191. Fax: (209) 383-2950. E-mail: ynavarro@radiomerced.com. Licensee: Mapleton Communications

Stations in the U.S. — Colorado

Developers & Brokers of Radio Properties — contact American Media Services at our suite: Philadelphia Marriott Downtown 215-625-2900 / 843-972-2200 / americanmediaservices.com / Charleston, SC / Dallas, TX • Chicago, Il • Austin, TX / American Media Services, LLC

LLC (group owner; acq 6-1-2002; grpsl). Leventhal, Senter & Lerman. Format: Mexican rgnl. Target aud: 25-49; Hispanic. ♦Kelly Leonard, gen mgr & opns mgr.

Woodlake

KFRR(FM)— September 1994: 104.1 mhz; 17 kw. 853 ft. TL: N36 38 12 W118 56 34. 1066 E. Shaw Ave., Fresno 93710. Phone: (559) 230-0104. Fax: (559) 230-0177. Licensee: Wilks License Co.-Fresno LLC. (acq 6-1-2005; grpsl). Arter & Hadden. Format: Alternative. Target aud: 18-34; young affluent adults. ♦Jody Rosen, gen mgr.

Woodland

KSFM(FM)—Licensed to Woodland. See Sacramento

KTKZ(AM)—See Sacramento

Yermo

KRSX-FM— December 1996: 105.3 mhz; 400 w. Ant 1,037 ft. TL: N34 48 30 W116 41 01. 12370 Hesperia Rd, Suite 105 Victorville 92395. Phone: (760) 241-1313. Fax: (760) 241-0205. Web Site: www.kissfm1053.com. Licensee: Citicasters Licenses L.P. Group owner: Clear Channel Communications Inc. (acq 5-4-99; grpsl). Pepper & Corazzini. Format: Oldies. News staff: one. Target aud: 18-49; young adults, families. ♦Larry Thornhill, gen mgr; Coleen Quinn, opns mgr.

KRXV(FM)— April 1980: 98.1 mhz; 1.1 kw. Ant 2,280 ft. TL: N34 59 43 W116 50 15. Stereo. Box 1668, 1611 E. Main St., Barstow 92312. Phone: (760) 256-0326. Fax: (760) 256-9507. E-mail: tim@highwayradio.com. Web Site: www.thehighwaystations.com. Licensee: KHWY Inc. Network: AP Radio. Hogan & Hartson. Format: Adult contemp. News staff: one; News: 28 hrs wkly. Target aud: 35 plus; travelers on I-15 & I-40 & loc communities. ♦Howard B. Anderson, CEO & pres; Kirk M. Anderson, exec VP & VP; Timothy B. Anderson, VP; Timothy B. Anderson, gen mgr; Judy Robinson, sls VP & gen sls mgr; John McNeil, mktg mgr & chief of engrg; Lance Todd, progmg dir.

Yreka

*KNYR(FM)— 1995: 91.3 mhz; 400 w. Ant 2,365 ft. TL: N41 36 36 W122 37 26. Jefferson Public Radio, 1250 Siskiyou Blvd., Ashland, OR 97520. Phone: (541) 552-6301. Fax: (541) 552-8565. Web Site: www.jeffnet.org. Licensee: The State of Oregon, Acting By and Through the State Board of Higher Education for the Benefit of Southern Oregon University. Network: Network: NPR, PRI. Ernest Sanchez. Format: Class, news. News staff: one; News: 35 hrs wkly. ♦Ronald Kramer, CEO & gen mgr; Bryon Lambert, opns dir; Paul Westhelle, dev dir & mktg dir; Eric Teel, progmg dir; Eric Alan, mus dir; Darin Ransom, engrg dir.

*KSYC(AM)— July 27, 1947: 1490 khz; 1 kw-U. TL: N41 43 28 W122 39 00. Jefferson Public Radio, 1250 Siskiyou Blvd., Ashland, OR 97520. Phone: (541) 552-6301. Web Site: www.jeffnet.org. Licensee: JPR Foundation Inc. (acq 8-8-02; $300,000. with KMJC(AM) Mount Shasta). Network: Network: NPR, PRI. Ernest Sanchez. News staff: one; News: 35 hrs wkly. ♦Mitchell Christian, CFO; Ronald Kramer, CEO & gen mgr; Bryon Lambert, opns dir; Paul Westhelle, dev dir & mktg dir; Eric Teel, progmg dir; Eric Alan, mus dir; Darin Ransom, engrg dir.

KSYC-FM— June 1, 1983: 103.9 mhz; 10 kw. 2,364 ft. TL: N41 43 28 W122 37 46. Stereo. Box 1729 96097. Secondary address: 316 Lawrence Ln. 96097. Phone: (530) 842-4158. Fax: (530) 842-7635. Licensee: Four Rivers Broadcasting Inc. (group owner; (acq 7-21-2005; grpsl). Baraff, Koerner & Olender. Format: Country. ♦John Anthony, gen mgr; Bill Jacobs, opns mgr.

Yuba City

KMYC(AM)—See Marysville

KOBO(AM)— June 1953: 1450 khz; 500 w-D, 1 kw-N. TL: N39 08 07 W121 36 41. Box 669, Marysville 95901. Phone: (530) 742-5555. Fax: (530) 741-3758. Licensee: Tom F. Huth. Group owner: Huth Broadcasting (acq 12-17-2003; $200,000). Format: Sp, ethnic. Spec prog: East Indian 3 hrs wkly. ♦Thomas Huth, CEO & gen mgr.

KUBA(AM)— January 1948: 1600 khz; 5 kw-D, 2.5 kw-N, DA-N. TL: N39 06 22 W121 39 18. Drawer 232 95992-0232. Secondary address: 1479 Sanborn Rd. 95992. Phone: (530) 673-1600. Fax: (530) 673-1917. E-mail: harlan@succeed.net. Web Site: www.kuba1600.com. Licensee: Scope Planning & Engineering Inc. Group owner: Nevada County Broadcasting Inc. (acq 8-9-2004; $500,000). Rep: Roslin. Koteen & Naftalin. Format: Adult standards, news. News staff: 2; News: 15 hrs wkly. Target aud: 35-64; community oriented. Spec prog: Farm 4 hrs, Punjabi Indian 4 hrs, gospel 2 hrs, relg 2 hrs wkly. ♦Dave Bear, opns mgr, prom dir, progmg dir & chief of engrg; Robert R. Harlan, gen mgr, sls dir, gen sls mgr & mktg dir; Chris Gilbert, news dir; Lucy Spears, pub affrs dir.

Yucaipa

*KLRD(FM)— July 15, 1986: 90.1 mhz; 300 w. 1,024 ft. TL: N34 02 19 W116 57 09. Village Plaza, 35225 Ave. A,, Suite 105 92399. Phone: (909) 790-1849. Fax: (909) 790-0228. E-mail: aramirez@emfbroadcasting.com. Licensee: Educational Media Foundation. Group owner: EMF Broadcasting (acq 1-22-99). Network: USA. Shaw Pittman. Format: Alternative rock, div. News: 7 hrs wkly. Target aud: 18-34; Christians. ♦Andy Ramirez, stn mgr.

Yucca Valley

KDGL(FM)— August 1988: 106.9 mhz; 4 kw. 1,371 ft. TL: N34 04 55 W116 20 32. Stereo. 1321 N. Gene Autry Trail, Palm Springs 92262. Phone: (760) 322-9890. Fax: (760) 322-5493. Web Site: www.desertfun.com. Licensee: MCC Radio LLC. Group owner: Morris Radio LLC (acq 1998; $2.25 million. with KXPS(AM) Thousand Palms). Network: USA. Format: Classic Hits. Target aud: 25 plus. ♦William Morris III, chmn & pres; Darrel Fry, CFO; Michael Oslehaut, sr VP & VP; Keith Martin, gen mgr; Larry Snider, opns dir.

Colorado

Alamosa

KALQ-FM—Listing follows KGIW(AM).

*KASF(FM)— 1967: 90.9 mhz; 17 w. 121 ft. TL: N37 28 20 W105 52 39. Stereo. Adams State College, 110 Richardson Ave. 81102. Phone: (719) 587-7871. Phone: (719) 587-7154. Fax: (719) 587-7522. Web Site: www.adams.edu. Licensee: Adams State College. Format: CHR, AOR, urban contemp. News: one hr wkly. Target aud: Community; college and local. Spec prog: Gospel 4 hrs, talk 6 hrs, blues/jazz 6 hrs, reggae 5 hrs wkly. ♦Beth Dussault, gen mgr.

KGIW(AM)— Feb 27, 1929: 1450 khz; 1 kw-U. TL: N37 28 20 W105 51 13. Box 179, 292 Santa Fe 81101. Phone: (719) 589-6644. Phone: (719) 589-6645. Fax: (719) 589-0993. Licensee: Community Broadcasting Corp. (acq 1964). Network: ABC Information & Entertainment. Format: Oldies. News staff: one; News: 25 hrs wkly. Target aud: 18-60. Spec prog: Sp 6 hrs, farm 6 hrs wkly. ♦Dale K. Burns, pres; Marilyn Burns, exec VP; Neil J. Hammer, gen mgr & progmg dir; Helen Lozoya, gen sls mgr; Mark Beatty, news dir; Will Williams, chief of engrg.

KALQ-FM—Co-owned with KGIW(AM). June 26, 1969: 93.5 mhz; 2.8 kw. 130 ft. TL: N37 28 20 W105 51 13. Stereo. Format: Country. ♦Patsy Garcia, opns mgr.

*KRZA(FM)— Oct 26, 1985: 88.7 mhz; 9.8 kw. 2,076 ft. TL: N36 51 32 W106 00 28. Stereo. 528 9th St. 81101. Phone: (719) 589-9057. Fax: (719) 587-0032. Web Site: www.krza.org. Licensee: Equal Representation of Media Advocacy Corp. Network: NPR. Format: News, jazz,various. News staff: one; News: 18 hrs wkly. Target aud: General; adult progsv community oriented rural area. Spec prog: Sp 14 hrs, Latin American 3 hrs, news 4 hrs wkly. ♦Christine Taylor, gen mgr & stn mgr.

Arvada

KDDZ(AM)— June 1998: 1690 khz; 10 kw-D, 1 kw-N. TL: N39 39 21 W105 04 27. 12136 W. Bayaud Ave., Suite 125, Lakewood 80228. Phone: (303) 783-0880. Fax: (303) 761-1774. Web Site: www.radiodisney.com. Licensee: Radio Disney Group LLC. Group owner: ABC Inc. (acq 7-16-98; $3.5 million. with KADZ Arvada). Network: Radio Disney. Format: Children. ♦Ronda Sheya, gen mgr.

Aspen

*KAJX(FM)— July 7, 1987: 91.5 mhz; 380 w horiz, 370 w vert. Ant -987 ft. TL: N39 11 48 W106 48 14. Stereo. 110 E. Hallam St., Suite 134 81611. Phone: (970) 925-5259. Fax: (970) 544-8002. Web Site: www.kajx.org. Licensee: Roaring Fork Public Radio Translators Inc. (acq 1996). Network: Network: NPR, PRI. Format: Class, jazz, news. News staff: one; News: 50 hrs wkly. Target aud: General; Aspen residents & tourists. Spec prog: Bluegrass, folk 4 hrs wkly. ♦Brent Gardner-Smith, gen mgr; Michael Waters, stn mgr.

KPVW(FM)— 2000: 107.1 mhz; 20.5 kw. Ant 361 ft. TL: N39 18 56 W106 57 32. Stereo. Entravision Holdings LLC, Suite 6000, 2425 Olympic Blvd., Santa Monica, CA 90404. Secondary address: 5700 Wilshire Blvd #250, Los Angeles, CA 90036-3659. Phone: (970) 927-6902. Fax: (970) 927-8001. E-mail: jeloy@entravision.com. Licensee: Entravision Holdings LLC. Group owner: Entravision Communications Corp. (acq 12-13-01; $57,500). Format: Rgnl Mexican. Target aud: Latino; 18-34. ♦Philip Wilkinson, COO; Walter Ulloa, CEO & chmn; Jeffery A. Liberman, pres; John DeLorenzo, CFO; Mario Carrera, gen mgr; Jesus Eloy Montes de Oca, stn mgr.

KSNO-FM—See Snowmass Village

KSPN-FM— Feb 14, 1970: 103.1 mhz; 3 kw. Ant -85 ft. TL: N39 13 33 W106 50 00. Stereo. Bldg 402 D, Airport Business Center 81611. Phone: (970) 925-5776. Fax: (970) 925-1142. E-mail: kspnlive@liveradio.com. Web Site: www.kspnradio.com. Licensee: NRC Mountain Division LLC. (group owner; (acq 7-9-2004; grpsl). Rep: Christal. Rosenman & Colin. Format: AAA. News staff: 2; News: 6 hrs wkly. Target aud: 25-49; affluent, well educated people who live in resort areas. ♦Colleen Barill, gen mgr; David Bach, chief of opns.

Aurora

KEZW(AM)— 1954: 1430 khz; 5 kw-U, DA-N. TL: N39 12 28 W104 55 46. Stereo. 4700 S. Syracuse St., Suite 1050, Denver 80237. Phone: (303) 967-2700. Fax: (303) 967-2747. Web Site: KEZW.com. Licensee: Entercom Denver License LLC. Group owner: Entercom Communications Corp. (acq 7-24-02; with KOSI(FM) Denver). Rep: Katz Radio. Format: Nostalgia, big band, MOR. News: 4 hrs wkly. Target aud: 35 plus; general. Spec prog: Adult standards. ♦Jerry McKenna, VP & gen mgr; Miles Schallert, gen sls mgr & rgnl sls mgr; Rick Crandall, progmg dir & progmg mgr; Jeff Garrett, chief of engrg.

KMXA(AM)—Licensed to Aurora. See Denver

KOSI(FM)—See Denver

Avon

KZYR(FM)— Dec 24, 1984: 97.7 mhz; 15 kw. Ant 440 ft. TL: N39 38 05 W106 26 47. Stereo. Box 6806 81620. Secondary address: 82 E. Beaver Creek Blvd., Suite 205 A 81620. Phone: (970) 845-8565. Fax: (970) 845-8612. Licensee: Cool Radio LLC (acq 12-3-2001; $1.5 million. with KSNO-FM Snowmass Village). Cole, Raywid & Braverman. Format: AAA. Target aud: 18-54. ♦Thomas Dobrez, CEO & pres; Tony Mauro, gen mgr.

Colorado

Basalt

KNFO(FM)— July 1995: 106.1 mhz; 2 kw. 364 ft. TL: N39 18 55 W106 57 36. 402D AABC, Aspen 81611. Phone: (970) 544-9100. Fax: (970) 925-1142. Licensee: NRC Mountain Division LLC. (group owner; (acq 7-9-2004); grpsl). Network: CBS. Rosenman & Colin. Format: News, talk, sports. News staff: 2; News: 13 hrs wkly. Target aud: 35-64. ◆Tim Brown, CEO; Ray Skibitsky, pres; Dave Rogers, CFO; Steve Wodlinger, gen mgr; Colleen Barill, stn mgr; David Bach, chief of opns.

Bayfield

KLJH(FM)— July 2003: 107.1 mhz; 100 kw horiz. Ant 1,870 ft. TL: N37 21 49 W107 47 30. (CP: Ant 1,883 ft. TL: N37 21 46 W107 47 40). Voice Ministries of Farmington Inc., 1105 W. Apache, Farmington, NM 87401. Phone: (505) 327-7202. Fax: (505) 327-2163. E-mail: kljh@kljh.org. Web Site: www.kljh.org. Licensee: Voice Ministries of Farmington Inc. Format: Praise & worship-Christian. ◆Fareed W. Ayoub, gen mgr.

Bennett

KSIR-FM— 1978: . Stn currently dark 107.1 mhz; 100 kw. Ant 1,932 ft. TL: N39 55 22 W103 58 18. Denver Radio Co. LLC, 9229 W. Sunset Blvd., Suite 900, Los Angeles, CA 90069. Phone: (310) 276-7439. Licensee: KSIR-FM LLC (acq 7-20-2005; $14 million). ◆Luis G. Nogales, CEO & gen mgr.

Boulder

KBCO-FM— Oct 1, 1955: 97.3 mhz; 100 kw. Ant 1,541 ft. TL: N39 54 48 W105 17 32. Stereo. 2500 Pearl St., Suite 315 80302. Phone: (303) 444-5600. Fax: (303) 449-3057. E-mail: kbco@clearchannel.com. Licensee: Citicasters Licenses L.P. Group owner: Clear Channel Communications Inc. Format: AAA. ◆Mark Remington, gen mgr; Kenny Marks, natl sls mgr; Greg Hoffman, rgnl sls mgr.

KCFC(AM)— Feb 15, 1947: 1490 khz; 1 kw-U. TL: N40 01 42 W105 15 06. 7409 S. Alton Ct., Centennial 80112. Phone: (303) 871-9191. Fax: (303) 733-3319. Web Site: www.cpr.org. Licensee: Public Broadcasting of Colorado Inc. (acq 8-17-01; $1.1 million). Network: Westwood One. Format: News. Target aud: 30 plus; listeners interested in news, info & entertainment (loc progmg). ◆Max Wycisk, pres & gen mgr; Sue Coughlin, dev VP.

*****KGNU-FM**— May 22, 1978: 88.5 mhz; 1.3 kw. 215 ft. TL: N39 59 32 W105 09 10. Stereo. 4700 Walnut St., Suite 100 80301-2548. Phone: (303) 449-4885. E-mail: marty@kgnu.org. Web Site: www.kgnu.org. Licensee: Boulder Community Broadcast Association Inc. Network: Network: PRI, NPR. Haley, Bader & Potts. Format: Var/div. News staff: one; News: 30 hrs wkly. Target aud: General. Spec prog: Black 7 hrs, folk 20 hrs, Sp 3 hrs, jazz 15 hrs, class 13 hrs wkly. ◆Marty Durlin, gen mgr & stn mgr; Evan Perkins, opns mgr; Joanne Cole, dev dir.

KRCN(AM)—See Longmont

KRKS-FM— Mar 15, 1971: 94.7 mhz; 100 kw. 984 ft. TL: N40 04 19 W105 21 14. (CP: Ant 1,745 ft. TL: N39 40 33 W105 29 07). Stereo. 3131 S. Vaughn Way, Suite 601, Aurora 80014-3510. Phone: (303) 750-5687. Fax: (303) 696-8063. Web Site: www.krks.com. Licensee: Salem Media of Colorado Inc. Group owner: Salem Communications Corp. (acq 12-15-93; $5 million; 11-15-93). Format: Relg. ◆Edward Atsinger, pres; Rob Adair, VP; Brian Taylor, gen mgr; Carrie Lakey, gen sls mgr; Ryan Kloberdanz, progmg dir.

KVCU(AM)— Nov 14, 1973: 1190 khz; 5 kw-D. TL: N39 57 54 W105 14 05. Stereo. Box 207, University of Colorado 80309. Phone: (303) 492-5031. Fax: (303) 492-1369. Web Site: www.radio1190.org. Licensee: The University of Colorado Foundation. Haley, Bader & Potts. Format: Mus. News staff: 3; News: 3 hrs wkly. Target aud: 25-44. Spec prog: Jazz 3 hrs wkly. ◆Sean Choi, gen mgr; John Quigley, stn mgr.

Breckenridge

KSMT(FM)— Sept 12, 1975: 102.3 mhz; 3 kw. -230 ft. TL: N39 29 44 W106 01 44. Stereo. Box 7069 80424. Secondary address: 130 Ski Hill Rd., Suite 240 80424. Phone: (970) 453-2234. Fax: (970) 453-5425. E-mail: ksmt@ksmtradio.com. Web Site: www.ksmtradio.com. Licensee: NRC Mountain Division LLC. Group owner: American General Media (acq 7-9-2004; grpsl). Format: Adult rock, alternative News staff: one; News: 12 hrs wkly. Target aud: 18-44; upscale adults, heavy ski & outdoor industry consumers. Spec prog: Sp 2 hrs, Reggae 2 hrs wkly. ◆Lisa Korry-Cheek, gen mgr & stn mgr.

Brighton

KLDC(AM)— Apr 26, 1956: 800 khz; 1 kw-D, DA. TL: N40 01 41 W104 49 21. (CP: 2.5 kw-D, 200 w-N. TL: N39 41 06 W105 04 05). 2150 W. 29th Ave., Suite 300, Denver 80211. Phone: (303) 433-5500. Fax: (303) 433-1555. Web Site: www.crawfordbroadcasting.com. Licensee: KLZ Radio Inc. Group owner: Crawford Broadcasting Co. (acq 12-10-93; $700,000; 1-10-94). Format: Gospel. Target aud: 24-55; general. Spec prog: Black 2 hrs wkly. ◆Donald B. Crawford, pres; Leon Owens Jr., gen mgr.

Broomfield

KDJM(FM)— June 1967: 92.5 mhz; 57 kw. 1,237 ft. TL: N40 05 47 W104 54 04. Stereo. 1560 Broadway, Suite 1100, Denver 80202. Phone: (303) 832-5665. Fax: (303) 832-7000. Web Site: www.jammin925.com. Licensee: Infinity Radio Inc. Group owner: Infinity Broadcasting Corp. (acq 12-14-00; grpsl). Format: Classic soul. News staff: one; News: 2 hrs wkly. Target aud: 35-64; educated, upscale, active professionals, ethnic. ◆Lisa Petrone, gen sls mgr; Derrick Brown, progmg dir & mus dir; Barry Walters, chief of engrg.

Brush

*****KBWA(FM)**—Not on air, target date: unknown: 89.5 mhz; 6 kw. Ant 328 ft. TL: N40 11 32 W103 35 07. Box 64500, Colorado Springs 80962. Phone: (719) 533-0300. Fax: (719) 278-4339. Web Site: kxwa.wayfm.com. Licensee: WAY-FM Media Group Inc. (acq 2-23-2005; $25,000. for CP). ◆Robert D. Augsburg, pres.

KPRB(FM)—Listing follows KSIR(AM).

KSIR(AM)— Aug 1, 1977: 1010 khz; 25 kw-D, 280 w-N. TL: N40 18 50 W103 35 30. Box 917, Fort Morgan 80701. Secondary address: 220 State St., Suite 106, Fort Morgan 80701. Phone: (970) 867-7271. Fax: (970) 867-2676. E-mail: ksir@necolorado.com. Web Site: www.ksir.com. Licensee: Northeast Colorado Broadcasting LLC (group owner; acq 7-1-2003; grpsl). Network: Network: ABC Daytime Direction, CBS Radio. Format: Talk, agriculture, sports. News staff: 2; News: 5 hrs wkly. Target aud: 25-65; farmers, ranchers, sports fans. ◆Alec Creighton, gen mgr; Larrie Boyer, progmg dir; Marcus Kammer, news dir.

KPRB(FM)— Co-owned with KSIR(AM). Nov 2, 1998: 106.3 mhz; 6 kw. 201 ft. TL: N40 18 50 W103 35 30. Stereo. E-mail: b106@necolorado.com. Web Site: www.b106.com. Network: CBS Radio. Format: Hot adult contemp. News staff: one; News: one hr wkly. Target aud: 18-45; females. ◆Alec Creighton, CEO & gen mgr; Marcus Kammer, news dir.

Buena Vista

KBVC(FM)— Jan 1, 1997: 104.1 mhz; 600 w. 1,187 ft. TL: N38 44 45 W106 11 55. 7600 County Rd. 120, Salida 81201. Phone: (719) 539-2575. Fax: (719) 539-4851. E-mail: kbvc@bresnan.net. Web Site: www.kbvcfm.com. Licensee: Headwaters Media L.L.C. (acq 2-11-00; $150,000). Format: Country. ◆Michael Kerrigan, gen mgr.

KSKE(AM)— Aug 22, 1986: 1450 khz; 1 kw-U. TL: N38 49 07 W106 09 01. 614 Kimbark St., Longmont 80501. Phone: (303) 776-2323. Fax: (303) 776-1377. Web Site: www.radiocoloradonetwork.com. Licensee: Pilgrim Communications Inc. (acq 12-11-97). Format: News/talk. ◆P. Gene Hood, pres; Ron Nickell, sr VP.

Burlington

KNAB(AM)— July 11, 1967: 1140 khz; 1 kw-D. TL: N39 17 28 W102 15 45. Box 516, 17534 County Rd., No. 49 80807. Phone: (719) 346-8600. Phone: (719) 346-5566. Fax: (719) 346-8656. E-mail: knab@centurytel.net. Licensee: KNAB Inc. (acq 9-6-91). Network: ABC Information & Entertainment. Fletcher, Heald & Hildreth. Format: Adult standards, farm. Target aud: 18 plus. ◆Bette Bailly, CEO, pres, gen mgr & chief of engrg.

KNAB-FM— Mar 7, 1980: 104.1 mhz; 50.7 kw. 358 ft. TL: N39 17 41 W102 15 37. Stereo. Network: ABC Information & Entertainment. Format: Country, agriculture.

Canon City

KRLN(AM)— Aug 15, 1947: 1400 khz; 1 kw-U. TL: N38 27 35 W105 13 26. 1615 Central 81212. Phone: (719) 275-7488. Fax: (719) 275-5132. E-mail: star@krln.cc. Licensee: Royal Gorge Broadcasting LLC. (acq 3-31-00; $715,000 with co-located FM). Network: CBS. Format: Oldies, news/talk. News staff: one; News: 25 hrs wkly. Target aud: 25-54; two income families & older discretionary income. ◆Ed Norden, gen mgr, news dir & pub affrs dir; Joan Wood, sls dir & adv mgr; Dave Moore, prom dir; Kyle Horne, progmg dir; Dan Thomas, chief of engrg.

KSTY(FM)—Co-owned with KRLN(AM). June 1, 1975: 104.5 mhz; 6 kw. 46 ft. TL: N38 18 54 W105 12 40. Stereo. Format: Country. Target aud: 25-60. ◆Kyle Horne, stn mgr; Melissa Nunn, adv mgr; Joan Wood, progmg mgr; Gregg Royce, mus dir & news dir.

*****KTLC(FM)**— May 2001: 89.1 mhz; 1.15 kw. Ant 1,476 ft. TL: N38 45 21 W105 13 02. 1665 Briargate Blvd., Suite 100, Colorado Springs 80920. Phone: (719) 593-0600. Fax: (719) 593-2399. E-mail: lightpraise@ktlf.org. Web Site: www.ktlf.org. Licensee: Make a Difference Foundation Inc. (acq 12-27-01). Network: Salem Radio Network. Format: Christian. Target aud: 45-60; Christian. ◆Karen Veazey, gen mgr & stn mgr; Kevin Waldren, progmg dir.

Carbondale

*****KCJX(FM)**— Sept 6, 2004: 88.9 mhz; 4 kw horiz, 3.5 kw vert. Ant 2,542 ft. TL: N39 25 08 W107 22 10. 110 E. Hallam St., Suite 134, Aspen 81611. Phone: (970) 925-6445. Fax: (970) 544-8002. Web Site: www.kajx.org. Licensee: Roaring Fork Public Radio Translator Inc. (acq 4-16-2002). Format: Div. ◆Brent Gardner-Smith, gen mgr; Michael Waters, stn mgr; Andrea Lee, news dir.

KUUR(FM)—Not on air, target date: unknown: 96.7 mhz; 90 w. Ant 2,507 ft. TL: N39 25 08 W107 22 10. Box 1223, Aspen 81612. Phone: (866) 250-6422. Licensee: Marcos Rodriguez. ◆Marcos Rodriguez, gen mgr.

*****KVOV(FM)**— Apr 15, 1983: 90.5 mhz; 215 w. Ant 2,798 ft. TL: N39 25 35 W107 22 48. 7409 S. Alton Ct., Centennial 80112. Phone: (303) 871-9191. Fax: (303) 733-3319. Web Site: www.cpr.org. Licensee: Public Broadcasting of Colorado Inc. (acq 10-29-2004; exchange for KDNK(FM) Glenwood Springs). Format: Classical music. ◆Max Wycisk, pres.

Castle Rock

KJMN(FM)— Feb 26, 1978: 92.1 mhz; 30 w. 627 ft. TL: N39 25 15 W104 39 15. (CP: 32.5 kw, ant 600 ft.). Stereo. 777 Grant St., 5th Fl., Denver 80203. Phone: (303) 823-0050. Fax: (303) 832-3410. Web Site: www.denverspanishradio.com. Licensee: Entravision Holdings LLC. Group owner: Entravision Communications Corp. (acq 3-14-00; grpsl). Rep: Caballero. Wiley, Rein & Fielding. Format: Sp. Target aud: 25-54. ◆Mario Carrera, gen mgr.

Colona

KAVP(AM)— Sept 30, 2000: 1450 khz; I kw-U. TL: N38 15 59 W107 51 07. 751 Horizon Ct. , Suite 225, Grand Junction 81506. Phone: (970) 241-6460. Fax: (970) 241-6452. Web Site: www.kisssradio.com. Licensee: WS Communications LLC. Group owner: Western Slope Communications LLC. Format: Classic rock. ◆Ken Bench, gen mgr.

*****KTMH(FM)**—Not on air, target date: unknown: 89.9 mhz; 4 kw vert. Ant 1,633 ft. TL: N38 23 15 W107 40 31. 1665 Briargate Blvd., Suite 200, Colorado Springs 80920. Phone: (719) 593-0600. Fax: (719) 593-2399. Licensee: Educational Communications of Colorado Springs Inc. Format: Christian. Target aud: 40-65; Christian. ◆Karen Veazey, gen mgr; Steve Howard, opns mgr; John Hayes, mus dir; Harry Russell, chief of engrg.

Colorado Springs

KBIQ(FM)—See Manitou Springs

KCCY(FM)—See Pueblo

KCMN(AM)— Feb 9, 1964: 1530 khz; 15 kw-D, 15 w-N, 1 kw-CH. TL: N38 49 08 W104 46 32. 5050 Edison Dr. 80915. Phone: (719) 570-1530. Fax: (719) 570-1007. E-mail:

Stations in the U.S.   Colorado

Developers & Brokers of Radio Properties — contact American Media Services at our suite: Philadelphia Marriott Downtown 215-625-2900 • 843-972-2200 • americanmediaservices.com • Charleston, SC • Dallas, TX · Chicago, Il · Austin, TX — American Media Services, LLC

kcmninfo@crawfordbroadcasting.com. Web Site: www.crawfordbroadcasting.com. Licensee: KLZ Radio Inc. Group owner: Crawford Broadcasting Co. (acq 1999; $750,000 with KCBR(AM) Monument). Network: Network: CNN Radio, Westwood One. Format: Oldies. Target aud: 40 plus. Spec prog: Relg 3 hrs wkly. ♦ Don Crawford Jr., CEO, VP & gen mgr; Tron Simpson, opns mgr.

*KEPC(FM)— Feb 15, 1957: 89.7 mhz; 10 kw. Ant -256 ft. TL: N38 45 41 W104 47 04. Stereo. 5675 S. Academy Blvd. 80906. Phone: (719) 540-7489. Fax: (719) 540-7487. E-mail: kepc@ppcc.edu. Web Site: kepc.cjb.net. Licensee: Pikes Peak Community College. Format: Var/div. Target aud: General. ♦ Sharon Hogg, gen mgr & pub affrs dir.

KILO(FM)— Jan 21, 1966: 94.3 mhz; 83 kw. 2,110 ft. TL: N38 44 44 W104 51 43. (CP: 94.3 mhz). Stereo. Box 2080 80906. Secondary address: 1805 E. Cheyenne Rd. 80906. Phone: (719) 634-4896. Fax: (719) 634-5837. Web Site: www.kilo943.com. Licensee: Bahakel Communications. (group owner; acq 8-14-84). Format: AOR. ♦ Lou Mellini, gen mgr; Rich Hawk, opns mgr; Karen Gonzalez, gen sls mgr & prom dir.

KKCS-FM— Jan 28, 1967: 101.9 mhz; 72 kw. Ant 2,280 ft. TL: N38 44 43 W104 51 41. Box 39102 80949. Secondary address: 3515 N. Chestnut St. 80907. Phone: (719) 633-9200. Fax: (719) 667-1831. Web Site: www.kkcscountry.com. Licensee: Superior Broadcasting of Denver LLC (group owner; (acq 12-24-2003; $18 million). Cohn & Marks. Format: Country. News staff: 4. Target aud: 25-54. ♦ Henry Tippie, gen mgr; Kalya Holt, opns mgr; Ron Mitchell, gen sls mgr.

KKFM(FM)— 1958: 98.1 mhz; 72 kw. 2,300 ft. TL: N38 44 36 W104 51 44. Stereo. 6805 Corporate Dr., Suite 130 80919-1977. Phone: (719) 593-2700. Fax: (719) 593-2727. Web Site: www.kkfm.com. Licensee: Citadel Broadcasting Co. Group owner: Citadel Broadcasting Corp. (acq 1-86; $2.5 million;. FTR: 8-16-82). Rep: McGavren Guild. Format: Classic rock. News: one hr wkly. Target aud: 25-54. ♦ Farid Suleman, CEO; Judy Ellis, COO; Bill Figenshu, pres; Brenda Goodrich, gen mgr.

KKLI(FM)—(Widefield). Mar 23, 1987: 106.3 mhz; 1.6 kw. 2,224 ft. TL: N38 44 41 W104 51 46. Stereo. 2864 S. Circle Dr., Suite 150 80906. Phone: (719) 540-9200. Fax: (719) 579-0882. Web Site: www.kkli.com. Licensee: Capstar TX L.P. Group owner: Clear Channel Communications Inc. (acq 8-30-00; grpsl). Rep: Clear Channel. Format: Soft adult contemp. News staff: one; News: 4 hrs wkly. Target aud: 25-54; family-oriented, educated. ♦ Bob Gourley, gen mgr.

KKML(AM)— Sept 22, 1922: 1300 khz; 5 kw-D, 1 kw-N. TL: N38 48 46 W104 48 51. 6805 Corporate Dr., Suite 130 80919-1977. Phone: (719) 593-2700. Fax: (719) 593-2727. Licensee: Citadel Broadcasting Co. Group owner: Citadel Broadcasting Corp. (acq 1999; grpsl). Rep: McGavren Guild. Format: Talk. News staff: 2; News: 2 hrs wkly. Target aud: 51-62. ♦ Farid Suleman, CEO; Bill Figenshu, pres; Brenda Goodrich, gen mgr.

*KRCC(FM)— Oct 2, 1951: 91.5 mhz; 2.1 kw. 2,103 ft. TL: N38 44 43 W104 51 42. Stereo. 912 N. Weber St. 80903. Phone: (719) 473-4801. Fax: (719) 473-7863. E-mail: krcc@coloradocollege.edu. Web Site: www.krcc.org. Licensee: The Colorado College. Network: Network: NPR, PRI. Garvey, Schubert & Barer. Format: Div. news. News: 42 hrs wkly. Target aud: 25-54; general. Spec prog: Celtic 5 hrs, reggae 6 hrs, jazz 15 hrs, blues 5 hrs wkly. ♦ Mario B. Valdes, gen mgr; Mike Procell, opns mgr; Denise Vienne, dev mgr; Jeff Bieri, prom dir.

KRDO(AM)— March 1947: 1240 khz; 1 kw-U. TL: N38 49 42 W104 50 15. Box 1457 80901. Secondary address: 3 S. Seventh St. 80905. Phone: (719) 632-1515. Phone: (719) 635-8455. Fax: (719) 520-9374. Fax: (319) 575-6245. E-mail: m.lewis@krdotv.com. Licensee: Pikes Peak Broadcasting Co. (group owner): ABC Information & Entertainment. Rep: D & R Radio. Fletcher, Heald & Hildreth. Format: Sports. News: one hr wkly; News: 2 hrs wkly. Target aud: 25-54; mmen. ♦ Harry W. Hoth Jr., chmn; Patti Hoth, pres; Neil O. Klockziem, gen mgr; Pat Carey, natl sls mgr & rgnl sls mgr; Mike Lewis, progmg mgr; Charles Upton, chief of engrg.

KRDO-FM— Oct 1, 1969: 95.1 mhz; 96 kw. 2,010 ft. TL: N38 44 47 W104 51 37. Stereo. 3 S. 7th St. 80905. Secondary address: Box 1457 80901. Web Site: peak951.com. Network: ABC Information & Entertainment. Format: Bright adult contemp. ♦ Mike Lewis, CEO & progmg dir. Co-owned TV: KRDO-TV affil.

KSKX(FM)—See Security

KSPZ(FM)—Listing follows KVOR(AM).

*KTLF(FM)— Feb 27, 1989: 90.5 mhz; 20 kw. Ant 2,178 ft. TL: N38 44 43 W104 51 39. Stereo. 1665 Briargate Blvd., Suite 100 80920. Phone: (719) 593-0600. Fax: (719) 593-2399. E-mail: lightpraise@ktlf.org. Web Site: www.lightpraise.org. Licensee: Educational Communications of Colorado Springs Inc. Format: Christian music. News: 12 hrs wkly. Target aud: 25-49. ♦ Dr. Ron Johnson, chmn; Karen Veazey, stn mgr; Steve Howard, opns mgr; Kevin Walden, progmg dir.

KVOR(AM)— Sept 22, 1922: 740 khz; 3.3 kw-D, 1.5 kw-N, DA-2. TL: N39 05 02 W104 42 41. Stereo. 6805 Corporate Dr., Suite 130 80919. Phone: (719) 593-2700. Fax: (719) 527-2727. Licensee: Citadel Broadcasting Co. Group owner: Citadel Broadcasting Corp. (acq 1999; grpsl). Network: Network: Network: CBS, Wall Street, ABC News/Talk. Format: News/talk, sports. Target aud: General. ♦ Brenda Goodrich, gen mgr; Nada Gutierrez, gen sls mgr; Laurie White, prom dir; Jim Arthur, progmg dir; Joe Meyers, news dir.

KSPZ(FM)—Co-owned with KVOR(AM). Feb 1, 1960: 92.9 mhz; 53 kw. 2,130 ft. TL: N38 44 44 W104 51 39. Stereo. Format: Oldies. Target aud: 25-54. ♦ Jim Berry, progmg dir.

KWYD(AM)— June 22, 1957: 1580 khz; 10 kw-D. TL: N38 43 11 W104 43 16. 490 Willow Springs Rd., Fountain 80817-2722. Phone: (719) 392-4219. Fax: (719) 392-3307. Web Site: www.radiocoloradonetwork.com. Licensee: Pilgrim Communications Inc. (acq 6-1-98; $450,000). Format: Conservative talk, Christian. News staff: one; News: 2 hrs wkly. Target aud: General. ♦ P. Gene Hood, pres; Dot Rich, gen mgr; Ron Nickles, progmg dir; Ron Crider, chief of engrg.

KZNT(AM)— Dec 15, 1956: 1460 khz; 5 kw-D, 500 w-N, DA-N. TL: N38 49 36 W104 44 30. 7150 Campus Dr., Suite 150 80920. Phone: (719) 531-5438. Fax: (719) 531-5588. Licensee: Bison Media Inc. Group owner: Salem Communications Corp. (acq 10-6-03; $1.5 million). Format: News/talk. ♦ Phil Lewis, gen mgr.

Commerce City

KLTT(AM)— 1996: 670 khz; 50 kw-D, 1.4 kw-N, DA-2. TL: N39 57 20 W104 43 50. 2150 W. 29th Ave., Suite 300, Denver 80211. Phone: (303) 433-5500. Fax: (303) 433-1551. E-mail: klttinfo@crawfordbroadcasting.com. Web Site: www.crawfordbroadcasting.com. Licensee: KLZ Radio Inc. Group owner: Crawford Broadcasting Co. (acq 1995; $750,000). Format: Relg, Christian, conservative talk. Target aud: 30 plus; general. ♦ Mike Triem, gen mgr & stn mgr.

Cortez

KISZ-FM— Sept 28, 1978: 97.9 mhz; 100 kw. 1,360 ft. TL: N37 21 48 W108 09 00. Stereo. 212 W. Apache St., Farmington, NM 87401-6235. Secondary address: 2402 Hawkins 81321. Phone: (505) 325-3541. Fax: (505) 327-5796. Web Site: www.kisscountry979fm.com. Licensee: Winton Road Broadcasting Co. LLC (group owner; (acq 5-3-01; grpsl). Fleischman & Walsh. Format: Country. News staff: one; News: 4 hrs wkly. Target aud: 18-49; young sophisticated adults. ♦ Sara Olsen, gen mgr.

KRTZ(AM)—Listing follows KVFC(AM).

*KSJD(FM)— July 1990: 91.5 mhz; 145 w. -417 ft. TL: N37 21 10 W108 26 07. Stereo. 33057 Hwy. 160, Mancos 81328. Phone: (970) 565-9121. Phone: (970) 565-8457. Fax: (970) 565-6160. Licensee: San Juan Basin Technical School. Format: Rock, alternative, country.

News staff: one. Target aud: 16-30; college level. Spec prog: Relg one hr wkly. ♦ Anthony Valdez, gen mgr; Jeff Pope, progmg dir.

KVFC(AM)— Feb 27, 1955: 740 khz; 1 kw-D, 250 w-N, DA-N. TL: N37 20 58 W108 32 29. Box 1299 81321. Secondary address: 2402 Hawkins 81321. Phone: (970) 565-6565. Fax: (970) 565-8567. E-mail: feedback@kvfcradio.com. Web Site: www.kvfcradio.com. Licensee: Winton Road Broadcasting Co. LLC (group owner; acq 12-18-01; with co-located FM). Network: Network: ABC, CNN Radio, Westwood One. Format: News/talk. News staff: 2; News: 15 hrs wkly. Target aud: 18-54; young adults. ♦ Anthony Brandon, CEO; L. Rogers Brandon, COO; Sara Olsen, gen mgr; Kelly Turner, opns mgr & news dir; Cindy Allen, sls dir & gen sls mgr; Nihla McCabe, pub affrs dir; Jim Burt, chief of engrg.

KRTZ(FM)—Co-owned with KVFC(AM). December 1981: 98.7 mhz; 27 kw. 2,900 ft. TL: N37 13 10 W108 48 26. Stereo. E-mail: sales@krtzradio.com. Web Site: hitsand favorites.com. Network: ABC Information & Entertainment. Format: Adult contemp. News staff: one; News: 3 hrs wkly. Target aud: 20-55. Spec prog: American Indian one hr, gospel one hr wkly. ♦ Cindy Allen, stn mgr; Kelly Turner, chief of opns; Nihla McCabe, prom mgr & progmg dir; Jim Burt, engrg dir.

Craig

*KPYR(FM)—Not on air, target date: unknown: 88.3 mhz; 250 w. Ant 889 ft. TL: N40 33 50 W107 36 40. Colorado Public Radio, Bridges Broadcast Center, 7409 S. Alton Ct., Centennial 80112. Phone: (303) 871-9191. Fax: (303) 733-3319. Licensee: Public Broadcasting of Colorado Inc. ♦ Max Wycisk, pres & gen mgr.

KQZR(FM)— Mar 1, 2005: . Stn currently dark 102.5 mhz; 100 kw. Ant 1,243 ft. TL: N40 11 45 W107 56 00. Box 772850, Steamboat Springs 80477. Phone: (970) 870-0900. Fax: (970) 879-5843. Licensee: Craig Broadcasting LLC. Format: Classic rock. ♦ Brian Harvey, gen mgr.

KRAI(AM)— 1948: 550 khz; 5 kw-D, 500 w-N, DA-N. TL: N40 32 45 W107 31 52. Stereo. Box 65 81626. Secondary address: 1111 W. Victory Way. 81626. Phone: (970) 824-6574. Fax: (970) 826-4581. E-mail: frank@krai.com. Licensee: Wild West Radio Inc. (acq 5-89). Network: Westwood One. Format: Country. News: 12 hrs wkly. Target aud: 25-54. Spec prog: Farm one hr wkly. ♦ Frank R. Hanel Jr., pres, gen mgr & chief of engrg.

KRAI-FM— April 1976: 93.7 mhz; 100 kw. 980 ft. TL: N40 34 35 W107 36 29. Stereo. Web Site: www.krai.com. Format: Adult contemp. Target aud: 18-49.

Crested Butte

*KBUT(FM)— Dec 20, 1986: 90.3 mhz; 250 w. -667 ft. TL: N38 52 19 W106 58 44. Stereo. Box 308 81224. Secondary address: 508 Maroon Ave. 81224. Phone: (970) 349-5225. Phone: (970) 349-7444. Fax: (970) 349-6440. E-mail: kbut@kbut.org. Web Site: www.kbut.org. Licensee: Crested Butte Mountain Educational Radio Inc. Network: Network: NPR, PRI. Garvey, Schubert & Barer. Format: Educational, diversified music, news/talk. News staff: one; News: 72 hrs wkly. Target aud: General. ♦ Kim Carroll-Bosler, gen mgr & stn mgr; Josh Elmer, dev dir.

Delta

KDTA(AM)— Jan 14, 1955: 1400 khz; 1 kw-U. TL: N38 45 38 W108 05 28. 1360 E. Sherwood Dr., Grand Junction 81501-7575. Phone: (970) 254-5565. Fax: (970) 254-5550. E-mail: info@kjol.org. Web Site: www.kjol.org. Licensee: United Ministries. (group owner; (acq 11-16-2004; $88,000). Format: Christian talk, music. ♦ Ken Andrews, gen mgr.

KKNN(FM)— December 1985: 95.1 mhz; 100 kw. 969 ft. TL: N38 52 40 W108 13 30. Stereo. 315 Kennedy Ave., Grand Junction 81501. Phone: (970) 242-7788. Fax: (970) 243-0567. Web Site: www.coloradowest.com. Licensee: Cumulus Licensing Corp. Group owner: Cumulus Media Inc. (acq 1-00). Rep: Katz Radio. Format: Classic rock. News staff: one; News: 6 hrs wkly. Target aud: 18-49;

Broadcasting & Cable Yearbook 2006

men. ♦Lewis Dickey Jr., CEO & pres; John Dickey, exec VP; Marco Comacho, VP; Pat Cantwell, gen mgr; Mike Shafer, opns mgr; Julie Shafer, gen sls mgr.

***KPRU(FM)**— 2001: 103.3 mhz; 12 kw. Ant 987 ft. TL: N38 52 40 W108 13 32. Colorado Public Radio, Bridges Broadcast Center, 7409 S. Alton Ct., Centennial 80112. Phone: (303) 871-9191. Fax: (303) 733-3319. Web Site: www.cpr.org. Licensee: Public Broadcasting of Colorado Inc. Format: Classical. ♦Max Wycisk, pres & gen mgr; Ed Trudeau, stn mgr & progmg dir; Sue Coughlin, dev VP; Arlene Wayland, prom dir; Bob Hensler, chief of engrg.

Denver

KALC(FM)— June 21, 1965: 105.9 mhz; 100 kw. 900 ft. TL: N39 43 59 W105 14 12. Stereo. 4700 S. Syracuse St., Suite 1050 80237. Phone: (303) 967-2700. Fax: (303) 967-2747. Web Site: www.alice106.com. Licensee: Entercom Denver License LLC. Group owner: Entercom Communications Corp. (acq 5-1-2002; $88 million). Rep: Christal. Format: Hot adult contemp. Target aud: 18-34; women. ♦Jerry McKenna, VP & gen mgr; Gerry Jones, gen sls mgr; Mark Edwards, natl sls mgr; Amber Pope, mktg dir; Sara Williams, prom mgr; B.J. Harris, progmg dir; Kevin Koske, mus dir; Jeff Garrett, engrg dir; Mark Smith, chief of engrg.

KBJD(AM)— 2001: 1650 khz; 10 kw-D, 1 kw-N. TL: N39 47 56 W104 58 12. 3131 S. Vaughn Way, Suite 601, Aurora 80114. Phone: (303) 750-5687. Fax: (303) 696-8063. E-mail: production@salemdenver.com. Web Site: www.710knus.com. Licensee: Salem Media of Colorado Inc. Group owner: Salem Communications Corp. Format: Conservative news/talk. News staff: 3; News: 15 hrs wkly. ♦Brian Taylor, gen mgr.

KBNO(AM)— May 15, 1948: 1280 khz; 5 kw-U, DA-2. TL: N39 36 05 W104 58 49. 600 Grant St., Suite 600 80203. Phone: (303) 733-5266. Fax: (303) 733-5242. E-mail: kbno.net@kbno.net. Web Site: www.kbno.net. Licensee: Latino Communications LLC (group owner; acq 11-21-00; $3.3 million). Network: Network: Westwood One, CBS. Format: Sp. News: 21 hrs wkly. Target aud: 25-54; male. Spec prog: Spanish - 168 hrs wkly. ♦Michael Ferrufino, VP & opns VP; Zee Ferrufino, CEO, CFO, sr VP, gen mgr & stn mgr.

KBPI(FM)— June 19, 1962: 106.7 mhz; 100 kw. 987 ft. TL: N39 43 59 W105 14 12. Stereo. 4695 S. Monaco St. 80237. Phone: (303) 713-8000. Fax: (303) 713-8744. Web Site: www.kbpi.com. Licensee: Citicasters Licenses Inc. (NEW). Group owner: Clear Channel Communications Inc. (acq 5-4-99; grpsl). Network: ABC. Format: AOR. Target aud: 25-34; men. ♦Mark Remington, gen mgr & gen sls mgr; Ron Smith, gen mgr & opns mgr; Willie Hung, progmg dir.

***KCFR(AM)**— Mar 4, 1956: 1340 khz; 1 kw-U. TL: N39 39 34 W105 00 44. (CP: TL: N39 41 01 W105 00 25). 7409 S. Alton Ct., Centennial 80112. Phone: (303) 871-9191. Fax: (303) 733-3319. Web Site: www.cpr.org. Licensee: Public Broadcasting of Colorado Inc. (acq 11-30-00; $4.2 million). Format: NPR news. ♦Max Wycisk, pres & gen mgr; Sue Coughlin, dev VP.

KEZW(AM)—See Aurora

***KGNU(AM)**— Jan 1, 1954: 1390 khz; 5 kw-D, DA. TL: N39 39 29 W105 00 49. Stereo. 930 West 7th Ave. 80204. Phone: (303) 623-1390. Fax: (303) 595-0131. Web Site: www.lajota1390.com. Licensee: Boulder Community Broadcast Association Inc. (acq 11-26-2004; $4.2 million). Format: Rgnl Mexican. ♦Arleigh Benenson-Stranahan, chmn; Kris Roberts, gen mgr.

KHOW(AM)— 1925: 630 khz; 5 kw-U, DA-2. TL: N39 54 36 W104 54 50. Stereo. 4695 S. Monaco 80237. Phone: (303) 713-8000. Fax: (303) 713-8738. Web Site: www.clearchannel.com. Licensee: Citicasters Licenses L.P. Group owner: Clear Channel Communications Inc. (acq 5-4-99; grpsl). Format: Talk. Target aud: 25-54. ♦Lee Larsen, gen mgr; Jan Whitbeck, prom dir & prom mgr; Elizabeth Estes-Cooper, progmg dir; Jeff Gulick, chief of engrg.

KMGG(FM)—Co-owned with KHOW(AM). Mar 31, 1968: 95.7 mhz; 100 kw. 725 ft. TL: N39 43 59 W105 14 10. Stereo. Web Site: www.975kissfm.com. Format: Adult contemp. Target aud: General.

KIMN(FM)— Aug 1, 1959: 100.3 mhz; 100 kw. 331 ft. TL: N39 41 06 W105 04 05. (CP: Ant 1,705 ft. TL: N39 54 48 W105 17 32). Stereo. 1560 Broadway, Suite 1100 80202. Phone: (303) 832-5665. Fax: (303) 832-7000. Web Site: www.mix100.com. Licensee: Infinity Radio Inc. Group owner: Infinity Broadcasting Corp. (acq 8-24-00; grpsl). Rep: Christal. Format: Hot adult contemp. Target aud: 35-44; women. Spec prog: Pub affrs 2 hrs wkly. ♦Drew Hilles, VP & gen mgr.

KKFN(AM)— July 4, 1922: 950 khz; 5 kw-U, DA-1. TL: N39 52 30 W104 56 00. Stereo. 1095 S. Monaco Pkwy. 80224. Phone: (303) 321-0950. Fax: (303) 321-3383. Licensee: Jefferson-Pilot Communications Co. (group owner) Network: Network: CBS, ABC Daytime Direction. Rep: CBS Radio. Format: All sports, talk. Target aud: 25-54; men. ♦Robert Call, VP & gen mgr; Steve Price, gen sls mgr; Randy Weidner, natl sls mgr; Larry Nettingham, rgnl sls mgr; Mark Etchason, mktg dir; Dwayne Taylor, prom dir; Tim Spence, progmg dir; Jennifer Page, news dir & pub affrs dir; Brad Hart, engrg dir.

KYGO-FM—Co-owned with KKFN(AM). Dec 1, 1953: 98.5 mhz; 100 kw. 1,820 ft. TL: N39 40 35 W105 29 09. Stereo. Web Site: www.kygo.com. Format: Country. Target aud: 25-54. ♦John St. John, progmg dir; Tad Svendsen, mus dir.

KKZN(AM)—See Thornton

KLDC(AM)—See Brighton

KLDV(FM)—See Morrison

KLVZ(AM)— June 5, 1954: 1220 khz; 660 w-D, 11 w-N. TL: N39 41 00 W105 00 24. 2150 W. 29th Ave., Suite 300 80211. Phone: (303) 433-5500. Fax: (303) 433-1555. Web Site: www.crawfordbroadcasting.com. Licensee: KLZ Radio Inc. Group owner: Crawford Broadcasting Co. (acq 8-11-99; $1.5 million). Fisher, Wayland, Cooper, Leader & Zaragoza L.L.P. Format: Radio & Victoria. Target aud: 18-49. ♦Mike Triem, gen mgr.

KLZ(AM)— Mar 10, 1922: 560 khz; 5 kw-U, DA-1. TL: N39 50 36 W104 57 14. 2150 W. 29th Ave., Suite 300 80211. Phone: (303) 433-5500. Fax: (303) 433-1555. E-mail: klzinfo@crawfordbroadcasting.com. Web Site: www.z560.com. Licensee: KLZ Radio Inc. Group owner: Crawford Broadcasting Co. (acq 6-30-92; $1.5 million;. FTR: 7-20-92). Network: ABC. Format: Sports. Target aud: 25-54; men. ♦Donald B. Crawford Jr., VP & gen mgr; Gregory C. Gates, stn mgr & natl sls mgr; Ian McGee, prom dir & chief of engrg; Jim Ortega, gen sls mgr & progmg dir.

KMXA(AM)—(Aurora). Sept 12, 1972: 1090 khz; 50 kw-D, 500 w-N, DA-2. TL: N39 39 53 W104 39 24. Stereo. 777 Grant St., 5th Floor 80203. Phone: (303) 832-0050. Fax: (303) 832-3410. Web Site: www.denverspanishradio.com. Licensee: Entravision Holdings LLC. Group owner: Entravision Communications Corp. (acq 3-14-00; grpsl). Rep: Caballero. Format: Sp. Target aud: 18-54; Hispanics. ♦Maseo Carrera, gen mgr.

KNRV(AM)—See Englewood

KNUS(AM)— 1941: 710 khz; 5 kw-U, DA-1. TL: N39 57 19 W104 51 01. 3131 S. Vaughn Way, Suite 601, Aurora 80014. Phone: (303) 750-5687. Fax: (303) 696-8063. E-mail: production@salemdenver.com. Web Site: www.710knus.com. Licensee: Salem Media of Colorado Inc. Group owner: Salem Communications Corp. (acq 1996; $1.2 million). Network: CNN Radio. Format: News/talk. News staff: 3; News: 15 hrs wkly. Target aud: 35-54; Adults. ♦Brian Taylor, gen mgr.

KOA(AM)— Dec 15, 1924: 850 khz; 50 kw-U. TL: N39 30 22 W104 45 57. 4695 S. Monaco St. 80237. Phone: (303) 713-8000. Phone: (303) 713-8500 (News). Fax: (303) 713-8424. Web Site: www.850koa.com. Licensee: Citicasters Licenses Inc. (NEW). Group owner: Clear Channel Communications Inc. (acq 5-4-99; grpsl). Network: Network: CBS, ABC Information & Entertainment. Format: News/talk, sports. Target aud: 25-54. ♦Barry Remington, gen mgr.

KRFX(FM)—Co-owned with KOA(AM). June 1, 1961: 103.5 mhz; 100 kw. 1,045 ft. TL: N39 43 50 W105 14 07. Stereo. Fax: (303) 713-8743. Web Site: www.thefox.com. Format: Classic rock. Target aud: 25-54. ♦Don Howe, VP, gen mgr & progmg dir; Barry Remington, gen sls mgr & adv mgr; Mike O'Connor, progmg dir.

KOSI(FM)— Mar 3, 1968: 101.1 mhz; 100 kw. 1,624 ft. TL: N39 43 45 W105 14 06. Stereo. 4700 S. Syracuse, Suite 1050 80237. Phone: (303) 967-2700. Fax: (303) 967-2747. Web Site: www.kosi101.com. Licensee: Entercom Denver License LLC. Group owner: Entercom Communications Corp. (acq 7-24-02; with KEZW(AM) Aurora). Format: Adult contemp. News staff: one; News: 5 hrs wkly. Target aud: 25-54; women/families. ♦Jerry E. McKenna, VP & gen mgr.

***KPOF(AM)**— Mar 9, 1928: 910 khz; 5 kw-D, 1 kw-N. TL: N39 50 47 W105 01 59. 3455 W. 83rd Ave., Westminster 80031. Phone: (303) 428-0910. Fax: (303) 429-0910. Web Site: www.am910.org. Licensee: Pillar of Fire Corp. (group owner; acq 1928). Network: Moody. Format: Christian. Target aud: 18-plus; mature adult and families. ♦Robert Dallenbach, pres; Jack H. Pelon, gen mgr; Jerry Bauer, opns mgr.

KQKS(FM)—See Lakewood

KQMT(FM)— Oct 2, 1959: 99.5 mhz; 100 kw. 279 ft. TL: N39 41 01 W105 00 25. (CP: Ant 1,311 ft.). Stereo. 4700 S, Syracuse St., Suite 1050 80237. Phone: (303) 967-2700. Fax: (303) 967-2747. Web Site: www.995themountain.com. Licensee: Entercom Denver License LLC. Group owner: Entercom Communications Corp. (acq 3-21-03). Format: Timeless rock. News: 4 hrs wkly. Target aud: 25-54; upscale, educated. ♦Jerry E. McKenna, VP & gen mgr.

KRKS(AM)— Aug 1, 1953: 990 khz; 5 kw-D, 390 w-N, DA-N. TL: N39 41 06 W105 04 05. 3131 S. Vaughn Way, Suite 601, Aurora 80114. Phone: (303) 750-5687. Fax: (303) 696-8063. Web Site: www.salemdenver.com. Licensee: Salem Media of Colorado Inc. Group owner: Salem Communications Corp. (acq 10-93; $400,000). Network: Superadio. Format: Relg. Target aud: 25 plus. ♦Brian Taylor, gen mgr & stn mgr.

***KUVO(FM)**— Aug 29, 1985: 89.3 mhz; 22.5 kw. 910 ft. TL: N39 43 49 W105 14 59. Stereo. PO Box 2040 80201-2040. Secondary address: 2900 Welton St., Suite 200 80205. Phone: (303) 480-9272. Phone: (303) 291-0666. Fax: (303) 291-0757. E-mail: info@kuvo.org. Web Site: www.kuvo.org. Licensee: Denver Educational Broadcasting. Network: Network: NPR, PRI. Haley, Bader & Potts. Format: Jazz. Target aud: 25-49. Spec prog: Sp 15 hrs wkly. ♦Florence Hernandez-Ramos, CEO, pres & gen mgr; Tina Cartagena, dev dir.

***KVOD(FM)**— November 1970: 90.1 mhz; 50 kw. Ant 910 ft. TL: N39 43 49 W105 14 59. Stereo. 7409 S.Alton Ct., Centennial 80112. Phone: (303) 871-9191. Fax: (303) 733-3319. E-mail: info@cpr.org. Web Site: www.cpr.org. Licensee: Public Broadcasting of Colorado Inc. (acq 1991; 10-28-91). Network: NPR. Arter & Hadden. Format: Classical. News staff: 8; News: 50 hrs wkly. Target aud: General. ♦Max Wycisk, pres; Jenny Gentry, exec VP; Ed Trudeau, gen mgr; Sue Coughlin, dev VP; Sean Nethery, mktg VP; Carlo Walker, progmg dir; Robert Hensler, engrg VP.

KXKL-FM— Dec 1, 1956: 105.1 mhz; 100 kw. 1,200 ft. TL: N39 36 00 W105 12 35. (CP: Ant 1,168 ft.). 1560 Broadway, Suite 1100 80202. Phone: (303) 832-5665. Fax: (303) 832-7000. Web Site: www.kool105.com. Licensee: Infinity Radio Inc. Group owner: Infinity Broadcasting Corp. (acq 8-24-00; grpsl). Format: Oldies. ♦Drew Hilles, gen mgr; Lisa Petrone, gen sls mgr & mktg dir; Marci Crum, prom dir; Keith Abrams, progmg dir; Steve Alexander, news dir; Barry Walters, chief of engrg.

Dolores

KKDC(FM)—Not on air, target date: unknown: 93.3 mhz; 50 kw. Ant 338 ft. TL: N37 27 59 W108 31 28. 185 Suttle St., Suite 203, Durango 81301. Phone: (970) 259-4444. Fax: (970) 247-1005. E-mail: joy@radiodelores.com. Web Site: www.radiodelores.com. Licensee: Four Corners Broadcasting L.L.C. (group owner). Target aud: 35-54. ♦Ward S. Holmes, gen mgr; Jay Baldwin, stn mgr.

***KTCF(FM)**— 2004: 89.5 mhz; 500 w. Ant 174 ft. TL: N37 28 07 W108 32 48. 1665 Briargate Blvd., Suite 100, Colorado Springs 80920. Phone: (719) 593-0600. Fax: (719) 593-2399. E-mail: lightpraise@ktlf.org. Web Site: www.ktlf.org. Licensee: Educational Communications of Colorado Springs Inc. Format: Christian/inspirational. News staff: 12.

Durango

KDGO(AM)— Apr 18, 1958: 1240 khz; 1 kw-U. TL: N37 18 17 W107 51 10. 1911 Main Ave., Suite 100 81301. Phone: (970) 247-1240. Fax: (970) 247-1771. E-mail: smatthews@americageneralmedia.com. Licensee: Winton Road Broadcasting Co. LLC. (group owner; (acq 6-1-2001; grpsl). Network: ABC. Format: Sports, news/talk. News staff: one. Target aud: 35-55. ♦Sara Olsen, gen mgr; Scott Matthews, opns mgr & progmg dir.

KPTE(FM)—Co-owned with KDGO(AM). July 1, 1995: 99.7 mhz; 9.2 kw. 1,128 ft. TL: N37 19 59 W107 49 13. E-mail: kpte@997thepoint.com. Web Site: 997thepoint.com. Format: Hot adult contemp. Target aud: 18-44.

Stations in the U.S. — Colorado

Developers & Brokers of Radio Properties

contact American Media Services at our suite:
Philadelphia Marriott Downtown
215-625-2900
843-972-2200
americanmediaservices.com
Charleston, SC
Dallas, TX · Chicago, Il · Austin, TX

American Media Services, LLC

*KDUR(FM)— 1975: 91.9 mhz; 225 w. -447 ft. TL: N37 16 31 W107 52 00. Stereo. Fort Lewis College, 1000 Rim Dr. 81301. Phone: (970) 247-7634. Web Site: www.kdur.org. Licensee: Board of Trustees for Fort Lewis College. Network: PRI. Format: Div. Spec prog: Bluegrass 6 hrs, blues 6 hrs, class 6 hrs, jazz 9 hrs, Native American folk 3 hrs wkly. ♦Nancy Stoffer, gen mgr; Jessie Caldwell, opns dir; David Smith, dev dir.

KIQX(FM)— Oct 15, 1982: 101.3 mhz; 100 kw. 439 ft. TL: N37 15 45 W107 54 07. Stereo. Box X 81301. Secondary address: 185 Suttle St., Suite 203 81301. Phone: (970) 259-4444. Fax: (970) 247-1005. E-mail: fcb@frontier.net. Web Site: www.radiodurango.com. Licensee: Four Corners Broadcasting L.L.C. (group owner) Network: CBS. Akin, Gump, Strauss, Hauer & Feld. Format: Adult contemp. News staff: 2; News: 5 hrs wkly. Target aud: 25-49; mainstream business professionals & families. Spec prog: Jazz 7 hrs wkly. ♦Allen H. Brill, chmn; Ward Holmes, VP; Kristin Dills, opns dir.

KIUP(AM)— Dec 10, 1935: 930 khz; 5 kw-D, 1 kw-N, DA-N. TL: N37 13 45 W107 51 49. 185 Suttle St., Suite 203 81303. Phone: (970) 259-4444. Fax: (970) 247-1005. E-mail: fcb@frontier.net. Web Site: www.radiodurango.com. Licensee: Four Corners Broadcasting LLC. (group owner; acq 4-1-96; with co-located FM). Network: CBS. Akin, Gump, Strauss, Hauer & Feld. Format: Full service, MOR, news/talk. News staff: 2; News: 5 hrs wkly. Target aud: 35-64. Spec prog: Jazz 4 hrs, sports 4 hrs, class 2 hrs, Opera 4 hrs wkly. ♦Allen Brill, CEO; Ward S. Holmes, VP.

KRSJ(FM)— Co-owned with KIUP(AM). Dec 4, 1972: 100.5 mhz; 100 kw. 200 ft. TL: N37 15 46 W107 53 45. Stereo. Web Site: www.radiodurango.com. Network: CBS Radio. Format: C&W. News staff: 2. Target aud: 25 plus.

Eagle

KTUN(FM)— Apr 16, 1984: 101.7 mhz; 12 kw. Ant 2,211 ft. TL: N39 44 18 W106 47 58. Stereo. Box 7205, Avon 81620. Phone: (970) 949-0140. Fax: (970) 949-4318. Licensee: NRC Mountain Division LLC. (group owner; acq 7-9-2004; grpsl). Arter & Hadden. Format: Classic rock. News staff: 2; News: 4 hrs wkly. Target aud: 25-63; affluent locals & tourists. ♦Steve Wodlinger, gen mgr, opns mgr & pub affrs dir.

Eaton

*KLCQ(FM)— Dec 23, 2003: 88.9 mhz; 640 w. Ant -3 ft. TL: N41 08 17 W104 47 30. Stereo. 5700 W. Oaks Blvd., Rocklin, CA 95765. Phone: (916) 251-1600. Fax: (916) 251-1650. E-mail: klove@klove.com. Web Site: www.klove.com. Licensee: Educational Media Foundation. Group owner: EMF Broadcasting. Network: K-Love. Shaw Pittman. Format: Contemp Chrisitan. News staff: 3. Target aud: 25-44; Judeo Christian, female. ♦Richard Jenkins, pres; Mike Novak, VP; Lloyd Parker, gen mgr; Ed Lenane, opns dir; Keith Whipple, dev dir.

El Jebel

KCUF(FM)— Not on air, target date: unknown: 100.5 mhz; 6 kw. Ant 295 ft. TL: N39 18 56 W106 57 32. c/o Alice Puente, 207 W. Norgate St., Glendora, CA 91740. Phone: (323) 930-1000. Licensee: Simon T. ♦Simon T, gen mgr.

Englewood

KNRV(AM)— 1951: . Stn currently dark 1150 khz; 5 kw-D, 1 kw-N, DA-2. TL: N39 36 18 W104 50 25. (CP: 50 kw-D, 1 kw-N, DA-2). 1201 18th St., Suite 200, Denver 80202. Phone: (303) 296-7025. Fax: (303) 296-7030. E-mail: info@knrcradio.com. Licensee: New Radio Venture Inc. (group owner; acq 7-6-2005; $5.53 million). ♦Dave Rogers, CFO; Dave Zobl, VP; Ray Skibitsky, gen mgr.

Estes Park

KEZZ(AM)— Aug 19, 1967: 1470 khz; 1 kw-D, 53 w-N. TL: N40 20 15 W105 31 36. Box 2690 80517. Secondary address: 184 E. Elkhorn Ave. 80517. Phone: (970) 586-9555. Fax: (970) 586-9561. E-mail: info@estesparkradio.com. Licensee: MK Inc. (acq 11-00; $185,000). Format: AC Hot/Rock Hits. News staff: one; News: 35 hrs wkly. Target aud: General. ♦Melody Sanders, gen mgr.

KXDC(FM)— Apr 6, 1998: 102.1 mhz; 175 w. Ant 1,007 ft. TL: N40 04 19 W105 21 11. 8975 E. Kenyon Ave., Denver 80237. Phone: (720) 529-1431. Fax: (720) 529-1418. Web Site: www.1021thundercountry.com. Licensee: Superior Broadcasting of Denver LLC. (group owner; acq 3-29-2000; $12 million). Network: ABC. Rep: Allied Radio Partners. Format: Classic country. Target aud: Urban adults 19-34; Black, Hispanic, White. ♦Chris Devine, pres.

Evergreen

KXPK(FM)— June 8, 1994: 96.5 mhz; 93 kw. 328 ft. TL: N39 40 18 W105 13 12. 777 Grant St., 5th Fl., Denver 80203. Phone: (303) 832-0050. Fax: (303) 832-3410. Web Site: www.denverspanishradio.com. Licensee: Entravision Holdings LLC. Group owner: Entravision Communications Corp. (acq 5-1-02; $47.5 million). Format: Rgnl Mexican. News staff: one. ♦Mario Carrera, gen mgr.

Fort Collins

KCOL(AM)— (Wellington). Jan 12, 1959: 600 khz; 1 kw-D, 100 w-N, DA-2. TL: N40 35 34 W105 06 18. 1612 La Porte Ave. 80521. Phone: (970) 482-5991. Fax: (970) 484-5451. E-mail: kcol600@hotmail.com. Web Site: www.kcol.com. Licensee: Jacor Broadcasting of Colorado Inc. Group owner: Clear Channel Communications Inc. (acq 5-8-98; $6.1 million. with co-located FM). Rep: McGavren Guild. Format: News/talk. Target aud: 35 plus. Spec prog: Farm 2 hrs, relg one hr, sports talk 7 hrs wkly. ♦Stu Haskell, stn mgr; Kenton Skeels, gen sls mgr; Rebecca Kneipp, prom dir; Rich Bircumshaw, news dir; Jim Mross, chief of engrg.

KTCL(FM)— Co-owned with KCOL(AM). September 1965: 93.3 mhz; 100 kw. 1,328 ft. TL: N40 32 57 W105 11 49. Stereo. 4695 S. Monaco St., Denver 80237. Phone: (303) 713-8000. Web Site: www.area93.com. Format: Alternative. Target aud: 18 plus. Spec prog: Comedy one hr, loc bands one hr, reggae 2 hrs wkly. ♦Greg Hoffman, adv mgr; John Hayes, progmg dir.

*KCSU-FM— Sept 20, 1964: 90.5 mhz; 10 kw. -355 ft. TL: N40 36 00 W105 09 21. Stereo. Lory Student Ctr., Box 13 80523. Phone: (970) 491-7611. Fax: (970) 491-7612. E-mail: program@colostate.edu. Web Site: www.kcsufm.com. Licensee: Colorado State Board of Agriculture. Arter & Hadden. Format: Progsv. News: 3 hrs wkly. Target aud: 18-34; general. Spec prog: Hip-hop 3 hrs, jazz 3 hrs, Black 3 hrs wkly. ♦Jeff Browne, gen mgr.

KIIX(AM)— Mar 1, 1947: 1410 khz; 1 kw-U, DA-N. TL: N40 35 34 W105 06 18. 1612 Laporte Ave. 80521. Phone: (970) 482-5991. Fax: (970) 482-5994. Licensee: Citicasters Licenses Inc. (NEW). Group owner: Clear Channel Communications Inc. (acq 5-4-99; grpsl). Network: ABC Information & Entertainment. Format: Sports. News staff: 2; News: 35 hrs wkly. Target aud: 18-54; educated, affluent, professional. ♦Stu Haskell, VP & gen mgr; Rebecca Sponheimer, sls dir; Ron Barnhart, natl sls mgr & rgnl sls mgr; Colleen Miller, prom VP & prom dir; Chris Christman, progmg dir; Randy Barnard, progmg dir; Rich Bircumshaw, news dir; Jim Mross, chief of engrg.

KPAW(FM)— Co-owned with KIIX(AM). July 27, 1975: 107.9 mhz; 100 kw. 470 ft. TL: N40 40 50 W104 56 32. Stereo. Web Site: www.1079thebear.com. Format: Classic rock. Target aud: 25-54; men. ♦Stu Haskell, stn mgr; Jefferson Chase, opns VP & progmg dir; Kenton Skeels, sls VP; Collen Taylor, prom dir; Chris Kelly, progmg dir; Steve Payne, mus dir; Rich Bircumshaw, news dir.

*KLHV(FM)— 2005: 88.3 mhz; 1 w horiz, 90 w vert. Ant 941 ft. TL: N40 29 36 W105 10 52. 5700 W. Oaks Blvd., Rocklin, CA 95765. Phone: (916) 251-1600. Fax: (916) 251-1650. E-mail: klove@klove.com. Web Site: www.klove.com. Licensee: Educational Media Foundation. Group owner: EMF Broadcasting (acq 10-2-03; grpsl). Network: K-Love. Shaw Pittman. Format: Contemp Christian. News staff: 3. Target aud: 25-44; Judeo Christian female. ♦Richard Jenkins, pres; Mike Novak, VP; Lloyd Parker, gen mgr; Ed Lenane, opns dir; Keith Whipple, dev dir.

*KRFC(FM)— Not on air, target date: unknown: 88.9 mhz; 10 w horiz, 3 kw vert. Ant 216 ft. TL: N40 34 53 W104 54 20. 619 S. College Ave., Suite #4 80524. Phone: (970) 221-5075. E-mail: brianh@krfcfm.org. Web Site: www.krfcfm.org. Licensee: Public Radio for the Front Range. Format: Var/div. ♦Beth Flowers, stn mgr; Dawn Paepke, dev dir; Louis Fowler, mus dir.

Fort Morgan

KBRU-FM— May 1, 1968: . Stn currently dark 101.7 mhz; 3 kw. Ant 135 ft. TL: N40 15 31 W103 51 07. (CP: COL Strasburg. 101.5 mhz; 97 kw horiz, ant 2,050 ft. TL: N39 55 22 W103 58 18). Stereo. Denver Radio Co. LLC, 9229 W Sunset Blvd., Suite 900, Los Angeles, CA 90069. Phone: (310) 276-7439. Licensee: KBRU-FM LLC (group owner; acq 7-20-2005; $15.5 million). ♦Luis G. Nogales, CEO & gen mgr.

KFTM(AM)— May 22, 1949: 1400 khz; 1 kw-U. TL: N40 15 31 W103 51 07. Box 430 80701. Secondary address: 16041 Hwy. 34 80701. Phone: (970) 867-5674. Fax: (970) 542-1023. E-mail: kftm@aginformation.com. Web Site: kftm.net. Licensee: Media Logic LLC (group owner; acq 9-29-03; $415,000). Network: AP Radio, Jones Radio Networks. Format: Adult contemporary, Sp, news/talk. News staff: one; News: 16 hrs wkly. Target aud: General; the people of (Morgan county) Colorado. Spec prog: Farm news 6 hrs, talk 5 hrs, sports 10 hrs, Christian progmg 6 hrs, Spanish 9 hrs wkly. ♦Wayne Johnson, pres & gen mgr; Keith Lippolt, gen sls mgr; John Waters, progmg dir.

KSIR(AM)— See Brush

Fountain

KIBT(FM)— Sept 25, 1992: 96.1 mhz; 460 w. Ant 2,168 ft. TL: N38 44 44 W104 51 42. Stereo. 2864 So. Circle Dr., Suite 150, Colorado Springs 80906. Phone: (719) 540-9200. Fax: (719) 579-0882. Web Site: www.beatcolorado.com. Licensee: AMFM Radio Licenses LLC. Group owner: Clear Channel Communications Inc. (acq 7-1-2000; grpsl). Rep: Clear Channel. Format: Urban. News staff: one; News: 4 hrs wkly. Target aud: 25-44; men. Spec prog: Blues 3 hrs wkly. ♦Bob Gourley, gen mgr; Bob Richards, opns dir.

KJME(AM)— Not on air, target date: unknown: 890 khz; 5.5 kw-D, 500 w-N, DA-2. TL: N38 33 47 W104 36 20. 965 S. Irving St., Denver 80219. Phone: (303) 935-1156. Licensee: Timothy C. Cutforth. ♦Timothy C. Cutforth, gen mgr.

Frisco

KYSL(FM)— May 27, 1988: 93.9 mhz; 560 w. 1,050 ft. TL: N39 33 22 W106 06 53. Stereo. Box 27 80443. Secondary address: 719 Ten Mile Dr. 80443. Phone: (970) 668-0292. Fax: (970) 668-3667. Web Site: www.krystal93.com. Licensee: Krystal Broadcasting Inc. Network: AP Radio. Rep: Interep. Format: AAA. News staff: one; News: 8 hrs wkly. Target aud: 25-49; upscale adults. ♦Ann Penny, pres; Maureen Bennett, gen mgr.

Fruita

KEKB(FM)— Licensed to Fruita. See Grand Junction

Glenwood Springs

*KDNK(FM)— 2004: 88.1 mhz; 1.2 kw. Ant 2,542 ft. TL: N39 25 08 W107 22 10. Box 1388, Carbondale 81623. Phone: (970) 963-0139. Fax: (970) 963-0810. E-mail: kdnk@kdnk.org. Web Site: www.kdnk.org. Licensee: Carbondale Community Access Radio Inc. (acq 10-29-2004; exchange for KVOV(FM) Carbondale). Network: NPR. Haley, Bader &

Potts. Format: News. News: 21 hrs wkly. ♦Shawna Claiborne, stn mgr; Amy Kimberly, dev dir; Wick Moses, adv dir; Luke Nestler, mus dir.

KGLN(AM)— May 14, 1950: 980 khz; 1 kw-D, 225 w-N. TL: N39 33 10 W107 19 48. Box 1028 81602. Phone: (970) 945-9124. Fax: (970) 945-5409. Licensee: Colorado West Broadcasting Inc. (acq 6-93). Format: News/talk. Target aud: 45 plus. ♦Gabe Chenoweth, pres, gen mgr, opns dir, progmg dir & chief of engrg; Kimberly Henrie, sls dir & prom dir; Ron Milhorn, news dir.

KMTS(FM)—Co-owned with KGLN(AM). June 6, 1977: 99.1 mhz; 3 kw. -301 ft. TL: N39 32 36 W107 17 49. (CP: 10 kw). Stereo. Network: ABC Information & Entertainment. Format: Country. Target aud: 25-50.

KKCH(FM)— Sept 1, 1997: 92.7 mhz; 58 kw. 2,470 ft. TL: N39 25 05 W107 22 01. Box 7205, Avon 81620. Phone: (970) 949-0140. Fax: (970) 949-4318. Licensee: NRC Mountain Division LLC. (group owner; (acq 7-9-2004; grpsl). Format: Adult contemp. ♦Steve Wodlinger, gen mgr.

***KLXV(FM)**— August 1995: 91.9 mhz; 1 w horiz, 250 w vert. Ant 2,660 ft. TL: N39 25 30 W107 22 46. 5700 W. Oaks Blvd., Rocklin, CA 95765. Phone: (916) 251-1600. Fax: (916) 251-1650. E-mail: klove@klove.com. Web Site: www.klove.com. Licensee: Educational Media Foundation. Group owner: EMF Broadcasting (acq 12-28-00; grpsl). Network: K-Love. Shaw Pittman. Format: Contemp Christian. News staff: 3. Target aud: 25-44; Judeo Christian, female. ♦Richard Jenkins, pres; Mike Novak, VP; Lloyd Parker, gen mgr; Ed Lenane, stn mgr & opns mgr; Keith Whipple, dev dir.

KRVG(FM)— Oct. 1, 2000: 95.5 mhz; 70 w. 2,709 ft. TL: N39 25 30 W107 22 46. 751 Horizon Ct., Suite 225, Grand Junction 81506. Phone: (970) 241-6460. Fax: (970) 241-6452. Web Site: www.kissradio.com.Jones Rock Classics Licensee: Western Slope Communications LLC. (group owner) Format: Classic Rock. News staff: one; News: 20 hrs wkly. ♦Ken Bench, gen mgr.

Granby

KRKY(AM)— July 3, 1986: 930 khz; 4.5 kw-D. TL: N40 02 26 W105 56 11. Box 999, Dillon 80435. Phone: (970) 887-1100. Fax: (970) 468-2384. E-mail: comment@highcountryradio.com. Web Site: www.highcountryradio.com. Licensee: Granby Mountain Broadcasting LLC. Group owner: Kona Coast Radio LLC (acq 12-10-2003; grpsl). Network: ABC. Format: Country. News staff: 2; News: 5 hrs wkly. Target aud: 24-49; adults. Spec prog: Agriculture one hr, sp one hr. ♦M.R. Murray, VP & gen mgr.

KSPN-FM—See Aspen

Grand Junction

***KAFM(FM)**— 1999: 88.1 mhz; 20 w. 1,240 ft. TL: N39 04 00 W108 44 41. Stereo. 1310 Ute Ave. 81501. Phone: (970) 241-8801. Fax: (970) 241-0995. E-mail: kafm@kafmradio.org. Web Site: www.kafmradio.org. Licensee: Grand Valley Public Radio Co. Inc. Format: Community, edu, community radio. Target aud: 25-80. Spec prog: American Indian 3 hrs, Black 3 hrs, folk 10 hrs, Sp 3 hrs wkly. ♦Peter Trosclair, stn mgr; Jill Comstock, opns mgr; Julia Hall, dev dir & dev mgr.

KBKL(FM)— 1993: 107.9 mhz; 100 kw. 1,305 ft. TL: N39 04 00 W108 44 41. (CP: Ant 1,460 ft.). Stereo. 315 Kennedy Ave. 81501. Phone: (970) 242-7788. Fax: (970) 243-0567. Web Site: www.kool1079.com. Licensee: Cumulus Licensing Corp. Group owner: Cumulus Media LLC (acq 3-10-98; grpsl). Format: Oldies. Target aud: 25-54. ♦Lewis Dickey Jr., CEO; Jonathan Pinch, COO; Marty Gausvik, CFO; John Dickey, exec VP; Marco Camacho, VP; Mike Shafer, opns mgr.

***KCIC(FM)**— Mar 4, 1979: 88.5 mhz; 450 w. -431 ft. TL: N39 04 38 W108 30 38. Stereo. 3102 E Rd. 81504. Phone: (970) 434-4113. Licensee: Pear Park Baptist Schools. Format: Educ, relg. Spec prog: Class 14 hrs wkly. ♦Randy David, pres; Glenn Gardner, gen mgr & progmg dir.

KEKB(FM)—(Fruita). May 24, 1984: 99.9 mhz; 79 kw. 1,380 ft. TL: N39 03 56 W108 44 52. (CP: Ant 1,542 ft.). Stereo. 315 Kennedy Ave. 81501. Phone: (970) 242-7788. Fax: (970) 243-0567. Web Site: www.coloradowest.com. Licensee: Cumulus Licensing Corp. Group owner: Cumulus Media Inc. (acq 7-9-98; grpsl). Format: Country. News staff: 2; News: 6 hrs wkly. Target aud: 25-54. ♦Lewis Dickey Jr., CEO; Marty Gausvik, CFO; John Dickey, exec VP; Dave Noll, VP; Martiey Miller, gen mgr; Mike Shafer, opns mgr.

KEXO(AM)— 1942: 1230 khz; 1 kw-U. TL: N39 05 41 W108 34 41. 315 Kennedy Ave. 81501. Phone: (970) 242-7788. Fax: (970) 243-0567. Web Site: www.coloradowest.com.La Maguina Musical Licensee: Cumulus Licensing Corp. Group owner: Cumulus Media Inc. (acq 1-00). Format: Sp. News staff: one. Target aud: General. ♦Lewis Dickey Jr., CEO; Marty Gausvik, CFO; John Dickey, exec VP; Mike Shafer, opns mgr.

KJOL(AM)— June 19, 1957: 620 khz; 5 kw-U. TL: N39 07 35 W108 38 13. 1360 E. Sherwood Dr. 81501-7575. Phone: (970) 254-5565. Fax: (970) 254-5550. E-mail: info@kjol.org. Web Site: www.kjol.org. Licensee: United Ministries. (acq 5-1-2003). Format: Christian, talk, music. ♦Ken Andrews, gen mgr.

KJYE(FM)—Listing follows KNZZ.

***KLFV(FM)**— Apr 24, 1982: 90.3 mhz; 1.5 kw. 1,296 ft. TL: N30 03 57 W108 44 48. Stereo. 5700 W. Oaks Blvd., Rocklin, CA 95765. Phone: (916) 251-1600. Fax: (916) 251-1650. E-mail: klove@klove.com. Web Site: www.klove.com. Licensee: Educational Media Foundation. Group owner: EMF Broadcasting (acq 12-28-00; grpsl). Network: K-Love. Shaw Pittman. Format: Contemp Christian. News staff: 3. Target aud: 25-44; Judeo Christian, female. Spec prog: Sp 2 hrs wkly. ♦Richard Jenkins, pres; Mike Novak, VP; Lloyd Parker, gen mgr; Ed Lenane, opns dir; Keith Whipple, dev dir.

KMGJ(FM)— Nov 1, 1973: 93.1 mhz; 100 kw. 1,433 ft. TL: N39 03 59 W108 44 41. Stereo. 1360 E. Sherwood Dr. 81501. Phone: (970) 254-2100. Fax: (970) 245-7551. Web Site: gjradio.com. Licensee: M.B.C. Grand Broadcasting, Inc. (group owner; acq 5-94; with co-located AM). Format: CHR. News staff: one; News: 6 hrs wkly. Target aud: 18-49; women. ♦Richard C. Dean, pres; Jim Terlouw, gen mgr; Robert St. John, opns mgr; Dave Beck, gen sls mgr & natl sls mgr; Amanda Walker, prom mgr; Chris Britt, progmg dir; Randy Hampton, news dir; Dwight Morgan, chief of engrg.

KTMM(AM)—Co-owned with KMGJ(FM). 1959: 1340 khz; 1 kw-U. TL: N39 05 35 W108 35 51. Web Site: gjradio.com. Format: Sports. News staff: one; News: 10 hrs wkly. Target aud: 25-54; men. ♦Jim Davis, progmg dir; Dwight Morgan, chief of engrg.

KMOZ-FM— Mar 27, 1999: 100.7 mhz; 42 kw. 1,302 ft. TL: N39 04 00 W108 44 41. Stereo. 1360 E. Sherwood Dr. 81501. Phone: (970) 254-2100. Fax: (970) 245-7551. Web Site: www.gjradio.com. Licensee: MBC Grand Broadcasting Inc. (group owner) Format: Country. News staff: 2; News: 2 hrs wkly. Target aud: 25-54. ♦Richard C. Dean, pres; Jim Terlouw, gen mgr.

***KMSA(FM)**— Feb 18, 1975: 91.3 mhz; 3 kw. Ant -382 ft. TL: N39 04 48 W108 33 09. Stereo. 1100 North Ave. 81501. Phone: (970) 248-1442. Fax: (970) 248-1199. Fax: (970) 248-1834. E-mail: rtucci@mesastate.edu. Web Site: www.kmsa.com. Licensee: Mesa State College. Format: Adult alternative, hip hop, reggae. News staff: 2; News: 10 hrs wkly. Target aud: 18-60; college students and gen pub. Spec prog: Black 6 hrs, folk 2 hrs, jazz 12 hrs wkly. ♦Nathan King, pres & gen mgr.

KMXY(FM)— 1996: 104.3 mhz; 100 kw. 1,296 ft. (CP: Ant 1,460 ft.). 315 Kennedy Ave. 81501. Phone: (970) 242-7788. Fax: (970) 243-0567. Web Site: www.cumulus.com. Licensee: Cumulus Licensing Corp. Group owner: Cumulus Media Inc. (acq 7-9-98; grpsl). Format: Adult contemp. ♦Lewis Dickey Jr., CEO; Marty Gausvik, CFO; John Dickey, exec VP; Dave Noll, VP.

KNZZ(AM)— May 1, 1926: 1100 khz; 50 kw-D, 10 kw-N, DA-N. TL: N38 57 06 W108 25 10. 1360 E. Sherwood Dr. 81501. Phone: (970) 254-2100. Fax: (970) 245-7551. Web Site: www.knzz.com. Licensee: MBC Grand Broadcasting Inc. (group owner; acq 8-30-89). Network: AP Network News. Format: News/talk. News staff: 3; News: 44 hrs wkly. Target aud: 25-64; upscale adults. ♦Richard C. Dean, pres; Jim TerLouw, gen mgr & progmg mgr; Dave Beck, gen sls mgr; Libby Jackson, news dir; Dwight Morgan, chief of engrg.

KJYE(FM)—Co-owned with KNZZ. May 1, 1960: 92.3 mhz; 100 kw. 1,378 ft. TL: N39 04 00 W108 44 41. Stereo. Web Site: www.gjradio.com. Format: Adult contemp. News: 8 hrs wkly. Target aud: Adults; 25-54.

***KPRN(FM)**— April 1985: 89.5 mhz; 10 kw. 1,191 ft. TL: N39 03 57 W108 44 45. (CP: Ant 1,233 ft.). Stereo. 7409 S. Alton Ct., Centennial 80112. Phone: (303) 871-9191. Fax: (303) 733-3319. E-mail: info@cpr.org. Web Site: www.cpr.org. Licensee: Public Broadcasting of Colorado Inc. Network: NPR. Arter & Hadden. Format: News. News staff: one; News: 28 hrs wkly. Target aud: 25 plus. ♦Max Wycisk, pres; Jenny Gentry, exec VP; Ed Trudeau, gen mgr; Sue Coughlin, dev VP; Sean Nethery, mktg VP; Carlo Walker, progmg dir; Robert Hensler, engrg VP & chief of engrg.

Greeley

KFKA(AM)— May 21, 1921: 1310 khz; 5 kw-D, 1 kw-N, DA-N. TL: N40 21 56 W104 43 56. 820 11th Ave 80632. Phone: (970) 356-1310. Fax: (970) 356-1314. E-mail: info@1310kfka.com. Web Site: 1310kfka.com. Licensee: Music Ventures LLC dba Broadcast Media LLC (acq 11-1-2002; $1.6 million). Network: CBS Radio. Format: News/talk. News staff: 2; News: 25 hrs wkly. Target aud: 25-54; community-minded, active people. Spec prog: Farm 15 hrs, Ger one hr, relg 4 hrs wkly. ♦Damon Sasso, pres & opns mgr; Justin Sasso, gen mgr.

KGRE(AM)— Aug 24, 1948: 1450 khz; 1 kw-U. TL: N40 26 15 W104 43 25. 1020 9th St., Suite 201 80631. Phone: (970) 356-1452. Fax: (970) 356-8522. E-mail: kgre@msn.com. Web Site: www.tigre1450.com. Licensee: Greely Broadcasting Corp. (acq 3-24-98). Format: Sp. Target aud: 25-54; Hispanic. Spec prog: Bienvenidos a America one hr wkly. ♦Ricardo Salazar, pres & gen mgr.

KSME(FM)— Dec 25, 1975: 96.1 mhz; 100 kw. 660 ft. TL: N40 40 50 W104 56 32. Stereo. 1612 Laporte Ave., Fort Collins 80521. Phone: (970) 482-5991. Fax: (970) 482-5994. Web Site: www.kissfmcolorado.com. Licensee: Citicasters Licenses Inc. (NEW). Group owner: Clear Channel Communications Inc. (acq 5-4-99; grpsl). Network: ABC. Format: Top-40. News staff: 2. Target aud: 10-44. ♦Stu Haskell, VP & gen mgr; Kathy Arias, sls dir & gen sls mgr.

***KUNC-FM**— Jan 1, 1967: 91.5 mhz; 81 kw. Ant 692 ft. TL: N40 38 31 W104 49 03. Stereo. 822 Seventh St., Suite 530 80631. Phone: (970) 378-2579. Fax: (970) 378-2580. E-mail: mailbag@kunc.org. Web Site: www.kunc.org. Licensee: Community Radio for Northern Colorado (acq 8-01; $1.9 million). Network: Network: NPR, PRI. Format: Div, news. News staff: 3; News: 65 hrs wkly. Target aud: General. ♦Neil Best, gen mgr & stn mgr; Michelle Kormnich, dev dir; Kirk Mowens, progmg dir; Jim Beers, news dir; Larry Selzle, chief of engrg.

Gunnison

KEJJ(FM)— 1980: 98.3 mhz; 3 kw. Ant 304 ft. TL: N38 31 22 W106 54 28. Stereo. Box 1288 81230. Phone: (970) 641-4000. Fax: (970) 641-3300. Licensee: John Harvey Rees (acq 2-6-2001; $275,000). Format: Oldies. News staff: 2. Target aud: 25-54. ♦John Harvey Rees, CEO & pres.

KPKE(AM)— Aug 23, 1960: 1490 khz; 1 kw-U. TL: N38 33 57 W106 55 32. Box 1288 81230. Phone: (970) 641-4000. Fax: (970) 641-3300. E-mail: kpkeharv@hotmail.com. Licensee: John Harvey Rees. Network: ABC Information & Entertainment. Format: Country. News staff: one; News: 2 hrs wkly. Target aud: 25-54. ♦John Harvey Rees, CEO & gen mgr; Matt Rees, opns VP.

KVLE-FM— Apr 18, 1980: 102.3 mhz; 3 kw. 200 ft. TL: N38 33 53 W106 55 38. Stereo. Box 884, 1445 N. Hwy. 135 81230. Phone: (970) 641-3600. Fax: (970) 641-4566. E-mail: kvle@pcrs.net. Licensee: Pilgrim Communications Inc. (acq 4-30-98; $300,000). Network: CBS. Format: Classic rock. Target aud: General. ♦Dot Rich, gen mgr.

***KWSB-FM**— Jan 26, 1968: 91.1 mhz; 135 w. 304 ft. TL: N38 31 22 W106 54 28. Stereo. Taylor Hall, Western State College 81231. Phone: (970) 943-2036. Phone: (970) 943-2117. Fax: (970) 943-7069. Web Site: www.western.edu. Licensee: Western State College of Colorado. Network: AP Radio. Format: Var. News: 2 hrs wkly. Target aud: 18-25. Spec prog: Jazz 3 hrs, reggae 6 hrs, blues 3 hrs, 60s hits 3 hrs, Sp one hr wkly. ♦Justin Maloy, gen mgr & mus dir.

Gypsum

***KLRY(FM)**— 2003: 91.3 mhz; 800 w. Ant 1,036 ft. TL: N39 39 20 W106 40 39. 5700 W. Oaks Blvd., Rocklin, CA 95765. Phone: (916) 251-1600. Fax: (916) 251-1650. E-mail: klove@klove.com. Web Site: www.klove.com. Licensee: Educational Media Foundation. Group owner: EMF Broadcasting (acq 10-2-03; grpsl). Network: K-Love. Shaw Pittman. Format: Contemp Christian. News staff: 3. Target aud: 25-44; Judeo Christian female. ♦Richard Jenkins, pres; Mike Novak, VP & progmg dir; Lloyd Parker, gen mgr; Ed Lenane, opns dir & news

Stations in the U.S. — Colorado

Developers & Brokers of Radio Properties — contact American Media Services at our suite: Philadelphia Marriott Downtown 215-625-2900. 843-972-2200. americanmediaservices.com. Charleston, SC. Dallas, TX • Chicago, Il • Austin, TX. American Media Services, LLC

dir; Keith Whipple, dev dir; Chris Joyce, prom dir; David Pierce, progmg mgr; Jon Rivers, mus dir; Sam Wallington, engrg dir.

Hayden

*KHCO(FM)—Not on air, target date: unknown: 90.1 mhz; 10 kw. Ant 522 ft. TL: N40 31 36 W107 15 52. 5700 West Oaks Blvd., Rocklin, CA 95765. Phone: (916) 251-1600. Fax: (916) 251-1650. Licensee: Educational Media Foundation. (acq 6-8-2005; $25,000. for CP). ♦ Richard Jenkins, pres.

KIDN-FM— Feb 15, 1985: 95.9 mhz; 1.8 kw. 1,181 ft. TL: N40 25 46 W107 05 34. Stereo. Box 772850, Steamboat Springs 80477. Phone: (970) 879-5368. Fax: (970) 879-5843. Licensee: NRC Mountain Division LLC. Group owner: American General Media (acq 7-9-2004; grpsl). Format: Modern rock. Target aud: 21-54. ♦ Brian Harvey, gen mgr & stn mgr.

KRMR(FM)— 2000: 107.3 mhz; 29 kw. Ant 649 ft. TL: N40 31 16 W107 17 46. Box 772850, Steamboat Springs 80477. Phone: (970) 879-5368. Fax: (970) 879-5843. E-mail: krmrtalk@yahoo.com. Web Site: krmrradio.com. Licensee: NRC Mountain Division LLC. (group owner; acq 7-9-2004; grpsl). Format: News/talk. ♦ Brian Harvey, gen mgr.

Holyoke

KSTH(FM)— 2002: 92.3 mhz; 100 kw. Ant 567 ft. TL: N40 51 42 W103 23 35. Box 333, McCook, NE 69001. Phone: (308) 345-5400. Fax: (308) 345-4720. Licensee: Julesburg/Holyoke Media Association (acq 6-24-2004; $50,000. for 50% with KJBL(FM) Julesburg). Format: Adult contemp. ♦ David M. Stout, gen mgr; Connie Stout, sls dir; Ben Korn, progmg dir.

Ignacio

*KSUT(FM)— June 9, 1976: 91.3 mhz; 425 w. Ant 18 ft. TL: N37 05 51 W107 37 32. Stereo. Box 737 81137. Secondary address: 123 Capote Dr. 81137. Phone: (970) 563-0255. Web Site: www.ksut.org. Licensee: Kute Inc. Network: Network: NPR, PRI. Format: Native American. News: 30 hrs wkly. Target aud: 24 plus; public radio audience. Spec prog: American Indian 7 hrs, class 8 hrs, jazz 15 hrs wkly. ♦ Beth Warren, gen mgr.

*KUTE(FM)— June 1998: 90.1 mhz; 3 kw. 1,965 ft. TL: N37 21 51 W107 46 56. Box 737 81137. Phone: (970) 563-0255. Web Site: www.ksut.org. Licensee: KUTE Inc. Network: Network: NPR, PRI. Format: Eclectic, talk, music blend. ♦ Beth Warren, gen mgr.

Johnstown

KHNC(AM)— January 1993: 1360 khz; 10 w-D, 450 w-N, DA-N. TL: N40 23 11 W104 54 19. (CP: 10 kw-D, 1 kw-N, DA-N). Box 1750 80534-1750. Phone: (970) 587-5175. Fax: (970) 587-5450. E-mail: don@americanewsnet.com. Web Site: www.americanewsnet.com. Licensee: Donald A. and Sharon A. Wiedeman. Format: Conservative news/talk. ♦ Donald Wiedeman, pres & gen mgr; Michael Golden, opns mgr.

Julesburg

KJBL(FM)— 2002: 96.5 mhz; 100 kw. Ant 567 ft. TL: N40 51 42 W103 23 35. Box 333, McCook, NE 69001. Phone: (308) 345-5400. Fax: (308) 345-4720. Licensee: Julesburg/Holyoke Media Association (acq 6-24-2004; $50,000. for 50% with KSTH(FM) Holyoke). Format: Country. ♦ David M. Stout, gen mgr.

Kremmling

KZMV(FM)— Nov 1, 1987: 106.3 mhz; 2.5 kw. 1,050 ft. TL: N40 00 18 W106 26 57. Stereo. Box 999, Dillon 80435. Secondary address: 124 Main St., Suite 105, Dillon 80435. Phone: (970) 468-2353. Fax: (970) 468-2384. E-mail: comments@highcountryradio.com. Web Site: www.highcountryradio.com. Licensee: Granby Mountain Broadcasting LLC. Group owner: Kona Coast Radio LLC (acq 12-10-2003; grpsl). Network: ABC. Format: Oldies. News staff: 2; News: 5 hrs wkly. Target aud: 24-49. ♦ Vic Michael, pres; M.R. Murray, gen mgr.

La Junta

KBLJ(AM)— July 23, 1937: 1400 khz; 1 kw-U. TL: N37 59 14 W103 34 01. 116 Dalton 81050. Phone: (719) 384-5456. Fax: (719) 384-5450. Licensee: CCR-La Junta IV LLC. Group owner: Cherry Creek Radio LLC (acq 12-19-2003; grpsl). Network: Westwood One. Format: Oldies. Target aud: 30 plus; general. ♦ Pat McGee, gen mgr.

KTHN(FM)—Co-owned with KBLJ(AM). Aug 28, 1974: 92.1 mhz; 3 kw. 300 ft. TL: N37 59 15 W103 34 02. Stereo. Format: Country.

KFVR-FM—Not on air, target date: unknown: 106.5 mhz; 100 kw. Ant 512 ft. TL: N37 39 31 W103 27 55. Superior Broadcasting of Denver LLC, 8975 E. Kenyon Ave., Denver 80237. Phone: (720) 529-1431. Fax: (720) 529-1418. Licensee: Superior Broadcasting of Denver LLC. (group owner; (acq 5-15-2000; $2 million. for CP with CP for KOOO(FM) Rocky Ford). Duncan, Weinberg, Miller & Pembroke, P.C. ♦ Cindy Adcock, gen mgr.

*KRLJ(FM)— August 2002: 89.1 mhz; 740 w. 298 ft. TL: N37 58 43 W103 34 48. c/o KRCC(FM), 912 N. Weber St., Colorado Springs 80906. Phone: (719) 473-4801. Fax: (719) 473-7863. E-mail: info@krcc.org. Licensee: The Colorado College. ♦ Delaney Viterback, VP; Mario B. Valdes, gen mgr; Mike Procell, opns mgr; Denise Vienne, dev mgr; Jeff Bieri, prom dir; Joel Belik, chief of engrg.

Lakewood

KCKK(AM)— Jan 8, 1955: 1600 khz; 5 kw-U, DA-N. TL: N39 39 20 W105 04 28. Stereo. 1095 S. Monaco Pkwy., Denver 80224. Phone: (303) 321-0950. Fax: (303) 333-2987. Web Site: www.kckk1043.com. Licensee: Jefferson-Pilot Communications Co. (group owner; acq 11-24-92; $6.1 million with co-located FM; 12-14-92). Network: CBS. Rep: CBS Radio. Format: Classic country. Target aud: 35-64. ♦ Clarke Brown, pres; Bob Call, sr VP & gen mgr; John St. John, opns dir; Steve Price, sls dir; Randy Weidner, natl sls mgr; Mark Etchason, mktg dir; Garrott Doll, prom dir; Chuck St. John, progmg dir; Doug Olipra, news dir & pub affrs dir; Brad Hart, engrg dir.

KQKS(FM)—Co-owned with KCKK(AM). July 9, 1966: 107.5 mhz; 100 kw. 670 ft. TL: N39 41 45 W105 09 54. Stereo. Fax: (303) 321-3383. Web Site: www.ks1075.com. Format: Hip-hop, rhythm and blues. Target aud: 12-34. ♦ Dave Zobl, rgnl sls mgr; Jennifer Wilde, progmg dir; Jennifer Page, news dir.

*KFDN(FM)— 2005: 88.1 mhz; 430 w vert. Ant 1,053 ft. TL: N39 40 18 W105 13 05. 5700 W. Oaks Blvd., Rocklin, CA 95765. Phone: (916) 251-1600. Fax: (916) 251-1650. E-mail: klove@klove.com. Web Site: www.klove.com. Licensee: Educational Media Foundation. Group owner: EMF Broadcasting (acq 10-2-03; grpsl). Network: K-Love. Shaw Pittman. Format: Contemp Christian. News staff: 3. Target aud: 25-44; Judeo Christian, female. ♦ Richard Jenkins, pres; Mike Novak, VP; Lloyd Parker, gen mgr; Ed Lenane, opns dir; Keith Whipple, dev dir.

Lamar

KLMR(AM)— December 1948: 920 khz; 5 kw-D, 500 w-N, DA-N. TL: N38 06 53 W102 37 16. Box 890 81052. Secondary address: 7650 US Hwy. 50 81052. Phone: (719) 336-2206. Licensee: CCR-Lamar IV LLC. Group owner: Cherry Creek Radio LLC (acq 12-19-2003; grpsl). Network: ABC Information & Entertainment. Rep: Interep. Format: Classic country. News: 12 hrs wkly. Target aud: 25-54. ♦ Pat Gittings, gen mgr & stn mgr; Ty Hormon, gen sls mgr & progmg mgr; Eric Mullens, news dir.

KLMR-FM— November 1978: 93.3 mhz; 100 kw. 498 ft. TL: N38 02 10 W102 35 58. Stereo. 7350 U.S. Hwy. 50 81052. E-mail: klmr@hotmail.com. Network: CBS. Format: Classic hits. Target aud: 25-54.

KVAY(FM)— Aug 5, 1991: 105.7 mhz; 100 kw. 545 ft. TL: N38 06 44 W102 57 37. (CP: Ant 479 ft.). Stereo. Box 1176, 224 S. Main 81052. Phone: (719) 336-8734. Fax: (719) 336-5977. E-mail: bobd@kvay.com. Web Site: kvay.com. Licensee: Beacon Broadcasting LLC (acq 1-3-03; $825,000). Network: AP Radio. Leventhal, Senter & Lerman. Format: Country. News staff: one. Target aud: 25-55. Spec prog: Gospel 4 hrs, classic rock 4 hrs wkly. ♦ Robert Delancey, gen mgr, stn mgr & opns dir.

Las Animas

KRKV(FM)—Not on air, target date: unknown: 107.3 mhz; 100 kw. Ant 384 ft. TL: N38 06 44 W102 57 39. 19801 Huntsville-Brownferry Rd., Tanner, AL 35671. Phone: (256) 345-2478. Licensee: Alleycat Communications. ♦ Richard W. Dabney, gen mgr.

Limon

KAVD(FM)— 2003: 103.1 mhz; 100 kw. Ant 443 ft. TL: N39 28 12 W103 38 14. Stereo. Box 1023, Strassburg 81136. Phone: (303) 622-4888. Fax: (303) 622-9258. Licensee: High Peak Broadcasting LLC (acq 6-15-01). Duncan, Weinberg, Miller & Pembroke, P.C. Format: Country. ♦ Billy Seeger, gen mgr, sls dir & progmg dir; Quinn Morrison, chief of engrg.

KLIM(AM)— May 8, 1984: . Stn currently dark 1120 khz; 250 w-D. TL: N39 16 27 W103 42 49. 165 E Ave. 80828. Phone: (719) 775-8199. Licensee: Roger L. Hoppe II (acq 3-7-96; $8,000). Miller & Neely. Format: Oldies. ♦ Roger Hoppe II, pres; Alan Olson, gen mgr.

Littleton

KCUV(FM)— Aug 22, 1957: 1510 khz; 10 kw-D, 1.3 kw-N, DA-2. TL: N39 33 08 W105 02 00. 1201 18th St., Suite 220, Denver 80202. Phone: (303) 296-7025. Fax: (303) 296-7030. Web Site: www.kcuvradio.com. Licensee: People's Wireless Inc. Group owner: NRC Broadcasting Inc. (acq 4-26-2002; $2.7 million). Format: Americana. ♦ Tim Brown, CEO; Dave Rogers, CFO; Ray Skibitsky, gen mgr.

Longmont

*KGUD(FM)— September 1975: 90.7 mhz; 100 w. Ant 270 ft. TL: N40 14 24 W105 03 19. Stereo. Box 1534 80502-1534. Secondary address: Studio: 457 Fourth Ave. 80501. Phone: (303) 485-9811. E-mail: baskos_george@stvrain.k12.co.us. Licensee: Longmont Community Radio (acq 10-31-2003). Format: Btfl music. Target aud: 45 plus; retirees. ♦ George N. Baskos, gen mgr; James R. Boynton Sr., stn mgr.

KJCD(FM)— September 1964: 104.3 mhz; 5.8 kw. 1,204 ft. TL: N40 05 47 W104 54 04. Stereo. 1095 S. Monaco Pkwy., Denver 80224. Phone: (303) 321-0950. Fax: (303) 321-3383. Web Site: www.1043.com. Licensee: Jefferson-Pilot Communications Co. (group owner; acq 11-25-96; $15 million). Network: Westwood One. Rep: Allied Radio Partners. Wiley, Rein & Fielding. Format: Smooth jazz. Target aud: 18-34; hip. ♦ Bob Call, gen mgr; Michael Fischer, opns mgr, opns mgr, gen sls mgr & progmg dir; Cheryl Holbeck, gen sls mgr; Dwayne Taylor, mktg mgr; Steve Conklin, prom dir; Steve Price, progmg dir & mus dir; Brad Hart, chief of engrg.

KRCN(AM)— December 1949: 1060 khz; 50 kw-D, 100 w-N. TL: N40 11 28 W105 07 35. 614 Kimbark St. 80501. Phone: (303) 776-2323. Fax: (303) 776-1377. Web Site: www.radiocoloradonetwork.com. Licensee: Pilgrim Communications Inc. (acq 5-27-98; $575,000). Network: ABC Daytime Direction. Format: Talk. News staff: one; News: 20 hrs wkly. Target aud: 30-60; news & sports listeners. Spec prog: Sp one hr, farm one hr wkly. ♦ Gene Hood, pres; Ron Nickell, sr VP & stn mgr.

Loveland

KSXT(AM)— Jan 21, 1955: 1570 khz; 1 kw-D. TL: N40 23 31 W105 05 51. 1270 Boston Ave., Longmont 80501. Phone: (970) 612-1570. Fax: (970) 612-0137. E-mail: sfmtaylor@yahoo.com. Licensee: O.J. &

Colorado

Carol Pratt (acq 5-23-02). Format: News/talk. ◆Wes Hood, gen mgr & chief of opns; Mike Taylor, progmg dir.

KTRR(FM)— Feb 5, 1966: 102.5 mhz; 50 kw. 410 ft. TL: N40 27 19 W104 55 25. Stereo. 600 Main St., Windsor 80550. Phone: (970) 686-2791. Fax: (970) 686-7491. Web Site: www.tri102.com. Licensee: Regent Broadcasting of Ft. Collins Inc. Group owner: Regent Communications Inc. (acq 2-25-03). Format: Adult contemp. Target aud: 25-54. ◆Cal Hall, gen mgr; Mark Callaghan, opns mgr; Lisa Scheider, gen sls mgr.

*KXWA(FM)— 2005: 89.7 mhz; 45 w horiz, 36 w vert. Ant 1,220 ft. TL: N40 37 03 W105 19 40. Box G, Boulder 80306. Phone: (719) 533-0300. Fax: (303) 485-1929. Web Site: wayfm.com. Licensee: WAY-FM Media Group Inc (group owner; acq 11-19-2002). Format: Contemp Christian. ◆Robert D. Augsburg, pres; Zach Cochran, stn mgr; Dusty Rhodes, chief of opns; Scott Viegel, progmg dir.

Manitou Springs

KBIQ(FM)— May 1952: 102.7 mhz; 100 kw. 2,000 ft. TL: N38 44 47 W104 51 37. Stereo. 7150 Campus Dr., Suite 150, Colorado Springs 80920. Phone: (719) 531-5438. Fax: (719) 531-5588. Web Site: www.positiveq102.com. Licensee: Bison Media Inc. Group owner: Salem Communications Corp. (acq 10-8-96; $2.825 million). Format: Christian, adult contemp. News: one hr wkly. Target aud: 18-54. ◆Phil Lewis, gen mgr.

*KCME(FM)— Sept 1, 1979: 88.7 mhz; 8.9 kw. Ant 2,191 ft. TL: N38 44 40 W104 51 41. Stereo. 1921 N. Weber, Colorado Springs 80907-6903. Phone: (719) 578-5263. Fax: (719) 578-1033. E-mail: kcme@kcme.org. Web Site: www.kcme.org. Licensee: Cheyenne Mt. Public Broadcast House Inc. Format: Class, jazz. Target aud: 45 plus; upper-middle class, mostly college graduates. Spec prog: World music. ◆Joseph Reich Jr., pres; Jeanna Wearing, gen mgr, opns dir & mktg VP; Cynthia Bullock, dev VP.

KXRE(AM)— November 1956: 1490 khz; 500 w-D, 250 w-N. TL: N38 51 43 W104 55 32. 600 Grant St., Denver 80203. Phone: (303) 733-5266. Fax: (303) 733-5242. E-mail: kbno@kbno.net. Web Site: www.kbno.net. Licensee: Latino Communications LLC (group owner); acq 1-23-03; $350,000. with KAVA(AM) Pueblo). Format: Rgnl Mexican. ◆Zee Ferrufino, gen mgr.

Meeker

KAYW(FM)— Sept 30, 2000: 98.1 mhz; 100 kw horiz. 1,191 ft. TL: N39 58 18 W108 02 23. 751 Horizon Ct., Suite 225, Grand Junction 81506. Phone: (970) 241-6460. Fax: (970) 241-6452. E-mail: kiss@kissradio.com. Web Site: www.kissradio.com. Licensee: Western Slope Communications LLC (group owner) Format: Country. News: 20 hrs wkly. ◆Ken Bench, gen mgr.

Monte Vista

KSLV(AM)— February 1954: 1240 khz; 1 kw-U. TL: N37 36 10 W106 08 58. Box 631, 109 Adams St. 81144. Phone: (719) 852-3581. Fax: (719) 852-3583. E-mail: kslv@amigo.com. Web Site: www.kslvradio.com. Licensee: San Luis Valley Broadcasting Inc. (acq 4-1-79). Cohn & Marks. Format: Country. News staff: one; News: 6 hrs wkly. Target aud: 25-54. Spec prog: Sp 10 hrs, farm one hr, gospel 4 hrs wkly. ◆Gerald Vigil, gen mgr; Linda Pacheco, news dir.

KSLV-FM— 1986: 95.3 mhz; 6 kw. 89 ft. TL: N37 36 10 W106 08 58. Stereo. Web Site: www.kslvradio.com. Format: Soft adult contemp. News: 2 hrs wkly.

Montrose

KKXK(FM)—Listing follows KUBC(AM).

*KPRH(FM)— October 1998: 88.3 mhz; 5 kw. 1,535 ft. TL: N38 20 01 W107 39 52. Colorado Public Radio, Bridges Broadcast Center, 7409 S. Alton Ct., Centennial 80112. Phone: (303) 871-9191. Phone: (800) 722-4449. Fax: (303) 733-3319. Web Site: www.cpr.org. Licensee: Public Broadcasting of Colorado Inc. Network: NPR. Arter & Hadden. Format: News. Target aud: General. ◆Max Wycisk, pres; Arlene Wayland, prom mgr; Ed Trudeau, progmg dir; Robert Hensler, engrg VP.

KSTR-FM— Apr 10, 1980: 96.1 mhz; 100 kw. 1,099 ft. TL: N38 52 40 W108 13 33. Stereo. 2808 North Ave., Suite 440, Grand Junction 81501. Phone: (970) 242-5787. Fax: (970) 245-6585. Web Site: www.kstr.com. Licensee: Leggett Broadcasting Inc. (acq 8-1-94; $650,000; with KSTR(AM) Grand Junction). Network: Westwood One. Rep: McGavren Guild. Format: Modern rock. Target aud: 18-49. ◆Brad Leggett, pres & gen mgr; John Dane, opns mgr & sls.

KUBC(AM)— Sept 25, 1947: 580 khz; 5 kw-D, 1 kw-N, DA-N. TL: N38 25 32 W107 52 57. Box 970 81402. Secondary address: 106 Rose Ln. 81401. Phone: (970) 249-4546. Fax: (970) 249-2229. Web Site: www.coloradoradio.com. Licensee: CCR-Montrose IV LLC. (group owner; (acq 8-19-2004); grpsl). Network: ABC. Rep: Interep. Garvey, Schubert & Barer. Format: Country. News: 4 hrs wkly. Target aud: 35-54. Spec prog: Sports 5 hrs, relg 3 hrs wkly. ◆Joseph D. Schwartz, pres; John Craft, gen mgr.

KKXK(FM)— Co-owned with KUBC(AM). December 1976: 94.1 mhz; 90 kw. 1,748 ft. TL: N38 20 16 W107 38 23. Stereo. Web Site: www.94kix.com. News staff: one; News: 4 hrs wkly. Target aud: 25-54.

*KVMT(FM)— 1999: 89.1 mhz; 3 kw. Ant 1,748 ft. TL: N38 18 52 W108 12 02. Box 1350, Paonia 81428. Phone: (970) 527-4866. Fax: (970) 527-4865. Web Site: www.kvnf.org. Licensee: North Fork Valley Public Radio Inc. Format: News, music. ◆Sally Kane, gen mgr.

Monument

KCBR(AM)— July 20, 1986: 1040 khz; 15 kw-D. TL: N38 49 08 W104 46 32. Stereo. 5050 Edison Ave., Suite 218, Colorado Springs 80915. Phone: (719) 570-1530. Fax: (719) 570-1007. E-mail: kcbrinfo@crawfordbroadcasting.com. Web Site: www.crawfordbroadcasting.com. Licensee: KLZ Radio Inc. Group owner: Crawford Broadcasting Co. (acq 1999; $750,000 with KCMN(AM) Colorado Springs). Format: Christian talk. Target aud: 25-54; 70% male, upper-middle income or higher. ◆Don Crawford, Sr., pres; Don Crawford Jr., VP & gen mgr; Tron Simpson, opns mgr, progmg VP & progmg dir.

Morrison

*KLDV(FM)— Mar 27, 1971: 91.1 mhz; 100 kw. Ant 1,168 ft. TL: N39 36 00 W105 12 35. (CP: ant 1,207 ft). Stereo. 5700 W. Oaks Blvd., Rocklin, CA 95765. Phone: (916) 251-1600. Fax: (916) 251-1650. E-mail: klove@klove.com. Web Site: www.klove.com. Licensee: Educational Media Foundation. Group owner: EMF Broadcasting (acq 12-28-00; grpsl). Network: K-Love. Shaw Pittman. Format: Contemp Christian. News staff: 3. Target aud: 25-44; Judeo Christian, female. ◆Richard Jenkins, pres; Mike Novak, VP; Lloyd Parker, gen mgr; Ed Lenane, opns dir; Keith Whipple, dev dir.

New Castle

KCUV-FM— 2005: 94.5 mhz; 25 kw. Ant -397 ft. TL: N39 33 56 W107 32 01. 1201 18th St., Suite 250, Denver 80202-1869. Phone: (303) 675-4698. Fax: (303) 296-7030. Licensee: Wildcat Communications LLC. ◆Timothy Brown, gen mgr.

Norwood

KRYD(FM)— January 1998: 104.9 mhz; 16 kw. 1,607 ft. TL: N37 59 57 W107 57 42. Stereo. 475 Water St., Montrose 81401. Phone: (970) 249-8989. Fax: (970) 240-0909. E-mail: wes@krydradio.com. Licensee: Rocky III Investments Inc. Wood, Maine & Brown, Chartered. Format: Country. Target aud: 25 plus. ◆Bill Varecha, CEO; Debbie Varecha, CFO; Wes Smith, opns mgr; Carol Heiner, gen sls mgr.

Oak Creek

KFMU-FM— Sept 22, 1975: 104.1 mhz; 1.4 kw. 1,073 ft. TL: N40 14 10 W106 52 30. Stereo. Box 772850, 2955 Village Dr., Steamboat Springs 80477. Phone: (970) 879-5368. Fax: (970) 879-5843. Web Site: www.kfmu.com. Licensee: NRC Mountain Division LLC. (group owner; (acq 7-9-2004); grpsl). Network: CBS. Format: Adult progsv, rock. News staff: 2; News: 10 hrs wkly. Target aud: 21-54. Spec prog: Jazz 4 hrs, modern mus 4 hrs wkly. ◆Brian Harvey, gen mgr.

Otis

KATR-FM— Sept 1, 1983: 98.3 mhz; 100 kw. Ant 554 ft. TL: N40 25 13 W102 58 10. Stereo. Box 354, Wray 80758. Secondary address: 804 S. Ash St., Yuma 80759. Phone: (970) 848-3525. Phone: (970)

332-4171. Fax: (970) 332-4172. Fax: (970) 542-1173. E-mail: krdzkatr@plains.net. Web Site: www.katcountry983.com. Licensee: Media Logic LLC (group owner; acq 10-28-2002; $700,000). Format: Country. News staff: 3; News: 15 hrs wkly. Target aud: 16-70; males & females. ◆Wayne Johnson, gen mgr & opns mgr.

Ouray

KWGL(FM)— June 16, 1986: 105.7 mhz; 7 kw. -23 ft. TL: N38 01 22 W107 40 12. (CP: 25 kw, ant 203 ft. TL: N38 15 59 W107 51 07). Stereo. 751 Horizon Ct., Suite 225, Grand Junction 81506. Phone: (970) 241-6460. Fax: (970) 241-6452. Web Site: www.kissradio.com. Licensee: WS Communications L.L.C. (acq 1-95; 5-22-95). Network: Jones Radio Networks. Format: Classic rock. News staff: one; News: 15 hrs wkly. ◆Ken Bench, gen mgr.

Pagosa Springs

*KPGS(FM)— Not on air, target date: unknown: 88.1 mhz; 375 w vert. Ant 1,309 ft. TL: N37 11 32 W107 05 56. Box 737, Ignacio 81137-0737. Phone: (970) 563-0255. Web Site: www.ksut.org. Licensee: KUTE Inc. ◆Eddie Box Jr., pres; Beth Warren, gen mgr.

*KTPS(FM)— Not on air, target date: unknown: 89.7 mhz; 200 w. Ant 1,273 ft. TL: N37 11 35 W107 05 58. 1665 Briargate Blvd., Colorado Springs 80920. Phone: (719) 593-0600. Fax: (719) 593-2399. Licensee: Educational Communications of Colorado Springs Inc. Format: Christian. ◆Karen Veazey, gen mgr; Steve Howard, opns mgr; John Hayes, mus dir; Harry Russell, chief of engrg.

KWUF-FM— May 1, 1986: 106.3 mhz; 255 w. 1,280 ft. TL: N37 11 32 W107 05 55. Stereo. Box 780 81147. Secondary address: 702 S. 10th St. 81147. Phone: (970) 264-5983. Fax: (970) 264-5129. E-mail: kwuf@pagosa.net. Web Site: www.kwuf.com. Licensee: Wolf Creek Broadcasting L.L.C. (acq 1999; with co-located AM). Network: Westwood One. Format: Adult contemp. News: 10 hrs wkly. Target aud: 18 plus. Spec prog: Blues 10 hrs, jazz 10 hrs wkly. ◆Christie Spears, VP; Beth Porter, sls dir; Will Spears, CEO, pres, gen mgr & progmg mgr; Peter Mergens, chief of engrg.

KWUF(AM)— Aug 27, 1975 1400 khz; 1 kw-U. TL: N37 15 24 W107 01 06. Web Site: www.kwuf.com. Network: Westwood One. Format: Country, news/talk, sports. News: 10 hrs wkly. Target aud: General.

Paonia

*KVNF(FM)— Oct 5, 1979: 90.9 mhz; 3 kw. Ant -171 ft. TL: N38 52 20 W107 39 45. Stereo. Box 1350, 213 Grand Ave. 81428. Phone: (970) 527-4866. Fax: (970) 527-4865. Web Site: www.kvnf.org. Licensee: North Fork Valley Public Radio Inc. (acq 1-27-78). Network: NPR. Format: News, music. Spec prog: Class 15 hrs, jazz 17 hrs, blues 3 hrs, C&W 5 hrs, new age 6 hrs, Sp 2 hrs, gospel 3 hrs wkly. ◆Sally Kane, gen mgr.

Pierce

KJMP(AM)— 2004: 870 khz; 1.2 kw-D, 320 w-N, DA-2. TL: N40 36 25 W104 41 19. Radio Frontier Broadcasting LLC, 6807 Foxglove Dr., Cheyenne, WY 82009. Phone: (307) 778-9318. Fax: (307) 632-9349. Licensee: White Park Broadcasting Inc (acq 9-6-2005; $350,000). Format: Adult contemporary. ◆Victor Michael Jr., gen mgr.

Placerville

*KTEI(FM)— Not on air, target date: unknown: 90.7 mhz; 250 w. Ant 1,486 ft. TL: N37 59 29 W107 58 21. 1665 Briargate Blvd., Colorado Springs 80920. Phone: (719) 593-0600. Fax: (719) 593-2399. Licensee: Educational Communications of Colorado Springs Inc. ◆Karen Veazey, gen mgr.

Pueblo

KAVA(AM)— June 1963: 1480 khz; 1 kw-D, DA. TL: N38 18 56 W104 37 03. 600 Grant St., Denver 80203. Phone: (303) 733-5266. Fax: (303) 733-5242. E-mail: kbno@kbno.net. Web Site: www.kbno.net. Licensee: Latino Communications LLC (group owner; acq 1-23-03; $350,000. with KXRE(AM) Manitou Springs). Format: Rgnl Mexican. ◆Zee Ferrufino, gen mgr & opns dir.

KCCY(FM)— Aug 23, 1975: 96.9 mhz; 100 kw. 320 ft. TL: N38 21 32 W104 58 13. 2864 S. Circle Dr., Suite 150 80906. Phone: (719)

Stations in the U.S. Colorado

Developers & Brokers of Radio Properties — contact American Media Services at our suite: Philadelphia Marriott Downtown 215-625-2900 — 843-972-2200 — americanmediaservices.com — Charleston, SC — Dallas, TX · Chicago, IL · Austin, TX — American Media Services, LLC

540-9200. Fax: (719) 543-9898. Web Site: www.y969.com. Licensee: Clear Channel Radio Licenses, Inc. Group owner: Clear Channel Communications Inc. (acq 11-22-00; with KDZA-FM Pueblo). Rep: Christal. Format: C&W. Target aud: 25-54; general. ◆Bob Gourley, gen mgr.

*KCFP(FM)— June 1986: 91.9 mhz; 600 w. 633 ft. TL: N38 22 23 W104 33 42. Stereo. 7409 S. Alton Ct., Centennial 80112. Phone: (303) 871-9191. Fax: (303) 733-3319. Web Site: www.cpr.org. Licensee: Public Broadcasting of Colorado Inc. Network: NPR. Arter & Hadden. Format: Class, news. News staff: 8; News: 50 hrs wkly. Target aud: General. ◆Max Wycisk, pres; Sue Coughlin, dev VP.

KCSJ(AM)— 1947: 590 khz; 1 kw-U, DA-N. TL: N38 21 30 W104 38 13. 106 W. 24th St. 81003. Phone: (719) 545-2080. Fax: (719) 543-9898. Web Site: www.590kcsj.com. Licensee: Clear Channel Broadcasting Licenses Inc. Group owner: Clear Channel Communications Inc. (acq 6-14-01; with KGHF(AM) Pueblo). Network: ABC. Rep: Christal. Format: News/talk, sports. News staff: 2; News: 41 hrs wkly. Target aud: 35-64; upscale. ◆Olene Greenwood, gen mgr.

KDZA-FM— Mar 3, 1987: 107.9 mhz; 100 kw. 239 ft. TL: N37 56 40 W104 59 56. Stereo. 106 W. 24th St. 81003. Phone: (719) 545-2080. Fax: (719) 543-9898. Web Site: www.kdzafm.com. Licensee: Capstar TX L.P. Group owner: Clear Channel Communications Inc. (acq 11-22-00; with KCCY(FM) Pueblo). Format: Oldies. ◆Olene Greenwood, gen mgr; Mark Warren, gen sls mgr; Margaret Thornberg, prom dir.

KFEL(AM)— August 1956: 970 khz; 3.2 kw-D, 184 w-N. TL: N38 15 57 W104 40 44. 3305 N. Elizabeth St., Suite B 81008. Phone: (719) 543-7506. Fax: (719) 543-0432. E-mail: kfel970am@aol.com. Licensee: Wellspring Harvest Ministries Inc. (acq 11-4-98; $390,000). Format: Relg. Target aud: 25 plus. ◆Allen Bickle, gen mgr.

*KFRY(FM)—Not on air, target date: unknown: 89.9 mhz; 870 w. Ant 2,122 ft. TL: N38 02 29 W105 11 05. Family Stations Inc., 4136 Northgate Blvd., Suite 1, Sacramento, CA 95834-1226. Phone: (916) 641-8191. Fax: (510) 568-6190. Licensee: Family Stations Inc. ◆Harold Camping, gen mgr.

KGFT(FM)— Mar 31, 1988: 100.7 mhz; 72.4 kw. 2,217 ft. TL: N38 44 44 W104 51 39. Stereo. 7150 Campus Drive, Ste 150, Colorado Springs 80920. Phone: (719) 531-5438. Fax: (719) 531-5588. Licensee: Salem Communications Corp. (group owner; acq 1996; $3 million). Network: Network: UPI, AP Radio. Format: Christian, news/talk, relg. News staff: one; News: 4 hrs wkly. Target aud: 25 plus; Christian. Spec prog: Gospel 3 hrs, old time radio 11 hrs wkly. ◆Phil Lewis, gen mgr; Bob Medran, gen sls mgr.

KGHF(AM)— February 1928: 1350 khz; 5 kw-D, 1 kw-N, DA-N. TL: N38 18 29 W104 38 24. Stereo. 106 W. 24th St. 81003. Phone: (719) 545-2080. Fax: (719) 543-9898. Web Site: www.1350thezone.com. Licensee: Clear Channel Broadcasting Licenses Inc. Group owner: Clear Channel Communications Inc. (acq 6-14-01; with KCSJ(AM) Pueblo). Network: ABC Information & Entertainment. Rep: Allied Radio Partners. Haley, Bader & Potts. Format: Sports. News staff: one; News: one hr wkly. Target aud: 35 plus. ◆Olene Greenwood, gen mgr.

KILO(FM)—See Colorado Springs

KKMG(FM)— Jan 1, 1967: 98.9 mhz; 100 kw. 1,715 ft. TL: N38 44 32 W104 51 41. (CP: 56 kw, ant 2,299 ft.). Stereo. 6805 Corporate Dr., Suite 130, Colorado Springs 80919-1977. Phone: (719) 593-2700. Fax: (719) 593-2727. Web Site: www.989magicfm.com. Licensee: Citadel Broadcasting Co. Group owner: Citadel Broadcasting Corp. (acq 3-21-94; $912,500;. FTR: 4-18-94). Rep: McGavren Guild. Reed, Smith, Shaw & McClay. Format: Top-40. Target aud: 18-49. ◆Brenda Goodrich, gen mgr.

KKPC(AM)— Dec 29, 1947: 1230 khz; 1 kw-U. TL: N38 16 38 W104 39 13. Colorado Public Radio, 7409 S. Alton Ct., Centennial 80112. Phone: (303) 871-9191. Fax: (303) 733-3319. E-mail: info@cpr.org. Web Site: www.cpr.org. Licensee: Public Broadcasting of Colorado Inc. (acq 6-21-01; $275,000). Format: News and info. ◆Jenny Gentry, exec VP; Max Wycisk, pres & gen mgr; Ed Trudeau, progmg VP.

KNKN(FM)— November 1979: 106.9 mhz; 27.5 kw. Ant 666 ft. TL: N38 06 22 W104 29 18. Stereo. 30 N. Electronic Dr., Pueblo West 81007. Phone: (719) 547-0411. Fax: (719) 547-9301. E-mail: elgatonnegro@amigo.net. Licensee: Metropolitan Radio Group Inc. (group owner; (acq 8-1-97; $725,000. with co-located AM). Format: Sp Contemp. Target aud: 18-54. ◆Mark L. Acker, pres & gen mgr; Lup Brown, stn mgr.

KRMX(AM)— 1958: 690 khz; 250 w-D, 24 w-N. TL: N38 17 48 W104 38 47. Stereo. 30 N. Electronic Dr., Pueblo West 81007. Phone: (719) 545-2883. E-mail: elgatonnegro@amigo.net. Licensee: Metropolitan Radio Group Inc. (group owner; acq 10-97; $171,500). Format: Rgnl Mexican. Target aud: General; Hispanic families. ◆Lupe Brown, gen mgr.

*KTPL(FM)— 2005: 88.3 mhz; 65 kw. Ant 226 ft. TL: N37 56 40 W104 59 56. 1665 Briargate Blvd., Colorado Springs 80920. Phone: (719) 593-0600. Fax: (719) 593-2399. E-mail: lightpraise@ktlf.irg. Web Site: www.ktlf.org. Licensee: Educational Communications of Colorado Springs Inc. (acq 12-2-02; $6,251. for CP). Format: Inspirational Christian. ◆Karen Veazey, gen mgr.

*KTSC-FM— October 1970: 89.5 mhz; 9.8 kw. 165 ft. TL: N38 18 38 W104 34 40. Stereo. Univ. of Southern Colorado, 2200 Bonforte Blvd. Rm #120 81001. Phone: (719) 549-2822. Fax: (719) 549-2120. Licensee: University of Southern Colorado. Format: Top 40. ◆Sam Lovato, stn mgr.

KVUU(FM)— 1976: 99.9 mhz; 57. 2,200 ft. TL: N33 44 47 W104 51 37. Stereo. 2864 S. Circle Dr., Suite 150, Colorado Springs 80906. Phone: (719) 540-9200. Fax: (719) 579-0882. Web Site: www.my999radio.com. Licensee: Capstar TX L.P. Group owner: Clear Channel Communications Inc. (acq 8-30-00; grpsl). Rep: Clear Channel. Format: Hits of the 90s. News staff: one; News: 3 hrs wkly. Target aud: 25-54; upscale young adults. ◆Bob Gourley, chmn & gen mgr.

KYZX(FM)—(Pueblo West). 1993: 103.9 mhz; 1.75 kw. Ant 2,158 ft. TL: N38 44 40 W104 51 41. Stereo. 1805 E. Cheyenne Rd., Colorado Springs 80906. Phone: (719) 634-4896. Fax: (719) 634-5837. Web Site: www.theeagle.com. Licensee: Colorado Springs Radio Broadcasters Inc. Group owner: Bahakel Communications (acq 2-22-99; grpsl). Format: Class rock. News staff: one; News: one hr wkly. Target aud: 25-49; general. ◆Lou Mellini, gen mgr; Rich Hawk, opns mgr.

Pueblo West

KYZX(FM)—Licensed to Pueblo West. See Pueblo

Ridgway

KBNG(FM)— 2002: 103.7 mhz; 4.1 kw. Ant 1,574 ft. TL: N38 23 15 W107 40 31. Box 970, Montrose 81402. Phone: (970) 249-4546. Fax: (970) 249-2229. Web Site: www.coloradoradio.com. Licensee: CCR-Montrose IV LLC. (group owner; (acq 8-19-2004); grpsl). Format: Hot adult contemp. Target aud: 18-44; female. ◆Joseph D. Schwartz, pres; John H. Craft, gen mgr; Scott Stacey, progmg dir.

Rifle

KRGS(AM)— June 9, 1967: 690 khz; 1 kw-D. TL: N39 32 55 W107 46 10. 751 Horizon Ct., Suite 200, Grand Junction 81506. Phone: (970) 241-6460. Fax: (970) 241-6452. Licensee: Western Slope Communications L.L.C. (group owner) Akin, Gump, Strauss, Hauer & Feld. Format: Sports. Target aud: 18-54; males. ◆John Monroe, gen mgr; Marc Kanter, prom dir & progmg dir; Rich Cron, chief of engrg.

Rocky Ford

KPHT(FM)— 2002: 95.5 mhz; 100 kw. Ant 735 ft. TL: N37 54 08 W104 16 00. 106 W. 24th St., Pueblo 81003. Phone: (719) 545-2080. Fax: (719) 543-9898. Licensee: Capstar TX L.P. Group owner: Clear Channel Communications Inc. (acq 2-12-2001; $1 million). Format: Adult contemp. ◆Olene Greenwood, gen mgr.

Rye

KRYE(FM)—Not on air, target date: unknown: 104.9 mhz; 25 kw. Ant 64 ft. TL: N37 56 40 W104 59 56. 3611 Cherry Hill Dr., Greensboro, NC 27410. Phone: (336) 286-2087. Licensee: United States CP LLC. ◆W. Philip Robinson, gen mgr.

*KRYI(FM)—Not on air, target date: unknown: 89.7 mhz; 9.8 kw. Ant 679 ft. TL: N37 32 34 W104 22 31. Box 711 81069. Phone: (719) 622-9108. Licensee: Harvest Radio Corp. ◆Larry Perry, pres.

*KXWY(FM)—Not on air, target date: unknown: 90.9 mhz; 11.3 kw. Ant 113 ft. TL: N37 56 40 W104 59 56. Box 64500, Colorado Springs 80962. Phone: (719) 533-0300. Licensee: WAY-FM Media Group Inc. (acq 6-17-2005; $200,000 for CP). ◆Robert Augsburg, pres.

Salida

KSBV(FM)— 2002: 93.7 mhz; 1 kw. Ant 2,722 ft. TL: N38 26 47 W106 00 37. Stereo. Arkansas Valley Broadcasting LLC, 115 E. 2nd St. 81201. Phone: (719) 539-9377. Fax: (719) 539-7904. E-mail: ksbvradio@chaffee.net. Web Site: www.ksbv.com. Licensee: Arkansas Valley Broadcasting L.L.C. Gammon & Grange. Format: Classic rock. Target aud: 25-65. ◆Marc Scott, pres & gen mgr.

KVRH(AM)— Dec 10, 1948: 1340 khz; 1 kw-U. TL: N38 31 55 W106 00 54. 7600 County Rd. 120 81201. Phone: (719) 539-2575. Fax: (719) 539-4851. E-mail: kbvc@amigo.net. Web Site: www.kvrh.com. Licensee: Three Eagles Communications LLC. (acq 9-23-59). Format: News/talk, info. News staff: one; News: 7 hrs wkly. Target aud: 25-54; general. Spec prog: Class 3 hrs, relg 2 hrs wkly. ◆Michael Kerrigan, gen mgr; Gayle Dudley, stn mgr & progmg dir; Jorian Sartorius, gen sls mgr; Mary Rose, news dir.

KVRH-FM— 1971: 92.3 mhz; 13.5 kw. -655 ft. TL: N38 30 26 W106 01 22. Stereo. Web Site: www.kvrh.com. Format: Hot adult contemp.

Security

KSKX(FM)— Apr 8, 1973: 105.5 mhz; 409 w. 2,230 ft. TL: N38 44 40 W104 51 41. Stereo. Box 1457, Colorado Springs 80901. Secondary address: 3 S. 7th St., Colorado Springs 80901. Phone: (719) 578-1055. Fax: (719) 635-8455. E-mail: m.lewis@krdotv.com. Licensee: Optima Communications Inc. (acq 1989). Network: Jones Radio Networks. Mullin, Rhyne, Emmons & Topel. Format: Smooth jazz. News: one hr wkly. Target aud: 25-54; middle America. ◆J.B. McCoy III, pres; James R. Bond Jr., CFO; Edward L. Klimek, VP; Neil O. Klockziem, gen mgr.

Snowmass Village

KSNO-FM— April 1985: 103.9 mhz; 6 kw. Ant 325 ft. TL: N39 14 51 W106 55 13. Stereo. 225 N. Mill St., Suite L-100, Aspen 81611. Phone: (970) 925-4111. Fax: (970) 925-7190. E-mail: news@thesoundfm.com. Web Site: www.ksno.us. Licensee: Radio America Ltd. (acq 8-18-2005; grpsl). Rep: Katz Radio. Cole, Raywid & Braverman. Format: AAA. News staff: one; News: 2 hrs wkly. Target aud: 25-54. ◆Tony Mauro, gen mgr & opns mgr; Meredith Cohen, news dir; Pete Barnes, sls.

Steamboat Springs

KBCR(AM)— Aug 1, 1976: 1230 khz; 1 kw-U. TL: N40 29 19 W106 50 57. Box 774050 80477. Secondary address: 2110 Mt. Werner Rd. 80487. Phone: (970) 879-2270. Fax: (970) 879-1404. Licensee: Radio America Ltd. (acq 8-18-2005; grpsl). Network: ABC Information & Entertainment. Format: Oldies, sports, country, news. News staff: one. Target aud: 24-55. ◆Thomas Palmer, gen mgr, prom mgr & progmg dir.

KBCR-FM— July 25, 1974: 96.9 mhz; 10 kw. 666 ft. TL: N40 27 43 W106 50 57. Stereo. Network: ABC. Format: Country, news.

Broadcasting & Cable Yearbook 2006

Colorado

KFMU-FM—See Oak Creek

*KLBV(FM)—Not on air, target date: unknown: 89.3 mhz; 6.5 kw. Ant 1,676 ft. TL: N40 27 04 W106 45 04. 5700 W. Oaks Blvd., Rocklin, CA 95765. Phone: (916) 251-1600. Fax: (916) 251-1650. E-mail: klove@klove.com. Web Site: www.klove.com. Licensee: Educational Media Foundation. Group owner: EMF Broadcasting (acq 10-2-03; grpsl). Network: K-Love. Shaw Pittman. Format: Contemp Christian. News staff: 3. Target aud: 25-44; Judeo Christian, female. ◆Richard Jenkins, pres; Mike Novak, VP; Lloyd Parker, gen mgr; Ed Lenane, opns dir; Keith Whipple, dev dir.

*KTAH(FM)—Not on air, target date: unknown: 88.5 mhz; 240 w. Ant 600 ft. TL: N40 27 43 W106 50 57. 1665 Briargate Blvd., Suite 200, Colorado Springs 80920. Phone: (719) 590-1866. Fax: (719) 593-2399. Licensee: Educational Communications of Colorado Springs Inc.

Sterling

*KDRE(FM)—Not on air, target date: unknown:. Stn currently dark 90.7 mhz; 50 kw. Ant -66 ft. TL: N40 37 35 W103 12 13. Broadcasting for the Challenged Inc., 188 S. Bellevue, Suite 222, Memphis, TN 38104. Phone: (901) 726-8970. Licensee: Broadcasting for the Challenged Inc. ◆George S. Flinn Jr., pres.

*KLZV(FM)—Not on air, target date: unknown: 91.3 mhz; 6 kw. Ant 423 ft. TL: N40 08 56 W103 17 04. 5700 W. Oaks Blvd., Rocklin, CA 95765. Phone: (916) 251-1600. Fax: (916) 251-1650. E-mail: klove@klove.com. Web Site: www.klove.com. Licensee: Educational Media Foundation. Group owner: EMF Broadcasting (acq 10-2-2003; grpsl). Network: K-Love. Shaw Pittman. Format: Contemp Christian. News staff: 3. Target aud: 25-44; Judeo Christian, female. ◆Richard Jenkins, pres; Mike Novak, VP & progmg dir; Lloyd Parker, gen mgr; Ed Lenane, opns dir & news dir; Keith Whipple, dev dir; Eric Allen, natl sls mgr; Roger Chapman, rgnl sls mgr; Chris Joyce, prom dir; David Pierce, progmg mgr; Jon Rivers, mus dir; Sam Wallington, engrg dir.

KNNG(FM)—Listing follows KSTC(AM).

KPMX(FM)— Aug 19, 1983: 105.7 mhz; 12 kw. Ant 479 ft. TL: N40 31 57 W103 07 22. Stereo. 117 Main St. 80751. Phone: (970) 522-4800. Phone: (970) 522-4801. Fax: (970) 522-3997. Web Site: www.kpmx.com.Jones Licensee: Northeast Colorado Broadcasting LLC (group owner; acq 7-1-2003; grpsl). Rep: Allied Radio Partners. Booth, Freret, Imlay & Tepper. Format: Adult contemp. Target aud: 18-54. ◆Alec Crighton, gen mgr.

KSTC(AM)— Jan 3, 1925: 1230 khz; 1 kw-U. TL: N40 37 04 W103 10 31. Box 830, 803 W. Main 80751. Phone: (970) 522-1607. Fax: (970) 522-1322. E-mail: knng@plains.net. Licensee: Track 1 Media of Sterling LLC (group owner; acq 4-7-2004; grpsl). Network: ABC Information & Entertainment. Format: Classic oldies. News staff: one; News: 12 hrs wkly. Target aud: General. Spec prog: Farm 15 hrs wkly. ◆Betty Carlson, gen mgr, opns mgr & gen sls mgr; Tommie Witt, mus dir.

KNNG(FM)—Co-owned with KSTC(AM). Feb 8, 1974: 104.7 mhz; 100 kw. 500 ft. TL: N40 34 57 W103 01 56. (CP: 1.8 kw, and 424 ft.). Stereo. Phone: (970) 522-1609. Network: ABC Information & Entertainment. Format: Colorado country. News staff: one; News: 10 hrs wkly. Target aud: General; country listeners.

*KTAD(FM)—Not on air, target date: unknown: 90.3 mhz; 5 kw. Ant 407 ft. TL: N40 28 48 W103 05 47. 1665 Briargate Blvd., Suite 100, Colorado Springs 80920. Fax: (719) 593-2399. Licensee: Educational Communications of Colorado Springs Inc. ◆Karen Veazey, gen mgr.

Strasburg

KJEB(FM)— July 19, 1995: 102.3 mhz; 6 kw. Ant 328 ft. TL: N39 36 23 W104 19 42. (CP: COL Greenwood Village. Ant 210 ft. TL: N39 39 55 W104 51 38). Stereo. Box 1023 80136. Secondary address: 2349 Paris St., Aurora 80010. Phone: (303) 622-4888. Fax: (303) 622-9258. Licensee: KAGM LLC. Format: Country, relg, news. Target aud: General. ◆Lenora Alexander, CEO; F.C. Harris, pres.

Telluride

*KOTO(FM)— October 1975: 91.7 mhz; 2.35 kw. -187 ft. TL: N37 55 59 W107 49 59. Stereo. Box 1069, 207 N. Pine St. 81435. Phone: (970) 728-4334. Fax: (970) 728-4326. Licensee: San Miguel Educational Fund. (acq 7-22-86). Network: Network: NPR, PRI. Format: Free-form.

News staff: 2. Target aud: General; community. Spec prog: Class 9 hrs, country 12 hrs jazz 9 hrs, blues 7 hrs, drama 3 hrs wkly. ◆Bob Biener, chmn & pres; Ben Kerr, gen mgr & progmg dir; Steve Kennedy, dev dir; Jim Dolan, mus dir; Stephen Barrett, news dir.

Thornton

KKZN(AM)— May 30, 1987: 760 khz; 5 kw-D, 1 kw-N, DA-2. TL: N39 36 18 W104 50 25. 4695 S. Monaco St., Denver 80237. Phone: (303) 713-8000. Fax: (303) 713-8743. Web Site: www.am760.com. Licensee: Citicasters Licenses Inc. (NEW). Group owner: Clear Channel Communications Inc. (acq 5-4-99; grpsl). Format: Talk, sports. ◆Mark Remington, gen mgr.

Timnath

KJAC(FM)— Apr 10, 1989: 105.5 mhz; 58 kw. Ant 1,217 ft. TL: N40 37 03 W105 19 40. Stereo. 1201 18th St., Denver 80202. Phone: (307) 745-5208. Phone: (303) 296-7025. Fax: (303) 296-7030. Web Site: www.1055jackfm.com. Licensee: NRC Broadcasting Inc. (group owner; acq 4-13-2004; $15 million). Network: Westwood One. Rep: Target Broadcast Sales. Eugene T. Smith. Format: Var. News: 10 hrs wkly. Target aud: 18-54; general. ◆Ray Skibitsky, gen mgr.

Trimble

*KTDU(FM)— May 2, 2005: 88.5 mhz; 2.2 kw. Ant 302 ft. TL: N37 15 46 W107 53 45. 1665 Briargate Blvd., Suite 100, Colorado Springs 80920. Phone: (719) 593-0600. Fax: (719) 593-2399. Web Site: www.ktlf.org. Licensee: Educational Communications of Colorado Springs Inc. Format: Christian. ◆Karen Veazey, gen mgr.

Trinidad

KCRT(AM)— May 21, 1946: 1240 khz; 250 w-U. TL: N37 08 45 W104 30 42. 100 Fisher Dr. 81082. Phone: (719) 846-3355. Fax: (719) 846-4711. E-mail: kcrt@adelphia.net. Licensee: Phillips Broadcasting Inc. (group owner; acq 3-30-92; $235,000. with co-located FM; FTR: 4-20-92). Network: Network: ABC, Jones Radio Networks. Format: Country. News staff: one; News: 15 hrs wkly. Target aud: General. Spec prog: Farm one hr, relg 5 hrs wkly. ◆Anita Phillips, pres & opns VP; Lory Phillips, gen mgr & gen sls mgr; David Phillips, stn mgr, mktg dir, progmg VP, news dir & pub affrs dir; Rick Neurater, adv dir.

KCRT-FM— August 1981: 92.5 mhz; 38.5 kw. Ant 1,020 ft. TL: N36 59 33 W104 28 24. Stereo. Format: Classic rock. Target aud: 25-54.

Vail

*KPRE(FM)— Sept 1, 1994: 89.9 mhz; 1.5 kw. 295 ft. TL: N39 38 05 W106 26 47. 7409 S. Alton Ct., Centennial 80112. Phone: (303) 871-9191. Fax: (303) 733-3319. E-mail: info@cpr.org. Web Site: cpr.org. Licensee: Public Broadcasting of Colorado Inc. Network: NPR. Arter & Hadden. Format: Class, news, info. News staff: 8; News: 50 hrs wkly. Target aud: General. ◆Max Wycisk, pres; Sue Coughlin, dev VP.

KSKE-FM— 1997: 104.7 mhz; 100 kw. 394 ft. TL: N39 38 08 W106 26 46. Stereo. Box 7205, Avon 81620. Secondary address: 182 Avon Rd., Avon 81620. Phone: (970) 949-0140. Fax: (970) 949-1464. E-mail: kske@vail.net. Licensee: NRC Mountain Division LLC. (group owner; acq 7-9-2004; grpsl). Format: Country. ◆Steve Wodinger, gen mgr & opns mgr; Holli Snyder, gen sls mgr; Brian Wilder, progmg dir; David Bach, news dir; Ken Laughlin, chief of engrg.

KVLE(AM)— July 25, 1983: 610 khz; 5 kw-D, 217 w-N. TL: N39 34 47 W106 24 54. 614 Kimbark St., Longmont 80501. Phone: (303) 776-2323. Fax: (303) 776-1377. Web Site: radiocoloradonetwork.com Licensee: Pilgrim Communications Inc. (group owner; acq 3-2-2000; $150,000). Format: Talk. ◆Gene Hood, pres; Ron Nickell, sr VP & gen mgr.

Walsenburg

KSPK(FM)— March 1985: 102.3 mhz; 100 kw. Ant 430 ft. TL: N37 37 39 W104 49 17. Stereo. 516 Main 81089. Phone: (719) 738-3636. Fax: (719) 738-2010. E-mail: info@kspk.com. Web site: www.kspk.com. Licensee: Mainstreet Broadcasting Co. Inc. (acq 9-12-90; $275,000;. FTR: 10-8-90). Network: ABC. Format: Sports, country, farm. News staff: 2; News: 3 hrs wkly. Target aud: 24-59; upwardly mobile, two-income families. Spec prog: Relg 2 hrs wkly. ◆Paul Richards, gen mgr; Kim Lucero, gen sls mgr; Larry Patrick, news dir.

Wellington

KCOL(AM)—Licensed to Wellington. See Fort Collins

KKQZ(FM)— 2003: 94.3 mhz; 8.7 kw. Ant 551 ft. TL: N40 55 41 W105 08 36. 600 Main St., Windsor 80550. Phone: (970) 493-1170. Fax: (970) 686-7491. Web Site: www.z943.com. Licensee: Regent Broadcasting of Ft. Collins Inc. Group owner: Regent Communications Inc. (acq 2-25-03). Format: Classic rock. ◆Cal Hall, gen mgr; Mark Callaghan, opns mgr; Lisa Schneider, gen sls mgr; Bill Cody, progmg dir; Todd Harding, news dir; Quinn Morrison, chief of engrg.

Widefield

KKLI(FM)—Licensed to Widefield. See Colorado Springs

Windsor

KJJD(AM)— Apr 12, 1969: 1170 khz; 1 kw-D. TL: N40 27 46 W104 54 47. Box 597 80550. Secondary address: 9217 Eastman Park Dr., Suite 124 B 80550. Phone: (970) 686-1170. Fax: (970) 686-7700. Web Site: www.laley1170.com. Licensee: Rodriguez-Gallegos Broadcasting Corporation. (acq 3-19-85). Rep: Caballero. Fisher, Wayland, Cooper, Leader & Zaragoza L.L.P. Format: Sp, music. News: 5 hrs wkly. Target aud: 18-54; general. Spec prog: Pub affrs. ◆Jesse Rodriguez, gen mgr; Danny Casas, stn mgr.

KUAD-FM— May 31, 1975: 99.1 mhz; 100 kw. Ant 836 ft. TL: N40 38 31 W104 49 03. Stereo. 600 Main St. 80550. Phone: (970) 686-2791. Fax: (970) 686-7491. Web Site: www.k99.com. Licensee: Regent Broadcasting of Ft. Collins Inc. Group owner: Regent Communications Inc. (acq 2-25-03). Dow, Lohnes & Albertson. Format: Country. Target aud: 25-54; upscale country listeners, 60% women. ◆Cal Hall, gen mgr; Mark Callaghan, opns mgr & progmg dir; Shelley Heier, gen sls mgr, mktg dir & prom dir.

Winter Park

KZMV(FM)—See Kremmling

Wray

KRDZ(AM)— Jan 11, 1978: 1440 khz; 5 kw-D, 200 w-N. TL: N56 04 00 W102 11 25. Box 354 80758. Secondary address: 32992 Hwy. 34 80758. Phone: (970) 332-4171. Fax: (970) 332-4172. E-mail: krdzkatr@plains.net. Licensee: Media Logic LLC (group owner; acq 10-31-2002). Network: Network: ABC Daytime Direction, Jones Radio Networks. Format: Classic hits. News: 10 hrs wkly. Target aud: Farmers & ranchers. Spec prog: Focus on family 2 hrs, farm 10 hrs wkly. ◆Wayne Johnson, gen mgr & opns mgr.

Yuma

KNEC(FM)— 1999: 100.9 mhz; 23 kw. Ant 348 ft. TL: N40 00 33 W102 45 35. Box 285 80759. Phone: (970) 848-2302. Fax: (970) 848-2240. E-mail: knec@plains.net. Web Site: www.knec.net. Licensee: Track 1 Media of Sterling LLC (group owner; acq 4-7-2004; grpsl). Format: Light rock. ◆Betty Carlson, gen mgr; Tammy Sewell, stn mgr.

Connecticut

Ansonia

WADS(AM)— May 8, 1956: 690 khz; 1 kw-D, 33 w-N, DA-2. TL: N41 20 48 W73 06 56. (CP: 3.5 kw-D, 200 w-N). 261 Portsea St., New Haven 06519. Phone: (203) 777-7690. Phone: (203) 782-3564. Fax: (203) 782-3565. E-mail: radioamorwads@aol.com. Licensee: Radio Amor Inc. (acq 12-30-93; $450,000; 1-17-94). Shaw Pittman. Format: Relg, educ, Sp. News: 3.5 hrs wkly. Target aud: General. ◆Rev. Moses Mercedes, pres; Rev. Luis Rivera, VP; Abraham Hernandez, gen mgr.

Berlin

*WERB(FM)— Jan 12, 1979: 94.5 mhz; 27.5 w. 95 ft. TL: N41 37 18 W72 45 13. (CP: 94.5 mhz). Stereo. Berlin High School Media Center, 139 Patterson Way 06037. Phone: (860) 828-0606. Phone: (860) 828-6577. Fax: (860) 829-0526. E-mail: werb@berlinschools.org. Web

Stations in the U.S.   Connecticut

Developers & Brokers of Radio Properties

contact American Media Services at our suite:
Philadelphia Marriott Downtown
215-625-2900
843-972-2200
americanmediaservices.com
Charleston, SC
Dallas, TX · Chicago, Il · Austin, TX

American Media Services, LLC

Site: www.berlinwall.org. Licensee: Berlin Board of Education. Format: Educ/Rock. Teenage listeners from Berlin High School. ♦ Chris Wolfe, gen mgr.

Bloomfield

WDZK(AM)— February 1964: 1550 khz; 5 kw-D, 2 kw-N, DA-2. TL: N41 51 47 W72 44 01. 160 Chapel Rd., Manchester 06040. Phone: (860) 947-3000. Fax: (860) 947-3005. Web Site: www.radiodisney.com. Licensee: Radio Disney Group LLC. Group owner: ABC Inc. (acq 11-21-00; grpsl). Format: Children, lt. News staff: one; News: 11 hrs wkly. Target aud: 18-80; general. ♦ Heather Lee, gen mgr.

Bridgeport

WCUM(AM)— September 1941: 1450 khz; 1 kw-U. TL: N41 12 40 W73 11 28. Box 3975 06605. Phone: (203) 335-1450. Fax: (203) 337-1220. E-mail: radiocumbre1450@aol.com. Web site: www.radiocumbre.com. Licensee: Radio Cumbre Broadcasting Inc. (acq 4-89; $550,000; 4-24-89). Network: CNN Radio. Rep: Caballero. Format: Sp, tropical. News staff: 2; News: 14 hrs wkly. Target aud: 25 plus. ♦ Pablo De Jesus Colon Hijo, CEO & pres; Migdalia Ramos Colon, VP; Allison Sheahan, gen mgr.

WDJZ(AM)— Apr 30, 1977: 1530 khz; 5 kw-D, DA. TL: N41 10 09 W73 13 14. 177 State St., 06604. Phone: (203) 368-4392. Fax: (203) 367-4551. Licensee: People's Broadcast Network LLC (acq 7-10-01). Format: Foreign/Ethnic, gospel. Target aud: 35 plus. ♦ Milford Edwards Sr., gen mgr.

WEZN-FM— Oct 24, 1960: 99.9 mhz; 27.6 kw. 669 ft. TL: N41 16 46 W73 11 09. Stereo. 440 Wheelers Farms Rd., Milford 06460. Phone: (203) 783-8200. Fax: (203) 783-8383. Web Site: www.star999.com. Licensee: CXR Holdings L.L.C. Group owner: Cox Broadcasting (acq 3-28-97; grpsl). Format: Adult contemp. Target aud: 25-54. ♦ Kim Guthrie, exec VP & gen mgr; Helaine Greenbaum, natl sls mgr; Stuart Gorlick, rgnl sls mgr; Marit Spisany, prom dir; Steve Marcus, progmg dir; Randye Kaye, news dir; Dom Bordonaro, chief of engrg.

WICC(AM)— 1926: 600 khz; 1 kw-D, 500 w-N, DA-2. TL: N41 09 36 W73 09 53. Stereo. 2 Lafayette Sq. 06604-6000. Phone: (203) 366-6000. Fax: (203) 384-0600. E-mail: wicc600@aol.com. Web site: www.wicc600.com. Licensee: Cumulus Licensing Corp. Group owner: Cumulus Media Inc. (acq 3-14-02; grpsl). Rep: Christal, Wiley, Rein & Fielding. Format: Talk. News staff: 5; News: 25 hrs wkly. Target aud: 35-64. Spec prog: lt 5 hrs wkly. ♦ Ann McManus, VP & gen mgr; Curt Hansen, opns VP.

*****WPKN(FM)**— Oct 10, 1963: 89.5 mhz; 10 kw. 550 ft. TL: N41 16 43 W73 11 08. Stereo. 244 University Ave. 06604. Phone: (203) 331-9756. Web Site: www.wpkn.org. Licensee: WPKN Inc. (acq 12-10-97). Format: Div. Spec prog: Class 2 hrs, Sp 4 hrs, Black 4 hrs, Fr 2 hrs, jazz 16 hrs wkly. ♦ Henry Minot, gen mgr.

Bristol

WPRX(AM)— October 1948: 1120 khz; 1 kw-D, 500 w-N, DA-N. TL: N41 39 29 W72 56 51. 330 Main St., Hartford 06106. Phone: (860) 524-0001. Fax: (860) 727-0849. E-mail: wprx1120@aol. Web Site: members.aol.com/wprx 1120. Licensee: Nievezquez Productions Inc. (acq 4-28-99; $925,000). Network: Network: CNN Radio, Westwood One. Format: News/talk, Sp tropical. News staff: 2; News: 12 hrs wkly. Target aud: 23-54; Hispanic adults. Spec prog: Pol 2 hrs wkly. ♦ Oscar Nieves, pres; Joe Velazquez, exec VP & VP; Felix Viera, gen mgr.

Brookfield

WINE(AM)— May 9, 1966: 940 khz; 1 kw-D, 4 w-N. TL: N41 29 35 W73 25 47. 1004 Federal Rd. 06804. Phone: (203) 775-1212. Fax: (203) 775-6452. Web Site: www.cumulus.com. Licensee: Cumulus Licensing Corp. Group owner: Cumulus Media Inc. (acq 1-23-2002; grpsl). Network: ESPN Radio. Haley, Bader & Potts. Format: Sports.

Target aud: 25-54. ♦ Robert Mordente, gen mgr; C. Moore, sls dir; Matt Carey, prom dir; Tim Sheehan, progmg dir; Rob Smith, news dir; Peter Partenio, chief of engrg.

WRKI(FM)—Co-owned with WINE(AM). Dec 24, 1976: 95.1 mhz; 50 kw. 500 ft. TL: N41 29 35 W73 25 47. Stereo. Web Site: www.i95rock.com. Format: Classic rock.

Danbury

WDAQ(FM)—Listing follows WLAD(AM).

*****WFAR(FM)**— July 19, 1981: 93.3 mhz; 18 w. 210 ft. TL: N41 23 44 W73 25 24. Stereo. 25 Chestnut St. 06810. Phone: (203) 748-0001. Fax: (203) 746-4262. Web Site: www.radiofamilia.com. Licensee: Danbury Community Radio Inc. (acq 7-81). Format: Educ, Por, relg. Spec prog: lt one hr, East Indian one hr wkly. ♦ David Abrantes, pres & gen mgr; Helena Abrantes, opns mgr; Joe Mingachos, news dir.

WINE(AM)—See Brookfield

WLAD(AM)— October 1947: 800 khz; 1 kw-D, 287 w-N. TL: N41 22 27 W73 26 47. Stereo. 198 Main St. 06810. Phone: (203) 744-4800. Fax: (203)778-4655. E-mail: radio80wlad@aol.com. Web Site: www.wlad.com. Licensee: Berkshire Broadcasting Corp. (group owner) Network: CNN Radio. Rep: D & R Radio. Cohn & Marks. Format: Full service. News staff: 3. Target aud: General. ♦ James B. Lee Jr., pres; Mary Lu Orteig, exec VP; Irving J. Goldstein, VP & gen mgr.

WDAQ(FM)—Co-owned with WLAD(AM). December 1953: 98.3 mhz; 1.3 kw. 460 ft. TL: N41 22 27 W73 26 47. Stereo. E-mail: radio@98q.com. Web Site: www.98q.com. Format: Hot adult contemp. Target aud: 25-54.

WREF(AM)—See Ridgefield

WRKI(FM)—See Brookfield

*****WXCI(FM)**— Feb 10, 1973: 91.7 mhz; 1.2 kw. 205 ft. TL: N41 23 44 W73 25 24. (CP: 3 kw, ant 201 ft.). Stereo. Student Ctr., 181 White St. 06810. Phone: (203) 837-8635. Fax: (203) 837-8599. E-mail: wxci@yahoo.com. Web Site: www.wcsu.edu/wxci. Licensee: Western Connecticut State University Board of Trustees. (acq 3-73). Format: New wave. News: 3 hrs wkly. Target aud: 14-25. Spec prog: Club mus 3 hrs, jazz 3 hrs, reggae 2 hrs, new age 3 hrs, metal 3 hrs, classic rock 3 hrs wkly. ♦ Adeline Gronkowski, gen mgr; Jessica Minor, prom dir; Jesse Gosselin, progmg dir; Gretchen Schmidlin, mus dir; Nancy London, news dir; Tonya White, pub affrs dir; Bob Marino, chief of engrg.

East Lyme

WNLC(FM)— Apr 1, 1994: 98.7 mhz; 5.5 kw. 269 ft. TL: N41 20 48 W72 06 50. Stereo. 89 Broad St., New London 06320. Phone: (860) 442-5328. Fax: (860) 442-6532. E-mail: arussell@hallradio.com. Web Site: www.wnlc.com. Licensee: Hall Communication Inc. (group owner; acq 6-16-97; $2 million). Network: Westwood One. Fletcher, Heald & Hildreth. Format: Lite AC/Nostalgia. Target aud: 35 plus; today's upcoming citizens who have discretionary income. ♦ Bonnie H. Rowbotham, chmn; Arthur J. Rowbotham, pres; Bill Baldwin, sr VP; Andy Russell, gen mgr & stn mgr.

Enfield

WPKX(FM)— July 1990: 97.9 mhz; 2.22 kw. 528 ft. TL: N42 05 05 W72 42 14. 1331 Main St., Springfield, MA 01103. Phone: (413) 781-1011. Fax: (413) 734-4434. Web Site: www.979.com. Licensee: Capstar TX L.P. Group owner: Clear Channel Communications Inc. (acq 8-30-00; grpsl). Format: Contemp country. Target aud: 25-54. ♦ Tom McConnell, gen mgr; Pat McKay, opns mgr.

Fairfield

*****WSHU(FM)**— February 1964: 91.1 mhz; 20 kw. Ant 624 ft. TL: N41 16 45 W73 11 09. Stereo. 5151 Park Ave. 06825. Phone: (203) 365-6604. Fax: (203) 371-7991. E-mail: lombardi@wshu.org. Web Site: www.wshu.org. Licensee: Sacred Heart University Inc. (acq 1-5-90). Network: Network: NPR, PRI. Format: Class, news. News staff: 4; News: 43 hrs wkly. Target aud: General; all ages. Spec prog: Folk 5 hrs, new age 6 hrs wkly. ♦ George Lombardi, gen mgr; Barbara Bashar, opns mgr; Gillian Anderson, dev dir.

*****WVOF(FM)**— Sept 1, 1970: 88.5 mhz; 100 w. 35 ft. TL: N41 09 32 W73 15 35. Stereo. Box R, Campus Ctr., N. Benson Rd. 06430. Phone: (203) 254-4144. Fax: (203) 254-4224. E-mail: centralstaff@wvof.org. Web Site: www.wvof.org. Licensee: Fairfield University. Format: Var/div, progsv. News staff: 5; News: 4 hrs wkly. Target aud: 18-35. Spec prog: Sp 12 hrs, Pol 3 hrs, Hungarian 2 hrs, Ger 2 hrs, lt one hr wkly. ♦ Matt Dinnan, gen mgr; Mike Wood, opns dir; Chris Anders, gen sls mgr; Steve Sennett, mktg dir; Dave McGovern, progmg dir; Katie Marzy, mus dir.

Greenwich

WGCH(AM)— Sept 14, 1964: 1490 khz; 1 kw-U. TL: N41 01 37 W73 37 59. Stereo. 1490 Dayton Ave. 06830. Phone: (203) 869-1490. Fax: (203) 869-3636. Web Site: www.wgch.com. Licensee: The Greenwich Broadcasting Corp. (acq 6-18-2003; $1.1 million). Network: CNN Radio. Format: News, business talk, sports. News staff: 2; News: 35 hrs wkly. Target aud: 35 plus; very upscale, active, athletic, community-minded. Spec prog: High school sports 6 hrs, educ 2 hrs, Pol one hr, relg 3 hrs, lt one hr wkly. ♦ Jeff Weber, exec VP & progmg dir; Michael Metter, CEO, chmn, pres & gen mgr.

Groton

WQGN-FM—Listing follows WSUB(AM).

WSUB(AM)— July 26, 1958: 980 khz; 1 kw-D. TL: N41 23 05 W72 04 13. 7 Governor Winthrop Blvd., New London 06320-6437. Phone: (860) 443-1980. Fax: (860) 444-7970. Web Site: www.wsub.com. Licensee: Citadel Broadcasting Co. Group owner: Citadel Broadcasting Corp. (acq 4-26-2001; grpsl). Network: ABC. Format: All sports. Target aud: 25-49; middle income professionals. ♦ Wayne Leland, exec VP; Bob Cox, stn mgr; Kevin O'Connor, progmg VP & progmg dir; Frank Doremus, chief of engrg.

WQGN-FM—Co-owned with WSUB(AM). 1971: 105.5 mhz; 3 kw. 275 ft. TL: N41 23 05 W72 04 13. Stereo. Web Site: www.q105.fm. Format: CHR. Target aud: 18-49. ♦ Shawn Murphy, mus dir.

Guilford

*****WGRS(FM)**— Dec 27, 1993: 91.5 mhz; 3.1 kw. 82 ft. TL: N41 17 19 W72 39 32. (CP: 6 kw). Stereo. Box 920, Monroe 06468. Phone: (203) 268-9667. E-mail: staff@wmnr.org. Web site: www.wmnr.org. Licensee: Monroe Board of Education. Network: PRI. Format: Class. Spec prog: Big band 8 hrs, folk 2 hrs, new age one hr, Broadway one hr wkly. ♦ Kurt Anderson, gen mgr; Jane Stadler, opns mgr; Carol Babina, dev dir.

Hamden

WAVZ(AM)—See New Haven

WKCI-FM—Licensed to Hamden. See New Haven

WQAQ(FM)—Listing follows WQUN(AM).

WQUN(AM)— July 17, 1960: 1220 khz; 1 kw-D, 305 w-N, DA-1. TL: N41 22 32 W72 55 54. Stereo. Quinnipiac University, 275 Mt. Carmel Ave. 06518. Phone: (203) 582-8984. Fax: (203) 582-5372. Web Site: www.wqun.com. Licensee: Quinnipiac University (acq 9-12-96; $500,000). Network: Network: CBS, Jones Radio Networks. Shook, Hardy &

Broadcasting & Cable Yearbook 2006
D-111

Connecticut

Bacon. Format: News, nostalgia, loc info. News staff: 2. Target aud: General; community, business & cultural leaders. Spec prog: Irish 2 hrs wkly. ♦ Michael Collins, gen mgr & pub affrs dir; Ray Andrewsen, opns dir; Greg Little, news dir; Clif Mills, chief of engrg.

WQAQ(FM)—Co-owned with WQUN(AM). February 1973: 98.1 mhz; 16 w. -82 ft. TL: N41 25 10 W72 53 41. Stereo. Box 59, Quinnipiac Univ., 275 Mt. Casnad Ave. 06518. Phone: (203) 582-5278. Fax: (203) 582-8098. Web Site: www.angelfire.com/ct2/wqaqradio/. Format: AOR, news/talk, alternative rock. News: 10 hrs wkly. Target aud: 18-30. ♦ Chris Cooper, gen mgr; Carlos Lanesee, prom dir; Sally Densa, adv VP; Glenn Giangrande, progmg dir; Jessie Elgarten, progmg mgr; Alison Keller, news dir; Bill Shoulders, pub affrs dir.

Hartford

WCCC-FM—Listing follows WTMI(AM).

WDRC(AM)— Dec 10, 1922: 1360 khz; 5 kw-U, DA-N. TL: N41 48 45 W72 41 44. 869 Blue Hills Ave., Bloomfield 06002. Phone: (860) 243-1115. Fax: (860) 286-8257. E-mail: wdrc@talkofconnecticut.com. Web Site: talkofconnecticut.com. Licensee: Buckley Broadcasting of Connecticut LLC. Group owner: Buckley Broadcasting Corp. (acq 8-1-59). Network: Network: Westwood One, AP Radio. Rep: McGavren Guild. Format: News/talk. News staff: one. Target aud: 40+. ♦ Richard D. Buckley, pres; Wayne G. Mulligan, VP & gen mgr.

WDRC-FM— 1939: 102.9 mhz; 19.5 kw. Ant 810 ft. TL: N41 33 44 W72 50 40. Stereo. E-mail: bighits@drcfm.com. Web Site: drcfm.com. Format: Classic hits. News staff: one. Target aud: 25-64. ♦ Grahame Winters, prom mgr; Dave Nagel, progmg dir & mus dir; Mike Stevens, engrg mgr.

WHCN(FM)— 1939: 105.9 mhz; 16 kw. 867 ft. TL: N41 33 47 W72 50 42. Stereo. 10 Columbus Blvd. 06106. Phone: (860) 723-6000. Fax: (860) 723-6106. Web Site: www.whcn.com. Licensee: Capstar TX L.P. Group owner: Clear Channel Communications Inc. (acq 8-30-00; grpsl). Rep: Christal. Format: Rock/AOR. ♦ Manuel Rodriguez, gen mgr; Joe Graham, sls dir; Fran Knights, gen sls mgr; Todd Thomas, prom dir & progmg dir; Rick Walsh, engrg VP & chief of engrg.

WPOP(AM)—Co-owned with WHCN(FM). July 1935: 1410 khz; 5 kw-U, DA-2. TL: N41 41 35 W72 43 50. Fax: (860) 723-6195. Web Site: www.espnradio1410.com. Network: ESPN Radio. Format: Sports. News staff: 8; News: 25 hrs wkly. Target aud: 35 plus. ♦ Andrew Tartaglia, gen sls mgr; Bob Plante, progmg dir.

***WJMJ(FM)**— Oct 18, 1976: 88.9 mhz; 7.2 kw. 580 ft. TL: N41 45 09 W72 59 40. Stereo. St. Thomas Seminary, 467 Bloomfield Ave., Bloomfield 06002. Phone: (860) 242-8800. Fax: (860) 242-4886. Web Site: wjmj.org. Licensee: St. Thomas Seminary-Archdiocese of Hartford. Network: ABC Information & Entertainment. Garvey, Schubert & Barer. Format: Btfl music, class, relg. News staff: one; News: 10 hrs wkly. Target aud: 40-65; working, middle-class, family group. Spec prog: Educ, foreign one hr wkly. ♦ Archbishop Henry Mansell, pres; John L. Ellinger, gen mgr.

WKND(AM)—See Manchester

WKSS(FM)— June 1947: 95.7 mhz; 16.5 kw. 880 ft. TL: N41 33 41 W72 50 39. Stereo. Hartford Sq. N., 10 Columbus Blvd. 06106-1944. Phone: (860) 723-6000. Fax: (860) 493-7090. Web Site: kiss957.com. Licensee: Capstar TX L.P. Group owner: Clear Channel Communications Inc. (acq 8-30-00; grpsl). Rep: Christal. Format: CHR. Target aud: 18-34. ♦ Manuel Rodriguez, exec VP & gen mgr.

WLAT(AM)—See New Britain

WNEZ(AM)—See Windsor

WPHH(FM)—See Waterbury

***WQTQ(FM)**— November 1971: 89.9 mhz; 120 w. 86 ft. TL: N41 47 47 W72 41 42. Weaver High School, 415 Granby St. 06112. Phone: (860) 722-8661. Phone: (860) 695-1899. Fax: (860) 286-9909. E-mail: wqtqfm@hotmail.com. Web Site: www.wqtq.com/wqtq. Licensee: Hartford Board of Education. Network: UPI. Format: Educ, urban contemp, ballads, rhythm and blues. Target aud: 15-45; literate, professional, quality mus listeners. Spec prog: Gospel 12 hrs, clean hip hop rap 19

hrs, reggae/calypso 4 hrs, jazz 12 hrs wkly. ♦ Thomas G. Smith, CEO; Connie Coles, pres & gen mgr; Shirley Minnifield, CFO; Tom Smith, chief of opns.

WRCH(FM)—See New Britain

***WRTC-FM**— February 1958: 89.3 mhz; 300 w. 95 ft. TL: N41 45 06 W72 41 29. Stereo. c/o Trinity College, 300 Summit St. 06106. Phone: (860) 297-2450. Phone: (860) 297-2439. Fax: (860) 987-6214. Web Site: www.wrtcfm.com. Licensee: Trustees of Trinity College. Format: Div. Target aud: 15 plus. Spec prog: Class 4 hrs, gospel 6 hrs, West Indian 6 hrs, Pol 3 hrs, Por 8 hrs, Sp 6 hrs wkly. ♦ Bob Poisak, gen mgr; Joshua Cerretti, gen mgr; Mike Caputo, progmg dir.

WTIC(AM)— Feb 10, 1925: 1080 khz; 50 kw-U, DA-N. TL: N41 46 39 W72 48 19. Stereo. 10 Executive Dr., Farmington 06032. Phone: (860) 677-6700. Fax: (860) 284-9842. Web Site: www.wtic.com. Licensee: Infinity Radio Inc. Group owner: Infinity Broadcasting Corp. (acq 11-13-98; grpsl). Network: CBS. Format: Full service, news/talk. News: 30 hrs wkly. Target aud: 35-59; intelligent, mature adults. ♦ Suzanne McDonald, VP & gen mgr; Steve Salhany, opns mgr; Kathy Browne, gen sls mgr; Geri DeRosa, natl sls mgr; Tristano Korlov, mktg dir & prom dir; Dana Whalen, news dir & chief of engrg; Jeff Hugabone, chief of engrg.

WTIC-FM— Feb 5, 1940: 96.5 mhz; 20 kw. 810 ft. TL: N41 46 27 W72 48 20. Stereo. Fax: (860) 678-3952. Web Site: www.ticfm.com. Format: Hot adult contemp. News: 8 hrs wkly. Target aud: 18-34; intelligent, spirited, youthful adults.

WTMI(AM)—(West Hartford). 1947: 1290 khz; 490 w-D. TL: N41 47 48 W72 47 50. 1039 Asylum Ave. 06105. Phone: (860) 525-1069. Fax: (860) 246-9084. Licensee: Marlin Broadcasting of Hartford LLC (acq 5-18-2000; grpsl). Akin, Gump, Strauss, Hauer & Feld. Format: Class. Target aud: 18-54. ♦ Woody Tanger, CEO; Boyd E. Arnold, VP & gen mgr; Michael Picozzi, opns mgr; Jay Schultz, sls dir & gen sls mgr; Michelle Bassoss, natl sls mgr; Nicole Godburn, prom dir; John Ramsey, chief of engrg.

WCCC-FM—Co-owned with WTMI(AM). June 7, 1960: 106.9 mhz; 23 kw. 730 ft. TL: N41 47 51 W72 47 52. Stereo. Web Site: www.wccc.com. Akin, Gump, Strauss, Hauer & Feld. Format: Active rock. Target aud: 18-49; adult men. ♦ Jon Skonieczny, prom dir.

WWUH(FM)—See West Hartford

WWYZ(FM)—See Waterbury

WZMX(FM)— 1939: 93.7 mhz; 17 kw. Ant 850 ft. TL: N41 33 42 W72 50 41. Stereo. 10 Executive Dr., Farmington 06032. Phone: (860) 677-6700. Fax: (860) 674-8427. Web Site: www.hot937.com. Licensee: Infinity Radio Inc. Group owner: Infinity Broadcasting Corp. (acq 6-8-98; grpsl). Format: Hip-hop. Target aud: 18-34; adults in Hartford & New Haven. ♦ Suzanne McDonald, VP & gen mgr; Steve Salhany, opns mgr.

Ledyard

WBMW(FM)— Dec 24, 1992: 106.5 mhz; 3.1 kw. Ant 459 ft. TL: N41 27 43 W72 01 27. Stereo. 758 Colonel Ledyard Hwy. 06339. Phone: (860) 464-1065. Fax: (860) 464-8143. E-mail: wbmwandwjjf@aol.com. Web Site: www.wbmw.com. Licensee: Redwolf Broadcasting Corp. (acq 1-25-94). Network: USA. Smithwick & Belendiuk. Format: Hot adult contemp. News staff: one. Target aud: 20-49. ♦ John J. Fuller, gen mgr; Scott Bradshaw, opns dir.

Litchfield

WZBG(FM)— July 8, 1992: 97.3 mhz; 3 kw. 328 ft. TL: N41 48 08 W73 09 50. Box 1497, Litchfield Commons, 49 Commons Dr. 06759. Phone: (860) 567-3697. Fax: (860) 567-3292. E-mail: info@wzbg.com. Web Site: www.wzbg.com. Licensee: Local Girls & Boys Broadcasting Corp. Network: CBS. Format: News & info, adult contemp. News staff: 3. Target aud: 25-54. Spec prog: Motor racing, jazz 2 hrs wkly. ♦ Jennifer L. Parsons, gen mgr.

Manchester

WKND(AM)— May 18, 1958: 1230 khz; 1 kw-U. TL: N41 46 34 W72 33 27. 330 Main St., 1st Fl., Hartford 06106-1622. Phone: (860) 524-0001. Fax: (860) 548-1922. E-mail: msanchez@freedomcommct.com. Licensee: Freedom Communications of Connecticut Inc. (acq 6-1-2004;

$3 million. with WLAT(AM) New Britain). Format: Urban contemp, rhythm and blues. ♦ Melvin Sanchez, gen mgr.

Meriden

WMMW(AM)— 1946: 1470 khz; 2.5 kw, DA-2. TL: N41 33 14 W72 48 07. 869 Blue Hills Ave., Bloomfield 06002. Phone: (860) 243-1115. Fax: (860) 286-8257. Web Site: www.talkofconnecticut.com. Licensee: Buckley Broadcasting of Connecticut LLC. Group owner: Buckley Broadcasting Corp. (acq 10-21-98; $630,000). Network: Network: Westwood One, AP Radio, ABC. Rep: McGavren Guild. Format: News, talk. Target aud: 40 plus; middle income, grassroots America. ♦ Richard D. Buckley, pres; Wayne Mulligan, VP & gen mgr; Laura Kittell, opns mgr; Ron Pell, sls VP & gen sls mgr; Donna Banhs, prom dir; Dave Nagel, progmg dir; Don Lovallo, news dir; Scott Baron, chief of engrg.

***WPKT(FM)**— June 11, 1978: 90.5 mhz; 18.5 kw horiz, 13.5 kw vert. 1,148 ft. TL: N41 33 42 W72 50 41. Stereo. Box 260240, 240 New Britain Ave., Hartford 06106-0240. Phone: (860) 278-5310. Fax: (860) 244-9624. Fax: (860) 278-2157. E-mail: info@wnpr.org. Web Site: www.wnpr.org. Licensee: Connecticut Public Television & Radio. Network: Network: NPR, PRI. Schwartz, Woods and Miller. Format: Class, news, info. News staff: 5; News: 26 hrs wkly. ♦ Jerry Franklin, CEO & pres; Kim Grehn, stn mgr & progmg mgr; Steve Futernick, dev VP; Nancy Bauer, mktg VP; John Nowacki, mus dir; John Dankosky, news dir; Joseph Zareski, chief of engrg.

Middlefield

WPKT(FM)—See Meriden

Middletown

***WESU(FM)**— September 1939: 88.1 mhz; 1.5 kw. 38 ft. TL: N41 33 16 W72 39 30. Stereo. 45 Broad St. 06457. Phone: (860) 685-7703/685-7700/685-7707. E-mail: wesu@wesufm.org. Web Site: www.wesufm.org. Licensee: Wesleyan University (acq 3-27-2003). Format: Free-form. Target aud: General. Spec prog: Blues 10 hrs, gospel 6 hrs, reggae 10 hrs, metal 5 hrs wkly. ♦ Benjamin Michael, gen mgr.

***WIHS(FM)**— Oct 11, 1969: 104.9 mhz; 3 kw. 300 ft. TL: N41 30 18 W72 39 32. 1933 S. Main St. 06457. Phone: (860) 346-1049. Fax: (860) 347-1049. E-mail: wihs@snet.net. Web Site: www.wihsradio.org. Licensee: Connecticut Radio Fellowship Inc. Network: Moody. Format: Christian. News: 18 hrs wkly. Target aud: General. Spec prog: Children 9 hrs wkly. ♦ William Bacon, pres; G.J. Gerard, gen mgr; Paul A. Kretschmer, opns mgr.

WMRD(AM)— Dec 12, 1948: 1150 khz; 2.5 kw-D, 46 w-N. TL: N41 11 33 W72 37 13. 777 River Rd. 06457. Phone: (860) 347-9673. Phone: (860) 347-2565. Fax: (860) 347-7704. E-mail: radio@wliswmrd.net. Web Site: www.wliswmrd.net. Licensee: Crossroads Communications L.L.C. (acq 1996; $320,000). Shook, Hardy & Bacon. Format: MOR, news/talk. News staff: one; News: 8 hrs wkly. Target aud: 25-54; adults. Spec prog: Pol 2 hrs, lt 2 hrs, Celtic one hr, Caribbean one hr, Jewish one hr wkly. ♦ Don DeCesare, pres & gen mgr.

Milford

WADS(AM)—See Ansonia

WFIF(AM)— Sept 4, 1965: 1500 khz; 5 kw-D, DA. TL: N41 11 33 W73 06 05. 90 Kay Ave. 06460. Phone: (203) 878-5915. E-mail: wfif@aol.com. Web Site: www.wfif.net. Licensee: K.W. Dolmar Broadcasting Co. Inc. Group owner: Blount Communications Group (acq 4-82; $425,000; 1-19-81). Network: Salem Radio Network. Format: Relg. Target aud: General. Spec prog: Black 6 hrs wkly. ♦ Dave Young, exec VP & opns VP; William Blount, pres & gen mgr; Jon Vaught, stn mgr; William Barnett, mus dir & chief of engrg.

Monroe

***WMNR(FM)**— Jan 31, 1974: 88.1 mhz; 5 kw. 403 ft. TL: N41 19 08 W73 15 13. Stereo. Box 920 06468. Phone: (203) 268-9667. E-mail: staff@wmnr.org. Web Site: www.wmnr.org. Licensee: Monroe Board of Education. Network: PRI. Format: Class. Spec prog: Big band 8 hrs, folk 2 hrs, new age one hr, Broadway one hr wkly. ♦ Kurt Anderson, gen mgr; Jane Stadler, opns dir; Carol Babina, dev dir.

Stations in the U.S. — Connecticut

Developers & Brokers of Radio Properties — contact American Media Services at our suite: Philadelphia Marriott Downtown 215-625-2900 / 843-972-2200 / americanmediaservices.com / Charleston, SC / Dallas, TX · Chicago, Il · Austin, TX — American Media Services, LLC

Naugatuck

WFNW(AM)— Feb 26, 1961: 1380 khz; 5 kw-D, 500 w-N, DA-2. TL: N41 30 35 W73 03 20. Stereo. 182 Grand St., Suite 215, Waterbury 06702. Phone: (203) 755-4960. Fax: (203) 755-4957. E-mail: galaxia1380@yahoo.com. Web Site: www.galaxia1380.com. Licensee: Candido Dias Carrelo. (acq 6-90; $350,000; 6-25-90). Format: Sp, tropical. ♦Placido Acevedo, pres; Candido Carrelo, gen mgr.

New Britain

*****WFCS(FM)**— Oct 17, 1972: 107.7 mhz; 50 w. 160 ft. TL: N41 41 36 W72 45 49. Stereo. Student Center, 1615 Stanley St. 06050-4010. Phone: (860) 832-1883. Fax: (860) 832-3757. Web Site: www.wfcs.ccsu.edu. Licensee: Trustees of Central Connecticut State University. Network: ABC Information & Entertainment. Format: Alternative, diversified. News staff: 4; News: 10 hrs wkly. Target aud: 14-50. Spec prog: Blues 12 hrs, Sp 2 hrs wkly. ♦Joe Carcand, gen mgr; Don Eldred, dev dir; Kenny Albert, progmg dir; John Ramsey, chief of engrg.

WLAT(AM)— May 20, 1949: 910 khz; 5 kw-U, DA-N. TL: N41 42 58 W72 48 38. Stereo. 330 Main St., 1st Fl., Hartford 06106. Phone: (860) 524-0001. Fax: (860) 548-1922. E-mail: msanchez@freedomcommct.com. Licensee: Freedom Communications of Connecticut Inc. (acq 6-1-2004; $3 million. with WKND(AM) Manchester). Format: Spanish tropical. ♦Melvin Sanchez, gen mgr.

WRCH(FM)— July 1, 1968: 100.5 mhz; 7.5 kw. Ant 1,250 ft. TL: N41 42 13 W72 49 57. Stereo. 10 Executive Dr., Farmington 06032. Phone: (860) 677-6700. Fax: (860) 677-5483. E-mail: wrch@cbs.com. Web Site: www.wrch.com. Licensee: Infinity Radio Inc. Group owner: Infinity Broadcasting corp. (acq 6-8-98; grpsl). Format: Soft adult contemp. Target aud: 25-54; women, adults. ♦Suzanne McDonald, VP & gen mgr; Steve Salhany, opns mgr; James Gomes, gen sls mgr.

WRYM(AM)— August 1946: 840 khz; 1 kw-D, 208 w-N. TL: N41 41 15 W72 43 46. 1056 Willard Ave., Newington 06111. Phone: (860) 666-5646. Fax: (860) 666-5647. Web Site: www.wrymradio.com. Licensee: Eight Forty Broadcasting Corp. (acq 4-8-2004; $1.06 million). Network: CNN en Espanol. Rep: Caballero. Format: Sp. News staff: 4; News: 8 hrs wkly. Target aud: General; Hispanic. Spec prog: Pol 5 hrs wkly. ♦Lucio Ruzzier, pres; Walter Martinez, VP & gen mgr.

New Canaan

*****WSLX(FM)**— 1975: 91.9 mhz; 10 w horiz. 518 ft. TL: N41 11 32 W73 29 46. (CP: 19 w vert, ant 171 ft.). Stereo. 377 N. Wilton Rd. 06840. Phone: (203) 972-3894. Licensee: St. Luke's Foundation Inc. Format: Class, div. ♦Dan Mecca, gen mgr.

New Fairfield

WDBY(FM)—See Patterson, NY

New Haven

WAVZ(AM)— September 1947: 1300 khz; 1 kw-U, DA-N. TL: N41 17 16 W72 56 48. 495 Benham St., Hamden 06514. Phone: (203) 248-8114. Fax: (203) 281-2795. Web site: www.wavz.com. Licensee: Clear Channel Broadcasting Licenses Inc. Group owner: Clear Channel Communications Inc. (acq 12-18-92; $10. with WKCI-FM; FTR: 1-11-93). Network: ABC Information & Entertainment. Rep: Clear Channel. Format: Sports. News staff: one; News: 14 hrs wkly. Target aud: 35 plus. ♦Massimo Rosati, sls dir; Brooke Blasko, natl sls mgr; Paula Wilmer, gen sls mgr & natl sls mgr; Brett Charest, mktg dir; Jerry Kristafer, progmg dir; Paul Pacelli, news dir; Fred Santore, chief of engrg.

WKCI-FM—Co-owned with WAVZ(AM). Feb 10, 1969: 101.3 mhz; 15 kw. 876 ft. TL: N41 25 22 W72 57 06. Stereo. Web Site: www.kc101.com. Licensee: Clear Channel Radio Licenses Inc. (acq 7-24-92). Format: CHR, top 40.

WELI(AM)— October 1935: 960 khz; 5 kw-U, DA-N. TL: N41 22 14 W72 56 15. Stereo. 495 Benham St., Hamden 06514. Phone: (203) 281-9600. Phone: (203) 288-8814. Fax: (203) 407-4652. E-mail: comments@weli.com. Web Site: www.weli.com. Licensee: Clear Channel Broadcasting Licenses Inc. (group owner, (acq 8-5-85). Network: ABC Information & Entertainment. Rep: Clear Channel. Format: News/talk. Target aud: 18 plus. ♦L. Lowry Mays, pres; Paula Wilmer, gen mgr; Susan Ambrusco, gen sls mgr & mktg dir; Harry Christopher, progmg dir.

WPLR(FM)— 1944: 99.1 mhz; 15 kw. 905 ft. TL: N41 25 23 W72 57 06. Stereo. 440 Wheelers Farm Rd., Suite 302, Milford 06460. Phone: (203) 783-8200. Fax: (203) 783-8373. Web Site: www.wplr.com. Licensee: CXR Holdings Inc. Group owner: Cox Broadcasting (acq 8-00; grpsl). Format: Rock/AOR. ♦Jackie Rinker, gen sls mgr; Samuel Tilery, prom mgr; Ed Sabatino, progmg dir.

WQUN(AM)—See Hamden

WYBC(AM)— 1944: 1340 khz; 1 kw-U. TL: N41 17 32 W72 57 12. 142 Temple St., Stuite 203 06510. Phone: (203) 776-4118. Fax: (203) 776-2446. Licensee: Yale Broadcasting Co. Inc. (acq 7-24-98; $775,000). Format: College. Spec prog: Sp one hr wkly. ♦Caroline Nathan, gen mgr; Wayne Schmidt, opns mgr; Juan Castillo, progmg dir.

WYBC-FM— Mar 9, 1959: 94.3 mhz; 1.8 kw. 325 ft. TL: N41 20 58 W72 58 27. Stereo. Licensee: Yale Broadcasting Co. Network: ABC. Format: Urban contemp. News: 10 hrs wkly. Target aud: Urban & college age listeners. Spec prog: Gospel 8 hrs, jazz 8 hrs, folk 3 hrs wkly. ♦Matthew Loucheim, VP & gen mgr; Emad Abdelnaby, progmg dir; Juan Castillo, pub affrs dir.

New London

*****WCNI(FM)**— 1974: 90.9 mhz; 2 kw vert. Ant 187 ft. TL: N41 22 53 W72 06 28. Stereo. Box 4972, Connecticut College, 270 Mohegan Ave. 06320. Phone: (860) 439-2853 (office). Phone: (860) 439-2850 ext 52 (studio). Fax: (860) 439-2805. E-mail: wnci@conncoll.edu. Web Site: wcni.radio.org. Licensee: Connecticut College Broadcasting Association Inc. Format: Var/div. Target aud: General; all musical audiences except pop. Spec prog: Black 3 hrs, class 6 hrs, folk 9 hrs, gospel 3 hrs, jazz 9 hrs, Pol 3 hrs, Sp 3 hrs, women's 3 hrs wkly. ♦Charles A. Butkiewicz, pres; Jana Savanapirdi, gen mgr; Ross Morin, progmg dir; Mark Warren, mus dir; Jenny Faries, pub affrs dir; Craig Mellon, chief of engrg.

WKNL(FM)— Jan 1, 1970: 100.9 mhz; 3 kw. 328 ft. TL: N41 26 27 W72 08 29. Stereo. Box 1031 06320. Secondary address: 89 Broad St. 06320. Phone: (860) 442-5328. Fax: (860) 442-6532. E-mail: arussell@hallradio.com. Web Site: www.kool101fm.com. Licensee: Hall Communications Inc. (group owner; acq 1-19-95; $3.5 million with co-located AM; 3-20-95). Network: ABC. Rep: D & R Radio. Fletcher, Heald & Hildreth. Format: Oldies. News: 2 hrs wkly. Target aud: 25-54. ♦Bonnie Rowbotham, chmn; Arthur J. Rowbotham, pres; Bill Baldwin, sr VP; Andy Russell, gen mgr & stn mgr.

WQGN-FM—See Groton

WSUB(AM)—See Groton

Norfolk

*****WSGG(FM)**— May 17, 2001: 89.3 mhz; 100 w. Ant 167 ft. TL: N41 59 30 W73 12 46. Box 4594, Hartford 06147. Phone: (860) 232-6425. Licensee: Revival Christian Ministries Inc. Format: Christian. ♦Samuel Girona, gen mgr & progmg dir.

Norwalk

WEFX(FM)—Listing follows WNLK(AM).

WNLK(AM)— 1948: 1350 khz; 1 kw-D, 500 w-N, DA-N. TL: N41 06 54 W73 26 06. 444 Westport Ave. 06851. Phone: (203) 845-3030. Fax: (203) 845-3097. Web Site: www.wstcwnlk.com. Licensee: Cox Radio Inc. Group owner: Clear Channel Communications Inc. (acq 8-25-2000; grpsl). Format: News/talk. News staff: 4; News: 16 hrs wkly. Target aud: 25-54. ♦Robin Saller, gen mgr.

WEFX(FM)—Co-owned with WNLK(AM). 1966: 95.9 mhz; 3 kw. 299 ft. TL: N41 06 54 W73 26 06. Stereo. Web Site: thefoxonline.com. Format: Rock.

Norwich

WCTY(FM)—Listing follows WICH(AM).

WICH(AM)— September 1946: 1310 khz; 5 kw-U, DA-2. TL: N41 33 10 W72 04 34. Box 551, Cuprak Rd. 06360-0551. Phone: (860) 887-3511. Fax: (860) 886-7649. Web Site: www.wich.com. Licensee: WICH Inc. Group owner: Hall Communications Inc. (acq 7-1-65). Rep: D & R Radio. Fletcher, Heald & Hildreth. Format: Full service. News staff: 4. Target aud: 35 plus. Spec prog: Pol one hr wkly. ♦Bonnie H. Rowbotham, chmn; Arthur J. Rowbotham, pres; Bill Baldwin, sr VP; James J. Reed, gen mgr; Karen Dole, opns dir, rgnl sls mgr & pub affrs dir; Bob Reed, prom dir; Jimmy Lane, progmg dir; Roger Arnold, chief of engrg.

WCTY(FM)—Co-owned with WICH(AM). May 1968: 97.7 mhz; 1.9 kw. 410 ft. TL: N41 28 28 W72 06 14. Stereo. Web Site: www.wcty.com. Network: ABC FM Connection. Format: Country. Target aud: 25-54. ♦James J. Reed, prom dir.

*****WNPR(FM)**— Oct 17, 1981: 89.1 mhz; 5.1 kw. 590 ft. TL: N41 31 11 W72 10 04. Stereo. Box 260240, Hartford 06106-0240. Secondary address: 240 New Britain Ave., Hartford 06106-0240. Phone: (860) 278-5310. Fax: (860) 244-9624. Fax: (860) 278-5310. E-mail: info@wnpr.org. Web Site: www.wnpr.org. Licensee: Connecticut Public Television & Radio. Network: Network: NPR, PRI. Schwartz, Woods and Miller. Format: Class, news, info. News staff: 15. News: 38 hrs wkly. Target aud: General. ♦Jerry Franklin, CEO & pres; Kim Grehn, stn mgr & progmg dir; Steve Futernick, dev VP; Nancy Bauer, mktg VP; Evette Cook, prom mgr; John Nowacki, mus dir; John Dankosky, news dir; Joe Zareski, engrg mgr & chief of engrg.

Old Saybrook

WLIS(AM)— Sept 27, 1956: 1420 khz; 5 kw-D, 500 w-N, DA-N. TL: N41 19 38 W72 23 21. 777 River Rd. 06457. Phone: (860) 388-1420. Fax: (860) 347-7704. E-mail: radio@wliswmrd.net. Web Site: www.wliswmrd.net. Licensee: Crossroads Communications of Old Saybrook L.L.C. (acq 10-96). Network: CBS. Format: Talk personalities. News: 15 hrs wkly. Target aud: 25-64; Adults. Spec prog: Jazz 4 hrs wkly. ♦Don DeCesare, pres & gen mgr.

Pawcatuck

WWRX(FM)— Nov 30, 1995: 107.7 mhz; 1.4 kw. Ant 492 ft. TL: N41 27 35 W71 55 40. Stereo. 758 Colonel Ledyard Hwy., Ledyard 06339. Phone: (860) 464-1065. Phone: (860) 723-1063. Fax: (860) 464-8143. Web Site: www.jammin1077.com. Licensee: Fuller Broadcasting International LLC (acq 12-13-2002; $3.75 million). Fisher, Wayland, Cooper, Leader & Zaragoza. Format: Top 40 hits. News: one hr wkly. Target aud: 25-54; mobile, upscale. ♦John J. Fuller, pres & gen mgr; Scott Bradshaw, opns mgr.

Pomfret

*****WBVC(FM)**— 2001: 91.1 mhz; 100 w. Ant 289 ft. TL: N41 53 27 W71 57 24. Box 128, 398 Pomfret St. 06258. Phone: (860) 963-5919. Web Site: www.pomfretschool.org. Licensee: Pomfret School. Format: Var. ♦Bill Pratt, gen mgr.

Putnam

WINY(AM)— May 3, 1953: 1350 khz; 5 kw-D, 79 w-N. TL: N41 54 10 W71 53 43. Stereo. Box 231, 45 Pomfret St. 06260. Phone: (860) 928-1350. Fax: (860) 928-7878. E-mail: info@winyradio.com. Web Site: www.winyradio.com. Licensee: Osbrey Broadcasting Co. (acq

Connecticut

5-31-01; $2 million). Network: Network: AP Radio, Jones Radio Networks. Miller & Miller. Format: Adult contemp. News staff: 3; News: 18 hrs wkly. Target aud: 25-54 plus; adults. Spec prog: Talk 10 hrs wkly. ♦Gary W. Osbrey, pres & gen mgr; Karen Osbrey, VP; Marc Allard, news dir.

Ridgefield

WREF(AM)— Mar 15, 1985: 850 khz; 2.5 kw. TL: N41 17 27 W73 29 16. Stereo. 198 Main St., Danbury 06810. Phone: (203) 744-4800. Fax: (203) 778-4655. E-mail: trueoldies850@hotmail.com. Licensee: The Berkshire Broadcasting Corp. Group owner: Berkshire Broadcasting Corp. (acq 3-31-97; $550,000). Network: ABC. Rep: D & R Radio. Cohn & Marks. Format: Oldies. Target aud: 35-64. ♦James B. Lee Jr., pres; Mary Lu Orteig, exec VP; Irv Goldstein, VP & gen mgr.

Salisbury

WKZE-FM— Sept 1, 1992: 98.1 mhz; 1.8 kw. 604 ft. TL: N41 58 35 W73 31 27. Stereo. 67 Main St., Sharon 06069. Phone: (860) 364-5800. Fax: (860) 364-0129. E-mail: info@wkze.com. Web Site: www.wkze.com. Licensee: Johnson Development Inc. (acq 2-14-97; $850,000 with WKZE(AM) Sharon). Network: AP Radio. Format: AAA. News staff: one; News: 2 hrs wkly. Target aud: 25-54. ♦Scott R. Johnson, CEO & pres; Dave Doud, gen mgr; Pete Nugent, sls VP & gen sls mgr; Paul Higgins, sls; Dennis Sanger, mktg.

Sharon

WKZE(AM)— Dec 23, 1986: 1020 khz; 2.5 kw-D. TL: N41 58 35 W73 31 27. Stereo. 67 Main St. 06069. Phone: (860) 364-5800. Fax: (860) 364-0129. E-mail: info@wkze.com. Licensee: Johnson Development Inc. (acq 2-14-97; $350,000 with WKZE-FM Salisbury). Network: AP Radio. Format: Triple A. News staff: one; News: 2 hrs wkly. Target aud: 25-54. ♦Scott R. Johnson, CEO & gen mgr; Dave Doud, stn mgr & opns mgr; Dennis Sanger, progmg VP & sls; Pete Nugent, engrg VP & sls; Paul Higgins, sls.

WQQQ(FM)— Oct 3, 1994: 103.3 mhz; 1.5 kw. 640 ft. TL: N41 55 03 W73 33 32. Stereo. Box 446, Lakeville 06039-0446. Phone: (860) 435-3333. Phone: (860) 435-0103. Fax: (860) 435-3334. E-mail: q103fm@yahoo.com. Web Site: www.wqqq.com. Licensee: The Ridgefield Broadcasting Corp. (acq 7-20-01). Cohn & Marks. Format: Adult contemp, hits of the 70s, 80s & 90s. News staff: one; News: 14 hrs wkly. Target aud: Upscale adults; 25-54. Spec prog: Jazz 3 hrs, 50's/60's oldies 5 hrs, standards 3 hrs, country 3 hrs, sports talk 2 hrs wkly. ♦Dennis Jackson, chmn; Joe Loverro, exec VP & gen mgr.

Shelton

*****WRXC(FM)**— 1977: 90.1 mhz; 45 w. 482 ft. TL: N41 21 43 W73 06 48. Stereo. Box 920, Monroe 06468. Phone: (203) 268-9667. E-mail: staff@wmnr.org. Web Site: www.wmnr.org. Licensee: Monroe Board of Education. Network: PRI. Format: Class. Spec prog: Big band 8 hrs, folk 2 hrs, new age one hr, Broadway one hr wkly. ♦Kurt Anderson, gen mgr; Jane Stadler, opns dir; Carol Babina, dev dir.

Somers

*****WDJW(FM)**— Oct 6, 1986: 89.7 mhz; 9.2 w. -58 ft. TL: N41 57 43 W72 27 51. Somers High School, 9th District Rd. 06071. Phone: (860) 749-2501. Phone: (860) 749-0719. Fax: (860) 749-9264. Licensee: Somers Board of Education. Format: Jazz, folk, alternative. ♦Peter Stone, pres & gen mgr.

South Kent

*****WGSK(FM)**— Dec 25, 1987: 90.1 mhz; 77 w. Ant 128 ft. TL: N41 40 54 W73 29 13. Stereo. Box 920, Monroe 06468. Phone: (203) 268-9667. E-mail: staff@wmnr.org. Web Site: www.wmnr.org. Licensee: Monroe Board of Education. Network: PRI. Format: Class. Spec prog: Big band 8 hrs, folk 2 hrs, new age one hr, Broadway one hr wkly. ♦Kurt Anderson, gen mgr; Jane Stadler, opns dir; Carol Babina, dev dir.

Southington

WXCT(AM)— Sept 2, 1969: 990 khz; 2.5 kw-D, 80 w-N, DA-2. TL: N41 34 59 W72 53 01. 440 Old Turnpike Rd. 06489. Phone: (860) 548-9410. Fax: (860) 548-1855. E-mail: office@wxct.com. Web Site: www.wxct.com. Licensee: Davidson Media Station WXCT LLC. Group owner: Davidson Media Group LLC (acq 4-30-2004; $1.4 million). New

England. Format: Sp. Spec prog: It 4.5 hrs. ♦Peter Davidson, pres; Charlie Profit, gen mgr & opns VP.

Stamford

*****WEDW-FM**— Feb 17, 1992: 88.5 mhz; 2 kw horiz, 1.8 kw vert. 302 ft. TL: N41 02 49 W73 31 36. Stereo. 240 New Britain Ave., Hartford 06106. Phone: (860) 278-5310. Fax: (860) 244-9624. Web Site: www.wnpr.org. Licensee: Connecticut Public Broadcasting Inc. Format: Class, news. ♦Kim Grehn, gen mgr, stn mgr & progmg dir; Evette Cook, mktg VP & prom mgr; Nancy Bauer, mktg VP; John Nowacki, mus dir; John Dankosky, news dir; Joe Zareski, engrg VP.

WKHL(FM)— Oct. 18, 1974: 96.7 mhz; 3 kw. 328 ft. TL: N41 02 49 W73 31 36. Stereo. 444 Westport Ave., Norwalk 06851. Phone: (203) 845-3030. Fax: (203) 845-3097. Web Site: kool967.com. Licensee: Cox Radio Inc. Group owner: Cox Broadcasting (acq 8-25-00; grpsl). Rep: Katz Radio. Format: Oldies. Target aud: 25-54; upscale. ♦Robin Faller, gen mgr; Jim Stagnitti, gen sls mgr; Helaine Greenbaum, natl sls mgr; Brian Schutz, rgnl sls mgr; Steve Soyland, prom dir; Peter Delloro, progmg dir; Clark Burgard, chief of engrg.

WSTC(AM)— Co-owned with WKHL(FM). Sept 18, 1941: 1400 khz; 1 kw-U. TL: N41 02 49 W73 31 36. Stereo. Web Site: wstcwnlk.com. Network: CNN Radio, Westwood One. Rep: Katz Radio. Format: News/talk. News staff: 4; News: 16 hrs wkly. Target aud: 25-54. ♦Lisa Lacerra, progmg dir & news dir; Tyler Scalzi, prom.

Stonington

WXLM(FM)— November 1981: 102.3 mhz; 3 kw. 328 ft. TL: N41 24 23 W71 50 15. Stereo. 7 Governor Winthrop Blvd., New London 06320. Phone: (860) 443-1980. Fax: (860) 444-7970. Web Site: www.wxlm.fm. Licensee: Citadel Broadcasting Co. Group owner: Citadel Broadcasting Corp. (acq 4-26-01; grpsl). Rep: D & R Radio. Bryan Cave. Format: News, talk, sports. News staff: 2; News: 5 hrs wkly. Target aud: 21-54; adults who grew up in the 60s & 70s. Spec prog: Jazz 2 hrs wkly. ♦Fahrid Sulman, pres; Judy Ellis, VP; Bob Cox, gen mgr; Kelly Fernandez, sls VP; Tim Burrows, gen sls mgr; Kevin O'Connor, prom mgr, prom mgr & news dir; Kevin Palana, progmg dir; Frank Doremus, chief of engrg.

Storrs

*****WHUS(FM)**— 1956: 91.7 mhz; 3.16 kw. 360 ft. TL: N41 48 48 W72 15 33. Stereo. Box U-8R, 2110 Hillside Rd. 06269-3008. Phone: (860) 486-4007. Fax: (860) 486-2955. E-mail: whvsfm@uconn.edu. Web Site: www.whusfm.org. Licensee: Board of Trustees University of Connecticut. Format: Div. Spec prog: Sp 3 hrs wkly. ♦John Murphy, gen mgr.

Torrington

*****WAPJ(FM)**— 1997: 89.9 mhz; 40 w. Ant 276 ft. TL: N41 48 08 W73 09 50. 40 Water St. 06790. Phone: (860) 489-9033. Fax: (860) 482-7614. Licensee: The I.B. and Zena H. Temkin Foundation Inc. (acq 9-30-2004). Format: Educ, adult contemp, MOR, talk. News: 10 hrs wkly. Target aud: General; any and all. Spec prog: Children 1 hr, country/farm 3 hrs, gospel 1 hr, sports, 2-8, music 4 hrs wkly.

WSNG(AM)— Jan 29, 1948: 610 khz; 1 kw-D, 500 w-N, DA-2. TL: N41 45 28 W73 03 06. Box 657 06790. Secondary address: 64 Hungerford Ln., Harwinton 06791. Phone: (860) 689-8050. Fax: (860) 286-8257. E-mail: wsng@talkofconn. Web Site: www.wdrc.com. Licensee: Buckley Broadcasting of Connecticut LLC. Group owner: Buckley Broadcasting Corp. (acq 12-18-96; $425,000). Network: Westwood One. Erwin Krasnow. Format: Talk. News staff: 3; News: 25 hrs wkly. Target aud: 25-54. ♦Wayne Mulligan, gen mgr; Laura Kittell, opns mgr; Ron Pell, gen sls mgr; Dave Nagel, progmg dir; Scott Baron, chief of engrg.

Vernon

*****WCTF(AM)**— Nov 21, 1982: 1170 khz; 1 kw-D, DA. TL: N41 52 38 W72 28 43. (CP: 2.5 kw-D). WCTF c/o WFSI, 918 Chesapeake Ave., Annapolis, MD 21403. Secondary address: 45 1/2 East St. 06066. Phone: (860) 871-2526. Web Site: www.familyradio.com. Licensee: Family Stations Inc. (group owner; acq 1-86; $136,000; 9-23-85). Format: Relg. ♦Harold Camping, pres.

Wallingford

*****WWEB(FM)**— Nov 10, 1976: 89.9 mhz; 10 w. 230 ft. TL: N41 27 34 W72 48 48. Choate Rosemary Hall Foundation, 333 Christian St. 06492. Phone: (203) 697-2506. Fax: (203) 697-2186. E-mail: cbielizna@choate.edu. Web Site: www.student.choate.edu/wweb. Licensee: Choate Rosemary Hall Foundation. Format: Var/div. Target aud: High school students. Spec prog: Class 2 hrs, C&W 2 hrs wkly. ♦Chris Bielizna, gen mgr.

Waterbury

WATR(AM)— June 15, 1934: 1320 khz; 5 kw-D, 1 kw-N, DA-2. TL: N41 32 12 W73 01 52. One Broadcast Ln. 06706. Phone: (203) 755-1121. Fax: (203) 574-3025. E-mail: talkback@watr.com. Web Site: www.watr.com. Licensee: WATR Inc. Network: CBS. Format: News/talk. News staff: 2; News: 15 hrs wkly. Target aud: 35-64. Spec prog: Pol 2 hrs, It 3 hrs wkly. ♦Tom Chute, gen mgr.

WPHH(FM)— Dec 25, 1967: 104.1 mhz; 50 kw. 859 ft. TL: N41 33 41 W72 50 39. Stereo. 10 Columbus Blvd., Hartford 06106. Phone: (860) 723-6000. Fax: (860) 493-7090. Web Site: power1041.com. Licensee: Capstar TX L.P. Group owner: Clear Channel Communications Inc. (acq 8-30-00; grpsl). Network: ABC. Rep: Christal. Format: Modern rock. Target aud: 18-49. ♦Manuel Rodriguez, exec VP & gen mgr; Todd Thomas, opns mgr.

WWCO(AM)— 1946: 1240 khz; 1 kw-U. TL: N41 33 59 W73 03 23. Box 99 06720. Secondary address: 20 Main St., Suite 8 B, Oakville 06779. Phone: (860) 243-1115. Fax: (860) 274-9734. E-mail: wwco@talkofconnecticut.com. Web Site: www.talkofconnecticut.com. Licensee: Buckley Broadcasting of Connecticut LLC. Group owner: Buckley Broadcasting Corp. (acq 4-97; $500,000). Format: Talk/news. News staff: 2. Target aud: 35 plus. Spec prog: NY Yankee games. ♦Richard Buckley, pres; Wayne Mulligan, gen mgr & stn mgr; Laura Kittell, opns mgr.

WWYZ(FM)— Aug 1, 1961: 92.5 mhz; 17.8 kw. 879 ft. TL: N41 33 43 W72 50 41. Stereo. 10 Columbus Blvd., Hartford 06106. Phone: (860) 723-6000. Fax: (860) 493-7090. Web Site: www.country925.com. Licensee: Capstar TX L.P. Group owner: Clear Channel Communications Inc. (acq 8-30-00; grpsl). Network: Westwood One. Rep: Christal. Format: Country. News staff: one; News: 5 hrs wkly. Target aud: 25-54. ♦Manuel Rodriguez, exec VP & gen mgr; Todd Thomas, opns mgr.

West Hartford

WRYM(AM)—See New Britain

WTMI(AM)—Licensed to West Hartford. See Hartford

*****WWUH(FM)**— July 15, 1968: 91.3 mhz; 440 w. 784 ft. TL: N41 46 27 W72 48 20. Stereo. Univ. of Hartford, 200 Bloomfield Ave. 06117. Phone: (860) 768-4701. Phone: (860) 768-4703. Fax: (860) 768-5701. E-mail: wwuh@hartford.edu. Web Site: www.wnuh.org. Licensee: University of Hartford. Format: Var/div. News: 8 hrs wkly. Target aud: General. Spec prog: It 3 hrs, Por 3 hrs, Pol 3 hrs, It 3 hrs, foreign/ethnic 14 hrs wkly. ♦John N. Ramsey, pres & gen mgr; Kate Horrigan, opns dir; Susan Mullis, dev dir.

West Haven

*****WNHU(FM)**— 1973: 88.7 mhz; 1.7 kw. 150 ft. TL: N41 17 29 W72 57 40. Stereo. Maxy Hall, 300 Orange Ave. 06516. Phone: (203) 934-8888/934-9296. Fax: (203) 931-6055. E-mail: wnhu@charger.newhaven.edu. Web Site: www.wnhu.org. Licensee: University of New Haven Inc. Dow, Lohnes & Albertson. Format: Alternative, big band, Black. News: 12 hrs wkly. Target aud: General. Spec prog: Jazz 12 hrs, folk 6 hrs, Irish 5 hrs, metal 9 hrs, class 9 hrs, gospel 4 hrs wkly. ♦Steven A. Raucher, gen mgr.

Westport

WEBE(FM)— Sept 1, 1962: 107.9 mhz; 50 kw. 383 ft. TL: N41 10 14 W73 11 05. Stereo. 2 Lafayette Sq., Bridgeport 06604-6000. Phone: (203) 333-9108. Fax: (203) 384-0600. Fax: (203) 394-6000. Web Site: www.webe108.com. Licensee: Cumulus Licensing Corp. Group owner: Cumulus Media Inc. (acq 3-14-02; grpsl). Rep: Christal. Format: Adult contemp. News staff: one; News: 3 hrs wkly. Target aud: 25-54; upscale females. Spec prog: Talk one hr wkly. ♦Ann Surface McManus, gen mgr; Curtis Hansen, opns VP & opns mgr.

Stations in the U.S. Delaware

*WSHU(AM)— Apr 15, 1959: 1260 khz; 1 kw-D, DA. TL: N41 07 44 W73 23 20. Stereo. 5151 Park Ave., Fairfield 06825. Phone: (203) 365-6604. Fax: (203) 371-7991. E-mail: info@wshu.org. Web Site: www.wshu.org. Licensee: Sacred Heart University Inc. (acq 11-28-97; $325,000. as donation). Network: Network: Network: USA, NPR, PRI. Format: News/talk. News staff: 2; News: 45 hrs wkly. Target aud: General. ♦George Lombardi, gen mgr; Julie Freddino, opns dir & opns mgr; Gillian Anderson, dev dir.

*WWPT(FM)— 1975: 90.3 mhz; 330 w. 110 ft. TL: N41 10 19 W73 19 43. Stereo. Staples High School, 70 N. Ave. 06880. Secondary address: 110 Myrtle Ave. 06880. Phone: (203) 341-1381. Phone: (203) 341-1200. Fax: (203) 226-6875. Licensee: Board of Education, Town of Westport. Format: Free-form. Target aud: 14-24; youth. Spec prog: Slovak 3 hrs wkly. ♦Jack Lapick, gen mgr.

Willimantic

*WECS(FM)— Feb 6, 1982: 90.1 mhz; 421 w. 380 ft. TL: N41 41 00 W72 12 59. 83 Windham St. 06226. Phone: (860) 465-5354. Fax: (860) 465-5073. E-mail: wecs@hotmail.com. Web Site: www.easternct.edu. Licensee: Eastern Connecticut State University. Format: Urban contemp, rock/AOR. Spec prog: Jazz 16 hrs, relg 3 hrs, Sp 9 hrs wkly. ♦John L. Zatowski, gen mgr.

WILI(AM)— Oct 5, 1957: 1400 khz; 1 kw-U. TL: N41 42 55 W72 11 23. 720 Main St. 06226. Phone: (860) 456-1111. Fax: (860) 456-9501. Web Site: www.wili.com. Licensee: Nutmeg Broadcasting Co. (acq 7-11-2005; $1.8 million with co-located FM). Network: Network: Westwood One, ABC Information & Entertainment. Format: Full service, adult contemp, news/talk. News staff: 3; News: 10 hrs wkly. Target aud: 25 plus; general. Spec prog: Ukrainian one hr, Sp one hr, relg 2 hrs, Jewish one hr wkly. ♦Colin K. Rice, VP.

WILI-FM— June 16, 1975: 98.3 mhz; 1.05 kw. 525 ft. TL: N41 41 00 W72 13 01. Stereo. Web Site: www.wili.com. Network: Superadio. Format: CHR. News staff: one; News: 6 hrs wkly. Target aud: 22-44; college students, young married couples, young families.

Windsor

WNEZ(AM)— May 4, 1961: 1480 khz; 500 w-D, DA. TL: N41 51 10 W72 40 43. 330 Main St., Hartford 06106. Phone: (860) 524-0001. Fax: (860) 548-1922. Web Site: www.wknd1480.com. Licensee: Freedom Communications of Connecticut Inc. (acq 11-29-2004). Network: ABC. Format: Gospel. Target aud: General; greater Hartford's minority population. Spec prog: Gospel 5 hrs, jazz 3 hrs wkly. ♦Richard Weaver-Bey, pres; Marion Anderson, gen mgr; Eddie Jordan, opns dir & prom mgr.

Delaware

Bethany Beach

WJKI(FM)— 1996: 103.5 mhz; 1.45 kw. Ant 479 ft. TL: N38 34 21 W75 06 58. 20200 DuPont Blvd., Georgetown 19947. Phone: (302) 856-2567. Fax: (302) 856-7633. Web Site: www.hitsandfavorites.com. Licensee: Great Scott Broadcasting. (group owner) Format: Lite rock. ♦Mitchell Scott, gen mgr.

WOSC(FM)— 1974: 95.9 mhz; 10.5 kw. Ant 469 ft. TL: N38 25 20 W75 08 23. Stereo. Gateway Crossing, 351 Tilghman Rd., Salisbury, MD 21804. Phone: (410) 742-1923. Fax: (410) 742-2329. Web Site: www.96rocksyou.com. Licensee: Capstar TX L.P. Group owner: Clear Channel Communications Inc. (acq 8-7-2000; grpsl). Rep: Clear Channel. Format: Active rock. Target aud: 18-34. ♦Frank Hamilton, gen mgr; Brian Cleary, opns mgr & progmg dir; Dixie Penner, prom dir.

Christiana

*WXHL-FM— Aug 1, 1994: 89.1 mhz; 1 w horiz, 1.2 kw vert. 67 ft. TL: N39 40 38 W75 39 47. 179 Stanton-Christiana Rd., Newark 19702. Phone: (302) 731-0690. Fax: (302) 738-3090. Web Site: www.thereachfm.com. Licensee: Priority Radio Inc. (group owner; acq 12-10-99). Format: Adult contemp Christian mus. ♦Steve Hare, gen mgr; Dan Edwards, opns mgr; Larry Humm, gen sls mgr; Dave Kirby, progmg dir.

Dover

WDOV(AM)— 1948: 1410 khz; 5.4 kw, DA-2. TL: N39 12 03 W75 33 13. 1575 McKee, Suite 206 19904. Phone: (302) 793-4200. Fax: (302) 674-2049. E-mail: mail@wdov.com. Web Site: www.wdov.com. Licensee: Capstar TX L.P. Group owner: Clear Channel Communications Inc. (acq 8-30-00; grpsl). Network: Westwood One. Rep: McGavren Guild. Format: News/talk. News staff: 2; News: 162 hrs wkly. Target aud: 25-54. ♦Bob Walton, opns dir & progmg dir; Phil Feliciangeli, news dir & pub affrs dir.

WRDX(FM)— Co-owned with WDOV(AM). 1956: 94.7 mhz; 50 kw. 377 ft. TL: N39 12 03 W75 33 55. Stereo. 3001 Philadelphia Pike, Claymont 19703. Fax: (302) 793-4200. E-mail: mail@river947.com. Web Site: www.river947.com. Network: Westwood One. Latham & Watkins. Format: Hot adult contemp. ♦Joe Puglise, gen sls mgr; Bob Walton, progmg dir.

WKEN(AM)— Aug 2, 1957: 1600 khz; 5 kw-D, 1 kw-N, DA-2. TL: N39 10 11 W75 33 13. Box 272, Bethel 19931. Phone: (302) 731-7600. Fax: (302) 731-7673. E-mail: wams1260amgk@aol.com. Licensee: East Coast Broadcasting Inc. (acq 2-22-2001). Format: Black Gospel. ♦Vincent Klepac, CEO; George Krementz, gen mgr.

*WRTX(FM)— Apr 5, 1995: 91.7 mhz; 580 w. 315 ft. TL: N39 12 03 W75 33 55. Stereo. 2020 N. 13th St., 1509 Cecil B. Moore Ave., Philadelphia, PA 19122. Phone: (215) 204-8405. Fax: (215) 204-4870. E-mail: comments@wrti.org. Web Site: www.wrti.org. Licensee: Temple University of the Commonwealth System of Higher Education. Network: NPR, AP Radio. Format: Jazz, class. News staff: one; News: 15 hrs wkly. Target aud: 30-65. ♦Dave Conant, exec VP; Tobias Poole, gen mgr & opns dir; Brick Torpey, gen sls mgr.

Fenwick Island

WLBW(FM)— Apr 1, 1994: 92.1 mhz; 3 kw. Ant 469 ft. TL: N38 25 20 W75 08 23. Stereo. 351 Tilghman Rd., Salisbury, MD 21804. Phone: (410) 742-1923. Fax: (410) 742-2329. E-mail: wave@intercom.net. Web Site: www.isurfthewave.com. Licensee: Capstar TX L.P. Group owner: Clear Channel Communications Inc. (acq 8-7-00; grpsl). Format: Oldies. Target aud: 25-54. ♦Frank Hamilton, gen mgr.

Georgetown

WJWL(AM)— June 23, 1951: 900 khz; 10 kw-D, 1 w-N, DA-1. TL: N38 42 31 W75 24 25. Stereo. 20200 DuPont Blvd. 19947. Phone: (302) 856-2567. Fax: (302) 856-6839. Licensee: Great Scott Broadcasting Ltd. Group owner: Great Scott Broadcasting Cohn & Marks. Format: Adult contemp. News staff: one; News: 10 hrs wkly. Target aud: 25-54; mature adults. Spec prog: Relg 6 hrs wkly. ♦Faye Scott, pres; Mitchell Scott, gen mgr.

WZBH(FM)—Co-owned with WJWL(AM). July 4, 1969: 93.5 mhz; 11 kw. Ant 485 ft. TL: N38 31 24 W75 17 55. (CP: COL Millsboro. 50 kw, ant 492 ft.). 20200 DuPont Blvd. 19947. Phone: (302) 856-2567. Format: Contemp rock. Target aud: Adults; baby boomers. ♦Shawn Murphy, progmg dir; Terry Dalton, chief of engrg.

Laurel

WKDB(FM)— Nov 19, 1991: 95.3 mhz; 6 kw. 328 ft. TL: N38 30 12 W75 39 39. Stereo. 20200 DuPont Blvd., Georgetown 19947. Phone: (302) 856-2567. Fax: (302) 856-7633. Web Site: www.musicontheb.com. Licensee: Great Scott Broadcasting (group owner; acq 2-13-98; $1.5 million). Format: Adult contemp. News: 6 hrs wkly. Target aud: 25-49. ♦Mitchell Scott, gen mgr & stn mgr.

Lewes

WXJN(FM)— June 1, 1991: 105.9 mhz; 6 kw. 341 ft. TL: N38 38 36 W75 13 00. Stereo. Box 909, Salisbury, MD 21803. Phone: (410) 219-3500. Phone: (410) 548-1543. Web Site: www.catcountryradio.com. Licensee: Delmarva Broadcasting Co. (group owner; acq 6-26-97; grpsl). Rep: Katz Radio. Hogan & Hartson. Format: Country. News staff: one; News: 3 hrs wkly. Target aud: 25-54. Spec prog: NASCAR. ♦Mike Reath, gen mgr; Joe Edwards, opns mgr; Joe Beail, gen sls mgr; Jeff Twilley, engrg dir & chief of engrg.

Milford

WAFL(FM)— May 19, 1973: 97.7 mhz; 6 kw. 328 ft. TL: N38 55 39 W75 29 20. Stereo. Box 808 19963. Secondary address: 1666 Blairs Pond Rd. 19963. Phone: (302) 422-7575. Fax: (302) 422-3069. E-mail: staff@eagle977.com. Web Site: www.eagle977.com. Licensee: Delmarva Broadcasting Co. (group owner; acq 6-26-97; grpsl). Network: Westwood One. Hogan & Hartson. Format: Adult contemp. Target aud: 18-54; active, affluent adults in central & southern Delaware. Spec prog: Southern gospel 2 hrs wkly. ♦Melody Booker, gen mgr; Dee Dee Du Pre', sls dir; Mike Sommers, progmg mgr; Jeff Twilly, chief of engrg.

WYUS(AM)—Co-owned with WAFL(FM). 1953: 930 khz; 500 w-D, 100 w-N, DA-1. TL: N38 55 39 W75 29 20. Phone: (302) 422-2428. Rep: Caballero. Format: Sp. Target aud: 18 plus; Hispanic. Spec prog: Relg 10 hrs, Haitian 3 hrs wkly. ♦Rafael Dosman, progmg dir.

WNCL(FM)— Nov 5, 1990: 101.3 mhz; 3 kw. Ant 328 ft. TL: N38 51 21 W75 29 02. Stereo. Box 808, 1666 Blairs Pond Rd. 19963. Phone: (302) 422-7575. Fax: (302) 422-3069. E-mail: lightfm@wxpz.com. Web Site: www.eagle977.com. Licensee: Delmarva Broadcasting Co. (group owner; acq 1-17-2003; $1.6 million). Gammon & Grange. Format: Greatest hits of the 60s and 70s. News: 7 hrs wkly. Target aud: 25-49; women. ♦Julian H. Booker, pres; Melody Gardner, gen mgr.

Newark

WAMS(AM)— Aug 17, 1964: 1260 khz; 1 kw-D, 42 w-N, DA-2. TL: N39 38 39 W75 41 33. 25 S. Old Baltimore Pike 19702. Phone: (302) 731-7600. Licensee: East Coast Broadcasting Inc. (acq 3-11-2002; $140,000). Network: Network: ABC, AP Radio. Format: Gospel. ♦Vincent Klepac, pres; Alfred R. Campagnone, gen mgr.

*WVUD(FM)— Oct 4, 1976: 91.3 mhz; 1 kw. 135 ft. TL: N39 41 26 W75 45 23. Stereo. Univ. of Delaware, Perkins Student Ctr. 19716. Phone: (302) 831-2701. Fax: (302) 831-1399. Web Site: www.wvud.org. Licensee: University of Delaware. Network: AP Radio. Format: Progsv, div, educ. Target aud: General. Spec prog: Class 10 hrs, Black 10 hrs, jazz 15 hrs, folk 15 hrs, Sp 2 hrs wkly. ♦Chuck Tarver, stn mgr.

Ocean View

WZEB(FM)— Jan 12, 1986: 101.7 mhz; 3 kw. 328 ft. TL: N38 29 20 W75 12 01. Stereo. 20200 DuPont Blvd., Georgetown 19947. Phone: (302) 856-2567. Fax: (302) 856-7633. Web Site: www.musicontheb.com. Licensee: Great Scott Broadcasting. (group owner; acq 5-29-98; $1.5 million). Format: CHR. ♦Shawn Murphy, opns mgr.

Pike Creek

*WMHS(FM)— April 2000: 88.1 mhz; 90 w vert. 121 ft. TL: N39 45 27 W75 40 02. Red Clay Consolidated School District, 2916 Duncan Rd., Wilmington 19808. Phone: (302) 636-5652. Fax: (302) 992-5525. Licensee: Red Clay Consolidated School District. Format: Oldies. News staff: 11; News: 20 hrs wkly. Target aud: 25-54; adults-baby boomers. ♦Fran Kulas, gen mgr.

Rehoboth Beach

WGMD(FM)— Sept 21, 1975: 92.7 mhz; 3 kw. 300 ft. TL: N38 42 05 W75 11 58. Stereo. Box 530 19971. Phone: (302) 945-2050. Fax: (302) 945-3781. Web Site: www.wgmd.com. Licensee: Resort Broadcasting Co. L.L.C. (acq 7-25-80). Rep: ABC Radio Sales. Format: News/talk. News staff: 3; News: 16 hrs wkly. Target aud: 35 plus. Spec prog: Farm 2 hrs, jazz 2 hrs, relg 2 hrs wkly. ♦Dan Gaffney, gen mgr; Jared Morris, opns mgr; Marie Moulinier, gen sls mgr.

Seaford

WGBG(FM)— February 1972: 98.5 mhz; 6 kw. 321 ft. TL: N38 36 47 W75 35 12. Stereo. 20200 DuPont Blvd., Georgetown 19947. Phone: (302) 856-2567. Fax: (302) 856-6839. Web Site: www.bigclassichits.com. Licensee: Great Scott Broadcasting. (group owner; acq 4-27-98; $1.2 million with co-located AM). Network: CBS. Mullin, Rhyne, Emmons & Topel. Format: Classic rock. News: 4 hrs wkly. Target aud: 18-49; secondary 25-54, tertiary 35 plus. Spec prog: Farm one hr wkly. ♦Mitch Scott, gen mgr; Shawn Murphy, opns mgr; Sue Timmons, gen sls mgr; Sean Murphy, progmg dir; Terry Dalton, chief of engrg.

WJWK(AM)—Co-owned with WGBG(FM). 1955: 1280 khz; 840 w-D, 250 w-N. TL: N38 37 03 W75 35 09. Format: Big band. News: 4 hrs wkly. Target aud: Black adults. ♦Eric Littleton, progmg mgr.

Selbyville

WOCM(FM)— March 1993: 98.1 mhz; 3 kw. Ant 469 ft. TL: N38 25 20 W75 08 23. 117th W. 49th St., Ocean City, MD 21842. Phone: (410) 723-3683. Fax: (410) 723-4347. Web Site: www.irieradion.com. Licensee: Irie Radio Inc. (acq 9-27-02; $1.08 million). Cohen & Berfield. Format: AAA. Target aud: 25-54; seasonal, beach residents & loc urban/farm. Spec prog: Bluegrass one hr wkly. ♦Leighton Moore, pres; David Rothner, stn mgr & chief of engrg.

Smyrna

WDSD(FM)— Nov 10, 1993: 92.9 mhz; 1.7 kw. 377 ft. TL: N39 16 08 W75 31 28. Stereo. 1575 McKee Rd., Dover 19904. Phone: (302) 674-1410. Fax: (302) 674-5978. Web Site: www.wdsd.com. Licensee: Capstar TX L.P. Group owner: Clear Channel Communications Inc. (acq 8-30-00; grpsl). Network: Jones Radio Networks. Latham & Watkins. Format: Country. News staff: one; News: 2 hrs wkly. Target aud: 18-49. ♦Bob Walton, opns mgr.

Wilmington

WDEL(AM)— 1922: 1150 khz; 5 kw-U, DA-2. TL: N39 48 54 W75 31 47. Box 7492, 2727 Shipley Rd. 19803. Phone: (302) 478-2700. Fax: (302) 478-0100. E-mail: wdel@wdel.com. Licensee: Delmarva Broadcasting Co. Inc. (group owner) Network: Westwood One. Rep: Katz Radio. Hogan & Hartson. Format: Full service, news/talk. News staff: 10; News: 70 hrs wkly. Target aud: 35-64. Spec prog: Sp 2 hrs wkly. ♦Julian H. Booker, CEO, pres & gen mgr.

WSTW(FM)—Co-owned with WDEL(AM). 1950: 93.7 mhz; 50 kw. 490 ft. TL: N39 48 57 W75 31 31. Stereo. Format: Hot adult contemp. News: 10 hrs wkly. Target aud: 25-54. Spec prog: Relg one hr, pub affrs one hr wkly.

WFAI(AM)—(Salem).NJ Sept 1, 1966: 1510 khz; 2.5 kw-D, DA. TL: N39 34 58 W75 27 39. First Federal Plaza Bldg., 704 King St., Suite 604 19801. Phone: (302) 622-8895. Fax: (302) 622-8678. E-mail: tonya@faith1510.com. Web Site: www.faith1510.com. Licensee: QC Communication Inc. (acq 3-17-97; $1.8 million with WJKS(FM) Canton). Format: Gospel. News staff: 2; News: 3 hrs wkly. Target aud: 18 plus. Spec prog: Farm 8 hrs wkly. ♦Tony Quartarone, gen mgr; Manuel Mena, progmg dir.

WILM(AM)— Oct 1, 1923: 1450 khz; 1 kw-U. TL: N39 43 46 W75 33 07. 1215 French St. 19801. Phone: (302) 656-9800. Fax: (302) 655-1450. Web Site: www.wilm.com. Licensee: Citicasters Licenses L.P. (acq 10-29-2004; $3,986,000). Network: Network: CBS, Wall Street. Rep: Savalli. Format: All news/talk. News staff: 25; News: 168 hrs wkly. Target aud: 25 plus; educated people who care about Delaware & the world. ♦Bob Walton, gen mgr.

WJBR-FM— January 1957: 99.5 mhz; 50 kw. 499 ft. TL: N39 50 03 W75 31 25. Stereo. 812 Philadelphia Pike 19809. Phone: (302) 765-1160. Fax: (302) 765-1192. E-mail: info@wjbr.com. Web Site: www.wjbr.com. Licensee: NM Licensing LLC. Group owner: NextMedia Group L.L.C. (acq 3-7-00; $32.4 million). Network: ABC. Rep: Christal. Liebowitz & Associates. Format: Adult contemp. News staff: one. Target aud: 25-54. ♦Steven Dinetz, CEO; Carl E. Hirsch, chmn; Skip Weller, pres; Sean Stover, CFO; Jeff Dinetz, exec VP; Jane E. Bartsch, VP; Jane Bartsch, gen mgr; Michael Waite, opns VP.

***WMPH(FM)**— October 1969: 91.7 mhz; 100 w. 143 ft. TL: N39 46 23 W75 30 25. Stereo. 5201 Washington St. Ext. 19809. Phone: (302) 762-7199. E-mail: radio@wmph.org. Web Site: www.wmph.org. Licensee: Brandywine School District, Brd of Educ Format: Rythmic contemp hit/dance. News staff: one; News: 2 hrs wkly. Target aud: 13-27; high school & college students. ♦Bruce Harter, CEO; Gregg Robinson, pres; Clint Dantinne, gen mgr.

WTMC(AM)— 1947: 1380 khz; 5 kw-D, 1 kw-N. TL: N39 48 12 W75 37 42. (CP: 520 w-D, 4.2 kw-N. TL: N39 43 46 W75 33 07 day, N39 48 41 W75 46 20 night). 169 Brick Stone Landing Rd., Smyrna 19977. Phone: (302) 659-2412. Fax: (302) 659-6128. E-mail: rbrittingham @mail.dot.state.de.us. Web Site: www.deldot.net. Licensee: State of Delaware Department of Transportation. (acq 11-4-99). Format: Talk. ♦Ray Brittingham, CEO & pres; Chris Marsh, chmn; Reza Moghissi, sr VP; Bob Garbacz, VP; Skip Lemieux, gen mgr; Glenn Molinari, stn mgr.

WWTX(AM)— Apr 21, 1947: 1290 khz; 2.5 kw-U. TL: N39 44 03 W75 31 44. 3001 Philadelphia Pike, Claymont 19703. Phone: (302) 793-4200. Fax: (302) 793-4204. E-mail: mail@1290theticket.com. Web Site: www.1290theticket.com. Licensee: Capstar TX L.P. Group owner: Clear Channel Communications Inc. Format: Sports. ♦Joe Puglise, gen mgr; Bob Walton, opns mgr.

District of Columbia

Washington

WABS(AM)—See Arlington, VA

WACA(AM)—See Wheaton, MD

***WAMU(FM)**— Oct 23, 1961: 88.5 mhz; 50 kw. 500 ft. TL: N38 56 09 W77 05 33. Stereo. The American Univ., Brandywine Bldg., 4400 Massachuetts Ave., N.W. 20016-8082. Phone: (202) 885-1200. Fax: (202) 885-1269. E-mail: feedback@wamu.org. Web Site: www.wamu.org. Licensee: American University. Network: Network: NPR, PRI. Format: News/talk, bluegrass, culture. News staff: 6; News: 120 hrs wkly. Target aud: 25-54. Spec prog: Vintage radio 4 hrs, country 4 hrs, jazz 5 hrs wkly. ♦Caryn Mathis, gen mgr.

WARW(FM)—See Bethesda, MD

WASH(FM)— 1948: 97.1 mhz; 26 kw. 690 ft. TL: N38 57 21 W77 04 57. Stereo. 1801 Rockville Pike, Rockville, MD 20852. Phone: (301) 984-9710. Fax: (301) 255-4314. Web Site: www.washfm.com. Licensee: AMFM Radio Licenses LLC. Group owner: Clear Channel Communications Inc. (acq 8-30-00; grpsl). Format: Adult Contemp. ♦Bennett Zier, VP, gen mgr & opns mgr; Loretta Lage, gen sls mgr; Mark Lapidus, mktg dir; Bill Hess, progmg dir.

WAVA(FM)—(Arlington).VA Aug 1, 1948: 105.1 mhz; 41 kw. 541 ft. TL: N38 53 44 W77 08 04. Stereo. 1901 N. Moore St., Suite 200, Arlington, VA 22209. Phone: (703) 807-2266. Fax: (703) 807-2248. E-mail: comment@wava.com. Web Site: www.wava.com. Licensee: Salem Media of Virginia Inc. Group owner: Salem Communications Corp. (acq 2-13-92; $20 million; 11-18-91). Network: Salem Radio Network. Rep: Salem. Fletcher, Heald & Hildreth. Format: Adult contemp, Christian, talk. News: 4 hrs wkly. Target aud: 25-54. ♦Edward Atsinger, CEO & chief of engrg; Stu Epperson, chmn; David Evans, CFO; Joe Davis, exec VP; David Ruleman, VP & gen mgr.

WBIG-FM— June 3, 1994: 100.3 mhz; 36 kw. 574 ft. TL: N38 53 44 W77 08 04. Stereo. 6th Fl., 1801 Rockville Pike, Rockville, MD 20852. Phone: (301) 468-1800. Fax: (301) 770-0236. Web Site: www.big100.com. Licensee: AMFM Radio Licenses LLC. Group owner: Clear Channel Communications Inc. (acq 8-30-00; grpsl). Network: ABC FM Connection. Format: Oldies. News staff: 2; News: one hr wkly. Target aud: 35-54; professional, college, upscale. ♦Bennett Zier, gen mgr.

***WCSP-FM**— May 8, 1982: 90.1 mhz; 50 kw. 450 ft. TL: N38 57 44 W77 01 36. 400 N. Capitol St. N.W., Suite 650 20001. Phone: (202) 737-3220. Fax: (202) 737-5554. Web Site: www.c-span.org. Licensee: National Cable Satellite Corp. (acq 1997). Format: Pub affrs. Target aud: General. ♦Brian P. Lamb, CEO; Robert Spence, gen mgr.

WCTN(AM)—See Potomac-Cabin John, MD

WDCT(AM)—See Fairfax, VA

***WETA(FM)**— Apr 19, 1970: 90.9 mhz; 75 kw. Ant 610 ft. TL: N38 53 30 W77 07 55. Stereo. 2775 S. Quincy St., Arlington, VA 22206-2269. Phone: (703) 998-2600. Fax: (703) 824-7288. E-mail: radio@weta.com. Web Site: www.weta.org. Licensee: Greater Washington Educational Telecommunications Association Inc. Network: Network: NPR, PRI. Dow, Lohnes & Albertson. Format: News, pub affrs. Target aud: General; educated adults. ♦Sharon Percy Rockefeller, CEO & pres; Polly Heath, CFO; Dan Devany, sr VP, VP & stn mgr; DeLinda Mrowka, prom mgr; Ingrid Lakey, progmg dir; David Ginder, mus dir. Co-owned TV: *WETA-TV affil

WFAX(AM)—(Falls Church).VA September 1948: 1220 khz; 5 kw-D, 100 w-N. TL: N38 52 47 W77 10 18. 161 Hillwood Ave., Suite B, Falls Church, VA 22046-2983. Phone: (703) 532-1220. Fax: (703) 533-7572. E-mail: wfax@wfaxam.com. Web Site: www.wfax.com. Licensee: Newcomb Broadcasting Corp. Arent, Fox, Kintner, Plotkin & Kahn. Format: Relg. News: one hr wkly. Target aud: 34-54. Spec prog: Black 15 hrs, It one hr wkly. ♦Doris N. Newcomb, pres & gen mgr; R. C. Woolfenden, opns dir.

WFED(AM)—(Silver Spring).MD Dec 7, 1946: 1050 khz; 1 kw-D, 44 w-N. TL: N39 00 50 W77 01 46. 3400 Idaho Ave. N.W. 20016. Phone: (202) 895-5000. Fax: (202) 895-5144. Web Site: www.federalnewsradio.com. Licensee: Bonneville Holding Co. (group owner; (acq 12-1-2004; $4 million). Format: Federal news. ♦M. Farrell Benson, pres; Joel Oxley, gen mgr.

WGMS-FM— September 1948: 103.5 mhz; 44 kw. 518 ft. TL: N38 56 09 W77 05 33. Stereo. 3400 Idaho Ave. N.W. 20016. Phone: (202) 895-5000. Fax: (202) 895-4167. Web Site: www.wgmsclassical1035.com. Licensee: Bonneville Holding Co. Group owner: Bonneville International Corp. (acq 1-30-98; grpsl). Network: Westwood One. Rep: Katz Radio. Format: Class. News: 4 hrs wkly. Target aud: 35-64; affluent, educated, professionals. ♦Bruce Reese, pres; Glenn Larkin, CFO; Joel Oxley, gen mgr; Patti Fears, gen sls mgr; Steve Nicklin, mktg dir; Laura Higgins, prom dir; Jim Allison, progmg dir; Scott Thureen, asst music dir.

WGTS(FM)—See Takoma Park, MD

WHUR-FM— Dec 10, 1971: 96.3 mhz; 16.5 kw. Ant 800 ft. TL: N38 57 01 W77 04 47. Stereo. 529 Bryant St. N.W. 20059. Phone: (202) 806-3500. Fax: (202) 806-3522. Web Site: www.whur.com. Licensee: Howard University Board of Trustees. Network: Network: CNN Radio, ABC. Rep: D & R Radio. Format: Urban adult contemp. News staff: 3; News: 7 hrs wkly. Target aud: 25-54. Spec prog: Gospel 14 hrs, Caribbean 6 hrs wkly. ♦Dr. H. Patrick Swygert, pres; Millard J. Watkins III, gen mgr; Jeanette Tyce, gen sls mgr; David Dickinson, progmg dir.

WIHT(FM)— 1960: 99.5 mhz; 22 kw. Ant 751 ft. TL: N38 57 49 W77 06 18. 1801 Rockville Pike, 6th Fl., Rockville, MD 20852. Phone: (301) 468-9429. Phone: (301) 587-7100. Fax: (301) 770-3541. Web Site: www.hot995.com. Licensee: AMFM Radio Licenses L.L.C. Group owner: Clear Channel Communications Inc. (acq 9-00). Format: CHR. ♦Bennett Zier, VP, gen mgr & opns mgr; Melissa Kelly, gen sls mgr; Jessica Ritch, prom dir; Jeff Wyatt, progmg dir.

WILC(AM)—See Laurel, MD

WJFK-FM—(Manassas).VA Apr 8, 1968: 106.7 mhz; 22.5 kw horiz, 18.5 kw vert. 731 ft. TL: N38 52 28 W77 13 24. (CP: 22 kw, ant 745 ft.). Stereo. 10800 Main St., Fairfax, VA 22030. Phone: (703) 691-1900. Fax: (703) 934-9896. Web Site: www.1067wjfk.com. Licensee: Infinity Broadcasting of Washington D.C. Inc. Group owner: Infinity Broadcasting Corp. (acq 10-86; $13 million; 9-22-86). Format: Personality, sports. News staff: one; News: 3 hrs wkly. Target aud: 25-54. ♦Ken Stevens, gen mgr; Jeremy Coleman, opns mgr; David Hain Line, natl sls mgr; Tammy Sacks, prom dir; Buzz Burbank, news dir; Mike Elston, pub affrs dir; Dan Ryson, chief of engrg.

WJZW(FM)—(Woodbridge).VA Dec 25, 1958: 105.9 mhz; 28 kw. Ant 648 ft. TL: N38 52 28 W77 13 24. Stereo. 4400 Jennifer St. 20015. Phone: (202) 686-3100. Fax: (202) 686-3064. Web Site: www.smoothjazz1059.com. Licensee: WMAL Inc. Group owner: ABC Inc. (acq 1997; $105 million. with WDRQ(FM) Detroit, MI). Format:

Stations in the U.S.　　　Florida

Smooth jazz. ♦Jeff Boden, gen mgr; Kenny King, opns dir; Laura Gonzalez, gen sls mgr; Diane Pelton, natl sls mgr; Robert Minton, mktg dir; Meredith Groban, prom mgr; Carl Anderson, progmg dir; Renee DePuy, mus dir; Thomas Grooms, news dir & pub affrs dir; Dave Sproul, chief of engrg.

WKDL(AM)—(Alexandria).VA Dec 10, 1945: 730 khz; 8 kw-D, 25 w-N. TL: N38 44 43 W77 05 58. Stereo. 8121 Georgia Ave., 10th Fl., Silver Spring, MD 20910. Phone: (301) 588-6200. Fax: (301) 589-9772. Web Site: www.megasepega.com. Licensee: Mega Communications of Alexandria Licensee LLC. Group owner: Mega Communications Inc. (acq 1999; $11 million. with WZHF(AM) Arlington). Network: CNN Radio. Rep: Christal. Format: Mexican rgnl. News: 4 hrs wkly. ♦Maria Elena Verdugo, gen mgr.

WKIK(AM)—See La Plata, MD

WKYS(FM)— Aug 1, 1947: 93.9 mhz; 24 kw. 707 ft. TL: N38 56 24 W77 04 54. Stereo. 5900 Princess Garden Pkwy., Lanham, MD 20706. Phone: (301) 306-1111. Phone: (301) 429-2626. Fax: (301) 306-9609. Licensee: Radio One Licenses LLC. Group owner: Radio One Inc. (acq 6-95; $34 million;. FTR: 2-27-95). Rep: McGavren Guild. Format: Urban contemp. News staff: 3; News: 4 hrs wkly. Target aud: 25-54; upscale Black adults. ♦Michele Williams, gen mgr; Jack Murray, sls dir; Ezio Torres, natl sls mgr; Darryl Huckaby, progmg dir; Iran Waller, mus dir; Taylor Thomas, news dir; Tim White, chief of engrg.

WOL(AM)— Co-owned with WKYS(FM). 1924: 1450 khz; 1 kw-U. TL: N38 54 16 W77 00 25. (Acq 6-95). Network: ABC Information & Entertainment. Format: News/talk. ♦Karen Jackson, gen sls mgr; Vaughn Holmes, prom dir; Ron Thompson, progmg dir.

WLXE(AM)—See Rockville, MD

WMAL(AM)— Oct 12, 1925: 630 khz; 5 kw-U, DA-2. TL: N39 00 55 W77 08 30. Stereo. 4400 Jenifer St. N.W., 4th Floor 20015. Phone: (202) 686-3100. Fax: (202) 686-3061. Licensee: WMAL Inc. Group owner: ABC Inc. (acq 3-5-77). Network: ABC Information & Entertainment. Rep: ABC Radio Sales. Format: News/talk. ♦Chris Berry, pres & gen mgr; Randall Bloomquist, opns dir; Ernie Fears Jr., sls dir; John Matthews, news dir; David Sproul, engrg dir.

WRQX(FM)—Co-owned with WMAL(AM). May 15, 1948: 107.3 mhz; 19.5 kw. Ant 807 ft. TL: N38 57 01 W77 04 47. Stereo. Fax: (202) 686-3091. Network: ABC. Format: Hot adult contemp. ♦Jeff Boden, pres & gen mgr; Carol Parker, mus dir; Chilli Amar, news dir; Mike Kaufman, pub affrs mgr; David Sproul, engrg mgr.

WMMJ(FM)—See Bethesda, MD

WMZQ-FM— September 1968: 98.7 mhz; 50 kw. 490 ft. TL: N38 53 12 W77 12 05. Stereo. 1801 Rockville Pike, 6th Fl., Rockville, MD 20852. Phone: (301) 231-8231. Fax: (301) 984-4895. Web Site: www.wmzq.com. Licensee: Clear Channel Radio Licenses, Inc. Group owner: Clear Channel Communications Inc. (acq 8-30-00; grpsl). Rep: Christal. Latham & Watkins. Format: Country. News staff: one. Target aud: 25-54. ♦Bennett Zier, VP, gen mgr & opns mgr; Shelley Rose, rgnl sls mgr & mus dir; Mark Lapidus, mktg mgr; Wendie Vestfall, prom dir; George King, progmg dir; Greg Gallagher, engrg mgr & chief of engrg.

*****WPFW(FM)**— Feb 28, 1977: 89.3 mhz; 50 kw. 410 ft. TL: N38 56 09 W77 05 33. Stereo. 2390 Champlain St. N.W. 20009. Phone: (202) 588-0999. Fax: (202) 588-0561. E-mail: bmwpfw@aol.com. Web Site: www.wpfw.org. Licensee: Pacifica Foundation Inc. Group owner: Pacifica Radio Haley, Bader & Potts. Format: Jazz, news/talk, world mus. News: 9 hrs wkly. Target aud: 25-55. Spec prog: Oldies 3 hrs, women 3 hrs, health one hr wkly. ♦Ron Pinchback, gen mgr; Tiffany Jordan, dev dir.

WPGC(AM)—See Morningside, MD

WPGC-FM—See Morningside, MD

WTEM(AM)— Aug 1, 1923: 980 khz; 50 kw-D, 5 kw-N, DA-2. TL: N38 57 43 W76 58 24. 8750 Brookville Rd., Silver Spring, MD 20910. Phone: (301) 231-7798. Fax: (301) 881-8030. Web Site: www.sportstalk980.com. Licensee: AMFM Radio Licenses L.L.C. Group owner: Clear Channel Communications Inc. (acq 8-30-00; grpsl). Network: ESPN Radio. Format: Sports/talk. Target aud: 25-54; men. ♦Bennett Zier, VP.

WTNT(AM)—See Bethesda, MD

WTOP(AM)— Sept 25, 1926: 1500 khz; 50 kw-U, DA-2. TL: N39 02 30 W77 02 45. 3400 Idaho Ave. N.W. 20016. Phone: (202) 895-5000. Fax: (202) 895-5140. Fax: (202) 895-4149. E-mail: newsroom@wtopnews.com. Web Site: www.wtopnews.com. Licensee: Bonneville Holding Co. Group owner: Bonneville International Corp. (acq 4-27-98; grpsl). Network: CBS. Wilkinson, Barker, Knauer & Quinn. Format: News. News staff: 30; News: 168 hrs wkly. Target aud: General. ♦Joel Oxley, VP & gen mgr.

WUST(AM)— 1949: 1120 khz; 20 kw-D, 3 kw-CH. TL: N38 54 15 W77 09 54. 2131 Crimmins Ln., Falls Church, VA 22043. Phone: (703) 532-0400. E-mail: mail@wust1120.com. Web Site: www.wust1120.com. Licensee: New World Radio Inc. (acq 10-26-92; $1.15 million; 8-24-92). Format: Multicultural, ethnic. Spec prog: Fr 15 hrs, Sp 15 hrs, Ger 7 hrs, Ethiopian 6 hrs, Farsi 5 hrs, Russian 5 hrs wkly. ♦Alan Pendleton, gen mgr; Brian Edwards, opns mgr.

WWDC-FM— 1947: 101.1 mhz; 22.5 kw. 760 ft. TL: N38 59 59 W77 03 27. Stereo. 1801 Rockville Pike, Suite 405, Rockville, MD 20852. Phone: (301) 587-7100. Fax: (301) 587-0225. Web Site: www.dc101.com. Licensee: AMFM Radio Licenses L.L.C. Group owner: Clear Channel Communications Inc. (acq 8-30-00; grpsl). Format: Rock. ♦Bennett Zier, gen mgr; Joe Bivilacua, progmg dir; Tom Shedlick, chief of engrg.

WWGB(AM)—See Indian Head, MD

WWRC(AM)— 1941: 1260 khz; 5 kw-U, DA-2. TL: N38 59 59 W77 03 27. Stereo. 8750 Brookville Rd., Silver Spring, MD 20910. Phone: (301)231-7798. Fax: (301)881-8030. Web Site: www.wrcam1260.com. Licensee: AMFM Radio Licenses L.L.C. Group owner: Clear Channel Communications Inc. (acq 8-30-2000; grpsl). Network: Westwood One. Rep: Clear Channel. Format: Progressive talk. Target aud: 25-54; adults. ♦Bennett Zier, gen mgr; Tod Castleberry, opns dir; Kaiya Ramsey, sls dir & gen sls mgr; Jerry Phillips, mus dir, news dir & pub affrs dir; Shaun Sandoval, chief of engrg.

WWZZ(FM)—See Waldorf, MD

WYCB(AM)— 1978: 1340 khz; 1 kw-U. TL: N38 55 04 W77 01 27. (CP: TL: N38 51 50 W76 54 38). 5900 Princess Garden Pkwy., Lanham, MD 20706. Phone: (301) 306-1111. Fax: (301) 306-9510. Licensee: Radio One Licenses LLC. Group owner: Radio One Inc. (acq 11-8-01; grpsl). Network: American Urban. Format: Gospel. ♦Alfred Liggins, CEO; Cathy Hughes, chmn; Alfred Liggins, pres; Scott Royster, CFO; Michele Williams, gen mgr; Karen Jackson, gen sls mgr; Tim White, chief of engrg.

WZHF(AM)—See Arlington, VA

Florida

Alachua

WNDT(FM)— 1996: 92.5 mhz; 3.2 kw. Ant 443 ft. TL: N29 44 22 W82 23 09. 4020 Newberry Rd., Gainesville 32607. Phone: (352) 373-6644. Fax: (352) 375-1700. E-mail: windfm@aol.com. Web Site: www.windfm.com. Licensee: Ocala Broadcasting Corp. L.L.C. Group owner: Wooster Republican Printing Co. (acq 10-22-97; $675,000 for stock). Format: Classic Rock. ♦Jim Robertson, VP & gen mgr; Robert Kassi, gen sls mgr; Kevin Davis, progmg dir.

Altamonte Springs

WORL(AM)— 1986: 660 khz; 10 kw-D, DA. TL: N28 32 21 W80 58 26. 6600 N. Andrews Ave., Ste 160, Fort Lauderdale 33309. Phone: (954) 315-1515. Fax: (954) 315- 1555. Licensee: JCE Licenses L.L.C. Group owner: James Crystal Inc. (acq 6-21-00). Fletcher, Heald & Hildreth. Format: Business. ♦James C. Hilliard, pres; Rick Hindes, CFO; Steve Lapa, gen mgr; John Trybulec, stn mgr.

Apalachicola

WFCT(FM)— November 1997: 105.5 mhz; 50 kw. 315 ft. TL: N29 45 02 W84 52 18. Stereo. Box 1005, Port St. Joe 32457. Phone: (850) 227-9048. Fax: (850) 227-9298. E-mail: wfct@gtcom.net. Web Site: www.vcoast105.com. Licensee: Williams Communications Inc. (group owner; acq 3-27-02; $650,000). Format: Adult standards, contemp. ♦Dennis Tidwell, gen mgr.

WOYS(FM)— July 1988: 100.5 mhz; 12 kw. Ant 476 ft. TL: N29 43 57 W84 53 24. Stereo. Point Mall 35 Island Dr. #16, Eastpoint 32328-3264. Phone: (850) 670-8450. Fax: (850) 670-8492. Web Site: www.oysterradio.com. Licensee: Richard L. Plessinger Sr. Group owner: Plessinger Radio Group (R.L. Plessinger Holding Co.). Network: ABC Information & Entertainment. Format: Adult contemp/beach music. News staff: one. Target aud: General. ♦Richard L. Plessinger Sr., pres; Rick Plessinger, gen mgr; Michael Allen, stn mgr, prom mgr & news dir; William Denton, gen sls mgr.

Apopka

WHIM(AM)— May 4, 1964: 1520 khz; 5 kw-D, 350 w-N, DA. TL: N28 39 08 W81 29 40. 1188 Lake View Dr., Altamonte Springs 32714. Phone: (407) 682-9494. Phone: (407) 682-9595. Fax: (407) 682-7005. E-mail: whim1520@aol.com. Web Site: www.wtln.com. Licensee: Alton Rainbow Corp. Rep: Salem. Holland & Knight. Format: Relg, southern gospel, talk. Target aud: 25-54; general. ♦Thomas H. Moffit Sr., pres; Thomas H. Moffit Jr., gen mgr; Janice Willis, stn mgr; Lee Brandell, opns dir.

Arcadia

WFLN(AM)— Sept 3, 1955: 1480 khz; 1 kw-D. TL: N27 13 43 W81 51 28. 201 Asbury St. 34266. Phone: (863) 993-1480. Fax: (863) 499-1485. E-mail: wzzs@desoto.net. Licensee: Integrity Radio of Florida LLC (acq 8-9-2005; $119,000 for 49% of the membership interests). Network: USA. Format: News/talk, talk. Target aud: 24-44; upscale adults. ♦George Kalman, pres & gen mgr.

Atlantic Beach

WFYV-FM— Mar 10, 1980: 104.5 mhz; 100 kw. 984 ft. TL: N30 16 34 W81 33 53. Stereo. 8000 Belfort Pkwy., Jacksonville 32256. Phone: (904) 245-8500. Fax: (904) 245-8501. Licensee: Cox Radio Inc. Group owner: Cox Broadcasting (acq 2000; grpsl). Network: AP Radio. Rep: Christal, Katz Radio. Format: Classic Rock. News: 20 hrs wkly. Target aud: 18-49; male oriented. ♦Dick Williams, gen mgr; Cat Thomas, opns dir; Lindley Tolbert, sls dir & gen sls mgr; Michele Michaels, prom mgr; David Moore, progmg dir.

WQOP(AM)— Jan 30, 1958: 1600 khz; 5 kw-D, 90 w-N. TL: N30 19 30 W81 25 42. Box 51585, Jacksonville Beach 32246. Secondary address: 391 S. 14th Ave., Jacksonville Beach 32250. Phone: (904) 241-3311. Fax: (904) 241-1402. E-mail: radioqop@aol.com. Web Site: www.qopradio.com. Licensee: Queen of Peace Radio, Inc. (acq 6-5-97; $350,000). Network: USA. Format: Talk, relg. ♦C. Williams, pres; Tom Moran, gen mgr.

Auburndale

WTWB(AM)— Oct 10, 1956: 1570 khz; 5 kw-D, 13 w-N. TL: N28 04 32 W81 49 19. 127 Glenn Road 33823. Phone: (863) 967-1570. Fax: (206) 350-6874. E-mail: wtwb@talks1570.com. Web Site: www.talks1570.com. Licensee: Carpenter's Home Church Inc. LMA - Breidenbach Media Group (acq 12-5-2002). Network: ABC Information

Florida

& Entertainment. News staff: one; News: 13 hrs wkly. Target aud: 30 plus; middle income, 2-income family. ♦Lynne Breidenbach, pres; Greg Gillman, gen mgr; Kevin MacKenzie, progmg dir.

Avon Park

WAVP(AM)— Oct 1, 1970: 1390 khz; 1 kw-D, 770 w-N. TL: N27 37 08 W81 29 27. 801 Hwy. 27 S., Suite 5 33825. Phone: (863) 295-9411. Phone: (863) 453-3423. Fax: (863) 453-3423. Licensee: Anscombe Broadcasting Group Ltd. (acq 9-5-01). Network: Jones Radio Networks. Format: Gospel. News staff: one; News: 12 hrs wkly. Target aud: 18-54; Sp audience. ♦Joe Fisher, pres & gen mgr; Robert Jones, opns mgr.

WWOJ(FM)— August 1982: 99.1 mhz; 10 kw. Ant 515 ft. TL: N27 30 39 W81 31 54. Stereo. 3750 U.S. 27 N., Suite One, Sebring 33870. Phone: (863) 382-9999. Fax: (863) 382-1982. E-mail: cohanradiogroup@htn.net. Web Site: www.cohanradiogroup.com. Licensee: Cohan Radio Group Inc. (group owner; acq 11-1-98; $910,000 with WWTK(AM) Lake Placid). Network: ABC. Rgnl Reps Latham & Watkins. Format: Country. News staff: one; News: 7 hrs wkly. Target aud: 18 plus. Spec prog: Bluegrass one hr wkly. ♦Peter L. Coughlin, pres; Michael Taylor, opns dir.

Baker

*WTJT(FM)— May 1987: 90.1 mhz; 50 kw. Ant 417 ft. TL: N30 49 19 W86 42 37. 957 Hwy. C-4A 32531. Phone: (850) 537-2009. Fax: (850) 537-4663. Licensee: Okaloosa Public Radio Inc. Network: USA. Format: educ. Target aud: 35 plus. ♦Earl Thompson, pres & gen mgr; Jessica Walker, stn mgr & opns mgr; Ruth Thompson, mus dir; Randy Henry, chief of engrg.

Baldwin

WHJX(FM)— July 30, 1992: 105.7 mhz; 25 kw. Ant 328 ft. TL: N30 22 28 W82 01 42. Stereo. Tama Broadcasting Inc., 9550 Regency Square Blvd., Jacksonville 32225. Phone: (904) 680-1050. Fax: (904) 680-1051. E-mail: jacksproduction@tamabroadcasting.com. Web Site: www.tamabroadcasting.com. Licensee: Tama Radio Licenses of Jacksonville, FL, Inc. Group owner: Tama Broadcasting Inc. (acq 12-2-2001; $1.5 million). Format: Urban adult contemp. ♦Linda Davis-Fructuoso, gen mgr; Joel Widdows, opns mgr.

Bartow

WQXM(AM)— Sept 28, 1953: 1460 khz; 1 kw-D, 155 w-N. TL: N27 54 34 W81 51 29. Box 820 33831. Secondary address: 1355 N. Maple Ave. 33830. Phone: (863) 533-9227/533-2658. Fax: (863) 519-9514. E-mail: Jordan@classiccountry1460.com. Web Site: www.classiccountry1460.com. Licensee: Florida Broadcasting Media LLC (acq 5-17-2004; $325,000). Network: CBS. Format: Traditional country. Target aud: General. ♦Armando Gutierrez, gen mgr; Osvaldo Vega, opns mgr.

WWBF(AM)— Sept 16, 1969: 1130 khz; 2.5 kw-D, 500 w-N, DA-N. TL: N27 54 34 W81 49 35. Stereo. 1130 Radio Rd. 33830. Phone: (863) 533-0744. Fax: (863) 533-8546. E-mail: tom@wwbf.com. Web site: www.wwbf.com. Licensee: Thornburg Communications Inc. (acq 1-27-84; $220,000; 2-6-84). Network: CNN Radio. Format: Oldies. News staff: one; News: 10 hrs wkly. Target aud: 35-54; affluent adults. Spec prog: Sports. ♦Jeffrey A. Thornburg, VP; Thomas N. Thornburg, pres & gen mgr; Susan E. Thornburg, stn mgr.

Belle Glade

WBGF(FM)— May 31, 1965: 93.5 mhz; 5 kw. 269 ft. TL: N26 42 43 W80 40 59. Stereo. Box 1505 33430. Secondary address: 2001 State Rd. 715 33430. Phone: (561) 996-2063. Fax: (561) 996-1852. E-mail: hairglo@gatenet. Licensee: BGI Broadcasting LP. Network: ABC. Interep Format: Country, sports. Target aud: 25-54. Spec prog: Farm 5 hrs wkly. ♦Phil Haire, gen mgr & gen sls mgr; Mike Diagostine, progmg dir.

WSWN(AM)— Oct 7, 1947: 900 khz; 1 kw-D, 26 w-N. TL: N26 42 54 W80 40 58. (CP: TL: N26 42 56 W80 40 58). Box 1505 33430. Secondary address: 2001 State Rd. 715 33430. Phone: (561) 996-2063. Fax: (561) 996-1852. E-mail: wswnwbgfa@bellsouth.net. Licensee: BGI Inc. (acq 1996). Network: ABC, Jones Radio Networks. Rep: Interep. Format: Relg, Gospel. Target aud: 25-54. Spec prog: Sports. ♦Phil Haire, gen mgr; Harvey J. Poole Jr., progmg dir; Rick Rieke, chief of engrg.

Belleview

*WWKO(FM)— Apr 2001: 91.3 mhz; 200 w horiz, 1.1 kw vert. 328 ft. TL: N29 10 31 W82 09 09. Box 6090, Ocala 34478. Secondary address: 1124 SW 6th Ave., Ocala 34474. Phone: (352) 690-7799. Fax: (352) 690-7841. E-mail: kgospelradio@kgospelradio.net. Web Site: www.kgospelradio.net. Licensee: Walker Information and Education Institute Inc. Format: Southern gospel. News: 14 hrs wkly. Target aud: General; 18-65 yrs. ♦Keith Walker, pres; Joe Ruggiero, gen mgr; Cherrietta Prince, progmg dir; Frank Strnad, chief of engrg.

Beverly Hills

WINV(AM)— Sept 1, 1965: 1560 khz; 5 kw-D, 4.1 kw-CH. TL: N28 50 30 W82 22 16. Stereo. 4554 S. Suncoast Blvd., Homosassa 34446. Phone: (727) 849-2285. Fax: (727) 781-4375. E-mail: staff@citrus95radio.com. Web Site: www.citrus95radio.com. Licensee: WGUL-FM Inc. (acq 11-26-97; $5,000). Network: USA. Michael Wilhelm. Format: News/talk. Target aud: 25-65. ♦Carl J. Marcocci, CEO & chmn; David Marcocci, gen mgr.

Big Pine Key

WWUS(FM)— Sept 22, 1980: 104.1 mhz; 100 kw. 433 ft. TL: N24 39 38 W81 25 10. Stereo. 30336 Overseas Hwy. 33043. Phone: (305) 872-9100. Fax: (305) 872-8930. E-mail: us1radio@aol.com. Web Site: www.us1radio.com. Licensee: Vox Communications Group LLC. (acq 7-28-2005; grpsl). Network: AP Radio. Katten Muchin Rosenman LLP. Format: Adult contemp, classic rock. News staff: one; News: 2 hrs wkly. Target aud: 30-50. Spec prog: Island mus 4 hrs wkly. ♦Kevin Leroux, gen mgr; Laura Lewis, stn mgr; Gina Dietrich, gen sls mgr; Chris Todd, prom mgr; Dana Hunt, progmg dir; Bob Soos, mus dir; Bill Becker, news dir; Randy Perry, chief of engrg.

Bithlo

WNTF(AM)— July 31, 1974: 1580 khz; 2.1 kw-D. TL: N28 32 11 W81 05 06. Box 680889, Orlando 32868. Secondary address: 805 N. Dixie Ave., Titusville 32796. Phone: (407) 523-2770. Phone: (407) 383-1000. Fax: (407) 523-2888. Licensee: Rama Communications Inc. (group owner; (acq 10-29-2002; $600,000. with WGAF(AM) Alachua). Format: Sp. ♦Sabita Persaud, pres; Kris Persaud, gen mgr; Steve De Lay, chief of engrg.

Blountstown

WPHK(FM)—Listing follows WYBT(AM).

WYBT(AM)— Sept 8, 1962: 1000 khz; 5 kw-D. TL: N30 27 15 W85 02 32. 20872 N.E. Kelley Ave. 32424. Phone: (850) 674-5101. Fax: (850) 674-2965. Licensee: Blountstown Communications (acq 6-26-86; $103,000;. FTR: 4-14-86). Format: Country, Christian. Spec prog: Gospel & relg 15 hrs wkly. ♦Harry S. Hagen, pres; Cathy Hagen, progmg dir.

WPHK(FM)— Co-owned with WYBT(AM). Dec 18, 1968: 102.7 mhz; 13 kw. Ant 318 ft. TL: N30 27 15 W85 02 32. Stereo. Format: Modern country. ♦Harry S. Hagen, gen mgr.

Boca Raton

WKIS(FM)—Licensed to Boca Raton. See Miami

WSBR(AM)— April 1965: 740 khz; 2.5 kw-D, 940 w-N, DA-2. TL: N26 20 06 W80 15 55. 6699 N. Federal Hwy., Suite 200 33487. Phone: (561) 997-0074. Fax: (561) 997-0476. Web Site: www.wsbrmoneytalkradio.com. Licensee: WWNN License LLC. Group owner: Beasley Broadcast Group (acq 3-14-2000; grpsl). Network: ABC Information & Entertainment. Format: Financial talk. ♦Bob Morency, VP & gen mgr; Greg Cooper, opns mgr.

Bonifay

WYYX(FM)— Apr 23, 1983: 97.7 mhz; 100 kw. 830 ft. TL: N30 30 41 W85 29 24. Stereo. 7106 Laird St., Suite 102, Panama City Beach 32408. Phone: (850) 233-6606. Fax: (850) 233-1541. Web Site: www.wyyx.com. Licensee: Styles Media Group LLC (group owner; acq 9-30-02; grpsl). Format: Active rock, AOR. News staff: one. Target aud: 18-49. ♦J.P. Ferrell, gen sls mgr; Kim Styles, gen mgr, opns mgr & engrg mgr.

Bonita Springs

WRXK-FM— Sept 1, 1974: 96.1 mhz; 100 kw. 1,122 ft. TL: N26 26 53 W81 48 54. Stereo. Box 307, Estero 33928. Secondary address: 20125 S. Tamiami Tr., Estero 33928. Phone: (239) 495-2100. Fax: (239) 992-8165. Web Site: www.96krock.com. Licensee: Beasley Broadcasting of Western Florida Inc. Group owner: Beasley Broadcast Group (acq 8-12-86). Network: ABC. Rep: Katz Radio. Format: Classic rock. Target aud: 18-49. ♦George G. Beasley, pres; Brad Beasley, gen mgr; Shane Reilly, opns mgr; Robert Hallman, gen sls mgr; Ronnie Kabansky, prom dir; John Rozz, progmg dir; Nicole Wilcox, news dir; Richard Gallow, chief of engrg.

Boynton Beach

WLVJ(AM)— Jan 23, 1973: 1040 khz; 25 kw-D, 1.2 kw-N, DA-2. TL: N26 28 26 W80 12 11. Stereo. 6600 N. Andrews Ave., Suite 160, Fort Lauderdale 33309. Phone: (954) 315-1515. Fax: (954) 315-1555. Web Site: www.wlvj.com. Licensee: JCE Licenses L.L.C. Group owner: James Crystal Inc. (acq 12-26-00). Format: Relg. ♦James C. Hilliard, pres; Rick Hindes, CFO; Steve Lapa, gen mgr.

*WRMB(FM)— Apr 15, 1979: 89.3 mhz; 100 kw. 500 ft. TL: N26 31 07 W80 10 17. Stereo. 1511 W. Boynton Beach Blvd. 33436. Phone: (561) 737-9762. Fax: (561) 737-9899. Web Site: www.wrmb.org. Licensee: Moody Bible Institute of Chicago. (group owner) Network: Moody. Format: Relg. Target aud: General. ♦Michael Easley, pres; Jennifer Etterson, stn mgr & mus dir.

WXEL(FM)—See West Palm Beach

Bradenton

WFUS(FM)— October 1963: 103.5 mhz; 100 kw. 1,358 ft. TL: N27 50 32 W82 15 46. Stereo. 4002 W. Gandy Blvd., Tampa 33611. Phone: (813) 832-1000. Fax: (813) 832-1943. Licensee: Citicasters Licenses L.P. Group owner: Clear Channel Communications Inc. (acq 6-99; grpsl). Network: ABC. Format: Country. Target aud: 25-54; men. ♦Dan DiLoreto, gen mgr; Brad Hardin, opns mgr; Chris Soechtig, gen sls mgr.

*WJIS(FM)— 1989: 88.1 mhz; 100 kw. 397 ft. TL: N27 07 54 W82 23 29. 6469 Parkland Dr., Sarasota 34243. Phone: (941) 753-0401. Fax: (941) 753-2963. E-mail: thejoyfm@thejoyfm.com. Web Site: www.thejoyfm.com. Licensee: WJIS FM Radio. (acq 8-17-89; grpsl; 9-11-89). Format: Adult Contemp Christian music. ♦Jeff McFarlane, gen mgr & stn mgr; Carmen Brown, prom dir; Steve Swanson, progmg dir; Steve Rieker, chief of engrg.

WLLD(FM)—See Holmes Beach

WWPR(AM)— 1946: 1490 khz; 1 kw-U. TL: N27 30 00 W82 34 25. 5910 Cortez Rd. W., Suite 130 34210. Phone: (941) 761-8843. Fax: (941) 761-8683. E-mail: vivuan@1490wwpr.com. Web Site: 1490wwpr.com. Licensee: Greenrose Broadcasting Services Inc. (acq 9-19-97; $265,000). Pepper & Corazzini. Format: Oldies. Target aud: 45-64; general. Spec prog: Talk 15 hrs, relg 6 hrs, gospel 6 hrs, wkly. ♦Raymond Green, CEO, pres & gen mgr; Steve Seeler, CFO; Mike Dougherty, opns mgr.

Brandon

WLCC(AM)— February 1988: 760 khz; 10 kw-D, 1 kw-N, DA-2. TL: N28 01 29 W82 17 02. 1915 N. Dale Mabry Hwy., Suite 200, Tampa 33607. Phone: (813) 871-1819. Fax: (813) 871-1155. Licensee: Mega Communications of Tampa Licensee L.L.C. Group owner: Mega Communications Inc. (acq 4-24-98). Format: Rgnl Mexican. Target aud: 25-54. ♦Rafael Grullon, VP & gen mgr; Ricardo Villalona, gen mgr.

Brooksville

WWJB(AM)— Oct 11, 1958: 1450 khz; 1 kw-U. TL: N28 33 02 W82 25 02. Box 1507 34605. Secondary address: 55 W. Fort Dade Ave. 34605-1507. Phone: (352) 796-7469. Fax: (352) 796-5074. E-mail: wwjb@innet.com. Licensee: Hernando Broadcasting Co. (acq 3-1-82; 4-5-82). Network: Westwood One, ABC Information & Entertainment. Rep: Dora-Clayton. Gardner, Carton & Douglas. Format: News/talk, sports. News staff: one. Target aud: 25 plus. ♦Steve Manuel, pres & gen mgr; Bob Haa, opns mgr; Bill Willamson, gen sls mgr; Jason Yungmann, prom dir & prom mgr; Bob Penrod, news dir.

Stations in the U.S. — Florida

Developers & Brokers of Radio Properties

contact American Media Services at our suite:
Philadelphia Marriott Downtown
215-625-2900
843-972-2200
americanmediaservices.com
Charleston, SC
Dallas, TX · Chicago, Il · Austin, TX

American Media Services, LLC

Bushnell

WKFL(AM)— Jan 1, 1987: 1170 khz; 1 kw-D. TL: N28 42 31 W82 07 36. 5224 State Rt. 46, Ste. 354, Sanford 32771. Phone: (352) 330-4033. Fax: (801) 858-5647. Web Site: www.talknsports.net. Licensee: TalknSports Inc. (acq 6-22-2004). Network: Salem Radio Network. Format: Sports, news/talk. News staff: one; News: 8 hrs wkly. Target aud: 18-54; those who enjoy family programming. ♦ Bruce Cox, pres; Jan Hall, gen mgr.

Callahan

WEWC(AM)— 1999: 1160 khz; 5 kw-D, 250 w-N, DA-D. TL: N30 34 47 W87 17 18. 610 N. Julia St., Jacksonville 32202. Phone: (904) 549-2218. Fax: (904) 359-0070. Web Site: www.1160latinohits.com. Licensee: Circle Broadcasting of America Inc. (acq 3-24-93; $11,160;. FTR: 4-12-93). Format: Sp. ♦ George Lopez, gen mgr.

WPLA(FM)—Licensed to Callahan. See Jacksonville

Callaway

WAKT-FM— February 1990: 103.5 mhz; 100 kw. 475 ft. TL: N30 03 18 W85 18 09. (CP: Ant 748 ft. TL: N30 13 45 W85 23 20). Stereo. 118 Gwyn Dr., Panama City Beach 32408. Phone: (850) 234-8858. Fax: (850) 234-1181. E-mail: pgeorge@waittradio.com. Web Site: www.maxcountry1035.com. Licensee: Double O Radio Corp. (group owner; acq 3-10-2004); grpsl). Rep: Christal. Format: Country. ♦ Steve Green, gen mgr.

Cantonment

WNVY(AM)—Licensed to Cantonment. See Pensacola

Cape Coral

WXKB(FM)— 1975: 103.9 mhz; 100 kw. 981 ft. TL: N26 47 43 W81 48 04. Stereo. 20125 S. Tamiami Tr., Estero 33928. Phone: (239) 495-2100. Fax: (239) 948-0785. Web Site: www.b103.com. Licensee: Beasley Broadcasting. Group owner: Beasley Broadcast Group (acq 11-18-94; $3.7 million;. FTR: 1-2-95). Format: CHR. Target aud: General. ♦ George G. Beasley, pres; Brad Beasley, gen mgr; Shane Reilly, opns mgr; Matt Johnson, progmg dir.

Carrabelle

WOCY(FM)— 1999: 106.5 mhz; 100 kw. Ant 361 ft. TL: N29 43 57 W84 53 24. Stereo. Point Mall 35 Island Dr. #16, Eastpoint 32328-3264. Phone: (850) 670-8450. Fax: (850) 670-8492. E-mail: woyswocy@tcom.net. Web Site: www.woyswocy.homestead.com. Licensee: Richard L. Plessinger Sr. Group owner: Plessinger Radio Group Format: Country. ♦ Richard L. Plessinger Sr., pres & gen mgr; Michael Allen, stn mgr & news dir; William Denton, gen sls mgr; Billy Denton, mus dir.

Cedar Creek

*WKSG(FM)— 1999: 89.5 mhz; 2 kw. Ant 308 ft. TL: N29 11 20 W81 52 52. (CP: 30 kw vert, ant 341 ft). 7 E. Silver Springs Blvd., Suite 102, Ocala 34471. Phone: (352) 369-8950. Fax: (352) 369-1109. E-mail: daystar@ocalapro.com. Web Site: www.daystarradio.com. Licensee: Daystar Public Radio Inc. (acq 1-5-98). Format: Adult contemp Christian. ♦ Gary Linkus, gen mgr.

Cedar Key

WRGO(FM)— Sept 1996: 102.7 mhz; 12.5 kw. Ant 459 ft. TL: N29 11 45 W82 59 46. 1929 N.W. Hwy. 19, Crystal River 34428. Phone: (352) 795-1027. Fax: (352) 795-0002. Licensee: Jablamo License Holdings LLC. (group owner; (acq 7-6-2004); grpsl). Network: Jones Radio Networks. Booth, Freret, Imlay & Tepper. Format: Oldies. Target aud: 25-64. ♦ Dave Cobb, gen mgr.

Century

WPFL(FM)— July 1989: 105.1 mhz; 25 kw. 328 ft. TL: N30 52 12 W87 20 05. Box 967, Flomaton, AL 36441. Secondary address: 2059 Old Fannie Rd., Flomaton, AL 36441. Phone: (251) 296-1051. Fax: (251) 296-1055. Web Site: www.oldiesradioonline.com. Licensee: Tri-County Broadcasting Inc. (acq 4-10-01; $575,000. including $50,000 ad credit). Format: Oldies. ♦ Walter Douglas, gen mgr, opns mgr & progmg dir; Howard Macht, chief of engrg.

Charlotte Harbor

WIKX(FM)—Licensed to Charlotte Harbor. See Punta Gorda

Chattahoochee

WTCL(AM)— Nov 1, 1963: 1580 khz; 5 kw-D. TL: N30 40 14 W84 50 08. (CP: 10 kw-D, 500 w-N, DA-N). Box 96 32324. Phone: (850) 663-2857. Fax: (850) 663-8543. Licensee: Metz Inc. (acq 1-9-97; $55,000). Network: USA. Format: Gospel, ministries. Target aud: General. ♦ Don Metz, pres; Todd J. Van Dyke, gen mgr; Chris Starr, opns dir; Jeff Sailway, progmg dir & chief of engrg.

Chiefland

WLQH(AM)— June 6, 1968: 940 khz; 1 kw-D. TL: N29 31 00 W82 53 11. Stereo. 12750 Old Fanning Springs Rd. 32626. Phone: (352) 493-4940. Fax: (352) 493-9909. Licensee: Ocala Broadcasting Corp. (acq 11-2-99; with co-located FM). Format: Adult contemp. Spec prog: Relg 9 hrs wkly. ♦ Bob Moody, stn mgr.

WNDN(FM)— Co-owned with WLQH(AM). 1991: 107.9 mhz; 6 kw. Ant 328 ft. TL: N29 31 00 W82 53 11. Network: Jones Radio Networks. Format: Plastic Rock.

Chipley

WBGC(AM)— Apr 10, 1956: 1240 khz; 1 kw-U. TL: N30 46 19 W85 33 31. 1513 S. Blvd. 32428. Phone: (850) 638-0234. Fax: (850) 638-4333. Licensee: Jacquelyn Collier Pembroke (acq 5-28-02; with WALD(AM) Walterboro). Rep: Keystone (unwired net). Format: Var. ♦ Todd Burnett, gen mgr.

Clearwater

WBTP(FM)— Aug 19, 1963: 95.7 mhz; 90 kw. Ant 607 ft. TL: N27 52 00 W82 37 27. Stereo. 4002 Gandy Blvd., Tampa 33611. Phone: (813) 832-1000. Fax: (813) 832-1090. Web Site: www.957thebeat.com. Licensee: Clear Channel Broadcasting Licenses Inc. Group owner: Clear Channel Communications Inc. (acq 10-94). Network: AP Radio. Format: Hot adult contemp/urban. News staff: one. Target aud: 18-49; upwardly mobile adults. ♦ Dave Reinhart, gen mgr; Jeff Kapugi, opns mgr; J.J. Paone, prom dir; Ron Shepard, progmg dir.

WLVU(AM)—See Dunedin

WTAN(AM)— June 1948: 1340 khz; 1 kw-U. TL: N27 57 49 W82 24 14. 706 N. Myrne Ave. 33755. Phone: (727) 726-8247. Fax: (727) 799-8866. E-mail: lola@tantalk.net. Web Site: www.tantalk1340.com. Licensee: Wagenvoord Advertising Group Inc. (group owner; acq 12-29-99; $100,000). Format: Talk/news. News staff: 2; News: 12 hrs wkly. Target aud: 25-45; Greek community. Spec prog: Big band 2 hrs wkly. ♦ Dave Wagenvoord, CEO & pres; Lola Wagenvoord, gen mgr.

WXTB(FM)— Dec 1, 1967: 97.9 mhz; 100 kw. 1,345 ft. TL: N28 10 56 W82 46 06. Stereo. 4002 Gandy Blvd., Tampa 33611. Phone: (813) 832-1000. Fax: (813) 831-9898. E-mail: brianmedlin@clearchannel.com. Web Site: www.98rock.com. Licensee: Citicasters Licenses L.P. Group owner: Clear Channel Communications Inc. (acq 5-6-99; grpsl). Format: Rock. News staff: one; News: 2 hrs wkly. Target aud: 18-49; men. Spec prog: Pub affrs 4 hrs wkly. ♦ Daniel DiLoreto, pres & gen mgr; Brad Hardin, opns dir; Brian Medlin, progmg dir & chief of engrg.

WYUU(FM)—See Tampa

Clermont

WWFL(AM)— 1962: 1340 khz; 1 kw-U. TL: N28 33 06 W81 46 45. c/o Carl Bauer, Central Florida Investments Inc., 5601 Windover Dr., Orlando 32819. Phone: (407) 351-3350. Fax: (407) 370-3524. Web Site: www.cflradio.net. Licensee: Central Florida Investments Inc. Format: MOR. ♦ Jack Spangler, CEO; Mark Waltrip, gen mgr.

*WWKG(FM)— July 18, 1997: 88.7 mhz; 1 kw. Ant 505 ft. TL: N28 37 37 W81 43 49. Stereo. 4540 Curry Ford Rd., Orlando 32812-2711. Phone: (407) 208-0333. Fax: (407) 208-0633. Web Site: www.lamegaorlando.com. Licensee: Hispanic Broadcast System Inc. James L. Oyster. Format: Black gospel. ♦ Idalia Arzuaga, pres; Jose Arzuaga, sr VP; Noah Chapanno, gen mgr.

Clewiston

WAFC(AM)— Feb 16, 1988: 590 khz; 930 w-D, 470 w-N. TL: N26 43 47 W80 54 45. 530 E. Alverdez Ave. 33440-3901. Phone: (863) 983-6106. Fax: (863) 983-6109. E-mail: robbiec@gladesmedia.com. Web Site: www.radiofiesta.com. Licensee: Glades Media Co. Network: CNN en Espanol. Rep: Interep. Leibowitz & Associates. Format: Hispanic. News: 10 hrs wkly. Target aud: General; adult Hispanics. ♦ Jim Johnson, CFO; Robert Castellanos, CEO & gen mgr; Larry Parrish, sls dir; Alfredo Hernandez, progmg dir.

WAFC-FM— July 2, 1979: 99.5 mhz; 12 kw. Ant 472 ft. TL: N26 41 27 W80 47 18. Stereo. Phone: (863) 902-0995. Fax: (863) 983-5904. Web Site: www.wafcfm.com. Network: Network: Westwood One, CNN Radio. Rep: Interep. Leibowitz & Associates. Format: Modern country. News staff: one; News: 5 hrs wkly. Target aud: 18-49. ♦ Will Skinner, opns mgr & progmg dir.

*WJCB(FM)—Not on air, target date: unknown: 88.5 mhz; 3 kw. Ant 292 ft. TL: N26 43 46 W80 54 49. 1150 W. King St., Cocoa 32922. Phone: (321) 632-1000. Fax: (321) 636-0000. Licensee: Black Media Works Inc. (group owner).

Cocoa

WLRQ-FM—Listing follows WMMV(AM).

*WMIE(FM)— December 1984: 91.5 mhz; 20 kw horiz, 19 kw vert. 98 ft. TL: N28 21 21 W80 44 47. Stereo. 1150 W. King St. 32922. Phone: (407) 632-1000. Fax: (407) 636-0000. Web Site: www.wjfp.com. Licensee: National Christian Network. Format: Modern worship. Target aud: 18-49. ♦ Raymond A. Kassis, pres; Jim Conn, gen mgr & progmg dir; Jan Ferguson, chief of engrg.

WMMV(AM)— Oct 4, 1957: 1350 khz; 1 kw-U, DA-N. TL: N28 21 58 W80 45 08. Stereo. 1388 S. Babcock St., Melbourne 32901. Phone: (321) 733-1000. Fax: (321) 733-0904. Web Site: www.wmmvdm.com. Licensee: Capstar TX L.P. Group owner: Clear Channel Communications Inc. (acq 8-30-00; grpsl). Network: Network: ABC, Westwood One. Format: Adult standards, news/talk radio. ♦ Barbara Latham, gen mgr.

WLRQ-FM— Co-owned with WMMV(AM). June 15, 1967: 99.3 mhz; 1.2 kw. 500 ft. TL: N28 16 42 W80 42 03. (CP: 50 kw, ant 492 ft.). Stereo. Web Site: www.wlrqfm.com. Format: Lite rock.

WWBC(AM)— July 1965: 1510 khz; 1 kw-D. TL: N28 21 30 W80 42 38. (CP: COL: Rockledge, 770 khz, 1 kw-D, 480 w-N, DA-2, TL: N28 20 05 W80 46 56). 1150 W. King St. 32922. Phone: (321) 632-1510. Fax: (321) 636-0000. E-mail: wwbc@juno.com. Web Site: wwww.wmieefm.com. Licensee: Astro Enterprises. (acq 3-1-76). Format: Relg. Target aud: 25 plus. ♦ Ray Kassis, pres; Paul Esposito, gen mgr.

Cocoa Beach

WJRR(FM)— July 19, 1962: 101.1 mhz; 100 kw. 1,598 ft. TL: N28 34 51 W81 04 32. Stereo. 2500 Maitland Ctr. Pkwy., Suite 401, Maitland

Florida

32751. Phone: (407) 916-7800. Phone: (407) 916-1011. Fax: (407) 916-0329. Web Site: www.realrock1011.com. Licensee: Clear Channel Radio Licenses Inc. Group owner: Clear Channel Communications Inc. (acq 11-21-97; grpsl). Format: AOR, alternative rock. Target aud: 18-34; men. ♦ Linda Byrd, pres; Chris Kampmeier, opns VP; Josh Egolf, prom mgr; Rick Everett, natl sls mgr & progmg dir.

WTIR(AM)— June 22, 1959: 1300 khz; 5 kw-D, 1 kw-N, DA-2. TL: N28 20 38 W80 46 06. 3765 N. John Young Pkwy., Orlando 32804. Phone: (407) 523-2770. Fax: (407) 523-2888. Web Site: www.tirn.com. Licensee: Rama Communications Inc. (group owner; (acq 10-13-93; $950,000. with WOKB(AM) Winter Garden; FTR: 11-8-93). Cohn & Marks. Format: Tourism radio. ♦ Sabeta Persaud, pres; Steve January, gen mgr.

WTKS-FM—Licensed to Cocoa Beach. See Orlando

Coral Cove

WSRZ-FM— Mar 25, 1995: 107.9 mhz; 47 kw. Ant 508 ft. TL: N27 09 03 W82 27 51. Stereo. 1779 Independence Blvd., Sarasota 34234. Phone: (941) 552-4800. Fax: (941) 552-4900. Web Site: www.oldies108.com. Licensee: Citicasters Licenses L.P. Group owner: Clear Channel Communications Inc. (acq 5-4-99; grpsl). Format: Oldies. Target aud: 25-54. ♦ Sherri Carlson, gen mgr.

Coral Gables

WHQT(FM)— Nov 15, 1958: 105.1 mhz; 100 kw. 1,049 ft. TL: N25 57 59 W80 12 33. (CP: Ant 1,007 ft.). Stereo. 2741 N. 29th Ave., Hollywood 33020. Phone: (305) 444-4404. Fax: (954) 847-3240. Web Site: www.hot105fm.com. Licensee: Cox Radio Inc. Group owner: Cox Broadcasting (acq 12-28-92; 1-11-93). Rep: Christal. Dow, Lohnes & Albertson. Format: Urban adult contemp. Target aud: 18-49. ♦ Jerry Rushin, gen mgr; Janine DuPont, prom mgr; Derrick Brown, progmg dir.

WRHC(AM)— 1963: 1550 khz; 10 kw-D, 500 k-N, DA-2. TL: N25 39 02 W80 09 36. 330 S.W. 27th Ave., Suite 207, Miami 33135. Phone: (305) 541-3300. Fax: (305) 541-7470. E-mail: ana670@aol.com. Web Site: www.wrhc.com. Licensee: WRHC Broadcasting Corp. (acq 3-23-93; 4-5-93). Schwartz, Woods & Miller. Format: Sp, news/talk, entertainment, sports. ♦ Jorge Rodriguez, pres; Ana M. Vidal Rodriguez, VP & gen mgr.

WVCG(AM)— Feb 18, 1949: 1080 khz; 50 kw-D, 20 kw-N, DA-2. TL: N25 44 53 W80 32 47. 2828 W. Flagler St., Miami 33135. Phone: (305) 644-0800. Fax: (305) 644-0030. E-mail: msilva@radio-one.com. Licensee: Radio One Licenses LLC. Group owner: Radio One Inc. (acq 11-8-01; grpsl). Format: Urban. ♦ Alfred Liggins, CEO & pres; Michael L. Silva, gen mgr.

*WVUM(FM)— May 1968: 90.5 mhz; 100 w horiz, 1.3 kw vert. 175 ft. TL: N25 43 02 W80 16 48. Stereo. Box 248191, Univ. Ctr., 1306 Stanford Dr., U.C. 110 33124. Phone: (305) 284-3131. Fax: (305) 284-3132. E-mail: info@wvum.org. Web Site: www.wvum.org. Licensee: WVUM Inc. Format: Alternative music. News staff: one; News: 3 hrs wkly. Target aud: 13-plus. Spec prog: Sports 5 hrs, Black 7 hrs, relg 6 hrs, Sp 2 hrs, oldies 5 hrs wkly. ♦ Jesse Agler, gen mgr; Paulo Mendez, prom mgr; Brian Hunker, mus dir; Dara Upton, news dir.

Crawfordville

WAKU(FM)— January 1996: 94.1 mhz; 3 kw. 459 ft. TL: N30 04 34 W84 18 05. Stereo. Box 941 32326. Secondary address: 218 Ochlockonee St. 32327. Phone: (850) 926-9258. Phone: (850) 926-8000. Fax: (850) 926-2000. E-mail: mail@wave94.com. Web Site: www.wave94.com. Licensee: Altrua Investments International Corp. (acq 7-14-98; $550,000). Network: Network: Motor Racing Net, USA. Koteen & Naftalin. Format: Contemp christian. News staff: one; News: 10 hrs wkly. Target aud: 18-55; general. Spec prog: Jam 3 hrs wkly. ♦ Mike Floyd, CEO, pres & gen mgr; Rocky Russell, opns dir & progmg mgr.

Crestview

WAAZ-FM—Listing follows WJSB(AM).

WJSB(AM)— Sept 15, 1954: 1050 khz; 5 kw-D. TL: N30 45 56 W86 35 06. (CP: 3.1 kw-D, 500 w-N, DA-N; TL: N30 46 00 W86 35 08). Box 267 32536. Secondary address: 506 W. First Ave. Phone: (850) 682-3040. Phone: (850) 682-4623. Fax: (850) 682-5232. Licensee: Crestview Broadcasting Co. (acq 8-11-98). Network: CBS. Format: C&W, MOR. ♦ James T. Whitaker, pres, gen mgr & chief of engrg.

WAAZ-FM—Co-owned with WJSB(AM). July 15, 1965: 104.7 mhz; 100 kw. Ant 485 ft. TL: N30 46 01 W86 35 07.

Cross City

WKZY(FM)—Listing follows WYNY(AM).

*WWLC(FM)—Not on air, target date: unknown: 88.5 mhz; 33 kw horiz, 70 kw vert. Ant 180 ft. TL: N29 36 35 W83 08 03. Spirit Radio of North Florida Inc., 500 N.E. 16th Ave., Gainesville 32601. Phone: (352) 372-4641. Fax: (352) 376-0575. Licensee: Spirit Radio of North Florida Inc. Format: Christian. ♦ Fr. Roland M. Julien, gen mgr; Chuck Kramer, progmg dir.

WYNY(AM)— November 1985: 1240 khz; 1 kw-U. TL: N29 36 35 W83 08 03. Box 1430, Trenton 32693. Secondary address: 8749 S.W. 25th Ave., Trenton 32693. Phone: (352) 463-1345. Fax: (352) 463-9966. Licensee: Jablamo License Holdings LLC. (group owner; (acq 7-6-2004; grpsl). Format: Country. Spec prog: Relg 5 hrs wkly. ♦ Tom Hunt, gen mgr.

WKZY(FM)—Co-owned with WYNY(AM). Nov 16, 1987: 106.9 mhz; 4.5 kw. 184 ft. TL: N29 24 07 W83 08 10. Stereo. Web Site: www.literock1069.com. Format: Music of the 80s. ♦ Bruce Cherry, progmg dir.

Crystal River

*WAQV(FM)— 1999: 90.9 mhz; 3 kw. 331 ft. TL: N29 01 52 W82 27 05. 3343 E Silver Springs Blvd., Ocala 34470. Phone: (352) 351-8810. Fax: (352) 351-8917. Web Site: www.thejoyfm.com. Licensee: Radio Training Network Inc. (acq 10-5-01; $80,000. with WHIJ(FM) Ocala). Format: Adult contemp, christian. ♦ Jeff MacFarlane, gen mgr & progmg mgr; Joe Cerreta, opns mgr; Carmen Brown, prom dir; Steve Rieker, chief of engrg.

*WHGN(FM)— November 1992: 91.9 mhz; 41 kw horiz, 39.3 kw vert. Ant 541 ft. TL: N28 50 29 W82 30 21. (CP: 41 kw). 1566 N. Meadowcrest Blvd. 34429. Phone: (352) 564-0002. Fax: (352) 564-8750. Licensee: The Moody Bible Institute of Chicago (group owner; acq 4-11-03; $500,000). Format: Christian. ♦ David Boyer, gen mgr; Mike Gleichman, opns mgr; Pierre Chestang, stn mgr & progmg dir; John Stortz, chief of engrg.

WKTK(FM)— Feb 13, 1976: 98.5 mhz; 100 kw. 1,332 ft. TL: N29 15 32 W82 34 03. (CP: 44 kw). Stereo. 1566 N.W. 43rd St., Suite B, Gainesville 32606-8127. Phone: (352) 377-0985. Fax: (352) 377-1884. E-mail: mleopord@entercom.com. Web Site: www.ktk985.com. Licensee: Entercom Gainesville License LLC. Group owner: Entercom Communications Corp. (acq 11-13-86; $3.6 million; 7-21-86). Network: Westwood One Lerman. Format: Adult contemp. News staff: one; News: 6 hrs wkly. Target aud: 25-54. ♦ Joseph Field, CEO & chmn; David Field, pres; Joe Nicholson, sr VP, prom dir, mktg & prom; Mark Leopord, VP & gen mgr; Bruce Cherry, progmg dir.

WXCV(FM)—See Homosassa Springs

Cypress Gardens

WHNR(AM)—Licensed to Cypress Gardens. See Winter Haven

Cypress Quarters

*WREH(FM)— 2004: 90.5 mhz; 100 kw horiz, 91.7 kw vert. Ant 249 ft. TL: N27 20 51 W80 57 04. Reach Communications Inc., 2701 W. Cypress Creek Rd., Fort Lauderdale 33309. Phone: (954) 315-4315. Fax: (954) 315-4231. Web Site: www.reachfm.org. Licensee: Reach Communications Inc. (acq 4-2-2003; $1 million. for CP). Format: Christian. ♦ Carl Mims, gen mgr; Barry Case, progmg dir; John Boone, opns mgr & mus dir.

Dade City

WDCF(AM)— December 1954: 1350 khz; 1 kw-D, 500 w-N, DA-N. TL: N28 20 04 W82 11 23. 37905 WDCF Dr. 33525-5735. Secondary address: 2360 N.E. Coachman Rd., Clearwater 33765. Phone: (352) 567-1350. Fax: (352) 567-5532. E-mail: lola@tantalk1340.com. Web Site: www.tantalk1340.com. Licensee: Wagenvoord Advertising Group Inc. (group owner; acq 2-13-02). Network: ABC. Format: News/talk. Target aud: 25 plus; basic country demographics. Spec prog: Interview shows 16 hrs, farm 2 hrs, relg 6 hrs, gospel 6 hrs, Sp 3 hrs wkly. ♦ Dave Wagenvoord, pres; Lola Wagenvoord, sr VP & gen mgr; Jeff Collins, stn mgr.

WTMP-FM— Sept 3, 1993: 96.1 mhz; 2.8 kw. 413 ft. TL: N28 28 22 W82 17 45. (CP: 2.75 kw, ant 485 ft.). 5207 Washington Blvd., Tampa 33619. Phone: (813) 620-1300. Fax: (813) 628-0713. E-mail: info@tamabroadcasting.com. Web Site: www.wtmp.com. Licensee: Tama Radio Licenses of Tampa, FL, Inc. Group owner: Tama Broadcasting Inc. (acq 12-21-2001; $4.1 million). Rep: Caballero. Format: Rhythm and blues, class song. Target aud: 35 plus; general. Spec prog: Gospel 20 hrs wkly. ♦ Glenn Cherry, CEO & gen mgr; Floran Thomas, CFO; Louis Muhammad, opns mgr; Nicole Goltes, prom mgr; Lynn Tolliver, progmg dir.

Davie

WAVS(AM)— Aug 21, 1970: 1170 khz; 5 kw-D, 250 w-N, DA-N. TL: N26 04 39 W80 13 03. 6360 S.W. 41st Pl. 33314. Phone: (954) 584-1170. Phone: (305) 948-6991. Fax: (954) 581-6441. E-mail: isd@wavs1170.com. Web Site: www.wavs1170.com. Licensee: Alliance Broadcasting Inc. (acq 7-28-2004; $2 million). Koerner & Olender PC. Format: Caribbean. News staff: one; News: 5 hrs wkly. Target aud: General; West Indians/Dade, Broward, Palm Beach Counties, Bahamas. Spec prog: Black. ♦ Emmanuel Cherubin, pres.

Daytona Beach

WCFB(FM)— March 1947: 94.5 mhz; 100 kw. 1,469 ft. TL: N28 58 55 W81 27 18. Stereo. 4192 John Young Pkwy., Orlando 32804. Phone: (407) 422-9696. Fax: (407) 422-5883. Web Site: www.star94fm.com. Licensee: Cox Radio Inc. Group owner: Cox Broadcasting (acq 3-28-97; grpsl). Format: Adult contemp, urban contemp. ♦ Todd Dickerson, gen mgr; Steve Holbrook, opns dir.

WELE(AM)—See Ormond Beach

WJHM(FM)— Nov 1, 1967: 101.9 mhz; 28 kw. 1,584 ft. TL: N28 55 16 W81 19 09. (CP: 61 kw). Stereo. 1800 Pembroke Dr., Suite 400, Orlando 32810. Phone: (407) 919-1000. Fax: (407) 919-1136. Web Site: www.102jamzorlando.com. Licensee: Infinity Radio Inc. Group owner: Infinity Broadcasting Corp. (acq 8-7-00; grpsl). Network: AP Radio. Format: Rhythmic CHR. Target aud: 18-34. ♦ Earnest Jones, sr VP & gen mgr; Dawn Campbell, prom dir & prom; Stevie DeMann, progmg dir.

WMFJ(AM)— Apr 16, 1935: 1450 khz; 1 kw-U. TL: N29 13 30 W81 01 30. 4295 Ridgewood Ave., Port Orange 32127. Phone: (386) 756-9000. Fax: (386) 760-7107. E-mail: thecornerstone@cornerstoneministry.org. Web Site: www.cornerstoneministry.org. Licensee: Cornerstone Broadcasting Corp. (acq 1996; $225,000). Network: Network: Moody, USA. Format: Relg. Target aud: General. ♦ William Powell, gen mgr.

WNDB(AM)— April 1948: 1150 khz; 1 kw-U, DA-N. TL: N29 14 06 W81 04 19. 126 W. International Speedway Blvd. 32174. Phone: (386) 239-0033. Phone: (386) 255-9300. Fax: (386) 239-0966. Fax: (386) 239-0966. Web Site: www.wndb.am. Licensee: Black Crow LLC. Group owner: Black Crow Media Group LLC (acq 9-21-2001; grpsl). Network: Network: CBS, Motor Racing Net. Rep: Allied Radio Partners. Dow, Lohnes & Albertson. Format: News/talk, sports. News staff: 2. Target aud: 25-64; general. Spec prog: Relg 5 hrs, NASCAR auto racing wkly. ♦ J. Michael Linn, pres; Stacey Knerler, gen mgr; Frank Scott, opns mgr.

WNUE-FM— (Titusville). September 1968: 98.1 mhz; 100 kw. 462 ft. TL: N28 50 54 W80 51 44. Stereo. 337 S North Lake Blvd., Ste. 1100, Altamonte Springs 32701. Phone: (407) 331-1777. Fax: (407) 830-6223. E-mail: jeff@lanueva981.com. Web Site: www.mega981.com. Licensee: Mega Communications of Daytona Beach Licensee LLC. Group owner: Mega Communications Inc. (acq 8-7-00; $15 million). Rep: SBS/Interep. Format: CHR, Sp. News staff: one; News: 2 hrs wkly. Target aud: 25-54; Hispanic adults 25-54. ♦ George Lindemann, CEO; Adam Lindemann, chmn & pres; Eran Schrerber, CFO; Jeff Stein, gen mgr & sls VP; Rafael Grullon, exec VP & gen mgr.

WPUL(AM)—See South Daytona

WROD(AM)— 1947: 1340 khz; 1 kw-U. TL: N29 11 19 W81 00 28. Box 211340, South Daytona 32121-1340. Secondary address: 2400 S. Ridgewood Ave., Suite 51, South Daytona 32119. Phone: (386)

Stations in the U.S. Florida

253-0000. Fax: (386) 255-3178. E-mail: wrod@cfc.rr.com. Web Site: www.wrod.net. Licensee: Gore-Overgaard Broadcasting Inc. (group owner; acq 1-8-99; $1.01 million). Network: ABC Information & Entertainment. Haley, Bader & Potts. Format: Mus of Your Life, adult standards. News staff: one; News: 15 hrs wkly. Target aud: 50 plus; senior community. ♦ Hal Gore, CEO & chmn; Cordell Overgaard, pres; Tony Welch, gen mgr.

De Funiak Springs

*WAKJ(FM)— January 1996: 91.3 mhz; 300 w. 57 ft. TL: N30 44 18 W86 06 22. Stereo. Box 127 32435. Secondary address: 295 Hwy. 90 W. 32435. Phone: (850) 892-2107. Fax: (850) 892-2381. E-mail: wakj913@earthlink.net. Web Site: www.fbcdfs.org. Licensee: First Baptist Church Inc. Network: USA. Format: Christian classic's. ♦ Zane Welch, gen mgr & opns mgr.

WGTX(AM)— Mar 1, 1956: 1280 khz; 2.5 kw-D. TL: N30 42 41 W86 06 25. Box 459 32435. Phone: (850) 951-1280. Fax: (850) 951-1282. E-mail: wgtx@wgtx.com. Web Site: www.wgtx.com. Licensee: Beebe Communications LLC (acq 9-15-2003; $220,000). Format: Oldies, news/talk. Target aud: 25-54. ♦ John Beebe, pres & progmg dir; Joey Beebe, VP & stn mgr; John H. Beebe, gen mgr; Terry Reeves, CEO & gen sls mgr; David Miniard, chief of engrg.

WMXZ(FM)— November 1974: 103.1 mhz; 50 kw. 482 ft. TL: N30 30 53 W86 13 12. Stereo. 743 Hwy. 98 E., Suite 6, Destin 32541. Phone: (850) 654-1031. Fax: (850) 654-6510. Licensee: Qantum of Fort Walton Beach License Co. LLC. Group owner: Qantum Communications Corp. (acq 7-2-2003; grpsl). Format: Top-40. News staff: one; News: 20 hrs wkly. Target aud: 18-49; general. ♦ Diane Augram, gen mgr; Fox Feltman, opns mgr & progmg dir; Suzy Nicholson-Hunt, sls dir & natl sls mgr; Cindy O'Shea, progmg dir & news dir; Curtis Blount, chief of engrg.

WZEP(AM)— October 1955: 1460 khz; 10 kw-D, 186 w-N. TL: N30 43 45 W86 07 04. 449 N. 12th St. 32433. Secondary address: Box 627 32435. Phone: (850) 892-3158. Phone: (800) 881-1460. Fax: (850) 892-9675. E-mail: wzep@wzep1460.com. Web Site: www.wzep1460.com. Licensee: Walton County Broadcasting Inc. (acq 6-1-93; $60,000; 6-21-93). Network: CBS. Timothy K. Brady. Format: Full service, news/talk, country, oldies. News staff: one; News: 47 hrs wkly. Target aud: General; residents & visitors to Walton & Holmes counties. Spec prog: Gospel 10 hrs wkly. ♦ Arthur F. Dees, pres & gen mgr; Martha K. Dees, VP; Marty Dees, stn mgr; Kevin Chilcutt, news dir.

De Land

WNDA(AM)— Sept 10, 1948: 1490 khz; 1 kw-U. TL: N29 00 58 W81 17 10. 126 W. International Speedway Blvd., Daytona Beach 32114. Phone: (386) 257-1150. Phone: (386) 255-9300. Fax: (386) 236-0966. Licensee: Black Crow Radio LLC. Group owner: Black Crow Media Group LLC (acq 9-21-2001; grpsl). Network: ABC Information & Entertainment. Format: News/talk, community affrs, sports. Target aud: 35 plus. ♦ Mike Linn, pres; Stacey Knerler, gen mgr; Frank Scott, stn mgr & opns mgr.

WOCL(FM)— July 10, 1967: 105.9 mhz; 96 kw. 1,581 ft. TL: N28 55 16 W81 19 09. Stereo. 1800 Pembrook Dr., Suite 400, Orlando 32810. Phone: (407) 919-1000. Fax: (407) 919-1136. E-mail: contactus@orock105.listenersnetwork.com. Web Site: www.orock1059.com. Licensee: Infinity Radio Inc. Group owner: Infinity Broadcasting Corp. (acq 8-7-00; grpsl). Rep: Christal. Leibowitz & Associates. Format: Rock alternative. News staff: one; News: 20 hrs wkly. Target aud: 25-54. ♦ Earnest James, sr VP; Jacqueline Landry, gen mgr & gen sls mgr; Bobby Smith, progmg dir; Scott Mangan, prom.

WYND(AM)— Dec 7, 1956: 1310 khz; 5 kw-D, 95 w-N. TL: N28 59 57 W81 17 55. 316 E. Taylor Rd. 32724. Phone: (386) 734-1310. Licensee: Buddy Tucker Association Inc. (acq 12-30-86; $255,000; 12-1-86). Network: USA. Format: Christian, news/talk. News staff: one; News: 45 hrs wkly. Target aud: 25-55. ♦ Buddy Tucker, gen mgr; Art Taylor, chief of engrg.

Delray Beach

WDJA(AM)— February 1952: 1420 khz; 5 kw-D, 500 w-N, DA-2. TL: N26 27 22 W80 05 58. 6600 N. Andrews Ave., Suite 160, Fort Lauderdale 33309. Phone: (954) 315-1515. Phone: (561) 686-1100. Fax: (954) 315-1555. Web Site: www.wdja.com. Licensee: James Crystal Delray Beach Inc. Group owner: James Crystal Inc. (acq 3-1-03; $1.55 million. with WJBW(AM) Jupiter). Network: Network: CBS, UPI. Format: Business talk. Target aud: 35 plus. ♦ James C. Hilliard, pres; Rick Hindes, CFO; Steve Lapa, gen mgr.

Destin

WFFY(FM)— Sept 24, 1981: 92.1 mhz; 25 kw. 279 ft. TL: N30 23 08 W86 24 52. Stereo. 21 Miracle Strip Pkwy. S.E., Fort Walton Beach 32548-4166. Phone: (850) 244-1400. Fax: (850) 243-1471. Licensee: Gulf Breeze Media Inc., debtor in posserssion (acq 6-28-2004). Rep: Roslin. Format: Classic rock. ♦ Ron Hale Sr., gen mgr; Frank Hale, opns mgr; David Kuntz, gen sls mgr & progmg dir; Adan McClosky, progmg dir; Ronald Hill Jr., chief of engrg.

WNWF(AM)— 2000: 1120 khz; 1 kw-D. TL: N30 30 34 W86 28 34. Box 1120 32540. Secondary address: 415 Mountain Dr., Suite 7 32541. Phone: (850) 654-4040. Fax: (850) 650-9440. E-mail: dale@fox1120.com. Web Site: www.fox1120.com. Licensee: Flagship Communications Inc. (acq 8-28-03; $400,000). Format: News/talk. News staff: one. Target aud: 35-64. ♦ Dale Riddick, gen mgr & progmg dir; Steve Williams, news dir; Max Howell, sls.

Dogwood Lakes Estate

*WJED(FM)— Jan 15, 1992: 91.1 mhz; 700 w. 180 ft. TL: N30 51 34 W85 47 45. Box 537, Bonifay 32425. Phone: (850) 547-9405. Fax: (334) 793-4344. E-mail: wjed911fm@bethanybc.edu. Licensee: Bethany Bible College & Bethany Theological Seminary Inc. Network: USA. Format: Educ, relg, gospel. Target aud: General; college students & relg community. ♦ Dr. H.D. Shuemake, CEO & gen mgr; Dr. Steve Shuemake, pres & stn mgr; Sylvia Green, opns mgr.

Dunedin

WLVU(AM)— 1955: 1470 khz; 5 kw-D, 500 w-N. TL: N28 03 24 W82 44 16. 402 N. Reo St., Suite 204, Tampa 33609. Phone: (813) 281-1040. Fax: (813) 281-1948. Web Site: www.wlvu1470.com. Licensee: Genesis Communications of Tampa Bay Inc. Group owner: Genesis Communications Inc. (acq 3-5-2001; $2 million). Network: ESPN Radio. Rep: D & R Radio. Format: Sports. Spec prog: Relg 2 hrs wkly. ♦ Bruce Maduri, CEO; Jeff Lebhar, pres & gen mgr; Jeff Taylor, opns dir; Carol Azaravich, progmg dir; Jerry Smith, chief of engrg.

WNTR(AM)—Licensed to Dunedin. See Tampa

Dunnellon

WTRS(FM)— Mar 11, 1969: 102.3 mhz; 3 kw. 300 ft. TL: N29 11 16 W82 23 39. (CP: 50 kw, ant 489 ft.). Stereo. 3357 S.W. 7th St., Ocala 34474. Phone: (352) 732-9877. Fax: (352) 622-6675. E-mail: shane@thundercountry.net. Web Site: www.asteriskcommunications.com/wtrs. Licensee: Asterisk Communications Inc. Format: Country. ♦ Shane Finch, opns dir & progmg dir; Dave Tyler, mus dir & pub affrs dir.

Eatonville

WRLZ(AM)—Licensed to Eatonville. See Orlando

Eau Gallie

WBVD(FM)—See Melbourne

WINT(AM)—See Melbourne

WMEL(AM)—See Melbourne

WMMB(AM)—See Melbourne

Ebro

WBPC(FM)— July 2005: 95.1 mhz; 25 kw. Ant 285 ft. TL: N30 34 06 W85 48 28. Box 27272, Panama City Beach 32411. Phone: (850) 235-2195. Fax: (850) 235-2795. Licensee: Bay Broadcasting LLC. Format: Adult contemp. ♦ Charles Shapiro, pres & gen mgr; Bob DeCarlo, opns mgr; Cheryl Adams, prom dir.

Edgewater

WKRO-FM— 1993: 93.1 mhz; 14.9 kw. 427 ft. TL: N28 54 52 W80 53 48. 126 W. International Speedway Blvd., Daytona Beach 32114. Phone: (386) 255-9300. Fax: (386) 239-0966. Web Site: www.wkro.fm. Licensee: Black Crow LLC. Group owner: Black Crow Media Group LLC (acq 9-21-2001; grpsl). Format: Country. ♦ Stacey Knerler, gen mgr.

*WKTO(FM)— November 1997: 88.7 mhz; 4 kw vert. 298 ft. TL: N29 02 29 W81 03 23. 900 Old Mission Rd., New Smyrna Beach 32168. Phone: (386) 427-1095. Fax: (386) 427-8970. Web Site: www.wkto.org. Licensee: Mims Community Radio Inc. Format: Relg. Target aud: 18-50. Spec prog: Jazz 4 hrs, Pol 1.5 hrs, Ger 1.5 hrs, Sp 2 hr wkly. ♦ Carol Henry, CEO, chmn, pres, CFO & gen mgr.

Egypt Lake

WTMP(AM)—Licensed to Egypt Lake. See Tampa

Englewood

WENG(AM)— Nov 15, 1964: 1530 khz; 1 kw-D. TL: N26 58 15 W82 19 24. Box 2908 34295-2908. Secondary address: 1355 S. River Rd. 34223. Phone: (941) 474-3231. Fax: (941) 475-2205. E-mail: kenb@1530weng.com. Web Site: www.1530weng.com. Licensee: Viper Communications Inc. Group owner: Viper Communications Broadcast Group (acq 10-21-02). Network: ABC. Pepper & Corazzini. Format: News/talk, listener participation. News staff: one; News: 50 hrs wkly. Target aud: 18 plus; securely established, financially independent. Spec prog: Gospel 2 hrs wkly. ♦ Kenneth W. Kuenzie, pres; Dennis Klautzer, exec VP; Kenneth A. Birdsong, gen mgr; Scott Holcomb, opns dir.

*WSEB(FM)— May 1989: 91.3 mhz; 62 kw horiz, 60 kw vert. 282 ft. TL: N26 51 48 W87 17 54. Stereo. 135 W. Dearborne Ave. 34223. Phone: (941) 475-9732. Fax: (941) 473-7308. E-mail: comments@wsebfm.com. Web Site: www.wsebfm.net. Licensee: Suncoast Educational Broadcasting Corp. Format: Christian. Target aud: 35 plus; Christian families. ♦ Kenneth C. Lindow, pres; Joy Clark, gen mgr; Roger Johnson, progmg dir & mus dir.

WTZB(FM)— Apr 5, 1999: 105.9 mhz; 4.3 kw. 394 ft. TL: N27 06 01 W82 22 18. 1779 Indenpeudee Blvd., Sarasota 34236. Phone: (941) 552-4800. Fax: (941) 552-4900. Web Site: www.1059thebuzz.com. Licensee: Citicasters Licenses L.P. Group owner: Clear Channel Communications Inc. (acq 5-4-99; grpsl). Format: Alternative rock. ♦ Sherri Carlson, gen mgr; Ron White, opns mgr.

Estero

WRQC(FM)— Dec 16, 1978: 92.5 mhz; 6.8 kw. Ant 620 ft. TL: N26 19 00 W81 47 13. Stereo. 2824 Palm Beach Blvd., Ft. Myers 33916. Phone: (239) 337-2346. Fax: (239) 332-0767. E-mail: realrockvince@hotmail.com. Web Site: www.realrock925.com. Licensee: Meridian Broadcasting Inc. (group owner; acq 9-14-00; $7 million). Leibowitz & Associates. Format: AOR. Target aud: 18-49; general. ♦ Joseph C. Schwartzel, chmn, pres & gen mgr; Wayne Simons, exec VP & sls dir; Matt Francis, prom dir; Keith Stuhlman, engrg dir.

Florida

Eustis

WKIQ(AM)— June 1955: 1240 khz; 790 w-U. TL: N28 50 19 W81 41 46. Rama Communications Inc., 3765 N. John Young Pkwy., Orlando 32804. Phone: (407) 523-2770. Fax: (407) 523-2888. Licensee: Rama Communications Inc. (group owner; acq 10-15-2004; $180,000. with WQBQ(AM) Leesburg). Format: Gospel; R & B. ♦Sabeta Persaud, pres; Steve January, gen mgr.

WLBE(AM)—See Leesburg

Fernandina Beach

WJSJ(FM)— 2000: 105.3 mhz; 3.9 kw. Ant 410 ft. TL: N30 30 04 W81 35 14. 9550 Regency Sq. Blvd., Suite 200, Jacksonville 32225. Phone: (904) 680-1050. Fax: (904) 680-1051. Web Site: www.smoothjazz.com. Licensee: Tama Radio Licenses of Jacksonville, FL, Inc. Group owner: Tama Broadcasting Inc. (acq 2-28-2003; $8.5 million. with WSJF(FM) Saint Augustine Beach). Format: Jazz. ♦ Linda Davis-Fructuoso, gen mgr; Joel Widdows, opns mgr; George Sample, gen sls mgr.

***WNLE(FM)**— Oct 6, 1985: 91.7 mhz; 32 kw. 223 ft. TL: N30 37 20 W81 31 48. (CP: 26 kw, ant 312 ft). Stereo. 464059 State Rd. 200, Yulee 32097. Phone: (904) 277-2256. Phone: (904) 277-1569. Fax: (904) 277-1569. E-mail: wnle@adelphia.net. Licensee: Nassau Baptist Ministries. Network: USA. Southmayd & Miller. Format: Christian, relg, southern gospel. News: 11 hrs wkly. Target aud: General. ♦ Truman Blankenship, CEO; Truman Bankenship, pres; Robert Moughton, gen mgr & chief of opns; Greg Chapman, progmg dir & chief of engrg.

WVOJ(AM)— 1955: 1570 khz; 10 kw-D, 30 w-N. TL: N30 40 33 W81 27 35. 8384 Baymeadows Rd., Suite 1, Jacksonville 32256. Phone: (904) 743-6234. Fax: (904) 739-9409. Licensee: Norsan Consulting and Management Inc. (acq 6-1-2005; $2.1 million. with WNNR(AM) Jacksonville). Format: Sp CHR. ♦Norberto Sanchez, pres; Bernie Daigle, gen mgr.

Five Points

WCJX(FM)— 1996: 106.5 mhz; 4.2 kw. 328 ft. TL: N30 14 40 W82 40 11. 1305 Helvenston St., Live Oak 32064. Secondary address: North 41 Hwy., Lake City 32056. Phone: (386) 755-9259. Fax: (386) 755-1557. Web Site: www.wcjx.com. Licensee: RTG Radio LLC. Group owner: Black Crow Media Group LLC (acq 11-9-2001; grpsl). Network: ABC. Format: Classic rock. ♦R.T. Ganzak, pres; Dean Blackwell, gen mgr; Steve Johnson, stn mgr.

Flagler Beach

***WJLH(FM)**— Aug 23, 1996: 90.3 mhz; 2 kw vert. 184 ft. TL: N29 22 18 W81 10 45. 4295 Ridgewood Ave., Port Orange 32127. Phone: (386) 756-9094. Fax: (386) 760-7107. E-mail: thecornerstone @cornerstoneministry.org. Web Site: www.cornerstoneministry.org. Licensee: Cornerstone Broadcasting Corp. (acq 3-20-97; $27,044). Format: Christian. ♦William Powell, gen mgr; Dave Purin, progmg dir; Sandra Leisner, pub affrs dir.

Florida City

***WMFL(FM)**— Oct 1, 1998: 88.5 mhz; 8 kw vert. Ant 134 ft. TL: N25 05 50 W80 26 12. Family Stations Inc., 290 Hegenberger Rd., Oakland, CA 94621. Phone: (510) 568-6200. Fax: (510) 568-6190. Web Site: www.familyradio.com. Licensee: Family Stations Inc. (group owner; acq 11-15-00; $75,000). Network: Family Radio. Format: Christian, relg. ♦ Bill Musser, gen mgr.

Fort Lauderdale

***WAFG(FM)**— 1974: 90.3 mhz; 3 kw. 280 ft. TL: N26 11 48 W80 06 45. Stereo. 5555 N. Federal Hwy. 33308. Phone: (954) 776-7705. Fax: (954) 771-2633. E-mail: wafg@crpc.org. Web Site: www.wafg.com. Licensee: Westminster Academy. Network: Network: USA, Salem Radio Network. Gammon & Grange. Format: Christian, news/talk, relg. News: 10 hrs wkly. Target aud: 30 plus; general. ♦ Dolores King-St.George, gen mgr & dev dir; Scott Blakely, opns mgr; Lesley Hurst, progmg dir.

WBGG-FM— July 1960: 105.9 mhz; 100 kw. Ant 1,030 ft. TL: N25 59 34 W80 10 27. Stereo. 7601 Riviera Blvd., Miramar 33023. Phone: (954) 862-2000. Fax: (954) 862-4013. Web Site: www.big1059.com. Licensee: Clear Channel Radio Licenses Inc. Group owner: Clear Channel Communications Inc. (acq 2-24-94; $14 million; 3-14-94). Format: Classic rock. ♦Ronna Woulfe, gen mgr.

WEXY(AM)—See Wilton Manors

WFLL(AM)— Sept 16, 1946: 1400 khz; 1 kw-U. TL: N26 09 13 W80 10 11. 6600 N. Andrews Ave., Suite 160 33309. Phone: (954) 315-1515. Fax: (954) 315-1555. Web Site: www.wftl.com. Licensee: James Crystal Licenses L.L.C. Group owner: James Crystal Inc. (acq 6-17-98; grpsl). Format: Sports. Target aud: 25 plus. ♦ Richard Hindes, CFO; Steve Lapa, gen mgr & sls VP.

WHSR(AM)—See Pompano Beach

WHYI-FM— July 31, 1960: 100.7 mhz; 100 kw. 928 ft. TL: N25 59 34 W80 10 27. (CP: Ant 1,007 ft. TL: N25 57 59 W80 12 33). 7601 Riviera Blvd., Miramar 33023. Phone: (954) 862-2000. Fax: (954) 862-4013. Web Site: www.y100.7miami.com. Licensee: Clear Channel Radio Licenses Inc. Group owner: Clear Channel Communications Inc. (acq 11-94; grpsl). Rep: McGavren Guild. Format: CHR. ♦ Ronna Woulfe, gen mgr.

WMIB(FM)— Oct 17, 1959: 103.5 mhz; 100 kw. 1,007 ft. TL: N25 57 59 W80 12 33. Stereo. 7601 Riviera Blvd., Miramar 33023. Phone: (954) 862-2000. Web Site: www.mega1035.cc. Licensee: Clear Channel Broadcasting Licenses Inc. Group owner: Clear Channel Communications Inc. (acq 11-21-97; grpsl). Format: Hip hop, rhythm and blues. ♦David Ross, gen mgr.

WMXJ(FM)—See Pompano Beach

WRMA(FM)— Aug 15, 1962: 106.7 mhz; 100 kw. 984 ft. TL: N25 59 34 W80 10 27. Stereo. 1001 Ponce DeLeon Blvd., Coral Gables 33134. Phone: (305) 446-3900. Phone: (305) 620-1067. Fax: (305) 569-9439. E-mail: jacinbs@hotmail.com. Web Site: www.romance106fm.com. Licensee: WRMA Licensing Inc. Group owner: Spanish Broadcasting System Inc. (acq 7-11-97; $110 million with WXDJ(FM) North Miami Beach). Rep: D & R Radio. Format: Sp, adult contemp. News staff: one. Target aud: 18-54; Hispanic adults. ♦ Raoul Alarcon, pres; Greg Alexander, gen mgr & gen sls mgr; Jackie Nosti-Cambo, gen mgr; German Estrada, progmg dir; Tomas Regalado, news dir; Yoli Machado, pub affrs dir; Ralph Chambers, chief of engrg.

WSRF(AM)— 1955: 1580 khz; 10 kw-D, 5 kw-N, DA-2. TL: N26 04 54 W80 13 34. 4431 Rock Island Rd. 33314. Phone: (954) 587-1035. Phone: (954) 731-1855. Fax: (954) 731-1833. E-mail: lhudson@wsrf.com. Web Site: www.wsrf.com. Licensee: Urban Radio of Florida L.L.C. Group owner: Inner City Broadcasting (acq 6-17-99; $1.5 million). Network: American Urban Renaissance. Format: Caribbean, Talk. News staff: 2. Target aud: 18-54. ♦ Carl Nelson, pres & gen mgr; Lynda Hudson, gen mgr; Joe Cheatum, opns mgr; Ron Burke, progmg dir.

WWNN(AM)—See Pompano Beach

Fort Meade

WWRZ(FM)— Mar 7, 1977: 98.3 mhz; 26 kw. 686 ft. TL: N27 38 38 W81 48 00. Stereo. 404 W. Lime St., Lakeland 33815-4651. Phone: (863) 682-8184. Fax: (863) 683-2409. E-mail: info@rosefm.com. Web Site: www.rosefm.com. Licensee: Hall Communications Inc. (group owner; acq 10-1-96; $1,750,000). Fletcher, Heald & Hildreth. Format: Adult contemp. News staff: 2; News: 2 hrs wkly. Target aud: 25-54; women. Spec prog: Women. ♦ Arthur L. Rowbotham, pres & gen mgr; William S. Baldwin, sr VP; Steve Howard, stn mgr; Tunie Moss, prom dir; Brian Bruchey, progmg dir.

Fort Myers

WARO(FM)—See Naples

***WAYJ(FM)**— October 1987: 88.7 mhz; 75 kw. Ant 1,007 ft. TL: N26 25 22 W81 37 49. Stereo. Box 61275 33906. Secondary address: 1860 Boy Scout Dr., Suite 202 33906. Phone: (239) 936-1929. Fax: (239) 936-5433. Web Site: www.wayfm.com. Licensee: WAY-FM Media Group Inc. (group owner). Network: USA. Gammon & Grange. Format: Contemp Christian. News staff: one; News: one hr wkly. Target aud: 18-34. ♦ Bob Augsburg, pres & gen mgr; Cobi Knight, stn mgr & prom dir; Jeff Taylor, stn mgr; Steve Shore, progmg dir.

WCRM(AM)— Aug 22, 1964: 1350 khz; 1 kw-D, 150 w-N. TL: N26 37 31 W81 50 29. (CP: 5 kw-D.) 3448 Canal St. 33916. Phone: (239) 334-1350. Fax: (239) 332-8890. E-mail: radio1350office@aol.com. Web Site: www.aleluya.com/1350_am.htm. Licensee: Manna Christian Missions Inc. (acq 6-89). Network: USA. Schwartz, Woods & Miller. Format: Sp, Christian. News staff: one; News: 5 hrs wkly. Target aud: General. ♦ Salvador Santana, gen mgr.

***WGCU-FM**— Sept 12, 1983: 90.1 mhz; 100 kw. 813 ft. TL: N26 48 54 W81 45 44. Stereo. 10501 FGCU Blvd. 33965-6565. Phone: (239) 590-2500. Fax: (239) 590-2511. Licensee: Board of Trustees, Florida Gulf Coast University (acq 11-16-01). Network: Network: NPR, PRI. Cohn & Marks. Format: Class, jazz, news. News staff: 2; News: 28 hrs wkly. Target aud: 24 plus. ♦ Kathleen Davey, gen mgr & stn mgr; Terry Brennen, dev dir; Christine Hause, rgnl sls mgr; Toby Cooke, progmg dir; Valerie Alker, news dir; Joe Maggio, engrg dir.

WINK(AM)— Mar 1, 1940: 1240 khz; 1 kw-U. TL: N26 37 28 W81 49 52. 2824 Palm Beach Blvd. 33916. Phone: (239) 337-2346. Fax: (239) 479-5579. Web Site: www.winkwnog.com. Licensee: Fort Myers Broadcasting Co. (group owner) Network: CBS Radio. Rep: McGavren Guild. Leibowitz & Spencer. Format: News/talk. Target aud: 35 plus. ♦ Brian A. McBride, pres; Gary Gardner, gen mgr.

WINK-FM—Listing follows WPTK(AM).

***WJYO(FM)**— 1988: 91.5 mhz; 3 kw. 285 ft. TL: N26 30 18 W81 51 14. Stereo. Box 61721 33906. Secondary address: 4050 Colonial Blvd. 33907. Phone: (239) 275-9785. Phone: (706) 886-6831. Fax: (239) 275-3112. E-mail: wjyo@aol.com. Web Site: airwavesforJesus.com. Licensee: Airwaves for Jesus Inc. (acq 3-8-2004; $500,000. with WBIY(FM) La Belle). Format: Bible teaching, light Christian Praise/worship music. News: 10 hrs wkly. Target aud: 44 plus; traditional minded persons. Spec prog: Children 5 hrs wkly. ♦ Art Ramos, CEO, pres & gen mgr; Jasmin Ramos, VP; Bill Simon, stn mgr; Joe Scoggins, opns mgr & pub affrs dir.

WMYR(AM)— Nov 11, 1952: 1410 khz; 5 kw-U, DA-N. TL: N26 37 24.9 W81 51 16.7. 12470 Woodtimber Ln. 33913. Phone: (239) 768-9256. Fax: (239) 768-9256. E-mail: wmyr@relevantradio.com. Web Site: www.relevantradio.com. Licensee: Starboard Media Foundation Inc. Group owner: Relevant Radio (acq 9-22-2004; $1.5 million). Format: Catholic talk. ♦ Patricia Gedra, gen mgr.

WOLZ(FM)— January 1970: 95.3 mhz; 79 kw. 453 ft. TL: N26 37 25 W82 06 56. Stereo. 13320 Metro Pkwy. 33912. Phone: (239) 225-4300. Fax: (239) 225-4329. Web Site: www.wolz.com. Licensee: Clear Channel Radio Licenses Inc. Group owner: Clear Channel Communications Inc. (acq 2-18-97; grpsl). Rep: Clear Channel. Format: Oldies. News staff: one; News: 2 hrs wkly. Target aud: 35-54; upbeat, fun oldies, strong at work and in-car listening. ♦ Jim Keating, gen mgr.

WPTK(AM)—(Pine Island Center). Feb 20, 1986: 1200 khz; 10 kw-D, 2.5 kw-N. TL: N26 42 52 W82 02 46. 2824 Palm Beach Blvd. 33916. Phone: (239) 337-2346. Fax: (239) 332-0767. Licensee: Fort Myers Broadcasting Co. (group owner) Network: ABC. Rep: McGavren Guild. Leibowitz & Associates. Format: News, talk. Target aud: 35 plus; listeners with buying power. ♦Brain A. McBride, pres; Joseph C. Schwartzel, gen mgr; Wayne Simons, sls dir; Tracy Ruyle, prom mgr; Jim Watkins, progmg dir; Keith Stuhlmann, engrg dir.

WINK-FM—Co-owned with WPTK(AM). Oct 10, 1964: 96.9 mhz; 100 kw. 1,322 ft. TL: N26 38 40 W081 52 10. Stereo. Phone: (239) 334-1111. Fax: (239) 334-0744. Web Site: www.winkfm.com. Rep: McGavren Guild. Leibowitz & Associates. Format: Adult contemp. News: 8 hrs wkly. Target aud: 25-54; females. ♦Brian A. McBride, pres; Gary Gardner, gen mgr; Tracy Ruyle, prom mgr; Bob Grissinger, progmg dir. Co-owned TV: WINK-TV affil

WRXK-FM—See Bonita Springs

WWGR(FM)— Dec 2, 1969: 101.9 mhz; 100 kw. 1,020 ft. TL: N26 25 23 W81 37 07. Stereo. 10915 K-Nine Dr., 2nd Fl., Suite 210, Bonita Springs 34135. Phone: (239) 495-8383. Fax: (239) 495-0883. Web Site: www.gatorioia.com. Licensee: Renda Broadcast Corp. Group owner: Renda Broadcasting Corp.-Renda Radio Inc. (acq 7-13-94; $4 million; 8-1-94). Format: Country. ♦ Kelley McGrath, gen mgr.

WZJZ(FM)—See Lehigh Acres

Fort Myers Beach

WJBX(FM)— 1983: 99.3 mhz; 50 kw. 476 ft. TL: N26 30 18 W81 51 14. Stereo. 20125 S. Tamiami, Estero 33928. Phone: (239) 495-2100.

Developers & Brokers of Radio Properties
contact American Media Services at our suite: Philadelphia Marriott Downtown 215-625-2900
843-972-2200
americanmediaservices.com
Charleston, SC
Dallas, TX - Chicago, Il - Austin, TX
American Media Services, LLC

Fax: (239) 992-8165. Web Site: www.99xwjax.com. Licensee: Dillon License L.P. Group owner: Beasley Broadcast Group (acq 10-16-97; $6 million). Leventhal, Senter & Lerman. Format: Alternative/new rock. Target aud: 18-49; adults. ♦Brad Beasley, gen mgr.

Fort Myers Villas

WJPT(FM)— July 31, 1991: 106.3 mhz; 50 kw. 472 ft. TL: N26 29 16 W81 55 49. 20125 S. Tamiami Trail, Estero 33928. Phone: (239) 495-2100. Fax: (239) 948-0785. E-mail: randy@morningshow.net. Licensee: WJST License L.P. Group owner: Beasley Broadcast Group (acq 12-11-97; $5 million). Format: Adult standards. Target aud: 45 plus. ♦Brad Beasley, gen mgr; Shane Reilly, opns mgr.

Fort Pierce

WIRA(AM)— May 18, 1946: 1400 khz; 1 kw-U. TL: N27 26 07 W80 21 41. 6803 So. Federal Hwy., Port St. Lucie 34952. Phone: (772) 460-9356. Fax: (772) 460-2700. Web Site: www.1400wira.com. Licensee: Team One Media LLC (acq 2-11-2004; $375,000). Network: ABC. Format: Urban gospel. Target aud: 45 plus; male & female. Spec prog: Relg one hr, pub affrs one hr wkly. ♦Al Richards, opns mgr; Barbara Marshall, gen mgr & opns mgr.

***WJFP(FM)**— Jan 15, 1995: 91.1 mhz; 6 kw. 157 ft. 2192 North U.S. Hwy #1., Ft. Pierce 34946. Phone: (772) 467-2400. Phone: (772) 467-0312. Fax: (772) 467-9400. Web Site: www.wjfp.com. Licensee: Black Media Works Inc. (group owner; acq 1-21-98). Format: Urban contemp, relg, educ. Target aud: 12-49. Spec prog: Sp 2 hrs, Haitian 8 hrs wkly. ♦Kimberly Kassis, pres; Joseph Jenkins, opns mgr, gen sls mgr & progmg dir.

WJNX(AM)— Dec 24, 1952: 1330 khz; 5 kw-D, 1 kw-N, DA-2. TL: N27 27 20 W80 22 02. Stereo. 8245 Business Park Dr., Port St. Lucie 34952. Phone: (772) 340-1590. Fax: (772) 340-3245. E-mail: wpsl@wpsl.com. Web Site: www.lagigante1330.com. Licensee: Port St. Lucie Broadcasters Inc. (acq 3-31-2004; $400,000). Network: CNN en Espanol. Leventhal, Senter & Lerman. Format: Sp news/talk. News staff: one. Target aud: 25-54. ♦Carol Wyatt, CEO & pres; Greg Wyatt, gen mgr.

WKGR(FM)— May 1, 1961: 98.7 mhz; 100 kw. 1,381 ft. TL: N27 07 20 W80 23 21. Stereo. 3071 Continental Dr., West Palm Beach 33407. Phone: (561) 616-6600. Fax: (561) 616-6677. E-mail: katenorem@clearchannel.com. Web Site: www.gater.com. Licensee: Clear Channel Radio Licenses Inc. Group owner: Clear Channel Communications Inc. (acq 9-16-97; grpsl). Format: Classic rock. Target aud: 25-54. ♦John Hunt, gen mgr; Dave Denver, opns dir & opns mgr; Roger Koch, sls dir.

WLDI(FM)— Oct 30, 1969: 95.5 mhz; 100 kw. 981 ft. TL: N27 07 20 W80 23 21. Stereo. 3071 Continental Dr., West Palm Beach 33407. Phone: (561) 616-6600. Fax: (561) 616-6677. Web Site: www.wild955.com. Licensee: Clear Channel Radio Licenses Inc. Group owner: Clear Channel Communications Inc. (acq 6-17-98; grpsl). Format: CHR. Target aud: 18-49; active, contemp. ♦John Hook, gen mgr; Dave Denver, opns dir.

***WQCS(FM)**— April 1982: 88.9 mhz; 100 kw. 436 ft. TL: N27 25 17 W80 21 23. Stereo. 3209 Virginia Ave. 34981. Phone: (772) 462-4744. Fax: (772) 462-4743. Licensee: Indian River Community College. Network: Network: Network: NPR, PRI, AP Radio. Format: Class, news. ♦Jim Holmes, stn mgr & progmg dir; Michelle Rhinesmith, opns mgr.

Fort Walton Beach

WBAU(AM)— 1956: 1400 khz; 1 kw-U. TL: N30 24 38 W86 37 23. 21 Miracle Strip Pkwy. S.E. 32548. Phone: (850) 244-1400. Fax: (850) 243-1471. Licensee: Star Broadcasting Inc. (acq 7-11-2005). Format: Memories. Target aud: 50 plus. Spec prog: Gospel 2 hrs wkly. ♦Ron Hale Sr., gen mgr; David Kuntz, gen sls mgr; Frank Hale, progmg dir & chief of engrg.

WFSH(AM)—See Valparaiso-Niceville

WFTW(AM)— Nov 20, 1953: 1260 khz; 2.5 kw-D, 131 w-N. TL: N30 24 49 W86 37 40. Box 2347, 225 N.W. Hollywood Blvd. 32548. Phone: (850) 243-7676. Fax: (850) 243-6806. E-mail: wftw@radiopeople.net. Web Site: www.wftw.com. Licensee: Cumulus Licensing Corp. Group owner: Cumulus Media Inc. (acq 1-10-03; grpsl). Format: News/talk. ♦Lou Dickey, pres; Ron Raybourne, gen mgr; Georgia Edmiston, gen sls mgr; Lisa Captain, prom dir & prom mgr; Steve Williams, progmg dir; Bruce Campbell, chief of engrg.

WKSM(FM)—Co-owned with WFTW(AM). May 28, 1965: 99.5 mhz; 50 kw. Ant 440 ft. TL: N30 24 50 W86 37 40. (CP: ant 438 ft). Stereo. Web Site: www.wftw.com. Format: Rock. ♦Lee Leonard, rgnl sls mgr; Steve O'Day, prom mgr; Nicci Garmon, progmg dir; Anthony Proffitt, mus dir; Aimee Shaffer, news dir & pub affrs dir.

***WPSM(FM)**— July 1, 1985: 91.1 mhz; 383 w. 120 ft. TL: N30 25 14 W86 36 43. Stereo. Box 10 32549. Secondary address: 23 N. Hill Ave. 32548. Phone: (850) 244-7667. Fax: (850) 244-3254. E-mail: wpsmradio@aol.com. Web Site: www.wpsm.com. Licensee: Fort Walton Beach Educ. Broadcasting Corp. Network: USA. Format: Christian. News staff: one; News: 14 hrs wkly. Target aud: 25-55; young to middle-age adult Christians. ♦Terry Thorne, gen mgr.

WTKE(FM)—(Holt). July 1950: 98.1 mhz; 100 kw. Ant 482 ft. TL: N30 24 38 W86 37 22. Stereo. 21 Miracle Strip Pkwy. S.E. 32548. Phone: (850) 244-1400. Fax: (850) 994-7191. Web Site: www.sportsradio.com. Licensee: Star Broadcasting Inc. Group owner: Qantum Communications Corp. (acq 2-14-2003). Rep: Roslin. Wiley, Rein & Fielding. Format: Sports, talk. Target aud: 25-54. ♦Paula Peterson, gen mgr; Mike Carr, gen sls mgr; Lynn West, prom dir.

WZNS(FM)— 1997: 96.5 mhz; 100 kw. 440 ft. TL: N30 24 50 W86 37 40. 225 N.W. Hollywood Blvd. 32548. Phone: (850) 243-2323. Fax: (850) 243-6806. E-mail: sales@z96.com. Web Site: www.z96.com. Licensee: Cumulus Licensing Corp. Group owner: Cumulus Media Inc. (acq 1-10-03; grpsl). Format: CHR. ♦Ron Raybourne, gen mgr; Lisa Captain, prom mgr; Hayden Green, progmg mgr.

Gainesville

WAJD(AM)— May 31, 1961: 1390 khz; 5 kw-D, 51 w-N. TL: N29 39 56 W82 17 26. 7120 S.W. 24th Ave. 32607. Phone: (352) 331-2200. Fax: (352) 331-0401. Web Site: www.kiss1053.com. Licensee: Gillen Broadcasting Corp. (acq 9-22-87; $1.9 million with co-located FM; 8-17-87). Format: Radio Disney. Target aud: 12-49. ♦Douglas Gillen, pres, gen mgr & gen sls mgr.

WYKS(FM)—Co-owned with WAJD(AM). May 4, 1970: 105.3 mhz; 3 kw. 466 ft. TL: N29 37 52 W82 25 18. (CP: 105.3 mhz, 6 kw). Web Site: www.kiss1053.com. Format: Top 40.

WDVH(AM)— October 1954: 980 khz; 5 kw-D, 166 w-N. TL: N29 37 26 W82 17 19. 249 W. Universtiy Ave., Suite B 322601. Secondary address: 3135 27th St. S.E., Gainsville 32641. Phone: (352) 372-2528. Fax: (352) 372-0851. E-mail: jim@wdvh.org. Web Site: www.wdvh.org. Licensee: Jablamo License Holdings LLC. (group owner; (acq 7-6-2004; grpsl). Rep: Roslin. Format: Country legends. News: 2 hrs wkly. Target aud: 35 plus. ♦Eric Jewell, gen mgr.

WGGG(AM)— February 1948: 1230 khz; 1 kw-U. TL: N29 40 56 W82 24 48. 343 N.E. First Ave., Ocala 34470. Phone: (352) 732-2010. Fax: (352) 629-1614. E-mail: sales@floridasportstalk.com. Web Site: www.floridasportstalk.com. Licensee: Florida Sportstalk Inc. (acq 2-5-97; $300,000). Format: All sports. ♦Gordon Smith, gen mgr; Jeff Francis, opns dir.

***WJLF(FM)**— Aug 26, 1990: 91.7 mhz; 2 kw. 400 ft. TL: N29 38 34 W82 25 13. Stereo. 2925 N.W. 39th Ave. 32605. Phone: (352) 373-9553. Fax: (352) 373-9888. E-mail: thejoyfm@thejoyfm.com. Web Site: thejoyfm.com. Licensee: Radio Training Network Inc. (acq 10-1-2004; $1 million). Gammon & Grange. Format: Christian. News staff: one; News: 2 hrs wkly. Target aud: 18-49; young adults & young families. Spec prog: Youth 5 hrs, jazz 2 hrs, children 1 hr wkly. ♦James L. Campbell, pres; Andy Haynes, gen mgr & stn mgr.

WKTK(FM)—See Crystal River

WNDD(FM)—(Silver Springs). Feb 1, 1991: 95.5 mhz; 6 kw. 340 ft. TL: N29 16 55 W82 02 50. Stereo. 3602 N.E. 20th Pl., Ocala 34470. Phone: (352) 622-9500. Fax: (352) 622-1900. Web Site: www.windfm.com. Licensee: Ocala Broadcasting Corp. L.L.C. Group owner: Wooster Republican Printing Co. (acq 9-1-97). Format: Classic rock. Target aud: 25-44; upscale young adults. ♦Jim Robertson, gen mgr; Bob Kassi, gen sls mgr; Kevin Davis, progmg dir.

WRUF-FM— 1948: 103.7 mhz; 100 kw. 768 ft. TL: N29 42 34 W82 23 40. Stereo. Box 14444 32604. Secondary address: Univ. of Florida, 3200 Wiemer Hall 32611. Phone: (352) 392-0771. Fax: (352) 392-0519. Web Site: www.rock104.com. Licensee: University of Florida, Board of Trustees. Format: Contemp rock. News staff: 3; News: 5 hrs wkly. Target aud: 25-34; urban rockers. Spec prog: Alternative 6 hrs wkly. ♦Larry Dankner, gen mgr & gen sls mgr; Harry Guscott, opns mgr & progmg dir; Cathy Ferguson, news dir; Tom Kyrnski, news dir; Don Rice, chief of engrg.

WRUF(AM)— 1928: 850 khz; 5 kw-U, DA-N. TL: N29 38 34 W82 25 13. Web Site: www.am850.com. Network: Network: CBS, Westwood One. Format: News/talk, sports. News staff: 3; News: 54 hrs wkly. Target aud: 35-54; middle-to-upper income, decision makers. Spec prog: Black 4 hrs wkly. ♦Robert Lawrence, opns mgr; Larry Dankner, dev dir, mktg dir & progmg mgr; Tom Ksynski, news dir & pub affrs dir; Don Rice, chief of engrg. Co-owned TV: WUFT-TV, WLUF-TV affils.

WTMG(FM)—See Williston

WTMN(AM)— January 1990: 1430 khz; 2.5 kw-D. TL: N29 37 26 W82 17 19. 249 W. University Ave., Suite B 32601. Phone: (352) 371-1980. Fax: (352) 338-0566. E-mail: shinds@sunshinebroadcasting.com. Licensee: Jablamo License Holdings LLC. (group owner; (acq 7-6-2004; grpsl). Irwin, Campbell, Crowe & Tannenwald. Format: Gospel. ♦Eric Jewell, gen mgr; Bruce Cherry, opns VP; Bob Lima, gen sls mgr; Scott Hinds, progmg dir; C. Thompson, pub affrs dir.

***WUFT-FM**— Sept 27, 1981: 89.1 mhz; 100 kw. 771 ft. TL: N29 42 34 W82 23 40. Stereo. 2206 Weimer Hall, Univ. of Florida 32611. Phone: (352) 392-5200. Fax: (352) 392-5741. E-mail: info@woft.org. Web Site: www.wuft.org. Licensee: Board of Trustees, University of Florida. Network: Network: NPR, PRI. Schwartz, Woods & Miller. Format: Class, jazz, pub affrs. News staff: 3; News: 15 hrs wkly. Target aud: 35-65; general, educated (some college or degree). Spec prog: Black 4 hrs, folk one hr, gospel one hr wkly. ♦Richard A. Lehner, gen mgr; Henri Pensis, stn mgr; Steve Seipp, opns mgr; Brent Williams, dev dir. Co-owned TV: *WUFT-TV affil.

WXJZ(FM)— May 1, 1982: 100.9 mhz; 3 kw. 300 ft. TL: N29 38 02 W82 18 50. Stereo. 4424 N.W. 13th St., Suite C-5 32609. Phone: (352) 375-1317. Fax: (352) 375-6961. E-mail: feedback@wxjz.fm. Web Site: www.wxjz.fm. Licensee: Asterisk Communications Inc. Group owner: Asterisk Inc. (acq 10-4-93; $1.4 million;. FTR: 10-25-93). Network: ABC Information & Entertainment. Rep: McGavren Guild. Format: Smooth jazz. Target aud: 25-54; upscale, affluent, sophisticated. ♦John Starr, gen mgr & adv mgr; Bill Elliott, progmg dir.

***WYFB(FM)**— Aug 4, 1985: 90.5 mhz; 100 kw. 679 ft. TL: N29 52 08 W82 12 04. (CP: 96.81 kw). Stereo. 5553 S.E. 3rd Ave., Keystone Heights 32656. Phone: (800) 888-7077. Phone: (352) 473-7077. Fax: (352) 437-7077. E-mail: wyfb@bbnradio.org. Web Site: www.bbnradio.org. Licensee: Bible Broadcasting Network Inc. (group owner) Network: Network: Bible Bcstg Net, USA. Format: Relg. News: 12 hrs wkly. Target aud: General. ♦Lowell Davey, pres; David Nichols, chief of opns; Hank Farrior, progmg mgr; Hal Mashburn, chief of engrg.

WYGC(FM)—(High Springs). Jan 31, 1984: 104.9 mhz; 3.2 kw. 450 ft. TL: N29 49 16 W82 34 28. Stereo. 3357 S.N.W. 7h St., Suite C5, Ocala 34474. Phone: (352) 732-9877. Fax: (352) 375-6961. E-mail: dean@thundercountry.net. Web Site: www.asteriskcommunications.com /wtrs/business.htm. Licensee: Asterisk Communications Inc. Group

Broadcasting & Cable Yearbook 2006

D-123

Florida

owner: Asterisk Inc. (acq 2-99; $825,000). Network: Network: CNN Radio, Westwood One. Larry Perry. Format: Country. News: 4 hrs wkly. Target aud: 25-54. ♦ Fred Ingraham, pres; John Rutledge, gen mgr; Dean Johnson, gen sls mgr; Bill Elliott, chief of engrg; Shane Finch, opns.

Gifford

WSYR-FM— June 1994: 94.7 mhz; 25 kw. 295 ft. TL: N27 33 21 W80 22 08. Box 0093, Port St. Lucie 34985. Phone: (772) 335-9300. Fax: (772) 335-3291. E-mail: star947@clearchannel.com. Web Site: www.star947.com. Licensee: Capstar TX L.P. Group owner: Clear Channel Communications Inc. (acq 8-30-00; grpsl). Format: Adult contemp. Target aud: 25-54. ♦ Mark Bass, gen mgr; Andrew Bednar, prom dir; Mike Michaels, opns mgr & progmg dir.

Goulds

WRTO-FM—Licensed to Goulds. See Miami

Graceville

WTOT-FM— 1996: 101.7 mhz; 6 kw. 328 ft. TL: N30 57 21 W85 29 53. 285 E. Broad St., Ozark, AR 36360. Phone: (334) 774-9323. Fax: (334) 774-6450. Licensee: GFR Inc. Network: ABC. Format: News, talk. Target aud: 25+; female. ♦ Jack Mizell, pres.

Green Cove Springs

WJBT(FM)— 1978: 92.7 mhz; 2.6 kw. Ant 505 ft. TL: N30 04 08 W81 38 50. Stereo. 11700 Central Pkwy., Jacksonville 32224. Phone: (904) 636-0507. Fax: (904) 997-7713. Web Site: www.wjbt.com. Licensee: Citicasters Licenses L.P. Group owner: Clear Channel Communications Inc. (acq 5-4-99; grpsl). Format: Urban contemp. Target aud: 12-54; the young & young-at-heart. ♦ Norm Feuer, gen mgr; Gail Austin, opns mgr; April Johnson, gen sls mgr; Rhonda Hernandez, news dir; Phil Tuck, chief of engrg.

Greenville

*WYJC(FM)—Not on air, target date: unknown: 90.3 mhz; 47.8 kw. Ant 328 ft. TL: N30 20 51 W83 47 26. CSN International, 3232 W. MacArthur Blvd., Santa Ana, CA 92704. Phone: (714) 825-9663. Fax: (714) 825-9660. Licensee: CSN International (group owner). Format: Christian. ♦ Mike Kespler, gen mgr.

Gretna

WGWD(FM)— Oct 2, 1989: 93.3 mhz; 3 kw. 328 ft. TL: N30 33 24 W84 36 05. (CP: 6 kw). Stereo. Box 919, Quincy 32353. Secondary address: 8 W. Washington, Quincy 32351. Phone: (850) 627-7086. Fax: (850) 627-3422. Licensee: De Col Inc. (acq 9-18-91; $75,000; 10-7-91). Network: USA. Format: Classic country. News: 21 hrs wkly. Target aud: 25-54. Spec prog: Black 20 hrs wkly. ♦ Monte Bitner, gen mgr & progmg dir; Pat Bitner, opns mgr; Cindy Burdick, gen sls mgr; Jan Rogers, news dir; Jeff Fallaway, chief of engrg.

Gulf Breeze

WNRP(AM)— Feb 1, 1998: 1620 khz; 10 kw-D, 1 kw-N. TL: N30 26 12 W87 13 13. 7251 Plantation Rd., Pensacola 32504. Phone: (850) 494-2800. Fax: (850) 494-0778. E-mail: catsplashfever@catcountry987.com. Web Site: www.catcountry987.com. Licensee: ADX Communications of Escambia (acq 11-16-2000). Format: Country. ♦ Mary Hoxeng, gen mgr; Kevin King, opns dir; Dana Cervanies, prom dir.

WRRX(FM)—Not on air, target date: unknown: 106.1 mhz; 6565 N. W St., Pensacola, PA 32505. Phone: (850) 478-6011. Fax: (850) 478-3971. Web Site: www.cumulus.com. Licensee: Cumulus Licensing Corp. Format: Urban contemp. ♦ Liz Hanlon, gen mgr; Debbie Dingwall, opns mgr.

Haines City

*WLVF-FM— Apr 11, 1986: 90.3 mhz; 800 w. 265 ft. TL: N28 09 28 W81 37 34. (CP: 1.2 kw, ant 308 ft.). Stereo. 810 E. Hinson Ave 33844. Phone: (863) 422-9583. Fax: (863) 422-0110. E-mail: wlvf@gate.net. Web Site: www.gospel903.com. Licensee: Landmark Baptist Church. Network: USA. Format: Southern gospel. ♦ Steven Carter, gen mgr; Lewis Cruz, opns mgr & progmg dir; Bobby Ogden, gen sls mgr; Jeff Crews, chief of engrg.

WLVF(AM)— Sept 9, 1960: 930 khz; 500 w-D, DA. TL: N28 04 52 W81 38 23. E-mail: wlvf@gate.net. Format: Southern gospel. Target aud: General.

Havana

WHTF(FM)— 1986: 104.9 mhz; 47 kw. 494 ft. TL: N30 35 11 W84 14 11. Stereo. 3000 Olson Rd., Tallahassee 32308. Phone: (850) 386-8004. Fax: (850) 442-1897. Web Site: www.hot1049.com. Licensee: Opus Broadcasting Tallahassee LLC. Group owner: Triad Broadcasting Co. LLC (acq 7-11-2005; grpsl). Rep: McGavren Guild. Format: CHR. Target aud: 18-49. ♦ Chris Knight, gen mgr; Tom Watson, opns mgr.

Hernando

WRZN(AM)— June 1989: 720 khz; 10 kw-D, 250 w-N, DA-N. TL: N28 55 21 W82 22 21. 249 W. University Ave., Suite B, Gainsville 32601. Secondary address: 3938 N. Roscoe Rd. 34442. Phone: (352) 726-7221. Fax: (352) 726-3172. Licensee: Jablomo License Holdings LLC. (group owner; (acq 7-6-2004); grpsl). Format: Adult standards. Target aud: 45 plus. Spec prog: Loc news 4 hrs wkly. ♦ Eric Jewell, gen mgr.

Hialeah

WACC(AM)—Licensed to Hialeah. See Miami

WCMQ-FM— Dec 22, 1969: 92.3 mhz; 31 kw. 617 ft. TL: N25 46 29 W80 11 19. Stereo. 1001 Ponce De Leon Blvd., Coral Gables 33134. Phone: (305) 444-9292. Fax: (305) 461-4466. E-mail: saludos@classica92fm.com. Web Site: www.lamusica.com. Licensee: WCMQ Licensing Inc. Group owner: Spanish Broadcasting System Inc. (acq 12-22-86; grpsl; 9-29-86). Format: Adult contemp, Sp. ♦ Jackie Nosti-Combo, gen mgr; Albert Rodriguez, gen sls mgr; German Estrada, progmg dir.

High Springs

WYGC(FM)—Licensed to High Springs. See Gainesville

Hobe Sound

WOLL(FM)— 2002: 105.5 mhz; 50 kw. Ant 456 ft. TL: N26 45 42 W80 04 42. 3071 Continental Dr., West Palm Beach 33407. Phone: (561) 616-6600. Fax: (561) 616-6677. Web Site: www.1055online.com. Licensee: Clear Channel Broadcasting Licenses Inc. Group owner: Clear Channel Communications Inc. (acq 6-17-98; grpsl). Format: Oldies. Target aud: 25-54. ♦ John Hunt, gen mgr; Dave Denver, opns dir.

Holiday

WSUN-FM— 1979: 97.1 mhz; 3.3 kw. 300 ft. TL: N28 16 51 W82 42 52. Stereo. 11300 4th St. N., Suite 300, St. Petersburg 33716. Phone: (727) 579-2000. Fax: (727) 579-2662. E-mail: 97xcomments@97xonline.com. Web Site: www.97xonline.com. Licensee: Cox Radio Inc. Group owner: Cox Broadcasting (acq 11-20-98). Reddy, Begley & McCormick. Format: Alternative/new rock. Target aud: 35 plus. ♦ Bob Neil, CEO & pres; Jay O'Connor, gen mgr; Paul Ciliano, opns mgr; Keith Lawless, gen sls mgr; Dan Connelly, prom mgr.

Holly Hill

*WAPN(FM)— October 1985: 91.5 mhz; 1.8 kw. 285 ft. TL: N29 15 06 W81 02 53. Stereo. Box 250-311, 1508 State Ave. 32125. Phone: (386) 677-4272. Phone: (386) 672-3333. Fax: (386) 673-3715. E-mail: wapn@wapn.net. Web Site: www.wapn.net. Licensee: Public Radio Capital Florida (acq 5-16-03; $1.5 million). Format: Gospel. Target aud: General. Spec prog: Sp 4 hrs wkly. ♦ Earlyne Lund, gen sls mgr, prom mgr & news dir; Shellye Lund-Vallance, gen mgr & progmg dir.

*WEAZ(FM)— Aug 20, 1999: 88.1 mhz; 5.1 kw vert. 114 ft. TL: N29 16 44 W81 11 25. 1065 Rainer Dr., Altamonte Springs 32714-3847. Phone: (407) 869-8000. E-mail: zcrew@zradio.org. Web Site: www.zradio.org. Licensee: Central Florida Educational Foundation Inc. (acq 6-8-99; $75,000). Format: Contemp Christian. ♦ James Hoge, gen mgr & opns mgr.

WVYB(FM)— 1997: 103.3 mhz; 3 kw. 328 ft. TL: N29 15 05 W81 07 23. (CP: Ant 315 ft.). 126 W. International Speedway Blvd., Daytona Beach 32114. Phone: (386) 257-6900. Fax: (386) 239-0966. Web Site: www.wvyb.fm. Licensee: Black Crow LLC. Group owner: Black Crow Media Group LLC (acq 9-21-2001; grpsl). Format: Hot adult contemp, CHR. News: 2 hrs wkly. Target aud: 18-49. ♦ Stacey Knerler, gen mgr.

Hollywood

WLQY(AM)— April 1953: 1320 khz; 5 kw-U, DA-2. TL: N26 01 53 W80 16 42. 10800 Biscayne Blvd., Suite 810, Miami 33161. Phone: (945) 587-5075. Fax: (305) 891-1583. Web Site: www.entravision.com. Licensee: Entravision Holdings LLC. Group owner: Entravision Communications Corp. (acq 7-28-00; grpsl). Format: Ethnic. Target aud: 35 plus; female. ♦ Jeff Liberman, pres; Rick Santos, gen mgr.

Holmes Beach

WLLD(FM)— Jan 27, 1992: 98.7 mhz; 3 kw. 328 ft. TL: N27 27 49 W82 35 32. Stereo. 9721 Executive Center Dr. N., Suite 200, St. Petersburg 33702-2439. Phone: (727) 579-1925. Fax: (727) 579-8888. E-mail: beata@infinitybroadcasting.com. Web Site: www.wild987.com. Licensee: Infinity Radio Inc. Group owner: Infinity Broadcasting Corp. (acq 11-13-98; grpsl). Network: CNN Radio. Leventhal, Senter & Lerman. Format: CHR. Target aud: 25 plus; professional, educated, upscale audience. Spec prog: Jazz 3 hrs wkly. ♦ Charlie Ochs, gen mgr; Joe Corbett, gen sls mgr; Orlando Davis, progmg dir & mus dir; Ross Block, opns mgr & progmg dir.

Holt

WTKE(FM)—Licensed to Holt. See Fort Walton Beach

Homestead

WOIR(AM)— Nov 4, 1957: 1430 khz; 5 kw-D, 500 w-N, DA-N. TL: N25 27 09 W80 30 57. 13077 S.W. 133rd Ct., Miami 33186. Phone: (305) 969-3884. Fax: (305) 969-3825. Licensee: Amanecer Christian Network Inc. (acq 5-17-2001; $2.58 million). Format: Sp, relg. ♦ Frank Lopez, gen mgr.

*WRGP(FM)— 1999: 88.1 mhz; 165 w. Ant 423 ft. TL: N25 32 24 W80 28 07. Florida International University, 11200 S.W. 8th Ast., University Park Campus GC 319, Miami 33199. Phone: (305) 348-3071. Fax: (305) 348-6665. E-mail: wrgp@fiu.edu. Web Site: www.wrgp.fiu.edu. Licensee: Florida International University. Format: Var. News: 4 hrs wkly. Target aud: General; young adults, mainly university students. Spec prog: Hip hop 12 hrs, news 3 hrs, raggae 3 hrs wkly. ♦ Brennan Forsyth, gen mgr; Susy Vela, prom dir; Jennifer Mojena, progmg dir; Annette Estevill, mus dir; Jackie Diaz, news dir.

Homosassa Springs

WXCV(FM)— March 1983: 95.3 mhz; 6 kw. 328 ft. TL: N28 53 14 W82 31 39. Stereo. 4554 S. Suncoast Blvd. 34446. Phone: (352) 795-9595. Fax: (352) 628-4450. Web Site: www.citrus95radio.com. Licensee: Westwind Broadcasting Inc. Network: ABC Information & Entertainment. Gardner, Carton & Douglas. Format: Adult contemp. News staff: one; News: 7 hrs wkly. Target aud: 25-54. Spec prog: Jazz 7 hrs, oldies 6 hrs wkly. ♦ David Marcocci, gen mgr; Margie McNeal, gen sls mgr.

Immokalee

WAFZ(AM)— Oct 14, 1964: 1490 khz; 1 kw-U. TL: N26 25 27 W81 26 32. 2105 Immokalee Dr. 34142. Phone: (239) 658-1490. Fax: (239) 658-6109. E-mail: robbie@gladesmedia.com. Web Site: www.radiofiesta.com. Licensee: Glades Media Company LLP (acq 8-21-89; $210,000). Format: Regional Mexican, Tejano. ♦ Robbie Castellanos, pres; Gary Holloway, gen mgr, opns mgr & engrg dir.

WAFZ-FM— 1995: 92.1 mhz; 6 kw. 397 ft. TL: N26 21 19 W81 21 03. 2105 Immokalee Dr. 34142. Phone: (239) 658-1490. Fax: (239) 658-6109. E-mail: robbie@gladesmedia.com. Web Site: www.radiofiesta.com. Licensee: Glades Media Co. LLC (acq 5-18-2004). Network: USA. Format: Sp. Target aud: 18 plus; general. ♦ Gary Holloway, gen mgr & opns mgr; Robbie Castellanos, pres & sls dir; Larry Parrish, prom dir.

Indian River Shores

WOSN(FM)— 1996: 97.1 mhz; 6 kw. 328 ft. TL: N27 44 06 W80 27 27. 1235 16th Street, Vero Beach 32960. Phone: (772) 567-0937. Fax: (772) 562-4747. Web Site: www.wosnfm.com. Licensee: Vero Beach

Stations in the U.S.　　　Florida

Developers & Brokers of Radio Properties
contact American Media Services at our suite: Philadelphia Marriott Downtown 215-625-2900
843-972-2200
americanmediaservices.com
Charleston, SC
Dallas, TX · Chicago, Il · Austin, TX
American Media Services, LLC

Broadcasters LLC (group owner; acq 2-15-01; $4.1 million). Format: Adult standards. ♦Jim Davis, gen mgr; Hamp Elliott, progmg dir; Lynne Glass, opns mgr & prom.

Indian Rocks Beach

WPOI(FM)—See Saint Petersburg

WXYB(AM)— May 11, 1963: 1520 khz; 1 kw-D, DA. TL: N27 50 26 W82 46 10. (CP: 600 w. TL: N27 50 45 W82 46 21). 109 Bayview Blvd., Suite A, Oldsmar 34677. Phone: (727) 725-5555. Phone: (813) 814-7575. Fax: (813) 814-7500. E-mail: wpso@wpso.com. Web Site: www.wpso.com. Licensee: ASA Broadcasting Inc. (acq 5-24-93; $31,000; 6-14-93). Format: Ethnic, Greek, news/talk, educ. News: 7 hrs wkly. Target aud: General; international, ethnic. Spec prog: Hillsborough Community College progmg, Indian 3 hrs, Serbian 3 hrs, Colombian 2 hrs, Ger 2 hrs, It 2 hrs, Pol 2 hrs, Chinese one hr, Filipino one hr, East Indian one hr, relg 8 hrs wkly. ♦Sam Agelatos, pres; Angelo Agelatos, gen mgr, stn mgr & opns dir.

Indiantown

WPBZ(FM)— July 4, 1965: 103.1 mhz; 90 kw. 974 ft. TL: N27 01 32 W80 10 43. Stereo. 901 Northpoint Pkwy., Suite 400, West Palm Beach 33407. Phone: (561) 616-4600. Fax: (561) 684-6311. Web Site: www.buzz103.com. Licensee: Infinity Radio Inc. Group owner: Infinity Broadcasting Corp. (acq 12-14-00; grpsl). Rosenman & Colin. Format: Alternative. News staff: one; News: 12 hrs wkly. Target aud: 18-34; men. ♦Lee K. Strasser, gen mgr; John O'Connell, opns dir & progmg dir; Fran Marcone, gen sls mgr; Susan Oland, natl sls mgr; Lynette Shady, prom dir; Nik Rivers, mus dir; Chuck Herlihey, engrg dir & chief of engrg.

Inglis

WIFL(FM)— Oct 1, 1994: 104.3 mhz; 4.4 kw. Ant 380 ft. TL: N29 01 18 W82 41 20. Stereo. 1566 N. Meadowcrest Blvd., Crystal River 34429. Phone: (352) 564-0002. Fax: (352) 564-8750. E-mail: wifl@xtalwind.net. Licensee: Nature Coast Broadcasting Inc. (acq 2-9-2004; $525,000). Gammon & Grange. Format: Mix adult contemp, CHR. News: one hr wkly. Target aud: 25-54. ♦Lisa Cuppelli, CEO, gen mgr & stn mgr; Sab Cupelli, pres; Jon Kay, opns mgr; Jeremy Howard, gen sls mgr.

Inverness

*WJUF(FM)— Oct 1, 1995: 90.1 mhz; 4.5 kw. 354 ft. TL: N28 52 09 W82 26 47. c/o WUFT-FM, 2206 Weimer Hall, Univ. of Florida, Gainesville 32611. Phone: (352) 392-5200. Fax: (352) 392-5741. E-mail: info@wuft.org. Web Site: www.wuft.org. Licensee: Board of Trustees, University of Florida. (acq 10-14-94; 12-5-94). Network: NPR. Schwartz, Woods & Miller. Format: Classic rock, jazz, pub affrs. News staff: 3; News: 15 hrs wkly. Target aud: General. Spec prog: Gospel one hr wkly. ♦Richard A. Lehner, gen mgr; Henri Pensis, stn mgr; Steve Seipp, opns mgr; Brent Williams, dev dir. Co-owned TV: *WUFT-TV affil.

Jacksonville

WAPE-FM— April 1949: 95.1 mhz; 100 kw. 460 ft. TL: N30 17 09 W81 44 52. Stereo. 8000 Belfort Pkwy, 32256. Phone: (904) 245-8500. Fax: (904) 245-8501. E-mail: contest@wape951.com. Web Site: www.wape951.com. Licensee: Cox Radio Inc. Group owner: Cox Broadcasting (acq 8-00; grpsl). Rep: Christal. Format: CHR. ♦Dick Williams, gen mgr; Cat Thomas, progmg dir.

WAYR(AM)—See Orange Park

WBWL(AM)— Dec 9, 1933: 600 khz; 5 kw-D, 5.4 kw-N, DA-N. TL: N30 18 00 W81 45 34. 10245 Centurion Pkwy., Suite 109 32256. Phone: (904) 783-3711. Fax: (904) 646-1117. Web Site: www.radiodisney.com. Licensee: Radio Disney Group LLC. Group owner: ABC Inc. (acq 8-1-02; $2.5 million). Network: Radio Disney

Format: Children. ♦Jean-Paul Coloco, pres; Jean-Paul Colaco, gen mgr; Jay Schneider, stn mgr; Sarah Stone, mktg VP; Robin Jones, progmg VP.

WCGL(AM)— 1948: 1360 khz; 5 kw-D. TL: N30 16 33 W81 38 12. 6050-6 Moncrief Rd. 32209. Phone: (904) 766-9955. Fax: (904) 765-9214. E-mail: info@wcgl1360.com. Web Site: www.wcgl1360.com. Licensee: JBD Communications Inc. (acq 12-27-89; $510,000; 1-15-90). Pepper & Corazzini. Format: Relg. Target aud: 25 plus. ♦Deborah Maiden, pres & gen mgr; Kelvin Postell, opns mgr.

*WCRJ(FM)— Mar 16, 1984: 88.1 mhz; 8 kw. Ant 495 ft. TL: N30 16 34 W81 33 53. Stereo. 2361 Cortez Rd. 32246. Phone: (904) 641-9626. Fax: (904) 645-9626. E-mail: calvin@fm88.org. Web Site: www.riverradio.org. Licensee: New Covenant Educational Ministries Inc. Network: Christian contemp. ♦Henry Hoot, VP; Calvin Grabau, gen mgr & opns mgr.

WEJZ(FM)— 1949: 96.1 mhz; 100 kw. 984 ft. TL: N30 19 22 W81 38 34. Stereo. 6440 Atlantic Blvd. 32211. Phone: (904) 727-9696. Fax: (904) 721-9322. Web Site: www.wejz.com. Licensee: Renda Broadcasting Corp. (group owner; acq 6-90; grpsl; 6-25-90). Rep: McGavren Guild. Format: Soft adult contemp. Target aud: 25-54; office, home & in-the-car audience. ♦Tony Renda Sr., CEO & pres; Bill Scull, gen mgr.

WFXJ(AM)— November 1925: 930 khz; 5 kw-U, DA-N. TL: N30 17 09 W81 44 52. 11700 Central Pkwy 32224-2600. Phone: (904) 636-0507. Phone: (904) 642-3030. Fax: (904) 997-7713. E-mail: victoriagowan @clearchannel.com. Web Site: www.930thefox.com. Licensee: Clear Channel Radio Licenses Inc. Group owner: Clear Channel Communications Inc. Format: Sports. Target aud: 25-49; men. ♦Norm Feuer, gen mgr; Gail Austin, opns mgr; Victoria Gowan, gen sls mgr.

WIOJ(AM)—See Jacksonville Beach

WJAX(AM)—Listing follows WKTZ-FM.

WJBT(FM)—See Green Cove Springs

*WJCT-FM— Apr 17, 1972: 89.9 mhz; 100 kw. 835 ft. TL: N30 16 53 W81 34 15. Stereo. 100 Festival Park Ave. 32202. Phone: (904) 353-7770. Fax: (904) 358-6352. E-mail: info@wjct.org. Web Site: www.wjct.org. Licensee: WJCT Inc. Network: Network: NPR, PRI. Schwartz, Woods & Miller. Format: Class, news/talk. ♦Michael Boylan, CEO & pres; Tom Patton, stn mgr. Co-owned TV: *WJCT-TV affil.

*WJFR(FM)— Sept 15, 1987: 88.7 mhz; 8 kw. 380 ft. TL: N30 16 53 W81 34 15. Stereo. Box 40345 32203. Phone: (510) 568-6200. Fax: (510) 633-7983. Web Site: www.familyradio.com. Licensee: Family Stations Inc. Format: Relg. Target aud: Conservative Christians. ♦Harold Camping, pres; Harold Camping, gen mgr; Marcy Morrison-Pearce, progmg dir & news dir; Phyllis Johnston, mus dir.

WJGL(FM)—Listing follows WOKV(AM).

WJGR(AM)— 1945: 1320 khz; 5 kw-U, DA-N. TL: N30 17 50 W81 44 35. Stereo. 4190 Belfort Rd., Suite 450 32216. Phone: (904) 470-4615. Fax: (904) 470-4646. Web Site: www.1320thepatriotr.com. Licensee: Caron Broadcasting Inc. Group owner: Salem Communications Corp. (acq 5-30-03; grpsl). Network: ABC Daytime Direction. Format: News/talk. Target aud: 25-54. ♦Edward Atsinger, CEO & pres; Steve Griffin, gen mgr; Steve Fox, opns mgr.

WJXR(FM)— (Macclenny). September 1978: 92.1 mhz; 25 kw. 328 ft. TL: N30 17 54 W82 00 55. Stereo. Box One 32234. Phone: (904) 772-7200. Phone: (904) 358-2265. Fax: (904) 772-0004. Fax: (904) 259-4488. Web Site: www.wjxr.com. Licensee: WJXR Inc. (acq 1-8-85; $335,000; 2-4-85). Network: ABC Daytime Direction. Rothman, Gordon, Foreman & Groudine. Format: Talk. News staff: one; News: 7 hrs wkly. Target aud: 25-54; middle class & upscale families. ♦Gregory G. Perich, CEO, pres, gen mgr, stn mgr, opns mgr & sls VP.

*WKTZ-FM— Feb 8, 1973: 90.9 mhz; 50 kw. Ant 500 ft. TL: N30 16 36 W81 33 47. Stereo. 5353 Arlington Expwy. 32211. Phone: (904) 743-1122. Web Site: www.wktz.jones.edu. Licensee: Jones College. (acq 2-7-86). Network: AP Radio. Format: Easy listening/smooth jazz. Target aud: 40 plus; mature adults. ♦Kenneth Jones, gen mgr, gen sls mgr & prom dir; Tom Buetow, mus dir; Dick Jones, chief of engrg.

WJAX(AM)—Co-owned with WKTZ-FM. 1958: 1220 khz; 1 kw-D, 37 w-N. TL: N30 19 30 W81 34 15. Web Site: www.wjax.jones.edu. Network: CNN Radio. Format: Swing mus. Target aud: 40 plus.

WMXQ(FM)— November 1965: 102.9 mhz; 100 kw. 984 ft. TL: N30 16 34 W81 33 53. Stereo. 8000 Belfort Pky. 32256. Phone: (904) 783-3711. E-mail: thepoint@10291.com. Web Site: www.1029i.com. Licensee: Cox Radio Inc. Group owner: Cox Communications Inc. (acq 2-23-00; grpsl). Rep: Christal. Format: Adult contemp. News staff: one; News: 7 hrs wkly. Target aud: 25-49. Spec prog: Jazz 4 hrs wkly. ♦Dick Williams, gen mgr.

WNNR(AM)— Jan 1, 1969: 970 khz; 1 kw-U, DA-1. TL: N30 23 08 W81 40 04. 8384 Bay Meadow Rd., Suite 1 32256. Phone: (904) 739-3660. Fax: (904) 739-9409. Web Site: www.970thewinner.com. Licensee: Norsan Consulting and Management Inc. (acq 6-1-2005; $2.1 million with WVOJ(AM) Fernandina Beach). Format: Sports. Target aud: General. ♦Norberto Sanchez, pres; Bernie Daigle, gen mgr & stn mgr; Colleen Kogos, gen sls mgr; Gary Murphy, progmg dir & chief of engrg; Marci Koziolek, news dir & pub affrs dir.

WOKV(AM)— November 1925: 690 khz; 50 kw-D, 10 w-N, DA-N. TL: N30 18 27 W81 56 28. 8000 Belfort Pkwy. 32206. Phone: (904) 245-8500. Fax: (904) 245-8501. E-mail: wokv.news@cox.com. Web Site: www.wokv.com. Licensee: Cox Radio Inc. Group owner: Cox Broadcasting (acq 2-28-2000; grpsl). Network: CBS. Cohn & Marks. Format: News/talk. ♦Dick Williams, gen mgr; Cat Thomas, opns mgr; Lindley Tolbert, sls dir; Allison Misora, prom dir; Mike Dorwart, progmg dir; Roxy Tyler, pub affrs dir; Dick Jones, engrg dir.

WJGL(FM)—Co-owned with WOKV(AM). July 1, 1969: 96.9 mhz; 98 kw. Ant 1,014 ft. TL: N30 16 34 W81 33 53. Stereo. Web Site: www.cool969.com. Format: Oldies. News staff: one. Target aud: 25-54. ♦Scott Walker, progmg dir.

WPLA(FM)—(Callahan). June 1, 1983: 93.3 mhz; 50 kw. 462 ft. TL: N30 33 22 W81 33 13. Stereo. 11700 Central Pkwy. 32224. Phone: (904) 636-0507. Fax: (904) 997-7713. E-mail: rhondagroff @clearchannel.com. Web Site: www.planetradio933.com. Licensee: Clear Channel Radio Licenses Inc. Group owner: Clear Channel Communications Inc. (acq 11-21-97; grpsl). Format: Alternative. Target aud: 18-45. ♦Norm Feuer, gen mgr; Gail Austin, opns dir; Chad Chumley, progmg dir.

WQIK-FM— September 1964: 99.1 mhz; 100 kw. 1,050 ft. TL: N30 16 34 W81 33 53. Stereo. Norm Feuer, 11700 Central Pkwy. 32224. Phone: (904) 642-3030. Fax: (904) 997-7707. E-mail: tanderson@ccjax.com. Web Site: www.wqik.com. Licensee: Citicasters Licenses L.P. Group owner: Clear Channel Communications Inc. (acq 5-4-99; grpsl). Network: ABC. Format: Country. News staff: one; News: 4 hrs wkly. Target aud: 18-54. ♦John Hogan, sr VP; Norm Feuer, gen mgr; Gail Austin, opns dir & progmg dir; Tony Anderson, prom dir.

WROO(FM)— May 9, 1977: 107.3 mhz; 100 kw. 705 ft. TL: N30 21 48 W81 45 09. Stereo. 11700 Central Pkwy 32224-2600. Phone: (904) 636-0507. Fax: (904) 997-7713. Web Site: www.roostercountry1073.com. Licensee: Clear Channel Radio Licenses Inc. Group owner: Clear Channel Communications Inc. (acq 11-21-97; grpsl). Rep: Clear Channel. Format: Country. News staff: one. Target aud: 25-49. Spec prog: Relg 2 hrs wkly. ♦Norm Feuer, gen mgr; Gail Austin, opns mgr. Co-owned TV: WAWS-TV affil

WROS(AM)— July 1955: 1050 khz; 5 kw-D, DA. TL: N30 21 14 W81 44 21. 5590 Rio Grande Ave. 32254. Phone: (904) 353-1050. Fax: (904) 353-7076. E-mail: wros@wros.net. Web Site: www.wros.net. Licensee: The Rose of Jacksonville (acq 6-1-85; FTR: 4-1-85).

Broadcasting & Cable Yearbook 2006

Format: Family oriented, Christian. Target aud: 25-65; Christians & secular. ♦Dean Hall, exec VP; Elwyn V. Hall, CEO, pres & gen mgr; Dean Hall, opns VP.

WSOL-FM—(Brunswick).GA Sept 1, 1966: 101.5 mhz; 100 kw. 239 ft. TL: N31 08 40 W81 34 56. (CP: Ant 1,463 ft.). Stereo. 11700 Central Pkwy. 32224. Phone: (904) 996-0400. Fax: (904) 997-7713. E-mail: lisa@v1015.com. Web Site: www.v1015.com. Licensee: Citicasters Licenses L.P. Group owner: Clear Channel Communications Inc. (acq 5-4-99; grpsl). Format: Adult urban contemp. ♦Norm Fever, gen mgr.

WYMM(AM)— Nov 18, 1976: 1530 khz; 50 kw-D, DA. TL: N30 21 50 W81 44 54. 5900 Pickettville Rd. 32254. Phone: (904) 786-2820. Fax: (904) 786-2661. Licensee: Word Broadcasting Network Inc. (group owner; (acq 7-29-2003; $1.25 million. with WYRM(AM) Norfolk, VA). Format: Talk. ♦Raymond Burkhart, gen mgr.

WZAZ(AM)— July 4, 1950: 1400 khz; 1 kw-U. TL: N30 19 43 W81 41 42. Stereo. 4190 Belfort Rd., Suite 450 32216. Phone: (904) 470-4615. Fax: (904) 296-1683. Web Site: www.1400wzaz.com. Licensee: Caron Broadcasting Inc. Group owner: Salem Communications Corp. (acq 5-30-03; grpsl). Rep: Roslin. Format: Gospel. News staff: 2; News: 5 hrs wkly. Target aud: 25-54; adult Black listeners. ♦Edward G. Atsinger, CEO & pres; Steve Griffin, gen mgr; Octavius Davis, progmg dir.

WZNZ(AM)— August 1942: 1460 khz; 5 kw-U, DA-N. TL: N30 19 40 W81 44 49. Stereo. 4190 Belfort Rd., Suite 450 32216. Phone: (904) 470-4615. Fax: (904) 296-1683. Web Site: www.espn1560.com. Licensee: Caron Broadcasting Inc. Group owner: Salem Communications Corp. (acq 5-30-03; grpsl). Rep: Clear Channel. Format: Sports. Target aud: 25-54. ♦Edward G. Atsinger, CEO & pres; Steve Griffin, gen mgr; Chris Wayne, progmg dir.

Jacksonville Beach

WIOJ(AM)— 1946: 1010 khz; 10 kw-D, 143 w-N, DA-2. TL: N30 17 21 W81 33 01. 10055 Beach Blvd., Jacksonville 32246. Phone: (904) 641-1010. Fax: (904) 641-1022. E-mail: wioj@wioj.net. Web Site: www.wioj.net. Licensee: McEntee Broadcasting of Florida Inc. (acq 4-1-96). Network: Network: Salem Radio Network, USA. Garvey, Schubert & Barer. Format: Variety & talk. News staff: one; News: 5 hrs wkly. Target aud: 25 plus; adult Christian. Spec prog: Black. ♦William McEntee Jr., CEO & pres; Marion Luther, gen mgr.

Jensen Beach

WMBX(FM)— Dec 10, 1980: 102.3 mhz; 100 kw. 974 ft. TL: N27 01 32 W80 10 43. (CP: 100 kw). Stereo. 901 Northpoint Pkwy., Suite 400, West Palm Beach 33407. Phone: (561) 616-4600. Fax: (561) 684-6311. Web Site: www.mix1023.com. Licensee: Infinity Radio Operations Inc. Group owner: Infinity Broadcasting Corp. (acq 12-14-00; grpsl). Rosenman & Colin. Format: Modern adult contemp. News staff: one; News: 17 hrs wkly. Target aud: 25-54; women. ♦Patricia A. Larschan, VP & gen mgr; John O'Connell, opns mgr & progmg dir; Mark Krieger, gen sls mgr & natl sls mgr; Danelle Sarvas, prom mgr; Jeff Clarke, mus dir; Pam Crosby, news dir & pub affrs dir; Scott Paxson, chief of engrg.

Jupiter

WJBW(AM)— 1997: 1000 khz; 650 w-D, DA. TL: N26 56 40 W80 05 30. 6600 N. Andrews Ave., Suite 160, Fort Lauderdale 33309. Phone: (954) 315-1515. Fax: (954) 315-1555. Licensee: James Crystal Jupiter Inc. Group owner: James Crystal Inc. (acq 2-3-03; $1.55 million. with WDJA(AM) Delray Beach). Format: News/talk. ♦James C. Hilliard, pres; Steve Lapa, gen mgr.

WJBW-FM— Oct 15, 1971: 106.3 mhz; 19 kw. Ant 374 ft. TL: N26 47 59 W80 04 33. 701 Northpoint Pkwy., Suite 500, West Palm Beach 33407. Phone: (561) 684-7400. Fax: (561) 686-9505. Web Site: www.infinityradio.com. Licensee: Infinity Radio Inc. Group owner: Infinity Broadcasting Corp. (acq 8-30-01; $20 million). Format: Urban adult contemp. ♦Lee Strasser, gen mgr; Mark McCray, opns mgr.

Kendall

WRHB(AM)— August 1999: 1020 khz; 8.9 kw-D, 980 w-N, DA-2. TL: N25 37 09 W80 31 00. 2828 Coral Way, Suite 110, Miami 33145. Phone: (305) 446-5444. Fax: (305) 446-1009. Web Site: www.radiocarnivale.com/wrhb. Licensee: New World Broadcasting Inc. (acq 12-20-01; $260,000. for stock for 52%). Format: Creole progmg. Target aud: 25-55; adult. ♦Mervyn Moore, gen mgr.

Key Colony Beach

WKYZ(FM)— April 15, 1999: 101.3 mhz; 50 kw. 276 ft. TL: N24 41 30 W81 06 31. Box 500940, Marathon 33050. Phone: (305) 289-1013. Fax: (305) 743-9441. Licensee: Keys Media Co. Inc. Format: Classic Rock. Target aud: 25-54. ♦Joe Nascone, gen mgr.

Key Largo

***WGES(FM)**— 2004: 90.9 mhz; 33 kw. Ant 308 ft. TL: N25 14 07 W80 19 35. Box 820814, South Florida 33082-0814. Phone: (305) 551-6590. Fax: (305) 551-2737. Licensee: Genesis Broadcasting Network Corp. Format: Christian, Sp. ♦Edwin Lemuel Ortiz, pres; Kenny Reyes, gen mgr.

***WMKL(FM)**— Oct 1, 1998: 91.7 mhz; 50 kw. Ant 308 ft. TL: N25 14 07 W80 19 35. Stereo. Box 561832, Miami 33256-1832. Phone: (305) 662-7736. Fax: (305) 251-2293. E-mail: callfm@callfm.com. Web Site: www.callfm.com. Licensee: Call Communications Group Inc. (acq 11-4-99; $295,000). Gammon & Grange. Format: Christian. Target aud: 13-25. ♦Robert Robbins, pres & gen mgr; Kelly Downing, dev dir & mus dir; Jim Sorensen, chief of engrg.

WZMQ(FM)— Jan 20, 1990: 106.3 mhz; 6 kw. 150 ft. TL: N25 05 29 W80 26 37. (CP: 50 kw, ant 239 ft. TL: N21 01 35 W80 30 30). Stereo. 1001 Ponce De Leon Blvd., Coral Gables 33134. Phone: (305) 444-9292. Fax: (305) 461-4466. Licensee: South Broadcasting System Inc. (acq 1-27-00; $1 million. with WMFM(FM) Key West). Format: Adult contemp, Sp. ♦Raul Alarcon Jr., pres; Maria Llansa, gen mgr; Victor Aleman, stn mgr; Madeline Rodriquez, gen sls mgr; Thomas Garcia Fuste, news dir; Ralph Chambers, chief of engrg.

Key West

WAIL(FM)— December 1978: 99.5 mhz; 100 kw. 991 ft. TL: N24 39 25 W81 32 18. (CP: Ant 239 ft.). Stereo. 5450 McDonald Ave, Suite 10 33040. Phone: (305) 296-7511. Fax: (305) 296-0358. E-mail: kenmackenzie@clearchannel.com. Web Site: www.wail995.com. Licensee: Clear Channel Radio Licenses Inc. Group owner: Clear Channel Communications Inc. (acq 6-5-98; $2.6 million with WEOW(FM) Key West). Format: Classic rock. Target aud: 25-54; men. ♦Dave Harris, VP, gen mgr & gen mgr; Sherry Russo, stn mgr; Ken MacKenzie, opns dir.

***WAVQ(FM)**— June 1, 2005: 88.3 mhz; 180 w. Ant 110 ft. TL: N24 33 07 W81 47 53. 6910 N.W. 2nd Terr., Boca Raton 33487. Phone: (561) 912-9002. Licensee: Educational Public Radio Inc.

WCNK(FM)— January 1986: 98.7 mhz; 100 kw. 300 ft. TL: N24 34 42 W81 44 49. Stereo. 30336 Overseas Hwy., Big Pine Key 33043. Phone: (305) 872-0474. Fax: (305) 872-8930. Licensee: Vox Communications Group LLC. (acq 7-28-2005; grpsl). Format: Smooth jazz. News: one hr wkly. Target aud: 24-55; military, baby boomers & largest income holders. Spec prog: Armed Forces news one hr wkly. ♦Ken Barlow, gen mgr & stn mgr.

WEOW(FM)— February 1967: 92.7 mhz; 100 kw. Ant 551 ft. TL: N24 40 35 W81 30 41. Stereo. 5450 MacDonald Ave., Suite 10 33040. Phone: (305) 296-7511. Fax: (305) 296-0358. E-mail: kenmackenzie@clearchannel.com. Web Site: www.weow927.com. Licensee: Clear Channel Radio Licenses Inc. Group owner: Clear Channel Communications Inc. (acq 6-5-98; $2.6 million with WAIL(FM) Key West). Format: CHR, Top-40. ♦Lowery Mays, pres; Dave Harris, VP & gen mgr; Ken Mackenzie, opns mgr & progmg dir; Sherry Russo, stn mgr & sls dir.

WIIS(FM)— June 1978: 107.1 mhz; 3 kw. 200 ft. TL: N24 33 18 W81 48 07. Stereo. 1075 Duval St., Suite C-17 33040. Phone: (305) 292-1133. Phone: (305) 292-1071. Fax: (305) 292-6936. E-mail: johnrussin@hotmail.com. Web Site: www.island107.com. Licensee: The Keyed Up Communications Co. (acq 1995; $275,000). Fletcher, Heald & Hildreth. Format: Alternative. News staff: one; News: 5 hrs wkly. Target aud: 18-44; young, educated, active spenders for goods & services. Spec prog: Reggae 4 hrs, Metropolitan opera 4 hrs wkly. ♦John Russin, CEO & sls dir; Linda Russin, COO; Linda Hamlin, mktg dir; Vinnie Montalto, mus dir; Jerry Coleman, pub affrs dir; Kirk Sheldon, chief of engrg.

***WJIR(FM)**— December 1986: 90.9 mhz; 390 w. 121 ft. TL: N24 33 07 W81 47 53. (CP: 3 kw, ant 105 ft.). Stereo. 1209 United St. 33040. Phone: (305) 294-9547. Fax: (305) 294-9547. E-mail: info@sosradio.net. Web Site: www.sossnetwork.org. Licensee: Key West Educational Broadcasting. (acq 12-15-85). Format: Relg, educ, Christian. News: 12 hrs wkly. Target aud: General. ♦Ernie DeLoach, stn mgr & opns mgr.

WKEY-FM— Nov 17, 1985: 93.5 mhz; 32 kw. Ant 138 ft. TL: N24 34 17 W81 44 25. Stereo. 5450 MacDonald Ave. 33040. Phone: (305) 296-7511. Fax: (305) 296-1155. E-mail: kenmackenzie@clearchannel.com. Web Site: www.key93.com. Licensee: Clear Channel Broadcasting Licenses Inc. Group owner: Clear Channel Communications Inc. (acq 11-21-97; grpsl). Rep: Clear Channel. Format: Adult contemp. News staff: one; News: 8 hrs wkly. Target aud: 25-54; affluent, upscale, culturally supportive. Spec prog: Classical 4 hrs, jazz 4 hrs, Sp 3 hrs wkly. ♦David Harris, gen mgr; John Stuempfig, prom dir; Sherry Russo, stn mgr, gen sls mgr & adv mgr.

WKIZ(AM)— Feb 2, 1959: 1500 khz; 250 w-U, DA-1. TL: N24 34 01 W81 44 54. Stereo. 5016 Fifth Ave. 33040. Phone: (305) 293-9536. Fax: (305) 293-1793. E-mail: wkizradio@aol.com. Web Site: www.wkizradio.com. Licensee: Seattle Streaming Radio L.L.C. Network: CBS. Format: News/talk. ♦David Drucker, pres; Jacques Combeau, gen mgr & progmg dir; Oscar Ibarra, sls dir; Drew Lassiter, chief of engrg.

WKWF(AM)— October 1945: 1600 khz; 500 w-U. TL: N24 34 30 W81 44 01. 5450 MacDonald Ave., Ste. 10 33040. Phone: (305) 296-7511. Fax: (305) 296-0358. E-mail: Toddswofford@clearchannel.com. Web Site: www.keysradio.com. Licensee: Spottswood Partners II Ltd. (acq 10-27-97; with co-located FM). Format: Prime sports. ♦Dave Harris, VP; Dave Harris, gen mgr; Sherry Russo, stn mgr & sls dir; Todd Swofford, progmg dir.

***WKWR(FM)**—Not on air, target date: unknown: 90.1 mhz; 25 kw. Ant 102 ft. TL: N24 34 10 W81 45 09. Broadcasting for the Challenged Inc., 6080 Mount Moriah Ext., Memphis, TN 38115. Phone: (901) 375-9324. Fax: (901) 375-0041. Licensee: Broadcasting for the Challenged Inc. ♦George Flinn Jr., gen mgr.

WMFM(FM)— 1995: 107.9 mhz; 100 kw. 548 ft. TL: N24 39 08 W81 32 04. 1001 Ponce de Leon Blvd., Coral Gables 33134. Phone: (305) 447-9595. Fax: (305) 461-4466. Licensee: South Broadcasting System Inc. (acq 1-27-00; $1million with WZMQ(FM) Key Largo). Format: Sp. ♦Jackie Nosti Combo, gen mgr; Albert Rodriguez, gen sls mgr.

Kissimmee

WHOO(AM)— April 1965: 1080 khz; 10 kw-D, DA. TL: N28 20 35 W81 20 22. (CP: 19 kw-D, 10 kw-CH, DA-2). 1160 S Semoran Blvd., Suite B, Orlando 32807. Phone: (407) 380-9255. Fax: (407) 382-7565. E-mail: studio@espn1080.com. Web Site: www.espn1080.com. Licensee: Genesis Communications I Inc. Group owner: Genesis Communications Inc. (acq 10-19-99). Network: ESPN Radio. Rep: Interep. Booth, Freret, Imlay & Tepper. Format: Sports talk. Target aud: 25-54; men. Spec prog: Creole 2 hrs wkly. ♦Bruce Maduri, pres; Don Childress, sr VP; Sandra Culver, VP; Jeff Taylor, opns mgr; Joe Nichols, gen sls mgr; Chris Visser, progmg VP.

***WLAZ(FM)**— 2000: 89.1 mhz; 1.1 kw vert. Ant 535 ft. TL: N28 10 27 W81 17 01. 415 W. Vine St. 34741. Phone: (407) 518-7150. Fax: (407) 518-0062. E-mail: contacto@gensis89.com. Web Site: www.genesis89.net. Licensee: Caguas Educational TV Inc. (acq 5-3-02; $1.5 million). James L. Oyster. Format: Christian, Sp. News staff: 2; News: 10 hrs wkly. ♦Rodolfo Font Ruiz, pres; Ricky Rosado, sr VP.

WOTS(AM)— Oct 23, 1978: 1220 khz; 1 kw-D. TL: N28 19 27 W81 23 44. 222 Hazard St., Orlando 32804-3030. Phone: (407) 841-8282. Fax: (407) 841-8250. Licensee: J&V Communications Inc. (group owner; acq 1-12-99). Leibowitz & Associates. Format: Sp, relg. News staff: one. Tourists. Spec prog: Imus in the Morning. ♦John Torrado, CEO, pres, gen mgr & progmg dir; Frank Vaught, opns mgr & mktg dir; Homan Machuca, prom mgr & news dir; Lou Mueller, chief of engrg.

La Belle

***WBIY(FM)**— 1999: 88.3 mhz; 3 kw. Ant 161 ft. TL: N26 44 26 W81 27 46. c/o WJYO(FM), Box 61721, Fort Myers 33906. Phone: (239) 275-9785. Fax: (239) 275-3112. Web Site: www.kingdom.fm. Licensee: Airwaves for Jesus Inc. (acq 1-23-2004; $500,000. with WJYO(FM) Fort Myers). Format: Contemp Christian. ♦Art Ramos, pres.

Stations in the U.S. Florida

La Crosse

WBXY(FM)— October 1993: 99.5 mhz; 2.2 kw. 472 ft. TL: N29 44 22 W82 23 09. Stereo. 4424 N.W.13th St., Gainesville 32609. Phone: (352) 372-3700. Fax: (352) 375-6961. E-mail: star99@thestar.com. Web Site: www.thestar.fm. Licensee: Asterisk Communications Inc. (acq 7-23-98; $1.15 million). Network: Westwood One. Format: Oldies. Target aud: 25-54; primarily baby boomers-upscale. ♦ John Starr, gen mgr.

Lafayette

WEGT(FM)—Licensed to Lafayette. See Tallahassee

Lake City

WDSR(AM)— May 6, 1946: 1340 khz; 1 kw-U. TL: N30 09 20 W82 38 14. Box 3299 32056. Secondary address: 3507 S. Marion St. 32055. Phone: (386) 752-1340. Phone: (386) 961-9494. Fax: (386) 755-9369. E-mail: wnfb@mix943.com. Web Site: www.mix943.com. Licensee: Newman Media Inc. (acq 9-3-98; $750,000 with co-located FM). Network: CBS. Florida's Radio Net. Format: Sports. Target aud: 18-54; upscale males. Spec prog: Black 2 hrs wkly. ♦ John R. Newman, pres, gen mgr & gen sls mgr; Ryan Walker, progmg dir; Barry Cole, chief of engrg.

WNFB(FM)—Co-owned with WDSR(AM). May 28, 1969: 94.3 mhz; 50 kw. 492 ft. TL: N30 07 44 W82 52 49. Stereo. Format: Adult contemp. ♦ Cesta Newman, VP; John Newman, stn mgr; Steve Johnson, sls dir.

WGRO(AM)— Nov 14, 1958: 960 khz; 500 w-D, 1 kw-N, DA-N. TL: N30 11 47 W82 40 48. (CP: 1 kw-U, DA-N). 820 N.W. Frontier Dr. 32055. Phone: (386) 755-4102. Fax: (386) 752-9861. E-mail: bandk@ISgroup.net. Licensee: Power Country Inc. (acq 9-20-95). Format: Nostalgia. ♦ Louis Bolton II, pres; Bob Hendrickson, gen mgr.

*WOLR(FM)— Sept 11, 1986: 91.3 mhz; 18 kw vert. 285 ft. TL: N30 02 56 W82 48 44. 3332 220th Pl. 32024. Phone: (386) 935-3300. Fax: (386) 935-2684. Web Site: www.christianhitradio.net. Licensee: WOLR 91.3 FM Inc. (acq 6-25-93; $75,000; 7-19-93). Format: Christian. ♦ Rita Loos, gen mgr; Shane Stanton, chief of engrg.

Lake Placid

WWTK(AM)— 1989: 730 khz; 500 w-D, 340 w-N, DA-1. TL: N27 24 25 W81 25 56. 3750 U.S. 27 N., Suite One, Sebring 33870. Phone: (863) 382-9999. Fax: (863) 382-1982. E-mail: cohanradiogroup@htn.net. Web Site: www.cohanradiogroup.com. Licensee: Cohan Radio Group Inc. (group owner; (acq 11-1-98; $910,000. with WWOJ(FM) Avon Park). Network: Network: Network: ABC News/Talk, USA, Premiere Focus, CBS Radio. Interep Latham & Watkins. Format: Talk. News staff: one; News: 120 hrs wkly. Target aud: 35+. Spec prog: U of Fla Football & Basketball Sports Show 1 hr. per wk Sat 12n-1pm; Rel Su 6-11am; Local Talk Show M-F 8-10am. ♦ Peter L. Coughlin, pres & gen sls mgr; Michael Taylor, opns dir; Libby Coughlin, rgnl sls mgr; Barry Foster, news dir; Phil Scott, chief of engrg.

Lake Wales

WIPC(AM)— July 1951: 1280 khz; 1 kw-D, 500 w-N, DA-N. TL: N27 55 34 W81 36 04 (D), N27 55 30 W81 36 16 (N). 630 Mountain Lake Cut/Off Rd., Suite A 33859. Phone: (863) 679-7178. Fax: (863) 679-9395. E-mail: wipc1280@yahoo.com. Licensee: Siber Media Group Inc. (acq 4-30-02; $73,000). Donald E. Martin. Format: Sp. News staff: one; News: 10 hrs wkly. Target aud: 18+ Hispanics. ♦ Carl Czuchaj, VP, opns mgr & gen sls mgr; Robert Cubero, pres & gen mgr; Edward Olivares, progmg dir; Agustin E. Olivares, mus dir.

Lake Worth

WWRF(AM)— May 1, 1959: 1380 khz; 1 kw-D, 500 w-N. TL: N26 37 23 W80 04 20. 2326 S. Congress Ave., Suite 2A, W. Palm Beach 33406-7614. Phone: (561) 585-1380. Phone: (561) 721-9950. Fax: (561) 721-9973. E-mail: jesus@gladesmedia.com. Web Site: www.radiofiesta.com. Licensee: Radio Fiesta Inc. (acq 2-24-00; $400,000). Network: CNN en Espanol. Format: Regional Mexican. News staff: one. Target aud: 25-54; Hispanic. Spec prog: Sp relg 4 hrs wkly. ♦ Jesus Lobo, pres & gen mgr; Robbie Castellanos, pres & stn mgr.

Lakeland

*WKES(FM)— May 20, 1975: 91.1 mhz; 100 kw. 500 ft. TL: N28 04 46 W82 02 27. (CP: 420 ft.). Stereo. 5800 100th Way N., St. Petersburg 33708. Phone: (727) 391-9994. Fax: (727) 397-6425. E-mail: wkesmovingon@hotmail.com. Web Site: www.wkes.org. Licensee: The Moody Bible Institute of Chicago. (group owner; acq 10-10-96; $5 million). Southmayd & Miller. Format: Relg, educ. ♦ Dr. Joseph Stowell III, pres; Michael Gleichman, opns mgr & pub affrs dir; Pierre Chestang, stn mgr & progmg dir; John Stoltz, chief of engrg.

WLKF(AM)— 1936: 1430 khz; 5 kw-D, 1 kw-N. TL: N28 02 27 W81 56 08. Box 2038 33815. Secondary address: 404 W. Lime St. 33815-4651. Phone: (863) 682-8184. Fax: (863) 683-2409. E-mail: talk1430@wlkf.com. Web Site: www.wlkf.com. Licensee: Hall Communications Ltd. Group owner: Hall Communications Inc. (acq 10-1-96; $550,000). Rep: D & R Radio. Fletcher, Heald & Hildreth. Format: News/talk. News: 15 hrs wkly. Target aud: 35 plus; middle to upper income adults. ♦ Bonnie H. Rowbotham, chmn; Arthur J. Rowbotham, pres; Bill Baldwin, sr VP; Steve Howard, stn mgr.

WONN(AM)— Sept 15, 1949: 1230 khz; 1 kw-U. TL: N28 02 23 W81 57 39. Stereo. Box 2038 33806. Secondary address: 404 W. Lime St. 33815-4651. Phone: (863) 682-8184. Phone: (407) 297-1201. Fax: (863) 683-2409. E-mail: wonn@wonn.com. Web Site: www.wonn.com. Licensee: Hall Communications Inc. (group owner; acq 10-1-81; $2 million with co-located FM; 8-10-81). Network: CNN Radio. Rep: D & R Radio. Fletcher, Heald & Hildreth. Format: MOR. News: 20 hrs wkly. Target aud: 35 plus. Spec prog: Relg 2 hrs wkly. ♦ Bonnie H. Rowbotham, chmn; Arthur J. Rowbotham, pres & gen mgr; Bill Baldwin, sr VP; Steve Howard, stn mgr.

WPCV(FM)—Co-owned with WONN(AM). 1962: 97.5 mhz; 100 kw. 1,017 ft. TL: N28 07 35 W81 33 03. Stereo. E-mail: wpcv@wpcv.com. Web Site: www.wpcv.com. Format: Country. News staff: one; News: 4 hrs wkly. Target aud: 25-54.

WSJT(FM)— Sept 11, 1967: 94.1 mhz; 100 kw. 1,059 ft. TL: N27 59 56 W81 53 16. (CP: Ant 1,492 ft.). Stereo. 9721 Executive Center Dr. N., Suite 200, St. Petersburg 33702-2439. Phone: (727) 568-0941. Fax: (727) 568-9758. E-mail: smoothjazz@wsjt.com. Web Site: www.wsjt.com. Licensee: Infinity Radio Inc. Group owner: Infinity Broadcasting Corp. (acq 1999; grpsl). Rep: Clear Channel. Format: Jazz. News staff: one. Target aud: 25-54; middle to upper income adults, skews towards females. ♦ Charlie Ochs, gen mgr & sls mgr; Rose Bobier, prom dir; Ross Block, opns mgr & progmg dir.

WWAB(AM)— September 1957: 1330 khz; 1 kw-D. TL: N28 02 40 W81 58 28. Box 65 33802. Secondary address: 1203 Chase St. 33802. Phone: (863) 682-2998. E-mail: frankclark859@mybluelight.com. Licensee: WWAB Inc. (acq 1-16-73). Format: Rhythm and blues, talk, gospel. Target aud: 18-49. Spec prog: Gospel 12 hrs wkly. ♦ Jerry Hughes, gen mgr; Hugh Hughes, stn mgr & gen sls mgr; Frank Clark, opns mgr & progmg dir.

*WYFO(FM)— March 1988: 91.9 mhz; 25 kw horiz, 23 kw vert. 328 ft. TL: N27 56 35 W81 54 45. 755 Creative Dr., Suite 3, North Carolina 33813. Phone: (863) 648-5516. Fax: (863) 648-5516. E-mail: wyfo@bbnradio.org. Web Site: www.bbnradio.org. Licensee: Bible Broadcasting Network Inc. (group owner; acq 9-21-89; $200,000; 10-16-89). Format: Christian, educ. ♦ Doug Roby, stn mgr.

Lantana

WPBR(AM)— 1941: 1340 khz; 1 kw-U. TL: N26 36 41 W80 02 17. (CP: TL: N26 33 26 W80 04 20). 1217 S. Military Trail, Suite E, West Palm Beach 33415-4600. Phone: (561) 641-8882. Fax: (561) 641-8629. E-mail: adminandsales@1340wpbr.com. Web Site: www.talkwpbr1340am.com. Licensee: Omni-Lingual Broadcasting Corp. (acq 3-4-94; $700,000;. FTR: 5-9-94). Network: USA. Format: News/talk, community progmg. Target aud: 35-64. Spec prog: Financial 9 hrs, medical 8 hrs, Jewish 3 hrs, Creole 30 hrs wkly. ♦ Emil Antonoff, pres; Markes Pierre Louis, gen mgr; Virginia C. Martinez, gen mgr & stn mgr.

Largo

WMGG(AM)— May 29, 1972: 820 khz; 50 kw-D, 1 kw-N, DA-2. TL: N27 54 30 W82 46 51. 1916 N. Dale Mabry Hwy., Suite 200, Tampa 33607. Phone: (813) 871-1819. Fax: (813) 871-1155. Licensee: Mega Communications of St. Petersburg. Group owner: Mega Communications Inc. (acq 1999; grpsl). Format: Sp, tropical. Target aud: 25-54. ♦ Ricardo Villalona, gen mgr; Tex Meyer, gen sls mgr; Rafael Grullon, progmg dir; Robert Hailey, chief of engrg.

Lecanto

*WLMS(FM)— September 1992: 88.3 mhz; 3.8 kw. Ant 259 ft. TL: N28 52 55 W82 31 30. Box 18081, Tampa 33629. Secondary address: 3816 Morrison Ave. 33629. Phone: (813) 289-8040. Fax: (813) 282-3580. E-mail: contact@spiritfm905.com. Web Site: www.spiritfm905.com. Licensee: Bishop of the Diocese of St. Petersburg. Format: Relg.

Leesburg

WLBE(AM)— August 1949: 790 khz; 5 kw-D, 1 kw-N, DA-N. TL: N28 49 00 W81 46 45. 32900 Radio Rd. 34788. Phone: (352) 787-7900. Fax: (352) 787-1402. E-mail: 790wlbe@comcast.net. Licensee: WLBE 790 Inc. Network: CBS. Rep: Dora-Clayton. Format: 50% talk, 50% music. News: 25 hrs wkly. Target aud: 45 plus. Spec prog: Black 3 hrs, farm 3 hrs, gospel 4 hrs, Pol 2 hrs wkly. ♦ MJ McNair, gen mgr.

WQBQ(AM)— Sept 12, 1962: 1410 khz; 5 kw-D, 90 w-N. TL: N28 47 13 W81 53 26. Stereo. Rama Communications Inc., 3765 N. John Young Pkwy., Orlando 32804. Phone: (407) 523-2770. Fax: (407) 523-2888. Licensee: Rama Communications Inc. (group owner; (acq 10-15-2004; $180,000. with WKIQ(AM) Eustis). Format: Spanish. ♦ Sabeta Persaud, pres; Steve January, gen mgr.

WVLG(AM)—(Wildwood). September 1987: 640 khz; 830 w-D, 980 w-N. TL: N28 51 19 W81 58 12. 1153 Main St., The Villages 32159. Phone: (352) 753-1119. Fax: (352) 259-4819. E-mail: wvlg@thevillagesmedia.com. Licensee: Senior Broadcasting Corp. (acq 9-12-00; $1.05 million). Format: Var/div. Target aud: 18 plus; general. ♦ Skip Diegel, gen mgr; Chris English, opns mgr.

WXXL(FM)—(Tavares). Feb 12, 1969: 106.7 mhz; 100 kw. 823 ft. TL: N28 33 31 W81 35 38. Stereo. 2500 Maitland Center Pkwy., Suite 401, Maitland 32751-7407. Phone: (407) 916-7800. Fax: (407) 916-7510. Web Site: www.wxxl.com. Licensee: AMFM Radio Licenses L.L.C. Group owner: Clear Channel Communications Inc. (acq 8-30-00; grpsl). Fisher, Wayland, Cooper, Leader & Zaragoza. Format: CHR. News staff: one. Target aud: 18-49; general. Spec prog: Alternative 6 hrs wkly. ♦ Linda Byrd, VP & gen mgr; Adam Cook, opns dir & progmg dir; Sam Nein, sls dir; Richard Rectanus, natl sls mgr; Rick Everett, mktg dir & prom dir; Bobbi King, prom mgr; Pete deGraaff, mus dir; Grace Vasquez, news dir; Mike Spry, engrg dir; Dave Chambers, chief of engrg.

Lehigh Acres

WWCL(AM)— Apr 29, 1970: 1440 khz; 5 kw-D, 1 kw-N, DA-2. TL: N26 36 05 W81 33 30. 7573 N.W. First St. 33972. Phone: (239) 337-1440. Fax: (239) 369-3386. E-mail: energi1440@aol.com. Licensee: Olbota Communications, Inc. (acq 1-1-79). Format: Sp, Mexican. ♦ Angel Ramos, gen mgr.

WZJZ(FM)— Jan 1, 1976: 107.1 mhz; 23.5 kw. Ant 722 ft. TL: N26 19 00 W81 47 13. Stereo. 13320 Metro Pkwy., Fort Myers 33912. Phone: (239) 225-4300. Fax: (239) 275-4669. Web Site: www.wdrr.com. Licensee: Clear Channel Broadcasting Licenses Inc. Group owner:

Florida   Directory of Radio

Clear Channel Communications Inc. (acq 1996; grpsl). Rep: Clear Channel. Format: Smooth jazz. Target aud: 25-54. ♦ Jim Keating, gen mgr.

Live Oak

WQHL(AM)— June 16, 1949: 1250 khz; 1 kw-D, 83 w-N. TL: N30 17 14 W82 57 56. 1305 Helvenston St. SE 32064-3465. Phone: (386) 362-1250. Phone: (386) 364-3502. Fax: (386) 364-3504. Web Site: www.wqhlcounrty.com. Licensee: RTG Radio LLC. Group owner: Black Crow Media Group LLC (acq 11-9-2001; grpsl). Network: ABC Information & Entertainment. Format: ESPN sports. News: 12 hrs wkly. Target aud: General. Spec prog: Gospel 7 hrs, relg 6 hrs wkly. ♦ Dean Blackwell, gen mgr; R.T. Ganzak, pres & news dir.

WQHL-FM— October 1973: 98.1 mhz; 50 kw. 420 ft. TL: N30 17 14 W82 57 56. Stereo. E-mail: dean@wqhlcountry.com. Web Site: wqhlcountry.com. Network: ABC Information & Entertainment. Format: Country. Target aud: General.

Macclenny

WJXR(FM)—Licensed to Macclenny. See Jacksonville

Madison

*WAPB(FM)— 2005: 91.7 mhz; 200 w. Ant 224 ft. TL: N30 27 13 W83 24 17. 1508 State Ave., Holly Hill 32117. Phone: (386) 677-4272. Fax: (386) 673-3715. Web Site: wapb.org. Licensee: Public Radio Inc. Format: Relg. ♦ Gordon C. Lund, pres.

WMAF(AM)— Dec 6, 1956: 1230 khz; 1 kw-U. TL: N30 28 23 W83 26 09. Box 621 32341. Secondary address: 2 Country Club Rd. 32341. Phone: (850) 973-3233. Fax: (850) 973-3097. E-mail: countrywmaf@warthlink.net. Web Site: radiowmaf.com. Licensee: Geneva Walker. (acq 1996). Format: Classic country. Spec prog: Oldies, gospel. ♦ James Sealey, gen mgr.

WXHT(FM)— November 2000: 102.7 mhz; 19 kw. Ant 377 ft. TL: N30 38 23 W83 26 52. Stereo. 1711 Ellis Dr., Valdosta, GA 31602. Phone: (229) 244-8642. Fax: (229) 242-7620. Web Site: www.hot10227wxnt.com. Licensee: RTG Radio L.L.C. Group owner: Black Crow Media Group LLC (acq 6-4-2004; $3.4 million. with WSTI-FM Quitman, GA). Rini Coran PC. Format: Contemporary hits. Target aud: Adults 18-49. ♦ Robert Ganzak, gen mgr; Carrie Alop, prom.

Maitland

WPYO(FM)— Sept 1, 1968: 95.3 mhz; 12 kw. Ant 472 ft. TL: N28 34 27 W81 27 46. 4192 N. John Young Pkwy., Orlando 32804. Phone: (407) 299-9595. Fax: (407) 578-5933. Web Site: www.power953.com. Licensee: CXR Holdings L.L.C. Group owner: Cox Broadcasting (acq 1999; $14.5 million). Format: Rhythm and blues. Target aud: General. ♦ Brian Elam, gen mgr.

Marathon

WAVK(FM)— 2002: 97.7 mhz; 50 kw horiz, 49 kw vert. Ant 213 ft. TL: N24 46 02 W80 56 42. Stereo. 11399 Overseas Hwy. 33050. Phone: (305) 743-3434. Fax: (305) 743-9091. E-mail: mail@wave-fm.com. Web Site: www.wave-fm.com. Licensee: Vox Communications Group LLC. (acq 7-28-2005; grpsl). Format: Hot adult contemp. ♦ Kathy Koury, gen mgr.

WFFG(AM)— Apr 7, 1962: 1300 khz; 2.5 kw-U, DA-1. TL: N24 41 28 W81 06 30. Box 500940, One Boot Key 33050. Phone: (305) 743-5563. Phone: (305) 743-5564. Fax: (305) 743-9441. E-mail: keysradiogroup@aol.com. Licensee: The Great Marathon Radio Co. (acq 11-5-90; grpsl; 11-26-90). Network: Westwood One. Format: News/talk, sports. News: 10 hrs wkly. Target aud: 25-54; general. ♦ Joe Mascone, pres & gen mgr; Vince Cacone, engrg dir & chief of engrg.

*WHWY(FM)—Not on air, target date: unknown: 91.5 mhz; 89.3 kw. Ant 308 ft. TL: N24 39 02 W81 18 36. 172 N.E. 15th St., Miami 33132-1348. Phone: (305) 995-1717. Fax: (305) 995-2299. Licensee: The School Board of Miami-Dade County, FL. ♦ John LaBonia, gen mgr.

WWWK(FM)— Oct 15, 1984: 105.5 mhz; 26 kw. Ant 115 ft. TL: N24 43 44 W81 02 05. Stereo. 11399 Overseas Hwy. 33050. Phone: (305) 743-3434. Fax: (305) 743-9091. Licensee: LSM Radio Partners LLC (acq 6-24-2004; with WAVK(FM) Marathon). Network: ABC. Format: Oldies. ♦ Kevin Leroux, gen mgr.

Marco

WAVV(FM)— May 30, 1987: 101.1 mhz; 100 kw. 981 ft. TL: N26 10 57 W81 34 32. Stereo. 11800 Tamiami Tr. E., Naples 34113. Phone: (239) 793-1011. Fax: (239) 793-7000. E-mail: wavvfm101@earthlink.net. Licensee: Alpine Broadcasting Corp. (group owner; acq 4-84; $95,000;. FTR: 4-23-84). Network: AP Radio. Rep: Christal. Format: Modern, easy lstng. News: 8 hrs wkly. Target aud: 35 plus; an economically qualified audience that is somewhat more affluent. Spec prog: Jazz 3 hrs wkly. ♦ Norman Alpert, pres; Donna Alpert, CFO; Jeff Alpert, VP & gen mgr; Kenny Lamb, opns mgr.

WGUF(FM)— 1990: 98.9 mhz; 6 kw. Ant 328 ft. TL: N26 01 50 W81 38 33. Stereo. 10915 K-Nine Dr., 2nd Fl., Suite 316, Bonita Springs 34135. Phone: (239) 495-8383. Fax: (239) 495-0883. Web Site: www.thegulf989.com. Licensee: Renda Broadcasting Corp. of Nevada. Group owner: Renda Broadcasting Corp. (acq 4-17-97; $2 million). Format: News/talk. News: 7 hrs wkly. Target aud: 35 plus; affluent southwest FL residents. ♦ Kelly McGrath, gen mgr.

*WMKO(FM)— Feb 8, 1999: 91.7 mhz; 25 kw. 140 ft. TL: N25 55 43 W81 43 49. Florida Gulf Coast University, 10501 FGCU Blvd., Fort Myers 33965. Phone: (941) 590-2500. Fax: (941) 590-2511. E-mail: wgcufm@fgcu.edu. Licensee: Board of Trustees, Florida Gulf Coast University (acq 11-16-01). Format: Great Music, Classical, Jazz & NPR News. ♦ Gene Craven, stn mgr; Jeff Highsmith, opns mgr; Jill Erickson, dev dir & mktg dir; Terry Brennen, rgnl sls mgr; Taylor Lewis, progmg dir; Amy Tardif, news dir; Hal Kneller, chief of engrg.

Marco Island

WCNZ(AM)— May 1999: 1660 khz; 10 kw-D, 1 kw-N. TL: N25 59 30 W81 37 30. Stereo. 5043 E. Tamiami Tr., Naples 34113. Phone: (239) 732-9369. Fax: (239) 732-7267. E-mail: bladd@relevantradio.com. Web Site: www.newsradio1660.com. Licensee: Starboard Media Foundation Inc. (acq 5-19-2005; $2 million. with WVOI(AM) Marco Island). Network: ABC. Arter & Hadden. Format: News/talk. News staff: 2; News: 51 hrs wkly. Spec prog: Vintage Radio. ♦ Bob Ladd, opns dir.

WTLT(FM)—See Naples

WVOI(AM)— Jan 1, 1975: 1480 khz; 1 kw-U, DA-2. TL: N25 59 30 W81 37 30. 5043 E. Tamiami Tr., Naples 34113. Phone: (239) 732-9369. Fax: (239) 732-7267. E-mail: bladd@relevantradio.com. Licensee: Starboard Media Foundation Inc. (acq 5-19-2005; $2 million. with WCNZ(AM) Marco Island). Network: ABC. Arter & Hadden. Format: Btfl mus. News staff: 2; News: 5.5 hrs wkly. Target aud: 45+; Upscale and professional adults. Spec prog: Vintage radio 6.5 hrs wkly. ♦ Bob Ladd, opns VP.

Marianna

WJAQ(FM)—Listing follows WTOT(AM).

*WJNF(FM)— May 1985: 88.3 mhz; 25 kw vert. Ant 262 ft. TL: N30 46 57 W85 06 30. Stereo. Box 450 32447-0450. Secondary address: 2914 Jefferson St. 32446. Phone: (904) 526-4477. Fax: (904) 526-1831. E-mail: wjnf@phonL.com. Web Site: www.wjnf.org. Licensee: Marianna Educational Broadcasting Foundation. Network: Moody. Format: Relg, adult contemp, Christian. News staff: one; News: 6 hrs wkly. Target aud: Families. ♦ Jack Hollis, pres; Rene Parton, gen mgr, progmg dir & news dir; Shellie Hollis, VP, mktg dir & prom mgr; Charles Wooten, chief of engrg.

WTOT(AM)— Sept 24, 1958: 980 khz; 1 kw-D, 500 w-N. TL: N30 47 01 W85 15 18. Box 569, 4376 Lafayette St., Suite A 32446. Phone: (850) 482-3046. Fax: (850) 482-3049. Licensee: MFR Inc. (acq 10-8-96; with co-located FM). Network: ABC. Format: Btfl mus, big band, oldies. Target aud: 25 plus. ♦ John Biddinger, CEO; Ed Cearley, pres, gen mgr & gen mgr; Don Moore, sls dir, news dir & pub affrs dir; Curtis Blount, chief of engrg.

WJAQ(FM)— Co-owned with WTOT(AM). Sept 1, 1964: 100.9 mhz; 5.9 kw horiz. 331 ft. TL: N30 47 01 W85 15 18. Stereo. 4376 Lafayette St., Suite A 32446. Phone: (850) 482-3046. Network: ABC. Format: Country. News staff: one; News: 3 hrs wkly. Target aud: General.

WTYS(AM)— Apr 3, 1947: 1340 khz; 1 kw-U. TL: N30 45 49 W85 13 52. Box 777 32447. Secondary address: 2725 Jefferson St. 32448. Phone: (850) 482-2131. Fax: (850) 526-3687. E-mail: wtysradio@earthlink.net. Web Site: www.wtys.cc. Licensee: James L. Adams Jr. (acq 12-1-98; $250,000. with WTYS-FM Marianna). Format: Classic country. News staff: one; News: 7 hrs wkly. Target aud: 25-64; adults in Jackson County & the surrounding area. Spec prog: Farm one hr, gospel 11 hrs wkly. ♦ Jimmy Adams, gen mgr; Tom O'Brien, opns dir.

WTYS-FM— Aug 4, 1995: 94.1 mhz; 4.4 kw. Ant 384 ft. TL: N30 45 47 W85 13 52. Stereo. Box 777 32447. Secondary address: 2725 Jefferson St. 32448. Phone: (850) 482-2131. Fax: (850) 526-3687. E-mail: wtysradio@earthlink.net. Web Site: www.wtys.cc. Licensee: James L. Adams Jr. (acq 12-1-98; with WTYS(AM) Marianna). Network: CBS. Format: Southern gospel. News staff: one; News: 5 hrs wkly. Target aud: 25-64; adults in Jackson county, FL & surrounding area. ♦ James L. Adams, gen mgr; Tom O'Brien, opns mgr & news dir.

Mary Esther

WYZB(FM)— May 1986: 105.5 mhz; 6 kw. 328 ft. TL: N30 24 42 W86 37 14. Stereo. 225 N.W. Hollywood Blvd., Fort Walton Beach 32548. Phone: (850) 244-1055. E-mail: sales@wyzb.com. Web Site: www.wyzb.com. Licensee: Cumulus Licensing Corp. Group owner: Cumulus Media Inc. (acq 1-10-03; grpsl). Format: Country. Target aud: 25-54. ♦ Georgia Edmiston, gen mgr.

Mayo

*WGSG(FM)— 1991: 89.5 mhz; 2.5 kw horiz, 20 kw vert. 249 ft. TL: N30 02 30 W83 07 45. Box 644, Whispering Oaks 32066. Phone: (386) 294-2525. Fax: (386) 294-2525. Licensee: True Concepts of Levy County Inc. Format: Relg. ♦ Terri Simmons, gen mgr.

Melbourne

WAOA-FM—Listing follows WINT(AM).

WBVD(FM)—Listing follows WMMB(AM).

WCIF(FM)— Jan 1, 1980: 106.3 mhz; 3 kw. 230 ft. TL: N28 04 40 W80 39 26. Stereo. Box 366 32902. Secondary address: 3301 Dairy Rd. 32904. Phone: (321) 725-9243. E-mail: info@wcif.com. Web Site: www.wcif.com. Licensee: First Baptist Church Inc. Format: Relg. ♦ Lee J. Martinez, gen mgr; Martha Root, opns mgr.

*WFIT(FM)— April 1975: 89.5 mhz; 900 w horiz, 4.6 kw vert. 112 ft. TL: N28 03 51 W80 37 25. (CP: 700 w, ant 151 ft.). Stereo. 150 W. University Blvd. 32901. Phone: (321) 674-8140. Fax: (321) 674-8139. E-mail: wfit@fit.edu. Web Site: www.wfit.org. Licensee: Florida Institute of Technology. Format: News. News: 40 hrs wkly. Target aud: 25-54; Public Radio Listeners. Spec prog: Jazz 20 hrs, class 3 hrs, folk 5 hrs, reggae 2 hrs, Latin 2 hrs wkly. ♦ Terri Wright, gen mgr.

WINT(AM)— Mar 8, 1968: 1560 khz; 5 kw-D. TL: N28 07 40 W80 42 29. 1775 W. Hibiscus Blvd., Suite 301 32901. Phone: (321) 984-1000. Fax: (321) 724-1565. Licensee: Cumulus Licensing Corp. Group owner:Cumulus Media Inc. (acq 5-23-2001; with co-located FM). Network: ABC News/Talk. Erwin Krasnow. Format: Music of your life. News staff: 2; News: 25 hrs wkly. Target aud: 35-64. ♦ Dan Carelli, gen mgr; Ted Turner, opns mgr.

WAOA-FM— Co-owned with WINT(AM). Nov 9, 1972: 107.1 mhz; 100 kw. 500 ft. TL: N28 08 14 W80 42 11. Stereo. Web Site: www.wa1a.com. Format: CHR. Target aud: 25-54.

WMEL(AM)— Jan 4, 1956: 920 khz; 5 kw-D, 1 kw-N, DA-3. TL: N28 08 11 W80 41 20. Stereo. 1800 Turtleward Rd. 32934. Phone: (321) 254-2282. Fax: (321) 254-1199. E-mail: jharper@920wmel.com. Web Site: www.920wmel.com. Licensee: David Ryder, receiver (acq 7-29-2005). Network: Network: CBS Radio, Westwood One. Rep: Savalli. Format: News/talk, sports. News staff: 2; News: 144 hrs wkly. Target aud: 35-64; decision making men & women. Spec prog: Relg 6 hrs, Jewish 2 hrs wkly. ♦ John Harper, gen mgr.

WMMB(AM)— 1947: 1240 khz; 1 kw-U. TL: N28 04 40 W80 35 55. (CP: 940 w-U. TL: N28 04 42 W80 35 56). 1388 S. Babcock St. 32901. Phone: (321) 733-1000. Fax: (321) 725-6821. E-mail: wmmb1240@aol.com. Web Site: www.wmmbam.com. Licensee: Capstar TX L.P. Group owner: Clear Channel Communications Inc. (acq 8-30-00; grpsl). Network: Network: Westwood One, ABC Information & Entertainment.

Broadcasting & Cable Yearbook 2006

Rep: Allied Radio Partners. Robert A. DePont. Format: Adult standards, swing. News staff: 3; News: 4 hrs wkly. Target aud: 35 plus. ♦ Barbara Latham, gen mgr; Larry Brewer, progmg dir.

WBVD(FM)—Co-owned with WMMB(AM). Dec 25, 1965: 95.1 mhz; 6 kw. 250 ft. TL: N28 04 42 W80 35 56. (CP: Ant 253 ft.). Stereo. Web Site: www.951thebeat.com. Format: Urban CHR. News: one hr wkly. Target aud: 25-54. ♦ Jeff McKeel, sls dir; Doug Remington, engrg dir.

Merritt Island

WWBC(AM)—See Cocoa

Mexico Beach

WPBH(FM)— Nov 28, 1990: 99.3 mhz; 50 kw. 519 ft. TL: N30 00 21 W85 20 36. Stereo. Box 59288, Panama City 32412. Phone: (850) 769-1408. Fax: (850) 769-0659. Web Site: www.beachfm.com. Licensee: Clear Channel Radio Licenses Inc. Group owner: Clear Channel Communications Inc. (acq 11-21-97; grpsl). Lukas, McGowan, Nace & Gutierrez. Format: Oldies. Target aud: 30 plus; professional adults. ♦ Jimmy Vineyard, gen mgr.

Miami

WACC(AM)—(Hialeah). Dec 1, 1987: 830 khz; 1 kw-U, DA-2. TL: N25 46 22 W80 25 16. Stereo. Box 421500 33142. Secondary address: 1779 N.W. 28th St. 33142. Phone: (305) 638-9729. Fax: (305) 636-3976. E-mail: pax@paxcc.org. Web Site: www.paxcc.org. Licensee: Radio Peace Catholic Broadcasting Inc. (acq 11-27-96; $2.55 million). Thiemain & Evenas. Format: Relg, talk, Sp. News staff: 5; News: 18 hrs wkly. Target aud: 25-54; adults. Spec prog: Sports. ♦ Father Jose L. Hernando, pres; Father Alberto R. Cutie, gen mgr & opns mgr; Ivette Acosta, stn mgr; Ivetta Acosta, opns mgr; Mary Lou Cutie, sls dir; Marite Alfonso, progmg dir; Jose Francisco Nunez, news dir.

WAMR-FM— June 7, 1974: 107.5 mhz; 95 kw horiz, 80 kw vert. 1,007 ft. TL: N25 57 59 W80 12 33. Stereo. 800 Douglas Rd., Suite 111, Coral Gables 33134. Phone: (305) 447-1140. Fax: (305) 443-4701. Licensee: WQBA-FM License Corp. Group owner: Univision Radio (acq 9-22-2003; grpsl). Format: Sp, adult contemp. ♦ Claudia Puig, gen mgr.

WAQI(AM)— 1939: 710 khz; 50 kw-U, DA-2. TL: N25 58 07 W80 22 44. 800 Douglas Rd., Suite 111, Coral Gables 33134. Phone: (305) 447-1140. Fax: (305) 443-3601. E-mail: gferandez@univisionradio.com. Web Site: www.univisionradio.com. Licensee: Licensee Corporation #1. Group owner: Univision Radio (acq 9-22-2003; grpsl). Rep: Caballero. Format: Sp, news/talk, entertainment. ♦ Claudia Puig, sr VP & gen mgr; Yvette Sanguilty, sls dir; Monica Rabassa, mktg dir & prom dir; Armando Perez-Roura, progmg dir; Augustine Tamargo, news dir; Max Fitero, chief of engrg.

WAXY(AM)—See South Miami

WBGG-FM—See Fort Lauderdale

WCMQ-FM—See Hialeah

*****WDNA(FM)**— June 10, 1980: 88.9 mhz; 7.4 kw. 1,145 ft. TL: N25 32 24 W80 28 07. Stereo. Box 558636, 4848 S.W. 74 Ct. 33255. Phone: (305) 662-8889. Fax: (305) 662-1975. E-mail: feedback@wdna.org. Web Site: www.wdna.org. Licensee: Bascomb Memorial Broadcasting Foundation Inc. (acq 1971). Haley, Bader & Potts. Format: Jazz, Sp. News: 10 hrs wkly. Target aud: General; minorities. Spec prog: World music 10 hrs wkly. ♦ Luis W. Fernandez, pres; Margarita Pelleya, stn mgr; Joe Cassala, opns mgr & sls dir; Raymond M. Ball Jr., chief of engrg.

WEDR(FM)— May 18, 1963: 99.1 mhz; 100 kw. 926 ft. TL: N25 57 30 W80 12 44. (CP: TL: N25 57 59 W80 12 33). Stereo. 2741 N. 29th Ave., Hollywood 33020. Phone: (305) 623-7711. Fax: (305) 624-2736. Web Site: www.wedr.com. Licensee: Cox Radio Inc. Group owner:

Cox Broadcasting (acq 8-00; grpsl). Smithwick & Belendiuk. Format: Hip-hop. ♦ Jerry Rushin, gen mgr; Maestro Powell, prom dir; Cedric Hollywood, progmg dir.

WFLC(FM)— July 20, 1951: 97.3 mhz; 100 kw. 800 ft. TL: N25 57 30 W80 12 44. Stereo. 2741 N. 29th Ave., Hollywood 33020. Phone: (305) 444-4404. Fax: (954) 847-3223. E-mail: mike.disney@cox.com. Web Site: www.coastfm.com. Licensee: Cox Radio Inc. Group owner: Cox Communications Inc. Rep: Christal. Format: Hot adult contemp. Target aud: 25-54. ♦ Bob Neil, CEO; Rich Reis, VP; Mike G. Disney, gen mgr; David Isreal, opns dir & progmg dir; John Lynch, gen sls mgr; Derek Pitts, mktg dir.

WHDR(FM)— Nov 1, 1960: 93.1 mhz; 100 kw. Ant 1,007 ft. TL: N25 58 03 W80 12 34. Stereo. 2741 N. 29th Ave., Hollywood 33020. Phone: (305) 444-4404. Fax: (954) 847-3201. Web Site: 93rock.com. Licensee: Cox Radio - Miami LLC. Group owner: Cox Communications Inc. (acq 5-18-2000; grpsl). Rep: Christal. Format: Active rock. Target aud: 18-49; upscale, educ adults with hip active lifestyles. ♦ Bob Neil, CEO; Michael Disney, VP & gen mgr; David Isreal, opns mgr; Marc Telsey, gen sls mgr; Derick Pitts, mktg dir; Phil Michaels, progmg dir.

WHYI-FM—See Fort Lauderdale

WINZ(AM)— 1946: 940 khz; 50 kw-D, 10 kw-N. TL: N25 57 36 W80 16 13. 7601 Riviera Blvd., Miramar 33023. Phone: (954) 862-2000. Fax: (954) 862-4012. Web Site: www.am940southflorida.com. Licensee: Clear Channel Broadcasting Licenses Inc. Group owner: Clear Channel Communications Inc. (acq 11-21-97; grpsl). Network: ABC. Rep: Clear Channel. Format: Progsv talk. News staff: 20. Target aud: 35-64; upscale, professional, managerial adults. ♦ Ronna Woulfe, gen mgr; David Ross, opns.

WIOD(AM)— Jan 19, 1926: 610 khz; 10 kw-U, DA-N. TL: N25 50 58 W80 09 18. Stereo. 7601 Riviera Blvd, Miramar 33023. Phone: (954) 862-2000. Fax: (954) 862-4012. E-mail: newsradio610@ccmiami.com. Web Site: www.newsradio610.com. Licensee: Clear Channel Radio Licenses Inc. Group owner: Clear Channel Communications Inc. (acq 11-21-97; grpsl). Format: News/talk. Target aud: 25-64. ♦ Ronna Woulfe, gen mgr; David Ross, opns VP; Peter Bolger, progmg dir.

WJCC(AM)—(Miami Springs). 1997: 1700 khz; 10 kw-D, 1 kw-N. TL: N25 54 02 W80 21 50. Stereo. 1590 N.E. 162 St., Suite 600, N. Miami 33162. Phone: (305) 940-1700. Fax: (305) 919-1750. E-mail: eduardor@msbi.net. Web Site: www.planet17radio.com. Licensee: Multicultural Radio Broadcasting Licensee LLC. Group owner: Multicultural Radio Broadcasting Inc. (acq 2-4-2004; grpsl). Format: Sp relg, Haitian. ♦ Eduardo Rueda, opns mgr.

WKAT(AM)—See North Miami

WKIS(FM)—Listing follows WQAM(AM).

*****WLRN-FM**— February 1948: 91.3 mhz; 47 kw. Ant 935 ft. TL: N25 58 46 W80 11 46. Stereo. 172 N.E. 15th St. 33132. Phone: (305) 995-1717. Fax: (305) 995-2299. E-mail: info@wlrn.org. Web Site: www.wlrn.org. Licensee: School Board of Miami Dade County Florida. Network: NPR, PRI. Leibowitz & Associates. Format: News/talk info. News staff: 3; News: 50 hrs wkly. Target aud: General; well educated, moderate to high income bracket. Spec prog: Haitian 3 hrs wkly. ♦ Karen Echols, CFO; John Labonia, gen mgr; Ted Eldredge, stn mgr; Clyde Pinder, opns dir; Jack F. Yaghdjian, chief of engrg. Co-owned TV: *WLRN-TV affil.

WLYF(FM)— 1948: 101.5 mhz; 100 kw. 810 ft. TL: N25 57 59 W80 12 44. Stereo. 20450 N.W. 2nd Ave. 33169-2505. Phone: (305) 521-5100. Fax: (305) 652-0098. E-mail: litefm@litemiami.com. Web Site: www.litemiami.com. Licensee: Jefferson-Pilot Communications Co. of Florida. Group owner: Jefferson-Pilot Communications Co. (acq 1979). Rep: Interep. Format: Adult contemp. News: 2 hrs wkly. Target aud: 25-54; women. ♦ Dennis Glass, CEO; Theresa Stone, pres; Joseph Weatherly, CFO; Dennis P. Collins, sr VP & gen mgr; Rob Sidney, opns dir, sls dir & progmg dir; Rosemary Zimmerman, natl sls mgr; Danielle Webb, rgnl sls mgr; Tammy Moye, mktg dir & prom dir; Gary Blau, engrg dir.

WMBM(AM)—See Miami Beach

*****WMCU(FM)**— Aug 24, 1970: 89.7 mhz; 100 kw. 1,014 ft. TL: N25 32 24 W80 28 07. Stereo. 600 S.W. 3rd St., Suite 2270, Pompano Beach 33060. Phone: (305) 381-7400. Fax: (305) 381-7413. E-mail: mp@897spiritfm.com. Web Site: www.897spiritfm.com. Licensee: Trinity International Foundation Inc. (acq 11-6-01). Network: USA. Dow, Lohnes & Albertson. Format: Relg, educ, Christian. News staff: one. Target aud: 25-54. ♦ Merryan Padron, stn mgr & chief of engrg; Dwight Taylor, progmg dir; Donna Matthews, news dir; Mike Schloman, dev dir & news dir.

WMGE(FM)—See Miami Beach

WMIB(FM)—See Fort Lauderdale

WMYM(AM)— Aug 15, 1997: 990 khz; 5 kw-U. TL: N25 50 34 W80 25 12. 2150 W. 68th St., Suite 202, Hialeah 33016. Phone: (305) 823-0990. Fax: (305) 823-9322. Web Site: www.ontheradio.net /radiostations/wmymam.aspx. Licensee: Radio Disney Group LLC. Group owner: ABC Inc. (acq 7-30-99; $7.4 million). Format: Radio Disney, top 40. Kids and families. ♦ Rudy Renaud, gen mgr.

WNMA(AM)—(Miami Springs). May 18, 1958: 1210 khz; 25 kw-D, 2.5 kw-N, DA-2. TL: N25 54 00 W80 21 49. 7250 N.W. 58th St. 33166. Phone: (786) 497-3414. Fax: (786) 497-3412. E-mail: eduardor@mrbi.net. Licensee: Multicultural Radio Broadcasting Licensee LLC. Group owner: Multicultural Radio Broadcasting Inc. (acq 2-4-2004; grpsl). Format: Sp, talk, sports. ♦ Eduardo Rueda, gen mgr.

WOCN(AM)— Dec 22, 1956: 1450 khz; 1 kw-U. TL: N25 50 24 W80 11 20. 350 N.E. 71 St. 33138. Phone: (305) 759-7280. Fax: (305) 759-2276. E-mail: richardvega@wocn.net. Web Site: www.wocn.net. Licensee: Minority Broadcasters Inc. (acq 6-26-84). Gunsten, Yonkley. Format: Sp, news/talk. Target aud: General. Spec prog: Creole 84 hrs wkly. ♦ Pablo Vega, pres & VP; Richard Vega, pres, VP & gen mgr.

WPOW(FM)— June 15, 1985: 96.5 mhz; 100 kw. 1,007 ft. TL: N25 57 59 W80 12 33. Stereo. 20295 N.W. 2nd Ave., Suite 300 33169. Fax: (305) 770-1456. Licensee: Beasley FM Acquisition Corp. Group owner: Beasley Broadcast Group (acq 8-94). Format: CHR. ♦ George Beasley, pres; Greg Reed, gen mgr; Mathew Bell, gen sls mgr; Kid Curry, natl sls mgr & opns.

WQAM(AM)— May 1921: 560 khz; 5 kw-D, 1 kw-N. TL: N25 44 36 W80 09 14. Stereo. 20295 N.W. 2nd Ave. 33169. Phone: (305) 653-6796. Fax: (305) 770-1456. Web Site: www.wqam.com. Licensee: Beasley-Reed Broadcasting. Group owner: Beasley Broadcast Group Winston & Strawn. Format: Sports. Target aud: 25-54; males. Spec prog: Relg 4 hrs wkly. ♦ Greg Reed, gen mgr; Dorene Alberts, rgnl sls mgr & prom dir; Duff Lindsey, progmg dir; George Corso, chief of engrg.

WKIS(FM)—Co-owned with WQAM(AM). October 1965: 99.9 mhz; 100 kw. 986 ft. TL: N25 59 34 W80 10 27. Stereo. 194 N.W.187th St. 33169. Phone: (305) 654-1700. Fax: (305) 654-1718. Web Site: www.wkis.com. Format: Country. News staff: one; News: 2 hrs wkly. Target aud: 25-54. ♦ George Corso, CEO; Joe Bell, VP; Carole Bowen, gen sls mgr; Bob Barnett, progmg dir.

WQBA(AM)— 1947: 1140 khz; 50 kw-D, 10 kw-N, DA-2. TL: N25 45 46 W80 29 03. 800 Douglas Rd., Annex 1, Suite 111, Coral Gables 33134. Phone: (305) 447-1140. Fax: (305) 441-2454. E-mail: wqba@univisionradio.com. Web Site: www.wqba.com. Licensee: WQBA-AM License Corp. Group owner: Univision Radio (acq 9-22-2003; grpsl). Format: News/talk, Sp. ♦ Claudia Puig, VP & gen mgr; Teresa Montoya, progmg dir.

WRHC(AM)—See Coral Gables

WRMA(FM)—See Fort Lauderdale

WRTO-FM—(Goulds). February 1976: 98.3 mhz; 1.1 kw. 462 ft. TL: N25 32 24 W80 28 07. (CP: 100 kw, ant 1,627 ft.). Stereo. 800

Florida

Douglas Rd., Suite 111, Coral Gables 33134. Phone: (305) 445-4020. Fax: (305) 529-6631. Licensee: License Corp. #2. Group owner: Univision Radio (acq 9-22-2003; grpsl). Network: UPI. Format: Latin/tropical, Sp. ◆Claudia Puig, gen mgr; Elisa Alfonso, mktg dir; Cesar Canales, progmg dir; Miguel Triay, chief of engrg.

WSUA(AM)— June 20, 1969: 1260 khz; 5 kw-U, DA-2. TL: N25 46 23 W80 25 17. 2100 Coral Way, Suite 201 33145. Phone: (305) 285-1260. Fax: (305) 858-5907. E-mail: ycuello@carcolusa.com. Web Site: www.caracolusa.com. Licensee: WSUA Broadcasting Corp. (acq 7-28-2005; $72,000 for 24% of stock). Format: Sp, News/talk. News staff: 7; News: 31 hrs wkly. Target aud: 18-54; Latin American audience. ◆Felipe Santo Domingo, CEO; Malule Gonzalez, gen mgr.

WVUM(FM)—See Coral Gables

WWFE(AM)— July 1989: 670 khz; 50 kw-D, 2.5 kw-N, DA-2. TL: N25 51 27 W80 28 52. Stereo. 330 S.W. 27th Ave., Suite 207 33135. Phone: (305) 541-3300. Fax: (305) 541-7470. E-mail: info@lapoderosa.com. Web Site: www.lapoderosa.com. Licensee: Fenix Broadcasting Corp. (acq 6-22-93; $2.7 million; 7-12-93). Mullin, Rhyne, Emmons & Topel. Format: Sp, var/div. News: 27 hrs wkly. Target aud: 25-54. ◆Jorge Rodriguez, CEO; Ana M. Vidal Rodriguez, VP; Jorge A. Rodriguez, pres & gen mgr; Gina Garcia, sls dir & prom dir.

Miami Beach

WLVE(FM)— July 1, 1968: 93.9 mhz; 96 kw, 1,006 ft. TL: N25 57 59 W80 12 33. (CP: 100 kw horiz, 82 kw vert). Stereo. 7601 Riviera Blvd, Miramar 33023. Phone: (954) 862-2000. Fax: (954) 862-4013. Web Site: www.love94.com. Licensee: Clear Channel Radio Licenses Inc. Group owner: Clear Channel Communications Inc. (acq 11-21-97; grpsl). Rep: Allied Radio Partners. Wiley, Rein & Fielding. Format: Smooth jazz. Target aud: 25-54. ◆Ronna Woulfe, gen mgr.

WMBM(AM)— 1949: 1490 khz; 1 kw-U. TL: N25 46 10 W80 08 11. 13242 NW 7 Avenue, North Miami 33168. Phone: (305) 769-1100. Fax: (305) 769-9975. E-mail: wmbm@wmbm.com. Web Site: www.wmbm.com. Licensee: New Birth Broadcasting Corp. (acq 3-8-95; 5-8-95). Network: Network: American Urban, Westwood One. Pepper & Corazzini. Format: Gospel, community talk. News staff: one; News: 3 hrs wkly. Target aud: 25 plus; mature Black, self-motivated, Christian, professionals. ◆Caroline Kelly, sr VP; Victor T. Curry, pres & gen mgr; Claudette Freeman, stn mgr; Grey Cooper, progmg mgr.

WMGE(FM)— 1961: 94.9 mhz; 100 kw, 1,007 ft. TL: N25 46 29 W80 11 19. Stereo. 7601 Riviera Blvd., Miramar 33023. Phone: (954) 862-2000. Fax: (305) 862-4013. Web Site: www.mega949.com. Licensee: Clear Channel Broadcasting Licenses Inc. Group owner: Clear Channel Communications Inc. (acq 11-21-97; grpsl). Network: Westwood One. Format: Latino. Target aud: 18-34. ◆David Ross, pres & gen mgr; Juan Arroyo, stn mgr.

Miami Springs

WJCC(AM)—Licensed to Miami Springs. See Miami

WNMA(AM)—Licensed to Miami Springs. See Miami

Micanopy

WSKY-FM— Sept 7, 1985: 97.3 mhz; 2.6 kw. 495 ft. TL: N29 32 08 W82 19 17. (CP: 13.5 kw, ant 948 ft.). Stereo. 3600 N.W. 43rd St., Suite B, Gainesville 32606-8127. Phone: (352) 377-0985. Fax: (352) 337-2968. Web Site: www.thesky973.com. Licensee: Entercom Gainesville License L.L.C. Group owner: Entercom Communications Corp. (acq 3-18-98; $2.8 million). Rep: Christal. Fisher, Wayland, Cooper, Leader & Zaragoza. Format: News/talk. Target aud: 18-54. ◆Mark Leopold, gen mgr; Dick O'Neil, gen sls mgr; Nancy Parish, prom dir; T.J. Hart, progmg dir & news dir.

Midway

WBWT(FM)— 1996: 100.7 mhz; 11.3 kw. 489 ft. TL: N30 32 22 W84 21 54. Bldg. G, 325 John Knox Rd., Tallahassee 32303. Phone: (850) 383-0741. Licensee: Clear Channel Broadcasting Licenses Inc. Group owner: Clear Channel Communications Inc. (acq 11-21-97; grpsl). Format: Hip hop, rhythm and blues. ◆Judy Bailey, gen mgr; Jeff Horn, opns mgr; Ryan Philips, prom dir; Vanessa Jerome, progmg dir.

Milton

WEBY(AM)— 1978: 1330 khz; 25 kw-D, 79 w-N, DA-D. TL: N30 31 05 W87 04 56. Stereo. 7179 Printers Alley 32583. Phone: (850) 983-2242. Fax: (850) 983-3231. E-mail: weby@1330weby.com. Web Site: www.1330weby.com. Licensee: Spinnaker License Corp. (acq 5-28-02). Network: Jones Radio Networks. Format: Talk, news. News: 15 hrs wkly. Target aud: 35 plus; affluent, educated adults. Spec prog: Christian 7 hrs wkly / Florida State football. ◆Mike Bates, pres & gen mgr; Jeff Johnson, opns mgr; Dave Daughtry, news dir.

WECM(AM)— Dec 18, 1957: 1490 khz; 1 kw-U. TL: N30 37 30 W87 02 54. 6583 Berryhill Rd. 32570. Phone: (850) 623-1490. Fax: (850) 623-6818. E-mail: mike@memories1490.com. Web Site: www.memories1490.com. Licensee: Worldlink Technologies Group Inc. (acq 9-29-03). Network: USA. Format: Oldies, Big Band, beautiful music. News: 12 hrs wkly. Target aud: General; Adults 45 and older. ◆Michael Pfost, gen mgr.

***WEGS(FM)**— Oct 15, 1985: 91.7 mhz; 2 kw. 300 ft. TL: N30 37 29 W87 05 08. Stereo. 1836 Olive Rd., Pensacola 32514. Secondary address: 505 Josephine St., Titusville 32796. Phone: (850) 476-1932. Fax: (850) 447-9650. E-mail: dtalley@olivebaptist.org. Web Site: www.olivebaptist.org. Licensee: Florida Public Radio Inc. Format: Talk, adult Christian contemp. ◆Dave Talley, gen mgr & chief of engrg.

WXBM-FM— Apr 28, 1964: 102.7 mhz; 100 kw. 1,328 ft. TL: N30 35 18 W87 33 16. Stereo. 6085 Quintet Rd., Pace 32571. Phone: (850) 994-5357. Fax: (850) 994-7191. E-mail: feedback@wxbm.com. Web Site: www.wxbm.com. Licensee: 6 Johnson Road Licenses Inc. Group owner: Pamal Broadcasting Ltd. (acq 10-19-2001; grpsl). Format: Country. ◆Dave Cobb, gen mgr.

Mims

WPGS(AM)— May 5, 1986: 840 khz; 250 w-D. TL: N28 44 17 W80 52 52. Stereo. 7232 Sand Lake Rd., Ste 300, Orlando 32819. Phone: (407) 903-1061. Fax: (407) 226-1047. E-mail: wpgs840@aol.com. Web Site: www.wpgsam840.com. Licensee: WPGS Inc. (acq 3-93; $65,000; 3-29-93). Network: USA. Format: Regional Mexican. News: 12 hrs wkly. Target aud: 35 plus; working Americans, upscale NASA employees & loc retirement community. Spec prog: Talk show one hr, big band 4 hrs, gospel 4 hrs wkly. ◆Ed Shiflett, pres.

Miramar Beach

WSBZ(FM)— Oct 18, 1994: 106.3 mhz; 3 kw. 328 ft. TL: N30 23 07 W86 18 03. 10859 Emerald Pkwy. W., Suite 4-415, Destin 32541. Phone: (850) 267-3279. Fax: (850) 231-1775. E-mail: office@wsbz.com. Web Site: www.wsbz.com. Licensee: Carter Broadcasting Inc. (acq 9-10-99). Format: Smooth jazz (new adult contemp). ◆Renee Carter, CFO; Mark Carter, gen mgr.

Monticello

***WFRF-FM**— December 1996: 105.7 mhz; 16 kw. Ant 410 ft. TL: N30 23 08 W83 50 05. Box 181000, Tallahassee 32318-0009. Phone: (850) 201-1070. Fax: (850) 201-1071. Web Site: www.faithradio.us. Licensee: Faith Radio Network Inc. (acq 1-26-2004; $800,000). Network: CBS. Format: Relg. Target aud: 12+. ◆Van Willson, gen mgr.

***WKVH(FM)**— March 2003: 91.9 mhz; 1.5 kw. Ant 1,322 ft. TL: N30 40 13 W83 56 26. Stereo. 2351 Sunset Blvd., Suite 170-218, Rocklin, CA 95765. Phone: (916) 434-8400. Fax: (916) 251-1650. E-mail: klove@klove.com. Web Site: www.klove.com. Licensee: Educational Media Foundation. Group owner: EMF Broadcasting. Network: K-Love. Shaw Pittman. Format: Contemp Christian. News staff: 3. Target aud: 25-44; Judeo Christian, female. ◆Richard Jenkins, pres; Mike Novak, VP; Lloyd Parker, gen mgr.

Mount Dora

WMGF(FM)— 1966: 107.7 mhz; 100 kw. 1,584 ft. TL: N28 55 16 W81 19 09. Stereo. 2500 Maitland Ctr. Pkwy., Suite 401, Maitland 32751. Phone: (407) 916-7800. Fax: (407) 916-0329. Web Site: www.magic107.com. Licensee: Clear Channel Broadcasting Licenses Inc. Group owner: Clear Channel Communications Inc. (acq 11-21-97; grpsl). Rep: Allied Radio Partners. Format: Soft adult contemp. News staff: one; News: 2 hrs wkly. Target aud: 25-54; working women. Spec prog: Contemp Christian mus 20 hrs wkly. ◆Linda Byrd, gen mgr.

Murdock

WBCG(FM)— Oct 22, 2001: 98.9 mhz; 5.5 kw. Ant 341 ft. TL: N27 00 09 W82 10 54. Concord Media Group Inc., 11521 Innfields Dr., Odessa 33556. Secondary address: Studio 3151 Cooper St., Ste. 56, Putna Gorda 33950. Phone: (813) 926-9260. Phone: (941) 639-1112. Fax: (941) 637-6187. E-mail: wbcgbeachradio@cs.com. Licensee: Concord Media Group Inc. (acq 8-28-2001). Rosenman & Colin, L.L.P. Format: Adult contemp. News: 2 hrs wkly. Target aud: Adults 25+; core 35-54 female. ◆Mark W. Jorgenson, gen mgr; David Ayres, gen sls mgr; Kerri Black, prom dir; Michael G. Keating, progmg dir & mus dir; Gale West, pub affrs dir.

Naples

WARO(FM)—Listing follows WNOG(AM).

***WBGY(FM)**— August 2004: 88.1 mhz; 110 w vert. Ant 59 ft. TL: N25 51 56 W81 23 09. 297 Fillmore St. 34104. Phone: (239) 404-9849. E-mail: wbby@earthlink.net. Licensee: Everglades City Broadcasting Co. Inc. (acq 3-30-2004; $25,000). Format: Country. ◆Robert Ladd, pres.

WNOG(AM)— Oct 14, 1954: 1270 khz; 5 kw-D, 1.9 kw-N, DA-2. TL: N26 15 26 W81 40 33. 2824 Palm Beach Blvd., Fort Myers 33916. Phone: (239) 337-2346. Fax: (239) 332-0767. Web Site: www.winkwnog.com. Licensee: Meridian Broadcasting Inc. (group owner; (acq 12-1-96; grpsl). Network: CBS. Rep: McGavren Guild. Leibowitz & Associates. Format: News/talk. Target aud: 35 plus. ◆Joseph C. Schwantzel, pres; Paul Thomas, gen mgr; Wayne Simons, sls dir; Jim Watkins, progmg dir; Keith Stulhmann, engrg dir.

WARO(FM)—Co-owned with WNOG(AM). May 8, 1962: 94.5 mhz; 100 kw. 1,049 ft. TL: N26 20 26 W81 42 48. Stereo. Web Site: www.arrow945.com. Format: Classic rock. Target aud: 25-54; men. Spec prog: Relg 2 hrs wkly. ◆Mike Allen, progmg dir.

WSGL(FM)— May 10, 1980: 104.7 mhz; 14 kw. 450 ft. TL: N26 07 34 W81 43 18. Stereo. 10915 K-Nine Dr., 2nd Fl., Bonita Springs 34135. Phone: (239) 495-8383. Fax: (239) 495-0883. Web Site: www.wsgl1047.com. Licensee: Renda Broadcasting Corp. of Nevada. Group owner: Renda Broadcasting Corp. (acq 11-10-98; $3.65 million). Format: Hot adult contemp. News: one hr wkly. Target aud: 25-54; women. Spec prog: 70s & 80s mus 5 hrs wkly. ◆Kelly McGrath, gen mgr.

***WSOR(FM)**— 1989: 90.9 mhz; 36 kw. Ant 902 ft. TL: N26 20 29 W81 42 38. 5800 100th Way N. St, Saint Peterburg 33708. Phone: (727) 391-9994. Fax: (727) 397-6425. E-mail: wkes@moody.edu. Web Site: www.wkes.fm. Licensee: Moody Bible Institute. (acq 1996). Network: USA. Format: MOR, inspirational. News staff: one. Target aud: 40 plus. ◆Pierre Chestang, gen mgr; Bill Simon, progmg dir; Ron Maxwell, mus dir; Dave Coffman, chief of engrg.

***WSRX(FM)**— August 1988: 89.5 mhz; 20 kw. 223 ft. TL: N26 07 33 W81 43 37. 3805 The Lords Way 34114. Phone: (239) 775-8950. Fax: (239) 774-5889. E-mail: praisefm895@msn.com. Web Site: www.praisefm.com. Licensee: Shadowlawn Association Inc. (acq 1-95; $236,000; 2-27-95). Format: Christian. Target aud: 18-40. ◆Arnie Coones, gen mgr.

WTLT(FM)— Dec 1, 1971: 93.7 mhz; 21 kw. 328 ft. TL: N26 19 00 W81 47 13. Stereo. 2824 Palm Beach Blvd., Fort Myers 33916. Phone: (239) 337-2346. Fax: (239) 332-0767. E-mail: john.conrad@lite937.com. Web Site: www.lite973.com. Licensee: Meridian Broadcasting Inc. (group owner; acq 12-1-96; grpsl). Rep: McGavren Guild. Leibowitz & Associates. Format: Adult contemp. News staff: 3; News: 2 hrs wkly. Target aud: 25-54; women. ◆Joseph C. Schwantzel, CEO & gen mgr; Wayne Simons, sls dir; Matt Francis, prom mgr; John DeHine, progmg dir; Keith Stulhmann, engrg dir.

Naples Park

WBTT(FM)— Oct 22, 1987: 105.5 mhz; 950 w. 584 ft. TL: N26 19 00 W81 47 13. (CP: 6.3 kw, ant 649 ft.). Stereo. 13320 Metro Pkwy., Suite 1, Fort Myers 33912. Phone: (239) 225-4300. Fax: (239) 225-4329. Web Site: www.1055thebeat.com. Licensee: Clear Channel Radio Licenses Inc. Group owner: Clear Channel Communications Inc. (acq 1996; grpsl). Format: Rhythmic CHR. Target aud: 18-34. ◆Jim Keating, gen mgr.

Stations in the U.S. — Florida

Navarre

WGCX(FM)—Not on air, target date: unknown: 95.7 mhz; 25 kw. 282 ft. TL: N30 27 02 W86 51 59. 2070 N. Palafax, Pensacola 32501. Phone: (850) 434-1230. Fax: (850) 469-9698. E-mail: mglin@aol.com. Web Site: www.praise95.net. Licensee: 550 AM Inc. Format: Christian. ◆Dara Glinter, exec VP & opns VP; Michael Glinter, pres, gen mgr & progmg VP.

Neptune Beach

WFKS(FM)— August 1965: 97.9 mhz; 12.5 kw. Ant 991 ft. TL: N30 16 51 W81 34 12. Stereo. 11700 Central Parkway, Jacksonville 32224. Phone: (904) 636-0507. Fax: (904) 997-7713. Web Site: www.979kissfm.com. Licensee: Clear Channel Broadcasting Licenses Inc. Group owner: Clear Channel Communications Inc. (acq 11-21-97; grpsl). Format: Top 40. News staff: one; News: one hr wkly. Target aud: 35-54; general. ◆Norm Feuer, stn mgr; Gail Austin, opns mgr.

New Port Richey

WDUV(FM)—Licensed to New Port Richey. See Tampa

***WLPJ(FM)**— Apr 10, 1985: 91.5 mhz; 22 kw. Ant 230 ft. TL: N28 16 41 W82 43 06. Stereo. 6214 Springer Dr. 34668. Phone: (727) 848-9150. Fax: (727) 848-1233. E-mail: jeff@thejoyfm.com. Web Site: www.thejoyfm.com. Licensee: Radio Training Network Inc. (acq 1995; $100,000). Gammond & Grange. Format: Adult contemp, Christian. ◆James L. Campbell, pres; Jeff MacFarlane, gen mgr; Carmen Brown, prom dir; Steve Rieker, chief of engrg.

WPSO(AM)— Oct 31, 1963: 1500 khz; 250 w-D. TL: N28 15 32 W82 43 54. 109 Bayview Blvd., #A, Oldsmar 34677. Phone: (727) 725-3500. Phone: (727) 725-5555. Fax: (813) 814-7500. E-mail: wpso@wpso.com. Web Site: www.wpso.com. Licensee: AKMA Broadcast Network Inc. (acq 1993; $250,000; 9-13-93). Format: News/talk, Greek. News staff: one; News: 35 hrs wkly. Target aud: General; international, ethnic. Spec prog: Pol two hrs, quiz/trivia program, relg 8 hrs, East Indian one hr, lt 3 hrs wkly. ◆Sam Agelatos, pres & gen mgr; Angelo Agelatos, chief of opns.

New Smyrna Beach

***WJLU(FM)**— Sept 7, 1989: 89.7 mhz; 5 kw. 328 ft. TL: N29 00 32 W80 58 27. (CP: 10 kw). Stereo. 4295 Ridgewood Ave., Port Orange 32127. Phone: (904) 756-9094. Fax: (904) 760-7107. E-mail: thecornerstone @cornerstoneministry.org. Web Site: www.cornerstoneministry.org. Licensee: Cornerstone Broadcasting Corp. Network: Network: USA, Moody. Format: Relg. News: 18 hrs wkly. Target aud: General; families. ◆William Powell, gen mgr; Dave Purin, progmg dir; Sandra Leisner, pub affrs dir; William A. Leisner, chief of engrg.

WSBB(AM)— 1950: 1230 khz; 1 kw-U. TL: N29 01 57 W80 55 03. Box 1128, Daytona Beach 32115. Secondary address: 175 N. Causeway 32169. Phone: (386) 428-9091. Fax: (386) 428-7835. E-mail: wsbb@cfl.rr.com. Web Site: www.wsbb.com. Licensee: T.K. Radio Inc. (acq 10-7-91; $50,000; 10-28-91). Format: Adult standard. News: 120 hrs wkly. Target aud: 45 plus. Spec prog: Pol one hr, relg 5 hrs wkly. ◆Brian Tolby, pres & gen mgr; Bob Knight, opns mgr.

Newberry

WHHZ(FM)— February 1999: 100.5 mhz; 44 kw. Ant 469 ft. TL: N29 36 29 W82 51 01. 3135 S.E. 27th St., Grainesville 32641. Phone: (352) 372-2528. Fax: (352) 372-0851. E-mail: themorningbuzz2004@yahoo.com. Web Site: www.1005thebuzz.com. Licensee: Jablamo License Holdings LLC. (group owner; (acq 7-6-2004); grpsl). Format: Modern rock. ◆Jim Flannery, gen mgr.

Niceville

WNCV(FM)— May 1, 1993: 100.3 mhz; 3.5 kw. 440 ft. TL: N30 29 20 W86 25 16. Box 2347, 225 Hollywood Blvd. N.W., Ft. Walton Beach 32548. Phone: (850) 243-2323. Fax: (850) 243-6806. E-mail: coastoffice@wncv.com. Web Site: www.wncv.com. Licensee: Cumulus Licensing Corp. Group owner: Cumulus Media Inc. (acq 1-10-03; grpsl). Network: Jones Radio Networks. Format: Adult contemp, soft hits. Target aud: 25-54; upscale income. ◆Ron Raybourne, gen mgr & stn mgr; Jim Wellem, opns mgr.

Nocatee

WZSP(FM)— Aug 27, 1998: 105.3 mhz; 6 kw. 328 ft. TL: N27 11 01 W81 56 57. Heartland Broadcasting Corp., 7891 U.S. Highway 17 S., Zolfo Springs 33890. Phone: (863) 494-4111. Fax: (863) 494-4443. E-mail: wzsp@desoto.net. Web Site: www.wzsp1053.com. Licensee: Heartland Broadcasting Corp. Network: CNN Radio. Rgnl Reps Kaye, Scholer, Fierman, Hays & Handler. Format: Sp. Target aud: General; Spanish speaking audience, Charlotte, Desoto, Hardee, Sarasota & Highlands counties. Spec prog: Children. ◆Harold Kneller Jr., pres; Sherry Good, gen mgr & opns mgr; Carolyn Francoletti, engrg dir & sls.

North Fort Myers

WWCN(AM)— Dec 17, 1983: 770 khz; 10 kw-D, 1 kw-N, DA-2. TL: N26 46 30 W81 50 51. Stereo. 20125 S. Tamiami Tr., Estero 33928. Phone: (239) 495-2100. Fax: (239) 992-8165. Web Site: www.am770.com. Licensee: Beasley Radio Co. Group owner: Beasley Broadcast Group (acq 12-16-87). Format: Talk, sports. ◆George Beasley, pres; Bradley C. Beasley, gen mgr; John Rozz, opns mgr.

North Miami

WKAT(AM)— November 1937: 1360 khz; 5 kw-D, 1 kw-N. TL: N25 44 36 W80 09 14. 3191 Coral Way, Suite 1000, Miami 33145. Phone: (305) 503-1340. Fax: (305) 503-1349. E-mail: info@classical1360.com. Web Site: www.classical1360.com. Licensee: Caron Broadcasting Inc. (acq 12-10-2004; $10 million). Bob Healey. Format: Classical. Target aud: 30-50. ◆Edward G. Atsinger III, pres; Andy Korge, gen mgr.

North Miami Beach

WXDJ(FM)— 1986: 95.7 mhz; 40 kw. 531 ft. TL: N25 46 29 W80 11 19. Stereo. 1001 Ponce deLeon Blvd., Coral Gables 33134. Phone: (305) 444-3900. Licensee: WXDJ Licensing Inc. Group owner: Spanish Broadcasting System Inc. (acq 7-11-97; $110 million with WRMA(FM) Fort Lauderdale). Wiley, Rein & Fielding. Format: Salsa. News: 4 hrs wkly. Target aud: 18-54; Hispanic Adults. ◆Marielena Johnson, gen mgr.

North Palm Beach

WGGT(AM)—Not on air, target date: 7/01/05: 960 khz; 5 kw-D, 250 w-N, DA-D. TL: N26 49 01 W80 15 07. Intermart Broadcasting Southwest Florida Inc., 3434 S.W. 26th Pl., Cape Coral 33914. Phone: (239) 542-4200. Fax: (239) 542-4221. E-mail: swfradio@aol.com. Licensee: Intermart Broadcasting Southwest Florida Inc. ◆Patricia S. Woods, VP & gen mgr.

Ocala

WCFI(FM)— 1939: 1290 khz; 5 kw-D, 1 kw-N, DA-N. TL: N29 11 51 W82 10 57. 3621 N.W. Tenth St. 34475. Fax: (352) 351-9307. E-mail: wcfi1290@wcfi1290.com. Web Site: www.wcfi1290.com. Licensee: Vector Communications Inc. (acq 9-24-99; $250,000). Format: News/talk. News staff: one; News: 20 hrs wkly. Target aud: 35 plus. Spec prog: Loc talk 13, farm 5 hrs wkly. ◆Robert J. Maines Jr., gen mgr & stn mgr; Tom Duff, opns mgr.

***WHIJ(FM)**— Mar 30, 1990: 88.1 mhz; 1.25 kw. 394 ft. TL: N29 14 17 W82 07 17. Stereo. 3343 E. Silver Springs Blvd. 34470. Phone: (352) 351-8810. Fax: (352) 351-8917. E-mail: thejoyfm@thejoyfm.com. Web Site: www.thejoyfm.com. Licensee: Radio Training Network Inc. (acq 10-5-01; $80,000. with WAQV(FM) Crystal River). Gammon & Grange. Format: Adult contemp, educ, Christian. Target aud: 20-50. ◆Jeff Macfariano, gen mgr; Joe Cerreta, stn mgr.

WMFQ(FM)— July 11, 1977: 92.9 mhz; 50 kw. 476 ft. TL: N29 04 45 W82 05 35. Stereo. 3357 S.W. 7th St. 34474. Phone: (352) 732-2442. Fax: (352) 622-6675. E-mail: feedback@bigoldies929.com. Web Site: www.wmfq.fm. Licensee: Asterisk Communications Inc. Group owner: Asterisk Inc. (acq 1995; $2.1 million). Rep: McGavren Guild. Reddy, Begley & McCormick. Format: Adult Oldies. News staff: one; News: 5 hrs wkly. Target aud: 35 plus; upscale. Spec prog: Black 2 hrs wkly. ◆Frederick H. Ingham, pres; John Rutledge, gen mgr; Shane Finch, opns dir.

WMOP(AM)— Dec 18, 1953: 900 khz; 5 kw-D, 23 w-N. TL: N29 14 17 W82 07 17. Stereo. Box 3930 34478-3930. Secondary address: 343 N.E. First Ave. 34470. Phone: (352) 732-2010. Fax: (352) 629-1614. E-mail: sales@floridasportstalk.com. Web Site: www.floridasportstalk.com. Licensee: Florida Sportstalk Inc. (acq*11-14-96; $350,000). Network: ABC. Rep: Dora-Clayton. Pepper & Corazzini. Format: Sports, talk. News staff: one; News: 3 hrs wkly. Target aud: 35 plus. ◆Gordon Smith, gen mgr.

WOCA(AM)— May 1957: 1370 khz; 5 kw-D. TL: N29 12 04 W82 09 07. Box 1056 34478. Secondary address: 1515 E. Silver Springs Blvd., Suite 134 34470. Phone: (352) 732-8000. Phone: (352) 622-9622. Fax: (352) 732-0174. E-mail: woca@woca.com. Web Site: www.woca.com. Licensee: Westshore Broadcasting Inc. Network: ABC Daytime Direction. Format: News/talk. News staff: two; News: 16 hrs wkly. Target aud: 35 plus. Spec prog: Black 2 hrs wkly. ◆Tishia A. Moeller, gen mgr; Larry Whitler, opns mgr.

WOGK(FM)— Nov 7, 1960: 93.7 mhz; 100 kw. 1,348 ft. TL: N29 16 06 W82 04 51. Stereo. 3602 N.E. 20th Pl. 34470. Phone: (352) 622-5600. Fax: (352) 622-3998. E-mail: terry@937kcountry.com. Web Site: www.93kcountry.com. Licensee: Ocala Broadcasting L.L.C. Group owner: Wooster Republican Printing Co. (acq 9-27-86). Format: Country. News staff: one; News: 3 hrs wkly. Target aud: 25-54; general. ◆G. Charles Dix, pres; Jim Robertson, VP & gen mgr.

Ocoee

WUNA(AM)— Oct 25, 1962: 1480 khz; 1 kw-D, 71 w-N. TL: N28 33 27 W81 32 29. Stereo. 749 S. Bluford Ave. 34761. Phone: (407) 656-9823. Fax: (407) 656-2092. E-mail: WUNA1480orlando@juno.com. Licensee: Way Broadcasting Licensee LLC (acq 4-20-2000; grpsl). Format: Sp contemp. ◆Juan Nieves, gen mgr & chief of engrg; Sheila Rodriguez, sls dir; Jose Lopez, progmg dir.

Okeechobee

WOKC(AM)— Feb 6, 1962: 1570 khz; 1 kw-D, 14 w-N. TL: N27 12 59 W80 49 53. Stereo. 210 W. North Park St., Suite 102 34974. Phone: (863) 467-1570. Fax: (863) 763-3171. E-mail: wokc@gladesmedia.com. Web Site: www.wokc.com. Licensee: Glades Media Co. LLC (acq 7-31-01; $200,000). Format: Classic country. News staff: one; News: 10 hrs wkly. Target aud: General. ◆Robbie Castellanos, CEO, pres & gen mgr.

Orange Park

***WAYR(AM)**— May 28, 1960: 550 khz; 5 kw-D, 500 w-N, DA-1. TL: N30 04 21 W81 47 24. 2500 Russell Rd., Green Cove Springs 32043-9492. Phone: (904) 284-1111. Phone: (904) 284-2500. Fax: (904) 284-2501. E-mail: lstephens@wayradio.org. Web Site: www.wayradio.org. Licensee: Good Tidings Trust Inc. Wiley, Rein & Fielding. Relg. Target aud: 45 plus; mature Christian. ◆Bill Tidwell, pres & chief of engrg; Luke Stephens, gen mgr; Bart Wagner, progmg dir; Jim Collins, pub affrs dir.

Orlando

WAMT(AM)—See Pine Castle-Sky Lake

WDBO(AM)— May 24, 1924: 580 khz; 5 kw-U, DA-N. TL: N28 37 12 W81 24 34. 4192 John Young Pkwy. 32804. Phone: (407) 295-5858. Fax: (407) 291-4879. Web Site: www.wdbo.com. Licensee: Cox Radio Inc. Group owner: Cox Broadcasting (acq 3-28-97; grpsl). Network: ABC Information & Entertainment. Format: News/talk. ◆Bill Hendrich,

Florida

gen mgr; Steve Holbrook, opns mgr; Tom Interrante, gen sls mgr; Steve Avellone, natl sls mgr; Rich Mastroberte, prom dir; Kipper McGee, progmg dir; Marsha Taylor, news dir; Steve Fluker, chief of engrg.

WDYZ(AM)— Dec 5, 1947: 990 khz; 50 kw-D, 5 kw-N, DA-2. TL: N28 34 28 W81 27 48. Stereo. 610 Sycamore St., Suite 220, Celebration 34747. Phone: (407) 566-2033. Fax: (407) 566-2034. E-mail: paul.t.proly@ABC.com. Web Site: www.radiodisney.com. Licensee: Radio Disney Group LLC. Group owner: ABC Inc. (acq 1-23-01; $5 million. cash). Network: Radio Disney. Format: Children. Target aud: 45 plus; adults. ◆Jean-Paul Colaco, pres; Paul T. Proly, gen mgr; Salan Stone, mktg VP; Robin Jones, progmg VP.

WFLF(AM)—See Pine Hills

WHTQ(FM)— 1952: 96.5 mhz; 100 kw. 1,600 ft. TL: N28 34 51 W81 04 32. Stereo. 4192 John Young Parkway 32804. Phone: (407) 422-9696. Fax: (407) 422-5883. Web Site: www.whtq.com. Licensee: Cox Radio Inc. Group owner: Cox Broadcasting (acq 1997). Format: Classic rock. News staff: one; News: 2 hrs wkly. Target aud: 25-54; adult male. ◆Debbie Morel, VP & gen mgr.

***WMFE-FM**— July 14, 1980: 90.7 mhz; 100 kw. 731 ft. TL: N28 36 08 W81 05 37. Stereo. 11510 E. Colonial Dr. 32817-4699. Phone: (407) 273-2300. Fax: (407) 273-8462. Fax: (407) 273-3613. Web Site: www.wmfe.org. Licensee: Community Communications Inc. Network: Network: PRI, NPR. Format: Class, news & info. News staff: 4; News: 48 hrs wkly. Target aud: 35 plus; well-educated, executive, professional, upper-income. Spec prog: New instrumental 4 hrs wkly. ◆Stephen M. Steck, CEO & pres; Patrick Dalton, opns mgr; Bethany Mott, sls VP & sls dir; Philip Kuhn, progmg VP; David Glerum, mus dir; Pat Duggins, news dir; Mike Simmons, engrg dir.

WMGF(FM)—See Mount Dora

WMMO(FM)— Aug 19, 1990: 98.9 mhz; 44 kw. 522 ft. TL: N28 34 27 W81 27 46. Stereo. 4192 John Young Pkwy. 32804. Phone: (407) 422-9890. Phone: (407) 422-5883. Web Site: www.wmmo.com. Licensee: Cox Radio Inc. Group owner: Cox Broadcasting Rep: Christal. Format: Adult contemp, soft rock. News: one hr wkly. Target aud: 25-49. ◆Debbie Morel, VP & gen mgr; Fleetwood Gruver, opns mgr.

WOKB(AM)—See Winter Garden

WOMX-FM— Aug 15, 1967: 105.1 mhz; 95 kw. 1,309 ft. TL: N28 36 17 W81 05 13. (CP: Ant 1,597 ft.). Stereo. 1800 Pembrook Dr., Suite 400 32810. Phone: (407) 919-1000. Fax: (407) 919-1138. Web Site: www.mix1051.com. Licensee: Infinity Radio Inc. Group owner: Infinity Broadcasting Corp. (acq 12-14-00; grpsl). Leibowitz & Associates. Format: Adult contemp. News staff: one. ◆Michele Holland, CEO & gen sls mgr.

WPCV(FM)—See Lakeland

WPRD(AM)—See Winter Park

WQTM(AM)— 1947: 740 khz; 50 kw-U, DA-2. TL: N28 28 53 W81 39 43. 2500 Maitland Center Pkwy., Suite 401, Maitland 32751. Phone: (407) 916-7800. Fax: (407) 916-0329. E-mail: programdirector@7400theteam.com. Web Site: www.740theteam.com. Licensee: Clear Channel Radio Licenses Inc. Group owner: Clear Channel Communications Inc. (acq 11-21-97; grpsl). Network: CBS. Format: Talk, sports. Target aud: 25-54; adult male. ◆Linda Byrd, gen mgr; Chris Kampmeier, opns dir; Rick Everett, mktg dir; Bill Alverson, prom mgr.

WRLZ(AM)—(Eatonville). 1957: 1270 khz; 5 kw-U, DA-N. TL: N28 34 03 W81 25 38. Box 593642 32859-3642. Secondary address: 6106 B Hoffner Ave. 32822. Phone: (407) 345-0700. Fax: (407) 345-1492. E-mail: info@radioluz1270.com. Web Site: www.radioluz1270.com. Licensee: Radio Luz Inc. (acq 1996; $378,500). Format: Sp, contemp. Target aud: General; Family. ◆Saturnino Gonzalez, pres; John Maldonado, gen mgr.

WRMQ(AM)— Oct 21, 1985; 1140 khz; 4.1 kw-D. TL: N28 30 42 W81 14 09. 1033 Semoran Blvd., Suite 253, Casselberry 32707. Phone: (407) 830-0800. Fax: (407) 260-6100. E-mail: wonq1030@aol.com. Licensee: Florida Broadcasters. Rep: Caballero. Roy F. Perkins. Format: Talk, Sp. Target aud: 25-54. ◆George M. Arroyo, pres & gen mgr.

WRUM(FM)— July 1, 1971: 100.3 mhz; 100 kw. Ant 1,597 ft. TL: N28 36 08 W81 05 37. Stereo. 2500 Maitland Ctr. Pkwy., Suite 401, Maitland 32751. Phone: (407) 916-7800. Fax: (407) 916-7400. Web Site: www.rumba1003.com. Licensee: Clear Channel Broadcasting Licenses Inc. Group owner: Clear Channel Communications Inc. (acq 1997; grpsl). Format: Sp/tropical. Target aud: 18-44. ◆Linda Byrd, pres & gen mgr; Chris Kampmeier, opns dir.

WSDO(AM)—See Sanford

WTKS-FM—(Cocoa Beach). May 8, 1962: 104.1 mhz; 100 kw. 1,609 ft. TL: N28 34 51 W81 04 32. Stereo. 2500 Maitland Ctr. Pkwy., Suite 401, Maitland 32751. Phone: (407) 916-7800. Fax: (407) 916-7511. Web Site: www.wtks.com. Licensee: Clear Channel Broadcasting Licenses Inc. Group owner: Clear Channel Communications Inc. (acq 11-21-97; grpsl). Format: Entertainment talk. News staff: 7; News: 6 hrs wkly. Target aud: Adults; 25-54. ◆Linda Byrd, gen mgr & chief of engrg.

WTLN(AM)— April 1, 1940: 950 khz; 12 kw-U, DA-N. TL: N28 32 08 W81 26 55. 1188 Lake View Dr., Altamonte Springs 32714. Phone: (407) 682-9494. Fax: (407) 682-7005. Web Site: www.wtln.com. Licensee: TM2 Inc. (acq 7-14-98; $500,000). Rep: Salem. Holland & Knight. Format: Christian, talk. Target aud: 25-44; general. ◆Thomas H. Moffit Jr., pres; Janice Willis, stn mgr, gen sls mgr & progmg dir.

***WUCF-FM**— Jan 30, 1978: 89.9 mhz; 40 kw. 194 ft. TL: N28 36 00 W81 12 05. Stereo. Box 162199 32816-2199. Secondary address: Bldg. 75, 4000 Central Florida Blvd., Room 130 32816. Phone: (407) 823-0899. Fax: (407) 823-6364. Web Site: wucf.cf.ucf.edu. Licensee: University of Central Florida. Network: Network: NPR, PRI. Cohn & Marks. Format: Jazz. News staff: 10; News: 16 hrs wkly. Spec prog: Fr one hr, It one hr, Indian 5 hrs, blues 6 hrs, bluegrass 3 hrs, Irish one hr wkly. ◆John Hitt, pres; Kayonne Riley, gen mgr; Bruce Duerie, engrg dir & chief of engrg.

WXXL(FM)—See Leesburg

Orlovista

WEUS(AM)—Not on air, target date: 10/05: 810 khz; 1 kw-D, 400 w-N, DA-2. TL: N28 33 39 W81 30 23. 357 Ocean Shore Blvd., Ormond Beach 32176. Phone: (386) 672-2723. Fax: (386) 673-9795. Licensee: Star Over Orlando Inc. ◆Carl Como, pres.

Ormond Beach

WELE(AM)— Aug 1, 1957: 1380 khz; 5 kw-D, 2.5 kw-N, DA-2. TL: N29 16 09 W81 04 54. 432 S. Nova Rd. 32174. Phone: (386) 677-4122. Fax: (386) 677-4123. E-mail: doug@wele1380.com. Web Site: www.wele1380.com. wele1380.com Licensee: Wings Communications Inc. (acq 9-90; $175,000; 9-24-90). Network: Network: CNN Radio, Westwood One. Format: News/talk. Target aud: General; mature, adults interested in sports & local current events. ◆F. Douglas Wilhite, pres & gen mgr; Sherry White, opns mgr.

Ormond-by-the-Sea

WHOG-FM— 1995: 95.7 mhz; 25 kw. 328 ft. TL: N29 14 10 W81 04 23. 126 W. International Speedway Blvd., Daytona Beach 32114. Phone: (386) 257-1150. Fax: (386) 239-0966. Web Site: www.whog.fm. Licensee: Black Crow LLC. Group owner: Black Crow Media Group LLC (acq 9-21-2001; grpsl). Format: Classic rock, AOR. ◆Stacey Knerler, gen mgr; Donna Fillion, sls dir & progmg dir.

Oviedo

WONQ(AM)— Nov 21, 1992: 1030 khz; 10 kw-D, 1.7 kw-N, DA-2. TL: N28 40 31 W81 10 01. 1033 Semoran Blvd., Suite 253, Casselberry 32707. Phone: (407) 830-0800. Fax: (407) 260-6100. E-mail: wonq1030@aol.com. Licensee: Florida Broadcasters. Network: CNN en Espanol. Rep: Caballero. Roy F. Perkins. Format: Sp music, news, contemp Latin hits. Target aud: 25-54. ◆George M. Arroyo, pres & gen mgr; George Mier, opns VP.

Palatka

WGNE-FM— Dec 13, 1973: 99.9 mhz; 100 kw. 1,201 ft. TL: N29 31 08 W81 19 02. Stereo. 801 W. Granada Blvd., Ormond Beach 32174. Phone: (386) 672-9210. Fax: (386) 677-2252. Web Site: www.999frog.com. Licensee: Renda Broadcasting Corp. Group owner: Renda Broadcasting Corp.-Renda Radio Inc. (acq 1996; $6.5 million. with WKQL(FM)

Directory of Radio

Brunswick, GA). Haley, Bader & Potts. Format: Country. Target aud: 18-49. ◆Toney Renda, pres; B. J. Nielson, gen mgr, sls dir & gen sls mgr.

***WHIF(FM)**— Mar 29, 1996: 91.3 mhz; 1.7 kw. 318 ft. TL: N29 38 54 W81 39 42. 201 S. Palm Ave. 32177. Phone: (386) 325-3334. Fax: (386) 325-0934. E-mail: whif@gbso.net. Web Site: http://www.whif.org. Licensee: Putnam Radio Ministries Inc. Format: Adult contemp, Christian. Target aud: 25-54; family-oriented, middle-class. Spec prog: Relg educ 10 hrs wkly. ◆Robin Toole, gen mgr & progmg dir.

WIYD(AM)— Feb 14, 1947: 1260 khz; 1 kw-D, 500 w-N, DA-N. TL: N29 38 23 W81 38 26. Box 918 32178-0918. Phone: (386) 325-4556. Fax: (386) 328-5161. E-mail: wiyd@atlantic.net. Licensee: Hall Broadcasting Co. (acq 2-14-57; $100,000). Format: C&W. News staff: one; News: 6 hrs wkly. Target aud: 18-49; rich & powerful. Spec prog: Relg 5 hrs wkly. ◆Ronald G. Tumlin, pres; Suzanne Tumlin, gen mgr; Mary Makie Connor, stn mgr, sls VP, prom VP, news dir & pub affrs dir; Bob Henry, progmg VP & mus dir.

WPLK(AM)— 1957: 800 khz; 1 kw-D, 334 w-N. TL: N29 37 40 W81 34 35. (CP: TL: N29 39 07 W81 35 32). Stereo. Box 335 32178. Secondary address: 1428 St. John's Ave. 32177. Phone: (386) 325-5800. Fax: (386) 328-8725. E-mail: wplk@wplk.com. Licensee: Radio Palatka Inc. (acq 4-28-98; $250,000 for stock). Network: ABC. Format: Oldies. News staff: one; News: 2 hrs wkly. Target aud: General. ◆Wayne Bullock, pres & gen mgr.

Palm Bay

***WEJF(FM)**— 1993: 90.3 mhz; 2 kw. 295 ft. TL: N28 02 54 W80 40 34. 2824B Palm Bay Rd. 32905. Secondary address: 505 Josephine St., Titusville 32796. Phone: (321) 722-9998/267-3000. Fax: (321) 724-0845. E-mail: wejf@bellsouth.net. Web Site: www.wejf.com. Licensee: Florida Public Radio Inc. (acq 7-95; $40,000). ◆Eric Sabo, gen mgr.

***WWIA(FM)**— July 1997: 88.5 mhz; 600 w vert. 108 ft. TL: N28 02 54 W80 40 34. Stereo. Victory Christian Academy, 100 Emerson Dr. N.W. 32907. Phone: (321) 953-9942. Fax: (321) 768-6265. Licensee: Victory Christian Academy. Format: Praise & worship. Target aud: Christian. ◆L. Mark Ostrander, pres & gen mgr.

Palm Beach

WBZT(AM)—See West Palm Beach

WRMF(FM)—Licensed to Palm Beach. See West Palm Beach

Palm City

***WCNO(FM)**— Apr 1, 1990: 89.9 mhz; 100 kw. 613 ft. TL: N27 07 20 W80 23 21. 2960 S.W. Mapp Rd. 34990-2737. Phone: (772) 221-1100. Fax: (772) 221-8716. E-mail: wcno@wcno.com. Web Site: www.wcno.com. Licensee: National Christian Network Inc. Format: Christian, adult contemp. ◆Tom Craton, gen mgr.

Palmetto

WBRD(AM)— October 1957: 1420 khz; 2.5 kw-D, 1 kw-N, DA-2. TL: N27 32 42 W82 34 28. Stereo. Box 144, Oneco 34264. Phone: (941) 955-1420. Fax: (941) 752-4794. E-mail: wbrdradio@aol.com. Web Site: www.wbrd.com. Licensee: Metropolitan Radio Group Inc. (group owner; acq 6-96). Format: Southern Gospel. Target aud: 35 plus. ◆Mark Acker, pres; Bill Bailey, gen mgr & opns dir; Roy Smith, progmg dir; T. Michael Craft, chief of engrg & engr.

Panama City

WDIZ(AM)— April 1940: 590 khz; 1.7 kw-D, 2.5 kw-N, DA-N. TL: N30 10 20 W85 36 49. Stereo. Box 5288 32412. Secondary address: 1834 Lisenby Ave. 32405. Phone: (850) 769-6161. Fax: (850) 769-0659. Licensee: Clear Channel Broadcasting Licenses Inc. Group owner: Clear Channel Communications Inc. (acq 11-21-97; grpsl). Rep: Allied Radio Partners. Format: Nostalgia. ◆Peter Nordan, gen mgr.

WFSY(FM)— Co-owned with WDIZ(AM). October 1971: 98.5 mhz; 100 kw. 1,090 ft. TL: N30 30 41 W85 29 24. Stereo. Format: Adult contemp. Target aud: 25-54.

Stations in the U.S.   Florida

Developers & Brokers of Radio Properties — contact American Media Services at our suite: Philadelphia Marriott Downtown 215-625-2900   843-972-2200   americanmediaservices.com   Charleston, SC   Dallas, TX · Chicago, Il · Austin, TX   American Media Services, LLC

*WFFL(FM)—Not on air, target date: unknown: 91.7 mhz; 310 w. Ant 207 ft. TL: N30 10 47 W85 38 11. Box 2440, Tupelo, MS 38803-2440. Phone: (662) 844-8888. Fax: (662) 842-6791. Web Site: www.afr.net. Licensee: American Family Association. ♦Marvin Sanders, gen mgr.

*WFSW(FM)— 1995: 89.1 mhz; 100 kw. 403 ft. TL: N30 22 02 W85 55 29. 1600 Red Barber Plaza, Tallahassee 32310. Phone: (850) 487-3086. Fax: (850) 487-3293. Web Site: www.wfsu.org. Licensee: Florida State University. Network: NPR. Format: News, talk. ♦Pat Keating, gen mgr; Caroline Austin, stn mgr; Aron Myers, prom dir; Marshall Griffen, news dir; Andy Hanus, engrg dir.

WILN(FM)— Apr 11, 1985: 105.9 mhz; 50 kw. Ant 406 ft. TL: N30 10 44 W85 46 55. Stereo. 7106 Laird St., Suite 102, Panama City Beach 32408. Phone: (850) 230-5855. Fax: (850) 230-6988. E-mail: kimstyles@aol.com. Web Site: www.island106.com. Licensee: Styles Media Group LLC (group owner; acq 1-31-03; grpsl). Format: CHR. News staff: one; News: 2 hrs wkly. Target aud: 18-49. ♦Kim Styles, CEO & gen mgr; Mike Preble, opns VP.

*WJTF(FM)— Oct 15, 1998: 89.9 mhz; 100 kw. 213 ft. TL: N30 10 20 W85 40 20. 835A S. Berthe 32404. Phone: (850) 874-9900. Fax: (850) 874-9930. E-mail: wjtf@bellsouth.net. Web Site: www.wjtf.org. Licensee: Joy Public Broadcasting Corp. (acq 5-4-93; $11,000; 5-24-93). Network: Moody. Hill & Welch. Format: Relg, educ. Target aud: 35-90; general. ♦Kelly Dickson, opns mgr; Lowell M. Bush, pres, gen mgr & dev dir.

*WKGC-FM— October 1982: 90.7 mhz; 100 kw. 336 ft. TL: N30 13 05 W85 51 16. Stereo. 5230 W. Hwy. 98 32401. Phone: (850) 873-3500. Fax: (850) 913-3299. E-mail: fsundram@gulfcoast.edu. Web Site: www.wkgc.org. Licensee: Gulf Coast Community College. Network: Network: NPR, PRI. Dow, Lohnes & Albertson. Format: News. Target aud: General. Spec prog: Black 6 hrs wkly. ♦Robert Spadden, pres; Frank Sundram, gen mgr; Reed Kinney, opns mgr.

WLTG(AM)— Dec 11, 1949: 1430 khz; 5 kw-U, DA-2. TL: N30 09 55 W85 35 19. Box 15635 32406. Secondary address: 3100 E. 15th St., Springfield 32405. Phone: (850) 784-9873. Fax: (850) 784-6908. Licensee: Williams Communications Inc. (group owner; acq 8-12-03; $500,000). Format: News/talk, sports, info. Target aud: General. Spec prog: Black gospel 7 hrs wkly. ♦John Gay, gen mgr, sls dir & progmg dir.

WPAP-FM— Mar 30, 1967: 92.5 mhz; 100 kw. 930 ft. TL: N30 22 05 W85 12 24. Stereo. Caller Box 59288 32412. Secondary address: 1834 Lisenby Ave. 32405. Phone: (850) 769-1408. Fax: (850) 769-0659. Web Site: www.wpapfm.com. Licensee: Clear Channel Radio Licenses Inc. Group owner: Clear Channel Communications Inc. (acq 11-21-97; grpsl). Rep: McGavren Guild. Format: Modern country. Target aud: 25-54. ♦Pete Norden, gen mgr; Jim Radford, opns mgr.

WPBH(FM)—See Mexico Beach

WPFM-FM— September 1963: 107.9 mhz; 100 kw. 781 ft. TL: N30 26 00 W85 24 51. (CP: 98.4 kw, ant 954 ft. TL: N30 13 45 W85 23 20). Stereo. 118 Gwyn Dr., Panama City Beach 32407. Phone: (850) 234-8858. Fax: (850) 234-6592. Licensee: Double O Radio Corp. (group owner; acq 3-10-2004; grpsl). Rep: Christal. Format: Contemp hit/Top-40. Target aud: 18-49; active lifestyle, young adult audience. ♦Steve Green, gen mgr.

WYOO(FM)—(Springfield). Mar 2, 1993: 101.1 mhz; 5.2 kw. 236 ft. TL: N30 12 12 W85 36 57. (CP: 25 kw). Stereo. 7106 Laird St., Suite 102, Panama City Beach 32408. Phone: (850) 230-5855. Fax: (850) 230-6988. Web Site: www.talkradio101.com. Licensee: Styles Media Group LLC (group owner; acq 9-30-02; grpsl). Rep: Christal. Richard Hayes. Format: Talk. News staff: one; News: 28 hrs wkly. Target aud: 25-54; educated, upscale. ♦Thomas DiBacco, chmn; Kim Styles, pres & gen mgr; Mike Preble, opns dir & adv mgr.

Panama City Beach

WASJ(FM)— January 1993: 105.1 mhz; 50 kw. 335 ft. TL: N30 10 44 W85 46 55. Stereo. 118 Gwyn Dr., Panama City 32408. Phone: (850) 234-8858. Fax: (850) 234-6592. E-mail: sstevegreen@panamacityradio.com. Web Site: www.smoothjazz1051.com. Licensee: Double O Radio Corp. (group owner; acq 3-10-2004; grpsl). Rep: Christal. Format: Smooth Jazz. ♦Kevin Harlan, gen mgr; Steve Larson, progmg dir.

WFSY(FM)—See Panama City

*WKGC(AM)— June 25, 1965: 1480 khz; 500 w-D, 87 w-N. TL: N30 10 33 W85 48 03. 5230 W. Hwy. 98, Panama City 32401. Phone: (850) 873-3500. Fax: (850) 913-3299. E-mail: fsundram@gnfcoast.edu. Web Site: www.wkgc.org. Licensee: Gulf Coast Community College. (acq 12-1-72). Network: NPR. Format: Easy listening. News: 25 hrs wkly. Target aud: General; college students & older high school students. Spec prog: Folk 2 hrs, educ 8 hrs wkly. ♦Robert McSpadden, pres; Frank Sundram, gen mgr & stn mgr; Reed Kinney, opns mgr.

WPCF(AM)— Sept 23, 1958: 1290 khz; 270 w-D, 1 kw-N. TL: N30 10 44 W85 46 55. 7106 Laird St., Suite 102 32408. Phone: (850) 230-5855. Fax: (850) 230-6988. E-mail: kimstyles@aol.com. Licensee: Styles Media Group L.L.C. (group owner; acq 9-30-02; grpsl). Format: Sports. ♦Kim Styles, CEO, gen mgr & gen mgr; Peter Gunn, stn mgr; Mike Preble, opns mgr.

WVVE(FM)— June 1988: 100.1 mhz; 12 kw. Ant 403 ft. TL: N30 10 44 W85 46 55. Stereo. 7106 Laird St., Suite 102 32408. Phone: (850) 230-5855. Fax: (850) 230-6988. E-mail: kimstyles@aol.com. Licensee: Styles Media Group LLC (group owner; acq 9-30-02; grpsl). Format: Adult contemp. ♦Kim Styles, CEO, CEO & gen mgr; Mike Piebie, opns mgr.

Parker

WFBX(FM)— August 1977: 94.5 mhz; 100 kw. 991 ft. TL: N29 49 09 W85 15 34. Stereo. Box 59288, Panama City 32412. Phone: (850) 769-1408. Fax: (850) 769-6620. Web Site: www.945thefox.com. Licensee: Clear Channel Broadcasting Licenses Inc. Group owner: Clear Channel Communications Inc. (acq 11-21-97; grpsl). Format: Soft rock. Target aud: 25 plus; adults. Spec prog: Relg 5 hrs wkly. ♦Pete Norden, gen mgr.

Pennsuco

*WIRP(FM)— 1999: 88.3 mhz; 2.25 kw. Ant 282 ft. TL: N25 52 24 W80 28 59. (CP: 6 kw). Stereo. 1400 N.W. 107 Ave., Suite 306, Miami 33172. Phone: (305) 406-2883. Fax: (305) 406-3030. E-mail: info@pariso883.com. Web Site: www.paraiso883.com. Licensee: Genesis Radio Network Inc. (acq 4-11-2005; $1.69 million). Format: Christian, Sp. News staff: one; News: 3 hrs wkly. Target aud: 18-35; Hispanic Christians. Spec prog: Children 6 hrs. ♦Edwin L. Ortiz, pres; Ricardo Ballesteros, gen mgr; Mauricio Quintana, stn mgr.

Pensacola

WBSR(AM)— Sept 1, 1946: 1450 khz; 1 kw-U. TL: N30 25 44 W87 14 27. Box 19047 32523. Secondary address: 1601 N. Pace Blvd. 32505. Phone: (850) 438-4982. Fax: (850) 433-7932. E-mail: wbsr@wbsr.com. Licensee: Easy Media Inc. (acq 2-23-85; $330,000; 2-25-85). Format: Soft adult contemp. Target aud: 35-54. ♦Frederic T.C. Brewer, pres; Gene Pfalzer, stn mgr.

WCOA(AM)— Feb 3, 1926: 1370 khz; 5 kw-U, DA-N. TL: N30 26 57 W87 15 46. 6565 N. W St. 32505. Phone: (850) 478-6011. Fax: (850) 478-3971. Licensee: Cumulus Licensing Corp. Group owner: Cumulus Media Inc. (acq 10-25-99; with co-located FM). Network: Network: Moody, ABC Information & Entertainment. Rep: McGavren Guild. Format: News/talk. Target aud: 25-54. Spec prog: Relg 6 hrs wkly. ♦Curt Peterson, gen mgr; Chris Peddie, progmg dir & news dir; Yancy McNair, chief of engrg.

WJLQ(FM)—Co-owned with WCOA(AM). Sept 1, 1965: 100.7 mhz; 100 kw. 1,555 ft. TL: N30 37 35 W87 38 50. Stereo. Format: Music, hot adult comtemp. Target aud: 25-44. ♦Mark Dagwell, progmg dir.

WMEZ(FM)— Nov 11, 1960: 94.1 mhz; 100 kw. 1,328 ft. TL: N30 35 18 W87 33 16. Stereo. 1101 Gulf Breeze Pkwy., Suite 102, Gulf Breeze 32561. Phone: (850) 916-9222. Fax: (850) 916-9266. Web Site: www.softrock941.com. Licensee: 6 Johnson Road Licenses Inc. Group owner: Pamal Broadcasting Ltd. (acq 10-19-2001; grpsl). Network: Westwood One. Format: Soft rock. Target aud: 25-54. ♦Dave Cobb, gen mgr; Kevin Peterson, progmg mgr; Gerald Wilson, chief of engrg.

WNVY(AM)—(Cantonment). December 1955: 1090 khz; 10 kw-D (2.3 kw-CH). TL: N30 34 47 W87 17 18. 2070 N. Palafox 32501. Phone: (850) 434-1230. Fax: (850) 469-9698. E-mail: mglin@aol.com. Web Site: www.pensacolachristianradio.com. Licensee: 1090-AM. (acq 4-7-97). Format: Black gospel. ♦Michael Glinter, gen mgr.

*WPCS(FM)— June 22, 1971: 89.5 mhz; 95 kw. Ant 1,358 ft. TL: N30 35 16 W87 33 13. Stereo. Box 18000, 250 Brent Ln. 32523. Phone: (850) 479-6570. Fax: (850) 969-1638. E-mail: rbn@rejoice.org. Web Site: www.rejoice.org. Licensee: Pensacola Christian College Inc. Format: Relg, educ. ♦Arlin Horton, pres & gen mgr; Ted Nadaskay, chief of engrg; Paul Stimer, opns.

WPNN(AM)— October 1956: 790 khz; 1 kw-D. TL: N30 27 18 W87 14 22. 3801 N. Pace Blvd. 32505. Phone: (850) 433-1141. Fax: (850) 433-1142. Web Site: www.cnnpensacola.com. Licensee: Miracle Radio Inc. (acq 4-1-81). Smithwick & Belendiuk. Format: Local news, CNN Headline News. ♦Gerald Schroeder, pres; Don Schroeder, gen mgr; Michael Schroeder, stn mgr.

WRNE(AM)— November 1957: 980 khz; 4 kw-D, 1 kw-N, DA-N. TL: N30 29 08 W87 05 01. Stereo. 312 E. Nine Mile Rd., Suite 27-D 32514. Phone: (850) 478-6000. Fax: (850) 484-8080. E-mail: hill@wrne980.com. Web Site: www.wrne980.com. Licensee: Media One Communications Inc. (acq 11-15-90; 11-19-90). Rep: Dora-Clayton. Dennis J. Kelly. Format: Urban contemp; Gospel; Hispanic. News staff: one; News: 5 hrs wkly. Target aud: 25-54; minorities. Spec prog: Gospel, talk. ♦Robert Hill, pres & gen mgr.

WTKX-FM— 1971: 101.5 mhz; 100 kw. Ant 1,328 ft. TL: N30 35 18 W87 33 16. Stereo. 6485 Pensacola Blvd. 32505. Phone: (850) 473-0400. Fax: (850) 473-0907. E-mail: radio@tk101.com. Web Site: www.tk101.com. Licensee: Clear Channel Broadcasting Licenses Inc. Group owner: Clear Channel Communications Inc. (acq 11-21-97; grpsl). Wiley, Rein & Fielding. Format: Active rock. Target aud: 18-49; general. ♦Lowry Mays, CEO & chmn; Mark Mays, pres; Randall Mays, CFO.

*WUWF(FM)— January 1981: 88.1 mhz; 100 kw. 617 ft. TL: N30 24 09 W86 59 35. Stereo. 11000 University Pkwy. 32514. Phone: (904) 727-9696. E-mail: wuwf@wuwf.org. Web Site: www.wuwf.org. Licensee: Board of Trustees, University of West Florida (acq 12-4-01). Network: Network: PRI, NPR. Format: Class, news, adult alternative. News staff: one; News: 34 hrs wkly. Target aud: General. ♦Patrick Crawford, gen mgr; Sandra Averhart, news dir.

WVTJ(AM)— Nov 1, 1959: 610 khz; 500 w-D, 142 w-N. TL: N30 26 52 W87 15 30. 2070 N. Palafox Ave. 32501. Phone: (850) 434-1230. Fax: (850) 469-9698. E-mail: mglin@aol.com. Web Site: wvtj.net. Licensee: 610-AM. (acq 6-26-98; $130,000). Network: Network: UPI, USA. Format: Relg, praise, worship. Target aud: 18-64. ♦Michael Glinter, pres, gen mgr & dev VP.

WXBM-FM—See Milton

WYCL(FM)— Nov 10, 1976: 107.3 mhz; 100 kw. Ant 1,407 ft. TL: N30 42 20 W87 19 00. Stereo. 6485 Pensacola Blvd. 32505. Phone: (850) 473-0400. Fax: (850) 473-0907. Web Site: www.cool107.com. Licensee: Clear Channel Broadcasting Licenses Inc. Group owner: Clear Channel Communications Inc. (acq 9-30-2003; $2.2 million). Rep: McGavren Guild. Format: 60s & 70s. News staff: 2; News: 15 hrs wkly. Target aud: 25-54. ♦Jeanie Hufford, gen mgr; Eddie Hill, stn mgr & gen sls mgr; Steve Powers, opns dir.

WYCT(FM)— Nov 28, 2003: 98.7 mhz; 100 kw. Ant 981 ft. TL: N30 37 30 W87 26 39. Stereo. 7251 Plantation Rd. 32504. Phone: (850)

Florida | Directory of Radio

494-2800. Fax: (850) 494-0778. Web Site: www.catcountry987.com. Licensee: ADX Communications of Pensacola. Dan Alpert. Format: Country. ◆David E. Hoxeng, CEO; Mary Hoxeng, gen mgr; Susan Nieman, sls dir; Kevin King, opns.

WZNO(AM)— 1947: 1230 khz; 1 kw-U. TL: N30 25 57 W87 13 07. 2070 N. Palasox St. 32501. Phone: (850) 434-1230. Phone: (850) 433-9489. Fax: (850) 469-9698. E-mail: mglin@aol.com. Web Site: www.wzno.net. Licensee: 1230-AM Broadcasting Corp. Network: Motor Racing Net. Format: Southern gospel. News: 28 hrs wkly. Target aud: 25-54. ◆Michael Glinter, pres & gen mgr.

Perry

WNFK(FM)— December 1989: 92.1 mhz; 2.45 kw. 345 ft. TL: N30 07 36 W83 36 28. Stereo. 5450 Hwy. 27 E. 32347. Phone: (850) 584-9210. Fax: (850) 223-3492. E-mail: powercountry921@yahoo.com. Licensee: Taylor County Broadcasting Inc. (acq 4-19-00). ◆Bob Hendrickson, gen mgr; Jerry Allen, progmg dir.

WPRY(AM)— 1953: 1400 khz; 1 kw-U. TL: N30 06 27 W83 34 00. 872 Hwy. 27 E. 32347. Phone: (850) 223-1400. Fax: (850) 223-3501. Web Site: www.wpry.com. Licensee: HF Broadcasting Perry LC (acq 4-1-2004; $150,000). Format: Classic hits. News: 15 hrs wkly. Target aud: 18 plus. Spec prog: Black 2 hrs wkly. ◆Gary Williams, gen mgr.

Pine Castle-Sky Lake

WAMT(AM)— Jan 28, 1977: 1190 khz; 5 kw-D. TL: N28 27 58 W81 22 30. 1160 S. Semoran Blvd., Suite A, Orlando 32807. Phone: (407) 380-9255. Fax: (407) 382-7565. E-mail: studio@wamt1190.com. Web Site: www.wamt1190.com. Licensee: Genesis Communications I Inc. Group owner: Genesis Communications Inc. (acq 3-20-2000; $2.1 million). Network: Network: ABC, Westwood One. Rep: Interep. Booth, Freret, Imlay, & Tepper. Format: News/talk. Target aud: 25-65; general. ◆Bruce Maduri, pres; Don Childress, sr VP & gen sls mgr; Mike Burgess, opns mgr; Joe Nuchols, gen sls mgr; Chris Visse, progmg VP & progmg dir; Bill Smith, progmg dir & chief of engrg.

Pine Hills

WFLF(AM)— Sept 9, 1955: 540 khz; 50 kw-U, DA-2. TL: N28 07 57 W81 43 16. 2500 Maitland Center Pkwy., Suite 407, Maitland 32751. Phone: (407) 916-7800. Fax: (407) 661-1940. Web Site: www.540wfla.com. Licensee: Clear Channel Radio Licenses Inc. Group owner: Clear Channel Communications Inc. (acq 11-21-97; grpsl). Network: CBS. Format: News/talk. News staff: 5. Target aud: 35-64. Spec prog: Univ. of Central Florida football & basketball, Florida Marlins, Miami Dolphins. ◆Linda Byrd, gen mgr; Chris Kampmeier, opns VP & progmg VP; Mark Kanak, sls VP; Joe Russo, natl sls mgr; Rick Everett, prom dir; Bobbi King, prom mgr; Tom Benson, opns mgr & progmg dir; Larry Spilman, news dir; Mike Spry, engrg dir & chief of engrg; Dave Chambers, chief of engrg.

Pine Island Center

WPTK(AM)—Licensed to Pine Island Center. See Fort Myers

Pinellas Park

WTBN(AM)— Nov 12, 1966: 570 khz; 5 kw-D, DA-2. TL: N28 12 40 W82 31 46. 5211 W. Laurel St., Tampa 33607. Phone: (813) 639-1903. Fax: (813) 639-1272. E-mail: info@bayword.com. Web Site: www.bayword.com. Licensee: Common Ground Broadcasting Inc. Group owner: Salem Communications Corp. (acq 8-7-2001; $6.75 million). Network: Network: Network: CBS, CNN Radio, AP Radio. Format: Christian Talk Radio. News staff: 2; News: 30 hrs wkly. Target aud: 25-64. Spec prog: College (USF) sports football & basketball. ◆Chris Gould, gen mgr; Chris Turner, opns mgr; Phil Jimenez, gen sls mgr.

WWBA(AM)—Licensed to Pinellas Park. See Tampa

Plant City

WTWD(AM)— July 1949: 910 khz; 5 kw-D, DA-1. TL: N27 59 26 W82 12 31. 5211 Laurel St., Tampa 33607. Phone: (813) 639-1903. Fax: (850) 639-1272. E-mail: info@baywood.com. Web Site: www.baywood.com. Licensee: South Texas Broadcasting Inc. Group owner: Salem Communications Corp. (acq 7-27-00; grpsl). Network: ABC. Rep: Christal. Format: Talk. Target aud: 25-54. ◆Christopher Gould, Sr., gen mgr; Chris Turner, opns mgr.

Plantation Key

WCTH(FM)— July 1969: 100.3 mhz; 100 kw. 440 ft. TL: N24 57 30 W80 34 30. Stereo. 93351 Overseas Hwy., Tavernier 33070. Phone: (305) 852-9085. Fax: (305) 852-5586. Web Site: www.thundercountry.com. Licensee: Clear Channel Radio Licenses Inc. Group owner: Clear Channel Communications Inc. (acq 2-99; $1.8 million). Network: Network: Westwood One, Motor Racing Net, Premiere Action. Rep: Clear Channel. Format: Country. News staff: one; News: 4 hrs wkly. Target aud: 25-54; residents & tourists. Spec prog: NASCAR 3 hrs wkly. ◆John Hogan, CEO; David Harris, VP & gen mgr; Dave Donahue, progmg dir & progmg mgr.

WFKZ(FM)— Jan 2, 1984: 103.1 mhz; 25 kw. 250 ft. TL: N25 01 35 W80 30 30. 93351 Overseas Hwy., Tavernier 33070. Phone: (305) 852-9085. Fax: (305) 852-5586. E-mail: info@keysradio.net. Web Site: www.sun103.com. Licensee: Clear Channel Radio Licenses Inc. Group owner: Clear Channel Communications Inc. (acq 11-21-97; grpsl). Format: Adult rock. News staff: 2; News: 8 hrs wkly. Target aud: 21-54; adults, active, community interest, expendable income. ◆Dave Harris, VP; Jack Niedbalski, gen mgr & stn mgr.

Pompano Beach

WHSR(AM)— 1959: 980 khz; 5 kw-D, 1 kw-N, DA-D. TL: N26 14 26 W80 10 07. 6699 N. Federal Hwy., Boca Raton 33487. Phone: (561) 997-0074. Fax: (561) 997-0476. Web Site: www.whsrentertainmentradio.com. Licensee: WWNN License L.L.C. Group owner: Beasley Broadcast Group (acq 3-17-2000; grpsl). Jason Shrinsky. Format: Foreign, ethnic, talk. Target aud: 25-54; baby boomers weaned on electronic media as an info source. ◆Bob Morency, VP & gen mgr; Greg Cooper, opns mgr.

WMXJ(FM)— 1960: 102.7 mhz; 100 kw. 1,007 ft. TL: N25 57 59 W80 12 33. Stereo. 20450 N.W. 2nd Ave., Miami 33169-2505. Phone: (305) 521-5100. Fax: (305) 652-1888. Web Site: www.majic1027.com. Licensee: Jefferson-Pilot Communications Co. (acq 1994). Format: Oldies. Target aud: 35-64. ◆Dennis Collins, sr VP & gen mgr; Daryl Leoce, sls dir & gen sls mgr; Jonny Rose, prom dir; Robert Hamilton, progmg dir.

WWNN(AM)— 1959: 1470 khz; 5 kw-D, 2.5 kw-N, DA-1. TL: N26 10 46 W80 13 15. (CP: 50 kw-D). 6699 N. Federal Hwy., Boca Raton 33487. Phone: (561) 997-0074. Fax: (561) 997-0476. Web Site: www.wnnhealthtalkradio.com. Licensee: WWNN License LLC. Group owner: Beasley Broadcast Group (acq 3-14-2000; grpsl). Format: Health & wealth. ◆Bob Morency, VP & gen mgr; Greg Cooper, opns mgr.

Ponte Vedra Beach

WBGB(FM)— 1996: 106.5 mhz; 6 kw. 328 ft. TL: N30 16 34 W81 33 58. Stereo. 11700 Central Pkwy., 4190 Belfort Rd., Suite 450, Jacksonville 32216. Phone: (904) 470-4615. Fax: (904) 296-1683. Web Site: www.1065thepromise.com. Licensee: Caron Broadcasting Inc. Group owner: Salem Communications Corp. (acq 5-30-03; grpsl). Format: Christian. Target aud: 25-44. ◆Steve Griffin, gen mgr; Steve Fox, opns VP & opns dir; Gary Walsh, progmg dir.

Port Charlotte

WCKT(FM)— Oct 1, 1976: 100.1 mhz; 100 kw. 476 ft. TL: N26 37 25 W82 06 58. Stereo. 3151 Cooper St., Suite 56, Punta Gorda 33912. Secondary address: 13320 Metro Pkwy., Suite 1, Fort Myers 33912. Phone: (239) 225-4300. Fax: (293) 225-4329. Web Site: www.catcountryonlinecom. Licensee: Clear Channel Broadcasting Licenses Inc. Group owner: Clear Channel Communications Inc. (acq 2-18-97; grpsl). Kaye, Scholer, Fierman, Hays & Handler L.L.P. Format: Country. News staff: one; News: 20 hrs wkly. Target aud: 25-54. ◆Lowry Mays, chmn; Mark Mays, pres; Randall Mays, CFO; Jay Meyers, sr VP; Jim Keating, gen mgr; Steve Amari, opns dir; Robin Craig, sls dir; Jerry stagg, gen sls mgr; Joe Turner, mktg dir; Buzzy Ford, prom mgr; Jo Johnson, progmg dir; Dave Logan, mus dir; Church Morgan, news dir; Dick Parrish, chief of engrg.

WKII(AM)—Co-owned with WCKT(FM). Nov 19, 1986: 1070 khz; 3.1 kw-D, 260 w-N. TL: N26 54 40 W82 02 12. Stereo. 3151 Cooper St., Suite 56, Punta Gorda 33912. Phone: (941) 639-1112. Fax: (941) 637-6187. Web Site: www.catcountryonline.com. Format: Adult standards. News staff: one; News: 2 hrs wkly. Target aud: 35 plus. ◆Mike Moody, stn mgr, progmg dir & news dir; David Ayres, sls dir; Paul Wolf, chief of engrg.

*WVIJ(FM)— July 26, 1987: 91.7 mhz; 380 w. 130 ft. TL: N26 58 48 W82 04 03. (CP: 2 kw, ant 118 ft.). Stereo. 3279 Sherwood Rd. 33980. Phone: (941) 624-5000. Fax: (775) 243-0586. E-mail: wvij@wvij.com. Web Site: www.wvij.com. Licensee: Port Charlotte Educational Broadcasting Foundation Inc. Format: Educ, relg. Target aud: 35 plus. ◆Daniel P. Kolenda Jr., gen mgr.

Port Richey

WSUN-FM—See Holiday

Port St. Joe

WEBZ(FM)— Mar 12, 1990: 93.5 mhz; 14.5 kw. 659 ft. TL: N29 49 09 W85 15 34. Box 59288, Panama City 32405. Phone: (850) 769-1408. Fax: (850) 769-0659. Web Site: www.935thebeat.com. Licensee: Citicasters Licenses L.P. Group owner: Clear Channel Communications Inc. (acq 8-26-99; $1 million). Format: Urban. Target aud: 35 plus; upscale, white collar professionals. ◆Pete Norton, stn mgr; Eddie Rupp, opns mgr.

Port St. Lucie

WHLG(FM)— Nov 16, 1998: 101.3 mhz; 6 kw. 328 ft. TL: N27 16 04 W80 16 49. Stereo. Horton Broadcasting Co. Inc., 1670 N.W. Federal Hwy., Stuart 34994. Phone: (772) 692-9454. Fax: (772) 692-0258. E-mail: info@coast1013.com. Web Site: www.coast1013.com. Licensee: Horton Broadcasting Co. Inc. Format: Adult contemp. Target aud: 25-54; female/male 60/40%, 35 years old. ◆George Metcalf, CEO; Helen Horton, pres; Phil Scott, gen mgr.

WPSL(AM)— Oct 26, 1985: 1590 khz; 5 kw-D, 64 w-N. TL: N27 18 28 W80 18 26. Stereo. 8245 Business Park Dr. 34952. Phone: (772) 340-1590. Fax: (772) 340-3245. E-mail: wpsl@wpsl.com. Web Site: www.wpsl.com. Licensee: Port St. Lucie Broadcasters Inc. (acq 4-12-93; $200,000;. FTR: 4-26-93). Network: Network: CBS, ESPN Radio. Leventhal, Senter & Lerman. Format: News/talk, sports. News staff: one; News: 4 hrs wkly. Target aud: 45 plus; established families. Spec prog: Relg 6 hrs wkly. ◆Carol Wyatt, CEO & pres; Greg Wyatt, VP & gen mgr.

Punta Gorda

WCCF(AM)— Sept 15, 1961: 1580 khz; 1.25 kw-D, 122 w-N. TL: N26 53 37 W82 03 01. 4810 Deltona Dr. 33950. Phone: (941) 639-1188. Fax: (941) 639-6742. Licensee: Citicasters Licenses L.P. Group owner: Clear Channel Communications Inc. (acq 2-1-99; grpsl). Network: ABC Information & Entertainment. Format: News/talk. Target aud: 45 plus. ◆Michael Moody, gen mgr & opns mgr; Greg Schmaltz, progmg dir.

WIKX(FM)—Co-owned with WCCF(AM). Sept 1, 1970: 92.9 mhz; 100 kw. 807 ft. TL: N26 53 47 W82 14 27. Stereo. Network: ABC Information & Entertainment. Format: Country. News: 10 hrs wkly. Target aud: 25-54.

Punta Rassa

WTLQ-FM— May 3, 1999: 97.7 mhz; 14.5 kw. 430 ft. TL: N26 29 16 W81 55 46. Stereo. 2824 Palm Beach Blvd., Ft. Myers 33916. Phone: (239) 334-1111. Fax: (239) 334-0744. Web Site: www.latinotropical.com. Licensee: Fort Myers Broadcasting Co. (group owner; acq 9-13-00; $7 million). Rep: McGavren Guild. Liebowitz & Associates. Format: Sp. Target aud: 18-49; adults. ◆Brian A. McBride, pres & exec VP; Gary Gardner, gen mgr; Tracy Ruyle, gen mgr & prom dir; Wayne Simons, sls dir; Tim Spires, rgnl sls mgr; Bob Grissinger, progmg dir; Keith Stuhlmann, engrg dir.

Quincy

WWSD(AM)— Mar 15, 1948: 1230 khz; 1 kw-U. TL: N30 34 55 W84 35 59. 1732 W. Elm St. 32351. Phone: (904) 627-1230. Licensee: Tuff-Starr Jam Commuication Inc.

WXSR(FM)— December 1966: 101.5 mhz; 50 kw. 476 ft. TL: N30 31 08 W84 27 04. Bldg. G, 325 John Knox Rd., Tallahassee 32303. Phone: (850) 422-3107. Fax: (850) 383-0747. Web Site: www.x1015.com. Licensee: Clear Channel Radio Licenses Inc. Group owner: Clear Channel Communications Inc. (acq 11-21-97; grpsl). Network: Westwood One. Rep: Christal. Format: Alternative, new rock. Target aud: 18-34. ◆Judy Bailey, VP & gen mgr; Jeff Horn, opns mgr & gen sls mgr.

Florida

Developers & Brokers of Radio Properties — contact American Media Services at our suite: Philadelphia Marriott Downtown 215-625-2900 / 843-972-2200 / americanmediaservices.com / Charleston, SC / Dallas, TX · Chicago, IL · Austin, TX / American Media Services, LLC

Riviera Beach

WMNE(AM)— Aug 17, 1959: 1600 khz; 5 kw-D, 4.7 kw-N, DA-2. TL: N26 44 55 W80 08 02. Stereo. 824 US Hwy. 1, North Palm Beach 33408. Phone: (561) 694-7636. Fax: (561) 694-7574. Web Site: www.radiodisney.com. Licensee: Radio Disney Group LLC. Group owner: ABC Inc. (acq 8-22-00; grpsl). Rep: Roslin. Format: Family. News staff: 2; News: 30 hrs wkly. Local Blacks & Hispanics. Spec prog: Sp. ◆ Tim Bryan, gen mgr.

WZZR(FM)—Licensed to Riviera Beach. See West Palm Beach

Rock Harbor

WKLG(FM)— Nov 1, 1984: 102.1 mhz; 50 kw. 450 ft. TL: N25 05 29 W80 26 37. Stereo. 1452 N. Krome Ave., Suite 103 E., Key Largo 33034. Phone: (305) 451-2202. Fax: (305) 453-2265. Licensee: WKLG Inc. Leibowitz & Associates. Format: Adult contemp. Target aud: 25-54; majority are female 18 plus. ◆ David W. Freeman, VP; Douglas D. LaRue, pres & gen mgr.

Rockledge

WHKR(FM)— Nov 25, 1989: 102.7 mhz; 50 kw. 492 ft. TL: N28 35 03 W80 50 56. Stereo. 1775 W. Hibiscus Blvd., Suite 301, Melbourne 32901. Phone: (321) 984-1000. Fax: (321) 724-1565. Web Site: www.thehitkicker.com. Licensee: Cumulus Licensing Corp. Group owner: Cumulus Media Inc. (acq 8-7-2000; grpsl). Format: Modern country. News staff: 2; News: 6 hrs wkly. Target aud: 25-54. Spec prog: Pub service one hr wkly. ◆ Dan Casell, gen mgr.

Royal Palm Beach

WJNA(AM)— April 1987: 640 khz; 25 kw-D, 4.5 w-N, DA-1. TL: N26 45 34 W80 22 11. 6600 N. Andrews Ave., Suite 160, Fort Lauderdale 33309. Phone: (954) 315-1515. Fax: (954) 315-1555. Web Site: www.wjna.com. Licensee: JCE Licenses L.L.C. Group owner: James Crystal Inc. (acq 11-18-99; $3,945,500. for stock). Network: ABC. Format: Adult standards. News: 4 hrs wkly. Target aud: 25-55; middle-aged, married Christians with children. Spec prog: Black 2 hrs, Sp 2 hrs wkly. ◆ James C. Hilliard, gen mgr.

WPSP(AM)— February 1991: 1190 khz; 1 kw-U, DA-N. TL: N26 44 14 W80 16 23. 5730 Corporate Way, Suite 210, West Palm Beach 33407. Phone: (561) 687-9350. Phone: (561) 687-9345. Fax: (561) 687-3398. E-mail: wpspradio@aol.com. Licensee: George M. Arroyo. (acq 5-87; $75,000; 5-11-87). Roy F. Perkins. Format: Sp talk. News staff: 2; News: 20 hrs wkly. Target aud: 25-54. ◆ George M. Arroyo, pres; Lissette M. Diaz, gen mgr & opns dir.

Safety Harbor

WYUU(FM)—Licensed to Safety Harbor. See Tampa

Saint Augustine

WAOC(AM)— December 1953: 1420 khz; 2.18 kw-D, 250 w-N. TL: N29 51 00 W81 19 50. Box 3847 32085. Secondary address: 567 Lewis Point Rd. Ext. 32086. Phone: (904) 797-4444. Fax: (904) 797-3446. E-mail: wfoy@aug.com. Licensee: Shull Broadcasting Co. Inc. (acq 11-26-2003). Network: ABC Information & Entertainment. Rep: Rgnl Reps. Rgnl Reps Alan Campbell. Format: Country. News: 8 hrs wkly. Target aud: 26 plus; affluent adults. Spec prog: Florida State Univ. football & basketball; nascar. ◆ Douglas H. Shull, pres & gen mgr; Rose Napolitano, opns VP; Dave O'Dell, progmg dir.

***WAYL(FM)**— May 22, 1994: 91.9 mhz; 5 kw. 200 ft. TL: N29 54 26 W81 18 51. Box 127 32085. Secondary address: 1485 US Rt. 1 S. 32086. Phone: (904) 829-9200. Fax: (904) 829-9202. E-mail: waylfm@aug.com. Web Site: www.riverradio.org. Licensee: New Covenant Educational Ministries Inc. (acq 6-14-02). Network: Salem Radio Network. Fletcher, Heald & Hildreth. Format: Contemp Christian. News staff: 2; News: 10 hrs wkly. Target aud: 25-45. ◆ David Oglesby, stn mgr; Jerry Smith, engrg mgr.

***WFCF(FM)**— Nov 1, 1993: 88.5 mhz; 6 kw. 141 ft. TL: N29 54 27 W81 18 49. Box 1027, Flagler College 32085. Phone: (904) 829-6481, EXT. 313. Phone: (904) 829-6940. Fax: (904) 826-3471. Web Site: www.flagler.edu. Licensee: Flagler College. Caressa D. Bennet. Format: Div. News: one hr wkly. Target aud: General. Spec prog: Sp 4 hrs, new age 4 hrs, folk 3 hrs, reggae 4 hrs, world 4 hrs, blues 4 hrs wkly. ◆ Daniel McCook, stn mgr.

WFOY(AM)— July 7, 1936: 1240 khz; 1 kw-U. TL: N29 54 26 W81 18 51. Box 3847 32085. Secondary address: 567 Lewis Point Rd. Ext. 32086. Phone: (904) 797-1955. Phone: (904) 797-4444. Fax: (904) 797-3446. E-mail: wfoy@aug.com. Licensee: Shull Broadcasting Co. Inc. (acq 4-84). Network: CBS Radio. Rep: Rgnl Reps. Rgnl Reps Alan Campbell. Format: News/talk, sports. News staff: one; News: 8 hrs wkly. Target aud: 26 plus; affluent adults. Spec prog: Univ. of FL & Jaguars. ◆ Douglas Shull, pres & gen mgr; Rose Napolitano, opns VP. Co-owned TV: WFOY-TV affil

WSOS-FM— July 17, 1982: 94.1 mhz; 25 kw. Ant 302 ft. TL: N29 57 57 W81 28 36. Stereo. 6440 Atlantic Blvd., Jacksonville 32211. Phone: (904) 824-0833. Phone: (904) 824-0834. Fax: (904) 825-0105. Fax: (904) 721-9322. E-mail: drunk@rendabroadcasting.com. Web Site: www.wsosfm.com. Licensee: Renda Broadcasting Corp. of Nevada. (acq 4-27-2005; $7.75 million). Network: Westwood One. Format: Adult contemp. News staff: one. Target aud: 25-54; upscale audience. ◆ Bill Scull, gen mgr; Ron Runk, gen sls mgr.

Saint Augustine Beach

WSJF(FM)— Sept 1, 1995: 105.5 mhz; 16 kw. Ant 410 ft. TL: N29 51 00 W81 19 50. Stereo. 9550 Regency Sq. Blvd., Suite 200, Jacksonville 32225. Phone: (904) 680-1050. Fax: (904) 680-1051. E-mail: jaxproduction@tamabroadcasting.com. Web Site: www.tamabroadcasting.com. Licensee: Tama Radio Licenses of Jacksonville, FL, Inc. Group owner: Tama Broadcasting Inc. (acq 2-28-2003; $8.5 million. with WJSJ(FM) Fernandina Beach). Format: Jazz. Target aud: 20-45; general. ◆ Linda Fructuoso, gen mgr; Joel Widdows, opns mgr & prom dir; Gerry Smith, chief of engrg.

WSOS(AM)— Oct 15, 1986: 1170 khz; 710 w-D. TL: N29 55 05 W81 23 26. 2715 Stratton Blvd., St. Augustine 32084. Phone: (904) 824-0833. Fax: (904) 825-0105. E-mail: wsosam@wsosfm.com. Web Site: wsosfm.com/am. Licensee: 3 Point Media - Florida LLC. (acq 7-1-2003; $4 million. with WSOS-FM Saint Augustine). Format: 50s, 60s, 70s oldies. ◆ Don Runk, gen mgr, opns dir, sls VP, news dir & adv; Andy Calvert, prom dir; Gary Hart, progmg dir; Michelle Raiman, mus dir; Frank Everett, pub affrs dir; Alan Alsobrook, chief of engrg.

Saint Catherine

***WKFA(FM)**— 2005: 89.3 mhz; 100 w. Ant 295 ft. TL: N28 32 22 W82 04 48. 505 Josephine St., Titusville 32796. Phone: (321) 267-3000. Fax: (321) 264-9370. E-mail: wpio@gate.net. Web Site: www.noncomradio.com. Licensee: Florida Public Radio Inc. (acq 4-12-03). ◆ Randy Henry, pres & gen mgr.

Saint Cloud

WOYE(AM)—Not on air, target date: November 2003: 1160 khz; 2.5 kw-D, 500 w-N, DA-2. TL: N28 16 15 W81 20 00. Box 1553, Quebradillas, PR 00678. Secondary address: 4540 Turryford Rd., Orlando 32812. Phone: (787) 895-2725. Fax: (787) 895-4198. E-mail: magic973@prtc.net. Licensee: Jose J. Arzuaga Jr. dba Ammedia. Format: Spanish. ◆ Jose J. Arzuaga Jr., gen mgr.

Saint Marks

***WUJC(FM)**—Not on air, target date: unknown: 91.1 mhz; 100 kw. Ant 492 ft. TL: N30 20 51 W83 47 26. CSN International, 3232 W. MacArthur Blvd., Santa Ana, CA 92704. Fax: (714) 825-9660. Licensee: CSN International (group owner). ◆ Jeffrey W. Smith, gen mgr.

Saint Petersburg

WDAE(AM)— Nov 1, 1927: 620 khz; 5 kw-D, 5.4 kw-N, DA-N. TL: N27 52 37 W82 35 26. Stereo. 4002 Gandy Blvd., Tampa 33611. Phone: (813) 832-1000. Fax: (813) 831-3299. Web Site: www.620wdae.com. Licensee: Clear Channel Broadcasting Licenses Inc. (acq 11-20-98; $9.75 million). Format: Sports. ◆ Dan Diloreto, gen mgr.

WFLA(AM)—See Tampa

WFLZ-FM—See Tampa

***WFTI-FM**— June 1988: 91.7 mhz; 3 kw. 282 ft. TL: N27 46 15 W82 38 19. Stereo. 360 Central Ave., Suite 1240 33701. Phone: (727) 823-1140. E-mail: WFTI@hotmail.com. Web Site: www.familyradio.com. Licensee: Family Stations Inc. (group owner; acq 11-19-88). Network: Family Radio. Format: Relg. News: 9 hrs wkly. Target aud: General. ◆ Bob Barnes, stn mgr.

WHPT(FM)—See Sarasota

WMTX(FM)—See Tampa

WPOI(FM)— July 1, 1961: 101.5 mhz; 100 kw. 1,358 ft. TL: N27 50 32 W82 15 46. Stereo. Cox Radio Inc., 11300 4th St. N., Suite 300 33716-2941. Phone: (727) 579-2000. Fax: (727) 578-1015. E-mail: comments@1015thepoint.com. Web site: www.1015thepoint.com. Licensee: CXR Holdings L.L.C. Group owner: Cox Communications Inc. (acq 1999; grpsl). Rep: Clear Channel. Format: Hits of the 80s. Target aud: 25-54. ◆ Howard Tuuri, VP, gen mgr & stn mgr; Tom Paleveda, opns mgr; Bernadette Van Osdal, gen sls mgr; Gerry Brauer, prom mgr.

WQYK-FM— May 1958: 99.5 mhz; 100 kw. 590 ft. TL: N27 56 50 W82 27 35. Stereo. 5510 W. Gray St., Tampa 33609. Phone: (813) 287-0995. Fax: (813) 636-0995. Web Site: www.wqyk.com. Licensee: Infinity Broadcasting Corp. of Florida. Group owner: Infinity Broadcasting Corp. (acq 12-1-86; 10-6-86). Network: CBS. Leventhal, Senter & Lerman. Format: Contemp country. News staff: one; News: 6 hrs wkly. Target aud: 25-54. ◆ Charlie Ochs, sr VP; Luis Albertini, gen mgr; Mike Culotta, opns mgr.

WRBQ-FM—See Tampa

WRMD(AM)— May 5, 1950: 680 khz; 690 w-D, 125 w-N. TL: N27 51 24 W82 37 26. 402 N. Reo Street, Suite 218, Tampa 33609. Phone: (813) 319-5757. Fax: (813) 319-0029. Licensee: ZGS Broadcasting of Tampa Inc. (acq 1-18-91; $200,000; 2-4-91). Katz Hispanic Media Format: Tropical/Spanish. Target aud: General; adults 18-49. ◆ Maria Chacon, gen mgr.

WWMI(AM)— 1939: 1380 khz; 5 kw-U, DA-N. TL: N27 52 15 W82 37 03. 11300 4th St. N., Suite 143, St. Petersburg 33716. Phone: (727) 577-4500. Fax: (727) 579-1340. Web Site: www.radiodisney.com. Licensee: Radio Disney Group LLC. Group owner: ABC Inc. (acq 1999; grpsl). Network: ABC FM Connection. Rep: Clear Channel. Format: Top- 40. News staff: 2. Target aud: 25-54. ◆ Drew Rashbaum, gen mgr; Ted Wolfe, stn mgr.

WWRM(FM)—(Tampa). 1958: 94.9 mhz; 100 kw. 1,289 ft. TL: N27 49 09 W82 14 26. Stereo. 11300 4th St. N., Suite 300, St. Petersburg 33716-2941. Phone: (727) 579-2000. Fax: (727) 579-2662. Web Site: www.949online.com. Licensee: Cox Radio Inc. Group owner: Cox Communications Inc. (acq 7-1-88). Rep: Christal. Format: Adult contemp. Target aud: 25-54. ◆ Howard Tuuri, gen mgr; Tom Paleveda, opns mgr; Mark Kanak, gen sls mgr & natl sls mgr; Julia Freeman, prom mgr.

WXGL(FM)— 1958: 107.3 mhz; 100 kw. 649 ft. TL: N27 51 24 W82 37 26. Stereo. 11300 4th St. N., Suite 300 33716. Phone: (727) 577-2000. Fax: (727) 579-2280. Web Site: www.1073theeagle.com. Licensee: Cox Radio Inc. Group owner: Cox Communications Inc. (acq 7-1-88). Rep: Christal. Format: Classic Hits. ◆ Jay O'Connor, VP & gen mgr; Chantal L. Jeanrenaud, gen sls mgr; Tom Paleveda, opns mgr & natl sls mgr.

Florida | Directory of Radio

Saint Petersburg Beach

WRXB(AM)— 1957: 1590 khz; 5 kw-D, 1 kw-N, DA-2. TL: N27 44 03 W82 41 08. 2060 First Ave. N., St. Petersburg 33713. Phone: (727) 821-9967. Fax: (727) 321-3025. E-mail: wrxb@juno.com. Web Site: www.wrxb.com. Licensee: Metropolitan Radio Group of Florida Inc. Group owner: Metropolitan Radio Group Inc. Format: Adult contemp, urban contemp. Target aud: 23-54; urban contemp. Spec prog: Jazz 15 hrs wkly. ♦Juanita Dials, gen mgr.

San Carlos Park

WUSV(FM)— 1995: 98.5 mhz; 18.5 kw. Ant 371 ft. TL: N26 30 18 W81 51 14. Stereo. 2824 Palm Beach Blvd., Ft. Myers 33916. Phone: (239) 334-1111. Fax: (239) 479-5553. Web Site: us985.com. Licensee: Ave Maria University Inc. (acq 2-9-2004; $4.9 million). Format: Country. ♦Joe Schwartzel, gen mgr.

Sanford

WSDO(AM)— May 20, 1947: 1400 khz; 1 kw-U. TL: N28 48 04 W81 15 06. 222 Hazard St., Orlando 32804-3030. Phone: (407) 841-8282. Phone: (407) 322-1400. Fax: (407) 841-8250. Licensee: J & V Communications Co. (acq 6-5-92; $300,000; 6-22-92). Network: Westwood One. Format: Sp news/talk. Target aud: 21 plus. Spec prog: Relg 3 hrs wkly. ♦John Torrado, CEO, pres & gen mgr; Frank Vaught, opns mgr.

Santa Rosa Beach

WWAV-FM— Apr 3, 1985: 102.1 mhz; 18 kw. TL: N30 23 17 W86 17 55. 743 Hwy. 98 E., Suite 6, Destin 32541-2574. Phone: (850) 654-1031. Fax: (850) 654-6510. Web Site: www.wave1021.com. Licensee: Qantum of Fort Walton Beach License Co. LLC. Group owner: Root Communications (acq 7-2-2003; grpsl). Format: Classic rock. News: one hr wkly. Target aud: 25-54; general. ♦Frank Osborne, pres; Diane Augram, gen mgr; Suzie Nicholson-Hunt, gen sls mgr.

Sarasota

WBRD(AM)—See Palmetto

WCTQ(FM)—Listing follows WSRQ(AM).

WHPT(FM)— 1973: 102.5 mhz; 100 kw. 1,776 ft. TL: N27 29 08 W82 32 00. Stereo. 11300 4th St. N., Suite 300, St. Petersburg 33716. Phone: (727) 579-2000. Fax: (727) 579-2662. Web Site: theboneonline.com. Licensee: CXR Holdings L.L.C. Group owner: Cox Broadcasting (acq 5-99; grpsl). Rep: Clear Channel. Format: Class rock. Target aud: 25-54. ♦Jay O'Connor, gen mgr.

WIBQ(AM)— Jan 1, 1961: 1220 khz; 1 kw-D, 600 w-N, DA. TL: N27 19 27 W82 29 47. 1476 Main St. 34236. Phone: (941) 952-1220. Fax: (941) 365-2900. E-mail: 1220@newstalk1220.com. Web Site: www.newstalk1220.com. Licensee: Nova Broadcasting Co. (acq 9-9-02; $450,000). Format: News/talk. Target aud: 25-64; men. ♦James Grady, pres & gen mgr.

*****WKZM(FM)**— Oct 21, 1974: 104.3 mhz; 6 kw. Ant 266 ft. TL: N27 16 30 W82 28 54. Box 8888, St. Petersburg 33738. Phone: (727) 391-9994. Fax: (727) 397-6425. E-mail: wkes@moody.edu. Web Site: www.wkes.org. Licensee: The Moody Bible Institute of Chicago. (group owner; acq 10-15-99). Format: Inspirational, educ. News: 14 hrs wkly. Target aud: General. ♦Michael Gleichman, gen mgr; Pierre Chestang, stn mgr.

WLLD(FM)—See Holmes Beach

WLSS(AM)— May 23, 1949: 930 khz; 5 kw-D, 3 kw-N, DA-2. TL: N27 21 17 W82 23 06. 5211 W. Laurel St., Tampa 33607. Phone: (813) 639-1903. Fax: (813) 639-1272. E-mail: wlss@wlssradio.com. Web Site: www.wlssradio.com. Licensee: Caron Broadcasting Inc. Group owner: WGUL-FM, Inc. (acq 8-12-2005; $9.5 million. with WNTR(AM) Dunedin). Format: News/talk. ♦Chris Gould, gen mgr.

*****WSMR(FM)**— 1993: 89.1 mhz; 50 kw. 462 ft. TL: N27 06 00 W82 22 19. 240 N. Washington Blvd., Suite 490 34236. Phone: (941) 906-9767. Fax: (941) 362-0377. Web Site: www.wsmr.org. Licensee: Northwestern College. Group owner: Northwestern College & Radio (acq 10-4-96; $400,000). Format: Christian lite contemp. News: 6 hrs wkly. Target aud: 30-55; with kids still at home. ♦Dr. Alan Cureton, CEO & pres; Harv Hendrickson, gen mgr; Douglas Poll, stn mgr; Dale Davis, opns VP; Joe Smith, dev VP.

WSRQ(AM)— Dec 7, 1939: 1450 khz; 1 kw-ND. TL: N27 20 12 W82 34 25. 1779 Independence Blvd. 34234. Phone: (941) 552-4800. Fax: (941) 552-4900. E-mail: news@1450wsrq.com. Web Site: www.1450wsrq.com. Licensee: Citicasters Licenses L.P. Group owner: Clear Channel Communications Inc. (acq 5-4-99; grpsl). Format: News/talk. News staff: 3; News: 40 hrs wkly. Target aud: 25-54; general. ♦Sherri Carlson, VP & gen mgr.

WCTQ(FM)—Co-owned with WSRQ(AM). June 30, 1965: 106.5 mhz; 25 kw. 280 ft. TL: N27 20 12 W82 34 25. Stereo. Web Site: www.1065ctq.com. Format: Country. News: one hr wkly. Target aud: 25-54. ♦Mark Wilson, opns mgr & progmg dir; Tracy Black, pub affrs dir; Matt Howell, engrg dir; Maverick Johnson, chief of engrg.

WTMY(AM)— Dec 2, 1961: 1280 khz; 500 w-D, 340 w-N, DA-2. TL: N27 21 21 W82 29 13. 2101 Hammock Pl. 34235. Phone: (941) 954-1280. Fax: (941) 955-9062. E-mail: wtmy@juno.com. Web Site: www.wtmy.com. Licensee: Metropolitan Radio Group Inc. (group owner; acq 8-96). Format: Money talk, health talk, talk. Target aud: 40 plus; wealth & health oriented. Spec prog: Pol one hr, gospel 6 hrs, full service 2 hrs wkly. ♦Mark Acker, pres; Valerie Silver, gen mgr.

Sebastian

WSJZ-FM— 2001: 95.9 mhz; 25 kw. Ant 289 ft. TL: N27 49 05 W80 37 18. 1775 W. Hibiscus Blvd., Suite 101, Melbourne 32901. Phone: (321) 984-1000. Fax: (321) 724-1565. Web Site: www.pirate959.com. Licensee: Cumulus Licensing LLC. (acq 11-8-2004; $5 million). Format: Rock. ♦Dan Carelli, gen mgr.

Sebring

WAVP(AM)—See Avon Park

WITS(AM)— Nov 24, 1959: 1340 khz; 1 kw-U. TL: N27 30 30 W81 25 20. 3750 U.S. 27 N., Suite 1 33870. Phone: (863) 382-9999. Fax: (863) 382-1982. E-mail: cohanradiogroup@htn.net. Web Site: www.cohanradiogroup.com. Licensee: Cohan Radio Group Inc. (group owner; (acq 11-1-98; $585,000. with co-located FM). Network: ABC Music Radio. Intercep Latham & Watkins. Format: MOR. News staff: one; News: 5 hrs wkly. Target aud: 40 plus; mature adults. ♦Peter Coughlin, pres & gen mgr; Libby Coughlin, gen sls mgr.

WWLL(FM)—Co-owned with WITS(AM). July 1967: 105.7 mhz; 19 kw. 351 ft. TL: N27 21 29 W81 28 22. Stereo. Web Site: www.cohanradiogroup.com. (Acq 11-1-98.). Format: Adult contemp. News staff: one; News: 2 hrs wkly. Target aud: 25-54; adults.

WJCM(AM)— May 22, 1950: 1050 khz; 1 kw-D, 11 w-N. TL: N27 30 30 W81 25 20. 3750 U.S. 27 N. 33870. Phone: (863) 382-9999. Fax: (863) 382-1982. E-mail: cohanradiogroup@htn.net. Web Site: www.cohanradiogroup.com. Licensee: Cohan Radio Group Inc. (group owner; acq 11-1-98; $150,000). Interep Latham & Watkins. Format: Oldies. News staff: one; News: 8 hrs wkly. Target aud: 45+. Spec prog: Sp one hr wkly. ♦Peter Coughlin, gen mgr & gen sls mgr; Libby Coughlin, rgnl sls mgr; Alan Gray, progmg mgr; Timothy Saenz, news dir; Phil Scott, chief of engrg.

WWOJ(FM)—See Avon Park

WWTK(AM)—See Lake Placid

Seffner

WBZZ(AM)—Licensed to Seffner. See Tampa

Silver Springs

WNDD(FM)—Licensed to Silver Springs. See Gainesville

Solana

WCVU(FM)— 1994: 104.9 mhz; 6 kw. 318 ft. TL: N26 53 37 W82 03 03. 24100 Tiseo Blvd., Unit 10, Port Charlotte 33980. Phone: (941) 206-1188. Fax: (941) 206-9296. Web Site: www.clearchannel.com. Licensee: Citicasters Licenses L.P. Group owner: Clear Channel Communications Inc. (acq 2-1-99; grpsl). Network: CNN Radio.

Format: Soft adult contemp. ♦Michael Moody, gen mgr; David Ayres, sls dir; Todd Matthews, progmg mgr.

WKII(AM)—Licensed to Solana. See Port Charlotte

South Daytona

WPUL(AM)— June 13, 1957: 1590 khz; 1 kw-D. TL: N29 09 16 W81 01 20. 427 S. Martin L. King Blvd., Daytona Beach 32114. Phone: (386) 239-7080 (Studio). Phone: (386) 226-2398. Fax: (386) 254-7510. E-mail: ccherry2@aol.com. Licensee: PSI Communications Inc. (acq 2-1-89; $250,000; 1-23-89). Network: American Urban. Format: Gospel. Target aud: General. ♦Charles W. Cherry II, CEO & gen mgr; Tamala Powell, progmg mgr.

South Miami

WAXY(AM)— Sept 15, 1947: 790 khz; 25 kw-U, DA-2. TL: N25 46 25 W80 38 13. Stereo. 20450 N.W. 2nd Ave., Miami 33169. Phone: (305) 521-5100. Fax: (305) 521-1416. Web Site: www.waxy.com. Licensee: Jefferson-Pilot Communications Co. (group owner; acq 10-23-85; 7-29-85). Rep: CBS Radio. Format: Sports talk. Target aud: 35 plus. ♦Dennis P. Collins, sr VP & gen mgr; Gary Aybar, opns mgr.

Spring Hill

WJQB(FM)— October 1992: 106.3 mhz; 25 kw. Ant 315 ft. TL: N28 31 41 W82 32 45. 35048 US Hwy. 19 N., Palm Harbor 34684. Phone: (727) 442-4027. Fax: (727) 781-4375. E-mail: staff@wjqb.com. Web Site: www.wjqb.com. Licensee: WGUL-FM Inc. Format: Oldies. ♦Steve Schurdell, VP & gen mgr; Dale Smrekar, chief of engrg.

Springfield

WRBA(FM)— June 1986: 95.9 mhz; 50 kw. 300 ft. TL: N30 12 12 W85 36 57. 118 Gwyn Dr., Panama City Beach 32408. Phone: (850) 234-8858. Fax: (850) 234-6592. E-mail: billyoung@panamacityradio.com. Web Site: www.arrow959.com. Licensee: Double O Radio Corp. (group owner; acq 3-10-2004; grpsl). Format: Classic rock. Target aud: 30-54; general. ♦Bill Young, gen mgr & opns mgr; Steve Green, gen mgr.

WYOO(FM)—Licensed to Springfield. See Panama City

Starke

*****WTLG(FM)**— 1982: 88.3 mhz; 7 kw. 285 ft. TL: N29 54 34 W82 06 02. Stereo. Box 1258, 163 W. Jefferson at Clarke 32091. Phone: (904) 964-9854. Fax: (904) 964-2968. E-mail: wtlg-radio@earthlink.net. Licensee: Starke Christian Educational Radio & TV. Network: Moody. Format: Southern gospel, relg. Target aud: General. ♦Terry Blakeslee, gen mgr; Hal Mashburn, chief of engrg.

Stuart

WAVW(FM)— Dec 24, 1964: 92.7 mhz; 50 kw. 482 ft. TL: N27 16 30 W80 17 12. Stereo. Drawer 0093, Port St. Lucie 34985. Phone: (772) 335-9300. Fax: (772) 335-3291. Web Site: www.wavw.com. Licensee: Capstar TX L.P. Group owner: Clear Channel Communications Inc. (acq 8-30-00; grpsl). Format: Country. ♦Mark Bass, gen mgr; Layne Ryan, gen sls mgr; Richard Dickerson, progmg dir; Woody Maxwell, mus dir; Mike Kerley, chief of engrg.

WSTU(AM)— Dec 9, 1954: 1450 khz; 1 kw-U. TL: N27 12 53 W80 15 24. 8245 Business Park Dr., Port St. Lucie 34952. Phone: (772) 220-9788. Fax: (772) 340-3245. E-mail: wpsl@wpsl.com. Web Site: www.wstu1450.com. Licensee: Treasure Coast Broadcasters Inc. (acq 2-13-02; $500,000). Network: Network: ABC Information & Entertainment, ESPN Radio. Leventhal, Senter & Lerman. Format: News/talk, sports. News staff: 2. Target aud: 35+. ♦Carol Wyatt, pres.

*****WWFR(FM)**— 1988: 91.7 mhz; 2.65 kw. Ant 499 ft. TL: N27 07 14 W80 23 59. Stereo. Box 277, Okeechobee 34972. Secondary address: 508 2nd Ave., Okeechobee 34972. Phone: (863) 763-5454. Fax: (863) 763-8867. E-mail: wwfr@okeechobee.com. Web Site: www.familyradio.com. Licensee: Family Stations Inc. (group owner) Network: Family Radio. Format: Relg. News: 11 hrs wkly. Target aud: General. Spec prog: Pub affrs 2 hrs wkly. ♦Ed Dearborn, chief of opns.

Stations in the U.S. — Florida

Developers & Brokers of Radio Properties
contact American Media Services at our suite: Philadelphia Marriott Downtown
215-625-2900
843-972-2200
americanmediaservices.com
Charleston, SC
Dallas, TX · Chicago, Il · Austin, TX
American Media Services, LLC

Summerland Key

WPIK(FM)— December 1991: 102.5 mhz; 50 kw. Ant 413 ft. TL: N24 40 35 W81 30 41. Stereo. 631 Whitehead St., Keywest 33040. Licensee: Summerland Media LLC (acq 6-3-2005; $1.85 million). Format: Hot adult contemp. News staff: one; News: one hr wkly. Target aud: 25-54; upscale adult listeners. Spec prog: Relg one hr, country currents one hr wkly. ◆ Keith Thomas, CFO; Connie Rice, gen mgr & opns mgr.

Sunrise

*WKPX(FM)— Feb 14, 1983: 88.5 mhz; 3 kw. 100 ft. TL: N26 10 38 W80 15 23. Stereo. 8000 N.W. 44th St. 33351. Phone: (954) 572-1321. Fax: (954) 572-1344. Licensee: School Board of Broward County. Format: Modern rock, alternative. Target aud: 15-35; people interested in alternative progmg. Spec prog: Black 3 hrs, blues 3 hrs wkly. ◆ Pat Swank, stn mgr; Jim Sorensen, chief of engrg.

Tallahassee

WAIB(FM)— June 17, 1976: 103.1 mhz; 50 kw. 295 ft. TL: N30 29 43 W84 13 51. (CP: 42 kw, ant 541 ft. TL: N30 29 39 W84 14 00). Stereo. Opus Broadcasting, 3000 Olson Rd. 32308. Phone: (850) 386-8004. Phone: (850) 422-1896. Fax: (850) 422-1897. E-mail: hkestenbaum @opusbroadcasting.com. Web Site: www.newcountryb103.com. Licensee: Opus Broadcasting Tallahassee LLC. Group owner: Triad Broadcasting Co. LLC (acq 7-11-2005; grpsl). Rep: McGavren Guild. Format: Country. Target aud: 25-54. ◆ Hank Kestenbaum, gen mgr; Tom Waston, opns dir.

*WANM(FM)— November 1976: 90.5 mhz; 1.6 w. 167 ft. TL: N30 25 49 W84 17 27. Stereo. Florida A&M Univ., 314 Tucker Hall 32307. Phone: (850) 599-3083. Fax: (850) 561-2829. E-mail: theflavastation@hotmail.com. Web Site: www.famu.edu/famcast. Licensee: The Board of Trustees of Florida A&M University. Network: AP Radio. Format: News, sports. News: 5 hrs wkly. Target aud: General; urban African-American in area. Spec prog: Reggae 3 hrs wkly. ◆ Keith Miles, gen mgr; Ebonee Rudolph, opns mgr; Travon McCall, chief of engrg.

WBZE(FM)—Listing follows WHBT(AM).

WCVC(AM)— Nov 5, 1953: 1330 khz; 5 kw-D. TL: N30 29 03 W84 17 13. 117 1/2 Henderson Rd. 32312. Phone: (850) 386-1330. Fax: (850) 386-2138. E-mail: wcvc65@hotmail.com. Web Site: www.wcvc1330.com. Licensee: WCVC Inc. (acq 10-4-85; $500,000; 8-12-85). Network: USA. In house-Alan McCall News: 7 hrs wkly. Target aud: 25-54. ◆ Wendell H. Borrink, pres; Erwin O'Conner, gen mgr, opns mgr & progmg dir.

WEGT(FM)—(Lafayette). Dec 17, 1989: 99.9 mhz; 50 kw. 492 ft. TL: N30 20 59 W83 59 53. Stereo. North Florida Broadcasting, 3000 Olson Rd. 32308. Phone: (850) 386-8004. Fax: (850) 422-1897. Web Site: www.theoldies999.com. Licensee: Opus Broadcasting Tallahassee LLC. Group owner: Triad Broadcasting Co. LLC (acq 7-11-2005; grpsl). Rep: McGavren Guild. Format: Classic hits of the 60s, 70s, etc. News: 2 hrs wkly. Target aud: 25-54. ◆ Chris Knight, gen mgr; Tom Watson, opns dir.

*WFRF(AM)— August 1974: 1070 khz; 10 kw-D. TL: N30 30 34 W84 20 07. Box 181000 32318. Secondary address: 4015 N. Monroe St. 32301. Phone: (850) 201-1070. Fax: (850) 201-1071. E-mail: mailbox@faithradio.us. Web Site: www.faithradio.us. Licensee: Faith Radio Network Inc. (acq 9-30-97; $150,000). Format: Christian. Target aud: 12+.

*WFSQ(FM)— May 1954: 91.5 mhz; 100 kw. 663 ft. TL: N30 21 29 W84 36 39. Stereo. Public Broadcast Ctr., 1600 Red Barber Plaza 32310. Phone: (850) 487-3086. Fax: (850) 487-2611. Web Site: www.wfsu.org. Licensee: The Board of Regents of Florida acting for and on behalf of Florida State University. Network: Network: NPR, PRI. Format: Class. News: one hr wkly. Target aud: 35 plus; highly educated. ◆ Patrick Keating, gen mgr; Caroline Austin, stn mgr & prom dir; Andy Hanus, engrg dir.

*WFSU-FM— Oct 14, 1990: 88.9 mhz; 95 kw. 1,243 ft. TL: N30 40 13 W83 56 26. Stereo. Public Broadcast Ctr., 1600 Red Barber Plaza 32310. Phone: (850) 487-3086. Fax: (850) 487-2611. Web Site: www.wfsu.org. Licensee: The Board of Regents of Florida acting for and on behalf of Florida State University. Network: Network: NPR, PRI. Cohn & Marks. Format: News/talk. News staff: 9. Target aud: 35-54; highly educated. Spec prog: Jazz 8 hrs wkly. ◆ Pat Keating, gen mgr; Caroline Austin, stn mgr; Ann Meyers, prom dir; Carl Tinsley, chief of engrg.

WGLF(FM)— December 1967: 104.1 mhz; 100 kw. 1,359 ft. TL: N30 27 09 W84 00 50. Stereo. 3411 W. Tharpe St., Tallahasse 32303. Phone: (850) 201-3000. Phone: (850) 201-3009. Fax: (850) 561-8903. Web Site: www.gulf104.com. Licensee: Cumulus Licensing Corp. Group owner: Cumulus Media Inc. (acq 6-22-99; $4 million). Rep: McGavren Guild. Arent, Fox, Kintner, Plotkin & Kahn. Format: Classic rock, AOR. Target aud: 25-54. ◆ John Columbus, gen mgr; Scott Less, progmg dir.

WHBT(AM)— Aug 6, 1959: 1410 khz; 5 kw-D, 39 w-N. TL: N30 29 35 W84 17 00. (CP: N30 29 03 W84 17 13). 3411 W. Tharpe St. 32303. Phone: (850) 201-3000. Fax: (850) 561-8903. Licensee: Cumulus Licensing Corp. Group owner: Cumulus Media Inc. (acq 10-28-97; grpsl). Arent, Fox, Kintner, Plotkin & Kahn. Format: Urban gospel, sports. Target aud: 18-54. ◆ John Columbus, gen mgr; Dave Smith, opns mgr; Steve Curtis, gen sls mgr; Rick Anderson, rgnl sls mgr; Marvin Emilien, prom dir; Peter Walkowiak, chief of engrg.

WBZE(FM)—Co-owned with WHBT(AM). July 15, 1962: 98.9 mhz; 100 kw. 390 ft. TL: N30 29 35 W84 16 55. Stereo. Web Site: www.mystar98.com. Format: Adult contemp, urban contemp. Target aud: 25-54. ◆ John Emilien, progmg dir.

WHBX(FM)— June 28, 1982: 96.1 mhz; 37 kw. 479 ft. TL: N30 16 08 W84 16 32. Stereo. 3411 West Tharpe St. 32303. Phone: (850) 201-3000. Fax: (850) 561-8903. Web Site: 961jamz.com. Licensee: Cumulus Licensing Corp. Group owner: Cumulus Media Inc. (acq 10-28-97; grpsl). Rep: McGavren Guild. Arent, Fox, Kintner, Plotkin & Kahn. Format: Urban contemp. Target aud: 25-54. ◆ John Columbus, gen mgr; Dave Smith, opns mgr.

WHTF(FM)—See Havana

WNLS(AM)—Listing follows WTNT-FM.

WTAL(AM)— 1935: 1450 khz; 1 kw-U. TL: N30 26 20 W84 15 30. 1363 E. Tennesse Street 32308. Phone: (850) 671-1450. Fax: (850) 877-5110. E-mail: wtaal@nettally.com. Web Site: www.wtal1450.com. Licensee: Live Communications Inc. (acq 9-14-01; $400,000). Network: CBS. Rep: Roslin. Reddy, Begley & McCormick. Format: News/talk, Christian, relig. News staff: 4; News: 21 hrs wkly. Target aud: 25-54; educated, intelligent, affluent, involved, conservative. ◆ Dr. R.B. Holmes Jr., CEO & pres; Rebecca Johnson, gen mgr.

WTLY(FM)—(Thomasville).GA 1971: 107.1 mhz; 100 kw. 981 ft. TL: N30 43 55 W84 08 45. Stereo. Bldg. G, 325 John Knox Rd. 32303. Phone: (850) 422-3107. Fax: (850) 383-0747. Fax: (850) 514-4443. E-mail: jeffhorn@clearchannel.com. Web Site: www.magic1071.com. Licensee: Clear Channel Radio Licenses Inc. Group owner: Clear Channel Communications Inc. (acq 11-21-97; grpsl). Rep: Christal. Format: Hot adult contemp. News staff: one; News: 5 hrs wkly. Target aud: 25-54. ◆ Judy Bailey, gen mgr; Jeff Horn, opns mgr; Belinda Bininger, sls VP & natl sls mgr; Vanessa Jerome, prom mgr; Steve Cannon, progmg VP; Randall Moore, chief of engrg.

WTNT-FM— July 24, 1967: 94.9 mhz; 100 kw. 840 ft. TL: N30 34 43 W84 15 49. Stereo. Bldg. G, 325 John Knox Rd. 32303. Phone: (850) 422-3107. Fax: (850) 383-0747. Web Site: www.wtntfm.com. Licensee: Clear Channel Radio Licenses Inc. Group owner: Clear Channel Communications Inc. (acq 11-21-97; grpsl). Network: ABC Daytime Direction. Rep: Christal. Format: Country. News: one hr wkly. Target aud: 25-54. ◆ Judy Bailey, gen mgr & natl sls mgr; Kris Van Dyke, opns mgr, progmg VP & progmg dir; Belinda Bininger, sls VP; Jonathan Faulkner, prom dir; Woody Hayes, mus dir; J. L. Dunbar, news dir & pub affrs dir; Rick Flagg, news dir; Randy Moore, engrg dir.

WNLS(AM)—Co-owned with WTNT-FM. Oct 15, 1946: 1270 khz; 5 kw-U, DA-N. TL: N30 25 38 W84 19 46. Web Site: www.wnls.com. Network: Network: ABC, Sporting News Radio Network. Rep: Christal. Format: News/talk. News staff: one; News: 25 hrs wkly. Spec prog: Florida State Univ. sports. ◆ J. L. Dunbar, progmg dir.

WUTL(FM)— May 1992: 106.1 mhz; 3 kw. 328 ft. TL: N30 28 37 W84 20 07. Opus Broadcasting, 3000 Olson Rd. 32308. Phone: (850) 386-8004. Fax: (850) 422-1897. E-mail: hkestenbaum @opusbroadcasting.com. Web Site: www.u1061.com. Licensee: Opus Broadcasting Tallahassee LLC. Group owner: Triad Broadcasting Co. LLC (acq 7-11-2005;. grpsl). Format: Classic rock. Target aud: 18-49. ◆ Chris Knight, VP; Hank Kestenbaum, gen mgr; Tom Watson, opns mgr.

*WVFS(FM)— September 1987: 89.7 mhz; 2.7 kw. 174 ft. TL: N30 26 22 W84 17 29. Florida State Univ., 420 Diffenbaugh 32306-1550. Phone: (850) 644-3871. Fax: (850) 644-8753. E-mail: wvfs@wvfs.fsu.edu. Web Site: www.wvfs.fsu.edu. Licensee: Florida State University. Format: Div. News: 2 hrs wkly. Target aud: General. Spec prog: Black 8 hrs, folk 3 hrs, Sp 2 hrs wkly. ◆ Dr. Misha Laurents, gen mgr.

Tampa

WAMA(AM)— 1961: 1550 khz; 10 kw-D, 125 w-N. TL: N27 55 16 W82 23 41. Box 152164 33684. Secondary address: 402 N. Reo St., Ste 218 33609. Phone: (813) 289-1552. Fax: (813) 289-1554. E-mail: oscarrojas@lainvasora1550.com. Web Site: www.lainvasora1550.com. Licensee: WAMA Inc. (acq 10-15-97; $2 million). Drinker, Biddle & Reath. Format: Mexican. News staff: one. Target aud: 18-49; Hispanic females. ◆ Ron Gordon, chmn & pres; Joshua Mednick, VP; Oscar Rojas, gen mgr.

WBTP(FM)—See Clearwater

*WBVM(FM)— May 27, 1986: 90.5 mhz; 100 kw. 958 ft. TL: N27 49 09 W82 14 26. Stereo. Box 18081 33679. Secondary address: 3816 Morrison Ave. 33629. Phone: (813) 289-8040. Fax: (813) 282-3580. E-mail: contact@spiritfm905.com. Web Site: www.spiritfm905.com. Licensee: The Bishop of the Diocese of St. Petersburg. Format: Contemp Christian. Target aud: 35 plus; families. Spec prog: Black 4 hrs, Greek one hr, children 4 hrs, Sp 4 hrs wkly. ◆ John Morris, VP & gen mgr; Chris Sampson, opns mgr.

WBZZ(AM)—(Seffner). Nov 7, 1960: 1010 khz; 50 kw-D, 5 kw-N, DA-2. TL: N27 59 25 W82 15 06. Stereo. 5510 W. Gray St., Suite 130 33609. Phone: (813) 637-8326. Fax: (813) 636-0995. Web Site: www.sportsradio1010.com. Licensee: Infinity Broadcasting Corp. of Tampa. Group owner: Infinity Broadcasting Corp. (acq 11-21-87). Network: Network: Westwood One, CBS. Rep: Infinity Radio Sales. Leventhal, Senter & Lerman. Format: All sports. News staff: one; News: 35 hrs wkly. Target aud: 25-54. ◆ Charlie Ochs, sr VP & gen mgr; Mike Culotta, opns mgr; Michael Remaley, gen sls mgr.

WYUU(FM)—Co-owned with WBZZ(AM). October 1983: 92.5 mhz; 50 kw. Ant 489 ft. TL: N27 50 32 W82 48 52. Stereo. Phone: (813) 287-1047. Fax: (813) 287-1833. Web Site: lanueva925.com. Licensee: Infinity Radio Inc. (acq 10-15-98; $75 million. with WLLD(FM) Holmes Beach). Leventhal, Senter & Lerman. Format: Sp. ◆ John Fennessy, gen sls mgr.

WDAE(AM)—See Saint Petersburg

WDUV(FM)—(New Port Richey). Sept 19, 1969: 105.5 mhz; 46 kw. Ant 1,345 ft. TL: N28 10 56 W82 46 06. (CP: 6.7 kw, ant 1,050 ft.). Stereo. 11300 4th St. N., Suite 300, St. Petersburg 33716-2941. Phone: (727) 579-2000. Fax: (727) 568-9388. Web Site: www.wduv.com. Licensee: CXR Holdings L.L.C. Group owner: Cox Communications

Florida

Inc. (acq 5-99). Format: Soft adult contemp. Target aud: 25-54. Spec prog: It one hr wkly. ◆Howard Tuuri, VP & gen mgr; Tom Paleveda, opns mgr & gen sls mgr.

WFLA(AM)— 1924: 970 khz; 5 kw-U, DA-2. TL: N28 01 14 W82 36 34. 4002A Gandy Blvd. 33611. Phone: (813) 839-9393. Fax: (813) 831-4475. Fax: (813) 837-0300. Web Site: www.970wfla.com. Licensee: Citicasters Licenses L.P. Group owner: Clear Channel Communications Inc. (acq 5-4-99; grpsl). Network: ABC Information & Entertainment. Hogan & Hartson. Format: News/talk. Target aud: 25-54. ◆David Reinhart, VP & gen mgr; Sue Treccase, progmg dir; Wilson Welch, chief of engrg.

WFLZ-FM—Co-owned with WFLA(AM). 1948: 93.3 mhz; 99 kw. 1,358 ft. TL: N27 50 32 W82 15 46. Stereo. Web Site: www.933flz.com. Format: CHR. Target aud: 18-34. ◆Dave Reinhart, gen mgr; Jeff Kapugi, progmg dir; Wilson Welch, chief of engrg.

WHNZ(AM)— May 15, 1922: 1250 khz; 5 kw-U, DA-1. TL: N28 00 41 W82 29 53. 4002 Gandy Blvd. 33611. Phone: (813) 839-9393. Fax: (813) 831-3299. Web Site: www.whnz.com. Licensee: Citicasters Licenses L.P. Group owner: Clear Channel Communications Inc. (acq 5-4-99; grpsl). Rep: McGavren Guild. Format: News/talk. Target aud: 25-54. ◆Dan DiLorette, pres & gen mgr; Gene Lindsey, progmg dir; Wilson Welch, chief of engrg.

WMTX(FM)—Co-owned with WHNZ(AM). November 1947: 100.7 mhz; 100 kw. 1,358 ft. TL: N28 02 21 W82 39 21. (CP: TL: N27 50 32 W82 15 46). Stereo. Web Site: www.wmtx.com. Format: Top 40, adult contemp. ◆Dan DiLoreto, gen mgr; Tony Florentino, progmg dir; Wilson Welch, chief of engrg.

WHPT(FM)—See Sarasota

*WMNF(FM)— Sept 14, 1979: 88.5 mhz; 70 kw. 520 ft. TL: N27 49 04 W82 14 31. 1210 E. Martin Luther King Jr. Blvd. 33603. Phone: (813) 238-8001. E-mail: wmnf@wmnf.org. Web Site: www.wmnf.org. Licensee: The Nathan B. Stubblefield Foundation. Network: NPR. Haley, Bader & Potts. Format: Div. News staff: 2; News: 15 hrs wkly. Target aud: General. ◆Sheila Cowley, opns mgr; Vicki Santa, stn mgr & dev dir; Randy Wynne, progmg dir; Bill Brown, chief of engrg.

WNTR(AM)— (Dunedin). Nov 21, 1959: 860 khz; 5 kw-D, 1.5 kw-N, DA-2. TL: N27 59 55 W82 42 01. 5211 W. Laurel St. 33607. Phone: (813) 639-1903. Fax: (813) 639-1272. Web Site: www.860wntr.com. Licensee: Caron Broadcasting Inc. WGUL FM Inc. (acq 8-12-2005; $9.5 million with WLSS(AM) Sarasota). Format: News/talk. ◆Chris Gould, gen mgr.

WQBN(AM)—(Temple Terrace). 1956: 1300 khz; 5 kw-D, 1 kw-N, DA-2. TL: N28 03 44 W82 19 44. Box 151300 33684. Secondary address: 5203 N. Armenia Ave. 33603. Phone: (813) 871-1333. Fax: (813) 876-1333. E-mail: superq1300@hotmail.com. Licensee: Radio Tropical Inc. Format: Sp, variety. News staff: 3; News: 20 hrs wkly. Target aud: 25 plus; Hispanics. ◆Efrain Archilla, pres; Marc L. Vila, VP & gen mgr.

WRBQ-FM— 1954: 104.7 mhz; 100 kw. Ant 561 ft. TL: N27 56 50 W82 27 35. Stereo. 9721 Executive Center Dr. N., Suite 200, Saint Petersburg 33702. Phone: (727) 579-1925. Fax: (727) 579-8888. Web Site: www.oldies1047.com. Licensee: Infinity Radio Inc. Group owner: Infinity Broadcasting Corp. (acq 5-99). Format: Oldies. Target aud: 18-49. ◆Charlie Ochs, gen mgr; Mason Dixon, progmg dir.

WTIS(AM)— 1946: 1110 khz; 10 kw-D, DA. TL: N27 52 26 W82 37 53. 311 112th Ave. N.E., St. Petersburg 33716. Phone: (727) 576-2234. Fax: (727) 577-3814. Licensee: WTIS-AM Inc. (acq 12-13-89; $1.7 million;. FTR: 1-1-90). Format: Relg, ethnic. Target aud: 25-54. Spec prog: Sp one hr wkly. ◆Ron Roseman, pres; Ed Roseman, exec VP; Mike Smith, gen mgr & opns mgr; Robert Kansnicki, progmg dir.

WTMP(AM)—(Egypt Lake). 1954: 1150 khz; 10 kw-D, 500 w-N. TL: N28 00 42 W82 29 53. 5207 Washington Blvd. 33619-3437. Phone: (813) 620-1300. Fax: (813) 628-0713. E-mail: info@tamabroadcasting.com. Web Site: www.wtmp.com. Licensee: Tama Radio Licenses of Tampa, FL, Inc. Group owner: Tama Broadcasting Inc. (acq 12-18-2001). Network: American Urban. Format: Rhythm and Blues. Target aud: 18-49; urban contemporary music listeners & adults. Spec prog: Gospel 20 hrs wkly. ◆Dr. Glenn Cherry, CEO, pres & CFO; Glenn Cherry, gen mgr; Louis Muhammad, opns mgr; Lynn Tolliver, progmg dir.

*WUSF(FM)— September 1963: 89.7 mhz; 71 kw. Ant 941 ft. TL: N27 50 53 W82 15 48. Stereo. WRB 219, 4202 E. Fowler Ave. 33620-6870. Phone: (813) 974-8700. Fax: (813) 974-5016. E-mail: jurofsky@usf.org. Web Site: www.wusf.org. Licensee: Board of Trustees, University of South Florida. Network: Network: NPR, PRI. Cohn & Marks. Format: Class, news, jazz. News staff: 5; News: 38 hrs wkly. Target aud: General. ◆Jo Ann Urofsky, gen mgr; Tom Dollenmayer, stn mgr; Cathy Cocca, dev mgr. Co-owned TV: *WUSF-TV affil

WWBA(AM)—(Pinellas Park). November 1948: 1040 khz; 5 kw-D, 500 w-N, DA-N. TL: N27 50 50 W82 46 21. 402 N. Reo St., Suite 204 33609. Phone: (813) 281-1040. Fax: (813) 281-1948. Web Site: www.wwba1040.com. Licensee: Genesis Communications of Tampa Bay Inc. Group owner: Genesis Communications Inc. (acq 12-17-97; $1.5 million). Format: News/talk. News staff: 1; News: 14 hrs wkly. Target aud: 25-54. ◆Bruce Maduri, CEO; Bambi Arnold, CFO; Sandra Culver, opns VP; Carol Azaravich, opns mgr.

WWRM(FM)—Licensed to Tampa. See Saint Petersburg

WXGL(FM)—See Saint Petersburg

WXTB(FM)—See Clearwater

Tarpon Springs

*WYFE(FM)— June 14, 1988: 88.9 mhz; 50 kw. 500 ft. TL: N28 24 07 W82 36 30. (CP: 60 kw, ant 449 ft.). Stereo. 5553 S.E. 3rd Ave., Keystone Heights 32656. Fax: (877) 939-9933. Web Site: www.bbnradio.org. Licensee: Bible Broadcasting Network Inc. (group owner; acq 8-11-89). Format: Relg. Target aud: General; Christians. ◆Lowell Davey, pres; Jack Long, gen mgr; Ron Muffley, chief of engrg.

Tavares

WXXL(FM)—Licensed to Tavares. See Leesburg

Tavenier

WKEZ-FM— 1999: 96.9 mhz; 6 kw. 220 ft. TL: N25 01 35 W80 30 30. 93351 Overseas Hwy. 33070. Phone: (305) 852-9085. Fax: (305) 852-5586. Web Site: www.easy969.com. Licensee: Clear Channel Broadcasting Licenses Inc. Group owner: Clear Channel Communications Inc. (acq 3-16-99; $849,900). Format: Easy lstng. ◆Dave Harris, VP; Jack Niedbalski, stn mgr; Scott Hamilton, opns mgr.

Temple Terrace

WQBN(AM)—Licensed to Temple Terrace. See Tampa

Tequesta

WEFL(AM)— Aug 1, 2002: 760 khz; 3 kw-D, 1.5 kw-N, DA-2. TL: N26 59 43 W80 11 34. 2090 Palm Beach Lakes Blvd., Ste 701, West Palm Beach 33409. Phone: (561) 697-8353. Fax: (561) 697-8525. E-mail: sports@espn.com. Web Site: www.@spn760.com. Licensee: Star of the Palm Beaches Inc. (acq 7-30-02). Network: Network: ESPN Radio, Westwood One. Format: Sports. ◆Craig Karmazin, CEO; Steve Politziner, gen mgr; Lance Davis, opns dir.

Tice

WJGO(FM)— March 2000: 102.9 mhz; 50 kw horiz, 48 kw vert. Ant 466 ft. TL: N26 29 16 W81 55 46. 10914 K-Nine Dr., 2nd Fl., Bonita Springs 34135. Phone: (239) 495-8383. Fax: (239) 495-0883. Web Site: www.groovingoldies.com. Licensee: Renda Broadcasting Corp. of Nevada. Group owner: Renda Broadcasting Corp. (acq 8-10-00; $7 million). Format: Rhythmic oldies. ◆Kelley McGrath, gen mgr.

Titusville

WIXC(AM)— Nov 20, 1957: 1060 khz; 10 kw-D, 5 kw-N, DA-2. TL: N28 39 47 W80 55 17. (CP: 50 kw-D, 17 kw-CH, DA-3). 6305 Hwy. 46, Mims 32754. Phone: (321) 264-1060. Phone: (321) 264-9700. Fax: (321) 264-4246. E-mail: gregsherlock@wixc1060.com. Licensee: Genesis Communications Inc. Group owner: Genesis Communications Inc. (acq 4-19-00; $650,000). Network: ESPN Radio. Format: Sports. Target aud: 35 plus. Spec prog: Relg 6 hrs wkly. ◆Bruce C. Maouri, CEO; Greg Sherlock, gen mgr & news dir; Steve Potter, gen sls mgr; Jerry Smith, chief of engrg.

WNUE-FM—Licensed to Titusville. See Daytona Beach

WORL(AM)—See Altamonte Springs

*WPIO(FM)— Oct 19, 1975: 89.3 mhz; 10 kw. 300 ft. TL: N28 34 49 W80 51 00. Stereo. 505 Josephine St. 32796. Phone: (321) 267-3000. Fax: (321) 264-9370. Web Site: www.noncomradio.com. Licensee: Florida Public Radio Inc. Format: Inspirational mus, pub affrs. ◆Randy Henry, pres & gen mgr.

Trenton

WDVH-FM— February 1988: 101.7 mhz; 3 kw. 328 ft. TL: N29 36 40 W82 51 14. Stereo. 3135 S. E. 27th St., Gainesville 32641. Phone: (352) 372-2528. Fax: (352) 372-0851. Licensee: Jablamo License Holdings LLC. (group owner; acq 7-6-2004; grpsl). Format: Country. News: 7 hrs wkly. Target aud: 25 plus; working class & professionals. Spec prog: Farm 2 hrs wkly. ◆Gordon Obarski, gen mgr & mus dir; Jim Brand, gen mgr & opns mgr.

Union Park

*WPOZ(FM)— Aug 9, 1995: 88.3 mhz; 2.5 kw. 1,469 ft. TL: N28 36 08 W81 05 37. (CP: 14.5 kw, ant 1,273 ft.). 1065 Rainer Dr., Altamonte Springs 32714. Phone: (407) 869-8000. Fax: (407) 869-0380. E-mail: zcrew@zradio.org. Web Site: www.zradio.org. Licensee: Central Florida Educational Foundation Inc. Joseph E. Dunne III. Format: Contemp Christian. Target aud: 25-44. ◆James S. Hoge, chmn, pres & gen mgr.

Valparaiso-Niceville

WFSH(AM)— November 1958: 1340 khz; 1 kw-U. TL: N30 30 34 W86 28 34. Box 1120, Destin 32540. Secondary address: 415 Mountain Dr., Suite 7, Destin 32541. Phone: (850) 654-4000. Fax: (850) 650-9440. E-mail: dale@fox1120.com. Licensee: Flagship Communications Inc. (acq 8-28-03; $225,000). Network: ESPN Radio. News staff: one. Target aud: 25-54. Spec prog: Sports. ◆Dale Riddick, gen mgr; Max Howell, gen sls mgr; Steve Williams, news dir.

Venice

WDDV(AM)— Feb 1, 1960: 1320 khz; 5 kw-D, 1 kw-N, DA-4. TL: N27 06 20 W82 24 01. 1779 Independence Blvd., Sarasota 34234. Phone: (941) 552-4800. Fax: (941) 552-4900. Web Site: www.1320wamr.com. Licensee: Citicasters Licenses L.P. Group owner: Clear Channel Communications Inc. (acq 5-4-99; grpsl). Format: Sports. Target aud: 25-54; active, upscale, affluent. Spec prog: Sp. ◆Sherri Carlson, gen mgr & mktg mgr.

WLTQ-FM—Co-owned with WDDV(AM). Mar 1, 1974: 92.1 mhz; 11.5 kw. Ant 476 ft. TL: N27 09 03 W82 27 51. Stereo. Web Site: www.921online.com. Format: Rock of 80's. Target aud: 25-54; female. ◆Randy Wanek, sls dir; Jeff Lynn, progmg dir.

Vero Beach

WCZR(FM)— May 29, 1986: 101.7 mhz; 1.48 kw. 471 ft. TL: N27 32 46 W80 22 08. Drawer 0093, Port St. Lucie 34985. Phone: (772) 335-9300. Fax: (772) 335-3291. Web Site: www.wzzr.com. Licensee: Capstar TX L.P. Group owner: Clear Channel Communications Inc. (acq 8-30-00; grpsl). Format: Talk. ◆Mark Bass, gen mgr.

WGNX(FM)— 1995: 99.7 mhz; 50 kw. 321 ft. TL: N27 46 38 W80 27 17. 1235 16th St. 32960. Phone: (561) 567-0937. Fax: (561) 562-4747. E-mail: info@wgnxfm.com. Web Site: www.wgnxfm.com. Licensee: Vero Beach FM Radio Partnership. (acq 2-11-2002). Format: 80s, 90s & now. ◆Jim Davis, gen mgr.

WGYL(FM)—Listing follows WTTB(AM).

WQOL(FM)— Sept 1, 1979: 103.7 mhz; 50 kw. 476 ft. TL: N27 33 21 W80 22 08. Stereo. Box 0093, Port St. Lucie 34985. Secondary address: 3771 S.E. Jennings Rd., Port St. Lucie 34952. Phone: (772) 335-9300. Fax: (772) 335-3291. Web Site: www.wqolfm.com. Licensee: Capstar TX L.P. Group owner: Clear Channel Communications Inc. (acq 8-30-00; grpsl). Network: Westwood One. Format: Oldies. Target aud: 35-64; baby boomers. ◆Mark Bass, gen mgr; Mike Michaels, opns mgr & chief of opns; Heath West, progmg mgr & mus dir; Mike Kerley, engrg mgr.

WSCF-FM— Feb 1, 1990: 91.9 mhz; 15.5 kw. 305 ft. TL: N27 38 10 W80 27 59. 6767 20th St. 32966. Phone: (561) 569-0919. Fax: (561) 562-4892. Licensee: Central Educational Broadcasting Inc. (acq 2-15-89). Network: USA. Format: Christian, hit radio. ♦ Jon Hamilton, VP & gen mgr; Brad Bacon, dev VP; Paul Tipton, progmg dir; Bruce Douglas, news dir.

WTTB(AM)— June 7, 1954: 1490 khz; 1 kw-U. TL: N27 37 12 W80 25 01. 1235 16th St. 32960. Phone: (772) 569-1490. Fax: (772) 562-4747. Web Site: www.wgylfm.com. Licensee: Vero Beach Broadcasters LLC (group owner; acq 6-19-00; $5.15 million. with co-located FM). Network: ABC. Rep: Allied Radio Partners. Format: Music of Your Life, talk. Target aud: General. ♦ Jim Davis, gen mgr.

WGYL(FM)—Co-owned with WTTB(AM). November 1970: 93.7 mhz; 50 kw. 475 ft. TL: N27 36 04 W80 23 33. Stereo. Web Site: www.wgylfm.com. Format: Soft adult contemp, smooth jazz. Target aud: 35-64; upscale adult. ♦ Jim Davis, opns mgr.

WZTA(AM)— May 1954: 1370 khz; 1 kw-D. TL: N27 36 01 W80 23 33. Box 0093, Port St. Lucie 34985. Secondary address: 3771 S.E. Jennings Rd., Port St. Lucie 34952. Phone: (772) 335-9300. Fax: (772) 335-3291. Licensee: Capstar TX L.P. Group owner: Clear Channel Communications Inc. (acq 8-30-2000; grpsl). Format: Talk. ♦ Mark Bass, gen mgr; Mike Michaels, opns mgr.

Watertown

WQLC(FM)— Oct 6, 1990: 102.1 mhz; 9 kw. 531 ft. TL: N30 13 58 W82 48 18. 820 N.W. Frontier Dr., Lake City 32055. Phone: (386) 755-4102. Fax: (386) 752-9861. E-mail: webmaster@powercountry102.com. Web Site: www.powercountry102.com. Licensee: Power Country Inc. Format: Hot country. Target aud: 18-54. Spec prog: Gospel 4 hrs wkly. ♦ L.D. Bolton II, CEO; Bob Hendrickson, pres & gen mgr; Scott Burns, chief of opns.

Wauchula

WAUC(AM)— Jan 7, 1958: 1310 khz; 5 kw-D, 500 w-N, DA-2. TL: N27 31 48 W81 49 08. Box 471 33873. Secondary address: 1310 S. Florida Ave. 33873. Phone: (863) 773-5008. Phone: (863) 773-9282. Fax: (863) 773-2032. E-mail: wauc.radiostation@earthlink.net. Licensee: Dora A. Cruz. (acq 12-1-97; $25,000). Format: Mexican. Target aud: 35-54. ♦ Robert Ayala, gen mgr.

West Palm Beach

*WAYF(FM)— Nov 11, 1993: 88.1 mhz; 50 w horiz, 50 kw vert. Ant 1,053 ft. TL: N26 35 20 W80 12 44. Box 881 33402. Secondary address: 800 Northpoint Pkwy., Suite 881 33407. Phone: (561) 881-1929. Fax: 840-1929. E-mail: jim@wayfm.com. Web Site: www.wayfm.com. Licensee: WAY-FM Media Group Inc. (group owner). Format: Contemp Christian. Target aud: 18-34; teens, young adults & young families. ♦ Bob Augsburg, pres; Jim Marshall, stn mgr.

WBZT(AM)— July 31, 1936: 1230 khz; 1 kw-U. TL: N26 43 36 W80 03 03. (CP: 800 w-N). 3071 Continental Dr. 33407. Phone: (561) 616-6600. Fax: (561) 616-6677. Web Site: www.wbzt.com. Licensee: Capstar TX L.P. Group owner Clear Channel Communications Inc. (acq 9-27-00; grpsl). Format: Talk. ♦ John Hunt, gen mgr; Dave Denver, opns dir.

WEAT-FM— Aug 30, 1969: 104.3 mhz; 100 kw. 1,273 ft. TL: N26 34 37 W80 14 32. Stereo. 701 Northpoint Pkwy., Suite 500 33407. Phone: (561) 686-9505. Fax: (561) 686-9579. Web Site: www.sunny1043.com. Licensee: Infinity Radio Inc. Group owner: Infinity Broadcasting Inc. (acq 11-13-98; grpsl). Leibowitz & Associates. Format: Soft adult contemp. Target aud: 25-54. ♦ Lee K. Strasser, gen mgr.

WFTL(AM)— 1948: 850 khz; 50 kw-D, 24 kw-N, DA-2. TL: N26 32 30 W80 44 30. 6600 N. Andrews Ave., Fort Lauderdale 33309. Phone: (954) 315-1515. Fax: (954) 315-1555. Licensee: JCE Licenses L.L.C. Group owner: James Crystal Inc. (acq 5-15-98; $1.5 million). Format: News/talk. Target aud: 35 plus. ♦ James C. Hilliard, pres; Rick Hindes, CFO; Steve Lapa, gen mgr; Lupe Soto, opns mgr; Tim Reever, gen sls mgr; Ken Pauli, news dir; Rick Reike, chief of engrg.

WIRK-FM— Aug 1, 1965: 107.9 mhz; 100 kw. Ant 426 ft. TL: N26 45 47 W80 12 19. Stereo. 701 Northpoint Pkwy., Suite 500 33407. Phone: (561) 686-9505. Fax: (561) 686-0157. Web Site: www.wirk.com. Licensee: Infinity Radio Inc. Group owner: Infinity Broadcasting Corp. (acq 11-13-98; grpsl). Format: Hot new country. ♦ Lee K. Strasser, gen mgr; Tony Bonvini, gen sls mgr; Doreen Rogers, mktg dir.

WJNO(AM)— July 15, 1947: 1290 khz; 5 kw-U, DA-N. TL: N26 37 55 W80 07 07. (CP: 10 kw-D, 4.9 kw-N. TL: N26 45 50 W80 12 17). 3071 Continental Drive 33407. Phone: (561) 616-6600. Fax: (561) 616-6677. Web Site: www.wjno.com. Licensee: Clear Channel Radio Licenses Inc. Group owner: Clear Channel Communications Inc. (acq 9-16-97; grpsl). Network: ABC Information & Entertainment. Rep: Clear Channel. Format: News/talk, sports. Target aud: Adults; 25-64. ♦ John Hunt, gen mgr; Dave Denver, opns dir; Bill Brady, gen sls mgr; Steve Nicholl, progmg dir & progmg mgr; Jim Leifer, chief of engrg.

WKGR(FM)—See Fort Pierce

WLVJ(AM)—See Boynton Beach

WRLX(FM)— Dec 13, 1975: 92.1 mhz; 7.2 kw. Ant 498 ft. TL: N26 47 58 W80 04 33. Stereo. 3071 Continental Dr. 33407. Phone: (561) 616-6600. Fax: (561) 616-6677. Web Site: www.classic921.com. Licensee: Clear Channel Broadcasting Licenses Group owner: Clear Channel Communications Inc. (acq 9-27-00; grpsl). Rep: Clear Channel. Format: Soft adult contemp. Target aud: 35-64. ♦ John Hunt, pres & gen mgr; Dave Denver, opns dir & opns mgr.

WRMF(FM)—(Palm Beach). 1957: 97.9 mhz; 100 kw. 1,350 ft. TL: N26 34 37 W80 14 32. (CP: Ant 417 ft.). 2406 S. Congress Ave. 33406. Phone: (561) 868-1100. Fax: (561) 868-1111. Licensee: PPB Licenses LLC (acq 7-1-02; $70 million). Rep: McGavren Guild. Latham & Watkins. Format: Adult contemp. Target aud: 25-54; general. ♦ Mike Catchall, CEO; Chet Tart, pres & gen mgr; Doris Dupee, CFO; Elizabeth Hamma, sls dir; Dennis Winslow, progmg dir; Tammy Hayes, prom.

*WXEL(FM)— Nov 24, 1969: 90.7 mhz; 38 kw. Ant 1,115 ft. TL: N26 35 20 W80 12 44. Stereo. Box 6607 33405. Secondary address: 3401 S. Congress Ave., Boynton Beach 33405. Phone: (561) 737-8000. Fax: (561) 369-3067. E-mail: jcarr@wxel.org. Web Site: www.wxel.org. Licensee: Barry Telecommunications Inc. (acq 4-16-97). Network: NPR. Schwartz, Woods & Miller. Format: Class, news info. News staff: 7. Target aud: 35 plus; career oriented (news & info). ♦ Jerry Carr, CEO & pres; Bernard Henneberg, exec VP & VP; Joanna Marie, opns mgr; Fred Flaxman, dev VP.

WZZR(FM)—(Riviera Beach). 1971: 94.3 mhz; 50 kw. Ant 456 ft. TL: N26 45 42 W80 04 42. Box 0093, Port St. Lucie 34985. Secondary address: 3771 S.E. Jennings Rd., Port St. Lucie 34952. Phone: (772) 335-9300. Fax: (772) 335-3291. Web Site: www.wzzr.com. Licensee: Clear Channel Broadcasting Licenses Inc. Group owner: Clear Channel Communications Inc. (acq 11-21-97; grpsl). Format: Talk. Target aud: 25-54. ♦ Mark Bass, gen mgr; Mike Michaels, opns mgr.

White City

WFLM(FM)— Dec 1, 1993: 104.7 mhz; 25 kw. 328 ft. TL: N27 26 05 W80 21 42. 6803 S. Federal Hwy., Port St. Lucie 34952. Phone: (772) 460-9356. Fax: (772) 460-2700. Licensee: Midway Broadcasting Co. Format: Rhythm and blues. Target aud: 18-54. Spec prog: Gospel 5 hrs, jazz 5 hrs, reggae 5 hrs wkly. ♦ Alice Lee, pres; Mark Fitzmayer, gen mgr.

Wildwood

WVLG(AM)—Licensed to Wildwood. See Leesburg

Williston

WTMG(FM)— July 1, 1983: 101.3 mhz; 3.5 kw. 433 ft. TL: N29 25 04 W82 32 58. Stereo. 249 W. University, Gainesville 32601. Phone: (352) 371-1980. Fax: (352) 338-0566. E-mail: info@magic1013.com. Web Site: www.magic1013.com. Licensee: Jablamo License Holdings LLC. (group owner; (acq 7-6-2004); grpsl). Format: Urban AC. News staff: one; News: 2 hrs wkly. ♦ Gordon Obarski, gen mgr; Scott Hinds, opns mgr; Michael Slack, prom dir.

Wilton Manors

WEXY(AM)— June 1963: 1520 khz; 3.5 kw-D, 250 w-N, DA-N. TL: N26 10 26 W80 09 27. 412 W. Oakland Park Blvd., Fort Lauderdale 33311. Phone: (954) 561-1520. Fax: (954) 561-9830. Licensee: Multicultural Radio Broadcasting Licensee LLC. Group owner: Multicultural Radio Broadcasting Inc. (acq 4-4-03; $2.75 million). Network: American Urban. Format: Gospel. ♦ Arthur Liu, CEO & pres; Jim Glogowski, VP; Doug DeVos, gen mgr & opns mgr; Eduardo Ruedo, gen mgr.

Windermere

WUNA(AM)—See Ocoee

Winter Garden

WLAA(AM)— Feb 22, 2000: 1680 khz; 10 kw-D, 1 kw-N. TL: N28 34 08 W81 31 08. 1801 Clark Rd., Ocoee 34761. Phone: (407) 523-2770. Phone: (407) 996-6542. Fax: (407) 481-0751. Licensee: Rama Communications Inc. (group owner). Format: Sp. ♦ Sabita Persaud, pres; Kris Persaud, gen mgr.

WOKB(FM)— Jan 1, 1958: 1600 khz; 5 kw-U, DA-2. TL: N28 34 06 W81 31 09. 1801 Clark Rd., Ocoee 34761. Phone: (407) 523-2770. Phone: (407) 291-1395. Fax: (407) 523-2888. E-mail: jchsamek@yahoo.com. Web Site: www.gospelrama.com. Licensee: Rama Communications Inc. (group owner; acq 10-13-93; $950,000 with WXXU(AM) Cocoa Beach; 11-8-93). Cohn & Marks. Format: Gospel. News staff: one. Target aud: 25-54. Spec prog: Fr 7 hrs, gospel 12 hrs wkly. ♦ Sabita Persaud, pres; Earl Harvey, gen mgr; Steve January, opns mgr.

Winter Haven

WHNR(AM)—(Cypress Gardens). Nov 29, 1958: 1360 khz; 5 kw-D, 2.5 kw-N, DA-2. TL: N28 01 16 W81 42 02. Box 7742, 1505 Dundee Rd. 33883. Phone: (863) 299-1141. Fax: (863) 293-6397. E-mail: info@whnr1360.com. Web Site: www.whnr1360.com. Licensee: GB Enterprises Communication Corp. (acq 8-1-95; $250,000). Network: ABC Information & Entertainment. Format: Urban AC. News staff: one; News: 20 hrs wkly. Target aud: 55 plus. Spec prog: Relg 10 hrs wkly. ♦ Frankie Grover, CEO & pres; P.J. Allen, stn mgr & gen sls mgr.

WLKF(AM)—See Lakeland

WPCV(FM)—Licensed to Winter Haven. See Lakeland

WSIR(AM)— Feb 14, 1947: 1490 khz; 1 kw-U. TL: N28 00 50 W81 45 02. 665 South Lake Howard Dr. S.W. 33880-2577. Phone: (863) 295-9411. Fax: (863) 401-9365. Web Site: www.rejoice1490.com. Licensee: Anscombe Broadcasting Group Ltd. (acq 9-5-01). Format: Gospel, rhythm and blues classics. News: 5 hrs wkly. Target aud: 25 plus. Spec prog: Relg 14 hrs, Sp 10 hrs wkly. ♦ Steve Reszka, CEO & pres; Joe Fisher, VP, gen mgr & gen mgr; Tony Charles, mus dir.

Winter Park

WLOQ(FM)— 1966: 103.1 mhz; 2.65 kw. 351 ft. TL: N28 32 22 W81 26 46. Stereo. 2301 Lucien Way, Suite 180, Maitland 32751. Phone: (407) 647-5557. Fax: (407) 647-4495. E-mail: frontdesk@wloq.com. Web Site: www.wloq.com. Licensee: Gross Communications Corp. (group owner; (acq) 1977). Rep: Interep, Allied Radio Partners. Pepper & Corazzini. Format: Jazz. Target aud: 25-54; white collar/professionals. ♦ Herbert Paul Gross, pres; John Gross, CFO; Rick Weinkauf, VP & gen mgr; Ken Marks, gen sls mgr.

Florida

WPRD(AM)—September 1954: 1440 khz; 5 kw-D, 1 kw-N, DA-N. TL: N28 35 18 W81 22 53. Stereo. 222 Hazard St., Orlando 32804-3030. Phone: (407) 841-8282. Fax: (407) 841-8250. E-mail: wprd1440@hotmail.com. Licensee: J & V Communications Inc. (group owner; acq 11-94; $300,000). Larry Perry. Format: Sp, news/talk. Target aud: 25-64; upscale. ◆John Torrado, CEO, pres & gen mgr; Frank Vaught, opns mgr.

*WPRK(FM)—Dec 10, 1952: 91.5 mhz; 1.32 kw. 89 ft. TL: N28 35 40 W81 20 07. Stereo. Box 2745, Rollins College, 1000 Holt Ave. 32789-4499. Phone: (407) 646-2915. Fax: (407) 646-2241. Fax: (407) 646-1560. Web Site: www.rollins.edu/wprk. Licensee: Rollins College. Format: Class, progsv, urban contemp. News: 2 hrs wkly. Target aud: General; non-traditional class and/or rock listeners. Spec prog: Jazz 3 hrs wkly. ◆Dan Seeger, gen mgr; Margo DeGuenery, pub affrs dir.

Woodville

WJZT(FM)—September 2003: 97.9 mhz; 6 kw. Ant 328 ft. TL: N30 16 30 W84 07 39. 435 St. Francis St., Tallahassee 32301. Phone: (850) 561-8400 (studio). Phone: (407) 227-3642. E-mail: epetrone@wjztfm.com. Web Site: www.wjztfm.com. Licensee: 97.9 WJZTFM Inc. Format: Smooth jazz. ◆Ernest Petrone, gen mgr.

Yankeetown

WXOF(FM)—1998: 96.3 mhz; 6 kw. 285 ft. TL: N29 01 18 W82 41 20. 4554 S. Suncoast Blvd., Homosassa Springs 34446. Phone: (352) 628-4444. Fax: (352) 628-4450. E-mail: staff@citrus95radio.com. Licensee: WGUL-FM Inc. (acq 1-22-99). Format: Classic hits. ◆David Marcocci, gen mgr.

Zephyrhills

WZHR(AM)—May 9, 1962: 1400 khz; 1 kw-U. TL: N28 16 54 W82 12 30. 2360 N.E. Coachman Rd., Clearwater 33765. Phone: (727) 441-3311. Fax: (727) 441-1300. E-mail: lola@tantalk1340.com. Web Site: www.tantalk1340.com. Licensee: Wagenvoord Advertising Group Inc. (group owner; acq 2-13-02). Network: Network: CNN Radio, CBS Radio. Format: News/talk/sports. Target aud: 35-64; men & women. Spec prog: CHR 10 hrs wkly. ◆Dave Wagenvoord, CEO & pres; Lola Wagenvoord, VP & gen mgr.

Zolfo Springs

WZZS(FM)—November 1992: 106.9 mhz; 6 kw. 328 ft. TL: N27 21 59 W81 47 52. 7891 U.S. Hwy. 17 S. 33890. Phone: (863) 494-4111. Fax: (863) 494-4443. E-mail: wzzs@desoto.net. Web Site: www.wzzs1069.com. Licensee: Heartland Broadcasting Corp. Format: Country. News staff: one; News: one hr wkly. Target aud: General; DeSoto, Hardee and Highlands counties. Spec prog: Gospel 2 hrs, farm one hr wkly. ◆Harold Kneller Jr., pres; Sherry Good, opns mgr; Carolyn Francoletti, mktg dir & sls.

Georgia

Adel

WDDQ(FM)—October 1979: 92.1 mhz; 6 kw. Ant 298 ft. TL: N31 08 15 W83 23 41. Stereo. 1203 W. 4th St., Suite 11 31620. Phone: (229) 896-4572. Licensee: Adventure Radio Group LLC (acq 12-30-02; $435,000). Format: Adult contemp, oldies. Target aud: 18-50. ◆Ron Hester, gen mgr & progmg mgr.

Albany

WALG(AM)—1940: 1590 khz; 5 kw-D, 1 kw-N, DA-2. TL: N31 37 19 W84 09 09. 1104 W. Broad Ave. 31707. Phone: (912) 888-5000. Fax: (912) 888-5960. Web Site: www.cumulus.com. Licensee: Cumulus Licensing Corp. Group owner: Cumulus Media Inc. (acq 11-3-98; grpsl). Network: ABC. Rep: Katz Radio. Format: News/talk. Target aud: General. ◆George Francis, pres & VP; Bill Jones, progmg dir; Jenna McKay, pub affrs dir; Joey Falgout, chief of engrg.

WNUQ(FM)—Co-owned with WALG(AM). Dec 17, 1972: 101.7 mhz; 3 kw. Ant 300 ft. TL: N31 37 15 W84 09 11. Stereo. Web Site: www.cumulus.com. Format: CHR. ◆Ken O'Brien, opns mgr; Mark McGee, progmg dir; Jenna McKay, news dir.

WEGC(FM)—(Sasser). 1995: 107.7 mhz; 11.5 kw. 312 ft. TL: N31 38 42 W84 21 15. 1104 W. Broad Ave. 31707. Phone: (229) 888-5000. Fax: (229) 888-5960. Web Site: www.mix107albany.com. Licensee: Cumulus Licensing Corp. Group owner: Cumulus Media Inc. (acq 7-7-98). Format: Adult contemp, lite rock favorites. ◆Paul Bucurel, gen mgr.

WGPC(AM)—1933: 1450 khz; 1 kw-U. TL: N31 34 55 W84 11 58. Stereo. 1104 W. Broad Ave. 31707. Phone: (229) 888-5000. Fax: (229) 888-5960. Web Site: www.cumulus.com. Licensee: Cumulus Licensing Corp. Group owner: Cumulus Media Inc. (acq 11-3-98; $2.25 million. with co-locatd FM). Network: CBS. Holland & Knight. Format: Easy Istng. News: 20 hrs wkly. Target aud: 25 plus; middle to upper income. ◆George Francis, pres & gen mgr; Bill Jones, progmg dir; Joey Falgout, chief of engrg.

WKAK(FM)—Co-owned with WGPC(AM). Feb 22, 1963: 104.5 mhz; 100 kw. Ant 981 ft. TL: N31 32 57 W84 00 19. Stereo. Web Site: www.cumulus.com. Format: Country. News: 25 hrs wkly. ◆Claire Peeples, gen sls mgr.

WJIZ-FM—Listing follows WJYZ(AM).

WJYZ(AM)—November 1952: 960 khz; 5 kw-D, DA. TL: N31 37 06 W84 10 33. Stereo. Box 3106 31706. Secondary address: 809 S. Westover Blvd. 31707. Phone: (229) 439-9704. Fax: (229) 439-1509. Licensee: Clear Channel Broadcasting Licenses Inc. Group owner: Clear Channel Communications Inc. (acq 7-12-00; grpsl). Rep: D & R Radio. Format: Gospel. Target aud: 25-54. ◆John Richards, gen mgr; Ken O'Brien, opns mgr.

WJIZ-FM—Co-owned with WJYZ(AM). January 1965: 96.3 mhz; 100 kw. 469 ft. TL: N31 39 20 W84 10 30. (CP: Ant 466 ft. N31 39 16 W84 10 36). Stereo. Box 3106 31706. Secondary address: 809 Westover Blvd. 31707. Phone: (912) 439-9704. Fax: (912) 439-1509. Network: American Urban. Format: Urban contemp. ◆Tom Collins, gen mgr; Adrian Guyton, progmg dir.

WOBB(FM)—(Tifton). 1975: 100.3 mhz; 100 kw. 1,100 ft. TL: N31 25 49 W83 45 22. Stereo. 809 S. Westover Blvd. 31707. Phone: (229) 439-9704. Fax: (229) 439-1509. E-mail: johnrichards@clearchannel.com. Licensee: Clear Channel Broadcasting Licenses Inc. Group owner: Clear Channel Communications Inc. (acq 7-12-00; grpsl). Rep: Christal. Bechtel & Cole. Format: Country. News: 2 hrs wkly. Target aud: 25-49. ◆John Richards, gen mgr; Kurt Baker, progmg dir.

WSRA(AM)—July 10, 1962: 1250 khz; 1 kw-D, 53 w-N. TL: N31 37 00 W84 09 32. 2804 N. Jefferson St. 31701. Phone: (229) 432-1250. Fax: (229) 436-0544. Licensee: Agape Life Ministries Inc. (acq 8-11-2004; $150,000). Format: Sports radio. Target aud: 25-54. ◆Livingston W. Fulton, pres; Sharon Shernisky, gen mgr.

*WUNV(FM)—1990: 91.7 mhz; 3 kw. 328 ft. TL: N31 40 20 W84 03 27. Stereo. 260 14th St. N.W., Atlanta 30318-5360. Phone: (404) 685-2690. Fax: (404) 685-2684. E-mail: ask@gpb.org. Web Site: www.gpb.org. Licensee: Georgia Public Telecommunications Commission. Network: Network: PRI, NPR. Format: Class, news. News staff: 6; News: 40 hrs wkly. Target aud: 35 plus; professional, college educated. ◆Nancy Hall, CEO; Bonnie Bean, CFO; Ryan Fowler, opns mgr; St. John Flynn, progmg dir; Susanna Capelouto, news dir.

*WWXC(FM)—July 12, 1990: 90.7 mhz; 3 kw. 328 ft. TL: N31 38 42 W84 21 15. 280 June Ln., Dawson 31742. Phone: (229) 698-5866. Fax: (775) 249-6757. E-mail: wgnp@alltel.net. Web Site: www.wwxc.com. Licensee: Lamad Ministries Inc. (acq 7-89). Format: Relg. News: 4 hrs wkly. Target aud: 35 plus. ◆C. William Eidenire, pres; Bob Nichols, gen mgr.

Alma

WAJQ(AM)—October 1957: 1400 khz; 1 kw-U. TL: N31 31 50 W82 27 45. Drawer F 31510. Phone: (912) 632-1000. Fax: (912) 632-9696. Licensee: Blueberry Broadcasting Co. Inc. (acq 10-5-94; $12,000 with co-located FM; 10-31-94). Format: Southern gospel. News staff: one; News: 6 hrs wkly. Target aud: General. Spec prog: Farm 2 hrs wkly. ◆Debra Deen, gen mgr.

WAJQ-FM—May 14, 1987: 104.3 mhz; 4.5 kw. 371 ft. TL: N31 36 26 W82 32 46. Stereo. Format: Country. Target aud: General. ◆Bob Sass, prom dir.

Alpharetta

WLTA(AM)—Aug 25, 1986: 1400 khz; 1 kw-U. TL: N34 03 49 W84 16 34. 2970 Peachtree Rd. N.W., Suite 700, Atlanta 30305. Phone: (404) 365-0970. Fax: (404) 816-0748. E-mail: wniv@wniv.com. Web Site: www.wniv.com. Licensee: Salem Media of Georgia Inc. Group owner: Salem Communications Corp. (acq 11-17-99; $8 million with WNIV(AM) Atlanta). Group owner: Booth, Freret, Imlay & Tepper. Format: Relg, talk/news. Target aud: 25-49; upper middle to upper income. ◆Allen Power, gen mgr; Mike Moran, stn mgr; Jim Sutton, opns dir.

Americus

*WBJY(FM)—2002: 89.3 mhz; 65 kw vert. Ant 613 ft. TL: N31 38 22 W83 44 58. 113 College Ave., Ashburn 31714. Phone: (229) 567-8081. Fax: (229) 567-9045. Web Site: www.free893.com. Licensee: American Family Association. Group owner: American Family Radio Format: Christian. ◆Marvin Sanders, gen mgr.

WDEC-FM—Sept 12, 1964: 94.7 mhz; 25 kw. 328 ft. TL: N31 53 52 W84 18 53. Stereo. Box 727 31709. Secondary address: 1028 Adderton St. 31709. Phone: (229) 924-1390. Fax: (229) 928-2337. Web Site: www.americusradio.com. Licensee: Sumter Broadcasting Co. Group owner: Sumter Broadcasting Co. Inc. (acq 1994; with co-located AM). Rep: Rgnl Reps. Format: Hot adult contemp. News staff: 2; News: 2 hrs wkly. Spec prog: Black 5 hrs, farm one hr wkly. ◆Steve Lashley, pres & gen mgr; Thurston Clary, progmg dir.

*WFRP(FM)—Not on air, target date: unknown: 88.5 mhz; 2 kw vert. Ant 285 ft. TL: N32 05 34 W84 16 56. Family Stations Inc., 4135 Northgate Blvd., Suite 1, Sacramento, CA 95834. Phone: (916) 641-8191. Fax: (916) 641-8238. Web Site: www.familyradio.com. Licensee: Family Stations Inc. Format: Relg.

WISK(AM)—Aug 28, 1962: 1390 khz; 5 kw-D, 1 kw-N. TL: N32 04 51 W84 15 20. Box 727, 1028 Adderton St. 31709. Phone: (229) 924-1390. Phone: (229) 924-6500. Fax: (229) 928-2337. Web Site: www.americusradio.com. Licensee: Sumter Broadcasting Co. Inc. (group owner) Format: Oldies. News staff: one. Target aud: 19-65. ◆Steve Lashley, gen mgr; Donnie McCreary, news dir.

WISK-FM—September 1973: 98.7 mhz; 25 kw. 302 ft. TL: N32 04 51 W84 15 20. Stereo. Rep: Rgnl Reps. Format: Country.

Ashburn

WFFM(FM)—December 1989: 105.7 mhz; 6 kw. Ant 328 ft. TL: N31 41 17 W83 38 38. 400 Dunbar Lane., Albany 31707. Phone: (229 776-9565. Fax: (229) 446-9279. Licensee: On Top Communications Inc. (group owner; acq 1-8-2002; grpsl). Rep: Allied Radio Partners. Format: Urban contemp. Target aud: 18-49; adults. ◆Steve Hegwood, CEO, chmn & gen mgr; Audra Coley, opns mgr; Mary Beth Bateman, sls dir & mktg mgr.

Athens

WBKZ(AM)—(Jefferson). Sept 15, 1984: 880 khz; 5 kw-D. TL: N34 00 52 W83 27 11. Box 88 30603. Secondary address: 1186 W. Broad 30606. Phone: (706) 548-8800. Fax: (706) 549-1340. E-mail: mbgeter@aol.com. Licensee: Brown Broadcasting System Inc. (acq 9-29-93; $270,000; 10-18-93). Format: Var/div. ◆Melvin Geter, gen mgr & opns mgr.

WFSH-FM—Licensed to Athens. See Atlanta

WGAU(AM)—May 1, 1938: 1340 khz; 1 kw-U. TL: N33 56 28 W83 24 13. 850 Bobbin Mill Rd. 30606. Phone: (706) 549-1340. Fax: (706) 353-1220. E-mail: wgau@negia.net. Web Site: www.1340wgau.net. Licensee: Southern Broadcasting of Pensacola Inc. Group owner: Southern Broadcasting Companies Inc. (acq 8-6-99). Leventhal, Senter & Lerman. Format: News/talk. News staff: 3; News: 25 plus; educated, middle to upper-income, news & info oriented. Spec prog: Univ. of Georgia sports, Atlanta Braves. ◆Paul Stone, pres & VP; Scott Smith, opns mgr.

*WMSL(FM)—October 1987: 88.9 mhz; 20 kw. 315 ft. TL: N33 54 25 W83 29 35. Stereo. 2121 Ruth Jackson Rd., Bogart 30622. Phone: (770) 725-0889. Fax: (678) 753-0089. E-mail: gm@wmsl.fm. Web Site: www.wmsl.fm. Licensee: Prince Avenue Baptist Christian School. Network: USA. Haley, Bader & Potts. Format: Contemp Christian.

News staff: one; News: 11 hrs wkly. Target aud: 25-54; women. ♦James O. Hutto, gen mgr & mus dir; Dianne M. Hutto, dev dir; Nathan Collins, news dir.

WPUP(FM)—(Royston). Dec 1, 1988: 103.7 mhz; 25 kw. 328 ft. TL: N34 14 13 W83 16 03. Stereo. 1010 Tower Pl., Bogart 30622. Phone: (706) 549-6222. Fax: (706) 353-1967. Web Site: www.rock1037fm.com. Licensee: Southern Broadcasting of Athens Inc. Group owner: Southern Broadcasting Companies Inc. (acq 2-21-97; grpsl). Format: Active rock. News staff: 2. Target aud: 18-24. ♦Paul Stone, pres, gen mgr & stn mgr; Scott Smith, stn mgr.

WRFC(AM)— May 1, 1948: 960 khz; 5 kw-D, 2.5 kw-N, DA-N. TL: N33 59 58 W83 26 00. Stereo. 1010 Tower Pl., Bogart 30622. Phone: (706) 549-6222. Fax: (706) 353-1967. Web Site: www.960theref.com. Licensee: Southern Broadcasting of Athens Inc. Group owner: Southern Broadcasting Companies Inc. (acq 2-21-97; grpsl). Network: Network: CBS, ABC Information & Entertainment. Format: Sports, Talk. News staff: 3; News: 10 hrs wkly. Target aud: 25-54; community-minded adults. Spec prog: Black 15 hrs wkly. ♦Paul Stone, pres & gen mgr; Scott Smith, opns mgr & chief of engrg.

***WUGA(FM)**— Aug 28, 1987: 91.7 mhz; 6 kw. 328 ft. TL: N33 55 13 W83 14 46. Stereo. Georgia Public Radio (HQ), 260 14th St. N.W., Atlanta 30318. Phone: (404) 685-2690. Fax: (404) 685-2684. E-mail: ask@gpb.org. Web Site: www.gpb.org. Licensee: Georgia Public Telecommunications Commission. Network: Network: Network: PRI, NPR, AP Radio. Format: Class, news. News staff: 3; News: 5 hrs wkly. Target aud: 35-65; college educ. Spec prog: Folk 4 hrs, jazz 4 hrs wkly. ♦Nancy Hall, CEO & gen mgr; Bonnie Bean, CFO; Ryan Fowler, opns mgr; St. John Flynn, progmg mgr; Susanna Capelouto, news dir.

***WUOG(FM)**— Oct 16, 1972: 90.5 mhz; 9.5 kw. 180 ft. TL: N33 57 00 W83 22 02. (CP: 26 kw, ant 179 ft. TL: N33 56 59 W83 22 58). Stereo. Box 2065, Tate Student Ctr., University of Georgia 30602. Phone: (706) 542-7100. Fax: (706) 542-0070. Web Site: www.uga.edu/wuog. Licensee: University of Georgia. Format: Alternative. News staff: 3; News: 4 hrs wkly. Target aud: 18-25; students & faculty of Univ. ♦Alison Taffel, gen mgr; Justin Waller, prom dir; Brian Crews, adv dir; Jackie Steele, news dir; Beth Orcult, pub affrs dir; Wilbur Harrington, chief of engrg.

WXAG(AM)— June 10, 1957: 1470 khz; 1 kw-D, 176 w-N. TL: N33 59 14 W83 20 17 (D), N33 55 03 W83 22 39 (N). 855 Sunset Dr., Suite 16 30606. Phone: (706) 552-1470. Fax: (706) 452-0847. Licensee: Mecca Communications Inc. (acq 9-8-94; 9-26-94). Format: Gospel. ♦Michael Thurmond, gen mgr.

Atlanta

***WABE(FM)**— Sept 13, 1948: 90.1 mhz; 96 kw. Ant 821 ft. TL: N33 45 32 W84 20 07. Stereo. 740 Bismark Rd. N.E. 30324. Phone: (678) 686-0321. Fax: (678) 686-0356. Web Site: www.wabe.org. Licensee: Board of Education of the City of Atlanta. Network: Network: NPR, PRI. Schwartz, Woods & Miller. Format: News/talk, class. News staff: 3; News: 9 hrs wkly. Target aud: 35-54; news advocates, class music enthusiasts. Spec prog: Jazz 5 hrs wkly. ♦Milton Clipper, CEO & pres; Irene Wreen, CFO; Earl Johnson, VP, gen mgr & stn mgr; Lisa Williams, opns mgr & dev dir. Co-owned TV: *WPBA-TV affil

WAEC(AM)— 1947: 860 khz; 5 kw-D, 500 w-N. TL: N33 43 45 W84 19 19. 1465 Northside Dr., Suite 218 30318. Phone: (404) 355-8600. Fax: (404) 355-4156. E-mail: waec@love86am.com. Web Site: www.love86am.com. Licensee: WAEC License L.P. (acq 10-29-99). Format: Contemp Christian, Relg. Total Christian community. ♦George Beasley, chmn; Brian Beasley, pres & exec VP; Caroline Beasley, CFO; Chris Edmonds, gen mgr.

WAFS(AM)— Sept 1, 1955: 1190 khz; 10 kw-D. TL: N33 48 35 W84 21 14. Stereo. 2970 Peachtree Rd. N.W., Suite 700 30305. Phone: (404) 365-0970. Fax: (404) 816-0748. E-mail: wniv@wniv.com. Web Site: www.wniv.com. Licensee: Salem Media of Georgia Inc. Group owner: Salem Communications Corp. (acq 4-4-2000; $8 million). Rep: CMBS. Format: Southern gospel. Target aud: 35-64. ♦Allen Power, gen mgr; Jim Sutton, opns dir; Jeff Carter, opns mgr.

WALR(AM)— Nov 20, 1965: 1340 khz; 1 kw-U. TL: N33 44 56 W84 24 26. 3535 Piedmont Rd., Bldg. 14, Suite 1200 30305. Phone: (404) 688-0068. Fax: (404) 995-4045. E-mail: jimmypowers@680thefan.com. Web Site: www.talkradio1340.com. Licensee: Dickey Broadcasting Co. (group owner; acq 8-31-00; grpsl). Network: Network: Network: CBS Radio, AP Radio, Sporting News Radio Network. Rep: McGavren Guild. Holland & Knight. Format: Talk. News staff: 2; News: 10 hrs wkly. Target aud: 25-64; Black adults. Spec prog: Natre Dame football (fall). ♦David Dickey, gen mgr; Jimmy Powers, opns dir; Lee Killian, sls dir; John Levinson, mktg dir, prom dir & chief of engrg.

WALR-FM—See La Grange

WAOK(AM)— Mar 15, 1954: 1380 khz; 5 kw-U, DA-N. TL: N33 45 36 W84 28 45. (CP: 4.2 kw-N). 1201 Peachtree St., Suite 800 30361. Phone: (404) 898-8900. Fax: (404) 898-8916. E-mail: slgosnell@cbs.com. Web Site: www.waok.com. Licensee: Infinity Broadcasting East Inc. Group owner: Infinity Broadcasting Corp. (acq 1996; grpsl). Network: CBS. Format: News/talk. News staff: 5; News: 50 hrs wkly. Target aud: 25-54. ♦Mel Karmazin, CEO & pres; Monique McCoy, VP & prom mgr; Val Carolin, gen mgr & sls dir; Rick Caffey, mktg mgr; Tasha Brown, prom dir & pub affrs dir; Tasha Love, progmg dir; Tony Brown, progmg dir; Sid Daniel, chief of engrg.

WVEE(FM)—Co-owned with WAOK(AM). July 1, 1948: 103.3 mhz; 100 kw. 1,022 ft. TL: N33 45 35 W84 20 07. Stereo. Web Site: www.v-103.com. Network: Westwood One. Format: Urban contemp. News staff: 2. Target aud: 18-49. ♦Monique McCoy, prom mgr; Denise Dunbar, progmg dir; Linda Looney, mus dir; Tasha Love, mus dir; Jean Ross, news dir.

WATB(AM)—See Cumming

***WCLK(FM)**— Apr 10, 1974: 91.9 mhz; 6 kw. Ant 308 ft. TL: N33 44 56 W84 24 26. Stereo. 111 James P. Brawley Dr. S.W. 30314. Phone: (404) 880-8284. Phone: (404) 880-8278. Fax: (404) 880-8869. E-mail: wclkfm@cau-edu. Web Site: www.wclk.com. Licensee: Clark Atlanta University. Network: Network: NPR, PRI. Format: Jazz. News staff: 16. Target aud: 25-49; upscale, college educated, primarily African American. Spec prog: Gospel 17 hrs, reggae 3 hrs, blues 3 hrs, info/talk 12 hrs wkly. ♦Wendy Williams, gen mgr; Tammy Nobles, stn mgr; Glen Simmonds, opns mgr; Roxane Hurley, mktg dir; Shelley Trotter, prom mgr & pub affrs dir; Shelley Wynter, adv mgr; Bill Clark, progmg dir; Renee Williams, mus dir; Juanita Vasser, pub affrs dir; Gary Owens, chief of engrg.

WCNN(AM)—(North Atlanta). Dec 4, 1967: 680 khz; 50 kw-D, 10 kw-N, DA-2. TL: N33 57 42 W84 15 48. 3535 Piedmont Rd., Bldg. 14, Suite 1200 30305. Phone: (404) 688-0068. Fax: (404) 995-4045. Web Site: www.680thefan.com. Licensee: Dickey Broadcasting Co. (group owner; acq 8-31-00; grpsl). Format: News, sports. ♦David Dickey, pres & gen mgr; Robert Hasson, gen sls mgr; Jimmy Powers, progmg dir.

WDWD(AM)— July 1, 1938: 590 khz; 5 kw-U, DA-N. TL: N33 49 34 W84 18 56. (CP: 4.5 kw-N, DA-2). 6th Fl., 210 Interstate Pkwy. N. 30339. Phone: (770) 541-0590. Fax: (770) 952-7461. Web Site: www.radiodisney.com. Licensee: Radio Disney Atlanta LLC. Group owner: ABC Inc. (acq 5-17-85; $6.85 million;. FTR: 6-3-85). Network: ABC. Rep: ABC Radio Sales. Format: Radio Disney. Target aud: Children. Spec prog: Children. ♦Victor Sansone, pres & gen mgr; Kellye Harbison, sls dir; Jay Bowden, natl sls mgr; Melissa Cordwell, prom dir; Russell Smith, chief of engrg.

WKHX-FM—Co-owned with WDWD(AM). November 1960: 101.5 mhz; 100 kw. Ant 1,079 ft. TL: N33 48 26 W84 20 22. Stereo. Phone: (404) 521-1015. Fax: (404) 499-1015 (news/on-air). Web Site: www.kick1015.com. Licensee: ABC Radio Atlanta LLC (acq 11-81). Network: ABC. Format: Country. News staff: one. Target aud: 25-54. ♦Mark Richards, opns mgr & progmg dir; Rick Mack, sls dir; Matt Scarano, rgnl sls mgr; Tammy Elliot, rgnl sls mgr; Christy Ullman, prom mgr; Johnny Gray, mus dir.

WFOM(AM)—See Marietta

WFSH-FM—(Athens). January 1964: 104.7 mhz; 24 kw. Ant 1,656 ft. TL: N33 52 02 W83 49 44. Stereo. 2970 Peachtree Rd. N.W., Suite 700 30305. Phone: (404) 365-0970. Fax: (404) 816-0748. Web Site: www.thefishatlanta.com. Licensee: South Texas Broadcasting Inc. Group owner: Salem Communications Corp. (acq 7-27-2000; grpsl). Holland & Knight. Format: CHR. Spec prog: Gospel 2 hrs wkly. ♦Mike Moran, stn mgr; David Koon, gen sls mgr; Mike Stoudt, natl sls mgr & mus dir; Taylor Scott, prom dir & prom mgr; Kevin Avery, progmg dir; C. J. Jackson, chief of engrg.

WFTD(AM)—See Marietta

WGKA(AM)— Mar 17, 1922: 920 khz; 5 kw-D, 488 w-N. TL: N33 48 35 W84 21 23. 2970 Peachtree Rd. N.W., Suite 700 30305. Phone: (404) 365-0970. Fax: (404) 816-0748. Web Site: www.themighty1190.com. Licensee: Pennsylvania Media Associates Inc. Group owner: Salem Communications Corp. (acq 6-28-2004; $16.4 million). Format: News/talk. Target aud: General. ♦Allen Power, gen mgr; Mike Moran, stn mgr; Jeff Carter, opns mgr; David Koon, gen sls mgr.

WGST(AM)— Apr 7, 1988: 640 khz; 50 kw-D, 1 kw-N, DA-2. TL: N33 45 43 W84 27 29. 1819 Peachtree Rd., Suite 700 30309. Phone: (404) 367-0640. Fax: (404) 367-1100. Web Site: www.wgst.com. Licensee: Citicasters Licenses L.P. Group owner: Clear Channel Communications Inc. Network: ABC Information & Entertainment. Format: News/talk. Target aud: 25-54. ♦Pat McDonnell, VP & gen mgr; Tim Dukes, opns mgr; Jared Blass, gen sls mgr; Jim Oktavec, mktg dir; Pam Rahal, prom dir & prom mgr; Tom Parker, progmg dir; Paul Mann, news dir; Mike Lawing, chief of engrg.

WLTM(FM)—Co-owned with WGST(AM). Feb 18, 1962: 94.9 mhz; 100 kw. Ant 984 ft. TL: N33 48 27 W84 20 26. Stereo. Phone: (404) 367-0949. Fax: (404) 367-9490. Web Site: www.949litefm.com. Network: ABC. Format: Soft adult contemp. Target aud: 25-64. ♦Cheryl Ervin, gen sls mgr; Scott Baker, mktg mgr; Louis Kaplan, progmg dir; Steve Goss, mus dir.

WGUN(AM)—Licensed to Atlanta. See Tucker

***WJSP-FM**—(Warm Springs). Feb 3, 1985: 88.1 mhz; 100 kw. 975 ft. TL: N32 51 08 W84 42 04. Stereo. 260 14th St. N.W. 30318-5360. Phone: (404) 685-2690. Fax: (404) 685-2684. E-mail: ask@gpb.org. Web Site: www.gpb.org. Licensee: Georgia Public Telecommunications Commission. Network: Network: NPR, PRI. Format: News, class, talk. News staff: 4; News: 40 hrs wkly. Target aud: 35-54; NPR-demo. ♦Nancy Hall, CEO; Bonnie Bean, CFO; St. John Flynn, progmg dir; Susanna Capelouto, news dir & chief of engrg.

WKLS(FM)— Dec 2, 1960:: 96.1 mhz; 99 kw. 984 ft. TL: N33 48 27 W84 20 26. Stereo. 1819 Peachtree St., Suite 700 30309. Phone: (404) 325-0960. Fax: (404) 367-1155. Web Site: www.96rock.com. Licensee: Citicasters Licenses L.P. Group owner: Clear Channel Communications Inc. (acq 5-4-99; grpsl). Format: AOR. News: 7 hrs wkly. Target aud: 25-49; primarily male. ♦Jerry Del Core, gen mgr & gen sls mgr; Mike Wheeler, opns mgr & prom dir; Jeff McMurray, progmg dir; Susan De Bonis, mktg dir & pub affrs dir.

WNIV(AM)— 1948: 970 khz; 5 kw-D, 39 w-N. TL: N33 48 35 W84 21 14. 2970 Peachtree Rd. N.W., Suite 700 30305. Phone: (404) 365-0970. Fax: (404) 816-0748. E-mail: wniv@wniv.com. Web Site: www.wniv.com. Licensee: Salem Media of Georgia Inc. Group owner: Salem Communications Corp. (acq 11-17-99; $8 million with WLTA(AM) Alpharetta). Cohn & Marks. Format: Christian, talk. News staff: one; News: 7 hrs wkly. Target aud: 25-49; educated adults, upper middle to upper income. ♦Stuart W. Epperson, chmn; Edward G. Atsinger III, pres; Allen Power, gen mgr; Mike Moran, stn mgr; Jim Sutton, opns VP, opns mgr, progmg dir & progmg mgr; David Koon, sls VP & gen sls mgr; Kathy Van Meter, prom dir; C. J. Jackson, chief of engrg.

WNNX(FM)— November 1963: 99.7 mhz; 100 kw. 1,032 ft. TL: N33 46 57 W84 23 20. Stereo. 780 Johnson Ferry Rd., Suite 500 30342. Phone: (404) 497-4700. Fax: (404) 497-4735. Web Site: www.99x.com. Licensee: WNNX Lico Inc. Group owner: Susquehanna Radio Corp. (acq 2-28-74). Rep: McGavren Guild. Format: Alternative. Target aud: 18-49; trend-setting young adults. ♦Mark Renier, gen mgr; Lisa Kelly, opns dir & natl sls mgr; Leslie Fram, gen sls mgr & progmg dir.

WQXI(AM)— October 1947: 790 khz; 28 kw-D, 1 kw-N, DA-N. TL: N33 48 42 W84 21 13. Stereo. 3350 Peachtree Rd. N.E., Suite 1610 30326. Phone: (404) 237-0079. Fax: (404) 231-5923. E-mail: asaltzman@790thezone.com. Web Site: www.790thezone.com. Licensee: Jefferson Pilot Communications Co. (group owner: Big League Broadcasting (acq 3-1-74). Network: UPI. Format: Talk, sports. Target aud: 18-54; men. ♦Andrew Saltzman, pres & gen mgr; Stephen "Steak" Shapiro, opns mgr.

***WRAS(FM)**— Jan 18, 1971: 88.5 mhz; 100 kw. 436 ft. TL: N33 41 04 W84 17 23. Stereo. Georgia State University, Rm. 226, 95 Piedmont Ave. 30303. Phone: (404) 651-2240. Phone: (404) 463-9021. Fax: (404) 651-1705. Web Site: www.wras.org. Licensee: Georgia State University. Network: ABC Daytime Direction. Format: College rock. News: 6 hrs wkly. Target aud: 18-34; college students. Spec prog: Classical 3 hrs, world 3 hrs, reggae 4 hrs, new age 3 hrs, rap/hip-hop 6 hrs wkly. ♦Dr. Kurt Keppler, CEO; Brady Rainey, gen mgr; Michael Valania, prom dir; Andy Hawley, progmg dir; Todd Wiese, mus dir; Tom Taylor, chief of engrg.

***WREK(FM)**— Apr 1, 1968: 91.1 mhz; 40 kw. 340 ft. TL: N33 46 41 W84 24 22. Stereo. Georgia Tech., 350 Ferst Dr., Suite 2224 30332. Phone: (404) 894-2468. Fax: (404) 894-6872. E-mail: wrek@gatech.edu. Web Site: www.wrek.org. Licensee: Radio Communications Board, Georgia Institute of Technology. Format: Progsv, div, Ethnic music. Target aud: General. Spec prog: Experimental 18 hrs, jazz 15 hrs, class 15 hrs wkly. ♦Aakash Jariwala, gen mgr; Jeremy Varner, opns mgr; Steve Fenton, progmg dir.

***WRFG(FM)**— July 15, 1973: 89.3 mhz; 100 kw. 279 ft. TL: N33 44 56 W84 24 26. Stereo. 1083 Austin Ave. N.E. 30307. Phone: (404) 523-3471. Fax: (404) 523-8990. E-mail: info@wrfg.org. Web Site: www.wrfg.org. Licensee: Radio Free Georgia Broadcasting Foundation Inc. Haley, Bader & Potts. Format: Eclectic. News: 3 hrs wkly. Target aud: 18-45; socially conscious African-Americans. Spec prog: , Indian 3 hrs, Sp 5 hrs wkly. ♦Joan Baptist, stn mgr; Wanique Shabazz, opns dir.

WSB(AM)— Mar 15, 1922: 750 khz; 50 kw-U. TL: N33 50 43 W84 15 12. 1601 W. Peachtree St. N.E. 30309. Phone: (404) 897-7500. Fax: (404) 897-7363. Licensee: CXR Holdings L.L.C. Group owner: Cox Broadcasting Rep: Christal. Dow, Lohnes & Albertson. Format: News/talk. News staff: 9; News: 168 hrs wkly. Target aud: 25-54. Spec prog: Relg 3 hrs, minorities one hr wkly. ♦Marc W. Morgan, sr VP; David Meszaros, VP, gen mgr & gen sls mgr; Neal Maziar, sls dir; Neil Williamson, mktg dir; Michael Dobson, prom dir; Pete Spriggs, progmg dir & progmg mgr; Chris Camp, news dir; Mike Kavanagh, pub affrs dir; Charles Kinney, chief of engrg.

WSBG(FM)—Co-owned with WVPO(AM). Oct 1, 1964: 93.5 mhz; 550 w. 764 ft. TL: N40 56 56 W57 09 29. Stereo. Format: Hot adult contemp, rock & hip. Target aud: 18-49. Spec prog: Modern rock 3 hrs wkly.

WSB-FM— Nov 10, 1944: 98.5 mhz; 100 kw. 1,027 ft. TL: N33 45 33 W84 20 05. Stereo. Web Site: www.b985.com. Format: Adult contemp. News staff: one; News: 3.5 hrs wkly. Target aud: 25-54. ♦Will Gara, prom dir; Tom Paleveda, progmg dir; Kelly McCoy, progmg mgr; Nancy Richards, news dir. Co-owned TV: WSB-TV affil

WSTR(FM)—See Smyrna

WTJH(AM)—See East Point

WYZE(AM)— June 1957: 1480 khz; 5 kw-D, 44 w-N. TL: N33 43 25 W84 22 08. 1111 Boulevard S.E. 30312. Phone: (404) 622-7802. Fax: (404) 622-6767. E-mail: am1480wyze@aol.com. Web Site: www.wyze1480.com. Licensee: GHB Broadcasting Inc. Group owner: GHB Radio Group Format: Black gospel. ♦George H. Buck Jr., pres; Jacob E. Bogan, stn mgr.

WZGC(FM)— Sept 1, 1965: 92.9 mhz; 100 kw. 910 ft. TL: N33 45 34 W84 23 19. Stereo. 1100 Johnson Ferry Rd. N.E., Suite 593 30342. Phone: (404) 851-9393. Fax: (404) 843-3541. E-mail: acc@z93.com. Web Site: www.z93.com. Licensee: Infinity Broadcasting Corp. of Atlanta. Group owner: CBS Radio (acq 11-13-98; grpsl). Network: Westwood One. Format: Classic rock. News staff: one; News: 2 hrs wkly. Target aud: 25-54; upscale baby boomers; male skew. ♦Rick Caffey, sr VP; Michael Hughes, gen mgr; Val Carolin, sls dir; Barbara Natoli, natl sls mgr; Monte Carlo, news dir & pub affrs dir; Jeremy Siscoe, engrg mgr; Robert Lafore, chief of engrg.

Augusta

***WACG-FM**— June 2, 1970: 90.7 mhz; 25 kw. 400 ft. TL: N33 24 15 W81 50 19. Stereo. 260 14th St. N.W., Atlanta 30318-5360. Secondary address: 2500 Walton Way 30904. Phone: (404) 685-2690. Fax: (404) 685-2684. E-mail: gpr@gpb.org. Web Site: www.gpb.org. Licensee: Georgia Public Telecommunications Commission. (acq 4-87). Network: Network: PRI, NPR. Format: Classical, News. News staff: 6; News: 40 hrs wkly. Target aud: 35 plus; upscale, professional, educated, affluent. Spec prog: Jazz 18 hrs wkly. ♦James Lyle, CEO; Bonnie Bean, CFO; John Hughes, exec VP; Alan Cooke, gen mgr; Chuck Miller, gen mgr; Shelease Whitaker, chief of opns; Anne Bramlette, sls dir; Marcia Killingsworth, prom dir; St. John Flynn, progmg mgr; Terrance McKnight, mus dir; Mark Fehlig, engrg dir.

WBBQ-FM— March 1955: 104.3 mhz; 100 kw. 1,003 ft. TL: N33 36 41 W81 56 30. Stereo. 2743 Perimeter Pkwy., Bldg. 100, Suite 200 30909. Phone: (706) 396-6000. Fax: (706) 396-6010. Web Site: www.wbbq.com. Licensee: Clear Channel Broadcasting Licenses Inc. Group owner: Clear Channel Communications Inc. (acq 12-19-2000; grpsl). Format: Adult contemp, loc news. News staff: 8; News: 7 hrs wkly. Target aud: General. ♦Barry Kaye, gen mgr; Mike Kramer, opns mgr; Bobby Boggs, gen sls mgr; Steve Cherry, progmg dir; Earl Welch, chief of engrg.

WSGF(AM)—Co-owned with WBBQ-FM. Jan 12, 1947: 1340 khz; 1 kw-U. TL: N33 27 46 W82 00 29. Holland & Knight. Format: All sports. Target aud: Children.

WEKL(FM)—Listing follows WPCH(AM).

WFAM(AM)— Mar 10, 1952: 1050 khz; 5 kw. TL: N33 27 21 W81 56 20. 552 Laney-Walker Blvd. Ext. 30901. Phone: (706) 722-6077. Fax: (706) 722-7066. E-mail: wfam@wilkinsradio.com. Web Site: www.wilkinsradio.com. Licensee: J.J. & B. Broadcasting Inc. Group owner: Wilkins Communications Network Inc. (acq 11-22-96; $330,000). Format: Relg. News: 2 hrs wkly. Target aud: 25 plus; general. ♦Robert L. Wilkins, pres; Thomas Hardie, gen mgr, stn mgr & opns mgr.

WFXA-FM— July 11, 1968: 103.1 mhz; 3 kw. 299 ft. TL: N33 30 00 W81 56 03. Stereo. Box 1584 30903. Secondary address: 104 Bennett Ln., North Augusta, SC 29841. Phone: (803) 279-2330. Fax: (803) 279-8149. Licensee: Radio One of Augusta LLC. Group owner: Radio One Inc. (acq 5-30-00; grpsl). Network: ABC FM Connection. Format: Black, urban contemp. Target aud: 25-34; females. ♦Dennis Jackson, gen mgr; Ron Thomas, opns mgr & progmg dir; Dianne Mutimer, gen sls mgr; Lakeshia Collins, news dir; Walter Brumbeloe, chief of engrg.

WTHB(AM)—Co-owned with WFXA-FM. May 1960: 1550 khz; 5 kw-D. TL: N33 30 00 W81 56 03. Network: American Urban. Rep: Allied Radio Partners. Format: Gospel. ♦Mary Kingcannon, progmg dir.

WGAC(AM)— 1940: 580 khz; 5 kw-D, 1 kw-N, DA-N. TL: N33 30 41 W82 04 44. Box 211045 30917. Secondary address: 432 S. Belair Rd., Martinez 30907. Phone: (706) 394-7000. Fax: (706) 394-7100. E-mail: wgac@wgac.com. Web Site: www.wgac.com. Licensee: Beasley Broadcasting of Augusta Inc. Group owner: Beasley Broadcast Group (acq 5-19-92; assumption of debt; 6-8-92). Network: CBS. Rep: D & R Radio. Format: News/talk, sports. News staff: 5. Target aud: 35-65. Spec prog: Farm 4 hrs, military 3 hrs wkly. ♦George Beasley, chmn; Kent Dunn, VP, gen mgr & gen sls mgr; Harley Drew, opns dir & progmg dir; Mary Liz Nolan, news dir; Charlie McCoy, chief of engrg.

***WGPH(FM)**—(Vidalia). 1988: 91.5 mhz; 40 kw. 508 ft. TL: N32 14 02 W82 28 52. Stereo. 2278 Wortham Ln, Grovetown 30813. Phone: (706) 309-9609. Fax: (706) 309-9669. E-mail: ctbarinowski@comcast.net. Web Site: www.gnnradio.org. Licensee: Augusta Radio Fellowship. Format: Christian. News: 12 hrs wkly. Target aud: General. ♦C.T. Barinowski, pres; Mark Barinowski, VP; Pratt Johnson, chief of engrg.

WGUS(AM)— July 1930: 1480 khz; 5 kw-U, DA-N. TL: N33 31 00 W82 00 36. Stereo. Box 211045 30917. Secondary address: 4051 Jimmie Dyess Pkwy. 30909. Phone: (706) 396-7000. Fax: (706) 396-7100. Licensee: WCHZ License LLC. Group owner: Beasley Broadcast Group Inc. (acq 5-3-2000; $800,000. with WGAC-FM Warrenton). Format: Southern Gospel. Target aud: 18-49; well educated. ♦Connie Sansom, gen mgr; Harley Drew, chief of opns.

WIBL(FM)— Mar 10, 1952: 105.7 mhz; 100 kw. Ant 1,168 ft. TL: N33 25 15 W81 50 19. Stereo. 2743 Perimeter Pkwy., Suite 300 30909. Phone: (706) 396-6000. Fax: (803) 510-3121. Web Site: www.bullcountry.com. Licensee: Clear Channel Broadcasting Licenses Inc. Group owner: Clear Channel Communications Inc. (acq 12-19-2000; grpsl). Network: AP Radio. Holland & Knight. Format: Country. News staff: one; News: 3 hrs wkly. Target aud: 18-34. ♦Barry Kaye, gen mgr; Mike Kramer, opns VP; Bobby Boggs, sls VP & sls dir.

WKDG(FM)—See Martinez

WKSP(FM)—See Aiken, SC

WKXC-FM—See Aiken, SC

WKZK(AM)—See North Augusta, SC

***WLPE(FM)**— Nov 17, 1984: 91.7 mhz; 1.15 kw. Ant 589 ft. TL: N33 34 21 W81 55 23. Stereo. 2278 Wortham Ln., Grovetown 30813. Phone: (706) 309-9609. Fax: (706) 309-9669. E-mail: ctbarinowski@comcast.net. Web Site: www.gnnradio.org. Licensee: Augusta Radio Fellowship Institute Inc. Format: Christian. News: 12 hrs wkly. Target aud: General. ♦C.T. Barinowski, pres; Mark Barinowski, VP; Jim Cook, chief of engrg.

WNRR(AM)— November 1993: 1230 khz; 1 kw-U. TL: N33 27 14 W82 01 47. 1802 Killingsworth Rd. 30904. Secondary address: Box 6811 30916-6811. Phone: (706) 738-1992. Fax: (706) 738-1973. Licensee: Eastern Broadcasting Group Inc. (group owner; acq 11-3-2003; $425,000). Network: ESPN Radio. Format: Talk, sports. ♦Tom McCoy, gen mgr.

WPCH(AM)—(North Augusta).SC July 30, 1958: 1380 khz; 4 kw-D, 70 w-N. TL: N33 29 17 W81 56 46. 2743 Perimeter Pkwy., Bldg. 100, Suite 200 30909. Phone: (706) 396-6000. Fax: (706) 396-6010. Licensee: Capstar TX L.P. Group owner: Clear Channel Communications Inc. (acq 12-19-2000; grpsl). Wiley, Rein & Fielding. Format: Classic country. News staff: one; News: 7 hrs wkly. ♦Barry Kaye, gen mgr.

WEKL(FM)—Co-owned with WPCH(AM). Nov 11, 1967: 102.3 mhz; 1.5 kw. Ant 666 ft. TL: N33 26 15 W82 05 27. Stereo. Web Site: eagle102.com. Format: Classic rock. Target aud: 18-44.

WRDW(AM)— 2001: 1630 khz; 10 kw-D, 1 kw-N. TL: N33 31 00 W82 00 36. Box 211045 30917. Secondary address: 4051 Belair Rd. 30909. Phone: (706) 396-7000. Fax: (706) 396-7100. Web Site: wrdw.com. Licensee: WCHZ License LLC. Group owner: Beasley Broadcast Group Inc. (acq 2-23-2000). Format: Sports, news/talk. ♦Kent Dunn, gen mgr; Harley Drew, opns mgr.

WYFA(FM)—(Waynesboro). Aug 1, 1991: 107.1 mhz; 6 kw. 328 ft. TL: N33 10 42 W81 59 24. Stereo. 1388 Old Waynesboro Rd., Waynesboro 30830. Phone: (706) 554-3942. Fax: (704) 522-1967. E-mail: wyfa@bbnradio.org. Web Site: www.bbnradio.org. Licensee: Bible Broadcasting Network Inc. (group owner; acq 8-26-92; $225,000; 9-21-92). Format: Relg. ♦George Quick, gen mgr; Richard Johnson, progmg dir.

Austell

WAOS(AM)— Apr 16, 1968: 1600 khz; 20 kw-D, 67 w-N. TL: N33 48 34 W84 39 25. Box 746, 5815 Westside Rd. 30106. Secondary address: 5815 Westside Rd. 30106. Phone: (770) 944-0900. Fax: (770) 944-9794. E-mail: gracie@radiolafavorita.com. Web Site: www.radiolafavorita.com. Licensee: La Favorita Inc. (group owner; acq 1-24-90). Rep: Caballero. Format: Sp. Target aud: 18 plus; Hispanics in metro Atlanta & northeast GA. ♦Samuel Zamarron, CEO, pres & gen mgr; Gracie Zamarron, stn mgr.

WXEM(AM)—(Buford). Dec 12, 1957: 1460 khz; 5 kw-D. TL: N34 07 15 W83 58 35. Box 746 30106. Secondary address: 5815 Westside Rd. 30106. Phone: (770) 944-0900. Fax: (770) 944-9794. E-mail: sammy@radiofavoita.com. Web Site: www.radiolafavorita.com. Licensee: La Favorita Inc. (group owner; acq 6-12-91; 7-1-91). Format: Sp. Target aud: Hispanic. ♦Samuel Zamarron, CEO, pres & gen mgr; Gracie Zamarron, stn mgr; Juan Prieto, opns mgr.

Avondale Estates

WWAA(AM)— November 2003: 1690 khz; 10 kw-D, 1 kw-N. TL: N33 47 13 W84 14 55. Box 13087, Atlanta 30324. Secondary address: 2695 Buford Hwy. N.E. 30324. Phone: (404) 846-0305. Fax: (404) 842-9535. E-mail: 1690airatlanta@usa.com. Licensee: Intermart Broadcasting of Georgia Inc. (acq 11-4-99; $265,000. with WBIT(AM) Adel). Format: Talk. ♦Gil Moor, gen mgr; John Ervin, opns mgr.

Stations in the U.S. — Georgia

Developers & Brokers of Radio Properties — contact American Media Services at our suite: Philadelphia Marriott Downtown, 215-625-2900. 843-972-2200. americanmediaservices.com. Charleston, SC. Dallas, TX · Chicago, IL · Austin, TX. American Media Services, LLC.

Bainbridge

WBGE(FM)— May 2001: 101.9 mhz; 5.3 kw. Ant 351 ft. TL: N30 54 36 W84 33 45. 521 S. Scott St. 39819. Phone: (229) 246-7776. Fax: (229) 246-9995. E-mail: kevin@live1019.com. Web Site: www.live1019.com. Licensee: Flint Media Inc. (acq 7-15-2005; $485,000). Format: Hot adult contemp. ♦ Kevin Dowdy, gen mgr.

WMGR(AM)— Aug 17, 1947: 930 khz; 5 kw-D, 500 w-N. TL: N30 54 25 W84 33 02. 203 W. Shotwell St. 39819. Phone: (229) 246-1650. Fax: (229) 246-1403. E-mail: wmgr@wmgr.net. Licensee: Decatur Broadcasting Inc. (acq 6-10-2005; for 50% of stock). Network: ABC Information & Entertainment. Format: Oldies. News: 10 hrs wkly. Target aud: 30 plus. ♦ Dewey Robinson, pres; Coley Voyles, exec VP & gen mgr.

WRAK-FM— Dec 20, 1967: 97.3 mhz; 100 kw. 1,200 ft. TL: N31 09 12 W84 32 42. 809 S. Westover Blvd., Albany 31707. Phone: (229) 439-9704. Fax: (229) 439-1509. Web Site: www.magic973radio.com. Licensee: Clear Channel Broadcasting Licenses Inc. Group owner: Clear Channel Communications Inc. (acq 7-11-00; grpsl). Rep: Christal. Format: Adult contemp. News: 2 hrs wkly. Target aud: 18-49. ♦ John Richards, gen mgr; Jasmine Phoenix, progmg dir.

Barnesville

WBAF(AM)— July 23, 1966: 1090 khz; 1 kw-D. TL: N33 03 13 W84 08 07. 645 Forsyth St. 30204. Phone: (770) 358-1090. Fax: (770) 358-1090. Licensee: Barnesville Broadcasting Inc. Reddy, Begley & McCormick. Format: C&W, relg. Spec prog: Loc 5 hrs wkly. ♦ Charles Waters, pres & gen mgr.

Baxley

WBYZ(FM)—Listing follows WUFE(AM).

WUFE(AM)— December 1954: 1260 khz; 5 kw-D. TL: N31 48 00 W82 24 40. Box 390 31515. Secondary address: Hwy. 341 W. 31515. Phone: (912) 367-3000. Fax: (912) 367-9779. Licensee: South Georgia Broadcasters Inc. (acq 1-19-82; $240,000;. FTR: 2-8-82). Network: ABC Information & Entertainment. Fletcher, Heald & Hildreth. Format: Relg. News: 6 hrs wkly. Target aud: General. ♦ Al Graham, pres & pub affrs dir; Peggy C. Miles, gen mgr, gen sls mgr, prom mgr & adv mgr; Larry Ring, chief of engrg.

WBYZ(FM)—Co-owned with WUFE(AM). July 1983: 94.5 mhz; 100 kw. 1,014 ft. TL: N31 47 10 W82 27 03. Stereo. Box 390 31515. Secondary address: 4005 Golden Isles W. 31515. E-mail: peggy@wbyz94.com. Web Site: www.wbyz.com. Network: ABC Information & Entertainment. Format: Modern country. Target aud: 20-55; those with buying power. ♦ Peggy C. Miles, mktg mgr; Al Graham, progmg mgr; Cody West, mus dir; Cole Younger, news dir.

Blackshear

WFNS(AM)— Mar 10, 1961: 1350 khz; 2.5 kw-D. TL: N31 18 44 W82 14 00. 1701 Boulevard Ave., Waycross 31501. Phone: (912) 285-5002. Fax: (912) 285-3877. E-mail: thefanradio@aol.com. Web Site: www.fandog.net. Licensee: MarMac Communications LLC (acq 7-19-2001; $60,000). Network: USA. Format: All sports. Target aud: General; families. Spec prog: Black 10 hrs, farm 10 hrs wkly. ♦ Gary Moss Marmitt, pres & gen mgr.

WKUB(FM)— Dec 1, 1979: 105.1 mhz; 50 kw. Ant 308 ft. TL: N31 15 49 W82 17 30. Stereo. Box 112, 2132 Hwy. 84 31516. Secondary address: Box 1472, Waycross 31502. Phone: (912) 449-3391. Fax: (912) 449-6284. E-mail: wkub@almatel.net. Licensee: Mattox Broadcasting Inc. Network: ABC. Rep: Dora-Clayton. Fletcher, Heald & Hildreth. Format: Country. News: 4 hrs wkly. Target aud: 25 plus. ♦ G. Troy Mattox, pres & gen mgr.

Blakely

WBBK(AM)— Oct 22, 1959: 1260 khz; 1 kw-D. TL: N31 21 11 W84 56 50. Box 87, Donalsonville 31745. Secondary address: Hwy. 62 W. 31745. Phone: (229) 723-2677. Fax: (229) 524-5123. Fax: (229) 723-2678. Fax: (229) 524-2265. E-mail: wbbk@alltel.net. Licensee: Styles Media Group LLC (group owner; acq 3-17-2004); grpsl). Format: Country, talk. Target aud: 25-49. ♦ Gil Kelley, gen mgr.

WBBK-FM— November 1984: 93.1 mhz; 45 kw. Ant 328 ft. TL: N31 17 55 W85 03 18. Stereo. Box 879 39823. E-mail: wbbk@surfsouth.com.

Blue Ridge

WPPL(FM)— 1971: 103.9 mhz; 6 kw. 400 ft. TL: N34 52 03 W84 20 02. (CP: 6 kw, ant 400 ft.). Stereo. Box 938, 333 W. Highland St. 30513. Phone: (706) 632-9775. Fax: (706) 632-5922. E-mail: mcwolf@tds.net. Web Site: www.mountaincountryradio.com. Licensee: Fannin County Broadcasting Co. Inc. (acq 12-12-97; $200,000 for stock). Format: Country. Target aud: 25-54; adults. ♦ Tim White, pres; Dalton Davis, gen mgr & opns dir.

Bolingbroke

WWWD(FM)— 2005: 102.1 mhz; 4.5 kw. Ant 377 ft. TL: N32 54 30 W83 46 37. 6080 Mount Moriah Ext., Memphis, TN 38115. Phone: (901) 375-9324. Fax: (901) 375-0041. Web Site: www.flinn.com. Licensee: George S. Flinn Jr. ♦ George S. Flinn Jr., gen mgr.

Boston

WTUF(FM)— July 18, 1988: 106.3 mhz; 6 kw. 328 ft. TL: N30 47 40 W83 46 54. Stereo. Box 129, Thomasville 31799. Secondary address: 117 Remington Ave., Thomasville 31792. Phone: (229) 225-1063. Fax: (229) 226-1361. E-mail: lenrob@rose.net. Web Site: www.wtufradio.com. Licensee: Boston Radio Co. Network: AP Network News. Rep: Rgnl Reps. Format: Classic country. Target aud: 18-65; adults. Spec prog: Bluegrass 5 hrs, gospel 7 hrs wkly. ♦ Len Robinson, pres; Wade Scaffe, opns dir & opns mgr.

Bostwick

WMOQ(FM)— 1994: 92.3 mhz; 3 kw. 328 ft. TL: N33 44 58 W83 33 30. Box 649, Monroe 30655. Secondary address: 1610 Launius Rd., Good Hope Phone: (770) 267-0923. Fax: (770) 342-8135. Web Site: www.wmoqfm.com. Licensee: Bostwick Broadcasting Group Inc. Format: Classic country. ♦ Grace Morris, gen mgr; David Malcolm, opns mgr.

Bowdon

WBZY(FM)— Dec 9, 1996: 105.3 mhz; 61 kw. Ant 1,204 ft. TL: N33 24 41 W84 49 48. 1819 Peachtree Rd., Atlanta 30309. Phone: (404) 367-0640. Licensee: Clear Channel Broadcasting Licenses Inc. Group owner: Clear Channel Communications Inc. (acq 11-24-2000; at least $7 million). Format: Sp contemp music. ♦ Pat McDonnell, gen mgr.

Bremen

WGMI(AM)— October 1957: 1440 khz; 2.5 kw-D. TL: N33 42 56 W85 09 34. 613 Tallapoosa St. 30110. Phone: (770) 537-0840. Phone: (770) 537-9464. Fax: (770) 537-0220. E-mail: wgmi@wgmiradio.com. Web Site: www.wgmiradio.com. Licensee: Garner Ministries Inc. (acq 11-10-93; $150,000; 11-29-93). Reddy, Begley & McCormick. Format: Relg, southern gospel, Christian country. News staff: one; News: 3 hrs wkly. Target aud: 25-54; majority married women with children. ♦ Horace Garner, CEO & stn mgr; Peggy Garner, opns mgr.

Broxton

WULS(FM)— Nov 1, 1993: 103.7 mhz; 6 kw. 328 ft. TL: N31 33 26 W82 52 10. 702 N. Madison Ave., Douglas 31533. Phone: (912) 384-9857. Phone: (912) 384-1037. Fax: (912) 384-0016. Licensee: WULS Inc. Format: Southern gospel. ♦ Wyndel Bunnsed, pres; Leona M. Bunnsed, exec VP; Candace M. Bunnsed, VP; Scott Bender, gen mgr & sls dir; Clyde Scott, chief of engrg.

Brunswick

*WAYR-FM— 1996: 90.7 mhz; 2.3 kw. 312 ft. TL: N31 11 39 W81 29 30. Stereo. 2500 Russell Rd., Green Cove Springs, FL 32043. Phone: (904) 272-1111. Fax: (904) 284-2501. E-mail: LStephens@wayradio.org. Web Site: www.wayradio.org. Licensee: Good Tidings Trust Inc. (acq 3-13-98; $100,000). Format: Christian. Target aud: 45-70. ♦ Bill Tidwell, gen mgr & chief of engrg; Luke Stephens, stn mgr; Bart Wagner, progmg dir.

WBGA(FM)—Listing follows WMOG(AM).

WGIG(AM)— Mar 5, 1949: 1440 khz; 5 kw-D, 1 kw-N, DA-N. TL: N31 10 07 W81 32 14. 3833 U.S. Hwy. 82 31523. Phone: (912) 267-1025. Fax: (912) 264-5462. E-mail: ryfun@adelphia.net. Web Site: www.1440wgig.com. Licensee: Qantum of Brunswick License Co. LLC. Group owner: Qantum Communications Corp. (acq 7-2-03; grpsl). Network: CBS. Format: News/talk. ♦ Jonathan Havens, gen mgr; Scott Rygun, opns dir.

WHFX(FM)—See Darien

WKQL(FM)— Nov 8, 1965: 100.7 mhz; 62 kw. Ant 1,473 ft. TL: N30 49 16 W81 44 14. Stereo. 6440 Atlantic Blvd., Jacksonville, FL 32216. Phone: (904) 727-9696. Fax: (904) 721-9322. Licensee: Renda Broadcasting Corp. Group owner: Renda Broadcasting Corp.-Renda Radio Inc. (acq 1996; $6.5 million with WGNE-FM Palatka, FL). Haley, Bader & Potts. Format: Oldies. Target aud: 25-54; Adult men. ♦ Tony Renda Sr., CEO; Bill Scull, gen mgr.

WMOG(AM)— June 1940: 1490 khz; 1 kw-U. TL: N31 09 55 W81 28 28. (CP: 600 w-U, TL: N31 09 42 W81 28 28). 3833 Hwy. 82 31523. Phone: (912) 267-1025. Fax: (912) 264-5462. Licensee: Qantum of Brunswick License Co. LLC. Group owner: Qantum Communications Corp. (acq 7-2-2003; grpsl). Network: ABC Information & Entertainment. Rep: McGavren Guild. Format: Nostalgia, news/talk, sports. News staff: one; News: 20 hrs wkly. Target aud: 35 plus. Spec prog: Black 8 hrs, class one hr wkly. ♦ Larry Landrum, gen mgr; Scott Ryfun, progmg dir.

WBGA(FM)—Co-owned with WMOG(AM). Jan 1, 1990: 92.7 mhz; 6 kw. 340 ft. TL: N31 09 55 W81 28 28. Stereo. Phone: (912) 265-9300. Network: ABC. Format: Urban. Target aud: 24-45. ♦ Jonthan Havens, gen mgr.

WRJY(FM)— June 30, 1994: 104.1 mhz; 4.2 kw. 390 ft. TL: N31 11 39 W81 29 30. 185 Benedict Rd. 31520. Phone: (912) 261-1000. Fax: (912) 265-8391. Web Site: www.coastalcountry.com. Licensee: Golden Isles Broadcasting LLC (acq 3-23-2001; $2.8 million. with WXMK(FM) Dock Junction). Rep: Rgnl Reps. Format: Country. News: 168 hrs wkly. Target aud: 25-54; urban female. ♦ Everett Armstrong, pres & opns mgr; Traci Long, gen mgr; Jenna McNeal, progmg dir.

WSFN(AM)— Sept 1, 1966: 790 khz; 500 w-D, 115 w-N, DA-2. TL: N31 08 40 W81 34 56. 7515 Blythe Island Hwy. 31523. Phone: (912) 264-6251. Fax: (912) 264-9991. E-mail: thefanradio@aol.com. Web Site: www.fandog.net. Licensee: MarMac Communications L.L.C. (acq 4-98; $350,000). Network: ABC. Format: Sports. ♦ Gary Moss Marmitt, pres & gen mgr.

WSOL-FM—Licensed to Brunswick. See Jacksonville FL

*WWIO-FM— Feb 28, 1993: . Stn currently dark 88.9 mhz; 7 kw. 135 ft. TL: N31 11 19 W81 28 10. (CP: 5.5 kw, ant 154 ft.). Stereo. 260 14th St. N.W., Atlanta 30318-5360. Phone: (404) 685-2690. Fax: (404) 685-2684. E-mail: gpr@gpb.org. Web Site: www.gpb.org. Licensee: Georgia Public Telecommunications Commission. Network: Network: NPR, PRI. Format: Classical, News. News staff: one; News: 51 hrs wkly. Target aud: 45 plus. ♦ James Lyle, CEO; Bonnie Bean, CFO; John Hughes, exec VP; Chuck Miller, gen mgr; Teresa Sanders, opns mgr; Shelease Whitaker, chief of opns & chief of engrg; Anne

Broadcasting & Cable Yearbook 2006

D-143

Georgia

Bramlette, sls dir; Marcia Killingsworth, prom dir; St. John Flynn, progmg mgr; Terrance McKnight, mus dir; Mark Fehlig, engrg dir.

WWSN(FM)—(Waycross). June 3, 1972: 103.3 mhz; 100 kw. 1,100 ft. TL: N31 15 42 W82 19 26. (CP: TL: N31 09 22 W81 58 19). Stereo. 3833 US Hwy. 82 31525. Phone: (912) 267-1025. Fax: (912) 264-5462. E-mail: ryfun@adelphia.net. Web Site: www.sunny103.com. Licensee: Qantum of Brunswick License Co. LLC. Group owner: Qantum Communications Corp. (acq 7-2-03; grpsl). Rep: McGavren Guild. Format: Adult contemp. Target aud: 25-54. Spec prog: Jazz 5 hrs wkly. ♦ Jonathan Havens, gen mgr; Scott Ryfun, opns mgr.

WYNR(FM)—(Waycross). Oct 10, 1971: 102.5 mhz; 100 kw. 980 ft. TL: N31 09 13 W81 58 00. Stereo. 3833 Hwy. 82 31525. Phone: (912) 267-1025. Fax: (912) 264-5462. E-mail: joeportagee@hotmail.com. Web Site: www.1025wynr.com. Licensee: Qantum of Brunswick License Co. LLC. Group owner: Qantum Communications Corp. (acq 7-2-03; grpsl). Rep: McGavren Guild. Smithwick & Belendiuk. Format: Country. Target aud: 25-54. ♦ Frank Osborne, pres & exec VP; Mike Mangen, CFO; Jonathan Brewster, exec VP; Jonathan Havens, gen mgr; Joe Sousa, stn mgr & opns mgr.

Buckhead

WPMA(FM)— December 2002: 102.7 mhz; 7.5 kw. Ant 594 ft. TL: N33 30 09 W83 15 37. Stereo. 2278 Wortham Ln, Grovetown 30813. Phone: (706) 309-9609. Fax: (706) 309-9669. E-mail: ctbarinowski@comcast.net. Web Site: www.gnnradio.org. Licensee: Barinowski Investment Co., a Georgia L.P. Group owner: Good News Network. Format: Christian. ♦ C.T. Barinowski, gen mgr.

Buena Vista

WEAM-FM— June 21, 2001: 100.7 mhz; 2.6 kw. Ant 502 ft. TL: N32 20 33 W84 39 18. Box 1998, Columbus 31902-1998. Phone: (706) 576-3565. Fax: (706) 576-3683. Licensee: Davis Broadcasting Inc. of Columbus. Group owner: Davis Broadcasting Inc. (acq 7-30-2003). Format: Gospel. ♦ Gregory Davis, CEO; Janet Armstead, gen mgr; Carl Conner, opns VP; Cheryl Davis, opns mgr; Angela Verdago, gen sls mgr.

Buford

WLKQ-FM— Jan 1, 1970: 102.3 mhz; 4.2 kw. Ant 390 ft. TL: N34 07 16 W83 58 35. Stereo. 3235 Satellite Blvd., Duluth 30096. Phone: (770) 623-8772. Fax: (770) 623-4722. Web Site: www.laraza1023.com. Licensee: Davis Broadcasting of Atlanta L.L.C. Group owner: Davis Broadcasting Inc. (acq 9-30-2003; $5.25 million). Kenkel & Associates. Format: Sp. News staff: 2; News: 6 hrs wkly. Target aud: 35-54; upper-middle class professionals. ♦ Gregory A. Davis, pres.

WXEM(AM)—Licensed to Buford. See Austell

Byron

***WPWB(FM)**— 1988: 90.5 mhz; 16.5 kw. 453 ft. TL: N32 40 56 W83 22 11. Stereo. 2278 Wortham Ln., Grovetown 30813-5103. Phone: (706) 309-9609. Fax: (706) 309-9669. E-mail: ctbarinowski@comcast.net. Web Site: www.gnnradio.org. Licensee: Augusta Radio Fellowship Institute Inc. Format: Christian. News: 12 hrs wkly. Target aud: General. ♦ C.T. Barinowski, pres; Mark Barinowski, VP; Glenn Finney, chief of engrg.

Cairo

WGRA(AM)— October 1949: 790 khz; 1 kw-D. TL: N30 54 08 W84 14 03. Box 120 39828. Secondary address: 1809 U.S. 84 W. 39828. Phone: (229) 377-4392. Fax: (229) 377-4564. E-mail: summerhillstudio@msn.com. Licensee: Lovett Broadcasting Enterprises Inc. (acq 1-84; $450,000;. FTR: 4-23-84). Rep: Rgnl Reps. Format: News/talk. Target aud: 30 plus; mainly women. Spec prog: Black 6 hrs wkly. ♦ Jeffrey Lovett, pres & gen mgr.

WWLD(FM)— June 1983: 102.3 mhz; 27 kw. Ant 604 ft. TL: N30 29 32 W84 17 02. Stereo. 3411 W. Tharpe St., Tallahassee, FL 32303-1139. Phone: (850) 201-3000. Fax: (850) 561-8903. Web Site: blazin1023.com. Licensee: Cumulus Licensing LLC. Group owner: Cumulus Media Inc. (acq 10-10-01; $1.5 million. including noncompete agreement). Arent, Fox, Kintner, Plotkin & Kahn. Format: Black, hip hop/rhythm and blues. Target aud: 18-34. ♦ John Columbus, gen mgr; Ed Sylvain, progmg dir.

Calhoun

WEBS(AM)— Nov 1, 1966: 1030 khz; 5 kw-D, 3 w-N. TL: N34 29 25 W84 55 04. Box 1299 30703. Secondary address: 427 S. Wall St. 30703. Phone: (706) 629-2238. Fax: (706) 629-7092. Licensee: Radio WEBS Inc. (acq 7-1-80). Network: Jones Radio Networks. Format: Oldies. Target aud: 18-52. Spec prog: Black 2 hrs wkly. ♦ Ken D. Payne, pres & gen mgr.

WJTH(AM)— June 16, 1977: 900 khz; 1 kw-D, 266 w-N. TL: N34 27 40 W84 53 44. Box 1119 30703. Secondary address: 329 Richardson Rd. S.E. 30701. Phone: (706) 629-6397. Fax: (706) 629-8463. E-mail: am900@wjth.com. Web Site: www.wjth.com. Licensee: Cherokee Broadcasting Co. Network: ABC. Rep: Rgnl Reps. Format: C&W, loc news & info. News staff: one; News: 20 hrs wkly. Target aud: 18-64; general. Spec prog: Farm one hr, gospel 2 hrs, relg 16 hrs wkly. ♦ Sam Thomas, gen mgr; Keith Thomas, stn mgr; Gloria Cooley, gen sls mgr.

Camilla

WQVE(FM)— April 1977: 105.5 mhz; 6 kw. Ant 300 ft. TL: N31 18 51 W84 12 18. Stereo. 1104 W. Broad Ave., Albany 31707. Phone: (229) 888-5000. Fax: (912) 888-5960. Web Site: www.v105albany.com. Licensee: Cumulus Licensing Corp. Group owner: Cumulus Media Inc. (acq 8-27-99; $675,000). Rep: Rgnl Reps. Format: Urban contemp. News staff: one; News: 3 hrs wkly. Target aud: 25-54; female. Spec prog: Blues 5 hrs, gospel 16 hrs wkly. ♦ Paul Bucuriel, gen mgr.

Canton

WCHK(AM)— Apr 11, 1957: 1290 khz; 5 kw-D, 500 w-N, DA-N. TL: N34 15 08 W84 27 49. Box 1290 30169. Secondary address: 2189 Marietta Hwy. Phone: (770) 479-2101. Fax: (770) 479-1134. E-mail: wchk@mindspring.com. Web Site: www.wchk.am. Licensee: Cherokee Broadcasting Co. Inc. Format: Classic country, bluegrass. Target aud: 35 plus; residents of Cherokee & Pickens counties. ♦ Rebecca Johnston, gen mgr.

WWVA-FM— Aug 1, 1964: 105.7 mhz; 20 kw. Ant 781 ft. TL: N34 03 58 W84 27 15. Stereo. 1819 Peachtree Rd., N.E., Suite 700, Atlanta 30309. Phone: (404) 367-1336. Fax: (404) 367-1100. Licensee: Clear Channel Broadcasting Licenses Inc. Group owner: Clear Channel Communications Inc. (acq 3-29-2004; $31 million). Format: Sp contemp. ♦ Pat McDonnell, gen mgr.

Carrollton

WBTR-FM— 1964: 92.1 mhz; 580 w. 636 ft. TL: N33 33 54 W85 01 02. Stereo. 102 Parkwood Cir. 30117-8353. Phone: (770) 832-9685. Fax: (770) 830-1027. Licensee: WYAI Inc. (acq 6-7-01). Format: Country. News staff: one; News: 3 hrs wkly. Target aud: 25-49. Spec prog: Black 5 hrs wkly. ♦ Steven L. Gradick, pres & opns VP; Jim Row, gen sls mgr.

WLBB(AM)— Nov 19, 1975: 1330 khz; 500 w-D. TL: N33 34 17 W85 03 02. 808 Newnan Rd. 30117. Phone: (678) 601-1330. Fax: (678) 601-8256. Web Site: www.newstalk1330.com. Licensee: WYAI Inc. (acq 6-7-01). Network: CBS. Format: News/talk. News staff: 2. Spec prog: Gospel 7 hrs wkly. ♦ Steve Gradick, pres & gen mgr.

***WUWG(FM)**— Feb 19, 1973: 90.7 mhz; 500 w. 494 ft. TL: N33 33 50 W85 01 04. Stereo. 260 14th St. N.W., Atlanta 30318-5360. Phone: (404) 685-2690. Fax: (404) 685-2684. E-mail: gpr@gpb.org. Web Site: www.gpb.org. Licensee: Georgia Public Telecommunications Commission (acq 8-9-2004). Network: Network: NPR, PRI. Format: Classical, News. News staff: 6; News: 25-30 hrs wkly. Target aud: General; students & area residents. Spec prog: Folk 2 hrs, bluegrass 2 hrs, new age 3 hrs. ♦ James Lyle, CEO; Bonnie Bean, CFO; John Hughes, exec VP; Chuck Miller, gen mgr; Kevin Sanders, stn mgr; Shelease Whitaker, opns mgr; Marcia Killingsworth, prom dir; St. John Flynn, progmg mgr; Terrance McKnight, mus dir; Mark Fehlig, engrg mgr.

Cartersville

WBHF(AM)— July 17, 1946: 1450 khz; 1 kw-U. TL: N34 11 09 W84 48 13. 7 N. Wall St. 30120. Phone: (770) 386-1450. Fax: (770) 382-5390. E-mail: news@wbhfradio.org. Licensee: Anverse Inc. (acq 7-5-00). Network: Network; ABC, AP Radio. Format: Oldies, loc news/sports. News staff: 3; News: 10 hrs per wk. ♦ Matt Santini, gen mgr; Ernestine Young Jones, opns mgr.

Directory of Radio

***WCCV(FM)**— Jan 24, 1983: 91.7 mhz; 910 w. 537 ft. TL: N34 11 35 W84 45 31. Stereo. Box 1000 30120-1000. Phone: (770) 387-0917. Fax: (770) 387-2856. E-mail: onair@ibn.org. Web Site: www.ibn.org. Licensee: Immanuel Broadcasting. Format: Relg. ♦ Ed Tuten, pres; Jane Tuten, VP; Chris Isbell, progmg dir & progmg mgr; Jimmy Hardee, mus dir.

WYXC(AM)— Sept 21, 1961: 1270 khz; 2 kw-D, 187 w-N. TL: N34 34 W84 47 49. Box 200399 30121. Phone: (770) 382-1306. Fax: (770) 936-1967. E-mail: chuck@newstalk1270.com. Web Site: www.wyxcradio.com. Licensee: Clarion Communications Inc. (acq 6-14-2005; $500,000). Format: News, talk, sports. Target aud: 25-55. ♦ Charles Shiflett, pres; Jim Adams, gen mgr & stn mgr; Connie Dixon, gen sls mgr & prom dir; Charles Brachel, progmg dir & news dir; Allen Schmelz, chief of engrg; Manny Garrett, chief of engrg.

Cedartown

WGAA(AM)— 1941: 1340 khz; 1 kw-U. TL: N34 02 06 W85 15 04. Box 167 30125. Secondary address: 413 Lakeview Dr. 30125. Phone: (770) 748-1340. Fax: (770) 748-4539. E-mail: jmerricko@wgaaradio.com. Web Site: www.wgaaradio.com. Licensee: Burgess Broadcasting Corp. (acq 12-13-93; $100,000. purchased from bankruptcy ct.; FTR: 8-25-86) Rgnl Reps. Format: Cassic hits. Target aud: General. Spec prog: College football, loc sports. ♦ Frank H. Burgess Jr., pres; Bob Shannon, gen mgr; Jordan Merrick, progmg dir & chief of engrg.

Chatsworth

WQMT(FM)— Nov 13, 1976: 98.9 mhz; 6 kw. 311 ft. TL: N34 49 42 W84 53 41. Box 1284, 613 Silver Cir., Dalton 30721. Phone: (706) 278-5511. Fax: (706) 278-9917. Web Site: www.georgia99.com. Licensee: Clear Channel Broadcasting Licenses Inc. Group owner: Clear Channel Communications Inc. (acq 8-17-00; grpsl). Leventhal, Senter & Lerman. Format: Country. News staff: 3. Target aud: General. ♦ Mark Cooper, gen mgr.

Chauncey

WQIL(FM)— Oct 20, 1995: 101.3 mhz; 50 kw. 492 ft. TL: N32 21 37 W83 08 28. (CP: 33 kw, ant 413 ft.). Stereo. Box 130, Dublin 31040-0130. Fax: (912) 365-7799. Licensee: GSW Inc. (acq 1994; $95,000). Format: Southern gospel. Target aud: 30 plus; Christians. ♦ Ted White, gen mgr.

Clarkesville

WCHM(AM)— December 1989: 1490 khz; 1 kw-U. TL: N34 36 27 W83 32 15. Box 368 30523. Secondary address: 1331 Washington St. 30523. Phone: (706) 754-6272. Fax: (706) 754-8621. E-mail: northgeorgiaradio@hemc.net. Licensee: Brian Rothell. (acq 11-21-95; $70,000). Network: USA. Reynolds & Manning. Format: Contemp Christian. News staff: one; News: 5 hrs wkly. Target aud: 25-62. ♦ Brian Rothell, gen mgr, gen sls mgr & progmg dir; Bill Nobels, opns dir; Sherry Rothell, rgnl sls mgr; Jimmy Dillard, chief of engrg.

WMJE(FM)— 1990: 102.9 mhz; 16 kw. 413 ft. TL: N34 29 05 W83 38 24. Stereo. Box 10, Gainesville 30503. Secondary address: 1102 Thompson Bridge Rd. N.E., Gainesville 30501. Phone: (770) 532-9921. Fax: (770) 532-0506. E-mail: rreece@wmje.com. Web Site: www.accessnorthga.com. Licensee: JWJ Properties Inc. Group owner: Jacobs Media Corp. (acq 3-19-92). Network: Westwood One. Format: Oldies. Target aud: 25-54; females with a median age of 41. ♦ John W. Jacobs III, CEO & pres; John W. Jacobs Jr., chmn; Joel Williams, stn mgr; Jones Andrews, gen mgr & gen sls mgr.

Claxton

WCLA(AM)— July 20, 1958: 1470 khz; 1 kw-D, 260 w-N. TL: N32 10 12 W81 53 56. 316 N. River St. 30417. Phone: (912) 739-3035. Fax: (912) 739-0050. Licensee: Progressive United Communications Inc. (group owner; acq 2-18-97; $330,000. with co-located FM). Format: Gospel. Target aud: 25-60; religious. ♦ L. Perry McNeal, gen mgr, opns mgr, progmg dir & chief of engrg.

WMCD(FM)— Sept 15, 1972: 107.3 mhz; 25 kw. Ant 328 ft. TL: N32 10 01 W81 54 07. Stereo. Box 958, Statesboro 30458. Secondary address: 561 E. Olliff St., Statesboro 30458. Phone: (912) 764-5446. Fax: (912) 764-8827. E-mail: wwnswmcd@enia.net. Web Site: www.radiostatesboro.com. Licensee: Communications Capital Co. of Georgia LLC. Group owner: Communications Capital Managers LLC (acq 11-20-2003; $525,000). Network: Westwood One. Rgnl Reps

Broadcasting & Cable Yearbook 2006

Stations in the U.S.   Georgia

Richard Helmick. Format: Adult contemp. News staff: one; News: 7 hrs wkly. Target aud: 25-50; general. ◆ Buddy Horne, gen mgr & opns dir; Nate Hirsch, gen mgr.

Clayton

WGHC(AM)— June 28, 1961: 1370 khz; 2.5 kw-D. TL: N34 51 41 W83 24 25. Box 1149, 18 Radio Ln. 30525. Phone: (706) 782-4251. Phone: (706) 782-1041. Fax: (706) 782-4252. E-mail: rabunradio@hotmail.com. Web Site: www.rabunradio.com. Licensee: Sutton Radiocasting Corp. Group owner: Georgia-Carolina Radiocasting Companies (acq 12-14-2001; grpsl). Network: CBS Radio. Format: Talk, MOR. News staff: one; News: 5 hrs wkly. Target aud: 35 plus. ◆ Douglas M. "Art" Sutton Jr., pres; Adam Wright, VP & gen mgr; Timothy C. Stephens, chief of engrg.

WRBN(FM)—Co-owned with WGHC(AM). June 11, 1990: 104.1 mhz; 370 w. Ant 1,296 ft. TL: N34 54 24 W83 24 56. 18 Radio Lane 30525. E-mail: sky104@rabun.net. Format: Adult contemp. News staff: one; News: 2 hrs wkly. Target aud: 25-54.

Cleveland

WAZX-FM— 1989: 101.9 mhz; 6 kw. 410 ft. TL: N34 33 49 W83 38 26. Stereo. 2460 N. Atlanta Rd., Smyrna 30080. Phone: (770) 436-6171. Fax: (770) 436-0100. Web Site: www.radiolaquebuena.com. Licensee: WAZX-FM Inc. (acq 4-20-01; $60,000. for 80%). Network: CBS. Format: Regional Mexican. Target aud: 21-48. ◆ Javier Macias, pres; Humberto Izquierdo, gen mgr.

WRWH(AM)— Sept 27, 1958: 1350 khz; 1 kw-D. TL: N34 35 11 W83 46 01. Box 181 30528. Secondary address: 681 Hood St. 30528. Phone: (706) 865-3181. Fax: (706) 865-0421. E-mail: wrwh@hemc.net. Web Site: wrwh.com. Licensee: Newsic Inc. (acq 5-17-89). Reddy, Begley & McCormick. Format: Country, gospel. Target aud: 35 plus. ◆ Dean Dyer, pres, gen mgr & gen sls mgr.

Cochran

*WDCO-FM— Feb 4, 1985: 89.7 mhz; 100 kw. 1,010 ft. TL: N32 28 11 W83 15 17. Stereo. 260 14th St. N.W., Atlanta 30318-5360. Phone: (404) 685-2690. Fax: (404) 685-2684. E-mail: gpr@gpb.org. Web Site: www.gpb.org. Licensee: Georgia Public Telecommunications Commission. Network: Network: NPR, PRI. Format: Classical, News. News staff: 6; News: 40 hrs wkly. Adults 35+. ◆ James Lyle, CEO; Bonnie Bean, CFO; John Hughes, exec VP; Chuck Miller, gen mgr; Shelease Whitaker, chief of opns; Anne Bramlette, sls dir; Marcia Killingsworth, prom dir; St. John Flynn, progmg mgr; Terrance McKnight, mus dir; Mark Fehlig, engrg dir.

WDXQ(AM)— July 4, 1965: 1440 khz; 1 kw-D. TL: N32 24 43 W83 21 42. 7080 Industrial Hwy., Macon 31216. Phone: (478) 934-4548. Fax: (478) 781-6711. E-mail: taylor@ham.net. Licensee: Communications Capital Co. of Georgia LLC. Group owner: Communications Capital Managers LLC (acq 10-17-2003; $675,000. with co-located FM). Format: Country. Target aud: 18-54; adults. Spec prog: Black 6 hrs, farm 3 hrs, gospel 6 hrs wkly. ◆ Jerry Kerstina, CFO; Rick Humphrey, gen mgr; Carl Strandell, sls dir; Jerry Jennings, natl sls mgr; Kyle Taylor, mus dir; James Gay, chief of engrg.

WDXQ-FM— July 4, 1968: 96.7 mhz; 3 kw. 319 ft. TL: N32 24 43 W83 21 42. Stereo. Phone: (478) 781-1063. Network: ABC. Rep: Clear Channel. Target aud: Adults 18-54. ◆ Carl Strandell, sls VP.

College Park

WWWQ(FM)— April 1947: 100.5 mhz; 3 kw. Ant 954 ft. TL: N33 45 34 W84 23 19. Stereo. 780 Johnson Ferry Rd., Suite 500, Atlanta 30342. Phone: (404) 497-4700. Fax: (404) 497-4735. Web Site: www.q100atlanta.com. Licensee: WNNX Lico Inc. Group owner: Susquehanna Radio Corp. (acq 1-27-97; with co-located AM). Format: Top-40. ◆ Mike Fowler, gen mgr; Lisa Kelly, opns mgr; Scott Kinney, progmg dir.

Columbus

WCGQ(FM)—Listing follows WRCG(AM).

WDAK(AM)— August 1940: 540 khz; 5 kw-D, 500 w-N, DA-N. TL: N32 27 08 W85 03 18. Stereo. Box 687 31902. Secondary address: 1501 13th Ave. 31901. Phone: (706) 576-3000. Fax: (706) 576-3010. E-mail: scottmiller@clearchannel.com. Web Site: wdakonline.com. Licensee: Clear Channel Broadcasting Licenses Inc. Group owner: Clear Channel Communications Inc. (acq 5-9-03; $2.73 million. with WSTH-FM Alexander City, AL). Network: Network: USA, Westwood One. Format: News. Target aud: 18-49; men. ◆ Jim Martin, gen mgr; Brian Waters, opns mgr.

WEAM(AM)— December 1954: 1580 khz; 2.3 kw-D, 1 kw-N, DA-N. TL: N32 27 55 W85 01 22. Box 1998 31902-1998. Phone: (706) 576-3565. Fax: (706) 576-3683. Licensee: Davis Broadcasting Inc. of Columbus. Group owner: Davis Broadcasting Inc. (acq 4-20-01; $400,000). Network: USA. Reddy, Begley & McCormick. Format: Sports. News: 15 hrs wkly. Target aud: General. ◆ Gregory Davis, CEO; Janet Armstead, gen mgr; Carl Conner, opns VP; Cheryl Davis, opns mgr; Heidi Smith, sls dir; Angela Verdejo, gen sls mgr.

*WFRC(FM)— June 14, 1985: 90.5 mhz; 8.5 kw. 248 ft. TL: N32 27 37 W85 00 30. Stereo. 1010 7th Pl., Phenix City, AL 36867. Phone: (334) 291-0399. Phone: (800) 543-1495. Fax: (510) 633-7983. Web Site: www.familyradio.com. Licensee: Family Stations Inc. (group owner) Format: Relg. Spec prog: Call-in 8 hrs wkly. ◆ Harold Camping, pres; Sandra Salewski, opns mgr.

WFXE(FM)—Listing follows WOKS(AM).

WGSY(FM)—(Phenix City).AL Mar 4, 1971: 100.1 mhz; 6 kw. 328 ft. TL: N32 30 42 W85 00 41. Stereo. Box 687 39102. Secondary address: 1501 13th Ave. 31901. Phone: (706) 576-3000. Fax: (706) 576-3010. Web Site: www.sunny100columbus.com. Licensee: Clear Channel Broadcasting Licenses Inc. Group owner: Clear Channel Communications Inc. (acq 2-21-02; grpsl). Rep: McGavren Guild. Reddy, Begley & McCormick. Format: Adult contemp. Target aud: 25-54; women. ◆ Jim Martin, gen mgr & stn mgr.

WHAL(AM)—(Phenix City).AL 1951: 1460 khz; 5 kw-D, 1 kw-N, DA-N. TL: N32 29 50 W85 00 20. (CP: 4 kw-D, 140 w-N). Stereo. 1501 13th Ave. 31901. Secondary address: Box 687 31902. Phone: (706) 576-3000. Fax: (706) 576-3010. E-mail: marshawhitney@clearchannel.com. Licensee: Clear Channel Broadcasting Licenses Inc. Group owner: Clear Channel Communications Inc. (acq 2-21-02; grpsl). Rep: McGavren Guild. Format: Southern gospel. Target aud: 25 plus. ◆ Jim Martin, gen mgr.

WVRK(FM)—Co-owned with WHAL(AM). Nov 16, 1946: 102.9 mhz; 100 kw. 1,521 ft. TL: N32 19 25 W84 46 46. Stereo. E-mail: brianwaters@clearchannel.com. Web Site: www.rock103online.com. Format: AOR, classic rock. ◆ Jerri Northington, gen sls mgr; Brian Waters, progmg dir.

WJSP-FM—See Atlanta

WOKS(AM)— Mar 2, 1959: 1340 khz; 1 kw-U. TL: N32 27 07 W84 58 25. Box 1998 31902-1998. Secondary address: 2203 Wynnton Rd. 31906. Phone: (706) 576-3565. Fax: (706) 576-3683. Licensee: Davis Broadcasting Inc. (group owner; acq 7-24-92). Network: American Urban. Rep: Katz Radio. Format: Black gold & gospel. Target aud: 35-64. ◆ Gregory Davis, pres & gen mgr; Bernie Corcoran, stn mgr; Cheryl Davis, opns VP; Angela Verdejo, gen sls mgr; Michael Soul, progmg dir; Nicole Gates, prom VP & news dir.

WFXE(FM)—Co-owned with WOKS(AM). Sept 22, 1969: 104.9 mhz; 6 kw. 289 ft. TL: N32 27 37 W85 00 30. Stereo. Network: ABC FM Connection. Format: Urban contemp. ◆ Gregory A. Davis, CEO; Bernie Corcoran, CFO.

WRCG(AM)— May 10, 1928: 1420 khz; 5 kw-U, DA-N. TL: N32 29 52 W85 02 48. 1353 13th Ave. 31901. Phone: (706) 327-1217. Fax: (706) 596-4600. Web Site: www.wrcg.com. Licensee: ABG Georgia LLC. Group owner: Archway Broadcasting Group (acq 4-25-03; grpsl). Network: Network: CBS, ABC Information & Entertainment. Rep: Christal. Format: Sports, news/talk. News staff: one; News: 24 hrs wkly. Target aud: 35 plus; adults with discretionary income. Spec prog: Farm 3 hrs wkly. ◆ Chuck Thompson, gen mgr; Bob Quick, opns dir.

WCGQ(FM)—Co-owned with WRCG(AM). July 15, 1966: 107.3 mhz; 100 kw. 1,011 ft. TL: N32 27 59 W85 03 23. Stereo. Web Site: www.q1073.com. Format: Top 40. Target aud: 18-49. ◆ Chuck Thompson, mktg dir; Al Haynes, progmg dir.

WSHE(AM)— 1947: 1270 khz; 5 kw. TL: N32 26 16 W85 01 10. Box 687 31902. Secondary address: 1501 13th Ave. 31901. Phone: (706) 576-3000. Fax: (706) 576-3010. E-mail: scottmiller@clearchannel.com. Web Site: www.WMLFonline.com. Licensee: Clear Channel Broadcasting Licenses Inc. Group owner: Clear Channel Communications Inc. (acq 2-21-02; grpsl). Rep: McGavren Guild. Reddy, Begley & McCormick. Format: Gospel, sports, Latino. News: 20 hrs wkly. Target aud: 35-60. ◆ Jim Martin, gen mgr; Brian Waters, opns mgr.

WSTH-FM—See Alexander City, AL

*WTJB(FM)— Dec 15, 1984: 91.7 mhz; 5 kw. 298 ft. TL: N32 25 20 W85 01 50. Wallace Hall, Troy State Univ., Troy, AL 36082. Phone: (334) 670-3268. Fax: (334) 670-3934. E-mail: wtsu@troy.edu. Web Site: www.troy.edu. Licensee: Troy State University. Network: Network: NPR, PRI. Format: Class, news. News: 25 hrs wkly. Target aud: General. Spec prog: Children one hr wkly. ◆ James Clower, mgr; Judy Davis, opns mgr; Fred Azbell, progmg dir.

*WYFK(FM)— July 1987: 89.5 mhz; 50 kw. 439 ft. TL: N32 40 03 W84 57 19. Stereo. 75 Raymond Dr., Cataula 31804. Phone: (706) 322-1980. Licensee: Bible Broadcasting Network Inc. (group owner) Format: Relg. Target aud: General. ◆ Lowell Davey, pres; Jeff Blodgett, gen mgr; Shannon Dyess, stn mgr.

Commerce

WJJC(AM)— June 27, 1957: 1270 khz; 5 kw-D. TL: N34 12 57 W83 26 09. Box 379 30529. Secondary address: 1801 N. Elm St. 30529. Phone: (706) 335-3155. Phone: (706) 335-1270 (Request Line). Fax: (706) 335-1905. E-mail: wjjc@alltel.net. Licensee: Banks-Jackson Broadcasting Inc. (acq 1996). Rep: Rgnl Reps. Format: Americana/country. News: 30 hrs wkly. Target aud: 25-55. Spec prog: Farm 2 hrs, bluegrass 13 hrs wkly. ◆ Rob Jordan, gen mgr; Keith Parnell, progmg dir.

Conyers

WPBS(AM)— November 1979: 1040 khz; 12 kw-D, 5 kw-CH. TL: N33 40 48 W84 01 44. 6171 Neely Farm Dr., Norcross 30092. Phone: (404) 932-5006. E-mail: amkorea2000@yahoo.com. Licensee: Pacific Star Broadcasting Inc. (acq 5-11-2005; $2.25 million.) ◆ Charles Kim, gen mgr.

Coosa

WSRM(FM)— 2005: 95.3 mhz; 6 kw. Ant 72 ft. TL: N34 11 51 W85 21 21. 20 John Davenport Dr., Rome 30165. Phone: (706) 291-9496. Fax: (706) 235-7107. E-mail: info@wrgarome.com. Web Site: www.wrgarome.com. Licensee: Coosa Broadcasting Corp. (acq 5-31-2005; $1.1 million). Format: News/talk. ◆ Paul Stone, pres; Randy Quick, gen mgr.

Cordele

*WAEF(FM)— 2001: 90.3 mhz; 11 kw vert. Ant 505 ft. TL: N31 38 22 W83 44 58. Box 3206, American Family Radio, Tupelo, MS 38803. Phone: (662) 844-8888. Fax: (662) 842-6791. Web Site: www.afr.net. Licensee: American Family Association. Group owner: American Family Radio Format: Inspirational Christian. ◆ Marvin Sanders, gen mgr.

Broadcasting & Cable Yearbook 2006

Georgia

WQSY(AM)—Not on air, target date: unknown: 1490 khz; 1 kw-U. TL: N31 57 24 W83 48 20. Box 667 31010. Phone: (229) 271-8983. Fax: (229) 273-4900. Licensee: Staton Broadcasting Inc. (acq 11-12-2003; grpsl). ♦John Long, gen mgr.

WQXZ(FM)— Feb 22, 1969: 98.3 mhz; 4.2 kw. 410 ft. TL: N31 57 26 W83 46 08. Stereo. Box 667 31010. Phone: (229) 271-8983. Fax: (229) 273-4900. E-mail: wqxzfm@mchsl.com. Licensee: Staton Broadcasting Inc. (group owner; (acq 11-12-2003; grpsl). Network: Network: Motor Racing Net, Jones Radio Networks. Dan Alpert. Format: Oldies. News staff: one; News: 15 hrs wkly. Target aud: 35-64. ♦Cecil Staton, pres; John Long, exec VP, gen mgr & opns dir; Michael Harman, opns mgr.

Cornelia

WCON(AM)— Mar 28, 1953: 1450 khz; 1 kw-U. TL: N34 30 57 W83 32 20. Box 100 30531. Secondary address: 540 N. Main St. 30531. Phone: (706) 778-2241. Fax: (706) 778-0576. Web Site: www.wconfm.com. Licensee: Habersham Broadcasting Co. (acq 2-1-61). Network: ABC Information & Entertainment. Format: Gospel, country. News staff: one. Target aud: Adults. ♦Bobbie C. Foster, pres & gen mgr; John C. Foster, VP; Brandon Reed, news dir; Jimmy Dillard, chief of engrg.

WCON-FM— Mar 27, 1965: 99.3 mhz; 50 kw. 808 ft. TL: N34 31 24 W83 40 46. Stereo. E-mail: bobbiefoster@alltel.net. Web Site: www.wconfm.com. News staff: one. Target aud: 18 plus.

Covington

WGFS(AM)— Oct 9, 1946: 1430 khz; 3.9 kw-D, 212 w-N. TL: N33 37 14 W83 53 04. Stereo. Box 2419 30015. Secondary address: 1151 Hendricks St. 30014. Phone: (770) 786-1430. Fax: (770) 784-9892. Licensee: Multicultural Radio Broadcasting Licensee LLC. Group owner: Multicultural Radio Broadcasting Inc. (acq 11-21-03; $700,000). Network: CBS. Mullin, Rhyne, Emmons & Topel. Format: Oldies of 50s & 60s. News staff: one; News: 20 hrs wkly. Target aud: General. Spec prog: Georgia Southern and local football in season, relg 8 hrs wkly. ♦Arthur Liu, pres; Mike Shumate, stn mgr.

Crawford

WGMG(FM)— April 1990: 102.1 mhz; 6 kw. 328 ft. TL: N33 55 18 W83 14 14. (CP: 25 kw). 1010 Tower Pl., Bogart 30622. Phone: (706) 369-7223. Fax: (706) 353-1967. E-mail: mornings@southernbroadcasting.com. Web Site: www.magic1021fm.com. Licensee: New Broadcast Investment Properties Inc. Group owner: Southern Broadcasting Companies Inc. (acq 2-11-02). Format: Adult contemp. Target aud: 18-49; general. ♦Paul Stone, pres; Scott Smith, opns mgr.

Cumming

WATB(AM)—(Decatur). July 19, 1958: 1420 khz; 1 kw-D, DA. TL: N33 47 13 W84 14 53. 3589 N. Decatur Rd., Scottdale 30079. Phone: (404) 508-1420. Fax: (404) 508-8930. E-mail: watb1420@yahoo.com. Licensee: Way Broadcasting Licensee LLC (acq 6-13-00; grpsl). Format: Multi-cultural. Target aud: General; ethnic groups from around the world. ♦Benjamin F. Vannoy Jr., gen mgr; H.R. Garrison, opns mgr; H. R. Garrison, progmg dir; Skipper Marshall, chief of engrg.

***WWEV-FM**— Dec 4, 1981: 91.5 mhz; 8.9 kw. 960 ft. TL: N34 14 13 W84 09 36. Stereo. Box 248 30028. Secondary address: 1705 Sawnee Dr. 30040. Phone: (770) 781-9150. Fax: (770) 781-5003. E-mail: wwev@wwev.org. Web Site: www.wwev.org. Licensee: Curriculum Development Foundation Inc. Format: Relg. Target aud: 18-49; the family unit. ♦N. Barry Holt, gen mgr & progmg dir; Ray Haynes, prom dir.

Cuthbert

WCUG(AM)— Dec 1, 1971: 850 khz; 500 w-D. TL: N31 46 26 W84 50 16. Box 348 39840. Phone: (229) 732-3725. Licensee: Mullis Communications Inc. Format: Country, Gospel, Oldies. Spec prog: Black 4 hrs, farm 8 hrs wkly. ♦N. Scott Mullis, gen mgr.

Dahlonega

WDGR(AM)— Mar 1, 1982: . Stn currently dark 1210 khz; 10 kw-D. TL: N34 31 45 W84 00 23. 6972 Buford Hwy., Suite 2000, Atlanta 30342. Phone: (770) 300-0999. Fax: (770) 300-3082. E-mail: uskradio@yahoo.com. Web Site: www.uskradio.com. Licensee: USK Broadcasting Inc. (acq 11-25-2003; $500,000). ♦Hye Kim, pres & gen mgr.

WKHC(FM)— Dec 16, 1996: 104.3 mhz; 3.7 kw. Ant 417 ft. TL: N34 29 56 W84 08 32. Stereo. 1376 Ben Higgins Rd. 30533. Phone: (706) 867-9542. Fax: (706) 864-4364. E-mail: wkhc@alltel.net. Web Site: www.realcountryonline.com. Licensee: Williams Communications Inc. (group owner; acq 8-22-02; $1.1 million). Network: ABC. Format: Real country. Target aud: 25-54; general. Spec prog: American Indian one hr wkly. ♦Walt Williams Jr., CEO; Walt Williams III, pres; Rick Morris, gen mgr, stn mgr & opns mgr; Trudy Austin, dev mgr.

***WNGU(FM)**— 1998: 89.5 mhz; 750 w. 459 ft. TL: N34 31 29 W83 59 50. Stereo. 260 14th St. N.W., Atlanta 30318-5360. Phone: (404) 685-2690. Fax: (404) 685-2684. E-mail: gpr@gpb.org. Web Site: www.gpb.org. Licensee: Georgia Public Telecommunications Commission. Network: Network: NPR, PRI. Format: Classical, News. News staff: 6; News: 40 hrs wkly. ♦James Lyle, CEO; Bonnie Bean, CFO; John Hughes, exec VP; Chuck Miller, gen mgr; Shelease Whitaker, chief of opns; Anne Bramlette, sls dir; Marcia Killingsworth, prom dir; St. John Flynn, progmg mgr; Terrance McKnight, mus dir; Mark Fehlig, engrg dir.

Dallas

WDPC(AM)— Sept 21, 1979: 1500 khz; 1 kw-D, DA. TL: N33 56 40 W84 49 28. c/o WDCY(AM), 8451 S. Cherokee Blvd., Suite B, Douglasville 30134. Phone: (770) 920-1520. Fax: (770) 920-4600. Licensee: Word Christian Broadcasting Inc. (acq 7-96; $25,000). Format: Old time relg, Southern gospel. Target aud: General. ♦Ken Johns, pres, gen mgr & progmg dir; Ford Berry, mus dir; Tom Taylor, chief of engrg.

Dalton

WBLJ(AM)— Apr 8, 1940: 1230 khz; 1 kw-U. TL: N34 45 23 W84 57 02. 613 Silver Cir. 30721. Phone: (706) 278-5511. Fax: (706) 226-8766. Web Site: www.wbljnewstalk1230.com. Licensee: Clear Channel Broadcasting Licenses Inc. Group owner: Clear Channel Communications Inc. (acq 8-17-00; grpsl). Network: CBS Radio. Format: News/talk. News staff: 2; News: 28 hrs wkly. Target aud: 18-54. Spec prog: Relg mus. ♦Alene Grevey, sr VP; Mark Cooper, gen mgr; Rich Phillips, opns dir; Larry Gibson, progmg mgr.

WDAL(AM)— Oct 1, 1954: 1430 khz; 2.5 kw, 72 w-N. TL: N34 47 23 W84 57 12. Stereo. Box 1284 30722. Secondary address: 613 Silver Cir. 30721. Phone: (706) 278-5511. Fax: (706) 278-3300. Fax: (706) 278-7966. Licensee: Clear Channel Broadcasting Licenses Inc. Group owner: Clear Channel Communications Inc. (acq 8-17-00; grpsl). Network: CBS. Rep: Rgnl Reps. Leventhal, Senter & Lerman. Format: Mexican. News staff: 3; News: 30 hrs wkly. Target aud: 25-45. ♦Rich Phillips, gen mgr.

WYYU(FM)— Co-owned with WDAL(AM). August 1995: 104.5 mhz; 3 kw. 328 ft. TL: N34 49 42 W84 53 41. Format: Adult contemp. News staff: 3.

WTTI(AM)— June 17, 1965: 1530 khz; 10 kw-D, 10 kw-CH, DA-CH. TL: N34 47 09 W85 02 40. Box 216 30722. Secondary address: 111 W. Crawford St. 30720. Phone: (706) 277-7117. Phone: (706) 277-5188. Fax: (706) 277-7180. E-mail: wtti1530@alltel.net. Licensee: Troy L. Hall. Network: USA. Format: Southern gospel. Target aud: 25-54; family, relg. Spec prog: Southern gospel. ♦Troy Hall, CEO & gen mgr; C. W. Queen, stn mgr.

Darien

WHFX(FM)— May 13, 1993: 107.7 mhz; 50 kw. 403 ft. TL: N31 10 09 W81 32 14. 3833 Hwy. 82, Brunswick 31523. Phone: (912) 267-1025. Fax: (912) 264-5462. Licensee: Qantum of Brunswick License Co. LLC. Group owner: Qantum Communications Corp. (acq 7-2-2003; grpsl). Network: ABC Information & Entertainment. Rep: McGavren Guild. Format: Oldies 1963-1978. News staff: one; News: 4 hrs wkly. Target aud: 25 plus; general. ♦Larry W. Landrum, gen mgr; Gerri Landrum, sls dir; Bryan Thomas, progmg dir; Dick Boekeloo, chief of engrg.

Dawson

WMRZ(FM)— June 2005: 98.1 mhz; 6 kw. Ant 328 ft. TL: N32 14 W84 28 50. Staton Broadcasting Inc., 6316 Peake Rd., Macon 31210. Phone: (478) 757-0564. Licensee: Staton Broadcasting Inc. (group owner; acq 11-12-2003; grpsl). ♦Cecil Staton, pres.

Decatur

WATB(AM)—Licensed to Decatur. See Cumming

WLTM(FM)—See Atlanta

WPBC(AM)— Aug 11, 1964: 1310 khz; 500 w-D. TL: N33 46 22 W84 16 55. 4900 Rupert Ln., La Canada, CA 91011. Phone: (323) 559-8869. Licensee: Chang Soo Kim (acq 2-28-2005; $3.3 million). ♦Chang Soo Kim, gen mgr.

Demorest

***WPPR(FM)**— 1997: 88.3 mhz; 6 kw. 640 ft. TL: N34 31 24 W83 40 46. Stereo. 260 14th St. N.W., Atlanta 30318-5360. Phone: (404) 685-2690. Fax: (404) 685-2684. E-mail: gpr@gpb.org. Web Site: www.gpb.org. Licensee: Georgia Public Telecommunications Commission. Network: Network: NPR, PRI. Format: News, class. News staff: 6; News: 40 hrs wkly. Adults 35+. ♦James Lyle (GPB), CEO; Bonnie Bean, CFO; John Hughes, exec VP; Chuck Miller, gen mgr; Shelease Whitaker, opns mgr; Anne Bramlette, sls dir; Marcia Killingsworth, prom dir; St. John Flynn, progmg mgr; Terrance McKnight, mus dir; Mark Fehlig, engrg dir.

Dock Junction

WXMK(FM)— May 1, 1991: 105.9 mhz; 15 kw. 489 ft. TL: N31 10 09 W81 32 14. Stereo. 185 Benedict Rd., Brunswick 31520. Phone: (912) 261-1000. Fax: (912) 265-8391. E-mail: jenna@magic1059.com. Web Site: www.magic1059.com. Licensee: Golden Isles Broadcasting L.L.C. (acq 3-23-2001; $2.8 million. with WRJY(FM) Brunswick). Pepper & Corazzini. Format: CHR, adult contemp. Target aud: 25-54; women. ♦Traci Long, gen mgr; Everett Armstrong, opns mgr; Jenna McNeal, progmg dir.

Donalsonville

WGMK(FM)—Listing follows WSEM(AM).

WSEM(AM)— Feb 12, 1963: 1500 khz; 1 kw-D. TL: N31 04 26 W84 52 47. Box 87 31745. Secondary address: 91 North Way 31743. Phone: (229) 524-5123. Fax: (229) 524-2265. E-mail: wgmk@alltel.net. Licensee: Styles Media Group LLC (group owner; acq 3-17-2004; grpsl). Format: Country, talk, Black gospel. Target aud: 25-49. ♦Gilbert M. Kelley Sr., pres; Gilbert M. Kelley Jr., gen mgr; Grace Kelley, gen sls mgr; Gilbert M. Kelley Jr., progmg dir & news dir.

WGMK(FM)— Co-owned with WSEM(AM). Sept 1, 1980: 106.3 mhz; 5.9 kw. Ant 331 ft. TL: N31 04 26 W84 52 47. Format: Hot adult contemp.

WWGF(FM)— Aug 1, 1998: 107.5 mhz; 6 kw. 315 ft. TL: N30 58 36 W84 55 51. Stereo. 2278 Wortham Lane, Grovetown 30813-5103. Phone: (706) 309-9610. Fax: (706) 309-9669. E-mail: ctbarinowski@comcast.net. Web Site: www.gnnradio.org. Licensee: Barinowski Investment Co., a Georgia L.P. Group owner: Good News Network (acq 1-21-99). Format: Christian. Target aud: All. ♦C. T. Barinowski, gen mgr.

Doraville

WBTS(FM)— May 1948: 95.5 mhz; 74 kw. Ant 1,115 ft. TL: N34 07 32 W83 51 32. Stereo. 1601 W. Peachtree St. N.E., Atlanta 30309. Phone: (404) 897-7500. Fax: (404) 897-7363. Web Site: www.955thebeat.com. Licensee: CXR Holdings L.L.C. Group owner: Cox Broadcasting (acq 7-19-99; $78 million). Format: Top-40. Target aud: 25-54; blue collar to executive, modern country mus lovers. Spec prog: Univ. of Georgia sports, country classic oldies 5 hrs, NASCAR 2 hrs wkly. ♦Dan Kearney, gen mgr.

Douglas

WDMG(AM)— March 1947: 860 khz; 5 kw-U, DA-N. TL: N31 30 26 W82 48 46. (CP: TL: N31 30 23 W82 49 10). 620 E. Ward St. 31533. Phone: (912) 389-0995. Fax: (912) 383-8552. E-mail: wdmgamfm@charter.net. Licensee: RTG Radio LLC. Group owner: Black Crow Media Group LLC (acq 11-9-2001; grpsl). Network: USA.

Stations in the U.S. — Georgia

Format: Sports. News staff: one; News: 20 hrs wkly. Target aud: 25-54. Spec prog: Farm 4 hrs, relg 6 hrs wkly. ◆John Higgs, stn mgr.

WOKA(AM)— Dec 10, 1962: 1310 khz; 3.9 kw-D, 39 w-N. TL: N31 31 24 W82 52 22. 1310 W. Walker St. 31533. Phone: (912) 384-8153. Fax: (912) 383-6328. Licensee: Coffee County Broadcasters Inc. (acq 2-13-98; with co-located FM). Format: Solid gold oldies. Target aud: General. ◆Jim Squires, CEO, gen mgr & gen sls mgr; Dwayne Gillis, pres; Paul Sullivan, opns mgr; Michael Van Cleave, news dir.

WOKA-FM— July 1971: 106.7 mhz; 100 kw. 1,000 ft. TL: N31 31 24 W82 52 22. Phone: (912) 384-8153. Phone: (912) 389-1067. Fax: (912) 383-6328. E-mail: production@accessatc.net. Web Site: www.dixiecountry.com. Format: Country. Target aud: Adults 25-54. Spec prog: Gospel 4 hrs wkly.

Douglasville

WDCY(AM)— May 5, 1993: 1520 khz; 2.5 kw-D. TL: N33 45 48 W84 44 28. 8451 S. Cherokee Blvd., Suite B 30134. Phone: (770) 920-1520. Phone: (770) 920-1521. Fax: (770) 920-4600. Licensee: Word Christian Broadcasting Inc. (acq 5-7-93; $95,000; 4-12-93). Format: Old time relg, Southern gospel. News: 10 hrs wkly. Target aud: General. ◆Ken Johns, pres, gen mgr, opns mgr & progmg dir; Ford Berry, mus dir; Tom Taylor, chief of engrg.

Dry Branch

WMWR(AM)— Apr 15, 1998: 1670 khz; 10 kw-D, 1 kw-N. TL: N32 48 16 W83 36 16. 7080 Industrial Hwy., Macon 31216. Phone: (478) 781-1063. Fax: (478) 781-6711. Licensee: AMFM Radio Licenses LLC. Group owner: Clear Channel Communications Inc. (acq. 2-15-2001; grpsl). Rep: Clear Channel. Format: News/talk. Target aud: General; adults. ◆Rick Humphrey, gen mgr; Carl Strandell, sls dir; Carey Brown, gen sls mgr; Robbie Brown, gen sls mgr; Leslie Harriell-Turner, progmg dir; James Gay, chief of engrg.

Dublin

***WAWH(FM)**— 2000: 88.3 mhz; 400 w. Ant 82 ft. TL: N32 32 27 W82 57 27. Box 3206, American Family Radio, Tupelo, MS 38803. Phone: (662) 844-8888. Fax: (662) 842-6791. Web Site: www.afr.net. Licensee: American Family Association. Group owner: American Family Radio Format: Inspirational Christian. ◆Marvin Sanders, gen mgr.

WKKZ(FM)— Apr 4, 1967: 92.7 mhz; 50 kw. 417 ft. TL: N32 31 21 W82 54 00. Stereo. Box 967 31040. Secondary address: 1006 Martin Luther King Blvd. 31021. Phone: (478) 272-9270. Fax: (478) 275-3592. Licensee: Kirby Broadcasting Co. (acq 9-18-2003). Network: ABC. Rep: Dora-Clayton. Format: CHR. ◆Mike Kirby, pres, gen mgr & opns VP; Jason Kirby, adv mgr.

WMLT(AM)— Jan 12, 1945: 1330 khz; 5 kw-D, 500 w-N, DA-N. TL: N32 33 50 W82 52 00. Box 130 31040. Secondary address: 807 Bellevue Ave. 31021. Phone: (478) 272-4422. Fax: (478) 275-4657. Licensee: State Broadcasting Corporation. Network: ABC Information & Entertainment. Rep: Rgnl Reps. Format: Adult standards, news/talk, sports. Target aud: 25-54. Spec prog: Farm 6 hrs wkly. ◆Mac Davis, gen mgr & gen sls mgr.

WQZY(FM)— Co-owned with WMLT(AM). 1978: 95.9 mhz; 88 kw. 1,023 ft. TL: N32 33 51 W82 52 18. Stereo. Web Site: www.wqzyfm.com. Format: Hot country. Target aud: 18-54. ◆Morgan Dowdy, pres; Mac Davis, gen sls mgr.

WXLI(AM)— Mar 16, 1958: 1230 khz; 1 kw-U. TL: N32 31 21 W82 54 00. Box 967 31040. Secondary address: 1006 Martin Luther King Blvd. 31021. Phone: (478) 272-4282. Fax: (478) 275-3592. Licensee: Laurens County Broadcasting Co. (acq 8-10-03). Network: CBS. Rep: Dora-Clayton. Format: Country. ◆Mike Kirby, gen mgr.

East Dublin

WELT(FM)—Licensed to East Dublin. See Swainsboro

East Point

WMLB(AM)— Oct 9, 1994: 1160 khz; 50 kw-D, 160 w-N, DA-2. TL: N33 49 34 W84 36 20. 225 Corey Center S.E., Atlanta 30312. Phone: (404) 681-9307. Fax: (404) 659-1329. E-mail: bnewman@am1160.net. Web Site: www.am1160.net. Licensee: JW Broadcasting Inc. (acq 8-11-2004; $10.4 million). Network: AP Radio. Holland & Knight. Format: Music of your life. News: 14 hrs wkly. Target aud: 50 plus; senior citizens. Spec prog: Relg music 4 hrs wkly. ◆Brigham Newman, gen mgr; Michael Kay, chief of opns.

WTJH(AM)— December 1949: 1260 khz; 5 kw-D. TL: N33 41 47 W84 28 29. 2146 Dodson Dr. 30344. Phone: (404) 344-2233. Fax: (404) 346-0647. Licensee: Christian Broadcasting of East Point Inc. Group owner: Willis Broadcasting Corp. Format: Inspirational, gospel. ◆Bishop L.E. Willis Sr., pres; R.J. Lovett, gen mgr.

Eastman

WUFF(AM)— Sept 1, 1961: 710 khz; 2.5 kw-D. TL: N32 13 35 W83 13 10. Box 4097 31023. Secondary address: 855 College St. Phone: (478) 374-3437. Fax: (478) 374-3585. E-mail: news@wolfradio.com. Licensee: Dodge Broadcasting Inc. Format: Country. Spec prog: Black 5 hrs wkly. ◆Mike Lowe, gen mgr & stn mgr; Mike Shipman, gen sls mgr & pub affrs dir; James Clinton, chief of engrg.

WUFF-FM— 1976: 97.5 mhz; 2 kw. 371 ft. TL: N32 13 35 W83 13 10. (CP: 4.6 kw, ant 364 ft.). Stereo.

Eatonton

WKVQ(AM)— Dec 15, 1966: 1520 khz; 1 kw-D. TL: N33 19 19 W83 25 03. Box 3965 31024. Phone: (706) 485-8792. Fax: (706) 485-3555. Licensee: Craig Baker. Format: Adult standards. Target aud: General. ◆Craig Baker, pres & gen mgr.

WMGZ(FM)— Feb 8, 1988: 97.7 mhz; 8.5 kw. 554 ft. TL: N33 20 41 W83 13 41. Stereo. Box 832, Milledgeville 31061. Secondary address: 156 Lake Laurel Rd., Milledgeville 31061. Phone: (478) 453-9406. Fax: (478) 453-3298. E-mail: z97mail@yahoo.com. Licensee: Southern Stone Broadcasting Inc. (acq 7-6-2005; $1.1 million with WKGQ(AM) Milledgeville). Network: ABC. Format: Hot adult contemp. News staff: one; News: 4 hrs wkly. Target aud: 18-49. ◆Paul C. Stone, pres; Tom Ptak, gen mgr, opns mgr & prom dir; Tony Taylor, sls.

Elberton

WLVX(FM)— May 15, 1998: 105.1 mhz; 6 kw. 328 ft. TL: N33 59 22 W82 46 23. Box 340 30635. Secondary address: 562 Jones St. 30635. Phone: (706) 213-1051. Fax: (706) 283-8710. E-mail: gibson@gacaradio.com. Web Site: www.elbertonradio.com. Licensee: Georgia-Carolina Radiocasting Co. LLC. Group owner: Georgia-Carolina Radiocasting Companies (acq 12-19-2001; grpsl). Network: ABC. Format: Adult urban. News staff: one; News: 2 hrs wkly. Target aud: 25-54; general. ◆Douglas M. Sutton Jr., pres; Sean Gibson, VP & gen mgr; Ron Shuller, opns mgr.

WSGC(AM)— 1946: 1400 khz; 1 kw-U. TL: N34 06 45 W82 52 52. Box 340, 562 Jones St. 30635. Phone: (706) 283-1400. Fax: (706) 283-8710. E-mail: gibson@gacaradio.com. Web Site: www.elbertonradio.com. Licensee: Georgia-Carolina Radiocasting Co. LLC. Group owner: Georgia-Carolina Radiocasting Companies (acq 12-19-01; grpsl). Network: ABC. Dan J. Alpert. News staff: one; News: 6 hrs wkly. Target aud: 35+. ◆Douglas M. Sutton Jr., pres; Sean Gibson, VP & stn mgr; Ron Shuller, opns mgr; Tim Stephens, chief of engrg.

WSGC-FM— 1973: 92.1 mhz; 3 kw. Ant 299 ft. TL: N31 04 45 W82 55 16. Box E, Toccoa 30577. Secondary address: 562 Jones St. 30635. Phone: (706) 297-7264. Fax: (706) 297-7266. Licensee: Radio Elberton Inc. Group owner: Georgia-Carolina Radiocasting Companies (acq 3-30-01; at least $478,000. debt). Format: Country. ◆Sean Gibson, gen mgr.

Ellijay

WLJA-FM—Listing follows WPGY.

WPGY(AM)— May 10, 1978: 1560 khz; 1 kw-D. TL: N34 42 14 W84 28 35. Box 545141, Tabor St., Jasper 30143. Secondary address: 134 S. Main St., Jasper 30143. Phone: (706) 276-2016. Fax: (706) 635-1018. E-mail: wlja@ellijay.com. Licensee: Tri-State Communications Inc. (acq 10-21-98; $500,000 with co-located FM). Format: MOR, country. Target aud: 18-75. ◆Randy D. Grauley, VP, gen mgr & gen sls mgr; Byron Dobbs, news dir.

WLJA-FM—Co-owned with WPGY. Nov 1, 1985: 93.5 mhz; 6 kw. 272 ft. TL: N34 42 59 W84 30 50. Format: Country & gospel. Target aud: 18-75. ◆Byron L. Dobbs, chmn & gen mgr; Randy D. Grauley, CFO & exec VP; Jackie Grizzle, chief of engrg.

Evans

WAEG(FM)— November 1991: 92.3 mhz; 3 kw. 328 ft. TL: N33 35 25 W82 13 52. Box 1584, Augusta 30903-2429. Secondary address: 104 Bennett Lane, North Augusta, SC 29841. Phone: (803) 279-2330. Fax: (803) 279-8149. Web Site: www.waeg923.com. Licensee: Radio One of Augusta LLC. Group owner: Radio One Inc. (acq 11-8-01; grpsl). Rep: Christal. Shaw Pittman. Format: Alternative. Target aud: Teen-49. ◆Ron Tomel, opns mgr & prom dir.

Fayetteville

WPZE(FM)—Licensed to Fayetteville. See Griffin

Fitzgerald

WBHB(AM)— Oct 8, 1946: 1240 khz; 1 kw-U. TL: N31 42 23 W83 15 40. 601 W. Roanoke Dr. 31750. Phone: (229) 423-2077. Fax: (229) 423-8313. E-mail: jank@rtgmedia.net. Licensee: RTG Radio LLC. Group owner: Black Crow Media Group LLC (acq 11-9-2001; grpsl). Network: Westwood One. Format: Black Gospel. Target aud: General. Spec prog: Black 4 hrs, farm 6 hrs, gospel 10 hrs wkly. ◆Robert Ganzak, pres; John Higgs, stn mgr.

WRDO(FM)— 1991: 96.9 mhz; 6 kw. 328 ft. TL: N31 44 33 W83 14 41. 232 North Central, Tifton 31794. Phone: (229) 386-9898. Fax: (229) 386-9866. E-mail: jank@rtgmedia.net. Licensee: RTG Radio LLC. Group owner: Black Crow Media Group LLC (acq 11-9-2001; grpsl). Network: USA. Roy F. Perkins. Format: Adult contemp-soft hits. News staff: one. Target aud: 25-55; baby boomers. Spec prog: Gospel 6 hrs wkly. ◆Robert Ganzak, pres; John Higgs, gen mgr; Jan Kicklighter, gen sls mgr.

Folkston

***WATY(FM)**— 2000: 91.3 mhz; 600 w. Ant 321 ft. TL: N30 52 29 W82 01 10. Box 777 31537. Secondary address: 104 N. First St. 31537. Phone: (912) 496-4484. Fax: (912) 496-4086. E-mail: maysj@alltel.net. Licensee: Okefenokee Educational Foundation Inc. Format: Traditional country. ◆Jack R. Mays, CEO & gen mgr.

***WECC-FM**— 2002: 89.3 mhz; 16 kw. Ant 282 ft. TL: N30 55 54 W81 42 30. (CP: 30 kw, ant 479 ft). 5465 Hwy. 40 E., St. Marys 31558. Phone: (912) 882-8930. Fax: (912) 882-9322. E-mail: paul@weccradio.org. Web Site: www.weccradio.org. Licensee: Lighthouse Christian Broadcasting Corp. Format: Christian. ◆Paul Hafer, gen mgr; John M. DillonHafer, progmg dir.

WFJO(FM)— November 1989: 92.5 mhz; 6 kw. 324 ft. TL: N30 43 45 W81 56 21. (CP: Ant 328 ft.). Stereo. Box 777 31537. Secondary address: 104 N. First St. 31537. Phone: (904) 680-1050. E-mail:

Georgia

maysj@plantell.net. Licensee: Tama Radio Licenses of Jacksonville, FL, Inc. Group owner: Tama Broadcasting Inc. (acq 6-4-2003). Rep: Rgnl Reps. Stan Emert. Format: Oldies of the 50s, 60s, 70s. News staff: one. Target aud: General. Spec prog: Gospel 5 hrs wkly. ◆Jack R. Mays, gen mgr, sls dir & pub affrs dir.

Forsyth

WQMJ(FM)— Nov 22, 1973: 100.1 mhz; 3 kw. 209 ft. TL: N32 58 31 W83 52 11. (CP: 2 kw, ant 574 ft. TL: N32 55 41 W83 52 37). Stereo. 6174 Hwy. 57, Macon 31217. Phone: (478) 745-3301. Fax: (478) 742-2293. Licensee: Roberts Communications Inc. (group owner; acq 5-23-97; $550,000 with WXKO(AM) Fort Valley). Format: Urban contemp, gospel. ◆Mike Roberts, stn mgr.

Fort Gaines

***WJWV(FM)**— Feb 28, 1993: 90.9 mhz; 85 kw. 267 ft. TL: N31 36 16 W85 02 02. 260 14th St. N.W., Atlanta 30318-5360. Phone: (404) 685-2690. Fax: (404) 685-2684. E-mail: ask@gpb.org. Web Site: www.gpb.org. Licensee: Georgia Public Telecommunications Commission. (group owner) Format: Class, news. Spec prog: Jazz 4 hrs, Latin 3 hrs. ◆Nancy Hall, CEO; Bonnie Bean, CFO; St. John Flynn, progmg mgr; Susanna Capelouto, news dir.

Fort Valley

WIBB-FM—Licensed to Fort Valley. See Macon

***WJTG(FM)**— Mar 1, 1989: 91.3 mhz; 100 kw. 459 ft. TL: N32 41 27 W83 51 45. Stereo. 3214 Richardson Mill Rd. 31030. Phone: (478) 825-0085. Fax: (478) 825-9911. E-mail: wjtg@wjtg.org. Licensee: Joy Public Broadcasting Corp. Network: USA. Format: Gospel. Target aud: General. ◆Wally Vander Zwaag, gen mgr & progmg dir; Richard Hamilton, chief of engrg.

WQBZ(FM)—Licensed to Fort Valley. See Macon

WXKO(AM)— June 1951: 1150 khz; 1 kw-D, 60 w-N. TL: N32 34 34 W83 54 17. 1675 Hwy. 341 N. 31030. Phone: (478) 825-5547. Phone: (478) 827-1274. Fax: (478) 827-1273. E-mail: jjohnsonwxko@bellsouth.net. Licensee: Roberts Communications Inc. (group owner, acq 5-23-97; $550,000 with WFXM-FM Forsyth). Booth, Freret, Imlay & Tepper P. Format: Gospel. News staff: one; News: 10 hrs wkly. Target aud: 25 plus; Black. ◆Jamie Johnson, gen mgr.

Gainesville

***WBCX(FM)**— 1977: 89.1 mhz; 875 w. 544 ft. TL: N34 19 01 W83 49 45. Stereo. Brenau Univ., 500 Washington St. S.E. 30501. Phone: (770) 538-4708. Fax: (770) 538-4558. E-mail: sfugate@lib.brenau.edu. Web Site: www.brenau.edu. Licensee: Brenau University. Network: Network: PRI, Jones Radio Networks. Format: Eclectic. Target aud: 14-85. Spec prog: Black 12 hrs, American Indian 4 hrs, Gospel 6 hrs wkly. ◆J. Scott Fugate, gen mgr, opns dir & dev dir.

WDUN(AM)— Apr 2, 1949: 550 khz; 5 kw-D, 2.5 kw-N, DA-N. TL: N34 20 11 W83 47 41. Stereo. Box 10 30503. Secondary address: 1102 Thompson Bridge Rd. N.E. 30501. Phone: (770) 532-9921. Fax: (770) 532-0506. E-mail: news@wdun.com. Web Site: www.wdun.com. Licensee: JWJ Properties Inc. Group owner: Jacobs Media Corp. (acq 9-83; FTR: 9-5-83). Network: Network: CBS, ABC Information & Entertainment. Format: News/talk, sports. Target aud: 25-65. ◆John W. Jacobs III, CEO & pres; John W. Jacobs Jr., chmn; Jones Andrews, gen mgr; Joel Williams, stn mgr & progmg dir.

WFOX(FM)— Nov 1, 1965: 97.1 mhz; 97 kw. 1,571 ft. TL: N34 07 32 W83 51 31. Stereo. 1601 W. Peachtree St., Suite 797, Atlanta 30309. Phone: (404) 897-7500. Fax: (404) 897-7380. Web Site: www.971jamz.com. Licensee: Cox Radio Inc. Group owner: Cox Broadcasting (acq 8-16-00; grpsl). Format: Urban contemp. News: 3 hrs wkly. Target aud: 35-54; baby boomers. ◆Tony Kidd, gen mgr.

WGGA(AM)— Oct 10, 1941: 1240 khz; 1 kw-U. TL: N34 19 01 W83 49 45. Stereo. Box 10 30503. Secondary address: 1102 Thompson Bridge Rd. N.E. 30501. Phone: (770) 532-9921. Fax: (770) 532-0506. Web Site: www.am1240wgga.com. Licensee: JWJ Properties Inc. Group owner: Jacobs Media Corp. (acq 4-20-93; $360,000;. FTR: 5-10-93). Network: CBS. Format: Sports. News staff: 2; News: 31 hrs wkly. Target aud: 25-54; middle, upper income adults. ◆John W. Jacobs III, CEO & pres; John W. Jacobs Jr., chmn; Jones Andrews, gen mgr; Joel Williams, stn mgr.

WGTJ(AM)—(Murrayville). Nov 1, 1986: 1330 khz; 1 kw-D. TL: N34 22 16 W83 56 47. Box 907038 30503. Secondary address: 1716 Cleveland Hwy. 30501. Phone: (770) 297-7485. Fax: (770) 297-8030. E-mail: mail@glory1330.com. Web Site: www.glory1330.com. Licensee: Vision Communications Inc. (acq 1999; $120,000). Format: Christian music. News staff: one. Target aud: General. ◆Mike Wofford, pres & stn mgr.

WLBA(AM)— Jan 26, 1957: 1130 khz; 10 kw-D. TL: N34 16 45 W83 46 33. Box 746, Austell 30106. Secondary address: 213 Jesse Jewel Pkwy., Austell 30503. Phone: (770) 532-6331. Fax: (770) 532-2672. E-mail: ariel@radiolafavorita.com. Web Site: www.radiolafavorita.com. Licensee: La Favorita Inc. (group owner; acq 2-18-97; $275,000). Format: Sp. ◆Samuel Zamarron, CEO, pres & gen mgr; Ariel Zamarron, stn mgr; Juan Prieto, opns mgr.

WMJE(FM)—See Clarkesville

WYAY(FM)— Apr 3, 1949: 106.7 mhz; 99 kw. 1,400 ft. TL: N34 07 32 W83 51 31. Stereo. 6th Fl., 210 Interstate N., Atlanta 30339. Phone: (404) 521-1007. Fax: (404) 499-1067 (NEWS FAX). Licensee: ABC Radio Atlanta LLC. Group owner: ABC Inc. (acq 7-30-93; grpsl; FTR: 8-23-93). Network: ABC. Rep: ABC Radio Sales. Format: Country. Target aud: 25-54. ◆Steve Mitchell, progmg dir.

Glennville

WOAH(FM)— Nov 18, 1977: 106.3 mhz; 6 kw. Ant 394 ft. TL: N32 00 27 W81 54 51. Stereo. 120C Liberty St., Hinesville 31313. Phone: (912) 408-1063. Fax: (912) 876-6920. E-mail: jimlewis@coastalnow.net. Licensee: Broadcast Executives Corp. (acq 3-29-2002; $250,000). Format: Hip-hop, rhythm and blues. ◆James Lewis, pres & gen mgr.

Gordon

WFXM(FM)—Listing follows WXJO.

WXJO(AM)— Sept 1, 1969: 1120 khz; 10 kw-D, 2.5 kw-CH. TL: N32 50 59 W83 28 38. 6174 Georgia Hwy. 57, Macon 31217. Phone: (478) 745-3301. Phone: (478) 745-1077. Fax: (478) 742-2293. Licensee: Roberts Communication Inc. (group owner; acq 2-14-97; $575,000 with co-located FM). Format: Gospel. ◆Mike Roberts, gen mgr.

WFXM(FM)—Co-owned with WXJO. Mar 30, 1976: 107.1 mhz; 2.25 kw. 541 ft. TL: N32 51 43 W83 21 56. Stereo. E-mail: info@foxie107.com. Web Site: www.foxie107.com. Format: Mainstream urban contemp. Target aud: Middle & upper class Georgians. Spec prog: Jazz 3 hrs wkly.

Gray

WYNF(FM)— January 1994: 96.5 mhz; 7.6 kw. 414 ft. TL: N32 59 03 W83 33 16. Stereo. 7080 Industrial Hwy., Macon 31216. Phone: (478) 781-1063. Fax: (478) 781-6711. Web Site: www.965thebuzz.net. Licensee: AMFM Radio Licenses LLC. Group owner: Clear Channel Communications Inc. (acq 2-1-2001; grpsl). Format: AOR. Target aud: 18-54; adults. ◆Bill Clark, gen mgr.

Grayson

WPLO(AM)—Licensed to Grayson. See Lawrenceville

Greensboro

WDDK(FM)— July 12, 1980: 103.9 mhz; 5.3 kw. 328 ft. TL: N33 28 29 W83 14 46. 1271-B E. Broad St. 30642. Phone: (706) 453-4140. Licensee: Wyche Services Corp. (acq 2-28-2005). Network: ABC. Format: Talk, oldies. News staff: one; News: 4 hrs wkly. Target aud: 24-60. Spec prog: Talk, Atlanta Braves baseball, Univ. of Georgia sports, relg 6 hrs wkly. ◆Chip Lyness, VP & gen mgr; K.B. Travis, opns dir.

Greenville

WIOL(FM)— July 4, 1994: 95.7 mhz; 3.4 kw. Ant 876 ft. TL: N32 50 48 W84 41 27. Box 1998, Columbus 31902. Phone: (706) 576-3565. Fax: (706) 576-3683. Licensee: Davis Broadcasting of Columbus Inc. Group owner: Davis Broadcasting Inc. (acq 11-4-97; $450,000). Network: CBS. McCampbell & Young, P. Format: Classic rock. News

staff: 2; News: 6 hrs wkly. Target aud: 18-49; females 18-35 specifically. ◆Gregory A. Davis, CEO, CFO & gen mgr; Bernie Corcoran, stn mgr.

Griffin

WEKS(FM)—See Zebulon

WHIE(AM)— Dec 15, 1952: 1320 khz; 5 kw-D, 83 w-N. TL: N33 14 30 W84 18 17. 1000 Memorial Dr. 30223. Phone: (770) 227-9451. Fax: (770) 229-2291. E-mail: info@whieam1320.com. Web Site: www.whieam1320.com. Licensee: Chappell Communications L.L.C. (acq 6-30-98; $240,000). Format: Country, news/talk, sports. ◆Robert E. Chappell Jr., pres & gen mgr; D. C. Crawley, stn mgr.

WKEU(AM)— 1933: 1450 khz; 1 kw-U. TL: N33 14 25 W84 14 54. Box 997 30224. Secondary address: 1000 Memorial Dr. 30224. Phone: (770) 227-5507. Fax: (770) 229-2291. E-mail: wkeu@aol.com. Web Site: www.wkeuradio.com. Licensee: WLT & Associates L.P. Network: ABC Information & Entertainment. Rep: Rgnl Reps. Format: Oldies, news. Target aud: 25 plus. ◆William Taylor, pres & gen mgr.

***WMVV(FM)**— Apr 16, 1995: 90.7 mhz; 18 kw. Ant 472 ft. TL: N33 22 12 W84 08 00. Stereo. Box 2020 30224. Secondary address: 100 S. Hill St., Suite 100 30223. Phone: (770) 229-2020. Fax: (770) 229-4820. E-mail: contactus@wmvv.com. Web Site: www.wmvv.com. Licensee: Life Radio Ministries Inc. (acq 1996; $75,000). Format: Relg, Christian. ◆Joseph C. Emert, pres; Douglas J. Doran, VP, gen mgr, dev dir & chief of engrg; James Stewart, opns dir; Glenn Finney, engrg dir.

WPZE(FM)—(Fayetteville). Mar 8, 1966: 97.5 mhz; 8.5 kw. 554 ft. TL: N33 29 22 W84 34 07. (CP: 6.6 kw, ant 636 ft.). Stereo. 75 Piedmont Ave., 10th Floor, Atlanta 30303. Phone: (404) 765-9750. Fax: (404) 688-7686. Web Site: www.praise975.com. Licensee: ROA Licenses LLC. Group owner: Radio One Inc. (acq 11-8-01; grpsl). Network: ABC. Format: Gospel. ◆Mary Catherine Sneed, COO & VP; Wayne Brown, gen mgr & progmg dir.

Hahira

WTHV(AM)— 1990: 810 khz; 2.5 kw-D. TL: N30 52 25 W83 15 07. Stereo. 2352 Jaycee Shack Rd., Valdosta 31602. Phone: (229) 245-9848. Fax: (229) 242-0809. E-mail: wthv810am@yahoo.com. Licensee: Eternal Life Ministries Inc. (acq 8-13-2003; $180,000). Format: Southern gospel. Target aud: 24-55. Spec prog: Spanish 5 hrs wkly. ◆Cody Fender, pres, gen mgr & stn mgr; Phyllis Fender, VP.

Hampton

WHTA(FM)— Oct 19, 1973: 107.9 mhz; 27 kw. Ant 577 ft. TL: N33 29 24 W84 34 07. Stereo. 75 Piedmont Ave., 10th Fl., Atlanta 30303. Phone: (404) 765-9750. Fax: (404) 688-7686. Web Site: www.hot1079atl.com. Licensee: Radio One Licenses LLC. Group owner: Radio One Inc. (acq 8-20-01; $60 million). Format: Hip hop. ◆Wayne Brown, gen mgr.

Hapeville

WWWE(AM)— Jan 7, 1947: 1100 khz; 1 kw-D. TL: N33 36 34 W85 05 13. (CP: COL: Hapeville. 5 kw-D, 3.8 kw-CH. TL: N33 43 43 W84 19 20). 1465 North Side Dr., Suite 218, Atlanta 30318. Phone: (404) 355-8600. Fax: (404) 355-0291. Web Site: www.radiovidaatlanta.org. Licensee: WAEC License L.P. Group owner: Beasley Broadcast Group (acq 10-29-99; $10 million with WAEC(AM) Atlanta). Format: Sp, relg. News staff: one; News: 8 hrs wkly. Target aud: 35 plus; mature audience. Spec prog: Relg 12 hrs, news/talk 14 hrs, East Indian 2 hrs, Ethiopian 2 hrs wkly. ◆George Beasley, chmn; Bruce Beasley, pres; Caroline Beasley, CFO; Brian Beasley, exec VP; Chris Edmonds, gen mgr.

Harlem

WCHZ(FM)— Nov 23, 1992: 95.1 mhz; 5.7 kw. 440 ft. TL: N33 31 34 W82 15 55. Box 211045, Augusta 30917. Secondary address: 432 S. Belair Rd., Martinez 30907. Phone: (706) 855-9494. Fax: (706) 396-7100. Web Site: www.95rock.com. Licensee: WCHZ License LLC Group owner: Beasley Broadcast Group Inc. (acq 1-13-97; $1.2 million). Format: Rock. Target aud: 18-34; well-educated adults, upper demographics. ◆Ken Dunn, gen mgr.

Stations in the U.S.   Georgia

Developers & Brokers of Radio Properties
contact American Media Services at our suite: Philadelphia Marriott Downtown 215-625-2900
843-972-2200
americanmediaservices.com
Charleston, SC
Dallas, TX • Chicago, Il • Austin, TX
American Media Services, LLC

Hartwell

WKLY(AM)— Sept 5, 1947: 980 khz; 1 kw-D, 140 w-N. TL: N34 21 28 W82 58 35. (CP: 149 w-N). Box 636, Bowersville Hwy. 30643. Phone: (706) 376-2233. Phone: (706) 376-3363. Fax: (706) 376-3100. E-mail: wklyradio@hartcom.net. Web Site: www.wklyradio.com. Licensee: WKLY Broadcasting Co. (acq 11-18-88; FTR: 12-19-88). Format: Mainstream country, southern gospel, talk. News staff: 2; News: 18 hrs wkly. Target aud: 30 plus; middle class, working adults. Spec prog: Agriculture 1 hrs wkly. ♦Bruce Hicks, CFO; Bryan Hicks, gen mgr & opns mgr.

Hawkinsville

WCEH(AM)— Dec 11, 1952: 610 khz; 500 w-D. TL: N32 16 50 W83 26 37. Stereo. Box 1398, Hwy. 341 S. 31036. Phone: (478) 892-9061. Fax: (478) 892-9063. Licensee: Staton Broadcasting Inc. (acq 11-12-2003; grpsl). Network: ABC Daytime Direction. Dan Alpert. Format: Pop standards, sports, talk. News staff: 2; News: 30 hrs wkly. Target aud: 35 plus. Spec prog: Sports, farm 10 hrs, relg one hr wkly. ♦John Long, gen mgr; Bill Boys, progmg dir.

WRPG(FM)— Co-owned with WCEH(AM). Sept 26, 1968: 103.9 mhz; 25 kw. Ant 492 ft. TL: N32 16 50 W83 26 31. (CP: Ant 500 ft.). Stereo. 4027 Watson Blvd., Suite 260, Warner Robins 31093. Phone: (478) 971-0103. Fax: (478) 971-2136. Format: News/talk.

Hazlehurst

WVOH(AM)— Sept 6, 1962: 920 khz; 500 w-D, 39 w-N. TL: N31 51 15 W82 34 00. Stereo. Box 645, 546 Baxley Hwy. 31539. Phone: (912) 375-4511. Fax: (912) 375-4512. Licensee: Jeff Davis Broadcasters Inc. Network: USA. Format: Gospel. Spec prog: Farm 2 hrs wkly. ♦Tony DeLoach, gen mgr.

WVOH-FM— Dec 9, 1975: 93.5 mhz; 50 kw. 315 ft. TL: N31 51 15 W82 34 00. Format: Classic country. ♦Tony DeLoach, gen mgr.

Helen

WHEL(FM)— Dec 6, 1993: 105.1 mhz; 1.7 kw. Ant 613 ft. TL: N34 44 55 W83 43 43. Stereo. Box 256, Bruckenstrasse at Edelweiss, Suite 201 30545. Phone: (706) 878-1051. Phone: (800) 725-0932. Fax: (706) 878-1433. E-mail: monikademuth@clearchannel.com. Licensee: Radio Seoul Georgia LLC Group owner: Clear Channel Communications Inc. (acq 7-15-2005). Format: Sp contemp music. Target aud: 25-49. ♦Mike Lawing, chief of opns & chief of engrg; Monica Demuth, gen mgr & prom mgr; Bruce Collins, progmg dir.

*****WTFH(FM)**— February 2001: 89.9 mhz; 10 w. Ant 561 ft. TL: N34 44 55 W83 43 43. Stereo. TFC Radio Network, Box 780, Toccoa Falls 30598. Secondary address: 292 Old Clarksville Hwy., Toccoa Falls 30577. Phone: (706) 282-6030. Phone: (800) 251-8326. Fax: (706) 282-6090. E-mail: tfcm@tfc.edu. Licensee: Toccoa Falls College. Format: Christian. ♦Wayne Gardner, CEO; David Cornelius, gen mgr; Bryan Race, stn mgr; Bob Biermann, chief of engrg.

Hinesville

WGML(AM)— Dec 9, 1958: 990 khz; 250 w-D, 76 w-N. TL: N31 51 01 W81 36 04. Box 615 31310. Secondary address: 308 Rolland St. 31313. Phone: (912) 368-3399. Fax: (912) 368-4191. E-mail: wgml@coastalnow.net. Licensee: Powerhouse of Deliverance Church Inc. (acq 10-12-94; 10-31-94). Borsari & Paxson. Format: Gospel, relg. News: 10 hrs wkly. Target aud: General. Spec prog: One hr wkly. ♦Bishop Raymond Napper, pres; Elder Mary Napper, exec VP; Emanuel White, gen mgr; Sharon Paschal, stn mgr; Lawanna Stewart, opns mgr.

WSGA(FM)— 1994: 104.7 mhz; 12 kw. Ant 469 ft. TL: N31 51 18 W81 44 28. Stereo. Box 29 31310. Secondary address: 120 D Liberty St. 31313. Phone: (912) 368-9258. Fax: (912) 368-5526. E-mail: wssjfm@coastalnwo.net. Web Site: www.freedom1047.com. Licensee: Tama Broadcasting Inc. (group owner; acq 4-8-2004). Format: Adult hits. ♦Yvonne Clark, gen mgr.

WSSJ(FM)— Aug 2, 1982: 92.3 mhz; 50 kw. 482 ft. TL: N31 41 37 W81 23 27. Stereo. Box 29 31310. Secondary address: 120 D Liberty St. 31313. Phone: (912) 368-9258. Fax: (912) 368-5526. E-mail: wssjfm@coastalnow.net. Web Site: www.smoothjazz923.com. Licensee: Tama Radio Licenses of Savannah, GA, Inc. Group owner: Tama Broadcasting Inc. (acq 4-8-2004; $2.79 million). Rep: Rgnl Reps. Miller & Miller. Format: Smooth jazz. News: 2 hrs wkly. Target aud: 25-54; Savannah, Hinesville, Brunswick, 15 county area. ♦Glenn Cherry, pres; Yvonne Clark, gen mgr.

Hogansville

WMGP(FM)— Sept 3, 1992: 98.1 mhz; 25 kw. 328 ft. TL: N33 03 54 W84 57 23. (CP: 25 kw). Box 1114, La Grange 30241. Secondary address: 300 Mooty Bridge Rd., Suite 204, LaGrange 30240. Phone: (706) 882-9699. Phone: (770) 253-9670. Fax: (706) 882-0421. E-mail: magic981@charter.net. Licensee: Citicasters Licenses L.P. Group owner: Clear Channel Communications Inc. (acq 1999; grpsl). David Tillotson. Format: Classic rock. News staff: one; News: 20 hrs wkly. Target aud: 17-64; non-country listeners. ♦Joe Pedicino, gen mgr; Ed Miranda, gen sls mgr; Chris East, progmg dir; Jackie Steele, news dir.

WVCC(FM)— Co-owned with WMGP(FM). Aug 12, 1985: 720 khz; 7.97 kw-D. TL: N33 03 54 W84 57 23. E-mail: newsradio720@charter.net. Rep: Rgnl Reps. Format: News/talk. News staff: one. Target aud: 10 plus; Black. ♦Joe Pedicino, pres.

Homerville

WBTY(FM)— December 1980: 98.7 mhz; 6 kw. Ant 298 ft. TL: N31 02 04 W82 51 50. Stereo. Box 9, Dupont 31630-0009. Secondary address: Intersection of Hwy's 168 & 37 31634. Phone: (912) 487-3412. Fax: (912) 487-3414. Licensee: Southern Broadcasting & Investments. (acq 3-9-90; $100,000; 4-30-90). Format: Classic Hits. Target aud: General. ♦Jim Strickland, opns mgr & chief of engrg; Nancy K. Strickland, pres, gen mgr & gen sls mgr.

Irwinton

WVKX(FM)— September 1995: 103.7 mhz; 3 kw. 328 ft. TL: N32 52 48 W83 11 07. Box 569 31042. Phone: (478) 946-3445. Fax: (478) 946-2406. E-mail: love1037@alltel.net. Licensee: Wilkinson Broadcasting Inc. (acq 8-10-92; $60,000; 8-31-92). Format: Rhythm and blues, gospel, urban contemp. ♦Star Carter, gen mgr.

Jackson

WJGA-FM— Apr 24, 1967: 92.1 mhz; 2.15 kw. Ant 374 ft. TL: N33 16 37 W83 57 59. Stereo. Box 878, 940 Brownlee Rd. 30233. Phone: (770) 775-3151. Fax: (770) 775-3153. Licensee: Earnhart Broadcasting Co. Inc. (acq 8-90; $800,000; 8-27-90). Rep: Keystone (unwired net). Rgnl Reps. Format: Adult contemp, Black. News staff: one; News: 20 hrs wkly. Target aud: General. Spec prog: Gospel 15 hrs wkly. ♦Don Earnhart, pres & gen mgr.

Jasper

*****WNEE(FM)**— 1999: 88.3 mhz; 100 w. 3 ft. TL: N34 28 01 W84 25 49. Stereo. Box 6767, Athens 30604. Phone: (706) 425-1830. Fax: (706) 425-1868. E-mail: communitypublicradio@prodigy.net. Licensee: Community Public Radio Inc. Format: Btfl music, Christian. Target aud: 35-55; upper middle class, educated, Christian. ♦Penny Jackson, pres.

WYYZ(AM)— May 25, 1973: 1490 khz; 1 kw-U. TL: N34 28 32 W84 26 13. Box 280 30143. Phone: (706) 692-4100. Fax: (706) 692-4012. Licensee: Mark Hellinger. (acq 1-1-95; $60,000). Network: CBS. Format: Var/div. ♦Mark Hellinger, pres & gen mgr.

Jefferson

WBKZ(AM)—Licensed to Jefferson. See Athens

Jeffersonville

WPEZ(FM)— Sept 27, 1993: 93.7 mhz; 50 kw. 490 ft. TL: N32 54 49 W83 29 47. Stereo. 544 Mulberry St., Macon 31202. Phone: (478) 746-6286. Fax: (478) 742-8061. Web Site: www.z937.com. Licensee: Cumulus Licensing Corp. Group owner: Cumulus Media Inc. (acq 12-20-02; grpsl). Format: Lite Rock. News: one hr wkly. Target aud: 25-54. ♦Bill Hazen, gen mgr.

Jesup

WIFO-FM—Listing follows WLOP(AM).

WLOP(AM)— July 12, 1949: 1370 khz; 5 kw-D, 36 w-N. TL: N31 36 06 W81 56 00. Box 647 31598. Secondary address: 2420 Waycross Hwy 31545. Phone: (912) 427-3711. Fax: (912) 530-7717. E-mail: butch@bigdogcountry.com. Licensee: Jesup Broadcasting Corp. (group owner; acq 3-31-92). Network: ABC Information & Entertainment. Rep: Rgnl Reps. Format: News/talk, sports. Target aud: General. Spec prog: Farm 5 hrs, gospel 5 hrs wkly. ♦Charles Hubbard Jr., pres & gen mgr.

WIFO-FM—Co-owned with WLOP(AM). July 1, 1968: 105.5 mhz; 25 kw. Ant 308 ft. TL: N31 36 06 W81 56 00. Stereo. Format: Country. Target aud: General.

*****WLPT(FM)**— 1988: 88.3 mhz; 30 kw. 800 ft. TL: N31 40 27 W81 53 12. Stereo. 2278 Wortham Ln, Grovetown 30813. Phone: (706) 309-9609. Fax: (706) 309-9669. E-mail: ctbarinowski@comcast.net. Web Site: www.gnnradio.org. Licensee: Georgia Radio Fellowship. Format: Christian. News: 12 hrs wkly. Target aud: General.

*****WTLD(FM)**— January 2004: 90.5 mhz; 6 kw. Ant 171 ft. TL: N31 35 49 W81 56 14. Box 515, Jessup 31598. Phone: (912) 695-7169. Phone: (912) 588-1821. Fax: (912) 588-1822. E-mail: lsmall7629@aol.com. Licensee: Resurrection House Ministries Inc. Format: Gospel. ♦Dr. Leonard Small, CEO; Marie Butler, gen mgr.

Kingsland

WKBX(FM)— Feb 23, 1987: 106.3 mhz; 6 kw. 330 ft. TL: N30 48 04 W81 40 43. Stereo. Box 2525, 111 N. Grove Blvd. 31548. Phone: (912) 729-6106. Phone: (912) 729-5229. Fax: (912) 729-4106. E-mail: wkbx@k-bay106.com. Web Site: www.k-bay106.com. Licensee: Radio Kings Bay Inc. (acq 7-1-89; $1 million; 5-29-89). Network: ABC. Wolf, Block, Schorr, & Solis-Cohen. Format: Country. News staff: one; News: one hr wkly. Target aud: 18-54; contemp country audience. ♦James Steele, pres & gen mgr; Wendy Steele, exec VP; John Fluery, progmg dir & progmg mgr; Dave Smith, news dir.

La Fayette

WQCH(AM)— November 1954: 1590 khz; 5 kw-D. TL: N34 42 57 W85 16 06. Box 746 30728. Phone: (706) 638-3276. Fax: (706) 638-3896. E-mail: q-country@juno.com. Licensee: Radix Broadcasting Inc. (acq 6-1-88). Network: AP Network News. Rep: Rgnl Reps. Format: Country, news. News staff: one; News: 10 hrs wkly. Target aud: 25 plus. Spec prog: Farm 2 hrs wkly. ♦Rich Gwyn, pres & gen mgr.

La Grange

WALR-FM— Sept 1, 1947: 104.1 mhz; 60 kw. Ant 1,217 ft. TL: N33 24 43 W84 50 03. Stereo. 1601 W. Peachtree St., Atlanta 30309. Phone: (404) 897-7500. Fax: (404) 897-6495. Web Site: www.kiss1041fm.com. Licensee: CXR Holdings L.L.C. Group owner: Cox Broadcasting (acq 8-2000; $280 million). Rep: McGavren Guild. Format: Urban & adult contemp. Target aud: 25-54. ♦Tony Kidd, gen mgr.

Georgia

WELR-FM—See Roanoke, AL

WLAG(AM)— May 1, 1941: 1240 khz; 1 kw-U. TL: N33 02 24 W85 01 27. Box 1429 30241. Secondary address: 304 Broome St. 30240. Phone: (706) 845-1023. Fax: (706) 845-8642. E-mail: wlag@eagle1023.com. Web Site: www.eagle1023.com. Licensee: Eagle's Nest Inc. (group owner; acq 4-3-92; $10; 4-27-92). Format: Sports. News staff: one; News: 4 hrs wkly. Target aud: 25-54; general. Spec prog: Black one hr, gospel 3 hrs, relg 2 hrs wkly. ♦ Jim Vice, gen mgr & stn mgr; Coleman Vice, stn mgr; Kay Vice, opns mgr.

***WOAK(FM)**— June 11, 1984: 90.9 mhz; 3.4 kw. 299 ft. TL: N32 57 57 W84 59 08. 1921 Hamilton Rd. 30241. Phone: (706) 884-2950. Fax: (706) 884-2930. E-mail: info@woak.org. Web Site: www.woak.org. Licensee: Oakside Christian School. Network: USA. Format: Educ, relg. ♦ Rick Varnum, gen mgr; Deena Brand, progmg dir.

WTRP(AM)— Jan 9, 1953: . Stn currently dark 620 khz; 1 kw-D, 127 w-N. TL: N33 03 33 W85 01 40. 806 New Franklin Rd. 30240. Phone: (706) 884-7022. Fax: (706) 884-7806. E-mail: wtrp@charter.net. Web Site: www.WTRP.com. Licensee: Casey Network LLC (group owner; acq 11-13-02). Format: Music of the 50s, 60s & 70s. ♦ Larry Fairall, gen mgr; Glenn Buxton, progmg dir; Brandon Jarrell, news dir; Terry Harper, chief of engrg.

Lakeland

WVGA(FM)— 1994: 105.9 mhz; 6 kw. 328 ft. TL: N31 04 55 W83 10 47. Stereo. 1711 Ellis Dr., Valdosta 31601. Phone: (229) 244-8642. Phone: (229) 241-1059. Fax: (229) 242-7620. E-mail: scottjames@rtgmedia.com. Web Site: www.newstalk1059wvga.com. Licensee: RTG Radio LLC. Group owner: Black Crow Media Group LLC (acq 11-9-2001; grpsl). Format: News/talk. ♦ Robert Ganzak, pres; Robert T. Ganzak, gen mgr; Scott James, stn mgr.

Lawrenceville

WPLO(AM)—(Grayson). Jan 7, 1959: 610 khz; 1.5 kw-D, 225 w-N. TL: N33 57 11 W83 58 15. Stereo. 239 Ezzard St. 30045. Phone: (770) 237-9897. Fax: (770) 237-8769. E-mail: tesquivel@radiomex610atlanta.com. Web Site: www.radiomex610.com. Licensee: Teresa Prieto (acq 6-1-96). Format: Sp, Mexican rgnl music. ♦ Ana I. Esquivel, opns VP & pub affrs dir; Luis E. Garcia, chief of opns & engrg mgr; Marilu Rabago, sls dir & mktg mgr; Teresa Esquivel-Prieto, CEO, pres, stn mgr, gen sls mgr & natl sls mgr; Otto Samayoa, rgnl sls mgr; Mauricio Monreal, news dir.

Leesburg

WJAD(FM)— October 1989: 103.5 mhz; 12.5 kw. 460 ft. TL: N31 39 09 W84 05 20. 1104 W. Broad Ave., Albany 31707. Phone: (229) 888-5000. Fax: (229) 888-5960. Web Site: www.wjad.com. Licensee: Cumulus Licensing Corp. Group owner: Cumulus Media Inc. (acq 7-7-98). Format: Rock. Target aud: 25-40; Generation X, tail end of baby boomers. ♦ Bill Jones, opns mgr.

Louisville

WPEH(AM)— Sept 10, 1960: 1420 khz; 1 kw-D, 159 w-N. TL: N33 00 48 W82 23 33. Box 425, 5442 Middleground Rd. 30434. Phone: (912) 625-7248. Fax: (912) 625-7249. E-mail: wpeh@jeffersonenergy.com. Licensee: Peach Broadcasting Co. Inc. Holland & Knight. Format: Country. News: 11 hrs wkly. Target aud: General. ♦ Ottis G. Stephens, pres, gen mgr & gen sls mgr; Sue Stephens, prom mgr; John D. Reid, mus dir; Wendell F. Stephens, progmg dir, news dir & chief of engrg.

WPEH-FM— May 6, 1971: 92.1 mhz; 3 kw. 296 ft. TL: N33 00 48 W82 23 33. Target aud: 25 plus.

Lumber City

***WMOC(FM)**— April 1997: 88.7 mhz; 50 kw. 210 ft. TL: N31 55 48 W82 41 06. Box 520, 412 Renwick St. 31549. Phone: (912) 363-4502. Fax: (912) 363-2106. E-mail: wmoc887@yahoo.com. Licensee: Full Gospel Church of God Written in Heaven. Format: Southern gospel. ♦ Eddie Conaway, gen mgr & progmg dir.

Lumpkin

WKCN(FM)— Nov 6, 1992: 99.3 mhz; 50 kw. 492 ft. TL: N32 09 25 W85 05 51. Stereo. 1353 13th Ave., Columbus 31901. Phone: (706) 596-9000. Fax: (706) 596-4600. Web Site: www.kissin993.com. Licensee: ABG Georgia LLC. Group owner: Archway Broadcasting Group (acq 4-25-03; grpsl). Rep: Christal. Fletcher, Heald & Hildreth. Format: New hot country. Target aud: 25-54; general. ♦ Chuck Thompson, gen mgr; Bob Quick, opns mgr.

***WTMQ(FM)**—Not on air, target date: unknown: 88.5 mhz; 10 kw. Ant 328 ft. TL: N32 04 07 W84 51 55. Box 9382, Columbus 31908. Licensee: Spanish Cultural Education Inc.

Lyons

WBBT(AM)— Mar 12, 1959: 1340 khz; 1 kw-U. TL: N32 12 50 W82 19 51. Stereo. Box 629, 473 N. Victory Dr. 30436. Phone: (912) 526-8122. Phone: (912) 526-6333. Fax: (912) 526-9155. E-mail: rday@tcbbroadcasting.com. Web Site: www.tcbbroadcasting.com.ABC Classic R&B Licensee: T.C.B. Broadcasting Inc. (acq 6-16-97; $400,000 with co-located FM). Network: ABC. Format: Classic rhythm and blues, Black. News staff: 2; News: 20 hrs wkly. Target aud: General. ♦ Ray Bilbrey, CEO, pres, gen mgr, stn mgr & gen sls mgr; Robin Watson, progmg dir.

WLYU(FM)—Co-owned with WBBT(AM). Jan 1, 1989: 100.9 mhz; 6 kw. Ant 328 ft. TL: N32 06 48 W82 23 52. Stereo. Web Site: www.tcbbroadcasting.com. Format: Modern country. News staff: 3; News: 8 hrs wkly. Target aud: General. ♦ Ralph Trapnell, exec VP; Toni Thompson, opns mgr & sls VP; Ray Bilbrey, chief of engrg.

Mableton

WAMJ(FM)— 2001: 102.5 mhz; 3 kw. Ant 469 ft. TL: N33 41 20 W84 30 38. 75 Piedmont Ave., 10th Fl., Atlanta 30303. Phone: (404) 765-9750. Fax: (404) -688-7686. Web Site: www.classic102.com. Licensee: New Mableton Broadcasting Corp. Group owner: Radio One Inc. (acq 7-8-2004; $31.5 million). Format: Urban oldies. ♦ Wayne Brown, gen mgr.

Macon

WAYS(AM)— August 1967: 1500 khz; 1 kw-D. TL: N32 48 47 W83 37 36. Box 900 31202. Secondary address: 544 Mulberry St., Suite 500 31201. Phone: (478) 745-3383. Fax: (478) 745-9693. Fax: (478) 741-8811. Licensee: Cumulus Licensing Corp. Group owner: Cumulus Media Inc. (acq 12-20-2002; grpsl). Network: Westwood One. Rep: Christal. Format: Country. Target aud: 25-54. ♦ Steve Hazen, exec VP & gen mgr; Vickie Nahum, gen sls mgr; Gerry Marshall, progmg dir; Laura Starling, mus dir; Ken Mann, news dir; Joe Meredith, chief of engrg.

WIFN(FM)—Co-owned with WAYS(AM). June 10, 1968: 105.5 mhz; 6.1 kw. Ant 659 ft. TL: N32 53 48 W83 32 05. Stereo. Phone: (478) 746-6286. Fax: (478) 742-8061. Format: Oldies. ♦ Jim Jones, rgnl sls mgr; David Nolin, mus dir.

***WBKG(FM)**— 2002: 88.9 mhz; 5.5 kw. Ant 502 ft. TL: N32 45 51 W83 33 32. Box Drawer 2440, Tupelo, MS 38803-2440. Phone: (662) 844-8888. Fax: (662) 842-6791. Web Site: www.afr.net. Licensee: American Family Association. Group owner: American Family Radio Format: Adult contemp. ♦ Marvin Sanders, gen mgr; John Riley, progmg dir.

WBML(AM)— Oct 15, 1940: 900 khz; 2 kw-D, 145 w-N. TL: N32 50 58 W83 36 06. Box 6298 31208-6298. Secondary address: 735 Reese St. 31217. Phone: (478) 743-5453. Fax: (478) 743-9265. Licensee: WBML Inc. Group owner: Rodgers Broadcasting Corp. Format: Relg. Target aud: 35 plus. ♦ David A. Rogers, pres.

WDDO(AM)— Nov 25, 1957: 1240 khz; 1 kw-U. TL: N32 50 18 W83 39 02. 544 Mulberry St., Suite 500 31201. Phone: (478) 746-6286. Fax: (478) 742-8061. Fax: (478) 745-4383. Licensee: Cumulus Licensing Corp. Group owner: Cumulus Media Inc. (acq 12-20-02; grpsl). Network: American Urban. Rep: Christal. Format: Black gospel. ♦ Bill Hazen, gen mgr; Jeff Silvers, opns mgr.

WDEN-FM—Listing follows WMAC(AM).

WIBB-FM—(Fort Valley). Mar 3, 1993: 97.9 mhz; 10.5 kw. 499 ft. TL: N32 34 12 W83 45 26. Stereo. 7080 Industrial Hwy. 31216. Phone: (478) 781-1063. Fax: (478) 781-6711. Web Site: www.wibb.com. Licensee: AMFM Radio Licenses LLC. Group owner: Clear Channel Communications Inc. (acq 2-15-2001; grpsl). Format: Urban contemp. News staff: one; News: 14 hrs wkly. Target aud: 18-44. ♦ Lowery Mays, pres; Rick Humphrey, VP & gen mgr; Jerry Kersting, stn mgr; Carl Strandell, sls VP & sls dir; Carey Brown, gen sls mgr; Tammy Vaughan, natl sls mgr; Mike Williams, progmg dir; James Gay, chief of engrg.

WLCG(AM)— November 1948: 1280 khz; 5 kw-D, 99 w-N. TL: N32 48 16 W83 36 16. 7080 Industrial Hwy. 31216-7538. Phone: (478) 781-1063. Fax: (478) 781-6711. E-mail: ccw@clearchannel.com. Licensee: AMFM Radio Licenses LLC. Group owner: Clear Channel Communications Inc. (acq 2-15-2001; grpsl). Rep: Clear Channel. Format: Black gospel. Target aud: General. ♦ John Hogan, CEO; Lowery Mays, chmn; Randy Michaels, pres; Jerry Kersting, CFO; Bill Clark, gen mgr; Erich West, opns mgr; Chris Williams, progmg dir.

WLZN(FM)— August 1992: 92.3 mhz; 3 kw. 328 ft. TL: N32 46 26 W83 38 15. Box 500 31202. Secondary address: 544 Mulberry St., Suite 500 31201. Phone: (478) 746-6286. Fax: (478) 742-8061. Licensee: Cumulus Licensing Corp. Group owner: Cumulus Media Inc. (acq 12-20-2002; grpsl). Format: Hip hop rhythm and blues. News: one hr wkly. ♦ Bill Hazen, gen mgr; Brian Rayes, progmg dir; Joe Meredith, engrg VP & chief of engrg.

WMAC(AM)— Oct 30, 1922: 940 khz; 50 kw-D, 10 kw-N, DA-N. TL: N32 53 06 W83 43 50. Stereo. Box 900 31202. Secondary address: 544 Mulberry St., Suite 500 31201. Phone: (478) 746-6286. Fax: (478) 742-8061. Licensee: Cumulus Licensing Corp. Group owner: Cumulus Media Inc. (acq 12-20-02; grpsl). Network: ABC Daytime Direction. Rep: McGavren Guild. Format: News/talk, sports. News staff: 2; News: 40 hrs wkly. Target aud: 40 plus; upscale, college educated, household income $50K plus. Spec prog: Relg 4 hrs wkly. ♦ Bill Hazen, gen mgr; Beth Edmonson, prom mgr; Kenny Burgamy, progmg dir; Ken Mann, news dir; Joe Meredith, chief of engrg.

WDEN-FM—Co-owned with WMAC(AM). Feb 17, 1947: 99.1 mhz; 100 kw. Ant 581 ft. TL: N32 45 51 W83 33 32. Stereo. Network: ABC FM Connection. Rep: Christal. Format: Country. News staff: one; News: 4 hrs wkly. Target aud: 25-54; female/male split, median age 37. ♦ Gerry Marshall, progmg dir; Laura Starling, mus dir.

WMWR(AM)—See Dry Branch

WNEX(AM)— April 1945: 1400 khz; 1 kw-U. TL: N32 51 07 W83 39 12. 1691 Forsyth St. 31201. Phone: (478) 745-5858. Fax: (478) 745-0500. E-mail: phil@upga.tv. Web Site: www.radiodisney.com. Licensee: Radio Peach Inc. (acq 1-31-00). Network: Radio Disney. Format: Children. ♦ Lowell Register, CEO & pres; Debbie Hart, gen mgr; Bob Clark, stn mgr.

WNNG(AM)—See Warner Robins

WQBZ(FM)—(Fort Valley). Apr 6, 1981: 106.3 mhz; 50 kw. 426 ft. TL: N32 45 31 W83 44 49. Stereo. 7080 Industrial Hwy. 31216. Phone: (478) 781-1063. Fax: (478) 781-6711. Web Site: www.q106.fm. Licensee: AMFM Radio Licenses LLC. Group owner: Clear Channel Communications Inc. (acq 2-15-2001; grpsl). Format: Classic rock. Target aud: 18-49. ♦ Lowery Mays, pres; Bill Clark, VP & gen mgr.

WRBV(FM)—See Warner Robins

Madison

WYTH(AM)— June 1955: 1250 khz; 1 kw-D. TL: N33 34 45 W83 28 40. 1281 Eatonton Rd. 30650. Phone: (706) 342-1250. Fax: (706) 342-1752. Licensee: Central Georgia Broadcasting Co. (acq 9-1-59). Format: News/talk, oldies. News staff: one; News: 15 hrs wkly. Target aud: General. Spec prog: Farm 15 hrs, class one hr, Black 13 hrs, talk 15 hrs wkly. ♦ Pamala Bryan, pres & gen mgr; Richard Bryan, stn mgr.

Manchester

WFDR(AM)—Listing follows WVFJ-FM.

WVFJ-FM— 1967: 93.3 mhz; 100 kw. 1,250 ft. TL: N32 50 40 W84 37 25. Stereo. 120 Peachtree E. Shopping Ctr., Peachtree City 30269. Phone: (770) 487-4500. Fax: (770) 486-6400. Web Site: www.j933.com. Licensee: Provident Broadcasting Co. (acq 8-81; $790,000 with co-located AM; 9-7-81). Rep: Rgnl Reps. Brown, Nietert & Kaufman. Format: Contemporary, Christian. Target aud: 25-45. ♦ Rick Davison, gen mgr & opns mgr; Jeanette Rader, gen sls mgr; Don Schaeffer, progmg mgr; Tiffany Thorpe, news dir; Brian Chin, chief of engrg.

Stations in the U.S. — Georgia

WFDR(AM)—Co-owned with WVFJ-FM. June 1957: 1370 khz; 1 kw-D. TL: N32 53 14 W84 35 54. Box 510 31816. Target aud: 35-65. Co-owned TV: WSB-TV affil

Marietta

WFOM(AM)— Oct 13, 1946: 1230 khz; 1 kw-U. TL: N33 55 38 W84 30 08. 3535 Piedmont Rd., Bldg. 14, Suite 1200, Atlanta 30305. Phone: (404) 688-0068. Fax: (404) 995-4045. E-mail: jimmypowers@680thefan.com. Web Site: www.talkradio1340.com. Licensee: Dickey Broadcasting Co. (group owner; acq 8-31-00; grpsl). Network: Network: CBS Radio, Sporting News Radio Network, Westwood One. Rep: McGavren Guild. Holland & Knight. Format: Talk. News staff: 2; News: 10 hrs wkly. Target aud: 25-64. Spec prog: Notre Dame football (fall). ♦David Dickey, gen mgr; Jimmy Powers, opns dir; Lee Killian, sls dir; John Devinson, mktg dir; John Levinson, prom dir.

WFTD(AM)— Nov 14, 1955: 1080 khz; 10 kw-D, DA. TL: N34 01 25 W84 40 04. 2865 Amwiler Rd., Suite 650, Doraville 30360. Phone: (770) 825-0095. Fax: (770) 246-0054. Licensee: Prieto Enterprises Inc. (acq 12-20-01). David Tillotson. Format: Spanish. Target aud: 21-45. ♦Filiberto Prieto, pres & gen mgr.

WKHX-FM—Licensed to Marietta. See Atlanta

Martinez

WKDG(FM)— May 31, 1984: 93.9 mhz; 25 kw. 328 ft. TL: N33 26 17 W82 05 19. Stereo. 4051 Jimmie Dyess Pkwy., Augusta 30909. Phone: (706) 396-7000. Fax: (706) 396-7100. Web Site: www.bigdoglive.com. Licensee: WGOR License LLC. (acq 11-10-92; $810,000;. FTR: 11-30-92). Format: Legendary country. Target aud: 25 plus. ♦Kent Dunn, VP; Coni Samson, gen mgr; T. Gentry, opns dir.

WPRW-FM— 1994: 107.7 mhz; 50 kw. 492 ft. TL: N33 38 35 W82 19 50. 2743 Perimeter Pky., Bldg. 100, Suite 200, Augusta 30909. Phone: (706) 396-6000. Fax: (706) 396-6010. Web Site: www.power107.net. Licensee: Clear Channel Comm. Group owner: Cumulus Media Inc. (acq 6-30-97; grpsl). Format: Urban Contemp. ♦Barry Kaye, gen mgr.

McDonough

WKKP(AM)— Apr 2, 1979: 1410 khz; 2.5 kw-D. TL: N33 25 47 W84 07 52. Box 878, Jackson 30233. Secondary address: 940 Brownlee Rd., Jackson 30233. Phone: (770) 504-8410. Fax: (770) 775-3153. Licensee: Henry County Radio Co. Inc. (acq 3-30-92; $65,000;. FTR: 4-20-92). Rep: Rgnl Reps. Format: Gospel. News: 20 hrs wkly. Target aud: General. ♦Susanne Earnhart, pres; Don Earnhardt, gen mgr; Tom Lynde, opns dir.

McRae

WYIS(AM)— July 27, 1957: 1410 khz; 1 kw-D. TL: N32 03 25 W82 51 56. Box 247, Hwy. 341 S. 31055. Phone: (229) 868-5611. Fax: (229) 868-7552. Licensee: Cinecom Broadcasting Systems Inc. (acq 8-31-99; $220,000 with co-located FM). Network: ABC Information & Entertainment. Rep: Rgnl Reps. Format: Oldies. Target aud: 25-50; mature, wage earners. Spec prog: Black 4 hrs wkly. ♦Jimmy Hussey, gen mgr.

WYSC(FM)—Co-owned with WYIS(AM). Aug 3, 1979: 102.7 mhz; 3 kw. 289 ft. TL: N32 03 25 W82 51 56.

Metter

WBMZ(FM)—Listing follows WHCG(AM).

WHCG(AM)— Dec 22, 1961: 1360 khz; 1 kw-D. TL: N32 23 56 W82 02 36. Box 238 30439. Secondary address: 1075 E. Lillian St. 30439. Phone: (912) 685-2136. Fax: (912) 685-2137. Web Site: www.wbmzfm.com. Licensee: Radio Metter Inc. Reddy, Begley & McCormick. Format: Southern gospel. Target aud: General. Spec prog: Gospel 4 hrs wkly. ♦Jimmy Page, pres, gen mgr & gen sls mgr.

WBMZ(FM)—Co-owned with WHCG(AM). Aug 1, 1971: 103.7 mhz; 3 kw. 299 ft. TL: N32 23 56 W82 02 36. Stereo. Format: Classic hits. Target aud: General. ♦Jimmy Page, CEO.

Midway

WGCO(FM)—Licensed to Midway. See Savannah

Milan

WMCG(FM)— 1982: 104.9 mhz; 36 kw. Ant 564 ft. TL: N32 07 16 W83 16 05. Stereo. Box 130, Dublin 31040-0130. Phone: (478) 272-4422. Fax: (478) 274-4657. Licensee: Tel-Dodge Broadcasting Inc. Network: ABC Information & Entertainment. Format: Country. Target aud: 25-54; mature country fans. Spec prog: Farm one hr wkly. ♦Mac Davis, gen mgr.

Milledgeville

*WGUR(FM)— August 1975: 88.9 mhz; 38 w. 110 ft. TL: N33 04 44 W83 13 55. (CP: 91.9 mhz). Box 3124, Georgia State University 31061. Phone: (912) 445-4101. Phone: (912) 445-4102. Fax: (912) 445-1483. Licensee: Georgia College. (acq 8-75). Format: Alternative. Target aud: 18-24; college students. Spec prog: Jazz 12 hrs, class 7 hrs, gospel 10 hrs wkly. ♦Billy Johnson, gen mgr.

WKGQ(AM)— Mar 6, 1975: 1060 khz; 1 kw-D. TL: N33 05 45 W83 11 36. Box 832 31061. Secondary address: 156 Lake Laurel Rd. 31061. Phone: (478) 453-9406. Fax: (478) 453-3298. E-mail: 297mail@yahoo.com. Licensee: Southern Stone Broadcasting Inc. (acq 7-6-2005; $1.1 million with WMGZ(FM) Eatonton). Format: Urban gospel. Target aud: 25 plus. ♦Tom Ptak, pres, gen mgr & opns mgr.

WKZR(FM)—Listing follows WMVG(AM).

WLRR(FM)— July 24, 1990: 100.7 mhz; 3 kw. 328 ft. TL: N33 06 50 W83 13 08. Box 3965, Eatonton 31024. Phone: (706) 485-8792. Fax: (706) 485-3555. Licensee: Preston W. Small. Format: Adult standards. Target aud: 18-35. ♦Craig Baker, gen mgr & opns VP.

WMVG(AM)— Mar 29, 1946: 1450 khz; 1 kw-U. TL: N33 04 58 W83 15 01. Box 519, 1250 W. Charlton St. 31061. Phone: (478) 452-0586. Fax: (478) 452-5886. Licensee: WMVG Inc. (acq 7-8-99; $258,230 for 80% with co-located FM). Network: ABC Information & Entertainment. Rep: Rgnl Reps. Format: Sports, news. News staff: one; News: 25 hrs wkly. Target aud: 18-49. Spec prog: Black 4 hrs wkly. ♦Randy Beasley, pres & gen mgr.

WKZR(FM)—Co-owned with WMVG(AM). June 30, 1966: 102.3 mhz; 3.3 kw. 300 ft. TL: N33 04 58 W83 15 01. Stereo. Format: Country.

Millen

WHKN(FM)— Dec 4, 1989: 94.9 mhz; 14.5 kw. 400 ft. TL: N32 43 57 W81 51 43. Stereo. 35 E. Main St., Statesboro 30458. Phone: (912) 764-1029. Fax: (912) 489-3959. E-mail: radiocenter@frontiernet.net. Licensee: Staton Broadcasting Inc. (group owner; acq 11-12-2003; grpsl). Network: ABC. Dan Alpert. Format: Country. News staff: one; News: 8 hrs wkly. Target aud: 25-54; adults. Spec prog: Farm 10 hrs, relg 2 hrs wkly. ♦Cecil Staton, pres; John Long, sr VP; Jeff Anderson, gen mgr; Mike Mull, news dir.

Monroe

WKUN(AM)— Feb 4, 1971: 1490 khz; 1 kw-U. TL: N33 48 37 W83 42 01. Box 649 30655. Secondary address: 1610 Launius Rd., Good Hope 30641. Phone: (770) 267-0923. Fax: (706) 342-8135. Licensee: B.R. Anderson Sr. dba Radio Station WKUN (acq 6-96). Format: Southern gospel. News: 3 hrs wkly. Target aud: 25-65. ♦B. R. Anderson Sr., pres; Melanie Jackson, gen mgr.

Montezuma

WMGB(FM)— Aug 10, 2001: 95.1 mhz; 46 kw. 390 ft. TL: N32 33 20 W83 44 14. Stereo. 544 Mulberry St., Suite 500, Macon 31201. Phone: (478) 746-6286. Fax: (478) 742-8061. Web Site: www. all the hitsB951.com. Licensee: Cumulus Licensing Corp. Group owner: Cumulus Media Inc. (acq 12-20-02; grpsl). Network: Westwood One. Format: CHR. ♦Bill Hazen, gen mgr.

WMNZ(AM)— Nov 29, 1961: 1050 khz; 250 w-D, 42 w-N. TL: N32 17 58 W84 01 34. (CP: TL: N32 17 53 W84 02 02). Box 610 31063. Secondary address: 115 1/2 Cherry St. 31063. Phone: (478) 472-8386. Fax: (478) 472-8296. Licensee: Macon County Broadcasting Co. Format: Country, oldies, gospel. ♦Danny Blizzard, pres & gen mgr.

Morrow

WSSA(AM)— November 1956: 1570 khz; 5 kw-D, 50 w-N. TL: N33 36 05 W84 18 40. 2424 Old Rex Morrow Rd., Ellenwood 30296. Phone: (404) 361-1570. Fax: (404) 366-9772. Web Site: www.wssathelight1570am.com. Licensee: South Atlanta Broadcasting Inc. (acq 9-23-98; $380,000 for stock). Format: Gospel, Christian. Target aud: 24-55. ♦Paul Ploener, gen mgr; Leah St. Cyr, stn mgr.

Moultrie

WHBS(AM)— 2002: 1400 khz; 1 kw-U. TL: N31 09 56 W83 46 01. 1643 South Blvd. 31768. Phone: (229) 890-2900. Fax: (229) 890-1497. Licensee: Sailor Broadcasting of Georgia Inc. (acq 3-3-2005; $195,000). ♦W. Ron Sailor, gen mgr; Marion Sailor, gen sls mgr.

WMTM(AM)— Nov 10, 1953: 1300 khz; 5 kw-D. TL: N31 12 54 W83 47 13. Stereo. Box 788 31776. Secondary address: 100 WMTM Rd. 31768. Phone: (229) 985-1300. Fax: (229) 890-0905. Licensee: Colquitt Broadcasting Co. L.L.C. Network: ABC News/Talk. Rep: Rgnl Reps. Smithwick & Belendiuk. Format: Southern gospel. News staff: one. Target aud: General. Spec prog: Farm 16 hrs wkly. ♦Jim Turner, pres & gen mgr.

WMTM-FM— Nov 17, 1964: 93.9 mhz; 100 kw. 555 ft. TL: N31 12 54 W83 47 13. Stereo. Format: Oldies. ♦Jim Turner, opns mgr & mktg mgr.

Mount Vernon

WYUM(FM)— Aug 3, 1998: 101.7 mhz; 6 kw. 325 ft. TL: N32 12 44 W82 27 48. Box 900, Vidalia 30475. Phone: (912) 537-9202. Fax: (912) 537-4477. E-mail: zfowler@vidaliacommunications.com. Web Site: www.vidaliacommunications.com. Licensee: Vidalia Communications Corp. (group owner) Rgnl Reps. Format: Country. Target aud: 25-49. ♦John Ladson III, pres; Zack Fowler, gen mgr; Collins Knightor, opns dir.

Mountain City

WALH(AM)— May 1, 1986: 1340 khz; 1 kw-U. TL: N34 56 16 W83 23 27. Box F 30562. Phone: (706) 746-2256. Fax: (706) 746-2259. E-mail: walh@alltel.net. Web Site: www.wolfcreekbroadcasting.com. Licensee: Mountain City Broadcasting Inc. (acq 1-19-2005; $275,000). Format: Country, bluegrass, gospel. Target aud: 30-50; blue collar. Spec prog: Farm 2 hrs wkly. ♦A.D. Frazier Jr., pres; Rebecca St. John, gen mgr; Loraine Savage, progmg dir; W.L. Savage, gen sls mgr, mus dir & news dir; E.O. Holden, chief of engrg.

Murrayville

WGTJ(AM)—Licensed to Murrayville. See Gainesville

Nashville

WJYF(FM)—Licensed to Nashville. See Tifton

Georgia
Directory of Radio

Newnan

WCOH(AM)— December 1947: 1400 khz; 1 kw-U. TL: N33 21 53 W84 48 42. 154 Boone Dr. 30263. Phone: (770) 252-3509. Phone: (770) 683-7234. Fax: (770) 683-9846. E-mail: wcoh@charter.net. Web Site: www.wcoh.com. Licensee: Citicasters Licenses L.P. Group owner: Clear Channel Communications Inc. (acq 5-4-99; grpsl). Miller & Miller, P.C. Format: Classic country. Target aud: 25-54. ♦Joe Pedicino, gen mgr.

WNEA(AM)— Apr 18, 1962: 1300 khz; 1 kw-D. TL: N33 22 31 W84 47 08. 8451 South Cherokee Blvd., Suite B, Douglasville 30134. Phone: (770) 920-1520. Fax: (770) 920-4600. Web Site: www.wordchristianbroadcasting.com. Licensee: Word Christian Broadcasting Inc. (acq 2-28-96; 3-11-96). Format: Christian. Target aud: 18-64. Spec prog: Black, relg, gospel 15 hrs wkly. ♦Ken Johns, CEO, gen mgr & opns dir.

North Atlanta

WCNN(AM)—Licensed to North Atlanta. See Atlanta

Ochlocknee

WJEP(AM)— June 4, 1984: 1020 khz; 10 kw-D. TL: N30 54 00 W83 59 55. Box 90, Thomasville 31799. Secondary address: 540 Daisy Ln., Thomasville 31792. Phone: (229) 228-5683. Fax: (229) 228-0398. E-mail: wjep@rose.net. Web Site: www.lifelineministries.com. Licensee: Lifeline Ministries Inc. (acq 8-18-83). Network: UPI. Format: Christian contemp. Spec prog: Black 2 hrs, southern gospel 3 hrs wkly. ♦Henry Miller, pres & progmg dir.

Ocilla

WDMG-FM— December 1983: 97.7 mhz; 3.7 kw. Ant 417 ft. TL: N31 31 40 W83 20 01. (CP: COL Ambrose. 97.9 mhz; 3 kw, ant 316 ft. TL: N31 31 51 W82 54 34). Stereo. 232 No. Central Ave., Tifton 31794. Phone: (229) 386-9898. Fax: (229) 386-9866. Licensee: RTG Radio LLC. Group owner: Black Crow Media Group LLC (acq 11-9-2001; grpsl). Network: Network: ABC, Jones Radio Networks. Format: Oldies. ♦Bob Granzak, CEO; John Higgs, pres, gen mgr & stn mgr; Danny Hogan, opns dir; Jan Kicklighter, sls dir & gen sls mgr; Jay Matthews, progmg dir; Tony Mooney, chief of engrg.

WLPF(FM)— December 1993: 98.5 mhz; 2.3 kw. 521 ft. TL: N31 28 11 W83 14 11. Stereo. 2278 Wortham Ln., Grovetown 30813. Phone: (706) 309-9610. Fax: (706) 736-9669. E-mail: ctbarinowski@comcast.net. Web Site: www.gnnradio.org. Licensee: Barinowski Investment Co., a Georgia L.P. Group owner: Good News Network (acq 11-17-92; for CP; FTR: 12-7-92). Format: Christian. News: 12 hrs wkly. Target aud: General. ♦Clarence Barinowski, gen mgr.

Omega

WTIF-FM— April 1993: 107.5 mhz; 1.8 kw. 400 ft. TL: N31 27 17 W83 33 37. Box 968, Tifton 31793. Phone: (229) 382-1340. Fax: (229) 386-8658. Licensee: Three Trees Communications Inc. (group owner; acq 3-29-2004; grpsl). Format: Country. News staff: 6; News: 5 hrs wkly. Target aud: 18 plus. ♦Chris Beckham, pres & gen mgr.

Pavo

*****WVRI(FM)**— 2005: 90.5 mhz; 1 w horiz, 50 w vert. Ant 292 ft vert. TL: N31 09 26 W83 22 28. Air 1 Radio Network, 5700 W. Oaks Blvd., Rocklin, CA 95765. Phone: (916) 251-1600. Fax: (916) 251-1650. E-mail: info@air1.com. Web Site: www.air1.com. Licensee: Educational Media Foundation. Group owner: EMF Broadcasting. (acq 1-7-2004). Network: Air 1. Format: Christian. ♦Joe Miller, CFO; Keith Whipple, gen mgr.

Peachtree City

WVVA(FM)— 1948: 96.7 mhz; 1 kw. Ant 545 ft. TL: N33 26 22 W84 42 42. Stereo. 1819 Peachtree Rd. N.E., Suite 700, Atlanta 30309. Phone: (404) 367-0640. Fax: (404) 367-1055. E-mail: roach@buzzatlanta.com. Web Site: www.wild967.com. Licensee: Citicasters Licenses L.P. Group owner: Clear Channel Communications Inc. (acq 5-4-99; grpsl). Miller & Miller. Format: Rock/AOR. Target aud: 25-54. ♦Joe Pedicino, VP & gen mgr; Mike Copeland, sls dir & prom dir; Matt Bailey, progmg dir; Tom Taylor, chief of engrg.

Pearson

WPNG(FM)— August 1999: 101.9 mhz; 12.9 kw. Ant 459 ft. TL: N31 19 36 W82 51 54. Stereo. 2232 Old Douglas Hwy. 31642. Phone: (912) 422-6122. Fax: (912) 422-7840. E-mail: freedom1019@planttel.net. Web Site: www.hitsandfavorites.com. Licensee: KM Radio of Pearson L.L.C. Group owner: KM Communications Inc. (acq 5-3-99). Cohen, Dipple & Everist. Format: Adult contemp. Target aud: 25-49; women ages 25-49. ♦Myoung Hwa Bae, pres; Kevin Bae, gen mgr; Connie McCarty, stn mgr.

Pelham

WQLI(FM)— Sept 8, 2000: 92.3 mhz; 6 kw. 247 ft. TL: N31 04 50 W84 09 33. 2586 Old Pelham Rd. 31779. Phone: (229) 294-1909. Licensee: Mitchell County Television. Format: Adult contemp.

WQVE(FM)—See Camilla

Perry

WPGA(AM)— 1955: 980 khz; 5 kw-D, 270 w-N. TL: N32 26 40 W83 45 00. Stereo. 1691 Forsyth St., Macon 31201. Phone: (478) 745-5858. Fax: (478) 745-5800. Web Site: www.58abc.com. Licensee: Register Communications Inc. (acq 1996). Format: Children. News staff: one. Target aud: Children up to 12. ♦Debbie Hart, gen mgr; Loel Register, pres & gen sls mgr.

WPGA-FM— May 3, 1966: 100.9 mhz; 3 kw. 345 ft. TL: N32 33 20 W83 44 14. (CP: 2.15 kw, ant 551 ft.). Stereo. Phone: (478) 745-5500. Web Site: www.58abc.com. Format: Adult contemp. News staff: one. ♦Kristy Turner, gen sls mgr. Co-owned TV: WPGA-TV affil

Port Wentworth

*****WLFS(FM)**— 2001: 91.9 mhz; 6 kw. Ant 180 ft. TL: N32 09 17 W81 09 55. 5859 Abeerorn St., Suite 3, Savannah, SC 31405. Phone: (912) 353-9226. Fax: (912) 353-9325. Web Site: www.hisradio.com. Licensee: Radio Training Network Inc. Format: Christian contemp. ♦Allen Henderson, gen mgr.

Quitman

WSFB(AM)— Nov 19, 1955: 1490 khz; 1 kw-U. TL: N30 46 51 W83 34 30. Box 632 31643. Phone: (229) 263-4373. Fax: (229) 263-7693. Licensee: Jim Chion Productions. Format: Adult standards. Target aud: 30+. ♦Jim Chion, pres, gen mgr & opns dir.

WSTI-FM— Sept 12, 1986: 105.3 mhz; 3 kw. 300 ft. TL: N30 48 45 W83 31 18. Stereo. 2622 Madison Hwy., Valdosta 31601. Phone: (229) 244-8642. Fax: (229) 242-7620. Licensee: RTG Radio L.L.C. Group owner: Black Crow Media Group LLC (acq 6-4-2004; $3.4 million. with WXHT(FM) Madison, FL). Format: Adult contemp. Target aud: 25-54; white collar. Spec prog: Farm 5 hrs wkly. ♦Scott James, gen mgr.

Reidsville

WRBX(FM)—Listing follows WTNL(AM).

WTNL(AM)— June 25, 1976: 1390 khz; 500 w-D. TL: N32 05 14 W82 07 47. Box 69 30453. Secondary address: 125 Friartuck Cir. 30453. Phone: (912) 557-3777. Fax: (912) 557-6956. Licensee: WRBX/WTNL L.L.C. (acq 3-93; $35,000. with co-located FM; FTR: 2-15-93). Network: USA. Format: Southern gospel, talk. Target aud: General. ♦Truman Blankenship III, CEO; Larry Montgomery, pres; Gregory J. Lemon, VP, gen mgr, gen sls mgr & adv dir; Dawn Lemon, progmg dir; Bob Moughton, engrg VP & chief of engrg.

WRBX(FM)—Co-owned with WTNL(AM). July 1993: 104.1 mhz; 3 kw. 187 ft. TL: N32 05 14 W82 07 47. Network: USA. Target aud: 8 plus; religious. ♦Gregory J. Lemon, mus dir; Bob Moughton, chief of engrg.

Richmond Hill

WRHQ(FM)— May 13, 1991: 105.3 mhz; 11 kw. 485 ft. TL: N32 02 52 W81 07 26. Stereo. 1102 E. 52nd St., Savannah 31404. Phone: (912) 234-1053. Fax: (912) 354-6600. E-mail: qualityrock@wrhq.com. Web Site: www.wrhq.com. Licensee: Thoroughbred Communications Inc. Group owner: Thoroughbred Communications Rep: Christal. Shook,

Hardy & Bacon. Format: Rock, adult contemp. News: 2 hrs wkly. Target aud: 25-44; affluent. ♦Jerry Rogers, pres, gen mgr, gen sls mgr & adv mgr; Ray Williams, rgnl sls mgr & prom mgr; Keith Hendrix, progmg dir; Lyndy Brannan, pub affrs dir; Marty Foglia, chief of engrg.

Ringgold

WMPZ(FM)—Licensed to Ringgold. See Chattanooga TN

WTUN(FM)— March 1989: 101.9 mhz; 1.32 kw. Ant 702 ft. TL: N34 58 11 W85 05 10. 7413 Old Lee Hwy., Chattanooga, TN 37421. Phone: (423) 892-3333. Fax: (423) 553-9490. Licensee: Clear Channel Broadcasting Licenses Inc. Group owner: Clear Channel Communications Inc. (acq 10-1-2000; $2.5 milion). Format: Classic rock. ♦Sammy George, gen mgr.

Rockmart

WTSH-FM— August 1989: 107.1 mhz; 45 kw. Ant 518 ft. TL: N34 15 03 W84 59 05. 20 John Davenport Dr., Rome 3016s. Phone: (706) 232-3160. Licensee: Woman's World Broadcasting Inc. (acq 11-14-2003; $5.4 million). Format: Country. Target aud: 25-54. ♦Randy Quick, gen mgr.

WZOT(AM)— Aug 28, 1959: 1220 khz; 500 w-D, 150 w-N. TL: N34 00 14 W85 03 22. 602 W. Elm St. 30153. Phone: (770) 684-7848. Fax: (770) 684-7848. Licensee: Triple J's Broadcasting LLC (acq 9-1-2004; $346,804. with WGJK(AM) Rome). Format: Southern gospel. Target aud: 18-45. ♦Paul Stone, pres; Ned Ingle, stn mgr.

Rome

WGJK(AM)— Aug 1, 1962: 1360 khz; 500 w-D, 150 w-N. TL: N34 16 15 W85 11 00. Box 746 30162. Secondary address: 98 E. Callahan St. 30161. Fax: (706) 232-3160. Licensee: Triple J's Broadcasting LLC (acq 9-1-2004; $346,804. with WZOT(AM) Rockmart). Format: Classic country. News staff: one. Target aud: 25-54. Spec prog: Black gospel 19 hrs wkly. ♦Gregory Kamishlian, pres & gen mgr.

WKCX(FM)— May 22, 1965: 97.7 mhz; 25 kw. 790 ft. TL: N34 14 00 W85 14 02. Stereo. Box 1546 30162. Secondary address: 710 Turner McCall Blvd. 30165. Phone: (706) 291-9766. Fax: (706) 291-9706. E-mail: k98@k98radio.com. Web Site: www.k98radio.com. Licensee: Briar Creek Broadcasting Corp. (acq 5-85). Network: Network: Jones Radio Networks, CNN Radio. Rep: Rgnl Reps. Richard F. Swift. Format: Adult contemp. News staff: one; News: 10 hrs wkly. Target aud: 18-54; family-oriented, active in the community. ♦A. Mills Fitzner, pres & gen mgr.

WLAQ(AM)— 1947: 1410 khz; 1 kw-U, DA-N. TL: N34 15 43 W85 12 22. 2 Mount Alto Rd. 30165. Phone: (706) 232-7767. Fax: (706) 295-9225. E-mail: wlaq1410am@hotmail.com. Web Site: www.wlaq.com. Licensee: Cripple Creek Broadcasting Co. (acq 4-1-87). Network: CBS. Format: News/talk, sports. ♦Randy Davis, pres & gen mgr; Sandy Davis, exec VP.

WQTU(FM)—Listing follows WRGA(AM).

WRGA(AM)— November 1929: 1470 khz; 5 kw-U, DA-N. TL: N34 18 05 W85 09 19. Box 6008 30162. Secondary address: 20 John Davenport Rd. 30162. Phone: (706) 291-9496. Fax: (706) 235-7107. E-mail: south107@aol.com. Licensee: McDougald Broadcasting Corp. Group owner: Southern Broadcasting Companies Inc. (acq 1-28-2002; $1.6 million. with co-located FM). Network: ABC Information & Entertainment. Fletcher, Heald & Hildreth. Format: News/talk. News staff: 2; News: 168 hrs wkly. Target aud: General; upscale, involved, upwardly mobile. ♦Paul Stone, pres; Gregory Kamishlian, gen mgr; Randy Quick, stn mgr, sls dir & news dir; Brian Landrum, opns mgr; Rosemary Ringer, prom mgr; Doug Walker, news dir; Randy Rhodes, chief of engrg.

WQTU(FM)—Co-owned with WRGA(AM). May 2, 1966: 102.3 mhz; 6 kw. 804 ft. TL: N34 14 02 W85 13 50. Stereo. E-mail: q102rome@q102rome.com. Web Site: www.q102rome.com. Format: Adult contemp. News staff: one; News: 6 hrs wkly. Target aud: 25-54; upscale. ♦Ginger Prado, sls VP; Gregory Kamishlian, gen sls mgr; Kevin Daniels, mus dir; Randy Rhodes, mus dir.

WROM(AM)— Dec 26, 1946: 710 khz; 1 kw-D. TL: N34 15 30 W85 09 15. 1105 Calhoun Ave. 30161. Phone: (706) 234-7171. Fax: (706) 234-8043. E-mail: wromradio@comcast.net. Web Site: www.wromradio.com. Licensee: LGV Broadcasting (acq 1999; $150,000). Network:

Broadcasting & Cable Yearbook 2006

Stations in the U.S. — Georgia

USA. Maupin, Taylor, Ellis & Adams. Format: Southern gospel. News staff: one; News: 14 hrs wkly. Target aud: 35 plus; middle class families, women, homeowners. Spec prog: Christian teaching, contemp Christian mus. ♦ Mark Lumpkin, gen mgr; Robert Vinos, opns mgr.

Rossville

WRXR-FM—Listing follows WUUS.

WUUS(AM)— Nov 11, 1958: 980 khz; 500 w-D. TL: N34 58 03 W85 18 00. Box 8799, Chattanooga, TN 37414. Secondary address: 7413 Old Lee Hwy., Chattanooga 37421. Phone: (423) 892-3333. Fax: (423) 899-7224. Licensee: Capstar TX L.P. Group owner: Clear Channel Communications Inc. (acq 8-7-2000; grpsl). Rep: McGavren Guild. Format: Sports. News staff: one. Target aud: 25-54; males. ♦ Sammy George, gen mgr.

WRXR-FM—Co-owned with WUUS. June 8, 1966: 105.5 mhz; 1.55 kw. 646 ft. TL: N34 57 26 W85 17 33. Stereo. 7413 Old Lee Hwy., Chattanooga 37421. Format: Active Rock.

Roswell

WJZZ-FM— 1997: 107.5 mhz; 6 kw. 321 ft. TL: N33 55 48 W84 20 45. 75 Piedmont Ave., 10th Fl., Atlanta 30303. Phone: (404) 765-9750. Fax: (404) 688-7686. Web Site: www.1075wjzz.com. Licensee: ROA Licenses LLC. Group owner: Radio One Inc. (acq 11-8-01; grpsl). Format: Jazz. ♦ Wayne K. Brown, gen mgr; Frank Johnson, stn mgr; Dave Kosh, progmg dir.

Royston

WBIC(AM)— January 1971: 810 khz; 250 w-D. TL: N34 16 50 W83 07 09. 259 Turner St. 30662. Phone: (706) 245-6101. Fax: (706) 245-9571. Web Site: www.wbicradio.com. Licensee: Diane E. Hawkins (acq 4-3-2003; $50,000). . Format: Southern Gospel. News staff: one; News: 7 hrs wkly. Target aud: General. ♦ Louis Hawkins, gen mgr.

WPUP(FM)—Licensed to Royston. See Athens

Saint Mary's

WWIO(AM)— Oct 15, 1985: 1190 khz; 2.5 kw-D. TL: N30 45 48 W81 36 40. 260 14th St. N. W., Atlanta 30318-5360. Phone: (404) 685-2728. Fax: (404) 685-2684. Licensee: Lighthouse Christian Broadcasting Corp. (acq 12-21-99). Network: Network: USA, NPR. Rep: Rgnl Reps. Format: News/talk. News staff: 6; News: 40 hrs wkly. Target aud: General; 35 yrs +. Spec prog: Black 4 hrs wkly. ♦ Taylor Lewis, opns mgr; John Flynn, progmg dir.

Saint Simons Island

WBGA(FM)—Licensed to Saint Simons Island. See Brunswick

WGIG(AM)—See Brunswick

WKQL(FM)—See Brunswick

WSOL-FM—See Jacksonville, FL

Sandersville

WSNT(AM)— May 11, 1956: 1490 khz; 1 kw-U. TL: N32 58 23 W82 48 34. Box 150 31082. Secondary address: 312 Morningside Dr. 31082. Phone: (478) 552-5182. Fax: (478) 553-0800. Web Site: www.waco100fm.com. Licensee: Radio Station WSNT Inc. Format: Black gospel. ♦ Francis Brazzell, pres; Capers Brazzell, gen mgr.

WSNT-FM— 1975: 99.9 mhz; 3 kw. 184 ft. TL: N32 58 23 W82 48 34. Stereo. Web Site: www.waco100fm.com. Rgnl Reps. Format: "The real country.". ♦ Capers Brazzell, sls dir.

Sandy Springs

WFGM(AM)—Not on air, target date: unknown: 830 khz; 50 kw-D, 2.4 kw-N, DA-2. TL: N34 02 00 W84 19 09. 24180 Forest Dr., Forest Lake, IL 60047. Phone: (847) 540-5410. Licensee: Frank McCoy. ♦ Frank McCoy, gen mgr.

Sasser

WEGC(FM)—Licensed to Sasser. See Albany

Savannah

WAEV(FM)—Listing follows WSOK(AM).

WBMQ(AM)— Dec 29, 1939: 630 khz; 5 kw-U, DA-N. TL: N32 03 51 W81 00 52. 214 Television Cir. 31406. Phone: (912) 961-9000. Fax: (912) 961-7070. Web Site: www.wbmq.com. Licensee: Cumulus Licensing Corp. Group owner: Cumulus Media Inc. (acq 3-26-98; grpsl). Network: CBS. Format: News/talk. Target aud: 35 plus. ♦ Dale Powers, gen mgr.

WIXV(FM)—Co-owned with WBMQ(AM). Apr 24, 1972: 95.5 mhz; 100 kw. 900 ft. TL: N32 03 30 W81 20 20. Stereo. Web Site: www.rockofsavannah.com. Format: Classic rock. Target aud: 18-49.

WEAS-FM—Listing follows WJLG(AM).

WGCO(FM)—(Midway). 1974: 98.3 mhz; 100 kw. 1,047 ft. TL: N31 36 45 W81 21 37. Stereo. 401 Mall Blvd., Suite 101 D 31406. Phone: (912) 351-9830. Fax: (912) 352-4821. Web Site: www.oldies983fm.com. Licensee: Monterey Licenses LLC. Group owner: Triad Broadcasting Co. LLC (acq 9-1-00; grpsl). Rep: Christal. Format: Oldies. News staff: 3; News: 2 hrs wkly. Target aud: 25-54; yuppies. ♦ David Benjamin, pres; Robert Leonard, gen mgr & rgnl sls mgr; Susan Groves, gen mgr & opns mgr; Chuck Cannon, progmg dir.

*****WHCJ(FM)**— Aug 18, 1975: 90.3 mhz; 6 kw. 100 ft. TL: N32 01 23 W81 03 24. (CP: Ant 231 ft. TL: N32 01 29 W81 03 24). Box 20484 31404. Phone: (912) 356-2399/356-2381. Fax: (912) 356-2041. E-mail: cartert@savstate.edu. Web Site: www.savstate.edu/whcj. Licensee: Savannah State University. Network: UPI. Format: Var/div. Target aud: 17-65; interested in jazz, reggae, blues & gospel. ♦ Theron "Ike" Carter, gen mgr.

WHGM(AM)— May 1956: 1400 khz; 1 kw-U. TL: N32 04 18 W81 04 47. (CP: 650 w. TL: N32 04 29 W81 04 17). 4328 Augusta Rd., Garden City 31408. Phone: (912) 964-1362. Fax: (912) 964-1363. E-mail: whgm1400@aol.com. Licensee: WHGM Radio Inc. (acq 1999; $500,000). Format: Gospel. ♦ Ron Grant, gen mgr & progmg dir.

WJCL-FM— June 18, 1972: 96.5 mhz; 100 kw. 1,232 ft. TL: N32 03 30 W81 20 20. Stereo. 214 Television Cir. 31406. Phone: (912) 961-9000. Fax: (912) 961-7070. Web Site: www.kix96.com. Licensee: Cumulus Licensing Corp. Group owner: Cumulus Media LLC (acq 3-12-98; $7.25 million). Format: Hot country. News staff: one. Target aud: 25-54. ♦ Lewis W. Dickey Jr., CEO & pres; Martin R. Gausvik, CFO; Dale Powers, gen mgr; Sam Nelson, opns dir; Tom Hennessey, sls dir.

WJLG(AM)— Oct 6, 1950: 900 khz; 5 kw-D, 157 w-N. TL: N32 05 13 W81 05 35. (CP: TL: N32 04 30 W81 04 16). 214 Television Cir. 31406. Phone: (912) 961-9000. Fax: (912) 961-7070. Web Site: www.cumulus.com. Licensee: Cumulus Licensing Corp. Group owner: Cumulus Media Inc. (acq 7-29-98; $5.25 million with co-located FM). Format: Gospel. ♦ Dale Power, gen mgr.

WEAS-FM—Co-owned with WJLG(AM). August 1967: 93.1 mhz; 97 kw. 981 ft. TL: N32 02 48 W81 20 27. Stereo. Web Site: www.e93jamz.com. Format: Urban contemp.

*****WLXP(FM)**— Jan 1, 2002: 88.1 mhz; 1.5 kw. 361 ft. TL: N32 02 49 W81 04 42. Stereo. Air 1 Radio Network, 5700 W. Oak Blvd., Rocklin, CA 95765. Phone: (916) 251-1600. Fax: (916) 251-1650. E-mail: info@air1.com. Web Site: www.air1.com. Licensee: Christian Multimedia Network Inc. Network: Air 1. Shaw Pittman. Format: Contemp Christian. News staff: 3. Target aud: 18-35; Judeo-Christian, female. ♦ Joe Miller, CFO; Keith Whipple, gen mgr.

WQBT(FM)—Listing follows WTKS(AM).

WSOK(AM)— October 1946: 1230 khz; 1 kw-U. TL: N32 04 20 W81 04 35. 245 Alfred St. 31408. Phone: (912) 964-7794. Fax: (912) 964-9414. Licensee: Capstar TX L.P. Group owner: Clear Channel Communications Inc. (acq 8-30-00; grpsl). Network: American Urban. Format: Gospel. ♦ Jerry Stevens, CEO & VP; Sheryl Collison, sls dir; E. Larry McDuffie, progmg dir & progmg mgr; Marty Foglia, chief of engrg.

WAEV(FM)—Co-owned with WSOK(AM). Feb 4, 1969: 97.3 mhz; 100 kw. 1,000 ft. TL: N32 03 30 W81 20 20. Stereo. Network: Westwood One. Format: CHR. Target aud: 25-54; affluent. ♦ Chris Allen, opns mgr & progmg mgr; Sheryl Collison, natl sls mgr & rgnl sls mgr.

*****WSVH(FM)**— Apr 20, 1981: 91.1 mhz; 100 kw. 1,068 ft. TL: N32 03 32 W81 17 57. Stereo. 260 14th St. N.W., Atlanta 30318-5360. Secondary address: 12 Ocean Science Cir. 30602. Phone: (404) 685-2690 HQ. Fax: (404) 685-2684 HQ. E-mail: gpr@gpb.org. Web Site: www.gpb.org. Licensee: Georgia Public Telecommunications Commission. Network: Network: PRI, NPR. Format: Class, news, jazz. News staff: one; News: 51 hrs wkly. Target aud: 45 plus; Adults 35+. ♦ James Lyle, CEO; Bonnie Bean, CFO; John Hughes, exec VP; Chuck Miller, gen mgr; Eric Nauert, stn mgr; Russell Wells, opns mgr; Lisa Anne gaston, dev dir; Jeannie Allen, sls dir; Marcia Killingsworth, prom dir; St. John Flynn, progmg mgr; Terrance McKnight, mus dir; Mark Fehlig, engrg mgr.

WTKS(AM)— Oct 15, 1929: 1290 khz; 5 kw-U, DA-N. TL: N32 05 26 W81 08 55. Stereo. 245 Alfred St. 31408-3205. Phone: (912) 964-7794. Fax: (912) 964-9414. Licensee: Capstar TX L.P. Group owner: Clear Channel Communications Inc. (acq 8-30-00; grpsl). Network: ABC Information & Entertainment. Wiley, Rein & Fielding. Format: Talk. Target aud: 25-64. ♦ Jerry Storey, VP & gen mgr; Brad Kelly, opns mgr; Sheryl Collison, sls dir; Jeff Storey, mktg mgr; Brian Mudd, progmg dir; Marty Foglia, chief of engrg.

WQBT(FM)—Co-owned with WTKS(AM). Nov 29, 1946: 94.1 mhz; 100 kw. 1,320 ft. TL: N32 03 14 W81 21 01. Stereo. Format: Urban contemp. ♦ Jeff Storey, gen mgr; Bo Money, progmg dir.

*****WYFS(FM)**— Nov 1, 1986: 89.5 mhz; 100 kw. 630 ft. TL: N32 04 04 W81 21 17. Stereo. 156 Falcon Ln., Bloomingdale 31302-9338. Secondary address: Bible Broadcasting Network, Charlotte 28241-7300. Phone: (704) 522-1967. Phone: (704) 523-5555. Fax: (707) 522-1967. E-mail: wyfs@bbnradio.org. Web Site: www.bbnradio.org. Licensee: Bible Broadcasting Network Inc. (group owner) Format: Educ, relg, christian. Target aud: General; christian progmg for the entire family. ♦ Lowell Davey, pres; Richard Hunt, stn mgr; Harold Richards, mus dir & news dir; Ron Muffley, chief of engrg.

WZAT(FM)— Oct 19, 1971: 102.1 mhz; 98 kw. Ant 1,496 ft. TL: N32 03 37 W81 20 40. 214 Television Cir. 31406. Phone: (912) 961-9000. Fax: (912) 961-7070. E-mail: brian.rickman@z102.net. Web Site: www.z102.net. Licensee: Cumulus Licensing Corp. Group owner: Cumulus Media Inc. (acq 7-29-98; $3.5 million). Format: CHR, var. ♦ Lewis W. Dickey Jr., CEO & pres; Martin R. Gausvik, CFO; Dale Powers, gen mgr; Sam Nelson, opns dir; Robert Combs, sls dir & engr.

Smithville

WZIQ(FM)— 1996: 106.5 mhz; 2.45 kw. 515 ft. TL: N31 47 59 W84 14 54. Stereo. 2278 Wortham Ln., Grovetown 30813. Phone: (706) 309-9609. Fax: (706) 309-9669. E-mail: ctbarinowski@comcast.net. Web Site: www.gnnradio.org. Licensee: Barinowski Investment Co., a

Georgia

Georgia L.P. Group owner: Good News Network (acq 1-21-98). Format: Christian. ◆Clarence Barinowski, gen mgr.

Smyrna

WAZX(AM)— March 1962: 1550 khz; 50 kw-D, 500 w-N, DA-2. TL: N33 53 29 W84 31 19. Stereo. 2460 Atlanta Rd. 30080. Phone: (770) 436-6171. Fax: (770) 436-0100. E-mail: wazx@hotmail.com. Web Site: www.radiolaquebuena. Licensee: GA-MEX Broadcasting Inc. (acq 7-29-93; $1.1 million; 8-23-93). Format: Sp. Target aud: 12 plus; Sp. Spec prog: Regional Mexican. ◆Javier Macias, CEO; Humberto Izquierdo, VP, gen mgr, sls VP & gen sls mgr; Duncan Pearson, engrg VP & chief of engrg.

WSTR(FM)— May 1966: 94.1 mhz; 100 kw. 910 ft. TL: N33 45 34 W84 23 19. Penthouse, 3350 Peachtree Rd., Suite 1800, Atlanta 30326. Phone: (404) 261-2970. Fax: (404) 365-9026. E-mail: mark.kanov@star94.com. Web Site: www.star94.com. Licensee: Jefferson Pilot Communications Co. (group owner; acq 3-1-74). Format: CHR. Target aud: 18-49; general. ◆Don Benson, pres; Mark Kanov, gen mgr; Dan Bowen, progmg dir.

Soperton

WKTM(FM)— Nov 23, 1982: 106.1 mhz; 6 kw. 298 ft. TL: N32 25 31 W82 33 26. Stereo. 2278 Wortham Ln., Grovetown 30813. Phone: (706) 309-9610. Fax: (706) 309-9669. E-mail: ctbarinowski@comcast.net. Web Site: www.gnnradio.org. Licensee: Barinowski Investment Co., a Georgia L.P. Group owner: Good News Network (acq 1-21-99). Format: Sp. ◆C. Barinowski, gen mgr.

Sparta

***WJDS(FM)**—Not on air, target date: unknown: 88.7 mhz; 2 kw vert. 134 ft. TL: N33 18 48 W83 00 05. 2278 Wortham Ln, Grovetown 30813. Phone: (706) 309-9609. Fax: (706) 309-9669. E-mail: ctbarinowski@comcast.net. Web Site: www.gnnradio.org. Licensee: Augusta Radio Fellowship Institute I. Format: Spanish. ◆Clarence Barinowski, gen mgr.

Springfield

WTYB(FM)— Oct 1, 1977: 103.9 mhz; 14 kw. Ant 328 ft. TL: N32 16 48 W81 11 41. (CP: COL Tybee Island. 50 kw, ant 344 ft. TL: N32 03 33 W81 00 57). 214 Television Cir., Savannah 31406. Phone: (912) 961-9000. Fax: (912) 961-7070. Web Site: www.cumulus.com. Licensee: Cumulus Licensing Corp. Group owner: Cumulus Media Inc. (acq 3-26-98; grpsl). Format: R&B oldies, R&B, contemp gospel. ◆Tom Conolly, gen mgr.

Statenville

WHLJ(FM)— 1999: 97.5 mhz; 6 kw. 328 ft. TL: N30 46 47 W82 52 43. LaTaurus Productions Inc., Box 1305, Valdosta 31605. Phone: (229) 242-9997. Fax: (229) 249-9765. E-mail: whlj@surfsouth.com. Licensee: LaTaurus Productions Inc. Format: Rhythm and blues, hip-hop, urban contemp. ◆Warren Lee, gen mgr.

Statesboro

WMZD(FM)— May 1, 1967: 100.1 mhz; 50 kw. Ant 300 ft. TL: N32 27 21 W81 46 27. Stereo. Box 29, Hinesville 31313. Phone: (912) 368-9258. Fax: (912) 368-5526. Licensee: Tama Radio Licenses of Savannah, GA, Inc. Group owner: Tama Broadcasting Inc. (acq 4-28-2004). Format: Adult contemp. News staff: one. Target aud: 18-45. ◆Yvonne Clark, gen mgr.

WPMX(FM)— 1995: 102.9 mhz; 25 kw. 328 ft. TL: N32 26 43 W81 58 07. 35 E. Main St. 30458. Phone: (912) 764-1029. Fax: (912) 489-3959. E-mail: radiocenter@frontiernet.net. Licensee: Staton Broadcasting Inc. (group owner; acq 11-12-2003; grpsl). Network: ABC. Format: Adult contemp. Target aud: General. ◆Cecil Staton, pres; John Long, sr VP; Jeff Anderson, gen mgr; Jodi Chase, progmg mgr.

WPTB(AM)— Apr 4, 1976: 850 khz; 1 kw-U, DA-N. TL: N32 28 02 W81 50 07. Box 958 30458. Phone: (912) 764-6621. Fax: (912) 764-6622. Licensee: Communications Capital Co. II of Georgia LLC. Group owner: Communications Capital Managers LLC (acq 5-27-2003; $135,000). Rep: Dora-Clayton. Format: Sports. News staff: one; News: 7 hrs wkly. Target aud: General. Spec prog: Gospel 6 hrs wkly. ◆Bill Kent, gen mgr, stn mgr & opns mgr.

***WVGS(FM)**— 1975: 91.9 mhz; 1 kw. 161 ft. TL: N32 25 32 W81 46 58. Stereo. Box LB 8016, Georgia Southern Univ. 30460. Phone: (912) 681-0877. Phone: (912) 681-5507. Fax: (912) 486-7113. E-mail: wvgs@georgiasouthern.edu. Licensee: Board of Regents University System of Georgia. Format: Alternative, progsv, educ. Target aud: 18-25; college kids. Spec prog: Rap, jazz 5 hrs, reggae 3 hrs wkly. ◆Dennis Hightower, pres; Bill Neville, stn mgr & opns mgr.

WWNS(AM)— Dec 1, 1946: 1240 khz; 1 kw-U. TL: N32 27 21 W81 46 27. Box 958 30459. Secondary address: 561 E. Olliff St. 30458. Phone: (912) 764-5446. Fax: (912) 764-8827. E-mail: wwnswmcd@enia.net. Web Site: www.radiostatesboro.com. Licensee: Communications Capital Co. II of Georgia LLC. Group owner: Communications Capital Managers LLC (acq 4-28-2004; grpsl). Network: USA. Rgnl Reps Richard Helnick. Format: News/talk, sports. News staff: one; News: 20 hrs wkly. Target aud: 25-death. ◆Nate Hirsch, gen mgr; Buddy Horne, opns dir.

Summerville

WGTA(AM)— Aug 27, 1950: 950 khz; 5 kw-D, 140 w-N. TL: N34 27 53 W85 21 12. 339 Hwy. 100 30747. Phone: (770) 436-6171. Fax: (770) 436-0100. E-mail: radiobuena@hotmail.com. Web Site: www.radiolaquebuena.com. Licensee: TTA Broadcasting Inc. (acq 2-4-97; $50,000). Network: Westwood One. Cordon & Kelly. Format: Mexican. News staff: one; News: 15 hrs wkly. Target aud: 18 plus. Spec prog: Relg 12 hrs wkly. ◆Humberto Izquierdo, gen mgr; Javier Macias, pres & opns mgr.

WZQZ(AM)— (Trion). Apr 1, 1985: 1180 khz; 5 kw-D. TL: N34 28 22 W85 19 31. Box 735 30747. Secondary address: 2278 Wortham Ln., Grovetown 30813. Phone: (706) 857-5555. Fax: (706) 857-2006. E-mail: radio@wzqz.net. Web Site: wzqz.com. Licensee: Barinowski Investment Co., a Georgia L.P. Group owner: Good News Network. Network: Network: USA, CNN Radio. Format: Adult standards, Music of Your Life. Target aud: All ages; Northwest Georgia. ◆C.T. Barinowski, pres; Terry Adams, gen mgr & opns dir.

Swainsboro

WELT(FM)—Listing follows WJAT(AM).

WJAT(AM)— Jan 1, 1950: 800 khz; 1 kw-D, 500 w-N. TL: N32 35 08 W82 21 42. 2 Radio Loop 30401. Phone: (478) 237-1590. Fax: (478) 237-3559. Licensee: RadioJones LLC (group owner; acq 11-10-2003; grpsl). Rep: Dora-Clayton. Booth, Freret, Imlay, Tepper. Format: Gospel. News: 5 hrs wkly. Target aud: 18 plus; general. Spec prog: Farm 5 hrs, gospel 2 hrs wkly. ◆Dennis Jones, gen mgr; Jolly Martin, sls dir, prom dir & progmg dir; Jeff Wiggins, news dir & engrg dir.

WELT(FM)— Co-owned with WJAT(AM). Dec 18, 1966: 98.1 mhz; 9.6 kw. Ant 525 ft. TL: N32 32 55 W82 38 49. Stereo. Web Site: www.theradio@theradiogroup.com. Format: Contemp hit. Target aud: 18-35.

WXRS(AM)— Mar 10, 1978: 1590 khz; 2.5 kw-D, 25 w-N. TL: N32 33 25 W82 20 29. 2 Radio Loop 30401. Phone: (478) 237-1590. Fax: (478) 237-3559. Web Site: www.theradiojones.com. Licensee: RadioJones LLC. (group owner; acq 11-10-2003; grpsl). Network: ABC. Rep: Dora-Clayton. Format: Talk, sporrts, news. News staff: two; News: 7 hrs wkly. Target aud: 30 plus. ◆Jeff Wiggins, opns mgr, progmg dir, news dir & chief of engrg; Jolly Martin, rgnl sls mgr & prom dir.

WXRS-FM— Aug 2, 1982: 100.5 mhz; 3 kw. 300 ft. TL: N32 34 52 W82 23 14. Stereo. Format: Country. News staff: 3; News: 8 hrs wkly. Target aud: 25 plus.

Sylvania

WSYL(AM)— Dec 1, 1955: 1490 khz; 1 kw-U. TL: N32 43 51 W81 37 04. Box 519, 1526 Savannah Hwy. 30467. Phone: (912) 564-7461. Fax: (912) 564-7462. Licensee: Communications Capital Co. II of Georgia LLC. Group owner: Communications Capital Managers LLC (acq 4-28-2004; grpsl). Rep: Rgnl Reps. Format: Contemp country. News staff: 2; News: 7 hrs wkly. Target aud: 18-49; affluent. Spec prog: Farm 5 hrs wkly. ◆Nathan Hirsch, gen mgr.

WZBX(FM)—Co-owned with WSYL(AM). Sept 6, 1991: 106.5 mhz; 6 kw. 328 ft. TL: N32 43 53 W81 37 03. Format: Country. ◆Nate Hirsch, stn mgr.

Sylvester

WRXZ(FM)— Jan 27, 1993: 106.1 mhz; 6 kw. Ant 328 ft. TL: N31 30 15 W83 55 46. 400 Dunbar Ln., Albany 31701. Phone: (229) 776-9565. Fax: (229) 446-9279. E-mail: marybethbateman@bellsouth.net. Licensee: On Top Communications Inc. (group owner; (acq 1-8-02; grpsl). Network: American Urban. Taylor, Thiemann & Aitken. Format: Hip hop, rhythm and blues. ◆Steve Hegwood, pres; Lenny Rayford, CFO; Marybeth Batemen, gen mgr; Titus Miller, chief of engrg.

WZBN(FM)— Aug 1, 1999: 102.1 mhz; 6 kw. 276 ft. TL: N31 31 42 W83 50 29. 1104 W. Broad Ave., Albany 31707. Phone: (229) 888-5000. Fax: (229) 888-5960. E-mail: info18@cumulus.com. Web Site: www.cumulus.com. Licensee: Cumulus Licensing Corp. Group owner: Cumulus Media Inc. (acq 3-12-01; $550,000). Format: Blues, urban ceontemp. ◆Paul Bacurel, gen mgr; Roshon Vance, progmg dir.

Talking Rock

WNSY(FM)— 1999: 100.1 mhz; 1.4 kw. 663 ft. TL: N34 37 50 W84 29 29. Box 1290, Canton 30169. Secondary address: 2189 Marietta Hwy., Canton 30114. Phone: (770) 479-2101. Fax: (770) 479-1134. E-mail: wwnsy@mindspring.com. Web Site: www.sunny-100.com. Licensee: Dorothy McClure and Dean Copeland/Suntrust Bank Format: Oldies. ◆Rebecca Johnston, gen mgr; Scott Evans, progmg dir.

Tallapoosa

WKNG(AM)— Sept 1, 1977: 1060 khz; 11 kw-D, 5 kw-CH. TL: N33 44 06 W85 15 08. Box 626, Hwy. 78, Golf Course Rd. 30176. Phone: (770) 574-1060. Fax: (770) 574-1062. Web Site: www.wkng.com. Licensee: WKNG LLC. Network: ABC. Format: Classic country. Target aud: 25-54. ◆Steven L. Gradick, pres & gen mgr.

Tennille

WJFL(FM)— Oct 14, 1993: 101.9 mhz; 6 kw. 328 ft. TL: N32 54 49 W82 53 06. Box 36 31089. Phone: (478) 553-1019. Fax: (478) 553-1123. E-mail: wjfl@wjfl.com. Web Site: www.wjfl.com. Licensee: Fall Line Media Inc. (group owner; (acq 1996; $225,000). Format: Adult contemp. ◆Linda Fulghum, gen mgr & sls dir; Rachel Durden, prom dir & news dir; Michael Fulghum, engrg dir.

The Rock

***WKEU-FM**— 2000: 88.9 mhz; 5 kw. Ant 764 ft. TL: N32 59 11 W84 21 56. Box 997, Griffin 30224. Secondary address: 1000 Memorial Dr., Griffin 30224. Phone: (770) 227-5507. Fax: (770) 229-2291. E-mail: info@wkeuradio.com. Web Site: www.wkeuradio.com. Licensee: Georgia Public Radio Inc. Format: Classic rock. ◆William Taylor Jr., gen mgr.

Thomaston

WTGA(AM)— Nov 1, 1962: 1590 khz; 500 w-D, 25 w-N. TL: N32 53 45 W84 18 10. 208 S. Center St. 30286. Secondary address: Box 550 Phone: (706) 647-7121. Fax: (706) 647-7122. Web Site: www.wtga.com. Licensee: Radio Georgia Inc. (acq 1972). Network: ABC Information & Entertainment. Format: Soft hits. Spec prog: Black 4 hrs wkly. ◆David L. Piper, pres, gen mgr & progmg dir; Bill Chapman, gen sls mgr; Robert Lyons, chief of engrg.

WTGA-FM— Nov 15, 1982: 101.1 mhz; 6 kw. 308 ft. TL: N32 51 49 W84 25 10. Web Site: www.wtga.com. Format: Soft hits.

Thomasville

***WAYT(FM)**— 2003: 88.1 mhz; 35 kw. Ant 1,332 ft. TL: N30 40 06 W83 58 10. Box 4188, Tallahassee, FL 32315. Phone: (850) 422-1928. Fax: (850) 297-1888. E-mail: wayt@wayfm.com. Web Site: wayt.wayfm.com. Licensee: WAY-FM Media Group Inc. (group owner; acq 10-24-02). Format: Christian. ◆Steve Young, stn mgr.

***WFSL(FM)**— Mar 1, 2005: 90.7 mhz; 250 w. Ant 154 ft. TL: N30 50 12 W83 58 57. Florida State University, FSU Broadcasting Ctr., 1600 Red Barber Plaza, Tallahassee, FL 32310-6068. Phone: (850) 487-3086. Fax: (850) 487-3293. E-mail: wfsufm@wfsu.org. Web Site: www.wfsu.org. Licensee: Florida State University Board of Trustees. Format: Class. ◆Patrick Keating, gen mgr; Caroline Austin, opns mgr.

WHGH(AM)— Dec 15, 1987: 840 khz; 10 kw-D. TL: N30 47 54 W83 56 22. Box 2218 31799. Secondary address: 221 Pallbearer Rd.

Stations in the U.S. — Georgia

31792. Phone: (229) 228-4124. Fax: (229) 225-9508. Licensee: H.G.H. Investment Corp. Format: Hip hop, gospel. Target aud: 12 plus; Blacks. ◆Moses Gross, pres, gen mgr & stn mgr; Carlos Copeland, mus dir.

WPAX(AM)— Dec 27, 1922: 1240 khz; 1 kw-U. TL: N30 50 10 W83 59 19. Stereo. Box 129, 117 Remington Ave. 31799. Phone: (229) 226-1241. Fax: (229) 226-1361. E-mail: lenrob@rose.net. Web Site: www.wpaxradio.com. Licensee: LenRob Inc. (acq 10-85). Network: CBS. Rep: Rgnl Reps. Miller & Fields, P.C. Format: Adult standards, news. News staff: one; News: 20 hrs wkly. Target aud: 25 plus; mature with disposable income. Spec prog: Farm 2 hrs, gospel 7 hrs, relg 3 hrs wkly. ◆Len Robinson, pres & gen mgr.

WSTT(AM)— 1947: 730 khz; 5 kw-D, 27 w-N. TL: N30 48 50 W84 00 48. 2194 Hwy. 319 S. 31792. Phone: (229) 377-2337. Fax: (229) 377-0023. Licensee: Marion R. Williams. (acq 7-26-99; $300,000). Network: Network: CBS, UPI. Matthew McCormick. Format: Gospel. Target aud: 25-54; general. ◆Marion Williams, VP; Bill James, stn mgr.

WTLY(FM)—Licensed to Thomasville. See Tallahassee FL

Thomson

WTHO-FM— Feb 22, 1971: 101.7 mhz; 3 kw. 300 ft. TL: N33 28 21 W82 30 00. Stereo. Box 900, 788 Cedar Rock Rd. N.W. 30824. Phone: (706) 595-5122. Fax: (706) 595-3021. E-mail: wtho@classicsouth.net. Licensee: Camellia City Communications Inc. (acq 2-5-93; $110,000 with co-located AM; 3-1-93). Rep: Rgnl Reps Covington & Burling. Format: C&W. Target aud: 25-54. Spec prog: Farm 3 hrs, gospel one hr, relg 6 hrs wkly. ◆Lisa Kitchens, news dir; Mike Wall, gen mgr, opns dir, gen sls mgr, adv mgr, progmg dir, mus dir, news dir & chief of engrg.

WTWA(AM)— Co-owned with WTHO-FM. Jan 10, 1948: 1240 khz; 1 kw-U. TL: N33 28 20 W82 31 02. Phone: (706) 595-1561. E-mail: wtwa@classicsouth.net. Format: Adult Contemporary. Target aud: 35 plus.

Tifton

*WABR-FM**— December 1973: 91.1 mhz; 30 kw. 249 ft. TL: N31 29 30 W83 31 49. Stereo. 260 14th St. N.W., Atlanta 30318-5360. Phone: (404) 685-2690. Fax: (404) 685-2684. E-mail: ask@gpb.org. Web Site: www.gpb.org. Licensee: Georgia Public Telecommunications Commission. Network: NPR. Format: News, class. News staff: 6; News: 40 hrs wkly. ◆Nancy Hall, CEO; Bonnie Bean, CFO; St. John Flynn, progmg dir; Susanna Capelouto, news dir.

WJYF(FM)—Listing follows WTIF(AM).

WKZZ(FM)— 2000: 92.5 mhz; 20.5 kw. Ant 361 ft. TL: N31 31 40 W83 20 01. 232 N. Central Ave. 31794. Phone: (229) 386-9898. Fax: (229) 386-9866. E-mail: jank@rtgmedia.net. Licensee: RTG Radio LLC. Group owner: Black Crow Media Group LLC (acq 11-9-2001; grpsl). McCampbell & Young. Format: Adult contemp. ◆John Higgs, CEO, CEO & gen mgr; Jan Kicklighter, gen sls mgr.

WOBB(FM)—Licensed to Tifton. See Albany

*WPLH(FM)**— January 1988: 103.1 mhz; 29 w. 177 ft. TL: N31 28 51 W83 31 38. Stereo. Box 36, ABAC 31794. Phone: (229) 391-4977. Fax: (229) 386-7158. E-mail: wplh@abac.edu. Licensee: Abraham Baldwin Agriculture College. (acq 4-1-88). Format: Var.

WTIF(AM)— 1957: 1340 khz; 1 kw-U. TL: N31 28 16 W83 29 12. Box 968 31793. Secondary address: 104 E. 7th St. 31794. Phone: (229) 382-1340. Fax: (229) 386-8658. Licensee: Three Trees Communications Inc. (group owner; acq 3-29-2004; grpsl). Network: CBS. Format: Country. News staff: one; News: 15 hrs wkly. Target aud: 18 plus. Spec prog: Farm 5 hrs wkly. ◆James Andrew Howard, pres; Ron Yontz, gen mgr; Andy Reeves, stn mgr.

WJYF(FM)—Co-owned with WTIF(AM). Nov 26, 1986: 95.3 mhz; 9.7 kw. 500 ft. TL: N31 10 18 W83 21 57. Stereo. 113 N. College St., Ashburn Network: Westwood One. Format: Soft adult contemp. News staff: one; News: one hr wkly. Target aud: 30 plus.

Toccoa

WLET(AM)— May 1, 1941: 1420 khz; 5 kw-D. TL: N34 35 23 W85 19 11. Box 780, TFC Radio Network, Toccoa Falls 30598. Secondary address: 292 Old Clarsville Hwy. 30577. Phone: (800) 282-6030. Phone: (800) 251-8326. Fax: (706) 282-6090. E-mail: wlet@tfc.edu. Licensee: Toccoa Falls College. (acq 11-3-99). Format: Gospel. News staff: one; News: 10 hrs wkly. Target aud: 35 plus; Stephens county residents seeking news & community info. Spec prog: Black, gospel, relg. ◆David Cornelius, gen mgr; Rick Simon, stn mgr.

WNEG(AM)— Apr 21, 1956: 630 khz; 500 w-D, 44 w-N. TL: N34 34 15 W83 19 35. Box 1159 30577-0907. Phone: (706) 886-2191. Fax: (706) 282-0189. E-mail: hobbs@gacaradio.com. Web Site: www.wnegradio.com. Licensee: Georgia-Carolina Radiocasting Co. LLC. Group owner: Georgia-Carolina Radiocasting Companies (acq 12-19-01; grpsl). Network: Network: AP Radio, CBS Radio. Dan J. Alpert. Format: MOR, local news. News staff: 2; News: 18 hrs wkly. Target aud: General; adult working class. ◆Douglas M. Sutton Jr., pres; Phil Hobbs, VP & gen mgr; Connie Gaines, opns mgr; M.J. Kneiser, news dir; Tim Stephens, chief of engrg.

WNGC(FM)— November 1947: 106.1 mhz; 100 kw. 1,132 ft. TL: N34 43 46 W83 29 29. Stereo. 850 Bobbin Mill Rd., Athens 30606. Phone: (706) 549-1340. Fax: (706) 546-0441. E-mail: wngc@negia.net. Web Site: www.1061wngc.com. Licensee: Southern Broadcasting of Pensacola Inc. Group owner: Southern Broadcasting Companies Inc. (acq 1999; $2.2 million. with co-located AM). Format: Country. News staff: one; News: 10 hrs wkly. Target aud: 25-54; adults with disposable income. Spec prog: Gospel. ◆Paul Stone, pres; Scott Smith, opns mgr.

Toccoa Falls

*WRAF-FM**— Sept 4, 1980: 90.9 mhz; 100 kw. 564 ft. TL: N34 35 57 W83 21 55. Stereo. Box 780, TFC Radio Network 30598. Secondary address: 292 Old Clarksville Hwy., Toccoa 30577. Phone: (800) 251-8326. Fax: (706) 282-6090. E-mail: tfcrn@tfc.edu. Web Site: www.myfavoritestation.net. Licensee: Toccoa Falls College. Network: USA. Wiley, Rein & Fielding. Format: Relg, MOR. Target aud: General; families. ◆W. Wayne Gardner, CEO; David Cornelius, gen mgr, stn mgr & opns mgr; Bryan Race, stn mgr & prom dir.

*WTXR(FM)**— September 1996: 89.7 mhz; 100 w. -190 ft. Stereo. Box 780, TFC Radio Network 30598. Secondary address: 292 Old Clarksville Hwy., Toccoa 30577. Phone: (706) 886-7299, EXT. 5268. Fax: (706) 282-6027. E-mail: wtxr@tfc.edu. Web Site: www.wtxr.com. Licensee: Toccoa Falls College. Format: Christian. Target aud: 18-35; college students, young adults. ◆David Cornelius, gen mgr; Bryan Race, stn mgr & opns mgr.

Trenton

WBDX(FM)— 1989: 102.7 mhz; 320 w. 1,374 ft. TL: N34 51 48 W85 23 35. Box 9396, Chattanooga, TN 37412. Phone: (423) 892-1200. Fax: (423) 892-1633. E-mail: mailbag@j103.com. Web Site: www.j103.com. Licensee: Partners for Christian Media Inc. (acq 5-7-98; $1,189,395). Format: Adult contemp, Christian. Target aud: 18-49. ◆Bob Lubell, CEO, pres & gen mgr; David Skinner, CFO; Debbie Lubell, sls dir.

WKWN(AM)— Apr 4, 1982: 1420 khz; 2.5 w-D, 112 w-N. TL: N34 51 43 W85 29 59. Box 829, 12544 N. Main St. 30752. Phone: (706) 657-7594. Fax: (706) 657-6767. E-mail: kwntv7@yahoo.com. Licensee: Dade County Broadcasting Inc. (acq 11-20-97; $63,000). Format: News/talk radio. News staff: one; News: 6 hrs wkly. Target aud: 25-54; locals. Spec prog: Relg 6 hrs, gospel 12 hrs, loc sports 10 hrs wkly. ◆Evan Stone, CEO, chmn, pres, gen mgr & stn mgr.

Trion

WATG(FM)— January 1997: 95.7 mhz; 6 kw. 699 ft. TL: N34 28 10 W85 17 48. Box 200, Summerville 30747. Secondary address: 10143 Commerce St., Summerville 30747. Phone: (706) 857-2000. Phone: (706) 857-2467. Fax: (706) 857-3652. E-mail: oldies957@aol.com. Licensee: TTA Broadcasting Inc. (acq 10-19-99; up to $296,530). Network: ABC. Rep: Rgnl Reps. Cordon & Kelly. Format: Oldies. News: one hr wkly. Target aud: 25-54; general. ◆Jim Bojo, CFO & gen mgr; Randy Davis, pres & sr VP.

WZQZ(AM)—Licensed to Trion. See Summerville

Tucker

WGUN(AM)—(Atlanta). July 1947: 1010 khz; 50 kw-D, 300 w-N. TL: N33 41 55 W84 17 23. 2901 Mountain Industrial Blvd. 30084. Phone: (770) 491-1010. Fax: (770) 491-3019. E-mail: wgun@bellsouth.net. Web Site: wgunam.com. Licensee: Dee Rivers Group. Format: relg talk, info & inspiration. News: one hr wkly. Target aud: 25-54; working class. ◆Georgia Salva, CEO; Darrell Vick, gen mgr; Erwin Hill, opns mgr.

Unadilla

WQSA(FM)— June 1995: 99.9 mhz; 6 kw. 328 ft. TL: N32 18 29 W83 46 30. Stereo. 1006 First St., Perry 31069. Phone: (478) 218-7756. Fax: (478) 988-7977. E-mail: mail@wqsa.com. Web Site: www.wqsa.com. Licensee: Toccoa Falls College. Format: Talk. ◆Bob Biermann, gen mgr.

Valdosta

WAAC(FM)—Listing follows WGOV(AM).

WAFT(FM)— Nov 25, 1971: 101.1 mhz; 100 kw. 558 ft. TL: N30 51 50 W83 23 39. Stereo. 215 Waft Hill Ln. 31602-6512. Phone: (229) 244-5180. Fax: (229) 242-8808. E-mail: mail@waft.org. Web Site: www.waft.org. Licensee: Christian Radio Fellowship Inc. Format: Relg. News: 3 hrs wkly. Target aud: General. ◆Bill Tidwell, pres, gen mgr & chief of opns; Shelia Hofmeister, mus dir.

WFVR(AM)— Nov 3, 1951: 910 khz; 5 kw-U, DA-N. TL: N30 52 21 W83 20 36. 3765 N. John Young Pkwy., Orlando 32804. Phone: (407) 523-2770. Fax: (407) 523-2888. Web Site: www.travelersinformationradio.com. Licensee: Rama Communications Inc. (group owner; acq 2-28-2002; $255,000). Format: Travelers information. ◆Sabeta Persaud, pres; Kris Persaud, gen mgr; Steve January, gen sls mgr, mktg mgr, adv mgr & progmg dir; Steve Delay, chief of engrg.

WGOV(AM)— 1939: 950 khz; 5 kw-D, 1 kw-N, DA-N. TL: N30 48 09 W83 21 17. (CP: 5 kw-D, 630 w-N, DA-N). Box 1207 31603. Secondary address: 2973 Hwy. 84 W. 31601. Phone: (229) 244-9500. Fax: (229) 247-7676. Licensee: WGOV Inc. Group owner: Dee Rivers Group Rep: Rgnl Reps. Format: Urban contemp. News staff: one; News: 3 hrs wkly. Target aud: 18-45; Black. Spec prog: Gospel 14 hrs, oldies 10 hrs wkly. ◆Mr. Hanson, gen mgr & gen sls mgr.

WAAC(FM)—Co-owned with WGOV(AM). 1968: 92.9 mhz; 100 kw. 509 ft. TL: N30 48 13 W83 21 20. Stereo. Phone: (229) 242-4513. Web Site: www.waacradio.com. Network: ABC Information & Entertainment. Format: Country. Target aud: 25-54.

WGOV-FM— June 1985: 96.7 mhz; 3 kw. 300 ft. TL: N30 50 10 W83 12 40. (CP: 50 kw, ant 492 ft. TL: N30 48 37 W83 31 19). Stereo. Box 5406 31603-5406. Secondary address: 704 N. Ashly St. 31601. Phone: (229) 333-0755. Fax: (229) 333-0286. Licensee: CDJ Inc. (acq 7-1-91; 7-22-91). Format: Classic rock. Target aud: 18-49. ◆Mike Howard, gen mgr.

WQPW(FM)— September 1977: 95.7 mhz; 35.9 kw. 606 ft. TL: N30 50 11 W83 17 56. Stereo. 1700 Ellis Dr. 31601. Phone: (229)

Georgia

244-8642. Fax: (229) 242-7620. E-mail: scottjames@rtgmedia.net. Web Site: www.957themix.com. Licensee: RTG Radio LLC. Group owner: Black Crow Media Group LLC (acq 11-9-2001; grpsl). Borsari & Paxson. Format: Adult contemp. News staff: 14. Target aud: 18-44. ♦ Scott James, gen mgr.

*WVDA(FM)—Not on air, target date: unknown: 88.5 mhz; 25 kw vert. Ant 216 ft. TL: N30 47 50 W83 01 01. 113 E. College Ave., Ashburn 31714. Secondary address: 6080 Mt. Moriah Ext., Memphis 38115. Phone: (229) 567-9038. Licensee: AGT Communications Inc. (acq 6-1-2005; $100,000 for CP). ♦ James Andrew Howard, pres; George Flinn Jr., sr VP; Keith Parnell, gen mgr.

WVLD(AM)— Sept 3, 1959: 1450 khz; 1 kw-U. TL: N30 50 11 W83 17 56. 1711 Ellis Dr. 31601. Phone: (229) 244-8642. Fax: (229) 242-7620. Licensee: RTG Media. Group owner: Black Crow Media Group LLC (acq 11-9-2001; grpsl). Network: CBS. Borsari & Paxson. Format: Sports. News: 10 hrs wkly. Target aud: 35 plus. Spec prog: Gospel 2 hrs wkly. ♦ Robert Ganzack, pres & gen mgr.

*WVVS(FM)— July 26, 1971: 90.9 mhz; 5.3 kw. 68 ft. TL: N30 50 50 W83 17 26. Stereo. Box 142, VSU Student Union, 1500 N. Patterson 31698. Phone: (229) 333-5662. Fax: (229) 333-7313. Licensee: Valdosta State University. Format: Rock/AOR, hard rock. Target aud: 18-25; students of VSU, population at large. Spec prog: Gospel 2 hrs, jazz 2 hrs, relg 2 hrs, var/div music 16 hrs. ♦ Jimmy Hallsworth, gen mgr & stn mgr; Jason Maxwell, opns mgr; Lauren Aparilio, prom dir; Zinte Lovelace, progmg dir; Walter Johnson, news dir.

*WWET(FM)— December 1989: 91.7 mhz; 430 w vert. Ant 85 ft. TL: N30 49 35 W83 16 40. Stereo. 260 14th St. N.W., Atlanta 30318-5360. Phone: (404) 685-2690. Fax: (404) 685-2684. E-mail: gpr@gpb.org. Web Site: www.gpb.org. Licensee: Georgia Public Telecommunications Commission. Network: NPR, PRI. Format: Class, news. News staff: 6; News: 40 hrs wkly. Target aud: 35 plus; general. Spec prog: Jazz 4 hrs, Latin 3 hrs wkly. ♦ James Lyle, CEO; Bonnie Bean, CFO; John Hughes, exec VP; Chuck Miller, gen mgr; Shelease Whitaker, opns mgr; Anne Bramlette, sls dir; Marcia Killingsworth, prom dir; St. John Flynn, progmg mgr; Terrance McKnight, mus dir; Mark Fehlig, engrg dir.

WWRQ-FM— Feb 1, 1992: 107.9 mhz; 14 kw. Ant 315 ft. TL: N30 50 11 W83 17 56. (CP: 50 kw, ant 449 ft. TL: N31 03 46 W83 04 21). 1711 Ellis Dr. 31601. Phone: (229) 244-8642. Fax: (229) 247-7620. Licensee: RTG Radio LLC. Group owner: Black Crow Media Group LLC (acq 11-9-2001; grpsl). Miller & Miller. Format: Classic rock, AOR. Target aud: 25-49; upscale suburban couples. ♦ Scott James, gen mgr & progmg dir.

Vidalia

WBBT(AM)—See Lyons

WGPH(FM)—Licensed to Vidalia. See Augusta

WLYU(FM)—See Lyons

WTCQ(FM)—Listing follows WVOP(AM).

WVOP(AM)— Dec 2, 1946: 970 khz; 5 kw-D. TL: N32 13 12 W82 26 13. Stereo. Box 900 30475. Secondary address: 1501 Mt. Vernon Rd. 30474. Phone: (912) 537-9202. Fax: (912) 537-4477. E-mail: wtcq@vidaliacommunications.com. Licensee: Vidalia Communications Corp. (group owner) Network: ABC Information & Entertainment. Rep: Rgnl Reps. Fletcher, Heald & Hildreth. Format: Oldies, news, sports. News staff: one; News: 18 hrs wkly. Target aud: 25-54. Spec prog: Pub affrs 2 hrs, relg 8 hrs wkly. ♦ John Ladson, pres; Zack Fowler, stn mgr; Jim Perry, opns mgr; Marvin McIntyre, gen sls mgr; Dick Boekeloo, chief of engrg.

WTCQ(FM)— Co-owned with WVOP(AM). Mar 5, 1969: 97.7 mhz; 6 kw. 300 ft. TL: N32 13 12 W82 26 13. Stereo. Rep: Rgnl Reps. Format: Adult contemp. Target aud: 18-34. ♦ Zack Fowler, gen mgr; Marvin McIntyre, rgnl sls mgr.

Vienna

WKTF(AM)— Nov 17, 1979: 1550 khz; 1 kw-D, 23 w-N. TL: N32 07 44 W83 47 46. Box 188 31092. Phone: (229) 268-1550. Fax: (229) 268-4382. E-mail: imartinez@lenmedia.net. Licensee: LEN Radio Broadcasting of Vienna, Georgia LLC. (acq 11-19-2004; $230,000).

Format: Spanish. News staff: one; News: 15 hrs wkly. Target aud: 20 plus. ♦ Antonio Hernandez, gen mgr.

Warm Springs

WJSP-FM—Licensed to Warm Springs. See Atlanta

Warner Robins

WEBL(FM)— September 1994: 102.5 mhz; 4 kw. Ant 328 ft. TL: N32 34 20 W83 40 13. Stereo. 7080 Industrial Hwy., Macon 31216. Phone: (478) 781-1063. Fax: (478) 781-6711. Web Site: www.bull1025.com. Licensee: AMFM Radio Licenses LLC. Group owner: Clear Channel Communications Inc. (acq 2-1-2001; grpsl). Format: Country. Target aud: 25-64. ♦ Bill Clark, gen mgr.

WNNG(AM)— Oct 13, 1954: 1350 khz; 15 kw-D, 500 w-N, DA-N. TL: N32 37 00 W83 39 00. Stereo. 1350 Radio Loop 31088. Phone: (478) 923-3416. Fax: (478) 923-3236. Web Site: www.wnng1350.com. Licensee: Chase Broadcasting Inc. (acq 7-17-01). Network: Westwood One. Format: Adult Standards. News staff: one; News: 3 hrs wkly. Target aud: Target audience: 35-74, middle to upper class; working class, military, retired, business owners. ♦ Gordon Van Mol, pres; Anna McCloy, opns mgr.

WRBV(FM)— August 1969: 101.7 mhz; 4.9 kw. 350 ft. TL: N32 38 19 W83 38 33. Stereo. 7080 Industrial Hwy., Macon 31216. Phone: (478) 781-1063. Fax: (478) 781-6711. Web Site: www.1017.com. Licensee: AMFM Radio Licenses LLC. Group owner: Clear Channel Communications Inc. (acq 2-1-2001; grpsl). Network: ABC. Format: Urban contemp. News: one hr wkly. Target aud: 21-54. ♦ Bill Clark, gen mgr.

Warrenton

WGAC-FM— 1998: 93.1 mhz; 4.1 kw. Ant 400 ft. TL: N33 29 59 W82 37 09. Box 211045, Augusta 30917. Phone: (706) 396-7000. Fax: (706) 396-7100. Web Site: www.wgac.com. Licensee: WCHZ License LLC. Group owner: Beasley Broadcast Group Inc. (acq 5-3-2000; $800,000. with WGUS(AM) Augusta). Format: News/talk. ♦ Coni Sansom, gen mgr; Kent Dunn, gen mgr.

Washington

WLOV(AM)—Listing follows WXKT(FM).

WXKT(FM)— June 1, 1970: 100.1 mhz; 2.4 kw. 321 ft. TL: N33 43 50 W82 43 10. Stereo. 823 Berkshire Dr. 30673. Secondary address: 312 Old First National Bank Bldg., Elberton 30635. Phone: (706) 678-0100. Fax: (706) 678-3394. Licensee: Southern Broadcasting Companies Inc. (group owner; acq 8-28-01; $635,000. with co-located AM). Format: Country. Target aud: 25-54; baby boomers. ♦ Scott Smith, gen mgr; Mel Stovall, opns mgr, progmg dir & news dir; Julie Irby, gen sls mgr.

WLOV(AM)—Co-owned with WXKT(FM). Sept 1, 1955: 1370 khz; 1 kw-D. TL: N33 43 50 W82 43 10. Format: Timeless classics.

Waycross

*WASW(FM)— June 1998: 91.9 mhz; 1 kw. 148 ft. TL: N31 13 07 W82 21 34. Box 3206, American Family Radio, Tupelo, MS 38803. Phone: (662) 844-8888. Fax: (662) 842-6791. Web Site: www.afr.net. Licensee: American Family Radio. (group owner) Format: Inspirational Christian. ♦ Marvin Sanders, gen mgr; Rick Robertson, progmg dir.

WKUB(FM)—See Blackshear

WWGA(FM)— 2004: 1230 khz; 1 kw-U. TL: N31 12 45 W82 22 20. 1766 Memorial Dr., Suite 1 31501. Phone: (912) 285-5002. Fax: (912) 264-1991. E-mail: wgaradio@yahoo.com. Web Site: www.wgaradio.com. Licensee: MarMac Communications L.L.C. Format: News/talk. ♦ Gary Marmitt, gen mgr, gen sls mgr & progmg dir; Dick Eoekeloo, chief of engrg.

WWSN(FM)—Licensed to Waycross. See Brunswick

WWUF(FM)— Jan 25, 1986: 97.7 mhz; 6 kw. Ant 325 ft. TL: N31 11 05 W82 15 24. Stereo. Box 1472 31501. Secondary address: 2132 Hwy. 84, Blackshear 31516. Phone: (912) 449-3391. Fax: (912) 449-6284. E-mail: gtmattox@yahoo.com. Licensee: Mattox Broadcasting

Directory of Radio

Inc. (acq 5-16-2000). Network: ABC. Rep: Keystone (unwired net). Format: Oldies. Target aud: 25-54; general. ♦ Troy Mattox, pres & gen mgr; Ray Williamson, opns dir.

*WXVS(FM)— December 1985: 90.1 mhz; 79 kw horiz, 71 kw vert. 918 ft. TL: N31 13 17 W82 34 24. Stereo. 260 14th St. N.W., Atlanta 30318-5360. Phone: (404) 685-2690. Fax: (404) 685-2684. E-mail: gpr@gpb.org. Web Site: www.gpb.org. Licensee: Georgia Public Telecommunications Commission. Network: NPR, PRI. Format: Classical, News. News staff: 6; News: 40 hrs wkly. ♦ James Lyle, CEO; Bonnie Bean, CFO; John Hughes, exec VP; Chuck Miller, gen mgr; Shelease Whitaker, chief of opns; Anne Bramlette, sls dir; Marcia Killingsworth, prom dir; St. John Flynn, progmg mgr; Terrance McKnight, mus dir; Mark Fehlig, engrg dir.

WYNR(FM)—Licensed to Waycross. See Brunswick

Waynesboro

WTHB-FM— 1975: 100.9 mhz; 6 kw. 279 ft. TL: N33 05 15 W82 02 17. Stereo. Box 1584, Augusta 30903. Phone: (803) 279-2330. Fax: (803) 279-8149. Web Site: www.thbgospelalive.com. Licensee: Radio One of Augusta LLC. Group owner: Radio One Inc. (acq 11-8-01; grpsl). Rep: Allied Radio Partners. Fisher, Wayland, Cooper, Leader & Zaragoza. Format: Gospel. News staff: 2; News: 5 hrs wkly. Target aud: Teen-49. ♦ Ron Tomel, opns mgr.

WYFA(FM)—Licensed to Waynesboro. See Augusta

West Point

WCJM-FM— July 18, 1966: 100.9 mhz; 1.85 kw. 235 ft. TL: N32 53 42 W85 09 32. (CP: 6 kw, ant 177 ft., TL: N32 53 48 W85 09 24). 705 W. 4th Ave. 31833. Phone: (706) 645-2991. Fax: (706) 645-3364. E-mail: wjcm@qantumofauburn.com. Licensee: Qantum of Auburn License Co. LLC. Group owner: Qantum Communications Corp. (acq 7-2-03; grpsl). Format: Country. ♦ Steve Wheeler, gen mgr; Anthony Lovelady, progmg dir.

WPLV(AM)— August 1958: 1310 khz; 1 kw-D. TL: N32 53 42 W85 09 32. (CP: TL: N32 53 48 W85 09 24). 705 W. Fourth Ave., Westpoint 31833. Phone: (706) 645-1310. Fax: (706) 645-3364. E-mail: wcjm@quantumofauburn.com. Licensee: Qantum of Auburn License Co. LLC. Group owner: Qantum Communications Corp. (acq 7-2-03; grpsl). Network: ABC Information & Entertainment. Format: Talk radio. ♦ Steve Wheeler, gen mgr; Terry Harper, chief of engrg.

WRLA(AM)— May 1944: 1490 khz; 1 kw-U. TL: N32 52 26 W85 11 32. 503 W. 8th St., Suite 102 31833. Phone: (706) 645-1490. Fax: (706) 645-1497. E-mail: wrla@wrla1490.com. Licensee: Casey Network LLC (group owner; acq 11-18-02). Network: ABC Information & Entertainment. Gardner, Carton & Douglas. Format: Oldies. News staff: one; News: 9 hrs wkly. Target aud: 18-55. ♦ Vince Smith, gen mgr.

Willacoochee

WKAA(FM)— Apr 7, 1978: 99.5 kw; 43 kw. Ant 755 ft. TL: N31 10 18 W83 21 57. 1711 Ellis Dr., Valdosta 31601. Phone: (229) 244-8642. Fax: (229) 242-7620. Web Site: www.995kixcountry.com. Licensee: RTG Radio LLC. (acq 11-9-2001; grpsl). Format: Country. News staff: one; News: 10 hrs wkly. Target aud: 25-54. ♦ Bob Ganzak, pres.

Winder

WIMO(AM)— Nov 4, 1952: 1300 khz; 1 kw-D, 59 w-N. TL: N33 58 22 W83 42 40. 850 Arch Tanner Rd., Bethlehem 30620. Phone: (770) 867-1300. Fax: (770) 868-1962. E-mail: quincos@aol.com. Web Site: www.wimo1300am.com. Licensee: Mark Myers (acq 3-30-2004; $75,000). Network: ABC Information & Entertainment. Format: Talk, gospel. Target aud: General. ♦ Mark Myers, pres; Kim Mitchell, gen mgr; Kurt Andrews, progmg dir.

*WYFW(FM)— December 1987: 89.5 mhz; 530 w. 130 ft. TL: N33 59 32 W83 45 15. (CP: 6 kw). Stereo. 11530 Carmel Commons Blvd., Charlotte, NC 28226. Phone: (800) 888-7077. E-mail: wyfw@bbnradio.org. Web Site: www.bbnradio.org. Licensee: Bible Broadcasting Network Inc. (group owner; acq 6-24-93; $104,000; 6-28-93). Format: Relg, MOR. News: 7 hrs wkly. Target aud: 35-44. ♦ Lowell Davey, pres; Paul D. Montgomery, gen mgr.

Stations in the U.S.   Hawaii

Developers & Brokers of Radio Properties
contact American Media Services at our suite: Philadelphia Marriott Downtown 215-625-2900
843-972-2200
americanmediaservices.com
Charleston, SC
Dallas, TX · Chicago, Il · Austin, TX
American Media Services, LLC

Woodbine

WCGA(AM)— June 15, 1987: 1100 khz; 10 kw-D. TL: N30 55 54 W81 42 31. 714 Narrow Way, St. Simons Island 31522. Phone: (912) 634-4543. Fax: (912) 634-4804. E-mail: wescox@adelphia.net. Licensee: Cox Broadcast Group Inc. Format: News/talk. News staff: 2; News: 2 hrs wkly. Target aud: Adults; 35-64. ◆Wesley Cox, gen mgr.

Wrens

WAKB(FM)— June 10, 1979: 96.9 mhz; 1 kw. 489 ft. TL: N33 16 21 W82 25 32. (CP: 750 w, ant 1,364 ft.). Stereo. 104 Bennett Ln., North Augusta, SC 29841. Secondary address: Box 1584, Augusta 30903. Phone: (803) 279-2330. Fax: (803) 819-3781. Web Site: www.magic969.com. Licensee: Radio One of Augusta LLC. Group owner: Radio One Inc. (acq 11-8-01; grpsl). Format: Urban contemp. ◆Dennis Jackson, gen mgr.

Wrightsville

WDBN(FM)— May 27, 1986: 107.5 mhz; 3 kw. 295 ft. TL: N32 42 24 W82 43 08. Box 130, Dublin 31040. Phone: (478) 274-0108. Fax: (478) 275-4657. E-mail: macd@wqzy.com. Licensee: State Broadcasting Corp. (acq 5-29-89; $160,000; 5-29-89). Format: Rock. Target aud: 12 plus. ◆Mac Davis, gen mgr.

Yates

***WWBM(FM)**—Not on air, target date: unknown: 89.7 mhz; 1 kw. Ant 321 ft. TL: N33 27 47 W84 53 35. Best Media Inc., 3601 36th Ave., Long Island City 11106. Phone: (718) 784-8555. Fax: (718) 784-8901. Licensee: Best Media Inc. Scott Cinnamon Law Office. Format: South Asian Music News, educational, cultural programs. News staff: one; News: 5 hrs wkly. Asian, Indian, Pakistani, Bengladesh, and other audience. This rebroadcasts in our translator FM stations in Chicago, Houston, Detroit, & Long Island New York. ◆Banad Visuianatu, pres.

Young Harris

WYHG(AM)— May 1984: 770 khz; 750 w-D. TL: N34 56 26 W83 51 13. 1352 Main St., Suite 6 30582. Phone: (706) 379-3169. Fax: (706) 379-4104. E-mail: wyhg@brmemc.net. Web Site: www.wolkcreekbroadcasting.com.Solid Gospel Network Licensee: Young Harris Broadcasting Corp. (acq 4-30-03; $120,000). Format: Country, bluegrass, gospel. News staff: 2. Target aud: 30-60; mature adults. ◆Ad Frazier, pres; Clair Frazier, pres; Rebecca St. John, gen mgr.

Zebulon

WEKS(FM)— February 1994: 92.5 mhz; 6 kw. 328 ft. TL: N33 05 11 W84 19 11. Stereo. c/o Stephen D. Tarkenton, 1523 Kell Ln., Suite One, Griffin 30224. Phone: (770) 412-8700. Fax: (770) 412-8080. E-mail: bear925@bellsouth.net. Web Site: www.bear92.com. Licensee: Spalding Broadcasting Inc. Miller & Miller. Format: C&W. News staff: one. Target aud: 25-54. ◆Stephen D. Tarkenton, CEO; Les Reed, opns VP.

Hawaii

Aiea

KGMZ-FM— September 1992: 107.9 mhz; 100 kw-horiz, 79 kw-vert. 1,965 ft. TL: N21 23 51 W158 06 01. Stereo. 900 Fort St., Suite 700, Honolulu 96813. Phone: (808) 275-1079. Fax: (808) 536-2528. E-mail: onair@oldiesradio.net. Web Site: www.oldiesradio.net. Licensee: Salem Media of Hawaii Inc. (acq 1-3-2005 in exchange for KRTR(AM) Honolulu and KKNE(AM) Waipahu). Format: Oldies. News staff: one. Target aud: 35-54; adults. ◆Scott MacKenzie, gen mgr; Leslie Kahana, gen sls mgr; John Matthews, progmg dir.

Eleele

KUAI(AM)— June 30, 1965: 720 khz; 5 kw-U. TL: N21 53 37 W159 33 27. Box 720, 4469 Waialo Rd. 96705. Phone: (808) 335-3171. Fax: (808) 335-3834. E-mail: kuai@hawaiian.net. Licensee: Visionary Related Entertainment L.L.C. (group owner; acq 2-10-2004; grpsl). Format: Adult contemp, country, Hawaiian. News: 21 hrs wkly. Target aud: 25-65; loc long-time residents, blue & white collar. Spec prog: Hawaiian 5 hrs, jazz 4 hrs wkly. ◆John Detz, pres & gen mgr.

Haiku

KUAU(AM)— 1995: 1570 khz; 1 kw-D, 500 w-N. TL: N20 54 37 W156 17 15. (CP: 50 kw-U). 777 Mokulele Hwy., Kahului 96732. Phone: (808) 871-7311. Fax: (808) 871-9708. Web Site: www.kingscathedral.com. Licensee: First Assembly of God-Kahului, Maui Inc. (acq 6-30-99). Network: Westwood One. Rep: Western Regional Broadcast Sales. Baraff, Koerner & Olender. Format: Sports, talk, relg. News staff: one. Target aud: General; upscale. ◆Ron Moody, gen mgr & stn mgr.

Haliimaile

KPMW(FM)— 1994: 105.5 mhz; 6 kw. -512 ft. TL: N20 42 32 W156 21 33. 230 Hana Hwy. #2, Kahului 96732. Phone: (808) 871-6251. Fax: (808) 871-5670. E-mail: 105@maui.net. Web Site: www.wild105.com. Licensee: Rey-Cel Broadcasting Inc. Format: CHR/rhythmic top 40.

Hanalei

***KKCR(FM)**— Aug 2, 1997: 90.9 mhz; 950 w. Ant -308 ft. TL: N22 13 02 W159 28 53. Stereo. Box 825 96714. Phone: (808) 826-7774. Fax: (808) 826-7977. E-mail: kkcr@kkcr.org. Web Site: www.kkcr.org. Licensee: Kekahu Foundation Inc. Format: Hawaiian Pacifica, eclectic, educ. News: 5 hrs wkly. Target aud: General; Kauai County residents. ◆Harvey Cohen, pres & CFO; Gwen Squyres, gen mgr; Jessica Dofflemyer, dev dir; Donna Lewis Giarman, engrg VP.

Hilo

***KANO(FM)**: 2001: 91.1 mhz; 100 kw. 592 ft. TL: N19 47 02 W155 05 23. 738 Kaheka St., Honolulu 96814. Phone: (808) 955-8821. Fax: (808) 942-5477. Web Site: www.hawaiipublicradio.org. Licensee: Hawaii Public Radio. Network: Network: NPR, PRI. Paul, Hastings, Janofsky & Walker, L.L.P. Format: Class. News staff: 3; News: 35 hrs wkly. ◆Valerie Yee, VP; Michael Titterton, gen mgr; Charles Husson, opns dir.

KAPA(FM)— December 1988: 100.3 mhz; 74 kw. Ant -515 ft. TL: N19 50 19 W155 06 43. Stereo. 913 Kanoelehua St. 96720. Phone: (808) 961-0651. Licensee: Pacific Radio Group Inc. (group owner; acq 8-11-2005; grpsl). Format: Hawaiian. Target aud: 18-49. ◆Jeanine Atebare, gen mgr.

***KCIF(FM)**— July 1, 1998: 90.3 mhz; 14 kw. 164 ft. TL: N19 30 17 W155 10 40. 180 Kinoole St., Suite 310 96720. Phone: (808) 935-7434. Fax: (808) 961-6022. E-mail: kcifradio@turquoise.net. Licensee: Hilo Christian Broadcasting. Format: Christian, relg, educ. ◆Pastor David Shotwell, chmn & pres.

KHBC(AM)— October 1986: 1060 khz; 5 kw-U. TL: N19 41 48 W155 03 05. Box 515 96721. Phone: (808) 959-5700. Fax: (808) 959-5800. E-mail: happenings@khbcradio.com. Web Site: www.khbcradio.com. Licensee: Hilo Broadcasting L.L.C. (acq 1-31-03). Network: CNN Radio. Format: Adult contemp. Spec prog: Hawaiian culture & language. ◆Buddy Gordon, gen mgr & stn mgr; Robert Turner, chief of engrg.

KHLO(AM)— Apr 1, 1950: 850 khz; 5 kw-U. TL: N19 44 11 W155 02 07. 913 Kanoelehua Ave. 96720. Phone: (808) 961-0651. Fax: (808) 934-8088. E-mail: jatebare@pacificradiogroup.com. Licensee: Pacific Radio Group Inc. (group owner; acq 9-17-03; grpsl). Format: Sports. News staff: 2; News: 7 hrs wkly. Target aud: 25-54. ◆Jeanine Atebare, gen mgr.

KHWI(FM)— Sept 20, 1992: 92.7 mhz; 9 kw. Ant -256 ft. TL: N19 50 19 W155 06 43. 333 Kilauea Ave., Suite 201 96720. Phone: (808) 934-9444. Fax: (808) 934-9448. E-mail: frank@hawaiian927.com. Web Site: www.hawaiian927.com. Licensee: Aloha Radio Group LLC (acq 5-21-2004). Format: Hawaiian reggae. Target aud: 18-49; active lifestyle, above average income, family. ◆Frank Hooten, pres & gen mgr; Janette Hooton, CFO & gen mgr; Denyse Woo, prom dir; Alan Ada, progmg dir.

KIPA(AM)— Sept 10, 1947: 620 khz; 10 kw-U. TL: N19 51 03 W155 05 09. 74-5605 Luhia St., B-7, Kailua-Kona 96740. Phone: (808) 329-8090. Fax: (808) 443-0888. E-mail: info@lava105.com. Web Site: www.lava105.com. Licensee: Skynet Hawaii LLC (acq 3-11-2004; $75,000). Format: Adult Standards/Hawaiian. News staff: 2. Target aud: 35 plus. ◆Chip Begay, opns mgr.

KKBG(FM)— Aug 5, 1980: 97.9 mhz; 51 kw. Ant -65 ft. TL: N19 50 19 W155 06 43. 913 Kanoelehua 96720. Phone: (808) 961-0651. Fax: (808) 934-8088. E-mail: jatebare@pacificradiogroup.com. Licensee: Pacific Radio Group Inc. (group owner; (acq 9-17-2003; grpsl). Format: Adult contemp. News staff: one; News: 10 hrs wkly. ◆Jeanine Atebare, gen mgr.

KNWB(FM)— Aug 3, 1985: 97.1 mhz; 40 kw. -124 ft. TL: N19 45 33 W155 08 33. (CP: 38 kw. TL: N19 47 02 W155 05 25). Stereo. 1145 Kilauea Ave. 96720. Phone: (808) 935-5461. Fax: (808) 935-7761. E-mail: sales@kwxx.com. Web Site: www.B97Hawaii.com. Licensee: New West Broadcasting Corp. (group owner; acq 1995; $270,000). Format: Classic Hits. News staff: one; News: 8 hrs wkly. Target aud: 25-45. ◆Chris Leonard, pres & gen mgr; Gavin Tanouye, stn mgr.

KPUA(AM)— 1936: 670 khz; 10 kw-U. TL: N19 47 02 W155 05 25. (CP: 50 kw-U, DA-N). Stereo. 1145 Kilauea Ave. 96720. Phone: (808) 935-5461. Fax: (808) 935-7761. Web Site: www.kpua.net. Licensee: New West Broadcasting Corp. (group owner; acq 5-18-92; $370,000. with co-located FM; FTR: 6-8-92). Network: Network: CBS, Westwood One. Dan Alpert. Format: News/talk, sports. News staff: 3; News: 22 hrs wkly. Target aud: 25 plus; upscale adults with interest in news. Spec prog: Japanese 6 hrs wkly. ◆Christopher Leonard, gen mgr, sls dir, mktg mgr & prom dir; John Orozco, rgnl sls mgr; Triska LaRochell, rgnl sls mgr; Ken Hupp, progmg dir & news dir.

KWXX-FM—Co-owned with KPUA(AM). Dec 16, 1984: 94.7 mhz; 100 kw. -330 ft. TL: N19 43 02 W155 08 13. Stereo. Web Site: www.kwxx.com. Network: Westwood One. Format: Hot adult contemp, Hawaiian. News staff: one; News: 3 hrs wkly. Target aud: 25 plus; upscale adults. Spec prog: Contemp Hawaiian 20 hrs, reggae 20 hrs wkly. ◆Gavin Tawouye, progmg dir.

KPVS(FM)— 1995: 95.9 mhz; 50 kw. 230 ft. TL: N19 41 12 W155 09 04. (CP: 27 kw, ant -361 ft.). 913 Kanoelehua Ave. 96720. Phone: (808) 961-0651. Fax: (808) 934-8088. E-mail: jatebare@pacificradiogroup.com. Licensee: Pacific Radio Group Inc. (group owner; (acq 8-11-2005; grpsl). Cohen & Berfield. Format: Rhythmic adult contemp. Target aud: 25-54; women. ◆Jeanine Atebare, gen mgr.

Honolulu

KAIM-FM—Listing follows KHNR(AM).

KCCN-FM— May 21, 1990: 100.3 mhz; 100 kw horiz, 81 kw vert. 1,965 ft. TL: N21 23 51 W158 06 01. 900 Fort St., Suite 700 96813. Phone: (808) 536-2728. Fax: (808) 536-2528. E-mail: info@kccnfm100.com. Web Site: kccnfm100.com. Licensee: CXR Holdings L.L.C. Group owner: Cox Broadcasting (acq 3-15-2000; grpsl). Format: Contemp Hawaiian mus. ◆Mike Kelly, gen mgr; David Daniels, opns mgr & progmg dir.

KDNN(FM)— July 4, 1988: 98.5 mhz; 51 kw. Ant 59 ft. TL: N21 18 49 W157 51 43. Stereo. 650 Iwilei Road, Suite 400 96817. Phone: (808) 550-9200. Fax: (808) 550-9510. Web Site: www.island985.com. Licensee: Capstar TX L.P. Group owner: Clear Channel Communications Inc. (acq 8-30-00; grpsl). Rep: Clear Channel. Ginsburg, Feldman &

Broadcasting & Cable Yearbook 2006

Bress. Format: Island Rhythm. Target aud: 25-54; upscale, white collar, college educated. ♦John Hogan, CEO & pres; Charlie Rahilly, sr VP; Chuck Cotton, gen mgr.

KHBZ(AM)—Co-owned with KDNN(FM). Mar 18, 1957: 990 khz; 5 kw-U. TL: N21 17 59 W157 51 33. Web Site: khbz.com. Network: ABC. Rep: Clear Channel. Ginsburg, Feldman & Bress. Format: News/talk. News: 20 hrs wkly. Target aud: 25-54.

KGU(AM)— May 11, 1922: 760 khz; 10 kw-U. TL: N21 17 41 W157 51 49. 560 N. Nimitz Hwy., Suite 109 96817. Phone: (808) 533-0065. Fax: (808) 524-2104. E-mail: info@kguradio.com. Web Site: www.kguradio.com. Licensee: Salem Media of Hawaii Inc. Group owner: Salem Communications Corp. (acq 2-16-00). Network: Salem Radio Network. Rep: Salem. Fletcher, Heald & Hildreth. Format: Christian talk & teaching. News: 5 hrs wkly. Target aud: 35-54; general. ♦T.J. Malievsky, gen mgr; Jack Waters, opns mgr.

KHCM(AM)— December 1959: 1170 khz; 5 kw-U. TL: N21 17 08 W157 48 08. 560 N. Nimitz Hwy. #109 96817. Phone: (808) 533-0065. Fax: (808) 524-2104. Licensee: Salem Media of Hawaii Inc. Group owner: Salem Communications Corp. (acq 4-7-2004; $500,000). Dan J. Alpert. Format: Country. ♦Ed Atsinger, CEO & pres; Stewart Eperson, chmn; David Evans, CFO; T.J. Malievsky, opns VP.

KHNR(AM)— Aug 31, 1956: 870 khz; 50 kw-U, DA-1. TL: N21 10 56 W157 13 27. 560 N. Nimitz Hwy., Suite 109 96817. Phone: (808) 533-0065. Fax: (808) 524-2104. Licensee: Salem Media of Hawaii Inc. Group owner: Salem Communications Corp. (acq 11-10-99; with co-located FM). Shaw Pittman. Format: Relg. ♦T.J. Malievsky, gen mgr; Jack Waters, chief of opns, progmg dir & mus dir; David Serrone, gen sls mgr; Kathleen Friedman, prom dir; Bob Adams, chief of engrg.

KAIM-FM—Co-owned with KHNR(AM). Nov 1, 1953: 95.5 mhz; 100 kw. -23 ft. TL: N21 17 08 W157 48 08. (CP: 99 kw, ant 1,988 ft. TL: N21 23 42 W158 05 55). Stereo. Web Site: www.thefishhawaii.com. Network: Salem Radio Network. Format: Contemp Christian music. Target aud: 25-49; female. ♦Michael Shishido, progmg dir; Kim Harper, mus dir.

KHNR-FM— Mar 6, 1962: 97.5 mhz; 80 kw. Ant 46 ft. TL: N21 17 37 W157 50 32. Stereo. 560 N. Nimitz Hwy., Suite 109 96817. Phone: (808) 533-0065. Fax: (808) 524-2104. Web Site: www.khnr.com. Licensee: Salem Media of Hawaii Inc. Group owner: Salem Communications Corp. (acq 6-22-2004; $3.7 million. with KHUI(FM) Honolulu). Format: News/talk. ♦T.J. Malievsky, gen mgr; Jack Walters, opns mgr.

***KHPR(FM)**— Nov 13, 1981: 88.1 mhz; 44 kw. 2,000 ft. TL: N21 24 03 W158 06 10. Stereo. 738 Kaheka St. 96814. Phone: (808) 955-8821. Fax: (808) 942-5477. Web Site: www.hawaiipublicradio.org. Licensee: Hawaii Public Radio. Network: Network: NPR, PRI. Paul, Hastings, Janofsky & Walker. Format: Class, news, info. News staff: 3; News: 35 hrs wkly. Target aud: General. ♦Valerie Yee, VP; Michael Titterton, gen mgr; Charles Husson, opns mgr.

KHRA(AM)— March 1992: 1460 khz; 5 kw-U. TL: N21 19 26 W157 52 32. Stereo. 320 Ward Ave., Suite 207 96814. Phone: (808) 348-1986 (cell phone). Fax: (808) 591-1986. Licensee: Trade Center Management Inc. (acq 2-2-2002; $575,000). Format: Korean. ♦Ki Kim, gen mgr.

KHUI(FM)— Mar 1, 1993: 99.5 mhz; 100 kw. -386 ft. TL: N21 18 02 W157 51 53. Stereo. 1833 Kalakaua Ave., Suite 500 96815. Phone: (808) 533-0065. Fax: (808) 524-2104. Web Site: breezeofhawaii.com. Licensee: Salem Media of Hawaii Inc. Group owner: Salem Communications Corp. (acq 6-22-2004; $3.7 million. with KHNR-FM Honolulu). Rep: McGavren Guild. Format: 80s & 90s. ♦T.J. Malievsky, gen mgr.

KHVH(AM)— April 1951: 830 khz; 10 kw-U. TL: N21 19 26 W157 52 32. Stereo. 650 Iwilei Rd., Suite 400 96817. Phone: (808) 550-9200. Fax: (808) 550-9510. Web Site: www.khvh830am.com. Licensee: Capstar TX L.P. Group owner: Clear Channel Communications Inc. (acq 8-30-00; grpsl). Network: ABC News/Talk. Rep: Clear Channel. Ginsburg, Feldman & Bress. Format: News/talk, weather, traffic. News staff: 5; News: 21 hrs wkly. Target aud: 25-54. ♦John Hogan, CEO; Charlie Ramilly, sr VP; Chuck Cotton, gen mgr; Patti Milburn, gen sls mgr; Scott Hogle, sls dir & gen sls mgr; Jamie Hartnett, prom dir; Paul Wilson, progmg dir; Dave Curtis, news dir; Jerry Varoujean, chief of engrg.

KIKI-FM—Co-owned with KHVH(AM). Feb 14, 1979: 93.9 mhz; 100 kw. -44 ft. TL: N21 19 26 W157 52 32. Stereo. Web Site: www.hot939.com. Format: Rhythmic CHR. News staff: one; News: hrs wkly. Target aud: 18-34. ♦Paul Wilson, opns dir; Laurie Mizuno, gen sls mgr; Kamu Kanekoa, prom dir; Fred Rico, progmg dir; Dave Curtis, pub affrs dir; Dale Machado, chief of engrg.

KINE-FM— November 1988: 105.1 mhz; 100 kw. 1,948 ft. TL: N21 23 51 W158 06 01. Stereo. 900 Fort St. Mall, Suite 700 96813-3797. Phone: (808) 536-2728. Fax: (808) 536-2528. E-mail: info@hawaiian105.com. Web Site: www.hawaiian105.com. Licensee: CXR Holdings L.L.C. Group owner: Cox Broadcasting (acq 3-15-2000; grpsl). Rep: Major Market Broadcasters Ltd. Format: Contemp & traditional Hawaiian. Target aud: 25-44. ♦Michael Kelly, VP & gen mgr; John Aeto, sls dir; David Daniels, progmg dir.

***KIPO(FM)**— 1989: 89.3 mhz; 3.3 kw. 1,968 ft. TL: N21 24 03 W158 06 10. Stereo. 738 Kaheka St. 96814. Phone: (808) 955-8821. Fax: (808) 942-5477. Web Site: www.hawaiipublicradio.org. Licensee: Hawaii Public Radio. Network: Network: PRI, NPR. Paul, Hastings, Janofsky & Walker. Format: News & info, jazz, international mus. News staff: 3; News: 50 hrs wkly. Target aud: General. ♦Valerie Yee, VP; Michael Titterton, gen mgr; Charles Husson, opns dir.

KKEA(AM)— Nov 1, 1966: 1420 khz; 5 kw-U. TL: N21 19 26 W157 52 47. 900 Fort St., Suite 700 96813. Phone: (808) 275-1047. Phone: (808) 296-1420. Fax: (808) 275-1197. Fax: (808) 548-0608. Web Site: www.kkea1420am.com. Licensee: Blow Up LLC (acq 5-31-02; $750,000). Network: UPI. Format: Talk, sports. Target aud: 35-64 plus; male oriented, interested in sports/talk current events. Spec prog: Food show 10 hrs wkly. ♦Randall Ikeda, gen mgr; Chris Hart, progmg dir.

***KKUA(FM)**—(Wailuku). Apr 15, 1988: 90.7 mhz; 7 kw. 5,533 ft. TL: N20 42 41 W156 15 26. 738 Kaheka St. 96814. Phone: (808) 955-8821. Fax: (808) 942-5477. Web Site: www.hawaiipublicradio.org. Licensee: Hawaii Public Radio Inc. Network: Network: PRI, NPR. Format: Class, news, info. News staff: 3; News: 35 hrs wkly. Target aud: General. Spec prog: Hawaiian one hr, Pacific Island 2 hrs wkly. ♦Valerie Yee, VP; Michael Titterton, gen mgr; Charles Husson, opns dir.

KLHT(AM)— 1946: 1040 khz; 7.5 kw-U. TL: N21 17 08 W157 48 08. 98-1016 Komo Mai Dr., Aiea 96701. Phone: (808) 524-1040. Fax: (808) 524-0998. E-mail: klht@hawaii.rr.com. Licensee: Calvary Chapel of Honolulu Inc. (acq 5-85). Format: Bible teaching. Target aud: General. ♦Jake O'Neil, gen mgr.

KNDI(AM)— July 11, 1960: 1270 khz; 5 kw-U. TL: N21 19 26 W157 52 47. 1734 S. King St. 96826. Phone: (808) 946-2844. Fax: (808) 947-3531. E-mail: kndi.am@verizon.net. Web Site: www.kndi.com. Licensee: Leona Jona dba KNDI Radio. Rep: A/D. Format: Ethnic, Filipino 3 dialects. Spec prog: Togan 7 hr, Vietnamesel 2 hrs, Loatian 2 hrs wkly. ♦Harvey Weinstein, VP, opns mgr & mus dir; Leona Jona, pres & gen mgr.

KORL(AM)— May 14, 1947: 690 khz; 10 kw-U. TL: N21 17 41 W157 51 49. Stereo. 900 Fort Street Mall, Suite 450 96813. Phone: (808) 538-9690. Fax: (808) 538-9548. Licensee: Hochman-McCann Hawaii Inc. (acq 12-30-2003; $550,000). Format: Ethnic, local talk. ♦George Hochman, CEO & gen mgr.

KPOI-FM— Aug 3, 2000: 105.9 mhz; 97 kw. 1,968 ft. TL: N21 23 50 W158 06 06. Stereo. 765 Amana 96814. Phone: (808) 947-1500. Fax: (808) 947-1506. E-mail: kumu@kumu.com. Web Site: www.lavarock1059.com. Licensee: Visionary Related Entertainment LLC. (group owner; (acq 3-17-2004; grpsl). Thompson, Hine & Flory. Format: Classic rock. News staff: one; News: 23 hrs wkly. Target aud: 24-54; families, including single-parent families. ♦John Detz, gen mgr.

KQMQ-FM— Oct 1, 1967: 93.1 mhz; 100 kw. Ant 1,853 ft. TL: N21 23 45 W158 05 58. Stereo. 765 Amana St. 96814. Phone: (808) 947-1500. Fax: (808) 947-1506. Web Site: www.kqmq.net. Licensee: Visionary Related Entertainment L.L.C. (group owner; acq 7-1-2004; grpsl). Format: Hits of the 80s. ♦Jeff Coelho, gen mgr.

KREA(AM)— Apr 24, 1973: 1540 khz; 5 kw-D. TL: N21 19 27 W157 52 47. 1839 S. King St. 96826. Phone: (808) 955-1234. Licensee: JMK Communications Inc. (acq 3-10-00; $575,000). Format: Korean language stn.

KRTR(AM)— 1946: 650 khz; 10 kw-U. TL: N21 26 43 W158 03 49. 560 N. Nimitz Hwy., Suite109 96817. Phone: (808) 533-0065. Fax: (808) 524-2104. Web Site: www.khnr.com. Licensee: CXR Holdings LLC. Group owner: Salem Communications Corp. (acq 1-3-2005 with KKNE(AM) Waipahu in exchange for KGMZ-FM Aiea). Network: Network: CNN Radio, CBS Radio. Rep: Salem. Fletcher, Heald & Hildreth. Format: News, talk. News: 55 hrs wkly. Target aud: 25-54. ♦T.J. Malievsky, gen mgr; Jack Walters, chief of opns; Wayne Marla, progmg dir.

KRTR-FM—See Kailua

KRUD(AM)—Not on air, target date: June 1, 2005:. Stn currently dark 1130 khz; 10 kw-D, 5 kw-N. TL: N21 16 30 W157 49 25. 900 Fort Street Mall, Suite 450 96813. Phone: (808) 538-9690. Fax: (808) 538-9548. Licensee: Hochman-McCann Hawaii Inc. (acq 1-26-2005; $60,000. for CP). Format: Ethnic. Target aud: Adults 18-24. ♦George Hochman, pres & gen mgr; Donna Vincent, opns dir; Byron McCann, chief of engrg; Dianna Hochman, sls.

KSHK(FM)—(Kekaha). Aug 10, 1999: 103.3 mhz; 100 kw. 918 ft. TL: N21 56 11 W159 26 43. Box 1748, Lihue 96766. Phone: (808) 245-9527. E-mail: knog@hawaiian.net. Web Site: www.kongradio.com. Licensee: Visionary Related Entertainment L.L.C. (group owner; acq 2-10-2004; grpsl). Format: Top-40. ♦John Detz, pres; Jim McKeon, opns dir; Denise Roberts, prom dir.

KSSK(AM)— 1929: 590 khz; 7.5 kw-U. TL: N21 19 26 W157 52 32. 650 Iwilei Rd., Suite 400 96817. Phone: (808) 550-9200. Fax: (808) 550-9507. Web Site: www.ksskradio.com. Licensee: Capstar TX L.P. Group owner: Clear Channel (acq 3-12-99; grpsl). Rep: Clear Channel. Ginsburg, Feldman & Bress. Format: Adult contemp, personalities. News staff: 5; News: 15 hrs wkly. Target aud: 25-54. ♦Chuck Cotton, gen mgr.

KSSK-FM—See Waipahu

***KTUH(FM)**— Jan 1, 1969: 90.3 mhz; 3kw. -82 ft. TL: N21 18 14 W157 49 22. Stereo. 2445 Campus Rd., Suite 203 96822. Phone: (808) 956-7431. Phone: (808) 956-5288. Fax: (808) 956-5271. E-mail: gm@ktuh.org. Web Site: www.ktuh.org. Licensee: University of Hawaii. Target aud: 18-59; no target, all kinds of people listen. ♦Paul Zalate, gen mgr; Loriel Macalma, prom dir & prom mgr; Eric Rosenfeld, progmg dir; Allyson Ota, mus dir; Jared Lau, asst music dir; Dale Machado, chief of engrg.

KUMU-FM— Sept 1, 1967: 94.7 mhz; 100 kw. 78 ft. TL: N21 17 09 W157 50 19. Stereo. 765 Amana St., Suite 206 96814. Phone: (808) 947-1500. Fax: (808) 947-1506. E-mail: kumu@kumu.com. Licensee: Visionary Related Entertainment LLC (group owner; acq 3-17-2004; grpsl). Format: Lite rock, adult contemporary. Target aud: 25-54. ♦Bonnie Craig, pres & gen sls mgr; Jeff Coelho, gen mgr; Sumee Mikkelson, prom dir; Ed Kanoi, progmg dir; Ernie Nearman, chief of engrg.

KUMU(AM)— Mar 1, 1963: 1500 khz; 10 kw-U. TL: N21 17 08 W157 48 08. Network: Westwood One. Format: Talk. Target aud: 35-64.

KUPA(AM)—(Pearl City). May 2, 1990: 1370 khz; 6.2 kw-U. TL: N21 26 18 W157 59 29. Broadcasting Corp. of America, 4766 Holladay Blvd., Holladay, UT 84117. Phone: (808) 533-0065. Phone: (801) 273-9200. Licensee: Broadcasting Corp. of America. Group owner: Diamond Broadcasting Corp. (acq 8-18-2005; $650,000). Format: Hawaiian music. ♦Nathan W. Drage, pres.

KWAI(AM)— Jan 21, 1972: 1080 khz; 5 kw-U. TL: N21 17 41 W157 51 49. 100 N. Beretania St., Suite 401 96817. Phone: (808) 523-3868. Fax: (808) 531-6532. E-mail: kwai@hotmail.com. Licensee: Radio Hawaii Inc. (acq 2-85). Network: CNN Radio. Format: News/talk. News: 72 hrs wkly. Target aud: 25-64; general. Spec prog: Fillpino 7 hrs, Hawaiian 2hrs wkly. ♦Barry Wagenvoord, pres & gen mgr; Sam Wagenvoord, VP; Renee Rosehill, opns VP & opns dir.

KZOO(AM)— Oct 18, 1963: 1210 khz; 1 kw-U. TL: N21 17 59 W157 51 33. (CP: TL: N21 17 41 W157 51 49). Box 61335 96839-1335. Phone: (808) 988-8828. Fax: (808) 988-5882. E-mail: newsdesk@kzoohawaii.com. Web Site: www.kzoohawaii.com. Licensee: Polynesian Broadcasting Inc. (acq 8-4-2005). Format: Japanese, English. ♦David Furuya, pres & gen mgr.

Kahaluu

KLEO(FM)— 1992: 106.1 mhz; 7.3 kw. Ant 2,995 ft. TL: N19 43 16 W155 55 15. 913 Kanaoelehua Ave., Hilo 96720. Phone: (808) 961-0651. Fax: (808) 934-8088. E-mail: jatebare@pacificradiogroup.com. Licensee: Pacific Radio Group Inc. (group owner; acq 9-17-03; grpsl). Format: Adult contemp. ♦Jeanine Atebare, gen mgr.

Stations in the U.S. — Hawaii

Developers & Brokers of Radio Properties
contact American Media Services at our suite: Philadelphia Marriott Downtown 215-625-2900
843-972-2200
americanmediaservices.com
Charleston, SC
Dallas, TX · Chicago, Il · Austin, TX
American Media Services, LLC

Kahului

KAOI-FM—(Wailuku). June 1974: 95.1 mhz; 100 kw. 1,227 ft. TL: N20 38 12 W156 23 24. Stereo. Box 38 96732. Phone: (808) 244-9145. Licensee: Visionary Related Entertainment L.L.C. (group owner; (acq 2-10-2004); grpsl). Format: Adult contemp. News staff: one; News: 5 hrs wkly. Target aud: General. ♦John Detz, pres, gen mgr & opns mgr; Greg Everett, gen sls mgr; Jack Gist, progmg dir & news dir; Alex Kowalski, chief of engrg.

KAOI(AM)— Oct 11, 1979: 1110 khz; 5 kw-U. TL: N20 47 30 W156 28 21. Stereo. 1900 Main St., Wailuku 96793. Network: Network: CBS, Westwood One. Format: Talk/news, sports. Target aud: 25-54. ♦Alex Kowalski, chief of engrg.

KJKS(FM)—Listing follows KNUI(AM).

KNUI(AM)— Sept 14, 1962: 900 khz; 5 kw-U. TL: N20 47 30 W156 28 21. 311 Ano St. 96732. Phone: (808) 877-5566. Fax: (808) 877-2888. Fax: (808) 871-0666. E-mail: onair@knuiam900.com. Web Site: www.am900knui.com. Licensee: Pacific Radio Group Inc. (group owner; (acq 12-10-99); grpsl). Network: ABC Information & Entertainment. Format: Hawaiian, full service. News staff: one; News: 14 hrs wkly. Target aud: 35-54. Spec prog: Filipino 12 hrs wkly. ♦Eddie Johnson, CEO & CFO; Chuck Bergson, pres & CFO; Pamela Tsutsui, gen mgr; Jeff Hunter, opns mgr; Debbie Probst, gen sls mgr & rgnl sls mgr; Sherri Grimes, prom mgr; Wendy Osher, news dir; Earl Tolley, chief of engrg.

KJKS(FM)—Co-owned with KNUI(AM). June 22, 1984: 99.9 mhz; 100 kw. -540 ft. TL: N20 47 30 W156 28 21. Network: Westwood One. Format: Adult contemp. News staff: one. Target aud: 25-49. ♦Sherri Grimes, prom dir; Jeff Hunter, progmg dir.

Kailua

KRTR-FM— Oct 9, 1978: 96.3 mhz; 75 kw. 2,120 ft. TL: N21 19 49 W157 45 24. Stereo. 900 Fort St., 7th Fl., Honolulu 96813. Phone: (808) 275-1000. Fax: (808) 536-2528. Web Site: www.krater96.com. Licensee: CXR Holdings L.L.C. Group owner: Cox Broadcasting (acq 11-10-99); grpsl). Format: Adult contemp. Target aud: 25-54. ♦Bob Neil, CEO & pres; Marc Morgan, COO; Neil Johnston, CFO; Richard Ferguson, exec VP; Mike Kelly, gen mgr; John Aeto, sls dir; Mimi Beams, gen sls mgr; Corinne Webb, natl sls mgr & mus dir; Scott McKenzie, mktg dir; Aron Dotes, prom mgr; Wayne Maria, opns mgr & progmg dir; Jane Pascual, news dir; Chris Caughill, chief of engrg.

Kailua-Kona

KLUA(FM)— 1991: 93.9 mhz; 5.3 kw. 2,831 ft. TL: N19 43 15 W155 55 16. Stereo. 913 Kanoelehua Ave., Hilo 96720. Phone: (808) 961-0651. Fax: (808) 934-8088. E-mail: jatebare@pacificradiogroup.com. Licensee: Pacific Radio Group Inc. (group owner; (acq 8-11-2005); grpsl). Format: Rhythmic adult contemp. Target aud: 25-54; women. ♦Jeanine Atebare, gen mgr.

Kalaheo

KTOH(FM)— June 1, 2002: 99.9 mhz; 100 kw. 892 ft. TL: N21 56 11 W159 26 43. Box 929 96741. Secondary address: 4334 Rice St., Suite 204B, Lihue 96766. Phone: (808) 246-4444. Fax: (808) 246-4405. Licensee: Hochman Hawaii-One Inc. group owner: Hochman Hawaii-One Inc. (acq 6-23-2000); $125,000. for CP). Format: Oldies. News staff: one. Target aud: 25-54; adults. ♦Dianna Hochman, gen mgr & sls mgr; George Hochman, mktg mgr; Mark James, progmg dir.

Kaneohe

KPHW(FM)— Oct 17, 1997: 104.3 mhz; 73.5 kw. 2,116 ft. TL: N21 19 49 W157 45 24. 900 Fort St., 7th Fl., Honolulu 96813. Phone: (808) 275-1000. Fax: (808) 536-2528. E-mail: info@1043xme.com. Web Site: www.1043xme.com. Licensee: CXR Holdings L.L.C. Group owner: Cox Broadcasting (acq 11-10-99); grpsl). Format: CHR. Target aud: 18-34. ♦Bob Neil, CEO & pres; Marc Morgan, COO & VP; Neil Johnson, CFO; Richard Ferguson, exec VP; Mike Kelly, gen mgr; Wayne Maria, opns mgr; John Aeto, sls dir; Mark Haworth, gen sls mgr; Corinne Webb, natl sls mgr; Scott McKenzie, mktg dir & prom dir; Cy Shimabukuro, prom mgr; Kevin Akitake, progmg dir & mus dir; Chris Caughill, engrg mgr.

Kapaa

KITH(FM)— 1999: 98.9 mhz; 100 kw. Ant 918 ft. TL: N21 56 11 W159 26 43. 4334 Rice St., Suite. 204 B, Lihue 96766. Phone: (808) 246-4444. Fax: (808) 246-4405. Licensee: Hochman Hawaii-Two Inc. (acq 7-14-2000; $110,000. for CP). Format: Island music. News: 10 hrs wkly. ♦Dianna Hochman, gen mgr.

Kawaihae

KWYI(FM)— November 1993: 106.9 mhz; 5.5 kw. 341 ft. TL: N19 53 09 W155 39 28. Box 6540, 64-1040 Mamalahoa Hwy., Suite 4, Kamuela 96743. Phone: (808) 885-9866. Fax: (808) 885-6480. Licensee: Colin H. Naito. Format: Adult contemp. Target aud: 25-54. ♦Colin H. Naito, gen mgr.

Keaau

KBGX(FM)— Apr 16, 2004: 105.3 mhz; 25.26 kw. Ant 92 ft. TL: N19 43 18 W155 27 23. 74-5605 Luhia St. B-7, Kailua-Kona 96740. Phone: (808) 329-8090. Fax: (808) 443-0888. E-mail: info@lava105.com. Web Site: www.lava105.com. Licensee: Skynet Hawaii LLC (acq 12-10-03). Network: ABC. Shok, Hardy & Bacon. Format: Oldies. ♦Chip Begay, opns mgr.

Kealakekua

KAOY(FM)— Nov 11, 1982: 101.5 mhz; 6 kw. Ant 2,052 ft. TL: N19 31 10 W155 55 08. Stereo. c/o KWXX-FM, 1145 Kilauea Ave., Hilo 96720. Phone: (808) 935-5461. Fax: (808) 935-7761. E-mail: studio@kwxx.com. Web Site: www.kwxx.com. Licensee: New West Broadcasting Corp. (group owner; acq 4-16-2004; $500,000). Format: Adult contemp. Target aud: 18-49. ♦Christopher Leonard, gen mgr.

KKON(AM)— October 1963: 790 khz; 5 kw-U. TL: N19 31 10 W155 55 08. 913 Kanoelehua Ave., Hilo 96720. Phone: (808) 961-0651. Fax: (808) 935-0396. Web Site: www.pacificradiogroup.com. Licensee: Pacific Radio Group Inc. (group owner; (acq 8-11-2005); grpsl). Format: Sports. Target aud: 35 plus; general. Spec prog: Hawaiian mus. ♦Jeanine Atebara, gen mgr.

Kekaha

KSHK(FM)—Licensed to Kekaha. See Honolulu

Kihei

KAOI(AM)—Licensed to Kihei. See Kahului

Kilauea

__KAQA(FM)__— July 3, 1997: 91.9 mhz; 950 w. Ant 1,607 ft. TL: N21 58 41 W159 29 55. Stereo. Box 825, Hanalei 96714. Phone: (808) 826-7774. Fax: (808) 826-7977. E-mail: kkcr@kkcr.org. Web Site: www.kkcr.org. Licensee: Kekahu Foundation Inc. Format: Hawaiian Pacifica, eclectic, educ. Target aud: General; Kauai County residents. ♦Harvey Cohen, pres; Gwen Squyres, gen mgr, stn mgr & progmg dir; Jessica Dofflemyer, dev VP & engrg VP.

Kurtistown

KTBH-FM—Not on air, target date: unknown: 102.1 mhz; 50 kw horiz. Ant -207 ft. TL: N19 41 48 W155 03 05. Box 1730, Rohnert Park, CA 94927. Fax: (808) 244-8247. Licensee: Visionary Related Entertainment LLC. ♦John Detz, pres & gen mgr.

Lahaina

KLHI-FM— May 1984: 101.1 mhz; 100 kw. 745 ft. TL: N20 41 27 W156 22 07. Stereo. 311 Ano St., Kahului 96732. Phone: (808) 877-5566. Web Site: www.thepointfm101.com. Licensee: Pacific Radio Group Inc. (group owner; acq 12-10-99); grpsl). Dan Alpert. Format: Alternative rock. News staff: one; News: one hr wkly. Target aud: 18-49; general. ♦Pamela Tsutsui, gen mgr & stn mgr; Jeff Hunter, opns mgr.

KPOA(FM)— October 1984: 93.5 mhz; 1.4 kw. 1,305 ft. TL: N20 50 43 W156 54 04. (CP: 346 w, ant 2,421 ft.). Stereo. 311 Ano St., Kahului 96732. Phone: (808) 877-5566. Fax: (808) 877-2888. Fax: (808) 871-0666. Web Site: www.kpoa.com. Licensee: Pacific Radio Group Inc. (group owner; acq 12-10-99); grpsl). Kenkel & Associates. Format: Contemp Hawaiian Island sounds. News staff: one; News: one hr wkly. Target aud: Adults; 25-54. ♦Eddie Johnson, CFO; Pamela Tsutsui, gen mgr; Jeff Hunter, opns mgr.

Lanai City

KONI(FM)— Nov 1, 1993: 104.7 mhz; 69 kw. Ant 2,283 ft. TL: N20 39 36 W156 21 50. 300 Ohukai Rd.,, Suite C-318, Kihei 96753. Phone: (808) 875-8866. Fax: (808) 875-8870. E-mail: koni@hawaii.rr.com. Licensee: Hochman Hawaii Publishing Inc. (acq 6-17-2002; $1.15 million). Format: Oldies. News: one hr wkly. Target aud: 25-54; Maui county residents. ♦George Hochman, COO, chmn, pres, CFO & VP; Jim Carroll, gen mgr.

Lihue

KAWV(FM)— 2001: 98.1 mhz; 51 kw. Ant 13 ft. TL: N21 59 41 W159 24 36. O'Hana Radio Partners, 41-625 Eclectic St. J-1, Palm Desert, CA 92260. Licensee: O'Hana Radio Partners. ♦James L. Primm, pres.

KFMN(FM)— Mar 7, 1988: 96.9 mhz; 100 kw. 400 ft. TL: N21 59 54 W159 25 35. Stereo. Box 1566, 1860 Leleiona St. 96766-5566. Phone: (808) 246-1197. Fax: (808) 246-9697. E-mail: frontdesk@fm97radio.com. Licensee: FM 97 Associates. (acq 6-7-88; $600,000). Mullin, Rhyne, Emmons & Topel. Format: Adult contemp. News staff: one; News: 4 hrs wkly. Target aud: 25-54; island residents & visitors. ♦John Wada, gen mgr; Dianne Reynolds-Mikami, opns mgr.

__KHJC(FM)__—Not on air, target date: unknown: 88.9 mhz; 100 kw. 892 ft. TL: N21 56 11 W159 26 43. 2970 Kele St., Suite 117 96766. Secondary address: CSN International, 3000 W. MacArthur Blvd., 3rd Fl, Santa Ana, CA 92704. Phone: (808) 245-9696. Fax: (808) 245-9898. E-mail: khjc@csnradio.com. Web Site: www.csnradio.com. Licensee: CSN International (group owner) Format: Teaching.

KQNG(AM)— 1939: 570 khz; 1 kw-U. TL: N21 59 33 W159 24 24. Box 1748, KQNG Radio Bldg., 4271 Halenani St. 96766. Phone: (808) 245-9527. Fax: (808) 245-3563. E-mail: kong@hawaiian.net. Web Site: www.kongradio.com. Licensee: Visionary Related Entertainment L.L.C. (group owner; acq 2-10-2004; grpsl). Format: News/talk, sports. Target aud: 25-54. ♦John Detz, CEO & gen mgr; Ron Middac, progmg dir & chief of engrg.

KQNG-FM— Oct 17, 1983: 93.5 mhz; 100 kw. 226 ft. TL: N21 59 33 W159 24 24. Stereo. Format: Hot adult Comtemp. Target aud: 18-49. ♦John Detz, pres; Ron Wiley, opns mgr.

Makawao

KDLX(FM)— Dec 31, 1980: 94.3 mhz; 3 kw. -22 ft. TL: N20 50 48 W156 19 35. Stereo. Box 1437, Wailuku 96793. Phone: (808) 244-9145. Fax: (808) 244-8247. Licensee: Visionary Related Entertainment L.L.C. (group owner; acq 2-10-2004; grpsl). Format: Country. ♦John Detz, pres & gen mgr; Greg Everett, stn mgr.

Hawaii

Paauilo

KNUQ(FM)— 1995: 103.7 mhz; 100 kw. 1,209 ft. TL: N20 38 18 W156 23 01. Box 1437, Wailuku 96793. Phone: (808) 244-9145. Fax: (808) 244-8247. Web Site: www.q103maui.com. Licensee: Visionary Related Entertainment LLC (group owner; acq 2-10-2004; grpsl). Format: Contemp island music. News staff: one. Target aud: 18-49; young active adults. ♦John Detz, CEO & gen mgr; Greg Everett, stn mgr & prom mgr; Alex Kowalski, opns mgr & chief of engrg.

Pahala

*****KPHL(FM)**—Not on air, target date: unknown: 90.5 mhz; 50 kw. Ant -433 ft. TL: N19 16 26 W155 29 04. Broadcasting for the Challenged Inc., 6080 Mt. Moriah Ext., Memphis, TN 38115. Phone: (901) 375-9324. Fax: (901) 375-0041. Licensee: Broadcasting for the Challenged Inc. ♦George Flinn Jr., gen mgr.

Pearl City

KUCD(FM)— Feb 14, 1995: 101.9 mhz; 100 kw. 1,948 ft. TL: N21 23 51 W158 06 01. Stereo. 650 Iwilei Rd, Suite 400, Honolulu 96817. Phone: (808) 550-9200. Fax: (808) 550-9510. Web Site: www.star1019fm.com. Licensee: Capstar TX L.P. Group owner: Clear Channel Communications Inc. (acq 8-30-00; grpsl). Rep: Clear Channel. Ginsburg, Feldman & Bress. Format: Alternative. Target aud: 25-54; boomers & yuppies. ♦John Hogan, CEO; Charlie Rahilly, sr VP; Chuck Cotton, VP & gen mgr.

KUPA(AM)—Licensed to Pearl City. See Honolulu

Poipu

KSRF(FM)— Aug 14, 1999: 95.9 mhz; 100 kw. 918 ft. TL: N21 56 11 W159 26 43. Box 1748, Lihue 96766. Phone: (808) 245-9527. E-mail: kong@hawaiian.net. Web Site: www.kongradio.com. Licensee: Visionary Related Entertainment L.L.C. (group owner; acq 2-10-2004; grpsl). Format: Contemp Hawaiian. ♦John Detz, pres & gen mgr; Shelly Cobb, progmg dir & engrg dir.

Pukalani

KJMD(FM)— June 15, 1984: 98.3 mhz; 50 kw. 102 ft. TL: N20 42 19 W156 21 54. Stereo. 311 Ano St., Kahului 96732. Phone: (808) 877-5566. Fax: (808) 871-0666. Web Site: www.kjmd.com. Licensee: Pacific Radio Group Inc. (group owner; acq 12-10-99; grpsl). Network: ABC. Format: CHR. News staff: one. Target aud: 18-34; young active adults. ♦Chuck Bergson, CEO; Pamela Tsutsui, gen mgr; Jeff Hunter, opns mgr.

Volcano

KKOA(FM)— 1996: 107.7 mhz; 3 kw. 207 ft. TL: N19 29 08 W155 16 17. (CP: 18 kw). 74-5605 Luhia St., B-7, Kailua-Kona 96740. Phone: (808) 329-8090. Fax: (808) 443-0888. E-mail: info@lava105.com. Web Site: www.lava105.com. Licensee: Skynet Hawaii LLC (acq 5-3-2004; $350,000). Network: ABC. Format: Country. ♦Chip Begay, opns mgr.

Wailuku

KAOI-FM—Licensed to Wailuku. See Kahului

KJMD(FM)—See Pukalani

KKUA(FM)—Licensed to Wailuku. See Honolulu

KMVI(AM)— Mar 17, 1947: 550 khz; 5 kw-U. TL: N20 53 29 W156 29 23. 311 Ano St., Kahului 96732. Phone: (808) 877-5566. Fax: (808) 871-0666. Web Site: www.kmvi550.com. Licensee: Pacific Radio Group Inc. (group owner; acq 12-10-99; grpsl). Network: Network: ESPN Radio, ABC. Format: Sports radio. News staff: one. Target aud: Men 18+; residents/tourists, educated professionals. ♦Chuck Bergson, pres; Pamela Tsutsui, gen mgr; Jeff Hunter, opns mgr.

Waimea

KAGB(FM)— 2000: 99.1 mhz; 7.3 kw. Ant 2,990 ft. TL: N19 43 16 W155 55 15. 913 Kanoelehua Ave., Hilo 96720. Phone: (808) 961-0651. Licensee: Pacific Radio Group Inc. (group owner; (acq 8-11-2005; grpsl). Format: Hawaiian. ♦Jeanine Atebare, gen mgr.

Waipahu

KDDB(FM)— Nov 23, 1988: 102.7 mhz; 61 kw. 1,893 ft. TL: N21 23 49 W158 05 58. Stereo. 765 Amana St., Suite 200, Honolulu 96814. Phone: (808) 947-1500. Fax: (808) 947-1506. Licensee: Visionary Related Entertainment L.L.C. (group owner; acq 7-1-2004; grpsl). Rep: McGavren Guild. Reed, Smith, Shaw & McClay. Format: Top 40 hits. Target aud: 18-34; young adults who enjoy many different types of mus. ♦John Petz, gen mgr & stn mgr.

KKNE(AM)— Sept 20, 1950: 940 khz; 10 kw-U. TL: N21 26 43 W158 03 49. 900 Fort St., Suite 700, Honolulu 96813. Phone: (808) 533-0065 Ext. 731. Phone: (808) 257-1000. Fax: (808) 275-1195. Licensee: CXR Holdings LLC. Group owner: Salem Communications Corp. (acq 1-3-2005 with KRTR(AM) Honolulu in exchange for KGMZ-FM Aiea). Format: Country. Target aud: 25-44. ♦John Aeto, sls dir; Michael Kelly, gen mgr & sls dir; David Daniels, progmg dir.

KSSK-FM— Dec 30, 1976: 92.3 mhz; 100 kw. 1,630 ft. TL: N21 23 49 W158 05 58. (CP: Ant 1,950 ft.). Stereo. 650 Iwilei Rd., Suite 400, Honolulu 96817-5319. Phone: (808) 550-9200. Fax: (808) 550-9510. Web Site: ksskradio.com. Licensee: Clear Channel Broadcasting Licenses Inc. Clear Channel Communications Inc. (acq 9-1-00; grpsl). Rep: Clear Channel. Ginsburg, Feldman & Bress. Format: Adult contemp. News staff: 3; News: 6 hrs wkly. Target aud: 25-54. ♦John Hogan, CEO & VP; Charlie Rahilly, sr VP; Chuck Cotton, gen mgr; Scott Hogle, opns dir & sls dir; Patti Milburn, gen sls mgr; Jamie Hartnett, prom dir & prom mgr; Paul Wilson, progmg dir; Dave Curtis, news dir; Dale Machado, chief of engrg.

Idaho

American Falls

KORR(FM)— 1995: 104.1 mhz; 3 kw. 328 ft. TL: N42 45 24 W112 48 38. Box 97, Pocatello 83204-0097. Secondary address: 436 N. Main St., Pocatello 83204. Phone: (208) 234-1290. Fax: (208) 234-9451. E-mail: spots@kzbq.com. Web Site: www.idahobroadcasters.org. Licensee: Idaho Wireless Corp. (group owner; acq 1996). Format: Adult contemp. ♦Paul E. Anderson, gen mgr; Cyndi Colaianni, gen sls mgr; Paul Anderson, progmg dir.

Ammon

KUPI(AM)—Licensed to Ammon. See Idaho Falls

Blackfoot

KBLI(AM)— November 2000: 1620 khz; 10 kw-D, 1 kw-N. TL: N43 10 04 W112 22 08. Box 699 83221-0699. Phone: (208) 785-1400. Fax: (208) 785-0184. E-mail: jdressen@intermountainradio.com. Licensee: Bonneville Holding Co. Group owner: Bonneville International Corp. (acq 11-24-03; grpsl). Format: Sports. ♦Dave Cummings, gen mgr & progmg dir; Jeremy Dresen, gen sls mgr; Bill Troy, chief of engrg.

KCVI(FM)— Sept 22, 1994: 101.5 mhz; 100 kw. 1,512 ft. TL: N43 30 03 W112 39 43. Stereo. Box 699 83221. Phone: (208) 785-1400. Fax: (208) 785-0184. E-mail: scott@kbear.fm. Web Site: www.kbear.fm. Licensee: Bonneville Holding Co. Group owner: Bonneville International Corp. (acq 11-24-03; grpsl). Rep: McGavren Guild. Format: Active rock. News staff: one; News: 3 hrs wkly. Target aud: 25-44; male. ♦Delyn Hendricks, gen mgr; Jeremy Dresen, gen sls mgr; Scott Taylor, progmg dir; Bill Troy, chief of engrg.

KLCE(FM)—Listing follows KSLJ(AM).

KSLJ(AM)— November 1951: 690 khz; 1 kw-D, 43 w-N. TL: N43 10 70 W112 22 10. Box 699 83221. Phone: (208) 785-1400. Fax: (208) 785-0184. Licensee: Bonneville Holding Co. Group owner: Bonneville International Corp. (acq 11-24-2003; grpsl). Format: Talk. ♦Delyn Hendricks, gen mgr.

KLCE(FM)—Co-owned with KSLJ(AM). Oct 15, 1975: 97.3 mhz; 100 kw. 1,512 ft. TL: N43 30 03 W112 39 43. Stereo. Web Site: www.klce.com. Rep: McGavren Guild. Format: Adult contemp. Target aud: 18-49.

Boise

*****KAWS(FM)**—Not on air, target date: unknown: 89.1 mhz; 8.8 kw vert. Ant 2,189 ft. TL: N43 00 25 W116 42 13. 4002 N. 3300 E., Twin Falls 83301-0354. Phone: (208) 733-3133. Fax: (208) 736-1958. Licensee: Calvary Chapel of Twin Falls Inc. ♦Mike Kestler, pres & gen mgr.

KBOI(AM)— May 1, 1947: 670 khz; 50 kw-U, DA-N. TL: N43 25 44 W116 19 43. Stereo. Box 1280 83701. Secondary address: 1419 W. Bannock 83702. Phone: (208) 336-3670. Fax: (208) 336-3734 (Main). Fax: (208) 336-3735 (News). E-mail: andrew.paul@citcomm.com. Web Site: www.670kboi.com. Licensee: Citadel Broadcasting Co. Group owner: Citadel Broadcasting Corp. (acq 12-10-97; grpsl). Network: ABC Information & Entertainment. Rep: Katz Radio. Allied Radio Partners Format: News/talk. News staff: 3. Target aud: 25-54; white collar, upper income. ♦Kevin Godwin, gen mgr; Ken Weaver, sls dir & news dir; Linda Rupe, prom dir; Andrew Paul, progmg dir; Mike Owens, gen sls mgr & chief of engrg.

KQFC(FM)—Co-owned with KBOI(AM). Nov 1, 1960: 97.9 mhz; 47 kw. 2,499 ft. TL: N43 45 12 W116 06 08. (CP: 58 kw). Stereo. Format: Country. Target aud: 25-54; country lifestyle.

*****KBSU(AM)**— Dec 4, 1955: 730 khz; 15 kw-D, 500 w-N, DA-2. TL: N43 34 13 W116 20 45. Stereo. 213 SMITC, 1910 University Dr. 83725. Phone: (208) 426-3663. Fax: (208) 344-6631. Web Site: www.radio.boisestate.edu. Licensee: Idaho State Board of Education (Boise State University) (acq 12-30-91; donation;. FTR: 1-20-92). Dow, Lohnes & Albertson. Format: Class. Spec prog: Folk. ♦Steve Johnson, gen mgr; Hy Kloc, gen sls mgr; Jim East, progmg dir; Steve Jess, news dir; Tom Taylor, chief of engrg.

*****KBSU-FM**— Jan 16, 1977: 90.3 mhz; 19 kw. Ant 2,637 ft. TL: N43 35 41 W116 08 39. Stereo. Boise State Radio, 1910 University Dr. 83725. Phone: (208) 344-3961. Phone: (208) 947-5659. Fax: (208) 344-4080. E-mail: jeast@boisestate.edu. Web Site: radio.boisestate.edu. Licensee: Boise State Board of Education. (acq 12-30-91). Network: Network: PRI, NPR. Format: Class, news. News: 15 hrs wkly. Target aud: General. ♦John Hess, gen mgr & chief of engrg; Jim East, progmg dir; Steve Jess, news dir.

*****KBSX(FM)**— 1994: 91.5 mhz; 4 kw. 2,581 ft. TL: N43 45 18 W116 05 52. Boise State Radio, 1910 University Dr. 83725. Phone: (208) 344-3961. Fax: (208) 344-4080. Web Site: radio.boisestate.edu. Licensee: Idaho State Board of Education. Network: NPR. Format: News. ♦Jim East, gen mgr; Maureen Clark, opns mgr; Tom Taylor, chief of engrg.

KBXL(FM)—See Caldwell

KCIX(FM)—(Garden City). Jan 1, 1985: 105.9 mhz; 50 kw. 2,700 ft. TL: N43 45 18 W116 05 52. Stereo. 827 Park Blvd., Suite 201 83712. Phone: (208) 344-6363. Fax: (208) 385-9064. Web Site: www.mix106radio.com. Licensee: Citicasters Licenses L.P. Group owner: Clear Channel Communications Inc. (acq 5-4-99; grpsl). Rep: McGavren Guild. Format: Adult contemp. Target aud: 25-54. ♦Terry Tario, gen mgr; Susan Green, opns mgr; Jeff Cochran, progmg dir; Dave Burnett, news dir.

KFXD(AM)— Nov 9, 1928: 630 khz; 5 kw-U, DA-2. TL: N43 30 57 W116 19 43. (CP: TL: N43 30 56 W116 19 43). 827 E. Park Blvd. 83712-7782. Phone: (208) 344-6363. Fax: (208) 385-9064. E-mail: email@kfxd.com. Web Site: www.kfxd.net. Licensee: Citicasters L.P. Group owner: Clear Channel Communications Inc. (acq 5-4-99; grpsl). Network: ABC. Rep: Christal. Format: Classic country. Target aud: 35-64; managerial, professional, affluent. ♦Dick Lumenello, gen mgr; Mitch Pruitte, progmg dir; Lee Eichelberger, chief of engrg.

KLTB(FM)—Co-owned with KFXD(AM). Nov 2, 1979: 104.3 mhz; 52 kw. 2,574 ft. TL: N43 45 18 W116 05 52. Stereo. Web Site: www.koololdies1043.com. Format: Classic oldies. Target aud: 25-54; affluent, managerial, professional. ♦Jack Armstrong, progmg dir.

KGEM(AM)— 1945: 1140 khz; 10 kw-U, DA-N. TL: N43 35 54 W116 15 14. (CP: 50 kw-D). Stereo. 5257 Fairview Ave., Suite 260 83706. Phone: (208) 344-3511. Fax: (208) 947-6765. Licensee: Journal Broadcast Corp. Group owner: Journal Broadcast Group Inc. (acq 5-13-98; grpsl). Network: Westwood One. Rep: Katz Radio. Format: Original hits of the 40s, 50s & 60s. Target aud: 35 plus. ♦Bob Rosenthal, VP, gen mgr & opns mgr.

Stations in the U.S.
Idaho

Developers & Brokers of Radio Properties

contact American Media Services
at our suite:
Philadelphia Marriott Downtown
215-625-2900
843-972-2200
americanmediaservices.com
Charleston, SC
Dallas, TX · Chicago, Il · Austin, TX
American Media Services, LLC

KJOT(FM)—Co-owned with KGEM(AM). 1979: 105.1 mhz; 43 kw. 2,570 ft. TL: N43 45 19 W116 06 52. (CP: 52.5 kw). Stereo. Format: Classic rock. Target aud: 25-49.

KIDO(AM)—See Nampa

KIZN(FM)— Aug 1, 1968: 92.3 mhz; 44 kw. 2,500 ft. TL: N43 45 19 W116 05 52. Stereo. 1419 W. Bannock St. 83701. Phone: (208) 336-3670. Fax: (208) 336-3736. E-mail: rich.summers@citicomm.com. Web Site: www.kizn.com. Licensee: Citadel Broadcasting Co. Group owner: Citadel Broadcasting Corp. (acq 12-24-97; grpsl). Format: Country. News staff: one. Target aud: 25-54. ♦ Kevin Godwin, stn mgr; Rich Summers, opns VP & progmg dir; Brenda Mee, news dir; Bill Frahm, chief of engrg.

KNJY(AM)— Apr 8, 1961: 950 khz; 5 kw-D, 35 w-N. TL: N43 37 14 W116 17 57. Box 1600, Nampa 83653. Phone: (208) 463-1900. Licensee: First Western Inc. (acq 8-4-03; $150,000). Network: ABC Information & Entertainment. Format: Relg. Spec prog: Farm 5 hrs wkly. ♦ Steve Sumner, gen mgr.

KSAS-FM—See Nampa

KSPD(AM)— Apr 29, 1959: 790 khz; 1 kw-D, 61 w-N. TL: N43 33 57 W116 20 13. 1440 S. Weideman Ave. 83709. Phone: (208) 377-3790. Fax: (208) 377-3792. E-mail: info@myfamilyradio.com. Web Site: www.myfamilyradio.com. Licensee: KSPD Inc. (group owner; acq 3-24-83; FTR: 4-18-83). Network: Moody. Wiley, Rein & Fielding. Format: Christian, talk. Target aud: 18-54. ♦ Beth Schafer, exec VP; Lee Schafer, CEO, chmn, pres & gen mgr; David Schafer, stn mgr.

KZMG(FM)—(New Plymouth). Mar 17, 1982: 93.1 mhz; 50 kw. 2,630 ft. TL: N43 45 19 W116 05 52. Stereo. Box 1280 83701-1280. Secondary address: 1419 W. Bannock St. 83701. Phone: (208) 336-3670. Phone: (208) 424-9300. Fax: (208) 336-3734. E-mail: beau.richards@citcomm.com. Web Site: www.magic93.com. Licensee: Citadel Broadcasting Co. Group owner: Citadel Broadcasting Corp. (acq 12-24-97; grpsl). Rep: D & R Radio. Wiley, Rein, Fielding. Format: Contemporary hit/Top-40. News: 6 hrs wkly. Target aud: 18-34; women. ♦ Kevin Godwin, gen mgr & stn mgr; Mike Owens, gen sls mgr; Deb Course, progmg dir & news dir; Shelly Williams, pub affrs dir; Bill Frahm, chief of engrg.

Bonners Ferry

KBFI(AM)— Sept 1, 1977: 1450 khz; 1 kw-U. TL: N48 41 20 W116 20 04. 327 S. Marion, Sandpoint 83864. Phone: (208) 267-5234. Fax: (208) 267-5594. E-mail: prod@953kpnd.com. Licensee: Blue Sky Broadcasting. (acq 1996). Format: News/talk, sports. News staff: 1. Target aud: General. ♦ Bob Witte, gen mgr.

*KIBX(FM)— 2000: 92.1 mhz; 74 kw. Ant 2,749 ft. TL: N48 36 37 W116 15 24. Spokane Public Radio, Inc., 2319 N. Monroe St., Spokane, WA 99205-4586. Phone: (509) 328-5729. Fax: (509) 328-5764. E-mail: kpbx@kpbx.org. Web Site: kpbx.org. Licensee: Spokane Public Radio Inc. Format: Classical, news, jazz. ♦ Richard Kunkel, gen mgr; Brian Flick, progmg dir; Verne Windham, mus dir; Doug Nadvornick, news dir.

Buhl

*KTFY(FM)— 2005: . Stn currently dark 88.1 mhz; 60 kw vert. Ant 653 ft. TL: N42 43 48 W114 25 06. 16115 S. Montana Ave., Caldwell 83605. Phone: (208) 459-5879. Fax: (208) 459-3144. E-mail: magee@ktfy.org. Web site: www.881ktfy.org. Licensee: Southern Idaho Corp. of Seventh-Day Adventists dba Gem State Academy. Donald Martin. Format: Christian. Target aud: 25-54; women 25-54. ♦ Donald Klinger, chmn; Stephen L. McPherson, pres; Michael Agee, gen mgr; Jerry Woods, progmg dir.

Burley

KBAR(AM)— Aug 31, 1946: 1230 khz; 1 kw-U. TL: N42 32 05 W113 48 54. Stereo. 120 S. 300 W., Rupert 83350. Phone: (208) 678-2244. Fax: (208) 678-2246. E-mail: kimlee@cableone.net. Licensee: KART Broadcasting Co. Inc. and Eagle Rock Broadcasting Inc. as tenants-in-common. Group owner: Tri-Market Radio Broadcasters Inc. & Eagle Rock Broadcasting Inc. (acq 1-30-98; with co-located FM). Network: ABC Information & Entertainment. Format: Oldies, talk. ♦ Kim Lee, gen mgr.

KZDX(FM)—Co-owned with KBAR(AM). Feb 15, 1975: 99.9 mhz; 27 kw. Ant 2,450 ft. TL: N42 20 06 W113 36 15. Stereo. Network: ABC FM Connection. Format: AOR.

*KBSY(FM)— October 1998: 88.5 mhz; 440 w vert. 2,083 ft. TL: N42 21 42 W113 27 17. Boise State Radio, 1910 University Dr., Boise 83725. Phone: (208) 344-3961. Fax: (208) 344-4080. Web Site: radio.boisestate.edu. Licensee: Idaho State Board of Education. Network: NPR. Format: News. ♦ Jim East, gen mgr; Steve Johnston, progmg dir; Tom Taylor, chief of engrg.

Caldwell

KBGN(AM)— Oct 5, 1960: 1060 khz; 10 kw-D. TL: N43 43 13 W116 31 58. 3303 E. Chicago 83605. Phone: (208) 459-3635. E-mail: kbgn@kbgnradio.com. Web Site: www.kbgnradio.com. Licensee: Nelson M. Wilson & Karen E. Wilson. (acq 8-25-89; $188,000; 9-11-89). Network: USA. Format: Inspirational, Christian, talk. Target aud: General. Spec prog: Sp 5 hrs wkly. ♦ Nelson Wilson, gen mgr; Marnie Fillmore, opns dir.

KBXL(FM)— Feb 22, 1961: 94.1 mhz; 40 kw. Ant 2,634 ft. TL: N43 45 18 W116 05 52. Stereo. 1440 S. Weideman Ave., Boise 83709. Phone: (208) 377-3790. Fax: (208) 377-3792. E-mail: info@myfamilyradiol.com. Web Site: www.myfamilyradio.com. Licensee: KSPD Inc. (group owner; acq 4-26-89; FTR: 7-10-89). Network: AP Network News. Wiley, Rein & Fielding. Format: Relg, Christian talk. Target aud: 25-54. ♦ Lee Schafer, pres & gen mgr.

KCID(AM)— 1947: 1490 khz; 1 kw-U. TL: N43 39 51 W116 38 10. 5257 Fairview Ave., Suite 260, Boise 83706. Phone: (208) 344-3511. Fax: (208) 947-6765. Licensee: Journal Broadcast Corp. Group owner: Journal Broadcast Group Inc. (acq 5-13-98; grpsl). Network: ABC. Rep: Katz Radio. Dow, Lohnes & Albertson. Format: Oldies. Target aud: 25-54. Spec prog: Farm 16 hrs wkly. ♦ Bob Rosenthal, VP, gen mgr & chief of engrg.

KTHI(FM)—Co-owned with KCID(AM). Dec 1, 1983: 107.1 mhz; 52 kw. Ant 2,578 ft. TL: N43 45 18 W116 05 52. Stereo. Format: Super hits of 60's & 70's. Target aud: General. Spec prog: Farm 4 hrs wkly.

KSAS-FM—Licensed to Caldwell. See Nampa

*KTSY(FM)— Oct 14, 1990: 89.5 mhz; 8.3 kw. 2,601 ft. TL: N43 45 18 W116 05 52. (CP: Ant 2,594 ft.). Stereo. 16115 S. Montana Ave. 83607. Phone: (208) 459-5879. Fax: (208) 459-3144. Web Site: www.ktsy.org. Licensee: Gem State Adventist Academy. Donald E. Martin. Format: Contemp Christian mus. News: 4 hrs wkly. Target aud: 25-45. ♦ Donald Klinger, chmn; Stephen McPherson, pres; Michael Agee, gen mgr; Jerry Woods, progmg dir.

Chubbuck

KLLP(FM)— Nov 10, 1984: 98.5 mhz; 150 w. 1,350 ft. TL: N42 55 15 W112 20 40. (CP: 98.5 mhz, 6.24 kw). 259 E. Center St., Pocatello 83204. Phone: (208) 233-1133. Fax: (208) 232-1240. E-mail: kellymartinez@clearchannel.com. Web Site: www.985klite.com. Licensee: Citicasters Licenses L.P. Group owner: Clear Channel Communications Inc. (acq 5-4-99; grpsl). Format: Adult contemp. Target aud: General. Spec prog: Sp 4 hrs wkly. ♦ Tim Murphy, gen mgr; Kelly Martinez, progmg dir; Rhett Downing, chief of engrg.

KRTK(AM)— 1981: 1490 khz; 1 kw-U. TL: N42 55 38 W112 30 03. Stereo. Box 985, Pocatello 83204. Secondary address: 1633 Olympus Dr., Pocatello 83201. Phone: (208) 237-9500. Fax: (208) 237-4600. E-mail: krtk@ltlink.com. Web Site: www.krtk.com. Licensee: Broken Chains Inc. (acq 8-25-00). Network: ABC. Format: Christian. Target aud: 35-55. ♦ Stacy Dare, stn mgr & chief of opns; Andrew Burk, progmg dir.

Coeur d'Alene

KHTQ(FM)—Listing follows KVNI(AM).

KICR(FM)— Oct 12, 2001: 102.3 mhz; 6 kw. 1,843 ft. TL: N47 39 35 W116 57 12. Stereo. 327 Marion Ave., Sandpoint 83864. Phone: (208) 664-3241. Fax: (208) 665-7880. E-mail: dylanb@a53kpwd.com. Licensee: Great Northern Broadcasting Inc. (acq 8-17-01; $550,000). Smithwick & Belendiuk, PC. Format: Country. ♦ Dylan Benefield, gen mgr, opns dir & gen sls mgr; Jim Tomcheck, progmg dir; Mike Brown, news dir.

KVNI(AM)— Nov 1, 1946: 1080 khz; 10 kw-D, 1 kw-N, DA-N. TL: N47 36 57 W116 43 07. 504 E. Sherman 83814. Secondary address: 500 W. Boone Ave., Spokane, WA 99201. Phone: (208) 664-9271. Fax: (208) 667-0945. Licensee: QueenB Radio Inc. Rep: Katz Radio. Format: Doo Whopping Oldies, news. News staff: 2. Target aud: 25 plus. Spec prog: Relg 3 hrs wkly. ♦ Chris Garras, gen mgr & gen sls mgr; Tery Garras, sls dir; George Kessler, natl sls mgr; Brian Paul, mktg dir; Dick Haugen, progmg dir, news dir & pub affrs dir; Tim Anderson, chief of engrg.

KHTQ(FM)—Co-owned with KVNI(AM). Nov 1, 1991: 94.5 mhz; 100 kw. 1,883 ft. TL: N47 39 34 W116 57 48. Stereo. Web Site: rock945.com. Format: Active rock. Target aud: 24-54. ♦ Chris Garras, VP; Brew Michaels, opns dir; George Kressler, rgnl sls mgr; Ken Richards, progmg dir; Barry Bennet, mus dir.

Cottonwood

*KNWO(FM)— January 1994: 90.1 mhz; 250 w. 612 ft. TL: N46 04 09 W116 27 54. c/o Radio Stn KRFA-FM, Box 642530, 382 Murrow Communications Ctr., Pullman, WA 99164. Phone: (509) 335-6500. Fax: (509) 335-3772. E-mail: nwpr@wsu.edu. Web Site: www.nwpr.org. Licensee: Washington State University. Dow, Lohnes & Albertson. Format: Class, news. News staff: 0. News: 37 hrs wkly. Target aud: 25 plus. ♦ Karen Olstad, COO & gen mgr; Dennis Haarsager, gen mgr; Roger Johnson, stn mgr & sls dir; Scott Weatherly, opns mgr; Sarah McDaniel, dev dir; Mary Hawkins, progmg dir; Robin Rilette, mus dir; Ralph Hogan, engrg dir.

Donnelly

KMCL(AM)—Licensed to Donnelly. See McCall

Driggs

KCHQ(FM)— Feb 12, 2004: 102.1 mhz; 4 kw. Ant 1899 ft. TL: N43 42 42 W111 20 56. Stereo. Box 54 83422. Secondary address: 650 S. Centennial Mountain St., Suite 112 83422. Phone: (208) 354-4102. Fax: (208) 354-4104. E-mail: listen@q102fm.net. Web Site: www.q102fm.net. Licensee: Ted W. Austin Jr. Network: CNN Radio. Tacher Reddy, Begley & McCormick. News staff: one; News: 8 hrs wkly. Target aud: 25-54; adults. Spec prog: Farm one hr, classic country 3 hrs wkly. ♦ Ted W. Austin Jr., pres & gen mgr; Gwen Mielke, opns mgr; Dave Plourde, news dir.

Eagle

KXLT-FM— September 1994: 107.9 mhz; 45 kw. 2,683 ft. TL: N43 45 18 W116 05 52. 827 E. Park Blvd., Suite 201, Boise 83712. Phone: (208) 344-6363. Fax: (208) 327-8800. Web Site: www.lite108.com. Licensee: Citicasters Licenses L.P. Group owner: Clear Channel Communications Inc. (acq 5-4-99; grpsl). Rep: McGavren Guild. Format: Soft adult contemp, lite music. Target aud: 25-54. ♦ Terry Torio, gen mgr & stn mgr; Dave Burnett, gen sls mgr & news dir; Susan Green, prom dir; Tobin Jeffries, progmg dir.

Broadcasting & Cable Yearbook 2006

Idaho

Emmett

KDBI(FM)— Mar 12, 1973: 101.9 mhz; 57 kw. Ant 2,532 ft. TL: N43 45 18 W116 05 52. Stereo. 624 3rd St. S., Nampa 83651. Phone: (208) 463-2900. Web Site: www.bustosmedia.com. Licensee: First Western Inc. (acq 11-1-2003; $1.05 million). Format: Rgnl Mexican. ♦ Ed Distel, gen mgr.

Franklin

KFMS(FM)— Sept 6, 2005: 97.5 mhz; 68 kw. Ant 1,076 ft. TL: N41 44 54 W112 13 37. 515 S. 700 E., Suite 1C, Salt Lake City 84102. Phone: (801) 524-2600. Fax: (801) 521-9234. Licensee: 3 Point Media - Franklin LLC (acq 11-28-2001; $1.5 million. for CP). Format: News/talk. ♦ Steve Johnson, gen mgr.

Fruitland

KWEI-FM—Licensed to Fruitland. See Weiser

Garden City

KCIX(FM)—Licensed to Garden City. See Boise

Gooding

KISY(FM)— Dec 2, 1996: 100.7 mhz; 73 kw. Ant 2,191 ft. TL: N43 14 43 W115 26 12. 21361 Hwy. 30, Twin Falls 83301. Phone: (208) 735-8300. Web Site: www.sunny1007.com. Licensee: Locally Owned Radio LLC (group owner; acq 10-31-2003; grpsl). Format: Soft adult contemp. ♦ Shannon Neville, gen mgr.

KRXR(AM)— 1992: 1480 khz; 1 kw-D. TL: N42 54 54 W114 42 41. 501 S. Lincoln Ave., Jerome 83338. Phone: (208) 324-9267. Fax: (208) 324-9268. E-mail: krxr@cableone.net. Licensee: Maria Elena Juarez. (acq 1999; $200,000). Format: Sp. ♦ Efrain Ortega, gen mgr.

Grangeville

KORT(AM)— Oct 8, 1954: 1230 khz; 1 kw-U. TL: N45 55 52 W116 07 50. Box 510 83530. Phone: (208) 983-1230. Fax: (208) 983-2744. Licensee: 4-K Radio Inc. (group owner; acq 6-1-71). Format: Today's C&W. News staff: one; News: 8 hrs wkly. Target aud: General. Spec prog: Farm 2 hrs wkly. ♦ Mike Ripley, pres; Melinda Fischer, gen mgr, opns mgr, gen sls mgr & progmg dir; Brian Lee, mus dir & news dir; David Forsman, chief of engrg.

KORT-FM— Dec 1, 1979: 92.7 mhz; 360 w. 2,352 ft. TL: N45 51 48 W116 07 24. Stereo. Network: ABC. Format: Country.

Hailey

KSKI-FM—See Sun Valley

Hayden

KHTQ(FM)—Licensed to Hayden. See Coeur d'Alene

Homedale

KQTA(FM)— December 2004: 106.3 mhz; 100 kw. Ant 1,028 ft. TL: N43 37 15 W117 12 35. 2957 Stonebridge Tr., Reno, NV 89511. Phone: (775) 741-3777. E-mail: leoramos97035@aol.com. Licensee: R & S Media (acq 4-19-2000; $10 for 50% of stock).

Idaho Falls

*KAIO(FM)— Not on air, target date: unknown: 90.7 mhz; 43 w. Ant 508 ft. TL: N43 32 37 W111 53 07. 5700 West Oaks Blvd., Rocklin, CA 95765. Phone: (916) 251-1600. Fax: (916) 251-1650. Licensee: Educational Media Foundation. ♦ Richard Jenkins, pres.

KFTZ(FM)— May 24, 1986: 103.3 mhz; 100 kw. 659 ft. TL: N43 32 34 W111 53 07. Stereo. Box 699, Blackfoot 83221. Secondary address: 1190 Lincoln Rd. 83401. Phone: (208) 785-1400. Fax: (208) 785-0184. Web Site: www.z103.fm. Licensee: Bonneville Holding Co. Group owner: Bonneville International Corp. (acq 11-24-03; grpsl). Format: CHR top-40. Target aud: 18-34. ♦ Delyn Hendricks, gen mgr & opns dir.

KID(AM)— 1928: 590 khz; 5 kw-D, 1 kw-N, DA-N. TL: N43 33 35 W111 55 15. 1406 Commerce Way 83404. Phone: (208) 524-5900. Fax: (208) 522-9696. Licensee: Citicasters Licenses L.P. Group owner: Clear Channel Communications Inc. (acq 5-4-99; grpsl). Network: CBS. Rep: Target Broadcast Sales. Pepper & Corazzini. Format: News/talk. Target aud: 25-54; upscale decision-making professionals. Spec prog: Farm 18 hrs wkly. ♦ Tim Murphy, gen mgr.

KID-FM— May 1, 1965: 96.1 mhz; 100 kw. 1,500 ft. TL: N43 29 51 W112 39 50. Stereo. Format: Country.

KQEO(FM)— April 2003: 107.1 mhz; 82 kw. Ant 597 ft. TL: N43 32 33 W111 53 04. Box 570, Logan, UT 84323. Phone: (435) 752-1390. Licensee: Sand Hill Media Corp. (group owner; acq 9-7-01; $1.2 million. with KADQ-FM Rexburg plus 36-month employment agreement). Format: Classic rock. ♦ Jim Garshow, gen mgr.

KSSL(AM)— Sept 10, 1960: 1260 khz; 5 kw-D, 64 w-N. TL: N43 31 15 W111 59 33. Box 699, Blackfoot 83221. Phone: (208) 785-1400. Fax: (208) 785-0184. Licensee: Bonneville Holding Co. Group owner: Bonneville International Corp. (acq 11-24-2003; grpsl). Format: Talk. Target aud: 35 plus; upscale, mature adults. ♦ Delyn Hendricks, gen mgr; Matt Burgoyne, gen sls mgr & adv mgr; Jeremy Dressen, progmg dir; Bill Traue, chief of engrg.

KTHK(FM)— October 1993: 105.5 mhz; 100 kw. 659 ft. TL: N43 21 06 W112 00 22. Stereo. 1190 Lincoln Rd. 83401. Phone: (208) 523-3722. Fax: (208) 525-2575. Web Site: www.1055thehawk.net. Licensee: Bonneville Holding Co. Group owner: Bonneville International Corp. (acq 11-24-03; grpsl). Format: Country. ♦ Jeremy Dresen, gen mgr & sls.

KUPI(AM)— (Ammon). Nov 9, 1957: 980 khz; 5 kw-D, 1 kw-N, DA-2. TL: N43 31 23 W112 00 36. Stereo. 854 Lindsay Blvd., Ammon 83402. Phone: (208) 522-1101. Fax: (208) 522-6110. Licensee: Sandhill Media Group LLC. Group owner: Sand Hill Media Corp. (acq 1-9-2004; $2.65 million. with co-located FM). Rep: McGavren Guild. Haley, Bader & Potts. Format: Old country. Target aud: 25 plus. ♦ James Garshow, exec VP & gen mgr; Ken Walker, gen sls mgr & natl sls mgr.

KUPI-FM— Aug 16, 1975: 99.1 mhz; 100 kw. 1,513 ft. TL: N43 32 33 W111 53 04. Stereo. Format: Country.

Island Park

KWYS-FM— November 1998: 102.9 mhz; 46 kw. 2,732 ft. TL: N44 33 41 W111 26 32. Stereo. Box 2158, Ketchum 83340. Phone: (208) 535-1033. Fax: (208) 535-0761. Licensee: Chaparral Broadcasting Inc. Group owner: Chaparral Communications (acq 7-30-2004; grpsl). Cohn & Marks. Format: Classic rock. News staff: 2; News: 10 hrs wkly. Target aud: 18-45; Adults. ♦ Scott Parker, gen mgr.

Jerome

KART(AM)—Listing follows KMVX(FM).

KMVX(FM)— August 1970: 102.9 mhz; 100 kw. 760 ft. TL: N42 43 54 W114 25 04. Stereo. 47 N. 100 West 83338. Phone: (208) 324-8181. Fax: (208) 324-7124. Licensee: KART Broadcasting Co. Allied Radio Partners. Format: Adult contemp. Target aud: 25-54; general. ♦ Kent Lee, gen mgr & gen sls mgr; Karla Cunha, news dir; Jerry Tharton, chief of engrg.

KART(AM)— Co-owned with KMVX(FM). August 1956: 1400 khz; 1 kw-U. TL: N42 43 51 W114 32 17. (Acq 9-1-64). Network: CBS. Format: Real country. Target aud: 25 plus. ♦ Lamont Summers, progmg dir.

Ketchum

KIKX(FM)— Dec 2, 1996: 104.7 mhz; 100 kw. 1,578 ft. TL: N43 16 45 W114 09 14. 21361 Hwy. 30, Twin Falls 83301. Phone: (208) 735-8300. Fax: (208) 733-4196. Web Site: www.kikx.com. Licensee: Locally Owned Radio LLC (group owner; acq 10-31-2003; grpsl). Format: Classic rock. ♦ Larry Johnson, pres & gen mgr; Jerre Fender, opns dir; Deb Uvieu, gen sls mgr; Sierra Tattersall, progmg dir.

Kootenai

KTPO(FM)— Not on air, target date: unknown: 106.7 mhz; 1.3 kw. Ant 1,158 ft. TL: N48 13 45 W116 30 30. 1724 Hickory, Sandpoint 83864. Phone: (208) 265-5979. Licensee: Hellroaring Communications L.L.C. ♦ Dylan L. Benefield, gen mgr.

Kuna

*KARJ(FM)— 2005: 88.3 mhz; 23 kw vert. Ant 2,161 ft. TL: N43 00 26 W116 42 23. Stereo. 5700 W. Oaks Blvd., Rocklin, CA 95765. Phone: (916) 251-1600. Fax: (916) 251-1650. E-mail: info@air1.com. Web Site: www.air1.com. Licensee: Educational Media Foundation. Group owner: EMF Broadcasting. Network: Air 1. Shaw Pittman. Format: Contemp Christian. News staff: 3. Target aud: 18-35; Judeo-Christian, female. ♦ Richard Jenkins, pres; Mike Novak, VP; Lloyd Parker, gen mgr; Keith Whipple, dev dir; Mke Novak, progmg dir.

Lewiston

KATW(FM)— Oct 2, 1986: 101.5 mhz; 100 kw. 848 ft. TL: N46 27 38 W117 01 00. Stereo. 403 C St. 83501. Phone: (208) 743-6564. Fax: (208) 798-0110. E-mail: ryan@catfm.com. Web Site: www.catfm.com. Licensee: Pacific Empire Radio Corp. (group owner; acq 10-6-98; $788,500. with KBJX(FM) Shelley). Format: Hot adult contemp. News staff: one; News: 4 hrs wkly. Target aud: 25-54. ♦ Jay Mlazgar, pres, gen mgr & gen sls mgr; Jill Law, gen sls mgr; Ryan Cook, progmg dir & progmg mgr.

KCLK-FM—See Clarkston, WA

*KLHS-FM— October 1967: 88.9 mhz; 155 w horiz. Ant -810 ft. TL: N46 24 38 W117 00 54. Attn: Radio, 500 Eighth Ave. 83501. Phone: (208) 792-2418. Fax: (208) 792-2568. Web Site: www.lcsc.edu. Licensee: Lewis-Clark State College (acq 3-23-2005; $5,000). Format: Var/div. ♦ Tate Smith, gen mgr.

KMOK(FM)— March 1983: 106.9 mhz; 99 kw. 1,230 ft. TL: N46 27 33 W117 02 18. Stereo. 805 Stewart Ave. 83501. Phone: (208) 743-1551. Fax: (208) 743-4440. E-mail: sales@idavend.com. Licensee: Ida-Vend Co. Inc. Group owner: IdaVend Broadcasting Inc. Network: AP Radio. Format: Country. News staff: one; News: 3 hrs wkly. Target aud: 25-49; female. ♦ Robert Prasil, pres & gen mgr; Darin Siebert, opns mgr; Ben Bonnfield, gen sls mgr; Jim Nelly, progmg dir; John Thomas, news dir; Steve Frankel, mus dir & chief of engrg.

KOZE(AM)— Oct 6, 1955: 950 khz; 5 kw-D, 1 kw-N, DA-2. TL: N46 23 32 W117 02 03. Stereo. Box 936 83501. Phone: (208) 743-2502. Fax: (208) 743-1995. Licensee: 4-K Radio Inc. (group owner; acq 6-1-71). Network: ABC Information & Entertainment. Tacher Company. Format: Talk. News staff: 2. Target aud: 25-54. Spec prog: Farm 2 hrs wkly. ♦ Michael R. Ripley, pres; Chris Ripley, stn mgr & progmg VP; Jason Ford, news dir; David Forsman, chief of engrg.

KOZE-FM— Jan 17, 1961: 96.5 mhz; 25 kw. 741 ft. TL: N46 27 48 W117 00 01. Stereo. Format: Adult rock. Target aud: 18-49. ♦ Lee McVey, progmg dir.

KRLC(AM)— March 1935: 1350 khz; 5 kw-D, 1 kw-N, DA-N. TL: N46 23 39 W116 59 40. 805 Stewart Ave. 83501. Phone: (208) 743-1551. Fax: (208) 743-4440. E-mail: sales@idavend.com. Licensee: Ida-Vend Inc. Group owner: IdaVend Broadcasting Inc. (acq 11-1-81). Format: Country, news/talk, sports. News staff: one; News: 10 hrs wkly. Target aud: 25 plus; adults. Spec prog: Farm 5 hrs, radio auction one hr wkly. ♦ Robert Prasil, pres & gen mgr; Melva Prasil, stn mgr.

KVTY(FM)— July 20, 1998: 105.1 mhz; 500 w. 1,099 ft. TL: N46 27 33 W117 02 18. c/o KRLC(AM) and KMOK(FM), 805 Stewart Ave. 83501. Phone: (208) 743-1551. Fax: (208) 743-4440. E-mail: sales@idavend.com. Licensee: IdaVend Co. Inc. Group owner: IdaVend Broadcasting Inc. Network: AP Radio. Format: CHR. News staff: one; News: 1 hr wkly. Target aud: 18-44. ♦ Robert Prasil, pres & gen mgr; Melva Prasil, stn mgr; Ben Bonfield, gen sls mgr; Darin Siebert, progmg dir; John Thomas, news dir; Steve Franco, chief of engrg.

McCall

*KBSK(FM)— 2002: 89.9 mhz; 220 w. Ant 1,919 ft. TL: N45 00 38 W116 07 53. Boise State Radio, 1910 University Dr., Boise 83725-1915. Phone: (208) 426-3663. Fax: (208) 344-6631. Web Site: radio.boisestate.edu. Licensee: Idaho State Board of Education. Format: Jazz. ♦ John

Stations in the U.S. — Idaho

Developers & Brokers of Radio Properties — contact American Media Services at our suite: Philadelphia Marriott Downtown, 215-625-2900. 843-972-2200. americanmediaservices.com. Charleston, SC. Dallas, TX · Chicago, IL · Austin, TX. American Media Services, LLC

Hess, gen mgr; Hy Kloc, dev dir; Jim East, progmg dir; Steve Jess, news dir; Tom Taylor, chief of engrg.

*KBSM(FM)— Jan 20, 1991: 91.7 mhz; 220 w. 1,912 ft. TL: N45 00 38 W116 07 53. Stereo. Boise State Radio, 1910 University Dr., Boise 83725. Phone: (208) 426-3663. Fax: (208) 344-6631. Web Site: radio.boisestate.edu. Licensee: Idaho State Board of Education. Network: Network: PRI, NPR. Dow, Lohnes & Albertson. Format: Class, news, new age. News: 15 hrs wkly. Target aud: General. Spec prog: Jazz. ♦ John Hess, gen mgr; Hy Kloc, dev dir; Steve Jess, news dir.

*KBSQ(FM)—Not on air, target date: unknown: 90.7 mhz; 220 w. 1,919 ft. Boise State Radio, 1910 University Dr., Boise 83725. Phone: (208) 426-3663. Fax: (208) 344-6631. Web Site: radio.boisestate.edu. Licensee: Idaho State Board of Education. Format: News, div. ♦ Jim East, progmg dir.

KDZY(FM)— 2001: 98.3 mhz; 500 w horiz. Ant 1,922 ft. TL: N45 00 18 W116 08 01. 321 N. Third St., Suite 8 83638. Phone: (208) 377-3790. Phone: (208) 634-3781. Fax: (208) 634-3799. Licensee: KSPD Inc. (group owner; acq 4-15-02; $75,000). Format: Country. ♦ Lee Schafer, pres & gen mgr; Beth Schafer, exec VP; Monty Ivey, opns dir; Bunny Ivey, gen sls mgr; David Schafer, progmg dir.

KMCL-FM— Oct 22, 1990: 101.1 mhz; 3.9 kw. 1,873 ft. TL: N44 45 54 W116 11 54. Stereo. Box 813, 204 N. 3rd St. 83638. Phone: (208) 634-4777. Fax: (208) 634-3059. Licensee: Brundage Mountain Air Inc. (acq 7-15-94). Rep: Target Broadcast Sales. Format: Adult contemp. News staff: one; News: 5 hrs wkly. Target aud: 25-54; upper-middle class to white collar, young families & students. Spec prog: Sports, entertainment, business one hr, relg one hr wkly. ♦ David Eaton, gen mgr, gen sls mgr, prom dir, progmg dir & news dir; Linda Jackson, pub affrs dir; Rockwell Smith, chief of engrg.

KMCL(AM)— Oct 15, 1965: 1240 khz; 1 kw-U. TL: N44 46 52 W116 02 51. Licensee: Brundage Mountain Air Inc.

Meridian

KDJQ(AM)— May 1, 2005: 890 khz; 50 kw-D, 250 w-N, DA-N. TL: N43 27 36 W116 14 19. 1609 N. 22nd St., Boise 83702. Phone: (208) 388-4502. Licensee: Robert E. Combs (acq 5-14-2004; $425,000. for CP). Format: Sp. ♦ Robert E. Combs, gen mgr.

Montpelier

KVSI(AM)— July 20, 1965: 1450 khz; 1 kw-U. TL: N42 18 54 W111 18 38. Box 340, 24681 US 89 83254. Phone: (208) 847-1450. Fax: (208) 847-1451. E-mail: kvsi@dcdi.net. Web Site: kvsi.com. Licensee: Tri-States Broadcasting LLC (acq 11-1-68). Network: ABC Information & Entertainment. Rep: Sandeberg-Glenn. Format: Country. Spec prog: Farm 4 hrs, relg 2 hrs wkly. ♦ Keith Martindale, gen mgr.

Moscow

KQQQ(AM)—See Pullman, WA

*KRFA-FM— Sept 1, 1963: 91.7 mhz; 1.45 kw. 1,009 ft. TL: N46 40 54 W116 58 13. Stereo. Box 642530, 382 Murrow Communications Ctr., Washington State Univ., Pullman, WA 99164-2530. Phone: (509) 335-6500. Fax: (509) 335-6557. E-mail: nwpr@wsu.edu. Web Site: www.nwpr.org. Licensee: Washington State University. (acq 7-1-84). Network: Network: NPR, PRI. Don, Lohnes & Albertson. Format: Class, news. News staff: one; News: 37 hrs wkly. Target aud: General. Spec prog: Folk, jazz. ♦ Karen Olstad, COO & gen mgr; Dennis Haarsager, opns mgr; Roger Johnson, stn mgr & sls dir; Scott Weatherly, opns mgr; Sarah McDaniel, dev dir; Mary Hawkins, progmg dir; Robin Rilette, mus dir; Ralph Hogan, engrg dir & engrg mgr.

KRPL(AM)— May 20, 1947: 1400 khz; 1 kw-U. TL: N46 44 47 W117 01 06. Box 8849, 200 N. Almon 83843. Phone: (208) 882-2551. Fax: (208) 883-3571. Licensee: KRPL Inc. (acq 1-27-2004; $1 million. for two-thirds of the shares with co-located FM). Network: ABC Daytime Direction. Rep: McGavren Guild. Haley, Bader & Potts. Format: American adult standards, big band. News staff: one; News: 12 hrs wkly. Target aud: 25-54. Spec prog: Farm 4 hrs, relg 2 hrs wkly. ♦ Gary Cummins, pres.

KZFN(FM)—Co-owned with KRPL(AM). Feb 24, 1973: 106.1 mhz; 62 kw. 921 ft. TL: N46 40 51 W116 58 26. Stereo. Network: ABC Daytime Direction. Format: CHR. News staff: one; News: 5 hrs wkly. Target aud: 25-54. ♦ Gary Cummings, progmg mgr.

*KUOI-FM— November 1945: 89.3 mhz; 400 w. -92 ft. TL: N46 43 43 W117 00 11. Stereo. Student Union Bldg., 3rd Fl., Univ. of Idaho 83844-4272. Phone: (208) 885-6433. Phone: (208) 885-2218. Fax: (208) 885-2222. E-mail: kuoi@uidaho.edu. Web Site: www.kuoi.org. Licensee: University of Idaho. Format: Free-form, div. News staff: 3; News: 2 hrs wkly. Target aud: General; alternative mus listeners. Spec prog: Black 3 hrs, folk 3 hrs, jazz 4 hrs wkly. ♦ Sarah Long, stn mgr; Andy Olson, dev mgr & prom dir; Devin Barrett, progmg dir; James Yeary, mus dir; Jeff Kimberling, chief of engrg.

Mountain Home

KMHI(AM)— Mar 20, 1962: 1240 khz; 1 kw-U. TL: N43 09 03 W115 42 26. Box 704, 1795 Canyon Creek Rd. 83647. Phone: (208) 587-8424. Fax: (208) 587-8425. E-mail: barbara@kmhi1240.com. Web Site: www.kmhi.com. Licensee: Locally Owned Radio LLC (group owner; acq 10-31-2003; grpsl). Network: Westwood One. Format: Classic hit country. News staff: one; News: 15 hrs wkly. Target aud: General. Spec prog: Sp 7 hrs wkly. ♦ Larry Johnson, gen mgr; Barbara Lambert, stn mgr; Jerry Fender, opns mgr; Shannon Neville, gen sls mgr; Dale Metzger, progmg dir; Jeff Allen, chief of engrg.

KTPZ(FM)— 1982: 99.1 mhz; 73 kw. Ant 2,191 ft. TL: N43 14 43 W115 26 12. Stereo. 888 N. Cole Rd., Boise 83709. Phone: (208) 658-9806. Phone: (735) 735-0099. Fax: (208) 658-9808. E-mail: monsterdy@ktpz.com. Web Site: www.ktpz.com. Licensee: Locally Owned Radio LLC (group owner; acq 10-31-2003; grpsl). Format: 80s rock. Target aud: 18-34. ♦ Howard Mayhem, progmg dir.

Nampa

KIDO(AM)— May 17, 1920: 580 khz; 5 kw-U, DA-N. TL: N43 33 35 W116 24 02. 827 E. Park Blvd., Suite 201, Boise 83712. Phone: (208) 344-6363. Fax: (208) 385-9064. Web Site: www.kido.net. Licensee: Citicasters Licenses L.P. Group owner: Clear Channel Communications Inc. (acq 5-4-99; grpsl). Network: CBS. Format: News, talk. Target aud: 25-54. ♦ Terry Tario, gen mgr; Mitch Pruitte, stn mgr; Jeff Cochran, opns mgr & progmg mgr; David Levi, natl sls mgr; Dave Burnett, news dir.

KKGL(FM)— February 1977: 96.9 mhz; 44 kw. 2,520 ft. TL: N43 45 19 W116 05 52. Stereo. 1419 W. Bannock St., Boise 83702. Phone: (208) 336-3670. Fax: (208) 336-3734. Web Site: www.96-9meeagle.com. Licensee: Citadel Broadcasting Co. Group owner: Citadel Broadcasting Corp. (acq 12-10-97; grpsl). Rep: Katz Radio. Format: Classic rock. Target aud: 25-44; upscale baby boomers who listen to primarily 70s based rock. ♦ Kevin Godwin, gen mgr; Rich Summers, opns mgr; Rich Bryan, progmg dir; Bill Frahn, chief of engrg.

KRVB(FM)— Jan 10, 1975: 94.9 mhz; 49 kw. 2,692 ft. TL: N43 45 18 W116 05 52. Stereo. 5257 W. Fairview Ave., Suite 260, Boise 83706. Phone: (208) 344-3511. Fax: (208) 947-6765. Web Site: www.riverinteractive.com. Licensee: Journal Broadcast Corp. Group owner: Journal Communications Inc. (acq 4-11-00). Rep: Katz Radio. Format: AOR. Target aud: 18-64. ♦ Bob Rosenthal, CFO, VP & gen mgr; Dan McColly, opns mgr & progmg dir.

KSAS-FM—(Caldwell). Sept 28, 1982: 103.3 mhz; 54 kw. 2,578 ft. TL: N43 45 18 W116 05 52. Stereo. 827 E. Park Blvd., Suite 201, Boise 83712. Phone: (208) 344-6363. Fax: (208) 385-9064. Fax: (208) 344-1134. Web Site: www.1033kissfm.com. Licensee: Citicasters Licenses L.P. Group owner: Clear Channel Communications Inc. (acq 15-4-99; grpsl). Fletcher, Heald & Hildreth. Format: Top 40. News staff: one; News: one hr wkly. Target aud: 25-54; upscale, white collar. Spec prog: Class 2 hrs, jazz 4 hrs wkly. ♦ Terry Torio, stn mgr; David Levi, natl sls mgr; Aaron Traylor, progmg dir; Dave Burnett, news dir & chief of engrg.

KTIK(AM)— Nov 1, 1962: 1350 khz; 5 kw-D, 600 w-N. TL: N43 32 58 W116 24 38. Box 1280, 1419 W. Bannock St., Boise 83702. Phone: (208) 336-3670. Fax: (208) 336-3736. Web Site: www.ktik.com. Licensee: Citadel Broadcasting Co. Group owner: Citadel Broadcasting Corp. (acq 4-1-03; $750,000). Network: Network: ESPN Radio, Westwood One. Format: Sports, talk. News: one hr wkly. Target aud: 25-54; sports oriented men. ♦ Kevin Godwin, gen mgr; Mike Owens, gen sls mgr; Andrew Paul, progmg dir.

New Plymouth

KZMG(FM)—Licensed to New Plymouth. See Boise

Orofino

KLER(AM)— Oct 15, 1958: 1300 khz; 5 kw-D, 1 kw-U, DA-N. TL: N46 28 41 W116 14 34. Box 32, 3110 Upper Fords Creek Rd. 83544. Phone: (208) 476-5702. Fax: (208) 476-5703. E-mail: klerorofino@clearwater.net. Licensee: Central Idaho Broadcasting. (acq 12-7-92; $75,000 with co-located FM; 1-4-93). Network: ABC Information & Entertainment. Format: Country. News staff: news progmg 8 hrs wkly News: 2;. Target aud: General; family or logging industry-federal employee workers. ♦ Jeff Jones, gen mgr.

KLER-FM— Sept 20, 1979: 95.3 mhz; 2.3 kw. Ant 676 ft. TL: N46 28 09 W116 16 40. Stereo. Box 3110, Upper Fords Creek Rd. 83544. Format: Adult contemp. News staff: 2; News: 8 hrs wkly.

KZID(FM)— 2003: 98.5 mhz; 1.65 kw. Ant 630 ft. TL: N46 28 09 W116 16 40. Torro Broadcasting, 2307 Princess Anne St., Greensboro, NC 27408. Phone: (336) 286-2087. Licensee: Torro Broadcasting.

Payette

KIOV(AM)— Dec 20, 1957: 1450 khz; 1 kw-U. TL: N44 03 47 W116 54 27. 1406 N. Main St., Suite 107, Meridian 83642-1798. Phone: (208) 884-5330. Fax: (208) 888-9647. E-mail: sports@kiov.com. Web Site: www.kiov.com. Licensee: Media Enterprises LLC. (Acq 8-00). Tacher. Format: Sports. Target aud: 18-54; 65% male. ♦ David Combes, gen mgr; Marshill Sagu, opns mgr.

KQXR(FM)— Dec 1, 1978: 100.3 mhz; 98 kw. 708 ft. TL: N43 49 31 W116 30 29. Stereo. 5257 W. Fairview Ave., Suite 260, Boise 83706. Phone: (208) 344-3511. Fax: (208) 947-6765. E-mail: kqxr@hotmail.com. Web Site: www.xrock.com. Licensee: Journal Broadcast Corp. Group owner: Journal Broadcast Group Inc. (acq 5-13-98; grpsl). Rep: Katz Radio. Format: Rock, alternative. Target aud: 18-49. ♦ Bob Rosenthal, VP & gen mgr; Dan McColly, opns mgr.

Pocatello

*KISU-FM— Apr 15, 1998: 91.1 mhz; 410 w. 1,043 ft. TL: N42 51 46 W112 31 03. Stereo. Box 8014, Idaho State University 83209. Phone: (208) 236-3691. Fax: (209) 236-4600. E-mail: milljerr@isu.edu. Web Site: www.isu.edu/kisufm. Licensee: Idaho State University. Network: NPR, PRI. Format: Jazz, AAA. Spec prog: American Indian, Folk. ♦ Richard Bowen, pres; Jerry Miller, gen mgr; Jeremy Petersen, mus dir; Megan Clements, pub affrs dir; Vanessa Sutton, pub affrs dir; Royce Martin, engrg mgr; Nick Davidson, chief of engrg.

KLLP(FM)—See Chubbuck

KMGI(FM)—Listing follows KSEI(AM).

KOUU(AM)— Dec 20, 1956: 1290 khz; 1 kw-D. TL: N42 57 28 W112 25 46. Stereo. Box 97, 436 N. Main 83204. Phone: (208) 234-1290. Fax: (208) 234-9451. Licensee: Idaho Wireless Corp. (group owner; acq 3-86; with co-located FM; FTR: 12-9-85). Rep: Tacher. Format: Contemp country.

Idaho

KZBQ(FM)—Co-owned with KOUU(AM). Dec 27, 1969: 93.7 mhz; 100 kw. 984 ft. TL: N42 51 57 W112 30 46. Stereo.

KPKY(FM)—Listing follows KWIK(AM).

KPPC(FM)—Not on air, target date: unknown: 92.1 mhz; 6 kw. Ant 121 ft. TL: N42 54 49 W112 26 14. Intermart Broadcasting Pocatello Inc., 3434 S.W. 26th Pl., Cape Coral, FL 33914. Phone: (239) 542-4200. Fax: (239) 542-4221. E-mail: swfradio@aol.com. Licensee: Intermart Broadcasting Pocatello Inc. ♦Patricia Woods, VP & gen mgr.

KPTO(AM)—Not on air, target date: unknown: 1440 khz; 2.5 kw-D, 350 w-N, DA-2. TL: N42 56 30 W112 27 17. AM Radio 1441 Inc., Box 1450, St. George, UT 84771-1450. Secondary address: 210 North 1000 East, Box 1450, St. George, UT 84771-1450. Phone: 435-628-1000. Fax: 435-628-6636. Licensee: AM Radio 1440 Inc. Group owner: Diamond Broadcasting Corp. (acq 12-6-04). Network: CNN Radio. Dan J. Alpert. Format: Adult Standards. News staff: 2; News: news progm 1 hr wkly. Target aud: 18 - 64. ♦E. Morgan Skinner, Jr., CEO; E. Morgan Skinner Jr., pres.

KRTK(AM)—See Chubbuck

KSEI(AM)— Sept 23, 1926: 930 khz; 5 kw-U, DA-N. TL: N42 57 44 W112 29 50. Box 40 83204. Secondary address: 544 N. Arthur St. 83204. Phone: (208) 233-2121. Fax: (208) 234-7682. Licensee: Pacific Empire Radio Corp. (group owner; acq 8-28-97; $1.2 million. with co-located FM). Rep: Katz Radio. Format: Sporting news. Target aud: General. ♦Mark Bolland, gen mgr.

KMGI(FM)—Co-owned with KSEI(AM). Apr 1, 1978: 102.5 mhz; 100 kw. Ant 1,023 ft. TL: N42 51 57 W112 30 46. Stereo. 544 N. Arthur 83204. Web Site: www.classicrock102.fm. Network: Westwood One. Format: Classic rock. ♦Mark Bolland, pres; C.J. Morrison, progmg mgr.

KWIK(AM)— September 1946: 1240 khz; 1 kw-U. TL: N42 55 14 W112 27 17. Stereo. Box 998, 259 E. Center St. 83201. Phone: (208) 233-1133. Phone: (800) 582-1240. Fax: (208) 232-1240. E-mail: new1240@yahoo.com. Web Site: www.newsradio1240.com. Licensee: Citicasters Licenses L.P. Group owner: Clear Channel Communications Inc. (acq 5-4-99; grpsl). Network: ABC Information & Entertainment. Rep: Allied Radio Partners. Art Moore. Pepper & Corazzini. Format: Sports, news/talk. News staff: 3; News: 15 hrs wkly. Target aud: 45 plus. Spec prog: Farm 3 hrs, gospel 2 hrs, relg one hr, American Indian one hr wkly. ♦Tim Murphy, gen mgr.

KPKY(FM)—Co-owned with KWIK(AM). Aug 18, 1975: 94.9 mhz; 100 kw. 1,004 ft. TL: N42 52 26 W112 30 47. Stereo. Web Site: www.kpky.com. Format: Oldies. Target aud: 35 plus; general. ♦Marie Mccallister, progmg dir.

*KZJB(FM)—Not on air, target date: unknown: 90.3 mhz; 782 w horiz, 2.3 kw vert. Ant 1,371 ft. TL: N42 55 15 W112 20 44. CSN International, 3232 W. MacArthur Blvd., Santa Ana, CA 92704. Phone: (208) 734-6633. Fax: (208) 736-1958. E-mail: csn@csnradio.com. Web Site: www.csnradio.com. Licensee: CSN International (group owner). Format: Christian. ♦ Ray Garney, gen mgr; Don Mills, progmg dir; Kelly Carlson, chief of engrg.

Post Falls

KCDA(FM)—Licensed to Post Falls. See Spokane WA

Preston

KACH(AM)— Sept 4, 1948: 1340 khz; 1 kw-U. TL: N42 07 45 W111 51 00. 1133 E. Glendale Rd. 83263. Phone: (208) 852-1340. Fax: (208) 852-1342. E-mail: kach@nstep.net. Web Site: www.nstep.net/kach. Licensee: Alan J. White, Nelada G. White. (acq 5-13-98). Network: ABC. Format: Oldies. News: 12 hrs wkly. Target aud: 18-54; general. Spec prog: Farm. ♦ Alan White, gen mgr.

KKEX(FM)— Dec 9, 1993: 96.7 mhz; 105 w. 226 ft. TL: N47 07 45 W111 51 00. Box 3369, Radio Stn. KKEX(FM), Logan, UT 84323-3369. Secondary address: 810 W. 200 N., Logan, UT 84321. Phone: (435) 752-1390. Phone: (435) 753-9607. Fax: (435) 752-1392. E-mail: kkex@vradio.com. Web Site: www.kix96.fm. Licensee: Sun Valley Radio Inc. (group owner; acq 1994). Format: Country. ♦M. Kent Frandsen, pres; Jay Eubanks, gen mgr; Lynn Simmons, progmg dir & progmg mgr; Dan Baker, chief of engrg.

Rathdrum

*KWJT(FM)—Not on air, target date: unknown: 89.9 mhz; 10 kw vert. Ant 771 ft. TL: N48 12 42 W117 04 58. CSN International, 3232 W. MacArthur Blvd., Santa Ana, CA 92704. Phone: (208) 734-6633. Fax: (714) 825-9660. Licensee: CSN International (group owner). Format: Relg.

Rexburg

KADQ-FM— Aug 18, 1975: 94.3 mhz; 43 kw. Ant 522 ft. TL: N43 45 20 W111 57 56. Stereo. 854 Lindsay Blvd., Idaho Falls 83402. Phone: (208) 522-1101. Fax: (208) 522-6110. Licensee: Sand Hill Media Corp. (group owner; acq 9-7-01; $1.2 million. with KQEO(FM) Idaho Falls plus 36-month employment agreement). Network: Network: Jones Radio Networks, USA. Rep: Tacher. Format: Modern rock. ♦James Garshow, gen mgr; John Balginy, news dir.

*KBYI(FM)— Nov 13, 1972: 100.5 mhz; 100 kw. 692 ft. TL: N43 45 44 W111 57 30. Stereo. 102 RGS Bldg., BYU Idaho 83460-1700. Phone: (208) 496-2907. Fax: (208) 496-2912. E-mail: clarkjim@byui.edu. Web Site: www.kbyu.edu/kbyi. Licensee: Brigham Young University-Idaho. Network: Network: NPR, PRI. Format: Class, news. News staff: one; News: 33 hrs wkly. Target aud: General. ♦David Bednar, pres; Jim Clark, gen mgr; Dale Hillier, dev dir & progmg dir; Chris Hall, mktg mgr; Mark Bailey, gen sls mgr & news dir.

*KBYR-FM— 1993: 91.5 mhz; 100 w. -39 ft. TL: N43 49 09 W111 46 51. Ricks College, Spori Bldg. 83460-0105. Phone: (208) 356-2927. Fax: (208) 356-2390. Web Site: www.byui.edu/kbyr. Licensee: Ricks College Corp. Format: Mormon contemp. Target aud: General. ♦Ernie Riedelbach, gen mgr.

KGTM(FM)— Jan 17, 1986: 98.1 mhz; 3 kw. 299 ft. TL: N43 48 55 W111 46 09. (CP: 25 kw, ant 276 ft.). Stereo. 228 First St., Idaho Falls 83402. Phone: (208) 529-6926. Fax: (208) 529-6927. Licensee: Pacific Empire Radio Corp. (group owner; acq 7-25-2000; $495,000. with KRXK(FM) Rexburg). Fletcher, Heald & Hildreth. Format: Oldies. Target aud: 35 plus. ♦Mark Bolland, CEO & pres; Bill Keith, gen mgr.

KRXK(FM)— January 1951: 1230 khz; 1 kw-U. TL: N43 50 50 W111 47 03. 228 1st St., Idaho Falls 83401. Phone: (208) 529-6926. Fax: (208) 529-6927. E-mail: billkeith@pacempire.com. Licensee: Pacific Empire Radio Corp. (group owner; (acq 7-25-2000; $495,000. with KGTM(FM) Rexburg). Rep: Target Broadcast Sales. Format: Sports talk. News staff: 9. Target aud: 25-54; male. ♦Mark Bolland, CEO & pres; Bill Keith, stn mgr.

Rigby

*KLRI(FM)— 2005: 89.5 mhz; 78 kw vert. Ant 1,527 ft. TL: N43 30 04 W112 39 44. Stereo. 5700 W. Oaks Blvd., Rocklin, CA 95765. Phone: (916) 251-1600. Fax: (916) 251-1650. E-mail: klove@klove.com. Web Site: www.klove.com. Licensee: Educational Media Foundation. Group owner: EMF Broadcasting. Network: K-Love. Shaw Pittman. Format: Contemp Christian. News staff: 3. Target aud: 25-44; Judeo Christian, female. ♦Richard Jenkins, pres; Mike Novak, VP & progmg dir; Lloyd Parker, gen mgr; Ed Lenane, opns dir & news dir; Keith Whipple, dev dir.

Rupert

KFTA(AM)— Oct 12, 1955: 970 khz; 2.5 kw-D. TL: N42 37 08 W113 39 31. (CP: 900 w-D, DA-N. TL: N42 36 10 W113 43 21). 120 S. 300 W. 83350. Phone: (208) 436-4757. Fax: (208) 436-3050. E-mail: lafantastica970@quepasa.com. Licensee: Tri-Market Radio Broadcasters Inc. Group owner: Tri-Market Radio Broadcasters Inc. & Eagle Rock Broadcasting Inc. (acq 9-24-93; $700,000. with co-located FM; FTR: 10-11-93). Format: Sp. Spec prog: Sp. ♦ Kim Lee, gen mgr.

KKMV(FM)—Co-owned with KFTA(AM). Dec 5, 1978: 106.1 mhz; 25 kw. Ant 2,496 ft. TL: N42 20 06 W113 36 15. Format: Country.

Saint Anthony

KIGO(AM)— July 10, 1966: . Stn currently dark 1400 khz; 1 kw-U. TL: N43 58 23 W111 39 28. (CP: 1420 khz; 50 kw-D, 16 w-N). Box 17 83445. Secondary address: 2458 Radio Rd. 83445. Phone: (208) 624-3387. Licensee: Fremont Broadcasting Co. (acq 10-1-94; $85,000; assumption of previous sales contract). Format: Classic country. Target aud: 35-64. Spec prog: Farm & Sports. ♦ Ted Austin Jr., pres; Connie Austin, stn mgr & sls dir.

Saint Maries

KOFE(AM)— Mar 1, 1970: 1240 khz; 1 kw-D, 500 w-N. TL: N47 19 14 W116 32 50. Box 278, 201 N. 8th 83861. Phone: (208) 245-1240. Fax: (208) 245-6525. E-mail: kofeam@usamedia.tv. Web Site: www.koferadio.com. Licensee: Campbell River Holding Co. L.L.C. (acq 5-3-01; $1,000. for 70%). Network: ABC Information & Entertainment. Rep: Tacher. Format: Country. News staff: 2; News: 9 hrs wkly. Target aud: 25-55. Spec prog: Paul Harvey, loc sports 3 hrs wkly. ♦Sherry Janda, gen mgr, stn mgr, opns dir & gen sls mgr; Jim Sheldon, chief of engrg.

Salmon

KSRA(AM)— Mar 1, 1959: 960 khz; 1 kw-D. TL: N45 11 02 W113 52 12. 315 Hwy. 93 N. 83467. Phone: (208) 756-2218. Fax: (208) 756-2098. Licensee: Salmon River Communications Inc. (acq 6-19-00; $345,000. with co-located FM). Network: ABC Information & Entertainment. Format: Country, adult contemp. Spec prog: Farm 4 hrs, class one hr wkly. ♦Jim Hone, pres; Rick Sessions, gen mgr; Leo Marshall, gen sls mgr; Colby Smith, progmg dir; Tom Louther, engrg VP.

KSRA-FM— September 1979: 92.7 mhz; 1.5 kw. -880 ft. TL: N45 11 02 W113 52 12. Stereo. E-mail: ksra@ksrafm.com.

Sandpoint

KIBR(FM)— 1994: 102.5 mhz; 3 kw. 177 ft. TL: N48 15 22 W116 30 46. Stereo. 327 Marion Ave. 83864. Phone: (208) 263-2179. Fax: (208) 265-5440. E-mail: dylanb@953kpwd.com. Licensee: Benefield Broadcasting Inc. (acq 3-31-95; $250,000;. FTR: 5-22-95). Network: ABC. Format: Classic country. News staff: one. Target aud: 25-54. ♦Dylan Benefield, gen mgr, opns mgr & gen sls mgr; Jim Tomcheck, progmg dir & progmg mgr; Mike Brown, news dir.

KPND(FM)—Listing follows KSPT(AM).

KSPT(AM)— Mar 23, 1949: 1400 khz; 1 kw-U. TL: N48 18 16 W116 32 32. 327 Marion Ave. 83864. Phone: (208) 263-2179. Fax: (208) 265-5440. E-mail: prod@953kpno.com. Licensee: Blue Sky Broadcasting Inc. (acq 5-4-83; $250,000;. FTR: 5-30-85). Network: ABC, USA. Rep: Tacher. Smith & Belendiuk. Format: News/talk, sports. Target aud: 25 plus. Spec prog: Relg 2 hrs wkly. ♦Dylan Benefield, gen mgr & progmg dir; Conrad Agtee, chief of engrg.

KPND(FM)—Co-owned with KSPT(AM). May 19, 1980: 95.3 mhz; 9.8 kw. Ant 2,368 ft. TL: N48 22 40 W116 37 05. Stereo. Format: AAA.

Shelley

KBJX(FM)— October 1999: 106.3 mhz; 100 kw. 636 ft. TL: N43 06 45 W112 29 34. Stereo. 228 1st St., Idaho Falls 83401. Phone: (208) 529-6926. Fax: (208) 529-6927. E-mail: support@hot106.fm. Web Site: www.106kbjx.com. Licensee: Pacific Empire Radio Corp. (group owner; acq 10-6-98; $788,500. with KATW(FM) Lewiston). Format: Adult contemp. Target aud: 25-54; adults. ♦Mark Bolland, CEO & pres; Bill Keith, gen mgr.

Soda Springs

KBRV(AM)— Sept 22, 1957: 790 khz; 5 kw-D. TL: N42 38 30 W111 36 40. Box 777, 213 E. Second St. 83276. Phone: (208) 547-2500. Fax: (208) 547-4593. E-mail: kvsi@dcdi.net. Web Site: www.kvsi.com. Licensee: Caribou Broadcasting Inc. (acq 1-8-2001). Format: Country. ♦ Tom Mathis, gen mgr.

KITT(FM)— Sept 10, 1982: 100.1 mhz; 3 kw. Ant -174 ft. TL: N42 38 30 W111 36 40. Stereo. Box 1450, 210 North 1000 East, St. George, UT 84771-1450. Phone: (435) 628-1000. Fax: (435) 628-6636. E-mail: legacy1@infowest.com. Licensee: Tri-State Media Corp. Group owner: Legacy Communications Corp. (acq 7-8-2004; $234,000). Dan J. Alpert. Format: Hot country. ♦E. Morgan Skinner, Jr., CEO & pres.

Sun Valley

*KBSS(FM)— August 2004: 91.1 mhz; 700 w. Ant 1,870 ft. TL: N43 38 36 W114 23 49. Boise State Radio, 1910 University Dr., Boise 83725-1915. Phone: (208) 426-3663. Fax: (208) 344-6631. E-mail: radio@boisestate.edu. Web Site: radio.boisestate.edu. Licensee: Idaho State Board of Education. Network: NPR. Format: News, info. ♦Jim East, gen mgr; Steve Jess, news dir; Tom Taylor, engrg mgr.

Stations in the U.S. — Illinois

Developers & Brokers of Radio Properties
contact American Media Services at our suite:
Philadelphia Marriott Downtown
215-625-2900
843-972-2200
americanmediaservices.com
Charleston, SC
Dallas, TX · Chicago, Il · Austin, TX
American Media Services, LLC

KECH-FM— Nov 21, 1988: 95.3 mhz; 100 w. Ant 2,168 ft. TL: N43 39 42 W114 24 07. (CP: 16 kw, ant 1,909 ft. TL: N43 38 36 W114 23 49). Box 2158, Ketchum 83340. Phone: (208) 726-5324. Fax: (208) 726-5459. Web Site: www.kech95.com. Licensee: Chaparral Broadcasting Inc. Group owner: Chaparral Communications acq 7-30-2004; grpsl). Cohn & Marks. Format: Classic rock. News staff: one; News: 6 hrs wkly. Target aud: 25-54; upscale adults. Spec prog: Alternative 5 hrs, blues 8 hrs, jazz 6 hrs wkly. ♦ Scott Anderson, gen mgr; Cathy Nikolaisons, gen sls mgr; Bob Thompson, progmg dir; Sue Bailey, news dir.

KSKI-FM— Aug 3, 1977: 103.7 mhz; 53 kw. 1,905 ft. TL: N43 38 36 W114 23 49. Stereo. Box 2158, Ketchum 83340. Phone: (208) 726-5324. Fax: (208) 726-5459. Web site: www.ketsvidaho.net. Licensee: Chaparral Broadcasting Inc. Group owner: Chaparral Communications (acq 7-30-2004; grpsl). Chon & Marks. Format: Alt rock. News staff: one; News: 2 hrs wkly. Target aud: 18-49; affluent, upscale consumers. ♦ Scott Anderson, gen mgr; Cathy Nikolaisons, gen sls mgr & sls; Bob Thompson, progmg dir; Sue Bailey, news dir.

*KWRV(FM)— July 29, 1993: 91.9 mhz; 100 w. -512 ft. TL: N43 40 59 W114 20 52. Box 67, MN 83353. Phone: (208) 622-5999. Fax: (651) 290-1295. E-mail: molson@mpr.org. Web Site: www.mpr.org. Licensee: Minnesota Public Radio. Network: PRI. Format: Class. ♦ William Kling, pres; Craig Curtis, VP; Michael Orson, gen mgr; Anne Hovland, dev VP; Ginger Sisco, mktg VP; Vic Bremer, progmg VP.

KYZK(FM)—Not on air, target date: unknown: 107.5 mhz; 100 kw. 1,734 ft. TL: N43 16 50 W114 09 08. Box 2158, Ketchum 83340. Phone: (208) 726-5324. Fax: (208) 726-5459. Web site: www.swing107.com. Licensee: Chaparral Broadcasting Inc. Group owner: Chaparral Communications (acq 7-30-2004; grpsl). Network: ABC. Allied Radio Cohn & Marks. Format: Swing. ♦ Scott Anderson, gen mgr; Cathy Nikolaisons, gen sls mgr; Bob Thompson, progmg dir; Sue Bailey, news dir; Don Mussell, engrg dir.

Troy

KQZB(FM)—Not on air, target date: unknown: 100.5 mhz; 26.5 kw. Ant 686 ft. TL: N46 42 18 W116 55 25. 403 C St., Lewiston 83501. Phone: (208) 743-4560. Fax: (208) 798-0110. Licensee: Pacific Empire Radio Corp. ♦ Mike Bolland, pres.

Twin Falls

KART(AM)—See Jerome

*KAWZ(FM)— Apr 13, 1988: 89.9 mhz; 33 kw horiz, 100 kw vert. Ant 991 ft. TL: N42 43 47 W114 24 52. Stereo. Box 391 83303. Secondary address: 4002 N. 3300 E. 83301. Phone: (208) 734-4357. Fax: (208) 736-1958. E-mail: csn@csnradio.com. Web Site: www.csnradio.com. Licensee: Calvary Chapel of Twin Falls Inc. Format: Christian praise & worship, Bible teaching. News: 2 hrs wkly. Target aud: General; 18-80. ♦ Matt McNeilly, stn mgr; Don Mills, opns dir, opns mgr & progmg dir; Mike Kestler, pres, gen mgr & dev VP.

*KBSW(FM)— May 15, 1989: 91.7 mhz; 4.5 kw. Ant 492 ft. TL: N42 43 48 W114 25 06. Stereo. Boise State Univ., 1910 University Dr., Boise 83725. Phone: (208) 426-3663. Fax: (208) 344-6631. Web Site: radio.boisestate.edu. Licensee: Idaho State Board of Education. Network: Network: PRI, NPR. Dow, Lohnes & Albertson. Format: Talk, class. News staff: 2; News: 15 hrs wkly. Target aud: General. ♦ Don Wimberly, stn mgr; Steve Jess, news dir; Tom Taylor, engrg mgr.

*KCIR(FM)— Dec 12, 1982: 90.7 mhz; 20 kw. 2,519 ft. TL: N42 20 07 W113 36 17. Stereo. 1446 Filer Ave. E. 83301. Phone: (208) 734-5777. Fax: (208) 734-0331. Web Site: www.sosradio.net. Licensee: Faith Communications Corp. (acq 9-29-82). Network: USA. Format: Christian, educ. News: 5 hrs wkly. Target aud: 25-49; adults with families. Spec prog: Children 2 hrs wkly. ♦ Jack French, pres & gen mgr; Duane Luchsinger, stn mgr; Chris Staley, progmg dir & mus dir; Tim Hunt, chief of engrg.

*KEFX(FM)— 1996: 88.9 mhz; 3 kw. 20 ft. TL: N42 33 25 W114 28 18. Box 271 83303. Phone: (208) 734-4357. Fax: (208) 736-1958. E-mail: effectradio@effectradio.com. Web Site: www.effectradio.com. Licensee: Calvary Chapel of Twin Falls Inc. Group owner: CSN International Format: Christian, relg, bible teaching. ♦ Mike Kestler, pres & gen mgr; Matt McNeilly, stn mgr; Brian Harman, progmg dir; Ray Gorney, chief of engrg.

*KEZJ(AM)— 1946: 1450 khz; 1 kw-U. TL: N42 32 36 W114 28 14. Box 1238, College of Southern Idaho 83303-1238. Phone: (208) 736-3046. Phone: (888) 859-5278. Fax: (208) 736-2188. Licensee: College of Southern Idaho. Format: Multicultural, jazz. ♦ Don Wimberly, gen mgr.

KEZJ-FM— Mar 15, 1977: 95.7 mhz; 100 kw. Ant 620 ft. TL: N42 43 42 W114 24 48. Stereo. Box 1259 83301. Secondary address: 415 Park Ave. 83301. Phone: (208) 733-7512. Fax: (208) 733-7525. E-mail: bradweiser@clearchannel.com. Web Site: www.957kezj.com. Licensee: Citicasters Licenses L.P. Group owner: Clear Channel Communications Inc. (acq 5-99; grpsl). Network: ABC. Rep: Clear Channel. Format: Country. Target aud: 25-54. ♦ Janice Degner, VP & gen mgr; Brad Weiser, opns dir & progmg VP; Chris Mulvaney, gen sls mgr; Kelly Klaas, chief of engrg.

KLIX(AM)— Dec 12, 1946: 1310 khz; 5 kw-D, 2.5 kw-N, DA-N. TL: N42 33 30 W114 26 40. Box 1259, 415 Park Ave. 83303. Phone: (208) 733-1310. Fax: (208) 733-7525. Web Site: www.newsradio1310.com. Licensee: Citicasters Licenses L.P. Group owner: Clear Channel Communications Inc. Network: ABC. Format: News/talk. News staff: one; News: 12 hrs wkly. Target aud: 35-54. Spec prog: Farm 2 hrs wkly. ♦ Terry Tario, VP & gen mgr; Brad Weiser, opns mgr & progmg dir; Janice Degner, gen sls mgr; James Tidmarsh, news dir; Kelly Klaas, chief of engrg.

KLIX-FM— June 15, 1974: 96.5 mhz; 100 kw. 130 ft. TL: N42 33 05 W114 30 59. Stereo. Web Site: www.coololdies965.com. Format: Oldies. Target aud: 18-49. ♦ Brad Hollstrom, opns mgr & progmg dir; Janice Degner, sls dir.

KMVX(FM)—See Jerome

KSNQ(FM)— September 2004: 98.3 mhz; 100 kw. Ant 620 ft. TL: N42 43 42 W114 24 48. Intermart Broadcasting Twin Falls Inc., 3434 S.W. 26th Pl., Cape Coral, FL 33914. Phone: (239) 542-4200. Fax: (239) 542-4221. E-mail: swfradio@aol.com. Licensee: Intermart Broadcasting Twin Falls Inc. Format: Classic rock. ♦ Patricia Woods, VP & gen mgr.

KTFI(AM)— October 1928: 1270 khz; 5 kw-D, 1 kw-N. TL: N42 33 30 W114 32 00. Secondary address: 21361 Hwy 30 83301. Phone: (208) 733-1270. Fax: (208) 733-4196. Web Site: www.ktfi.com. Licensee: Locally Owned Radio LLC (group owner; acq 10-31-2003; grpsl). Format: Oldies. Target aud: 35 plus. Spec prog: Farm 3 hrs, relg 5 hrs, sports 3 hrs wkly. ♦ Larry Johnson, pres & gen mgr; Jerre Fender, opns dir; Deb Uvieu, gen sls mgr; Sierra Tattersall, progmg dir.

Victor

KKTN(FM)— May 2005: 103.7 mhz; 55 kw. Ant -476 ft. TL: N43 41 07 W111 06 54. 6807 Foxglove Dr., Cheyenne, WY 82009. Phone: (307) 778-9318. Fax: (307) 632-9349. Licensee: Michael Radio Group LLC. Format: Rock. ♦ Victor A. Michael Jr., gen mgr.

KMQS(FM)— May 2005: 92.3 mhz; 26 kw. Ant -508 ft. TL: N43 41 07 W111 06 54. 6807 Foxglove Dr., Cheyenne, WY 82009. Phone: (307) 778-9318. Fax: (307) 632-9349. Licensee: Michael Radio Group LLC. Format: Country. ♦ Victor A. Michael Jr., gen mgr.

Wallace

KIBG(FM)— 2001: . Stn currently dark 100.7 mhz; 500 w. Ant 2,207 ft. TL: N47 33 44 W115 50 33. (CP: 85 kw, ant 2,119 ft. TL: N47 46 25 W114 16 04). 581 N. Reservoir Rd., Polson, MT 59860. Phone: (406) 883-5255. Fax: (406) 883-4441. Licensee: Anderson Radio Inc. (group owner; acq 9-22-2003; grpsl). ♦ Dennis Anderson, gen mgr; Gary Meili, gen sls mgr; Dean August, progmg dir; Jeff Smith, news dir; Tony Mulligan, chief of engrg.

*KTWD(FM)— December 2000: 97.5 mhz; 1.6 kw. Ant -2212 ft. TL: N47 33 49 W115 50 01. Stereo. Box 1208, Airway Heights, WA 99001. Phone: (509) 244-5577. Fax: (509) 244-2232. E-mail: ktwd@csnradio.com. Licensee: CSN International (group owner; acq 2-24-2000; $50,000. for CP). Format: Relg. ♦ Barney Dasovich, gen mgr.

KWAL(AM)— May 1938: 620 khz; 1 kw-U, DA-N. TL: N47 30 29 W116 00 17. Stereo. Box 828, 120 First St., Osburn 83849. Phone: (208) 752-1141. Phone: (208) 752-1142. Fax: (208) 753-5111. E-mail: kwalradio@usamedia.tv. Licensee: Silver Valley Broadcasters Inc. (acq 1-1-73). Network: Jones Radio Networks. Rep: Tacher. Format: C&W. ♦ Paul Robinson, pres; Paul Robinson, gen mgr; George White, gen sls mgr; Larry Crigger, progmg dir & prom.

Weiser

KWEI-FM—(Fruitland). March 1984: 99.5 mhz; 8 kw. 2,634 ft. TL: N44 00 58 W116 24 15. Stereo. Box 45234, Boise 83704. Phone: (208) 367-1859. Fax: (208) 383-9170. E-mail: kweispanishradio@aol.com. Web Site: kweispanishradio.com. Licensee: Treasure Valley Broadcasting Co. (acq 1987). Format: Sp. News: 15 hrs wkly. Target aud: 25-54; mass appeal. ♦ Randall Williamson, gen mgr; Connie Weisgerber, gen sls mgr; Melvin Albeniz, progmg dir; Melvin Albenez, news dir; Rockwell Smith, chief of engrg.

KWEI(AM)— December 1947: 1260 khz; 1 kw-D, 60 w-N. TL: N44 14 00 W116 57 18. Box 791, 556 Hwy. S. 95 83672. Phone: (208) 549-0886. (Acq 1996). Format: News/talk. Target aud: 35-65; mass appeal.

Weston

KLZX(FM)—Not on air, target date: unknown: 95.9 mhz; Sun Valley Radio Inc., Box 570, Logan, UT 84323. Phone: (435) 752-1390. Fax: (435) 752-1392. Web Site: www.rock959.com. Licensee: Sun Valley Radio Inc. (group owner). Format: AOR. ♦ Alan Lewis, gen mgr.

Illinois

Albion

*WBJW(FM)— December 1997: 91.7 mhz; 6 kw. 328 ft. TL: N38 26 51 W88 05 07. (CP: 1.7 kw, ant 499 ft. TL: 38 19 14 W88 02 37). Box 4164, Evansville, IN 47724. Phone: (812) 386-3342. Phone: (800) 264-5550. Fax: (812) 768-5552. Web Site: www.thyword.org. Licensee: Music Ministries Inc. Format: Relg. ♦ Floyd E. Turner, gen mgr; Dave Rigg, opns mgr.

Aledo

WRMJ(FM)— June 12, 1979: 102.3 mhz; 3 kw. 300 ft. TL: N41 12 29 W90 46 10. Stereo. Box 187, 2104 S.E. 3rd St. 61231. Phone: (309) 582-5666. Fax: (309) 582-5667. E-mail: wrmj@mcol.net. Web Site: wrmj.com. Licensee: Western Illinois Broadcasting Co. (acq 8-83; $200,000; 8-1-83). Network: ABC Daytime Direction. Koerner & Olender. Format: Country, news. News staff: one; News: 20 hrs wkly. Target aud: 25-54. Spec prog: Relg 3 hrs wkly. ♦ John Hoscheidt, gen mgr.

Alton

KATZ-FM— September 1961: 100.3 mhz; 50 kw. 482 ft. TL: N38 55 44 W90 13 03. (CP: 50 kw). Stereo. 1001 Highlands Plaza Dr. W/, St. Louis, MO 63110. Phone: (314) 333-8000. Web Site: www.katzfm.com. Licensee: Citicasters Licenses L.P. Group owner: Clear Channel Communications Inc. (acq 5-4-99; grpsl). Format: Rhythm & blues, hip hop. News staff: 2; News: 7 hrs wkly. Spec prog: Black, relg 2 hrs wkly. ♦ Lee Armstrong Clear, gen mgr & VP; Chuck Atkins, opns mgr.

WBGZ(AM)— 1948: 1570 khz; 1 kw-D, 74 w-N. TL: N38 55 44 W90 13 03. Box 615, 227 Market St. 62002. Phone: (618) 465-3535. Fax:

(618) 465-3546. E-mail: wbgz@wbgzradio.com. Web Site: www.wbgzradio.com. Licensee: Metroplex Communications Inc. (acq 12-6-2004); $70,000. for 39% of stock). Network: USA. Format: News/talk. News staff: 2; News: 20 hrs wkly. Target aud: General. Spec prog: Gospel 4 hrs, relg 3 hrs wkly. ◆Sam Stemm, gen mgr; Nancy Birens, gen sls mgr; Dennis Laird, progmg dir; Mark Ellebracht, news dir.

Anna

WIBH(AM)— Jan 10, 1957: 1440 khz; 500 w-D, 109 w-N. TL: N37 26 45 W89 15 00. 330 S. Main St. 62906. Phone: (618) 833-9424. Fax: (618) 833-9091. E-mail: wibh@ajinternet.net. Web Site: www.wibhradio.com. Licensee: WIBH Inc. (acq 3-2-98; $315,000). Network: Network: UPI, ABC Information & Entertainment. Format: Classic country. News staff: one; News: 3 hrs wkly. Target aud: 25-69. ◆Maury Bass, VP; Moury Bass, gen mgr, stn mgr & progmg dir; Ronald Ellis, pres & gen mgr; Rick Campbell, gen sls mgr.

WKIB(FM)— Jan 13, 1958: 96.5 mhz; 22.5 kw. 745 ft. TL: N37 26 45 W89 15 00. (CP: 20 kw, ant 780 ft.). Stereo. 901 S. Kingshighway, Cape Girardeau, MO 63703. Phone: (573) 339-7000 (business). Fax: (573) 651-4100. Web Site: www.withersradio.com. Licensee: Withers Broadcasting Co. of Missouri LLC. Group owner: Withers Broadcasting Co. (acq 10-22-2001; $2 million). Format: Pop contemp hit radio. News staff: one; News: 10 hrs wkly. Target aud: 18-45. ◆Rick Lambert, gen mgr; Marla Stover, gen sls mgr; Steve Thomas, progmg dir.

Arcola

WXET(FM)—Licensed to Arcola. See Mattoon

Arlington Heights

*****WCLR(FM)**— Nov 1, 2003: 88.3 mhz; 1 w horiz, 1 kw vert. Ant 59 ft. TL: N42 06 45 W87 58 58. Educational Media Foundation, 5700 W. Oaks Blvd., Rocklin, CA 95765. Phone: (916) 251-1732. Fax: (916) 251-1650. E-mail: info@air1.com. Web Site: www.air1.com. Licensee: Educational Media Foundation. Group owner: EMF Broadcasting (acq 8-13-03). Network: Air 1. Shaw Pittman LLP. Format: Contemp Christian. News staff: 3. Target aud: 18-35; Judeo Christian, female. ◆Richard Jenkins, pres; Mike Novak, VP; Keith Whipple, dev dir.

WKIE(FM)—Licensed to Arlington Heights. See Chicago

Arthur

WXET(FM)—See Mattoon

Atlanta

WLCN(FM)— Apr 13, 2001: 96.3 mhz; 5.4 kw. Ant 266 ft. TL: N40 14 39 W89 15 51. Stereo. 1779 2250th St. 61723. Phone: (217) 648-5510; (847) 674-0864. Fax: (217) 648-2499; (847) 674-9188. E-mail: wmnw2002@yahoo.com. Web Site: www.wmnw.net. Licensee: KM Radio of Atlanta L.L.C. Group owner: KM Communications Inc. (acq 5-3-99). Format: Country. ◆Jim Ash, gen mgr; Tamera Turner, sls.

Auburn

WCVS-FM—See Springfield

Augusta

*****WAHI-FM**— May 10, 1995: . Stn currently dark 98.5 mhz; 1 kw. Ant 154 ft. TL: N40 16 03 W90 57 10. Rt. 1 Box 72, Plymouth 62367. Phone: (217) 392-2340. Licensee: Good News Broadcasters Inc. Target aud: General. ◆Francis L. Hollon, gen mgr.

Aurora

WAUR(AM)—(Sandwich). May 1986: 930 khz; 2.5 kw-D, 4.2 kw-N, DA-2. TL: N41 36 26 W88 27 11. 130 S. Jefferson, Ste 200, Chicago 60661. Phone: (312) 648-1621. Web Site: www.waur.relevantradio.com. Licensee: Starboard Media Foundation Inc. Group owner: Relevant Radio (acq 5-4-2004); $3.5 million). Network: ABC Information & Entertainment. Format: Catholic/talk. Target aud: 25-54. Spec prog: Farm 15 hrs wkly. ◆Mike Kendall, stn mgr.

WBIG(AM)— Dec 13, 1938: 1280 khz; 1 kw-D, 500 w-N, DA-2. TL: N41 46 10 W88 14 44. 620 Eola Rd. 60504. Phone: (630) 851-5200. Fax: (630) 851-5286. Web Site: wbig1280.com. Licensee: Big Broadcasting Co. Group owner: McNaughton-Jakle Stations (acq 1-94; $550,000). Leonard S. Joyce. Format: News/talk, sports. News staff: one; News: 10 hrs wkly. Target aud: 25-54; professional, upscale, suburbanites with children. Spec prog: Relg 6 hrs wkly. ◆Rick Jakle, pres; Steve Marten, exec VP & gen mgr; Jack Davis, opns mgr; Jim Sauers, gen sls mgr; Brian Felsten, progmg dir; Brien Prenevost, chief of engrg.

WERV-FM— Feb 12, 1961: 95.9 mhz; 3 kw. 338 ft. TL: N41 26 12 W88 16 03. Stereo. 1884 Plain Ave. 60505. Phone: (630) 898-1580. Fax: (630) 898-2463. Web Site: www.959theriver.fm. Licensee: NM Licensing LLC. Group owner: NextMedia Group L.L.C. (acq 11-26-01; grpsl). Rep: McGavren Guild. Leibowitz & Associates. Format: Classic hits. News staff: one; News: 5 hrs wkly. Target aud: 25-54; suburban Chicago adults. ◆Dennis Mockler, gen mgr; Dana Jang, opns dir; Chip Ramsey, opns mgr.

WKKD(AM)— Sept 21, 1960: 1580 khz; 170 w-D, 200 w-N, DA-2. TL: N41 46 12 W88 16 03. Stereo. 2100 Lee St., Evanston 60202. Phone: (847) 475-1590. Fax: (847) 475-1590. Licensee: Kovas Communications of Indiana Inc. (group owner; (acq 2-28-2002). Format: Health talk. ◆Connie Walburn, gen mgr.

WLEY-FM— 1965: 107.9 mhz; 21 kw. 761 ft. TL: N41 56 01 W88 04 23. Stereo. 150 N. Michigan Ave., Suite 1040, Chicago 60601. Phone: (312) 920-9500. Fax: (312) 920-9516. E-mail: info@laley1079.com. Web Site: www.laley1079.com. Licensee: WLEY Licensing Inc. Group owner: Spanish Broadcasting System Inc. (acq 12-26-96; $33 million). Format: Rgnl Mexican. News staff: one. Target aud: 25-54. ◆Jeff Schrinsky, gen mgr & natl sls mgr; Mario Paez, gen mgr; Joe McKay, gen sls mgr & mktg dir; Marylu Ramos, progmg dir; Sam Palerno, chief of engrg.

Ava

WXAN(FM)— Jan 11, 1982: 103.9 mhz; 2.9 kw horiz, 2.9 kw vert. 675 ft. TL: N37 51 19 W89 28 06. Stereo. 9077 Ava Rd. 62907. Phone: (618) 426-3308. Phone: (618) 426-3309. Fax: (618) 426-3310. E-mail: wxan@egyptian.net. Web Site: www.wxan.net. Licensee: Southern Gospetality LLC. Format: Relg, southern gospel. News: 10 hrs wkly. Target aud: 30-55; Christians & family-oriented listeners. ◆Harold Lawder, pres; Doug Apple, gen mgr.

Bartonville

WIXO(FM)— February 1997: 99.9 mhz; 1.5 kw. 584 ft. TL: N40 36 23 W89 32 20. 120 Eaton St., Peoria 61603. Phone: (309) 676-5000. Fax: (309) 694-2600. Web Site: www.99xrocks.com. Licensee: Regent Broadcasting of Peoria Inc. Group owner: Regent Communications Inc. (acq 7-6-01; grpsl). Rep: Katz Radio. Pepper & Corazzini. Format: Modern Rock. Target aud: 18-34; young active, primarily men. ◆Bill Hurley, gen mgr; Ric Morgan, opns mgr; Bob Swinehart, sls dir & gen sls mgr; Matt Bahan, progmg dir; Jerry Scott, chief of engrg.

Beardstown

WRMS(AM)— Nov 1, 1959: 790 khz; 500 w-D, 59 w-N, DA-2. TL: N40 00 11 W90 23 51. Covenant Network, 3515 Hampton Ave., St. Louis, MO 63139. Phone: (314) 752-7000. E-mail: office@covenantnet.net. Licensee: Covenant Network (acq 7-21-2004). Format: Christian, relg, inspirational. ◆Tony Holman, pres & gen mgr.

WRMS-FM— 1976: 94.3 kw. 6 kw. Ant 298 ft. TL: N40 04 45 W90 25 58. 108 E. Main St. 62618. Phone: (217) 323-1790. Fax: (217) 323-1705. E-mail: wrmsfm@casscomm.com. Licensee: Conner Family Broadcasting Inc. (acq 3-87). Format: Country. ◆John Conner, gen mgr, gen sls mgr & progmg dir; Glen Hopkins, chief of engrg.

Belleville

WSDZ(AM)— July 13, 1947: 1260 khz; 5 kw-U, DA-2. TL: N38 27 28 W89 57 43. 638 Westport Plaza, St. Louis, MO 63146. Phone: (314) 682-1260. Fax: (314) 682-1190. Web Site: www.radiodisney.com. Licensee: Radio Disney Group LLC. Group owner: ABC Inc. (acq 9-22-98; $2.5 million). Network: ABC. Format: Children. News staff: one; News: 20 hrs wkly. Target aud: 35 plus; affluent, well-educated, business & professional. Spec prog: Farm 3 hrs, sports/talk 13 hrs wkly. ◆Jason Miller, progmg dir.

WVRV(FM)—See East St. Louis

Belvidere

WXRX(FM)— Feb 27, 1971: 104.9 mhz; 4 kw. 333 ft. TL: N42 19 21 W88 57 15. Stereo. 2830 Sandy Hollow Rd., Rockford 61109. Phone: (815) 874-7861. Fax: (815) 874-2202. Web Site: www.wxrx.com. Licensee: Maverick Media of Rockford License LLC. Group owner: RadioWorks Inc. (acq 4-27-2005); grpsl). Shaw, Pittman. Format: Rock/AOR. Target aud: 18-49. ◆Gary Rozynek, pres.

Benton

WQRL(FM)— Oct 1, 1973: 106.3 mhz; 12.5 kw. 328 ft. TL: N37 55 51 W88 40 52. (CP: Ant 459 ft.). Stereo. Box 818, 303 N. Main 62812. Secondary address: 303 N. Main St. 62812. Phone: (618) 435-8100. Fax: (618) 435-8102. E-mail: wwqrlfm@shawneelink.net. Licensee: Dana Communications Corp. (acq 4-28-92; $250,000; 5-18-92). Format: Oldies. News staff: 2; News: 15 hrs wkly. Target aud: 25-49; adults & young adults preferring new country. Spec prog: Farm 3 hrs wkly. ◆Dana Withers, CEO, pres, gen mgr & opns mgr; Bleu Withers, exec VP; Gloria Holland, stn mgr; Janet Jensen, gen sls mgr; Steve Browning, natl sls mgr & mktg mgr; Michael Steele, prom dir; Travis Clark, mus dir; Dean Cramer, asst music dir & news dir; Jeff Oestreich, chief of engrg & chief of engrg.

Bethalto

WFUN-FM— April 1991: 95.5 mhz; 6 kw. 328 ft. TL: N38 49 39 W90 00 53. Stereo. 9666 Olive Blvd., Suite 610, St. Louis, MO 63132. Phone: (314) 989-9550. Fax: (314) 989-9551. Web Site: www.foxy995.net. Licensee: Radio One Licenses LLC. Group owner: Radio One Inc. (acq 11-8-01; grpsl). Brown, Nietert & Kaufman. Format: Rhythm and blues. News: 2 hrs wkly. Target aud: General; families. ◆Alfred Liggins, pres; Linda O'Connor, gen mgr; Bri Kruezer, gen sls mgr; Garth Adams, progmg mgr; Gary Bennett, engrg VP & chief of engrg.

Bloomington

WBNQ(FM)—Listing follows WJBC(AM).

WBWN(FM)—See Le Roy

*****WESN(FM)**— 1972: 88.1 mhz; 120 w. 98 ft. TL: N40 29 28 W88 59 37. Stereo. Box 2900 61701. Phone: (309) 556-2638. Fax: (309) 556-3411. E-mail: wesn@iwu.edu. Web Site: www.wesn.org. Licensee: Illinois Wesleyan University. Network: PRI. Format: Div. Spec prog: Black 18 hrs, class 6 hrs, jazz 6 hrs wkly. ◆Camm Rowland, stn mgr.

WIHN(FM)—See Normal

WJBC(AM)— 1925: 1230 khz; 1 kw-U. TL: N40 27 32 W89 00 38. 236 Greenwood Ave. 61704. Phone: (309) 829-1221. Fax: (309) 827-8071. Web Site: www.wjbc.com. Licensee: Regent Broadcasting of Lancaster Inc. Group owner: Regent Communications Inc. (acq 5-12-2004); grpsl). Network: ABC Information & Entertainment. Rep: McGavren Guild. Reddy, Begley & McCormick. Format: Full service. Spec prog: Farm 13 hrs wkly. ◆Red Pitcher, gen mgr; R.C. McBride, opns mgr & progmg dir; Julie Penn, gen sls mgr & natl sls mgr; Colleen Reynolds, news dir; Ron Schott, chief of engrg.

WBNQ(FM)— Co-owned with WJBC(AM). 1947: 101.5 mhz; 50 kw. 460 ft. TL: N40 27 32 W89 00 38. Stereo. Web Site: www.wbnq.com. Licensee: Regent Licensee of Erie Inc. Format: CHR. Spec prog: Farm one hr wkly. ◆Dan Westhoff, stn mgr; Tony Travatto, gen sls mgr; Chad Fasig, progmg mgr; Russell Rush, mus dir.

Breese

WDLJ(FM)— 2003: 97.5 mhz; 2.5 kw. Ant 512 ft. TL: N38 36 33 W89 23 35. KM Radio of Breese L.L.C., 3654 W. Jarvis Ave., Skokie 60076. Phone: (847) 674-0864. Fax: (847) 674-9188. Web Site: www.wdlj.net. Licensee: KM Radio of Breese L.L.C. Format: Classic rock. ◆Dave Collier, gen mgr.

Brookport

WNTX(AM)— October 1987: 750 khz; 500 w-D. TL: N37 08 31 W88 38 58. 6120 Waldo Church Rd., Metropolis 62960-4903. Phone: (618) 564-2171. Fax: (618) 564-3202. Licensee: Daniel S. Stratemeyer (acq 9-20-2002). Format: Talk. ◆Samuel Stratemeyer, gen mgr.

Stations in the U.S. — Illinois

Developers & Brokers of Radio Properties

contact American Media Services at our suite:
Philadelphia Marriott Downtown
215-625-2900

843-972-2200
americanmediaservices.com
Charleston, SC
Dallas, TX · Chicago, Il · Austin, TX

American Media Services, LLC

Bushnell

WLMD(FM)— August 1992: 104.7 mhz; 3 kw. 328 ft. TL: N40 32 52 W90 26 25. Stereo. 119 W. Carroll, Macomb 61455. Phone: (309) 833-5561. Fax: (309) 833-3460. E-mail: wlmd@macomb.com. Web Site: www.radiomacomb.com. Licensee: WPW Broadcasting Inc. (group owner; (acq 12-27-99); grpsl). Network: Network: ABC, Jones Radio Networks. Format: Country. News staff: one; News: 2 hrs wkly. Target aud: 25-54; general. Spec prog: Farm 3 hrs wkly. ♦ Don Davis, CEO; David Madison, pres; Vanessa Wetterling, stn mgr; Rick Bulger, opns mgr.

Cairo

*WBEL(FM)— 2002: 88.5 mhz; 64 kw vert. Ant 558 ft. TL: N36 59 32 W88 59 19. Box 3206, American Family Radio, Tupelo, MS 38803. Phone: (662) 844-8888. Fax: (662) 842-6791. Web Site: www.afr.net. Licensee: American Family Association. Group owner: American Family Radio Format: Christian. ♦ Marvin Sanders, gen mgr.

WKRO(AM)— Jan 8, 1942: 1490 khz; 1 kw-U. TL: N37 02 36 W89 11 02. Box 311, Hwy. 37 N. 62914. Phone: (618) 734-1490. Fax: (618) 734-0884. E-mail: djman75@hotmail.com. Licensee: Alexander Broadcasting Corp. (acq 3-22-01; $20,500). Network: ABC. Format: Urban adult contemp. News staff: one; News: 12 hrs wkly. Target aud: 25-54; general. Spec prog: Gospel 12 hrs, farm 12 hrs wkly. ♦ Danny McDonald, gen mgr & opns mgr; Marti Nicholson, gen sls mgr & adv dir.

Canton

WBYS(AM)— Oct 5, 1947: 1560 khz; 250 w-D. TL: N40 32 43 W90 01 08. Box 600, 1000 E. Linn St. 61520. Phone: (309) 647-1560. Fax: (309) 647-1563. Web Site: www.wbysradio.com. Licensee: WPW Broadcasting Inc. (group owner; (acq 1999); $210,000. for stock with co-located FM). Network: ABC Information & Entertainment. Richard F. Swift. Format: Hits of the 50's & 60's. News staff: one; News: 20 hrs wkly. Target aud: 30 plus; community-oriented with above average income. Spec prog: Farm 10 hrs wkly. ♦ David Madison, CEO & pres; David Klockenga, stn mgr.

WCDD(FM)— Co-owned with WBYS(AM). Oct 7, 1968: 107.9 mhz; 25 kw. 265 ft. TL: N40 32 43 W90 01 08. Stereo. Format: Classic hits. News staff: one; News: 10 hrs wkly. Target aud: 25-54; primarily females.

Carbondale

WCIL(AM)— Nov 14, 1946: 1020 khz; 1 kw-D. TL: N37 43 31 W89 15 25. 1431 Country Aire Dr., Carterville 62918. Phone: (618) 985-4843. Fax: (618) 985-6529. E-mail: mail@magic951.com. Web Site: www.wjpf.com. Licensee: MRR License LLC. Group owner: MAX Media L.L.C. (acq 3-29-2004); grpsl). Network: ABC Information & Entertainment. Rep: Christal. Format: Sports, news/talk. News staff: 2; News: 10 hrs wkly. Target aud: 35 plus. Spec prog: Farm one hr wkly. ♦ Brian Schimmel, gen mgr; Rusty James, opns dir; Steve Falat, gen sls mgr; Dave Kuffel, rgnl sls mgr; Kristen Lewis, prom mgr; Ryan Patrick, adv mgr; Roz Rice, progmg dir & news dir; Tim Deterding, engrg dir.

WCIL-FM— July 1968: 101.5 mhz; 50 kw. 430 ft. TL: N37 43 31 W89 15 25. Stereo. Web Site: www.cilfm.com. Format: Top 40 hit music. Target aud: 18-34; adult females. ♦ Rusty James, stn mgr.

*WDBX(FM)— February 1996: 91.1 mhz; 3 kw. Ant 131 ft. TL: N37 43 43 W89 12 57. Stereo. 224 N. Washington St. 62901. Phone: (618) 457-3691. Phone: (618) 529-5900. E-mail: wdbx@globaleyes.net. Web Site: www.wdbx.org. Licensee: Heterodyne Broadcasting Co. Format: Div. ♦ Francis Murphy, pres; Brian R. Powell, stn mgr.

*WSIU(FM)— Sept 15, 1958: 91.9 mhz; 50 kw. 299 ft. TL: N37 42 29 W89 14 05. Stereo. Mail code 6602, Southern Illinois Univ.-Carbondale 62901. Phone: (618) 453-4343. Fax: (618) 453-6186. E-mail: lisa.morrisette@wsiu.com. Web Site: wsiu.org. Licensee: Board of Trustees Southern Illinois University. Network: Network: NPR, PRI.

Cohn & Marks. Format: Class, news. News staff: 3; News: 36 hrs wkly. Target aud: 35-64; highly educated, upper income, socially conscious. Spec prog: New age 4 hrs, big band 4 hrs, folk 3 hrs wkly. ♦ Candis Isberner, CEO; Delores Kerstein, CFO; Jeff Williams, gen mgr; Mike Zelten, opns mgr & progmg dir; Renee Dillard, dev dir; Jack Hammer, chief of engrg. Co-owned TV: *WSIU-TV affil

WTAO(FM)— (Murphysboro). August 1972: 105.1 mhz; 25 kw. 308 ft. TL: N37 45 15 W89 19 14. Stereo. Box 127, 1822 N. Court St., Marion 62959. Phone: (618) 997-8123. Fax: (618) 993-2319. Web Site: www.105tao.com. Licensee: Clear Channel Broadcasting Licenses Inc. Group owner: Clear Channel Communications Inc. (acq 1-18-01; grpsl). Format: Rock/active rock. Target aud: 18-49. ♦ Jerry Crouse, gen mgr; Paxton Guy, opns mgr; Matt Mellon, progmg dir.

Carlinville

*WIBI(FM)— Sept 30, 1975: 91.1 mhz; 50 kw. 476 ft. TL: N39 20 58 W89 48 16. Stereo. 17387 Cottonwood Ln., Box 140 Phone: (217) 854-4800. Phone: (800) 707-9191. Fax: (217) 854-4810. E-mail: wibi@wibi.org. Web Site: www.wibi.org. Licensee: Illinois Bible Institute Inc. (group owner) Gammon & Grange. Format: Adult contemp Christian. Target aud: 25-49. ♦ Jessica Barton, prom dir; Paul Anthony, gen mgr, opns mgr, sls dir, mktg dir & progmg dir.

*WOLG(FM)— Dec 8, 1990: 95.9 mhz; 6 kw. 325 ft. TL: N39 14 25 W89 54 26. Stereo. Covenant Network, 3515 Hampton, St. Louis, MO 63139. Licensee: Covenant Network. (acq 8-10-98; $300,000). Format: Relg.

*WTSG(FM)— Aug 11, 1997: 90.1 mhz; 3 kw. 295 ft. TL: N39 20 58 W89 48 16. Box 140 62626-0140. Phone: (217) 854-4851. Fax: (217) 854-4810. E-mail: staff@wtsg.org. Web Site: www.wtsg.org. Licensee: Illinois Bible Institute Inc. (group owner) Gammon & Grange. Format: Southern gospel mus, relg. Target aud: 25-44. ♦ Jessica Barton, prom dir; Paul Anthony, gen mgr, opns mgr & progmg dir.

Carmi

WROY(AM)—Listing follows WRUL(FM).

WRUL(FM)— 1951: 97.3 mhz; 50 kw. 496 ft. TL: N38 04 54 W88 12 04. Stereo. Box 400, 101 N. Church St. 62821. Phone: (618) 382-4161. Phone: (618) 382-2345. Fax: (618) 382-4162. E-mail: wrul973@shawneelink.net. Web Site: www.wrul.com. Licensee: Carmi Broadcasting Co. Network: ABC. Format: Country. News staff: 2; News: 8 hrs wkly. Target aud: 25-55. ♦ John Strader, gen mgr & gen sls mgr.

WROY(AM)—Co-owned with WRUL(FM). Dec 13, 1948: 1460 khz; 1 kw-D, 85 w-N. TL: N38 04 54 W88 12 04. Web Site: www.wrul.com. Format: Hits of the 50s, 60s, 70s & 80s. News staff: 2; News: 25 hrs wkly. Target aud: 35 plus; general. Spec prog: Farm 6 hrs wkly.

Carrier Mills

*WBVN(FM)— Jan 8, 1990: 104.5 mhz; 6 kw. 328 ft. TL: N37 46 25 W88 44 20. Stereo. Box 1126, Marion 62959. Secondary address: Sherlock Homes, Rte. 13E, Marion 62959. Phone: (618) 252-2999. Fax: (618) 997-3194. E-mail: wbvn@shawneclink.net. Web Site: www.wbvn.org. Licensee: Kenneth W. and Jane A. Anderson (acq 2-28-00). Format: Contemp Christian. News staff: 3. Target aud: 18-45; general. ♦ Ken Anderson, pres & gen mgr.

Carterville

WUEZ(FM)— Apr 2, 1992: 95.1 mhz; 17.6 kw. Ant 390 ft. TL: N37 43 31 W89 15 25. 1431 Country Arc Dr. 62918. Phone: (618) 985-4843. Fax: (618) 985-6529. E-mail: mail@magic951.com. Web Site: www.magic951.com. Licensee: MRR License LLC. Group owner: MAX Media L.L.C. (acq 3-29-2004); grpsl). Format: Adult contemp. News staff: 3; News: 18 hrs wkly. Target aud: 25-49; 60% women, 40% men, good spendable income; mgrs, supvrs, professionals. Spec prog: Dick Clark countdown, Solid Gold Saturday Night. ♦ Brian Schimmel, gen

mgr; Chad Elliot, chief of opns; Steve Salat, gen sls mgr; Pat Benton, progmg dir; Tim Deterding, chief of engrg.

Carthage

WCAZ(AM)— 1922: 990 khz; 1 kw-D, 9 w-N. TL: N40 24 30 W88 12 04. Box 498 62321. Secondary address: 86 S. Madison 62321. Phone: (217) 357-3128. Fax: (217) 357-2014. E-mail: wcazam@adamas.net. Web Site: www.wcazam990.com. Licensee: Ralla Broadcasting Co. Inc. (acq 1993). Network: UPI. Format: Talk.

WCEZ(FM)— 2001: 93.9 mhz; 6 kw. Ant 328 ft. TL: N40 24 54 W91 15 11. 108 Washington St., Keokuk, IA 52632. Secondary address: 303 N. Main 62812. Phone: (217) 357-9800. Fax: (319) 524-7275. E-mail: gmfolluo@interl.net. Licensee: Dana R. Withers. ♦ Dana Withers, CEO & pres; Gary M. Folluo, gen mgr.

WQKQ(FM)— Nov 1, 1978: 92.1 mhz; 25 kw. Ant 328 ft. TL: N40 35 37 W91 06 48. Stereo. 2850 Mount Pleasant St., Burlington, IA 52601. Phone: (319) 752-5402. Fax: (319) 752-4715. E-mail: johnp@burlingtonradio.com. Licensee: Pritchard Broadcasting Co. (acq 12-1-99). Format: Classic hits. News staff: one; News: 3 hrs wkly. Target aud: 25-54. ♦ John T. Pritchard, pres, VP & gen mgr; Kathy Vance, opns mgr; Chet Young, gen sls mgr.

Casey

WCBH(FM)— Sept 19, 1988: 104.3 mhz; 11.2 kw. 495 ft. TL: N39 16 24 W87 55 39. 208 W. Jefferson St., Effington 62401. Phone: (217) 342-4141. Phone: (217) 342-4142. Fax: (217) 342-4143. E-mail: wcrc@wcrc975.com. Licensee: Two Petaz Inc. Group owner: The Cromwell Group Inc. (acq 1-9-02; grpsl). Format: Christian. ♦ Bud Walters, CEO; Marvin Phillips, gen mgr; Gail Willison, opns dir, progmg dir & progmg dir; Marvin Phillips, gen sls mgr; David Wilson, chief of engrg.

WKZI(AM)— Dec 14, 1963: 800 khz; 250 w-U. TL: N39 18 14 W87 58 15. 18889 N. 23rd 50th St., Dennison 62423. Phone: (217) 826-9673. E-mail: wkzi@rr1.net. Web Site: www.rr1.net/users/wkzi. Licensee: Word Power Inc. (acq 5-4-93; $152,400;. FTR: 5-24-93). Network: Moody. Shook, Hardy & Bacon. Format: Christian. News: 17 hrs wkly. Target aud: General; 12 plus. ♦ Eleanor Jean Ford, progmg dir; Mark Stephen Ford, engrg dir; Paul Dean Ford, pres, gen mgr, gen sls mgr, news dir & chief of engrg.

WLHW(FM)—Co-owned with WKZI(AM).Not on air, target date: unknown: 91.5 mhz; 6 kw. Ant 197 ft. TL: N39 18 14 W87 58 15.

Centralia

WILY(AM)— Aug 15, 1946: 1210 khz; 10 kw-D, 3 w-N, 1.1 kw-CH, DA-2. TL: N38 28 55 W89 08 56. Box 528 62801. Phone: (618) 533-5700. Fax: (618) 533-5737. E-mail: wrxx@mvn.net. Licensee: Withers Broadcasting Co. of West Virginia. Group owner: Withers Broadcasting Co. (acq 11-4-97; $527,500. with co-located FM). Network: ABC Information & Entertainment. Dennis Kelly. Format: Oldies. News staff: 2; News: 60 hrs wkly. Target aud: 25-54. Spec prog: Business news. ♦ Russ Withers, pres; Dana Withers, gen mgr & progmg dir; Brenda Robinson, opns mgr.

WRXX(FM)—Co-owned with WILY(AM). Dec 24, 1964: 95.3 mhz; 3 kw. 217 ft. TL: N38 34 44 W89 06 46. Stereo. Network: ABC. Format: Rock. News staff: 2; News: 2 hrs wkly. Target aud: 18-49.

Champaign

WBCP(AM)—See Urbana

*WBGL(FM)— Oct 31, 1982: 91.7 mhz; 20 kw. 500 ft. TL: N40 09 09 W88 06 56. Stereo. 2108 W. Springfield St. 61821. Phone: (217) 359-8232. Fax: (217) 359-7374. E-mail: wbgl@wbgl.org. Web Site: www.wbgl.org. Licensee: Illinois Bible Institute Inc. (group owner) Network: USA. Format: Educ, relg. News staff: one. Target aud: 25-44.

Broadcasting & Cable Yearbook 2006
D-167

♦Barry Copeland, gen mgr; Jeff Scott, stn mgr; Meridith Foster, opns mgr & progmg dir; Joe McCall, chief of engrg & engr.

WCFF(FM)—See Urbana

WDWS(AM)— Jan 24, 1937: 1400 khz; 1 kw-U. TL: N40 05 04 W88 14 53. Stereo. Box 3939 61826. Phone: (217) 351-5300. Fax: (217) 351-5385. E-mail: talk@wdws.com. Web Site: www.wdws.com. Licensee: D.W.S. Inc. Network: ABC. Rep: Christal. Format: News/talk, sports. News staff: 4; News: 26 hrs wkly. Target aud: 35-64; adults. Spec prog: Farm 10 hrs, relg 4 hrs wkly. ♦Mike Halle, gen mgr; Steve Khachaturian, VP & gen mgr; Jim Lewis, opns mgr; Dave Burns, gen sls mgr; Carol Vorel, news dir.

WHMS-FM—Co-owned with WDWS(AM). 1948: 97.5 mhz; 50 kw. 358 ft. TL: N40 05 04 W88 14 53. Stereo. E-mail: literock@whms.com. Web Site: www.whms.com. Format: Adult contemp. News staff: 4; News: 10 hrs wkly. Target aud: 25-54; adults. ♦Ryan Aurthur, opns mgr.

WEBX(FM)—(Tuscola). Sept 30, 1970: 93.5 mhz; 6 kw. 308 ft. TL: N39 54 24 W88 16 35. Stereo. 4108 Fieldstone Rd., Suite C 61822. Phone: (217) 367-1195. Fax: (217) 367-3291. Web Site: www.935953therock.com. Licensee: AAA Entertainment Licensing LLC. Group owner: AAA Entertainment L.L.C. (acq 6-12-00; grpsl). Kaye, Scholer, Fierman, Hays & Handler. Format: Modern/extreme rock. Target aud: 18-49; adult professionals & college students. ♦Peter Ottmar, CEO; John Maguire, pres; John Ginzky, gen mgr & prom dir; Linda Bosch, gen sls mgr; Jon Mayotte, progmg dir.

***WEFT(FM)**— Sept 21, 1981: 90.1 mhz; 10 kw. 135 ft. TL: N40 10 51 W88 19 04. Stereo. 113 N. Market St. 61820-4004. Phone: (217) 359-9338. E-mail: weft@weftfm.org. Web Site: www.weftfm.org. Licensee: Prairie Air Inc. Network: Network: NPR, PRI. Haley, Bader & Potts. Format: Var/div. News: 10 hrs wkly. Target aud: General. Spec prog: Black 8 hrs, blues 10 hrs, folk 10 hrs, pub affrs 5 hrs, Sp 3 hrs wkly. ♦Mick Woolf, gen mgr & stn mgr.

WEVX(FM)—(Rantoul). Mar 15, 1972: 95.3 mhz; 3 kw. 425 ft. TL: N40 13 05 W88 06 55. Stereo. 4108 Fieldstone Rd., Suite C 61822. Phone: (217) 367-1195. Fax: (217) 367-3291. Web Site: 935953therock.com. Licensee: AAA Entertainment Licensing LLC. Group owner: AAA Entertainment L.L.C. (acq 4-21-00; grpsl). Network: Westwood One. Format: AOR/extreme rock. News staff: one. Target aud: 18-49. ♦John Ginzkey, gen mgr.

WILL(AM)—See Urbana

WILL-FM—See Urbana

WIXY(FM)— June 1, 1992: 100.3 mhz; 13 kw. Ant 453 ft. TL: N40 00 45 W88 08 29. 2603 W. Bradley Ave. 61821. Phone: (217) 355-2222. Fax: (217) 352-1256. Web Site: www.wixy.com. Licensee: Saga Communications of Illinois LLC. Group owner: Saga Communications Inc. (acq 11-4-92; $250,000;. FTR: 11-30-92). Rep: Katz Radio. Format: Country. News: 5 hrs wkly. Target aud: 25 plus. ♦Ed Christian, CEO & chmn; Sam Bush, CFO; Steven Goldstein, exec VP; Alan Beck, gen mgr.

WJCI(AM)—(Rantoul). Feb 1, 1963: 1460 khz; 500 w-D, 65 w-N, DA-1. TL: N40 18 37 W88 12 54. 129 N. Garrard, Rantoul 61866. Phone: (217) 893-1460. Fax: (217) 893-0884. E-mail: fanmail@1460sports.com. Web Site: www.1460sports.com. Licensee: Hooterville Broadcasting Inc. (acq 1-20-2005; $215,000). Network: ESPN Radio. Format: Sports. Target aud: General. ♦Gary Voss, gen mgr.

WLRW(FM)— January 1963: 94.5 mhz; 50 kw. Ant 390 ft. TL: N40 07 35 W88 17 25. Stereo. 2603 W. Bradley 61821. Phone: (217) 352-4141. Fax: (217) 352-1256. Web Site: www.mix945.com. Licensee: Saga Communications of Illinois LLC. Group owner: Saga Communications Inc. (acq 10-86; grpsl; FTR: 7-7-86). Format: Hot adult contemp. Target aud: 18-49. ♦Alan Beck, gen mgr; Jonathan Drake, progmg dir.

***WPCD(FM)**— January 1978: 88.7 mhz; 10.5 kw. Ant 338 ft. TL: N40 08 14 W88 17 10. Stereo. Parkland College, 2400 W. Bradley Ave. 61821. Phone: (217) 351-2450. Fax: (217) 373-3899. E-mail: wpcd@eudoramail.com. Web Site: www.parkland.edu/wpcd/. Licensee: Parkland College Community College District No. 505. Network: AP Radio. Format: Classic rock, AOR, urban comtemp. News: 8 hrs wkly. Target aud: General. Spec prog: News 8 hrs, alternative 4 hrs wkly. ♦Dan Hughes, gen mgr.

WPGU(FM)—See Urbana

WQQB(FM)—See Urbana

Charleston

WEIC(AM)— Dec 10, 1954: 1270 khz; 1 kw-D, 500 w-N, DA-3. TL: N39 30 18 W88 12 54. 2560 W. State St. 61920. Phone: (217) 345-2148. Fax: (217) 348-7036. Licensee: Eastern Illinois Christian Broadcasting Inc. (acq 9-9-03). Format: Southern gospel. Spec prog: Farm 8 hrs wkly. ♦Brad Lee, gen mgr; Steve Hamm, chief of engrg.

***WEIU(FM)**— July 1, 1985: 88.9 mhz; 4 kw. 166 ft. TL: N39 28 43 W88 10 21. Stereo. 600 Lincoln Ave. 61920. Phone: (217) 581-5956. Fax: (217) 581-6650. E-mail: hitmix@weiu.net. Web Site: www.weiuhitmix.net. Licensee: Eastern Illinois University. Cohn & Marks. Format: mix/var. News staff: one; News: 3 hrs wkly. Target aud: 12 plus; 25-55 women. Spec prog: Folks 4 hrs, jazz 4 hrs wkly. ♦Denis Roche, gen mgr; Jeff Owens, stn mgr & dev dir. Co-owned TV: *WEIU-TV affil

WWGO(FM)— Oct 1, 1965: 92.1 mhz; 6 kw. 140 ft. TL: N39 30 18 W88 12 54. Stereo. 209 Lakeland Blvd., Mattoon 61938. Phone: (217) 348-9292. Phone: (217) 235-5624. Fax: (217) 235-6624. E-mail: bub@radiomattoon.com. Licensee: The Cromwell Group Inc. of Illinois. Group owner: The Cromwell Group Inc. (acq 1993). Network: ABC. Pepper & Corazzini. Format: Rock. News staff: one; News: 20 hrs wkly. Target aud: 25-54; upscale, educated adults. ♦Bayard H. Walters, pres; Carol Floyd, gen mgr, gen sls mgr & news dir; Bub McCullough, progmg dir; Josh Jamison, chief of engrg.

Chester

KPNT(FM)—See Sainte Genevieve, MO

KSGM(AM)— July 5, 1947: 980 khz; 1 kw-D, 500 w-N, DA-N. TL: N37 51 24 W89 49 44. Box 428, St. Genevieve, MO 63670. Phone: (573) 883-2980. Fax: (573) 883-2866. E-mail: suntimesnews@brick.net. Web Site: www.suntimesnews.com. Licensee: Donze Communications Inc. (acq 6-20-89; $200,000; 7-10-89). Reddy, Begley & McCormick. Format: Country, news/talk. News staff: 2; News: 14 hrs wkly. Target aud: General; adults. Spec prog: Farm 2 hrs, relg 6 hrs wkly. ♦Don Pritchard, gen mgr & news dir.

Chicago

WAIT(AM)— 1941: 820 khz; 5 kw-D. TL: N41 56 18 W87 45 05. Stereo. 5625 N. Milwaukee Ave. 60646. Phone: (773) 792-1121. Fax: (873) 792-2904. E-mail: 820am@relevantradio.com. Web Site: 820am.relevantradio.com. Licensee: WYPA Inc. Group owner: Newsweb Corp. (acq 2-15-2001; $10.5 million). Format: Relg. ♦Mark Pinski, gen mgr; Michael Kendall, stn mgr; Michael Tillermann, gen sls mgr; Danny Zederman, progmg dir; Mike McCarthy, chief of engrg.

WBBM(AM)— Nov 14, 1923: 780 khz; 50 kw-U. TL: N41 59 32 W88 01 36. 630 N. McClurg Ct. 60611. Phone: (312) 944-6000. Fax: (312) 202-3205. Web Site: www.wbbm780.com. Licensee: Infinity Broadcasting East Inc. Group owner: Infinity Broadcasting Corp. (acq 1931). Network: CBS. Format: News. ♦David Belmonte, rgnl sls mgr; Rod Zimmerman, VP, gen mgr & progmg dir; Mike Krauser, news dir; Mark Williams, chief of engrg.

WBBM-FM— Dec 7, 1941: 96.3 mhz; 6.2 kw. 1,174 ft. TL: N41 53 56 W87 37 23. (CP: 4.2 kw, ant 1,554 ft.). Stereo. Phone: (312) 951-3497. Fax: (312) 951-3876. Web Site: www.b96.com. Network: CBS. Rep: Infinity Radio Sales. Format: CHR. ♦Dave Robbins, VP; Paul Agase, gen sls mgr; Thad Gentry, rgnl sls mgr; Michael Biemolt, mktg dir & prom mgr; Todd Cavanah, progmg dir; Eric Bradley, mus dir; Louis Segura, news dir; Tony Kelly, chief of engrg.

***WBEZ(FM)**— 1942: 91.5 mhz; 8.3 kw. 1,180 ft. TL: N41 53 56 W87 37 23. Stereo. Navy Pier, 848 E. Grand Ave. 60611. Phone: (312) 948-4600. Fax: (312) 832-3100. E-mail: questions@wbez.org. Web Site: www.chicagopublicradio.org. Licensee: The WBEZ Alliance Inc. (acq 9-7-90; 10-1-90). Network: NPR. Format: Jazz, pub affrs, news. News staff: 5; News: 45 hrs wkly. Target aud: General; people who want to know about the world around them. ♦Merrill Smith, chmn; Donna Moore, CFO; Torey Malatia, chmn, pres & gen mgr.

WBGX(AM)—See Harvey

WCFJ(AM)—See Chicago Heights

WCGO(AM)—See Chicago Heights

WCKG(FM)—See Elmwood Park

***WCRX(FM)**— July 29, 1975: 88.1 mhz; 100 w. 150 ft. TL: N41 52 22 W87 38 52. 600 S. Michigan Ave. 60605. Secondary address: 33 E. Congress 60605. Phone: (312) 344-8155. Phone: (312) 344-8163. Fax: (312) 663-5204. Web Site: wcrx.net. Licensee: Columbia College. (acq 10-5-82). Network: AP Radio. Dow, Lohnes & Albertson. Format: Sports, news. News staff: 2; News: 20 hrs wkly. Target aud: 18-24; Men. Spec prog: Reggae, Rock, Alt. Reggae. ♦Cheryl Langston, gen mgr; Tony Kwiecinski, stn mgr; Dave Dennis, chief of engrg.

WDRV(FM)— July 9, 1955: 97.1 mhz; 8.4 kw. 1,196 ft. TL: N41 53 08 W87 37 15. Stereo. 875 N. Michigan, Suite 1510 60611. Phone: (312) 274-9710. Fax: (312) 274-1304. Web Site: www.wdrv.com. Licensee: Bonneville Holding Co. Group owner: Bonneville International Corp. (acq 1-25-01; $165 million. with WWDV(FM) Zion). Rep: Katz Radio. Format: Classic timeless rock. ♦Jerry Schnacke, VP & gen mgr; Chris Winston, gen sls mgr; Eileen Elliot, gen sls mgr; Patty Martin, progmg dir; Mike Rugen, chief of engrg.

WFMT(FM)— Dec 13, 1951: 98.7 mhz; 16 kw. 1,170 ft. TL: N41 53 56 W87 37 23. Stereo. 5400 N. St. Louis Ave. 60625-4698. Phone: (773) 279-2000. Fax: (773) 279-2199. E-mail: finearts@wfmt.com. Web Site: www.networkchicago.com. Licensee: Window to the World Communications Inc. (acq 3-5-70). Schwartz, Woods & Miller. Format: Class. News: 7 hrs wkly. Target aud: 25-54; upscale, professional, college educated, upper income adults. Spec prog: Folk 4 hrs, jazz 5 hrs wkly. ♦Dan Schmidt, CEO & pres; Steve Robinson, sr VP & gen mgr; Don Mueller, opns mgr; Paul Ansell, gen sls mgr; Peter Whorf, mus dir; Gordon Carter, engrg dir. Co-owned TV: WTTW(TV) affil

WGCI-FM—Listing follows WGRB(AM).

WGN(AM)— June 1, 1924: 720 khz; 50 kw-U. TL: N42 00 42 W88 02 07. 435 N. Michigan Ave. 60611. Phone: (312) 222-4700. Fax: (312) 222-5165. E-mail: tlangmyer@wgnradio.com. Web Site: www.wgnradio.com. Licensee: WGN Continental Broadcasting Co. Group owner: Tribune Broadcasting Co. Network: ABC Information & Entertainment. Format: News/talk, sports. Target aud: General. Spec prog: Cubs, Northwestern play-by-play. ♦Dennis FitzSimons, chmn; Pat Mullen, pres; Tom Langmyer, gen mgr; Wendi Power, sls dir & gen sls mgr; Len Weiner, progmg dir; Jim Garollo, chief of engrg. Co-owned TV: WGN-TV affil

WGRB(AM)— 1924: 1390 khz; 5 kw-U, DA-2. TL: N41 44 13 W87 42 00. 233 N. Michigan Ave., Suite 2800 60601. Phone: (312) 540-2000. Fax: (312) 938-4477. Web Site: www.wgci.com. Licensee: AMFM Broadcasting Licenses LLC. Group owner: Clear Channel Communications Inc. (acq 8-30-2000; grpsl). Rep: Christal. Format: Gospel. ♦Marv Dyson, pres; Sandra Robinson, progmg dir.

WGCI-FM—Co-owned with WGRB(AM). Dec 11, 1958: 107.5 mhz; 33 kw. 600 ft. TL: N41 52 57 W87 38 15. Stereo. Web Site: www.wgci.com. Format: R&B hip hop. ♦Elroy Smith, progmg dir.

***WHPK-FM**— Mar 15, 1968: 88.5 mhz; 100 w. 121 ft. TL: N41 47 40 W87 35 55. Stereo. 5706 S. University Ave. 60637. Phone: (773) 702-8289. Fax: (773) 834-1488. E-mail: whpk@uchicago.edu. Web Site: whpk.uchicago.edu. Licensee: The University of Chicago. Format: Div, educ, jazz. News: 5 hrs wkly. Spec prog: Class 10 hrs, African one hr, Haitian 3 hrs, Israeli one hr, Irish one hrs wkly. ♦Lisa C. Neimand, stn mgr; Tammy Ghatlas, prom dir; Pat Reisinger, progmg dir; Grin Chug, mus dir; Paul Gazzero, asst music dir; Lucia Cantero, pub affrs dir; Mark O'Drobinak, chief of engrg.

***WIIT(FM)**— June 1974: 88.9 mhz; 17 w. 90 ft. TL: N41 50 04 W87 37 43. Stereo. 3300 S. Federal St. 60616. Phone: (312) 567-3087. Phone: (312) 567-3088. Fax: (312) 567-7042. E-mail: wiit@iit.edu. Licensee: Illinois Institute of Technology. Crowell & Moring. Format: Var/div. News: 5 hrs wkly. Target aud: 15-35; college & young urban community. Spec prog: Jazz 9 hrs, Ger 3 hrs, relg 2 hrs, Sp 5 hrs wkly. ♦Patrick Schneider, stn mgr; Chris Curtis, progmg dir; Diana Goluch, mus dir.

WILV(FM)— 1947: 100.3 mhz; 5.7 kw. Ant 1,394 ft. TL: N41 53 56 W87 37 23. Stereo. One Prudential Plaza, Suite 2780, 130 E. Randolph 60601. Phone: (312) 297-5100. Fax: (312) 297-5111. E-mail: davidj@lovefm.fm. Web Site: www.wnnd.com. Licensee: Bonneville Holding Co. Group owner: Bonneville International Corp. (acq 6-13-97; $75 million). Format: Adult contemp. Target aud: 25-49; women. ♦Barry James, exec VP, VP, gen mgr & progmg dir; Tracey Thomas, gen sls mgr; Keith Warner, chief of engrg.

WIND(AM)— 1927: 560 khz; 5 kw-U, DA-2. TL: N41 33 54 W87 25 11. 25 Northwest Point Blvd., Suite 400, Elk Grove Village 60007. Phone: (847) 437-5200. Fax: (847) 956-5040. Web Site: www.560wind.com. Licensee: Salem Media of Illinois LLC. Group owner: Univision Radio (acq 1-7-2005; with KNIT(AM) Dallas and KKHT-FM Winnie, both TX, in exchange for WPPN(FM) Des Plaines, IL). Format: Conservative news/talk. ♦Stuart Epperson, CEO; Edward Atsinger, pres; Eric Halvorson, CFO; David Santrella, gen mgr; Eric Thomas, opns dir.

WJMK(FM)—Listing follows WSCR(AM).

WKIE(FM)—(Arlington Heights). Mar 10, 1960: 92.7 mhz; 3 kw. Ant 299 ft. TL: N42 07 50 W87 58 59. Stereo. 6012 S. Pulaski Rd. 60629. Phone: (773) 767-1000. Fax: (773) 767-1100. Web Site: www.ninechicago.com. Licensee: WKIE Inc. Group owner: Spanish Broadcasting System Inc. (acq 11-15-2004; grpsl). Format: Var. Target aud: 18-49. ♦Frank Shenz, gen mgr; Bill Cavanaugh, gen sls mgr; Mike McCarthy, chief of engrg.

***WKKC(FM)**— 1975: 89.3 mhz; 250 w. 112 ft. TL: N41 46 15 W87 37 48. Stereo. Kennedy-King College, 6800 S. Wentworth Ave. 60621. Phone: (773) 602-5540. Fax: (773) 602-5532. Web Site: www.ccc.edu. Licensee: District 508 City College of Chicago. Format: Urban contemp, educ, var/div. Target aud: 15-50. ♦Kevin Brown, gen mgr.

WKQX(FM)— 1948: 101.1 mhz; 8.3 kw. 1,710 ft. TL: N41 53 56 W87 37 23. Box 3404 60654. Secondary address: 230 Merchandise Mart Plaza 60654. Phone: (312) 245-1200. Fax: (312) 527-3620. Web Site: www.q101.com. Licensee: Emmis Radio License LLC. Group owner: Emmis Communications Corp. Rep: D & R Radio. Format: Alternative rock. Target aud: 18-34. ♦Marv Nyren, VP & gen mgr; Lance Richard, gen sls mgr; Mike Stern, progmg dir; Patrick Berger, chief of engrg.

WKSC-FM— November 1957: 103.5 mhz; 4.3 kw. 1,548 ft. TL: N41 52 44 W87 38 10. Stereo. 233 N. Michigan, Suite 2800 60601. Phone: (312) 540-2000. Fax: (312) 938-0712. Web Site: www.kisschicago.com. Licensee: AMFM Broadcasting Licenses LLC. Group owner: Clear Channel Communications Inc. (acq 8-30-2000; grpsl). Format: CHR. News staff: one; News: 15 hrs wkly. Target aud: 18-34; upscale. ♦Patrick Kelly, gen mgr; Rod Phillips, progmg dir; Bob Fukuda, chief of engrg.

WLIT-FM— Apr 7, 1958: 93.9 mhz; 4 kw. 1,581 ft. TL: N41 52 44 W87 38 10. Stereo. 233 N. Michigan Ave., Suite 2800 60601. Phone: (312) 540-2000. Fax: (312) 938-0111. Web Site: www.wlit.com. Licensee: AMFM Broadcasting Licenses LLC. Group owner: Clear Channel Communications Inc. (acq 8-30-2000; grpsl). Rep: Clear Channel. Format: Adult contemp. News: one hr wkly. Target aud: 25-54; affluent adults. ♦John Gehron, VP; Bob Kaake, natl sls mgr & progmg dir; Ken Denton, gen sls mgr & rgnl sls mgr; Eric Richeke, mus dir & news dir; Bob Fukuda, chief of engrg.

WLS(AM)— Apr 12, 1924: 890 khz; 50 kw-U. TL: N41 33 21 W87 50 54. Stereo. 190 N. State St. 60601. Phone: (312) 984-0890. Fax: (312) 984-5305. Web Site: www.wlsam.com. Licensee: WLS Inc. Group owner: ABC Inc. (acq 6-86; grpsl; FTR: 7-15-85). Network: Network: ABC Daytime Direction, ABC Information & Entertainment. Format: News/talk. Target aud: 35-64; listeners involved in Chicago news & community affairs. ♦Zemira Jones, pres & gen mgr; Bill Gamble, progmg dir; Carol O'Keefe, pub affrs dir.

WZZN(FM)—Co-owned with WLS(AM). Apr 1, 1949: 94.7 mhz; 4.4 kw. 1,535 ft. TL: N41 53 56 W87 37 23. Stereo. Phone: (312) 984-9923. Fax: (312) 984-5357. Web Site: www.947zone.com. Licensee: ABC Chicago FM Radio Inc. Format: Alternative. Target aud: 18-34. ♦Jim Pastor, pres & gen mgr. Co-owned TV: WLS-TV affil

WLUP-FM— 1942: 97.9 mhz; 4 kw. Ant 1,394 ft. TL: N41 53 56 W87 37 23. Stereo. 37th Fl., 875 N. Michigan Ave. #3750 60611. Phone: (312) 440-5270. Fax: (312) 440-9377. E-mail: wlup_fm@wlup.com. Web Site: www.wlup.com. Licensee: Emmis Radio License LLC. Group owner: Bonneville International Corp. (acq 12-15-2004; swap for KMVP(AM) and KTAR(AM)-KKLT(FM) Phoenix, AZ). Rep: D & R Radio. Format: Rock. Target aud: 18-49. ♦Marv Nyren, gen mgr.

***WLUW(FM)**— Sept 19, 1978: 88.7 mhz; 100 w. 230 ft. TL: N42 00 04 W87 39 36. Stereo. 6525 N. Sheridan Rd. 60626. Phone: (773) 508-8080. Fax: (773) 508-8082. E-mail: wluwradio@wluw.org. Web Site: www.wluw.org. Licensee: Loyola University, Chicago. Network: ABC Information & Entertainment. Format: Div, progsv, rock. News: 8 hrs wkly. Target aud: General. Spec prog: Sp 5 hrs, Haitian 2 hrs, world mus 5 hrs, Korean 6 hrs, gospel 4 hrs, jazz 2 hrs, children 2 hrs, folk 2 hrs, Bulgarian one hr, Vietnamese one hr wkly. ♦Craig Kois, gen mgr; Sean Campbell, progmg dir; Matt Malooly, news dir.

***WMBI-FM**— July 25, 1960: 90.1 mhz; 100 kw. 440 ft. TL: N41 55 35 W88 00 22. Stereo. 820 N. LaSalle Blvd. 60610. Phone: (312) 329-4300. Fax: (312) 329-4468. E-mail: wmbi@moody.edu. Web Site: www.wmbi.org. Licensee: The Moody Bible Institute of Chicago. (group owner) Network: Moody. Southmayd & Miller. Format: Relg, educ, Christian. News staff: 2. Target aud: 35-54; Christian. ♦Michael Easely, pres; Wayne Pederson, gen mgr.

WMBI(AM)— July 28, 1926: 1110 khz; 5 kw-D (L-WBT Charlotte, NC; KFAB Omaha). TL: N41 55 35 W88 00 22. Network: Moody. Format: Urban contemp. Target aud: 35-54; Hispanic Christians, children, English-speaking. Spec prog: Sp 12 hrs wkly.

WMVP(AM)— June 25, 1926: 1000 khz; 50 kw-U, DA-2. TL: N41 49 04 W87 59 17. 190 N. State St., 7th Fl. 60601. Phone: (312) 980-1000. Fax: (312) 980-1020. E-mail: james.pastor@abc.com. Web Site: www.espnradio.com. Licensee: Sports Radio Chicago LLC. Group owner: ABC Inc. (acq 4-1-99; $21 million). Latham & Watkins. Format: Sports, comedy, talk. Target aud: 25-54. ♦Steve Lieberman, CEO & gen sls mgr; James Pastor, gen mgr; Tom Serritella, progmg dir; John Hurni, chief of engrg.

WNTD(AM)— May 1922: 950 khz; 1 kw-D, 5 kw-N, DA-N. TL: N41 38 29 W87 33 14. 541 N. Fairbanks Ave., Suite 1260 60611. Phone: (312) 467-9755. Fax: (312) 467-9603. Web Site: www.radiounica.com. Licensee: Multicultural Radio Broadcasting Licensee LLC. Group owner: Multicultural Radio Broadcasting Inc. (acq 2-4-2004; grpsl). Format: Sp contemp. Target aud: 25-54.

WNUA(FM)— Mar 9, 1959: 95.5 mhz; 8.3 kw. 1,174 ft. TL: N41 53 56 W87 37 23. Stereo. 233 N. Michigan Ave., Suites 2700 & 2800 60601. Phone: (312) 540-2000. Web Site: www.wnua.com. Licensee: AMFM Broadcasting Licenses LLC. Group owner: Clear Channel Communications Inc. (acq 8-30-2000; grpsl). Format: Smooth jazz, adult contemp. Target aud: 25-54. ♦Ralph Sherman Jr., VP; Patrick Kelly, gen mgr; Bob Kake, opns mgr.

WOJO(FM)—See Evanston

***WRTE(FM)**— Dec 1, 1969: 90.5 mhz; 8 w. 56 ft. TL: N41 20 26 W87 43 05. (CP: 17 w, ant 85 ft.). 1401 W. 18th St. 60608. Secondary address: c/o Mexican Fine Arts Ctr. Museum, 1852 W. 19th St. 60608-2706. Phone: (312) 455-9455. Phone: (312) 738-1503. Fax: (312) 455-9755. E-mail: wrte@radioarte.org. Web Site: www.radioarte.org. Licensee: Mexican Fine Arts Center Museum. Shaw Pittman. Format: Var/div. Target aud: 15-35. ♦Jorge Valdivia, gen mgr & prom dir; Monica Ferro, progmg dir; Germaine Resendiz, news dir; Gloria Guaderrama, pub affrs dir.

WRTO(AM)— December 1988: 1200 khz; 10 kw-D, 1 kw-N, DA-2. TL: N41 42 14 W87 35 47. Stereo. 625 N. Michigan Ave., 3rd Fl. 60611. Phone: (312) 981-1800. Fax: (312) 981-1806. Licensee: WLXX-AM License Corp. Group owner: Univision Radio (acq 9-22-2003; grpsl). Rep: Caballero, McGavren Guild. Shaw Pittman. Format: Sp. News staff: 4; News: 10 hrs wkly. Target aud: Urban Spanish. ♦Jerry Ryan, gen mgr.

WSBC(AM)— 1925: 1240 khz; 1 kw-U. TL: N41 56 18 W87 45 05. 5625 N. Milwaukee Ave. 60646. Phone: (773) 792-1121. Fax: (773) 792-2904. E-mail: wsbc@wsbcradio.com. Licensee: WSBC Inc. (acq 2-23-98). Format: Var/div. Target aud: General. ♦Harvey Wells, VP; Mark Pinski, gen mgr; Dan Zederman, opns mgr; Diana Rodino, gen sls mgr & mktg dir; Mike McCarthy, progmg dir & chief of engrg.

WSCR(AM)— April 1922: 670 khz; 50 kw-U. TL: N41 56 01 W88 04 23. Stereo. NBC Tower, 455 N. Cityfront Plaza 60611. Phone: (312) 245-6000. Fax: (312) 245-6143. Web Site: www.wscr670am.com. Licensee: Infinity Broadcasting East Inc. Group owner: Infinity Broadcasting Corp. (acq 11-13-98; grpsl). Format: Sports. Target aud: 25-54. ♦Rod Zimmerman, VP & gen mgr; Drew Hayes, opns dir & opns mgr; Paul Agase, gen sls mgr; Mary Lou Compton, natl sls mgr; Cher Ames, mktg dir, prom dir & prom mgr; Matt Fishman, progmg dir; George Offman, news dir; Jesse Rogers, pub affrs dir; Greg Davis, chief of engrg.

WJMK(FM)—Co-owned with WSCR(AM). Jan 2, 1961: 104.3 mhz; 4.1 kw. 1,575 ft. TL: N41 52 44 W87 38 10. Stereo. 180 N. Stetson, Suite 900 60601. Phone: (312) 870-6400. Fax: (312) 977-1859. E-mail: wjmk@wjmk.com. Web Site: www.wjmk.com. Licensee: Infinity Broadcasting Corp. of Illinois. Format: Oldies. Target aud: 25-54. ♦Dave Robbins, VP & gen mgr; Terry Hardin, natl sls mgr; Lisa Piovosi, mktg dir; Charlie Lake, progmg dir; John Galenta, chief of engrg.

***WSSD(FM)**— Sept 15, 1987: 88.1 mhz; 10 w. 100 ft. TL: N41 52 22 W87 38 52. Stereo. 515 W. 111th St. 60628-4221. Phone: (773) 928-8800. Fax: (773) 928-9009. Licensee: Lakeside Communications Inc. Lauren A. Colby. Format: Blues, gospel, talk. Target aud: 25 plus; Black. Spec prog: Gospel, jazz, talk. ♦Huey Williams, pres & gen mgr; Steven McKinney, stn mgr & gen sls mgr; Willie McPhatter, progmg dir & progmg mgr; Suebee Graham, mus dir; James Kelly, news dir & chief of engrg.

WUSN(FM)— 1940: 99.5 mhz; 8.3 kw. 1,174 ft. TL: N41 53 56 W87 37 23. Stereo. 2 Prudential Plaza, Suite 1000 60601. Phone: (312) 649-0099. Web Site: www.us99.com. Licensee: Infinity Broadcasting Corp. of Chicago. Group owner: CBS Radio (acq 1996; grpsl). Format: Country. Target aud: 25-54. ♦Angela Ingram, gen mgr & stn mgr.

WXRT-FM— 1959: 93.1 mhz; 6.7 kw. 1,309 ft. TL: N41 53 56 W87 37 23. Stereo. 4949 W. Belmont Ave. 60641. Phone: (773) 777-1700. Fax: (773) 777-5031. Web Site: www.93xrt.com. Licensee: Infinity Broadcasting East Inc. Group owner: Infinity Broadcasting Corp. (acq 11-13-98; grpsl). Rep: CBS Radio. Format: Rock/AOR, alternative. News staff: one. Target aud: 25-54; upscale adults. ♦Michael Damsky, VP & gen mgr; John Farneda, opns mgr & mktg dir; Dan Manella, gen sls mgr; Adrienne Szarmack, rgnl sls mgr; Norm Winer, progmg VP & progmg dir; Mark Nielson, chief of engrg.

WYLL(AM)— Oct 13, 1924: 1160 khz; 50 kw-D, 5 kw-N, DA-2. TL: N42 02 30 W87 51 57. (CP: 50 kw-U, DA-2). 25 North West Point Blvd., Suite 400, Elk Grove Village 60007. Phone: (847) 956-5030. Fax: (847) 956-5040. Web Site: www.wyll.com. Licensee: SCA License Corp. Group owner: Salem Communications Corp. (acq 12-20-00; $29 million). Format: Relg. Target aud: 25-54; Upscale income adults. ♦David Santrella, gen mgr.

***WZRD(FM)**— July 8, 1974: 88.3 mhz; 100 w. 76 ft. TL: N41 58 56 W87 43 07. Stereo. 5500 N. St. Louis Ave. 60625. Phone: (773) 442-4586. Fax: (773) 442-4900. E-mail: livewire909@hotmail.com. Web Site: www.zap.to/wizard_wzrd. Licensee: Northeastern Illinois University. Format: Div, educ. News staff: 29; News: 12 hrs wkly. Target aud: General. ♦Dan Gonzalez, stn mgr; Beth Turkin, progmg dir.

Chicago Heights

WCFJ(AM)— Aug 15, 1963: 1470 khz; 1 kw-U, DA-2. TL: N41 25 29 W87 38 27. 5625 N. Milwaukee Ave., Chicago 60646. Phone: (773) 792-1121. Fax: (773) 792-2904. E-mail: wsbc@wsbcradio.com. Licensee: WCFJ Inc. (acq 2-23-98). Format: var/div. General. ♦Harvey Wells, VP; Mark Pinski, gen mgr; Dan Zederman, opns mgr; Diana Rodino, gen sls mgr & mktg dir; Mike McCarthy, progmg dir & chief of engrg.

WCGO(AM)— Aug 29, 1959: 1600 khz; 1 kw-D, 23 w-N, DA-2. TL: N41 31 05 W87 35 11. Stereo. 222 Vollmer Rd., Suite 2AA 60411. Phone: (708) 755-5900. Fax: (708) 755-5941. E-mail: wcgo1600am@aol.com. Licensee: Kovas Communications of Indiana

Illinois   **Directory of Radio**

Inc. (group owner; (acq 10-25-2002; $750,000). Network: ABC. Format: Adult contemp. Target aud: 25-54. ♦ Frank Kovas, pres; Keith Middleton, VP & gen mgr.

WYCA(FM)—See Crete

Chillicothe

WPMJ(FM)— May 16, 1977: 94.3 mhz; 6 kw. 300 ft. TL: N40 49 48 W89 29 54. (CP: 1.3 kw). Stereo. Box 180, 3641 Meadowbrook Rd., Peoria 61650-0180. Phone: (309) 685-5975. Fax: (309) 685-7150. E-mail: studio@magic943.com. Web Site: www.magic943.com. Licensee: Kelly Communications Inc. (acq 1-2-2003; $1.5 million. value part of cash/swap for WXCL(FM) Pekin). McGavren Guild. Format: Smooth jazz. News: 2 hrs wkly. Target aud: 25-54; affluent adults. ♦ Bob Kelly, CEO, chmn, pres, CFO & gen mgr; Joyce Powell, sr VP & prom dir.

Christopher

WXLT(FM)— Dec 25, 1990: 103.5 mhz; 6 kw. 328 ft. TL: N37 55 55 W88 57 28. 1431 Country Aire Dr., Carterville 62918. Phone: (618) 985-4843. Fax: (618) 985-6529. E-mail: mail@wxlt.com. Web Site: www.wxlt.comm. Licensee: MRR License LLC. Group owner: MAX Media L.L.C. (acq 3-29-2004; grpsl). Format: Rock. ♦ Brian Schimmel, gen mgr; Chad Elliott, opns mgr; Steve Fallat, gen sls mgr; Dana Lucas, progmg dir; Rick Gregg, news dir; Steve Sine, news dir; Jim Deterding, chief of engrg.

Cicero

WCEV(AM)— Oct 1, 1979: 1450 khz; 1 kw-U (ST: WVON[AM]). TL: N41 49 57 W87 42 40. 5356 W. Belmont Ave., Chicago 60641-4192. Phone: (773) 282-6700. Phone: (773) 777-1450. Fax: (773) 282-0123. E-mail: wcev@earthlink.net. Web site: www.wcev145.com. Licensee: Migala Communications Corp. Format: Multiethnic. News: 7 hrs wkly. Target aud: Adult ethnic Americans. Spec prog: Lithuanian 9 3/4 hrs, Arabic 2, Czech 2 hrs, Polish 12 hrs , Ukrainian one hr wkly. ♦ Estelle Migala, pres; George Migala, stn mgr; Lucyna Migala, progmg dir; Sam Palermo, chief of engrg.

WLUP-FM—See Chicago

WVON(AM)— 1979: 1450 khz; 1 kw-U (ST: WCEV[AM]). TL: N41 49 57 W87 42 20. 3350 S. Kedzie Ave., Chicago 60623. Phone: (773) 247-6200. Fax: (773) 247-5336. Web Site: www.wvon.com. Licensee: Midway Broadcasting Corp. Network: ABC. Format: Talk. News staff: one; News: 32 hrs wkly. Target aud: 25-54; urban talk listeners. ♦ Pervis Spann, CEO; Melody Spann-Cooper, pres & gen mgr; Bridget Goins, opns mgr.

Clinton

WHOW(AM)— Aug 1, 1947: 1520 khz; 5 kw-D, 1 kw-CH. TL: N40 05 43 W88 57 51. R.R. 2, Box 117M 61727. Phone: (217) 935-9590. Fax: (217) 935-9909. Licensee: WHOW Radio LLC (acq 1-26-2004; $300,000. with co-located FM). Format: Talk. ♦ Jim Sauers, gen mgr.

WHOW-FM— Dec 15, 1975: 95.9 mhz; 3 kw. Ant 300 ft. TL: N40 05 43 W88 57 51. Stereo. Format: Light rock.

Coal City

WRXQ(FM)— Feb 8, 1991: 100.7 mhz; 1.4 kw. 482 ft. TL: N41 17 39 W88 10 15. Stereo. 2410-B Caton Farm Rd., Crest Hill 60435. Phone: (815) 556-0100. Fax: (815) 577-9231. Web Site: www.100.7rxq.com. Licensee: NM Licensing LLC. Group owner: NextMedia Group L.L.C. (acq 11-26-01; grpsl). Rep: McGavren Guild. Format: Classic rock. News: 5 hrs wkly. Target aud: 35-50; adults. ♦ Dennis Mockler, gen mgr; Ryan Snow, opns mgr; Todd Elbrink, gen sls mgr; Rob Creighton, progmg dir.

Colchester

WMQZ(FM)— 1999: 104.1 mhz; 6 kw. Ant 328 ft. TL: N40 32 01 W90 51 45. 31 East Side Sq., Macomb 61455. Phone: (309) 833-2121. Fax: (309) 836-3291. E-mail: wjeq@macomb.com. Web Site: www.wmqz.com. Licensee: Colchester Radio Inc. Format: Oldies. ♦ Jerry Johnson, gen mgr; Mandy Pierson, progmg dir; Bruce Foster, chief of engrg.

Colfax

WRPW(FM)— 1997: 92.9 mhz; 6 kw. 328 ft. TL: N40 29 28 W88 43 14. 108 Borykens Pl., Normal 61761. Phone: (309) 888-4496. Fax: (309) 452-9677. Web Site: www.power92.net. Licensee: AAA Entertainment Licensing LLC. Group owner: AAA Entertainment L.L.C. (acq 8-7-01). Format: CHR/rythmic. ♦ John Maguire, CEO & pres; Peter Ottmar, chmn; John Riccardi, CFO; Patti Donsbach, gen mgr; Kevin Trueblood, opns mgr; Amber Goodwin, prom dir; Don Black, progmg dir.

Columbia

KMJM-FM— Feb 15, 1964: 104.9 mhz; 11.5 kw. 480 ft. TL: N38 34 24 W90 19 30. Stereo. 1001 Highland Plaza Dr. W., St. Louis, MO 63110. Phone: (314) 333-8000. Web Site: www.majic105fm.com. Licensee: Citicasters Licenses L.P. Group owner: Clear Channel Communications Inc. (acq 5-4-99; grpsl). Format: Urban adult contemp. News: one hr wkly. Target aud: 25-49; women & their families. ♦ Lee Clear, gen mgr; Chuck Atkins, opns mgr.

Crest Hill

WCCQ(FM)—Licensed to Crest Hill. See Joliet

Crete

*WBMF(FM)— 2002: 88.1 mhz; 90 w. Ant 374 ft. TL: N41 25 17 W87 38 39. Box 3206, American Family Radio, Tupelo, MS 38803. Phone: (662) 844-8888. Fax: (662) 842-6791. Web Site: www.afr.net. Licensee: American Family Association. Group owner: American Family Radio Format: Christian. News: 2 hrs wkly.

WYCA(FM)— Sept 5, 1965: 102.3 mhz; 1 kw. 299 ft. TL: N41 18 53 W87 37 11. Stereo. 6336 Calumet Ave., Hammond, IN 46324. Phone: (773) 734-4455. E-mail: wybainfo@crawfordbroadcasting.com. Web Site: www.crawfordbroadcasting.com. Licensee: Dontron Inc. Group owner: Crawford Broadcasting Co. (acq 8-26-97; $1.8 million). Format: Christian talk. Target aud: 35 plus; adult, African-Americans. ♦ Donald B. Crawford, CEO; Taft Harris, gen mgr; Yolanda Brown, opns mgr.

Crystal Lake

WCPT(AM)— Oct 1, 1965: 850 khz; 2.5 kw-D, DA. TL: N42 15 30 W88 21 48. Stereo. 6012 S. Pulaski Rd., Chicago 60629. Phone: (773) 767-1000. Fax: (773) 767-1100. Licensee: Chicago Newsweb Corp. Group owner: Newsweb Corp. (acq 9-16-2003; $8.25 million). Format: Progressive talk. ♦ Harvey Wells, gen mgr.

WZSR(FM)—See Woodstock

Danville

KUUL(FM)—See East Moline

WDAN(AM)— October 1938: 1490 khz; 1 kw-U. TL: N40 08 58 W87 37 35. 1501 N. Washington Ave 61832. Phone: (217) 442-1700. Fax: (217) 431-1489. Licensee: Neuhoff Family L.P. (group owner; acq 11-5-03; grpsl). Rep: McGavren Guild. Format: News/talk, sports. News staff: one; News: 20 hrs wkly. Target aud: 25-54. Spec prog: Farm 20 hrs wkly. ♦ Roger Neuhoff, pres; Geoffery Newhoff, exec VP; Michael Hulvey, VP & gen mgr; Michelle Campbell, sls dir & adv mgr; Tom Barnes, opns mgr, prom mgr & progmg dir; Bill Pickett, news dir; Don Russel, chief of engrg.

WDNL(FM)—Co-owned with WDAN(AM). May 1967: 102.1 mhz; 50 kw. 380 ft. TL: N40 08 58 W87 37 35. Stereo. Format: Adult contemp. News: 2 hrs wkly. Target aud: 18-49. ♦ Michael Hulvey, opns VP; Tom Barnes, progmg mgr; Carole Wade, mus dir.

WITY(AM)— Nov 24, 1953: 980 khz; 1 kw-U, DA-1. TL: N40 04 42 W87 38 19. Box 142 61834. Secondary address: Hegeler La. 61832. Phone: (217) 446-1312. Fax: (217) 446-1314. Licensee: Vermilion Broadcasting Corporation. (acq 1981). Network: Network: Westwood One, ABC Information & Entertainment. Format: Adult standards. Target aud: 35 plus; general. Spec prog: Relg 6 hrs, farm 6 hrs wkly. ♦ Donald E. Ward, pres; David W. Brown, exec VP, VP & gen mgr; Scot C. Medlin, gen sls mgr; Jim Jordan, news dir; Marvin Wells, pub affrs dir; George Dudich, chief of engrg.

WRHK(FM)— November 1992: 94.9 mhz; 6 kw. 328 ft. TL: N40 10 40 W87 28 55. 1501 N. Washington 61832. Phone: (217) 442-1700. Fax:

(217) 431-1489. Licensee: Neuhoff Family L.P. (group owner; acq 11-5-03; grpsl). Rep: McGavren Guild. Schwartz, Wood & Miller. Format: Classic rock. News: 5 hrs wkly. Target aud: 18-49. ♦ Roger Neuhoff, chmn; Pat Odea, CFO; Geoffery Neuhoff, exec VP; Michael Hulvey, gen mgr & opns VP; Michelle Campbell, gen sls mgr; Tom Barnes, progmg dir; Don Russell, chief of engrg.

WXTT(FM)— Mar 2, 1970: 99.1 mhz; 50 kw. Ant 500 ft. TL: N40 08 52 W87 46 20. 2603 W. Bradley Ave., Champaign 61821. Phone: (217) 352-4141. Fax: (217) 352-1256. Licensee: Saga Communications of Illinois LLC. Group owner: Saga Communications Inc. (acq 6-30-2004; $3.25 million). Rep: D & R Radio. Format: Classic rock. ♦ Alan Beck, gen mgr.

De Kalb

WDEK(FM)— Dec 17, 1961: 92.5 mhz; 20 kw. Ant 495 ft. TL: N41 52 33 W88 45 16. Stereo. 6012 S. Pulaski Rd., Chicago 60629. Phone: (773) 767-1000. Fax: (773) 767-1100. Web Site: www.ninechicago.com. Licensee: WDEK Inc. Group owner: Spanish Broadcasting System Inc. (acq 11-15-2004; grpsl). Format: Adult contemp. Target aud: 25-44. ♦ Harvey Wells, gen mgr; Bill Cavanaugh, gen sls mgr; Matt Duviel, progmg mgr; Mike McCarthy, chief of engrg.

WDKB(FM)— Aug 13, 1990: 94.9 mhz; 3 kw. 328 ft. TL: N41 56 58 W88 53 33. 2201 N. 1st St., Suite 95 60115. Phone: (815) 758-0950. Phone: (815) 758-4926. Fax: (815) 758-6226. Web Site: www.b95fm.com. Licensee: De Kalb County Radio Ltd. Shaw Pittman. Format: Adult contemp. News staff: one; News: 3hrs wkly. Target aud: 25-54; adults with moderate to upper incomes. Spec prog: Relg one hr wkly. ♦ Tana S. Knetsch, pres & gen mgr.

WLBK(AM)— Dec 7, 1947: 1360 khz; 1 kw-D. TL: N41 56 18 W88 45 03. Box 448 60115. Secondary address: 1325 Sycamore Rd. 60115. Phone: (815) 758-8686. Fax: (815) 756-9723. Licensee: WPW Broadcasting Inc. (group owner; (acq 4-12-2000). Network: UPI. Dow, Lohnes & Albertson. Format: Adult contemp, news/talk. News staff: 3; News: 21 hrs wkly. Target aud: General. Spec prog: Farm 12 hrs, big band 5 hrs, relg 6 hrs wkly. ♦ Norm Miller, gen mgr.

*WNIJ(FM)— October 1954: 89.5 mhz; 50 kw. 421 ft. TL: N42 00 55 W89 00 07. Stereo. NIU Broadcast Ctr., 801 N. First St., DeKalb 60115. Phone: (815) 753-9000. Fax: (815) 753-9938. E-mail: npr@niu.edu. Web Site: www.northernpublicradio.org. Licensee: Northern Illinois University. Network: Network: PRI, NPR. Arter & Hadden. Format: News, jazz. News staff: 2; News: one hr wkly. Target aud: General. Spec prog: Folk 4 hrs wkly. ♦ Tim Emmons, gen mgr; Jan Kilgard, dev dir; Bill Drake, progmg dir.

WNIU(FM)—See Rockford

Decatur

WDZ(AM)— Mar 17, 1921: 1050 khz; 1 kw-U. TL: N39 48 54 W89 00 05. 337 N. Water St. 62523. Phone: (217) 423-9744. Fax: (217) 423-9764. Web Site: www.magic1050am.com. Licensee: NM Licensing LLC. Group owner: NextMedia Group L.L.C. (acq 11-26-01; grpsl). Format: Urban. ♦ Joel Fletcher, gen mgr; Tricia LeVeck, progmg dir.

WDZQ(FM)—Co-owned with WDZ(AM). Nov 1, 1976: 95.1 mhz; 50 kw. 500 ft. TL: N39 37 36 W89 04 49. Stereo. Web Site: www.95q.com. Rep: Allied Radio Partners. Format: Country. ♦ Brad Wells, progmg dir.

*WJMU(FM)— Mar 10, 1971: 89.5 mhz; 1 kw. 95 ft. TL: N39 50 39 W88 58 29. (CP: 1.66 kw). Stereo. 1184 W. Main St. 62522. Phone: (217) 424-6377. Phone: (217) 424-6369. Fax: (217) 424-3993. E-mail: wjmu@mail.millikin.edu. Licensee: Millikin University. Format: Progsv. News: 8 hrs wkly. Target aud: 20 plus; students, surrounding community. ♦ Dove Zemke, pres; Chris Bullock, gen mgr.

WSOY-FM— November 1946: 102.9 mhz; 54 kw. 495 ft. TL: N39 52 40 W88 56 30. Stereo. 1100 E. Pershing Rd. 62526. Phone: (217) 877-5371. Fax: (217) 877-8777. Web Site: www.wsoy.com. Licensee: NM Licensing LLC. Group owner: NextMedia Group L.L.C. (acq 11-26-01; grpsl). Network: CBS. Wilmer, Cutler & Pickering. Format: CHR. News staff: 3; News: 3 hrs wkly. Target aud: 25-54. ♦ Joel Fletcher, gen mgr; Roy Jaynes, progmg dir.

Stations in the U.S. — Illinois

Developers & Brokers of Radio Properties
contact American Media Services at our suite:
Philadelphia Marriott Downtown
215-625-2900
843-972-2200
americanmediaservices.com
Charleston, SC
Dallas, TX · Chicago, Il · Austin, TX

American Media Services, LLC

WSOY(AM)— 1925: 1340 khz; 1 kw-U. TL: N39 52 40 W88 56 30. Web Site: www.wsoy.com. Format: News/talk, sports. News staff: 3; News: 13 hrs wkly. Target aud: 25 plus. ♦ Joel Fletcher, VP; Ryan Forden, progmg dir.

WYDS(FM)— 1993: 93.1 mhz; 6 kw. 328 ft. TL: N39 48 35 W88 59 31. 410 N. Water St., Suite C 62523. Phone: (217) 428-4487. Fax: (217) 428-4501. E-mail: theparty@family-net.net. Licensee: WEJT Inc. (acq 4-9-93; $750,000; 5-3-93). Format: Top-40 contemporary Hit. News staff: one. Target aud: 18-49; females average age of 26. ♦ Mike Topoll, gen mgr; Chris Bullock, opns mgr; Jerry Scott, gen sls mgr & chief of engrg.

Deerfield

WEEF(AM)—See Highland Park

WVIV-FM—See Highland Park

Des Plaines

WPPN(FM)— Dec 3, 1971: 106.7 mhz; 50 kw. Ant 423 ft. TL: N42 08 10 W87 58 55. Stereo. 625 N. Michigan Ave. 3rd Fl., Chicago 60611. Phone: (312) 981-1800. Fax: (312) 981-1806. Web Site: www.univision.com. Licensee: Univision Radio License Corp. Group owner: Salem Communications Corp. (acq 12-21-2004; asset exchange agreement). Format: Sp. ♦ McHenry Tichenor, pres; Jerry Ryan, gen mgr; Jose Lopez, gen sls mgr; Victor Cerdo, mus dir; Roberto Lopez, chief of engrg.

Dixon

WIXN(AM)— July 1961: 1460 khz; 1 kw-D, DA. TL: N41 49 38 W89 29 11. 1460 S. College Ave. 61021. Phone: (815) 288-3341. Phone: (815) 626-3091. Fax: (815) 284-1017. Web Site: www.wixn.com. Licensee: NewRadio Group LLC (group owner; acq 12-20-2002; grpsl). Network: ABC Information & Entertainment. Miller & Fields, P.C. Format: News, oldies. News staff: 2; News: 14 hrs wkly. Target aud: 25-54. Spec prog: Farm 11 hrs wkly. ♦ Al Knickrehm, gen mgr & stn mgr.

WRCV(FM)—Co-owned with WIXN(AM). Sept 1, 1965: 101.7 mhz; 6 kw. 300 ft. TL: N41 49 29 W89 29 51. Stereo. Web Site: www.wixn.com. Network: ABC Information & Entertainment. Format: Country. News staff: 2; News: 10 hrs wkly. ♦ Steve Marco, progmg dir.

Dorsey

*WDRS(FM)—Not on air, target date: unknown: 89.5 mhz; 350 w. Ant 36 ft. TL: N38 57 36 W89 58 06. Broadcasting for the Challenged Inc., 188 S. Bellevue, Suite 222, Memphis, TN 38104. Phone: (901) 726-8970. Phone: (901) 375-9324 (station). Licensee: Broadcasting for the Challenged Inc.

Downers Grove

*WDGC-FM— Feb 28, 1969: 88.3 mhz; 250 w. 130 ft. TL: N41 48 16 W88 00 44. Stereo. 4436 Main St. 60515. Phone: (630) 795-8490. Phone: (630) 795-8400. Fax: (630) 795-8499. E-mail: wdgcfm@hotmail.com. Web Site: www.csd99.k12.il.us/wdgc. Licensee: High School District No. 99 Dupage County. Format: Div. News: 5 hrs wkly. Target aud: General; all age groups. Spec prog: Community affrs 6 hrs wkly. ♦ John Waite, gen mgr & opns mgr.

Du Quoin

WDQN(AM)— 1951: 1580 khz; 170 w-D, 7 w-N. TL: N38 01 56 W89 14 30. Box 190 62832. Secondary address: 2337 US Rt. 51 62832. Phone: (618) 542-3894. Fax: (618) 542-4514. Licensee: Du Quoin Broadcasting Co. Network: ABC Information & Entertainment. Format: Adult contemp, country. Target aud: 25-64; male & female. Spec prog: Farm 3 hrs, relg 5 hrs wkly. ♦ Greg Showalter, gen mgr.

WDQN-FM—Sept 1, 1969: 95.9 mhz; 6 kw. Ant 328 ft. TL: N38 01 56 W89 14 30. Box 220, West Frankfort 62896. Secondary address: 3391 Charley Good Rd., West Frankfort 62896. Phone: (618) 627-4651. Fax: (618) 627-2726. Web Site: www.3abn.org. Licensee: Three Angels Broadcasting Network Inc. (acq 7-16-2003; $600,000). Format: Christian. ♦ Danny Shelton, pres; Mollie Steenson, gen sls mgr; Jim Morris, gen sls mgr; Sandra Juarez, progmg dir; Moses Primo, chief of engrg.

Dundee

WWYW(FM)— June 8, 1967: 103.9 mhz; 2.55 kw. Ant 321 ft. TL: N42 06 21 W88 22 37. Stereo. 8800 Rt. 14, Crystal Lake 60012. Phone: (815) 459-7000. Fax: (815) 459-7027. Web Site: www.y1039.com. Licensee: NM Licensing LLC. Group owner: NextMedia Group L.L.C. (acq 5-19-2004; $5 million). Leibowitz & Associates. Format: News/talk. ♦ Don Oberbillig, gen mgr; Mark Anthony, chief of engrg; Chuck Barham, sls; Bobby Knight, progmg.

Dwight

WJEZ(FM)— June 9, 1997: 98.9 mhz; 1.3 kw. Ant 489 ft. TL: N41 02 06 W88 26 11. 315 N. Mill St., Pontiac 61764. Phone: (815) 844-6101. Fax: (815) 844-7235. Web Site: www.wjez.com. Licensee: Livingston County Broadcasters Inc. Group owner: Regent Communications Inc. (acq 5-12-2004; grpsl). Format: Adult contemp. Target aud: 18-49; general. ♦ Red Pitcher, gen mgr; Glenn Schaefer, gen sls mgr; Eric Miller, progmg dir; Lane Lindstrom, chief of engrg.

Earlville

WMKB(FM)— Feb 3, 2003: . Stn currently dark 102.9 mhz; 2.15 kw. Ant 558 ft. TL: N41 37 16 W89 05 20. 4756 E. 4th Rd., Mendota 61342. Phone: (815) 538-7500. Fax: (815) 538-7505. E-mail: info@wmkbradio.com. Web Site: www.wmkbradio.com. Licensee: KM Radio of Earlville L.L.C. Group owner: KM Communications Inc. Network: ABC. Format: Class rock. News: 2 hrs wkly. Target aud: 25-54. Spec prog: Blues 5 hrs wkly. ♦ Bryan Spies, gen mgr; Lizzi Neal, opns dir; Bryan Spies, progmg dir.

East Moline

KUUL(FM)— Feb 23, 1976: 101.3 mhz; 50 kw. 500 ft. TL: N41 37 10 W90 17 41. Stereo. 3535 E. Kimberly Rd., Davenport, IA 52807. Phone: (563) 344-7000. Fax: (563) 359-8524. Web Site: www.kuul.com. Licensee: Citicasters Licenses L.P. Group owner: Clear Channel Communications Inc. (acq 11-15-00; grpsl). Rep: Katz Radio. Format: Classic rock, hits of the 60s & 70s. Target aud: 25-54; contemp, upscale adults. Spec prog: Pub affrs 6 hrs, farm one hr wkly. ♦ Larry R. Rosmilso, VP & gen mgr; Scott Bitting, sls dir & gen sls mgr; Bo J. Spates, progmg dir; Kevin Allensworth, chief of engrg.

*WDLM(FM)— Apr 3, 1960: 960 khz; 1 kw-D, 102 w-N, DA-2. TL: N41 24 57 W90 23 54. Box 149 61244. Phone: (309) 234-5111. Fax: (309) 234-5114. E-mail: wdlm@moody.edu. Web Site: www.mbn.org. Licensee: Moody Bible Institute of Chicago. (group owner) Format: Relg. ♦ Lane D. Morgan, gen mgr.

WDLM-FM— Jan 20, 1980: 89.3 mhz; 100 kw. 500 ft. TL: N41 32 52 W90 28 30. Web Site: www.mbn.com.

East St. Louis

*WCBW-FM— 2001: 89.7 mhz; 250 w. Ant 187 ft. TL: N38 37 53 W90 12 09. New Life Evangelistic Center Inc., 1411 Locust St., St. Louis, MO 63103. Phone: (314) 421-3020. Fax: (314) 436-2434. E-mail: larryr@hereshelpnet.org. Web Site: www.hereshelpnet.org. Licensee: New Life Evangelistic Center Inc. Format: Relg. ♦ Larry Rice, gen mgr.

WESL(AM)— Aug 1, 1934: 1490 khz; 1 kw-U, DA-2. TL: N38 37 16 W90 09 36. Stereo. 149 S. 8th St. 62201. Phone: (618) 271-7687. Fax: (618) 875-4315. Licensee: Simmons-Austin LS LLC (acq 2-16-2005;

$1.15 million). Network: American Urban. Rep: Katz Radio. Format: Gospel, rhythm & blues. Target aud: 23-55. ♦ Craig Hanson, pres; Robert Riggins, gen mgr.

WVRV(FM)— June 6, 1965: 101.1 mhz; 44 kw. Ant 525 ft. TL: N38 45 11 W90 07 09. Stereo. 11647 Olive Blvd., St. Louis, MO 63141. Phone: (314) 983-6000. Fax: (314) 994-9447. E-mail: feedback@wvrv.com. Web Site: www.wvrv.com. Licensee: Bonneville Holding Co. Group owner: Bonneville International Corp. (acq 9-26-00; grpsl). Rep: McGavren Guild. Format: Rock-based adult contemp. Target aud: 25-49. Spec prog: Blues 1 hr wkly. ♦ Bruce Reese, CEO & pres; Bob Johnson, CFO; John Kijowski, VP & gen mgr; Emily Bushman, gen sls mgr; Marty Link, progmg dir; Trish Gazzal, news dir; Marshall Rice, chief of engrg.

Edwardsville

*WRYT(AM)— Nov 20, 1987: 1080 khz; 500 w-D, DA. TL: N38 47 58 W89 57 45. (CP: 250 w-N, DA-2, TL: N38 38 30 W89 57 45). 3515 Hampton Ave., St. Louis, MO 63139. E-mail: covenantnetwork@juno.com. Licensee: Covenant Network. (acq 10-2-97). Format: Catholic, relg. Target aud: General. ♦ John A. Holman, pres; Tony Holman, gen mgr.

*WSIE(FM)— Sept 4, 1970: 88.7 mhz; 37 kw. 567 ft. TL: N38 47 06 W89 59 10. Stereo. Box 1773, So. Illinois Univ. at Edwardsville 62026. Phone: (618) 650-2228. Fax: (618) 650-2233. Web Site: www.siue.edu.wsie. Licensee: Board of Trustees, Southern Illinois University. Network: Network: NPR, PRI. Dow, Lohnes & Albertson. Format: Jazz. News staff: one; News: 20 hrs wkly. Target aud: 25-49; adults seeking a sophisticated alternative. Spec prog: New age 10 hrs wkly. ♦ Frank Akers, gen mgr; Tom Dehner, news dir; David Caires, chief of engrg.

Effingham

WCRA(AM)— June 8, 1947: 1090 khz; 1 kw-D. TL: N39 06 26 W88 33 44. Box 60 62401. Phone: (217) 342-4141. Fax: (217) 342-4143. Licensee: Two Petaz Inc. Group owner: The Cromwell Group Inc. (acq 1-9-02; grpsl). Network: CBS. Format: News/talk. Target aud: 25-54. ♦ Bayard Walters, pres; Gil Rosenwald, gen sls mgr; Bruce Enrigetto, progmg dir; Scott Ealy, news dir.

WCRC(FM)—Co-owned with WCRA(AM). June 14, 1963: 95.7 mhz; 50 kw. 480 ft. TL: N39 06 26 W88 33 44. Stereo. Web Site: www.wcrc957.com. Format: Country.

WXEF(FM)— Oct 4, 1982: 97.9 mhz; 6 kw. 300 ft. TL: N39 07 25 W88 38 28. Stereo. Box 988, 206 S. Willow 62401. Phone: (217) 347-5518. Fax: (217) 347-5519. E-mail: info@thexradio.com. Web Site: www.thexradio.com. Licensee: Premier Broadcasting Inc. (acq 11-3-93; $380,000; 11-22-93). Format: Adult contemp. News: 15 hrs wkly. Target aud: General. Spec prog: High school sports. ♦ T. David Ring, pres; Greg Sapp, stn mgr & opns dir; Tonya Siner, opns VP; George Flexter, opns mgr.

Eldorado

WEBQ-FM— April 1972: 102.3 mhz; 3 kw. 296 ft. TL: N37 49 14 W88 27 11. Stereo. 701 S. Commercial, Harrisburg 62946. Phone: (618) 252-6307. Fax: (618) 252-2366. E-mail: webq@yourclearwave.com. Licensee: W. Russell Withers Jr. Group owner: Withers Broadcasting Co. (acq 7-28-2004; $450,000. with WEBQ(AM) Harrisburg). Network: ABC. Format: Adult contemp. News staff: one; News: 6 hrs wkly. Target aud: 25-45; young middle class adults. ♦ Cathy Horton, gen mgr, stn mgr & progmg dir; Sonny Dotson, gen sls mgr; Wyatt Drake, news dir; Bob Romonosky, chief of engrg.

Elgin

*WEPS(FM)— 1950: 88.9 mhz; 740 w. Ant 100 ft. TL: N42 02 17 W88 16 15. 355 E. Chicago St. 60120. Phone: (847) 888-5000. Fax: (847) 888-0272. E-mail: jackieolsonkold@u-46.org. Licensee: Board of Education, Union School District 46. Format: Div, educ. Target aud: Parents of students. Spec prog: Class 5 hrs, jazz 6 hrs, community affrs 3 hrs, educ 13 hrs wkly. ♦ Jackie Olson Kold, stn mgr.

Illinois

WJKL(FM)—Listing follows WRMN(AM).

WRMN(AM)— 1949: 1410 khz; 1 kw-D, 500 w-N, DA-N. TL: N42 00 21 W88 17 55. 14 Douglas Ave. 60120. Phone: (847) 741-7700. Fax: (847) 888-4227. Web Site: www.radioshoppingshow.com. Licensee: Elgin Broadcasting Co. Group owner: McNaughton-Jakle Stations (acq 1952). Blair, Joyce & Silva. Format: News/talk. Target aud: General. Spec prog: Sp 10 hrs wkly. ♦Richard Jakle, CEO, chmn, pres & gen mgr; Jack Davis, stn mgr.

WJKL(FM)—Co-owned with WRMN(AM). September 1960: 94.3 mhz; 6 kw. 350 ft. TL: N42 02 43 W88 15 35. Stereo. Web Site: www.klove.com. Format: Christian. Target aud: 25-49.

Elmhurst

WJJG(AM)— Oct 10, 1974: 1530 khz; 500 w-D, DA. TL: N41 52 03 W87 55 07. (CP: 760 w). Stereo. 5629 St. Charles Rd., Suite 208, Berkeley 60163. Phone: (708) 493-1530. Fax: (708) 493-1537. Web Site: www.wjjg.com. Licensee: Joseph J. Gentile Inc. (acq 7-6-94; $700,000). Format: News/talk. Target aud: 45 plus; affluent adults.

*****WRSE(FM)**— Dec 7, 1962: 88.7 mhz; 100 w. 95 ft. TL: N41 53 46 W87 56 45. Stereo. Frick Center # 028, 190 Prospect Ave. 60126-3296. Phone: (630) 617-3729. Fax: (630) 617-3313. Web Site: www.elmhurst.edu /~wrse/contact.html. Licensee: Board of Trustees Elmhurst College. Format: Alternative, rock. Target aud: 12-26; high school & college. Spec prog: Jazz 6 hrs, metal 9 hrs, oldies 9 hrs wkly. ♦Tony White, gen mgr; Jon Magan, stn mgr; Ken Steininger, chief of engrg.

Elmwood

WFYR(FM)— Aug 2, 1993: 97.3 mhz; 23.5 kw. 338 ft. TL: N40 46 22 W89 44 50. Stereo. 120 Eaton St., Peoria 61603. Phone: (309) 676-5000. Fax: (309) 676-2600. E-mail: jgreeley@regentcomm.com. Web Site: www.973rivercountry.com. Licensee: Regent Broadcasting of Peoria Inc. Group owner: Regent Communications Inc. (acq 7-6-01; grpsl). Rep: Katz Radio. Reddy, Begley & McCormick. Format: Country. News: one hr wkly. Target aud: 25-54; adults, family oriented & skewing female. ♦J.R. Greeley, gen mgr; Ric Morgan, opns dir.

Elmwood Park

WCKG(FM)— 1947: 105.9 mhz; 4.2 kw. 1,575 ft. TL: N41 52 44 W87 38 10. Stereo. 2 Prudential Plaza, Suite 1059, Chicago 60601. Phone: (312) 240-7900. Fax: (312) 565-3181. Web Site: www.wckg.com. Licensee: Infinity Holdings Corp. of Orlando. Group owner: CBS Radio (acq 1996). Network: Westwood One. Format: Personality talk. News staff: one; News: one hr wkly. Target aud: 25-54. ♦Michael G. Disney, VP & gen mgr.

Elsah

*****WTPC(FM)**— Dec 1, 1970: 105.3 mhz; 17 w. 210 ft. TL: N38 56 52 W90 20 57. Stereo. Merrick Wing, Principia College 62028. Phone: (618) 374-4934. Licensee: Principia College Communications. (acq 3-5-90). Network: UPI. Format: Diversified. Target aud: 18-25. Spec prog: Reggae 6 hrs, class 3 hrs, jazz 3 hrs, hardcore 3 hrs, dance rock 3 hrs, new age 3 hrs, female artists 3 hrs, rap/hip hop 3 hrs wkly.

Eureka

WPIA(FM)— 1989: 98.5 mhz; 3 kw. 328 ft. TL: N40 44 20 W89 16 13. Stereo. 120 Easton St., Peoria 61603. Phone: (309) 676-5000. Fax: (309) 676-2600. Web Site: www.9851011theparty.com. Licensee: Regent Broadcasting of Peoria Inc. Group owner: Regent Communications Inc. (acq 7-6-01; grpsl). Network: Westwood One. Format: Contemp Christian. Target aud: 18-49. ♦Tim Ylineu, progmg dir.

Evanston

WKTA(AM)— 1953: 1330 khz; 5 kw-D, 17 w-N, DA-1. TL: N42 08 23 W87 53 09. 4320 Dundee Rd., Northbrook 60062. Phone: (847) 498-3350. Fax: (847) 498-5743. E-mail: wkta@inc-us.com. Web Site: www.pclradio.com. Licensee: Polnet Communications Ltd. (group owner; acq 5-5-86; $1.66 million;. FTR: 2-17-86). Wiley, Rein and Fielding. Format: AOR/rock, Russian, Korean. News: 5 hrs wkly. Target aud: 18-54; Russian, Korean and German speaking audience. Spec prog: Ger 5 hrs wkly. ♦Walter K. Kotaba, pres; Bolek Barka, gen mgr; Scott Davidson, opns mgr & progmg dir.

*****WNUR-FM**— May 8, 1950: 89.3 mhz; 7.2 kw. 100 ft. TL: N42 03 12 W87 40 33. Stereo. 1920 Campus Dr. 60208-2280. Phone: (847) 491-7101. Phone: (847) 491-2234. Fax: (847) 467-2058. E-mail: gm@wnur.org. Web Site: www.wnur.org. Licensee: Northwestern University. Format: Progsv, jazz, new mus. News: 3 hrs wkly. Target aud: 18-34; general. Spec prog: Folk 3 hrs, world mus 10 hrs, reggae 4 hrs wkly. ♦Henry Bienen, pres; Mike Corsa, gen mgr; John Hanauer, opns mgr; Alex Freedman, progmg dir & pub affrs dir; Raysh Weisss, prom dir & news dir.

WOJO(FM)— 1946: 105.1 mhz; 5.7 kw. Ant 1,394 ft. TL: N41 53 56 W87 37 23. (CP: 5.7 kw, ant 1,394 ft). Stereo. 625 N. Michigan Ave., Suite 300, Chicago 60611-3110. Phone: (312) 981-1800. Fax: (312) 981-1806. Web Site: www.netmio.com/radio/wojo. Licensee: Tichenor License Corp. Group owner: Univision Radio (acq 9-22-2003; grpsl). Rep: Katz Radio. Format: Sp contemp hit. News staff: one; News: 2 hrs wkly. Target aud: 18-35; regional/Mexican. ♦Jerry Ryan, gen mgr; Cesar Canales, progmg dir; Paul Easter, genrg mgr.

WONX(AM)— 1947: 1590 khz; 1 kw-D, 2.5 kw-N, DA-N. TL: N42 01 20 W87 42 43. (CP: 3.5 kw-D, DA). 2100 Lee St. 60202. Phone: (847) 475-1590. Licensee: Kovas Communications Inc. (acq 12-1-75). Format: Ethnic, Sp. News: 8 hrs wkly. Target aud: General. Spec prog: Greek 2 hrs, Indian 8 hrs, Assyrian 15 hrs, Haitian 5 hrs, Lithuanian one hr, Korean 20 hrs wkly. ♦Frank Kovas, pres & gen mgr; Bob Richards, stn mgr.

Fairbury

WYST(FM)— Aug 8, 2000: 107.7 mhz; 22.5 kw. Ant 351 ft. TL: N40 37 45 W88 46 52. 108 Boeykens Pl., Normal 61761. Phone: (309) 888-4496. Fax: (309) 452-9677. E-mail: star1077@aaabloomingron.com. Web Site: www.star1077.net. Licensee: AAA Entertainment Licensing LLC. Group owner: AAA Entertainment L.L.C. (acq 2-22-02; $1.7 million). Network: AP Radio. Format: Adult contemp. News staff: 1; News: 2 hrs wkly. Target aud: 25+; women. ♦John Maguire, CEO & pres; Peter Ottmar, chmn; John Riccardi, CFO; Patti Donsbach, gen mgr; Kevin Trueblood, opns mgr & progmg dir.

Fairfield

WFIW(AM)— Aug 21, 1953: 1390 khz; 710 w-D, 58 w-N. TL: N38 22 46 W88 19 33. Box 310, Hwy. 15 E. 62837. Phone: (618) 842-2159. Fax: (618) 847-5907. E-mail: wf.wwokz@fairfieldwireless.net. Web Site: www.wfiwradio.com. Licensee: Wayne County Broadcasting Co. (group owner) Network: ABC. Format: News/talk. News staff: one; News: 22 hrs wkly. Target aud: 45 plus; small town rural, business, farm, older adults. Spec prog: Farm 16 hrs wkly. ♦Thomas S. Land, chmn; David H. Land, pres, gen mgr, gen sls mgr & progmg dir; Margaret H. Land, VP; Tom Lavine, mus dir; Len Wells, news dir; Kirk Wallace, chief of engrg.

WFIW-FM— 1965: 104.9 mhz; 4.9 kw. 364 ft. TL: N38 22 46 W88 19 33. Stereo. Web Site: www.wfiwradio.com. Format: Adult contemp. News staff: one; News: 16 hrs wkly. Target aud: 25-49; small town rural, young, middle age, business, farm. Spec prog: Farm 12 hrs wkly. ♦David H. Land, opns VP & sls dir.

WOKZ(FM)— September 1996: 105.9 mhz; 6 kw. 328 ft. TL: N38 22 46 W88 19 33. Stereo. Box 310, Hwy. 15 E. 62837. Phone: (618) 842-2159. Fax: (618) 847-5907. E-mail: wfiiwwokz@fairfieldwireless.net. Web Site: www.wokz.com. Licensee: Wayne County Broadcasting Co., Inc. (group owner) Format: Country. News staff: one; News: 20 hrs wkly. Target aud: 25-54; small town rural, business, farm. ♦Thomas S. Land, chmn; David H. Land, pres & gen mgr.

Farmer City

WWHP(FM)— Oct 1, 1983: 98.3 mhz; 3 kw. 300 ft. TL: N40 16 54 W88 32 00. Stereo. 407 N. Main 61842. Phone: (309) 928-9876. Fax: (309) 928-3708. E-mail: wwhp@farmwagon.com. Web Site: www.wwhp.com. Licensee: WMS1 Inc. Format: Americana. Target aud: 18-65; reach city, suburbs & rural listeners in east central Illinois. Spec prog: Gospel 3 hrs, sports 5 hrs wkly. ♦Rory O'Connor, pres; Larry Williams, gen mgr & stn mgr; Lori Allen, gen sls mgr; Charles Williams, progmg dir; Darren Martin, chief of engrg.

Farmington

WWCT(FM)— 1997: 96.5 mhz; 4.3 kw. 377 ft. TL: N40 40 10 W89 53 31. 4234 N. Brandywine, Suite D, Peoria 61614. Phone: (309) 282-7625. Phone: (309) 686-0101. Fax: (309) 686-0111. E-mail: studio@rock965.com. Web Site: www.rock965.com. Licensee: AAA Entertainment Licensing LLC. Group owner: AAA Entertainment L.L.C. (acq 5-31-00; grpsl). Format: Rock. ♦John Maguire, pres; Michael Rea, gen mgr; Rick Hirschmann, opns mgr; Gabe Reynolds, progmg dir.

Fisher

*****WGNN(FM)**— Apr 7, 1996: 102.5 mhz; 6 kw. 328 ft. TL: N40 20 21 W88 24 18. Stereo. Box 12345, Champaign 61826. Secondary address: 2421 N. 1450 E. Rd., White Heath 61884. Phone: (217) 897-6333. E-mail: staff@greatnewsradio.org. Web Site: www.greatnewsradio.org. Licensee: Good News Radio Inc. (acq 4-7-96; $225,000). Network: Network: Moody, USA. Format: Educ, relg, news/talk. Target aud: 35 plus; general. ♦David B. Herriott, chmn; Mark Burns, pres & gen mgr; Carrie Burns, opns dir.

Flora

WNOI(FM)— May 21, 1971: 103.9 mhz; 3.3 kw. 300 ft. TL: N38 40 42 W88 29 14. Stereo. Box 368, 1001 N. Olive Rd. 62839. Phone: (618) 662-8331. Fax: (618) 662-2407. E-mail: info@wnoi.com. Web Site: www.wnoi.com. Licensee: H&R Communications Inc. (acq 10-16-88). Network: Jones Radio Networks. Format: Adult contemp. News staff: one; News: 12 hrs wkly. Target aud: General. ♦Steven S. Lovellette, pres; Randy Poole, gen mgr; Patrick Garret, opns dir; Brenda Miller, gen sls mgr; Patrick Garrett, progmg dir; Kirk Wallace, chief of engrg.

Flossmoor

*****WHFH(FM)**— January 1965: 88.5 mhz; 1.5 kw. 92 ft. TL: N41 32 43 W87 41 30. Stereo. 999 Kedzie Ave. 60422. Phone: (708) 798-9434. Fax: (708) 799-3033. E-mail: sean@whfh.org. Web Site: www.whfh.org. Licensee: Community High School District No. 233. Format: Rock. News: 4 hrs wkly. Target aud: Teens-Adult. Spec prog: News/talk one hr, sports talk one hr, live sports 4 hrs wkly. ♦Robert Comstock, pres & gen mgr; Sean Powers, gen mgr & stn mgr; Tracy Calablese, progmg dir.

Freeport

WFPS(FM)— Nov 1, 1970: 92.1 mhz; 3.6 kw. 300 ft. TL: N42 19 41 W89 43 32. (CP: 6 kw, ant 312 ft.). Stereo. Box 747, 834 N. Tower Rd. 61032. Phone: (815) 235-7191. Fax: (815) 235-4318. E-mail: countrylegends @radioworks.net. Web Site: www.921wfps.com. Licensee: Maverick Media of Freeport License LLC. Group owner: RadioWorks Inc. (acq 4-27-2005; grpsl). Format: Country. News staff: one; News: 15 hrs wkly. Target aud: 25-49. ♦Gary Rozynek, pres; David McAley, VP; David Nelson, sls dir; Curt Baumann, prom dir; Chuck Ingle, chief of engrg.

WFRL(AM)—Co-owned with WFPS(FM). Oct 28, 1947: 1570 khz; 5 kw-D, 500 w-N, DA-2. TL: N42 18 45 W89 35 38. Network: ABC. Format: Adult standards. News staff: one; News: 24 hrs wkly. Target aud: 35 plus. ♦Curt Baumann, opns mgr; Chuck Ingle, engrg dir.

*****WNIE(FM)**— 1999: 89.1 mhz; 6 kw. Ant 361 ft. TL: N42 18 45 W89 35 38. Stereo. NIU Broadcast Ctr., 801 N. First St., De Kalb 60115. Phone: (815) 753-9000. Fax: (815) 753-9938. E-mail: npr@niu.edu. Web Site: www.northernpublicradio.org. Licensee: Northern Illinois University. Network: Network: PRI, NPR. Arter & Hadden. Format: News, class. News staff: 2. Target aud: General. ♦Tim Emmons, gen mgr; Jan Kilgard, dev VP; Bill Drake, progmg dir.

WXXQ(FM)— Apr 11, 1965: 98.5 mhz; 50 kw. 450 ft. TL: N42 18 45 W89 35 38. Stereo. 3901 Brendewood Rd., Rockford 61107-2246. Phone: (815) 399-2233. Fax: (815) 399-8148. Web Site: www.wxxq.com. Licensee: Cumulus Licensing Corp. Group owner: Cumulus Media Inc. (acq 3-15-00). Format: Contemp country. News staff: one. Target aud: 25-54. ♦Greg Sher, gen mgr & mktg mgr.

Galatia

WISH-FM— 2001: 98.9 mhz; 4.1 kw. Ant 400 ft. TL: N37 55 52 W88 40 50. 303 North Main, Benton 62812. Phone: (618) 643-2311. Fax: (618) 643-3299. Licensee: W. Russell Withers Jr. Group owner: Withers Broadcasting Co. Format: CHR, adult contemp. ♦Dana Withers, gen mgr.

Galena

WDBQ-FM— February 1989: 107.5 mhz; 6 kw. 328 ft. TL: N42 24 02 W90 23 55. Stereo. 5490 Saratoga Rd., Dubuque, IA 52002. Phone:

Stations in the U.S. **Illinois**

Developers & Brokers of Radio Properties
contact American Media Services at our suite: Philadelphia Marriott Downtown 215-625-2900
843-972-2200
americanmediaservices.com
Charleston, SC
Dallas, TX · Chicago, Il · Austin, TX
American Media Services, LLC

(563) 557-1040. Fax: (563) 583-4535. Licensee: Cumulus Licensing Corp. Group owner: Cumulus Media Inc. (acq 12-17-98; grpsl). Format: Oldies. News staff: one. Target aud: 25-54. ♦Scott Lindahl, mktg mgr.

Galesburg

WAAG(FM)—Listing follows WGIL(AM).

WAIK(AM)— 1957: 1590 khz; 5 kw-D, 50 w-N, DA-3. TL: N40 57 43 W90 18 30. Box 429 61401. Phone: (309) 342-3161. Fax: (309) 342-0199. E-mail: waik@knoxnet.net. Licensee: WPW Broadcasting Inc. (group owner; acq 7-9-98; $439,500). Network: ABC Information & Entertainment. Fisher, Wayland, Cooper, Leader & Zaragoza L.L.P. Format: MOR, big band, nostalgia. News staff: 3; News: 24 hrs wkly. Target aud: 25 plus. Spec prog: Talk 10 hrs, loc sports 10 hrs, relg 6 hrs wkly. ♦Don Davis, CEO & news dir; David Klockenga, gen mgr; Heidi Sights, opns dir; Kit Osborn, gen sls mgr; Greg Ford, progmg dir; Aaron Winski, chief of engrg.

WGIL(AM)— June 12, 1938: 1400 khz; 740 w-U. TL: N40 56 34 W90 20 39. Box 1227 61402-1227. Secondary address: 154 E. Simmons 61401. Phone: (309) 342-5131. Fax: (309) 342-0840. E-mail: wgil@wgil.com. Web Site: www.wgil.com. Licensee: Galesburg Broadcasting Co. (group owner). Network: Westwood One. Rep: Allied Radio Partners. Edmondson & Edmondson. Format: News/talk, sports. News staff: 4; News: 20 hrs wkly. Target aud: 25-54. Spec prog: Farm 10 hrs, relg 4 hrs, sports 15 hrs wkly. ♦John T. Pritchard, pres; Roger Lundeen, gen mgr.

WAAG(FM)—Co-owned with WGIL(AM). Dec 15, 1966: 94.9 mhz; 50 kw. Ant 492 ft. TL: N40 56 34 W90 20 39. Stereo. E-mail: fm95@fm95online.com. Web Site: www.fm95online.com. Format: Country. News staff: 4; News: 2 hrs wkly. Target aud: 25-54. ♦Brian Prescott, mus dir.

WLSR(FM)— Jan 17, 1979: 92.7 mhz; 3.8 kw. Ant 371 ft. TL: N40 57 43 W90 18 30. (CP: 4.2 kw, ant 380 ft. TL: N40 56 34 W90 20 39). Stereo. Box 1227, 154 E. Simmons St. 61401. Phone: (309) 342-5131. Fax: (309) 342-0840. E-mail: thelaser@thelaseronline.com. Web Site: www.thelaseronline.com. Licensee: Galesburg Broadcasting Co. (group owner; acq 7-3-97). Rep: Allied Radio Partners. Edmundson & Edmundson. Format: AOR. News staff: 4; News: one hr wkly. Target aud: 18-34. Spec prog: Relg 2 hrs wkly. ♦John T. Pritchard, pres; Roger Lundeen, gen mgr; Brian Prescott, prom dir, progmg dir, opns & progmg.

***WVKC(FM)**— Apr 12, 1961: 90.7 mhz; 1 kw. 98 ft. TL: N40 56 46 W90 22 11. Knox College, Box K 254, 2 E. South St. 61401-4999. Phone: (309) 341-7266 (staff). Phone: (309) 341-7000 (switchboard). Fax: (309) 341-7090. E-mail: wvkc@knox.edu. Web Site: www.knox.edu/wvkc.xml. Licensee: Knox College. Format: Var/div. Spec prog: Black 6 hrs, jazz 15 hrs, class 18 hrs wkly.

Galva

WGEN(AM)—Listing follows WJRE(FM).

WJRE(FM)— Oct 15, 1997: 102.5 mhz; 3 kw. Ant 328 ft. TL: N41 07 38 W90 02 27. Stereo. Box 266, Kewanee 61443-0266. Secondary address: 133 .E. Division St., Kewanee 61443. Phone: (309) 853-4471. Fax: (309) 853-4474. E-mail: wkei@insightbb.com. Web Site: www.1025wjre.com. Licensee: Virden Broadcasting Corp. Group owner: Miller Media Group (acq 3-31-2003; $475,000. with WGEN(AM) Geneseo). Rep: Commercial Media Sales. Womble, Carlyle, Sandridge & Rice. Format: Hot adult contemp. Target aud: 18-49. ♦Randal J. Muller, pres; Gary Peterson, gen mgr; Danielle Arch, progmg dir.

WGEN(AM)—Co-owned with WJRE(FM). 1964: 1500 khz; 250 w-D. TL: N41 26 23 W90 09 18. Phone: (309) 944-1500. Fax: (309) 853-4474. Web Site: www.randyradio.com. Format: News/talk. News staff: one; News: 13 hrs wkly. Target aud: 25 plus; community oriented adults.

Geneseo

KBOB-FM— Jan 12, 1977: 104.9 mhz; 3.3 kw. 280 ft. TL: N41 25 47 W90 16 34. (CP: COL De Witt, IA. 12.5 kw, ant 469 ft. TL: N41 43 11 W90 34 13). Stereo. 1229 Brady St., Davenport, IA 52803. Phone: (563) 326-2541. Fax: (563) 326-1819. Web Site: www.bobcountry.com. Licensee: Cumulus Licensing Corp. Group owner: Cumulus Media Inc. (acq 10-2-00; grpsl). Format: Classic country. ♦Jack Swart, gen mgr; Julie Derrer, gen sls mgr; Ryan Chase, progmg dir; Andy Anderson, chief of engrg.

***WAXR(FM)**— 2001: 88.1 mhz; 3 kw vert. Ant 321 ft. TL: N41 28 47 W90 16 08. 3316 Avenue of the Cities, Moline 61265. Phone: (309) 736-9297. Fax: (309) 277-3122. E-mail: info@waxr.org. Web Site: www.waxr.org. Licensee: American Family Association. Group owner: American Family Radio Format: Inspirational Christian. ♦Ron Cook, gen mgr.

WGEN(AM)—Licensed to Geneseo. See Galva

Geneva

WSPY(AM)— Nov 11, 1961: 1480 khz; 1 kw-D, 500 w-N, DA-2. TL: N41 54 25 W88 17 43. 1 Broadcast Center, Plano 60545. Phone: (630) 552-1000. Fax: (630) 552-9300. E-mail: wspy@nelsonmultimedia.net. Licensee: Nelson Multi Media Inc. (acq 9-30-01). Miller and Miller. Format: Adult contemp. News staff: one; News: 2 hrs wkly. Target aud: 35-65; baby boomers. ♦Larry Nelson, pres, gen mgr & gen mgr; Beth Perry, gen sls mgr & progmg dir; Sonny Nelson, mus dir; Lane Lindstrom, chief of engrg.

Genoa

WYRB(FM)— 2001: 106.3 mhz; 6 kw. Ant 213 ft. TL: N42 04 28 W88 49 24. 6336 Calumet Ave., Hammond, IN 46324. Phone: (773) 734-4455. Fax: (303) 433-1555. E-mail: wycainfo@crawfordbroadcsting.com. Web Site: www.crawfordbroadcasting.com. Licensee: Dontron Inc. Group owner: Crawford Broadcasting Co. (acq 9-28-01; $1.5 million). Format: Gospel, Christian talk & music. ♦Larry Nelson, gen mgr.

Gibson City

WGCY(FM)— Nov 28, 1983: 106.3 mhz; 6 kw. Ant 292 ft. TL: N40 34 01 W88 20 41. (CP: Ant 321 ft.). Stereo. Box 192, 607 S. Sangamon Ave. 60936. Phone: (217) 784-8661. Fax: (217) 784-8677. Licensee: F & G Broadcasting Inc. (acq 12-30-86; $225,000; 11-24-86). Network: USA. Format: Easy lstng. News staff: one. Target aud: 35 plus. ♦Fred McCullough, pres; Gary McCullough, gen mgr.

Girard

WCVS-FM—See Springfield

Glasford

WVEL-FM— 2000: 101.1 mhz; 3.3 kw. Ant 449 ft. TL: N40 39 00 W89 46 46. Stereo. 120 Eaton St., Peoria 61603. Phone: (309) 676-5000. Fax: (309) 676-2600. Web Site: wvel.com. Licensee: Regent Broadcasting of Peoria Inc. Group owner: Regent Communications Inc. (acq 7-6-01; grpsl). Rep: Katz Radio. Format: Gospel. Target aud: 18-34; adults, skewing female.

Glen Ellyn

***WDCB(FM)**— July 5, 1977: 90.9 mhz; 5 kw. 300 ft. TL: N41 50 36 W88 05 00. Stereo. College of DuPage, 425 Fawell Blvd. 60137. Phone: (630) 942-4200. Fax: (630) 942-2788. E-mail: wdcbmktg@cdnet.cod.edu. Web Site: www.wdcb.org. Licensee: College of DuPage. Network: Network: PRI, UPI. Cohn & Marks. Format: Jazz, news, blues. News staff: 3; News: 13 hrs wkly. Target aud: General. Spec prog: College classes 12 hrs, folk 12 hrs, gospel 2 hrs, var music 7 hrs wkly. ♦Scott Wager, stn mgr; Jim Barker, sls dir & gen sls mgr; Ken Scott, mktg dir; Mary Pat LaRue, progmg dir; Paul Abella, mus dir; Brian O'Keefe, news dir.

Glenview

***WGBK(FM)**— Jan 13, 1979: 88.5 mhz; 185 w. 100 ft. TL: N42 04 30 W87 49 23. Stereo. c/o Glenbrook S. High School, 4000 W. Lake Ave. 60025. Phone: (847) 486-4487. Phone: (847) 486-4573. Fax: (847) 486-4439. E-mail: wgbk@glenbrook.k12.il.us. Licensee: Glenbrook High School District 225. (acq 1996; $110,000). Format: Alternative, educ, sports. News: 1 hr wkly. Target aud: General; teens & adults. Spec prog: Sports talk 5 hrs, live sports 4 hrs. ♦Dr. Daniel Oswald, gen mgr.

Godfrey

***WLCA(FM)**— 1974: 89.9 mhz; 1.5 kw. Ant 394 ft. TL: N38 56 57 W90 11 47. 5800 Godfrey Rd. 62035. Phone: (618) 466-8936. Fax: (618) 466-7458. Licensee: Lewis and Clark Community College. Network: USA. Format: Progsv, AOR, alt rock. ♦Mike Lemons, gen mgr.

Golconda

WLIE-FM— Nov 22, 1990: 94.3 mhz; 3.1 kw. 449 ft. TL: N37 14 04 W88 29 48. Stereo. Box 2250, One Executive Blvd., Paducah, KY 42002-2250. Phone: (270) 247-5122. Fax: (270) 247-4207. E-mail: wlie@hcis.net. Web Site: www.willieradio.com. Licensee: Bristol Broadcasting Co. Inc. (group owner; acq 2-20-2004; grpsl). Format: Classic country. News staff: one; News: 5 hrs wkly. Target aud: 25-55. Spec prog: Relg 1 hr wkly. ♦Pete Ninninger, pres; Gary Morse, gen mgr.

Granite City

WARH(FM)—Licensed to Granite City. See Saint Louis MO

WGNU(AM)—Licensed to Granite City. See Saint Louis MO

Greenville

WGEL(FM)— Dec 20, 1984: 101.7 mhz; 3 kw. 300 ft. TL: N38 48 11 W89 20 56. Stereo. Box 277, 309 W. Main 62246. Phone: (618) 664-3300. Fax: (618) 664-3318. Web Site: www.wgel.com. Licensee: Bond Broadcasting. (acq 6-1-85; $170,000; 6-10-85). Network: USA. Format: Country. Target aud: 25-64. Spec prog: Farm 19 hrs wkly. ♦John Kennedy, pres & gen mgr; John Goldsmith, progmg dir; Ryan Mifflin, news dir.

***WGRN(FM)**— Sept 26, 1966: 89.5 mhz; 300 w. 206 ft. TL: N38 53 43 W89 24 30. Stereo. 315 E. College Ave. 62246. Phone: (618) 664-2800, EXT. 4895. Phone: (618) 644-2800. Fax: (618) 664-1373. Web Site: wgrn.greenville.edu. Licensee: Greenville College. Format: Christian hit radio. Target aud: 16-24. ♦Nathan Milner, stn mgr; Cary Holman, opns mgr; Ben Snider, progmg dir; Scott Wight, chief of engrg.

Harrisburg

WEBQ(AM)— September 1923: 1240 khz; 1 kw-U. TL: N37 43 03 W88 32 37. 701 S. Commercial St. 62946. Phone: (618) 253-7282. Fax: (618) 252-2366. E-mail: webq@yourclearwave.com. Web Site: www.realcountrynlin.com. Licensee: W. Russell Withers Jr. Group owner: Withers Broadcasting Co. (acq 7-28-2004; $450,000. with WEBQ-FM Eldorado). Format: Country. News staff: one; News: 6 hrs wkly. Target aud: Older area residents. Spec prog: Farm 6 hrs wkly. ♦Cathy Horton, gen mgr & progmg dir; Bob Romonoski, chief of engrg; Sonny Dotson, sls.

WOOZ-FM— September 1947: 99.9 mhz; 32 kw. 650 ft. TL: N37 36 45 W88 52 03. Stereo. 1431 Countryaire Dr., Carterville 62918. Phone: (618) 985-4843. Phone: (800) 455-3243. Fax: (618) 985-6529. E-mail: mail@z100fm.com. Web Site: www.z100fm.com. Licensee: MRR License LLC. Group owner: MAX Media L.L.C. (acq 3-29-2004; grpsl). Fletcher, Heald & Hildreth. Format: Country. Target aud: 18-49. ♦Brian Schimmel, gen mgr; Chad Elliott, opns mgr; Dean Fallat, gen sls mgr; Tracy McKeown, progmg dir; Jim Deterding, chief of engrg.

Harvard

WMCW(AM)— 1955: 1600 khz; 500 w-D, 19 w-N. TL: N42 26 07 W88 36 39. 67 N. Ayer 60033. Phone: (815) 943-3100. Fax: (815) 943-5120. E-mail: wmcw1600@yahoo.com. Licensee: Kovas Communications of Indiana Inc. (group owner; acq 1-23-2004; $650,000). Network: CNN Radio. Format: Adult standards. News: 12 hrs wkly. Target aud: 35+. Spec prog: ♦Constance Kovas, pres; Fred Brandt, gen mgr; Bill Marquis, opns mgr.

Harvey

WBGX(AM)— 1955: 1570 khz; 1 kw-D, 500 w-N, DA-2. TL: N41 36 14 W87 40 45. Great Lakes Radio-Chicago, 5956 S. Michigan Ave., Chicago 60637. Phone: (773) 752-1570. Fax: (773) 752-2242. E-mail: gospel1570@aol.com. Licensee: Great Lakes Radio-Chicago LLC (acq 10-7-03; $1.78 million). Format: Gospel. Target aud: 18-64; affluent Americans. ♦Mike Gallagher, chmn; Tim Gallagher, pres.

Havana

WDUK(FM)— Feb 27, 1970: 99.3 mhz; 3 kw. 300 ft. TL: N40 18 43 W90 03 19. 901 N. Promenade 62644. Phone: (309) 543-3331. Licensee: Illinois Valley Radio. (acq 3-5-73). Brownfield. Format: C&W, div. Target aud: General. Spec prog: Farm 8 hrs wkly. ♦Edwin Stimpson, pres.

Henry

WRVY-FM— July 30, 1990: 100.5 mhz; 3 kw. 328 ft. TL: N41 04 32 W89 21 10. Stereo. Box 69, Princeton 61356. Phone: (815) 875-8014. Phone: (309) 364-4411. Fax: (815) 872-0308. Licensee: WZOE Inc. (group owner; acq 5-8-98). Network: CBS. Shaw Pittman. Format: Classic rock. News staff: 3; News: 3 hrs wkly. Target aud: 25-45. Spec prog: Farm 4 hrs wkly. ♦Steve Samet, gen mgr; Mary Harmon, opns dir.

Herrin

WDDD(AM)—See Johnston City

WJPF(AM)— Aug 28, 1940: 1340 khz; 1 kw-U. TL: N37 50 03 W89 01 37. (CP: 770 w-U). 1431 Countryaire Dr., Carterville 62918. Phone: (618) 985-4843. Phone: (800) 455-3243. Fax: (618) 985-6529. E-mail: mail@wjpf.com. Web Site: www.wjpf.com. Licensee: MRR License LLC. Group owner: MAX Media L.L.C. (acq 3-29-2004; grpsl). Network: Westwood One, ABC News/Talk. Format: News/talk, Sports. News staff: 3; News: 10 hrs wkly. Target aud: 35 plus; mature, middle-income wage earners. ♦Brian Schimmel, gen mgr; Chad Elliot, chief of opns; Steve Falat, sls dir & gen sls mgr; Tom Miller, progmg dir; Rick Gregg, news dir; Steve Sine, news dir; Tom Deterding, chief of engrg.

WVZA(FM)— March 1994: 92.7 mhz; 3.3 kw. 433 ft. TL: N37 45 15 W88 56 05. Box 127, 1822 N. Court St., Marion 62959-0127. Phone: (618) 997-8123. Fax: (618) 993-2319. Web Site: www.kissfm927.com. Licensee: Clear Channel Broadcasting Licenses Inc. Group owner: Clear Channel Communications Inc. (acq 1-18-01; grpsl). Rep: Katz Radio. Format: Contemp hit. Target aud: 18-34. ♦Jerry Crouse, gen mgr; Paxton Guy, opns dir & progmg dir; Steve Browning, gen sls mgr & natl sls mgr; April Ruebke, news dir; Brett Blankenship, chief of engrg.

Heyworth

WBBE(FM)—Not on air, target date: unknown: 97.9 mhz; 5.4 kw. Ant 344 ft. TL: N40 27 08 W88 57 48. 520 N. Center St., Bloomington 61701-2902. Licensee: Connoisseur Media LLC. Shaw Pittman LLP. ♦Larry Weiss, gen mgr.

Highland

WCBW(AM)— Dec 2, 1963: 880 khz; 1 kw-D, DA. TL: N38 45 23 W89 39 18. (CP: 1.7 kw-D, 160 w-N, DA-2). Box 303, 13063 Winu Dr. 62249. Phone: (618) 654-7521. Fax: (618) 654-6333. E-mail: hhnjim@hereshelpnet.org. Licensee: New Life Evangelistic Center Inc. (acq 11-5-98); $1.25 million with WDID(AM) Highland). Format: Christian. News staff: one; News: 18 hrs wkly. Target aud: General; mature adults. Spec prog: Farm 3 hrs, Ger one hr wkly. ♦Larry Rice, pres; Charlie Hale, gen mgr; Bernard Turner, opns dir.

WDID(AM)— 2000: 1510 khz; 1 kw-D, DA. TL: N38 44 56 W89 34 10. Box 303 62249. Secondary address: 13063 WINU Dr. 62249. Phone: (618) 654-7521. Fax: (618) 654-6333. E-mail: 1510wcbw@mail.com. Licensee: New Life Evangelistic Center Inc. (acq 11-5-98; $1.25 million with WCBW(AM) Highland). Format: Southern gospel, christian. ♦Larry Rice, pres; Charlie Hale, gen mgr; Bernard Turner, opns dir.

Highland Park

WEEF(AM)— Aug 15, 1963: 1430 khz; 1 kw-D, 29 w-N, DA. TL: N42 10 53 W87 57 05. 210 Skokie Valley Rd. 60035. Phone: (847) 831-5440. Fax: (847) 831-5479. E-mail: weefam1430@aol.com. Licensee: Polnet Communications Ltd. (group owner; acq 5-20-2003; $1 million). Dow, Lohnes & Albertson. Format: It, Greek. Target aud: General; ethnic. Spec prog: Assyrian, Jewish, East Indian, Romanian, Russian, mus/talk. ♦Chris Bagat, stn mgr.

WVIV-FM— Aug 15, 1963: 103.1 mhz; 3 kw. Ant 241 ft. TL: N42 09 24 W87 48 20. Stereo. 625 N. Michigan Ave., Suite 300, Chicago 60611. Phone: (312) 981-1800. Fax: (312) 981-1850. E-mail: ayudachi@netmio.com. Web Site: wviv.netmio.com. Licensee: HBC License Corp. Group owner: Univision Radio (acq 9-22-2003; grpsl). Rep: Allied Radio Partners. Format: Sp. Target aud: 25-54. Spec prog: Asian, Pol, Ger, Greek. ♦Jerry Ryan, gen mgr; David Miranda, prom dir; Cesar Canales, progmg dir; Armando Reyes, mus dir; Robert Lopez, chief of engrg.

Hillsboro

WXAJ(FM)— Sept 1, 2000: 99.7 mhz; 50 kw. 492 ft. TL: N39 20 14 W89 32 04. 3055 S. 4th St., Springfield 62703. Phone: (217) 528-3033. Fax: (217) 528-5348. Web Site: www.997kissfm.com. Licensee: Clear Channel Broadcasting Licenses Inc. Group owner: Clear Channel Communications Inc. (acq 8-6-01; $2.8 million). Rep: Clear Channel. Format: Contemporary Hit/Top 40. Target aud: Adults; 18-49. ♦Kevin O'Dea, gen mgr; Frank Reed, gen sls mgr; Michelle Mitchell, prom dir; Michael Theriac, progmg dir; Jeff Hofmann, chief of engrg.

Hinsdale

***WHSD(FM)**— Dec 6, 1970: 88.5 mhz; 200 w. 131 ft. TL: N41 47 25 W87 55 11. Stereo. Hinsdale Central High School, 55th & Grant St. 60521. Phone: (630) 570-8463. Fax: (630) 887-1362. Licensee: Hinsdale Twsp. High School District 86. Format: Var. Target aud: General.

Hoopeston

WHPO(FM)— May 29, 1979: 100.9 mhz; 3 kw. 280 ft. TL: N40 28 36 W87 41 36. Stereo. 912 S. Dixie Hwy. 60942. Phone: (217) 283-7744. Fax: (217) 283-6090. E-mail: whporadio@whporadio.com. Web Site: www.whporadio.com. Licensee: Market Street Broadcasting LLC (acq 12-27-00; $900,000). Format: Country. News staff: one; News: 6 hrs wkly. Target aud: 25 plus; rural middle class. Spec prog: Southern gospel 7 hrs, big band 2 hrs wkly. ♦Gary Voss, pres & gen mgr; Blanche M. Voss, opns mgr; Becky Voss, progmg dir.

Jacksonville

WJIL(AM)— November 1961: 1550 khz; 1 kw-D, 10 w-N, DA-2. TL: N39 43 20 W90 11 43. Box 1055, Rt. 4, E. Morton Rd. 62651. Phone: (217) 245-5119. Fax: (217) 245-1596. Licensee: Morgan County Broadcasting Co. Inc. (acq 5-1-93; with co-located FM). Network: Network: Westwood One, ABC Information & Entertainment, ABC News/Talk. Rep: Roslin. Fisher, Wayland, Cooper, Leader & Zaragoza L.L.P. Format: News/talk, btfl music. News staff: one; News: 9 hrs wkly. Target aud: 35-64. Spec prog: Farm 8 hrs wkly. ♦Sarah Hautala, gen mgr; Diana McCutcheon, sls dir; Mike Viles, prom mgr; Julie Ann Cambridge, mus dir; Glen Hopkiins, chief of engrg.

WJVO(FM)— Co-owned with WJIL(AM). Sept 1, 1986: 105.5 mhz; 6 kw. 340 ft. TL: N39 43 20 W90 11 43. Stereo. 1251 East Morton, South Jacksonville Network: Network: Westwood One, ABC. Format: Country. News staff: one; News: 4 hrs wkly. Target aud: 25-54.

WLDS(AM)— Dec 9, 1941: 1180 khz; 1 kw-D. TL: N39 44 06 W90 11 50. Box 1180, 2161 Old State Rd. 62651. Phone: (217) 245-7171. Fax: (217) 245-6711. E-mail: wlds@wlds.com. Web Site: www.wlds.com. Licensee: Jerdon Broadcasting. (acq 8-1-89; $650,000; 6-5-89). Network: CBS. Kaye, Scholer, Fierman, Hays & Handler. Format: Adult contemp, news/talk. News staff: 3; News: 23 hrs wkly. Target aud: 35 plus; business & professional people, farmers & housewives. Spec prog: Farm 20 hrs wkly. ♦Jerry Symons, CEO & gen mgr.

WYMG(FM)—Licensed to Jacksonville. See Springfield

Jerseyville

WJBM(AM)— Oct 11, 1959: 1480 khz; 500 w-D, 32 w-N, DA-2. TL: N39 06 46 W90 18 43. 1010 Shipman Rd. 62052. Phone: (618) 498-2185. Fax: (618) 498-9830. E-mail: wjbm@wjbmradio.com. Web Site: www.wjbmradio.com. Licensee: DJ Two Rivers Radio Inc. (acq 1-9-2004; $320,000. with WBBA-FM Pittsfield). Network: ABC Daytime Direction. Format: Oldies. Target aud: 25 plus; general market through retirement. Spec prog: Farm 18 hrs, sports 13 hrs, relg 3 hrs wkly.

WRDA(FM)— Oct 10, 1967: 104.1 mhz; 50 kw. 500 ft. TL: N38 51 36 W90 18 38. Stereo. 800 St. Louis Union Station, The Power House, St. Louis, MO 63013. Phone: (314) 621-0400. Fax: (314) 621-3000. E-mail: feedback@1041themall.com. Web Site: www.red1041.com. Licensee: Emmis Radio License LLC. Group owner: Emmis Communications Corp. (acq 2-11-97; grpsl). Format: New American Standards. News staff: one; News: 2 hrs wkly. Target aud: 25-54; families with children, singles. Spec prog: Heartland issues one hr, today's issues one hr, pub agenda one hr wkly. ♦John Beck, VP; Lisa Sesti, stn mgr & gen sls mgr.

Johnston City

WDDD(AM)— July 1, 1979: 810 khz; 250 w-U, DA-N. TL: N37 51 14 W88 52 12. (CP: 300 w-U, DA-N). Box 127, Marion 62959. Secondary address: 1822 N. Court, Marion 62959. Phone: (618) 997-8123. Fax: (618) 993-2319. Web Site: www.foxsports810.com. Licensee: Clear Channel Broadcasting Licenses Inc. Group owner: Clear Channel Communications Inc. (acq 12-19-00; grpsl). Format: talk, sports. News: 2 hrs wkly. Target aud: 18-49; Adults. ♦Jerry Crouse, gen mgr; Steve Browning, gen sls mgr; Paxton Guy, progmg dir; April Rebke, news dir; Brett Blankenship, chief of engrg.

WRLL(AM)— Oct 7, 2003: 1690 khz; 10 kw-D, 1 kw-N. TL: N37 46 28 W89 05 50. (CP: COL Berwyn. TL: N41 44 14 W87 42 04). 233 N. Michigan Ave., Suite 2800, Chicago 60601. Phone: (312) 540-2000. Fax: (312) 938-0111. Licensee: Clear Channel Broadcasting Licenses Inc. Group owner: Clear Channel Communications Inc. (acq 1-18-01). Format: Oldies. ♦John Gehron, gen mgr; Tommy Edwards, opns dir; Rod Phillips, progmg dir.

Joliet

WCCQ(FM)—(Crest Hill). Jan 28, 1976: 98.3 mhz; 3 kw. 300 ft. TL: N41 27 55 W88 07 33. 2410-B Canton Farm Rd. 60435. Phone: (815) 556-0100. Web Site: www.wccq.com. Licensee: Three Eagles of Joliet Inc. Group owner: Three Eagles Communications (acq 1-13-97; grpsl). Network: ABC. Dow, Lohnes & Albertson. Format: Country. Target aud: 25-54; general. ♦Dennis Mockler, VP & gen mgr; Roy Gregory, progmg dir.

***WCSF(FM)**— Sept 5, 1988: 88.7 mhz; 100 w. 108 ft. TL: N41 31 58 W88 05 54. Stereo. 500 N. Wilcox St. 60435. Phone: (815) 740-3425. Phone: (815) 740-3214. Fax: (815) 740-3697. E-mail: webmaster@st.francis.edu. Web Site: www.stfrancis.edu. Licensee: University of St. Francis. Format: AOR. Target aud: 18-45; males. Spec prog: Black 2 hrs, jazz 2 hrs, talk 4 hrs, requests 4 hrs, classic rock 4 hrs wkly. ♦Don Burke, pres; Rick Lawrence, gen mgr.

***WJCH(FM)**— Apr 25, 1986: 91.9 mhz; 50 kw. 460 ft. TL: N41 24 55 W88 16 19. Stereo. 13 Fairlane Dr. 60435. Phone: (815) 725-1331. Licensee: Family Stations Inc. (group owner) Format: Relg. Spec prog: Class 2 hrs wkly. ♦Harold Camping, pres & gen mgr; Virginia Beehn, opns mgr.

WJOL(AM)— 1924: 1340 khz; 1 kw-U. TL: N41 32 10 W88 03 15. 2410-B Caton Farm Rd., Crest Hill 60435. Phone: (815) 556-0100. Fax: (815) 577-9231. Web Site: www.wjol.com. Licensee: NM Licensing LLC. Group owner: NextMedia Group L.L.C. (acq 11-26-01; grpsl). Network: ABC Information & Entertainment. Rep: McGavren Guild. Ill. Radio Net. Format: Talk. News staff: 2; News: 40 hrs wkly. Target aud: 35 plus. Spec prog: Farm 3 hrs, gospel one hr, Pol one hr wkly. ♦Steven Dinetz, CEO; Skip Wellar, pres; Dennis Mockler, gen mgr.

WSSR(FM)— Co-owned with WJOL(AM). Feb 6, 1960: 96.7 mhz; 3 kw. 300 ft. TL: N41 32 10 W88 03 15. Stereo. Web Site: www.star967.net. Format: Adult contemp. News staff: one. Target aud: 25-44; men.

Stations in the U.S. Illinois

Developers & Brokers of Radio Properties
contact American Media Services at our suite:
Philadelphia Marriott Downtown
215-625-2900
843-972-2200
americanmediaservices.com
Charleston, SC
Dallas, TX · Chicago, Il · Austin, TX
American Media Services, LLC

WVIX(FM)— Apr 17, 1960: 93.5 mhz; 6 kw. Ant 328 ft. TL: N41 36 39 W88 00 33. Stereo. 625 N. Michigan Ave., Suite 300, Chicago 60611. Phone: (312) 981-1800. Fax: (312) 981-1806. Licensee: HBC License Corp. Group owner: Univision Radio (acq 9-22-2003; grpsl). Format: Sp contemp. News staff: one; News: one. ♦ Jerry Ryan, gen mgr; Cesar Canales, opns mgr; Paul Easter, engrg mgr.

WWHN(AM)— Apr 10, 1964: 1510 khz; 1 kw-D. TL: N41 30 50 W88 03 10. Stereo. 10321 S. Halsted, Chicago 60628. Phone: (773) 239-2300. Fax: (773) 239-9921. E-mail: wwhn@aol.com. Licensee: Hawkins Broadcasting Co. (acq 12-89; $250,000; 12-4-89). Format: Gospel. Target aud: 18-54; affluent adults. Spec prog: Sp one hr wkly. ♦ Raymond E. Hawkins, pres; Toni Hawkins, gen mgr.

Kankakee

*WAWF(FM)— 2000: 88.3 mhz; 1.25 kw. Ant 285 ft. TL: N41 04 39 W87 45 22. Box 3206,, American Family Radio, Tupelo, MS 38803. Phone: (662) 844-8888. Fax: (662) 842-6791. Web Site: www.afr.net. Licensee: American Family Radio. (group owner) Format: Inspirational Christian. ♦ Marvin Sanders, gen mgr.

WKAN(AM)— June 1, 1947: 1320 khz; 1 kw-D, 500 w-N, DA-N. TL: N41 08 08 W87 49 10. 70 Meadowview Ctr., Suite 400 60901. Phone: (815) 935-9555. Fax: (815) 935-9593. Web Site: www.wkan.com. Licensee: STARadio Corp. (acq 2-7-94; $1.31 million with co-located FM; 3-28-94). Network: UPI. Pepper & Corazzini. Format: Talk. News staff: one; News: 20 hrs wkly. Target aud: 25-54. Spec prog: Farm 10 hrs wkly. ♦ Robert L. Kersmarki, pres & gen mgr; Brendan Micheals, opns mgr & progmg dir; Larry Regnier, gen sls mgr.

*WKCC(FM)— June 1, 1992: 91.1 mhz; 1.75 kw. Ant 305 ft. TL: N41 09 24 W87 52 16. 1270 Larry Power Rd., Bourbonnais 60914. Phone: (815) 802-8100. Fax: (815) 935-5169. Licensee: Kankakee Community College. Format: Educ, tourism. Target aud: General; travelers in northern IL. ♦ William Yohnka, gen mgr.

WKIF(FM)— Sept 21, 1986: 92.7 mhz; 3 kw. Ant 300 ft. TL: N41 07 22 W87 53 35. Stereo. 6012 S. Pulaski Rd., Chicago 60629. Phone: (773) 767-1000. Fax: (773) 767-1100. Licensee: WKIF Inc. Group owner: Spanish Broadcasting System Inc. (acq 11-15-2004; grpsl). Network: CNN Radio. Format: News. ♦ Gary Wright, gen mgr & progmg dir.

*WONU(FM)— 1966: 89.7 mhz; 35 kw. 421 ft. TL: N41 09 24 W87 52 16. Stereo. One University Ave., Bourbonnais 60914. Phone: (815) 939-5330. Fax: (815) 939-5087. E-mail: shinefm@wonu.fm. Web Site: www.shine.fm. Licensee: Olivet Nazarene University. Miller & Miller. Format: Christian Pop. Target aud: 25-49; female, predominantly conservative. ♦ Justin Knight, gen mgr; Johnathon Eltrevoog, prom dir & progmg dir; Don Johnson, chief of engrg.

WVLI(FM)— Oct 22, 1992: 95.1 mhz; 3 kw. Ant 328 ft. TL: N41 04 39 W87 45 22. Stereo. Box 758, Bourbonnais 60914-0756. Secondary address: 292 N. Convent, Bourbonnais 60914. Phone: (815) 933-9287. Fax: (815) 933-8696. E-mail: wvli951@aol.com. Licensee: Milner Broadcasting Co. (acq 3-17-95; $400,000). Network: AP Network News. Womble, Carlyle, Sandridge & Rice. Format: Greatest hits & artists. News staff: 2; News: 20 hrs wkly. Target aud: 25+. Spec prog: Chicago Bears (NFL) Football Games. ♦ Tim Milner, pres, gen mgr & stn mgr; Jim Brandt, opns mgr.

Kewanee

WKEI(AM)— Sept 11, 1952: 1450 khz; 500 w-D, 1 kw-N. TL: N41 13 37 W89 56 08. Box 266 61443-0266. Secondary address: 133 E. Division St. 61443. Phone: (309) 853-4471. Fax: (309) 853-4474. Web Site: www.randyradio.com. Licensee: Virden Broadcasting Corp. Group owner: Miller Media Group (acq 11-8-94; $400,000. with co-located FM; FTR: 1-2-95). Network: CBS Radio. Rep: Commercial Media Sales. Womble Carlyle. Format: News/talk. News staff: one. Spec prog: Farm 20 hrs, relg 6 hrs wkly. ♦ Randal J. Miller, pres & sls dir; Gary Petersen, gen mgr; Bob McKee, adv mgr, news dir & pub affrs dir; Danielle Arch, progmg dir; Wayne R. Miller, chief of engrg.

WYEC(FM)—Co-owned with WKEI(AM). May 20, 1966: 93.9 mhz; 3.1 kw. Ant 453 ft. TL: N41 16 40 W89 55 15. Stereo. Web Site: www.randyradio.com. Network: CNN Radio. Format: Soft adult contemp. Target aud: 35-64. ♦ Gary Petersen, stn mgr; Randal J. Miller, sls VP.

Knoxville

WKAY(FM)— Dec 13, 2001: 105.3 mhz; 3.1 kw. Ant 456 ft. TL: N41 01 49 W90 13 14. 154 E. Simmons, Galesburg 61401. Phone: (309) 342-5131. Fax: (309) 342-0840. E-mail: kfm@1053kfm.com. Web Site: www.1053kfm.com. Licensee: Galesburg Broadcasting Co. Group owner: Galesburg Broadcasting Co. (acq 4-1-99). Rep: Allied Radio Partners. Edmundson & Edmundson. Format: Adult contemp. News staff: 4; News: one hr wkly. Target aud: 25-54; Adults. ♦ Roger Lundeen, gen mgr; Brian Prescott, opns dir.

La Grange

*WLTL(FM)— Jan 5, 1968: 88.1 mhz; 180 w. 138 ft. TL: N41 48 45 W87 52 51. Stereo. 100 S. Brainard Ave. 60525. Phone: (708) 482-9585. Fax: (708) 482-7051. E-mail: wltl@lths.net. Web Site: www.wltl.net. Licensee: Lyons Township High School. Format: Var, rock. News: 10 hrs wkly. Target aud: 14-35; young adults. Spec prog: Sports 5 hrs, news & views 10 hrs wkly. ♦ Chris Thomas, gen mgr; Robert Wieghmann, progmg dir; Ross Johnson, chief of engrg.

WRDZ(AM)— October 1950: 1300 khz; 5 kw-D, 500 w-N, DA-2. (CP: 4 kw-N. TL: N41 40 29 W87 45 45). 190 N. State St., Chicago 60601. Phone: (312) 683-1300. Fax: (312) 577-5994. Licensee: Radio Disney Chicago LLC. Group owner: ABC Inc. (acq 5-12-99; with WPJX(AM) Zion). Network: ABC. Format: Children. Children, mom's & dad's. ♦ Zemiro Jones, gen mgr; Karyn Esken, stn mgr.

La Salle

WAJK(FM)—Listing follows WLPO(AM).

WLPO(AM)— Nov 16, 1947: 1220 khz; 1 kw-D, 500 w-N, DA-2. TL: N41 18 14 W89 05 44. 1 Broadcast Ln., Oglesby 61348. Phone: (815) 223-3100. Fax: (815) 223-3095. E-mail: wlpo@ivnet.com. Web Site: wlpo.net. Licensee: La Salle County Broadcasting Co. (group owner) (acq 8-1-49). Format: News/talk, sports. News staff: 3; News: 35 hrs wkly. Target aud: 30 plus. ♦ Peter Miler, pres; Joyce McCullough, VP & gen mgr; Dave Ebener, sls VP.

WAJK(FM)—Co-owned with WLPO(AM). Dec 4, 1964: 99.3 mhz; 11 kw. 500 ft. TL: N41 18 15 W89 05 46. Stereo. Web Site: wajk.com. Format: Hot adult contemp. Target aud: 25-49. ♦ John Spencer, progmg dir.

*WNIW(FM)— November 1998: 91.3 mhz; 8 kw. Ant 331 ft. TL: N41 26 44 W89 00 42. Stereo. NIU Broadcast Ctr., 801 N. First St., DeKalb 60115. Phone: (815) 753-9000. Fax: (815) 753-9938. E-mail: npr@niu.edu. Web Site: www.northernpublicradio.org. Licensee: Northern Illinois University. Network: PRI, NPR. Arter & Hadden. Format: News, classical. News staff: 2. Target aud: General. ♦ Tim Emmons, gen mgr; Jan Kilgard, dev dir; Bill Drake, progmg dir.

Lake Forest

*WMXM(FM)— Sept 10, 1973: 88.9 mhz; 300 w. 100 ft. TL: N42 15 00 W87 49 45. Stereo. 555 N. Sheridan Rd. 60045. Phone: (847) 735-5220 (office). Phone: (847) 735-6038 (studio). Fax: (847) 735-6291. Web Site: www.lfcradio.com. Licensee: Lake Forest College. Format: Div, classic rock, progsv. News staff: 2; News: 5 hrs wkly. Target aud: 18-25; students. Spec prog: Black 6 hrs, class 3 hrs, gospel 3 hrs, jazz 6 hrs wkly. ♦ Ethan Helm, gen mgr.

Lansing

WSRB(FM)— Aug 28, 1961: 106.3 mhz; 2 kw. Ant 397 ft. TL: N41 34 44 W87 32 46. 6336 Calumet Ave., Hammond, IN 46324. Phone: (773) 734-4455. Fax: (219) 933-0323. E-mail: wycainfo@crawfordbroadcasting.com. Web Site: www.crawfordbroadcasting.com. Licensee: Dontron Inc. Group owner: Crawford Broadcasting Co. (acq 4-10-97; $14.8 million). Network: ABC. Format: Gospel, Christian, old school music. Target aud: 12-34; adult, African-American. ♦ Donald B. Crawford, CEO; Taft Harris, gen mgr.

Lawrenceville

WAKO(AM)— June 9, 1959: 910 khz; 500 w-D, 59 w-N, DA-2. TL: N38 43 23 W87 39 13. Box 210 62439. Phone: (618) 943-3354. Fax: (618) 943-4173. Licensee: Lawrenceville Broadcasting Co. Inc. (acq 5-31-73). Network: Westwood One. Format: Adult contemp, country. News staff: one; News: 12 hrs wkly. Target aud: 20-65+. ♦ Stuart Kent Lankford, pres & stn mgr.

WAKO-FM— March 1965: 103.1 mhz; 6 kw. 328 ft. TL: N38 43 23 W87 39 13. Stereo. E-mail: wakoradio@yahoo.com. ♦ Stuart Kent Lankford, gen mgr; Steve Anderson, news dir.

Le Roy

WBWN(FM)— Oct 15, 1979: 104.1 mhz; 25 kw. 328 ft. TL: N40 25 25 W88 51 28. (CP: .80 kw, ant 413 ft. TL: N40 27 01 W89 00 42). Stereo. 236 Greenwood Ave., Bloomington 61704. Phone: (309) 829-1221. Fax: (309) 662-8598. Web Site: www.wbwn.com. Licensee: Regent Broadcasting of Lancaster Inc. Group owner: Regent Communications Inc. (acq 5-12-2004; grpsl). Rep: McGavren Guild. Format: Country. Target aud: 25-45. ♦ Red Pitcher, stn mgr; Dan Westhoff, progmg dir.

Lena

WQLF(FM)— Aug 2, 2002: 102.1 mhz; 5.2 kw. Ant 351 ft. TL: N42 20 31 W89 48 21. W4765 Radio Ln., Monroe, WI 53566. Phone: (608) 325-2161. Fax: (608) 325-2164. E-mail: wekz@wekz.com. Web Site: www.wekz.com. Licensee: Lena Radio Broadcasting (acq 2-26-02). Classic hits (rock). Target aud: 20-49. ♦ Scott Thompson, gen mgr & gen sls mgr; Wyatt Herrmann, progmg dir; Don Jacobson, news dir; Todd Hauser, chief of engrg.

Lexington

WDQZ(FM)— 2004: 99.5 mhz; 6 kw. Ant 328 ft. TL: N40 34 30 W88 50 15. 108 Boeykens Place, Normal 61761. Phone: (309) 888-4496. Fax: (309) 452-9677. Web Site: www.eagleclassichits.com. Licensee: AAA Entertainment Licensing LLC. Group owner: AAA Entertainment L.L.C. (acq 9-8-00; $1.3 million. for CP). Format: Classic Rock. News staff: 1; News: 2 hrs wkly. Target aud: 25-54. ♦ Patti Donsbach, gen mgr.

Lincoln

WLLM(AM)— April 1951: 1370 khz; 1 kw-D, 35 w-N. TL: N40 08 24 W89 23 10. c/o WLUJ(FM), 600 W. Mason St., Springfield 62702. Phone: (217) 528-2300. Fax: (217) 528-2400. Web Site: www.wluj.org. Licensee: Cornerstone Community Radio Inc. (acq 4-7-03; $275,000). Format: Christian talk. ♦ Richard Van Zandt, gen mgr; John McBride, stn mgr; Howard Fouks, opns VP.

*WLNX(FM)— Jan 28, 1974: 88.9 mhz; 225 w. Ant 68 ft. TL: N40 09 23 W89 21 40. Stereo. 300 Keokuk St. 62656. Phone: (217) 732-3155. Fax: (217) 732-3715. Licensee: Lincoln University. Womble, Carlyle, Sandridge & Rice. Format: Classical. ♦ John Malone, gen mgr.

Lincolnshire

*WAES(FM)— 2002: 88.1 mhz; 150 w. Ant 49 ft. TL: N42 11 59 W87 56 49. Adlai E. Stevenson High School, Two Stevenson Dr. 60069. Phone: (847) 634-4000 ext. 1710. Fax: (847) 634-0983. Licensee: Adlai E. Stevenson High School District No. 125. Format: Var. ♦ Greg Sherwin, gen mgr.

Broadcasting & Cable Yearbook 2006

Litchfield

WSMI(AM)— Nov 2, 1950: 1540 khz; 1 kw-D. TL: N39 10 21 W89 34 14. Box 10, WSMI Bldg, E. Rt. 16 62056. Secondary address: 6308 IL Rt. 16, Hillsboro 62049. Phone: (217) 324-5921. Fax: (217) 532-2431. E-mail: wsmi@wsmiradio.com. Web Site: wsmiradio.com. Licensee: Talley Broadcasting Corp. Group owner: Talley Radio Stations Network: CNN Radio. Rep: Christal. Format: Farm, country, news/talk. News staff: 3; News: 15 hrs wkly. Target aud: General. Spec prog: Farm 18 hrs wkly. ♦Hayward L. Talley, chmn & gen mgr.

WSMI-FM— Mar 5, 1960: 106.1 mhz; 50 kw. 500 ft. TL: N39 15 21 W89 36 48. Stereo. Format: Contemp country. News staff: 3. ♦Hayward Talley, pres; Brian Talley, VP.

Lockport

***WLRA(FM)**— November 1972: 88.1 mhz; 250 w. 95 ft. TL: N41 36 06 W88 04 51. Stereo. c/o Lewis Univ., 500 Independence Blvd., Romeoville 60446. Phone: (815) 836-5214. Fax: (815) 838-9149. E-mail: wlraradio@lewisu.edu. Web Site: www.thestartradio.com. Licensee: Lewis University. Format: Educ, div. News: 2 hrs wkly. Target aud: 13-30; college bound or post-college. Spec prog: Black 15 hrs, class 6 hrs, jazz 15 hrs, sports 15 hrs, talk 10 hrs wkly. ♦Samuel D. Enyia, chmn; John Carey, pres; Wayne J. Draudt, exec VP; Peter Turano, gen mgr; Nick Hoeppner, opns dir; Stuart Lang, dev VP.

Loves Park

***WGSL(FM)**— Mar 28, 1988: 91.1 mhz; 4 kw. 400 ft. TL: N42 19 18 W89 00 42. Stereo. Box 2730, Rockford 61132-2730. Secondary address: 5375 Pebble Creek Tr. 61111. Phone: (815) 654-1200. Fax: (815) 282-7779. E-mail: home@radio91.com. Web Site: www.radio91.com. Licensee: Christian Life Center School. Network: USA. Wilkinson Barker Knauer. Format: Relg, contemp praise. Target aud: 35-50; older families. ♦Paul Youngblood, gen mgr; Ron Tietsort, opns mgr.

WKGL-FM— Mar 25, 1964: 96.7 mhz; 3 kw. Ant 300 ft. TL: N42 19 48 W89 04 58. Stereo. 3901 Brendenwood Rd., Rockford 61107. Phone: (815) 399-2233. Fax: (815) 399-8148. Web Site: www.cumulus.com. Licensee: Cumulus Licensing Corp. Group owner: Cumulus Media Inc. (acq 3-12-2001). Format: Classic rock. ♦Greg Sher, gen mgr; Paul Miller, gen sls mgr; Steve Brill, opns dir & progmg dir; Paul Hannigan, news dir; Michael Hayden, chief of engrg.

WLUV(AM)— Sept 29, 1962: 1520 khz; 500 w-D. TL: N42 19 48 W89 04 58. (CP: 12.5 w). Box 2616 61132. Secondary address: 2272 Elmwood Rd., Rockford 61103. Phone: (815) 877-9588. Fax: (815) 877-9649. Licensee: Loves Park Broadcasting Co. Network: ABC Information & Entertainment. Format: Classic country, sports. Target aud: 25-60; blue collar workers. Spec prog: Farm 6 hrs, polka 6 hrs wkly. ♦Joe Salvi, gen mgr.

Lynnville

WEAI(FM)— Nov 15, 1989: 107.1 mhz; 6 kw. 328 ft. TL: N39 37 16 W90 15 28. Stereo. Box 1180, Jacksonville 62651. Secondary address: 2161 Old State Rd., Jacksonville 62651. Phone: (217) 243-2800. Fax: (217) 245-6711. E-mail: weai@weai.com. Web Site: www.weai.com. Licensee: Jerdon Broadcasting. Kaye, Scholer, Fierman, Hays & Handler. Format: Contemp hit, oldies. News staff: 3; News: 6 hrs wkly. Target aud: 20-40; Active Young Adults. ♦Jerry Symons, gen mgr & opns mgr; Don Hamilton, gen sls mgr; Perry Brown, progmg dir; Gary Scott, news dir; John Coe, chief of engrg.

Macomb

***WIUM(FM)**— May 23, 1956: 91.3 mhz; 50 kw. 485 ft. TL: N40 25 40 W90 40 58. Stereo. 515 Univ. Svcs. Bldg., Western Illinois Univ. 61455. Phone: (309) 298-2424. Phone: (309) 298-1873. Fax: (309) 298-2133. E-mail: publicradio@wiu.edu. Web Site: www.tristatesradio.com. Licensee: Western Illinois University. Network: Network: NPR, PRI. Cohn & Marks. Format: Class, news. News staff: 2; News: 58 hrs wkly. Target aud: General. Spec prog: Folk/blues 7 hrs, jazz 5 hrs wkly. ♦Dorothy Vallillo, gen mgr & progmg dir; Ken Thermon, opns dir; Sharon Faust, dev dir; Rich Egger, news dir; Greg Manfroi, chief of engrg.

***WIUS(FM)**— Feb 1, 1982: 88.3 mhz; 120 w. 83 ft. TL: N40 27 47 W90 41 00. Stereo. Sallee Hall, One University Cir., Western Ill. Univ. 61455-1390. Phone: (309) 298-3217 (request). Fax: (309) 298-2133. Web Site: www.wiu.edu/the dog/. Licensee: Western Illinois University. Cohn & Marks. Format: Progsv new mus, urban contemp, alternative. Target aud: 18-30. Spec prog: Jazz 2 hrs, Sp 3 hrs, blues 4 hrs wkly. ♦Dr. Roger Sadler, stn mgr & progmg dir.

WJEQ(FM)— February 1983: 102.7 mhz; 25 kw. 269 ft. TL: N40 29 00 W90 38 19. Stereo. 31 E. Side Sq. 61455-2248. Phone: (309) 833-2121. Fax: (309) 836-3291. E-mail: wjeq@macomb.com. Web Site: www.wjeq.com. Licensee: Central Illinois Broadcasting. (acq 6-14-89). Format: Classic rock. News staff: one; News: 10 hrs wkly. Target aud: 18-49. Spec prog: Farm one hr wkly. ♦Bruce Foster, pres & chief of engrg; Nancy Foster, gen mgr; Jerry Johnson, stn mgr, gen sls mgr & progmg dir; Brad Choate, news dir.

WKAI(FM)—Listing follows WLRB(AM).

WLRB(AM)— July 4, 1947: 1510 khz; 1 kw-D. TL: N40 29 50 W90 40 30. Box 250, 119 W. Carroll 61455. Phone: (309) 833-5561. Fax: (309) 833-3460. E-mail: wlrb@macomb.com. Web Site: www.radiomacomb.com. Licensee: WPW Broadcasting Inc. (group owner; acq 12-27-99; grpsl). Network: Network: Network: Westwood One, ABC Daytime Direction, Jones Radio Networks. Format: Music of Your Live. News staff: one; News: 6 hrs wkly. Target aud: 45 plus. Spec prog: Farm 1.25 hrs wkly. ♦Don Davis, pres; Vanessa Wetterling, gen mgr & gen sls mgr.

WKAI(FM)—Co-owned with WLRB(AM). June 6, 1966: 100.1 mhz; 3.08 kw. 463 ft. TL: N40 26 57 W90 42 22. Stereo. E-mail: wkai@macomb.com. Web Site: www.radiomacomb.com. Network: ABC Daytime Direction. Format: Adult contemp. News staff: one; News: 5 hrs wkly. Target aud: 35 plus.

WNLF(FM)— 2003: 95.9 mhz; 6 kw. 328 ft. TL: N40 25 03 W90 36 51. c/o WJEQ Radio, 31 E Side Sq. 61455. Phone: (309) 833-2121. Fax: (309) 836-3291. Web Site: www.modernrock959.com. Licensee: Nancy L. Foster. Format: Modern rock. ♦Bruce Foster, pres & chief of engrg; Nancy Foster, gen mgr; Jerry Johnson, gen sls mgr & progmg dir; Brad Choate, news dir.

Macon

WZUS(FM)— May 5, 1977: 100.9 mhz; 6 kw. Ant 328 ft. TL: N39 47 11 W88 59 29. Stereo. 410 N. Water St., Decatur 62523. Phone: (217) 428-4487. Fax: (217) 428-4501. Licensee: The Cromwell Group Inc. of Illinois. Group owner: The Cromwell Group Inc. (acq 4-16-02; $900,000). Network: Westwood One. Pepper & Corazzini. Format: Country. Target aud: General. Spec prog: Farm 5 hrs wkly. ♦Chris Bullock, opns mgr, progmg dir & news dir; Mike Topoll, gen mgr & gen sls mgr; Jerry Scott, chief of engrg.

Mahomet

WGKC(FM)— Dec 15, 1990: 105.9 mhz; 1.25 kw. 512 ft. TL: N40 13 27 W88 17 56. 4108 Fieldstone Rd., Suite C, Champaign 61822. Phone: (217) 367-1195. Fax: (217) 367-3291. Web Site: www.wgkc.net. Licensee: AAA Entertainment Licensing LLC. Group owner: AAA Entertainment L.L.C. (acq 5-31-00; grpsl). Network: ABC. Format: Classic rock. News staff: one. Target aud: 25-54; adult men. ♦John Ginzkey, gen mgr; Linda Bosch, gen sls mgr & prom dir; Marty Booth, progmg dir; Mark Garrett, chief of engrg.

Marion

***WAWJ(FM)**— 2001: 90.1 mhz; 3 kw vert. Ant 344 ft. TL: N37 51 23 W89 08 22. Drawer 3206, Tupelo, MS 38803. Phone: (662) 844-8888. Fax: (662) 842-6791. Web Site: www.afr.net. Licensee: American Family Association. Group owner: American Family Radio Format: Inspirational Christian. ♦Marvin Sanders, gen mgr.

WDDD(AM)—See Johnston City

WDDD-FM— Nov 22, 1970: 107.3 mhz; 50 kw. 500 ft. TL: N37 45 15 W88 56 05. Stereo. Box 127, 1822 Broadcast N. Ctr. 62959. Phone: (618) 997-8123. Fax: (618) 993-2319. Web Site: www.w3dcountry.com. Licensee: Clear Channel Broadcasting Licenses Inc. Group owner: Clear Channel Communications Inc. (acq 1-18-01; grpsl). Format: Country. News staff: 3; News: 5 hrs wkly. Target aud: 25 plus. ♦Jerry Crouse, gen mgr; Paxton Guy, gen sls mgr & progmg dir.

WGGH(AM)— Sept 24, 1949: 1150 khz; 5 kw-D, 44 w-N DA-1. TL: N37 43 47 W88 53 44. Box 340, 1801 E. Main St. 62959. Phone: (618) 993-8102. Phone: (618) 997-2305. Fax: (618) 997-2307. E-mail: wggh@shawneelink.net. Licensee: Vine Broadcasting Inc. (acq 4-7-92; 6-9-92). Network: USA. Format: Southern gospel, relg, talk. News: one hr wkly. Target aud: 18 plus; general. ♦Elaine Gomez, gen mgr & sls; Jean Turner, progmg dir; Johnny Gomez, chief of engrg.

Maroa

WDKR(FM)— May 1996: 107.3 mhz; 3 kw. 456 ft. TL: N39 57 56 W89 03 27. 120 Wildwood Dr., Mt. Zion 62549. Phone: (217) 875-9357. Phone: (217) 864-4141. Fax: (217) 864-4727. Licensee: WDKR Inc. (acq 3-6-02). Format: Oldies. Target aud: 25-54; general. ♦Mary Ellen Burns, gen mgr.

Marseilles

WKOT(FM)— March 1992: 96.5 mhz; 3 kw. 328 ft. TL: N41 18 40 W88 49 07. Stereo. 1 Broadcast Ln., Oglesby 61348. Phone: (815) 434-4000. Fax: (815) 434-4055. E-mail: wajk@ivnet.com. Web Site: wkot.com. Licensee: La Salle County Broadcasting Corp. (group owner; acq 6-99; $550,000). Network: ABC. Format: Oldies. News staff: one; News: 8 hrs wkly. Target aud: 35-54. ♦Joyce McCullough, VP; Peter Miller, pres & gen mgr; Joe Hogan, opns dir.

Marshall

WMMC(FM)— Oct 2, 1989: 105.9 mhz; 2.3 kw. Ant 528 ft. TL: N39 21 09 W87 49 19. Stereo. Box 158 62441. Secondary address: 627 1/2 Archer Ave. 62441. Phone: (217) 826-8017. Fax: (217) 826-8519. Licensee: JDL Broadcasting Inc. (acq 9-10-98; $300,000). Network: ABC. Format: Adult contemp. News: 8 hrs wkly. Target aud: 25-54; career-oriented men and women. ♦J. D. Spangler, pres & gen mgr; Lori Spangler, opns mgr.

Mattoon

WLBH(AM)— Nov 26, 1946: 1170 khz; 5 kw-D, DA. TL: N39 31 05 W88 22 15. Box 1848, N. Rt. 45 (2 mi) 61938-1848. Phone: (217) 234-6464. Fax: (217) 234-6019. E-mail: wlbh@wlbh.com. Web Site: www.wlbh.com. Licensee: Mattoon Broadcasting Co. Group owner: J.R. Livesay Group Network: ABC Information & Entertainment. Format: Farm, news/talk, MOR. News staff: 3; News: 20 hrs wkly. Target aud: 25 plus. Spec prog: Relg 5 hrs wkly. ♦J.R. Livesay II, CEO & pres; S.L. Herrington, CFO; Adam Kennedy, news dir.

WLBH-FM— August 1949: 96.9 mhz; 50 kw. 500 ft. TL: N39 31 02 W88 22 13. Stereo. Web Site: www.wlbh.com. Network: ABC Information & Entertainment. Format: Adult contemp. News staff: 3; News: 18 hrs wkly. Target aud: 25 plus.

***WLKL(FM)**— Jan 20, 1975: 89.9 mhz; 1.3 kw. 203 ft. TL: N39 25 07 W88 22 55. Stereo. 5001 Lakeland Blvd. 61938. Phone: (217) 234-5373. Fax: (217) 234-5506. E-mail: kbeno@lakeland.cc.il.us. Web Site: www.wlkl.net. Licensee: Community College District 517 Lake Land College. Format: CHR, AOR. News staff: one; News: 6 hrs wkly. Target aud: 18-34; general. ♦Bryan Minnigerode, opns mgr & prom dir; Ken Beno, gen mgr & gen sls mgr.

WMCI(FM)— Aug 24, 1989: 101.3 mhz; 14.5 kw. 433 ft. TL: N39 31 39 W88 21 23. Stereo. 209 Lakeland Blvd. 61938. Phone: (217) 235-5624. Phone: (217) 348-9292. Fax: (217) 235-6624. Web Site: www.radiomattoon.com. Licensee: The Cromwell Group Inc. of Illinois. Group owner: The Cromwell Group Inc. Katz Format: Country. News staff: one; News: 10 hrs wkly. Target aud: 25-54. Spec prog: Farm 5 hrs wkly. ♦Bayard H. Walters, pres; Bub McCullough, opns mgr & progmg dir; Carol Floyd, gen mgr, stn mgr & gen sls mgr.

WXET(FM)—(Arcola). Dec 19, 1974: 107.9 mhz; 2.5 kw. Ant 492 ft. TL: N39 34 15 W88 18 17. Stereo. Box 988, 206 S. Willow St., Effingham 62401. Secondary address: 401 Lakeland Blvd. 61938. Phone: (217) 258-6060. Fax: (217) 258-6077. E-mail: info@thexradio.com. Web Site: www.thexradio.com. Licensee: Premier Broadcasting Inc. (acq 8-12-97; $80,000). Format: Adult contemp. News staff: one; News: 10 hrs wkly. Target aud: 25-54. Spec prog: Loc news and sports. ♦David Ring, pres & CFO; Greg Sapp, gen mgr; Tonya Siner, opns VP.

McLeansboro

WMCL(AM)— Jan 26, 1968: 1060 khz; 2.5 kw-D, DA. TL: N38 06 16 W88 33 48. Box 46 A R.R. 1 62859. Phone: (618) 643-2311. Fax: (618) 643-3299. Licensee: Dana Communications Corp. (acq 7-23-98; $245,000). Network: CNN Radio. Bryan Cave. Format: Country, agriculture news. Target aud: 25-65; agricultural community. ♦Dana Withers, pres & gen mgr; Gloria Holland, opns mgr.

Developers & Brokers of Radio Properties

contact American Media Services at our suite:
Philadelphia Marriott Downtown
215-625-2900
843-972-2200
americanmediaservices.com
Charleston, SC
Dallas, TX · Chicago, Il · Austin, TX

American Media Services, LLC

Mendota

WGLC-FM— Sept 1, 1965: 100.1 mhz; 6 kw. 328 ft. TL: N41 32 16 W89 06 25. Stereo. 4162 E. 3rd Rd. 61342. Secondary address: 3905 Progress Blvd., Peru 61354. Phone: (815) 224-2100. Fax: (815) 225-2066. E-mail: wglcfm@theramp.net. Web Site: wglc.net. Licensee: Mendota Broadcasting Inc. Group owner: Studstill Broadcasting (acq 4-8-88). Network: Network: ABC Daytime Direction, Jones Radio Networks. Rep: Rgnl Reps. Booth, Freret, Imlay & Tepper. Format: Country. Target aud: 35 plus. ♦Lee Studstill, CEO & gen mgr; Owen L. Studstill, pres; Cole Studstill, VP; Stuart Hall, opns dir; Chris Turnow, opns mgr.

Metropolis

WMOK(AM)— Feb 4, 1951: 920 khz; 1 kw-D, 73 w-N. TL: N37 09 13 W88 42 30. Stereo. Box 720, 339 Fairgrounds Rd. 62960. Phone: (618) 524-4400. Fax: (618) 524-3133. Licensee: Withers Broadcasting Co. of Paducah LLC. Group owner: Withers Broadcasting Co. (acq 9-11-97; grpsl). Format: Country. News staff: one. Target aud: General. Spec prog: Relg 5 hrs wkly. ♦Rick Lambert, gen mgr; Kathy Duncan, gen sls mgr & rgnl sls mgr; Steve Bunyard, progmg dir; Smokey King, chief of engrg.

WREZ(FM)—Co-owned with WMOK(AM). Dec 12, 1988: 105.5 mhz; 6 kw. 328 ft. TL: N37 10 25 W88 42 29. Stereo. Box 7501, Paducah, KY 42002. Phone: (270) 538-5251. Fax: (270) 415-0599. Format: Adult contemp. ♦Steve Thompson, progmg dir.

WRIK-FM— July 11, 1984: 98.3 mhz; 100 kw. 699 ft. TL: N36 45 09 W88 29 58. Stereo. 6120 Waldo Church Rd. 62960-4903. Phone: (618) 564-2171. Fax: (618) 564-3202. E-mail: K98@hitsandfavs.com. Licensee: Sun Media Inc. Format: Adult contemp. ♦Samuel K. Stratemeyer, pres & gen mgr.

Milford

*****WJCZ(FM)**— 2005: 91.3 mhz; 25 kw. Ant 89 ft. TL: N40 35 07 W87 57 47. CSN International, 4002N. 3300E., Twin Falls, ID 83301. Phone: (208) 734-6633. Fax: (208) 736-1958. E-mail: csn@csnradio.com. Web Site: www.csnradio.com. Licensee: CSN International (group owner). Format: Christian. ♦Ray Garney, gen mgr.

Moline

WFXN(AM)— 1946: 1230 khz; 1 kw-U. TL: N41 28 54 W90 31 49. 3535 E. Kimberly Rd., Davenport, IA 52807. Phone: (563) 344-7000. Fax: (563) 359-8524. Licensee: Citicasters Licenses L.P. Group owner: Clear Channel Communications Inc. (acq 11-15-00; grpsl). Format: Country. News staff: one; News: 6 hrs wkly. Target aud: 25-54; upscale/contemp. Spec prog: Sports 8 hrs, pub affrs 4 hrs, farm one hr wkly. ♦Larry R. Rosmilso, VP & gen mgr; Scott Bitting, sls dir & gen sls mgr; Dan Kennedy, progmg dir; Kevin Allensworth, chief of engrg.

WXLP(FM)— Nov 22, 1970: 96.9 mhz; 50 kw. 499 ft. TL: N41 20 16 W90 22 46. Stereo. 1229 Brady St., Davenport, IA 52803. Phone: (563) 326-2541. Fax: (563) 326-1819. Fax: (319) 326-0844. Web Site: www.97rock.net. Licensee: Cumulus Licensing Corp. Group owner: Cumulus Media Inc. (acq 3-15-00; grpsl). Network: Westwood One. Rep: Allied Radio Partners. Putbrese, Hunsaker & Trent. Format: Active rock. Target aud: 25-54. ♦Lew Dickey, CEO; Julie Derrer, pres & gen sls mgr; Jack Swart, gen mgr; Dave Levora, progmg dir; Andy Andreson, chief of engrg.

Monee

*****WJCG(FM)**— Nov 1, 1995: 88.9 mhz; 100 w vert. 82 ft. TL: N41 27 58 W87 47 35. 820 N. La Salle Dr., Chicago 60610. Phone: (312) 329-4300. Fax: (312) 329-4339. E-mail: mbn@moody.edu. Web Site: www.wjcg.org. Licensee: The Moody Bible Institute of Chicago. (group owner) Southmayd & Miller. Format: Christian, relg. Target aud: General. ♦Dr. Michael Easley, pres; Richard Campbell, CFO; Ed Cannon, exec VP; Robert Neff, VP; John E. Maddex, gen mgr; Doug Hastings, stn mgr; Pamela McCain, opns mgr.

Monmouth

WMOI(FM)—Listing follows WRAM(AM).

WRAM(AM)— May 1957: 1330 khz; 1 kw-D, 50 w-N, DA-2. TL: N40 56 59 W90 34 19. Box 885, 55 Public Sq. 61462. Phone: (309) 734-9452. Phone: (309) 734-2111. Fax: (309) 734-3276. Web Site: www.977wmoi.com. Licensee: WPW Broadcasting Inc. (group owner; acq 12-24-97; $1.7 million with co-located FM). Network: ABC. Format: Country. News staff: 3; News: 20 hrs wkly. Target aud: General; adult, mature. Spec prog: Farm 18 hrs, relg 3 hrs wkly. ♦David Klockenga, gen mgr; Don Davis, pres & gen mgr.

WMOI(FM)—Co-owned with WRAM(AM). Dec 6, 1967: 97.7 mhz; 3.36 kw. 439 ft. TL: N40 53 25 W90 36 31. Stereo. Format: Adult contemp. News staff: 3; News: 40 hrs wkly. Target aud: General.

Monticello

WCZQ(FM)— Jan 18, 1972: 105.5 mhz; 3 kw. 300 ft. TL: N40 02 52 W88 34 22. Stereo. 337 N. Water St., Decatur 62523. Phone: (217) 429-9595. Fax: (217) 423-9764. E-mail: wczq@piatt.com. Web Site: www.wczq.piatt.com. Licensee: NM Licensing LLC. Group owner: NextMedia Group L.L.C. (acq 11-26-01; grpsl). Network: ABC. Format: Urban contemp. News: 5 hrs wkly. Target aud: 25-65; upscale suburban & prosperous farm. Spec prog: Farm 11 hrs wkly. ♦Joel Fletcher, gen mgr & stn mgr; Wendy Tohill, gen sls mgr; Jamie Pendleton, progmg dir; Frank Konwinski, chief of engrg.

Morris

*****WBEQ(FM)**— November 2003: 90.7 mhz; 6 kw. Ant 321 ft. TL: N41 13 48 W88 27 24. 848 E. Grand Ave., Navy Pier, Chicago 60611. Phone: (312) 948-4600. Fax: (312) 832 3100. Web Site: www.chicagopublicradio.org. Licensee: The WBEZ Alliance Inc. Network: NPR. Format: Jazz, news/talk. ♦Merrill Smith, chmn; Donna Moore, CFO; Torey Malatia, pres & gen mgr.

*****WCFL(FM)**— 1962: 104.7 mhz; 50 kw. 496 ft. TL: N41 21 17 W88 29 55. Stereo. 1802 N. Division, Suite 403 60450. Phone: (815) 942-4400. Fax: (815) 942-4401. E-mail: wbgl@wbgl.org. Web Site: www.wbgl.org. Licensee: Illinois District Council of Assembly. (acq 4-16-94). Network: USA. Gammon & Grange. Format: Adult contemp, Christian. Target aud: 24-39. ♦Jeff Scott, gen mgr & progmg dir.

WCSJ(AM)— Jan 15, 1964: . Stn currently dark 1550 khz; 250 w-D, 6 w-N. TL: N41 20 20 W88 25 20. 219 W. Washington St. 60450. Phone: (815) 941-1000. Fax: (815) 941-9300. Licensee: Grundy County Broadcasters Inc. (acq 7-22-97; $425,000). ♦Larry Nelson, pres; Jack Daly, gen mgr; Susan Pellegrini, gen sls mgr.

WCSJ-FM— 1993: 103.1 mhz; 6 kw. Ant 328 ft. TL: N41 17 35 W88 20 04. 219 W. Washington St. 60450. Phone: (815) 941-1000. Fax: (815) 941-9300. Licensee: Grundy County Broadcasters Inc. (acq 11-5-2003; $426,000). Network: ABC. Format: MOR, news/talk. News staff: one; News: 20 hrs wkly. Target aud: 25 plus; community oriented. Spec prog: Farm 10 hrs wkly. ♦Larry Nelson, pres; Jack Daly, gen mgr; Kevin Schramm, opns mgr.

Morrison

WZZT(FM)— Apr 10, 1991: 102.7 mhz; 6 kw. Ant 328 ft. TL: N41 50 16 W89 55 29. 3101 Freeport Rd., Sterling 61081-8612. Phone: (815) 625-3400. Fax: (815) 625-6940. E-mail: wsdr1240@theramp.net. Licensee: Withers Broadcasting Co. of Rock River LLC. Group owner: Withers Broadcasting Co. (acq 1-21-98; grpsl). Network: ABC. Rep: Christal. Format: Classic rock, sports. Target aud: 25-54; adults/men. ♦Brian Zschiesche, gen mgr & gen sls mgr; Kathy Wagner, progmg dir & mus dir; Mary Carlson, news dir; Arnold Taylor, chief of engrg.

Morton

WDQX(FM)— Nov 28, 1976: 102.3 mhz; 6 kw. 300 ft. TL: N40 38 27 W89 24 33. 4234 N. Brandywine Dr., Suite D, Peoria 61614-5507. Phone: (309) 686-0101. Fax: (309) 686-0111. Web Site: www.eagleclassichits.com. Licensee: AAA Entertainment Licensing LLC. Group owner: AAA Entertainment L.L.C. (acq 10-18-00; $2.75 million. with WCNL(FM) Chillicothe). Network: Network: Westwood One, CBS, ABC News/Talk. Format: Classic hits. News staff: one; News: 10 hrs wkly. Target aud: 25 plus; active, affluent males. Spec prog: Relg one hr wkly. ♦Rick Hirschmann, pres & opns mgr; Michael Rea, gen mgr; Becky Riojas, sls dir & gen sls mgr; Scott Robbins, progmg dir; Jon Symmonds, chief of engrg.

Mount Carmel

*****WVJC(FM)**— July 23, 1973: 89.1 mhz; 50 kw. 331 ft. TL: N38 26 29 W87 45 26. Stereo. 2200 College Dr. 62863. Phone: (618) 262-8989. Phone: (618) 262-8641. Fax: (618) 262-7317. E-mail: peachk@iecc.edu. Web Site: www.iecc.cc.il.us/wvjc. Licensee: Illinois Eastern Community Colleges. Arent, Fox, Kintner, Plotkin & Kahn. Format: Educational, alternative. News: 11/4 hrs wkly. Target aud: General; Persons 12-24. ♦Kyle J. Peach, gen mgr.

WVMC(AM)— Dec 1, 1948: 1360 khz; 500 w-D, 20 w-N. TL: N38 26 58 W87 46 12. 606 Market St. 62863. Phone: (618) 262-4102. Fax: (618) 262-4103. E-mail: wsjd@midwest.net. Licensee: Wabash Communications Inc. (acq 12-5-01; $85,000). Format: Adult standards. News staff: 2. Target aud: General; Adults 35 yrs plus. Spec prog: Farm 5 hrs wkly. ♦Kevin Williams, pres; Kevin Madden, gen mgr; Scott Allen, stn mgr.

WYNG(FM)— Nov 28, 1960: 94.9 mhz; 50 kw. Ant 425 ft. TL: N38 23 57 W87 47 18. Stereo. 1133 Lincoln Ave., Evansville, IN 47714. Phone: (812) 425-4226. Fax: (812) 421-0005. Web Site: www.949theriver.com. Licensee: Regent Broadcasting of Evansville/Owensboro Inc. Group owner: Regent Communications Inc. (acq 12-3-2003; grpsl). Network: ESPN Radio. Format: Sports. Target aud: 18-49. ♦Mark Thomas, gen mgr; Mike Sanders, opns mgr; Angie Ross, gen sls mgr; John Story, progmg dir & news dir; Rick Crago, chief of engrg.

Mount Sterling

WPWQ(FM)— September 1995: 106.7 mhz; 25 kw. 328 ft. TL: N39 56 33 W90 57 44. Quincy Regional Airport, 1645 Hwy. 104, Suite G, Quincy 62305. Phone: (217) 224-4653. Fax: (217) 885-3233. E-mail: wpwq106@adams.net. Web Site: www.oldies1067.com. Licensee: WPW Broadcasting Inc. (group owner; acq 12-6-99; $550,000. with WKXQ(FM) Rushville). Format: Oldies. ♦Don Davis, pres; Phil Alexander, gen mgr & gen sls mgr; Chuck Yates, progmg dir.

Mount Vernon

*****WAPO(FM)**— 1997: 90.5 mhz; 500 w. Ant 203 ft. TL: N38 18 39 W88 56 11. (CP: 1.25 kw). Box 3206, American Family Radio, Tupelo, MS 38803. Phone: (662) 844-8888. Fax: (662) 842-6791. Web Site: www.afr.net. Licensee: American Family Association. Group owner: American Family Radio Format: Inspirational Christian. ♦Marvin Sanders, gen mgr; John Riley, progmg mgr.

*****WBMV(FM)**— Sept 30, 1997: 89.7 mhz; 6.2 kw. 492 ft. TL: N38 22 15 W88 55 20. Box 140, Carlinville 62626. Phone: (217) 854-4800. Fax: (217) 854-4810. E-mail: panthony@wibi.org. Licensee: Illinois Bible Institute Inc. (group owner) Format: Adult contemp, Christian mus. Target aud: 29-45. ♦Reverend Larry Griswold, pres; Barry Copeland, gen mgr; Jessica Barton, opns dir & prom dir; Paul Anthony, opns dir & sls dir.

WIBV(FM)— 2001: 102.1 mhz; 10.5 kw. Ant 508 ft. TL: N38 24 07 W89 08 09. 6120 Waldo Church Rd., Metropolis 62960. Phone: (618) 564-2171. Fax: (618) 564-3202. E-mail: K98@hitsandfavs.com. Licensee: Benjamin Stratemeyer (acq 4-26-02; $1.25 million). Format: Christian alt. ♦Benjamin Stratemeyer, gen mgr; Jason Crockett, opns mgr.

Broadcasting & Cable Yearbook 2006

Illinois

WMIX(AM)— 1947: 940 khz; 5 kw-D, 1.5 kw-N, DA-2. TL: N38 21 15 W89 00 29. Box 1508 62864. Secondary address: 3501 Broadway 62864. Phone: (618) 242-3500. Fax: (618) 242-4444. Fax: (618) 242-2490. E-mail: wmix@mvn.net. Licensee: Withers Broadcasting Co. of Illinois LLC. Group owner: Withers Broadcasting Co. (acq 5-30-73). Network: Westwood One. Dennis Kelly. Format: Talk, great memories. News staff: 2; News: 15 hrs wkly. Target aud: 25 plus. Spec prog: Farm 18 hrs wkly. ◆ Dana Withers, gen mgr; W. Russell Withers Jr., pres & sls dir; Nicholas Lemay, news dir.

WMIX-FM— 1946: 94.1 mhz; 50 kw. 550 ft. TL: N38 22 14 W88 55 20. Stereo. Format: C&W. ◆ Russell Withers, CEO; Craig Warner, news dir.

*WVSI(FM)—Not on air, target date: unknown: 88.9 mhz; 1.9 kw horiz, 4 kw vert. Ant 338 ft. TL: N38 21 13 W88 56 32. SIUC Broadcasting Service, 1003 Communications Bldg., Southern Illinois University, Carbondale 62901. Phone: (618) 453-4343. Fax: (618) 453-6186. Licensee: The Board of Trustees of Southern Illinois University. ◆ Candis S. Isberner, CEO & stn mgr; Mike Zelten, opns mgr; Renee Dillard, dev dir.

Mount Zion

WXFM(FM)— October 1984: 99.3 mhz; 1.15 kw. 495 ft. TL: N39 48 35 W88 59 31. Stereo. 120 Wildwood 62549. Phone: (217) 864-4141. Fax: (217) 864-4727. Licensee: Technicom Inc. Format: Adult contemp. News: 5 hrs wkly. Target aud: Free spending, affluent adults. ◆ Mary Ellen Burns, pres & gen mgr.

Murphysboro

WINI(AM)— Sept 15, 1954: 1420 khz; 420w-D, 500 w-N, DA-N. TL: N37 45 30 W89 14 02. 1677 Business Hwy. 13 62966. Phone: (618) 684-2128. Fax: (618) 687-4318. E-mail: wini@intrnet.net. Licensee: Radio Station WINI. (acq 7-28-00). Network: UPI. Eugene T. Smith. Format: News/talk. News: 22 hrs wkly. Target aud: 25-59. Spec prog: Relg 6 hrs wkly. ◆ Dale Adkins, gen mgr, gen sls mgr & chief of engrg; Nancy Engel, opns mgr.

WTAO(FM)—Licensed to Murphysboro. See Carbondale

Naperville

WBIG(AM)—See Aurora

WERV-FM—See Aurora

*WONC(FM)— July 1, 1968: 89.1 mhz; 1.5 w. 163 ft. TL: N41 46 45 W88 08 25. Stereo. Box 3063 60566. Secondary address: 30 N. Brainard St. 60566. Phone: (630) 637-8989. Fax: (630) 637-5900. E-mail: jvmadormo@noctrl.edu. Web Site: www.wonc.org. Licensee: North Central College. Format: Rock/AOR. Target aud: 18-34. Spec prog: Relg 4 hrs, alternative 10 hrs wkly. ◆ John Madormo, gen mgr.

Nashville

WNSV(FM)— July 10, 1994: 104.7 mhz; 3 kw. 328 ft. TL: N38 20 38 W89 20 59. 168 E. St. Louis St. 62263. Phone: (618) 327-4444. Fax: (618) 327-3716. E-mail: wnsvfm@papadocs.com. Licensee: Dana K. Withers. (acq 1-16-92; $60,000; 2-10-92). Format: Adult contemp. Target aud: 30 plus. ◆ Dana Withers, pres & gen mgr; Gloria Holland, opns mgr.

Neoga

WHQQ(FM)— September 1996: 98.9 mhz; 2.9 kw. Ant 482 ft. TL: N39 14 59 W88 22 48. Stereo. Box 150846, The Cromwell Group Inc., Nashville, TN 37215. Secondary address: 209 Lakeland Blvd., Mattoon 61938. Phone: (615) 361-7560. Phone: (217) 235-5624 (stn). Fax: (615) 366-4313. Fax: (217) 235-6624 (stn).Westwood One Oldies Licensee: WSHY Inc. Group owner: The Cromwell Group Inc. Network: Westwood One. Format: Oldies. News: 15 hrs wkly. Target aud: 25-54; adults. Spec prog: Farm 7 hrs wkly. ◆ Bayard Walters, chmn & pres; Tommy Crocker, CFO; Carol Floyd, gen mgr & stn mgr; Bub McCullough, opns mgr.

Newton

WIKK(FM)— May 4, 1992: 103.5 mhz; 25 kw. 328 ft. TL: N38 59 23 W88 11 19. Stereo. 4667 Radio Tower Ln., Olney 62450. Phone: (618) 783-8000. Phone: (618) 392-2156. Fax: (618) 783-4040. E-mail: wikk1035@psbnewton.com. Web Site: www.1035theeagle.com. Licensee: V.L.N. Broadcasting Inc. Group owner: Key Broadcasting Inc. (acq 6-25-02; $600,000). Classic rock (66). News staff: one; News: 8 hrs wkly. Target aud: 25-49. ◆ Terry Forcht, CEO; Deb Burnett, stn mgr; Mike Shipman, opns VP, progmg dir & mus dir.

Normal

WBNQ(FM)—See Bloomington

*WGLT(FM)— Feb 4, 1966: 89.1 mhz; 25 kw. 377 ft. TL: N40 28 46 W89 03 12. Stereo. Box 8910, Illinois State Univ. 61790-8910. Phone: (309) 438-2255. Fax: (309) 438-7870. E-mail: wglt@ilstu.edu. Web Site: www.wglt.org. Licensee: Illinois State University. Network: NPR. Dow, Lohnes & Albertson. Format: Jazz, blues, pub affrs. News staff: 3; News: 40 hrs wkly. Target aud: 35-54. Spec prog: Folk 6 hrs, musical theater 3 hrs wkly. ◆ Bruce Bergethon, gen mgr; Kevin Conlin, opns dir & pub affrs dir; Kathryn Carter, dev dir; Mike McCurdy, progmg dir; Jon Norton, mus dir; Willis Kern, news dir; Mark Hill, chief of engrg.

WIHN(FM)— Dec 21, 1973: 96.7 mhz; 3.9 kw. Ant 410 ft. TL: N40 28 34 W89 02 02. Stereo. 108 Boeykens Pl. 61761. Phone: (309) 888-4496. Fax: (309) 452-9677. Web Site: www.967irock.com. Licensee: AAA Entertainment Licensing LLC. Group owner: AAA Entertainment L.L.C. (acq 8-7-01). Network: ABC. Rep: Christal. Putbrese, Hunsaker & Trent. Format: Rock. News staff: one; News: 9 hrs wkly. Target aud: 18-44. ◆ John Maguire, CEO & pres; Peter Ottmar, chmn; Patti Dunsbach, gen mgr; Ron West, opns mgr; Dean Peterson, sls dir; Fred Koebel, sls dir; Ed Chandler, prom dir & progmg dir; Ben Stone, mus dir; Jon Symmonds, chief of engrg.

WVMG(FM)— Aug 12, 2005: 100.7 mhz; 4.2 kw. Ant 344 ft. TL: N40 27 08 W88 57 48. 520 N. Center St., Bloomington 61701-2902. Licensee: Connoisseur Media LLC. Shaw Pittman LLP. Format: Adult contemp. ◆ Larry Weiss, gen mgr; Bob Vandergrift, progmg dir.

Oak Lawn

WNWI(AM)— Dec 31, 1965: 1080 khz; 1.9 kw-D. TL: N41 38 36 W87 38 45. Box 34978, Riverdale 60827. Secondary address: 934 W. 138th St., Riverdale 60827. Phone: (708) 201-9600. Fax: (248) 557-2950. E-mail: infomacja@wietrzneradio.com. Licensee: Birach Broadcasting Corp. (group owner; (acq 6-30-95; $375,000). Format: Foreign language, Pol. ◆ Sima Birach, pres & gen mgr; John Marinocovich, progmg dir.

Oak Park

WPNA(AM)— Oct 7, 1950: 1490 khz; 1 kw-U. TL: N41 52 52 W87 47 38. Box 3878 60303. Secondary address: 408 S. Oak Park Ave. 60302. Phone: (708) 848-8980. Phone: (708) 524-9762. Fax: (708) 848-9220. E-mail: email@wpna1490am.com. Web Site: www.wpna1490am.com. Licensee: Alliance Communications Inc. (acq 5-1-87). Format: Ethnic, Polish. News: 7 hrs wkly. Target aud: General. Spec prog: Polka 15 hrs, gospel 2 hrs, relg 4 hrs, Irish 4 hrs, Ukranian 2 hrs wkly. ◆ Frank Spula, pres; Emily Leszczynski, gen mgr; Alan Kearns, chief of opns; Jerry Obrecki, gen sls mgr; Len Petrulis, progmg mgr & news dir.

WVAZ(FM)— Oct 17, 1950: 102.7 mhz; 6 kw. 1,170 ft. TL: N41 53 56 W87 37 23. (CP: 9 kw). Stereo. 233 N. Michigan Ave., 28th Fl., Chicago 60601. Phone: (312) 540-2000. Fax: (312) 938-4404. Web Site: www.wvaz.com. Licensee: AMFM Broadcasting Licenses LLC. Group owner: Clear Channel Communications Inc. (acq 8-30-2000; grpsl). Network: UPI. Format: Black adult contemp. News staff: 2; News: one hr wkly. Target aud: 25-54; Black adults. Spec prog: Gospel 4 hrs, pub affrs 2 hrs wkly. ◆ Anita Genes, gen mgr, gen sls mgr & natl sls mgr; Elroy Smith, opns mgr; Angela Fleming, prom dir; Armando Rivera, mus dir; Wanda Wells, news dir & pub affrs dir; Tim Wright, chief of engrg.

Oglesby

WALS(FM)— February 1993: 102.1 mhz; 1.35 kw. 482 ft. TL: N41 18 05 W88 57 11. 3905 Progress Blvd., Peru 61354. Phone: (815) 224-2100. Fax: (815) 224-2066. E-mail: walls102@theradiogroup.net. Licensee: Laco Radio Inc. Group owner: Studstill Broadcasting Booth, Freret, Imlay & Tepper. Format: Country. News: 5 hrs wkly. Target aud: 25-55. ◆ Doris A. Studstill, CEO, pres & gen mgr; Cole C. Studstill, CFO; Lamar Studstill, chmn & stn mgr; Judy Miller, gen sls mgr.

Olney

*WPTH(FM)— July 1992: 88.1 mhz; 133 w. 203 ft. TL: N38 41 50 W88 02 15. (CP: 720 w). 817 Orchard Dr. 62450. Phone: (618) 863-2765. Fax: (618) 395-7064. Licensee: Olney Voice of Christian Faith Inc. Format: Christian, talk. ◆ Dr. Thomas E. Benson, pres & gen mgr; Ron James, VP.

WSEI(FM)—Listing follows WVLN(AM).

*WUSI(FM)— Nov 1, 1992: 90.3 mhz; 25 kw. 472 ft. TL: N38 50 18 W88 07 46. Stereo. Rm. 1003, Communications Bldg., Carbondale 62901-6602. Phone: (618) 453-4343. Fax: (618) 453-6186. Web Site: www.wsiu.org. Licensee: Southern Illinois University. (group owner) Network: Network: NPR, PRI. Cohn & Marks. Format: Class, news. News staff: 3; News: 36 hrs wkly. Target aud: 35-64; highly educated, upper income, socially conscious. ◆ Candis Isberner, CEO; Jeff Williams, stn mgr, news dir & chief of engrg; Mike Zelten, opns mgr.

WVLN(AM)— Nov 11, 1947: 740 khz; 250 w-D, 7 w-N. TL: N38 42 00 W88 04 53. Box L, Radio Tower Rd. 62450. Phone: (618) 393-2156. Fax: (618) 392-4536. Licensee: V.L.N. Broadcasting Inc. Group owner: Key Broadcasting Inc. (acq 7-21-87; $1.12 million with co-located FM; 6-8-87). Network: ABC. Rep: Rgnl Reps. Format: News/talk. Spec prog: Farm 10 hrs wkly. ◆ Terry E. Forcht, pres; Mike Lowe, gen mgr, sls VP & adv VP; Mike Shipman, opns mgr; Deb Burnett, sls dir & prom VP; Mark Weiler, news dir; Kirk Wallace, chief of engrg.

WSEI(FM)—Co-owned with WVLN(AM). 1953: 92.9 mhz; 50 kw. 552 ft. TL: N38 42 00 W88 04 49. Stereo. Format: Country. Target aud: 25-54. ◆ Mike Lowe, stn mgr; Mike Shipman, pub affrs dir.

Oregon

WSEY(FM)— Dec 27, 1999: 95.7 mhz; 3.2 kw. Ant 358 ft. TL: N42 04 19 W89 25 08. c/o WIXN-AM-FM, 1460 S. College Ave., Dixon 61021. Phone: (815) 288-3341. Fax: (815) 284-1017. E-mail: wixnstaff@wixn.com. Licensee: NewRadio Group LLC (group owner; acq 12-20-2002; grpsl). Format: Oldies. ◆ Allan Knickrehm, gen mgr & gen sls mgr; Steve Marco, progmg dir; Danette Dallgas-Frey, news dir; Mark Baker, chief of engrg.

Ottawa

WCMY(AM)— Mar 5, 1952: 1430 khz; 500 w-D, 38 w-N. TL: N41 20 53 W88 48 15. 216 W. Lafayette 61350. Phone: (815) 434-6050. Fax: (815) 434-5311. E-mail: info@wcmy1430.com. Licensee: NewRadio Group LLC. (group owner; (acq 12-20-2002; grpsl). Network: Network: CBS Radio, Westwood One. Rep: Interep. Format: Adult contemp, news/talk. News staff: 2; News: 35 hrs wkly. Target aud: 25 plus. Spec prog: Farm 9 hrs wkly.

WRKX(FM)—Co-owned with WCMY(AM). Sept 1, 1964: 95.3 mhz; 4.3 kw. 200 ft. TL: N41 23 00 W88 51 16. Stereo. Format: Modern adult contemp.

*WWGN(FM)— Sept 24, 1994: 88.9 mhz; 1.5 kw. 646 ft. TL: N41 16 51 W88 56 13. Stereo. 807 La Salle St. 61350. Phone: (815) 433-6000. Fax: (815) 433-6100. E-mail: wwgn@afo.net. Web Site: www.afr.net. Licensee: American Family Association Group owner: American Family Radio (acq 1-4-99; $250,000). Format: Relg, educ. News staff: 2; News: 14 hrs wkly. Target aud: General. ◆ Tim Wildmon, pres; Dan Hennenfent, gen mgr, stn mgr, progmg dir & engrg dir.

Palatine

*WHCM(FM)— 2003: 88.3 mhz; 100 w. Ant 56 ft. TL: N42 04 54 W88 04 23. William Rainey Harper College, 1200 W. Algonquin Rd. 60067. Phone: (847) 925-6000. Phone: (847) 925-6488. Web Site: www.harpercollege.edu. Licensee: William Rainey Harper College. Format: College, div. ◆ Dave Dluger, gen mgr.

Pana

WMKR(FM)— July 12, 1996: 94.3 mhz; 5.6 kw. Ant 341 ft. TL: N39 27 08 W89 17 10. Stereo. Box 169, 918 E. Park St., Taylorville 62568-0169. Phone: (217) 824-3395. Fax: (217) 824-3301. Web Site: www.randyradio.com. Licensee: Miller Communications Inc. Group owner: Miller Media Group Network: Westwood One. Womble, Carlyle, Sandridge & Rice. Format: Country. Target aud: 25-54. ◆ Randal J. Miller, pres & gen mgr; Kami Payne, stn mgr.

Stations in the U.S. Illinois

*WZRS(FM)—Not on air, target date: unknown: 89.3 mhz; 500 w. Ant 233 ft. TL: N39 22 19 W89 04 51. Drawer 3206, Tupelo, MS 38803. Phone: (662) 844-8888. Fax: (662) 842-6791. Web Site: www.afr.net. Licensee: American Family Association. Group owner: American Family Radio. Format: Inspirational Christian.

Paris

WACF(FM)—Listing follows WPRS(AM).

WPRS(AM)— 1951: 1440 khz; 1 kw-D, 250 w-N. TL: N39 36 21 W87 43 35. Stereo. Box 277, Rt. 133 W. 61944. Phone: (217) 465-6336. Fax: (217) 466-1408. E-mail: wacf@comwares.net. Licensee: P.R.S. Broadcasting Inc. Group owner: Key Broadcasting Inc. (acq 1-28-94; $675,000; 4-11-94). Format: Talk, sports, news. News staff: one. Target aud: General. ♦Terry E. Forcht, pres; Phil Johnson, gen mgr & gen sls mgr; Lisa Adams, opns mgr; Jason Murphy, progmg dir; Teresa Keys, news dir.

WACF(FM)—Co-owned with WPRS(AM). 1952: 98.5 mhz; 50 kw. 500 ft. TL: N39 36 21 W87 43 35. Stereo. Format: Modern country. Target aud: 18 plus. ♦Al Larcher, progmg dir.

Park Forest

WRZA(FM)— Jan 5, 1962: 99.9 mhz; 50 kw. Ant 492 ft. TL: N41 18 04 W87 49 35. Stereo. 6012 S Pulaski Rd, Chicago 60629. Phone: (773) 767-1000. Fax: (773) 767-1100. Web Site: www.ninechicago.com. Licensee: WCLR Inc. Group owner: Newsweb Corp. (acq 3-16-2004; $24 million. with WNDZ(AM) Portage, IN). Format: Var. News staff: one. Target aud: 18-49. ♦Harvey Wells, gen mgr.

Park Ridge

*WMTH(FM)— May 22, 1960: 90.5 mhz; 100 w. 103 ft. TL: N42 02 14 W87 51 30. 2601 W. Dempster St. 60068. Phone: (847) 692-8484. Phone: (847) 692-8266. Fax: (847) 692-8499. Licensee: Board of Education School District No. 207. Network: UPI. Format: Eclectic. Spec prog: Class 4 hrs, jazz 2 hrs wkly. ♦Jim Wunderlich, gen mgr; Ana Bolotin, stn mgr; Dom Burdi, mus dir; Vicki Chan, news dir.

Paxton

WPXN(FM)— Oct 1, 1984: 104.9 mhz; 3 kw. 298 ft. TL: N40 27 11 W88 06 11. 361 N. Railroad Ave. 60957. Phone: (217) 379-4333. Phone: (217) 892-9796. Fax: (217) 379-4334. Licensee: Paxton Broadcasting Corp. (acq 7-84). Network: CBS. Rep: Roslin, Borsari & Paxson. Format: Adult contemp. News staff: one; News: 8 hrs wkly. Target aud: 25-49. Spec prog: Farm 10 hrs wkly. ♦Dan Daugherity, pres, gen mgr & gen sls mgr; Joel Cluver, stn mgr & progmg VP.

Pekin

*WBNH(FM)— Dec. 1988: 88.5 mhz; 8.8 kw. 524 ft. TL: N40 38 38 W89 32 38. Stereo. Box 1132 61555. Phone: (309) 347-8850. Fax: (309) 353-8850. E-mail: wbnh@wbnh.org. Web Site: www.wbnh.org. Licensee: Central Illinois Radio Fellowship Inc. Network: Moody. Southmayd & Miller. Format: Relg. Target aud: General. ♦Don Rice, pres; Scott Krus, stn mgr.

*WCIC(FM)— Nov 2, 1983: 91.5 mhz; 35 kw. 338 ft. TL: N40 33 24 W89 34 04. Stereo. 3902 W. Baring Trace, Peoria 61615. Phone: (309) 282-9191. Fax: (309) 282-9192. E-mail: wcic@wcicfm.org. Web Site: www.wcicfm.org. Licensee: Illinois Bible Institute. (group owner) Format: Relg, adult contemp, Christian. News: 2 hrs wkly. Target aud: 25-49. ♦Dave Brooks, gen mgr; Grayson Long, progmg dir; Debbie McMorrow, mus dir; Morgan Grammer, chief of engrg.

WGLO(FM)—Listing follows WVEL(AM).

WVEL(AM)— Apr 21, 1948: 1140 khz; 5 kw-D, 3.2 kw-CH. TL: N40 36 08 W89 37 32. 28 S. 4th St. 61554. Phone: (309) 346-2134. Fax: (309) 346-2662. Licensee: Regent Broadcasting of Peoria Inc. Group owner: Regent Communications Inc. (acq 7-6-01; grpsl). Format: Relg, Black. Target aud: General. ♦Ric Morgan, opns VP & opns mgr; Robert Caruth, gen mgr, sls VP, sls dir, progmg VP & progmg dir; Jerry Scott, chief of engrg.

WGLO(FM)—Co-owned with WVEL(AM). Nov 18, 1971: 95.5 mhz; 25 kw. 620 ft. TL: N40 36 23 W89 32 20. Stereo. 120 Eaton St., Peoria 61603-4217. Phone: (309) 676-5000. Fax: (309) 676-2600. Web Site: www.955glo.com. Rep: D & R Radio. Format: Classic rock. Target aud: 18-49. ♦Steve Young, gen sls mgr; Matt Bahan, progmg dir.

WXCL(FM)— 1973: 104.9 mhz; 3 kw. 328 ft. TL: N40 38 34 W89 32 28. Stereo. 4234 Brandywine Dr., Suite D, Peoria 61614-5507. Phone: (309) 686-0101. Fax: (309) 686-0111. E-mail: studio@wxcl.com. Web Site: www.wxcl.com. Licensee: AAA Entertainment Licensing L.L.C. Group owner: AAA Entertainment L.L.C. (acq 10-31-02; swap for WPMJ(FM) Chillicothe). McGavren Guild. Format: Country. News staff: 2. Target aud: 25-54; affluent adults. ♦Michael Rea, gen mgr; Rick Hirschmann, pres, CFO & opns mgr.

Peoria

*WCBU(FM)— January 1970: 89.9 mhz; 50 kw. 650 ft. TL: N40 37 44 W89 34 12. Stereo. 1501 W. Bradley Ave. 61625. Phone: (309) 677-3690. Fax: (309) 677-3462. E-mail: wcbu@bradley.edu. Web Site: www.wcbufm.org. Licensee: Bradley University. Network: NPR. Format: Class, news. ♦Thomas Hunt, gen mgr; Jackie Benitz, opns mgr; Heather Binder, gen sls mgr; Nathan Irwin, progmg dir; Jonathan Ahl, news dir; David Schenk, chief of engrg.

WGLO(FM)—See Pekin

WIRL(AM)— 1947: 1290 khz; 5 kw-U, DA-2. TL: N40 37 24 W89 35 27. Stereo. 331 Fulton St., Suite 1200 61602. Phone: (309) 637-3700. Fax: (309) 686-8655. Web Site: www.foxsportsradio1290.com. Licensee: Monterey Licenses LLC. Group owner: JMP Media LLC (acq 3-25-2003; grpsl). Rep: Christal. Format: Sports. Target aud: 25-54; men. ♦David J. Benjamin III, pres; Mike Wild, gen mgr; Mark Bretsck, sls dir & prom mgr; Brian Rowell, gen sls mgr; John Malone, progmg dir; Dave Dahl, news dir; Wayne Miller, chief of engrg.

WSWT(FM)—Co-owned with WIRL(AM). 1964: 106.9 mhz; 50 kw. 480 ft. TL: N40 43 22 W89 30 40. Stereo. 331 Fulton St., 12th Fl. 61602. Phone: (309) 637-3700. Fax: (309) 673-7538. Web Site: www.literock107.com. Format: Adult contemp. News staff: 3; News: 1.25 hrs wkly. Target aud: 25-54. ♦Jack Everette, CEO; Randy Rundle, opns dir & progmg dir; Mark Bretsch, gen sls mgr; Stephanie Aaron, prom dir; Dave Dahl, news dir.

WMBD(AM)— 1927: 1470 khz; 5 kw-U, DA-2. TL: N40 34 22 W89 32 00. Stereo. 331 Fulton St., Suite 1200 61602. Phone: (309) 637-3700. Fax: (309) 673-9562. Web Site: www.1470wmbd.com. Licensee: Monterey Licenses LLC. Group owner: JMP Media LLC (acq 3-25-2003; grpsl). Network: ABC Information & Entertainment. Rep: Christal. Shaw Pittman. Format: News/talk. News staff: 5; News: 40 hrs wkly. Target aud: 35-64; upscale, well educated, professional. Spec prog: Farm 15 hrs wkly. ♦David J. Benjamin III, pres; Mike Wild, gen mgr & stn mgr.

WPBG(FM)—Co-owned with WMBD(AM). 1947: 93.3 mhz; 41 kw. 548 ft. TL: N40 38 07 W89 32 19. Stereo. Web Site: www.bigoldies933.com. Format: Oldies. Target aud: 25-54; baby boomers.

WOAM(AM)— Feb 8, 1960: 1350 khz; 1 kw-U, DA-2. TL: N40 35 41 W89 35 40. Box 180 61604. Secondary address: 3641 Meadowbrook Rd. 61604. Phone: (309) 685-1350. Fax: (309) 685-9095. E-mail: studio@1350woam.com. Web Site: www.1350woam.com. Licensee: Kelly Communications Inc. (acq 12-1-86; $500,000;. FTR: 9-29-86). Network: ABC. Rep: McGavren Guild. Format: Adult standards. News staff: 2; News: 10 hrs wkly. Target aud: 45 plus; upscale business leaders. Spec prog: Jazz 2 hrs wkly. ♦Bob Kelly, stn mgr & news dir.

WPEO(AM)— 1946: 1020 khz; 1 kw-D. TL: N40 41 53 W89 31 31. 1708 Highview Rd., East Peoria 61611. Secondary address: Box 1 61650. Phone: (309) 698-9736. Fax: (309) 698-9740. E-mail: wpeo@wpeo.com. Web Site: www.wpeo.com. Licensee: Pinebrook Foundation Inc. (acq 1-6-70). Wood, Maines & Brown. Format: Relg, talk. Target aud: 35 plus. ♦Richard T. Crawford, pres; Robert Ulrich, gen mgr; Roger Bennington, gen sls mgr; Nelson Hostetler, progmg dir.

WPMJ(FM)—See Chillicothe

WVEL(AM)—See Pekin

WXCL(FM)—See Pekin

WXMP(FM)— May 14, 1972: 105.7 mhz; 32 kw. Ant 555 ft. TL: N40 43 25 W89 29 04. Stereo. 4234 Brandywine Dr., Suite D 61614. Phone: (309) 686-0101. Fax: (309) 686-0111. E-mail: studio@mix1057.com. Web Site: www.mix1057.com. Licensee: AAA Entertainment Licensing LLC. Group owner: AAA Entertainment L.L.L. (acq 4-18-00; $7.5 million). Rep: Christal. Format: Hot adult contemp. ♦Rick Hirschmann, pres; Michael Rea, gen mgr & opns mgr.

WZPW(FM)— November 1992: 92.3 mhz; 19.2 kw. Ant 374 ft. TL: N40 47 10 W89 47 01. 4234 N. Brandywine Dr., Suite D 61614-5507. Phone: (309) 686-0101. Fax: (309) 686-0111. E-mail: studio@power92.net. Web Site: www.power92.net. Licensee: B&G Broadcasting Inc. Group owner: AAA Entertainment L.L.C. (acq 10-4-00; $2.3 million). Format: Top 40, CHR. ♦Michael Rea, gen mgr; Rick Hirschmann, pres & opns mgr.

Peru

WBZG(FM)— Mar 15, 1970: 100.9 mhz; 3 kw. 328 ft. TL: N41 18 09 W89 14 11. Stereo. 3905 Progress Blvd. 61354. Phone: (815) 224-2100. Fax: (815) 224-2066. E-mail: wbzg@theradiogroup.net. Web Site: wbzg.net. Licensee: Mendota Broadcasting Inc. Group owner: Studstill Broadcasting (acq 7-17-97; $700,000. with WIVQ(FM) Spring Valley). Rep: Rgnl Reps. Booth, Freret, Imlay & Tepper. Format: Classic rock. News staff: 2. Target aud: 18-54. ♦Lamar Studstill, chmn; Cole Charles Studstill, CFO & VP; Owen L. Studstill, CEO, pres & gen mgr; Doris Studstill, opns VP; Cole Studstill, opns mgr.

WXAN(FM)—See Ava

Petersburg

*WLWJ(FM)— Oct 7, 2001: 88.1 mhz; 6 kw. 328 ft. TL: N40 00 05 W89 41 49. 600 W. Mason St., Springfield 62702. Phone: (217) 528-2300. Fax: (217) 528-2400. Web Site: www.wluj.org. Licensee: Cornerstone Community Radio Inc. Format: Christian talk, inspirational music. ♦Richard Van Zandt, gen mgr; John McBride, stn mgr & progmg dir; Howard Fouks, opns mgr; Richard Beaman, gen sls mgr.

WYVR(FM)— March 1987: 97.7 mhz; 6 kw. Ant 328 ft. TL: N40 00 05 W09 41 49. (CP: N39 54 35 W89 43 01). Stereo. Box 460, Springfield 62705. Phone: (217) 629-7077. Fax: (217) 629-7952. Web Site: www.theriver.fm. Licensee: Long-Nine Inc. Group owner: The Mid-West Family Broadcast Group (acq 7-27-01; $3 million). Shaw Pittman. Format: CHR. Target aud: 18-34; female. Spec prog: Relg 5 hrs wkly. ♦Glen Gardner, pres & gen mgr; Dave Doetsch, gen sls mgr; Kellie Michaels, progmg dir; Jim Leach, news dir; Greg Stephens, chief of engrg.

Pittsfield

WBBA(AM)— Dec 1, 1954: . Stn currently dark 1580 khz; 250 w-D, 15 w-N. TL: N39 34 53 W90 47 52. Stereo. Box 150 62363. Licensee: Brown Radio Group Inc. (acq 1996; with co-located FM). ♦Gary Brown, pres.

WBBA-FM— Aug 1, 1966: 97.5 mhz; 10 kw. Ant 300 ft. TL: N39 34 53 W90 47 52. Stereo. Box 312 62363. Phone: (217) 285-5975. Fax: (217) 285-5977. Licensee: DJ Two Rivers Radio Inc. (acq 1-9-2004;

Broadcasting & Cable Yearbook 2006

D-179

Illinois

$320,000. with WJBM(AM) Jerseyville). Format: Country. Target aud: General. ◆ David Fuhler, gen mgr.

*WIPA(FM)— Jan 4 1993: 89.3 mhz; 50 kw. 492 ft. TL: N39 43 25 W90 41 09. Stereo. Box 19243, CBM-130, Univ. of Illinois at Springfield, Springfield 62703-5407. Phone: (217) 206-6516. Fax: (217) 206-6527. E-mail: wuis@uis.org. Web Site: www.wuis.org. Licensee: University of Illinois at Springfield. Network: Network: NPR, PRI. Dow, Lohnes & Albertson. Format: News, class, jazz. News staff: 4; News: 45 hrs wkly. Target aud: 25-54. ◆ Bradley Swanson, gen mgr; Sinta Seiber, opns mgr; Lisa Clemmons Stott, dev dir; Jim Dunn, engrg mgr & chief of engrg.

Plano

WSPY-FM— Jan 19, 1974: 107.1 mhz; 1.5 kw. 466 ft. TL: N41 39 55 W88 34 34. Stereo. One Broadcast Ctr. 60545. Phone: (630) 552-1000. Fax: (630) 552-9300. E-mail: wspy@nelsonmultimedia.net. Licensee: Nelson Enterprises Inc. Network: ABC Information & Entertainment. Format: Easy listening. Target aud: 25-54. Spec prog: Farm 18 hrs wkly. ◆ Larry Nelson, pres & opns mgr; Carol Barrows, CFO; Pam Nelson, gen mgr; Beth Pierre, gen sls mgr & progmg dir; Lane Lindstrom, chief of engrg.

Polo

WLLT(FM)— Dec 12, 1989: 107.7 mhz; 1.35 kw. 476 ft. TL: N41 53 52 W89 36 20. Stereo. 260 Illinois Rt. 2, Dixon 61021. Phone: (815) 284-1077. Licensee: Sauk Valley Broadcasting Co. Format: Soft adult contemp. ◆ Bob Burns, gen mgr; Bob Thomas Burns, pres & gen mgr; Andy Jackson, opns mgr.

Pontiac

*WPJC(FM)— 2003: 88.3 mhz; 500 w. Ant 207 ft. TL: N40 56 42 W88 38 46. 150 Lincoln Way, Suite 2001, Valparaiso, IN 46383. Phone: (219) 548-8956. Fax: (219) 548-5808. E-mail: wpjc@csnradio.com. Licensee: CSN International (group owner; acq 12-31-2001; $25,000. for CP). Format: Christian talk. ◆ Jim Motshagen, gen mgr.

WTRX-FM— July 1969: 93.7 mhz; 12 kw. Ant 472 ft. TL: N40 45 27 W88 37 40. Stereo. 315 N. Mill St. 61764. Phone: (815) 844-6101. Fax: (815) 844-7235. Web Site: www.thunder937.com. Licensee: Livingston County Broadcasters Inc. Group owner: Regent Communications Inc. (acq 5-12-2004; grpsl). Format: Classic rock. News staff: one. Target aud: 25-54. ◆ Red Pitcher, gen mgr & gen sls mgr.

Princeton

*WPRC(FM)—Not on air, target date: unknown: 88.3 mhz; 150 w vert. Ant 315 ft. TL: N41 16 53 W89 35 12. c/o WCIC, 3902 S. Baring Trace, Peoria 61615. Phone: (309) 282-9191. Fax: (309) 282-9192. E-mail: wcic@wcicfm.org. Licensee: Illinois Bible Institute Inc. (group owner). Format: Christian talk. ◆ Dave Brooks, gen mgr; Tracey Moushon, prom dir; Debbie McMorrow, progmg dir.

WZOE(AM)— Oct 25, 1961: 1490 khz; 1 kw-U. TL: N41 21 08 W89 28 05. Box 69, Broadcast Ctr. 61356. Secondary address: S. Main St. 61356. Phone: (815) 875-8014. Licensee: WZOE Inc. (group owner; acq 11-1-73). Network: CBS. Shaw Pittman. Format: News/talk, sports. News staff: 3; News: 84 hrs wkly. Spec prog: Farm 15 hrs wkly. ◆ Steve Samet, pres & gen mgr; Paul Bomleny, opns dir; Chris Compton, sls dir; Tommy Rose, progmg dir; Jennifer Nagle, news dir; Nedda Simon, pub affrs dir; Greg Stephens, chief of engrg.

WZOE-FM— July 1, 1980: 98.1 mhz; 6 kw. 300 ft. TL: N41 21 49 W89 23 36. Stereo. Format: Oldies. News staff: 3; News: 8 hrs wkly.

Quincy

KGRC(FM)—See Hannibal, MO

KPCR(AM)— Dec 13, 1966: 1530 khz; 1.4 kw-D, 290 w-CH. TL: N39 55 51 W91 25 46. Stereo. Box 431, Bowling Green 63334. Secondary address: 15894 Hwy. 54, Bowling Green 63334. Phone: (573) 324-2283. Fax: (573) 324-2670. Licensee: Bick Broadcasting Co. (group owner; acq 10-14-2003). Network: UPI. Format: Country. News: 12 hrs wkly. Target aud: General; fun-loving, adult listeners. Spec prog: Farm 9 hrs wkly.

WCOY(FM)—Listing follows WTAD(AM).

*WGCA-FM— Sept 20, 1987: 88.5 mhz; 40 kw. 449 ft. TL: N39 58 18 W91 19 42. Stereo. 525 Main, Suite 10 62306. Phone: (217) 224-9422. Fax: (217) 228-0504. E-mail: themix@wgca.org. Web Site: www.wgca.org. Licensee: Great Commission Broadcasting Corp. Network: USA. Format: Christian contemp. Target aud: 25-45. ◆ Jim Taylor, gen mgr & opns mgr; Bruce Rice, progmg dir; John T. Ingraham IV, chief of engrg.

WGEM(AM)— Jan 1, 1948: 1440 khz; 5 kw-D, 1 kw-N, DA-2. TL: N39 58 47 W91 19 27. Stereo. Box 80 62306. Secondary address: 513 Hampshire 62301. Phone: (217) 228-6600. Fax: (217) 228-6670. Fax: TWX: 910-246-3209. E-mail: mansger@wgem.com. Web Site: wgem.com. Licensee: Quincy Broadcasting Co. Group owner: Quincy Newspapers Inc. Network: ABC Information & Entertainment. Rep: Christal. Wilkinson, Barker & Knauer. Format: Sports. News: 40 hrs wkly. Target aud: 25-54; general. ◆ Thomas A. Oakley, CEO; Ralph M. Oakley, COO & opns dir; Thomas Oakley, pres; Leo T. Henning, VP & gen mgr.

WGEM-FM— 1947: 105.1 mhz; 27.5 kw. 500 ft. TL: N39 57 03 W91 19 54. Stereo. Web Site: www.wgem.com. Network: ABC Information & Entertainment. Rep: Christal. Wilkinson, Barker, Knauer & Quinn. Format: News. News: 110 hrs wkly. Target aud: 25-54. Spec prog: Farm 10 hrs wkly. Co-owned TV: WGEM-TV affil

WQCY(FM)— May 8, 1989: 103.9 mhz; 1.8 kw. Ant 436 ft. TL: N39 56 30 W91 35 03. 329 Maine St. 62301. Phone: (217) 224-4102. Phone: (217) 228-2800. Fax: (217) 224-4133. Fax: (217) 228-1031. E-mail: wqcy@staradio.com. Web Site: www.wqcy.com. Licensee: STARadio Corp. (group owner; acq 8-13-98; grpsl). Network: CBS. Format: Hot 80s. Target aud: 18-44; general. ◆ Michael J. Moyers, gen mgr; Brenda Park, gen sls mgr; Jim Dewey, progmg dir & progmg; Mary Griffith, mus dir & news dir; Phillip Reilly, chief of engrg.

*WQUB(FM)— April 1974: 90.3 mhz; 28 kw. 417 ft. TL: N39 57 22 W91 23 22. Stereo. 1800 College Ave. 62301. Phone: (217) 228-5410. Fax: (217) 228-5616. Web Site: www.wqub.org. Licensee: Quincy University Corp. Network: Network: NPR, PRI. Wilkinson Barker Knauer. Format: Class, news, jazz. News staff: 2; News: 31 hrs wkly. Target aud: 25-64; male & female. Spec prog: Folk 2 hrs, blues 2 hrs, alternative rock 12 hrs, hip hop 2 hrs, oldies 2 hrs wkly. ◆ Mick Freeman, progmg dir & mus dir; Jim Cate, engrg mgr & chief of engrg.

WTAD(AM)— July 25, 1925: 930 khz; 5 kw-D, 1 kw-N, DA-N. TL: N39 53 31 W91 25 25. Lincoln-Douglas, 329 Maine St. 62306. Phone: (217) 224-4102. Fax: (217) 224-4133. Web Site: www.wtad.com. Licensee: STARadio Corp. (group owner; acq 8-13-98; grpsl). Network: CBS. Rep: McGavren Guild. Format: News/talk. News staff: one; News: 22 hrs wkly. Target aud: 35 plus; general. ◆ Michael J. Moyers, gen mgr.

WCOY(FM)—Co-owned with WTAD(AM). 1948: 99.5 mhz; 100 kw. Ant 489 ft. TL: N39 56 30 W91 35 03. Network: CBS. Format: Hot country classics. ◆ Mike Moyers, progmg dir.

Ramsey

*WJLY(FM)— 1999: 88.3 mhz; 25 kw. 502 ft. TL: N39 08 06 W89 06 02. Box 456 62080. Secondary address: R.R. 2 Box 51A Phone: (618) 423-2082. Fax: (618) 423-2394. E-mail: wjly@swetlandcom.com. Licensee: Countryside Broadcasting. Network: Moody. Format: Christian. News: 14 hrs wkly. Target aud: 35 plus. ◆ Richard Wheeler, gen mgr; Ralph Rounds, gen sls mgr; Steve Curll, progmg dir; Henry Voss, chief of engrg.

WTRH(FM)— Nov 21, 1990: 93.3 mhz; 3 kw. Ant 466 ft. TL: N39 08 06 W89 06 02. Stereo. R.R. 2, Box 51A 62080. Secondary address: Box 456 62080. Phone: (618) 423-2082. Fax: (618) 423-2394. E-mail: wtrh@swetlandcom.com. Licensee: Countryside Broadcasting Inc. Format: Oldies, talk. News: 14 hrs wkly. Target aud: 35 plus; men & women who love old radio prgms & mus. ◆ Henry Voss, pres & chief of engrg; Richard Wheeler, gen mgr & opns mgr.

Rantoul

WEVX(FM)—Licensed to Rantoul. See Champaign

WJCI(AM)—Licensed to Rantoul. See Champaign

WQQB(FM)—Licensed to Rantoul. See Urbana

Directory of Radio

River Grove

*WRRG(FM)— Mar 10, 1975: 88.9 mhz; 100 w. 128 ft. TL: N41 54 56 W87 50 12. 2000 N. 5th Ave., R113 60171. Phone: (708) 583-3110. Fax: (708) 583-3120. E-mail: info@wrrg.org. Web Site: www.wrrg.org. Licensee: Triton College. Format: CHR, alternative. News: 2 hrs wkly. Target aud: 18-34. Spec prog: Jazz 5 hrs, loc 4 hrs, metal 4 hrs, world mus 3 hrs, oldies 11 hrs, classic rock 2 hrs wkly. ◆ Rick Linus, gen mgr & progmg mgr.

Robinson

WTAY(AM)— Jan 9, 1956: 1570 khz; 250 w-D. TL: N39 00 29 W87 46 41. Box 245, Rt. 33 W. 62454. Phone: (618) 544-2191. Fax: (618) 544-3621. E-mail: wtaywtye@yahoo.com. Licensee: Ann Broadcasting Corp. (acq 1994). Network: ABC. Format: Adult contemp. News staff: one; News: 15 hrs wkly. Spec prog: C&W 12 hrs, farm 3 hrs, polka 3 hrs, big band 10 hrs wkly. ◆ Jerry F. Tye, pres & gen mgr.

WTYE(FM)—Co-owned with WTAY(AM). Jan 4, 1963: 101.7 mhz; 1.45 kw. 449 ft. TL: N39 00 29 W87 46 41. Stereo.

Rochelle

WRHL(AM)— Sept 16, 1966: 1060 khz; 250 w-D, DA. TL: N41 55 24 W89 03 30. Box 177 61068. Secondary address: 400 May Mart Dr. 61068. Phone: (815) 562-7001. Fax: (815) 562-7002. E-mail: wrhlamfm@rochelle.net. Web Site: www.wrhl.net. Licensee: Rochelle Broadcasting Co. Inc. (acq 10-11-70). Network: AP Network News. Format: News/talk. News staff: 2; News: 140 hrs wkly. Target aud: 25-75. ◆ David Van Drew, gen mgr; Kurt Baker, gen sls mgr; Jeremiah Beck, progmg dir; Jeffrey Leon, news dir; Rob Whipple, pub affrs dir; Doug White, chief of engrg.

WRHL-FM— Oct 5, 1973: 102.3 mhz; 4.6 kw. 180 ft. TL: N41 55 24 W89 03 30. Stereo. E-mail: jb@wrhl.net. Web Site: www.hitsandfavorites.com. Network: ABC. Format: Adult contemp. News: one hr wkly. Target aud: 25-54; female.

Rock Falls

WSDR(AM)—See Sterling

Rock Island

WHTS(FM)—Listing follows WKBF(AM).

WKBF(AM)— Feb 16, 1925: 1270 khz; 5 kw-U, DA-N. TL: N41 29 40 W90 28 00. 3535 E. Kimberly Rd., Davenport, IA 52807. Phone: (563) 344-9487. Fax: (563) 344-7037. E-mail: info@wkbf.com. Web Site: www.wkbf.com. Licensee: Mercury Broadcasting Co. Inc. (group owner; acq 11-27-01; $510,000. for 51% of stock with co-located FM). Rep: Katz Radio. Format: Air America. Target aud: 35 plus; women. Spec prog: Relg one hr wkly. ◆ Larry Rofmilso, gen mgr & stn mgr; Ron Evans, progmg dir.

WHTS(FM)—Co-owned with WKBF(AM). October 1947: 98.9 mhz; 39 kw. 900 ft. TL: N41 19 40 W90 22 47. Stereo. Phone: (563) 355-9890. E-mail: info@allhit989.com. Web Site: www.allhit989.com. Format: Urban contemp. News staff: one; News: 2 hrs wkly. ◆ Teri Van Dyke, gen sls mgr; Caressa Clearman, mktg dir; Tony Waitekus, progmg dir; Joey Tack, mus dir; Mark Minnick, news dir.

*WVIK(FM)— Feb 25, 1963: 90.3 mhz; 31 kw. 1,096 ft. TL: N41 32 52 W90 28 29. Stereo. Augustana College, 639 38th St. 61201. Phone: (309) 794-7500. Fax: (309) 794-1236. Web Site: www.wvik.org. Licensee: Augustana College. Network: NPR. Dow, Lohnes & Albertson. Format: Class, news. News staff: 2; News: 35 hrs wkly. Target aud: General. Spec prog: Jazz 9 hrs wkly. ◆ Lowell Dorman, gen mgr; David Garner, opns dir; Sonita Oldfield-Carlson, dev dir; Mindy Heusel, gen sls mgr & mus dir; Herb Trix, news dir.

Rockford

*WFEN(FM)— Aug 25, 1991: 88.3 mhz; 8.5 kw. 575 ft. TL: N42 21 51 W89 08 15. 4701 S. Main St. 61102. Phone: (815) 964-9336. Fax: (815) 964-9318. E-mail: fred@wfen.org. Web Site: www.wfen.org. Licensee: Faith Center (acq 10-2-91; FTR: 10-28-91). Format: Contemp Christian, praise & worship. Target aud: 35-54. Spec prog: Sp one hr wkly. ◆ Fred Tscholl, gen mgr.

Stations in the U.S.   Illinois

Developers & Brokers of Radio Properties

contact American Media Services at our suite:
Philadelphia Marriott Downtown
215-625-2900

843-972-2200
americanmediaservices.com
Charleston, SC
Dallas, TX · Chicago, Il · Austin, TX

American Media Services, LLC

WGFB(FM)—See Rockton

WLUV(AM)—See Loves Park

WNIJ(FM)—See De Kalb

*WNIU(FM)— Apr 28, 1991: 90.5 mhz; 50 kw. 367 ft. TL: N42 00 55 W89 00 07. Stereo. NIU Broadcast Ctr., 801 N. First St., DeKalb 60115. Secondary address: Riverfront Museum Park, 711 N. Main St. 61103. Phone: (815) 753-9000. Phone: (815) 961-8000. Fax: (815) 753-9938. Fax: (815) 963-5374. E-mail: npr@niu.edu. Web Site: www.northernpublicradio.org. Licensee: Northern Illinois University. Network: Network: PRI, NPR. Arter & Hadden. Format: Classical. News staff: 2; News: 52 hrs wkly. Target aud: General. Spec prog: New age 2 hrs, blues 4 hrs wkly. ♦Tim Emmons, gen mgr; Jan Kilgard, dev dir; Bill Drake, progmg dir; Susan Stephens, news dir; Jeff Glass, chief of engrg.

WNTA(AM)— Dec 24, 1953: 1330 khz; 1 kw-D, 91 w-N, DA-2. TL: N42 13 32 W89 02 47. 2830 Sandy Hollow Rd. 61109. Secondary address: 2830 Sandy Hollow Rd. 61109. Phone: (815) 874-7861. Fax: (815) 874-2202. E-mail: wnta@wnta.com. Web Site: www.wnta.com. Licensee: Maverick Media of Rockford License LLC. Group owner: RadioWorks Inc. (acq 4-27-2005; grpsl). Shaw Pittman. Format: MOR, news, talk. News staff: 2; News: 2 hrs wkly. Target aud: 35 plus. Spec prog: Gospel 20 hrs wkly. ♦Gary Rozynek, pres; David W. McAley, VP & gen mgr; Ken DeCoster, progmg dir, news dir & chief of engrg.

WQFL(FM)— May 2, 1974: 100.9 mhz; 6 kw. 500 ft. TL: N42 19 17 W89 00 47. Stereo. Box 2730 61132-2730. Secondary address: 5375 Pebble Creek Tr., Loves Park 61111. Phone: (815) 654-1200. Fax: (815) 282-7779. E-mail: positive@101qfl.com. Web Site: www.101qfl.com. Licensee: Quest for Life Inc. (acq 6-80; $590,000;. FTR: 6-2-80). Network: UPI. Wilkinson, Barker, Knauer, L.L.P. Format: Christian prog. News staff: one; News: one hr wkly. Target aud: 25-44; female dominant, educated, upscale & middle class. ♦Paul Youngblood, gen mgr; Nick Guzzardo, gen sls mgr & prom dir; Rick Hall, progmg dir; John Burkholder, chief of engrg.

WROK(AM)— 1923: 1440 khz; 5 kw-D, 270 w-N, DA-D. TL: N42 16 50 W89 02 16. Stereo. 3901 Brendenwood Rd. 61107. Phone: (815) 399-2233. Fax: (815) 399-8148. Web Site: www.cumulus.com. Licensee: Cumulus Licensing Corp. Group owner: Cumulus Media Inc. (acq 10-2-00; grpsl). Network: ABC Daytime Direction. Rep: McGavren Guild. Wiley, Rein & Fielding. Format: News/talk. Target aud: 35 plus. ♦David Bevins, gen mgr; Mary Gerard, rgnl sls mgr; Erika Mohr, prom dir; Jesse Garcia, progmg dir; Kelly Dukes, chief of engrg.

WZOK(FM)—Co-owned with WROK(AM). 1949: 97.5 mhz; 50 kw. 235 ft. TL: N42 16 50 W89 02 16. (CP: Ant 429 ft.). Stereo. Web Site: www.97zok.com. Format: CHR. Target aud: 25-34. ♦J.J. Morgan, progmg dir.

WXRX(FM)—See Belvidere

WYHY(FM)—See Winnebago

Rockton

WGFB(FM)— March 1963: 103.1 mhz; 1.2 kw. 525 ft. TL: N42 22 02 W89 05 13. Stereo. 2830 Sandy Hollow Rd., Rockford 61109. Secondary address: 4570 E. Rockton Rd., Roscoe 61073. Phone: (815) 874-7861. Fax: (815) 874-2202. Web Site: www.B103fm.com. Licensee: Maverick Media of Rockford License LLC. Group owner: RadioWorks Inc. (acq 4-27-2005; grpsl). Rep: Katz Radio. Shaw Pittman. Format: Adult contemp. Target aud: 25-54; adult women. ♦Gary Rozynek, pres; David McAley, VP & gen mgr; Dave Nelson, gen sls mgr; Doug Daniels, progmg dir; Chuck Ingle, chief of engrg.

Rushville

WKXQ(FM)— May 1, 1985: 92.5 mhz; 6 kw. 328 ft. TL: N40 08 20 W90 39 26. Stereo. Box 196 62681. Secondary address: 109 N. Liberty 62681. Phone: (217) 322-9300. Fax: (217) 322-4925. E-mail: wkxq92@frontiernet.net. Licensee: WPW Broadcasting Inc. (group owner; acq 12-6-99; $550,000. with WPWQ(FM) Mount Sterling). Network: CNN Radio. Reddy, Begley & McCormick. Format: Oldies. News staff: one; News: 12 hrs wkly. Target aud: 18-54. Spec prog: Relg 6 hrs, farm 6 hrs wkly. ♦David Madison, CEO & pres; Vanessa Wetterling, sr VP; Jamie Friend, gen mgr & rgnl sls mgr; Chuck Keller, stn mgr & opns dir.

Saint Joseph

*WGNJ(FM)— 1999: 89.3 mhz; 50 kw. Ant 351 ft. TL: N40 05 16 W87 53 42. Stereo. Box 12345, Champaign 61826. Secondary address: 2421 N. 1450 E. Rd., White Heath 61884. Phone: (217)897-6333. E-mail: staff@greatnewsradio.org. Web Site: www.greatnewsradio.org. Licensee: Good News Radio Inc. Format: Christian, religious, talk. Target aud: 35 plus; general. ♦David Herriott, chmn; Mark Burns, pres & gen mgr; Carrie Burns, opns dir.

Salem

WJBD(AM)— Dec 16, 1956: 1350 khz; 430 w-D, 60 w-N. TL: N38 37 56 W88 55 02. Box 70, 310 W. McMackin St. 62881. Secondary address: 221 E. Broadway, Suite 107, Centralia 62801. Phone: (618) 548-2000. Phone: (618) 532-9600. Fax: (618) 548-2079. E-mail: wjbd@accessus.net. Licensee: NewRadio Group LLC (group owner; acq 12-20-2002; grpsl). Format: Country. News staff: 3; News: 30 hrs wkly. Target aud: General. Spec prog: Farm 4 hrs, relg 6 hrs wkly. ♦Bruce Kropp, gen mgr, opns VP, sls VP, progmg dir & news dir.

WJBD-FM— June 1, 1972: 100.1 mhz; 1.5 kw. 450 ft. TL: N38 33 45 W88 59 57. Stereo. E-mail: wjbd@accessus.net. Format: Adult contemp, news. ♦Matt Tackett, opns mgr.

*WSLE(FM)— 2005: 91.3 mhz; 900 w. Ant 154 ft. TL: N38 37 34 W88 56 41. Drawer 3206, Tupelo, MS 38803. Phone: (662) 844-8888. Fax: (662) 842-6791. Licensee: American Family Association. Group owner: American Family Radio. Format: Christian. ♦Marvin Sanders, gen mgr; John Riley, progmg dir.

Sandwich

WAUR(AM)—Licensed to Sandwich. See Aurora

Savanna

WCCI(FM)— Nov 7, 1971: 100.3 mhz; 25 kw. 450 ft. TL: N42 07 49 W90 08 24. Stereo. Box 310, 316 Main 61074. Phone: (815) 273-7757. Fax: (815) 273-2760. E-mail: wccifm@internetni.com. Web Site: www.wcciradio.com. Licensee: Carroll County Communications Inc. (acq 9-1-76). Network: Jones Radio Networks. Rini & Coran. Format: New hit country, news. News staff: one; News: 35 hrs wkly. Target aud: 25-54. ♦John L. Miller, pres & gen mgr; Edward F. Bock, VP; Brian Reusch, stn mgr; Leslie Smith, progmg dir; Mark Schoening, news dir.

Seneca

WJDK-FM— 1993: 95.7 mhz; 3 kw. 328 ft. TL: N41 13 12 W88 32 27. Stereo. 219 W. Washington St., Morris 60450. Phone: (815) 941-1000. Fax: (815) 941-9300. Licensee: Grundy County Broadcasters Inc. (acq 4-20-98). Network: ABC. Format: Adult contemp. News staff: one; News: 14 hrs wkly. Target aud: 25-49. ♦Larry Nelson, pres; Jack Daly, gen mgr.

Shelbyville

WEJT(FM)— Dec 31, 1969: 105.1 mhz; 13 kw. 459 ft. TL: N39 35 39 W88 50 44. Stereo. 410 N. Water, Suite C, Decatur 62523. Phone: (217) 428-4487. Fax: (217) 428-4501. Web Site: www.wejt.com. Licensee: Cromwell Group Inc. of Illinois. Group owner: The Cromwell Group Inc. (acq 8-1-89; $320,000 with co-located AM; 7-31-89). Rep: D & R Radio. Pepper & Corazzini. Format: Adult contemp. Target aud: 25-54; baby boomers. ♦Mike Topoll, gen mgr.

WINU(AM)— Nov 24, 1972: 870 khz; 500 w-D, DA. TL: N39 29 14 W88 57 31. 126 W. Main St. 62565. Phone: (217) 774-5277. Fax: (217) 774-5280. Web Site: www.hereshelpnet.org. Licensee: New Life Evangelistic Center Inc. (acq 7-31-98; $75,000). Format: Southern gospel. Target aud: 25-54. Spec prog: Farm 5 hrs, big band 2 hrs wkly. ♦Hank Zeniewicz, gen mgr.

Sherman

WABZ(FM)— May 10, 1971: 93.9 mhz; 15 kw. Ant 430 ft. TL: N39 59 25 W89 30 46. 3501 E. Sangamon Ave., Springfield 62707. Phone: (217) 735-5400 (business). Fax: (217) 753-7902. Licensee: Saga Communications of Illinois LLC. Group owner: Saga Communications Inc. (acq 7-96; grpsl). Format: Continuous soft favorites. Target aud: 25-54. ♦Leanne Arndt, gen mgr; Kevin Anfield, gen sls mgr; Jane Cochran, progmg dir.

Skokie

WTMX(FM)— Aug 18, 1961: 101.9 mhz; 4.2 kw. 1,561 ft. TL: N41 52 44 W87 38 10. Stereo. One Prudential Plaza, Suite 2700, Chicago 60601. Phone: (312) 946-1019. Fax: (312) 946-4747. Web Site: www.wtmx.com. Licensee: Bonneville International Corp. (group owner; (acq 8-70). Rep: Katz Radio. Format: Adult contemp. News staff: one. ♦Drew Horowitz, pres & gen mgr; Barry James, stn mgr; Jessy Ferdman, prom mgr; Mary Ellen Kachinske, progmg VP & progmg dir; Barry Keefe, news dir & pub affrs dir; Chris Lufitz, chief of engrg.

South Beloit

WTJK(AM)—Licensed to South Beloit. See Beloit WI

South Jacksonville

WJVO(FM)—Licensed to South Jacksonville. See Jacksonville

Sparta

WHCO(AM)— February 1955: 1230 khz; 1 kw-U. TL: N38 07 25 W89 43 20. Box 255, 1230 W. Broadway 62286. Secondary address: 47 W. Maine, Mascoutah 62258. Phone: (618) 443-2121. Fax: (618) 443-2800. Licensee: Hirsch Communication Engineering Co. Network: Network: CBS, Westwood One. Format: News/talk, sports. News staff: 2; News: 10 hrs wkly. Target aud: 25-65. Spec prog: Pol 2 hrs, farm 20 hrs, relg 10 hrs wkly. ♦Jack L. Scheper Sr., pres & gen mgr.

Spring Valley

WIVQ(FM)— December 1993: 103.3 mhz; 4.9 kw. 361 ft. TL: N41 18 09 W89 14 11. 3905 Progress Blvd., Peru 61354. Phone: (815) 224-2100. Fax: (815) 224-2066. E-mail: q@theradiogroup.net. Web Site: qhitmusic.com. Licensee: Mendota Broadcasting Inc. Group owner: Studstill Broadcasting (acq 7-17-97; $700,000. with WBZG(FM) Peru). Rep: Rgnl Reps. Booth, Freret, Imlay & Tepper. Format: Top-40, adult contemp. Target aud: 18-44. ♦Lamar Studstill, chmn; Cole Charles Studstill, CFO; Owen L. Studstill, CEO, pres & gen mgr; Cole Studstill, stn mgr & opns mgr; Doris Studstill, opns VP.

*WSOG(FM)— 12/2002: 88.1 mhz; 4 kw vert. Ant 262 ft. TL: N41 17 32 W89 07 59. Box 34 61362. Phone: (815) 220-1929. Fax: (815) 220-1929. E-mail: wsog881@hotmail.com. Licensee: Spirit Education Association Inc. ♦Louis J. Perona, pres.

Springfield

WCVS-FM—(Virden). May 10, 1982: 96.7 mhz; 6 kw. Ant 328 ft. TL: N39 38 26 W89 39 24. Stereo. 3055 S. 4th St. 62703. Phone: (217) 528-3033. Fax: (217) 528-5348. E-mail: wcvs@wcvs.com. Web Site: www.wcvsfm.com. Licensee: Capstar TX L.P. Group owner: Clear Channel Communications Inc. (acq 8-30-00; grpsl). Dow, Lohnes & Albertson. Format: Classic hits, rock. News staff: one. Target aud: 25-54. ♦Kevin O'Dea, VP, gen mgr & gen sls mgr.

Broadcasting & Cable Yearbook 2006

WDBR(FM)—Listing follows WTAX(AM).

WFMB(AM)— 1922: 1450 khz; 1 kw-U. TL: N39 45 36 W89 39 05. 3055 S. 4th St. 62703. Phone: (217) 528-3033. Phone: (217) 544-9855. Fax: (217) 528-5348. E-mail: sportsradio1450@sportsradio1450.com. Web Site: www.sportradio1450.com. Licensee: Capstar TX L.P. Group owner: Clear Channel Communications Inc. (acq 8-30-00; grpsl). Network: ABC Information & Entertainment. Rep: Clear Channel. Format: Sports/personality. News staff: 2; News: 5 hrs wkly. Target aud: 25-54; upscale professionals. ♦Kevin O'Dea, gen mgr.

WFMB-FM— July 1965: 104.5 mhz; 43 kw. 465 ft. TL: N39 45 36 W89 39 05. Stereo. Format: Country. Target aud: Professional adults. ♦Kevin O'Dea, VP.

***WLUJ(FM)**— May 24, 1995: 89.7 mhz; 20 kw. 328 ft. TL: N39 48 30 W89 37 30. (CP: 10 kw). Stereo. 600 W. Mason St. 62702. Phone: (217) 528-2300. Fax: (217) 528-2400. E-mail: wluj897@ameritech.net. Web Site: www.wluj.org. Licensee: Cornerstone Community Radio Inc. Network: Moody. Format: Christian talk. Target aud: General. ♦Richard Van Zandt, pres; Arthur Gregg, sr VP; Dick Reed, VP; John McBride, stn mgr; Howard Fouks, opns mgr.

WMAY(AM)— Oct 15, 1950: 970 khz; 1 kw-D, 500 w-N, DA-2. TL: N39 51 42 W89 32 32. Stereo. Box 460 62705. Secondary address: 1510 N. Third, Riverton 62561. Phone: (217) 629-7077. Fax: (217) 629-7952. Web Site: www.wmay.com. Licensee: Long Nine Inc. Group owner: The Mid-West Family Broadcast Group (acq 12-7-76). Network: ABC Information & Entertainment. Rep: D & R Radio. Fisher, Wayland, Cooper, Leader & Zaragoza. Format: News/talk. Target aud: 25-64. Spec prog: Big band 5 hrs wkly. ♦Glen Gardner, gen mgr; Dave Doetsch, sls VP; Amanda Johnson, prom dir; Jim Leach, news dir; Greg Stephens, chief of engrg.

WNNS(FM)—Co-owned with WMAY(AM). Nov 1, 1980: 98.7 mhz; 50 kw. 500 ft. TL: N39 41 59 W89 46 55. Stereo. Web Site: www.wnns.com. Format: Adult contemp. Spec prog: Jazz 6 hrs wkly. ♦Kellie Michaels, progmg dir & pub affrs dir; Greg Stephens, engrg dir.

***WQNA(FM)**— Aug 31, 1979: 88.3 mhz; 250 w. Ant 256 ft. TL: N39 44 03 W89 38 18. Stereo. Capital Area Career Ctr., 2201 Toronto Rd. 62707. Phone: (217) 529-5431. Fax: (217) 529-7861. E-mail: info@wqna.org. Web Site: www.wqna.org. Licensee: Capital Area Vocational Center. Shaw Pittman. Format: Div. News: 6 hrs wkly. Target aud: 13-24; high school & college students. Spec prog: Varied. ♦J.G. Reynolds PhD., chmn; Jim Grimes, gen mgr; Kerri Donovan, CEO & opns dir.

WQQL(FM)— Nov 15, 1993: 101.9 mhz; 50 kw. 300 ft. TL: N39 42 39 W89 38 42. Stereo. 3501 E. Sangamon Ave. 62707. Phone: (217) 753-5400. Fax: (217) 753-7902. Web Site: www.cool1019.com. Licensee: Saga Communications of Illinois LLC. Group owner: Saga Communications Inc. (acq 9-10-93; $1.44 million;. FTR: 10-4-93). Rep: Katz Radio. Smithwick & Belendiuk. Format: Oldies. News: 2 hrs wkly. Target aud: 25 plus; upscale educated adults. ♦Leanne Arndt, gen mgr; Kevin Anfield, gen sls mgr & prom dir; Joey McLaughlin, progmg dir & progmg mgr; R.D. Miller, engrg dir & chief of engrg.

***WSCT(FM)**— November 1993: 90.5 mhz; 3.8 kw. Ant 410 ft. TL: N39 38 38 W89 30 51. Stereo. Box 140, Carlinville 62626. Phone: (217) 854-4800. Fax: (217) 854-4810. E-mail: wibi@wibi.org. Web Site: www.wibi.org. Licensee: Illinois Bible Institute. Format: Christian. News: 5 hrs wkly. Target aud: 25-44; Christian & seeking non-Christians. ♦Reverend Larry Griswold, pres; Paul Anthony, opns mgr; Jessica Barton, mktg dir & prom dir; Lori Walder, mus dir; Tracey Barton, chief of engrg.

WTAX(AM)— 1930: 1240 khz; 1 kw-U. TL: N39 47 36 W89 36 18. 3501 E. Sangamon Ave. 62707. Phone: (217) 753-5400. Fax: (217) 753-7902. Web Site: www.wtax.com. Licensee: Saga Communications of Illinois LLC. Group owner: Saga Communications Inc. (acq 1996). Network: Network: Network: Moody, CBS, ABC News/Talk. Rep: Christal. Format: News/talk, sports. News staff: 3; News: 20, hrs wkly. Target aud: 30 plus. Spec prog: Farm 16 hrs wkly. ♦Leanne Arndt, gen mgr.

WDBR(FM)—Co-owned with WTAX(AM). April 1948: 103.7 mhz; 50 kw. 320 ft. TL: N39 47 36 W89 36 18. (CP: 20 kw, ant 768 ft.). Web Site: www.wdbr.com. Format: CHR. Target aud: 18-49; general.

***WUIS(FM)**— Jan 3, 1975: 91.9 mhz; 50 kw. 524 ft. TL: N39 47 00 W89 26 46. Stereo. Box 19243, CBM-130, Univ. of Illinois at Springfield 62794-9243. Secondary address: One University Plaza, MS CBM-130 62703. Phone: (217) 206-6516. Fax: (217) 206-6527. E-mail: wuis@uis.edu. Web Site: www.wuis.org. Licensee: University of Illinois at Springfield. Network: Network: NPR, PRI. Dow, Lohnes & Albertson. Format: News, class, jazz. News staff: 4; News: 45 hrs wkly. Target aud: 25-54. Spec prog: NPR entertainment 15 hrs, Celtic one hr, bluegrass 2 hrs, Singer/Songwriter 2 hrs, ambient 2 hrs wkly. ♦Rich Bradley, gen mgr; Sinta Seiber, opns mgr; Lisa Clemmons-Stott, dev dir; Karl Scroggin, mus dir.

WYMG(FM)—(Jacksonville). March 1948: 100.5 mhz; 50 kw. 500 ft. TL: N39 39 40 W89 55 18. Stereo. 3501 E. Sangamon Ave. 62707. Phone: (217) 753-5400. Fax: (217) 753-7902. E-mail: wymg@wymg.com. Web Site: www.wymg.com. Licensee: Saga Communications of Illinois LLC. Group owner: Saga Communications Inc. (acq 10-1-86). Format: Classic rock. Target aud: 18-49. Spec prog: Jazz 2 hrs, comedy one hr wkly. ♦Dana Harmon, VP & gen mgr.

Staunton

WAOX(FM)— December 1, 1999: 105.3 mhz; 6 kw. Ant 285 ft. TL: N39 02 37 W89 44 56. Stereo. Box 10, Litchfield 62056. Phone: (217) 532-2085. Fax: (217) 532-2431. E-mail: waox@theox1053.com. Web Site: www.waox.com. Licensee: Talley Broadcasting Corp. Group owner: Talley Radio Stations Format: Adult contemp. ♦Hayward L. Talley, pres & gen mgr; Brian Talley, opns VP.

Sterling

***WNIQ(FM)**— unknown: 91.5 mhz; 2.1 kw. 331 ft. TL: N41 53 12 W89 35 43. Stereo. NIU Broadcast Ctr., 801 N. First St., DeKalb 60115. Phone: (815) 753-9000. Fax: (815) 753-9938. E-mail: npr@niu.edu. Web Site: www.northernpublicradio.org. Licensee: Northern Illinois University. Network: Network: PRI, NPR. Arter & Hadden. Format: News/talk, class. News: 2 hrs wkly. Target aud: General. ♦Tim Emmons, gen mgr; Jan Kilgard, dev dir; Bill Drake, progmg dir.

WSDR(AM)— Aug 21, 1949: 1240 khz; 500 w-D, 1 kw-N. TL: N41 48 59 W89 40 13. 3101 Freeport Rd. 61081. Phone: (815) 625-3400. Fax: (815) 625-6940. E-mail: wsdr1240@theramp.net. Licensee: Withers Broadcasting Co. of Rock River LLC. Group owner: Withers Broadcasting Co. (acq 1-21-98; grpsl). Network: Network: CBS, ABC. Rep: Christal. Format: News, sports, talk. News staff: 2; News: 10 hrs wkly. Target aud: 25 plus. Spec prog: Farm 16 hrs, Sp 4 hrs wkly. ♦Michael McCulloch, gen mgr; Brian Zschiesche, progmg dir.

WSSQ(FM)—Co-owned with WSDR(AM). August 1966: 94.3 mhz; 6 kw. 309 ft. TL: N41 51 06 W89 42 38. Stereo. Network: Network: Westwood One, ABC. Rep: Christal. Format: Adult contemp. Target aud: 25-54; women. ♦Jay Pauley, progmg dir.

Streator

WSPL(AM)— Sept 26, 1953: 1250 khz; 500 w-D, 100 w-N, DA-D. TL: N41 09 30 W88 50 13. Box 377 61364. Phone: (815) 672-2947. Fax: (815) 673-1833. Licensee: Mendota Broadcasting Inc. Group owner: Studstill Broadcasting (acq 5-30-00; grpsl). Network: ABC Information & Entertainment. Format: News/talk, sports. News staff: 3; News: 25 hrs wkly. Target aud: 35 plus. ♦Lamar Studstill, chmn; Owen L. Studstill, pres; Cole Studstill, VP & opns mgr; Lee Studstill, gen mgr; Cheryl Knirlberger, sls dir; Dave Noesen, news dir; Mark Baker, chief of engrg.

WSTQ(FM)—Co-owned with WSPL(AM). Sept 15, 1964: 97.7 mhz; 6 kw. Ant 328 ft. TL: N41 10 49 W88 52 06. Stereo. 3905 Progress Blvd., Peru 61354. Phone: (815) 224-2100. Fax: (815) 224-2066. E-mail: edsytrits106@theradiogroup.net. Format: CHR. Target aud: 18-44. ♦Owen Studstill, pres; Cole Studstill, gen mgr & progmg dir.

WYYS(FM)— 1995: 106.1 mhz; 3 kw. 292 ft. TL: N41 10 49 W88 52 06. Box 377 61634. Secondary address: 1317 N. 300 Rd. 61634. Phone: (815) 672-2947. Fax: (815) 673-1833. E-mail: wyys@theradiogroup.net. Licensee: Mendota Broadcasting Inc. Group owner: Studstill Broadcasting (acq 3-8-00; grpsl). Network: ABC. Rep: Rgnl Reps. Format: Lite hits. ♦Lamar Studstill, chmn; Cole Studstill, CFO; Lee Studstill, pres & gen mgr.

Sugar Grove

***WSRI(FM)**— 2005: 88.7 mhz; 250 w. Ant 129 ft. TL: N41 47 01 W88 26 14. 5700 W. Oaks Blvd., Rocklin, CA 95765. Phone: (916) 251-1600. Fax: (916) 251-1650. E-mail: klove@klove.com. Web Site: www.klove.com. Licensee: Educational Media Foundation. Group owner: EMF Broadcasting. Network: K-Love. Shaw Pittman. Format: Contemp Christian. News staff: 3. Target aud: 25-44; female-Judeo/Christian. ♦Richard Jenkins, pres; Mike Novak, VP; Ed Lenane, opns dir; Keith Whipple, dev dir.

Sullivan

WZNX(FM)— April 1992: 106.7 mhz; 9.5 kw. 550 ft. TL: N39 36 38 W88 41 32. 410 N. Water St., Suite C, Decatur 62523. Phone: (217) 428-4487. Fax: (217) 428-4501. Web Site: www.wznx.com. Licensee: WSHY Inc. Group owner: The Cromwell Group Inc. (acq 2-14-97; $750,000). Format: Classic rock. News staff: one. Target aud: 25-54; strong men. ♦Mike Topoll, gen mgr; Chris Bullock, opns dir.

Summit

***WARG(FM)**— January 1976: 88.9 mhz; 500 w. 98 ft. TL: N41 46 36 W87 48 17. Stereo. 7329 W. 63rd St. 60501. Phone: (708) 728-8368. Fax: (708) 728-3155. Licensee: Community High School District No. 217. Format: Alternative, rock. Target aud: General; alternative subculture. Spec prog: World beat, metal mus, blues 6 hrs, jazz 6 hrs wkly. ♦Ilene Tokarz, gen mgr.

Sycamore

WDEK(FM)—See De Kalb

WLBK(AM)—See De Kalb

WSQR(AM)— June 11, 1981: 1560 khz; 250 w-D, 18 w-N. TL: N42 00 24 W88 40 40. (CP: 210 w-N. TL: N41 52 44 W88 42 59). 1851 Coltonville Rd. 60178. Phone: (630) 552-1000. Fax: (630) 552-9300. E-mail: wspy-news@nelsonmultimedia.net. Licensee: De kalb County Broadcasters Inc. (acq 9-94). Network: ABC. Format: News info, full service. Target aud: 35-55. Spec prog: Farm 6 hrs wkly. ♦Larry Nelson, pres; Beth Pierre, gen mgr & sls VP; Pam Nelson, CFO & gen mgr.

Taylorville

***WIHM(AM)**— 1952: 1410 khz; 1 kw-D, 63 w-N, DA-1. TL: N39 32 38 W89 16 36. 3515 Hampton Ave., St. Louis, MO 63139. Phone: (314) 752-7000. E-mail: office@covenantnet.net. Web Site: www.covenantnet.net. Licensee: Covenant Network (acq 7-31-98; $60,000). Format: Christian; Religious; inspirtional. ♦Tony Holman, pres & gen mgr.

WQLZ(FM)— December 1967: 92.7 mhz; 11.5 kw. 482 ft. TL: N39 38 38 W89 30 51. Stereo. Box 460, Springfield 62705. Secondary address: 1510 N. Third, Riverton 62561. Phone: (217) 629-7077. Fax: (217) 629-7952. Web Site: www.wqlz.com. Licensee: Long Nine Inc. Group owner: Mid-West Family Stations (acq 2-3-93; $1 million; 2-22-93). Fisher, Wayland, Cooper, Leader & Zaragoza. Format: AOR. News staff: 4; News: 3 hrs wkly. Target aud: 18-34. ♦Glen Gardner, gen mgr; Dave Doetsch, gen sls mgr; Jim Leach, news dir; Greg Stephens, chief of engrg.

WTIM-FM— Nov 13, 1997: 97.3 mhz; 4.6 kw. Ant 374 ft. TL: N39 27 08 W89 17 10. Box 169 62568-0169. Secondary address: 918 E. Park St. 62568. Phone: (217) 824-3395. Fax: (217) 824-3301. Web Site: www.randyradio.com. Licensee: Miller Communications Inc. Group owner: Miller Media Group Network: Westwood One. Rep: Commercial Media Sales. Womble, Carlyle, Sandridge & Rice. Format: News/talk. News staff: one; News: 25 hrs wkly. Target aud: 25 plus. Spec prog: Farm 20 hrs, relg 4 hrs wkly. ♦Randal J. Miller, pres & gen mgr; Kami Payne, stn mgr.

Teutopolis

WKJT(FM)— 1994: 102.3 mhz; 6 kw. 328 ft. TL: N39 08 30 W88 33 36. 206 S. Willow, Effingham 62401. Phone: (217) 347-5518. Fax: (217) 347-5519. E-mail: info@kjcountry.com. Web Site: www.kjcountry.com. Licensee: Kirby Broadcasting Inc. Format: Country. ♦John W. Kirby, pres.

Tower Hill

WRAN(FM)— Nov 25, 1997: 98.3 mhz; 3.7 kw. 420 ft. TL: N39 16 48 W88 58 22. Stereo. 918 E. Park, Box 169, Taylorville 62568. Phone: (217) 824-3395. Fax: (217) 824-3301. Web Site: www. randyradio.com. Licensee: Kaskaskia Broadcasting Inc. Group owner: Miller Media Group Network: CBS. Rep: Commercial Media Sales. Womble, Carlyle, Sandridge & Rice. Format: Soft adult contemp music. News

Developers & Brokers of Radio Properties

contact American Media Services at our suite:
Philadelphia Marriott Downtown
215-625-2900
843-972-2200
americanmediaservices.com
Charleston, SC
Dallas, TX · Chicago, Il · Austin, TX

American Media Services, LLC

staff: one; News: 25 hrs wkly. Target aud: 35—64. Spec prog: Farm 6 hrs, relg 3 hrs wkly. ♦ Randal J. Miller, pres & gen mgr.

Tuscola

WEBX(FM)—Licensed to Tuscola. See Champaign

Urbana

WBCP(AM)— 1948: 1580 khz; 250 w-D, 10 w-N. TL: N40 07 32 W88 17 29. Unit D, 904 N. 4th St., Champaign 61820. Phone: (217) 359-1580. Fax: (217) 359-1583. E-mail: wbcpradio@sbcglobal.net. Licensee: WBCP Inc. (acq 12-89; $135,000; 12-4-89). Network: Network: American Urban, ABC. Format: Gospel, rhythm and blues, smooth jazz. Spec prog: ''''. ♦ Lonnie Clark, pres; J.W. Pirtle, VP & gen mgr; Sam Britten, stn mgr, opns VP & progmg dir; Jill Clements, gen sls mgr; Steve Hamm, chief of engrg.

WCFF(FM)— Dec 4, 1967: 92.5 mhz; 11.5 kw. 485 ft. TL: N40 01 29 W88 08 28. Stereo. 2603 W, Bradley Ave., Champaign 61821. Phone: (217) 352-1040. Fax: (217) 352-1256. E-mail: studio@wkio.com. Web Site: www.wkio.com. Licensee: Saga Communications of Illinois LLC. Group owner: Saga Communications Inc. (acq 2000; $7 million). Rep: Katz Radio. Format: Oldies. Target aud: 35-64. ♦ Ed Christian, CEO & chmn; Steve Goldstein, exec VP; Alan Beck, gen mgr; Mark Bretsch, sls dir & gen sls mgr; Mark Spalding, chief of engrg.

***WILL(AM)**— Mar 28, 1922: 580 khz; 5 kw-D, DA-D. TL: N40 04 53 W88 14 18. Campbell Hall for Public Telecommunications, 300 N. Goodwin Ave. 61801-2316. Phone: (217) 333-0850. Fax: (217) 244-9586. Fax: (217) 333-7151. E-mail: willamfm@uiuc.edu. Web Site: www.will.uiuc.edu. Licensee: University of Illinois Board of Trustees. Network: Network: NPR, PRI. Dow, Lohnes & Albertson. Format: News/talk, div. News staff: 3; News: 115 hrs wkly. Target aud: 25-60; educated, upper middle income, professionals. Spec prog: Farm 7 hrs wkly. ♦ Donald P. Mullally, gen mgr; Jay H. Pearce, stn mgr & progmg dir; Deborah Day, dev dir; Tom Rogers, news dir; Rick Finnie, chief of engrg.

WILL-FM— Sept 1, 1941: 90.9 mhz; 105 kw. 850 ft. TL: N40 06 52 W88 13 27. Stereo. Network: Network: NPR, PRI. Format: Class. News: 2 hrs wkly. Target aud: 35-70. ♦ Jake Schumacher, progmg dir. Co-owned TV: *WILL-TV affil

WLRW(FM)—See Champaign

WPGU(FM)— Apr 17, 1967: 107.1 mhz; 3 kw. 235 ft. TL: N40 06 34 W88 14 06. Stereo. 24 E. Green St., Suite 107, Champaign 61820-7903. Phone: (217) 244-3000. Fax: (217) 244-3001. E-mail: wpgu@wpgu.com. Web Site: www.wpgu.com. Licensee: Illini Media Co. Fisher, Wayland, Cooper, Leader & Zaragoza. Format: Alternative Rock. News: 7 hrs wkly. Target aud: 18-34. ♦ Mary Cory, gen mgr; Michelle Gabris, opns mgr; Rebecca Lalez, prom dir; Jim Finnerty, progmg dir; Jon Hansen, news dir; Scott S. Downs, sls dir & chief of engrg.

WQQB(FM)—(Rantoul). January 1993: 96.1 mhz; 3.8 kw. 403 ft. TL: N40 12 27 W88 17 56. Stereo. 4108 Fieldstone Rd., Suite C, Champaign 61822. Phone: (217) 367-3700. Fax: (217) 367-3291. E-mail: will@aaa-champaign.com. Web Site: www.wqqb.com. Licensee: AAA Entertainment Licensing LLC. Group owner: AAA Entertainment LLC (acq 4-21-00; grpsl). Format: CHR. Target aud: 18-49. ♦ Peter Ottmar, CEO; John Ginzkey, gen mgr; Linda Bosch, gen sls mgr & rgnl sls mgr; Will Sterrett, progmg dir; Mark Garrett, engrg dir & chief of engrg.

Vandalia

WKRV(FM)—Listing follows WPMB(AM).

WPMB(AM)— Dec 9, 1963: 1500 khz; 250 w-D. TL: N38 57 30 W89 07 27. Box 100 62471. Secondary address: 232 S. 4th St. 662471. Phone: (618) 283-2325. Phone: (618) 283-2355. Fax: (618) 283-1503. E-mail: wkrv@fgi.net. Licensee: Two Petaz Inc. (acq 2-3-2005;

$350,000. with co-located FM). Network: ABC Music Radio. Format: Big band, adult standards. News staff: one; News: 8-10 hrs wkly. Target aud: General. Spec prog: Farm 4 hrs, gospel 3 hrs wkly. ♦ Bayard H. Walters, pres; John D. Harris, gen mgr; Todd Stapleton, opns mgr & news dir.

WKRV(FM)—Co-owned with WPMB(AM). May 28, 1974: 107.1 mhz; 6 kw. Ant 164 ft. TL: N38 57 30 W89 07 27. Stereo. Format: CHR, adult contemp. News staff: one; News: 10 hrs wkly. Target aud: 20-45.

***WVNL(FM)**— 10/7/2002: 91.7 mhz; 100 w. 164 ft. Box 140, Carlinville 62626. Phone: (217) 854-4800. Fax: (217) 854-4810. E-mail: wibi@wibi.org. Web Site: www.wibi.org. Licensee: Illinois Bible Institute Inc. ♦ Richard C. Whitworth, gen mgr.

Vernon Hills

WNVR(AM)— Mar 1, 1988: 1030 khz; 5 kw-D, 120 w-N, DA-N. TL: N42 15 10 W88 23 45. 3656 W. Belmont, Chicago 60618. Phone: (773) 588-6300. Fax: (773) 267-4913. E-mail: polskieradio@polskieradio.com. Web Site: www.polskieradio.com. Licensee: Polnet Communications Ltd. (group owner; acq 3-15-91; $495,000;. FTR: 1-25-93). Wiley, Rein and Fielding. Format: Polish language. News staff: 7; News: 20 hrs wkly. Target aud: 18-54; Polish speaking audience. ♦ Kent Gustafson, CEO; Walter Kotaba, pres.

Virden

WCVS-FM—Licensed to Virden. See Springfield

Virginia

WVIL(FM)— February 1998: 101.3 mhz; 4 kw. 390 ft. TL: N40 00 52 W90 19 55. Stereo. Box 101, Jacksonville 62650. Secondary address: #7 Dunlap Ct., Jacksonville 62650. Phone: (217) 245-5700. Fax: (217) 245-5701. E-mail: lbostwick@mchsi.com. Web Site: www.wvilfm.com. Licensee: Mark J. Langston. Gammon & Grange. Format: All sports. News staff: one; News: one hr wkly. Target aud: 18-65; general. ♦ Larry Bostwick, gen mgr.

Warsaw

***WIUW(FM)**— May 17, 1995: 89.5 mhz; 10 kw. 449 ft. TL: N40 20 44 W91 24 11. 515 Univ. Svcs. Bldg., Western Illinois Univ., Macomb 61455. Phone: (309) 298-2424. Phone: (309) 298-1873. Fax: (309) 298-2133. E-mail: publicradio@wiu.edu. Web Site: www.tristatesradio.com. Licensee: Western Illinois University. Cohn & Marks. Format: Class, news. News staff: 2; News: 58 hrs wkly. Target aud: General. ♦ Dorothy Vallillo, gen mgr; Ken Thermon, opns dir; Sharon Faust, dev dir; Ken Zahnie, progmg dir & mus dir; Rich Egger, news dir.

Watseka

WGFA-FM— Mar 2, 1962: 94.1 mhz; 50 kw. Ant 364 ft. TL: N40 47 37 W87 45 17. Stereo. 1973 E. 1950 North Rd. 60970. Phone: (815) 432-4955. Fax: (815) 432-4957. E-mail: 941fm@wgfaradio.com. Web Site: www.wgfaradio.com. Licensee: Iroquois County Broadcasting Co. Network: ABC Information & Entertainment. Borsari & Paxson. Format: Adult contemp. News staff: one; News: 12 hrs wkly. Target aud: 25-54. Spec prog: Farm 18 hrs, business 2 hrs, sports 18 hrs wkly. ♦ Margaret Martin, gen mgr, dev dir & prom mgr; Michelle Ferguson, stn mgr, gen sls mgr & natl sls mgr; Justin Kaiser, opns dir, progmg dir & progmg dir; M'lissa Long, rgnl sls mgr & pub affrs dir; Carl Gerdovich, news dir; Stacey Smith, pub affrs dir; Mark Spalding, chief of engrg.

WGFA(AM)— Sept 1, 1961: 1360 khz; 1 kw-D, DA. TL: N40 47 48 W87 45 11. Web Site: www.wgfaradio.com. Format: Big band, easy lstng. News staff: 6. Target aud: 30-65; wealthy, retiring, entrepreneurs. Spec prog: Talk 5 hrs wkly. ♦ Margaret Martin, mktg dir, prom dir, adv dir & progmg VP.

Waukegan

WKRS(AM)— Sept 25, 1949: 1220 khz; 1 kw-D, DA. TL: N42 20 59 W87 52 53. (CP: 99 w-N). 3250 Belvidere Rd. 60085. Phone: (847) 336-7900. Fax: (847) 336-1523. Web Site: www.wkrs.com. Licensee: NM Licensing LLC. Group owner: NextMedia Group LLC (acq 11-26-01; grpsl). Network: ABC Daytime Direction. Rep: Allied Radio Partners. Format: News/talk. News staff: 4; News: 40 hrs wkly. Target aud: 25 plus. ♦ Kira La Foud, gen mgr.

WXLC(FM)—Co-owned with WKRS(AM). May 1963: 102.3 mhz; 3 kw. 322 ft. TL: N42 20 59 W87 52 53. Stereo. Web Site: www.1023xlc.com. Format: Adult contemp. Target aud: 25-44. ♦ Kim Ciesco, prom dir; Trent Erickson, progmg dir.

West Frankfort

WFRX(AM)— May 2, 1951: 1300 khz; 1 kw-D. TL: N37 53 04 W88 55 44. Box 127, 1822 N. Court St., Marion 62959. Phone: (618) 997-8123. Phone: (618) 932-8121. Fax: (618) 993-2319. Web Site: www.wfrx.com. Licensee: Clear Channel Broadcasting Licenses Inc. Group owner: Clear Channel Communications Inc. (acq 1-18-01; grpsl). Format: News, big band. News staff: one; News: 20 hrs wkly. Target aud: Adult. ♦ Jerry Crouse, gen mgr; Paxton Guy, progmg dir & news dir; Clarence Larson, chief of engrg.

WQUL(FM)—Co-owned with WFRX(AM). Mar 14, 1972: 97.7 mhz; 3.5 kw. 433 ft. TL: N37 45 15 W88 56 05. Web Site: www.thebear977fm.com. Format: Pure classic rock. News: 2 hrs wkly. Target aud: 25-54; adult. ♦ D. T. Brown, progmg dir.

Wheaton

***WETN(FM)**— Feb 27, 1962: 88.1 mhz; 250 w. 140 ft. TL: N41 52 09 W88 05 56. Stereo. Wheaton College 60187. Phone: (630) 752-5074. Fax: (630) 752-5286. E-mail: wetn@wheaton.edu. Web Site: www.wetn.org. Licensee: Trustees of Wheaton College. Format: Christian , classical. News: 2 hrs wkly. Target aud: 18-49. Spec prog: Live sports 5 hrs, live church svcs 3 hrs, live concerts 2 hrs wkly. ♦ Dr. A. Duane Litfin, pres; John Rorvik, gen mgr; Mark Bartlebaugh, stn mgr.

Wilmington

WYKT(FM)— Sept 29, 1980: 105.5 mhz; 1.3 kw. 482 ft. TL: N41 17 11 W88 14 23. Stereo. 70 Meadowview Ctr., Kamkakee 60901. Phone: (815) 727-9555. Fax: (815) 724-1025. Web Site: www.1055thepickle.com. Licensee: STARadio Corp. (group owner; acq 7-6-98). Format: Hits of the 60s & 70s. News staff: one; News: 4 hrs wkly. Target aud: 25-54. Spec prog: Gospel 4 hrs, pub service 4 hrs, sports 12 hrs wkly. ♦ Brendan Michaels, opns mgr & progmg dir; Larry Regnler, gen sls mgr & chief of engrg; Robert Kersmarki, VP, gen mgr & mktg VP.

Winnebago

WYHY(FM)— 1971: 95.3 mhz; 1.25 kw. 512 ft. TL: N42 17 26 W89 09 51. Stereo. 2830 Sandy Hollow Rd., Rockford 61109. Phone: (815) 874-7861. Fax: (815) 874-2202. Licensee: Maverick Media of Rockford License LLC. Group owner: RadioWorks Inc. (acq 4-27-2005; grpsl). Rep: Katz Radio. Shaw Pittman. Format: Classic hits. Target aud: 25-54. ♦ Gary Rozynek, pres; David W. McAley, VP & gen mgr.

Winnetka

***WNTH(FM)**— Dec 10, 1960: 88.1 mhz; 100 w. 105 ft. TL: N42 05 40 W87 43 07. Stereo. 385 Winnetka Ave. 60093. Phone: (847) 501-6302. Fax: (847) 501-6400. Web Site: www.newtrier.kiz.il.us. Licensee: New Trier Township Board of Education. (acq 1960). Format: Div. ♦ Nina Lynn, stn mgr.

Illinois

Wood River

KFNS(AM)— Oct 5, 1961: 590 khz; 1 kw-U, DA-2. TL: N38 55 43 W90 05 08.KFNS-FM, Troy/St. Louis, Missouri, 100% 8045 Big Bend Blvd., Webster Groves, MO 63119. Phone: (314) 962-0590. Fax: (314) 962-7576. Web Site: www.kfns.com. Licensee: Big Stick One LLC. Group owner: Big League Broadcasting LLC (acq 7-13-2004; grpsl). Rep: Interep. Format: Sports. Target aud: 25-54; men. ◆Evan Crocker, VP & gen mgr; Jim Goessling, gen sls mgr; Jason Komito, prom dir; Rob Weingarten, progmg dir; John Masters, chief of engrg.

Woodlawn

WDML(FM)— Nov 5, 1993: 106.9 mhz; 3 kw. 328 ft. TL: N38 21 29 W89 05 56. Stereo. Box 1591, 3501 Broadway, Mount Vernon 62864. Phone: (618) 242-3333. Fax: (618) 242-3334. E-mail: wdml@mvn.net. Web Site: www.wdml.com. Licensee: Volunteer Broadcasting of Illinois Inc. Network: Westwood One. Dennis Kelly. Format: Adult rock. News staff: one; News: one hr wkly. Target aud: 30 plus; male. Spec prog: Christian rock 3 hrs wkly. ◆David M. Lister, CEO, pres & gen mgr; Ryan Roddy, COO & stn mgr.

Woodstock

WZSR(FM)— May 24, 1974: 105.5 mhz; 3 kw. 429 ft. TL: N42 15 30 W88 21 48. (CP: 1.95 kw, ant 567 ft. TL: N42 15 34 W88 21 45). Stereo. 8800 Rt. 14, Crystal Lake 60012. Phone: (815) 459-7000. Fax: (815) 459-7027. Web Site: www.star105.com. Licensee: NM Licensing LLC. Group owner: NextMedia Group L.L.C. (acq 11-26-01; grpsl). Format: Adult contemp. Target aud: 25-54; female. Spec prog: Relg one hr wkly. ◆Kira Lefond, gen mgr; Jim Johnson, opns dir; Don Oberbillig, gen sls mgr; Bobby Knight, progmg VP & progmg dir; Stew Cohen, news dir & chief of engrg.

Zion

WPJX(AM)— Sept 19, 1967: 1500 khz; 250 w-D, DA. TL: N42 27 18 W87 54 01. 190 N. State St., Chicago 60601. Phone: (312) 683-1300. Fax: (312) 577-5994. Web Site: www.radiodisney.com. Licensee: ABC Inc. (group owner; acq 3-30-99; grpsl). Format: Radio Disney. Target aud: 18-40. ◆Zemira Jones, pres; Karyn Esken, stn mgr.

WWDV(FM)— 1962: 96.9 mhz; 50 kw. 500 ft. TL: N42 30 36 W87 53 11. Stereo. 875 N. Michigan Ave., Suite 1510, Chicago 60611. Phone: (312) 274-9710. Fax: (312) 274-1304. Web Site: www.wdrv.com. Licensee: Bonneville Holding Co. Group owner: Bonneville International Corp. (acq 1-25-01; $165 million. with WDRV(FM) Chicago). Format: Classic rock. ◆Jerry Schnacke, pres, VP & gen mgr; Greg Solk, opns VP.

Indiana

Alexandria

WHTI(FM)— Sept 3, 1980: 96.7 mhz; 2.5 kw. Ant 351 ft. TL: N40 10 38 W85 40 23. Stereo. 800 E. 29th St., Muncie 47302. Phone: (866) 516-1278. Phone: (765) 288-4403. Fax: (765) 288-0429. E-mail: maxstudio@maxrocks.net. Web Site: www.maxrocks.net. Licensee: Indiana Sabrecom Inc. Group owner: Backyard Broadcasting LLC (acq 12-1-02; grpsl). Network: Motor Racing Net. Format: Classic rock. News staff: one; News: 2 hrs wkly. Target aud: 25-54. ◆Steve Lindell, VP & gen mgr; Elaine Merritt, gen sls mgr; Brian Thomas, prom mgr & progmg dir; Tom Hammond, news dir; Sean Mattingly, chief of engrg.

Anderson

*WBSB(FM)— December 1996: 89.5 mhz; 400 w. 364 ft. TL: N40 10 38 W85 40 23. c/o WBST(FM), Ball State Univ., Muncie 47306-0550. Phone: (765) 285-5888. Fax: (765) 285-8937. E-mail: ipr@bsu.edu. Web Site: www.bsu.edu/ipr. Licensee: Ball State University. Format: Class, news. News staff: one. ◆Anthony Hunt, gen mgr, gen sls mgr, progmg dir & mus dir; Robert Mittendorf, chief of engrg.

*WGNR-FM— Sept 11, 1973: 97.9 mhz; 50 kw. 489 ft. TL: N40 03 43 W85 42 34. Stereo. 2000 W. 53rd St. 46013. Phone: (765) 642-2750. Fax: (765) 642-4033. E-mail: wgnr@moody.edu. Web Site: www.wgnr.org. Licensee: Moody Bible Institute of Chicago. Group owner: The Moody Bible Institute of Chicago (acq 12-17-97; $5.5 million with co-located AM). Format: Inspirational, Christian. News staff: one. Target aud: 35-54. ◆Dr. Joe Stowell, pres; Ray Hashley, gen mgr & stn mgr; Tom Winn, progmg dir & progmg mgr; Sam Sundin, news dir; Jim Wagner, chief of engrg.

WGNR(AM)— 1946: 1470 khz; 1 kw-D, 35 w-N. TL: N40 03 43 W85 42 37. E-mail: wgnr@moody.com. Web Site: www.wgnr.org. Format: Christian talk. Target aud: 35-54. ◆Ray Hashley, gen mgr.

WHBU(AM)— April 1923: 1240 khz; 1 kw-U. TL: N40 06 17 W85 40 45. 9821 S. 800 West, Daleville 47334. Phone: (765) 378-2080. Fax: (765) 378-2090. Licensee: Indiana Sabrecom Inc. Group owner: Backyard Broadcasting LLC (acq 12-1-02; grpsl). Format: News/talk, sports. News staff: one; News: 40 hrs wkly. Target aud: 25-54. Spec prog: Purdue sports, Indy 500, NASCAR, Indiana University. ◆Steve Lindell, VP & gen mgr; Elaine Merritt, gen sls mgr; Leland Franklin, progmg dir; Tom Hammond, news dir; Sean Mattingly, chief of engrg.

WQME(FM)— Nov 29 1990: 98.7 mhz; 4.5 kw. 400 ft. TL: N39 58 59 W85 42 41. Stereo. 1100 E. 5th St. 46012-3495. Phone: (765) 641-4349. Fax: (765) 641-3825. E-mail: email@wqme.com. Web Site: www.wqme.com. Licensee: Anderson University Inc. Fletcher, Heald & Hildreth. Format: Adult contemp, Christian. News staff: one; News: 8 hrs wkly. Target aud: 25-54. Spec prog: Relg 9 hrs wkly. ◆Donald Boggs, gen mgr; Gerald Longenbaugh, gen sls mgr; Matt Rust, progmg dir; Kristy Deer, news dir; Jerry Morton, chief of engrg & engr; Jill O'Malia, mktg.

Angola

*WEAX(FM)— September 1979: 88.3 mhz; 920 w. Ant 151 ft. TL: N41 37 53 W85 00 37. Stereo. Stewart Hall, 935 Park St. 46703-1750. Secondary address: 1 University Ave. 46703. Phone: (260) 665-4288. Fax: (260) 665-4765. E-mail: weaxfm@tristate.edu. Web Site: www.88xonline.com. Licensee: Tri-State University. Network: CNN Radio. Reddy, Begley & McCormick. Format: Classic rock, AOR, heavy metal. News staff: one; News: 10 hrs wkly. Target aud: 16-54; general. Spec prog: Class 4 hrs, Black 2 hrs, jazz 2 hrs wkly. ◆Jim Carlyle, gen mgr & opns mgr; Patrick Zillmer, chief of engrg.

WLKI(FM)— July 15, 1974: 100.3 mhz; 4 kw. Ant 393 ft. TL: N41 40 51 W85 00 05. Stereo. Box 999 46703. Secondary address: 2655 State Rd. 127N 46703. Phone: (260) 665-9554. Fax: (260) 665-9064. E-mail: wlki@wlki.com. Web Site: www.wlki.com. Licensee: Lake Cities Broadcasting Corp. Network: ABC FM Connection. Format: Hot adult contemp. Target aud: 25-49; adults with youthful outlook, skews female. ◆Bill Kerner, VP; Thomas R. Andrews, pres & gen mgr; Greg Case, chief of engrg.

Attica

*WFWR(FM)—Not on air, target date: unknown: 91.5 mhz; 160 w. 171 ft. TL: N40 16 47 W87 14 50. 909 S. McDonald St. 47918. Phone: (765) 764-1934. Licensee: Fountain Warren Community Radio Corp. Format: Var.

WSHP(AM)— April 1990: 95.7 mhz; 3.1 kw. Ant 433 ft. TL: N40 23 02 W87 07 55. Stereo. 3824 S. 18th St., Lafayette 47909. Phone: (765) 474-1410. Fax: (765) 474-3442. Licensee: Artistic Media Partners L.P. Group owner: Artistic Media Partners Inc. (acq 10-3-94; $410,000;. FTR: 10-17-94). Rep: Christal. Rosenman & Colin. Format: Classic rock. Target aud: 25-54. ◆Arthur A. Angotti, pres; Arthur Angotti III, exec VP & gen mgr; Bob Henning, gen sls mgr & chief of engrg; Mike Warner, progmg dir.

Auburn

WGLL(AM)— Sept 3, 1968: 1570 khz; 500 w-D, 151 w-N, DA-2. TL: N41 20 01 W85 03 08. 5446 C. R. 29, Fort Wayne 46706. Phone: (260) 925-4300. Fax: (260) 432-0986. Licensee: Kovas Communications of Indiana Inc. (acq 11-9-01; grpsl). Network: CBS. Rep: Rgnl Reps. Lauren A. Colby. Format: Relg progmg. Target aud: 25-54. ◆Raymond Alexander, pres & gen mgr.

WXTW(FM)— Apr 10, 1967: 102.3 mhz; 3 kw. 300 ft. TL: N41 20 01 W85 03 08. Stereo. 2000 Lower Huntington Rd., Fort Wayne 46819. Phone: (260) 747-1511. Fax: (260) 747-3999. E-mail: kfoate@summitcityradio.com. Web Site: x102fm.com. Licensee: Travis Broadcasting LLC. Group owner: Summit City Radio Group (acq 6-18-2002; grpsl). Rep: McGavren Guild. Format: CHR, Rock. ◆Kristine Foate, CEO & gen mgr.

Aurora

WSCH(FM)— Oct 29, 1970: 99.3 mhz; 1.15 kw. 525 ft. TL: N38 57 55 W84 56 51. Stereo. 6857 Salem Ridge Rd. 47001. Phone: (812) 438-2777. Fax: (812) 438-3495. E-mail: wsch@one.net. Licensee: Columbus Radio Inc. (acq 12-2-02; with WXCH(FM) Versailles). Network: ABC. Format: Young country. News staff: one; News: 10 hrs wkly. Target aud: 25-plus. Spec prog: Farm 3 hrs wkly. ◆Marty Pierattt, pres; Bill Reinberger, gen mgr; Jamin Tuttle, progmg dir & mus dir; Bob Shannon, news dir; Robert Hawkins, chief of engrg.

Austin

WJAA(FM)— 1991: 96.3 mhz; 3 kw. 328 ft. TL: N38 50 39 W85 49 26. 1531 W. Tipton St., Seymour 47274. Phone: (812) 523-3343. Fax: (812) 523-5116. E-mail: coolbus@wjaa.net. Web Site: www.wjaa.net. Licensee: Midland Media Inc. (acq 6-28-91; $15,000; 7-22-91). Network: Network: ABC, Westwood One. Format: AOR, classic rock. News staff: News progmg 5 hrs wkly Target aud: 25-54; men & women. ◆Robert Becker, gen mgr; Tony Starkey, gen sls mgr; Shanno Pyle, progmg dir.

WJCP(FM)— December 1993: 92.7 mhz; 2 kw. 400 ft. TL: N38 49 23 W85 47 24. Stereo. 2470 N. Hwy. 7, North Vernon 47265. Phone: (812) 346-1927. Fax: (812) 346-9722. Licensee: Pieratt Communications Inc. (acq 7-2-97; $275,000). Network: USA. Format: Country. News staff: one; News: 21 hrs wkly. Target aud: 25-65. ◆Marty Pieratt, gen mgr.

Batesville

WRBI(FM)— May 14, 1977: 103.9 mhz; 1.95 kw. 360 ft. TL: N39 13 22 W85 15 28. Stereo. 133 S. Main St. 47006. Phone: (812) 934-5111. Fax: (812) 934-2765. E-mail: wrbi@wrbiradio.com. Web Site: www.wrbiradio.com. Licensee: White River Broadcasting Co. Inc. Group owner: The Findlay Publishing Co. (acq 7-31-97; grpsl). Rep: Rgnl Reps Rgnl Reps Format: Country. News staff: one; News: 10 hrs wkly. Target aud: General. Spec prog: Farm 5 hrs wkly. ◆Davis Glass, VP; Ronald E. Green, gen mgr.

Battle Ground

WASK-FM— Mar 11, 1993: 98.7 mhz; 4.4 kw. 384 ft. TL: N40 29 57 W86 52 25. Stereo. Box 7880, Lafayette 47903-7880. Secondary address: 3575 McCarty Ln., Lafayette 47905. Phone: (765) 447-2186. Fax: (765) 448-4452. Web Site: www.wask.com. Licensee: WASK Inc. Group owner: Schurz Communications Inc. (acq 3-6-95; $860,000; 6-26-95). Rep: Christal. Rgnl Reps. Hogan & Hartson. Format: Oldies. News staff: 4; News: 20 hrs wkly. Target aud: 35 plus; general. ◆John A. Trent, pres, gen mgr & gen sls mgr; Randy Jones, opns mgr; Brian Green, gen sls mgr; Mark Allen, progmg dir & progmg mgr; Eric Burch, news dir; Steve Truex, chief of engrg.

Bedford

WBIW(AM)— October 1948: 1340 khz; 1 kw-U. TL: N38 52 23 W86 28 34. 424 Heltonville Rd. 47421. Phone: (812) 275-7555. Fax: (812) 279-8046. E-mail: wbiw1340am@yahoo.com. Web Site: www.wbiw.com. Licensee: Ad-Venture Media Inc. (acq 1-30-89; $1 million with co-located FM; 1-30-89). Network: Network: Westwood One, USA. Rep: Rgnl Reps. Reed, Smith, Shaw & McClay. Format: Sports, news, talk. News staff: 2; News: 28 hrs wkly. Target aud: 25 plus; general. Spec prog: Sports, weather, farm 3 hrs wkly. ◆Dean Spencer, pres & gen mgr.

Beech Grove

WNTS(AM)— Dec 10, 1956: 1590 khz; 5 kw-D, 500 w-N, DA-3. TL: N39 44 21 W86 05 29. 4800 E. Raymond St., Indianapolis 46203. Phone: (317) 359-5591. Fax: (317) 359-3885. Web Site: wnts1590am.com. Licensee: S & M Broadcasting Co. Inc. (acq 4-15-74). Network: Network: USA, Salem Radio Network. Wiley, Rein & Fielding. Format: Relg & spiritual, southern gospel. Target aud: 25-54. ◆Jack N. Marsella, pres; James S. Wilson, gen mgr.

Berne

WZBD(FM)— Aug 27, 1993: 92.7 mhz; 4.1 kw. 394 ft. TL: N40 46 15 W85 56 05. 1891 W. State Rd. 97, Portland 47371. Secondary address: 955 US 27 N. 46711. Phone: (260) 726-8729. Fax: (260) 726-4311. E-mail: wpgw@jayco.net. Licensee: Adams County Radio

Stations in the U.S. — Indiana

Inc. (acq 3-11-99). Format: Adult contemp, local news. Target aud: General. ♦ Rob Weaver, pres & gen mgr; David A. Giltner, opns mgr.

Bicknell

WUZR(FM)—Licensed to Bicknell. See Vincennes

Bloomington

WBWB(FM)— July 17, 1978: 96.7 mhz; 1.65 kw. 439 ft. TL: N39 09 46 W86 28 21. Stereo. Box 7797 47407. Secondary address: 304 State Rd. 446 47401. Phone: (812) 336-8000. Fax: (812) 336-7000. E-mail: wbwb@wbwb.com. Web Site: www.wbwb.com. Licensee: Artistic Media Partners L.P. Group owner: Artistic Media Partners Inc. (acq 1-89; grpsl; 1-23-89). Rep: McGavren Guild. Rgnl Reps. Haley, Bader & Potts. Format: CHR. News staff: one. Target aud: 18-49. ♦ Art Angotti, pres; Sandy Zehr, gen mgr; Dale Clark, gen sls mgr; Jeremy Gray, news dir; Bob Henning, chief of engrg.

*****WFHB(FM)**— December 1992: 91.3 mhz; 2.5 kw horiz, 2.45 kw vert. 266 ft. TL: N39 01 55 W86 36 33. Box 1973 47402. Secondary address: 108 W. 4th St. 47404. Phone: (812) 323-1200. Fax: (812) 323-0320. E-mail: wfhb@wfhb.org. Web Site: www.wfhb.org. Licensee: Bloomington Community Radio Inc. Format: Div, news, pub affrs. News staff: one; News: 5 hrs wkly. Target aud: General. Spec prog: Folk 10 hrs, Latin 3 hrs, Finnish 3 hrs wkly. ♦ Jim Krause, pres; Ryan Bruce, CEO & stn mgr.

*****WFIU(FM)**— Sept 30, 1950: 103.7 mhz; 29 kw. Ant 646 ft. TL: N39 08 31 W86 29 43. Stereo. Radio-TV Ctr., Indiana Univ., 1229 E. 7th St. 47405. Phone: (812) 855-1357. Fax: (812) 855-5600. E-mail: wwfiu@indiana.edu. Web Site: www.indiana.edu/~wfiu. Licensee: Trustees of Indiana University. Network: NPR. Crowell & Moring. Format: Class, jazz, news. News staff: one; News: 7 hrs wkly. Target aud: General. ♦ Christina Kuzmych, stn mgr; Will Murphy, news dir; Bradley Howard, chief of engrg. Co-owned TV: *WTIU(TV) affil.

WGCL(AM)— Mar 11, 1949: 1370 khz; 5 kw-D, 500 w-N, DA-2. TL: N39 11 25 W86 38 02. Stereo. 400 One City Ctr. 47404. Phone: (812) 332-3366. Fax: (812) 331-4570. Web Site: www.am1370wgll.com. Licensee: Sarkes Tarzian Inc. (group owner) Network: ABC Information & Entertainment. Rep: Christal. Format: News/talk. News staff: 3; News: 5 hrs wkly. Target aud: 30 plus. ♦ Ron Tarsi, gen mgr; Don Pratt, progmg dir; Marc Antonetti, chief of engrg.

WTTS(FM)—Co-owned with WGCL(AM). Jan 7, 1960: 92.3 mhz; 37 kw. 1,090 ft. TL: N39 24 27 W86 08 52. Stereo. Web Site: www.wttsfm.com. Rep: Christal. Format: AAA. News staff: one. Target aud: 25-54. Spec prog: Blues 2 hrs, acoustic show 4 hrs wkly. ♦ Roger Ingram, gen sls mgr & prom dir; Laura Duncan, news dir.

Bluffton

WNUY(FM)— Dec 10, 1963: 100.1 mhz; 5.2 kw. 351 ft. TL: N40 44 50 W85 10 21. Stereo. Box 321 46714. Phone: (260) 824-2804. Fax: (260) 824-2805. E-mail: wnuy@wnuy.com. Web Site: www.wnuy.com. Licensee: Wells County Radio Corp. (acq 4-10-86). Format: Adult contemp. News staff: one; News: 3 hrs wkly. Target aud: 25-49; professional women. Spec prog: Relg 4 hrs wkly. ♦ Joe Shanley, gen mgr & gen sls mgr; Rob Caylor, progmg dir; Rob Taylor, prom dir & news dir; Rick Elwell, chief of engrg.

Boonville

WBNL(AM)— Sept 10, 1950: 1540 khz; 250 w-D. TL: N38 03 58 W87 16 27. Box 270 47601. Secondary address: 2177 N. Hwy. 61, 47601. Phone: (812) 897-2080. Fax: (812) 897-2130. E-mail: rtradio@sigecom.net. Web Site: www.radio1540.net. Licensee: Turpen Communications LLC (acq 8-22-01). Network: USA. Format: MOR, adult contemp. News staff: one; News: 14 hrs wkly. Target aud: 25-54; Women 25-54. Spec prog: Gospel 5 hrs wkly. ♦ Ralph E. Turpen, pres & gen mgr.

WYXY(FM)— Dec 19, 1967: 107.1 mhz; 3 kw. 185 ft. TL: N38 03 58 W87 16 27. Box 3848, Evansville 47736. Secondary address: 1162 Mt. Auburn Rd., Evansville 47720. Phone: (812) 424-8284. Fax: (812) 426-7928. E-mail: tim@sccradio.com. Licensee: Boonville Broadcasting Co. Inc. Group owner: South Central Communications Corp. (acq 8-14-00; $400,000 for stock. with co-located AM). Format: Contemp Christian. ♦ John P. Engelbrecht, CEO; Tim Huelsing, VP & gen mgr; Cindy Miller, progmg mgr; Kevin Potter, chief of engrg.

Brazil

WSDM-FM— Nov 13, 1973: 97.7 mhz; 6 kw. Ant 300 ft. TL: N39 30 43 W87 08 19. Stereo. 1301 Ohio St., Terre Haute 47807. Phone: (812) 234-9770. Fax: (812) 238-1576. E-mail: wsdm@wsdm.com. Web Site: www.oldiesradioonline.com. Licensee: Crossroads Investments LLC. (acq 8-1-90; with co-located AM). Network: ABC. Rep: Roslin. Booth, Freret, Imlay & Tepper. Format: Pure gold, oldies. News staff: one; News: 2 hrs wkly. Target aud: 35-64; baby boomers living in Terre Haute market. ♦ Dan Lacy, CFO; Michael Petersen, pres & gen mgr.

WSDX(AM)—Co-owned with WSDM-FM. 1959: 1130 khz; 500 w-D, 20 w-N. TL: N39 30 44 W87 08 18. Licensee: Crossroads Communications Inc. Web Site: espnsportsradio.com. Group owner: Crossroads Communications Inc. Rep: Roslin. Rgnl Reps. Booth, Freret, Imlay & Tepper. Format: Sports. News staff: one. Target aud: General; sports fans.

Bremen

WHPZ(FM)— Mar 1, 1993: 96.9 mhz; 2.99 kw. Ant 462 ft. TL: N41 26 37 W86 01 18. 61300 S. Ironwood Rd., South Bend 46614. Phone: (574) 291-8200. Fax: (574) 291-9043. E-mail: thale@lesea.com. Web Site: www.pulsefm.com. Licensee: Le Sea Broadcasting Corp. Group owner: Le Sea Broadcasting Corp. (acq 1-4-2000; $280,296). Format: Contemp Christian. ♦ Tony Hale, CFO; Anna Riblet, gen sls mgr; Zach Anders, progmg dir; Wes Hylton, chief of engrg.

Brookston

WLFF(FM)— Apr 16, 1967: 95.3 mhz; 2.3 kw. Ant 505 ft. TL: N40 32 48 W86 50 59. Stereo. 3824 S. 18th Street, Lafayette 47909. Phone: (765) 474-1410. Fax: (765) 474-3442. Web Site: www.wlff.com. Licensee: Artistic Media Partners Inc. (group owner; (acq 9-1-98; $1.8 million). Rosenman & Colin. Format: Country. News staff: one; News: 14 hrs wkly. Target aud: 35 plus; affluent, educated & upscale. ♦ Doug Kern, pres; Arthur Angotti III, gen mgr; Steve Clark, progmg dir & mus dir; Bob Henning, chief of engrg.

Brownsburg

WKLU(FM)— Mar 23, 1992: 101.9 mhz; 3.7 kw. Ant 252 ft. TL: N39 49 07 W86 22 40. Stereo. 733 N. Green St. 46112. Secondary address: Box 532219, Indianapolis 46253. Phone: (317) 852-9119. Fax: (317) 852-8018. E-mail: mark@wklu.net. Web Site: www.kool-1019.com. Licensee: Indy Radio LLC (acq 7-30-2004; $6.2 million). Format: Classic rock, sports. News staff: 2; News: 10 hrs wkly. Target aud: 25-54. Spec prog: Sports, talk. ♦ Mark Clark, gen mgr; Libby Farr, opns mgr & progmg dir.

Cannelton

WLME(FM)— July 1990: 102.9 mhz; 12.5 kw. Ant 466 ft. TL: N37 46 57 W86 36 26. Stereo. 1115 Tamarock Rd., Suite 500, Owensboro, KY 42301. Phone: (270) 683-5200. Fax: (270) 688-0108. Licensee: WLME Inc. Group owner: The Cromwell Group Inc. Network: ABC. Rep: Rgnl Reps. Pepper & Corazzini. Format: Oldies. News staff: one; News: 10 hrs wkly. Target aud: 25-54; general. Spec prog: Sports 9 hrs wkly. ♦ Bayard H. Walters, pres; Corky Norcia, gen mgr.

Carmel

*****WHJE(FM)**— September 1963: 91.3 mhz; 400 w. 100 ft. TL: N39 58 45 W86 07 10. Stereo. 520 E. Main St. 46032. Phone: (317) 571-4055. Phone: (317) 846-7721. Fax: (317) 571-4066. E-mail: whje@spitfire.net. Web Site: www.whje.com. Licensee: Carmel Clay Schools. Network: UPI. Format: Classic rock, alternative. Target aud: 12 plus. ♦ Tom Schoeller, gen mgr.

Centerville

WHON(AM)—Licensed to Centerville. See Richmond

Chandler

WLFW(FM)— Apr 2, 1994: 93.5 mhz; 3.2 kw. Ant 446 ft. TL: N38 01 27 W87 21 43. Box 3848, Evansville 47736. Secondary address: 1162 Mt. Auburn Rd., Evansville 47720. Phone: (812) 424-8284. Fax: (812) 426-7928. Web Site: www.935thewolf.com. Licensee: South Central Communications Corp. (group owner; (acq 1996; $860,000). Network: Westwood One. Format: Country. News staff: 3. Target aud: 35-49. ♦ John D. Englebrecht, chmn; Craig Jacobus, pres; La Donne Craig, gen mgr & gen sls mgr; Tim Huelsing, gen mgr; James Ashley, prom dir; Rusty James, progmg dir.

Charlestown

WEGK(FM)— Apr 7, 1998: 104.3 mhz; 3 kw. Ant 328 ft. TL: N38 28 55 W85 37 33. Stereo. 520 S. 4th St., 2nd Fl., Louisville, KY 40202. Phone: (502) 625-1220. Fax: (502) 625-1257. Web Site: www.eagle1043.com. Licensee: Blue Chip Broadcasting Licenses Ltd. Group owner: Radio One Inc. (acq 2-14-2003; $2 million). Format: Rhythmic CHR. ♦ Dale Schaefer, gen mgr.

Chesterton

*****WBEW(FM)**— 2001: 89.5 mhz; 7 kw. Ant 216 ft. TL: N41 42 58 W86 51 47. (CP: 23 kw, ant 187 ft.). 848 E. Grand Ave., Navy Pier, Chicago, IL 60611-3462. Phone: (312) 948-4600. Fax: (312) 948-4837. E-mail: tmalatia@chicagopublicradio.org. Web Site: www.chicagopublicradio.org. Licensee: The WBEZ Alliance Inc. (acq 10-4-02; $550,000). Format: News, talk, jazz. ♦ Torey Malatia, pres & gen mgr; Greg Salustro, dev VP.

*****WDSO(FM)**— November 1976: 88.3 mhz; 400 w. 135 ft. TL: N41 36 29 W87 03 37. Stereo. Chesterton High School, 2125 S. 11th St. 46304. Phone: (219) 983-3777. Phone: (219) 983-3730. Fax: (219) 983-3773. Web Site: www.wdso.org. Licensee: Duneland School Corp. Format: Rock. News: 6 hrs wkly. Target aud: General. Spec prog: Class one hr, specialty rock 8 hrs wkly. ♦ Brent Barber, stn mgr & chief of engrg; Michele Stipanovich, opns mgr.

Churubusco

WNHT(FM)— August 1994: 96.3 mhz; 6.7 kw. 554 ft. TL: N41 06 13 W85 10 44. 2000 Lower Huntington Rd., Fort Wayne 46819. Phone: (260) 747-1511. Fax: (260) 747-3999. Web Site: hits963.com. Licensee: Travis Broadcasting LLC. Group owner: Summit City Radio Group (acq 6-18-2002; grpsl). Rep: McGavren Guild. Format: Top 40, hip hop, rock. Target aud: 18-34; men. ♦ Kris Foate, CEO & gen mgr; Dave Wisniewski, gen sls mgr; Dave B. Goode, progmg dir.

Cicero

*****WJCY(FM)**— 2005: 91.5 mhz; 475 w vert. Ant 193 ft. TL: N40 11 53 W86 07 44. CSN International, 4002N. 3300E., Twin Falls, ID 83301. Phone: (208) 734-6633. Licensee: CSN International. (group owner).

Clarksville

WTFX-FM— 1998: 93.1 mhz; 2.15 kw. Ant 387 ft. TL: N38 17 02 W85 54 17. 4000 #1 Radio Dr., Louisville, KY 40218. Phone: (502) 479-2222. Fax: (502) 479-2223. Web Site: www.foxrocks.com. Licensee: Clear Channel Radio Licenses Inc. Group owner: Clear Channel Communications Inc. Format: Acitve rock. ♦ Earl Jones, gen mgr.

Clinton

WAXI(FM)—See Rockville

*****WPFR-FM**— 1998: 93.9 mhz; 2.3 kw. 531 ft. TL: N39 33 18 W87 28 40. Stereo. 18889 N. 2350th St., Dennison, IL 62423. Phone: (217)

Indiana

826-9673. E-mail: wkzi@rr1.net. Licensee: Word Power Inc. Network: Moody. Vinson & Elkins. Format: Christian. News: 17 hrs wkly. Target aud: 12 plus. ♦ Paul Dean Ford, pres & gen mgr; Mark S. Ford, opns dir; Dan Watson, chief of opns.

Cloverdale

*WSPM(FM)— 2003: 89.1 mhz; 25 w horiz, 49 kw vert. Ant 298 ft. TL: N39 41 19 W86 42 03. 3500 DePauw Blvd., Suite 2085, Indianapolis 46268. Phone: (317) 870-8400 ext 21. Fax: (317) 870-8404. E-mail: jim@catholicradioindy.org. Web Site: www.catholicradioindy.org.org. Licensee: Hoosier Broadcasting Corp. Format: Relg-Catholic. ♦ James J. Ganley, gen mgr.

Columbia City

WDDB(FM)— Oct 13, 1968: 106.3 mhz; 5.6 kw. Ant 339 ft. TL: N41 12 49 W85 12 04. Stereo. 2100 Goshen Rd., Suite 332, Fort Wayne 46808. Phone: (260) 482-9288. Fax: (260) 482-8655. E-mail: info@sunny106fm.com. Web Site: www.sunny106fm.com. Licensee: Artistic Media Partners Inc. (group owner; (acq 7-30-2004; $2.61 million). Tierney & Swift. Format: Hot adult contemp. Target aud: 35 plus. ♦ John Henry, gen mgr; Kenny Edwards, opns mgr; Ron Gregory, progmg dir; Bob Henning, chief of engrg.

*WJHS(FM)— Aug 12, 1985: 91.5 mhz; 2.65 kw. 219 ft. TL: N41 10 04 W85 29 41. Stereo. 600 N. Whitley St. 46725. Phone: (260) 248-8915. Phone: (260) 244-6136. Fax: (260) 244-5610. E-mail: comments@wjhs915.org. Web Site: www.wjhs915.org. Licensee: Whitley County Consolidated Schools Board of Control. Format: Adult alternative. Target aud: Men 25-54; general. Spec prog: Sports events. ♦ Krystal Walker Zoltek, stn mgr; Mike Peters, chief of engrg.

Columbus

WCSI(AM)— 1950: 1010 khz; 500 w-D, 19 w-N. TL: N39 11 05 W85 57 17. Stereo. Box 1789 47202-1789. Secondary address: 3212 Washington St. 47203. Phone: (812) 372-4448. Fax: (812) 372-1061. Licensee: White River Broadcasting Co. Group owner: The Findlay Publishing Co. (acq 11-1-57). Rgnl Reps. Format: News/talk, weather, sports. News staff: 3. Target aud: 35 plus. ♦ Kurt P. Kah, pres; David P. Glass, VP; John Foster, opns mgr, progmg dir & pub affrs dir; Tasha Mann, gen mgr & gen sls mgr; Kevin Keith, news dir.

WKKG(FM)—Co-owned with WCSI(AM). 1958: 101.5 mhz; 50 kw. 492 ft. TL: N39 11 05 W85 57 17. Stereo. E-mail: wkkg@wkkg.com. Web Site: wkkg.com. Format: Country. Target aud: 25-54. ♦ Scott Michaels, progmg dir.

WINN(FM)— Jan 30, 1975: 104.9 mhz; 6 kw. 300 ft. TL: N39 11 09 W85 57 37. Stereo. Box 1789 47202-1789. Secondary address: 3212 Washington St. 47203. Phone: (812) 372-4448. Fax: (812) 372-1061. E-mail: fun@goodtimeoldies.com. Web Site: www.goodtimeoldies.com. Licensee: White River Broadcasting Co. Inc. Group owner: The Findlay Publishing Co. (a 1-8-02). Network: ABC Daytime Direction. Format: Oldies. News staff: 3. Target aud: 35-65; baby-boomers. Spec prog: Farm 2 hrs, new age 3 hrs wkly. ♦ Kurt Kah, pres; David Glass, VP; Tasha Mann, gen mgr; John Foster, opns mgr; Rich Anthony, progmg dir; Kevin Keith, news dir; Chuck Weber, chief of engrg.

WRZQ-FM—See Greensburg

WYGS(FM)— Feb 27, 2003: 91.1 mhz; 380 w vert. Ant 328 ft. TL: N39 13 35 W85 44 47. Box 2626 47202. Secondary address: 825 Washington St. 47201. Phone: (812) 373-9947. Fax: (812) 375-2555. Web Site: www.wygs.org. Licensee: Good Shepherd Radio Inc. Format: Southern gospel. ♦ Keith Reising Jr., CEO & gen mgr.

Connersville

WCNB(AM)— Apr 5, 1948: 1580 khz; 250 w-D, 5 w-N. TL: N39 38 18 W85 08 54. Box 619 47331. Secondary address: 406 Central Ave. Phone: (765) 825-6411. Phone: (765) 825-8561. Fax: (765) 825-2411. Web Site: www.wifefm.com. Licensee: Rodgers Broadcasting Corp. (group owner; (acq 8-88; grpsl; 8-29-88). Rgnl Reps. Format: Country. News staff: 2; News: 3 hrs wkly. Target aud: 25-54; affluent, middle-aged country listeners. Spec prog: Relg 12 hrs wkly. ♦ David A. Rodgers, pres; John Trine, gen mgr; Mike Reese, progmg dir; Barry Welsh, mus dir; Kristin Deiwert, news dir & pub affrs dir; Mike Peacock, engrg mgr; Bob Hawkins, chief of engrg.

WIFE(FM)—Co-owned with WCNB(AM). Feb 27, 1948: 100.3 mhz; 28 kw. 215 ft. TL: N39 38 15 W85 08 45. Stereo. Web Site: www.wifefm.com. News staff: rwo. Target aud: Affluent; young to middle aged men & women. Spec prog: Gospel 6 hrs wkly.

Corydon

WOCC(AM)— May 22, 1964: 1550 khz; 250 w-D. TL: N38 11 26 W86 08 00. Box 838 47112. Phone: (812) 738-9622. Fax: (812) 738-1676. Licensee: Richard Lee Brabandt. (acq 4-15-97). Rep: Rgnl Reps. Format: Classic oldies. News staff: one; News: 18 hrs wkly. Target aud: 34-55; baby boomers. ♦ Richard Lee Brabandt, pres; MaryAnn Brabandt, gen mgr & progmg dir; Joe Pollock, chief of engrg.

WSFR(FM)— 1994: 107.7 mhz; 8.2 kw. 567 ft. TL: N38 10 25 W85 54 50. (CP: 36 kw). Stereo. 612 4th Ave., Suite 100, Louisville, KY 40202. Phone: (502) 589-4800. Fax: (502) 583-4820. Web Site: www.1077sfr.com. Licensee: CXR Holdings L.L.C. Group owner: Cox Broadcasting (acq 5-99). Dow, Lohnes & Albertson. Format: Classic rock. ♦ Rolf Pepple, VP & gen mgr.

Covington

*WFOF(FM)— June 17, 1984: 90.3 mhz; 19 kw. 265 ft. TL: N40 09 08 W87 27 58. Stereo. Box 227 47932-0227. Secondary address: 610 3rd St. 47932. Phone: (765) 793-4088. Fax: (765) 793-4039. E-mail: wfof@wfof.org. Web Site: www.wfof.org. Licensee: Doxa Inc. Format: Relg. ♦ Ray McDaniel, pres; Ogle Snider, gen mgr; Barbara Snelling, progmg dir; Alan Woodrum, chief of engrg.

WKZS(FM)— June 1, 1982: 103.1 mhz; 3 kw. 300 ft. TL: N40 08 46 W87 27 15. Stereo. Box 67, Danville, IL 61834. Secondary address: 820 Railroad St. 47932. Phone: (217) 443-4004. Phone: (765) 793-4823. Fax: (765) 793-4644. E-mail: kiss1031@aol.com. Web Site: www.kisscountry.allrounddanville.com. Licensee: Benton-Weatherford Broadcasting Inc. of Indiana. (acq 7-12-85; $325,000; 6-3-85). Network: Jones Radio Networks. Rep: Roslin. Borsari & Paxson. Format: Country. News: 10 hrs wkly. Target aud: 18-49. ♦ Larry Weatherford, pres & opns dir; Rhea Benton-Weatherford, gen mgr; Greg Green, stn mgr.

Crawfordsville

WCDQ(FM)— Aug 13, 1953: 106.3 mhz; 3.4 kw. 440 ft. TL: N40 03 19 W86 55 57. Stereo. Box 603 47933. Secondary address: 1800 N. 175 W. 47933. Phone: (765) 362-8200. Phone: (765) 364-1063. Fax: (765) 364-1550. E-mail: cd1063@keybroadcasting.net. Web Site: www.keybroadcasting.com. Licensee: C.V.L. Broadcasting Inc. Group owner: Key Broadcasting Inc. (acq 12-13-99; $400,000). Arter & Hadden. Format: Hot adult contemp. News staff: 2; News: 48 hrs wkly. Target aud: 25-49; middle & upper class, educated, socially aware. ♦ Chris Aldridge, CEO & pres; Stephen R. White, gen mgr; Bob Lee, opns mgr; Howdy Bell, gen sls mgr & news dir; Jared Allen, progmg mgr; Mike Rabey, chief of engrg.

WCVL(AM)— Dec 12, 1964: 1550 khz; 250 w-U, DA-N. TL: N40 03 54 W86 56 00. Box 603 47933-0603. Phone: (765) 362-8200. Fax: (765) 364-1550. Licensee: C.V.L. Broadcasting Inc. Group owner: Key Broadcasting Inc. (acq 1986). Network: ABC Information & Entertainment. Rep: Rgnl Reps. Format: Music of Your Life. Target aud: 45 plus. Spec prog: Farm 5 hrs wkly. ♦ Howdy Bell, gen mgr; Jared Allen, progmg dir.

WIMC(FM)—Co-owned with WCVL(AM). June 1, 1974: 103.9 mhz; 1.35 kw. 500 ft. TL: N40 08 05 W86 54 12. Stereo. Format: Classic hits. Target aud: 25-49.

*WNDY(FM)— 1997: 91.3 mhz; 2.2 kw. 194 ft. TL: N40 03 19 W86 55 57. Box 352 47933. Secondary address: 301 W. Wabash 47933. Phone: (765) 361-6240. Phone: (765) 361-6038. Fax: (765) 361-6437. Web Site: www.wabash.edu. Licensee: Wabash College Radio Inc. Format: College eclectic. ♦ Kevin Gore, gen mgr; Michael Ritter, progmg dir; James Jared, mus dir.

Crothersville

*WOJC(FM)— 2005: 89.9 mhz; 300 w vert. Ant 244 ft. TL: N38 50 39 W85 49 26. CSN International, 4002N. 3300E., Twin Falls, ID 83301. Phone: (208) 734-6633. Licensee: CSN International. (group owner).

Crown Point

WXRD(FM)— Nov 10, 1972: 103.9 mhz; 3 kw. 330 ft. TL: N41 19 24 W87 21 22. Stereo. 2755 Sager Rd., Valpraiso 46383. Phone: (219) 462-4880. Fax: (219) 467-4880. Web Site: www.xrock1039.com. Licensee: Porter County Broadcasting Holding Corporation, LLC. Group owner: Porter County Broadcasting Corp. (acq 2-6-2004; $4.9 million. with WZVN(FM) Lowell). Network: ABC. Reddy, Begley & McCormick. Format: Classic rock. News staff: one; News: 12 hrs wkly. Target aud: 25-54; women. ♦ Leigh Ellis, pres & gen mgr.

Danville

WEDJ(FM)— Jan 10, 1975: 107.1 mhz; 6 kw. 604 ft. TL: N39 48 06 W86 34 24. Stereo. 1800 N. Meridian, Suite 605, Indianapolis 46202. Phone: (317) 924-1071. Fax: (317) 924-7766. Web Site: www.wedjfm.com. Licensee: Continental Broadcast Group Inc. (acq 12-30-93; grpsl; 1-24-94). Rep: CMBS. Putbrese, Hunsaker & Trent. Format: Hispanic. Target aud: 35-64; very upscale, professionals. ♦ Dwight Barnette, gen mgr; Tom Posz, progmg dir; Phil Alexander, chief of engrg.

Decatur

WADM(AM)— May 22, 1964: 1540 khz; 250 w-D. TL: N40 49 14 W84 55 12. Box 586 46733-0586. Secondary address: Box 321, 118 S. Main St., Bufftton 46714. Phone: (260) 724-7161. Fax: (260) 824-2805. Licensee: Wells County Radio Corp. (acq 8-25-94; $27,500; 9-5-94). Format: Adult contemp. ♦ Joe Shanley, gen mgr.

WQHK-FM— Nov 8, 1966: 105.1 mhz; 2 kw. 397 ft. TL: N40 49 14 W84 55 12. (CP: 13.4 kw, ant 449 ft.). Stereo. 2915 Maples Rd., Fort Wayne 46816. Phone: (260) 447-5511. Fax: (260) 447-7546. Web Site: www.k105fm.com. Licensee: Jam Communications Inc. Group owner: Federated Media. Format: Country. ♦ Mark DePrez, gen mgr; Rob Kelley, opns mgr; Bob Swinehart, gen sls mgr; Dean McNeil, progmg dir; Michael O'Shea, news dir; Jack Didier, chief of engrg.

Delphi

WXXB(FM)— May 24, 1989: 102.9 mhz; 2.2 kw. 420 ft. TL: N40 34 57 W86 38 26. Stereo. Box 7093, Lafayette 47903. Secondary address: 711 N. Earl Ave., Lafayette 47904. Phone: (765) 448-1566. Fax: (765) 448-1348. E-mail: erica.condict@radio-works.net. Web Site: www.b1029.com. Licensee: Stay Tuned Broadcasting Corp. Group owner: RadioWorks Inc. (acq 10-00; $1 million). Shaw Pittman. Format: CHR/Top 40. News staff: one. Target aud: 18-49. ♦ Robert Rhea, pres; Ernie Caldemone, VP & gen mgr; Anthony Bannon, progmg dir.

Earl Park

WIBN(FM)— Oct 15, 1983: 98.1 mhz; 25 kw. 328 ft. TL: N40 34 22 W87 27 42. Stereo. Box 25, Oxford 47971. Phone: (765) 385-2373. Fax: (765) 385-2374. E-mail: wib@981wibn.com. Web Site: www.981wibn.com. Licensee: Brothers Broadcasting Corp. (group owner; acq 8-95; $100,000). Format: Oldies. ♦ John Balvich, pres, gen mgr & gen sls mgr; Dan McKay, progmg dir; Ken Stapleton, news dir; Don Kerawac, chief of engrg.

Edinburgh

WYGB(FM)— Aug 24, 2000: 102.9 mhz; 6 kw. 328 ft. TL: N39 15 37 W86 06 21. Edinburgh Radio, 825 Washington St., Columbus 47201. Phone: (812) 348-1029. Fax: (812) 375-2555. E-mail: korncountry @korncountry.com. Web Site: www.korncountry.com. Licensee: Edinburgh Radio. Format: Country. Target aud: 25-54; Bartholomew & Johnson County folks. ♦ Keith Reising Jr., CEO & gen mgr; Mike King, stn mgr; Dave Wineland, opns mgr.

Elkhart

WAUS(FM)—See South Bend

WBYT(FM)—Listing follows WTRC(AM).

WFRN-FM— June 10, 1963: 104.7 mhz; 50 kw. 488 ft. TL: N41 37 18 W85 57 37. Stereo. Box 307 46517. Secondary address: 25802 County Rd. 26 46515. Phone: (574) 875-5166. Fax: (574) 875-6662. E-mail: moore@wfrn.com. Web Site: www.wfrn.com. Licensee: Progressive Broadcasting System Inc. (group owner). Network: USA. Reddy, Begley & McCormick. Format: Contemp Christian. News staff: one.

Stations in the U.S. — Indiana

Target aud: 25-54; families-primarily women. ♦ Edwin Moore, pres & gen mgr; Joanne Matthews, prom dir.

WFRN(AM)— Mar 16, 1956: 1270 khz; 5 kw-D, 1 kw-N, DA-2. TL: N41 37 16 W85 57 40. Web Site: www.wfrm.com. Format: Christian relg, talk. Target aud: 30 plus. ♦ Doug Moore, progmg dir.

WTRC(AM)— Nov 18, 1931: 1340 khz; 1 kw-U. TL: N41 40 28 W85 56 51. Box 699 46515. Secondary address: 58096 CR 7 S. 46517. Phone: (574) 293-5611. Fax: (574) 389-5101. Web Site: www.am1340.com. Licensee: Pathfinder Communications Corp. Group owner: Federated Media Network: ABC. Rep: Christal. Format: News/talk. News staff: 2; News: 21 hrs wkly. Target aud: 35-64; Elkhart County residents. ♦ John Dille III, pres; Julie Lockhard, gen mgr; Tom Bugg, gen sls mgr; Tom Forde, news dir.

WBYT(FM)— Co-owned with WTRC(AM). Apr 1, 1947: 100.7 mhz; 15 kw. 910 ft. TL: N41 36 58 W86 11 38. Stereo. 237 Edison Rd., Mishawaka 46545. Phone: (574) 674-5951. Fax: (574) 258-0930. E-mail: bloo@b100.com. Web Site: www.b100.com. Rep: Christal. Format: Country. Target aud: 25-54. Spec prog: Relg 2 hrs wkly. ♦ Brad Williams, gen mgr; Barb Deniston, gen sls mgr; Clint Marsh, progmg dir.

*****WVPE(FM)**— May 1972: 88.1 mhz; 10 kw. 400 ft. TL: N41 36 20 W86 12 46. (CP: 10.5 w, ant 554 ft. TL: N41 36 59 W86 11 43). Stereo. EACC, 2424 California Rd. 46514. Phone: (574) 262-5660. Phone: (574) 674-9873. Fax: (574) 262-5520. E-mail: wvpe@wvpe.org. Web Site: www.wvpe.org. Licensee: Elkhart Community Schools Corp. Network: Network: PRI, NPR. Format: Jazz, news/talk. News staff: one; News: 13 hrs wkly. Target aud: 25-55. Spec prog: Blues 15 hrs, folk 9 hrs. ♦ Jon Howard, gen mgr; Claudia Russell, progmg dir; Bob Henning, news dir & chief of engrg; Jason White, news dir.

WZOW(FM)—See Goshen

Ellettsville

WHCC(FM)— 1992: 105.1 mhz; 6 kw. 328 ft. TL: N39 11 32 W86 41 46. Box 7797, Bloomington 47407. Secondary address: 304 State Rd. 446, Bloomington 47401. Phone: (812) 336-8000. Phone: (812) 335-1051. Fax: (812) 336-7000. Web Site: www.whcc105.com. Licensee: Artistic Media Partners L.P. Group owner: Artistic Media Partners Inc. (acq 7-96; $675,000). Network: Jones Radio Networks. Russ Dodge Haley, Bader & Potts. Format: Country. News staff: 2. Target aud: 25-54. ♦ Art Angotti, pres; Sandy Zehr, stn mgr; Rick Evans, opns dir; Jeff Gross, gen sls mgr; Jeremy Gray, news dir; Bob Henning, chief of engrg.

Elwood

WURK(FM)— July 1964: 101.7 mhz; 3 kw. 328 ft. TL: N40 16 33 W85 51 44. 800 E. 29th St., Muncie 47302. Secondary address: 9821 S. 800 W., Daleville 47334. Phone: (765) 378-2080. Phone: (765) 288-4403. Fax: (765) 378-2090. Fax: (765) 765-2091. Web Site: www.werkfm.com. Licensee: Indiana Sabrecom Inc. Group owner: Backyard Broadcasting LLC (acq 12-1-02; grpsl). Network: ABC. Format: Oldies. News staff: one; News: 2 hrs wkly. Target aud: 25-54; adult buying public. Spec prog: Gospel 4 hrs wkly. ♦ Dave Koffee, gen mgr; Steve Lindell, opns VP & opns dir; Elaine Merritt, gen sls mgr; Jay Garrison, progmg dir; Tom Hammond, news dir; Sean Mattingly, chief of engrg.

Evansville

WABX(FM)— 1997: 107.5 mhz; 2.35 kw. 518 ft. TL: N37 59 21 W87 35 48. Box 3848 47736. Secondary address: 20 N.W. 3rd St. 47728. Phone: (812) 424-8284. Fax: (812) 426-7928. Web Site: www.wabx.net. Licensee: South Central Communications Corp. (group owner) Rep: Katz Radio. Format: Classic rock. Target aud: 25-49; men. ♦ John P. Engelbrecht, CEO; Craig Jacobus, pres; Tim Huelsing, gen mgr; Paul Brayfield, gen sls mgr; Jason Mack, progmg dir.

WEOA(AM)— 1935: 1400 khz; 1 kw-U. TL: N37 56 17 W87 31 51. Stereo. 1100 W. Lloyd Expwy., Suite 419 47708. Phone: (812) 424-8864. Fax: (812) 424-9946. Licensee: South Central Communications Corp. (group owner; acq 11-81). Bryan Cave. Format: Urban adult contemp. News staff: 3; News: 2 hrs wkly. Target aud: 25-49; general. ♦ Ed Lander, pres, gen sls mgr & progmg dir; Ron Lyles, news dir.

WIKY-FM—Co-owned with WEOA(AM). Aug 28, 1948: 104.1 mhz; 39 kw. 571 ft. TL: N37 59 21 W87 35 48. Stereo. 1162 Mt. Auburn Rd. 47720. Phone: (812) 424-8284. Fax: (812) 426-7928. Web Site: www.wiky.com. Licensee: South Central Communications corp. (Acq 1948). Format: Adult contemp. Target aud: 25-54; females, workplace. Spec prog: Farm 17 hrs wkly. ♦ John P. Engelbrecht, CEO; Craig Jacobus, pres; Tim Huelsing, gen mgr; LaDonne Craig, gen sls mgr; Nora Mitz, mktg dir; Stephanie Todich, prom mgr; Mark Baker, progmg dir; Randy Wheeler, news dir; Chris Myers, chief of engrg.

WGBF(AM)— Nov 22, 1923: 1280 khz; 5 kw-D, 1 kw-N, DA-N. TL: N37 59 53 W87 28 33. Stereo. Secondary address: 1133 Lincoln Ave. 47714. Phone: (812) 425-4226. Fax: (812) 421-0005. Web Site: iuhoosiers.com/iuradionetwork.html. Licensee: Regent Broadcasting of Evansville/Owensboro Inc. Group owner: Regent Communications Inc. (acq 12-3-2003; grpsl). Network: Network: CNN Radio, Westwood One. Rep: Katz Radio. Format: News/talk. News staff: one; News: 10 hrs wkly. Target aud: 25-54; affluent, mature. ♦ Mark Thomas, gen mgr.

WGBF-FM—See Henderson, KY

WJLT(FM)— Dec 22, 1964: 105.3 mhz; 50 kw. Ant 480 ft. TL: N38 04 47 W87 36 36. Stereo. Box 78 47701. Secondary address: 1133 Lincoln Ave. 47714. Phone: (812) 425-4226. Fax: (812) 421-0005. Web Site: www.lite1053.com. Licensee: Regent Broadcasting of Evansville/Owensboro Inc. Group owner: Regent Communications Inc. (acq 12-3-2003; grpsl). Format: Oldies. Target aud: 25-54. ♦ Mike Sanders, CFO & opns mgr; Mark Thomas, gen mgr; Jeff Walker, prom dir & news dir; Cindy Patrick, progmg dir; Rick Craago, gen mgr & chief of engrg.

*****WNIN-FM**— Feb 1, 1982: 88.3 mhz; 17 kw. Ant 840 ft. TL: N37 59 01 W87 16 13. Stereo. 405 Carpenter St. 47708. Phone: (812) 423-2973. Fax: (812) 428-7548. E-mail: wnin@wnin.org. Web Site: www.wnin.org. Licensee: Tri-State Public Teleplex Inc. Network: Network: PRI, NPR. Dow, Lohnes & Albertson. Format: Class, news. News: 20 hrs wkly. Target aud: General. ♦ David L. Dial, pres & gen mgr; Jean Noyes, stn mgr; Daniel Moore, opns VP; Rosi Weatherwax, dev VP.

*****WPSR(FM)**— September 1957: 90.7 mhz; 14 kw. 130 ft. TL: N38 01 45 W87 34 42. Stereo. 5400 First Ave. 47710. Phone: (812) 435-8241. Fax: (812) 435-8241. E-mail: wpsr@907wpsr.com. Web Site: www.907wpsr.com. Licensee: Evansville Vanderburg School Corp. (acq 9-57). Network: UPI. Format: Div, educ, var music. News: 3 hrs wkly. Target aud: General. ♦ Michael H. Reininga, gen mgr & dev dir.

*****WSWI(AM)**— Aug 6, 1947: 820 khz; 250 w-D. TL: N37 57 53 W87 40 06. Liberal Arts Bldg., 8600 University Blvd. 47712. Phone: (812) 465-1665. Fax: (812) 461-5261. E-mail: wswi@usi.edu. Web Site: www.usi.edu/wswi. Licensee: University of Southern Indiana. (acq 11-3-81). Format: College alternative. News staff: News progmg 3 hrs wkly Target aud: 18-54; students, faculty & community members. ♦ John Morris, gen mgr; Chad Connor, progmg dir.

*****WUEV(FM)**— Apr 1, 1951: 91.5 mhz; 6.1 kw. 150 ft. TL: N37 58 24 W87 31 48. Stereo. 1800 Lincoln Ave. 47722. Phone: (812) 479-2022. Fax: (812) 479-2320. E-mail: wuev@evansville.edu. Web Site: wuev.evansville.edu. Licensee: University of Evansville. Network: UPI. Format: Div, jazz. News staff: 3; News: 10 hrs wkly. Spec prog: Children 5 hrs, American Indian one hr wkly. ♦ Mike Crowley, gen mgr & opns mgr; Phil Bailey, chief of engrg.

WVHI(AM)— Oct 31, 1948: 1330 khz; 5 kw-D, 1 kw-N, DA-N. TL: N38 03 12 W87 35 40. Box 3636 47735. Phone: (812) 425-2221. Fax: (812) 425-2078. Web Site: www.wvhi.com. Licensee: Word Broadcasting Network. (acq 3-17-99). Format: Relg, adult contemp. Target aud: General. ♦ Jim Fraser, gen mgr; Christy Denton, gen sls mgr.

WYNG(FM)—See Mount Carmel, IL

Ferdinand

WQKZ(FM)— Nov 1, 1997: 98.5 mhz; 6 kw. 328 ft. TL: N38 10 02 W86 49 49. 1978 S. WITZ Rd., Jasper 47546. Phone: (812) 482-2131. Fax: (812) 482-9609. E-mail: wqkz@psci.net. Licensee: Gem Communications L.L.P. (acq 4-17-98). Network: Jones Radio Networks. Format: Country. ♦ G. Earl Metzger, pres; Gene Kuntz, gen mgr; Bob Boyles, gen sls mgr; Walt Ferber, progmg dir & progmg mgr; Frank Hertel, chief of engrg.

Fishers

WISG(FM)— February 1993: 93.9 mhz; 2.95 kw. Ant 476 ft. TL: N39 49 39 W85 58 51. 6810 N. Shadeland Ave., Indianapolis 46220. Phone: (317) 842-9550. Fax: (317) 577-3361. Web Site: www.retro939.fm. Licensee: Indy Lico Inc. Group owner: Susquehanna Radio Corp. (acq 5-27-97; $4.3 million). McFadden, Evans & Sill. Format: 80s hits. Target aud: 35 plus; mature, upscale adults. Spec prog: Hymns of praise 3 hrs, family values one hr wkly. ♦ David E. Kennedy, pres; Charlie Morgan, gen mgr; Eric Wnnenverg, gen sls mgr; David Wood, progmg dir; Mike Orr, news dir; Max Turner, chief of engrg.

Fort Branch

*****WBGW(FM)**— July 20, 1990: 101.5 mhz; 1 kw. 561 ft. TL: N38 10 45 W87 29 13. Stereo. Box 4164, Evansville 47724. Secondary address: Box 71A, R.R. 2, County Rd.1200 S., Haubstadt 47629. Phone: (812) 386-3342. Fax: (812) 768-5552. E-mail: goodnews@evansville.net. Web Site: www.thyword.org. Licensee: Music Ministries Inc. Network: Network: Moody, USA. Format: Relg. News: 12 hrs wkly. Target aud: 35-54. ♦ Donald C. Chagle, pres; Floyd E. Turner, gen mgr; Dave Rigg, opns dir & progmg dir.

Fort Wayne

WAJI(FM)— August 1959: 95.1 mhz; 39 kw. 680 ft. TL: N41 06 13 W85 11 28. Stereo. 347 W. Berry, Suite 417 46802. Phone: (260) 423-3676. Fax: (260) 422-5266. Licensee: Sarkes Tarzian Inc. (group owner) Format: Adult contemp. News staff: one. Target aud: 25-54; women. ♦ Thomas Tarzian, CEO; R. Geoffrey Vargo, pres; Robert Davis, CFO; Candace A. Wendling, gen mgr; Lee Tobin, opns mgr; Daryl McIntire, gen sls mgr; Barb Richards, progmg dir; Amy Collins, news dir; Ed Didier, chief of engrg.

*****WBCL(FM)**— Jan 8, 1976: 90.3 mhz; 26 kw. Ant 692 ft. TL: N41 06 13 W85 11 46. Stereo. 1025 W. Rudisill Blvd. 46807. Phone: (260) 745-0576. Fax: (260) 456-2913. E-mail: wbcl@wbcl.org. Web Site: www.wbcl.org. Licensee: Taylor University Broadcasting Inc. (acq 6-24-92; FTR: 7-20-92). Format: Contemp Christian. ♦ Char Binkley, gen mgr; Craig Albrecht, opns mgr & chief of engrg; Scott Tsuleff, progmg dir.

*****WBOI(FM)**— June 15, 1978: 89.1 mhz; 34 kw. Ant 604 ft. TL: N41 06 13 W85 10 44. Stereo. Box 8459 46898-8459. Secondary address: 3204 Clairmont Ct. 46808. Phone: (260) 452-1189. Fax: (260) 452-1188. Web Site: www.nipr.fm. Licensee: Public Broadcasting of Northeastern Indiana Inc. (acq 1-15-82). Network: Network: PRI, NPR, AP Radio. Dow, Lohnes & Albertson. Format: News/talk, jazz. Target aud: 25 plus. ♦ Bruce Haines, gen mgr; Collen Condron, opns dir & opns mgr; Karen Fraser, dev VP & prom dir; Jeanette Dillon, progmg dir.

WBTU(FM)—(Kendallville). Dec 16, 1964: 93.3 mhz; 50 kw. 450 ft. TL: N41 23 55 W85 15 08. Stereo. 2100 Goshen Rd., Suite 232 46808. Phone: (260) 482-9288. Fax: (260) 482-8655. E-mail: pd@wbtu.fm. Web Site: www.wbtu.fm. Licensee: Artistic Media Partners Inc. (acq 1-16-97). Format: Country. Target aud: 18-54; upscale, young audience. ♦ Arthur Angotti, stn mgr; Linda Bradley, gen mgr & stn mgr; Kenny Edwards, opns dir; Bob Henning, chief of engrg.

WFCV(AM)— June 17, 1968: 1090 khz; 2.5 kw-D, 1 kw-CH, DA-2. TL: N41 05 01 W85 04 32. 3737 Lake Ave. 46805-5554. Phone: (260) 423-2337. Fax: (260) 423-6355. Web Site: www.bottradionetwork.com. Licensee: Bott Broadcasting. (group owner; acq 5-1-80). Network: USA. Format: Christian info. Target aud: 25-54; family oriented. ♦Richard P. Bott, pres; Richard Bott II, VP; Dale Gerke, stn mgr; Kathy McClish, opns mgr.

WFWI(FM)— Mar 4, 1993: 92.3 mhz; 2.2 kw. Ant 544 ft. TL: N41 06 39 W85 11 44. 1005 Production Rd. 46808. Phone: (260) 471-5100. Fax: (260) 471-5224. Web Site: www.923thefort.com. Licensee: Pathfinder Communications Corp. Group owner: Federated Media (acq 3-1-97). Network: ABC. Format: Classic rock. News staff: one; News: 6 hrs wkly. Target aud: 25-54; men and adults. ♦John Dille, pres; Jim Allgeier, gen mgr; Billy Elvis, progmg dir; Mogan David, engrg mgr & chief of engrg.

WGL(AM)— Jan 24, 1924: 1250 khz; 2.5 kw-D, 1.4 kw-N, DA-2. TL: N41 01 16 W85 09 46. 2000 Lower Huntington Rd. 46819. Phone: (260) 747-1511. Fax: (260) 747-3999. Web Site: foxsports1250.com. Licensee: Summit City Radio Group LLC. Group owner: Summit City Radio Group (acq 6-18-2002;. grpsl). Network: CBS. Format: Fox sports. News: 2 hrs wkly. ♦Kris Foate, CEO & gen mgr; B.J. Steele, progmg dir.

WKJG(AM)— November 1947: 1380 khz; 5 kw-U, DA-2. TL: N41 00 15 W85 05 57. Stereo. 2915 Maples Rd. 46816. Phone: (260) 447-5511. Fax: (260) 447-7546. Web Site: www.wise33.com. Licensee: Pathfinder Communications Corp. Group owner: Federated Media. Network: ABC. Rep: Christal. Format: All sports. ♦Mark DePrez, gen mgr & gen sls mgr; Tony Richards, COO & gen mgr; Jim Tighe, sls dir; Mark Osborn, gen sls mgr; Sean Bratton, prom dir; Dean McNeal, progmg dir & news dir; Jack Didion, engrg VP; Mogan David, chief of engrg.

WMEE(FM)—Co-owned with WKJG(AM). Feb 5, 1965: 97.3 mhz; 26 kw. 689 ft. TL: N41 06 42 W85 11 43. Stereo. 2915 Maples Rd. 46816. Phone: (260) 447-5511. Fax: (260) 447-7546. E-mail: info@wmee.com. Web Site: www.wmee.com. Format: Hot adult contemp. News: one hr wkly. Target aud: 25-54. ♦John Dille, pres; Bob Watson, CFO; Mark Evans, opns mgr & progmg dir; Mark Osborn, sls dir; Joel Pyle, gen sls mgr; Chris Cage, mus dir; Erika Taylor, news dir; Jack Didier, engrg dir.

***WLAB(FM)**— Aug 23, 1976: 88.3 mhz; 7 kw. 341 ft. TL: N41 05 58 W85 08 43. Stereo. 6600 N. Clinton St., 8 Martin Luther Dr. 46825. Phone: (260) 483-8236. Fax: (260) 482-7707. E-mail: melissa@star883.org. Web Site: www.star883.org. Licensee: The Indiana District Lutheran Church-Missouri Synod Inc. (acq 4-24-87). Network: Salem Radio Network. Shaw Pittman. Format: Adult contemp Christian. Target aud: 25-44; Christian. ♦Melissa Montana, gen mgr; Don Buettner, progmg dir.

WLDE(FM)— Aug 24, 1970: 101.7 mhz; 3 kw. 328 ft. TL: N41 04 58 W85 04 22. Stereo. 347 W. Berry, Suite 417 46802. Phone: (260) 423-3676. Fax: (260) 422-5266. Licensee: Sarkes Tarzian Inc. (group owner; acq 2-16-93; 3-8-93). Format: Oldies. Target aud: 35-64. ♦Thomas Tarzian, CEO; R. Geoffrey Vargo, pres; Robert Davis, CFO; Candace A. Wendling, gen mgr; Shelly Steckler, gen sls mgr; Lee Tobin, progmg dir; Ed Didier, chief of engrg.

WLYV(AM)— Mar 28, 1948: 1450 khz; 1 kw-U. TL: N41 04 14 W85 07 10. Stereo. 4705 Illinois Rd., Suite 104 46804. Phone: (260) 432-6179. Licensee: Christian Broadcasting System Ltd. (group owner; acq 12-12-94; $90,000;. FTR: 2-20-95). Network: USA. Format: Christian, religious. Target aud: 25-54; Christian adults. Spec prog: Spanish one hr wkly. ♦Jon R. Yinger, CEO & pres.

WOWO(AM)— Mar 31, 1925: 1190 khz; 50 kw-U, DA-N. TL: N40 59 47 W85 21 06. (CP: 9.8 kw-N). Stereo. 2915 Maples Rd. 46816. Phone: (260) 447-5511. Fax: (260) 447-7546. E-mail: info@wowo.com. Web Site: www.wowo.com. Licensee: Pathfinder Communications Corp. Group owner: Federated Media Network: CBS. Rep: Christal. Format: News/talk, sports. News staff: 5. Target aud: 25-54. ♦Tony Richards, COO; John Dille, pres; Bob Watson, CFO; Mark DePrez, gen mgr; Jon Zimney, opns mgr, prom mgr & progmg mgr; Jim Tighe, gen sls mgr & progmg dir; Mogan David, chief of engrg.

WYLT(FM)— May 6, 1976: 103.9 mhz; 3 kw. Ant 380 ft. TL: N41 06 31 W85 09 56. Stereo. 2000 Lower Huntington Rd. 46819. Phone: (260) 747-1511. Fax: (260) 747-3999. E-mail: dbgoode@summitradio.com. Web Site: www.my1039fm.com. Licensee: Travis Broadcasting LLC. Group owner: Summit City Radio Group (acq 5-30-2003; $4 million. with WXKE(FM) Huntington). Rep: D & R Radio. Format: Adult contemp. News staff: one. Target aud: 18-44; females & young families. ♦Kris Foati, gen mgr; Dave Wisniewski, sls dir; David B. Goode, progmg dir.

Frankfort

WILO(AM)— Nov 23, 1953: 1570 khz; 250 w-U. TL: N40 16 40 W86 29 07. Box 545 46041. Secondary address: 1401 Barner St. 46041-1506. Phone: (765) 659-3338. Fax: (765) 659-3338. Web Site: www.wilo.net. Licensee: Kaspar Broadcasting Co. Inc. Group owner: Kaspar Broadcasting Group (acq 10-1-59). Rep: Rgnl Reps. Format: Community svc, nostalgia. Spec prog: Farm 12 hrs wkly. ♦Vernon Kaspar, pres; Russ Kaspar, gen mgr & stn mgr; Vernon Kasper, gen mgr.

WSHW(FM)—Co-owned with WILO(AM). Sept 14, 1962: 99.7 mhz; 50 kw. 460 ft. TL: N40 25 14 W86 24 47. Stereo. 1804 1/2 S. Plate St., Kokomo 46902-5730. Phone: (800) 447-4463. Fax: (765) 452-0299. Fax: (765) 452-0399. Web Site: www.wshw.com. Format: Adult contemp. Spec prog: Farm 8 hrs wkly. ♦Randy Lawson, progmg dir.

Franklin

***WFCI(FM)**— Oct 15, 1960: 89.5 mhz; 1.15 kw. Ant 140 ft. TL: N39 24 29 W86 08 52. Stereo. Franklin College / WCFI, 501 E. Monroe St., Shirk Hall 46131. Phone: (317) 738-8205. Phone: (317) 738-8204. Fax: (317) 738-8233. Web Site: www.franklincollege.edu. Licensee: Franklin College of Indiana. Format: CHR. Target aud: 12-24; college & high school students. ♦LaCinda Bray, gen mgr; Tara Hettinger, opns dir; Charles Sears, chief of engrg.

WIJY(FM)— Dec 15, 1961: 95.9 mhz; 3 kw. 300 ft. TL: N39 30 49 W86 04 07. Stereo. 645 Industrial Dr. 46131. Phone: (317) 736-4040. Fax: (317) 736-4781. Web Site: www.joy96.com. Licensee: Pilgrim Communications LLC (acq 7-2-99). Network: Network: ABC, American Urban. Rep: Rgnl Reps. Format: Christian, business talk, sports. Target aud: 25-49; families. Spec prog: Jazz 10 hrs wkly. ♦Dr. Gene Hood, CEO; Randy Tipmore, gen mgr, opns dir & progmg dir.

French Lick

WFLQ(FM)— Apr 12, 1983: 100.1 mhz; 6 kw. 300 ft. TL: N38 35 41 W86 36 48. Stereo. Box 100 47432. Phone: (812) 936-9100. Fax: (812) 936-9495. E-mail: wflqfm@smithville.net. Web Site: www.wflq.com. Licensee: W.G. Willis dba Willtronics Broadcasting. Network: ABC. Format: Modern country. News staff: one; News: 11 hrs wkly. Target aud: 25 plus. Spec prog: Farm 3 hrs, relg 6 hrs, Gospel 4 hrs wkly. ♦Col. W.G. Willis, CEO & gen mgr; Catherine Willis, opns mgr; Bill Willis, gen sls mgr & chief of engrg; Randall Hamm, progmg dir & mus dir; Joe Randolph, news dir.

Gary

***WGVE(FM)**— January 1954: 88.7 mhz; 2.1 kw. 91 ft. TL: N41 33 15 W87 19 05. 1800 E. 35th Ave. 46409. Phone: (219) 962-9483. Fax: (219) 962-3726. E-mail: wgve887fm@yahoo.com. Licensee: Gary Community School Corp. Format: Educ, pub affrs. ♦Sarita Stevens, gen mgr; Eric Johnson, progmg dir.

WLTH(AM)— Nov 5, 1950: 1370 khz; 1 kw-D, 500 w-N, DA-N. TL: N41 34 17 W87 19 02. 1563 E. 85th Ave., Merrillville 46410. Phone: (219) 794-1370. Fax: (219) 794-1377. Licensee: WLTH Radio Inc. (acq 4-21-98; $750,000). Network: CNN Radio. Format: News/talk, sports. ♦Pluria Marshall Jr., gen mgr.

WWCA(AM)— Dec 7, 1949: 1270 khz; 1 kw-U, DA-1. TL: N41 31 38 W87 22 36. Box10745, Meriville 46411-0745. Phone: (219) 309-9327. Web Site: www.ca@revelantradio.com. Licensee: Starboard Media Foundation Inc. Group owner: Relevant Radio (acq 7-1-2004; $1.5 million). Format: Talk radio. ♦Armand Ciabattari, stn mgr.

Goshen

***WGCS(FM)**— Oct 2, 1958: 91.1 mhz; 6 kw. 220 ft. TL: N41 33 29 W85 51 06. Stereo. 1700 S. Main 46526. Phone: (574) 535-7488. Phone: (574) 535-7688. Fax: (574) 535-7293. E-mail: globe@goshen.edu. Web Site: globeradio.org. Licensee: Goshen College Broadcasting Corp. Network: PRI. Reddy, Bagley, McCormick. Format: Folk. News: 8 hrs wkly. Target aud: Adults 25-49. Spec prog: Sp 8 hrs, news 8 hrs, sports 10 hrs wkly. ♦Jason Samuel, gen mgr; Kimberlee Roher, stn mgr; Brandie Dalton, progmg dir.

WKAM(AM)— 1954: 1460 khz; 2.5 kw-D, 500 w-N, DA-N. TL: N41 35 24 W85 48 56. 930 E. Lincoln Ave. 46528. Phone: (574) 533-1460. Fax: (574) 534-3698. Web Site: www.wkam1460.com. Licensee: Fulmer Communications LLC (acq 5-16-02; $100,000). Network: USA. Rep: Katz Radio, Rgnl Reps. Format: Adult contemp, Latin. News staff: one; News: 20 hrs wkly. Target aud: 30-65; mature, family oriented, goal oriented. Spec prog: Southern gospel 6 hrs wkly. ♦Kent Fulmer, gen mgr.

WZOW(FM)— Jan 17, 1977: 97.7 mhz; 3 kw. 482 ft. TL: N41 36 04 W85 55 41. Stereo. 3371 Cleveland Rd., Suite 300, South Bend 46628. Phone: (574) 273-9300. Fax: (574) 273-9090. E-mail: michael@wzow.com. Web Site: www.wzow.com. Licensee: Artistic Media Partners Inc. (group owner; acq 2-12-02; $925,000). Format: Classic rock. Target aud: 25-54. ♦Michael Stone, gen mgr & stn mgr.

Granger

WRBR-FM—See South Bend

Greencastle

***WGRE(FM)**— Apr 25, 1949: 91.5 mhz; 1 kw. 160 ft. TL: N39 39 16 W86 51 40. Stereo. Ctr. for Contemporary Media, 609 S. Locust 46135. Phone: (765) 658-4642. Phone: (765) 658-4637. Fax: (765) 658-4693. E-mail: newton@depauw.edu. Web Site: www.wgre.org. Licensee: DePauw University. Network: AP Radio. Format: Alternative. News: 12 hrs wkly. Target aud: 18-25; college campus & loc community. Spec prog: Jazz 3 hrs, Intl 2 hrs, regl 2 hrs wkly. ♦Jeff McCall, pres & gen mgr; Chris Newton, opns mgr; Greg Stephan, chief of engrg.

***WIKL(FM)**—Not on air, target date: unknown: 90.5 mhz; 22 kw vert. Ant 253 ft. TL: N39 41 19 W86 42 03. 3500 DePauw Blvd., Suite 2085, Indianapolis 46268. Phone: (317) 870-8400. Licensee: Hoosier Broadcasting Corp. Format: Christian. ♦William Shirk Poorman, gen mgr.

WREB(FM)— May 16, 1966: 94.3 mhz; 3 kw. 165 ft. TL: N39 39 38 W86 53 34. Stereo. 2468 W. County Rd. 25 N. 46135. Phone: (765) 653-9717. Fax: (765) 653-6677. Web Site: www.theoriginalco.com. Licensee: The Original Co. Group owner: The Original Co. Inc. (acq 6-22-94; $200,000; 7-11-94). Format: Country, loc news, sports. News staff: one; News: 37 hrs wkly. Target aud: General. Spec prog: Farm 5 hrs wkly. ♦Mark Lange, gen mgr.

Greenfield

***WRGF(FM)**— 2001: 89.7 mhz; 750 w horiz, 2 kw vert. Ant 164 ft. TL: N39 44 55 W85 40 50. Greenfield Central Comm. School Corp., 110 W. North St. 46140. Secondary address: 810 N. Broadway 46140. Phone: (317) 462-9211. Fax: (317) 467-6755. E-mail: wrgf@insight66.com. Web Site: gcsc.k12.in.us. Licensee: Greenfield Central Community School Corp. Format: Old & new rock. ♦Tim Renshaw, gen mgr.

WZPL(FM)— June 1, 1962: 99.5 mhz; 12.5 kw. 991 ft. TL: N39 46 03 W86 00 12. Stereo. 9245 N. Meridian, Suite 300, Indianapolis 46260. Phone: (317) 816-4000. Fax: (317) 816-4080. Web Site: www.wzpl.com. Licensee: Entercom Indianapolis License LLC. (acq 8-26-2004; grpsl). Rep: McGavren Guild. Format: Modern adult contemp. Target aud: 18-49. ♦Joseph M. Field, chmn; David J. Field, pres; Tim Medland, CFO, VP, gen mgr & mktg mgr.

Greensburg

***WAUZ(FM)**— Sept 1, 1998: 89.1 mhz; 1.2 kw vert. 420 ft. TL: N39 14 13 W85 34 00. c/o WYGS(FM), 825 Washington St., Columbus 47201. Secondary address: Box 487 47201. Phone: (812) 373-9947. Fax: (812) 375-2555. E-mail: ygs@wygs.org. Web Site: www.wygs.org. Licensee: Good Shepherd Radio Inc. Format: Christian/ southern Gospel. Target aud: 25-40. ♦Keith Reising, pres; Tom Rust, gen mgr; Rena Coomer, opns mgr.

WRZQ-FM—Listing follows WTRE(AM).

WTRE(AM)— July 1, 1968: 1330 khz; 500 w-D, 41 w-N, DA-2. TL: N39 19 41 W85 30 06. Box 487, 1217 W. Park Rd. 47240. Phone: (812) 663-3000. Fax: (812) 663-8355. E-mail: wtre@hsonline.net. Web Site: www.treecountry.com. Licensee: WTRE Inc. (acq 8-13-99; with co-located FM). Network: ABC Daytime Direction. Format: Country, div, news/talk. News staff: one; News: 24 hrs wkly. Target aud: 25 plus. Spec prog: Farm 10 hrs, relg 3 hrs wkly. ♦Keith Reising

Jr., pres; Dave Peach, sls dir; Sandy Biddinger, stn mgr, gen sls mgr & news dir; Robert Hawkins, chief of engrg.

WRZQ-FM—Co-owned with WTRE(AM). December 1962: 107.3 mhz; 41.8 kw. 531 ft. TL: N39 14 13 W85 34 00. Stereo. Radio Bldg., 825 Washington St., Columbus 47201. Phone: (812) 379-1077. Fax: (812) 375-2555. E-mail: qmix@qmix.com. Web Site: www.qmix.com. Format: Adult contemp. News staff: one; News: 4 hrs wkly. Target aud: 18-49. ♦ Keith Reising Jr., pres & gen mgr; Dave Wineland, opns dir; Dale Marks, sls dir; Mike King, mktg dir; Matt Joyce, prom dir; Trent Michaels, progmg dir; Liz Thomas, news dir; Jim Burgan, engrg dir.

Greenwood

WTLC-FM— 1994: 106.7 mhz; 3 kw. 328 ft. TL: N39 42 42 W86 08 45. 21 E. Saint Joseph St., Indianapolis 46204. Phone: (317) 266-9600. Fax: (317) 328-3870. Web Site: www.wtlc.com. Licensee: Radio One of Indiana LLC. Group owner: Radio One Inc. (acq 2-15-01; grpsl). Format: Oldies, rhythm and blues. ♦ Charles T. Williams, VP & gen mgr.

Hagerstown

*****WBSH(FM)**— December 1996: 91.1 mhz; 300 w. 216 ft. TL: N39 56 31 W85 11 41. c/o WBST(FM), Ball State Univ., Muncie 47306. Phone: (765) 285-5888. Fax: (765) 285-8937. E-mail: ipr@bsu.edu. Web Site: www.bsu.edu/ipr. Licensee: Ball State University. Format: Class, news. News staff: one; News: 33 hrs wkly. Target aud: General. ♦ Anthony Hunt, gen mgr; Pam Coletti, gen sls mgr; Carol Trimmer, prom mgr; Steven Turpin, progmg dir & mus dir.

Hammond

WJOB(AM)— 1928: 1230 khz; 1 kw-U. TL: N41 35 46 W87 28 42. 6405 Olcott Ave. 46320. Phone: (219) 844-1230. Fax: (219) 844-6190. Web Site: www.flicklives.com/radio/wjob/wjob.htm. Licensee: Vazquez Development LLC (acq 12-4-03; $1.2 million. with WIMS(AM) Michigan City). Martin & McCormick. Format: News/talk. News staff: 10; News: 17 hrs wkly. Target aud: 25-49; general. Spec prog: Sports, Pol 2 hrs, relg 2 hrs, Greek one hr wkly. ♦ Alexis Vazquez Dedelow, gen mgr; Rick Federighi, gen sls mgr; John Rush, progmg dir.

WPWX(FM)— Sept 14, 1959: 92.3 mhz; 50 kw horiz, 44 kw vert. 492 ft. TL: N41 37 50 W87 31 40. Stereo. 6336 Calumet Ave. 46324. Phone: (219) 933-4455. Phone: (708) 957-0105. Fax: (219) 933-0323. E-mail: wpwxinfo@crawfordbroadcasting.com. Web Site: www.crawfordbrodcasting.com. Licensee: Dontron Inc. Group owner: Crawford Broadcasting Co. (acq 9-14-59). Format: Relg, gospel, adult contemp. Target aud: 18-49; young, adult Christian. Spec prog: Black. ♦ Donald Crawford, pres; Taft Harris, gen mgr & stn mgr; Jay Allen, progmg dir.

Hanna

*****WHLP(FM)**— 2001: 89.9 mhz; 8 kw. Ant 505 ft. TL: N41 26 09 W86 50 48. 150 Lincoln Way, Suite 2001, Valparaiso 46383. Phone: (219) 548-8956. Fax: (219) 548-5808. E-mail: whlp@csnradio.com. Web Site: csnradio.com. Licensee: CSN International (group owner). Format: Relg. ♦ Jim Motshagen, gen mgr; Kathy Motshagen, progmg dir.

Hardinsburg

WKLO(FM)— 2002: 96.9 mhz; 3.5 kw. Ant 433 ft. TL: N38 28 21 W86 24 39. 514 N. JFK Ave., Loogootee 47553. Phone: (812) 295-9480. Licensee: Hembree Communications Inc. (acq 11-26-2003; $350,000). Format: Hot adult contemp. ♦ Larry Hembree, gen mgr.

Hartford City

*****WHCI(FM)**— 2003: 88.1 mhz; 100 w. 72 ft. Blackford County School Corp., 2392 N. SR 3 N. 47348. Phone: (765) 348-7560. Fax: (765) 348-7568. Web Site: www.bcs.k12.in.us. Licensee: Blackford County School Corp. Format: Var. ♦ Harry Anderson, gen mgr.

WHTY(FM)— Feb 26, 1965: 93.5 mhz; 3.04 kw. 456 ft. TL: N40 25 16 W85 25 40. 800 E. 29th St., Muncie 47302. Phone: (866) 516-1278. Fax: (765) 378-2091. E-mail: maxstudio@maxrocks.com. Web Site: www.maxrocks.net. Licensee: Indiana Sabrecom Inc. Group owner: Backyard Broadcasting LLC (acq 1-1-02; grpsl). Network: Westwood One. Rep: Rgnl Reps. Format: Classic rock. News staff: one; News: one hr wkly. Target aud: 25-54. ♦ Steve Lindell, opns VP & opns mgr.

Howe

*****WHWE(FM)**— May 1, 1970: 89.7 mhz; 100 w. 68 ft. TL: N41 43 32 W85 25 30. Stereo. Box 240, Howe Military School 46746. Phone: (219) 562-2131. Fax: (219) 562-3678. Licensee: Howe Military School. Format: Educ, CHR, div. Target aud: 7-20; high school. ♦ Steve Clark, stn mgr.

*****WQKO(FM)**— 1994: 91.9 mhz; 3 kw. Ant 298 ft. TL: N41 38 59 W85 21 12. 6200 E. SR 120 46746. Phone: (260) 562-2242. E-mail: wqko@earthlink.net. Web Site: www.jesusfanatic.com. Licensee: CSN International (group owner; (acq 7-13-98; $80,000). Format: Christian praise & worship, teaching. ♦ Banner Kidd, gen mgr.

Huntingburg

WBDC(FM)—Licensed to Huntingburg. See Jasper

Huntington

WBZQ(AM)— May 25, 1957: 1300 khz; 500 w-D, DA. TL: N40 52 31 W85 28 27. Box 5570, Fort Wayne 46895. Phone: (219) 482-8500. Licensee: Larko Communications Inc. (acq 8-31-00; $16,500). Format: Oldies. Target aud: 25-65. ♦ Chris Larko, gen mgr; Susan Derr, stn mgr.

*****WVSH(FM)**— Jan 1, 1950: 91.9 mhz; 920 w. 110 ft. TL: N40 53 32 W85 30 38. Stereo. 450 MacGahan St. 46750. Phone: (260) 356-2019. Fax: (260) 358-2210. E-mail: reds@fwi.com. Licensee: Huntington County Community School Corp. Format: CHR. ♦ Bill Walker, gen mgr.

WXKE(FM)— Sept 1, 1965: 102.9 mhz; 4.7 kw. Ant 298 ft. TL: N40 55 33 W85 23 15. Stereo. 200 Lowea Hunting Rd., Ft. Wayne 46819. Phone: (260) 747-1511. Fax: (260) 747-3999. Web Site: www.1029theriver.com. Licensee: Travis Broadcasting LLC. Group owner: Summit City Radio Group (acq 5-30-2003; $4 million. with WYLT(FM) Fort Wayne). Network: CBS. Rep: D & R Radio. Format: Soft adult contemp. News staff: one. Target aud: 25-54. ♦ Kris Foate, CEO & gen mgr; Bill Stewart, progmg dir.

Indianapolis

*****WBDG(FM)**— Sept 13, 1965: 90.9 mhz; 400 w. 78 ft. TL: N39 47 05 W86 17 27. Stereo. 1200 N. Girls School Rd. 46214. Phone: (317) 244-9234. Fax: (317) 243-5506. E-mail: jon.easter@wayne.k12.in.us. Web Site: www.wayne.k12.in.us/bdwbdg. Licensee: Metropolitan School District of Wayne Township. Format: Contemp hit, rock/AOR, urban contemp. News: 10 hrs wkly. Target aud: 12-49. ♦ Jon Easter, gen mgr; Matt Reedy, progmg dir; Rob Woock, progmg dir; Paul McDonald, news dir; Kevin Van Wyk, chief of engrg & chief of engrg.

WBRI(AM)— Mar 10, 1964: 1500 khz; 5 kw-D, DA. TL: N39 52 14 W86 05 17. 4802 E. 62nd St. 46220. Phone: (317) 255-5484. Fax: (317) 255-8592. E-mail: wbri@wilkinsradio.com. Licensee: Heritage Christian Radio Inc. (acq 7-1-2003; $1.5 million). Network: Network: USA, Moody. Kaye, Scholer, Fierman, Hays & Handler. Format: Christian talk & info. Target aud: 35 plus. ♦ Keith Smiley, opns mgr & progmg mgr.

*****WEDM(FM)**— Sept 14, 1970: 91.1 mhz; 180 w vert. Ant 216 ft. TL: N39 47 29 W85 59 53. Stereo. c/o Walker Career Ctr., 9651 E. 21st St. 46229. Phone: (317) 532-6301. Fax: (317) 532-6199. Licensee: Metropolitan School District of Warren Township. Format: CHR. News: 3 hrs wkly. Target aud: General; Warren Township residents. ♦ Daniel J. Henn, stn mgr; Mike Rabey, chief of engrg.

WFBQ(FM)—Listing follows WNDE(AM).

WFMS(FM)— Mar 17, 1957: 95.5 mhz; 13 kw. 1,000 ft. TL: N39 46 03 W86 00 12. Stereo. 6810 N. Shadeland Ave. 46220. Phone: (317) 842-9550. Fax: (317) 577-3361. Web Site: www.wfms.com. Licensee: WFMS Lico Inc. Group owner: Susquehanna Radio Corp. (acq 11-20-72). Format: Modern country. ♦ David E. Kennedy, pres; Charlie Morgan, gen mgr; David Wood, opns mgr & progmg dir; Laureen Colley, gen sls mgr; Mike Orr, news dir & pub affrs dir; Max Turner, chief of engrg.

*****WFYI-FM**— Oct 1, 1954: 90.1 mhz; 10 kw. Ant 560 ft. TL: N39 53 59 W86 12 01. Stereo. 1401 N. Meridian St. 46202-2389. Phone: (317) 636-2020. Fax: (317) 397-2976. E-mail: webmaster@wfyi.org. Web Site: www.wfyi.org. Licensee: Metropolitan Indianapolis Public Broadcasting Inc. (acq 12-1-86). Network: Network: PRI, NPR. Indiana Public Broadcasting Stations Format: Class, news/talk. News: 41 hrs wkly. Target aud: 25-64; general. Spec prog: Black 5 hrs, blues 4 hrs wkly.Lloyd Wright, pres; Anthony Lorenz, CFO; Alan Cloe, exec VP & sr VP; Jeanelle Adamak, exec VP & VP; Jed Duvall, stn mgr; Jay Zochowski, opns mgr; Theresa Tetrault, dev dir; Susanne McAlister, sls VP, natl sls mgr & rgnl sls mgr; Rena Barraclough, prom VP & adv VP; Lori Plummer, prom mgr; Michael Toulouse, mus dir; Steve Jensen, engrg VP; Nate Pass, engrg dir . Co-owned TV: *WFYI-TV affil.

WHHH(FM)— Oct 28, 1991: 96.3 mhz; 3.3 kw. 285 ft. TL: N39 46 32 W86 09 10. Stereo. 21 E. St. Joseph 46204. Phone: (317) 266-9600. Fax: (317) 328-3870. Web Site: www.hot963.com. Licensee: Radio One of Indiana LLC. Group owner: Radio One Inc. (acq 11-8-01; grpsl). Network: CNN Radio. Format: CHR, Urban Hip Hop, R&B. Target aud: 18-49. ♦ Alfred Liggins, CEO & pres; Charles Williams, VP & gen sls mgr; Charles T. Williams, gen mgr.

WIBC(AM)— 1938: 1070 khz; 50 kw-D, 10 kw-N, DA-2. TL: N39 57 21 W86 21 30. Stereo. 40 Monument Cir., Suite 400, One Emmis Plaza 46204. Phone: (317) 266-9422. Fax: (317) 684-2022. Web Site: www.wibc.com. Licensee: Emmis Radio License LLC. Group owner: Emmis Communications Corp. (acq 6-9-94; $26 million. with co-located FM). Network: ABC Information & Entertainment. Rep: D & R Radio. Format: News/talk, sports. News staff: 12. Target aud: 25-54; white collar, above average income & education. ♦ Jeff Smulyan, CEO; Tom Severino, VP & gen mgr; Jon Quick, opns dir, progmg dir & news dir; Jay Chapman, sls dir; Patty England, gen sls mgr & natl sls mgr; Ashley Harris, prom mgr; Maure Baumeister, prom mgr; Jeff Dinsmore, chief of engrg.

WNOU(FM)—Co-owned with WIBC(AM). Dec 5, 1960: 93.1 mhz; 13.5 kw. Ant 991 ft. TL: N39 46 03 W86 00 12. Stereo. 40 Monument Cr. 46204. Phone: (317) 236-9300. Fax: (317) 971-6469. Format: CHR. Target aud: 18-34; adults. ♦ Jeff Simulyan, pres & stn mgr; David Edgar, opns dir; Jo Robinson, gen sls mgr & mktg dir; Chris Burnham, prom mgr; Chris Edge, progmg dir; David Hood, chief of engrg.

*****WICR(FM)**— Aug 20, 1962: 88.7 mhz; 5 kw. 1,000 ft. TL: N39 53 59 W86 12 02. Stereo. 1400 E. Hanna Ave. 46227. Phone: (317) 788-3280. Fax: (317) 788-3490. E-mail: wicr@uindy.edu. Web Site: wicr.uindy.edu. Licensee: University of Indianapolis. Network: PRI. John D. Pellegrin. Format: Class, jazz. News: 5 hrs wkly. Target aud: 35 plus; Educated, Affluent, Older. ♦ Beverley Pitts, pres; Scott Uecker, gen mgr; Russell Maloney, chief of engrg.

*****WJEL(FM)**— Sept 3, 1975: 89.3 mhz; 1 kw. 115 ft. TL: N39 54 34 W86 07 39. Stereo. 1901 E. 86th St. 46240. Phone: (317) 259-5278. Fax: (317) 259-5298. Web Site: www.geocities.com/wjelpower. Licensee: Metropolitan School District of Washington Township. Network: ABC Daytime Direction. Format: Var. ♦ John R. King, gen mgr; Robert L. Hendrix, progmg dir; Mike Rabey, chief of engrg.

WJJK(FM)—(Noblesville). Sep 25, 1950: 104.5 mhz; 50 kw. Ant 492 ft. TL: N39 50 25 W86 10 34. Stereo. 6810 N. Shadeland Ave. 46220. Phone: (317) 842-9550. Fax: (317) 577-3361. Web Site: www.gold1045.com. Licensee: Indy Lico Inc. Group owner: Susquehanna Radio Corp. (acq 10-7-93; $7.15 million;. FTR: 11-8-93). Haley, Bader & Potts. Format: Oldies. News staff: one. Target aud: 25-54. ♦ David E. Kennedy, pres;

Charlie Morgan, VP; Jenny Skjodt, gen mgr; David Wood, opns mgr; Lauren Colley, gen sls mgr; Mike Orr, news dir; Max Turner, chief of engrg.

WNDE(AM)— Oct 23, 1924: 1260 khz; 5 kw-U, DA-N. TL: N39 51 54 W86 03 43. 6161 Fall Creek Rd. 46220. Phone: (317) 257-7565. Fax: (317) 253-6501. Web Site: www.wnde.com. Licensee: Capstar TX L.P. Group owner: Clear Channel Communications Inc. (acq 8-30-00; grpsl). Network: Network: AP Radio, ESPN Radio. Rep: Clear Channel. Format: Sports, talk. Target aud: 25-54. Spec prog: 0. ♦Christopher Wheat, gen mgr; Marty Bender, opns mgr; Lee Anne Brooks, gen sls mgr; Helen Zimmerman, prom dir; Drew Carey, progmg dir; Dan Mettler, engrg mgr; Scott Fenstermaker, chief of engrg.

WFBQ(FM)—Co-owned with WNDE(AM). Nov 26, 1959: 94.7 mhz; 58 kw. Ant 804 ft. TL: N39 53 43 W86 12 04. Web Site: www.wfbq.com. Network: AP Radio. Format: Classic rock. ♦Helen Zimmerman, sls VP & mktg mgr; Tad Williams, prom dir; Mike Thomas, progmg dir.

***WRFT(FM)**— June 6, 1978: 91.5 mhz; 130 w. 180 ft. TL: N39 40 39 W86 00 58. Stereo. 6215 S. Franklin Rd. 46259. Phone: (317) 803-5552. Fax: (317) 862-7262. Licensee: Franklin Township Community School Corp. Format: Educ, div. Target aud: General. ♦Steve George, gen mgr; Danielle Searcy, opns dir.

WRZX(FM)— May 15, 1964: 103.3 mhz; 18 kw. 850 ft. TL: N39 53 43 W86 12 04. Stereo. 6161 Fall Creek Rd. 46220. Phone: (317) 257-7565. Fax: (317) 254-9619. Web Site: www.x103.com. Licensee: Capstar TX L.P. Group owner: Clear Channel Communications Inc. (acq 8-30-00; grpsl). Format: Modern rock. ♦Christopher J. Wheat, gen mgr; Marty Bender, opns mgr; Lee Anne Brooks, gen sls mgr; Scott Jameson, prom mgr & progmg dir; Dan Mettler, chief of engrg.

WSYW(AM)— May 15, 1963: 810 khz; 250 w-D. TL: N39 43 32 W86 11 08. 1800 N. Meridian St., Suite 603 46202-1433. Phone: (317) 924-1071. Fax: (317) 924-7766. Licensee: Continental Broadcast Group Inc. (acq 12-30-93; grpsl; 1-24-94). Rep: CMBS. Format: Sp. News: 3 hrs wkly. Target aud: 6-13. Spec prog: Loc children's show 5 hrs wkly. ♦Dwight Barnette, VP & gen mgr.

WTLC(AM)— July 27, 1941: 1310 khz; 5 kw-D, 1 kw-N, DA-N. TL: N39 43 08 W86 10 33. Stereo. 21 E. Saint Joseph St. 46204. Phone: (317) 266-9600. Fax: (317) 261-4664. Web Site: www.1310thelight.com. Licensee: Radio One of Indiana LLC. Group owner: Radio One Inc. (acq 11-8-01; grpsl). Network: ABC. Rep: D & R Radio. Format: Gospel, talk. News: one hr wkly. Target aud: 35 plus; black females. ♦Vince Fruge, gen mgr.

WTPI(FM)— Oct 15, 1984: 107.9 mhz; 22 kw. 762 ft. TL: N39 53 43 W86 12 04. Stereo. 9245 N. Meridian St., Suite 300 46260. Phone: (317) 816-4000. Fax: (317) 816-4050. E-mail: akeddie@mystar.com. Web Site: www.wtpi.com. Licensee: Entercom Indianapolis License LLC. (group owner; (acq 8-26-2004; grpsl). Rep: Christal. Fletcher, Heald & Heldreth. Format: Adult contemp. News staff: 3. Target aud: 25-54. Spec prog: Jazz 6 hrs wkly. ♦David J. Field, pres; Alex Keddie, opns VP & engrg dir; Greg Morris, sls VP; Steve Hartley, sls dir; Tami Wellbaum, prom dir; Gary Havens, progmg VP & mus dir; Steve Cooper, asst music dir; Kelly Vaughn, news dir; Jerry Curtis, pub affrs dir.

WXNT(AM)—Co-owned with WTPI(FM). 1923: 1430 khz; 5 kw-U, DA-N. TL: N39 50 17 W86 11 53. Stereo. Web Site: newstalk1430.com. Format: News/talk. News staff: one; News: 18 hrs wkly. Target aud: 35-64. Spec prog: Big band 2 hrs wkly. ♦Tim Medland, gen mgr; Kim Hurst, opns dir, opns mgr, pub affrs dir & chief of engrg; Greg Morris, sls dir; Drew Medland, adv mgr & news dir; Gary Havens, progmg dir.

WXLW(AM)— August 1948: 950 khz; 5 kw-D, 117 w-N, DA-2. TL: N39 51 05 W86 14 39. 54 Monument Cir., Suite 250 46204. Phone: (317) 655-9999. Fax: (317) 655-9995. E-mail: david@espn950.com. Web Site: www.espn950.com. Licensee: Pilgrim Communications L.L.C. (acq 10-1-95). Network: Network: ABC, ESPN Radio. Format: Sports. News: 7 hrs wkly. Target aud: 25-54; men, secondary women. Spec prog: Gospel 5 hrs wkly. ♦Dr. Gene Hood, CEO; Randy Hood, pres; Scott Taylor, VP; Russ Dodge, gen mgr & news dir; Greg Rakestraw, progmg dir.

WYXB(FM)— Jan 22, 1968: 105.7 mhz; 50 kw. 445 ft. TL: N39 48 01 W86 04 39. Stereo. One Emmis Plaza, 40 Monument Cir. 46204. Phone: (317) 684-1057. Fax: (317) 684-2021. E-mail: music@b1057.com. Web Site: www.b1057.com. Licensee: Emmis Radio License LLC. Group owner: Emmis Communications Corp. (acq 9-8-97; with co-located AM). Rep: D & R Radio. Format: Soft Rock. News staff: one; News: 3 hrs wkly. Target aud: 25-34; adults, (secondary is 25-54). Spec prog: Gospel 10 hrs wkly. ♦Jeffrey H. Smulyan, pres; David Edgar, opns dir; J. Chapman, gen sls mgr; Mary Young, mktg dir; Tom Severino, gen mgr & mktg mgr; Greg Duncan, progmg dir; Dave Hood, chief of engrg.

WZPL(FM)—See Greenfield

Jasper

WBDC(FM)—(Huntingburg). Dec 22, 1975: 100.9 mhz; 11 kw. 500 ft. TL: N38 12 31 W86 54 00. Stereo. Box 1009, 511 Newton St., 2nd Fl. 47547-1009. Secondary address: Box 330, 501 Old State Rd., Huntingburg 47542-0330. Phone: (812) 683-4144. Phone: (812) 634-9232. Fax: (812) 683-5891. E-mail: wbdc@psci.net. Web Site: www.dcbroadcasting.com.JRN Licensee: Dubois County Broadcasting Inc. Group owner: DCBroadcasting Inc. Network: Network: CNN Radio, Jones Radio Networks. Miller & Miller. Format: Country. News staff: 2; News: 10 hrs wkly. Target aud: 18-54. Spec prog: Farm 5 hrs, relg 5 hrs, sports 6 hrs, Sp .5 hr wkly. ♦Paul Knies, pres & gen mgr; Ron Spaulding, sls dir & gen sls mgr; Jason Lents, progmg dir; Dave Ferguson, chief of engrg.

WITZ-FM— Nov 1, 1954: 104.7 mhz; 50 kw. 490 ft. TL: N38 21 02 W86 56 26. Stereo. Box 167, 1978 S. WITZ Rd. 47546. Phone: (812) 482-2131. Fax: (812) 482-9609. E-mail: witzamfm@psci.net. Web Site: www.witzamfm.com. Licensee: Jasper On The Air Inc. Network: ABC Daytime Direction. Rep: Rgnl Reps. Format: Adult contemp. Target aud: 18-54. Spec prog: Paul Harvey 3 hrs wkly. ♦Earl Metzger, gen mgr; Bob Boyles, gen sls mgr; Walt Ferber, progmg dir; Reed Parker, news dir; Jeri Weisheit, chief of engrg.

WITZ(AM)— July 4, 1948: 990 khz; 1 kw-D. TL: N38 21 02 W86 56 26. Stereo. Web Site: www.witzamfm.com.

***WKJR(FM)**—Not on air, target date: unknown: 91.7 mhz; 3.8 kw. Ant 180 ft. TL: N38 26 08 W86 47 50. 1680 Hwy. 62 N.E., Corydon 47112. Phone: (812) 738-3482. Licensee: Good Samaritan Educational Radio Inc. ♦Steve Reising, gen mgr.

Jeffersonville

WAVG(AM)— June 26, 1961: 1450 khz; 1 kw-U. TL: N38 17 41 W85 45 07. Box 726, 213 Magnolia Ave. 47130. Phone: (812) 283-3577. Fax: (812) 285-5060. E-mail: wavg1450@inoightbb.com. Web Site: www.wavg1450.com. Licensee: Sunnyside Communications Inc. Group owner: Susquehanna Radio Corp. (acq 3-30-01; grpsl). Network: Jones Radio Networks. Rgnl Reps. Dow, Lohnes & Albertson. Format: Classic hit country. News staff: one. Target aud: 35 plus; general. ♦Blair W. Trask, pres & stn mgr; Kelly Trask, gen mgr & prom dir; Kelly Anderson, mktg dir; Ron Chilton, progmg dir; Gil Daugherty, news dir; Bill Brown, chief of engrg.

WQMF(FM)— Apr 25, 1974: 95.7 mhz; 28.5 kw. 643 ft. TL: N38 08 06 W85 56 05. Stereo. 4000 Radio Rd., Suite 1, Louisville, KY 40218. Phone: (502) 479-2222. Fax: (502) 479-2227. Web Site: www.wqmf.com. Licensee: Clear Channel Radio Licenses Inc. Group owner: Clear Channel Communications Inc. (acq 1-23-97; $13.5 million). Format: Classic Rock. ♦Earl Jones, gen mgr; Kevin Hughes, stn mgr.

Kendallville

WAWK(AM)— Nov 9, 1955: 1140 khz; 250 w-D. TL: N41 27 16 W85 15 48. 931 East Ave. 46755. Phone: (260) 347-2400. Phone: (260) 347-2401. Fax: (260) 347-2524. E-mail: wawk@locl.net. Web Site: www.wawk.com. Licensee: Northeast Indiana Broadcasting Inc. Network: USA. Irwin, Campbell. Format: Var, hits of the 50s to present. News: 7 hrs wkly. Target aud: 25-54. Spec prog: Big Band 2 hrs, bluegrass 2 hrs, Farm one hr wkly. ♦Don Moore, pres, VP & gen mgr; Karen White, sls dir & gen sls mgr; Scott Paul, progmg dir; Mike Shultz, news dir; Greg Case, chief of engrg.

WBTU(FM)—Licensed to Kendallville. See Fort Wayne

Kentland

WIVR(FM)— 2000: 101.7 mhz; 3.2 kw. Ant 453 ft. TL: N40 51 52 W87 35 14. Stereo. 202 E. Walnut, Watseka, IL 60970. Phone: (815) 432-0700. Phone: (815) 933-9287. Fax: (815) 432-6112. E-mail: wvliradio@comcast.net. Licensee: Milner Broadcasting Enterprises LLC (acq 12-11-00). Network: AP Network News. Womble, Carlyle, Sandridge & Rice. Format: Traditional country. News staff: 2; News: 168 bcsts wkly. Target aud: 12 plus; anthology country with current & recurrent hits. Spec prog: Chicago Bears Football. ♦Jim Brandt, gen mgr & opns mgr; Chris Swain, gen sls mgr; Mickey Milner, progmg dir; Ken Zyre, news dir; Don Kerouac, chief of engrg.

Knightstown

***WKPW(FM)**— Sept 7, 1993: 90.7 mhz; 4.4 kw. TL: N39 46 08 W85 31 05. 10892 N. State Rd., 140 46148. Phone: (765) 345-9070. Fax: (765) 345-7039. E-mail: wkpw@knightstown.net. Web Site: www.wkpw.net. Licensee: IN Soldiers' & Sailors' Childrens' HME. Booth, Freret, Imlay & Tepper. Format: Country. Target aud: General. Spec prog: Gospel. ♦Dr. John Wittkamper, pres; Paul Wilkinson, gen mgr; Mike York, progmg dir; Bob Hawkins, chief of engrg.

Knox

WKVI(AM)— June 30, 1969: 1520 khz; 250 w-D. TL: N41 19 20 W86 36 17. (CP: 1.8 kw-D). Box 10, 400 W. Culver Rd. 46534. Phone: (574) 772-6241. Fax: (574) 772-5920. Web Site: www.wkvi.com. Licensee: Kankakee Valley Broadcasting Co. Inc. Format: Adult contemp. ♦Ted Hayes, gen mgr; Tim Price, progmg dir.

WKVI-FM— July 21, 1969: 99.3 mhz; 3 kw. 303 ft. TL: N41 19 20 W86 36 17. Stereo. Web Site: www.wkvi.com.

Kokomo

WIOU(AM)— July 16, 1948: 1350 khz; 5 kw-D, 1 kw-N, DA-2. TL: N40 25 00 W86 06 49. Box 2208 46904-2208. Secondary address: 671 E. 400 S. 46902. Phone: (765) 453-1212. Fax: (765) 455-3882. E-mail: newsroom.wzwz.wiou@sbcglobal.net. Licensee: Mid-America Radio Group Inc. (group owner; acq 3-24-93; $1.21 million. with co-located FM; FTR: 4-12-93). Network: CBS. Format: Sports, news/talk. News staff: 2; News: 9 hrs wkly. Target aud: 25-54. ♦Steve Lamar, gen mgr.

WZWZ(FM)—Co-owned with WIOU(AM). Nov 20, 1964: 92.5 mhz; 6 kw. 324 ft. TL: N40 28 18 W86 09 52. Stereo. E-mail: wzwz@comteck.com. Licensee: Mid-America Radio Group of Kokomo Inc. Format: Adult contemp. News: 4 hrs wkly. Target aud: 18-49.

***WIWC(FM)**— September 1993: 91.7 mhz; 2.1 kw. 299 ft. TL: N40 36 00 W86 18 08. c/o WGNR, 2000 W. 53rd St., Anderson 46013. Phone: (765) 642-2750. Fax: (765) 642-4033. E-mail: wiwc@moody.edu. Web Site: wiwc.mbn.org. Licensee: The Moody Bible Institute of Chicago. (group owner) Format: Relg. Target aud: 34-55; general. ♦Ray Hashley, gen mgr; Tom Winn, progmg dir; Sam Sundin, news dir; Jim Wagner, chief of engrg.

WWKI(FM)— Oct 21, 1962: 100.5 mhz; 50 kw. 480 ft. TL: N40 27 04 W86 02 12. Stereo. 519 N. Main St. 46901-4661. Phone: (765) 459-4191. Fax: (765) 456-1111. Fax: (765) 456-1112. Licensee: Citadel Broadcasting Co. Group owner: Citadel Broadcasting Corp. (acq 6-30-99; grpsl). Network: AP Radio. Rep: Katz Radio. Rgnl Reps. Leventhal, Senter & Lehrman. Format: Country. News staff: 2; News: 13 hrs wkly. Target aud: 25-54. ♦Mike Christopher, gen mgr.

La Porte

WCOE(FM)—Listing follows WLOI(AM).

WLOI(AM)— 1948: 1540 khz; 250 w-D. TL: N41 37 55 W86 45 43. 1700 Lincolnway Pl., Suite 8 46350. Phone: (219) 362-6144. Phone: (219) 872-8986. Fax: (219) 324-7418. E-mail: wcoe@csinet.net. Licensee: La Porte County Broadcasting Company Inc. (acq 1955). Network: Network: ABC, Westwood One. Rep: Rgnl Reps. Wiley, Rein & Fielding. Format: Adult standards, MOR. News staff: 2; News: 26 hrs wkly. Target aud: 35 plus. Spec prog: Farm 8 hrs wkly. ♦Kenneth S. Coe, pres, gen mgr & gen sls mgr; Norma Sabie, sls dir & prom mgr; Dennis Siddall, progmg dir.

WCOE(FM)—Co-owned with WLOI(AM). Jan 23, 1964: 96.7 mhz; 3 kw. 265 ft. TL: N40 37 55 W86 45 43. Stereo. Phone: (219) 362-5290. Web Site: www.eaglewcoe.com. Format: Hot country. News staff: 2; News: 19 hrs wkly. Target aud: 35-54; upper income, middle aged. ♦Norma Sabie, adv dir; Kenneth S. Coe, adv mgr; Dennis Sidall, mus dir; Donna Eichelberg, pub affrs dir; Carl Fletcher, engrg dir.

Ladoga

*WJCJ(FM)—Not on air, target date: unknown: 88.9 mhz; 50 kw. Ant 207 ft. TL: N40 31 19 W87 30 58. CSN International, 4002N. 3300E., Twin Falls, ID 83301. Phone: (208) 734-6633. Web Site: www.csnradio.com. Licensee: CSN International (group owner;

Lafayette

WASK(AM)— 1942: 1450 khz; 1 kw-U. TL: N40 24 08 W86 50 59. Box 7880 47903. Secondary address: 3575 McCarty Ln. 47903. Phone: (765) 447-2186. Fax: (765) 448-4452. Web Site: www.wask.com. Licensee: WASK Inc. Group owner: Schurz Communications Inc. (acq 1-28-91; $8.25 million. with co-located FM; FTR: 1-28-91). Network: CBS. Rep: Christal. Hogan & Hartson. Format: Oldies. News staff: 6; News: 15 hrs wkly. Target aud: 25-54; affluent, well-educated adults. Spec prog: Farm 2 hrs wkly. ◆John Trent, pres & gen mgr; Randy Jones, progmg dir; Steve Truex, news dir & chief of engrg.

WKOA(FM)—Co-owned with WASK(AM). Sept 28, 1964: 105.3 mhz; 50 kw. 375 ft. TL: N40 24 08 W86 50 59. Stereo. Web Site: www.wkoa.com. Group owner: Lafayette Broadcasting Inc. Network: ABC Information & Entertainment. Format: Country. News staff: 3; News: 12 hrs wkly. Target aud: 25-54. Spec prog: Farm 3 hrs wkly. ◆Bob Miller, mktg dir & prom dir; Mark Allen, progmg dir.

WAZY-FM— March 1965: 96.5 mhz; 50 kw. 500 ft. TL: N40 23 02 W87 07 55. Stereo. 3824 S. 18th St. 47909. Phone: (765) 474-1410. Fax: (765) 474-3442. Web Site: www.wazy.com. Licensee: Artistic Media Partners L.P. Group owner: Artistic Media Partners Inc. (acq 10-86; $2 million;. FTR: 9-22-86). Network: ABC. Rep: Christal. Rosenman & Colin L.L.P. Format: Top-40, CHR. News staff: one; News: 4 hrs wkly. Target aud: 18-34. ◆Doug Kein, pres & sls mgr; Arthur Angotti, gen mgr; Zack Tylor, gen sls mgr & prom dir; J.J. Davis, progmg dir; Bob Henning, chief of engrg.

WLAS(AM)—Co-owned with WAZY-FM. Nov 28, 1959: 1410 khz; 1 kw-D, 65 w-N, DA-1. TL: N40 21 38 W86 52 38. Licensee: Artistic Media Partners Inc. (acq 9-30-98; $275,000). Format: Country. News: 3 hrs wkly. Target aud: 25-49. ◆Justin Kaiser, progmg dir.

*WJEF(FM)— Feb 7, 1972: 91.9 mhz; 250 w. 100 ft. TL: N40 23 52 W86 52 26. Stereo. 1801 S. 18th St. 47905. Secondary address: 2300 Cason St. 47904. Phone: (765) 772-4700. E-mail: rbrist@lsc.k12.in.us. Web Site: www.jeff92.org. Licensee: Lafayette School Corp. Format: Oldies. News: 6 hrs wkly. Target aud: General. ◆Randall J. Brist, gen mgr.

WKHY(FM)— Jan 1, 1970: 93.5 mhz; 6 kw. 311 ft. TL: N40 23 13 W86 58 10. Stereo. Box 7093 47903. Secondary address: 711 N. Earl Ave. 47904. Phone: (765) 448-1566. Fax: (765) 448-1348. Web Site: www.wkhy.com. Licensee: Stay Tuned Broadcasting Corp. Group owner: RadioWorks Inc. (acq 5-12-99; grpsl). Network: AP Radio. Rep: Katz Radio. Shaw Pittman. Format: Classic rock/AOR. News staff: one. Target aud: 25-54; adults that are active, mobile & moderately affluent. ◆Robert Rhea Jr., pres; John Schurz, gen sls mgr; Liz Hahn, prom dir; Jeff Strange, progmg dir; Steve Truey, chief of engrg.

*WQSG(FM)—Not on air, target date: unknown: 90.7 mhz; 17 kw vert. Ant 328 ft. TL: N40 22 13 W86 30 06. Drawer 2440, Tupelo, MS 38803. Phone: (662) 844-8888. Fax: (662) 842-6791. Licensee: American Family Association. Group owner: American Family Radio (acq 7-29-03). ◆Marvin Sanders, gen mgr.

Lafayette Township

*WCYT(FM)— 1995: 91.1 mhz; 200 w. 213 ft. TL: N40 58 58 W85 17 42. Stereo. Homestead High School, 4310 Homestead Rd., Fort Wayne 46814. Phone: (260) 431-2299. Phone: (260) 431-2911. Fax: (260) 431-2330. Web Site: www.wcyt.org. Licensee: Southwest Allen County Schools. Format: Modern rock, alternative, contemporary hit. Target aud: General. Spec prog: Oldies 2 hrs wkly, blues 2 hrs wkly. ◆Adam Schenkel, stn mgr; Joe Asher, progmg dir; Andy Dunn, mus dir.

Lagrange

WTHD(FM)— Sept 2, 1994: 105.5 mhz; 2.4 kw. Ant 522 ft. TL: N41 37 24 W85 20 49. 206 S. High St. 46761. Phone: (260) 463-8500. Phone: (800) 856-1055. Fax: (260) 463-8580. E-mail: wthd@wthd.net. Web Site: www.wthd.net. Licensee: Lake Cities Broadcasting Inc. (acq 7-14-93; FTR: 8-9-93). Network: ABC. Format: Country. News staff: one; News: 2 hrs wkly. Target aud: 25-54. ◆Penny Mitchell, opns mgr; Tim Murray, gen mgr & news dir; Thomas Andrews, chief of engrg.

Lanesville

WGZB-FM— June 20, 1988: 96.5 mhz; 1.6 kw. Ant 638 ft. TL: N38 10 25 W85 54 50. Stereo. 520 S. 4th St., Louisville, KY 40202. Phone: (502) 625-1220. Fax: (502) 625-1257. Web Site: www.b96jams.com. Licensee: Blue Chip Broadcasting Licenses II Ltd. Group owner: Radio One Inc. (acq 4-30-2001; grpsl). Format: Urban contemp. ◆Dale Schafer, gen mgr; Holly Bussey, gen sls mgr; Mark Gunn, progmg dir; Valerie Sickles, news dir; Don Backherms, chief of engrg.

Lebanon

*WIRE(FM)— 2001: 91.1 mhz; 3.2 kw vert. Ant 220 ft. TL: N40 03 48 W86 26 36. Stereo. 3500 DePauw Blvd., Suite 2085, Indianapolis 46268-6103. Phone: (317) 870-8400. Fax: (317) 870-8404. Web Site: www.radiomom.fm. Licensee: Hoosier Broadcasting Corp. Format: Adult contemp. Target aud: 25-54; adults. ◆William Shirk Poorman, pres; Annie Martin, CFO; Chuck Cunningham, VP & gen mgr; Tom Gibson, mktg mgr.

WYJZ(FM)— May 28, 1967: 100.9 mhz; 6 kw. 328 ft. TL: N39 54 55 W86 23 38. 21 E. St. Joseph, Indianapolis 46204. Phone: (317) 266-9600. Fax: (317) 328-3870. Web Site: www.wyjzradio.com. Licensee: Radio One of Indiana LLC. Group owner: Radio One Inc. (acq 11-8-01; grpsl). Network: ABC. Rep: Katz Radio. Format: Smooth jazz, new adult contemp. News staff: 2; News: 12 hrs wkly. Target aud: General. Spec prog: F. ◆Alfred Liggins, pres; Charles Williams, VP, gen mgr & progmg dir; Brian Harrington, gen sls mgr; Jeff Crave, rgnl sls mgr & chief of engrg.

Ligonier

WLEG(FM)—Licensed to Ligonier. See Warsaw

Linton

*KXJH(FM)—Not on air, target date: unknown: 90.1 mhz; 400 w. Ant 141 ft. TL: N39 02 22 W87 07 33. American Family Radio, Box 3206, Tupelo, MS 38803. Phone: (662) 844-8888. Fax: (662) 842-6791. Web Site: www.afr.net. Licensee: American Family Association. Group owner: American Family Radio. Format: Inspirational Christian. ◆Marvin Sanders, gen mgr.

WBTO(AM)— Oct 10, 1953: 1600 khz; 500 w-D, 32 w-N. TL: N39 03 57 W87 11 19. Box 242, Vincennes 47591. Phone: (812) 847-4474. Fax: (812) 847-0167. Web Site: www.wqtyfm.com. Licensee: The Original Co. Inc. (group owner; acq 6-11-99; $350,000 with co-located FM). Network: Moody. Rep: Rgnl Reps. Format: Country. ◆Mark Lange, pres & gen mgr; Michelle York, sls dir.

WQTY(FM)—Co-owned with WBTO(AM). Sept 14, 1970: 93.3 mhz; 12 kw. 475 ft. TL: N39 00 46 W87 22 23. Stereo. Web Site: www.wqtyfm.com.

*WYTJ(FM)—Not on air, target date: Aug 2003: 89.3 mhz; 1 kw. Ant 292 ft. TL: N39 05 59 W87 10 59. R.R. 3, Box 1034 47441. Phone: (812) 847-7222. Licensee: Bethel Baptist Church. Format: Relg. ◆Doug Cassel, gen mgr.

Logansport

WLHM(FM)—Listing follows WSAL(AM).

WSAL(AM)— Feb 24, 1949: 1230 khz; 1 kw-U. TL: N40 45 16 W86 18 40. Box 719 46947. Phone: (574) 722-4000. Fax: (574) 722-4010. Web Site: www.wsal.com. Licensee: Logansport Radio Corp. (acq 12-11-85; $850,000; 11-4-85). Network: ABC Daytime Direction. Rep: Rgnl Reps. Format: Adult contemp, news/talk. News staff: 2; News: 14 hrs wkly. Target aud: General. Spec prog: Farm 10 hrs wkly. ◆John P. Jenkins, CEO & pres; Andy Eubank, gen mgr; Lynne Ness, gen sls mgr; Joe Ulary, news dir; Jeff Smith, chief of engrg.

WLHM(FM)—Co-owned with WSAL(AM). May 11, 1965: 102.3 mhz; 3 kw. 300 ft. TL: N40 45 16 W86 18 40. Stereo. Web Site: www.102fm.com. Format: CHR. News staff: 2; News: 5 hrs wkly. Target aud: 18-49. ◆Andy Eubank, progmg dir.

*WWTS(FM)—Not on air, target date: unknown: 89.5 mhz; 5 w horiz, 24 kw vert. Ant 400 ft. TL: N40 40 08 W86 41 44. CSN International, 4002N. 3300E., Twin Falls, ID 83301. Phone: (208) 734-6633. Licensee: CSN International (group owner).

Loogootee

*WBHW(FM)— September 1995: 88.7 mhz; 1.7 kw. 761 ft. TL: N38 38 30 W86 59 57. Box 4164, Evansville 47724. Secondary address: Box 71A, R.R.2, County Rd. 1200 S., Haubstadt 47629. Phone: (812) 386-3342. Fax: (812) 768-5552. E-mail: goodnews@evansville.net. Web Site: www.thyword.org. Licensee: Music Ministries Inc. Format: Relg. ◆Floyd E. Turner, gen mgr; Dave Rigg, progmg dir.

WRZR(FM)— Dec 6, 1984: 94.5 mhz; 1.8 kw. 426 ft. TL: N38 37 09 W86 58 27. Stereo. Box 1009, Jasper 47547. Phone: (812) 634-9232. Fax: (812) 482-3696. E-mail: wrzr@psci.net. Licensee: Hembree Communications Inc. Group owner: DCBroadcasting Inc. (acq 8-97). Network: Jones Radio Networks. Ron Spaulding Miller & Miller. Format: Classic rock. News staff: one; News: 2 hrs wkly. Target aud: 24-45. Spec prog: Farm 2 hrs wkly. ◆Paul Knies, pres, gen mgr & gen sls mgr; Alan Williams, opns mgr; Jason Lents, progmg dir; Steve Kulb, news dir; David Ferguson, chief of engrg.

Lowell

*WTMK(FM)—Not on air, target date: unknown: 88.5 mhz; 1.5 kw. Ant 167 ft. TL: N41 04 59 W87 10 47. CSN International, 4002N. 3300E., Twin Falls, ID 83301. Phone: (208) 734-6633. Licensee: CSN International (group owner).

WZVN(FM)— Nov 24, 1972: 107.1 mhz; 1.29 kw. 499 ft. TL: N41 21 09 W87 24 12. 2755 Sager Rd., Valparaiso 46383. Phone: (219) 462-6111. Fax: (219) 462-4880. Web Site: www.z1071.com. Licensee: Porter County Broadcasting Holding Corp. LLC. Group owner: Porter County Broadcasting Corp. (acq 2-6-2004; $4.9 million. with WXRD(FM) Crown Point). Network: ABC. Wilmer, Cutler & Pickering. Format: Adult contemp. Target aud: 25-54. ◆Leigh Ellis, pres; Marty J. Wielgos, sr VP & gen mgr; George Stevens, stn mgr; O.J. Jackson, gen sls mgr; Scott Wagner, progmg dir & progmg mgr; Laura Walszko, news dir.

Madison

WIKI(FM)—See Carrollton, KY

WORX-FM—Listing follows WXGO(AM).

WXGO(AM)— March 1956: 1270 khz; 1 kw-D, 58 w-N, DA-2. TL: N38 44 28 W85 21 41. Box 95, 1224 E. Telegraph Hill Rd. 47250. Phone: (812) 265-3322. Fax: (812) 273-5509. E-mail: worxwxgo@seidata.com. Web Site: www.worxradio.com. Licensee: Dubois County Broadcasting Inc. Group owner: DCBroadcasting Inc. Network: USA. Rep: Rgnl Reps. Format: News, oldies. Target aud: General. Spec prog: Farm 3 hrs, relg 6 hrs wkly. ◆Paul Knies, pres; Bill Potter, gen mgr.

WORX-FM—Co-owned with WXGO(AM). March 1950: 96.7 mhz; 3 kw. 320 ft. TL: N38 44 30 W85 21 41. Stereo. Web Site: www.worxradio.com. Format: Adult contemp. News staff: one; News: 20 hrs wkly. Spec prog: Agriculture business 3 hrs wkly.

Indiana

Marengo

*WBRO(FM)— 2000: 89.9 mhz; 1 kw. Ant 279 ft. TL: N38 21 49 W86 25 13. Box 181 47140. Phone: (812) 365-9276. Fax: (812) 365-2127. E-mail: wbrofm@aol.com. Web Site: www.wbro.org. Licensee: Crawford County Community Radio Inc. (acq 6-25-01). Format: Var. ♦ Shawn Scott, gen mgr.

Marion

WBAT(AM)— June 7, 1947: 1400 khz; 1 kw-U. TL: N40 33 40 W85 41 30. Box 839, 120 N. Miller Ave. 46952. Phone: (765) 664-6239. Fax: (765) 662-0730. E-mail: wbat@comteck.com. Web Site: www.wbat.com. Licensee: Mid-America Radio Group. Group owner: Mid-America Radio Group Inc. (acq 12-88; grpsl; 12-19-88). Network: Network: CBS, ESPN Radio. Regional Reps Format: Sports, oldies. News staff: one; News: 7 hrs wkly. Target aud: 25-54. ♦ David Keister, pres; David Poehler, exec VP; Carolyn Bush, gen mgr; James F. Brunner, gen sls mgr; Tim George, progmg dir; Mike Jenkins, news dir; Warren Arnett, chief of engrg.

*WBSW(FM)— 1997: 90.9 mhz; 1 kw horiz, 2.4 kw vert. 308 ft. TL: N40 40 01 W85 37 50. c/o WBST(FM), Ball State Univ., Muncie 47306-0550. Phone: (765) 285-5888. Fax: (765) 285-8937. E-mail: ipr@bsu.edu. Web Site: www.bsu.edu/ipr. Licensee: Ball State University. Format: Class, news. News staff: one; News: 33 hrs wkly. Target aud: General. ♦ Anthony Hunt, gen mgr; Pam Coletti, gen sls mgr; Carol Trimmer, prom mgr; Steven Turpin, progmg dir & mus dir; Terry Heifetz, news dir; Robert Mittendorf, chief of engrg.

WCJC(FM)— (Van Buren). Aug 28, 1989: 99.3 mhz; 3 kw. 328 ft. TL: N40 40 01 W85 37 50. Stereo. Box 839, 120 N. Miller Ave. 46952. Phone: (765) 664-6239. Fax: (765) 662-0730. E-mail: wcjc@comteck.com. Web Site: www.wcjc.com. Licensee: Mid-America Radio Group Inc. (group owner; acq 12-19-88; grpsl; FTR: 12-19-88). Network: ABC. Regional Reps Format: Country. News staff: 2; News: 25 hrs wkly. Target aud: 25-54; consumer-oriented modern country fans. Spec prog: Relg 3 hrs wkly. ♦ David Keister, pres; David Poehler, VP & stn mgr; Carolyn Bush, gen mgr; Tim George, opns mgr & progmg dir; James F. Brunner, gen sls mgr; Warren Arnett, chief of engrg.

WGOM(AM)— May 11, 1955: 860 kg; 1 kw-D, 500 w-N, DA-2. TL: N40 33 12 W85 38 45. Box 1538 46952. Phone: (765) 664-7396. Phone: (765) 664-9466. Fax: (765) 668-6767. Licensee: Mid-America Radio of Indiana Inc. Group owner: Mid-America Radio Group Inc. (acq 5-12-2003; with co-located FM). Format: Talk, sports. Target aud: 25-54. ♦ David Poehler, pres; Rich Coolman, opns mgr; Gloria Millspaugh, gen sls mgr; Kyle Charters, news dir & pub affrs dir; Jack Elmore, chief of engrg.

WMRI(FM)— Co-owned with WGOM(AM). Dec 19, 1948: 106.9 mhz; 50 kw. 499 ft. TL: N40 35 52 W85 39 21. Stereo. E-mail: wmri@wmri.com. Web Site: www.wrmi.com. Network: CNN Radio. Format: Adult contemp. Target aud: 25-54.

Martinsville

WCBK-FM—Listing follows WMCB(AM).

WMCB(AM)— Apr 18, 1967: 1540 khz; 500 w-D. TL: N39 24 31 W86 25 10. Box 1577 46151. Secondary address: 1639 Burton Ln. 46151-3004. Phone: (765) 342-3394. Fax: (765) 342-5020. Web Site: www.wcbk.com. Licensee: Mid-America Radio Group Inc. (group owner; acq 8-4-97; with co-located FM). Network: USA. Format: Country. Target aud: 25-54. Spec prog: Farm one hr wkly. ♦ David Keister, gen mgr; Jeff Hancock, gen sls mgr; Dave Stanley, progmg dir.

WCBK-FM—Co-owned with WMCB(AM). Oct 15, 1968: 102.3 mhz; 3 kw. 300 ft. TL: N39 26 18 W86 27 54. Stereo. Web Site: www.wcbk.com.

Michigan City

WEFM(FM)— Sept 15, 1966: 95.9 mhz; 3 kw. Ant 230 ft. TL: N41 42 58 W86 51 47. Stereo. 1903 Springland Ave. 46360. Phone: (219) 879-8201. Fax: (219) 879-8202. E-mail: wefm@yahoo.com. Licensee: Michigan City FM Broadcasters Inc. Network: USA. Format: Adult contemp, oldies. Target aud: General. Spec prog: Farm, relg 4 hrs wkly. ♦ Thomas Burns, pres; Ronald Miller, stn mgr; Jim Spevak, gen sls mgr; Tod Allen, progmg dir & progmg mgr; Tim Volckmann, chief of engrg.

Directory of Radio

WIMS(AM)— Aug 10, 1947: 1420 khz; 5 kw-U, DA-2. TL: N41 40 26 W86 55 58. 6405 Olcott Ave., Hammond 46320. Phone: (219) 844-1230. Fax: (219) 989-8516. Web Site: www.wimsradio.com. Licensee: Vazquez Development LLC (acq 12-4-2003); $1.2 million. with WJOB(AM) Hammond). Rep: Rgnl Reps. Format: Full service. Target aud: 30 plus; general. Spec prog: Pol 3 hrs wkly. ♦ Ric Federighi, gen mgr; Bill Baker, gen sls mgr; Michael Stewart, progmg dir.

Mitchell

*WMBL(FM)—Not on air, target date: unknown: 88.1 mhz; 1 kw. Ant 400 ft. TL: N38 45 50 W86 31 15. 820 N. LaSalle Blvd., Chicago, IL 60610. Phone: (312) 329-4438. Phone: (800) 246-0691. Web Site: www.mbn.org. Licensee: The Moody Bible Institute of Chicago. Format: Relg.

WQRJ(FM)— Aug 17, 1991: 102.5 mhz; 6 kw. 282 ft. TL: N38 38 16 W86 27 11. Box 1307, Bedford 47421. Phone: (812) 275-7555. Fax: (812) 279-8046. E-mail: realcountry1025@yahoo.com. Web Site: realcountryonline.com. Licensee: Mitchell Community Broadcast Co. (acq 2-26-92; $8,000. for CP; FTR: 3-16-92). Network: Network: ABC, Jones Radio Networks. Rep: Rgnl Reps. Reed, Smith, Shaw & McClay. Format: Real country. News staff: one; News: 2 hrs wkly. Target aud: General. ♦ Dean Spencer, CEO & gen mgr.

Monticello

WMRS(FM)— March 1989: 107.7 mhz; 4.4 kw. 500 ft. TL: N40 45 03 W86 48 17. Stereo. 132 N. Main 47960. Phone: (574) 583-8121. Phone: (574) 583-8933. Fax: (574) 583-8933. E-mail: kevinp@wmrsradio.com. Web Site: www.wmrsradio.com. Licensee: Monticello Community Radio Inc. (acq 1-15-91; FTR: 2-11-91). Network: Network: USA, Jones Radio Networks. Format: Adult contemp, div, talk. News staff: 2; News: 20 hrs wkly. Target aud: 25-60; motivated, intelligent, diverse. Spec prog: Gospel 5 hrs wkly. ♦ Kevin Page, gen mgr; Bruce Quinn, opns mgr & dev dir.

WXXB(FM)—See Delphi

Montpelier

*WJCO(FM)—Not on air, target date: unknown: 91.3 mhz; 350 w vert. Ant 196 ft. TL: N40 33 21 W85 17 39. CSN International, 4002N. 3300E., Twin Falls, ID 83301. Phone: (208) 734-6633. Licensee: CSN International (group owner).

Morgantown

*WCJL(FM)—Not on air, target date: unknown: 90.9 mhz; 1 kw horiz, 13.6 kw vert. Ant 213 ft. TL: N39 19 17 W86 31 08. CSN International, 3000 W. MacArthur Blvd., Santa Ana, CA 92704-6916. Fax: (714) 825-9661. Licensee: CSN International (group owner). ♦ Jeffrey W. Smith, VP & gen mgr.

Morristown

*WJCF(FM)— 2000: 88.1 mhz; 2.7 kw vert. Ant 151 ft. TL: N39 45 01 W85 33 19. Box 846, Greenfield 46140. Secondary address: 15 Wood St., Greenfield 46140-2162. Phone: (317) 467-1064. Fax: (317) 467-1065. E-mail: wjcfradio@aol.com. Web Site: www.wjcfradio.com. Licensee: Indiana Community Radio Corp. Format: Community radio. ♦ Jennifer Cox-Hensley, pres; Mary Hensley, gen mgr.

Mount Vernon

WRCY(AM)— Aug 21, 1955: 1590 khz; 500 w-D, 35 w-N. TL: N37 56 03 W87 55 42. 7109 Upton Rd. 47620-9483. Phone: (812) 838-4484. Fax: (812) 838-6434. Licensee: The Original Co. Inc. (group owner; acq 1999; $360,000 with co-located FM). Format: Real country. Target aud: 25 plus; loc county. Spec prog: Farm 5 hrs wkly. ♦ Mark Lange, pres; John Curry, gen mgr; Frank Hertel, chief of engrg.

Muncie

*WBST(FM)— Sept 12, 1960: 92.1 mhz; 3 kw. 300 ft. TL: N40 12 48 W85 27 36. Stereo. Ball State Univ. 47306-0550. Phone: (765) 285-5888. Fax: (765) 285-8937. E-mail: ipr@bsu.edu. Web Site: www.bsu.edu/ipr. Licensee: Ball State University. Network: Network: PRI, NPR. Format: Classical, news. News staff: one; News: 33 hrs wkly. Target aud: General. ♦ Anthony Hunt, gen mgr; Pam Coletti, sls

dir & gen sls mgr; Carol Trimmer, prom mgr; Steven Turpin, progmg dir & mus dir; Terry Heifetz, news dir; Robert Mittendorf, chief of engrg.

WERK(FM)— Jan 16, 1986: 104.9 mhz; 3 kw. 328 ft. TL: N40 09 19 W85 25 48. Stereo. 800 E. 29th St. 47302. Phone: (765) 378-0291. Fax: (765) 378-0291. E-mail: werkstudio@werkradio.com. Web Site: www.werkradio.com. Licensee: Indiana Sabrecom Inc. Group owner: Backyard Broadcasting LLC (acq 12-1-02; grpsl). Format: Oldies. ♦ Jay Garrison, progmg dir & news dir.

WLBC-FM—Listing follows WXFN(AM).

WLHN(AM)— Feb 14, 1965: 990 khz; 250 w-D, 2 w-N, DA-1. TL: N40 06 54 W85 22 02. Stereo. 3611 S. Post Rd. 47302. Phone: (765) 747-6970. Fax: (765) 747-5054. E-mail: wlhn990@yahoo.com. Web Site: wlhnradio.com. Licensee: Electronic Applications Radio Service Inc. (acq 3-16-99). Rep: Roslin, Rgnl Reps. Harris, Beach & Wilcox. Format: Southern gospel. Target aud: 25-54; upscale adults & families, professional & blue collar. ♦ Steven Dugger, gen mgr.

WMDH-FM—See New Castle

*WWDS(FM)— 1978: 90.5 mhz; 100 w. Ant 174 ft. TL: N40 16 42 W85 20 52. Stereo. 3400 E. State Rd. 28 47303. Phone: (765) 288-5597. Fax: (765) 288-8498. E-mail: fclark@delcomschools.org. Web Site: www.delcomschools.org. Licensee: Delaware Community School Corp. Format: Adult contemp. ♦ Ford Clark, stn mgr.

*WWHI(FM)— 1950: 91.3 mhz; 310 w. 79 ft. TL: N40 09 45 W85 22 45. 1601 E. 26th St. 47302. Phone: (765) 747-5339. Fax: (765) 747-5325. Licensee: Ball State University (acq 2-13-2004). Format: Educ. ♦ Ken Wickliffe, gen mgr.

*WWMU(FM)—Not on air, target date: unknown: 88.3 mhz; 200 w vert. Ant 295 ft. TL: N40 05 06 W85 23 52. Box 2440, Tupelo, MS 38803-2440. Phone: (662) 844-8888. Fax: (662) 842-6791. Web Site: www.afr.net. Licensee: American Family Association. (acq 5-13-2005; $10 for CP). ♦ Marvin Sanders, gen mgr.

WXFN(AM)— November 1926: 1340 khz; 1 kw-U. TL: N40 09 42 W85 22 41. 800 E. 29th St. 47302. Phone: (765) 288-4403. Fax: (765) 288-0429. Licensee: Indiana Sabrecom Inc. Group owner: Backyard Broadcasting LLC (acq 12-1-2002; grpsl). Network: Network: ABC, ESPN Radio, Sporting News Radio Network. Format: Sports. News staff: 2; News: 12 hrs wkly. Target aud: 25-54. Spec prog: Black 3 hrs wkly. ♦ Barry Drake, CEO; Robin Smith, CFO; Steve Lindell, VP & gen mgr; Tom Hammond, news dir; Sean Mattingly, chief of engrg.

WLBC-FM—Co-owned with WXFN(AM). October 1947: 104.1 mhz; 50 kw. 420 ft. TL: N40 09 38 W85 22 42. Stereo. E-mail: steve@wlbc.com. Web Site: www.wlbc.com. Format: News. News staff: one; News: 19 hrs wkly. Target aud: 18-49; female. ♦ Elaine Merritt, stn mgr; Steve Lindell, progmg VP.

Nappanee

WYPW(FM)— Dec 16, 1991: 95.7 mhz; 1.4 kw. 500 ft. TL: N41 24 43 W86 01 51. Stereo. Box 370, 12478 N. 950 W. 46550. Phone: (574) 773-7989. Web Site: www.power957.com. Licensee: Talking Stick Communications LLC. (group owner; acq 8-25-2000). Network: Network: ABC, CBS. Format: Adult contemp. News: 10 hrs wkly. Target aud: 35-70; secretaries, bankers. ♦ Marilyn S. Cobb, pres; James W. Cobb, exec VP & gen mgr.

Nashville

WVNI(FM)— August 1997: 95.1 mhz; 1.6 kw. 636 ft. TL: N39 13 39 W86 25 05. (CP: 2.3 kw, ant 472 ft.). Box 1628, Bloomington 47402. Secondary address: 4317 E.3rd St., Bloomington 47401. Phone: (812) 335-9500. Fax: (812) 335-8880. E-mail: todayschristianmusic @spirit95fm.com. Web Site: www.sprint95fm.com. Licensee: Brown County Broadcasters Inc. Group owner: Mid-America Radio Group Inc. (acq 10-29-97; $20,000 for 51% of stock). Format: Contemp Christian. Target aud: 25-54. ♦ Diana Nuchols, gen mgr; Todd Youmans, opns dir.

New Albany

WFIA-FM— Jan 1, 1996: 94.7 mhz; 6 kw. 328 ft. TL: N38 17 02 W85 54 17. Stereo. 9960 Corporate Campus Dr., Suite 3600, Louisville, KY 40223. Phone: (502) 339-9470. Fax: (502) 423-3139. E-mail:

Stations in the U.S. — Indiana

listeners@salemradiogroup.com. Web Site: www.salemradiogroup.com. Licensee: Salem Media of Kentucky Inc. Group owner: Salem Communications Corp. (acq 1999; $5 million with WRVI(FM) Valley Station, KY). Format: Talk, teaching, Southern gospel, Christian. Target aud: 30 plus. ♦ Gordon Marcy, gen mgr.

WNAS(FM)— May 28, 1949: 88.1 mhz; 2.85 kw. 3 ft. TL: N38 17 56 W85 48 45. 1020 Vincennes St. 47150. Phone: (812) 949-4272. Fax: (812) 949-6926. Web Site: www.wnas.org. Licensee: New Albany-Floyd County Consolidated School Corp. Format: Educ, Top-40. ♦ Lee Kelly, gen mgr.

WWSZ(AM)— June 15, 1949: 1570 khz; 1.5 kw-D, 233 w-N. TL: N38 19 40 W85 46 56. 8700 Westport Rd., Suite 107, Louisville, KY 40242. Phone: (502) 240-0400. Fax: (502) 412-0993. Web Site: www.wszradio.com. Licensee: New Albany Broadcasting Co. Inc. Group owner: Mortenson Broadcasting Co. (acq 1-27-2005; $1 million). Network: Network: CBS Radio, ESPN Radio. Format: All sports. Target aud: 35-54; blues and true jazz listeners. ♦ Archie Dale, gen mgr.

New Carlisle

WOZW(FM)— July 2, 1991: 102.3 mhz; 2 kw. 397 ft. TL: N41 43 38 W86 24 30. Stereo. 3371 Cleveland Rd., Suite 300, South Bend 46628. Phone: (574) 273-9300. Fax: (574) 273-9090. E-mail: michael@wzow.com. Web Site: www.wzow.com. Licensee: Artistic Media Partners Inc. (group owner; acq 2-18-2002; $1.5 million). Format: Classic rock. ♦ Michael Stone, gen mgr & stn mgr.

New Castle

WMDH(AM)— Nov 14, 1960: 1550 khz; 250 w-U, DA-2. TL: N39 55 57 W85 24 24. Box 690, 1134 W. St. Rd. 38 47362. Phone: (765) 529-2600. Fax: (765) 529-1688. Web Site: www.wmdh.com. Licensee: Citadel Broadcasting Co. Group owner: Citadel Broadcasting Corp. (acq 7-1-99; grpsl). Network: UPI. Rep: McGavren Guild. Format: Adult standards. Target aud: 49 plus. Spec prog: Farm 2 hrs, relg 2 hrs wkly. ♦ Paulette Lees, gen mgr & gen sls mgr; Clint Marsh, progmg dir.

WMDH-FM— Aug 6, 1976: 102.5 mhz; 50 kw. 500 ft. TL: N40 03 18 W85 23 05. Stereo. Web Site: www.wmdh.com. Format: Country. News staff: one; News: 2 hrs wkly. Target aud: 25-49; upper middle class. Spec prog: Farm one hr wkly.

New Haven

WJFX(FM)— April 1990: 107.9 mhz; 3.2 kw. Ant 453 ft. TL: N41 01 26 W85 03 51. Stereo. 5936 E. State Blvd., Fort Wayne 46815. Phone: (260) 493-9539. Fax: (260) 749-5151. Web Site: www.hot1079online.com. Licensee: Fort Wayne Radio Corp. (acq 12-1-98; $1.3 million). Rep: Interep. Wiley, Rein & Fielding. Format: CHR. Target aud: 18-49; adults. ♦ Russ Oasis, pres; Roger Diehm, VP & gen mgr.

New Paris

WVXR(FM)—See Richmond

New Washington

WSOH(FM)— 1994: 88.3 mhz; 1 kw. Ant 272 ft. TL: N38 35 51 W85 28 04. (CP: 1.2 kw, ant 256 ft. TL: N38 35 52 W85 29 49). Stereo. 5700 W. Oaks Blvd., Rocklin, CA 95765. Phone: (916) 251-1600. Fax: (916) 251-1650. E-mail: info@air1.com. Web Site: www.air1.com. Licensee: Educational Media Foundation. Group owner: EMF Broadcasting (acq 10-2-03; grpsl). Network: Air 1. Shaw Pittman. Format: Contemp Christian. News staff: 3. Target aud: 18-35; Judeo Christian, female. ♦ Richard Jenkins, pres; Mike Novak, VP; Lloyd Parker, gen mgr; Keith Whipple, dev dir.

Newburgh

WDKS(FM)— Feb 11, 1991: 106.1 mhz; 6 kw. 328 ft. TL: N37 57 16 W87 25 07. Stereo. Box 78, Evansville 47701. Secondary address: 1133 Lincoln Ave., Evansville 47714. Phone: (812) 425-4226. Fax: (812) 421-0005. E-mail: mthomas@regentcomm.com. Web Site: www.kissevansville.com. Licensee: Regent Broadcasting of Evansville/Owensboro Inc. Group owner: Regent Communications Inc. (acq 12-3-2003; grpsl). Network: ABC. Format: Top 40. News staff: one. Target aud: 18-34; women. ♦ Mark Thomas, gen mgr; Bobby Gates, prom dir; Cat Michaels, progmg dir; Warren Korff, news dir; Rick Crazo, chief of engrg.

WGAB(AM)— Mar 5, 1984: 1180 khz; 670 w-D. TL: N37 57 16 W87 25 07. 1180 Maple Ln. 47630. Phone: (812) 853-9422. Fax: (812) 474-4483. E-mail: faithmusicbb@aol.com. Licensee: Faith Broadcasting LLC (acq 12-1-2004; $300,000). Network: Network: Network: Network: ABC, Jones Radio Networks, Salem Radio Network, Westwood One. Format: Christian progmg. Target aud: 18-54; men & women. ♦ Gayle Russ, gen mgr, opns VP & opns mgr.

Noblesville

WJJK(FM)—Licensed to Noblesville. See Indianapolis

North Manchester

WBKE-FM— May 1967: 89.5 mhz; 3 kw. 80 ft. TL: N41 00 40 W85 45 45. Stereo. Box 19, Manchester College, 604 E. College Ave. 46962. Phone: (260) 982-5424. Fax: (260) 982-5043. E-mail: wbke@manchester.edu. Web Site: www.wbke.manchester.edu. Licensee: Manchester College. Format: Div, free form. News staff: one; News: 10 hrs wkly. Target aud: General. Spec prog: Class 10 hrs, Sp one hr, classic rock 6 hrs, AOR 6 hrs, Top 40/rap 10 hrs, alternative 7 hrs wkly. ♦ Sunday Isang, gen mgr; Logan Condon, stn mgr; Kelly Creech, progmg dir.

North Vernon

WNVI(AM)— Jan 8, 1955: 1460 khz; 1 kw-D, 92 w-N. TL: N38 59 46 W85 39 02. Stereo. 2470 N. State Hwy. 7 47265-7184. Phone: (812) 346-1927. Fax: (812) 346-9722. Licensee: Columbus Radio Inc. (acq 11-20-01; swap for WWWY(FM) Columbus plus $1.2 million). Format: Sports. ♦ Marty Pieratt, gen mgr.

WWWY(FM)— Mar 19, 1963: 106.1 mhz; 50 kw. 486 ft. TL: N39 04 02 W85 42 10. Stereo. Box 1789, Columbus 47202-1789. Secondary address: 3212 Washington St., Columbus 47203. Phone: (812) 372-4448. Fax: (812) 372-1061. E-mail: rockme@106.com. Web Site: www.106.com. Licensee: White River Broadcasting Co. Inc. Group owner: The Findlay Publishing Co. (acq 8-1-97; grpsl). Format: Classic rock. News staff: 3. Target aud: 25-54. ♦ Kurt Kah, pres; David Glass, VP; Tasha Mann, gen mgr; John Foster, opns mgr; Scott Michaels, progmg dir; Kevin Keith, news dir; Chuck Weber, chief of engrg.

Notre Dame

WSND-FM— Sept 17, 1962: 88.9 mhz; 3.4 kw. 361 ft. TL: N41 36 20 W86 12 46. Stereo. Office of Student Activities, LaFortune Student Ctr. 46556. Phone: (574) 631-7342. Fax: (574) 631-3653. E-mail: mcfadden.20@nd.cdn. Web Site: www.nd.edu/~wsnd. Licensee: Voice of the Fighting Irish Inc. Format: Class. ♦ Laurie McFadden, gen mgr; Ed Jaroszewski, progmg dir.

Oolitic

WMYJ(FM)—Not on air, target date: unknown: 88.9 mhz; 5.2 kw vert. Ant 256 ft. TL: N38 59 14 W86 27 31. Box 1970, Martinsville 46151. Phone: (765) 349-1485. Fax: (765) 342-3569. Licensee: Spirit Educational Radio Inc. (acq 6-30-2005; $45,000 for CP). ♦ David Keister, chmn.

Orland

WBNI-FM— Feb 2, 2002: 91.3 mhz; 2 kw. Ant 298 ft. TL: N41 44 36 W85 05 48. Stereo. Box 8459, Fort Wayne 46898. Phone: (260) 452-1189. Fax: (260) 452-1188. E-mail: ccondron@nipr.fm. Web Site: www.nipr.fm. Licensee: Northeast Indiana Public Radio Inc. Format: Classical. News staff: . ♦ Bruce Haines, gen mgr & prom dir; Colleen Condron, opns dir; Karen Fraser, dev VP; Janice Furtner, mus dir; Jeanette Dillon, news dir.

Paoli

WSEZ(AM)— Nov 7, 1963: 1560 khz; 250 w-D. TL: N38 32 25 W86 28 42. Box 26, 192 S. Court St. 47454. Phone: (812) 723-4484. Fax: (812) 723-4966. E-mail: wume@blueriver.net. Web Site: hitsandfavorites.com. Licensee: Ironic Broadcasting Inc. (acq 3-21-97; with co-located FM). Rep: Rgnl Reps. Haley, Bader & Potts. Format: Oldies. News staff: one; News: 7 hrs wkly. Target aud: General. Spec prog: Farm 7 hrs wkly. ♦ Imojean Apple, pres, gen mgr, chief of opns, gen sls mgr, mktg mgr & prom dir; Jason Archer, progmg mgr & pub affrs dir; Dave Dedrick, news dir; Todd Edwards, chief of engrg.

WUME-FM—Co-owned with WSEZ(AM). September 1972: 95.3 mhz; 3 kw. 300 ft. TL: N38 32 25 W86 28 42. Stereo. Web Site: hitsandfavorites.com. Network: ABC. Rgnl Reps Format: Comtemp hit. News staff: one; News: 9 hrs wkly. Target aud: General.

Pendleton

WEEM(FM)— Nov 1, 1971: 91.7 mhz; 1.2 kw. 154 ft. TL: N39 59 52 W85 44 07. Stereo. One Arabian Dr. 46064. Phone: (765) 778-2161, EXT. 236. Fax: (765) 778-2161, EXT. 237. Fax: (765) 778-0605. Licensee: South Madison Community School Corp. Format: Oldies, educ. Spec prog: High school sports 10 hrs, Sp 5 hrs wkly. ♦ Robert Zimmerman, pres; Jeff Dupont, gen mgr; Ashley Ford, prom dir & progmg dir; Rachel Lewis, mus dir & news dir; Steve Longenecker, chief of engrg.

Peru

WARU(AM)— Sept 12, 1954: 1600 khz; 1 kw-D. TL: N40 45 53 W86 02 26. Box 1010 46970. Secondary address: 1711 E. Wabash Rd. 46970. Phone: (765) 473-4448. Fax: (765) 473-4449. E-mail: waru@sbcglobal.net. Web Site: www.the80sstation.com. Licensee: Miami County Broadcasting Inc. Group owner: Mid-America Radio Group Inc. (acq 1996; $360,000. with WMYK(FM) Peru). Network: AP Radio. Rep: Rgnl Reps. Format: 80s Hits. News staff: one; News: 20 hrs wkly. Target aud: 25-54. ♦ David Keister, pres; David Poehler, VP; Tom Bugg, gen mgr & stn mgr.

WARU-FM— 2001: 101.9 mhz; 3.6 kw. Ant 423 ft. TL: N40 48 30 W85 56 07. Stereo. 1711 E. Wabash Rd. 46970. Web Site: www.classichits.org. Licensee: Mid-America Radio Group Inc. News staff: one; News: 4 hrs wkly.

WMYK(FM)— Apr 5, 1965: 98.5 mhz; 6 kw. Ant 328 ft. TL: N40 37 46 W86 02 28. Stereo. Box 2208, Kokomo 46904-2208. Secondary address: 671 E. 400 S., Kokomo 46902. Phone: (765)455-9850. Fax: (765) 455-3882. E-mail: classichits@radio.fm. Web Site: www.classichits.org. Licensee: Miami County Broadcasting Inc. Group owner: Mid-America Radio Group Inc. (acq 1996; $360,000. with WARU(AM) Peru). Network: Network: ABC Music Radio, ABC News/Talk. Format: Classic rock. News staff: one. ♦ Steve LaMar, gen mgr; Bryan Michaels, opns mgr.

Petersburg

WBTO-FM— Oct 8, 1984: 102.3 mhz; 3 kw. 321 ft. TL: N38 30 33 W87 17 28. Stereo. Box 616, Washington 47501. Secondary address: Box 242, Vincennes 47591. Phone: (812) 254-4300. Phone: (812) 882-6060. Fax: (812) 254-4361. Fax: (812) 885-2604. Web Site: www.wbtofm.com. Licensee: The Original Co. Inc. (group owner; acq 11-24-99; $400,000). Rep: Rgnl Reps. Format: Classic rock. News: 9 hrs wkly. Target aud: General. ♦ Mark Lange, pres.

Plainfield

WRDZ-FM— Aug 16, 1964: 98.3 mhz; 3 kw. 300 ft. TL: N39 45 33 W86 22 30. Stereo. 630 W. Carmel Dr., Indianapolis 46032. Phone: (317) 574-2000. Fax: (317) 581-1985. Web Site: www.radiodisney.com.

Indiana

Licensee: Radio Disney Group LLC. Group owner: ABC Inc. (acq 7-1-03; $5.6 million). Network: Network: USA, Salem Radio Network. Format: Children's. News staff: one; News: 20 hrs wkly. Target aud: 24-54. ♦ Jim McCondville, gen mgr; Laura Sanchez, prom mgr & chief of engrg.

Plymouth

*WRXH(FM)— 2005: 89.3 mhz; 400 w. Ant 249 ft. TL: N41 20 51 W86 20 23. Drawer 3206, Tupelo, MS 38803. Phone: (662) 844-8888. Fax: (662) 842-6791. Web Site: www.afr.net. Licensee: American Family Association. Group owner: American Family Radio. Format: Inspirational Christian. ♦ Marvin Sanders, gen mgr.

WTCA(AM)— Aug 18, 1964: 1050 khz; 250 w-U, DA-2. TL: N41 19 06 W86 18 41. 112 W. Washington St. 46563. Phone: (574) 936-4096. Fax: (574) 936-6776. Licensee: Community Service Broadcasters Inc. (acq 11-27-98). Reddy, Begley & McCormick. Format: Oldies. Target aud: 25-65. Spec prog: Farm 11 hrs wkly. ♦ Kathryn E. Bottorff, stn mgr.

WZOC(FM)— July 20, 1966: 94.3 mhz; 11.5 kw. 492 ft. TL: N41 31 41 W86 15 53. Stereo. 112 W. Washington St. 46563. Phone: (574) 936-4096. Fax: (574) 936-6776. Licensee: Plymouth Broadcasting Inc. (acq 9-12-96; $575,000). Format: Oldies. ♦ James Kunze, stn mgr.

Portage

WNDZ(AM)— May 13, 1987: 750 khz; 2.5 kw-D, DA. (CP: 17 kw-D). 6012 S. Pulaski Rd., Chicago, IL 60629. Phone: (773) 767-1000. Fax: (773) 767-1100. Licensee: WNDZ Inc. Group owner: Newsweb Corp. (acq 3-16-2004; $24 million. with WRZA(FM) Park Forest, IL). Format: Relg, ethnic. Target aud: General. Spec prog: Ger 2 hrs, gospel 2 hrs, Serbian 2 hrs, Lithuanian 4 hrs, Bosnian one hr wkly. ♦ Harvey Wells, gen mgr.

Portland

*WBSJ(FM)— December 1996: 91.7 mhz; 2.1 kw. 210 ft. TL: N40 24 26 W85 02 15. c/o WBST(FM), Ball State Univ., Muncie 47306-0550. Phone: (765) 285-5888. Fax: (765) 285-8937. E-mail: ipr@bsu.edu. Web Site: www.bsu.edu/ipr. Licensee: Ball State University. Format: Class, news. News staff: one; News: 33 hrs wkly. Target aud: General. ♦ Anthony Hunt, gen mgr; Terry Heifetz, news dir; Robert Mittendorf, chief of engrg.

WPGW(AM)— Jan 14, 1951: 1440 khz; 500 w-D, 35 w-N, DA-1. TL: N40 26 10 W85 00 56. 1891 W. State Rd 67 47371. Phone: (260) 726-8729. Fax: (260) 726-4311. E-mail: wpgw@jayco.net. Licensee: WPGW Inc. (acq 8-1-74). Rep: Rgnl Reps. Format: Adult contemp. Target aud: General. ♦ Robert A. Weaver, pres & gen mgr.

WPGW-FM— May 19, 1975: 100.9 mhz; 4.6 kw. 180 ft. TL: N40 26 10 W85 00 54. Stereo. Format: Country. Target aud: General.

Princeton

WRAY(AM)— Dec 16, 1950: 1250 khz; 1 kw-D, 59 w-N. TL: N38 21 25 W87 35 25. Stereo. Box 8, 1900 W. Broadway 47670-0008. Phone: (812) 386-1250. Fax: (812) 386-6249. E-mail: wray@wrayradio.com. Web Site: www.wrayradio.com. Licensee: Princeton Broadcasting Co. Inc. Format: News, talk. News staff: 3. Target aud: 25-54. ♦ Richard Langford, pres; Lynn Davis, gen sls mgr & prom mgr; Stephen R. Langford, gen mgr, opns mgr & progmg dir; Rodger Beard, news dir; Floyd Turner, chief of engrg.

WRAY-FM— May 15, 1960: 98.1 mhz; 50 kw. 420 ft. TL: N38 21 25 W87 35 25. Stereo. Web Site: www.wrayradio.com. Format: Country. ♦ Dave Kunkel, progmg dir.

WSJD(FM)— Oct 1, 1994: 100.5 mhz; 6 kw horiz, 5.5 kw vert. Ant 328 ft. TL: N38 23 24 W87 34 23. Stereo. 606 Market St., Mount Carmel, IL 62863. Phone: (618) 262-4102. Fax: (618) 262-4103. E-mail: wsjd@midwest.net. Web Site: www.wsjd.com. Licensee: WSJD Inc. Group owner: Southern Wabash Communications Corp. (acq 8-3-01). Format: Classic rock. News staff: 2; News: 20 hrs wkly. Target aud: 35-54. ♦ Randolph V. Bell, pres; Sally Dorgan Potts, exec VP; Kevin Madden, gen mgr.

Rensselaer

WLQI(FM)—Listing follows WRIN(AM).

*WPUM(FM)— Sept 6, 1977: 90.5 mhz; 10 w. 190 ft. TL: N40 55 12 W87 09 27. Stereo. Box 651, St. Joseph's College 47978. Phone: (219) 866-6000. E-mail: wpum@saintjoe.edu. Web Site: www.saintjoe.edu/rdept20/wpum. Licensee: St. Joseph's College. (acq 8-1-76). Network: Superadio. Format: Rock. News staff: one; News: 10 hrs wkly. Target aud: 18-34; general. Spec prog: Country 3 hrs, classical 3 hrs, blues 3 hrs, talk 1 hr wkly. ♦ Sally Nesselroad, stn mgr.

WRIN(AM)— Sept 14, 1963: 1560 khz; 1 kw-D, 500 w-CH. TL: N40 57 41 W87 09 07. Box D 47978. Secondary address: 560 W. Amster Rd. Phone: (219) 866-5105. Phone: (219) 866-4104. Fax: (219) 866-5106. Web Site: www.1560wrin.com. Licensee: Brothers Broadcasting Corp. (acq 6-18-86). Network: ABC Daytime Direction. Rep: Rgnl Reps. Format: Oldies. Target aud: 25-54. Spec prog: Farm 12 hrs, gospel 2 hrs, relg 10 hrs wkly. ♦ John Balvich, pres & gen mgr; Bob Burt, progmg dir.

WLQI(FM)— Co-owned with WRIN(AM). 1973: 97.7 mhz; 3.3 kw. 300 ft. TL: N40 58 14 W87 09 10. Stereo. Network: Network: ABC Daytime Direction, Jones Radio Networks. Cohn & Marks. Format: Adult contemp. News staff: one. Target aud: 25 plus.

Richmond

*WECI(FM)— September 1964: 91.5 mhz; 400 w. 106 ft. TL: N39 49 22 W84 54 39. Stereo. Drawer 45, Earlham College 47374. Phone: (765) 962-3541. Phone: (765) 983-1246. Fax: (765) 983-1641. E-mail: hennja@earlham.edu. Web Site: www.earlham.edu/~weci. Licensee: Earlham College. Format: Class, country, var/div. Spec prog: Bluegrass/folk 19 hrs, classic rock 16 hrs, progressive 18 hrs wkly. ♦ Amanda Lewis, prom dir; Jason Henn, stn mgr & chief of engrg.

WFMG(FM)—Listing follows WKBV(AM).

WHON(AM)— (Centerville). Feb 17, 1964: 930 khz; 500 w-D, 114 w-N, DA-2. TL: N39 53 33 W84 56 09. Box 1647 47375. Phone: (765) 962-1595. Fax: (765) 966-4824. Licensee: Brewer Broadcasting Corp. (group owner; acq 11-20-97). Rep: Rgnl Reps. Format: News/talk. News staff: one. Target aud: 35 plus. ♦ Dave Strycker, gen mgr; Troy Derengowski, progmg dir.

WQLK(FM)— Co-owned with WHON(AM). Oct 15, 1973: 96.1 mhz; 50 kw. 350 ft. TL: N39 53 33 W84 56 09. Stereo. Web Site: www.kicks96.com. Format: Hot country. News staff: one. Target aud: 25-54. ♦ Steve Baker, progmg dir.

WKBV(AM)— Sept 27, 1926: 1490 khz; 1 kw-U. TL: N39 49 30 W84 55 50. (CP: N39 49 41 W84 55 57). Box 1646, 2301 W. Main St. 47374. Phone: (765) 962-6533. Fax: (765) 966-1499. Licensee: Rodgers Broadcasting Corp. (group owner; acq 8-4-97; with co-located FM). Network: ABC Information & Entertainment. Format: News/talk. News staff: 2. Target aud: 25-54. Spec prog: Farm 4 hrs wkly. ♦ David Rodgers, pres; Steve Frey, sls dir; Rick Duncan, progmg dir.

WFMG(FM)— Co-owned with WKBV(AM). Dec 17, 1960: 101.3 mhz; 50 kw. 280 ft. TL: N39 49 30 W84 55 50. Stereo. Format: Hot adult contemp. News staff: 2. Target aud: 18-44. ♦ Sheri Snapp, progmg mgr.

*WVXR(FM)— Dec 24, 1988: 89.3 mhz; 4.2 kw. Ant 187 ft. TL: N39 52 08 W84 47 47. Stereo. c/o WVXU(FM), 1223 Central Pkwy., Cincinnati, OH 45214. Phone: (513) 352-9170. Fax: (513) 241-8456. E-mail: wvxu@cinradio.org. Web Site: www.wvxu.org. Licensee: Cincinnati Classical Public Radio Inc. (acq 8-22-2005; grpsl). Network: Network: PRI, NPR. Baker & Hostetler LLP. Format: News and info. ♦ Richard Eiswerth, gen mgr.

Rising Sun

WSCH(FM)—See Aurora

Roann

WARU-FM—Licensed to Roann. See Peru

Directory of Radio

Roanoke

WCKZ(FM)— 1991: 94.1 mhz; 6 kw. Ant 340 ft. TL: N40 58 51 W85 16 48. 2000 Lower Huntington Rd., Fort Wayne 46819. Phone: (260) 747-1511. Fax: (260) 747-3999. Licensee: Travis Broadcasting LLC. Group owner: Summit City Radio Group (acq 6-18-2002; grpsl). Rep: McGavren Guild. Format: Classic rock. Target aud: 25-49; women. ♦ Kris Foate, gen mgr; Bill Stewart, gen sls mgr & progmg dir.

Rochester

*WHNI(FM)— Not on air, target date: unknown: 88.5 mhz; 250 w. Ant 171 ft. TL: N41 03 14 W86 16 12. Drawer 2440, Tupelo, MS 38803. Phone: (662) 844-8888. Fax: (662) 842-6791. Licensee: American Family Association. Group owner: American Family Radio. ♦ Marvin Sanders, gen mgr.

WROI(FM)— Aug 29, 1971: 92.1 mhz; 4.2 kw. 240 ft. TL: N41 03 02 W86 15 39. Stereo. 110 E. 8th St. 46975. Phone: (574) 223-6059. Fax: (574) 223-2238. E-mail: wroi@rtcol.com. Licensee: Bair Communications Inc. (acq 10-21-92; 10-19-92). Network: Network: ABC Information & Entertainment, Jones Radio Networks. Rep: Rgnl Reps. Format: Oldies. News staff: one; News: 20 hrs wkly. Target aud: General. Spec prog: Farm 10 hrs, relg 6 hrs wkly. ♦ Tom Bair, pres & gen mgr.

Rockville

WAXI(FM)— August 1977: 104.9 mhz; 3 kw. 400 ft. TL: N39 43 44 W87 17 56. Stereo. 1301 Ohio St., Terre Haute 47807. Phone: (812) 234-9770. Fax: (812) 238-1576. E-mail: waxi@waxi.com. Web Site: www.waxi.com. Licensee: Crossroads Investments LLC. Group owner: Crossroads Communications Inc. (acq 4-20-98; $485,000). Network: ABC. Rep: Rgnl Reps. Booth, Freret, Imlay & Tepper. Format: Adult standards. News staff: one; News: 10 hrs wkly. Target aud: 35 plus; local to Parke, Vermillion counties, affluent boomers & seniors in Terre haute market. Spec prog: Gospel 2 hrs, Cubs baseball & sports. ♦ Mike Peterson, gen mgr & prom dir.

Royal Center

WHZR(FM)— Oct 16, 1989: 103.7 mhz; 6 kw. 328 ft. TL: N40 48 43 W86 21 56. Stereo. Box 103, 2100 E. Market St., Logansport 46947. Secondary address: Box 1970, Corp. Hqtrs., Martinsville 46151. Phone: (574) 732-1037. Fax: (574) 739-1037. E-mail: hoosiercountry@lneti.com. Licensee: Mid-America Radio Group of Logansport-Peru Inc. Group owner: Mid-America Radio Group Inc. (acq 5-1-95; $450,000;. FTR: 6-5-95). Format: Country. News staff: one; News: 6 hrs wkly. Target aud: 18-49; mass appeal. ♦ David Keister, pres; David Poehler, VP; Julie Plummer, news dir; Jack Elmore, chief of engrg.

Rushville

WKWH-FM— Aug 5, 1971: 94.3 mhz; 1.05 kw. 561 ft. TL: N39 42 22 W85 29 41. Stereo. 102 N. Perkins St. 46173. Phone: (765) 932-3983. Phone: (765) 932-3409. Fax: (765) 938-1916. E-mail: wkwh-fm@wkwhradio.com. Licensee: RSE Broadcasting LLC. (acq 11-4-99). Rep: Christal, Rgnl Reps. Format: Country. Target aud: 35 plus. Spec prog: Farm 18 hrs wkly. ♦ David Sheets, pres; Scott Huber, gen mgr; Kevin Stone, gen sls mgr; Scott Murray, progmg dir; Douglas Raab, engrg mgr & chief of engrg; Martha Swain, chief of engrg.

Salem

WSLM(AM)— Feb 14, 1953: 1220 khz; 5 kw-D, 384 w-N, DA-2. TL: N38 36 55 W86 05 10. Box 385 47167. Phone: (812) 883-5750. Fax: (812) 883-2797. Licensee: Don H. Martin. Rep: Rgnl Reps. Baraff, Koerner & Olender. Format: Farm, C&W, gospel. News staff: 5; News: 12 hrs wkly. Target aud: 21-70. ♦ Don H. Martin, pres, gen mgr & gen sls mgr; Becky L. White, adv dir; David Stuart, mus dir; J.R. Martin, stn mgr, prom mgr & chief of engrg.

WSLM-FM— 1992: 97.9 mhz; 3 kw. 220 ft. TL: N38 38 07 W86 10 37. Stereo. Licensee: Rebecca L. White. Format: News, talk shows. Target aud: 18-65. ♦ David Stuart, progmg dir; Don H. Martin, adv mgr & progmg mgr.

WZKF(FM)— 1962: 98.9 mhz; 50 kw. 300 ft. TL: N38 35 59 W86 05 17. (CP: Ant 492 ft. TL: N38 21 56 W85 58 55). Stereo. 4000 Radio Dr., Suite 1, Louisville, KY 40218-4568. Phone: (502) 479-2222. Fax: (502) 479-2227. Web Site: www.kiss989fm.com. Licensee: Clear

Stations in the U.S. — Indiana

Channel Radio License Inc. Group owner: Clear Channel Communications Inc. (acq 12-31-96). Format: CHR. Target aud: 18-54; country music listeners. ♦Lowry Mays, CEO & pres; Bill Gentry, gen mgr; Doug James, stn mgr; C. L. Matthews, opns VP.

Santa Claus

WAXL(FM)— July 30, 1996: 103.3 mhz; 3 kw. 462 ft. TL: N38 12 31 W86 54 00. Stereo. Box 1009, Jasper 47547. Secondary address: 501 Old State Rd., Huntingburg 47547. Phone: (812) 683-1215. Phone: (800) 522-1033. Fax: (812) 683-5891. E-mail: waxl@psci.net. Web Site: www.dcbroadcasting.com.ABC Licensee: Dubois County Broadcasting Inc. Group owner: DCBroadcasting Inc. (acq 7-25-97). Network: ABC. Miller & Miller, P.C. Format: Adult contemp. News staff: one; News: 3 hrs wkly. Target aud: 24-49. Spec prog: Agriculture 3 hrs wkly. ♦Paul Knies, pres & gen mgr; Ron Spaulding, stn mgr, sls dir & gen sls mgr; Jason Lents, progmg VP & progmg dir.

Scottsburg

WMPI(FM)— Dec 16, 1966: 105.3 mhz; 2.2 kw. 511 ft. TL: N38 37 12 W85 45 15. Stereo. Box 270, 22 E. McClain Ave. 47170. Phone: (812) 752-5612. Fax: (812) 752-2345. E-mail: Ray@scottsburg.com. Web Site: www.i1053.com. Licensee: D. R. Rice Broadcasting Inc. (acq. 1987). Network: ABC Daytime Direction. Rep: Rgnl Reps. Format: C&W. News staff: one; News: 5 hrs wkly. Target aud: 25-54. ♦Donald R. Rice, pres; Raymond Rice, gen mgr; Tom Cull, stn mgr.

Seelyville

WWSY(FM)— Sept 12, 1996: 95.9 mhz; 6 kw. 100 ft. (CP: 4.1 kw, ant 397 ft.). 824 S. 3rd St., Terre Haute 47807. Phone: (812) 232-4161. Fax: (812) 234-9999. E-mail: chadedwards@xsthe.net. Web Site: www.y96.net. Licensee: Bright Tower Communications Inc. (acq 8-5-99; $665,000). Network: Jones Radio Networks. Format: Hot Adult Contempo. Target aud: 18-49. ♦Bob Swanson, gen mgr; Kathleen Walker, sls VP & gen sls mgr; Chad Edwards, progmg dir; Jerry Arnold, chief of engrg.

Seymour

***WJLR(FM)**— August 1995: 91.5 mhz; 5.6 kw. Ant 351 ft. TL: N38 49 23 W85 47 24. Stereo. EMF Broadcasting, 5700 West Oaks Blvd., Rocklin, CA 95765. Phone: (916) 251-1600. Fax: (916) 251-1650. Licensee: Educational Media Foundation. (acq 11-9-2004; $150,000). Network: K-Love. Shaw Pittman LLP. Format: Christian info & educ. Target aud: 30-80; family oriented. ♦Lloyd Parker, gen mgr.

WQKC(FM)—Listing follows WZZB(AM).

WZZB(AM)— Nov 4, 1949: 1390 khz; 1 kw-D, 74 w-N. TL: N38 58 23 W85 53 20. Box 806 47274. Secondary address: 1534 Ewing St. 47274. Phone: (812) 522-1390. Fax: (812) 522-9541. Licensee: SCI Broadcasting Inc. Group owner: Susquehanna Radio Corp. (acq 5-25-01; grpsl). Network: Network: USA, Jones Radio Networks. Rgnl Reps. Dow, Lohnes & Albertson. Format: Full service, news, sports, adult contemp, oldies. News staff: 2; News: 17 hrs wkly. Target aud: 25 plus; community oriented. Spec prog: Farm 2 hrs, relg 6 hrs wkly. ♦Blair W. Trask, pres, gen mgr & gen sls mgr; Bud Shippee, opns dir, progmg dir & news dir; Bob Hawkins, chief of engrg.

WQKC(FM)—Co-owned with WZZB(AM). Feb 23, 1961: 93.7 mhz; 25 kw horiz, 24.5 kw vert. Ant 699 ft. TL: N38 58 22 W86 10 03. Stereo. Network: Jones Radio Networks. Format: Country. News staff: one; News: 7 hrs wkly. Target aud: General. ♦Bud Shippee, pub affrs dir.

Shelbyville

WKWH(AM)— Jan 14, 1961: 1520 khz; 1 kw-D, 250 w-N, DA-2. TL: N39 33 25 W85 46 18. 60 E. Washington St. Suite A 46176-1380. Phone: (317) 398-9757. Fax: (317) 392-3292. Web Site: www.wkwhradio.com. Licensee: RSE Broadcasting LLC. (acq 11-4-99).

Format: Classic hits. ♦Dave Sheets, pres; Scott A. Huber, gen mgr; Kevin Stone, gen sls mgr & news dir; Sean Craig, progmg dir; Marty Hensley, chief of engrg.

WLHK(FM)— Nov 6, 1964: 97.1 mhz; 23 kw. 739 ft. TL: N39 40 02 W86 01 51. Stereo. One Emmis Plaza, 40 Monument Cir., Suite 600, Indianapolis 46204. Phone: (317) 266-9700. Fax: (317) 684-2021. Web Site: www.real971.com. Licensee: Emmis Radio License LLC. Group owner: Emmis Communications Corp. (acq 6-81). Rep: D & R Radio. Gardner, Carton & Douglas. Format: Adult contemp. News staff: one. Target aud: 25-54; female. ♦Jeffrey H. Smulyan, pres; Tom Severino, gen mgr; David Edgar, opns dir, progmg dir & news dir; Dave Hood, chief of engrg.

South Bend

***WAUS(FM)**—(Berrien Springs).MI 1971: 90.7 mhz; 50 kw. 492 ft. TL: N41 57 42 W86 21 02. Stereo. Waus Berrien Spring, Berrien Springs, MI 49104-0240. Phone: (269) 471-3400. Fax: (269) 471-3804. E-mail: waus@andrews.edu. Web Site: www.waus.org. Licensee: Andrews Broadcasting Corp. Network: PRI. Donald E. Martin. Format: Class. News: 3 hrs wkly. Target aud: 35 plus; listeners with interest in classical music. Spec prog: Relg 10 hrs wkly. ♦Niels-Erik Andreasen, chmn; Sharon Dudgeon, gen mgr; Bill Brent, opns dir.

WBYT(FM)—See Elkhart

WDND(AM)— Dec 22, 1947: 1580 khz; 10 kw-D, 500 w-N, DA-N. TL: N41 41 09 W86 09 53. 3371 Cleveland Rd., Suite 310 46628. Phone: (574) 273-9300. Fax: (574) 273-9090. E-mail: u93@u93.com. Web Site: www.artisticradio.com. Licensee: Artistic Media Properties Inc. (acq 11-23-99). Network: Westwood One. Lauren A. Colby. Format: MOR, oldies. News: 5 hrs wkly. Target aud: 35-64. Spec prog: Pol one hr, relg 2 hrs wkly. ♦Greg DeRue, gen mgr & stn mgr.

***WETL(FM)**— Nov 17, 1958: 91.7 mhz; 3 kw. 200 ft. TL: N41 37 24 W86 14 15. Stereo. 635 S. Main St. 46601. Phone: (574) 283-8076. Fax: (574) 283-8059. E-mail: jovermyer@sbcsc.k12.in.us. Licensee: South Bend Community School Corp. (acq 11-17-58). Format: Educ, instructional. Target aud: General; student in the South Bend community school and community. ♦Anita Brown, gen mgr; Allen Wujcik, chief of engrg.

WHLY(AM)— Nov 6, 1998: 1620 khz; 10 kw-D, 1 kw-N. TL: N41 38 11 W86 17 06. 3371 Cleveland Rd., Suite 310 46628. Phone: (574) 273-9300. Fax: (574) 273-9090. E-mail: u93@u93.com. Licensee: Artistic Media Properties Inc. (acq 11-23-99). Format: Sports. Target aud: 25-54. ♦Greg DeRue, stn mgr.

WHME(FM)— January 1968: 103.1 mhz; 3 kw. 300 ft. TL: N41 36 11 W86 12 51. 61300 Ironwood Rd. 46614. Phone: (574) 291-8200. Fax: (574) 291-9043. E-mail: thale@lesea.com. Web Site: www.lesea.com. Licensee: Le Sea Broadcasting Corp. Group owner: Le Sea Broadcasting Gardner, Carton & Douglas. Format: Adult contemp Christian. News: 3 hrs wkly. Target aud: 24-36; general. ♦Peter Sumrall, pres; Tony Hale, CFO; Zach Anders, stn mgr; Anna Riblet, gen sls mgr & natl sls mgr; Wes Hylton, chief of engrg. Co-owned TV: WHME-TV affil.

WNDV(AM)— 1944: 1490 khz; 1 kw-U. TL: N41 41 38 W86 13 50. Box 1616, 3371 Cleveland Rd., Suite 310 46628. Phone: (574) 273-9300. Fax: (574) 273-9090. E-mail: u93@u93.com. Web Site: www.u93.com. Licensee: Artistic Media Partners Inc. (group owner; acq 10-22-98; $6,123,180 with co-located FM). Network: Westwood One. Rep: McGavren Guild. Format: CHR. Target aud: 25-54. Spec prog: Notre Dame football, basketball, hockey. ♦Arthur A. Angotti, pres; Greg Derue, gen mgr; Mike Sullivan, stn mgr; Kasey Daniels, progmg dir.

WNDV-FM— 1962: 92.9 mhz; 12.5 kw. 800 ft. TL: N41 36 20 W86 12 45. Stereo. Web Site: www.u93.com. Target aud: 25-44; women. Spec prog: Notre Dame football & basketball, Rick Dees 4 hrs wkly.

WNSN(FM)—Listing follows WSBT(AM).

WRBR-FM— 1965: 103.9 mhz; 3 kw. 328 ft. TL: N41 41 53 W86 09 20. Stereo. 237 W. Edison Rd., Suite 200, Mishawaka 46545. Phone: (574) 258-5483. Fax: (574) 258-0930. Web Site: www.wrbr.com. Licensee: Hicks Broadcasting of Indiana LLC (acq 6-5-2002; $840,879). Rep: Christal. Format: Hard rock. Target aud: 25-54; affluent, older people. ♦Brad Williams, gen mgr; George Trobridge, chief of engrg.

WSBT(AM)— April 1922: 960 khz; 5 kw-U, DA-2. TL: N41 37 00 W86 13 01. 300 W. Jefferson Blvd. 46601. Phone: (574) 233-3141. Fax: (574) 289-7382. Web Site: www.wsbtradio.com. Licensee: WSBT Inc. Group owner: Schurz Communications Inc. Network: CBS. Rep: Katz Radio. Format: News/talk, sports. News staff: 3; News: 10 hrs wkly. Target aud: 25-54. Spec prog: Relg 2 hrs wkly. ♦Sally Brown, VP & gen mgr. Co-owned TV: WSBT-TV affil

WNSN(FM)—Co-owned with WSBT(AM). Aug 1, 1962: 101.5 mhz; 13 kw. 970 ft. TL: N41 37 00 W86 13 01. Stereo. Web Site: www.sunny1015.com. Format: Adult contemp. News staff: one; News: 2 hrs wkly. Target aud: 25-54; adults. Co-owned TV: WSBT-TV affil

***WUBS(FM)**— 1993: 89.7 mhz; 1.5 kw. 79 ft. TL: N41 40 51 W86 15 34. Box 3931 46619. Phone: (574) 287-4700. Fax: (574) 287-2478. E-mail: broshane@wubs.org. Licensee: Interfaith Christian Union Inc. Format: Inspirational. ♦Rev Sylvester Williams Jr., gen mgr; Shane R. Williams, progmg dir; Brian Hoover, chief of engrg.

WUBU(FM)— October 1992: 106.3 mhz; 3 kw. 292 ft. TL: N41 44 11 W86 17 19. 237 Edison Rd., Suite 200, Mishawaka 46545. Phone: (574) 258-5483. Fax: (574) 258-0930. Web Site: www.smooth1063.com. Licensee: Partnership Radio LLC (acq 7-15-99). Network: Jones Radio Networks. Rep: Interep, McGavren Guild. Wiley, Rein & Fielding. Format: Smooth jazz. Target aud: 35-64; adults. ♦Abe Thompson, gen mgr; Gene Walker, opns mgr; Emily Wideman, gen sls mgr.

WZOW(FM)—See Goshen

South Whitley

WLZQ(FM)— Dec 2, 1992: 101.1 mhz; 6 kw. Ant 328 ft. TL: N41 04 42 W85 31 20. Stereo. Box 5570, Ft. Wayne 46895. Phone: (260) 482-8500. E-mail: q101@wlzq.com. Licensee: Larko Communications. Network: ABC. Format: Hot adult contemp. Target aud: 25-44. ♦Chris Larko, CEO & gen mgr; Susan Derr, stn mgr.

Spencer

WSKT(FM)— Sept 15, 1983: 92.7 mhz; 1 kw. 480 ft. TL: N39 15 18 W86 51 51. Stereo. 201 N. VanDalia Ave. 47460. Phone: (812) 829-9393. Fax: (812) 829-9747. E-mail: wsktfm@smithville.net. Licensee: Mid-America Radio of Indiana Inc. Group owner: Mid-America Radio Group Inc. (acq 11-13-02; $321,100). Network: Westwood One. Format: Mainstream country. Spec prog: Relg 6 hrs wkly. ♦Jeff Hancock, stn mgr; Tony Kale, opns mgr; Johnnie Robbins, gen sls mgr & mktg; Pam McGuire, progmg dir; Lacinda Bray, news dir; Steve Ross, chief of engrg.

Sullivan

WNDI(AM)— Oct 7, 1963: 1550 khz; 250 w-D. TL: N39 04 32 W87 23 57. 556 E. State Rd. 54 47882. Phone: (812) 268-6322. Fax: (812) 268-6652. Licensee: JTM Broadcasting Corp. (acq 7-13-94; $237,000 with co-located FM; 8-1-94). Format: Country. Target aud: 24-54. Spec prog: Farm 6 hrs wkly. ♦John Montgomery, gen mgr.

WNDI-FM— Aug 10, 1982: 95.3 mhz; 6 kw. Ant 328 ft. TL: N39 09 36 W87 32 32.

Syracuse

WAWC(FM)— May 31, 1991: 103.5 mhz; 3 kw. 328 ft. TL: N41 22 57 W85 41 35. Stereo. 10129 N. 800 E. 46567. Phone: (574) 457-8181. Phone: (800) 779-1094. Fax: (574) 457-4488. E-mail: bill@hoosier1035.com. Web Site: hoosier1035.com. Licensee: William Andrew Dixon. Network:

CBS. Format: Adult contemp. News staff: one; News: 7 hrs wkly. Target aud: 25-54; people in Kosciusko, Elkhart & Noble counties. Spec prog: Relg 4 hrs wkly. ♦Bill Dixon, gen mgr & news dir; Todd Lucas, progmg dir; Brent Randall, pub affrs dir; Greg Stoddard, chief of engrg.

Tell City

WTCJ(AM)— Feb 1, 1948: 1230 khz; 1 kw-U. TL: N37 56 16 W86 45 28. 1115 Tamarack Rd., Suite 500, Owensboro, KY 42301. Phone: (812) 547-2345. Fax: (812) 547-2346. Web Site: www.wtcjradio.com. Licensee: Hancock Communications Inc. Group owner: The Cromwell Group Inc. (acq 10-29-99; $25,000). Network: ABC. Rep: Rgnl Reps. Format: Soft adult contemp. News staff: one. Target aud: 25-54; community-oriented listeners. Spec prog: Gospel 6 hrs wkly. ♦Bayard Walter, pres; Corky Norcia, gen mgr; Kevin Rickey, sls dir & gen sls mgr; Jeff Morgan, progmg dir & news dir.

WTCJ-FM— May 2001: 105.7 mhz; 4.8 kw. Ant 364 ft. TL: N37 55 33 W86 43 19. Phone: (270) 683-5200. Phone: (270) 688-0108. E-mail: wbioradio@adelphia.net. Format: CHR. ♦Bayard Walters, CEO; Kevin Rickey, opns mgr; Rob Nichols, mus dir.

Terre Haute

WBOW(AM)— May 23, 1958: 1300 khz; 500 w-D, 75 w-N. TL: N39 28 01 W87 25 34. 1301 Ohio St. 47807. Phone: (812) 234-9770. Fax: (812) 238-1576. E-mail: score@espnsportsradio.com. Web Site: www.espnsportsradio.com. Licensee: Crossroads Investments LLC. Group owner: Crossroads Communications Inc. (acq 9-10-97; $57,500. assumption of debt). Network: ESPN Radio. Rep: Roslin. Rgnl Reps. Booth, Freret, Imlay & Tepper. Format: All sports. News: 5 hrs wkly. Target aud: 25-64; Sports Fans. ♦Dan Lacy, CFO; Michael A. Petersen, pres & gen mgr; Ed Ice, gen sls mgr; John Sherman, progmg dir & news dir.

WBOW-FM— Sept 11, 1962: 102.7 mhz; 28 kw. 659 ft. TL: N39 20 13 W87 28 00. Stereo. 1301 Ohio St. 47807. Phone: (812) 234-9770. Fax: (812) 238-1576. E-mail: wbow@literock1027.com. Web Site: www.literock1027.com. Licensee: Crossroads Investments LLC (acq 3-14-03; $2.09 million). Rep: Roslin. Rgnl Reps Booth, Freret, Imlay & Tepper. Format: Soft adult contemp. News: 2 hrs wkly. Target aud: Adults 25-54. ♦Michael Peterson, pres & gen mgr; Ed Ice, gen sls mgr.

***WCRT(FM)**— January 1992: 88.5 mhz; 550 w. 308 ft. TL: N39 30 14 W87 26 37. 2108 W. Springfield, Champaign, IL 61821. Phone: (217) 359-8232. Fax: (217) 359-7374. E-mail: wbgl@wbgl.org. Web Site: www.wbgl.org. Licensee: Illinois Bible Institute. Format: Adult contemp Christian. ♦Jeff Scott, stn mgr; Meredith Foster, opns dir; Jennifer Wagoner, prom dir; Joe Buchanan, mus dir.

***WHOJ(FM)**— 1997: 91.9 mhz; 1 kw. Ant 95 ft. TL: N39 28 06 W87 23 56. Covenant Network, 3515 Hampton Ave., St. Louis, MO 63139. Phone: (314) 752-7000. Web Site: www.covenantnet.net. Licensee: Covenant Network (acq 3-30-2004; $112,500. with KBKC(FM) Moberly, MO). Format: Christian, relg, talk. ♦John Anthony Holman, pres.

***WISU(FM)**— Sept 13, 1964: 89.7 mhz; 13.5 kw. 512 ft. TL: N39 30 26 W87 31 50. Stereo. Rm. 217, 217 N. 6th St. 47809. Phone: (812) 237-3248. Phone: (812) 237-3252. Fax: (812) 237-8970. Fax: (812) 237-3241. E-mail: cmwisufm@ruby.indstate.edu. Web Site: wisu.indstate.edu. Licensee: Indiana State University Board of Trustees. Crowell & Moring. Format: Urban contemp, AOR. News: 4 hrs wkly. Target aud: 18-25; young professionals, students. ♦Lloyd Benjamin, pres; Steven Pontius, CFO; David Sabaini, gen mgr & progmg dir; Jeremy Willis, opns dir & mus dir; Rick Vincent, dev mgr; Marissa Kelly, prom dir, news dir & pub affrs dir; Dan Watson, chief of engrg.

WMGI(FM)— June 13, 1960: 100.7 mhz; 50 kw. 500 ft. TL: N30 27 22 W87 28 50. Stereo. 824 S. 3rd St. 47807. Phone: (812) 232-4161. Fax: (812) 234-9999. E-mail: mixfm@1007mixfm.com. Web Site: www.1007mixfm.com. Licensee: Bright Tower Communications Inc. (acq 9-14-99). Network: Westwood One. Format: CHR. Target aud: 25-54. ♦Donald E. Foster, pres; Marvin Frank, VP; Bob Swanson, gen mgr; Kathleen Walker, gen sls mgr; Matt Luecking, progmg dir; Jerry Arnold, chief of engrg.

***WMHD-FM**— 1981: 90.7 mhz; 160 w. 79 ft. TL: N39 28 57 W87 19 33. Stereo. 5500 Wabash Ave. 47803. Phone: (812) 872-6923. Fax: (812) 872-6926. E-mail: wmhd@wmhd.rose-hulman.edu. Web Site: wmhd.rose-hulman.edu. Licensee: Rose Hulman Institute of Technology. Format: Educ, AOR, progsv. News: 2 hrs wkly. Target aud: General; loc & college audience. Spec prog: Classical 4 hrs, bluegrass 1 hr, Jazz 2 hrs, contemp Christian 2 hrs wkly. ♦Brooks Borchers, gen mgr; Rachel Young, progmg dir.

WPFR(AM)— Jan 6, 1948: 1480 khz; 5 kw-D, 1 kw-N, DA-2. TL: N39 30 02 W87 23 10. 18889 N. 23 50th St., Dennison, IL 62423. Phone: (217) 826-9673. E-mail: wpfr@abcs.com. Licensee: Word Power Inc. (acq 1-1-00; $350,000 donation). Network: Moody. Vinson & Elkins. Format: Christian. ♦Paul Dean Ford, gen mgr; Mark S. Ford, opns VP; Dan Watson, chief of opns.

WTHI-FM— October 1948: 99.9 mhz; 50 kw. 494 ft. TL: N39 27 57 W87 24 12. Box 1486 47808. Secondary address: 918 Ohio St. 47808. Phone: (812) 232-9481. Fax: (812) 234-0089. E-mail: jconner@wthi.emmis.com. Web Site: www.hi99.com. Licensee: Emmis Radio License LLC. Group owner: Emmis Communications Corp. (acq 1998 grpsl). Network: ABC. Rep: Interep, D & R Radio. Format: Country. ♦David Bailey, sr VP; James Conner, stn mgr; Barry Kent, opns mgr; Robert Rhodes, sls dir & gen sls mgr; Chris Perrot, prom dir & progmg mgr. Co-owned TV: WTHI-TV affil

WWVR(FM)—See West Terre Haute

Union City

***WJYW(FM)**— 1997: 88.9 mhz; 4.1 kw. 285 ft. TL: N40 11 32 W84 47 58. Box 445 47390. Secondary address: 505 S. Division St., OH 45390. Phone: (937) 968-5633. Fax: (937) 968-3320. E-mail: office@899joyfm.com. Web Site: www.889joyfm.com. Licensee: Positive Alternative Radio Inc. Network: Salem Radio Network. Booth, Freret, Imlay & Tepper. Format: Contemp Christian music. ♦Vernon H. Baker, CEO; Dan Franks, gen mgr.

Upland

***WTUR(FM)**— Sept 4, 1995: 89.7 mhz; 150 w. 112 ft. TL: N40 25 02 W85 29 31. 236 W. Reade Ave. 46989-1001. Phone: (765) 998-5263. Phone: (765) 998-2751. Fax: (765) 998-4810. Web Site: www.tayloru.edu. Licensee: Taylor University. Format: Contemp Christian music. Target aud: College age. ♦Tim Walter, progmg dir.

Valparaiso

WAKE(AM)— Nov 4, 1964: 1500 khz; 1 kw-D, 25 w-N, DA-2. TL: N41 26 36 W87 02 54. 2755 Sager Rd. 46383. Phone: (219) 462-6111. Fax: (219) 462-4880. Licensee: Porter County Broadcasting Holding Corp. LLC. Group owner: Porter County Broadcasting Corp. Miller & Fields, P.C. Format: Adult pop standards. News staff: 2; News: 21 hrs wkly. Target aud: 30 plus; community oriented, middle to middle-upper class. ♦Leigh Ellis, chmn, pres & gen mgr; O.J. Jackson, stn mgr & gen sls mgr; Scott Wagner, progmg dir; Laura Waluszko, news dir; Carl Fletcher, chief of engrg.

WLJE(FM)—Co-owned with WAKE(AM). Oct 6, 1967: 105.5 mhz; 1.25 kw. 513 ft. TL: N41 31 28 W87 01 08. Stereo. Phone: (219) 462-8125. Web Site: www.indiana105.com. Network: ABC Daytime Direction. Format: Country. Target aud: 25-55; family, middle income. ♦Scott Wagner, mus dir.

***WVUR-FM**— Sept 25, 1966: 95.1 mhz; 36 w. 125 ft. TL: N41 27 57 W87 02 29. Stereo. 1809 Chapel Dr. 46383. Phone: (219) 464-5383. Fax: (219) 464-6742. E-mail: wvur@valpo.edu. Web Site: www.valpo.edu/wvur. Licensee: The Lutheran University Association Inc. Format: Free-form. News staff: 2; News: 8 hrs wkly. Target aud: 18-34. Spec prog: Class 3 hrs, jazz 3 hrs, urban contemp 3 hrs, metal 3 hrs, classic rock 3 hrs wkly. ♦Andrew Viano, gen mgr; Ken LaVicka, gen mgr.

Van Buren

WCJC(FM)—Licensed to Van Buren. See Marion

Veedersburg

WSKL(FM)— July 15, 1999: 92.9 mhz; 4.5 kw. 269 ft. TL: N40 08 46 W87 27 15. Box 67, Danville, IL 61834. Phone: (765) 793-4823. Fax: (765) 793-4644. E-mail: fmkool929@aol.com. Web Site: www.kool929.allrounddanville.com. Licensee: Zona Communications Inc. (acq 10-29-99). Network: Network: AP Radio, Jones Radio Networks. Format: Oldies. News staff: one; News: 5 hrs wkly. Target aud: 35-65. ♦Rhea Benton-Weatherford, pres; Rhea Banton-Weatherford, gen mgr.

Versailles

***WKRY(FM)**— Apr 11, 2003: 88.1 mhz; 600 w. Ant 233 ft. TL: N39 03 55 W85 19 00. 825 Washington St., Columbus 47201. Phone: (812) 663-3000. Fax: (812) 375-2555. Licensee: Good Shepherd Radio Inc. Format: Relg. ♦Keith Reising, CEO.

WXCH(FM)— Nov 15, 1984: 103.1 mhz; 3 kw. 328 ft. TL: N39 10 38 W85 17 00. Stereo. 6857 Salem Ridge Rd., Aurora 47001. Phone: (812) 438-2777. Fax: (812) 438-3495. E-mail: wsch@one.net. Licensee: Columbus Radio Inc. (acq 12-2-02; with WSCH(FM) Aurora). Format: Country. ♦Marty Pieratt, CEO; Allen Willis, gen mgr; Dennis Drees, opns VP; Bob Shannon, news dir.

Vevay

WKID(FM)— Sept 6, 1974: 95.9 mhz; 2.7 kw. 308 ft. TL: N38 50 12 W85 01 48. Stereo. 118 W. Main St. 47043. Phone: (812) 427-9590. Fax: (812) 427-2492. Web Site: www.k959froggy.com. Licensee: Dial Broadcasting Inc. (acq 1996). Network: Jones Radio Networks. Regl Reps Kaye, Scholer, Fierman, Hays & Handler. Format: Country. News: 7 hrs wkly. Target aud: 25-49; middle-income families. ♦Ken Trimble, gen mgr.

Vincennes

WAOV(AM)— Oct 22, 1940: 1450 khz; 1 kw-U. TL: N38 42 26 W87 29 42. Box 242 47591-0242. Phone: (812) 882-6060. Fax: (812) 885-2604. E-mail: wzdm@wvc.net. Web Site: www.waovam.com. Licensee: Old Northwest Broadcasting Inc. Group owner: The Original Co. Inc. (acq 9-28-93; $250,000 with WWBL(FM) Washington; 10-18-93). Rep: Rgnl Reps. Format: News/talk, sports. News staff: 2; News: 56 hrs wkly. Target aud: 25 plus. ♦Mark R. Lange, pres, gen mgr & progmg dir; Jim Evans, news dir & chief of engrg.

***WATI(FM)**— 2002: 89.9 mhz; 500 w. Ant 157 ft. TL: N38 41 47 W87 26 27. Box 3206, American Family Radio, Tupelo, MS 38803. Phone: (662) 844-8888. Fax: (662) 842-6791. Web Site: www.afr.net. Licensee: American Family Association. Group owner: American Family Radio Format: Relg (Christian), inspirational. ♦Marvin Sanders, gen mgr.

WFML(FM)— May 16, 1965: 96.7 mhz; 3 kw. 377 ft. TL: N38 42 26 W87 29 42. Stereo. Box 882, 1200 N. 2nd 47591. Phone: (812) 888-4950. Fax: (812) 888-4955. E-mail: kdoades@hot96wfml.com. Web Site: hot96wfml.com. Licensee: The Vincennes University Foundation (acq 8-29-86). Network: ABC Daytime Direction. Rgnl Reps Format: Contemp country. News staff: 2; News: 2 hrs wkly. Target aud: 18-54. ♦Keith Doades, pres & gen mgr; Kevin Watson, progmg dir; John Szink, news dir; Steve McClure, chief of engrg.

WUZR(FM)—(Bicknell). June 4, 1991: 105.7 mhz; 1.8 kw. 426 ft. TL: N38 43 47 W87 24 44. Stereo. Box 242, Historic Brevoort House, 522 Busseron St. 47591. Phone: (812) 882-6060. Fax: (812) 885-2604. E-mail: wzdm@wvc.net. Web Site: www.wuzr.com. Licensee: The Original Co. Inc. (group owner; acq 4-20-98; $682,000). Format: Good time rock and roll oldies. News staff: one; News: 7 hrs wkly. Target aud: 25-54. Spec prog: Loc news, high school sports, Univ. of Evansville basketball. ♦Mark Lange, pres & gen mgr; Brad Deetz, opns dir.

***WVUB(FM)**— Dec 7, 1970: 91.1 mhz; 50 kw. 500 ft. TL: N38 39 06 W87 28 37. Stereo. Davis Hall #64, Vincennes Univ. 47591-5201. Phone: (812) 888-5830. Phone: (812) 888-5354. Fax: (812) 882-2237. E-mail: blazerwvub@hotmail.com. Licensee: Board of Trustees for Vincennes University. Network: PRI. Format: Hot adult contemp/CHR. Spec prog: Class 6 hrs wkly. ♦Phil Smith, stn mgr. Co-owned TV: WVUT(TV) affil

WZDM(FM)— September 1988: 92.1 mhz; 4.1 kw. 400 ft. TL: N38 43 18 W87 33 37. Stereo. Box 242, Historic Brevoort House, 522 Busseron St. 47591. Phone: (812) 882-6060. Fax: (812) 885-2604. E-mail: wzdm@wvc.net. Web Site: www.wzdm.com. Licensee: The Original Co. Inc. (group owner) Format: Adult contemp. News staff: 2; News: 10 hrs wkly. Target aud: 25-54; upscale. ♦Mark R. Lange, pres & gen mgr; Tom Lee, news dir.

Wabash

WJOT-FM— July 1, 1993: 105.9 mhz; 3 kw. 318 ft. TL: N40 47 11 W85 49 19. 1360 S. Wabash St. 46992. Phone: (260) 563-1161. Fax: (260) 563-0883. E-mail: wjot@comtek.com. Licensee: Mid-America Radio of Wabash Inc. Group owner: Mid-America Radio Group Inc. (acq

Stations in the U.S. — Iowa

Developers & Brokers of Radio Properties
contact American Media Services at our suite:
Philadelphia Marriott Downtown
215-625-2900
843-972-2200
americanmediaservices.com
Charleston, SC
Dallas, TX · Chicago, Il · Austin, TX
American Media Services, LLC

7-1-98; $190,000 with co-located AM). Network: Westwood One. Rgnl Reps. Fletcher, Heald & Hildreth. Format: Oldies. Target aud: 25-64. ♦ Bill Barrows, opns dir, opns mgr & news dir; Wade Weaver, gen mgr, gen sls mgr & progmg dir; Deb Dale, pub affrs dir; Jack Elmore, chief of engrg.

WJOT(AM)— November 1971: 1510 khz; 250 w-D. TL: N40 47 11 W85 49 19. Network: Westwood One. ♦ Wade Weaver, prom mgr & progmg dir.

WKUZ(FM)— Apr 1, 1965: 95.9 mhz; 4.2 kw. 394 ft. TL: N40 41 54 W85 45 03. Stereo. Box 342, 1864 S. Wabash St. 46992. Phone: (260) 563-4111. Fax: (260) 563-4425. E-mail: wkuz@kconline.com. Web Site: www.wkuz.com. Licensee: Upper Wabash Broadcasting Corp. Network: USA. Format: Country. News staff: one; News: 10 hrs wkly. Target aud: General. Spec prog: Farm 5 hrs wkly. ♦ Toni Adams, pres & CFO; Mark Lamey, exec VP & gen mgr; Dawn Hughes, stn mgr; Amber Childers, opns mgr & sls.

Wadesville

*WRFM(FM)— 2005: 90.1 mhz; 4.5 kw vert. Ant 285 ft. TL: N37 56 03 W87 55 35. Box 846, Greenfield 46140. Secondary address: 15 Wood St., Greenfield 46140-2162. Phone: (317) 467-1062. Fax: (317) 467-1065. E-mail: hensleym31@aol.com. Licensee: Indiana Community Radio Corp. Format: Adult contemp, Christian. ♦ Jennifer Cox-Hensley, pres & gen mgr.

Walton

WFRR(FM)— 1995: 93.7 mhz; 6 kw. 328 ft. TL: N40 43 30 W86 10 30. Stereo. c/o WFRN-FM Box 307, Elkhart 46515. Secondary address: 25802 CR 26, Elkhart 46517. Phone: (574) 875-5166. Phone: (574) 674-6626. Fax: (574) 875-6662. E-mail: moore@wfrn.com. Web Site: www.wfrn.com. Licensee: Christian Friends Broadcasting Inc. Network: USA. Reddy, Begley & McCormick. Format: Contemp Christian. News staff: one. Target aud: 25-54; general. ♦ Edwin Moore, pres & gen mgr; James Carter, progmg dir; Stephen Aldridge, gen sls mgr & mus dir; Don Wagner, news dir.

Warsaw

WLEG(FM)—(Ligonier). June 10, 1991: 102.7 mhz; 2 kw. Ant 394 ft. TL: N41 27 52 W85 44 40. Stereo. Box 699, Elkhart 46515. Secondary address: 421 S. 2nd St., Elkhart 46516. Phone: (574) 389-5100. Fax: (574) 389-5101. E-mail: kuebler@federatedmedia.com. Web Site: www.ilovemyfroggy.com. Licensee: Pathfinder Communications Corp. Group owner: Federated Media (acq 9-26-2002; $550,000). Format: Hot adult contemp. ♦ Kathy Uebler, gen mgr; George Trobridge, chief of engrg.

WRSW(AM)— 1951: 1480 khz; 1 kw-D, 500 w-N. TL: N41 13 21 W85 50 17. Stereo. 216 W. Market St. 46580. Secondary address: Box 1448 46581. Phone: (574) 372-3064. Phone: (574) 267-3111. Fax: (574) 267-2230. Web Site: www.wrsw.net. Licensee: Talking Stick Communications LLC. (group owner; (acq 12-19-2003; $1.2 million. with co-located FM). Network: Westwood One. Format: Sports. News staff: one; News: 18 hrs wkly. Target aud: General; 60% male, 40% female. Spec prog: Farm 11 hrs, Sp 2 hrs wkly. ♦ Patrick Brown, gen mgr & progmg dir.

WRSW-FM— 1948: 107.3 mhz; 50 kw. 293 ft. TL: N41 13 21 W85 50 17. Stereo. Network: Westwood One. Rep: Rgnl Reps. Rgnl reps. Format: Oldies, Sp, classic rock. Target aud: General; affluent adults. Spec prog: Sp 2 hrs, farm 2 hrs wkly.

Washington

WAMW(AM)— January 1955: 1580 khz; 500 w-D, DA-D. TL: N38 39 04 W87 09 55. 104 E. Main St., Box 779 47501. Phone: (812) 254-6761. Fax: (812) 254-3940. E-mail: wamw@charter.net. Web Site: www.wamwamfm.com. Licensee: Greene Electronics. Network: Salem Radio Network. Format: Christian. News staff: one. Target aud: 25+. ♦ Dave Crooks, gen mgr; Andy Morrison, opns mgr & news dir; Stacey Ramsey, gen sls mgr.

WAMW-FM— Nov 20, 1989: 107.9 mhz; 3 kw. 328 ft. TL: N38 38 47 W87 16 47. Stereo. Web Site: www.wamwamfm.com. Network: ABC. Format: Soft adult contemp. News staff: one; News: 10 hrs wkly. Target aud: 25+; soft adult contemporary. Spec prog: Cincinnati Reds, Notre Dame Basketball, Indy 500, Backyard 400.

WWBL(FM)— February 1948: 106.5 mhz; 50 kw. 340 ft. TL: N38 39 04 W87 09 55. Stereo. Box 616 47501-0616. Secondary address: Box 242, Vincennes 47591-0242. Phone: (812) 254-4300. Phone: (812) 882-6060. Fax: (812) 254-4361. Fax: (812) 885-2604. Web Site: www.wwbl.com. Licensee: Old Northwest Broadcasting Inc. Group owner: The Original Co. Inc. (acq 10-93; $250,000 with WAOV(AM) Vincennes; 10-18-93). Network: ABC. Rep: Rgnl Reps. Format: Country. News staff: one; News: 15 hrs wkly. Target aud: 18 plus. Spec prog: Farm 15 hrs wkly. ♦ Mark Lange, pres; Ken Booth, opns mgr.

West Lafayette

*WBAA(AM)— Apr 4, 1922: 920 khz; 5 kw-D, 1 kw-N, DA-N. TL: N40 20 29 W86 53 01. Purdue Univ., 712 3rd St. 47907-1740. Phone: (765) 494-5920. Fax: (765) 496-1542. E-mail: mail@wbaa.org. Web Site: www.wbaa.org. Licensee: Purdue University. Network: PRI, NPR. Wiley, Rein & Fielding. Format: Jazz, news/talk. News staff: one; News: 33 hrs wkly. Target aud: 30 plus; general. Spec prog: Black one hr, mixed nationality one hr, jazz 18 hrs, folk 5 hrs, Indian one hr wkly. ♦ Dan Skinner, gen mgr; Tracie Heughes, mktg dir & prom dir; David Bunte, progmg dir; Maurice Mogridge, chief of engrg.

WBAA-FM— February 1993: 101.3 mhz; 5 kw. 358 ft. TL: N40 17 50 W86 54 05. Web Site: www.wbaa.org. (Acq 2-22-91; 3-25-91). Network: PRI. Format: Classic rock. News: 5 hrs wkly. ♦ Brandi Parisi, mus dir.

WGLM(FM)— June 15, 1992: 106.7 mhz; 6 kw. 328 ft. TL: N40 31 20 W86 58 57. 2700-A Kent Ave. 47906. Phone: (765) 497-9456. Fax: (765) 497-3299. E-mail: ron@wglm.fm. Web Site: www.wglm.fm. Licensee: KVB Broadcasting. Network: CNN Radio. Format: Adult contemp. News staff: one; News: 8 hrs wkly. Target aud: 25-54. ♦ Kelly Busch, CEO & gen mgr; Ron Schuessler, stn mgr, sls dir & gen sls mgr.

*WHPL(FM)— Sept 10, 1993: 89.9 mhz; 2 kw. 328 ft. TL: N40 17 50 W86 54 05. P.O. Box 5508, Lafayette 47903-5508. Phone: (765) 449-0899. Fax: (765) 448-3025. E-mail: whpl@moody.edu. Web Site: www.whpl.org. Licensee: The Moody Bible Institute of Chicago. (group owner; acq 6-20-97). Network: Moody. Southmayd & Miller. Format: Relg. News: 14 hrs wkly. Target aud: 35 plus; relg. ♦ Brenda D. Campbell, stn mgr.

WLFF(FM)—See Brookston

West Terre Haute

WWVR(FM)— Jan 20, 1967: 105.5 mhz; 3.3 kw. 314 ft. TL: N39 27 15 W87 28 18. Box 1486, Terre Haute 47808. Secondary address: 918 Ohio St., Terre Haute 47808. Phone: (812) 232-9481. Fax: (812) 234-0089. E-mail: jconner@wthi.emmis.com. Web Site: www.1055theriver.net. Licensee: Emmis Radio License LLC. Group owner: Emmis Communications Corp. Format: Classic rock. News: 6 hrs wkly. Target aud: 35-64. Spec prog: Gospel, news/talk, Black 6 hrs wkly. ♦ David Bailey, gen mgr; James Conner, stn mgr & gen sls mgr; Chris Perrot, prom dir & prom mgr; Barry Kent, progmg dir; Jeff Tucker, chief of engrg.

Winamac

WFRI(FM)— 1998: 100.1 mhz; 6 kw. 328 ft. TL: N41 02 21 W86 30 55. Stereo. Box 307, Elkhart 46515. Phone: (219) 875-5166. Fax: (219) 875-6662. E-mail: comments@wfrn.com. Web Site: www.wfrn.com. Licensee: Progressive Broadcasting System Inc. (group owner). Network: USA. Format: Contemp Christian. Target aud: 25-54. ♦ Edwin Moore, pres & gen mgr.

Winchester

WZZY(FM)— May 1967: 98.3 mhz; 3 kw. 300 ft. TL: N40 05 23 W84 56 13. Stereo. Box 427 47394. Secondary address: 2301 W. Main St., Richmond 47374. Phone: (765) 962-6533. Fax: (765) 966-1499. Licensee: Rodgers Broadcasting Corp. (group owner; acq 1-1-00). Rgnl Reps. Format: Full service, adult contemp. News staff: 2; News: 10 hrs wkly. Target aud: 25-54; general. ♦ David Rodgers, pres & gen mgr; Rick Duncan, opns dir & progmg dir; Steve Frey, gen sls mgr; Steve Douglas, news dir; Dave Gill, chief of engrg.

Iowa

Adel

*KIHS(FM)— 2004: 88.9 mhz; 10 kw. Ant 154 ft. TL: N41 36 12 W94 02 53. CSN International, 4002N. 3300E., Twin Falls, ID 83301. Phone: (208) 734-6633. Fax: (208) 736-1958. E-mail: csn@csnradio.com. Web Site: www.csnradio.com. Licensee: CSN International (group owner). Format: Christian. ♦ Ray Garney, gen mgr.

Albia

KLBA-FM— June 15, 1995: 96.7 mhz; 10 kw. Ant 508 ft. TL: N41 01 47 W92 47 12. Stereo. 10 N. Clinton 52531. Phone: (641) 932-2112. Fax: (641) 932-2113. Licensee: H&H Broadcasting Corp. Format: Country, hits of the 50s & 60s. ♦ Harold Mick, pres; Larry Mikesell, gen mgr & gen sls mgr; Sue Mikesell, prom dir & progmg dir; Joe Milledge, chief of engrg.

Algona

KLGA(AM)— 1956: 1600 khz; 5 kw-D, 500 w-N, DA-2. TL: N43 03 52 W94 18 13. Box 160 50511. Secondary address: 2102 80th Ave. 50511. Phone: (515) 295-2475. Fax: (515) 295-3851. Web Site: www.waittmedia.com. Licensee: Waitt Radio Inc. Group owner: Waitt Broadcasting Inc. (acq 9-30-99; with co-located FM). Network: ABC. Bryan Cave. Format: Adult contemp. News staff: one; News: 44 hrs wkly. Target aud: 25-54. Spec prog: Farm, news, weather. ♦ Bob Ketchum, gen mgr; Dana Myee, progmg dir.

KLGA-FM— Aug 17, 1970: 92.7 mhz; 3.5 kw. 449 ft. TL: N43 04 05 W94 12 08. Stereo. Web Site: www.waittmedia.com. Network: ABC Information & Entertainment. ♦ Mark Hedberg, CEO.

Alta

KBVU-FM— 1999: 97.5 mhz; 6 kw. Ant 315 ft. TL: N42 38 05 W95 10 10. Buena Vista University, 610 W. 4th St., Storm Lake 50588. Phone: (712) 749-1234. Fax: (712) 749-1211. Web Site: edge.bvu.edu. Licensee: Buena Vista University. Format: Alternative rock. Target aud: 18-25; college students. ♦ Bruce Ellingson, gen mgr.

Ames

KASI(AM)— 1948: 1430 khz; 1 kw-D, 32 w-N. TL: N42 02 15 W93 41 21. 415 Main St. 50010. Phone: (515) 232-1430. Fax: (515) 232-1439. Web Site: www.1430kasi.com. Licensee: Citicasters Licenses L.P. Group owner: Clear Channel Communications Inc. (acq 8-24-99; with co-located FM). Network: ABC. Format: Oldies, news/talk. News staff: 2; News: 25 hrs wkly. Target aud: 25 plus. ♦ Joel McCrea, gen mgr; Tony Calumet, gen sls mgr; Linda Thede, progmg dir; Trent Rice, news dir; Mike Stover, chief of engrg.

KCCQ(FM)—Co-owned with KASI(AM). June 20, 1968: 105.1 mhz; 25 kw. 328 ft. TL: N42 04 33 W93 38 54. Stereo. Web Site: 1051channelq.com. Format: CHR. Target aud: 18-40. ♦ Linda Thede, opns dir.

Broadcasting & Cable Yearbook 2006
D-197

Iowa

KLTI-FM— June 2, 1967: 104.1 mhz; 100 kw. 1,026 ft. TL: N41 54 09 W93 54 15. (CP: Ant 1,009 ft.). Stereo. 1416 Locust St., Des Moines 50309. Phone: (515) 280-1350. Fax: (515) 280-3011. E-mail: jms720@aol.com. Web Site: www.lite1041.com. Licensee: Saga Communications of Iowa LLC. Group owner: Saga Communications Inc. (acq 1-1-97; $3.2 million). Smithwick & Belendiuk. Format: Soft adult. News staff: one. ♦ Ed Christian, CEO; Bill Wells, gen mgr; Jim Schaefer, opns dir; Celia Rodine, natl sls mgr; Marianne Kaye, prom dir.

*****KURE(FM)**— Apr 17, 1970: 88.5 mhz; 250 w. 100 ft. TL: N42 01 24 W93 39 00. Stereo. 1199 Friley Hall, Iowa State Univ. 50012. Phone: (515) 294-4332. Fax: (515) 294-9292. E-mail: generalmanager@kure885.org. Web Site: www.kure885.org. Licensee: Residence Associations Broadcasting Service Inc. Format: Var/div. News: 10 hrs wkly. Target aud: 18-25; Iowa State Univ students & Ames community. ♦ Rob McMahon, gen mgr; Rezza Rahmoni, opns dir; Katherine Beaver, mktg dir; James Bishop, progmg dir.

*****WOI(AM)**— 1922: 640 khz; 5 kw-D, 1 kw-N, DA-N. TL: N41 59 34 W93 41 27. 2022 Communicatons Bldg., Iowa State Univ. 50011. Phone: (515) 294-2025. Fax: (515) 294-1544. Web Site: www.woi.org. Licensee: Iowa State University. Network: Network: NPR, PRI. Dow, Lohnes & Albertson. Format: News/talk. News staff: 3; News: 40 hrs wkly. Target aud: General. Spec prog: Jazz 7 hrs, blues 3 hrs wkly. ♦ Gregory Geoffroy, pres; William A. McGinley, gen mgr; Dave Becker, progmg dir; David Knippel, chief of engrg.

WOI-FM— July 1, 1949: 90.1 mhz; 100 kw. 1,490 ft. TL: N41 48 33 W93 36 53. Stereo. Web Site: www.woi.org. Format: Class, jazz. News staff: 3; News: 12 hrs wkly. Target aud: General.

Ankeny

KDRB(FM)— July 1, 1991: 106.3 mhz; 6 kw. 328 ft. TL: N41 40 45 W93 35 46. 1801 Grand Ave., Des Moines 50309. Phone: (515) 242-3500. Fax: (515) 242-3798. Licensee: Citicasters Licenses L.P. Group owner: Clear Channel Communications Inc. (acq 5-4-99; grpsl). Format: Smooth jazz. Target aud: 35 plus. ♦ Joel McCrea, gen mgr; Andy Roat, gen sls mgr; J.D. Stites, natl sls mgr; Cathy Erickson, prom dir; Molly Pins, prom mgr; Cindy Chance, adv mgr; Greg Chance, progmg dir; Jared Goldberg, mus dir; Jim Boyd, news dir; Raleigh Rubenking, chief of engrg.

Asbury

WJOD(FM)— Mar 31, 1994: 103.3 mhz; 6.6 kw. 643 ft. TL: N42 34 19 W90 30 55. Stereo. 5490 Saratoga Rd., Dubuque 52002-2593. Phone: (563) 557-1040. Fax: (563) 583-4535. Web Site: www.103wjod.com. Licensee: Cumulus Licensing Corp. Group owner: Cumulus Media Inc. (acq 2-6-98). Network: Jones Radio Networks. Wiley, Rein & Fielding. Format: Country. Target aud: 18-49. ♦ Scott Lindahl, gen mgr; Ken Peiffer, opns mgr & progmg VP.

Atlantic

KJAN(AM)— September 1950: 1220 khz; 250 w-D, 86 w-N. TL: N41 25 02 W95 00 15. Stereo. Box 389, N. Olive St. 50022. Phone: (712) 243-3920. Fax: (712) 243-3937. E-mail: kjan@metc.net. Web Site: www.kjan.com. Licensee: Wireless Communications Corp. (acq 1-13-88; 11-16-87). Network: ABC Information & Entertainment. Format: Adult contemp, MOR, news. News staff: 1; News: 40 hrs wkly. Target aud: 25 plus; general. Spec prog: Farm 12 hrs wkly. ♦ J.C. Van Ginkel, chmn; Merlyn Christensen, pres; James M. Field, gen mgr.

KSWI(FM)— July 2000: 95.7 mhz; 20 kw. Ant 358 ft. TL: N41 26 07 W94 50 00. Stereo. 413 Chestnut St. 50022. Phone: (712) 243-6885. Fax: (712) 243-1691. E-mail: ksom@metc.net. Web Site: www.iowasuperstation.com. Licensee: Meredith Communications L.C. Format: CHR. ♦ Stephen O. Meredith, pres; Larry Tiarks, gen mgr; Ryan Wendt, opns mgr.

Audubon

KSOM(FM)— August 1995: 96.5 mhz; 100 kw. 528 ft. TL: N41 26 07 W94 50 00. Stereo. 413 Chestnut St., Atlantic 50022. Phone: (712) 243-6885. Fax: (712) 243-1691. E-mail: ksom@metc.net. Web Site: www.iowasuperstation.com. Licensee: Meredith Communications L.C. Format: Country. News staff: 2; News: 6 hrs wkly. Target aud: General; upscale & farmers. ♦ Larry Tiarks, gen mgr; Ryan Wendt, opns mgr.

Belle Plaine

KZAT-FM— May 30, 1997: 95.5 mhz; 4.4 kw. 384 ft. TL: N41 56 35 W92 23 51. Box 357, Tama 52339. Secondary address: 303 McClellan St., Tama 52339. Phone: (641) 484-5958. Fax: (641) 484-5962. E-mail: kzat@kzat.com. Web Site: www.kzat.com. Licensee: Camrory Broadcasting Inc. (acq 8-27-2004). Network: Network: Network: CBS, Westwood One, ABC. Katten Muchin Zavis Rosenman. Format: Classic hits. News staff: one; News: 6 hrs wkly. Target aud: 25-54; listeners who are professionals, laborers, commuters, tourists & truckers. Spec prog: Polka 2 hrs, Sp 2 hrs wkly. ♦ Catherine A. Campbell Currier, pres & gen mgr.

Bettendorf

KQCS(FM)— July 7, 1984: 93.5 mhz; 6 kw. 300 ft. TL: N41 35 59 W90 24 33. Stereo. 1229 Brady St., Davenport 52803. Phone: (563) 326-2541. Fax: (563) 326-0844. Web Site: www.93rock.net. Licensee: Cumulus Licensing Corp. Group owner: Cumulus Media Inc. (acq 3-15-00; grpsl). Rep: Allied Radio Partners. Putbrese, Hunsaker & Trent. Format: Active rock. Target aud: 18-34. ♦ Jack Swart, gen mgr.

Bloomfield

KOJY(FM)— June 26, 1982: 106.9 mhz; 14 kw. Ant 367 ft. TL: N40 46 39 W92 23 54. Stereo. Box 186 52537. Secondary address: 22620 195th St. 52537. Phone: (641) 664-3721. Fax: (641) 664-3721. E-mail: kojy@netins.net. Web Site: kojyfm.com. Licensee: Horizon Broadcasting Inc. (acq 7-24-89; FTR: 7-24-89). Network: ABC Daytime Direction. Linda Hamilton Format: Southern gospel. Target aud: 20-55; upper middle class. ♦ Doug Smiley, pres; Linda Hamilton, gen mgr; Noelle Bales, opns mgr.

Boone

*****KFFF(AM)**— 1927: 1260 khz; 5 kw-D, 33 w-N, DA-2. TL: N42 02 55 W93 53 54. 924 W. 2nd St. 50036. Phone: (515) 432-6805. Phone: (515) 432-2092. Fax: (515) 432-6805. Licensee: Boone Biblical Ministries Inc. Format: Relg. ♦ Robert Stumbo, pres; Jamie Johnson, gen mgr & progmg dir; Bob Pink, chief of engrg.

KFFF-FM— 1950: 99.3 mhz; 5.2 kw. 351 ft. TL: N42 02 55 W93 53 54. Format: Relg. ♦ Jamie Johnson, progmg dir.

KWBG(AM)— Jan 15, 1950: 1590 khz; 1 kw-D, 500 w-N, DA-N. TL: N42 01 22 W93 52 36. 724 Story St. 50036. Phone: (515) 432-2046. Fax: (515) 432-1448. E-mail: kwbg@waittradio.com. Web Site: www.kwbg.com. Licensee: WMMP LLC. Group owner: Waitt Broadcasting Inc. (acq 9-10-99; grpsl). Network: ABC Information & Entertainment. Rep: Farmakis. Format: News/talk. News staff: one; News: 36 hrs wkly. Target aud: 35 plus; Boone county, Iowa residents. Spec prog: Farm 15 hrs wkly. ♦ Carol Kuster, gen mgr; Mark McDowell, progmg dir; Jim Turbes, news dir.

KWQW(FM)— May 15, 1975: 98.3 mhz; 41 kw. 525 ft. TL: N42 01 22 W93 52 36. Stereo. 4143 109th St., Urbandale 50322. Phone: (515) 331-9200. Fax: (515) 331-9292. Licensee: Citadel Broadcasting Co. Group owner: Citadel Broadcasting Corp. (acq 8-29-2003; grpsl). Shaw Pittman. Format: Talk. News: 15 hrs wkly. Target aud: 25-54. ♦ Terry Peters, gen mgr; Jack O'Brien, opns VP.

Britt

KHAM(FM)—Not on air, target date: unknown: 99.5 mhz; 6 kw. Ant 253 ft. TL: N43 06 05 W93 55 10. 1296 Marian Ln., Green Bay, WI 54304. Phone: (920) 494-6310. Licensee: Lyle Robert Evans. ♦ Lyle R. Evans, gen mgr.

Brooklyn

KSKB(FM)— Mar 1, 1988: 99.1 mhz; 50 kw. 175 ft. TL: N41 42 36 W92 27 54. Stereo. Box 440 52211. Secondary address: 505 Josephine St., Titusville, FL 32796. Phone: (641) 522-7202. E-mail: wpio@gate.net. Web Site: www.gate.net/~wpio. Licensee: Florida Public Radio Inc. (acq 1-8-90). Format: Adult contemp Christian mus. Target aud: General. Spec prog: Ger one hr, Pol one hr wkly. ♦ Bill Korns, gen mgr.

Burlington

*****KAYP(FM)**— Nov 1, 2000: 89.9 mhz; 9 kw vert. Ant 440 ft. TL: N40 47 59 W91 32 35. 14267 Washington Rd., West Burlington 52655. Phone: (319) 758-6911. Fax: (319) 758-6922. E-mail: kayp@mchsi.com. Web Site: www.afr.net. Licensee: American Family Association. Group owner: American Family Radio Format: Christian adult contemp. ♦ Marvin Sanders, gen mgr.

KBUR(AM)— July 1941: 1490 khz; 1 kw-U. TL: N40 49 26 W91 08 33. Stereo. Box 70, 1411 N. Roosevelt Ave. 52601. Phone: (319) 752-2701. Fax: (319) 752-5287. Web Site: www.kbur.com. Licensee: Citicasters Licenses L.P. Group owner: Clear Channel Communications Inc. (acq 5-4-99; grpsl). Network: ABC Information & Entertainment. Rep: Clear Channel. Format: Adult contemp, MOR, news/talk. News staff: 3; News: 28 hrs wkly. Target aud: 25 plus; general. Spec prog: Farm 19 hrs wkly. ♦ Steve Staebell, gen mgr & natl sls mgr; Steve Hexom, progmg dir; Carl Lensgraf, mus dir; J.K. Martin, news dir; Brad Bostrom, engrg mgr.

KGRS(FM)—Co-owned with KBUR(AM). Nov 27, 1968: 107.3 mhz; 100 kw. 429 ft. TL: N40 49 26 W91 08 33. Stereo. Web Site: www.kgrsfm.com. Format: Adult contemp. News staff: 3; News: 15 hrs wkly. Target aud: 25-45. ♦ Cosmo Leone, progmg dir.

KCPS(AM)— July 30, 1965: 1150 khz; 500 w-D, 67 w-N, DA-1. TL: N40 51 11 W91 08 10. Box 946, 208 Jefferson 52601. Phone: (319) 754-6698. Fax: (319) 754-8899. E-mail: kcps@aol.com. Web Site: www.kcps.com. Licensee: John Giannettino. (acq 1-88). Network: Network: CBS, Westwood One, ABC. Rep: Katz Radio. Shaw Pittman. Format: Talk. News staff: one; News: 7 hrs wkly. Target aud: 25-54; middle-aged, upscale & well-informed adults. Spec prog: Agri-business 10 hrs, pro sports 10 hrs wkly. ♦ John Giannettino, gen mgr.

KDMG(FM)— July 19, 1993: 103.1 mhz; 12 kw. 445 ft. TL: N40 44 04 W91 15 16. Stereo. #112, 2850 Mt. Pleasant St. 52601. Phone: (319) 752-5402. Fax: (319) 752-4715. E-mail: johnp@burlingtonradio.com. Licensee: Pritchard Broadcasting Co. Rep: Allied Radio Partners. Format: Country. News staff: one; News: 3 hrs wkly. Target aud: 25-54. ♦ John T. Pritchard, pres & gen mgr; Kathy Jolly Vance, opns mgr; Chet Young, gen sls mgr.

KKMI(FM)— Oct 22, 1981: 93.5 mhz; 6.0 kw. 305 ft. TL: N40 49 11 W91 07 02. Stereo. Suite 112, 2850 Mt. Pleasant St. 52601. Phone: (319) 752-5402. Fax: (319) 752-4715. E-mail: johnp@burlingtonradio.com. Licensee: Pritchard Broadcasting Co. (acq 8-5-91). Rep: Allied Radio Partners. Format: Adult contemp. News staff: one; News: 3 hrs wkly. Target aud: 25-55; upscale. Spec prog: Pu. ♦ John T. Pritchard, pres & gen mgr; Kathy Vance, opns mgr; Chet Young, gen sls mgr.

Carroll

KCIM(AM)— June 8, 1950: 1380 khz; 1 kw-U, DA-2. TL: N42 02 29 W94 53 06. 1119 E. Plaza Dr. 51401. Phone: (712) 792-4321. Fax: (712) 792-6667. E-mail: kcimkkrl@win-4-u.net. Licensee: Carroll Broadcasting Co. (group owner; acq 8-1-85; $1.5 million with co-located FM; 5-20-85). Network: CBS. Format: Adult contemp. ♦ Mary Collison, CEO; Neil Trobak, gen mgr; Kim Hackett, natl sls mgr; John Ryan, progmg mgr; Bob Grote, chief of engrg.

KKRL(FM)—Co-owned with KCIM(AM). Jan 18, 1967: 93.7 mhz; 100 kw. 300 ft. TL: N42 03 14 W94 53 06. Stereo. ♦ John Ryan, progmg dir.

*****KWOI(FM)**—Not on air, target date: unknown: 90.7 mhz; 10 kw. Ant 289 ft. TL: N42 07 14 W94 48 49. 2022 Communications Bldg. ISU, WOI Radio Group, Ames 50011-3241. Phone: (515) 294-2025. Fax: (515) 294-1544. E-mail: woi@iastate.edu. Web Site: www.woi.org. Licensee: Iowa State University of Science and Technology. Network: NPR. Format: Class, news. ♦ William A. McGinley, gen mgr; Don Wirth, dev dir; Dave Becker, progmg dir.

Castana

*****KILV(FM)**— 2001: 107.5 mhz; 25 kw. Ant 328 ft. TL: N42 12 26 W96 07 26. Stereo. Air 1 Radio Network, 5700 W. Oaks Blvd., Rocklin, CA 95765. Phone: (916) 251-1600. Fax: (916) 251-1650. E-mail: klove@klove.com. Web Site: www.klove.com. Licensee: Educational Media Foundation. Group owner: EMF Broadcasting (acq 10-26-01). Network: K-Love. Shaw Pittman. Format: Contemp Christian. News

Stations in the U.S. — Iowa

staff: 3. Target aud: 25-44; female-Judeo/Christian. ♦ Richard Jenkins, pres; Joe Miller, CFO; Mike Novak, VP; Keith Whipple, gen mgr; Ed Lenane, opns dir.

Cedar Falls

KCNZ(AM)— September 1998: 1650 khz; 10 kw-D, 1 kw-N. TL: N42 24 47 W92 26 15. Stereo. Box 248 50613. Phone: (319) 277-1918. Fax: (319) 277-5202. E-mail: kcnz@kcnzam.com. Web Site: www.kcnzam.com. Licensee: Fife Communications Co. LLC. Network: CBS. Format: Sports/talk. News staff: 2; News: 25 hrs wkly. Target aud: 25-54; eastern Iowa adults. Spec prog: Farm 6 hrs. ♦ Jim Coloff, gen mgr.

KDNZ(AM)— Feb 2, 1958: 1250 khz; 500 w-U, DA-2. TL: N42 32 41 W92 29 16. Box 248, 721 Shirley St. 50613. Phone: (319) 277-1918. Fax: (319) 277-5202. E-mail: kcnz@kcnzam.com. Licensee: Fife Communications L.C. (acq 1995; $90,000). Format: Sp. ♦ Jim Coloff, pres & gen mgr; Tony Coloff, VP; Sue Coloff, opns VP.

***KHKE(FM)**— Apr 1, 1974: 89.5 mhz; 10 kw. 410 ft. TL: N42 23 58 W92 19 15. (CP: Ant 417 ft. TL: N42 23 55 W92 19 34). Stereo. 324 Communications Arts Center, Univ. of Northern Iowa 50614-0359. Phone: (319) 273-6400. Fax: (319) 273-7911. E-mail: kuni@uni.edu. Web Site: www.khke.org. Licensee: University of Northern Iowa. Format: Class. News staff: 3; News: 9 hrs wkly. Target aud: General. ♦ Wayne Jarvis, gen mgr & progmg dir.

KOEL-FM— Jan 7, 1994: 98.5 mhz; 25 kw. 328 ft. TL: N42 28 09 W92 29 05. 501 Sycamore St., Suite 300, Blacks Bldg., Waterloo 50703. Phone: (319) 833-4800. Phone: (319) 833-4985 (Contest line). Fax: (319) 833-4866. Web Site: www.k985.com. Licensee: Cumulus Licensing Corp. Group owner: Cumulus Media Inc. (acq 3-15-00; grpsl). Format: Country. News staff: one; News: one hr wkly. Target aud: 18-49; general. ♦ Lew Dickey, pres; William Hathaway, gen mgr.

***KUNI(FM)**— Sept 15, 1960: 90.9 mhz; 100 kw. 1,782 ft. TL: N42 18 59 W91 51 31. Stereo. 324 Communications Art Center, Univ. of Northern Iowa 50614-0359. Phone: (319) 273-6400. Fax: (319) 273-7911. E-mail: kuni@uni.edu. Web Site: www.kuniradio.org. Licensee: University of Northern Iowa. Network: Network: NPR, PRI. Format: News, talk. News staff: 3; News: 35 hrs wkly. Target aud: General. Spec prog: Folk 15 hrs, rhythm and blues 8 hrs wkly. ♦ Wayne Jarvis, prom dir & progmg dir.

Cedar Rapids

***KCCK-FM**— Sept 5, 1972: 88.3 mhz; 10 kw. 420 ft. TL: N41 54 33 W91 39 17. Stereo. Box 2068, 214 Linn Hall, 6301 Kirkwood Blvd. S.W. 52406. Phone: (319) 398-5446. Fax: (319) 398-5492. E-mail: studio@kcck.org. Web Site: www.kcck.org. Licensee: Kirkwood Community College. Network: Network: PRI, AP Radio. Wilkinson, Barker & Knauer. Format: Jazz. News staff: one; News: 8 hrs wkly. Target aud: 25-54; educated, affluent, active in community. Spec prog: New age 7 hrs wkly. ♦ Cheryle Mitvalsky, exec VP; Dennis Green, gen mgr; George Dorman, opns dir.

KCRG(AM)— 1947: 1600 khz; 5 kw-U, DA-N. TL: N41 58 21 W91 32 04. Stereo. Box 816 52406. Secondary address: 501 2nd Ave. S.E. 52401. Phone: (319) 395-9999. Fax: (319) 398-8378. Web Site: www.thezone1600.com. Licensee: Cedar Rapids TV Co. Wiley, Rein & Fielding. Format: Sports. News staff: 20; News: 164 hrs wkly. Target aud: 25 plus. ♦ John Phelan, gen mgr; Demetrios Hadjis, gen sls mgr; Scott Unash, progmg dir. Co-owned TV: KCRG-TV affil

KDAT(FM)— May 1971: 104.5 mhz; 100 kw. 500 ft. TL: N42 04 51 W91 41 45. Stereo. 4th Fl., 425 Second St. S.E. 52401. Phone: (319) 365-9431. Fax: (319) 363-8062. E-mail: kdat@kdat.com. Web Site: www.kdat.com. Licensee: Cumulus Licensing Corp. Group owner: Cumulus Media Inc. (acq 8-7-00; grpsl). Latham & Watkins. Format: Light rock. Target aud: 25-54. ♦ Jim Worthington, gen mgr.

KFMW(FM)—See Waterloo

KHAK(FM)— July 1, 1961: 98.1 mhz; 100 kw. 485 ft. TL: N41 55 28 W91 36 55. Stereo. 425 Second St. S.E., 4th Fl. 52401. Phone: (319) 365-9431. Phone: (319) 365-3698. Fax: (319) 363-8062. E-mail: khak@khak.com. Web Site: www.khak.com. Licensee: Cumulus Licensing Corp. Group owner: Cumulus Media Inc. (acq 8-7-00; grpsl). Latham & Watkins. Format: Modern country. Target aud: 25-54; general. ♦ Jim Worthington, gen mgr; Dick Stadlen, opns mgr.

KMJM(AM)— July 1, 1961: 1360 khz; 1 kw-D, 124 w-N, DA-1. TL: N41 55 28 W91 36 55. 600 Old Marion Rd. N.E. 52402. Phone: (319) 395-0530. Fax: (319) 393-9600. Licensee: Capstar TX L.P. Group owner: Clear Channel Communications Inc. (acq 8-30-2000; grpsl). Format: Sports. ♦ John Laton, gen mgr.

KMRY(AM)— August 1949: 1450 khz; 1 kw-U. TL: N42 00 25 W91 42 29. (In-band On-channel). 1957 Blairsferry Rd. N.E. 52402. Phone: (319) 393-1450. Fax: (319) 393-1407. E-mail: kmry@kmryradio.com. Web Site: www.kmry/radio.com. Licensee: Sellers Broadcasting Inc. (acq 3-5-98; $475,000). Network: CBS. Lauren A. Colby. Format: Adult standards. News staff: one; News: 20 hrs wkly. Target aud: 40 plus; affluent, upscale adults with large disposable income. Spec prog: 50's oldies 3 hrs, polka 3 hrs, big band 2 hrs weekly. ♦ Kevin Alexander, pres; Rick Sampson, opns mgr; Eric Christopher, progmg dir & progmg mgr.

KZIA(FM)— Apr 29, 1975: 102.9 mhz; 100 kw. 853 ft. TL: N42 03 25 W91 41 42. Stereo. 1110 26th Ave. S.W. 52404-3430. Phone: (319) 363-2061. Fax: (319) 363-2948. E-mail: kzia@kzia.com. Web Site: www.kzia.com. Licensee: KZIA Inc. (acq 5-13-94; $2 million; 2-25-85). Rep: D & R Radio. Dow, Lohnes & Albertson. Format: CHR. News staff: one; News: one hr wkly. Target aud: 18-49. ♦ Eliot A. Keller, pres & gen mgr; Robert K. Norton Jr., exec VP & opns mgr; Greg Runyon, progmg dir.

WMT(AM)— 1922: 600 khz; 5 kw-U, DA-N. TL: N42 03 40 W91 32 44. Stereo. 600 Old Marion Rd. N.E. 52406. Phone: (319) 395-0530. Fax: (319) 393-0918. Web Site: www.wmtradio.com. Licensee: Citicasters Licenses L.P. Group owner: Clear Channel Communications Inc. (acq 5-4-99; grpsl). Network: CBS. Format: Full svc, news/talk. Target aud: 35 plus. Spec prog: Farm 19 hrs wkly. ♦ John Laton, gen mgr; Andy Roat, gen sls mgr; Lisa Pucelik, mktg dir; Teisha Welsh, mktg dir; Randy Lee, progmg mgr; Jeff Schmidt, news dir; Tom Spaight, chief of engrg.

WMTX(FM)—Co-owned with WHNZ(AM). November 1947: 100.7 mhz; 100 kw. 1,358 ft. TL: N28 02 21 W82 39 21. (CP: TL: N27 50 32 W82 15 46). Stereo. Web Site: www.wmtx.com. Format: Top 40, adult contemp. ♦ Dan DiLoreto, gen mgr; Tony Florentino, progmg dir; Wilson Welch, chief of engrg.

WMTC-FM— Jan 1, 1991: 99.9 mhz; 6 kw. Ant 328 ft. TL: N37 36 23 W83 26 48. Stereo. Phone: (606) 666-5006. E-mail: wmtc@asburyusa.net. Format: Christian, relg. Spec prog: Farm one hr wkly.

WMTD-FM— Oct 1, 1985: 102.3 mhz; 160 w. 1,008 ft. TL: N37 42 56 W80 56 55. (CP: 368 w, ant 1,273 ft.). Stereo. News staff: one; News: 1 hr wkly. Target aud: Adults 18-49.

WMTM-FM— Nov 17, 1964: 93.9 mhz; 100 kw. 555 ft. TL: N31 12 54 W83 47 13. Stereo. Format: Oldies. ♦ Jim Turner, opns mgr & mktg mgr.

WMT-FM— Feb 16, 1963: 96.5 mhz; 100 kw. 540 ft. TL: N42 01 43 W91 38 27. Stereo. Web Site: www.mix965.com. Network: CBS. Format: Adult contemp. Target aud: 25-49. ♦ Randy Lee, progmg dir.

Centerville

KCOG(AM)— Mar 1, 1949: 1400 khz; 500 w-D, 1 kw-N. TL: N40 44 40 W92 54 32. 402 N. 12th St. 52544. Phone: (641) 437-4242. E-mail: kcogam@lisco.net. Web Site: www.kmgo.com. Licensee: KCOG Inc. (acq 6-1-84; $406,000; 4-16-84). Network: USA. Format: Adult contemp. ♦ Fred Jenkins, gen mgr & progmg dir.

KMGO(FM)—Co-owned with KCOG(AM). Oct 1, 1974: 98.7 mhz; 100 kw. 500 ft. TL: N40 47 34 W92 52 47. Stereo. Phone: (641) 856-3996. Fax: (641) 856-3337. E-mail: kmgofm@lisco.net. Web Site: www.kmgo.com. Licensee: KMGO Inc. (acq 6-5-85). Network: USA. Format: Country. ♦ Larry Stout, progmg dir.

Chariton

KELR-FM— Nov 15, 1979: 105.5 mhz; 50 kw. 390 ft. TL: N41 00 50 W93 17 23. Stereo. 215 N. Main St. 50049. Phone: (641) 774-8494. Fax: (641) 774-8495. E-mail: KELR@lisco.com. Licensee: FMC Broadcasting (acq 6-15-99). Network: Westwood One. Format: Adult contemp. News staff: one; News: 30 hrs wkly. Target aud: 28 plus. Spec prog: Gosp 5 hrs wkly. ♦ Thomas A. Palen, CEO & pres; Cindy Spidle, adv mgr; Nick Hoffman, progmg VP & asst music dir; Fred Jenkins, engrg VP.

Charles City

KCHA(AM)— November 1949: 1580 khz; 500 w-D, 10 w-N. TL: N43 03 05 W92 40 00. 207 N. Main St. 50616. Phone: (641) 228-1000. Fax: (641) 228-1200. Web Site: www.kchafm.com. Licensee: Clear Channel Broadcasting Licenses Inc. Group owner: Clear Channel Communications Inc. (acq 9-25-00; grpsl). Rep: Farmakis. Format: Info, talk. Target aud: General. Spec prog: Farm 12 hrs wkly. ♦ Charlie Thomas, gen mgr; Mark Dorenkamp, progmg dir.

KCHA-FM— October 1971: 95.9 mhz; 3 kw. 300 ft. TL: N43 03 05 W92 40 00. Stereo. Web Site: www.kchafm.com. Format: EZ listening.

Cherokee

KCHE(AM)— January 1953: 1440 khz; 500 w-D. TL: N42 47 21 W95 33 06. Box 1440, 201 S. 5th 51012. Phone: (712) 225-2511. Fax: (712) 225-2513. E-mail: kche1@nen.net. Web Site: www.kcheradio.com. Licensee: J & J Broadcasting Corp. (acq 11-14-03; $600,000. with co-located FM). Network: ABC. Format: Oldies. News staff: 2; News: 14 hrs wkly. Target aud: 45-80; general. Spec prog: Farm 12 hrs, Sp one hr wkly. ♦ Jeff Fuller, pres, gen mgr & gen sls mgr; Curt Carlson, VP, gen mgr & sls VP; Dick Keane, chief of opns & chief of engrg; Bill Beroni, progmg dir; Greg Slotsky, news dir; Lynn Dittmer, prom dir & pub affrs dir.

KCHE-FM— Dec 9, 1976: 92.1 mhz; 3 kw. 302 ft. TL: N42 47 21 W95 33 06. Stereo. Web Site: www.kcheradio.com. Network: ABC. Rep: Farmakis. Format: Adult contemp. News staff: 2; News: 28 hrs wkly.

Clarinda

KKBZ(FM)— Sept 25, 1990: 99.3 mhz; 50 kw. 492 ft. TL: N40 33 12 W95 07 18. Stereo. Box 960, 209 N. Elm, Shenandoah 51601. Phone: (712) 246-5270. Fax: (712) 246-5275. Web Site: www.kmakkbz.com. Licensee: May Broadcasting Co. Network: Westwood One. Format: Adult Contemp. News staff: 2; News: 5 hrs wkly. Target aud: 25-44. ♦ Edward W. May, pres; Don Hansen, stn mgr.

Clarion

KIAQ(FM)— May 18, 1964: 96.9 mhz; 100 kw. 578 ft. TL: N42 40 18 W94 09 11. Stereo. 1014 Central Ave., Fort Dodge 50501. Phone: (515) 573-5748. Fax: (515) 573-3376. Licensee: Three Eagles of Ft. Dodge Inc. Group owner: Three Eagles Communications (acq 4-22-97; $1,244,117). Format: Country. Target aud: 25-54. ♦ Gary Buchanan, pres; Patrick Kolar, gen mgr & gen sls mgr; Gregg Ellendson, opns mgr; Travis Reeves, gen mgr & progmg mgr.

Clear Lake

KLKK(FM)— Feb 16, 1978: 103.7 mhz; 25 kw. Ant 187 ft. TL: N43 03 35 W93 22 47. Stereo. 341 Yorktown Pike, Mason City 50401. Phone: (641) 424-1300. Fax: (641) 423-2906. Web Site: www.klkkfm.com. Licensee: Clear Channel Broadcasting Licenses Inc. Group owner: Clear Channel Communications Inc. (acq 9-25-00; grpsl). Rep: Clear

Broadcasting & Cable Yearbook 2006

Iowa Directory of Radio

Channel. Format: Classic rock. News staff: one; News: 42 hrs wkly. Target aud: 25-54. ♦Hal Hofman, gen mgr.

Clinton

KCLN(AM)— Dec 21, 1956: 1390 khz; 1 kw-D, 91 w-N, DA-2. TL: N41 54 32 W90 13 16. 1853 442nd Ave. 52732. Phone: (563) 243-1390. Fax: (563) 242-4567. E-mail: kcln@kcln.com. Web Site: www.kcln.kcln.com. Licensee: WPW Broadcasting Inc. (group owner; acq 4-29-99; $800,000 with co-located FM). Network: ABC Information & Entertainment. Miller & Fields. Format: Mus of the 40s, 50s & 60s, big band. News staff: one; News: 2 hrs wkly. Target aud: 40 plus. Spec prog: Farm 10 hrs wkly. ♦David Madison, pres; Penny Helm, gen mgr; Chris Streets, stn mgr, opns dir & progmg dir; Chris Lake, gen sls mgr; Brad Seward, news dir; Bill Dieckman, chief of engrg.

KMXG(FM)— July 1974: 96.1 mhz; 100 kw. 980 ft. TL: N41 37 58 W90 24 38. Stereo. 3535 E. Kimberly Rd., Davenport 52807. Phone: (563) 344-7000. Fax: (563) 344-7006. Web Site: www.kmxg.com. Licensee: Citicasters Licenses L.P. Group owner: Clear Channel Communications Inc. (acq 11-15-00; grpsl). Rep: Christal. Format: Hot adult contemp. News staff: one; News: 3 hrs wkly. Target aud: 25-54; yuppies, baby boomers, upscale professional females. Spec prog: Jazz 3 hrs wkly. ♦Larry Rosmilso, VP & gen mgr; Joanne Kerschieter, opns mgr; Jim O'Hara, progmg dir.

KROS(AM)— Sept 28, 1941: 1340 khz; 1 kw-U. TL: N41 51 36 W90 12 18. Stereo. Box 0518, William Scott Broadcast Ctr., 870 13th Ave. N. 52733-0518. Phone: (563) 242-1252. Fax: (563) 242-4825. E-mail: kros@clinton.net. Licensee: KROS Broadcasting Inc. (acq 7-28-98; $23,000 for 28). Format: Full service. News staff: one; News: 38 hrs wkly. Target aud: General; loc audience. Spec prog: Folk 2 hrs, jazz one hr, blues one hr, gospel one hr, women 5 hrs. ♦Brad Parker, pres; Wayne Larkey, gen mgr.

Council Bluffs

KHLP(AM)—See Omaha, NE

***KIWR(FM)**— Nov 23, 1981: 89.7 mhz; 100 kw. 1,100 ft. TL: N41 18 40 W96 01 37. Stereo. 2700 College Rd. 51503. Phone: (712) 325-3254. Fax: (712) 325-3391. E-mail: sjohn@iwcc.edu. Web Site: www.897theriver.com. Licensee: Iowa Western Community College. Format: Progsv. News: 5 hrs wkly. Target aud: 18-34; well-educated, upper & middle-upper income. Spec prog: Var/div 16 hrs wkly. ♦Dan Kinney, pres; Tom Johnson, CFO; Sophia John, gen mgr.

KLNG(AM)— 1947: 1560 khz; 1 kw-D. TL: N41 12 28 W95 54 04. 120 S. 35th St., Suite 2 51501. Phone: (712) 323-0100. Fax: (712) 323-0022. Web Site: www.wilkinsweb.com. Licensee: Wilkins Communications Network Inc. (group owner; acq 4-89; $250,000). Format: Bible teaching, Christian talk. Target aud: 25-54. Spec prog: Sp 10 hrs, Black 6 hrs wkly. ♦Charles Yates, stn mgr.

KQKQ-FM— 1969: 98.5 mhz; 100 kw. Ant 1,102 ft. TL: N41 18 25 W96 01 37. Stereo. 5011 Capitol Ave., Omaha, NE 68132. Phone: (402) 342-2000. Fax: (402) 342-5874. Fax: (402) 827-5293. Web Site: www.q985fm.com. Licensee: Waitt Omaha LLC. (group owner; (acq 1-7-2002; grpsl). Format: CHR. Target aud: 18-44. ♦Chuck DuCoty, COO & mus dir; Mary Quass, CEO, pres & sr VP; Ken Fearnow, VP, gen mgr & chief of engrg; Mark Todd, prom dir & progmg VP.

KSRZ(FM)—See Omaha, NE

Cresco

KCZQ(FM)— Apr 1, 1991: 102.3 mhz; 3 kw. Ant 328 ft. TL: N43 25 47 W92 09 49. Stereo. 116 First Ave. W. 52136-1514. Phone: (563) 547-1000. Phone: (563) 547-3366. Fax: (563) 547-2200. E-mail: superc@iowatelecom.net. Licensee: Mega Media Ltd. Rep: Farmakis. Format: Adult contemp. Target aud: General. Spec prog: Farm 12 hrs wkly. ♦James B. Hebel, pres, gen mgr & gen sls mgr; Debra Lowe, opns mgr; Jim Bernard, progmg dir; Stan McHenry, mus dir.

Creston

***KLOX(FM)**—Not on air, target date: unknown: 90.9 mhz; 100 kw vert. Ant 335 ft. TL: N41 04 29 W94 22 35. 505 Josephine St., Titusville, FL 32796. Phone: (321) 267-3000. Fax: (321) 264-9370. E-mail: wpio@gate.net. Web Site: www.gate.net/~wpio. Licensee: Florida Public Radio Inc. Format: Adult contemp Christian. ♦Archie Shetler, exec VP; Randy Henry, pres & gen mgr.

KSIB(AM)— Dec 7, 1946: 1520 khz; 1 kw-D. TL: N41 02 16 W94 23 38. Box 426 50801. Phone: (641) 782-2155. Fax: (641) 782-6963. Licensee: G.O. Radio Ltd. (acq 2-82; grpsl; FTR: 2-22-82). Network: ABC. Format: C&W. Target aud: General. ♦Dave Rieck, pres & gen mgr; Ben Walter, progmg dir; Mark Saylor, news dir; Charlie Maley, chief of engrg.

KSIB-FM— March 1966: 101.3 mhz; 3 kw. 255 ft. TL: N41 03 41 W94 22 30. (CP: 18.75 kw, ant 364 ft.). Stereo. Network: ABC Daytime Direction. Target aud: General.

Davenport

***KALA(FM)**— Nov 4, 1967: 88.5 mhz; 100 w. 110 ft. TL: N41 32 28 W90 34 57. Stereo. 518 W. Locust St. 52803. Phone: (563) 333-6219. Fax: (563) 333-6218. E-mail: kala@sau.edu. Web Site: www.sau.edu/kala. Licensee: St. Ambrose University. (acq 11-4-67). Format: Jazz, progsv, urban contemp. News staff: one; News: 34.5 hrs wkly. Target aud: General. Spec prog: Sp 15 hrs, gospel 13 hrs wkly. ♦David Baker, gen mgr & opns mgr.

KBEA-FM—(Muscatine). February 1949: 99.7 mhz; 100 kw. 895 ft. TL: N41 26 43 W91 04 36. Stereo. 1229 Brady St. 52803. Phone: (563) 326-2541. Fax: (563) 326-1819. Licensee: Cumulus Licensing Corp. Group owner: Cumulus Media Inc. (acq 3-15-00; grpsl). Rep: Allied Radio Partners. Putbrese, Hunsaker & Trent. Format: Top 40. News staff: one. Target aud: 25-54. ♦Jack Swart, pres & gen mgr.

KCQQ(FM)— Sept 1, 1996: 106.5 mhz; 100 kw. 210 ft. TL: N41 32 14 W90 34 30. Stereo. 3535 E. Kimberly Rd. 52807. Phone: (563) 344-7000. Fax: (563) 359-8524. E-mail: dorks@2dorks.com. Web Site: www.kcqq.com. Licensee: Citicasters Licenses L.P. Group owner: Clear Channel Communications Inc. (acq 11-15-00; grpsl). Format: Classic rock. News staff: one; News: 2 hrs wkly. Target aud: 25-54. Spec prog: Relg one hr wkly. ♦Larry R. Rosmilso, gen mgr; Jim Hunter, stn mgr & progmg dir; Teri Van Dyke, gen sls mgr.

KJOC(AM)— 1947: 1170 khz; 1 kw-U, DA-2. TL: N41 23 22 W90 31 08. 1229 Brady St. 52803. Phone: (563) 326-2541. Fax: (563) 326-1819. Web Site: www.kjoc.com. Licensee: Cumulus Licensing Corp. Group owner: Cumulus Media Inc. (acq 3-15-00; grpsl). Network: CBS. Rep: Allied Radio Partners. Putbrese, Hunsaker & Trent, P. Format: Sports. Target aud: 18-49. ♦Jack Swart, gen mgr.

WFXN(AM)—See Moline, IL

WLLR-FM—Listing follows WOC(AM).

WOC(AM)— February 1922: 1420 khz; 5 kw-U, DA-2. TL: N41 33 00 W90 28 37. 3535 E. Kimberly Rd. 52807. Phone: (563) 344-7000. Fax: (563) 344-7065. Web Site: www.woc1420.com. Licensee: Citicasters Licenses L.P. Group owner: Clear Channel Communications Inc. (acq 11-15-2000; grpsl). Network: ABC Information & Entertainment. Rep: Christal. Baker & Hostetler. Format: News/talk, info. News staff: 5. Target aud: 35-64; info-oriented adults. Spec prog: Farm 10 hrs wkly. ♦Larry Rosmilso, gen mgr; Scott Bitting, gen sls mgr; Caressa Clearman, prom dir; Dan Kennedy, progmg dir; Kevin Allensworth, chief of engrg.

WLLR-FM—Co-owned with WOC(AM). October 1948: 103.7 mhz; 100 kw. 1,191 ft. TL: N41 32 49 W90 28 35. Stereo. Phone: (563) 359-9557. Fax: (563) 344-7016. E-mail: jimohara@clearchannel.com. Web Site: www.wllr.com. Format: Country. News: 2 hrs wkly. Target aud: 25-54. ♦Mike Weindruch, gen sls mgr; Carrie Clearman, prom dir; Jim O'Hara, progmg dir; Kevin Allensworth, engrg dir.

Decorah

KDEC-FM— Sept 2, 1986: 100.5 mhz; 30 kw. Ant 420 ft. TL: N43 19 26 W91 47 04. Stereo. Box 27 52101. Secondary address: 110 Highland Dr. 52101. Phone: (563) 382-4251. Fax: (563) 382-9540. E-mail: kdec@kdecradio.com. Web Site: www.kdecradio.com. Licensee: Decorah Broadcasting Inc. (acq 3-1-96; $696,500). Reddy, Begley & McCormick. Format: Adult contemp. News: 3 hrs wkly. Target aud: 25-54. ♦Bob Holtan, pres & gen mgr; Colleen Holtan, VP; Jennifer Grouws, opns dir.

KDEC(AM)— May 1947: 1240 khz; 1 kw-U. TL: N43 19 26 W91 47 04. Network: Network: Westwood One, ABC Daytime Direction. Rep: Farmakis. Format: MOR. News staff: 2; News: 12 hrs wkly. Target aud: 35 plus.

***KLCD(FM)**— July 15, 1977: 89.5 mhz; 100 w. 140 ft. TL: N43 18 56 W91 47 18. Stereo. 206 S. Broadway, Suite 735, Rochester, MN 55904. Phone: (507) 282-0910. Fax: (507) 282-2107. E-mail: mail@mpr.org. Web Site: www.mpr.org. Licensee: Minnesota Public Radio Inc. Network: Network: NPR, PRI. Format: Class. ♦Chris Cross, gen mgr; Mary Stapek, dev dir; Erin Galbally, news dir.

***KLNI(FM)**— 1993: 88.7 mhz; 100 w. -36 ft. TL: N43 18 35 W91 48 30. 206 S. Broadway, Suite 735, Rochester, MN 55904. Phone: (507) 282-0910. Fax: (507) 282-2107. E-mail: mail@mpr.org. Web Site: www.mpr.org. Licensee: Minnesota Public Radio (group owner; (acq 6-10-92). Network: NPR. Format: News & info. News staff: 2. ♦Chris Cross, gen mgr; Mary Stapek, dev dir; Erin Galbally, news dir; Jeryl Komejan, pub affrs dir; Craig Erpestad, chief of engrg.

***KWLC(AM)**— December 1926: 1240 khz; 1 kw-U. TL: N43 18 38 W91 48 41. 700 College Dr. 52101. Phone: (563) 387-1240. Fax: (563) 387-1489. Web Site: kwlc.luther.edu. Licensee: Luther College. Format: Div, progsv. Target aud: General. Spec prog: Classic rock, class, educ, jazz, relg, folk, blues, reggae, sports 6 hrs wkly.

Denison

KDSN(AM)— Apr 11, 1956: 1530 khz; 500 w-D, 13 w-N. TL: N42 02 10 W95 19 44. Box 670 51442. Secondary address: 1530 Ridge Rd. 51442. Phone: (712) 263-3141. Fax: (712) 263-2088. E-mail: info@kdsnradio.com. Web Site: www.kdsnradio.com. Licensee: M & J Radio Corp. (acq 8-3-93; $450,000. with co-located FM; FTR: 8-23-93). Network: ABC Daytime Direction. Rep: Farmakis. Format: Country, adult contemp, farm markets. News staff: one; News: 8 rs wkly. Target aud: General. Spec prog: Farm 12 hrs, polka 4 hrs, Sp 3 hrs wkly. ♦Michael Dudding, pres, exec VP & gen mgr; Phyllis Rohlin, exec VP & gen mgr.

KDSN-FM— Aug 1, 1968: 107.1 mhz; 6 kw. 300 ft. TL: N42 02 11 W95 19 50. Stereo. Web Site: www.kdsnradio.com. Format: Adult contemp. News staff: one; News: 8 hrs wkly. Target aud: 25-54. ♦Michael Dudding, adv dir; Dick Keane, engrg dir.

Des Moines

KBGG(AM)— 1998: 1700 khz; 10 kw-D, 1 kw-N. TL: N41 35 30 W93 31 43. 4143 109th St., Urbandale 50322. Phone: (515) 331-9200. Phone: (515) 278-4117. Fax: (515) 331-9292. Fax: (515) 254-1037. E-mail: laley1700@yahoo.com. Web Site: www.laleyiowa.com. Licensee: Citadel Broadcasting Co. Group owner: Citadel Broadcasting Corp. (acq 8-29-03; grpsl). Rep: McGavren Guild. Format: Spanish. Target aud: 25 plus. ♦Joel Garcia, gen mgr.

***KDFR(FM)**— Mar 24, 1989: 91.3 mhz; 32 kw. 446 ft. TL: N41 36 59 W93 31 36. Stereo. Box 57023 50317. Secondary address: 2350 N.E. 44th Ct. 50317. Phone: (515) 262-0449. E-mail: kdfr@familyradio.org. Web Site: www.familyradio.com. Licensee: Family Stations Inc. (group owner) Format: Relg, inspirational. News staff: one; News: 6 hrs wkly. Target aud: 25 plus; general. Spec prog: Class 2 hrs wkly. ♦Harold Camping, pres; Larry Vavroch, opns mgr.

KGGO(FM)— May 31, 1964: 94.9 mhz; 100 kw. 1,059 ft. TL: N41 37 54 W93 27 24. Stereo. 4143 109th St., Urbandale 50322. Phone: (515) 331-9200. Fax: (515) 312-9292. E-mail: kggo@kggo.com. Web Site: www.kggo.com. Licensee: Citadel Broadcasting Co. Group owner: Citadel Broadcasting Corp. (acq 8-29-03; grpsl). Format: Classic Rock. ♦Jack O'Brien, gen mgr & progmg dir.

KHKI(FM)— July 4, 1964: 97.3 mhz; 115 kw. 449 ft. TL: N41 39 47 W93 45 21. Stereo. 4143 109th St., Urbandale 50322. Phone: (515) 331-9200. Fax: (515) 331-9292. Web Site: 973thehawk.com. Licensee: Citadel Broadcasting Co. Group owner: Citadel Broadcasting Corp. (acq 8-29-03; grpsl). Format: Country. Target aud: 18-49. ♦Terry Peters, gen mgr; Jack O'Brian, opns VP & progmg dir.

KIOA(FM)— Sept 18, 1964: 93.3 mhz; 100 kw. 1,063 ft. TL: N41 37 54 W93 27 24. Stereo. 1416 Locust St. 50309. Phone: (515) 280-1350. Fax: (515) 280-3011. Web Site: www.kioa.com. Licensee: Saga Communications of Iowa LLC. Group owner: Saga Communications Inc. (acq 4-19-93; $2.7 million. with co-located AM; FTR: 5-3-93). Smithwick & Belendiuk. Format: Oldies. News staff: one. Target aud: 25-54. ♦Bill Wells, gen mgr; Jeff Delvaux, sls dir; Jill Olsen, prom mgr; Don Tool, adv mgr; Tim Fox, progmg dir; Polly Carverkimm, news dir; Joe Farrington, chief of engrg.

Stations in the U.S. — Iowa

KPSZ(AM)—Co-owned with KIOA(FM). April 1947: 940 khz; 10 kw-D, 5 kw-N, DA-2. TL: N41 28 35 W93 22 26. Network: ABC Information & Entertainment. Format: Christian contemp mus, talk. ♦ Mary Sayre, sls dir; Joe Acker, prom dir; Steve Gibbons, progmg mgr.

KJJY(FM)—(West Des Moines). Feb 4, 1978: 92.5 mhz; 41 kw. Ant 541 ft. TL: N41 39 53 W93 45 24. Stereo. 4143 109th St., Urbandale 50322. Phone: (515) 331-9200. Fax: (515) 331-9292. Web Site: www.kjjy.com. Licensee: Citadel Broadcasting Co. Group owner: Citadel Broadcasting Corp. (acq 8-29-03; grpsl). Format: Country. Target aud: 25-54; general. ♦ Scott Farkas, gen mgr; Andy Elliott, mktg dir & progmg dir.

*KJMC(FM)— May 1999: 89.3 mhz; 7.1 kw. Ant 200 ft. TL: N41 39 21 W93 35 51. Stereo. 1169 25th St. 50311. Phone: (515) 279-1811. Fax: (515) 279-1802. Licensee: Minority Communications Inc. Network: ABC. Format: Urban contemp, hits, oldies. ♦ Larry Rollins, gen mgr; Larry Neville, opns VP; John Farington, chief of opns.

KKDM(FM)— Aug 22, 1995: 107.5 mhz; 100 kw. 705 ft. TL: N41 38 36 W93 17 21. 2141 Grand Ave. 50312. Phone: (515) 245-8900. Fax: (515) 245-8906. Web Site: www.kkdm.com. Licensee: Clear Channel Broadcasting Licenses Inc. Group owner: Clear Channel Communications Inc. (acq 9-1-99; $7.35 million). Rep: Clear Channel. Format: CHR. Target aud: 18-49. ♦ Joel McCrea, gen mgr; Greg Chance, opns mgr; Andy Poat, gen sls mgr; Andy Reat, adv mgr.

KMXD(FM)—Listing follows WHO(AM).

KRNT(AM)—Listing follows KSTZ(FM).

KSTZ(FM)— 1970: 102.5 mhz; 100 kw. 1,248 ft. TL: N41 48 01 W93 36 27. Stereo. 1416 Locust St. 50309. Phone: (515) 280-1350. Fax: (515) 280-3011. E-mail: jms720@aol.com. Web Site: www.star1025.com. Licensee: Saga Communications of Iowa LLC. Group owner: Saga Communications Inc. (acq 8-88; $3.2 million with co-located AM; 8-1-88). Network: CNN Radio. Smithwick & Belendiuk. Format: Hot adult contemp. News staff: one. Target aud: 25-54; emphasis on upscale women. ♦ Jeremy Dresen, gen mgr & sls.

KRNT(AM)—Co-owned with KSTZ(FM). Mar 17, 1935: 1350 khz; 5 kw-U, DA-N. TL: N41 33 34 W93 34 40. E-mail: krntpdsteve@hotmail.com. Web Site: www.1350krnt.com. Network: CBS. Smithwick & Belendiuk. Format: MOR. News staff: one. Target aud: 50 plus. ♦ Jill Olsen, mktg dir, prom dir & adv dir; Steve Gibbons, progmg dir.

KWKY(AM)— Feb 2, 1948: 1150 khz; 1 kw-U, DA-2. TL: N41 27 07 W93 40 44. Box 662 50303. Secondary address: 6626 Dubuque Trail, Norwalk 50211. Phone: (515) 981-0981. Fax: (515) 981-0840. Web Site: www.kwky.com. Licensee: Putbrese Communications Ltd. (acq 4-22-02). Network: Network: USA, Salem Radio Network. Format: Relg, talk, sports. Target aud: General. ♦ John Putbrese, pres; Charles E. Putbrese, gen mgr; Jerry Chiaramonte, stn mgr; Pat Pedigo, opns mgr; Dennis Ray, mus dir; Richard Fowler, chief of engrg.

KXNO(AM)— July 21, 1921: 1460 khz; 5 kw-U, DA-N. TL: N41 38 45 W93 32 12. Stereo. 1801 Grand Ave. 50309-3309. Phone: (515) 242-3500. Fax: (515) 222-0033. E-mail: kxno@clearchannel.com. Web Site: www.kxno.com. Licensee: Capstar TX L.P. Group owner: Clear Channel Communications Inc. (acq 8-30-00; grpsl). Format: Sports. Target aud: 35 plus; 25-54 Male. ♦ Joel McCrea, gen mgr & gen sls mgr; Geoff Conn, opns mgr; Andy Roat, natl sls mgr; Cathy Erickson, prom dir; Van Harden, progmg dir; Jim Boyd, news dir; Raleigh Rubenking, chief of engrg.

WHO(AM)— Apr 10, 1924: 1040 khz; 50 kw-U. TL: N41 39 10 W93 21 01. 1801 Grand Ave. 50309. Phone: (515) 242-3500. Fax: (515) 242-3798. Fax: (515) 242-3553. Web Site: www.whoradio.com. Licensee: Citicasters Licenses L.P. Group owner: Clear Channel Communications Inc. (acq 5-4-99; grpsl). Network: ABC. Rep: Christal. Format: News/talk. Target aud: General; info seeking adults. Spec prog: Farm 15 hrs wkly. ♦ Cheryl Pannier, opns mgr; Cathy Erickson, prom dir; Van Harden, progmg dir; Jim Boyd, news dir; Bonnie Lucas, pub affrs dir; Raleigh Ruben King, chief of engrg.

KMXD(FM)—Co-owned with WHO(AM). Feb 1, 1948: 100.3 mhz; 100 kw. 1,700 ft. TL: N41 48 33 W93 36 53. Stereo. Network: Westwood One. Format: Hot adult contemp. Target aud: 25-54.

Dubuque

KATF(FM)—Listing follows KDTH(AM).

KDTH(AM)— May 4, 1941: 1370 khz; 5 kw-U, DA-N. TL: N42 29 06 W90 38 39. Box 659 52004-0659. Secondary address: 8th & Bluff Sts. 52001. Phone: (563) 690-0800. Fax: (563) 588-5688. E-mail: kdth@kdth.com. Web Site: www.kdth.com. Licensee: Radio Dubuque Inc. (group owner; acq 7-1-00; $3.68 million. with co-located FM). Network: CBS. Rep: Katz Radio. Pepper & Corazzini. Format: Full service. News staff: 3; News: 25 hrs wkly. Target aud: 35 plus; responsible adults with established careers & households. Spec prog: Farm 17 hrs wkly. ♦ Thomas Parsley, stn mgr; Perry Mason, gen sls mgr & natl sls mgr; Michael Kaye, progmg dir; Rob Kundert, news dir.

KATF(FM)—Co-owned with KDTH(AM). June 25, 1967: 92.9 mhz; 89.7 kw. Ant 1,014 ft. TL: N42 31 44 W90 36 58. Stereo. Phone: (563) 690-0800. Format: Adult contemp. News: 3 hrs wkly. Target aud: 25-54; adults establishing families, careers & households. ♦ Thomas Parsley, gen mgr.

*KDUB(FM)—Not on air, target date: unknown: 90.1 mhz; 810 w. Ant 522 ft. TL: N42 36 17 W90 47 44. 324 Communications Arts Center, Univ. of Northern Iowa, Cedar Falls 50614. Phone: (319) 273-6400. Fax: (319) 273-2682. E-mail: kuni@uni.edu. Licensee: University of Northern Iowa. ♦ Wayne Jarvis, progmg dir.

*KIAD(FM)—Not on air, target date: unknown: 88.5 mhz; 750 w vert. Ant 518 ft. TL: N42 24 16 W90 34 12. Drawer 2440, Tupelo, MS 38803. Phone: (662) 844-8888. Fax: (662) 842-6791. Web Site: www.afr.net. Licensee: American Family Association. ♦ Marvin Sanders, gen mgr.

KLYV(FM)—Listing follows WDBQ(AM).

KXGE(FM)— Mar 8, 1980: 102.3 mhz; 2.4 kw. 410 ft. TL: N42 32 28 W90 36 46. Stereo. 5490 Saratoga Rd., Box 1280 52002. Phone: (563) 557-1040. Fax: (563) 583-4535. Web Site: www.cumulus.com. Licensee: Cumulus Licensing Corp. Group owner: Cumulus Media Inc. (acq 12-17-98; grpsl). Network: ABC. Format: Classic rock. News staff: one; News: 2 hrs wkly. Target aud: 18-49; in high school or college in the 60s & 70s. ♦ Dan Sullivan, gen mgr; Doris Garius, gen sls mgr; Scott Thomas, progmg dir; Tom Berryman, news dir.

WDBQ(AM)— Oct 30, 1933: 1490 khz; 1 kw-U. TL: N42 30 10 W90 42 24. Stereo. Box 1280 52004. Secondary address: 5490 Saratoga Rd. 52002. Phone: (563) 557-1040. Fax: (563) 583-4535. Web Site: www.cumulus.com. Licensee: Cumulus Licensing Corp. Group owner: Cumulus Media Inc. (acq 12-17-98; grpsl). Network: ABC Daytime Direction. C. Reynolds. Format: News, talk, sports. ♦ Jack Kilcoyne, progmg dir & news dir.

KLYV(FM)—Co-owned with WDBQ(AM). Sept 1, 1965: 105.3 mhz; 50 kw. 330 ft. TL: N42 30 10 W90 42 11. Stereo. Web Site: www.cumulus.com. Format: CHR. Target aud: 18-49. ♦ Scott Thomas, progmg dir.

Dyersville

KDST(FM)— Aug 25, 1985: 99.3 mhz; 3 kw. 298 ft. TL: N42 25 43 W91 12 50. Stereo. 1931 20th Ave. S.E. 52040. Phone: (563) 875-8193. Fax: (563) 875-6001. E-mail: kdst993@iowatelecom.net. Web Site: www.realcountryonline.com. Licensee: Design Homes Inc. (acq 12-88; $22,079; 12-26-88). Network: ABC. Miller & Miller. Format: Country. News staff: one. Target aud: 45-60. Spec prog: Farm. ♦ Randy Weeks, CEO; Franklin Weeks, pres; Doug Langston, stn mgr & opns mgr.

Eagle Grove

*KJYL(FM)— Feb 20, 1994: 100.7 mhz; 25 kw. 328 ft. TL: N42 40 18 W94 09 11. Box 325, 103 W. Broadway 50533. Phone: (515) 448-4588. Fax: (515) 448-5267. Web Site: www.kjyl.org. Licensee: Minn-Iowa Christian Broadcasting Inc. (group owner). Format: Christian. News staff: one. Target aud: 30-55. ♦ Jay Rudolph, opns mgr.

Eddyville

KKSI(FM)— July 30, 1990: 101.5 mhz; 49 kw. 498 ft. TL: N41 07 57 W92 46 12. Stereo. 416 E. Main St., Ottumwa 52501. Phone: (641) 684-5563. Fax: (641) 684-5832. E-mail: kiss@kissclassicrock.com. Web Site: www.kissclassicrock.com. Licensee: "O"-Town Communications Inc. (acq 12-10-99; $162,400). Miller & Neely, P.C. Format: Classic rock. News staff: one; News: 4 hrs wkly. Target aud: 25-54. ♦ Greg H. List, pres; Bruce Linder, VP; Jeff Downing, opns dir.

Eldon

KRKN(FM)— 1996: 104.3 mhz; 23.5 kw. Ant 341 ft. TL: N40 52 06 W92 18 20. Stereo. 416 E. Main St., Ottumwa 52501. Phone: (641) 684-5563. Fax: (641) 684-5832. E-mail: glist@krknnewcountry.com. Web Site: www.krknnewcountry.com. Licensee: O-Town Communications Inc. (acq 12-10-99; $162,400). Miller & Neely, P.C. Format: New country. News staff: one; News: 4 hrs wkly. Target aud: 18-49; general. ♦ Greg H. List, pres & stn mgr; Bruce Linder, VP; Jeff Downing, opns mgr.

Eldora

KDAO-FM— June 1, 1992: 99.5 mhz; 3 kw. 328 ft. TL: N42 15 49 W93 03 57. Stereo. Box 538, Marshalltown 50158. Secondary address: 1930 N. Center St., Marshalltown 50158. Phone: (641) 752-4122. Fax: (641) 752-5121. Licensee: Eldora Broadcasting Co. Inc. (acq 12-18-91; $15,000 for CP; 1-13-92). Network: ABC. Format: Adult contemp. Target aud: 25-54. ♦ Mark Osmundson, gen mgr.

Elkader

KADR(AM)— May 15, 1983: 1400 khz; 1 kw-U. TL: N42 50 57 W91 24 43. Box 990 52043. Phone: (563) 245-1400. Fax: (563) 245-1402. Web Site: www.hitsandfavorites.com. Licensee: KADR-AM 14, div of Design Homes Inc. (acq 3-20-85). Rep: Farmakis. Format: Adult contemp. ♦ Dan Berns, gen mgr; Troy Thein, chief of opns.

KCTN(FM)—See Garnavillo

Emmetsburg

KDWD(FM)— Jan 10, 1977: 100.1 mhz; 16 kw. 300 ft. TL: N43 01 20 W94 41 59. Stereo. 2303 W. 18th St., Spencer 51301. Phone: (712) 264-1074. Fax: (712) 264-1077. Licensee: Jim Dandy Broadcasting Inc. (acq 12-30-02; $2.5 million. with KKIA(FM) Ida Grove). Network: ABC Daytime Direction. Rep: Farmakis. Format: CHR. News staff: one; News: 11 hrs wkly. Target aud: 25 plus. Spec prog: Farm 10 hrs, auto racing one hr wkly. ♦ Mike Puetz, gen mgr.

Epworth

KGRR(FM)— Dec 10, 1994: 97.3 mhz; 19 kw. 380 ft. TL: N42 26 13 W90 50 43. Box 659, Dubuque 52004. Secondary address: 346 W. 8th St., Dubuque 52004. Phone: (563) 690-0800. Fax: (563) 588-5688. E-mail: kgrr@kgrr.com. Web Site: www.kgrr.com. Licensee: Radio Dubuque Inc. (group owner; acq 7-1-00; $1.5 million). Rep: Katz Radio. Format: Classic hits, classic rock. News staff: one; News: 2 hrs wkly. Target aud: 25-54; families. ♦ Don Rabbitt, CEO; Paul Hemmer, VP; Thomas Parsley, pres, gen mgr & progmg dir.

Estherville

KILR(AM)— Dec 23, 1967: 1070 khz; 250 w-D, 48 w-N, DA-2. TL: N43 25 45 W94 49 23. Box 453, 3875 150th St. 51334. Secondary

Iowa

address: 3875 150th St. 51334. Phone: (712) 362-2644. Fax: (712) 362-5951. E-mail: ubcbroadcast@netins.net. Licensee: Jacobson Broadcasting Co. Inc. (acq 7-1-82; $610,000 with co-located FM; 7-5-82). Network: ABC. Rep: Farmakis. Lauren A. Colby. Format: News/talk. News staff: one; News: 24 hrs wkly. Target aud: 29-65; loc baby boomers. Spec prog: Farm 9 hrs, relg 11 hrs wkly. ♦ Barbara J. Jacobson, CFO; Peggy Zahrt, opns mgr; Ed Funston, news dir; Roger J. Jacobson, pres, gen mgr, gen sls mgr, prom dir, progmg dir & chief of engrg.

KILR-FM— Oct 17, 1969: 95.9 mhz; 20 kw. Ant 325 ft. TL: N43 25 45 W94 49 23. Stereo. 3875 150th St. 51334. E-mail: kilrprod@netins.net. Rep: Salem. Format: Country, sports. Target aud: 25-54.

Fairfield

*KHOE(FM)— 1994: 90.5 mhz; 100 w. 98 ft. TL: N41 00 59 W91 58 09. Stereo. Box 1017, 1000 N. 4th St. 52557. Phone: (641) 469-5463. E-mail: khoe@mum.edu. Licensee: Fairfield Educational Radio Station. Format: World music, class, educ. News: 2 hrs wkly. Target aud: 18-35; University audience, College. Spec prog: Children 3 hrs, Folk 6 hrs, Gospel 3 hrs, Jazz 2 hrs, Spanish 2 hrs wkly. ♦ Bill Goldstein, CEO; Jeffrey Hedquist, pres; Stan Stansberry, gen mgr.

KIIK-FM— Listing follows KMCD(AM).

KMCD(AM)— Mar 3, 1958: 1570 khz; 250 w-D, 108 w-N. TL: N41 00 25 W92 00 50. Box 648, 57 S. Court St. 52556. Phone: (641) 472-4191. Fax: (641) 472-2071. E-mail: jay.mitchell@radiovillage.com. Web Site: www.radiovillage.com. Licensee: Fairfield Media Group Inc. (group owner; acq 2-28-94; $200,000. with co-located FM; FTR: 5-2-94). Network: ABC Information & Entertainment. Format: News/talk. News staff: 2; News: 22 hrs wkly. Target aud: 30 plus; community leaders & Jefferson County. Spec prog: Farm 10 hrs wkly. ♦ Jay Mitchell, pres & gen mgr; Scott Krause, gen sls mgr; Steve Smith, progmg dir.

KIIK-FM— Co-owned with KMCD(AM). 1977: 95.9 mhz; 6 kw. 400 ft. TL: N40 58 47 W92 05 45. (CP: 4.1 kw). Stereo. Web Site: www.radiovillage.com. Network: ABC. Format: Adult contemp. News staff: one; News: 12 hrs wkly. Target aud: 25-54.

Forest City

KIOW(FM)— Nov 8, 1978: 107.3 mhz; 25 kw. 328 ft. TL: N43 17 02 W93 37 50. Stereo. Box 308 50436. Secondary address: 18643 360th St. 50436. Phone: (641) 585-1073. Fax: (641) 585-2990. E-mail: kiow@kiow.com. Web Site: www.kiow.com. Licensee: Pilot Knob Broadcasting Inc. Network: CNN Radio. Rep: Farmakis. Format: Country, adult contemp, news. News staff: one; News: 15 hrs wkly. Target aud: General; Adults 25 +. Spec prog: Farm 15 hrs, contemp hits 19 hrs wkly. ♦ Susan I. Coloff, CFO; Tony Coloff, pres & gen mgr.

Fort Dodge

*KEGR(FM)— 2005: 89.5 mhz; 17 kw vert. Ant 364 ft. TL: N42 40 18 W94 09 11. Box 286, Shenandoah 51601. Phone: (712) 246-5151. Fax: (712) 246-5152. E-mail: kyfr@familyradio.org. Web Site: www.shenessex.heartland.net/kyfr. Licensee: Family Stations Inc. (group owner). Network: Family Radio. Format: Relg. ♦ Mike DeStefano, stn mgr.

*KICB(FM)— September 1971: 88.1 mhz; 200 w. 130 ft. TL: N42 29 27 W94 12 01. Stereo. 330 Ave. M 50501. Phone: (515) 576-6049. Fax: (515) 576-5656. Licensee: Iowa Central Community College. Format: Alternative. Target aud: 13-34; young men & women with progsv tastes. ♦ Robert Paxton, pres; Amy Simpson, gen mgr; Chris Tasler, mus dir; Mark Lumsden, chief of engrg.

KKEZ(FM)— Listing follows KWMT(AM).

*KTPR(FM)— Sept 15, 1980: 91.1 mhz; 100 kw. Ant 1,052 ft. TL: N42 49 03 W94 24 41. Stereo. WOI Radio Group, 2022 Communications Bldg., Ames 50011-3241. Phone: (515) 294-2025. E-mail: woi@iastate.edu. Web Site: www.woi.org. Licensee: Iowa State University of Science and Technology. Network: NPR. Format: Class, jazz, news. News staff: 2; News: 41 hrs wkly. Target aud: General; educated, affluent. Spec prog: Black 4 hrs, new age 10 hrs wkly. ♦ William McGinley, gen mgr; Don Wirth, opns mgr & dev dir; Dave Becker, progmg dir.

KUEL(FM)— Listing follows KVFD(AM).

KVFD(AM)— Dec 24, 1939: 1400 khz; 1 kw-U. TL: N42 28 44 W94 12 10. Box Y, 200 N. 10th St. 50501. Phone: (515) 955-1400. Fax: (515) 955-5844. Licensee: Three Eagles of Joliet Inc. Group owner: Three Eagles Communications (acq 6-18-2004; grpsl). Network: ABC. Format: Sports, news, oldies. ♦ Gary Buchanan, pres; Dennis Martin, gen mgr; Jay Alexander, opns mgr; Mike Laughter, engrg VP.

KUEL(FM)— Co-owned with KVFD(AM). July 28, 1975: 92.1 mhz; 3 kw. 300 ft. TL: N42 28 44 W94 12 10. (CP: Ant 321 ft.). Stereo. Phone: (515) 955-5656. Format: Adult contemp. ♦ Rolland C. Johnson, chmn; Jay Alexander, progmg dir; Mike Laughter, engrg dir.

KWMT(AM)— April 1956: 540 khz; 5 kw-D, 200 w-N, DA-2. TL: N42 22 94 W94 12 27. Box 508 50501. Secondary address: 540 A St. 50501. Phone: (515) 576-7333. Fax: (515) 955-4250. Web Site: www.kwmt.com. Licensee: Clear Channel Broadcasting License Inc. Group owner: Clear Channel Communications Inc. (acq 7-19-99; $7.5 million. with co-located FM). Rep: McGavren Guild. Reddy, Begley & McCormick. Format: Country. Target aud: General. Spec prog: Farm. ♦ Ron Revere, gen mgr; Lindy Kaye, progmg dir; Jerry Sheeder, news dir; Barry Walsh, chief of engrg.

KKEZ(FM)— Co-owned with KWMT(AM). 1966: 94.5 mhz; 100 kw. 640 ft. TL: N42 29 43 W94 12 33. Stereo. E-mail: kkez@clearchannel.com. Web Site: www.kkez.com. Format: Rock. News staff: 3; News: 5 hrs wkly. Target aud: 18-49. ♦ Linda Kaye, mus dir.

Fort Madison

KBKB(AM)— Feb 6, 1948: 1360 khz; 1 kw-D, 35 w-N. TL: N40 39 30 W91 16 20. Box 70, Burlington 52601. Secondary address: 2060 Hwy. 61, Burlington 52601. Phone: (319) 372-5252. Fax: (319) 752-5287. Web Site: www.1360kbkb.com. Licensee: Citicasters Licenses L.P. Group owner: Clear Channel Communications Inc. (acq 5-4-99; grpsl). Network: ABC. Rep: Farmakis. Fisher, Wayland, Cooper, Leader & Zaragoza L.L.P. Format: News/talk. News staff: 2; News: 30 hrs wkly. Target aud: 30-55. ♦ Steve Staebell, gen mgr; Steve Hexom, progmg dir; J.K. Martin, news dir; Brad Bostrom, chief of engrg.

KBKB-FM— June 1, 1973: 101.7 mhz; 50 kw. 466 ft. TL: N40 43 25 W91 13 49. Stereo. Web Site: www.1017thebull.com. Network: ABC. Format: Country. News staff: 2; News: 7 hrs wkly. ♦ Kosmo Leone, progmg dir.

Garnavillo

KCTN(FM)— Dec 6, 1982: 100.1 mhz; 3 kw. 300 ft. TL: N42 53 06 W91 19 11. Stereo. Box 990, Elkader 52043. Phone: (563) 245-1400. Fax: (563) 245-1402. E-mail: kctn@alpinecom.net. Web site: www.kctn.com. Licensee: KCTN-FM 100 div of Design Homes Inc. Rep: Farmakis. Format: Country. News staff: one. Target aud: 24-55; farmers & rural communities. Spec prog: Farm. ♦ Randy Weeks, CEO; Dan Berns, gen mgr & opns mgr; Troy Thein, chief of opns.

Glenwood

KXKT(FM)— Apr 8, 1966: 103.7 mhz; 100 kw horiz, 82 kw vert. 1,014 ft. TL: N41 18 40 W96 01 37. Stereo. 5010 Underwood Ave., Omaha, NE 68132. Phone: (402) 561-2000. Fax: (402) 556-8937. E-mail: request@thekat.com. Web site: www.thekat.com. Licensee: Capstar TX L.P. Group owner: Clear Channel Communications Inc. (acq 8-30-00; grpsl). Haley, Bader & Potts. Format: Country. News staff: one. Target aud: 18-54; general. ♦ Donna Baker, gen mgr; Mitch Baker, opns mgr.

Grinnell

KGRN(AM)— Nov 15, 1957: 1410 khz; 500 w-D, 47 w-N. TL: N41 44 44 W92 42 36. (CP: 300 w-D, 33 w-N. TL: N41 46 35 W92 38 56). Box 660 50112. Phone: (641) 236-6106. Fax: (641) 236-8896. E-mail: kgm@iowatelecom.net. Web Site: www.kgm1410.com. Licensee: Crawford Broadcasting Co. (acq 12-5-97; $560,000 for stock). Rep: Farmakis. Format: Adult Contemp. Spec prog: Farm 12 hrs, C&W 12 hrs wkly. ♦ Russ Crawford, pres & gen mgr.

KRTI(FM)— May 1993: 106.7 mhz; 50 kw. 492 ft. TL: N41 48 16 W92 40 09. Box 306 50112. Secondary address: 1801 N. 13th Ave. E., Newton 50208. Phone: (641) 792-5262. Fax: (641) 792-8403. Web Site: www.energy1067.com. Licensee: Central Iowa Broadcasting Inc. (acq 12-6-93; $350,000; 1-3-94). Format: CHR mainstream. ♦ Frank Liebl, gen mgr; Tim Graves, opns dir.

Grundy Center

KCRR(FM)— Oct 8, 1983: 97.7 mhz; 16 kw. 407 ft. TL: N42 23 28 W92 13 57. Stereo. 501 Sycamore St., Suite 300 Black's Bldg., Waterloo 50703. Phone: (319) 833-4800. Fax: (319) 833-4866. Licensee: Cumulus Licensing Corp. Group owner: Cumulus Media Inc. (acq 3-15-00; grpsl). Format: Classic rock. News staff: 2; News: 3 hrs wkly. Target aud: 25-54. ♦ Lew Dickey, CEO; William Hathaway, gen mgr; Dick Stadlen, opns mgr.

Hampton

KLMJ(FM)— May 16, 1983: 104.9 mhz; 6 kw. 255 ft. TL: N42 49 45 W93 11 10. Stereo. Box 495, 1509 Fourth St. N.E. 50441. Phone: (641) 456-5656. Fax: (641) 456-5655. E-mail: klmj@klmj.com. Web Site: www.klmj.com. Licensee: C.D. Broadcasting Inc. (acq 10-93; $60,000; 10-11-93). Network: ABC Daytime Direction. Rep: Farmakis. Fletcher, Heald & Hildreth, P.L.C. Format: Adult contemp,country, oldies. News staff: 2; News: 14 hrs wkly. Target aud: 25 plus; general. Spec prog: Iowa State & Univ. of Northern Iowa, farm 8 hrs wkly. ♦ Craig Donnelly, gen mgr; Marlin Burrier, opns dir.

Harlan

KNOD(FM)— Nov 12, 1979: 105.3 mhz; 25 kw. 300 ft. TL: N41 37 00 W95 16 10. Stereo. Box 723 51537. Phone: (712) 755-3883. Fax: (712) 755-7511. E-mail: knodnews@harlannet.com. Web Site: knodfm.com. Licensee: Wireless Broadcasting L.L.C. (acq 5-23-02). Network: ABC Daytime Direction. Format: Oldies. News staff: one; News: 5 hrs wkly. Target aud: 25-50. Spec prog: Farm 3 hrs, relg 2 hrs wkly. ♦ Judy Storm, gen mgr & gen sls mgr; Richard Keane, chief of opns; Jason Dinesen, news dir.

Hiawatha

*KWOF-FM— 2002: 89.1 mhz; 400 w vert. Ant 400 ft. TL: N42 03 13 W91 44 35. 3232 Osage Rd., Waterloo 50703. Phone: (319) 378-8600. Phone: (319) 236-5700. Fax: (319) 236-8777. E-mail: studio@891thespirit.com. Web Site: www.891thespirit.com. Licensee: Friendship Communications Inc. Format: Christian hit radio. ♦ Michael James, stn mgr.

Hudson

KCVM(FM)— Aug 27, 1997: 96.1 mhz; 6 kw. 312 ft. TL: N42 23 33 W92 30 44. Stereo. Box 248, 721 Shirley St., Cedar Falls 50613. Phone: (319) 277-1918. Phone: (319) 266-6499. Fax: (319) 277-5202. E-mail: themix@mix96.net. Web site: www.mix96.net. Licensee: Fife Communications Co. L.C. Format: Adult contemp. News staff: one; News: 2 hrs wkly. Target aud: 25-54; eastern Iowa adult females. ♦ Jim Coloff, pres, gen mgr, opns VP & opns mgr; Tony Coloff, VP.

Humboldt

KHBT(FM)— Aug 5, 1970: 97.7 mhz; 5.8 kw. 275 ft. TL: N42 43 57 W94 12 23. Stereo. Box 217 50548. Secondary address: 2196 Montana Ave. 50548. Phone: (515) 332-4100. Fax: (515) 332-2723. E-mail: thebolt@waittradio.com. Licensee: WMMP LLC. (group owner; acq 6-1-2000; $500,000). Pepper & Corazzini. Format: Adult contemp. News staff: one; News: 30 hrs wkly. Target aud: 30-65; general. Spec prog: Farm 10 hrs wkly. ♦ Bob Ketchum, gen mgr.

Ida Grove

KKIA(FM)— September 1981: 92.9 mhz; 25 kw. 328 ft. TL: N42 29 23 W95 17 40. Stereo. Box 108, 606 1/2 Lake Ave., Storm Lake 50588. Phone: (712) 732-3520. Fax: (712) 732-1746. E-mail: themoose@waittradio.com. Licensee: Jim Dandy Broadcasting Inc. (acq 12-30-02; $2.5 million. with KDWD(FM) Emmetsburg). Rep: Farmakis. Format: Hot country. News staff: one; News: 5 hrs wkly. Target aud: 18-54. Spec prog: Farm 10 hrs wkly. ♦ Buzz Paterson, stn mgr; Matt Fisher, prom mgr; Brad Stensgaard, progmg dir.

Independence

KQMG(AM)— Dec 10, 1959: 1220 khz; 250 w-D, 166 w-N. TL: N42 28 34 W91 52 31. 1812 Third Ave. S.E. 50644. Phone: (319) 334-3300. Fax: (319) 334-6158. E-mail: lite953@indyte.com. Web Site: www.lite953.com. Licensee: KM Radio of Independence L.L.C. Group owner: KM Communications Inc. (acq 10-9-03; $500,000. with co-located FM). Network: ABC. Format: Adult contemp. ♦ Noel Showers, mus dir; Rick Peters, chief of engrg.

KQMG-FM— Jan 1, 1972: 95.3 mhz; 2.9 kw. 410 ft. TL: N42 28 34 W91 52 31. Stereo. ♦Noel Showers, progmg dir.

Indianola

KSTM(FM)— Apr 15, 1994: 88.9 mhz; 100 w. 124 ft. TL: N41 22 00 W93 33 57. Simpson College, 701 N. C St. 50125. Phone: (515) 961-1747. Phone: (515) 961-1803. Fax: (515) 961-1674. E-mail: KSTM@storm.simpson.edu. Licensee: Simpson College. Format: Alt. ♦Rich Ramos, gen mgr.

KXLQ(AM)— July 22, 1963: . Stn currently dark 1490 khz; 500 w-D, 1 kw-N. TL: N41 21 24 W93 35 16. Box 228, Pella 50219. Phone: (515) 263-1490. Fax: (515) 263-1500. Licensee: KXLQ Insight Sports LLC (acq 1-24-2005; $360,000). Format: Sports. Target aud: 18-48; male. ♦Bob Dyer, gen mgr.

Iowa City

KCJJ(AM)— Oct 14, 1998: 1630 khz; 10 kw-D, 1 kw-N. TL: N41 36 03 W91 30 04. Stereo. Box 2118 52244-2118. Phone: (319) 354-1242. Fax: (319) 354-1921. E-mail: kcjjam@aol.com. Web Site: www.1630kcjj.com. Licensee: River City Radio Inc. (acq 9-1-94; $650,000). Network: Network: ABC, CBS. Format: Hot talk, hot hits. News staff: 4. Target aud: 25-54. ♦Tom Suter, gen mgr.

KKRQ(FM)—Listing follows KXIC(AM).

KRNA(FM)— Oct 4, 1974: 94.1 mhz; 100 kw. 981 ft. TL: N41 45 00 W91 50 16. Stereo. 4th Floor, 425 2nd St. S.E, Cedar Rapids 52401-1819. Phone: (319) 365-9431. Fax: (319) 363-8062. Web Site: www.krna.com. Licensee: Cumulus Licensing Corp. Group owner: Cumulus Media Inc. (acq 2000; grpsl). Rep: D & R Radio. Dow, Lohnes & Albertson. Format: Classic Rock. News staff: 2; News: 2 hrs wkly. Target aud: 18-49. ♦Jim Worthington, mgr; Dick Stadlen, progmg dir.

KRUI-FM— Mar 28, 1984: 89.7 mhz; 100 w. 90 ft. TL: N41 39 29 W91 32 40. Stereo. 379 Iowa Memorial Union 52242. Phone: (319) 335-9525. Fax: (319) 335-9526. E-mail: krui@uiowa.edu. Web Site: www.uiowa.edu/~krui. Licensee: Student Broadcasters Inc. Format: Div, educ, progsv. News: 7 hrs wkly. Target aud: 18-34; Univ. Spec prog: Black 12 hrs, jazz 3 hrs, blues 3 hrs, reggae 2 hrs, heavy metal 3 hrs, dance 3 hrs, Sp 3 hrs wkly. ♦Jennie Guyan, gen mgr; Bradley Harris, mktg dir; Brian Anstey, prom dir; Valerie Wild, progmg dir; Ben High, mus dir; Bill Penisten, news dir; Aaron Roemig, pub affrs dir; Adam Erickson, chief of engrg.

KSUI(FM)—Listing follows WSUI(AM).

KXIC(AM)— June 7, 1948: 800 khz; 1 kw-D, 199 w-N, DA-2. TL: N41 41 15 W91 32 39. 3365 Dubuque St. N.E. 52240-7970. Phone: (319) 354-9500. Fax: (319) 354-9504. Web Site: www.kxic.com. Licensee: Citicasters Licenses L.P. Group owner: Clear Channel Communications Inc. (acq 5-4-99; grpsl). Network: ABC Information & Entertainment. Format: News & info. ♦John Laton, gen mgr; Roy Justis, news dir.

KKRQ(FM)—Co-owned with KXIC(AM). May 1, 1966: 100.7 mhz; 100 kw. 981 ft. TL: N41 45 26 W91 31 31. Stereo. Web Site: www.thesox.com. Format: Classic rock.

WSUI(AM)— 1919: 910 khz; 5 kw-U, DA-N. TL: N41 39 45 W91 34 30. 710 S. Clinton St. Bldg., Univ. of Iowa 52242-1030. Phone: (319) 335-5730. Fax: (319) 335-6116. E-mail: wsui@uiowa.edu. Web Site: wsui.uiowa.edu. Licensee: The University of Iowa. Network: NPR. Format: News/talk. ♦John Monick, gen mgr; Dennis Reese, progmg dir; Jim Davis, chief of engrg.

KSUI(FM)—Co-owned with WSUI(AM). 1948: 91.7 mhz; 100 kw. 1,292 ft. TL: N41 43 15 W91 20 30. Web Site: ksui.uiowa.edu. Format: Fine arts, class. ♦Joan Kjaer, progmg dir; Jim Davies, engrg dir.

Iowa Falls

KIFG(AM)— July 22, 1962: 1510 khz; 1 kw-D, 500 w-CH. TL: N42 30 49 W93 12 57. 406 Stevens St. 50126. Phone: (641) 648-4281. Phone: (641) 648-4282. Fax: (641) 648-4606. E-mail: kifg@iafalls.com. Licensee: Times-Citizen Communications Inc. (acq 9-99; $320,000. with co-located FM). Network: Network: CNN Radio, Westwood One. Rep: Keystone (unwired net). Reddy, Begley & McCormick. Format: Adult contemp. News staff: one. Target aud: 25 plus. Spec prog: Farm 5 hrs wkly. ♦T.J. Norman, gen mgr & progmg dir.

KIFG-FM— Oct 1, 1965: 95.3 mhz; 6 kw. 194 ft. TL: N42 30 49 W93 12 57. Stereo. Web Site: www.kifgradio.com. Format: Sports, news, weather. News staff: one. ♦Ann Denholm, prom dir & prom mgr.

Jefferson

KGRA(FM)— Oct 1, 1981: 98.9 mhz; 11 kw. 499 ft. TL: N42 00 59 W94 22 26. Stereo. 116 E. State 50129. Phone: (515) 386-2222. Fax: (515) 386-2215. E-mail: kg98@netins.net. Web Site: www.realcountryonline.com. Licensee: Coon Valley Communications. (acq 1-19-94; 3-28-94). Network: ABC. Format: Country. News staff: one; News: 9 hrs wkly. Target aud: 35 plus; rural farm community, middle class adults. Spec prog: Farm 2 hrs, sports 3 hrs wkly. ♦Patrick Delaney, pres, CFO, sls dir & chief of engrg; Sue Thomsen, gen mgr & stn mgr.

Keokuk

KMDY(FM)— 2001: 90.9 mhz; 30 w. Ant 321 ft. TL: N40 23 56 W91 26 03. (CP: 940 w). Box 124 52632-0124. Phone: (319) 526-7007. Fax: (319) 526-7008. Licensee: The Moody Bible Institute of Chicago. (group owner) Format: Christian. ♦Michael Easley, pres; Robert Neff, VP; Dale Thomas, stn mgr.

KOKX(AM)— Oct 19, 1947: 1310 khz; 1 kw-D, 500 w-N, DA-N. TL: N40 22 50 W91 21 09. Box 427, 108 Washington St. 52632. Phone: (319) 524-5410. Fax: (319) 524-7275. E-mail: gmfolluo@interlinet. Licensee: Withers Broadcasting of Iowa. Group owner: Withers Broadcasting Co. (acq 7-15-81; $900,000 with co-located FM; 7-13-81). Format: Adult standards, news/talk, sports. News staff: 2; News: 25 hrs wkly. Target aud: 25-54. Spec prog: Farm 6 hrs wkly. ♦W. Russell Withers Jr., pres; Gary M. Folluo, gen mgr, opns mgr & adv mgr; Greg Ikerd, progmg dir.

KOKX-FM— Jan 30, 1973: 95.3 mhz; 100 kw. Ant 804 ft. TL: N40 24 01 W91 35 09. Stereo. 108 Washington St., Box108 52632. Network: ABC. Format: Var/div. News staff: 2; News: 4 hrs wkly. Target aud: 25-54; women 50% Men 50%. ♦Jim Worrell, news dir.

KRNQ(FM)— 1999: 96.3 mhz; 19 kw. Ant 804 ft. TL: N40 24 01 W91 35 09. 108 Washington St. 52632. Phone: (319) 524-1111. Fax: (319) 524-7275. Licensee: David M. Lister. Format: Classic rock. ♦Gary M. Folluo, gen mgr.

Knoxville

KNIA(AM)— Aug 30, 1960: 1320 khz; 500 w-D, 222 w-N. TL: N41 19 40 W93 06 34. Box 31 50138. Secondary address: 1610 N. Lincoln 50138. Phone: (641) 842-3161. Fax: (641) 842-5606. E-mail: kniaakrls@kniakrls.com. Web Site: www.kniakrls.com. Licensee: M & H Broadcasting Inc. (acq 2-23-93; $768,000 with co-located FM; 3-15-93). Network: ABC Music Radio. Format: Real country. News staff: 3; News: 25 hrs wkly. Target aud: 25-54; female. Spec prog: Relg 18 hrs wkly. ♦Jim Butler, gen mgr.

Lake City

KIKD(FM)— 1997: 106.7 mhz; 25 kw. 328 ft. TL: N42 07 14 W94 48 49. Box 886, Carroll 51401-0886. Secondary address: 1119 East Plaza Dr., Carroll 51401. Phone: (712) 792-4321. Fax: (712) 792-6667. E-mail: kikd@carrollbroadcasting.com. Licensee: Carroll Broadcasting Co. (group owner; acq 1999; $975,000). Format: Country. Target aud:

18-49; contemporary country with strong families. Spec prog: Sports. ♦Mary Collison, pres; Kim Hackett, gen mgr.

Lamoni

KOWI(FM)— 2000: 97.9 mhz; 50 kw. Ant 492 ft. TL: N40 48 52 W93 50 15. WOI Radio Group, 2022 Communications Bldg., Iowa State University, Ames 50011-3241. Phone: (515) 294-2025. Fax: (515) 294-1544. E-mail: woi@iastate.edu. Web Site: www.woi.org. Licensee: Iowa State University of Science and Technology (acq 7-30-2004; $450,000). Format: Class, news. ♦William A. McGinley, gen mgr; Don Wirth, dev dir.

Le Mars

KKMA(FM)—Listing follows KLEM.

KLEM(AM)— Oct 12, 1954: 1410 khz; 1 kw-D, 63 w-N. TL: N42 49 05 W96 10 00. 37 2nd Ave. N.W. 51031. Phone: (712) 546-4121. Fax: (712) 546-9672. E-mail: daveg@lemarscomm.net. Web Site: www.klem1410.com. Licensee: Powell Broadcasting Co Inc. (acq 7-6-99; w/kkma-fm). Format: Adult contemp, news, sports. News staff: 2. Spec prog: Farm 18 hrs wkly. ♦Tom Spies, pres; Dennis Bullock, gen mgr; Dave Grosenheider, stn mgr & gen sls mgr; Dave Ruden, progmg dir; Larry Schmitz, news dir; Stan Culley, chief of engrg.

Madrid

KNWM(FM)— Aug. 21, 1997: 96.1 mhz; 2.5 kw. Ant 515 ft. TL: N41 58 49 W93 44 23. 3737 Woodland Ave., Suite 111, Des Moines 50366. Phone: (515) 327-1071. Fax: (515) 327-1073. Licensee: Northwestern College. Group owner: Northwestern College & Radio (acq 12-30-2003; $1.8 million. with KNWI(FM) Osceola). Format: Christian. ♦Richard Whitworth, gen mgr.

Manchester

KMCH(FM)— Dec 5, 1991: 94.7 mhz; 6 kw. 328 ft. TL: N42 31 42 W91 22 53. Stereo. Box 497, 212 E. Main St. 52057. Phone: (563) 927-6249. Fax: (563) 927-4372. E-mail: kmchradio@iowatelecom.net. Web Site: www.kmch.com. Licensee: Fife Communication Co. L.C. Network: CBS. Format: Adult contemp, C&W. News staff: one; News: 20 hrs wkly. Target aud: 25-64; northeast Iowa adults & farm population. Spec prog: Farm 7 hrs, sports 7 hrs, relg 4 hrs wkly. ♦Anthony G. Coloff, pres; James A. Coloff, VP & gen mgr; Jackie Coates, stn mgr & opns mgr.

Maquoketa

KMAQ(AM)— Aug 26, 1958: 1320 khz; 500 w-U. TL: N42 05 26 W90 37 43. Box 940, 129 N. Main St. 52060. Phone: (563) 652-2426. Fax: (563) 652-6210. Licensee: Maquoketa Broadcasting Co. (acq 1965). Network: USA. Rep: Farmakis. Miller & Fields, P.C. Format: C&W. News staff: one; News: 28 hrs wkly. Target aud: General; adults, high percentage of farmers. Spec prog: Farm 10 hrs, polka 3 hrs wkly. ♦Dennis W. Voy, pres, gen mgr & progmg dir; Leighton Hepker, opns dir & sls dir; Tom Messerli, chief of engrg.

KMAQ-FM— Sept 1, 1967: 95.1 mhz; 6 kw. 328 ft. TL: N42 05 26 W90 37 43. Stereo. News staff: one; News: 28 hrs wkly. ♦Leighton Hepker, adv dir.

Marshalltown

KDAO(AM)— Dec 16, 1978: 1190 khz; 250 w-D. TL: N42 04 17 W92 55 19. 1930 N. Center St. 50158. Phone: (641) 752-4122. Fax: (641) 752-5121. Web Site: www.kdao.com. Licensee: MTN Broadcasting Inc. Format: Adult standards. Target aud: 25-54. ♦Mark K. Osmundson, gen mgr. Co-owned TV: KDAO-TV affil

KFJB(AM)— June 1923: 1230 khz; 1 kw-U. TL: N42 04 01 W92 58 10. Box 698, 123 W. Main St. 50158. Phone: (641) 753-3361. Fax: (641) 752-7201. E-mail: office@marshalltownbroadcasting.com. Web

Iowa

Site: www.1230kfjb.com. Licensee: Marshalltown Broadcasting Inc. (acq 12-29-86). Network: ABC Information & Entertainment. Rep: Katz Radio. Format: News/talk. News staff: 2; News: 12 hrs wkly. Target aud: 25-54. ◆David L. Nelson, pres; Clark L. Wideman, gen mgr.

KXIA(FM)—Co-owned with KFJB(AM). January 1968: 101.1 mhz; 100 kw. 649 ft. TL: N42 00 19 W92 55 45. Stereo. Web Site: www.kixweb.com. Format: Country. News staff: 2; News: 6 hrs wkly.

Mason City

*KBDC(FM)— 2001: 88.5 mhz; 1.8 kw vert. Ant 230 ft. TL: N43 03 35 W93 22 47. Box 3206, American Family Radio, Tupelo, MS 38803. Phone: (662) 844-8888, EXT. 204. Fax: (662) 842-6791. Licensee: American Family Association. Group owner: American Family Radio Format: Adult contemp. ◆Marvin Sanders, gen mgr.

*KCMR(FM)— May 3, 1979: 97.9 mhz; 6 kw. 300 ft. TL: N43 07 18 W93 11 32. (CP: Ant 315 ft.). Stereo. Box 979 50402-0979. Secondary address: 600 First St. N.W. 50401. Phone: (641) 424-9300. Fax: (641) 423-2221. Licensee: TLC Broadcasting Corp. (acq 5-24-2004). Format: Easy lstng, inspirational. Target aud: Over 30. Spec prog: Class 5 hrs, nostalgia 10 hrs wkly. ◆Bill Schickel, gen mgr; Bob Miller, dev dir.

KGLO(AM)— Jan 17, 1937: 1300 khz; 5 kw-U, DA-2. TL: N43 03 15 W93 12 17. Box 1300, 341 Yorktown Pike 50401. Phone: (641) 423-1300. Fax: (641) 423-2906. Web Site: www.rivercitysquare.com. Licensee: Clear Channel Broadcasting Licenses Inc. Group owner: Clear Channel Communications Inc. (acq 9-25-00; grpsl). Network: CBS. Format: Talk. News staff: 3. Target aud: 25-35; adults. Spec prog: Farm 15 hrs wkly. ◆Charlie Thomas, gen mgr; Tim Fleming, stn mgr; Tim Fleming, opns dir & progmg dir; Hall Hofman, gen sls mgr; Andy Roat, natl sls mgr; Tami Ramon, mktg dir; Jamie Larson, prom dir; Tim Renshaw, news dir; Greg Gade, chief of engrg.

KIAI(FM)—Co-owned with KGLO(AM). November 1985: 93.9 mhz; 100 kw. Ant 790 ft. TL: N43 10 04 W93 06 05. Stereo. E-mail: jbrooks@clearchannel.com. Web Site: kiaifm.com. Format: Country. News: 2 hrs wkly. Target aud: 24-54. ◆J. Brooks, progmg dir.

KLSS-FM—Listing follows KRIB.

KRIB(AM)— April 1948: 1490 khz; 1 kw-U. TL: N43 08 05 W93 12 30. Stereo. 402 19th St. S.W. 50401. Phone: (641) 423-8634. Fax: (641) 423-8206. E-mail: krib@kribradio.com. Web Site: www.kribradio.com. Licensee: Three Eagles of Mason City Inc. Group owner: Three Eagles Communications (acq 5-2-97; $3.596 million with co-located FM). Network: ABC Information & Entertainment. Rep: McGavren Guild. Format: Adult standards, oldies. News staff: 2; News: 25 hrs wkly. Target aud: 35 plus; married up-scale adults, financially secure with two incomes or retired. Spec prog: Relg 5 hrs wkly. ◆Gary Buchanan, pres; Dalena Barz, gen mgr & natl sls mgr; John Swinton, progmg dir; Bob Fisher, news dir; Christi Lyman, pub affrs dir; Ron Schacts, chief of engrg.

KLSS-FM—Co-owned with KRIB. Nov 1, 1967: 106.1 mhz; 100 kw. 315 ft. TL: N43 08 31 W93 06 40. Stereo. E-mail: klss@klssradio.com. Web Site: www.klssradio.com. Network: ABC. Format: Adult contemp. Target aud: 18-54. ◆John Swinton, opns mgr; Pam Dzick, gen sls mgr; Harry O'Neil, mus dir.

*KRNI(AM)— Mar 1, 1948: 1010 khz; 1 kw-D, 16 w-N. TL: N43 08 31 W93 06 40. c/o KUNI-FM, Univ. of Northern Iowa, Cedar Falls 50614-0359. Phone: (319) 273-6400. Fax: (319) 273-2682. E-mail: kuni@uni.edu. Web Site: www.kuniradio.org. Licensee: University of Northern Iowa. (acq 10-30-98; grpsl). Network: PRI, NPR. Format: Div, class, news, progsv. News staff: 3; News: 14 hrs wkly. Target aud: General. Spec prog: Folk 15 hrs, blues 8 hrs wkly. ◆John Hess, gen mgr & dev dir; David Hays, mktg dir; Wayne Jarvis, progmg dir; Al Schares, mus dir; Greg Shanley, news dir; Steve Schoon, engrg dir.

Milford

KUQQ(FM)—Licensed to Milford. See Spirit Lake

Mitchellville

*KDMR(FM)—Not on air, target date: unknown: 88.9 mhz; 1 kw. Ant 236 ft. TL: N41 40 05 W93 19 43. University of Northern Iowa, 324 Communications Arts Center, Cedar Falls 50614. Phone: (319) 273-6400. Fax: (319) 273-2682. Licensee: University of Northern Iowa. ◆John Hess, gen mgr.

Mount Pleasant

KILJ(AM)— December 1974: 1130 khz; 250 w-D. TL: N40 57 32 W91 35 01. 2411 Radio Dr. 52641. Phone: (319) 385-8728. Fax: (319) 385-4517. Web Site: www.inter.net/~kiljamfm.com. Licensee: KILJ Inc. (acq 10-29-2003; $1.01 million. with co-located FM). Network: ABC Daytime Direction. Format: Oldies. ◆John R. Kuhens, gen mgr, stn mgr, sls dir & progmg dir; Bob Maltocks, news dir; Leo Septen, chief of engrg.

KILJ-FM— October 1970: 105.5 mhz; 24 kw. 338 ft. TL: N40 56 32 W91 34 08. (CP: 3.3 kw). Stereo. Network: ABC Daytime Direction. Format: Country. Target aud: 25-54.

Mount Vernon

*KRNL-FM— Apr 1, 1948: 89.7 mhz; 36 w. 167 ft. TL: N41 55 24 W91 25 18. Stereo. 810 Commons Cir. 52314. Phone: (319) 895-4431. Phone: (319) 895-5765. E-mail: krnl@cornellcollege.edu. Web Site: www.cornellcollege.edu/krnl. Licensee: Cornell College. Network: USA. Format: Free-form, progsv. Target aud: 18-25; collegians & those seeking an alternative to coml radio. Spec prog: Folk 2 hrs, Ger 2 hrs, jazz 2 hrs, Sp one hr wkly. ◆Aly Johnston, gen mgr; Sarah Altmann, stn mgr.

Muscatine

KBEA-FM—Licensed to Muscatine. See Davenport

KWCC(FM)—Listing follows KWPC(AM).

KWPC(AM)— Jan 5, 1947: 860 khz; 250 w-D, 8 w-N. TL: N41 26 43 W91 04 36. Stereo. 3218 Mulberry Ave. 52761. Phone: (563) 263-2442. Fax: (563) 263-9206. E-mail: mail@voiceofmuscatine.com. Web Site: www.voiceofmuscatine.com. Licensee: WPW Broadcasting Inc. (group owner; (acq 11-5-99; $2.2 million. with co-located FM). Network: USA. Fletcher, Heald & Hildreth. Format: Adult contemp, news/talk. News staff: 2; News: 20 hrs wkly. Target aud: 25-54. ◆Don Davis, pres & mus dir; Terri Forbes, CFO; DeWayne Hopkins, gen mgr.

KWCC(FM)—Co-owned with KWPC(AM). June 16, 1996: 93.1 mhz; 4.4 kw. 384 ft. TL: N41 26 34 W91 04 33. Stereo. Network: Network: USA, AP Radio. Format: Country. News: 6 hrs wkly. Target aud: 25-54.

New Hampton

KCZE(FM)— Dec 1, 1992: 95.1 mhz; 5.5 kw. 328 ft. TL: N43 02 46 W92 18 09. Stereo. 207 N. Main St., Charles City 50616. Phone: (641) 228-1000. Fax: (641) 228-1200. E-mail: kcze@clearchannel.com. Web Site: www.951thebull.com. Licensee: Clear Channel Broadcasting Licenses Inc. Group owner: Clear Channel Communications Inc. (acq 9-25-00; grpsl). Rep: Farmakis. Format: Country. Target aud: General. Spec prog: Farm 12 hrs wkly. ◆Hal Hofman, gen mgr; J. Brooks, opns mgr.

New London

KKNL(FM)— Oct 5, 2001: 97.3 mhz; 3.8 kw. Ant 410 ft. TL: N40 47 53 W91 26 22. Stereo. 2850 Mt. Pleasant St., Burlington 52601. Phone: (319) 752-5402. Fax: (319) 752-4715. E-mail: johnp@burlingtonradio.com. Licensee: Pritchard Broadcasting Co. (acq 12-27-99; $25,000. for CP). Format: Adult contemp. News staff: one; News: 3 hrs wkly. Target aud: 25-54. ◆John T. Pritchard, pres & gen mgr; Kathy Jolly Vance, opns mgr; Chet Young, gen sls mgr.

New Sharon

KCWN(FM)— Oct 16, 1995: 99.9 mhz; 25 kw. 297 ft. Box 999, Pella 50219. Secondary address: 304 Oskaloosa St., Pella 50219. Phone: (641) 628-9999. Phone: (800) 506-4562. Fax: (641) 628-9229. E-mail: kcwnfm@lisco.com. Web Site: www.kcwnfm.org. Licensee: Crown Broadcasting Co. Format: Adult contemp Christian. ◆Marion L. Vink, CEO, pres & gen mgr; Beverly DeVries, stn mgr.

Newton

KCOB(AM)— Sept 15, 1955: 1280 khz; 1 kw-D, 500 w-N. TL: N40 44 11 W93 01 12. Box 66, 1801 N. 13th Ave. E. 50208. Phone: (641) 792-5262. Fax: (641) 792-8403. Web Site: kcobradio.com. Licensee: Central Iowa Broadcasting Inc. Format: Country, news. Target aud: 25-50. Spec prog: Farm 2 hrs wkly. ◆Frank Liebl, CEO, pres, gen mgr & gen sls mgr; Terry Walter, progmg dir; Randy Van, news dir; Phil Benjamin, chief of engrg.

KCOB-FM— Jan 3, 1969: 95.9 mhz; 2.5 kw. 354 ft. TL: N41 44 11 W93 01 12. (CP: 5.1 kw). Stereo. Web Site: kcobradio.com.

*KNNU(FM)—Not on air, target date: unknown: 88.3 mhz; 1.1 kw. Ant 108 ft. TL: N41 40 56 W92 58 40. Broadcasting for the Challenged Inc., 6080 Mt. Moriah Ext., Memphis, TN 38115. Phone: (901) 375-9324. Fax: (901) 375-0041. Licensee: Broadcasting for the Challenged Inc. ◆George Flinn Jr., gen mgr.

Northwood

KYTC(FM)— Oct 15, 1990: 102.7 mhz; 25 kw. 318 ft. TL: N43 29 18 W93 14 12. Stereo. 402 19th St. S.W., Mason City 50401. Phone: (800) 598-2858. Phone: (641) 423-8634. Fax: (641) 423-8206. E-mail: steveg@klssradio.com. Web Site: www.ky102.net. Licensee: Three Eagles of Mason City Inc. Group owner: Three Eagles Communications (acq 5-21-99). Format: Country. News staff: one; News: 6 hrs wkly. Target aud: 25-64; primary audience men and women 35+. Spec prog: Gospel one hr, relg 2 hrs wkly. ◆Rolland Johnson, CEO; Gary Buchanan, pres; Dalena Barz, gen mgr & stn mgr; Henry O'Neil, chief of opns.

Oelwein

KKHQ-FM—Listing follows KOEL(AM).

KOEL(AM)— July 23, 1950: 950 khz; 5 kw-D, 500 w-N, DA-2. TL: N42 39 26 W91 54 02. 2502 S. Frederick 50662. Phone: (319) 283-1234. Fax: (319) 283-3615. Licensee: Cumulus Licensing Corp. Group owner: Cumulus Media Inc. (acq 3-15-00; grpsl). Network: ABC Information & Entertainment. Rep: Allied Radio Partners. Format: News/talk, sports. News staff: 2; News: 30 hrs wkly. Target aud: 35 plus. Spec prog: Farm 16 hrs wkly. ◆Jeffrey D. Warshaw, pres; Jeff Dientz, VP; Rob Murthum, gen mgr & mktg mgr; Dick Stadlen, opns mgr; Craig Friedrich, gen sls mgr; Bob Fisher, natl sls mgr; April Walker, prom mgr; Rich Calvert, progmg dir & progmg mgr; Matt Kelly, mus dir; Roger King, news dir & pub affrs dir; Arnold Zaruba, chief of engrg.

KKHQ-FM—Co-owned with KOEL(AM). Dec 29, 1971: 92.3 mhz; 100 kw. 1,000 ft. TL: N42 40 53 W91 52 52. (CP: 95.3 mhz, ant 991 ft.). Stereo. Box 720, Blacks Bldg., 501 Sycamore St., Waterloo 50703. Phone: (319) 833-4800. Phone: (800) 923-5635. Fax: (319) 833-4866. Rep: Allied Radio Partners. Format: Country. News staff: one; News: 2 hrs wkly. Target aud: 35 plus. ◆Mark Anderson, gen sls mgr; April Walker, prom dir & mus dir; Bill Knight, progmg mgr; Elwin Huffman, news dir; Wes Davis, chief of engrg.

Okoboji

*KOJI(FM)— 2002: 90.7 mhz; 4.5 kw. Ant 371 ft. TL: N43 09 53 W95 19 29. 4647 Stone Ave., Sioux City 51106-1997. Phone: (712) 274-6406. Fax: (712) 274-6411. E-mail: gondekg@witcc.com. Web Site: www.kwit-koji.org. Licensee: Western Iowa Tech Community College. Format: Classical, news/talk, Sp. Spec prog: Triple A 12 hrs, blues 2 hrs, jazz 17 hrs wkly. ◆Gretchen Gondek, gen mgr; Steve Smith, opns mgr.

Onawa

KZSR(FM)— Nov 6, 1995: 102.3 mhz; 100 kw. 643 ft. TL: N42 10 29 W96 23 13. 100 Gold Cir., Dakota Dunes, SD 57049. Phone: (712) 258-5655. Fax: (712) 258-1511. Web Site: www.star1023.com. Licensee: Waitt Radio Inc. Format: Adult contemp. Target aud: 25-54. ◆Jerry Haack, gen mgr.

Osage

KSMA-FM— July 9, 1980: 98.7 mhz; 25 kw. Ant 328 ft. TL: N43 21 53 W93 02 53. Stereo. 341 S. Yorktown Pike, Mason City 50401. Phone: (641) 423-1300. Fax: (641) 423-2906. E-mail: patrickgwin

Stations in the U.S. — Iowa

@clearchannel.com. Web Site: www.kiss987.com. Licensee: Clear Channel Broadcasting Licenses Inc. Group owner: Clear Channel Communications Inc. (acq 9-25-00; grpsl). Rep: Farmakis. Format: Adult contemp, CHR. Target aud: General; 12-25. ♦Charlie Thomas, gen mgr; Tim Fleming, opns dir; Hall Hofman, gen sls mgr; Tami Ramon, mktg dir; Jamie Larson, prom dir; Patrick Gwin, progmg dir; Greg Gade, chief of engrg; Tim Renshaw, chief of engrg.

Osceola

*KNWI(FM)— Oct 4, 1982: 107.1 mhz; 27 kw. Ant 649 ft. TL: N41 01 34 W93 51 43. Stereo. 3737 Woodland Ave., Suite 111, West Des Moines 50266. Phone: (515) 327-1071. Fax: (515) 327-1073. E-mail: knwi@desmoines.fm. Web Site: www.desmoines.fm. Licensee: Northwestern College. Group owner: Northwestern College & Radio. (acq 12-30-2003; $1.8 million. with KNWM(FM) Madrid). Network: ESPN Radio. Format: Christian. News staff: 2; News: 4 hrs wkly. Target aud: 18-44; men. Spec prog: Farm 8 hrs wkly. ♦Richard Whitworth, gen mgr.

Oskaloosa

KBOE(AM)— Nov 15, 1950: 740 khz; 250 w-D, 12 w-N. TL: N41 19 15 W92 38 44. Box 380, Hwy. 63 N. 52577. Phone: (515) 673-3493. Fax: (515) 673-3495. E-mail: kboe@kboeradio.com. Web Site: www.kboeradio.com. Licensee: Jomast Corp. Network: ABC Daytime Direction. Format: Country. News staff: one; News: 15 hrs wkly. Target aud: 25-50. Spec prog: Gospel 9 hrs wkly. ♦Brad Muhl, pres; Scott Ewing, gen mgr & gen sls mgr; Jamie Brockman, news dir; Gary Wilson, chief of engrg.

KBOE-FM— Feb 7, 1964: 104.9 mhz; 50 kw. 492 ft. TL: N41 19 15 W92 38 44. Stereo. Web Site: www.kboeradio.com. Format: News/talk.

*KIGC(FM)— 1975: 88.7 mhz; 230 w. 93 ft. TL: N41 18 37 W92 38 49. (CP: Ant 123 ft.). Stereo. William Penn University, 201 Trueblood Ave. 52577. Phone: (641) 673-1095. Fax: (641) 673-1396. Licensee: William Penn University Format: Oldies, alternative, black. News: one hr wkly. Target aud: 13-25. Spec prog: Jazz 12 hrs, gospel 12 hrs wkly. ♦Larz G. Roberts, gen mgr; James Roberts, progmg dir.

Ottumwa

KBIZ(AM)— 1941: 1240 khz; 1 kw-U. TL: N41 00 00 W92 23 23. Box 190, Broadcast Ctr., 209 S. Market 52501. Phone: (641) 682-4535. Fax: (515) 684-5892. Licensee: Fairfield Media Group Inc. (group owner; acq 1-4-02; $950,000. with co-located FM). Network: CBS. Format: Classic oldies. Target aud: 25-54. Spec prog: Farm 12 hrs, relg 4 hrs wkly. ♦Jay Mitchell, pres & opns mgr; Judy Bushong, gen mgr; Mike Buchanan, news dir; Phil Benjamin, chief of engrg.

KTWA(FM)— Co-owned with KBIZ(AM). December 1984: 92.7 mhz; 50 kw. 318 ft. TL: N41 01 29 W92 28 09. Format: Adult contemp. ♦Judy Bushong, gen mgr & stn mgr; Phil Benjamin, chief of engrg.

KLEE(AM)— Aug 1, 1954: 1480 khz; 500 w-D, 33 w-N. TL: N41 01 27 W92 28 56. Stereo. 601 W. 2nd St. 52501. Phone: (641) 682-8711. Phone: (641) 682-8712. Fax: (641) 682-8482. Licensee: FMC Broadcasting Inc. (acq 1-16-92; $400,000 with co-located FM; 2-10-92). Network: Westwood One. Format: Country, news/talk. News staff: one; News: 28 hrs wkly. Target aud: General; people on the move. Spec prog: Gospel 6 hrs, polka one hr wkly. ♦Thomas A. Palen, pres, gen mgr & gen sls mgr; Marcia Wagner, prom dir; Dave Michaels, progmg dir; Mike Dixon, news dir; Fred Jenkins, chief of engrg.

KOTM-FM— Co-owned with KLEE(AM). Mar 22, 1976: 97.7 mhz; 6 kw. 200 ft. TL: N41 01 27 W92 28 56. Stereo. Web Site: www.kotm.com. Network: Westwood One. Format: CHR. Target aud: Teens-50.

*KUNZ(FM)— Not on air, target date: unknown: 91.1 mhz; 1.9 kw. Ant 400 ft. TL: N40 57 40 W92 22 11. University of Northern Iowa, 324 Communications Arts Center, Cedar Falls 50614-0359. Phone: (319) 273-6325. Fax: (319) 273-2682. Web Site: www.kuniradio.org. Licensee: University of Northern Iowa. ♦John Hess, gen mgr.

Parkersburg

KQCR-FM— Oct 18, 2000: 98.9 mhz; 6 kw. 328 ft. TL: N42 33 48 W92 57 22. Stereo. 1509 4th St. N.E., Hampton 50441-0495. Phone: (641) 456-5656. Fax: (641) 456-5655. E-mail: kqcr@kqcr.fm. Web Site: www.kqcr.fm. Licensee: CD Broadcasting Inc. Fletcher, Heald & Hildreth, P.L.C. Format: Adult contemp. News staff: 2; News: 12 hrs wkly. Target aud: 25-45; Light, Soft AC 70's, 80's, 90's. ♦Craig Donnelly, gen mgr; Marlin Burrier, opns dir.

Pella

KAZR(FM)— Aug 1, 1976: 103.3 mhz; 100 kw. 745 ft. TL: N41 32 18 W93 17 58. (CP: 98 kw, ant 1,043 ft.). Stereo. 1416 Locust St., Des Moines 50309. Phone: (515) 280-1350. Fax: (515) 280-3011. Web Site: www.lazer1033.com. Licensee: Saga Communications of Iowa LLC. Group owner: Saga Communications Inc. (acq 9-17-96; $2.7 million). Format: Active rock. News staff: one; News: 4 hrs wkly. Target aud: 25-44. Spec prog: Jazz 6 hrs wkly. ♦Bill Wells, gen mgr; Jim Schaefer, opns mgr; Celia Rodine, natl sls mgr; Scott Allen, mktg mgr.

KNIA(AM)— See Knoxville

Perry

KDLS(AM)— May 10, 1961: 1310 khz; 500 w-D, 300 w-N, DA-2. TL: N41 49 58 W94 02 15. Box 548 50220. Secondary address: 2260 141st Dr. 50220. Phone: (515) 465-5357. Fax: (515) 465-3952. E-mail: kdls@prairieinet.net. Licensee: Perry Broadcasting Co. (acq 8-27-2004; $750,000. with co-located FM). Network: Westwood One, CNN Radio. Rep: Farmakis. Format: Var. News staff: one; News: 25 hrs wkly. Target aud: General. ♦Steve Whitehead, pres; Tom Quinlan, VP; Patrick Graney, gen mgr & gen sls mgr; John Patrick, opns dir, progmg dir & news dir; Bob Pink, chief of engrg.

KDLS-FM— Feb 26, 1971: 105.5 mhz; 6 kw. 305 ft. TL: N41 50 03 W94 02 12. Stereo. Format: Var.

Postville

*KPVL(FM)— 2003: 89.1 mhz; 250 w. Ant 246 ft. TL: N43 05 20 W91 33 54. Box 875 52162-0875. Secondary address: 210 S. Ogden St. 52162. Phone: (563) 864-7945. Fax: (563) 864-7940. E-mail: radiopostville@netins.net. Web Site: www.kpvl.org. Licensee: Postville Chamber of Commerce. Format: Educ. ♦Bob Dehli, gen mgr.

Red Oak

KCSI(FM)— Listing follows KOAK(AM).

KOAK(AM)— Aug 16, 1968: 1080 khz; 250 w-D. TL: N41 01 00 W95 12 46. Box 465, 1991 Ironwood 51566. Phone: (712) 623-2584. Fax: (712) 623-2583. E-mail: kcsifm@yahoo.com. Licensee: Hawkeye Communications Inc. (acq 7-1-94). Network: ABC. Format: Contemp country. ♦Jerry V. Dietz, pres & gen mgr; Melanie L. West, gen sls mgr.

Rock Valley

KIHK(FM)— 1998: 106.9 mhz; 25 kw. 328 ft. TL: N43 20 28 W96 19 03. Box 298, Sioux Center 51250. Phone: (712) 722-1090. Fax: (712) 722-1102. E-mail: ksou@waittradio.com. Web Site: www.ksoufm.com. Licensee: Sorenson Broadcasting Corp. (group owner; acq 6-18-2004; grpsl). Format: Country. Spec prog: Gospel bluegrass 3 hrs wkly. ♦Craig Aukes, gen mgr.

Sageville

KIYX(FM)— 1999: 106.1 mhz; 4.1 kw. 397 ft. TL: N42 41 27 W90 37 26. Stereo. PO Box 1, Platteville, WI 53818. Phone: (608) 348-2775. Fax: (608) 348-2780. E-mail: superhits@queenbradio.com. Licensee: Queen B Radio Wisconsin Inc. (acq 6-8-99). Network: Westwood One. Format: Adult contemp. News staff: one. ♦Dan Sullivan, gen mgr.

Saint Ansgar

KJCY(FM)— September 2001: 95.5 mhz; 6 kw. Ant 328 ft. TL: N43 21 12 W93 02 48. Box 1069, Mason City 50402. Phone: (641) 424-5529. Fax: (641) 424-5597. E-mail: kjcy@kjcy.com. Web Site: www.kjcy.com. Licensee: Minn-Iowa Christian Broadcasting Inc. (group owner; acq 3-20-01; $200,000). Format: Christian. ♦Matt Dorfner, exec VP; Rick Boyd, stn mgr & opns mgr.

Sheldon

KIWA(AM)— Oct. 27, 1961: 1550 khz; 283 w-D, 6 w-N. TL: N43 10 53 W95 51 56. 411 9th St. 51201. Phone: (712) 324-2597. Fax: (712) 324-2340. E-mail: kiwa@ncn.net. Web Site: www.kiwa-fm.com. Licensee: Sheldon Broadcasting Co. Inc. (acq 10-27-61). Network: ABC Information & Entertainment. Rep: Farmakis. Format: Country, div. News staff: one; News: 15 hrs wkly. Target aud: General; adult. ♦Frank Luepke, gen mgr & gen sls mgr; Walt Pruiksma, sls dir, gen sls mgr & prom mgr; Tom Traughber, progmg dir & chief of engrg; Scott Neff, mus dir.

KIWA-FM— Oct 1, 1971: 105.3 mhz; 50 kw. 292 ft. TL: N43 11 00 W95 52 05. Stereo. E-mail: kiwa@ncn.net. Web Site: www.kiwafm.com. Rep: Farmakis. Format: Country. News staff: one; News: 15 hrs wkly. Target aud: General. ♦Frank Luepke, stn mgr & adv mgr; Tom Traughber, mus dir.

Shenandoah

KMA(AM)— Aug 12, 1925: 960 khz; 5 kw-U, DA-N. TL: N40 46 48 W95 21 23. Box 960, 209 N. Elm 51601. Phone: (712) 246-5270. Fax: (712) 246-5275. E-mail: marke@kmakkbz.com. Web Site: www.kma960.com. Licensee: May Broadcasting Co. Network: ABC Information & Entertainment. Format: News/talk. News staff: 2; News: 15 hrs wkly. Target aud: 35-54. Spec prog: Farm. ♦Edward W. May, pres; Mark Eno, gen mgr; Don Hansen, stn mgr.

*KYFR(FM)— 1924: 920 khz; 5 kw-D, 2.5 w-N, DA-2. TL: N40 37 22 W95 14 42. Box 286 51601. Secondary address: 700 W. Sheridan Ave. 51601. Phone: (712) 246-5151. Fax: (712) 246-5152. E-mail: kyfr@familyradio.org. Web Site: www.shenessex.heartland.net/kyfr. Licensee: Family Stations Inc. (group owner; (acq 1976). Network: Family Radio. Format: Christian. ♦Harold Camping, pres; Mike DeStefano, stn mgr.

Sioux Center

*KDCR(FM)— Aug 16, 1968: 88.5 mhz; 100 kw. 320 ft. TL: N43 05 00 W96 09 50. Stereo. Dordt College Campus, 498 4th Ave. N.E. 51250. Phone: (712) 722-0885. Fax: (712) 722-6244. E-mail: kdcr@dordt.edu. Web Site: www.kdcrdordt.edu. Licensee: Dordt College Inc. (acq 1-19-90). Network: USA. Format: Relg. Spec prog: Farm 2 hrs, Dutch one hr wkly. ♦Dennis DeWaard, gen mgr.

KSOU(AM)— Nov 17, 1969: 1090 khz; 500 w-D, DA. TL: N43 03 22 W96 10 17. Box 298, 128 20th St. S.E. 51250. Phone: (712) 722-1090. Phone: (712) 722-1091. Fax: (712) 722-1102. Web Site: www.ksoufm.com. Licensee: Sorenson Broadcasting Corp. (group owner; (acq 6-18-2004); grpsl). Rep: Farmakis. Format: Contempory Christian. News staff: one; News: 17 hrs wkly. Target aud: General. ♦Craig Aukes, gen mgr; Dan Bonnema, gen sls mgr; James DeBoer, progmg dir; Doug Broek, news dir; Steve Heaton, chief of engrg.

KSOU-FM— Oct 17, 1974: 93.9 mhz; 3 kw. 300 ft. TL: N43 03 22 W96 10 17. (CP: 50 kw, ant 492 ft.). Stereo. Network: ABC. Format: Adult contemp. ♦Scott France, progmg VP & progmg dir; Steve Heaton, chief of opns & engrg VP.

Sioux City

KGLI(FM)— Listing follows KWSL(AM).

KKYY(FM)— See Whiting

KMNS(AM)— May 1, 1949: 620 khz; 1 kw-U, DA-2. TL: N42 22 15 W96 27 00. Box 3009 51102. Secondary address: 1113 Nebraska St. 51102. Phone: (712) 258-0628. Fax: (712) 252-2430. Web Site: www.620kmns.com. Licensee: AMFM Radio Licenses LLC. Group owner: Clear Channel Communications Inc. (acq 10-1-2002; grpsl). Network: ABC Information & Entertainment. Rep: Christal. Format: News/talk, farm. Target aud: 35 plus; rural, farm & country. Spec prog: Farm 20 hrs wkly. ♦Rich Schorg, gen mgr; Laura Schiltz, sls dir; Steve George, progmg dir.

KSEZ(FM)—Co-owned with KMNS(AM). Feb 6, 1960: 97.9 mhz; 100 kw. 643 ft. TL: N42 29 48 W96 18 55. Stereo. Phone: (712) 258-5595. Web Site: www.298rocks.com. Network: Network: ABC, Westwood One. Leventhal, Senter & Lerman. Format: Classic rock. Target aud: 18-49. ♦Chris Thomas, progmg dir; Steve George, chief of engrg.

***KMSC(FM)**— April 1978: 88.3 mhz; 10 w. 105 ft. TL: N42 28 28 W96 21 34. Library Bldg., 1501 Morningside Ave. 51106. Phone: (712) 274-5331. Phone: (712) 274-5241. Fax: (712) 274-5664. E-mail: fusion@morningside.edu. Web Site: webs.morningside.edu/kmsc. Licensee: Morningside College Board of Directors. Format: Alternative. Target aud: 12-24; high school, college students. Spec prog: Womens mus 5 hrs, techno 4 hrs, rock/AOR 4 hrs, urban contemp 4 hrs wkly. ♦Ross Fuglsang, pres; Ron Jorgensen, CFO; Bill Deeds, exec VP; Dr. Mark J. Heistad, gen mgr; Bob Deutsch, stn mgr; Matt Black, opns dir & opns mgr; Liz Barrett, sls dir; Brian Hamilton, prom dir; Libby Green, mus dir; Ashley Lewis, asst music dir; Sheila Partaridge, news dir.

KSCJ(AM)— 1927: 1360 khz; 5 kw-D, 1 kw-N, DA-N. TL: N42 33 24 W96 20 12. 2000 Indian Hills Dr. 51104. Phone: (712) 239-2100. Fax: (712) 239-3346. Web Site: www.kscj.com. Licensee: Powell Broadcasting Co. (acq 1996; $3.8 million with KSUX(FM) Winnebago, NE). Network: CBS. Rep: Allied Radio Partners. Format: News/talk, sports. News staff: 2; News: 40-42 hrs wkly. Target aud: 35-64; Educated, higher income, issues-oriented. Spec prog: Relg 5 hrs. ♦Dennis J. Bullock, gen mgr; Dave Grossenherder, sls dir & gen sls mgr; Willie Clark, progmg dir; Randy Renshaw, news dir.

KTFC(FM)— July 1, 1965: 103.3 mhz; 100 kw. 669 ft. TL: N42 29 26 W96 18 21. Stereo. 1534 Buchanan Ave. 51106. Phone: (712) 252-4621. Licensee: Donald A. Swanson. Network: USA. Format: Gospel, all bible. Spec prog: Farm one hr, news 10 hrs, children 5 hrs wkly. ♦Donald A. Swanson, pres & gen mgr.

***KWIT(FM)**— Jan 31, 1978: 90.3 mhz; 100 kw. Ant 910 ft. TL: N42 28 56 W96 15 30. Stereo. 4647 Stone Ave. 51106-1997. Phone: (712) 274-6406. Fax: (712) 274-6411. E-mail: gondekg@witcc.com. Web Site: www.kwit-koji.org. Licensee: Western Iowa Tech Community College. Network: Network: PRI, NPR. Format: Class, news/talk, Sp. News staff: one; News: 36 hrs wkly. Target aud: 25-54. Spec prog: Blues 2 hrs, Triple A 12 hrs, Sp 20 hrs wkly. ♦Gretchen Gondek, gen mgr; Steve Smith, opns mgr.

KWSL(AM)— April 1938: 1470 khz; 5 kw-U, DA-2. TL: N42 24 42 W96 25 30. Stereo. Box 3009 51102. Phone: (712) 255-1470. Fax: (712) 252-2430. Licensee: AMFM Radio Licenses LLC. Group owner: Clear Channel Communications Inc. (acq 10-1-2002; grpsl). Rep: Christal. Leventhal, Senter & Lerman. Format: Sp. Target aud: 35 plus. ♦Rick Schorg, gen sls mgr; Curtis Anderson, progmg dir.

KGLI(FM)—Co-owned with KWSL(AM). Mar 11, 1974: 95.5 mhz; 100 kw. 900 ft. TL: N42 30 53 W96 18 13. Stereo. Phone: (712) 258-5595. Fax: (712) 252-2430. Format: Hot adult contemp. Target aud: 18-49. ♦Rob Powers, progmg dir.

Sioux Rapids

KTFG(FM)— 1991: 102.9 mhz; 50 kw. 479 ft. TL: N42 54 34 W95 09 35. 1534 Buchanan Ave., Sioux City 51106. Phone: (712) 252-0327. Licensee: Donald A. Swanson. Network: USA. Format: Gospel. Spec prog: Children 5 hrs wkly. ♦Donald A. Swanson, gen mgr.

Spencer

KICD(AM)— December 1942: 1240 khz; 1 kw-U. TL: N43 10 00 W95 08 45. Box 260, 2600 N. Hwy. Blvd. 51301. Phone: (712) 262-1240. Fax: (712) 262-2076. Web Site: www.cd1077fm.com. Licensee: Saga Communications of Iowa LLC. Group owner: Saga Communications Inc. (acq 11-22-99; grpsl). Network: CBS. Format: Talk. News staff: one; News: 26 hrs wkly. Target aud: 35 plus. ♦David Putnam, gen mgr & gen sls mgr; Bill Campbell, opns mgr & progmg dir; Chris Swanson, gen sls mgr; Brent Palm, news dir; Dave Inqualson, pub affrs dir; Joseph Schloss, chief of engrg.

KICD-FM— Sept 17, 1965: 107.7 mhz; 100 kw. 310 ft. TL: N43 10 00 W95 08 45. Stereo. Web Site: www.cd1077fm.com. Network: CBS. Format: Country. News staff: one. Target aud: 25 plus. ♦Rhoda Wede King, progmg dir.

KLLT(FM)— February 1979: 104.9 mhz; 25 kw. 279 ft. TL: N43 17 13 W95 08 34. Stereo. Box 260, 2600 N. Hwy. Blvd. 51301. Phone: (712) 262-1240. Fax: (712) 262-2076. Fax: (712) 262-5821. E-mail: lite1049@ncn.net. Web Site: www.lite1049.com. Licensee: Saga Communications of Iowa LLC. Group owner: Saga Communications Inc. (acq 11-22-99; grpsl). Format: Light Rock. News: one hr wkly. Target aud: 25-54. ♦Edward Christian, CEO & pres; Dave Putnam, gen mgr; Bill Campbell, opns dir & opns mgr.

Spirit Lake

***KJIA(FM)**—Not on air, target date: unknown: 88.9 mhz; 50 kw. Ant 272 ft. TL: N43 20 34 W95 12 24. Box 738, Okoboji 51355. Secondary address: 7 S. Okoboji Grove Rd., Arnolds Park 51331. Phone: (712) 332-7184. Fax: (712) 332-2428. E-mail: kjia@kjiaradio.com. Web Site: www.kjiaradio.com. Licensee: Minn-Iowa Christian Broadcasting Inc. (group owner). Format: Christian. ♦Matt Dorfner, gen mgr.

KUOO(FM)— Apr 1, 1985: 103.9 mhz; 50 kw. 492 ft. TL: N43 20 34 W93 12 24. Stereo. Box 528, 1039 Radio Dr. 51360. Phone: (712) 336-5800. Fax: (712) 336-1634. Licensee: Sorenson Broadcasting Corp. (group owner; acq 6-18-2004; grpsl). Network: ABC. Format: Adult contemp. News staff: 2; News: 16 hrs wkly. Target aud: 25-54. ♦Dean Sorenson, pres; Mike Puetz, gen mgr; George Bower, opns mgr.

KUQQ(FM)—(Milford). Oct 1, 1996: 102.1 mhz; 50 kw. 420 ft. TL: N43 20 34 W93 12 24. Box 528, 1039 Radio Dr. 51360. Phone: (712) 336-5877. Fax: (712) 336-1634. Licensee: Sorenson Broadcasting Corp. (group owner; acq 6-18-2004; grpsl). Format: Classic rock. Target aud: 18-44. ♦Dean Sorenson, pres; Mike Puetz, gen mgr; George Bower, opns mgr.

Storm Lake

KAYL(AM)— November 1948: 990 khz; 250 w-D. TL: N42 37 56 W95 09 54. (CP: TL: N42 38 05 W95 10 10). Box 1037 50588. Secondary address: 606 1/2 Lake Ave. 50588. Phone: (712) 732-3520. Fax: (712) 732-1746. E-mail: kayl@waittradio.com. Licensee: Sorenson Broadcasting Corp. (group owner; acq 6-24-2004; grpsl). Network: ABC Information & Entertainment. Format: Farm, easy listening. News staff: one; News: 30 hrs wkly. Target aud: 50 plus. Spec prog: Farm 5 hrs, Sp 3 hrs wkly. ♦Dean Sorenson, pres; Buzz Paterson, gen mgr.

KAYL-FM— February 1949: 101.7 mhz; 50 kw. 400 ft. TL: N42 38 05 W95 10 10. Stereo. Format: Adult contemp, news, sports. News staff: one; News: 15 hrs wkly. Target aud: 25-54; male & female.

Stuart

KKRF(FM)— Aug 11, 1993: 107.9 mhz; 12.kw. Ant 472 ft. TL: N41 30 25 W94 18 06. Stereo. 204 S. Division St. 50250. Phone: (515) 523-1107. Fax: (515) 523-1817. E-mail: kkrf1079@aol.com. Web Site: RealCountryOnline.Com. Licensee: Coon Valley Communications Inc. Network: ABC. Format: Country. News staff: 2; News: 10 hrs wkly. Target aud: 25-64; general. Spec prog: Farm 5 hrs wkly. ♦Pat Delaney, pres & CFO; Jeanette Woodson, gen mgr & stn mgr; Sue Thomsen, gen mgr; John France, opns mgr & progmg dir.

Twin Lakes

KTLB(FM)— Oct 5, 1975: 105.9 mhz; 25 kw. 328 ft. TL: N42 32 09 W94 40 48. Stereo. 1014 Central Ave., Fort Dodge 50501. Phone: (515) 573-5748. Fax: (515) 573-3376. Licensee: Three Eagles of Ft. Dodge Inc. Group owner: Three Eagles Communications (acq 4-22-97; $248,883). Network: ABC Daytime Direction. Format: Oldies. News staff: one; News: 15 hrs wkly. Target aud: 35-54; baby boomers. Spec prog: Farm 15 hrs, gospel 2 hrs, relg 2 hrs wkly. ♦Gary Buchanan, pres; Pat Kolar, gen mgr & gen sls mgr; Greg Allenson, opns mgr & gen sls mgr; Travis Reeves, gen mgr & opns mgr.

Vinton

KROJ(FM)— 2005: 107.1 mhz; 2.5 kw. Ant 371 ft. TL: N42 08 56 W91 52 50. 6080 Mt. Moriah Ext., Memphis, TN 38115. Phone: (901) 375-9324. Fax: (901) 375-0041. Web Site: www.flinn.com. Licensee: George S. Flinn Jr. ♦George Flinn Jr., gen mgr.

Wapello

***KLRX(FM)**—Not on air, target date: unknown: 88.9 mhz; 1 w hoirz, 32.5 kw vert. Ant 318 ft vert. TL: N41 05 00 W91 10 10. Air 1 Radio Network, 5700 W. Oaks Blvd., Rocklin, CA 95765. Phone: (916) 251-1600. Fax: (916) 251-1650. E-mail: klove@klove.com. Web Site: www.klove.com. Licensee: Educational Media Foundation. Group owner: EMF Broadcasting. Network: K-Love. Shaw Pittman. Format: Contemp Christian. News staff: 3. Target aud: 25-44; Judeo Christian, female. ♦Richard Jenkins, pres; Joe Miller, CFO; Mike Novak, VP; Keith Whipple, gen mgr; Ed Lenane, opns dir; Eric Allen, natl sls mgr; John D. Burkholder, rgnl sls mgr.

Washington

KCII(AM)— Nov 12, 1961: 1380 khz; 500 w-D. TL: N41 18 18 W91 42 36. Box 524, 110 E. Main St. 52353. Phone: (319) 653-2113. Fax: (319) 653-3500. Licensee: Home Broadcasting Inc. (acq 9-3-96; $800,000 with co-located FM). Network: AP Radio. Shaw Pittman. Format: News, adult contemp. News staff: one; News: 14 hrs wkly. Target aud: 25-54; females. ♦Jack Davison, gen mgr; Joe Nichols, gen sls mgr; Ben Tyler, progmg dir; Jeremy Aitken, news dir.

KCII-FM— 1975: 95.3 mhz; 3 kw. 300 ft. TL: N41 18 18 W91 42 36. Stereo. Format: News, oldies.

Waterloo

***KBBG(FM)**— July 26, 1978: 88.1 mhz; 9.5 kw. 150 ft. TL: N42 30 35 W92 19 35. Stereo. 918 Newell St. 50703-2720. Phone: (319) 234-1441. Phone: (319) 235-1515. Fax: (319) 234-6182. E-mail: lou@kbbg.org. Web Site: www.kbbgfm.org. Licensee: Afro-American Community Broadcasting Inc. Network: American Urban. Format: Educ, gospel, rhythnm & blues, jazz. Target aud: General. Spec prog: Gospel. ♦Jimmie Porter, CEO; Lou Porter, pres; Beverly Douglas, stn mgr; Lou Lou Porter, dev dir & news dir.

KFMW(FM)—Listing follows KWLO(AM).

***KNWS(AM)**— 1953: 1090 khz; 1 kw-D. TL: N42 26 38 W92 17 58. 4880 Texas 50702. Phone: (319) 296-1975. Fax: (319) 296-1977. E-mail: knws@knws.org. Web Site: www.knws.org. Licensee: Northwestern College. Group owner: Northwestern College & Radio (acq 4-2-53). Format: Relg, Christian, talk. Target aud: 35 plus. ♦Wayne Pederson, exec VP; Doug Smith, gen mgr; Brent Manion, progmg dir & asst music dir; David Dobes, chief of engrg.

KNWS-FM— 1965: 101.9 mhz; 100 kw. 1,010 ft. TL: N42 24 48 W92 00 25. Stereo. Web Site: www.knws.org. (acq 1965). Network: AP Radio. Format: Inspirational, relg. Target aud: 30-50; women.

KOKZ(FM)—Listing follows KXEL(AM).

KWLO(AM)— November 1947: 1330 khz; 5 kw-U, DA-2. TL: N42 28 56 W92 16 16. Stereo. Box 1540 50704. Secondary address: 514 Jefferson St. 50704. Phone: (319) 234-2200. Fax: (319) 234-0149. Web Site: www.star1330.com. Licensee: KXEL Broadcasting Co. Inc. Group owner: Bahakel Communications (acq 8-16-96; grpsl). Network: ABC. Brooks, Pierce, McLendon, Humphrey & Leonard. Format: Btfl mus, big band. News staff: 3. Target aud: 35 plus. ♦Cy N. Bahakel, pres; Tim Mathews, gen mgr; Dennis Lowe, opns dir, progmg dir & news dir; James Patrick, prom dir; Mark Schumacher, chief of engrg.

KFMW(FM)—Co-owned with KWLO(AM). November 1968: 107.9 mhz; 100 kw. 1,850 ft. TL: N42 24 04 W91 50 43. Stereo. Web Site: www.rock108.com. Format: AOR. Target aud: 18-34; men. ♦Michael Cross, opns mgr; Mark Chapman, progmg dir; Dolly Fortier, pub affrs dir.

KWOF(AM)— Oct 31, 1972: 850 khz; 500 w-D, DA. TL: N42 28 56 W92 16 16. 3232 Osage Rd. 50703. Phone: (319) 378-8600. Fax: (319) 236-8777. E-mail: studio@891thespirit.com. Web Site: www.891thesprint.com. Licensee: Friendship Communications Inc. (acq 2-23-95; FTR: 5-22-95). Format: Christian hit radio. Target aud: 18-45; Christian, interdenominational. ♦Michael James, gen mgr.

KXEL(AM)— July 14, 1942: 1540 khz; 50 kw-U, DA-N. TL: N42 10 47 W92 18 38. Stereo. Box 1540, 514 Jefferson St. 50701. Phone: (319) 234-2200. Fax: (319) 234-0149. Web Site: www.kxel.com. Licensee: KXEL Broadcasting Co. Inc. Group owner: Bahakel Communications (acq 1-11-58). Network: ABC Information & Entertainment. Format:

Stations in the U.S. — Kansas

News/talk. News staff: 3; News: 28 hrs wkly. Target aud: 45-65. Spec prog: Rush Limbaugh 15 hrs, relg 20 hrs wkly. ♦ Cy N. Bahakel, pres; Tim Mathews, gen mgr; Dennis Lowe, opns dir, progmg dir & news dir; James Patrick, prom dir; Mark Schumacher, chief of engrg.

KOKZ(FM)— Co-owned with KXEL(AM). Nov 21, 1962: 105.7 mhz; 100 kw. 1,403 ft. TL: N42 24 35 W92 05 10. Stereo. Web Site: www.cool1057.com. Format: Oldies. Target aud: 25-54. ♦ Dolly Fortier, pub affrs dir.

Waukon

KHPP(AM)—Listing follows KNEI-FM.

KNEI-FM— Sept 1, 1968: 103.5 mhz; 37 kw. Ant 574 ft. TL: N43 18 28 W91 27 18. Stereo. 14 W. Main St. 52172. Phone: (563) 568-3476. Phone: (563) 568-3477. Fax: (563) 568-3391. E-mail: knei@direcway.com. Licensee: Wennes Communications Stations Inc. (acq 4-5-2002; grpsl). Network: CBS Radio. Sam Miller. Format: Real country. News: one hr wkly. Target aud: 25-45. ♦ Greg Wennes, CEO; Chuck Bloxham, gen mgr, opns dir & gen sls mgr.

KHPP(AM)—Co-owned with KNEI-FM. July 1, 1967: 1160 khz; 880 w-D, 26 w-N. TL: N43 17 13 W91 28 06. Network: ESPN Radio. Format: Sports.

Waverly

*KWAR(FM)— Sept 15, 1951: 89.1 mhz; 40 w. 125 ft. TL: N42 43 24 W92 28 05. Wartburg College, 100 Wartburg Blvd. 50677. Phone: (319) 352-8209/352-8306. Fax: (319) 352-8610. E-mail: business@kwar.org. Web Site: www.kwar.org. Licensee: Wartburg College. Format: Educ, div. News staff: one; News: 3 to 5 hrs wkly. Target aud: General. Spec prog: Folk 3 hrs, classical 3 hrs, jazz 5 hrs, world music 3 hrs, news public affairs 3 hrs wkly. ♦ Steven Murray, stn mgr; Adam Van Briesen, progmg dir.

KWAY(AM)— May 6, 1958: 1470 khz; 1 kw-D, 61 w-N, DA-2. TL: N42 42 13 W92 28 21. Box 307 50677. Phone: (319) 352-3550. Fax: (319) 352-3601. E-mail: kwayradio@kwayradio.com. Web Site: www.kwayradio.com. Licensee: Al Suhr Enterprises. Format: Classic country. ♦ Al Suhr, pres, gen mgr & chief of engrg; Steven Hatter, opns mgr.

KWAY-FM— Dec 21, 1971: 99.3 mhz; 3 kw. 180 ft. TL: N42 42 13 W92 28 21. Format: Adult contemp.

*KWVI(FM)—Not on air, target date: unknown: 88.9 mhz; 15 kw vert. Ant 328 ft. TL: N42 46 20 W92 08 58. Drawer 2440, Tupelo, MS 38801. Phone: (662) 844-8888. Fax: (662) 842-6791. Web Site: www.afr.net. Licensee: American Family Association. ♦ Marvin Sanders, gen mgr.

Webster City

KQWC(AM)— Feb 5, 1950: 1570 khz; 250 w-D, 132 w-N. TL: N42 27 45 W93 48 05. (CP: 147 w). Box 550 50595. Phone: (515) 832-1570. Fax: (515) 832-2079. Licensee: Waitt Radio Inc. Group owner: Waitt Broadcasting Inc. (acq 9-10-99; grpsl). Network: ABC Daytime Direction. Rep: Farmakis. Format: Btfl mus, big band. News staff: one; News: 45 hrs wkly. Target aud: 50 plus; affluent with max spendable income. Spec prog: Farm 8 hrs wkly. ♦ Mike Delick, CFO; Mary Harris, stn mgr; Eli Savoie, opns mgr; Tracey Williams, gen sls mgr; Pat Powers, news dir.

KQWC-FM— 1969: 95.7 mhz; 25 kw. 328 ft. TL: N42 28 04 W93 47 48. Stereo. 1020 E. 2nd St. 50595. Web Site: www.kqradio.com. Format: Adult Contemp. News staff: one; News: 35 hrs wkly.

West Des Moines

KJJY(FM)—Licensed to West Des Moines. See Des Moines

*KWDM(FM)— March 1976: 88.7 mhz; 100 w. 170 ft. TL: N41 35 25 W93 45 10. Stereo. 1140 35th St. 50266. Phone: (515) 226-2660. Phone: (515) 226-2600. Fax: (515) 226-2609. E-mail: kwdmfm@hotmail.com. Web Site: www.wdm.k12.ia.us/kwdm. Licensee: West Des Moines Community School District. Reddy, Begley & McCormick. Format: Alternative. News: 3 hrs wkly. Target aud: 12-25; educ facility-var progmg. Spec prog: Sports 3 hrs wkly. ♦ Mack Wzie Carey, stn mgr; Marianne Coppock, dev dir; Nicole Faust, mktg dir & progmg dir.

Whiting

KKYY(FM)— Dec 11, 1979: 101.3 mhz; 50 kw. Ant 492 ft. TL: N42 21 25 W96 08 02. Stereo. 101 Gold Circle Dr., Dakota Dunes, SD 57050. Phone: (712) 258-5655. Fax: (712) 258-1511. E-mail: country101.5@huntel.net. Licensee: Waitt Radio Inc. Group owner: Waitt Broadcasting Inc. (acq 7-17-2000; $950,000). Network: Network: Network: Motor Racing Net, Westwood One, ABC. Format: Country. News staff: one; News: 20 hrs wkly. Target aud: 18-54; adult men & women. ♦ Jerry Haack, gen mgr; Kelli Erickson, gen sls mgr; Eric Morgan, progmg dir; Pam Guntz, chief of engrg.

Winterset

KZZQ(FM)— March 1994: 99.5 mhz; 6 kw. 328 ft. TL: N41 24 02 W93 54 58. Stereo. 3317 335th St., Waukee 50263. Phone: (515) 987-9995. Fax: (515) 987-9808. Web Site: www.kzzq.com. Licensee: Positive Impact Media Inc. (acq 1-11-94; $600,000; 1-31-94). Format: Contemp Christian mus. Target aud: Families. ♦ David Nadler Jr., gen mgr; David St. John, progmg dir.

Kansas

Abilene

KABI(AM)— Apr 8, 1963: 1560 khz; 250 w-D, 58 w-N. TL: N38 55 46 W97 14 46. 200 N. Broadway 67410. Phone: (785) 263-1560. Fax: (785) 263-0166. Web Site: www.ebclink.com. Licensee: MCC Radio LLC. Group owner: Morris Radio LLC (acq 1-30-2004; grpsl). Network: ABC. Format: Adult contemp, adult standards, big band. News staff: one; News: 2 hrs wkly. Target aud: 35 plus; loc residents of Dickinson County. Spec prog: Relg 4 hrs wkly. ♦ Larry Riggins, VP; Clarke Sanders, opns mgr; Billy Hansen, progmg dir; John Anderson, news dir.

KSAJ-FM—Co-owned with KABI(AM). Dec 10, 1968: 98.5 mhz; 100 kw. 443 ft. TL: N38 47 50 W97 13 01. Stereo. Box 80, Salina 67402. Secondary address: 131 N. Santa Fe, Salina 67401. Phone: (785) 823-1111. Fax: (785) 823-2034. Web Site: www.ebclink.com. Network: ABC. Format: Oldies. Target aud: 25-54; baby boomers. ♦ Brett Muarry, gen mgr & prom mgr; Danielle Norwood, engrg mgr.

Andover

KDGS(FM)— Nov 1, 1993: 93.9 mhz; 25 kw. 328 ft. TL: N37 37 00 W97 20 11. 2120 N. Woodlawn, Suite 352, Wichita 67206. Phone: (316) 685-2121. Fax: (316) 685-3408. E-mail: info@power939.com. Web Site: www.power939.com. Licensee: Entercom Wichita License LLC. Group owner: Entercom Communications Corp. (acq 4-21-00; $3.15 million). Format: CHR rhythmic. Target aud: 18-34. ♦ David Field, CEO; Jackie Wise, CFO & gen mgr; Greg Williams, progmg dir.

Arkansas City

KACY(FM)— February 1999: 102.5 mhz; 6 kw. 328 ft. TL: N37 05 01 W96 55 46. 106 N. Summitt 67005. Phone: (620) 442-1102. Fax: (620) 442-8102. Licensee: Third Coast Broadcasting. Format: AAA, AOR. ♦ Robert W. Fisher, pres & gen mgr; Cindy Fisher, gen sls mgr; Jerry Ford, progmg dir.

*KAXR(FM)— 2001: 91.3 mhz; 13.5 kw. Ant 321 ft. TL: N36 55 32 W97 01 34. Box 3206, American Family Radio, Tupelo, MS 38803. Phone: (662) 844-8888. Fax: (662) 842-6791. E-mail: comments@afr.net.

Web Site: www.afr.net. Licensee: American Family Association. Group owner: American Family Radio. Format: Inspirational Christian. ♦ Marvin Sanders, gen mgr.

KSOK(AM)— Jan 1, 1947: 1280 khz; 1 kw-D, 100 w-N. TL: N37 05 19 W97 01 56. Box 1014, 334 East Radio Lane 67005. Phone: (620) 221-1440. Fax: (620) 442-5401. E-mail: brianc@ksokfm.com. Licensee: Cowley County Broadcasting Inc. (acq 9-3-02; with KSOK-FM Winfield). Format: Classic Country. News staff: one; News: 10 hrs wkly. Target aud: 34 plus; agriculturally oriented listeners seeking info. Spec prog: Farm 10 hrs, relg 5 hrs wkly. ♦ Marty Mutti, gen mgr; Brian Cunningham, chief of opns.

KYQQ(FM)— Nov 1, 1979: 106.5 mhz; 100 kw. Ant 1,278 ft. TL: N37 21 24 W96 57 55. Stereo. 4200 N. Old Lawrence Rd., Wichita 67219. Phone: (316) 838-9141. Fax: (316) 832-9755. Licensee: Journal Broadcast Corp. Group owner: Journal Broadcast Group Inc. (acq 6-11-99; grpsl). Shaw Pittman. Format: Mexican. Target aud: 18-49; Hispanic. ♦ Rob Burton, VP & gen mgr; Beverlee Brannigan, progmg dir.

Atchison

KAIR(AM)— July 28, 1939: 1470 khz; 1 kw-U, DA-1. TL: N39 37 09 W94 59 27. Box G, 5th & Kansas Sts. 66002. Phone: (913) 367-1470. Phone: (913) 367-7021. E-mail: kair@lunworth.com. Licensee: Mark V Media Group Inc. (group owner; (acq 12-16-2004; $1.55 million. with KAIR-FM Horton). Format: Country. Target aud: General; 25-65. Spec prog: Farm 7 hrs wkly. ♦ Mark Oppold, pres.

Augusta

KFXJ(FM)— Apr 1, 1992: 104.5 mhz; 45 kw. Ant 515 ft. TL: N37 48 15 W97 15 56. 4200 N. Old Lawrence Rd., Wichita 67219. Phone: (316) 838-9141. Fax: (316) 832-9755. Web Site: www.1045thefox.com. Licensee: Journal Broadcast Corp. Group owner: Journal Broadcast Group Inc. (acq 6-11-99; grpsl). Format: Classic rock hits. Target aud: 25-54. ♦ Rob Burton, VP & gen mgr; Ron Eric Taylor, opns mgr.

Baldwin City

*KNBU(FM)— Nov 29, 1965: 89.7 mhz; 100 w. 118 ft. TL: N38 46 45 W95 11 15. Box 65 66006. Phone: (785) 594-6451, EXT. 300. Phone: (785) 594-8300. Fax: (785) 594-3570. Licensee: Baker University. Spec prog: Jazz 15 hrs wkly. ♦ Tom Hedrick, gen mgr.

Baxter Springs

KMOQ(FM)— Feb 1, 1980: 107.1 mhz; 6 kw. 300 ft. TL: N37 07 34 W94 42 12. Stereo. 2510 W. 20th St., Joplin, MO 64804. Phone: (417) 781-1313. Fax: (417) 781-1316. Licensee: FFD Holdings I Inc. (acq 12-20-2004; grpsl). Network: ABC. Format: CHR. Target aud: 25-54. ♦ Kathleen Pike, gen mgr; Dave Clemons, gen sls mgr; Chris Yeager, progmg dir; Jerry Tibbets, chief of engrg.

Belle Plaine

KANR(FM)— Mar 4, 1996: 92.7 mhz; 12 kw. 469 ft. TL: N37 20 15 W97 27 56. 2120 N. Woodlawn, Wichita 67208. Phone: (316) 652-9275. Fax: (316) 683-0818. Web Site: www.fly927.com. Licensee: Daniel D. Smith (acq 2-16-93; $10,700;. FTR: 3-8-93). Network: AP Radio. Format: Modern rock. News: 168 hrs wkly. Target aud: 25 plus; general. ♦ Daniel D. Smith, pres; Daniel Smith, gen mgr; Joe Roach, progmg dir.

Belleville

KREP(FM)— June 26, 1984: 92.1 mhz; 6 kw. 300 ft. TL: N39 45 00 W97 36 48. Stereo. 2307 US Hwy. 81 66935. Phone: (785) 527-2266. Phone: (785) 527-2267. Fax: (785) 527-5919. E-mail: kr-92@nckcn.com. Licensee: First Republic Broadcasting Corp. (acq 6-84; 1-84). Network: ABC. Format: Country. News staff: one; News: 20 hrs wkly. Target aud:

Kansas   **Directory of Radio**

25-55. ♦Deborah Sasser, pres, gen mgr, progmg dir & news dir; Christine Strutt, gen sls mgr & mktg dir; Marvin Hoffman, chief of engrg.

Beloit

KVSV(AM)— Nov 21, 1979: 1190 khz; 2.3 kw-D, 90 w-N, DA. TL: N39 26 53 W98 04 45. Box 7, E. Hwy. 24 67420. Phone: (785) 738-2206. Web Site: www.kvsvradio.com. Licensee: McGrath Publishing Co. (acq 11-1-99; $500,000 with co-located FM). Network: ABC Information & Entertainment. Format: Adult Top-40. News staff: one; News: 11 hrs wkly. Target aud: General. Spec prog: Farm 9 hrs wkly. ♦John Swanson, gen mgr & progmg dir.

KVSV-FM— Nov 11, 1980: 105.5 mhz; 50 kw. 443 ft. TL: N39 28 09 W98 05 37. Stereo. Web Site: www.kvsvradio.com. Format: Btfl mus, easy lstng. ♦John Swanson, progmg dir.

Bronson

*KBJQ(FM)— 2002: 88.3 mhz; 99 kw. Ant 380 ft. TL: N37 53 56 W95 00 09. Drawer 3206, Tupelo, MS 38803. Phone: (662) 844-8888 ext. 204. Fax: (662) 842-6791. Licensee: American Family Association. Group owner: American Family Radio Format: Relg. ♦Marvin Sanders, gen mgr.

Burlington

KSNP(FM)— June 14, 1990: 97.7 mhz; 6 kw. 349 ft. TL: N38 10 08 W95 39 07. Box 233, 1910 S. 6th 66839. Phone: (620) 364-8807. Fax: (620) 364-2047. E-mail: ksnp@kans.com. Licensee: Southeast Kansas Broadcasting Co. (group owner; acq 1999; $230,000). Format: Hot country. News staff: one; News: 5 hrs wkly. Target aud: 25-45; industrial employees. Spec prog: Farm 8 hrs, relg 3 hrs wkly. ♦Peg Downard, stn mgr, sls dir & gen sls mgr; Mindy Ryan, progmg dir.

Caney

KEOJ(FM)— Oct 15, 1992: 101.1 mhz; 3 kw. 328 ft. TL: N36 58 19 W95 53 47. Stereo. City Plex Towers, 2448 E. 81 St., Tulsa, OK 74137. Phone: (918) 492-2660. Fax: (918) 492-8840. E-mail: kxoj@kxoj.com. Web Site: www.kxoj.com. Licensee: KXOJ Inc. Group owner: Adonai Radio Group (acq 4-29-92; grpsl). Network: UPI. Format: Contemp Christian. Target aud: 18-35; young married Christians. ♦Mike Stephens, pres; Joy Stephens, VP; David Stephens, gen mgr & stn mgr; Bob Thornton, sls dir & progmg dir; Joe Hancock, chief of engrg.

Cawker City

KZDY(FM)— 1999: 96.3 mhz; 13 kw. Ant 230 ft. TL: N39 30 29 W98 18 57. Box 88, Glen Elder 67446. Phone: (785) 545-3220. Fax: (785) 545-3220. Licensee: Waconda Broadcasting Corp. Group owner: Hoeflicker Stns. Network: Network: Jones Radio Networks, AP Radio. Kenkel & Associates. Format: Oldies. News staff: 4. Target aud: 25-60. ♦Ruby J. Hoeflicker, gen mgr.

Chanute

KKOY(AM)— Nov 17, 1952: 1460 khz; 1 kw-D, 57 w-N. TL: N37 41 25 W95 28 08. Box 788 66720-0788. Secondary address: 702 N. Plummer Sts. 66720. Phone: (620) 431-3700. Fax: (620) 431-4643. Web Site: www.kkoy.com. Licensee: Southeast Kansas Broadcasting Co. Inc. (group owner; acq 5-21-97; $464,447. with co-located FM). Network: Network: ABC Information & Entertainment, ABC News/Talk. Format: News/talk. News staff: one. Target aud: 25-54. ♦Phil McComb, gen mgr; Matt Clark, progmg dir.

KKOY-FM— Jan 1, 1971: 105.5 mhz; 4.3 kw. 170 ft. TL: N37 41 25 W95 28 08. Stereo. E-mail: sales@kkoy.com. Web Site: www.kkoy.com. Network: ABC. Format: Hot adult contemp.

Clay Center

KCLY(FM)— Jan 6, 1978: 100.9 mhz; 6 kw. 255 ft. TL: N39 21 53 W97 05 32. Stereo. Box 16, 1815 Meadowlark Rd. 67432. Phone: (785) 632-5661. Fax: (785) 632-5662. Web Site: www.kclyradio.com. Licensee: Taylor Communications. (acq 8-94; 1-78). Network: ABC Daytime Direction. Format: C&W, adult contemp, relg. Target aud: 24-55; general. ♦Kyle Bauer, gen mgr; Joyce Beck, gen sls mgr; Jamie Bloom, progmg dir; Rod Keen, engrg mgr.

Clearwater

KFH-FM—Licensed to Clearwater. See Wichita

Coffeyville

KGGF(AM)— 1930: 690 khz; 10 kw-D, 5 kw-N, DA-2. TL: N37 08 58 W95 28 27. Box 1087, 306 W. 8th St. 67337. Phone: (620) 251-3800. Fax: (620) 251-9210. Licensee: KGGF-KUSN Inc. Group owner: Mahaffey Enterprises Inc. (acq 12-26-90; $750,000. with co-located FM; FTR: 1-14-91). Network: ABC. Format: News/talk. News staff: one; News: 5 hrs wkly. Target aud: 35 plus. ♦John Leonard, gen mgr; Kevin Taylor, progmg dir.

KKRK(FM)—Co-owned with KGGF(AM). Sept 1, 1983: 98.9 mhz; 6 kw. 305 ft. TL: N37 06 28 W95 43 22. Stereo. Licensee: KGGF-KUSN, Inc. Format: Classic rock. News staff: one. Target aud: 35-54.

Colby

KQLS(FM)—Listing follows KXXX(AM).

*KTCC(FM)— May 1974: 91.9 mhz; 3 kw. 199 ft. TL: N39 22 34 W101 03 08. Stereo. 1255 S. Range 67701. Phone: (785) 462-3984, EXT. 309. Fax: (785) 462-4600. Web Site: www.colbycc.edu. Licensee: Colby Community College. Format: CHR. News staff: one; News: 14 hrs wkly. Target aud: 18-25; young adults. Spec prog: Sports 3 hrs, classic rock 3 hrs, hard rock 7 hrs, hip hop 4 hrs wkly. ♦Corey Sorenson, stn mgr.

KWGB(FM)— Sept 1, 1998: 97.9 mhz; 100 kw. Ant 712 ft. TL: N39 23 19 W101 33 34. 3023 W. 31st St., Goodland 67765. Phone: (785) 899-2309. Fax: (785) 899-3062. Licensee: Melia Communications Inc. (group owner) Format: Country. ♦Martin K. Melia, pres & gen mgr; Martin Melia, gen sls mgr; Curtis Duncan, progmg dir.

KXXX(AM)— August 1947: 790 khz; 5 kw-D. TL: N39 23 35 W101 00 06. 1065 S. Range 67701. Phone: (785) 462-3305. Fax: (785) 462-3307. E-mail: kxkq@colbyweb.com. Licensee: Waitt Radio Inc. Group owner: Waitt Broadcasting Inc (acq 5-3-01; grpsl). Network: Westwood One. Format: Contemp country. News: 5 hrs wkly. Target aud: 35-55; male, female, city & rural. ♦Michael Delich, pres; Mike Pell, gen mgr & stn mgr; Joe Vyzourek, progmg dir; Mike Hendrickson, engrg mgr.

KQLS(FM)—Co-owned with KXXX(AM). September 1971: 100.3 mhz; 100 kw. 610 ft. TL: N39 28 50 W100 54 34. Stereo. Phone: (785) 462-3306. Network: ABC. Format: Adult contemp. Target aud: 18-49; general. ♦Mike Pell, stn mgr.

Columbus

KJML(FM)— Dec 25, 1982: 105.3 mhz; 6.1 kw. 308 ft. TL: N37 14 47 W94 44 52. (CP: 25 kw, ant 210 ft. TL: N37 01 57 W94 49 44). Stereo. 2510 W. 20th St., Joplin, MO 64804. Phone: (417) 781-1313. Phone: (417) 624-7601. Fax: (417) 781-1316. Licensee: FFD Holdings I Inc. Group owner: Petracom Media L.L.C. (acq 12-20-2004; grpsl). Network: ABC. Format: Modern rock. News staff: one; News: 2 hrs wkly. Target aud: 18-49; growing families with needs for a wide range of goods & svcs. ♦Dave Clemons, CFO & gen sls mgr; Kathleen Pike, VP; Johnny Duratt, progmg dir; Jerry Tibbets, mus dir & chief of engrg.

Concordia

KCKS(FM)—Listing follows KNCK(AM).

KNCK(AM)— Feb 6, 1954: 1390 khz; 500 w-D, 54 w-N. TL: N39 33 58 W97 41 04. Box 629, Rt. 1 W. 11th St. 66901. Phone: (785) 243-1414. Licensee: KNCK Inc. (acq 10-18-89; $190,000 with co-located FM; 11-6-89). Format: Country. Target aud: 45 plus. ♦Joe Jindra, pres, gen mgr & progmg dir; Brian Strait, opns mgr; Marvin Hoffman, chief of engrg.

*KVCO(FM)— May 1, 1977: 88.3 mhz; 127 w. 77 ft. TL: N39 33 17 W97 39 48. Stereo. Box 1002, 2221 Campus Dr. 66901. Phone: (785) 243-1435. Fax: (785) 243-1043. Licensee: Cloud County Community College. Network: CNN Radio. Format: Div/var. Target aud: 16-30 plus; students & young adults. ♦John Chapin, gen mgr.

Copeland

*KHYM(FM)— Dec 23, 1997: 103.9 mhz; 100 kw. 702 ft. TL: N37 28 35 W100 35 59. Stereo. Box 991, 909 W. Carthage, Meade 67864-0991. Phone: (620) 873-2991. Fax: (620) 873-2755. E-mail: khym@khym.org. Web Site: www.khym.org. Licensee: Great Plains Christian Radio Inc. Format: Relg, Christian. ♦Don Hughes, CEO, pres & gen mgr; David Hayes, opns dir & sls dir; Peggy Burdick, dev dir; Steve Larsen, chief of engrg.

*KJIL(FM)— Sept 5, 1992: 99.1 mhz; 100 kw. 935 ft. TL: N37 23 35 W100 35 59. Stereo. Box 991, 909 W. Carthage, Meade 67864-0991. Phone: (620) 873-2991. Fax: (620) 873-2755. E-mail: kjil@kjil.com. Web Site: www.kjil.com. Licensee: Great Plains Christian Radio Inc. Network: Network: Moody, USA. Format: Contemp Christian, relg. Target aud: 25-60; Evangelical Christians. ♦Don Hughes, pres & gen mgr; Michael Luskey, opns dir; Steve Larsen, chief of engrg.

KSKZ(FM)— May 1, 1994: 98.1 mhz; 100 kw. Ant 666 ft. TL: N37 30 00 W100 40 00. Box 759, 1402 E. Kansas Ave., Garden City 67846. Phone: (620) 276-2366. Fax: (620) 276-3568. Web Site: www.wksradio.com. Licensee: Ingstad Broadcasting Inc. Group owner: Robert Ingstad Broadcast Properties (acq 1-27-95; FTR: 3-20-95). Format: Hot adult contemp. Target aud: 25-54. ♦Gil Wohler, gen mgr & gen sls mgr; James Jander, progmg dir; Andrew Mahoney, news dir; Tom Dial, chief of engrg.

Dearing

KUSN(FM)— Oct 1, 1999: 98.1 mhz; 9.7 kw. 495 ft. TL: N37 06 28 W95 43 22. Stereo. Box 4584, Springfield, MO 65808. Secondary address: 306 W. 8th St., Coffeyville 67337. Phone: (417) 883-9180. Fax: (417) 883-9095. Licensee: KGGF-KUSN Inc. Group owner: Mahaffey Enterprises Inc. (acq 12-26-90). Format: Country. Target aud: 18-49. ♦Robert B. Mahaffey, pres; John Leonard, gen mgr.

Derby

KZCH(FM)— 1978: 96.3 mhz; 50 kw. 492 ft. TL: N37 37 03 W97 20 11. Stereo. 9323 E. 37th St. N., Wichita 67226. Phone: (316) 494-6600. Fax: (316) 494-6730. Licensee: Clear Channel Broadcasting Licenses Inc. Group owner: Clear Channel Communications Inc. (acq 8-30-2000; grpsl). Network: CBS. Rep: D & R Radio. Format: Chr. Target aud: 25-54; baby boomers. ♦Dick Harlow, gen mgr.

Dodge City

*KAIG(FM)—Not on air, target date: unknown: 89.9 mhz; 45 kw vert. Ant 590 ft. TL: N37 55 56 W100 19 02. 5700 West Oaks Blvd., Rocklin, CA 95765. Phone: (916) 251-1600. Fax: (916) 251-1650. Licensee: Educational Media Foundation. ♦Richard Jenkins, pres.

KDCC(AM)— 1992: 1550 khz; 1 kw-D, 90 w-N, DA-2. TL: N37 47 14 W100 01 55. 3004 N. 14th 67801-2007. Phone: (316) 225-6783. Phone: (316) 225-6720. Fax: (316) 225-0918. Licensee: Dodge City Community College. (acq 6-7-92; $11,400; 7-27-92). Format: Educ, news, sp. News: 35 hrs wkly. Target aud: 18 plus. Spec prog: Christian, Sp. ♦Chris Bowen, opns mgr & news dir; John Ewy, gen mgr & sls dir; Jesus Garcia, progmg dir; James Reisfelt, news dir & pub affrs dir; Chuck Stark, chief of engrg.

KONQ(FM)—Co-owned with KDCC(AM). Apr 26, 1978: 91.9 mhz; 2.6 kw. 123 ft. TL: N37 46 33 W100 02 12. Phone: (316) 225-6720. Phone: (316) 225-6783. Fax: (316) 225-0918. Web Site: www.dodgecitycommunitycollege.com. Format: Var/div, educ, MOR. News: 7 hrs wkly. Spec prog: Black 10 hrs, sports 5 hrs wkly. ♦Chris Bowen, engrg dir.

KGNO(AM)— June 30, 1930: 1370 khz; 5 kw-D, 230 w-N. TL: N37 45 36 W100 05 53. 2601 Central Ave., Suite C, Village Plaza 67801. Phone: (620) 225-8080. Fax: (620) 225-6655. E-mail: rockswks@sbcgobal.net. Licensee: Waitt Radio Inc. Group owner: Waitt Broadcasting Inc. (acq 5-3-01; grpsl). Format: News, sports, talk radio. Target aud: 25-54. Spec prog: Farm 15 hrs wkly. ♦Jeff Ogden, gen mgr; Erik Carl, progmg dir.

KOLS(FM)—Co-owned with KGNO(AM). May 1966: 95.5 mhz; 100 kw. 570 ft. TL: N37 38 28 W100 20 40. (CP: 24 kw, ant 59 ft.). Stereo. Format: Adult contemp. News: 5 hrs wkly. Target aud: 25-49.

KZRD(FM)— December 1997: 93.9 mhz; 100 kw. 511 ft. TL: N38 00 07 W101 14 45. 2601 Central Ave., Village Plaza Suite C 67801. Phone: (620) 225-8080. Fax: (620) 225-6655. Licensee: Waitt Radio

Stations in the U.S. — Kansas

Developers & Brokers of Radio Properties
contact American Media Services at our suite:
Philadelphia Marriott Downtown
215-625-2900
843-972-2200
americanmediaservices.com
Charleston, SC
Dallas, TX · Chicago, Il · Austin, TX
American Media Services, LLC

Inc. Group owner: Waitt Broadcasting Inc. (acq 5-3-01; grpsl). Format: Classic rock. ◆ George DeMarco, gen mgr & gen sls mgr; Eric Carl, opns mgr; Keith Tallent, progmg dir.

Downs

KDNS(FM)— Apr 11, 1994: 94.1 mhz; 28 kw. Ant 292 ft. TL: N39 30 29 W98 18 57. Stereo. Box 88, West Hwy. 24, Glen Elder 67446. Phone: (785) 545-3220. Web Site: www.kdnskzdy@nckcn.com. Licensee: Hoeflicker Broadcasting Corp. Network: Jones Radio Networks. Format: Country. News staff: one; News: 4 hrs wkly. Target aud: 25-54. Spec prog: Farm 6 hrs, gospel 5 hrs wkly. ◆ Herbert R. Hoeflicker, gen mgr.

El Dorado

KAHS(AM)— Nov 16, 1953: 1360 khz; 1 kw-D. TL: N37 48 47 W96 48 44. Box 50 67042. Secondary address: 1612 S.E. River Rd. 67042. Phone: (316) 320-1360. Fax: (316) 320-1360. E-mail: kahs@kahs.kscoxmail.com. Web Site: www.1360kahs.com. Licensee: SMP Communications Inc. (group owner; acq 7-6-2005; $400,000). Network: Network: CNN Radio, Westwood One. Format: Contemp, adult standards. Target aud: 35-69. Spec prog: Jazz. Jazz 2 hrs wkly ◆ Stan Tacker, pres & gen mgr; David S. Ellis, opns mgr.

***KBTL(FM)**— March 1998: 88.1 mhz; 400 w. 92 ft. TL: N37 48 16 W96 53 02. Stereo. Butler County Community College, 901 S. Haverhill Rd. 67042. Phone: (316) 222-3194. Licensee: Butler County Community College. Format: Div. ◆ Lance D. Hayes, gen mgr.

KTLI(FM)— Feb 15, 1972: 99.1 mhz; 100 kw. Ant 617 ft. TL: N37 56 22 W96 59 20. Stereo. 125 N. Market, Suite 1900, Wichita 67202. Phone: (316) 303-9999. Fax: (316) 303-9900. Web Site: k-love.com. Licensee: Adonai Radio Group Inc. Group owner: KXOJ Inc. (acq 11-5-2004; $2.95 million). Format: Adult contemp, Christian. Target aud: 25-54; women. ◆ Crystal Wojtecko, gen mgr & rgnl sls mgr.

Emporia

***KANH(FM)**— 2002: 89.7 mhz; 3 kw. Ant 262 ft. TL: N38 21 45 W96 07 00. 1120 W. 11th St., Lawrence 66044. Phone: (785) 864-4530. Fax: (785) 864-5278. Web Site: www.kpr.ku.edu. Licensee: University of Kansas. Format: Class, jazz. ◆ Janet Campbell, gen mgr.

KANS(FM)— April 1998: 96.1 mhz; 6 kw. Ant 318 ft. TL: N38 24 21 W96 14 13. 1811 W. 6th Ave. 66801. Phone: (620) 343-9393. Fax: (620) 342-7617. E-mail: kans@ksradio.com. Web Site: www.ksradio.com. Licensee: C&C Consulting Inc. (acq 11-14-97; $10,000. for CP). Format: Soft hits. ◆ Brook Reed, pres; Marty Hill, gen mgr, opns mgr & dev dir; Andie Boden, progmg dir; Edward Lipson, chief of engrg.

KFFX(FM)—Listing follows KVOE(AM).

***KNGM(FM)**— Jan 11, 1987: 91.9 mhz; 3 kw. Ant 263 ft. TL: N38 24 35 W96 13 30. Stereo. Box 506, 815 Graham 66801. Phone: (620) 343-9292. E-mail: kngm@osprey.net. Licensee: Christian Action Team Inc. (acq 8-86; 1-87). Format: Contemp Christian. News staff: one. Target aud: Young families and adults. ◆ Jeff Shirley, pres & sr VP; April Reitmann, VP; Steve Pearson, gen mgr.

***KPOR(FM)**— 2002: 90.7 mhz; 2 kw. Ant 328 ft. TL: N38 26 50 W96 07 42. Family Stations Inc., 4135 Northgate Blvd., Sacramento, CA 95834. Phone: (916) 641-8191. Licensee: Family Stations Inc. (group owner) Format: Relg. ◆ Scott Miller, opns mgr.

KVOE(AM)— Jan 21, 1939: 1400 khz; 1 kw-U. TL: N38 23 10 W96 10 36. Box 968, 1420 C of E Dr. 66801. Phone: (620) 342-1400. Fax: (620) 342-0804. E-mail: kvoe@kvoe.com. Licensee: Emporia Radio Stations Inc. Group owner: Emporia's Radio Stations Inc. (acq 1-7-87). Network: ABC Information & Entertainment. Irwin, Campbell & Tannenwald. Format: Adult contemp, oldies, news. Target aud: 35-54. Spec prog: Sp 3 hrs wkly. ◆ Lee Schroeder, gen mgr.

KFFX(FM)—Co-owned with KVOE(AM). June 15, 1966: 104.9 mhz; 3 kw. Ant 279 ft. TL: N38 23 10 W96 10 36. Stereo. Format: Hot adult contemp. News: 4 hrs wkly. Target aud: 20-40.

KVOE-FM— Jan 16, 1985: 101.7 mhz; 3.2 kw. Ant 298 ft. TL: N38 21 45 W96 07 00. Stereo. 1420 C of E Dr. 66801. Phone: (620) 342-1400. Fax: (620) 342-0804. E-mail: kvoe@kvoe.com. Licensee: Emporia Radio Stations Inc. Group owner: Emporia's Radio Stations Inc. (acq 1994). Irwin, Campbell & Tannenwald. Format: Country. News staff: 2; News: 7 hrs wkly. Target aud: 25-54. ◆ Erren Harter, pres & prom mgr; Steve Sauder, CEO, pres & gen sls mgr; Jef O'Dell, news dir & chief of engrg.

Enterprise

***KBMP(FM)**— Mar 6, 2002: 90.5 mhz; 250 w. Ant 171 ft. TL: N38 54 03 W97 05 40. American Family Radio, Box 3206, Tupelo, MS 38803. Phone: (626) 844-8888. Web Site: www.afr.net. Licensee: American Family Association. Group owner: American Family Radio (acq 8-17-99). Format: Christian. ◆ Marvin Sanders, gen mgr.

Eureka

KOTE(FM)— October 1988: 93.5 mhz; 3 kw. 321 ft. TL: N37 47 29 W96 17 25. Stereo. Box 350 67045. Secondary address: 326 Village Ln. 67045. Phone: (620) 583-7414. Fax: (620) 583-7233. E-mail: info@kotefm.com. Web Site: www.kotefm.com. Licensee: Niemeyer Communications LLC (acq 8-12-2005; $125,000). Network: Jones Radio Networks. Format: Classic rock, country. Target aud: General. Spec prog: Blues 2 hrs, oldies 6 hrs wkly. ◆ David Niemeyer, gen mgr.

Fairway

KCNW(AM)— Apr 16, 1953: 1380 khz; 2.5 kw-D, 29 w-N. TL: N39 04 19 W94 40 58. 4535 Metropolitan Ave., Kansas City 66106. Phone: (913) 384-1380. Fax: (913) 236-9583. Web Site: www.wilkinsradio.com. Licensee: Kansas City Radio Inc. Group owner: Wilkins Communications Network Inc. (acq 1-17-01; $725,000). Network: Westwood One. Format: Talk radio. News staff: one. Target aud: 24-55; adults involved in community & family. ◆ Anthony Norman, gen mgr & stn mgr.

Fort Scott

KMDO(AM)— Oct 8, 1954: 1600 khz; 1 kw-D, 50 w-N. TL: N37 48 35 W94 42 22. (CP: TL: N37 48 27 W94 42 33). Box 72, 2 N. National 66701. Phone: (620) 223-4500. Phone: (620) 223-4501. Fax: (620) 223-5662. Licensee: Fort Scott Broadcasting Co. (acq 2-1-60). Format: Oldies, rock. Target aud: General; 30 plus. ◆ Tim McKenney, pres & gen mgr; Jon Hart, prom dir.

KOMB(FM)—Co-owned with KMDO(AM). Jan 23, 1981: 103.9 mhz; 2 kw. 400 ft. TL: N37 48 27 W98 42 33. Stereo.

***KVCY(FM)**— November 1983: 104.7 mhz; 16 kw. 410 ft. TL: N37 47 47 W94 42 20. Stereo. 3434 W. Kilbourn Ave., Milwaukee, WI 53208. Phone: (414) 935-3000. Fax: (414) 935-3015. E-mail: kvcy@vcyamerica.org. Web Site: www.vcyamerica.org. Licensee: VCY America Inc. (group owner) Network: Network: USA, Moody. Format: Relg, Christian. ◆ Vic Eliason, VP & gen mgr.

Fredonia

KGGF-FM— July 14, 1997: 104.1 mhz; 6 kw. 328 ft. TL: N37 31 36 W95 49 39. 200 Arco Pl., Suite 345, Independence 67301. Phone: (620) 331-8444. Fax: (620) 331-8444. Licensee: KGGF-KUSN Inc. Group owner: Mahaffey Enterprises Inc. Format: Adult contemp. ◆ John Leonard, gen mgr.

Galena

KCAR-FM— June 29, 2000: 104.3 mhz; 6 kw. Ant 328 ft. TL: N37 03 13 W94 42 12. 2510 W. 20th St., Joplin, MO 64804. Phone: (417) 781-1313. Fax: (417) 781-1316. Licensee: FFD Holdings I Inc. Group owner: Petracom Media L.L.C. (acq 12-20-2004; grpsl). Format: Classic rock, oldies. ◆ Dave Clemens, gen mgr; Steve Smith, gen mgr.

Garden City

***KANZ(FM)**— June 29, 1980: 91.1 mhz; 100 kw. 650 ft. TL: N37 46 40 W100 52 08. Stereo. Box 1176 67846-5519. Secondary address: 210 N. 7th St. 67846-5519. Phone: (620) 275-7444. Fax: (620) 275-7496. Web Site: www.hppr.org. Licensee: KANZA Society Inc. (acq 11-77; 7-80). Network: Network: PRI, NPR. Format: Div, educ, class. News: 39 hrs wkly. Target aud: General. Spec prog: Jazz 15 hrs, folk 6 hrs, Sp 6 hrs wkly. ◆ Robert Kirby, progmg dir.

KBUF(AM)—(Holcomb). 1948: 1030 khz; 25 kw-D, 1 kw-N, DA-2. TL: N38 00 01 W100 53 54. Box 759, 1402 E. Kansas 67846. Phone: (620) 276-2366. Fax: (620) 276-3568. Licensee: KBUF Partnership. Group owner: Robert Ingstad Broadcast Properties (acq 11-1-79). Network: ABC Information & Entertainment. Fisher, Wayland, Cooper, Leader & Zaragoza L.L.P. Format: C&W, talk. News staff: one. Target aud: 25-54; people interested in class country & info progmg. Spec prog: Farm 15 hrs wkly. ◆ James Janda, progmg mgr.

KKJQ(FM)—Co-owned with KBUF(AM). Nov 20, 1962: 97.3 mhz; 100 kw. 850 ft. TL: N37 46 48 W100 27 36. Stereo. Network: ABC. Format: Country, adult contemp. Target aud: 18-49.

KIUL(AM)— May 20, 1935: 1240 khz; 1 kw-U. TL: N37 59 52 W100 54 25. 1402 E.Kansas Ave. 67846. Phone: (620) 276-3251. Fax: (620) 276-3568. Web Site: www.wksradio.com. Licensee: Dakota Communications Ltd. (group owner; acq 9-27-96; $258,820). Network: Network: CBS, Westwood One. Dow, Lohnes & Albertson. Format: Sports, news/talk. Target aud: 45 plus; upscale adults. Spec prog: Farm 5 hrs wkly. ◆ Gil Wohler, gen mgr.

KWKR(FM)—See Leoti

Girard

KSEK-FM— Sept 1, 1988: 99.1 mhz; 6 kw. Ant 325 ft. TL: N37 29 02 W94 51 08. 202 E. Centenial Dr., Suite 2B, Pittsburg 66762. Phone: (620) 232-9912. Fax: (620) 232-9915. Licensee: Southeast Kansas Independent Living Resource Center Inc. (group owner; acq 10-20-2004; $700,000. with KSEK(AM) Pittsburg). Network: AP Network News. Format: Classic rock. News: 10 hrs wkly. Target aud: 25-54; resident adults & university students. ◆ Lynn Meredith, pres & gen mgr.

Goodland

***KGCR(FM)**— Mar 1, 1988: 107.7 mhz; 100 kw. 446 ft. TL: N39 22 03 W101 26 44. Stereo. Box 9, Brewster 67732. Secondary address: 3410 Rd. 66, Brewster 67732. Phone: (785) 694-2877. Fax: (785) 694-2875. Licensee: The Praise Network Inc. (acq 7-2-98). Network: Moody, USA. Format: Relg. News staff: one; News: 30 hrs wkly. Target aud: 25-54; Christian families. Spec prog: Farm 2 hrs wkly. ◆ Lloyd Mintzmyer, CEO & pres.

KKCI(FM)—Listing follows KLOE(AM).

KLOE(AM)— 1947: 730 khz; 1 kw-D, 20 w-N. TL: N39 20 04 W101 45 28. Box 569, 3023 W. 31st St. 67735-0569. Phone: (785) 899-2309. Fax: (785) 899-3062. Web Site: www.kloe.com. Licensee: Melia Communications Inc. (group owner; acq 1-26-96; $990,000 with co-located FM). Network: CBS. Format: News/talk, country, farm. Target aud: General. ◆ Martin K. Melia, pres & gen mgr.

KKCI(FM)—Co-owned with KLOE(AM). Sept 15, 1990: 102.5 mhz; 100 kw. 712 ft. TL: N39 23 19 W101 33 34. Stereo. (Acq 4-90; $40,000; 5-21-90). Network: Jones Radio Networks. Format: Oldies, sports, jazz. Target aud: 25-55.

Kansas — Directory of Radio

Great Bend

*KBDA(FM)— 1999: 89.7 mhz; 250 w. Ant 112 ft. TL: N38 20 16 W98 45 48. American Family Radio Assoc., Box 3206, Tupelo, MS 38803. Phone: (662) 844-8888, EXT. 204. Fax: (662) 842-6791. Web Site: www.afr.net. Licensee: American Family Association. Group owner: American Family Radio Format: Inspirational Christian. ♦Marvin Sanders, gen mgr.

*KHCT(FM)— Aug 3, 1992: 90.9 mhz; 50 kw. 781 ft. TL: N38 37 04 W98 56 32. 815 N. Walnut St., Suite 300, Hutchinson 67501. Phone: (620) 662-6646. Licensee: Hutchinson Community College. Network: NPR. Format: Class, new age, news. ♦David Horning, gen mgr; Geralyn Drumgold, opns dir; Sharon Webb, dev dir.

KHOK(FM)—(Hoisington). 1978: 100.7 mhz; 100 kw. 430 ft. TL: N38 32 49 W98 45 59. Stereo. Box 609, 1200 Baker St. 67530. Phone: (620) 792-3647. Fax: (620) 792-3649. Web Site: www.eagleradio.net. Licensee: Eagle Communications Inc. Group owner: Eagle Communications Group (acq 9-1-86; grpsl; FTR: 4-8-91). Format: Country. News staff: one. Target aud: 18-44. Spec prog: Relg 2 hrs wkly. ♦Gary Shorman, CEO, chmn & pres; Rick Nulton, gen mgr.

KVGB(AM)— Mar 10, 1937: 1590 khz; 5 kw-U, DA-N. TL: N38 18 50 W98 47 35. Box 609, 1200 Baker St. 67530. Phone: (620) 792-4637. Fax: (620) 792-3649. Web Site: eagleradio.net. Licensee: Eagle Communications Inc. Group owner: Eagle Communications Group (acq 4-95). Network: ABC. Format: News, talk, sports. Target aud: 28 plus. Spec prog: Farm 7 hrs, relg 2 hrs wkly. ♦Rick Nulton, gen mgr; Randy Goering, sls dir.

KVGB-FM— Jan 17, 1977: 104.3 mhz; 96 kw. 810 ft. TL: N38 25 54 W98 46 18. Stereo. Web Site: eagleradio.net. Network: ABC. Format: Classic rock. ♦Randy Goering, sls VP.

*KWBI(FM)— Oct 10, 2001: 91.9 mhz; 1.8 kw. Ant 259 ft. TL: N38 20 16 W98 45 48. Stereo. 5700 W. Oaks Blvd., Rocklin, CA 95765. Phone: (916) 251-1600. Fax: (916) 251-1650. E-mail: klove@klove.com. Web Site: www.klove.com. Licensee: Educational Media Foundation. Group owner: EMF Broadcasting. Network: K-Love. Shaw Pittman. Format: Contemp Christian. News staff: 3. Target aud: 25-44; Judeo Christian, female. ♦Richard Jenkins, pres; Mike Novak, VP; Lloyd Parker, gen mgr; Ed Lenane, opns dir; Keith Whipple, dev dir.

KZLS(FM)— Feb 3, 1986: 107.9 mhz; 100 kw. 886 ft. TL: N38 46 16 W98 44 17. Stereo. 5501 10th St., Great W. Bend 67530. Phone: (620) 792-7108. Fax: (620) 792-7051. E-mail: kzls@waittradio.com. Licensee: Waitt Radio Inc. Group owner: Waitt Broadcasting Inc. (acq 5-3-01; grpsl). Blooston, Mordkofsky, Jackson & Dickens. Format: Adult contemp. News staff: one; News: 5 hrs wkly. Target aud: 25-54. ♦Ken Schwamborn, gen mgr; Josh Boor, opns dir & progmg VP; Mike Hendrickson, chief of engrg.

Hays

KAYS(AM)—Listing follows KHAZ(FM).

KHAZ(FM)— May 1, 1985: 99.5 mhz; 100 kw. 515 ft. TL: N38 56 29 W99 21 22. Stereo. Box 6 67601. Secondary address: 2300 Hall St. 67601. Phone: (785) 625-2578. Fax: (785) 625-3632. Licensee: Eagle Communications Inc. Group owner: Eagle Communications Group Network: ABC. Format: Country. News staff: 2; News: 4 hrs wkly. Target aud: 25-54. Spec prog: Farm 10 hrs, gospel 3 hrs wkly. ♦Todd Nelson, gen mgr; Dwayne Detter, gen sls mgr.

KAYS(AM)—Co-owned with KHAZ(FM). Oct 15, 1948: 1400 khz; 1 kw-U. TL: N38 53 29 W99 22 03. Stereo. Box 817, 2300 Hall St. 67601. (Acq 3-20-91; grpsl; 4-8-91). Format: Oldies. News staff: one; News: 6 hrs wkly. Target aud: Adults. ♦John Pennington, news dir.

KJLS(FM)— June 27, 1974: 103.3 mhz; 100 kw. 994 ft. TL: N39 01 15 W99 28 12. Stereo. Box 6 67601. Secondary address: 2300 Hall 67601. Phone: (785) 625-2578. Fax: (785) 625-3632. Licensee: Eagle Communications Inc. Group owner: Eagle Communications Group (acq 9-12-00; with KKQY(FM) Hill City). Network: ABC Information & Entertainment. Format: Adult contemp. News staff: one; News: 8 hrs wkly. Target aud: 25-49; 60% female, 40% male. ♦Todd Nelson, VP & gen mgr.

*KPRD(FM)— 1994: 88.9 mhz; 83 kw. 636 ft. TL: N38 46 16 W98 44 17. 301 W. 13th St., Suite 409 67601. Phone: (785) 628-6300. Fax: (785) 628-6389. E-mail: kprd@kprd.org. Web Site: www.kprd.org. Licensee: The Praise Network Inc. Format: Relg. Target aud: 20-48. ♦Lloyd Mintzmyer, CEO.

*KZAN(FM)—Not on air, target date: unknown: 91.7 mhz; 1.25 kw. Ant 246 ft. TL: N38 56 28 W99 21 20. Kanza Society Inc., 207 N. 7th St., Garden City 67846. Phone: (800) 678-7444. Fax: (620) 275-7496. Licensee: Kanza Society Inc. Network: Network: NPR, PRI. Format: Var.

Haysville

KFBZ(FM)— Aug 25, 1985: 105.3 mhz; 100 kw. 1,000 ft. TL: N37 46 40 W97 30 37. Stereo. 2120 N. Woodlawn, Suite 352, Wichita 67208-1847. Phone: (316) 685-2121. Fax: (316) 685-3408. Web Site: www.1053thebuzz.com. Licensee: Entercom Wichita License LLC. Group owner: Entercom Communications Corp. (acq 2000; grpsl). Format: Hot AC. News: 2 hrs wkly. Target aud: 25-54. Spec prog: Relg 2 hrs wkly. ♦Jackie Wise, gen mgr.

Herington

KJRL(FM)— Sept 6, 1997: 105.7 mhz; 12.5 kw. 500 ft. TL: N38 37 01 W96 59 09. Stereo. Box 389, 165 Trail Rd. 67449. Phone: (785) 258-2660. Fax: (785) 258-2777. E-mail: kjrl@kjrl.org. Web Site: www.kjrl.org. Licensee: Great Plains Christian Radio Inc. (acq 9-5-01). Network: Salem Radio Network. Format: AC Christian. News: 16 hrs wkly. Target aud: 18-54; farmers, railroad & transportation workers, military & professional. ♦Don Hughes, CEO & gen mgr; Lee Issaac, chmn; Doug Wedekind, stn mgr; Mark Erdman, opns dir; Dave Scott, dev dir.

Hiawatha

KNZA(FM)— Aug 18, 1977: 103.9 mhz; 50 kw. 492 ft. TL: N39 34 41 W95 33 46. Stereo. Box 104 66434-0104. Secondary address: 1828 Hwy. 73 66434-0104. Phone: (785) 547-3461. Fax: (785) 547-9900. E-mail: knza@rainbowtel.net. Licensee: KNZA Inc. (group owner; acq 6-83; 6-20-83). Network: ABC Daytime Direction. Format: Country. News staff: one; News: 10 hrs wkly. Target aud: 18-54; general. Spec prog: Farm 14 hrs wkly. ♦Greg Buser, gen mgr; Robert Hilton, opns mgr.

Hill City

KKQY(FM)— Aug 29, 1997: 101.9 mhz; 97 kw. 994 ft. TL: N39 01 15 W99 28 13. Stereo. Box 6, Hays 67601. Phone: (785) 625-2578. Fax: (785) 625-3632. Licensee: Eagle Communications Inc. Group owner: Eagle Communications Group (acq 9-12-00; with KJLS(FM) Hays). Format: Country. News: 5 hrs wkly. Target aud: 25-54. ♦Todd Nelson, gen mgr; Steve Klitzke, gen sls mgr; Scott Bommer, progmg dir.

*KZNA(FM)— 1986: 90.5 mhz; 100 kw. 600 ft. TL: N39 15 56 W99 49 48. Stereo. 210 N. 7th St., Garden City 67846-5519. Phone: (620) 275-7444. Fax: (620) 275-7496. E-mail: hppr@hppr.org. Web Site: www.hppr.org. Licensee: Kanza Society Inc. (acq 11-77; 7-80). Network: PRI, NPR. Format: Educ, class, news/talk. News: 39 hrs wkly. Target aud: 25-80; educated. Spec prog: Jazz 15 hrs, folk 6 hrs, Sp 6 hrs wkly. ♦Bob Kirby, opns dir, opns mgr & progmg dir; Diana Aguilar-Sinclair, dev dir.

Hoisington

KHOK(FM)—Licensed to Hoisington. See Great Bend

Holcomb

KBUF(AM)—Licensed to Holcomb. See Garden City

Horton

KAIR-FM— Jan 25, 1995: 93.7 mhz; 25 kw. Ant 328 ft. Stereo. Box G, Atchison 66002. Secondary address: 200 N. 5th St., Atchinson 66002. Phone: (913) 367-1470. Fax: (913) 367-7021. E-mail: thewakeupcrew@hotmail.com. Licensee: Mark V Media Group Inc. (group owner)(acq 12-16-2004; $1.55 million. with KAIR(AM) Atchison). Network: AP Radio. Format: Country. News staff: 4; News: 133 hrs wkly. Target aud: 25-54. ♦Mark A. Oppold, pres.

Hugoton

KFXX-FM— Sept 16, 1983: 106.7 mhz; 35 kw. Ant 259 ft. TL: N37 19 03 W101 20 16. Stereo. 2917 S. Colorado, Ulysses 67880. Phone: (620) 276-2366. Fax: (620) 356-3635. Licensee: KBUF Partnership. Group owner: Robert Ingstad Broadcast Properties. Baraff, Koerner & Olender. Format: Rgnl Mexican. ♦Eddie Ochoa, gen mgr.

Humboldt

KINZ(FM)— September 1998: 95.3 mhz; 24 kw. Ant 335 ft. TL: N37 44 52 W95 33 39. Stereo. 117 S. Grant St., Chanute 66720. Phone: (620) 431-1333. Fax: (620) 431-1943. E-mail: mike@kinz.biz. Web Site: www.kinz.biz. Licensee: Sutcliffe Communications LLC. Network: CNN Radio. Format: Classic rock. Target aud: 25-55. Spec prog: Gospel 3 hrs wkly. ♦Mike Sutcliffe, CEO & gen mgr; Sheri Sutcliffe, VP.

Hutchinson

*KHCC-FM— Sept 11, 1972: 90.1 mhz; 100 kw. 1,080 ft. TL: N38 03 40 W97 45 49. 815 N. Walnut, Suite 300 67501-6217. Phone: (620) 662-6646. Web Site: www.radiokansas.org. Licensee: Hutchinson Community College. Network: NPR. Format: Class, new age, news. News: 27 hrs wkly. ♦David M. Hornming, gen mgr; Geralyn Drumgold, opns dir; Sharon Webb, dev dir.

KHUT(FM)—Listing follows KWBW(AM).

KSKU(FM)— 1998: 97.1 mhz; 13.5 kw. Ant 449 ft. TL: N37 57 54 W97 49 26. (CP: 50 kw, ant 492 ft. TL: N37 48 03 W97 56 49). 106 N. Main St. 67501-5219. Phone: (620) 665-5758. Fax: (620) 665-6655. Licensee: Ad Astra Per Aspera Broadcasting Inc. (group owner; acq 9-16-98). Format: Contemp. Target aud: 12-49. ♦Cliff C. Shank, gen mgr; Mike Hill, stn mgr; Aaron West, opns mgr.

KWBW(AM)— May 28, 1935: 1450 khz; 1 kw-U. TL: N38 04 02 W97 57 53. Box 1036 67504-1036. Phone: (620) 662-4486. Fax: (620) 662-5357. Web Site: www.khutfm.com. Licensee: Eagle Communications Inc. Group owner: Eagle Communications Group (acq 11-4-91; with co-located FM). Format: Talk, new/sports. Spec prog: Black 2 hrs, gospel 11 hrs wkly. ♦Dan Deming, gen mgr & progmg dir.

KHUT(FM)—Co-owned with KWBW(AM). Mar 15, 1972: 102.9 mhz; 28.5 kw. 496 ft. TL: N38 02 36 W98 00 53. (CP: N38 02 39 W98 00 56). Web Site: www.khutfm.com. Format: C&W. ♦Jason Younger, progmg dir.

KZSN(FM)— Oct 7, 1968: 102.1 mhz; 100 kw. 1,032 ft. TL: N37 47 47 W97 31 59. Stereo. 2402 E. 37th St. N., Wichita 67219. Phone: (316) 832-9600. Web Site: www.kzsn.com. Licensee: Capstar TX L.P. Group owner: Clear Channel Communications Inc. (acq 8-30-00; grpsl). Format: Country. News staff: one. Target aud: General. ♦John Walker, gen mgr & gen sls mgr.

Independence

*KARF(FM)— 1997: 91.9 mhz; 250 w. Ant 180 ft. TL: N37 15 54 W95 39 26. Box 3206, Tupelo, MS 38803. Phone: (662) 844-8888. Fax: (662) 842-6791. Web Site: www.afr.net. Licensee: American Family Association. Group owner: American Family Radio Format: Adult contemp. ♦Marvin Sanders, gen mgr.

*KBQC(FM)— 2002: 88.5 mhz; 13 kw vert. Ant 476 ft. TL: N37 03 11 W96 06 07. Drawer 2440, Tupelo, MS 38801. Phone: (662) 844-8888. Fax: (662) 842-6791. Licensee: American Family Association. Group owner: American Family Radio (acq 12-18-00; buyer paid construction & bcst costs of CP). Format: Christian. ♦Marvin Sanders, gen mgr.

KIND(AM)— Dec 8, 1947: 1010 khz; 250 w-D, 32 w-N. TL: N37 13 07 W95 43 30. 122 W. Myrtle 67301. Phone: (620) 331-3000. Fax: (620) 331-8008. E-mail: patti@radiokind.com. Licensee: Central Broadcasting Inc. (acq 3-12-2001; $20,000. for stock with co-located FM). Network: Westwood One. Format: Adult Standards. Target aud: 35-65; baby boomers. Spec prog: Big band 2 hrs, class 3 hrs wkly. ♦Bill Kurtis, CEO; Patti McCormick, gen mgr.

KIND-FM— May 10, 1969: 102.9 mhz; 25 kw. Ant 272 ft. TL: N37 15 42 W95 45 59. Network: CNN Radio. Format: Hot adult contemp. Target aud: 22-44. Spec prog: Alternative 4 hrs, Christian hot AC 2 hrs wkly.

Stations in the U.S. — Kansas

Ingalls

KSSA(FM)— July 1, 1999: 105.9 mhz; 100 kw. 666 ft. TL: N37 46 48 W100 27 36. 1402 E. Kansas Ave., Garden City 67846. Phone: (620) 276-3251. Fax: (620) 276-3568. E-mail: kssa@wksradio.com. Licensee: KBUF Partnership. Group owner: Robert Ingstad Broadcast Properties (acq 1999; $250,000). Shaw Pittman. Format: Sp. ♦G.L. Wohler, gen mgr.

KSSH(FM)— Jan 1, 2001: 96.3 mhz; 100 kw. 659 ft. TL: N37 38 28 W100 20 40. Stereo. 2601 Central, Suite C, Dodge City 67801. Phone: (620) 225-8080. Fax: (620) 225-6655. Licensee: Waitt Radio Inc. (group owner; acq 3-17-03; swap for KHMY(FM) Pratt). ♦George DeMarco, gen mgr.

Iola

KALN(AM)— July 25, 1961: 1370 khz; 500 w-D, 62 w-N, DA. TL: N37 54 07 W95 24 26. Box 710 66749. Phone: (620) 365-3151. Fax: (620) 365-5431. Licensee: Iola Broadcasting Inc. (acq 9-1-73). Format: Oldies. ♦Michael P. Russell, pres & gen mgr; Lovetta R. Russell, CFO; Tom Norris, stn mgr & progmg dir.

KIKS-FM—Co-owned with KALN(AM). June 9, 1977: 101.5 mhz; 11.5 kw. Ant 289 ft. TL: N37 54 04 W95 24 04. Stereo. Format: Adult contemp.

Junction City

KJCK(AM)— May 15, 1949: 1420 khz; 1 kw-D, 500 w-N, DA-N. TL: N39 01 33 W96 48 36. Box 789, W. Ash & Hwy. 77 66441. Phone: (785) 762-5525. Fax: (785) 762-5387. E-mail: platinum@kjck.com. Web Site: www.kjck.com. Licensee: Platinum Broadcasting Inc. (group owner; acq 9-4-86). Network: Network: ABC Information & Entertainment, Jones Radio Networks. Format: C&W. News staff: one; News: 15 hrs wkly. Target aud: 35-54. Spec prog: Relg 4 hrs wkly. ♦Mark Ediger, gen mgr, opns dir & gen sls mgr; Gary McIntyre, opns dir & progmg dir; Ben Bennett, prom dir; Dewey Terrill, news dir; Randy Stewart, chief of engrg.

KJCK-FM— July 22, 1965: 97.5 mhz; 100 kw. Ant 630 ft. TL: N39 00 53 W96 52 15. Stereo. Web Site: www.kjck.com. Format: Top-40. News staff: one; News: 10 hrs wkly. Target aud: 18-34; young adults. ♦Wende Horton, progmg dir; Brad Jepsen, mus dir.

Kansas City

KCKN(AM)— 1925: 1340 khz; 1 kw-U. TL: N39 06 50 W94 40 05. 11131 Colorado Ave., MO 64137. Phone: (816) 763-2040. Fax: (816) 966-1055. Web Site: www.kc1340am.com. Licensee: KCKN LLC (acq 7-20-2004; $1.6 million). News staff: 2. Target aud: 25-64; upscale, affluent, well educated. ♦Michael Carter, gen mgr; Andre Carson, opns mgr.

KFKF-FM— May 28, 1963: 94.1 mhz; 100 kw. 994 ft. TL: N39 00 57 W94 30 24. Stereo. 4717 Grand Ave., Suite 600, MO 64112. Phone: (816) 753-4000. Fax: (816) 753-4045. Web Site: www.kfkf.com. Licensee: Infinity Radio Holdings Inc. Group owner: Infinity Broadcasting Corp. (acq 12-14-00; grpsl). Format: Contemp country. ♦Hendon Hasty, gen mgr.

KKHK(AM)— 1926: 1250 khz; 25 kw-D, 3.7 kw-N, DA-N. TL: N39 11 06 W94 27 28. 6220 Kansas Ave. 66611. Phone: (913) 788-1255. Fax: (913) 788-1254. Web Site: www.lasupeerx1250.com. Licensee: Entercom Kansas City License LLC. Group owner: Entercom Communications Corp. (acq 3-3-99; $2.75 million). Format: Mexican rgnl. ♦Michael H. Payne, gen mgr.

KUDL(FM)— Oct 9, 1959: 98.1 mhz; 100 kw. 994 ft. TL: N39 04 23 W94 29 06. Stereo. 4935 Belinder Rd., Westwood 66205. Phone: (913) 677-8998. Fax: (913) 677-8981. Web Site: www.kudl.com. Licensee: Entercom Kansas City License L.L.C. Group owner: Entercom Communications Corp. (acq 10-17-97; grpsl). Format: Adult contemp. News staff: one. Target aud: 25-44; women. ♦Cindy Schloff, gen mgr.

KXTR(AM)— 2001: 1660 khz; 10 kw-D, 1 kw-N. TL: N39 06 50 W94 40 45. 4935 Belinder Rd., Westwood 66205. Phone: (913) 677-8998. Fax: (913) 677-8980. Web Site: www.kxtrlive.com. Licensee: Entercom Kansas City License LLC. Group owner: Entercom Communications Corp. Format: Classical. ♦Cindy Schloss, gen mgr; Patrick Nease, progmg dir; John Verlin, sls.

Kingman

KCVW(FM)— December 1997: 94.3 mhz; 50 kw. 492 ft. TL: N37 48 03 W97 56 49. Mezzanine, 100 N. Main, Hutchinson 67501. Phone: (620) 663-0943. Fax: (620) 663-0913. E-mail: kcvw@bottradionetwork.com. Web Site: www.bottradionetwork.com. Licensee: Bott Communications Inc. Group owner: Bott Radio Network Network: USA. Format: Christian talk. ♦Richard P. Bott II, exec VP.

KTCM(FM)— Sept 15, 1989: 100.3 mhz; 48 kw. 505 ft. TL: N37 29 59 W98 10 24. Stereo. 315 W. D Ave. 67010. Phone: (620) 532-1190. Fax: (620) 264-0562. Licensee: Maria L. Salazar. (acq 2-26-96; 3-11-96). Format: Sp, salsa. ♦Tony Delgado, gen mgr.

Larned

KBGL(FM)— 2001: 106.9 mhz; 100 kw. Ant 485 ft. TL: N38 27 06 W99 10 03. 1200 Baker St., Great Bend 67530. Phone: (620) 792-3647. Fax: (620) 792-3649. Web Site: www.eagleradio.net. Licensee: Hull Broadcasting Inc. (acq 9-12-00; with KFIX(FM) Plainville). Format: Oldies. ♦Rick Nulton, gen mgr.

KGTR(FM)—Listing follows KNNS(AM).

KNNS(AM)— Nov 4, 1963: 1510 khz; 1 kw-D, TL: N38 09 54 W99 06 05. 5501 W. 10 St., Great Bend 67530. Phone: (620) 792-7108. Fax: (620) 792-7051. Licensee: Waitt Radio Inc. Group owner: Waitt Broadcasting Inc. (acq 5-3-01; grpsl). Format: ESPN sports. Target aud: General; people looking for loc info. Spec prog: Farm 10 hrs, gospel 6 hrs, relg 5 hrs wkly. ♦George Pelletier, pres; Joyce Marshall, gen mgr; Jim Hill, opns mgr & progmg dir; Mike Hendrickson, chief of engrg.

KGTR(FM)—Co-owned with KNNS(AM). Nov 1, 1965: 96.7 mhz; 3 kw. 290 ft. TL: N38 09 54 W99 06 05. (CP: Ant 265 ft.). Stereo. Format: Oldies. Target aud: 30-60; baby boomers with disposable income.

Lawrence

***KANU(FM)**— Sept 15, 1952: 91.5 mhz; 100 kw. 698 ft. TL: N38 57 18 W95 15 57. Stereo. 1120 W. 11th St. 66044. Phone: (785) 864-4530. Fax: (785) 864-5278. Web Site: www.kpr.ku.edu. Licensee: University of Kansas. Network: Network: PRI, NPR. Arter & Hadden. Format: Class, jazz. News staff: 3; News: 35 hrs wkly. Target aud: 25-49; upscale. Spec prog: Bluegrass 4 hrs, Celtic 2 hrs, blues 4 hrs wkly. ♦Janet Campbell, gen mgr; Cordelia Brown, opns dir.

***KJHK(FM)**— 1975: 90.7 mhz; 2.9 kw. 163 ft. TL: N38 57 30 W95 15 00. Stereo. Phone: (785) 864-4746. Fax: (785) 864-5173. E-mail: kjhk@mail.ku.edu. Web Site: www.kjhk.org. Licensee: University of Kansas. Network: ABC Information & Entertainment. Format: Rock, jazz. News: 15 hrs wkly. Target aud: 18-34; Univ & community population. Spec prog: Reggae 3 hrs, blues 2 hrs wkly. ♦Andy Dierks, gen mgr; Brent Stevens, stn mgr.

KLWN(AM)— Feb 22, 1951: 1320 khz; 500 w-D, 250 w-N. TL: N38 56 05 W95 17 12. 3125 W. 6th St. 66049-3101. Phone: (785) 843-1320. Fax: (785) 841-5924. Fax: (785) 843-4585. E-mail: mail@lazer.com. Web Site: www.1320sports.com. Licensee: Zimmer Radio of Mid-Missouri Inc. Group owner: Zimmer Radio Group (acq 9-1-98; $3 million. with co-located FM). Fletcher, Heald & Hildreth. Format: News/talk, sports. News staff: 2; News: 10 hrs wkly. Target aud: 25-59; adults. Spec prog: Relg 4 hrs wkly. ♦John Flood, progmg dir.

KLZR(FM)—Co-owned with KLWN. Aug 20, 1963: 105.9 mhz; 100 kw. 771 ft. TL: N39 02 21 W95 26 59. Stereo. Web Site: www.lazer.com. Format: CHR, top 40. News staff: 2; News: one hr wkly. Target aud: 18-34; young adults.

Leavenworth

KKLO(AM)— 1946: 1410 khz; 5 kw-D, 500 w-N, DA-2. TL: N39 16 24 W94 54 27. 481 Muncie Rd. 66048. Phone: (913) 351-1410. Fax: (913) 351-1410. Web Site: www.hereshelpnet.org. Licensee: New Life Evangelistic Center Inc. (acq 10-29-99). Format: Christian. Target aud: 25-49; upscale, educated, loyal Christian listeners. ♦Charlie Hale, stn mgr; Larry Rice, CEO, chmn, pres, gen mgr & progmg dir.

KQRC-FM—Licensed to Leavenworth. See Kansas City MO

Leoti

KWKR(FM)— Nov 1, 1983: 99.9 mhz; 100 kw. Ant 395 ft. TL: N38 16 39 W101 17 50. Stereo. Box 759, Garden City 67846. Secondary address: 1402 E. Kansas, Garden City 67846. Phone: (620) 276-3251. Fax: (620) 276-3568. Web Site: www.wksradio.com. Licensee: KBUF Partnership. Group owner: Robert Ingstad Broadcast Properties (acq 12-1-97; $841,170). Network: Westwood One. Dow, Lohnes & Albertson. Format: Classic rock. Target aud: 25-44. Spec prog: Sp 3 hrs wkly. ♦James Janda, VP; Gil Wohler, gen mgr.

Liberal

KLDG(FM)— October 1994: 102.7 mhz; 100 kw. 466 ft. TL: N37 02 45 W101 06 11. 1410 Northwestern Ave. 67901. Phone: (620) 624-3891. Fax: (620) 624-7885. Web Site: www.kscb.net. Licensee: Seward County Broadcasting Co. Inc. (group owner) Network: Jones Radio Networks. Rep: Roslin. Shaw Pittman. Format: Country. News staff: 2; News: 2 hrs wkly. Target aud: 18-49; young, mobile & impulsive consumers. ♦John Landon, chmn; Don Ford, pres; Bob Larrabee, VP; Stuart Melchert, gen mgr; Terry Miller, opns mgr; Kevin Colvin, sls dir & gen sls mgr.

KSCB(AM)— July 25, 1948: 1270 khz; 1 kw-D, 30 w-N. TL: N37 03 15 W100 53 39. 1410 N. Western Ave. 67901. Phone: (620) 624-3891. Fax: (620) 624-9472. E-mail: kscb@kscb.net. Web Site: www.kscb.net. Licensee: Seward County Broadcasting Co. Network: Network: ABC, Westwood One. Rep: Roslin. Wiley, Rein & Felding. Format: News/talk. News staff: 3. Target aud: 35 plus. Spec prog: Farm 6 hrs wkly. ♦Stuart Melchert, gen mgr; Terry Miller, VP, VP & opns mgr; Lisa Hatcher, gen sls mgr; Joe Nicks, news dir; John Mulhurn, engrg dir & chief of engrg.

KSCB-FM— July 10, 1978: 107.5 mhz; 100 kw. 511 ft. TL: N37 02 45 W101 06 11. Stereo. Web Site: www.kscb.net. Network: Network: ABC Information & Entertainment, Jones Radio Networks. Rep: Roslin. Format: Adult contemp. News staff: 2; News: 7 hrs wkly. Target aud: 25-49; young adults.

KSLS(FM)—Listing follows KYUU(AM).

KYUU(AM)— Sept 15, 1960: 1470 khz; 1 kw-D, 125 w-N. TL: N37 03 17 W100 53 06. 224 N. Kansas Ave. 67905. Phone: (620) 624-8156. Fax: (620) 624-4606. Web Site: www.kslskyuu.com. Licensee: Waitt Radio Inc. Group owner: Waitt Broadcasting Inc. (acq 5-3-01; grpsl). Rep: McGavren Guild. Format: Sp. News: one hr wkly. Target aud: 25-54; Spanish speaking. ♦Kevin Colvin, gen mgr; Matt Younkin, progmg dir.

KSLS(FM)—Co-owned with KYUU(AM). July 1978: 101.5 mhz; 100 kw. 550 ft. TL: N37 03 20 W100 48 40. Stereo. Web Site: www.kslskyuu.com. Format: Country.

KZQD(FM)— October 1997: 105.1 mhz; 50 kw. 492 ft. TL: N37 17 39 W100 51 38. (CP: Ant 387 ft. TL: N37 02 53 W100 54 34). Box 2636 67905. Phone: (620) 626-8282. Fax: (620) 626-6062. Web Site: www.kzqdradiolibertad.com. Licensee: Mario Loredo. (acq 3-8-94; 5-9-94). Format: Christian. ♦Mario Loredo, gen mgr.

Kansas   Directory of Radio

Lindsborg

KQNS-FM— Oct 8, 1985; 95.5 mhz; 15.5 kw. Ant 417 ft. TL: N38 40 00 W97 41 30. Stereo. 1825 S. Ohio, Salina 67401-4573. Phone: (785) 827-2100. Fax: (785) 827-3503. Web Site: www.0295.com. Licensee: B-B Broadcasting Inc. (acq 9-15-94; 10-24-94). Format: Adult contemp. News: 2 hrs wkly. Target aud: 25-49. ♦ Steven Johns, gen mgr.

Lyons

KXKU(FM)— Apr 10, 1970; 106.1 mhz; 100 kw. 659 ft. TL: N38 16 33 W98 12 11. Stereo. 106 N. Main St., Hutchinson 67501-5219. Phone: (620) 665-5758. Fax: (620) 665-6655. Licensee: Ad Astra Per Aspera Broadcasting Inc. (group owner; acq 9-17-86); $366,816; 6-9-86). Format: Country. News staff: one; News: 2 hrs wkly. Target aud: 25-64; listeners throughout central KS. ♦ Cliff C. Shank, pres; Mike Hill, VP, stn mgr & sls VP; Cheryl Dinwiddie, rgnl sls mgr.

Manhattan

KJCK-FM—See Junction City

KMAN(AM)— June 1950; 1350 khz; 500 w-D, 40 w-N. TL: N39 13 00 W96 33 30. Stereo. Box 1350 66502. Secondary address: 2414 Casement Rd. 66502. Phone: (785) 776-1350. Phone: (785) 776-4851. Fax: (785) 539-1000. Web Site: www.1350kman.com. Licensee: Manhattan Broadcasting Co. Group owner: Seaton Stations Network: Network: CBS, ESPN Radio, Westwood One. Shaw Pittman. Format: News/talk, sports. News staff: one; News: 60 hrs wkly. Target aud: 30 plus. ♦ Richard Seaton, chmn; Richard T. Wartell, pres & gen mgr; Eric Weber, opns mgr & gen sls mgr; Eric Webber, sls dir; Matt Walters, progmg dir; Cathy Dawes, news dir; Kevin Block, chief of engrg.

KMKF(FM)— Co-owned with KMAN(AM). Sept 1, 1972; 101.5 mhz; 39 kw. 577 ft. TL: N39 15 55 W96 27 56. Stereo. Phone: (785) 776-1015. Web Site: www.purerock.com. Format: Rock/AOR. News staff: one; News: 2 hrs wkly. Target aud: 18-35. ♦ Corey Dean, progmg dir; Kevin Block, engrg dir.

KQLA(FM)— (Ogden). Feb 14, 1986; 103.5 mhz; 50 kw. 660 ft. TL: N39 09 21 W96 36 44. (CP: 103.5 mhz, 50 kw). Stereo. Box 789, Junction City 66441. Secondary address: US Hwy. 77 & W. Ash, Junction City 66441. Phone: (785) 587-0103. Phone: (785) 762-5525. Fax: (785) 762-5387. E-mail: platinum@kjck.com. Web Site: www.kjck.com. Licensee: Platinum Broadcasting Co. (group owner; acq 9-24-97; $650,000). Network: ABC. Format: Hot Adult Contemp. News staff: one; News: 10 hrs wkly. Target aud: 18-44; mobile, educated persons with quality income. ♦ Mark Ediger, gen mgr.

***KSDB-FM**— 1950: 91.9 mhz; 1.4 kw. 290 ft. TL: N39 09 49 W96 31 54. Stereo. A.Q. Miller School of Journalism, Rm. 104, Kedzie Hall 66506. Phone: (785) 532-2971. Fax: (785) 532-5484. E-mail: radio@ksu.edu. Web Site: www.wildcatradio.ksu.edu. Licensee: Kansas State University. Format: Progsv, rock, urban contemp. News: 12 hrs wkly. Target aud: 18-34; young adults. Spec prog: Black 4 hrs, gospel 3 hrs, jazz 3 hrs wkly. ♦ Todd Simon, pres; Candace L. Walton, gen mgr; Sara Roland, mus dir; Gary Pettet, chief of engrg.

KXBZ(FM)— September 1994; 104.7 mhz; 20 kw. 502 ft. TL: N39 15 55 W96 27 56. 2414 Casement Rd. 66502. Phone: (785) 776-1350. Fax: (785) 539-1000. E-mail: dubs@purerock.com. Web Site: www.b1047.com. Licensee: Manhattan Broadcasting Co. Inc. Group owner: Seaton Stations (acq 3-2-99). Network: Westwood One. Format: Hot country. Target aud: 18-35; men & women. ♦ Richard T. Wartell, pres & gen mgr.

Marysville

KNDY(AM)— July 10, 1956; 1570 khz; 250 w-D. TL: N39 51 02 W96 38 52. R.R. 3, 1212 Eleventh St., Marysville 66508. Phone: (785) 562-2361. Fax: (785) 562-2188. Licensee: Dierking Communications Inc. (group owner; acq 9-6-88). Network: ABC Daytime Direction. Format: Farm, C&W. News: 24 hrs wkly. Target aud: General. ♦ Bruce Dierking, pres, gen mgr, gen sls mgr & progmg dir.

KNDY-FM— July 23, 1974; 95.5 mhz; 25 kw. Ant 328 ft. TL: N39 57 36 W96 44 05. Stereo. Network: ABC Daytime Direction. Format: C&W. ♦ Myron Nolind, chief of engrg.

McPherson

KBBE(FM)—Listing follows KNGL(AM).

KNGL(AM)— Jan 4, 1949: 1540 khz; 250 w-D. TL: N38 20 30 W97 40 12. Box 1069 67460. Phone: (316) 241-1504. Fax: (316) 241-3196. E-mail: kbbeingl@earthlink.net. Web Site: midkansasmedia.com. Licensee: Davies Communications Inc. (acq 10-1-85; $589,000 with co-located FM; 8-19-85). Format: Oldies. News staff: 2; News: 25 hrs wkly. Target aud: 25-54. Spec prog: Relg 5 hrs wkly. ♦ Jerry Davies, pres; Diane Davies, exec VP, prom dir & progmg dir; Claude Hughes, stn mgr & gen sls mgr; Chris Swick, news dir; Shawn White, engrg dir; Rod Rogers, chief of engrg.

KBBE(FM)—Co-owned with KNGL(AM). Jan 12, 1974; 96.7 mhz; 6 kw. 245 ft. TL: N38 20 30 W97 40 12. Stereo. 1137 14th Ave. 67460. Web Site: midkansasmedia.com. Format: Adult contemp. News staff: one. ♦ Claude Hughes, sls VP.

Medicine Lodge

KREJ(FM)— January 1990; 101.7 mhz; 50 kw. 492 ft. TL: N37 13 58 W98 39 43. 301 S. Main St. 67104-1513. Phone: (316) 886-3537. Licensee: Florida Public Radio Inc. (acq 5-90; 6-11-90). Network: Moody. Format: Relg. Target aud: General. ♦ Mike Henry, gen mgr; Randy Henry, chief of engrg.

***KSNS(FM)**— April 1999; 91.5 mhz; 25 kw. 462 ft. TL: N37 14 02 W98 39 55. 301 S. Main 67104-1513. Secondary address: 505 Josephine St., Titusville, FL 32796. Phone: (316) 886-3537. Web Site: www.gate.net/~wpio. Licensee: Florida Public Radio Inc. Format: Contemp Christian mus. ♦ Mike Henry, gen mgr.

Minneapolis

KILS(FM)— Feb 24, 1993; 92.7 mhz; 50 kw. 492 ft. TL: N39 00 52 W97 37 42. 1825 S. Ohio, Salina 67401. Phone: (785) 827-2100. Fax: (785) 827-3503. Web Site: www.927thezoo.com. Licensee: Waitt Radio Inc. Group owner: Waitt Broadcasting Inc. (acq 5-3-01; grpsl). Format: Classic rock. Target aud: 18-54. ♦ Steven Johns, gen mgr.

Mission

KCNW(AM)—See Fairway

KCZZ(AM)— October 1957; 1480 khz; 1 kw-D, 500 w-N, DA-2. TL: N39 04 05 W94 42 09. 1701 S. 55th St., Kansas City 66106. Phone: (913) 287-1480. Fax: (913) 287-5881. E-mail: jim_macdonald771@hotmail.com. Web Site: www.aranbaonline.com. Licensee: Davidson Media Station KCZZ Licensee LLC. (acq 1-28-2005; $3.9 million. with KAKS(FM) Huntsville, AR). Rep: Lotus Entravision Reps LLC. Format: Sp. Target aud: 18-49; adults. ♦ Jim MacDonald, gen mgr; Carlos Mercado, opns dir.

KRBZ(FM)—See Kansas City, MO

Newton

KJRG(AM)— May 24, 1953; 950 khz; 500 w-D, 147 w-N. TL: N38 02 45 W97 22 24. Box 567 67114. Phone: (316) 283-5150. Fax: (316) 284-2684. Licensee: KJRG Inc. Format: Relg. ♦ Daisyann Anderson, gen mgr & gen sls mgr.

KMXW(FM)— 1959: 92.3 mhz; 100 kw. Ant 650 ft. TL: N38 01 09 W97 23 01. Stereo. 4200 N. Old Lawrence Rd., Wichita 67219. Phone: (316) 838-9141. Fax: (316) 832-9755. Web Site: www.thenew923.com. Licensee: Journal Broadcast Corp. Group owner: Journal Communications Inc. (acq 3-20-00; $4.25 million). Format: Hot adult contemp. Target aud: 18-34; adults. ♦ Rob Burton, VP & gen mgr; Ray Micheals, progmg dir.

North Fort Riley

KBLS(FM)— Jan 1, 1993; 102.5 mhz; 100 kw. 492 ft. TL: N38 57 05 W96 47 45. Stereo. 5008 Skyway Dr., Manhattan 66503. Phone: (785) 537-3232. Fax: (785) 587-9495. Licensee: MCC Radio LLC. Group owner: Morris Radio LLC (acq 1-14-2004; grpsl). Format: Adult contemp. News staff: 5. Target aud: 25-54; women. ♦ William S. Morris IV, pres; John Leifheit, gen mgr & stn mgr; Tom Clay, opns mgr; John Anderson, progmg dir.

North Newton

***KBCU(FM)**— Apr 6, 1989; 88.1 mhz; 149 w. 56 ft. TL: N38 04 26 W97 20 35. 300 E. 27th St. 67117. Phone: (316) 284-5228. Phone: (316) 284-5271. Fax: (316) 284-5286. Licensee: Bethel College. Format: Var/div. News: 5 hrs wkly. Target aud: General; college students & Harvey County. Spec prog: Sp 2 hrs wkly. ♦ Christine Crouse-Dick, gen mgr & stn mgr.

Norton

KQNK(AM)— Oct 30, 1963; 1530 khz; 1 kw-D. TL: N38 35 04 W95 15 57. 1530 KQNK Road 67654. Phone: (785) 877-3378. Fax: (785) 877-3379. Licensee: Dierking Communications Inc. (group owner; acq 7-13-99; $165,000 with co-located FM). Network: ABC Information & Entertainment. Rep: Keystone (unwired net). Format: Soft adult contemp. ♦ Bruce Dierking, pres; Dina Wente, progmg dir & chief of engrg.

KQNK-FM— Mar 1, 1993; 106.7 mhz; 51 kw. 92 ft. TL: N39 49 37 W99 52 08. Format: Adult contemp. ♦ Marvin Matchett, progmg dir.

Oberlin

KFNF(FM)— July 1977; 101.1 mhz; 100 kw. 420 ft. TL: N39 49 33 W100 39 09. Stereo. Box 116 C, R.R. 2, 6 Miles W. of Oberlin 67749. Phone: (785) 475-2225. Phone: (785) 475-2226. Fax: (785) 475-2510. Web Site: www.bestcountryaround.com. Licensee: McCook Radio Group LLC. (group owner; (acq 11-5-2003; $400,000). Network: ABC. Format: Country. Target aud: 25-65; farmers. Spec prog: Gospel 3 hrs wkly. ♦ Bryan Loker, stn mgr; Adam Kadavy, chief of opns.

Ogden

KQLA(FM)—Licensed to Ogden. See Manhattan

Olathe

KCCV-FM— Dec 1, 1993; 92.3 mhz; 8.3 kw. 564 ft. TL: N38 56 10 W94 50 41. Stereo. 10550 Barkley, Suite 112, Overland Park 66212. Phone: (913) 642-7600. Fax: (913) 642-2424. E-mail: kccv@bottradionetwork.com. Web Site: www.bottradionetwork.com. Licensee: Bott Broadcasting Co. (group owner; acq 7-1-92; $537,500; 8-3-92). Network: USA. Format: Christian talk. Target aud: 25-54; family oriented. ♦ Richard Bott II, exec VP & VP; Ebsen Fowler, gen mgr.

Olsburg

***KANV(FM)**— 2003: 91.3 mhz; 6 kw. Ant 328 ft. TL: N39 00 55 W96 53 55. 1120 W. 11th St., Lawrence 66044. Phone: (785) 864-4530. Fax: (785) 864-5278. Web Site: www.kpr.ku.edu. Licensee: The University of Kansas. Format: Class, jazz. ♦ Janet Campbell, gen mgr; Cordelia Brown, opns mgr.

Osage City

KMXN(FM)— July 26, 1982; 92.9 mhz; 7.9 kw. Ant 538 ft. TL: N38 48 21 W95 42 58. (CP: 36 kw, ant 564 ft. TL: N38 31 47 W96 05 09). Stereo. 3125 W. 6th St., Lawrence 66049. Phone: (785) 843-1320. Fax: (785) 841-5924. Web Site: www.wild929.com. Licensee: Viking Enterprises LLC (acq 1-31-2005; $3.1 million). Format: Rhythmic CHR. ♦ Ron Convert, gen mgr.

Ottawa

KCHZ(FM)— Mar 1, 1962; 95.7 mhz; 100 kw. 987 ft. TL: N38 50 15 W95 29 51. (CP: 98.6 kw). 4240 Blueridge Blvd., Suite 820, Kansas City, MO 64133. Phone: (816) 356-2400. Fax: (816) 356-2479. Web Site: www.z957.net. Licensee: Cumulus KC Licensing Corp. Group owner: Cumulus Media Inc. (acq 11-26-03; $25 million). Format: Modern CHR. ♦ Lewis W. Dickey Jr., chmn; Marty Gaysuik, CFO; John Dickey, exec VP; Jon Pinch, exec VP; Mike Payne, gen mgr; Maurice DeVoe, opns mgr.

KOFO(AM)— Sept 24, 1949; 1220 khz; 250 w-D, 40 w-N. TL: N38 35 04 W95 15 57. 320 E. Radio Rd. 66067. Phone: (785) 242-1220. Fax: (785) 242-1442. E-mail: kofo@kofo.com. Web Site: www.kofo.com. Licensee: Brandy Communications Inc. Network: ABC Information &

Stations in the U.S.   Kansas

Developers & Brokers of Radio Properties — contact American Media Services at our suite: Philadelphia Marriott Downtown 215-625-2900. 843-972-2200. americanmediaservices.com. Charleston, SC. Dallas, TX · Chicago, Il · Austin, TX. American Media Services, LLC

Entertainment. Format: C&W. News staff: one; News: 7 hrs wkly. Target aud: 25-54. Spec prog: Farm 2 hrs wkly. ♦ Brad Howard, pres & gen mgr.

*KRBW(FM)— 1997: 90.5 mhz; 250 w. 187 ft. TL: N38 35 04 W95 15 57. American family Radio, 320 E. Radio Rd. 66067. Phone: (785) 242-9050. Fax: (662) 842-6791. Web Site: www.afr.net. Licensee: American Family Association Group owner: American Family Radio (acq 1-24-97). Format: Comtemporary Christian. ♦ Marvin Sanders, gen mgr.

*KTJO-FM— May 1951: 88.9 mhz; 145 w. 66 ft. TL: N38 36 16 W95 15 49. Stereo. Box 110, Ottawa Univ., 1001 S. Cedar 66067. Phone: (785) 242-5200. Fax: (785) 242-7429. Licensee: Ottawa University. Format: Div, CHR, Contemp Christian. News: 5 hrs wkly. Target aud: General; Ottawa Univ community & City of Ottawa, KS. ♦ Bradley A. Howard, CEO; Ben Weiss, engrg VP.

Overland Park

KCCV(AM)— 1962: 760 khz; 6 kw-D, 200 w-N, DA-2. TL: N39 02 26 W94 30 34. 10550 Barkley, Suite 112 66212. Phone: (913) 642-7600. Fax: (913) 642-2424. E-mail: kccv@bottradionetwork.com. Web Site: www.bottradionetwork.com. Licensee: Bott Broadcasting Co. Group owner: Bott Radio Network (acq 1962). Network: USA. Format: Christian talk, Christian, relg, news/talk. Target aud: 25-54; family-oriented. ♦ Richard P. Bott II, exec VP; Eben Fowler, gen mgr.

Parsons

KLKC(AM)— 1948: 1540 khz; 250 w-D. TL: N37 20 35 W95 13 55. Box 853, 24020 Queens Rd. 67357-0853. Phone: (620) 421-6400. Fax: (620) 421-5570. E-mail: judyvance@klkc.com. Web Site: klkc.com. Licensee: Acme Broadcasting LLC (acq 1-15-2004; $250,000. with co-located FM). Format: Oldies, adult contemp. News: 28 hrs wkly. Target aud: 12-60; general. Spec prog: Farm 2 hrs, relg 2 hrs, big band 3 hrs wkly. ♦ Mike Cobb, gen mgr; Ed Hernandez, gen sls mgr & sls; Steve Lardy, progmg dir; Terry Blackburn, mus dir; Annette Tucker, news dir & chief of engrg.

KLKC-FM— October 1978: 93.5 mhz; 3 kw. 267 ft. TL: N37 20 35 W95 13 55. Format: Oldies.

Phillipsburg

KKAN(AM)— Dec 31, 1959: 1490 khz; 1 kw-U. TL: N39 47 32 W99 19 55. Box 548 67661. Phone: (785) 543-2151. Phone: (785) 543-6593. Web Site: www.kkankqma.com. Licensee: Walter C. Seidel. (acq 3-29-88). Format: Div, news. Target aud: General; rural population & small towns. Spec prog: Farm 10 hrs, gospel 12 hrs wkly. ♦ Bob Yates, gen mgr & stn mgr.

KQMA-FM—Co-owned with KKAN(AM). July 14, 1984: 92.5 mhz; 100 kw. 510 ft. TL: N39 37 02 W99 17 55. Stereo. 205 F St. 67661. Web Site: www.kkankqma.com. Format: Var. ♦ Tad Felts, asst music dir.

Pittsburg

KKOW(AM)— Oct 11, 1937: 860 khz; 10 kw-D, 5 kw-N, DA-N. TL: N37 24 46 W94 38 16. 1162 E. Hwy. 126 66762. Phone: (620) 231-7200. Fax: (620) 231-3321. E-mail: kkow@kkowradio.com. Web Site: www.kkowam.com. Licensee: American Media Investment Inc. (acq 6-89; $400,000 with co-located FM; 6-26-89). Network: CBS. Rep: McGavren Guild. Format: Classic country. News staff: 2; News: 5 hrs wkly. Target aud: General. ♦ Chris Kelly, gen mgr & prom dir.

KKOW-FM— Apr 20, 1975: 96.9 mhz; 100 kw. 278 ft. TL: N37 23 44 W94 40 42. Stereo. 1162 E. Hwy. 126 66762. Phone: (620) 231-7200. Fax: (620) 231-3321. E-mail: kkow@kkowradio.com. Web Site: www.kkowfm.com. Licensee: American Media Investments Inc. Format: Contemp country. ♦ Chris Kelly, gen mgr.

*KRPS(FM)— Apr 29, 1988: 89.9 mhz; 100 kw. 1,000 ft. TL: N37 18 44 W94 48 58. Stereo. Box 899 66762. Phone: (620) 235-4288. Fax: 620(235-4290). E-mail: krps@pittstate.edu. Web Site: www.krps.org. Licensee: Pittsburg State University. Network: Network: NPR, PRI. Format: Class, jazz, news. News: 39 hrs wkly. Spec prog: Folk 3 hrs. ♦ Missi Kelly, gen mgr; Vicki Pritchett, dev dir.

KSEK(AM)— 1948: 1340 khz; 1 kw-U. TL: N37 23 44 W94 40 42. 202 E. Centenial Dr., Suite 2B 66762. Phone: (620) 232-1340. Fax: (620) 232-9915. Licensee: Southeast Kansas Independent Living Resource Center Inc. (group owner; (acq 10-20-2004; $700,000. with KSEK-FM Girard). Network: Network: ESPN Radio, AP Network News. Format: Sports. News: 10 hrs wkly. Target aud: 25 plus. Spec prog: High school basketball & football. ♦ Lynn Meredith, gen mgr.

Plainville

KFIX(FM)— May 11, 1998: 96.9 mhz; 10.5 kw. 876 ft. TL: N39 01 15 W99 28 13. Stereo. Box 6, Hays 67601. Secondary address: 2300 Hall, Hays 67601. Phone: (785) 625-2578. Fax: (785) 625-3632. E-mail: studio@kfix.com. Web Site: www.kfix.com. Licensee: Hull Broadcasting Inc. (acq 9-12-00); with KBGL(FM) Larned). Format: AOR. Target aud: 25-64. ♦ Richard C. Hull, pres; Nancy E. Baumrucker, gen mgr; Cameron Perry, progmg dir.

Pratt

KHMY(FM)— July 1, 1965: 93.1 mhz; 100 kw. Ant 1,007 ft. TL: N37 55 50 W98 19 04. Stereo. Box 1036, Hutchinson 67504-1030. Phone: (620) 662-5900. Fax: (620) 662-5797. Licensee: Eagle Communications Inc. Group owner: Eagle Communications Group (acq 3-17-03; swap for KSSH(FM) Ingalls). Rep: McGavren Guild. Format: Adult contemp. ♦ Mark Trotman, gen mgr & sls dir.

KWLS(AM)— Sept 19, 1963: 1290 khz; 5 kw-D, 500 w-N, DA-2. TL: N37 38 34 W98 40 39. Box 486, 30129 E. Hwy. 54 67124. Phone: (620) 672-5581. Fax: (620) 672-5583. E-mail: kwls@socencom.net. Licensee: Waitt Radio Inc. Group owner: Waitt Broadcasting Inc. (acq 5-3-01; grpsl). Network: ABC Information & Entertainment. Rep: McGavren Guild. Fisher, Wayland, Cooper, Leader & Zaragoza L.L.P. Format: Oldies 60s & 70s. News staff: one; News: 3 hrs wkly. Target aud: 25 plus; rural.

Riley

KACZ(FM)— Sept 16, 2003: 96.3 mhz; 11.5 kw. Ant 479 ft. TL: N39 13 34 W96 37 00. Box 1350, 2414 Casement Rd., Manhattan 66502. Phone: (785) 776-1350. Fax: (785) 539-1000. Web Site: www.z963.com. Licensee: Manhattan Broadcasting Co. Inc. Group owner: Seaton Stations. Format: CHR. News staff: 3; News: 4 hrs wkly. Target aud: 18-59; woman. ♦ Richard T. Wartell, pres & gen mgr.

Rozel

KKCV(FM)—Not on air, target date: unknown: 102.5 mhz; 100 kw horiz, 100.1 kw vert. Ant 525 ft. TL: N37 57 28 W99 25 46. 10550 Barkley, Suite 108, Overland Park 66212. Phone: (913) 642-7770. Fax: (913) 642-1319. Licensee: Bott Communications Inc. ♦ Richard P. Bott II, VP & gen mgr.

Russell

KCAY(FM)—Listing follows KRSL(AM).

KRSL(AM)— Jan 11, 1956: 990 khz; 250 w-D, 30 w-N. TL: N38 54 22 W98 51 39. Box 666, 1984 N. Main St. 67665. Phone: (785) 483-3121. Fax: (785) 483-6511. E-mail: wayne@krsl.com. Web Site: www.krsl.com. Licensee: West Central Radio Inc. (acq 10-24-89; $404,000. with co-located FM; FTR: 11-13-89). Format: Adult contemp. Target aud: 24 plus; general. Spec prog: Polka 4 hrs, farm 2 hrs wkly. ♦ Wayne Grabbe, gen mgr; Gordon Gorton, stn mgr & progmg dir; Carol McKenna, news dir.

KCAY(FM)—Co-owned with KRSL(AM). July 1, 1965: 95.9 mhz; 1.35 kw. Ant 487 ft. TL: N38 54 22 W98 51 39. Stereo. Web Site: www.krsl.com. Format: Adult contemp. ♦ Robert Musgrave, VP; Melody Vance, dev dir.

Saint Marys

KQTP(FM)— Dec 4, 1994: 102.9 mhz; 50 kw. 320 ft. TL: N39 05 34 W95 47 05. 825 S. Kansas Ave., Topeka 66612. Phone: (785) 272-2122. Fax: (785) 272-6219. E-mail: oldieskqtp@aol.com. Web Site: www.cumulus.com. Licensee: Cumulus Licensing Corp. Group owner: Cumulus Media Inc. (acq 4-13-01; with KWIC(FM) Topeka). Format: Classic country. Target aud: 35-54. ♦ Kevin Kline, gen mgr; Jeff Peterson, opns mgr.

Salina

*KAKA(FM)— 2002: 88.5 mhz; 46 kw. Ant 394 ft. TL: N39 04 12 W97 51 14. American Family Radio, Box 2440, Tupelo, MS 38803. Phone: (662) 844-8888. Fax: (662) 842-6791. Web Site: www.afr.net. Licensee: American Family Association. Group owner: American Family Radio Format: Relg. ♦ Marvin Sanders, stn mgr.

*KCVS(FM)— 1994: 91.7 mhz; 11.5 kw. Ant 748 ft. TL: N38 39 58 W97 41 30. 3434 W. Kilbourn Ave., Milwaukee, WI 53208. Phone: (414) 935-3000. Fax: (414) 935-3015. E-mail: kcvs@vcyamerica.org. Web Site: www.vcyamerica.org. Licensee: VCY/America Inc. (group owner; acq 7-2-97; $260,000). Network: Network: Moody, USA. Format: Christian. ♦ Vic Eliason, VP & gen mgr.

KFRM(AM)— 1947: 550 khz; 5 kw-D, 110 w-N, DA-2. TL: N39 26 10 W97 39 40. 1815 Meadowlark Rd., Clay Center 67432. Phone: (785) 632-5661. Fax: (785) 632-5662. E-mail: kbauen@kfrm.com. Web Site: kfrm.com. Licensee: Taylor Communications Inc. (acq 9-12-96; $500,000). Format: Farm, talk. News staff: 2; News: 6 hrs wkly. Target aud: 25-55; agricultural. Spec prog: Farm 5 hrs, gospel 5 hrs wkly. ♦ Kyle Bauer, gen mgr; Rod Keen, opns mgr.

*KHCD(FM)— Jan 28, 1988: 89.5 mhz; 100 kw. 925 ft. TL: N39 06 16 W97 23 15. Stereo. 815 N. Walnut, Suite 300, Hutchinson 67501. Phone: (620) 662-6646. Licensee: Hutchinson Community College. Network: NPR. Format: Class, new age, news. ♦ David M. Horning, gen mgr; Geralyn Drumgould, opns dir; Sharon Webb, dev dir.

KINA(AM)—Listing follows KSKG(FM).

KSAL(AM)— May 18, 1937: 1150 khz; 5 kw-U, DA-N. TL: N38 53 08 W97 30 58. Box 80 67402. Secondary address: 131 N. Santa Fe 67401. Phone: (785) 823-1111. Fax: (785) 823-2034. Web Site: www.ksal.com. Licensee: MCC Radio LLC. Group owner: Morris Radio LLC (acq 1-30-2004; grpsl). Network: ABC Information & Entertainment. Format: News/talk. News staff: 5; News: 20 hrs wkly. Target aud: General. Spec prog: Farm 6 hrs wkly. ♦ John Leifheit, gen mgr & stn mgr; Tom Clay, opns mgr & gen sls mgr; Rich Alexander, progmg dir; Todd Pittenger, news dir.

KYEZ(FM)—Co-owned with KSAL(AM). May 1, 1975: 93.7 mhz; 100 kw. 510 ft. TL: N38 57 14 W97 36 29. Stereo. Web Site: www.y937.com. Format: Country. Target aud: 25-54. ♦ Bill Ray, progmg dir.

KSAL-FM— October 1988: . Stn currently dark 104.9 mhz; 14 kw. 440 ft. TL: N38 53 23 W97 38 46. Stereo. Box 80 67402-0080. Phone: (785) 823-1111. Fax: (785) 823-2034. Web Site: www.ebclink.com. Licensee: MCC Radio LLC. Group owner: Morris Radio LLC (acq 1-14-2004; grpsl). Format: Contemp classic hits. News staff: 5. Target aud: 18-34. ♦ John Leifheit, gen mgr & stn mgr; Tom Clay, opns mgr; J.J. Hill, progmg dir.

KSKG(FM)— 1961: 99.9 mhz; 100 kw. 570 ft. TL: N38 47 36 W97 31 33. 1825 S. Ohio St. 67401-0198. Phone: (785) 825-4631. Fax: (785) 825-4600. Licensee: Eagle Communications Inc. Group owner: Eagle Communications Group. Format: Modern country. Target aud: 25-54; 51% female, 49% male (baby boomers). Spec prog: Gospel 3 hrs wkly. ♦ Gary Shorman, pres; Steven Johns, gen mgr & gen sls mgr;

Kansas

Bill Ray, opns mgr; Sky Phillips, progmg dir; Randy Picking, news dir; Tammie Henson, pub affrs dir; Jay Thouvenall, chief of engrg.

KINA(AM)—Co-owned with KSKG(FM). Apr 20, 1964: 910 khz; 500 w-D, 29 w-N, DA-2. TL: N38 45 52 W97 32 30. (Acq 11-1-95; $235,000). Network: CNN Radio. Format: News/talk, sports. Target aud: 45 plus; middle to upper income adults. ♦ Sky Phillips, opns mgr; Dave Foor, progmg dir.

Scott City

KFLA(AM)— Oct 13, 1962: 1310 khz; 500 w-D, 147 w-N. TL: N38 31 35 W100 54 42. Box 246 67871. Phone: (620) 872-5345. Licensee: Dakota Communications Ltd. (group owner; acq 5-1-98). Format: Relg. Spec prog: Farm 5 hrs wkly. ♦ Gil Wohler, gen mgr.

KSKL(FM)— Nov 9, 1964: 94.5 mhz; 100 kw. Ant 345 ft. TL: N38 31 35 W100 34 42. Stereo. Box 246 67871. Phone: (620) 872-5345. Fax: (620) 872-5422. Web Site: www.wksradio.com. Licensee: Western Kansas Wireless Inc. Group owner: Robert Ingstad Broadcast Properties (acq 3-26-93; $175,000. with co-located AM; FTR: 4-12-93). Format: Oldies. ♦ Gil Wohler, gen mgr.

Seneca

KMZA(FM)— Oct 15, 1992: 92.1 mhz; 4.5 kw. 377 ft. TL: N39 49 50 W96 02 39. Stereo. 28 S. 4th St. 66538. Phone: (785) 336-6166. Fax: (785) 336-3600. Web Site: www.kmzaseneca.com. Licensee: KNZA Inc. (group owner) Network: ABC Daytime Direction. Format: Country, loc. News staff: one; News: 10 hrs wkly. Target aud: General. Spec prog: Farm 7 hrs wkly. ♦ Greg Buser, pres & gen mgr; Robert Hilton, opns mgr.

Silver Lake

KCVT(FM)— 1996: 92.5 mhz; 6.7 kw. 387 ft. TL: N39 08 42 W95 55 37. 534 S. Kansas, Suite 930, Topeka 66603. Phone: (785) 233-9250. Fax: (785) 233-9260. E-mail: kcvt@bottradionetwork.com. Web Site: www.bottradionetwork.com. Licensee: Richard P. Bott II. Group owner: Bott Radio Network: USA. Format: Christian talk. ♦ Richard P. Bott II, VP & gen mgr.

Sterling

KGGG(FM)— June 12, 1995: 94.7 mhz; 20 kw. 312 ft. TL: N38 16 33 W98 12 11. 106 N. Main St., Hutchinson 67501-5219. Phone: (620) 665-5758. Fax: (620) 665-6655. E-mail: ksku@ourtownusa.com. Licensee: Ad Astra Per Aspera Broadcasting Inc. (group owner) Network: ABC. Format: Oldies. News staff: one; News: 2 hrs wkly. Target aud: 25-54; general. ♦ Cliff C. Shank, pres; Mike Hill, VP, stn mgr & sls VP; Cheryl Dinwiddie, natl sls mgr.

Topeka

*KBUZ(FM)— 1994: 90.3 mhz; 11 kw. 840 ft. TL: N39 00 19 W96 02 58. 2800 S.W. Wanamaker Rd., Suite 196 66614. Phone: (785) 272-6191. Fax: (785) 272-2132. Licensee: American Family Association. Group owner: American Family Radio (acq 12-30-94; 3-20-95). Format: Relg. ♦ Bob Faulkner, stn mgr, sls VP & progmg VP; Jennie Crable, prom VP; George McGurk, chief of engrg.

KDVV(FM)—Listing follows KTOP(AM).

*KJTY(FM)— Aug 31, 1985: 88.1 mhz; 100 kw. 350 ft. TL: N39 11 25 W95 39 29. Stereo. 1005 S.W. 10th St. 66604. Phone: (785) 357-8888. Fax: (785) 357-0100. E-mail: joy88@joy88.org. Web Site: www.joy88.org. Licensee: Joy Public Broadcasting Corp. Network: USA. Format: Relg. News: 15 hrs wkly. Target aud: 25-49. Spec prog: Children 5 hrs wkly. ♦ Lowell M. Bush, pres; Dr. Jack Jacob, gen mgr & opns mgr.

KMAJ(AM)— July 1947: 1440 khz; 5 kw-D, 1 kw-N, DA-1. TL: N39 01 17 W95 34 15. 5315 S.W. Seventh St. 66606-2514. Phone: (785) 272-2122. Fax: (785) 272-6219. Web Site: www.kmaj.com. Licensee: Cumulus Licensing Corp. Group owner: Cumulus Media Inc. (acq 7-31-98). Network: ABC Information & Entertainment. Rep: Allied Radio Partners. Format: News/talk, sports. Target aud: General. ♦ Don Pollnow, gen mgr; Kurt Boney, gen sls mgr; Chris Rundel, progmg dir.

KMAJ-FM— July 1, 1971: 107.7 mhz; 100 kw. 1,214 ft. TL: N39 01 34 W95 54 58. Stereo. Web Site: www.kmaj.com. Format: Adult contemp. ♦ Rose Diehl, progmg dir.

KTOP(AM)— July 1947: 1490 khz; 1 kw-U. TL: N39 04 39 W95 40 46. 5315 S.W. Seventh St. 66606. Phone: (785) 272-2122. Fax: (785) 272-6219. Web Site: www.cumulus.com. Licensee: Cumulus Licensing Corp. Group owner: Cumulus Media Inc. (acq 7-31-98; grpsl). Format: Sports, talk, adult standard. Target aud: 45 plus. ♦ Don Pollnow, gen mgr.

KDVV(FM)—Co-owned with KTOP(AM). May 29, 1960: 100.3 mhz; 100 kw. 984 ft. TL: N38 57 15 W95 54 43. Stereo. Web Site: www.v100rocks.com. Format: Classic rock. Target aud: 18-54.

KTPK(FM)— Nov 25, 1974: 106.9 mhz; 100 kw. Ant 1,210 ft. TL: N39 01 34 W95 55 01. Stereo. 2121 S.W. Chelsea 66614. Phone: (785) 273-1069. Phone: (785) 297-1069. Fax: (785) 273-0123. Web Site: www.ktpk1069.com. Licensee: JMJ Broadcasting Co. Inc. (acq 11-24-2004; $5.7 million). Network: ABC Daytime Direction. Rep: McGavren Guild. Format: Country. News staff: 2; News: 6 hrs wkly. Target aud: 25-49; mobile, family-oriented, high-income professional adults. ♦ Herbert W. McCord, pres; Jim Allan, gen mgr & adv VP; Gene Owen, sls dir; Keith Van Sickle, prom dir.

KWIC(FM)— Oct 15, 1993: 99.3 mhz; 6 kw. 292 ft. TL: N39 02 56 W95 40 32. 825 S. Kansas Ave., Suite 100 66612. Phone: (785) 272-2122. Fax: (785)2726219. Web Site: www.eagle993.com. Licensee: Cumulus Licensing Corp. Group owner: Cumulus Media Inc. (acq 4-13-01; with KQTP(FM) Saint Marys). Format: Classic rock. ♦ Kevin Klein, gen mgr.

WIBW(AM)— May 8, 1927: 580 khz; 5 kw-U, DA-N (ST-KKSU). TL: N39 05 05 W95 46 58. 1210 S.W. Executive Dr. 66615. Phone: (785) 272-3456. Fax: (785) 228-7282. Web Site: www.580radio.com. Licensee: Morris Communications Corp. Group owner: Morris Communications Inc. (acq 12-22-97; grpsl). Network: ABC. Wiley, Rein & Fielding. Format: News/talk, sports. News staff: 4. Target aud: 25 plus. Spec prog: Relg 6 hrs wkly. ♦ Michael Osterhaus, VP; Craig Colboch, gen mgr; Dan Lindquist, gen sls mgr; Carla Newman, prom dir; Liz Montano, news dir; Ed O'Donnell, chief of engrg.

WIBW-FM— Sept 1, 1961: 94.5 mhz; 100 kw. Ant 1,161 ft. TL: N39 01 34 W95 55 01. Stereo. Web Site: www.580radio.com. Format: Country. News staff: 4; News: 4 hrs wkly. Target aud: 25-54. ♦ Trey Cooler, progmg dir; Patti Cheek, mus dir.

Ulysses

KULY(AM)— Mar 1, 1965: 1420 khz; 1 kw-D, 500 w-N, DA-N. TL: N37 14 28 W101 21 49. Box 1420 67880. Phone: (620) 276-2366. Fax: (620) 356-3635. Web Site: realcountryonline.com. Licensee: KBUF Partnership. Group owner: Robert Ingstad Broadcast Properties. Network: Network: Westwood One, ABC Daytime Direction. Fisher, Wayland, Cooper, Leader & Zaragoza. Format: Country. News staff: one; News: 24 hrs wkly. Target aud: 21-65; middle to upper class workers, farmers & housewives. Spec prog: Farm 12 hrs, Sp 3 hrs wkly.

Wamego

KHCA(FM)— Mar 6, 1986: 95.3 mhz; 6 kw. 328 ft. TL: N39 12 35 W96 21 05. Stereo. Box 1471, Manhattan 66505. Secondary address: 103 N. 3rd, Manhattan 66502. Phone: (785) 537-9595. Fax: (785) 537-2955. E-mail: angel95@kansas.net. Web Site: www.angel95.com. Licensee: KHCA Inc. (acq 9-18-91; $126,000; 10-7-91). Network: Salem Radio Network. Format: Christian, adult contemp, rock. ♦ Jerry Hutchinson, pres & gen mgr.

Wellington

KLEY(AM)— Nov 19, 1966: 1130 khz; 250 w-D, 1 w-N. TL: N37 14 28 W97 24 04. 338 S. Kley Dr. 67152. Phone: (316) 326-3341. Fax: (316) 326-8512. E-mail: kley@sutv.com. Licensee: Johnson Enterprises Inc. (acq 5-1-89; $575,000 with co-located FM; 3-27-89). Network: USA. Format: Talk, news. News staff: one; News: 20 hrs wkly. Target aud: General. Spec prog: Farm 10 hrs, relg 4 hrs wkly. ♦ E. Gordon Johnson, pres, gen mgr & gen sls mgr; Travis Turner, opns mgr, prom mgr, progmg dir & news dir; Larry Waggoner, engrg dir & chief of engrg.

KWME(FM)—Co-owned with KLEY(AM). Aug 27, 1979: 93.5 mhz; 6 kw. 321 ft. TL: N37 14 28 W97 24 04. Network: USA. Format: Oldies. News staff: one. Target aud: 35-64. ♦ Travis Turner, progmg mgr.

Wichita

*KCFN(FM)— Apr 23, 1978: 91.1 mhz; 100 kw. 345 ft. TL: N37 48 01 W97 17 50. Stereo. 4000 N. Old Lawrence Rd. 67219. Phone: (316) 831-9111. Fax: (316) 831-9119. E-mail: kcfn@afo.net. Web Site: www.kcfn.net. Licensee: American Family Association Group owner: American Family Radio (acq 5-94). Format: Christian. News: 2 hrs wkly. Target aud: 35-65; general. Spec prog: Relg, news/talk. ♦ Don Wildmon, chmn; Tim Widmon, pres; Marvin Sanders, gen mgr; Cindy Kreyer, stn mgr & opns dir; Karen Myers, mus dir.

KEYN-FM— October 1968: 103.7 mhz; 95 kw. 859 ft. TL: N37 46 37 W97 31 01. Stereo. 2120 N. Woodlawn, Suite 352 67208. Phone: (316) 685-2121. Fax: (316) 685-3408. Web Site: www.keyn.com. Licensee: Entercom Wichita License LLC. Group owner: Entercom Communications Corp. (acq 2000; grpsl). Network: ABC. Format: Oldies. News: 5 hrs wkly. Target aud: 25-54; baby boomers. Spec prog: Dr. Demento 2 hrs wkly. ♦ Jackie Wise, gen mgr.

KFDI-FM—Listing follows KFTI(AM).

KFH(AM)— Oct 28, 1947: 1240 khz; 637 w-U. TL: N37 43 06 W97 19 05. 2120 N. Woodlawn, Suite 352 67208. Phone: (316) 685-2121. Fax: (316) 685-3408. E-mail: letters@kfhradio.com. Web Site: www.kfhradio.com. Licensee: Entercom Wichita License L.L.C. Group owner: Entercom Communications Corp. (acq 2000; grpsl). Network: Network: CBS, ABC News/Talk. Rep: D & R Radio. Format: Hot talk. Target aud: 35 plus; professionals. ♦ Jackie Wise, gen mgr.

KFH-FM—(Clearwater). July 4, 1995: 98.7 mhz; 50 kw. Ant 492 ft. TL: N37 24 11 W97 35 22. Stereo. 2120 N. Woodlawn, Suite 352 67208. Phone: (316) 685-2121. Fax: (316) 685-3408. E-mail: letters@kfhradio.com. Web Site: www.kfhradio.com. Licensee: Entercom Witicha License LLC. Group owner: Entercom Communications Corp. (acq 5-8-00; $2 million). Format: Sports, talk. Target aud: 18-49; general. ♦ Jackie Wise, gen mgr; Steve McIntosh, sls dir & news dir; Jason Schlitz, gen sls mgr & mus dir; Tony Duesing, progmg VP & progmg dir; Jessie Yearout, pub affrs dir; Craig Maudlin, chief of engrg.

KFRM(AM)—See Salina

KFTI(AM)— September 1923: 1070 khz; 10 kw-D, 1 kw-N, DA-N. TL: N37 42 47 W97 19 59. Stereo. Box 1402 67201. Secondary address: 4200 N. Old Lawrence Rd. 67219. Phone: (316) 838-9141. Fax: (316) 832-9755. E-mail: ccrawford@kfdi.com. Web Site: www.kfdi.com. Licensee: Journal Broadcast Corp. Group owner: Journal Communications Inc. (acq 6-11-99; grpsl). Network: ABC. Dow, Lohnes & Albertson. Format: C&W, oldies. News staff: 7. Target aud: 25-54. ♦ Beverlee Brannigan, progmg dir; Pat James, mus dir; Dan Dillon, news dir; Bill Nolan, engrg dir.

KFDI-FM—Co-owned with KFTI(AM). June 6, 1963: 101.3 mhz; 100 kw. Ant 1,139 ft. TL: N37 47 47 W97 31 59. Stereo. Format: Modern country. Target aud: 25-54; adults.

KGSO(AM)— 1950: 1410 khz; 5 kw-D, 1 kw-N, DA-2. TL: N37 44 05 W97 21 06. 1632 S. Maize Rd. 67209. Phone: (316) 721-4407. Fax: (316) 721-8276. Web Site: www.kgso.com. Licensee: Steckline Communications Inc. (acq 7-1-2005; $1.3 million). Format: Sports. ♦ Rick Betzen, gen mgr.

KICT-FM— Apr 28, 1972: 95.1 mhz; 100 kw. 1,026 ft. TL: N37 47 45 W97 31 58. Stereo. 4200 N. Old Lawrence Rd. 67219. Phone: (316) 838-9141. Fax: (316) 838-3607. Web Site: www.t95.com. Licensee: Journal Broadcast Corp. Group owner: Journal Broadcast Group Inc. (acq 6-14-99; grpsl). Format: Active rock. News staff: 2; News: 15 hrs wkly. Target aud: 18-44. ♦ Rob Burton, gen mgr; Ray Michaels, progmg dir.

*KMUW(FM)— Apr 26, 1949: 89.1 mhz; 100 kw. 450 ft. TL: N37 45 01 W97 18 12. Stereo. 3317 E. 17th St. 67208. Phone: (316) 978-6789. Fax: (316) 978-3946. E-mail: info@kmuw.org. Web Site: www.kmuw.org. Licensee: Wichita State University. Network: Network: NPR, PRI. Schwartz, Woods & Miller. Format: Class, jazz, news. News staff: one; News: 95 hrs wkly. Target aud: General. Spec prog: Gospel 3 hrs, Sp 2 hrs, folk 6 hrs, AAA 14 hrs wkly. ♦ Mark McCain, gen mgr.

Stations in the U.S.
Kentucky

KNSS(AM)— May 26, 1922: 1330 khz; 5 kw-U, DA-N. TL: N37 42 47 W97 14 51. Stereo. 2120 N. Woodlawn St., Suite 352 67208-1847. Phone: (316) 685-2121. Fax: (316) 685-3408. Web Site: www.knssradio.com. Licensee: Entercom Wichita License LLC. Group owner: Entercom Communications Corp. (acq 2000; grpsl). Network: CBS. Format: News/talk. Target aud: 25-54. ♦Jackie Wise, gen mgr.

KQAM(AM)— 1936: 1480 khz; 5 kw-D, 1 kw-N, DA-2. TL: N37 44 21 W97 16 14. 5610 E. 29th St. N. 67220. Phone: (316) 686-5726. Fax: (316) 686-5728. Licensee: Radio Disney Group LLC. Group owner: ABC Inc. (acq 7-29-02; $2 million). Network: Radio Disney. Format: Children. ♦Shelly Beckham, gen mgr.

KRBB(FM)— Sept 19, 1948: 97.9 mhz; 100 kw. 993 ft. TL: N37 42 47 W97 14 51. Stereo. 9323 E. 37th St. N. 67226. Phone: (316) 832-9600. Fax: (316) 832-0443. Web Site: www.698fm.com. Licensee: Capstar TX L.P. Group owner: Clear Channel Communications Inc. (acq 8-30-00; grpsl). Rep: Christal. Format: Adult contemp. News staff: one. Target aud: 28-48; working & family oriented. Spec prog: Jazz 2 hrs, Sp 3 hrs, love songs 18 hrs wkly. ♦Lindsay Morgan, prom dir & pub affrs dir.

KSGL(AM)— August 1957: 900 khz; 250 w-D, 28 w-N, DA-2. TL: N37 41 33 W97 22 54. 3337 W. Central 67203. Phone: (316) 942-3231. Fax: (316) 942-9314. E-mail: ksgl900@aol.com. Licensee: Agape Communications Inc. (acq 1977). Network: USA. Format: Relg, big band. ♦Don Clifford, pres; Norbert Atherton, sr VP; Terry Atherton, gen mgr.

KTHR(FM)— Apr 17, 1967: 107.3 mhz; 100 kw. 884 ft. TL: N37 46 37 W97 31 01. Stereo. 9323 E. 37th N. 67226. Phone: (316) 494-6600. Fax: (316) 494-6730. Licensee: Capstar TX L.P. Group owner: Clear Channel Communications Inc. (acq 8-30-2000; grpsl). Format: Classic rock. ♦Dick Harlow, gen mgr.

***KYFW(FM)**— Sept 24, 1988: 88.3 mhz; 17 kw. 141 ft. TL: N37 40 22 W97 20 08. Stereo. 239 Harral, Derby 67037. Phone: (316) 788-7883. Fax: (316) 788-7883. E-mail: kyfw@bbnradio.org. Web Site: www.bbnradio.org. Licensee: Bible Broadcasting Network. (group owner; acq 6-26-89). Format: Christian mus & progmg. Target aud: General. ♦Lowell Davey, pres; Matt Johnson, gen mgr.

KYQQ(FM)—See Arkansas City

***KYWA(FM)**— Mar 25, 1990: 90.7 mhz; 25 kw horiz, 23 kw vert. 335 ft. TL: N37 21 53 W97 20 30. 1600 W. 40th St. N. 67204-4225. Phone: (316) 436-1091. Fax: (316) 838-0691. E-mail: email@kzzd.org. Web Site: www.kzzd.org. Licensee: WAY-FM Media Group Inc. (group owner; acq 4-12-2004; $485,000). Format: Sp, relg talk, CHR, modern rock. News: 10 hrs wkly. Target aud: 25-54; upscale females. ♦Robert D. Augsburg, pres; Dan Wemmer, stn mgr.

KZCH(FM)—See Derby

Winfield

***KBDD(FM)**— 2000: 91.9 mhz; 48 kw. Ant 492 ft. TL: N37 22 56 W96 57 20. Box 262550, Baton Rouge, LA 70826. Phone: (225) 768-3102. Licensee: Family Worship Center Church Inc. (group owner; acq 6-10-2004; $1.15 million). Format: Christian classics. ♦Jimmy Swaggart, pres; Marvin Sanders, gen mgr.

KKLE(AM)— Aug 19, 1963: 1550 khz; 250 w-D, 52 w-N. TL: N37 14 21 W97 00 43. Box 249, Wellington 67152. Phone: (316) 221-3341. Fax: (620) 326-8512. Licensee: Johnson Enterprises Inc. (group owner; acq 1990). Network: Network: ESPN Radio, USA. Format: Talk, news/talk, sports. News staff: one; News: 36 hrs wkly. Target aud: General. ♦Gordon Johnson, pres & gen mgr.

KSJM(FM)— 1980: 107.9 mhz; 50 kw. 397 ft. TL: N37 14 42 W96 54 19. Stereo. 7701 E. Kellogg, Suite 107, Wichita 67207. Phone: (316) 612-1079. Fax: (316) 612-1077. E-mail: hot107.9jamz@aol.com. Licensee: Carter-Sherman Broadcast Group Inc. Group owner: Carter Broadcast Group Inc. (acq 5-17-2004; $900,000). . Arter & Hadden.

Format: Rhythm and blues, hip hop. News staff: one; News: 10 hrs wkly. Target aud: 25-54. ♦Don Sherman, pres & gen mgr.

KSOK-FM— 1996: 95.9 mhz; 15.2 kw. Ant 420 ft. TL: N37 04 32 W96 56 13. 334 E. Radio Ln., Arkansas City 67005. Phone: (620) 442-5400. Fax: (620) 442-5401. E-mail: ksok@ksokradio.com. Web Site: www.ksok.com. Licensee: Cowley County Broadcasting Inc. (acq 9-3-02; with KSOK(AM) Arkansas City). Format: Today's best country. ♦Marty Mutti, gen mgr.

***KSWC(FM)**— November 1967: 100.3 mhz; 10 w. 70 ft. TL: N37 14 42 W96 54 19. 100 College St. 67156. Phone: (620) 229-6337. Fax: (620) 229-6382. Web Site: www.sckans.edu. Licensee: Southwestern College. Format: College rock. Target aud: 21 & younger. ♦William DeArmond, gen mgr.

Kentucky

Albany

WANY(AM)— Oct 25, 1958: 1390 khz; 1 kw-D. TL: N36 41 54 W85 09 00. Box 400 42602. Phone: (606) 387-5186. Fax: (606) 387-6595. Licensee: Pamela Allred dba Albany Broadcasting Co. (acq 11-13-01; with co-located FM). Network: UPI. Rep: Keystone (unwired net). Format: Country. Spec prog: Farm 2 hrs, gospel 6 hrs wkly. ♦Randy Speck, gen mgr, prom mgr, progmg dir & news dir; Larry Nelson, chief of engrg.

WANY-FM— Apr 18, 1966: 106.3 mhz; 2.7 kw. 155 ft. TL: N36 41 54 W85 09 00. Format: Country.

Allen

WMDJ-FM— Sept 1, 1984: 100.1 mhz; 1.3 kw. 492 ft. TL: N37 35 12 W82 42 57. (CP: 2.6 kw). Stereo. Box 1530, Martin 41649. Phone: (606) 874-8005. Phone: (606) 874-8006. Fax: (606) 874-0057. Licensee: Floyd County Broadcasting Co. Inc. (acq 12-84; grpsl; FTR: 12-31-84). Rep: Katz Radio. Format: Country, oldies. Target aud: 25-65. Spec prog: Solid Gold Saturday nights, gospel. ♦Dale McKinney, pres; Rick Caudill, stn mgr; Mona Dingus, gen sls mgr.

Ashland

WCMI(AM)— 1935: 1340 khz; 1 kw-U. TL: N38 28 02 W82 35 50. 401 11th St., Suite 200, Huntington, WV 25701. Phone: (304) 523-8401. Web Site: www.wcmi.am. Licensee: Fifth Avenue Broadcasting Co. Inc. Group owner: Kindred Communications Inc. (acq 1-26-98; with WRVC-FM Catlettsburg). Network: Network: Westwood One, CBS. Format: Sports. ♦Mike Kirtner, pres & gen mgr; Cameron Smith, opns VP.

WDGG(FM)— 1948: 93.7 mhz; 100 kw. 741 ft. TL: N38 23 14 W82 39 45. Stereo. 401 11th St., Suite 200, Huntington, WV 25701. Phone: (304) 523-8401. Fax: (304) 523-4848. Web Site: www.wdgg.fm. Licensee: Fifth Avenue Broadcasting Co. Inc. Group owner: Kindred Communications Inc. (acq 1988). Arent, Fox, Kintner, Plotkin & Kahn. Format: Country. Target aud: 25-49; male. ♦Mike Kirtner, pres & gen mgr.

WRVC-FM—See Catlettsburg

WTCR-FM—See Huntington, WV

Auburn

***WAYD(FM)**— 2005: 88.1 mhz; 1 kw. Ant 371 ft. TL: N36 57 37 W86 32 49. WAY-FM, 1012 McEwen Dr., Franklin, TN 37067. Phone: (615) 261-9293. Fax: (615) 261-3967. E-mail: waym@wayfm.com. Web Site: www.wayfm.com. Licensee: WAY-FM Media Group Inc. (group owner). Format: Christian. ♦Matt Austin, gen mgr.

WBVR-FM— May 1965: 96.7 mhz; 45 kw. Ant 423 ft. TL: N36 50 35 W86 15 30. Stereo. 2465 Russellville Rd., Suite 2, Bowling Green 42101. Phone: (270) 843-3333. Fax: (270) 843-0454. E-mail: bhogan@beaverfm.com. Web Site: www.beaverfm.com. Licensee: Forever Communications Inc. (group owner; acq 12-31-02; grpsl). Network: ABC. Rgnl Reps Corp.- Cincinneti, Oh. Format: Country. Target aud: 18-54. ♦Brad Hogan, VP, gen mgr & stn mgr; Christine Hillard, pres & opns dir.

Barbourville

WKKQ(FM)—Listing follows WYWY(AM).

WYWY(AM)— Dec 13, 1955: 950 khz; 1 kw-D. TL: N36 50 26 W83 52 16. 222 Daniel Boone Dr. 40906. Phone: (606) 546-4128. Fax: (606) 546-4138. Licensee: Barbourville Community Broadcasting Co. (acq 11-66). Format: Relg. ♦Mildfred Engle, pres; Tad Engle, gen mgr; Pat Jordan, opns mgr; Orville Burnett, chief of engrg.

WKKQ(FM)—Co-owned with WYWY(AM). Oct 2, 1974: 96.1 mhz; 25 kw. 300 ft. TL: N36 51 55 W83 53 55. Stereo. Format: Country. Target aud: 25-34. ♦Randy Brock, gen sls mgr.

Bardstown

WBRT(AM)— December 1954: 1320 khz; 1 kw-D. TL: N37 49 09 W85 29 10. 106 S. 3rd St. 40004. Phone: (502) 348-3943. Fax: (502) 348-4043. E-mail: wbrt@commonwealthbroadcasting.com. Licensee: CBC of Nelson County Inc. Group owner: Commonwealth Broadcasting Corp. (acq 12-12-97; $400,000. with co-located FM). Network: ABC Information & Entertainment. Rep: Rgnl Reps. Format: C&W, info. Target aud: 20 plus. Spec prog: Farm 10 hrs wkly. ♦Kenny Fogle, gen mgr.

Beattyville

WLJC(FM)— May 12, 1965: 102.1 mhz; 1.2 kw. 520 ft. TL: N37 36 23 W83 41 16. 219 Radio Stn. Loop 41311. Phone: (606) 464-3600. Fax: (606) 464-5021. E-mail: wljc@wljc.com. Web Site: www.wljc.com. Licensee: Hour of Harvest Inc. Rep: Rgnl Reps. Format: Relg. ♦Margaret Drake, pres; Jonathan Drake, gen mgr.

Beaver Dam

WAIA(AM)—Licensed to Beaver Dam. See Hartford

WKLX(FM)— 2000: 100.7 mhz; 6 kw. 328 ft. TL: N37 21 11 W86 43 14. 661F 31W Bypass, Bowling Green 42101. Phone: (270) 846-0222. Fax: (270) 783-8829. Web Site: www.bowlinggreenstar.com. Licensee: Charles M. Anderson. Leventhal, Senter & Lerman. Format: Hot adult contemp. ♦Darron Steenbergen, gen mgr.

WXMZ(FM)—See Hartford

Benton

***WAAJ(FM)**— 1996: 89.7 mhz; 3.7 kw vert. 298 ft. TL: N36 48 31 W88 13 26. Box 281, Hardin 42048. Phone: (270) 437-4095. Fax: (270) 437-4098. Web Site: www.heartlandradio.org. Licensee: Heartland Ministries. Format: Christian hit radio. ♦Cecil Glass, gen mgr.

WCBL(AM)— Dec 13, 1954: 1290 khz; 5 kw-D. TL: N36 51 30 W88 20 13. Box 387, 1039 Eggners Ferry Rd. 42025. Phone: (270) 527-3102. Fax: (270) 527-5606. Licensee: Jim W. Freeland. (acq 11-17-98; with co-located FM). Format: Country. News staff: one; News: 7 hrs wkly. Target aud: General. ♦Jim Freeland, gen mgr; Sherry Rickman, opns mgr; Chris Freeland, gen sls mgr; Gregg Leath, progmg dir; Stephanie Waters, news dir; Lowell Coal, chief of engrg.

WCBL-FM— Mar 3, 1966: 99.1 mhz; 3 kw. 298 ft. TL: N36 51 30 W88 20 13. (CP: 3.3 kw). Format: Oldies.

Broadcasting & Cable Yearbook 2006

Kentucky

*WTRT(FM)— December 1998: 88.1 mhz; 600 w. 253 ft. TL: N36 47 53 W88 20 50. Stereo. Box 281, Hardin 42048. Phone: (270) 437-4095. Fax: (270) 437-4098. E-mail: wtrt@heartlandradio.org. Web Site: www.heartlandradio.org/wtrt. Licensee: Heartland Ministries Format: Inspirational. ◆ Cecil Glass, stn mgr.

*WVHM(FM)— June 1989: 90.5 mhz; 8 kw. 351 ft. TL: N36 48 31 W88 13 26. Box 281, Hardin 42048. Secondary address: 219 College St., Hardin 42048. Phone: (270) 437-4095. Fax: (270) 437-4098. E-mail: wvhm@heartlandradio.com. Web Site: www.heartlandradio.org/wvhm. Licensee: Heartland Ministries. Network: USA. Format: Gospel. Target aud: 18-49. ◆ Darrell Gibson, pres; Cecil Glass, gen mgr & stn mgr; Justin Patton, opns mgr.

Berea

WKXO(AM)— July 18, 1971: 1500 khz; 250 w-D. TL: N37 35 12 W84 18 04. Box 822, 128 Big Hill Ave., Richmond 40475. Phone: (606) 723-5138. Fax: (859) 623-1341. Licensee: Wallingford Communications LLC. Group owner: Wallingford Broadcasting Co. (acq 1999; grpsl). Network: Network: ABC Information & Entertainment, Jones Radio Networks. Format: Oldies, talk. News staff: one; News: 3 hrs wkly. Target aud: 21 plus. Spec prog: Gospel 12 hrs, relg 12 hrs wkly. ◆ Kelly Wallingford, gen mgr & stn mgr; Abby Anglin, news dir.

WLFX(FM)— Co-owned with WKXO(AM). Sept 27, 1990: 106.7 mhz; 1.95 kw. 584 ft. TL: N37 30 15 W84 12 58. Stereo. Network: ABC Information & Entertainment. Format: Classic rock. Spec prog: Gospel 12 hrs wkly.

Bowling Green

WBGN(AM)— Nov 24, 1959: 1340 khz; 1 kw-U. TL: N37 00 34 W86 27 09. 901 Lehman Ave., Suite 1 42101. Phone: (270) 842-1638. Fax: (270) 782-0767. E-mail: wbgn@sirque.net. Licensee: Forever Communications Inc. (group owner; acq 12-31-02; grpsl). Network: CBS. Rep: Rgnl Reps. Pepper & Corazzini. Format: Sports. News staff: one; News: 20 hrs wkly. Target aud: 35-54. ◆ Brad Hogan, gen mgr; Chris Idle, opns dir.

*WCVK(FM)— Apr 22, 1986: 90.7 mhz; 14 kw. 448 ft. TL: N37 00 18 W86 31 19. Stereo. 1407 Scottsville Rd. 42104. Phone: (270) 781-7326. Fax: (270) 781-8005. Web Site: www.christianfamilyradio.com. Licensee: Bowling Green Community Broadcasting Inc. Network: USA. Format: Relg, MOR, adult contemp Christian. Target aud: 25-54; Christian men & women. Spec prog: Black 2 hrs wkly. ◆ Mike Wilson, gen mgr.

WDNS(FM)—Listing follows WKCT(AM).

WGGC(FM)— June 23, 1961: 95.1 mhz; 100 kw. Ant 987 ft. TL: N36 54 43 W86 11 21. Box 70163 42101. Secondary address: 1727 US 31-W. Bypass 42101. Phone: (270) 651-2142. Phone: (270) 782-9595. Fax: (270) 783-8665. E-mail: wggc@wggc.com. Web Site: www.wggc.com. Licensee: Heritage Communications Inc. (acq 10-20-97; $400,000. for stock). Format: Country. ◆ Bill Evans, gen mgr; Darrin Evans, stn mgr.

WKCT(AM)— Nov 1, 1947: 930 khz; 5 kw-D, 500 w-N, DA-N. TL: N37 01 53 W86 26 18. Box 930, 804 College St. 42101-0930. Phone: (270) 781-2121. Fax: (270) 842-0232. E-mail: alan@wdnsfm.com. Web Site: www.wdnsfm.com. Licensee: Daily News Broadcasting Co. Network: CBS. Format: News/talk, info. News staff: one; News: 25 hrs wkly. Target aud: 25 plus. ◆ John Gaines, chmn; Pipes Gaines, pres; Alan Cooper, gen mgr.

WDNS(FM)—Co-owned with WKCT(AM). Mar 12, 1973: 93.3 mhz; 12 kw. 472 ft. TL: N36 56 39 W86 15 11. Stereo. Web Site: www.wdnsfm.com. Format: Classic Rock. News staff: one; News: 7 hrs wkly. Target aud: 18-54.

*WKYU-FM— November 1980: 88.9 mhz; 100 kw. 721 ft. TL: N37 05 22 W86 38 05. Stereo. Western Kentucky Univ., 1901 College Heights Blvd. 42101. Phone: (270) 745-5489. Fax: (270) 745-6272. E-mail: wkyufm@wku.edu. Web Site: www.wku.edu/wkyu-fm. Licensee: Western Kentucky University. Network: Network: NPR, PRI. Leventhal, Senter & Lerman. Format: Class, news. News staff: 3; News: 35 hrs wkly. Target aud: General. Spec prog: Folk 5 hrs, jazz 15 hrs wkly. ◆ Peter Bryant, gen mgr; Charolene Burden, opns mgr. Co-owned TV: *WKYU-TV affil

*WWHR(FM)— Aug 18, 1988: 91.7 mhz; 100 w. 10 ft. TL: N36 59 00 W86 27 24. Stereo. Western Kentucky Univ., 1901 College Heights Blvd. 42101. Phone: (270) 745-5439. Phone: (270) 745-5350. Fax: (270) 745-2084. Web Site: www.revolution.fm. Licensee: Western Kentucky University. Format: College progsv. News: 3 hrs wkly. Target aud: Adults 18-34. Spec prog: Black 2 hrs, punk 2 hrs, gothic 2 hrs, local 2 hrs wkly. ◆ Marjorie Yambor, gen mgr; Ryan Johnson, stn mgr.

Brandenburg

WMMG(AM)— July 1984: 1140 khz; 250 w-D. TL: N37 59 05 W86 09 24. Box 505, 1715 Bypass Rd. 40108. Phone: (270) 422-3961. Fax: (270) 422-3464. Licensee: Meade County Communications Inc. Rep: Rgnl Reps. Format: Country. Spec prog: Relg 8 hrs wkly. ◆ Gwen Blevins, gen mgr; Dave Clark, prom mgr & news dir; Calvin Bader, chief of engrg.

WMMG-FM— Aug 23, 1972: 93.5 mhz; 3.4 kw. 290 ft. TL: N37 59 05 W86 09 24. Stereo. Web Site: www.wmmgradio.com. Rep: Rgnl Reps. Target aud: 18-65. ◆ Gwen Blevins, gen sls mgr & adv mgr; Dave Clark, progmg mgr & pub affrs dir.

Buffalo

WXAM(AM)— Nov 26, 1974: 1430 khz; 1 kw-D. TL: N37 31 49 W85 42 49. Box 177, Hodgenville 42748. Secondary address: 216 S. Lincoln Blvd., Hodgenville 42748. Phone: (270) 358-4707. Fax: (270) 358-4755. Licensee: Mark Goodman Productions Inc. (acq 2-1-89; $99,292; 2-13-89). Network: USA. Format: Country. ◆ Mark Goodman, VP; Carolyn Goodman, gen mgr.

Burkesville

WKYR-FM— October 1988: 107.9 mhz; 6 kw. Ant 312 ft. TL: N36 47 26 W85 22 47. Stereo. Box 340 42717. Secondary address: Hwy. 90 E. 42717. Phone: (270) 433-7191. Fax: (270) 433-7195. E-mail: wkyr@mchsi.com. Licensee: WKYR Inc. Network: Network: ABC, Jones Radio Networks. Format: Country. ◆ Pam Prewitt, gen mgr & gen sls mgr.

Burnside

WSEK(FM)—Listing follows WSFE(AM).

WSFE(AM)— Feb 28, 1984: 910 khz; 500 w-D. TL: N37 01 46 W84 36 28. Box 740, Somerset 42502. Secondary address: 101 First Radio Ln., Somerset 42501. Phone: (606) 678-5152. Fax: (606) 678-2026. E-mail: thefirstradiogroup@.com. Licensee: Capstar TX L.P. Group owner: Clear Channel Communications Inc. (acq 12-8-2000; grpsl). Format: Southern gospel. News staff: one; News: 5 hrs wkly. Target aud: 25-54. ◆ Michael S. Tarter, gen mgr & stn mgr.

WSEK(FM)—Co-owned with WSFE(AM). Aug 17, 1985: 93.9 mhz; 50 kw. 492 ft. TL: N37 09 15 W84 27 35. Stereo. Format: Adult contemp.

Cadiz

WKDZ(AM)— Apr 8, 1966: 1110 khz; 1 kw-D. TL: N36 52 57 W87 50 44. Box 1900 42211-0316. Secondary address: 1487 Will Jackson Rd. 42211-0316. Phone: (270) 522-3232. Fax: (270) 522-1110. Licensee: Ham Broadcasting Co. Inc. (acq 1-22-91; $200,000 with co-located FM; 2-11-91). Network: Network: ABC, CNN Radio. Format: News/talk. News staff: 3; News: 18 hrs wkly. Target aud: 25-54. Spec prog: Farm 2 hrs wkly. ◆ D.J. Everett III, pres; Beth A. Mann, gen mgr; Alan Watts, news dir.

WKDZ-FM— May 18, 1972: 106.5 mhz; 1.4 kw. 321 ft. TL: N36 52 57 W87 50 44. Stereo. Network: ABC. Format: Real country. News staff: 2; News: 20 hrs wkly. Target aud: 35-64.

Calvert City

WCCK(FM)— 1993: 95.7 mhz; 960 w. 505 ft. TL: N37 04 21 W88 15 04. Box 1116 42029. Phone: (270) 395-5133. Fax: (270) 395-5231. E-mail: wcck@charter.net. Licensee: Jim Freeland DBA Freeland Broadcasting. Network: CBS. Format: Classic Country. News: 10 hrs wkly. Target aud: 30 plus; professionals and retired. ◆ Jim Freeland, CEO, gen mgr & gen sls mgr; Sherry Darnall, opns dir; Greg Leath, progmg dir; Loal D. Cole, chief of engrg.

Campbellsville

*WAPD(FM)— 1996: 91.7 mhz; 2.323 kw vert. Ant 216 ft. TL: N37 19 59 W85 19 53. St. Andrew United Methodist Church, 1001 S. Central Ave. 42718. Phone: (270) 465-7559. Licensee: American Family Association. Group owner: American Family Radio Format: Christian. ◆ Linda Collins, gen mgr.

WCKQ(FM)— Dec 1, 1964: 104.1 mhz; 17 kw. 374 ft. TL: N37 19 29 W85 18 36. Stereo. 50 Friendship Pike 42718. Secondary address: Box 1053 42719. Phone: (270) 789-2401. Fax: (270) 789-1450. E-mail: wckq@commonwealthbroadcasting.com. Licensee: CBC of Marion and Taylor Counties Inc. Group owner: Commonwealth Broadcasting Corp. (acq 6-30-97; $720,000 with co-located AM). Network: Network: ABC, Jones Radio Networks. Rep: Rgnl Reps. Haley, Bader & Potts. Format: Adult contemp. News staff: one. Target aud: 18-54. ◆ Steve Newberry, pres; Barb Smith, stn mgr & gen sls mgr; Marty Bagby, opns mgr & news dir; Rob Collins, prom mgr & progmg dir; Mike Graham, chief of engrg.

WTCO(AM)— Co-owned with WCKQ(FM). March 1948: 1450 khz; 1 kw-U. TL: N37 20 07 W85 22 33. Phone: (270) 469-9826. Format: All Sports (ESPN radio). News staff: one. Target aud: 25-64.

WGRK-FM—See Greensburg

Campton

WCBJ(FM)— 1999: 103.7 mhz; 6 kw. 328 ft. TL: N37 44 23 W83 33 59. 129 College St., West Liberty 41472. Phone: (606) 743-3145. Fax: (606) 743-9557. Licensee: Morgan County Industries Inc. (group owner) Format: Rock. ◆ Paul Lyons, gen mgr.

Cannonsburg

WOKT(AM)— December 1987: 1040 khz; 2.5 kw-D, DA-D. TL: N38 23 39 W82 41 53. 3027 Lester Ln., Ashland 41102. Phone: (606) 928-3778. Licensee: Big River Radio Inc. Group owner: Baker Family Stations (Positive Radio Group) Format: Sports/talk. Target aud: General. ◆ Dickie Tiller, stn mgr.

Carlisle

WBVX(FM)— December 1994: 92.1 mhz; 32 kw. Ant 610 ft. TL: N38 11 19 W84 22 13. Stereo. 401 W. Main, Suite 301, Lexington 40507. Phone: (859) 233-1515. Fax: (859) 233-1517. Licensee: L.M. Communications of Kentucky LLC. Group owner: L.M. Communications Inc. (acq 8-17-01; $4.8 million). Format: Adult contemp. Target aud: General. ◆ Lynn Martin, pres; James MacFarlane, gen mgr; Bill May, gen sls mgr; Bill Clary, progmg dir; Mary Lynn, news dir.

Carrollton

WIKI(FM)— Apr 12, 1968: 95.3 mhz; 3 kw. 423 ft. TL: N38 39 58 W85 16 51. Stereo. 2470 N. State Hwy. 7, North Vernon, IN 47265. Phone: (812) 273-3139. Phone: (800) 953-9454 (OH, IN, KY). Fax: (812) 265-4536. Licensee: Star Media Inc. (acq 1999; $550,000). Network: Network: Jones Radio Networks, CNN Radio. Rep: Rgnl Reps. Pepper & Corazzini. Format: Country. News: 10 hrs wkly. Target aud: 10-90; general. ◆ Marty Pieratt, CEO, pres & gen mgr; Juliette Knola, gen sls mgr; Larry Duke, prom dir; Jamur Tuttle, progmg dir.

Catlettsburg

WRVC-FM— Jan 19, 1972: 92.7 mhz; 3 kw. 298 ft. TL: N38 27 58 W82 35 27. Stereo. 401 11th St., Suite 200, Huntington, WV 25701. Phone: (304) 523-8401. Fax: (304) 523-4848. Web Site: www.wrvc.fm. Licensee: Fifth Avenue Broadcasting Co. Inc. Group owner: Kindred Communications Inc. (acq 7-7-98; with WCMI(AM) Ashland). Network: ABC Information & Entertainment. Format: Rock. ◆ Mike Kirtner, pres & gen mgr.

Cave City

WPTQ(FM)— Sept 2, 1988: 103.7 mhz; 13.5 kw. 449 ft. TL: N37 06 39 W85 58 41. Stereo. 113 W. Public Sq., Suite 400, Glasgow 42141. Phone: (270) 651-6060. Fax: (270) 651-7666. E-mail: wptq@commonwealthbroadcasting.com. Licensee: Commonwealth Broadcasting Corp. (acq 11-25-97). Network: Westwood One. Pepper

Stations in the U.S.   Kentucky

& Corazzini. Format: Classic rock. News staff: one; News: 7 hrs wkly. Target aud: 25-44. ♦Darren Steenbergen, gen mgr; Alex Parocai, opns mgr.

Central City

WMTA(AM)— Feb 19, 1955: 1380 khz; 500 w-D, 23 w-N. TL: N37 16 34 W87 08 39. Stereo. Box 2463, Evansville, IN 47728. Phone: (812) 479-1762. Fax: (812) 474-0483. Web Site: www.faith1380.com. Licensee: WMTA LLC (acq 2-26-2004; $65,000). Fisher, Wayland, Cooper, Leader & Zaragoza. Format: Christian. News: 20 hrs wkly. Target aud: General. ♦Gayle Russ, CEO.

WNES(AM)— Jan 1, 1955: 1050 khz; 1 kw-D, 172 w-N. TL: N37 16 09 W87 08 32. Box 471 42330. Phone: (270) 754-3000. Fax: (270) 754-9484. Licensee: Starlight Broadcasting. (acq 9-28-89). Network: CBS. Format: Sports, talk. Spec prog: Farm 7 hrs wkly. ♦Andy Anderson, pres & gen mgr; Stan Barnett, progmg mgr.

WQXQ(FM)—Co-owned with WNES(AM). Dec 18, 1956: 101.9 mhz; 100 kw. 215 ft. TL: N37 16 09 W87 08 32. (CP: Ant 676 ft.). Format: Hot adult contemp.

Clinton

WLLE(FM)— 1997: 102.1 mhz; 12.5 kw. 476 ft. TL: N36 44 22 W88 47 13. Box 2397, Paducah 42002. Secondary address: 1176 State Rt. 45 N., Mayfield 42066. Phone: (270) 247-5122. Fax: (270) 554-5468. E-mail: roth@wkyx.com. Licensee: Bristol Broadcasting Co. Inc. (group owner; acq 2-20-2004; grpsl). Format: Country. ♦Gary Morse, gen mgr; Roth Stratton, opns VP.

Coal Run

WPKE-FM— Sept 21, 1974: 103.1 mhz; 1.2 kw. Ant 741 ft. TL: N37 27 57 W82 33 04. Stereo. Box 2200, Pikeville 41502. Secondary address: 1240 Radio Dr., Pikeville 41501. Phone: (606) 437-4051. Fax: (606) 432-2809. E-mail: wpke@wpke.com. Licensee: East Kentucky Broadcasting Corp. (group owner; acq 6-94; $480,000. with WBPA(AM) Elkhorn City). Network: ABC. Rgnl Reps Womble, Carlyle, Sandridge & Rice. Format: Rock. News staff: one. Target aud: General. ♦Keith Casebolt, gen mgr.

Columbia

WAIN(AM)— Aug 1, 1951: 1270 khz; 1 kw-D, 68 w-N. TL: N37 06 36 W85 16 42. Box 69 42728. Secondary address: 1521 Liberty Rd. 42728. Phone: (270) 384-2134. Fax: (270) 384-6722. E-mail: wain@keybroadcasting.net. Licensee: Tri-County Radio Broadcasting Corp. Group owner: Key Broadcasting Inc. Network: ABC Information & Entertainment. Rep: Rgnl Reps. Rgnl Reps Format: Oldies 50s, 60s, 70s. News staff: one; News: 8 hrs wkly. Target aud: 16-65. Spec prog: Farm 2 hrs. ♦Louise Wooten, gen mgr.

WAIN-FM— Mar 1, 1968: 93.5 mhz; 5.2 kw. 220 ft. TL: N37 06 36 W85 16 42. Stereo. Network: ABC. Format: Country. News staff: one. Target aud: 16-65. ♦Louise Wooten, gen mgr & mktg mgr.

WHVE(FM)—See Russell Springs

Corbin

WCTT(AM)— May 9, 1947: 680 khz; 1 kw-U, DA-N. TL: N36 54 09 W84 04 50. Box 742 40702-0742. Secondary address: 821 Adams Rd. 40701. Phone: (606) 528-4717. Fax: (606) 528-4487. Licensee: Encore Communications Inc. (acq 5-95; with co-located FM; 6-22-81). Network: ABC. Rep: Rgnl Reps. Shaw Pittman. Format: Talk/news, oldies, MOR. News staff: one. ♦Stephanie Waggoner, gen mgr.

WCTT-FM— June 1, 1967: 107.3 mhz; 50 kw. 492 ft. TL: N36 54 09 W84 04 55. Stereo. Rep: Rgnl Reps. Format: Adult contemp. News: one hr wkly. Target aud: 18-54.

*WEKF(FM)— June 24, 2003: 88.5 mhz; 21 kw vert. Ant 499 ft. TL: N37 01 13 W84 23 41. Stereo. 102 Perkins Bldg., 521 Lancaster Ave., Richmond 40475-3102. Phone: (859) 622-1660. Fax: (859) 622-6276. Web Site: www.weku.fm. Licensee: Eastern Kentucky University. Network: Network: NPR, PRI. Hardy, Carey & Chautin. Format: News, classical. News staff: 3; News: 35 hrs wkly. ♦Tim Singleton, stn mgr; Mary Ellyn Cain, opns mgr; Carol Siler, dev dir; Marie Mitchell, news dir.

WKDP(AM)— Nov 23, 1961: 1330 khz; 5 kw-D, DA. TL: N36 56 20 W84 04 44. Box 742 40702. Secondary address: 821 Adams Rd. 40701. Phone: (606) 528-6617. Fax: (606) 528-4487. E-mail: swaggoner@wkdp.com. Licensee: Eubanks Broadcasting Inc. (acq 12-28-89). Network: ABC Information & Entertainment. Rep: Rgnl Reps. Format: Relg, news/talk. Target aud: 30-64. ♦Dallas R. Eubanks, pres; Stephanie Waggoner, gen mgr; Derek Eubanks, chief of engrg.

WKDP-FM— 1967: 99.5 mhz; 50kw. 709 ft. TL: N36 57 14 W84 58 41. Stereo. 821 Adams Rd. 40701. Network: ABC. Fisher, Wayland, Cooper, Leader & Zaragoza. Format: Country. Target aud: General.

Covington

WCVG(AM)— Oct 29, 1965: 1320 khz; 500 w-D, 430 w-N, DA-2. TL: N39 02 44 W84 30 30. Box 15034, 135 W. 38th St., Latonia 41015. Phone: (859) 291-2255. Fax: (859) 655-4345. E-mail: gospel1320@aol.com. Web Site: www.wcvg.com. Licensee: Richard L. Plessinger Sr. Group owner: Plessinger Radio Group (R.L. Plessinger Holding Co.) (acq 1987). Network: Network: USA, American Urban. Format: Black, gospel, Christian, relg. News: 7 hrs wkly. Target aud: 25-54; African-American females. ♦Tracie Hunter, gen mgr; Jeff Eldred, opns mgr; Avery Corbin, prom dir & prom mgr; John Jones, mus dir.

Cumberland

WCPM(AM)— October 1951: 1280 khz; 1 kw-D. TL: N36 58 25 W82 59 15. 101 Keller St. 40823. Phone: (606) 589-4623. Licensee: Cumberland City Broadcasting Inc. (acq 8-22-2003; with co-located FM). Network: Jones Radio Networks. Format: C&W, relg. News: 9 hrs wkly. Target aud: 18-49; general. Spec prog: Black 3 hrs, farm one hr wkly. ♦George Bibb, gen mgr.

WVEK-FM— December 1994: 102.7 mhz; 175 w. Ant 1,824 ft. TL: N36 54 59 W82 54 02. 101 Keller St. 40823. Phone: (606) 589-4623. Licensee: JBL Broadcasting Inc. (acq 5-24-2005; $265,000). Network: Jones Radio Networks. Format: Country. News: 4 hrs wkly. Target aud: 18-49; young adults. ♦Susan Burton, gen mgr; George Bibb, adv mgr.

Cynthiana

WCYN(AM)— Sept 1, 1956: 1400 khz; 500 w-D, 1 kw-N. TL: N38 24 20 W84 17 32. 111 Court St. 41031. Phone: (859) 234-1400. Fax: (859) 234-1425. Web Site: www.wcyn.com. Licensee: WCYN Broadcasting Inc. (acq 12-29-2004; $122,000). Rep: Keystone (unwired net), Rgnl Reps. Format: Oldies. Target aud: General. Spec prog: Farm 15 hrs, relg 11 hrs wkly. ♦Chris Winkle, gen mgr.

WCYN-FM— June 1, 1970: 102.3 mhz; 3.4 kw. Ant 400 ft. TL: N38 24 39 W84 19 07. 300 W. Vine St., Lexington 40507. Phone: (859) 253-5900. Fax: (859) 253-5940. Web Site: www.k93fm.com. Licensee: Cumulus Licensing LLC. (acq 11-26-2002). Format: Classic country. ♦Chris Clendenen, gen mgr.

Danville

*WDFB(FM)— Sept 1992: 88.1 mhz; 170 w. 328 ft. TL: N37 35 46 W84 50 19. Box 106 40423-0106. Secondary address: 3596 Alum Springs Rd. 40422. Phone: (859) 236-9333. Fax: (859) 236-3348. E-mail: wdfb@searnet.com. Web Site: www.wdfb.com. Licensee: Alum Springs Educational Corp. (acq 6-8-92). Network: USA. Format: Educ, Christian. Target aud: General. ♦Donald A. Drake, pres; Jim Gaskin, gen sls mgr; Mildred Drake, exec VP, gen mgr & progmg dir.

WHIR(AM)— Oct 27, 1947: 1230 khz; 1 kw-U. TL: N37 40 28 W84 46 06. 2063 Shakertown Rd. 40422. Phone: (859) 236-2711. Fax: (859) 236-1461. E-mail: hometownradio@bellsouth.net. Licensee: Hometown Broadcasting of Danville Inc. (acq 1995; $525,000. with co-located FM). Network: Network: Westwood One, CBS Radio. Rep: Rgnl Reps. Format: News/talk. News staff: one; News: 2 hrs wkly. Target aud: 25-54; business owners, sports fans, housewives. Spec prog: Farm one hr, relg 8 hrs, sports 20 hrs wkly. ♦Bruce Leslie, pres; Robert Wagner, gen mgr; Jim Parman, opns dir.

WHIR-FM— Oct 27, 1969: 107.1 mhz; 4.9 kw. Ant 158 ft. TL: N37 40 28 W84 46 06. Stereo. 2063 Shakertown Rd. 40422. Phone: (859) 236-2711. Fax: (859) 236-1461. Licensee: Vernon R. Baldwin Inc. (group owner; (acq 8-2-2004; $1 million). Network: ABC. Format: Relg. News staff: one; News: 2 hrs wkly. Target aud: General; Central KY country fans. ♦Robert Wagner, gen mgr.

Drakesboro

WNTC(FM)— 2001: 103.9 mhz; 1.95 kw. Ant 407 ft. TL: N37 06 50 W87 03 52. 2514 Eugenia Ave., Nashville, TN 37211. Phone: (615) 844-1039. Phone: (615) 251-1222. Fax: (615) 313-9933. Licensee: Nashville's SportsRadio Inc. Group owner: Southern Wabash Communications Corp. (acq 10-17-01). Format: Mexican. ♦Randolph V. Bell, pres; Wayne DeSylvia, gen mgr & stn mgr.

Eddyville

WWLK(AM)— May 2, 1981: . Stn currently dark 900 khz; 1 kw-D, 120 w-N, DA-2. TL: N37 04 26 W88 04 48. Box 90 42038. Licensee: Tilent Inc. (acq 7-20-89; $65,000;. FTR: 8-14-89). ♦Jim Baggett, pres.

Edmonton

WHSX(FM)— Apr 5, 1990: 99.1 mhz; 3 kw. 328 ft. TL: N37 01 33 W85 33 14. Stereo. Box 377 42129. Phone: (270) 432-0991. Fax: (270) 432-0993. Licensee: Hart County Communications Inc. (acq 7-5-2001; $350,000). Format: Country. News staff: one; News: 10 hrs wkly. Target aud: 25-54. Spec prog: Farm 15 hrs wkly. ♦Jessie Crantree, gen mgr.

Elizabethtown

WIEL(AM)— Oct 1, 1950: 1400 khz; 1 kw-U. TL: N37 41 11 W85 52 19. Box 1206 42701. Secondary address: 406 S. Mulberry 42701. Phone: (270) 763-0800. Fax: (270) 769-6349. Licensee: Elizabethtown CBC Inc. Group owner: Commonwealth Broadcasting Corp. (acq 5-12-00; grpsl). Network: ABC. Rep: Rgnl Reps. Format: ESPN. News staff: one; News: 24 hrs wkly. Target aud: 24-54; upscale adult. ♦John Wright, gen mgr.

WKMO(FM)—See Hodgenville

*WKUE(FM)— Oct 15, 1990: 90.9 mhz; 5.2 kw. 633 ft. TL: N37 44 46 W85 53 18. Stereo. Western Kentucky Univ., 1906 College Heights Blvd., Bowling Green 42101. Phone: (270) 745-5489. Fax: (270) 745-6272. Web Site: www.wku.edu/wkyu-fm. Licensee: Western Kentucky University. Network: Network: NPR, PRI. Leventhal, Senter & Lerman. Format: Class, news. News staff: 3; News: 30 hrs wkly. Target aud: General. Spec prog: Jazz 15 hrs, folk 5 hrs wkly. ♦Gary Randsall, pres; Peter Bryant, gen mgr; Terry Reagan, dev dir.

WQXE(FM)— Nov 24, 1969: 98.3 mhz; 8.5 kw. Ant 531 ft. TL: N37 43 18 W86 02 10. Stereo. 233 W. Dixie Ave. 42701. Phone: (270) 737-8000. Fax: (270) 737-7229. E-mail: bill@wqxe.com. Web Site: www.wqxe.com. Licensee: Skytower Communications E'town Inc. Network: Westwood One. Format: Hot adult contemp. Target aud: 25-54; upscale, dual income families. ♦Billy R. Evans, pres & gen mgr; Marilyn Evans, prom mgr; Lee Bramblett, news dir; Greg Happel, chief of engrg.

Broadcasting & Cable Yearbook 2006

Kentucky

Elkhorn City

WEKB(AM)— Nov 24, 1979: 1460 khz; 5 kw-D, 114 w-N. TL: N37 18 25 W82 19 53. Box 2200, Pikeville 41502. Secondary address: 1240 Radio Dr., Pikeville 41501. Phone: (606) 437-4051. Fax: (606) 432-2809. E-mail: wdhr@wdhr.com. Licensee: East Kentucky Broadcasting Corp. (group owner; acq 6-94; $480,000. with co-located FM). Network: ABC. Rgnl Reps Womble, Carlyle, Sanridge & Rice. Format: Oldies. Target aud: 25-49. ♦ Keith Casebolt, VP, gen mgr & opns mgr; Debbie Lawson, dev mgr; Pat Hall, sls dir, mktg dir, prom mgr & adv mgr; Walter E. May, CEO, pres, prom mgr & progmg dir; Randy Jones, progmg mgr; Shannon Deskins, news dir; Paul Manuel, engrg mgr; Walter Dingus, engrg mgr.

Elkton

WEKT(AM)— July 21, 1977: 1070 khz; 500 w-D. TL: N36 48 33 W87 09 38. Box 577 42220. Phone: (270) 265-5636. E-mail: wektan1070@yahoo.com. Licensee: M&R Broadcasting Inc. (acq 1-22-98; $55,000 for 50% of stock). Network: USA. Format: Southern gospel. Spec prog: Southern gospel, country gospel, bluegrass.

Eminence

WTSZ(AM)— June 1, 1956: 1600 khz; 500 w-D, 48 w-N. TL: N38 21 02 W85 11 11. 11864 Capital Way, Louisville 40299-6332. Phone: (502) 420-2494. Fax: (502) 420-2495. Licensee: Metro East CBC Inc. Group owner: Commonwealth Broadcasting Corp. (acq 4-13-00; $600,000. with WTSZ-FM Eminence). Format: Sports. Target aud: 25-54. ♦ Scott Thompson, gen mgr.

WTSZ-FM— July 4, 1988: 105.7 mhz; 3 kw. Ant 325 ft. TL: N38 21 09 W85 11 09. 300 Distillery Commons. Suite 200, Louisville 40206. Phone: (502) 583-6200. Fax: (502) 587-2979. E-mail: wthg@cbcradio.net. Licensee: Metro East CBC Inc. Group owner: Commonwealth Broadcasting Corp. (acq 4-13-00; $600,000. with WTSZ(AM) Eminence). Format: Sp contemp. ♦ Scott Thompson, gen mgr.

Erlanger

WIZF(FM)— Sept 22, 1965: 100.9 mhz; 1.25 kw. 508 ft. TL: N39 06 18 W84 33 24. (CP: 2.25 kw, ant 518 ft.). Stereo. 705 Central Ave., Suite 200, Cincinnati, OH 45202. Phone: (513) 679-6000. Fax: (513) 679-6014. Web Site: www.wize.com. Licensee: Blue Chip Broadcasting Licenses II Ltd. Group owner: Radio One Inc. (acq 4-30-01; grpsl). Format: Urban mainstream. Target aud: 18-54. ♦ Alfred Wiggins, CEO; Rick Porter, gen mgr.

Falmouth

WIOK(FM)— June 1981: 107.5 mhz; 6 kw. 695 ft. TL: N38 43 15 W84 22 27. Stereo. Box 50 41040. Phone: (859) 472-1075. Fax: (859) 472-2875. E-mail: wiok@fuse.net. Web Site: www.wiok.com. Licensee: Hammond Broadcasting Inc. (acq 1993). Network: USA. Rep: Rgnl Reps. Format: Gospel, relg. News: 12 hrs wkly. Target aud: 25-64; women. ♦ Gil Hammond, pres; Jan Hammond, VP & gen mgr; John Kent, progmg dir.

Flemingsburg

WFLE(AM)— November 1981: 1060 khz; 1 kw-D, DA. TL: N38 27 01 W83 44 06. Rt. 3, One Radio Dr. 41041. Phone: (606) 849-4433. Fax: (606) 845-9353. Licensee: DreamCatcher Communications Inc. (group owner; acq 5-23-02; $607,491. with co-located FM). Format: C&W. Target aud: 25-54. ♦ Ernest Sparkman, pres; Carl Haight, gen mgr & news dir; Kim Hestler, gen sls mgr; Eddie Plummer, prom mgr; Brent Mulliken, progmg dir; Jim Hay, chief of engrg.

WFLE-FM— February 1993: 95.1 mhz; 1.61 kw. 449 ft. TL: N38 24 42 W83 34 41.

Florence

WBOB(AM)— September 1984: 1160 khz; 5 kw-D, 990 w-N, DA-2. TL: N38 58 09 W84 40 56. 635 W. 7th St., Suite 400, Cincinnati, OH 45203. Phone: (513) 533-2500. Fax: (513) 533-2527. Web Site: www.wbob.com. Licensee: Caron Broadcasting Inc. Group owner: Salem Communications Corp. (acq 8-24-00; grpsl). Network: Salem Radio Network. Format: News/talk. News: 6 hrs wkly. Target aud: 25-54; adults. ♦ Edward Atsinger, CEO; Dan Craig, gen mgr & prom mgr.

Fort Campbell

WCVQ(FM)—Listing follows WJQI(AM).

WJQI(AM)— July 27, 1963: 1370 khz; 1 kw-D, 53 w-N. TL: N36 38 28 W87 26 04. 1640 Old Rosselville Pike, Clarksville, TN 37043. Phone: (931) 431-4984. Fax: (931) 648-7769. E-mail: q108@q108.com. Web Site: www.q108.com. Licensee: Saga Communications of Tuckessee L.L.C. Group owner: Saga Communications Inc. (acq 2-1-2001; grpsl). Format: Adult contemp. News staff: one; News: 14 hrs wkly. Target aud: 18-34. Spec prog: Gospel 10 hrs, relg 4 hrs wkly. ♦ Scott Farkas, pres; Susan Quesenberry, gen mgr; Lee Erwin, prom dir; J.C. Morrow, chief of engrg.

WCVQ(FM)—Co-owned with WJQI(AM). August 1969: 107.9 mhz; 100 kw. 950 ft. TL: N36 32 23 W87 39 45. Stereo. Phone: (931) 648-7720. E-mail: q108@q108.com. Web Site: www.q108.com. News staff: one; News: 2 hrs wkly. Target aud: 25-40. ♦ Lee Erwin, prom mgr.

Fort Knox

WLVK(FM)— Oct 1, 1967: 105.5 mhz; 6 kw. 299 ft. TL: N37 46 57 W85 54 38. Stereo. 519 N. Miles St., Elizabethtown 42701. Phone: (270) 766-1035. Fax: (270) 769-1052. Licensee: Big Cat Broadcasting Inc. (acq 6-26-00; $900,000). Miller & Miller. Format: Country. Target aud: 25-49; young & middle age country fans. ♦ Bill Walters, pres; Rene Bell, gen mgr; Cale Tharp, opns mgr & chief of engrg.

Fort Thomas

WAQZ(FM)— Apr 18, 1994: 97.3 mhz; 2.55 kw. Ant 508 ft. TL: N39 12 01 W84 31 22. Stereo. 2060 Reading Rd., Cincinnati, OH 45202. Phone: (513) 699-5959. Fax: (513) 699-5000. Web Site: www.newrock973.com. Licensee: Infinity Radio Inc. Group owner: Infinity Broadcasting Corp. (acq 11-13-98; grpsl). Tierney & Swift. Format: Alternative, rock. News: 8 hrs wkly. Target aud: 25-49. ♦ Mike Fredrick, gen mgr; Rob McClacken, gen sls mgr; Jeff Nagel, prom dir.

Frankfort

WFKY(AM)— February 1946: 1490 khz; 1 kw-U. TL: N38 12 46 W84 52 31. Box 4130, 115 W. Main St. 40601. Phone: (502) 875-1130. Fax: (502) 875-1225. E-mail: wfky@clearchannel.com. Licensee: Clear Channel Broadcasting Licenses Inc. Group owner: Clear Channel Communications Inc. (acq 8-27-2001; grpsl). Network: Westwood One. Rep: Rgnl Reps. Format: Full service, oldies. News staff: 2; News: 12 hrs wkly. Target aud: 25-55. Spec prog: Relg 6 hrs wkly. ♦ Ray Holbrook, gen mgr; Teresa Johnson, opns mgr; Joel Adams, news dir.

WKYW(FM)—Co-owned with WFKY(AM). Jan 1, 1967: 104.9 mhz; 3 kw. 300 ft. TL: N38 13 19 W84 54 55. Stereo. E-mail: wkyw@cbcradio.net. Format: News. News staff: 2; News: 168 hrs wkly. Target aud: 25-54.

WKED-FM— Apr 15, 1991: 103.7 mhz; 2.5 kw. 350 ft. TL: N38 13 17 W84 54 52. Stereo. 115 W. Main St. 40601-1840. Phone: (502) 875-1130. Fax: (502) 875-1225. Licensee: Clear Channel Broadcasting Licenses Inc. Group owner: Clear Channel Communications Inc. (acq 8-27-01; grpsl). Network: Westwood One. Format: Adult contemp. News staff: 2; News: 4 hrs wkly. Target aud: 25-54. ♦ Dave Colin, gen mgr.

Franklin

WFKN(AM)— Apr 25, 1954: 1220 khz; 250 w-D, 90 w-N. TL: N36 44 20 W86 34 42. 103 N. High St. 42135-0390. Phone: (270) 586-4481. Fax: (270) 586-6031. Licensee: WFKN LLC (acq 11-27-01). Network: ABC Information & Entertainment. Rep: Rgnl Reps. Format: Country. News staff: 2; News: 16 hrs wkly. Target aud: General. Spec prog: Relg, farm 6 hrs wkly. ♦ Ben Sheroan, gen mgr.

Fulton

WFUL(AM)— July 8, 1951: 1270 khz; 1 kw-D, 54 w-N. TL: N36 30 54 W88 54 16. Stereo. 8807 Middle Rd. State Rt. 166 E. 42041. Phone: (270) 472-1270. Fax: (270) 472-1189. E-mail: wfulradio@yahoo.com. Licensee: River County Broadcasting Inc. (acq 8-23-2004; $350,000). Network: ABC Information & Entertainment. Format: Country, gospel. Target aud: 40 plus. ♦ Max Mcdade, gen mgr.

WWKF(FM)— September 1954: 99.3 mhz; 3.3 kw. 337 ft. TL: N36 27 59 W88 56 47. Stereo. 1729 Nailling Dr., Union City, TN 38261. Phone: (731) 885-1240. Fax: (731) 885-3405. Web Site: www.kf99kq105.com. Licensee: WENK of Union City Inc. Group owner: WENK Broadcast Group Inc. (acq 10-1-82; $473,131; 10-18-82). Rep: Rgnl Reps. Format: CHR. News staff: one. Target aud: 18-34. ♦ Terry L. Hailey, pres & gen mgr.

Garrison

WOKE(FM)— Sept 7, 1998: 98.3 mhz; 5.2 kw. 492 ft. TL: N38 36 19 W83 03 37. 492 Main St. 41175. Phone: (606) 932-2223. Fax: (606) 932-6132. E-mail: info@wokejoyfm.org. Web Site: www.wokejoyfm.org. Licensee: Big River Radio Inc. (acq 10-25-94; 11-14-94). Booth, Freret, Imlay & Tepper. Format: Southern gospel. ♦ Paul Hunt, gen mgr.

Georgetown

*****WRVG(FM)**— Oct 1, 1963: 89.9 mhz; 50 kw. Ant 410 ft. TL: N38 12 15 W84 32 51. 5700 W. Oaks Blvd., Rocklin, CA 95765. Phone: (916) 251-1600. Fax: (916) 251-1650. Web Site: www.klove.com. Licensee: Educational Media Foundation. Group owner: EMF Broadcasting (acq 3-12-2004; $1.7 million). Format: Christian. ♦ Richard Jenkins, pres & progmg dir.

WXRA(AM)— Sept 6, 1957: 1580 khz; 10 kw-D, 45 w-N, DA-2. TL: N38 10 05 W84 35 37. 2601 Nicholasville Rd., Lexington 40503. Phone: (859) 422-1000. Fax: (859) 422-1038. Web Site: www.sunny1580.com. Licensee: Citicasters Licenses L.P. Group owner: Clear Channel Communications Inc. (acq 6-30-97; grpsl). Rep: Christal. Format: All sports. News: 2 hrs wkly. Target aud: 45-70. ♦ Keith Yarber, gen mgr.

WXZZ(FM)— Sept 10, 1973: 103.3 mhz; 1.8 kw. 607 ft. TL: N38 02 07 W84 27 02. Stereo. 300 W. Vine St., Lexington 40507. Phone: (859) 253-5900. Fax: (859) 253-5940. Web Site: www.zrock103.com. Licensee: Cumulus Licensing Corp. Group owner: Cumulus Media Inc. (acq 7-22-99; grpsl). Format: Rock. News staff: 3. Target aud: 18-34. ♦ Chris Clendenen, gen mgr & prom dir.

Glasgow

WCDS(AM)—Listing follows WOVO(FM).

WCLU(AM)— Sept 25, 1946: 1490 khz; 1 kw-U. TL: N37 00 19 W85 54 42. Box 1628 42142. Phone: (270) 651-9149. Fax: (270) 651-9222. Web Site: www.wcluradio.com. Licensee: Royse Radio Inc. Network: CBS. Format: Full service. Target aud: 30 plus; listeners with disposable income. ♦ Henry Royse, pres & gen mgr.

WLYE-FM— 1997: 94.1 mhz; 4.5 kw. Ant 298 ft. TL: N36 59 02 W85 52 20. Stereo. 2465 Russellville Rd., Bowling Green 42101. Phone: (270) 843-3333. Fax: (270) 843-0454. E-mail: bhogan@beaverfm.com. Licensee: Forever Communications Inc. (group owner; acq 9-3-03). Format: Country. News staff: one; News: 6 hrs wkly. Target aud: 25-54; adults, serving southern central Kentucky. ♦ Christine Hillard, pres; Brad Hogan, VP & gen mgr.

WOVO(FM)— July 14, 1972: 105.3 mhz; 25 kw. 318 ft. TL: N36 54 50 W85 43 20. Stereo. Box 457 42142-0457. Secondary address: 113 W. Public Sq., Suite 400 42141. Phone: (270) 651-6050. Fax: (270) 651-7666. E-mail: wovo@cbcradio.net. Licensee: Newberry Broadcasting Inc. Group owner: Commonwealth Broadcasting Corp. (acq 11-25-97; grpsl). Format: Oldies. ♦ Derron Steenbergen, gen mgr & gen sls mgr; Alex Chase, opns mgr; Scott Jackson, progmg dir; Jay Turner, news dir; Mike Graham, news dir & chief of engrg.

WCDS(AM)—Co-owned with WOVO(FM). Oct 1, 1962: 1440 khz; 5 kw-D. TL: N36 58 10 W85 56 24. E-mail: wcds@cbsradio.net. Licensee: Newberry Broadcasting Inc. Format: Sports. ♦ Alex Chase, progmg dir.

*****WSGP(FM)**— 2002: 88.3 mhz; 13 kw. Ant 298 ft. TL: N36 49 05 W85 41 30. Box 1423, Somerset 42502. Phone: (606) 679-6300. Fax: (606) 679-1342. Web Site: www.kingofkingsradio.net. Licensee: Somerset Educational Broadcasting Foundation. Format: Christian. ♦ S. David Carr, gen mgr.

Stations in the U.S.   Kentucky

Developers & Brokers of Radio Properties

contact American Media Services at our suite:
Philadelphia Marriott Downtown
215-625-2900
843-972-2200
americanmediaservices.com
Charleston, SC
Dallas, TX · Chicago, Il · Austin, TX

American Media Services, LLC

Grayson

WGOH(AM)— June 1, 1959: 1370 khz; 5 kw-D, 21 w-N. TL: N38 19 44 W82 58 33. Box 487, 150 Radio Hill 41143. Phone: (606) 474-5144. Phone: (606) 474-5145. Fax: (606) 474-7777. E-mail: mail @wgohwugo.com. Web Site: www.wgohwugo.com. Licensee: Carter County Broadcasting Co. Network: CBS. Rep: Rgnl Reps. Booth, Freret, Imlay & Tepper. Format: Classic country, bluegrass, news. News staff: one; News: 30 hrs wkly. Target aud: 35-65. Spec prog: Bluegrass 13 hrs, gospel 8 hrs wkly. ♦ Francis M. Nash, gen mgr; Jeff Roe, opns dir & opns mgr; Melodie Carter, progmg dir; Mike Phillips, mus dir; Jim Phillips, news dir; William H. Craig, chief of engrg & engr.

WUGO(FM)—Co-owned with WGOH(AM). February 1967: 102.3 mhz; 4.8 kw. 360 ft. TL: N38 19 44 W82 58 33. Stereo. Format: Adult contemp, oldies, sports. News: 30 hrs wkly. Target aud: 25-54. Spec prog: Sports.

Greensburg

WAKY(AM)— Mar 15, 1972: 1540 khz; 1 kw-D. TL: N37 15 34 W85 30 57. Box 1053, Campbellsville 42719. Secondary address: 50 Friendship Pike, Campbellsville 42719. Phone: (270) 932-7401. Phone: (270) 789-1464. Fax: (270) 789-1450. Licensee: Green County CBC Inc. (acq 10-30-97; $600,000 with co-located FM). Network: Network: ABC, Jones Radio Networks. Rep: Rgnl Reps. Format: Country. Target aud: 25-54. Spec prog: Farm 15 hrs wkly. ♦ Steve Newberry, pres; Barb Smith, stn mgr & gen sls mgr; Marty Bagby, opns mgr; Andy Colley, progmg dir; Mike Graham, chief of engrg.

WGRK-FM—Co-owned with WAKY(AM). Dec 15, 1977: 103.1 mhz; 2.2 kw. 375 ft. TL: N37 15 34 W85 30 57. (CP: 4.6 kw). Stereo. Format: Mainstream country hits. News staff: one.

Greenup

WLGC-FM— Sept 1, 1982: 105.7 mhz; 12.5 kw. Ant 466 ft. TL: N38 35 44 W82 51 22. Stereo. Box 685 41144. Phone: (606) 920-9565. Fax: (606) 920-9523. Licensee: Greenup County Broadcasting Inc. Format: Country. News staff: one; News: 3 hrs wkly. Target aud: 25-54; middle income listeners. ♦ Bob Hall, gen mgr; Scott Martin, gen sls mgr; Mark Justice, progmg dir.

WLGC(AM)— Apr 1, 1985: 1520 khz; 5 kw-D. TL: N38 35 44 W82 51 20. Stereo. Network: ABC Daytime Direction.

Greenville

WKYA(FM)— Dec 11, 1981: 105.5 mhz; 3 kw. 300 ft. TL: N37 11 45 W87 12 38. Stereo. 464 St. Rt. 189 S. 42345. Phone: (270) 338-6655. Fax: (270) 338-7388. Licensee: Starlight Broadcasting Co. (group owner; acq 1996; grpsl). Network: ABC Information & Entertainment. Format: Good time oldies. Target aud: 18-40. ♦ Jowanna Bandy, gen mgr.

Hardinsburg

WULF(FM)— July 9, 1970: 94.3 mhz; 43 kw. 290 ft. TL: N37 45 40 W86 26 22. (CP: Ant 525 ft.). Stereo. 233 W. Dixie Ave., Elizabethtown 42701. Phone: (270) 351-0943. Fax: (270) 737-7229. E-mail: bill@wqxe.com. Licensee: Skytower Communications - 94.3 LLC (acq 12-12-01; $1.15 million). Format: Country. ♦ Bill Evans, pres & stn mgr; Jodie Thompson, opns mgr.

WXBC(FM)— Aug 15, 1992: 104.3 mhz; 3 kw. 328 ft. TL: N37 45 12 W86 26 08. Stereo. Box 104, 110 S. Main St. 40143. Phone: (270) 756-1043. Fax: (270) 756-1086. E-mail: wxbc@bbtel.com. Licensee: Breckinridge Broadcasting Co. Inc. Network: ABC Daytime Direction. Booth, Freret, Imlay & Tepper. Format: Classic hit country. News staff: one; News: 15 hrs wkly. Target aud: 25-55. Spec prog: Farm 5 hrs, relg 7 hrs, news 15 hrs wkly. ♦ Jo Ann Keenan, CEO, pres, CFO & gen mgr; Dennis Day, chief of opns.

Harlan

WFSR(AM)— April 1976: 970 khz; 5 kw-D, 94 w-N. TL: N36 50 59 W83 23 41. Box 818 40831-0818. Secondary address: 125 S. Main 40831. Phone: (606) 573-1470. Fax: (606) 573-1473. E-mail: live105@harlanonline.net. Licensee: Eastern Broadcasting Co. (acq 5-26-98; $400,000 with co-located FM). Format: Southern gospel. Target aud: 25-54; adult purchasers. ♦ Jeff Capps, gen mgr & gen sls mgr.

WTUK(FM)—Co-owned with WFSR(AM). June 26, 1991: 105.1 mhz; 270 w. 1,037 ft. TL: N36 54 09 W83 18 01. Format: Country.

WHLN(AM)— May 30, 1941: 1410 khz; 5 kw-D, 94 w-N. TL: N36 52 02 W83 19 36. Box 898 40831. Secondary address: 100 Eversole St., Suite 1 40831. Phone: (606) 573-2540. Fax: (606) 573-7557. E-mail: whln@harlanonline.net. Licensee: Radio Harlan Inc. (acq 6-1-56). Rep: Rgnl Reps. Format: Oldies. ♦ James T. Morgan, pres; James O. Morgan, VP & gen mgr.

Harold

WXLR(FM)— January 1994: 104.9 mhz; 370 w. 922 ft. TL: N37 31 59 W82 29 40. Box 1049 41635. Phone: (606) 478-1200. Fax: (606) 478-1050. Licensee: Adam D. Gearheart. Format: Classic rock, oldies. ♦ Adam D. Gearheart, pres & gen mgr.

Harrodsburg

WHBN(AM)— June 25, 1955: 1420 khz; 1 kw-D, 46 w-N. TL: N37 44 03 W84 48 50. 2063 Shakertown Rd., Danville 40422. Phone: (859) 236-2711. Fax: (859) 236-1461. E-mail: hometownradio@bellsouth.net. Web Site: www.1420wbhn.com. Licensee: Hometown Broadcasting of Harrodsburg Inc. (acq 1-4-01). Network: Jones Radio Networks. Rgnl Reps. Format: C&W, var, rel. News staff: one; News: 21 hrs wkly. Target aud: General; residents of Mercer county. Spec prog: Farm 3hrs wkly, Gospel 12 hrs wkly. ♦ Robert Wagner, gen mgr.

Hartford

WAIA(AM)—(Beaver Dam). June 21, 1969: 1600 khz; 1 kw-D. TL: N37 26 36 W86 53 57. Box 106, Beaver Dam 42347. Phone: (270) 298-3268. Phone: (270) 298-3269. Fax: (270) 298-9326. Licensee: Starlight Broadcasting Co. (group owner; acq 1996; grpsl). Rep: Rgnl Reps. Format: News/talk, sports. Target aud: General. ♦ Andy Anderson, pres, gen mgr, opns mgr, gen sls mgr, progmg dir & chief of engrg.

WXMZ(FM)—Co-owned with WAIA(AM). May 18, 1972: 106.3 mhz; 3 kw. 280 ft. TL: N37 26 36 W86 53 57. Stereo. Web Site: www.wxmzfm.com. Format: Classic rock.

Hawesville

WKCM(AM)— Nov 7, 1972: 1160 khz; 2.5 kw-D, 1 kw-N, DA-N. TL: N37 54 20 W86 45 30. Stereo. 1115 Tamarack Rd., Suite 500, Owensboro 42301. Phone: (270) 683-5200. Fax: (270) 688-0108. E-mail: wbio@apex.net. Web Site: www.owensbororadio.com. Licensee: Hancock Communications Inc. Group owner: The Cromwell Group Inc. Format: Real country. News staff: one; News: 10 hrs wkly. Target aud: 25-54; general. Spec prog: Farm 3 hrs, sports 6 hrs wkly. ♦ Bayard H. Walters, pres; Corky Norcia, gen sls mgr; Jeff Morgan, progmg dir.

WXCM(FM)—Co-owned with WKCM(AM). May 1993: 97.1 mhz; 4 kw. Ant 403 ft. TL: N37 54 10 W86 59 28. Web Site: www.owensbororadio.com. Licensee: The Cromwell Group Inc. of Kentucky. (acq 1993; $170,000;. FTR: 9-6-93). Format: Rock. Target aud: Males in 30's. ♦ Bayard H. Walters, CEO; Kevin Rickey, opns mgr.

Hazard

*****WEKH(FM)**— February 1985: 90.9 mhz; 33 kw. 1,004 ft. TL: N37 11 34 W83 11 16. Stereo. 102 Perkins Bldg., 521 Lancaster Ave., Richmond 40475-3102. Phone: (859) 622-1660. Fax: (859) 622-6276.

Web Site: www.weku.fm. Licensee: Board of Regents, Eastern Kentucky University. Network: Network: NPR, PRI. Hardy, Carey & Chautin. Format: Class, news magazine, info. News staff: 3; News: 35 hrs wkly. Target aud: General. ♦ Tim Singleton, stn mgr; Mary Ellyn Cain, opns mgr; Carol Siler, dev dir; Marie Mitchell, news dir; Bill Browning, chief of engrg.

WJMD(FM)— July 26, 1989: 104.7 mhz; 2.5 kw. 1,135 ft. TL: N37 11 36 W83 11 04. Stereo. Box 7001 41702. Secondary address: 125 Main St. 41701. Phone: (606) 439-3358. Fax: (606) 439-3371. Web Site: wjmdfm.com. Licensee: Hazard Broadcasting Services (acq 4-13-01; $250. for 25%). Network: Salem Radio Network. Format: Relg. News staff: 2; News: 7 hrs wkly. Target aud: General. ♦ Michael R. Barnett, gen mgr.

WKIC(AM)— Nov 23, 1947: 1390 khz; 5 kw-D. TL: N37 14 19 W83 12 41. Stereo. Box 7428, 516 Main St. 41702. Phone: (606) 436-2121. Fax: (606) 436-4172. Licensee: Mountain Broadcasting Service Inc. (acq 12-67). Network: Network: Westwood One, ABC Information & Entertainment. Rep: Rgnl Reps. Format: CHR. ♦ Faron Sparkman, gen mgr & gen sls mgr.

WSGS(FM)—Co-owned with WKIC(AM). Feb 3, 1959: 101.1 mhz; 100 kw. 1,463 ft. TL: N37 11 38 W83 10 52. Stereo. Box 7428, Radio Bldg., 101 Morgan St. 41701. Network: ABC. Format: Country. ♦ Faron Sparkman, pres.

WQXY(AM)— Mar 1, 1988: 1560 khz; 1 kw-D, 500 w-CH, DA. TL: N37 16 27 W83 11 29. Stereo. Box 864, Hidman 41822. Phone: (606) 439-0156. Fax: (606) 785-0106. Licensee: Black Gold Broadcasting. (acq 8-90; $97,500; 9-24-90). Network: Network: Jones Radio Networks, AP Radio, CNN Radio. Format: Oldies. Target aud: 25-54; educated, mobile, child-rearing couples in suburbs, blue collar workers.

Henderson

WGBF-FM— Dec 1, 1971: 103.1 mhz; 6 kw. 460 ft. TL: N37 46 54 W87 37 24. (CP: 3.16 kw, ant 453 ft.). Stereo. 1133 Lincoln Ave., Evansville, IN 47714. Phone: (812) 425-4226. Fax: (812) 421-0005. Web Site: www.103gbfrocks.com. Licensee: Regent Broadcasting of Evansville/Owensboro Inc. Group owner: Regent Communications Inc. (acq 12-3-2003; grpsl). Network: ABC. Format: Rock/AOR. News staff: one. Target aud: 18-49. ♦ Mark Thomas, gen mgr.

WKDQ(FM)— 1947: 99.5 mhz; 100 kw. 944 ft. TL: N37 49 36 W87 33 00. Stereo. 1133 Lincoln N.E., Evansville, IN 47714. Phone: (812) 425-4226. Web Site: www.wkdq.com. Licensee: Regent Broadcasting of Evansville/Owensboro Inc. Group owner: Regent Communications Inc. (acq 2-25-03; grpsl). Network: ABC Information & Entertainment. Rep: Christal. Format: Country. News staff: 2. Target aud: 25-54. ♦ Mike Sanders, opns mgr.

*****WKPB(FM)**— Apr 1, 1990: 89.5 mhz; 43 kw. 377 ft. TL: N37 51 06 W87 19 43. Stereo. Western Kentucky Univ., 1906 College Heights Blvd., Bowling Green 42101. Phone: (270) 745-5489. Fax: (270) 745-2084. E-mail: wkyufm@wku.edu. Web Site: www.wku.edu/wkyu-fm. Licensee: Western Kentucky University. Network: Network: NPR, PRI. Leventhal, Senter & Lerman. Format: News. News staff: 3; News: 35 hrs wkly. Target aud: General. Spec prog: Folk 5 hrs wkly. ♦ Gary Randsall, pres; Peter Bryant, gen mgr; Terry Reagan, dev dir.

WSON(AM)— Dec 17, 1941: 860 khz; 500 w-U, DA-N. TL: N37 51 11 W87 32 12. Stereo. Box 418 42419-0418. Secondary address: 230 2nd St. 42420. Phone: (270) 826-3923. Fax: (270) 826-7572. Licensee: Henry G. Lackey (acq 7-31-79). Rep: Rgnl Reps. Format: Adult standards. News staff: one; News: 8 hrs wkly. Target aud: 35+. Spec prog: Farm 2 hrs wkly. ♦ Henry G. Lackey, pres & gen mgr; Bill Stephens, news dir.

Highland Heights

*****WNKU(FM)**— Apr 29, 1985: 89.7 mhz; 12 kw. 318 ft. TL: N39 02 21 W84 27 57. Stereo. Box 337 41076. Secondary address: Northern

Broadcasting & Cable Yearbook 2006

D-219

Kentucky

Kentucky Univ., Rm. 301, Nunn Dr. 41099. Phone: (859) 572-6500. Fax: (859) 572-6604. E-mail: wnku@nku.edu. Web Site: www.wnku.org. Licensee: Northern Kentucky University. Network: Network: PRI, NPR. Arter & Hadden. Format: AAA, news. News staff: 2; News: 40 hrs wkly. Target aud: 35-49. Spec prog: Celtic 3 hrs, blues 6 hrs, bluegrass 3 hrs wkly. ◆Benjamin Singleton, gen mgr; Aaron Sharpe, dev dir; Grady Kirkpatrick, progmg dir.

Hindman

WKCB(AM)— Jan 26, 1971: 1340 khz; 6 kw-U. TL: N37 19 45 W83 00 17. Box 864 41822. Phone: (606) 785-3129. Fax: (606) 785-0106. Web Site: www.wkcb.com. Licensee: Hindman Broadcasting Corp. (acq 9-15-89; $100,000 with co-located FM; 10-23-89). Network: ABC Information & Entertainment. Rep: Rgnl Reps. Format: Christian. ◆Randy Thompson, pres, gen mgr & news dir.

WKCB-FM— Dec 13, 1974: 107.1 mhz; 770 w. 650 ft. TL: N37 19 56 W82 56 52. Stereo. Box 864 41822. Web Site: www.wkcb.com. Format: Heart of rock.

Hodgenville

WKMO(FM)— March 1974: 106.3 mhz; 3 kw. 400 ft. TL: N37 40 21 W85 44 34. Stereo. 406 S. Mulberry St., Elizabethtown 42701. Phone: (270) 763-0800. Fax: (270) 769-6349. Web Site: www.1063thebear.com. Licensee: Elizabethtown CBC Inc. Group owner: Commonwealth Broadcasting Corp. (acq 7-1-00; grpsl). Network: ABC Information & Entertainment. Rep: Keystone (unwired net), Rgnl Reps. Verner, Liipfert, Bernhard, McPherson & Hand. Format: Mainstream country. Target aud: 24-65. Spec prog: Farm 2 hrs wkly. ◆Steve Newberry, pres; Dale Thornhill, VP; John Wright, stn mgr.

WXAM(AM)— See Buffalo

Hopkinsville

WHOP(AM)— Jan 8, 1940: 1230 khz; 830 w-U. TL: N36 52 54 W87 30 44. Box 709, 220 Dink Embry's Buttermilk Rd. 42241-0709. Phone: (270) 885-5331. Fax: (270) 885-2688. E-mail: whopamfm@bellsouth.net. Web Site: www.lite987whop.com. Licensee: Hop Broadcasting Inc. (acq 10-28-99; with co-located FM). Network: CBS. Rep: Rgnl Reps. Format: News/talk. News staff: 2. Target aud: 25-65. ◆Roger E. Jeffers, gen mgr.

WHOP-FM— May 1948: 98.7 mhz; 100 kw. Ant 620 ft. TL: N36 55 41 W87 32 50. Stereo. Format: Adult contemp. Target aud: 18-54.

WHVO(AM)— Sept 19, 1954: 1480 khz; 1 kw-D, 24 w-N. TL: N36 52 15 W87 30 43. Oldies Radio, Box 1900, Cadiz 42211-1900. Phone: (270) 886-1480. Fax: (270) 886-6286. E-mail: oldies@oldies1480.com. Web Site: www.oldies1480.com. Licensee: Ham Broadcasting Inc. (acq 10-95). Network: Network: AP Network News, Jones Radio Networks. Rep: Rgnl Reps. Format: Oldies. News staff: two; News: 3 hrs wkly. Target aud: 35-54; Upscale Baby-boomers. Spec prog: Relg 6 hrs, gospel 3 hrs wkly. ◆D.J. Everett, pres; Amy Hougland, gen mgr.

***WNKJ(FM)—** Aug 3, 1981: 89.3 mhz; 12 kw. 330 ft. TL: N36 48 34 W87 24 20. Stereo. Box 1029 42241-1029. Secondary address: 1100 E. 18th St. 42240. Phone: (270) 886-9655. Fax: (270) 885-7210. E-mail: gm@wnkj.org. Web Site: www.wnkj.org. Licensee: Pennyrile Christian Community Inc. Network: Moody. Format: Christian. News: 12 hrs wkly. Target aud: General. Spec prog: Black 7 hrs, Korean one hr, Sp one hr wkly. ◆Jim Dozier Adams, gen mgr.

WVVR(FM)— July 1, 1960: 100.3 mhz; 100 kw. 1,000 ft. TL: N36 56 58 W87 40 18. Stereo. 1640 Old Russellville Pike, Clarksville, TN 37043. Phone: (931) 648-7720. Fax: (931) 648-7769. Web Site: www.thebeaver.com. Licensee: Saga Communications of Tuckessee LLC. Group owner: Saga Communications Inc. (acq 11-27-00; $7 million). Network: ABC FM Connection. Rgnl Reps. Format: Country. News staff: one; News: 7 hrs wkly. Target aud: 18-54; working class. ◆Susan Quesenberry, gen mgr.

WZZP(FM)— Feb 28, 2001: 97.5 mhz; 6 kw. Ant 328 ft. TL: N36 45 47 W87 26 59. 1640 Old Russellville Pike, Clarksville 37043. Phone: (931) 648-7720. Fax: (931) 648-7769. Web Site: www.z975.com. Licensee: Saga Communications of Tuckessee L.L.C. Group owner: Saga Communications Inc. (acq 2-1-01; grpsl). Format: Rock. ◆Susan Quesenberry, gen mgr.

Horse Cave

WHHT(FM)— Sept 19, 1994: 106.7 mhz; 2.9 kw. 476 ft. TL: N37 13 57 W85 52 06. Box 457, Glasgow 42142-0457. Secondary address: 113 W. Public Sq., Suite 400, Glasgow 42141. Phone: (270) 651-6050/651-6060. Fax: (270) 651-7666. E-mail: magic@magic1067.net. Licensee: Commonwealth Broadcasting Corp. (acq 11-25-97; grpsl). Network: Westwood One. Format: Adult Contemp. ◆Derron Steenbergen, gen mgr, stn mgr, opns mgr & gen sls mgr; Alex Parocai, opns mgr & progmg mgr; Jay Turner, news dir.

Hyden

WZQQ(FM)— Nov 7, 1988: 97.9 mhz; 1.75 kw. 1,207 ft. TL: N37 11 36 W83 11 04. Stereo. Box 7280, Hazard 41702. Secondary address: 516 Main St., Hazard 41701. Phone: (606) 436-9898. Fax: (606) 436-4172. E-mail: wzqq@alltel.net. Licensee: Leslie County Broadcasting Inc. (acq 4-3-01; $50. for 50%). Network: ABC. Format: Hot adult contemp, CHR. Target aud: General. ◆Stuart Shane Sparkman, CEO; Mike Reeves, gen mgr & gen sls mgr; Bob Hale, chief of engrg.

Inez

WBTH(AM)— See Williamson, WV

WXCC(FM)— See Williamson, WV

Irvine

WCYO(FM)— Listing follows WIRV(AM).

WIRV(AM)— July 2, 1960: 1550 khz; 1 kw-D. TL: N37 42 26 W83 58 15. (CP: TL: N37 42 57 W83 58 29). Box 281, 1030 Winchester Rd. 40336. Phone: (606) 723-5138. Fax: (606) 723-5180. Licensee: Kentucky River Broadcasting Co Inc. Rep: Rgnl Reps. Format: Oldies. ◆Kelly T. Wallingford, pres, gen mgr & gen sls mgr.

WCYO(FM)— Co-owned with WIRV(AM). August 1991: 100.7 mhz; 9.2 kw. 505 ft. TL: N37 39 40 W84 08 55. Network: ABC Daytime Direction. Format: Country. ◆David Adams, pub affrs dir.

Jackson

WEKG(AM)— Mar 7, 1969: 810 khz; 5 kw-D. TL: N37 34 41 W83 24 19. 1501 Hargas Ln., Suite 2 41339. Phone: (606) 666-7531. Fax: (606) 666-4946. Licensee: Intermountain Broadcasting Co. Format: Country. ◆Doug Neace, gen mgr.

WJSN-FM— Co-owned with WEKG(AM). Jan 1, 1979: 106.5 mhz; 638 w. 610 ft. TL: N37 32 46 W83 23 42. (CP: 895 w, ant 827 ft.). Stereo. ◆Gloria Hay, stn mgr.

Jamestown

WJKY(AM)— Sept 3, 1967: 1060 khz; 1 kw-D. TL: N37 01 31 W85 04 23. Box 800, 2804 South US Hwy 127 42629. Phone: (270) 866-3487. Fax: (270) 343-4444. Fax: (270) 866-2060. Licensee: Lake Cumberland Broadcasters. (acq 7-1-70). Format: Country. ◆Mae Hoover, gen mgr & gen sls mgr.

WJRS(FM)— Co-owned with WJKY(AM). Sept 3, 1966: 104.9 mhz; 2 kw. 360 ft. TL: N37 01 31 W85 04 23. Box 800 42629. Phone: (502) 343-4444. Fax: (502) 866-2060.

Jeffersontown

WMJM(FM)— Dec 1, 1978: 101.3 mhz; 2 kw. 194 ft. TL: N38 13 42 W85 38 22. Stereo. 520 S. 4th St., Suite 200, Louisville 40202. Phone: (502) 625-1220. Fax: (502) 625-1259. Web Site: www.1013online.com. Licensee: Blue Chip Broadcasting Licenses II Ltd. Group owner: Radio One Inc. (acq 4-30-01; grpsl). Format: Urban adult contemp. ◆Dale Schaefer, gen mgr; Holly Bussey, sls dir.

Jenkins

WIFX-FM— May 10, 1975: 94.3 mhz; 4.2 kw. 1,565 ft. TL: N37 06 38 W82 44 18. 32 Cowan St., Whitesburg 41858. Phone: (606) 633-9430. Fax: (606) 633-3314. E-mail: wifx@kintelwireless.com. Licensee: Letcher County Broadcasting Inc. (acq 7-1-93; $37,000; 7-26-93).

Henry Crawford. Format: Adult rock. News: 2 hrs wkly. Target aud: 25-45. Spec prog: Oldies. ◆Ernestine Kincer, pres; G.C. Kincer, gen mgr.

WKVG(AM)— Feb 1, 1970: 1000 khz; 1 kw-D. TL: N37 09 59 W82 37 13. Box 613, Pound, VA 24279-0613. Secondary address: Box 1474 41537. Phone: (606) 832-4655. Fax: (606) 832-4656. Licensee: Martins and Assoc. Inc. (acq 6-15-92; $40,000; 6-7-92). Format: Gospel, relg. News: 9 hrs wkly. Target aud: General. ◆Jerry Martin, gen mgr.

Junction City

WDFB(AM)— May 20, 1985: 1170 khz; 1 kw-D, DA. TL: N37 35 46 W84 50 19. Box 106, Danville 40423-0106. Secondary address: 3596 Alum Springs Rd., Danville 40422. Phone: (859) 236-9332. Fax: (859) 236-3348. E-mail: wdfb@searnet.com. Web Site: www.wdfb.com. Licensee: Alum Springs Vision and Outreach Corp. Network: USA. Format: Relg. Target aud: General. ◆Donald A. Drake, pres; Mildred Drake, exec VP & gen mgr.

Keavy

***WVCT(FM)—** January 1984: 91.5 mhz; 100 w. 341 ft. TL: N36 58 21 W84 07 28. Stereo. 968 W. City Dam Rd. 40737. Phone: (606) 528-4671. Fax: (606) 526-0589. E-mail: csivley@bellsouth.net. Licensee: Victory Training School Corp. Format: Educ, relg. ◆Brenda Sivley, exec VP; Charles Sivley, pres & gen mgr.

Keene

WJMM-FM— Dec 9, 1969: 99.1 mhz; 4.5 kw. Ant 384 ft. TL: N37 57 37 W84 32 42. Stereo. 3270 Blazer Pkwy., Suite 101, Lexington 40509. Phone: (859) 264-9700. Fax: (859) 264-9705. Licensee: Mortenson Broadcasting Co. of Central Kentucky L.L.C. Network: USA. Rep: Salem. Rgnl Reps Format: Relg. Target aud: 25-54; women. ◆Ed Lewis, opns mgr; Dennis Smith, gen sls mgr; Dennis Blais, chief of engrg.

Lancaster

WRNZ(FM)— Oct 1, 1988: 105.1 mhz; 3 kw. 325 ft. TL: N37 36 06 W84 34 27. Stereo. 2063 Shakertown Rd., Danville 40422. Phone: (859) 236-2711. Fax: (859) 236-1461. E-mail: hometownradio@bellsouth.net. Licensee: Hometown Broadcasting of Lancaster Inc. Rgnl Reps Format: CHR, adult contemp. News staff: one; News: 2 hrs wkly. Target aud: 25-54; upscale, white collar, baby boomers, business owners. Spec prog: Relg 4 hrs wkly. ◆Robert Wagner, gen mgr.

Lawrenceburg

WKYL(FM)— May 11, 1993: 102.1 mhz; 6 kw. Ant 328 ft. TL: N38 01 37 W84 52 59. Stereo. 1010 Industry Rd., Frankfort 40342. Phone: (502) 839-1021. Licensee: Davenport Broadcasting Inc. (acq 1-16-97; $525,000). Network: Jones Radio Networks. Pepper & Corazzini. Format: Soft adult contemp, weekend jazz. Target aud: 30-50; higher income; especially at-work listeners. Spec prog: Relg 2 hrs wkly. ◆C. Michael Davenport, CEO.

Lebanon

WLBN(AM)— October 1954: 1590 khz; 1 kw-D, 74 w-N, DA-1. TL: N37 35 55 W85 14 47. Box 680, 480 Radio Station Rd. 40033. Phone: (270) 692-3126. Fax: (270) 692-6003. Licensee: CBC of Marion County Inc. Group owner: CBC of Marion and Taylor Counties Inc. (acq 7-3-97; $360,000. with co-located FM). Network: Jones Radio Networks. Rep: Rgnl Reps. Leonard S. Joyce. Format: Adult standards. News staff: one; News: 13 hrs wkly. Target aud: 35-64. Spec prog: Gospel 5 hrs, open mike 5 hrs wkly. ◆Barb Smith, gen mgr; Misty Monroe, opns mgr, progmg mgr & mus dir; Lisa Kearnes, gen sls mgr, prom mgr & adv dir; Steve Meredith, news dir; Mike Graham, chief of engrg.

WLSK(FM)— Co-owned with WLBN(AM). Oct 1, 1979: 100.9 mhz; 16.5 kw. Ant 410 ft. TL: N37 41 43 W85 19 06. Stereo. Box 680 40033. Secondary address: 480 Radio Station Rd. 40033. Phone: (270) 692-3126. Fax: (270) 692-6003. E-mail: wlsk@commonwealthbroadcasting.com. Format: Classic hits. News staff: one; News: 9 hrs wkly. Target aud: 30-49. ◆Lisa Kearnes, mktg dir; Misty Russell, opns mgr, sls VP & progmg dir.

Stations in the U.S. — Kentucky

Lebanon Junction

WTHX(FM)— October 1979: 107.3 mhz; 6 kw. Ant 321 ft. TL: N37 44 26 W85 49 28. Stereo. Box 1206, Elizabethtown 42701. Phone: (270) 763-0800. Fax: (270) 769-6349. Web Site: www.mosthitsmostfun.com. Licensee: Elizabethtown CBC Inc. Group owner: Commonwealth Broadcasting Corp. (acq 12-23-02; $900,000). Format: Hot adult contemp. Target aud: 18-44; females. ♦Steve Newberry, CEO & chmn; Dale Thornhill, sr VP; John Wright, gen mgr; Dan Diaz, opns VP.

Ledbetter

*****WHMR(FM)**— 2004: 90.1 mhz; 1 kw vert. Ant 328 ft. TL: N37 06 10 W88 24 15. Box 281, Hardin 42048. Phone: (270) 437-4095. Fax: (270) 437-4098. Web Site: www.heartlandradio.org. Licensee: Heartland Ministries Inc. Format: Southern gospel. ♦Cecil Glass, gen mgr.

Leitchfield

WKHG(FM)—Listing follows WMTL(AM).

WMTL(AM)— Jan 17, 1959: 870 khz; 500 w-D. TL: N37 30 40 W86 17 15. 2160 Brandenburg Rd. 42754. Phone: (270) 259-3165. Fax: (270) 259-5693. E-mail: k105@k105.com. Licensee: Heritage Media of Kentucky Inc. (acq 1-26-95; $350,000 with co-located FM; 3-20-95). Format: Bluegrass. ♦Mark Buckles, pres, gen mgr & gen sls mgr; Steve Meredith, progmg dir; Ed Thomas, chief of engrg.

WKHG(FM)—Co-owned with WMTL(AM). Oct 29, 1967: 104.9 mhz; 3.5 kw. 250 ft. TL: N37 30 40 W86 17 15. Stereo. Phone: (270) 259-5692. Web Site: www.k105.com. Network: ABC Information & Entertainment. Format: Adult contemp. ♦Mark Buckles, progmg dir.

Lerose

*****WOCS(FM)**— March 1999: 88.3 mhz; 1 kw. Ant 321 ft. TL: N37 36 23 W83 41 16. Owsley County High School, Hwy. 28/Shepherd Ln., Booneville 41314. Phone: (606) 593-5185. Fax: (606) 593-6312. E-mail: tburns@owsley.k12.ky.us. Web Site: www.owsley.k12.ky.us. Licensee: Board of Regents - Morehead State University (acq 4-13-01; $15,000). Format: Div. Target aud: 12-35; poor & uneducated in need of information. ♦Diana Gross, chmn; Stephen F. Jackson, CEO & pres; Jerry McIntosh, CFO; Dan Conti, gen mgr; Bill Hodges, mus dir.

Lewisport

WKCM(AM)—See Hawesville

Lexington

WBUL-FM— July 15, 1969: 98.1 mhz; 100 kw. 561 ft. TL: N38 02 07 W84 27 02. Stereo. 2601 Nicholasville Rd. 40503. Phone: (859) 422-1000. Web Site: www.wbul.com. Licensee: Citicasters Licenses L.P. Group owner: Clear Channel Communications Inc. (acq 5-4-99; grpsl). Format: Country. Target aud: 25-49; baby boomers who grew up with Stones and Beatles. ♦Keith Yarber, gen mgr.

WGKS(FM)—Listing follows WLXG(AM).

WLAP(AM)—Listing follows WMXL(FM).

WLXG(AM)— 1946: 1300 khz; 2.5 kw-D, 1 kw-N, DA-N. TL: N38 05 50 W84 31 45. 1300 Greendale Rd. 40511. Secondary address: Box 11788 40578. Phone: (859) 233-1515. Fax: (859) 233-1517. E-mail: jmac@lmcomm.com. Web Site: www.wxlg.com. Licensee: L.M. Communications Inc. (group owner; acq 7-1-84). Format: Sports radio. Target aud: 25-54; adults. Spec prog: Cincinnati Reds baseball, Cincinnati Bengals football, SCC Game of the Week. ♦Lynn Martin, pres; James E. MacFarlane, gen mgr; Chris Cross, progmg mgr.

WGKS(FM)—Co-owned with WLXG(AM). June 5, 1968: 96.9 mhz; 50 kw. 492 ft. TL: N38 07 32 W84 21 12. Stereo. Web Site: www.wxlg.com. Network: ABC. Format: Adult contemp. News staff: one; News: 15 hrs weekly. ♦Skip Elliot, progmg dir.

WLXX(FM)—Listing follows WVLK(AM).

WMXL(FM)— 1940: 94.5 mhz; 100 kw. 640 ft. TL: N38 07 25 W84 26 45. Stereo. 2601 Nicholasville Rd. 40503. Phone: (859) 422-1000. Fax: (859) 422-1038. Web Site: www.wmxl.com. Licensee: Citicasters Licenses L.P. Group owner: Clear Channel Communications Inc. (acq 5-4-99; grpsl). Format: Adult contemp. News: 3 hrs wkly. Target aud: 25-54; women. ♦Keith Yarber, gen mgr; Barry Fox, opns mgr; Gene Guinn, gen sls mgr; Michael Jordan, mktg dir & prom dir; Dale O'Brien, progmg dir; Gerry Westerberg, mus dir & chief of engrg; Karyn Czar, news dir.

WLAP(AM)—Co-owned with WMXL(FM). September 1922: 630 khz; 5 kw-D, 1 kw-N, DA-2. TL: N38 07 25 W84 26 45. Web Site: www.wlap.com. Network: CBS. Rep: Christal. Format: News. News staff: one. Target aud: 18-49; men. ♦Kevin Bell, progmg dir; Wydine Cruse, progmg dir; Karyn Czar, news dir.

*****WRFL(FM)**— Mar 3, 1988: 88.1 mhz; 250 w. 289 ft. TL: N38 02 19 W84 30 16. Box 777, University Stn. 40506-0025. Phone: (859) 257-4636. Fax: (859) 323-1039. E-mail: wrfl@pop.uky.edu. Licensee: Radio Free Lexington Inc. Format: Alternative, free-form. Spec prog: Christian 3 hrs, folk 3 hrs, blues 3 hrs, jazz 3 hrs wkly. ♦Leslia Lemaster, gen mgr; Wesley Belts, sls dir; Kris McNeil, progmg dir; Mike Connelly, mus dir; Mary Lynn Lanius, news dir.

*****WUKY(FM)**— Mar 13, 1941: 91.3 mhz; 95 kw. 1,004 ft. TL: N37 47 18 W84 40 49. Stereo. Univ. of Kentucky, 340 McVey 40506-0045. Phone: (859) 257-3221. Phone: (859) 257-9600. Fax: (859) 257-6291. Web Site: www.wuky.org. Licensee: University of Kentucky. Network: Network: NPR, PRI, AP Radio. Sanchez Law Firm. Format: News, AAA music. News staff: 2; News: 62 hrs wkly. Target aud: 35-54. ♦Tom Godell, gen mgr; John Lumagui, opns mgr; Gail Bennett, dev dir & mus dir.

WVLK(AM)— October 1947: 590 khz; 5 kw-D, 1 kw-N, DA-2. TL: N38 06 42 W84 34 36. (CP: 1.6 kw-N). Stereo. 300 W. Vine St. 40507. Phone: (859) 253-5900. Fax: (859) 253-5903. Web Site: www.wvlkam.com. Licensee: Cumulus Licensing Corp. Group owner: Cumulus Media Inc. (acq 7-22-99; grpsl). Network: CBS. Rep: Allied Radio Partners. Latham & Watkins. Format: News/talk, sports. News staff: 5. Target aud: 25-54. Spec prog: Farm one hr wkly. ♦Darren Smith, gen mgr; Robert Lindsey, opns mgr & progmg dir; Mike Fell, gen sls mgr; Leisje Coyle, rgnl sls mgr; Kat Weisenberger, prom dir; Joe Gillespie, news dir; Tom Devine, chief of engrg.

WLXX(FM)—Co-owned with WVLK(AM). February 1962: 92.9 mhz; 100 kw. Ant 854 ft. TL: N38 02 22 W84 24 11. Stereo. Fax: (859) 253-5940. Web Site: www.k93fm.com. Format: Country. ♦Chris Clendenen, gen mgr; John Sebastian, progmg dir.

Lexington-Fayette

WLKT(FM)— July 30, 1992: 104.5 mhz; 50 kw. 492 ft. TL: N38 05 54 W84 18 38. 2601 Nicholasville Rd., Lexington 40503. Phone: (859) 422-1000. Fax: (859) 422-1038. Web Site: www.wlkt.com. Licensee: Citicasters Licenses L.P. Group owner: Clear Channel Communications Inc. (acq 5-4-99; grpsl). Format: Contemp hit. ♦Keith Yarber, gen mgr.

Liberty

WKDO(AM)— November 1963: 1560 khz; 1 kw-D. TL: N37 18 22 W84 55 02. Box 990, Hwy. 1649 42539. Phone: (606) 787-7331. Phone: (606) 787-7838. Fax: (606) 787-2166. Licensee: Radio Station WKDO. (acq 11-27-75). Network: USA. Format: Country, relg. Target aud: 18-49. ♦Carlos Wesley, pres, gen mgr & gen sls mgr.

WKDO-FM— January 1977: 98.7 mhz; 25 kw. 239 ft. TL: N37 18 22 W84 55 02. Stereo. Format: Modern country, oldies. News staff: 3; News: 21 hrs wkly. Target aud: 15-35.

London

WFTG(AM)— Sept 1, 1955: 1400 khz; 1 kw-U. TL: N37 08 28 W84 04 45. Box 1988 40743-0647. Secondary address: 534 Tobacco Rd. 40741. Phone: (606) 864-2148. Phone: (606) 864-2048. Fax: (606) 864-0645. E-mail: wftg@kih.net. Licensee: F.T.G. Broadcasting Inc. Group owner: Key Broadcasting Inc. (acq 8-5-92; $410,000; 8-24-92). Format: Talk. News staff: one. Target aud: 40 plus. Spec prog: Loc sports. ♦Chris Aldrich, pres; Frances Wilhoit, gen mgr.

WWEL(FM)—Co-owned with WFTG(AM). Sept 15, 1970: 103.9 mhz; 3 kw. 190 ft. TL: N37 08 28 W84 04 45. Stereo. Phone: (606) 864-2048. Format: Modern country. News staff: one; News: 21 hrs wkly. Target aud: 18-50. ♦Terry Harris, opns mgr.

WGWM(AM)— Aug 8, 1981: 980 khz; 900 w-D, 109 w-N. TL: N37 10 16 W84 06 39. 948 Moriah Church Rd. 40741-7635. Phone: (606) 878-0980. Licensee: WGWM Broadcasting Inc. (acq 1996; $35,000). Network: ABC Information & Entertainment. Format: Gospel. News: 5 hrs wkly. Target aud: 25-54; male/female. Spec prog: Relg 6 hrs wkly. ♦Elmer Oakley, gen mgr.

WYGE(FM)— 1994: 92.3 mhz; 5.2 kw. 722 ft. TL: N37 09 01 W83 59 32. 201 E. 2nd St. 40741. Phone: (606) 877-1326. Fax: (606) 864-3702. E-mail: gnoutreach@sun-spot.com. Licensee: Ethel Huff Broadcasting LLC. Network: Network: Salem Radio Network, USA. Format: Relg. Spec prog: Children 7 hrs wkly. ♦Ethel Huff, chmn; Gene Huff, gen mgr.

Louisa

WBTH(AM)—See Williamson WV

WXCC(FM)—See Williamson WV

WZAQ(FM)— May 17, 1991: 92.3 mhz; 4.48 kw. 377 ft. TL: N38 10 33 W82 37 39. 112 Madison St. 41230. Phone: (606) 638-9203. Fax: (606) 638-9210. E-mail: wsac923@foothills.net. Licensee: Louisa Communications Inc. Format: Contemp rock. ♦Harold Britton, pres.

Louisville

WAMZ(FM)—Listing follows WHAS-TV.

WAVG(AM)—See Jeffersonville, IN

WDJX(FM)— Aug 1, 1963: 99.7 mhz; 24 kw. 720 ft. TL: N38 21 53 W85 50 18. Stereo. 520 S. 4th, 2nd Fl. 40202. Phone: (502) 625-1220. Fax: (502) 625-1256. Web Site: www.wdjx.com. Licensee: Blue Chip Broadcasting Licenses II Ltd. Group owner: Radio One Inc. (acq 4-30-01; grpsl). Format: Adult CHR. ♦Dale Schaefer, gen mgr; Kim Combest, sls dir; Doug James, natl sls mgr.

WFIA(AM)— March 1947: 900 khz; 1 kw-U. TL: N38 16 12 W85 42 25. Stereo. Suite 3600, 9960 Corporate Campus Dr. 40223. Phone: (502) 339-9470. Fax: (502) 423-3139. Web Site: www.salemradiogroup.com. Licensee: SCA License Corp. Group owner: Salem Communications Corp. (acq 1-24-01; $1.75 million). Rep: Salem. Format: Christian teaching, talk. News: 2 hrs wkly. Target aud: 30 plus; general. ♦Gordon Marcy, gen mgr.

*****WFPK(FM)**— Oct 4, 1954: 91.9 mhz; 100 kw. 236 ft. TL: N38 14 40 W85 45 27. Stereo. 619 S. Fourth St. 40202. Phone: (502) 814-6500. Fax: (502) 814-6599. Web Site: www.prp.org. Licensee: Kentucky Public Radio Inc. Network: Network: PRI, NPR. Format: AAA, jazz. Target aud: 25 plus. Spec prog: Bluegrass 3 hrs wkly. ♦Brian Conn, opns mgr; Gray Smith, gen sls mgr; Stacy Owen, progmg dir & mus dir; Thomas Dula, chief of engrg.

***WFPL(FM)**— Feb 20, 1950: 89.3 mhz; 21 kw. 774 ft. TL: N38 21 55 W85 50 24. Stereo. 619 S. Fourth St. 40202. Phone: (502) 814-6500. Fax: (502) 814-6599. Web Site: www.prp.org. Licensee: Kentucky Public Radio Inc. Network: Network: NPR, PRI. Format: News/talk. News staff: 3; News: 124 hrs wkly. Target aud: General. ♦Brian Conn, opns dir.

WGTK(AM)— Dec 30, 1933: 970 khz; 5 kw-U, DA-2. TL: N38 19 05 W85 44 39. Stereo. 9960 Campus Dr., Suite 3600 40223. Phone: (502) 339-9470. Fax: (502) 423-3139. Web Site: www.wgtk.net. Licensee: Salem Media of Kentucky Inc. (group owner; (acq 10-4-2000). Brooks, Pierce, McLendon, Humphrey & Leonard. Format: News/talk. News staff: one; News: 21 hrs wkly. Target aud: 35 plus; people with most discretionary incomes. ♦Gordon Marcy, gen mgr.

WHAS(AM)— July 18, 1922: 840 khz; 50 kw-U. TL: N38 15 40 W85 25 43. Stereo. 4000 #1 Radio Dr. 40218. Phone: (502) 479-2222. Fax: (502) 479-2224. Web Site: www.whas.com. Licensee: Clear Channel Radio Licenses Inc. (acq 8-86; with co-located FM). Network: ABC Information & Entertainment. Rep: Clear Channel. Cohn & Marks. Format: News/talk. News staff: 12; News: 14 hrs wkly. Target aud: 25-54. Spec prog: Farm 1 hr, relg 2 hrs wkly. ♦Bill Gentry, gen mgr; Mark Thomas, stn mgr; Kelly Carls, opns VP, opns dir & progmg dir; Rick Wookie, natl sls mgr & sls; Ron Fisher, prom dir; Ted Werbin, news dir; Jerry Snapp, chief of engrg.

WKJK(AM)— November 1948: 1080 khz; 10 kw-D, 1 kw-N, DA-2. TL: N38 18 29 W85 49 45. 4000 Radio Dr. 40218. Phone: (502) 479-2222. Fax: (502) 479-2225. Web Site: www.talkradio1080.com. Licensee: Clear Channel Radio Licenses Inc. Group owner: Clear Channel Communications Inc. (acq 9-13-96; $1 million. with intellectual property of WSFR(FM) Corydon, IN) Network: ABC. Rep: Clear Channel. Format: Talk. Target aud: 18-34; women. ♦Bill Gentry, gen mgr.

WKRD(AM)—Listing follows WLUE(FM).

WLLV(AM)— June 1940: 1240 khz; 1 kw-U. TL: N38 14 49 W85 42 19. 2001 W. Broadway 40203. Phone: (502) 776-1240. E-mail: wlovwllv@juno.com. Licensee: Mortenson Broadcasting Co. of Louisville Inc. Group owner: Mortenson Broadcasting Co. (acq 12-8-93; $375,000;. FTR: 1-3-94). Format: Black gospel. ♦Archer Dale, gen mgr.

WLOU(AM)— 1948: 1350 khz; 5 kw-U, DA-N. TL: N38 13 45 W85 46 47. (CP: 2.2 kw). 2001 W. Broadway 40203. Phone: (502) 776-1240. Fax: (502) 776-1250. E-mail: wlouwllv@juno.com. Licensee: Mortenson Broadcasting Co. of Louisville Inc. Group owner: Mortenson Broadcasting Co. (acq 1996; $490. for 49% of stock). Network: American Urban. Format: Black, urban contemp. Target aud: 25-54; mature adults. ♦Jack Mortenson, pres; Archer Dale, gen mgr.

WLUE(FM)— June 7, 1993: 100.5 mhz; 37.4 kw. Ant 554 ft. TL: N38 03 49 W85 43 52. 4000 #1 Radio Dr. 40218. Phone: (502) 479-2222. Fax: (502) 479-2308. Web Site: www.louieonline.com. Licensee: Clear Channel Broadcasting Licenses Inc. Group owner: Clear Channel Communications Inc. (acq 9-13-96; $6.9 million. with co-located AM). Format: Hot adult contemp. Target aud: 18-49; general. ♦Earl Jones, gen mgr & gen sls mgr.

WKRD(AM)—Co-owned with WLUE(FM). 1936: 790 khz; 5 kw-D, 1 kw-N, DA-2. TL: N38 11 34 W85 31 14. Stereo. Fax: (502) 479-2225. Web Site: www.wxxa.com. (Acq 1996). Rep: Clear Channel. Format: Sports. Target aud: 25-54. ♦Doug Wethington, stn mgr; Jim Fenn, progmg dir.

WMJM(FM)—See Jeffersontown

WPTI(FM)— 1974: 103.9 mhz; 1.35 kw. Ant 490 ft. TL: N38 15 20 W85 45 28. Stereo. 612 4th Ave., Suite 100 40202. Phone: (502) 589-4800. Fax: (502) 587-0212. Web Site: newcountry1039.com. Licensee: CXR Holdings L.L.C. Group owner: Cox Broadcasting (acq 8-26-99; $1.77 million). Dow, Lohnes & Albertson. Format: Country. News: one hr wkly. Target aud: 25-54; emphasis on 25-44. ♦Rolf Pepple, VP & gen mgr; Dave Bestler, sls dir; Julie Bruner-Sells, gen sls mgr & natl sls mgr.

WQMF(FM)—See Jeffersonville, IN

WTMT(AM)— Aug 20, 1958: 620 khz; 500 w-U, DA-2. TL: N38 18 59 W85 42 08. 300 Distillery Commons, Suite 200 40206-1913. Phone: (502) 583-6200. Fax: (502) 589-2979. E-mail: info@wtmt.com. Web Site: wtmt.com. Licensee: Jefferson Broadcasting Co. Format: Rgnl Mexican. ♦Lee Stinson Jr., pres & gen mgr; Paul Fink, stn mgr; Patty Scoggins, gen sls mgr; Bianca Baker, progmg dir.

***WUOL(FM)**— Dec 20, 1976: 90.5 mhz; 21 kw. Ant 774 ft. TL: N38 21 55 W85 50 24. Stereo. 619 S. Fourth St. 40202. Phone: (502) 814-6500. Fax: (502) 814-6599. Web Site: www.wuol.org. Licensee: Kentucky Public Radio Inc. Format: Class. News: 2 hrs wkly. Target aud: General; those interested in quality mus & info.

WVEZ(FM)— Apr 1, 1967: 106.9 mhz; 24.5 kw. 670 ft. TL: N38 22 20 W85 49 32. Stereo. 612 4th Ave., Suite 100 40202. Phone: (502) 589-4800. Fax: (502) 583-4820. Web Site: www.lite1069.com. Licensee: CXR Holdings L.L.C. Group owner: Cox Broadcasting (acq 5-99). Dow, Lohnes & Albertson. Format: Lite music. Target aud: 24-54; upper-scale, working women. ♦Don Nordin, progmg dir.

WWSZ(AM)—See New Albany, IN

WXMA(FM)— October 1964: 102.3 mhz; 3 kw. 300 ft. TL: N38 14 37 W85 45 34. 520 S. 4th Ave., Suite 200 40202-2532. Phone: (502) 625-1220. Fax: (502) 625-1258. Web Site: www.themaxfm.com. Licensee: Blue Chip Broadcasting Licenses II Ltd. Group owner: Radio One Inc. (acq 8-10-01; grpsl). Network: ABC FM Connection. Format: Hot adult contemp. Target aud: 25-49; young adults who enjoy modern/alternative rock. ♦Dale Schaefer, gen mgr; Tom Ulmer, sls dir; Doug James, natl sls mgr; Katrina Blair, prom dir.

Madisonville

WFMW(AM)— January 1947: 730 khz; 500 w-D, 215 w-N. TL: N37 21 03 W87 29 25. Stereo. Box 338 42431. Secondary address: 2380 N. Main St. 42431. Phone: (502) 821-4096. Fax: (502) 821-5954. E-mail: wfmw@charter.net. Web Site: www.wfmw.net. Licensee: Sound Broadcasters Inc. Network: CNN Radio. Rep: Rgnl Reps. Format: C&W. News staff: one; News: 13 hrs wkly. Target aud: 18 plus. ♦Robert T. Kelley, pres & gen mgr; Danny Koeber, progmg dir; Chris Gardener, news dir; Chris Meyers, chief of engrg.

WKTG(FM)—Co-owned with WFMW(AM). Apr 19, 1949: 93.9 mhz; 50 kw. 584 ft. TL: N37 21 05 W87 29 25. Stereo. Phone: (270) 821-1156. E-mail: wktg@charter.net. Web Site: www.wktg.com. Network: USA. Pepper & Corazzini. Format: AOR, classic rock. News staff: one; News: 3 hrs wkly. Target aud: 20-45. ♦Robert T. Kelley, stn mgr; Bill McClone, progmg dir.

***WSOF-FM**— February 1977: 89.9 mhz; 39.4 kw. 282 ft. TL: N37 19 11 W87 30 57. Stereo. 1415 Island Ford Rd. 42431. Phone: (270) 821-9684. Phone: (270) 825-3004. Fax: (270) 825-3005. E-mail: comments@wsof.org. Web Site: www.wsof.org. Licensee: Madisonville Christian School a division of Madisonville Baptist Temple Inc. Network: USA. Format: Christian educ. Target aud: General; Christian. ♦Doug Bell, progmg dir; Gary Hall, pres, gen mgr & chief of engrg.

WTTL(AM)— Sept 16, 1956: 1310 khz; 1.5 kw-D, 500 w-N, DA-N. TL: N37 20 12 W87 32 41. 265 S. Main St. 42431. Phone: (270) 821-1310. Fax: (270) 825-3260. Licensee: Madisonville CBC Inc. Group owner: Commonwealth Broadcasting Corp. (acq 2-8-00; $1.31 million with co-located FM). Format: News, talk, sports. Target aud: 25-54. ♦Tom Rogers, gen mgr & opns mgr; Marion Miller, gen sls mgr & adv mgr; Keith Farrell, news dir.

WYMV(FM)—Co-owned with WTTL(AM). Sept 7, 1992: 106.9 mhz; 2 kw. 528 ft. TL: N37 22 51 W87 28 04. Stereo. Network: Network: ABC, Jones Radio Networks. Format: Adult contemp. Target aud: 25-34. ♦Tom Rogers, progmg dir.

Manchester

WKLB(AM)— Sept 26, 1981: 1290 khz; 50 kw-U. TL: N37 09 29 W83 47 06. Stereo. Box 448, 106 Richmond Rd. 40962. Phone: (606) 598-2445. Phone: (606) 598-2653. Fax: (606) 598-2653. E-mail: wklb1stchoice@yahoo.com. Licensee: Barker Broadcasting Co. Group owner: Larry Barker (acq 1981). Network: ABC Information & Entertainment. Rep: Rgnl Reps. Barker Broadcasting Robert Olender. Format: Country. News staff: one; News: 8 hrs wkly. Target aud: 24-65; working people. Spec prog: Farm one hr, gospel 4 hrs wkly. ♦Larry Barker, pres & gen mgr.

WTBK(FM)— October 1989: 105.7 mhz; 7.5 kw. 462 ft. TL: N37 08 57 W83 45 09. Stereo. 107 Dickerson St. 40962. Phone: (606) 598-7588/598-7559. Fax: (606) 598-7598. E-mail: wtbkradio@yahoo.com. Licensee: Manchester Communications Inc. (acq 3-24-89). Network: Westwood One, ABC. Format: Classic rock. News staff: one; News: 10 hrs wkly. Target aud: General; 18 plus in the morning, 16-45 at night. Spec prog: Talk 8 hrs wkly. ♦Tim Finley, gen mgr.

WWLT(FM)— Aug 9, 1967: 103.1 mhz; 1.1 kw. Ant 538 ft. TL: N37 04 30 W83 49 14. Stereo. 100 Thompson-Poynter Rd., London 40741. Phone: (606) 878-9958. Fax: (606) 864-9958. Licensee: Wilderness Hills Broadcasting Co. Group owner: Vernon R. Baldwin Inc. (acq 1956). Network: K-Love. Format: Adult contemp, Christian. Target aud: 18-49; females. ♦Tom Cody, gen mgr.

WWXL(AM)— 1956: 1450 khz; 1 kw-U. TL: N37 09 04 W83 45 45. 1450 Radio Hill Rd. 40962. Phone: (606) 598-9995. Fax: (606) 598-9995. Licensee: Juanita H. Nolan (acq 12-9-03). Format: Oldies. News staff: one; News: 3 hrs wkly. Target aud: 35-54; programmed for adults 35-54. Spec prog: University of Kentucky Football/Basketball, Cincinnati Reds Baseball. ♦Junita H. Nolan, CEO; James Nolan, chmn & pres; Phil Lindsey, gen mgr & opns mgr.

Mannsville

WVLC(FM)— Dec 31, 1994: 99.9 mhz; 11 kw. 492 ft. TL: N37 10 04 W85 11 26. Stereo. Box 4190, Campbellsville 42719. Secondary address: 101 East Main St., Campbellsville 42719. Phone: (270) 789-0099. Phone: (270) 789-4998. Fax: (270) 789-4584. E-mail: bigdawg@wvlc.com. Web Site: www.wvlc.com. Licensee: Patricia Rodgers. Network: Network: Jones Radio Networks, CNN Radio. Format: Country. News staff: one. Target aud: General. ♦Bryan McFarland, gen mgr; Greg Gribbins, opns VP & news dir; Janie M. Smith, sls VP; Kevin Johnson, progmg dir & mus dir.

Marion

WMJL(AM)— July 10, 1968: 1500 khz; 250 w-D. TL: N37 20 11 W88 04 12. Stereo. Box 68, 251 Club Dr. 42064. Phone: (270) 965-2271. Licensee: Joe Myers Production Inc. Rep: Rgnl Reps. Format: Oldies. News staff: one; News: 12 hrs wkly. Target aud: General. Spec prog: Loc news, farm 3 hrs, community announcements one hr wkly. ♦Barbara Myers, news dir; Joe Myers, pres, gen mgr, gen sls mgr & chief of engrg.

WMJL-FM— June 1993: 102.7 mhz; 6 kw. 328 ft. TL: N37 20 16 W88 04 03. Stereo. (Acq 3-12-91; 4-1-91). Format: Oldies.

Mayfield

WNGO(AM)— Jan 7, 1947: 1320 khz; 1 kw-D, 97 w-N. TL: N36 45 37 W88 38 20. Box 679, 1176 US Hwy 45 N. 42066. Phone: (270) 247-5122. Fax: (270) 247-4207. Licensee: Bristol Broadcasting Co. Inc. (group owner; acq 2-20-2004; grpsl). Network: ABC Daytime Direction. Mullin, Rhyne, Emmons & Topel. Format: News/talk. News staff: one; News: 12 hrs wkly. Target aud: 24-54. Spec prog: Farm 4 hrs, relg 10 hrs wkly. ♦Dita Dillinger, gen mgr; Tim Hopwood, prom dir; Jeremy Wilkison, chief of engrg.

WQQR(FM)—Co-owned with WNGO(AM). Nov 2, 1955: 94.7 mhz; 32 kw. 442 ft. TL: N36 45 59 W88 38 55. (CP: 31.5 kw, ant 443 ft.). Stereo. Box 679, 1176 US Hwy 46 N. 42066. Rgnl Reps. Format: Class country. Target aud: 25 plus. ♦Jennifer Abernathy, sls dir; Randy Gardner, adv mgr; Becky Thatcher, progmg dir; Tim Hopwood, asst music dir & pub affrs dir.

WYMC(AM)— Oct 18, 1976: 1430 khz; 1 kw-U, DA-N. TL: N36 47 12 W88 39 16. Box V, 197 WYMC Rd. 42066. Phone: (270) 247-1430. Fax: (270) 247-1825. E-mail: wymc@wk.net. Licensee: JDM Communications Inc. (acq 12-31-90; $277,649; 1-21-91). Wiley, Rein & Fielding. Format: MOR. News staff: one. Target aud: 35-64; affluent, business oriented. ♦Jim Moore, gen mgr, gen sls mgr & mktg mgr; Joe Jackson, news dir; Allen Fowler, chief of engrg.

Maysville

WFTM(AM)— Jan 1, 1948: 1240 khz; 1 kw-U. TL: N38 38 10 W83 45 38. Box 100 41056. Phone: (606) 564-3361. Fax: (606) 564-4291. E-mail: wftmnews@maysvilleky.net. Licensee: Standard Tobacco Co. Rep: Keystone (unwired net), Rgnl Reps. Format: Music of your life. News staff: 2; News: 10 hrs wkly. Target aud: 18-55. Spec prog: Farm 6 hrs, gospel 5 hrs, relg 5 hrs wkly. ♦J.A. Finch, pres; Jeff Cracraft, VP; Doug McGill, gen mgr, gen sls mgr & chief of engrg; Erin McGill, news dir.

Stations in the U.S.   Kentucky

Developers & Brokers of Radio Properties — contact American Media Services at our suite: Philadelphia Marriott Downtown 215-625-2900 843-972-2200 americanmediaservices.com Charleston, SC Dallas, TX · Chicago, Il · Austin, TX American Media Services, LLC

WFTM-FM— Oct 26, 1965: 95.9 mhz; 3 kw. 207 ft. TL: N38 38 04 W83 46 48. Stereo. Network: AP Radio. Format: Soft hits. ♦ Danny Weddle, sls dir; Robert Roe, mus dir.

McDaniels

*WBFI(FM)— Sept 7, 1987: 91.5 mhz; 5 kw. 190 ft. TL: N37 36 06 W86 22 13. Box 2, Hwy. 259 S. 40152. Secondary address: 18424 Leitchfield Rd., Leitchfield 42754. Phone: (270) 257-2689. Fax: (270) 257-8344. Web Site: www.thenewwbfi.org. Licensee: Bethel Fellowship Inc. Reddy, Begley & McCormick. Format: Relg, educ, news/talk. News: 20 hrs wkly. Target aud: General; Christians. ♦ Ronald W. Miller, pres; Roger Goostree, gen mgr & opns mgr; Daryl Cook, progmg dir; James Coates, mus dir & engrg mgr.

McKee

WWAG(FM)— Nov 1, 1990: 107.9 mhz; 3.9 kw. 400 ft. TL: N37 23 39 W83 54 32. 1680 State Rd. 1071, Tyner 40486-9543. Phone: (606) 287-9924. E-mail: 1079fm@prtcnet.org. Licensee: Dandy Broadcasting Inc. (acq 1994). Network: ABC. Rep: Rgnl Reps. Lauren A. Colby. Format: Country. News staff: one; News: 10 hrs wkly. Target aud: General. Spec prog: Bluegrass 9 hrs wkly. ♦ Dan Brockman, pres; Sherry Handy, gen mgr.

Middlesboro

WFXY(AM)— Mar 1, 1969: 1490 khz; 1 kw-U. TL: N36 36 47 W83 42 34. Stereo. Box 999, 2118 Cumberland Ave. 40965. Phone: (606) 248-1560. Fax: (606) 248-1574. Licensee: Country-Wide Broadcasters Inc. (acq 5-1-01). Network: ABC Daytime Direction, Jones Radio Networks. Rep: Rgnl Reps. Bechtel & Cole. Format: Adult contemp. News staff: 2; News: 20 hrs wkly. Target aud: 25-54; community-oriented. Spec prog: Black 2 hrs, gospel 3 hrs, relg 3 hrs .wkly.

WMIK(AM)— Nov 15, 1948: 560 khz; 500 w-D, 88 w-N. TL: N36 37 38 W83 42 52. (CP: 2.5 kw-D). Box 608 40965. Phone: (606) 248-5842. Fax: (606) 248-7660. Licensee: Gateway Broadcasting Inc. Network: UPI. Format: Southern gospel. Spec prog: Farm one hr, gospel 2 hrs wkly. ♦ Trevor Barden, gen mgr.

WMIK-FM— June 4, 1971: 92.7 mhz; 130 w. 1,438 ft. TL: N36 35 50 W83 47 49. Stereo. Network: UPI. Format: Contemp gospel.

Midway

WBTF(FM)— 1998: 107.9 mhz; 6 kw. 328 ft. TL: N38 11 41 W84 38 25. 401 W. Main, Suite 301, Lexington 40507. Phone: (859) 233-1515. Fax: (859) 233-1517. Licensee: L.M. Communications of Kentucky L.L.C. Group owner: L.M. Communications Inc. (acq 4-10-01). Format: Urban contemp, CHR. ♦ Lynn Martin, CEO; James MacFarlane, gen mgr.

Monticello

WFLW(AM)— May 19, 1955: 1360 khz; 1 kw-D. TL: N36 49 30 W84 51 20. Box 696, 150 Worsham Ln. 42633. Phone: (606) 348-8427. Phone: (606) 348-7083. Fax: (606) 348-3867. Licensee: Stephen Staples Jr. (acq 11-9-94; with co-located FM; 1-2-95). Rep: Rgnl Reps. Format: Gospel. News staff: one. Target aud: General. Spec prog: Farm 5 hrs, news/talk 10 hrs wkly. ♦ Stephen Staples Jr., gen mgr; Debbie Brown, mus dir; Bruce Correll, chief of engrg.

WKYM(FM)— Co-owned with WFLW(AM). Dec 19, 1965: 101.7 mhz; 1.75 kw. 617 ft. TL: N36 48 08 W84 50 51. Stereo. E-mail: wkymmail@wkym.com. Web Site: www.wkym.com. Rep: Rgnl Reps. Format: Classic rock. Target aud: 18-50; baby boomers. ♦ Stephen Staples Jr., progmg dir.

WMKZ(FM)— June 1, 1990: 93.1 mhz; 2.15 kw. 558 ft. TL: N36 48 29 W84 50 46. Stereo. 183 Old Hwy. 90 42633. Phone: (606) 348-3393. Fax: (606) 348-3330. Web Site: www.wmkz.com. Licensee: Monticello-Wayne County Media Inc. Network: USA. Format: Country. News: 9 hrs wkly. Target aud: 24-55; general. ♦ Joel Catron, gen mgr.

Morehead

*WBMK(FM)— 2002: 88.5 mhz; 600 w. Ant 522 ft. TL: N38 10 38 W83 24 24. Box 3206, Tupelo, MS 38803. Phone: (662) 844-8888. Web Site: www.afr.net. Licensee: American Family Association. Group owner: American Family Radio (acq 11-26-99). Format: Christian. ♦ Marvin Sanders, gen mgr.

WIVY(FM)— July 1, 1994: 96.3 mhz; 6 kw. Ant 328 ft. TL: N38 10 56 W83 26 56. Stereo. 123 E. First St. 40351. Phone: (606) 784-9966. Fax: (606) 674-6700. Licensee: Gateway Radio Works Inc. (group owner). Network: ABC. William Silva. Format: Unforgettable Favorites. News staff: one. Target aud: 25 plus; afluent, well educ, mature adult, higher spendable income. ♦ Hays McMakin, pres; Jeff Ray, gen mgr & stn mgr.

WKCA(FM)—See Owingsville

*WMKY(FM)— June 1965: 90.3 mhz; 37 kw. Ant 895 ft. TL: N38 10 38 W83 24 18. Stereo. 132 Brenwick Hall, Morehead State Univ. 40351. Phone: (606) 783-2001. E-mail: wmky@moreheadstate.edu. Web Site: www.msuradio.com. Licensee: Morehead State University. Network: Network: PRI, NPR. Format: Class, news, Americana. News staff: 2; News: 53 hrs wkly. Target aud: 25-54; high education level (58% college or beyond). Spec prog: Jazz 3 hrs, bluegrass 3 hrs, rhythm and blues 3 hrs, folk 2 hrs, Celtic 2 hrs wkly. ♦ Paul W. Hitchcock, gen mgr & stn mgr; Greg Jenkins, opns dir.

WMOR(AM)— Feb 18, 1955: 1330 khz; 1 kw-D. TL: N38 10 12 W83 26 02. Box 338, 129 College St., West Liberty 41472. Phone: (606) 784-1029. Fax: (606) 743-9557. Licensee: Morgan County Industries Inc. (group owner; acq 3-16-99; $300,000 with co-located FM). Network: Network: Moody, ABC Information & Entertainment. Format: Country. ♦ C.C. Smith, pres, pres & gen mgr.

WMOR-FM— June 15, 1965: 106.1 mhz; 8 kw. 348 ft. TL: N38 10 56 W83 26 56. Format: Adult contemp.

Morganfield

WMSK(AM)— Nov 21, 1960: 1550 khz; 250 w-D. TL: N37 40 00 W87 55 40. Box 369 42437. Phone: (270) 389-1550. Fax: (270) 389-1553. E-mail: wmsk@vci.net.Jones U.S. Country Licensee: Union County Broadcasting Inc. Network: ABC Information & Entertainment. Rep: Rgnl Reps. Format: Relg, country. Target aud: General; adults 25-64. ♦ J.B. Crawley, pres; John Robinson, gen mgr, gen sls mgr, adv VP & progmg dir; Don Sheridan, sls VP & news dir; Rhonda Gibson, mus dir.

WMSK-FM— Aug 8, 1967: 95.3 mhz; 6 kw. Ant 298 ft. TL: N37 40 00 W87 55 40. (CP: 25 kw, ant 256 ft). Stereo. 1339 Hwy. 60 42437. Secondary address: Box 36 42437. Phone: (270) 389-1551.Jones Network: ABC Information & Entertainment. Rep: Rgnl Reps. Pepper & Corazzini. Target aud: 25-64; general. ♦ J.B. Crawley, CEO; Rhonda Gibson, opns mgr; John Robinson, mktg dir, prom dir & adv dir.

Morgantown

WLBQ(AM)— 1976: 1570 khz; 1 kw-D, 150 w-N. TL: N37 14 10 W86 42 29. (CP: TL: N37 13 09 W86 41 21). Box 130 42261. Phone: (270) 526-3321. Fax: (270) 526-5393. Licensee: Butler County Broadcasting Co. Network: ABC. Format: C&W. News staff: one; News: 8 hrs wkly. Target aud: General; residents of Morgantown & Butler County, KY. Spec prog: Relg 9 hrs, farm 3 hrs, gospel 3 hrs, sports 3 hrs wkly. ♦ Charles Black, pres; Jan Embry, VP; Mary Alice Black, gen mgr; Howard Phelps, stn mgr.

Mt. Sterling

*WAXG(FM)— 1998: 88.1 mhz; 300 w. 174 ft. TL: N38 03 39 W83 57 20. Box 2440, American Family Radio, Tupelo, MS 38803. Phone: (662) 844-8888. Fax: (662) 842-6791. Web Site: www.afr.net. Licensee: American Family Association. Group owner: American Family Radio Format: Relg. ♦ Marvin Sanders, gen mgr.

WKCA(FM)—See Owingsville

WMKJ(FM)— May 28, 1968: 105.5 mhz; 3 kw. 300 ft. TL: N38 05 36 W83 56 39. Stereo. 2601 Nicholasville Rd., Lexington 40503-3307. Phone: (859) 422-1000. Fax: (859) 422-1038. Web Site: www.majicoldies.com. Licensee: Citicasters Co. Group owner: Clear Channel Communications Inc. (acq 4-13-01). Format: Oldies. ♦ Keith Yarber, gen mgr.

WMST(AM)— Oct 17, 1957: 1150 khz; 500 w-D, 54 w-N. TL: N38 02 41 W83 54 05. 22 West Main 40353. Phone: (859) 498-1150. Fax: (859) 498-7930. Licensee: Gateway Radio Works Inc. (group owner; acq 1-1-00). Network: ABC Information & Entertainment. Rep: Rgnl Reps. William Silva. Format: Timeless Classics, news/talk. News staff: one; News: 37 hrs wkly. Target aud: 25 plus; affuent, mature adult, high spendalbe income, well educated. Spec prog: Farm 2 hrs wkly. ♦ Hays McMakin, pres; Jeff Ray, gen mgr; Vernice Taylor, stn mgr.

Mt. Vernon

WRVK(AM)— April 30, 1957: 1460 khz; 500 w-D. TL: N37 23 49 W84 19 45. Box 7, Renfro Valley 40473. Phone: (606) 256-2146. Fax: (606) 256-9146. Licensee: Saylor Broadcasting Inc. (acq 2-1-02). Network: UPI. Format: Classic country, country gospel. Target aud: General. Spec prog: Call-in talk show 15 hrs wkly. ♦ Charles W. Saylor, pres; Charles Saylor, gen mgr; Charles Napier, sls VP & gen sls mgr.

Mt. Washington

WLCR(AM)— Oct 29, 1955: 1040 khz; 1.5 kw-D. TL: N38 00 11 W85 40 51. Stereo. 3600 Goldsmith Ln., Louisville 40220. Phone: (502) 451-9527. Web Site: www.wlcr.net. Licensee: LCR Partners L.P. (acq 1999; $162,500). Format: Southern gospel, relg, talk. Target aud: General; Those interested in the existance of God. ♦ Vince Heuser, gen mgr.

Munfordville

WCLU-FM— Aug 1, 1964: 102.3 mhz; 3 kw. 99 ft. TL: N37 16 30 W85 55 00. Box 1628, Glasgow 42142. Phone: (270) 651-9149. Fax: (270) 651-9222. Web Site: www.wcluradio.com. Licensee: Royse Radio Inc. (acq 3-9-98; $225,000. with co-located AM). Format: Adult contemp. ♦ Henry Royse, gen mgr.

WLOC(AM)— February 1993: 1150 khz; 1 kw-D, 61 w-N. TL: N37 16 30 W85 55 00. Box 98, Horse Cave 42749. Phone: (270) 786-4400. Fax: (270) 786-4402. E-mail: wloc@scrtc.com. Web Site: www.am1150wloc.com. Licensee: Forbis Communications Inc. (acq 12-5-2003; $120,000). Format: Country. Target aud: 25 plus; serve entire area. Spec prog: Gospel 20 hrs, farm 2 hrs wkly. ♦ DeWayne Forbis, pres, gen mgr & gen sls mgr; Chris Jessie, progmg dir.

Murray

WFGE(FM)—Listing follows WRKY(AM).

*WKMS-FM— May 11, 1970: 91.3 mhz; 100 kw. 602 ft. TL: N36 55 18 W88 05 50. Stereo. Box 2018, University Stn. 42071. Phone: (800) 599-4737. Phone: (270) 762-4359. Fax: (270) 762-4667. E-mail: wkms@murraystate.edu. Web Site: www.wkms.org. Licensee: Board of Regents, Murray State University. Network: Network: NPR, PRI. Don Martin. Format: Class, jazz, news. News staff: 2; News: 72 hrs wkly. Target aud: 35 plus; upscale, well-educated, curious people. Spec prog: New age 3 hrs, blues 2 hrs, urban contemp 3 hrs, classic rock 2 hrs, big band 2 hrs wkly. ♦ Kate Lochte, stn mgr; Tracy Ross, opns mgr; Rhonda Gibson, dev dir & dev mgr; Allen Fowler, prom mgr & chief of engrg; Mark Welch, progmg dir & mus dir.

WNBS(AM)— July 1948: 1340 khz; 1 kw-U. TL: N36 37 42 W88 18 04. Box 1707 42071. Phone: (270) 753-2400. Fax: (270) 753-9434.

Broadcasting & Cable Yearbook 2006

Kentucky — Directory of Radio

Licensee: Forever Communications Inc. (group owner; acq 12-31-02; grpsl). Network: ABC. Rgnl Reps. Format: News, talk. News staff: one; News: 10 hrs wkly. Target aud: 25-55. Spec prog: Farm 6 hrs wkly. ♦ Debbie Howard, gen mgr.

WRKY(AM)— Sept 12, 1978: 1130 khz; 2.5 kw-D, 250 w-N, DA-2. TL: N36 38 09 W88 19 12. 1500 Diuguid Dr. 42071. Phone: (270) 753-2400. Fax: (270) 753-9434. Licensee: Forever Communications Inc. (group owner; acq 12-31-02; grpsl). Network: CBS. Rgnl reps. Format: Oldies. News staff: 2; News: 20 hrs wkly. Target aud: 35 plus. ♦ Greg Delaney, gen mgr.

WFGE(FM)— Co-owned with WRKY(AM). June 23, 1967: 103.7 mhz; 100 kw. 659 ft. TL: N36 32 58 W88 19 52. Stereo. Web Site: www.froggy103.com. Network: Westwood One. Format: Country. News staff: one; News: 4 hrs wkly. Target aud: 18-45. ♦ Greg Delaney, stn mgr.

Neon

WEZC(AM)— Aug 31, 1956: 1480 khz; 5 kw-D. TL: N37 11 54 W82 42 42. 1268 Bill Moore Branch Rd., Kona 41858. Phone: (606) 855-4232. Fax: (606) 855-7888. E-mail: jci@kih.net. Licensee: Jesus Communications Inc. Format: Relg. Target aud: 24-60; general. ♦ Frank Holbrook, pres.

Newburg

WDRD(AM)— 1992: 680 khz; 1.3 kw-D, 450 w-N, DA-2. TL: N38 05 31 W85 40 56. 11700 Commonwealth Dr., Suite 800, Louisville 40299. Phone: (502) 240-0602. Fax: (502) 240-0940. E-mail: john.salzman@abc.com. Web Site: www.radiodisney.com. Licensee: Radio Disney Group LLC. Group owner: ABC Inc. (acq 2-14-02; $1.92 million). Format: Children. Target aud: Age 25-44 mothers of children; Mothers of children younger than 15. ♦ John Salzman, gen mgr.

Newport

WNOP(AM)— Aug 21, 1948: 740 khz; 2.5 kw-D, 30 w-N, DA-2. TL: N39 05 41 W84 34 59. Stereo. 5440 Moeller Ave., Norwood, OH 45212. Phone: (513) 731-7740. Fax: (513) 731-6465. Licensee: Catholic Radio Foundation of Greater Cincinnati Inc. (acq 9-10-01). Format: Catholic relg. ♦ Bill Levitt, stn mgr.

Nicholasville

WCGW(AM)— Sept 15, 1986: 770 khz; 1 kw-D. TL: N37 53 07 W84 31 46. Stereo. 3270 Blazer Pkwy., Suite 101, Lexington 40509-1847. Secondary address: 3950 Lexington Rd., Versailles 40383. Phone: (859) 264-9700. Fax: (859) 264-9705. Licensee: Mortenson Broadcasting Co. (group owner) Network: USA. Format: Southern gospel. Target aud: 25-54; above average in education, family size, income. ♦ Ed Wright, gen mgr.

WLTO(FM)— Aug 29, 1988: 102.5 mhz; 2 kw. Ant 400 ft. TL: N37 49 52 W84 30 18. Stereo. 300 W. Vine St., Lexington 40507. Phone: (859) 253-5900. Fax: (859) 253-5940. Licensee: Cumulus Licensing Corp. Group owner: Cumulus Media Inc. (acq 7-22-99; grpsl). Format: Classic country. ♦ Darren Smith, gen mgr.

WWFT(AM)— December 1962: 1250 khz; 500 w-D, 59 w-N. TL: N37 54 18 W84 33 25. 3270 Blazer Pkwy., Lexington 40509. Phone: (859) 264-9700. Fax: (859) 264-9705. Licensee: Mortenson Broadcasting Co. of Kentucky LLC. Group owner: Mortenson Broadcasting Co. (acq 7-2-98; $150,000). Target aud: 12 plus. ♦ Jack Mortenson, pres; Dennis Smith, gen mgr; Ed Lewis, opns mgr.

Oak Grove

WEGI(FM)— Aug 31, 1964: 94.3 mhz; 6 kw. Ant 256 ft. TL: N36 38 28 W87 26 01. Stereo. 1640 Old Russellville Pike, Clarksburg, TN 37043. Phone: (931) 648-7720. Fax: (931) 648-7769. Web Site: eagle943.com. Licensee: Saga Communications of Tuckessee LLC. Group owner: Saga Communications Inc. (acq 10-4-2002; $1.5 million. with co-located AM). Format: Classic hits. News staff: one; News: 5 hrs wkly. Target aud: 25-54. ♦ Susan Quesenberry, gen mgr.

Okolona

***WJIE-FM)**— Jan 1, 1988: 88.5 mhz; 24.5 kw. 623 ft. TL: N38 01 59 W85 45 16. Stereo. 5400 Minors Ln., Louisville 40219. Secondary address: Box 197309, Louisville 40259. Phone: (502) 968-1220. Fax: (502) 962-3143. Web Site: www.wjie.org. Licensee: Evangel Schools Inc. Network: Moody, Pepper & Corazzini. Format: Relg. News: 7 hrs wkly. Target aud: 25-49; Christian adults. ♦ Robert W. Rodgers, pres; Greg Holt, gen mgr & opns VP.

Owensboro

WBKR(FM)— Listing follows WOMI(AM).

***WJVK(FM)**— 2004: 91.7 mhz; 100 w. Ant 174 ft. TL: N37 44 48 W87 06 58. 1407 Scottsville Rd., Bowling Green 42104. Phone: (270) 781-7326. Fax: (270) 781-8005. Web Site: www.christianfamilyradio.com. Licensee: Bowling Green Community Broadcasting Inc. Format: Christian. ♦ Mike Wilson, gen mgr; Dale McCubbins, progmg dir; Geoffrey Powviriya, mus dir.

***WKWC(FM)**— Jan 21, 1983: 90.3 mhz; 5 kw. 100 ft. TL: N37 44 37 W87 07 12. Stereo. 601 E. 14th 42303. Phone: (270) 926-3111 EXT. 5270. Fax: (270) 926-3196. Fax: (270) 926-8205. Licensee: Kentucky Wesleyan College. Format: Relg. News: 2 hrs wkly. Target aud: 12 plus. ♦ Pam Gray, gen mgr & progmg dir; Brandon Bartlett, news dir; Rick Graves, chief of engrg.

WOMI(AM)— Mar 7, 1938: 1490 khz; 830 w-U. TL: N37 44 29 W87 06 58. 3301 Frederica St. 42301.6082. Phone: (270) 683-1558. Fax: (270) 685-2500. Web Site: www.wbkr.com. Licensee: Regent Broadcasting of Evansville/Owensboro Inc. Group owner: Regent Communications Inc. (acq 2-25-03; with co-located FM). Rep: Christal. Format: News/talk. News staff: 2. Target aud: 35-64. ♦ Bill Stakelin, CEO; Gary Exline, pres & gen mgr; Kristen Hardesty, prom dir; Jim Williamson, progmg dir; Lee Denney, news dir; Rick Crago, engrg dir.

WBKR(FM)— Co-owned with WOMI(AM). 1948: 92.5 mhz; 91 kw. 1,049 ft. TL: N37 36 29 W87 03 15. (CP: 96 kw, ant 1,000 ft. TL: N37 46 20 W87 21 27). Stereo. Format: Country. News staff: 3. Target aud: 25-54. Spec prog: Farm 2 hrs wkly. ♦ Gary Exline, gen sls mgr & prom VP; A.J. Martin, progmg dir; Dave Spenser, mus dir; Rick Crago, engrg mgr.

WSTO(FM)— June 7, 1948: 96.1 mhz; 100 kw. 1,000 ft. TL: N37 46 20 W87 21 27. Stereo. 111 S.E. 3rd St., Suite 201, Evansville, IN 47708. Phone: (812) 421-9696. Fax: (812) 421-3273. Web Site: www.hot96.com. Licensee: South Central Communications Corp. (group owner; (acq 12-30-2003; $13 million). Format: CHR. Target aud: 18-34. ♦ Robert Shirel, CFO; Tim Huelsing, VP; Paul Brayfield, stn mgr.

WVJS(AM)— Nov 26, 1947: 1420 khz; 5 kw-D, 1 kw-N, DA-2. TL: N37 46 32 W87 09 31. Stereo. 1115 Tamarack Rd., Suite 500 42301. Phone: (270) 683-5200. Fax: (270) 688-0108. Licensee: Cromwell Group Inc. of Kentucky. Group owner: The Cromwell Group Inc. (acq 11-20-02; $300,000). Format: Adult standards, memories. Target aud: 35-54. Spec prog: Farm one hr wkly. ♦ Leonard "Corky" Norcia, gen mgr.

Owingsville

WKCA(FM)— Dec 1, 1983: 107.7 mhz; 6 kw. 370 ft. TL: N38 11 16 W83 46 34. Stereo. 17 S. Court St. 40360. Phone: (606) 674-2266. Fax: (606) 674-6700. Licensee: Gateway Radio Works Inc. (group owner). Network: ABC. William Silva. Format: Real country. News staff: one; News: 10 hrs wkly. Spec prog: Farm 3 hrs, Bluegrass 3 hrs, Gospel 4 hrs wkly. ♦ Hays McMakin, pres; Jeff Ray, gen mgr; Becky Young-Black, opns mgr.

Paducah

WDDJ(FM)— Nov 26, 1946: 96.9 mhz; 100 kw. 340 ft. TL: N37 05 55 W88 37 19. (CP: Ant 777 ft. TL: N37 02 56 W88 36 52). Stereo. Box 2397, 6000 WKYQ-WKYX Rd. 42002. Phone: (270) 534-9690. Fax: (270) 554-4613. Fax: (270) 554-5468. Licensee: Bristol Broadcasting Co. Inc. Group owner: Nininger Stations (acq 6-24-97; $2.7 million. with co-located AM). Format: Adult top 40. News staff: 2; News: 2 hrs wkly. Target aud: 18-49; active, white & blue collar adults. ♦ W.L. Nininger, chmn & pres; Gary Morse, gen mgr, gen sls mgr & natl sls mgr; Bobby Cook, opns mgr; Jamie Futrell, rgnl sls mgr; Mark Summer, prom VP & progmg dir; Donna Groves, news dir & pub affrs dir; Greg Walker, chief of engrg.

WPAD(AM)— Co-owned with WDDJ(FM). Aug 23, 1930: 1560 khz; 10 kw-D, 5 kw-N, DA-3. TL: N37 03 08 W88 36 03. Network: Westwood One. Format: Oldies, adult standards. News staff: 2; News: 22 hrs wkly. Target aud: 35-64; upscale, white-collar. Spec prog: Relg 7 hrs wkly.

WDXR(AM)— Dec 24, 1957: 1450 khz; 1 kw-U. TL: N37 05 55 W88 37 19. Stereo. Box 2397 42002. Phone: (270) 554-8255. Fax: (270) 554-5468. Licensee: Bristol Broadcasting Co. Inc. (group owner; acq 2-20-2004; grpsl). Network: ABC. Rosenman & Colin L.L.P. Format: Urban contemp. News staff: one; News: 5 hrs wkly. Target aud: 30-65. ♦ Randy Gardner, gen mgr & stn mgr.

***WGCF(FM)**— December 1996: 89.3 mhz; 12 kw. 492 ft. TL: N37 11 31 W88 58 41. Box 7931 42002-7931. Secondary address: 605 Broadway 42002-7931. Phone: (270) 443-3241. Fax: (270) 443-8219. E-mail: info@wgcf.org. Licensee: American Family Association. Group owner: American Family Radio (acq 11-25-2003; $200,000). Format: Adult contemp, CHR, contemp Christian. ♦ Frank Williams, chmn.

WKYQ(FM)— Listing follows WKYX(AM).

WKYX(AM)— 1946: 570 khz; 1 kw-D, 500 w-N, DA-2. TL: N37 00 53 W88 36 46. Stereo. Box 2397 42002. Secondary address: 6000 WKYX/WKYQ Rd. 42003. Phone: (270) 554-8255. Phone: (270) 554-0093. Fax: (270) 554-5468. Fax: (270) 554-4613. Web Site: www.wkyx.com. Licensee: Bristol Broadcasting Co. Inc. Group owner: Nininger Stations (acq 11-23-71). Rep: Christal. Fisher, Wayland, Cooper, Leader & Zaragoza L.L.P. Format: News/talk, sports. News staff: 3; News: 20 hrs wkly. Target aud: 25-54; middle to upper income. Spec prog: Gospel 2 hrs, NASCAR 8 hrs wkly. ♦ Gary Morse, gen mgr & gen sls mgr.

WKYQ(FM)— Co-owned with WKYX(AM). 1947: 93.3 mhz; 100 kw. 915 ft. TL: N37 00 53 W88 36 46. Stereo. E-mail: production@wkyq.com. Web Site: wkyq.com. Network: ABC Information & Entertainment. Format: Country. News staff: 3. Target aud: 25-54. ♦ Bobby Cook, opns mgr; Jamie Futrell, gen sls mgr; Bobbi Sue Tucker, prom dir; Jeff Lawrence, progmg dir; Mark Summer, mus dir; Donna Groves, news dir; John Lowery, pub affrs dir; Greg Walker, chief of engrg.

WREZ(FM)— See Metropolis, IL

WRIK-FM— See Metropolis, IL

WZZL(FM)— See Reidland

Paintsville

WKLW-FM— Listing follows WKYH.

WKYH(AM)— Mar 18, 1985: 600 khz; 5 kw-D, 500 w-N. TL: N37 47 19 W82 47 07. Stereo. 330 2nd St 41240-1834. Phone: (606) 789-3333. Fax: (606) 789-6939. Web Site: www.wkyhnews.com. Licensee: Highlands Broadcasting Corp. (acq 11-18-99). Network: Westwood One. Midlen & Guillot. Format: News/talk. Target aud: 25-49; middle to upper class adults. ♦ Charles K. Belhasen, gen mgr, pres, opns mgr, gen sls mgr, progmg dir, news dir & chief of engrg.

WKLW-FM— Co-owned with WKYH. June 18, 1993: 94.7 mhz; 4.9 kw. 731 ft. TL: N37 42 42 W82 48 03. Stereo. Drawer 1407, Suite 6, Woodland Pl. 41240. Phone: (606) 789-6664. Fax: (606) 789-6669. Web Site: www.wklw.com. Licensee: B & G Broadcasting Inc. Format: Hot adult contemp. ♦ Alan Burton, stn mgr.

WSIP(AM)— April 24, 1949: 1490 khz; 1 kw-U. TL: N37 48 21 W82 46 01. Box 597, 124 Main St. 41240. Phone: (606) 789-5311. Fax: (606) 789-7200. Licensee: S.I.P. Broadcasting Inc. Group owner: Key Broadcasting Inc. (acq 2-84). Rep: Rgnl Reps. Format: Southern Gospel. Target aud: General. ♦ Spike Berkhimer, gen mgr.

WSIP-FM— Jan 12, 1965: 98.9 mhz; 94 kw. 600 ft. TL: N37 47 45 W82 48 04. Stereo.

Paris

WGKS(FM)— Licensed to Paris. See Lexington

***WPTJ(FM)**— August 2003: 90.7 mhz; 6 kw. Ant 328 ft. TL: N38 17 24 W84 10 13. 1811 Cynthiana, Millersburg Rd. 40361. Secondary address: Lay Witness Broadcasting, Box 7 40362-0007. Phone: (859)

Stations in the U.S. — Kentucky

Developers & Brokers of Radio Properties — contact American Media Services at our suite: Philadelphia Marriott Downtown 215-625-2900, 843-972-2200, americanmediaservices.com, Charleston, SC. Dallas, TX · Chicago, IL · Austin, TX. American Media Services, LLC

484-9691. E-mail: thewind@wptj.com. Web Site: www.wptj.org. Licensee: Lay Witness Outreach Inc. Format: Relg. ♦ John Smith, gen mgr; John Wesley Brett, progmg dir.

WYGH(AM)— January 1993: 1440 khz; 1 kw-D, 25 w-N. TL: N38 13 30 W84 14 59. Box 50, Falmouth 41040. Phone: (859) 472-1075. Fax: (859) 472-2875. Licensee: Hammond Broadcasting Inc. Format: Relg. Spec prog: Spanish. ♦ Jan Hammond, gen mgr.

Philpot

WBIO(FM)— Nov 18, 1993: 94.7 mhz; 3 kw. 328 ft. TL: N37 41 51 W86 59 26. Stereo. 1115 Tamarack Rd., Suite 500, Owensboro 42301. Phone: (270) 683-5200. Fax: (270) 688-0108. E-mail: wbioradio@adelphia.net. Web Site: www.wbio.com. Licensee: Hancock Communications Inc. Group owner: The Cromwell Group Inc. (acq 6-17-93; $90,565; 7-5-93). Format: Country. News staff: one; News: 2 hrs wkly. ♦ Bayard Walters, CEO; Leonard "Corky" Norcia, gen mgr; Kevin Rickey, opns mgr.

Pikeville

WBTH(AM)—Williamson WV

WDHR(FM)—Listing follows WPKE(AM).

*WJSO(FM)— Apr 1989: 90.1 mhz; 3.8 kw. 455 ft. TL: N37 27 52 W82 32 45. Box 3237 41502. Phone: (606) 432-0351. Phone: (312) 329-4300. Fax: (312) 329-8980. E-mail: wjso@moody.edu. Web Site: wjso.mbn.org. Licensee: Moody Bible Institute of Chicago. (group owner; acq 12-18-91; donation; 1-13-92). Format: Relg. News: 15 hrs wkly. Target aud: 35-55. ♦ Dr. Joseph Stowell, pres; Ed Cannon, CFO; Bob Neff, VP; John E. Maddex, gen mgr; Pamela McCain, stn mgr.

WLSI(AM)— Jan 20, 1949: 900 khz; 5 kw-D. TL: N37 29 06 W82 32 44. Box 2200 41502. Phone: (606) 437-4051. Fax: (606) 432-2809. Licensee: East Kentucky Broadcasting Corp. (acq 5-14-2003; $531,273. with WZLK(FM) Virgie). Format: Country. News staff: one; News: 21 hrs wkly. Target aud: 25-49. ♦ Keith Casebolt, gen mgr.

WPKE(AM)— July 31, 1949: 1240 khz; 1 kw-U. TL: N37 28 53 W82 31 27. Stereo. Box 2200 41502. Secondary address: 1240 Radio Dr. 41501. Phone: (606) 437-4051. Fax: (606) 432-2809. E-mail: wdhr@wdhr.com. Web Site: www.wdhr.com. Licensee: East Kentucky Broadcasting Corp. (group owner; acq 1962). Network: ABC Information & Entertainment. Rep: Rgnl Reps. Rgnl Reps Womble, Carlylee, Sandridge & Rice. Format: Oldies. News staff: one; News: 5 hrs wkly. Target aud: General. ♦ Keith Casebolt, VP, gen mgr & opns mgr; Debbie Lawson, dev mgr; Pat Hall, sls dir, mktg mgr, prom mgr & adv mgr; Randy Jones, progmg dir & progmg mgr; Paul Manuel, engrg mgr; Walter Dingus, engrg mgr.

WDHR(FM)— Co-owned with WPKE(AM). Mar 25, 1966: 93.1 mhz; 22 kw. Ant 758 ft. TL: N37 27 57 W82 33 04. Stereo. Phone: (606) 432-8103. Web Site: www.wdhr.com. Network: ABC. Format: Country. News staff: 2. ♦ Walter E. May, CEO & pres; Keith Casebolt, opns VP; Randy Jones, mus dir.

WXCC(FM)—Williamson WV

Pineville

WANO(AM)— Mar 16, 1957: 1230 khz; 1 kw-U. TL: N36 46 07 W83 42 59. Box 999, Middlesboro 40965. Phone: (606) 337-2100. Fax: (606) 248-6397. Licensee: Cumberland Media Group Inc. (acq 5-1-01). Format: Oldies.

WRIL(FM)— Feb 24, 1973: 106.3 mhz; 350 w. 750 ft. TL: N36 45 15 W83 42 23. (CP: 1.05 kw, ant 768 ft.). Box 693 40977. Phone: (606) 337-5200. Fax: (606) 337-8020. Licensee: Pine Hills Broadcasting Inc. (acq 2-22-84; $300,000; 3-5-84). Network: ABC Information & Entertainment. Format: Country. ♦ Gil McPherson, gen mgr.

Pippa Passes

*WWJD(FM)— Nov 1, 1986: 91.7 mhz; 7.3 kw. 544 ft. TL: N37 19 45 W82 52 30. Stereo. Alice Lloyd College, 100 Purpose Rd. 41844. Phone: (606) 368-6131. Phone: (606) 368-6150. Fax: (606) 368-6017. E-mail: wwjd@alc.com. Licensee: Alice Lloyd College. Format: Adult contemp, Christian. Target aud: 13-25. ♦ Mike Sexton, gen mgr.

Prestonsburg

WDOC(AM)— November 1957: 1310 khz; 5 kw-D, 25 w-N. TL: N37 41 45 W82 45 24. Box 345, 95 Jackson 41653. Phone: (606) 886-2338. Phone: (606) 886-8409. Fax: (606) 886-1026. E-mail: q95fm@eastky.net. Licensee: WDOC Inc. Network: ABC Information & Entertainment. Rep: Rgnl Reps. Format: Country, talk. Target aud: 25-64. ♦ Gormon Collins Jr., pres & gen mgr; Samantha Osborne, gen sls mgr.

WQHY(FM)— Co-owned with WDOC(AM). Feb 11, 1968: 95.5 mhz; 100 kw. 1,000 ft. TL: N37 41 45 W82 45 24. Stereo. Network: ABC. Format: Adult contemp. News staff: one; News: 2 hrs wkly. Target aud: 18-34. ♦ Chris Slone, progmg dir; Ron Webb, mus dir; Russ Lafforty, chief of engrg.

WPRT(AM)— Dec 5, 1952: 960 khz; 5 kw-D. TL: N37 40 14 W82 45 14. Box 2200, Pikeville 41502. Phone: (606) 437-4051. Fax: (606) 432-2809. E-mail: radio@thexxx.com. Web Site: www.thexxx.com. Licensee: East Kentucky Radio Network Inc. (group owner; acq 10-26-01). Format: Oldies. ♦ Keith Casebolt, gen mgr.

WXKZ-FM— Feb 10, 1967: 105.3 mhz; 4.7 kw. Ant 371 ft. TL: N37 39 24 W82 45 58. Stereo. Box 1049, Harold 41635. Phone: (606) 478-1200. Fax: (606) 478-1050. E-mail: radio@thedoublex.com. Web Site: www.thedoublex.com. Licensee: Adam Gearheart dba WXLR-FM (acq 1-17-97; with co-located AM). Format: Oldies. ♦ Barry Boyd, gen mgr & gen sls mgr; Beau Daniels, progmg dir.

Princeton

WAVJ(FM)—Listing follows WPKY(AM).

WPKY(AM)— Mar 15, 1950: 1580 khz; 250 w-D. TL: N37 07 14 W87 51 31. Box 270 42445. Phone: (270) 365-2072. Fax: (270) 365-2073. E-mail: wavj@cbcradio.net. Licensee: Caldwell County CBC Inc. (acq 6-25-98; $362,000 with co-located FM). Format: Lite rock. News staff: one; News: 11 hrs wkly. Target aud: General. ♦ Tom Rogers, gen mgr & opns mgr; Larry Smith, progmg dir & news dir.

WAVJ(FM)— Co-owned with WPKY(AM). Apr 1, 1969: 104.9 mhz; 3 kw. 187 ft. TL: N37 07 14 W83 51 31. Stereo. E-mail: wavj@cbcradio.net. Format: Lite rock.

Providence

WWKY(AM)— Apr 9, 1976: 97.7 mhz; 6 kw. 328 ft. TL: N37 24 52 W87 34 23. Stereo. Box 1310,, 265 S. Main St., Madisonville 42431. Phone: (270) 825-9779. Fax: (270) 825-3260. E-mail: wwky@commonwealthbroadcasting.com. Licensee: Hopkins-Webster CBC Inc. Group owner: Commonwealth Broadcasting Corp. (acq 5-21-98; $425,000). Network: CNN Radio. Leonard S. Joyce. Format: Oldies. News staff: 2; News: 21 hrs wkly. Target aud: 25-54. ♦ Marion Miller, gen sls mgr & adv mgr; Tom Rogers, gen mgr, opns mgr & progmg dir.

Radcliff

WASE(FM)— July 25, 1995: 103.5 mhz; 15.5 kw. 449 ft. TL: N37 46 57 W85 54 38. Stereo. Box 2087, Elizabethtown 42702. Secondary address: 519 N. Miles, Elizabethtown 42701. Phone: (270) 766-1035. Fax: (270) 769-1052. E-mail: rbell@wase.org. Licensee: W & B Broadcasting Inc. Network: ABC. Miller & Miller. Format: Oldies. News: 4 hrs wkly. Target aud: 25-54; baby boomers. ♦ Bill Walters, pres; Renee Bell, gen mgr; Cale Tharp, opns mgr & chief of engrg.

Reidland

WZZL(FM)— October 1992: 106.7 mhz; 1.35 kw. 492 ft. TL: N37 03 23 W88 27 22. Box 7501, Paducah 42002-8123. Phone: (270) 538-5251. Fax: (270) 415-0599. E-mail: wzzl@withers.net. Licensee: Withers Broadcasting Co. of Paducah LLC. Group owner: Withers Broadcasting Co. (acq 9-11-97; grpsl). Format: Rock/AOR. Target aud: 18-45. ♦ Rick Lambert, pres & gen mgr.

Richmond

WCBR(AM)— March 1969: 1110 khz; 250 w-D. TL: N37 44 09 W84 16 05. Box 570 40476-0570. Secondary address: 509 Leighway Dr. 40475. Phone: (859) 623-1235. Fax: (859) 623-7094. E-mail: wcbr-radio@bellsouth.net. Licensee: WCBR Inc. (acq 3-12-2004). Network: USA. Format: Southern gospel. News: 5 hrs wkly. Target aud: 35 plus; older adult listener. Spec prog: Loc talk shows, news, sports & relg talk 35 hrs wkly. ♦ Bill Robbins, pres; David L. Humes, exec VP & gen mgr.

*WEKU(FM)— September 1968: 88.9 mhz; 50 kw. 720 ft. TL: N37 52 45 W84 19 33. Stereo. 102 Perkins Bldg., 521 Lancaster Ave. 40475-3102. Phone: (859) 622-1660. Fax: (859) 622-6276. Web Site: www.weku.fm. Licensee: Board of Regents, Eastern Kentucky University. Network: Network: NPR, PRI. Hardy, Carey & Chautin. Format: Class, news magazine, info. News staff: 3; News: 35 hrs wkly. Target aud: General. ♦ Tim Singleton, stn mgr; Mary Ellyn Cain, opns mgr; Carol Siler, dev dir; Marie Mitchell, news dir.

WEKY(AM)— Oct 17, 1953: 1340 khz; 1 kw-U. TL: N37 43 00 W84 18 25. 128 Big Hill Ave. 40475. Phone: (859) 623-1340. Phone: (859) 985-1500. Fax: (859) 623-1341. E-mail: coyote@chpl.net. Web Site: www.wcyo.com. Licensee: Wallingford Communications Inc. Group owner: Wallingford Broadcasting Co. (acq 1999; grpsl). Network: UPI. Rep: Rgnl Reps. Format: News/talk. News staff: one; News: 3 hrs wkly. Target aud: 25-54. Spec prog: Black 12 hrs, relg 6 hrs wkly. ♦ Kelly Wallingford, CEO, pres & gen mgr; Ray White, opns mgr.

WLRO(FM)— May 12, 1972: 101.5 mhz; 7.2 kw. 541 ft. TL: N37 52 45 W84 19 33. Stereo. 300 W. Vine St., Suite 3, Lexington 40592-1814. Phone: (606) 253-5900. Fax: (606) 253-5940. Licensee: Cumulus Licensing Corp. Group owner: Cumulus Media Inc. (acq 10-5-99; grpsl). Format: Rock and roll classics. News staff: one; News: 6 hrs wkly. Target aud: 25-54; mid to upper scale adults. ♦ Darren Smith, gen mgr.

Russell Springs

WHVE(FM)— 1993: 92.7 mhz; 6 kw. 328 ft. TL: N37 00 31 W85 12 14. Box 927, Columbia 42728. Secondary address: 7955 Russell Springs Rd. 42642. Phone: (270) 384-7979. Fax: (270) 384-6244. E-mail: thewave@ridingthewave.com. Web Site: www.ridingthe wave.com. Licensee: Shoreline Communications Inc. (group owner; acq 5-2002; $525,000). Format: Adult contemp. ♦ Alan W. Reed, gen mgr.

WIDS(AM)— Oct 14, 1982: 570 khz; 500 w-D. TL: N37 05 42 W85 05 05. Box 50, Falmouth 41040. Phone: (859) 472-1075. Fax: (859) 472-2875. E-mail: wiok@fuse.net. Web Site: www.wiok.com. Licensee: Hammond Broadcasting Inc. (acq 8-16-94; 8-29-94). Format: Southern gospel. ♦ Jan Hammond, gen mgr.

WJKY(AM)—See Jamestown

WJRS(FM)—See Jamestown

Russellville

WRUS(AM)— Aug 28, 1953: 610 khz; 2.5 kw-D, 73 w-N. TL: N36 48 51 W86 52 50. (CP: 500 w-N, TL: N36 52 29 W86 52 56 (night)). Box 1740 42276. Phone: (270) 726-2471. Fax: (270) 726-3095. Licensee: Logan Radio Inc. (acq 10-24-02). Network: ABC Daytime Direction. Format: News/talk, classic country. ♦ Chris McGinnis, gen mgr & gen sls mgr; Don Neagle, gen mgr & news dir; Mack Mallory, progmg dir.

Broadcasting & Cable Yearbook 2006

Kentucky
Directory of Radio

WUBT(FM)— Mar 28, 1965: 101.1 mhz; 47 kw. 1,289 ft. TL: N36 31 36 W86 41 14. Stereo. 55 Music Sq. W., Nashville, TN 37203. Phone: (615) 664-2400. Fax: (615) 664-2457. Web site: www.101thebeat.com. Licensee: Capstar TX L.P. Group owner: Clear Channel Communications Inc. (acq 8-30-00; grpsl). Format: Urban contemp. ◆ David Alpert, gen mgr; Bill Reed, sls dir; Keith Kaufman, mktg dir.

Saint Matthews

WRKA(FM)— Oct 19, 1964: 103.1 mhz; 6 kw. 312 ft. TL: N38 16 03 W85 41 53. Stereo. 612 4th Ave., Suite 100, Louisville 40202. Phone: (502) 589-4800. Fax: (502) 587-0212. Web Site: www.wrka.com. Licensee: CXR Holdings L.L.C. Group owner: Cox Broadcasting Network: ABC. Rep: Christal. Dow, Lohnes & Albertson. Format: Oldies. Target aud: 35-49. ◆ Rolf Pepple, VP & gen mgr; Dave Bestler, sls dir; Mike Crusham, gen sls mgr.

Salyersville

WRLV(AM)— September 1979: 1140 khz; 1 kw-D. TL: N37 44 58 W83 05 19. Box 550, 225 S. Church St. 41465. Phone: (606) 349-6125. Fax: (606) 349-6126. Fax: (606) 349-6129. E-mail: Coyote2@foothills.net. Licensee: Wallingford Broadcasting Co. Inc. (acq 4-20-98; $270,000 with co-located FM). Network: ABC Information & Entertainment. Rep: Rgnl Reps. Format: Gospel, relg. News staff: 2; News: 5 hrs wkly. Target aud: 35-65; middle age to elderly. ◆ Kelly T. Wallingford, pres; Kathy Puckett, gen mgr, gen sls mgr, mktg VP, prom mgr & adv VP; Beverley Crace, sls dir; Cecelia Russell, prom dir; Teresa Witten, progmg dir & progmg dir; Sanford Baca, news dir; Paul Manuel, chief of engrg.

WRLV-FM— Aug 25, 1989: 97.3 mhz; 5.2 kw. 350 ft. TL: N37 45 30 W83 03 52. Stereo. 225 S. Church St. 41465. Format: Country. News staff: 2; News: 5 hrs wkly. Target aud: 18-80; young to elderly. ◆ Cecelia Russell, prom VP; Kathy Puckett, stn mgr, sls VP & adv dir; Bryan Russell, mus dir.

Scottsville

WLCK(AM)— Feb 27, 1958: 1250 khz; 1 kw-D. TL: N36 44 24 W86 10 20. Box 158, 104.5 Public Sq. 42164. Phone: (270) 237-3149. Fax: (270) 237-3533. Licensee: Sherandan Broadcasting Co. (acq 7-3-85). Network: USA. Hardy & Carey. Format: Relg. News staff: one; News: 12 hrs wkly. Target aud: General. Spec prog: Farm 3 hrs wkly. ◆ Danny Tabor, pres & gen mgr; Don Meador, mus dir; Chris Nelson, news dir.

Shelbyville

WCND(AM)— June 3, 1964: 940 khz; 250 w-D. TL: N38 13 00 W85 09 45. 115 W. Main St., Frankfort 40601. Phone: (502) 647-2101. Fax: (502) 875-1225. Licensee: Clear Channel Broadcasting Licenses Inc. Group owner: Clear Channel Communications Inc. (acq 2-1-2002; with co-located FM). Format: Oldies. News staff: one; News: one hr wkly. Target aud: 35-64; upscale, white collar. Spec prog: Farm 6 hrs, Sp 2 hrs wkly. ◆ Dave Colvin, gen mgr.

WJZO(FM)— Sept 30, 1989: 101.7 mhz; 6 kw. Ant 328 ft. TL: N38 12 48 W85 10 16. Stereo. 4000 #1 Radio Dr., Louisville 40218. Phone: (502) 479-2222. Fax: (502) 479-2223. Web Site: www.foxrocks.com. Licensee: Clear Channel Broadcasting Licenses Inc. (acq 2-1-2002; with co-located AM). Format: Active rock. ◆ Earl Jones, gen mgr.

Shepherdsville

WLRS(FM)— 1993: 105.1 mhz; 2.2 kw. Ant 446 ft. TL: N38 02 54 W85 46 04. 520 S. Fourth Ave., 2nd Fl., Louisville 40202. Phone: (502) 625-1220. Fax: (502) 584-1051. Web site: www.wlrs.com. Licensee: Blue Chip Broadcasting Licenses II Ltd. Group owner: Radio One Inc. (acq 4-30-01; grpsl). Format: New rock. ◆ Dale Schaeffer, gen mgr.

Smiths Grove

WUHU(FM)— Dec 1, 1986: 107.1 mhz; 50 kw. 492 ft. TL: N36 50 35 W86 15 30. Stereo. 901 Lehman Ave., Suite 1 42101. Phone: (270) 843-0107. Fax: (270) 782-0767. Web site: www.allhitwuhu107.com. Licensee: Forever Communications Inc. (group owner; acq 12-31-02; grpsl). Rep: Rgnl Reps. Pepper & Corazzini. Format: Top-40 main stream. News staff: 2; News: 5 hrs wkly. Target aud: 25-49. ◆ Chris Hillard, pres; Brooke Summers, opns dir.

Somerset

***WDCL-FM**— July 1985: 89.7 mhz; 100 kw. 570 ft. TL: N37 09 29 W85 09 50. Stereo. Western Kentucky Univ., 1901 College Heights Blvd., Bowling Green 42101. Phone: (270) 745-5489. Fax: (270) 745-6272. Web Site: www.wku.edu/wkyu-fm. Licensee: Western Kentucky University. Network: Network: PRI, NPR. Leventhal, Senter & Lerman. Format: Class, news. News staff: 3; News: 35 hrs wkly. Target aud: General. Spec prog: Folk 5 hrs, jazz 15 hrs wkly. ◆ Gary Randsall, pres; Peter Bryant, gen mgr; Terry Reagan, dev dir.

WKEQ-FM—Listing follows WSFC(AM).

***WKVY(FM)**— 2004: 88.1 mhz; 6.1 kw vert. Ant 453 ft. TL: N37 04 42 W84 48 37. Stereo. 5700 W. Oaks Blvd., Rocklin, CA 95765. Phone: (916) 251-1600. Fax: (916) 251-1650. E-mail: klove@klove.com. Web Site: www.klove.com. Licensee: Educational Media Foundation. Group owner: EMF Broadcasting. Network: K-Love. Shaw Pittman. Format: Contemp Christian. News staff: 3. Target aud: 25-44; Judeo Christian, female. ◆ Richard Jenkins, pres; Mike Novak, VP.

WLLK-FM— Aug 14, 1989: 102.3 mhz; 6 kw. 328 ft. TL: N37 04 41 W84 40 39. Box 740 42502. Secondary address: 101 First Radio Ln. 42503. Phone: (606) 679-2394. Fax: (606) 678-2026. E-mail: wsek@clearchannel.com. Web site: www.firstradio.com. Licensee: Capstar TX L.P. Group owner: Clear Channel Communications Inc. (acq 12-8-2000; grpsl). Format: Hot adult contemp. News staff: one; News: 6 hrs wkly. Target aud: 25-54. ◆ Richard Dills, gen mgr.

WSFC(AM)— Dec 14, 1947: 1240 khz; 790 w-U. TL: N37 07 06 W84 36 44. Stereo. Box 740 42502-0740. Secondary address: 101 First Radio Ln. 42501. Phone: (606) 678-5151. Fax: (606) 678-2026. Licensee: Capstar TX L.P. Group owner: Clear Channel Communications Inc. (acq 12-8-2000; grpsl). Network: ABC Information & Entertainment. Rep: Rgnl Reps. Latham & Watkins. Format: Talk. News staff: one; News: 15 hrs wkly. Target aud: General. Spec prog: Farm 2 hrs wkly. ◆ Nolan Kenner, pres; Michael S. Tarter, gen mgr & stn mgr; Joella Shelly, sls dir; James Mercer, chief of engrg.

WKEQ-FM— Co-owned with WSFC(AM). Sept 1, 1964: 97.1 mhz; 27.5 kw. 659 ft. TL: N36 57 40 W84 34 07. Stereo. Format: C&W.

***WTHL(FM)**— July 16, 1987: 90.5 mhz; 50 kw. 590 ft. TL: N37 07 52 W84 33 15. Stereo. Box 1423 42502. Secondary address: 93 Rainbow Terr. 42503. Phone: (606) 679-6300. Fax: (606) 679-1342. Web Site: www.kingofkingsradio.net. Licensee: Somerset Educational Broadcasting Foundation. Network: Moody. Format: Conservative, traditional relg, educ. Target aud: 40 plus; people with conservative, traditional & relg values & interests. ◆ S. David Carr, gen mgr, gen sls mgr & progmg dir.

WTLO(AM)— Nov 1, 1958: 1480 khz; 1 kw-D. TL: N37 05 15 W84 38 14. Stereo. 290 WTLO Rd. 42502. Phone: (606) 678-8151. Fax: (606) 678-8152. E-mail: wtlo@usa.com. Web Site: www.wtloradio.com. Licensee: Cumberland Communications Inc. (acq 11-6-74; $255,000). Rep: Keystone (unwired net). Format: Unforgettable oldies, rhythm, news/talk. Target aud: 45 plus; upscale & highly mobile. Spec prog: Farm one hr, relg 4 hrs wkly. ◆ Brooke Cary, gen mgr & opns mgr; J.J. Johnson, gen sls mgr; J. Allen Brown, news dir; Bruce Corell, chief of engrg.

Springfield

WAKY-FM— Feb 17, 1989: 102.7 mhz; 4 kw. Ant 354 ft. TL: N37 41 43 W85 19 06. 106 S. 3rd St., Bardstown 40004. Phone: (502) 348-3943. Fax: (502) 348-4043. E-mail: kfogle@commonwealthbroadcashieg.com. Licensee: Washington County CBC Inc. Group owner: Commonwealth Broadcasting Corp. (acq 10-30-97; $350,000). Network: ABC. Format: Oldies, news. News staff: 4; News: 20 hrs wkly. Target aud: 25-55. Spec prog: Sports 12 hrs, farm 10 hrs wkly. ◆ Kenny Fogle, gen mgr, gen sls mgr & adv dir.

Stamping Ground

WLXO(FM)— Dec 15, 1994: 96.1 mhz; 6 kw. Ant 328 ft. TL: N38 12 15 W84 32 51. 401 W. Main, Suite 301, Lexington 40507. Phone: (859) 233-1515. Fax: (859) 233-1517. Web Site: www.supertalk961.com. Licensee: Clarity Communications Inc. (acq 8-7-01; $400,000). Format: Talk. ◆ Lynn Martin, pres; James MacFarlane, gen mgr.

Stanford

WRSL(AM)— Nov 1, 1961: 1520 khz; 1 kw-D. TL: N37 33 03 W84 38 45. Stereo. Box 300 40484. Fax: (606) 365-7979. E-mail: generalstore@wxkyfm.com. Web site: www.wxkyfm.com. Licensee: Lincoln-Garrard Broadcasting Co. Inc. (acq 2-11-2002; with co-located FM). Format: Country. News staff: 2. Target aud: 25-54; young Christian families. Spec prog: Farm & community affrs 4 hrs wkly. ◆ Johnathan Smith, pres; Renee Schoebel, gen mgr; David Smith, chief of engrg.

WXKY-FM— May 22, 1967: 96.3 mhz; 12.5 kw. Ant 472 ft. TL: N37 31 27 W84 52 12. 5700 W. Oaks Blvd., Rocklin, CA 95765. Phone: (916) 251-1600. Fax: (916) 251-1650. Web site: www.klove.com. Licensee: Educational Media Foundation. (acq 10-20-2004; $800,000). Network: K-Love. Shaw Pittman LLP. Format: Christian music. ◆ Richard Jenkins, pres.

Stanton

WBFC(AM)— June 21, 1975: 1470 khz; 850 w-D, 82 w-N. TL: N37 53 14 W83 52 58. Box 577 40380. Phone: (606) 663-6631. Fax: (606) 663-2267. E-mail: beverly@wbfcam.com. Web Site: www.wbfcam.com. Licensee: Combs Broadcasting Inc. (acq 10-13-98; $70,000). Format: Southern gospel. ◆ James Harold Combs, pres; William Combs, gen mgr; Beverly Combs, opns dir.

WSKV(FM)— Aug 10, 1974: 104.9 mhz; 440 w. 680 ft. TL: N37 45 43 W83 50 36. Stereo. 28 W. Hall's Rd. 40380. Phone: (606) 663-2811. Fax: (606) 663-2895. E-mail: wskv@setel.com. Licensee: Moore Country 104 LLC (acq 12-16-2004; $650,000). Format: Classic Country. Target aud: General. ◆ A.C. Moore, gen mgr.

Sturgis

WEZG(FM)— Not on air, target date: unknown: 101.3 mhz; 6 kw. Ant 276 ft. TL: N37 40 00 W87 55 40. 427 Starks Bldg., 455 S. 4th Ave., Louisville 40202. Phone: (502) 589-0060. Licensee: Henson Media Inc. ◆ Ed Henson, pres & gen mgr.

Tompkinsville

WKWY(FM)— 2003: 102.7 mhz; 6 kw. Ant 315 ft. TL: N36 43 27 W85 40 53. 341 Radio Station Rd. 42167. Phone: (270) 487-6119. Fax: (270) 487-8462. Licensee: J.K. Whittimore. Format: Country. News staff: 2; News: 20 wkly. All age group. Spec prog: Bluegrass 6 hrs, gospel 7 hrs wkly. ◆ Bernice Whittimore, gen mgr.

WTKY(AM)— May 28, 1960: 1370 khz; 2.1 kw-D. TL: N36 43 27 W85 40 53. Stereo. 341 Radio Station Rd. 42167. Phone: (270) 487-6119. Fax: (270) 487-8462. Licensee: Whittimore Enterprises Inc. (acq 6-10-2004). Network: CBS. Format: C&W. News staff: 2; News: progmg 17 hrs wkly. Target aud: All age groups. Spec prog: Bluegrass 6 hrs, gospel 8 hrs, bargain time 1 hr wkly. ◆ Bernice Whittimore, gen mgr.

WTKY-FM— Jan 20, 1972: 92.1 mhz; 6 kw. 328 ft. TL: N36 43 27 W85 40 53. Stereo. News staff: 2; News: 20 hrs wkly.

Upton

***WJCR-FM**— February 1990: 90.1 mhz; 100 kw. 383 ft. TL: N37 25 57 W86 01 50. Stereo. Box 91 42784-0091. Secondary address: 13101 Raider Hollow Rd. 42784. Phone: (270) 369-8614. Fax: (270) 369-7402. E-mail: wjcrfm@earthlink.net. Licensee: FM 90.1 Inc. Reddy, Begley & McCormick. Format: Southern gospel mus. Target aud: General. ◆ Don Powell, pres & gen mgr; Gerri Powell, exec VP, gen sls mgr & adv mgr; Gary Richardson, progmg dir; Larry Baysinger, engrg dir.

Valley Station

WRVI(FM)— 1982: 105.9 mhz; 1.9 kw. 413 ft. TL: N38 08 16 W85 56 06. 9960 Corporate Campus Dr., Suite 3600, Louisville 40223. Phone: (502) 339-9470. Fax: (502) 423-3139. Licensee: Salem of Kentucky Inc. Group owner: Salem Communications Corp. (acq 1999; $5 million. with WFIA-FM New Albany, IN). Format: Christian. ◆ Gordon Marcy, gen mgr.

Stations in the U.S. — Louisiana

Vanceburg

WKKS(AM)— June 1, 1958: 1570 khz; 1 kw-D. TL: N38 35 50 W83 20 50. 1106 Fairlane Dr. 41179. Phone: (606) 796-3031. Fax: (606) 796-6186. Licensee: Brown Communications Inc. (acq 1984). Format: Classic country. Spec prog: Gospel 16 hrs, oldies 7 hrs wkly. ♦ Dennis Brown, pres, gen mgr & progmg dir.

WKKS-FM— 1983: 104.9 mhz; 3 kw. 298 ft. TL: N38 36 19 W83 19 57. Format: Top 40 country.

Vancleve

WMTC(AM)— June 1948: 730 kHz; 5 kw-D, DA. TL: N37 36 12 W83 26 39. Box 8 41385. Secondary address: 1036 KY 541, Jackson 41339. Phone: (606) 666-5006. Phone: (606) 666-9512. Fax: (606) 666-7534. E-mail: wmtc@kih.net. Licensee: Kentucky Mountain Holiness Assn. Network: USA. Pepper & Corazzini. Format: Relg, Christian. News: 14 hrs wkly. Spec prog: Farm one hr wkly. ♦ John Eldon Neihof, pres; Seldon Short, VP, gen mgr & sls dir; Jennifer Cox, progmg dir; Gordon Sampsel, mus dir; Kenneth Amspaugh, chief of engrg.

WMTC-FM— Jan 1, 1991: 99.9 mhz; 6 kw. Ant 328 ft. TL: N37 36 23 W83 26 48. Stereo. Phone: (606) 666-5006. E-mail: wmtc@asburyusa.net. Format: Christian, relg. Spec prog: Farm one hr wkly.

Versailles

WCDA(FM)— July 16, 1973: 106.3 mhz; 3 kw. Ant 316 ft. TL: N38 02 44 W84 39 29. Stereo. 401 W. Main, Suite 301, Lexington 40507. Phone: (859) 233-1515. Fax: (859) 233-1517. Web Site: www.cd1063.com. Licensee: L.M. Communications Inc. (group owner; acq 9-3-98). Network: USA. Format: Hot adult contemp. News: 2 hrs wkly. Target aud: 25-49; female. ♦ Lynn Martin, pres; James E. Macfarlane, gen mgr.

Vine Grove

WRZI(FM)— Oct 5, 1993: 101.5 mhz; 6 kw. 328 ft. TL: N37 35 07 W85 50 20. Stereo. 406 S. Mulberry St., Elizabethtown 42701. Phone: (270) 763-0800. Fax: (270) 769-6349. Web Site: wrzi.net. Licensee: Elizabethtown CBC Inc. Group owner: Commonwealth Broadcasting Corp. (acq 7-1-00); grpsl). Rgnl Reps. Verner, Liipfert, Bernhard, McPherson & Hand. Format: Classic rock. News staff: one; News: 3 hrs wkly. Target aud: 25-45; males. ♦ Steve Newberry, pres; John Wright, gen mgr, sls VP, prom dir & adv mgr; Chris Bratcher, opns VP, opns dir & progmg dir; Jerry Shouse, engrg dir.

Virgie

WZLK(FM)— Nov 15, 1992: 107.5 mhz; 580 w. TL: N37 22 47 W82 34 11. (CP: 1.12 kw). Box 2200, Pikeville 41502. Phone: (606) 437-4051. Fax: (606) 432-2801. Licensee: East Kentucky Broadcasting Corp. (acq 5-14-2003; $531,273. with WLSI(AM) Pikeville). Format: Top 40s. ♦ Keith Caseboit, gen mgr.

Warsaw

WKID(FM)—See Vevay, IN

West Liberty

WLKS(AM)— July 25, 1965: 1450 khz; 1 kw-U. TL: N37 55 36 W83 16 41. Stereo. Box 338, 129 College St. 41472. Phone: (606) 743-3145. Fax: (606) 743-9557. Licensee: Morgan County Industries Inc. (group owner) Rep: Rgnl Reps. Format: Oldies. News staff: one; News: 35 hrs wkly. Target aud: General. Spec prog: Farm 5 hrs wkly. ♦ Paul Lyons, gen mgr.

WLKS-FM— Jan 1, 1994: 102.9 mhz; 6 kw. 328 ft. TL: N37 55 36 W83 16 41. 129 College St. 41472. Phone: (606) 743-1029. Format: Country.

Whitesburg

***WMMT(FM)**— Nov 1, 1985: 88.7 mhz; 1 kw horiz 15 kw vert. 1,469 ft. TL: N37 06 38 W82 44 15. Stereo. 91 Madison Ave. 41858. Phone: (606) 633-0108. Fax: (606) 633-1009. E-mail: wmmtfm@appalshop.org. Web Site: www.appalshop.org. Licensee: Appalshop Inc. Format: Div. Target aud: General. Spec prog: Oldies, bluegrass, american indian,. ♦ Cheryl Marshall, stn mgr & dev dir.

WTCW(AM)— Feb 19, 1953: 920 khz; 5 kw-D, 47 w-N. TL: N37 08 04 W82 46 08. (CP: TL: N37 08 46 W82 46 01). Box 288, Mayking 41837. Phone: (606) 633-4434. Phone: (606) 633-2711. Fax: (606) 633-4445. Licensee: T.C.W. Broadcasting Co. Inc. Group owner: Key Broadcasting Inc. (acq 1-1-86; $765,000 with co-located FM; 10-7-85). Network: CBS. Rep: Rgnl Reps. Format: News/talk. Target aud: 30 plus. Spec prog: Bluegrass 10 hrs wkly. ♦ Kevin Day, gen mgr.

WXKQ(FM)— Co-owned with WTCW(AM). Nov 25, 1964: 103.9 mhz; 145 w. Ant 1,499 ft. TL: N37 06 38 W82 44 15. Stereo. Format: Modern country.

Whitesville

WXCM(FM)—Licensed to Whitesville. See Hawesville

Whitley City

WHAY(FM)— Dec 1, 1990: 98.3 mhz; 5.1 kw. Ant 354 ft. TL: N36 39 40 W84 26 53. Box 69 42653. Phone: (606) 376-2218. Fax: (606) 376-5146. Web Site: www.hay98.com. Licensee: Tim Lavender. Format: Americana. News: 5 hrs wkly. Target aud: 30 plus. ♦ Dave Shelley, gen mgr.

Wickliffe

WBCE(AM)— Jan 4, 1981: 1200 khz; 1 kw-D. TL: N36 58 54 W89 04 39. Box 128 42087. Phone: (270) 335-5171. Fax: (270) 335-5172. Licensee: WBCE Inc. Format: Relg. Target aud: General. Spec prog: Southern gospel mus. ♦ David Courtney, gen mgr.

WGKY(FM)— January 1987: 95.9 mhz; 3 kw. 759 ft. TL: N36 56 24 W88 57 59. Stereo. 930 Wickliffe Rd. 42087. Phone: (270) 335-3696. Fax: (270) 335-3698. E-mail: wgky@brtc.net. Web Site: www.96classiccountry.com. Licensee: Wickliffe Rental Properties Inc. (acq 7-9-98; $270,000). Network: Jones Radio Networks. Rgnl Reps. Miller & Miller. Format: Classic country. News: 5 hrs wkly. Target aud: 24-54; rural homeowners, farmers. Spec prog: Gospel 5 hrs, bluegrass 6 hrs, news 5 hrs wkly. ♦ Keith Kelley, CEO, chmn & pres; Kolleen Kelley, CFO; Larry Kelley, gen mgr & opns mgr.

Williamsburg

WEKC(AM)— Sept 21, 1981: 710 khz; 4.2 kw-D. TL: N36 46 28 W84 10 05. Stereo. Box 419 40769. Secondary address: 402 Main St. 40769. Phone: (606) 549-3000. Phone: (606) 549-3033. Fax: (606) 539-0916. E-mail: wekc@wekc.net. Licensee: Gerald Parks (acq 6-21-00). Network: USA. Format: Religious and gospel only. News: 5 hrs wkly. Target aud: General; young adults, All ages, race & creed. Spec prog: Tri-county spotlite, relg 7 hrs wkly. ♦ Gerald Parks, CEO, chmn, pres & CFO; Helen Park, exec VP; Kay Meadors, gen mgr, opns mgr, progmg mgr & mus dir; Kay Parks, gen mgr & stn mgr.

WEZJ(AM)— Mar 7, 1959: 1440 khz; 2.5 kw-D, 500 w-N, DA-1. TL: N36 43 48 W84 09 04. 522 Main St. 40769. Phone: (606) 549-2285. Fax: (606) 549-5565. Licensee: Whitley Broadcasting Co. Inc. (group owner; acq 5-23-02; grpsl). Network: ABC Information & Entertainment. Rep: Rgnl Reps. Format: Modern country. Target aud: General. Spec prog: Sports. ♦ David Estes, gen mgr.

WEZJ-FM— November 1990: 104.3 mhz; 1.4 kw. 656 ft. TL: N36 44 43 W84 11 24. Network: ABC Information & Entertainment.

Williamstown

WNKR(FM)— Apr 1, 1992: 106.5 mhz; 1.41 kw. 476 ft. TL: N38 40 54 W84 39 33. Stereo. Box 182, 118 S. Main St., Dry Ridge 41035. Phone: (859) 824-9106. Phone: (800) 925-1220. Fax: (859) 824-9835. E-mail: prod@wnkr.net. Licensee: Grant County Broadcasters Inc. (acq 1992). Rep: Rgnl Reps. Koerner & Olender. Format: Country. News: 6 hrs wkly. Target aud: 25-54; adults. ♦ Robert Wallace, pres; Jeffrey K. Ziesmann, gen mgr; Brad Mundstock, opns mgr; Laura Ziesmann, sls dir & gen sls mgr; Katherine Marshall, pub affrs dir; Jim Stitt, chief of engrg.

Wilmore

WVRB(FM)— Sept 18, 1995: 95.3 mhz; 4.1 kw. Ant 397 ft. TL: N37 57 37 W84 32 42. 105 C Edgewood Plaza Dr., Nicholasville 40356. Phone: (859) 885-7109. Fax: (859) 885-7332. Web Site: www.klove.com. Licensee: Vernon R. Baldwin Inc. (group owner; acq 7-26-94; FTR: 8-8-94). Network: K-Love. Format: Contemp Christian. Target aud: 20-45; baby boomers, Christians. ♦ Tom Cody, gen mgr & stn mgr.

Winchester

WKQQ(FM)— 1974: 100.1 mhz; 32 kw. 490 ft. TL: N38 07 25 W84 26 45. Stereo. 2601 Nicholasville Rd., Lexington 40503. Phone: (859) 422-1000. Web Site: www.wkqq.com. Licensee: Citicasters Licenses L.P. Group owner: Clear Channel Communications Inc. (acq 5-4-99; grpsl). Format: Classic rock. News staff: one; News: 3 hrs wkly. Target aud: 18-49; women. ♦ Michael Jordan, prom dir.

WMJR(AM)— Oct 19, 1954: 1380 khz; 2.5 kw-D, 40 w-N. TL: N38 00 46 W84 09 38. 195 Moore Dr., Lexington 40503-2918. Phone: (859) 278-0894. Fax: (859) 278-0426. Web Site: www.wmjr.net. Licensee: Thy Kingdom Come Network Inc. (acq 1999; $583,000). Pepper & Corazzini. Format: Christian. Target aud: 35-64. ♦ Leo Brown, pres & progmg dir.

Louisiana

Abbeville

KPEL-FM—Listing follows KROF(AM).

KROF(AM)— July 9, 1948: 960 khz; 1 kw-D, 95 w-N. TL: N30 00 40 W92 07 21. Box 62630, Lafayette 70506. Phone: (337) 233-6000. Fax: (337) 234-7360. Licensee: Regent Broadcasting of Lafayette Inc. Group owner: Regent Communications Inc. (acq 10-17-01; grpsl). Format: Country, Fr/Cajun. ♦ Mike Grimsley, gen mgr.

KPEL-FM—Co-owned with KROF(AM). June 1, 1974: 105.1 mhz; 25 kw. 300 ft. TL: N30 00 40 W92 07 21. (CP: Ant 292 ft.). Stereo. Format: Oldies. ♦ Mike Calamari, mus dir.

Alexandria

***KAPM(FM)**— June 1998: 91.7 mhz; 1 kw. 128 ft. TL: N31 16 04 W92 26 24. Box 3206, American Family Radio, Tupelo, MS 38803. Phone: (662) 844-8888. Fax: (662) 842-6791. Web Site: www.afr.net. Licensee: American Family Association. Group owner: American Family Radio Format: Inspirational Christian. ♦ Marvin Sanders, gen mgr.

KBCE(FM)—(Boyce). Mar 29, 1982: 102.3 mhz; 21 kw. Ant 289 ft. TL: N31 22 21 W92 38 09. 1605 Murray St., Suite 216 71301. Phone: (318) 445-0800. Fax: (318) 445-1445. Licensee: Trinity Broadcasting Corp. (acq 7-2-98; $26,248). Network: American Urban. Rep: D & R Radio. Format: Urban contemp. Target aud: General. Spec prog: Gospel 19 hrs, jazz 3 hrs, blues one hr, talk one hr wkly. ♦ Alison Randolf, pres; James Alexander, gen mgr.

KDBS(AM)— December 1953: 1410 khz; 1 kw-D, 30 w-N. TL: N31 16 25 W92 25 43. 1515 Jackson St. 71301. Phone: (318) 443-7454. Fax:

Louisiana

(318) 442-2747. Licensee: Capstar TX L.P. Group owner: Clear Channel Communications Inc. (acq 8-30-00; grpsl). Network: Network: Westwood One, ABC Information & Entertainment. Pepper & Corazzini. Format: Sports. News staff: 2; News: 4 hrs wkly. Target aud: 25-54. ♦J. R. Greeley, gen mgr & sls dir; Scott Beyadt, opns mgr; Robby Greene, sls dir; Kellie Wilson, prom mgr; Monica Blake, news dir; Lyn Hare, chief of engrg.

KRRV-FM—Co-owned with KDBS(AM). May 11, 1969: 100.3 mhz; 100 kw. 1,055 ft. TL: N31 01 59 W92 30 08. Stereo. Web Site: www.krrv-fm.com. Format: Country. ♦Steve Casey, mus dir.

KEDG(FM)— 2001: 106.9 mhz; 6 kw. Ant 328 ft. TL: N31 25 35 W92 24 25. Box 7057 71306. Phone: (318) 445-1234. Web Site: www.kiss1069.com. Licensee: Flinn Broadcasting Corp. Format: Hip hop, rhythm and blues. ♦Taylor Thompson, gen mgr.

KEZP(FM)—(Bunkie). 1993: 104.3 mhz; 18 kw. 384 ft. TL: N31 05 14 W92 21 34. 1605 Murray 71301. Phone: (318) 449-1999. Fax: (318) 487-8173. Licensee: Opus Broadcasting Alexandria LLC. Group owner: Opus Media Partners LLC (acq 7-30-2004; $1.83 million). Network: Westwood One. Format: Oldies. News staff: one. Target aud: 35-64. ♦Mark Jones, gen mgr.

KJMJ(AM)— Sept 21, 1935: 580 khz; 5 kw-D, 1 kw-N, DA-N. TL: N31 18 25 W92 25 00. 601 Washington St. 71301. Phone: (318) 561-6145. Fax: (318) 449-9954. E-mail: info.usa@radiomaria.org. Web Site: www.radiomaria.us. Licensee: Radio Maria Inc. (group owner; acq 9-20-99). Putbrese, Hunsaker & Trent, P.C. Format: Christian, relg, talk. News: 8 hrs wkly. Homebound, prisoners & sick. Spec prog: Sports 15 hrs wkly. ♦Thomas Bordelon, gen mgr.

KLAA(FM)—(Tioga). May 25, 1984: 103.5 mhz; 50 kw. 476 ft. TL: N31 25 39 W92 24 18. Stereo. 92 W. Shamrock, Pineville 71360. Phone: (318) 448-8888. Phone: (318) 487-1035. Fax: (318) 487-1045. E-mail: chris@ia103.com. Web Site: www.la103.com. Licensee: Opus Broadcasting Alexandria LLC. Group owner: Opus Media Partners LLC (acq 9-30-2004; $3.38 million. with KBKK(FM) Ball). Rep: McGavren Guild. Dow, Lohnes & Albertson. Format: Country. News staff: one; News: 4 hrs wkly. Target aud: 25-54; working people, upscale professionals. ♦Gene Dickerson, gen mgr.

***KLSA(FM)**— 1987: 90.7 mhz; 100 kw. Ant 1,243 ft. TL: N31 33 56 W92 32 50. Box 5250, Shreveport 71135. Phone: (318) 797-5150. Phone: (800) 552-8502. Fax: (318) 797-5265. E-mail: listenermail @redriverradio.com. Web Site: www.redriverradio.com. Licensee: Board of Supervisors Louisiana State University & Agricultural Mechanical College. Network: Network: NPR, PRI. Format: Class, news. News: Nws progmg 40 hrs wkly. ♦Roy Gerritsen, gen mgr.

***KLXA-FM**— November 1998: 89.9 mhz; 3 kw. Ant 328 ft. TL: N31 22 40 W92 28 27. EMF Broadcasting, 5700 West Oaks Blvd., Rocklin, CA 95765. Phone: (916) 251-1600. Fax: (916) 251-1650. E-mail: klov@klove.com. Web Site: www.klove.com. Licensee: Educational Media Foundation. Group owner: EMF Broadcasting (acq 12-1-03; $125,000). Network: K-Love. Shaw Pittman. Format: Contemp Christian. News staff: 3. Target aud: 25-44; Judeo Christian, female. ♦Richard Jenkins, pres; Mike Novak, VP; Ed Lenane, opns dir; Keith Whipple, dev dir.

KMXH(FM)— February 1993: 93.9 mhz; 6 kw. Ant 328 ft. TL: N31 16 04 W92 26 24. 1605 Murray St., Suite 216 71301. Phone: (318) 445-0800. Fax: (318) 445-1445. Licensee: FM Broadcasting Corp. (acq 7-1-2005; $1.2 million). Format: Rhythm and blues, Southern soul. ♦James Alexander, gen mgr.

KQID(FM)—Listing follows KSYL(AM).

KSYL(AM)— Apr 1, 1947: 970 khz; 1 kw-U, DA-N. TL: N31 19 33 W92 29 17. Stereo. Box 7057 71306. Secondary address: 1115 Texas Ave. 71306. Phone: (318) 445-1234. Fax: (318) 445-7231. Licensee: Cenla Broadcasting Inc. (acq 8-1-80). Rep: Allied Radio Partners. Format: News/talk, sports. ♦Taylor Thompson, pres, gen mgr, stn mgr & gen sls mgr.

KQID(FM)—Co-owned with KSYL(AM). Sept 17, 1978: 93.1 mhz; 100 kw. 1,700 ft. TL: N31 38 20 W92 12 18. Stereo. Web Site: www.q93fm.com. Format: Top-40.

KTTP(AM)—(Pineville). Sept 13, 1974: 1110 khz; 2 kw-D. TL: N31 21 52 W92 27 15. Stereo. 3419 Hyson St. 71303. Phone: (318) 473-4388. Fax: (318) 449-1779. E-mail: kttpam1110@aol.com. Licensee: Benjamin-Dane LLC (acq 4-7-2005; $175,000). Format: Gospel. Target aud: 25-70. ♦Ronald Reeves, pres; Carolyn Frazier, gen mgr; Bob Wagner, gen sls mgr & chief of engrg.

KWDF(AM)—(Ball). 1986: 840 khz; 10 kw-D. TL: N31 22 41 W92 28 27. 3735 Rigoletto Rd., Pineville 71360. Phone: (318) 640-4373. Phone: (318) 640-9001. Fax: (318) 640-9001. E-mail: kwdf840@juno.com. Licensee: Educational Media Foundation. Group owner: EMF Broadcasting (acq 12-1-03; $375,000). Network: USA. Format: Southern gospel, relg.

KZMZ(FM)— 1947: 96.9 mhz; 100 kw. 1,450 ft. TL: N31 02 15 W92 29 45. Stereo. 1515 Jackson St. 71301. Phone: (318) 443-2543. Fax: (318) 443-7306. Web Site: www.kzmz.com. Licensee: Capstar TX L.P. Group owner: Clear Channel Communications Inc. (acq 8-30-00; grpsl). Network: ABC Information & Entertainment. Pepper & Corazzini. Format: Classic rock. News staff: one; News: 2 hrs wkly. Target aud: 18-49; baby boomers. ♦Lisa Ballance, gen mgr.

Amite

WABL(AM)— January 1956: 1570 khz; 500 w-D. TL: N30 42 31 W90 31 31. Box 8888, Metairie 70011. Phone: (985) 748-8385. Fax: (985) 748-3918. E-mail: wabl1570@hotmail.com. Licensee: Spotlight Broadcasting LLC (group owner); acq 6-8-01; $70,000). Format: News/talk, C&W. Target aud: 20-64. ♦Patrick Andras, pres; Charlie Hart, gen mgr.

WTGG(FM)— Mar 3, 1997: 96.5 mhz; 6 kw. 328 ft. TL: N30 41 39 W90 26 41. 200 E. Thomas, Hammond 70401. Phone: (985) 542-9844. Fax: (985) 542-6483. Web Site: www.tangi965.com. Licensee: Southwest Broadcasting Inc. (group owner; acq 4-8-98; $650,000). Network: Westwood One. Format: 50s, 60s & 70s oldies. News staff: one; News: one hr wkly. Target aud: 25-54; women. ♦Charles Dowdy, CEO; Elouise Dowdy, gen mgr.

Angola

***KLSP(FM)**— Aug 12, 1986: 91.7 mhz; 100 w. 90 ft. TL: N30 57 17 W91 35 45. Louisiana State Penitentiary, Hwy. 66 70712. Phone: (225) 655-2001. Web Site: www.corrections.state.la.us/lsp/klsp.htm. Licensee: Angola Educational Foundation Inc. Format: Div. Target aud: General. Spec prog: Black 10 hrs, C&W 6 hrs, jazz 7 hrs, poets corner one hr, legal wave 3 hrs wkly. ♦Burl Cain, gen mgr; Cheryl M. Ranatza, stn mgr.

Arcadia

KHCL(FM)— Jan 20, 2001: 92.5 mhz; 6 kw. 328 ft. TL: N32 27 27 W92 59 38. Houston Christian Broadcasters Inc., 2424 South Blvd., Houston, TX 77098. Phone: (713) 520-5200. Web Site: www.khcb.org. Licensee: Houston Christian Broadcasters Inc. (group owner) Format: Christian. ♦Bruce Munsterman, stn mgr; Bonnie BeMent, mus dir & news dir; Dan Wales, chief of engrg.

Atlanta

KCIJ(FM)— January 2002: 106.5 mhz; 25 kw. Ant 328 ft. TL: N31 48 29 W92 48 22. Stereo. 213 Renee St., Natchitoches 71457. Phone: (318) 354-4000. Fax: (318) 352-9598. Licensee: North Face Broadcasting L.L.C. (acq 5-9-2003; $348,000. with KNOC(AM) Natchitoches). Format: Classic Hits. Target aud: 25-54; general. ♦Bill Vance, gen mgr.

Baker

WTGE(FM)— June 16, 1994: 107.3 mhz; 4.6 kw. 328 ft. TL: N30 37 24 W91 09 50. Stereo. Box 2231, Baton Rouge 70821. Secondary address: 929-B Government St., Baton Rouge 70802. Phone: (225) 388-9898. Fax: (225) 344-3077. E-mail: owen.weber@gbcradio.com. Licensee: Guaranty Broadcasting Co. of Baton Rouge LLC. Group owner: Guaranty Broadcasting Co. (acq 2-5-97). Rep: D & R Radio. Wiley, Rein & Fielding. Format: Classic country. Target aud: 25-54; general. ♦George A. Foster Jr., chmn; Bridger Eglin, pres & gen mgr; Owen Weber, gen mgr.

Ball

KBKK(FM)— September 1998: 105.5 mhz; 6 kw. 318 ft. TL: N31 25 39 W92 24 18. 92 W. Shamrock, Pineville 71360. Phone: (318) 487-1035. Fax: (318) 487-1045. Web Site: www.1055kbuck.com. Licensee: Opus Broadcasting Alexandria LLC. Group owner: Opus Media Partners LLC (acq 9-30-2004; $3.38 million. with KLAA(FM) Tioga). Rep: McGavren Guild. Format: Classic country. ♦Kim Jones, pres.

KWDF(AM)—Licensed to Ball. See Alexandria

Basile

KQIS(FM)— May 4, 1990: 102.1 mhz; 3 kw. 328 ft. TL: N30 28 52 W92 35 50. Box 60571, Lafeyette 70596. Secondary address: 320 N. Parkerson Ave., Crowley 70526. Phone: (337) 783-2520. Fax: (337) 783-5744. E-mail: info@kqis.com. Web Site: www.kqis.com. Licensee: Third Partner Broadcasting Inc. (acq 3-21-94; $380,000; 5-30-94). Network: ABC. Format: MOR. News: 3 hrs wkly. Target aud: 25-55; middle-income. Spec prog: Fr 5 hrs, relg one hr wkly. ♦Phil Lizotte, gen mgr & gen sls mgr; Ed Perkins, progmg dir.

Bastrop

***KAXV(FM)**— 2000: 91.9 mhz; 12 kw. Ant 456 ft. TL: N32 49 22 W92 07 28. Box 3206, American Family Radio, Tupelo, MS 38803. Phone: (662) 844-8888. Fax: (662) 842-6791. E-mail: comments@afr.net. Web Site: www.afr.net. Licensee: American Family Radio. (group owner) Format: Inspirational Christian. ♦Marvin Sanders, gen mgr.

KJMG(FM)— 1996: 97.3 mhz; 6 kw. 328 ft. TL: N32 45 46 W91 57 35. 1109 Hudson Ln., Monroe 71201. Secondary address: Box 4808 71211. Phone: (318) 388-2323. Fax: (318) 388-0569. E-mail: kjmg@bayou.com. Web Site: www.majic97.com. Licensee: Holladay Broadcasting of Louisiana LLC (group owner; acq 9-30-98; $700,000). Rep: McGavren Guild. Latham & Watkins. Format: Urban adult contemp. Target aud: 25-54. Spec prog: Gospel 24 hrs wkly. ♦Bob Holladay, pres & gen mgr.

KRVV(FM)— 1977: 100.1 mhz; 50 kw. 490 ft. TL: N32 40 20 W91 55 06. Stereo. Box 4808, Monroe 71211. Secondary address: 1109 Hudson Ln., Monroe 71201. Phone: (318) 388-2323. Fax: (318) 388-0569. E-mail: krvv@bayou.com. Web Site: www.thebeat.net. Licensee: Holladay Broadcasting of Louisiana LLC (group owner; acq 10-15-91; $1 million;. FTR: 11-4-91). Rep: McGavren Guild. Latham & Watkins. Format: Urban. Target aud: 18-54; general. Spec prog: Gospel 4 hrs wkly. ♦Bob Holladay, pres & gen mgr.

KTRY-FM— Mar 1, 1974: 94.3 mhz; 25 kw. Ant 289 ft. TL: N32 49 06 W91 54 29. 328 W. Madison Ave. 71220. Phone: (318) 281-3333. Fax: (318) 283-0720. Licensee: Jamie Patrick Broadcasting Ltd. Format: Rhythm and blues. ♦Henry Cotton, pres; William Hendrix Jr., gen mgr.

Baton Rouge

KBRH(AM)—Listing follows WBRH(FM).

***KLSU(FM)**— October 1981: 91.1 mhz; 5 kw. 159 ft. TL: N30 24 37 W91 10 37. Stereo. LSU 39 Hodges Hall 70803. Phone: (225) 578-8688. Fax: (225) 388-1698. Fax: (225) 578-0579. E-mail: klsustationmanager@yahoo.com. Web Site: klsu.stumedia.lsu.edu. Licensee: Louisiana State University. Rep: Rgnl Reps. Format: Jazz, modern rock, blues, div. News: one hr wkly. Target aud: 18-25; university students & college age listeners. Spec prog: Class 3 hrs, blues 3 hrs, international 3 hrs, reggae 3 hrs wkly. ♦Linus Lee, stn mgr.

***WBRH(FM)**— September 1977: 90.3 mhz; 21 kw. Ant 197 ft. TL: N30 26 42 W91 09 33. Stereo. 2825 Government St. 70806. Phone: (225) 383-3243. Fax: (225) 379-7685. Licensee: East Baton Rouge Parish School Board. Network: NPR. Format: Jazz. Target aud: 25-54; men. Spec prog: Cajun one hr wkly. ♦Larry Davis, gen mgr & stn mgr; Lyn Kenyon, sls dir; Rob Payer, mus dir.

KBRH(AM)—Co-owned with WBRH(FM). 1953: 1260 khz; 5 kw-D, 127 w-N. TL: N30 27 38 W91 14 37. Phone: (225) 387-1260. (Acq 7-7-93; 8-2-93). Format: Classic rhythm and blues. Target aud: 35+. Spec prog: Cajun 2 hrs wkly.

WCDV(FM)—See Hammond

WDGL(FM)— Oct 1, 1968: 98.1 mhz; 100 kw. 1,550 ft. TL: N30 21 58 W91 12 47. Stereo. Box 2231 70821. Secondary address: 929-B Government St. 70802. Phone: (225) 388-9898. Fax: (225) 344-3077. E-mail: owen.weber@gbcradio.com. Licensee: Guaranty Broadcasting Co. of Baton Rouge LLC. Group owner: Guaranty Broadcasting Co.

Stations in the U.S.   Louisiana

Network: Westwood One. Rep: McGavren Guild. Wiley, Rein & Fielding. Format: Classic rock. Target aud: 25-54; general. ♦ George A. Foster Jr., chmn; Bridger Eglin, pres & VP; Owen Weber, VP & gen mgr.

WDVW(FM)—See La Place

WFMF(FM)—Listing follows WJBO(AM).

WIBR(AM)— July 18, 1948: 1300 khz; 5 kw-D, 1 kw-N, DA-2. TL: N30 28 25 W91 13 34. 650 Wooddale Blvd. 70806. Phone: (225) 926-1106. Fax: (225) 928-1606. Web Site: www.sports-animal.net. Licensee: Citadel Broadcasting Co. Group owner: Citadel Broadcasting Corp. (acq 1999; grpsl). Network: ABC. Rep: McGavren Guild. Format: News. Target aud: 25-50. Spec prog: Swamp pop Cajun mus 18 hrs wkly. ♦ Rebecca Breeding, gen mgr; Jeff Jarnigan, opns dir & opns mgr.

WJBO(AM)— Dec 11, 1934: 1150 khz; 5 kw-U, DA-1. TL: N30 27 47 W91 16 10. 5555 Hilton Ave., Suite 500 70808. Phone: (225) 231-1860. Fax: (225) 231-1873. E-mail: info@wjbo.com. Web Site: www.wjbo.com. Licensee: Capstar TX L.P. Group owner: Clear Channel Communications Inc. (acq 8-30-00; grpsl). Network: Network: CBS, Westwood One. Format: Talk, news, sports. Target aud: 20 plus. ♦ Dick Lewis, gen mgr.

WFMF(FM)—Co-owned with WJBO(AM). 1941: 102.5 mhz; 85 kw. 1,260 ft. TL: N30 17 49 W91 11 40. Stereo. Fax: (225) 231-1879. Format: CHR. Target aud: 18-34; female.

***WJFM(FM)**— June 1995: 88.5 mhz; 25.5 kw. Ant 269 ft. TL: N30 23 06 W91 05 28. Stereo. Box 262550 70826-2550. Secondary address: 8919 World Ministry Ave. 70810. Phone: (225) 768-3202. Phone: (225) 768-3227. Fax: (225) 768-3729. Web Site: www.jsm.org. Licensee: Family Worship Center Church Inc. (group owner; acq 12-15-99). Format: Gospel. News staff: one; News: 2 hrs wkly. Target aud: 25-54; full gospel Christians & anyone searching for hope. ♦ John Santiago, stn mgr & dev dir.

WNDC(AM)— Nov 1, 1946: 910 khz; 1 kw-U, DA-1. TL: N30 34 48 W91 07 50. 3000 Tecumseh St. 70805. Phone: (225) 357-4571. Phone: (225) 356-7700. Licensee: Church Point Ministries Inc. (acq 3-1-89). Format: Black gospel. Target aud: 18-59. ♦ Dwight Pate, pres; Sandra Pate, gen mgr.

WPFC(AM)—(Port Allen). 1963: 1550 khz; 5 kw-D. TL: N30 30 07 W91 12 39. 6943 Titian Dr. 70806. Phone: (225) 926-1506. Fax: (225) 926-6560. Licensee: Victory and Power Ministries Inc. (acq 11-15-94; $450,000; 12-12-94). Network: USA. Latham & Watkins. Format: Relg, gospel music. News staff: 2; News: 3 hrs wkly. Target aud: 35-59; middle-class female. ♦ Ralph N. Moore, gen mgr.

WPYR(AM)— 1956: 1380 khz; 5 kw-D, DA. TL: N30 27 39 W91 13 23. 5555 Hilton Ave., Suite 500 70808. Phone: (225) 231-1860. Fax: (226) 231-1879. Licensee: Capstar TX L.P. Group owner: Clear Channel Communications Inc. (acq 8-30-2000; grpsl). Network: Radio Disney. Format: Talk. ♦ Mark Kennedy, progmg dir.

***WRKF(FM)**— Jan 18, 1980: 89.3 mhz; 28 kw. 935 ft. TL: N30 22 22 W91 12 16. Stereo. 3050 Valley Creek 70808. Phone: (225) 926-3050. Fax: (225) 926-3105. Licensee: Public Radio Inc. Network: Network: NPR, PRI. Format: Class, news/talk. News staff: one; News: 35 hrs wkly. Target aud: General. ♦ Jim Engster, pres; Shirley Sands, opns dir; Malcolm Robinson, dev VP.

WXOK(AM)— February 1953: 1460 khz; 5 kw-D, 1 kw-N, DA-3. TL: N30 28 08 W91 12 24. 650 Wooddale Blvd. 70806. Phone: (225) 926-1106. Fax: (225) 922-7019. Web Site: www.citadelcommunications.com. Licensee: Citadel Broadcasting Co. Group owner: Citadel Broadcasting Corp. (acq 1-14-99). Network: ABC. Rep: Allied Radio Partners. Format: Gospel. Target aud: 18 plus. ♦ Rebecca Breeding, gen mgr.

WYNK-FM— Dec 7, 1968: 101.5 mhz; 97 kw. Ant 1,499 ft. TL: N30 19 34 W91 16 36. Stereo. 5555 Hilton Ave, Suite 500 70808. Phone: (225) 231-1860. Fax: (225) 231-1878. Web Site: www.wynk.com. Licensee: Capstar TX L.P. Group owner: Clear Channel Communications Inc. (acq 8-30-00; grpsl). Network: ABC Information & Entertainment. Format: Country. News staff: 2. Target aud: 18-54. ♦ Dick Lewis, gen mgr; Bob Murphy, opns mgr.

WYPY(FM)— Sept 10, 1966: 100.7 mhz; 97 kw. 1,499 ft. TL: N30 19 35 W91 16 36. Stereo. Box 2231 70821. Secondary address: 929-B Government St. 70802. Phone: (225) 388-9898. Fax: (225) 344-3077. E-mail: owen.weber@gbcradio.com. Licensee: Guaranty Broadcasting Co. of Baton Rouge LLC. Group owner: Guaranty Broadcasting Co. (acq 1996; $5.5 million). Network: ABC. Wiley, Rein & Fielding. Format: Country. Target aud: 25-54; general. ♦ George A. Foster Jr., chmn & VP; Bridger Eglin, pres; Owen Weber, gen mgr; Dave Dunway, progmg dir. Co-owned TV: WVLA(TV) affil

Bayou Vista

KQKI(FM)— Dec 31, 1976: 95.3 mhz; 16.5 kw. 400 ft. TL: N29 29 38 W91 17 41. 128 Pluto St. 70381. Phone: (985) 395-2853. Fax: (985) 395-5094. Web Site: www.kqki.com. Licensee: Teche Broadcasting Corp. Network: ABC. Format: Country. News staff: one; News: 17 hrs wkly. Target aud: 30 plus; general. Spec prog: Fr 4 hrs wkly. ♦ Paul J. Cook, pres & gen mgr; Ernest Dean Polk, stn mgr & news dir; Mac Bruno, progmg dir; Tony Evans, chief of engrg.

Belle Chasse

KMEZ(FM)— March 1990: 102.9 mhz; 4.7 kw. 604 ft. TL: N29 57 14 W89 56 58. 201 St. Charles Ave., Suite 201, New Orleans 70170. Phone: (504) 581-7002. Fax: (504) 566-4857. Web Site: www.oldschool1029.com. Licensee: Citadel Broadcasting Co. Group owner: Citadel Broadcasting Corp. (acq 8-29-03; grpsl). Dow, Lohnes & Albertson. Format: Rhythm & blues, oldies. Target aud: 35-54; female. ♦ Dave Siebert, gen mgr & mktg dir; Lee Killian, gen mgr.

Benton

KSYR(FM)— 1981: 92.1 mhz; 3 kw. 299 ft. TL: N32 39 19 W93 41 38. Stereo. 208 N. Thomas Dr., Shreveport 71107. Phone: (318) 222-3122. Phone: (318) 320-9292. Fax: (318) 459-1493. Licensee: Access. 1 Louisiana Holding Co. LLC. Group owner: Access.1 Communications Corp. (acq 5-5-00; grpsl). Network: ABC. Rep: Allied Radio Partners. Format: Lite rock. Target aud: 35 plus; upper income, upwardly mobile. ♦ Cary D. Camp, pres, gen mgr & stn mgr.

Berwick

KBZE(FM)— July 4, 1990: 105.9 mhz; 3.2 kw. Ant 403 ft. TL: N29 45 27 W91 10 25. Stereo. Box 1560, Morgan City 70381. Secondary address: 1320 Victor II Blvd., Morgan City 70380. Phone: (985) 385-6266. Fax: (985) 385-6268. E-mail: kbze@petronet.com. Web Site: ww.kbze.com. Licensee: HubCast Broadcasting Inc. (acq 6-6-94; $105,500). Network: ABC. Format: Urban adult contemp, relg. News staff: one; News: 10 hrs wkly. Target aud: 24-54; middle to upper income. ♦ Howard Castay Jr., pres & gen mgr; Darlene Castay, opns VP.

Blanchard

KDKS-FM— Oct 19, 1998: 102.1 mhz; 14 kw. 440 ft. TL: N32 35 57 W93 54 01. Box 7197, Shreveport 71107. Secondary address: 208 N. Thomas Dr., Shreveport 71107. Phone: (318) 222-3122. Fax: (318) 459-1493. Web Site: kdkshot102.fm. Licensee: Access. 1 Louisiana Holding Co. LLC. Group owner: Access.1 Communications Corp. (acq 6-30-00; $7.9 million. with KLKL(FM) Minden). Format: Urban contemp. ♦ John Mitchell, pres; Cary Camp, gen mgr; Quenn Echols, progmg dir.

***KOUZ(FM)**—Not on air, target date: unknown: 89.1 mhz; 20 kw vert. Ant 406 ft. TL: N32 18 28 W93 58 34. Box 6506, Shreveport 71136. Phone: (318) 686-1489. Licensee: Missionary Action Projects. ♦ William D. Franks, pres.

Bogalusa

WBOX(AM)— Mar 1, 1954: 920 khz; 1 kw, DA-N. TL: N30 50 29 W89 50 06. Box 280 70429. Secondary address: 22037 Hwy. 436 70427. Phone: (985) 732-4288. Phone: (985) 839-2990. Licensee: Best Country Broadcasting LLC (acq 4-18-02; $150,000. with WBOX-FM Varnado). Format: Country. ♦ Ben R. Strickland, pres & gen mgr.

WBOX-FM—See Varnado

WIKC(AM)— May 15, 1947: 1490 khz; 1 kw-U. TL: N30 47 30 W89 52 47. Box 638 70429. Secondary address: Rio Grande St. 70427. Phone: (985) 732-4190. Fax: (985) 732-7594. E-mail: timbadut@huntnet.net. Licensee: Timberlands Broadcasting Corp. (acq 6-29-82). Network: Network: USA, Reach Satellite. Format: Relg, gospel, news/talk. News: 30 hrs wkly. Target aud: General. ♦ G.S. Adams Jr., pres; Gardner Adams, gen mgr.

Bossier

KRMD(AM)—See Shreveport

KRMD-FM—See Shreveport

Bossier City

KBCL(AM)— September 1957: 1070 khz; 250 w-D. TL: N32 32 14 W93 43 28. 316 Gregg St., Shreveport 71104. Phone: (318) 861-1070. E-mail: kbcl_radio@juno.com. Licensee: Barnabas Center Ministries (acq 8-26-02; donation). Format: Contemp & traditional Christian mus, talk shows.

Boyce

KBCE(FM)—Licensed to Boyce. See Alexandria

Breaux Bridge

KFTE(FM)— May 1, 1993: 96.5 mhz; 22.5 kw. 328 ft. TL: N30 06 09 W91 59 30. Stereo. 1749 Bertrand Dr., Lafayette 70506-2054. Phone: (337) 232-2242. Fax: (337) 234-7360. Web Site: www.planet965.com. Licensee: Regent Broadcasting of Lafayette Inc. Group owner: Regent Communications Inc. (acq 10-17-01; grpsl). Rep: Allied Radio Partners. Wiley, Rein & Fielding. Format: Modern rock, alternative. ♦ Mike Grimsley, gen mgr.

Brusly

KRVE(FM)— Sept 9, 1989: 96.1 mhz; 43 kw. 449 ft. TL: N30 29 34 W91 00 15. Stereo. 5555 Hilton Ave., Suite 500, Baton Rouge 70808. Phone: (225) 231-1860. Fax: (225) 231-1869. E-mail: info@murphysamandjodi.com. Web Site: www.961theriver.com. Licensee: Capstar TX L.P. Group owner: Clear Channel Communications Inc. (acq 8-30-00; grpsl). Format: Lite adult contemp. News staff: 3. Target aud: 25-54; women. ♦ Dick Lewis, gen mgr; Jill Stokold, prom dir & pub affrs dir; Bob Murphy, progmg dir; Jodie Carson, mus dir.

Bunkie

***KAHJ(FM)**—Not on air, target date: unknown: 89.5 mhz; 15 kw. Ant 131 ft. TL: N30 57 11 W92 10 59. Broadcasting for the Challenged Inc., 188 S. Bellevue, Suite 222, Memphis, TN 38104. Phone: (901) 726-8970. Fax: (901) 375-0041. Licensee: Broadcasting for the Challenged Inc. ♦ George S. Flinn Jr., gen mgr.

KEZP(FM)—Licensed to Bunkie. See Alexandria

Buras

***KMRL(FM)**— Apr 22, 1995: 91.9 mhz; 3 kw. Ant 164 ft. TL: N29 20 15 W89 28 46. 3600 Manhattan Blvd., Harvey 70058. Phone: (504) 362-3379. Fax: (504) 362-3379. Licensee: White Dove Fellowship Inc.

Broadcasting & Cable Yearbook 2006

Louisiana

(acq 8-12-02; $25,000). Format: Inspirational gospel. Target aud: General. ◆ Mike Chaucin, gen mgr.

Clinton

WQCK(FM)— Sept 23, 1981: 92.7 mhz; 32 kw. Ant 604 ft. TL: N30 51 03 W91 04 31. Stereo. 5700 West Oaks Blvd., Rocklin, CA 95765. Phone: (916) 251-1600. Fax: (916) 251-1650. Licensee: Educational Media Foundation. (acq 6-13-2005; $3.2 million). Format: Contemp Christian. ◆ Richard Jenkins, pres; Lloyd Parker, gen mgr.

Columbia

KQLQ(FM)— Jan 21, 1980: 103.1 mhz; 25 kw. 348 ft. TL: N32 09 25 W92 10 58. Stereo. 1200 N. 18th St., Suite D, Monroe 71201. Phone: (318) 387-3922. Fax: (318) 322-4585. Web Site: 1031theparty.com. Licensee: Opus Broadcasting Monroe L.L.C. Group owner: Opus Media Partners LLC (acq 7-19-2004; grpsl). Format: Hip hop. ◆ Chris Zimmerman, gen mgr.

Coushatta

KRRP(AM)— May 1981: 950 khz; 500 w-D, 209 w-N, DA-2. TL: N31 56 49 W93 21 13. Stereo. Box 197, Rt. 4, Jordan Ferry Rd. 71019. Phone: (318) 932-6704. Fax: (318) 932-9700. E-mail: krrp@cp-tel.net. Licensee: Roberto Feliz (acq 12-1-2003; $350,000). Network: CBS. Cohn & Marks. Format: ESPN sports. News staff: one; News: 20 hrs wkly. Target aud: 35 plus; mature, educated, affluent listeners. Spec prog: Farm 3 hrs wkly. ◆ Luis Capote, gen mgr.

KSBH(FM)— Nov 15, 1992: 94.9 mhz; 25 kw. 328 ft. TL: N31 51 34 W93 13 00. Stereo. 213 Renee St., Natchitoches 71457. Phone: (318) 354-4000. Fax: (318) 352-9598. Licensee: KSBH L.L.C. (acq 6-3-98; $350,000). Format: Country. News staff: one; News: 2 hrs wkly. Target aud: 18-54. ◆ Rick Beck, gen mgr; John Brewer, opns mgr.

Covington

WASO(AM)— November 1953: 730 khz; 250 w-D, 25 w-N. TL: N30 29 37 W90 08 37. 3313 Kingman St., Metairie 70006. Phone: (504) 888-8255. Fax: (504) 888-8329. Licensee: America First Communications Inc. (acq 7-7-2005). Format: News/talk, sports. Target aud: 25 plus. ◆ Robert Namer, pres & gen mgr.

Crowley

KAJN-FM— Oct 1, 1977: 102.9 mhz; 95 kw. 1,499 ft. TL: N30 02 19 W92 22 15. Stereo. Box 1469 70527-1469. Secondary address: 110 W. 3rd St. 70526. Phone: (337) 783-1560. Fax: (337) 783-1674. Web Site: www.kajn.com. Licensee: Rice Capital Broadcasting. Network: USA. Shaw Pittman. Format: Relg. News staff: one; News: 3 hrs wkly. Target aud: 25-44; female, family oriented. Spec prog: Black 2 hrs wkly. ◆ Annette G. Thompson, VP; Barry D. Thompson, CEO, pres & gen mgr.

KSIG(AM)— May 1947: 1450 khz; 1 kw-U. TL: N30 13 50 W92 21 45. Box 228 70527. Secondary address: 320 N. Parkerson Ave. 70527. Phone: (337) 783-2520. Fax: (337) 783-5744. Licensee: Acadia Broadcast Partners Inc. (acq 12-7-92; $350,000; 1-4-93). Format: Memories, nostalgia. Spec prog: Fr 18 hrs, farm 5 hrs wkly. ◆ Phil Lizotte, pres, gen mgr & stn mgr.

De Quincy

KTSR(FM)— Nov 1, 1985: 92.1 mhz; 13.5 kw. Ant 448 ft. TL: N30 13 24 W93 18 36. Stereo. 900 N. Lakeshore Dr., Lake Charles 70601. Phone: (337) 433-1641. Fax: (337) 433-2999. Licensee: Apex Broadcasting Inc. (group owner; acq 11-6-2001). Format: Urban adult contemp. ◆ Bill May, gen mgr.

De Ridder

*KBAN(FM)— 2001: 91.5 mhz; 14 kw. Ant 361 ft. TL: N30 38 10 W93 02 33. American Family Radio, Box 3206, Tupelo, MS 38503. Secondary address: Quicken Ministries %AFR, 1411 Parish Rd., Lake Charles 70611. Phone: (662) 844-8888. Phone: (337) 217-0252. Fax: (662) 842-6791. Fax: (337) 217-0253. E-mail: comments@myafr.com. Web Site: www.afr.net. Licensee: American Family Association. Group owner: American Family Radio Format: Inspirational Christian. ◆ Marvin Sanders, gen mgr; Elizabeth Arrington, stn mgr.

KDLA(AM)— Nov 11, 1950: 1010 khz; 1 kw-D, 40 w-N. TL: N30 52 43 W93 17 25. 1825 Pelican Rd. 70634. Phone: (337) 462-1000. Fax: (337) 460-9099. Licensee: Christian Broadcasting of De Ridder Inc. (group owner; acq 2-18-98; $150,000). Network: Reach Satellite. Format: Gospel. Target aud: 18-54. ◆ Samuel Williams, gen mgr.

KQLK(FM)— Sept 6, 1991: 97.9 mhz; 50 kw. Ant 492 ft. TL: N30 36 57 W93 13 31. Stereo. 607 Ryan St., Lake Charles 70601. Phone: (337) 312-9790. Fax: (337) 312-9794. Web Site: www.kqlk.com. Licensee: Cumulus Licensing LLC. (group owner; acq 12-6-2004; $3 million. with KAOK(AM) Lake Charles). Format: CHR, top-40. ◆ Crash Kelly, gen mgr.

Delhi

KGGM(FM)— September 1991: 93.5 mhz; 3 kw. 328 ft. TL: N32 37 45 W91 33 13. 1707 Louisa St., Rayville 71269. Secondary address: 1204 Hwy. 80 71232. Phone: (318) 878-8255. Licensee: Kenneth W. Diebel (acq 9-10-2003; $120,000). Format: Southern gospel. ◆ Ken Diebel, pres.

Denham Springs

WSKR(AM)— Apr 15, 1959: 1210 khz; 10 kw-D, 1 kw-N, DA-N. TL: N30 31 20 W90 58 15. Stereo. 5555 Hilton Ave., Suite 500, Baton Rouge 70808. Phone: (225) 231-1860. Fax: (225) 231-1869. Web Site: www.thescore1210.com. Licensee: Capstar TX L.P. Group owner: Clear Channel Communications Inc. (acq 8-30-00; grpsl). Network: Westwood One. Format: Sports. News staff: 2. Target aud: 25-54. ◆ Dick Lewis, gen mgr.

Donaldsonville

KNXX(FM)— 1972: 104.9 mhz; 6 kw. Ant 299 ft. TL: N30 05 57 W91 00 13. 929 B Government St., Baton Rouge 70802. Phone: (225) 388-9898. Fax: (225) 499-9800. Fax: (225) 474-0073. E-mail: help@radiotraks.com. Web Site: www.x-1049.com. Licensee: Guaranty Broadcasting Co. of Baton Rouge LLC. Group owner: Guaranty Broadcasting Co. (acq 2-18-2000; $1.2 million). Format: Alternative, new rock. News: 2 hrs wkly. Target aud: 25-54. ◆ Owen Weber, gen mgr.

Dry Prong

*KVDP(FM)— Aug 13, 1985: 89.1 mhz; 4.5 kw. 295 ft. TL: N31 35 20 W92 30 59. Stereo. Box 249, 160 Bud Walker Rd. 71423. Phone: (318) 899-5837. Fax: (318) 899-7624. E-mail: coyandleta@kvcp.org. Web Site: www.kvdp.org. Licensee: Dry Prong Educational Broadcasting Foundation Inc. (acq 11-24-92; 12-21-92). Network: USA. Format: Relg, educ, Christian. ◆ Coy Edwards, pres; Leta Edwards, gen mgr; Darris Cline, mus dir & engr.

Dubach

KPCH(FM)— June 4, 1984: 97.7 mhz; 50 kw. Ant 464 ft. TL: N32 40 09 W92 37 58. Stereo. Box 430, Ruston 71270. Secondary address: 1319 N. Vienna, Ruston 71270. Phone: (318) 255-5000. Fax: (318) 255-5084. E-mail: thepeach@bayou.com. Web Site: www.thepeach977.com. Licensee: Communications Capital Co. II of Louisiana LLC. Group owner: Communications Capital Managers LLC (acq 5-27-03; $1.5 million). Format: Oldies, sports. ◆ William W. Brown, VP & gen mgr.

Empire

KNOU(FM)— June 2001: 104.5 mhz; 7.8 kw. Ant 850 ft. TL: N29 33 45 W89 49 46. 3501 N. Causeway Blvd., Suite 700, Metairie 70002. Secondary address: 4601 President Dr., Suite 120, Lanham, MD 20706. Phone: (504) 833-4456. Fax: (504) 832-0776. Web Site: www.hot1045no.com. Licensee: On Top Communications of Louisiana LLC. Group owner: On Top Communications Inc. (acq 1-6-03; $8.5 million). Format: Hip hop, rhythm and blues.

Erath

KRKA(FM)— April 1992: 107.9 mhz; 25 kw. 328 ft. TL: N30 02 54 W91 59 49. (CP: 10 kw, ant 469 ft.). Stereo. 1749 Bertrand Dr., Lafayette 70506-2054. Phone: (337) 233-7003. Phone: (337) 233-6000. Fax: (337) 234-7360. Web Site: www.1079ishot.com. Licensee: Regent Broadcasting of Lafayette Inc. Group owner: Regent Communications Inc. (acq 10-17-01; grpsl). Rep: Katz Radio. Format: Rhythmic CHR. News: 25 hrs wkly. Target aud: 12-34. ◆ Mike Grimsley, gen mgr.

Erwinville

*KPAE(FM)— Sept 30, 1985: 91.5 mhz; 5 kw. 167 ft. TL: N30 32 09 W91 24 52. Stereo. 13028 U.S. Hwy. 190 W., Port Allen 70767. Phone: (225) 627-4578. Fax: (225) 627-4970. Web Site: www.soundradio.org. Licensee: Port Allen Educational Broadcasting Foundation. Network: Moody. Format: Relg, educ. Target aud: General. Spec prog: Children 5 hrs, Gospel 15 hrs wkly. ◆ Willie F. Kennedy, pres.

Eunice

KEUN(AM)— October 1952: 1490 khz; 1 kw-U. TL: N30 28 17 W92 24 51. 330 W. Laurel 70535. Phone: (318) 457-3041. Fax: (318) 457-3081. E-mail: karl@keunworldwide.com. Web Site: www.keunworldwide.com. Licensee: Tri-Parish Broadcasting Co. Inc. (acq 5-12-2003; with co-located FM). Format: C&W, news, Fr Cajun. News staff: one; News: 5 hrs wkly. Target aud: 25 plus. Spec prog: Zydeco 6 hrs wkly. ◆ Karl Rene De Rouen, pres, gen mgr, natl sls mgr & prom mgr; Shane Marquardt, progmg dir; Steve Gauthier, opns mgr & news dir; Dave Grachin, chief of engrg.

KEUN-FM— Oct 22, 1981: 105.5 mhz; 1 kw. Ant 485 ft. TL: N30 26 16 W92 26 49. Stereo. Box 1049 70535. E-mail: karl@kjjbfm.com. Format: Real country. News staff: one; News: 10 hrs wkly. Target aud: 25-54. ◆ Johnette LaLonde, chief of engrg.

Farmerville

KWJM(FM)— Apr 19, 1979: 92.7 mhz; 6 kw. 328 ft. TL: N32 48 21 W92 22 24. Stereo. 1133 Old Hwy 15, W. Monroe 71241. Phone: (318) 397-0927. Fax: (318) 397-3132. Licensee: Union Broadcasting Co. Inc. Network: CBS. Format: Adult contemp. News: 18 hrs wkly. Target aud: 24-65; adult audience with incomes to buy. ◆ Don Barron, pres; Chuck Redden, gen mgr.

Ferriday

KFNV-FM— October 1971: 107.1 mhz; 18.5 kw. 233 ft. TL: N31 36 08 W91 32 27. Stereo. Box 1510 71334. Secondary address: 917 S. EEWallace Blvd. 71334. Phone: (318) 757-4200. Fax: (318) 757-7689. E-mail: info@kfnv.com. Web Site: www.kfnv.com. Licensee: Desi-Ray Productions. Group owner: The Radio Group Format: Adult contemp. News: 2 hrs wkly. Target aud: 25-55; baby boomers. Spec prog: Farm 2 hrs, Black 3 hrs, gospel 4 hrs, relg 4 hrs wkly. ◆ Desiree Smith, gen mgr.

Folsom

WJSH(FM)— March 1996: 104.7 mhz; 6 kw. Ant 328 ft. TL: N30 39 55 W90 04 49. 200 E. Thomas St., Hammond 70401. Phone: (985) 542-9844. Fax: (985) 542-9377. Licensee: Southwest Broadcasting. (acq 11-17-2000). Format: Smooth jazz. ◆ Charles Dowdy, gen mgr.

Franklin

KDDK(FM)— May 9, 1975: 105.5 mhz; 3 kw. 300 ft. TL: N29 50 14 W91 32 22. Stereo. 604 St. John St., Lafayette 70582. Phone: (337) 233-4262. Fax: (337) 235-9681. Licensee: Radio & Investments Inc. James Cooke. Format: Urban contemp. ◆ JeNelle Chargois, gen mgr.

KFRA(AM)— June 4, 1961: 1390 khz; 500 w-D. TL: N29 50 14 W91 32 22. Stereo. Box 27224, Richmond, VA 23261. Licensee: Radio & Investments Inc. (acq 4-15-97; with co-located FM). ◆ Kenneth R. Noble II, pres; Roger Robinson, gen mgr.

Franklinton

WOMN(AM)— Dec 5, 1966: 1110 khz; 1 kw-D. TL: N30 51 34 W90 09 57. Box 604 70438. Phone: (985) 839-4110. Fax: (985) 839-4800. E-mail: wfcg@huntnet.net. Licensee: Pittman Broadcasting Services LLC (group owner; acq 6-4-02; with co-located FM). Format: Diversified. Target aud: General. Spec prog: Black 5 hrs, gospel 10 hrs wkly. ◆ J.A. Gatewood, pres, gen sls mgr & chief of engrg; Vickie DeCarlo, natl sls mgr, prom dir, adv dir & mus dir.

WUUU(FM)— Co-owned with WOMN(AM). Mar 3, 1997: 98.9 mhz; 6 kw. 108 ft. TL: N30 51 34 W90 09 57. Format: C&W. ◆ Vickie DeCarlo, gen sls mgr & adv mgr; Amanda Stafford, progmg dir.

Broadcasting & Cable Yearbook 2006

Galliano

WTIX-FM—Licensed to Galliano. See Golden Meadow

Garyville

WCKW(AM)— Dec 22, 1970: 1010 khz; 500 w-D, 42 w-N. TL: N30 04 35 W90 37 17. Stereo. 5284 W. Airwine Hwy. 70051. Secondary address: Box 683, Mandeville 70470. Phone: (985) 535-2424. Fax: (985) 535-5706. E-mail: wckwam@wckw.com. Web Site: www.wckw.com/wckwam.htm. Licensee: River Parish Radio Inc. Format: Gospel, relg. Target aud: 18-54. ◆ Sidney J. Levet IV, pres; Darnetta Nelson, stn mgr.

Gibsland

KBEF(FM)— May 23, 2001: 104.5 mhz; 6 kw. Ant 328 ft. TL: N32 31 59 W93 11 34. Box 1240, Minden 71055. Phone: (318) 377-1240. Fax: (318) 377-4619. E-mail: staff@kbef.com. Web Site: www.kbef.com. Licensee: Amistad Communications Inc. (acq 7-12-2000; $375,000. for CP with KASO(AM) Minden). Format: Contemp Christian. ◆ Fred Caldwell, gen mgr; Cindy Wilson, opns mgr; Mike Griffith, gen sls mgr.

Golden Meadow

KLEB(AM)— May 13, 1963: 1600 khz; 5 kw-D, 250 w-N. TL: N29 22 41 W90 15 50. Drawer 1350, Larose 70373. Secondary address: 11603 Hwy. 308 70373. Phone: (985) 798-7792. Fax: (985) 798-7793. E-mail: klrz@mobiletel.com. Web Site: www.klrzfm.com. Licensee: Coastal Broadcasting of Larose Inc. (acq 1999; $250,000). Format: C&W, Fr, Oldies. Target aud: 25 plus; general. Spec prog: Cajun Fr mus & language 13 hrs wkly. ◆ Jerry J. Gisclair, pres & gen mgr; Andrea Galjour, opns mgr.

WTIX-FM—(Galliano). Nov 16, 1975: 94.3 mhz; 100 kw. 982 ft. TL: N29 33 46 W89 49 46. 3rd Fl., 4539 I-10 Service Rd., Metairie 70006. Phone: (504) 454-9000. Fax: (504) 454-9506. E-mail: mcostello@wtixfm.com. Web Site: wtixfm.com. Licensee: Fleur de Lis Broadcasting Inc. (acq 6-8-95; $600,000). Network: ABC. Reddy, Begley & McCormick. Format: Oldies. News: 4 hrs wkly. Target aud: 25-54. ◆ George Buck, pres; Michael Costello, exec VP & gen mgr.

Grambling

*KGRM(FM)— January 1974: 91.5 mhz; 50 kw. 492 ft. TL: N32 30 56 W92 43 27. Stereo. Box K 71245. Secondary address: Dunbar Hall, Room 220, Grambling State Univ. 71245. Phone: (318) 274-3244. Fax: (318) 274-3245. E-mail: evansjb@gram.edu. Licensee: Grambling State University. Format: Urban var, sports, talk, news. Target aud: Black community. Spec prog: Gospel 17 hrs jazz 15 hrs wkly. ◆ Joyce Evans, opns mgr.

Gretna

KGLA(AM)— Jan 6, 1969: 1540 khz; 1 kw-D. TL: N29 53 27 W90 05 05. Box 50790, New Orleans 70150-0790. Phone: (504) 347-8492. Fax: (504) 340-4737. E-mail: sales@tropical1540.com. Web Site: www.tropical1540.com. Licensee: Crocodile Broadcasting Corp. (acq 1-13-97). Network: UPI. Rep: Caballero. Format: Sp. ◆ Ernesto Schweikert, gen mgr.

KKNO(AM)— Sept 10, 1989: 750 khz; 250 w-D, DA. TL: N29 53 15 W90 05 03. 980 Avenue A, Marrero 70072. Phone: (504) 347-7775. Fax: (504) 347-7440. E-mail: kkno750am@aol.com. Licensee: Robert C. Blakes Enterprises Inc. (acq 6-24-93; $275,000; 7-12-93). Format: Christian gospel, relg. News: 10 hrs wkly. Target aud: General. ◆ Robert C. Blakes Sr., CEO & pres; Lois R. Blakes, exec VP & gen mgr; Stacey Blakes, opns mgr; John Poteate, gen sls mgr; Vernitra Blakes, prom dir; Devron J. Wilson, progmg dir; Olga Johnson, news dir; Eugene Cotton III, pub affrs dir; Ralph Hartwell, chief of engrg.

Hammond

*KSLU(FM)— Nov 11, 1974: 90.9 mhz; 3 kw. 143 ft. TL: N30 30 53 W90 27 59. Stereo. D. Vickers Hall Rm 112, SLU Box 10783 70402. Phone: (985) 549-2330. Phone: (985) 549-5758. Fax: (985) 549-3960. E-mail: kslu@selu.edu. Web Site: www.selu.edu/kslu. Licensee: Southeastern Louisiana University. Network: PRI. Format: Triple A. News staff: one; News: 30 hrs wkly. Target aud: General. Spec prog: Americana 10 hrs, blues 6 hrs wkly. ◆ Todd Delaney, gen mgr.

WCDV(FM)— Apr 3, 1965: 103.3 mhz; 100 kw. 1,004 ft. TL: N30 24 06 W90 50 43. Stereo. 650 Wooddale Blvd., Baton Rouge 70806-2930. Phone: (225) 926-1106. Fax: (225) 922-7019. Web Site: www.b103.fm. Licensee: Citadel Broadcasting Co. Group owner: Citadel Broadcasting Corp. (acq 1999; grpsl). Network: ABC. Rep: McGavren Guild. Format: Soft adult contemp. News staff: one; News: 3 hrs wkly. Target aud: 25-54. Spec prog: Cajun 3 hrs, Fr 4 hrs wkly. ◆ Ed Turner, stn mgr; Rebecca Breeding, gen mgr & sls dir.

WDVW(FM)—La Place

WFPR(AM)— Nov 15, 1947: 1400 khz; 1 kw-U. TL: N30 30 31 W90 30 18. 200 E. Thomas 70401. Phone: (504) 542-1400. Phone: (504) 345-0060. Fax: (504) 542-9377. E-mail: guaranty@i-55.com. Licensee: North Shore Broadcasting Co. Inc. (acq 12-4-2003; $1.85 million. with co-located FM). Network: CBS. Format: Classic hits, country. News staff: one; News: 7 hrs wkly. Target aud: 35-64. Spec prog: Farm one hr, gospel 12 hrs wkly. ◆ Wayne Dowdy, pres; Forrest Mills, CFO; Nanette C. Guerin, gen mgr & gen sls mgr; Ken Benitez, news dir; Bo Hoover, chief of engrg.

WHMD(FM)—Co-owned with WFPR(AM). Aug 26, 1974: 107.1 mhz; 6 kw. Ant 328 ft. TL: N30 25 32 W90 17 01. Stereo. Format: Hot country. ◆ Chris Powers, mus dir.

Haughton

KBTT(FM)— 1993: 103.7 mhz; 6 kw. 328 ft. TL: N32 31 20 W93 30 05. Box 7197, Shreveport 71107. Secondary address: 208 N. Thomas Dr., Shreveport 71107. Phone: (318) 222-3122. Fax: (318) 459-1493. Licensee: Access. 1 Louisiana Holding Co. LLC. Group owner: Access.1 Communications Corp. (acq 5-10-00; grpsl). Rep: Allied Radio Partners. Format: Hip hop. ◆ Cary D. Camp, gen mgr.

Homer

KYLA(FM)— March 1998: 106.7 mhz; 50 kw. 492 ft. TL: N32 37 03 W93 14 36. Box 7197, Shreveport 71107. Secondary address: 208 N. Thomas Dr., Shreveport 71107. Phone: (318) 222-3122. Fax: (318) 459-1493. Web Site: www.kyla106.fm. Licensee: Alfred T. Moore Jr. (acq 6-4-01). Format: Classic country. ◆ Alfred T. Moore Jr., exec VP & stn mgr; Cary D. Camp, gen mgr.

Houma

KCIL(FM)—Listing follows KJIN(AM).

KHEV(FM)— Nov 15, 1968: 104.1 mhz; 100 kw. Ant 1,945 ft. TL: N29 57 13 W90 43 25. Stereo. 929 Howard Ave., New Orleans 70113. Phone: (504) 260-1041. Fax: (504) 679-7358. Web Site: www.kissneworleans.com. Licensee: Clear Channel Broadcasting Licenses Inc. Group owner: Clear Channel Communications Inc. (acq 2-97; $6.75 million). Rep: Clear Channel. Format: CHR. News staff: one; News: 2 hrs wkly. Target aud: 25-54. ◆ Muriac Fuentes, pres & gen mgr.

KJIN(AM)— Apr 1, 1946: 1490 khz; 1 kw-U. TL: N29 34 14 W90 43 42. Box 2068 70361. Secondary address: 120 Prevost Dr. 70361. Phone: (985) 851-1020. Phone: (985) 851-1025. Fax: (985) 872-4403. Licensee: Guaranty Broadcasting Co. of Houma LLC. Network: ABC. Rep: Roslin. Wiley, Rein & Fielding. Format: MOR, nostalgia. News staff: one; News: 3 hrs wkly. Target aud: 35 plus. Spec prog: Sunday gospel, Braves baseball, high school football. ◆ George Foster, CEO Don Nelson, exec VP; Eric Gill, opns dir & progmg dir; Melanie Hotard, gen mgr & gen sls mgr; "Dr." Don, prom dir; Captain Glen, news dir & pub affrs dir; Bo Hoover, chief of engrg.

KCIL(FM)—Co-owned with KJIN(AM). Dec 31, 1965: 107.5 mhz; 100 kw. Ant 649 ft. TL: N29 26 48 W90 44 34. (CP: 28.8 kw). Stereo. Phone: (985) 851-1075. Web Site: www.1075kcil.net. Format: Country. News staff: one; News: 2 hrs wkly. Target aud: Adults; 25-54. ◆ Eric Gill, mus dir.

Jackson

WNXX(FM)— Oct 17, 2001: 104.5 mhz; 6 kw. 328 ft. TL: N30 43 07 W91 14 26. Stereo. Box 2231, Baton Rouge 70821. Secondary address: 929-B Government St., Baton Rouge 70802. Phone: (225) 388-9898. Fax: (225) 344-3077. E-mail: owen.webe@gbcradio.com. Licensee: Guaranty Broadcasting Co. of Baton Rouge LLC. Group owner: Guaranty Broadcasting Co. (acq 10-5-00; $1.044 million). Network: Westwood One. Rep: McGavren Guild. Wiley, Rein & Fielding. Format: Rock/AOR, alternative. Target aud: 18-34; general. ◆ George A. Foster Jr., chmn; Bridger Eglin, pres & gen mgr; Owen Weber, gen mgr.

Jena

*KAYT(FM)— Jan 1, 2001: 88.1 mhz; 15.5 kw horiz, 70 kw vert. 1,007 ft. TL: N31 33 54 W92 33 00. 5003 Masonic Dr., Suite 113, Alexandria 71301. Phone: (318) 484-2500. Fax: (318) 487-0909. Licensee: Black Media Works Inc. (group owner). Format: Relg. ◆ Raymond Kassis, gen mgr; Jocelyn Jacob, stn mgr & opns mgr; Darrell Ranel, progmg dir.

KJNA-FM— November 1976: 102.7 mhz; 6 kw. 298 ft. TL: N31 41 51 W92 05 43. Stereo. Box 2750 71342. Secondary address: 1791 N. 2nd St. 71342. Phone: (318) 992-4155. Fax: (318) 992-4479. Licensee: Little River Radio Co. Format: C&W. News staff: one; News: 20 hrs wkly. Target aud: 25-54. Spec prog: Farm 3 hrs wkly. ◆ Larry Evans, gen mgr.

Jennings

KHLA(FM)—Listing follows KJEF(AM).

KJEF(AM)— November 1950: 1290 khz; 1 kw-U. TL: N30 12 38 W92 39 55. Stereo. Drawer 1008, 1215 S. Lake Arthur Ave. 70546. Phone: (337) 824-2934. Fax: (337) 824-1384. E-mail: kjef@cfweb.net. Web Site: www.kjef.com. Licensee: Apex Broadcasting Inc. (group owner; acq 9-19-00; $864,800. with co-located FM). Format: C&W. Target aud: General. Spec prog: Fr 12 hrs, gospel 6 hrs wkly. ◆ Sarah Cormier, stn mgr.

KHLA(FM)—Co-owned with KJEF(AM). January 1963: 92.9 mhz; 33 kw. 600 ft. TL: N30 00 31 W92 46 47. Stereo. Web Site: www.la929.com. ◆ Gary Shannon, progmg dir.

Jonesboro

*KTOC-FM— Oct 1, 1967: 104.9 mhz; 25 kw. Ant 236 ft. TL: N32 13 28 W92 43 27. Stereo. Box 262550, Baton Rouge 70810. Phone: (225) 768-3102. Web Site: www.jsm.org/htm/radio.htm. Licensee: Family Worship Center Church Inc. (acq 9-25-2002; $200,000. with co-located AM). Format: Relg. ◆ Jimmy Swaggart, pres.

Jonesville

KTGV(FM)— 2001: 105.1 mhz; 6 kw. Ant 315 ft. TL: N31 36 21 W91 50 06. Box 768, Natchez, MS 39121. Secondary address: 2 Oferrall St., Natchez 39120-3000. Phone: (601) 442-4895. Fax: (601) 446-8260. Licensee: First Natchez Corp. Group owner: First Natchez Radio Group (acq 8-30-99; $150,000). Format: Urban contemp. ◆ Margaret Perkins, gen mgr; Mickey Alexander, progmg dir; Keith Sanders, chief of engrg.

Louisiana   Directory of Radio

Kaplan

*KCKR(FM)—Not on air, target date: unknown: 91.9 mhz; 12.5 kw. Ant 464 ft. TL: N30 17 05 W92 04 03. Box 563, Tanner, AL 35671-0563. Phone: (256) 345-2478. Licensee: North Alabama Educational Foundation. ♦ Richard W. Dabney, pres.

KMDL(FM)— Aug 1, 1981: 97.3 mhz; 42 kw. 535 ft. TL: N30 02 54 W91 59 49. Stereo. 1749 Bertrand Dr., Lafayette 70506-2054. Phone: (337) 232-2242. Phone: (337) 261-9797. Fax: (337) 234-7360. Web Site: www.973thedawg.com. Licensee: Regent Broadcasting of Lafayette Inc. Group owner: Regent Communications Inc. (acq 10-17-01; grpsl). Network: AP Radio. Rep: Allied Radio Partners. Wiley, Rein & Fielding. Format: Classic country. News: 7 hrs wkly. Target aud: 25-54. ♦ Mike Grimsley, gen mgr.

Kenner

WKBU(FM)— Sept 8, 1970: 105.3 mhz; 96 kw. Ant 1,004 ft. TL: N29 58 57 W89 57 09. Stereo. 1450 Poydras, Suite 500, New Orleans 70112. Phone: (504) 593-6376. Fax: (504) 593-2285. Web Site: www.1053thezone.com. Licensee: Entercom New Orleans License LLC. Group owner: Entercom Communications Corp. (acq 12-13-99; grpsl). Format: Hot adult contemp. ♦ Phil Hoover, gen mgr; Dan Harrison, progmg dir & chief of engrg.

Kentwood

WEMX(FM)— Dec 14, 1967: 94.1 mhz; 100 kw. 981 ft. TL: N30 51 18 W90 39 59. Stereo. 650 Wooddale Blvd., Baton Rouge 70806. Phone: (225) 926-1106. Fax: (225) 922-7019. E-mail: wemx.fm@citcomm.com. Web Site: www.max94one.com. Licensee: Citadel Broadcasting Co. Group owner: Citadel Broadcasting Corp. (acq 1-14-99; grpsl). Format: Rap, hip hop. ♦ Rebecca Breeding, gen mgr; Jeff Jarnigan, opns mgr.

La Place

WDVW(FM)— Jan 10, 1966: 92.3 mhz; 100 kw. Ant 1,945 ft. TL: N29 57 10 W90 43 26. Stereo. 201 St. Charles Ave., Suite 201, New Orleans 70170. Phone: (504) 581-7002. Fax: (504) 566-4857. Licensee: Citadel Broadcasting Co. Group owner: Citadel Broadcasting Corp. (acq 1-30-2004; $14.25 million). Rep: Christal. Christal Radio Format: Adult contemp. ♦ Dave Siebert, gen mgr.

Lacombe

WOPR(FM)— March 1996: 94.7 mhz; 5.3 kw horiz, 5.2 kw vert. Ant 348 ft. TL: N30 15 08 W89 45 46. 201 St. Charles Ave., Suite 201, New Orleans 70170. Phone: (504) 581-7002. Fax: (504) 566-4857. Web Site: www.praise949fm.com. Licensee: Southeastern Broadcasting Inc. (group owner; (acq 4-26-2005; $4.5 million. with WPRF(FM) Reserve). Format: Gospel. News staff: one; News: 2 hrs wkly. Target aud: 25-54; general. ♦ Dave Siebert, gen mgr & sls dir.

Lafayette

KFXZ(AM)— Nov 15, 1960: 1520 khz; 10 kw-D, 500 w-N, DA-N. TL: N30 16 51 W92 00 53. Stereo. 3225 Ambassador Caffery Pkwy. 70506. Phone: (337) 993-5500. Fax: (337) 993-5510. Web Site: www.kfxz.com. Licensee: Pittman Broadcasting Services LLC (group owner; acq 1-28-2004; grpsl). Format: Gospel. ♦ Michael Schutta, gen mgr.

*KIKL(FM)— Feb 7, 1988: 90.9 mhz; 6 kw. Ant 476 ft. TL: N30 17 08 W92 04 03. Stereo. 5700 W. Oaks Blvd., Rocklin, CA 95765. Phone: (916) 251-1600. Fax: (916) 251-1650. Licensee: Educational Media Foundation. Group owner: EMF Broadcasting (acq 4-25-2005; $1.5 million). Shaw Pittman LLP. Format: Christian. ♦ Lloyd Parker, gen mgr & stn mgr.

KJCB(AM)— Apr 9, 1982: 770 khz; 1 kw-D, 500 w-N, DA-N. TL: N30 17 55 W91 59 30. Stereo. 413 Jefferson St. 70501. Phone: (337) 233-4262. Fax: (337) 235-9681. Web Site: www.blackaction.net/kjcb.html. Licensee: R & M Broadcasting Inc. (acq 11-16-92; $100,000; 12-14-92). Network: ABC Information & Entertainment. Format: Urban contemp. Target aud: 25-54. Spec prog: Gospel, jazz. ♦ JeNelle Chargois, gen mgr.

KPEL(AM)— Jan 2, 1950: 1420 khz; 1 kw-D, 750 w-N, DA-N. TL: N30 16 38 W92 20 03 51. KPEL AM FM, 1749 Bertrand Dr. 70506. Phone: (337) 233-7003. Phone: (337) 233-6000. Fax: (337) 234-7360. Web Site: www.weareradio.com. Licensee: Regent Broadcasting of Lafayette Inc. Group owner: Regent Communications Inc. (acq 10-17-01; grpsl). Network: Network: ABC Information & Entertainment, ABC News/Talk. Rep: Christal. Format: Sports. Target aud: 35-54; male. ♦ Tom Galloway, CEO; Mike Grimsley, gen mgr; Michele Ezell, opns mgr; Bonnie Roberts, gen sls mgr; Ray Sutley, progmg dir; Joe Langlinais, news dir; Tony L. Evans, chief of engrg.

KTDY(FM)—Co-owned with KPEL(AM). Sept 15, 1966: 99.9 mhz; 100 kw. 984 ft. TL: N30 12 04 W91 46 33. Stereo. Web Site: www.weareradio.com. Format: Adult contemp. Target aud: 25-54; female. ♦ Mike Grinsley, gen sls mgr.

KRRQ(FM)— 1996: 95.5 mhz; 50 kw. 443 ft. TL: N30 21 08 W92 10 51. 3225 Ambassador Caffery Pkwy. 70506. Phone: (337) 981-0106. E-mail: krrq@krrq.com. Web Site: www.krrq.com. Licensee: Citadel Broadcasting Co. Group owner: Citadel Broadcasting Corp. (acq 1-14-99; grpsl). Format: Urban contemp/hip hop. ♦ Mary Galyean, gen mgr.

*KRVS(FM)— 1962: 88.7 mhz; 100 kw. 449 ft. TL: N30 15 25 W92 09 38. Stereo. UL Box 42171,, Hebrard Blvd. 70504-2171. Phone: (337) 482-5787. Fax: (337) 482-6101. E-mail: admin@krvs.org. Web Site: www.krvs.org. Licensee: University of Southwestern Louisiana. Network: NPR. Format: Cajun, Louisiana music. Target aud: General. ♦ Dave Spizale, gen mgr; James Herbert, opns mgr; Judith Meriwether, prom mgr.

KSMB(FM)— 1964: 94.5 mhz; 100 kw. Ant 1,079 ft. TL: N30 21 44 W92 12 53. Stereo. Box 3345 70502. Secondary address: 202 Galbert Rd. 70506. Phone: (337) 232-1311. Fax: (337) 233-3779. Web Site: www.ksmb.com. Licensee: Citadel Broadcasting Co. Group owner: Citadel Broadcasting Corp. (acq 4-26-01; grpsl). Format: Top-40, CHR. Target aud: 18-49; active on-the-go adults. ♦ Mary Galyean, gen mgr.

KVOL(AM)— May 18, 1935: 1330 khz; 5 kw-D, 1 kw-N, DA-2. TL: N30 14 29 W92 03 31. 3225 Ambassador Caffery Pkwy. 70506. Phone: (337) 233-1330. Phone: (337) 993-5510. Fax: (337) 233-3779. Web Site: www.kvolradio.com. Licensee: Pittman Broadcasting Services LLC (group owner; acq 1-28-2004; grpsl). Network: Westwood One. Rep: Allied Radio Partners. Format: Sports, talk. Target aud: 25-54; middle & upper income. ♦ Michael Schutta, gen mgr.

KXKC(FM)—See New Iberia

Lake Arthur

KJMH(FM)— Aug 1, 1998: 107.5 mhz; 50 kw. Ant 462 ft. TL: N30 12 07 W92 56 47. 900 North Lakeshore Dr., Lake Charles 70601. Phone: (337) 433-1641. Fax: (337) 433-2999. Web Site: www.107jamz.com. Licensee: Apex Broadcasting Inc. (group owner; acq 9-17-97; $74,300). Rep: Christal. Format: Hip Hop, rhythm and blues. News staff: one. Target aud: 25-54. ♦ Billy May, gen mgr.

Lake Charles

KAOK(AM)— May 10, 1947: 1400 khz; 1 kw-U. TL: N30 12 35 W93 12 43. 607 Ryan St. 70601. Phone: (337) 436-7541. Fax: (337) 436-7278. E-mail: programming@kaok.com. Web Site: www.kaok.com. Licensee: Cumulus Licensing LLC. Group owner: Pittman Broadcasting Services LLC (acq 12-6-2004; $3 million. with KQLK(FM) De Ridder). Network: Network: CBS, ABC Information & Entertainment. Format: News/talk, info & sports. News staff: one; News: 168 hrs wkly. Target aud: 24 plus; baby boomers. ♦ Lewis W. Dickey Jr., pres; Michael Schutta, gen mgr; Larry LeBlanc, stn mgr & opns mgr.

KBIU(FM)— Dec 1, 1976: 103.3 mhz; 35 kw. Ant 479 ft. TL: N30 14 41 W93 20 37. Stereo. 425 Broad St., Lakes Charles 70601. Phone: (337) 439-3300. Fax: (337) 433-7701. E-mail: b104@kbiu.com. Web Site: www.kbiu.com. Licensee: Cumulus Licensing Corp. Group owner: Cumulus Media Inc. (acq 12-17-98; grpsl). Rep: Bryan Cave. Format: Adult contemp. Target aud: 18-35. ♦ Jim Ray, gen mgr; Don Kellogg, opns mgr & progmg dir; Steven Hickox, gen sls mgr; Steve Hickox, adv mgr; Ron Alexander, news dir; Richard Rhodes, chief of engrg.

KXZZ(AM)—Co-owned with KBIU-FM. 1947: 1580 khz; 1 kw-U, DA-N. TL: N30 15 28 W93 11 55. Stereo. Web Site: www.cumulus.com. Network: American Urban. Format: Gospel. Target aud: 18-49.

KEZM(AM)—See Sulphur

KKGB(AM)—See Sulphur

KLCL(AM)—Listing follows KNGT(FM).

KNGT(FM)— Nov 8, 1965: 99.5 mhz; 100 kw. 984 ft. TL: N30 23 59 W93 00 10. Stereo. 900 N. Lake Shore Dr. 70601. Phone: (337) 433-1641. Fax: (337) 433-2999. Web Site: www.kbig99.com. Licensee: Apex Broadcasting Inc. (group owner; acq 7-26-2000; grpsl). Rep: Christal. Format: Country. Target aud: 25-54. ♦ Bill May, pres & gen mgr.

KLCL(AM)—Co-owned with KNGT(FM). May 12, 1935: 1470 khz; 5 kw-D, 500 w-N. TL: N30 15 31 W93 16 07. Web Site: www.la99.com. Format: News/talk, sports. Target aud: 18-64. Spec prog: Relg 2 hrs wkly.

*KOJO(FM)— 1990: 91.1 mhz; 4 kw horiz, 14 kw vert. Ant 387 ft. TL: N30 12 07 W92 56 47. Radio Maria Inc., 601 Washington St., Alexandria 71301. Phone: (318) 561-6145. Fax: (318) 449-9954. E-mail: info.usa@radiomaria.org. Web Site: www.radiomaria.us. Licensee: Radio Maria Inc. (group owner; acq 10-13-99). Format: Christian. Target aud: General; Christians seeking training & encouragement through Bible teaching programs. ♦ Father Duane Stenzel, gen mgr & mus dir; Danny Brou, chief of engrg.

KYKZ(FM)— January 1976: 96.1 mhz; 97 kw. 1,204 ft. TL: N30 17 26 W93 34 35. Stereo. 425 Broad St. 70601. Phone: (337) 439-3300. Fax: (337) 436-7278. Fax: (337) 433-7701. E-mail: eric@kykz.com. Web Site: www.kykz.com. Licensee: Cumulus Licensing Corp. Group owner: Cumulus Media Inc. (acq 12-17-98; grpsl). Network: ABC Information & Entertainment. Format: Modern country. News staff: 3; News: 8 hrs wkly. Target aud: General. ♦ Bill Bungerroth, pres; Susan Seifert, gen mgr & stn mgr.

*KYLC(FM)— 2001: 90.3 mhz; 80 kw vert. 469 ft. TL: N30 38 10 W93 02 33. American Family Radio, Box 3206, Tupelo, MS 38803. Phone: (662) 844-8888. Fax: (662) 842-6791. E-mail: comments@afr.net. Web Site: www.afr.net. Licensee: American Family Association. Group owner: American Family Radio (acq 3-14-01). Format: Inspirational Christian. ♦ Marvin Sanders, gen mgr.

Lake Providence

KLPL(AM)— June 27, 1957: . Stn currently dark 1050 khz; 250 w-D, 22 w-N. TL: N32 48 59 W91 12 22. Willis Broadcasting Corp., 645 Church St., Suite 400, Norfolk, VA 23510. Phone: (757) 622-4600. Fax: (757) 624-6515. Licensee: Willis Broadcasting Corp. (group owner; acq 4-21-98; $120,000. with co-located FM). Target aud: General.

KLPL-FM— Jan 28, 1975: . Stn currently dark 92.7 mhz; 3 kw. Ant 154 ft. TL: N32 48 59 W91 12 22. Stereo.

Larose

KLRZ(FM)— Mar 29, 1993: 100.3 mhz; 50 kw. 328 ft. TL: N29 32 46 W90 24 35. 11603 Hwy. 308 70373. Phone: (985) 798-7792. Fax: (985) 798-7793. E-mail: klrz@mobiletel.com. Web Site: www.klrzfm.com. Licensee: Citadel Broadcasting Co. (acq 7-28-2005; $6.5 million). Network: Westwood One. Format: All Louisiana all the time. News staff: one; News: 22 hrs wkly. Target aud: 25-54; professionals. ♦ Jerry Gisclair, pres, gen mgr & chief of engrg.

Leesville

KJAE(FM)—Listing follows KLLA(AM).

KLLA(AM)— September 1956: 1570 khz; 1 kw-D. TL: N31 06 24 W93 17 38. Box 1323 71446. Secondary address: 101 Lees Ln. 71446. Phone: (337) 239-3402. Fax: (337) 238-9283. Web Site: www.kjae935.com. Licensee: Pene Broadcasting Co. (acq 12-1-76). Format: Oldies. ♦ Penny Scogin, pres & gen mgr.

KJAE(FM)—Co-owned with KLLA(AM). October 1979: 93.5 mhz; 7.5 kw. 328 ft. TL: N31 08 28 W93 17 44. Stereo. Format: C&W.

KVVP(FM)— Jan 20, 1977: 105.7 mhz; 25 kw. 400 ft. TL: N31 00 17 W93 16 40. Stereo. 168 KVVP Dr. 71446. Phone: (337) 537-5887.

Developers & Brokers of Radio Properties

contact American Media Services at our suite:
Philadelphia Marriott Downtown
215-625-2900
843-972-2200
americanmediaservices.com
Charleston, SC
Dallas, TX · Chicago, Il · Austin, TX

American Media Services, LLC

Fax: (337) 537-4152. E-mail: kvvp@kvvp.com. Web Site: www.kvvp.com. Licensee: Stannard Broadcasting Co. Inc. James Popham. Format: New country. News staff: one; News: 15 hrs wkly. Target aud: 18-54; adults with spending power. Spec prog: Relg 9 hrs wkly. ◆John S. Stannard, pres; Doug Stannard, gen mgr & progmg dir; Robin Brians, prom dir; Jim Gore, mus dir; James Alexander, news dir.

Mamou

KBON(FM)— June 1997: 101.1 mhz; 25 kw. Ant 328 ft. TL: N30 39 33 W92 19 00. 109 S. 2nd St., Eunice 70535. Phone: (337) 546-0007. Fax: (337) 546-0097. E-mail: 101.1@kbon.com. Web Site: www.kbon.com. Licensee: Rose Ann Marx. (acq 9-8-98; $70,000). Format: Var. ◆Paul Marx, gen mgr.

Mansfield

KJVC(FM)— September 1976: 92.7 mhz; 3 kw. 299 ft. TL: N32 01 18 W93 44 18. Stereo. Box 268 71052. Phone: (318) 697-4000. Fax: (318) 697-4004. E-mail: korifm@wnonline.net. Web Site: www.korifm.com. Licensee: Metropolitan Radio Group Inc. (group owner; acq 10-97; $85,000). Format: Southern gospel. ◆Gene Fields, gen mgr.

*KMSL(FM)—Not on air, target date: unknown: 91.7 mhz; 12 kw vert. Ant 328 ft. TL: N32 10 57 W93 55 01. Box 2440, Tupelo, MS 38803-2440. Phone: (662) 844-8888. Fax: (662) 842-6791. Web Site: www.afr.net. Licensee: American Family Association. (acq 5-13-2005; $10 for CP). ◆Marvin Sanders, gen mgr.

KORI(FM)— May 1994: 104.7 mhz; 25 kw. 328 ft. TL: N31 57 49 W93 53 58. Box 700, Logansport 71049. Phone: (318) 697-4000. Fax: (318) 697-4004. E-mail: korifm@wnonline.net. Web Site: www.korifm.com. Licensee: Metropolitan Radio Group Inc. (group owner; acq 1-30-98; $390,250). Format: Country. ◆Gene Fields, gen mgr & opns dir.

Mansura

KZLG(FM)— July 2000: 95.9 mhz; 6 kw. 328 ft. Box 516, Moreauville 71355. Secondary address: 10586 Hwy. 1, Moreauville 71355. Phone: (318) 985-3070. Fax: (318) 985-2995. E-mail: klil@kricket.net. Licensee: Amy M. Coco. Format: Adult Top 40. ◆Janice Armond, gen mgr.

Many

*KAVK(FM)— June 1998: 89.7 mhz; 1 kw. 430 ft. TL: N31 32 06 W93 25 21. Box 3206, American Family Radio, Tupelo, MS 38803. Phone: (662) 844-8888. Fax: (662) 842-6791. E-mail: comments@afr.net. Web Site: www.afr.net. Licensee: American Family Radio. Group owner: American Family Radio Format: Inspirational Christian. ◆Marvin Sanders, gen mgr.

KWLA(AM)— August 1962: 1400 khz; 1 kw-U. TL: N31 34 30 W93 29 47. Stereo. 605 San Antonio 71449. Phone: (318) 256-5177. Licensee: Baldridge-Dumas Communications Inc. (group owner; acq 1-10-00; with co-located FM). Format: Talk. News: 5 hrs wkly. Target aud: General; 38 plus. Spec prog: Gospel 8 hrs wkly. ◆Rhonda Benson, gen mgr, sls VP & adv VP; Tommy O'Con, news dir; Kenny Carter, chief of engrg.

KWLV(FM)—Co-owned with KWLA(AM). Nov 12, 1977: 107.1 mhz; 25 kw. 253 ft. TL: N31 36 27 W93 24 05. Phone: (318) 256-5924. Fax: (318) 256-0950. Format: Country. Target aud: 20 plus.

Marksville

KAPB-FM— Aug 14, 1971: 97.7 mhz; 6 kw. 328 ft. TL: N31 07 27 W92 04 40. Stereo. 520 Chester 71351. Phone: (318) 253-5272. Fax: (318) 253-5262. E-mail: kapbfm@yahoo.com. Licensee: Three Rivers Radio Co. Group owner: The Radio Group Network: CNN Max. Format: Classic hit country. ◆Pamela Couvillion, gen mgr; Larry Young, news dir & chief of engrg.

Maurice

KKSJ(FM)— June 13, 1985: 106.3 mhz; 1.3 kw. Ant 495 ft. TL: N30 04 16 W92 11 53. Stereo. 3225 Ambassador Caffery Pkwy., Lafayette 70506. Phone: (337) 993-5500. Fax: (337) 993-5510. Licensee: Pittman Broadcasting Services LLC (group owner; acq 1-28-2004; grpsl). Format: Smooth jazz. ◆Michael Schutta, gen mgr.

Minden

KASO(AM)— Apr 1, 1952: 1240 khz; 1 kw-U. TL: N32 37 50 W93 16 56. Box 1240 71058. Secondary address: 410 Lakeshore Dr. 71055. Phone: (318) 377-1240. Fax: (318) 377-4619. E-mail: kasoradio@yahoo.com. Licensee: Amistad Communications Inc. (acq 10-2000; $375,000. with CP for KBEF(FM) Gibsland). Network: Jones Radio Networks. Format: Adult standards, local news. News: 102 hrs wkly. Target aud: 35-64; male & female. ◆Fred Caldwell Sr., pres; Mike Griffith, gen mgr; Mark Cheerve, opns mgr.

KLKL(FM)—Licensed to Minden. See Shreveport

Monroe

*KBMQ(FM)— Aug. 15, 2000: 88.7 mhz; 25 kw horiz, 24.5 kw vert. Ant 458 ft. TL: N32 24 15 W92 02 07. Stereo. Media Ministries Inc., 1700 Parkview Dr. 71202. Phone: (318) 651-8870. E-mail: thecross@mediaministries.com. Web Site: www.mediaministries.com. Licensee: Media Ministries Inc. Format: Christian. News: one hr wkly. Target aud: 25-54; women. ◆Tony Davis, pres; Mike Downhour, gen mgr.

*KEDM(FM)— Apr 23, 1991: 90.3 mhz; 87.1 kw. 863 ft. TL: N32 39 38 W91 59 28. Stereo. 225 Stubbs Hall-ULM 71209-6805. Phone: (318) 342-5556. Fax: (318) 342-5570. E-mail: kedm@ulm.edu. Web Site: www.kedm.org. Licensee: University of Louisiana at Monroe. Network: NPR, PRI. Dow, Lohnes & Albertson. Format: News, class, jazz. News staff: one; News: 40 hrs wkly. Target aud: 35 plus; involved, upscale, educated, movers & shakers. Spec prog: New age 6 hrs wkly, blues 4 hrs wkly. ◆Mark Simmons, gen mgr & progmg dir; Ray Davidson, opns mgr.

KJLO-FM— July 1946: 104.1 mhz; 100 kw. Ant 1,017 ft. TL: N32 39 36 W92 05 15. Stereo. Box 4808 71211. Secondary address: 1109 Hudson Ln. 71201. Phone: (318) 388-2323. Fax: (318) 388-0569. Web Site: www.kjlo.com. Licensee: New South Communications Inc. (group owner; acq 12-15-86). Network: ABC Information & Entertainment. Format: Country. News staff: one. Spec prog: Gospel 4 hrs wkly. ◆Robert H. Holladay, pres.

KLIC(AM)— 1950: 1230 khz; 1 kw-U. TL: N32 29 16 W92 05 25. Stereo. 1700 Parkview Dr. 71202. Phone: (318) 387-1230. Fax: (318) 387-8856. E-mail: thesource@mediaministries.net. Web Site: www.mediaministries.net. Licensee: Media Ministries Inc. (acq 10-28-92; $165,000; 11-23-92). Network: Salem Radio Network. Format: Christian, talk. News staff: 0; News: 14 hrs wkly. Target aud: 25-54; Adults 35 +. ◆Tony Davis, pres; Mike Downhour, gen mgr & progmg dir; Diane Osborne, sls dir & mktg dir; Naomi Thompson, news dir & pub affrs dir; Ernie Sandidge, engrg dir.

KLIP(FM)— April 1993: 105.3 mhz; 50 kw. 433 ft. TL: N32 33 08 W92 08 33. Stereo. Box 4808 71211. Secondary address: 1109 Hudson Ln. 71201. Phone: (318) 388-2323. Fax: (318) 388-0569. E-mail: la105@bayou.com. Web Site: www.la105.com. Licensee: Holladay Broadcasting of Louisiana LLC (group owner; acq 11-21-2003; grpsl). Rep: McGavren Guild. Latham & Watkins. Format: Classic hits. News: 2 hrs wkly. Target aud: 25-54. ◆Bob Holladay, pres & gen mgr.

KMLB(AM)— July 1, 1930: 1440 khz; 5 kw-D, 1 kw-N, DA-N. TL: N32 33 10 W92 04 24. Box 4808 71211. Secondary address: 1109 Hudson Ln. 71201. Phone: (318) 388-2323. Fax: (318) 388-0569. E-mail: kmlb@bayou.com. Web Site: www.kmlb.com. Licensee: Holladay Broadcasting of Louisiana LLC (group owner; acq 11-21-2003; grpsl). Network: ABC. Rep: McGavren Guild. Latham & Watkins. Format: Talk/news. Target aud: 25 plus. ◆Bob Holladay, pres & gen mgr; Cynthia Halladay, gen sls mgr; Tory Crow, progmg dir.

KNOE(AM)— Oct 4, 1944: 540 khz; 5 kw-D, 1 kw-N, DA-2. TL: N32 32 36 W92 10 45. Box 4067 71211. Secondary address: 1400 Oliver Rd. 71201. Phone: (318) 388-8888. Fax: (318) 325-9466. Licensee: Noe Corp. L.L.C. Format: News/talk, sports. ◆James A. Noe Jr., pres; Randy Minter, gen mgr; Bobby Richards, opns mgr; Jerry Harkins, chief of engrg.

KNOE-FM— Jan 29, 1967: 101.9 mhz; 97 kw horiz, 96 kw vert. 1,670 ft. TL: N32 11 45 W92 04 10. Stereo. Format: CHR. ◆Bobby Richards, mus dir. Co-owned TV: KNOE-TV affil

KRJO(AM)— May 2001: 1680 khz; 10 kw-D, 1 kw-N. TL: N32 27 24 W92 01 06. Stereo. Box 4808 71211. Secondary address: 1109 Hudson Ln. 71201. Phone: (318) 338-2323. Fax: (318) 388-0569. E-mail: rejoice@bayou.com. Web Site: www.krjo.com. Licensee: Holladay Broadcasting of Louisiana LLC (group owner; acq 11-21-2003; grpsl). Network: ABC. Rep: McGavren Guild. Latham & Watkins. Format: Gospel. ◆Bob Holladay, pres & gen mgr; Mike Blakeney, opns dir.

KRVV(FM)—See Bastrop

KXRR(FM)— Nov 15, 1965: 106.1 mhz; 97 kw. Ant 1,017 ft. TL: N32 39 36 W92 05 15. Stereo. 1200 N. 18th St., Suite D 71201. Phone: (318) 387-3922. Fax: (318) 322-4585. Licensee: Opus Broadcasting Monroe L.L.C. Group owner: Opus Media Partners LLC (acq 7-19-2004; grpsl). Rep: Christal. Format: Rock. Target aud: 25-49. ◆Chris Zimmerman, gen mgr & stn mgr; Ric Petterson, prom dir; Barbara Dawson-Monk, adv mgr; Rick Knighten, progmg dir & news dir; Mark Wilson, chief of engrg.

*KXUL(FM)— May 9, 1973: 91.1 mhz; 8.5 kw. 716 ft. TL: N32 39 38 W91 59 28. Stereo. 130 Stubbs Hall 71209-8821. Phone: (318) 342-5985. Phone: (318) 342-5986. Web Site: www.kxul.com. Licensee: University of Louisiana at Monroe. Dow, Lohnes & Albertson. Format: Alternative, rock. News: 2 hrs wkly. Target aud: 12-34. ◆Joel Willer, gen mgr.

*KYFL(FM)— Oct 8, 1992: 89.5 mhz; 25 kw. Ant 377 ft. TL: N32 33 08 W92 08 33. Stereo. 11530 Carmel Commons Blvd., Charlotte, NC 28226. Phone: (704) 523-5555. E-mail: kyfl@bbnradio.org. Web Site: www.bbnradio.org. Licensee: Bible Broadcasting Network Inc. Group owner: Bible Broadcasting Network. Format: Conservative Christian. News: 3 hrs wkly. Target aud: General. ◆Michael Thomson, gen mgr.

Moreauville

KLIL(FM)— July 25, 1980: 92.1 mhz; 6 kw. 300 ft. TL: N31 02 53 W91 59 47. Stereo. Box 365, 10586 Hwy. 1 71355. Phone: (318) 985-2929. Fax: (318) 985-2995. E-mail: klil@kricket.net. Licensee: Cajun Broadcasting Inc. Format: Oldies. Target aud: 20 plus; working adults. Spec prog: Cajun Fr 5 hrs wkly. ◆Louis B. Coco Jr., pres & gen mgr.

Morgan City

KBZZ-FM— Aug 1, 1967: 96.7 mhz; 12 kw. Ant 476 ft. TL: N29 41 39 W90 59 58. Stereo. 120 Prevost Dr., Houma 70364. Phone: (985) 851-1020. Fax: (985) 872-4403. E-mail: info@softrock967.com. Web Site: www.967thebuzz.com. Licensee: Guaranty Broadcasting Co. of Houma L.L.C. (acq 8-28-98; $460,000 with co-located AM). Network: Jones Radio Networks. Format: Adult comtemp. News: 2 hrs wkly. Target aud: 18-34; majority women. Spec prog: Gospel 6 hrs wkly. ◆Melanie Hotard, gen mgr.

KMRC(AM)— April 1954: 1430 khz; 500 w-D, 100 w-N. TL: N29 45 03 W91 10 24. 409 Duke St. 70381. Phone: (985) 384-1430. Fax: (985) 384-2351. E-mail: kmrc@kmrc1430.com. Web Site: www.kmrc1430.com. Licensee: Spotlight Broadcasting L.L.C. (group owner; acq 2-1-00; $109,000). Format: Contemp hits, talk. News staff: one; News: 5 hrs wkly. Target aud: 25-54; middle to upper income. Spec prog: Gospel 10 hrs wkly. ◆Patrick Andras, CEO, pres, gen mgr & news dir.

Moss Bluff

KZWA(FM)— Aug 12, 1994: 104.9 mhz; 25 kw. Ant 328 ft. TL: N30 27 15 W93 08 20. 305 Enterprise Blvd., Lake Charles 70601. Phone: (337) 491-9955. Fax: (337) 433-8097. Web Site: www.kzwa.com. Licensee: B & C Broadcasting Inc. Format: Urban mainstream. Target aud: 18-34. ♦Faye Brown-Blackwell, CEO & gen mgr.

Natchitoches

***KBIO(FM)**— July 2, 2002: 89.7 mhz; 100 w. Ant 295 ft. TL: N31 47 13 W93 07 52. Radio Maria Inc., 601 Washington St., Alexandria 71301. Phone: (318) 561-6145. Fax: (318) 449-9954. E-mail: info.usa@radiomaria.org. Web Site: www.radiomaria.us. Licensee: Radio Maria Inc. (group owner; acq 9-6-01). Format: Christian. ♦Daune Stenzel, gen mgr; Danny Brou, chief of engrg.

KDBH(FM)— July 1, 1965: 97.3 mhz; 25 kw. Ant 220 ft. TL: N31 48 17 W93 01 27. Stereo. 720 Front St. 71457. Phone: (318) 354-4000. Fax: (318) 357-9595. Licensee: Baldridge-Dumas Communications Inc. (group owner; acq 5-14-01; $340,000. with co-located AM including two-year noncompete agreement). Network: ABC Information & Entertainment. Kaye, Scholer, Fierman, Hays & Handler. Format: Adult contemp. ♦Rhonda Benson, gen mgr & stn mgr; Gordon Rivet, news dir; Kenny Carter, chief of engrg.

KNOC(AM)— May 1, 1947: 1450 khz; 1 kw-U. TL: N31 45 47 W93 03 47. 213 Renee St. 71457. Phone: (318) 354-4000. Fax: (318) 352-9598. Licensee: North Face Broadcasting L.L.C. (acq 5-9-2003; $348,000. with KCIJ(FM) Atlanta). Network: ABC Information & Entertainment. Format: News/talk. News staff: 1; News: 20 hrs wkly. Target aud: 35+; upper-middle class. ♦Jeff Johnson, opns dir; John Brewer, opns dir & natl sls mgr; Rick Beck, gen mgr & sls dir; George Sluppick, news dir; George Sluppick, pub affrs dir.

***KNWD(FM)**— September 1975: 91.7 mhz; 255 w horiz. 164 ft. TL: N31 44 51 W93 05 47. Stereo. 109 Kyser Hall, NSU, Northwestern State Univ. 71497. Phone: (318) 357-4180. Phone: (318) 357-5693. Fax: (318) 357-4398. E-mail: knwd917@yahoo.com. Web Site: www.nsula.edu/thedemon. Licensee: Northwestern State University of Louisiana. Format: Modern rock, alternative, urban. News staff: one; News: 3 hrs wkly. Target aud: 18-25. Spec prog: Gospel 3 hrs, heavy metal 12 hrs, blues 6 hrs wkly. ♦Warner Tureaud, gen mgr & stn mgr; Jennifer Anderson, opns mgr.

KZBL(FM)— Oct 8, 1985: 100.7 mhz; 3 kw. 299 ft. TL: N31 48 18 W93 01 29. Stereo. 1115 Washington St. 71458. Phone: (318) 357-1007. Fax: (318) 357-9595. Licensee: Baldridge-Dumas Communications Inc. (group owner; acq 6-21-99; $400,000). Format: Oldies. News: 10 hrs wkly. Target aud: 25-50. ♦Rhonda Benson, gen mgr & stn mgr.

New Iberia

KANE(AM)— August 1946: 1240 khz; 1 kw-U. TL: N30 01 03 W91 50 10. Stereo. 2316 E. Main 70560. Phone: (337) 365-3434. Fax: (337) 365-9117. Licensee: Coastal Broadcasting of Lafourche L.L.C. (acq 12-31-01). Network: ABC Information & Entertainment. News: 30 hrs wkly. Target aud: 25-54. Spec prog: Sports, farm 2 hrs wkly.

KNIR(AM)— June 1, 1951: 1360 khz; 1 kw-D, 209 w-N. TL: N30 01 32 W91 49 20. Radio Maria Inc., 601 Washington St., Alexandria 71301. Phone: (318) 561-6145. Fax: (318) 449-9954. E-mail: info.usa@radiomaria.org. Web Site: www.radiomaria.us. Licensee: Radio Maria Inc. (group owner; (acq 6-10-2003; $45,000). Format: Christian. ♦Daune Stenzel, gen mgr.

KRDJ(FM)— 1991: 93.7 mhz; 100 kw. Ant 971 ft. TL: N30 20 19 W91 31 23. 650 Wooddale Blvd., Baton Rouge 70806. Phone: (225) 926-1106. Fax: (225) 922-7019. E-mail: krdj.fm@citcomm.com. Web Site: www.red937.com. Licensee: Citadel Broadcasting Co. Group owner: Citadel Broadcasting Corp. (acq 10-8-99; $9.5 million). Format: Classic rock. Target aud: 18-44; men. ♦Rebecca Breeding, gen mgr.

KXKC(FM)— January 1969: 99.1 mhz; 100 kw. 1,039 ft. TL: N30 12 06 W91 46 37. Stereo. Citadel Broadcasting, 202 Galbert Rd., Lafayette 70506. Phone: (337) 232-1311. E-mail: office@kxkc.com. Web Site: www.kxkc.com. Licensee: Citadel Broadcasting Co. Group owner: Citadel Broadcasting Corp. (acq 12-5-2003; $7.6 million). Rep: Allied Radio Partners. Format: Country. Target aud: 18-49. ♦Mary Galyean, gen mgr.

New Orleans

KGLA(AM)—See Gretna

WBOK(AM)— February 1951: 1230 khz; 1 kw-U. TL: N29 59 18 W90 02 45. 1639 Gentilly Blvd. 70119. Phone: (504) 943-4600. Fax: (504) 944-4662. Licensee: Christian Broadcasting of New Orleans Inc. Group owner: Willis Broadcasting Corp. (acq 1983; $700,000; 7-4-83). Rep: Roslin. Format: Gospel. Target aud: 25 plus. ♦Annette G. Pete, gen mgr.

***WBSN-FM**— Feb 5, 1979: 89.1 mhz; 8.5 kw. Ant 623 ft. TL: N29 56 59 W89 57 27. Stereo. 3939 Gentilly Blvd. 70126. Phone: (504) 816-8000. Phone: (888) 480-3600. Fax: (504) 816-8580. E-mail: onair@lifesongs.com. Web Site: www.wbsn.com. Licensee: Providence Educational Foundation. Format: Contemp Christian. Target aud: 25-49; active, Christian oriented families. ♦Stan Watts, gen mgr.

WBYU(AM)— 1950: 1450 khz; 1 kw-U. TL: N29 57 27 W90 09 47. 3330 W. Esplanade Ave., Metairie 70002. Phone: (504) 841-2800. Fax: (504) 841-2805. Licensee: Radio Disney Group LLC. Group owner: ABC Inc. (acq 2-5-2003; $1.5 million). Network: ABC. Rep: Roslin. Format: Children.

WDVW(FM)—See La Place

WEZB(FM)— Sept 1, 1945: 97.1 mhz; 100 kw. 984 ft. TL: N29 55 11 W90 01 29. Stereo. 1450 Poydras, Suite 500 70112-6010. Phone: (504) 593-6376. Fax: (504) 593-2205. Web Site: www.b97.com. Licensee: Entercom New Orleans License LLC. Group owner: Entercom Communications Corp. (acq 12-13-99; grpsl). Format: CHR, hot AC. Target aud: 18-34; females. ♦Phil Hoover, gen mgr; Patrick Galloway, gen sls mgr; Mike Kaplan, progmg dir; Dave Cohen, news dir.

WGSO(AM)— Jan 27, 1946: 990 khz; 1 kw-D, 400 w-N. TL: N29 57 24 W90 04 34. 111 Veterans Blvd., Metairie 70005. Phone: (504) 832-3555. Fax: (504) 838-7700. E-mail: wgso@mcmediallc.com. Web Site: bizneworleans.com. Licensee: WGSO L.L.C. (acq 4-3-03). Network: CNN Radio. Rep: D & R Radio. Format: News/talk. News staff: 4; News: 168 hrs wkly. Target aud: 35 plus. ♦Bill Metcalf, pres; Bob Charlestians, opns mgr.

WLMG(FM)—Listing follows WWL-TV.

WLNO(AM)— 1925: 1060 khz; 50 kw-D, 5 kw-N, DA-2. TL: N29 52 46 W89 59 51. Stereo. Oakwood Corporate Center, 401 Whitney Ave., #160, Gretna 70056. Phone: (504) 362-9800. Fax: (504) 362-5541. E-mail: wlno@i-55.com. Web Site: www.wlno.com. Licensee: Communicom Co. of Louisiana L.P. (acq 1-25-95; $700,000; 3-20-95). Format: Christian, Religious. Target aud: General. ♦D. Gayril Gibson, gen mgr; Jay Whitehurst, opns dir.

WNOE-FM— Sept 15, 1968: 101.1 mhz; 100 kw. 1,004 ft. TL: N29 58 57 W89 57 09. Stereo. 929 Howard Ave. 70113. Phone: (504) 679-7300. Fax: (504) 679-7343. Web Site: www.wnoe.com. Licensee: Clear Channel Communications Inc. (group owner: Clear Channel Communiaction Inc. acq 1996; grpsl). Network: Network: ABC, Westwood One. Rep: Clear Channel. Verner, Liipfert, Bernhard, McPherson & Hand. Format: Country. News staff: one. Target aud: 25-54. ♦Muriac Fueutes, gen mgr.

WODT(AM)— July 23, 1923: 1280 khz; 5 kw-U, DA-1. TL: N29 53 43 W90 00 16. Stereo. 929 Howard Ave. 70113. Phone: (504) 679-7300. Fax: (504) 679-7345. Web Site: www.blues1280.com. Licensee: Clear Channel Radio Licenses Inc. Group owner: Clear Channel Communications Inc. (acq 7-24-92). Network: ESPN Radio. Riley & Fielding. Format: Sports. News: one hr wkly. Target aud: 35 plus; general. ♦Muriel Funches, gen mgr; Jim Owen, opns mgr & progmg dir; Michael Breaver, prom dir.

WQUE-FM—Co-owned with WODT(AM). Jan 1, 1949: 93.3 mhz; 93 kw. 459 ft. TL: N29 57 24 W90 04 31. (CP: 100 kw, ant 984 ft. TL: N29 55 11 W90 01 29). Stereo. Format: Urban contemp. ♦Connie Macera, gen sls mgr; Metra Gilliard, prom dir; Muriel Funches, VP & progmg dir; Angela Harrison Watson, mus dir; Monica Pierre, news dir & pub affrs dir.

***WRBH(FM)**— 1980: 88.3 mhz; 54 kw. 600 ft. TL: N29 57 01 W89 57 29. 3606 Magazine St. 70115. Phone: (504) 899-1144. Fax: (504) 899-1165. Web Site: www.wrbh.org. Licensee: Radio for the Blind and Print Handicapped Inc. Format: Radio reading svc, news. News: 28 hrs wkly. Target aud: Blind & print handicapped. ♦Dori Orr, gen mgr; Natalia Gonzalez, dev dir; Jackie Bullock, progmg dir; Ernie Kain, chief of engrg.

WRNO-FM— Oct 17, 1967: 99.5 mhz; 100 kw. 1,004 ft. TL: N29 58 57 W89 57 09. Stereo. 929 Howard Ave. 70113. Phone: (504) 679-7300. Fax: (504) 679-7343. Web Site: www.wrno.com. Licensee: Clear Channel Broadcasting Licenses Inc. Group owner: Clear Channel Communications Inc. (acq 8-8-02; swap for KKND(FM) Port Sulphur). Network: ABC FM Connection. Dow, Lohnes & Albertson. Format: Classic rock. Target aud: 35-54; men. ♦Muriel Funches, gen mgr; Jim Owen, opns mgr.

WSHO(AM)— 1926: 800 khz; 1 kw-D, 233 w-N, DA-1. TL: N29 50 42 W90 06 39. 1001 Howard Ave., Suite 4304 70113. Phone: (504) 527-0800. Fax: (504) 527-0881. E-mail: whso@compuserve.com. Web Site: www.wsho.com. Licensee: Shadowlands Communications L.L.C. (acq 1996). Network: Salem Radio Network. Format: Christian mus & talk. Target aud: 25-54. ♦William Ainsworth, pres, gen mgr & opns mgr; Marc Musgrove, chief of engrg.

WSLA(AM)—See Slidell

WSMB(AM)— Apr 21, 1925: 1350 khz; 5 kw-U, DA-2. TL: N29 55 27 W90 02 04. 1450 Poydras, Suite 500 70112. Phone: (504) 593-2100. Fax: (504) 593-2099. Licensee: Entercom New Orleans License LLC. Group owner: Entercom Communications Corp. (acq 12-13-99; grpsl). Format: Sports, news. ♦Mal Pelham, gen mgr; Bobby Martinez, gen sls mgr; Diane Newman, progmg dir.

WTIX(AM)— 1948: 690 khz; 10 kw-D, 5 kw-N, DA-2. TL: N29 57 53 W89 57 31. Box 8386, Metairie 70011. Secondary address: 4539 N. I-10 Service Rd., Suite 205, Metaire 70006. Phone: (504) 885-4690. Fax: (504) 885-4671. E-mail: feedback@wtix690.com. Web Site: www.wtic690am.com. Licensee: WTIX Inc. Group owner: GHB Radio Group (acq 2-12-92; $800,000; 3-16-92). Cohn & Marks. Format: News/talk. News staff: 6; News: 30 hrs wkly. Target aud: 25 plus; affluent, educated, professional. ♦Daniel Frazier, gen mgr.

WTKL(FM)— February 1953: 95.7 mhz; 100 kw. 984 ft. TL: N29 55 11 W90 01 29. Stereo. 1450 Poydras, Suite 500 70112. Phone: (504) 593-6376. Fax: (504) 593-1850. E-mail: mail@entercom.com. Web Site: www.kool957.com. Licensee: Entercom New Orleans License LLC. Group owner: Entercom Communications Corp. (acq 12-13-99; grpsl). Latham & Watkins. Format: Oldies. Target aud: 25-54. ♦Phil Hoover, gen mgr; Suzanne Montgomery, gen sls mgr; Andy Holt, progmg dir; Dave Cohen, news dir; Joe Pollet, chief of engrg.

***WTUL(FM)**— Nov 14, 1974: 91.5 mhz; 1.5 kw. 161 ft. TL: N29 56 18 W90 07 07. Stereo. Tulane Univ. Ctr. 70118. Phone: (504) 865-5887. Phone: (504) 865-5885. Fax: (504) 862-3072. E-mail: wtul@wtul.fm. Web Site: www.wtul.fm. Licensee: Tulane Educational Fund. Format: Progsv. News: 3 hrs wkly. Target aud: General. Spec prog: Class 15 hrs, country 3 hrs, reggae 4 hrs, New Orleans music 2 hrs, wkly. ♦Jeremy Kutner, gen mgr; Tom Conner, gen mgr & chief of opns.

WVOG(AM)— Apr 23, 1964: 600 khz; 1 kw-D. TL: N29 57 25 W90 09 33. 2730 Loumour Ave., Metairie 70001. Phone: (504) 831-6941. E-mail: radiowvog@aol.com. Web Site: www.wwcr.com/wvog.html. Licensee: F.W. Robbert Broadcasting Co. Inc. (group owner; acq 6-28-74). Format: Christian talk. News: 2 hrs wkly. Target aud: 30 plus. ♦Fred P. Westenberger, CEO; Chris Westenberger, pres; Eric Westenberger, exec VP, gen mgr & opns VP.

WWL(AM)— Mar 31, 1922: 870 khz; 50 kw-U, DA-1. TL: N29 50 14 W90 07 55. 1450 Poydras, Suite 500 70112. Phone: (504) 593-6376. Fax: (504) 593-1850. Licensee: Entercom New Orleans License LLC. Group owner: Entercom Communications Corp. (acq 12-13-99; grpsl). Network: CBS. Rep: D & R Radio. Format: News/talk, sports. ♦Phil Hoover, VP & gen mgr; Diane Newman, opns mgr & progmg mgr; Helen Centani, prom dir & prom mgr; Dave Cohen, news dir; Joe Pollet, chief of engrg.

WLMG(FM)—Co-owned with WWL-TV. Mar 15, 1970: 101.9 mhz; 100 kw. 984 ft. TL: N29 55 11 W90 01 29. Stereo. Format: Adult contemp. ♦Patrick Galloway, gen sls mgr; Malorie Hood, prom dir; Nick Ferrara, progmg dir; Johnny Scott, mus dir.

***WWNO(FM)**— Feb 20, 1972: 89.9 mhz; 85 kw vert. Ant 748 ft. TL: N29 55 11 W90 01 29. Stereo. Univ. of New Orleans, 2000 Lakeshore Dr. 70148. Phone: (504) 280-7000. Fax: (504) 280-6061. E-mail: info@wwno.org. Web Site: www.wwno.org. Licensee: Louisiana State University. Network: Network: PRI, NPR. Format: Class, news. News:

Stations in the U.S. — Louisiana

39 hrs wkly. Target aud: 35 plus; well-educated professionals, mgrs, artists & art patrons. Spec prog: Jazz 6 hrs, prairie home companion 4 hrs wkly. ♦Ron C. Curtis, opns dir; Karen Anklam, dev dir & prom mgr; Fred Kasten, progmg dir.

*WWOZ(FM)— Dec 6, 1980: 90.7 mhz; 19 w. 279 ft. TL: N29 57 01 W90 09 16. (CP: 4 kw, ant 508 ft. TL: N29 57 24 W90 04 31). Stereo. Box 51840 70151. Secondary address: 1201 St. Phillip 70116. Phone: (504) 568-1234. Phone: (504) 568-1238. Fax: (504) 558-9332. E-mail: wwoz@wwoz.org. Web Site: www.wwoz.org. Licensee: Friends of WWOZ Inc. (acq 10-14-86). Haley, Bader & Potts. Format: Jazz, rhythm and blues. News staff: one; News: 5 hrs wkly. Target aud: 35-55; upscale & educated males. ♦David Freedman, gen mgr.

WYLD(AM)— 1949: 940 khz; 10 kw-D, 500 w-N, DA-2. TL: N29 54 00 W90 00 17. 2228 Gravier St. 70119. Phone: (504) 679-7300. Fax: (504) 679-7345. Web Site: www.am940.com. Licensee: Clear Channel Radio Licenses Inc. Group owner: Clear Channel Communications Inc. (acq 3-25-93; 3-20-95). Network: ABC. Rep: Clear Channel. Wiley, Rein & Fielding. Format: Gospel. Target aud: 25-54. ♦Carla Boatner, gen mgr.

WYLD-FM— 1971: 98.5 mhz; 100 kw. 984 ft. TL: N29 55 11 W90 01 29. (CP: Ant 902 ft.). Stereo. Fax: (504) 827-6045. Web Site: www.wyldfm.com. Format: Urban adult contemp. News staff: 2; News: 5 hrs wkly.

New Roads

KQXL-FM— Oct 1, 1979: 106.5 mhz; 50 kw. 485 ft. TL: N30 37 24 W91 09 50. Stereo. 650 Wooddale Blvd., Baton Rouge 70806. Phone: (225) 926-1106. Fax: (225) 928-1606. Web Site: www.q106dot5.com. Licensee: Citadel Broadcasting Co. Group owner: Citadel Broadcasting Corp. (acq 1-14-99; grpsl). Network: Network: CBS, ABC FM Connection. Format: Urban contemp. News staff: one. Target aud: 18-54; Black adults. ♦Donnie Picou, gen mgr; Denise Johnson, gen sls mgr; Tiffany Rivet, mktg dir.

Norco

WFNO(AM)— 1987: 830 khz; 5 kw-D, 750 w-N, DA-2. TL: N30 03 00 W90 22 41. 111 Veterans Blvd., Suite 1810, Metairie 70005. Phone: (504) 832-3555. Fax: (504) 838-7700. E-mail: wfno@mcmediallc.com. Licensee: WFNO L.L.C. (acq 4-3-03). Network: CNN en Espanol. Format: Sp contemp. News staff: 2; News: 12 hrs wkly. Target aud: 18-44. ♦William Metcalf Jr., pres; Miguel Soler, gen mgr & progmg dir; Juan Carlos Ramos, sls VP; Danny Miller, chief of engrg.

*WPDD(FM)—Not on air, target date: unknown: 91.1 mhz; 1 kw vert. Ant 56 ft. TL: N29 59 50 W90 24 48. Broadcasting for the Challenged Inc., 188 S. Bellevue, Suite 222, Memphis, TN 38104. Phone: (901) 726-8970. Fax: (901) 375-0041. Licensee: Broadcasting for the Challenged Inc. ♦George S. Flinn Jr., gen mgr.

North Fort Polk

KUMX(FM)— May 10, 1995: 106.7 mhz; 6 kw. 328 ft. TL: N31 03 46 W93 16 11. Stereo. 421 Tilly Rd., Leesville 71446. Phone: (318) 537-2111. Web Site: www.kumx1067.com. Licensee: West Central Broadcasting Co. Inc. (acq 3-8-02; $208,000). Network: USA. Format: Christian. Target aud: 22-42. ♦Roscoe Burwell, gen mgr.

Oak Grove

KWCL-FM— Jan 30, 1973: 96.7 mhz; 23 kw. Ant 341 ft. TL: N32 51 32 W91 21 22. Stereo. 230 E. Main St. 71263. Phone: (318) 428-9670. Fax: (318) 428-2476. E-mail: kwcl@bellsouth.net. Licensee: KWCL-FM Broadcasting Co. Inc. (acq 12-10-90). Network: Network: ABC, Jones Radio Networks. Miller & Miller. Format: Good time oldies. News staff: one; News: 17 hrs wkly. Target aud: General. ♦Irene Robinson, pres & gen mgr; Rita Brown, gen sls mgr; Ivy Robinson, engrg dir & chief of engrg.

Oakdale

KKST(FM)— 1972: 98.7 mhz; 34 kw. 1,053 ft. TL: N30 48 30 W92 38 30. Stereo. 1515 Jackson St., Alexandria 71301. Phone: (318) 443-7454. Fax: (318) 442-2747. Web Site: www.kkst-fm.com. Licensee: Capstar TX L.P. Group owner: Clear Channel Communications Inc. (acq 8-30-00; grpsl). Network: ABC Information & Entertainment. Format: Adult contemp. News staff: one; News: 20 hrs wkly. Target aud: 18-49; women. ♦J.R. Greeley, gen mgr; Scott Bryant, opns mgr; Cindy B. Goode, progmg dir; Lyn Hare, chief of engrg.

Oil City

KQHN(FM)— 1968: . Stn currently dark 107.9 mhz; 24.5 kw. Ant 533 ft. TL: N32 29 36 W93 45 55. Stereo. 270 Plaza Loop, Bossier City 71111. Phone: (318) 549-8500. Fax: (318) 549-8505. Licensee: Cumulus Licensing LLC. Group owner: Cumulus Media Inc. (acq 11-1-2002; $1.75 million). ♦C.J. Jones, gen mgr.

Opelousas

KOGM(FM)—Listing follows KSLO(AM).

KSLO(AM)— September 1947: 1230 khz; 1 kw-U. TL: N30 31 31 W92 06 17. Box 1150 70571-1150. Secondary address: 216 N. Court 70570. Phone: (337) 942-2633. Fax: (337) 942-2635. E-mail: kslokogm@bellsouth.net. Web Site: www.kslokogm-fm.com. Licensee: KSLO Broadcasting Co. Inc. Network: ABC Information & Entertainment. Format: C&W, Black, news/talk. Spec prog: Fr 18 hrs wkly. ♦Wandell Allegood, pres & gen mgr.

KOGM(FM)— Co-owned with KSLO(AM). June 18, 1965: 107.1 mhz; 3 kw. 203 ft. TL: N30 31 31 W92 06 17. Stereo. Web Site: www.kslokogm-fm.com. Network: ABC Information & Entertainment. Format: C & W. Target aud: 25 plus.

KTSJ(FM)— Aug 3, 1989: 105.9 mhz; 3.4 kw. Ant 433 ft. TL: N30 27 53 W92 04 31. 3225 Ambassador Caffery Pkwy., Lafayette 70506. Phone: (337) 993-5500. Fax: (337) 993-5510. Licensee: Pittman Broadcasting Services LLC (group owner; acq 1-28-2004; grpsl). Format: Smooth jazz. ♦Michael Schutta, gen mgr.

Pineville

KTTP(AM)—Licensed to Pineville. See Alexandria

Plaquemine

*KPAQ(FM)—Not on air, target date: unknown: 88.1 mhz; 4.5 kw. Ant 295 ft. TL: N30 18 00 W91 24 03. Drawer 2440, Tupelo, MS 38803. Phone: (662) 844-8888. Fax: (662) 842-6791. Licensee: American Family Association. ♦Marvin Sanders, gen mgr.

Port Allen

WPFC(AM)—Licensed to Port Allen. See Baton Rouge

Port Sulphur

KAGY(AM)— Aug 17, 1966: 1510 khz; 1 kw-D. TL: N29 29 03 W89 42 15. Box 8888, Metairie 70011. Secondary address: 4401 Veterons Hwy., Metairle 70011. Phone: (504) 309-7260. Fax: (504) 309-7262. Licensee: Spotlight Broadcasting of New Orleans LLC Group owner: Spotlight Broadcasting LLC (acq 12-30-2002; $250,000). Format: Swamp pop. Target aud: 24-54; general. ♦Patrick Andras, CEO; P.E. Gilligan, gen mgr.

KKND(FM)— July 4, 1989: 106.7 mhz; 100 kw. Ant 981 ft. TL: N29 48 30 W89 45 42. 201 St. Charles Ave., Suite 201, New Orleans 70170. Phone: (504) 581-7002. Fax: (504) 566-4857. E-mail: morningtrainwreck@1067theend.com. Web Site: www.106theend.com. Licensee: Citadel Broadcasting Co. Group owner: Citadel Broadcasting Corp. (acq 8-29-03; grpsl). Rep: Clear Channel. Format: New rock. News staff: one. Target aud: 25-54. ♦Lee Killian, pres & VP; Jessica Debate, prom; Ernie Kain, engr.

*KSUL(FM)—Not on air, target date: unknown: 91.5 mhz; 100 w. Ant 184 ft. TL: N29 30 52 W89 43 48. Drawer 2440, Tupelo, MS 38803. Phone: (662) 844-8888. Fax: (662) 842-6791. Web Site: www.afr.com. Licensee: American Family Association. Group owner: American Family Radio. Format: Christian. ♦Marvin Sanders, chmn.

Rayne

KBEB-FM— 1993: 106.7 mhz; 3 kw. 328 ft. TL: N30 18 17 W92 20 47. Box 228, Crowley 70527. Secondary address: 320 N. Parkerson Ave., Crowley 70527. Phone: (337) 783-2520. Fax: (337) 783-5744. E-mail: info@b1067.com. Web Site: www.b1067.com. Licensee: Broadcast Partners Inc. (acq 12-18-92; $60,000;. FTR: 1-11-93). Format: Adult classics. ♦Phil Lizotte, gen mgr.

Rayville

KMYY(FM)— September 1984: 92.3 mhz; 26 kw. 492 ft. TL: N32 27 51 W91 39 10. Stereo. 1200 N. 18th St., Suite D, Monroe 71201. Phone: (318) 387-3922. Fax: (318) 322-4585. Web Site: www.realcountry923.com. Licensee: Opus Broadcasting Monroe L.L.C. Group owner: Opus Media Partners LLC (acq 7-19-2004; grpsl). Format: Real country. ♦Chris Zimmerman, gen mgr.

Reserve

WPRF(FM)— August 1991: 94.9 mhz; 14 kw. Ant 440 ft. TL: N30 02 56 W90 28 28. 201 St. Charles Ave., Suite 201, New Orleans 70170. Phone: (504) 581-7002. Fax: (504) 566-4857. Licensee: Southeastern Broadcasting Inc. Group owner: Citadel Broadcasting Corp. (acq 4-26-2005; $4.5 million. with WOPR(FM) Lacombe). Format: Inspirational/gospel music. News: 2 hrs wkly. Target aud: 25-54; general. ♦Paris Suleman, CEO; Eric Logan, pres; Lee Killian, gen mgr.

Richwood

KHLL(FM)— March 1995: 100.9 mhz; 6 kw. 328 ft. TL: N32 24 25 W92 04 13. 704 C Trenton St., West Monroe 71291. Phone: (318) 323-5994. Phone: (318) 323-2000. Fax: (318) 323-6680. E-mail: hillradio@centurytel.net. Web Site: www.hillradio.com. Licensee: Dan Gilliland. (acq 3-95). Format: Christian hit radio. ♦Rick Godley, gen mgr.

Ruston

*KAPI(FM)— February 1998: 88.3 mhz; 300 w. Ant 197 ft. TL: N32 33 08 W92 39 21. Box 3206, American Family Radio, Tupelo, MS 38803. Phone: (662) 844-8888. Fax: (662) 842-6791. E-mail: comments@afr.net. Web Site: www.afr.net. Licensee: American Family Association. Group owner: American Family Radio Format: Inspirational Christian. ♦Marvin Sanders, gen mgr.

*KLPI-FM— 1973: 89.1 mhz; 4 kw. 285 ft. TL: N32 31 09 W92 39 02. (CP: 20 kw). Phone: (318) 257-4851. Phone: (318) 257-3689. Fax: (318) 257-5073. Web Site: www.891klpi.org. Licensee: Louisiana Tech University. Format: Alternative. Target aud: 18-24; college students. Spec prog: Black 6 hrs, class 3 hrs, oldies 12 hrs, reggae 6 hrs, gospel 3 hrs wkly. ♦Josh McDaniel, gen mgr; Denton Saurels, progmg dir.

KNBB(FM)— 1999: 99.3 mhz; 15.5 kw. Ant 328 ft. TL: N32 28 53 W92 40 37. 500 N. Monroe St. 71270. Phone: (318) 255-6993. Fax: (318) 255-5084. Web Site: www.hitsandfavorites.com. Licensee: Communications Capital Co. II of Louisiana LLC. Group owner: Communications Capital Managers LLC (acq 3-4-02; grpsl). Format: Adult Contemporary. ♦Gary McKenney, gen mgr; Drew Labord, mus dir; Tommy Gray, chief of engrg.

KRUS(AM)— Nov 7, 1947: 1490 khz; 1 kw-U. TL: N32 30 48 W92 39 56. Box 430, 500 N. Monroe St. 71270. Phone: (318) 255-5000. Fax: (318) 255-5084. Licensee: Communications Capital Co. II of Louisiana LLC. Group owner: Communications Capital Managers LLC (acq 3-4-02; grpsl). Format: Blues, Black gospel. Target aud: 25-55; Black. ♦Gary McKenney, gen mgr, stn mgr & sls VP; James Cooper, opns dir & mus dir; Mary Poe, prom mgr.

KXKZ(FM)—Co-owned with KRUS(AM). June 29, 1966: 107.5 mhz; 98 kw. 1,066 ft. TL: N32 26 38 W92 42 42. Stereo. Format: Country. News staff: one; News: 7 hrs wkly. Target aud: 25-54. ♦Don Winston, progmg dir; Matt McKenney, mus dir.

Saint Martinville

***KSJY(FM)**— 2005: 89.9 mhz; 30 kw. Ant 466 ft. TL: N30 08 03 W91 51 46. Box 3206, American Family Radio, Tupelo, MS 38803. Phone: (662) 844-8888. Fax: (662) 842-6791. E-mail: comments@afr.net. Web Site: www.afr.net. Licensee: American Family Association. Group owner: American Family Radio. Format: Inspirational Christian. ♦Marvin Sanders, gen mgr.

Shreveport

***KDAQ(FM)**— Dec 21, 1984: 89.9 mhz; 100 kw. 932 ft. TL: N32 40 41 W93 55 35. Stereo. Box 5250 71135. Secondary address: One University Pl. 71115. Phone: (318) 797-5150. Phone: (800) 552-8502. Fax: (318) 797-5153. E-mail: listenermail@redriverradio.com. Web Site: www.redriverradio.com. Licensee: Louisiana State University Board of Supervisors. Network: Network: NPR, PRI. Format: Class, news. News: 40 hrs wkly. Target aud: General. ♦Roy Gerritsen, gen mgr.

KEEL(AM)— 1922: 710 khz; 50 kw-D, 5 kw-N, DA-2. TL: N32 40 35 W93 51 35. 6341 Westport Ave. 71129. Phone: (318) 688-1130. Fax: (318) 687-8574. E-mail: erinmccarty@clearchannel.com. Web Site: www.710keel.com. Licensee: Citicasters Licenses L.P. Group owner: Clear Channel Communications Inc. (acq 5-4-99; grpsl). Rep: D & R Radio. Format: News, sports, talk. News staff: 5; News: 6 hrs wkly. Target aud: 25-54; men. ♦Gary McCoy, opns dir; Lisa Janes, gen sls mgr; Lisa Slade, gen mgr & prom mgr; Erin McCarty, progmg dir; John Lee, news dir.

KXKS-FM—Co-owned with KEEL(AM). May 17, 1968: 93.7 mhz; 95 kw. 1,010 ft. TL: N32 40 39 W93 55 41. Stereo. Web Site: www.kisscountry937.com. Format: Country. Target aud: 25-54; 30 yr old female. ♦Lisa Janes, sls dir; Lisa Slade, prom dir; Russ Winston, progmg mgr.

KIOU(AM)— 1950: 1480 khz; 1 kw-D. TL: N32 31 30 W93 48 30. 4149 George Rd. 71107. Phone: (318) 227-1990. Fax: (318) 222-0271. Licensee: Metropolitan Radio Group Inc. (group owner; acq 10-97; $70,500). Format: Christian. Target aud: General. ♦Steve Bradley, gen mgr.

KLKL(FM)—(Minden). July 1, 1978: 95.7 mhz; 50 kw. 469 ft. TL: N32 33 24 W93 31 45. Stereo. Box 7197 71107. Secondary address: 208 N. Thomas Dr. 71107. Phone: (318) 222-3122. Fax: (318) 459-1493. Web Site: www.oldies957.fm. Licensee: Access. 1 Louisiana Holding Co. LLC. Group owner: Access.1 Communications Corp. (acq 6-30-00; $7.9 million. with KDKS-FM Blanchard). Format: Oldies. Target aud: 25-54. ♦Cary D. Camp, gen mgr; Howard Clark, opns mgr.

KMJJ-FM— Dec 5, 1976: 99.7 mhz; 50 kw. 462 ft. TL: N32 30 24 W93 45 13. 270 Plaza Loop, Bossier City 71111. Phone: (318) 549-8500. Fax: (318) 549-8505. E-mail: cj.jones@cumulus.com. Web Site: www.997kmjj.com. Licensee: Cumulus Licensing Corp. Group owner: Cumulus Media Inc. (acq 8-7-00; grpsl). Format: Urban contemp. News: one hr wkly. Target aud: 18-49; African American & general. ♦C.J. Jones, gen mgr; Gary Robinson, opns dir & prom dir; Al Weeden, progmg dir.

KOKA(AM)— Aug 1, 1954: 980 khz; 5 kw-D. TL: N32 34 18 W93 44 39. 208 N. Thomas Dr. 71107. Phone: (318) 222-3122. Phone: (318) 221-9802. Fax: (318) 459-1493. Licensee: Access. 1 Louisiana Holding Co. LLC. Group owner: Access.1 Communications Corp. (acq 12-20-02; grpsl). Rep: D & R Radio. Format: Relg, Black. Target aud: 25-64; middle-aged, middle class, Black adults. ♦Cary D. Camp, gen mgr; Howard Toole, gen sls mgr; Eddie Giles, progmg dir.

KRMD-FM— August 1948: 101.1 mhz; 98 kw. Ant 1,119 ft. TL: N32 41 08 W93 56 00. (CP: 100 kw, ant 1,627 ft). Stereo. 270 Plaza Loop, Bossier City 71111. Phone: (318) 549-8500. Fax: (318) 549-8505. Web Site: www.krmd.com. Licensee: Cumulus Licensing Corp. Group owner: Cumulus Media Inc. (acq 8-7-2000; grpsl). Format: Contemp country. News staff: 2. Target aud: 25-54. ♦C.J. Jones, gen mgr; Lisa Winans, opns mgr & sls dir; Bridget Erwin, rgnl sls mgr; Brandon Keene, prom mgr; James Anthony, mus dir & asst music dir; Tony King, news dir.

KRMD(AM)— June 1928: 1340 khz; 1 kw-U. TL: N32 29 36 W93 45 55. Stereo. Web Site: www.supertalk1340.com. Format: Sports, news, talk. ♦Brandon Keene, prom dir; John Sherman, progmg dir; James Jeansonne, chief of engrg.

KRUF(FM)—Listing follows KWKH(AM).

***KSCL(FM)**— Mar 11, 1976: 91.3 mhz; 150 w. 79 ft. TL: N32 29 01 W93 43 53. Stereo. 2911 Centenary Blvd. 71134. Phone: (318) 869-5296. Phone: (318) 869-5011. Fax: (318) 869-5294. E-mail: kscl@centenary.edu. Web Site: www.centenary.edu. Licensee: Centenary College of Louisiana. Format: College alternative, div. News staff: one; News: 4 hrs wkly. Target aud: General; college students & adults interested in div music. Spec prog: Black 3 hrs, folk 6 hrs, jazz 3 hrs, reggae 4 hrs, Fr 2 hrs, blues one hr, world beat 3 hrs wkly. ♦Katie Howell, stn mgr; Sammy Williams, opns dir.

KSYB(AM)— July 10, 1975: 1300 khz; 5 kw-D. TL: N32 31 48 W93 48 16. 2097 N. Hearne Ave. 71107. Phone: (318) 222-2744. Fax: (318) 425-7507. Licensee: Amistad Communications Inc. (acq 10-26-2000; $900,000). Format: Christian, sports, news. Spec prog: Gospel 8 hrs wkly. ♦Priscilla Myres, chief of opns & chief of engrg.

KTUX(FM)—(Carthage).TX Apr 1, 1985: 98.9 mhz; 100 kw. 1,049 ft. TL: N32 23 19 W94 01 10. Stereo. 6341 Westport Ave. 71129. Phone: (318) 688-1130. Fax: (318) 687-8574. E-mail: tedferguson@clearchannel.com. Licensee: Citicasters Licenses L.P. Group owner: Clear Channel Communications Inc. (acq 4-18-00). Format: New rock. Target aud: 18-49; super-active adults. ♦Charley Thomas, gen mgr; Kevin West, opns mgr & progmg dir; Rick Shelton, chief of engrg.

KVKI-FM— May 1959: 96.5 mhz; 95 kw. 797 ft. TL: N32 35 38 W93 51 39. Stereo. 6341 Westport Ave. 71129. Phone: (318) 688-1130. Fax: (318) 687-7363. Web Site: www.965kvki.com. Licensee: Citicasters Licenses L.P. Group owner: Clear Channel Communications Inc. (acq 5-4-99; grpsl). Rep: D & R Radio. Format: Adult contemp. News staff: one. Target aud: 25-54; female. ♦Gary McCoy, opns mgr.

KVMA-FM— 2001: 102.9 mhz; 42 kw. Ant 535 ft. TL: N32 29 36 W93 45 55. 270 Plaza Loop, Bossier City 71111. Phone: (318) 549-8500. Fax: (318) 549-8505. Web Site: magic1029fm.com. Licensee: Cumulus Licensing Corp. Group owner: Cumulus Media Inc. (acq 10-23-2000). Format: Urban contemp. ♦C.J. Jones, gen mgr.

KWKH(AM)— September 1925: 1130 khz; 50 kw-U, DA-N. TL: N32 42 15 W93 52 52. 6341 Westport Ave. 71129. Phone: (318) 688-1130. Fax: (318) 687-8574. Licensee: Citicasters Licenses L.P. Group owner: Clear Channel Communications Inc. (acq 5-4-99; grpsl). Rep: D & R Radio. Format: Country. News staff: 4; News: 18 hrs wkly. Target aud: Male 25-54. ♦Gary McCoy, opns mgr; Lisa Janes, gen sls mgr; Barney Cannon, progmg dir; Lisa Slade, progmg mgr; John Lee, news dir; Bess Maxwell, pub affrs dir.

KRUF(FM)—Co-owned with KWKH(AM). Nov 5, 1948: 94.5 mhz; 100 kw. Ant 1,096 ft. TL: N32 40 13 W93 55 59. (CP: Ant 1,666 ft. TL: N32 39 57 W93 55 58). Stereo. E-mail: chriscallaway@clearchannel.com. Format: CHR. ♦Gary McCoy, stn mgr & opns dir; Lisa Slade, prom dir.

Slidell

WSLA(AM)— Dec 5, 1963: 1560 khz; 1 kw-U, DA-N. TL: N30 15 08 W89 45 46. Stereo. Box 1175 70459. Secondary address: 38230 Coast Blvd. 70458. Phone: (985) 643-1560. Fax: (985) 649-9822. Licensee: MAPA Broadcasting L.L.C. (acq 7-2-93; 8-2-93). Network: USA. Format: ESPN programming. Target aud: 25 plus; news intensive audience & sports fans. Spec prog: Sports, Folk/Cajun 5 hrs, Relg 5 hrs wkly. ♦George Mayoral, gen mgr; Jim Sommers, opns mgr.

South Fort Polk

KROK(FM)— Feb 22, 2003: 95.7 mhz; 6 kw. Ant 289 ft. TL: N31 03 05 W93 16 41. 168 KVVP Dr., Leesville 71446. Phone: (337) 537-9292. Fax: (337) 537-4152. E-mail: krok@krok.com. Web Site: www.krok.com. Licensee: West Central Broadcasting Co. Inc. (acq 1-25-02). Format: Adult album alternative. Target aud: 18-54. ♦Alan Taylor, CFO; Doug Stannard, pres & gen mgr.

Springhill

KBSF(AM)—Listing follows KTKC(FM).

KTKC(FM)— Sept 5, 1975: 92.9 mhz; 40 kw. 548 ft. TL: N33 00 30 W93 28 38. Stereo. Box 127, 541 N. Main St. 71075. Secondary address: c/o Metropolitan Radio Group Inc., 318 E. Pershing St., Springfield, MO 65806. Phone: (318) 539-4616. Phone: (417) 581-5595. Fax: (318) 539-2356. Web Site: www.metropolitanradio.com. Licensee: Metropolitan Radio Group Inc. (group owner; acq 6-97; with co-located AM). Network: ABC. Format: Black, religious. Target aud: 35-54. ♦Ernest Pickings, gen mgr, opns dir & progmg dir.

KBSF(AM)—Co-owned with KTKC(FM). June 30, 1954: 1460 khz; 1 kw-D, 220 w-N. TL: N33 00 02 W93 28 43. Spec prog: Gospel 15 hrs wkly.

Sulphur

KEZM(AM)— 1955: 1310 khz; 500 w-D, 50 w-N, DA-1. TL: N30 13 27 W93 22 44. Stereo. 101 W. Napoleon 70663. Phone: (337) 527-3611. Fax: (337) 527-0213. E-mail: kezm1310am@structurex.net. Licensee: Merchant Broadcasting Inc. (acq 1-30-98; $75,000). Network: Sporting News Radio Network. Cohn & Marks. Format: Sports. News staff: one; News: 5 hrs wkly. Target aud: 25-54; upscale baby-boomers. Spec prog: Fr (Cajun) 5 hrs, gospel 5 hrs , local sports 12 hrs wkly. ♦Bruce L. Merchant, pres & engr; Kathy Soileau, sls dir & gen sls mgr; Kristen Merchant, prom dir; Duane Bergeron, news dir.

***KHBQ(FM)**—Not on air, target date: unknown: 89.1 mhz; 3 kw vert. Ant 197 ft. TL: N30 18 44 W93 20 17. 6080 Mt. Moriah Ext., Memphis, TN 38115. Phone: (901) 375-9324. Licensee: Broadcasting for the Challenged Inc. ♦George S. Flinn Jr., pres & gen mgr.

KKGB(FM)— Dec 17, 1977: 101.3 mhz; 12 kw. Ant 479 ft. TL: N30 14 41 W93 20 37. Stereo. 425 Broad St., Lake Charles 70601-4225. Phone: (337) 439-3300. Fax: (337) 436-7278. Web Site: www.kkgb.com. Licensee: Cumulus Licensing Corp. Group owner: Cumulus Media Inc. (acq 12-17-98; grpsl). Rep: Christal. Kaye, Scholer, Fierman, Hays & Handler. Format: Classic rock. News staff: one. Target aud: General; baby boomers. ♦Don Kellogg, opns dir.

KYKZ(FM)—See Lake Charles

Tallulah

KBYO(AM)— Sept 4, 1954: 1360 khz; 500 w-D. TL: N32 25 37 W91 13 15. Box 1112, Hwy. 80 W. 71282. Phone: (318) 574-1500. Fax: (601) 638-0869. Licensee: Holladay Broadcasting of Louisiana LLC (acq 1-10-03; $450,000. with co-located FM). Format: Urban contemp, relg. Target aud: 18-54. ♦Robert H. Holladay, pres; Ron Anderson, gen mgr & progmg dir; Russell Kendrick, chief of engrg.

KBYO-FM— Apr 29, 1983: 104.5 mhz; 3 kw. 320 ft. TL: N29 45 35 W90 49 30. (CP: 104.5 mhz, 25 kw). Stereo. Network: ABC Information & Entertainment. Format: Rock/AOR. ♦Kurt Rushing, adv mgr.

KTJZ(FM)—Not on air, target date: unknown: 97.5 mhz; 6 kw. Ant 302 ft. TL: N32 25 42 W91 18 47. 3313 Government St., Baton Rouge 70806-5629. Phone: (225) 334-7490. Licensee: Mid South Communications Co. Inc. ♦Ernest L. Johnson, chmn & pres.

Thibodaux

***KNSU(FM)**— Feb 15, 1972: 91.5 mhz; 250 w vert. 148 ft. TL: N29 47 29 W90 48 07. (CP: 91.3 mhz, 3 kw, ant 285 ft. TL: N29 45 35 W90 49 30). Box 2664, Nicholls State Univ. 70310. Phone: (985) 448-4447. Fax: (985) 449-7106. E-mail: knsu@nicholls.edu. Web Site: www.nicholls.edu/knsu. Licensee: Board of Trustees, Nicholls State University. Format: Modern. News: 10 hrs wkly. Target aud: 18 plus. Spec prog: Black 8 hrs, gospel 4 hrs, jazz one hr, world 2 hrs wkly. ♦Caae Viosin, stn mgr; Josh Byrnes, progmg dir; John Zeringue, news dir.

KTIB(AM)— Dec 24, 1953: 640 khz; 5 kw-D, 1 kw-N, DA-2. TL: N29 50 05 W90 54 48. Stereo. 108 Green St. 70301. Phone: (985) 447-9006. Fax: (985) 446-2338. Web Site: www.oldies640.com.

Stations in the U.S.   Maine

Licensee: LaTerr Broadcasting Corp. (acq 11-16-73). Format: News, oldies. News staff: 2. Target aud: 35 plus. ♦ Linda Bellanger, gen mgr.

KTLN(FM)— May 1995: 90.5 mhz; 200 w. 357 ft. TL: N29 43 18 W90 46 33. Stereo. Univ. of New Orleans, New Orleans 70148. Phone: (504) 280-7000. Fax: (504) 280-6061. E-mail: info@wwno.org. Web Site: www.wwno.org. Licensee: Board of Supervisors of Louisiana State University and Agricultural and Mechanical College, University of New Orleans. Network: Network: NPR, PRI. Format: Class, news. News: 39 hrs wkly. Target aud: 35-70; well educated professionals, managers, artists & arts patrons. Spec prog: Jazz 6 hrs, prairie home companion 4 hrs wkly. ♦ Ronald C. Curtis, opns dir; Fred Kasten, prom mgr & progmg dir.

KXOR-FM— May 1, 1966: 106.3 mhz; 25 kw. Ant 328 ft. TL: N29 38 52 W90 41 34. Stereo. 120 Prevost Dr., Houma 70364. Secondary address: Box 2068, Houma 70361. Phone: (985) 851-1021. Fax: (985) 872-4403. E-mail: info@eagle1063.com. Web Site: www.eagle-1063.com. Licensee: Guaranty Broadcasting Co. of Houma L.L.C. (acq 7-23-98; $875,000). Network: ABC FM Connection. Format: Classic rock. News: 20 hrs wkly. Target aud: 18-54. Spec prog: LSU sports, loc high school football. ♦ Melanie Hotard, gen mgr.

Tioga

KLAA(FM)—Licensed to Tioga. See Alexandria

Varnado

WBOX-FM— November 1985: 92.9 mhz; 3 kw. 321 ft. TL: N30 54 10 W89 57 36. Stereo. Box 280, Bogalusa 70429. Phone: (985) 732-4288. Fax: (985) 732-4288. Licensee: Best Country Broadcasting LLC (acq 4-18-02; $150,000. with WBOX(AM) Bogalusa). Format: Contemp country. ♦ Ben R. Strickland, pres & gen mgr.

Vidalia

WQNZ(FM)—See Natchez, MS

Ville Platte

KVPI-FM— Feb 26, 1967: 92.5 mhz; 3.9 kw horiz. Ant 220 ft. TL: N30 41 39 W92 18 46. Stereo. Box J 70586. Secondary address: 809 W. LaSalle St. 70586. Phone: (337) 363-2124. Fax: (337) 363-3574. Web Site: www.oldies925.com. Licensee: Ville Platte Broadcasting Co. (acq 12-18-2001). Network: Network: CNN Radio, AP Radio. Format: Oldies. News staff: one; News: 12 hrs wkly. Target aud: 32-65. ♦ Roland Fink, CEO & pres; Rhonda Moser, sr VP; Mark Layne, gen mgr.

KVPI(AM)— November 1953: 1050 khz; 250 w-D, 10 w-N. TL: N30 41 39 W92 18 46. E-mail: kvpi@centurytel.net. Network: AP Radio. News staff: one; News: 12 hrs wkly. Target aud: General. Spec prog: Cajun 12 hrs wkly.

Vivian

KNCB(AM)— Apr 9, 1966: 1320 khz; 5 kw-D. TL: N32 54 08 W93 58 59. Box 1072 71082. Secondary address: 17525 Hwy. 1 N. 71082. Phone: (318) 375-3278. Fax: (318) 375-3329. E-mail: rjc1072@cs.com. Licensee: North Caddo Broadcasting Co. (acq 4-9-66). Format: Country, gospel. Target aud: General. ♦ Ruby J. Collins, gen mgr.

KNCB-FM— Sept 28, 1996: 105.3 mhz; 3.2 kw. 449 ft. TL: N32 55 54 W93 54 22. Stereo. (Acq 9-27-96.). Network: ABC. Format: Real country.

Washington

KNEK(AM)— Aug 18, 1980: 1190 khz; 250 w-D. TL: N30 35 09 W92 04 00. 3225 Ambassador Caffrey Pkwy., Lafayette 70506. Phone: (337) 981-0106. Fax: (337) 988-0443. Web Site: www.knek.com. Licensee: Citadel Broadcasting Co. Group owner: Citadel Broadcasting Corp. (acq 1-14-99; grpsl). Format: Zydeco & blues. Target aud: 25-54. Spec prog: Farm 4 hrs wkly. ♦ Mary Galyean, gen mgr.

KNEK-FM— 1989: 104.7 mhz; 3 kw. 223 ft. TL: N30 26 45 W92 09 24. (CP: 25 kw, ant 364 ft.). Stereo. Web Site: www.knek.com. Format: Adult contemp.

West Monroe

KMBS(AM)— August 1956: 1310 khz; 5 kw-D, 49 w-N. TL: N32 29 02 W92 09 10. Box 547 71294. Phone: (318) 397-0927. Phone: (318) 323-1310. Fax: (318) 397-3132. Licensee: Red Bear Broadcasting. (acq 6-10-93; $200,000; 6-28-93). Network: ABC. Format: Sports. ♦ Chuck Redden, gen mgr.

KZRZ(FM)— Aug 1, 1967: 98.3 mhz; 50 kw. 492 ft. TL: N32 39 38 W91 59 28. Stereo. 1200 N. 18th St., Suite D, Monroe 71201. Phone: (318) 387-3922. Fax: (318) 322-4585. Web Site: www.monroeradio.com. Licensee: Opus Broadcasting Monroe L.L.C. Group owner: Opus Media Partners LLC (acq 7-19-2004; grpsl). Format: Adult contemp. Target aud: 18-54; mid to upper income. ♦ Chris Zimmerman, gen mgr; Mike Dawnhour, gen sls mgr.

White Castle

KKAY(AM)— November 1976: 1590 khz; 1 kw-D. TL: N30 11 01 W91 06 27. 706 Railroad Ave., Donaldsonville 70346. Phone: (225) 473-6397. Fax: (225) 473-5764. Web Site: www.harry@kkay1590.com. Licensee: Cactus Communications LLC. Format: Varied. ♦ Harry Hoyler, gen mgr, opns mgr & progmg dir.

Winnfield

KVCL(AM)— Dec 17, 1955: 1270 khz; 820 w-D. TL: N31 56 54 W92 37 37. Stereo. Box 548, Harrison Bcstg. Org. Bldg., 304 KVCL Rd. 71483. Phone: (318) 628-5822. Fax: (318) 628-7355. Licensee: Harrison Broadcast Organization Inc. (acq 3-7-90; $475,000 3-26-90). Format: New adult contemp, jazz, talk. News staff: 2; News: 21 hrs wkly. Target aud: General; financially able persons, blacks and professionals. Spec prog: Black 3 hrs, relg 15 hrs, gospel 5 hrs, big band 4 hrs wkly. ♦ George B. Harrison PhD., CEO, pres, gen mgr, news dir & engrg VP; Leigh Anne Harrison, natl sls mgr & adv mgr; Patricia J. Harrison PhD., exec VP, prom mgr & pub affrs dir.

KVCL-FM— Nov 3, 1966: 92.1 mhz; 6 kw. 210 ft. TL: N31 56 54 W92 37 37. Stereo. (Acq 3-7-90; $595,000). Format: Country, black, relg. News staff: 2; News: 22 hrs wkly. Target aud: 24-60; professional financially able persons, blacks & general. Spec prog: Black 20 hrs, gospel 20 hrs wkly.

Winnsboro

KMAR-FM— August 1969: 95.9 mhz; 3 kw. 171 ft. TL: N32 11 40 W91 45 30. Stereo. 1823 Hwy. 618 71295. Phone: (318) 435-5141. Fax: (318) 435-5749. E-mail: kmar@3g.quik.com. Licensee: Boeuf River Broadcasting Co. Group owner: The Radio Group (acq 11-89; $200,000 with co-located AM; 11-6-89). Network: ABC. Format: Country. News staff: one; News: 20 hrs wkly. Target aud: 30-60; adults. Spec prog: Farm 5 hrs, southern gospel 20 hrs wkly. ♦ Tom Gay, pres, gen mgr & stn mgr.

Maine

Auburn

WFNK(FM)—See Portland

WLAM(AM)—See Lewiston

WTHT(FM)— February 1977: 99.9 mhz; 50 kw. 492 ft. TL: N43 57 07 W70 17 46. Stereo. 477 Congress St., Suite 3 A, Portland 04101. Phone: (207) 782-1800. Phone: (207) 797-0780. Fax: (207) 783-7371. Fax: (207) 253-1971. Licensee: Nassau Broadcasting III L.L.C. Group owner: Nassau Broadcasting Partners L.P. (acq 4-6-2004; grpsl). Format: Country. Target aud: Women 18-34, women 25-54; Maine's kiss 99.9. ♦ Tim Gatz, gen mgr & gen sls mgr; Stan Manning, progmg dir; Peter Magee, chief of engrg.

Augusta

WABK-FM—See Gardiner

WFAU(AM)—See Gardiner

WJZN(AM)— Feb 23, 1932: 1400 khz; 1 kw-U. TL: N44 17 30 W69 46 27. 52 Western Ave. 04330. Phone: (207) 623-4735. Fax: (207) 626-5948. E-mail: 92moose@midmaine.com. Licensee: Citadel Broadcasting Co. Group owner: Citadel Broadcasting Corp. (acq 4-26-2001; grpsl). Rep: D & R Radio. Format: Nostalgia. News staff: one. Target aud: 20-40; young adults. ♦ Al Perry, gen mgr; Julie Crocker, gen sls mgr; Renee Nelson, news dir; Bob Perry, chief of engrg.

WMME-FM—Co-owned with WJZN(AM). Jan 14, 1981: 92.3 mhz; 50 kw. Ant 500 ft. TL: N44 20 07 W69 41 01. Stereo. Web Site: www.92moose.fm. Format: CHR.

WKCG(FM)— July 1961: 101.3 mhz; 50 kw. Ant 321 ft. TL: N44 18 51 W69 50 03. 150 Whitten Rd. 04330. Phone: (207) 623-9000. Fax: (207) 623-9007. E-mail: kellyslater@clearchannel.com. Licensee: Capstar TX L.P. Group owner: Clear Channel Communications Inc. (acq 1-18-01; grpsl). Format: Adult contemp. ♦ Kelly Slater, gen mgr; Steve Smith, opns dir; Rick Dougle, gen sls mgr.

WMDR(AM)— Oct 2, 1946: 1340 khz; 1 kw-U. TL: N44 19 43 W69 45 53. 160 Riverside Dr 04330. Phone: (207) 622-1340. Fax: (207) 623-2874. E-mail: wmdr@adelphia.net. Web Site: www.wmdr.org. Licensee: Light of Life Ministries Inc. (acq 12-94; 2-13-95). Format: Christian, educ, children. News: 5 hrs wkly. Target aud: General. Spec prog: Gospel, relg. ♦ Denise LaFountain, gen mgr; Randy Todd, progmg dir.

Bangor

WABI(AM)— 1924: 910 khz; 5 kw-U, DA-N. TL: N44 46 44 W68 44 22. 184 Target Industrial Circle 04410. Phone: (207) 947-9100. Fax: (207) 942-8039. Licensee: Clear Channel Broadcasting Licenses Inc. Group owner: Clear Channel Communications Inc. acq 6-28-01; $3.75 million. including five-year noncompete agreement with co-located FM). Rep: Allied Radio Partners. Davis Wright Tremaine. Format: Local sports, nostalgia. News staff: one; News: 4 hrs wkly. Target aud: 35 plus. ♦ George Hale, opns dir; Jim Herron, gen mgr & gen sls mgr.

WWBX(FM)—Co-owned with WABI(AM). Mar 15, 1961: 97.1 mhz; 5 kw. 1,230 ft. TL: N44 42 13 W69 04 07. Stereo. Web Site: www.b97hits.com. (Acq 7-30-01). Format: Contemp hit. News staff: one; News: 2 hrs wkly. Target aud: General. ♦ Michael W. Hale, opns mgr & progmg dir.

WBFB(FM)—See Belfast

WEZQ(FM)— June 9, 1976: 92.9 mhz; 20 kw. 787 ft. TL: N44 45 35 W68 33 55. Stereo. 49 Acme Rd., Brewer 04412. Phone: (207) 989-5631. Fax: (207) 989-5685. E-mail: blacey@jpc.com. Web Site: www.wezq-fm.com. Licensee: Cumulus Licensing Corp. Group owner: Cumulus Media Inc. (acq 3-1-99; grpsl). Rep: D & R Radio. Fisher, Wayland, Cooper, Leader & Zaragoza. Format: Easy listening. News staff: one. Target aud: 25-54. ♦ Tom Preble, gen mgr; Paul Dupuius, opns VP & opns mgr; Undy Campbell, progmg dir.

WHCF(FM)— Aug 10, 1981: 88.5 mhz; 100 kw. 1,604 ft. TL: N45 07 46 W68 21 28. (CP: 35 kw, ant 1,620 ft.). Stereo. Box 5000 04402-5000. Secondary address: 1476 Broadway 04401. Phone: (207) 947-2751. Fax: (207) 947-0010. E-mail: whcf@whcf.cc. Web Site: whcf.cc. Licensee: Bangor Baptist Church. Network: Network: USA, Moody. Format: Inspirational Christian, gospel. News: 7 hrs wkly.

Maine

Target aud: Female; mid 40's. Spec prog: Childdren 6 hrs wkly. ♦ Scott Stewart, chmn; Jerry Mick, pres; Kathy Schroeher, opns mgr; Ed Paradis, chief of opns; Tom Obey, dev dir; Wayne Frost, gen mgr & progmg dir; Hal Welch, chief of engrg.

*WHSN(FM)— September 1974: 89.3 mhz; 140 w. 69 ft. TL: N44 49 30 W68 47 48. Stereo. One College Cir. 04401. Phone: (207) 941-7116. Phone: (207) 973-1011. Fax: (207) 947-3987. E-mail: whsn@nescom.edu. Web Site: www.nescom.edu. Licensee: Husson College Board of Trustees. Format: Alternative. News staff: one; News: 7 hrs wkly. Target aud: 12-25; high school & college students. ♦ Ben Haskell, gen mgr; Mark Nason, progmg VP & progmg dir; Susan Patten, news dir & chief of engrg.

WKIT-FM—See Brewer

*WMEH(FM)— Sept 14, 1970: 90.9 mhz; 13.5 kw. 850 ft. TL: N44 45 36 W68 33 59. Stereo. 65 Texas Ave. 04401. Secondary address: 1450 Lisbon St., Lewiston 04240. Phone: (207) 874-6570. Fax: (207) 942-2857. Fax: (207) 761-0318. E-mail: cbeck@mpn.com. Web Site: www.mainepublicradio.org. Licensee: Maine Public Broadcasting Corp. (acq 6-23-92; 7-13-92). Network: Network: NPR, PRI. Dow, Lohnes & Albertson. Format: Class, pub affrs, news. ♦ Mary Anne Alhadeff, CEO & pres; Christopher F. Amann, CFO; Charles Beck, VP & stn mgr; Deb Turner, dev VP.

WWMJ(FM)—See Ellsworth

WZON(AM)— December 1926: 620 khz; 5 kw-U, DA-N. TL: N44 49 44 W68 47 08. Box 1929 04402. Phone: (207) 990-2800. Fax: (207) 990-2444. E-mail: wzon@zoneradio.com. Web Site: www.zoneradio.com. Licensee: The Zone Corp. (group owner; acq 9-1-93; $236,200; 9-27-93). Format: Sports, talk. News staff: one; News: 18 hrs wkly. Target aud: General; info & entertainment seekers. ♦ Stephen King, pres; Bobby Russell, gen mgr & stn mgr; Ken Wood, sls dir & gen sls mgr; Scotty Moore, progmg dir.

Bar Harbor

WBQI(FM)— May 6, 1995: 107.7 mhz; 11.5 kw. 489 ft. TL: N44 33 13 W68 05 40. Stereo. 169 Port Rd., Kennebunk 04043. Phone: (207) 967-0993. Fax: (207) 967-8671. Web Site: www.1077.com. Licensee: Nassau Broadcasting III L.L.C. Group owner: Nassau Broadcasting Partners L.P. (acq 4-6-2004; grpsl). Network: Network: CBS, Westwood One. Format: Classic rock, jazz, sports. News staff: one; News: 6 hrs wkly. Target aud: 25-54; baby boomers. Spec prog: Blues 15 hrs wkly. ♦ Robert Scott Hogg Sr., pres; Pat Collins, gen mgr.

WLKE(FM)— June 1, 1992: 99.1 mhz; 45 kw. 400 ft. TL: N44 32 53 W68 18 53. Stereo. 184 Target Cir., Bangor 04401-5718. Phone: (207) 667-7573. Fax: (207) 667-9494. E-mail: larryjulius@clearchannel.com. Web Site: www.lucky99.net. Licensee: Clear Channel Broadcasting Licenses Inc. Group owner: Clear Channel Communications Inc. (acq 10-23-00; grpsl). Network: ABC. Rep: Christal. Dow, Lohnes & Albertson. Format: Country. News staff: one. Target aud: General. ♦ Larry Julius, gen mgr; Jeffrey Pierce, opns mgr, gen sls mgr & mus dir; Josh Scroggins, gen sls mgr.

Bath

WBCI(FM)— June 1971: 105.9 mhz; 50 kw. 499 ft. TL: N44 04 09 W69 55 28. Stereo. Box 359, Topsham 04086. Secondary address: 122 Main St., Topsham 04086. Phone: (207) 725-9224. Fax: (207) 725-2686. E-mail: wbci@gwi.net. Web Site: www.wbci.net. Licensee: Blount Communications Inc. Group owner: Blount Communications Group (acq 4-20-95; $375,000). Network: Salem Radio Network. Rep: Salem. Format: Talk, Christian. Target aud: 25-54; 60% men, 40% women. ♦ Bill Blount, pres; Deborah Blount, exec VP; David Young, sr VP; Janice Murphy, stn mgr.

WCME(FM)—See Boothbay Harbor

WJTO(AM)— Sept 30, 1957: 730 khz; 1 kw-D, 29 w-N. TL: N43 52 39 W69 50 49. Box 308 04530. Phone: (207) 443-6671. E-mail: bob@wjto.com. Licensee: Blue Jey Broadcasting Co. Group owner: Bob Bittner Broadcasting Inc. (acq 2-28-97; $150,000). Format: Adult Standards. News staff: one; News: 2 hrs wkly. Target aud: 35 plus; adults along the Maine coastline. ♦ Bob Bittner, gen mgr.

Belfast

WBFB(FM)— Mar 7, 1986: 104.7 mhz; 10 kw. 1,099 ft. TL: N44 34 51 W68 53 51. Stereo. 184 Target Industrial Circle, Bangor 04401. Phone: (207) 947-9100. Fax: (207) 942-8039. Web Site: www.1047the bear.com. Licensee: Clear Channel Broadcasting Licenses Inc. Group owner: Clear Channel Communications Inc. (acq 10-23-00; grpsl). Dow, Lohnes & Albertson. Format: Country. News staff: 2. Target aud: 18-49. ♦ Larry Julius, gen mgr.

Biddeford

WCYY(FM)— August 1972: 94.3 mhz; 12 kw. 472 ft. TL: N43 32 34 W70 24 12. Stereo. One City Ctr., Portland 04101. Phone: (207) 774-6364. Fax: (207) 774-8707. E-mail: mike.sambrook@citcomm.com. Web Site: www.wcyy.com. Licensee: Citadel Broadcasting Co. Group owner: Citadel Broadcasting Corp. (acq 7-7-99; grpsl). Rep: Katz Radio. Format: Modern rock. News staff: one. Target aud: 25-44; educated, affluent. ♦ Michael Sambrook, VP & gen mgr; Herbert Ivy, opns VP & opns mgr; Micah Malloy, sls dir; Wendell Clough, prom dir; Brian James, mus dir; Celeste Nadeau, news dir; Eugene Terwilliger, chief of engrg.

WVAE(AM)— 1948: 1400 khz; 1 kw-U. TL: N43 28 52 W70 29 08. 4020 Western Ave., South Portland 04106. Phone: (207) 774-4561. Fax: (207) 774-3788. E-mail: service@amoldies.com. Web Site: www.ilovethebay.com. Licensee: Saga Communications of New England LLC. Group owner: Saga Communications Inc. (acq 11-17-03; $350,000). Network: Network: ABC Information & Entertainment, Jones Radio Networks. Format: Adult standards. News staff: one. Target aud: 35 plus; upscale professional. Spec prog: Relg 2 hrs wkly.

Blue Hill

*WERU-FM— June 1, 1988: 89.9 mhz; 15 kw. 899 ft. TL: N44 26 04 W68 35 25. Stereo. Box 170, East Orland 04431-0170. Secondary address: 1186 Acadia Hwy., East Orland 04431. Phone: (207) 469-6600. Fax: (207) 469-8961. E-mail: info@weru.org. Web Site: www.weru.org. Licensee: Salt Pond Community Broadcasting Co. Format: Div, educ. Target aud: General. Spec prog: Class 5 hrs, jazz 18 hrs, folk 15 hrs, blues 5 hrs, reggae 4 hrs, Afro-beat 4 hrs, pub affrs 9 hrs wkly. ♦ Joel Mann, gen mgr & progmg dir; Denis Howard, dev dir; Maggie Overton, mus dir.

Boothbay Harbor

WCME(FM)— Apr 1, 1984: 96.7 mhz; 25 kw. 449 ft. TL: N44 01 31 W69 34 17. Stereo. 15 Payne Ave., Rockland 04841. Phone: (207) 594-9400. Fax: (207) 594-2234. E-mail: donshieldsjr@clearchannel.com. Licensee: Capstar TX L.P. Group owner: Clear Channel Communications Inc. (acq 1-18-01; grpsl). Brown, Nietert & Kaufman. Format: News/talk. News staff: one; News: 12 hrs wkly. Target aud: 25-49. ♦ Kelly Slater, gen mgr; Don Shields, opns dir; Steve Smith, progmg dir; Rick Dugal, chief of engrg & sls.

Brewer

WKIT-FM— Feb 14, 1979: 100.3 mhz; 50 kw. 850 ft. TL: N44 40 39 W68 45 15. Stereo. Box 1929, 861 Broadway, Bangor 04402. Phone: (207) 990-2800. Fax: (207) 990-2444. E-mail: wkit@zoneradio.com. Web Site: www.zoneradio.com. Licensee: The Zone Corp. (group owner; acq 9-95; $800,000 with co-located AM). Fisher, Wayland, Cooper, Leader & Zaragoza. News staff: 2. Target aud: 18-49. ♦ Stephen King, CEO; Bobby Russell, gen mgr & progmg dir; Ken Wood, gen sls mgr.

WQCB(FM)— Jan 20, 1986: 106.5 mhz; 98 kw. 1,079 ft. TL: N45 03 26 W69 11 27. Stereo. Box 100 04412. Secondary address: 49 Acme Rd. 04412. Phone: (207) 989-5631. Fax: (207) 989-5685. E-mail: tom.preble@midmaine.com. Web Site: www.wqcb-fm.com. Licensee: Cumulus Licensing Corp. Group owner: Cumulus Media LLC (acq 2-20-98; $6.4 million with WBZN(FM) Old Town). Rep: McGavren Guild. Format: Country. News staff: 2; News: 4 hrs wkly. Target aud: 25-54; general. ♦ Tom Preble, gen mgr; Paul Dupuis, opns mgr; Cindy Campbell, progmg dir.

Brunswick

WBCI(FM)—See Bath

*WBOR(FM)— April 1957: 91.1 mhz; 300 w. 154 ft. TL: N43 54 34 W69 57 43. Stereo. WBOR 91.1 FM, 6200 College Stn., Bowdoin College 04011-8462. Phone: (207) 725-3210. Phone: (207) 725-3250. Fax: (207) 725-3510. E-mail: wbor@bowdoin.edu. Web Site: www.wbor.org/wbor. Licensee: Trustees of Bowdoin College. Format: Div. Target aud: General. Spec prog: Class 8 hrs, jazz 20 hrs, folk 12 hrs, urban contemp 15 hrs, reggae 10 hrs, other 10 hrs, childrens 3 hrs wkly. ♦ Steve Seabrook, stn mgr; Burgwell Howard, opns VP & opns mgr.

WCLZ(FM)— Apr 11, 1965: 98.9 mhz; 48 kw. 400 ft. TL: N43 55 40 W69 59 43. Stereo. One City Ctr., Portland 04101. Phone: (207) 774-6364. Fax: (207) 774-8707. E-mail: wclz@989wclz.com. Web Site: www.989wclz.com. Licensee: Citadel Broadcasting Corp. Group owner: Citadel Broadcasting Corp. (acq 7-7-99; grpsl). Rep: Christal. Format: Progsv. ♦ Michael Sambrook, gen mgr; Michelle Morel, adv.

WJJB(AM)— December 1955: 900 khz; 1 kw-D, 66 w-N. TL: N43 55 40 W69 59 43. Atlantic Coast Radio, 779 Warren Ave., Portland 04103-1007. Phone: (207) 773-9695. Fax: (207) 761-4406. E-mail: morningjab@yahoo.com. Web Site: www.thebigjab.com. Licensee: Atlantic Coast Radio L.L.C. (group owner; acq 9-99). Rep: Christal. Format: Sports, talk. News staff: 2; News: 4 hrs wkly. Target aud: 25-54. ♦ Jon VanHoogenstyn, gen mgr; David Shamacher, progmg dir.

Calais

*WMED(FM)— November 1983: 89.7 mhz; 30 kw. 525 ft. TL: N45 01 44 W67 19 25. Stereo. 65 Texas Ave., Bangor 04401. Secondary address: 1450 Lisbon St., Lewiston 04240. Phone: (207) 874-6570. Fax: (207) 761-0318. E-mail: cbeck@mpbc.com. Web Site: www.mainepublicradio.org. Licensee: Maine Public Broadcasting Corp. (acq 6-23-92). Network: Network: NPR, PRI. Format: Class, pub affrs, news. ♦ Charles Beck, pres, VP & stn mgr; Mary Anne Alhadeff, CEO & pres; Chris Amann, CFO; Deb Turner, dev VP.

WQDY-FM— Jan 14, 1976: 92.7 mhz; 3 kw. Ant 299 ft. TL: N45 10 02 W67 16 38. Stereo. Box 403 04619. Secondary address: 637 Main St. 04619. Phone: (207) 454-7545. Fax: (207) 454-3062. E-mail: wqdy@wqdy.fm. Web Site: www.wqdy.fm. Licensee: WQDY Inc. (acq 11-26-96; for stock). Network: Network: ABC Information & Entertainment, Jones Radio Networks. Cyr Associates Fletcher, Heald & Hildreth. Format: Adult contemp, classic rock. News staff: one. ♦ Bill McVicar, pres; Roger Holst, chief of engrg.

Camden

*WMEP(FM)— Oct 2002: 90.5 mhz; 2 kw vert. 1,178 ft. TL: N44 12 40 W69 09 06. 65 Texas Ave., Bangor 04401. Secondary address: 1450 Lisbon St., Lewiston 04240. Phone: (207) 874-6570. Fax: (207) 761-0318. E-mail: cbeck@mpbn.net. Web Site: www.mpbc.org. Licensee: Maine Public Broadcasting Corp. Format: Class, pub affrs, news/talk. ♦ Chris Amann, CFO; Mary Anne Alhadeff, pres & gen mgr; Charles Beck, stn mgr & progmg dir; Deb Turner, dev dir; John Likshis, mktg dir.

WQSS(FM)— May 1988: 102.5 mhz; 7.9 kw. 1,201 ft. TL: N44 12 40 W69 09 06. Stereo. 15 Payne Ave., Rockland 04841-2117. Phone: (207) 594-9400. Fax: (207) 594-2234. E-mail: kellyslater@clearchannel.com. Web Site: www.1025thepeak.com. Licensee: Clear Channel Broadcasting Licenses Inc. Group owner: Clear Channel Communications Inc. (acq 5-3-02; $1.72 million). Network: ABC. Rep: McGavren Guild. Format: Classic rock. News staff: one; News: 10 hrs wkly. Target aud: 25-54. ♦ Kelly Slater, gen mgr; Steve Smith, opns dir; Rick Dougle, gen sls mgr; Don Shields, progmg dir; Marc Fisher, chief of engrg.

Caribou

WBPW(FM)—See Presque Isle

WCXU(FM)— Nov 15, 1986: 97.7 mhz; 20 kw. 328 ft. TL: N46 47 26 W67 55 07. Stereo. 152 E. Green Ridge Rd. 04736. Phone: (207) 473-7513. Fax: (207) 472-3221. E-mail: channelxradio@yahoo.com. Web Site: www.channelxradio.com. Licensee: The Canxus Broadcasting Corp. (group owner) Rep: Savalli. Cyr Associates. Koteen & Naftalin. Format: Adult contemp, news, oldies. News staff: one; News: 21 hrs wkly. Target aud: 25-54; educated, div occupations, affluent. ♦ Dennis H. Curley, CEO, chmn, pres & CFO; Richard Chandler, gen mgr & opns mgr; Mark Stewert, progmg dir.

*WFST(AM)— July 15, 1956: 600 khz; 5 kw-D, 127 w-N. TL: N46 53 12 W68 02 44. (CP: TL: N46 45 52 W67 59 23). Box 600, 670 Sweden St. 04736. Phone: (207) 492-6000. Fax: (207) 493-3268. E-mail: wfst@mfx.net. Web Site: www.wfst.net. Licensee: Northern Broadcast Ministries Inc. (acq 6-8-93; $54,000; 6-28-93). Format: Christian,

Stations in the U.S. **Maine**

gospel, relg. Target aud: General. ♦Donald Flewelling, pres; Tom Hale, VP; John Stephenson, gen mgr.

Dennysville

WCRQ(FM)— May 1998: 102.9 mhz; 100 kw. 456 ft. TL: N45 01 44 W67 19 25. Stereo. 637 Main St., Calais 04619. Phone: (207) 454-7545. Fax: (207) 454-3062. E-mail: wcrq@wqdy.fm. Licensee: WQDY Inc. (acq 5-30-03; $195,000). Fletcher, Heald & Hildreth. Format: Hot adult contemp. News: 6 hrs wkly. Target aud: 18-49; mass appeal. ♦Bill McVicar, pres; Bill Conley, mus dir.

Dexter

WGUY(FM)— 1993: 102.1 mhz; 50 kw. 672 ft. TL: N45 02 40 W69 15 01. Stereo. 184 Target Industrial Cir., Bangor 04401. Phone: (207) 947-9100. Fax: (207) 942-8039. Licensee: Clear Channel Broadcasting Licenses Inc. Group owner: Clear Channel Communications Inc. acq 10-20-03; $1.2 million). Rep: Cyr Associates. Format: Hits of the 50s, 60s, & 70s. News staff: one; News: 2 hrs wkly. Target aud: 25-54. ♦Larry Julius, gen mgr.

Dover Foxcroft

WDME-FM— November 1980: 103.1 mhz; 4.8 kw. 385 ft. TL: N45 12 58 W69 14 34. Stereo. Box 1929, Bangor 04402. Phone: (207) 990-2800. Fax: (207) 990-2444. E-mail: wdme@zoneradio.com. Web Site: zoneradio.com. Licensee: The Zone Corp. (group owner; acq 2-16-01; $175,100). Network: ABC. Rep: New England. Verner, Liipfert, Bernhard, McPherson & Hand. Format: Adult contemp. News staff: one. Target aud: General. Spec prog: Beatles one hr, 70s mus 2 hrs, 60s mus one hr, 50s mus one hr, countdown shows, 80s mus 2 hrs wkly. ♦Bobby Russell, VP, stn mgr & progmg dir; Howard Soule, chief of engrg; Ken Woods, pub affrs dir & sls.

Eastport

*WSHD(FM)— April 1984: 91.7 mhz; 12 w. Ant 115 ft. TL: N44 54 30 W66 59 24. Stereo. Shead High School, 89 High St. 04631. Phone: (207) 853-6254. Fax: (207) 853-2919. Licensee: Shead High School. Format: Classic hits. Target aud: General. ♦Raffy Hopkins, gen mgr.

Ellsworth

WDEA(AM)— Dec 13, 1958: 1370 khz; 5 kw-U, DA-2. TL: N44 28 00 W68 28 11. Box 100, 49 Acme Rd., Brewer 04412. Phone: (207) 989-5631. Fax: (207) 989-5685. Web Site: www.cumulus.com. Licensee: Cumulus Licensing Corp. Group owner: Cumulus Media Inc. (acq 1999; grpsl). Network: CBS. Rep: D & R Radio. Shaw Pittman. Format: Nostalgia. Target aud: 35 plus. ♦Fred Miller, opns VP & progmg dir; Tom Preble, gen mgr, sls VP & gen sls mgr; Michael O'Hara, prom dir; Allison Bankston, news dir; Richard Hyatt, chief of engrg.

WWMJ(FM)— Co-owned with WDEA(AM). Dec 27, 1965: 95.7 mhz; 11.5 kw. Ant 1,029 ft. TL: N44 39 31 W68 36 20. Stereo. E-mail: q1065@midmaine.com. Web Site: www.wwmj-fm.com. Network: ABC Information & Entertainment. Format: Classic hits. Target aud: 25-54. ♦Bob Duchesne, opns mgr; Fred Miller, progmg VP.

WKSQ(FM)— May 27, 1982: 94.5 mhz; 11.5 kw. 1,027 ft. TL: N44 39 31 W68 36 17. Stereo. 184 Target Cir., Bangor 04401-5718. Phone: (207) 667-7573. Fax: (207) 667-9494. E-mail: larryjulius@clearchannel.com. Web site: www.kiss945.com. Licensee: Clear Channel Broadcasting Licenses Inc. Group owner: Clear Channel Communications Inc. (acq 10-23-00; grpsl). Rep: Christal. Dow, Lohnes & Albertson. Format: Adult contemp. News staff: 3; News: 7 hrs wkly. Target aud: 25-54. ♦Larry Julius, gen mgr; Jeff Pierce, opns dir; Josh Scroggins, gen sls mgr & natl sls mgr.

Fairfield

WCTB(FM)— November 1993: 93.5 mhz; 13.5 kw. 440 ft. TL: N44 44 07 W69 41 18. Stereo. 150 Witten Rd., Augusta 04330. Phone: (207) 623-9000. Fax: (207) 623-9035. Licensee: Mountain Wireless Inc. (group owner; acq 4-20-94; $60,000. FTR: 7-4-94). Schwartz, Woods & Miller. Format: Classic country. Target aud: 35-44. ♦Jim Herron, gen mgr; Alisa Smith, progmg dir; Marc Fisher, chief of engrg.

Farmington

WKTJ-FM— Aug 21, 1973: 99.3 mhz; 1.5 kw. 400 ft. TL: N44 39 22 W70 11 48. Box 590 04938. Phone: (207) 778-3400. Fax: (207) 778-3000. E-mail: wktj@wktj.com. Web Site: www.wktj.com. Licensee: Franklin Broadcasting Corp. Format: Adult contemp. News: 12 hrs wkly. Target aud: 25-54. ♦Nelson Doak, gen mgr & mus dir; Steve Bull, gen sls mgr; Marc Fisher, chief of engrg.

*WUMF-FM— February 1972: 100.1 mhz; 13 w. Ant -190 ft. TL: N44 40 09 W70 09 00. Stereo. 111 South St. 04938. Phone: (207) 778-7352. Fax: (207) 778-7113. E-mail: wumf@umf.maine.edu. Web Site: http://wumf.umf.maine.edu. Licensee: University of Maine System. Format: AOR, progsv, div. Target aud: 18-45; college students & local residents. Spec prog: Jazz 15 hrs, techno/industrial 15 hrs wkly. ♦Megan Littlefield, gen mgr & stn mgr; Will McArthur, progmg dir; Rob Graham, mus dir.

Fort Kent

WMEF(FM)— March 1994: 106.5 mhz; 25 kw. 302 ft. TL: N47 15 30 W68 33 30. 65 Texas Ave., Bangor 04401. Secondary address: 1450 Lisbon St., Lewiston 04240. Phone: (207) 941-1010/783-9101. Fax: (207) 942-2857/783-5193. Web Site: www.mpbn.org. Licensee: Maine Public Broadcasting Corp. Network: PRI. Format: Class, pub affrs, news/talk. ♦Charles Beck, CFO, VP & stn mgr; Chris Amann, CFO; Mary Anne Alhadeff, pres & gen mgr.

WUFK(FM)— July 1974: 92.1 mhz; 14 w. -321 ft. TL: N47 15 02 W68 35 25. 25 Pleasant St. 04743. Phone: (207) 834-7500. Fax: (207) 834-7879. Web Site: www.quadphonic.com. Licensee: University of Maine. Format: AAA. Target aud: 12-35. Spec prog: Irish/Gaelic folk show 3 hrs wkly.

Freeport

*WMSJ(FM)— Dec 1, 1997: 89.3 mhz; 7.5 kw vert. 394 ft. TL: N43 45 45 W70 19 30. Box 287 04032. Phone: (207) 865-3448. Fax: (207) 865-1763. E-mail: wmsj@wmsj.org. Web Site: www.wmsj.org. Licensee: Downeast Christian Communications Inc. Format: Contemp Christian mus. Target aud: 25-48. ♦John Libby, pres; Chris Scotland, stn mgr & prom; Liz Boissonneault, opns mgr; Joe Polek, progmg dir; Paula Kay, gen mgr & progmg dir.

Gardiner

WABK-FM—Listing follows WFAU(AM).

WFAU(AM)— Sept 23, 1968: 1280 khz; 5 kw-U, DA-N. TL: N44 14 53 W69 48 51. Stereo. 150 Whitten Rd., Augusta 04330. Phone: (207) 623-9000. Fax: (207) 623-9035. Licensee: Capstar TX L.P. Group owner: Clear Channel Communications Inc. (acq 1-18-01; grpsl). Network: ABC Information & Entertainment. Reddy, Begley & McCormick. Format: Adult contemp, news/talk. News staff: one; News: 34 hrs wkly. Target aud: 25-54. ♦Jim Herron, gen mgr.

WABK-FM—Co-owned with WFAU(AM). Apr 1, 1974: 104.3 mhz; 50 kw. 492 ft. TL: N44 18 36 W69 49 51. Stereo. Format: Oldies. ♦Mark Jackson, progmg dir.

Gorham

WLVP(AM)— Mar 3, 1980: 870 khz; 10 kw-D, 1 kw-N. TL: N43 41 19 W70 30 34. Box 8, Auburn 04212-0008. Secondary address: 99 Danville Comer Rd. 04210. Phone: (207) 782-1800. Fax: (207) 797-0780. Fax: (207) 783-7371. Web Site: wmtw.com. Licensee: Nassau Broadcasting III L.L.C. Group owner: Nassau Broadcasting Partners L.P. (acq 4-6-2004; grpsl). Network: ABC. Format: News, News/talk, sports. ♦David Kaufman, gen mgr; Jay C. Champaign, opns dir & opns mgr; Bill Whitten, gen sls mgr; Sean Baker, progmg dir & progmg mgr; Jennifer Sullivan, news dir; Peter Magee, chief of engrg.

*WMPG(FM)— Sept 1, 1973: 90.9 mhz; 110 w horiz, 1 kw vert. 233 ft. TL: N43 40 50 W70 26 59. Stereo. Box 9300, 96 Falmouth St., Portland 04104. Phone: (207) 780-4943. Fax: (207) 780-4590. E-mail: stationmanager@wmpg.org. Web Site: www.wmpg.org. Licensee: Trustees University of Maine. Format: Div, community. News: 5 hrs wkly. Target aud: General; any group currently underserved by other loc stns. Spec prog: Sp 2 hrs, Indian 2 hrs, Cambodian 2 hrs, Swedish one hr, African one hr, Irish 2 hrs wkly. ♦James Rand, stn mgr & mus dir; Tom Flynn, dev dir; Dave Bunker, progmg dir.

Harpswell

*WYFP(FM)— July 8, 1993: 91.9 mhz; 6 kw. 144 ft. TL: N43 44 14 W69 59 39. 14 Maine St., Suite 206, Brunswick 04011. Phone: (207) 729-9919. Fax: (207) 729-9919. E-mail: wyfp@bbnradio.org. Web Site: www.bbnradio.org. Licensee: Bible Broadcasting Network Inc. (group owner; acq 9-30-97; $150,000). Network: USA. Format: Bible teaching, religious. Target aud: 25-49. Spec prog: Christian rock 4 hrs, praise & worship 3 hrs wkly. ♦T. A. Smith, gen mgr.

Hermon

WNZT(AM)—Not on air, target date: unknown: 1230 khz; 1 kw-D, 660 w-N. TL: N44 48 10 W68 54 03. Box 8526, Bangor 04401-8526. Secondary address: 379 Riverside Dr., Eddington 04428. Phone: (207) 947-9697. Fax: (207) 989-5251. Licensee: Daniel F. Priestley. Group owner: Daniel F. Priestley Stns. Network: CNN Radio. Cyr Associates Fletcher, Heald & Hildreth. ♦Jocelynn Priestley, stn mgr.

Houlton

WHOU-FM— Jan 13, 1976: 100.1 mhz; 9.6 kw. 525 ft. TL: N46 08 35 W68 06 50. Box 40 04730. Secondary address: 39 Court St., Suite 215 04730. Phone: (207) 532-3600. Fax: (207) 521-0056. E-mail: sales@whoufm.com. Web Site: www.whoufm.com. Licensee: County Communications Inc. (acq 4-96; $350,000). Network: ABC. Crowell & Moring. Format: Adult contemp. News: 8 hrs wkly. Target aud: 25-54. Spec prog: Sacred one hr wkly. ♦David Moore, pres & gen mgr; Jacqueline Spencer, opns mgr; George Kelley, progmg dir; Barrett Quinn, chief of engrg.

Howland

WVOM(FM)— June 1993: 103.9 mhz; 54 kw. 1,509 ft. TL: N45 07 46 W68 21 28. 184 Target Industrial Cir., Bangor 04401. Phone: (207) 942-3311. Fax: (207) 942-8039. E-mail: wvom@midmaine.com. Web Site: www.thevoicemaine.com. Licensee: Clear Channel Communications Inc. (acq 3-12-97). Network: Network: CBS, Westwood One. Format: News/talk. Target aud: 25-64; upper income, professional, managerial. ♦Jeffery Pierce, CEO & opns dir; Jim Herron, gen mgr; Susan Patten, progmg dir & news dir.

Islesboro

WBYA(FM)— 1999: 105.5 mhz; 20 kw. Ant 305 ft. TL: N44 18 58 W68 58 12. 1119 Tillson Ave., Rockland 04841. Phone: (207) 594-9283. Fax: (207) 594-1620. E-mail: jlynch@nassaubroadcasting.com. Web Site: www.frank1055fm.com. Licensee: Nassau Broadcasting III L.L.C. Group owner: Nassau Broadcasting Partners L.P. (acq 4-6-2004; grpsl). Format: Classic hits. News staff: one; News: 7 hrs wkly. Target aud: 50 plus. ♦Pat Collins, gen mgr; Stan Manning, opns mgr; Joe Lynch, gen sls mgr.

Kennebunk

WBQQ(FM)— November 1991: 99.3 mhz; 3 kw. 324 ft. TL: N43 24 16 W70 26 15. Unit 99.3, 169 Port Rd. 04043. Phone: (207) 797-0780. Fax: (207) 967-8671. E-mail: wbach@wbach.fm. Web Site: www.wbachradio.com. Licensee: Nassau Broadcasting III L.L.C. Group owner: Nassau Broadcasting Partners L.P. (acq 4-6-2004; grpsl).

Broadcasting & Cable Yearbook 2006

Maine

Network: ABC. Rep: CMBS. Format: Class. Target aud: 35-64; upscale. ◆ Pat Collins, pres & gen mgr; Scott Hooper, progmg dir; Stan Manning, opns mgr & mus dir.

Kennebunkport

WHXQ(FM)— Dec 1, 1994: 104.7 mhz; 6 kw. 292 ft. TL: N43 26 36 W70 26 38. 477 Congress St., Suite 3 A, Portland 04101. Phone: (207) 797-0780. Fax: (207) 797-0368. E-mail: portlandspots @nassaubroadcasting.com. Web Site: www.boneradio.com. Licensee: Nassau Broadcasting III L.L.C. Group owner: Nassau Broadcasting Partners L.P. (acq 4-6-2004); grpsl). Format: Classic rock. ◆ Pat Collins, VP & gen mgr; Stan Manning, opns mgr, progmg dir & chief of engrg.

Kittery

WSHK(FM)— October 1992: 105.3 mhz; 2.2 kw. 371 ft. TL: N43 10 28 W70 46 50. Stereo. Box 576, Dover, NH 03821-0576. Secondary address: 292 Middle Rd., Dover, NH 03820-4901. Phone: (603) 749-9750. Fax: (603) 749-1459. E-mail: shark.mail@citicomm.com. Web Site: www.shark1053.com. Licensee: Citadel Broadcasting Co. Group owner: Citadel Broadcasting Corp. (acq 7-7-99; grpsl). Network: CNN Radio. Rep: Christal, Wiley, Rein & Fielding. Format: Classic rock. News staff: 2. Target aud: 25-54. ◆ Farid Suleman, CEO; Judy Ellis, pres; Marty Lessard, gen mgr; Mark Ericson, opns mgr; Bill Elliott, progmg dir.

Lewiston

WCNM(AM)— Aug 21, 1938: 1240 khz; 1 kw-U. TL: N44 06 55 W70 14 56. 555 Center St., Auburn 04210. Phone: (207) 784-5868. Fax: (207) 784-4700. E-mail: dick@gleasonradio.com. Web Site: www.gleasonradio.com. Licensee: Mountain Valley Broadcasting Inc. Group owner: Gleason Radio Group (acq 11-28-90). Network: USA. Rep: Cyr Associates. Pepper & Corazzini. Format: CNN Headline News. News staff: one; News: 168 hrs wkly. Target aud: General. ◆ Richard D. Gleason, pres & VP; Jennifer Williams, stn mgr.

WCYI(FM)— Feb 29, 1948: 93.9 mhz; 27.5 kw. 633 ft. TL: N44 08 40 W70 01 22. One City Ctr., Portland 04101. Phone: (207) 774-6364. Fax: (207) 774-8707. E-mail: mike.sambrook@citcomm.com. Web Site: www.wcyy.com. Licensee: Citadel Broadcasting Corp. Group owner: Citadel Broadcasting Corp. (acq 8-19-99; grpsl). Rep: Christal. Format: Morden rock. Target aud: General. ◆ Mike Sambrook, gen mgr; Herb Ivy, progmg dir; Michelle Morel, pub affrs dir & adv; Gene Terwilliger, chief of engrg.

WFNK(FM)— Licensed to Lewiston. See Portland

WLAM(AM)— Sept 4, 1947: 1470 khz; 5 kw-U, DA-1. TL: N44 03 47 W70 15 00. Box 8, Auburn 04212-0008. Phone: (207) 784-4300. Fax: (207) 797-0368. Web Site: www.wmtw.com. Licensee: Nassau Broadcasting III L.L.C. Group owner: Nassau Broadcasting Partners L.P. (acq 4-6-2004); grpsl). Network: Network: Westwood One, ABC Information & Entertainment. Rep: D & R Radio. Format: News/talk, news. Spec prog: Fr 2 hrs wkly. ◆ Pat Collins, sr VP & gen mgr; David Kaufman, gen mgr; Stan Manning, opns dir.

*WRBC(FM)— Oct 6, 1958: 91.5 mhz; 150 w. 16 ft. TL: N44 06 18 W70 12 32. Stereo. 31 Frye St. 04240. Phone: (207) 777-7532. Fax: (207) 795-8793. E-mail: mgraham3@bates.edu. Web Site: www.bates.edu/wrbc. Licensee: President and Trustees of Bates College. Format: Div, rock. Target aud: General; anyone searching for something different. Spec prog: Fr 2 hrs, jazz 4 hrs, metal 4 hrs, classic rock 11 hrs, folk 6 hrs wkly. ◆ Molly Graham, gen mgr; Drew Faller, progmg dir; Bill Morse, mus dir.

Lincoln

*WHMX(FM)— Apr 1, 1975: 105.7 mhz; 50 kw. 413 ft. TL: N45 20 34 W68 30 25. Stereo. Box 5000, Bangor 04402-5000. Secondary address: 1476 Broadway, Bangor 04401. Phone: (207) 262-1057. E-mail: contact@solutionfm.com. Web Site: www.solutionfm.com. Licensee: Bangor Baptist Church. (acq 12-31-96; $80,000 with co-located AM). Fletcher, Heald & Hildreth. Format: Contemp Christian. Target aud: 18-35. ◆ Pencil Boone, stn mgr; Jolie Littlefield, prom dir & chief of engrg; Tim Collins, progmg dir.

WSYY(AM)— See Millinocket

Machias

WALZ-FM— Nov 25, 1978: 95.3 mhz; 3 kw. 220 ft. TL: N44 44 08 W67 30 11. Stereo. East Main St., Suite 5, Machais 04654. Phone: (207) 255-4652. Fax: (207) 454-3062. E-mail: wqdy@wqdy.fm. Web Site: www.wqdy.fm. Licensee: William McVicar & Roger Holst, general partnership (acq 10-26-01). Format: classic hits. ◆ William G. Mcvicar, gen mgr; Roger Holst, opns dir.

Madawaska

WCXX(FM)— Jan 30, 1988: 102.3 mhz; 1.75 kw. 384 ft. TL: N47 19 54 W68 20 31. Stereo. 152 E. Greenridge Rd., Caribou 04736. Phone: (207) 473-7513. Fax: (207) 472-3221. E-mail: channelxradio@yahoo.com. Web Site: www.channelradio.com. Licensee: Canxus Broadcasting Corp. Network: CNN Radio. Rep: Savalli. Cyr Associates. Koteen & Naftalin. Format: Adult contemp, news. News staff: one; News: 16 hrs wkly. Target aud: 18-54. ◆ Dennis H. Curley, pres; Richard Chandler, gen mgr; Mark Stewart, opns mgr & mus dir.

Madison

WIGY(FM)— 1995: 97.5 mhz; 6 kw. 328 ft. TL: N44 47 32 W69 58 10. Stereo. 150 Whitten Rd., Augusta 04330. Phone: (207) 623-9000. Fax: (207) 623-9035. E-mail: kellyslater@clearchannel.com. Licensee: Clear Channel Radio Licenses, Inc Group owner: Clear Channel Communications Inc. (acq 1-18-01; grpsl). Cyr Associates. Fletcher, Heald & Hildreth. Format: Sports. Target aud: 25-54. ◆ Kelly Slater, gen mgr & progmg mgr; Rick Dugal, gen sls mgr; Donald Shield, progmg dir.

Mexico

WTBM(FM)— Sept 15, 1988: 100.7 mhz; 850 w. Ant 1,273 ft. TL: N44 34 56 W70 37 59. Stereo. Box 72,, 243 Main St., Norway 04268. Phone: (207) 743-5911. Fax: (207) 743-5913. E-mail: info@woxo.com. Web Site: www.woxo.com. Licensee: Mountain Valley Broadcasting Inc. Group owner: Gleason Radio Group (acq 12-90; FTR: 10-22-90). Network: USA. Rep: Cyr Associates. Format: Country, sports. News staff: 2; News: 12 hrs wkly. Target aud: General. ◆ Richard Gleason, pres & gen mgr; Vic Hodgkins, stn mgr; Jeremy Rush, opns mgr; Jay Philips, progmg dir.

Milbridge

WRMO(FM)— Not on air, target date: unknown: 93.7 mhz; 50 kw. Ant 210 ft. TL: N44 33 10 W67 49 10. 1296 Marian Ln., Green Bay, WI 54304-2338. Phone: (920) 494-6310. Licensee: Lyle Robert Evans. ◆ Lyle Robert Evans, gen mgr.

Millinocket

WSYY(AM)— Dec 7, 1963: 1240 khz; 1 kw-U. TL: N45 40 24 W68 43 07. Box 1240 04462. Phone: (207) 723-9657. Fax: (207) 723-5900. E-mail: calendar@themountain949.com. Web Site: www.themountain949.com. Licensee: Katahdin Communications Inc. (acq 12-29-86; $295,000 with co-located FM; 11-10-86). Cyr Associates. Format: Country. Target aud: General. ◆ James N. Talbot, pres; Bob Kubera, gen mgr; Karen Rush, chief of engrg.

WSYY-FM— Apr 12, 1978: 94.9 mhz; 23.5 kw. 692 ft. TL: N45 52 58 W68 47 54. Stereo. Box 1240 04462. Phone: (207) 723-9657. Fax: (207) 723-5900. E-mail: calendar@themountain949.com. Web Site: www.themountain949.com. Format: Country. Target aud: 20-45.

Monticello

WREM(AM)— Sept 2, 1981: 710 khz; 5 kw-D. TL: N46 20 30 W67 49 04. 274 Britton Rd. 04760. Secondary address: 97 High St., Kennebunk 04769. Phone: (207) 538-9180. E-mail: wbco@gwi.net. Licensee: Allan H. Weiner (acq 2-12-02). Format: Talk. Target aud: 25-54; women 43%, men 57%. ◆ Allan H. Weiner, pres & gen mgr.

North Windham

WHXR(FM)— 1996: 106.7 mhz; 810 w. 623 ft. TL: N43 51 06 W70 19 40. Stereo. Box 8, Auburn 04210. Secondary address: 99 Danville Corner Rd. 04210. Phone: (207) 782-1800. Fax: (207) 783-7371. E-mail: www.wmtw.com. Web Site: www.wmtw.com. Licensee: Nassau Broadcasting III L.L.C. Group owner: Nassau Broadcasting Partners L.P. (acq 4-6-2004); grpsl). Network: Network: AP Radio, ABC News/Talk. Format: News. Target aud: 35 plus; general. ◆ David

Directory of Radio

Kaufman, gen mgr; Bill Whitten, gen sls mgr; Scan Baker, progmg mgr; Jennifer Sullivan, news dir; Peter Magec, chief of engrg.

Norway

WOXO-FM— Dec 12, 1970: 92.7 mhz; 2 kw. 360 ft. TL: N44 12 24 W70 33 18. Stereo. Box 72,, 243 Main St. 04268. Phone: (207) 743-5911. Fax: (207) 743-5913. E-mail: info@woxo.com. Web Site: www.woxo.com. Licensee: Mountain Valley Broadcasting Inc. Group owner: Gleason Radio Group (acq 12-12-75). Network: USA. Rep: Cyr Associates. Pepper & Corazzini. Format: Country, sports. News staff: 2; News: 12 hrs wkly. Target aud: General. ◆ Richard D. Gleason, pres & gen mgr; Vic Hodgkins, stn mgr; Jeremy Rush, opns mgr; Jay Philips, progmg dir & chief of engrg.

Oakland

*WMDR-FM— Not on air, target date: unknown: 88.9 mhz; 600 w vert. Ant 666 ft. TL: N44 42 48 W69 43 39. 160 Bangor St., Augusta 04330. Phone: (207) 622-1340. Fax: (207) 623-2874. Licensee: Light of Life Ministries Inc. ◆ Ray Bouchard, gen mgr.

Old Town

WBZN(FM)— Jan 1, 1995: 107.3 mhz; 50 kw. 308 ft. TL: N45 02 06 W68 40 57. Box 100, Brewer 04412. Secondary address: 49 Acme Rd., Brewer 04412. Phone: (207) 989-5631. Fax: (207) 989-5685. E-mail: z1073@midmaine.com. Web Site: www.wbzn-fm.com. Licensee: Cumulus Licensing Corp. Group owner: Cumulus Media Inc. (acq 2-20-98; $6.4 million with WQCB(FM) Brewer). Format: CHR. ◆ Tom Preble, gen mgr; Paul Dupois, opns dir; Dan Cashman, progmg dir & mus dir; Dick Hyatt, chief of engrg.

Orono

*WMEB-FM— Apr 1, 1963: 91.9 mhz; 380 w. 66 ft. TL: N44 54 04 W68 40 07. Stereo. 5748 Memorial Union 04469. Phone: (207) 581-4340. Phone: (207) 581-2333. Fax: (207) 581-4343. Web Site: www.umaine.edu/wmeb. Licensee: Board of Trustees, University of Maine. Format: Progsv, rock, div. Target aud: General. Spec prog: Heavy metal 10 hrs, blues 7 hrs, rap 5 hrs, folk 4 hrs, Fr 4 hrs, international 3 hrs wkly. ◆ Thomas Grucza, stn mgr.

Pittsfield

WJCX(FM)— December 1993: 99.5 mhz; 6 kw. 328 ft. TL: N44 48 11 W69 10 06. 2881 Ohio St., Suite 8, Bangor 04401. Phone: (207) 884-6052. Fax: (207) 884-6052. E-mail: wjcx@calvarychapel.com. Licensee: CSN International. (acq 1996; $87,500). Format: News/talk, Christian. Target aud: 18-34; young adults. ◆ Mike Archer, gen mgr, stn mgr, progmg dir & mus dir.

Portland

WBAE(AM)— March 1946: 1490 khz; 1 kw-U. TL: N43 39 48 W70 16 16. 420 Western Avenue 04106. Phone: (207) 774-4561. Fax: (207) 774-3788. E-mail: feedback@ilovethebay.com. Web Site: www.ilovethebay.com. Licensee: Saga Communications of New England LLC. Group owner: Saga Communications Inc. (acq 1996; $10 million. with co-located FM). Network: CNN Radio. Format: Music of your life. News staff: 5. Target aud: 25-54; general. ◆ Cary Pahigian, pres & gen mgr.

WPOR(FM)— Co-owned with WBAE(AM). Oct 31, 1967: 101.9 mhz; 32.5 kw. 606 ft. TL: N43 45 45 W70 19 30. Stereo. E-mail: wpor@wpor.com. Web Site: www.wpor.com. Format: Country.

WBLM(FM)— February 1966: 102.9 mhz; 100 kw. 1,460 ft. TL: N43 55 28 W70 29 28. Stereo. One City Ctr. 04101. Phone: (207) 774-6364. Fax: (207) 774-8707. Web Site: www.wblm.com. Licensee: Citadel Broadcasting Co. Group owner: Citadel Broadcasting Corp. (acq 7-7-99; grpsl). Rep: Katz Radio. Format: AOR. Target aud: 25-54; active, involved, fun-loving. ◆ Michael Sambrook, gen mgr; Michelle Morel, adv.

WFNK(FM)— (Lewiston). Mar 1, 1973: 107.5 mhz; 100 kw. Ant 928 ft. TL: N44 00 12 W70 25 24. Stereo. 477 Congress St., Ste. 3B 04101. Phone: (207) 797-0780. Fax: (207) 797-0368. E-mail: portlandspots @nassaubroadcasting.com. Web Site: www.1075frankfm.com. Licensee: Nassau Broadcasting III L.L.C. Group owner: Nassau Broadcasting

Stations in the U.S. Maine

Partners L.P. (acq 4-6-2004; grpsl). Rep: D & R Radio. Format: Classic rock. ♦ Pat Collins, VP & gen mgr; Tim Gatz, gen mgr; Stan Manning, opns mgr.

WGAN(AM)— Aug 3, 1938: 560 khz; 5 kw-U, DA-2. TL: N43 41 22 W70 19 00. (CP: 4.8 kw-U, DA-1). 420 Western Ave., S. Portland 04106. Phone: (207) 774-4561. Fax: (207) 774-3788. E-mail: wgan@wgan.com. Web Site: www.wgan.com. Licensee: Saga Communications of New England LLC. Group owner: Saga Communications Inc. (acq 6-2-92; grpsl, including co-located FM). Network: CNN Radio. Format: News/talk. ♦ Cary Pahigian, CEO, pres, VP & gen mgr.

WMGX(FM)—Co-owned with WGAN(AM). June 10, 1977: 93.1 mhz; 50 kw. 443 ft. TL: N43 41 27 W70 15 25. Stereo. Format: Adult contemp.

WHOM(FM)—See Mt. Washington, NH

WJBQ(FM)— June 1, 1960: 97.9 mhz; 16 kw. 889 ft. TL: N43 51 06 W70 19 40. (CP: 37.5 kw, ant 567 ft. TL: N43 45 32 W70 19 14). Stereo. One City Center 04101. Phone: (207) 774-6364. Fax: (207) 774-8087. Web Site: www.wjbq.com. Licensee: Citadel Broadcasting Co. Group owner: Citadel Broadcasting Corp. (acq 7-7-99; grpsl). Rep: Christal. Format: CHR. Target aud: 25-44; female listeners. ♦ Michael Sambrook, gen mgr; Tim Moore, opns mgr.

WLOB(AM)— Feb 2, 1957: 1310 khz; 5 kw-U, DA-2. TL: N43 41 22 W70 20 06. 779 Warren Ave. 04103-1007. Phone: (207) 773-9695. Fax: (207) 761-4406. E-mail: newstalkWLOB@yahoo.com. Licensee: Atlantic Coast Radio L.L.C. (group owner; acq 9-8-00; grpsl). Network: USA. Format: News/talk. News: 17 hrs wkly. Target aud: General. ♦ J.J. Jeffrey, pres & opns mgr; Jon VanHoogenstyn, gen mgr; Jon Van Hoogenstyn, progmg dir.

*WMEA(FM)— April 1974: 90.1 mhz; 49 kw. 1,919 ft. TL: N43 51 33 W70 42 43. Stereo. 65 Texas Ave., Bangor 04401. Secondary address: 1450 Libson St., Lewiston 04240. Phone: (207) 874-6570. Fax: (207) 761-0318. E-mail: cbeck@mpbn.net. Web Site: www.mpbc.org. Licensee: Maine Public Broadcasting Corp. (acq 6-23-92). Network: NPR, PRI. Format: Class, pub affrs, news/talk. News staff: 8; News: 20 hrs wkly. Target aud: 25-64. ♦ Christopher Amann, CFO; Mary Anne Alhadeff, pres & gen mgr; Charles Beck, stn mgr; Deb Turner, dev dir; John Likshis, mktg dir.

WPKQ(FM)—See North Conway, NH

WTHT(FM)—See Auburn

WYNZ(FM)—See Westbrook

WZAN(AM)— July 13, 1925: 970 khz; 5 kw-U, DA-N. TL: N43 36 19 W70 19 18. 420 Western Ave., S. Portland 04106. Phone: (207) 774-4561. Fax: (207) 774-3788. E-mail: feedback@970wzan.com. Web Site: www.970wzan.com. Licensee: Saga Communications of New England LLC. Group owner: Saga Communications Inc. (acq 6-23-93; $350,000. with WYNZ-FM Westbrook; FTR: 7-12-93). Network: Network: CBS, CNN Radio. Rep: Katz Radio. Format: Talk. Target aud: 25-54 Males. ♦ Cary Pahigian, pres & gen mgr; Chris McGorrill, opns.

Presque Isle

WBPW(FM)— September 1973: 96.9 mhz; 100 kw. 440 ft. TL: N46 45 52 W67 59 23. Box 312, 427 Caribou Rd., US Rt. 1 04769. Phone: (207) 769-6600. Fax: (207) 764-5274. E-mail: wbpw.radio@citcomm.com. Licensee: Citadel Broadcasting Co. Group owner: Citadel Broadcasting Corp. (acq 4-26-00; grpsl). Network: Westwood One. Rep: Katz Radio. Format: Hot country. News: 2 hrs wkly. Target aud: 25-54. ♦ Lisa Miles, gen mgr & gen sls mgr.

WEGP(AM)— June 24, 1960: 1390 khz; 5 kw-U, DA-N. TL: N46 39 17 W68 03 01. Box 4088 04769. Phone: (207) 762-6700. Fax: (207) 762-3319. E-mail: wegp@mfx.net. Web Site: www.wegp.net. Licensee: Decelles/Smith Media Inc. (acq 9-18-00). Network: USA. Format: Talk,

news. Target aud: Adults; Mature listeners over age 29. ♦ McDonnell Smith, pres & gen mgr; Patrick Patterson, opns dir.

*WMEM(FM)— 1975: 106.1 mhz; 99 kw. 1,079 ft. TL: N46 33 06 W67 48 38. 65 Texas Ave., Bangor 04401. Secondary address: 1450 Lisbon St., Lewiston 04240. Phone: (207) 874-6570. Phone: (800) 884-1717. Fax: (207) 942-2857. E-mail: cbeck@mpbn.net. Web Site: www.mpbc.org. Licensee: Maine Public Broadcasting Corp. (acq 6-23-92). Network: Network: NPR, PRI. Dow, Lohnes & Albertson. Format: Class, pub affrs, news/talk. ♦ Charles Beck, CFO, VP & stn mgr; Chris Amann, CFO; Mary Anne Alhadeff, pres & gen mgr; Deb Turner, dev dir; John Likshis, mktg dir.

WOZI(FM)— Feb 2, 1981: 101.9 mhz; 7.9 kw. Ant 1,207 ft. TL: N46 32 51 W67 48 35. Stereo. Box 312 04769. Secondary address: 427 Caribou Rd. Hwy. US Rt. 1 04769. Phone: (207) 769-6600. Fax: (207) 764-5274. E-mail: wozi.radio@citcomm.com. Web Site: www.oldies1019.com. Licensee: Citadel Broadcasting Co. Group owner: Citadel Broadcasting Corp. (acq 4-26-01; grpsl). Network: ABC. Rep: Katz Radio. Format: Oldies. News staff: one; News: 2 hrs wkly. Target aud: 25-54. ♦ Lisa Miles, gen mgr.

WQHR(FM)— 1981: 96.1 mhz; 95 kw. 1,309 ft. TL: N46 32 55 W67 48 35. Stereo. Box 312, 427 Caribou Hwy. 04769. Secondary address: 427 Caribou Rd. US Rt. 1 04769. Phone: (207) 769-6600. Fax: (207) 764-5274. E-mail: wqhr.radio@citcomm.com. Licensee: Citadel Broadcasting Co. Group owner: Citadel Broadcasting Corp. (acq 4-26-01; grpsl). Network: ABC. Rep: Katz Radio. Format: Hot adult contemp. News: 2 hrs wkly. Target aud: 18-49. ♦ Lisa Miles, gen mgr.

*WUPI(FM)— July 26, 1973: 92.1 mhz; 17 w. -39 ft. TL: N46 40 15 W68 01 00. c/o Univ. of Maine, 181 Main St., Box 525 04769. Phone: (207) 768-9711. Phone: (207) 768-9741. Fax: (207) 768-9742. Web Site: www.umpi.maine.edu. Licensee: University of Maine Trustees. Network: Westwood One. Format: Div. News staff: 2; News: 3 hrs wkly. Target aud: 16-35. Spec prog: Black 2 hrs, Russian 2 hrs, Kenyan 2 hrs, Indian 2 hrs wkly. ♦ Dr. Nancy Hensel, pres; Tim Cramer, stn mgr.

Rockland

WMCM(FM)—Listing follows WRKD(AM).

WRKD(AM)— Oct 1, 1952: 1450 khz; 1 kw-U. TL: N44 06 22 W69 06 31. Stereo. 15 Payne Ave., Rt. 1 S. 04841. Phone: (207) 594-1450. Phone: (207) 594-9400. Fax: (207) 594-2234. Licensee: Clear Channel Broadcasting Licenses Inc. Group owner: Clear Channel Communications Inc. (acq 2-12-01; $3.5 million. with co-located FM including two-year, $5,000 noncompete agreement). Network: Westwood One. Rep: Cyr Associates. Wilmer, Cutler & Pickering. Format: News/talk. News staff: one; News: 11 hrs wkly. Target aud: 35 plus. Spec prog: Loc high school sports. ♦ Jim Herron, gen mgr; Don Shields, opns dir, progmg dir & news dir; Peter K. Orne, gen sls mgr.

WMCM(FM)—Co-owned with WRKD(AM). Apr 16, 1968: 103.3 mhz; 20.5 kw. 771 ft. TL: N44 07 35 W69 08 18. Stereo. Format: Country. News staff: one. Target aud: General. ♦ D.J. McCoy, progmg dir.

Rumford

WLOB-FM— Nov 15, 1975: 96.3 mhz; 100 kw. Ant 1,433 ft. TL: N44 34 56 W70 37 59. (CP: 36 kw, ant 1,453 ft. N44 15 06 W70 25 24). Stereo. 779 Warren Ave., Portland 04103. Phone: (207) 773-9695. Fax: (207) 761-4406. E-mail: wlob@yahoo.com. Licensee: Atlantic Coast Radio L.L.C. (group owner; acq 9-8-00; grpsl). Format: News/talk. ♦ John Van Hoogenstyn, gen mgr.

WTME(AM)— Aug 21, 1953: 780 khz; 10 kw-D, 18 w-N. TL: N44 30 53 W70 31 01. Box 72, 243 Main St., Norway 04268. Phone: (207) 743-5911. Fax: (207) 743-5913. E-mail: info@woxo.com. Web Site: www.wtme.com. Licensee: Mountain Valley Broadcasting Inc. Group owner: Gleason Radio Group (acq 11-2-00; $50,000). Network: Network: CNN Radio, Westwood One. Rep: Cyr Associates. Format:

Relg, news. Target aud: General. ♦ Richard Gleason, pres & gen mgr; Jeremy Rush, opns mgr & progmg dir; Jay Philips, progmg dir & chief of engrg.

Saco

WCYY(FM)—See Biddeford

WRED(FM)— July 18, 1982: 95.9 mhz; 4.1 kw. Ant 397 ft. TL: N43 32 33 W70 24 17. Stereo. 779 Warren Ave., Portland 04103. Phone: (207) 773-9695. Fax: (207) 761-4406. E-mail: info@redhot959.com. Web Site: www.redhot959.com. Licensee: Atlantic Coast Radio L.L.C. (group owner; acq 7-12-99; $1.15 million). Network: Westwood One. Rep: McGavren Guild. Rick Hayes. Format: Hip-Hop, rhythm and blues, CHR. Target aud: 18-34. ♦ J.J. Jeffrey, pres; Lisa Menconi, CFO; John Van Hoogenstyn, gen mgr & sls dir; Buzz Bradley, stn mgr & opns VP; E.T. 'Gene' Terwilliger, chief of engrg; Linda Petrin, chief of engrg.

WVAE(AM)—See Biddeford

Sanford

WPHX(AM)— Nov 9, 1957: 1220 khz; 1 kw-D, 234 w-N. TL: N43 25 53 W70 45 44. 482 Congress St., Suite 501, Portland 04101. Phone: (207) 773-8900. Fax: (207) 773-8905. Licensee: FNX Broadcasting LLC. Group owner: Phoenix Media Communications Group (acq 5-17-99; $1.025 million. with co-located FM). Format: News/talk. ♦ Sam Pseifle, gen mgr.

WPHX-FM— Oct 10, 1975: 92.1 mhz; 1.2 kw. 525 ft. TL: N43 35 24 W70 22 20. Stereo. Web Site: www.fnxradio.com. Format: Alternative. News staff: one. Target aud: General. Spec prog: Blues 3 hrs, reggae 2 hrs wkly. ♦ Andy Kingston, gen mgr; Nadia Behring, mktg dir; Michael Santos, prom dir; Peter Vernaglia, engrg mgr.

*WSEW(FM)— Mar 2, 1992: 88.5 mhz; 100 w. 387 ft. TL: N43 25 11 W70 48 09. Stereo. Box 398, New Durham, NH 03855. Phone: (603) 859-9170. Fax: (603) 859-8172. E-mail: wsew@wsew.org. Web Site: www.wsew.org. Licensee: Word-Radio Educational Foundation. Network: USA. Format: Relg. ♦ Sharon Malone, gen mgr.

Scarborough

WBQW(FM)— 1960: 106.3 mhz; 3 kw. 299 ft. TL: N43 35 24 W70 22 20. Stereo. 169 Port Rd., Kennebunk 04043. Phone: (207) 797-0780. Fax: (207) 967-8671. E-mail: wbach@wbach.fm. Web Site: www.wbach.fm. Licensee: Nassau Broadcasting III L.L.C. Group owner: Nassau Broadcasting Partners L.P. (acq 4-6-2004; grpsl). Network: AP Radio. Rep: CMBS. Format: Class. Target aud: 25-54; upscale, affluent, management, professionals. Spec prog: Jazz 5 hrs wkly. ♦ Pat Collins, pres, pres & gen mgr; Scott Hooper, progmg dir; Stan Manning, mus dir.

Searsport

WFZX(FM)— Oct 10, 1994: 101.7 mhz; 2.65 kw. Ant 1,004 ft. TL: N44 34 51 W68 53 47. 184 Target Industrial Cir., Bangor 04401. Phone: (207) 947-9100. Fax: (207) 942-8039. E-mail: susanfaloon @clearchannel.com. Web: www.wfzxfm.com. Licensee: Clear Channel Broadcasting Licenses Inc. (group owner); (acq 10-8-98; $265,000). Format: Classic rock. ♦ Jeffrey Pierce, stn mgr; Josh Scroggins, gen sls mgr; Larry Julius, gen mgr & mktg dir.

Skowhegan

WHQO(FM)— September 1989: 107.9 mhz; 6 kw. Ant 666 ft. TL: N44 42 46 W69 43 36. Stereo. Box 159 04976. Phone: (207) 474-5171. Fax: (207) 474-2399. E-mail: maine.radio@verizon.net. Licensee: Mountain Wireless Inc. (group owner; (acq 11-20-97; $222,355). Format: Talk. Target aud: 25-54; baby boomers who grew up with Top-40 radio. ♦ Rick Davis, pres; Jay Hansen, gen mgr & opns VP.

WSKW(AM)— 1956: 1160 khz; 10 kw-D, 1 kw-N. TL: N44 44 43 W69 41 36. Box 159 04976. Secondary address: 208 Middle Rd. 04976. Phone: (207) 474-5171. Fax: (207) 474-2399. E-mail: maine.radio@verizon.net. Licensee: Mountain Wireless Inc. (group owner; (acq 1999; $1.6 million. with WCTB(FM) Fairfield). Format: Sports/ESPN. Target aud: 12 plus; loc sports fans. Spec prog: High school sports, Univ. of Maine sports, relg. ♦Rick Davis, pres; Jay Hanson, gen mgr & opns mgr; Melody Price, pub affrs dir.

WTOS-FM— Nov 13, 1969: 105.1 mhz; 50 kw. 2,431 ft. TL: N45 01 54 W70 18 50. Stereo. 150 Whitten Rd., Augusta 04330. Phone: (207) 623-9000. Fax: (207) 623-9035. E-mail: reverend@clearchannel.com. Web Site: www.wtosfm.com. Licensee: Capstar TX L.P. Group owner: Clear Channel Communications Inc. (acq 1-18-01; grpsl). Format: Active Rock. News staff: one; News: 3 hrs wkly. Target aud: 18-49. ♦Kelly Slater, mktg mgr; Steve Smith, progmg dir.

South Paris

WKTQ(AM)— Oct 28, 1955: 1450 khz; 1 kw-U. TL: N44 13 16 W70 31 43. Box 72, 243 Main St., Norway 04268. Phone: (207) 743-5911. Fax: (207) 743-5913. E-mail: info@woxo.com. Web Site: www.wtme.com. Licensee: Mountain Valley Broadcasting Inc. Group owner: Gleason Radio Group (acq 7-27-76). Network: Network: CNN Radio, Westwood One. Rep: Cyr Associates. Format: Relg, news. News: 126 hrs wkly. Target aud: General. ♦Richard D. Gleason, pres & gen mgr; Victor Hodgkins, stn mgr; Jeremy Rush, opns dir & progmg dir; Vic Hodgkins, sls VP; Bob Perry, chief of engrg.

WOXO-FM—See Norway

Standish

***WSJB-FM**— Apr 1, 1984: 91.5 mhz; 360 w. 85 ft. TL: N43 49 32 W70 29 03. Stereo. St. Joseph's College, 278 White's Bridge Rd. 04084. Phone: (207) 892-6766. Fax: (207) 893-7873. Web Site: www.homestead.com/wsjb/915. Licensee: Trustees of St. Joseph's College. Format: CHR. News: 3 hrs wkly. Target aud: College students. Spec prog: Class 2 hrs, C&W 3 hrs, jazz 3 hrs wkly. ♦Bill Yates, gen mgr.

Thomaston

WBQX(FM)— May 29, 1992: 106.9 mhz; 29.5 kw. 633 ft. TL: N44 06 30 W69 09 28. Stereo. 119 Tillson Ave., Suite 101A, Rockland 04841. Phone: (207) 594-9283. Fax: (207) 594-1620. E-mail: jlynch@nassaubroadcasting.com. Web Site: www.wbach.fm. Licensee: Nassau Broadcasting III L.L.C. Group owner: Nassau Broadcasting Partners L.P. (acq 4-6-2004; grpsl). Kettell-Carter. Smithwick & Belendiuk. Format: Class. News: 4 hrs wkly. Target aud: 35 plus; affluent, upscale adults. Spec prog: Jazz 2 hrs, children one hr wkly. ♦Louis F. Mercatanti, pres; Pat Collins, VP; Joe Lynch, gen mgr; Scott Hooper, progmg dir & mus dir.

Topsham

WJJB-FM— 1993: 95.5 mhz; 6 kw. 456 ft. TL: N43 54 12 W70 02 13. 779 Warren Ave., Portland 04103. Phone: (207) 773-9695. Fax: (207) 761-4406. E-mail: morningjab@yahoo.com. Web Site: www.bigjab.com. Licensee: Atlantic Coast Radio L.L.C. (group owner; acq 9-30-99). Network: Westwood One. Arter & Hadden. Format: Sports, talk. News staff: one; News: 4 hrs wkly. Target aud: 25-49; middle class, active lifestyle with discretionary income. ♦Carla Thibodeau, chmn; J. J. Jeffrey, pres; Bruce Biette, stn mgr; David Schumacher, opns mgr & progmg mgr; Gene Terwilliger, engrg dir & chief of engrg.

Veazie

WNZS(AM)— August 2002: 1340 khz; 1 kw-D, 630 w-N. TL: N44 51 10 W68 40 44. Box 8526, Bangor 04402. Secondary address: 379 Riverside Dr, Eddington 04428. Phone: (207) 947-9697. Fax: (207) 989-5251. Licensee: Waterfront Communications Inc. Group owner: Daniel F. Priestley Stns. Network: CNN Radio. Rep: Commercial Media Sales. Cyr Association Fletcher, Healld & Hildreth. Format: News. News staff: 2; News: 168 hrs wkly. Target aud: 25-54; 35-64; Adults in metro Banger area. Spec prog: Maine news. ♦Jocelynn Priestley, stn mgr.

WWNZ(AM)— August 2004: 1400 khz; 1 kw-D, 810 w-N. TL: N44 50 50 W68 40 48. Box 8526, Bangor 04402. Secondary address: 379 Riverside Dr., Eddington 04428. Phone: (207) 947-9697. Fax: (207) 989-5251. Licensee: Waterfront Communications Inc. Group owner: Daniel F. Priestley Stns. Network: USA. Rep: Commercial Media Sales. Cyr Associates Fletcher, Heald & Hildreth. Format: News/talk. News: 50+. Target aud: 25-54; 35-64; Banger metro area adults 25 plus. ♦Daniel F. Priestley, pres; Jocelynn Priestley, stn mgr.

Waterville

WEBB(FM)—Listing follows WTVL(AM).

***WMEW(FM)**— November 1983: 91.3 mhz; 3 kw. 299 ft. TL: N44 29 23 W69 39 05. Stereo. 65 Texas Ave., Bangor 04401. Secondary address: 1450 Lisbon St., Lewiston 04240. Phone: (207) 783-9101. Phone: (207) 941-1010. Fax: (207) 942-2857. E-mail: cbeck@mpbn.net. Web Site: www.mpbn.net. Licensee: Maine Public Broadcasting Corp. (acq 6-23-92; 7-13-92). Network: Network: NPR, PRI. Dow, Lohnes & Albertson. Format: Class, pub affrs, news/talk. News staff: 8; News: 20 hrs wkly. Target aud: 25-64. ♦Christopher Amann, CFO; Mary Anne Alhadeff, pres & gen mgr; Charles Beck, stn mgr & progmg dir; Kirk Hamill, dev dir; John Likshis, mktg dir.

***WMHB(FM)**— Oct 1, 1974: 89.7 mhz; 110 w. 98 ft. TL: N44 33 57 W69 39 49. Stereo. Colby College, 4000 Mayflower Hill Dr. 04901-8840. Phone: (207) 872-3686. Phone: (207) 872-3348. Fax: (207) 872-3785. E-mail: wmhb@colby.edu. Web Site: www.colby.edu/wmhb. Licensee: Mayflower Hill Broadcasting Corp. Format: Div. News: 2.5 hrs wkly. Target aud: 5-100; we cater to everyone. Spec prog: Folk 12 hrs, Black 8 hrs, jazz 8 hrs, world 6 hrs wkly. ♦Marc Bouchard, gen mgr.

WTVL(AM)— June 19, 1946: 1490 khz; 1 kw-U. TL: N44 33 52 W69 36 39. Box 5070, Augusta 04330. Secondary address: 52 Western Ave., Augusta 04330. Phone: (207) 623-4735. Fax: (207) 626-5948. E-mail: b98.5@midmaine.com. Web Site: www.b985.fm. Licensee: Citadel Broadcasting Co. Group owner: Citadel Broadcasting Corp. (acq 4-26-2001; grpsl). Format: Country favorites. Target aud: 25-54. ♦Farid Suleman, CEO; Bob Proffitt, pres; Julie Crocker, gen sls mgr; Al Perry, rgnl sls mgr; Mac Dickson, prom dir; Andy Capwell, progmg dir; Renee Nelson, news dir & pub affrs dir; Bob Perry, chief of engrg.

WEBB(FM)—Co-owned with WTVL(AM). Mar 26, 1968: 98.5 mhz; 50 kw. 305 ft. TL: N44 33 52 W69 36 39. Stereo. Web Site: www.b985.fm. Fisher, Wayland, Cooper, Leader & Zaragoza. News staff: one.

Westbrook

WBQW(FM)—See Scarborough

WJAE(AM)— Nov 8, 1959: 1440 khz; 5 kw-D, 1 kw-N, DA-1. TL: N43 40 50 W70 22 47. 779 Warren Ave., Portland 04103. Phone: (207) 773-9695. Fax: (207) 761-4406. E-mail: shoe@thebigjab.com. Web Site: www.thebigjab.com. Licensee: Atlantic Coast Radio L.L.C. (group owner; (acq 9-99). Network: Westwood One. Roslin Format: Sports, talk. News staff: News progmg 6 hrs wkly Target aud: General; male. ♦Bruce Biette, gen mgr; Dave Shoe, opns mgr.

WYNZ(FM)— February 1976: 100.9 mhz; 25 kw. Ant 305 ft. TL: N43 41 26 W70 19 05. Stereo. 420 Western Ave., South Portland 04106. Phone: (207) 774-4561. Fax: (207) 774-3788. E-mail: oldies@oldies1009.com. Web Site: www.oldies1009.com. Licensee: Saga Communications of New England LLC. Group owner: Saga Communications Inc. (acq 6-23-93; $350,000. with WYNZ(AM) Portland; FTR: 7-12-93). Network: CNN Radio. Rep: Katz Radio. Format: Oldies. Target aud: 25-54. ♦Cary Pahigian, pres & gen mgr; Chris McGorrill, opns mgr, mktg VP & prom mgr; Tina Segerstrom, sls VP; Tina Sewistna, gen sls mgr; Randi Kirshbaun, progmg dir; Doug Tribou, news dir; Andy Armstrong, engrg VP.

Winslow

WWWA(FM)— Apr 23, 1999: 95.3 mhz; 12 kw. Ant 672 ft. TL: N44 42 48 W69 43 39. 160 Bangor St., Augusta 04330. Phone: (207) 622-1340. Fax: (207) 623-2874. E-mail: wwwa@adelphia.net. Web Site: www.wwwafm.org. Licensee: Light of Life Ministries Inc. Format: Christian. ♦Ryan Gagne, gen mgr & progmg dir.

Winter Harbor

WNSX(FM)— 1999: 97.7 mhz; 50 kw. Ant 489 ft. TL: N44 33 13 W68 05 40. 184 Target Industrial Cir., Bangor 04401. Phone: (207) 947-9100. Fax: (207) 942-8039. E-mail: larryjulius@clearchannel.com. Web Site: www.thefoxthatrocks.com. Licensee: Stony Creek Broadcasting LLC Group owner: Clear Channel Communications Inc. (acq 7-18-2005; $800,000). Format: Sports, talk. ♦Larry Julius, gen mgr; Jeffrey Pierce, opns mgr; Joshua Scroggins, gen sls mgr.

Yarmouth

***WYAR(FM)**— Nov 16, 1998: 88.3 mhz; 100 w horiz. 79 ft. TL: N43 45 56 W70 08 27. Box 219, Heritage Radio Society Inc., Cousins St. 04096. E-mail: wyar@maine.rr.com. Licensee: Heritage Radio Society Inc. Format: Btfl music, big band, oldies, class, educ. Target aud: General; senior citizens & young people. ♦Gary D. King Sr., CEO, pres, opns dir, mus dir, pub affrs dir & chief of engrg; Lois B. King, gen mgr, opns VP & asst music dir.

York Center

WUBB(FM)— June 1987: 95.3 mhz; 1.4 kw. 682 ft. TL: N43 13 24 W70 41 35. Stereo. 815 Lafayette Rd., Portsmouth, NH 03801. Phone: (603) 436-7300. Fax: (603) 430-9415. E-mail: ianhorne@clearchannel.com. Web Site: www.wubbfm.com. Licensee: Clear Channel Communications Group owner: Clear Channel Communications Inc. (acq 8-30-00; grpsl). Rep: Katz Radio. Format: Country. News staff: one; News: 7 hrs wkly. Target aud: 25-54. ♦Ian Horne, progmg dir.

Maryland

Aberdeen

WAMD(AM)— May 1, 1957: 970 khz; 500 w-U, DA-2. TL: N39 30 35 W76 11 38. 400 Miob Ln. 21001. Phone: (410) 272-4400. Fax: (410) 575-6890. Licensee: First Broadcasting Investment Partners LLC (group owner; (acq 6-13-2005; grpsl). Network: ABC. Format: Oldies. News: 24 hrs wkly. Target aud: 35+; primarily female. ♦Steve Clendenin, opns dir; Chuck McKay, gen sls mgr; Steve Clendenin, progmg dir.

Annapolis

WBIS(AM)— Jan 10, 1947: 1190 khz; 10 kw-D, DA. TL: N38 56 32 W76 28 54. (CP: COL Garrison. 5 kw-D, 7 kw-N, DA-2. TL: N39 24 29 W76 46 32). Stereo. 1610 West St., Suite 209 21401. Phone: (410) 269-0700. E-mail: wbis@businessradio.net. Web Site: www.wbis1190.com. Licensee: Nations Radio L.L.C. (acq 3-31-98; $400,000). Reynolds & Manning. Format: Business talk. ♦Alan Pendelton, gen mgr.

***WFSI(FM)**— May 16, 1960: 107.9 mhz; 50 kw. 500 ft. TL: N38 59 45 W76 39 27. Stereo. 918 Chesapeake Ave. 21403. Phone: (410) 268-6200. Fax: (410) 268-0931. Licensee: Family Stations Inc. (group owner; acq 1-7-72). Network: Family Radio. Format: Relg, educ. ♦W.A. Sadlier, stn mgr.

WLZL(FM)— 1947: 99.1 mhz; 50 kw. Ant 459 ft. TL: N38 59 46 W76 39 26. Stereo. 4200 Parliament Pl., Suite 300, Lanham 20706. Phone: (301) 306-0991. Fax: (301) 731-0431. Web Site: www.elzol991.com. Licensee: Infinity Broadcasting East Inc. Group owner: Infinity Broadcasting Corp. (acq 11-13-98; grpsl). Rep: Infinity Radio Sales. Leventhal, Senter & Lerman. Format: Sp. News staff: one. Target aud: 18-34; upscale professionals. ♦Michael Hughes, gen mgr; Areacely Rivera, progmg dir.

WNAV(AM)— 1949: 1430 khz; 5 kw-D, 1 kw-N, DA-N. TL: N38 59 00 W76 31 21. Box 6726 21401. Phone: (410) 263-1430. Fax: (410) 268-5360. E-mail: stevehopp@wnav.com. Web Site: www.wnav.com. Licensee: Sajak Broadcasting Corp. (acq 5-26-98; $2.2 million). Network: Network: CBS Radio, Westwood One. Format: Adult contemp, full service. News staff: 2. Target aud: 35 plus. Spec prog: Baltimore Orioles baseball, Naval Academy sports. ♦Patrick L. Sajak, pres; Steve Hopp, VP & gen mgr; Bill Lusby, mus dir.

WRNR-FM—(Grasonville). Apr 1, 1980: 103.1 mhz; 6 kw. 328 ft. TL: N38 56 37 W76 10 43. Stereo. 112 Main St. 21401. Phone: (410) 626-0103. Fax: (410) 267-7634. E-mail: info@wrnr.com. Web Site: www.wrnr.com. Licensee: Empire Broadcasting System Inc. (acq 6-17-97; $2.15 million). Network: CBS Radio. Leventhal, Senter & Lerman. Format: Progressive/diversified. News staff: one; News: 2 hrs wkly. Target aud: 25-54; adults. ♦Don Cavaleri, chmn; Jon Peterson, opns mgr & mus dir; Steve Kingston, CEO, gen mgr & pub affrs dir; Judy Buddensick, sls.

WYRE(AM)— 1946: 810 khz; 250 w-D. TL: N38 58 13 W76 30 28. 112 Main St. 3rd Fl. 21401. Phone: (410) 295-0722. Phone: (410) 626-7810. Fax: (815) 371-1625. Web Site: wyreradio.com. Licensee: Bay Broadcasting Corp. (acq 2-28-02). Network: ABC Information &

Stations in the U.S.   Maryland

Entertainment. Baraff, Koerner & Olender. Format: Sp. Target aud: 35-54; upscale, mature audience. ◆Jake Einstein, gen mgr.

Baltimore

WBAL(AM)— Nov 2, 1925: 1090 khz; 50 kw-U, DA-N. TL: N39 22 33 W76 46 21. 3800 Hooper Ave. 21211. Phone: (410) 467-3000. Fax: (410) 338-6483. Web Site: www.wbal.com. Licensee: WBAL Div., The Hearst Corp. (acq 1-14-35). Network: CBS Radio. Rep: D & R Radio. Brooks, Pierce, McLendon, Humphrey & Leonard. Format: News/talk, sports. Target aud: 25-54. ◆Bob Cecil, VP & sls dir; Edward C. Kiernan, gen mgr; Jeffrey Beauchamp, stn mgr; Kerry Plackmayer, opns mgr; Steve Hartman, natl sls mgr; Arthur Hawkins, rgnl sls mgr; Suzy Roeser, prom mgr; Mark Miller, news dir; Hank Volpe, chief of engrg.

WIYY(FM)—Co-owned with WBAL(AM). Dec 7, 1958: 97.9 mhz; 13.5 kw. 945 ft. TL: N39 20 05 W76 39 03. Stereo. Web Site: www.98online.com. Format: AOR. Target aud: 18-49. ◆Hughes Jean, gen sls mgr; Steve Hartman, rgnl sls mgr; Lori Smyth, prom mgr; Dave Hill, progmg dir; Robert Heckman, mus dir; Bob Lopez, news dir. Co-owned TV: WBAL-TV affil

WBGR(AM)— July 27, 1955: 860 khz; 2.5 kw-D, 66 w-N, DA-2. TL: N39 18 43 W76 29 26. 918 Chesapeake, 4th Flr., Annapolis 21403. Phone: (410) 821-9000. Fax: (410) 268-0931. Licensee: Family Stations Inc. Group owner: Infinity Broadcasting Corp. (acq 3-2-2005; $7.5 million. with WBMD(AM) Baltimore). Format: Gospel, black. Target aud: 18-49. ◆Herold Camping, gen mgr.

WBIS(AM)—See Annapolis

*WBJC(FM)— Apr 6, 1951: 91.5 mhz; 50 kw. 500 ft. TL: N39 23 11 W76 43 52. Stereo. 6776 Riesterstown Rd. 21215. Phone: (410) 462-8444. Fax: (410) 333-7016. E-mail: info@wbjc.com. Web Site: www.wbjc.com. Licensee: Baltimore City Community College. (acq 4-22-91). Network: PRI. Format: Class. ◆Cary Smith, gen mgr; Kati Kershaw, opns dir & opns mgr; Jim Ward, dev dir.

WBMD(AM)— Dec 7, 1947: 750 khz; 1 kw-D. TL: N39 19 26 W76 32 56. 918 Chesapeake Ave., Annapolis 21203. Phone: (410) 821-9000. Fax: (410) 268-0931. Licensee: Family Stations Inc. Group owner: Infinity Broadcasting Corp. (acq 3-2-2005; $7.5 million. with WBGR(AM) Baltimore). Format: Relg. Target aud: 12 plus. Spec prog: Ger one hr, Pol 2 hrs, Greek 2 hrs, Lithuanian one hr wkly. ◆Herold Camping, gen mgr.

WCAO(AM)— May 8, 1922: 600 khz; 5 kw-U, DA-1. TL: N39 25 47 W76 45 42. 711 W. 40th St., Suite 350 21211. Phone: (410) 366-7600. Fax: (410) 467-0011. E-mail: yourvoice@heaven600.com. Web Site: www.heaven600.com. Licensee: Citicasters Licenses L.P. Group owner: Clear Channel Communications Inc. (acq 5-99; grpsl). Format: Contemporary Black gospel. ◆Jim Dolan, VP, gen mgr & mktg mgr; Bill Hopkinson, sls dir & gen sls mgr; Lee Michaels, progmg dir; Danielle Brown, mus dir & news dir.

WCBM(AM)— 1924: 680 khz; 10 kw-D, 5 kw-N, DA-2. TL: N39 24 30 W76 46 34. Hilton Plaza, 1726 Reisterstown Rd., Suite 117 21208. Phone: (410) 580-6800. Fax: (410) 580-6810. E-mail: am680@wcbm.com. Web Site: www.wcbm.com. Licensee: M-10 Broadcasting (acq 9-5-95). Network: CBS. Fisher, Wayland, Cooper, Leader & Zaragoza L.L.P. Format: Talk. News staff: 3; News: 11 hrs wkly. Target aud: 25-54; informed adults with major purchasing power. ◆Nick Mangione Jr., sr VP; Bob Pettit, gen mgr; Marc Beavin, gen sls mgr; Niles Seaberg, progmg dir; Eddie Applefeild, prom.

*WEAA(FM)— Jan 10, 1977: 88.9 mhz; 12.5 kw. 220 ft. TL: N39 20 31 W76 35 13. Stereo. Benjamin Bannexer, Bldg R Rm. 401, 1700 East Coldspring Ln. 21251. Phone: (443) 885-3564. Fax: (443) 885-8206. E-mail: weaa@moac.morgan.edu. Web Site: www.weaa.org. Licensee: Morgan State University. Network: NPR. Schwartz, Woods & Miller. Format: Jazz, news/talk. News staff: one; News: 10 hrs wkly. Target aud: 25-49; 85% Black. Spec prog: Urban oldies 5 hrs, Caribbean 7 hrs, Africian world 4 hrs, gospel 13 hrs, hip hop 5 hrs

wkly. ◆Dr. Preston Blakely, gen mgr; Sandi Mallony, progmg dir & progmg mgr; Kayona Ebony Brown, mus dir & chief of engrg.

WERQ-FM— 1960: 92.3 mhz; 37 kw. 571 ft. TL: N39 20 20 W76 40 02. Stereo. 100 St. Paul St. 21202. Phone: (410) 332-8200. Fax: (410) 783-4791. Web Site: www.92qjams.com. Licensee: Radio One Licenses LLC. Group owner: Radio One Inc. (acq 6-21-93; $9 million. with co-located AM; FTR: 7-19-93). Rep: Allied Radio Partners. Arent, Fox, Kintner, Plotkin & Kahn. Format: Urban contemp. Target aud: 18-34; young adults. ◆Alfred Liggins, CEO & prom dir; Mary Catherine Sneed, COO; Kathy Hughes, chmn; Howard Mazer, gen mgr; Jeff Spokes, sls dir & natl sls mgr; Neke Howse, mus dir & asst music dir; Karl Goehring, chief of engrg.

WOLB(AM)—Co-owned with WERQ-FM. Nov 25, 1947: 1010 khz; 1 kw-D, 27 w-N. TL: N39 16 38 W76 37 59. Format: News/talk. News: 5 hrs wkly. Target aud: 35 plus; African American adults. Spec prog: Relg 2 hrs, Sp 2 hrs wkly. ◆Keller Wynder, prom mgr.

WHFS(FM)—See Catonsville

WITH(AM)— Mar 1, 1941: 1230 khz; 1 kw-U. TL: N39 18 58 W76 36 03. Stereo. c/o WAVA-FM, 1901 N. Moore St., Suite 200, Arlington, VA 22209. Phone: (703) 807-2266. Fax: (703) 807-2248. E-mail: youropinioncounts@1230amwith.com. Web Site: www.1230amwith.com. Licensee: Caron Broadcasting Inc. Group owner: Salem Communications Corp. (acq 5-16-97; grpsl). Network: Network: Salem Radio Network, Wall Street. Rep: Salem. Fletcher, Heald,& Hildreth. Format: News/talk. News: 4 hrs wkly. Target aud: 25-54; contemporary Christian. Spec prog: Relg 4 hrs wkly-weekends. ◆Edward Atsinger, CEO & pres; Stu Epperson, chmn; David Evans, CFO; Joe Davis, exec VP; David Ruleman, VP, gen mgr & opns VP.

WJFK(AM)— June 8, 1922: 1300 khz; 5 kw-U, DA-2. TL: N39 20 00 W76 46 13. 600 Washington Ave., Suite 201, Towson 21204. Phone: (410) 825-5400. Fax: (410) 821-5482. Web Site: www.1300wjfk.com. Licensee: Infinity WLIF-AM Inc. (group owner; Infinity Broadcasting Corp. acq 5-29-89; $32 million with co-located FM; 4-24-89). Network: Westwood One. Rep: Infinity Radio Sales. Leventhal, Senter & Lerman. Format: Talk, sports. Target aud: 18-49; men. ◆Mel Karmazin, pres; Bob Philips, opns mgr.

WLIF(FM)—Co-owned with WJFK(AM). Dec 24, 1970: 101.9 mhz; 13.5 kw. 960 ft. TL: N39 25 02 W76 33 23. Stereo. Web Site: www.1019litefm.com. Format: Lite adult contemp. Spec prog: Jazz 8 hrs wkly.

WNST(AM)—See Towson

WPOC(FM)— 1959: 93.1 mhz; 16 kw. Ant 860 ft. TL: N39 17 13 W76 45 16. Stereo. 711 W. 40th St., Suite 350 21211. Phone: (410) 366-7600. Fax: (410) 235-3899. E-mail: kboesen@wpoc.com. Web Site: www.wpoc.com. Licensee: Citicasters Licenses L.P. Group owner: Clear Channel Communications Inc. (acq 4-29-99; grpsl). Format: Country. ◆Jim Dolan, VP, gen mgr & mktg dir; Gary LaFrance, natl sls mgr; Lew Munza, mktg mgr; Steve Reus, prom dir & prom mgr; Ken Boesen, progmg dir.

WQSR(FM)— Dec 15, 1947: 102.7 mhz; 50 kw. 436 ft. TL: N39 23 11 W76 43 52. Stereo. 600 Washington Ave., Suite 201, Towson 21204-3913. Phone: (410) 825-1000. Fax: (410) 823-0816. Web Site: www.wqsr.com. Licensee: Infinity Broadcasting Corp. of Chesapeake. Group owner: Infinity Broadcasting Corp. (acq 11-13-98; grpsl). Format: Mixed/automated. ◆Robert Philips, VP & gen mgr; Dave Labrozzi, progmg dir.

WRBS(FM)— Aug 1, 1964: 95.1 mhz; 50 kw. 499 ft. TL: N39 15 21 W76 40 29. Stereo. 3600 Georgetown Rd. 21227. Phone: (410) 247-4100. Fax: (410) 247-4533. E-mail: info@wrbs.com. Web Site: www.wrbs.com. Licensee: Peter and John Radio Fellowship Inc. (acq 9-64). Format: Contemp Christian. News staff: one; News: 6 hrs wkly. ◆Steven D. Lawhon, gen mgr.

WSMJ(FM)— 1949: 104.3 mhz; 50 kw. 420 ft. TL: N39 25 46 W76 27 01. Stereo. 711 W. 40th St., Suite 350 21211. Phone: (410) 366-7600. Fax: (410) 235-3899. E-mail: wsmj@smoothjazz1043.com. Web Site: www.smoothjazz1043.com. Licensee: Citicasters Licenses L.P. Group owner: Clear Channel Communications Inc. (acq 5-4-99; grpsl). Rep: Katz Radio. Format: Smooth jazz. Target aud: 25-44. ◆Jim Dolan, VP, gen mgr & mktg mgr; Bill Hopkinson, sls dir; Chuck Allen, gen sls mgr; Lori Lewis, progmg dir.

WWIN(AM)— 1951: 1400 khz; 1 kw-U. TL: N39 19 21 W76 36 33. Stereo. Licensee: Radio One Licenses LLC. Group owner: Radio One Inc. (acq 1-23-92; 7.5 million. with WWIN-FM Glen Burnie). Rep: D & R Radio. Allied Radio Partners. Verner, Liipfert, Bernhard, McPherson & Hand. Format: Gospel. News staff: one; News: one hr wkly. Target aud: 25-54; Black, relg.

WWIN-FM—See Glen Burnie

WWMX(FM)— 1960: 106.5 mhz; 7.4 kw. 1,217 ft. TL: N39 20 10 W76 38 59. Stereo. 600 Washington Ave., Suite 201 21204-3913. Phone: (410) 825-1065. Fax: (410) 321-4548. E-mail: dave.labrozzi @infinitybroadcasting.com. Web Site: mix1065.fm. Licensee: Infinity Radio Inc. Group owner: Infinity Broadcasting Corp. Format: Adult contemp. Target aud: 25-54. ◆Bill Hooper, VP & gen mgr; Tracy Brandys, sls dir; Dave Labrozzi, natl sls mgr & progmg VP; Dave Burgess, prom dir & prom mgr; Josh Medlock, progmg dir. Co-owned TV: WJZ-TV

*WYPR(FM)— May 23, 1979: 88.1 mhz; 10 kw. 360 ft. TL: N39 19 53 W76 39 28. Stereo. 2216 N. Charles St. 21218. Phone: (410) 235-1660. Fax: (410) 235-1161. E-mail: tbrandon@wypr.org. Web Site: www.wypr.org. Licensee: WYPR License Holding LLC (acq 1-16-02). Network: Network: NPR, PRI. Format: Jazz, news/talk. ◆Anthony Brandon, pres & gen mgr; Andy Bienstock, progmg dir.

Bel Air

*WHFC(FM)— 1972: 91.1 mhz; 1.10 kw. 226 ft. TL: N39 33 22 W76 16 48. Stereo. Harford Community College, 401 Thomas Run Rd. 21015-1698. Phone: (410) 836-4151. Phone: (410) 836-4305. Fax: (410) 836-4180. E-mail: whfc@harford.edu. Web Site: www.whfc911.org. Licensee: Harford Community College. Format: Var. Target aud: 24-42; upwardly mobile professionals. Spec prog: AAA 15 hrs, class 18 hr, jazz 18 hrs, Christian 6 hrs, Americain Indian 3 hrs wkly. ◆Gary Helton, gen mgr.

Berlin

WOCQ(FM)— June 25, 1981: 103.9 mhz; 3 kw. 328 ft. TL: N38 22 58 W75 18 58. Stereo. 20200 DuPont Blvd., Georgetown 19947-3105. Phone: (410) 641-0001. Fax: (410) 641-1294. Web Site: www.oc104.com. Licensee: Great Scott Broadcasting. (group owner; acq 11-7-97; $2.775 million). Network: ABC Information & Entertainment. Rep: Allied Radio Partners. Format: Rap, Hip-Hop. News staff: one; News: 4 hrs wkly. Target aud: 18-49. Spec prog: Casey's Top-40 4 hrs, Top-20 Double Play with Albie Dee 3 hrs wkly. ◆Cathy Deighan, gen mgr & opns mgr.

Bethesda

WARW(FM)— October 1959: 94.7 mhz; 20.5 kw. 771 ft. TL: N38 57 49 W77 06 18. Stereo. 5912 Hubbard Dr., Rockville 20852. Phone: (301) 683-0947. Fax: (301) 881-8746. Web Site: www.classicrock947.com. Licensee: Infinity Broadcasting East Inc. Group owner: Infinity Broadcasting Corp. (acq 8-1-85; grpsl; FTR: 6-10-85). Network: CNN Radio. Rep: Infinity Radio Sales. Format: Classic rock. Target aud: 25-49. ◆Michael Hughes, gen mgr.

WGMS-FM—See Washington, DC

WMMJ(FM)— Nov 12, 1961: 102.3 mhz; 2.9 kw. 480 ft. TL: N38 56 09 W77 05 33. Stereo. 5900 Princess Garden Pkwy. #800, Lanham 20706. Phone: (301) 306-1111. Fax: (301) 306-9510. Licensee: Radio One Licenses LLC. Group owner: Radio One Inc. (acq 11-8-01; grpsl).

Broadcasting & Cable Yearbook 2006

Maryland

Format: Adult contemp, motown. ♦ Alfred Liggins, CEO & pres; Catherine Hughes, chmn; Scott Royster, CFO; Michele Wiliams, gen mgr.

WTNT(AM)— Jan 2, 1946: 570 khz; 5 kw-D, 1 kw-N, DA-2. TL: N39 02 07 W77 10 11. 8750 Brookville Rd., Silver Spring 20910. Phone: (301) 231-7798. Fax: (301) 881-8030. E-mail: contact@wtntam570.com. Web Site: www.wtntam570.com. Licensee: AMFM Radio Licenses LLC. Group owner: Clear Channel Communications Inc. (acq 8-30-00; grpsl). Rep: Clear Channel. Format: Talk. Target aud: 25-54. ♦ Tod Castleberry, opns dir; Kaiya Ramsey, gen sls mgr; Kevin Cannady, prom dir & prom mgr.

WUST(AM)—See Washington, DC

Braddock Heights

WWVZ(FM)— Apr 8, 1972: 103.9 mhz; 380 w. 910 ft. TL: N39 27 50 W77 29 44. Stereo. 3400 Idaho Ave. N.W., Washington, DC 20016. Phone: (202) 895-5000. Web Site: www.moremusic104.com. Licensee: Bonneville Holding Co. Group owner: Bonneville International Corp. (acq 1996; grpsl). Rep: Roslin. Format: Hot AC. News staff: one; News: 5 hrs wkly. Target aud: 25-49. ♦ Joel Oxley, gen mgr; Mike Spacciapolli, gen sls mgr; Sammy Simpson, progmg dir; Sean Sellers, mus dir.

Brunswick

WTRI(AM)— Oct 2, 1966: 1520 khz; 9.3 kw-D, 14 kw-CH. TL: N39 18 45 W77 36 31. Stereo. 214 13th Ave. 21716. Phone: (301) 834-1991. Web Site: www.vegas-radio.com. Licensee: WTRI Holding LLC (acq 10-20-2004; $1.6 million). Format: Sp, top 40, contemp. Target aud: 20-45. Spec prog: Talk 2 hrs, farm 2 hrs, sports 5 hrs wkly. ♦ Martin F. Sheehan, pres; Alfred Hammond, gen mgr.

California

WKIK-FM— December 1994: 102.9 mhz; 3.7 kw. 407 ft. TL: N38 20 53 W76 37 40. Stereo. Box 2908, La Plata 20646. Secondary address: 28095 Three Notch Rd., Suite 2-B, Mechanicsville 20659. Phone: (301) 870-5550. Phone: (301) 884-5550. Fax: (301) 884-0280. E-mail: wsmdfm@aol.com. Licensee: Somar Communications Inc. (group owner; acq 1993; $130,000;. FTR: 5-24-93). Format: Country. Target aud: 25-54. ♦ Roy Robertson, pres & gen mgr; Terrell Soellner, opns mgr; Sharon McGuire, gen sls mgr.

Cambridge

WCEM(AM)— 1947: 1240 khz; 1 kw-U. TL: N38 35 02 W76 04 56. Stereo. Box 237, 2 Bay St. 21613. Phone: (410) 228-4800. Fax: (410) 228-0130. Web Site: www.mtslive.com. Licensee: MTS Broadcasting L.C. Group owner: MTS Broadcasting (acq 6-20-93; $1.8 million with co-located FM; 8-9-93). Network: Network: Westwood One, ABC Information & Entertainment. Format: ESPN radio. News staff: one. Target aud: 25-54. Spec prog: Relg 5 hrs wkly. ♦ Troy D. Hill, gen mgr; Joel Scott, opns mgr & prom mgr; John Harris, progmg dir; Norm Elliott, news dir; Al Miller, pub affrs dir; Josh Bohn, engrg dir.

WCEM-FM— Jan 29, 1968: 106.3 mhz; 6 kw. 325 ft. TL: N38 35 02 W76 04 56. Stereo. 2 Bay Street 21613. Secondary address: Box 237 21613. E-mail: theheat@intercom.net. Web Site: www.mtslive.com. (Acq 1993; 8-23-93). Format: Hot Adult contemp. Target aud: 18-49.

WINX-FM— 2000: 94.3 mhz; 4.6 kw. Ant 3617 ft. TL: N38 37 49 W76 03 24. Stereo. Box 943, Easton 21601. Phone: (800) 353-9430. E-mail: info@shorecountry943.com. Web Site: www.winxfm.com. Licensee: CWA Broadcasting Inc. Format: Country. ♦ Roy Deutschman, gen mgr.

Catonsville

WHFS(FM)— Nov 22, 1963: 105.7 mhz; 50 kw. 492 ft. TL: N39 19 26 W76 32 56. Stereo. 600 Washington Ave., Suite 202, Towson 21204. Phone: (410) 825-5400. Fax: (410) 825-5404. Web Site: www.live1057.com. Licensee: Infinity Radio Inc. Group owner: Infinity Broadcasting Corp. (acq 11-13-98; grpsl). Rep: Christal. Format: Talk. News staff: one. Target aud: 25-54. ♦ Robert Philips, VP, gen mgr & stn mgr.

Chestertown

WCTR(AM)— June 16, 1963: 1530 khz; 1 kw-D, 270 w-CH. TL: N39 13 35 W76 05 20. Box 700, 231 Flatland Rd. 21620. Phone: (410) 778-1530. Fax: (410) 778-4800. E-mail: wctr@wctr.com. Web Site: www.wctr.com. Licensee: WCTR Broadcasting LLC (acq 5-12-2004; $340,000). Network: ABC. Rgnl Reps Format: Adult contemp. News: 10 hrs wkly. Target aud: 35+. ♦ Richard Gelfman, pres; John Link, opns mgr; Richard Myers, gen mgr, progmg dir & news dir.

College Park

***WMUC-FM**— Sept 10, 1979: 88.1 mhz; 10 w. 3 ft. TL: N38 58 59 W76 56 37. Stereo. Box 3130, South Campus Dining Hall, Univ. of Maryland 20742-8431. Phone: (301) 314-7865. Phone: (301) 314 7868. Fax: (301) 314-7879. Web Site: wmuc.umd.edu. Licensee: University of Maryland. Format: Var/div. News: 5 hrs wkly. Target aud: College students. ♦ Mark Burdett, CFO; Anton Kropp, gen mgr; Nestor Diaz, opns mgr.

Crisfield

WBEY-FM— July 1995: 97.9 mhz; 4.3 kw. Ant 379 ft. TL: N38 01 45 W75 45 05. 1637 Dunn Swamp Rd., Pocomoke 21851. Phone: (410) 957-6081. Fax: (410) 957-6080. E-mail: wbey@direcway.com. Web Site: www.easternshoreradio.com. Licensee: Bay Broadcasting. Format: Adult country. ♦ Michael Powell, gen mgr, opns mgr & gen sls mgr; Adam Riggin, progmg dir.

Cumberland

WCBC(AM)— June 24, 1953: 1270 khz; 5 kw-D, 1 kw-N, DA-2. TL: N39 40 28 W78 46 48. Box 1290 21501. Secondary address: 35 Baltimore Street 21502. Phone: (301) 724-5000. Fax: (301) 722-8336. E-mail: dnorman@wcbc1270am.com. Web Site: www.wcbc1270am.com. Licensee: Cumberland Broadcasting Co. Inc. (acq 4-8-76). Network: Network: ABC, Westwood One. Format: News/talk. News staff: 2; News: 3 hrs wkly. Target aud: 25 plus. ♦ David N. Aydelotte Sr., pres; Jim Robey, gen mgr & stn mgr; Mary Clites, gen mgr.

WCMD(AM)—Listing follows WROG(FM).

WKGO(FM)—Listing follows WTBO(AM).

WROG(FM)— 1948: 102.9 mhz; 32 kw. Ant 1,440 ft. TL: N39 34 56 W78 53 53. Stereo. 516 White Ave. 21502. Phone: (301) 777-5400. Fax: (301) 777-5404. E-mail: mail@hitcoutry1029.com. Web Site: www.hitcountry1029.com. Licensee: Broadcast Communications Inc. (group owner; (acq 1-8-2004; $2 million. with co-located AM). Shaonis & Peltzman. Format: Country. Target aud: 25-49. ♦ Eva Geiger, gen mgr & sls; Grant Garland, progmg dir & news dir.

WCMD(AM)—Co-owned with WROG(FM). 1948: 1230 khz; 1 kw-U. TL: N39 38 36 W78 44 35. Web Site: www.hotcountry1029.com. Shaonis & Peltzman. Format: Oldies memories. News staff: 2; News: 20 hrs wkly. Target aud: 25-54.

WTBO(AM)— Dec 13, 1928: 1450 khz; 1 kw-U. TL: N39 38 43 W78 45 05. Stereo. Box 1644, 350 Byrd Ave. 21502. Phone: (301) 722-6666. Fax: (301) 722-0945. Licensee: WTBO-WKGO Corp. LLC. Group owner: Dix Communications (acq 11-1-77). Network: CSN. Baker & Hostetler. Format: Nostalgia, adult standards. News staff: one; News: 20 hrs wkly. Target aud: 40 plus. ♦ G. Charles Dix II, pres; Richard L. Cornwell, gen mgr & gen sls mgr; Tom Martin, prom dir & progmg dir; Jim Van, news dir; Mark Workman, chief of engrg.

WKGO(FM)—Co-owned with WTBO(AM). April 1962: 106.1 mhz; 4 kw. 1,400 ft. TL: N39 34 54 W78 53 58. (CP: 5.4 kw, ant 1,410 ft.). Stereo. Network: Westwood One. Format: Adult contemp. News staff: one; News: one hr wkly. Target aud: 25-54. ♦ Richard Cornwell, adv mgr.

Denton

WKDI(AM)— Dec 27, 1988: 840 khz; 1 kw-D, DA. TL: N38 53 53 W75 51 10. Stereo. Box 309 21629. Secondary address: 24580 Station Rd. 21629. Phone: (410) 479-2288. Fax: (410) 479-5188. E-mail: wkdi@broadcast.net. Licensee: Bayshore Communications Inc. Format: Christian/talk. News: 12 hrs wkly. Target aud: 25-49; middle-income Christians. ♦ Edward Baker, CEO; Michael A. McCoy, gen mgr & progmg dir.

Easton

WCEI-FM—Listing follows WEMD(AM).

WEMD(AM)— Sept 29, 1960: 1460 khz; 1 kw-D, 500 w-N, DA-2. TL: N38 46 13 W76 04 55. Stereo. 306 Port St. 21601. Phone: (410) 822-3301. Fax: (410) 822-0576. E-mail: sandy@wceiradio.com. Web Site: www.wceiradio.com. Licensee: First Media Radio L.L.C. (group owner; acq 11-30-99; $4 million. with co-located FM). Network: Jones Radio Networks. Dow, Lohnes & Albertson. Format: Music of your Life. Target aud: 45 plus; mature adults. ♦ Matt Spence, CEO & progmg dir.

WCEI-FM—Co-owned with WEMD(AM). May 14, 1975: 96.7 mhz; 25 kw. 245 ft. TL: N38 46 13 W76 04 55. Stereo. Web Site: www.wceiradio.com. Format: Adult contemp. News staff: one. Target aud: 25-54. ♦ Alex Kolbiaski, CEO; Sandy Reeves, gen mgr & sls dir.

Elkton

***WOEL-FM**— September 1978: 89.9 mhz; 3 kw. 259 ft. TL: N39 35 35 W75 51 49. Box 246 21922. Phone: (410) 398-3764. Fax: (410) 392-3229. E-mail: adp.saved@juno.com. Web Site: www.mbcmin.org. Licensee: Maryland Baptist Bible College. Network: USA. Format: Religious-Educational. ♦ Ray Linzy, gen mgr.

WSRY(AM)— Aug 22, 1963: 1550 khz; 1 kw-D, 10 w-N, DA-2. TL: N39 35 45 W75 47 50. Box 372, Wilmington, DE 19899. Phone: (302) 731-7270. Fax: (302) 738-3090. E-mail: wxhl@wxhl.com. Web Site: www.wxhl.com. Licensee: Priority Radio Inc. (group owner; (acq 12-10-99). Network: ABC Information & Entertainment. Format: Christian, contemporary. Target aud: 25-64. Spec prog: Relg 3 hrs, farm one hr wkly.

Emmittsburg

***WMTB-FM**— Oct 1, 1977: 89.9 mhz; 100 w. 144 ft. TL: N39 41 02 W77 21 25. Mount Saint Mary's College, 16300 Old Emmittsburg Rd. 21727-7799. Phone: (301) 447-5239. Web Site: www.msmary.edu/wmtb. Licensee: Mount Saint Mary's College. Format: Classic rock, new age, alternative. News: 2 hrs wkly. Target aud: General; college & community. Spec prog: Folk one hr, gospel one hr, relg 4 hrs wkly.

Federalsburg

WTDK(FM)— Dec 2, 1978: 107.1 mhz; 3.9 kw. 408 ft. TL: N38 46 02 W75 44 46. Box 1495, Cambridge 21613. Phone: (410) 288-4800. Fax: (410) 228-0130. Web Site: www.mtslive.com. Licensee: MTS Broadcasting. (group owner; acq 1-30-97). Network: Network: USA, Westwood One. Format: Hits of the 50s 60s & 70s. News: 4 hrs wkly. Target aud: 25-54; affluent listeners. ♦ Thomas Mulitz, pres; Troy Hill, gen mgr; Joel Scott, opns mgr.

Frederick

WFMD(AM)—Listing follows WFRE(FM).

WFRE(FM)— Feb 19, 1961: 99.9 mhz; 7.9 kw. Ant 1,164 ft. TL: N39 29 59 W77 29 58. Stereo. 5966 Grove Hill Rd. 21703. Phone: (301) 663-4337. Fax: (301) 682-8018. Web Site: www.wfre.com. Licensee: Capstar TX L.P. (acq 8-30-2000; grpsl). Rep: Clear Channel. Format: Country. News staff: 3; News: one hr wkly. Target aud: 25-54. ♦ Doug Hillard, gen mgr; Blaine Young, sls dir.

WFMD(AM)—Co-owned with WFRE(FM). Jan 1, 1936: 930 khz; 5 kw-D, 2.5 kw-N, DA-2. TL: N39 24 55 W77 27 41. 5966 Grove Hill Rd. 21703-6012. Phone: (301) 663-4181. Web Site: www.wfmd.com. Group owner: Clear Channel Communications Inc. Network: ABC. Format: News/talk, sports. News staff: 3. Target aud: 35-64. ♦ Frank Mitchell, opns mgr, prom dir & progmg dir; Renee Dutton-O'Hara, news dir.

WWEG(FM)—See Hagerstown

WXTR(AM)— Dec 15, 1960: 820 khz; 4.3 kw-D, 430 w-N, DA-N. TL: N39 24 42 W77 28 20. 6633 Mt. Phillip Rd. 21703. Phone: (202) 895-5000. Fax: (202) 895-5149. E-mail: wtopnews@wtopnews.com. Web Site: www.wtopnews.com. Licensee: Bonneville Holding Co. Group owner: Bonneville International Corp. (acq 1996; grpsl). Network: ABC Information & Entertainment. Rep: Roslin. Format: News. News staff: one; News: 15 hrs wkly. Target aud: 25-54. ♦ Joel Oxley, gen mgr.

Broadcasting & Cable Yearbook 2006

Developers & Brokers of Radio Properties

contact American Media Services at our suite: Philadelphia Marriott Downtown 215-625-2900
843-972-2200
americanmediaservices.com
Charleston, SC
Dallas, TX · Chicago, Il · Austin, TX

American Media Services, LLC

WYPF(FM)— May 1991: 88.1 mhz; 4 kw. Ant 554 ft. TL: N39 25 05 W77 30 03. Stereo. Box 319, 4707 E. Schley Ave., Braddock Heights 21714. Phone: (301) 662-9090. Phone: (301) 371-8888. Fax: (301) 371-1777. E-mail: wjtm@wjtm.org. Web Site: www.wjtm.org. Licensee: Your Public Radio Corp. (acq 11-24-2004; $1.2 million). Network: USA. Format: Christian, talk, music. Target aud: General. ♦Anthony S. Brandon, pres; Michael Payne, gen mgr.

Frostburg

WFRB(AM)— Dec 20, 1958: 560 khz; 5 kw-D. TL: N39 41 02 W78 57 57. 242 Finzel Rd., Frostburg 21532. Phone: (301) 689-8871. Phone: (301) 722-6666. Fax: (301) 689-8880. E-mail: wfrb@wfrb.com. Licensee: WTBO-WKGO Corp. L.L.C. Group owner: Dix Communications (acq 6-1-97; $3.5 million. with co-located FM). Format: Adult standards, relg, news/talk. News staff: one; News: 10 hrs wkly. Target aud: 40 plus; those gainfully employed in the market for goods & svcs. Spec prog: Middle of the road. ♦G. Charles Dix II, pres; Richard Cornwell, gen mgr & gen sls mgr; Hannah Ford, prom dir; Carson Yoder, progmg dir; Tim Martin, progmg mgr; Jim Van, news dir & pub affrs dir; Mark Workman, engrg mgr.

WFRB-FM— Oct 1, 1965: 105.3 mhz; 16.5 kw. 960 ft. TL: N39 41 02 W78 57 57. Stereo. Web Site: www.wrb.com. Format: Country. News staff: 2; News: 5 hrs wkly.

*WFWM(FM)— April 1986: 91.9 mhz; 255 w horiz, 1.3 kw vert. Ant 1,424 ft. TL: N39 34 54 W78 53 53. Stereo. Stangle Bldg., Frostburg State Univ. 21532. Phone: (301) 687-4143. Fax: (301) 687-7040. E-mail: wfwm@frostburg.edu. Web Site: www.wfwm.org. Licensee: Frostburg State University. Network: NPR. Format: Classical, jazz, alternative, NPR. News staff: one; News: 2 hrs wkly. Target aud: General. Spec prog: Educ 11 hrs wkly. ♦Rene G. Atkinson, gen mgr; Chuck Dicken, progmg dir & progmg mgr.

*WLIC(FM)— October 1989: 97.1 mhz; 3 kw, 1,401 ft. TL: N39 34 56 W78 53 53. (CP: 150 w, ant 1,355 ft.). Stereo. Box 540, Grantsville 21536-0540. Secondary address: He's Alive Corp. Offices, 34 Springs Rd., Grantsville 21536. Phone: (301) 895-3292. Fax: (301) 895-3293. E-mail: hesalive@hesalive.net. Web Site: www.hesalive.net. Licensee: He's Alive Inc. (group owner) Network: USA. Format: Gospel, Christian, relg. Target aud: 18-35. ♦Dewayne Johnson, pres; Monte Palmer, stn mgr.

Fruitland

WKHI(FM)— 1972: 107.5 mhz; 18.5 kw. Ant 339 ft. TL: N38 11 54 W75 40 50. Stereo. 20200 Dupont Blvd, Georgetown, DE 19947. Phone: (302) 856-2567. Fax: (302) 856-7633. E-mail: sue@greatscottbroadcasting.com. Web Site: www.literockdelmarva.com. Licensee: Great Scott Broadcasting. (group owner; acq 7-16-99; $700,000 with WKHW(FM) Pocomoke City, MD). Network: NBC. Cohn & Marks. Format: Adult contemp. Target aud: 25-54. Spec prog: Black 5 hrs, gospel 5 hrs wkly. ♦Faye Scott, pres; Sue Timmonds, gen mgr; Sue Scott, gen sls mgr; Adam Davis, progmg dir.

Gaithersburg

WMET(AM)— Jan 31, 1983: 1160 khz; 50 kw-D, 1.5 kw-N, DA-2. TL: N39 11 16 W77 12 56. 1850 Main St. N.W., Suite 350, Washington, DC 20036. Phone: (301) 921-2194. Fax: (301) 216-2194. E-mail: wmet@powertalk1150.com. Web Site: www.1160wmet.com. Licensee: Beltway Acquisition Corp. (acq 7-24-2002; $7.03 million). Format: News/talk info. Target aud: 35-65; upscale, educated with disposable income. Spec prog: Indian 4 hrs wkly.

Glen Burnie

WFBR(AM)— May 15, 1963: 1590 khz; 1 kw-U, DA-2. TL: N39 10 36 W76 37 20. 159 8th Ave. N.W. 21061. Phone: (410) 761-1590. Fax: (410) 761-9220. Licensee: Way Broadcasting Licensee LLC (group owner; (acq) 8-1-2005; exchange for WKDV(AM) Manassas, VA). Format: Black gospel. ♦Arthur S. Liu, pres; Keith Baldwin, gen mgr.

WWIN-FM— Sept 15, 1964: 95.9 mhz; 3 kw horiz, 2.55 kw vert. 299 ft. TL: N39 12 16 W76 34 07. 1705 Whitehead Rd., Baltimore 21207. Phone: (410) 332-8200. Fax: (410) 944-1282. Web Site: www.magic959baltimore.com. Licensee: Radio One Licenses LLC. Group owner: Radio One Inc. (acq 1-23-92; $7.5 million. with WWIN(AM) Baltimore). Rep: Allied Radio Partners. Verner, Liipfert, Bernhard, McPherson & Hand. Format: Urban contemp. News staff: one; News: one hr wkly. Target aud: 35-54; Black adult. ♦Howard Mazer, gen mgr & natl sls mgr.

Grantsville

*WAIJ(FM)— October 1984: 90.3 mhz; 10kw. 561 ft. TL: N39 42 14 W79 05 31. Stereo. Box 540 21536-0540. Secondary address: He's Alive Corp. Offices, 34 Springs Rd. 21536. Phone: (301) 895-3292. Fax: (301) 895-3293. E-mail: hesalive@hesalive.net. Web Site: www.hesalive.net. Licensee: He's Alive Inc. (group owner) Network: USA. Format: Gospel, Christian, relg. Target aud: 18-35. ♦Dewayne Johnson, pres; Tim Eutin, progmg dir.

Grasonville

WRNR-FM—Licensed to Grasonville. See Annapolis

Hagerstown

WARK(AM)— July 20, 1947: 1490 khz; 925 w-U. TL: N39 37 36 W77 42 40. 880 Commonwealth Ave. 21740. Phone: (301) 733-4500. Phone: (800) 222-9279. Fax: (301) 733-0040. E-mail: webmaster@wark.am. Licensee: Nassau Broadcasting III L.L.C. (acq 2-25-2005; $18 million. with co-located FM). Shaw Pittman. Format: Talk, oldies. News staff: 2; News: 8 hrs wkly. Target aud: 25-54. Spec prog: Jazz 2 hrs wkly. ♦Eugene J. Manning, gen mgr; J. Frederick Manning, opns VP; Marcia Cason, gen sls mgr; Roger Lide, engrg dir.

WWEG(FM)— Co-owned with WARK(AM). March 1957: 106.9 mhz; 15.5 kw. Ant 853 ft. TL: N39 29 57 W77 36 42. Stereo. Web Site: www.warx.com. Network: Westwood One. Format: Classic hits. News staff: 2.

WAYZ(FM)— 1946: 104.7 mhz; 8.3 kw. 1,379 ft. TL: N39 41 47 W77 30 47. Stereo. Box 788, Greencastle, PA 17225. Phone: (717) 597-9200. Fax: (717) 597-9210. E-mail: info@wayz.com. Web Site: www.wayz.com. Licensee: H.J.V. L.P. (acq 8-28-2000; $2.5 million. and WWMD(FM) Waynesboro, PA). Format: Country. Target aud: 25-54. Spec prog: Relg 3 hrs wkly. ♦Dottie Hedglin, gen mgr & pub affrs dir; Gary Kirtley, gen sls mgr; Chris Maestle, progmg dir; Toni Anderson, mus dir.

WDLD(FM)—Listing follows WHAG(AM).

*WETH(FM)— June 15, 1993: 89.1 mhz; 900 w. Ant 1,338 ft. TL: N39 41 39 W77 30 50. 2775 S. Quincy, Arlington, VA 22206-2304. Phone: (703) 998-2790. Fax: (703) 824-7288. Web Site: www.weta.org. Licensee: Greater Washington Education Telecommunication Association. Network: Network: NPR, PRI. Format: News, pub affrs. Target aud: General; educated adults. ♦Joseph Bruns, COO & sr VP; Sharon Rockefeller, CEO & chmn; Polly Heath, CFO; Dan De Vany, VP & gen mgr; Cynthia Cotton, opns mgr; Adam Gronski, mktg mgr; DeLinda Mrowka, prom dir; Ingrid Lakey, progmg dir; David Ginder, mus dir; Mitra Keykhah, asst music dir; Ed Kennedy, engrg dir; Mike Byrnes, chief of engrg.

WHAG(AM)—(Halfway). June 9, 1962: 1410 khz; 1 kw-D, 99 w-N, DA-2. TL: N39 37 03 W77 44 17. 1250 Maryland Ave. 21740. Phone: (301) 797-7300. Fax: (301) 797-2659. Licensee: MLB-Hagerstown-Chambersburg IV LLC. (group owner; (acq 7-20-2005; grpsl). Network: ABC News/Talk. Format: News/talk. News staff: 2; News: 7 hrs wkly. Target aud: 25-64; news-talk information profile; older, upscale. ♦Rich Bateman, gen mgr.

WDLD(FM)—Co-owned with WHAG(AM). January 1965: 96.7 mhz; 4.8 kw. 164 ft. TL: N39 37 03 W77 44 17. Network: ABC. Format: New & classic rock, AOR. Target aud: 18-54; adults, young families.

WICL(FM)—See Williamsport

WJEJ(AM)— October 1932: 1240 khz; 1 kw-U. TL: N39 40 00 W77 43 30. 1135 Haven Rd. 21742. Phone: (301) 739-2323. Fax: (301) 797-7408. E-mail: wjej@myactv.net. Web Site: www.wjejradio.com. Licensee: Hagerstown Broadcasting Co. Inc. (acq 12-21-72). Network: CBS. Baraff, Koerner & Olender. Format: Easy listiening/pop standards. News staff: one; News: 21 hrs wkly. Target aud: 35 plus. Spec prog: Farm one hr, talk 8 hrs wkly. ♦John T. Staub, pres & gen mgr; Joanna C. Staub, opns dir; Robert V. Tantillo, gen sls mgr & rgnl sls mgr; Louis J. Scally, progmg dir & chief of engrg; Tom Bradley, news dir.

Halfway

WDLD(FM)—Licensed to Halfway. See Hagerstown

WHAG(AM)—Licensed to Halfway. See Hagerstown

Havre de Grace

WJSS(AM)— May 15, 1948: 1330 khz; 5 kw-D, 500 w-N, DA-N. TL: N39 33 55 W76 07 08. 1605 Level Rd. 21078. Phone: (410) 939-0800. Fax: (410) 939-2156. Licensee: Benjamin-Dane LLC (acq 5-12-2004; $350,000). Format: Multi-culture Christian, relg. Target aud: General. Spec prog: Black, gospel, children one hr wkly. ♦Ronald Reeves, pres; Horace Tittle, gen mgr.

WXCY(FM)— June 19, 1960: 103.7 mhz; 50 kw. 341 ft. TL: N39 33 55 W76 07 08. Stereo. Box 269, 707 Revolution St. 21078. Secondary address: 2727 Shipley Rd., Wilmington, DE 19803. Phone: (410) 939-1100. Fax: (888) 766-1037. E-mail: wxcy@wxcyfm.com. Web Site: www.wxcyfm.com. Licensee: Delmarva Broadcasting Co. (group owner) Format: Modern country. News staff: 2. Target aud: 25-54. Spec prog: Relg 2 hrs, NASCAR info updates on race day 6 hrs wkly. ♦Pete Booker, CEO & pres; Willis Schenk, chmn; Bob Bloom, gen mgr; Bob Mercer, opns dir.

Hurlock

WAAI(FM)— June 1, 1989: 100.9 mhz; 1.3 kw. 502 ft. TL: N38 37 28 W75 53 20. Stereo. Box 1495, Cambridge 21613. Secondary address: 2 Bay St., Cambridge 21613. Phone: (410) 228-4800. Fax: (410) 228-0130. E-mail: waai@intercom.net. Web Site: www.mtslive.com. Licensee: MTS Broadcasting. (group owner; acq 1-30-97). Network: USA. Format: Country. News staff: one; News: 6 hrs wkly. Target aud: 25-54; general. Spec prog: Gospel 3 hrs wkly. ♦Thomas Mulitz, pres; Troy Hill, gen mgr; Joel Scott, opns mgr & progmg dir; Thomas Latimer, sls dir; Chris Singleton, chief of engrg.

Indian Head

WWGB(AM)— June 1986: 1030 khz; 50 kw-D, DA. TL: N38 33 53 W76 49 01. Stereo. 5210 Auth Rd., Suite 500, Suitland 20746. Phone: (301) 899-1444. Fax: (301) 899-7244. E-mail: info@wwgb.com. Web Site: www.wwgb.com. Licensee: Good Body Media LLC (acq 7-15-02). Roy F. Perkins. Format: Sp, Christian. ♦Ruth Salmeron, stn mgr.

La Plata

WKIK(AM)— October 1965: 1560 khz; 1 kw-D. TL: N38 32 36 W76 59 37. Box 2908 20646. Phone: (301) 884-5550/870-5550. Fax: (301) 884-0280. E-mail: wsmdfm@aol.com. Licensee: Somar Communications Inc. (group owner; acq 4-12-91; $65,000;. FTR: 5-6-91). Network: ABC. Format: Country. News: 5 hrs wkly. Target aud: 25-54. Spec prog: Local news, Baltimore Ravens football. ♦Jimmy R. Pyle, gen mgr; Roy Robertson, gen mgr; Terrell Soellner, opns mgr.

Laurel

WILC(AM)— Dec 23, 1965: 900 khz; 1.9 kw-D, 500 w-N. TL: N39 04 57 W76 50 19. 13499 Baltimore Ave., Suite 200 20707. Phone: (301) 419-2122. Fax: (301) 419-2409. E-mail: viva900@tvcontacto.net. Web Site: www.radiovivc900.com. Licensee: ZGS Radio Inc. (acq 2-11-02; $5.5 million). Rep: Caballero. Format: Sp, adult contemp, news. News

Broadcasting & Cable Yearbook 2006

Maryland

staff: 2; News: 15 hrs wkly. Target aud: General. ♦Mark O'Brien, gen mgr; Patricia Omana, gen sls mgr; Sergio Uriola, mus dir; Andrea Sarralde, news dir.

Lexington Park

WMDM-FM— Dec 16, 1976: 97.7 mhz; 3 kw. 273 ft. TL: N38 16 57 W76 33 35. Stereo. Box 2908, La Plata 20646. Phone: (301) 884-5550. Fax: (301) 884-0280. E-mail: wmdmfm@aol.com. Licensee: Somar Communications Inc. (group owner; acq 2-12-01; $2.25 million. with WPTX(AM) Lexington Park including three-year, $100,000 noncompete agreement). Network: ABC FM Connection. Format: Oldies. Target aud: 25-54. ♦Roy Robertson, gen mgr & progmg dir; Sharon Robertson, sr VP & gen sls mgr.

WPTX(AM)— July 1998: 1690 khz; 10 kw-D, 1 kw-N. TL: N38 16 57 W76 33 35. Box 2908, La Plata 20646. Phone: (301) 884-5550. Phone: (301) 870-5550. E-mail: wsmdfm@aol.com. Licensee: Somar Communications Inc. (group owner; acq 2-12-01; $2.25 million. with WMDM-FM Lexington Park including three-year, $100,000 noncompete agreement). Format: News/talk. ♦Roy Robertson, gen mgr & progmg dir; Terrell Soellner, opns mgr; Sharon Maguire, sls.

Mechanicsville

WSMD-FM— Sept 1, 1988: 98.3 mhz; 3 kw. 328 ft. TL: N38 24 49 W76 46 31. Stereo. Box 2908, La Plata 20646. Secondary address: 28095 Three Notch Rd., Suite 2-B 20659. Phone: (301) 870-5550. Phone: (301) 884-5550. Fax: (301) 884-0280. E-mail: wsmdfm@aol.com. Licensee: Somar Communications Inc. (group owner). Network: ABC. Format: Classic rock. News staff: one; News: 6 hrs wkly. Target aud: 25-54. Spec prog: Local news. ♦Roy Robertson, pres, gen mgr & progmg dir; Terrell Soellner, opns mgr; Sharon Robertson, gen sls mgr.

Middletown

WAFY(FM)— May 7, 1990: 103.1 mhz; 1 kw. Ant 571 ft. TL: N39 25 05 W77 30 03. Stereo. 5742 Industry Ln., Frederick 21704. Phone: (301) 620-7700. Phone: (301) 620-1031. Fax: (301) 696-0509. Web Site: www.wafy.com. Licensee: Nassau Broadcasting III L.L.C. (acq 2-14-2005; $15.7 million). Dickstein Shapiro Morin & Oshinsky. Format: Adult contemp. News staff: 2. Target aud: 25-54; upscale, well-educated, great radio commitment. ♦Brian Unger, sls dir; Rob Marmet, gen mgr & mktg dir; Caroline Wood, news dir; Fred Klimes, chief of engrg.

Morningside

WPGC(AM)— October 1954: 1580 khz; 50 kw-D, 250 w-N, DA. TL: N38 52 07 W76 53 48. 4200 Parliament Place, Suite 300, Lanham 20706. Phone: (301) 918-0955. Fax: (301) 459-9509. Web Site: www.heaven1580am.com. Licensee: Infinity WPGC(AM) Inc. (group owner; (acq 1994); with co-located FM). Leventhal, Senter & Lerman. Format: Gospel. News staff: one; News: 3 hrs wkly. Target aud: 25-54. ♦Sam Rogers, gen mgr.

WPGC-FM— February 1959: 95.5 mhz; 50 kw. 500 ft. TL: N38 51 48 W76 54 38. Stereo. Web Site: www.wpgc955.com. Licensee: Infinity Broadcasting Corp. of Maryland. Format: CHR. Target aud: 18-54.

Mountain Lake Park

WKHJ(FM)— July 9, 1990: 104.5 mhz; 1.5 kw. 663 ft. TL: N39 24 57 W79 17 15. Stereo. Box 2337 21550. Phone: (301) 344-4272. Phone: (301) 334-2086. Fax: (301) 334-2152. E-mail: wkhj@verizon.net. Licensee: Southern Highlands Inc. Network: CNN Radio. Format: Adult contemp. News staff: one; News: 12 hrs wkly. Target aud: 18-49. ♦Pam Trickett, prom mgr; Terry King, gen mgr, opns mgr, gen sls mgr & mus dir; James Shaffer, news dir; Roger L. Ruff, chief of engrg.

Oakland

WKHJ(FM)—See Mountain Lake Park

WMSG(AM)— May 19, 1963: 1050 khz; 1 kw-D, 75 w-N. TL: N39 25 15 W79 25 00. Box 449 21550. Phone: (301) 334-3800. Fax: (301) 334-2152. Licensee: Oakland Media Group Inc. (acq 2-21-95; $200,000 with co-located FM; 5-8-95). Network: CBS. Format: Adult standard. Target aud: General. ♦Paul Mullan, gen mgr & opns mgr.

WWHC(FM)—Co-owned with WMSG(AM). 1966: 92.3 mhz; 1.4 w. 689 ft. TL: N39 26 41 W79 31 42. Stereo. Network: ABC. Format: Country.

Ocean City

WKHZ(AM)— July 1, 1960: 1590 khz; 1 kw-D, 500 w-N, DA-2. TL: N38 24 16 W75 07 37. 11500 Coastal Hwy., Sea Watch Suite #1 21842. Secondary address: 12216 Parklawn Dr., Suite 203, Rockville 20852. Phone: (410) 723-9100. Fax: (410) 723-6561. E-mail: 1590news@verizon.net. Web Site: khzradio.com. Licensee: Radio Broadcast Communications Inc. (acq 2-2001). Format: News. News: 23 hrs wkly. Target aud: 25-54; active, thinking, responsive, affluent adults, with high disposable income. ♦Bill Parris, pres; John Acosta, VP.

WOCQ(FM)—See Berlin

WOSC(FM)—See Bethany Beach, DE

WRXS(FM)— Apr 15, 1994: 106.9 mhz; 6 kw. 303 ft. TL: N38 20 57 W75 11 07. 12010 Industrial Park Rd., Suite 6, Bishopville 21813. Phone: (410) 352-0001. Fax: (410) 352-0005. E-mail: skip@x1069.com. Web Site: www.x1069.com. Licensee: Atlantic Radio Broadcasting L.L.C. (acq 4-98). Format: Alternative. Target aud: 18-34. ♦Crystal Layton, VP & stn mgr; Ronald J. Gillenardo, gen mgr; Skip Dixxon, opns mgr & progmg dir.

***WSDL(FM)—** Feb 13, 1998: 90.7 mhz; 15 kw. Ant 331 ft. TL: N38 30 06 W75 10 07. Stereo. Box 2596, Salisbury 21802. Phone: (410) 543-6895. Web Site: www.wscl.org. Licensee: Salisbury State University Foundation Inc. Network: Network: NPR, PRI. Format: News/talk. News staff: one; News: 24 hrs wkly. Target aud: General. ♦Fred Marino, gen mgr.

WWFG(FM)— June 30, 1978: 99.9 mhz; 38 kw. Ant 469 ft. TL: N38 25 20 W75 08 23. Gateway Crossing, 351 Tilghman Rd., Salisbury 21804. Phone: (410) 742-1923. Fax: (410) 742-2329. E-mail: froggyemail@yahoo.com. Web Site: www.froggy999 .com. Licensee: Capstar TX L.P. Group owner: Clear Channel Communications Inc. (acq 8-7-00; grpsl). Rep: Clear Channel. Format: Country. Target aud: 25-54; affluent, upwardly mobile. ♦Frank Hamilton, gen mgr; Brian Cleary, opns mgr; Dixie Penner, prom dir.

Ocean City-Salisbury

WQHQ(FM)—Licensed to Ocean City-Salisbury. See Salisbury

Ocean Pines

WQJZ(FM)— March 1994: 97.1 mhz; 4.6 kw. 374 ft. TL: N38 22 75 W75 10 32. Stereo. Box 909, Salisbury 21803. Secondary address: 919 Ellegood St., Salisbury 21801. Phone: (410) 219-3500. Fax: (410) 548-1543. E-mail: wqjz@radiocenter.com. Web Site: www.wqjz.com. Licensee: Delmarva Broadcasting Co. (group owner; acq 6-26-97; grpsl). Rep: Katz Radio. Hogan & Hartson. Format: Smooth jazz. News staff: 3. Target aud: 30-60. ♦Michael Reath, gen mgr; Joe Edwards, opns mgr; Joe Beail, gen sls mgr.

Owings Mills

WCBM(AM)—See Baltimore

Pikesville

WWLG(AM)— Apr 5, 1955: 1370 khz; 50 kw-D, 7.7 kw-N, DA-2. TL: N39 26 23 W76 21 20. 1726 Reisterstown, Suite 117, Baltimore 21208. Phone: (410) 580-6800. Fax: (410) 580-6810. E-mail: bpettit680@yahoo.com. Web Site: www.wcbm.com. Licensee: M-10 Broadcasting Inc. (acq 6-12-98; $1.1 million with WJSS(AM) Havre de Grace). Network: American Urban. Format: MOR, big band, nostalgia, adult standards. Target aud: 50 plus. ♦Nick Mangione Jr., sr VP & opns mgr; Bob Pettit, gen mgr; Marc Beavin, gen sls mgr; Niles Seaberg, progmg dir; Eddie Applefeild, prom.

Pocomoke City

WGOP(AM)— Aug 1, 1955: 540 khz; 500 w-D, 243 w-N. TL: N38 03 11 W75 34 11. (CP: COL: Damascus, 1 kw-U, DA-2. TL: N39 17 46 W77 13 12). 1637 Dunn Swamp Rd. 21851. Phone: (410) 957-6081. Fax: (410) 957-6080. E-mail: wbey@direcway.com. Licensee: Birach Broadcasting Corp. (group owner; acq 11-25-92; $127,500;. FTR:

12-14-92). Pepper & Corazzini. Format: Adult standards. ♦Michael Powell, gen mgr; Chuppy Layton, opns dir & mus dir.

WKHW(FM)— May 1, 1992: 106.5 mhz; 1.8 kw. 341 ft. TL: N37 58 38 W75 32 36. 1508 Market St. 21851. Phone: (410) 957-4300. Fax: (410) 957-6080. E-mail: sue@greatscottbroadcasting.com. Licensee: Great Scott Broadcasting. (group owner; acq 7-16-99; $700,000 with WKHI(FM) Fruitland). Cohn & Marks. Format: Oldies. Target aud: 25-54. Spec prog: Gospel 5 hrs, bluegrass 4 hrs wkly. ♦Michael Powell, gen mgr.

WXMD(FM)— October 2000: 92.5 mhz; 2.95 kw. Ant 472 ft. TL: N38 08 35 W75 39 53. Box 909, Salisbury 21803. Phone: (410) 219-3500. Fax: (410) 548-1543. E-mail: max925@radiocenter.com. Web Site: www.max925.com. Licensee: Delmarva Broadcasting Co. (group owner; acq 7-10-00; $425,000). Rep: Katz Radio. Hogan & Hartson. Format: Adult contemp, rock. News staff: one; News: 2 hrs wkly. Target aud: Adults 35-54; baby boomers. ♦Michael Reath, gen mgr; Joe Edwards, opns mgr & progmg mgr; Bill Reddish, news dir; Jeff Twilley, chief of engrg.

Poolesville

WDMV(AM)— December 1994: 700 khz; 25 kw-D. TL: N39 17 46 W77 13 12. Birach Broadcasting Corp., 21700 Northwestern Hwy., Tower 14, Suite 1190, Southfield, MI 48075. Phone: (703) 934-6300. Web Site: www.dcradio700.com. Licensee: Birach Broadcasting Corp. (group owner; (acq 9-95). Format: Talk. ♦Sima Birach Jr., pres & gen mgr.

Potomac-Cabin John

WCTN(AM)— 1965: 950 khz; 2.5 kw-D, 47 w-N, DA-2. TL: N39 02 12 W77 12 09. 7825 Tuckerman Ln., Suite 211, Potomac 20854. Phone: (301) 299-7026. Fax: (301) 299-5301. E-mail: wctn@wctn.net. Web Site: www.wctn.net. Licensee: Win Radio Broadcasting Corp. (acq 1-15-2004); $2.2 million). Network: USA. Fisher, Wayland, Cooper, Leader & Zaragoza L.L.P. Format: Adult contemp, Christian. News: 8 hrs wkly. Target aud: 25-45. ♦Richard S. Yoon, pres; Steve Sparks, VP; John Vogt, gen mgr; Regis Vogt, opns mgr.

Prince Frederick

WBZS-FM— August 1971: 92.7 mhz; 2.85 kw. Ant 476 ft. TL: N38 40 26 W76 35 40. Stereo. 8121 Georgia Ave., 10th Fl., Silver Spring 20910. Phone: (301) 588-6200. Fax: (301) 589-4376. Licensee: Mega Communications of Prince Frederick Licensee LLC. Group owner: Mega Communications Inc. (acq 3-2-00; $5.145 million). Format: Sp. ♦Rafael Grullon, pres; Maria Elena Verdugo, gen mgr.

Princess Anne

***WESM(FM)—** Mar 29, 1987: 91.3 mhz; 50 kw. 347 ft. TL: N38 12 37 W75 40 56. Stereo. Univ. of Maryland Eastern Shore, Backbone Rd. 21853. Phone: (410) 651-8001. Fax: (410) 651-8005. E-mail: wesm913@umes.edu. Web Site: www.umes.edu/wesm. Licensee: University of Maryland Eastern Shore. Network: Network: NPR, PRI. Format: Jazz, blues, NPR. News staff: one; News: 15 hrs wkly. Target aud: General. Spec prog: Blues 5 hrs, reggae 2 hrs, big band 10 hrs, gospel 20 hrs wkly. ♦Dr. Thelma B. Thompson, pres; Marva Copeland, gen mgr & mktg dir; Angel Resto Jr., opns VP; Brian Daniels, mktg mgr & progmg; Yancy Carrigan, mus dir.

WOLC(FM)— Dec 24, 1976: 102.5 mhz; 50 kw. 500 ft. TL: N38 06 43 W75 39 14. Stereo. Box 130, 11890 Crisfield Ln. 21853. Phone: (410) 543-9652. Fax: (410) 651-9652. E-mail: wolc@wolc.org. Web Site: www.wolc.org. Licensee: Maranatha Inc. Network: USA. Shairis - Peltzman. Format: Relg. News: 5 hrs wkly. Target aud: 35-64; Christian listeners & ministries. ♦Robert L. Shores, pres; Deborah G. Byrd, gen mgr; Jennifer Burke, gen sls mgr; Greg Fentress, progmg dir; Mark Bohnett, chief of engrg.

Rockville

WLXE(AM)— November 1951: 1600 khz; 1 kw-D, 500 w-N, DA-N. TL: N39 05 51 W77 09 07. Radio Ctr., 12216 Parklawn Dr., Suite 203 20852. Phone: (301) 424-9292. Fax: (301) 424-8266. Licensee: Multicultural Radio Broadcasting Licensee LLC. Group owner: Multicultural Radio Broadcasting Inc. (acq 7-31-01; $800,000). Format: Sp. ♦Bill Parris, gen mgr.

Stations in the U.S.   Massachusetts

Developers & Brokers of Radio Properties

contact American Media Services
at our suite:
Philadelphia Marriott Downtown
215-625-2900
843-972-2200
americanmediaservices.com
Charleston, SC
Dallas, TX · Chicago, Il · Austin, TX

American Media Services, LLC

Salisbury

*WDIH(FM)— June 1990: 90.3 mhz; 378 w. 180 ft. TL: N38 24 28 W75 36 16. Box 186 21801. Phone: (410) 860-5000. Fax: (410) 546-7772. E-mail: biscope@acninc.net. Licensee: Salisbury Educational Broadcasting Foundation. Format: Christian preaching & mus, info progmg. ♦Bishop Dr. George Copeland, gen mgr.

WDKZ(FM)— July 25, 1982: 105.5 mhz; 2.1 kw. Ant 384 ft. TL: N38 24 26 W75 35 57. Stereo. Gateway Crossing, 351 Tilghman Rd. 21804. Phone: (410) 742-1923. Fax: (410) 742-2329. E-mail: kissfm@kiss1055.com. Web Site: www.kiss1055.com. Licensee: Capstar TX L.P. Group owner: Clear Channel Communications Inc. (acq 8-25-2000; grpsl). Rep: Clear Channel. Format: Top-40. News staff: one. Target aud: 18-44. ♦Frank Hamilton, gen mgr; Brian Cleary, opns mgr; Dixie Penner, prom dir.

WGOP(AM)—See Pocomoke City

WICO(AM)— September 1957: 1320 khz; 1 kw-D, 36 w-N. TL: N38 21 39 W75 37 00. Box 909 21803. Secondary address: 919 Ellegood St. 21801. Phone: (410) 219-3500. Fax: (410) 548-1543. E-mail: wico@radiocenter.com. Web Site: www.wicoam.com. Licensee: Delmarva Broadcasting Co. (group owner; acq 6-26-97; grpsl). Network: ABC. Rep: Katz Radio. Hogan & Hartson. Format: News/talk, sports. News staff: 2; News: 18 hrs wkly. Target aud: 35-64. Spec prog: Farm one hr wkly. ♦Michael Reath, gen mgr; Joe Edwards, opns mgr & progmg dir; Joe Beail, gen sls mgr; Bill Reddish, news dir & pub affrs dir; Jeff Twilley, chief of engrg.

WICO-FM— Sept 3, 1969: 97.5 mhz; 4.5 kw. 299 ft. TL: N38 21 39 W75 37 00. Stereo. E-mail: catcountry@radiocenter.com. Web Site: www.catcountryradio.com. Format: Country. News staff: one; News: 3 hrs wkly. Target aud: 25-54. ♦Joe Edwards, chief of opns; E.J. Foxx, prom dir & mus dir; Bill Reddish, news dir.

WJDY(AM)—Listing follows WSBY-FM.

WQHQ(FM)—Listing follows WTGM(AM).

WSBY-FM— Dec 13, 1989: 98.9 mhz; 6 kw. 328 ft. TL: N38 18 00 W75 37 41. Gateway Crossing, 351 Tilghman Rd. 21804. Phone: (410) 742-1923. Fax: (410) 742-2329. E-mail: kennylove@clearchannel.com. Web Site: www.wsby.com. Licensee: Capstar TX L.P. Group owner: Clear Channel Communications Inc. (acq 8-7-00; grpsl). Mullin, Rhyne, Emmons & Topel. Format: Urban contemp. News staff: one. Target aud: 25-54. ♦Frank Hamilton, gen mgr; Brian Cleary, opns mgr, progmg dir & news dir; Ed Sennestyn, gen sls mgr; Chris Kelly, chief of engrg.

WJDY(AM)—Co-owned with WSBY-FM. Mar 14, 1958: 1470 khz; 5 kw-D, 500 w-N, DA-D. TL: N38 23 30 W75 38 48. Web Site: www.wjdy.com. Format: Gospel. Target aud: 04-12.

*WSCL(FM)— May 29, 1987: 89.5 mhz; 33 kw. 600 ft. TL: N38 39 15 W75 36 42. Stereo. Box 2596 21802. Secondary address: S. Salisbury Blvd. 21802. Phone: (410) 543-6895. Fax: (410) 548-3000. E-mail: prd@salisbury.edu. Web Site: www.wscl.org. Licensee: Salisbury State University Foundation Inc. Network: Network: Network: NPR, PRI, AP Radio. Format: Class, news. News staff: one; News: 29 hrs wkly. Target aud: General. ♦Fred Marino, gen mgr; Pamela Andrews, progmg dir; Bill Bukowski, opns.

WTGM(AM)— Sept 13, 1940: 960 khz; 5 kw-U, DA-2. TL: N38 25 44 W75 37 26. Stereo. 351 Tilghman Rd. 21804-1891. Phone: (410) 742-1923. Fax: (410) 742-2329. Web Site: www.delmarvaradio.com. Licensee: Capstar TX L.P. Group owner: Clear Channel Communications Inc. (acq 8-7-00; grpsl). Format: Sports. News staff: one. Target aud: 25-64. ♦Doug Hillard, gen mgr.

WQHQ(FM)—Co-owned with WTGM(AM). July 31, 1965: 104.7 mhz; 33 kw. 610 ft. TL: N38 23 15 W75 17 30. Stereo. Arent, Fox, Kintner, Plotkin & Kahn. Format: Adult contemp. Target aud: 25-54.

WWFG(FM)—See Ocean City

Silver Spring

WFED(AM)—Licensed to Silver Spring. See Washington DC

WIHT(FM)—See Washington, DC

WWRC(AM)—See Washington, DC

Snow Hill

WQMR(FM)— October 2002: 101.1 mhz; 1.2 kw. Ant 489 ft. TL: N38 12 57 W75 19 21. Snow Hill Broadcasting L.L.C., 7200 Coastal Hwy., Suite 101, Ocean City 21842. Phone: (410) 524-6862. Fax: (410) 524-6808. E-mail: studio@wqmr.com. Web Site: www.wqmr.com. Licensee: Snow Hill Broadcasting L.L.C. (acq 5-21-2004; $200,000). Format: News/talk, sports. ♦Jack Gillen, pres & gen mgr; Kevin Brenahan, VP; Corey Duices, progmg dir.

Takoma Park

*WGTS(FM)— May 8, 1957: 91.9 mhz; 29.5 kw. 165 ft. TL: N38 59 12 W77 00 04. Stereo. 7600 Flower Ave. 20912. Phone: (301) 891-4200. Fax: (301) 270-9191. E-mail: wgts@wgts919.org. Web Site: www.wgts.org. Licensee: Columbia Union College Broadcasting Inc. Format: Educ, relg. Target aud: General. Spec prog: Inspirational. ♦Gerry Fuller, chmn; John Konrad, gen mgr; Becky Wilson Ali Gray, progmg dir.

Towson

WLIF(FM)—See Baltimore

WNST(AM)— Oct 27, 1955: 1570 khz; 5 kw-D, 236 w-N. TL: N39 25 04 W76 33 23. 1550 Hart Rd., Baltimore 21286. Phone: (410) 821-9678. Fax: (410) 828-4698. E-mail: nasty@wnst.net. Web Site: www.wnst.net. Licensee: Nasty 1570 Sports LLC. (acq 1-11-01; $1 million). Format: Sports. ♦Paul Kopleke, gen mgr; Steve Hennessey, gen sls mgr.

*WTMD(FM)— Feb 12, 1976: 89.7 mhz; 10.16 kw. 236 ft. TL: N39 23 45 W76 36 29. Stereo. 8000 York Rd. 21252. Phone: (410) 704-8938. Fax: (410) 704-2609. E-mail: wtmd@towson.edu. Web Site: www.wtmd.org. Licensee: Towson University. Format: AAA. News: 6 hrs wkly. Target aud: 25-64. Spec prog: Folk 2 hrs, polks 2 hrs, blues 2 hrs, reggae 2 hrs, Irish 2 hrs, world one hr wkly, doo wop 2 hrs weekly. ♦Stephen Yasko, gen mgr; Jeri Jenkins, dev dir; Dan Reed, progmg dir; Mike Matthews, mus dir; T. Scott Dunbar, chief of engrg.

Waldorf

WWZZ(FM)— February 1965: 104.1 mhz; 22 kw. 764 ft. TL: N38 37 07 W76 50 42. Stereo. 3400 Idano Ave. N.W., Washington, DC 20016. Phone: (703) 522-1041. Web Site: www.wwzz104radio.com. Licensee: Bonneville Holding Co. Group owner: Bonneville International Corp. (acq 1996; grpsl). Network: Network: ABC, AP Radio. Format: Hot AC. News staff: one; News: 28 hrs wkly. ♦Bruce Reese, CEO & pres; Joel Oxley, gen mgr; Mike Spacciapolli, gen sls mgr; Sammy Simpson, progmg dir; Sean Sellers, mus dir; Ken Sleeman, chief of engrg.

Westernport

WWPN(FM)— Oct 1, 1993: 101.1 mhz; 6 kw. -541 ft. TL: N39 29 14 W79 03 13. Stereo. Box 3382, Lavale 21502. Phone: (301) 463-5100. Licensee: Ernest F. Santmyire. Format: Relg, contemp Christian. Target aud: 18-45; working class. ♦Ernest F. Santmyire, CEO & gen mgr.

Westminster

WTTR(AM)— July 1953: 1470 khz; 1 kw-U, DA-N. TL: N39 34 37 W77 01 21. 101 WTTR Ln. 21158. Phone: (410) 876-1515. Fax: (410) 876-5095. E-mail: wttr@toad.com. Web Site: www.wttr.com. Licensee: Sajak Broadcasting Corp. (acq 12-20-2004; $540,000). Network: ABC Daytime Direction. Format: Oldies. News staff: one; News: 12 hrs wkly. Target aud: 35-64. Spec prog: Farm 4 hrs wkly. ♦Steve Hopp, gen mgr; Dwight Dingle, stn mgr & mus dir; Mark Woodworth, news dir & pub affrs dir.

WZBA(FM)— Nov 1, 1959: 100.7 mhz; 27 kw. Ant 660 ft. TL: N39 27 01 W76 46 37. Stereo. 11350 McCormick Rd.,, Executive Plaza 3, Suite 701, Hunt Valley 21031. Phone: (410) 771-8484. Fax: (410) 771-1616. E-mail: jlaird@thebayonline.com. Web Site: www.wzbathebay.com. Licensee: Shamrock Communications Inc. (group owner; (acq 4-7-81; $1.74 million. with co-located AM; FTR: 5-4-81). Network: ABC FM Connection. Rep: Allied Radio Partners. Format: Classic rock. News: one hr wkly. Target aud: 25-49; men & women active in the country life group. ♦Jeff Laird, gen mgr; Mark Sheely, gen sls mgr; Jon McGann, progmg dir; Fred Klims, chief of engrg.

Wheaton

WACA(AM)— 1954: 1540 khz; 5 kw-D. TL: N39 00 50 W77 01 46. 11141 Georgia Ave., Suite 310 20902. Phone: (301) 942-3500. Fax: (301) 942-7798. E-mail: news@radioamerican.net. Web Site: www.radioamerican.net. Licensee: Entravision Holdings LLC. Group owner: Entravision Communications Corp. (acq 3-14-00; grpsl). Rep: Katz Hispanic. Leventhal, Senter & Lerman. Format: Sp. Target aud: General; Hispanic, Central & Latin American, Caribbean listeners. ♦Alejandro Carrasco, gen mgr.

WASH(FM)—See Washington, DC

Williamsport

*WCRH(FM)— July 24, 1976: 90.5 mhz; 10 kw. Ant 884 ft. TL: N39 39 34 W77 57 56. Stereo. Box 439 21795. Secondary address: 12146 Cedar Ridge Rd. 21798. Phone: (301) 582-0285. Fax: (301) 582-2707. E-mail: wcrh@wcrh.org. Web Site: www.cedarridge.org. Licensee: Cedar Ridge Children's Home and School Inc. Network: Moody. Hardy, Carey & Chautin, L.L.P. Format: Relg. News staff: one; News: 9 hrs wkly. Target aud: 25-45. ♦David Swacina, CEO; Jeff Ward, opns mgr.

WICL(FM)— Nov 15, 1972: 95.9 mhz; 3 kw. 300 ft. TL: N39 36 17 W77 46 49. Stereo. 1606 W. King St., Martinsburg, WV 25401. Phone: (304) 263-8868. Fax: (304) 263-8906. Web Site: www.cool959.com. Licensee: Prettyman Broadcasting Co. (group owner; (acq 3-10-98; $1.05 million). Southmayd & Miller. Format: Hits of the 60s & 70s. News: 15 hrs wkly. Target aud: 35-64. ♦Yogi Yoder, gen mgr; Chuck Thornton, gen sls mgr; Ron Bauer, progmg dir.

Worton

*WKHS(FM)— Mar 28, 1974: 90.5 mhz; 17.5 kw. 215 ft. TL: N39 16 55 W76 05 26. Stereo. Box 905 21678. Secondary address: Rts. 297 & 298 21678. Phone: (410) 778-4249. Fax: (410) 778-3802. E-mail: wkhs@kent.k12.md.us. Licensee: Board of Education of Kent County. Format: Div. Target aud: 12 plus. Spec prog: Oldies 6 hrs, children 5 hrs, country 2 hrs, big band 2 hrs, rhythm and blues 2 hrs, jazz 2 hrs wkly. ♦Steve Kramarck, gen mgr.

Massachusetts

Acton

*WHAB(FM)— Aug 1, 1979: 89.1 mhz; 9.1 w. 53 ft. TL: N42 28 48 W71 27 28. 96 Hayward Rd. 01720. Phone: (978) 264-4700, EXT. 3470. Web Site: www.quadphonic.com. Licensee: Acton-Boxborough Regional School District. Format: Div, news. ♦Dan Drinkwater, gen mgr.

Allston

WGBH(FM)—See Boston

Amherst

***WAMH(FM)**— 1955: 89.3 mhz; 150 w. 718 ft. TL: N42 21 51 W72 25 24. Stereo. Box 2171, Amherst College, AC# 1907Campus Center 01002. Phone: (413) 542-2224. Phone: (413) 542-2288. E-mail: wamh@amherst.edu. Web Site: www.amherst.edu/~wamh. Licensee: Trustees of Amherst College. Format: Alternative, div. News: 6 hrs wkly. Target aud: 16-32; youth of today. Spec prog: Black 12 hrs, class 3 hrs, jazz 8 hrs, Sp 2 hrs, Japanese 2 hrs, comedy 3 hrs, talk 2 hrs wkly.

***WFCR(FM)**— May 6, 1961: 88.5 mhz; 13 kw. 895 ft. TL: N42 21 49 W72 25 24. Stereo. 131 County Circle, Hampshire House, Univ. of Mass. 01003-9257. Phone: (413) 545-0100. Fax: (413) 545-2546. E-mail: radio@wfcr.org. Web Site: www.wfcr.org. Licensee: University of Massachusetts. Network: Network: PRI, NPR. Wiley, Rein & Fielding. Format: NPR News, Classical, Jazz. News staff: 3; News: 40 hrs wkly. Target aud: General. Spec prog: Sp 4 hrs, folk 4 hrs wkly. ♦Martin Miller, gen mgr; Ellen Kennedy, dev dir; Michael Rathke, progmg dir.

***WMUA(FM)**— 1949: 91.1 mhz; 1 kw. 26 ft. TL: N42 23 31 W72 31 13. Stereo. Univ. of Mass., 105 Campus Ctr. 01003. Phone: (413) 545-2876. Fax: (413) 545-0682. E-mail: adviser@wmua.org. Web Site: www.wmua.org. Licensee: Board of Trustees of University of Massachusetts. Format: Rock, jazz, var/div. News: 3 hrs wkly. Target aud: General; Univ. Spec prog: Pol 6 hrs, Sp 9 hrs, folk 15 hrs, gospel 9 hrs, blues 15 hrs, intl 12 hrs wkly. ♦Jen Moskal, gen mgr.

WPNI(AM)— Apr 2, 1963: 1430 khz; 5 kw-D, DA. TL: N42 21 25 W72 29 13. 3rd Fl., 98 Lower Westfield Rd., Holyoke 01040-2712. Phone: (413) 536-1105. Fax: (413) 536-1153. Licensee: 6 Johnson Road Licenses Inc. Group owner: Pamal Broadcasting Ltd. (acq 5-29-03; $8 million. with co-located FM). Ginsburg, Feldman & Bress. Format: News. News staff: 2; News: 126 hrs wkly. Spec prog: Class 2 hrs wkly. ♦Martin Miller, gen mgr.

WRNX(FM)—Co-owned with WPNI(AM). Nov 12, 1990: 100.9 mhz; 1.35 kw. 692 ft. TL: N42 18 24 W72 31 59. Web Site: www.wrnx.com. Format: Adult rock.

Ashland

WSRO(AM)— May 1967: 650 khz; 250 w-D. TL: N42 17 17 W71 25 53. 100 Mt. Wayte Ave., Framingham 01701. Phone: (508) 820-2430. Fax: (508) 820-2473. E-mail: wsroam650@yahoo.com. Web Site: wsro.wsro.com. Licensee: Langer Broadcasting Group L.L.C. (group owner; acq 1996; $10,000). Format: Talk, relg. Target aud: 20-80; general. Spec prog: Indian 2 hrs wkly. ♦Carl Abrams, gen mgr.

Athol

WJOE(AM)—See Orange-Athol

WNYN-FM— Dec 4, 1989: 99.9 mhz; 1.85 kw. Ant 407 ft. TL: N42 35 39 W72 12 02. Stereo. 362 Green St., Gardner 01440. Phone: (978) 630-8700. Fax: (978) 630-3011. Web Site: www.999theeagle.com. Licensee: County Broadcasting Co. LLC. Group owner: Northeast Broadcasting Company Inc. (acq 10-6-2003; $650,000. with WJOE(AM) Orange-Athol). Network: ABC. Format: Classic rock. ♦Chris Thompson, gen mgr; William Curtis III, opns dir.

Attleboro

WARL(AM)— Oct 8, 1950: 1320 khz; 5 kw-U, DA-2. TL: N41 57 33 W71 19 37. 127 Dorrance St., 5th Fl., Providence, RI 02903. Phone: (508) 989-5013. Fax: (401) 521-5878. E-mail: scott@spojo.com. Web Site: www.1320thedrive.com. Licensee: The ADD Radio Group Inc. (acq 6-1-98; $600,000). Arent, Fox, Kintner, Plotkin & Kahn. Format: News/talk, sports radio. Target aud: 18 plus; middle to upper middle class. ♦Scott MacPherson, gen mgr.

Barnstable

WQRC(FM)— July 20, 1970: 99.9 mhz; 50 kw. 378 ft. TL: N41 41 19 W70 20 49. Stereo. 737 W. Main St., Hyannis 02601. Phone: (508) 771-1224. Fax: (508) 775-2605. Web Site: www.wqrc.com. Licensee: Sandab Communications Inc. (group owner; acq 4-16-92; grpsl; 1-13-92). Network: AP Radio. Rep: Clear Channel. Covington & Burling. Format: Full service, adult contemp. News staff: 4; News: 32 hrs wkly. Target aud: 25-54. ♦Gregory D. Bone, gen mgr; Wayne White, opns mgr; Stephen Colella, gen sls mgr; Michelle Dodd, prom mgr; Angella King, news dir.

Beverly

WNSH(AM)— Dec 23, 1963: 1570 khz; 1 kw-U, DA-2. TL: N42 33 08 W70 55 43. Box 403, Longmeadow Way, Hamilton 01936-0403. Phone: (978) 921-1570. Fax: (978) 468-1954. E-mail: kwillcox@wnsh.com. Web Site: www.wnsh.com. Licensee: Willow Farm Inc. (acq 9-24-97; $50,000). Format: News/talk. News staff: 2; News: 15 hrs wkly. Target aud: 35 plus. Spec prog: Pub affrs 2 hrs wkly. ♦Keating Willcox, pres & gen mgr.

Boston

WBCN(FM)— May 1968: 104.1 mhz; 20.9 kw. 771 ft. TL: N42 20 50 W71 04 59. Stereo. 1265 Boylston St. 02215. Phone: (617) 266-1111. Fax: (617) 247-2266. Web Site: www.wbcn.com. Licensee: Hemisphere Broadcasting Corp. Group owner: Infinity Broadcasting Corp. (acq 11-13-98; grpsl). Network: CBS. Format: Alternative. Target aud: 18-34; men. ♦Mel Karmazin, pres; Tony Berardini, gen mgr.

WBMX(FM)— 1948: 98.5 mhz; 9 kw. 1,145 ft. TL: N42 18 27 W71 13 27. Stereo. 1200 Soldiers Field Rd. 02134. Phone: (617) 779-2000. Fax: (617) 779-2002. Web Site: www.mix985.com. Licensee: Infinity Radio Inc. Group owner: Infinity Broadcasting Corp. (acq 6-5-98; grpsl). Network: CBS. Rep: Christal. Format: Modern adult contemp, var. ♦Mark Hannon, gen mgr; Greg Strassell, progmg dir.

WBOS(FM)—See Brookline

***WBUR-FM**— March 1950: 90.9 mhz; 7.2 kw. Ant 1,046 ft. TL: N42 18 27 W71 13 27. Stereo. 890 Commonwealth Ave. 02215. Phone: (617) 353-0909. Fax: (617) 353-4747. Web Site: www.wbur.org. Licensee: Executive Committee of the Trustees of Boston University. Network: Network: NPR, PRI. Format: News, talk. Target aud: 25-54; intelligent adults interested in news natl, internatl & local. Spec prog: Sp 5 hrs wkly. ♦Jane Christo, gen mgr & progmg dir; Thomas Terry, opns mgr & chief of opns.

WBZ(AM)— Sept 19, 1921: 1030 khz; 50 kw-U, DA-1. TL: N42 16 44 W70 52 34. Stereo. 1170 Soldiers Field Rd. 02134. Phone: (617) 787-7000. Phone: (617) 254-1050. Fax: (617) 787-5969. E-mail: tjordan@cbs.boston.com. Web Site: www.wbz1030.com. Licensee: Infinity Broadcasting East Inc. Group owner: Infinity Broadcasting Corp. Network: Network: ABC, CBS. Rep: CBS Radio. Format: News/talk. Target aud: 25-54. Spec prog: Relg 2 hrs. ♦Ted Jordan, gen mgr; Laurie Lamper, prom dir & progmg mgr; Peter Casey, progmg dir & news dir.

WCRB(FM)—See Waltham

WEEI(AM)— Dec 1, 1926: 850 khz; 50 kw-U, DA-2. TL: N42 16 41 W71 16 02. 20 Guest St., 3rd Flr., Brighton 02135-2040. Phone: (617) 779-3500. Fax: (617) 779-3557. Web Site: www.weei.com. Licensee: Entercom Boston License L.L.C. Group owner: Entercom Communications Corp. (acq 10-15-98; $82 million with WRKO(AM) Boston). Network: CBS. Format: Sports, talk. News staff: 6. Target aud: 25-54. ♦Jason Wolfe, progmg dir & progmg; Craig Berkel, engrg dir & mktg; Jim Rushton, chief of engrg & adv.

***WERS(FM)**— Nov 14, 1949: 88.9 mhz; 4 kw. 614 ft. TL: N42 21 08 W71 03 25. Stereo. c/o Emerson College, 120 Boylston St. 02116. Phone: (617) 824-8894. Fax: (617) 824-8804. E-mail: music@wers.org. Web Site: www.wers.org. Licensee: Emerson College. Format: Div. News: 3.5 hrs wkly. Spec prog: Black 15 hrs, blues 15 hrs, jazz 15 hrs, Broadway 4 hrs, relg one hr wkly. ♦Jack Casey, gen mgr; Alden Fertig, opns mgr.

WEZE(AM)— Sept 29, 1924: 590 khz; 5 kw-U, DA-1. TL: N42 24 24 W71 05 14. 308 Victory Rd., North Quincy Phone: (617) 328-0880. Fax: (617) 328-0375. E-mail: mnillas@wezeradio.com. Web Site: www.wezeradio.com. Licensee: New England Continental Media Inc. Group owner: Salem Communications Corp. (acq 1-31-97; $6 million). Network: ABC. Irwin, Campbell, Crowe & Tannenwald. Format: Relg, talk. News: 5 hrs wkly. Target aud: 25 plus. ♦Edward G. Atsinger III, pres; Alex Canavan, gen mgr.

***WGBH(FM)**— Oct 6, 1951: 89.7 mhz; 98 kw. 650 ft. TL: N42 12 42 W71 06 51. Stereo. 125 Western Ave. 02134. Phone: (617) 300-2000. Phone: (617) 300-2300. Fax: (617) 300-1026. E-mail: wgbh@wgbh.org. Web Site: www.wgbh.org. Licensee: WGBH Educational Foundation. Network: Network: PRI, NPR. Format: Class, jazz, news. News: 22 hrs wkly. Target aud: General. Spec prog: Folk 10 hrs, blues 8 hrs, Irish 2 hrs, cultural 3 hrs wkly. ♦Henry Becton, pres; Marita Rivero, gen mgr. Co-owned TV: *WGBH-TV, *WGBX-TV affils

WHRB(FM)—See Cambridge

WILD(AM)— 1946: 1090 khz; 5 kw-D. TL: N42 24 40 W71 04 28. 500 Victory Rd., Quincy 02179. Phone: (617) 472-9447. Fax: (617) 472-9474. Web Site: wild1090.com/home.asp. Licensee: Radio One of Boston Licenses LLC. Group owner: Radio One Inc. (acq 12-20-00; $5 million. in cash & stock merger). Network: ABC. Rep: Roslin. Format: Classic soul, R&B. Target aud: General. ♦Frank Kelley, pres & gen mgr.

WJIB(AM)—(Cambridge). 1948: 740 khz; 250 w-D, 5 w-N. TL: N42 23 13 W71 08 21. Stereo. 443 Concord Ave., Cambridge 02138. Phone: (617) 868-7400. Web Site: www.wjib740.com. Licensee: Bob Bittner Broadcasting Inc. (group owner; acq 9-12-91). Format: Adult Standards. News: 3 hrs wkly. Target aud: 40-75; locally-programmed for those enjoying good adult mus. Spec prog: French 10 hrs, gospel 4 hrs wkly. ♦Bob Bittner, pres & gen mgr.

WJMN(FM)— Mar 31, 1948: 94.5 mhz; 11.5 kw. 1,053 ft. TL: N42 18 27 W71 13 27. Stereo. 10 Cabot Rd., Suite 302, Medford 02155. Phone: (781) 663-2500. Fax: (781) 290-0722. E-mail: management@jamn945.com. Web Site: www.jamn945.com. Licensee: AMFM Radio Licenses L.L.C. Group owner: Clear Channel Communications Inc. (acq 8-30-00; grpsl). Rep: Katz Radio. Latham & Watkins. Format: Top-40. Target aud: 12-44. Spec prog: Pub affrs 2 hrs wkly. ♦Jake Karger, gen mgr.

WKLB-FM—See Lowell

WMJX(FM)— Jan 6, 1982: 106.7 mhz; 21.5 kw. 750 ft. TL: N42 20 50 W71 04 59. Stereo. 55 Morrissey Blvd. 02125. Phone: (617) 822-9600. Fax: (617) 822-6231. E-mail: dkelley@magic1067.com. Web Site: www.magic1067.com. Licensee: Greater Boston Radio Inc. Group owner: Greater Media Inc. (acq 2-85). Rep: McGavren Guild. Format: Adult contemp, soft rock. ♦Peter Smyth, pres & sr VP; Matt Mills, VP & gen mgr; Rob Hogan, prom dir; Don Kelley, progmg VP & progmg dir; Candy O'Terry, progmg dir.

WMKI(AM)— 1922: 1260 khz; 5 kw-U, DA-N. TL: N42 16 30 W71 02 31. 226 Lincoln St., Allston 02134. Phone: (617) 787-0146. Fax: (617) 787-1236. Web Site: www.disney.com. Licensee: Radio Disney Group LLC. Group owner: ABC Inc. (acq 8-22-00; grpsl). Network: USA. Format: Family. Target aud: 6-14. Spec prog: Sp one hr, Black 2 hrs, Por one hr, Haitian 2 hrs, children 18 hrs wkly. ♦Scott Halstead, gen mgr; Lison Zapach, prom dir.

WNTN(AM)—See Newton

WODS(FM)— 1948: 103.3 mhz; 16.5 kw. 938 ft. TL: N42 18 27 W71 13 27. Stereo. 83 Leo Birmingham Pkwy. 02135. Phone: (617) 787-7500. Fax: (617) 787-7523. E-mail: bmpage@boston.cbs.com. Web Site: www.oldies1033.com. Licensee: Infinity Broadcasting East Inc. Group owner: Infinity Broadcasting Corp. (acq 11-13-98; grpsl). Rep: CBS Radio. Format: Oldies. ♦Ted Jordan, gen mgr; Tina Murley, gen sls mgr; Brian Page, prom dir; Pete Falconi, progmg dir.

WQSX(FM)—(Lawrence). April 1960: 93.7 mhz; 50 kw. 430 ft. TL: N42 40 26 W71 11 26. (CP: 29.5 kw, ant 640 ft. TL: N42 35 42 W71 02 18). Stereo. Entercom Boston, 20 Guest St., 3rd Floor, Brighton 02135. Phone: (617) 779-5300. Fax: (617) 931-7827. Web Site: www.star937fm.com. Licensee: Entercom Boston II License L.L.C. Group owner: Entercom Communications Corp. (acq 10-15-98; grpsl). Format: Dance Hits. Target aud: 25-54. ♦Amy Caplan, gen mgr.

***WRBB(FM)**— October 1970: 104.9 mhz; 10.9 w. 89 ft. TL: N42 20 19 W71 05 28. 360 Huntington Ave. 02115. Phone: (617) 373-4338. Fax: (617) 373-5095. Web Site: www.wrbbradio.org. Licensee: Northeastern University. Format: Alternative rock, urban contemp. News staff: one; News: 2 hrs wkly. Target aud: 12-35; college, urban. Spec prog: Sp 4 hrs, relg 4 hrs, West Indian 5 hrs, gospel 8 hrs, jazz 8 hrs, talk 6 hrs wkly. ♦Kristen Aldrich, gen mgr.

WRKO(AM)— 1922: 680 khz; 50 kw-U, DA-2. TL: N42 29 25 W71 13 05. 20 Guest St., 3rd Fl., Brighton 02135. Phone: (617) 779-3400. Web Site: www.wrko.com. Licensee: Entercom Boston License L.L.C. Group owner: Entercom Communications Corp. (acq 10-15-98; $82 million with WEEI(AM) Boston). Network: ABC. Format: Talk. Target

Stations in the U.S.   Massachusetts

Developers & Brokers of Radio Properties

contact American Media Services at our suite:
Philadelphia Marriott Downtown
215-625-2900
843-972-2200
americanmediaservices.com
Charleston, SC
Dallas, TX · Chicago, IL · Austin, TX

American Media Services, LLC

aud: 25-54. Spec prog: Relg one hr, gardening 4 hrs, restaurant/food 4 hrs wkly. ♦Tom Baker, gen mgr.

WROL(AM)— Oct 8, 1950: 950 khz; 5 kw-D, 500 w-N. TL: N42 26 15 W70 59 40. Box 9121, Marina Bay 02171-9121. Phone: (617) 328-0880. Fax: (617) 328-0375. E-mail: acanavan@wezeradio.com. Web Site: www.wrolradio.com. Licensee: SCA License Corp. Group owner: Salem Communications Corp. (acq 3-2-01; $11 million). Format: Talk, relg, Irish. Target aud: Adults. Spec prog: Fr 15 hrs, Sp 10 hrs wkly. ♦Alex Canavan, gen mgr.

WROR-FM—See Framingham

WTKK(FM)— 1945: 96.9 mhz; 12.5 kw, 1,010 ft. TL: N42 18 12 W71 13 08. (CP: 22.5 kw, ant 735 ft.). Stereo. 55 Morrissey Blvd. 02125. Phone: (617) 822-9600. Fax: (617) 822-6859. Web Site: www.969fmtalk.com. Licensee: Greater Boston Radio Inc. Group owner: Greater Media Inc. (acq 3-31-93; $11.65 million; 4-19-93). Rep: Katz Radio. Format: Talk. ♦Peter Smyth, CEO; Matt Mills, VP & gen mgr.

WTTT(AM)— Jan 1, 1979: 1150 khz; 5 kw-U, DA-2. TL: N42 24 48 W71 12 40. Stereo. Box 9121 02171-9121. Phone: (617) 328-0880. Fax: (617) 328-0375. Web Site: www.talk1150.com. Licensee: Pennsylvania Media Associates Inc. Group owner: Salem Communications Corp. (acq 10-31-2003; $8.6 million). Format: Talk. ♦Alex Canavan, gen mgr.

*****WUMB-FM**— Sept 19, 1982: 91.9 mhz; 320 w. 207 ft. TL: N42 15 27 W71 01 44. Stereo. Univ. of Massachusetts Boston, 100 Morrissey Blvd. 02125-3393. Phone: (617) 287-6900. Fax: (617) 287-6916. E-mail: wumb@umb.edu. Web Site: www.wumb.org. Licensee: The University of Massachusetts. (group owner) Network: Network: PRI, NPR. Format: Folk, rhythm and blues, world mus. News: 5 hrs wkly. Target aud: 25-40. ♦Patricia A. Monteith, gen mgr; Brian Quinn, progmg dir; Marilyn Rea Beyer, mus dir; Grady Moates, chief of engrg.

WUNR(AM)—(Brookline). 1947: 1600 khz; 5 kw-U, DA-1. TL: N42 17 20 W71 11 22. 160 N. Washington St. 02114. Phone: (617) 367-9003. Fax: (617) 367-2265. Licensee: Champion Broadcasting System Inc. Rep: Caballero. Format: Ethnic, Sp. Spec prog: It 1hrs, Pol 1 hrs, Irish 2 hrs, Greek 2 hrs, Black 2 hrs wkly. ♦Matthew B. Hoffman, pres; Steve Lalli, gen mgr; Roger Houston, opns mgr; Velma May, pub affrs dir.

WWZN(AM)— 1934: 1510 khz; 50 kw-U, DA-2. TL: N42 23 10 W71 12 01. Stereo. 1 Van De Graaff Dr., Suite 300, Burlington 01803-5171. Phone: (781) 221-7878. Fax: (781) 221-7877. E-mail: wwzn@1510thezone.com. Web Site: 1510thezone.com. Licensee: Rose City Radio Corp. (group owner; acq 3-23-01; grpsl). Network: Sporting News Radio Network. Haley, Bader & Potts. Format: Sports. Target aud: 25-54. Spec prog: Boston Celtics, NASCAR. ♦Michael S. Winn, gen mgr; Anthony Pepe, mktg dir; Tony Palmisano, sls.

WXKS-FM—See Medford

WZLX(FM)— Jan 1, 1979: 100.7 mhz; 21.5 kw. 777 ft. TL: N42 20 50 W71 04 59. Stereo. 800 Boylston St., Suite 2450, Prudential Tower 02199. Phone: (617) 267-0123. Fax: (617) 421-9305. E-mail: songrequests@wzlx.com. Web Site: www.wzlx.com. Licensee: Infinity Broadcasting Corp. of Boston. Group owner: Infinity Broadcasting Corp. (acq 11-13-98; grpsl). Network: CBS. Rep: CBS Radio. Format: Classic rock. Target aud: 25-54; males. ♦Mark Hannon, sr VP, gen mgr & gen mgr; Beau Raines, progmg dir & progmg mgr; Joe Soucise, chief of engrg.

Boxford

*****WBMT(FM)**— Jan 30, 1978: 88.3 mhz; 710 w. 17 ft. TL: N42 37 39 W70 58 21. 20 Endicott Rd., Topsfield 01983. Phone: (978) 887-8830. Fax: (978) 887-7243. E-mail: gwalker@masconomet.org. Licensee: Masconomet Regional High School System. Format: AOR. ♦Glenn Walker, gen mgr.

Brewster

WZAI(FM)—Not on air, target date: unknown: 94.3 mhz; 4.7 kw. Ant 372 ft. TL: N41 46 36 W70 00 40. 125 Western Ave., Boston 02134. Phone: (617) 300-4405. Fax: (508) 548-5517. Licensee: GBH Telecommunications Inc. ♦Eric A. Brass, gen mgr.

Bridgewater

*****WBIM-FM**— November 1972: 91.5 mhz; 180 w. 71 ft. TL: N41 59 15 W70 58 21. Stereo. Campus Ctr. 109,, Bridgewater State College 02325. Phone: (508) 531-1303. Phone: (508) 531-1366. Fax: (508) 531-1786. E-mail: wbim@bridgew.edu. Web Site: www.bridgew.edu/wbim. Licensee: Bridgewater State College. Format: Div, progsv. News staff: one; News: 14 hrs wkly. Target aud: 18-35; college students & loc residents. Spec prog: Classic/AOR rock 6 hrs, dance 9 hrs, retro 80s 3 hrs, indie label 3 hrs, urban 9 hrs wkly. ♦Catherine Dussault, gen mgr & stn mgr; Jim McKellar, opns dir; Shelby Harris, opns mgr; Jen Janulewicz, prom dir; Mark Lilly, progmg dir; Kevin Kennedy, mus dir.

Brockton

WBET(AM)— Nov 27, 1946: 1460 khz; 5 kw-D, 1 kw-N, DA-N. TL: N42 04 23 W71 02 39. 60 Main St. 02301. Phone: (508) 587-2400. Fax: (508) 587-4786. Web Site: www.wbet.com. Licensee: KJI Broadcasting L.L.C. (acq 11-25-97; $1.5 million with co-located FM). Format: News/talk, sports. Target aud: 35 plus; general. Spec prog: Gospel one hr, It 2 hrs, Pol 2 hrs, Irish 2 hrs wkly. ♦Charles K. Bergeron, gen mgr.

WBOT(FM)— July 21, 1948: 97.7 mhz; 2 kw. Ant 567 ft. TL: N42 12 42 W71 06 51. 500 Victory Rd., Quincy 02171. Phone: (617) 427-9447. Fax: (617) 472-9581. Web Site: www.radio-one.com. Licensee: Radio One Licenses LLC. Group owner: Radio One Inc. (acq 11-8-01; grpsl). Format: Hip-Hop, rhythm and blues. ♦Frank Kelley, gen mgr.

WMSX(AM)— July 17, 1961: 1410 khz; 1 kw-D, DA. TL: N42 03 30 W71 02 40. 288 Linwood St. 02301. Phone: (508) 587-1410. Fax: (508) 584-9678. Web Site: www.wnsh.com. Licensee: Hispanic Broadcasters Inc. (acq 2-12-2004; $1.43 million). Format: News/talk. ♦Willie Nunez, gen mgr.

Brookline

WBOS(FM)— 1955: 92.9 mhz; 8.8 kw, 1,100 ft. TL: N42 18 27 W71 13 27. Stereo. 55 Morrissey Blvd., Boston 02125. Phone: (617) 822-9600. Fax: (617) 822-6759. Web Site: www.wbos.com. Licensee: Greater Los Angeles Radio Inc. Group owner: Greater Media Inc. (acq 7-23-97). Rep: Major Market Broadcasters Ltd. Format: AAA. News staff: one; News: 3 hrs wkly. Target aud: 25-49; baby boomers seeking diverse quality mus. ♦Peter Smyth, CEO; Matt Mills, gen mgr; Buzz Knight, opns mgr; Chris Paquin, gen sls mgr; David Douglas, progmg dir.

WUNR(AM)—Licensed to Brookline. See Boston

Cambridge

WHRB(FM)— May 1957: 95.3 mhz; 3 kw. 110 ft. TL: N42 22 20 W71 07 09. (CP: 1.55 kw, ant 508 ft.). Stereo. 389 Harvard St. 02138. Phone: (617) 495-4818. Fax: (617) 496-3990. E-mail: mail@whrb.org. Web Site: www.whrb.org. Licensee: Harvard Radio Broadcasting Co. Inc. Format: Class, jazz, AOR. News: 4 hrs wkly. Spec prog: Black 14 hrs, blues 4 hrs, country 4 hrs wkly. ♦Dan Anderson, pres.

WJIB(AM)—Licensed to Cambridge. See Boston

*****WMBR(FM)**— Apr 10, 1961: 88.1 mhz; 360 w. 285 ft. TL: N42 21 42 W71 05 03. Stereo. 3 Ames St. 02142. Phone: (617) 253-4000. Phone: (617) 253-8810. Fax: (617) 232-1384. E-mail: info@wmbr.mit.edu. Web Site: www.wmbr.mit.edu. Licensee: Technology Broadcasting Corp. Format: Div, underground progsv, rock. Target aud: General.

Spec prog: Black 15 hrs, Fr 2 hrs, Chinese 2 hrs, Brazilian 2 hrs, Haitian 2 hrs wkly. ♦Josh McDermott, gen mgr; Generoso Fiero, stn mgr.

WTKK(FM)—See Boston

Charlton

*****WYCM(FM)**— 1976: 90.1 mhz; 100 w. Ant 390 ft. TL: N42 08 01 W71 57 26. Stereo. Box 573 01507. Phone: (508) 248-0049. Fax: (508) 248-4518. E-mail: christianvintage@wycm.com. Web Site: www.wycm.com. Licensee: Christian Mix Radio Inc. (acq 3-17-2004; $200,000). Format: Christian music. ♦Stephen Binley, stn mgr.

Chatham

WFCC-FM— Mar 24, 1987: 107.5 mhz; 50 kw. 341 ft. TL: N41 44 14 W70 00 40. Stereo. 582 Rt. 28, W. Yarmouth 02673. Phone: (508) 790-3772. Fax: (508) 790-3773. E-mail: mail@wfcc.com. Web Site: www.wfcc.com. Licensee: Charles River Broadcasting Co. (acq 9-1-96; $1.19 million). Rep: CMBS. Format: Class. News: 2 hrs wkly. Target aud: 25 plus; upscale, affluent, educated adults. Spec prog: Children one hr wkly. ♦Christopher Jones, pres; Jan D'Antuono, gen mgr.

Chicopee

WACE(AM)— Dec 1, 1946: 730 khz; 5 kw-U. TL: N42 10 01 W72 37 31. Box 1, Springfield 01101. Secondary address: 326 Chicopee St. 01101. Phone: (413) 594-6654. Licensee: Carter Broadcasting Corp. (acq 12-24-86). Format: Relg, talk. Spec prog: Pol one hr, Irish 2 hrs, Por one hr wkly. ♦Ken Carter, pres & gen mgr; Michael Durocher, opns mgr.

Concord

WBNW(AM)— Aug 28, 1989: 1120 khz; 5 kw-D, 1 kw-N, DA-2. TL: N42 26 54 W71 25 39. 144 Gould St. Suite 155, Needham 02494. Phone: (781) 433-0001. Web Site: www.moneymattersradio.net. Licensee: Money Matters Radio Inc. (acq 6-17-98; $550,000). New England. Format: Business, personal finance. News: 17 hrs wkly. Target aud: 35 plus; upscale, suburban families. ♦Barry Armstrong, pres; Paul Hundley, gen mgr & opns mgr.

*****WIQH(FM)**— December 1971: 88.3 mhz; 100 w. 30 ft. TL: N42 26 48 W71 20 49. Stereo. 500 Walden St. 01742. Phone: (978) 318-1417. Phone: (978) 369-2440. Web Site: www.wiqh.org. Licensee: Concord-Carlisle Regional School District. Format: AOR, progsv. Target aud: 12-21; teenagers. ♦Ned Roos, gen mgr & stn mgr; Paul O'Neill, gen mgr.

Danvers

WNSH(AM)—See Beverly

Dedham

WAMG(AM)— Oct 1, 1994: 890 khz; 25 kw-D, 3.4 kw-N, DA-2. TL: N42 14 49 W71 25 30. 529 Main St., Suite 200, Charlestown 02129-1119. Phone: (617) 242-8173. Fax: (617) 241-0017. Web Site: www.iaamegasepega.com. Licensee: J Sports Boston LLC Group owner: Mega Communications Inc. (acq 6-22-2005; $9 million. with WLLH(AM) Lowell). Network: ESPN Radio. Format: Sports. ♦Ulysses Arrigoitia, gen mgr.

Deerfield

*****WGAJ(FM)**— May 1982: 91.7 mhz; 100 w. 314 ft. TL: N42 32 05 W72 35 32. Stereo. Deerfield Academy 01342. Phone: (413) 772-1812. Fax: (413) 772-1100. Web Site: wgaj.dearfield.edu. Licensee: Trustees of Deerfield Academy. Format: Rock/Top 40. Target aud: 10-20; teens, young adults, pre-teens. Spec prog: Black 5 hrs, jazz 2 hrs wkly. ♦Sean Terwilliger, gen mgr & stn mgr.

Broadcasting & Cable Yearbook 2006

Massachusetts

Dudley

WXRB(FM)— 1975: 95.1 mhz; 15 w. 125 ft. TL: N42 02 40 W71 55 52. Nichols College, Box 5000, Center Rd. 01571-5000. Phone: (508) 213-1560. Phone: (508) 213-2157. E-mail: wnrc@nichols.edu. Web Site: www.nichols.edu/wnrc/index.html. Licensee: Nichols College. Format: Eclectic. ◆ Andrea Becker, stn mgr.

East Longmeadow

WHNP(AM)— 1947: 1600 khz; 5 kw-D, 2.5 kw-N, DA-2. TL: N42 04 30 W72 31 40. 45 Fisher Ave. 01028. Phone: (413) 586-7400. Fax: (413) 525-4334. Licensee: Saga Communications of New England LLC. Group owner: Saga Communications Inc. (acq 6-2-92; grpsl). Format: News/talk. Target aud: 18-49; upscale young adults. ◆ Larry Goldberg, gen mgr.

Easton

WSHL-FM— Jan 1, 1973: 91.3 mhz; 100 w. 66 ft. TL: N42 03 27 W71 04 47. Stereo. Stonehill College, 320 Washington St., North Easton 02357. Phone: (508) 238-2612. Fax: (508) 238-5722. E-mail: wshl@stonehill.edu. Web Site: www.stonehill.edu/wshl. Licensee: Stonehill College. Format: Div. Target aud: 19-30. ◆ Ryan Delenunt, gen sls mgr; Megan Manshield, rgnl sls mgr.

Everett

WXKS(AM)—Licensed to Everett. See Medford

Fairhaven

WFHN(FM)— Mar 1, 1989: 107.1 mhz; 6 kw. 325 ft. TL: N41 37 43 W71 00 24. Stereo. 22 Sconticutneck Rd. 02719. Phone: (508) 999-6690. Fax: (508) 999-1420. Web Site: www.fun107.com. Licensee: Citadel Broadcasting Co. Group owner: Citadel Broadcasting Corp. (acq 2-23-00; grpsl). Rep: McGavren Guild. Format: CHR. Target aud: 18-49. ◆ Wayne Leland, exec VP; Gail Leblanc, gen mgr.

Fall River

WCTK(FM)—See Providence, RI

WHTB(AM)— May 13, 1948: 1400 khz; 1 kw-U. TL: N41 41 23 W71 08 43. 1 Home St., Somerset 02725. Phone: (508) 678-9727. Fax: (508) 673-0310. Licensee: SNE Broadcasting Ltd. (acq 5-8-89; $650,000; 5-29-89). Rep: McGavren Guild. Format: Ethnic talk. Target aud: 25-64; Portuguese (ethnic). Spec prog: English 10 hrs, Pol one hr, Cambodian one hr, Fr one hr wkly. ◆ Robert S. Karam, pres; Hector Gauthier, stn mgr & chief of opns.

WSAR(AM)— 1921: 1480 khz; 5 kw-U, DA-1. TL: N41 43 26 W71 11 21. One Home St., Somerset 02725. Phone: (508) 678-9727. Fax: (508) 673-0310. E-mail: paul@wsar.com. Web Site: www.wsar.com. Licensee: Bristol County Broadcasting Inc. (acq 1992; FTR: 11-23-92). Network: ABC Daytime Direction. Format: News/talk, sports. Target aud: 25 plus. Spec prog: Por 3 hrs wkly. ◆ Hector A. Gauthier Jr., gen mgr; Paul Giammarco, opns mgr & progmg dir.

Falmouth

WCIB(FM)— 1970: 101.9 mhz; 50 kw. 479 ft. TL: N41 33 31 W70 35 46. Stereo. 154 Barnstable Rd., Hyannis 02601. Phone: (508) 778-2888. Fax: (508) 790-4967. E-mail: info@cool102.com. Web Site: www.cool102.com. Licensee: Qantum of Cape Cod License Co. LLC. Group owner: Qantum Communications Corp. (acq 6-11-03; grpsl). Network: ABC Daytime Direction. Rep: Katz Radio. Format: Classic rock. Target aud: 25-54. ◆ Vince Cremora, gen mgr; Steve McVie Solomon, opns dir; Larry Eagan, progmg dir.

WFPB-FM— 1996: 91.9 mhz; 300 w. 177 ft. TL: N41 36 50 W70 35 56. Univ. of Massachusetts, 100 Morrissey Blvd., Boston 02125. Phone: (617) 287-6900. Fax: (617) 287-6916. E-mail: wumb@umb.edu. Web Site: www.wumb.org. Licensee: University of Massachusetts. Network: NPR. Format: Acoustic/folk, rhythm and blues, world mus. ◆ Patricia A. Monteith, gen mgr; Brian Quinn, progmg dir.

Fitchburg

WEIM(AM)— Oct 6, 1941: 1280 khz; 5 kw-D, 1 kw-N, DA-1. TL: N42 35 40 W71 50 12. 762 Water St. 01420. Phone: (978) 343-3766. Fax: (978) 345-6397. E-mail: radio@weim.com. Web Site: www.weim.com. Licensee: LiveAir Communications Inc. (acq 2-01; $777,500. including $2,500 five-year non-compete agreement). Network: ABC. Format: Adult contemp, news/talk, sports. News staff: 2; News: 28 hrs wkly. Target aud: 35 plus; loc listeners. Spec prog: Finnish 25 hrs wkly. ◆ David M. Wang, pres & gen mgr; Deborah Wang, mktg VP & prom VP.

WFGL(AM)— February 1950: 960 khz; 2.5 kw-D, 1 kw-N, DA-2. TL: N42 35 24 W71 49 41. 356 Broad St. 01420-3030. Phone: (978) 342-5025. E-mail: mail@wfgl.org. Web Site: www.wfgl.org. Licensee: CSN International. (group owner; acq 1993). Format: Christian. Target aud: 25-54; college & career age, young families. ◆ George Small, gen mgr; Steve Bessette, stn mgr.

WXLO(FM)—Licensed to Fitchburg. See Worcester

WXPL(FM)— August 1985: 91.3 mhz; 100 w. 134 ft. TL: N42 35 18 W71 47 26. Stereo. 160 Pearl St. 01420. Phone: (978) 665-3692. Phone: (978) 665-4848. Fax: (978) 665-3693. E-mail: wxpl@fsc.edu. Licensee: Fitchburg State College. Format: Progsv. Target aud: 16-25. Spec prog: Class 2 hrs, jazz 4 hrs, sports 2 hrs wkly. ◆ Ken Sears, stn mgr.

Framingham

WBIX(AM)—See Natick

WDJM-FM— 1973: 91.3 mhz; 100 w. 89 ft. TL: N42 17 44 W71 26 18. Stereo. 100 State St., Suite 514 01701. Phone: (508) 626-4622. Phone: (508) 626-4623. Fax: (508) 626-4939. Licensee: Framingham State College. Format: Alternative. Target aud: 15-35; college, surrounding community & commuters. Spec prog: Jazz 3 hrs, Sp 8 hrs, rap 3 hrs, industrial 4 hrs wkly. ◆ Ken Arienti, gen mgr.

WKOX(AM)— April 1947: 1200 khz; 10 kw-D, 1 kw-N, DA-N. TL: N42 17 17 W71 25 53. (CP: COL Newton. 50 kw-U, DA-2. TL: N42 17 20 W71 11 21). 99 Rivera Beach Pkwy., Medford 02155. Phone: (508) 820-2400. Fax: (508) 820-2458. Web Site: www.am1430wxks.com. Licensee: Capstar TX L.P. Group owner: Clear Channel Communications Inc. (acq 2-15-2001; $10 million). Rep: Allied Radio Partners. Haley, Bader & Potts. Format: Progressive talk. News staff: 2; News: 15 hrs wkly. Target aud: 25-54; upscale suburban/metropolitan Boston residents. Spec prog: It one hr. ◆ Jake Karger, VP & gen mgr.

WROR-FM— 1959: 105.7 mhz; 8.5 kw. 1,144 ft. TL: N42 18 27 W71 13 27. Stereo. 55 Morrissey Blvd., Boston 02125. Phone: (617) 822-9600. Fax: (617) 822-6459. E-mail: kwest@wror.com. Web Site: www.wror.com. Licensee: Greater Washington Radio Inc. Group owner: Greater Media Inc. (acq 10-11-96). Format: Classic hits. Target aud: 25-54. ◆ Matt Mills, gen mgr; Buzz Knight, opns mgr & prom mgr; Peter Smyth, CEO & gen sls mgr; Ken West, progmg dir & news dir.

Franklin

WGAO(FM)— 1975: 88.3 mhz; 125 w. 174 ft. TL: N42 05 08 W71 23 54. Stereo. 99 Main St. 02038. Phone: (508) 541-1650. Fax: (508) 541-1922. Web Site: www.dean.edu. Licensee: Dean College. Network: AP Radio. Format: Classic rock, CHR. Target aud: 15-25. Spec prog: Relg 8 hrs wkly. ◆ Vic Michaels, gen mgr & opns dir; Michael Katic, news dir.

Gardner

WGAW(AM)— 1946: 1340 khz; 1 kw-U. TL: N42 35 33 W71 59 20. 362 Green St., NH 01440. Phone: (978) 630-8700. Fax: (978) 632-1332. Fax: (603) 577-8682. E-mail: wotw900am@hotmail.com. Licensee: County Broadcasting Co. LLC. Group owner: Northeast Broadcasting Company Inc. (acq 12-2-2003; $235,000). Network: ABC. Format: News/talk. ◆ Chris Thompson, gen mgr; William B. Curtis, opns dir; Chuck Wright, progmg dir & chief of engrg.

WJWT(FM)—Not on air, target date: unknown: 91.7 mhz; 850 w. Ant 276 ft. TL: N42 33 29 W72 03 06. CSN International, 3232 W. MacArthur Blvd., Santa Ana, CA 92704. Phone: (714) 929-9663. Fax: (714) 825-9661. Licensee: CSN International (group owner).

Gloucester

WBOQ(FM)— Sept 14, 1964: 104.9 mhz; 3.2 kw. 446 ft. TL: N42 35 36 W70 43 28. Stereo. 8 Enon St., North Beverly 01915. Phone: (978) 927-1049. Fax: (978) 921-2635. Web Site: www.wboq.com. Licensee: Westport Communications L.P. Akin, Gump, Strauss, Hauer & Feld. Format: Classic hits. News: 3 hrs wkly. Target aud: 25-54; mass appeal classical favorites. ◆ Todd Tanger, gen mgr; Sam Koffman, opns mgr.

Great Barrington

WAMQ(FM)— November 1988: 105.1 mhz; 730 w. 918 ft. TL: N42 09 36 W73 28 48. Stereo. 318 Central Ave., Box 66600, Albany, NY 12206-6600. Phone: (518) 465-5233. Fax: (518) 432-6974. E-mail: mail@wamc.org. Web Site: www.wamc.org. Licensee: WAMC. Group owner: WAMC/Northeast Public Radio (acq 3-5-93; $325,000; 3-29-93). Network: Network: NPR, PRI. Dow, Lohnes & Albertson. Format: News/talk. Target aud: General. Spec prog: Folk 7 hrs, jazz 13 wkly. ◆ Alan Chartock, CEO; David Gallery, VP & progmg dir; Dona Frank, dev dir.

WSBS(AM)— December 1956: 860 khz; 2.7 kw-D. TL: N42 12 52 W73 20 45. Box 297, Stockbridge Rd., Rt. 7 01230. Secondary address: 425 Stockbridge Rd. 01230. Phone: (413) 528-0860. Fax: (413) 528-2162. E-mail: wsbs@b.c.n.net. Web Site: www.wsbs.com. Licensee: Berkshire Broadcasting Co. Group owner: Vox Radio Group L.P. (acq 2-13-2004; grpsl). Network: AP Radio. Rep: D & R Radio. Wilkinson Barker Knauer. Format: Adult contemp, community radio. News staff: 3; News: 10 hrs wkly. Target aud: 25 plus; general. Spec prog: Farm one hr, relg one hr wkly. ◆ Donald A. Thurston, pres; Corydon L. Thurston, gen mgr; David L. Winchester, stn mgr.

Greenfield

WHAI(FM)—Listing follows WHMQ(AM).

WHMQ(AM)— May 15, 1938: 1240 khz; 1 kw-U. TL: N42 35 21 W72 37 08. 81 Woodard Rd. 01301. Phone: (413) 774-4301. Fax: (413) 773-5637. Licensee: Saga Communications of New England LLC. Group owner: Saga Communications Inc. (acq 4-1-01; $2.2 million. with co-located FM). Network: CBS. Wiley, Rein & Fielding. Format: News/talk. News staff: 2; News: 20 hrs wkly. Target aud: 35 plus. Spec prog: Oldies 13 hrs wkly. ◆ Dan Guin, gen mgr; Chris Collins, progmg dir & news dir.

WHAI(FM)—Co-owned with WHMQ(AM). May 15, 1948: 98.3 mhz; 2 kw. 403 ft. TL: N42 34 15 W72 38 42. Stereo. E-mail: info@whai.com. Web Site: whai.com. Format: Adult contemp. News staff: one. Target aud: 25-54. ◆ Nick DeRuiter, progmg dir; Hugh Massey, news dir.

WINQ(FM)—See Winchester NH

WIZZ(AM)— Aug 26, 1980: 1520 khz; 10 kw-D, DA. TL: N42 36 12 W72 36 21. Box 983 01302. Phone: (413) 774-5757. Fax: (413) 625-8274. E-mail: info@wizzradio. Web Site: www.wizzradio.com. Licensee: P. & M. Radio LLC (acq 1-31-03; $150,000). Network: AP Network News. Format: Nostalgia. ◆ Phillip G. Drumheller, pres & gen mgr.

WPVQ(FM)— July 26, 1981: 95.3 mhz; 320 w. 780 ft. TL: N42 41 50 W72 36 20. Stereo. Box 268, North Hampton 01061. Phone: (413) 585-9555. Fax: (413) 585-0927. E-mail: info@bear953.com. Web Site: www.wpvq.com. Licensee: Saga Communications of New England LLC. Group owner: Saga Communications Inc. (acq 2-13-2004; grpsl). Format: Country. Target aud: 18-45. Spec prog: Class 6 hrs, jazz 6 hrs, C&W 6 hrs, oldies 5 hrs. ◆ Sean O'Mealy, gen mgr.

Harwich

WCCT-FM— May 1988: 90.3 mhz; 160 w horiz, 640 w vert. 125 ft. TL: N41 42 40 W70 04 34. Cape Cod Tech., 351 Pleasant Lake Ave. 02645. Phone: (508) 432-4500. Fax: (508) 432-7916. E-mail: burtfisher@capetech.us. Licensee: Cape Cod Regional Technical High School. (acq 11-11-87). Network: NPR. Format: Div, educ. News: 30 hrs wkly. Target aud: 20-65; educated adults. ◆ Tim Carroll, CEO; John Ganss, gen mgr.

Harwichport

WDVT(FM)— May 11, 1989: 93.5 mhz; 3 kw. 328 ft. TL: N41 44 19 W70 00 40. Stereo. 278 S. Sea Ave., W. Yarmouth 02673. Phone: (508) 760-5252. Fax: (508) 862-6329. Web Site: www.thewave1011.com. Licensee: Cape Cod Trust (Mark O. Hubbard, trustee) Group owner: Boch Broadcasting (acq 7-27-2005; with WTWV(FM) Mashpee). Network: Westwood One. Format: Oldies. Target aud: 35-64. ◆ Carolyn Bernhardt, VP & gen mgr.

Stations in the U.S. — Massachusetts

Haverhill

WCCM(AM)— 1947: 1490 khz; 1 kw-U. TL: N42 46 22 W71 06 01. 462 Merrimac St., Methuen 01844. Phone: (978) 683-7171. Fax: (978) 687-1180. E-mail: pjc@1490wccm.com. Web Site: www.1490wccm.com. Licensee: Costa-Eagle Radio Ventures L.P. (group owner; acq 1998). Rep: Roslin. Bryan Cave. Format: News/talk. News staff: 2; News: 25 hrs wkly. Target aud: General. Spec prog: Community call-in on pub affrs 2 hrs wkly. ◆ Patrick J. Costa, CEO, gen mgr & gen mgr; John Bassett, stn mgr; Bruce Arnold, progmg dir & mus dir; Dana Esmel, news dir.

WXRV(FM)— June 1959: 92.5 mhz; 25 kw. 710 ft. TL: N42 46 23 W71 06 01. Stereo. 30 How St. 01830. Phone: (978) 374-4733. Fax: (978) 373-8023. E-mail: theriver@wxrv.com. Web Site: www.wxrv.com. Licensee: Beanpot Broadcasting Corp. Group owner: Northeast Broadcasting Co. Inc. (acq 1981). Format: AAA, adult contemp. Target aud: 25-54. Spec prog: Radio shopping, community call-in on pub affrs one hr wkly. ◆ Dana Marshall, progmg dir & mus dir; Steve Young, gen sls mgr & chief of engrg.

Holliston

*****WHHB(FM)**— Apr 17, 1979: 99.9 mhz; 10 w. 52 ft. TL: N42 12 29 W71 26 19. (CP: 170 w, ant 203 ft.). Holliston High School, 370 Hollis St. 01746. Phone: (508) 429-0677. Fax: (508) 429-8225. E-mail: info@whhbfm.com. Web Site: www.whhbfm.com. Licensee: Holliston High School. Format: Div. ◆ Mary Casserly, gen mgr & stn mgr.

Holyoke

*****WCCH(FM)**— 1977: 103.5 mhz; 10 w. 258 ft. TL: N42 11 55 W72 38 27. 303 Homestead Ave. 01040. Phone: (413) 552-2488. E-mail: wcch1035@hotmail.com. Licensee: Holyoke Community College. Format: Progsv. Spec prog: Class 2 hrs, jazz 2 hrs, Sp 2 hrs, rhythm & blues 6 hrs wkly. ◆ Adam Roberts, gen mgr.

Hyannis

WCOD-FM— June 2, 1967: 106.1 mhz; 50 kw. 450 ft. TL: N41 43 46 W70 10 01. Stereo. 278 S. Sea Ave., W. Yarmouth 02673. Phone: (508) 775-5678. Fax: (508) 862-6329. Licensee: Qantum of Cape Cod License Co. LLC. Group owner: Boch Broadcasting (acq 4-11-2005; grpsl). Rep: Christal. Format: Adult contemp. News staff: 2. Target aud: 25-54. ◆ Carolyn Bernhardt, gen mgr; Gregg Cassidy, opns mgr, gen sls mgr & progmg dir; Larry Beavers, chief of engrg.

WPXC(FM)— Jan 9, 1987: 102.9 mhz; 6 kw. 325 ft. TL: N41 41 19 W70 20 49. Stereo. 154 Barnstable Rd. 02601. Phone: (508) 778-2888. Fax: (508) 790-4967. E-mail: info@pixy103.com. Web Site: www.pixy103.com. Licensee: Cape Cod Trust (Mark O. Hubbard, trustee) Group owner: Qantum Communications Corp. (acq 7-27-2005). Rep: McGavren Guild. Format: Rock. News staff: 3; News: 4 hrs wkly. Target aud: General. ◆ Vince Cremona, gen mgr; Steve McVie Solomon, opns dir; Suzanne Tonaire, progmg dir.

WQRC(FM)—See Barnstable

Lawrence

WLLH(AM)—See Lowell

WNNW(AM)— August 1947: 800 khz; 1 kw-D, 250 w-N. TL: N42 40 26 W71 11 26. 462 Merrimack St., Methuen 01844. Phone: (978) 683-7171. Phone: (978) 686-9966. Fax: (978) 687-1180. Web Site: www.poder800am.com. Licensee: Costa-Eagle Radio Ventures L.P. (group owner; acq 3-27-98; $405,000). Network: CNN Radio. Rep: Lotus Entravision Reps LLC. Bryan Cave. Format: Sp. News staff: 2; News: 10 hrs wkly. Target aud: 35-64; general. Spec prog: It 2 hrs, Pol one hr, Sp 10 hrs wkly. ◆ Patrick Costa, pres & gen mgr; John Bassett, stn mgr & gen sls mgr; Johnny McKenzie, opns mgr.

WQSX(FM)—Licensed to Lawrence. See Boston

Leicester

WVNE(AM)— June 19, 1991: 760 khz; 25 kw-D. TL: N42 14 57 W72 04 41. 70 James St., Suite 201, Worcester 01603. Phone: (508) 831-9863. Fax: (508) 831-7964. E-mail: info@wvne.net. Web Site: www.wvne.net. Licensee: Blount Masscom Inc. Group owner: Blount Communications Group (acq 5-15-90; 6-4-90). Network: Salem Radio Network. Rep: Salem. Format: Relg. Target aud: 25-54. ◆ William A. Blount, pres; Deborah C. Blount, exec VP; David O. Young, VP & gen mgr; Steve Tuzeneu, stn mgr & opns mgr.

Leominster

WCMX(AM)— Nov 13, 1967: 1000 khz; 1 kw-D. TL: N42 31 25 W71 44 07. 194 Electric Ave., Lunenburg 01462. Phone: (978) 582-8282. Fax: (978) 582-4978. E-mail: nate@hopewoo.com. Web Site: hope1000.com. Licensee: Twin City Baptist Temple Inc. (acq 1-95). Network: Salem Radio Network. Format: Southern Christian, gospel, worship. News: 7 hrs wkly. Target aud: 35-54 women. ◆ Pastor Erven Burke, gen mgr; Nathan Burke, stn mgr; Lauren Ford, opns mgr.

WEIM(AM)—See Fitchburg

Lowell

WCAP(AM)— June 10, 1951: 980 khz; 5 kw-U, DA-2. TL: N42 39 16 W01 21 43. 243 Central St. 01852. Phone: (978) 454-0404. Fax: (978) 458-9124. Web Site: www.wcap.net. Licensee: Northeast Radio Inc. Network: Westwood One. Richard J. Hayes Jr. Format: Talk, news, sports. News: 19.5 hrs wkly. Target aud: 25 plus; Business people, professionals, factory workers, housewives. ◆ Maurice Cohen, pres & gen mgr; Ryan Johnston, progmg dir.

WKLB-FM— 1947: 99.5 mhz; 27 kw. Ant 653 ft. TL: N42 39 14 W71 13 02. Stereo. 55 Morrissey Blvd., Boston 02125. Phone: (617) 822-9600. Fax: (617) 822-6659. Web Site: www.wklb.com. Licensee: Greater Boston Radio Inc. Group owner: Greater Media Inc. (acq 7-23-97). Rep: D & R Radio. Format: Country. Target aud: 25-54. ◆ Alan Chartrand, VP, sls dir & chief of engrg; Matt Mills, gen mgr.

WLLH(AM)— 1934: 1400 khz; 1 kw-U. TL: N42 39 29 W71 19 04. 529 Main St., Suite 200, Charlestown 02129-1119. Phone: (617) 242-8173. Fax: (617) 241-0017. Web Site: www.latinboston.com/iamegasepega. Licensee: J Sports Boston LLC Group owner: Mega Communications Inc. (acq 6-22-2005; $9 million. with WAMG(AM) Dedham). Network: ESPN Radio. Format: Sports. ◆ Ulysses Arrigoitia, gen mgr.

*****WUML(FM)**— Nov 6, 1967: 91.5 mhz; 1.4 kw. 207 ft. TL: N42 39 07 W71 19 15. Stereo. One University Ave. 01854. Phone: (978) 934-4970. Phone: (978) 934-4975. Fax: (978) 934-3031. E-mail: wuml@wuml.org. Web Site: www.wuml.org. Licensee: University of Massachusetts-Lowell Board of Trustees. Format: Div, progsv rock. Target aud: 16-25. Spec prog: Black 2 hrs, reggae 4 hrs. ◆ Glen J. Anderson, pres; Nate Osit, gen mgr; Dan Bennett, prom dir; Julius Hayden, progmg dir.

Lynn

WFNX(FM)— Aug 5, 1963: 101.7 mhz; 1.65 kw. 440 ft. TL: N42 25 52 W71 05 20. Stereo. 25 Exchange St. 01901. Phone: (781) 595-6200. Fax: (781) 595-3810. E-mail: fnx@fnxradio.com. Web Site: www.fnxradio.com. Licensee: MCC Broadcasting Inc. Group owner: Phoenix Media Communications Group (acq 11-10-82; FTR: 11-29-82). Rep: McGavren Guild. Rubin, Winston, Diercks, Harris & Cooke. Format: Alternative rock. News staff: one; News: 2 hrs wkly. Target aud: 18-49; well-educated, affluent & socially active trend setters. Spec prog: Jazz 8 hrs, "Sound System" 3 hrs, One In Ten (gay talk show) 2 hrs, loc mus 2 hrs wkly. ◆ Stephen Mindich, CEO & chmn; H. Barry Morris, pres; Charlie Walter, CFO; Andy Kingston, gen mgr & news dir; Max Tolkkoff, progmg dir & chief of engrg.

WLYN(AM)— November 1947: 1360 khz; 700 w-D, 76 w-N. TL: N42 27 17 W70 58 44. Stereo. 500 W. Cummings Park, Suite 2600, Woburn 01801. Phone: (781) 938-0869. Fax: (781) 938-0933. E-mail: jeffk@mrbi.net. Licensee: Multicultural Radio Broadcasting Licensee LLC. Group owner: Multicultural Radio Broadcasting Inc. (acq 8-7-02; $1.78 million). Network: ABC Information & Entertainment. Format: Ethnic - Leased Time. Spec prog: It 4 hrs, Pol 2 hrs, Greek 4 hrs wkly. ◆ Jeff Kline, stn mgr.

Marion

*****WWTA(FM)**— 1996: 88.5 mhz; 19 w horiz, 100 w vert. 53 ft. TL: N41 42 32 W70 45 57. 66 Spring St. 02738. Phone: (508) 748-2000. Fax: (508) 291-6666. E-mail: kkistler@taboracademy.org. Web Site: www.taboracademy.org. Licensee: Tabor Academy. Format: Eclectic. ◆ Karl Kistler, gen mgr.

Marshfield

WATD-FM— Dec 5, 1977: 95.9 mhz; 2.8 kw. 350 ft. TL: N42 06 40 W70 42 14. Stereo. 130 Enterprise Dr. 02050. Phone: (781) 837-1166. Fax: (781) 837-1978. E-mail: news@959watd.com. Web Site: www.959watd.com. Licensee: Marshfield Broadcasting Co. Format: Adult contemp, blues, oldies. News staff: 2; News: 10 hrs wkly. Target aud: 25-64; South Shore residents. Spec prog: Accoustic, Irish 6 hrs wkly. ◆ Edward F. Perry Jr., pres.

Mashpee

WTWV(FM)— Feb 12, 1987: 101.1 mhz; 3.7 kw. 253 ft. TL: N41 36 50 W70 35 56. Stereo. 278 South Sea Ave., West Yarmouth 02673. Phone: (508) 775-5678. Fax: (508) 862-6329. Licensee: Cape Cod Trust (Mark O. Hubbard, trustee) Group owner: Boch Broadcasting (acq 7-27-2005; with WDVT(FM) Harwichport). Network: Westwood One. Rep: D & R Radio. Format: Oldies. News staff: one. Target aud: 18-49. ◆ Bob Wakely, CFO; Carolyn Bernhardt, gen mgr.

Maynard

*****WAVM(FM)**— April 1973: 91.7 mhz; 16 w. -7 ft. TL: N42 25 18 W71 27 02. Stereo. Maynard High School, One Tiger Dr. 01754. Phone: (978) 897-5213. Phone: (978) 897-5179. Fax: (978) 897-6089. E-mail: studio@wavm.org. Web Site: www.wavm.org. Licensee: Maynard Public Schools. Format: Div. Target aud: General. Spec prog: Oldies one hr wkly. ◆ Joseph P. Magno, stn mgr.

Medford

*****WMFO(FM)**— March 1971: 91.5 mhz; 125 w. 135 ft. TL: N42 24 27 W71 07 15. Stereo. Box 65 02153. Secondary address: 474 Boston Ave. 02153. Phone: (617) 625-0800/627-3800. Fax: (617) 625-6072. E-mail: wmfo@wmfo.org. Web Site: www.wmfo.org. Licensee: Tufts University. Format: Free-form. Spec prog: Black 12 hrs, Por 3 hrs, Native American 6 hrs, Sp 3 hrs, Haitian 4 hrs, Brazilian 4 hrs wkly. ◆ Emily Ryan, gen mgr.

WXKS(AM)—(Everett). Jan 20, 1952: 1430 khz; 5 kw-D, 1 kw-N, DA-N. TL: N42 24 11 W71 04 29. 99 Revere Beach Pkwy. 02155. Phone: (781) 396-1430. Fax: (781) 391-3064. Web Site: www.am1430wxks.com. Licensee: AMFM Radio Licenses L.L.C. Group owner: Clear Channel Communications Inc. (acq 8-30-2000; grpsl). Format: Progressive talk. Target aud: 35 plus. ◆ Janet Karter, gen mgr.

WXKS-FM— Sept 1, 1960: 107.9 mhz; 20.5 kw. 771 ft. TL: N42 20 50 W71 04 59. Stereo. Format: Adult CHR. Target aud: 18-34.

Middleborough Center

WVBF(AM)— 1993: 1530 khz; 1 kw-D. TL: N41 55 28 W70 56 10. Box 329 02346. Phone: (781) 834-4400. Fax: (781) 834-7716. Licensee: Steven J. Callahan. Format: Info. ◆ Steven Callahan, gen mgr; Jamie Richards, progmg dir.

Massachusetts

Milford

WMRC(AM)— Oct 6, 1956: 1490 khz; 1 kw-U. TL: N42 08 12 W71 30 50. Box 421, 258 Main St. 01757. Phone: (508) 473-1490. Fax: (508) 478-2200. Licensee: Thomas M. McAuliffe. (acq 7-23-90; $250,000; 8-13-90). Format: Adult contemp, var radio. News staff: 2; News: 32 hrs wkly. Target aud: 25-54. Spec prog: Por 2 hrs wkly. ♦ Thomas M. McAuliffe Sr., pres; Thomas M. McAuliffe II, gen mgr.

Milton

*****WMLN-FM**— Apr 1, 1975: 91.5 mhz; 170 w. 98 ft. TL: N42 14 27 W71 06 52. 1071 Blue Hill Ave. 02186. Phone: (617) 333-0311. Fax: (617) 333-2123. E-mail: afrank@curry.edu. Web Site: www.curry.edu. Licensee: Curry College. Network: CNN Radio. Format: News/talk, adult contemp, div. News: 15 hrs wkly. Target aud: General. Spec prog: Reggae 8 hrs, pub affairs 2 hrs, jazz 3 hrs, Sp 7 hrs, black 4 hrs, gospel 3 hrs wkly. ♦ Alan H. Frank, gen mgr.

Nantucket

*****WNAN(FM)**— Mar. 15, 2000: 91.1 mhz; 2 kw. 72 ft. TL: N41 18 22 W70 00 28. Box 82, Woods Hole 02543. Secondary address: 3 Water St., Woods Hole 02543. Phone: (617) 300-2300. Fax: (508) 548-5517. Web Site: www.cainan.org. Licensee: WGBH Educational Foundation. (acq 12-31-97; $25,000 with WCAI(FM) Woods Hole). Network: NPR. Format: News/talk. ♦ Henry Becton, gen mgr.

*****WNCK(FM)**— June 28, 2002: 89.5 mhz; 78 w horiz, 500 w vert. Ant 118 ft. TL: N41 17 06 W70 08 39. Nantucket Public Radio Inc., Box 2185 02534. Phone: (508) 825-8951. Fax: (508) 325-0030. E-mail: wnck895@aol.com. Web Site: www.nantucketpublicradio.org. Licensee: Nantucket Public Radio Inc. Target aud: 40 plus. ♦ Lois K. Shapiro, pres; Jeffrey Shapiro, VP; Robert Shapiro, stn mgr.

WRZE(FM)— June 15, 1981: 96.3 mhz; 50 kw. Ant 430 ft. TL: N41 16 50 W70 10 10. Stereo. 154 Barnstable Rd., Hyannis 02601. Phone: (508) 778-2888. Fax: (508) 790-4967. E-mail: info@therose.net. Web Site: www.therose.net. Licensee: Qantum of Cape Cod License Co. LLC. Group owner: Qantum Communications Corp. (acq 6-11-03; grpsl). Rep: McGavren Guild. Format: CHR. News staff: 2; News: 8 hrs wkly. Target aud: 18-49. ♦ Shane Blue, gen mgr & progmg dir; Steve McVie Solomon, opns dir.

Natick

WBIX(AM)— November 1972: 1060 khz; 40 kw-D, 2.5 kw-N, 22 kw-CH, DA-3. TL: N42 17 17 W71 25 55. Nixon Peabody LLP, 100 Summer St., Boston 02110. Phone: (617) 345-1177. Licensee: David A. Vicinanzo, receiver Group owner: Langer Broadcasting Group L.L.C. (acq 1-14-2005). ♦ David A. Vicinanzo, gen mgr.

New Bedford

WBSM(AM)— July 17, 1949: 1420 khz; 5 kw-D, 1 kw-N, DA-2. TL: N41 39 02 W70 54 58. 22 Sconticut Neck Rd., Fairhaven 02719. Phone: (508) 993-1767. Fax: (508) 999-1420. E-mail: petebraley@wbsm.com. Web Site: www.wbsm.com. Licensee: Citadel Broadcasting Co. Group owner: Citadel Broadcasting Corp. (acq 4-26-01; grpsl). Rep: Christal. Format: News/talk, sports. ♦ Gail Le Blanc, gen mgr; Rhona Robitaille, prom dir; Pete Braley, progmg dir.

WCTK(FM)— Licensed to New Bedford. See Providence RI

*****WFHL(FM)**— 2003: 88.1 mhz; 300 w vert. Ant 134 ft. TL: N41 38 15 W70 52 19. Box 3025 02741. Secondary address: 71 William 02740. Phone: (508) 991-7600. E-mail: radio@radiowfhl.com. Web Site: www.radiowfhl.com. Licensee: New Bedford Christian Radio Inc. Format: Sp, English. ♦ Manuel Pereira, gen mgr.

WJFD-FM— Feb 22, 1949: 97.3 mhz; 50 kw. 500 ft. TL: N41 38 20 W70 52 27. Stereo. 270 Union St. 02740. Phone: (508) 997-2929. Fax: (508) 990-3893. E-mail: jorge@wjfd.com. Web Site: www.wjfd.com. Licensee: Edmund Dinis, trustee (acq 12-18-2001). Format: Ethnic. Target aud: General; Portuguese-speaking community. ♦ Edmund Dinis, pres.

WNBH(AM)—Licensed to New Bedford. See Providence RI

Newburyport

WNBP(AM)— Mar 10, 1957: 1450 khz; 1 kw-U. TL: N42 49 23 W70 51 42. Box 1450, 44 Merrimac St. 01950. Phone: (978) 462-1450. Fax: (978) 462-0333. E-mail: wnbp.radio@verizon.net. Web Site: www.wnbp.com. Licensee: Westport Communications L.P. (acq 11-23-2004; $500,000). Network: AP Radio. Rep: New England. Format: Adults Standards. News staff: one; News: 5 hrs wkly. Target aud: 25-54. Spec prog: Irish 4 hrs wkly. ♦ Al Mozier, gen mgr; Matt Stevens, opns mgr, prom dir, progmg mgr & pub affrs dir; Bill Wayland, gen sls mgr; William Fuller, mus dir; Win Damon, sls dir & news dir; Dan Guy, engrg dir.

*****WNEF(FM)**— 91.7 mhz; 400 w vert. 354 ft. TL: N42 51 56 W70 56 18. University of Massachusetts, 100 Morrissey Blvd., Boston 02125. Phone: (617) 287-6900. Fax: (617) 287-6916. E-mail: wumb@umb.edu. Web Site: www.wumb.org. Licensee: University of Massachusetts. Format: Acoustic/folk, rhythm and blues, world mus. ♦ Patricia A. Monteith, gen mgr.

Newton

WNTN(AM)— Apr 1, 1968: 1550 khz; 10 kw-D. TL: N42 21 27 W71 14 30. 143 Rumford Ave. 02466. Phone: (617) 969-1550. Web Site: www.wntn.com. Licensee: Colt Communications Inc. (acq 12-23-98; $602,800). Format: Var, Greek, Haitian. Target aud: 40 plus. Spec prog: Irish 6 hrs, Indian 2 hrs wkly. ♦ Rob Rudnick, gen mgr; Paul Roberts, opns dir.

*****WZBC(FM)**— April 1974: 90.3 mhz; 1 kw. 220 ft. TL: N42 20 05 W71 10 31. Stereo. Boston College, 107 McElroy Commons, Chestnut Hill 02467. Phone: (617) 552-3511. Fax: (617) 552-1738. Fax: (617) 552-0050. Web Site: www.wzbc.org. Licensee: Trustees of Boston College. Format: Underground rock. Target aud: 18-34. Spec prog: Haitian 4 hrs, industrial 2 hrs, Celtic 2 hrs, urban contemp 3 hrs, reggae 4 hrs, metal 3 hrs wkly. ♦ Leana Siochi, gen mgr; Mike Brady, opns dir & opns mgr.

Norfolk

WDIS(AM)— Mar 20, 1978: 1170 khz; 1 kw-D, DA. TL: N42 05 32 W71 18 13. 100 Pond St. 02056. Phone: (508) 384-8255. Fax: (508) 384-1530. E-mail: wdismgmt@aol.com. Licensee: Discussion Radio Inc. (acq 8-12-92; $65,000; 9-7-92). Network: USA. Format: News/talk. Target aud: 35-64. Spec prog: Big band one hr wkly. ♦ Corine Slade, gen mgr; Dan Collier, progmg dir.

North Adams

*****WJJW(FM)**— Sept 5, 1973: 91.1 mhz; 423 w. -830 ft. TL: N42 41 27 W73 06 16. Stereo. Mass. College of Liberal Arts, Murdock Hall, 375 Church St. 01247. Phone: (413) 662-5405. Fax: (413) 662-5010. E-mail: webmaster@mcla.edu. Web Site: www.mcla.edu. Licensee: Massachusetts College of Liberal Arts. Format: Progsv. Spec prog: Jazz 4 hrs, Pol 3 hrs, class 3 hrs wkly. ♦ Alisha Cropper, gen mgr; Nick Strassel, progmg dir; Paul Wiley, chief of engrg.

WMNB(FM)—Listing follows WNAW(AM).

WNAW(AM)— Nov 23, 1947: 1230 khz; 1 kw-U. TL: N42 41 03 W73 06 23. Box 707, 466 Curran Hwy. 01247-0707. Phone: (413) 663-6567. Fax: (413) 662-2143. E-mail: wnaw@wnaw.com. Web Site: www.wnaw.com. Licensee: Berkshire Broadcasting Co. Inc. Group owner: Vox Radio Group L.P. (acq 2-13-2004; grpsl). Rep: McGavren Guild. Wilkinson Barker Knauer. Format: Full service, adult contemp. News: 2. Target aud: Adults. ♦ David Luyk, gen mgr & gen sls mgr; Joyce Marshall, mktg mgr & progmg mgr.

WMNB(FM)—Co-owned with WNAW(AM). July 12, 1964: 100.1 mhz; 3 kw. Ant 501 ft. TL: N42 41 51 W73 03 52. Stereo. Web Site: www.wmnbfm.com. Format: Oldies. Target aud: 35 plus.

North Dartmouth

*****WSMU-FM**— September 1973: 91.1 mhz; 1.2 kw. 300 ft. TL: N41 37 43 W71 00 24. Stereo. 285 Old Westport Rd. 02747. Phone: (508) 999-8149. Phone: (508) 999-8150. Fax: (508) 999-8173. E-mail: wsmu@umassd.edu. Web Site: www.wsmu.org. Licensee: University of Massachusetts. Format: Progsv, alternative rock, techno. News: 12 hrs wkly. Target aud: 13-60; general, high school, college, community. Spec prog: Folk 11 hrs, gospel 2 hrs, jazz 10 hrs, hip hop/rap 14 hrs, reggae 10 hrs, blues 7 hrs, world beat 3 hrs, metal 4 hrs wkly. ♦ Jennifer Mulcare-Sullivan, gen mgr.

Northampton

WEIB(FM)— 2001: 106.3 mhz; 3 kw. Ant 289 ft. TL: N42 22 25 W72 40 26. Stereo. 8 North King St. 01060. Phone: (413) 585-1112. Fax: (413) 585-9138. E-mail: weibfm@aol.com. Web Site: www.weibfm. Licensee: Cutting Edge Broadcasting Inc. Format: Smooth jazz. ♦ Carol Moore Cutting, pres & gen mgr; Drew Dawson, progmg dir.

WHMP(AM)— December 1950: 1400 khz; 1 kw-U. TL: N42 19 36 W72 39 28. 15 Hampton Ave. 01061. Phone: (413) 586-7400. Fax: (413) 585-0927. Web Site: www.whmp.com. Licensee: Saga Communications of New England LLC. Group owner: Saga Communications Inc. (acq 2000; $12 million. with co-located AM). Network: CBS Radio, CNN Radio. Rep: Katz Radio. Format: Sports, news/talk. News staff: 4; News: 40 hrs wkly. Target aud: 35 plus; upscale, well edu. Spec prog: Pol 3 hrs wkly. ♦ Glenn Cardinal, gen mgr.

WLZX(FM)— Nov 1, 1956: 99.3 mhz; 3 kw. 321 ft. TL: N42 22 29 W72 40 24. (CP: 6 kw). Stereo. 45 Fisher Ave, East Longmeadow 01028. Phone: (413) 525-4141. Fax: (413) 525-4334. E-mail: comments@lazer993.com. Web Site: www.lazer993.com. Licensee: Saga Communications of New England LLC. Group owner: Saga Communications Inc. (acq 2000; $12 million. with co-located AM). Format: Rock/Active. News staff: 2. Target aud: 18-34; male. ♦ Larry Goldberg, gen sls mgr; Sarah Milewski, prom dir; Neal Mirsky, progmg dir.

*****WOZQ(FM)**— 1981: 91.9 mhz; 200 w. 115 ft. TL: N42 19 13 W72 38 14. Stereo. Smith College, Davis Ctr. 01063. Phone: (413) 585-4956. Phone: (413) 585-4977. Fax: (413) 585-2075. E-mail: mstern@email.smith.edu. Web Site: www.wozq.org. Licensee: Trustees of Smith College. Format: Educ, div, urban contemp. Target aud: 15 plus; college students & area businesses. Spec prog: Black 20 hrs, class 2 hrs, folk 4 hrs, jazz 6 hrs, Sp 2 hrs, country 2 hrs, disco 2 hrs wkly. ♦ Meredith Stern, stn mgr; Jackie Kim, progmg dir.

Northfield

*****WNMH(FM)**— Sept 10, 1984: 91.5 mhz; 235 w. 308 ft. TL: N42 42 52 W72 26 38. Stereo. Box WNMH, Northfield Mt. Hermon School, 206 Main St. 01360. Phone: (413) 498-3603. Fax: (413) 498-3664. Licensee: Northfield Mount Hermon School. Network: ABC Information & Entertainment. Format: Div. Target aud: Student body & surrounding communities. Spec prog: Class 2 hrs, jazz 10 hrs, Sp 4 hrs, Black 8 hrs, Fr 2 hrs wkly. ♦ Bill Hattendorf, opns VP & opns mgr.

Orange

WJDF(FM)— 1995: 97.3 mhz; 3 kw. 328 ft. TL: N42 37 19 W72 21 58. (CP: 5.8 kw, ant 82 ft.). Box 973 01364. Phone: (978) 544-5335. Phone: (978) 544-0957. Fax: (978) 544-2131. E-mail: info@wjdf.com. Web Site: www.wjdf.com. Licensee: Deane Brothers Broadcasting Corp. Format: Adult contemp. ♦ Donn Deane, gen mgr; Jay Deane, progmg dir.

Orange-Athol

WJOE(AM)— May 13, 1956: 700 khz; 2.5 kw-D. TL: N42 35 06 W72 16 56. Box 90, 660 E. Main St., Orange 01364. Phone: (978) 544-2321. Phone: (978) 544-2322. Fax: (978) 544-6977. Licensee: County Broadcasting Co. LLC. Group owner: Northeast Broadcasting Company Inc. (acq 10-6-2003; $650,000. with WNYN-FM Athol). Format: Christian Sp music. Target aud: 45 plus. ♦ Chris Thompson, gen mgr; Billy Curtis, progmg dir.

Orleans

WFPB(AM)— Apr 10, 1970: 1170 khz; 1 kw-D, DA. TL: N41 46 48 W70 00 36. WUMB-FM, 100 Morrissey Blvd., Boston 02125-3393. Phone: (617) 287-6900. Fax: (617) 287-6916. E-mail: wumb@umb.edu. Web Site: www.wumb.org. Licensee: University of Massachusetts. (acq 10-30-98). Format: Folk radio. ♦ Patricia Monteith, gen mgr; Brian Quinn, progmg dir.

WKPE-FM— July 25, 1974: 104.7 mhz; 50 kw. 504 ft. TL: N41 46 48 W70 00 36. Stereo. 582 Main St., W. Yarmouth 02673. Phone: (508) 790-3772. Fax: (508) 790-3773. E-mail: cat@rocket1047.com. Web Site: www.1047-the rocket.com. Licensee: Charles River Broadcasting

Stations in the U.S.   Massachusetts

Developers & Brokers of Radio Properties — contact American Media Services at our suite: Philadelphia Marriott Downtown 215-625-2900 · 843-972-2200 · americanmediaservices.com · Charleston, SC · Dallas, TX · Chicago, Il · Austin, TX — American Media Services, LLC

WKPE License Corp. (acq 9-99; $2.8 million). Garvey, Schubert & Barer. Format: Classic Rock. Target aud: 25-54; Males. ♦ Jan D'Antuono, gen mgr.

Pittsfield

WBEC(AM)— March 1947: 1420 khz; 1 kw-U, DA-N. TL: N42 26 40 W73 16 43. 211 Jason St. 01201-5907. Phone: (413) 499-3333. Fax: (413) 442-1590. Licensee: Vox Communications Group LLC. Group owner: Vox Radio Group L.P. (acq 9-13-2002; grpsl). Network: ABC Information & Entertainment. Rep: Allied Radio Partners. Smithwick & Belendiuk. Format: News/talk, sports. News staff: 2; News: 15 hrs wkly. Target aud: 25-55; 60% male, 40% female. Spec prog: Relg 3 hrs wkly. ♦ Laura Freed, gen mgr.

WBEC-FM— October 1967: 105.5 mhz; 950 w. Ant 590 ft. TL: N42 24 44 W73 17 05. Stereo. 211 Jason St. 01201-5907. Phone: (413) 499-3333. Fax: (413) 442-1590. Licensee: 6 Johnson Road Licenses Inc. (acq 7-12-2005; $7 million). Format: Hot adult contemp. News staff: 2; News: 2 hrs wkly. Target aud: 25-44; male & female. ♦ Laura Freed, gen mgr.

WBRK(AM)— Feb 20, 1938: 1340 khz; 1 kw-U. TL: N42 27 00 W73 12 55. 100 North St. 01201. Phone: (413) 442-1553. Fax: (413) 445-5294. E-mail: wbrk1340@aol.com. Web Site: www.wbrk.com. Licensee: WBRK Inc. (acq 6-30-84). Network: Network: CBS, Westwood One. Rep: D & R Radio. Drinker, Biddle & Reath. Format: Full service. News staff: 2. Target aud: 35 plus. Spec prog: Pol 2 hrs, Irish one hr, relg 2 hrs wkly. ♦ Willard H. Hodgkins III, CEO & pres; John Campoli, exec VP; Daniel Salzarulo, stn mgr & chief of engrg; Michael J. Bunn, opns VP & opns mgr; Cheryl Tripp, prom dir; Rick Beltaire, progmg VP & progmg dir.

WBRK-FM— Oct 10, 1970: 101.7 mhz; 3 kw. 145 ft. TL: N42 28 31 W73 16 07. Stereo. Web Site: www.wbrk.com. Network: ABC. Format: Adult contemp. Target aud: 25-54.

WUHN(AM)— Sept 9, 1971: 1110 khz; 5 kw-D, DA. TL: N42 26 22 W73 17 30. 211 Jason St., . 01201. Phone: (413) 499-3333. Fax: (413) 442-1590. E-mail: wupe@wupe.com. Web Site: www.wuhn.com. Licensee: Vox Communications Group LLC. (acq 12-8-2003; $2.83 million with co-located FM). Network: ABC. Rep: D & R Radio. Pepper & Corazzini. Format: Country. News staff: one; News: 14 hrs wkly. Target aud: 25-54; baby boomers. ♦ Joyce Marshall, gen mgr; David Isby, opns mgr & prom dir; Dick Savage, sls dir; Larry Kratka, news dir; Dan Salzarulo, chief of engrg.

WUPE(FM)— Co-owned with WUHN(AM). 1975: 95.9 mhz; 1 kw. Ant 560 ft. TL: N42 24 44 W73 17 05. Stereo. Web Site: www.wupe.com. Network: Westwood One. Format: Oldies. News staff: one; News: 28 hrs wkly. Target aud: 25-54; young adults with families.

Plymouth

WPLM(AM)— Aug 8, 1955: 1390 khz; 5 kw-U, DA-2. TL: N41 58 05 W70 42 06. 17 Columbus Rd. 02360. Secondary address: Box 1390 02362. Phone: (508) 746-1390. Fax: (508) 830-1128. Licensee: Plymouth Rock Broadcasting Co. Inc. Network: UPI. Rep: Roslin. Arent, Fox, Kintner, Plotkin & Kahn. Format: Soft adult contemp, news. ♦ Dr. Laurie Campbell, pres; Alan Anderson, gen mgr & gen sls mgr; Pat Cronin, chief of opns; Sean Casey, prom dir & progmg dir; Dick Jolls, chief of engrg.

WPLM-FM— June 25, 1961: 99.1 mhz; 50 kw. 430 ft. TL: N41 58 02 W70 42 04. Format: Adult contemp.

Provincetown

*WOMR(FM)— Mar 21, 1982: 92.1 mhz; 6 kw. Ant 161 ft. TL: N42 03 54 W70 09 31. Stereo. Box 975, 494 Commercial St. 02657. Phone: (508) 487-2106. Fax: (508) 487-5524. E-mail: info@womr.org. Web Site: www.womr.org. Licensee: Lower Cape Communications Inc. Garvey, Schubert, Baker. Format: Rock, jazz. News: 5 hrs wkly. Target aud: General; diverse. Spec prog: Bluegrass 3 hrs, Black 3 hrs, Class 16 hrs, educ 10 hrs, folk 17 hrs, oldies 9 hrs wkly. ♦ Tina Lynde, pres; Dave Willard, VP; Bob Seay, gen mgr; Diana Fabbri, opns mgr.

Quincy

WJDA(AM)— Sept 13, 1947: 1300 khz; 1 kw-D, 72 w-N. TL: N42 15 35 W70 58 36. Box 690626 02269-0626. Secondary address: 29 Brackett St. Phone: (617) 479-1300. Fax: (617) 479-0622. E-mail: info@wjda1300.com. Web Site: www.wjda1300.com. Licensee: South Shore Broadcasting Co. Network: ABC. Format: ABC " Memories ". News staff: 2; News: 10 hrs wkly. Target aud: 35 plus. Spec prog: Cantonese 3 hrs wkly. ♦ Joe Catalano, progmg dir; Mike Logan, news dir.

Rockland

*WRPS(FM)— Feb 8, 1974: 88.3 mhz; 100 w. 120 ft. TL: N42 07 43 W70 55 01. Stereo. 34 MacKinlay Way 02370. Phone: (781) 871-0724. Fax: (781) 982-1483. E-mail: wrps883@yahoo.com. Licensee: Rockland Public Schools. Format: Public service, educ, adult contemp. Target aud: General. ♦ David J. Cable-Murphy, gen mgr; Robert Mulligan, chief of engrg.

Salem

WESX(AM)— Jan 1, 1939: 1230 khz; 1 kw-U. TL: N42 31 06 W70 51 41. Box 710 01970. Secondary address: 27 Naugus Ave., Marblehead 01945. Phone: (978) 744-1230. Fax: (978) 744-1853. E-mail: info@wesx1230.com. Web Site: www.wesx1230.com. Licensee: North Shore Broadcasting Corp. (acq 4-1-50). Network: Network: ABC, Westwood One. Format: MOR, news/talk. News staff: 2; News: 25 hrs wkly. Target aud: 35 plus; general. Spec prog: Auto repair 2 hrs, gardening 2 hrs, home improvement 2 hrs, restaurant/dining 2 hrs, Pol 2 hrs wkly. ♦ James D. Asher, pres & gen mgr; Christopher Culkeen, opns mgr, progmg dir & progmg mgr; Bill Cooksly, news dir.

*WMWM(FM)— 1976: 91.7 mhz; 130 w. 132 ft. TL: N42 30 14 W70 53 26. Stereo. Campus Ctr., 352 Lafayette St. 01970-5353. Phone: (978) 745-9401. Phone: (978) 745-9170. Fax: (978) 741-9433. Web Site: www.wmwm.org. Licensee: Salem State College. Format: Diversified. Target aud: General. Spec prog: Black 16 hrs, jazz 3 hrs, relg 3 hrs, Sp 3 hrs, Celtic 3 hrs wkly. ♦ Johnny Jimenez, gen mgr; Rebecca Jimenez, gen mgr.

Sandwich

*WSDH(FM)— 1976: 91.5 mhz; 310 w. 150 ft. TL: N41 44 06 W70 27 35. Sandwich High School, 365 Quaker Meetinghouse Rd., East Sandwich 02537. Phone: (508) 888-0420. Fax: (508) 833-8392. Licensee: Sandwich Public Schools. Format: CHR, classic rock, educ. News: 4 hrs wkly. Target aud: 12-40. ♦ Leonard Gobeil, gen mgr & mus dir.

Scituate

*WSMA(FM)—Not on air, target date: unknown: 90.5 mhz; 5 w horiz, 21.6 kw vert. Ant 289 ft. TL: N41 56 02 W70 35 10. CSN International, 3232 W. MacArthur Blvd., Santa Ana, CA 92704. Phone: (714) 825-9663. Fax: (714) 825-9661. Licensee: CSN International (group owner).

Sheffield

*WBSL-FM— September 1973: 91.7 mhz; 250 w. 50 ft. TL: N42 06 57 W73 25 00. Berkshire School, 245 N. Undermountain Rd. 01257-9672. Phone: (413) 229-8511. Fax: (413) 229-1014. E-mail: jharris@berkshireschool.org. Web Site: www.berkshireschool.org. Licensee: Berkshire School Inc. Format: Div. Target aud: General. Spec prog: Jazz 15 hrs, Black 2 hrs, folk 2 hrs, Sp 2 hrs, Pol one hr wkly. ♦ James Harris, gen mgr.

South Hadley

*WMHC(FM)— May 14, 1957: 91.5 mhz; 100 w. Ant -18 ft. TL: N42 15 12 W72 34 40. Stereo. Box 9010, Mt. Holyoke College 01075. Secondary address: Mt. Holyoke College, Blanchard Campus Center 01075. Phone: (413) 538-2044. Phone: (413) 538-2019. Fax: (413) 538-2431. E-mail: amlewis@mtholyoke.edu. Web Site: www.mtholyoke.edu/org/wmhc. Licensee: President & Trustees of Mount Holyoke College. Network: AP Radio. Format: Rock, urban contemp, var/div. Target aud: General; Mount Holyoke College Community. Spec prog: Black one hrs, folk 3 hrs, African 2 hrs, gospel 1 hr wkly. ♦ Alexis Lewis, gen mgr; Ingrid Cobb, gen mgr.

South Yarmouth

WOCN-FM— August 1994: 103.9 mhz; 5.5 kw. 341 ft. TL: N41 41 30 W70 08 43. 737 W. Main St., Hyannis 02601. Phone: (508) 778-6200. Phone: (508) 771-1224. Fax: (508) 775-2605. E-mail: wocn@cape.com. Web Site: www.ocean104.com. Licensee: Sandab Communications L.P. II. (group owner; acq 6-19-98; $1.2 million). Network: CBS. Rep: Clear Channel. Covington & Burling. Format: MOR, soft adult contemp. News staff: one; News: 16 hrs wkly. Target aud: 25 plus. ♦ Gregory D. Bone, gen mgr; Wayne White, opns mgr; Stephen Colella, gen sls mgr; Michelle Dodd, prom mgr; Angella King, news dir.

Southbridge

WESO(AM)— Mar 20, 1955: 970 khz; 1 kw-D, 21 w-N. TL: N42 03 59 W71 59 28. 100 Foster St. 01550. Phone: (508) 764-4381. Fax: (508) 764-2682. Web Site: thespirit970.com. Licensee: Money Matters Inc. (acq 4-11-01; $250,000). Network: CBS. Format: Pop country, local news. News staff: 2; News: 30 hrs wkly. Target aud: 34-59. Spec prog: Pol 3 hrs. ♦ Dick Vaughn, COO & pres; Dick Vaughan, gen mgr; J.D. Page, opns mgr.

WWFX(FM)— Nov 1, 1968: 100.1 mhz; 2.85 kw. 295 ft. (CP: 1.74 kw, ant 590 ft.). 250 Commercial St., Worcester 01608. Secondary address: WBA Inc., 295 Bridle Trail Rd, Needham 02192. Phone: (508) 752-1045. Fax: (508) 770-9964. Web Site: www.thefoxfm.com. Licensee: Citadel Broadcasting Co. Group owner: Citadel Broadcasting Corp. (acq 4-26-01; grpsl). Network: Jones Radio Networks. Rep: D & R Radio. Format: Main Stream Rock. News staff: 2; News: 10 hrs wkly. Target aud: 25-54. ♦ Joe Flynn, gen mgr; JayBeau Jones, opns mgr; Alex Byrne, prom dir.

Springfield

WACE(AM)—See Chicopee

WACM(AM)—See West Springfield

*WAIC(FM)— February 1967: 91.9 mhz; 230 w. 66 ft. TL: N42 06 44 W72 33 29. Stereo. 1000 State St. 01109. Phone: (413) 205-3941. Fax: (413) 205-3943. E-mail: techsupport@waic.com. Web Site: www.waic.com. Licensee: American International College. Format: Div. Target aud: 16-40. Spec prog: Gospel. ♦ Will Hughes, CEO, chmn & pres; Doc Holiday, gen mgr; Richard Innes, opns dir.

WAQY(FM)— Dec 17, 1966: 102.1 mhz; 50 kw. 780 ft. TL: N42 05 00 W72 42 16. Stereo. 45 Fisher Ave., East Longmeadow 01028. Phone: (413) 525-4141. Fax: (413) 525-4334. E-mail: lgoldberg@rock102.com. Web Site: www.rock102.com. Licensee: Saga Communications of New England LLC. Group owner: Saga Communications Inc. (acq 6-2-92; grpsl). Rep: Katz Radio. Smithwick & Belendiuk. Format: Classic rock. Target aud: General; upscale young adults with high income. ♦ Larry Goldberg, gen mgr; Neal Mirsky, gen sls mgr & progmg dir.

WHYN(AM)— 1941: 560 khz; 5 kw-D, 1 kw-N, DA-2. TL: N42 11 37 W72 41 02. Stereo. 1331 Main St. 01103-. Phone: (413) 781-1011. Fax: (413) 734-4434. Web Site: www.whynam560.com. Licensee: Clear Channel Broadcasting Licenses Inc. Group owner: Clear Channel Communications Inc. (acq 1996; grpsl). Network: ABC Information & Entertainment. Haley, Bader & Potts. Format: News/talk. News staff: 6. Target aud: General. ♦ Debbie Wagner, gen mgr.

Broadcasting & Cable Yearbook 2006

Massachusetts

WHYN-FM— 1946: 93.1 mhz; 8.9 kw. 1,000 ft. TL: N42 14 28 W72 38 56. Stereo. E-mail: fm@mix931.com. Web Site: www.mix931.com. Format: Adult contemp. Target aud: 25-54.

WMAS(AM)— Sept 1, 1932: 1450 khz; 1 kw-U. TL: N42 06 32 W72 36 44. Stereo. Box 9500 01102. Secondary address: 101 West St. 01104. Phone: (413) 737-1414. Fax: (413) 737-1488. E-mail: susanwmas@aol.com. Web Site: www.947wmas.com. Licensee: Citadel Broadcasting Co. Group owner: Citadel Broadcasting Corp. (acq 6-3-2004; $22 million. with co-located FM). Network: ABC. Format: Adult standards. Spec prog: Black one hr, relg 2 hrs wkly. ♦Susan Murray, VP, gen mgr & gen sls mgr; Dina Cox, prom dir & prom mgr; Paul Cannon, progmg dir & progmg mgr; Rob Anthony, news dir; Randy Place, chief of engrg.

WMAS-FM— Dec 1, 1947: 94.7 mhz; 50 kw. 194 ft. TL: N42 06 32 W72 36 44. Stereo. E-mail: wmas@947wmas.com. Web Site: www.947wmas.com. Format: Adult contemp. ♦Randy Place, engrg VP.

*WNEK-FM— Feb 17, 1976: 105.1 mhz; 13 w. -23 ft. TL: N42 06 55 W72 31 05. Stereo. Western New England College, 1215 Wilbraham Rd. 01119-2684. Phone: (413) 782-1582. Fax: (413) 796-2111. Licensee: Trustees of Western New England College. Format: Div. Target aud: 15-35; college community, greater Springfield area. Spec prog: Black 8 hrs wkly. ♦Ian Martin, opns dir.

WNNZ(AM)—(Westfield). July 8, 1987: 640 khz; 50 kw-D, 1 kw-N, DA-2. TL: N42 10 46 W72 45 05. Stereo. 1331 Main St., Suite 5 01103. Phone: (413) 781-1011. Fax: (413) 734-4434. Web Site: www.wnnz.com. Licensee: Clear Channel Radio Licenses Inc. Group owner: Clear Channel Communications Inc. (acq 11-24-98; $1.2 million). Network: Network: CBS, ABC. Akin, Gump, Strauss, Hauer & Feld. Format: Talk, sports. News staff: one; News: 10 hrs wkly. Target aud: 25-54; upscale adults.

*WSCB(FM)— Mar 1, 1958: 89.9 mhz; 100 w. 35 ft. TL: N42 05 59 W72 33 30. 263 Alden St. 01109. Phone: (413) 748-3722. Phone: (413) 748-3712. Fax: (413) 748-3473. Licensee: President & Trustees of Springfield College. Format: Div.

WSPR(AM)— June 1936: 1270 khz; 5 kw-D, 1 kw-N, DA-2. TL: N42 05 24 W72 36 11. 34 Sylvan St., West Springfield 01089. Phone: (413) 827-8484. Fax: (413) 734-2240. E-mail: pgois@aol.com. Web Site: wspr1270.com. Licensee: Davidson Media Station WSPR Licensee LLC. (acq 5-16-2005; $6.8 million with WACM(AM) West Springfield). Format: Spanish, tropical. ♦Antonio Gois, pres; Paul Gois, exec VP, gen mgr & opns dir.

*WTCC(FM)— Aug 19, 1971: 90.7 mhz; 4 kw. 92 ft. TL: N42 06 32 W72 34 45. Stereo. Box 9000 01103. Phone: (413) 746-9822. Fax: (413) 781-3747. E-mail: managerwtcc@stcc.edu. Web Site: www.wtccfm.org. Licensee: Springfield Technical Community College. Format: Div, multi-cultural. Target aud: General. Spec prog: Country 4 hrs, Greek 2 hrs, It 2 hrs, Pol 2 hrs, Sp 14 hrs wkly. ♦Denise Stewart, gen mgr & stn mgr; Mark Leak, progmg dir.

Sudbury

*WYAJ(FM)— September 1980: 97.7 mhz; 4 w. 220 ft. TL: N42 22 30 W71 24 28. 390 Lincoln Rd. 01776. Phone: (978) 443-9961. Fax: (978) 443-8824. E-mail: paul_sarapas@lsrhs.net. Web Site: www.lsrhs.net. Licensee: Lincoln-Sudbury Regional School District. Format: CHR, new age, classic rock. Target aud: General. Spec prog: Black 6 hrs, class 3 hrs, jazz 5 hrs, loc rock artists 3 hrs wkly.

Taunton

WPEP(AM)— Dec 22, 1949: 1570 khz; 1 kw-D, 227 w-N. TL: N41 53 00 W71 03 50. 41 Taunton Green 02780-3233. Phone: (508) 822-1570. Fax: (508) 822-6473. E-mail: info@wpep1570.com. Web Site: www.wpep1570.com. Licensee: Anastos Media Group Inc. (group owner; acq 7-6-01; grpsl). Network: Network: USA, Westwood One. Rep: New England. Leventhal, Senter & Lerman. Format: News/talk. News staff: 2; News: 20 hrs wkly. Target aud: 35 plus; male & female. Spec prog: Por 10 hrs, gospel 12 hrs wkly. ♦A.J. Nicholson, gen mgr.

WSNE-FM— Jan 26, 1966: 93.3 mhz; 30 kw. 620 ft. TL: N41 51 56 W71 17 22. Stereo. 75 Oxford St., Suite 302, Providence 02905. Phone: (401) 781-9979. Phone: (401) 224-1933. Fax: (401) 781-9329. E-mail: feedback@coast933.com. Web Site: www.wsne.com. Licensee:

Capstar TX L.P. Group owner: Clear Channel Communications Inc. (acq 8-30-00; grpsl). Network: AP Radio. Format: Adult contemp. Target aud: 25-54; mostly women. Spec prog: Pub affrs 4 hrs wkly. ♦James Corwin, gen mgr; Kevin Hickey, sls dir; Michelle Maker, prom mgr; Steve Peck, progmg VP & progmg dir.

Tisbury

WMVY(FM)— June 1, 1981: 92.7 mhz; 3 kw. 300 ft. TL: N41 26 17 W70 36 47. (CP: Ant 328 ft.). Stereo. Box 1148, Vineyard Haven 02568. Secondary address: 57 Carrolls Way, Vineyard Haven 02568. Phone: (508) 693-5000. Fax: (508) 693-8211. E-mail: pj@mvyradio.com. Web Site: www.mvyradio.com. Licensee: Aritaur Communications Inc. (acq 6-17-98; $1 million). Network: Network: Moody, AP Radio. Format: Album-Oriented Rock. News staff: one. Target aud: 25-49; upper income, active consumer group. Spec prog: Class 4 hrs, jazz 4 hrs wkly. ♦Greg Orcutt, gen mgr; Megan Ward, gen sls mgr & prom dir; P.J. Finn, progmg dir.

Truro

WCDJ(FM)— 2000: 102.3 mhz; 340 w. Ant 98 ft. TL: N42 01 03 W70 04 23. 300 Western Ave., Allsston 02134. Phone: (617) 254-6333. Licensee: Truro Wireless Inc. (acq 11-8-91).

Turners Falls

WRSI(FM)— July 1994: 93.9 mhz; 3 kw. Ant 328 ft. TL: N42 32 01 W72 35 34. Stereo. Box 268, Northampton 01061. Phone: (413) 585-9555. Fax: (413) 585-0927. E-mail: dj@wrsi.com. Web Site: www.wrsi.com. Licensee: Saga Communications of New England LLC. Group owner: Saga Communications Inc. (acq 2-13-2004; grpsl). Network: ABC. Format: AAA. News: 9 hrs wkly. Target aud: 18-54; young, educated, spend money. ♦Sean O'Mealy, gen mgr.

Waltham

*WBRS(FM)— Feb 5, 1968: 100.1 mhz; 25 w. 151 ft. TL: N42 22 09 W71 15 28. Stereo. Brandeis Univ., 415 South St. 02453-2728. Phone: (781) 736-5277. E-mail: info@wbrs.org. Web Site: www.wbrs.org. Licensee: Brandeis University. Format: Div. News: 5 hrs wkly. Target aud: General. Spec prog: Fr 2 hrs, Sp 4 hrs, Black 14 hrs, Yiddish 1 hr, blues 14 hrs wkly.

WCRB(FM)— 1948: 102.5 mhz; 8.1 kw. 1,151 ft. TL: N42 18 27 W71 13 27. Stereo. 750 South St. 02453-1496. Phone: (781) 893-7080. Fax: (781) 893-0038. E-mail: wcrb@wcrb.com. Web Site: www.wcrb.com. Licensee: Charles River Broadcasting WCRB License Corp. (acq 9-10-99). Format: Class. News staff: one. Target aud: 30-64; adults. Spec prog: Boston Symphony Orchestra concerts live from Symphony Hall, wkly. ♦Christopher Jones, pres; William Campbell, CEO, gen mgr & sls VP.

WRCA(AM)— 1948: 1330 khz; 5 kw-U, DA-2. TL: N42 21 16 W71 15 44. (CP: COL Watertown. 25 kw-D, 17 kw-N, DA-2). Stereo. 552 Massachusetts Ave., Suite 201, Cambridge 02139. Phone: (617) 621-1330. Fax: (617) 492-2800. Licensee: WRCA License LLC. Group owner: Beasley Broadcast Group Inc. (acq 5-2000; $6 million). Format: Sp, Haitian. News: 10 hrs wkly. Target aud: General. Spec prog: Indian 2 hrs, It 3 hrs wkly. ♦Stu Fink, gen mgr & opns mgr.

Ware

WARE(AM)— July 11, 1948: 1250 khz; 5 kw-D, 2.5 kw-N, DA-2. TL: N42 14 41 W72 12 30. 100 Foster St., Southbridge 01550. Phone: (508) 289-2300. Fax: (508) 289-2323. E-mail: info@realoldies1250.com. Web Site: www.realoldies1250.com. Licensee: Success Signal Broadcasting Inc. (acq 12-3-02; $250,000). Rep: D & R Radio. Cohn & Marks. Format: Country, sports, loc news. Target aud: 30 plus. Spec prog: Pol 4 hrs wkly. ♦John P. Slosek Jr., pres; Marshall Sanft, gen mgr; Joe Grivalsky, chief of opns.

Watertown

WAZN(AM)— January 1958: 1470 khz; 1.4 kw-D, 3.4 kw-N, DA-2. TL: N42 24 49 W71 12 40. 500 W. Cummings Park, Suite 2600, Woburn 01801. Phone: (781) 938-0869. Fax: (781) 938-0933. E-mail: Jeffk@mrbi.net. Licensee: Multicultural Radio Broadcasting Licensee LLC. Group owner: Multicultural Radio Broadcasting Inc. (acq 12-11-02; $1.8 million). Format: Multicultural - leased time. News staff: 3.

Directory of Radio

Webster

WGFP(AM)— Apr 1, 1980: 940 khz; 1 kw-D. TL: N42 03 17 W71 50 00. 27 Douglas Rd. 01570. Phone: (508) 943-9400. Fax: (508) 943-0405. Web Site: www.coolcountry940.com. Licensee: Just Because Inc. (acq 6-12-2003). Format: Country. News: 25 hrs wkly. Target aud: 25-54. Spec prog: Pol one hr, Greek one hr wkly. ♦Barry Sims, CEO.

WORC-FM— Apr 8, 1994: 98.9 mhz; 3 kw. 410 ft. TL: N42 02 30 W71 59 18. Stereo. 250 Commercial St., Suite 530 01608. Phone: (508) 752-1045. Fax: (508) 793-0824. E-mail: jaybeau.jones@citcomm.com. Web Site: www.oldies989.com. Licensee: Citadel Broadcasting Co. Group owner: Citadel Broadcasting Corp. (acq 6-8-99; $3.5 million). Network: Network: Westwood One, ABC. Format: Oldies. News: 8 hrs wkly. Target aud: 25-49. Spec prog: Sp one hr wkly. ♦Joe Flynn, gen mgr; Amy Wilfong, prom mgr; JayBeau Jones, progmg dir & progmg mgr.

Wellesley

*WZLY(FM)— Sept 20, 1976: 91.5 mhz; 10 w. 164 ft. TL: N42 17 35 W71 18 21. Stereo. Schneider Ctr., 106 Central St. 02181-8201. Phone: (781) 283-2690. Fax: (781) 237-4433. Licensee: Wellesley College. Network: AP Radio. Format: Div, progsv, AOR. Target aud: General; Wellesley town and college community. Spec prog: It one hr, Sp one hr, Japanese one hr, Chinese one hr, Russian one hr wkly. ♦Julia Luechtefeld, gen mgr.

Wellfleet

*WWTE(FM)—Not on air, target date: unknown: 90.7 mhz; 1 kw. Ant 154 ft. TL: N41 56 44 W70 01 06. Box 637, Bishop, CA 93515. Phone: (760) 872-4225. Fax: (760) 872-4155. Licensee: Living Proof Inc. ♦Daniel McClenaghan, pres & gen mgr.

West Barnstable

*WKKL(FM)— Sept 19, 1977: 90.7 mhz; 205 w. 71 ft. TL: N41 41 31 W70 20 16. Cape Cod Community College, Rt. 132 02668. Phone: (508) 375-4030. Phone: (508) 362-2131, EXT. 4684. Fax: (508) 375-4020. E-mail: wkkl247@yahoo.com. Web Site: www.geocities.com/wkkl247. Licensee: Board of Trustees Cape Cod Community Colleges. Format: Alternative. ♦Lisa Zinsius, gen mgr.

West Springfield

WACM(AM)— Aug 28, 1949: 1490 khz; 1 kw-U. TL: N42 06 06 W72 37 22. 34 Sylvan St. 01089. Phone: (413) 827-8484. Fax: (413) 734-2240. E-mail: pgois@aol.com. Web Site: www.wacm1490.com. Licensee: Davidson Media Station WACM Licensee LLC. (acq 5-16-2005; $6.8 million with WSPR(AM) Springfield). Rep: New England. Format: Sp. ♦Paul Gois, gen mgr; Antonio Gois, news dir & chief of engrg.

West Yarmouth

*WBUR(AM)— October 1940: 1240 khz; 1 kw-U. TL: N41 38 07 W70 14 06. 890 Commonwealth Ave., Boston 02215. Phone: (617) 353-0909. Fax: (617) 353-4747. Web Site: www.wbur.org. Licensee: The Executive Committee of the Board of Trustees of Boston University Group owner: WBUR Group (acq 12-17-96). Format: News/talk. News: 78 hrs wkly. Target aud: 25-54; intelligent adults interested in news & politics. Spec prog: Sp 5 hrs wkly. ♦Jane Christo, gen mgr.

WXTK(FM)— Dec 30, 1948: 95.1 mhz; 50 kw. 246 ft. TL: N41 38 08 W70 14 06. Stereo. 278 S. Sea Ave. 02673. Phone: (508) 775-5678. Fax: (508) 862-6329. E-mail: edanddan@95wxtk.com. Web Site: www.95wxtk.com. Licensee: Qantum of Cape Cod License Co. LLC. Group owner: Boch Broadcasting (acq 2005; grpsl). Rep: D & R Radio. Format: News/talk. Target aud: 25 plus. ♦Carolyn Bernhardt, VP, VP & gen mgr; Greg Cassidy, opns mgr.

Westfield

WNNZ(AM)—Licensed to Westfield. See Springfield

*WSKB(FM)— October 1974: 89.5 mhz; 100 w. 130 ft. TL: N42 07 55 W72 47 51. Stereo. Ely Hall, 577 Western Ave. 01086. Phone: (431) 572-5579. Fax: (413) 572-5625. E-mail: wskb89.5fm@yahoo.com. Web Site: wskb.nipod.com. Licensee: Westfield State College. Format: Talk, alt, div. Target aud: General. Spec prog: Class 3 hrs, folk 3 hrs,

Stations in the U.S.   Michigan

jazz 6 hrs, Sp 3 hrs, reggae 3 hrs wkly. ♦ Krissy Green, gen mgr; Barbara Hand, opns mgr; Dave Kowaiski, progmg dir.

Williamstown

*WCFM(FM)— Sept 8, 1958: 91.9 mhz; 440 w. Ant -836 ft. TL: N42 42 38 W73 12 06. Baxter Hall, Williams College 01267. Phone: (413) 597-3265. Fax: (413) 597-2259. E-mail: wcfmbd@wso.williams.edu. Web Site: wcfm.williams.edu. Licensee: The President & Trustees of Williams College. ♦ Adam Ain, gen mgr.

Winchendon

*WKMY(FM)—Not on air, target date: unknown: 91.1 mhz; 155 w. Ant 207 ft. TL: N42 42 09 W72 02 18. 5700 West Oaks Blvd., Rocklin, CA 95765. Phone: (916) 251-1600. Fax: (916) 251-1650. Licensee: Educational Media Foundation. (acq 6-16-2005; $15,000 for CP). ♦ Lloyd Parker, gen mgr.

WOQL(FM)— January 1983: 97.7 mhz; 6 kw. Ant 328 ft. TL: N42 47 24 W72 09 06. Stereo. 69 Stanhope Ave., Keene, NH 03431. Phone: (603) 352-9230. Fax: (603) 357-3926. E-mail: winq@monadrockradiogroup.com. Web Site: www.601977.com. Licensee: Saga Communications of New England LLC. Group owner: Saga Communications Inc. (acq 4-1-2003; $400,000). Format: Hot new country. News staff: 2; News: 7 hrs wkly. Target aud: 25-54; 60% female, 40% male. ♦ Bruce Lyons, gen mgr, Steve Hamel, opns mgr; Vicki Lenanan, prom dir.

Woods Hole

*WCAI(FM)— Sept. 25, 2000: 90.1 mhz; 6.5 kw. 298 ft. TL: N41 25 26 W70 40 20. Box 82 02543. Secondary address: 3 Water St. 02543. Phone: (508) 548-9600. Fax: (508) 548-5517. E-mail: cainan@wgbn.org. Web Site: www.cainan.org. Licensee: WGBH Educational Foundation (acq 12-31-97; $25,000 with WNAN(FM) Nantucket). Network: NPR. Format: News/talk. ♦ John Voci, gen mgr & stn mgr; Susan Larks, pres & dev dir; Steve Young, progmg dir.

Worcester

WAAF(FM)—Listing follows WVEI.

*WBPR(FM)— 1994: 91.9 mhz; 1 kw. 469 ft. TL: N42 15 11 W71 57 41. c/o WUMB-FM, Univ. of Mass., 100 Morrissey Blvd., Boston 02125-3393. Phone: (617) 287-6900. Fax: (617) 287-6916. E-mail: wumb@umb.edu. Web Site: www.wumb.org. Licensee: University of Massachusetts. Format: Acoustic/folk, rhythm and blues, world mus. Target aud: 25-45. Spec prog: News. ♦ Patricia A. Monteith, gen mgr.

*WCHC(FM)— Sept 12, 1977: 88.1 mhz; 100 w. -656 ft. TL: N42 14 15 W71 48 31. Box G, Holy Cross College, One College St. 01610. Phone: (508) 793-2475. Fax: (508) 793-2471. Web Site: www.college.holycross.edu/wchc. Licensee: Trustees of the College of the Holy Cross. Network: UPI. Winston & Strawn. Format: Progsv, diversified. News: 5 hrs wkly. Target aud: 12-35; adventurous. Spec prog: Black 8 hrs, class 6 hrs, jazz 6 hrs, metal 6 hrs, funk 3 hrs wkly. ♦ Michael Cunningham, gen mgr.

WCRN(AM)— Dec 5, 1994: 830 khz; 7 kw-D, 5 kw-N, DA-2. TL: N42 14 47 W71 55 51. 1049 Main St. 01603. Phone: (508) 792-5803. Fax: (508) 770-0659. E-mail: studio@wcrnradio.com. Web Site: www.mikerobertswebdesign.com/wcrn/. Licensee: Carter Broadcasting Corp. (acq 1-16-90). Format: Oldies. Target aud: 25-54. ♦ Ken Carter, pres; Kurt Carberry, gen mgr; Art Dufault, stn mgr.

*WCUW(FM)— Dec 4, 1973: 91.3 mhz; 630 w. 145 ft. TL: N42 15 46 W71 47 59. Stereo. 910 Main St. 01610. Phone: (508) 753-1012. E-mail: wcuw@wcuw.com. Web Site: www.wcuw.com. Licensee: WCUW Inc. Format: Div. News: one hr wkly. Target aud: General. Spec prog: Fr 2 hrs, Sp 19 hrs, Ger 2 hrs, Pol 2 hrs, ethnic 10 hrs wkly. ♦ Joe Cutroni, gen mgr.

*WICN(FM)— Nov 21, 1969: 90.5 mhz; 8.1 kw horiz, 7.2 kw vert. Ant 371 ft. TL: N42 20 07 W71 42 54. (CP: N42 20 09 W71 42 57). Stereo. 50 Portland St. 01608. Phone: (508) 752-0700. Fax: (508) 752-7518. E-mail: webmaster@winc.org. Web Site: www.wicn.org. Licensee: WICN Public Radio Inc. Network: NPR. Format: Jazz, big band, folk. News: 12 hrs wkly. Target aud: 35 plus; high education, high income. ♦ Mike Gorman, pres; Thomas Kenney, VP & mktg mgr; Brian Barlow, gen mgr; Kyle Warren, opns dir & opns mgr; Tyra Penn, dev dir.

WNEB(AM)— Dec 18, 1946: 1230 khz; 1 kw-U. TL: N42 16 23 W71 49 23. 70 James St., Suite 201 01603. Phone: (508) 831-9863. Fax: (508) 831-7964. E-mail: wneb1230@ifriendly.net. Web Site: www.wneb.net. Licensee: Blount Masscom Inc. Group owner: Blount Communications Group (acq 1-28-2004; $400,000). Format: Relg. Target aud: 18-54; teen & adult contemp. ♦ William A. Blount, pres; Stephen A. Binley, stn mgr & opns mgr.

WORC(AM)— February 1925: 1310 khz; 5 kw-D, 1 kw-N, DA-2. TL: N42 13 19 W71 49 02. Stereo. 19 Norwich St. 01608. Phone: (508) 791-1310. Fax: (508) 752-6897. E-mail: info@power1310.com. Web Site: www.power1310.com. Licensee: Antonio F. Gois. (acq 1-7-2005; $950,000). Network: Westwood One. Rep: McGavren Guild. Leventhal, Senter & Lerman. Format: News/talk. News staff: one. Target aud: 29-54; upscale male adults. Spec prog: Sports 6 hrs, Pol 4 hrs wkly, Sp one hr wkly. ♦ Brian Jakusik, gen mgr.

WSRS(FM)—Listing follows WTAG(AM).

WTAG(AM)— May 1, 1924: 580 khz; 5 kw-U, DA-2. TL: N42 20 13 W71 49 15. Stereo. 98 Stereo Ln., Paxton 01612. Phone: (508) 795-0580. Phone: (508) 757-9696. Fax: (508) 757-1779. Web Site: www.wtag.com. Licensee: Capstar TX L.P. Group owner: Clear Channel Communications Inc. (acq 8-30-00; grpsl). Network: CBS. Format: News/talk. News staff: 6; News: 40 hrs wkly. Target aud: 25-54. Spec prog: Sports. ♦ Steve Peck, gen mgr; Paul Haley, natl sls mgr; Kerry Mathieson, prom dir & prom mgr; George Brown, progmg dir; Paul Tuthill, news dir; Lynne MacNamee, pub affrs dir; Dan Kelleher, chief of engrg.

WSRS(FM)—Co-owned with WTAG(AM). June 17, 1940: 96.1 mhz; 14 kw. 863 ft. TL: N42 18 34 W71 54 10. Stereo. Phone: (508) 757-9696. Web Site: www.wsrs.com. Network: ABC. Format: Adult contemp. News staff: one; News: 5 hrs wkly. Target aud: 25-54. ♦ Jackie Brush, mus dir; Sarah Ryan, news dir.

WVEI(AM)— 1926: 1440 khz; 5 kw-U, DA-N. TL: N42 20 13 W71 49 15. 181 Moreland St. 01609-1049. Phone: (508) 752-5611. Fax: (508) 752-1006. Licensee: Entercom Boston II License LLC. Group owner: Entercom Communications Corp. (acq 10-15-98; grpsl). Network: ABC Daytime Direction. Rep: CBS Radio. Format: Sports. ♦ Tom Baker, gen mgr & stn mgr; Jim Rushton, sls dir & natl sls mgr; Jason Wolfe, progmg dir; Eric Fitch, chief of engrg.

WAAF(FM)—Co-owned with WVEI. June 15, 1961: 107.3 mhz; 18.6 kw. 820 ft. TL: N42 18 13 W71 53 51. Stereo. 20 Guest St., 3rd Fl., Boston 02135. Phone: (617) 779-5400. Web Site: waaf.com. Format: AOR. Target aud: 25-54. ♦ Tom Baker, gen mgr; Julie Kahn, stn mgr; Jim Vereault, gen sls mgr; Bob Goodell, rgnl sls mgr; Keith Hasting, progmg dir; Mike Hsu, news dir.

WVNE(AM)—See Leicester

WXLO(FM)—(Fitchburg). August 1960: 104.5 mhz; 37 kw. 563 ft. TL: N42 30 27 W71 49 37. Stereo. 250 Commercial St., Suite 530 01608. Phone: (508) 752-1045. Fax: (508) 793-0824. Web Site: www.wxlo.com. Licensee: Citadel Broadcasting Co. Group owner: Citadel Broadcasting Corp. Rep: McGavren Guild. Kaye, Scholer, Fierman, Hays & Handler. Format: Hot A/C. News: 5 hrs wkly. Target aud: 25-54. Spec prog: 70s mus 5 hrs wkly. ♦ Joe Flynn, VP & gen mgr; JayBeau Jones, progmg dir.

Michigan

Ada

WDSS(AM)— 1998: 1680 khz; 10 kw-D, 680 w-N. TL: N42 56 09 W85 27 26. Stereo. 3777 44th St. S.E., Kentwood 49512. Phone: (616) 554-5958. Fax: (616) 656-9326. Web Site: www.wjnz.com. Licensee: Goodrich Radio L.L.C. Network: Radio Disney. Target aud: 18-34. ♦ Robert Goodrich, chmn; Ross Pettinga, gen mgr.

Adrian

WABJ(AM)— Nov 13, 1946: 1490 khz; 1 kw-U. TL: N41 54 02 W84 00 51. 121 W. Maumee St. 49221. Phone: (517) 265-1500. Fax: (517) 263-4525. Licensee: Friends Communication of Michigan Inc. Group owner: Friends Communications Inc. (acq 10-1-90; grpsl; FTR: 10-29-90). Network: ABC Information & Entertainment. Michigan. Fletcher, Heald & Hildreth. Format: News/talk. News staff: 2; News: 9 hrs wkly. Target aud: General. Spec prog: Farm 7 hrs, relg 3 hrs wkly. ♦ Bob Elliot, chmn, gen mgr & gen mgr; John Sebastian, progmg dir.

WQTE(FM)—Co-owned with WABJ(AM). Sept 1, 1976: 95.3 mhz; 3 kw. 299 ft. TL: N41 48 15 W84 05 25. Stereo. Phone: (517) 265-9500. Format: Country. News: 2 hrs wkly. Target aud: 25-54. ♦ Greg Green, progmg dir.

WLEN(FM)— June 9, 1965: 103.9 mhz; 3 kw. 299 ft. TL: N41 54 11 W83 59 13. Stereo. Box 687 49221. Secondary address: 242 W. Maumee St. 49221. Phone: (517) 263-1039. Fax: (517) 265-5362. Web Site: www.wlen.com. Licensee: Lenawee Broadcasting Co. Network: CNN Radio. Format: Adult contemp. Target aud: 25-54. Spec prog: Sp 4 hrs wkly. ♦ Julie M. Koehn, pres & gen mgr.

*WVAC-FM— Feb 13, 1967: 107.9 mhz; 13 w horiz. 79 ft. TL: N41 53 55 W84 03 33. Adrian College, 110 S. Madison St. 49221. Phone: (517) 265-5161, EXT. 4540. Phone: (517) 264-3141. Fax: (517) 264-3331. Licensee: Adrian College Board of Trustees. Format: Div. Target aud: 18-23; those affiliated to the college lifestyle. ♦ Steven Shehan, gen mgr; Jennifer Fries, prom mgr; Bethany Martinus, progmg mgr; Darius Cunningham, pub affrs dir; Bill Kresbach, chief of engrg.

Albion

*WUFN(FM)— April 1971: 96.7 mhz; 3.2 kw. Ant 456 ft. TL: N42 15 56 W84 38 43. Stereo. 13799 Donovan Rd. 49224. Phone: (800) 776-1020. Fax: (517) 531-5009. E-mail: wufn@flc.org. Web Site: www.myflr.org. Licensee: Family Life Broadcasting System. (group owner) Network: Network: USA, AP Radio. Format: Inspirational, Christian. News staff: one; News: 6 hrs wkly. Target aud: 25-54; Christian families. ♦ Randy Carlson, pres; Dave Phelps, gen mgr; David Jones, opns mgr; Rod Robison, dev VP; Dave Dawson, prom dir & adv dir.

WWKN(FM)—(Marshall). Oct 1, 1968: 104.9 mhz; 3 kw. 300 ft. TL: N42 18 47 W84 55 46. 390 Golden Ave., Battle Creek 49015. Phone: (269) 963-5555. Fax: (269) 963-5185. Web Site: www.battlecreekradio.com. Licensee: Capstar TX L.P. Group owner: Clear Channel Communications Inc. Format: Classic hits. ♦ Jack McDevitt, gen mgr; John Patrick, progmg dir.

Allegan

WZUU(FM)— April 1991: 92.3 mhz; 860 w. 600 ft. TL: N42 34 52 W85 45 17. Stereo. Box 80, 706 E. Allegan St., Otsego 49078. Phone: (269) 343-1717. Fax: (269) 692-6861. E-mail: tflynn@wqxc.com. Web Site: www.wzuu.com. Licensee: Forum Communications Inc. (acq 6-1-97). Rep: Roslin. Michigan. Richard Hayes. Format: Classic rock. News staff: one; News: 2 hrs wkly. Target aud: 25-54; professionals. ♦ Robert Brink, pres; Tom Bontrager, gen sls mgr; Tom Flynn, gen mgr & progmg dir.

Allendale

*WGVU-FM— July 15, 1983: 88.5 mhz; 3 kw. 311 ft. TL: N43 03 24 W85 57 31. Stereo. Grand Valley State Univ., 301 W. Fulton, Grand Rapids 49504-6492. Phone: (616) 331-6666. Fax: (616) 331-6625. E-mail: wgvu@gvsu.edu. Web Site: www.wgvu.org. Licensee: Board of Control of Grand Valley State University. Network: Network: NPR, AP Radio. Cohn & Marks. Format: Jazz, news. News staff: 5; News:

Michigan

26 hrs wkly. Target aud: 25 plus; mid to upper educ & income levels. ♦Michael T. Walenta, gen mgr; Ken Kolbe, opns mgr; Richard Nelson, gen sls mgr; Pamela Holtz, prom mgr; Fred Martino, news dir.

Alma

WFYC(AM)— Aug 17, 1948: 1280 khz; 1 kw-D, 45 w-N. TL: N43 22 08 W84 36 19. Box 665 48801. Phone: (989) 463-3175. Fax: (989) 463-6674. Licensee: Jacom Inc. (acq 1996). Format: Sports. Target aud: 25-50. Spec prog: Farm 4 hrs wkly. ♦James Sommerville, pres, gen mgr & progmg dir; Susan Sommerville, prom mgr.

WQBX(FM)—Co-owned with WFYC(AM). November 1964: 104.9 mhz; 6 kw. Ant 328 ft. TL: N43 22 08 W84 36 19. Stereo. Web Site: www.wqbx.com. Network: ABC. Format: Adult contemp.

WMLM(AM)—See Saint Louis

***WQAC-FM**— Mar 27, 1993: 90.9 mhz; 100 w. 66 ft. TL: N43 22 50 W84 40 14. Van Dusen Student Ctr., 614 W. Superior St. 48801. Phone: (989) 463-7095. Fax: (989) 463-7277. E-mail: wqaccharts@blazemail.com. Web site: students.alma.edu/organizations/wqac. Licensee: Alma College. Format: Rock. News staff: one; News: 3 hrs wkly. Target aud: 13-24; high school & college students. Spec prog: Jazz 2 hrs, relg 2 hrs, hip hop/R&B 7 hrs, heavy metal 5 hrs, classic rock 2 hrs wkly. ♦Kat Lanphear, gen mgr; Kelly Gildersleeve, prom dir; Cailean Dinwoody, progmg dir; Mike Cruz, mus dir.

Alpena

WATZ(AM)— 1946: 1450 khz; 1 kw-U. TL: N45 03 58 W83 29 06. Box 536, 123 Prentiss 49707. Phone: (989) 354-8400. Fax: (989) 354-3436. Web Site: www.watz.com. Licensee: WATZ Radio Inc. Group owner: Midwestern Broadcasting Co. Network: ABC Information & Entertainment. Format: Talk. News staff: 2; News: 31 hrs wkly. Target aud: 35-64. Spec prog: Farm 3 hrs, Ger 2 hrs, Pol 2 hrs, relg 2 hrs wkly. ♦Mike Centala, gen mgr; Steve Wright, opns mgr; John Pines, news dir.

WATZ-FM— 1967: 99.3 mhz; 17 kw. 843 ft. TL: N44 51 25 W83 32 34. Stereo. Network: ABC Information & Entertainment. Format: Country. Target aud: 25-54. ♦Elaine Wils, mus dir.

WCML-FM— Apr 24, 1978: 91.7 mhz; 100 kw. 1,171 ft. TL: N45 08 17 W84 09 44. Stereo. Public Broadcasting Ctr., Central Michigan Univ., Mount Pleasant 48859. Phone: (989) 774-3105. Fax: (989) 774-4427. E-mail: cmuradio@cmich.edu. Web Site: www.wcmu.org. Licensee: Central Michigan University. Network: Network: NPR, PRI. Dow, Lohnes & Albertson. Format: Jazz, class, news & info. News staff: 2; News: 45 hrs wkly. Target aud: General. ♦Ed Grant, gen mgr & rgnl sls mgr. Co-owned TV: *WCML-TV affil

WHSB(FM)— May 1965: 107.7 mhz; 99 kw. 760 ft. TL: N45 03 40 W83 43 05. Stereo. 1491 M-32 W., Apena 49707. Phone: (989) 354-4611. Fax: (989) 354-4014. E-mail: thebay@1077thebay.com. Web Site: www.1077thebay.com. Licensee: Edwards Communications LC. Group owner: Northern Radio Network (acq 12-21-2004; grpsl). Rep: Michigan. Format: Adult contemp. Target aud: 25-54. ♦Jerry Edwards, pres; Darrel Kelly, progmg dir & chief of engrg; Kerwin Kitzman, mus dir.

WKJZ(FM)—(Hillman). December 1993: 94.9 mhz; 50 kw. 492 ft. TL: N45 01 33 W83 54 52. Box 549, Tawas City 48764. Phone: (989) 362-3417. Fax: (989) 362-4544. E-mail: wkjc@wkjc.com. Web site: www.wkjc.com. Licensee: Carroll Enterprises Inc. (group owner; acq 6-29-92; 7-27-92). Format: Classic rock. ♦John Carroll Jr., gen mgr.

Ann Arbor

WAAM(AM)— October 1947: 1600 khz; 5 kw-U, DA-2. TL: N42 11 32 W83 41 09. Stereo. 4230 Packard Rd. 48108. Phone: (734) 971-1600. Fax: (734) 973-2916. E-mail: waamradio@aol.com. Web Site: www.talkradio1600.com. Licensee: First Broadcasting Investment Partners LLC (group owner; (acq 6-13-2005; grpsl). Network: Westwood One. Bryan Cave. Format: MOR, news/talk. News staff: 4; News: 20 hrs wkly. Target aud: 35 plus; home owners & professionals. Spec prog: Relg 4 hrs, old time radio 6 hrs wkly. ♦Mabel Johnson, VP; Steve Ames, gen mgr; Greg Carson, opns mgr & progmg dir.

WCBN-FM— Jan 23, 1972: 88.3 mhz; 200 w. 177 ft. TL: N42 16 37 W83 44 07. Stereo. 530 Student Activities Bldg. 48109-1285. Phone: (734) 647-4122. Phone: (734) 763-3535. E-mail: fm@wcbn.org. Web Site: www.wcbn.org. Licensee: Regents of the University of Michigan. Format: Div. News staff: 0. Target aud: 18-49. Spec prog: Jazz 17 hrs, Sp 3 hrs, folk 2 hrs, pub affrs 5 hrs, gospel one hr, Fr one hr wkly. ♦Cindy Horng, gen mgr; Matthieu Goddeyne, dev dir.

WDEO(AM)—(Ypsilanti). Nov 16, 1962: 990 khz; 9.2 kw-D, 250 w-N. TL: N42 15 53 W83 36 47 (D), N42 15 55 W83 36 42 (N). Stereo. Box 504, One Ave Maria Dr. 48106. Phone: (734) 930-5200. Fax: (734) 930-3179. E-mail: hroot@wdeo.net. Web Site: www.wdeo.net. Licensee: Word Broadcasters Inc. 990 Investors LLC (acq 9-8-99; $2.5 million). Dennis Kelly Law Offices. Format: Christian, talk. News: 9 hrs wkly. Target aud: 21 plus; adult christian. Spec prog: Catholic talk. ♦Al Kresta, CEO; Michael Jones, gen mgr; Henry J. Root, opns mgr.

WQKL(FM)—Listing follows WTKA(AM).

WSDS(AM)—(Salem Township). 1962: 1480 khz; 750 w-D, 5 kw-N, DA-2. TL: N42 15 42 W83 37 10. 580 W. Clark Rd., Ypsilanti 48198. Phone: (734) 484-1480. Fax: (734) 484-5313. E-mail: wsds@wsds1480.com. Web site: www.wsds1480.com. Licensee: Birach Broadcasting Corp. (acq 1-25-2005; $1.5 million). Network: Westwood One. Format: Classic country, talk. News: 8 hrs wkly. Target aud: 25 plus. Spec prog: Bluegrass 6 hrs, Chinese 4 hrs, classic country 12 hrs, Greek 4 hrs wkly. ♦Sima Birach, pres; George Koch, gen mgr; Keith Jason, opns mgr, progmg mgr & mus dir; Hannah Koch, sls dir & prom mgr; John Petelka, pub affrs dir; Ralph Hines, chief of engrg.

WTKA(AM)— Apr 26, 1945: 1050 khz; 10 kw-D, 500 w-N, DA-2. TL: N42 08 46 W83 39 36. Box 300, Lobby D, 24 Frank Lloyd Wright Dr. 48106. Phone: (734) 302-8100. Fax: (734) 741-1071. Fax: (734) 930-9500. Licensee: Capstar TX L.P. Group owner: Clear Channel Communications Inc. (acq 8-7-00; grpsl). Network: ABC Information & Entertainment. Rep: Michigan. Format: News, talk, sports. Spec prog: Farm 9 hrs wkly.

WQKL(FM)— Co-owned with WTKA(AM). Feb 14, 1967: 107.1 mhz; 3 kw. 289 ft. TL: N42 16 41 W83 44 32. Format: Adult contemp. ♦Ray Nelson, stn mgr.

WUOM(FM)— 1948: 91.7 mhz; 93 kw. 780 ft. TL: N42 24 24 W83 54 54. Stereo. 535 W. William St. 48103. Phone: (734) 764-9210. Fax: (734) 647-3488. E-mail: michigan.radio@umich.edu. Web Site: www.michiganradio.org. Licensee: The Regents of University of Michigan. Network: Network: NPR, PRI. Dow, Lohnes & Albertson. Format: News/talk. News staff: 7; News: 140 hrs wkly. ♦Jon Hoban, stn mgr; Peggy J. Watson, opns mgr; Justin Edbright, dev dir.

WWWW(FM)— March 1962: 102.9 mhz; 49 kw horiz, 42 kw vert. 499 ft. TL: N42 15 04 W83 48 28. Stereo. 1100 Victors Wayl, Suite 100 48108. Phone: (734) 302-8100. Fax: (734) 213-7508. E-mail: programming@w4country.com. Web site: www.w4country.com. Licensee: Capstar TX L.P. Group owner: Clear Channel Communications Inc. (acq 8-7-00; grpsl). Rep: McGavren Guild. Format: Country. ♦Bob Bolak, gen mgr; Shannon Brown, gen sls mgr; Rob Walker, progmg dir; Tom Baker, mus dir.

Ashley

WJSZ(FM)— Mar 14, 1994: 92.5 mhz; 3 kw. 328 ft. TL: N43 10 55 W84 26 58. 103 N. Washington, Owosso 48867. Phone: (989) 725-1925. Phone: (800) 725-1925. Fax: (989) 725-7925. Web Site: www.z925.com. Licensee: Curwood Broadcasting Co. Corp. (acq 9-3-99). Baraff, Koerner & Olender. Format: Classic rock/new rock. Target aud: 25-54; general. ♦Alana Beamish, gen mgr & opns dir; Kevin Beamish, gen mgr.

Atlanta

WFDX(FM)—Licensed to Atlanta. See Petoskey

Auburn Hills

WAHS(FM)— 1975: 89.5 mhz; 100 w. 141 ft. TL: N42 37 42 W83 13 56. c/o Rick Kreinbring, 2800 Waukegan St. 48326. Phone: (248) 852-9247. Fax: (248) 852-0595. Licensee: Avondale School District. Format: CHR. ♦Rick Kreinbring, gen mgr.

WXOU(FM)—Licensed to Auburn Hills. See Rochester

Bad Axe

WLEW-FM— 1956: 102.1 mhz; 50 kw. Ant 492 ft. TL: N43 53 28 W83 07 26. Stereo. 935 S. Van Dyke Rd. 48413. Phone: (989) 269-9931. Fax: (989) 269-7702. Licensee: Thumb Broadcasting Inc. (acq 9-15-93; with co-located AM; 10-11-93). Format: Adult contemp, classic rock. News staff: 2; News: 18 hrs wkly. Target aud: 25-50. ♦Matthew Aymen, VP & sls VP; Craig Routzahn, gen mgr, news dir & pub affrs dir; Jack Vobbe, sls VP & chief of engrg; Richard Aymen, CEO, VP, gen mgr & progmg dir.

WLEW(AM)— 1950: 1340 khz; 1 kw-U, DA-D. TL: N43 47 56 W83 01 21. Format: Country. News staff: 2; News: 19 hrs wkly. Target aud: 18-50. ♦Richard Aymen, sls dir.

Baraga

WVCN(FM)— 1998: 104.3 mhz; 100 kw. Ant 859 ft. TL: N46 39 50 W88 23 06. 3434 W. Kilbourn Ave., Milwaukee, WI 53208. Phone: (414) 935-3000. Fax: (414) 935-3015. E-mail: wvcn@vcyamerica.org. Web Site: www.vcyamerica.org. Licensee: Keweenaw Bay Broadcasting Inc. Group owner: VCY/America Inc. (acq 7-8-99). Format: Christian. ♦Dr. Randall Melchert, pres; Vic Eliason, VP & gen mgr; Jim Schneider, progmg dir & pub affrs dir; Tom Schlueter, mus dir; Gordon Morris, news dir; Andy Eliason, chief of engrg.

Battle Creek

WBCK(AM)— July 9, 1948: 930 khz; 5 kw-D, 1 kw-N, DA-2. TL: N42 17 40 W85 11 00. 390 Golden Ave. 49015. Phone: (269) 963-5555. Fax: (269) 963-5185. Web Site: www.wbck930.com. Licensee: Capstar TX L.P. Group owner: Clear Channel Communications Inc. (acq 8-30-00; grpsl). Format: News/talk. Target aud: 25-54. ♦Jack McDevitt, gen mgr & stn mgr; Tim Collins, prom mgr & progmg mgr; Walker Sisson, chief of engrg.

WBXX(FM)—Co-owned with WBCK(AM). Feb 28, 1975: 95.3 mhz; 3 kw. Ant 269 ft. TL: N42 17 17 W85 09 54. Stereo. Web Site: www.wbck930.com. Network: UPI. Format: Adult contemp. Target aud: 18-49.

WKFR-FM— June 11, 1963: 103.3 mhz; 50 kw. 500 ft. TL: N42 21 19 W85 20 28. Stereo. Box 50911, Kalamazoo 49005-0911. Secondary address: 4154 Jennings Dr., Kalamazoo 49048. Phone: (269) 344-0111. Fax: (269) 344-4223. E-mail: radio@wkfr.com. Web Site: www.wkfr.com. Licensee: Cumulus Licensing Corp. Group owner: Cumulus Media Inc. (acq 5-26-98; grpsl). Format: CHR. News staff: one; News: 3 hrs wkly. Target aud: 25-54. ♦Lew Dickey, CEO & pres; John Pinch, COO; Martin Gausvik, CFO; John Sterling, gen mgr; Mic Kelly, opns mgr; Mi Rhee Vanderwall, gen sls mgr; Woody Houston, progmg dir.

WOLY(AM)— Nov 22, 1963: 1500 khz; 1 kw-D, DA. TL: N42 17 30 W85 10 08. 15074 6 1/2 Mile Rd. 49014. Phone: (269) 965-1515. Fax: (269) 965-1315. E-mail: wolyradio@sbcglobal.net. Licensee: Christian Family Network. (acq 1-89; $100,000; 1-23-89). Network: USA. Format: Traditional Christian mus & progmg. Target aud: General. ♦James Elsman, pres; Kurt Bertz, gen mgr & progmg dir.

WRCC(AM)— July 1, 1993: 1400 khz; 1 kw-U. TL: N42 18 15 W85 11 31. 390 Golden Ave. 49015. Phone: (269) 963-5555. Fax: (269) 963-5185. E-mail: bcnews@clearchannel.com. Web Site: www.battlecreekradio.com. Licensee: Capstar TX Limited Partnership Group owner: Clear Channel Communications Inc. (acq 8-30-00; grpsl). Format: Adult standards, big band. Target aud: 18-54; general. ♦Jack McDevitt, gen mgr; Tim Collins, progmg dir.

Bay City

WCHW-FM— Sept 1, 1973: 91.3 mhz; 110 w. 125 ft. TL: N43 35 19 W83 52 28. 1624 Columbus Ave. 48708. Phone: (989) 892-1741. Phone: (989) 892-5533. Fax: (989) 892-7946. E-mail: wchwonline@fnmail.com. Web Site: www.wchwonline.freewebspace.com. Licensee: School District Bay City. Format: AOR. ♦Brian Bishop, gen mgr; Joe Bowker, progmg dir.

WHNN(FM)— 1947: 96.1 mhz; 100 kw. 1,020 ft. TL: N43 33 10 W83 41 24. Stereo. 1740 Champagne Dr. N., Saginaw 48604. Phone: (989) 298-9466. Fax: (989) 754-9600. Web site: www.whnn.com. Licensee: Citadel Broadcasting Co. Group owner: Citadel Broadcasting Corp. (acq 4-26-01; grpsl). Format: Oldies. News staff: one; News: 6 hrs wkly. Target aud: 25-54. ♦Scott Meier, gen mgr.

Michigan

Developers & Brokers of Radio Properties

contact American Media Services at our suite:
Philadelphia Marriott Downtown
215-625-2900
843-972-2200
americanmediaservices.com
Charleston, SC
Dallas, TX · Chicago, Il · Austin, TX

American Media Services, LLC

WIOG(FM)— September 1969: 102.5 mhz; 86 kw. 860 ft. TL: N43 28 24 W83 50 40. Stereo. 1740 N. Champagne Dr., Saginaw 48604. Phone: (989) 776-2100. Fax: (989) 754-5990. Web Site: www.wiog.com. Licensee: Citadel Broadcasting Co. Group owner: Citadel Broadcasting Corp. (acq 2-8-99; grpsl). Network: ABC. Rep: McGavren Guild. Format: Adult contemp. News staff: one; News: 5 hrs wkly. Target aud: 25-54. ♦Scott Meier, VP & gen mgr; Bob Kolen, sls dir; Tom Clark, gen sls mgr; Brent Carey, progmg dir.

WMAX(AM)—Licensed to Bay City. See Saginaw

WSGW(AM)—See Saginaw

***WTRK(FM)**— July 25, 1993: 89.1 mhz; 2 kw. Ant 328 ft. TL: N43 35 04 W83 51 36. Stereo. Box 489 48707-0489. Phone: (989) 892-1189. Fax: (989) 892-6689. E-mail: wtrk@wtrk.com. Licensee: Beyond The Bay Media Group. Format: Hot CHR Christian, relg. News: one hr wkly. Target aud: 13-35. ♦Mark T. Dewitt, pres; Kathy D. Dewitt, CFO.

***WUCX-FM**— September 1989: 90.1 mhz; 30 kw. 479 ft. TL: N43 33 10 W83 41 24. Stereo. Public Broadcasting Ctr., 1999 E. Campus Dr., Mount Pleasant 48859. Phone: (989) 774-3105. Fax: (989) 774-4427. E-mail: cmuradio@radio.cmich.edu. Web Site: www.wcmu.org. Licensee: Central Michigan University. Network: Network: NPR, PRI. Dow, Lohnes & Albertson. Format: Class, jazz, news & info. Target aud: General. ♦Edward Grant, gen mgr; Ray Ford, progmg dir; David Nicholas, news dir & chief of engrg.

Bear Creek Township

***WTLI(FM)**— Sept 16, 1998: 89.3 mhz; 6 kw vert. 1,023 ft. TL: N45 10 12 W84 45 04. Box 388, Williamston 48895. Phone: (517) 381-0573. Fax: (877) 850-0881. E-mail: info@positivehits.com. Web Site: www.positivehits.com. Licensee: Superior Communications. Format: Adult Christian hit. ♦Edward Czelada, pres; Jenn Czelada, gen mgr.

Bear Lake

WCUZ(FM)— Nov 2, 1987: 100.1 mhz; 3 kw. 328 ft. TL: N44 25 18 W86 07 17. 1532 Forrester Rd., Frankfort 49635. Phone: (231) 352-9603. Fax: (231) 352-7877. E-mail: marc@wbnz.com. Web Site: www.wbnz.com. Licensee: Fort Bend Broadcasting Co. (group owner; acq 9-27-00; $590,000. with WOUF(FM) Beulah). Baraff, Koerner & Olender. Format: Adult contemp, soft rock. ♦Marc McGuire, pres & gen mgr.

Beaverton

WMRX-FM— Sept 15, 1980: 97.7 mhz; 4.1 kw. Ant 400 ft. TL: N43 53 16 W84 31 45. Stereo. Box 1689, Midland 48641-1689. Secondary address: 1510 Bayliss St., Midland 48640. Phone: (989) 631-1490. Fax: (989) 631-6357. E-mail: requests@wmpxwmrx.com. Web Site: www.wmpxwmrx.com. Licensee: Steel Broadcasting Inc. (acq 1990). Network: ABC. Format: Adult standards, big band, classic. News: 8 hrs wkly. Target aud: General; 35+. Spec prog: Sounds of Sinatra 2 hrs wkly. ♦Thomas Steel, pres & gen mgr; Darrell Jacobs, gen sls mgr.

Benton Harbor

WCNF(FM)— June 15, 1998: 94.9 mhz; 2.2 kw. 380 ft. TL: N42 04 19 W86 22 14. Box 107, St. Joseph 49085. Secondary address: 580 E. Napier Ave. 49022. Phone: (269) 925-1111. Fax: (269) 925-1011. Web Site: www.thecoast.fm. Licensee: WSJM Inc. Group owner: The Mid-West Family Broadcast Group Michigan Spot Sales Format: Adult contemp, hits of the 80s & 90s. ♦Joe Daguanno, VP & sls dir; Gayle Olson, gen mgr; Jim Gifford, opns dir; Sandie Lieberg, prom dir; Robb Rose, progmg dir.

WHFB-FM—Licensed to Benton Harbor. See Benton Harbor-St. Joseph

Benton Harbor-St. Joseph

WHFB(AM)— Sept 22, 1947: 1060 khz; 5 kw-D, 2.5 kw-CH. TL: N42 04 44 W86 28 00. 2100 Fairplain Ave., Benton Harbor 49022. Phone: (269) 925-9300. Fax: (269) 925-0065. Licensee: WHFB Broadcast Associates L.P. Group owner: WinCom Communications Group Inc. (acq 8-85). Format: Great talk. News staff: one. Target aud: General. ♦Bill Stanley, gen mgr & progmg dir.

WHFB-FM— Oct 10, 1947: 99.9 mhz; 50 kw. 497 ft. TL: N42 03 17 W86 27 31. Stereo. Format: Country. Target aud: 25-54.

WIRX(FM)—Listing follows WSJM(AM).

WSJM(AM)—(Saint Joseph). Nov 18, 1956: 1400 khz; 880 w-U. TL: N42 05 12 W86 26 40. Box 107, St. Joseph 49085. Secondary address: 580 E. Napier, Benton Harbor 49022. Phone: (269) 925-1111. Phone: (269) 925-9756. Fax: (269) 925-1011. Web Site: www.wsjm.com. Licensee: WSJM Inc. Group owner: The Mid-West Family Broadcast Group (acq 1-1-59). Network: ABC. Shaw Pittman. Format: Full service, news/talk, sports. Target aud: 35 plus. Spec prog: Black 5 hrs wkly. ♦Gayle Olson, pres & gen mgr; Jim Gifford, opns dir; Joe Daguanno, VP & sls dir; Bob Bucholtz, sls.

WIRX(FM)—Co-owned with WSJM(AM). June 20, 1966: 107.1 mhz; 1.2 kw. 498 ft. TL: N42 04 19 W86 22 14. Stereo. Box 107, St. Joseph 49085. Secondary address: 580 E. Napier Ave., Benton Harbor 49022. Phone: (269) 925-1111. Fax: (269) 925-1011. Web Site: wirx.com. Format: Rock. Target aud: 18-49. ♦Joe Daguanno, VP; Gayle Olson, gen mgr; Jim Gifford, opns mgr; Shelley Morgan, progmg dir.

Berrien Springs

WAUS(FM)—Licensed to Berrien Springs. See South Bend IN

Beulah

WOUF(FM)— January 1998: 92.1 mhz; 1.6 kw. 600 ft. TL: N44 30 54 W86 06 52. 13999 S.W. Bayshore Dr. 49684. Phone: (231) 947-3220. Fax: (231) 947-7201. Licensee: Fort Bend Broadcasting Co. (group owner; acq 9-27-00; $590,000. with WCUZ(FM) Bear Lake). Format: Adult contemp. ♦Laurie McFarlan, pres & gen mgr.

Big Rapids

WBRN(AM)— Jan 6, 1953: 1460 khz; 5 kw-D, 2.5 kw-N, DA-N. TL: N43 39 57 W85 28 59. Stereo. Box 1158 49307. Secondary address: 13574 Northland Dr. 49307. Phone: (231) 796-7684. Fax: (231) 796-6227. E-mail: wbrnfm@wbrn.com. Web Site: www.wbrn.com. Licensee: Mentor Partners Inc. (acq 6-21-2005; $850,000. with co-located FM). Network: ESPN Radio. Rep: Michigan. Format: News/talk, sports. News staff: one; News: 12 hrs wkly. Target aud: 35 plus; adults. ♦Jeffrey Scarpelli, pres; Robert J. Hampson Jr., gen mgr & sls dir; Scott Roman, prom dir; Karol Berry, news dir & pub affrs dir; George Keen, chief of engrg.

WWBR(FM)—Co-owned with WBRN(AM). September 1964: 100.9 mhz; 6 kw. 318 ft. TL: N43 39 49 W85 28 54. Stereo. Web Site: www.wbrn.com. Network: Network: Jones Radio Networks, AP Network News. Format: Adult contemp, classic rock. News staff: one; News: 10 hrs wkly. Target aud: 16-54. ♦Bill Beckwith, progmg dir.

WYBR(FM)— June 30, 1982: 102.3 mhz; 10.5 kw. 436 ft. TL: N43 41 01 W85 34 56. Stereo. 18720 16-Mile Rd. 49307. Phone: (231) 796-7000. Fax: (231) 796-7951. E-mail: wybr@tucker-usa.com. Web Site: www.wybr.com. Licensee: Mentor Partners Inc. (acq 8-10-98). Rep: Patt. Format: Hot adult contemp, CHR. News: 8 hrs wkly. Target aud: 25-54. Spec prog: Relg one hr wkly. ♦Jeffrey J. Scarpelli, pres & gen mgr.

Birmingham

WCSX(FM)— Mar 14, 1987: 94.7 mhz; 13.5 kw. 945 ft. TL: N42 27 13 W83 09 50. Stereo. 1 Radio Plaza, Ferndale 48220. Phone: (248) 398-9470. Fax: (248) 541-9279. Web Site: www.wcsx.com. Licensee: Greater Michigan Radio Inc. Group owner: Greater Media Inc. (acq 7-3-73). Rep: McGavren Guild. Format: Classic rock. Target aud: 25-54; males. ♦Tom Bender, VP & gen mgr.

Bloomfield Hills

***WBFH(FM)**— Oct 1, 1976: 88.1 mhz; 360 w. 100 ft. TL: N42 34 42 W83 17 10. Stereo. 4200 Andover Rd. 48302. Phone: (248) 341-5690. Fax: (248) 341-5679. E-mail: wbfh@bloomfield.org. Web Site: www.wbfh.fm. Licensee: Board of Education of Bloomfield Hills School District. Putbrese, Hunsaker & Trent, P.C. Format: Div, CHR, educ. Target aud: 12-34. Spec prog: Prep sports 6 hrs wkly. ♦Pete Bowers, gen mgr; Randy Carr, stn mgr; Barb Browne, dev dir.

Boyne City

WBCM(FM)— Apr 10, 1978: 93.5 mhz; 14.1 kw. 928 ft. TL: N45 10 44 W85 05 42. Stereo. 314 E. Front St., Traverse City 49684. Phone: (231) 947-7675. Fax: (231) 929-3988. E-mail: country@wtcmradio.com. Web Site: www.wtcmi.com. Licensee: Biederman Investments Inc. (acq 9-6-90; $250,000; 10-1-90). Network: ABC Information & Entertainment. Rep: Katz Radio. Cordon & Kelly. Format: Modern country. News staff: 4; News: 25 hrs wkly. Target aud: 25-54. Spec prog: Farm one hr wkly. ♦Ross Biederman, pres & gen mgr; Jack O'Malley, stn mgr & progmg dir; Joel Frank, news dir.

Bridgeport

WNEM(AM)— Nov 26, 1956: 1250 khz; 5 kw-D, 1.1 kw-N, DA-2. TL: N43 20 31 W83 53 57. Box 531, Saginaw 48606. Secondary address: 107 N. Franklin St., Saginaw 48607. Phone: (989) 755-8191. Fax: (989) 758-2110. E-mail: wnem@wnem.com. Web Site: www.wnem.com. Licensee: Meredith Corp. Group owner: Meredith Broadcasting Group, Meredith Corp. (acq 5-18-2004; $1.1 million). Format: Local news and info. ♦Kevin O'Brien, pres; Al Blinke, VP & gen mgr.

Bridgman

WYTZ(FM)— March 1993: 97.5 mhz; 3.8 kw. 413 ft. TL: N41 59 19 W86 31 46. Stereo. 580 E. Napier, Benton Harbor 48022. Phone: (269) 925-1111. Fax: (269) 925-1011. E-mail: robb@975country.com. Web Site: www.975country.com. Licensee: WSJM Inc. Group owner: The Mid-West Family Broadcasting Group (acq 1996; grpsl). Rep: Christal. Shaw Pittman. Format: Country. News staff: 5. Target aud: 25-54. ♦Joe Daguanno, VP & chief of engrg; Gayle Olson, gen mgr; Jim Gifford, opns dir; Bob Bucholtz, gen sls mgr; Sandie Lieberg, prom dir; Robb Rose, progmg dir.

Bronson

***WCVM(FM)**— 1998: 94.7 mhz; 4 kw. 403 ft. TL: N41 44 32 W85 14 34. 6200 E. State Rd. 120, Howe, IN 46746. Phone: (260) 562-3276. E-mail: wqko@wqko.com. Web Site: www.wqko.com. Licensee: CSN International. (group owner; acq 12-1-98; $80,000). Format: Cutting edge Christian music. ♦Banner Kidd, gen mgr.

Brooklyn

WKHM-FM— January 1994: 105.3 mhz; 2.2 kw. 377 ft. TL: N42 06 29 W84 22 46. 1700 Glenshire Dr., Jackson 49201. Phone: (517) 787-9546. Fax: (517) 787-7517. E-mail: bgoldsen@k1053.com. Web Site: www.k1053.com. Licensee: Jackson Radio Works Inc. (group owner; (acq 12-8-97; grpsl). Michigan. Shaw Pittman. Format: Adult contemp. News staff: 2. Target aud: 18-49. ♦Bruce I. Goldsen, pres & gen mgr; Sue Goldsen, VP; Jamie McKibbin, opns mgr & progmg dir; Michael Bradford, chief of engrg.

Michigan

Buchanan

WSMK(FM)— 1991: 99.1 mhz; 3 kw. 328 ft. TL: N41 52 51 W86 18 13. 925 N. 5th St., Niles 49120. Phone: (269) 683-4343. Fax: (269) 683-7759. E-mail: sales@wsmkradio.com. Web Site: www.wsmkradio.com. Licensee: Marion R. Williams. Format: Rhythmic CHR. Target aud: 18-34; females. ♦ Marion R. Williams, gen mgr.

Cadillac

WATT(AM)— September 1945: 1240 khz; 1 kw-U. TL: N44 13 27 W85 24 06. Box 520 49601. Secondary address: 7825 S. Mackinaw Trail 49601-0520. Phone: (231) 775-1263. Fax: (231) 779-2844. Web Site: www.watt1240.com. Licensee: MacDonald Garber Broadcasting Inc. (group owner; acq 11-17-98; grpsl). Network: Westwood One. Rep: McGavren Guild. McGavren Guild. Format: News/talk. Target aud: General. ♦ Phil Orth, gen mgr.

WCKC(FM)— Sept 15, 1985: 107.1 mhz; 2.75 kw. 482 ft. TL: N44 10 16 W85 20 13. Stereo. 1356 Mackinaw Ave., Cheboygan 49721. Phone: (231) 627-2341. Fax: (231) 627-7000. Web Site: www.classicrockthebear.com. Licensee: Northern Star Broadcasting L.L.C. (group owner; acq 9-10-98; grpsl). Format: Classic rock. Target aud: 25-54. ♦ Palmer Pyle, pres; Chris Monk, VP & gen mgr.

WJZQ(FM)— Oct 15, 1961: 92.9 mhz; 100 kw. Ant 912 ft. TL: N44 35 41 W85 11 53. Stereo. 314 E. Front St., Traverse City 49684. Phone: (231) 947-7675. Fax: (231) 929-3988. E-mail: wjzq@929thebreeze.com. Web Site: www.929thebreeze.com. Licensee: WKJF Radio Inc. Group owner: Midwestern Broadcasting Co. (acq 10-29-2001; with co-located AM). Format: Smooth jazz. News staff: one; News: 2 hrs wkly. Target aud: 35-64; affluent adults. ♦ John Dew, gen mgr; Steve Hibbard, opns mgr; Joel Franck, news dir; Eric Send, chief of engrg.

WLJW(AM)— Mar 15, 2004: 1370 khz; 5 kw-D, 1 kw-N, DA-N. TL: N44 13 54 W85 24 45. Stereo. Box 1400, Traverse City 49685. Fax: (231) 946-3959. E-mail: info@wljn.com. Web Site: www.wljn.com. Licensee: Good News Media Inc. (group owner; acq 3-5-2004; $85,001). Network: Network: Moody, Salem Radio Network. Rep: Katz Radio. Southmayd & Miller. Format: Christian talk, relg. Target aud: General. ♦ Brian Harcey, pres & gen mgr; Doug Knorr, pres; Bob Olsen, VP; Pete Lathrop, progmg dir.

***WOLW(FM)**— May 26, 1988: 91.1 mhz; 50 kw horiz, 28 kw vert. 700 ft. TL: N44 16 33 W85 42 49. Stereo. Box 695, Gaylord 49734-0695. Secondary address: 1511 M-32 E., Gaylord 49735. Phone: (800) 545-8867. Fax: (989) 732-8171. E-mail: ncr@ncradio.org. Web Site: www.ncradio.org. Licensee: Northern Christian Radio Inc. (group owner). Network: Moody. Southmayd & Miller. Format: Relg. News: 10 hrs wkly. Target aud: 35-54. ♦ George A. Lake Jr., CEO, gen mgr & chief of engrg; Joe Sereno, chmn.

Caro

WIDL(FM)— Listing follows WKYO(AM).

WKYO(AM)— May 19, 1962: 1360 khz; 1 kw-U, DA-2. TL: N43 27 32 W83 23 39. WKYO-WIDL Radio, 1521 W. Caro Rd. 48723-9260. Phone: (989) 672-1360. Fax: (989) 673-0256. Licensee: Edwards Communications L.C. (group owner; (acq 2-25-98; with co-located FM). Network: ABC Information & Entertainment. Format: Country. Spec prog: Farm 18 hrs wkly. ♦ Tom Devitt, gen mgr.

WIDL(FM)— Co-owned with WKYO(AM). Oct 16, 1974: 92.1 mhz; 6 kw. 318 ft. TL: N43 28 51 W83 20 31. Stereo. Format: Hot adult contemp.

Carrollton

WXQL(FM)— Licensed to Carrollton. See Saginaw

Cassopolis

WGTO(AM)— August 1988: 910 khz; 1 kw-D, 35 w-N, DA-1. TL: N41 57 14 W86 00 59. Stereo. 58176 O'Keefe Ave. 49031. Phone: (574) 258-8470. Web Site: www.wgtoradio.com. Licensee: Larry Langford Jr. Lauren A. Colby. Format: Golden oldies. Target aud: 25-49; middle class Black adults. Spec prog: Blues 4 hrs, gospel 10 hrs wkly. ♦ Larry Langford, pres & gen mgr.

Charlevoix

WCZW(FM)— Jan 31, 2003: 107.9 mhz; 5 kw. Ant 164 ft. TL: N45 20 00 W85 14 47. Radio Centre, 300 E. Front St., Suite 450, Traverse City 49684. Phone: (231) 946-6211. Fax: (231) 946-1914. Web Site: www.wccwi.com. Licensee: WCCW Radio Inc. Group owner: Midwestern Broadcasting Co. Network: ABC. Rep: Katz Radio. Format: Oldies. Target aud: 35 plus; baby boomers. ♦ Ross Brederman, pres; Hal Payne, gen mgr & sls dir; Brian Hale, opns mgr; Dave Gauthier, mus dir; Anne Mac, news dir; Jim Sofonia, chief of engrg.

WKHQ-FM— May 16, 1980: 105.9 mhz; 100 kw. Ant 892 ft. TL: N45 10 49 W85 05 50. Stereo. Box 286, Petoskey 49770. Secondary address: 2095 U.S. 131 S., Petoskey 49770. Phone: (231) 347-8713. Fax: (231) 347-8782. Web Site: www.106khq.com. Licensee: MacDonald Garber Broadcasting Co. (group owner; acq 11-17-98; grpsl). Network: ABC. Rep: McGavren Guild. Koteen & Naftalin. Format: Top 40. News staff: one. Target aud: 18-34. ♦ Phil Orth, gen mgr; Tom Clemens, gen sls mgr; Mark Elliott, progmg dir; Lisa Knight, news dir; Brian Brachel, engrg dir & chief of engrg.

WMKT(AM)— Co-owned with WKHQ-FM. July 20, 1974: 1270 khz; 5 kw-U, DA-N. TL: N45 16 22 W85 15 08. Format: News/talk. News staff: one. Target aud: 35 plus; listeners with spendable income. ♦ Eric Michaels, progmg dir; Lisa Knight, news dir.

***WTCK(FM)**— Not on air, target date: unknown: 90.9 mhz; 6 kw vert. Ant 43 ft. TL: N45 19 57 W85 13 17. Broadcasting for the Challenged Inc., 188 S. Bellevue, Suite 222, Memphis, TN 38104. Phone: (901) 375-9324. Fax: (901) 375-4612. Licensee: Broadcasting for the Challenged Inc.

Charlotte

WLCM(AM)— Aug 25, 1956: 1390 khz; 5 kw, DA-1. TL: N42 34 02 W84 51 58. Stereo. Box 338, 1613 W. Lawrence 48813. Phone: (517) 543-8200. Fax: (517) 543-7779. E-mail: wlcm@cablespeed.com. Licensee: Christian Broadcasting System Ltd. (group owner; acq 1-5-93; assumption of land contract;. FTR: 1-25-93). Format: Relg; Christian progmg. News: 2 hrs wkly. Target aud: 25-55; general. Spec prog: Gospel 3 hrs wkly. ♦ Jon R. Yinger, CEO & pres; Evelyn Shaw, VP; Jeff Frank, gen mgr, stn mgr & opns dir; Carol Smith, gen sls mgr & mus dir.

WQTX(FM)— Dec 29, 1965: 92.7 mhz; 1.5 kw. Ant 466 ft. TL: N42 38 31 W84 47 55. Stereo. 2495 N. Cedar, Suite 106, Holt 48842. Phone: (517) 699-0111. Fax: (517) 699-1880. E-mail: djohnson@mmrglansing.com. Web Site: www.ticketradio.net. Licensee: Rubber City Radio Group. Group owner: Rubber City Radio Group Inc. (acq 2-15-01; $600,000). Baraff, Koerner & Olender. Format: Sports talk. News: 3 hrs wkly. Target aud: 18-54; men/sports. ♦ Dave Johnson, pres & gen mgr; Joe Toranto, prom mgr; Paul Cashin, opns dir & progmg mgr.

Cheboygan

WCBY(AM)— Oct 28, 1954: 1240 khz; 1 kw-U. TL: N45 39 38 W84 29 26. 1356 Mackinaw Ave. 49721. Phone: (231) 627-2341. Fax: (231) 627-7000. Licensee: Northern Star Broadcasting L.L.C. (group owner; (acq 9-10-98; grpsl). Network: ABC Information & Entertainment. Rep: Michigan. Format: Nostalgia, big band. Target aud: 35-64. ♦ Palmer Pyle, pres; Chris Monk, gen mgr & gen sls mgr; Mike Grisdale, progmg dir & news dir.

WGFM(FM)— Co-owned with WCBY(AM). Aug 15, 1968: 105.1 mhz; 100 kw. 610 ft. TL: N45 26 50 W84 28 30. Stereo. Web Site: www.classicrockthebear.com. Format: Classic rock. ♦ Chris Monk, VP.

Clare

WCFX(FM)— June 28, 1967: 95.3 mhz; 6 kw. 328 ft. TL: N43 44 41 W84 48 09. Stereo. 5847 Venture Way, Mount Pleasant 48858. Phone: (989) 772-4173. Fax: (989) 773-1236. E-mail: kent@wcfx.com. Web Site: www.wcfx.com. Licensee: Grenax Broadcasting LLC (acq 2-2-04). Format: Adult/CHR. Target aud: 18-49. Spec prog: Relg one hr, oldies 3 hrs wkly. ♦ Greg Dinetz, pres; Bob Peters, gen mgr; Kent Bergstrom, opns mgr & progmg dir; Rob Ryan, prom dir.

Coldwater

WNWN-FM— Licensed to Coldwater. See Kalamazoo

Charlevoix (cont.)

WTVB(AM)— Aug 7, 1949: 1590 khz; 5 kw-D, 1 kw-N, DA-N. TL: N41 54 34 W85 00 21. 182 N. Angola Rd. 49036. Phone: (517) 279-1590. Fax: (517) 279-4695. E-mail: wtvb@wtvbam.com. Licensee: Midwest Communications Inc. (group owner; acq 6-1-95; grpsl). Network: ABC Information & Entertainment. Rep: Christal. Format: Oldies, full service. News staff: 2; News: 10 hrs wkly. Spec prog: Farm 6 hrs wkly. ♦ D.E. Wright, pres; Peter Tanz, gen mgr; Ken Delaney, stn mgr.

Coleman

***WPRJ(FM)**— Dec 7, 1992: 101.7 mhz; 4.6 kw. 374 ft. TL: N43 48 41 W84 27 57. Stereo. Box 236, 227 Jackson St. 48618. Phone: (989) 465-9775. Fax: (989) 465-1060. E-mail: wprj@wprj.org. Web Site: www.wprj.org. Licensee: Come Together Ministries Inc. (acq 11-9-89; $8,000; 11-27-89). Reddy, Begley & McCormick. Format: Full-time Christian adult contemp, CHR. Target aud: 18 plus; youth, young singles & married. ♦ Gary H. Bugh, pres & gen mgr; Connie Wieber, stn mgr & opns mgr.

Crystal Falls

WOBE(FM)— June 2000: 100.7 mhz; 100 kw. Ant 653 ft. TL: N45 49 15 W88 02 38. Stereo. 212 W. J St., Iron Mountain 49801. Phone: (906) 774-5731. Fax: (906) 774-4542. E-mail: trisha@frogcountry.com. Licensee: Results Broadcasting of Iron Mountain Inc. Group owner: Results Broadcasting (acq 11-1-2001; $800,000). Network: ABC. Format: Classic hits. News staff: one. Target aud: 25-65. ♦ Bruce Grassman, pres; Trisha Peterson, VP & gen mgr; Keith Huotari, progmg dir.

Dearborn

WDTW(AM)— Dec 29, 1946: 1310 khz; 5 kw-U, DA-2. TL: N42 15 50 W83 15 14. 27675 Halsted, Farmington Hills 48331. Phone: (248) 324-5800. Fax: (248) 848-0313. E-mail: elliotlerner@clearchannel.com. Web Site: www.1310wdtw.com. Licensee: AMFM Radio Licenses L.L.C. Group owner: Clear Channel Communications Inc. (acq 8-30-2000; grpsl). Network: Westwood One. Format: Talk, sports. News staff: 4; News: 27 hrs wkly. Target aud: 25-54; men 25-54. ♦ Dave Pugh, gen mgr; Dom Theodore, opns mgr.

***WHFR(FM)**— Dec 20, 1985: 89.3 mhz; 270 w. 98 ft. TL: N42 19 26 W83 14 09. Stereo. Henry Ford Community College, 5101 Evergreen Rd. 48128. Phone: (313) 845-9676. Phone: (313) 845-9842. Fax: (313) 317-4034. E-mail: whfr@hfcc.edu. Web Site: www.whfr.fm. Licensee: Henry Ford Community College. Network: PRI. Format: Var, alternative. News: one hr wkly. Target aud: General. Spec prog: Jazz 16 hrs, world mus 2 hrs, big band 5 hrs, blues 6 hrs wkly. ♦ Susan McGraw, gen mgr; Lara Hrycaj, opns mgr; Joseph Hallisey, dev dir.

WNIC(FM)— Licensed to Dearborn. See Detroit

Dearborn Heights

WNZK(AM)— Licensed to Dearborn Heights. See Detroit

Detroit

WCAR(AM)— See Livonia

***WDET-FM**— Feb 13, 1949: 101.9 mhz; 48 kw. Ant 554 ft. TL: N42 21 06 W83 03 48. Stereo. 4600 Cass Ave. 48201. Phone: (313) 577-4146. Fax: (313) 577-1300. E-mail: wdetfm@wdetfm.org. Web Site: www.wdetfm.org. Licensee: Wayne State University. (acq 5-52). Network: NPR. Paul, Weiss, Rifkind, Wharton & Garrison. Format: News, jazz, adult alternative acoustic. News staff: 6; News: 44 hrs wkly. Target aud: 35-52; sophisticated, varied mus tastes & news consumers. Spec prog: Folk 3 hrs, bluegrass 3 hrs, blues 10 hrs, reggae 2 hrs wkly. ♦ Caryn Mathes, gen mgr; Ken Munson, dev dir; Kevin Plotrowski, prom dir & prom mgr; Judy C. Adams, progmg dir; Martin Bandyke, mus dir; Malloy Farley, chief of engrg.

WDFN(AM)— Dec 17, 1939: 1130 khz; 50 kw-D, 10 kw-N, DA-2. TL: N42 06 39 W83 11 52. 27675 Halsted Rd., Farmington 48331. Phone: (248) 324-5800. Fax: (248) 848-0313. Web Site: www.wdfn.com. Licensee: AMFM Radio Licenses L.L.C. Group owner: Clear Channel Communications Inc. (acq 8-30-2000; grpsl). Network: Westwood One. Format: Sports talk. Target aud: 25-54. ♦ Dave Pugh, gen mgr; Nancy Wede, gen sls mgr.

Developers & Brokers of Radio Properties
contact American Media Services
at our suite:
Philadelphia Marriott Downtown
215-625-2900
843-972-2200
americanmediaservices.com
Charleston, SC
Dallas, TX · Chicago, Il · Austin, TX
American Media Services, LLC

WDTW-FM—Co-owned with WDFN(AM). Oct 16, 1960: 106.7 mhz; 61 kw. Ant 508 ft. TL: N42 19 55 W83 02 42. Fax: (313) 259-9817. Web Site: www.1067thedrive.com. Format: Rockin hits of the 70s, 80s, 90s.

WDMK(FM)— May 26, 1960: 105.9 mhz; 20 kw. 725 ft. TL: N42 28 16 W83 12 03. Stereo. 3250 Franklin St. 48207. Phone: (313) 259-2000. Fax: (313) 259-7011. E-mail: kyoung@radio-one.com. Web Site: www.kissdetroit.com. Licensee: Radio One of Detroit LLC. Group owner: Radio One Inc. (acq 11-8-2001; grpsl). Rep: Allied Radio Partners. Format: Hip hop, Rhythm and Blues. Target aud: 25-49. Spec prog: Sports 2 hrs, entertainment guide 2 hrs wkly. ♦Alfred Liggins, pres; Carol Lawrence-Dobrusin, gen mgr; Benita Gray, mus dir.

WDRQ(FM)— July 9, 1947: 93.1 mhz; 26.5 kw. 669 ft. TL: N42 28 16 W83 12 03. Stereo. Fisher Building, Suite 800, 311 West Grand Blvd. 48202-9816. Phone: (313) 871-9300. Phone: (313) 298-9393. Fax: (313) 872-0190. Web Site: www.drgradio.com. Licensee: ABC Radio Detroit LLC. Group owner: ABC Inc. (acq 8-11-97). Rep: ABC Radio Sales. Target aud: 25-54. ♦Steve Kosbau, pres & gen mgr; Alex Tear, progmg dir; Hal Buttermore, chief of engrg.

WDTK(AM)— 1926: 1400 khz; 1 kw-U. TL: N42 24 22 W83 06 44. 645 Griswold, Suite 2050 48226. Phone: (313) 965-4500. Fax: (313) 965-4608. E-mail: zaron@wdtkam.com. Web Site: www.wdtkam.com. Licensee: Pennsylvania Media Associates Inc. Group owner: Salem Communications Corp. (acq 9-30-2004; $4.75 million). Format: News/talk. ♦Christian D. MacCourtney, gen mgr; Zaron Frumin, opns mgr.

WDTW(AM)—See Dearborn

WDVD(FM)—Listing follows WJR(AM).

WGPR(FM)— 1961: 107.5 mhz; 50 kw. Ant 405 ft. TL: N42 21 28 W83 03 55. Stereo. 3146 Jefferson E. 48207. Phone: (313) 259-8862. Fax: (313) 259-6662. E-mail: wgprradioincs@aol.com. Web Site: www.wgprdetroit.com. Licensee: WGPR Inc. (acq 7-64). Network: American Urban. Hogan & Hartson. Format: "New AC Jazz". Target aud: 18-49. ♦George Mathews, CEO, pres & gen mgr; James O. Dogan, VP & stn mgr; Stefanie Bradley, gen sls mgr; Rosetta Hines, progmg dir. Co-owned TV: WGPR-TV affil

WJLB(FM)— 1926: 97.9 mhz; 50 kw. 489 ft. TL: N42 24 22 W83 06 44. Stereo. 645 Griswold, Suite 633 48226. Phone: (313) 965-2000. Fax: (313) 965-3965. E-mail: deansnyder@clearchannel.com. Web Site: www.fm98wjlb.com. Licensee: AMFM Radio Licenses L.L.C. Group owner: Clear Channel Communications Inc. (acq 8-30-00; grpsl). Format: Urban contemp. Target aud: 18-49; Black adults. ♦Dave Pugh, gen mgr; Dean Snyder, gen sls mgr; K. J. Holiday, progmg dir; Kris Kelley, mus dir; Charles Pugh, news dir; Thomas Christie, engrg mgr & chief of engrg.

WJR(AM)— May 4, 1922: 760 khz; 50 kw-U. TL: N42 10 07 W83 13 00. 3011 W. Grand Blvd., 760 Fisher Bldg., Suite 800 48202. Phone: (313) 875-4440. Fax: (313) 875-9022. Web Site: www.wjr.net. Licensee: ABC Radio Detroit LLC. Group owner: ABC Inc. (acq 1986). Network: ABC Information & Entertainment. Rep: ABC Radio Sales. Format: News. Target aud: 12 plus. ♦Mike Fezzey, pres & gen mgr; John Gallagher, sls dir; Tom O'Brien, progmg dir; Dick Haefner, news dir; Ed Buterbaugh, chief of engrg.

WDVD(FM)—Co-owned with WJR(AM). June 1, 1948: 96.3 mhz; 20 kw. 787 ft. TL: N42 27 13 W83 09 50. Stereo. Phone: (313) 871-3030. Fax: (313) 875-9636. Web Site: www.planet963.com. Format: AC/modern AC.

WKQI(FM)— Feb 12, 1949: 95.5 mhz; 100 kw. 437 ft. TL: N42 28 22 W83 11 59. Stereo. 27675 Halsted, Farmington Hill 48331. Phone: (248) 324-5800. Fax: (248) 848-0272. E-mail: davepugh@clearchannel.com. Web Site: www.channel955.com. Licensee: AMFM Radio Licenses L.L.C. Group owner: Clear Channel Communications Inc. (acq 8-30-00; grpsl). Rep: Christal. Latham & Watkins. Format: Top 40. Target aud: 18-49; active, upscale women. ♦Dave Pugh, VP & gen mgr; Beau Daniels, prom dir & mus dir; Dom Theodore, progmg dir.

WKRK-FM—Listing follows WWJ(AM).

WLQV(AM)— 1925: 1500 khz; 50 kw-D, 5 kw-N, DA-2. TL: N42 13 51 W83 11 55. Stereo. 29200 Vassar Dr., Suite 150, Livonia 48152. Phone: (248) 477-4600. Fax: (248) 477-6911. E-mail: victory1500@wlqv.net. Licensee: Christian Broadcasting System Ltd. (group owner; acq 9-1-93; $2.65 million;. FTR: 9-27-93). Network: USA. Format: Relg, Christian talk, info. Target aud: 25-65 plus; middle class. Spec prog: Black 10 hrs wkly. ♦Jon R. Yinger, CEO, pres & gen mgr; Ralph Van Luven, VP; Mark Ennis, stn mgr.

WMGC-FM— Mar 6, 1960: 105.1 mhz; 20 kw. 784 ft. TL: N42 28 16 W83 12 03. Stereo. One Radio Plaza 48220. Phone: (248) 414-5600. Fax: (248) 542-7700. Web Site: www.detroitmagic.com. Licensee: Greater Boston Radio Inc. Group owner: Greater Media Inc. (acq 12-5-96). Rep: CMBS. Format: Adult contemp. Target aud: General; professional, upscale, educated. ♦Peter Smyth, pres; Tom Bender, gen mgr.

WMUZ(FM)— Nov 11, 1958: 103.5 mhz; 50 kw. 500 ft. TL: N42 22 40 W83 14 32. 12300 Radio Pl. 48228. Phone: (313) 272-3434. E-mail: wmuzinfo@crawfordbroadcasting.com. Web Site: www.crawfordbroadcasting.com. Licensee: WMUZ Radio Inc. Group owner: Crawford Broadcasting Co. Format: Contemporary Christian Music. ♦Donald B. Crawford, pres; Frank Franciosi, gen mgr.

WMXD(FM)— Dec 8, 1964: 92.3 mhz; 45 kw. 479 ft. TL: N42 19 55 W83 02 42. Stereo. 645 Griswold, Suite 633 48226. Phone: (313) 965-2000. Fax: (313) 965-3965. E-mail: wxmd@wxmd923.com. Web Site: www.wmxd923.com. Licensee: AMFM Radio Licenses L.L.C. Group owner: Clear Channel Communications Inc. (acq 8-30-00; grpsl). Format: Urban adult contemp. ♦Dave Pugh, gen mgr; Anthony Keith, gen sls mgr; Jamillah Muhammad, progmg dir; Sheila Little, mus dir; Thomas Christie, engrg mgr & chief of engrg.

WNIC(FM)—(Dearborn). December 1946: 100.3 mhz; 32 kw. 600 ft. TL: N42 23 22 W83 08 53. Stereo. 27675 Halstead, Farmington Hills 48331. Phone: (248) 324-5800. Fax: (248) 848-0396. Web Site: www.wnic.com. Licensee: AMFM Radio Licenses L.L.C. Group owner: Clear Channel Communications Inc. (acq 8-30-00; grpsl). Latham & Watkins. Format: Easy lstng. News staff: one; News: 2 hrs wkly. Target aud: 25-54; female. ♦Dave Pugh, gen mgr.

WNZK(AM)—(Dearborn Heights). Oct 12, 1985: 690 khz-D; 2.5 kw-U, DA-2. TL: N42 05 55 W83 19 48. (Note: Stn operates on 680 khz-N). 21700 Northwestern Hwy., Suite 1190, Southfield 48075. Phone: (248) 557-3500. Fax: (248) 557-2950. E-mail: sima@birach.com. Web Site: www.birach.com/wnzk.html. Licensee: Birach Broadcasting Corp. (acq 1984). Format: Talk, news, ethnic. Target aud: General. ♦Sima Birach, gen mgr; Jim Henderson, opns mgr.

WOMC(FM)— Mar 5, 1948: 104.3 mhz; 190 kw. 361 ft. TL: N42 28 25 W83 06 56. Stereo. 2201 Woodward Heights Blvd., Ferndale 48220. Phone: (248) 546-9600. Fax: (248) 546-5446. E-mail: kpmurphy@cbs.com. Web Site: www.womc.com. Licensee: Infinity Broadcasting of Michigan. Group owner: Infinity Broadcasting Corp. (acq 4-28-88). Network: Westwood One. Format: Oldies. News staff: one; News: 4 hrs wkly. Target aud: 25-54; upscale. ♦Joel Hollander, pres; Jacques Tortoroli, CFO; Scott Herman, exec VP; Stephen Schram, sr VP; Kevin Murphy, gen mgr; Doug Johnston, gen sls mgr; Steve Allan, progmg dir.

***WRCJ-FM**— Feb 5, 1948: 90.9 mhz; 42 kw horiz, 38 kw vert. 437 ft. TL: N42 22 25 W83 06 50. Stereo. 9345 Lawton Ave. 48206. Phone: (313) 596-3507. Fax: (313) 596-3517. Web Site: wdtr.com. Licensee: Board of Education, City of Detroit. Format: Educ, var. Target aud: General; intergenerational-urban/suburban. Spec prog: Contemp hit 10 hrs, black 4 hrs, jazz 4 hrs, world mus 4 hrs, Gospel 4 hrs, oldies 3 hrs, Sp 2 hrs, techno-house 2 hrs,rock billy 2 hrs, blues one hr wkly. ♦Kathy Young-Welch, gen mgr, opns dir & gen sls mgr; Donald Walker, mktg dir & progmg dir; Aaron Alfano, prom mgr; Stephanie Davis, mus dir, news dir & pub affrs dir; Steve Johnson, chief of engrg.

WRIF(FM)— Jan 1, 1948: 101.1 mhz; 27.2 kw. 879 ft. TL: N42 28 15 W83 15 00. Stereo. One Radio Plaza St. 48220-2140. Phone: (248) 547-0101. Fax: (248) 542-8800. Web Site: wrif.com. Licensee: Greater Media Inc. (group owner; acq 12-15-87). Rep: Katz Radio. Format: Active rock. Target aud: 18-49; men. ♦Tom Bender, gen mgr.

WVMV(FM)— 1961: 98.7 mhz; 50 kw. 462 ft. TL: N42 23 42 W83 08 58. Stereo. 31555 W. Fourteen Mile Rd., Suite 102, Farmington Hills 48334. Phone: (248) 855-5100. Fax: (248) 855-1302. Web Site: www.wvmv.com. Licensee: Infinity Broadcasting East Inc. Group owner: Infinity Broadcasting Corp. (acq 12-89; grpsl; FTR: 12-11-89). Format: Smooth Jazz. ♦Debbie Kenyon, VP & gen mgr; Sheryl Coyne, gen sls mgr; Tom Sleeker, opns mgr & progmg dir.

WWJ(AM)— Aug 20, 1920: 950 khz; 5 kw-U, DA-N. TL: N42 26 47 W83 10 23. 26495 American Dr., Southfield 48034. Phone: (248) 455-7200. Fax: (248) 304-4970. Web Site: www.wwj.com. Licensee: Infinity Broadcasting East Inc. Group owner: Infinity Broadcasting Corp. (acq 3-9-89; FTR: 2-27-89). Network: CBS. Format: News. News staff: 32. Target aud: General. ♦Rich Homberg, VP & gen mgr; Tom O'Brien, stn mgr; Georgeann Herbert, opns mgr; Pete Towalski, gen sls mgr; Elizabeth Hollidge, natl sls mgr; Debbie Spatafora, prom mgr; Pam Woodley, progmg dir & news dir; Ralph Hunt, chief of engrg.

WKRK-FM—Co-owned with WWJ(AM). May 9, 1941: 97.1 mhz; 15 kw. 890 ft. TL: N42 28 59 W83 12 20. Stereo. 15600 W. 12 Mile Rd., Southfield 48076. Phone: (248) 423-7780. Fax: (248) 423-7725. Web Site: www.wwj.com. Format: FM talk. ♦Stephen Sinicropi, VP & gen mgr; Dan Zako, gen sls mgr; Melissa Ryzy, natl sls mgr; Terry Lieberman, progmg dir; Ken Sands, chief of engrg. Co-owned TV: WWJ-TV affil

WXYT(AM)— Oct 10, 1925: 1270 khz; 5 kw-U, DA-N. TL: N42 27 58 W83 15 00. 26495 American Dr., Southfield 48076. Phone: (248) 455-7350. Fax: (248) 455-7369. E-mail: wxyt@wxyt.com. Web Site: www.1270sports.com. Licensee: Infinity Broadcasting Corp. of Detroit. Group owner: Infinity Broadcasting Corp. (acq 11-13-98; grpsl). Network: Westwood One. Covington & Burling. Format: Sports talk. News staff: 3. Target aud: 25-54. ♦Rich Homberg, VP & gen mgr; Georgeann Herbert, opns mgr.

WYCD(FM)— May 4, 1960: 99.5 mhz; 21 kw horiz, 19 kw vert. 755 ft. TL: N42 28 16 W83 12 03. Stereo. 26555 Evergreen, Suite 675, Southfield 48076. Phone: (248) 799-0600. Fax: (248) 358-9216. E-mail: stephen.schram@infinitybroadcasting.com. Web Site: www.wycd.com. Licensee: Infinity Broadcasting Corp. of Michigan. Group owner: CBS Radio (acq 1-96; grpsl). Fisher, Wayland, Cooper, Leader & Zaragoza. Format: Country. Target aud: 12-34. ♦Steve Schram, gen mgr; Janet Jabionski, gen sls mgr & natl sls mgr.

Dewitt

WQHH(FM)— 1991: 96.5 mhz; 3 kw. 328 ft. TL: N42 51 06 W84 40 06. 1011 Northcrest Rd., Suite 4, Lansing 48906. Phone: (517) 484-9600. Fax: (517) 484-9699. E-mail: wqhh-fm@mindspring.com. Licensee: Mid Michigan FM Inc. Rep: Allied Radio Partners. Format: Urban contemp. Target aud: 18-49. ♦Helena Dubose, pres, sr VP & opns dir.

Dimondale

WXLA(AM)— Sept 20, 1982: 1180 khz; 1 kw-D, DA. TL: N42 39 01 W84 34 49. 1011 Northcrest, Suite 4, Lansing 48906. Phone: (517) 484-9600. Fax: (517) 484-9699. E-mail: wghh-fm@comcast.net. Licensee: Mid Michigan FM Inc. Format: Adult contemp, urban contemp. Target aud: 25-54; mature audience. Spec prog: Gospel 5 hrs, jazz 3 hrs, relg 5 hrs wkly. ♦Helena Dubose, pres & gen mgr.

Dowagiac

WAUS(FM)—South Bend IN

WDOW-FM— January 1971: 92.1 mhz; 3.3 kw. Ant 299 ft. TL: N41 59 52 W86 03 14. Stereo. Box 150, 26914 Marcellus Hwy. 49047. Phone: (269) 782-5106. Fax: (269) 782-5107. E-mail: q92radio@yahoo.com. Web Site: www.pulsefm.com. Licensee: LeSea Broadcasting Corp. (acq 2-14-2005; $950,000. with co-located AM). Rep: Michigan.

Michigan

Keorner & Olender. Format: Contemp Christian. Target aud: 25-64. ♦Joe Urbanski, gen mgr, gen sls mgr, progmg dir & chief of engrg; Mike Bruneau, news dir & engrg dir.

WDOW(AM)— September 1960: 1440 khz; 1 kw-D, 89 w-N. TL: N41 59 35 W86 05 10. Format: Sports. News staff: one. Target aud: 25-49.

Eagle

*****WJOM(FM)**—Not on air, target date: unknown: 88.5 mhz; 4.5 kw vert. Ant 89 ft. TL: N42 47 04 W84 50 18. Michigan Community Radio, 3302 N. Van Dyke, Imlay City 48444. Phone: (810) 721-0891. Licensee: Michigan Community Radio. ♦Ed Czelada, pres.

East Jordan

*****WICV(FM)**— June 25, 1989: 100.9 mhz; 2.8 kw. 489 ft. TL: N45 10 40 W85 05 57. Stereo. Box 199, One Lyon St., Interlochen 49643. Phone: (231) 276-4400. Fax: (231) 276-4417. Licensee: Interlochen Center for the Arts (acq 5-23-90). Network: Network: NPR, PRI, ABC. Haley, Bader & Potts. Format: Class. Target aud: 35-65; upper income, arts-oriented, civic-minded professionals. ♦Thom Paulson, VP & gen mgr; Billie Thompson, opns mgr.

East Lansing

*****WDBM(FM)**— Feb 24, 1989: 88.9 mhz; 2 kw. 279 ft. TL: N42 42 20 W84 28 30. Stereo. G-4 Holden Hall, Michigan State Univ. Campus 48825-1206. Phone: (517) 353-4414. Fax: (517) 355-6552. Web Site: www.mpact89fm.org. Licensee: Board of Trustees of Michigan State University. Format: Alternative rock. News: 10 hrs wkly. Target aud: 18-34; students of MSU. Spec prog: Blues 4 hrs, jazz 5 hrs, heavy metal 4 hrs, progsv country 4 hrs, Christian rock 4 hrs wkly. ♦Gary Reed, gen mgr.

WFMK(FM)— July 16, 1959: 99.1 mhz; 28 kw. 600 ft. TL: N42 40 33 W84 30 00. Stereo. Secondary address: 3420 Pine Tree Rd., Lansing 48911. Phone: (517) 394-3999. Fax: (517) 394-3391. E-mail: wfmk@acd.net. Web Site: www.99wfmk.com. Licensee: Citadel Broadcasting Co. Group owner: Citadel Broadcasting Corp. (acq 2000; grpsl). Rep: McGavren Guild. Leventhal, Senter & Lerman. Format: Adult contemp. News staff: one; News: 2 hrs wkly. Target aud: 25-54. ♦Rob Striker, gen mgr; Ray Marshall, opns mgr; Chris Reynolds, mus dir.

*****WKAR(AM)**— Aug 18, 1922: 870 khz; 10 kw-D, DA. TL: N42 42 19 W84 28 30. 283 Communication Arts Bldg., Michigan State Univ. 48824-1212. Phone: (517) 432-9527. Fax: (517) 353-7124. E-mail: mail@wkar.org. Web Site: www.wkar.org. Licensee: Board of Trustees of Michigan State University. Network: Network: NPR, PRI. Schwartz, Woods & Miller. Format: News/talk. News staff: 5; News: 25 hrs wkly. Spec prog: Sp 3 hrs wkly. ♦Steven Meuche, gen mgr; Harold Prentice, opns mgr & mus dir; Jayne Marsh, dev dir & gen sls mgr; Diane Hutchens, prom dir; Valerie Lee, adv dir; Curt Gilleo, progmg dir & news dir; Gary Blievernicht, engrg dir & engrg mgr.

WKAR-FM— Oct 10, 1948: 90.5 mhz; 86 kw horiz, 57 kw vert. 895 ft. TL: N42 42 08 W84 24 51. Format: Class, news. Spec prog: Jazz 7 hrs wkly. ♦Harold Prentice, progmg dir. Co-owned TV: *WKAR-TV affil

WMMQ(FM)—Listing follows WVFN(AM).

WQTX(FM)—See Charlotte

WVFN(AM)— September 1964: 730 khz; 500 w-D, 17.5 w-N, DA-2. TL: N42 38 45 W84 33 39. 3420 Pine Tree Rd., Lansing 48911. Phone: (517) 394-7272. Fax: (517) 394-3391. Web Site: www.730amthefan.com. Licensee: Citadel Broadcasting Co. Group owner: Citadel Broadcasting Corp. (acq 2000; grpsl). Network: ESPN Radio. Rep: Christal. Leventhal, Senter & Leman. Format: All sports, talk. Target aud: 25-54. ♦Farid Suleman, CEO & chmn; Rod Krol, gen mgr; Ray Marshall, opns mgr; Brian Olson, sls dir; Jack Robbins, progmg dir; Robert Bowe, chief of engrg.

WMMQ(FM)—Co-owned with WVFN(AM). Nov 16, 1963: 94.9 mhz; 49 kw. 499 ft. TL: N42 38 44 W84 33 38. Stereo. 3200 Pine Tree Rd., Lansing 48911. Phone: (517) 393-1010. Fax: (517) 394-3391. E-mail: wmmq@voyager.net. Web Site: www.wmmq.com. Network: CNN Radio. Format: Classic rock and roll. News staff: one. Target aud: 25-54; baby boomers who grew up listening to the Beatles, the Who & the Stones. ♦Farid Suleman, chmn; Ray Marshall, opns dir; Keith Pellegrini, prom mgr; Mark Stevens, progmg dir; Deb Hart, news dir.

East Tawas

*****WZHN(FM)**—Not on air, target date: unknown: 91.3 mhz; 5.4 kw vert. Ant 328 ft. TL: N44 20 25 W83 37 18. Box 695, Gaylord 49734-0695. Phone: (989) 732-6274. Fax: (989) 732-8171. E-mail: ncr@ncradio.org. Web Site: www.ncradio.org. Licensee: Northern Christian Radio Inc. ♦George A. Lake Jr., gen mgr.

Elkton

*****WJCE(FM)**—Not on air, target date: unknown: 88.9 mhz; 50 kw. Ant 262 ft. TL: N43 16 25 W82 35 16. CSN International, 4002 N. 3300 E., Twin Falls, ID 83301. Phone: (208) 734-6633. Fax: (208) 736-1958. Web Site: www.csnradio.com. Licensee: CSN International. ♦Michael Kestler, pres.

Elmwood Township

*****WLJN(AM)**— Dec 23, 1982: 1400 khz; 640 w-U. TL: N44 46 36 W85 39 43. Box 1400, Traverse City 49685. Secondary address: 1101 Cass St., Traverse City 49684. Phone: (231) 946-1400. Fax: (231) 946-3959. E-mail: info@wljn.com. Web Site: www.wljn.com. Licensee: Good News Media Inc. (group owner). Format: Relg, contemp, talk. News: 4 hrs wkly. Target aud: General. ♦Doug Knorr, pres; Bob Olsen, VP; Brian Harcey, gen mgr.

Elsie

WOES(FM)—See Ovid-Elsie

Escanaba

WCHT(AM)— Dec 1, 1958: 600 khz; 1 kw-D, 191 w-N, DA-2. TL: N42 40 28 W87 08 41. 524 Ludington St., Suite 300 49829. Phone: (906) 789-0600. Fax: (906) 789-0600. E-mail: wglq@yahoo.com. Web Site: www.radioresultsnetwork.com. Licensee: Lakes Radio Inc. (group owner) Network: ABC Information & Entertainment. Rep: Christal. Format: News/talk. Target aud: 25-54. Spec prog: Farm one hr, forestry one hr wkly. ♦Rick Duerson, opns dir & opns mgr.

WGLQ(FM)— Co-owned with WCHT(AM). Sept 11, 1976: 97.1 mhz; 100 kw. 1,070 ft. TL: N46 08 04 W85 56 02. Stereo. Phone: (906) 789-9700. Fax: (906) 789-0600. E-mail: wglq@yahoo.com. Web Site: www.radioresultsnetwork.com. Format: Adult contemp.

WDBC(AM)— Sept 4, 1941: 680 khz; 10 kw-D, 1 kw-N, DA-2. TL: N45 45 53 W87 05 48. 604 Ludington St. 49829. Phone: (906) 786-6144. Fax: (906) 789-9959. E-mail: wdbcam@chartermi.net. Licensee: KMB Broadcasting Co. Inc. (acq 12-31-88). Network: CBS. Rep: Katz Radio. Format: Full service, nostalgia. News staff: one; News: 12 hrs wkly. Target aud: 25-54. Spec prog: Relg 4 hrs, children one hr wkly. ♦Betsy Cooke, pres; Alice Sabuco, pres; Kim Rabitoy, gen sls mgr; Barry Zieglar, news dir.

WYKX(FM)— Co-owned with WDBC(AM). Dec 22, 1977: 104.7 mhz; 100 kw. 351 ft. TL: N45 55 41 W87 16 00. (CP: Ant 1,000 ft. TL: N45 52 40 W87 28 00). Stereo. Phone: (906) 786-3800. Web Site: kxcountry.net. Network: Network: Jones Radio Networks, AP Radio. Format: Country. News staff: one; News: 4 hrs wkly. Target aud: General.

Essexville

WMJO(FM)— Jan 1, 1992: 97.3 mhz; 3 kw. 328 ft. TL: N43 36 48 W83 45 51. Box 1776, Saginaw 48605. Secondary address: 2000 Whittier St., Saginaw 48601. Phone: (989) 752-8161. Fax: (989) 752-8102. E-mail: rickwalker@98fmxcq.com. Web Site: www.973jofm.com. Licensee: The MacDonald Broadcasting Co. Group owner: MacDonald Broadcasting Co. (acq 12-20-2001; grpsl). Interep. Fisher, Wayland, Cooper, Leader & Zaragoza. Format: Hits of the 80s, 90s & beyond. News staff: one; News: 3 hrs wkly. Target aud: 18-54; adults with a classic rock life style. Spec prog: Virtual shopping 8 hrs wkly. ♦Kenneth H. MacDonald Jr., pres & stn mgr; Rick Walker, opns mgr, progmg dir & mus dir.

Fenton

WCXI(AM)— Nov 15, 1985: 1160 khz; 1 kw-U, DA-1. TL: N42 38 30 W83 43 50. 15130 North Rd. 48430. Phone: (810) 750-1911. Phone: (248) 557-3500. Fax: (248) 557-2950. Fax: (810) 750-9028. E-mail: sima@birach.com. Web Site: www.wnzk.com. Licensee: Birach Broadcasting Corp. (group owner; acq 9-13-99; $708,000). Network: American Urban. Format: Traditional country. Target aud: General; average age 35, primarily female, average income $35,000. ♦Sima Birach, CEO; Brenda Charette, opns mgr; John Morris, progmg dir & mus dir.

Flint

*****WAKL(FM)**— September 1997: 88.9 mhz; 380 w. Ant 263 ft. TL: N42 58 49 W83 34 40. Stereo. 5700 W. Oaks Blvd., Rocklin, CA 95765. Phone: (916) 251-1600. Fax: (916) 251-1650. E-mail: klove@klove.com. Web Site: www.klove.com. Licensee: Educational Media Foundation. Group owner: EMF Broadcasting (acq 11-19-01; $450,000). Network: K-Love. Shaw Pittman. Format: Contemp Christian. News staff: 3. Target aud: 25-44; female-Judeo Christian. ♦Richard Jenkins, pres; Mike Novak, VP & progmg dir; Keith Whipple, dev dir; Eric Allen, natl sls mgr; Paul Goldsmith, rgnl sls mgr; Chris Joyce, prom dir.

WCRZ(FM)—Listing follows WFNT(AM).

WDZZ-FM— Sept 29, 1979: 92.7 mhz; 3 kw. Ant 260 ft. TL: N43 00 57 W83 41 24. Stereo. 6317 Taylor Dr. 48507. Phone: (810) 238-7300. Fax: (810) 743-2500. E-mail: jeff.wade@cumulus.com. Web Site: www.wdzz.com. Licensee: Cumulus Licensing Corp. Group owner: Cumulus Media Inc. (acq 3-15-00; grpsl). Format: Urban adult. Target aud: Adults. Spec prog: Gospel 8 hrs, teen talk one hr, concerned pastors one hr wkly. ♦Mike Chire, stn mgr; Jeff Wade, opns mgr & progmg dir.

WFBE(FM)— Oct 5, 1953: 95.1 mhz; 50 kw. 243 ft. TL: N43 01 13 W83 40 40. Stereo. Box 88, Swartz Creek 48473. Secondary address: 4511 Miller Rd. 48507. Phone: (810) 720-9510. Fax: (810) 720-9513. E-mail: james.glendening@citcomm.com. Web Site: www.b95.com. Licensee: Citadel Broadcasting Co. Group owner: Citadel Broadcasting Corp. (acq 4-26-01; grpsl). Network: PRI. Format: Country. News: 3 hrs wkly. Target aud: General; country mus listeners. ♦Farid Suleman, CEO; Judy Ellis, CFO; Scott Meier, gen mgr; Jim Glendening, stn mgr; Rusty Thomas, news dir.

WFDF(AM)— May 25, 1922: 910 khz; 5 kw-D, 1 kw-N, DA-2. TL: N42 58 22 W83 37 30. (CP: COL Farmington Hills. 50 kw-D, 1 kw-N, DA-2. TL: N42 03 57 W83 23 39). 6317 Taylor Dr. 48507. Phone: (810) 695-9333. Web Site: radio.disney.go.com/mystation/flint. Licensee: Radio Disney Group LLC. Group owner: ABC Inc. (acq 8-15-02; $3 million). Network: CBS Radio. Rep: Allied Radio Partners. Format: Children.

WFLT(AM)— Dec 5, 1955: 1420 khz; 500 w-D, 142 w-N, DA-2. TL: N43 01 15 W83 38 36. 317 S. Averill 48506. Phone: (810) 239-5733. Fax: (810) 239-7134. E-mail: wflt1420am@aol.com. Licensee: Metropolitan Missionary Baptist Church (acq 7-2-90; $225,000;. FTR: 7-23-90). Rep: Michigan. Format: Black gospel. ♦Sammie Jordan, gen mgr.

WFNT(AM)— Apr 10, 1953: 1470 khz; 5 kw-D, 1 kw-N, DA-2. TL: N42 58 22 W83 38 24. G 3338 E. Bristol Rd., Burton 48529. Phone: (810) 742-5170. Fax: (810) 742-5170. E-mail: wfnt@aol.com. Web Site: www.wfnt.com. Licensee: Regent Broadcasting of Flint Inc. Group owner: Regent Communications Inc. (acq 8-13-98; grpsl). Haley, Bader & Potts. Format: Nostalgia. News staff: 3. ♦Connie Marsack, sls VP; Maggie McColman, prom mgr; Chris Pavelich, news dir; Bill Sanderson, chief of engrg.

WCRZ(FM)— Co-owned with WFNT(AM). Nov 4, 1961: 107.9 mhz; 50 kw. 331 ft. TL: N42 58 49 W83 34 40. Stereo. Phone: (810) 743-1080. E-mail: wcrz@aol.com. Web Site: www.wcrz.com. Format: Adult contemp.

*****WFUM-FM**— Aug 23, 1985: 91.1 mhz; 18 kw. 489 ft. TL: N42 53 57 W83 27 42. Stereo. 535 W. William St., Suite 110, Ann Arbor 48103. Phone: (734) 764-9210. Fax: (734) 647-3488. E-mail: michigan.radio@umich.edu. Web Site: michiganradio.org. Licensee: Regents of the University of Michigan. Network: NPR. Format: News/talk. ♦Donovan Reynolds, gen mgr; Michael Coleman, stn mgr & dev dir; Peggy Watson, opns mgr; Justin Ebright, dev dir. Co-owned TV: *WFUM-TV affil

WSNL(AM)— Apr 26, 1946: 600 khz; 1 kw-D, 500 w-N, DA-1. TL: N42 56 23 W83 37 41. 5210 S. Saginaw St. 48507. Phone: (810) 694-4146. Fax: (810) 694-0661. Licensee: Christian Broadcasting System Ltd. (group owner; acq 1-22-93; $400,000;. FTR: 2-8-93). Format: Christian adult contemp. Target aud: 25-50; Followers of Christian beliefs. ♦Jon Yinger, pres; Evelyn Shaw, VP & gen mgr; Graham Parker, opns mgr & rgnl sls mgr.

Stations in the U.S. Michigan

Developers & Brokers of Radio Properties — contact American Media Services at our suite: Philadelphia Marriott Downtown 215-625-2900 843-972-2200 americanmediaservices.com Charleston, SC Dallas, TX · Chicago, Il · Austin, TX American Media Services, LLC

WTRX(AM)— Oct 1, 1947: 1330 khz; 5 kw-D, 1 kw-N, DA-2. TL: N42 58 24 W83 39 02. Stereo. G 4511 Miller Rd. 48507. Phone: (810) 720-9510. Fax: (810) 720-9513. Web Site: www.wtrxsports.com. Licensee: Citadel Broadcasting Co. Group owner: Citadel Broadcasting Corp. (acq 10-6-00; $180,000). Format: Sports, talk. 18-49 Males. ♦Scott Meyer, gen mgr; Doug Fisher, progmg dir.

WWCK(AM)— Nov 11, 1946: 1570 kHz; 1 kw-D, 238 w-N. TL: N43 00 38 W83 39 09. 6317 Taylor Dr. 48507. Phone: (810) 238-7300. Fax: (810) 238-7310. Web site: www.wwck.com. Licensee: Cumulus Licensing Corp. Group owner: Cumulus Media Inc. (acq 3-15-00; grpsl). Network: Westwood One. Rep: Allied Radio Partners. Format: CHR. Target aud: 18-34. ♦Nancy Dymond, gen mgr; Les Root, news dir; Dan Greer, chief of engrg.

WWCK-FM— September 1964: 105.5 mhz; 25 kw. 328 ft. TL: N43 00 39 W83 39 04. Stereo. Web Site: www.wwck.com.

Frankenmuth

WRCL(FM)— 2001: 93.7 mhz; 3.5 kw. 436 ft. TL: N43 18 16 W83 33 07. 3338 E. Bristol Rd., Burton 48529. Phone: (810) 742-1470. Fax: (810) 742-5170. E-mail: clover@regentflint.com. Web Site: www.club937.com. Licensee: Regent Broadcasting of Flint Inc. Group owner: Regent Communications Inc. (acq 11-9-01; $7 million. with WFGR(FM) Grand Rapids). Network: Network: CNN Radio, Westwood One. Format: Rhythmic CHR. Target aud: 12-34; children & adults. ♦Burdine Fly, gen mgr; J. Patrick, opns dir; Clay Church, mus dir; Nathan Reed, mus dir.

Frankfort

WBNZ(FM)— Oct 2, 1978: 99.3 mhz; 50 kw. 410 ft. TL: N44 36 38 W86 09 38. Stereo. 1532 Forrester Rd. 49635. Phone: (231) 352-9603. Fax: (231) 352-7877. E-mail: marc@wbnz.com. Web Site: www.wbnz.com. Licensee: Fort Bend Broadcasting Co. (group owner; acq 8-7-01). Rep: Patt. Format: Soft rock. News staff: one; News: 3 hrs wkly. Target aud: 25-54. Spec prog: Folk 2 hrs, big band 2 hrs wkly. ♦Marc McGuire, pres & gen mgr; Carol Rader, gen sls mgr & news dir.

Freeland

***WLKB(FM)—** 2005: 90.9 mhz; 240 w. Ant 213 ft. TL: N43 28 55 W84 04 23. 5700 West Oaks Blvd., Rocklin, CA 95765. Phone: (916) 251-1600. Fax: (916) 251-1650. Web Site: www.klove.com. Licensee: Educational Media Foundation. Group owner: American Family Radio. (acq 6-29-2005; $75,000). Network: K-Love. ♦Richard Jenkins, pres.

Fremont

WSHN(AM)— May 23, 1961: 1550 kHz; 1 kw-D. TL: N43 28 15 W85 56 25. Box 190 49412. Phone: (231) 924-4700. Fax: (231) 924-9746. Web Site: www.funcountry.com. Licensee: WSHN Inc. (acq 3-11-97; grpsl). Rep: Patt. Format: News, talk. ♦John Russell, news dir.

WVIB(FM)— Co-owned with WSHN(AM). 1971: 100.1 mhz; 3 kw. Ant 302 ft. TL: N43 28 17 W85 56 19. Stereo. Format: Country. Target aud: Adult. ♦John Russell, gen mgr.

Gaylord

***WBLW(FM)—** 2000: 88.1 mhz; 3 kw vert. Ant 128 ft. TL: N45 01 28 W84 43 44. Box 177 49734. Secondary address: 232 S. Townline Rd. 49735. Phone: (989) 732-5676. Fax: (989) 731-1122. E-mail: info@wblwradio.com. Web Site: www.gracebaptistministries.com. Licensee: Gaylord Baptist Christian School. Format: Christian.

WKPK(FM)— Nov 18, 1972: 106.7 mhz; 100 kw. 580 ft. TL: N45 02 42 W84 50 44. Stereo. Box 190, 28 Old Colony Rd. 49735. Secondary address: 1020 Hastings, Traverse City 49686. Phone: (231) 546-4485. Fax: (231) 546-4490. E-mail: wkpk@wkpk.com. Web Site: www.wkpk.com. Licensee: Northern Radio of Gaylord Inc. (acq 9-23-96; $1.4 million with WMLQ(FM) Rogers City). Rep: Christal. Format: Hot adult contemp. Target aud: 18-49; rgnl orientation including Traverse City, Petoskey, Cheboygan-active life style. ♦Richard Dills, pres & gen mgr; T.J. Clark, gen sls mgr; Heather Leigh, prom dir; Rob Weaver, progmg dir; Dennis Murray, chief of engrg.

WMJZ-FM— 1984: 101.5 mhz; 50 kw. Ant 492 ft. TL: N45 01 10 W84 24 28. Stereo. Box 1766 49734. Secondary address: 3687 Old US Hwy. 27 S. 49735. Phone: (989) 732-2341. Fax: (989) 732-6202. Licensee: Darby Advertising Inc. (acq 1-1-98; with co-located AM). Network: Network: Motor Racing Net, Jones Radio Networks. Irwin Campbell & Tanneweld. Format: Oldies, sports, news. Target aud: 25-54. ♦Kent D. Smith, pres & gen mgr.

***WPHN(FM)—** Apr 7, 1985: 90.5 mhz; 100 kw. 1,000 ft. TL: N45 08 17 W84 09 44. Stereo. Box 695 49734-0695. Secondary address: 1511 M-32 E. 49735. Phone: (989) 732-6274. Fax: (989) 732-8171. E-mail: ncr@ncradio.org. Web Site: www.ncradio.org. Licensee: Northern Christian Radio Inc. (group owner). Network: Network: Moody, USA. Southmayd & Miller. Format: Relg. News: 10 hrs wkly. Target aud: 25-55. ♦George A. Lake Jr., CEO & gen mgr; Joe Sereno, pres; Patrick Green, stn mgr & chief of engrg.

Gladstone

WGKL(FM)— Feb 15, 1999: 105.5 mhz; 4.6 kw. 377 ft. TL: N45 48 17 W87 10 15. 524 Ludington, Suite 300, Escanaba 49829. Phone: (906) 789-9700. Fax: (906) 789-9700. E-mail: kool105fm@chartermi.net. Web Site: www.radioresultsnetwork.com. Licensee: Lakes Radio Inc. (group owner) Format: Oldies. ♦Rick Duerson, gen mgr.

Gladwin

WGDN(AM)— Dec 7, 1974: 1350 khz; 1 kw-D, DA. TL: N43 57 03 W84 30 34. 3601 W. Woods Rd. 48624. Phone: (989) 426-1031. Licensee: Apple Broadcasting Co. Inc. (acq 3-87; with co-located FM; 12-22-86). Format: Relg. Target aud: 35 plus. ♦Steve Coston, gen mgr.

WGDN-FM— Feb 7, 1978: 103.1 mhz; 11.5 kw. 453 ft. TL: N43 57 03 W84 30 34. Stereo. Network: Westwood One. Format: Country.

Glen Arbor

WGFN(FM)— February 1991: 98.1 mhz; 7.9 kw. 590 ft. TL: N44 49 15 W85 59 42. (CP: 21 kw, ant 738 ft. TL: N44 49 16 W85 59 47). Stereo. 1356 Mackinaw Ave., Cheboygan 49721. Phone: (231) 627-2341. Fax: (231) 627-7000. Web Site: www.classicrockthebear.com. Licensee: Northern Star Broadcasting L.L.C. (group owner; acq 9-11-98; grpsl). Format: Classic rock. News staff: one. Spec prog: Jazz 4 hrs wkly. ♦Palmer Pyle, pres; Chris Monk, gen mgr.

WJZJ(FM)— Sept 1, 1997: 95.5 mhz; 23 kw. 695 ft. TL: N44 53 25 W85 59 59. Stereo. 1356 Mackinaw Ave., Cheboygan 49721. Phone: (231) 627-2341. Fax: (231) 627-7000. Web Site: www.modernrockthezone.com. Licensee: Northern Star Broadcasting L.L.C. (group owner; acq 9-11-98; grpsl). Format: Modern rock. ♦Palmer Pyle, pres; Chris Monk, gen mgr.

Good Hart

***WJOG(FM)—** Not on air, target date: unknown: 91.3 mhz; 7.2 kw vert. Ant 518 ft. TL: N45 30 43 W85 02 19. Michigan Community Radio, 3302 N. Van Dyke, Imlay City 48444. Phone: (810) 721-0891. Licensee: Michigan Community Radio.

Goodland Township

***WHYT(FM)—** 2004: 88.1 mhz; 400 w vert. Ant 581 ft. TL: N43 10 30 W83 04 02. Box 388, Williamston 48895. Phone: (517) 381-0573. Fax: (877) 850-0881. E-mail: info@positivehits.com. Web Site: www.positivehits.com. Licensee: Superior Communications. ♦Jenn Czelada, gen mgr.

Grand Haven

WGHN(AM)— July 16, 1956: 1370 khz; 500 w-D, 22 w-N. TL: N43 02 17 W86 13 46. Box 330, One S. Harbor 49417. Phone: (616) 842-8110. Fax: (616) 842-4350. Web Site: www.wghn.com. Licensee: WGHN Inc. (acq 2-14-83; $260,500 with co-located FM; 3-7-83). Network: CBS. Rep: Patt. Rothman, Gordon, Foreman & Groudine. Format: Adult contemp. News staff: 2; News: 30 hrs wkly. Target aud: 25-54. Spec prog: Agriculture & farm 5 hrs wkly. ♦William Struyk, pres, gen mgr & gen sls mgr.

WGHN-FM— Jan 28, 1969: 92.1 mhz; 3 kw. 246 ft. TL: N43 03 23 W86 14 27. Stereo.

Grand Rapids

***WAYG(FM)—** May 18, 1978: 89.9 mhz; 4.9 w. Ant 207 ft. TL: N42 58 40 W85 35 44. Stereo. 1159 E. Beltline Ave. N.E. 49525. Phone: (616) 942-1500. Fax: (616) 942-7078. Web Site: www.way.fm. Licensee: Cornerstone University (acq 1-21-98; $200,000). Format: Christian hits. News: 10 hrs wkly. Target aud: General. ♦Dr. Rex Rogers, pres; Lee Geysbeek, VP; Rich Anderson, stn mgr.

WBBL(AM)— Listing follows WLAV-FM.

WBCT(FM)— October 1951: 93.7 mhz; 320 kw. 781 ft. TL: N42 37 56 W85 32 16. Stereo. 77 Monroe Center, Suite 1000 49503. Phone: (616) 459-1919. Fax: (616) 242-9373. Web Site: www.b93.com. Licensee: Clear Channel Radio Inc. Group owner: Clear Channel Communications Inc. (acq 1996; grpsl). Rep: Clear Channel. Format: Country. News staff: one; News: 3 hrs wkly. Target aud: 25-49. ♦Skip Essick, VP & gen mgr; Rich Berry, gen sls mgr; Kani Alger, natl sls mgr.

WBFX(FM)— Listing follows WTKG(AM).

***WBLU-FM—** Aug 18, 1979: 88.9 mhz; 650 w. 400 ft. TL: N42 59 15 W85 37 26. Stereo. Blue Lake Fine Arts Camp, Twin Lake 49457. Phone: (231) 894-2616. Phone: (231) 458-9258. Fax: (231) 893-2457. Web Site: www.bluelake.org. Licensee: Blue Lake Fine Arts Camp. (acq 3-1-93; $200,000; 3-15-93). Network: Network: PRI, NPR. Format: Class, jazz, news. Target aud: Adults. Spec prog: Folk 5 hrs wkly. ♦William F. Stansell, pres; Dave Myers, gen mgr; Gordon Christensen, opns dir; Steve Albert, progmg dir; Bonnie Bierma, mus dir; Brad Aspey, pub affrs dir; Don Hoogeboom, chief of engrg.

***WCSG(FM)—** June 9, 1973: 91.3 mhz; 37 kw. 570 ft. TL: N42 47 46 W85 38 58. Stereo. 1159 E. Beltline Ave. N.E. 49525. Phone: (616) 942-1500. Fax: (616) 942-7078. E-mail: wcsg@wcsg.org. Web Site: www.wcsg.org. Licensee: Cornerstone University. Network: AP Radio. Format: Christian. News staff: 2; News: 5 hrs wkly. Target aud: 35-49. ♦Dr. Rex Rogers, pres; Lee Geysbeek, VP; Chris Lemke, gen mgr & progmg dir.

WFGR(FM)— Aug 9, 1992: 98.7 mhz; 2.75 kw. Ant 492 ft. TL: N43 01 57 W85 41 47. 50 Monroe N.W., Suite 500 49503. Phone: (616) 458-2600. Fax: (616) 451-0113. Web Site: www.wfgr.com. Licensee: Haith Broadcasting Corp. Group owner: Regent Communications Inc. (acq 9-25-01; $3.9 million. for stock). Rep: Allied Radio Partners. Format: Oldies. Target aud: 25 plus; affluent, well-educated professionals. ♦Terry Jacobs, pres; Phil Catlett, gen mgr; Rick Sarata, sls dir.

WFUR(AM)— November 1947: 1570 khz; 1 kw-D, 306 w-N. TL: N42 57 14 W85 41 52. Box 1808, 399 Garfield Ave. S.W. 49501. Phone: (616) 451-9387. Fax: (616) 451-8460. Licensee: Furniture City Broadcasting Corp. Group owner: Kuiper Stations (acq 3-10-50). Network: USA. Format: Relg. News: 5 hrs wkly. Target aud: 35 plus; 60% female, 30% male. ♦William E. Kuiper Sr., pres & gen mgr; Steven Kuiper, opns mgr & mus dir; Roger Peular, gen sls mgr; Dave Kuiper, news dir; Pat Deja, pub affrs dir; Bill Kuiper Jr., chief of engrg.

WFUR-FM— September 1960: 102.9 mhz; 50 kw. 492 ft. TL: N42 57 13 W85 41 55. Stereo. Network: USA. Format: Relg mus. News: 5 hrs

Broadcasting & Cable Yearbook 2006

Michigan

wkly. Target aud: 35-64; homeowners, Christian families, Christian mus listeners. ◆William Kuiper Jr., asst music dir.

WGRD-FM— Aug 1, 1962: 97.9 mhz; 13 kw. 590 ft. TL: N42 47 46 W85 38 58. Stereo. 50 Monroe N.W., Suite 500, Grands Rapids 49503. Phone: (616) 459-4111. Fax: (616) 451-0113. Web Site: www.wgrd.com. Licensee: Regent Broadcasting of Grand Rapids Inc. Group owner: Regent Communications Inc. (acq 8-7-00; grpsl). Format: Modern rock, alternative. News staff: one; News: 3 hrs wkly. Target aud: 18-49. ◆Terry Jacobs, pres; Phil Catlett, gen mgr.

*WGVU(AM)—(Kentwood). Dec 25, 1954: 1480 khz; 2 kw-D, 5 kw-N. TL: N42 57 13 W85 41 36. 301 W. Fulton 49504. Phone: (616) 331-6666. Fax: (616) 331-6625. Licensee: Grand Valley State Univ. (acq 4-7-92; $240,000 part sale & part gift; 4-27-92). Network: Network: NPR, PRI. Format: News, info. News staff: 3; News: 89 hrs wkly. Target aud: 35-44; college-educated men with average income. ◆Michael T. Walenta, gen mgr; Ken Kolbe, opns mgr; Michael Haitley, dev mgr; Richard Nelson, sls dir; Pamela Holtz, mktg mgr & prom mgr; Fred Martino, news dir; Bob Lumbert, chief of engrg.

WGVU-FM—See Allendale

WJNZ(AM)—See Kentwood

WKLQ(FM)—(Greenville). October 1989: 107.3 mhz; 50 kw. Ant 492 ft. TL: N43 01 10 W85 20 58. Stereo. 60 Monroe Ctr. N.W., 3rd Fl. 49503. Phone: (616) 774-8461. Fax: (616) 774-2491. Web Site: www.wklq.com. Licensee: Citadel Broadcasting Co. Group owner: Citadel Broadcasting Corp. (acq 5-30-2000; grpsl). Network: Westwood One. Rep: D & R Radio. Format: Active rock. News staff: one. Target aud: 25-54. ◆Matt Hanlon, gen mgr.

WLAV-FM— January 1947: 96.9 mhz; 50 kw. 499 ft. TL: N43 02 01 W85 31 15. Stereo. 60 Monroe Ctr. N.W., 3rd Fl 49502. Phone: (616) 774-8461. Fax: (616) 774-2491. Web Site: www.wlav.com. Licensee: Citadel Broadcasting Co. Group owner: Citadel Broadcasting Corp. (acq 5-30-00; grpsl). Network: ABC. Reddy, Begley & McCormick. Format: Classic rock. Target aud: 25-49. ◆Matthew R. Hanlon, VP; Matt Hanlon, gen mgr; Brent Alberts, opns dir & adv dir; Kat Conley, gen sls mgr; Rob Brant, news dir; Don Allen, chief of engrg.

WBBL(AM)—Co-owned with WLAV-FM. Sept 18, 1940: 1340 khz; 1 kw-U. TL: N42 57 02 W85 41 55. Web Site: www.wbbl.com. Network: ABC. Format: Sports. Target aud: 18-49; men. ◆Bret Bakita, progmg dir.

WLHT-FM—Listing follows WNWZ(AM).

WMJH(AM)—See Rockford

WNWZ(AM)— Nov 1, 1947: 1410 khz; 1 kw-D, 48 w-N. TL: N42 59 14 W85 37 76. Stereo. Box 96 49501. Phone: (616) 451-4800. Fax: (616) 451-0113. Web Site: www.gogrand.com. Licensee: Regent Broadcasting of Grand Rapids Inc. Group owner: Regent Communications Inc. (acq 8-7-00; grpsl). Format: Latin mix /Sp language. Target aud: 35 plus; professionals. ◆Phil Catlett, pres mgr; Bobby Duncan, opns mgr & progmg dir; Rick Sarata, sls dir; Kevin Curnow, prom dir; Mike Maciejewski, engrg mgr.

WLHT-FM—Co-owned with WNWZ(AM). Feb 28, 1962: 95.7 mhz; 40 kw. 551 ft. TL: N43 01 57 W85 41 47. Stereo. 50 Monroe Ave. 49503. Web Site: www.wlht.com. Network: ABC. Dow, Lohnes & Albertson. Format: Adult contemp. Target aud: 25-54. ◆Rick Sarata, gen sls mgr; Terry Jacobs, pres & gen sls mgr; Bruce Parrott, prom mgr & news dir; Bill Bailey, progmg dir; Mike Maciejewski, chief of engrg.

WOOD(AM)— 1924: 1300 khz; 20 kw-U, DA-2. TL: N42 45 22 W85 39 24. Stereo. 77 Monroe Ctr., Suite 1000 49503. Phone: (616) 459-1919. Fax: (616) 242-6599. E-mail: web@woodradio.com. Web Site: www.woodradio.com. Licensee: Clear Channel Radio Inc. Group owner: Clear Channel Communications Inc. (acq 5-10-96; grpsl). Network: ABC. Rep: Clear Channel. Format: News/talk. News staff: 6; News: 24 hrs wkly. Target aud: 35-54. ◆Skip Essick, VP & gen mgr; Phil Tower, opns dir & progmg dir; Henry Capogna, gen sls mgr & rgnl sls mgr; Kami Alger, natl sls mgr; Glenn Del Vecchio, prom dir; Rich Jones, news dir; Don Missad, chief of engrg.

WOOD-FM— 1962: 105.7 mhz; 265 kw. 810 ft. TL: N42 41 13 W85 30 35. Stereo. E-mail: web@star1057online.com. Web Site: www.star1057online.com. Format: Soft adult contemp. News: 10 hrs wkly. ◆Glenn Del Vecchio, prom mgr; John Patrick, opns dir & progmg dir.

WTKG(AM)— February 1945: 1230 khz; 1 kw-U. TL: N42 59 42 W85 40 36. Stereo. 77 Monroe Ctr., Suite 1000 49503. Phone: (616) 459-1919. Fax: (616) 242-6599. E-mail: web@wtkg.com. Web Site: www.wtkg.com. Licensee: Clear Channel Broadcasting Licenses Inc. Group owner: Clear Channel Communications Inc. (acq 1996; grpsl). Network: ABC Information & Entertainment. Rep: Clear Channel. Format: Talk, sports. News staff: 2; News: 7 hrs wkly. Target aud: 25-54; conservative. ◆Skip Essick, VP & gen mgr; Phil Tower, opns dir & progmg dir; Henry Capogna, gen sls mgr; Kami Alger, natl sls mgr; Glenn Delvecchio, prom mgr; Rich Jones, news dir; Don Missad, chief of engrg.

WBFX(FM)—Co-owned with WTKG(AM). 1965: 101.3 mhz; 50 kw. Ant 420 ft. TL: N43 02 28 W85 21 28. Stereo. E-mail: web@101thefoxrocks.com. Web Site: www.101thefoxrocks.com. Format: Classic rock. ◆Rich Berry, gen sls mgr; Glenn Delvecchio, prom dir; Doug Montgomery, progmg dir; Aris Hampers, mus dir.

WTNR(FM)—See Holland

*WVGR(FM)— Dec 7, 1961: 104.1 mhz; 108 kw. 600 ft. TL: N42 41 13 W85 30 35. Stereo. 535 W. William St., Suite 10, Ann Arbor 48103. Phone: (616) 956-7711. Phone: (734) 764-9210. Fax: (734) 647-3488. E-mail: michigan.radio@umich.edu. Web Site: www.michiganradio.org. Licensee: Regents of the University of Michigan. Network: Network: NPR, PRI. Dow, Lohnes & Albertson. Format: News/talk. News staff: 7; News: 140 hrs wkly. ◆Donovan Reynolds, gen mgr & stn mgr; Jon Hoban, stn mgr; Justin Ebright, dev dir; Peggy Watson, opns mgr & dev dir.

Grayling

WGRY(AM)— Aug 1, 1970: 1230 khz; 750 w-U. TL: N44 39 05 W84 44 18. 6514 Old Lake Rd. 49738. Phone: (989) 348-6171. Fax: (989) 348-6181. E-mail: radio@i2k.net. Web Site: www.gannonbroadcasting.com. Licensee: Gannon Broadcasting. Rep: Michigan. Format: Music of Your Life. News staff: one; News: 16 hrs wkly. Target aud: 25 plus. ◆William S. Gannon, pres & gen mgr; Pete Michaels, opns mgr.

WGRY-FM— June 16, 1977: 100.3 mhz; 50 kw. 436 ft. TL: N44 36 50 W84 41 05. Stereo. 6514 Old Lake Rd. 49738. Phone: (989) 348-6171. Fax: (989) 348-6181. E-mail: radio@i2k.net. Web Site: www.gannonbroadcasting.com. Licensee: Gannon Broadcasting Systems Inc. Network: ABC. Rep: Patt. Format: Country. Target aud: 25-54. ◆William Gannon, pres & gen mgr; Pete Michaels, opns mgr.

Greenville

*WDPW(FM)—Not on air, target date: unknown: 91.9 mhz; 6 kw vert. Ant 157 ft. TL: N43 05 27 W85 16 27. 6808 Hanna Lake S.E., Caledonia 49316. Phone: (616) 698-1831. Licensee: Larlen Communications Inc.

WKLQ(FM)—Licensed to Greenville. See Grand Rapids

WSCG(AM)— May 19, 1960: 1380 khz; 1 kw-D, 500 w-N, DA-N. TL: N43 09 18 W85 15 25. Box 578, 9181 S. Greenville Rd. 48838. Phone: (616) 754-3656. Fax: (616) 754-2390. E-mail: wscgradio@chartermi.net. Licensee: Stafford Broadcasting L.L.C. (acq 10-19-2004); with WSCG-FM Lakeview). Format: News, talk, sports. ◆Chris Loiselle, CFO; Bruce Bentley, gen mgr, opns mgr & progmg dir; John P. Clark, gen mgr & gen sls mgr; Ralph Hayne, chief of engrg.

Gulliver

WCMM(FM)— 1982: 102.5 mhz; 100 kw. 813 ft. TL: N45 58 01 W86 29 18. Stereo. 524 Ludington, Suite 300, Escanaba 49829. Phone: (906) 228-9700. Fax: (906) 789-9700. E-mail: countrymoose@chartermi.net. Web Site: www.radioresultsnetwork.com/wcmm. Licensee: Lakes Radio Inc. (group owner; acq 11-30-99; grpsl). Network: ABC. Format: Country. Target aud: 18-54; younger, contemp, mobile adult workers. ◆Rick Duerson, gen mgr.

Hancock

WGLI(FM)— Feb 11, 2003: 98.7 mhz; 100 kw. Ant 522 ft. TL: N47 06 13 W88 34 04. 805-B U.S. 41 S., Baraga 49908. Phone: (906) 353-ROCK. Fax: (906) 353-9200. E-mail: Rock985@up.net. Web Site: www.wglifm.com. Licensee: Keweenaw Bay Indian Community (acq 2-13-03). Network: Jones Radio Networks. Format: Rock/AOR. ◆Ed Janisse, gen mgr; Mary Tober, opns dir & progmg dir; John Preston, sls.

WKMJ-FM—Listing follows WMPL(AM).

WMPL(AM)— Mar 2, 1957: 920 khz; 1 kw-D, 206 w-N. TL: N47 06 05 W88 35 26. Box 547 49930. Phone: (906) 482-3700. Fax: (906) 482-1540. Licensee: Victor Broadcasting Corp. (acq 5-22-01; $237,500. with co-located FM). Network: USA. Rep: Michigan. Format: Talk/news, info, sports. News staff: one; News: 15 hrs wkly. Target aud: General. ◆John Vertin, pres; Kathy Vertin, VP; Matt Vertin, gen mgr; Marianne Schulze, gen sls mgr; Brian Keranen, progmg dir & chief of engrg; Mitchell Lake, news dir.

WKMJ-FM—Co-owned with WMPL(AM). 1968: 93.5 mhz; 3 kw. 249 ft. TL: N47 06 05 W88 35 26. (CP: 13.5 kw, ant 456 ft.). Network: Jones Radio Networks. Booth, Freret, Imlay & Tepper. Format: Adult contemp, CHR. News staff: one. Target aud: 18-45.

Harbor Beach

WCZE(FM)— 2005: 103.7 mhz; 50 kw. Ant 440 ft. TL: N43 41 25 W82 56 27. Box 388, Williamston 48895. Phone: (810) 721-0891. Web Site: www.smile.fm. Licensee: Jennifer & Edward Czelada. Format: Christian. ◆Jenn Czelada, gen mgr.

Harbor Springs

*WCMW-FM— Aug 15, 1988: 103.9 mhz; 28 kw. 663 ft. TL: N45 29 02 W84 58 00. Stereo. Public Broadcasting Ctr., Central Michigan Univ., Mount Pleasant 48859. Phone: (989) 774-3105. Fax: (989) 774-4427. E-mail: cmuradio@cmich.edu. Web Site: www.wcmu.org. Licensee: Central Michigan University. (acq 7-21-93; $325,000; 8-23-93). Network: Network: NPR, PRI. Dow, Lohnes & Albertson. Format: Class jazz, news, info. News staff: 2; News: 45 hrs wkly. ◆Ed Grant, gen mgr & rgnl sls mgr.

Harrietta

WKAD(FM)— 2003: 93.7 mhz; 4.3 kw. Ant 390 ft. TL: N44 16 41 W85 35 28. Box 520, Cadillac 49601. Phone: (231) 775-1263. Fax: (231) 779-2844. Licensee: Cadillac Broadcasting LLC (acq 1-4-02). Format: Oldies. ◆Trish Garber, CEO.

Harrison

WVXH(FM)— Mar 26, 1975: 92.1 mhz; 6 kw. Ant 298 ft. TL: N43 59 38 W84 50 13. c/o WVXU(FM), 1223 Central Pkwy., Cincinnati, OH 45214. Phone: (513) 352-9170. Fax: (513) 241-8456. E-mail: wvxu@cinradio.org. Web Site: www.wvxu.org. Licensee: Cincinnati Classical Public Radio Inc. (acq 8-22-2005; grpsl). Network: Network: NPR, PRI. Format: News and info. ◆Richard Eiswerth, gen mgr.

Harrisville

*WJOJ(FM)— December 2001: 89.7 mhz; 31 kw. Ant 469 ft. TL: N44 42 12 W83 31 27. Box 388, Williamston 48895. Phone: (810) 721-0891. E-mail: info@joyfm.net. Web Site: www.joyfm.net. Licensee: Northland Community Broadcasters. Format: Contemporary Christian. ◆Jennifer Czelada, gen mgr.

Hart

WCXT(FM)— Sept 14, 1983: 105.3 mhz; 28 kw. Ant 659 ft. TL: N43 40 34 W86 14 20. (CP: COL Coopersville. 50 kw, ant 479 ft. TL: N43 15 41 W86 02 01). Stereo. 3720 Polk Rd. 49420. Phone: (231) 873-7129. Fax: (231) 873-7120. E-mail: wcxt@lakeshore.net. Licensee: Waters Broadcasting Corp. Format: Adult contemp. Target aud: 25-54; adult women. ◆Nancy Waters, pres; Yvette Jernudd, stn mgr & gen sls mgr.

Hartford

WSPZ-FM— March 1996: 103.7 mhz; 3 kw. Ant 328 ft. TL: N42 18 02 W86 15 03. Stereo. Box 107, St. Joseph 49085. Secondary address: 580 E. Napier Ave., Benton Harbor 49022. Phone: (269) 925-1111. Fax: (269) 925-1011. Licensee: WSJM Inc. Group owner: The Mid-West Family Broadcast Group (acq 4-96; grpsl). Network: ABC.

Stations in the U.S. Michigan

Rep: Christal. Shaw Pittman. Format: Rhythm and blues, oldies. Target aud: 25-49. ♦Gayle Olson, gen mgr; Jim Gifford, opns mgr & progmg dir; Brent Dingman, gen sls mgr; Sandie Lieberg, prom dir; Annette Weston, news dir; Terry Green, engrg dir & chief of engrg.

Hastings

WBCH(AM)— November 1957: 1220 khz; 250 w-D, 48 w-N. TL: N42 37 36 W85 16 39. Box 88, 119 W. State St. 49058. Phone: (269) 945-3414. Fax: (269) 945-3470. E-mail: wbch@wbch.com. Web Site: www.wbch.com. Licensee: Barry Broadcasting Co. (acq 8-17-58). Network: ABC Information & Entertainment. Patt. Format: Country, news/talk. News staff: one; News: 16 hrs wkly. Target aud: 25-54. ♦Steve Randant, gen mgr.

WBCH-FM— December 1967: 100.1 mhz; 3 kw. 295 ft. TL: N42 37 36 W85 16 39. Stereo. Network: ABC. Format: Hit country.

Hemlock

WCEN-FM— Aug 8, 1963: 94.5 mhz; 100 kw. Ant 981 ft. TL: N43 43 36 W84 36 16. Stereo. 1795 Tittabawassee Rd., Saginaw 48604-9431. Phone: (989) 752-3456. Fax: (989) 754-5046. Web Site: www.945themoose.com. Licensee: NM Licensing LLC. Group owner: NextMedia Group L.L.C. (acq 12-30-02; grpsl). Shaw Pittman. Format: Hot country. Target aud: 25-54; medium income, rural & urban. ♦Floyd Evans, gen mgr; Dave Maurer, opns mgr.

Highland Park

***WHPR(FM)**— May 21, 1954: 88.1 mhz; 11 w. Ant 105 ft. TL: N42 24 50 W83 05 48. 15851 Woodward 48203. Phone: (313) 868-6612. Fax: (313) 868-8725. E-mail: tv68whpr@aol.com. Licensee: R.J.s Late Night Entertainment Corp. Format: Talk, CHR, oldies. Target aud: 21 & over; African Americans 40 plus politically aware & motivated. ♦Henry Tyler, VP; R. J. Watkins, sr VP & gen mgr; John Maxey, stn mgr.

Hillman

WKJZ(FM)—Licensed to Hillman. See Alpena

Hillsdale

WCSR(AM)— May 21, 1959: 1340 khz; 500 w-D, 1 kw-N. TL: N41 55 41 W84 38 10. Box 273 49242. Secondary address: 170 N. West St. 49242. Phone: (517) 437-4444. Fax: (517) 437-7461. E-mail: wcsr@qcnet.net. Web Site: www.radiohillsdale.com. Licensee: WCSR Inc. (acq 11-15-61). Format: Adult contemp. Target aud: 25 plus; county-wide. Spec prog: Farm 3 hrs, relg 10 hrs wkly. ♦Anthony Flynn, pres & gen mgr.

WCSR-FM— May 19, 1973: 92.1 mhz; 6 kw. 243 ft. TL: N41 55 41 W84 38 10. Stereo. Web Site: www.radiohillsdale.com.

Holland

WHTC(AM)— July 31,1948: 1450 khz; 1 kw-U. TL: N42 47 41 W86 06 22. 87 Central Ave. 49423. Phone: (616) 392-3121. Fax: (616) 392-8066. E-mail: whtc@whtc.com. Web Site: www.whtc.com. Licensee: Midwest Communications Inc. (group owner) (acq 8-1-00; grpsl). Network: CBS. Rep: Michigan. MRN, MFRN Format: News/talk, full service. News staff: one; News: 15 hrs wkly. Target aud: 25 plus. Spec prog: Sp 3 hrs wkly. ♦Duke Wright, pres; Peter Tanz, gen mgr; Karl Wertzler, gen sls mgr.

WJQK(FM)—(Zeeland). Aug 23, 1971: 99.3 mhz; 4.7 kw. 371 ft. TL: N42 48 59 W85 57 24. Stereo. 425 Centerstone Ct., Zeeland 49464. Phone: (616) 931-9930. Phone: (888) 993-1260. Fax: (616) 931-1280. Web Site: www.jq99.com. Licensee: Lanser Broadcasting Corp. (acq 1-1-87). Network: Network: ABC Daytime Direction, AP Radio. Rep: Salem. Format: Contemp Christian. News: 7 hrs wkly. Target aud: 25-49. ♦Les Lanser, pres; Brad Lanser, VP & gen mgr; Troy West, stn mgr.

***WTHS(FM)**— Oct 15, 1984: 89.9 mhz; 1 kw. 154 ft. TL: N42 47 16 W86 06 02. Stereo. DeWitt Ctr., Hope College, Box 9000 49423. Phone: (616) 395-7878. Phone: (616) 395-7880. Fax: (616) 395-7958. E-mail: wths@hope.edu. Licensee: Hope College Board of Trustees. Lauren A. Colby. Format: Alternative. News: 7 hrs wkly. Target aud: 15-30; students & adults. Spec prog: Jazz 6 hrs, relg 14 hrs, Sp 8 hrs wkly.

WTNR(FM)— Mar 21, 1961: 94.5 mhz; 50 kw. Ant 499 ft. TL: N42 51 20 W85 57 45. Stereo. 60 Monroe Ctr. N.W., 3rd Fl., Grand Rapids 49503. Phone: (616) 774-8461. Fax: (616) 774-2491. Licensee: Citadel Broadcasting Co. Group owner: Citadel Broadcasting Corp. (acq 4-26-2001; grpsl). Network: ABC. Rep: Katz Radio. Fletcher, Heald & Hildreth. Format: Country. Target aud: 18-34; men. ♦Matt Hanlon, gen mgr; Jeff Morton, rgnl sls mgr.

WVTI(FM)— September 1962: 96.1 mhz; 50 kw horiz, 45 kw vert. 492 ft. TL: N42 49 10 W85 52 09. Stereo. 77 Monroe Ctr., Suite 1000, Grand Rapids 49503. Phone: (616) 459-1919. Fax: (616) 235-9600. Web Site: www.i96.net. Licensee: Clear Channel Radio Licenses Inc. Group owner: Clear Channel Communications Inc. (acq 2-27-97; $4.1 million). Rep: Clear Channel. Format: Contemp hit. Target aud: 25-34; women. ♦Skip Essick, VP & gen mgr.

Holton

WVIB(FM)—Licensed to Holton. See Fremont

Honor

WKVK(FM)— 2002: 100.7 mhz; 4.7 kw. Ant 367 ft. TL: N44 39 41 W85 48 53. 28 Old Colony Rd., Gaylord 49735. Phone: (231) 546-4485. Fax: (213) 546-4490. E-mail: wkpk@wkpk.com. Web Site: www.wkpk.com. Licensee: Northern Radio of Michigan Inc. Format: Hot adult contemp. ♦Charlie Ferguson, gen mgr.

Houghton

WCCY(AM)— 1929: 1400 khz; 1 kw-U. TL: N47 08 06 W88 33 53. 313 Montezuma Ave. 49931. Phone: (906) 482-7700. Fax: (906) 482-7751. Web Site: www.wccy.com. Licensee: Heartland Communications License LLC. (acq 11-10-2004; grpsl). Network: ABC Information & Entertainment. Rep: Patt. Format: Easy lstng. News staff: one; News: 18 hrs wkly. Target aud: 25-65. Spec prog: Relg one hr, pub affrs one hr wkly. ♦Mac Marzke, gen mgr & gen sls mgr; Kevin Ericson, progmg dir.

WOLV(FM)—Co-owned with WCCY(AM). Mar 7, 1980: 97.7 mhz; 875 w. 508 ft. TL: N47 08 27 W88 32 26. Stereo. Web Site: www.thewolf.com. Network: ABC Daytime Direction. Format: Classic rock. Target aud: 18-45.

***WGGL-FM**— February 1982: 91.1 mhz; 100 kw. 809 ft. TL: N47 02 08 W88 41 43. Stereo. 45 E. 7th St., St. Paul, MN 55101. Phone: (651) 290-1500. Fax: (651) 290-1224. Web Site: www.mpr.org. Licensee: Minnesota Public Radio Inc. Network: Network: PRI, NPR. Format: Class, news. News staff: one. Target aud: General. ♦William H. Kling, pres; Erik Nycklemoe, gen mgr; Ralph Hornberger, chief of engrg.

WHKB(FM)— Sept 1, 1989: 102.3 mhz; 1.05 kw. 554 ft. TL: N47 06 13 W88 34 04. (CP: 35.5 kw, ant 492 ft.). Stereo. 313 E. Montezuma Ave. 49931. Phone: (906) 482-7700. Fax: (906) 482-7751. Web Site: www.kbear.com. Licensee: Heartland Communications License LLC. (acq 11-10-2004; grpsl). Network: ABC. Format: Country. Target aud: 18-60. Spec prog: Oldies 16 hrs wkly. ♦Dallas Bond, gen mgr; A.J. Coffey, opns dir & news dir; Jack Harvey, progmg VP & progmg dir; Joy Winsor, chief of engrg.

***WMTU-FM**— Jan 26, 1994: 91.9 mhz; 100 w. 18 ft. TL: N47 02 08 W88 41 43. Michigan Technological Univ. G03, W. Wadsworth Hall, 1703 Townsend Dr. 49931. Phone: (906) 487-2333. Phone: (908) 487-1600. Fax: (906) 487-3016. E-mail: wmtu@mtu.edu. Web Site: www.wmtu.mtu.edu. Licensee: Michigan Technological University. Format: Var. ♦Matthew Barr, gen mgr.

Houghton Lake

WUPS(FM)— July 1, 1961: 98.5 mhz; 100 kw. Ant 981 ft. TL: N44 17 18 W84 44 30. Stereo. Box 468, Prudenville 48651. Phone: (989) 366-5364. Fax: (989) 366-6200. E-mail: wupsfm@yahoo.com. Web Site: www.wups.com. Licensee: Coltrace Communications Inc. (acq 3-15-88; $900,000). Network: ABC. Format: Classic hits. News: 6 hrs wkly. Target aud: 25-54; general. ♦John M. Salov, pres & opns mgr; Sindy Winkler, sr VP.

Howell

WHMI-FM— Sept 1, 1977: 93.5 mhz; 5.2 kw. 354 ft. TL: N42 39 47 W83 56 23. Stereo. Box 935 48844. Secondary address: 1277 Parkway Dr. 48843. Phone: (517) 546-0860. Fax: (517) 546-1758. E-mail: whmi@whmi.com. Web Site: www.whmi.com. Licensee: The Livingston Radio Co. (acq 3-3-89). Network: ABC. Michigan Spot Sales Irwin, Campbell & Tannenwald. Format: Classic hits. News staff: 3; News: 10 hrs wkly. Target aud: 25-64. ♦Greg Jablonski, pres & gen mgr; Reed Kittredge, opns mgr; Debbie Platt, gen sls mgr; Jon King, prom mgr & news dir.

Hubbard Lake

***WKHN(FM)**—Not on air, target date: unknown: 88.1 mhz; 1.1 kw vert. Ant 367 ft. TL: N44 54 20 W83 32 10. 901 Elizabeth Ct., Mount Pleasant 48858. Phone: (989) 779-9178. Fax: (989) 779-1558. Licensee: Great Lakes Community Broadcasting Inc. Format: Oldies. ♦James J. McCluskey, gen mgr.

Hudson

WBZV(FM)— Mar 1, 1995: 102.5 mhz; 6 kw. 328 ft. TL: N41 53 03 W84 31 24. 121 W. Maumee St., Adrian 49221-2019. Phone: (517) 437-1025. Fax: (517) 263-4525. E-mail: friends@tc3net.com. Licensee: Friends Communications of Hudson Inc. Group owner: Friends Communications Inc. Network: ABC. Rep: Michigan. Fletcher, Heald & Hildreth. Format: Hot AC. News staff: one; News: 6 hrs wkly. Target aud: 25-54. ♦Bob Elliot, chmn, pres & gen mgr.

Imlay City

***WWKM(FM)**— December 2000: 89.1 mhz; 1.5 kw. Ant 171 ft. TL: N43 03 42 W83 05 44. Michigan Community Radio, Box 388, Williamston 48896. Phone: (810) 721-0891. Fax: (413) 410-9708. E-mail: info@joyfm.net. Web Site: www.joyfm.net. Licensee: Michigan Community Radio. Format: Contemporary Christian. ♦Jenn Czelada, gen mgr.

Inkster

WDMK(FM)—See Detroit

WMKM(AM)— November 1956: 1440 khz; 1 kw-U. TL: N42 15 22 W83 21 48. 2994 E. Grand Blvd., Detroit 48202. Phone: (313) 871-1440. Fax: (313) 871-6088. Licensee: Davidson Media Station WMKM LLC. Group owner: Davidson Media Group LLC (acq 5-28-2004; $5.75 million). Format: Black gospel. Target aud: 35 plus; adult Black church audience. ♦Peter Davidson, pres; Crystal D. Sampson, gen mgr.

Interlochen

***WIAA(FM)**— July 22, 1963: 88.7 mhz; 100 kw. Ant 1,033 ft. TL: N44 16 33 W85 42 49. Stereo. Box 199, Interlochen Ctr. for the Arts 49643. Secondary address: One Lyon St. 49643. Phone: (231) 276-4400. Fax: (231) 276-4417. E-mail: ipr@interlochen.org. Web Site: www.interlochen.org/ipr. Licensee: Interlochen Center for the Arts. Network: Network: NPR, PRI. Format: Classical, news. Target aud:

Michigan

35-65; professional, arts-oriented, upper-income. Spec prog: Jazz 3 hrs, folk 3 hrs wkly. ♦Thom Paulson, CFO, VP & stn mgr; Billie Thompson, opns dir; Joanne Hermann, dev dir.

Ionia

WION(AM)— Feb 1, 1953: 1430 khz; 5 kw-D, 330 w-N, DA-2. TL: N43 00 16 W85 05 09. Box 143 48846. Secondary address: 1153 Haynor Rd. 48846. Phone: (616) 527-9466. Fax: (616) 775-5908. E-mail: deb@wion.net. Licensee: Packer Radio WION LLC (acq 12-14-2004; $127,000). Network: ABC Information & Entertainment. Rep: Michigan. Format: Full svc. Spec prog: Farm 8 hrs wkly. ♦Jim Carlyle, gen mgr & stn mgr.

Iron Mountain

WHTO(FM)— 2003: 106.7 mhz; 1.7 kw. Ant 623 ft. TL: N45 49 15 W88 02 25. 127 S. Stephenson 49801. Phone: (906) 774-9486. Web Site: www.whtofm.com. Licensee: Results Broadcasting of Iron Mountain Inc. (acq 6-29-2005; $650,000).

WIMK(FM)— Dec 27, 1981: 93.1 mhz; 100 kw. 590 ft. TL: N45 49 16 W88 02 28. Stereo. 101 E. Kent St. 49801. Phone: (906) 774-4321. Fax: (906) 774-7799. Web Site: thebearonlinetripod.com. Licensee: Northern Star Broadcasting L.L.C. (group owner; acq 11-5-01; grpsl). Reddy, Begley & McCormick. Format: Classic rock, AOR. Target aud: 25-54. ♦Veronica Roberts, gen mgr; Kevin Lynch, opns mgr & progmg dir; Steve Ponchaud, opns mgr; Tommy Johnson, gen sls mgr; Tom Hill, news dir; Paul Buck, chief of engrg.

WMIQ(AM)— Co-owned with WIMK(FM). January 1947: 1450 khz; 1 kw-U. TL: N45 49 16 W88 03 16. Web Site: talk1450.tripod.com. Network: Network: USA, ABC Information & Entertainment. Rep: Patt. Format: News/talk. News staff: one; News: 24 hrs wkly. Target aud: 35-64; educated, middle to upper income listeners. ♦Pete Frecchio, progmg dir.

WJNR-FM— Aug 17, 1972: 101.5 mhz; 100 w. 620 ft. TL: N45 49 15 W88 02 38. (CP: 100 kw, ant 613 ft.). Stereo. 212 W. J St. 49801. Phone: (906) 774-5731. Fax: (906) 774-4542. E-mail: wjnr@chartermi.net. Web Site: www.resultsbroadcasting.com. Licensee: Results Broadcasting of Michigan Inc. Group owner: Results Broadcasting (acq 6-5-97). Network: ABC Information & Entertainment. Format: Hot new country. Target aud: 25-54. ♦Bruce Grassman, pres; Keith Huotari, opns mgr; Trisha Peterson, gen mgr & gen sls mgr; Aaron Harper, news dir; Rick Eby, engrg VP & chief of engrg.

*WVCM(FM)— Not on air, target date: unknown: 91.5 mhz; 500 w. 600 ft. TL: N45 49 15 W88 02 25. 3434 W. Kilbourn Ave., Milwaukee, WI 53208. Phone: (414) 935-3000. Fax: (414) 935-3015. E-mail: wvcm@vcyamerica.org. Web Site: www.vcyamerica.org. Licensee: VCY America Inc. Group owner: VCY/America Inc. Format: Christian. ♦Randall Melchert, pres; Vic Eliason, VP & gen mgr; Jim Schneider, progmg dir.

Iron River

WIKB(AM)— Nov 18, 1949: 1230 khz; 1 kw-U. TL: N46 03 55 W88 38 17. Box AC, 809 W. Genesee St. 49935. Phone: (906) 265-5104. Fax: (906) 265-3486. E-mail: wikb@up.net. Licensee: Heartland Communications License LLC. (group owner; acq 5-10-2004; $1.25 million. with co-located FM). Rep: Roslin. Format: Oldies. News staff: one; News: 15 hrs wkly. Target aud: General. ♦Bill Leonoff, opns mgr & news dir; Jay Barry, gen mgr, gen sls mgr & chief of engrg.

WIKB-FM— Sept 25, 1981: 99.1 mhz; 50 kw. 492 ft. TL: N46 06 03 W88 32 23. Stereo.

Ironwood

*WICE(FM)— Not on air, target date: unknown: 88.3 mhz; 10 kw vert. Ant 515 ft. TL: N46 26 28 W90 11 26. Broadcasting for the Challenged Inc., 188 S. Bellevue, Suite 222, Memphis, TN 38104. Phone: (901) 726-8970. Licensee: Broadcasting for the Challenged Inc. ♦George S. Flinn Jr., pres.

WIMI(FM)— Listing follows WJMS(AM).

WJMS(AM)— Nov 3, 1931: 590 khz; 5 kw-D, 1 kw-N, DA-N. TL: N46 25 25 W90 12 30. 222 E. Lawrence St. 49938. Phone: (906) 932-2411. Fax: (906) 932-2485. E-mail: wimi@broadcast.net. Web Site: www.wimifm.com. Licensee: Roberts Broadcasting Inc. Group owner: Badger Communications L.L.C. (acq 6-4-01; grpsl). Network: CBS. Rep: D & R Radio. Format: Country, talk. News staff: one. Target aud: 25 plus. ♦David Winters, pres; Scott Michaels, progmg dir; Richard Mertz, engrg mgr & chief of engrg.

WIMI(FM)— Co-owned with WJMS(AM). March 1976: 99.7 mhz; 100 kw. 561 ft. TL: N46 25 25 W90 14 53. Stereo. Format: Adult contemp.

WUPM(FM)— Oct 17, 1977: 106.9 mhz; 53 kw. 495 ft. TL: N46 28 18 W90 00 43. Box 107 49938. Secondary address: 209 Harrison 49938. Phone: (906) 932-5234. Fax: (906) 932-1548. E-mail: wupm@wupm-whry.com. Web Site: www.wupm-whry.com. Licensee: Big G Little O Inc. Network: ABC. Format: Adult contemp, CHR. ♦Charles H. Gervasio, pres & gen mgr; Laura Keller, progmg VP & progmg dir.

Ishpeming

WIAN(AM)— 1947: 1240 khz; 1 kw-U. TL: N46 30 16 W87 40 46. 1009 W. Ridge St., Marquette 49855. Phone: (906) 225-1313. Fax: (906) 225-1324. Licensee: Northern Star Broadcasting L.L.C. (group owner; acq 11-5-01; grpsl). Format: News/talk. ♦Veronica Roberts, gen mgr; Tammy Johnsen, rgnl sls mgr; Coral Howe, chief of engrg.

WJPD(FM)— Co-owned with WIAN(AM). May 15, 1975: 92.3 mhz; 100 kw. Ant 508 ft. TL: N46 30 51 W87 28 58. Stereo.

WMQT(FM)— Listing follows WZAM(AM).

WZAM(AM)— June 26, 1959:: 970 khz; 5 kw-D, 62 w-N. TL: N46 30 20 W87 32 24. Stereo. 121 N. Front St., Suite A, Marquette 49855. Phone: (906) 225-9100. Fax: (906) 225-5577. Licensee: Taconite Broadcasting Inc. (acq 7-25-2005; $827,300 with co-located FM). Format: News. Target aud: 25-54. ♦Tom Mogush, gen mgr & sls dir; Dennis Whitley, news dir.

WMQT(FM)— Co-owned with WZAM(AM). Jan 26, 1974: 107.7 mhz; 98 kw. Ant 639 ft. TL: N46 30 08 W87 38 52. Stereo. E-mail: tom@wmqt.com. Web Site: www.wmqt.com. Format: Adult contemp. News staff: 2. Target aud: 18-49. ♦Tom Mogush, opns dir, sls VP & gen sls mgr; Jim Koski, progmg dir.

Jackson

WIBM(AM)— 1925: 1450 khz; 1 kw-U. TL: N42 13 16 W84 26 03. 1700 Glenshire Dr. 49201. Phone: (517) 787-9546. Fax: (517) 787-7517. Web Site: www.espnradio1450.com. Licensee: Jackson Radio Works Inc. (group owner; acq 11-14-97; grpsl). Michigan Spot Sales Shaw, Pittman. Format: Sports. News staff: 2; News: one hr wkly. Target aud: 18-49; sports enthusiasts. Spec prog: Polish, Spanish. ♦Bruce I. Goldsen, pres; Jamie McKibbin, opns dir; Linda McDougall, gen sls mgr; Sue Goldsen, VP, sls VP & mktg VP; Scott Clow, progmg dir & progmg mgr; Michael Bradford, chief of engrg.

*WJCQ(FM)— 2004: 89.7 mhz; 500 w. Ant 121 ft. TL: N42 17 05 W84 18 40. 901 Elizabeth Ct., Mount Pleasant 48858. Phone: (989) 779-9178. Fax: (989) 779-1558. Licensee: Great Lakes Community Broadcasting Inc. Format: Oldies. ♦James J. McCluskey, gen mgr.

*WJKN(AM)— January 1962: . Stn currently dark 1510 khz; 5 kw-D, DA. TL: N42 11 10 W84 22 39. (CP: TL: N42 10 08 W84 23 30). Stereo. Spring Arbor University, 106 E. Main St., Spring Arbor 49283. Phone: (517) 750-9723. Fax: (517) 750-6619. E-mail: wsae@arbor.edu. Licensee: Spring Arbor University (acq 1-12-01). Network: Network: CBS, Westwood One. Rep: Patt. Format: Inspirational. ♦Michelle Dawson, gen mgr & progmg dir; Dave Beason, chief of engrg.

*WJKQ(FM)— 2004: 88.5 mhz; 100 w vert. Ant 112 ft. TL: N42 16 22 W84 21 27. 901 Elizabeth Ct., Mount Pleasant 48858. Phone: (989) 779-9178. Fax: (989) 779-1558. Licensee: Great Lakes Community Broadcasting Inc. Format: Oldies. ♦James McCluskey, gen mgr.

WJXQ(FM)— May 30, 1976: 106.1 mhz; 50 kw. 489 ft. TL: N42 23 28 W84 37 22. Stereo. 2495 N. Cedar, Suite 106, Holt 48842. Phone: (517) 699-0111. Fax: (517) 699-1880. Web Site: www.q106fm.com. Licensee: Rubber City Radio Group. Group owner: Rubber City Radio Group Inc. (acq 7-12-00; grpsl). Rep: Katz Radio. Format: AOR. News staff: one; News: one hr wkly. Target aud: 25-44; baby boomers with an inclination for rock and roll. ♦Dave Johnson, gen mgr; Paul Cashin, opns mgr & mus dir; Scott Truman, gen sls mgr; Bob Olson, progmg dir.

WKHM(AM)— Dec 7, 1951: 970 khz; 1 kw-U, DA-2. TL: N42 11 39 W84 25 50. 1700 Glenshire Dr. 49201. Phone: (517) 787-9546. Phone: (517) 787-3397. Fax: (517) 787-7517. E-mail: bgoldsen@klo53.com. Web Site: www.wkhm.com. Licensee: Jackson Radio Works Inc. (group owner; acq 12-8-97; grpsl). Network: ABC Information & Entertainment. Shaw, Pittman. Format: News/talk. News staff: one; News: 15 hrs wkly. Target aud: 25-64. ♦Bruce I. Goldsen, pres; Sue Goldsen, VP, sls VP & mktg VP; Jamie McKibbin, opns dir; Linda McDougall, gen sls mgr; Deanna Stocker, rgnl sls mgr; Scott Clow, progmg dir; Tim Durkee, news dir; Michael Bradford, chief of engrg.

WVIC(FM)— 1955: 94.1 mhz; 40 kw. 551 ft. TL: N42 23 32 W84 40 00. Stereo. 2495 N. Cedar, Holt 48842. Phone: (517) 699-0111. Fax: (517) 699-1880. Web Site: www.wvic.net. Licensee: Rubber City Radio Group. Group owner: Rubber City Radio Group Inc. (acq 7-12-00; grpsl). Rep: Katz Radio. Format: Classic hits. News staff: one; News: 17.5 hrs wkly. Target aud: 25-54; Female 25-49. ♦Dave Johnson, gen mgr; Paul Cashin, opns mgr & progmg dir; Scott Truman, gen sls mgr.

Kalamazoo

*WAYK(FM)— Feb 3, 1997: 88.3 mhz; 10 kw. 397 ft. TL: N42 18 23 W85 39 25. 161 E. Michigan Ave., Suite 600 49007. Phone: (269) 383-3600. Fax: (269) 381-0239. Web Site: www.way.fm. Licensee: Cornerstone University. Format: Christian hit radio. ♦Rich Anderson, gen mgr; Tom Bos, rgnl sls mgr; Brook Taylor, prom dir; Mike Couchman, progmg dir.

*WIDR(FM)— July 7, 1975: 89.1 mhz; 100 w. 158 ft. TL: N42 16 55 W85 37 05. Stereo. Western Michigan Univ., 1511 Faunce Student Ser. Building 49008-6301. Phone: (269) 387-6301. Phone: (269) 387-6303. Fax: (269) 387-2839. Web Site: www.widr.org. Licensee: Western Michigan University Board of Trustees. Format: Var/div, educ, progsv. News: 7 hrs wkly. Target aud: 18-25; college students. Spec prog: Black 18 hrs, Sp 3 hrs, gospel 3 hrs, relg 3 hrs, British 3 hrs, Celtic 3 hrs wkly. ♦Wendy Wise, gen mgr; Jason Olexa, progmg dir; Ben Jones, news dir.

*WKDS(FM)— October 1982: 89.9 mhz; 100 w. 150 ft. TL: N42 14 36 W85 34 19. Stereo. 606 E. Kilgore Rd. 49001. Phone: (269) 337-0200. Fax: (269) 337-0251. Licensee: Kalamazoo Board of Education. Arent, Fox, Kintner, Plotkin & Kahn. Format: Div, educ. News: 3 hrs wkly. Target aud: High school & college students.

WKFR-FM—See Battle Creek

WKLZ(AM)— Feb 4, 1956: 1470 khz; 800 w-D, 1 kw-N. TL: N42 21 41 W85 34 37. Stereo. 4200 W. Main St. 49006. Phone: (269) 345-7121. Fax: (269) 345-1436. Licensee: Fairfield Broadcasting Co. (acq 7-1-85; $175,000; 4-1-85). Network: CNN Radio. Rep: Katz Radio. Format: Talk. Target aud: 25-54; sports fans, primarily men. ♦Stephen C. Trivers, pres & gen mgr; William J. Wertz, sr VP; Ken Lanphear, opns VP & opns mgr; Dennis Martin, sls VP & gen sls mgr; Randy Rowley, prom dir & prom mgr; Laura Lehman, news dir; Geary Morrill, chief of engrg.

WQLR(FM)— Co-owned with WKLZ(AM). June 19, 1964: 106.5 mhz; 33 kw. 600 ft. TL: N42 28 32 W85 29 22. Stereo. Format: Adult contemp.

WKMI(AM)— August 1947: 1360 khz; 5 kw-D, 1 kw-N, DA-2. TL: N42 19 36 W85 31 39. Box 50911 49005-0911. Secondary address: 4154 Jennings Dr. 49048. Phone: (269) 344-0111. Fax: (269) 344-4223. E-mail: radio@wkmi.com. Web Site: www.wkmi.com. Licensee: Cumulus Licensing Corp. Group owner: Cumulus Media Inc. (acq 5-26-98; grpsl). Network: ABC Information & Entertainment. Format: News/talk. News staff: 1; News: 30 hrs wkly. Target aud: 25 plus. Spec prog: Sports. ♦Lew Dickey, CEO & pres; Jon Pinch, COO; Martin Gausvik, CFO; John Sterling, gen mgr; Mike McKelly, opns mgr; Mi Rhee Vanderwal, gen sls mgr; Sheri Moffitt, natl sls mgr; Stephanie John, prom dir; Andy Stone, progmg dir, news dir & pub affrs dir; Dale Schiesser, chief of engrg.

WKPR(AM)— Oct 20, 1960: 1420 khz; 1 kw-D, DA. TL: N42 18 46 W85 37 06. Box 50867 49005. Secondary address: 2244 Ravine Rd. 49004. Phone: (269) 381-1420. Fax: (269) 381-1420. Licensee: Kalamazoo Broadcasting Co. Group owner: Kuiper Stations Network:

Stations in the U.S. Michigan

Developers & Brokers of Radio Properties — contact American Media Services at our suite: Philadelphia Marriott Downtown 215-625-2900. 843-972-2200. americanmediaservices.com. Charleston, SC. Dallas, TX • Chicago, IL • Austin, TX. American Media Services, LLC

USA. Format: Relg. Target aud: 25 plus. ♦William E. Kuiper Sr., pres; William E. Kuiper Jr., gen mgr; Stan Gebben, stn mgr.

WKZO(AM)— Sept 10, 1931: 590 khz; 5 kw-U, DA-N. TL: N42 21 00 W85 33 43. 4200 W. Main St. 49006. Phone: (269) 345-7121. Fax: (269) 345-1436. Web Site: www.wkzo.com. Licensee: Fairfield Broadcasting Co. (acq 11-15-96; $900,000). Network: CBS. Format: News/talk. News staff: 5. Target aud: 25 plus; upscale, 60% male, 40% female. Spec prog: Farm 10 hrs, relg 5 hrs wkly. ♦Bill Wertz, exec VP; Stephen C. Trivers, pres & gen mgr; Ken Lanphear, opns VP & opns dir; Dennis Martin, sls VP & sls dir; Randy Rowley, prom dir; Dave Jaconette, progmg dir; Laura Lehman, news dir; Geary Morrillo, chief of engrg.

*WMUK(FM)— Jan 8, 1951: 102.1 mhz; 50 kw. 490 ft. TL: N42 25 03 W85 31 55. Stereo. 1903 W. Michigan Ave. 49008-5351. Phone: (269) 387-5715. Fax: (269) 387-4630. E-mail: wmukfm@wmich.edu. Web Site: www.wmuk.org. Licensee: Western Michigan University Board of Trustees. Network: Network: NPR, PRI. Format: Class, jazz, news/talk. News staff: 3; News: 38 hrs wkly. Target aud: General; educated, affluent adults. Spec prog: Bluegrass 4 hrs wkly. ♦Floyd Pientka, gen mgr; Vickie Langkam, dev dir; Michael Hahn, adv mgr; Klayton Woodworth, progmg dir; Andy Robins, news dir; Mark Tomlonson, chief of engrg.

WNWN(AM)—See Portage

WNWN-FM—(Coldwater). Nov 11, 1950: 98.5 mhz; 50 kw. 500 ft. TL: N42 03 28 W84 59 51. Stereo. 25 W. Michigan Ave., Battle Creek 49017. Phone: (269) 968-1991. Fax: (269) 968-1881. Web Site: www.wincountry.com. Licensee: Midwest Communications Inc. (group owner; acq 6-1-95; grpsl). Network: ABC Information & Entertainment. Rep: Christal. Format: Contemp country. News staff: 3; News: 5 hrs wkly. Target aud: 25-54. ♦D.E. Wright, pres; Peter Tanz, gen mgr; Cindy Ireland, gen sls mgr; P.J. Lacey, progmg dir & progmg.

WQSN(AM)— Sept 24, 1998: 1660 khz; 10 kw-D, 1 kw-N. TL: N42 14 11 W85 34 37. 4200 W. Main St. 49006. Phone: (269) 345-7121. Fax: (269) 345-1436. Web Site: www.wqsn.com. Licensee: Fairfield Broadcasting Co. Format: Sports. ♦Stephen C. Trivers, pres & gen mgr; William Wertz, exec VP; Ken Lanphear, opns VP & opns dir.

WRKR(FM)—(Portage). Oct 13, 1988: 107.7 mhz; 50 kw. 500 ft. TL: N42 07 43 W85 20 16. Stereo. Box 50911 49005-0911. Secondary address: 4154 Jennings Dr. 49001-1087. Phone: (269) 344-0111. Phone: (269) 964-7173. Fax: (269) 344-4223. E-mail: radio@wrkr.com. Web Site: www.wrkr.com. Licensee: Cumulus Licensing Corp. Group owner: Cumulus Media Inc. (acq 5-26-98; grpsl). Format: Classic rock, AOR. News staff: 2; News: 4 hrs wkly. Target aud: 25-54. Spec prog: Blues 5 hrs, jazz 4 hrs wkly. ♦Lew Dickey, CEO & pres; John Pinch, COO; Martin Gausvik, CFO; John Sterling, gen mgr; Mike McKelly, opns mgr; Mike Klein, gen sls mgr; Sheri Moffitt, natl sls mgr; Jay Deacon, progmg dir; Stephanie John, prom dir & news dir; Dale Schiesser, chief of engrg.

Kalkaska

WKLT(FM)— Apr 8, 1979: 97.5 mhz; 32 kw. 670 ft. TL: N44 47 29 W85 14 20. Stereo. 1020 Hastings St., Traverse City 49686. Phone: (231) 947-0003. Fax: (231) 947-7002. Web Site: www.wklt.com. Licensee: Northern Radio of Michigan (acq 1-82; $320,000;. FTR: 1-18-82). Rep: Christal. Fletcher, Heald & Hildreth. Format: Classic AOR. News: 2 hrs wkly. Target aud: 25-54; baby boomers & young adults. Spec prog: Sunday night classics, blues 2 hrs wkly. ♦Richard Dills, pres; Jackie Gordon, natl sls mgr; Terri Ray, progmg dir; Dennis Murray, chief of engrg.

Kentwood

WGVU(AM)—Licensed to Kentwood. See Grand Rapids

WJNZ(AM)— Sept 18, 1978: 1140 khz; 5 kw-D, DA. TL: N42 56 13 W85 27 20. 1919 Eastern Ave. S.E., Grand Rapids 49507. Phone: (616) 475-4299. Fax: (616) 475-4335. E-mail: mjs@wjnz.com. Web Site: www.wjnz.com. Licensee: WJNZ Radio L.L.C. (acq 9-22-2003;

$360,000). Network: Jones Radio Networks. Koerner, Baraff, Olender & Hochberg. Format: Urban, rhythm and blues. Target aud: 25-54; Baby Boomers. Spec prog: Jazz 6 hrs, gospel 4 hrs. ♦Mike St. Cyr, pres & gen mgr.

Kingsford

*WEUL(FM)— Feb 11, 1990: 98.1 mhz; 240 w. 482 ft. TL: N45 49 58 W88 04 57. 130 Carmen Dr., Marquette 49855. Phone: (906) 249-1423. Fax: (906) 249-4042. E-mail: gospelop@chartermi.net. Web Site: www.gospelopportunities.com. Licensee: Gospel Opportunities Inc. Format: Relg. News staff: 3. ♦W. Curtis Marker, gen mgr & progmg dir.

Kingsley

WLDR(AM)— Apr 17, 1947: 1210 khz; 50 kw-D, 2.5 kw-CH. TL: N44 33 34 W85 35 37. 118 S. Union St., Traverse City 49684. Phone: (231) 947-3220. Fax: (231) 947-7201. E-mail: wldr@wldr.com. Licensee: Fort Bend Broadcasting Co. (group owner; acq 5-14-01; $225,000). Format: News/talk. ♦Lori McFarlan, gen mgr, sls dir & gen sls mgr; Rich Nadeau, progmg dir; Dave Maxson, news dir.

Lake City

*WAIR(FM)—Not on air, target date: Fall 2003: 104.9 mhz; 1.6 kw. Ant 489 ft. TL: N44 14 56 W85 18 48. Box 388, Williamston 48895. Phone: (517) 381-0573. Fax: (877) 850-0881. E-mail: info@positivehits.com. Web Site: www.positivehits.com. Licensee: Superior Communications. ♦Jenn Czelada, gen mgr.

Lakeview

WSCG-FM— November 1989: 106.3 mhz; 3 kw. 328 ft. TL: N43 24 33 W85 15 53. Stereo. Box 578, Greenville 48838. Secondary address: 9181 S. Greenville Rd., Greenville 48838. Phone: (616) 754-3656. Fax: (616) 754-2390. Licensee: Stafford Broadcasting L.L.C. (acq 10-19-2004; with WSCG(AM) Greenville). Format: Country. ♦Bruce Bentley, gen mgr & opns mgr; John Clark, gen mgr.

L'Anse

WCUP(FM)— Jan 1, 1998: 105.7 mhz; 50 kw. 492 ft. TL: N46 46 48 W88 32 06. Stereo. 805 B US 41, Baraga 49908. Phone: (906) 353-9287. Fax: (906) 353-9200. E-mail: wcupprod@up.net. Web Site: www.wcupfm.com. Licensee: Keweenaw Bay Indian Community (acq 5-31-01; $176,000. for debt for 70%). Network: ABC. Format: Country. News: 1 hr wkly. Target aud: 18 plus. Spec prog: American Indian 2 hrs wkly. ♦Ed Janisse, gen mgr; John Preston, sls dir; Mary Tober, opns VP, opns dir, progmg dir & progmg mgr.

Lansing

WHZZ(FM)—Listing follows WILS(AM).

WILS(AM)— July 17, 1947: 1320 khz; 5 kw-D, 1 kw-N, DA-2. TL: N42 41 30 W84 33 38. Box 25008 48909. Secondary address: 600 W. Cavanaugh Rd. 48910. Phone: (517) 393-1320. Fax: (517) 393-0882. Licensee: MacDonald Broadcasting Co. (group owner; acq 12-20-2001); grpsl). Rep: D & R Radio. Format: Nostalgia. Target aud: 25-54. Spec prog: Smart shopper 5 hrs wkly. ♦Sharon Crane, gen mgr, gen sls mgr & gen sls mgr.

WHZZ(FM)—Co-owned with WILS(AM). January 1967: 101.7 mhz; 4 kw. 400 ft. TL: N42 43 42 W84 30 54. Stereo. Web Site: www.z101.7fm.com. Format: CHR. Target aud: 25-54; upscale adults. ♦Gary Harding, engrg dir.

WITL-FM— Apr 15, 1964: 100.7 mhz; 26.5 kw. 640 ft. TL: N42 40 33 W84 30 00. Stereo. 3200 Pine Tree Rd. 48911. Phone: (517) 393-1010. Fax: (517) 394-3391. E-mail: witl@acd.net. Web Site: www.witl.com. Licensee: Citadel Broadcasting Co. Group owner: Citadel Broadcasting Corp. (acq 2000; grpsl). Rep: Christal.

Leventhal, Senter & Lerman. Format: Country. News staff: one. Target aud: 25-54. ♦Farid Suleman, chmn; Rod Krol, gen mgr; Ray Marshall, opns mgr; Brian Olson, sls dir; Gordon Gray, rgnl sls mgr; Jordan Lee, prom mgr; Jay J. McCrae, progmg mgr; Robert Bowe, chief of engrg.

WJIM(AM)— 1934: 1240 khz; 1 kw-U. TL: N42 44 22 W84 30 39. (CP: 890 w). 3420 Pine Tree Rd. 48911. Phone: (517) 394-7272. Fax: (517) 394-3391. E-mail: wjim@acd.net. Web Site: www.newstalk1240.com. Licensee: Citadel Broadcasting Co. Group owner: Citadel Broadcasting Corp. (acq 2000; grpsl). Network: Network: Westwood One, ABC. Rep: Christal. Leventhal, Senter & Lerman. Format: News, info, talk. News staff: one; News: 4 hrs wkly. Target aud: 25-54. ♦Farid Suleman, CEO & chmn; Rod Krol, gen mgr; Ray Marshall, opns mgr; Brian Olson, sls dir; Jack Robbins, progmg dir; Gary Austin, news dir; Robert Bowe, chief of engrg.

WJIM-FM— June 1960: 97.5 mhz; 45 kw. 512 ft. TL: N42 40 33 W84 30 00. Stereo. E-mail: oldies975@acd.net. Web Site: www.oldies975.com. Network: CNN Radio. Format: Oldies. News staff: one; News: 2 hrs wkly. ♦Andy Warnock, prom dir; Mike Benson, progmg dir; Monica Harris, news dir.

WJXQ(FM)—See Jackson

*WLNZ(FM)— Feb 11, 1994: 89.7 mhz; 100 w. 98 ft. TL: N42 44 16 W84 33 09. Lansing Community College, 400 N. Capitol Ave., Suite 001 48933. Phone: (517) 483-1710. Phone: (517) 483-9897. Fax: (517) 483-1894. E-mail: wlnz@lansing.cc.mi.us. Web Site: www.lcc.edu/wlnz. Licensee: Lansing Community College. Network: Network: PRI, NPR. Format: Jazz, blues, AAA. Spec prog: Reggae 4 hrs, big band 3 hrs, folk 3 hrs, Sp 4 hrs wkly. ♦Dave Downing, gen mgr; Lyn Peraino, progmg dir; Dae Lowry, mus dir; Lyle Layin, chief of engrg.

WMMQ(FM)—See East Lansing

WQTX(FM)—See Charlotte

WTXQ(FM)—See Saint Johns

WVFN(AM)—See East Lansing

WWSJ(AM)—See Saint Johns

Lapeer

WLSP(AM)— Nov 16, 1962: 1530 khz; 5 kw-D, DA-D. TL: N43 01 35 W83 17 12. 3338 E. Bristol Rd., Burton 48529. Phone: (810) 743-1080. Fax: (810) 742-7170. Licensee: Regent Broadcasting of Flint Inc. Group owner: Regent Communications Inc. (acq 7-18-02; $1.3 million. with co-located FM). Network: Westwood One. Rep: Patt. Earl Stanley. Format: Sports. Target aud: 35 plus. ♦Mark Thomas, gen mgr.

WQUS(FM)—Co-owned with WLSP(AM). Feb 6, 1968: 103.1 mhz; 3 kw. 299 ft. TL: N43 04 49 W83 11 30. Stereo. Web Site: www.radiox103.com. Format: Adult rock. Target aud: 25-40; college educated men & women. Spec prog: AOR, gospel, blues. ♦David Corley, sls dir; Mr. Jordan Hayes, progmg dir; Tony LaBrie, mus dir.

*WMPC(AM)— Dec 6, 1926: 1230 khz; 1 kw-U. TL: N43 04 46 W83 18 35. Box 104, 1800 N. Lapeer Rd. 48446. Phone: (810) 664-6211. Fax: (810) 664-5361. E-mail: wmpc@chartermi.net. Web Site: http://lapeer.org/ServiceOrg/WMPC. Licensee: The Calvary Bible Church of Lapeer Inc. Format: Relg. News staff: one; News: 24 hrs wkly. Target aud: General. ♦Bob Baldwin, gen mgr & opns dir.

Leland

WFCX(FM)— Aug 9, 1991: 94.3 mhz; 3.6 kw. 426 ft. TL: N44 54 48 W85 49 18. (CP: 14.88 kw). Stereo. 1020 Hastings, Traverse City 49686. Phone: (231) 947-0003. Fax: (231) 947-7002. Web Site: www.classichitsthefox.com. Licensee: Northern Michigan Radio Inc. (acq 12-23-93; $1.1 million. with WFDX(FM) Atlanta, MI; FTR: 1-17-94). Rep: Christal. Fletcher, Heald & Hildreth. Format: Classic

Michigan

Hits. News staff: one; News: 7 hrs wkly. Target aud: 25-54. Spec prog: Relg one hr wkly. ♦Charlie Ferguson, gen mgr.

Leroy Township

*WLGH(FM)— December 1996: 88.1 mhz; 2.5 kw. 328 ft. TL: N42 42 20 W84 21 25. Box 388, Williamston 48895. Phone: (517) 381-0573. Fax: (877) 850-0881. E-mail: info@positivehits.com. Web Site: www.positivehits.com. Licensee: Superior Communications. Format: Adult, Christian hit radio. ♦Edward Czelada, pres; Jenn Czelada, gen mgr.

Lexington

WBTI(FM)—Licensed to Lexington. See Port Huron

Livonia

WCAR(AM)— Oct 23, 1963: 1090 khz; 250 w-D, 500 w-N, DA-2. TL: N42 19 46 W83 21 43. 32500 Park Ln., Garden City 48135. Phone: (734) 525-1111. Fax: (734) 525-3608. Web Site: www.catholicradio.org. Licensee: 1090 Investments L.L.C. (acq 7-6-98; $2 million). Format: Catholic. Target aud: 25 plus. Spec prog: Ethnic.

Ludington

WKLA(AM)— Oct 9, 1944: 1450 khz; 1 kw-U. TL: N43 57 05 W86 25 28. 5941 W. U.S. 10 49431. Phone: (616) 843-3438. Fax: (616) 843-1886. Licensee: Lake Michigan Broadcasting Inc. (group owner; (acq 9-20-96; grpsl). Network: ABC Information & Entertainment. Format: News/talk, adult standards, talk. News staff: one; News: 4 hrs wkly. Target aud: 40 plus; mature adults. ♦Brett Michaels, opns dir; Jason Wilder, opns mgr & mus dir; Mike K. Baerwolf, prom mgr, progmg dir & chief of engrg.

WKLA-FM— May 1971: 106.3 mhz; 6 kw. 400 ft. TL: N43 03 30 W86 24 59. Stereo. Phone: (414) 978-9000. Network: ABC. Patt Media Shaw Pittman. Format: Adult contemp. News staff: 2; News: 3 hrs wkly. Target aud: 25-50. ♦Mike Baerwolf, opns dir & progmg VP; Jason Wilder, prom VP; R. J. Wheaton, news dir.

WKZC(FM)—See Scottville

Mackinaw City

*WIAB(FM)— Oct 1, 2000: 88.5 mhz; 20 kw. Ant 430 ft. TL: N45 40 00 W84 38 05. Box 199, Interlochen 49643. Phone: (231) 276-4400. Fax: (231) 276-4417. Web Site: www.interlochen.org/pr. Licensee: Interlochen Center for the Arts (acq 3-14-2005; $580,000). Format: Classical, news. ♦Thom Paulson, stn mgr.

WLJZ(FM)— Sept 6, 1989: 94.5 mhz; 3 kw. 380 ft. TL: N45 40 02 W84 38 06. Stereo. 1356 Mackinaw Ave., Cheboygan 49721. Phone: (231) 627-2341. Fax: (231) 627-7000. Web Site: www.modernrockthezone.com. Licensee: Northern Star Broadcasting L.L.C. (group owner; acq 9-10-98; grpsl). Rep: Allied Radio Partners. Format: Modern rock. ♦Palmer Pyle, pres; Chris Monk, VP; Chris Monk, gen mgr.

Manistee

WMTE(AM)— June 7, 1951: 1340 khz; 1 kw-U. TL: N44 14 07 W86 19 05. 52 Greenbush St. 49660. Phone: (231) 723-9906. Phone: (231) 843-3438. Fax: (231) 723-9908. Licensee: Lake Michigan Broadcasting Inc. (group owner; (acq 9-20-96; grpsl). Network: ABC. Rep: Michigan. Format: News/talk. News staff: 1. Target aud: General. ♦Judith Ouvry, stn mgr.

WMTE-FM— June 22, 1994: 101.5 mhz; 3 kw. 115 ft. TL: N44 12 18 W86 17 22. Stereo. 52 Greenbush 49660. Phone: (231) 723-0010. Phone: (231) 723-9906. Fax: (231) 723-9908. E-mail: judy@wkla.com. Web Site: www.oldies1015.com. Licensee: Lake Michigan Broadcasting Inc. (group owner; (acq 2000; $300,000). Patt Media Format: Oldies. News staff: one. Spec prog: Pol 6 hrs, relg 2 hrs wkly. ♦Judith Ouvry, stn mgr, opns dir, sls dir & progmg dir; Mike Baerwolf, progmg dir.

*WVXM(FM)— Aug 1, 1970: 97.7 mhz; 2.5 kw. Ant 515 ft. TL: N44 12 40 W86 17 53. Stereo. c/o WVXU(FM), 1223 Central Pkwy., Cincinnati, OH 45214. Phone: (513) 352-9170. Fax: (513) 241-8456. E-mail: wvxu@cinradio.org. Web Site: www.wvxu.org. Licensee: Cincinnati Classical Public Radio Inc. (acq 8-22-2005; grpsl). Network: Network: NPR, PRI. Baker & Hostetler LLP. Format: News and info. ♦Richard Eiswerth, gen mgr.

Manistique

WMII(AM)—Not on air, target date: unknown: 650 khz; 30 kw-D, 212 w-N, 20 kw-CH, DA-3. TL: N45 55 57 W86 17 00. Box 60991, Palo Alto, CA 94306. Licensee: JNE Investments. ♦Jeffrey N. Eustis, gen mgr.

WPIQ(FM)— 2005: 99.9 mhz; 6 kw. Ant 151 ft. TL: N45 58 13 W86 11 06. 6130W U.S. Hwy. 2, Suite B 49854. Phone: (906) 341-7588. Fax: (906) 228-8128. E-mail: wpiq@upmail.com. Web Site: www.wpiqradio.com. Licensee: Todd Stuart Noordyk. Group owner: Great Lakes Radio Inc. Format: Talk. ♦Todd Noordyk, pres & gen mgr.

WTIQ(AM)— Feb 11, 1968: 1490 khz; 1 kw-U. TL: N45 57 51 W86 16 37. Stereo. 7876W County Rd. 442 49854-9000. Phone: (906) 341-8444. Fax: (906) 341-6222. E-mail: wtiq@chartermi.net. Web Site: www.radioresultsnetwork.com. Licensee: Lakes Radio Inc. (group owner; acq 11-30-99; grpsl). Meyer, Faller, Weisman & Rosenberg, P. Format: Oldies. Target aud: 25-54; blue & white collar. ♦Rick Duerson, gen mgr; L. David Vaughan, stn mgr.

Marine City

WHLX(AM)—Licensed to Marine City. See Port Huron

Marlette

WBGV(FM)— July 25, 1999: 92.5 mhz; 3 kw. TL: N43 17 10 W82 58 17. Stereo. 1260 Yosemite Blvd., Birmingham 48009. Secondary address: 19 S. Elk St., Sandusky 48422. Phone: (810) 648-2700. Phone: (810) 679-2276. Fax: (248) 540-3379. E-mail: gebv@aol.com. Licensee: GB Broadcasting Co. (acq 6-5-92). Network: ABC. Format: Country. News staff: one; News: 2 hrs wkly. Target aud: General. ♦George Benko, pres; Robert Armstrong, gen mgr & opns mgr.

*WMSQ(FM)— 2004: 89.3 mhz; 100 w. Ant 98 ft. TL: N43 22 06 W83 07 00. 901 Elizabeth Ct., Mount Pleasant 48858. Phone: (989) 779-9178. Licensee: Great Lakes Community Broadcasting Inc. Format: Oldies. ♦James McClusky, gen mgr.

Marquette

WDMJ(AM)— July 1, 1931: 1320 khz; 5 kw-D, 1 kw-N, DA-N. TL: N46 32 40 W87 26 42. 1009 W. Ridge St., Suite A 49855-3963. Phone: (906) 225-1313. Fax: (906) 225-1324. Web Site: www.wjpd.com. Licensee: Northern Star Broadcasting L.L.C. (group owner; acq 11-5-01; grpsl). Network: ABC Information & Entertainment. Rep: Michigan. Format: News/talk. Target aud: 25-54.

WFXD(FM)— Apr 6, 1974: 103.3 mhz; 100 kw. 544 ft. TL: N46 30 52 W87 28 37. Stereo. 2025 US 41 W. 49855. Phone: (906) 228-6800. Fax: (906) 228-8128. E-mail: todd@greatlakesradio.org. Web Site: www.greatlakesshopping.com. Licensee: Great Lakes Radio Inc. (group owner; acq 11-30-99; grpsl). Network: Network: Westwood One, Jones Radio Networks. Rep: Patt. Lukas, McGowan, Nace & Gutierrez. Format: Country. News staff: one; News: 12 hrs wkly. Target aud: 25-54. ♦Todd Noordyk, pres, gen mgr & gen sls mgr; Kevin Downey, progmg dir.

*WHWL(FM)— Dec 16, 1965: 95.7 mhz; 100 kw. Ant 531 ft. TL: N46 29 52 W87 24 59. Stereo. 130 Carmen Dr. 49855. Phone: (906) 249-1423. Fax: (906) 249-4042. E-mail: whwl@whwl.net. Web Site: www.whwl.net. Licensee: Gospel Opportunities Inc. (acq 4-19-76). Format: Relg. ♦W. Curtis Marker, gen mgr & progmg dir.

WIAN(AM)—See Ishpeming

*WNMU-FM— August 1963: 90.1 mhz; 100 kw. 930 ft. TL: N46 21 09 W87 51 32. Stereo. Learning Resources Ctr., Northern Michigan Univ., 1401 Presque Isle Ave. 49855. Phone: (906) 227-2600. Fax: (906) 227-2905. Web Site: www.nmu.edu/wnmufm. Licensee: Board of Trustees of Northern Michigan University. Network: Network: NPR, PRI. Cohn & Marks. Format: Class, jazz, news. News: 31 hrs wkly. Spec prog: Educ. ♦Eric Smith, gen mgr; Evelyn Massaro, stn mgr. Co-owned TV: *WNMU-TV affil

WUPK(FM)— May 1, 1992: 94.1 mhz; 4.4 kw. Ant 380 ft. TL: N46 30 51 W87 28 58. WDMJ WIAN, 1009 E. Ridge St., Suite A 49855-3963. Phone: (906) 774-4321. Fax: (906) 774-7799. Licensee: Northern Star Broadcasting L.L.C. (group owner; acq 11-5-01; grpsl). Rep: Patt. Reddy, Begley & McCormick. Format: Classic rock, AOR. News staff: one; News: 3 hrs wkly. Target aud: 25-54; baby boomers. ♦Chris Monk, VP; Veronica Roberts, gen mgr; Steve Ponchaud, opns mgr.

*WUPX(FM)— 1994: 91.5 mhz; 200 w. 138 ft. TL: N46 34 44 W87 23 42. Northern Michigan Univ., 1204 University Ctr. 49855. Phone: (906) 227-2348. Phone: (906) 227-1844. Fax: (906) 227-2344. E-mail: wupx@nmu.edu. Web Site: www.wupx.com. Licensee: Board of Control of Northern Michigan University. Format: Alternative. Target aud: College. Spec prog: Black 6 hrs, jazz 2 hrs wkly. ♦Troy Hanson, gen mgr. Co-owned TV: *WNMU-TV affil

Marshall

WWKN(FM)—Licensed to Marshall. See Albion

Mason

*WUNN(AM)— May 11, 1967: 1110 khz; 1 kw-D, DA. TL: N42 33 04 W84 24 15. 13799 Donovan Rd., Albion 49224. Phone: (517) 676-2488. Fax: (517) 531-5009. E-mail: wunn@flc.org. Web Site: www.solidgospel1.org. Licensee: Family Life Broadcasting System. (group owner; (acq 1-1-69). Network: Salem Radio Network. Format: Southern gospel. News staff: one; News: 5 hrs wkly. Target aud: 25-54; Christian families. ♦Randy Carlson, pres; Dave Phelps, gen mgr; David Jones, opns mgr; Rod Robison, dev dir; Dave Dawson, mus dir; Robert Parson, news dir; Dick Lindley, chief of engrg.

Menominee

WAGN(AM)— Nov 14, 1952: 1340 khz; 1 kw-U. TL: N45 06 27 W87 36 25. N 2880 Roosevelt Rd., Marinette, WI 54143. Phone: (906) 863-5551. Fax: (906) 863-5679. Licensee: Badger Communications L.L.C. (group owner; acq 8-6-98; grpsl). Network: Moody, ABC Information & Entertainment. McCabe & Allen. Format: Oldies. News staff: 2; News: 15 hrs wkly. Target aud: 30 plus; older, affluent adults. Spec prog: CBS radio sports 6 hrs, loc sports hrs wkly. ♦Jeff Wagner, gen mgr & stn mgr.

WHYB(FM)—Co-owned with WAGN(AM). Oct 24, 1984: 103.7 mhz; 3 kw. 300 ft. TL: N45 04 00 W87 39 55. (CP: 7.01 kw). Stereo. Format: Country. News staff: 2; News: 5 hrs wkly. Target aud: 35-64. ♦Don Kitokowski, gen mgr.

WMAM(AM)—See Marinette, WI

Midland

WKQZ(FM)— Dec 14, 1976: 93.3 mhz; 39.2 kw. 554 ft. TL: N43 50 46 W84 05 32. Stereo. 1740 Champagne Dr., Saginaw 48604. Phone: (989) 776-2100. Fax: (989) 754-5990. Web Site: www.z93kqz.fm. Licensee: Citadel Broadcasting Co. Group owner: Citadel Broadcasting Corp. (acq 2-8-99; grpsl). Rep: McGavren Guild. Reddy, Begley & McCormick. Format: Rock. Target aud: 25-44; males. ♦Scott Meier, pres, pres, VP & gen mgr; Bob Kolen, sls dir; Jerry Tarrants, progmg dir; Jay Randall, mus dir; Hal Maas, news dir; Bob Friedle, chief of engrg.

WMPX(AM)— Sept 11, 1948: 1490 khz; 1 kw-U, DA-2. TL: N43 36 48 W84 13 17. Box 1689 48641. Secondary address: 1510 Bayliss St. 48640. Phone: (989) 631-1490. Phone: (989) 631-2220. Fax: (989) 631-6357. E-mail: request@wmpxwmrx.com. Web Site: www.wmpxwmrx.com. Licensee: Steel Broadcasting Inc. (acq 8-19-81; $900,000; 8-24-81). Network: ABC. Rep: Patt. Format: Adult standards, big band. News staff: one; News: 9 hrs wkly. Target aud: General. Spec prog: Sounds of Sinatra 2 hrs wkly, relg 3 hrs wkly. ♦Thomas Steel, pres & gen mgr.

*WUGN(FM)— Dec 2, 1973: 99.7 mhz; 100 kw. 997 ft. TL: N43 30 56 W84 32 49. Stereo. 510 E. Isabella Rd. 48640. Phone: (989) 631-7060. Fax: (989) 631-4825. E-mail: 997@997.org. Web Site: www.997.org. Licensee: Family Life Communications System. (acq 1996). Network: Salem Radio Network. Format: Contemp Christian. News: 8 hrs wkly. Target aud: 35-54; female with young children. ♦Peter Brooks, gen mgr.

Stations in the U.S. | Michigan

Developers & Brokers of Radio Properties
contact American Media Services at our suite:
Philadelphia Marriott Downtown
215-625-2900
843-972-2200
americanmediaservices.com
Charleston, SC
Dallas, TX · Chicago, Il · Austin, TX
American Media Services, LLC

Mio

WAVC(FM)— Oct 1, 1994: 93.9 mhz; 50 kw. 433 ft. TL: N44 43 40 W84 21 35. Stereo. 1356 Mackinaw Ave., Cheboygan 49721. Phone: (231) 627-2341. Fax: (231) 627-7000. Web Site: www.bigcountry1029.com. Licensee: Northern Star Broadcasting L.L.C. (group owner; acq 9-10-98; grpsl). Format: Country. ◆ Palmer Pyle, pres; Chris Monk, VP & gen mgr.

Monroe

WCSX(FM)—See Birmingham

*WDTR(FM)— 2003: 88.1 mhz; 910 w. Ant 144 ft. TL: N41 55 08 W83 22 34. Box 388, Williamston 48895. Phone: (810) 721-0891. Fax: (413) 410-9708. E-mail: info@joyfm.net. Web Site: www.joyfm.net. Licensee: Northland Community Broadcasters. Format: Contemporary Christian. ◆ Ed Czelada, gen mgr.

WRDT(AM)— July 12, 1956: 560 khz; 500 w-D, 27 w-N. TL: N41 53 28 W83 25 39. (CP: 14 w-N). 12300 Radio Pl., Detroit 48228. Phone: (313) 272-3434. Web Site: wmuz.com. Licensee: WMUZ Radio Inc. Group owner: Crawford Broadcasting Co. (acq 6-16-97; $3.15 million). Rep: McGavren Guild. Format: Bible teaching. ◆ Frank Franciosi, gen mgr & gen sls mgr.

WTWR-FM— July 16, 1967: 98.3 mhz; 1.4 kw. 465 ft. TL: N41 50 43 W83 27 59. Stereo. 14930 Laplaisance Rd. Suite 113 48161. Phone: (734) 242-6600. Fax: (734) 242-6599. Web Site: www.tower98.com. Licensee: Cumulus Licensing Corp Group owner: Cumulus Media L.L.C. (acq 7-98; $2.8 million). Rep: Michigan. Crowell & Moring. Format: CHR. News staff: one; News: 3 hrs wkly. Target aud: 25-54. Spec prog: Relg 3 hrs wkly. ◆ Bill Bailey, gen mgr.

*WYDM(FM)— November 1978: 97.5 mhz; 8 w. Ant 135 ft. TL: N41 55 07 W83 26 12. Monroe High School, 901 Herr Rd. 48161. Phone: (734) 265-3550. Web Site: www.angelfire.com/mi/wejy. Licensee: Monroe Public Schools (acq 8-77). Format: Var/div. Target aud: 15-24. ◆ John Tyner, mus dir.

Mount Clemens

WHTD(FM)— Nov 6, 1960: 102.7 mhz; 50 kw. 499 ft. TL: N42 32 39 W82 54 09. Stereo. 3250 Franklin, Detroit 48207. Phone: (313) 259-2000. Fax: (313) 259-7011. Web Site: www.kissdetroit.com. Licensee: Radio One of Detroit LLC. Group owner: Radio One Inc. (acq 1999; $27 million). Network: ABC. Rep: D & R Radio. Format: Urban / AC. Target aud: 25-49; rock and rollers of all ages. ◆ Carol Lawrence, gen mgr.

Mount Pleasant

WCFX(FM)—See Clare

*WCMU-FM— Apr 6, 1964: 89.5 mhz; 100 kw. 423 ft. TL: N43 34 24 W84 46 21. Stereo. Public Broadcasting Ctr., 1999 E. Campus Dr. 48859. Phone: (989) 774-3105. Fax: (989) 774-4427. E-mail: cmuradio@radio.cmich.edu. Web Site: www.wcmu.org. Licensee: Central Michigan University. Network: Network: NPR, PRI. Dow, Lohnes & Albertson. Format: Class, jazz, news & info. News staff: 2; News: 30 hrs wkly. Target aud: General. ◆ Edward Grant, gen mgr. Co-owned TV: *WCMU-TV affil

WCZY-FM— Aug 20, 1991: 104.3 mhz; 3 kw. 328 ft. TL: N43 35 39 W84 49 26. Stereo. 4065 E. Wing Rd. 48858. Phone: (989) 772-9664. Fax: (989) 773-5000. E-mail: wczy@litehits104.com. Web Site: www.litehits104.com. Licensee: Central Michigan Communications Inc. Network: Jones Radio Networks. Rep: Michigan. Patt. Reddy, Begley & McCormick. Format: Easy lstng, adult contemp. News staff: one; News: 6 hrs wkly. Target aud: 30 plus. ◆ Mike Carey, pres, gen mgr & gen sls mgr; Carmi Crisci, progmg dir & news dir.

*WMHW-FM— Nov 20, 1972: 91.5 mhz; 307 w. 112 ft. TL: N43 35 12 W84 46 24. Stereo. 180 Moore Hall, Central Michigan Univ. 48859. Phone: (989) 774-7287. Phone: (989) 774-3851. Fax: (989) 774-2426. E-mail: wmhw@mail.cmich.edu. Web Site: www.bca.cmich.edu. Licensee: Board of Trustees, Central Michigan University. Irwin, Campbell & Tannenwald. Format: New age, progsv. News: 10 wkly. Target aud: 12-34. ◆ Peter B. Orlik, gen mgr; Jerry Henderson, opns mgr; Randy Kapenga, chief of engrg.

Munising

WQXO(AM)— Sept 20, 1955: 1400 khz; 1 kw-U. TL: N46 24 30 W86 38 22. 2025 US Hwy. 41 W., Marquette 49855. Phone: (906) 387-4000. Phone: (800) 236-4007. Fax: (906) 387-5161. E-mail: munising@greatlakesradio.org. Licensee: Great Lakes Radio Inc. (group owner; (acq 11-30-99; grpsl). Rep: Patt. Haley, Bader & Potts. Format: Big band, oldies. Target aud: 25-54. ◆ Todd Noordyk, gen mgr.

WRUP(FM)—Co-owned with WQXO(AM). June 21, 1974: 98.3 mhz; 32 kw. 357 ft. TL: N46 24 53 W86 40 27. Stereo. Web Site: www.oldies983.com. Network: Westwood One. Rep: Patt. Format: Hot country hits. Target aud: 18-54.

Muskegon

WGVS(AM)— 1926: 850 khz; 1 kw-U. DA-1. TL: N43 08 05 W86 15 14. c/o WGVU, 301 W. Fulton, Grand Rapids 49504-6492. Phone: (616) 771-6666. Fax: (616) 336-7204. E-mail: wgvu@gvsu.edu. Licensee: Grand Valley State University. (acq 4-9-99; with WGVS-FM Whitehall). Network: NPR, PRI. Cohn & Marks. Format: News, info. ◆ Michael T. Walenta, gen mgr; Ken Kolbe, opns mgr; Richard Nelson, gen sls mgr; Pamela Holtz, mktg & prom mgr; Scott Vander Werf, mus dir; Fred Martino, news dir & pub affrs dir; Bob Lumbert, engrg dir.

WGVS-FM— 1975: 95.3 mhz; 2 kw. 360 ft. TL: N43 21 14 W86 19 38. Stereo. Format: Jazz, news.

WKBZ(AM)— June 15, 1947: 1090 khz; 1 kw-D. TL: N43 16 35 W86 15 10. 3565 Green St. 49444. Phone: (231) 733-2600. Fax: (231) 733-7461. Web Site: www.wmus.com. Licensee: Clear Channel Broadcasting Licenses Inc. Group owner: Clear Channel Communications Inc. (acq 1-17-2001; grpsl). Network: ABC Daytime Direction. Rep: D & R Radio. John Garziglia. Format: Contemp country. News staff: one. Target aud: 25-54 primary; 35-64 secondary. ◆ Bart Brandmiller, gen mgr.

WMUS(FM)—Co-owned with WKBZ(AM). 1962: 106.9 mhz; 50 kw. Ant 479 ft. TL: N43 13 48 W86 05 03. Stereo.

*WMCQ(FM)— Mar 31, 2005: 91.7 mhz; 6 kw. Ant 328 ft. TL: N43 18 37 W85 54 44. Drawer 2440, Tupelo, MS 38801. Phone: (662) 844-8888. Fax: (662) 842-6791. Licensee: American Family Association. (acq 12-20-2002). Format: Chirstian. ◆ Marvin Sanders, gen mgr.

WMHG(AM)— 1949: 1600 khz; 5 kw-U, DA-N. TL: N43 11 50 W86 13 22. 3565 Green St. 49444. Phone: (231) 733-2126. Fax: (231) 739-9037. Licensee: Cumulus Licensing Corp. Group owner: Cumulus Media Inc. (acq 3-15-00; grpsl). Network: ABC. Rep: D & R Radio. Format: MOR. News: 2 hrs wkly. Target aud: 35 plus. ◆ Teresa Dellit, gen mgr; Caroljean Lindquist, opns mgr & prom VP; Greg Mckitrick, gen sls mgr; Andrea Sipka, natl sls mgr & mktg dir; Don Beno, progmg dir & pub affrs dir; Jason Stephenitch, engrg dir.

*WPQZ(FM)— 2003: 88.1 mhz; 580 w. Ant 344 ft. TL: N43 16 38 W86 20 05. 901 Elizabeth Ct., Mount Pleasant 48858. Phone: (989) 779-9178. Fax: (989) 779-1558. Licensee: Great Lakes Broadcast Academy Inc. (acq 1-13-2003). Format: Oldies. ◆ James McCluskey, pres & gen mgr.

WSHZ(FM)— February 1990: 107.9 mhz; 15 kw. 348 ft. TL: N43 17 41 W86 13 12. 3565 Green St. 49444. Phone: (231) 733-2600. Fax: (231) 739-9037. Fax: (213) 733-7461. Web Site: www.star108.com. Licensee: Clear Channel Broadcasting Licenses Inc. Group owner: Clear Channel Communications Inc. (acq 1-17-01; grpsl). Format: Adult contemp. Target aud: 18-49. ◆ Bart Brandmiller, gen mgr; Greg McKitrick, gen sls mgr; Don Beno, progmg dir; Ron Steenwyk, chief of engrg.

WSNX-FM— Nov 18, 1971: 104.5 mhz; 50 kw. 361 ft. TL: N43 12 13 W86 20 05. Stereo. (CP: 32 kw, ant 620 ft. TL: N43 12 16 W86 01 35). Stereo. 77 Monroe Ctr., Suite 1000, Grand Rapids 49503. Phone: (616) 459-1919. Fax: (616) 235-9104. E-mail: web@wsnx.com. Web Site: www.wsnx.com. Licensee: Clear Channel Broadcasting Licenses Inc. Group owner: Clear Channel Communications Inc. (acq 9-30-99). Network: ABC. Rep: Clear Channel. Format: CHR, urban contemp. News staff: one; News: news progrmg one hr wkly. Target aud: 18-34; women. ◆ Skip Essick, VP & gen mgr.

Muskegon Heights

WMRR(FM)— Mar 29, 1974: 101.7 mhz; 15 kw. 305 ft. TL: N43 16 38 W86 20 05. Stereo. 3565 Green St., Muskegon 49444. Phone: (231) 733-2600. Fax: (231) 739-9037. Web Site: www.wmrr.com. Licensee: Clear Channel Broadcasting Licenses Inc. Group owner: Clear Channel Communications Inc. (acq 1-17-01; grpsl). Network: Westwood One. Format: Classic rock. Target aud: 25-54; male. ◆ Bart Brandmiller, gen mgr.

Negaunee

WKQS-FM— Jan 5, 1998: 101.9 mhz; 12 kw. 535 ft. TL: N46 28 42 W87 37 21. Stereo. 2025 U.S. 41 W., Marquette 49855. Phone: (906) 228-6800. Fax: (906) 228-8128. E-mail: todd@greatlakesradio.org. Web Site: www.wkqsfm.com. Licensee: Great Lakes Radio Inc. (group owner) Network: ABC. Booth, Freret, Imlay & Tepper. Format: Adult contemp, CHR. ◆ Todd Noordyk, gen mgr.

WNGE(FM)— 2001: 99.5 mhz; 3.6 kw. Ant 430 ft. TL: N46 30 51 W87 28 58. 1009 W. Ridge St., Suite A, Marquette 49855-3963. Phone: (906) 225-1313. Fax: (906) 225-1324. Licensee: Northern Star Broadcasting L.L.C. (group owner; acq 11-5-01; grpsl). Format: Oldies. ◆ Veronica Roberts, gen mgr.

Newaygo

WKOQ(FM)—Not on air, target date: unknown: 92.5 mhz; 2.25 kw. Ant 543 ft. TL: N43 18 37 W85 54 44. Citadel Broadcasting Co., 7201 West Lake Mead Blvd., Suite 400, Las Vegas, NV 89128. Phone: (702) 804-5200. Fax: (702) 804-5936. Licensee: Citadel Broadcasting Co. (acq 7-8-2005). ◆ Randy L. Taylor, VP.

Newberry

WIHC(FM)— Apr 24, 1989: 97.9 mhz; 50 kw. 352 ft. TL: N46 18 53 W85 33 45. Stereo. 1356 Mackinaw Ave., Cheboygan 49721. Phone: (231) 627-2341. Fax: (231) 627-7000. Web Site: www.classicrockthebear.com. Licensee: Northern Star Broadcasting L.L.C. (group owner; acq 11-5-01; grpsl). Network: Westwood One. Format: Classic rock. Target aud: 18-44. ◆ Palmer Pyle, pres; Chris Monk, VP & gen mgr.

WNBY(AM)— May 16, 1966: 1450 khz; 1 kw-U. TL: N46 18 48 W85 30 38. Box 501, Hwy. S. M-123 49868. Phone: (906) 293-3221. Phone: (906) 293-5200. Fax: (906) 293-8275. E-mail: wnby@up.net. Licensee: Sovereign Communications LLC (acq 8-21-2003; $400,000. with co-located FM). Network: ABC Information & Entertainment. Rep: Patt. Format: Country gold. Target aud: 35 plus. Spec prog: Polka 2 hrs wkly. ◆ Sandy Feutz, gen mgr; Travis Freeman, opns mgr & chief of engrg.

WNBY-FM— 1977: 93.7 mhz; 3.5 kw. 262 ft. TL: N46 18 48 W85 30 38. (CP: 6 kw, ant 279 ft.). Stereo. Format: Adult contemp. Target aud: 25-45.

Michigan

Niles

WAOR(FM)—Listing follows WNIL(AM).

WAUS(FM)—See South Bend, IN

WNIL(AM)— Dec 6, 1956: 1290 khz; 500 w-D, 44 w-N. TL: N41 49 22 W86 17 03. Box 370, 237 Edison Rd., Mishawaka, IN 46545. Phone: (269) 683-6123. Fax: (269) 683-2758. Web Site: www.1290wnil.com. Licensee: Pathfinder Communications Corp. Group owner: Federated Media (acq 7-21-99; $2 million with co-located FM). Network: Jones Radio Networks. Wilkinson Barker Knauer. Format: Oldies. News: 5 hrs wkly. Target aud: 35-54 women; pro-active, community-involved people. Spec prog: Relg 6 hrs wkly. ◆ J. Eric Plym, pres; Patrick Redd, gen mgr; Pam Reed, gen sls mgr; Ric Clingaman, progmg dir; Sara Charisse, news dir; Bob Henning, chief of engrg.

WAOR(FM)— Co-owned with WNIL(AM). Sept 13, 1968: 95.3 mhz; 3.3 kw. 298 ft. TL: N41 49 22 W86 17 03. Stereo. E-mail: waor@waor.com. Web Site: www.waor.com. Format: Classic rock, rock/AOR. News: 5 hrs wkly. Target aud: 25-54; predominantly male, socially active, economically secure. ◆ Shelley Morgan, prom dir.

North Muskegon

WLCS(FM)— November 1983: 98.3 mhz; 1.6 kw. Ant 456 ft. TL: N43 18 50 W86 09 17. Stereo. 517 Beebe St., Fremont 49412-1301. Phone: (231) 924-4700. Fax: (231) 924-9746. E-mail: jtb@wlcsonline.com. Web Site: www.wlcsonline.com. Licensee: Unity Broadcasting Inc. (group owner; acq 12-16-2002; grpsl). Network: ABC. Kaye, Scholer, Fierman, Hays & Handler. Format: Oldies. News: one hr wkly. Target aud: 35-54; general. ◆ Don Noordyk, gen mgr; Karen Lakes, prom dir; Tony Burke, progmg dir.

Norway

WZNL(FM)— Mar 15, 1990: 94.3 mhz; 2.4 kw. 649 ft. TL: N45 49 15 W88 02 25. 101 E. Kent St., Iron Mountain 49801-8110. Phone: (906) 774-4321. Fax: (906) 774-7799. E-mail: star943@uplogon.com. Web Site: www.wznl.tripod.com. Licensee: Northern Star Broadcasting L.L.C. (group owner; acq 11-5-01; grpsl). Network: Westwood One. Format: Adult contemp. ◆ Veronica Roberts, gen mgr; Tom Hill, opns mgr.

Novi

*WOVI(FM)— Sept 4, 1978: 89.5 mhz; 100 w. 67 ft. TL: N42 27 49 W83 29 28. Stereo. Novi High School, 24062 Taft Rd. 48375. Phone: (248) 449-1526. Fax: (248) 449-1519. Web Site: hs.novi.k12.mi.us/wovi. Licensee: Board of Education Novi School District. (acq 3-8-76). Format: Alternative, classic rock. Target aud: General.

Olivet

*WOCR(FM)— Apr 22, 1975: 89.7 mhz; 110 w. 75 ft. TL: N42 26 31 W84 55 30. Stereo. Kirk Ctr., Olivet College, 320 S. Main St. 49076. Phone: (269) 749-7127. Fax: (269) 749-6603. E-mail: rcraig@olivetcollege.edu. Licensee: Olivet College. Format: CHR. News: one hr wkly. Target aud: College; high school and college-age, variety. ◆ Richard Craig, gen mgr; Nya Kwai Taryor Jr., stn mgr; Garth Sims, opns mgr & chief of engrg.

Onsted

*WAAQ(FM)— 2001: 88.3 mhz; 250 w vert. Ant 77 ft. TL: N42 03 33 W84 12 54. 901 Elizabeth Ct., Mount Pleasant 48858. Phone: (989) 779-9178. Fax: (989) 779-1558. Licensee: Great Lakes Community Broadcasting Inc. Format: Oldies. ◆ James J. McCluskey, gen mgr.

Ontonagon

*WOAS(FM)— Nov 15, 1978: 88.5 mhz; 10 w. 124 ft. TL: N46 52 30 W89 18 00. 701 Parker 49953. Phone: (906) 884-4433. Fax: (906) 884-2742. E-mail: kraisane@go150.k12.mi.us. Web Site: www.woas-fm.org. Licensee: Ontonagon Area School District. Format: Var/div. News staff: one. Target aud: General; local residents of the area. Spec prog: Sp one hr wkly. ◆ Ken Raisanen, gen mgr.

WUPY(FM)— 1987: 101.1 mhz; 30 kw. 620 ft. TL: N46 44 49 W89 11 27. Stereo. 610 Greenland Rd. 49953. Phone: (906) 884-9668. Fax: (906) 884-4985. E-mail: wupy@jamadots.com. Web Site: www.wupy101.com. Licensee: SNRN Broadcasting Inc. (acq 7-90). Network: Network: CBS, ABC. Format: Country. News staff: 2; News: 13 hrs wkly. Target aud: 25 plus. Spec prog: Oldies 4 hrs, relg 3 hrs, polka 2 hrs wkly. ◆ Robert Schulz, pres; Jackie Dobbins, opns mgr; Sandy Schulz, gen mgr & gen sls mgr.

Orchard Lake

*WBLD(FM)— May 28, 1974: 89.3 mhz; 10 w. 110 ft. TL: N42 33 56 W83 21 32. Stereo. 4925 Orchard Lake Rd., West Bloomfield 48323. Phone: (248) 865-6754. Fax: (248) 865-6756. E-mail: wbld@hotmail.com. Web Site: wbld893.tripod.com. Licensee: West Bloomfield Board of Education. Format: Div, rock. ◆ Paul S. Townley, stn mgr; Randy G. Long, chief of engrg.

Oscoda

*WCMB-FM— June 1998: 95.7 mhz; 25 kw. 699 ft. TL: N44 40 30 W83 31 06. Central Michigan Univ., 1999 E. Campus Dr., Mount Pleasant 48859. Phone: (989) 774-3105. Fax: (989) 774-4427. E-mail: cmuradio@radio.cmich.edu. Web Site: www.wcmu.org. Licensee: Central Michigan University. Network: Network: NPR, PRI. Format: Class, jazz, News. News staff: 2; News: 45 hrs wkly. ◆ Ed Graham, gen mgr; Art Curtis, rgnl sls mgr; Ann Blatte, prom mgr; Ray Ford, progmg dir; Randy Kapenga, chief of engrg.

WWTH(FM)— Aug 29, 1992: 100.7 mhz; 20.5 kw. 360 ft. TL: N44 34 42 W83 22 40. Stereo. 4429 N. US Hwy. 23 48750. Phone: (989) 345-4611. E-mail: sunny100.7@kwcom.net. Licensee: Edwards Communications LC. Group owner: Northern Radio Network (acq 12-21-2004; grpsl). Rep: Roslin. Michigan. Carter, Ledyard & Milburn. Format: Soft adult contemp. News staff: one; News: 4 hrs wkly. Target aud: 25-54. ◆ Lucky Osborn, gen mgr.

Otsego

WAKV(AM)— 1958: 980 khz; 1 kw-D. TL: N42 27 33 W85 43 58. 213 Gilkey St., Plainwell 49080. Phone: (269) 685-2438. E-mail: 980am@net-link.net. Web Site: www.980.com. Licensee: Vintage Radio Enterprises L.L.C. (acq 7-17-98; $17,500). Network: UPI. Format: Adult standards. ◆ Jim Higgs, gen mgr.

WQXC-FM— Apr 17, 1981: 100.9 mhz; 3 kw. 299 ft. TL: N42 30 31 W85 46 08. Stereo. Box 80 49078. Secondary address: 706 E. Allegan St. 49078. Phone: (269) 692-6851. Fax: (269) 692-6861. E-mail: tflynn@wqxc.com. Web Site: www.wqxc.com. Licensee: Forum Communications Inc. Format: Oldies. ◆ Robert Brink, pres; Deb Whiteman, CFO; Tom Flynn, gen mgr, gen sls mgr & progmg dir; Todd Overhuel, mus dir; Jim McKinney, news dir & pub affrs dir.

Ovid-Elsie

*WOES(FM)— Mar 21, 1978: 91.3 mhz; 553 w. 140 ft. TL: N43 02 44 W84 23 14. Stereo. 8989 Colony Rd., Elsie 48831. Phone: (989) 834-2271. Fax: (989) 862-4463. Licensee: Ovid-Elsie Area Schools. (acq 1978). Format: Polka. Spec prog: Class one hr, Pol one hr, Czech one hr, stage & screen one hr wkly. ◆ George Bishop, gen mgr; Kevin Somers, opns mgr.

Owosso

WOAP(AM)— Jan 1, 1948: 1080 khz; 1 kw-D. TL: N43 01 48 W84 10 39. Box 128, 2301 N., M-52 48867. Phone: (989) 725-8196. Fax: (989) 725-6626. Licensee: 1090 Investments L.L.C. (acq 2-18-00). Rep: Patt. Format: Nostalgia, big band, MOR. Target aud: 45 plus; adults with disposable income. Spec prog: Farm 2 hrs, polka 4 hrs, relg 4 hrs, Sp 6 hrs wkly. ◆ Clem Sellers, gen sls mgr & rgnl sls mgr; Linda Pierce, mus dir; Art Kinsey, chief of engrg.

WRSR(FM)— Dec 2, 1965: 103.9 mhz; 2.85 kw. 482 ft. TL: N42 59 44 W83 59 33. Stereo. 6317 Taylor Dr., Flint 48507. Phone: (810) 238-7300. Fax: (810) 238-7310. Web Site: www.classicfox.com. Licensee: Cumulus Licensing Corp. Group owner: Cumulus Media Inc. (acq 3-15-00; grpsl). Format: Classic Rock. Target aud: 25-54. Spec prog: Class one hr, relg one hr, sports 4 hrs wkly. ◆ Floyd Evans, gen mgr; Randy Thomas, sls dir & gen sls mgr; Sheri Moffit, natl sls mgr; Mishel Lynne, prom dir; Jeff Wade, progmg dir; Les Root, news dir; Dan Greer, chief of engrg.

Pentwater

WMOM(FM)— Sept 26, 1999: 102.7 mhz; 6 kw. Ant 328 ft. TL: N43 52 10 W86 21 32. 907 E. Ludington Ave., Ludington 49431. Phone: (231) 845-9666. Fax: (231) 845-9332. Web Site: www.wmom.fm. Licensee: Bay View Broadcasting Inc. Format: CHR. ◆ Patrick L. Lopeman, pres & gen mgr; Dawn Skaradzinski, CFO & exec VP; Jenifer Hullinger, stn mgr; Pat Martin, opns mgr; Michael LaBelle, progmg dir; Jana Rogers, mus dir; Mary Lynn Marshall, news dir; Tom Green, chief of engrg.

WWKR(FM)— July 1, 1995: 94.1 mhz; 13 kw. 462 ft. TL: N43 51 33 W86 18 27. Stereo. Box 855, Ludington 49431. Secondary address: 347 Hancock St. 49449. Phone: (231) 869-7402. Fax: (231) 869-7502. Web Site: www.94k-rock.com. Licensee: Synergy Media Inc. (acq 4-10-98; $250,000). Network: AP Network News. Rep: Michigan. Michigan Spot Sales Drinker, Biddle & Reath. Format: Classic rock. News staff: one; News: 2 hrs wkly. Target aud: 25-54; baby boomers. Spec prog: Relg 3 hrs wkly. ◆ Todd A. Mohr, pres & gen mgr; Barry Smith, opns mgr & progmg dir; Tom Green, chief of engrg.

Petoskey

WFDX(FM)—(Atlanta). Oct 20, 1988: 92.5 mhz; 100 kw. 868 ft. TL: N45 01 00 W84 21 10. Stereo. 1020 Hastings St., Traverse City 49686. Phone: (231) 947-0003. Fax: (231) 947-7002. E-mail: markelliot @classichitsthefox.com. Web Site: www.classichitsthefox.com. Licensee: Northern Michigan Radio Inc. (acq 12-23-93; $1.165 million. with WFCX(FM) Leland; FTR: 1-17-94). Rep: Christal. Format: Classic hits. News staff: one. Target aud: 25-54. ◆ T.J. Clark, gen sls mgr; Mark Elliot, progmg dir; Susan Meltons, mus dir.

WJML(AM)— Dec 6, 1966: 1110 khz; 10 kw-D, DA. TL: N45 20 05 W84 55 34. 2175 Click Rd. 49770. Phone: (231) 348-5000. Web Site: www.wjml.com. Licensee: Stone Communications Inc. (acq 10-8-91; $24,000; 1-6-92). Network: CBS. Rep: Patt. Reddy, Begley & McCormick. Format: News/talk. News: 72 hrs wkly. Target aud: 25 plus. Spec prog: Loc professional and college sports, relg 8 hrs wkly. ◆ Richard D. Stone, pres & gen mgr; Philip Clever, stn mgr.

WKHQ-FM—See Charlevoix

WKLZ-FM— Dec 7, 1965: 98.9 mhz; 50 kw. 800 ft. TL: N45 28 40 W84 57 04. Stereo. 1020 Hastings St., Traverse City 49686. Phone: (231) 947-0003. Fax: (231) 947-7002. Web Site: www.wklt.com. Licensee: Northern Radio of Petoskey Inc. (acq 8-15-91; $800,000). Network: ABC. Rep: Christal. Fletcher, Heald & Hildreth. Format: Classic, AOR. News: 2 hrs wkly. Target aud: 18-49; baby boomers. ◆ Richard Dills, pres & gen mgr; Jackie Gordon, natl sls mgr; Terri Ray, progmg dir; Dennis Murray, chief of engrg.

WLXT(FM)—Listing follows WMBN(AM).

WMBN(AM)— May 1946: 1340 khz; 1 kw-U. TL: N45 20 50 W84 58 01. Box 286 49770. Secondary address: 2095 U.S. 131 S. 49770. Phone: (231) 347-8713. Fax: (231) 347-9920. Licensee: MacDonald Garber Broadcasting Inc. (group owner; acq 11-17-98; grpsl). Rep: D & R Radio. Format: Easy lstng. News staff: 2; News: 2 hrs wkly. Target aud: 25 plus. ◆ Phill Orth, gen mgr; Ron Pritchard, progmg dir; Brian Brachel, chief of engrg.

WLXT(FM)—Co-owned with WMBN(AM). Jan 1, 1967: 96.3 mhz; 100 kw. 981 ft. TL: N45 19 17 W84 52 33. Stereo. Format: Oldies. ◆ Dave Thomas, progmg dir.

WWKK(AM)— June 16, 2000: 750 khz; 1 kw-D, 330 w-N, DA-2. TL: N45 20 05 W84 55 34. 2175 Click Rd. 49770. Phone: (231) 348-5000. Web Site: www.kool750.com. Licensee: Stone Communications Inc. Network: USA. Format: Talk, sports, news. Target aud: 25 plus. ◆ Richard D. Stone, pres & gen mgr; Philip Clever, stn mgr.

Pickford

WADW(FM)— Dec 22, 2000: 105.5 mhz; 55 kw. Ant 108 ft. TL: N46 17 24 W84 18 53. Box 10707, Green Bay, WI 54307. Phone: (920) 469-3021. Fax: (920) 469-3023. Licensee: Starboard Broadcasting Inc. (acq 6-7-2003; $750,000). Format: Relg. ◆ Mark C. Follett, chmn.

Stations in the U.S. — Michigan

Developers & Brokers of Radio Properties
contact American Media Services at our suite:
Philadelphia Marriott Downtown
215-625-2900
843-972-2200
americanmediaservices.com
Charleston, SC
Dallas, TX • Chicago, Il • Austin, TX
American Media Services, LLC

Pinconning

WSAG(FM)— Nov 1, 2002: 104.1 mhz; 4.6 kw. Ant 325 ft. TL: N43 43 30 W83 56 50. 6807 Foxglove Dr., Cheyenne, WY 48650. Phone: (307) 778-9318. Licensee: MacDonald Broadcasting Co. (acq 6-30-2005). Format: Oldies. ♦ Dick Michael, gen mgr.

WYLZ(FM)— Nov 15, 1983: 100.9 mhz; 2.6 kw. 495 ft. TL: N43 50 46 W84 05 32. Stereo. 1740 N. Champagne Dr., Saginaw 48604. Phone: (989) 776-2100. Fax: (989) 754-5990. Licensee: Citadel Broadcasting Co. Group owner: Citadel Broadcasting Corp. Rep: McGavren Guild. Format: Classic rock. Target aud: 25-54; general. ♦ Stuart Stanek, pres; Scott Meier, VP & gen mgr; Bob Kolen, sls dir; Jerry Tarrants, progmg dir; Bob Friedle, chief of engrg.

Pittsford

*WPCJ(FM)— Oct 23, 1985: 91.1 mhz; 270 w. Ant 184 ft. TL: N41 53 04 W84 28 15. 9400 Beecher Rd. 49271. Phone: (517) 523-3427. Fax: (517) 523-3427. E-mail: wpcj@freedomfarm.info. Web Site: www.freedomfarm.info. Licensee: Pittsford Educational Broadcasting Foundation. Network: Moody. Format: Educ, relg, Christian. News: 10 hrs wkly. Target aud: General; rural. ♦ Tim Neinas, stn mgr; Ed Trombley, chief of engrg.

Plymouth

*WSDP(FM)— Feb 14, 1972: 88.1 mhz; 200 w. 110 ft. TL: N42 20 50 W83 29 51. Stereo. 46181 Joy Rd., Canton 48187. Phone: (734) 416-7732. Phone: (734) 416-7745. Fax: (734) 416-7732. E-mail: keithb@pccs.klz.mi.us. Web Site: www.881theescape.com. Licensee: Plymouth Canton Community Schools. Format: New mus. News: 2 hrs wkly. Target aud: General. Spec prog: Heavy metal 2 hrs wkly. ♦ Bill Keith, gen mgr & stn mgr.

Port Huron

WBTI(FM)—Listing follows WPHM(AM).

WGRT(FM)— December 1991: 102.3 mhz; 3 kw. 318 ft. TL: N43 04 08 W82 28 48. 624 Grand River Ave. 48060. Phone: (810) 987-3200. Fax: (810) 987-3325. E-mail: wgrt@msn.com. Web Site: www.wgrt.com. Licensee: Port Huron Family Radio Inc. (acq 11-10-2004; $100,000). Network: ABC. Cohen & Berfield. Format: Adult contemp. Target aud: General. ♦ Martin Doorn, gen mgr.

WHLS(AM)— Aug 8, 1938: 1450 khz; 1 kw-U. TL: N42 58 37 W82 27 52. Box 807 48061-0807. Secondary address: 808 Huron Ave. 48060. Phone: (810) 982-9000. Fax: (810) 987-9380. Licensee: Liggett Communications L.L.C. (acq 1-1-56). Rep: Michigan. Format: Oldies. Target aud: 18-50; middle class. Spec prog: Black one hr, Sp one hr wkly. ♦ Robert Liggett, chmn; James A. Jensen, pres; Lawrence C. Smith, gen mgr; Kristine Sikkewa, sls dir & gen sls mgr; Jim McKenzie, progmg dir; Bill Gilmer, news dir; Craig Bowman, chief of engrg.

WSAQ(FM)—Co-owned with WHLS(AM). Aug 7, 1964: 107.1 mhz; 6 kw. 298 ft. TL: N42 58 37 W82 27 52. Stereo. Web Site: www.wsaq.net. Format: Country. Target aud: 25-55. ♦ Brian Harper, progmg dir.

WHLX(AM)—(Marine City). Dec 10, 1951: 1590 khz; 1 kw-D, 102 w-N, DA-1. TL: N42 43 42 W82 31 15. Box 807 48061-0807. Secondary address: 808 Huron Ave. 48060. Phone: (810) 982-9000. Fax: (810) 987-9380. Licensee: Liggett Communications LLC. Group owner: Liqqctt Communications (acq 5-1-2000). Network: ABC. Format: Adult contemp, oldies. Target aud: 25-54. ♦ Robert Liggett, chmn; James A. Jenson, pres; Lawrence C. Smith, gen mgr.

*WNFA(FM)— May 15, 1986: 88.3 mhz; 1.3 kw. 227 ft. TL: N42 59 36 W82 28 06. Stereo. 2865 Maywood Dr. 48060. Phone: (810) 985-3260. Fax: (810) 985-7712. Web Site: www.wnradio.com. Licensee: Ross Bible Church. Network: Network: Moody, USA. Southmayd & Miller. Format: Relg, inspirational. News: 14 hrs wkly. Target aud: 25-44; females. ♦ Sara Kenner, pub affrs dir.

*WORW(FM)— May 31, 1973: 91.9 mhz; 188 w. 78 ft. TL: N43 01 30 W82 26 10. (CP: 180 w). 1799 Krafft Rd. 48060. Phone: (810) 984-2675, EXT. 363. Fax: (810) 984-2747. Licensee: Port Huron Area School District. Format: Top-40. ♦ Kim Storey, gen mgr.

WPHM(AM)— Dec 6, 1947: 1380 khz; 5 kw-U, DA-2. TL: N42 51 50 W82 29 40. 808 Huron St. 48060. Phone: (810) 982-9000. Fax: (810) 987-9380. Web Site: wphm.net. Licensee: Liggett Communicaions L.L.C. (group owner; acq 5-1-2000; grpsl). Network: ABC Information & Entertainment. Rep: Patt. Format: Adult contemp, news/talk, sports. News: 40 hrs wkly. Target aud: 25-54. Spec prog: Farm one hr wkly. ♦ Robert Liggett, chmn; James A. Jewsen, pres; Lawrence C. Smith, gen mgr; Kristine Sikkema, sls dir & gen sls mgr; Paul Miller, progmg dir; Craig Bowman, engrg VP.

WBTI(FM)—Co-owned with WPHM(AM). July 13, 1991: 96.9 mhz; 3 kw. 380 ft. TL: N43 12 34 W82 32 10. Stereo. Box 807 48061-0807. Web Site: wbti.net. Rep: Patt. Format: Adult contemp, CHR. Target aud: 18-34. ♦ Jerry Noble, progmg mgr.

*WSGR-FM— October 1971: 91.3 mhz; 100 w. 87 ft. TL: N42 58 43 W82 25 45. Stereo. Box 5015, 323 Erie St. 48061-5015. Phone: (810) 989-5564. Fax: (810) 984-8991. Web Site: www.stclair.cc.mi.us. Licensee: St. Clair County Community College. Format: Pop jazz. Target aud: General; all age groups. Spec prog: Metal-hard rock 12 hrs, urban 6 hrs wkly. ♦ John Hill, gen mgr.

Portage

WFAT(FM)—Listing follows WNWN(AM).

WNWN(AM)— July 25, 1986: 1560 khz; 4.1 kw-D, DA. TL: N42 10 59 W85 35 30. 6021 S. Westnedge Ave., Kalamazoo 49002. Phone: (269) 327-7600. Fax: (269) 327-0726. Web Site: www.1560radio.com. Licensee: Midwest Communications Inc. (group owner; acq 1995; grpsl). Rep: Christal. Format: Urban contemp. News staff: 2; News: 5 hrs wkly. Target aud: 25-54; emphasis on 35-50 age group. Spec prog: Blues 3 hrs wkly. ♦ D.E. Wright, pres; Peter Tanz, gen mgr; Janine Seals, gen sls mgr; John McNeill, news dir; Walker Sisson, chief of engrg.

WFAT(FM)—Co-owned with WNWN(AM). June 1992: 96.5 mhz; 3 kw. 321 ft. TL: N42 12 55 W85 36 37. Web Site: www.wfat.com. Format: Classic hits. Target aud: 25-49. ♦ Bill Martin, progmg dir; Walker Sisson, engrg dir.

WRKR(FM)—Licensed to Portage. See Kalamazoo

Raco

*WJOH(FM)—Not on air, target date: unknown: 91.5 mhz; 3.8 kw. Ant 328 ft. TL: N46 23 28 W84 27 52. Michigan Community Radio, 3302 N. Van Dyke, Imlay City 48444. Phone: (810) 721-0891. Licensee: Michigan Community Radio. ♦ Ed Czelada, pres.

Reed City

WDEE-FM— Aug 16, 1997: 97.3 mhz; 2.85 kw. Ant 479 ft. TL: N43 46 53 W85 36 58. PMB #97 732 Perry Ave., Big Rapids 49307. Phone: (231) 832-9333. Fax: (231) 832-1600. Web Site: www.sunny973.com. Licensee: Steven V. Beilfuss. Format: Classic hits, oldies. Target aud: 35 plus; anyone who likes oldies. ♦ Steven V. Beilfuss, gen mgr.

WDEE(AM)— Oct 17, 1981: . Stn currently dark 1500 khz; 250 w-D. TL: N43 52 09 W85 29 04.

Rochester

*WXOU(FM)—(Auburn Hills). August 1995: 88.3 mhz; 110 w. 256 ft. TL: N42 42 35 W83 13 50. Stereo. 69 Oakland Ctr. 48309. Phone: (248) 370-4273. Fax: (248) 370-2846. E-mail: wxougm@oakland.edu. Web Site: www.wxou.org. Licensee: Oakland University. Format: Free-form. News: 13 hrs wkly. Target aud: General; univ & loc community not serviced by commercial media. ♦ Robert Frank, gen mgr.

Rockford

WMJH(AM)— 1965: 810 khz; 3.6 kw-D. TL: N43 07 03 W85 34 06. Stereo. 2422 Burton St. S.E., Grand Rapids 49546. Phone: (616) 949-8585. Fax: (616) 949-9262. E-mail: jeremy@cookmediagr.com. Licensee: Birach Broadcasting Corp. (group owner; acq 11-6-2001; $1.9 million. with WMFN(AM) Zeeland). Network: Network: CBS, Westwood One. Format: Nostalgia, adult standards. Target aud: 30 plus. ♦ John Shepard, CEO; Dick McKay, gen mgr; Jeremy Bolker, opns dir & opns mgr.

Rogers City

WHAK-FM— April 1994: 99.9 mhz; 50 kw. 476 ft. TL: N45 23 53 W83 55 19. 1491 M-32 W., Alpena 49707. Phone: (989) 354-4611. Fax: (989) 354-4014. E-mail: nsn@chartermi.net. Web Site: www.999thewave.com. Licensee: Edwards Communications LC. Group owner: Northern Radio Network (acq 12-21-2004; grpsl). Format: Oldies. ♦ Don Bernard, gen mgr; Stacie Rasche, gen sls mgr; Danny Stann, progmg dir; Sam Eiler, news dir; Darrel Kelly, chief of engrg.

WHAK(AM)— May 1949: 960 khz; 5 kw-D. TL: N45 23 53 W83 55 19. Rep: Michigan. Format: Talk. Target aud: 18-75. ♦ Mary Garrow, natl sls mgr; Darrell Kelly, progmg dir.

*WVXA(FM)— June 16, 1984: 96.7 mhz; 26 kw. Ant 383 ft. TL: N45 21 01 W83 47 00. Stereo. c/o WVXU(FM), 1223 Central Pkwy., Cincinnati, OH 45214. Phone: (513) 352-9170. Fax: (513) 241-8456. E-mail: wxu@cinradio.org. Web Site: www.wvxu.org. Licensee: Cincinnati Classical Public Radio Inc. (acq 8-22-2005; grpsl). Network: Network: NPR, PRI. Format: News and info. ♦ Richard Eiswerth, gen mgr.

Rogers Heights

*WAQQ(FM)— 2004: 88.1 mhz; 100 w. Ant 85 ft. TL: N43 37 05 W85 32 40. 901 Elizabeth Ct., Mount Pleasant 48858. Phone: (989) 779-9178. Fax: (989) 779-1558. E-mail: great@broadcastingschool.com. Licensee: Great Lakes Community Broadcasting Inc. Format: Oldies. ♦ James J. McCluskey, pres & gen mgr.

Roscommon

WQON(FM)— March 1990: 101.1 mhz; 3.4 kw. 444 ft. TL: N44 34 31 W84 42 19. Stereo. 6514 Old Lake Rd., Grayling 49738. Phone: (989) 348-6171. Fax: (989) 348-6181. E-mail: radio@i2k.net. Web Site: www.gannonbroadcasting.com. Licensee: Gannon Broadcasting Systems Inc. (acq 9-88). Rep: Michigan. Format: Adult contemp. News staff: one; News: 16 hrs wkly. Target aud: 25 plus. ♦ William Gannon, gen mgr; Pete Michaels, opns mgr.

Rose Township

*WMSD(FM)— 08/03/2000: 90.9 mhz; 9 kw vert. -3 ft. Stereo. Box 42, Lupton 48635. Phone: (989) 473-4616. E-mail: biblebaptist77@yahoo.com. Web Site: www.bbc.northern-michigan.net. Licensee: Bible Baptist Church. Format: Relg. ♦ Paul E. Heaton, pres & stn mgr.

Royal Oak

WEXL(AM)— October 1923: 1340 khz; 1 kw-U, DA-D. TL: N42 28 25 W83 06 56. 12300 Radio Pl., Detroit 48228. Phone: (313) 272-3434. Licensee: WMUZ Radio Inc. Group owner: Crawford Broadcasting Co. (acq 4-19-97; $3.5 million). Format: Gospel. Target aud: General. ♦ Frank Franciosi, gen mgr.

Broadcasting & Cable Yearbook 2006

Michigan

Saginaw

WGER(FM)—Listing follows WSGW(AM).

WHNN(FM)—See Bay City

WILZ(FM)— 1992: 104.5 mhz; 2.9 kw. 413 ft. TL: N43 23 34 W83 55 37. 1740 Champagne Dr. N. 48604. Phone: (989) 776-2100. Fax: (989) 754-5990. Web Site: www.wheelz.fm. Licensee: Citadel Broadcasting Co. Group owner: Citadel Broadcasting Corp. (acq 2-8-99). Rep: McGavren Guild. Reddy, Begley & McCormick. Format: Classic rock. Target aud: 35-54; adults. ♦ Scott Meier, VP & gen mgr; Bob Kolen, sls dir; Jerry Tarrants, progmg dir; Hal Maas, mus dir; Bob Friedle, chief of engrg.

WIOG(FM)—See Bay City

WKCQ(FM)—Listing follows WSAM(AM).

WMAX(AM)—(Bay City). June 5, 1925: 1440 khz; 5 kw-D, 2.5 kw-N, DA-2. TL: N43 31 27 W83 57 58. 1 Ave Maria Drive, Ann Arbor 98105. Phone: (989) 771-9485. Phone: Ann Arbor (734) 930-3200. Fax: (989) 771-9937. E-mail: hroot@avemariaradio.net. Web Site: www.avemariaradio.net. Licensee: 990 Investors L.L.C. (acq 6-01; $650,000). Network: USA. Format: Christian, talk. News staff: 2; News: 14 hrs wkly. Target aud: 25-54; adult Christian. ♦ Al Kresta, CEO; Michael P. Jones, exec VP & gen mgr; Henry Root, opns mgr; Tom Loewe, dev dir.

WSAM(AM)— 1940: 1400 khz; 1 kw-U. TL: N43 25 00 W83 55 05. Box 1776, 2000 Whittier 48601. Phone: (989) 752-8161. Fax: (989) 752-8102. Licensee: MacDonald Broadcasting Co. (group owner; acq 12-20-2001; grpsl). Network: ABC Daytime Direction. Rep: D & R Radio. Fletcher, Heald & Hildreth. Format: MOR, full service. Target aud: 25 plus. ♦ Kenneth MacDonald Jr., pres & gen mgr; Rick Walker, VP, opns mgr & progmg dir; Duane Alverson, sls VP & gen sls mgr; Barb Sheltraw, prom mgr; Shari Garcia, news dir; Gary Harding, chief of engrg.

WKCQ(FM)—Co-owned with WSAM(AM). 1947: 98.1 mhz; 50 kw. 500 ft. TL: N43 25 04 W83 58 06. Stereo. Web Site: www.98fmkcq.com. Format: Country. Spec prog: Ger 3 hrs wkly. ♦ Rick Walker, opns mgr; Barb Sheltraw, prom dir; Duane Alverson, adv dir.

WSGW(AM)— Aug 11, 1950: 790 khz; 5 kw-D, 1 kw-N, DA-2. TL: N43 27 40 W83 48 48. 1795 Tittabawassee 48604. Phone: (517) 752-3456. Fax: (517) 754-5046. Web Site: www.wsgw.com. Licensee: NM Licensing LLC. Group owner: NextMedia Group L.L.C. (acq 12-30-02; grpsl). Network: CBS. Rep: Interep. Format: News/talk. News staff: 5; News: 40 hrs wkly. Target aud: 35-54; general. Spec prog: Farm 10 hrs wkly. ♦ Mike Laviolette, gen mgr & adv dir; Dave Maurer, opns dir, progmg dir & news dir; John Sterling, sls dir; R. Bruce Smith, chief of engrg.

WGER(FM)— Co-owned with WSGW(AM). Feb 19, 1969: 106.3 mhz; 4.4 kw. Ant 380 ft. TL: N43 28 36 W83 57 06. Stereo. Web Site: www.magic106.com. Format: Soft rock. Target aud: 25-54; upscale, mid/high level income. ♦ Mike Laviolette, gen sls mgr; Jim Johnson, progmg dir; Bill Anders, asst music dir.

WTLZ(FM)— Nov 15, 1968: 107.1 mhz; 4.9 kw. 400 ft. TL: N43 21 14 W83 55 06. Stereo. 1795 Tittabawassee Rd. 48604. Phone: (989) 752-3456. Fax: (989) 754-5046. E-mail: brownerb@lflint.com. Web Site: www.hotwtlz.com. Licensee: NM Licensing LLC. Group owner: NextMedia Group L.L.C. (acq 12-30-02). Network: American Urban. Pepper & Corazzini. Format: Rhythm and blues. News: 6 hrs wkly. Target aud: 18-49; upscale, Blacks, women. Spec prog: Gospel 6 hrs wkly. ♦ Floyd Evans, gen mgr.

WXQL(FM)—(Carrollton). Mar 11, 1991: 100.5 mhz; 3 kw. 328 ft. TL: N43 33 43 W85 58 54. Stereo. 1795 Tittabauassee Rd. 48604. Phone: (989) 752-3456. Fax: (989) 754-5046. Web Site: www.thenewkoolradio.com. Licensee: NM Licensing LLC. Group owner: NextMedia Group L.L.C. (acq 12-30-02; grpsl). Format: Rhythmic oldies. News staff: one. Target aud: 18-49; women & teens. ♦ Floyd Evans, gen mgr; David Mauer, opns mgr; Jim Johnson, progmg dir.

Saint Ignace

WIDG(AM)— June 7, 1966: 940 khz; 5 kw-D. TL: N45 52 04 W84 47 09. 1356 Mackinaw Ave., Cheboygan 49721. Phone: (231) 627-2341. Fax: (231) 627-7000. Licensee: Northern Star Broadcasting L.L.C.

(group owner; acq 9-10-98; grpsl). Rep: Allied Radio Partners. Format: All sports. ♦ Palmer Pyle, pres; Chris Monk, gen mgr & gen sls mgr; Nate Rose, progmg dir.

Saint Johns

WTXQ(FM)— July 15, 1972: 92.1 mhz; 6 kw. Ant 400 ft. TL: N42 53 29 W84 34 27. Stereo. 2495 N. Cedar, Holt 48842. Phone: (517) 699-0111. Fax: (517) 699-1880. Web Site: www.wqtx.net. Licensee: Rubber City Radio Group. Group owner: Rubber City Radio Group Inc. (acq 7-12-2000; grpsl). Rep: Katz Radio. Format: Sports talk. ♦ Thomas Mandel, pres; Mark Biviano, exec VP; Nick Anthony, exec VP; Dave Johnson, gen mgr; Paul Cashin, progmg dir.

WWSJ(AM)— Sept 23, 1959: 1580 khz; 1 kw-D, DA. TL: N42 58 14 W84 32 59. Box 451, 1363 W. Parks Rd., St. John 48879. Phone: (989) 224-7911. Fax: (989) 224-4683. Web Site: www.wwsj.com. Licensee: L. Harp, H. Harp, W. Hill, Elmira Hill. (acq 1-97; $160,000; 3-20-95). Network: American Urban. Format: Urban gospel. ♦ Larry Harp, pres; Danielle Beckley, prom VP; Helen Harp, progmg dir; Dione Harp, mus dir; Ed Czelada, chief of engrg.

Saint Joseph

WHFB(AM)—See Benton Harbor-St. Joseph

WHFB-FM—See Benton Harbor-St. Joseph

WIRX(FM)—Licensed to Saint Joseph. See Benton Harbor-St. Joseph

WSJM(AM)—Licensed to Saint Joseph. See Benton Harbor-St. Joseph

Saint Louis

WFYC(AM)—See Alma

WMLM(AM)— Dec 15, 1977: 1520 khz; 1 kw-U, DA-2. TL: N43 21 08 W84 36 15. Box 17 48880. Secondary address: 4170 N. State Rd., Alma 48801. Phone: (989) 463-4013. Fax: (989) 463-4014. E-mail: wmlm@cmsinter.net. Web Site: www.wmlm.com. Licensee: Siefker Broadcasting Corp. Network: ABC. Format: Country. Target aud: 35 plus. Spec prog: Farm 5 hrs, big band 4 hrs, gospel 2 hrs wkly. ♦ Gregory Siefker, pres & gen mgr.

WQBX(FM)—See Alma

Salem Township

WSDS(AM)—Licensed to Salem Township. See Ann Arbor

Saline

WLBY(AM)— 1958: 1290 khz; 500 w-D, DA. TL: N42 12 17 W83 47 19. 1100 Victors Way, Suite 100, Ann Arbor 48108. Phone: (734) 302-8100. Fax: (734) 213-7508. E-mail: wcas@clearchannel.com. Licensee: Capstar TX L.P. Group owner: Clear Channel Communications Inc. (acq 8-7-2000; grpsl). Format: Talk/sports. ♦ Rob Walker, gen mgr & progmg dir; Shannon Brown, gen sls mgr.

Sandusky

WMIC(AM)— June 27, 1968: 660 khz; 1 kw-D, DA. TL: N43 23 34 W82 49 57. 19 S. Elk St. 48471. Phone: (810) 648-2700. E-mail: wmic@avc1.net. Licensee: Sanilac Broadcasting Co. Network: ABC Information & Entertainment. Format: Country, news/talk. News staff: 2; News: 20 hrs wkly. Target aud: 25 plus; general. Spec prog: Farm 12 hrs, Pol 5 wkly. ♦ George E. Benko, pres; Robert Benko, VP; Bob Armstrong, gen mgr & gen sls mgr; Stan Grabitz, mus dir; Renae Davis, news dir; Kevin Larke, chief of engrg.

WTGV-FM—Co-owned with WMIC. Aug 16, 1971: 97.7 mhz; 3 kw. 325 ft. TL: N43 23 33 W82 49 56. Stereo. Format: Adult contemp.

*****WNFR(FM)**— Feb 14, 1994: 90.7 mhz; 18 kw. 328 ft. TL: N43 27 32 W82 57 42. Stereo. Wonderful News Radio, 2865 Maywood Dr., Port Huron 48060. Phone: (810) 985-3260. Fax: (810) 985-7712. Web Site: www.wnradio.com. Licensee: Ross Bible Church. Network: Network: Moody, USA. Southmayd & Miller. Format: Relg, inspirational. Target

Directory of Radio

aud: 25-44; females. ♦ Lori McNaughton, opns mgr; Ellyn Davey, mus dir & news dir; Sara Kenner, pub affrs dir; Ed Czelada, chief of engrg.

Saugatuck

WYVN(FM)— July 4, 1987: 92.7 mhz; 2.15 kw. 387 ft. TL: N42 41 10 W86 10 05. Stereo. 87 Central Ave., Holland 49423. Phone: (616) 392-3121. Phone: (616) 396-0927. Fax: (616) 392-8066. E-mail: advertising@thevan.fm. Licensee: Midwest Communications Inc. (group owner; acq 9-5-01; $1.5 million). Format: Classic hits. News staff: one; News: one hr wkly. Target aud: 25-54. ♦ Duke Wright, CEO; Peter Tanz, gen mgr; Melissa Ryzy, gen sls mgr; Joe Daugherty, progmg mgr; Gary Stevens, news dir.

Sault Ste. Marie

*****WCMZ-FM**— July 13, 1990: 98.3 mhz; 25 kw. 328 ft. TL: N46 29 10 W84 13 49. Stereo. Central Michigan Univ., 1999 E. Campus Dr., Mount Pleasant 48859. Phone: (989) 774-3105. Fax: (989) 774-4427. E-mail: cmuradio@radio.cmich.edu. Web Site: www.wcmu.org. Licensee: Central Michigan University. Network: Network: NPR, PRI. Dow, Lohnes & Albertson. Format: Class, jazz, news. News staff: 2; News: 45 hrs wkly. Target aud: General. ♦ Thomas Hunt, gen mgr; Art Curtis, rgnl sls mgr; Ann Blatte, prom mgr; Ray Ford, progmg dir; Randy Kapenga, chief of engrg.

WKNW(AM)—Listing follows WYSS(FM).

*****WLSO(FM)**— 1995: 90.1 mhz; 100 w. 98 ft. TL: N46 29 31 W84 21 48. 650 W. Easterday Ave. 49783. Phone: (906) 635-2107. Phone: (906) 635-2863. Fax: (906) 635-2111. E-mail: wlso@gw.lssu.edu. Web Site: www.lssu.edu/wlso. Licensee: Lake Superior State University. Format: Var. ♦ Kahler Schuemann, gen mgr; Hollie Arman, stn mgr.

WSOO(AM)— June 1, 1940: 1230 khz; 1 kw-U. TL: N46 26 16 W84 22 42. Box 1230 49783. Phone: (906) 632-2231. Fax: (906) 632-4411. Web Site: www.sooradio.com. Licensee: Sovereign Communications LLC (acq 12-18-03; $2.6 million. with co-located FM). Network: ABC Information & Entertainment. Rep: Michigan. Format: Adult contemp. ♦ Tom Ewing, gen mgr.

WSUE(FM)—Co-owned with WSOO(AM). 1978: 101.3 mhz; 100 kw. 978 ft. TL: N46 26 16 W84 22 42. Format: Classic rock, rock/AOR.

*****WTHN(FM)**— Jan 29, 2005: 102.3 mhz; 22.5 kw. Ant 344 ft. TL: N46 29 08 W84 13 49. 1511 M-32 E., Gaylord 49735. Secondary address: Box 695, Gaylord 49734. Phone: (989) 732-6274. Fax: (989) 732-8171. E-mail: ncr@ncradio.org. Web Site: www.ncradio.org. Licensee: Northern Christian Radio Inc. (group owner). Format: Inspirational. ♦ George A. Lake Jr., CEO & gen mgr.

WYSS(FM)— July 12, 1972: 99.5 mhz; 26.5 kw. 275 ft. TL: N46 23 48 W84 23 52. (CP: 100 kw). Stereo. 1402 Ashmun St. 49783. Phone: (906) 635-0995. Fax: (906) 635-1216. Web Site: www.995yesfm.com. Licensee: Northern Star Broadcasting L.L.C. (group owner; acq 11-5-01; grpsl). Network: Westwood One. Cohn & Marks. Format: CHR. Target aud: 18-49. ♦ Keith Neve, gen mgr, gen sls mgr & gen sls mgr; Tim Ellis, progmg dir; John Bell, news dir.

WKNW(AM)—Co-owned with WYSS(FM). Aug 25, 1990: 1400 khz; 250 w-U. TL: N46 29 18 W84 19 45. Stereo. Web Site: www.talkradio1400.com. Format: Sports, news/talk. ♦ John Bell, progmg dir.

Schoolcraft

*****WOFR(FM)**— May 2003: 89.5 mhz; 10 kw. Ant 138 ft. TL: N42 06 38 W85 37 57. Family Stations Inc., 4135 Northgate Blvd., Suite 1, Sacramento, CA 95834. Phone: (510) 568-6200. Fax: (510) 568-6190. Web Site: www.familyradio.com. Licensee: Family Stations Inc. (group owner). Format: Relg. ♦ Harold Camping, gen mgr; Craig Hulsebos, progmg dir; Rick Prime, chief of engrg.

Scottville

WKZC(FM)— Feb 16, 1983: 94.9 mhz; 17 kw. 400 ft. TL: N44 03 27 W86 24 58. Stereo. 5941 W. U.S. 10, Ludington 49431. Phone: (231) 843-3438. Fax: (231) 843-1886. E-mail: brett@yourcountry95.com. Web Site: www.yourcountryz95.com. Licensee: Lake Michigan Broadcasting Inc. (group owner; acq 9-20-96; grpsl). Network: ABC. Rep: Patt. Shaw Pittman. Format: Country. News staff: one; News: 5 hrs wkly.

Stations in the U.S. Michigan

Developers & Brokers of Radio Properties

contact American Media Services at our suite:
Philadelphia Marriott Downtown
215-625-2900
843-972-2200
americanmediaservices.com
Charleston, SC
Dallas, TX · Chicago, Il · Austin, TX

American Media Services, LLC

Target aud: 25-54. ♦Lynn Baerwolf, pres & gen mgr; Judy Ouvry, gen sls mgr; Mike Baerwolf, opns mgr & prom VP.

Shepherd

WMMI(AM)— Feb 2, 1987: 830 khz; 1 kw-D. TL: N43 33 42 W84 45 00. Stereo. 4065 E. Wing Rd., Mount Pleasant 48858. Phone: (989) 772-9664. Fax: (989) 773-5000. E-mail: wczy@litehits104.com. Web Site: wwwlitehits104.com. Licensee: Central Michigan Communications Inc. (acq 8-15-88). Rep: Michigan. Patt. Reddy, Begley & McCormick. Format: Talk. Target aud: 25-54; general. ♦Mike Carey, pres; Dan Bragg, progmg dir; Carmie Crisci, news dir.

South Haven

WCSY-FM—Listing follows WSPZ(AM).

WSPZ(AM)— 1961: 940 khz; 1 kw-D, 6 w-N, DA-D. TL: N42 24 34 W86 16 01. 510 Williams St. 49090. Phone: (269) 637-6397. Fax: (269) 637-2675. Web Site: www.wgmy.com. Licensee: WSJM Inc. (group owner; acq 10-95; with co-located FM). Network: ABC Information & Entertainment. Format: Nostalgia. Target aud: 35-45; females. Spec prog: Breakfast club, farm 3 hrs wkly. ♦Gayle Olson, pres; Tom Ewing, gen mgr.

WCSY-FM—Co-owned with WSPZ(AM). Oct 31, 1981: 98.3 mhz; 2 kw. 400 ft. TL: N42 18 02 W86 15 03. Stereo. Web Site: www.wcsy.com. Format: Middle of the Road.

Southfield

*****WSHJ(FM)**— Feb 28, 1967: 88.3 mhz; 125 w. 43 ft. TL: N42 28 12 W83 15 50. Stereo. Southfield High School, 24675 Lasher Rd. 48034. Phone: (248) 746-8630. Phone: (248) 746-8631. Web Site: www.southfield.l12.mi.us/itc. Licensee: Board of Education Southfield Public Schools. Format: Oldies, hip-hop. Target aud: General; students & families. ♦Jamie Rudolph, gen mgr.

Spring Arbor

*****KTGG(AM)**— Aug 15, 1985: 1540 khz; 450 w-D. TL: N42 09 13 W84 32 58. Spring Arbor University, 106 Main St., Sayre Hall 49283. Phone: (517) 750-6540. Phone: (517) 750-9723. Fax: (517) 750-6619. Licensee: Spring Arbor University. Lauren A. Colby. Format: Inspirational, relg. Target aud: 18-49; rural to urban. ♦Hal Munn, pres; Michelle Dawson, stn mgr, opns dir & progmg dir; Carl Jacobson, dev dir; Peggy Kilgore, pub affrs dir; Dave Benson, chief of engrg.

WSAE(FM)—Co-owned with KTGG(AM). Oct 2, 1963: 106.9 mhz; 3.9 kw. Ant 349 ft. TL: N42 09 13 W84 32 58. Stereo. E-mail: wsae@admin.arbor.edu. Web Site: www.arbor.edu/wsae. Lauren A. Colby. Format: Christian contemp, relg. Target aud: 18-44. ♦Michelle Dawson, opns mgr.

*****WJKN-FM**— 2005: 89.3 mhz; 2.5 kw vert. Ant 272 ft. TL: N42 09 13 W84 32 57. Spring Arbor University, 106 E. Main St. 49283. Phone: (517) 750-6540. Fax: (517) 750-6619. E-mail: powerpraise@arbor.edu. Web Site: www.arbor.edu. Licensee: Spring Arbor University. Format: Christian. ♦Carl Fletcher, gen mgr; Rachel Ryder, mus dir; Dave Benson, chief of engrg.

Standish

WWCM(FM)— January 1990: 96.9 mhz; 3 kw. Ant 328 ft. TL: N44 02 08 W84 00 31. Stereo. Public Broadcasting Ctr., 1999 E. Campus Dr., Mount Pleasant 48859. Phone: (989) 774-3105. Fax: (989) 774-4427. E-mail: cmuradio@radio.cmich.edu. Web Site: www.wcmu.org. Licensee: Central Michigan University (acq 9-14-00). Format: Class, jazz, news & info. Target aud: General. ♦Edward Grant, gen mgr.

Stephenson

WMXG(FM)— 1999: 106.3 mhz; 50 kw. Ant 492 ft. TL: N45 38 36 W87 22 37. 1101 A Ludington St., Escanaba 49829. Phone: (906) 786-0060. Fax: (906) 786-2990. E-mail: mix106@chartermi.net. Web Site: www.wmxg.com. Licensee: Pacer Radio of the Near-North. Format: Hot adult contemp. ♦Mike DuBord, gen mgr.

Sterling Heights

*****WUFL(AM)**— Oct 26, 1988: 1030 khz; 5 kw-D, DA. TL: N42 36 19 W82 54 37. 42669 Garfield Rd., Suite 328, Clinton Township 48038. Secondary address: Box 1030 48311. Phone: (586) 263-1030. Fax: (586) 228-1030. E-mail: wufl@flc.org. Web Site: wufl.org. Licensee: Family Life Broadcasting System. (group owner; acq 10-25-88). Network: USA. Format: Relg, Christian. News staff: one. Target aud: 25-49; evangelical Christians. ♦Dawn Bumstead, gen mgr & progmg mgr; Greg Kinzy, opns mgr; Donald Aupperle, prom mgr; Gary Lundy, news dir & pub affrs dir.

Sturgis

WMSH(AM)— 1951: 1230 khz; 1 kw-U, DA-1. TL: N41 46 11 W85 25 09. (CP: 2.16 kw). Box 7080, 70808 S. Nottawa Rd. 49091. Phone: (269) 651-2383. Phone: (269) 651-2384. Fax: (269) 659-1111. E-mail: wmsh@wmshradio.com. Web Site: www.wmshradio.com. Licensee: Lake Cities Broadcasting Corp. (group owner; acq 1-12-98; $600,000 with co-located FM). Network: Network: ABC, Jones Radio Networks. Rep: Michigan. Format: News, sports. Target aud: 25-54. ♦Carter Snider, gen mgr & sls VP.

WMSH-FM— 1951: 99.3 mhz; 2.15 kw. 390 ft. TL: N41 46 11 W85 25 09. Stereo. Format: Oldies.

Tawas City

WHST(FM)— Nov 1, 1972: 106.1 mhz; 6 kw. 280 ft. TL: N44 16 27 W83 39 42. Stereo. Box 695, Gaylord 49734-0695. Secondary address: 1511 M-32 E., Gaylord 49735. Phone: (989) 732-6274. Fax: (989) 732-8171. E-mail: ncr@ncradio.org. Web Site: www.ncradio.org. Licensee: Northern Christian Radio Inc. (group owner; acq 7-19-01). Format: Religious. Target aud: 25-54. ♦George A. Lake Jr., gen mgr.

WIOS(AM)— Sept 27, 1958: 1480 khz; 1 kw-D, DA. TL: N44 15 48 W83 32 42. Box 549 48764. Secondary address: 523 Meadow Rd. 48763. Phone: (989) 362-3417. Phone: (989) 362-3627. Fax: (989) 362-4544. Licensee: Carroll Enterprises Inc. (group owner; acq 5-1-69). Network: ABC Information & Entertainment. Rep: Michigan. Booth, Freret, Imlay & Tepper P. Format: Easy lstng, talk. Target aud: 25 plus; general. Spec prog: Big band 6 hrs wkly. ♦John Carroll Jr., CEO, pres & gen mgr; John Carroll Sr., chmn; Tim Carroll, gen sls mgr.

WKJC(FM)—Co-owned with WIOS(AM). October 1979: 104.7 mhz; 50 kw. 492 ft. TL: N44 24 43 W83 37 17. Stereo. E-mail: wkjc@wkjc.com. Web Site: www.wkjc.com. Format: Modern C&W.

WQLB(FM)— July 1997: 103.3 mhz; 25 kw. 328 ft. TL: N44 21 06 W83 31 39. Box 549 48764. Phone: (989) 362-3417. Fax: (989) 362-4544. E-mail: wkjc@wkjc.com. Web Site: www.wkjc.com. Licensee: Carroll Broadcasting Inc. (acq 12-1-97). Booth,Freret, Imlay & Tepper. Format: Classic rock. ♦John Carroll Jr., gen mgr; Tim Carroll, gen sls mgr; Dennis Kirk, progmg dir; Marvin Walther, chief of engrg.

Taylor

WCHB(AM)— 1990: 1200 khz; 25 kw-D, 15 kw-N, DA-2. TL: N42 09 24 W83 19 56. 3250 Franklin St., Detroit 48207. Phone: (313) 259-2000. Fax: (313) 259-7011. Licensee: Radio One of Detroit LLC. Group owner: Radio One Inc. (acq 6-19-98; $34.2 million. with WDTJ(FM) Detroit). Format: News/Talk, gospel. ♦Alfred Liggins, pres; Dr. Wendell Cox, VP; Tamara Knechtel, gen mgr.

Three Rivers

WLKM(AM)— May 3, 1962: 1520 khz; 430 w-D, 8 w-N. TL: N41 55 43 W85 38 15. 59750 Constantine Rd. 49093-9394. Phone: (269) 278-1815. Fax: (269) 273-7975. E-mail: info@wlkm.com. Web Site: www.wlkm.com. Licensee: Impact Radio LLC (group owner; acq 8-1-2002; grpsl). Network: Westwood One, AP Radio. Rep: Patt. Reddy, Begley & McCormick. Format: Classic hit country. News staff: one; News: 14 hrs wkly. Target aud: General. ♦Dennis Rumsey, pres & gen mgr.

WLKM-FM— March 1975: 95.9 mhz; 3 kw. 315 ft. TL: N41 55 43 W85 38 15. Stereo. Web Site: www.wlkm.com. Network: CNN Radio. Format: Adult contemp. News staff: one; News: 13 hrs wkly. Target aud: 25-54.

Traverse City

WCCW(AM)— July 15, 1960: 1310 khz; 5 kw-D. TL: N44 46 11 W85 41 22. 115 Park St. 49684. Phone: (231) 946-4446. Phone: (231) 946-6211. Fax: (231) 946-1914. E-mail: wccw@tii.com. Licensee: Midwestern Broadcasting Co. (group owner; acq 9-16-96; $2.2 million with co-located FM). Network: ABC Information & Entertainment. Rep: Michigan, Katz Radio. Format: Sports, talk. ♦Hal Paine, gen mgr; Dave Gauthier, progmg dir; Annie Mac, news dir.

WCCW-FM— Nov 8, 1967: 107.5 mhz; 50 kw. 518 ft. TL: N44 46 11 W85 41 22. (CP: 660 w, ant 702 ft. TL: N44 46 02 W85 41 26). Stereo. Network: ABC Information & Entertainment. Format: Oldies. ♦Jim Sofonia, progmg dir.

*****WICA(FM)**— Sept 13, 2000: 91.5 mhz; 4 kw. Ant 748 ft. TL: N44 45 22 W85 40 42. Stereo. Box 199, Interlochen 49643. Phone: (231) 276-4400. Fax: (231) 276-4417. E-mail: ipr@interlochen.org. Licensee: Interlochen Center for the Arts. Format: News, talk. News staff: 4; News: 168 hrs wkly. Target aud: 25-80. ♦Thom Paulson, VP & stn mgr; Joanne Hermann, dev dir.

WLDR-FM— July 17, 1966: 101.9 mhz; 100 kw. 538 ft. TL: N44 46 13 W85 41 43. (CP: Ant 630 ft.). Stereo. 118 S. Union St. 49684. Phone: (231) 947-3220. Fax: (231) 947-7201. E-mail: wldr@wldr.com. Web Site: www.wldr.com. Licensee: Great Northern Broadcasting System Inc. Group owner: Fort Bend Broadcasting Co. (acq 4-10-01; $3.6 million. for stock). Format: Adult contemp. News staff: one. Target aud: 25-54. ♦Roy Henderson, CEO; Steve Smith, CFO; Lori McFarlan, stn mgr & gen sls mgr; Dave Maxson, opns dir, gen sls mgr, prom dir & news dir; Rich Nadeau, progmg dir; Vic Browning, mus dir; Dennis Murray, chief of engrg.

*****WLJN-FM**— Oct 1, 1989: 89.9 mhz; 39 kw vert. Ant 554 ft. TL: N44 46 36 W85 39 43. Stereo. Box 1400 49685. Secondary address: 13930 S. Morgan Hill Rd. 49684. Phone: (231) 946-1400. Fax: (231) 946-3959. E-mail: info@wljn.com. Web Site: www.wljn.com. Licensee: Good News Media Inc. (group owner). Format: Relg, Christian music. News: 4 hrs wkly. Target aud: General. ♦Bob Olsen, VP; Brian Harcey, gen mgr; Doug Knorr, pres & progmg dir.

WLXT(FM)—See Petoskey

*****WNMC-FM**— October 1967: 90.7 mhz; 600 w. 538 ft. TL: N44 46 36 W85 41 02. Stereo. 1701 E. Front St. 49686. Phone: (231) 995-2562. Phone: (231) 995-1090. Fax: (231) 922-8963. Web Site: www.wnmc.org. Licensee: Northwestern Michigan College. Format: Div, jazz, rock,blues. Spec prog: American Indian one hr, Black 20 hrs, folk 11 hrs, Sp 2 hrs wkly. ♦Eric Hines, gen mgr.

WTCM(AM)— 1941: 580 khz; 50 kw-D, 1.1 kw-N, DA-2. TL: N44 43 18 W85 42 18. Stereo. 314 E. Front St. 49684. Phone: (231) 947-7675. Fax: (231) 929-3988. Web Site: www.wtcmi.com. Licensee: WTCM Radio Inc. Group owner: Midwestern Broadcasting Co. Network: ABC Information & Entertainment. Cordon & Kelly. Format: News/talk. News staff: 4; News: 12 hrs wkly. Target aud: 25-54. Spec prog: Farm 5 hrs wkly. ♦Ross Biederman, pres & gen mgr.

Broadcasting & Cable Yearbook 2006

Michigan

WTCM-FM— Dec 13, 1965: 103.5 mhz; 100 kw. 989 ft. TL: N44 27 31 W85 42 02. Stereo. Web Site: www.wtcmi.com. Format: Country. Target aud: 25-54.

Trout Lake

*****WHWG(FM)**— 1999: 89.9 mhz; 500 w. Ant 390 ft. TL: N46 11 17 W84 56 46. 130 Carmen Dr., Marquette 49855. Phone: (906) 249-1423. Fax: (906) 249-4042. E-mail: gospelop@chartermi.net. Web Site: www.gospelopportunities.com. Licensee: Gospel Opportunities Inc. Format: Relg. ♦W. Curtis Marker, gen mgr & progmg dir.

Tuscola

WWBN(FM)— Sept 14, 1987: 101.5 mhz; 1.8 kw. Ant 489 ft. TL: N43 12 00 W83 33 30. Stereo. G-3338 E. Bristol Rd., Burton 48529. Phone: (810) 742-1470. Fax: (810) 742-5170. E-mail: banana1015@regentflint.com. Web Site: www.banana1015.com. Licensee: Regent Broadcasting of Flint Inc. Group owner: Regent Communications Inc. (acq 12-19-97; grpsl). Network: Westwood Edge. Rep: Katz Radio. Format: Rock/AOR. News staff: one; News: 20 hrs wkly. Target aud: 18-49; men. ♦Terry Jacobs, CEO; Bill Stakelin, pres; Fred Murr, sr VP; Mark Thomas, VP & gen mgr; J. Patrick, opns VP; Brian Beddow, progmg dir.

Twin Lake

*****WBLV(FM)**— July 3, 1982: 90.3 mhz; 100 kw. Ant 649 ft. TL: N43 33 00 W86 02 34. Stereo. Blue Lake Fine Arts Camp, 300 East Crystal Lake Rd. 49457-9592. Phone: (231) 894-2616. Fax: (231) 893-2457. Web Site: www.bluelake.org. Licensee: Blue Lake Fine Arts Camp. Network: Network: PRI, NPR. Booth, Freret, Imlay & Tepper. Format: Class, jazz, news. News: 20 hrs wkly. Target aud: Adult. Spec prog: Folk 5 hrs wkly. ♦William F. Stansell, pres; Dave Myers, gen mgr; Gordon Christensen, opns dir; Steve Albert, progmg dir; Bonnie Bierma, mus dir.

Vassar

WOWE(FM)— July 1, 1990: 98.9 mhz; 3 kw. 328 ft. TL: N43 17 56 W83 30 34. 126 W. Kearsley St., Flint 48502. Phone: (810) 234-4335. Fax: (810) 234-7286. E-mail: wowe98.9@netzero.com. Licensee: Praestantia Broadcasting Inc. Format: Urban contemp. ♦Michael Shumpert, pres, gen mgr, progmg dir & chief of engrg.

Walker

WTRV(FM)— June 15, 1993: 100.5 mhz; 3 kw. 328 ft. TL: N43 00 59 W85 44 24. 50 Monroe N.W., Suite 500, Grand Rapids 49503. Phone: (616) 451-4855. Fax: (616) 451-4899. Web Site: www.theriver-fm.com. Licensee: Regent Broadcasting of Grand Rapids Inc. Group owner: Regent Communications Inc. (acq 8-7-00; grpsl). Format: Soft adult contemp. Target aud: 35-64. ♦Terry Jacobs, pres; Phil Catlett, gen mgr; Rick Sarata, sls dir; Rob Wagley, gen sls mgr; Nikki Havner, prom dir; Bill Bailey, progmg dir; Gene Parker, mus dir; Chuck Latour, news dir; Mike Mackjewski, engrg dir.

Walled Lake

WPON(AM)— December 1954: 1460 khz; 1 kw-D, 760 w-N, DA-2. TL: N42 32 38 W83 29 58. 21700 Northwestern Hwy., Suite 1190, Southfield 48075. Phone: (248) 557-3500. Fax: (248) 557-4321. E-mail: wpon@wpon.com. Web Site: www.wpon.com. Licensee: Birach Broadcasting Corp. (group owner; acq 5-25-2004; $800,000). Format: Oldies, talk. News staff: . Target aud: 35-65; 35 and above. ♦Sima Birach, gen mgr; Andy Warnock, stn mgr & opns mgr.

Warren

*****WPHS(FM)**— Mar 20, 1964: 89.1 mhz; 100 w. Ant 98 ft. TL: N42 31 00 W83 00 36. Stereo. P.K. Cousino High School, 30333 Hoover Rd. 48093. Secondary address: Warren Consolidated Schools, 31300 Anita 48093. Phone: (586) 698-4501. E-mail: wphs@wphs.com. Web Site: www.wphs.com. Licensee: Warren Consolidated Schools. (acq 1963). Format: Techno. News staff: 2; News: 10 hrs wkly. Target aud: 12-27; males. Spec prog: Blues 3 hrs, Pol 2 hrs, news 5 hrs, country 4 hrs, Christian rock 4 hrs wkly. ♦Jenny S. Stanczyk, gen mgr.

West Branch

WBMI(FM)— Nov 7, 1977: 105.5 mhz; 3 kw. 312 ft. TL: N44 17 57 W84 15 59. Stereo. 3275 W. M 55 48661. Phone: (989) 345-9264. Fax: (989) 345-3996. Licensee: Independent Television Productions of Michigan Inc. (acq 10-2-01). Network: Jones Radio Networks. Format: Hot AC. Target aud: 25-54. Spec prog: Pol 6 hrs wkly. ♦Dan Vargas, gen mgr & opns mgr; Lucky Osborn, opns mgr, news dir & news dir.

White Star

*****WEJC(FM)**— July 2001: 88.3 mhz; 30 kw vert. 472 ft. TL: N43 57 18 W84 32 57. Superior Communications, Box 388, Williamson 48895. Phone: (517) 381-0573. Fax: (877) 850-0881. E-mail: info@positivehits.com. Web Site: www.positivehits.com. Licensee: Superior Communications. Format: Contemporary Christian. ♦Jenn Czelada, gen mgr.

Whitehall

WEFG-FM—Listing follows WODJ(AM).

WGVS-FM—Licensed to Whitehall. See Muskegon

WODJ(AM)— Oct 21, 1959: 1490 khz; 1 kw-U. TL: N43 23 04 W86 19 30. Stereo. Box 190, Fremont 49412-0190. Phone: (231) 924-4700. Fax: (231) 759-3410. E-mail: jtb@wlcfonline.com. Web Site: www.funcountry.com. Licensee: Unity Broadcasting Inc. (group owner; acq 12-16-2002; grpsl). Network: Jones Radio Networks. Rep: Patt. Kaye, Scholer, Fierman, Hays & Handler. Format: Music of your life, MOR, big band. News: 14 hrs wkly. Target aud: 55 plus. ♦Don Noordyk, gen mgr.

WEFG-FM— Co-owned with WODJ(AM). Apr 1, 1991: 97.5 mhz; 3 kw. 430 ft. TL: N43 23 04 W86 19 30. Stereo. Network: Westwood One. Format: Black, oldies. News: one hr wkly. Target aud: 25-49; male and female. ♦Bob Bolton, exec VP; Ernest Herrera, engrg VP.

Wyoming

*****WYCE(FM)**— Nov 1, 1983: 88.1 mhz; 7 kw. 167 ft. TL: N42 54 43 W85 41 00. Stereo. 711 Bridge St., Grand Rapids 49504. Phone: (616) 459-4788. Fax: (616) 742-0599. E-mail: comment@wyce.org. Web Site: www.wyce.org. Licensee: Grand Rapids Cable Access Center Inc. (acq 5-31-89; $30,616; 6-19-89). Format: Alternative, eclectic. Target aud: 25-54; general. Spec prog: Folk one hr, Sp 10 hrs. ♦Michael Packer, stn mgr.

WYGR(AM)— Nov 14, 1964: 1530 khz; 500 w-D. TL: N42 55 38 W85 44 50. Box 9591, 1303 Chicago Dr. S.W. 49509. Phone: (616) 475-9947. Phone: (616) 248-9947. Fax: (616) 248-0176. E-mail: wygr@compuserv.com. Web Site: www.wygr.com. Licensee: WYGR Broadcasting. (acq 3-18-89). Rep: Patt. Meyer, Faller, Weisman & Rosenberg. Format: Sp, var/div. Target aud: Sp speaking Hispanics. Spec prog: Polka 3 hrs wkly. ♦Roland Rusticus, gen mgr, stn mgr, gen sls mgr & prom mgr; Scott Richards, progmg mgr, news dir & pub affrs dir; Robert Van Prooyen, chief of engrg.

Ypsilanti

WDEO(AM)—Licensed to Ypsilanti. See Ann Arbor

*****WEMU(FM)**— Dec 8, 1965: 89.1 mhz; 15.5 kw. 289 ft. TL: N42 15 48 W83 37 34. Stereo. Box 980350 48198-0350. Secondary address: Eastern Michigan Univ., 426 King Hall 48197. Phone: (734) 487-2229. Phone: (734) 487-8936. Fax: (734) 487-1015. E-mail: wemu@emich.edu. Web Site: www.wemu.org. Licensee: Eastern Michigan University. Network: NPR. Cohn & Marks. Format: News, jazz, blues. News staff: 4; News: 39 hrs wkly. Target aud: General. ♦Arthur Timko, gen mgr; Michael Jewett, opns mgr; Mary Motherwell, dev dir; Clark Smith, progmg dir, progmg mgr & news dir; Linda Yohn, mus dir; Ray Cryderman, chief of engrg.

Zeeland

*****WGNB(FM)**— Jan 21, 1989: 89.3 mhz; 30 kw. 499 ft. TL: N42 50 14 W85 59 17. Stereo. Box 40, 3764 84th Ave. 49464. Phone: (616) 772-7300. Fax: (616) 772-9663. E-mail: wgnb@moody.edu. Web Site: www.wgnb.org. Licensee: The Moody Bible Institute of Chicago Inc. (group owner; acq 2-5-91; 2-25-91). Network: Network: Salem Radio Network, Moody. Southmayd & Miller. Format: Relg. News: 15 hrs wkly. Target aud: 35-54; evangelical Christians. ♦Dr. Joseph Stowell, pres; Larry Mercer, sr VP; Robert Neff, VP; Scott Curtis, opns dir & mus dir; Dave Senzig, chief of engrg.

WJQK(FM)—Licensed to Zeeland. See Holland

WMFN(AM)— February 1990: 640 khz; 1 kw-D, 250 w-N. TL: N42 48 59 W85 57 24. Stereo. 2422 Burton S.E., Grand Rapids 49546. Phone: (616) 949-8585. Fax: (616) 949-9262. E-mail: jerenny@cookmediagr.com. Licensee: Birach Broadcasting Corp. (group owner; acq 11-6-01; $1.9 million. with WMJH(AM) Rockford). Network: CBS. Format: News/talk, financial. Target aud: 25-54. ♦John Shepard, CEO & pres; Fred Barr, opns mgr.

WPNW(AM)— Nov 2, 1956: 1260 khz; 5 kw-D, 1 kw-N, DA-1. TL: N42 43 56 W86 06 06. 425 Centerstone Ct., Suite 1 49464. Phone: (616) 931-6620. Fax: (616) 931-1280. Web Site: www.wpnw.com. Licensee: Lanser Broadcasting Corp. (acq 11-1-83; $950,000; 10-3-83). Reddy, Begley & McCormick. Format: Christian/talk. News staff: one; News: 9 hrs wkly. Target aud: 35 plus; mature adults. Spec prog: Sp 2 hrs, farm one hr wkly. ♦Leslie J. Lanser, pres; Bradley Lanser, exec VP; Claire Rotman, gen sls mgr & rgnl sls mgr; Troy West, gen mgr, stn mgr & progmg dir.

Minnesota

Ada

KRJB(FM)— Sept 1, 1985: 106.3 mhz; 3 kw. 276 ft. TL: N47 18 41 W96 31 13. Stereo. 312 W. Main St. 56510. Phone: (218) 784-2844. Fax: (218) 784-3749. Web Site: www.krjbradio.com. Licensee: R & J Broadcasting. (acq 10-1-87). Format: Country. ♦Jim Birkemeyer, gen mgr & mktg VP.

Aitkin

KKIN(AM)— June 1, 1961: 930 khz; 2.5 kw-D, 400 w-N. TL: N46 32 26 W93 39 22. Stereo. Box 140 56431. Secondary address: 37208 U.S. Hwy. 169 56431. Phone: (218) 927-2344. Fax: (218) 927-4090. E-mail: kkin@mlecmn.net. Web Site: www.kkinradio.com. Licensee: Quarnstrom Media Group LLC (group owner; acq 1-2-01; grpsl). Network: Jones Radio Networks. Timothy K. Brady. Format: Music of Your Life. News staff: one. Target aud: General. ♦Al Quarnstrom, pres; Terry Dee, gen mgr.

KKIN-FM— Jan 3, 1972: 94.3 mhz; 14 kw. Ant 436 ft. TL: N46 41 18 W93 35 58. Stereo. Phone: (218) 927-2100. Web Site: kkinradio.com. Format: Classic country. News staff: one; News: 5 hrs wkly. Target aud: 35 plus.

Albany

KASM(AM)— Nov 20, 1950: 1150 khz; 2.5 kw-D, 23 w-N. TL: N45 37 59 W94 36 00. (CP: 2.1 kw. TL: N45 37 53 W94 36 00). Box 390 56307. Secondary address: 35223 238th Ave. Phone: (320) 845-2184. Fax: (320) 845-2187. Licensee: Starcom LLC (acq 1997; $1.25 million. with co-located FM). Rep: Allied Radio Partners. Hyett/Ramsland. Baker & Hostetler. Format: Country, news, polka. News staff: one; News: 2 hrs wkly. Target aud: 36 plus. Spec prog: Oldies, Ger mus 2 hrs, farm 6 hrs wkly. ♦Kevin Pierskalla, gen mgr & progmg dir.

KDDG(FM)— Co-owned with KASM(AM). October 1993: 105.5 mhz; 6 kw. 328 ft. TL: N45 37 53 W94 36 00. Format: Adult contemp.

Albert Lea

KATE(AM)— October 1937: 1450 khz; 1 kw-U. TL: N43 38 00 W93 22 15. Stereo. 305 S. 1st Ave. 56007. Phone: (507) 373-2338. Fax: (507) 373-4736. E-mail: copy@albertlearadio.com. Licensee: Three Eagles of Luverne Inc. Group owner: Three Eagles Communications (acq 5-21-99; with co-located FM). Network: ABC Information & Entertainment. Rep: McGavren Guild. Midwest Radio. Reynolds & Manning. Format: News/talk, MOR. News staff: 3; News: 30 hrs wkly. Target aud: 12 plus; general. Spec prog: Farm 18 hrs, Sp 2 hrs wkly. ♦Gary Buchanan, pres; Bill Lubke, gen mgr & progmg mgr; Courtnay Doyle, gen sls mgr; Steve Oman, news dir.

KQPR-FM— Aug 14, 1990: 96.1 mhz; 25 kw. 328 ft. TL: N43 34 54 W93 23 42. Stereo. Box 1106 56007-1106. Phone: (507) 373-9600. Fax: (507) 373-9045. E-mail: power96@chartermi.net. Web Site: www.power96rocker.com. Licensee: Hometown Broadcasting Inc. (acq 11-21-01; grpsl). Network: Jones Radio Networks. Rep: Allied Radio Partners. Format: Classic rock. News staff: one. Target aud: General. ♦Greg Jensen, CEO & CFO; Anna Rahn, gen mgr; Anna Rahn, stn mgr.

Stations in the U.S.   Minnesota

Alexandria

*KBHG(FM)—Not on air, target date: unknown: 89.5 mhz; 7.2 kw. 321 ft. TL: N45 55 55 W95 26 41. 515 E. Pike St. 56360. Phone: (320) 859-3000. Fax: (320) 859-3010. E-mail: david@praisefm.org. Licensee: Christian Heritage Broadcasting Inc. Format: Christian. ◆ David McIver, gen mgr.

KULO(FM)— 1976: 94.3 mhz; 12 kw. Ant 466 ft. TL: N45 56 25 W95 28 03. Stereo. Box 1024 56308. Secondary address: 604 3rd Ave. W. 56308. Phone: (320) 762-6534. Fax: (320) 762-2156. E-mail: dvagle@kikvfm.com. Web Site: www.cool943.com. Licensee: BDI Broadcasting Inc. Group owner: Omni Broadcasting Co. (acq 12-31-01; $700,000). Network: ABC. Format: Oldies. Target aud: 35-64. ◆ Lou Buron, pres; Dave Vagle, gen mgr.

KXRA(AM)— July 27, 1949: 1490 khz; 1 kw-U. TL: N45 52 05 W95 21 47. Box 69, 1312 Broadway 56308. Phone: (320) 763-3131. Fax: (320) 763-5641. E-mail: thefolks@kxra.com. Web Site: www.kxra.com. Licensee: Paradis Broadcasting of Alexandria Inc. (group owner; acq 10-1-88). Network: CNN Radio. Midwest Radio. Fletcher, Heald & Hildreth. Format: News/talk. News staff: one; News: 25 hrs wkly. Target aud: 35-64. Spec prog: Farm 5 hrs, relg 2 hrs wkly. ◆ Mel Paradis, chmn; Brett Paradis, pres & gen mgr; Bill Franzen, VP.

KXRA-FM— May 1, 1968: 92.3 mhz; 13.5 kw. 446 ft. TL: N45 52 30 W95 21 30. Stereo. Web Site: www.kxra.com. Format: Classic rock. News staff: one; News: 5 hrs wkly. Target aud: 25-45; young adults, dual income households.

KXRZ(FM)— Apr 2, 1984: 99.3 mhz; 6 kw. Ant 285 ft. TL: N45 52 47 W95 18 35. Stereo. 1312 Broadway 56308. Secondary address: Box 69 56308. Phone: (320) 763-3131. Fax: (320) 763-5641. E-mail: thefolks@kxra.com. Web Site: www.z99radio.com. Licensee: Paradis Broadcasting of Alexandria Inc. (group owner; acq 5-1-00; $900,000). Network: Jones Radio Networks. Midwest Radio. Fletcher, Heald & Hildreth. Format: Hits of the 80s, 90s & today. News staff: one; News: 5 hrs wkly. Target aud: 18-40; young adults. Spec prog: Relg 3 hrs wkly. ◆ Brett Paradis, pres & gen mgr; Bill Franzen, opns VP.

Anoka

KLBP(AM)—(Brooklyn Park). Apr 15, 1956: 1470 khz; 5 kw-U, DA-2. TL: N45 05 17 W93 22 59. 331 11th St. S., Minneapolis 55404. Phone: (612) 321-7200. Fax: (612) 321-7202. Web Site: www.klbbradio.com. Licensee: 1400 Inc. (acq 7-20-2005; $5.2 million with KLBB(AM) Saint Paul). Network: Westwood One. Format: Adult standards. ◆ James Rasmussen, VP & progmg VP; Tim Shears, gen mgr.

KQQL(FM)— Aug 1, 1968: 107.9 mhz; 100 kw. 1,080 ft. TL: N45 20 12 W93 23 28. Stereo. 160 Utica Ave. S., Suite 400, Minneapolis 55416. Phone: (952) 417-3000. Fax: (952) 417-3001. Web Site: www.kqql.com. Licensee: AMFM Broadcasting Licenses LLC. Group owner: Clear Channel Communications Inc. (acq 8-30-2000; grpsl). Latham & Watkins. Format: Super hits of the 60s & 70s. Target aud: 25-54; nice people, families, homeowners. ◆ Dan Seeman, gen mgr.

Appleton

*KNCM(FM)— February 1997: 88.5 mhz; 100 kw. 984 ft. TL: N45 10 03 W96 00 02. Saint Johns University, Box 7011, Collegeville 56321. Phone: (320) 363-7702. Fax: (320) 363-4948. E-mail: kncm@mpr.org. Licensee: Minnesota Public Radio. Format: News & info.William H. Kling, CEO & pres; Mark Alfuth, CFO; Thomas Kigin, exec VP; Mike Olson, gen mgr; John McTaggart, opns VP; Perry Carter, opns dir; Jon Gossett, dev VP; Tim Roesler, sls VP; Micki Moore, sls dir & rgnl sls mgr; Gary Osberg, gen sls mgr; Norma Cox, natl sls mgr; Sue Edberg, mktg VP; Nancy Berg, mktg dir; Patrick Whalen, mktg mgr; Erick Nycklemoe, progmg VP; Bill Buzenburg, news dir; Tony Bol, pub affrs dir; Doug Thompson, engrg dir

*KRSU(FM)— Oct 25, 1989: 91.3 mhz; 75 kw. 1,158 ft. TL: N45 10 03 W96 00 02. Stereo. 45 E. 7th St., St. Paul 55101. Phone: (800) 228-7123. Phone: (651) 290-1500. Fax: (651) 290-1224. Web Site: www.mpr.org. Licensee: Minnesota Public Radio Inc. Network: Network: NPR, PRI. Format: Class. ◆ William H. Kling, pres & gen mgr; Ralph Hornberger, engrg dir & chief of engrg.

Atwater

KKLN(FM)—Licensed to Atwater. See Litchfield

Austin

KAUS(AM)— May 30, 1948: 1480 khz; 1 kw-U, DA-2. TL: N43 37 20 W92 59 26. 18431 State Hwy. 105 55912. Phone: (507) 437-7666. Phone: (507) 437-1480. Fax: (507) 437-7669. E-mail: kaus@kaus.com. Web Site: www.kaus.com. Licensee: Three Eagles of Luverne Inc. Group owner: Three Eagles Communications (acq 4-1-00; grpsl). Network: NBC. Wiley, Rein & Fielding. Format: Oldies, adult contemp, news/talk. News staff: 2; News: 20 hrs wkly. Target aud: 25-54. ◆ Rolland Johnson, chmn; Gary Buchanan, pres; Bill Lubke, gen mgr; Gregory Soderberg, gen sls mgr; Aaron Worm, progmg dir; Dan Conradt, news dir; Ron Schat, engrg VP.

KAUS-FM— 1963: 99.9 mhz; 100 kw. 928 ft. TL: N43 37 42 W93 09 12. Stereo. Web Site: www.kaus.com. Format: Country. News staff: 2; News: 12 hrs wkly. Target aud: 25-54. ◆ Tim Allen, prom mgr & progmg mgr.

*KMSK(FM)— Jan 12, 1981: 91.3 mhz; 135 w. 221 ft. TL: N43 40 39 W93 00 04. Stereo. 205 AFC, Mankato State University, 1536 Warren St., Mankato 56001. Phone: (507) 389-5678. Fax: (507) 389-1705. Web Site: www.kmsu.org. Licensee: Mankato State University. (acq 12-23-91). Network: NPR. Cohn & Marks. Format: Pub affrs, educ, mus. News staff: one; News: 50 hrs wkly. Target aud: General; upscale, educated. Spec prog: Drama 3 hrs, folk/ethnic 5 hrs, new age 5 hrs wkly. ◆ Jim Gullickson, gen mgr; Karen Wright, opns dir.

KNFX(AM)— Apr 16, 1960: 970 khz; 5 kw-D, 500 w-N, DA-2. TL: N43 42 27 W92 56 45. Radio Station KMFX(FM), 1530 Greenview Dr. S.W., Rochester 55902. Phone: (507) 288-3888. Fax: (507) 288-7815. Licensee: Clear Channel Broadcasting Licenses Inc. Group owner: Clear Channel Communications Inc. (acq 9-25-00; grpsl). Format: Sports/talk. News staff: one; News: 10 hrs wkly. Target aud: 25-54. ◆ Bob Fox, gen mgr.

*KNSE(FM)— 90.1 mhz; 6 kw. Ant 318 ft. TL: N43 38 27 W93 08 51. Minnesota Public Radio, 45 E. 7th St., Saint Paul 55101. Phone: (651) 290-1500. Fax: (651) 290-1224. E-mail: mail@mpr.org. Web Site: www.mpr.org. Licensee: Minnesota Public Radio. Format: News. ◆ William H. Kling, pres & gen mgr.

Babbitt

KAOD(FM)— 1999: 106.7 mhz; 19.8 kw. 790 ft. TL: N47 41 18 W91 54 15. 501 Lake Ave. S., Suite 200A, Duluth 55802. Phone: (218) 722-0921. Fax: (218) 723-1499. Licensee: Red Rock Radio Corp. (group owner; acq 1-10-00; grpsl). Format: Classic new Rock. ◆ Bill Jones, gen mgr.

Bagley

KKCQ-FM— October 1997: 96.7 mhz; 25 kw. 328 ft. TL: N47 36 08 W95 32 18. Box 606, Fosston 56542. Phone: (218) 435-1071. Fax: (218) 435-1480. E-mail: info@q107fm.com. Web Site: www.q107fm.com. Licensee: Pine to Prairie Broadcasting Inc. (acq 6-16-97; $5,553 for CP). Network: ABC. Format: Country. News staff: one. Spec prog: Farm 10 hrs, relg 9 hrs wkly. ◆ Phil Ehlke, gen mgr; Karen Bingham, progmg dir.

Baxter

WWWI(AM)— Aug 29, 1987: 1270 khz; 5 kw-D, DA-N. TL: N46 17 55 W94 16 42. Box 783, 305 W. Washington St., Brainerd 56401. Phone: (218) 828-9994. Fax: (218) 828-8327. E-mail: wwwi@brainerd.net. Web Site: www.3wiradio.com. Licensee: Tower Broadcasting Corp. Network: CBS. Format: News/talk. News: 20 hrs wkly. Target aud: 25 plus. Spec prog: Sports. ◆ James R. Pryor, pres, gen mgr, gen sls mgr & chief of engrg; Mary Pryor, VP & pub affrs dir.

Bemidji

KBHP(FM)—Listing follows KBUN(AM).

*KBSB(FM)— Jan 19, 1970: 89.7 mhz; 115 w. 126 ft. TL: N47 29 00 W94 52 27. FM 90 KBSB Bemidji, State University Deputy Hall # 215, 1500 Birehmontn Dr. N.E. 56601. Phone: (218) 755-4120. Fax: (218) 755-4119. Web Site: www.fm90.org. Licensee: Bemidji State University. Format: CHR. Target aud: 12-28; teens to young adults. Spec prog: American Indian 3 hrs, folk 3 hrs wkly. ◆ Roger Paskvan, gen mgr; Josh Harvey, stn mgr.

KBUN(AM)— 1946: 1450 khz; 1 kw-U, DA-1. TL: N47 27 56 W94 54 37. Box 1656, 502 Beltrami Ave. 56619-1656. Phone: (218) 444-1500. Fax: (218) 751-8091. E-mail: kbunam@pbbroadcasting.com. Licensee: Paul Bunyan Broadcasting Co. Group owner: Omni Broadcasting Co. (acq 6-22-89; 6-26-89). Network: Westwood One. Garvey, Schubert & Barer. Format: Sports, talk. News staff: one. Target aud: 18-54. ◆ Louis H. Buron Jr., CEO, pres & gen mgr; Mary A. Campbell, CFO & VP; Kevin Jackson, opns dir, opns mgr & progmg dir; Peggy Hanson, gen sls mgr.

*KCRB-FM— Dec 22, 1982: 88.5 mhz; 95 kw. 994 ft. TL: N47 42 03 W94 29 15. 45 E. 7th St., St. Paul 55101. Phone: (651) 290-1500. Fax: (651) 290-1224. Web Site: www.mpr.org. Licensee: Minnesota Public Radio Inc. Network: PRI, NPR. Format: Class. News staff: one; News: 25 hrs wkly. ◆ William H. Kling, gen mgr & stn mgr.

KKBJ(AM)— Oct 31, 1977: 1360 khz; 5 kw-D, 2.5 kw-N, DA-N. TL: N47 26 32 W94 55 07. 2115 Washington Ave. S. 56601. Phone: (218) 751-7777. Fax: (218) 759-0658. Web Site: www.kkbj.com. Licensee: R.P. Broadcasting Corp. (acq 4-1-95). Network: AP Radio. Bechtel & Cole. Format: Talk. News staff: one; News: 15 hrs wkly. Target aud: 25-54. ◆ Roger Paskvan, pres & engrg VP; Daniel J. Voss, gen mgr & gen sls mgr; Chuck Sebastian, progmg dir; Shaun Michaels, news dir.

KKBJ-FM— Aug 8, 1983: 103.7 mhz; 100 kw. 460 ft. TL: N47 33 19 W94 47 59. Stereo. Format: Hot adult contemp. News staff: one; News: 20 hrs wkly. Target aud: 18-49; 40% male & 60% female. ◆ Tracy Bailey, prom dir; Daniel Voss, adv mgr.

KKZY(FM)— May 7, 1999: 95.5 mhz; 100 kw. 423 ft. TL: N47 22 12 W94 52 54. Box 1656, 502 Beltrami Ave. N.W. 55619-1656. Phone: (218) 444-1500. Fax: (218) 751-8091. E-mail: kkzy@pbbroadcasting.com. Licensee: BG Broadcasting Inc. Group owner: Omni Broadcasting Co. (acq 6-22-98). Network: ABC. Garvey, Schubert & Barer. Format: Adult contemp. News staff: one. Target aud: 25-54; adults. ◆ Louis H. Buron Jr., CEO, chmn & gen mgr; Mary A. Campbell, CFO & VP; Peggy Hanson, gen sls mgr; Todd Haugen, opns mgr & news dir.

*KNBJ(FM)— July 1, 1994: 91.3 mhz; 60 kw. 974 ft. 45 E. 7th St., St. Paul 55101. Phone: (651) 290-1500. Fax: (651) 290-1224. Web Site: www.mpr.org. Licensee: Minnesota Public Radio. Network: Network: PRI, NPR. Format: News. ◆ William H. Kling, gen mgr & stn mgr.

Benson

KBMO(AM)— December 1956: 1290 khz; 500 w-D. TL: N45 19 06 W95 33 48. 105 13th St. N. 56215. Phone: (320) 843-3290. Fax: (320) 843-3955. E-mail: kscr@info-link.net. Licensee: Quest Broadcasting Inc. (acq 5-2-94; $390,000. with co-located FM). Network: Jones Radio Networks. Shainis & Peltzman. Format: Music of your life. News staff: one; News: 25 hrs wkly. Target aud: 40 plus. Spec prog: Farm 10 hrs wkly. ◆ Paul Estenson, pres & gen mgr; Jason Brandt, progmg dir & news dir; Maynard Meyer, chief of engrg.

KSCR-FM—Co-owned with KBMO(AM). Apr 26, 1968: 93.5 mhz; 25 kw. Ant 328 ft. TL: N45 19 06 W95 33 48. Stereo. Format: Adult contemp. Target aud: 18-54.

Broadcasting & Cable Yearbook 2006
D-273

Minnesota

Blackduck

WBJI(FM)— 1991: 98.3 mhz; 50 kw. 456 ft. TL: N47 33 19 W94 47 59. Stereo. 2115 Washington Ave. S.E., Bemidji 56601-8942. Phone: (218) 751-7777. Fax: (218) 759-0658. E-mail: wbji@paulbunyon.net. Web Site: www.wbji.com. Licensee: R.P. Broadcasting Inc. Network: ABC. Bechtel & Cole. Format: Real country. News staff: one; News: 8 hrs wkly. Target aud: 35-64; adults with above average income. Spec prog: NASCAR 4 hrs wkly. ◆ Roger Paskvan, CEO; Marla Weckman, exec VP.

Blooming Prairie

KOWZ-FM— September 1995: 100.9 mhz; 100 kw. 620 ft. TL: N44 02 46 W93 23 03. 1929 S. Ceader Ave., Owatonna 55060. Phone: (507) 583-2191. Fax: (507) 444-9080. Licensee: Blooming Prairie Farm Radio Inc. Group owner: Linder Broadcasting Group. Format: Adult var. ◆ Lynn Ketelsen, gen mgr; Aaron Worm, progmg dir.

Blue Earth

KBEW(AM)— Aug 29, 1963: 1560 khz; 1 kw-D. TL: N43 38 48 W95 33 48. Box 278, Leland Pkwy. 56013. Phone: (507) 526-2181. Fax: (507) 526-7468. E-mail: kbew@bevcomm.net. Licensee: KBEW Radio Inc. Group owner: Result Radio Group (acq 2-1-81). Network: ABC. Rep: Katz Radio. Format: Oldies, news/talk. News staff: one; News: 17 hrs wkly. Target aud: Farming community. Spec prog: Farm 15 hrs wkly. ◆ Jerry Papenfuss, pres; Kevin Benson, stn mgr.

KBEW-FM— 1993: 98.1 mhz; 25 kw. 328 ft. TL: N43 38 44 W94 05 33. Stereo. 56013. Format: Country. News staff: one; News: 3 hrs wkly. Target aud: 18-54. ◆ Kevin Benson, gen mgr & mktg mgr.

KJLY(FM)— Nov 1, 1983: 104.5 mhz; 50 kw. 453 ft. TL: N43 39 41 W94 06 29. Stereo. Box 72 56013. Secondary address: 12089 380th Ave. 56013. Phone: (507) 526-3233. Fax: (507) 526-3235. E-mail: kjly@kjly.com. Web Site: www.kjly.com. Licensee: Minn-Iowa Christian Broadcasting Inc. (group owner). Network: Network: Moody, Salem Radio Network. Format: Inspirational relg. News: 21 hrs wkly. Target aud: 45-65. Spec prog: Farm 5 hrs, children 4 hrs wkly. ◆ Maurice Schwen, pres; Eugene Stallkang, VP; Gina Frandle, gen mgr & mus dir; Doug Johnson, progmg dir; Mark Croom, chief of engrg.

Brainerd

*KBPN(FM)—Not on air, target date: Fall 2003: 88.3 mhz; 5 kw. Ant 669 ft. TL: N46 25 21 W94 27 41. Box 578, Bemidji 56619. Secondary address: Minnesota Public Radio, 45 E. 7th St., Saint Paul 55101. Phone: (651)290-1500. Fax: (651) 290-1224. Web Site: www.mpr.org. Licensee: Minnesota Public Radio. Format: News. ◆ William H. Kling, gen mgr.

KBPR(FM)—Licensed to Brainerd. See Collegeville

KLIZ(AM)— Aug 6, 1946: 1380 khz; 5 kw-U, DA-N. TL: N46 19 56 W94 10 26. Box 980 56401. Secondary address: 602 Laurel St. 56401. Phone: (218) 829-2853. Fax: (218) 829-6983. Licensee: BL Broadcasting Inc. Group owner: Omni Broadcasting Co. (acq 1-26-2004; grpsl). Network: Network: USA, Westwood One. Rep: Hyett/Ramsland. Format: Talk. News: 12 hrs wkly. Target aud: 25-64. ◆ Mike Overton, VP & gen mgr; Danny Wild, opns mgr, prom dir, progmg dir & pub affrs dir; Jeff Hilborn, gen sls mgr; Mark Krier, mus dir.

KLIZ-FM— May 23, 1960: 107.5 mhz; 100 kw. 350 ft. TL: N46 19 56 W94 10 26. Stereo. Format: Classic rock. Target aud: 18-49.

KUAL-FM—Listing follows KVBR(AM).

KVBR(AM)— May 16, 1964: 1340 khz; 1 kw-U. TL: N46 20 51 W94 10 52. Box 980 56401. Secondary address: 602 Laurel St. 56401. Phone: (218) 829-2853. Fax: (218) 829-6983. Licensee: BL Broadcasting Inc. Group owner: Omni Broadcasting Co. (acq 1-26-2004; grpsl). Format: All sports. Target aud: 25-54. ◆ Mike Overton, gen mgr; Jeff Hilborn, gen sls mgr; Dan Wild, progmg dir.

KUAL-FM—Co-owned with KVBR(AM). June 3, 1994: 103.5 mhz; 20 kw. 279 ft. TL: N46 20 55 W94 13 29. Network: Westwood One. Format: Hot country. Target aud: 18-49; male/female.

WJJY-FM— July 21, 1978: 106.7 mhz; 100 kw. 448 ft. TL: N46 26 36 W94 22 58. Stereo. Box 746 56401. Secondary address: 701 Dogwood Dr. S., Baxter 56425. Phone: (218) 828-1244. Fax: (218) 828-1119. E-mail: production@brainerd.net. Licensee: BL Broadcasting Inc. Group owner: Omni Broadcasting Co. (acq 3-2-94; $900,000;. FTR: 5-2-94). Format: Full service adult contemp. News staff: one; News: 20 hrs wkly. Target aud: 25 plus. ◆ Louis H. Buron Jr., CEO, chmn & pres; Mary A. Campbell, VP; G. Michael Boen, gen mgr; Tom Albrecht, gen sls mgr; Mark Hegstrom, progmg dir; Nancy Carlson, news dir; Phyllis Schilling, chief of engrg.

Breckenridge

KBMW(AM)—Licensed to Breckenridge. See Wahpeton ND

KLTA(FM)— Feb 17, 1970: 105.1 mhz; 100 kw. 713 ft. TL: N46 32 41 W96 37 33. Stereo. Box 9919, Fargo, ND 58106. Secondary address: 2720 7th Ave. S., Fargo, ND 58103. Phone: (701) 237-4500. Fax: (701) 235-9082. E-mail: studio@fm1051.net. Web Site: www.fm105.net. Licensee: Monterey Licenses LLC. Group owner: Triad Broadcasting Co. LLC (acq 10-99; grpsl). Rep: Christal. Shaw Pittman. Format: Adult contemp. Target aud: 25-54; skews female. ◆ Tom Douglas, CEO; David Benjamin, pres; Nancy Odney, gen mgr.

Breezy Point

KLKS(FM)— June 14, 1984: 104.3 mhz; 50 kw. 492 ft. TL: N46 36 13 W94 15 04. Stereo. Box 300 56472. Secondary address: 7170 Ski Chatet Dr. 56472. Phone: (218) 562-4884. Phone: (218) 829-2997. Fax: (218) 562-4058. Fax: (218) 829-9341. E-mail: klakes@uslink.net. Web Site: www.klks.com. Licensee: Lakes Broadcasting Group Inc. Hogan & Hartson. Format: Adult standards, btfl mus, big band. News staff: 2; News: 25 hrs wkly. Target aud: 40 plus. ◆ Bob Bundgaard, CEO & pres; Allen Gray, chmn; Diane Anderson, CFO & opns VP; Marj Bundgaard, gen mgr; Thomas Kenow, sls VP; Bob Stafford, progmg dir; David Pundt, news dir.

Brooklyn Park

KLBP(AM)—Licensed to Brooklyn Park. See Anoka

Browerville

KXDL(FM)—Licensed to Browerville. See Long Prairie

Buffalo

KRWC(AM)— Nov 16, 1971: 1360 khz; 500 w-D. TL: N45 10 00 W93 55 11. Box 267 55313. Secondary address: 1472 10th St. N.W. 55313. Phone: (763) 682-4444. Fax: (763) 682-3542. E-mail: info@krwc1360.com. Web Site: www.krwc1360.com. Licensee: Donnell Inc. (acq 6-15-98; $460,000). Network: CNN Radio. Format: Country, oldies, adult contemp, news/talk. News staff: one; News: 16 hrs wkly. Target aud: 25 plus. ◆ Joe Carlson, pres, gen mgr & gen sls mgr; Tim Matthews, opns dir, progmg dir & news dir; John George, chief of engrg.

Buhl

*WIRN(FM)— 1997: 92.5 mhz; 39 kw. 558 ft. TL: N47 29 46 W92 47 05. Minnesota Public Radio, 224 Holiday Ctr., Duluth 55802. Phone: (218) 722-9411. Fax: (218) 720-4900. Web Site: www.mpr.org. Licensee: Minnesota Public Radio. Format: News & info. ◆ William Kling, pres; John Snee, gen mgr; Char Dobosenski, adv dir; Bob Kelleher, news dir; Doug Thompson, engrg dir; Aaron White, chief of engrg.

Caledonia

KCLH(FM)— Nov 14, 1994: 94.7 mhz; 1.9 kw. Ant 584 ft. TL: N43 41 24 W91 30 09. 201 State St., La Crosse, WI 54602. Phone: (608) 782-1230. Fax: (608) 782-1170. Web Site: www.classichits98.com. Licensee: Family Radio Inc. Group owner: The Mid-West Family Broadcast Group (acq 7-19-01; grpsl). Shaw Pittman. Format: Classic hits. News staff: 4; News: one hr wkly. Target aud: General; 25-54. ◆ Dick Record, pres; Brian Michaels, opns mgr & progmg dir; Dave Roberts, progmg dir; Kris Kody, prom.

Cambridge

WGVY(FM)— May 5, 1973: 105.3 mhz; 25 kw. 298 ft. TL: N45 31 17 W93 10 27. Stereo. 2000 S.E. Elm St., Minneapolis 55414. Phone: (612) 617-4000. Fax: (612) 676-8292. E-mail: comments@drive105.com. Web Site: www.drive105.com. Licensee: KQRS Inc. Group owner: ABC Inc. (acq 7-24-97; grpsl). Haley, Bader & Potts. Format: AAA.

Target aud: 18-34. Spec prog: Farm 8 hrs wkly. ◆ Amy Rosenthal, pres & stn mgr; Dave Hamilton, opns mgr; Pete Frisch, sls dir; Susan Larkin, gen sls mgr; Jeff Berman, natl sls mgr; Brook Johnson, mktg dir; Shelley Miller, prom dir & prom mgr; Jeff Collins, progmg dir; Ben Gnam, mus dir; Julie Honebrink, pub affrs dir; Dave Szaflarski, chief of engrg.

Cloquet

WKLK(AM)— Jan 31, 1950: 1230 khz; 1 kw-U, DA-1. TL: N46 44 58 W92 25 17. 1104 Cloquet Ave. 55720-1613. Phone: (218) 879-4534. Fax: (218) 879-1962. Web Site: www.wklkradio.com. Licensee: QB Broadcasting Ltd. (acq 5-12-92; $200,000. with co-located FM; FTR: 6-1-92). Format: Mus of your Life. News staff: one; News: 16 hrs wkly. Target aud: Community oriented. Spec prog: Polka 2 hrs, relg 5 hrs, talk one hr, health issues one hr, political one hr wkly. ◆ Al Quarstorom, gen mgr.

WKLK-FM— Apr 30, 1992: 96.5 mhz; 6 kw. 315 ft. TL: N46 44 58 W92 25 17. Web Site: www.wklkradio.com. Format: Adult hit.

*WSCN(FM)— Nov 17, 1975: 100.5 mhz; 100 kw. 875 ft. TL: N46 47 21 W92 06 51. Stereo. 224 Holiday Ctr., Duluth 55802. Phone: (218) 722-9411. Fax: (218) 720-4900. Web Site: www.minnesotapublicradio.org. Licensee: Minnesota Public Radio. (acq 12-88; $200,000; 12-19-88). Network: Network: PRI, NPR. Format: News. ◆ William H. Kling, pres & gen mgr; Char Dobosenski, dev dir.

Cold Spring

KMXK(FM)— Aug 30, 1968: 94.9 mhz; 50 kw. 492 ft. TL: N45 23 53 W94 25 15. Stereo. Box 220, St. Cloud 56302. Secondary address: 640 Lincoln Ave. S.E., St. Cloud 56304. Phone: (320) 251-4422. Fax: (320) 251-1855. Web Site: www.mix949.com. Licensee: Regent of St. Cloud Inc. Group owner: Regent Communications Inc. (acq 1-5-99; grpsl). Format: Adult contemp. Target aud: 35-54. ◆ Terry Jacobs, CEO; Bill Stakelin, pres; Fred Murr, sr VP; David Engberg, gen mgr & sls dir; T.J. Randall, progmg dir; Lee Voss, news dir; Mark Young, chief of engrg.

Coleraine

KGPZ(FM)— July 1, 1995: 96.1 mhz; 100 kw. 577 ft. TL: N47 19 31 W93 16 18. Box 447, Grand Rapids 55744-0447. Phone: (218) 327-3339. Fax: (218) 327-3425. E-mail: kgpz@paulbunyan.net. Web Site: www.kgpzfm.com. Licensee: Latto Northland Broadcasting Inc. Group owner: Lew Latto Group of Northland Radio Stations Network: ABC. Pepper & Corazzini. Format: Real country. Target aud: 35-64. ◆ Lew Latto, pres; Dory Butala, stn mgr; Dennis Yourczek, opns dir.

Collegeville

*KBPR(FM)— (Brainerd). February 1988: 90.7 mhz; 34.2 kw. 679 ft. TL: N46 25 21 W94 27 41. Stereo. 45 E. 7th St., St. Paul 55101. Phone: (651) 290-1500. Fax: (651) 290-1224. Web Site: www.mpr.org. Licensee: Minnesota Public Radio. Network: Network: PRI, NPR. Format: Class. News staff: 2. Target aud: General. ◆ William H. Kling, pres & gen mgr; Erik Nycklemoe, dev VP.

*KNSR(FM)— Aug 29, 1988: 88.9 mhz; 100 kw. 728 ft. TL: N45 29 52 W94 32 14. Stereo. Box 7011, St. John's Univ. 56321. Phone: (320) 363-7702. Fax: (320) 363-4948. E-mail: knsr@mpr.org. Web Site: www.minnesotapublicradio.org. Licensee: Minnesota Public Radio. Network: Network: PRI, NPR. Format: News. News staff: 2. Target aud: General. ◆ William H. Kling, pres & gen mgr; Char Dobosenski, dev VP & dev dir; Doug Thompson, engrg dir.

*KSJR-FM— Jan 21, 1967: 90.1 mhz; 100 kw. 700 ft. TL: N45 29 52 W94 32 14. Stereo. 45 E. 7th St., St. Paul 55101. Phone: (651) 290-1500. Fax: (651) 290-1224. Web Site: www.mpr.org. Licensee: Minnesota Public Radio. Network: PRI. Format: Class. News staff: 2. Target aud: General. ◆ William H. Kling, pres, gen mgr & stn mgr.

Coon Rapids

WFMP(FM)—Licensed to Coon Rapids. See Minneapolis-St. Paul

Crookston

KQHT(FM)—Licensed to Crookston. See Grand Forks ND

Stations in the U.S. — Minnesota

Developers & Brokers of Radio Properties
contact American Media Services at our suite: Philadelphia Marriott Downtown 215-625-2900
843-972-2200
americanmediaservices.com
Charleston, SC
Dallas, TX • Chicago, Il • Austin, TX
American Media Services, LLC

KROX(AM)— April 1948: 1260 khz; 1 kw-D, 500 w-N, DA-N. TL: N47 47 20 W96 35 40. 208 S. Main St. 56716-0620. Phone: (218) 281-1140. Fax: (218) 281-5036. E-mail: kroxam@hotmail.com. Web Site: www.kroxam.com. Licensee: Gopher Communications Co. (acq 5-11-87). Network: CNN Radio. Format: Soft adult contemp, country, MOR, talk. Target aud: 35 plus; general. Spec prog: Farm 10 hrs wkly. ♦Frank Fee, pres & gen mgr; Jeanette Fee, VP; Gerri Wheelhouse, opns mgr.

KYCK(FM)— Mar 4, 1980: 97.1 mhz; 100 kw. 360 ft. TL: N47 49 17 W96 49 03. Stereo. Box 13638, Grand Forks, ND 58208. Phone: (701) 775-4611. Fax: (701) 772-0540. E-mail: morningkyck@97kyck.com. Web Site: www.97kyck.com. Licensee: Leighton Enterprises Inc. (group owner). ♦Al Leighton, pres; Linn Hodgson, VP & gen mgr.

Crosby

KFGI(FM)— Oct 10, 1990: 101.5 mhz; 25 kw. 328 ft. TL: N46 33 39 W94 00 15. (CP: TL: N46 32 05 W93 52 41). Box 746, Brainerd 56401. Secondary address: 701 Dogwood Dr. S., Baxter 56425. Phone: (218) 828-1244. Fax: (218) 828-1119. E-mail: production@brainerd.net. Licensee: Quarnstrom Media Group LLC (group owner; acq 10-29-2003; $400,000). Format: Good time oldies. ♦G. Michael Boen, gen mgr; Al Davison, progmg dir & progmg dir; Nancy Carlson, news dir; Tim Mitchell, pub affrs dir.

Dassel

KARP-FM—Licensed to Dassel. See Hutchinson

Deer River

KBAJ(FM)— 2000: 105.5 mhz; 100 kw. 508 ft. TL: N47 20 22 W93 23 48. 501 Lake Ave. S., Suite 200, Duluth 55802. Phone: (218) 722-0921. Fax: (218) 723-1499. Licensee: Red Rock Radio Corp. (group owner; acq 1-10-00; grpsl). Format: Classic new rock. ♦Shawn Skramstad, gen mgr.

Detroit Lakes

KDLM(AM)— October 1951: 1340 khz; 1 kw-U. TL: N46 50 14 W95 50 17. Box 746 56502-0746. Phone: (218) 847-5624. Fax: (218) 847-7657. E-mail: kdlm1340@yahoo.com. Web Site: www.1340kdlm.com. Licensee: Leighton Enterprises Inc. (group owner) Network: CBS. Format: Sports, news/talk, adult contemp. News staff: one; News: 10 hrs wkly. Target aud: 30 plus. Spec prog: Farm one hr, relg 8 hrs wkly. ♦Alver Leighton, chmn; John Sowada, pres; Denny Niess, exec VP; Joel Swanson, gen mgr; Andy Lia, opns mgr.

KRCQ(FM)— July 4, 1994: 102.3 mhz; 50 kw. 492 ft. TL: N46 48 24 W95 46 23. Stereo. Box 556, 1119 Jackson Ave. 56502. Phone: (218) 847-2001. Fax: (218) 847-2271. E-mail: krcq@lakesnet.net. Licensee: Detroit Lakes Broadcasting Co. Inc. (acq 7-8-97; $1.2 million). Miller & Miller. Format: Real country. News staff: one; News: 10 hrs wkly. Target aud: General. ♦Robert D. Spilman, gen mgr.

KRVI(FM)— Jan 2, 1976: 95.1 mhz; 100 kw. 970 ft. TL: N46 40 27 W96 13 39. Stereo. 1020 25th St. S., Fargo, ND 58103. Phone: (701) 237-5346. Fax: (701) 235-4042. Web Site: www.river95.com. Licensee: Capstar TX L.P. Group owner: Clear Channel Communications Inc. (acq 10-30-00; grpsl). Format: Soft rock favorites. ♦Richard Voight, gen mgr.

Duluth

KDAL(AM)— Nov 26, 1936: 610 khz; 5 kw-U, DA-N. TL: N46 43 13 W92 10 34. 715 E. Central Entrance 55811. Phone: (218) 722-4321. Fax: (218) 722-5423. Licensee: Midwest Communications Inc. (group owner; acq 8-1-01; grpsl). Network: CBS. Hyett/Ramsland. Rosenman & Colin. Format: Div, news/talk. Target aud: 35-64. ♦Duke Wright, CEO & pres; Gary Tesch, CFO & exec VP; Jeff "Del" Delvaux, gen mgr, stn mgr & gen sls mgr; Mark Fleischer, opns dir & opns mgr; Angie Main, prom dir & prom mgr; Kerry Rodd, progmg dir & progmg mgr; Dave Standberg, mus dir; Ken Buehler, news dir; John Talcott, engrg mgr.

KDAL-FM— July 1985: 95.7 mhz; 100 kw. Ant 725 ft. TL: N46 47 15 W92 07 21. Stereo. Format: Adult contemp, gold. Target aud: 25-49. ♦Dale Johnson, gen sls mgr; Brad Ruprecht, prom dir; Justin Case, progmg dir.

KDNI(FM)—Licensed to Duluth. See Roseville

*KDNW(FM)— December 1993: 97.3 mhz; 40 kw. 548 ft. TL: N46 47 20 W92 07 04. Stereo. 1101 E. Central Entrance 55811. Phone: (218) 722-6700. Fax: (218) 722-1092. E-mail: kdnw@kdnw.fm. Web Site: www.kdnw.fm. Licensee: Northwestern College. Group owner: Northwestern College & Radio (acq 12-4-91; $20,000;. FTR: 1-6-92). Network: Network: AP Radio, UPI. Bryan Cave. Format: Contemp Christian music. Target aud: 25-54. ♦Paul Virts, sr VP; Paul Harkness, stn mgr.

KKCB(FM)—Listing follows WEBC(AM).

KLDJ(FM)— Jan 1, 1994: 101.7 mhz; 18.5 kw. Ant 823 ft. TL: N46 47 13 W92 07 17. 14 E. Central Entrance 55811. Phone: (218) 727-4500. Fax: (218) 727-9356. Web Site: www.kool1017.com. Licensee: Clear Channel Broadcasting Licenses Inc. Group owner: Clear Channel Communications Inc. (acq 5-2-2003; grpsl). Rep: Christal. Format: Oldies. Target aud: 25-54; general. ♦Ron Stone, gen mgr; Derek Moran, opns mgr; Ryan Barnholdt, prom dir; Pat Puchalla, progmg dir.

KQDS-FM— Apr 1, 1976: 94.9 mhz; 100 kw. 730 ft. TL: N46 47 41 W92 07 05. Stereo. 501 Lake Ave. S., Suite 200 55802. Phone: (218) 728-9500. Fax: (218) 723-1499. E-mail: production@redrockradio.org. Licensee: Red Rock Radio Corp. (group owner; acq 1-10-00; grpsl). Rep: McGavren Guild. O'Malley. Format: Classic rock, AOR. News: 2 hrs wkly. Target aud: 25-54. ♦Shawn Skramstad, gen mgr; Jeff Anderson, gen sls mgr; Bill Jones, progmg dir & news dir; Phil Longenecker, chief of engrg.

KQDS(AM)— Mar 11, 1963: 1490 khz; 1 kw-U. TL: N46 47 42 W92 07 08.

KTCO(FM)— June 14, 1972: 98.9 mhz; 100 kw. 600 ft. TL: N46 47 30 W92 06 59. Stereo. 715 E. Central Entrance 55811. Phone: (218) 722-4321. Fax: (218) 722-5423. E-mail: david@ktco.fm.net. Web Site: www.ktco.fm.com. Licensee: Midwest Communications Inc. (group owner; acq 8-1-01; grpsl). Hyett/Ramsland. Rosenman & Colin. Format: Country hits. Target aud: 25-49. ♦Duke Wright, pres; Gary Tesch, exec VP; David Drew, opns dir & progmg dir; Don Snyder, sls VP; Alicia Ridley, gen sls mgr, mktg mgr & sls; Jeff McCarthy, prom VP & progmg VP; David Kuharski, prom mgr; Dave Strandberg, news dir; John Talcott, chief of engrg.

*KUMD-FM— May 26, 1971: 103.3 mhz; 95 kw. 820 ft. TL: N46 47 31 W92 07 21. Stereo. 130 Humanities Bldg., University of Minnesota 55812. Phone: (218) 726-7181. Fax: (218) 726-6571. E-mail: kumd@kumd.org. Web Site: www.kumd.org. Licensee: Board of Regents of University of Minnesota. (acq 8-75). Network: PRI. Dow, Lohnes & Albertson. Format: Triple A. News: 12 hrs wkly. Target aud: 25-45. ♦Paul Schmitz, gen mgr; Paul Damberg, dev dir.

WDSM(AM)—See Superior, WI

WEBC(AM)— June 1924: 560 khz; 5 kw-U, DA-2. TL: N46 38 37 W91 59 09. 14 E. Central Entrance 55811-5508. Phone: (218) 727-4500. Fax: (218) 727-9356. Web Site: www.560webc.com. Licensee: Clear Channel Broadcasting Licenses Inc. Group owner: Clear Channel Communications Inc. (acq 5-2-2003; grpsl). Network: ABC Information & Entertainment. Rep: Christal. Format: News/talk, sports. ♦Ron Stone, gen mgr.

KKCB(FM)—Co-owned with WEBC(AM). 1966: 105.1 mhz; 100 kw. 789 ft. TL: N46 47 21 W92 06 51. Stereo. 14 E. Central Entrance 55811. Phone: (218) 727-4500. Fax: (218) 727-9356. Web Site: www.kkcb.com. Format: Country. Target aud: General.

WGEE(AM)—See Superior, WI

*WIRR(FM)—(Virginia-Hibbing). December 1985: 90.9 mhz; 21 kw. 552 ft. TL: N47 29 46 W92 47 05. Stereo. 224 Holiday Ctr. 55802. Phone: (218) 722-9411. Fax: (218) 720-4900. Web Site: www.mpr.org. Licensee: Minnesota Public Radio Inc. Network: Network: PRI, NPR. Format: Class. News staff: 3. Target aud: General. ♦William H. Kling, pres; John Snee, gen mgr.

*WJRF(FM)— Nov 1, 1982: 89.5 mhz; 2.85 kw vert. Ant 512 ft. TL: N46 47 21 W92 07 09. Stereo. 425 W. Superior St., Suite 300 55802. Phone: (218) 722-3017. Fax: (218) 722-1650. Web Site: www.refugeradio.com. Licensee: Refuge Media Group. Format: contemp Christian. News: 5 hrs wkly. Target aud: 18-34; female. ♦Brett M. Gibson, CEO & gen mgr; Paul Hitchcock, pres; Keith Johnson, VP.

*WSCD-FM— 1975: 92.9 mhz; 70 kw. 614 ft. TL: N46 47 20 W92 07 04. Stereo. 224 Holiday Ctr. 55802. Phone: (218) 722-9411. Fax: (218) 720-4900. Web Site: www.mpr.org. Licensee: Minnesota Public Radio. Format: Classical music. ♦William Kling, pres; John Snee, gen mgr.

WWJC(AM)— Apr 26, 1963: 850 khz; 10 kw-D. TL: N46 39 19 W92 12 40. 1120 E. McCuen St. 55808. Phone: (218) 626-2738. Fax: (603) 907-7881. E-mail: radio@wwjc.com. Web Site: www.wwjc.com. Licensee: WWJC Inc. Network: USA. Format: Solid gospel / talk. ♦Ted Elm, gen mgr.

Eagan

KKMS(AM)—See Minneapolis-St. Paul

East Grand Forks

KCNN(AM)— Aug 14, 1959: 1590 khz; 5 kw-D, 1 kw-N, DA-2. TL: N47 52 41 W97 00 24. Box 13638, Grand Forks 58208-3638. Secondary address: Old Belmont Rd. S., Grand Forks, ND 58201. Phone: (701) 772-2204. Fax: (701) 772-0540. E-mail: general@kcnn.com. Licensee: Leighton Enterprises Inc. (group owner; (acq 11-14-03; $2.5 million). Network: CBS. Format: News/talk. Target aud: 25-60. Spec prog: Farm 6 hrs wkly. ♦Linn Hodgson, gen mgr.

KZLT-FM—Co-owned with KCNN(AM). Apr 1, 1975: 104.3 mhz; 100 kw. 550 ft. TL: N47 48 37 W96 55 46. E-mail: general@kcnn.com. Format: Adult contemp.

KSNR(FM)—(Thief River Falls). May 1976: 100.3 mhz; 100 kw. 620 ft. TL: N47 58 38 W96 36 42. Stereo. 505 University Ave., Grand Forks, ND 58203. Phone: (701) 746-1417. Fax: (701) 746-1410. E-mail: koolradio@hotmail.com. Web Site: www.ksnrfm100.com. Licensee: Citicasters Licenses L.P. Group owner: Clear Channel Communications Inc. (acq 10-26-99; grpsl). Haley, Bader & Potts. Format: Oldies. News staff: one; News: 10 hrs wkly. Target aud: 25-54; boomers & kids. Spec prog: Farm one hr wkly. ♦Pat McLean, gen mgr & gen sls mgr; Susie Johnson, prom mgr; David Andrews, progmg dir; Ken Morgan, pub affrs dir; Dave Schroeder, engrg mgr & chief of engrg.

Eden Prairie

WGVZ(FM)— March 1993: 105.7 mhz; 6 kw horiz, 5.8 kw vert. Ant 239 ft. TL: N44 53 51 W93 24 22. 2000 S. Elm St., Minneapolis 55414. Phone: (612) 617-4000. Fax: (612) 676-8292. E-mail: comments@drive105.com. Web Site: www.drive105.com. Licensee: KQRS Inc. Group owner: ABC Inc. (acq 7-24-97; grpsl). Network: Westwood One. Format: AAA. ♦Amy Rosenthal, pres & gen mgr; Dave Hamilton, opns mgr; Pete Frisch, sls dir; Susan Larkin, gen sls mgr; Jeff Bermen, natl sls mgr; Brook Johnson, mktg dir; Shelley Miller, prom mgr; Jeff Collins, progmg dir; Ben Gnam, mus dir & pub affrs dir; Julie Honebrink, pub affrs dir; Dave Szaflarski, chief of engrg.

Ely

WELY(AM)— Oct 2, 1954: 1450 khz; 1 kw-U, DA-N. TL: N47 53 37 W91 51 59. (CP: TL: N47 53 40 W91 51 50). 133 E. Chapman St.

Minnesota

55731-1229. Phone: (218) 365-4444. Fax: (218) 365-3657. E-mail: wely@spacestar.net. Web Site: www.wely.com. Licensee: Bois Forte Tribal Council (acq 6-1-2005; $445,000. with co-located FM). Network: ABC Information & Entertainment. Rini & Coran. Format: Variety, talk & country. Target aud: General; senior citizens. Spec prog: C&W 6 hrs, relg 6 hrs, class 6 hrs wkly. ♦ Bill Roloff, gen mgr.

WELY-FM— July 25, 1992: 94.5 mhz; 6 kw. Ant 328 ft. TL: N47 53 40 W91 51 50. (CP: 14.5 kw, ant 338 ft). Stereo. E-mail: wely@spacestar.net. Web Site: www.wely.com.

Eveleth

KRBT(AM)— December 1948: 1340 khz; 1 kw-U. TL: N47 28 40 W92 32 00. Box 650, 906 Old Hwy. 53 55734. Phone: (218) 741-5922. Fax: (218) 741-7302. E-mail: weve@spacestar.net. Licensee: Iron Range Broadcasting Inc. Group owner: Lew Latto Group of Northland Radio Stations (acq 5-1-78). Network: ABC Information & Entertainment. Format: News/talk. Target aud: 25-54. Spec prog: Finnish one hr, polka 3 hrs wkly. ♦ Nancy Grummett, gen mgr & gen sls mgr; Dennis Jerrold, opns mgr & progmg dir; Steve Carlson, news dir; Dave Houston, chief of engrg.

WEVE-FM— Co-owned with KRBT(AM). June 26, 1978: 97.9 mhz; 71 kw. 555 ft. TL: N47 35 53 W92 13 26. Stereo. Format: Adult contemp. News staff: one; News: one hr wkly. ♦ Annie Wargowski, stn mgr.

Fairmont

KFMC(FM)—Listing follows KSUM(AM).

KSUM(AM)— Jan 1, 1949: 1370 khz; 1 kw-U, DA-2. TL: N43 37 45 W94 29 00. Stereo. Box 491 56031. Secondary address: 1371 W. Lair Rd. 56031. Phone: (507) 235-5595. Fax: (507) 235-5973. E-mail: ksum@bevcomm.net. Web Site: www.ksum.com. Licensee: Woodward Broadcasting Inc. (acq 11-1-62). Rep: Hyett/Ramsland. Booth, Freret, Imlay & Tepper. Format: Country. Target aud: General. Spec prog: Farm 18 hrs wkly. ♦ Charles Woodward, gen mgr.

KFMC(FM)— Co-owned with KSUM(AM). July 31, 1978: 106.5 mhz; 100 kw. 400 ft. TL: N43 37 45 W94 29 00. Stereo. Format: Hot adult contemp. Target aud: 25-54.

Faribault

KBGY(FM)— October 2001: 107.5 mhz; 48 kw. 394 ft. TL: N44 12 42 W93 20 18. Stereo. 14589 Grand Ave. N., Burnsville 55306. Phone: (952) 435-5777. Fax: (952) 435-3181. E-mail: info@spirit.fm. Web Site: www.spirit.fm. Licensee: Milestone Radio II LLC (acq 10-3-01; $2.2 million). Format: Christian music. News staff: one; News: 10 hrs wkly. Target aud: General; 25-54. ♦ Tom Payne, gen mgr.

KDHL(AM)— Jan 10, 1948: 920 khz; 5 kw-U, DA-2. TL: N44 15 47 W93 16 29. 601 Central Ave. 55021. Phone: (507) 334-0061. Fax: (507) 334-7057. Web Site: www.kdhlradio.com. Licensee: Cumulus Licensing Corp. Group owner: Cumulus Media Inc. (acq 7-21-98; grpsl). Network: ABC Information & Entertainment. Format: News, sports, farm. News staff: one; News: 8 hrs wkly. Target aud: 35 plus. ♦ Scott Lindahl, gen mgr, sls dir & gen sls mgr; John Taylor, progmg dir; Gordon Kosfeld, news dir.

KQCL(FM)—Co-owned with KDHL(AM). Jan 10, 1968: 95.9 mhz; 3 kw. 328 ft. TL: N44 21 25 W93 11 31. Stereo. Web Site: www.cumulus.com. Format: Class rock. Target aud: 18-49. ♦ Steve Winters, progmg dir.

Fergus Falls

KBRF(AM)— Oct 20, 1926: 1250 khz; 5 kw-D, 1 kw-N, DA-N. TL: N46 17 19 W96 06 17. (CP: 2.2 kw-N. TL: N46 17 53 W95 58 42). Box 495 56538. Secondary address: 728 Western Ave. N. 56537. Phone: (218) 736-7596. Fax: (218) 736-2836. E-mail: kbrfkzcr@prtel.com. Licensee: Result Radio Inc. Group owner: The Result Radio Group (acq 1-30-78). Network: Westwood One. Rep: Midwest Radio. Midwest Radio Network Format: Country, news/talk. News staff: one; News: 20 hrs wkly. Target aud: Adults 35+. Spec prog: Farm 15 hrs, relg 7 hrs wkly. ♦ Jerry Papenfuss, CEO, pres & opns mgr; Greg Brady, pres & opns mgr; Doug Gray, gen mgr; Karen Steel, prom mgr; Charlie Kampa, progmg dir; Brian Lokken, news dir; Mary Paulson, pub affrs dir.

KZCR(FM)—Co-owned with KBRF(AM). Jan 19, 1968: 103.3 mhz; 100 kw. 620 ft. TL: N46 28 06 W96 11 54. Stereo. News staff: one; News: 10 hrs wkly. Target aud: Adults 25-49. ♦ Doug Gray, stn mgr; Greg Brady, opns dir, natl sls mgr & progmg dir; David Bishop, pub affrs dir.

*KCMF(FM)— June 6, 2003: 89.7 mhz; 2.7 kw. Ant 216 ft. TL: N46 19 12 W96 05 32. Minnesota Public Radio, 45 E. 7th St., St. Paul 55101. Phone: (651) 290-1500. Fax: (651) 290-1224. Web Site: www.mpr.org. Licensee: Minnesota Public Radio. Format: Class. ♦ William H. Kling, gen mgr.

KJJK(AM)— Dec 1, 1986: 1020 khz; 2 kw-D, 370 kw-N. TL: N46 14 43 W95 58 46. Box 495, 728 Western Ave. N. 56537. Phone: (218) 736-7596. Fax: (218) 736-2836. E-mail: kbrfkzcr@prtel.com. Licensee: Result Radio Inc. Group owner: The Result Radio Group (acq 3-27-97; $1.1 million with co-located FM). Network: ABC Daytime Direction. Pepper & Corazzini. Format: Oldies. News staff: one; News: one hr wkly. Target aud: 35 plus; family, home owners, execs, mgrs, dual house income. Spec prog: Relg 3 hrs wkly. ♦ Jerry Papenfuss, CEO & pres; Doug Grey, gen mgr, gen sls mgr & gen sls mgr; Gary Michaels, opns mgr & progmg dir; Brian Lokken, news dir.

KJJK-FM— Oct 14, 1981: 96.5 mhz; 100 kw. 480 ft. TL: N46 14 43 W95 58 46. Stereo. Midwest Radio Network Format: Country. News staff: one; News: 3 hrs wkly. Target aud: 21-54; today's country music fans. ♦ Jeff Swedberg, progmg dir.

*KNWF(FM)— April 2003: 91.5 mhz; 100 w. 226 ft. TL: 45 E. 7th St., St. Paul 55101. Phone: (651) 290-1500. Fax: (651) 290-1224. Web Site: www.mpr.org. Licensee: Minnesota Public Radio. Format: News. ♦ William H. Kling, gen mgr.

Forest Lake

WLKX-FM— Oct 28, 1978: 95.9 mhz; 3 kw. 300 ft. TL: N45 17 40 W93 04 22. Stereo. 15226 W. Freeway Dr. 55025. Phone: (651) 464-6796. Fax: (651) 464-3638. Web Site: www.spirit.fm. Licensee: Lakes Broadcasting Co. Inc. Format: Adult contemp Christian. News staff: one; News: 20 hrs wkly. Target aud: 25-54; general. Spec prog: Auction show 9 hrs, relg 6 hrs wkly. ♦ Gary Kastner, gen mgr.

Fosston

KKCQ(AM)— Dec 12, 1966: 1480 khz; 5 kw-D, 2.5 kw-N, DA-N. TL: N47 33 44 W95 43 50. (CP: 90 w-N). Box 606, 35006 Hwy. 2 E. 56542. Phone: (218) 435-1919. Fax: (218) 435-1480. E-mail: q107@gitel.com. Web Site: www.christianradio.com/q107. Licensee: Pine to Prairie Broadcasting Inc. (acq 2-1-92; $335,000 with co-located FM; 2-10-92). Network: ABC Information & Entertainment. Eugene T. Smith. Format: Talk, oldies. News staff: one; News: 4 hrs wkly. Target aud: 25-54; family-oriented adults. Spec prog: Farm 5 hrs, relg 4 hrs wkly. ♦ Bob Overmoe, pres & gen mgr; Phil Ehlke, gen sls mgr; Tom Lano, progmg dir; Jamie Nesvold, mus dir; Karen Bingham, news dir & pub affrs dir; Jim Offerdahl, chief of engrg.

KKEQ(FM)— Co-owned with KKCQ(AM). June 13, 1969: 107.1 mhz; 50 kw. 482 ft. TL: N47 33 44 W95 43 30. Stereo. Network: ABC Information & Entertainment. Format: Christian. News: 2 hrs wkly. Target aud: 25-45. ♦ Larry Roed, CEO; Kevin Arvidson, prom VP & progmg dir.

Glencoe

KTTB(FM)— Sept 23, 1993: 96.3 mhz; 100 kw. Ant 577 ft. TL: N44 56 25 W93 55 43. 5300 Edina Industrial Blvd., Suite 200, Edina 55439. Phone: (952) 842-7200. Fax: (952) 842-1048. Web Site: www.b96online.com. Licensee: Blue Chip Broadcasting Licenses II Ltd. Group owner: Radio One Inc. (acq 8-10-2001; grpsl). Format: Rhythmic CHR. News staff: one. Target aud: 18-34; Adults. ♦ Steve Woodbury, VP, gen mgr & engrg VP.

Glenwood

KMGK(FM)— Mar 11, 1983: 107.1 mhz; 3 kw. 300 ft. TL: N45 36 53 W95 23 28. Stereo. Box 241 56334. Phone: (320) 634-5358. Fax: (320) 634-5359. E-mail: traffic@kmgk1071.com. Web Site: www.kmgk1071.com. Licensee: Branstock Communications Inc. Format: Adult contemp. News staff: one; News: 13 wkly. Target aud: 25-54. Spec prog: Rock weekend 70s. ♦ Steven R. Nestor, CEO; Jeff Thornton, gen mgr.

Directory of Radio

Golden Valley

KDIZ(AM)—Listing follows KQRS-FM.

KQRS-FM— Sept 1, 1963: 92.5 mhz; 100 kw. 900 ft. TL: N44 59 20 W93 21 06. (CP: Ant 1,033 ft.). Stereo. 2000 Elm St. S.E., Minneapolis 55414. Phone: (612) 617-4000. Fax: (612) 676-8292. Web Site: www.92kqrs.com. Licensee: KQRS Inc. Group owner: ABC Inc. Network: ABC. Rep: ABC Radio Sales. Format: Classic rock. ♦ Amy Waggoner, gen mgr; Susan Larkin, gen sls mgr; Dave Hamilton, progmg dir; Reed Endersbe, mus dir; David Szaflarski, chief of engrg.

KDIZ(AM)—Co-owned with KQRS-FM. May 13, 1948: 1440 khz; 5 kw-D, 500 w-N, DA-N. TL: N44 59 20 W93 21 06. 10800 Lyndale Ave. S., Suite 255, Bloomington 55420. Phone: (952) 886-3277. Fax: (952) 886-0434. Web Site: www.disney.com. (Acq 6-30-86). Rep: ABC Radio Sales. Format: Children. News staff: one; News: 5 hrs wkly. Target aud: 18-49; baby boomers/Generation X. ♦ Brian Acker, stn mgr; Tess Juntunen, prom dir; Laura Olson, progmg dir.

KYCR(AM)—Licensed to Golden Valley. See Minneapolis-St. Paul

Grand Marais

*WLSN(FM)—Not on air, target date: unknown: 89.7 mhz; 6 kw. 613 ft. 224 Holiday Ctr., Duluth 55802. Phone: (218) 722-9411. Fax: (218) 720-4900. Web Site: www.mpr.org. Licensee: Minnesota Public Radio. Format: News & info. ♦ William H. Kling, pres; John Snee, gen mgr.

*WMLS(FM)—Not on air, target date: unknown: 88.7 mhz; 6 kw. 613 ft. 224 Holiday Ctr., Duluth 55802. Phone: (218) 722-9411. Fax: (218) 720-4900. Web Site: www.mpr.org. Licensee: Minnesota Public Radio. Format: Classical. ♦ William Kling, pres; John Snee, gen mgr; Char Dobosenski, adv dir; Bob Kelleher, news dir; Doug Thompson, engrg dir; Aaron White, chief of engrg.

*WTIP(FM)— July 1, 1998: 90.7 mhz; 25 kw. 584 ft. TL: N47 46 09 W90 20 49. Box 1005 55604. Secondary address: 55 W. 5th St. 55604. Phone: (218) 387-1070. Fax: (218) 387-1120. E-mail: wtip@boreal.org. Web Site: www.wtip.org. Licensee: Cook County Community Radio Corp. Format: AAA, var, adult contemp. News: 15 hrs wkly. Target aud: General. Spec prog: Blues 15 hrs, AOR 15 hrs, progsv rock 15 hrs wkly. ♦ Ann Possis, pres; Mike Raymond, exec VP & VP; Deb Benedict, stn mgr; Jeanne Wright, dev dir; Cathy Quinn, progmg dir; Jeff Nemitz, engrg dir.

WXXZ(FM)— 1999: 95.3 mhz; 100 kw. 699 ft. TL: N47 39 55 W90 42 22. 501 Lake Ave. S., Suite 200A, Duluth 55802. Phone: (218) 722-0921. Fax: (218) 723-1499. Licensee: Red Rock Radio Corp. (group owner; acq 1-10-00; grpsl). Format: Classic rock. ♦ Shawn Skramstad, gen mgr.

Grand Rapids

*KAXE(FM)— Apr 23, 1976: 91.7 mhz; 100 kw. 460 ft. TL: N47 15 17 W93 26 03. Stereo. 1841 E. Hwy. 169 55744. Phone: (218) 326-1234. Fax: (218) 326-1235. E-mail: comments@kaxe.org. Web Site: www.kaxe.org. Licensee: Northern Community Radio Inc. Network: Network: NPR, PRI. Format: Div. Target aud: General. Spec prog: Folk 6 hrs, Black 2 hrs, class 2 hrs, C&W 3 hrs, jazz 6 hrs, Finnish 2 hrs, polka 2 hrs, American Indian 3 hrs, farm one hr wkly. ♦ Rick McDonald, pres; Maggie Montgomery, gen mgr; John Bauer, dev dir; Dan Houg, progmg dir & engrg dir; Eleanor St. John, news dir.

KMFY(FM)—Listing follows KOZY(AM).

KOZY(AM)— Jan 29, 1948: 1320 khz; 5 kw-U, DA-2. TL: N47 10 22 W93 27 10. Box 597 55744. Secondary address: 507 11th St. S.E. 55744. Phone: (218) 326-3446. Fax: (218) 326-3448. E-mail: kozykmfy@mchsi.com. Licensee: Itasca Broadcasting Inc. (acq 4-15-02; with co-located FM). Network: ABC. Format: Gold classics. News staff: 5. ♦ Mike Iaizzo, pres & gen mgr.

KMFY(FM)—Co-owned with KOZY(AM). Dec 5, 1975: 96.9 mhz; 100 kw. 450 ft. TL: N47 15 17 W93 26 03. Stereo. Format: Adult contemp. News staff: 5. Target aud: 35-54.

Developers & Brokers of Radio Properties

contact American Media Services at our suite:
Philadelphia Marriott Downtown
215-625-2900
843-972-2200
americanmediaservices.com
Charleston, SC
Dallas, TX · Chicago, IL · Austin, TX

American Media Services, LLC

Granite Falls

KKRC(FM)— Oct 5, 1993: 93.9 mhz; 6 kw. 262 ft. TL: N44 54 06 W95 32 53. Box 513, R.R.5 160 A, Montevideo 56001. Phone: (320) 269-8815. Fax: (320) 269-8449. E-mail: kdma@info-link.net. Web Site: www.kdrckmgmkkrc.com. Licensee: Iowa City Broadcasting Co. Group owner: Tom Ingstad Broadcasting Group Format: Oldies. ♦Deanna Hodge, gen mgr & stn mgr; Dwight Mulder, opns mgr.

KMGM(FM)—See Montevideo

Hastings

KDWA(AM)— Oct 24, 1963: 1460 khz; 1 kw-D, 45 w-N. TL: N44 42 49 W92 50 30. 514 Vermillion St. 55033. Phone: (651) 437-1460. Fax: (651) 438-3042. E-mail: dan@kdwa.com. Web Site: www.kdwaradio.com. Licensee: K & M Broadcasting Inc. (acq 6-30-92; $161,000; 7-20-92). Network: Network: CNN Radio, USA. Format: Loc news, sports, talk. News staff: 2; News: 18 hrs wkly. Target aud: 25-65; general. ♦Dan Massman, gen mgr.

Hermantown

WWAX(FM)— June 17, 1996: 92.1 mhz; 780 w. 905 ft. TL: N46 47 13 W92 07 17. 501 Lake Ave. S., Suite 200A, Duluth 55802. Phone: (218) 722-0921. Fax: (218) 723-1499. Licensee: Red Rock Radio Corp. (group owner; acq 1-10-00; grpsl). Format: Adult contemp. Target aud: 18-35; general. ♦Shawn Skramstad, gen mgr.

Hibbing

*KADU(FM)— July 18, 1994: 90.1 mhz; 100 w. Ant 220 ft. TL: N47 23 59 W92 57 47. (CP: 2.2 kw horiz, 22 kw vert, ant 371 ft. TL: N47 24 34 W92 57 02). 3309 6th Ave. W. 55746. Phone: (218) 263-4420. Licensee: Heartland Christian Broadcasters Inc. (acq 4-22-2005; $30,000). Format: Christian. ♦Steven Drees, pres & gen mgr.

KMFY(FM)—See Grand Rapids

WIRR(FM)—See Duluth

WMFG(AM)— 1935: 1240 khz; 1 kw-U. TL: N47 24 30 W92 57 04. 807 W. 37th St. 55746. Phone: (218) 263-7531. Fax: (218) 263-6112. Licensee: Midwest Communications Inc. (group owner; (acq 5-10-2004); grpsl). Format: Sports, talk. News staff: 2; News: 13 hrs wkly. Target aud: 25-55; men. Spec prog: Folk, relg 4 hrs, polka 4 hrs wkly. ♦Kristi Garrity, gen mgr, gen sls mgr, mktg dir, prom dir & adv dir; Ben Johnson, progmg dir; Dan Klasmat, engrg dir.

WMFG-FM— 1971: 106.3 mhz; 25 kw. 253 ft. TL: N47 24 30 W92 57 04. (CP: 25 kw, ant 259 ft.). Stereo. Format: Oldies. Target aud: 25-54. ♦Dennis Martin, gen sls mgr; Bill Meyes, chief of engrg.

WNMT(AM)—(Nashwauk). June 2, 1975: 650 khz; 10 kw-D, 500 w-N, DA-N. TL: N47 22 31 W93 00 56. (CP: 10 kw-D, 1 kw-N). 807 W. 37th St. 55746. Phone: (218) 263-7531. Fax: (218) 263-6112. Web Site: www.wnmtradio.com. Licensee: Midwest Communications Inc. (group owner; acq 5-10-2004; grpsl). Network: ABC Information & Entertainment. Format: News/talk. Target aud: 35 plus. Spec prog: Pol 2 hrs wkly. ♦Kristy Garrity, gen mgr; Jim Heitzman, gen sls mgr; Rich Collins, mus dir; Craig Holgate, news dir; Danny Klaysmat, chief of engrg.

WTBX(FM)—Co-owned with WNMT(AM). Dec 31, 1980: 93.9 mhz; 100 kw. 548 ft. TL: N47 22 31 W93 00 56. Stereo. Web Site: www.wtbx.com. Network: ABC FM Connection. Format: CHR. Target aud: 18-40. ♦Rich Collins, progmg dir.

Hutchinson

KARP-FM—Listing follows KDUZ(AM).

KDUZ(AM)— Sept 16, 1953: 1260 khz; 1 kw-D, 64 w-N. TL: N44 54 24 W94 21 59. 20132 Hwy. 15 N. 55350-5643. Phone: (320) 587-2140. Fax: (320) 587-5158. E-mail: kduz@hutchtel.net. Web Site: www.kduz.com. Licensee: Iowa City Broadcasting Co. Inc. Group owner: Tom Ingstad Broadcasting Group (acq 4-1-2000; grpsl). Network: ABC Information & Entertainment. Hyett/Ramsland. Format: Oldies, news, sports. News staff: 2; News: 21 hrs wkly. Target aud: 30 plus; general. Spec prog: Farm 18 hrs, gospel 3 hrs, polka 8 hrs, Sp one hr wkly. ♦Tom Ingstag, chmn; Jim Bartels, gen mgr & gen sls mgr; John Mons, opns mgr; Jim Ohnstad, progmg dir & pub affrs dir; Mark Wodarczyk, news dir; Duane Wawyrzniak, chief of engrg.

KARP-FM—Co-owned with KDUZ(AM). June 6, 1968: 106.9 mhz; 7 kw. 554 ft. TL: N45 02 43 W94 33 32. Stereo. E-mail: info@karpradio.com. Web Site: www.karpradio.com. Format: Country. News staff: 2; News: 3 hrs wkly. Target aud: 18 plus. ♦Jim Bartels, stn mgr.

International Falls

*KBHW(FM)— Jan 4, 1983: 99.5 mhz; 100 kw. Ant 580 ft. TL: N48 33 45 W93 49 22. Stereo. Box 433 56649. Secondary address: 4090 Hwy.11 56649. Phone: (218) 285-7398. Fax: (218) 285-7419. E-mail: studio@psalm995.org. Web Site: www.psalm995.org. Licensee: Heartland Christian Broadcasters. (acq 7-23-99; $1 with KXBR(FM) International Falls). Network: Network: USA, Moody. Format: Christian. News: 15 hrs wkly. Target aud: General. ♦Bruce Christopherson, gen mgr & chief of engrg.

KGHS(AM)— Sept 1, 1959: 1230 khz; 500 w-D, 250 w-N. TL: N48 35 29 W93 22 54. 519 3rd St. 56649. Phone: (218) 283-3481. Fax: (218) 283-3087. E-mail: kghsksdm@northwinds.net. Web Site: www.ksdmradio.com. Licensee: Quarnstrom Media Group LLC (group owner; acq 10-99; $1.15 million. with co-located FM). Network: Jones Radio Networks. Format: Adult contemp. News staff: one; News: 10 hrs wkly. ♦Al Quarnstrom, pres; Don Welch, VP; Dan Traska, gen mgr & gen sls mgr; Jerry Franzen, news dir; Bill Meys, chief of engrg.

KSDM(FM)—Co-owned with KGHS(AM). Mar 17, 1979: 104.1 mhz; 8.5 kw. 200 ft. TL: N48 35 39 W93 22 56. Stereo. Phone: (218) 283-2622. Web Site: www.ksdmradio.com. Network: ABC. Format: Country. News staff: one; News: 20 hrs wkly.

*KXBR(FM)— June, 2000: 91.9 mhz; 1.5 kw. 128 ft. TL: N48 34 15 W93 26 19. Box 433,, 4090 Hwy. 11 56649. Phone: (218) 285-9190. Fax: (218) 285-7419. E-mail: dj@edge919.com. Web Site: www.edge919.com. Licensee: Heartland Christian Broadcasters. (acq 7-23-99; $1 with KBHW(FM) International Falls). Format: Christian rock. ♦Bruce Christopherson, gen mgr & chief of engrg.

Jackson

KKOJ(AM)— July 10, 1980: 1190 khz; 5 kw-D, DA. TL: N43 31 45 W95 00 02. Box 29 56143. Secondary address: 71991 US Hwy. 71 56143. Phone: (507) 847-5400. Fax: (507) 847-5745. E-mail: kkoj@rconnect.com. Web Site: www.kkoj.com. Licensee: Kleven Broadcasting Co. of Minnesota. Format: Modern country. News staff: one; News: 20 hrs wkly. Target aud: General. Spec prog: Farm 15 hrs wkly. ♦Doug Johnson, pres, gen mgr & gen sls mgr; Dave Maschoff, news dir; Jerrie Johnson, chief of engrg.

KRAQ(FM)— Apr 25, 1994: 105.7 mhz; 25 kw. 328 ft. TL: N43 36 54 W94 57 48. Stereo. Box 29 56143. Secondary address: 71991 US Hwy. 71 56143. Phone: (507) 847-5400. Fax: (507) 847-5745. E-mail: kkoj@rconnect.com. Web Site: www.kkoj.com. Licensee: Kleven Broadcasting Co. of Minnesota. (acq 2-27-98). Network: AP Radio. Baraff, Koerner & Olender. Format: Oldies/Classic Rock. News staff: one; News: new progmg 18 hrs wkly. ♦Doug Johnson, pres, gen mgr & gen sls mgr; Dave Maschoff, news dir.

La Crescent

KQEG(FM)—Licensed to La Crescent. See La Crosse WI

*KXLC(FM)— Nov 24, 1991: 91.1 mhz; 230 w. 843 ft. TL: N43 48 16 W91 22 18. Stereo. 206 S. Broadway, Suite 735, Rochester 55904. Phone: (507) 282-0910. Fax: (507) 282-2107. Web Site: www.mpr.org. Licensee: Minnesota Public Radio. (acq 4-9-90). Network: Network: NPR, PRI. Format: News. News staff: 2; News: 24 hrs wkly. Target aud: General. ♦Chris Cross, gen mgr; Mary Stapek, dev dir.

Lake City

KLCH(FM)— December 2001: 94.9 mhz; 6 kw. Ant 328 ft. TL: N44 22 56 W92 22 05. 474 Guernsey Ln., Redwing 55066. Phone: (651) 388-7151. Fax: (651) 388-7153. E-mail: preding@waittradio.com. Web Site: lakehits95.com. Licensee: Waitt Radio Inc. (group owner; acq 7-3-02; $280,000). Format: Adult contemp. News staff: 2. Target aud: 25-54. ♦Mike Delich, CEO; George Pelletier, sr VP; Paul Reding, gen mgr; Tom Hughes, opns dir.

KMFX-FM— Feb 14, 1991: 102.5 mhz; 9.4 kw. 528 ft. TL: N44 16 45 W92 23 38. 1530 Greenview Dr., Rochester 55902. Phone: (507) 288-3888. Fax: (507) 288-7815. Web Site: www.rochestersquare.com. Licensee: Clear Channel Broadcasting Licenses Inc. Group owner: Clear Channel Communications Inc. (acq 10-2000; grpsl). Rep: D & R Radio. Format: Country. ♦Bob Fox, gen mgr.

Lake Crystal

KQYK(FM)—Not on air, target date: unknown: 95.7 mhz; 6 kw. Ant 328 ft. TL: N44 03 06 W94 17 59. 6130 Cheney Ridge Cir., Lincoln, NE 68516. Licensee: William C. Doleman. ♦William C. Doleman, gen mgr.

Lakeville

WGVX(FM)— February 1993: 105.1 mhz; 2.6 kw. 499 ft. TL: N44 42 05 W93 09 02. 2000 S. E. Elm Street, Minneapolis 55414. Phone: (612) 617-4000. Fax: (612) 676-8292. Web Site: www.drive105.com. Licensee: KQRS Inc. Group owner: ABC Inc. (acq 7-24-97; grpsl). Format: AAA. Target aud: 18-34. ♦Amy Rosenthal, pres & stn mgr; Dave Hamilton, opns mgr; Pete Frisch, stn dir; Susan Larkin, gen sls mgr; Jeff Berman, natl sls mgr; Brook Johnson, mktg dir; Shelley Miller, prom dir; Jeff Collins, progmg dir; Ben Gnam, mus dir; Julie Honebrink, pub affrs dir; Dave Szaflarski, chief of engrg.

Litchfield

KKLN(FM)—(Atwater). Nov 26, 1988: 94.1 mhz; 3 kw. Ant 328 ft. TL: N45 04 24 W94 45 20. Stereo. Kandi Mall, 1605 S. 1st St., Willmar 56201-4234. Phone: (320) 235-1194. Fax: (320) 235-6894. E-mail: info@kkln.com. Web Site: www.kkln.com. Licensee: Flagship Broadcasting. (acq 1999). Format: Classic rock. Target aud: General. ♦Rick Anderson, pres; Brian Bach, gen mgr; Nate Thomas, opns mgr.

KLFD(AM)— Jan 2, 1959: 1410 khz; 500 w-D, 47 w-N. TL: N45 07 02 W94 33 13. 234 N. Sibley Ave. 55355. Phone: (320) 693-3281. Fax: (320) 693-3283. E-mail: klfd@hutchtel.net. Licensee: Mid-Minnesota Broadcasting Co. (acq 11-26-91; 12-16-91). Leventhal, Senter & Lerman. Format: Full service. News staff: one; News: 10 hrs wkly. Target aud: 25-54. Spec prog: Loc sports progmg, farm 20 hrs, relg 3 hrs wkly. ♦Bob Greenhow, pres; Steve Neighbors, opns VP.

Little Falls

KFML(FM)—Listing follows KLTF(AM).

KLTF(AM)— October 1950: 960 khz; 5 kw-D, 35 w-N. TL: N46 00 16 W94 19 42. 16405 Haven Rd. 56345. Phone: (320) 632-2992. Fax: (320) 632-2571. Web Site: www.fallsradio.com. Licensee: Little Falls Radio Corp. (group owner, acq 6-28-2004; grpsl). Network: ABC. Format: Adult contemp, country, news/talk. News staff: one; News: 24 hrs wkly. Target aud: 35-65; loc audience who listen for news & info. Spec prog: Farm 8 hrs, relg one hr, big band 5 hrs wkly. ♦Rod Grams, pres; Jack Hansen, stn mgr, gen sls mgr & chief of engrg; Gary Block, progmg dir; Brian Patrick, news dir.

Broadcasting & Cable Yearbook 2006

Minnesota

KFML(FM)—Co-owned with KLTF(AM). November 1988: 94.1 mhz; 6 kw. 275 ft. TL: N46 00 16 W94 19 42. Stereo. Network: Westwood One. Format: The best of yesterday & today. News staff: one; News: 3 hrs wkly. Target aud: 25-54. ◆Jack Hansen, gen mgr; Mitch Ryan, prom dir.

WYRQ(FM)— May 19, 1980: 92.1 mhz; 3 kw. 299 ft. TL: N45 56 57 W94 17 48. Stereo. 16405 Haven Rd. 56345. Phone: (320) 632-2992. Fax: (320) 632-2571. Web Site: www.fallsradio.com. Licensee: Little Falls Radio Corp. (group owner; acq 6-28-2004; grpsl). Network: CNN Radio. Format: Agriculture, country, news/talk. News staff: one; News: 20 hrs wkly. Target aud: 25-54; farmers & working people. ◆Rod Grams, pres; Jack Hansen, gen mgr, natl sls mgr & chief of engrg; Al Windsperger, prom mgr & progmg dir; Brian Patrick, news dir.

Long Prairie

KEYL(AM)— Sept 15, 1959: 1400 khz; 1 kw-U. TL: N45 57 45 W94 52 09. Box 187, 221 Central Ave. 56347. Phone: (320) 732-2164. Fax: (320) 732-2284. E-mail: keyl@keylrealcountry.com. Licensee: Prairie Broadcasting Co. (acq 10-28-98; $375,000 for stock with KXDL(FM) Browerville). Network: ABC. Miller & Miller, P.C. Format: Country. News: 15 hrs wkly. Target aud: 25 plus. Spec prog: Farm 5 hrs, sports 10 hrs, relg 4 hrs wkly. ◆Gene Sullivan, pres & gen mgr.

KXDL(FM)—(Browerville). May 15, 1992: 99.7 mhz; 6 kw. 328 ft. TL: N46 03 15 W94 50 50. Box 187 56347. Phone: (320) 732-2164. Fax: (320) 732-2284. Licensee: Prairie Broadcasting Co. (acq 10-28-98; $375,000 for stock with KEYL(AM) Long Prairie). O'Malley. Miller & Miller. Format: Adult contemp. News: 4 hrs wkly. Target aud: 18-44; female. Spec prog: Sports 2 hrs wkly. ◆Gene Sullivan, pres & gen mgr; Clif Cline, opns mgr.

Luverne

KLQL(FM)—Listing follows KQAD.

KQAD(AM)— Mar 1, 1971: 800 khz; 500 w-D, 80 w-N, DA-2. TL: N43 39 01 W96 10 19. Stereo. Box 599, County Rd. 4 E. 56156. Phone: (507) 283-4444. Fax: (507) 283-4445. Web Site: www.kqad.net. Licensee: Three Eagles Communications, Luverne. Group owner: Three Eagles Communications (acq 1996; grpsl). Rep: Hyett/Ramsland. Format: Soft adult contemp. News staff: one; News: 5 hrs wkly. Target aud: 50 plus. Spec prog: Relg 5 hrs wkly. ◆Steve Graphenteen, gen mgr.

Madison

KLQP(FM)— Jan 31, 1983: 92.1 mhz; 25 kw. 300 ft. TL: N45 01 37 W96 11 15. Stereo. Box 70, 623 W. 3rd St. 56256. Phone: (320) 598-7301. Fax: (320) 598-7955. E-mail: klqpfm@farmerstel.net. Web Site: www.klqpfm.com. Licensee: Lac Qui Parle Broadcasting Co. Inc. Network: CNN Radio. Format: Country, oldies. News: 18 hrs wkly. Target aud: General. Spec prog: Farm 5 hrs wkly. ◆Maynard R. Meyer, CEO, pres & gen mgr; Kris Kuechenmeister, opns mgr.

Mahnomen

KRJM(FM)— Aug 27, 2001: 101.5 mhz; 25 kw. 328 ft. TL: N47 27 23 W96 07 57. 213 N. Main St. 56510. Phone: (218) 935-5355. Fax: (218) 935-9020. Web site: www.krjmradio.com. Licensee: R & J Broadcasting. (acq. 9-1-01; Format: Oldies. ◆Jim Birkemeyer, gen mgr.

Mankato

KDOG(FM)—Listing follows KTOE(AM).

KEEZ-FM— Apr 1, 1968: 99.1 mhz; 100 kw. 864 ft. TL: N43 56 14 W94 24 41. Stereo. 54934 210 Ln. 56001. Phone: (507) 345-4646. Fax: (507) 345-3299. E-mail: zdesk@keez.com. Web Site: www.keez.com. Licensee: Three Eagles of Luverne Inc. Group owner: Three Eagles Communications (acq 6-19-00; grpsl). Network: Westwood One. O'Malley. Format: Hot adult contemp. News staff: one. Target aud: 25-54. ◆Rick Prusator, gen mgr.

KGAC(FM)—See Saint Peter

*KMSU(FM)— Jan 7, 1963: 89.7 mhz; 20 kw. 400 ft. TL: N44 08 34 W94 00 08. Stereo. AF 205 Mankato State University, 1536 Warren St. 56001. Phone: (507) 389-5678. Fax: (507) 389-1705. Web Site: www.kmsu.org. Licensee: Mankato State University. Network: PRI. Cohn & Marks. Format: Pub affrs, educ, music. News staff: one; News: 50 hrs wkly. Target aud: General; upscale, educated. Spec prog: Drama 3 hrs, folk/ethnic 5 hrs, new age 5 hrs wkly. ◆Jim Gullickson, gen mgr; Karen Wright, opns dir.

KNGA(FM)—See Saint Peter

KTOE(AM)— 1950: 1420 khz; 5 kw-U, DA-N. TL: N44 10 06 W93 54 37. Box 1420 56002. Phone: (507) 345-4537. Fax: (507) 345-5364. Web Site: www.ktoe.com. Licensee: Minnesota Valley Broadcasting Co. Group owner: Linder Broadcasting Group Rep: Katz Radio. Format: Talk. News staff: news progmg 21 hrs wkly News: 3;. Target aud: 25-54. ◆John Linder, CEO; Mike Parry, gen mgr.

KDOG(FM)—Co-owned with KTOE(AM). Apr 1, 1985: 96.7 mhz; 18 kw. 390 ft. TL: N44 13 20 W94 07 03. Stereo. Phone: (507) 625-9197. Fax: (507) 345-5364. Web Site: www.kdog.com. Format: Adult contemp. News staff: one; News: 4 hrs wkly.

KXLP(FM)—(New Ulm). Nov 21, 1966: 93.1 mhz; 100 kw. 489 ft. TL: N44 07 44 W94 11 15. Stereo. 1807 Lee Blvd. 56003. Phone: (507) 388-2900. Fax: (507) 345-4675. Web Site: www.kxlpradio.com. Licensee: Clear Channel Broadcasting Licenses Inc. Group owner: Clear Channel Communications Inc. (acq 10-1-2000; grpsl). Format: Classic rock and roll. Target aud: 25-54. Spec prog: Oldies 15 hrs wkly. ◆Jo Guck Bailey, gen mgr.

KYSM(AM)—Licensed to Mankato. See North Mankato

KYSM-FM—Licensed to Mankato. See North Mankato

Maplewood

WCTS(AM)—Licensed to Maplewood. See Minneapolis-St. Paul

Marshall

KARZ(FM)— July 7, 1985: 107.5 mhz; 25 kw. 300 ft. TL: N44 24 37 W95 51 43. (CP: 15 kw, ant 430 ft. TL: N44 19 32 W95 52 19). Stereo. Box 61 56258. Secondary address: 1414 E. College Dr. 56258. Phone: (507) 537-0566. Fax: (507) 532-3739. Web Site: www.marshallradio.net. Licensee: KMHL Broadcasting Co. Inc. Group owner: Linder Broadcasting Group (acq 5-6-97; $450,000). Format: Classic rock. Target aud: 25-54. ◆Brad Strootman, gen mgr & sls VP; Keith Petermeier, chief of opns; Scott Schmeling, chief of engrg.

KKCK(FM)—Listing follows KMHL(AM).

KMHL(AM)— Nov 30, 1946: 1400 khz; 1 kw-U. TL: N44 26 55 W95 45 27. (CP: TL: N44 26 59 W95 45 43). Box 61, 1414 E. College Dr. 56258. Phone: (507) 532-2282. Fax: (507) 532-3739. Web Site: www.marshallradio.com. Licensee: KMHL Broadcasting Co. Group owner: Linder Broadcasting Group Network: ABC Daytime Direction, ABC. Rep: Katz Radio. Format: Farm, news/talk. News staff: one; News: 20 hrs wkly. Target aud: 27 plus. Spec prog: Relg 7 hrs wkly. ◆Donald Linder, pres; John Linder, VP; Brad Strootman, gen mgr & sls dir; Keith Petermeier, chief of opns; Justin Thordsen, progmg dir; Aaron Ziemer, pub affrs dir; Scott Jeffries, chief of engrg.

KKCK(FM)—Co-owned with KMHL(AM). Dec 13, 1967: 99.7 mhz; 100 kw. 925 ft. TL: N44 26 55 W95 45 27. Stereo. Web Site: marshallradio.net. Network: ABC FM Connection. Format: Hot adult contemp, rock. News staff: one; News: 8 hrs wkly. Target aud: 21-39. ◆Brad Stoutman, exec VP & adv VP; Keith Petermierer, prom mgr; Chris Grosshan, progmg mgr.

Minneapolis

KBEM-FM—Licensed to Minneapolis. See Minneapolis-St. Paul

KFAI(FM)—Licensed to Minneapolis. See Minneapolis-St. Paul

KFAN(AM)—Licensed to Minneapolis. See Minneapolis-St. Paul

KFXN(AM)—Licensed to Minneapolis. See Minneapolis-St. Paul

KJZI(FM)—Licensed to Minneapolis. See Minneapolis-St. Paul

KMOJ(FM)—Licensed to Minneapolis. See Minneapolis-St. Paul

KSJN(FM)—Licensed to Minneapolis. See Minneapolis-St. Paul

KTCZ-FM—Licensed to Minneapolis. See Minneapolis-St. Paul

KTIS(AM)—Licensed to Minneapolis. See Roseville

KTIS-FM—Licensed to Minneapolis. See Minneapolis-St. Paul

KUOM(AM)—Licensed to Minneapolis. See Minneapolis-St. Paul

KXXR(FM)—Licensed to Minneapolis. See Minneapolis-St. Paul

WCCO(AM)—Licensed to Minneapolis. See Minneapolis-St. Paul

WLOL(AM)—Licensed to Minneapolis. See Minneapolis-St. Paul

WLTE(FM)—Licensed to Minneapolis. See Minneapolis-St. Paul

WWTC(AM)—Licensed to Minneapolis. See Minneapolis-St. Paul

Minneapolis-St. Paul

*KBEM-FM—(Minneapolis). Oct 4, 1970: 88.5 mhz; 2.15 kw. 370 ft. TL: N44 58 38 W93 15 55. Stereo. 1555 James Ave. N., Minneapolis 55411. Phone: (612) 668-1735. Phone: (612) 529-5236. Fax: (612) 668-1766. E-mail: kbem@mpls.k12.mn.us. Web Site: www.jazz88fm.com. Licensee: Special School District No. 1, Board of Education. Network: Network: PRI, ABC Information & Entertainment. Format: Jazz. News staff: one; News: 14 hrs wkly. Target aud: 35 plus; jazz/progsv adults, club/audiophiles. Spec prog: Bluegrass 4 hrs, Sp 4 hrs wkly. ◆Colleen Kosloski, gen mgr; Ted Allison, dev dir.

KDIZ(AM)—See Golden Valley

KDWB-FM—(Richfield). 1969: 101.3 mhz; 100 kw. 1,033 ft. TL: N45 03 30 W93 07 27. 1600 Utica Ave. S., Suite 400, Minneapolis 55416. Phone: (952) 417-3000. Fax: (952) 417-3001. Web Site: www.kdwb.com. Licensee: AMFM Radio Licenses LLC. Group owner: Clear Channel Communications Inc. (acq 8-30-00; grpsl). Rep: Clear Channel. Latham & Watkins. Format: CHR. News staff: one. Target aud: 18-34; women. ◆Dan Seeman, gen mgr.

KEEY-FM—Listing follows KFAN(AM).

*KFAI(FM)—(Minneapolis). May 1, 1978: 90.3 mhz; 125 w. 440 ft. TL: N44 58 29 W93 16 17. Stereo. 1808 Riverside Ave., Minneapolis 55454-1035. Phone: (612) 341-3144. Fax: (612) 341-4281. Web Site: www.kfai.org. Licensee: Fresh Air Inc. Format: Div. News staff: one; News: 7 hrs wkly. Target aud: General; underserved, under-represented communities. Spec prog: Black 10 hrs, folk 6 hrs, Fr 2 hrs, jazz 12 hrs, Sp 8 hrs wkly. ◆Janis Lane-Ewart, gen mgr; Kim Jackson, opns mgr & dev mgr.

KFAN(AM)—(Minneapolis). 1923: 1130 khz; 50 kw-D, 25 kw-N, DA-2. TL: N44 38 48 W93 23 31. 1600 Utica Ave. S., Suite 400, Minneapolis 55416. Phone: (952) 417-3000. Fax: (612) 417-3001. Web Site: www.kfan.com. Licensee: AMFM Broadcasting Licenses LLC. Group owner: Clear Channel Communications Inc. (acq 8-30-2000; grpsl). Format: Sports talk. News: 20 hrs wkly. Target aud: 25-54; males. ◆Mick Anselmo, VP; Dan Seeman, gen mgr; Gregg Swedberg, opns mgr; Todd Kalman, gen sls mgr; Jeff Framke, natl sls mgr; John O'Connell, mktg mgr; Mark Duevel, prom dir; Doug Westerman, progmg mgr; John Jansen, pub affrs dir; Allan Brace, engrg VP; Jess Meyer, chief of engrg.

KEEY-FM—Co-owned with KFAN(AM). June 1, 1969: 102.1 mhz; 100 kw. 1,033 ft. TL: N45 03 30 W93 07 27. Stereo. Web Site: www.k102.com. Format: Country. News staff: one; News: 2 hrs wkly. Target aud: 25-54. ◆Todd Kalman, gen sls mgr; Matt Tell, prom dir; Gregg Swedberg, progmg dir; Travis Moon, mus dir.

KFXN(AM)—(Minneapolis). Apr 5, 1962: 690 khz; 500 w-D, DA. TL: N45 01 25 W93 22 58. (CP: 1.5 kw-D, 500 w-N. TL: N44 44 58 W92 59 35). Stereo. 1600 Utica Ave. S., Suite 400, Minneapolis 55416. Phone: (952) 417-3000. Fax: (952) 417-3001. Web Site: www.thescore690.com. Licensee: AMFM Broadcasting Licenses LLC. Group owner: Clear Channel Communications Inc. (acq 8-30-2000; grpsl). Format: Syndicated sports, talk. Target aud: 25-54. ◆Mick Anselmo, pres & exec VP; Dan Seeman, gen mgr; Gregg Swedberg,

Stations in the U.S. — Minnesota

Developers & Brokers of Radio Properties
contact American Media Services at our suite:
Philadelphia Marriott Downtown
215-625-2900
843-972-2200
americanmediaservices.com
Charleston, SC
Dallas, TX · Chicago, Il · Austin, TX
American Media Services, LLC

opns dir; Todd Kalman, gen sls mgr; John O'Connell, mktg dir; Mark Duevel, prom mgr; Doug Westerman, progmg dir; Jess Meyer, chief of engrg.

KTCZ-FM—Co-owned with KFXN(AM). 1956: 97.1 mhz; 100 kw. 1,033 ft. TL: N45 03 30 W93 07 27. Stereo. Web Site: cities97.com. Format: Adult contemp. ◆ Mick Anselmo, exec VP; Dan Seeman, gen mgr; Sonia Ungurman, gen sls mgr; Dave Sheets, prom dir; Lauren MacLeash, progmg dir; Mike Wolf, mus dir.

KJZI(FM)—(Minneapolis). June 26, 1965: 100.3 mhz; 97 kw. 905 ft. TL: N45 20 12 W93 23 28. (CP: Ant 922 ft.). Stereo. 1600 Utica Ave. S., Suite 400, Minneapolis 55416. Phone: (952) 417-3000. Fax: (952) 417-3001. Web Site: www.kjzi.com. Licensee: AMFM Broadcasting Licenses LLC. Group owner: Clear Channel Communications Inc. (acq 8-30-2000); grpsl). Latham & Watkins. Format: Adult contemp, smooth jazz. Target aud: 18-49. ◆ Dan Seeman, gen mgr.

KKMS(AM)—(Richfield). Oct 18, 1949: 980 khz; 5 kw-U, DA-1. TL: N44 47 18 W93 12 54. Stereo. 2110 Cliff Rd., Eagan 55122. Phone: (651) 405-8800. Fax: (651) 405-8222. Web Site: www.kkms.com. Licensee: Common Ground Broadcasting Inc. Group owner: Salem Communications Corp. (acq 9-27-96; $3 million). Format: Christian, talk. Target aud: 18-50. ◆ John Hunt, gen mgr.

KLBB(AM)—(Saint Paul). 1936: 1400 khz; 1 kw-U. TL: N44 57 28 W93 12 23. 4930 W. 77th St., Edina 55435. Phone: (952) 820-8520. Fax: (651) 820-8502. Web Site: www.klbbradio.com. Licensee: 1400 Inc. (acq 7-20-2005; $5.2 million with KLBP(AM) Brooklyn Park). Network: Westwood One. Format: Lite music. Target aud: 35 plus. ◆ Scott Murry, gen mgr & opns mgr.

*KMOJ(FM)—(Minneapolis). Sept 15, 1978: 89.9 mhz; 1 kw. 600 ft. TL: N44 59 00 W93 17 22. Stereo. 555 Girard Terr., Suite 130, Minneapolis 55405. Phone: (612) 377-0594. Fax: (612) 377-3990. Web Site: www.kmoj.net. Licensee: Center for Communication & Development. (acq 1975). Format: Urban contemp. News staff: 2; News: 4 hrs wkly. Target aud: General. ◆ Kelvin Quarales, gen mgr.

KNOF(FM)—(Saint Paul). Apr 10, 1960: 95.3 mhz; 3 kw. 200 ft. TL: N44 56 48 W93 09 26. Stereo. 1347 Selby Ave., St. Paul 55104. Phone: (651) 645-8271. Fax: (651) 645-4593. Licensee: Selby Gospel Broadcasting Co. Network: Salem Radio Network. Format: Gospel. News: 2 hrs wkly. Target aud: All ages. Spec prog: Black 5 hrs, Sp one hr, Russian one hr wkly. ◆ Grace Adam, pres & gen mgr; Phil Mullen, opns mgr; Andy Higgins, mus dir.

*KNOW-FM— July 1, 1967: 91.1 mhz; 100 kw. Ant 1,310 ft. TL: N45 03 44 W93 08 21. Stereo. 45 E. 7th St., St. Paul 55101. Phone: (651) 290-1500. Fax: (651) 290-1224. Web Site: www.mpr.org. Licensee: Minnesota Public Radio. Format: News. ◆ William H. Kling, pres & gen mgr; Erik Nycklemoe, opns dir.

KQRS-FM—See Golden Valley

*KSJN(FM)—(Minneapolis). 1956: 99.5 mhz; 100 kw. 1,033 ft. TL: N44 03 30 W93 07 27. Stereo. 45 E. 7th St., St. Paul 55101. Phone: (651) 290-1500. Fax: (651) 290-1224. Web Site: www.mpr.org. Licensee: Minnesota Public Radio Inc. Format: Class. ◆ William H. Kling, pres & gen mgr; Erik Nycklemoe, opns dir.

KSTP(AM)—(Saint Paul). April 1924: 1500 khz; 50 kw-U, DA-N. TL: N45 01 32 W93 03 06. 3415 University Ave., Minneapolis 55414. Phone: (651) 647-1500. Fax: (651) 649-1515. Web Site: www.am1500.com. Licensee: KSTP-AM L.L.C., a Delaware L.L.C. Group owner: Hubbard Broadcasting Inc. Network: ABC Information & Entertainment. Rep: Christal. Format: Talk. News: 5 hrs wkly. Target aud: 25-54; adults. ◆ Stanley S. Hubbard, CEO; Virginia H. Morris, pres; Todd Fisher, VP & gen mgr. Co-owned TV: KSTP-TV affil

KSTP-FM—Nov 1, 1965: 94.5 mhz; 100 kw. 1,225 ft. TL: N45 03 45 W93 08 22. Stereo. Phone: (651) 642-4141. Fax: (651) 642-4239. Web Site: www.ks95.com. Licensee: KSTP-FM L.L.C. a Delaware L.L.C. Network: ABC. Rep: Christal. Format: Adult contemp. Target aud: 25-54; female. ◆ Marc Kalman, gen mgr. Co-owned TV: KSTP-TV affil

*KTIS-FM—(Minneapolis). May 1949: 98.5 mhz; 100 kw. 1,033 ft. TL: N45 03 30 W93 07 27. Stereo. 3003 Snelling Ave. N., St. Paul 55113-1598. Phone: (651) 631-5000. Fax: (651) 631-5084. Web Site: www.ktis.fm. Licensee: Northwestern College. Group owner: Northwestern College & Radio. Network: AP Network News. Bryan Cave. Format: Inspirational. News staff: one; News: 20 hrs wkly. Target aud: 25-45. ◆ Cary Humphries, chmn; Dr. Alan Cureton, pres; Dr. Paul Virts, exec VP; Harv Hendrickson, VP; Jon Engen, gen mgr.

KTNF(AM)—See Saint Louis Park

*KUOM(AM)—(Minneapolis). Jan 13, 1922: 770 khz; 5 kw-D. TL: N44 59 54 W93 11 18. Univ. of Minn., 330 21st Ave. S., Minneapolis 55455-0415. Phone: (612) 625-3500. Fax: (612) 625-2112. E-mail: radiok@tc.umn.edu. Web Site: www.radiok.org. Licensee: University of Minnesota. Dow, Lohnes & Albertson. Format: Progsv. News staff: one; News: 5 hrs wkly. Target aud: 18-34. ◆ Andrew Marlow, stn mgr; Stuart Sanders, dev dir; Larry Oberg, chief of engrg.

KXXR(FM)—(Minneapolis). Jan 6, 1961: 93.7 mhz; 100 kw. 1,033 ft. TL: N45 03 30 W93 07 27. 2000 S. E. Elm Street, Minneapolis 55414. Phone: (651) 617-4000. Fax: (612) 676-8293. E-mail: amy@93x.com. Web Site: www.93x.com. Licensee: KQRS Inc. Group owner: ABC Inc. (acq 2-94). Format: Active rock. Target aud: 25-54. ◆ Amy Rosenthal, stn mgr; Pete Frisch, sls dir; Wade Linder, progmg dir.

KYCR(FM)—(Golden Valley). Oct 27, 1961: 1570 khz; 2.5 kw-D, 237 w-N. TL: N44 57 39 W93 21 25. 2110 Cliff Rd., Eagan 55122. Phone: (651) 405-8800. Fax: (651) 405-8222. E-mail: info@kycr.com. Web Site: www.kycr.com. Licensee: Common Ground Broadcasting Co. Inc. Group owner: Salem Communications Corp. (acq 7-2-98; $2.7 million with KTEK(AM) Alvin, TX). Putbrese, Hunsaker & Trent, P. Format: Religious, talk. News: 6 hrs wkly. Target aud: 25-49; 60% female, 40% male. Spec prog: Sp 14 hrs wkly. ◆ John Hunt, gen mgr.

WCCO(AM)—(Minneapolis). Oct 2, 1924: 830 khz; 50 kw-U. TL: N45 10 40 W93 20 55. (CP: 46 kw-N. TL: N45 05 06 W93 31 06). 625 2nd Ave. S., Minneapolis 55402. Phone: (612) 370-0611. Fax: (612) 370-0159. E-mail: admin@wccoradio.cbs.com. Web Site: www.wccoradio.com. Licensee: Infinity Media Corp. Group owner: Infinity Broadcasting Corp. (acq 11-13-98; grpsl). Network: CBS. Rep: Interep. Format: News/talk. News staff: 7; News: 25 hrs wkly. Target aud: General. ◆ Brian Whittemore, gen mgr; Chuck Dickemann, opns mgr; Mary Niemeyer, gen sls mgr; Scott Bretey, natl sls mgr; Gary Wilson, engrg mgr.

WLTE(FM)—Co-owned with WCCO-TV. Aug 27, 1973: 102.9 mhz; 100 kw. 1,033 ft. TL: N45 03 30 W93 07 27. Stereo. 625 2nd Ave. S., Suite 550, Minneapolis 55402. Phone: (612) 339-1029. Phone: (612) 339-1083. Fax: (612) 339-5653. Web Site: www.wlte.com. Format: Soft adult contemp. News: 5 hrs wkly. Target aud: 25-54. ◆ Mel Karmazin, chmn; Dick Carlson, VP & gen mgr; Lori Moen, gen sls mgr; John McMonagle, natl sls mgr; Amy Zindell, prom dir; Gary Nolan, progmg dir; Steve Brown, chief of engrg.

WCTS(AM)—(Maplewood). August 1964: 1030 khz; 50 kw-D, 1 kw-N, DA-2. TL: N44 52 01 W92 54 02. 900 Forestview Ln. N., Plymouth 55441-5934. Phone: (763) 417-8270. Fax: (763) 417-8278. E-mail: wcts@centralseminary.edu. Web Site: www.centralseminary.edu/wcts. Licensee: Central Baptist Theological Seminary of Plymouth. (acq 1-30-93; $1.5 million; 11-23-92). Network: USA. Format: Christian, relg. ◆ Dennis Whitehead, gen mgr.

WDGY(AM)—(Hudson).WI Sept 19, 1959: 630 khz; 1 kw-D, 2.5 kw-N, DA-2. TL: N44 52 01 W92 54 02. 2619 E. Lake St., Minneapolis 55406. Phone: (612) 729-3776. Fax: (612) 724-0437. E-mail: radiorey630am@yahoo.com. Web Site: www.radiorey630am.com. Licensee: 630 Radio Inc. Format: Spanish music. ◆ Guadalupe Gonzales, stn mgr.

WFMP(FM)—Listing follows WIXK(AM).

WIXK(AM)—(New Richmond).WI Sept 29, 1960: 1590 khz; 5 kw-D. TL: N45 05 10 W92 34 19. 125 E. 2rd St., New Richmond, WI 54017. Secondary address: Box 8, New Richmond, WI 54017. Phone: (715) 246-2254. Fax: (715) 246-7090. E-mail: jpetersen@hbi.com. Licensee: WIXK-AM LLC. Group owner: Hubbard Broadcasting Inc. (acq 5-18-2000; with co-located FM). Network: ABC. Miller & Miller. Format: Country. News staff: one; News: 9 hrs wkly. Target aud: 25-54. ◆ Stanley S. Hubbard, CEO; Virginia H. Morris, pres; Todd Fisher, gen mgr.

WFMP(FM)—Co-owned with WIXK(AM). Sept 1, 1968: 107.1 mhz; 22 kw. Ant 587 ft. TL: N45 03 45 W93 08 21. Stereo. Phone: (651) 642-4107. Fax: (651) 647-2932. Web Site: www.fm107.fm. Licensee: WFMP-FM LLC. (acq 12-21-2000; $27 million). Network: ABC Information & Entertainment. Rep: Christal. Format: Talk.

WLOL(FM)—(Minneapolis). 1939: 1330 khz; 9.7 kw-D, 5.1 kw-N, DA-2. TL: N44 47 02 W93 20 38. 1107 Hazeltine Blvd., Suite 520, Chaska 55318. Phone: (952) 361-0019. Fax: (952) 361-5529. E-mail: wlol@relevantradio.com. Licensee: Starboard Media Foundation Inc. Group owner: Relevant Radio (acq 3-16-2004; $6.75 million). Format: Catholic. ◆ Mark Follett, CEO; John Bitting, pres; Jerry Moore, CFO; Paul Sadek, stn mgr.

*WMCN(FM)—(Saint Paul). Sept 15, 1979: 91.7 mhz; 10 w. 1,004 ft. TL: N44 36 22 W93 10 04. Stereo. 1600 Grand Ave., St. Paul 55105. Phone: (651) 696-6082. Phone: (651) 696-6000. Fax: (651) 696-6689. E-mail: wmcn@macalester.edu. Web Site: www.macalester.edu/~wmcn. Licensee: Macalester College. Format: New rock, jazz. Target aud: All ages. Spec prog: Country 2 hrs, Latin 6 hrs, multicultural 10 hrs, class 4 hrs, folk 2 hrs, jazz 4 hrs, punk 4 hrs wkly. ◆ Patrick McGrath, gen mgr; Ethan Torrey, chief of engrg.

WWTC(AM)—(Minneapolis). Aug 10, 1925: 1280 khz; 5 kw-U, DA-N. TL: N44 57 41 W93 21 24. 2110 Cliff Rd., Eagan 55122. Phone: (651) 405-8800. Fax: (651) 405-8222. Web Site: www.am1280thepatriot.com. Licensee: SCA License Corp. Group owner: Salem Communications Corp. (acq 12-18-00; $7 million. with WRRD(AM) Jackson, WI). Format: News/talk. Target aud: 18-54.

Montevideo

*KBPG(FM)— July, 2002: 89.5 mhz; 500 w. 151 ft. TL: N44 54 50 W95 44 10. American Family Radio, Box 3206, Tupelo, MS 38803. Phone: (662) 844-8888. Fax: (662) 842-6791. Web Site: www.afr.net. Licensee: American Family Association. Group owner: American Family Radio (acq 11-26-99). Network: USA. Format: Inspirational. ◆ Don Wildman, gen mgr.

KDMA(AM)— Dec 21, 1951: 1460 khz; 1 kw-U, DA-N. TL: N44 56 05 W95 44 50. Box 738, R.R. 5 160 A 56265. Phone: (320) 269-8815. Phone: (320) 269-5131. Fax: (320) 269-8449. E-mail: kdma@info-link.net. Web Site: www.kdmaradio.com. Licensee: Iowa City Broadcasting Co. Group owner: Tom Ingstad Broadcasting Group (acq 10-21-97; grpsl). Network: ABC Information & Entertainment. O'Malley. Format: Country. News staff: one. Spec prog: Farm 7 hrs wkly. ◆ Deanna Hodge, gen mgr; Dwight Mulder, opns dir & progmg dir; Roger Hill, gen sls mgr.

KMGM(FM)—Co-owned with KDMA(AM). Oct 1, 1982: 105.5 mhz; 3 kw. 300 ft. TL: N44 51 24 W95 37 46. Stereo. Web Site: www.kdmaradio.com. Format: Soft hits. Target aud: 25-54.

Moorhead

*KCCD(FM)— June 1, 1992: 90.3 mhz; 100 kw. 495 ft. TL: N46 45 35 W96 36 26. 901 S. 8th St. 56562. Phone: (218) 299-3666. Fax: (218) 299-3418. Web Site: www.mpr.org. Licensee: Minnesota Public Radio. Network: Network: NPR, PRI. Format: News. News staff: 2. Target aud: General. ◆ William Kling, pres; Vern Goodin, gen mgr; Julia Beaton, dev dir.

*KCCM-FM— Oct 23, 1971: 91.1 mhz; 67 kw. 656 ft. TL: N46 45 35 W96 36 26. Stereo. Concordia College, 901 8th St. S. 56562. Phone: (218) 299-3666. Fax: (218) 299-3418. Web Site: www.mpr.org.

Minnesota   **Directory of Radio**

Licensee: Minnesota Public Radio Inc. Network: Network: NPR, PRI. Format: Class mus, cultural progmg. News staff: 2; News: one hr wkly. Target aud: General. ♦ William H. Kling, pres; Vern Goodin, gen mgr; Julia Beaton, dev dir.

KKBX(FM)—See Fargo, ND

KLTA(FM)—See Breckenridge

KQWB-FM—Licensed to Moorhead. See Fargo ND

KVOX(AM)— Nov 30, 1937; 1280 khz; 5 kw-D, 1 kw-N, DA-2. TL: N46 49 10 W96 45 56. 1020 25th St. S., Fargo, ND 58108-2966. Phone: (701) 237-5346. Fax: (701) 235-4042. Licensee: Capstar TX L.P. Group owner: Clear Channel Communications Inc. (acq 10-30-00; grpsl). Network: ABC Daytime Direction. Rep: Allied Radio Partners, Hyett/Ramsland. Format: Sports. News: 12 hrs wkly. Target aud: 35-64. ♦ Richard Voight, gen mgr.

KVOX-FM— Nov 30, 1966; 99.9 mhz; 100 kw. 444 ft. TL: N46 49 09 W96 45 56. Stereo. Box 9919, Fargo, ND 58106. Secondary address: 2720 7th Ave. St., Fargo, ND 58103. Phone: (701) 237-4500. Fax: (701) 235-9082. E-mail: studio@froggyweb.com. Web Site: www.froggyweb.com. Licensee: Monterey Licenses L.L.C. Group owner: Triad Broadcasting Co. LLC. Rep: Christal. Shaw Pittman. Format: Country. News: 7 hrs wkly. Target aud: 25-54; female skew. ♦ David Benjamin, pres; Nancy Odney, gen mgr.

Moose Lake

WMOZ(FM)— 2001: 106.9 mhz; 6 kw. Ant 118 ft. TL: N46 30 20 W92 41 10. Agate Broadcasting Inc., 1104 Cloquet Ave., Cloquet 55720. Phone: (218) 879-4534. Fax: (218) 879-1962. Web Site: www.wklkradio.com. Licensee: QB Broadcasting Ltd. Format: Oldies. ♦ Mark Senarighi, gen mgr; Alan Quarnstron, stn mgr.

Mora

KBEK(FM)— May 12, 1995: 95.5 mhz; 25 kw. 328 ft. TL: N45 44 33 W93 22 48. Stereo. Box 136, 1947 Dennis Rd. 55051. Phone: (320) 679-6955. Phone: (763) 689-5500. Fax: (320) 679-2348. E-mail: kbek@besttimes.com. Web Site: www.besttimes.com. Licensee: Colleen McKinney, personal representative (acq 11-5-2004). Format: Lite rock, golden oldies. News: 8 hrs wkly. Target aud: General. ♦ Colleen McKinney, gen mgr, opns mgr, gen sls mgr & news dir; Robin Riley, progmg dir & mus dir.

Morris

KKOK-FM—Listing follows KMRS(AM).

KMRS(AM)— Sept 16, 1956: 1230 khz; 1 kw-U. TL: N45 36 11 W95 53 14. Box 533 56267. Phone: (320) 589-3131. Fax: (320) 589-2715. E-mail: kmrskkok@info-link.net. Licensee: Iowa City Broadcasting Co. Group owner: Tom Ingstad Broadcasting Group (acq 1-11-2000; with co-located FM). Rep: McGavren Guild. Format: News/talk, MOR. News staff: one; News: 80 hrs wkly. Target aud: 35-64; farmers & agri-business people. ♦ Deb Mattheis, gen mgr.

KKOK-FM—Co-owned with KMRS(AM). Sept 16, 1976: 95.7 mhz; 100 kw. 474 ft. TL: N45 36 11 W95 53 14. Stereo. Format: Country.

*KUMM(FM)— Sept 17, 1970: 89.7 mhz; 225 w. Ant 56 ft. TL: N45 35 20 W95 54 22. Stereo. KUMM, 600 E. 4th St. 56267. Phone: (320) 589-6076. Fax: (320) 589-6084. E-mail: kumm@kumm.org. Web Site: www.kumm.org. Licensee: University of Minnesota. Dow, Lohnes & Albertson. Format: Progsv. News: 3 hrs wkly. Target aud: 18-30; primarily college students. Spec prog: Hip hop 2 hrs, class 3 hrs, jazz 3 hrs, reggae 2 hrs, blues 2 hrs, classic rock 2 hrs. ♦ Mike Doucette, gen mgr.

Nashwauk

KMFG(FM)— October 1997: 102.9 mhz; 25 kw. 253 ft. TL: N47 24 30 W92 57 05. 807 W. 37th St., Hibbing 55746. Phone: (218) 263-7531. Fax: (218) 263-6112. Licensee: Midwest Communications Inc. (group owner; acq 5-10-2004; grpsl). Network: ABC. Format: Classic rock. Target aud: 24-55. ♦ Kristi Garrity, gen mgr.

WMFG(AM)—See Hibbing

WNMT(AM)—Licensed to Nashwauk. See Hibbing

New Prague

KCHK(AM)— Sept 22, 1969: 1350 khz; 500 w-D, 70 w-N, DA-2. TL: N44 34 39 W93 30 16. Box 251 56071. Secondary address: 25821 Langford Ave. 56071. Phone: (952) 758-2571. Phone: (952) 758-2572. Fax: (952) 758-3170. Licensee: Ingstad Brothers Broadcasting LLC (group owner; acq 5-1-2004; grpsl). Network: ABC. Rosenman & Colin L.L.P. Format: Oldies, country. News: 7 hrs wkly. Target aud: 35-59. Spec prog: Old-time mus 18 hrs, Sp. 6 hrs, Pol, Czch, Ger 40 hrs wkly. ♦ Jack B. Ludescher, gen mgr & gen sls mgr; Bud Frost, progmg dir; Dave Douglas, engrg mgr.

KRDS-FM—Co-owned with KCHK(AM). Dec 1, 1990: 95.5 mhz; 3 kw. 328 ft. TL: N44 27 41 W93 35 21. Stereo. Target aud: 25-64; general. ♦ Jack Ludescher, prom dir.

New Ulm

KNUJ(AM)— May 1949: 860 khz; 1 kw-U. TL: N44 17 10 W94 25 50. Box 368, Grand Hotel Bldg. 56073. Phone: (507) 359-2921. Fax: (507) 359-4520. Web Site: www.knuj.net. Licensee: Ingstad Brothers Broadcasting LLC (group owner; acq 5-1-2004; grpsl). Format: Country. News staff: 2; News: 30 hrs wkly. Target aud: 30 plus. Spec prog: Old-time 8 hrs wkly. ♦ Jim Bartels, sr VP; Marj Frederickson, gen mgr.

KXLP(FM)—Licensed to New Ulm. See Mankato

Nisswa

KBLB(FM)— 2002: 93.3 mhz; 100 kw. Ant 558 ft. TL: N46 26 34 W94 22 55. Box 746, Brainerd 56401. Secondary address: 13225 Dogwood Dr. S., Baxter 56425. Phone: (218) 828-1244. Fax: (218) 828-1119. E-mail: production@brainerd.net. Licensee: BL Broadcasting Inc. Group owner: Omni Broadcasting Co. (acq 12-11-00). Format: Country. ♦ G. Michael Boen, gen mgr; Al Davison, progmg dir; Nancy Carlson, news dir; Tim Mitchell, pub affrs dir.

North Branch

*KMKL(FM)— Oct 6, 2001: 90.3 mhz; 195 w. Ant 364 ft. TL: N45 24 42 W92 54 27. Stereo. 5700 W. Oaks Blvd., Rocklin, CA 95765. Phone: (916) 251-1600. Fax: (916) 251-1650. E-mail: klove@klove.com. Web Site: www.klove.com. Licensee: Educational Media Foundation. Group owner: EMF Broadcasting. Network: K-Love. Shaw Pittman. Format: Contemp Christian. News staff: 3. Target aud: 25-44; Judeo Christian, female. ♦ Richard Jenkins, pres; Mike Novak, VP; Ed Lenane, opns dir; Keith Whipple, dev dir.

North Mankato

KDOG(FM)—Licensed to North Mankato. See Mankato

KYSM(AM)—(Mankato). July 25, 1938: 1230 khz; 1 kw-U. TL: N44 10 20 W94 02 23. Stereo. 1807 Lee Blvd. 56003. Phone: (507) 388-2900. Fax: (507) 345-4675. E-mail: jobailey@clearchannel.com. Web Site: www.kysmradio.com. Licensee: Clear Channel Broadcasting Licenses Inc. Group owner: Clear Channel Communications Inc. (acq 9-25-00; grpsl). Format: Hits of the 40s, 50s & 60s. News staff: 2; News: 20 hrs wkly. Target aud: 45 plus. ♦ Jo Guck Bailey, gen mgr; Chris Painter, sls dir & gen sls mgr; Mike Anderson, prom dir; Terry Cooley, progmg dir; Randall Harter, news dir; Doug Viste, engrg dir.

KYSM-FM— April 1948: 103.5 mhz; 81 kw. 530 ft. TL: N44 10 20 W94 02 23. (CP: 100 kw, ant 541 ft.). Stereo. Format: Hot country. News staff: one; News: one hr wkly.

Northfield

*KCMP(FM)— Apr 4, 1968: 89.3 mhz; 98 kw. Ant 768 ft. TL: N44 41 19 W93 04 22. Stereo. 206 S. Broadway, Suite 735, Rochester 55904. Phone: (507) 282-0910. Fax: (507) 282-2107. Web Site: www.mpr.org. Licensee: Minnesota Public Radio (acq 11-15-2004) $10.5 million. with KMSE(FM) Rochester. Format: AAA. ♦ Chris Cross, gen mgr; Steve Nelson, progmg dir.

*KRLX(FM)— Jan 25, 1975: 88.1 mhz; 100 w. 16 ft. TL: N44 27 39 W93 09 21. Stereo. Carleton College, One N. College St. 55057. Phone: (507) 646-4102. Web Site: krlxweb.carleton.edu. Licensee: Carleton College. Network: UPI. Cohn & Marks. Format: Eclectic. Target aud: General; college-associated people and rural. ♦ Jeremy Gantz, stn mgr.

KYMN(AM)— Sept 27, 1968: 1080 khz; 1 kw-D. TL: N44 29 12 W93 06 20. Stereo. Box 201 55057. Phone: (507) 645-5695. Fax: (507) 645-9768. E-mail: kymn@clear.lakes.com. Licensee: Ingstad Brothers Broadcasting LLC (group owner; acq 5-1-2004; grpsl). Network: Motor Racing Net, Westwood One. O'Malley. Pepper & Corazzini. Format: Adult contemp. News staff: 1; News: 72 hrs wkly. Target aud: 35-54; parents with school-age children, well-educated. Spec prog: Big band 3 hrs, farm 6 hrs, relg 2 hrs, Latin/Hispanic 2 hrs wkly. ♦ James Ingstad, CEO & pres; Jim Bartels, gen mgr; Ned Newberg, stn mgr.

Olivia

KOLV(FM)— June 27, 1983: 100.1 mhz; 6 kw. 285 ft. TL: N44 45 51 W94 55 45. Stereo. Box 6 56277. Phone: (320) 523-1017. Fax: (320) 523-1018. Web Site: www.k100realcountry.com. Licensee: Bold Radio Inc. Group owner: Linder Broadcasting Group (acq 3-18-98; $335,000). Rep: Keystone (unwired net). Format: Country, farm, div. Spec prog: Big band, adult contemp, oldies, Top-40. ♦ Steve Linder, pres; Doug Loy, gen mgr; Michael Schroeder, stn mgr.

Ortonville

KCGN-FM—Licensed to Ortonville. See Milbank SD

KDIO(AM)— July 23, 1956: 1350 khz; 1 kw-D, 57 w-N. TL: N45 20 58 W96 27 10. 47 N.W. Second St. 56278. Phone: (320) 839-2581. Fax: (320) 839-2571. Licensee: Big Stone Broadcasting Inc. Group owner: Robert Ingstad Broadcast Properties (acq 10-15-99; grpsl). Network: CBS. Richard Hayes. Format: Real country. Spec prog: Farm 18 hrs, relg 5 hrs wkly. ♦ Jeff Kurtz, pres & gen mgr.

KPHR(FM)—Co-owned with KDIO(AM). 1996: 106.3 mhz; 6 kw. 328 ft. TL: N45 20 59 W96 27 08. Format: Classic rock. ♦ Jeff Kurtz, opns mgr & gen sls mgr; Jody Heemster, news dir.

Osakis

KBHL(FM)— Mar 11, 1985: 103.9 mhz; 3 kw. 341 ft. TL: N45 50 24 W95 05 56. (CP: 6 kw, ant 328 ft.). Stereo. Box 247 56360. Secondary address: 515 E. Pike St. 56360. Phone: (320) 859-3000. Fax: (320) 859-3010. E-mail: mail@praisefm.org. Web Site: www.praisefm.org. Licensee: Christian Heritage Broadcasting Inc. (acq 3-85; $14,127; 3-4-85). Network: Moody. Format: Christian. ♦ David McIver, gen mgr.

Owatonna

KRFO(AM)— 1950: 1390 khz; 500 w-D, 100 w-N. TL: N44 04 29 W93 10 46. 18th St. 55060. Phone: (507) 451-2250. Fax: (507) 451-8837. Licensee: Cumulus Licensing Corp. Group owner: Cumulus Media Inc. (acq 7-21-98; grpsl). Network: UPI. Format: Oldies. News staff: one; News: 18 hrs wkly. Target aud: 35 plus. Spec prog: Sp 2 hrs wkly. ♦ Scott Lindell, gen mgr.

KRFO-FM— Dec 29, 1966: 104.9 mhz; 4.7 kw. 200 ft. TL: N44 04 29 W93 10 46. Stereo. Format: Country. News staff: one; News: 12 hrs wkly. Target aud: 25-54.

Park Rapids

KDKK-FM—Listing follows KPRM(AM).

KPRM(AM)— Dec 1, 1962: 870 khz; 25 kw-D, 1 kw-N, DA-N. TL: N46 55 42 W95 00 22. Stereo. Box 49, Hwy. 34 E. 56470. Phone: (218) 732-3306. Licensee: De La Hunt Broadcasting Corp. Network: CBS. Format: Country. Target aud: 25 plus. ♦ Cheryl Harle, pres; Ed DeLa Hunt, gen mgr.

KDKK-FM—Co-owned with KPRM(AM). December 1967: 97.5 mhz; 100 kw. 426 ft. TL: N46 55 42 W95 00 22. Stereo. Format: Music of your life. Target aud: 40 plus. ♦ E.P. De La Hunt, gen mgr & progmg dir.

KXKK(FM)— 1998: 92.5 mhz; 25 kw. 328 ft. TL: N46 55 42 W95 00 22. Box 49 56470. Phone: (218) 732-3306. Fax: (218) 732-3307. Licensee: Bernadine A. Schumacher. Format: Hot country. ♦ Bernadine A. Schumacher, gen mgr.

Stations in the U.S. — Minnesota

Developers & Brokers of Radio Properties

contact American Media Services at our suite:
Philadelphia Marriott Downtown
215-625-2900
843-972-2200
americanmediaservices.com
Charleston, SC
Dallas, TX · Chicago, Il · Austin, TX

American Media Services, LLC

Paynesville

KZPK(FM)— Dec 1, 1995: 98.9 mhz; 50 kw. 492 ft. TL: N45 23 15 W94 24 47. 619 W. Saint Germain, St. Cloud 56301. Secondary address: Box 1458, St. Cloud 56302. Phone: (320) 251-1450. Fax: (320) 251-8952. Web Site: www.wildcountry989.com. Licensee: Leighton Enterprises Inc. (group owner; acq 4-15-97; $1 million). Format: Country. ♦Al Leighton, CEO; John Sowada, gen mgr; Denny Niess, sls VP; Gary Foss, gen sls mgr; Anna Windjue, prom dir; Matt Senne, progmg dir; Brook Stephens, mus dir; Fred Colby, news dir; Alex Hartman, chief of engrg.

Pelican Rapids

KBOT(FM)— June 1994: 104.1 mhz; 50 kw. 492 ft. TL: N46 29 57 W96 05 10. Stereo. Box 746, Detroit Lakes 56502-0746. Secondary address: 128 Junius Ave. W., Fergus Falls 56537. Phone: (218) 847-5624. Fax: (218) 847-7657. E-mail: kbot1041@yahoo.com. Web Site: www.wild1041.com. Licensee: Leighton Enterprises Inc. (group owner; (acq 9-24-96; $700,000). Network: Westwood One. O'Malley. Format: Hot country. News: one hr wkly. Target aud: 25-54; Fargo-Moorhead, metro & TSA listeners. ♦Alver Leighton, CEO; John Sowada, pres & VP; Joel Swanson, gen mgr; Andy Lia, opns mgr.

Pequot Lakes

KTIG(FM)— Apr 30, 1978: 102.7 mhz; 40 kw. 541 ft. TL: N46 40 48 W94 25 02. Stereo. Box 409 56472. Phone: (218) 568-4422. Fax: (218) 568-5950. E-mail: radio@ktig.org. Web Site: www.ktig.org. Licensee: Minnesota Christian Broadcasters Inc. Network: Network: Moody, USA. Reddy, Begley & McCormick. Format: Christian inspirational, educ, adult contemp. News staff: one. Target aud: 35-55; general. ♦Jim Gammello, pres; Mike Heuberger, gen mgr; Joe Kimbler, progmg dir; Tom Bonar, news dir; Dwayne Walker, chief of engrg.

WZFJ(FM)— 2002: 100.1 mhz; 3.9 kw. Ant 407 ft. TL: N46 40 48 W94 25 02. Box 409 56472. Phone: (218) 568-4422. Fax: (218) 568-5950. Web Site: www.z100online.com. Licensee: Minnesota Christian Broadcasters Inc. Network: Network: Moody, USA. Format: Christian rock. ♦Jim Gammello, pres; Mike Heuberger, gen mgr; Joe Kimbler, progmg dir; Tom Bonar, news dir; Dwayne Walker, chief of engrg.

Perham

KPRW(FM)— Aug 26, 1996: 99.5 mhz; 6 kw. 328 ft. TL: N46 33 16 W95 27 12. Box 363 56573. Phone: (218) 346-7596. Fax: (218) 346-7595. E-mail: kprw@eot.com. Licensee: Jerry Papenfuss. Group owner: The Result Radio Group Format: Adult hit radio. Target aud: 25-54. ♦Jerry Papenfuss, gen mgr.

Pillager

WWWI-FM— 2000: 95.9 mhz; 6 kw. Ant 239 ft. TL: N46 15 03 W94 19 30. Box 49, Park Rapids 56470. Phone: (218) 732-3306. Fax: (218) 732-3307. Licensee: Tower Broadcasting Corp. (acq 5-28-2004; $360,000). Format: Hot country. ♦David De La Hunt, gen mgr.

Pine City

WCMP(AM)— June 13, 1957: 1350 khz; 1 kw-D. TL: N45 49 10 W92 59 45. 15429 Pokegama Lake Rd. 55063. Phone: (320) 629-7575. Fax: (320) 629-3933. E-mail: pinemill@ecenet.net. Web Site: www.radiowcmp.net. Licensee: Quarnstrom Media Group LLC (group owner; acq 9-22-03). Network: ABC Information & Entertainment. Blair, Joyce & Silva. Format: News, info, music of your life. News: 25 hrs wkly. Target aud: 30 plus; farmers, commuters, homemakers. Spec prog: Farm 6 hrs wkly. ♦Al Quarstrom, CEO, COO & pres; Kim Cool, CFO; Don Welch, exec VP; Mike Knoll, gen mgr, stn mgr & sls dir; Mike Hughes, opns mgr & progmg dir; Mike Knoll, adv dir; Bill Mayes, chief of engrg.

WCMP-FM— Oct 15, 1977: 100.9 mhz; 25 kw. Ant 300 ft. TL: N45 54 07 W92 57 25. Stereo. 15429 Pokegama Lake Rd. 55063. Phone: (320) 629-7575. Fax: (320) 629-3933. E-mail: pinemill@ecenet.com. Web Site: www.radiowcmp.com. Licensee: Quarnstrom Media Group LLC (group owner; acq 8-23-01; $1.2 million. with co-located AM including five-year noncompete agreement). Network: ABC Information & Entertainment. Format: Contemp country, sports, news. Target aud: 18 plus; commuters, working adults with families. ♦Mike Knoll, gen mgr.

Pipestone

KISD(FM)—Listing follows KLOH(AM).

KLOH(AM)— June 1955: 1050 khz; 9 kw-D, 400 w-N. TL: N43 59 32 W96 20 37. Stereo. Box 456 56164. Secondary address: 608 W. Hwy. 30 56164. Phone: (507) 825-4282. Fax: (507) 825-3364. E-mail: kloh@klohradio.com. Web Site: www.klohradio.com. Licensee: Wallace Christensen. (acq 8-1-76). Network: Network: ABC Daytime Direction, ABC. Format: Talk, news, C&W, farm,. Spec prog: Relg 5 hrs, Sp 2 hrs, big band 2 hrs wkly. ♦Collin Christensen, gen mgr, natl sls mgr & chief of engrg; Carmen Christensen, gen sls mgr; Mylan Ray, mus dir; Bernie Wieme, news dir; Diane Carlson, pub affrs dir.

KISD(FM)—Co-owned with KLOH(AM). Nov 20, 1968: 98.7 mhz; 100 kw. 1,014 ft. TL: N43 53 52 W95 56 50. Stereo. E-mail: kisd@kisdradio.com. Web Site: kisdradio.com. Network: ABC. Format: Oldies. Target aud: 18-65. ♦Wally Christensen, gen mgr.

Preston

KFIL(AM)— May 21, 1966: 1060 khz; 1 kw-D. TL: N43 40 48 W92 08 27. Box 370, 300 St. Paul St. S.W. 55965. Phone: (507) 765-3856. Fax: (507) 765-2738. Licensee: KFIL Inc. Group owner: Cumulus Media Inc. (acq 3-30-2004; grpsl). Format: C&W. ♦Michael Borgen, gen mgr.

KFIL-FM— Sept 1, 1970: 103.1 mhz; 6 kw. 270 ft. TL: N43 40 48 W92 08 27. Stereo. Format: Country.

Princeton

KLCI(FM)—Listing follows WQPM(AM).

WQPM(AM)— Feb 1, 1967: 1300 khz; 1 kw-D, 83 w-N. TL: N45 32 58 W93 34 52. Box 106, 32215 124th St. 55371. Phone: (763) 389-1300. Phone: (763) 633-4262. Fax: (763) 389-1359. Licensee: Milestone Radio L.L.C. (acq 9-30-98; $1 million with co-located FM). Network: ABC. Mullin, Rhyne, Emmons & Topel. Format: Contemp country. News staff: one; News: 20 hrs wkly. Target aud: 25-54. Spec prog: Farm 2 hrs wkly. ♦Dennis Carpenter, pres; Joe Matvick, sls VP; Neil Freeman, gen mgr, opns dir & progmg dir; Jim Erickson, news dir.

KLCI(FM)—Co-owned with WQPM(AM). Dec 1, 1974: 106.1 mhz; 35 kw. 620 ft. TL: N45 23 00 W93 42 30. Stereo. Format: Country. News: 7 hrs wkly.

Proctor

KBMX(FM)— 1994: 107.7 mhz; 7.7 kw. Ant 912 ft. TL: N46 47 13 W92 07 17. 14 E. Central Entrance, Duluth 55811. Phone: (218) 727-4500. Fax: (218) 727-9356. Web Site: www.mix108.com. Licensee: Clear Channel Broadcasting Licenses Inc. Group owner: Clear Channel Communications Inc. (acq 5-2-2003; grpsl). Format: Adult Contemp. News: one hr wkly. Target aud: 25-54; working adults & families. ♦Ron Stone, gen mgr; Johnny Lee WAlker, opns mgr; Pat Puchalla, progmg dir; Dave Huston, chief of engrg.

Red Wing

KCUE(AM)— Jan 29, 1949: 1250 khz; 1 kw-D, 110 w-N. TL: N44 32 20 W92 31 25. 474 Guernsey Ln. 55066. Phone: (651) 388-7151. Fax: (651) 388-7153. E-mail: preding@waittradio.com. Web Site: 1250kcue.com. Licensee: Sorenson Broadcasting Corp. (group owner; acq 6-81; $1.1 million with co-located FM; 6-22-81). Network: ABC Information & Entertainment. Format: News/talk, farm, relg. News staff: 2; News: 7 hrs wkly. Target aud: 35 plus; information consumer. ♦Dean Sorenson, pres; Paul Reding, gen mgr & gen sls mgr; Tom Hughes, opns mgr; Cory Kampschroer, progmg dir & news dir; Mike Hendrickson, chief of engrg.

KWNG(FM)—Co-owned with KCUE(AM). Aug 26, 1965: 105.9 mhz; 20 kw. 300 ft. TL: N44 29 15 W92 13 56. Stereo. Web Site: klung.com. Network: ABC FM Connection. Format: Rock classics of the 60s, 70s & 80s. News staff: 2; News: one hr wkly. Target aud: 25-44; family & yuppie. ♦Paul Reding, stn mgr & gen sls mgr; Tom Hughes, progmg dir & mus dir.

Redwood Falls

KLGR(AM)— November 1954: 1490 khz; 1 kw-U. TL: N44 32 33 W95 07 57. (CP: 470 w. TL: N44 32 35 W95 07 57). 639 W. Bridge 56283. Phone: (507) 637-2989. Fax: (507) 637-5347. Web Site: www.klgram.com. Licensee: Three Eagles of Luverne Inc. Group owner: Three Eagles Communications (acq 12-13-99; with co-located FM). Network: ABC Information & Entertainment. Format: Country. Target aud: General. ♦Mike Neudecker, gen mgr.

KLGR-FM— June 3, 1974: 97.7 mhz; 3 kw. 305 ft. TL: N44 32 33 W95 07 57. (CP: 60 kw, ant 289 ft.). Stereo. Format: Oldies.

Richfield

KDWB-FM—Licensed to Richfield. See Minneapolis-St. Paul

KKMS(AM)—Licensed to Richfield. See Minneapolis-St. Paul

Rochester

*****KFSI(FM)**— Apr 28, 1981: 92.9 mhz; 6 kw. Ant 318 ft. TL: N44 01 27 W92 32 36. Stereo. 4016 28th St. S.E. 55904. Phone: (507) 289-8585. Fax: (507) 529-4017. E-mail: shine@kfsi.org. Web Site: www.kfsi.org. Licensee: Faith Sound Inc. Network: Moody. Format: Adult contemp Christian. ♦Ray Logan, pres & gen mgr; Paul Logan, VP & progmg dir; Jim Royston, mus dir; Mike Anderson, asst music dir; Steve Schuh, engrg VP.

*****KLSE-FM**— Dec 17, 1974: 91.7 mhz; 100 kw. Ant 953 ft. TL: N44 02 26 W92 20 28. Stereo. 206 S. Broadway, Suite 735 55904. Phone: (507) 282-0910. Fax: (507) 282-2107. Web Site: www.mpr.org. Licensee: Minnesota Public Radio Inc. Network: Network: NPR, PRI. Format: Class. News staff: one. ♦Chris Cross, stn mgr; Mary Stapek, dev dir.

*****KMSE(FM)**— Aug 1, 1998: 88.7 mhz; 250 w. Ant 531 ft. TL: N44 02 32 W92 20 26. 206 S. Broadway, Suite 735 55904. Phone: (507) 282-0910. Fax: (507) 282-2107. Web Site: www.mpr.org. Licensee: Minnesota Public Radio (acq 11-15-2004; $10.5 million. with WCAL(FM) Northfield). Format: AAA. ♦Chris Cross, gen mgr; Steve Nelson, progmg dir.

KNXR(FM)— Dec 24, 1965: 97.5 mhz; 100 kw. 1,040 ft. TL: N44 02 28 W92 20 25. Stereo. 1620 Greenview Dr. S.W. 55902-1034. Phone: (507) 288-7700. Fax: (507) 288-4531. Licensee: United Audio Corp. Network: Network: CBS, Wall Street. Rep: D & R Radio. Miller & Neely. Format: Adult traditional. Target aud: 35 plus. Spec prog: Class 4 hrs, talk 2 hrs wkly. ♦Thomas H. Jones, pres & gen mgr.

KOLM(AM)— November 1963: 1520 khz; 10 kw-D, 800 w-N. TL: N43 59 13 W92 25 05. 1220 4th Ave. S.W. 55902. Phone: (507) 288-1971. Fax: (507) 288-1520. Licensee: Cumulus Licensing LLC. Group owner: Cumulus Media Inc. (acq 3-31-2004; grpsl). Network: Westwood One. Rep: McGavren Guild. Smithwick & Belendiuk. Format: Talk. News staff: 2; News: 3 hrs wkly. Target aud: 35-64; male 55%, female 45%. Spec prog: Farm 3 hrs, Cambodian one hr, Sp 2 hrs wkly. ♦Dick Radke, gen mgr; Sue Daily, gen sls mgr; John Russell, mktg mgr & adv mgr; John Harwick, news dir & pub affrs dir; Tim Gintz, chief of engrg.

KWWK(FM)—Co-owned with KOLM(AM). July 4, 1967: 96.5 mhz; 43 kw. 528 ft. TL: N44 01 59 W92 36 10. Stereo. E-mail: dickradke@yahoo.com. Web Site: kwwkfm.com. Format: Country. News: 2 hrs wkly. Target aud: 25-54; male & female 18-49, 25-54, 35-54. ♦Sue Daily, rgnl sls mgr; Julie Jones, mus dir.

KRCH(FM)—Listing follows KWEB(AM).

KROC(AM)— October 1935: 1340 khz; 1 kw-U. TL: N44 01 47 W92 29 31. 122 4th St. S.W. 55902. Phone: (507) 286-1010. Fax: (507) 286-9370. Fax: (507) 280-0000. Web Site: www.kroc.com. Licensee: Southern Minnesota Broadcasting Co. Group owner: Cumulus Media Inc. (acq 3-29-2004; grpsl). Network: ABC Information & Entertainment. Rep: Allied Radio Partners, Hyett/Ramsland. Format: News/talk. News staff: 3; News: 42 hrs wkly. Target aud: 30-64. Spec prog: Farm 12 hrs wkly. ♦Greg Gentling, pres & gen mgr; Brent Ackerman, opns mgr; Rosanne Rybak, gen sls mgr; Joe O'Brien, progmg dir.

KROC-FM— July 1, 1965: 106.9 mhz; 100 kw. 1,110 ft. TL: N43 34 15 W92 25 37. Phone: (507) 281-2400. Web Site: www.kroc.com. Format: Contemporary hit. Target aud: 18-54. ♦James Rabe, prom mgr; Brent Ackerman, progmg dir.

***KRPR(FM)**— 1976: 89.9 mhz; 3.2 kw. Ant 590 ft. TL: N44 02 28 W92 20 25. Stereo. Rochester Public Radio, 1620 Greenview Dr. S.W. 55902-1034. Phone: (507) 288-2376. Fax: (507) 288-4531. Licensee: Rochester Public Radio (acq 5-13-99). Miller & Neely. Format: Classic rock. Target aud: General. ♦Thomas H. Jones, pres; Todd D. Brakke, gen mgr & stn mgr.

KWEB(AM)— Nov 27, 1957: 1270 khz; 5 kw-D, 1 kw-N, DA-2. TL: N43 58 47 W92 26 51. 1530 Greenview Dr. S.W., Suite 200 55902. Phone: (507) 288-3888. Fax: (507) 288-7815. Web Site: www.rochestersquare.com. Licensee: Clear Channel Broadcasting Licenses Inc. Group owner: Clear Channel Communications Inc. (acq 9-25-00; grpsl). Network: CBS. Rep: D & R Radio. Format: Sports, talk. Target aud: Men. ♦Bob Fox, gen mgr & opns mgr; Mary Ann Nonn, gen sls mgr; Mark Clark, prom dir & progmg dir; Craig Erpestad, chief of engrg.

KRCH(FM)—Co-owned with KWEB(AM). 1972: 101.7 mhz; 39.1 kw. 554 ft. TL: N44 06 59 W92 41 22. Stereo. Format: Classic rock. Target aud: 25-54.

***KZSE(FM)**— February 1989: 90.7 mhz; 1.38 kw. Ant 259 ft. TL: N44 02 26 W92 20 28. 206 S. Broadway, Suite 735 55904. Phone: (507) 282-0910. Fax: (507) 282-2107. Web Site: www.mpr.org. Licensee: Minnesota Public Radio Inc. Network: Network: NPR, PRI. Format: News & info. News staff: 2. ♦Chris Cross, gen mgr; Mary Stapek, dev dir.

Roseau

KCAJ-FM— June 1996: 102.1 mhz; 50 kw. 285 ft. TL: N48 38 50 W95 44 10. 407 3rd St. N.W. 56751. Phone: (218) 463-3360. Fax: (218) 463-1977. Web Site: www.kj102.com. Licensee: Jack J. Swanson. Network: CNN Radio. Format: Adult contemp. Target aud: General. ♦Jack Swanson, gen mgr & opns VP.

KRWB(AM)— Apr 5, 1963: 1410 khz; 1 kw-U, DA-N. TL: N48 50 40 W95 43 41. 113 A Lake St. Center, Warroad 56763. Phone: (218) 386-3024. Fax: (218) 386-3090. Web Site: www.1410krwb.com. Licensee: Border Broadcasting L.P. (acq 10-1-00; $62,000). Network: CBS. Format: Classic Rock. News staff: one. Target aud: 25-54; general. ♦Mike Pederson, gen mgr.

Roseville

***KDNI(FM)**—(Duluth). Apr 16, 1983: 90.5 mhz; 2 kw. 728 ft. TL: N46 47 21 W92 06 51. Stereo. 1101 E. Central Entrance, Duluth 55811. Secondary address: Northwestern College, 3003 N. Snelling Ave. N. 55811. Phone: (218) 722-6700. Fax: (218) 722-1092. E-mail: kdnw@kdnw.fm. Web Site: www.kdnw.fm. Licensee: Northwestern College Radio Network. Group owner: Northwestern College & Radio (acq 12-18-92). Network: AP Radio. Bryan Cave. Format: Talk, classic praise music. News: 5 hrs wkly. Target aud: 25-54; baby boomers. ♦Paul Virts, sr VP & VP; Paul Harkness, stn mgr.

***KTIS(AM)**—(Minneapolis). Feb 7, 1949: 900 khz; 25 kw-D, 300 w-N, DA-2. TL: N44 59 51 W93 21 10. 3003 Snelling Ave. N., St. Paul 55113. Phone: (651) 631-5000. Web Site: www.ktis.fm. Licensee: Northwestern College. Group owner: Northwestern College & Radio. Format: Relg, Christian, news. News staff: 2; News: 20 hrs wkly. Target aud: 35-45. ♦Paul Virts, sr VP; Jon Engen, gen mgr; Marilyn Ryan, opns dir.

Rushford

KWNO-FM— Dec 18, 1991: 99.3 mhz; 11 kw. 495 ft. TL: N43 56 32 W91 45 30. Box 767, Winona 55987. Secondary address: 752 Bluffview Cir., Winona 55987. Phone: (507) 452-4154. Fax: (507) 452-9494. E-mail: jpapenfuss@winonaradio.com. Web Site: winonaradio.com. Licensee: KAGE Inc. Group owner: The Result Radio Group (acq 6-19-95; $1 million with KWNO(AM) Winona). Wiley, Rein & Fielding. Format: Hot country. News staff: one; News: one hr wkly. Target aud: 18-49; active young students & working persons. ♦Jerry Papenfuss, CEO, gen mgr & mktg VP; Les Guderian, sls dir; Pat Papenfuss, pres, exec VP, opns mgr & prom VP; Aaron Taylor, progmg dir; Darryl Smelser, news dir; Bob Sebo, pub affrs dir.

Saint Charles

KLCX(FM)— Apr 18, 1998: 107.7 mhz; 1.95 kw. 571 ft. TL: N44 02 25 W92 13 05. 1220 4th Ave. S.W., Rochester 55902. Phone: (507) 288-1971. Fax: (507) 286-9370. E-mail: brendt@kroc.com. Licensee: Cumulus Licensing LLC. Group owner: Cumulus Media Inc. (acq 3-31-2004; grpsl). Network: Westwood One. Rep: McGavren Guild. Smithwick & Belenduik. Format: Oldies. News staff: one; News: 2 hrs wkly. Target aud: 25-49. ♦Roseanne Rybak, gen mgr.

Saint Cloud

***KCFB(FM)**— Nov 17, 1986: 91.5 mhz; 15 kw. 348 ft. TL: N45 30 02 W94 14 31. Stereo. Box 409, Pequot Lakes 56472. Phone: (320) 252-4214. Fax: (320) 252-2027. Web Site: www.kcfbradio.org. Licensee: Minnesota Christian Broadcasters Inc. (acq 9-4-97; $250,000). Network: Moody. Reddy, Begley & McCormick. Format: Christian inspirational, educ, adult contemp. News staff: one; News: 14 hrs wkly. Target aud: General. ♦Mike Heuberger, gen mgr.

KCLD-FM—Listing follows KNSI(AM).

KKSR(FM)—(Sartell). Aug 26, 1988: 96.7 mhz; 50 kw. 453 ft. TL: N45 46 03 W94 08 04. Stereo. 640 S.E. Lincoln Ave., St. Cloud 56304. Phone: (320) 251-4422. Fax: (320) 251-1855. E-mail: studio@kiss96.com. Web Site: www.kiss96.com. Licensee: Regent Licensee of St. Cloud Inc. Group owner: Regent Communications Inc. (acq 5-8-2001; grpsl). Wiley, Rein & Fielding. Format: Adult contemp. News staff: one. Target aud: 25-54. ♦Dave Ensberg, gen mgr; Lee Voss, mus dir & news dir; Merk Young, chief of engrg.

KNSI(AM)— June 1938: 1450 khz; 1 kw-U. TL: N45 32 21 W94 10 05. Stereo. Box 1458 56302. Secondary address: 619 W. St. Germain St. 56302. Phone: (320) 251-1450. Fax: (320) 251-8952. Web Site: www.1450knsi.com. Licensee: Leighton Enterprises Inc. (group owner; acq 9-15-75). O'Malley. Format: News/talk. Target aud: 35 plus; males. ♦John J. Sowada, pres, VP & gen mgr; Denny Niess, sls VP; Gary Foss, sls dir; Anna Windjue, prom dir; Daniel Ochsner, progmg dir; Fred Colby, news dir; Alex Hartman, chief of engrg.

KCLD-FM—Co-owned with KNSI(AM). May 1, 1948: 104.7 mhz; 100 kw. 984 ft. TL: N45 34 03 W94 30 43. Stereo. Web Site: www.1047kcld.com. Format: CHR. ♦Denny Niess, VP; Gary Foss, gen sls mgr; Sam Stevens, progmg dir.

***KVSC(FM)**— May 10, 1967: 88.1 mhz; 16.5 kw. Ant 446 ft. TL: N45 31 00 W94 13 52. Stereo. St. Cloud State Univ., 27 Stewart Hall 56301-4498. Phone: (320) 308-3066. Fax: (320) 308-5337. E-mail: info@kvsc.org. Web Site: www.kvsc.org. Licensee: St. Cloud State University. Format: Var/div, progsv, educ. News staff: 5; News: 15 hrs wkly. Target aud: 17-60; educated, progsv. Spec prog: Native American 4 hrs, Black 6 hrs, folk 8 hrs, jazz 15 hrs, blues 6 hrs, classic rock 8 hrs wkly. ♦Roy Saigo, pres; Jo McMullen-Boyer, CFO & stn mgr; Gretchen Rude, sr VP; Roya Majid, CEO & gen mgr.

KXSS(AM)—See Waite Park

WJON(AM)— September 1950: 1240 khz; 1 kw-U. TL: N45 33 36 W94 08 20. Box 220 56302. Secondary address: 640 Lincoln Ave. S.E. 56304. Phone: (320) 251-4422. Fax: (320) 251-1855. E-mail: wjonradio@yahoo.com. Web Site: www.wjon.com. Licensee: Regent Licensee of St. Cloud Inc. Group owner: Regent Communications Inc. (acq 5-1-99; grpsl). Network: Network: CBS, ABC Information & Entertainment. Pepper & Corazzini. Format: News/talk, full service. News staff: 3; News: 30 hrs wkly. Target aud: 25 plus. ♦Dave Engberg, gen mgr & sls dir; Bill Fink, opns mgr; J.G. Preston, progmg dir; Lee Voss, news dir; Mark Young, chief of engrg.

WWJO(FM)—Co-owned with WJON(AM). 1975: 98.1 mhz; 97 kw. 1,000 ft. TL: N45 48 52 W94 01 38. Stereo. Web Site: www.98country.com. Network: ABC Information & Entertainment. Format: Country. Target aud: 18 plus. ♦Terry Jacobs, CEO; Bill Stakelin, pres; Fred Murr, sr VP; Lynn Larson, mktg VP, prom VP & chief of engrg; Bill Fink, progmg dir; Sandi Davis, asst music dir.

Saint James

KRRW(FM)— July 24, 1983: 101.5 mhz; 14 kw. 446 ft. TL: N43 52 29 W94 36 04. Stereo. Box 1420, Mankato 56002. Phone: (507) 375-3386. Fax: (507) 375-5050. E-mail: krrw@linderradio.com. Web Site: www.myoldiesfm.com. Licensee: Minnesota Valley Broadcasting Co. Group owner: Linder Broadcasting Group (acq 1996; $800,000 with KXAC(FM) St). Miller & Miller. Format: Modern country. News staff: one; News: 16 hrs wkly. Target aud: 25-54. Spec prog: Sp one hr wkly. ♦Mike Parry, gen mgr; Dwayne Megaw, chief of opns.

KXAC(FM)— Nov. 1, 1992: 100.5 mhz; 50 kw. 433 ft. TL: N43 52 29 W94 36 04. (CP: 34 kw, ant 590 ft. TL: N43 57 04 W94 23 27). Box 1420, Mankato 56002. Phone: (507) 345-4537. Fax: (507) 345-5364. E-mail: kxac@linderradio.com. Web Site: www.myoldiesfm.com. Licensee: Minnesota Valley Broadcasting Co. Group owner: Linder Broadcasting Group (acq 1996; $800,000 with KXAX(FM) St). Miller & Miller. Format: Oldies. News staff: one; News: 17 hrs wkly. Target aud: 25-58. ♦Mike Parry, gen mgr; Dwayne Megaw, chief of opns.

Saint Joseph

KCML(FM)— 1998: 99.9 mhz; 6 kw. 328 ft. TL: N45 32 21 W94 10 05. Box 1458, St. Cloud 56302. Secondary address: 619 W. Saint Germain, St. Cloud 56301. Phone: (320) 251-1450. Fax: (320) 251-8952. Web Site: www.lite999.com. Licensee: Leighton Enterprises Inc. (group owner) Format: Contemp lite. ♦Al Leighton, CEO; John Sowada, gen mgr; Denny Niess, sls VP; Gary Foss, gen sls mgr; Anna Windjue, prom dir; Ron Linder, progmg dir; Fred Colby, news dir; Alex Hartman, chief of engrg.

KKJM(FM)— May 7, 1996: 92.9 mhz; 25 kw. 328 ft. TL: N45 38 19 W94 22 23. Stereo. 1310 Second St. N., Sauk Rapids 56379. Phone: (320) 251-1780. Fax: (320) 257-1624. E-mail: info@spirit929.com. Web Site: www.spirit929.com. Licensee: Gabriel Communications Co., St. Cloud. (acq 11-30-99). Network: Salem Radio Network. Format: Christian adult contemp. News: 5 hrs wkly. Target aud: 25-54; females. ♦Andy Hilger, CEO & gen mgr.

Saint Louis Park

***KDXL(FM)**— Mar 17, 1977: 106.5 mhz; 10 w (ST: KUOM-FM). Ant 85 ft. TL: N44 56 36 W93 21 39. Stereo. Senior High School, 6425 W. 33rd St. 55426. Phone: (952) 928-6149. Web Site: www.slpschools.org/sh/kdxl. Licensee: Independent School District 283. Format: AOR, classic rock, progsv. Target aud: 15-30; high school students & loc residents. ♦Charlie Fiss, stn mgr.

KTNF(AM)— May 13, 1958: 950 khz; 1 kw-U, DA-2. TL: N44 52 08 W93 25 11. 11320 Valley View Rd., Eden Praire 55344. Phone: (952) 946-8885. Fax: (952) 946-0888. Licensee: JR Broadcasting LLC Group owner: Infinity Broadcasting Corp. (acq 10-21-2004; $3 million). Network: ABC Information & Entertainment. Rep: McGavren Guild. Format: Talk. Target aud: 25-54. ♦Janet Robert, gen mgr.

***KUOM-FM**— Feb 17, 2003: 106.5 mhz; 8 w (ST: KDXL(FM)). Ant 253 ft. TL: N44 56 46 W93 19 27. Stereo. Univ. of Minnesota, 330 21st Ave. S., Minneapolis 55455-0415. Phone: (612) 625-3500. Fax: (612) 625-2112. E-mail: radiok@umn.edu. Web Site: www.radiok.org. Licensee: Regents of the University of Minnesota. Dow, Lohnes & Albertson. Format: Alternative. News: 5 hrs wkl;y. Target aud: 18-34. ♦Andrew Marlow, stn mgr; Larry Oberg, chief of opns; Stuart Sanders, dev dir.

KZJK(FM)— July 1, 1962: 104.1 mhz; 89 kw. Ant 1,033 ft. TL: N45 03 30 W93 07 27. Stereo. 7001 France Ave. S., Suite 200 55435. Phone: (952) 836-1041. Fax: (952) 915-6781. Web Site: www.mix1041fm.com. Licensee: The Audio House Inc. Network: ABC Information & Entertainment. Format: Hits of the 80s. ♦Mary Niemeyer, gen mgr.

Stations in the U.S. — Minnesota

Saint Paul

KEEY-FM—Licensed to Saint Paul. See Minneapolis-St. Paul

KLBB(AM)—Licensed to Saint Paul. See Minneapolis-St. Paul

KNOF(FM)—Licensed to Saint Paul. See Minneapolis-St. Paul

KSTP(AM)—Licensed to Saint Paul. See Minneapolis-St. Paul

KSTP-FM—Licensed to Saint Paul. See Minneapolis-St. Paul

WMCN(FM)—Licensed to Saint Paul. See Minneapolis-St. Paul

Saint Peter

***KGAC(FM)**— Mar 29, 1985: 90.5 mhz; 75 kw. 708 ft. TL: N44 13 20 W94 07 03. Stereo. Minnesota Public Radio Inc., 45 E. 7th St., St. Paul 55101. Phone: (800) 652-9700. Fax: (651) 290-1295. E-mail: mail@mpr.org. Web Site: www.mpr.org. Licensee: Minnesota Public Radio Inc. Network: PRI. Format: Class, arts. News staff: 2. Target aud: General. Spec prog: Folk var 17 hrs wkly. ◆William H. Kling, pres & gen mgr.

***KNGA(FM)**— Mar 1, 1992: 91.5 mhz; 8.5 kw. 600 ft. TL: N44 13 20 W94 07 03. Minnesota Public Radio, 45 E. 7th St., Saint Paul 55101. Phone: (800) 228-7123. Fax: (507) 651-1295. E-mail: mail@mpr.org. Web Site: www.mpr.org. Licensee: Minnesota Public Radio. Network: Network: NPR, PRI. Format: News, info. News staff: 2. Target aud: General. ◆William H. Kling, gen mgr.

KRBI(AM)— Aug 5, 1957: 1310 khz; 1 kw-D, 343 w-N, DA-1. TL: N44 19 51 W93 58 19. 1031 W. Grace St. 56082. Secondary address: 112 1/2 N. Main St., Le Sueur 56082. Phone: (507) 931-3220. Phone: (507) 665-3336. Fax: (507) 931-4740. Fax: (507) 665-8960. E-mail: krbi@krbi.com. Web Site: www.krbi.com. Licensee: Three Eagles Communications LLC. Group owner: Three Eagles Communications (acq 4-21-03; $3.2 million. with co-located FM). Network: ABC Information & Entertainment. Midwest Radio Reddy, Begley & McCormick. Format: Country, news/talk, sports. News staff: 2; News: 3 hrs wkly. Target aud: 25 plus; people interested in loc & rgnl news, sports, weather & country music. ◆Dave Meffert, prom dir & asst music dir; Jason Mediger, mus dir; Bruce Davis, news dir; Rick Johnson, gen mgr, gen sls mgr, adv dir, progmg dir & chief of engrg.

KRBI-FM— Sept 1, 1966: 105.5 mhz; 25.kw. 200 ft. TL: N44 19 41 W93 58 17. Stereo. Web Site: www.krbi.com. Format: Classic hits. News staff: one; News: 1 hr wkly. Target aud: 25-54; people liking classic hits - 70's, 80's, 90's & small amounts of news, weather, & sports.

Sartell

KKSR(FM)—Licensed to Sartell. See Saint Cloud

Sauk Centre

KIKV-FM— Dec 25, 1970: 100.7 mhz; 100 kw. Ant 790 ft. TL: N45 41 10 W95 08 03. Stereo. Box 1024, Alexandria 56308. Phone: (320) 762-2154. Phone: (320) 763-5458. Fax: (320) 762-2156. E-mail: 100.7@kikvfm.com. Licensee: BDI Broadcasting Inc. Group owner: Omni Broadcasting Co. (acq 9-25-89; $855,000; 10-16-89). Network: Network: ABC Information & Entertainment, AP Radio. Format: Country. Target aud: 25-54. Spec prog: Farm 20 hrs wkly. ◆Lou Buron, pres; Dave Vagle, gen mgr; Trudy Blanshan, gen sls mgr; Rick Blanshan, progmg dir; Jim Rohn, news dir; Craig Bomgaars, chief of engrg.

Sauk Rapids

WBHR(AM)— Aug 3, 1963: 660 khz; 10 kw-D, 250 w-N, DA-2. TL: N45 36 18 W94 08 21. Box 366, 1010 2nd St. N. 56379. Phone: (320) 252-6200. Phone: (320) 251-7747. Fax: (320) 252-9367. Web Site: www.660wbhr.com. Licensee: Tri-County Broadcasting Inc. Network: Radio Disney. Format: Disney radio. Target aud: Children; kids & their families. ◆Herb M. Hoppe, pres & gen mgr; Gary E. Hoppe, opns mgr & chief of engrg; Doug Kurtz, gen sls mgr.

WHMH-FM—Co-owned with WBHR(AM). Oct 31, 1975: 101.7 mhz; 50 kw. 423 ft. TL: N45 35 48 W94 09 25. Stereo. Web Site: www.rockin101.com. Format: AOR, active rock.

WVAL(AM)— Mar 1, 1999: 800 khz; 2.6 kw-D, 850 w-N, DA-2. TL: N45 36 18 W94 08 21. Box 366 56379. Secondary address: 1010 2nd St. N. 56379. Phone: (320) 252-6200. Fax: (320) 252-9367. E-mail: original@800wval.com. Web Site: www.800wval.com. Licensee: Tri-County Broadcasting Inc. Format: Classical country. ◆Herb M. Hoppe, gen mgr.

Sebeka

*KOPJ(FM)—Not on air, target date: unknown: 89.3 mhz; 100 kw. Ant 872 ft. TL: N46 40 35.9 W94 43 02. Box 209, Vonore, TN 37885. Phone: (423) 884-2800. Fax: (423) 884-2802. E-mail: office@lifetalk.net. Web Site: www.lifetalk.net. Licensee: LifeTalk Radio Inc. ◆James Gilley, pres.

Shakopee

KSMM(AM)— Oct 6, 1963: 1530 khz; 8.6 kw-D, 10 w-N, DA-2. TL: N44 48 26 W93 33 25. 1107 Hazeltine Blvd., Suite 520, Chaska 55318. Phone: (952) 361-0019. Fax: (952) 361-5529. E-mail: wlol@relevantradio.com. Licensee: Starboard Media Foundation Inc. Group owner: Relevant Radio (acq 12-2-2002). Format: Catholic. Target aud: 25-54; young adults. ◆Mark Follett, CEO; John Bitting, pres; Paul Sadek, gen mgr & stn mgr.

Slayton

KJOE(FM)— 1993: 106.1 mhz; 13 kw. 971 ft. TL: N43 53 52 W95 56 50. 2660 Broadway Ave. 56172. Phone: (507) 836-6125. Phone: (507) 836-6126. Fax: (507) 836-6537. E-mail: kjoe@kjoeradio.com. Web Site: www.kjoeradio.com. Licensee: Wallace Christensen. Format: Country. ◆Wallace Christensen, pres; Collin Christensen, gen mgr; Carmen Christensen, gen sls mgr; Bernard Wieme, prom dir; Mylan Ray, mus dir; Heath Radke, asst music dir; Joel Herrig, news dir; Diane Masie, pub affrs dir.

Sleepy Eye

KNUJ-FM— June 1, 1995: 107.3 mhz; 1.9 kw. 400 ft. TL: N44 19 38 W94 43 42. Stereo. Box 368, New Ulm 56073. Phone: (507) 359-2921. Fax: (507) 359-4520. E-mail: knuj@knuj.net. Web Site: www.knuj.net. Licensee: Ingstad Brothers Broadcasting LLC (group owner; acq 5-1-2004; grpsl). Format: Adult contemp. News staff: one; News: 20 hrs wkly. Target aud: 18-49; slightly more females than males. ◆Jim Bartels, VP; Marj Frederickson, gen mgr.

Spring Grove

KQYB(FM)— Aug 2, 1980: 98.3 mhz; 33 kw. 607 ft. TL: N43 40 53 W91 45 28. Stereo. Box 308, Hwy. 44 W. 55974-0308. Phone: (507) 498-5720. Fax: (507) 498-5766. E-mail: email@kq98.com. Web Site: www.kq98.com. Licensee: Family Radio Inc. Group owner: The Mid-West Family Broadcast Group (acq 7-19-01; grpsl). Shaw Pittman. Format: Hot country. News staff: one; News: one hr wkly. Target aud: General. ◆Dick Record, CEO.

Spring Valley

KVGO(FM)— 1993: 104.3 mhz; 2.8 kw. 472 ft. TL: N43 33 46 W92 25 29. Box 370, Preston 55965. Phone: (507) 765-3856. Fax: (507) 765-2738. Licensee: KVGO Inc. Group owner: Cumulus Media Inc. (acq 3-30-2004; grpsl). Rep: D & R Radio. Format: Oldies. ◆Bruce Fishbaugher, gen mgr & stn mgr.

Springfield

KNSG(FM)— 1995: 94.7 mhz; 50 kw. Ant 472 ft. TL: N44 21 54 W95 19 27. Stereo. 1414 E. College Dr., Marshall 56258. Phone: (507) 532-2282. Fax: (507) 532-3739. Web Site: marshallradio.net. Licensee: KMHL Broadcasting Co. Group owner: Linder Broadcasting Group (acq 3-31-2004; $525,000). Network: Westwood One. Rep: Katz Radio. Format: Adult contemp. Target aud: 30 plus; women. Spec prog: Farm 15 hrs, women 3 hrs wkly. ◆Brad Strootman, gen mgr; Heath Radke, chief of opns.

Staples

KNSP(AM)— June 3, 1982: 1430 khz; 1 kw-D, 199 w-N. TL: N46 21 34 W94 46 55. Box 551, 201 1/2 S. Jefferson, Wadena 56482. Phone: (218) 631-1803. Fax: (218) 631-4557. E-mail: kwadkkws@arvig.net. Licensee: BL Broadcasting Inc. Group owner: Omni Broadcasting Co. (acq 1-26-2004; grpsl). Network: UPI. Format: Country. Spec prog: Farm 6 hrs wkly. ◆Rick Youngbauer, gen mgr; Dan Skogen, opns dir.

KSKK(FM)— Aug 1, 1994: 94.7 mhz; 50 kw. 469 ft. TL: N46 33 08 W94 39 03. Stereo. 11 S.E. Bryant Ave., Wadena 56482. Secondary address: Box 49, Hwy. 34 E., Park Rapids 56470. Phone: (218) 631-3441. Phone: (218) 732-3306. Fax: (218) 631-3414. Fax: (218) 732-3307. E-mail: kskk@eot.com. Web Site: www.dbcradio.com. Licensee: NorMin Broadcasting Co. Network: CBS. Format: Soft hits. News: 20 hrs wkly. Target aud: 30 plus. ◆David J. De LaHunt, CEO, chmn, pres & CFO; Joleen De LaHunt, VP & stn mgr; Gene Marie Kanten, gen mgr; Heidi Hutson, gen sls mgr; Dave Lee, progmg VP; Sam Morris, chief of engrg.

Starbuck

KRVY-FM— 2001: 97.3 mhz; 50 kw. Ant 492 ft. TL: N45 31 42 W95 32 52. Box 380, Willmar 56201. Secondary address: 730 N.E. Hwy. 71, Willmar 56201. Phone: (320) 231-1600. Fax: (320) 235-7010. Web Site: www.k-musicradio.com. Licensee: Iowa City Broadcasting Co. Group owner: Tom Ingstad Broadcasting Group (acq 7-19-99; $200,000. for stock). Format: Adult contemp, light rock. News staff: one; News: 8 hrs wkly. Target aud: 25-54; male & female. ◆Doug Hanson, gen mgr.

Stewartville

KYBA(FM)— Feb 1, 1993: 105.3 mhz; 50 kw. 492 ft. TL: N43 40 23 W92 41 54. 122 4th St. S.W., Rochester 55902-3320. Phone: (507) 286-1010. Fax: (507) 286-9370. Web Site: www.y105fm.com. Licensee: Southern Minnesota Broadcasting Co. Group owner: Cumulus Media Inc. (acq 3-29-2004; grpsl). Network: ABC. Rep: Allied Radio Partners. Hyett/Ramsland. Format: Adult contemp. Target aud: 25-54. ◆Roseanne Rybak, gen mgr.

Stillwater

WMGT(AM)— Mar 13, 1949: 1220 khz; 5 kw-D, 254 w-N. TL: N45 03 15 W92 49 42. c/o Endurance Broadcasting LLC, 104 N. Main St. 55082. Phone: (651) 439-5006. Fax: (651) 439-5015. E-mail: dan@mighty1220.com. Web Site: www.mighty1220.com. Licensee: Endurance Broadcasting LLC (acq 7-5-01). Network: Network: ABC, Westwood One. Miller & Miller, P.C. Format: Talk, variety. News staff: one. Target aud: 35-64. ◆Daniel Smith, CEO, pres, gen mgr & opns VP; Gretchen Smith, VP.

Sunburg

KLFN(FM)— 2003: 106.5 mhz; 2.3 kw. Ant 525 ft. TL: N45 22 25 W95 08 23. Box 838, Willmar 56201. Phone: (320) 235-3535. Fax: (320) 235-9111. Licensee: Lakeland Broadcasting Co. (acq 10-5-01). Format: Classic rock. ◆Doug Loy, gen mgr.

Thief River Falls

KKAQ(AM)— Nov 2, 1979: 1460 khz; 2.5 kw-U. TL: N48 07 21 W96 08 24. Box 40 56701. Secondary address: Hwy. 32 N., ThiefRiver Falls

Minnesota

56701. Phone: (218) 681-4900. Fax: (218) 681-3717. Licensee: Iowa City Broadcasting Co. Inc. Group owner: Tom Ingstad Broadcasting Group (acq 11-19-99; $620,000. with co-located FM). Network: ABC Information & Entertainment. Eugene T. Smith. Format: Country. News staff: one; News: 4 hrs wkly. Target aud: 25-54. Spec prog: Oldies 6 hrs wkly. ♦ John Praska, gen mgr; Mike Johnson, progmg dir.

KKDQ(FM)—Co-owned with KKAQ(AM). Nov 1, 1989: 99.3 mhz; 6.5 kw. 167 ft. TL: N48 07 25 W96 08 31. Stereo. ♦ Rob Raymond, progmg dir.

*KNTN(FM)— Dec 13, 1991: 102.7 mhz; 100 kw. 538 ft. TL: N47 58 38 W96 36 32. Stereo. c/o KCCM, 901 S. 8th St., Moorhead 56562. Phone: (218) 299-3666. Fax: (218) 299-3418. Web Site: www.mpr.org. Licensee: Minnesota Public Radio Inc. Network: Network: NPR, PRI. Format: News. News staff: 2. Target aud: General. ♦ William H. Kling, pres; Vern Goodin, gen mgr; Julia Beaton, dev dir.

*KQMN(FM)— Nov 26, 1990: 91.5 mhz; 100 kw. 449 ft. TL: N47 58 38 W96 36 32. Stereo. 901 S. 8th St., Concordia College, Moorhead 56562. Phone: (218) 299-3666. Fax: (218) 299-3418. Web Site: www.mpr.org. Licensee: Minnesota Public Radio. Network: Network: NPR, PRI. Format: Class mus, cultural progmg. News staff: 2. ♦ William H. Kling, pres; Vern Goodin, gen mgr.

KSNR(FM)—Licensed to Thief River Falls. See East Grand Forks

*KSRQ(FM)— Nov 15, 1971: 90.1 mhz; 24 kw. 338 ft. TL: N48 01 19 W96 22 12. Stereo. 1101 Hwy. 1 E. 56701. Phone: (218) 681-0770. Phone: (800) 959-6282. Fax: (218) 681-0774. E-mail: travis.ryder @northlandcollege.edu. Web Site: www.pioneer.fm. Licensee: Northland Community & Technical College. (acq 5-29-92). Network: CNN Radio. Format: Alternative, AAA. News: 10 hrs wkly. Target aud: 18-54; professionals. Spec prog: Sp one hr, adult standards 5 hrs, Americana 4 hrs, country 5 hrs wkly. ♦ Orley Gunderson, pres; Mark Johnson, gen mgr & progmg dir; Travis Ryder, gen mgr & dev dir; Stan Mueller, chief of engrg.

KTRF(AM)— Jan 30, 1947: 1230 khz; 1 kw-U. TL: N48 07 47 W96 11 11. Box 40 56701. Phone: (218) 681-1230. Fax: (218) 681-3717. E-mail: ktrf@mncable.net. Licensee: Iowa City Broadcasting Co. (acq 9-30-97; with KSNR(FM) Thief River Falls). Network: CBS. Haley, Bader & Potts. Format: MOR, news. News staff: 2; News: 35 hrs wkly. Target aud: General; 25 plus. Spec prog: Farm 12 hrs wkly. ♦ Jon Praska, gen mgr.

Tracy

KARL(FM)— July 19, 1994: 105.1 mhz; 45 kw. 390 ft. TL: N44 19 32 W95 52 19. Stereo. Box 61, KMHL Broadcasting Co., 1414 E. College Dr., Marshall 56258. Phone: (507) 629-3355. Phone: (507) 532-2282. Fax: (507) 532-3739. E-mail: karl@marshallradio.net. Web Site: karl.marshallradio.net. Licensee: KMHL Broadcasting Co. Group owner: Linder Broadcasting Group (acq 12-17-92; $22,100; 1-11-93). Network: ABC. Format: Hot country. News: 3 hrs wkly. Target aud: General. Spec prog: Farm 15 hrs wkly. ♦ Donald Linder, pres; John Linder, VP; Brad Strootman, gen mgr; Justin Thordson, opns mgr.

Two Harbors

KZIO(FM)— September 1995: 104.3 mhz; 50 kw. 233 ft. TL: N46 55 48 W91 53 01. Stereo. 501 Lake Ave. S., Suite 200A, Duluth 55802. Phone: (218) 722-0921. Fax: (218) 723-1499. Licensee: Red Rock Radio Corp. (group owner; acq 1-10-00; grpsl). Format: Active rock. ♦ Sean Skramstad, gen mgr.

Verndale

KVKK(AM)— 2005: 1070 khz; 10 kw-D, 5 kw-N, DA-N. TL: N46 23 43 W94 57 54 (D), N46 23 45 W94 57 52 (N). Box 49, Park Rapids 56470. Phone: (218) 732-3306. Fax: (218) 732-3307. Licensee: D & E Communications. Format: Country. ♦ Edward P. DeLaHunt Sr., gen mgr.

Virginia

WEEP(AM)— Oct 12, 1936: . Stn currently dark 1400 khz; 1 kw-D. TL: N47 30 33 W92 32 31. 705 Pierce St., Eveleth 55734. Phone: (218)744-0642. Licensee: Full Armor Ministries Inc. (acq 2-13-01; $52,000). Network: ABC Information & Entertainment. Rini & Coran. ♦ Kirby Young, gen mgr.

WUSZ(FM)— June 2, 1971: 99.9 mhz; 100 kw. Ant 567 ft. TL: N47 22 52 W92 57 18. Stereo. 807 W. 37th St., Hibbing 55746. Phone: (218) 262-4545. Fax: (218) 263-6112. Web Site: www.radiousa.com. Licensee: Midwest Communications Inc. (group owner; acq 5-10-2004; grpsl). Network: Network: USA, ABC Information & Entertainment. Format: Contemp country. News: one hr wkly. Target aud: 25-49; blue and white collar workers and families. ♦ Kristi Garrity, gen mgr & sls VP.

Virginia-Hibbing

WIRR(FM)—Licensed to Virginia-Hibbing. See Duluth

Wabasha

KMFX(AM)— April 1976: 1190 khz; 1 kw-D. TL: N44 20 44 W91 58 28. 1530 Greenview Dr. S.W., Rochester 55902. Phone: (507) 288-3888. Fax: (507) 288-7815. Web Site: www.foxcountry.net. Licensee: Clear Channel Broadcasting Licenses Inc. Group owner: Clear Channel Communications Inc. (acq 9-25-2000; grpsl). Format: Hot Country. Target aud: 18-54. ♦ Bob Fox, gen mgr; Craig Erpestad, opns dir & progmg dir; Mary Anne Nons, gen sls mgr.

Wadena

KKWS(FM)—Listing follows KWAD(AM).

KWAD(AM)— Apr 24, 1948: 920 khz; 1 kw-U. TL: N46 22 15 W95 08 58. Box 551 56482. Secondary address: 201 1/2 S. Jefferson S. 56482. Phone: (218) 631-1803. Fax: (218) 631-4557. E-mail: rick@kwadknsp.com. Web Site: www.kwadknsp.com. Licensee: BL Broadcasting Inc. Group owner: Omni Broadcasting Co. (acq 1-26-2004; grpsl). Network: ABC Information & Entertainment. Format: C&W. News staff: one; News: 20 hrs wkly. Target aud: General. Spec prog: Farm 10 hrs wkly. ♦ Jeff Hilborne, sls dir; Rick Young Bauer, gen mgr & gen sls mgr.

KKWS(FM)—Co-owned with KWAD(AM). Sept 23, 1968: 105.9 mhz; 100 kw. 564 ft. TL: N46 36 00 W94 54 03. Stereo. Web Site: www.superstationk106.com. Network: ABC Information & Entertainment. Format: Country. News staff: one.

Waite Park

KLZZ(FM)—Listing follows KXSS(AM).

KXSS(AM)— Jan 1, 1981: 1390 khz; 2.5 kw-D, 1 kw-N, DA-2. TL: N45 32 31 W94 15 41. Stereo. 640 S.E. Lincoln Ave., St. Cloud 56304. Phone: (320) 251-4422. Fax: (320) 251-1855. Licensee: Regent Licensee of St. Cloud Inc. Group owner: Regent Communications Inc. (acq 5-8-2001; grpsl). Format: Classic Country. Target aud: 18-49. ♦ William Stakelin, pres; David Engberg, gen mgr & gen sls mgr; Dick Nelson, progmg dir; Lee Voss, news dir; Mark Young, chief of engrg.

KLZZ(FM)—Co-owned with KXSS(AM). July 1989: 103.7 mhz; 3 kw. 328 ft. TL: N45 32 35 W94 15 41. (CP: 25 kw. TL: N45 29 02 W94 08 12). Web Site: www.1037theloon.com. Format: Classic rock. ♦ Don Monson, progmg dir.

Walker

KAKK(AM)— July 11, 1970: 1570 khz; 1 kw-D, 250 w-N. TL: N47 04 58 W94 35 21. Box 1022 56484. Phone: (218) 547-4000. Fax: (218) 547-4001. Licensee: Edward De La Hunt (acq 12-26-00). Format: Oldies. Target aud: General. ♦ Brad Walhof, gen mgr & gen sls mgr.

KLLZ-FM— May 6, 1984: 99.1 mhz; 100 kw. Ant 505 ft. TL: N47 12 52 W94 55 18. Stereo. Box 1656, Bemidji 56619-1656. Secondary address: 502 Beltrami Ave. N.W., Beltrami 56601. Phone: (218) 444-1500. Fax: (218) 751-8091. Licensee: BG Broadcasting Inc. Group owner: Omni Broadcasting Co. (acq 10-24-00). Network: ABC. Garvey, Schubert & Barer. Format: Classic rock. News staff: one; News: 3 hrs wkly. Target aud: 25-54; Adults. ♦ Lou Buron, CEO & pres; Mary Campbell, CFO & VP; Harry Hastings, stn mgr; Jack Hicks, progmg dir.

KQKK(FM)— May 1, 1999: 101.9 mhz; 50 kw. 328 ft. TL: N47 03 03 W94 28 12. Stereo. Box 1022, Hwy. 34 W. 56484. Phone: (218) 547-4000. Fax: (218) 547-4001. E-mail: kqkkkakk@eot.com. Web Site: www.dbcradionet.com/kqkk. Licensee: CJ Broadcasting. Network: CBS Radio. Format: Adult contemp. ♦ Bradley J. Walhof, gen mgr.

Directory of Radio

Warroad

KKWQ(FM)— August 1989: 92.5 mhz; 100 kw. 472 ft. TL: N48 49 41 W92 23 16. Stereo. 113A Lake St. Ctr., Box 69 56763. Phone: (218) 386-3024. Fax: (218) 386-3090. Web Site: www.kq92.com. Licensee: Border Broadcasting LP (acq 1996). Network: Network: ABC, Jones Radio Networks. Format: Country. Target aud: 25-54. ♦ Mike Pederson, pres & gen mgr.

Waseca

KOWZ(AM)— Dec 22, 1971: 1170 khz; 2.5 kw-D, 60 w-N, 1 kw-CH. TL: N44 02 45 W93 23 08 (D), N44 04 45 W93 30 24 (N). 222 N. State St. 56093. Phone: (507) 835-5555. Fax: (507) 835-2030. Licensee: Main Street Broadcasting Inc. Group owner: Linder Broadcasting Group (acq 12-26-01; with co-located FM). Miller & Miller. Format: News, talk. News staff: 2; News: 12 hrs wkly. Target aud: 30-65; general, farm. ♦ Lynn Ketelsen, gen mgr; Colleen Carlson, sls dir; Don White, progmg dir.

KRUE(FM)—Co-owned with KOWZ(AM). June 1972: 92.1 mhz; 25 kw. 286 ft. TL: N44 02 45 W93 23 08. Stereo. Web Site: www.star92radio.com. Rep: Interep. Format: Hit country. News staff: one; News: 4 hrs wkly. Target aud: 25-50.

Watertown

KZGX(AM)— May 16, 1996: 1600 khz; 5 kw-U, DA-1. TL: N44 55 23 W93 46 56. Box 192 55388. Phone: (952) 955-1606. Fax: (952) 955-1655. Web Site: www.kwom1600.com. Licensee: WM Broadcasting Inc. (acq 2-9-2004; $600,000). Network: ABC. Format: Oldies. News staff: one. Target aud: 35 plus; general. ♦ Mike Parry, gen mgr; Randy Asplund, opns mgr.

Willmar

*KBHZ(FM)— Feb 16, 1996: 91.9 mhz; 25 kw. 328 ft. TL: N45 00 40 W94 53 56. Box 247, Osakis 56360. Secondary address: 106 Litchfield Ave. W. 56201. Phone: (320) 859-3000. Fax: (320) 859-3010. E-mail: mail@praisefm.org. Web Site: www.praisefm.org. Licensee: Christian Heritage Broadcasting Inc. Format: Worship mus. ♦ David McIver, gen mgr.

KDJS(AM)— Mar 2, 1981: 1590 khz; 1 kw-D, 89 w-N, DA-2. TL: N45 05 07 W95 00 19. Box 380, 730 N.E. Hwy. 71 56201. Phone: (320) 231-1600. Fax: (320) 235-7010. Licensee: Iowa City Broadcasting Inc. (acq 4-1-2000; with co-located FM). Format: Oldies. News staff: one. Target aud: 25-54. Spec prog: Farm 5 hrs wkly. ♦ Doug Hanson, gen mgr & gen sls mgr.

KDJS-FM— May 17, 1993: 95.3 mhz; 50 kw. 436 ft. TL: N45 01 23 W95 15 57. Stereo. Hyett/Ramsland Format: Country. News staff: one. ♦ Steve Youngberg, engrg mgr.

*KKLW(FM)— Jan 29, 2004: 90.9 mhz; 400 w. Ant 423 ft. TL: N45 11 52 W94 56 58. Stereo. 5700 W. Oaks Blvd., Rocklin, CA 95765. Phone: (916) 251-1600. Fax: (916) 251-1650. E-mail: klove@klove.com. Web Site: www.klove.com. Licensee: Educational Media Foundation. Group owner: EMF Broadcasting. Network: K-Love. Shaw Pittman. Format: Contemp Christian. News staff: 3. Target aud: 25-44; Judeo Christian, female. ♦ Richard Jenkins, pres; Mike Novak, VP & progmg dir; Lloyd Parker, gen mgr; Ed Lenane, opns dir & news dir; Keith Whipple, dev dir; Eric Allen, natl sls mgr; John D. Burkholder, rgnl sls mgr; Chris Joyce, prom dir; David Pierce, progmg mgr; Jon Rivers, mus dir; Sam Wallington, engrg dir.

KQIC(FM)—Listing follows KWLM(AM).

KWLM(AM)— 1940: 1340 khz; 1 kw-U. TL: N45 08 00 W95 02 35. Box 838, 1340 N. 7th St. 56201. Phone: (320) 235-1340. Fax: (320) 235-9111. Web Site: www.kwlm.com. Licensee: Steven W. Linder. (acq 4-5-91; $691,937 with co-located FM; 4-22-91). Network: ABC Information & Entertainment. Format: News/talk. News staff: 3; News: 30 hrs wkly. Target aud: General. Spec prog: Farm 8 hrs wkly. ♦ J.P. Cola, gen mgr & news dir; Doug Loy, gen sls mgr; Pete Hoagland, chief of engrg.

KQIC(FM)—Co-owned with KWLM(AM). July 1, 1965: 102.5 mhz; 100 kw. 830 ft. TL: N45 11 40 W95 05 01. Stereo. Phone: (320) 235-3535. Web Site: www.1025fm.com. Format: Adult contemp. Target aud: 18-49. ♦ Doug Loy, gen mgr & engrg mgr; MaryElin Macht, mus dir.

Stations in the U.S.

Mississippi

Developers & Brokers of Radio Properties

contact American Media Services at our suite:
Philadelphia Marriott Downtown
215-625-2900
843-972-2200
americanmediaservices.com
Charleston, SC
Dallas, TX • Chicago, Il • Austin, TX
American Media Services, LLC

Windom

KDOM(AM)— Dec 28, 1958: 1580 khz; 1 kw-D, 2 w-N, DA-2. TL: N43 51 41 W95 05 50. Box 218 56101. Phone: (507) 831-3908. Fax: (507) 831-3913. Web Site: www.kdomradio.com. Licensee: Windom Radio Inc. (acq 4-89; with co-located FM; 4-14-80). Network: ABC Daytime Direction. Format: Country, news/talk, sports. News staff: one; News: 21 hrs wkly. Target aud: General; farm audience, housewives, business owners & laborers. ♦Dave Cory, gen mgr, gen sls mgr, adv mgr & progmg mgr; Dirk Abraham, news dir.

KDOM-FM— Dec 8, 1976: 94.3 mhz; 5.7 kw. 335 ft. TL: N43 53 06 W95 10 53. Stereo. Web Site: www.kdomradio.com. ♦Dave Cory, sls VP.

KQRB(FM)— February 2003: 89.9 mhz; 250 w. Ant 171 ft. TL: N43 51 15 W95 07 30. Box 3206, American Family Radio, Tupelo, MS 38803. Phone: (662) 844-8888. Fax: (662) 842-6791. Web Site: www.afr.net. Licensee: American Family Association. Group owner: American Family Radio. Network: USA. Format: Christian. ♦Roy Willoff, gen mgr.

Winona

KAGE(AM)— Feb 17, 1957: 1380 khz; 4 kw-D. TL: N44 02 13 W91 37 09. Box 767, 752 Bluffview Cir. 55987-0767. Phone: (507) 452-4000. Fax: (507) 452-2867. E-mail: jpapenfuss@winonaradio.com. Web Site: www.winonaradio.com. Licensee: KAGE Inc. Group owner: The Result Radio Group (acq 1-73). Wiley, Rein & Fielding. Format: C&W. News staff: one; News: 7 hrs wkly. Target aud: 35 plus; general. Spec prog: Farm, relg. ♦Pat Papenfuss, pres, opns mgr & progmg dir; Jerry Papenfuss, gen mgr; Les Guderian, sls dir & gen sls mgr; Darryl Smelser, news dir; Steve Schuh, chief of engrg.

KAGE-FM— Aug 14, 1971: 95.3 mhz; 11 kw. 495 ft. TL: N44 02 31 W91 40 47. Stereo. Web Site: www.winonaradio.com. Format: Adult contemp. News staff: one; News: 14 hrs wkly. Target aud: 25-54. ♦Jerry Papenfuss, CEO; Aaron Taylor, progmg dir.

KHME(FM)— June 4, 1992: 101.1 mhz; 25 kw. 741 ft. TL: N44 04 26 W91 34 38. Stereo. Box 767 55987. Secondary address: 752 Bluffview Cir. 55987. Phone: (507) 452-4000. Fax: (507) 452-9494. E-mail: khme@hbci.com. Web Site: www.winonaradio.com/khme101. Licensee: KAGE Inc. Group owner: The Result Radio Group (acq 10-19-01; $1 million). Format: Soft rock. News staff: 2; News: 21 hrs wkly. Target aud: 25-54; women. ♦Jerry Papenfuss, gen mgr; Les Guderian, gen sls mgr; Kersten Kappmeyer, progmg dir; Pat Papen Fuss, opns mgr & chief of engrg.

***KQAL(FM)**— Dec 12, 1975: 89.5 mhz; 1.8 kw. 628 ft. TL: N44 02 52 W91 38 40. Stereo. Box 5838, 175 W. Mark St. 55987-0838. Phone: (507) 453-2222. Fax: (507) 457-5226. Web Site: www.kqal.org. Licensee: Winona State University. Network: AP Radio. Format: Jazz, AOR. News: 5 hrs wkly. Target aud: General. Spec prog: Class 14 hrs, pub affrs 10 hrs wkly. ♦Ajit Daniel, gen mgr.

***KSMR(FM)**— Nov 1, 1978: 92.5 mhz; 4 w. -141 ft. TL: N42 02 47 W91 41 43. Stereo. St. Mary's University, #29, 700 Terrace Heights 55987-1399. Phone: (507) 457-1613. Fax: (507) 457-1439. Web Site: www.smumn.edu. Licensee: St. Mary's University Format: AOR, hip hop, varied. Target aud: 18-24. ♦Dean Beckman, gen mgr.

KWNO(AM)— January 1938: 1230 khz; 1 kw-U. TL: N44 01 52 W91 38 31. 752 Bluffview Cir. 55987-0767. Phone: (507) 452-4154. Fax: (507) 452-9494. E-mail: jrhyner@winonaradio.com. Web Site: www.winonaradio.com. Licensee: KAGE Inc. Group owner: The Result Radio Group (acq 6-19-95; $1 million with KWNO-FM Rushford). Network: ABC Information & Entertainment. Wiley, Rein & Fielding. Format: Oldies, news/talk, sports. News staff: one; News: 21 hrs wkly. Target aud: 35 plus; Sports fans. Spec prog: Polka 5 hrs wkly. ♦Jerry Papenfuss, CEO & gen mgr; Pat Papenfuss, chmn, exec VP, opns VP & opns mgr.

Worthington

***KBOJ(FM)**— 2002: 88.1 mhz; 250 w. Ant 144 ft. TL: N43 35 53 W95 37 30. Box 3206, American Family Radio, Tupelo, MS 38803. Phone: (662) 844-8888. Fax: (662) 842-6791. Web Site: www.afr.net. Licensee: American Family Association. Group owner: American Family Radio Network: USA. Format: Christian. ♦Marvin Sanders, gen mgr.

KITN(FM)— November 1994: 93.5 mhz; 50 kw. 466 ft. TL: N43 31 31 W95 24 47. 28779 County Hwy. 35 56187. Phone: (507) 376-9350. Phone: (800) 886-KITN. Fax: (507) 376-5071. E-mail: kitn@frontiernet.net. Web Site: www.935theeagle.com. Licensee: Three Eagles of Luverne Inc. Group owner: Three Eagles Communications (acq 12-23-99; grpsl). Network: ABC Information & Entertainment. Format: Classic rock. News staff: one; News: 15 hrs wkly. Target aud: 25-49. ♦Gary Buchanan, CFO & prom dir; Joel Koetke, gen mgr & stn mgr; Matt Widboom, opns mgr.

***KRSW(FM)**— December 1973: 89.3 mhz; 100 kw. Ant 554 ft. TL: N43 53 01 W95 55 44. Stereo. 1450 College Way 56187. Phone: (605) 335-6666. Fax: (605) 335-1259. Licensee: Minnesota Public Radio Inc. Network: Network: PRI, NPR. Format: Class. ♦William H. Kling, pres & gen mgr; Kara Hetland, news dir.

KWOA(AM)— Oct 11, 1947: 730 khz; 1 kw-U, 159 w-N. TL: N43 37 48 W95 40 32. 28779 County Hwy. 35 56187. Phone: (507) 376-6165. Fax: (507) 376-5071. E-mail: kwoa@rconnect.com. Web Site: www.kwoa.com. Licensee: Three Eagles of Luverne Inc. Group owner: Three Eagles Communications (acq 12-23-99; grpsl). Network: CBS. Rep: Hyett/Ramsland. Midwest Radio. Pepper & Corazzini. Format: News/talk. News staff: 2; News: 18 hrs wkly. Target aud: 35 plus. Spec prog: Farm. ♦Joel Koepke, gen mgr & gen sls mgr; Matt Widboom, progmg dir; Darrell Stitt, news dir.

KWOA-FM— May 3, 1961: 95.1 mhz; 100 kw. 660 ft. TL: N43 37 48 W95 40 32. Stereo. Format: Adult contemp. News staff: one; News: 10 hrs wkly. Target aud: 25-40. ♦Tony Winter, progmg dir & mus dir.

Worthington-Marshall

***KNSW(FM)**— 1979: 91.7 mhz; 99 kw. Ant 797 ft. TL: N43 53 01 W95 55 44. Minnesota Public Radio, 45 7th St. E., Saint Paul 55101-2202. Phone: (651) 290-1500. Fax: (651) 290-1224. Web Site: www.mpr.org. Licensee: Minnesota Public Radio. Format: News/talk. ♦William H. Kling, gen mgr.

Mississippi

Aberdeen

WACR-FM— June 1, 1975: 105.3 mhz; 30 kw. 295 ft. TL: N33 55 20 W88 33 25. Stereo. Box 3300, 5026 Cliff Gookin Blvd., Tupelo 38803. Phone: (662) 844-2134. Fax: (662) 842-0725. E-mail: rickstevens @clearchannel.com. Web Site: www.kz105.com. Licensee: Urban Radio Licenses LLC. (acq 4-26-2005; $1.1 million). Format: CHR. Target aud: 18-34 & 25-54. ♦Mark Maharrey, gen mgr; Rick Stevens, opns VP.

WWZQ(AM)— February 1952: 1240 khz; 1 kw-U. TL: N33 48 32 W88 32 33. Box 458, Amory 38821. Phone: (662) 256-9726. Fax: (662) 256-9725. E-mail: wamywafm@traceroad.net. Web Site: www.fm95radio.com. Licensee: Stanford Communications Inc. (group owner; acq 12-2-99; $51,000). Network: UPI. Format: Oldies. Spec prog: Gospel 8 hrs wkly. ♦Ed Stanford, gen mgr.

Ackerman

WFCA(FM)— 1986: 107.9 mhz; 100 kw. 1,007 ft. TL: N33 25 25 W89 24 13. Stereo. R.R. 1 Box 12, 155 Mecklin, French Camp 39745. Phone: (662) 547-6414. Fax: (662) 547-9451. E-mail: sales@wfcafm108.com. Web Site: www.wfcafm108.com. Licensee: French Camp Radio Inc. Format: Southern gospel. Target aud: General. ♦Charles S. Carroll, stn mgr.

Amory

WACR-FM—See Aberdeen

WAFM(FM)—Listing follows WAMY(AM).

WAMY(AM)— Oct 23, 1955: 1580 khz; 1 kw-D. TL: N33 58 33 W88 29 29. Box 458 38821. Secondary address: 521 Hwy.278 W. 38821. Phone: (662) 256-9726. Fax: (662) 256-9725. E-mail: wamywafm@traceroad.net. Web Site: fm95radio.com. Licensee: Stanford Communications Inc. (group owner; acq 9-21-92; $85,000 with co-located FM; 11-9-92). Network: USA. Format: Sports, talk/news. News staff: one. Target aud: Genral. Spec prog: Relg 6 hrs, Gospel 6 hrs wkly. ♦Ed Stanford, CEO, gen mgr, sls VP & news dir; Teresa Stanford, VP; Ken Wardlaw, opns mgr, progmg mgr & mus dir; Olen Booth, chief of engrg.

WAFM(FM)—Co-owned with WAMY(AM). 1974: 95.3 mhz; 6 kw. 272 ft. TL: N33 58 33 W88 29 29. Stereo. Web Site: www.fm95radio.com. Network: ABC Daytime Direction. Format: Oldies. Spec prog: Relg 2 hrs wkly. ♦Ken Wardlaw, mus dir; Olen Booth, engrg VP.

Artesia

WSMS(FM)— 1985: 99.9 mhz; 6 kw. Ant 328 ft. TL: N33 39 14 W88 37 15. 200 6th St. N., Suite 205, Columbus 39701. Phone: (662) 327-1183. Fax: (662) 328-1122. Web Site: www.999thefoxrocks.com. Licensee: Cumulus Licensing Corp. Group owner: Cumulus Media Inc. (acq 9-99; grpsl). Format: Classic rock. Target aud: 18-49. ♦Greg Benefield, gen mgr.

Baldwyn

WESE(FM)— Oct 1, 1980: 92.5 mhz; 5.4 kw. 328 ft. TL: N34 26 32 W88 41 11. Box 3300, Tupelo 38803. Secondary address: 5026 Cliff Gookin Blvd., Tupelo 38801. Phone: (662) 842-1067. Fax: (662) 842-0725. Web Site: www.925jamz.com. Licensee: Clear Channel Broadcasting Licenses Inc. Group owner: Clear Channel Communications Inc. (acq 12-19-00; grpsl). Network: ABC. Rep: Interep. Format: Urban contemp. Target aud: 18-54. Spec prog: Gospel 6 hrs, Blues 6 hrs wkly. ♦Mark Maharrey, gen mgr; Rick Stevens, opns VP.

Batesville

WBLE(FM)—Listing follows WJBI(AM).

WJBI(AM)— June 19, 1953: 1290 khz; 730 w-D, 91 w-N. TL: N31 18 13 W89 58 59. Box 1528 38606. Phone: (662) 563-1290. Fax: (662) 563-9002. Licensee: Batesville Broadcasting Co. Inc. (acq 4-1-78). Network: ABC Information & Entertainment. Format: Nostalgia. Target aud: 30 plus. Spec prog: Gospel. ♦J. Boyd Ingram, pres; John P. Ingram, gen mgr.

WBLE(FM)—Co-owned with WJBI(AM). Aug 1, 1978: 100.5 mhz; 50 kw. 492 ft. TL: N34 18 13 W89 58 59. Stereo. Format: Country. Target aud: 25 plus.

Bay Springs

WIZK(AM)—Not on air, target date: Aug 05, 2002: 1570 khz; 3.2 kw-D. TL: N31 57 56 W89 18 03. Box 548, 150 Bay Ave. 39422. Phone: (601) 764-9888. Licensee: M. Jerome Hughey (Acq 3-15-02.). Format: Traditional Country, Southern gospel, oldies,. Target aud: 25-54; baby boomers & older consumers. ♦Mitchell Jerome Hughey, CEO, pres & gen mgr; Mitchell ODell Hughey, opns VP; Tom Diaz, stn mgr & chief of engrg.

WKZW(FM)— July 7, 1975: 94.3 mhz; 3 kw. 328 ft. TL: N31 59 00 W89 13 50. (CP: 50 kw, ant 531 ft.). Stereo. Box 6408, Laurel 39441. Secondary address: Box 16596, Hattiesburg 39404. Phone: (601)

Broadcasting & Cable Yearbook 2006

Mississippi — Directory of Radio

649-0095. Fax: (601) 649-8199. E-mail: kz94@kz94.com. Web Site: www.kz94.c0m. Licensee: Blakeney Communications Inc. (group owner; acq 3-25-98; $553,000 for stock). Format: Hot adult contemp. Target aud: 18-60; average working people. ◆ Larry Blakeney, pres; Randy Blakeney, gen mgr & engrg dir; Stephen St. James, progmg dir.

Bay St. Louis

WBSL(AM)— March 1974: 1190 khz; 5 kw-D. TL: N30 19 25 W89 21 03. 1190 Casino Magic Dr. 39520. Phone: (228) 467-1190. Phone: (228) 467-7009. Fax: (228) 467-5295. Licensee: Hancock Broadcasting Corp. Format: Blues/talk. News staff: one; News: 6 hrs wkly. Target aud: Men 25-54; sports enthusiasts. Spec prog: Gospel 13 hrs wkly. ◆ Ira Hatchett, CEO; Benni Hatchett, pres; Barry Hatchett, exec VP; Delores Hatchett, VP.

WZKX(FM)— Licensed to Bay St. Louis. See Poplarville

Belzoni

WBYP(FM)— 1986: 107.1 mhz; 9.4 kw. Ant 531 ft. TL: N33 03 04 W90 37 51. Stereo. Box 130, Yazoo City 39194. Secondary address: 611 Center Park Ln., Yazoo City Phone: (662) 746-7676. Fax: (662) 746-1525. E-mail: zoobel@bellsouth.net. Web Site: www.zoobelbroadcasting.com. Licensee: Zoo-Bel Broadcasting LLC. Format: Country, southern gospel. News staff: 3; News: 18 hrs wkly. Target aud: 18-65; Adults. Spec prog: Black 7 hrs wkly. ◆ Colon Johnston, gen mgr, sls dir, progmg dir & chief of engrg.

WELZ(AM)— 1959: 1460 khz; 1 kw-D. TL: N33 10 24 W90 28 51. Box 130, Yazoo City 39194. Phone: (662) 746-7676. Fax: (662) 746-1525. Web Site: www.zoobelbroadcasting.com. Licensee: Zoo-Bel Broadcasting LLC. (acq 6-9-98; $200,000). Format: Southern gospel am, gospel pm. Target aud: 12 plus; general. Spec prog: Black 20 hrs wkly. ◆ Colon Johnston, gen mgr.

Biloxi

***WMAH-FM**— December 1983: 90.3 mhz; 100 kw. 1,410 ft. TL: N30 45 14 W88 56 44. Stereo. 3825 Ridgewood Rd., Jackson 39211. Phone: (601) 432-6565. Fax: (601) 432-6806. Web Site: www.mpbonline.org. Licensee: Mississippi Authority for Educational Television. Network: Network: PRI, NPR. Schwartz, Woods & Miller. Format: Class, news/talk, jazz. News staff: 5; News: 20 hrs wkly. Target aud: General. ◆ Marie Antoon, chmn; Gene Edwards, gen mgr; Bob Holland, opns mgr & progmg mgr; Ty Warren, dev mgr; Tippy Garner, rgnl sls mgr; Jennifer Griffin, prom mgr; Greg Waxberg, mus dir; Dick Rizzo, news dir; Keith Martin, engrg dir.

WMJY(FM)— July 11, 1966: 93.7 mhz; 100 kw. 1,012 ft. TL: N30 29 09 W88 42 53. Stereo. 286 Debuys Rd. 39531. Phone: (228) 388-2323. Fax: (228) 388-2362. E-mail: reggiebates@clearchannel.com. Web Site: www.magic937.com. Licensee: Clear Channel Broadcasting Licenses Inc. Group owner: Clear Channel Communications Inc. (acq 2-2-2004; grpsl). Network: Premiere Action. Format: Adult contemp. News staff: one; News: 5 hrs wkly. Target aud: 25-54. ◆ Reggie Bates, gen mgr.

WTNI(AM)— 2003: 1640 khz; 10 kw-D, 1 kw-N. TL: N30 28 27 W88 51 23. 1909 E. Pass Rd., Suite D-11, Gulfport 39507. Phone: (228) 388-2001. Fax: (228) 896-9114. Web Site: www.1640wtni.com. Licensee: Monterey Licenses LLC. Group owner: Triad Broadcasting Co. LLC (acq 5-16-00). Format: News/talk, info. ◆ Mary Bigelow, stn mgr.

WXBD(AM)— May 1948: 1490 khz; 1 kw-U. TL: N30 23 38 W88 59 58. 1909 E. Pass Rd., Suite D-11, Gulfport 39507. Phone: (228) 388-2001. Fax: (228) 896-9736. Fax: (228) 896-9114. E-mail: wxbd@sportsradiowxbd.com. Web Site: www.sportsradiowxbd.com. Licensee: Monterey Licenses LLC. Group owner: Triad Broadcasting Co. LLC (acq 6-30-99; grpsl). Shaw Pittman. Format: ESPN sports. ◆ Jay Taylor, opns mgr.

Booneville

WBIP(AM)— Sept 1, 1950: 1400 khz; 1 kw-U. TL: N34 38 21 W88 24 33. Box 356 38829-0356. Secondary address: 1101 So. Second St. 38829-2572. Phone: (662) 728-0200. Fax: (662) 728-2572. E-mail: wbipam@avsia.com. Licensee: Community Broadcasting Services of Mississippi Inc. (acq 8-31-98; $1,000. for 50% of stock with co-located FM). Format: Classic country. News: 7 hrs wkly. Target aud: 24-54. ◆ Larry Melton, pres; Jerry Thornton, VP; Larry Hill, gen mgr; Marty Williams, stn mgr, opns mgr & gen sls mgr & progmg dir.

WBVV(FM)— Jan 15, 1976: 99.3 mhz; 6 kw. Ant 300 ft. TL: N34 38 15 W88 34 45. Box 3300, Tupelo 38803. Phone: (662) 728-5301. Fax: (662) 728-2572. Licensee: Clear Channel Broadcasting Licenses Inc. Group owner: Clear Channel Communications Inc. (acq 9-27-2001; $700,000. including 5-year noncompete agreement). Network: Network: USA, Reach Satellite. Format: Contemp inspirational. ◆ Mark Maharrey, gen mgr.

***WMAE-FM**— December 1983: 89.5 mhz; 85 kw. Ant 660 ft. TL: N34 40 00 W88 45 05. Stereo. 3825 Ridgewood Rd., Jackson 39211. Phone: (601) 432-6565. Fax: (601) 432-6806. Web Site: www.mpbonline.org. Licensee: Mississippi Authority for Educational Television. Network: Network: PRI, NPR. Schwartz, Woods & Miller. Format: Music, news, info. News staff: 5; News: 20 hrs wkly. Target aud: General. ◆ Marie Antoon, chmn; Gene Edwards, gen mgr; Bob Holland, opns mgr.

Brandon

WRJH(FM)— Dec 1, 1974: 97.7 mhz; 6 kw. Ant 308 ft. TL: N32 09 55 W89 58 53. Stereo. 1985 Lakeland Dr., Suite 201, Jackson 39216. Phone: (601) 713-0977. Fax: (601) 713-2977. Web Site: www.hot977fm.com. Licensee: On Top Communications of Mississippi Inc. Group owner: On Top Communications Inc. (acq 1-8-02;. grpsl). Format: Hip hop, rhythm & blues. Target aud: 18-34. ◆ Bart Hocton, stn mgr.

WZQK(AM)— June 1967: 970 khz; 1 kw-D, DA. TL: N32 17 20 W89 59 50. 1111 Lakeland Dr., Jackson 39216-4702. Licensee: Jackson Radio LLC (acq 6-21-2005). ◆ Bobbye Imbragulio, gen mgr.

Brookhaven

WBKN(FM)— July 29, 1976: 92.1 mhz; 5.2 kw. 351 ft. TL: N31 36 00 W90 27 09. Stereo. Box 711 39602. Secondary address: 911 Hwy. 550 39602. Phone: (601) 833-9210. Fax: (601) 833-6221. E-mail: wbkn92@vis-com.tv. Licensee: Ole Brook Broadcasting Inc., debtor-in-possession (acq 9-22-2004). Network: ABC Daytime Direction. Fletcher, Heald & Hildreth. Format: Country. News: 5 hrs wkly. Target aud: 25-54. Spec prog: Gospel 3 hrs wkly. ◆ Bill Reynolds, pres; Ken Hollingsworth, gen mgr; Robbie Hamilton, sls dir & prom dir; Gaye Laird, progmg dir.

WCHJ(AM)— Aug 15, 1955: 1470 khz; 1 kw-D, 66 w-N. TL: N31 33 46 W90 26 51. Box 177 39602. Secondary address: 983 Sawmill Ln. 39601. Phone: (601) 823-9006. Fax: (601) 823-0503. E-mail: wchjgospel@netsouth.com. Licensee: Tillman Broadcasting Network Inc. (acq 4-9-99; $150,000). Network: ABC Information & Entertainment. Format: Black, gospel. News: one hr wkly. Target aud: 25-54. ◆ Charles Tillman, CEO, gen mgr & opns mgr.

Brooksville

WAJV(FM)— August 1995: 98.9 mhz; 5.8 kw. Ant 676 ft. TL: N33 20 40 W88 32 47. 608 Yellow Jacket Dr., Starkville 39759. Phone: (662) 338-5424. Fax: (662) 338-5436. Web Site: www.joy989.com. Licensee: Urban Radio Licenses LLC (acq 4-20-2001). Format: Urban contemp, gospel. News: 14 hrs wkly. Target aud: General. ◆ Kevin Wagner, pres & gen mgr; James Alexander, opns mgr; Ron Davis, progmg dir.

Bude

***WMAU-FM**— December 1983: 88.9 mhz; 100 kw. 960 ft. TL: N31 22 19 W90 45 05. Stereo. 3825 Ridgewood Rd., Jackson 39211. Phone: (601) 432-6565. Fax: (601) 432-6806. Web Site: www.mpbonline.org. Licensee: Mississippi Authority for Educational Television. Network: Network: NPR, PRI. Schwartz, Woods & Miller. Format: Class, news/talk, jazz. News staff: 5; News: 20 hrs wkly. Target aud: General. ◆ Marie Antoon, chmn; Gene Edwards, gen mgr; Bob Holland, opns mgr.

WMJU(FM)— Aug 30, 1999: 104.3 mhz; 25 kw. Ant 328 ft. TL: N31 33 33 W90 40 26. Stereo. Box 711, Brookhaven 39602. Secondary address: 911 Hwy. 550, Brookhaven 39601. Phone: (601) 833-9210. Fax: (601) 833-6221. E-mail: majic104@yahoo.com.Jonos Licensee: Ole Brook Broadcasting Inc., debtor-in-possession (group owner) (acq 9-22-2004). Format: Adult contemp. News staff: one; News: 10 hrs wkly. Target aud: 25-49; adults who are middle income & above. ◆ Bill Reynolds, pres; Ken Hollingsworth, gen mgr; Robbie Hamilton, sls dir & prom dir; Gaye Laird, progmg dir.

Burnsville

***WOWL(FM)**— 2000: 91.9 mhz; 18 kw. Ant 548 ft. TL: N34 55 47 W88 24 37. Stereo. 121 Front St., Iuka 38852. Phone: (662) 423-9919. Fax: (662) 423-9333. Licensee: Southern Community Services Inc. Rep: Rgnl Reps. Garvey, Schubert & Barer. Format: Adult contemp. ◆ Derrick Robinson, gen mgr.

Byhalia

***WKVF(FM)**— November 1994: 94.9 mhz; 6 kw. 403 ft. TL: N34 55 30 W89 40 57. Stereo. 5700 W. Oaks Blvd., Rocklin, CA 95765. Phone: (916) 251-1600. Fax: (916) 251-1650. E-mail: klove@klove.com. Web Site: www.klove.com. Licensee: Educational Media Foundation. Group owner: EMF Broadcasting (acq 2-1-00; $1.4 million). Network: K-Love. Shaw Pittman. Format: Contemp, Christian. News staff: 3. Target aud: 25-44; Judeo Christian, female. ◆ Richard Jenkins, pres; Mike Novak, VP; Lloyd Parker, gen mgr; Ed Lenane, opns dir; Keith Whipple, dev dir.

Canton

WMGO(AM)— Dec 9, 1954: 1370 khz; 1 kw-D, 280 w-N. TL: N32 37 36 W90 01 47. 107 W. Peace St. 39046. Phone: (601) 859-2373. Phone: (601) 859-2374. Fax: (601) 859-2664. Licensee: WMGO Broadcasting Corp. Inc. (acq 5-3-93; $100,000; 5-24-93). Format: Adult contemp, urban contemp, gospel. News staff: one; News: 12 hrs wkly. Target aud: 25-54; upscale & involved adults. ◆ Jerry Lousteau, pres, gen mgr & progmg VP.

WONG(AM)— April 1989: 1150 khz; 500 w-D. TL: N32 32 35 W90 03 36. 126 E. Sowell Rd. 39046. Phone: (601) 855-2035. Fax: (601) 855-2094. E-mail: wong1150am@cs.com. Licensee: Marion R. Williams. (acq 7-26-99; $50,000). Network: American Urban. Format: Gospel, blues. Target aud: 25 plus. ◆ Marion Williams, pres; Kaple Hill, gen mgr.

Carthage

WCKK(FM)— April 1979: 98.3 mhz; 20 kw. Ant 328 ft. TL: N32 43 29 W89 32 44. Box 1700, Kosciusko 39090. Secondary address: 1 Golf Course Rd., Kosciusko 39039. Phone: (662) 289-1340. Fax: (662) 289-7907. Licensee: Johnny Boswell Radio LLC (acq 8-15-2003; $450,000). Network: USA. Format: C&W. ◆ Johnny Boswell, gen mgr; Ann Sheen, stn mgr; Eric Matthews, opns mgr.

Centreville

***WPAE(FM)**— 1997: 89.7 mhz; 70 kw. 298 ft. TL: N31 05 56 W91 02 27. Box 1390 39631. Secondary address: 122 E. Main St. 39631. Phone: (601) 645-6515. Fax: (601) 645-9122. Licensee: Port Allen Educational Broadcasting Foundation. Network: Moody. Format: Relg, educ. Spec prog: Children 5 hrs, Gospel 15 hrs wkly. ◆ Willie F. Kennedy, gen mgr.

WZFL-FM— Nov 21, 1977: 104.9 mhz; 3 kw. Ant 298 ft. TL: N31 06 07 W91 02 27. (CP: 6 kw, ant 328 ft. TL: N31 05 56 W91 02 27). Box 1649, McComb 39649. Phone: (601) 684-4116. Fax: (601) 684-4654. Licensee: Southwest Broadcasting. Format: Classic country. ◆ Charles Dowdy, gen mgr.

Charleston

WTGY(FM)— Apr 1, 1986: 95.7 mhz; 6 kw. Ant 328 ft. TL: N33 53 28 W90 03 09. Stereo. Sunlife Radio, 8919 World Ministry Ave., Baton Rouge, LA 70826. Phone: (225) 768-8300. Fax: (225) 768-3729. E-mail: info@jsm.org. Web Site: jsm.org. Licensee: Family Worship Center Church Inc. (group owner; acq 7-15-02; $300,000). Format: Relg. ◆ John Santiago, gen mgr.

Clarksdale

WAID(FM)— July 1, 1978: 106.5 mhz; 30 kw. 296 ft. TL: N34 09 22 W90 37 52. Stereo. Box 668 38614. Phone: (662) 627-2281. Fax: (662) 624-2900. Web Site: www.missradio.com. Licensee: Radio Cleveland Inc. (group owner; acq 8-2-83; $185,000; 8-1-83). Network: USA. Format: Urban contemp. News staff: one; News: 2 hrs wkly. Target aud: General. ◆ Clint Webster, gen mgr; Greg Shurden, gen sls mgr; Jim Thomas, progmg dir; Houston McDavid, chief of engrg.

Stations in the U.S. — Mississippi

Developers & Brokers of Radio Properties
contact American Media Services at our suite: Philadelphia Marriott Downtown 215-625-2900
843-972-2200
americanmediaservices.com
Charleston, SC
Dallas, TX · Chicago, Il · Austin, TX

American Media Services, LLC

WKDJ-FM— Nov 1, 1988: 96.5 mhz; 6 kw. 180 ft. TL: N34 09 22 W90 37 52. Stereo. Box 668 38614. Phone: (662) 627-2281. Fax: (662) 624-2900. Web Site: www.missradio.com. Licensee: Clint Webster. (acq 12-3-93). Network: ABC Information & Entertainment. Format: Country. Target aud: 25-55. ♦ Clint Webster, gen mgr; Greg Shurden, stn mgr; Jim Thomas, progmg dir.

WKXY(FM)—Listing follows WROX(AM).

WROX(AM)— 1944: 1450 khz; 1 kw-U. TL: N34 12 40 W90 34 42. 330 Sunflower 38614. Phone: (662) 627-1450. Fax: (662) 621-1176. Licensee: Delta Radio LLC. Group owner: Contemporary Communications (acq 12-18-98; $54,000. with WQMA(AM) Marks). Wood, Maines & Brown. Format: Rhythm and Blues. News staff: one; News: 3 hrs wkly. Target aud: General. ♦ George Hinds, gen mgr; Bill Perry Sr., stn mgr.

WKXY(FM)—Co-owned with WROX(AM). 2003: 92.1 mhz; 500 w. Ant 141 ft. TL: N34 12 40 W90 34 42.

WWUN-FM— 1973: 101.5 mhz; 6 kw. Ant 177 ft. TL: N34 11 33 W90 34 17. Stereo. 301 S. State St. 38614. Phone: (662) 624-5144. Fax: (662) 621-1833. E-mail: wwun@csnradio.com. Web Site: www.csnradio.com. Licensee: CSN International (group owner; acq 8-27-01). Format: Relg, Christian. ♦ Charles W. Smith, pres; Jeffrey W. Smith, VP & gen mgr; Clayton Collier, stn mgr.

Cleveland

WCLD(AM)— 1949: 1490 khz; 1 kw-U. TL: N33 44 01 W90 42 50. Hwy. 61 S. 38732. Secondary address: Drawer 780 Phone: (662) 843-4091. Fax: (662) 843-9805. E-mail: wcld@tecinfo.com. Web Site: www.missradio.com. Licensee: Radio Cleveland Inc. (group owner; acq 1957). Format: Black gospel. Target aud: 18 plus. ♦ Clint L. Webster, gen mgr; Jim Thomas, opns mgr, progmg dir & news dir; Kevin Cox, gen sls mgr; Houston McDavitt, chief of engrg.

WCLD-FM— 1972: 103.9 mhz; 24.5 kw. 300 ft. TL: N33 44 01 W90 42 50. Stereo. Web Site: www.missradio.com. Fletcher, Heald & Hildreth. Format: Urban contemp. Target aud: 18 plus.

WDFX(FM)— 1993: 98.3 mhz; 25 kw. 328 ft. TL: N33 52 44 W90 43 04. Box 3206, American Family Radio, Tupelo 38803. Phone: (662) 844-8888. Fax: (662) 842-6791. Web Site: www.afr.net. Licensee: American Family Association Inc. (acq 5-3-93; $6,150; 5-24-93). Network: USA. Format: Christian. ♦ Don Wildman, gen mgr.

WDSK(AM)—Listing follows WDTL-FM.

WDTL-FM— May 22, 1970: 92.9 mhz; 50 kw. 492 ft. TL: N33 44 17 W90 39 29. Stereo. Box 1438, 309 N. Chrisman Ave. 38732. Phone: (662) 846-0929. Fax: (662) 843-1410. E-mail: mrsviradio@aol.com. Licensee: M.R.S. Ventures Inc. (group owner; acq 11-1-2003; grpsl). Wood, Maines & Brown. Format: Country. News staff: one; News: 3 hrs wkly. Target aud: 25-54. ♦ Wash Sellers Jr., opns VP, opns dir & progmg dir; Wendy Hodges, gen mgr, gen mgr, gen sls mgr & engrg dir.

WDSK(AM)—Co-owned with WDTL-FM. June 25, 1958: 1410 khz; 920 w-D, 23 w-N. TL: N33 45 56 W90 42 41. Stereo. Network: CBS Radio. Format: News/talk. Target aud: 35 plus; male & female.

WMJW(FM)— 1993: 107.5 mhz; 25 kw. 328 ft. TL: N33 43 36 W90 43 53. Stereo. Box 780 38732. Phone: (662) 843-4091. Fax: (662) 843-9805. Web Site: www.missradio.com. Licensee: Radio Cleveland Inc. (group owner; acq 7-18-95). Network: ABC Information & Entertainment. Fletcher, Heald & Hildreth. Format: Country. News: 8 hrs wkly. Target aud: 25-54; adults. ♦ Clint L. Webster, pres & gen mgr; Jim Thomas, opns mgr; Kevin W. Cox, VP, sls dir, gen sls mgr & prom dir; Jim Gregory, pub affrs dir.

WRKG(FM)—(Drew). June 1, 1971: 95.3 mhz; 2.65 kw. 492 ft. TL: N33 44 17 W90 39 29. Stereo. Box 1438, 309 N. Chrisman Ave. 38732. Phone: (662) 846-0929. Fax: (662) 843-1410. E-mail: mrsviradio@aol.com. Web Site: www.deltaradio.net. Licensee: M.R.S. Ventures Inc. (group owner; acq 11-1-2003; grpsl). Network: Jones Radio Networks. Wood, Maines & Brown. Format: Classic Rock. News staff: one; News: 2 hrs wkly. Target aud: General. ♦ Wendy Hodges, gen mgr.

WZYQ(FM)—(Mound Bayou). Oct 10, 1997: 101.9 mhz; 6 kw. 328 ft. TL: N33 52 49 W90 42 24. Stereo. Box 1438, 309 N. Chrisman Ave. 38732. Phone: (662) 846-0929. Fax: (662) 843-1410. E-mail: mrsviradio@aol.com. Web Site: www.deltaradio.net. Licensee: M.R.S. Ventures Inc. (group owner; acq 11-1-2003; grpsl). Network: Jones Radio Networks. Wood, Maines & Brown. Format: Contemporary Hit Radio. News staff: one. Target aud: General. ♦ Wendy Hodges, gen mgr.

Clinton

WHJT(FM)— 1974: 93.5 mhz; 6 kw. 328 ft. TL: N32 20 15 W90 19 47. Stereo. Box 4048 39058. Secondary address: 100 S. Jefferson 39058. Phone: (601) 925-3458. Fax: (601) 925-3337. Web Site: www.star93fm.com. Licensee: Mississippi College. Smithwick & Belendiuk. Format: CHR Christian. News: 7 hrs wkly. Target aud: 18-54; upper & middle class Christian listeners. Spec prog: Relg 6 hrs wkly. ♦ Billy Lytal, pres; Russ Robinson, gen mgr & stn mgr.

WTWZ(AM)— Oct 10, 1982: 1120 khz; 7.5 kw-D (2.5 kw-CH). TL: N32 21 03 W90 20 22. 4611 Terry Rd., Suite C, Jackson 39212. Phone: (601) 346-0074. Fax: (601) 346-0896. E-mail: wtwzam1120@jam.rr.com. Licensee: Terry E. Wood. Network: USA. Format: Bluegrass. News: 7 hrs wkly. Target aud: 18-50; 50% men & 50% women. ♦ Terry Wood, pres & gen mgr.

Coldwater

WVIM-FM— 1976: 95.3 mhz; 3.6 kw. Ant 423 ft. TL: N34 46 45 W89 58 01. Stereo. 5555 McCracken, Hernando 38632. Phone: (662) 429-1404. Fax: (662) 429-0704. E-mail: jmarasco@oldies953.net. Web Site: www.oldies953.net. Licensee: First Broadcasting Investment Partners LLC (group owner; acq 6-24-2004; $2.1 million). Format: Oldies. Target aud: 25-54. ♦ Gary M. Lawrence, pres; Rick Dames, gen mgr; Danny McGregor, opns mgr & progmg dir.

Collins

WKNZ(FM)— Aug 15, 1978: 107.1 mhz; 2.25 kw. Ant 541 ft. TL: N31 31 49 W89 30 29. Stereo. Box 15935, Hattiesburg 39404. Secondary address: 7501 Hwy. 49 N., Hattiesburg 39404. Phone: (601) 264-0443. Phone: (601) 268-1017. Fax: (601) 264-5733. Licensee: Educational Media Foundation. (acq 7-15-2005; $700,000). Network: K-Love. Format: Christian. Target aud: 25-54; upwardly mobile. ♦ Ted Tibbett, gen mgr.

Columbia

WCJU(AM)— Dec 20, 1946: 1450 khz; 1 kw-U. TL: N31 14 14 W89 50 24. Stereo. Box 472 39429. Phone: (601) 736-2616. Fax: (601) 736-2617. Licensee: WCJU Inc. (acq 6-69). Network: ABC. Rep: Keystone (unwired net). Format: News/talk, sports. News staff: 2; News: 30 hrs wkly. Target aud: 18-54. Spec prog: Gospel 4 hrs wkly. ♦ Pam Ball, opns dir & rgnl sls mgr; T. McDaniel, pres & gen sls mgr; John Pittman Jr., mus dir.

WFFF(AM)— Apr 14, 1961: 1360 khz; 1 kw-D, 159 w-N. TL: N31 15 44 W89 50 41. Box 550, 11 Gardner Shopping Ctr. 39429. Phone: (601) 736-1360. Fax: (601) 736-1361. E-mail: wfffradio@zzip.cc. Licensee: Haddox Enterprises Inc. (acq 10-9-91; $250,000 with co-located FM; 11-4-91). Network: ABC. Format: C&W, gospel. News staff: 4; News: 8 hrs wkly. Target aud: General. ♦ Ronnie Geiger, pres, gen mgr, gen sls mgr, gen sls mgr, progmg dir, news dir & chief of engrg; Terri Geiger, VP.

WFFF-FM— October 1966: 96.7 mhz; 3 kw. 400 ft. TL: N31 15 44 W89 50 41. Stereo. Format: Adult contemp. News staff: 4; News: 8 hrs wkly. Target aud: 25-54. ♦ Ronnie Geiger, opns VP & engrg dir.

***WPRG(FM)**—Not on air, target date: unknown: 89.5 mhz; 250 w. 177 ft. TL: N31 16 50 W89 51 12. American Family Radio, Box 3206, Tupelo 38803. Phone: (662) 844-8888. Fax: (662) 842-6791. Web Site: www.afr.net. Licensee: American Family Association. Group owner: American Family Radio (acq 10-1-01). Network: USA. Format: Christian. ♦ Marvin Sanders, gen mgr.

Columbus

***WCSO(FM)**—Not on air, target date: unknown: 90.5 mhz; 6 kw. Ant 312 ft. TL: N33 28 38 W88 16 25. Drawer 3206, Tupelo 38803. Phone: (662) 844-8888. Fax: (662) 842-6791. Licensee: American Family Association. ♦ Marvin Sanders, gen mgr.

WJWF(AM)— Nov 1, 1969: 1400 khz; 1 kw-U. TL: N33 29 30 W88 24 14. 601 2nd Ave. N. 39703. Phone: (662) 327-1183. Licensee: Cumulus Licensing Corp. Group owner: Cumulus Media Inc. (acq 2-14-02; with co-located FM). Format: Sports, news/talk. ♦ Don Troutt, gen mgr; Bill Lemonds, gen sls mgr; Stan Smith, progmg dir.

WMBC(FM)—Co-owned with WJWF(AM). Nov 1, 1969: 103.1 mhz; 22 kw. 754 ft. TL: N33 29 30 W88 24 14. Stereo. 601 2nd Ave. N. 39701. Phone: (662) 327-1183. Format: Contemp hit radio/Top 40.

WKOR-FM— Dec 16, 1992: 94.9 mhz; 29.5 kw. 492 ft. TL: N33 28 38 W88 16 25. Stereo. 200 6th St. N., Suite 205 39701. Phone: (662) 327-1183. Fax: (662) 328-1122. Web Site: www.k949.net. Licensee: Cumulus Licensing Corp. Group owner: Cumulus Media Inc. (acq 2-14-02; grpsl). Network: ABC. Format: Hot country. Target aud: 18-54. ♦ Greg Benefield, gen mgr.

WTWG(AM)— 1950: 1050 khz; 1 kw-D, 48 w-N, DA. TL: N33 30 36 W88 24 46. Box 1078 39703. Secondary address: 1910 14th Ave. N. 39703. Phone: (662) 328-1050. Fax: (662) 328-1054. Licensee: T & W Communications Inc. (acq 1997; $110,000. with co-located FM; FTR: 9-13-93). Format: Gospel. Target aud: 25-54; general. ♦ Edna Turner, gen mgr & gen sls mgr; J. Michael Bailey, progmg dir; Lloyd Mitchell, chief of engrg.

WWKZ(FM)— Dec 15, 1978: 103.9 mhz; 50 kw. Ant 492 ft. TL: N33 24 27 W88 08 27. (CP: COL Okolona. Ant 394 ft. TL: N34 12 18 W88 41 49). Stereo. Box 3300, Tupelo 38803. Phone: (662) 842-1067. Fax: (662) 842-0725. Licensee: Citicasters Licenses L.P. (acq 7-13-2005; $2.2 million). Network: American Urban. Format: Urban contemp. News: 6 hrs wkly. ♦ Mark Maharrey, gen mgr.

Como

WRBO(FM)— Sept 28, 1966: 103.5 mhz; 100 kw. Ant 587 ft. TL: N34 51 44 W89 52 42. Stereo. 5629 Murray Rd., Memphis, TN 38119. Phone: (901) 682-1106. Fax: (901) 680-0457. Web Site: www.soulclassics.com. Licensee: Citadel Broadcasting Co. Group owner: Citadel Broadcasting Corp. (acq 3-23-2004; grpsl). Network: Network: ABC, Westwood One. Format: Soul classics. Target aud: 18-49. ♦ Tony Yoken, pres & gen mgr.

Corinth

WADI(FM)— Oct 26, 1968: 95.3 mhz; 2.6 kw. 4720 ft. TL: N34 55 47 W88 24 37. Stereo. 121 Front St., Iuka 38852. Phone: (662) 423-9533. Fax: (662) 423-9333. E-mail: biddleandsons@crossroadsisp.com. Licensee: Power Valley Communications Inc. (acq 5-31-2002; $330,000. with co-located AM). Format: Country. ♦ Frederick A. Biddle, pres & CFO; Brian Biddle, stn mgr; Mike Cannon, opns dir; Rick Biddle, gen mgr & sls VP.

WKCU(AM)— Oct 24, 1965: 1350 khz; 900 w-D, 44 w-N. TL: N34 54 29 W88 30 06. 1608 S. Johns St. 38834. Phone: (662) 286-8451. Fax: (662) 286-8452. E-mail: wxrz@earthlink.net. Licensee: TeleSouth Communications Inc. (group owner; acq 12-20-02; $350,000. with co-located FM). Format: Today's Christian music. News: 12 hrs wkly. Target aud: 25-54; female. Spec prog: Black 2 hrs wkly. ♦ James H. Anderson, gen mgr.

Mississippi

WXRZ(FM)—Co-owned with WKCU(AM). January 1967: 94.3 mhz; 25 kw. 328 ft. TL: N34 48 36 W88 34 45. Stereo. Format: Super talk Mississippi. ♦James H. Anderson, stn mgr.

WTKN(AM)— Mar 1, 1946: . Stn currently dark 1230 khz; 1 kw-U. TL: N34 52 07 W88 31 17. 121 Front St., Iuka 38852. Phone: (662) 423-9533. Fax: (662) 423-9333. Licensee: New Mind Broadcasting LLC (acq 12-14-2004; $45,000). ♦Rick Biddle, gen mgr.

Crenshaw

WHKL(FM)— Mar 1, 1997: 106.9 mhz; 6 kw. 328 ft. TL: N34 26 51 W90 06 25. Box 1528, Batesville 38606. Phone: (662) 563-4664. Fax: (662) 563-9008. E-mail: country101radio@yahoo.com. Licensee: Batesville Broadcasting Co. Inc. Format: Oldies. ♦John Ingram, gen mgr & stn mgr.

De Kalb

WJXM(FM)— 1999: 105.7 mhz; 50 kw. Ant 384 ft. TL: N32 38 37 W88 40 29. Box 5797, Meridian 39302. Phone: (601) 693-2661. Fax: (601) 483-0826. E-mail: wjxm@wokk.com. Licensee: Mississippi Broadcasters L.L.C. (group owner). Format: Urban contemp. ♦Clay Holladay, gen mgr; Scott Stevens, opns mgr; Karen Bostick, sls dir; Van Mac, news dir & pub affrs dir; Scott Shepperd, chief of engrg.

Decatur

WZKR(FM)— 2001: 103.3 mhz; 4.8 kw. Ant 590 ft. TL: N32 21 46 W88 54 48. 1106 18th Ave., Meridian 39301. Phone: (601) 693-1103. Fax: (601) 693-9949. Licensee: Rainey Broadcasting Inc. Format: Classic rock. ♦Al Brown, gen mgr.

D'Iberville

WCPR-FM— December 1992: 97.9 mhz; 50 kw. 466 ft. TL: N30 36 59 W89 08 03. 1909 E. Pass Rd., Suite D-11, Gulfport 39507. Phone: (228) 388-2171. Fax: (228) 388-2771 (request line). Fax: (228) 896-9736. E-mail: wcpr@wcprfm.com. Web Site: www.wcprfm.com. Licensee: Monterey Licenses LLC. Group owner: Triad Broadcasting Co. LLC (acq 7-14-99; grpsl). Network: ABC. Format: Active Rock/alternative. ♦Buddy Burch, VP; Jay Taylor, opns dir.

Drew

WRKG(FM)—Licensed to Drew. See Cleveland

Duck Hill

*WAUM(FM)— 1998: 91.9 mhz; 3 kw. 466 ft. TL: N33 38 34 W89 29 59. Box 3206, American Family Radio, Tupelo 38803. Phone: (662) 844-8888. Fax: (662) 842-6791. Web Site: www.afr.net. Licensee: American Family Association. Group owner: American Family Radio Network: USA. Format: Relg. ♦Marvin Sanders, gen mgr.

Durant

WLIN-FM— 1997: 101.1 mhz; 4.8 kw. 371 ft. TL: N33 03 51 W89 36 12. Box1700, Kosciusko 39090. Phone: (662) 289-1050. Fax: (662) 289-7907. E-mail: breezy@kopower.com. Web Site: www.breezynews.com. Licensee: Boswell Radio LLC. Format: Adult contemp. ♦Johnny Boswell, gen mgr; Ann Steen, stn mgr; Jerry Price, gen sls mgr; Eric Matthews, progmg dir.

Ellisville

WJKX(FM)— Oct 5, 1973: 102.5 mhz; 50 kw. 492 ft. TL: N31 46 05 W89 10 12. Stereo. 2625 S. Memorial Dr., Suite A, Tulsa 74129. Phone: (210) 822-2828. Licensee: Clear Channel Broadcasting Licenses Inc. Group owner: Clear Channel Communications Inc. (acq 12-19-00; grpsl). Format: Urban. ♦Urica Pleas, gen mgr.

Eupora

WLZA(FM)—Licensed to Eupora. See Starkville

Fayette

WTYJ(FM)— Oct 17, 1983: 97.7 mhz; 6 kw. 500 ft. TL: N31 40 32 W91 06 18. (CP: 6 kw, 328 ft.). Stereo. 20 E. Franklin St., Natchez 39120. Phone: (601) 442-2522. Fax: (601) 446-9918. Licensee: Natchez Broadcasting Inc. (acq 4-86; $200,000; 4-14-86). Format: Gospel, blues. Target aud: General. ♦Dianna Nutter, pres; James B. Nutter, VP & stn mgr; L. Weir, gen mgr.

Flora

WFMN(FM)— July 7, 1997: 97.3 mhz; 19.5 kw. 367 ft. TL: N32 27 21 W90 15 32. TeleSouth Communications Inc., 6311 Ridgewood Rd., Jackson 39211. Phone: (601) 957-1700. Fax: (601) 956-5228. E-mail: pgallo@telesouth.com. Web Site: www.supertalkms.com. Licensee: TeleSouth Communications Inc. (group owner; acq 9-8-97; $700,000). Network: ABC. Format: Talk. ♦Steve Davenport, pres; Paul Gallo, gen mgr; John Winfield, opns mgr; Alexis Ramsey, gen sls mgr; Andi Peterson, progmg dir.

Flowood

WPBQ(AM)— January 1995: 1240 khz; 880 w-U. TL: N32 18 03 W90 08 12. 850 Brandon Ave., Jackson 39209. Phone: (601) 982-3210. Fax: (601) 420-4114. Licensee: PDB Corp. (acq 2-10-92; $4,000; 3-2-92). Haley, Bader & Potts. Format: News/talk, sports. News staff: 3; News: 10 hrs wkly. Target aud: 25-54. ♦Bill Fulgham, gen mgr, stn mgr & engrg dir.

Forest

*WMBU(FM)— Oct 3, 1997: 89.1 mhz; 10 kw horiz, 100 kw vert. 640 ft. TL: N32 18 54 W89 21 12. Stereo. Box 400, 5189 Lake Norris Rd., Lake 39092. Phone: (601) 775-3100. Fax: (601) 775-3400. E-mail: wmbu@moody.edu. Web Site: www.wmbu.org. Licensee: The Moody Bible Institute of Chicago. (group owner) Network: Moody. Southmayd & Miller. Format: Christian. Spec prog: Children 2 hrs wkly. ♦Bob Neff, sr VP; Rob Moore, gen mgr; John Rogers, progmg dir; Tammy Sumerlin, progmg mgr; Dee Etheridge, pub affrs dir; Stan Carter, engrg dir; Mark Williams, chief of engrg.

WQST(AM)— September 1955: . Stn currently dark 850 khz; 10 kw-D, DA. TL: N32 21 46 W89 25 09. 18844 Hwy. 80 E. 39074. Licensee: Ace Broadcasting Inc. (acq 1999; $45,000). Garvey, Schubert & Barer.

WQST-FM— September 1962: 92.5 mhz; 100 kw. 1,040 ft. TL: N32 21 48 W89 25 29. Stereo. Box 3206, American Family Radio, Jackson 39236. Phone: (601) 362-4277. Fax: (601) 362-1994. Web Site: www.afr.net. Licensee: American Family Association Inc. Group owner: American Family Radio Network: USA. Format: Christian. ♦Don Wildman, stn mgr.

*WQVI(FM)— July 20, 2004: 90.5 mhz; 60 kw vert. Ant 430 ft. TL: N32 42 51 W89 49 19. Box 3206, Tupelo 38803. Phone: (662) 844-8888. Fax: (662) 842-6791. Web Site: www.afr.net. Licensee: American Family Association. Group owner: American Family Radio. Network: USA. Format: Christian classics. ♦Marvin Sanders, gen mgr.

*WSQH(FM)—Not on air, target date: unknown: 91.7 mhz; 250 w. Ant 338 ft. TL: N32 21 48 W89 25 29. Box 3206, Tupelo 38803-3206. Phone: (662) 844-8888. Fax: (662) 842-6791. Web Site: www.afr.net. Licensee: Salt & Light Communications Inc. Network: USA. Format: Christian. ♦Marvin Sanders, gen mgr.

Fulton

WFTA(FM)—Licensed to Fulton. See Tupelo

Gluckstadt

WYOY(FM)— Jan 7, 1976: 101.7 mhz; 50 kw. 300 ft. TL: N32 30 03 W90 02 28. Stereo. 265 High Point Dr., Ridgeland 39157. Phone: (601) 956-0102. Fax: (601) 978-3980. Web Site: www.y101.com. Licensee: New South Radio Inc. Group owner: New South Communications Inc. (acq 11-10-94; $750,000 with WLRM(AM) Ridgeland; 12-12-94). Network: ABC Daytime Direction. Rep: McGavren Guild. Format: CHR. Target aud: 18-49. ♦Gwen Rakestraw, gen mgr; Bill Rakestraw, gen sls mgr; Scott Steel, prom dir; Nick Vance, progmg dir; David Herring, news dir.

Greenville

WBAD(FM)—See Leland

WBAQ(FM)— May 1, 1970: 97.9 mhz; 49 kw horiz. Ant 495 ft. TL: N33 23 50 W91 00 33. Stereo. Box 656 38702. Secondary address: 136 S. Broadway 38701. Phone: (662) 335-3383. Fax: (662) 335-3383. E-mail: wbaq@tecinfo.com. Licensee: The River Broadcasting Co. Inc. Group owner: The River Group (acq 3-14-00; $300,000). Network: ABC Information & Entertainment. Format: btfl music, easy lstng. News: 14 hrs wkly. Target aud: 25-54; quality-conscious adults with spendable income. Spec prog: Farm one hr, btfl sacred music 4 hrs wkly. ♦Paul Artman Sr., gen mgr.

WDMS(FM)—Listing follows WGVM(AM).

WESY(AM)—See Leland

*WFBI(FM)—Not on air, target date: unknown: 91.5 mhz; 25 w vert. Ant 220 ft. TL: N33 32 11 W91 19 45. Broadcasting for the Challenged Inc., 188 S. Bellevue, Suite 222, Memphis, TN 38104. Phone: (901) 516-8970. Licensee: Broadcasting for the Challenged Inc. ♦George S. Flinn Jr., pres.

WGVM(AM)— 1948: 1260 khz; 5 kw-D, 32 w-N. TL: N33 25 20 W91 01 41. Box 1438 38701. Secondary address: 1383 Pickett St. 38701. Phone: (662) 334-4550. Fax: (662) 332-1315. Web Site: www.tecinfo.com/~wgvm. Licensee: Mid-America Broadcasting Co. Format: ESPN. Target aud: General. Spec prog: Black 5 hrs wkly. ♦Bob Ghetti, gen mgr & news dir; Michelle Cochran, gen mgr & opns dir; Pam Cochrelle, gen sls mgr; Dallas Peel, progmg dir.

WDMS(FM)—Co-owned with WGVM(AM). December 1967: 100.7 mhz; 100 kw. 449 ft. TL: N33 24 20 W91 01 41. Stereo. 1383 Pickett St. 38701. Phone: (662) 334-4559. Web Site: www.wdmsradio.com. Format: Country.

WIQQ(FM)—See Leland

WJIW(FM)—Not on air, target date: unknown: 104.7 mhz; 31 kw. Ant 620 ft. TL: N33 28 10 W90 50 30. Mondy-Burke Broadcasting Network, 204 Moore St., Helena, AR 72342. Phone: (870) 338-2700. Fax: (870) 338-3166. Licensee: Mondy-Burke Broadcasting Network. Format: Christian gospel. ♦Elijah Mondy, VP; Belinda Mondy, gen mgr.

WNIX(AM)— August 1937: 1330 khz; 1 kw-D, 500 w-N, DA-N. TL: N33 24 36 W91 01 03. Box 1816 38702-1816. Secondary address: Unit 39 Delta Plaza Mall, 800 Hwy. 1 S. 38701. Phone: (662) 378-2617. Fax: (662) 378-8341. E-mail: wiqq@bellsouth.net. Licensee: The River Broadcasting Co. Inc. Group owner: The River Group (acq 8-31-79). Network: ABC. Rep: McGavren Guild. Baraff, Koerner & Olender. Format: Urban Contemporary, Farm. News staff: one; News: 3 hrs wkly. Target aud: 24-55; upper scale, multi-income. Spec prog: Relg 6 hrs, farm 10 hrs wkly. ♦George E. Pine III, pres; James P. Karr Jr., VP, gen mgr, prom dir & progmg dir; Linda McKee, opns mgr; Margret Kazen Karr, gen sls mgr; Donna Lewis, mktg dir; Ray Renfroe, mus dir; Paul Artman, pub affrs dir; Percy Kuhn, chief of engrg.

Greenwood

WABG(AM)— February 1950: 960 khz; 1 kw-D, 500 w-N, DA-N. TL: N33 33 45 W90 12 38. 2001 Garrard Ave. 38930. Secondary address: Box 408 38935-0408. Phone: (662) 453-7822. Fax: (662) 455-3311. Licensee: Greenwood Broadcasting Co. Inc. Group owner: Bahakel Communications Network: UPI. Format: Country, talk. News: 11 hrs wkly. Target aud: 35 plus. Spec prog: Black 4 hrs wkly. ♦Sherry Nelson, gen mgr.

WGNL(FM)— Dec 1, 1989: 104.3 mhz; 50 kw. 360 ft. TL: N33 31 30 W90 09 52. (CP: TL: N33 21 56 W90 14 59). Stereo. Box 1801 38930. Secondary address: 503 Ione St. 38930. Phone: (662) 453-1646. Fax: (662) 453-7002. Web Site: www.broadcasturban.net. Licensee: Team Broadcasting Co. Inc. Rep: Dora-Clayton. Mullin, Rhyne, Emmons & Topel. Format: Adult contemp. News staff: one; News: 12 hrs wkly. Target aud: 18 plus. Spec prog: Jazz 6 hrs wkly. ♦Maxine Hughes, opns mgr; Ruben C. Hughes, gen mgr & gen sls mgr; Al Briscoe, mktg VP & prom VP; Cyreio Hughes, progmg dir & news dir.

WGRM(AM)— 1937: 1240 khz; 1 kw-U. TL: N33 31 55 W90 11 38. (CP: 730 w). 1110 Wright St. 38930. Phone: (662) 453-1240. Fax: (662) 453-1241. Licensee: Christian Broadcasting of Greenwood Inc. (group owner; (acq 2-22-99; $500,000 with co-located FM). Format: Gospel. Target aud: 25-45. Spec prog: Black 2 hrs wkly. ♦Gwen Riley, mus dir & news dir; Lee Hall, gen mgr, gen sls mgr, progmg dir & chief of engrg.

Stations in the U.S.

Mississippi

Developers & Brokers of Radio Properties
contact American Media Services at our suite: Philadelphia Marriott Downtown
215-625-2900
843-972-2200
americanmediaservices.com
Charleston, SC
Dallas, TX • Chicago, Il • Austin, TX
American Media Services, LLC

WGRM-FM— July 17, 1989: 93.9 mhz; 3 kw. 328 ft. TL: N33 32 02 W90 11 42. (CP: 25 kw).

WKXG(AM)— Jan 1, 1987: 1540 khz; 1 kw-D. TL: N33 31 12 W90 08 28. Box 1686 38935-1686. Secondary address: 3192 Browning Rd. 38935. Phone: (662) 453-2174. Fax: (662) 455-5733. Licensee: TeleSouth Communications Inc. (group owner; acq 8-1-88). Rep: Rgnl Reps. Format: Gospel. News: 3 hrs wkly. Target aud: 18-44. ♦ Charlotte Baglan, sls dir; Ellen Benish, progmg dir & news dir; Wes Sterling, gen mgr, gen sls mgr & chief of engrg.

WYMX(FM)— Co-owned with WKXG(AM). June 15, 1965: 99.1 mhz; 100 kw. 1,029 ft. TL: N33 31 12 W90 08 28. Stereo. Phone: (662) 453-2174. Fax: (662) 455-5733. Format: Classic rock. ♦ Herman Anderson, mus dir.

*WMAO-FM— December 1983: 90.9 mhz; 100 kw. 880 ft. TL: N33 22 34 W90 32 32. Stereo. 3825 Ridgewood Rd., Jackson 39211. Phone: (601) 432-6565. Fax: (601) 432-6806. Web Site: www.mpbonline.org. Licensee: Mississippi Authority for Educational Television. Network: Network: PRI, NPR. Schwartz, Woods & Miller. Format: Class, news/talk, jazz. News staff: 5; News: 20 hrs wkly. Target aud: General. ♦ Marie Antoon, chmn; Gene Edwards, gen mgr; Bob Holand, opns mgr; Ty Warren, dev mgr; Tippy Garner, rgnl sls mgr; Jennifer Griffin, prom dir; Bob Holland, progmg dir; Greg Waxberg, mus dir; Dick Rizzo, news dir; Keith Martin, engrg dir.

WTCD(FM)— (Indianola). May 1990: 96.9 mhz; 12.5 kw. 469 ft. TL: N33 35 35 W90 32 30. Stereo. Box 1686 38935. Phone: (662) 453-2174. Fax: (662) 455-5733. E-mail: radio@wtcd.com. Web Site: www.supertalkms.com. Licensee: TeleSouth Communications Inc. (group owner; acq 5-28-97; $325,000). Network: USA. Smithwick & Belendiuk. Format: News/talk. News staff: one; News: 20 hrs wkly. Target aud: 35-64; strong family orientation, middle to upper incomes. Spec prog: Farm 5 hrs, relg 11 hrs, talk 10 hrs wkly. ♦ Wes Sterling, gen mgr.

Grenada

WMUT(FM)— 2004: 101.3 mhz; 6 kw. Ant 328 ft. TL: N33 49 20 W89 55 40. Box 2266 38902. Secondary address: 157 Dowdle Rd. 38901. Phone: (662) 226-3133. Fax: (662) 226-3233. E-mail: rock101@cableone.net. Licensee: George S. Flinn Jr. Network: Network: CNN Radio, Westwood One. Format: Classic rock. Target aud: 18-54. ♦ Will Stammerjohan, gen mgr; Connie Stammerjohan, gen sls mgr.

WOHT(FM)— 2003: 92.3 mhz; 4.1 kw. Ant 397 ft. TL: N33 51 33 W89 55 13. Box 2266 38902. Phone: (662) 226-3133. Fax: (662) 226-3233. E-mail: star92@star92fm.com. Licensee: Century Broadcasting L.L.C. (acq 4-18-03). Format: Oldies. ♦ Will Stammerjohan, gen mgr.

WQXB(FM)— Listing follows WYKC(AM).

WTGY(FM)— See Charleston

WYKC(AM)— February 1949: 1400 khz; 1 kw-U. TL: N33 46 48 W89 48 09. 1348 Sunset Dr. 38901. Phone: (662) 226-1400. Fax: (662) 226-1464. Licensee: Chatterbox Inc. (acq 1-16-81). Format: Country. ♦ Bob Evans Jr., pres & gen mgr.

WQXB(FM)— Co-owned with WYKC(AM). Oct 16, 1970: 100.1 mhz; 3 kw. 300 ft. TL: N33 46 36 W89 49 23. Stereo. (Acq 2-24-78). Format: Hot country.

Gulfport

*WAOY(FM)— 1999: 91.7 mhz; 78 kw. 1,089 ft. TL: N30 42 29 W89 05 06. Box 3206, American Family Radio, Tupelo 38803. Phone: (601) 844-8888. Fax: (601) 842-6791. Web Site: www.afr.net. Licensee: American Family Association Inc. Group owner: American Family Radio Network: USA. Format: Christian. Target aud: General. ♦ Marvin Sanders, pres & gen mgr.

WGCM(AM)— 1928: 1240 khz; 1 kw-U. TL: N30 22 38 W89 04 45. 10250 Lorrian 39503. Phone: (228) 896-5500. Fax: (228) 896-0458. Licensee: JMD Inc. (acq 11-15-94; $950,000. with co-located FM; FTR: 12-12-94). Format: Country. Target aud: 35 plus. ♦ Morgan Dowdy, pres & gen mgr; Buddy Baylor, opns mgr; Steve Spillman, gen sls mgr; Brian Rhodes, progmg dir; Gwen Wilson, news dir; Dave Melton, chief of engrg.

WGCM-FM— Nov 14, 1969: 102.3 mhz; 25 kw. 299 ft. TL: N30 22 28 W89 04 45. (CP: 16 kw, ant 358 ft.). Stereo. Format: Easy listening. Target aud: 25-54. ♦ Buddy Baylor, gen sls mgr; Pat McGowan, progmg dir.

WQFX(FM)— May 7, 1975: 1130 khz; 500 w-D. TL: N30 23 21 W89 06 23. 336 Rodenberg Ave., Biloxi 39531-3444. Phone: (228) 374-9739. Fax: (228) 374-9739. E-mail: wqfxradio@aol.com. Web Site: www.wqfx.net. Licensee: Walking by Faith Ministries Inc. (acq 1994). Format: Power gospel. ♦ James Black, gen mgr.

WROA(AM)— Feb 27, 1955: 1390 khz; 5 kw-U, DA-2. TL: N30 27 30 W89 04 45. Box 2639 39505. Phone: (228) 896-5500. Fax: (228) 896-0458. Licensee: Dowdy & Dowdy Partnership. (acq 12-19-86). Format: Music of your life. Spec prog: Farm one hr wkly. ♦ Charles W. Dowdy, pres; Morgan Dowdy, gen mgr.

WUJM(FM)— July 13, 1977: 96.7 mhz; 3 kw. 245 ft. TL: N30 23 21 W89 06 23. Stereo. 1909 E. Pass Rd., Suite D11 39507. Phone: (228) 388-2001. Fax: (228) 896-9736. E-mail: molly967@molly967.com. Web Site: www.molly967.com. Licensee: Monterey Licenses LLC. Group owner: Triad Broadcasting Co. LLC (acq 7-14-99; grpsl). Network: ABC. Format: Hot adult contemp. ♦ Buddy Burch, VP; Jay Taylor, opns dir & opns mgr.

WXYK(FM)— 1964: 107.1 mhz; 1.85 kw. 394 ft. TL: N30 27 32 W89 04 45. (CP: 2.8 kw, ant 400 ft.). Stereo. 1909 E. Pass Rd., Suite D-11 39507. Phone: (228) 388-2001. Fax: (228) 896-9736. E-mail: wxyk@monkeyradio.com. Web Site: www.monkeyradio.com. Licensee: Monterey Licenses LLC. Group owner: Triad Broadcasting Co. LLC (acq 7-14-99; grpsl). Network: ABC. Format: Top-40/CHR. ♦ Jay Taylor, opns dir & opns mgr.

WZKX(FM)— See Poplarville

Hattiesburg

*WAII(FM)— 1998: 89.3 mhz; 1 kw. 220 ft. TL: N31 16 59 W89 21 01. American Family Radio, Box 3206, Tupelo 38803. Phone: (662) 844-8888. Fax: (662) 842-6791. Web Site: www.afr.net. Licensee: American Family Association. Group owner: American Family Radio Network: USA. Format: Relg. ♦ Marvin Sanders, gen mgr.

WFOR(AM)— May 1924: 1400 khz; 1 kw-U. TL: N31 20 03 W89 19 08. One Commerce Dr., #106 39402. Phone: (601) 544-1400. Phone: (601) 296-9800. Fax: (601) 582-5481. Licensee: Capstar TX L.P. Group owner: Clear Channel Communications Inc. (acq 12-19-00; grpsl). Format: Sports/talk. Target aud: 35 plus. Spec prog: Relg 8 hrs wkly. ♦ Mike Comfort, gen mgr; Jack Walker, opns mgr & progmg dir; James Harris, gen sls mgr; Sherri Merringo, news dir; Glen Musgrove, chief of engrg.

WUSW(FM)— Co-owned with WFOR(AM). July 1, 1966: 103.7 mhz; 100 kw. 1,056 ft. TL: N31 31 37 W89 08 07. Stereo. Phone: (601) 544-1037. Fax: (601) 582-5481. Format: Rock. Target aud: 25-54.

WGDQ(FM)— Not on air, target date: unknown: 93.1 mhz; 6 kw. Ant 328 ft. TL: N31 22 58 W89 23 43. 704 River St. 39401. Phone: (601) 544-1941. Fax: (601) 544-1947. Licensee: Unity Broadcasters. ♦ Victor Floyd, gen mgr.

WHSY(AM)— Sept 1, 1954: . Stn currently dark 950 khz; 5 kw-D, 64 w-N. TL: N31 22 33 W89 19 49. 63 Braswell Rd. 39401. Phone: (601) 582-7078. Fax: (601) 582-7122. E-mail: whsy95@megagate.com. Web Site: www.whsy950.com. Licensee: Southern Air Communications Inc. (acq 9-5-2004). Format: News, talk, sport. ♦ Charlie W. Holt, pres; Sam Minor, gen mgr.

WJMG(FM)— Listing follows WORV(AM).

WORV(AM)— June 7, 1969: 1580 khz; 1 kw-D, 88 w-N. TL: N31 20 33 W89 17 53. 1204 Graveline St. 39401. Phone: (601) 544-1941. Fax: (601) 544-1947. Licensee: Vernon C. Floyd dba Circuit Broadcasting of Hattiesburg. Network: American Urban. Rep: Dora-Clayton. Format: Gospel. ♦ Vernon C. Floyd, pres & gen mgr.

WJMG(FM)— Co-owned with WORV(AM). May 10, 1982: 92.1 mhz; 6 kw. 300 ft. TL: N31 20 33 W89 17 53. Stereo. Format: Urban contemp.

*WUSM-FM— May 10, 1973: 88.5 mhz; 3 kw. 282 ft. TL: N31 21 02 W89 22 12. Stereo. USM-118 College Dr., #10045 39406-0045. Phone: (601) 266-4287. Phone: (601) 266-5649. Fax: (601) 266-4288. E-mail: wusmmik@yahoo.com. Web Site: www.wusm.usm.edu. Licensee: University of Southern Mississippi. Network: AP Radio. Format: Class, var/div, AAA. News staff: 4; News: 22 hrs wkly. Target aud: General; college students & upper income univ & community listeners. Spec prog: Blues 10 hrs, World 4 hrs, children 2 hrs, jazz 18 hrs, new age 10 hrs, opera 3 hrs, pub affrs 10 hrs wkly. ♦ Shelby Thames, pres; Dennis Webster, exec VP; Michael Davis, gen mgr.

WXRR(FM)— July 1, 1967: 104.5 mhz; 100 kw. 984 ft. TL: N31 25 50 W89 08 51. (CP: TL: N31 25 52 W89 08 51). Stereo. Box 16596 39404. Phone: (601) 544-0095. Fax: (601) 649-8199. E-mail: rock104fm@rock104fm.com. Web Site: www.rock104fm.com. Licensee: Blakeney Communications Inc. (group owner; acq 8-30-94; $450,000 with co-located AM; 10-24-94). Format: Classic rock. Target aud: General. ♦ Larry Blakeney, pres & gen mgr.

WZLD(FM)— See Petal

Hazlehurst

WDXO(FM)— Listing follows WOEG(AM).

WOEG(AM)— June 1, 1953: 1220 khz; 250 w-D, 46 w-N. TL: N31 53 34 W90 24 08. Box 2016, Monticello 39654. Phone: (601) 587-9363. Phone: (601) 587-7625. Fax: (601) 587-9401. Licensee: The O'Neal Broadcasting Corp. (group owner; acq 10-16-97; with co-located FM). Booth, Freret, Imlay & Tepper. Format: Urban gospel. Target aud: General; Black. ♦ Heather Thurgood, opns mgr & progmg dir; Robert Byrd, gen sls mgr; Randy Bullock, prom dir; Rusty O'Neal, stn mgr, news dir & chief of engrg.

WDXO(FM)— Co-owned with WOEG(AM). Dec 24, 1970: 92.9 mhz; 6 kw. 295 ft. TL: N31 53 34 W90 24 08. Stereo. Network: ABC. Format: Oldies. News: 3 hrs wkly. Target aud: 18-50. ♦ Rusty O'Neal, gen mgr.

Heidelberg

WHER(FM)— May 1, 1980: 99.3 mhz; 50 kw. 492 ft. TL: N31 49 17 W89 18 37. Stereo. 2414 W. 7th St., Hattiesburg 39401. Phone: (601) 296-9800. Fax: (601) 582-5481. E-mail: contact@eagle99.com. Web Site: www.eagle99.com. Licensee: Capstar TX L.P. Group owner: Clear Channel Communications Inc. (acq 12-19-00; grpsl). Network: USA. Format: Oldies. Target aud: General. ♦ Mike Comfort, gen mgr; Jackson Walker, opns mgr; Glenn Musgrove, chief of engrg.

Hickory

*WGTC(FM)— Not on air, target date: unknown: 91.3 mhz; 18 kw. Ant 518 ft. TL: N32 26 35 W88 24 54. CSN International, 3232 W. MacArthur Blvd., Santa Ana, CA 92704. Phone: (714) 825-9663. Fax: (714) 825-9660. Web Site: www.csnradio.com. Licensee: CSN International (group owner). ♦ Jeffrey W. Smith, VP.

Broadcasting & Cable Yearbook 2006

Holly Springs

WKRA(AM)— Sept 2, 1966: 1110 khz; 1 kw-D. TL: N34 47 11 W89 25 00. Box 398, 1400 Hwy. 4 E., Suite C 38635. Phone: (662) 252-6692. Fax: (662) 252-2739. E-mail: wkra@dixie-net.com. Licensee: Bill Autrey. (acq 8-10-94; $250,000 with co-located FM; 9-5-94). Network: UPI. Format: Urban gospel. News staff: one; News: 9 hrs wkly. Target aud: 25-55. Spec prog: Gospel 12 hrs wkly. ♦Ray Vaughn Autry, gen mgr & stn mgr; Larry Nelson, gen sls mgr; Tracey Davis, progmg dir.

WKRA-FM— June 30, 1976: 92.7 mhz; 3 kw. 299 ft. TL: N34 47 11 W89 25 00. Format: Black, gospel, urban contemp. News staff: one. Target aud: General; Black community. Spec prog: Blues 12 hrs wkly.

***WURC(FM)**— Oct 14, 1988: 88.1 mhz; 3 kw. 328 ft. TL: N34 46 53 W89 26 49. Brown Mass Communications, 150 Rust Ave. 38635. Phone: (662) 252-5881. Fax: (662) 252-8869. Licensee: Rust College Inc. Network: NPR. Format: Jazz, inspirational, info, news. Target aud: General; college students, alternative seekers, minority listeners. ♦David L. Beckley, pres; Sylvester W. Oliver Jr., gen mgr; Wayne A. Fiddis, opns mgr; Sharron G. Hill, mus dir.

Horn Lake

WHAL-FM— July 26, 1994: 95.7 mhz; 6 kw. Ant 289 ft. TL: N35 08 09 W89 58 17. 2650 Thousand Oaks Blvd., Suite 4100, Memphis, TN 38118. Phone: (901) 529-4300. Fax: (901) 259-6451. Licensee: Clear Channel Broadcasting Licenses Inc. Group owner: Clear Channel Communications Inc. (acq 1996; grpsl). Rep: Clear Channel. Format: Gospel. News: 3 hrs wkly. Target aud: 35-54; baby boomers. ♦Tim Davies, gen mgr.

Houston

WCPC(AM)— Oct 21, 1955: 940 khz; 50 kw-D, 250 w-N, DA-2. TL: N33 56 00 W89 00 33. 1189 N. Jackson St. 38851. Phone: (662) 456-3071. Fax: (662) 456-3072. Licensee: WCPC Broadcasting Co. Inc. Network: USA. Format: Christian, country, gospel, Black. News staff: one; News: 14 hrs wkly. Adults. Spec prog: Black 10 hrs, farm5 hrs, gospel 40 hrs wkly. ♦Robin H. Mathis, pres & gen mgr; Melanie Mathis Munlin, opns dir, opns mgr & mus dir; Don Tallent, news dir.

WSYE(FM)— Sept 19, 1968: 93.3 mhz; 100 kw. 1,804 ft. TL: N33 45 06 W88 52 40. Stereo. Box 410, Tupelo 38802. Secondary address: 2214 S. Gloster, Tupelo 38802. Phone: (662) 842-7658. Fax: (662) 842-0197. E-mail: sunny93@network-one.com. Web Site: www.sunny93fm.com. Licensee: JMD Inc. (acq 9-28-99). Rep: McGavren Guild. Format: Adult contemp. News staff: one; News: 2 hrs wkly. Target aud: 25-54. ♦Cindy Roberts, gen mgr & sls VP; Bob Green, stn mgr; Dave Dunaway, opns dir; Cathy Williams, mus dir; Lee Adams, progmg dir & news dir; Barry Walters, chief of engrg.

Indianola

WNLA(AM)— May 1953: 1380 khz; 500 w-D, 44 w-N. TL: N33 27 32 W90 37 45. Box 667, Hwy. 448 38751. Phone: (662) 887-1380. Fax: (662) 887-1396. E-mail: wnla@capital2.com. Licensee: Shamrock Broadcasting Inc. (acq 10-1-84; $675,000 with co-located FM; 8-25-84). Network: ABC Information & Entertainment. Format: Black gospel. Target aud: 21-55; Black. ♦Erin Ely, gen mgr & progmg dir; Gerry Brophy, pres, sls dir & engrg dir; Bob Taylor, chief of engrg.

WNLA-FM— Sept 1, 1969: 105.5 mhz; 4.4 kw. 200 ft. TL: N33 28 41 W90 38 28. Stereo. Format: Adult contemp. News: 21 hrs wkly. Target aud: 21-55.

WTCD(FM)—Licensed to Indianola. See Greenwood

***WYTF(FM)**— Aug 26, 2004: 88.7 mhz; 100 kw vert. Ant 636 ft. TL: N33 35 03 W90 36 13. Drawer 3206, Tupelo 38801. Phone: (662) 844-8888. Fax: (662) 842-6791. Web Site: www.afr.net. Licensee: American Family Association. Group owner: American Family Radio. Network: USA. Format: Christian. ♦Don Wildman, gen mgr.

Itta Bena

***WVSD(FM)**— June 23, 1991: 91.7 mhz; 3 kw. 292 ft. TL: N33 31 05 W90 20 38. MVSU Box 7221, Hwy. 82 W. 38941. Phone: (662) 254-3612. Phone: (662) 254-3716. Fax: (662) 254-3000. Licensee: Mississippi Valley State University. Format: Jazz, gospel, blues. Spec prog: R&B oldies 10 hrs, Reggae/Latin 3 hrs, other 2 hrs wkly. ♦Dr. Lester Newman, pres; Larz G. Roberts, gen mgr & progmg dir; Debra Harmon, progmg mgr.

Iuka

WFXO(FM)— Nov 5, 1970: 104.9 mhz; 50 kw. 443 ft. TL: N34 46 35 W88 23 40. 311 W. Eastport St. 38852. Phone: (662) 423-2369. Fax: (662) 423-6059. E-mail: fox@freedom2000net.com. Licensee: Billy R. McLain. (acq 11-4-91; with co-located AM). Network: ABC Information & Entertainment. Format: Country, rock. ♦Billy McLain, gen mgr, gen sls mgr & progmg dir.

Jackson

WHLH(FM)— Nov 19, 1973: 95.5 mhz; 100 kw. Ant 1,115 ft. TL: N32 14 26 W90 24 15. Stereo. 1375 Beasley Rd. 39206. Phone: (601) 982-1062. Fax: (601) 362-1905. Web Site: www.hallelujah955.com. Licensee: Capstar TX L.P. Group owner: Clear Channel Communications Inc. (acq 8-30-00; grpsl). Network: CBS. Rep: D & R Radio. Cohn & Marks. Format: Gospel. Target aud: 18-34; female. ♦Jenell Roberts, gen mgr & progmg dir.

WJDX(AM)— 1929: 620 khz; 5 kw-D, 1 kw-N, DA-N. TL: N32 22 56 W90 11 26. Stereo. Box 31999 39286. Secondary address: 1375 Beasley Rd. 39206. Phone: (601) 982-1062. Fax: (601) 362-1905. Web Site: www.wjdx.com. Licensee: Capstar TX L.P. Group owner: Clear Channel Communications Inc. (acq 8-30-00; grpsl). Network: ABC Daytime Direction. Rep: McGavren Guild. Format: Sports/talk. News staff: one; News: 10 hrs wkly. Target aud: 25-54; middle to upper income contemp adults. Spec prog: Farm 2 hrs wkly. ♦Kenneth E. Windham, gen mgr; Mary Ann Kirby, gen sls mgr; Randy Bell, progmg dir & news dir; Jason Black, chief of engrg.

WMSI(FM)—Co-owned with WJDX(AM). 1948: 102.9 mhz; 100 kw. 1,800 ft. TL: N32 12 46 W90 22 54. Stereo. Web Site: www.miss103.com. Network: ABC Information & Entertainment. Format: C&W. News: 4 hrs wkly. Target aud: 25 plus. Spec prog: Farm one hr wkly. ♦Sam McLeod, gen sls mgr; Rick Adams, progmg dir; Marshall Stewart, mus dir & news dir.

WJMI(FM)—Listing follows WOAD(AM).

***WJSU(FM)**— August 1975: 88.5 mhz; 3 kw. 203 ft. TL: N32 17 47 W90 12 23. Stereo. Box 18450, Jackson State Univ. 39217. Phone: (601) 979-2140. Phone: (601) 979-2285. Fax: (601) 979-2878. Web Site: www.jsums.edu. Licensee: Jackson State University. Network: NPR. Format: Jazz, news, world. Target aud: 25-54; middle-class multiracial who prefer jazz or alternative mus. Spec prog: Gospel 18 hrs, reggae 2 hrs, blues 2 hrs wkly. ♦Bobby Walker, gen mgr.

WKXI(AM)— 1947: 1400 khz; 1 kw-U. TL: N32 19 12 W90 11 25. Box 9446 39286. Secondary address: 731 S. Pear Orchard, Ridgeland 39157. Phone: (601) 957-1300. Fax: (601) 956-0516. Licensee: Urban Radio II L.L.C. Group owner: Inner City Broadcasting (acq 8-25-2000; grpsl). Rep: D & R Radio. Format: Blues. News staff: one; News: 30 hrs wkly. Target aud: 25-54. ♦Kevin Webb, gen mgr.

***WMPN-FM**— November 1984: 91.3 mhz; 100 kw. 760 ft. TL: N32 16 53 W90 17 41. Stereo. 3825 Ridgewood Rd. 39211. Phone: (601) 432-6565. Fax: (601) 432-6806. Web Site: www.mpbonline.org. Licensee: Mississippi Authority for Educational Television. Network: Network: PRI, NPR. Schwartz, Woods & Miller. Format: Music news, info. News staff: 5; News: 20 hrs wkly. Target aud: General. ♦Marie Antoon, chmn & pres; Gene Edwards, gen mgr; Bob Holland, opns mgr & progmg dir; Ty Warren, dev dir & dev mgr; Tippy Garner, rgnl sls mgr; Jennifer Griffin, prom dir; Greg Waxberg, mus dir; Dick Rizzo, news dir & pub affrs dir; Keith Martin, engrg mgr & chief of engrg.

***WMPR(FM)**— 1983: 90.1 mhz; 100 kw. 500 ft. TL: N32 11 33 W90 05 28. Stereo. Box 9782 39286. Phone: (601) 948-5835. Fax: (601) 948-6162. E-mail: wmpr@wmpr901.com. Web Site: www.wmpr901.com. Licensee: J.C. Maxwell Broadcasting Group Inc. Format: Blues, gospel, urban contemp. ♦Charles Evers, gen mgr & progmg dir; Sandra Henry, gen sls mgr.

WOAD(AM)— 1929: 1300 khz; 5 kw-D, 1 kw-N. TL: N32 23 12 W90 09 47. 731 S. Pear Orchard Rd., Suite 27, Ridgeland 39157. Phone: (601) 957-1300. Fax: (601) 956-0516. Web Site: www.woad.com. Licensee: Urban Radio II L.L.C. Group owner: Inner City Broadcasting (acq 8-25-2000; grpsl). Network: Network: American Urban, ABC. Format: Gospel. Target aud: 25-54. ♦Kevin Webb, gen mgr & gen sls mgr; Percy Davis, progmg dir; Emmett Rushing, chief of engrg.

WJMI(FM)—Co-owned with WOAD(AM). 1967: 99.7 mhz; 100 kw. 1,060 ft. TL: N32 16 39 W90 17 41. Stereo. Web Site: www.wjmi.com. Network: ABC FM Connection. Format: Urban hip-hop. News staff: one. Target aud: 18-49. ♦Stan Branson, progmg dir.

WSFZ(AM)— September 1938: 930 khz; 5 kw-U, DA-N. TL: N32 23 42 W90 09 14. No. 5 Twelve Oaks Cir., Suite A 39209. Phone: (601) 922-9307. Fax: (601) 922-5051. E-mail: espnradio930@espnradio930.com. Licensee: Sportsrad Inc. (acq 12-20-01; $222,500). Network: Westwood One. Rep: McGavren Guild. Format: Sports. ♦Bryan Eubank, gen mgr, stn mgr, opns dir & progmg dir; John Rainey, gen sls mgr.

WSTZ-FM—(Vicksburg). June 1968: 106.7 mhz; 100 kw. 1,365 ft. TL: N32 12 22 W90 24 50. (CP: Ant 1,059 ft. TL: N32 12 29 W90 24 50). Stereo. Box 31999 39286. Secondary address: 1375 Beasley Rd. 39206. Phone: (601) 982-1062. Fax: (601) 362-1905. E-mail: dougjones@clearchannel.com. Web Site: www.z106.com. Licensee: Capstar TX L.P. Group owner: Clear Channel Communications Inc. (acq 8-30-00; grpsl). Rep: D & R Radio. Format: Classic rock. Target aud: 25-54. ♦Kenneth Windham, gen mgr; Kevin Keith, progmg dir.

WUSJ(FM)— Sept 16, 1966: 96.3 mhz; 100 kw. 1,450 ft. TL: N32 14 26 W90 24 15. (CP: 100 kw, ant 1,059 ft. TL: N32 12 29 W90 24 56). Stereo. 265 High Point Dr., Ridgeland 39157. Phone: (601) 956-0102. Fax: (601) 978-3890. Web Site: www.us963.com. Licensee: New South Communications Inc. (group owner; acq 8-24-99; $5 million). Network: ABC Daytime Direction. Format: Country. ♦Gwen Rakestraw, gen mgr.

WWJK(FM)— Aug 10, 1971: 94.7 mhz; 100 kw. 1,168 ft. TL: N32 16 53 W90 17 41. Stereo. 222 Beasley Rd. 39206. Phone: (601) 957-3000. Fax: (601) 956-0370. E-mail: mail94@arrow94.com. Web Site: www.arrow94.com. Licensee: Backyard Broadcasting Mississippi LLC Group owner: Backyard Broadcasting LLC (acq 5-31-2002; $4,830,000. with WRXW(FM) Pearl). Rep: Christal. Fletcher, Heald & Hildreth. Format: Classic rock and roll. News staff: one; News: one hr wkly. Target aud: 25-54. ♦Barry Drake, pres; Chris Butterich, VP & gen mgr; Bob Rall, opns dir; Janna Hughs, sls dir; Nikki Brown, prom dir; Sam Blythe, progmg dir; Karen Jones, news dir; Emmit Rushing, chief of engrg.

WYOY(FM)—See Gluckstadt

WZQK(AM)—See Brandon

WZRX(AM)— Apr 8, 1965: 1590 khz; 5 kw-D, 1 kw-N, DA-N. TL: N32 22 01 W90 13 26. Stereo. Box 9734 39286. Secondary address: 2980 Forest Ave. Ext. 39286. Phone: (601) 981-9080. Fax: (601) 981-9093. E-mail: radioair@bellsouth.net. Licensee: Capstar MS L.P. Group owner: Clear Channel Communications Inc. (acq 5-29-98; grpsl). Network: American Urban. Format: Gospel. Target aud: 25 plus; general. ♦Carl Haynes, gen mgr & stn mgr; Maria Epps, sls dir & prom mgr; Val Blue, pub affrs dir; Emmitte Rushing, chief of engrg.

Kosciusko

***WJTA(FM)**— 1989: 91.7 mhz; 383 w. 171 ft. TL: N33 05 54 W89 30 33. Stereo. Box 888, 319 N. Madison 39090. Phone: (662) 289-5703. Fax: (662) 290-6080. Licensee: Kosciusko Educational Broadcasting Foundation. Format: Gospel. News: 6 hrs wkly. Target aud: General. ♦Dr. William G. Suratt, pres & gen mgr.

WKOZ(AM)— Oct 31, 1947: 1340 khz; 1 kw-U. TL: N33 03 51 W89 36 12. Box 1700 39090-1700. Phone: (662) 289-1340. Phone: (662) 289-1050. Fax: (662) 289-7907. E-mail: breezy@kopower.com. Web Site: www.breezynews.com. Licensee: Boswell Radio LLC (acq 6-1-62). William D. Silva. Format: News/talk. News staff: one. Target aud: 50 plus. ♦Johnny Boswell, gen mgr; Ann Steen, stn mgr; Eric Matthews, opns mgr; Jerry Price, gen sls mgr; Jay Taylor, news dir.

WQJQ(FM)— June 25, 1965: 105.1 mhz; 100 kw. 981 ft. TL: N32 41 25 W89 52 06. Stereo. Box 31999, Jackson 39268. Phone: (601) 982-1062. Fax: (601) 362-8270. Web Site: www.q1051.com. Licensee: Capstar TX L.P. Group owner: Clear Channel Communications Inc. (acq 8-30-00; grpsl). Format: Motown & Jammin Oldies. Target aud: 35-64. ♦Kenneth Windham, gen mgr; Steve Kelly, opns mgr.

Stations in the U.S. Mississippi

Developers & Brokers of Radio Properties
contact American Media Services at our suite:
Philadelphia Marriott Downtown
215-625-2900
843-972-2200
americanmediaservices.com
Charleston, SC
Dallas, TX • Chicago, Il • Austin, TX
American Media Services, LLC

Laurel

WAML(AM)— Oct 20, 1932: 1340 khz; 1 kw-U. TL: N31 40 01 W89 08 59. Box 6226, 1425 Ellisville Blvd. 39440. Fax: (601) 425-0016. Licensee: Walking by Faith Ministries Inc. (acq 10-1-99). Format: Gospel, relg. Target aud: General. ♦James Black, gen mgr.

*WATP(FM)— 1998: 90.7 mhz; 350 w. 489 ft. TL: N31 46 54 W89 09 31. American Family Radio, Box 3206, Tupelo 38803. Phone: (662) 844-8888. Fax: (662) 842-6791. Web Site: www.afr.net. Licensee: American Family Association. Group owner: American Family Radio Network: USA. Format: Relg. ♦Marvin Sanders, gen mgr.

WEEZ(AM)— Feb 27, 1957: 890 khz; 10 kw-D. TL: N31 31 29 W89 14 31. Stereo. One Commerce Dr., Suite 106, Hattiesburg 39402. Secondary address: 51 Victory Rd. 39443. Phone: (601) 296-9800. Fax: (601) 296-9838. Licensee: Clear Channel Broadcasting Licenses Inc. Group owner: Clear Channel Communications Inc. (acq 12-19-00; grpsl). Network: ABC FM Connection. Format: Blues. News staff: one; News: 4 hrs wkly. Target aud: General. ♦Jackson Walker, opns mgr; Mike Comfort, gen mgr & sls dir; James Harris, gen sls mgr; Denise Brooks, progmg dir; Glen Musgrove, chief of engrg.

WNSL(FM)—Co-owned with WEEZ(AM). Mar 10, 1959: 100.3 mhz; 100 kw. 1,050 ft. TL: N31 31 37 W89 08 07. Stereo. Network: ABC. Format: CHR. Target aud: 18-49. ♦Don King, progmg dir.

WIZK(AM)—See Bay Springs

WKZW(FM)—See Bay Springs

WMXI(FM)— April 1989: 98.1 mhz; 2.55 kw. Ant 512 ft. TL: N31 33 22 W89 09 09. Box 15935, Hattiesburg 39403. Secondary address: 7501 U.S. Hwy. 49, Hattiesburg 39403. Phone: (601) 261-0898. Fax: (601) 261-3798. E-mail: zoo107@bellsouth.net. Licensee: Rainey Broadcasting Inc. (acq 10-21-96; $75,000). Format: News/talk. ♦Ted Tibbett, gen mgr.

Leland

WBAD(FM)—Listing follows WESY(AM).

WESY(AM)— Apr 8, 1957: 1580 khz; 1 kw-D, 48 w-N. TL: N33 22 46 W90 55 47. (CP: 1 kw-N, DA-N). Box 5804, Greenville 38704. Secondary address: 126 Seven Oaks Rd., Greenville 38701. Phone: (662) 335-9265. Fax: (662) 335-5538. E-mail: wbad@tecinfo.com. Licensee: East Delta Communications Inc. (acq 1980). Network: American Urban. David Tillotson. Format: Blues, relg, gospel. Target aud: 18-54. ♦Stanley S. Sherman, exec VP & gen sls mgr; William D. Jackson, pres & gen mgr.

WBAD(FM)—Co-owned with WESY(AM). 1973: 94.3 mhz; 50 kw. 300 ft. TL: N33 24 55 W90 59 18. Stereo. Licensee: Interchange Communications Inc. (acq 5-12-73). Network: American Urban. Format: Urban contemp.

WIQQ(FM)— Sept 1, 1985: 102.3 mhz; 6 kw. 440 ft. TL: N33 23 50 W91 00 33. Stereo. Box 1816, Greenville 38702-1816. Secondary address: Unit 39, 800 Hwy. 1 S., Greenville 38702. Phone: (662) 378-2617. Fax: (662) 378-8341. E-mail: wiqq@sellsouth.net. Licensee: The River Broadcasting Co. Inc. Group owner: The River Group. Network: Network: USA, Jones Radio Networks. Rep: McGavren Guild. Baraff, Koerner & Olender. Format: Adult contemp. News staff: one; News: 4 hrs wkly. Target aud: 18-49; multi-paycheck & spendable income. Spec prog: Farm 6 hrs, relg 6 hrs wkly. ♦George E. Pine, pres; James P. Karr Jr., VP, gen mgr & prom VP; Linda McKee, opns mgr; Margret Kazen Karr, gen sls mgr & mktg dir; Ray Renfroe, progmg dir; Paul Artman, pub affrs dir; Percy Kuhn, chief of engrg.

Lexington

WAGR-FM— June 1, 1990: 102.5 mhz; 6 kw. 328 ft. TL: N33 09 06 W90 07 45. (CP: 12.5 kw, ant 459 ft.). Stereo. Box 369, 100 Radio Rd. 39095. Phone: (662) 834-1025. Phone: (662) 834-1254. Fax: (662) 834-1254. Licensee: Brad Maurice Cothran (acq 12-21-01). Format: Country, oldies. ♦Brad Maurice Cothran, gen mgr, progmg dir & news dir; Fanny Cothran, chief of engrg.

WXTN(AM)— Oct 23, 1959: 1000 khz; 5 kw-D. TL: N33 06 39 W90 02 21. Box 369 39095. Phone: (662) 834-1666. Fax: (662) 834-1254. Licensee: Brad Maurice Cothran (acq 12-21-01). Format: Gospel, Black. ♦Brad M. Cothran, gen mgr.

Liberty

WAZA(FM)— 1998: 107.7 mhz; 25 kw. Ant 328 ft. TL: N31 17 12 W90 47 53. 215 E. Bay St., Magnolia 39652. Phone: (601) 684-4116. Fax: (601) 684-4654. E-mail: sandow@telapak.net. Licensee: Southwest Broadcasting Inc. Format: Oldies. Target aud: 18-30; adult contemporary, retro 80's shows. ♦Charles Dowdy, gen mgr.

Long Beach

WJZD(FM)— Mar 20, 1994: 94.5 mhz; 6 kw. 321 ft. TL: N30 22 25 W89 06 38. Box 6216, Gulfport 39506. Secondary address: 10211 Southpark Dr., Gulfport 39503. Phone: (228) 896-5307. Fax: (228) 896-5703. E-mail: info@wjzd.com. Web Site: www.wjzd.com. Licensee: WJZD Inc. Network: ABC. Rep: Interep. Allied Radio Partners. Fletch, Heald & Hildreth. Format: Urban adult contemp, news/talk. News staff: 2; News: 2 hrs wkly. Spec prog: Gospel 20 hrs wkly. ♦Rip Daniels, CEO & gen mgr; Danielle Jewett, opns dir; Tamara Wingerfer, sls dir, gen sls mgr & natl sls mgr; Rob Neal, progmg dir; Tabari Daniels, mus dir; Judy Whitfield, pub affrs dir; Thomas Bradley, chief of engrg.

Lorman

*WPRL(FM)— Oct 12, 1987: 91.7 mhz; 3 kw. 300 ft. TL: N31 53 37 W91 08 54. Stereo. Box 269 39096. Secondary address: Alcorn State University, 1000 Alcorn Dr. 39096. Phone: (601) 877-6290. Phone: (601) 877-6613. Fax: (601) 877-2213. E-mail: lljunag@hotmail.com. Web Site: alconstateuniv.edu. Licensee: Alcorn State University. Network: Network: Network: PRI, NPR, AP Radio. Format: Gospel, Jazz, urban contemp, rhythm & blues, news info, sports. News staff: 1; News: 23 hrs wkly. Target aud: General; African-American, rural, University faculty & students. Spec prog: Gospel 16 hrs wkly. ♦Lijuana Weir, opns mgr.

Louisville

WLSM-FM— Apr 22, 1966: 107.1 mhz; 12.5 kw. 466 ft. TL: N33 07 20 W89 01 05. Stereo. Box 279 39339. Secondary address: 2142 Hwy. 14 E. 39339. Phone: (662) 773-3481. Fax: (662) 773-3482. E-mail: wlsm@louisvillems.com. Licensee: Harrison Communications Inc. Network: ABC Daytime Direction. Format: Country. Target aud: 18-54. ♦Phillip A. Harrison, pres, gen mgr, gen sls mgr, prom mgr & news dir; Stacy S. Harrison, stn mgr, natl sls mgr, adv mgr & progmg dir.

Lucedale

WRBE(AM)— Sept 3, 1960: 1440 khz; 5 kw-D. TL: N30 56 00 W88 36 20. (CP: TL: N30 55 58 W88 36 21). Box 827 39452. Secondary address: 3276 Hwy. 198 W. 39452. Phone: (601) 947-8151. Fax: (601) 947-8152. E-mail: jdl@datasync.com. Licensee: JDL Corp. (acq 2-24-98; $220,000 with co-located FM). Rep: Dora-Clayton, Keystone (unwired net). Format: Country, gospel. Target aud: General. ♦Larry Shirley, pres, gen mgr, progmg dir & news dir; Lillian Hodgel, gen sls mgr.

WRBE-FM— April 1993: 106.9 mhz; 6 kw. 258 ft. TL: N30 55 58 W88 36 21.

Lumberton

WZNF(FM)— Dec 10, 1983: 95.3 mhz; 50 kw. Ant 1,181 ft. TL: N30 44 48 W89 03 30. 10250 Lorraine Rd., Gulfport 39503. Phone: (228) 896-5500. Fax: (228) 896-0458. E-mail: patty@z95fm.com. Web Site: www.z95fm.com. Licensee: JMD Inc. (acq 1-11-00; $5 million). Format: Classic rock. ♦Morgan Dowdy, CEO, chmn & pres; Buddy Baylor, gen mgr; David Melton Jr., engrg mgr; Patty Steele, progmg dir & chief of engrg.

Magee

WKXI-FM— Apr 11, 1970: 107.5 mhz; 98 kw. 952 ft. TL: N32 15 28 W89 47 22. Stereo. 731 S. Pear Orchard Rd., Suite 27, Ridgeland 39157. Phone: (601) 957-1300. Fax: (601) 956-0516. Web Site: www.kixie107.com. Licensee: Urban Radio II L.L.C. Group owner: Inner City Broadcasting (acq 8-25-2000; grpsl). Format: Urban contemp. Target aud: 25-54. ♦Kevin Webb, VP & gen mgr; Kevin Webb, gen sls mgr; Stan Branson, opns mgr & progmg dir.

WSJC(AM)— July 5, 1957: 810 khz; 50 kw-D, 500 w-N, DA-N. TL: N31 52 00 W89 41 35. 130 Radio Station Dr. 39111. Phone: (601) 849-5838. Fax: (601) 849-5838. Licensee: Witko Broadcasting L.L.C. (acq 12-3-98). Format: Christian. ♦Margaret Butler, gen mgr.

Marion

WYYW(FM)— Mar 15, 1990: 95.1 mhz; 50 kw. 606 ft. TL: N32 26 08 W88 36 24. Stereo. 4307 Hwy. 39 N., Meridian 39301. Phone: (601) 693-2381. Fax: (601) 485-2972. Web Site: www.classicrock951.com. Licensee: Clear Channel Broadcasting Licenses Inc. Group owner: Clear Channel Communications Inc. (acq 3-16-01; grpsl). Format: Country. Target aud: 25-54. ♦Ron Harper, gen mgr.

Marks

WQMA(AM)— Dec 1, 1969: 1520 khz; 250 w-D. TL: N34 15 42 W90 17 18. 1820 W. Marks Rd. 38646. Phone: (662) 326-3555. E-mail: jason@q1520radio.com. Licensee: Jason Konarz. (acq 1999; $50,000). Pepper & Corazzini. Format: Oldies. Spec prog: Relg 4 hrs wkly. ♦Jason Konarz, pres, gen mgr & stn mgr.

McComb

WAKH(FM)—Listing follows WAPF(AM).

WAKK(AM)— Apr 18, 1948: 980 khz; 5 kw-D, 152 w-N. TL: N31 12 51 W90 27 42. 206 N. Front St. 39648. Secondary address: Drawer 1649 39648. Phone: (601) 684-7470. Fax: (601) 684-4654. Licensee: Southwest Broadcasting Inc. (group owner; acq 9-86; $600,000 with co-located FM; 7-28-86). Network: ABC. Format: News/talk, relg. Target aud: General. ♦Wayne Dowdy, pres; Charles Dowdy, gen mgr; David Hughes, progmg dir; Carl Lazenby, pub affrs dir.

WAPF(AM)— Apr 25, 1975: 1140 khz; 1 kw-D. TL: N31 14 51 W90 25 14. Box 1649 39649. Secondary address: 206 N. Front 39648. Phone: (601) 684-4116. Fax: (601) 684-4654. Licensee: Southwest Broadcasting Inc. (group owner; acq 8-5-93; $600,000; 8-23-93). Format: Var/gospel. Target aud: General. ♦Charles Dowdy, gen mgr, gen sls mgr & news dir; David Hughes, progmg dir; Ben Bickham, chief of engrg.

WAKH(FM)—Co-owned with WAPF(AM). Oct 15, 1978: 105.7 mhz; 100 kw. 489 ft. TL: N31 16 50 W90 27 05. Stereo. Format: Country. Target aud: General.

*WAQL(FM)— 1999: 90.5 mhz; 3.75 kw. 331 ft. TL: N31 16 40 W90 26 56. American Family Radio, Box 3206, Tupelo 38803. Phone: (662) 844-8888. Fax: (662) 842-6791. Web Site: www.afr.net. Licensee: American Family Association. Group owner: American Family Radio Network: USA. Format: Relg. ♦Marvin Sanders, gen mgr.

WHNY(AM)— 1939: 1250 khz; 5 kw-D, 1 kw-N, DA-N. TL: N31 16 07 W90 26 03. 1114 Hwy. 570 E. 39648. Phone: (601) 250-1250. Fax: (601) 250-1254. E-mail: whny@eaglepc.net. Licensee: C.W.H. Broadcasting Inc. (acq 1952; $43,000). Network: ABC. Format: News, talk, sports. ♦Sean Oliver, gen mgr.

Mississippi

McLain

WXAB(FM)— January 1999: 96.9 mhz; 4 kw. Ant 400 ft. TL: N31 06 56 W88 45 56. Stereo. Box 723, Wiggins 39577. Licensee: Tralyn Broadcasting Inc. (acq 2-19-97; grpsl). ♦ Mike Self, gen mgr.

Meridian

WALT(AM)— 1946: 910 khz; 5 kw-D, 1 kw-N. TL: N32 23 37 W88 40 08. Stereo. Box 5797 39302. Phone: (601) 693-2661. Fax: (601) 483-0826. Licensee: New South Communications Inc. (group owner; acq 4-1-57). Network: ABC Information & Entertainment. Rep: McGavren Guild. Format: Talk. Target aud: 18-49. ♦ F.E. Holladay, pres; Larry Torgerson, gen mgr.

WOKK(FM)—Co-owned with WALT(AM). August 1967: 97.1 mhz; 100 kw. 600 ft. TL: N32 19 45 W88 41 26. Stereo. Web Site: www.wokk.com. Format: Country. Target aud: 25-54.

WFFX(AM)— December 1957: 1450 khz; 1 kw-U. TL: N32 23 09 W88 41 36. 4307 Hwy. 39 N. 39301. Phone: (601) 693-2381. Phone: (601) 693-2383. Fax: (601) 485-2972. Web Site: www.sports1450.com. Licensee: Clear Channel Communications Licenses Inc. Group owner: Clear Channel Communications Inc. (acq 3-16-01; grpsl). ♦ Ron Harper, gen mgr; Pam Gray, sls dir & gen sls mgr; Lee Taylor, progmg dir.

WJDQ(FM)— February 1968: 101.3 mhz; 99 kw. 581 ft. TL: N32 18 43 W88 41 33. Stereo. 4307 Hwy. 39 N. 39301. Phone: (601) 693-2381. Fax: (601) 485-2972. Licensee: Clear Channel Broadcasting Licenses Inc. Group owner: Clear Channel Communications Inc. (acq 3-16-01; grpsl). Format: Adult contemp. ♦ Ron Harper, gen mgr & sls dir; David Day, progmg dir; Christina Andrews, mus dir; Joyce Franklin, news dir; Olen Booth, chief of engrg.

*****WMAW-FM**— December 1983: 88.1 mhz; 100 kw. 1,050 ft. TL: N32 08 18 W89 05 36. Stereo. 3825 Ridgewood Rd., Jackson 39211. Phone: (601) 432-6565. Fax: (601) 432-6806. Web Site: www.mpbonline.org. Licensee: Mississippi Authority for Educational Television. Network: Network: PRI, NPR. Schwartz, Woods & Miller. Format: Music, news, info. News staff: 5; News: 20 hrs wkly. Target aud: General. ♦ Marie Antoon, chmn; Gene Edwards, gen mgr; Bob Holland, opns mgr.

WMER(AM)— Oct 16, 1973: 1390 khz; 5 kw-D, 250 w-N. TL: N32 20 41 W88 41 32. 1106 18th Ave. 39301. Phone: (601) 693-9637. Fax: (601) 693-9637. Licensee: Michael H. Glass. (acq 1-9-98; $55,000). Network: USA. Format: Gospel, Christian. Target aud: 25-54; upscale, young families, non-working mothers.

WMMZ(FM)— 1994: 102.1 mhz; 800 w. 610 ft. TL: N32 21 51 W88 38 34. 3436 Hwy. 45 N. 39301. Phone: (601) 693-2661. Fax: (601) 483-0826. E-mail: wmmz@wokk.com. Licensee: Mississippi Broadcasters L.L.C. (group owner; acq 2-26-93; $243,500; FTR: 3-22-93). Format: Urban. ♦ Clay Holladay, pres & gen mgr; Scott Stevens, opns mgr; Karen Bostick, sls dir; Scott Shepperd, chief of engrg.

WMOX(AM)— Dec 1, 1945: 1010 khz; 10 kw-D, 1 kw-N, DA-2. TL: N32 23 42 W88 39 28. Box 5184 39302. Phone: (601) 693-1891. Phone: (601) 693-1010. Fax: (601) 483-1010. E-mail: wmox@wmox.net. Web Site: www.wmox.net. Licensee: Magnolia State Broadcasting Inc. (acq 12-27-98; $125,000; 1-25-93). Rep: Dora-Clayton. Format: Talk/news, sports. News staff: one. Target aud: 25 plus; College educated with 30k plus annual income. Spec prog: Relg 8 hrs wkly. ♦ Eddie Smith, pres & gen mgr; William T. Smith, VP, opns dir, gen sls mgr & prom dir.

WNBN(AM)— Nov 1, 1987: 1290 khz; 2.5 kw-D, 90 w-N. TL: N32 21 42 W88 37 26. 266 23rd St. 39301. Phone: (601) 483-3401. Phone: (601) 483-7930. Fax: (601) 483-3411. Web Site: www.wnbn.onlineyp.net. Licensee: Frank Rackley Jr. Format: Gospel, blues, talk. News: 61 hrs wkly. Target aud: 18-54. Spec prog: Black, women's, business, inspirational. ♦ Frank Rackley Jr., pres & mus dir; Trell Hampton, gen mgr; Elder Eric Sharpe, opns VP; John Shaw, gen sls mgr; Beverly Nelson, progmg dir; Nate Pringle, asst music dir; Terry Clayton, chief of engrg.

Mississippi State

*****WMAB-FM**— December 1983: 89.9 mhz; 63 kw. 1,080 ft. TL: N33 21 07 W89 08 56. Stereo. 3825 Ridgewood Rd., Jackson 39211. Phone: (601) 432-6565. Fax: (601) 432-6806. Web Site: www.mpbonline.org. Licensee: Mississippi Authority for Educational Television. Network: Network: PRI, NPR. Schwartz, Woods & Miller. Format: Music, news, info. News staff: 5; News: 20 hrs wkly. Target aud: General. ♦ Marie Antoon, chmn; Gene Edwards, gen mgr; Bob Holland, opns mgr.

Monticello

WMLC(AM)— 1969: 1270 khz; 1 kw-D, 53 w-N. TL: N31 33 24 W90 08 06. 20 WMLC Rd. 39654. Phone: (601) 587-1270. Fax: (601) 587-2119. E-mail: espnradio1270@bellsouth.net. Licensee: WMLC LLC (acq 7-21-2004; $45,000). Network: ESPN Radio. Format: Sports. ♦ Will Watson, gen mgr.

WRQO(FM)— Nov 19, 1990: 102.1 mhz; 50 kw. 500 ft. TL: N31 36 13 W90 12 26. Stereo. Box 2016, Q102 Rd. 39654. Secondary address: Box 1084 39654. Phone: (601) 587-9363. Phone: (601) 587-7625. Fax: (601) 587-9401. Fax: (601) 835-5005. E-mail: country@wrqo-q102.com. Licensee: The O'Neal Broadcasting Corp. (group owner) Network: CBS. Booth, Freret, Imlay & Tepper. Format: Traditional country. News: 15 hrs wkly. Target aud: 25-54. Spec prog: Farm one hr, relg 10 hrs wkly. ♦ Marcus Rusty O'Neal, pres, gen mgr, gen sls mgr & chief of engrg; Randy Bullock, opns mgr.

Morton

WQST(AM)—See Forest

Moss Point

WBUV(FM)—Licensed to Moss Point. See Pascagoula-Moss Point

Mound Bayou

WZYQ(FM)—Licensed to Mound Bayou. See Cleveland

Natchez

*****WASM(FM)**— 2001: 91.1 mhz; 1 kw. Ant 482 ft. TL: N31 29 10 W91 21 42. American Family Radio, Box 3206, Tupelo 38803. Phone: (662) 844-8888. Fax: (662) 842-6791. Web Site: www.afr.net. Licensee: American Family Association. Group owner: American Family Radio Network: USA. Format: Relg. ♦ Marvin Sanders, gen mgr.

WKSO(FM)— March 1993: 97.3 mhz; 1.45 kw. Ant 686 ft. TL: N31 30 33 W91 24 19. Box 768 39121. Secondary address: 2 O'Ferrall St. 39420. Phone: (601) 442-4895. Fax: (601) 446-8260. Licensee: Will Perk Broadcasting. Group owner: First Natchez Radio Group (acq 8-31-92; $36,000; FTR: 9-21-92). Network: ABC. Format: Adult contemp. ♦ Margaret Perkins, gen mgr.

WMIS(AM)— May 18, 1941: 1240 khz; 1 kw-U. TL: N31 31 14 W91 23 09. Box 1248 39121. Secondary address: 20 E. Franklin St. 39120. Phone: (601) 442-2522. Fax: (601) 446-9918. E-mail: wmiswtyj@aol.com. Licensee: Natchez Broadcasting Co. Network: American Urban. Format: Black, gospel, blues. Target aud: General; Black. Spec prog: Farm 6 hrs wkly. ♦ Diana Ewing Nutter, pres; James B. Nutter, VP, gen mgr & gen sls mgr; Lijuna Weir, stn mgr & progmg dir; George Lee, mus dir; Larry Bolland, chief of engrg.

WNAT(AM)— Dec 4, 1949: 1450 khz; 1 kw-U. TL: N31 33 24 W91 23 00. Stereo. Box 768 39121. Secondary address: 2 O'Ferral St. 39121. Phone: (601) 442-4895. Fax: (601) 446-8260. Web Site: www.wnat1450am.com. Licensee: First Natchez Corp. Group owner: First Natchez Radio Group (acq 11-28-58). Network: ABC Information & Entertainment. Schwartz, Woods & Miller. Format: News/talk, sports. News staff: 2. Target aud: 25-54. Spec prog: Gospel 18 hrs wkly. ♦ Marie Perkins, pres; Margaret Perkins, gen mgr, gen sls mgr & pub affrs dir; Mickey Alexander, progmg dir; Keith Sanders, news dir & chief of engrg.

WQNZ(FM)—Co-owned with WNAT(AM). Mar 1, 1968: 95.1 mhz; 98 kw. 1,056 ft. TL: N31 30 33 W91 24 19. (CP: ant 1,896 ft). Stereo. Web Site: www.wnat1450.com. Network: ABC Information & Entertainment. Format: Country. News staff: 2; News: 7 hrs wkly. Target aud: 25 plus.

WTYJ(FM)—See Fayette

New Albany

WNAU(AM)— Mar 27, 1955: 1470 khz; 500 w-U, DA-N. TL: N34 29 48 W89 00 52. Box 808 38652. Phone: (662) 534-8133. Fax: (662) 538-4183. Licensee: MPM Investment Group (acq 11-9-2004). Rep: Allied Radio Partners. Format: Oldies. Target aud: 25-54. Spec prog: Gospel. ♦ Ricky McCollum, exec VP & gen sls mgr; Terry Cook, pres, gen mgr & progmg dir; Hollis Brown, chief of engrg.

WWZD-FM— Mar 3, 1986: 106.7 mhz; 50 kw. 657 ft. TL: N34 26 08 W88 57 35. Stereo. Box 3300, Tupelo 38803. Secondary address: 5026 Cliff Gookin Blvd., Tupelo 38803. Phone: (662) 842-1067. Fax: (662) 842-0725. E-mail: rickstevens@clearchannel.com. Licensee: Clear Channel Broadcasting Licenses Inc. Group owner: Clear Channel Communications Inc. (acq 12-19-00; grpsl). Network: ABC. Rep: Interep. Format: Country. News staff: one. Target aud: 25-54. Spec prog: Southern gospel 4 hrs wkly. ♦ Mark Maharrey, gen mgr; Rick Stevens, opns VP; Gigi South, sls VP, rgnl sls mgr & adv dir; Melonie Kight, natl sls mgr, mktg dir & prom dir; Bill Hughes, progmg dir & news dir; Olen Booth, chief of engrg.

Newton

WMSO(FM)— Apr 17, 1975: 97.9 mhz; 11 kw. 492 ft. TL: N32 29 16 W89 01 23. 4307 Hwy. 39 N., Meridian 39301-9704. Phone: (601) 693-2381. Fax: (601) 485-2972. Licensee: Clear Channel Broadcasting Licenses Inc. Group owner: Clear Channel Communications Inc. (acq 3-16-01; grpsl). Format: Oldies. ♦ Ron Harper, gen mgr.

WMYQ(AM)— Mar 15, 1955: . Stn currently dark 1100 khz; 1 kw-D. TL: N32 19 55 W89 10 49. Pittman Broadcasting Services LLC, 307 S. Jefferson Ave., Covington, LA 70433. Phone: (985) 892-3661. Licensee: Pittman Broadcasting Services LLC (group owner; acq 1-23-2004; $150,000). ♦ Marcus L. Pittman, gen mgr & stn mgr.

Ocean Springs

WOSM(FM)— Feb 12, 1971: 103.1 mhz; 50 kw. Ant 459 ft. TL: N30 24 34 W88 42 23. (CP: 100 kw, ant 679 ft. TL: N30 36 42 W88 39 17). Stereo. 4720 Radio Rd. 39564. Phone: (228) 875-9031. Fax: (228) 875-6461. E-mail: wosm@wosmradio.com. Licensee: Charles H. Cooper. Network: AP Radio. Format: Southern gospel. News: 14 hrs wkly. Target aud: 18-54; family. ♦ Charles H. Cooper, gen mgr; Phil Moss, opns dir & prom dir; Margaret Cooper, progmg dir.

WQYZ(FM)— Sept 1, 1992: 92.5 mhz; 6 kw. 197 ft. TL: N30 23 40 W88 53 41. 286 DeBuys Rd., Biloxi 39531. Phone: (228) 388-2323. Fax: (228) 388-2362. Web Site: www.kissfm925.com. Licensee: Capstar TX L.P. (acq 5-26-2005; $1,287,200). Network: Premiere Action. Format: CHR / Top 40. News: one hr wkly. Target aud: 28-42; adult families/singles. ♦ Reggie Bates, gen mgr; Ron Hill, gen sls mgr; Alissa Cuevas, prom dir; Walter Brown, opns mgr & progmg dir.

Oxford

*****WAVI(FM)**— 2002: 91.5 mhz; 8.13 kw. Ant 574 ft. TL: N34 11 57 W89 49 09. American Family Radio, Box 3206, Tupelo 38803. Phone: (662) 844-8888. Fax: (662) 842-6791. Web Site: www.afr.net. Licensee: American Family Association. Group owner: American Family Radio Network: USA. Format: Christian. ♦ Marvin Sanders, gen mgr.

*****WMAV-FM**— December 1983: 90.3 mhz; 100 kw. 1,240 ft. TL: N34 17 26 W89 42 24. Stereo. 3825 Ridgewood Rd., Jackson 39211. Phone: (601) 432-6565. Fax: (601) 432-6806. Web Site: www.mpbonile.org. Licensee: Mississippi Authority for Educational Television. Network: Network: PRI, NPR. Schwartz, Woods & Miller. Format: Music, news, info. News staff: 5; News: news progmging 20 hrs wkly. Target aud: General. ♦ Marie Antoon, chmn; Larry Miller, pres; Gene Edwards, gen mgr; Bob Holland, opns mgr; Merrill McKewen, dev dir.

WOXD(FM)— October 1988: 95.5 mhz; 3 kw. 328 ft. TL: N34 18 10 W89 31 25. Stereo. 302 Hwy 7 S. 38655-9799. Phone: (662) 234-9634. Phone: (662) 234-9631. Fax: (662) 236-5390. E-mail: info@bullseye955.com. Web Site: www.bullseye955.com. Licensee: Taylor Communications. (acq 1996). Network: ABC. Rep: Rgnl Reps. Format: Classic Hits. News: 3 hrs wkly. Target aud: 25-54. Spec prog: Gospel 7 hrs wkly. ♦ Jason T. Plunk, pres; Ron Cox, gen mgr.

WQLJ(FM)— Dec 31, 1984: 93.7 mhz; 25 kw. 328 ft. TL: N34 20 05 W89 43 29. Stereo. Box 1077 38655-1077. Secondary address: 461 Hwy. 6 W. 38655. Phone: (662) 236-0093. Fax: (662) 234-5155. E-mail: q937@exceedtech.net. Web Site: www.wqlj.com. Licensee: TeleSouth Communications Inc. (group owner; acq 11-30-99; $1.4 million). Fletcher, Heald & Hildreth. Format: Adult contemp. News staff: one; News: one hrs wkly. Target aud: 18-45. Spec prog: Contemp

Stations in the U.S. Mississippi

Christian 9 hrs wkly. ♦Steve Davenport, CEO & pres; Rick Mize, gen mgr; Jim Martin, opns dir; Judy McCormick, progmg dir; Bryan Hadley, news dir.

WWMS(FM)— Jan 1, 1969: 97.5 mhz; 100 kw. 1,000 ft. TL: N34 10 05 W89 09 23. Stereo. Box 410, 2214 S. Gloster St., Tupelo 38801. Phone: (662) 842-7658. Fax: (662) 842-0197. Web Site: www.miss98.com. Licensee: San-Dow Broadcasting Inc. (acq 5-10-85). Format: Country. Target aud: General. Spec prog: Farm 2 hrs wkly. ♦Bob Gipson, VP; Sam Cousley, stn mgr.

Pascagoula

WKNN-FM— December 1964: 99.1 mhz; 100 kw. 1,012 ft. TL: N30 29 09 W88 42 53. Stereo. 286 Debuys, Biloxi 39531. Secondary address: Box 4606, Biloxi 39535. Phone: (228) 388-2323. Fax: (228) 388-2362. Web Site: www.k99fm.com. Licensee: Clear Channel Broadcasting Licenses Inc. Group owner: Clear Channel Communications Inc. (acq 2-2-2004); grpsl). Network: Premiere Action. Format: Country. News staff: one; News: 6 hrs wkly. Target aud: 25-54. ♦Reggie Bates, gen mgr; Ron Hill, gen sls mgr; Brian Bledsoe, natl sls mgr; Dan Weinhofer, rgnl sls mgr; Alissa Cuevas, prom dir; Kipp Greggory, progmg dir; Tom Scott, chief of engrg.

***WPAS(FM)**— Mar 25, 2004: 89.1 mhz; 60 kw. Ant 574 ft. TL: N30 33 03 W88 27 06. American Family Radio, Box 3206, Tupelo 33880. Phone: (662) 844-8888. Fax: (662) 842-6791. Web Site: www.afr.net. Licensee: American Family Association. Group owner: American Family Radio. Network: USA. Format: Christian. ♦Marvin Sanders, gen mgr.

WXRG(FM)—Licensed to Pascagoula. See Pascagoula-Moss Point

Pascagoula-Moss Point

WBUV(FM)—(Moss Point). June 1, 1964: 104.9 mhz; 33 kw. Ant 600 ft. TL: N30 34 08 W88 22 48. Stereo. 286 Debuys Rd., Biloxi, AL 39531. Phone: (228) 450-0100. Phone: (228) 388-2323. Fax: (228) 388-2362. E-mail: wdwg@ccmobile.com. Web Site: www.v1049.com. Licensee: Clear Channel Broadcasting Licenses Inc. Group owner: Clear Channel Communications Inc. (acq 12-7-98; $1.4 million. swap with WYOK(FM) Atmore, AL). Cohn & Marks. Format: Classic country. News staff: one; News: 5 hrs wkly. Target aud: 25-40. ♦Reggie Bates, gen mgr.

WPMP(AM)— September 1951: 1580 khz; 5 kw-D, 50 w-N, DA-2. TL: N30 23 01 W88 32 07. 5115 Telephone Rd., Pascagoula 39567. Phone: (228) 762-5683. Fax: (228) 762-1222. E-mail: wzzjam1580@aol.com. Licensee: Flagship Radio Group Inc. (acq 5-26-2005; $88,000). Network: USA. Format: Christian. News: 6 hrs wkly. Target aud: 25-54; Christian baby-boomers. Spec prog: Black gospel 3 hrs wkly. ♦Kevin Grady, gen mgr.

WXRG(FM)—(Pascagoula). June 1, 1976: 105.9 mhz; 25 kw. 312 ft. TL: N30 22 05 W88 44 35. Stereo. 109 E. Pass Rd., Suite D-11, Gulfport 39507. Phone: (228) 388-2001. Fax: (228) 896-9736. E-mail: wxrg@wxrgfm.com. Web Site: www.wxrgfm.com. Licensee: Monterey Licenses LLC. Group owner: Triad Broadcasting Co. LLC (acq 7-14-99; grpsl). Format: Classic rock. Target aud: 25-54; male. ♦Buddy Burch, gen mgr & sls VP; Charla Orr, opns VP & rgnl sls mgr; Jay Taylor, opns dir; Brian Monie, sls dir; Mitch Cry, prom dir; Kevin Harris, prom mgr; Wayne Watkins, progmg dir; Patty Davis, news dir & pub affrs dir; Gary Allen, engrg dir & chief of engrg.

Pearl

WJNT(AM)— Oct 28, 1980: 1180 khz; 50 kw-D, 500 w-N. TL: N32 17 43 W90 06 54. Box 1248, Jackson 39215-1248. Secondary address: 1985 Lakeland Dr., Suite 212, Jackson 39216. Phone: (601) 366-1150. Phone: (601) 366-1150. Fax: (601) 366-1627. E-mail: contactus@wjnt.com. Web Site: www.wjnt.com. Licensee: Buchanan Broadcasting Co. Inc. Network: Network: Network: CBS, ABC, Westwood One. Womble, Sandridge, Carlyle & Rice. Format: News/talk. News staff: one; News: 28 hrs wkly. Target aud: 35 plus; high income, college educated, home owners. ♦Bob Buchanan, pres; Stan Carter, chief of opns, progmg dir & chief of engrg; Thena Gunn, gen mgr & gen sls mgr; Rick Whitlow, news dir.

WRXW(FM)— Nov 7, 1994: 93.9 mhz; 6 kw. 328 ft. TL: N32 17 52 W89 59 56. Stereo. 222 Beasley Rd., Jackson 39206. Phone: (601) 957-3000. Fax: (601) 956-0370. E-mail: mail@wviv.com. Web Site: www.wviv.com. Licensee: Backyard Broadcasting Mississippi LLC Group owner: Backyard Broadcasting LLC (acq 5-31-2002; $4,830,000. with WWJK(FM) Jackson). Christal. Fletcher, Heald, Hildreth. Format: Adult standards, rock/AOR. News staff: one; News: one hr wkly. Target aud: 35 plus. ♦Chris Butterich, VP & gen mgr; Bob Rall, opns mgr; Janna Hughes, sls dir; Nikki Brown, mktg dir; Phil Conn, progmg mgr; Stan Carter, chief of engrg.

Petal

WZLD(FM)— January 1986: 106.3 mhz; 3 kw. 400 ft. TL: N31 23 02 W89 10 44. Stereo. 2414 W. Seventh St., Hattiesburg 39401. Secondary address: 6555 Hwy. 98 W., Suite 8, Hattiesburg 39402. Phone: (601) 296-9800. Fax: (601) 296-9838. E-mail: contact@wild1063.com. Web Site: www.wild1063.com. Licensee: Clear Channel Broadcasting Licenses Inc. Group owner: Clear Channel Communications Inc. (acq 12-19-00; grpsl). Format: Hip hop, R&B. News: 4 hrs wkly. Target aud: 25-54; upscale, educated & professional. Spec prog: Sports 3 hrs wkly. ♦Michael Comfort, gen mgr; Jackson Walker, opns mgr.

Philadelphia

WHOC(AM)— July 31, 1948: 1490 khz; 1 kw-U. TL: N32 45 52 W89 07 48. Box 26, 1016 W. Beacon St. 39350. Phone: (601) 656-1490. Fax: (601) 656-1491. E-mail: wwslfm@yahoo.com. Licensee: WHOC Inc. (acq 1-31-89; $300,000; 2-20-89). Format: Adult standard, talk. Target aud: General. Spec prog: Farm 2 hrs wkly. ♦Leah Jarrell, gen mgr; Joe Vines, opns mgr, gen sls mgr & progmg dir; Rex Smith, chief of engrg.

WWSL(FM)—Co-owned with WHOC(AM). Jan 1, 1981: 102.3 mhz; 4.9 kw. 364 ft. TL: N32 43 35 W89 05 56. Stereo. Phone: (601) 656-7102. Licensee: H & GC Inc. Network: Westwood One. Format: Adult contemp.

Picayune

WKSY(FM)— November 1973: 106.1 mhz; 50 kw. 492 ft. TL: N30 31 06 W89 38 41. Stereo. 200 E. Thomas St., Hammond, LA 70401. Phone: (985) 345-0060. Fax: (985) 542-9377. Licensee: Citadel Broadcasting Co. (acq 7-11-2005; $7 million). Format: Soft adult contemp. News staff: 2; News: 2 hrs wkly. Target aud: 18-45; young professionals. ♦Elouise Dowdy, gen mgr & gen sls mgr; Roger Gill, prom dir; Melissa Gates, progmg dir; Richard Wark, mus dir; Ken Benitez, news dir; Ben Bickham, chief of engrg.

WRJW(AM)— October 1949: 1320 khz; 5 kw-D, 75 kw-N. TL: N30 31 06 W89 38 41. Box 907 39466. Secondary address: 2438 Hwy. 43 S. 39466. Phone: (601) 798-4835. Fax: (601) 798-9755. E-mail: wrjw@datasync.com. Web Site: www.wrjw.com. Licensee: Pearl River Communications Inc. (acq 8-2-91). Network: ABC. Format: Country/southern gospel. News staff: 2; News: 10 hrs wkly. Target aud: 18-54; contemp country listeners. Spec prog: Black 8 hrs, farm 6 hrs, relg 16 hrs, sports 4 hrs wkly. ♦Dot Pigott, VP; Delores Wood, gen mgr, opns dir, gen sls mgr, adv dir & progmg dir; Denise Wilson, mktg dir & pub affrs dir; John Pigott, pres, dev dir & prom dir; Dainya Jaye, asst music dir; Joe Whatley, news dir; Danny Miller, chief of engrg.

Pickens

WOAD-FM— July 20, 1980: 105.9 mhz; 22.5 kw. 735 ft. TL: N32 40 54 W90 06 06. (CP: Ant 745 ft.). Stereo. 731 S. Pear Orchard, Suite 27, Ridgeland 39157. Phone: (601) 957-1300. Fax: (601) 956-0516. Web Site: www.1059themaxx.com. Licensee: Urban Radio II L.L.C. Group owner: Inner City Broadcasting (acq 2000; grpsl). Format: Oldies. ♦Kevin Webb, gen mgr; Bill Wilson, prom dir & progmg dir; Don Tyler, pub affrs dir; Emmit Rushing, chief of engrg.

Pontotoc

WSEL(AM)— Nov 30, 1962: 1440 khz; 890 w-D, DA. TL: N34 15 10 W88 57 36. Stereo. Box 3788, Tupelo 38803. Phone: (662) 489-0297. Fax: (662) 488-9735. Licensee: Ollie Collins Jr. (acq 5-5-92; $46,500 with co-located FM; 6-1-92). Format: Urban gospel. ♦Ollie Collins Jr., gen mgr, opns mgr & progmg dir; Jerry Campbell, chief of engrg.

WSEL-FM— Jan 1, 1966: 96.7 mhz; 3 kw. 299 ft. TL: N34 15 10 W88 57 36. Stereo. Format: Urban gospel.

Poplarville

WRPM(AM)— 1963: 1530 khz; 10 kw-D, 1 kw. TL: N30 48 55 W89 30 24. Box 352 39470. Phone: (601) 795-4900. Fax: (601) 795-0277. E-mail: wrpm@wrpm.com. Licensee: Charles W. and J. Morgan Dowdy (acq 3-87; $2.25 million. with co-located FM; FTR: 12-15-86). Network: ABC. Format: Southern gospel. Target aud: 22-54. ♦Steve Spillman, gen sls mgr; Thomas Vaughn, gen mgr, progmg dir & chief of engrg.

WZKX(FM)—Co-owned with WRPM(AM). Feb 14, 1966: 107.9 mhz; 92 kw. 1,460 ft. TL: N30 44 48 W89 03 30. Box 2639, Gulfport 39505. Phone: (228) 896-5500. Fax: (228) 896-3724. Web Site: www.usasingles.com/wrpm.htm. Format: Country. ♦Morgan Dowdy, gen mgr.

Port Gibson

***WATU(FM)**— 1999: 89.3 mhz; 40 kw vert. Ant 384 ft. TL: N32 07 56 W90 45 29. Box 3206, American Family Radio, Tupelo 38803. Phone: (662) 844-8888. Fax: (662) 842-6791. Web Site: www.afr.net. Licensee: American Family Association. Group owner: American Family Radio Network: USA. Format: Relg. ♦Marvin Sanders, gen mgr.

WRTM-FM— July 16, 1999: 100.5 mhz; 25 kw. Ant 285 ft. TL: N32 08 13 W90 55 12. Stereo. Box 820583, Vicksburg 39182. Secondary address: 1713 Clay St., Suite 7 39180. Phone: (601) 636-7944. Fax: (601) 981-9093. E-mail: radioair@bellsouth.net. Licensee: Commander Communications Corp. (acq 10-15-99). Format: Urban adult contemp. ♦Carl Haynes, gen mgr; Maria Epps, gen sls mgr; Marty Hart, progmg mgr; Val Blue, pub affrs dir; Emmette Rushing, engrg VP.

Potts Camp

WCNA(FM)— Oct 1, 1995: 95.9 mhz; 14 kw. 436 ft. TL: N34 35 51 W89 53 33. Stereo. Box 2116, Radio Bldg., 1241 Cliff Gookin Blvd., Tupelo 38803. Phone: (662) 842-7625. Fax: (662) 842-9568. Licensee: Olvie E. Sisk. Group owner: Air South Radio Inc. Format: Classic rock. News: 14 hrs wkly. ♦Gene Sisk, pres; Fred Blalock, stn mgr; Ivous Sisk, opns VP.

Prentiss

WCJU-FM— 2002: 104.9 mhz; 2.8 kw. Ant 436 ft. TL: N31 31 56 W89 56 17. Box 472, Columbia 39429. Phone: (601) 736-8889. Fax: (601) 736-2617. E-mail: wcju@zzip.cc. Licensee: Sunbelt Broadcasting Corp. (group owner) Format: Oldies. ♦Tommy McDaniel, gen mgr; Glenn Beach, stn mgr.

WJDR(FM)— June 1, 1982: 98.3 mhz; 6 kw. 325 ft. TL: N31 29 43 W89 53 33. Stereo. Box 351, 37 S. High School Ave., Columbia 39429. Phone: (601) 731-2298. Phone: (601) 792-2056. Fax: (601) 792-2057. Licensee: Sunbelt Broadcasting Corp. (group owner; acq 12-1-85). Network: ABC. Format: Hot country. News: 20 hrs wkly. Target aud: 25-54. Spec prog: Black 5 hrs wkly. ♦Thomas F. McDaniel, pres; Jody Fortenberry, stn mgr; Wayne White, chief of engrg.

Quitman

WQMS(AM)— Feb 2, 1968: 1500 khz; 1 kw-D. TL: N32 03 51 W88 43 29. Drawer 70 39355. Phone: (601) 776-2931. Fax: (601) 776-6762.

Broadcasting & Cable Yearbook 2006

Mississippi

Licensee: Conquer Communications Inc. (acq 12-27-01). Rep: Keystone (unwired net). Format: Light pop. Spec prog: Farm 2 hrs wkly. ◆Jason Dozier, gen mgr.

WYKK(FM)— July 31, 1981: 98.9 mhz; 25 kw. Ant 380 ft. TL: N32 03 51 W88 43 29. Stereo. Box 70 39355. Phone: (601) 776-2931. Fax: (601) 776-6762. E-mail: management@k98.com. Web Site: www.k98.com. Licensee: Quitman Broadcasting Inc. (acq 5-2-83; $215,000. with co-located AM; FTR: 5-23-83). Format: C&W.

Redwood

WVBG(FM)— 2005: 105.5 mhz; 1.95 kw. Ant 430 ft. TL: N32 23 22 W90 48 34. 1102 Newit Vick Dr., Vicksburg 39183. Phone: (601) 883-0848. Licensee: Lina Jones. Format: Oldies. ◆Lina H. Jones, gen mgr.

Richton

WXHB(FM)— 1995: 96.5 mhz; 6 kw. Ant 328 ft. TL: N31 21 01 W88 59 11. Box 6408, Laurel 39441. Phone: (601) 649-0095. Phone: (601) 544-0095. Fax: (601) 649-8199. Licensee: Blakeney Communications Inc. (group owner; acq 3-27-03; $650,000). Network: ABC Information & Entertainment. Format: Solid gospel. ◆Larry Blakeney, gen mgr.

Ridgeland

WIIN(AM)— Dec 1, 1984: 780 khz; 5 kw-D. TL: N32 25 36 W90 12 19. 265 Highpoint Dr. 39157. Phone: (601) 956-0102. Fax: (601) 978-3980. Licensee: New South Radio Inc. Group owner: New South Communications Inc. (acq 11-10-94; $750,000 with WLIN(FM) Gluckstadt; 12-12-94). Rep: McGavren Guild. Format: Nostalgia. Target aud: General; Adult professionals. ◆Gwen Rakestraw, gen mgr; Bill Rakestraw, gen sls mgr; Mark McCoy, opns mgr & progmg dir.

Ripley

WCSA(AM)— 1995: . Stn currently dark 1260 khz; 500 w-D, 38 w-N. TL: N34 43 15 W88 56 40. 4598 Appleville St., Memphis, TN 38109. Phone: (601) 837-2816. Licensee: Keyboard Broadcasting Communication.

WKZU(FM)— June 1, 1979: 102.3 mhz; 3.5 kw. Ant 433 ft. TL: N34 42 35 W88 50 36. Stereo. Box 572, 107 E. Spring St. 38663. Phone: (662) 837-1023. Phone: (662) 837-2990. Fax: (662) 837-2994. E-mail: scott@kudzu102.com. Web Site: www.kudzu102.com. Licensee: Kudzu Communications Inc. (acq 7-23-98). Miss. Net. Format: Classic country. News: 2 hrs wkly. Target aud: 25-54; 50% men & 50% women. Spec prog: Relg 2 hrs, gospel 6 hrs, bluegrass 2 hrs wkly. ◆Scott Peters, pres & gen mgr.

Sardis

KBUD(FM)— 2005: 102.1 mhz; 4 kw. Ant 403 ft. TL: N34 22 33 W89 45 52. 6080 Mt. Moriah Ext., Memphis, TN 38115. Phone: (901) 375-9324. Fax: (901) 375-0041. Web Site: www.flinn.com. Licensee: George S. Flinn Jr. Format: Top-40. ◆Keith Parnell, gen mgr; Edrick Kearney, stn mgr.

Senatobia

*WKNA(FM)— Jan 4, 1971: 88.9 mhz; 100 kw. 380 ft. TL: N34 37 39 W90 01 27. Stereo. Box 241880, Memphis, TN 38124. Secondary address: 900 Getwell Rd., Memphis, TN 38111. Phone: (901) 458-2521. Fax: (901) 325-6506. Web Site: www.wkno.org. Licensee: Mid-South Public Communications Foundation. Network: Network: NPR, PRI. Schwartz, Woods & Miller. Format: News/talk. News staff: one; News: 58 hrs wkly. Target aud: 35 plus. ◆Michael LaBonia, pres; Dan Campbell, gen mgr; Darel Snodgrass, opns mgr; Charles McLarty, dev dir; Susab Sowell, prom mgr; Kacky Walton, mus dir. Co-owned TV: *WKNO-TV affil.

WSAO(AM)— Aug 8, 1962: 1140 khz; 5 kw-D. TL: N34 36 56 W89 56 09. Box 190 38668-0190. Phone: (601) 562-4445. Fax: (662) 562-4445. Licensee: Jesse C. Ross and Earnestine A. Ross. (acq 3-95). Format: Christian, gospel, spiritual music. News staff: one. Target aud: General. Spec prog: Gospel. ◆Jesse Ross, gen mgr & stn mgr.

Southaven

WAVN(AM)— June 4, 1990: 1240 khz; 580 w-U. TL: N34 58 57 W90 00 45. 1336 Brookhaven Dr. 38671. Phone: (662) 393-8056. Fax: (662) 393-8066. Licensee: Arlington Broadcasting Co. Inc. (acq 8-31-92; $115,000; 9-21-92). Format: Traditional gospel. News: 7 hrs wkly. Target aud: 20-50; general. ◆Walter Stevens, gen mgr & progmg dir.

Starkville

*WJZB(FM)— 1999: 88.7 mhz; 430 w. Ant 243 ft. TL: N33 27 47 W88 49 01. American Family Radio, Box 3206, Tupelo 38803. Phone: (662) 844-8888. Fax: (662) 842-6791. Web Site: www.afr.net. Licensee: American Family Association Inc. Group owner: American Family Radio (acq 10-8-97). Network: USA. Format: Relg. ◆Marvin Sanders, gen mgr.

WKOR(AM)— July 5, 1968: 980 khz; 1 kw-D. TL: N33 28 44 W88 44 40. Court Square Towers, 601 Second Ave. N., Columbus 39701. Phone: (662) 327-1183. Fax: (662) 328-1122. Licensee: Cumulus Licensing Corp. Group owner: Cumulus Media Inc. (acq 2-14-02). Network: ABC Information & Entertainment. Format: Black. Target aud: General; business professionals. ◆Don Trout, gen mgr; Stan Smith, progmg dir; Olen Booth, chief of engrg.

WLZA(FM)— (Eupora). Sept 1, 1978: 96.1 mhz; 50 kw. 500 ft. TL: N33 28 18 W89 13 36. Stereo. Box 884, 1105 A Stark Rd 39760. Phone: (662) 324-9601. Fax: (662) 324-7400. E-mail: wlza@bellsouth.net. Licensee: Metro Radio. Group owner: Air South Radio Inc. Format: Adult contemp. Target aud: General. ◆Olvie E. Sisk, pres; Carolyn Jackson, gen mgr; David Ever, progmg dir.

WMSU(FM)— Sept 13, 1979: 92.1 mhz; 1.1 kw. 500 ft. TL: N33 25 49 W88 45 17. Stereo. 608 Yellowjacket Dr. 39759. Phone: (662) 338-5424. Fax: (662) 338-5436. Web Site: www.power92fm.net. Licensee: Urban Radio Licenses LLC. (acq 12-7-2000). Format: Mainstream urban. Target aud: 25-54. ◆Kevin Wagner, pres & progmg mgr; James Alexander, opns mgr, progmg mgr, news dir & pub affrs dir; Jeffrey Hedgemon, sls VP; Vanessa Robinson, natl sls mgr; Joy Stanfield, mktg dir & prom dir.

*WMSV(FM)— March 1994: 91.1 mhz; 14.1 kw. 449 ft. TL: N33 25 49 W88 45 17. Box 6210, Mississippi State Univ. 39762. Phone: (662) 325-8064. Fax: (662) 325-8037. E-mail: wmsv@msstate.edu. Web Site: www.wmsv.msstate.edu. Licensee: Mississippi State University. Format: Alternative. ◆Steve Ellis, gen mgr.

WMXU(FM)— Listing follows WSSO(AM).

WSSO(AM)— Nov 8, 1948: 1230 khz; 1 kw-U. TL: N33 27 09 W88 49 15. Court Square Towers, 601 Second Ave. N., Columbus 39701. Phone: (662) 327-1183. Fax: (662) 328-1122. Licensee: Cumulus Licensing Corp. Group owner: Cumulus Media Inc. (acq 1998; grpsl). Rep: Keystone (unwired net). Allied Radio Partners. Format: Talk. Spec prog: Black 12 hrs wkly. ◆Don Troutt, gen mgr; Wesley Burns, progmg dir; Olen Booth, chief of engrg.

WMXU(FM)— Co-owned with WSSO(AM). July 15, 1968: 106.1 mhz; 3 kw. 220 ft. TL: N33 17 38 W88 39 27. Stereo. 601 Second Ave. N., Columbus 39701. Phone: (662) 327-1183. Fax: (662) 328-1122. Format: Adult urban. ◆Bobby Wonder, progmg mgr.

State College

WQJB(FM)— Not on air, target date: unknown: 104.5 mhz; 25 kw. Ant 328 ft. TL: N33 24 14 W88 55 21. 6080 Mt. Moriah, Memphis, TN 38115. Phone: (901) 375-9324. Fax: (901) 375-0041. Web Site: www.flinn.com. Licensee: George S. Flinn Jr. Format: Classic country. ◆Melanie Henkin-Booth, gen mgr.

Stonewall

WKZB(FM)— 1998: 106.9 mhz; 2.55 kw. 508 ft. TL: N32 10 48 W88 40 22. Box 5797, Meridian 39302. Phone: (601) 693-2661. Fax: (601) 483-0826. E-mail: wmlv@wokk.com. Licensee: Mississippi Broadcasters L.L.C. (group owner). Latham & Watkins. Format: Adult contemp. Target aud: 25-54. ◆Clay Holladay, pres & gen mgr; Scott Stevens, opns mgr & progmg mgr; Karen Bostick, sls dir; Van Mac, news dir & pub affrs dir; Scott Shepperd, chief of engrg.

Sumrall

WFMM(FM)— 1998: 97.3 mhz; 1 kw. 200 ft. TL: N31 21 18 W89 31 19. Box 17531, Hattiesburg 39403. Phone: (601) 957-1700. Fax: (601) 956-5228. Web Site: www.supertalkms.com. Licensee: TeleSouth Communications Inc. (group owner; acq 1999; $200,000). Format: Talk. ◆Paul Gallo, gen mgr.

Taylorsville

WBBN(FM)— Mar 20, 1985: 95.9 mhz; 31 kw. 625 ft. TL: N31 37 59 W89 28 40. Stereo. Box 6408, Laurel 39441. Phone: (601) 649-0095. Phone: (601) 544-0095. Fax: (601) 649-8199. E-mail: b95@b95country.com. Web Site: www.b95country.com. Licensee: Blakeney Communications Inc. (group owner) Network: ABC Information & Entertainment. Format: Country. Target aud: 25-54. ◆Larry Blakeney, CEO, pres & progmg dir; Randall A. Blakeney, VP & chief of engrg; David Blakeney, gen mgr; Debbie Blakeney, gen sls mgr; Allyson Scott, prom dir & mus dir; Tom Colts, news dir.

Tchula

WGNG(FM)— 2001: 106.3 mhz; 7.1 kw. Ant 499 ft. TL: N33 18 06 W90 07 31. Box 1801 38930. Secondary address: 503 Ione St. 38930. Phone: (662) 453-1643. Phone: (662) 453-1646. Fax: (662) 453-7002. E-mail: rhuge4@bellsouth.net. Licensee: Team Broadcasting Co. Inc. Format: Urban contemporary. ◆Reuben C. Hughes, gen mgr.

Tunica

WYYL(FM)— 1998: 96.1 mhz; 25 kw. Ant 328 ft. TL: N34 43 36 W90 09 43. Y96.1, Flinn Broadcasting, 6080 Mt. Moriah, Memphis, TN 38115. Phone: (901) 375-9324. Fax: (901) 375-0041. E-mail: mail@y961.com. Web Site: www.y961.com. Licensee: Flinn Broadcasting Corp. (acq 10-20-99). Format: Hispanic. ◆Lloyd Hekzer, gen mgr.

Tupelo

*WAFR(FM)— Aug 31, 1991: 88.3 mhz; 50 kw. 492 ft. TL: N34 28 28 W88 43 41. (CP: 60 kw). Stereo. American Family Radio, Box 3206 38803. Phone: (662) 844-8888. Phone: (662) 844-8893. Fax: (662) 842-6791. Web Site: www.afr.net. Licensee: American Family Association. Network: USA. Format: Christian. News staff: one; News: 3 hrs wkly. Target aud: 30-60; conservative Christian. ◆Don Wildman, gen mgr.

*WAJS(FM)— 1996: 91.7 mhz; 23 kw. Ant 505 ft. TL: N33 55 35 W88 39 46. Box 3206, American Family Radio 38803. Phone: (662) 844-8888. Fax: (662) 842-6791. Web Site: www.afr.net. Licensee: American Family Association. Group owner: American Family Radio Network: USA. Format: Christian. ◆Marvin Sanders, gen mgr.

*WAQB(FM)— 1997: 90.9 mhz; 9.5 kw. Ant 426 ft. TL: N34 28 28 W88 43 41. American Family Radio, Box 3206 38803. Phone: (662) 844-8888. Fax: (662) 842-6791. Web Site: www.afr.net. Licensee: American Family Association. Group owner: American Family Radio Network: USA. Format: Classic gospel. ◆Don Wildman, gen mgr.

WELO(AM)— May 15, 1944: 580 khz; 1 kw-D, 500 w-N, DA-2. TL: N34 18 10 W88 42 17. Box 410, 2214 S. Gloster Ave. 38801. Phone: (662) 842-7658. Fax: (662) 842-0197. Licensee: JMD Inc. Format: Music of Your Life, big band. Target aud: 45 plus. Spec prog: Farm one hr wkly. ◆Bob Green, gen mgr & gen sls mgr; Dave Dunaway, opns mgr; Scott Kelly, progmg dir; Cathy Williams, news dir.

WZLQ(FM)— Co-owned with WELO(AM). September 1968: 98.5 mhz; 100 kw. 951 ft. TL: N34 10 05 W89 09 23. Stereo. Format: Adult contemp. Target aud: 25-54. ◆Steve Drumm, progmg dir.

WFTA(FM)— (Fulton). Aug 19, 1976: 101.9 mhz; 100 kw. 560 ft. TL: N34 15 46 W88 32 24. Stereo. Box 2116 38803. Secondary address: 1241 Cliff Gookin Blvd., Radio Bldg. 38801. Phone: (662) 842-7625. Fax: (662) 842-9568. Licensee: Air South Radio Inc. (group owner) Format: Adult contemp. News: 4 hrs wkly. Target aud: 14-44. ◆Gene Sisk, pres; Olvie E. Sisk, gen mgr; Fred Blalock, stn mgr & gen sls mgr.

WKMQ(AM)— Aug 25, 1972: 1060 khz; 1 kw-D, 33 w-N. TL: N34 15 19 W88 41 46. Box 3300 38803. Secondary address: 5026 Cliff Gookin Blvd. 38801. Phone: (662) 842-1067. Fax: (662) 842-0725. E-mail: rickstevens@clearchannel.com. Licensee: Capstar TX L.P. Group owner: Clear Channel Communications Inc. (acq 12-19-00;

Stations in the U.S. Missouri

grpsl). Format: Talk. Target aud: 35-54. ♦Mark Maharrey, gen mgr; Cynthia South, gen sls mgr; Rick Stevens, opns mgr & progmg dir; Jerry Mathis, chief of engrg.

WTUP(AM)— October 1953: 1490 khz; 1 kw-U. TL: N34 15 19 W88 41 46. Box 3300 38803. Secondary address: 5026 Cliff Gookin Blvd. 38801. Phone: (662) 842-1067. Fax: (662) 842-0725. E-mail: markmaharrey @clearchannel.com. Licensee: Capstar TX L.P. Group owner: Clear Channel Communications Inc. (acq 12-19-00; grpsl). Rep: Interep. Gurman, Blask & Freedman. Format: Sports. News staff: one; News: 12 hrs wkly. Target aud: 25-54; men. ♦Mark Maharrey, gen mgr; Gigi South, sls dir & adv VP; Melonie Kight, mktg dir & prom dir; Rick Stevens, opns dir & progmg dir; Olen Booth, chief of engrg.

Tylertown

WFCG(FM)—Not on air, target date: unknown: 107.3 mhz; 3.2 kw. Ant 457 ft. TL: N31 04 39 W90 04 46. 215 E. Bay St., Magnolia 39652. Phone: (601) 783-6600. Licensee: Southwest Broadcasting Inc. ♦C. Wayne Dowdy, pres.

WTYL(AM)— Feb 8, 1969: 1290 khz; 1 kw-D. TL: N31 07 50 W90 08 13. 930 Union Rd. 39667. Phone: (601) 876-2105. Fax: (601) 876-9551. Licensee: Tylertown Broadcasting Co. Format: Country. Spec prog: Farm 6 hrs wkly. ♦Carolyn Dillon, pres & gen mgr; Gail Ratcliff, progmg dir.

WTYL-FM— Apr 9, 1970: 97.7 mhz; 3 kw. 145 ft. TL: N31 07 50 W90 08 13.

Union

WZKS(FM)— October 1995: 104.1 mhz; 16 kw. 535 ft. TL: N32 29 53 W88 53 20. (CP: 19 kw). 4307 Hwy. 39 N., Meridian 39301. Phone: (601) 693-2381. Fax: (601) 485-2972. Licensee: Clear Channel Broadcasting Licenses Inc. Group owner: Clear Channel Communications Inc. (acq 3-16-01; grpsl). Format: Urban contemp. ♦Ron Harper, gen mgr.

University

WUMS(FM)— Apr 10, 1989: 92.1 mhz; 6 kw. 328 ft. TL: N34 21 29 W89 32 30. Stereo. 201 Bishop Hall, Oxford 38677. Phone: (662) 915-5503. Fax: (662) 915-5703. Web Site: www.olemiss.edu. Licensee: Student Media Center of the University of Mississippi. Network: Westwood One. Format: Community alternative. Target aud: 18-25. Spec prog: International 2 hrs, women one hr, the 80's 2 hrs wkly. ♦Melanie Store, pres; David Stil, stn mgr; Beth Vance, sls dir; Ty Tumlin, mus dir; Mike Staton, chief of engrg.

Utica

WJXN-FM— Aug 28, 1990: 100.9 mhz; 39 kw. Ant 551 ft. TL: N32 03 13 W90 20 23. Stereo. 1985 Lakeland Drive, Suite 201, Jackson 39216. Phone: (601) 713-0977. Fax: (601) 713-2977. Licensee: Flinn Broadcasting Corp. (acq 12-31-97). Network: USA. Format: Urban adult contemp. Target aud: 25 plus. ♦George S. Flinn, pres; Karen Porter, stn mgr; Steve Poston, stn mgr & progmg dir.

Vicksburg

WBBV(FM)— Aug 21, 1989: 101.3 mhz; 13 kw. Ant 394 ft. TL: N32 20 42 W90 52 55. Stereo. 1601 E. North Frontage Rd. 39180. Phone: (601) 638-0101. Phone: (601) 636-2340 (business). Fax: (601) 638-0869. Licensee: Bishop Broadcasting Inc. Group owner: New South Communications Inc. (acq 7-11-2005; $400,000 for stock). Format: Country. Target aud: 24-54. ♦Eddie Holladay, pres; Betsy Harris, gen mgr; Ron Anderson, opns mgr & progmg dir; Kurt Rushing, gen sls mgr & prom mgr; Russell Kendrick, chief of engrg.

WJKK(FM)— Mar 19, 1966: 98.7 mhz; 100 kw. 950 ft. TL: N32 12 29 W90 24 50. Stereo. 265 Highpoint Dr., Ridgeland 39157. Phone: (601) 956-0102. Fax: (601) 978-3980. Web Site: www.mix987.com. Licensee: New South Radio Inc. Group owner: New South Communications Inc.

(acq 1-89; $1.1 million; 1-23-89). Network: ABC Daytime Direction. Format: Soft adult contemp. News staff: one; News: one hr wkly. Target aud: 18-49; upper income & educ. ♦Gwen Rakestraw, gen mgr.

WQBC(AM)— 1931: 1420 khz; 5 kw-D, 500 w-N. TL: N32 19 56 W90 51 00. 3190 Porter's Chapel Rd. 39180. Secondary address: Box 820483 39182. Phone: (601) 636-1108. Fax: (601) 631-0087. E-mail: WQBC@WQBC.net. Web Site: www.WQBC.net. Licensee: Grace Media International LLC (acq 3-20-2001; $100,000). Network: Network: USA, Salem Radio Network. Format: News/talk, Sports. News staff: 2; News: 4 hrs wkly. Target aud: 35-55; Male & Female. ♦Jerry Rushins, gen mgr & gen sls mgr; Mike Corley, pres & opns dir.

WRTM(AM)— 1948: 1490 khz; 1 kw-U. TL: N32 21 27 W90 51 29. Box 820583 39182. Secondary address: 1713 Clay St., Ste 7 39180. Phone: (601) 636-7944. Fax: (601) 981-9093. E-mail: radioair@bellsouth.net. Licensee: Commander Communications Corp. (acq 5-11-99). Format: Gospel. Target aud: 25 plus. ♦Carl Haynes, gen mgr; Maria Epps, gen sls mgr; Marty Hart, progmg mgr; Val Blue, pub affrs dir; Emmitte Rushing, engrg dir.

WSTZ-FM—Licensed to Vicksburg. See Jackson

Walnut

WLRC(AM)— June 21, 1982: 850 khz; 963 w-D. TL: N34 56 46 W88 52 44. Box 37 38683. Secondary address: 7760 Hwy. 72 E. 38683. Phone: (662) 223-4071. Fax: (662) 223-4072. Web Site: www.wlrcradio.com. Licensee: B.R. & Martha S. Clayton. (acq 11-83; $100,000; 11-28-83). Format: Christian. Spec prog: Southern & country gospel mus, preaching & children's programs.

Water Valley

WTNM(FM)— Aug 1, 1996: 105.5 mhz; 4.7 kw. Ant 371 ft. TL: N34 12 45 W89 44 49. Stereo. Box 1077, Oxford 38655. Secondary address: 461 Hwy. 6 W., Oxford 38655. Phone: (662) 236-0073. Fax: (662) 234-5155. E-mail: supertalk1055@exceedtech.net. Web Site: www.supertalkms.com. Licensee: TeleSouth Communications Inc. (group owner; acq 3-17-00). Format: Talk. News staff: one; News: 3 hrs wkly. Target aud: 25 plus. Spec prog: Christian, contemp 4 hrs wkly. ♦Rick Mize, gen mgr; Jim Martin, opns mgr; Steve Davenport, CEO & engrg VP.

Waynesboro

WABO(AM)— Sept 11, 1954: 990 khz; 1 kw-D. TL: N31 40 48 W88 40 34. Box 507 39367. Secondary address: 6746 Hwy. 184 W. 39367. Phone: (601) 735-4331. Fax: (601) 735-4332. E-mail: waboradio@c-gate.net. Web Site: www.wabo105.com. Licensee: Martin Broadcasting Inc. (acq 12-18-61). Network: ABC Information & Entertainment. Format: Country, soul. ♦Nancy N. Martin, pres, gen mgr & gen sls mgr; Jamie Heathcock, progmg dir.

WABO-FM— June 13, 1973: 105.5 mhz; 3 kw. 145 ft. TL: N31 40 48 W88 40 34. Stereo. E-mail: waboradio@c-gate.net. Web Site: www.wabo105.com. Format: Hot country.

***WZKM(FM)**—Not on air, target date: unknown: 89.7 mhz; 67 kw. Ant 581 ft. TL: N31 50 09 W88 52 21. American Family Radio, Box 3206, Tupelo 38803. Phone: (662) 844-8888. Fax: (662) 842-6791. Web Site: www.afr.net. Licensee: American Family Association. Group owner: American Family Radio (acq 1-24-03). Network: USA. Format: Relg. ♦Don Wildman, gen mgr.

West Point

WKBB(FM)—Listing follows WROB(AM).

WROB(AM)— September 1947: 1450 khz; 1 kw-U. TL: N33 36 30 W88 39 15. Box 1336, 413 N. Forest St. 39773. Phone: (662) 494-1450. Fax: (662) 494-9762. E-mail: wrobwkbb@ebicom.net. Licensee: TeleSouth Communications Inc. (group owner; acq 12-5-2003; $900,000.

with co-located FM). Format: Urban gospel. Target aud: General. Spec prog: Gospel 2 hrs wkly. ♦Peggy Goode, pres; Greg Benefield, gen mgr, progmg dir & news dir; Bob McRaney Jr., gen sls mgr.

WKBB(FM)—Co-owned with WROB(AM). Apr 14, 1974: 100.9 mhz; 10 kw. Ant 515 ft. TL: N33 40 43 W88 48 18. Stereo. Format: News/talk, jazz. Target aud: 35-54.

Wiggins

WIGG(AM)— February 1968: 1420 khz; 5 kw-D. TL: N30 52 18 W89 09 00. Box 723 39577. Secondary address: 959 N. Magnolia Dr. 39577. Phone: (601) 928-7281. Fax: (601) 528-5011. Licensee: Tralyn Broadcasting Inc. (acq 7-1-97; grpsl). Format: Country. News: 5 hrs wkly. Target aud: 25-54; general. Spec prog: Gospel, sports. ♦John McLean, CEO & chmn; Mike Self, pres; Bill Brock, gen mgr & opns VP.

Winona

WONA(AM)— Oct 25, 1958: 1570 khz; 1 kw-D. TL: N33 27 52 W89 44 11. Box 746 38967. Phone: (662) 283-1570. Fax: (662) 283-1520. Licensee: Southern Electronics Co. Format: Country. ♦Johnny Pettit, pres; Seth Kent, opns mgr, gen sls mgr, progmg dir & chief of engrg; Sharon Kent, VP, gen mgr & news dir.

WONA-FM— Jan 4, 1976: 95.1 mhz; 3 kw. 328 ft. TL: N33 29 34 W89 45 17. Stereo.

Yazoo City

WJNS-FM— Dec 13, 1968: 92.1 mhz; 20 kw. 300 ft. TL: N32 50 48 W90 23 18. Stereo. 1405 Enchanted Dr. 39194. Phone: (662) 746-5921. Fax: (662) 746-5996. Licensee: Family Worship Center Church Inc. (group owner; acq 6-16-2004; $350,000). Format: Relg. Target aud: 25-54. Spec prog: Farm 16 hrs, weather 16 hrs wkly.

WYAB(FM)— August 1997: 93.1 mhz; 4.1 kw. Ant 394 ft. TL: N32 49 20 W90 16 46. 740 Hwy. 49, Suite R, Flora 39071. Phone: (601) 879-0093. Fax: (601) 427-8800. E-mail: matt@wyab.com. Web Site: www.wyab.com. Licensee: SSR Communications Inc. (acq 4-1-03; $207,500). Format: Oldies. News staff: one. Target aud: 25-64; div blend, not your typical oldies stn. ♦Matthew Wesolowski, CEO & engrg dir.

***WYAZ(FM)**—Not on air, target date: unknown: 89.5 mhz; 350 w. Ant 171 ft. TL: N32 56 07 W90 21 15. American Family Radio, Box 3206, Tupelo 38803. Phone: (662) 844-8888. Fax: (662) 842-6791. Licensee: American Family Association. Group owner: American Family Radio (acq 5-13-2004). ♦Marvin Sanders, gen mgr.

Missouri

Albany

KAAN-FM—See Bethany

Anderson

***KGSF(FM)**—Not on air, target date: unknown: 88.5 mhz; 350 w vert. Ant 278 ft. TL: N36 20 59 W94 20 54. 4002 N. 3300 E., Twin Falls, ID 83301. Phone: (208) 734-6633. Fax: (208) 736-1958. Web Site: www.csnradio.com. Licensee: CSN International. ♦Michael Kestler, pres.

Arcadia

KTNX(FM)—Not on air, target date: unknown: 103.9 mhz; 450 w. Ant 932 ft. TL: N37 34 23 W90 41 35. 540 Maple Valley Dr., Farmington 63640. Phone: (573) 701-9590. Fax: (573) 701-9696. Licensee: Dockins Communications Inc. ♦Fred M. Dockins Sr., pres.

Broadcasting & Cable Yearbook 2006

Missouri

Arnold

*KGNA-FM— Mar 26, 1987: 89.9 mhz; 150 w horiz, 84 w vert. Ant 131 ft. TL: N38 26 35 W90 24 00. Box 187, Washington 63090. Phone: (636) 239-0400. Fax: (636) 239-4448. Web Site: www.goodnewsvoice.com. Licensee: Missouri River Christian Broadcasting Inc. (acq 10-5-99). Network: Network: Network: Moody, Salem Radio Network, Premiere Focus. Format: Beautiful music, christian, talk, teaching. Target aud: General; Those concerned with doing the right thing. Spec prog: Children 7 hrs wkly. ♦ J.C. Goggan, pres & gen mgr; R Jones, chief of opns.

Asbury

KWXD(FM)— October 1993: 103.5 mhz; 16 kw. Ant 413 ft. TL: N37 23 44 W94 40 42. Box 383, 412 Locust St., Pittsburg, KS 66762. Phone: (620) 232-5993. Fax: (620) 232-5550. Licensee: Innovative Broadcasting Corp. (group owner) Lauren A. Colby. Format: Country. News staff: one; News: 20 hrs wkly. Target aud: 25-54. ♦ Bob Young, CEO & adv dir; Lance Sayler, pres & gen mgr.

Ash Grove

KSGF-FM— Mar 1, 1994: 104.1 mhz; 21.5 kw. Ant 354 ft. TL: N37 15 22 W93 41 14. 2330 W. Grand St., Springfield 65781. Phone: (417) 865-6614. Fax: (417) 865-9643. Web Site: www.ksgf.com. Licensee: Journal Broadcast Corp. Group owner: Journal Communications Inc. (acq 11-26-2003; $5 million. with KZRQ-FM Mount Vernon). Format: News, talk. ♦ Rex Hanson, gen mgr.

Ashland

KOQL(FM)— October 1993: 106.1 mhz; 69 kw. Ant 958 ft. TL: N38 45 01 W92 33 31. Stereo. 503 Old 63 N., Columbia 65201. Phone: (573) 449-4144. Fax: (573) 449-7770. Web Site: www.q1061.com. Licensee: Cumulus Licensing LLC. Group owner: Cumulus Media Inc. (acq 4-26-2004; grpsl). Rep: Katz Radio. Mullin, Rhyne, Emmons & Topel. Format: Top-40. ♦ Lewis W. Dickey Jr., pres; Jack Lawson, opns dir; Scott Boltz, VP & mktg mgr.

Aurora

KSWF(FM)— Feb 19, 1968: 100.5 mhz; 33 kw. 600 ft. TL: N37 05 39 W93 31 05. Stereo. 1856 S. Glenstone, Springfield 65804. Phone: (417) 890-5555. Fax: (417) 890-5050. E-mail: mycountry@mycountry.com. Web Site: www.1005thewolf.com. Licensee: Clear Channel Broadcasting Licenses Inc. Group owner: Clear Channel Communications Inc. (acq 10-10-2000; grpsl). Format: Country. Target aud: 18-54; general. ♦ Mary Fleenor, gen mgr; Paul Kelley, opns mgr.

KSWM(AM)— Oct 19, 1961: 940 khz; 1 kw-D, 30 w-N. TL: N36 59 39 W93 42 58. 126 S. Jefferson 65605. Phone: (417) 678-0416. Fax: (417) 678-4111. Web site: www.talonbroadcasting.com. Licensee: Falcon Broadcasting Inc. Group owner: Community Service Radio Group (acq 8-19-2005; $417,500). Fletcher, Heald & Hildreth. Format: News/talk. News staff: 2; News: 21 hrs wkly. Target aud: General. ♦ Dewayn Candy, gen mgr & engrg mgr; Lance Beamer, opns mgr.

Ava

KKOZ-FM— 1990: 92.1 mhz; 4 kw. 380 ft. TL: N36 55 48 W92 39 19. Box 386 65608. Phone: (417) 683-4191. Web Site: www.kkoz.com. Licensee: Corum Industries Inc. Format: News/talk, farm. News: 15 hrs wkly. Target aud: 45 plus; farm oriented. ♦ Joe Corum, pres & gen mgr; Art Corum, opns mgr, prom mgr & progmg dir; Bob Moore, engrg mgr & chief of engrg.

KKOZ(AM)— 1968: 1430 khz; 500 w-U. TL: N36 55 48 W92 39 19. Web Site: www.kkoz.com. (Acq 7-97; $11,200).

Ballwin

*KYMC(FM)— February 1978: 89.7 mhz; 120 w. 154 ft. TL: N38 37 15 W90 31 49. (CP: Ant 171 ft. TL: N38 37 23 W90 32 01). Stereo. Box 4038, 16464 Burkhardt Pl., Chesterfield 63005. Phone: (636) 532-6515. Phone: (636) 532-3100. Fax: (636) 530-7928. E-mail: nhall@ymcastlouis.org. Web Site: kymcradio.org. Licensee: YMCA of Greater St. Louis-W. County Branch. Womble, Carlyle, Sandridge & Rice. Format: Var/div. News staff: 3; News: 6 hrs wkly. Target aud: 12-35; families. Spec prog: Jazz 6 hrs, teens one hr, Christian rock 4 hrs, talk 3 hrs wkly. ♦ Natalie Hall, gen mgr & chief of opns.

Bethany

KAAN(AM)— Dec 3, 1983: 870 khz; 1 kw-D. TL: N40 15 23 W94 09 23. Box 447, Hwy. 69 S. 64424. Phone: (660) 425-6380. Fax: (660) 425-8148. Web Site: www.regionalradio.com. Licensee: KAAN Inc. Group owner: Shepherd Group Network: ABC Information & Entertainment. Format: Country, news. News staff: 3; News: 10 hrs wkly. Target aud: 25 plus. Spec prog: Farm 10 hrs, relg one hr wkly. ♦ Mike Mattson, gen mgr & sls dir; Denise Asher, gen sls mgr; Stuart Johnson, progmg dir; Stuart Johnson, news dir; Gregg Richwine, chief of engrg.

KAAN-FM— Oct 27, 1978: 95.5 mhz; 50 kw. 360 ft. TL: N40 15 23 W94 09 23. Web Site: www.regionalradio.com.

Birch Tree

KACE(AM)— Sept 14, 1981: . Stn currently dark 1310 khz; 1 kw-D, 60 w-N. TL: N36 59 07 W91 32 54. 932 County Rd. 448, Poplar Bluff 63901. Phone: (573) 686-3700. Fax: (573) 686-1713. Licensee: Eagle Bluff Enterprises. (group owner; (acq 9-8-99); grpsl). ♦ Steven Fuchs, gen mgr.

KBMV-FM— 1983: 107.1 mhz; 25 kw. Ant 328 ft. TL: N36 56 03 W91 43 07. Stereo. Box 107, West Plains 65775. Phone: (417) 255-0427. Fax: (417) 255-2907. Web Site: www.todaysbesthits.com. Licensee: Mountain Lakes Broadcasting Corp. (acq 9-8-2003; $175,000). Format: Hot adult contemp. ♦ Connie P. Feifer, gen mgr.

Bismarck

KHCR(FM)— 2005: 99.5 mhz; 4.2 kw. Ant 798 ft. TL: N37 38 52 W90 37 33. 627 State Hwy. 47, Bonne Terre 63628. Phone: (573) 358-7700. Licensee: Joseph W. & Donna M. Bollinger. ♦ Joseph W. Bollinger, gen mgr.

Blue Springs

KCWJ(AM)— Feb 2, 1984: 1030 khz; 1 kw-D, 500 w-N, DA-2. TL: N39 02 44 W94 14 06. 4240 Blue Ridge Blvd., Suite 530, Kansas City 64133. Phone: (816) 313-0049. Fax: (816) 313-1036. E-mail: info@1030thelight.com. Web Site: www.1030thelight.com. Licensee: Christian Broadcasting Associates L.P. (acq 1-13-99; $750,000). Format: Christian. News: 5 hrs wkly. Target aud: 18-49; family oriented Christian audience. ♦ D.T. Stayton, CEO; Ken Ball, gen mgr.

Bolivar

KYOO(AM)— November 1961: 1200 khz; 1 kw-D. TL: N37 41 50 W93 25 45. 205 N. Pike Ave. 65613-1550. Phone: (417) 326-5259. Phone: (417) 326-5257. Fax: (417) 326-5900. E-mail: kyooradio@aol.com. Web Site: www.realcountryonline.com. Licensee: KYOO Communications KYOO Communications (acq 7-29-97; $52,000. assumption of note). Network: ABC. Format: News, country. Target aud: 10-72 yrs. Spec prog: Farm 3 hrs, gospel 2 hrs wkly. ♦ Ann Paris, VP; Stephen Paris, pres & gen mgr.

Bonne Terre

KDBB(FM)— September 1989: 104.3 mhz; 790 w. 630 ft. TL: N37 48 04 W90 33 44. Box 36, Park Hills 63601. Phone: (573) 431-1000. Fax: (573) 431-0850. E-mail: radio@b104fm.com. Web Site: www.b104fm.com. Licensee: MKS Broadcasting Inc. (acq 9-6-94; $315,753;. FTR: 10-17-94). Network: Westwood One. Format: Rock. News staff: one; News: 20 hrs wkly. Target aud: 25-55. ♦ M.L. Steinmetz, pres; Larry D. Joseph, gen mgr; Kelly Valle, gen sls mgr; Greg Camp, progmg mgr; Gib Collins Jr., news dir & pub affrs dir.

Boonville

KCLR-FM— Oct 1, 1974: 99.3 mhz; 33.2 kw. 590 ft. TL: N38 46 34 W92 32 45. Stereo. 3215 Lemone Industrial Blvd., Suite 200, Columbia 65201. Phone: (573) 875-1099. Fax: (573) 875-2439. Web Site: www.clear99.com. Licensee: Zimmer Broadcasting Co. Format: Country. News staff: 3; News: 3 hrs wkly. Target aud: 25-54. ♦ Ron Covert, gen mgr.

KWRT(AM)— Aug 11, 1953: 1370 khz; 1 kw-D, 84 w-N. TL: N38 56 44 W92 34 30. 1600 Radio Hill Rd. 65233. Phone: (660) 882-6686. Fax: (660) 882-6688. E-mail: kwrt@undata.com. Licensee: Big Country of Missouri Inc. Network: Network: ABC Information & Entertainment, Jones Radio Networks. Format: Country. News staff: 2; News: 5 hrs wkly. Target aud: 35 plus; general. Spec prog: Farm 5 hrs wkly. ♦ Dick Billings, pres; Matt Billings, gen mgr, gen sls mgr, progmg dir & mus dir; Pat Billings, opns mgr; Ted Bleil, progmg dir, mus dir & news dir; Mike Mcgowan, chief of engrg.

KWRT-FM— Sept 15, 1999: 93.1 mhz; 3.8 kw. 413 ft. TL: N38 56 31 W92 34 30. Format: Btfl mus, big band, adult standards. ♦ Don Lynch, gen mgr; Matt Billings, progmg mgr.

Bowling Green

KPVR(FM)— Aug 1, 1975: 94.1 mhz; 7.5 kw. Ant 592 ft. TL: N39 15 45 W91 04 09. Stereo. 13358 Manchester Rd., Suite 100, Des Peres 63131. Phone: (314) 909-8569. Fax: (314) 835-9739. E-mail: info@joyfmonline.org. Web Site: www.joyfmonline.org. Licensee: Four Him Enterprises L.L.C. (acq 5-15-2001; $725,000. with co-located AM). Format: Contemp Christian. ♦ Sandi Brown, gen mgr.

Branson

*KLFC(FM)— July 1988: 88.1 mhz; 1.8 kw. Ant 390 ft. TL: N36 33 06 W93 14 17. Stereo. 205 W. Atlantic 65616-0921. Phone: (417) 334-5532. Fax: (417) 335-2437. E-mail: 881fm@klfcradio.com. Web Site: www.klfcradio.com. Licensee: Mountaintop Broadcasting Inc. (acq 6-1-01). Network: USA. Format: Christian. News: 7 hrs wkly. Target aud: General; resort & tourist community. ♦ Herb Smith, pres, gen mgr & stn mgr; Vicky Smith, opns dir; Darin Ahrends, news dir.

KOMC(AM)— Dec 21, 1956: 1220 khz; 1 kw-D, 53 w-N. TL: N36 37 12 W93 12 40. 202 Courtney St. 65616. Phone: (417) 334-6003. Phone: (417) 334-6012. Fax: (417) 334-7141. E-mail: krzk@krzk.com. Web Site: www.hometownradioonline.com. Licensee: Turtle Broadcasting Co. of Branson L.P. Group owner: Orr & Earls Broadcasting Inc. (acq 11-21-86; $335,000). Network: CBS. Format: Christian, relg. News staff: 2; News: 10 hrs wkly. Target aud: 40 plus. ♦ Charles C. Earls, pres; Scottie Earls, gen mgr, stn mgr & opns mgr; Steve Willoughby, stn mgr & mktg mgr; Scott McCaulley, progmg dir; Don Paul, news dir; Greg Pyron, chief of engrg.

KRZK(FM)— Co-owned with KOMC(AM). Mar 1, 1971: 106.3 mhz; 5.7 kw. 672 ft. TL: N36 43 52 W93 10 03. (CP: 100 kw, ant 564 ft.). Stereo. Network: ABC Daytime Direction. Format: Country. News staff: one; News: 7 hrs wkly. Target aud: 25-54; Branson & loc tourists. ♦ Charles C. Earles, CEO; Steve Willoughby, mktg dir; Scott Earls, engrg mgr & chief of engrg.

*KOZO(FM)— 1998: 89.7 mhz; 150 w horiz, 22 kw vert. Ant 426 ft. TL: N36 33 02 W93 14 46. (CP: 150 w horiz, 20 kw vert. TL: N36 33 04 W93 14 36). Stereo. 301 Gibson Rd., Hollister 65672. Phone: (918) 455-5693. Phone: (417) 339-3388. Fax: (417) 339-3410. E-mail: mail@oasisnetwork.org. Web Site: www.oasisnetwork.org. Licensee: Creative Educational Media Corp. Inc. Network: AP Radio. Rgnl Reps Format: Positive easy gospel, Christian. Target aud: General. Spec prog: Talk 5 hrs wkly. ♦ David Ingles, pres & gen mgr; Hartlen Coats, stn mgr; David Warren, progmg dir; Rick Norwood, engrg dir; Roger King, chief of engrg.

Brookfield

KFMZ(AM)— Feb 14, 1956: 1470 khz; 500 w-D, 20 w-N, DA. TL: N39 50 26 W93 04 52. 107 S. Main 64628. Phone: (660) 258-3383. Fax: (660) 258-7307. E-mail: kzbk@kzbkradio.com. Web Site: www.kzbkradio.com. Licensee: Best Broadcasting Inc. Group owner: Best Broadcast Group (acq 6-14-93; $70,000. with co-located FM; FTR: 6-28-93). Network: ABC. Bryan Cave. Format: Hot adult contemp. News: 4 hrs wkly. Target aud: 18-49; men & women with spendable income. ♦ Phillip A. Chirillo, pres; Dale A. Palmer, VP & gen mgr.

KZBK(FM)— Co-owned with KFMZ(AM). September 1981: 96.9 mhz; 50 kw. 492 ft. TL: N39 54 32 W93 04 34. Stereo.

Brookline

KQRA(FM)— May 28, 2002: 102.1 mhz; 4.9 kw. Ant 361 ft. TL: N37 12 39 W93 13 42. Stereo. 319 B E. Battlefield, Springfield 65807. Phone: (417) 886-5677. Fax: (417) 886-2155. E-mail: info@q1021.fm. Web Site: www.q1021.fm. Licensee: MW SpringMo Inc. Group owner: The Mid-West Family Broadcast Group. Rep: McGavren Guild. Shawn Pittman, progmg dir. Format: Rock, AOR. Target aud: 18-49; active adults. ♦ Rick McCoy, pres & gen mgr.

Stations in the U.S. **Missouri**

Buffalo

KBFL(FM)— 1965: 99.9 mhz; 3.10 kw. 476 ft. TL: N37 31 14 W93 06 14. Stereo. Box 1385 65622. Secondary address: 304 S. Pine 65622. Phone: (417) 345-2412. Fax: (417) 345-2410. Web Site: www.radiospringfield.com. Licensee: Meyer-Baldridge Inc. Group owner: Meyer Communications Inc. (acq 6-1-00; $550,000). Fletcher, Heald & Hildreth. Format: Music of Your Life, news/talk, sports. News staff: one; News: 15 hrs wkly. Target aud: 34-54; male-female adults. Spec prog: Gospel 3 hrs wkly. ♦ Kenneth E. Meyer, pres; Rob Evans, gen mgr.

Butler

KMAM(AM)— May 11, 1962: 1530 khz; 500 w-D. TL: N38 14 56 W94 19 18. 800 E. Nursery St. 64730. Phone: (660) 679-4191. Fax: (660) 679-4193. E-mail: news@fm92radio.com. Web Site: www.921kmoe.com. Licensee: Bates County Broadcasting Co. Network: ABC Daytime Direction. Format: Country. News staff: one; News: 15 hrs wkly. Target aud: General; family. Spec prog: Farm 15 hrs wkly. ♦ Melody A. Thornton, pres & gen mgr.

KMOE(FM)—Co-owned with KMAM(AM). Jan 15, 1975: 92.1 mhz; 4.7 kw. Ant 148 ft. TL: N38 14 56 W94 19 18. Stereo.

Cabool

*****KFFW(FM)**— 2003: 89.9 mhz; 10.5 kw. Ant 495 ft. TL: N37 05 32 W92 03 10. Stereo. First Free Will Baptist Church, 401 S. Main, Mountain Grove 65711. Phone: (417) 926-5396. Fax: (417) 926-7911. E-mail: info@kffw.org. Web Site: www.kffw.org. Licensee: First Free Will Baptist Church (acq 12-11-01). Network: Network: Salem Radio Network, American Family Radio. Format: Christian. News: 12 hrs wkly. ♦ Brian Hurst, gen mgr; Rick Jesse, opns mgr.

KOZX(FM)— May 1978: 98.1 mhz; 3 kw. 220 ft. TL: N37 07 58 W92 08 04. Stereo. 800 N. Hubbard, Mountain Grove 65711. Phone: (417) 926-4650. Fax: (417) 926-7604. Licensee: Quorum Radio Partners Inc. (group owner; acq 8-8-2002; grpsl). Format: Classic hits. Spec prog: Farm 2 hrs wkly. ♦ Rick Vermillion, gen mgr.

California

KATI(FM)— July 27, 1984: 94.3 mhz; 50 kw. 492 ft. TL: N38 31 25 W92 24 25. Stereo. 3109 S. Ten Mile Dr., Jefferson City 65109. Phone: (573) 893-5696. Fax: (573) 893-4137. E-mail: kati@zrgmail.com. Web Site: www.kat943.com. Licensee: Zimmer Radio of Mid-Missouri Inc. Group owner: Zimmer Radio Group (acq 11-19-99; grpsl). Network: ABC Daytime Direction. Format: Country. ♦ Ron Covert, gen mgr.

KRLL(AM)— July 27, 1984: 1420 khz; 500 w-D, 225 w-N. TL: N38 38 12 W92 35 00. 100 A.E. Buchanan 65018. Phone: (573) 796-3139. Fax: (573) 796-4131. E-mail: krll01@earthlink.net. Licensee: Moniteau Communications Inc. (acq 3-30-95; $50,000;. FTR: 6-19-95). Network: ABC Daytime Direction. Leibowitz & Spencer. Format: Country. News staff: one; News: 19 hrs wkly. Target aud: 20 plus. Spec prog: Farm 5 hrs wkly, gospel 3 hrs wkly. ♦ Jeffrey G. Shackleford, pres & gen mgr.

Camdenton

*****KCVO-FM**— Sept 23, 1985: 91.7 mhz; 10 kw. 435 ft. TL: N38 01 13 W92 45 27. Stereo. Box 800, Lake Rd. 5-92 65020. Phone: (573) 346-3200. Fax: (573) 346-1010. E-mail: email@spiritfm.org. Web Site: www.spiritfm.org. Licensee: Lake Area Educational Broadcasting Foundation. Format: Div, Christian. News: 7 hrs wkly. Target aud: 25-45. ♦ Alice McDermott, CFO; James J. McDermott, pres & gen mgr.

Cameron

KKWK(FM)—Listing follows KMRN(AM).

KMRN(AM)— February 1971: 1360 khz; 500 w-D, 25 w-N. TL: N39 41 05 W94 14 22. 607 E. Platt Clay Way 64429. Phone: (816) 632-6661. Fax: (816) 632-1334. Web Site: www.regionalradio.com. Licensee: KAAN Inc. Group owner: Shepherd Group (acq 7-13-99); with co-located FM). Network: ABC Daytime Direction. Erwin Krasnow. Format: News/talk. News staff: one; News: 40 hrs wkly. Target aud: General. Spec prog: Farm 12 hrs, relg 4 hrs wkly. ♦ Rodney Harris, gen mgr & gen sls mgr; Barry Piatt, progmg dir; Greg Richwine, chief of engrg.

KKWK(FM)—Co-owned with KMRN(AM). Apr 5, 1995: 100.1 mhz; 50 kw. 492 ft. TL: N39 57 28 W94 06 55. Web Site: www.regionalradio.com. Network: ABC. Format: Adult contemp. Target aud: 25-49. ♦ Barry Piatt, mus dir.

Campbell

KFEB(FM)— October 1998: 107.5 mhz; 17.5 kw. 390 ft. TL: N36 29 55 W89 51 16. Stereo. 932 CR Box 448, Poplar Bluff 63901. Phone: (573) 686-3700. Fax: (573) 686-1713. Licensee: Eagle Bluff Enterprises. (group owner) Format: Modern rock. ♦ Steven C. Fuchs, gen mgr.

Canton

KRRY(FM)— May 4, 1971: 100.9 mhz; 28 kw. 656 ft. TL: N40 07 33 W91 31 42. 408 N. 24th St., Quincy, IL 62301. Phone: (217) 223-5292. Fax: (217) 223-5299. E-mail: mail@y101radio.com. Web Site: www.y101radio.com. Licensee: Bick Broadcasting. Rep: McGavren Guild. Format: Hot adult contemp. ♦ Bud Janes, pres; Jeff Dorsey, gen mgr; Cheri Robertson, gen sls mgr; Dennis Oliver, progmg dir; Tom Holmes, chief of engrg.

Cape Girardeau

KAPE(AM)— 1951: 1550 khz; 5 kw-D, 50 w-N, DA-2. TL: N37 16 45 W89 33 28. Box 558 63702. Secondary address: 901 S. Kings Hwy. 63703. Phone: (573) 339-7000. Fax: (573) 651-4100. Licensee: Withers Broadcasting Co. of Missouri LLC. Group owner: Withers Broadcasting Co. (acq 6-72). Network: Westwood One. Format: Adult standards, big band, oldies. Target aud: 25-54; active, aware adults. ♦ W. Russell Withers Jr., pres; Rick Lambert, gen mgr; Melody Anderson, natl sls mgr; Jeremie Hughes, progmg dir; John Steele, news dir; Smokey King, chief of engrg.

KGMO(FM)—Co-owned with KAPE(AM). Mar 17, 1969: 100.7 mhz; 100 kw. 987 ft. TL: N37 22 16 W89 31 52. Stereo. Format: Classic rock. ♦ Jeremie Hughes, prom mgr & progmg mgr.

KCGQ-FM—Listing follows KGIR(AM).

KEZS-FM— Dec 10, 1970: 102.9 mhz; 100 kw. 947 ft. TL: N37 24 23 W89 33 44. Stereo. Box 1610, 324 Broadway 63702. Phone: (573) 335-8291. Fax: (573) 335-4806. E-mail: k103@zrgmail.com. Web Site: www.k103fm.com. Licensee: MRR License LLC. Group owner: MAX Media L.L.C. (acq 3-29-2004; grpsl). Network: ABC Information & Entertainment. Fletcher, Heald & Hildreth. Format: Country. News staff: one. Target aud: 25-54. ♦ Carla Leible, gen mgr & sls dir; Whitney Thomas, opns dir; Tim Jones, progmg dir; Jack Leverich, chief of engrg.

KZIM(AM)—Co-owned with KEZS-FM. 1925: 960 khz; 5 kw-D, 500 w-N, DA-N. TL: N37 18 59 W89 29 06. E-mail: kzim@zrgmail.com. Web Site: www.960kzim.com. Network: CBS. Format: News/talk. News staff: 5. Target aud: 35-64. ♦ Terry Hester, progmg dir.

KGIR(AM)— June 10, 1966: 1220 khz; 250 w-D, 140 w-N. TL: N37 18 03 W89 29 27. Stereo. Box 1610, 324 Broadway 63702. Phone: (573) 335-8291. Fax: (573) 335-4806. E-mail: kgir@kgir.com. Licensee: MRR License LLC. Group owner: MAX Media L.L.C. (acq 3-29-2004; grpsl). Network: USA. Leventhal, Senter & Lerman. Format: Sports, talk. News staff: one. Target aud: 18 plus; men. ♦ Carla Leibley, gen mgr & sls dir; Dawn Leibley, gen sls mgr; Don Lind, gen sls mgr; Erik Sean, progmg dir & news dir.

KCGQ-FM—Co-owned with KGIR(AM). 1978: 99.3 mhz; 4.2 kw. 390 ft. TL: N37 22 07 W89 35 34. Stereo. Phone: (573) 335-8291. E-mail: realrock@zrgmail.com. Web Site: www.realrock993.com. Format: Rock/AOR, classic rock. Target aud: 18-49; general. ♦ Mike Rennick, progmg dir; Mike Cossey, chief of engrg.

*****KRCU(FM)**— Mar 3, 1976: 90.9 mhz; 6 kw. 259 ft. TL: N37 18 37 W89 31 57. Stereo. One University Plaza 63701. Phone: (573) 651-5070. Fax: (573) 651-5071. E-mail: comments@krcu.org. Web Site: www.krcu.org. Licensee: Board of Regents of Southeast Missouri State University. Network: Network: NPR, PRI. Dow, Lohnes & Albertson. Format: Class, jazz, news. Target aud: General. Spec prog: Folk, radio reader 3 hrs, big band one hr, opera 3 hrs wkly. ♦ Danny J. Woods, gen mgr & opns dir; Bill Prost, dev dir.

KREZ(FM)—(Chaffee). July 1, 1990: 104.7 mhz; 7.7 kw. Ant 585 ft. TL: N37 09 46 W89 28 59. Stereo. 901 S. Kings Hwy. 63702-0558. Phone: (573) 339-7000. Fax: (573) 651-4100. Licensee: Dana R. Withers (acq 4-12-90; $33,587;. FTR: 5-7-90). Format: Adult contemp. Target aud: 18-49. ♦ Rick Lambert, gen mgr.

Carrollton

KAOL(AM)— Apr 18, 1959: 1430 khz; 500 w-U, 27 w-N. TL: N39 19 58 W93 32 15. KMZU Bldg., 102 N. Mason 64633. Phone: (660) 542-0404. Fax: (660) 542-0420. E-mail: kmzu@carolnet.com. Licensee: Kanza Inc. (acq 11-1-81; $665,000 with co-located FM; 11-23-81). Rep: McGavren Guild. Format: Country, farm. News staff: 2; News: 10 hrs wkly. Target aud: 25-54; farm families & those with agricultural backrounds. Spec prog: Sp 3 hrs wkly. ♦ Miles Carter, gen mgr; Rick Barton, gen sls mgr; Scott Powell, progmg dir; Jim Woods, mus dir; Chastity Anderson, news dir; Larry Tannons, chief of engrg.

KMZU(FM)—Co-owned with KAOL(AM). July 13, 1962: 100.7 mhz; 98.6 kw. 990 ft. TL: N39 22 05 W93 29 40. Stereo. ♦ Larry Timmons, engrg dir.

Carthage

KDMO(AM)— June 3, 1947: 1490 khz; 1 kw-U. TL: N37 10 58 W94 21 43. Box 426, 221 E. 4th St. 64836. Phone: (417) 358-6054. Phone: (417) 358-2648. Fax: (417) 358-1278. Licensee: Ronald L. Petersen. (acq 1-23-90). Network: CNN Radio. Format: Adult standards. News staff: one; News: 160 hrs wkly. Target aud: 55 plus. Spec prog: Sp 6 hrs wkly. ♦ Ronald L. Petersen, pres & gen mgr.

KMXL(FM)—Co-owned with KDMO(AM). Jan 10, 1972: 95.1 mhz; 50 kw. 472 ft. TL: N37 10 58 W94 21 35. Stereo. Format: Adult contemp. News staff: one; News: one hr wkly. Target aud: 18-34 & 25-54; young adults & baby-boomers.

Caruthersville

KCRV(AM)— Feb 22, 1950: 1370 khz; 1 kw-D, 63 w-N. TL: N36 12 50 W89 41 25. Box 509, Kennett 63857-0509. Phone: (573) 888-4616. Fax: (573) 888-4991. Licensee: Pollack Broadcasting Co. (group owner; acq 9-21-99; with co-located FM). Network: Moody. Format: Country, gospel, farm. Target aud: General; residents of Pemiscot county. Spec prog: Relg 20 hrs wkly. ♦ Perry Jones, gen mgr & progmg dir; Bill Page, news dir; Palmer Johnson, chief of engrg.

KCRV-FM— Apr 28, 1975: 105.1 mhz; 3 kw. 200 ft. TL: N36 12 50 W89 41 25. (CP: 6 kw, ant 328 ft.). Stereo. Phone: (573) 333-1376. Format: Oldies.

Cassville

KRMO(AM)—Licensed to Cassville. See Monett

Cedar Hill

*****KNLH(FM)**— October 1998: 89.5 mhz; 108 w. 390 ft. TL: N38 21 40 W90 32 54. New Life Evangelistic Center Inc., 1411 Locust St., St.

Broadcasting & Cable Yearbook 2006
D-297

Missouri

Louis 63103. Phone: (314) 436-2424. Fax: (314) 436-2434. E-mail: larryr@hereshelpnet.org. Web Site: www.hereshelpnet.org. Licensee: New Life Evangelistic Center Inc. Format: Adult contemp, gospel, talk. ♦ Victor Anderson, gen mgr.

Centralia

KMFC(FM)— Feb 3, 1986: 92.1 mhz; 1.85 kw. Ant 418 ft. TL: N39 09 58 W92 09 52. Stereo. 1249 E. Hwy. 22 65240. Phone: (573) 682-5525. Fax: (573) 682-2744. E-mail: info@kmfc.com. Web Site: www.kmfc.com. Licensee: Clair Broadcasting Co. Network: USA. Format: Relg, Christian contemp. Target aud: 25-50. Spec prog: Black 3 hrs, gospel 2 hrs, Sp one hr wkly. ♦ Jerry D. Clair, pres & gen mgr; Sharon Dollens, stn mgr.

Chaffee

KREZ(FM)—Licensed to Chaffee. See Cape Girardeau

Charleston

KCHR(AM)— 1953: 1350 khz; 1 kw-D, 79 w-N. TL: N36 55 30 W89 17 45. 205 E. Commercial St. 63834. Phone: (573) 683-6044. Licensee: South Missouri Broadcasting Co. Inc. Format: C&W, talk. News: one hr wkly. Target aud: General. Spec prog: Gospel 10 hrs, easy lstng 5 hrs wkly. ♦ James L. Byrd III, pres; Danny Adams, gen mgr.

KWKZ(FM)— February 1993: 106.1 mhz; 34 kw. 384 ft. TL: N36 57 29 W89 23 38. Stereo. 753 Enterpirse, Cape Girardeau 63703. Phone: (573) 334-7800. Fax: (573) 334-7440. Web Site: www.kwkz.com. Licensee: Anderson Broadcasting Co. Inc. (acq 7-30-92). Format: Country, oldies. News: 2 hrs wkly. Target aud: 18-44; 35-55 male, 30-45 female. Spec prog: Farm one hr, gospel 6 hrs wkly. ♦ Bill Anderson, CEO, pres, gen mgr & sls dir; Ann Anderson, chmn, sr VP & opns VP; Susan Bell, stn mgr, opns dir, dev VP, prom dir & progmg dir; Aaron Moore, mus dir; Wendy Amanda Jarrell, news dir; Palmer Johnson, engrg dir.

Chillicothe

KCHI(AM)— Mar 3, 1950: 1010 khz; 250 w-D, 37 w-N. TL: N39 45 51 W93 33 21. Box 227, 421 Washington St. 64601. Phone: (660) 646-4173. Fax: (660) 646-2868. Licensee: Livingston Broadcasting Inc. (acq 7-1-84). Network: ABC Information & Entertainment. Format: 70s & 80s. Target aud: 35-49. ♦ Dan Leatherman, gen mgr; Dan Leatherman, gen sls mgr; Randy Dean, progmg dir; Tom Tingerthal, news dir.

KCHI-FM— October 1976: 103.9 mhz; 4.1 kw. 400 ft. TL: N39 48 52 W93 35 20. Stereo.

***KRNW(FM)**— Aug 30, 1993: 88.9 mhz; 38 kw. 498 ft. TL: N39 48 50 W93 35 20. Stereo. Wells Hall, 800 University Dr., Maryville 64468. Phone: (660) 562-1163. Phone: (660) 562-1164. Fax: (660) 562-1832. E-mail: kxcv@mail.nwmissouri.edu. Web Site: www.kxcv.org. Licensee: Northwest Missouri State University. Format: News, class, jazz. News staff: 2; News: 39 hrs wkly. Target aud: General. ♦ Dean L. Hubbard, pres; Sharon C. Bonnett, gen mgr & stn mgr; Patty Holley, opns mgr.

Clayton

KFUO-FM— Jan 1, 1948: 99.1 mhz; 100 kw. 1,026 ft. TL: N38 39 08 W90 17 03. Stereo. 85 Founders Ln., St. Louis 63105. Phone: (314) 725-0099. Fax: (314) 725-3801. E-mail: classic99@classic99.com. Web Site: www.classic99.com. Licensee: Lutheran Church-Missouri Synod. Network: Network: Wall Street, CNN Radio. Rep: Interep. Shaw Pittman. Format: Class. Target aud: General; upscale, educated. ♦ Dennis Stortz, opns dir & chief of engrg; Jim Setchfield, sls dir & gen sls mgr; Jim Connett, progmg dir.

KFUO(AM)— Dec 14, 1924: 850 khz; 5 kw-D. TL: N38 38 20 W90 18 57. Phone: (314) 725-3030. Fax: (314) 725-2538. E-mail: webmaster@kfuo.org. Web Site: www.kfuo.org. Network: UPI. Format: Relg, talk. Target aud: General.

KSIV(AM)— 1946: 1320 khz; 4.6 kw-D, 270 w-N, DA-N. TL: N38 36 26 W90 21 14. 1750 S. Brentwood Blvd., Suite 811, St. Louis 63144. Phone: (314) 961-1320. Fax: (314) 961-7562. Web Site: www.bottradionetwork.com. Licensee: Bott Broadcasting. (group owner; acq 2-25-82; 3-15-82). Network: USA. Format: Christian info. Target aud: 25-54; family-oriented. ♦ Richard P. Bott, pres; Richard Bott II, VP; Michael McHardy, gen mgr; Joy Elder, sls dir & mktg dir.

***KWUR(FM)**— July 4, 1976: 90.3 mhz; 10 w. 136 ft. TL: N38 38 45 W80 19 07. Stereo. Washington Univ. Box 1205, One Brookings Dr., St. Louis 63105. Phone: (314) 935-5952. Web Site: www.kwur.wustl.edu. Licensee: Washington University. Format: Progressive/diversified. Target aud: 18 plus; those seeking alternative radio. ♦ Nitin Bhojraj, pres.

Cleveland

KCTO(AM)—Not on air, target date: unknown: 1160 khz; 215 w-U, DA-2. TL: N38 40 26 W94 36 28. 310 S. La Frenz Rd., Liberty 64068. Phone: (816) 792-1140. Fax: (816) 792-8258. ♦ Peter E. Schartel, pres & gen mgr.

Clinton

KDKD(AM)— 1951: 1280 khz; 1 kw-D, 58 w-N. TL: N38 23 55 W93 46 19. Box 448, 2201 N. Antioch Rd. 64735. Phone: (660) 885-6141. Fax: (660) 885-4801. E-mail: bob@kdkd.net. Web Site: www.kdkd.net. Licensee: Legend Communications of Missouri LLC. Group owner: Legend Communications L.L.C. (acq 10-7-03; with co-located FM). Network: ABC Information & Entertainment. Format: Oldies. News staff: one; News: 10 hrs wkly. Target aud: 25-55. ♦ Bob May, gen mgr.

KDKD-FM— 1975: 95.3 mhz; 14.5 kw. Ant 433 ft. TL: N38 22 18 W93 55 06. Stereo. E-mail: randy@kokd.net. Web Site: www.kdkd.net. Licensee: Legend Communications of Missouri LLC. (acq 5-28-1985). Network: Network: ABC, Motor Racing Net. Format: Hot new country, news, sports. News staff: one. Target aud: 25-55.

***KLRQ(FM)**— Oct 5, 1990: 96.1 mhz; 100 kw. Ant 987 ft. TL: N38 28 27 W93 30 28. 5700 W. Oaks Blvd., Rocklin, CA 95765. Phone: (916) 251-1600. Fax: (916) 251-1650. Web Site: www.klove.com. Licensee: Educational Media Foundation. Group owner: EMF Broadcasting (acq 12-23-2003; $1.9 million). Network: K-Love. Format: Contemp Christian. ♦ Richard Jenkins, pres.

Columbia

***KBIA(FM)**— 1972: 91.3 mhz; 100 kw. 610 ft. TL: N38 53 16 W92 15 48. Stereo. Univ. of Missouri, 409 Jesse Hall 65211. Phone: (573) 882-3431. Fax: (573) 882-2636. E-mail: dunnm@missouri.edu. Web Site: www.kbia.org. Licensee: Board of Curators, University of Missouri. Group owner: The Curators of the University of Missouri Network: Network: NPR, PRI. Fisher, Wayland, Cooper, Leader & Zaragoza. Format: News, class. News: 55 hrs wkly. Target aud: 25-64. ♦ Michael Dunn, gen mgr; Roger Karwoski, stn mgr; John Bailey, dev dir & progmg dir.

KBXR(FM)— Nov 11, 1994: 102.3 mhz; 88 kw. 420 ft. TL: N38 57 21 W92 16 24. Stereo. 503 Old 63 N. 65201. Phone: (573) 449-4141. Fax: (573) 449-7770. E-mail: bxr@bxr.com. Web Site: www.bxr.com. Licensee: Cumulus Licensing LLC. Group owner: Cumulus Media Inc. (acq 4-26-2004; grpsl). Rep: Katz Radio. Leonard Joyce. Format: Album adult alternative. News staff: 3; News: one hr wkly. Target aud: 29-59; educated professional/technical. ♦ Lewis W. Dickey Jr., pres; Jack Lawson, opns dir; Scott Boltz, gen mgr & mktg mgr.

KCMQ(FM)— Dec 3, 1967: 96.7 mhz; 18 kw. 344 ft. TL: N38 41 30 W92 05 44. (CP: 98 kw, ant 912 ft. TL: N38 41 30 W92 05 44). Stereo. 3215 LeMone Industrial, Suite 200 65201. Phone: (573) 875-1099. Fax: (573) 875-2439. Web Site: ktgr.com. Licensee: Zimmer Radio of Mid-Missouri Inc. (acq 7-15-93; $625,000 with co-located AM; 8-9-93). Format: AOR. News: one hr wkly. Target aud: 25-54; male. ♦ Nicci Garmon, opns dir & progmg dir; Tony Richards, gen mgr & opns dir; Stu Steinmetz, sls dir; Anna Quast, mktg dir; Mike Mayfield, engrg mgr & chief of engrg.

KTGR(AM)— Co-owned with KCMQ(FM). 1955: 1580 khz; 250 w-D, 19 w-N. TL: N38 58 01 W92 18 39. Web Site: ktgr.com. Network: Network: ABC, ESPN Radio. Format: Sports. Target aud: 18-34; male. ♦ Aric Bremer, progmg dir.

***KCOU(FM)**— Oct 31, 1973: 88.1 mhz; 435 w. 110 ft. TL: N38 56 23 W92 19 20. Stereo. Univ. of Missouri, 101-F Pershing Hall 65201. Phone: (573) 882-7820. Fax: (573) 882-6262. E-mail: kcou@mu.org. Web Site: www.kcou.mu.org. Licensee: The Curators of the University of Missouri. (acq 12-14-98; $80,000). Format: Progsv, rock. News: 5 hrs wkly. Target aud: 18-22; students & community members. Spec prog: Jazz 10 hrs, blues 2 hrs, reggae/African 2 hrs, punk/hardcore 2 hrs, industrial 2 hrs wkly. ♦ Jason Smith, gen mgr.

KFRU(AM)— Oct 10, 1925: 1400 khz; 1 kw-U. TL: N38 57 52 W92 18 26. 503 Old Hwy., 63 N. 65201. Phone: (573) 449-4141. Fax: (573) 449-7770. Fax: (573) 499-1414. E-mail: news@kfru.com. Web Site: www.kfru.com. Licensee: Cumulus Licensing LLC. Group owner: Cumulus Media Inc. (acq 4-26-2004; grpsl). Network: ABC News/Talk. Format: News/talk. News staff: 9; News: 40 hrs wkly. Target aud: General. ♦ Lewis W. Dickey Jr., pres; John Ott, VP & gen mgr; Timothy Murphy, opns VP.

***KOPN(FM)**— Mar 1, 1973: 89.5 mhz; 36 kw. 236 ft. TL: N38 59 53 W92 11 48. (CP: 36.4 kw). Stereo. 915 E. Broadway 65201-4857. Phone: (573) 874-1139. Fax: (573) 499-1662. E-mail: mail@kopn.org. Web Site: www.kopn.org. Licensee: New Wave Corp. Network: Network: NPR, PRI. Haley, Bader & Potts. Format: News/talk, Americana. Target aud: 25-54; well educated, upwardly mobile. Spec prog: Blues 13 hrs, Black 10 hrs, AAA 10 hrs, Grateful Dead 6 hrs, jazz 4 hrs, gospel 3 hrs, bluegrass 6 hrs, folk 2 hrs wkly. ♦ David Owens, gen mgr.

KPLA(FM)— Feb 23, 1983: 101.5 mhz; 100 kw. 1,062 ft. TL: N39 00 52 W92 16 32. Stereo. 503 Old 63 N. 65201. Phone: (573) 442-3116. Fax: (573) 449-7770. E-mail: studio@kpla.com. Web Site: www.kpla.com. Licensee: Cumulus Licensing LLC. Group owner: Cumulus Media Inc. (acq 4-26-2004; grpsl). Format: Adult contemp. News staff: 2; News: one hr wkly. Target aud: 25-54. ♦ Lewis W. Dickey Jr., pres; Jack Lawson, opns VP.

***KWWC-FM**— Feb 2, 1965: 90.5 mhz; 1.25 kw. 131 ft. TL: N38 57 12 W92 19 05. Stereo. Box 2114, Stephens College 65215. Phone: (573) 876-7297. Phone: (573) 876-7272. Fax: (573) 876-2330. E-mail: msmith@stephens.edu. Licensee: Stephens College. Format: Jazz. Target aud: 25-60; college educated, professional or retired with middle upper income. ♦ Dr. Marcia Kierscht, pres; Dr. Robert Badal, CEO & CFO; Mark Smith, gen mgr; John Blakemore, mktg dir; Max Ornles, chief of engrg.

Concordia

***KYRV(FM)**— 1998: 88.1 mhz; 1 kw. Ant 213 ft. TL: N38 52 10 W93 32 58. 712 Chaucer Ln., Warrensburg 64093. Phone: (660) 747-4155. Fax: (660) 747-4155. Licensee: Full Smile Inc. Format: Southern gospel. ♦ Jim McCollum, gen mgr.

Country Club

***KJCV(FM)**— 2005: 89.7 mhz; 3.9 kw. Ant 548 ft. TL: N39 42 35 W95 02 33. Bott Radio Network, 10550 Barkley, Overland Park, KS 66212. Phone: (913) 642-7600. Fax: (913) 642-1319. Web Site: www.bottradionetwork.com. Licensee: Community Broadcasting Inc. Group owner: Bott Radio Network. Format: Relg. ♦ Eben Fowler, gen mgr.

Crestwood

KSHE(FM)— Feb 11, 1961: 94.7 mhz; 100 kw. 1,019 ft. TL: N38 34 24 W90 19 30. Stereo. The Powerhouse, 800 St. Louis Union Stn., St. Louis 63103. Phone: (314) 621-0095. Fax: (314) 621-3428. Web Site: www.kshe95.com. Licensee: Emmis Radio License LLC. Group owner: Emmis Communications Corp. (acq 3-19-84; grpsl; FTR: 1-30-84). Rep: D & R Radio. Format: Classic rock, AOR. News staff: one; News: one hr wkly. Target aud: 18-40. ♦ John R. Beck Jr., gen mgr.

Cuba

KESY(FM)— 2005: 107.3 mhz; 6.7 kw. Ant 626 ft. TL: N37 55 17 W91 26 36. 3418 Douglas Rd., Florissant 63034. Phone: (314) 921-9330. Licensee: Twenty-One Sound Communications Inc. (acq 11-8-2004; $400,000. for CP). Format: Country. ♦ Randy Wachter, gen mgr.

***KGNN-FM**— Jan 26, 1997: 90.3 mhz; 6.30 kw. Ant 324 ft. TL: N38 05 11 W91 18 30. Box 187, Washington 63090-0187. Phone: (636) 239-0400. Fax: (636) 239-4448. Web Site: goodnewsvoice.org. Licensee: Missouri River Christian Broadcasting Inc. Network: Network: Moody, Salem Radio Network, Premiere Focus. Format: Beautiful music, Christian, news/talk. News: 14 hrs wkly. Target aud: General; inquisitive, conservative, philosophical. Spec prog: Children. ♦ James Goggan, pres & gen mgr.

Stations in the U.S.   Missouri

Developers & Brokers of Radio Properties
contact American Media Services at our suite: Philadelphia Marriott Downtown
215-625-2900
843-972-2200
americanmediaservices.com
Charleston, SC
Dallas, TX · Chicago, Il · Austin, TX
American Media Services, LLC

*KNLQ(FM)— 2004: 91.9 mhz; 5 kw. Ant 249 ft. TL: N38 02 14 W91 23 04. New Life Evangelistic Center Inc., 1411 Locust St., St. Louis 63103. Phone: (314) 421-3020. Fax: (314) 436-2434. Web Site: www.hereshelpnet.org. Licensee: New Life Evangelistic Center Inc. Format: Gospel. ◆ Rick Jesse, stn mgr.

De Soto

KDJR(FM)— Jan 29, 1991: 100.1 mhz; 4.8 kw. Ant 371 ft. TL: N38 01 25 W90 34 02. Stereo. 12 Carroll St., Westminster, MD 21157. Phone: (314) 337-5423. Licensee: Serendipity Ventures II LLC (acq 10-20-03; $350,000). ◆ John Kotmier, gen mgr.

KRFT(AM)— Nov 1, 1968: 1190 khz; 10 kw-D, 22 w-N, DA-2. TL: N38 42 25 W90 03 10. 8045 Big Bend Blvd., St. Louis 63119. Phone: (314) 962-0590. Fax: (314) 962-7576. Web site: www.kfns.com. Licensee: Big Stick Three LLC. Group owner: Big League Broadcasting LLC (acq 7-13-2004; grpsl). Network: Motor Racing Net. Format: Sports. Target aud: 25-64; sports fans, men 25-54. ◆ Mike Phares, gen mgr.

Deerfield

KBZI(FM)— May 18, 2000: 100.7 mhz; 17.5 kw. Ant 390 ft. TL: N37 43 08 W94 40 06. American Media Investments Inc., 1162 E. Hwy 126, Pittsburg, KS 66762. Phone: (620) 231-7200. Fax: (620) 231-3321. Web Site: www.kbzi.com. Licensee: American Media Investments Inc. Format: Adult contemp. ◆ Chris Kelly, gen mgr.

Dexter

KDEX-FM— July 17, 1969: 102.3 mhz; 6 kw. 279 ft. TL: N36 47 18 W89 54 22. Stereo. Box 249, 20487 State Hwy. 114 63841. Phone: (573) 624-3545. Fax: (573) 624-9926. E-mail: kdex1@dexter.net. Licensee: Dexter Broadcasting Inc. (acq 7-15-88). Network: ABC Daytime Direction. Fisher, Wayland, Cooper, Leader & Zaragoza. Format: Modern country. News staff: 2; News: 5 hrs wkly. Target aud: 25-54. ◆ Tony James, opns dir & progmg dir; Joeli Barbour, natl sls mgr; Walt Turner, gen mgr, gen sls mgr & rgnl sls mgr; Dave Obergoenner, chief of engrg.

KDEX(AM)— Feb 1, 1956: 1590 khz; 620 w-D, 78 w-N. TL: N36 47 20 W89 54 28. Box 249 63841. Secondary address: 20487 State Hwy 114 63841. Phone: (573) 624-3545. Fax: (573) 624-9926. E-mail: kdexl@dexter.net.

Dixon

*KCVZ(FM)— May 2003: 92.1 mhz; 6 kw. Ant 328 ft. TL: N37 57 59 W92 10 03. Stereo. Box 800, Camdenton 65020. Phone: (573) 346-3200. Fax: (573) 346-1010. E-mail: spiritfm@spiritfm.org. Web Site: www.spiritfm.org. Licensee: Lake Area Educational Broadcasting Foundation (acq 12-20-01). Format: Div, Christian. ◆ Alice McDermott, CFO; James McDermott, pres & gen mgr.

Doniphan

KDFN(AM)— Feb 4, 1963: 1500 khz; 2.5 kw-D, DA. TL: N36 36 53 W90 49 23. Box 426 63935. Phone: (573) 686-3700. Fax: (573) 996-5328. Licensee: Eagle Bluff Enterprises. (group owner; acq 9-8-99; grpsl). Network: ABC Information & Entertainment. Format: Classic rock. Target aud: General. Spec prog: Farm 5 hrs wkly. ◆ Steven Fuchs, gen mgr; Ken Hosler, news dir.

KOEA(FM)— Co-owned with KDFN(AM). Apr 11, 1975: 97.5 mhz; 50 kw. 577 ft. TL: N36 35 20 W90 49 10. Stereo. Format: Country. ◆ Steven Fuchs, gen sls mgr; Tammy Jameson, mktg mgr; Skeet Collins, progmg dir.

East Prairie

KYMO(AM)— Nov 15, 1965: 1080 khz; 500 w-D. TL: N36 47 42 W89 21 17. (CP: TL: N36 47 49 W89 21 19). Box 130 63845. Phone: (573) 649-3597. E-mail: kymo@bootheel.net. Licensee: Usher Broadcasting Inc. (acq 6-1-69). Format: Easy Listening. ◆ Barney L. Webster, pres & gen mgr; Michael Bennett, opns mgr; Barney L. wEBSTER, gen sls mgr; James Glanville, progmg dir.

KYMO-FM— Aug 5, 1991: 105.3 mhz; 3 kw. 207 ft. TL: N36 47 49 W89 21 19. Format: Oldies.

El Dorado Springs

KESM(AM)— July 18, 1961: 1580 khz; 500 w-D. TL: N37 51 51 W94 00 54. Stereo. 200 Radio Ln. 64744. Phone: (417) 876-2741. Phone: (417) 876-2742. Fax: (417) 876-2743. Licensee: Wildwood Communications Inc. (acq 12-17-85). Format: C&W, oldies. Target aud: General. ◆ Donald Kohn, pres, gen mgr, opns dir, news dir & engrg mgr; Cindy Bird, stn mgr & progmg dir; Jennifer Corbin, gen sls mgr; Darla Steward, mus dir.

KESM-FM— June 1, 1965: 105.5 mhz; 6.0 kw. 187 ft. TL: N37 51 51 W94 00 54. Stereo. (Acq 12-17-85; $200,000; 11-11-85).

Eldon

KLOZ(FM)— July 1, 1979: 92.7 mhz; 50 kw. Ant 620 ft. TL: N38 20 27 W92 35 33. Stereo. 160 Hwy 42, Kaiser 65047. Phone: (573) 348-1958. Fax: (573) 348-1923. E-mail: mclayton@mix927.com. Web Site: www.todaysbesthits.com. Licensee: Benne Broadcasting Co. L.L.C. Network: ABC Information & Entertainment. Format: Adult contemp. News staff: 3; News: one hr wkly. Target aud: 25-54; 70% female/30% male with average or above income. Spec prog: U.S. mus survey, Blockbuster Top-25 countdown 6 hrs wkly. ◆ Kelly Thomas, mktg mgr; Mike Clayton, gen mgr, prom dir, progmg dir, news dir & engrg mgr.

Ellington

KAUL(FM)— 1999: 106.7 mhz; 3 kw. 298 ft. TL: N37 13 58 W90 51 08. 1411 Locust St., St. Louis 63103. Phone: (314) 421-3020. Fax: (314) 436-2434. E-mail: larryr@hereshelpnet.org. Web Site: www.hereshelpnet.org. Licensee: New Life Evangelistic Center. Format: Adult contemp, gospel, pub affrs. ◆ Larry Rice, gen mgr; Judy Redlich, sls dir.

Excelsior Springs

KEXS(AM)— August 1968: 1090 khz; 1 kw-D. TL: N39 20 25 W94 14 26. 201 N. Industrial Park Rd. 64024. Phone: (816) 630-1090. Web Site: www.kexs.com. Licensee: Kansas City Catholic Network Inc. (acq 5-17-2004; $825,000). Network: USA. Format: Catholic radio. Target aud: 25-54. ◆ James E. O'Laughlin, pres; John Lewis, stn mgr & opns VP.

Farmington

KREI(AM)— Dec 7, 1947: 800 khz; 1 kw-D, 150 w-N. TL: N37 47 45 W90 24 30. Box 461, 1401 KREI Blvd. 63640. Phone: (573) 756-6476. Fax: (573) 756-1110. Fax: (573) 756-9127(NEWS). Web Site: www.krei.com. Licensee: KREI Inc. Group owner: Shepherd Group (acq 7-1-82; $160,000 with co-located FM; 5-17-82). Network: ABC Information & Entertainment. Format: News/talk. News staff: 12; News: 40 hrs wkly. Target aud: General. Spec prog: Farm 5 hrs wkly. ◆ Richard Womack, gen mgr; Kimberly Long, stn mgr; Scott Kubala, progmg dir; Kevin Brooks, chief of engrg.

KTJJ(FM)— Co-owned with KREI(AM). June 5, 1977: 98.5 mhz; 100 kw. 1,040 ft. TL: N37 43 07 W90 33 01. Stereo. Web Site: j98.com. Network: ABC Information & Entertainment. Format: Country. News: 16 hrs wkly. Target aud: General.

*KSEF(FM)—Not on air, target date: unknown: 88.9 mhz; 10 kw. Ant 636 ft. TL: N37 48 04 W90 33 44. Southeast Missouri State University, One University Plaza, Cape Girardeau 63701. Phone: (573) 651-5070. Fax: (573) 651-5071. Licensee: Board of Regents, Southeast Missouri State University. ◆ Dan Woods, gen mgr.

Fayette

KSSZ(FM)— July 15, 1994: 93.9 mhz; 25 kw. 328 ft. TL: N39 03 28 W92 28 49. Stereo. 3215 Lemone Industrial Blvd., Suite 200, Columbia 65201. Phone: (573) 875-1099. Fax: (573) 875-2439. E-mail: eagle939@zrgmail.com. Web Site: www.939theeagle.com. Licensee: Zimmer Radio of Mid-Missouri Inc. (acq 9-27-96; $550,000). Network: Network: Network: ABC, Jones Radio Networks, Westwood One. Format: News/talk. News staff: 2; News: 4 hrs wkly. Target aud: 25-54; adults. ◆ Jason Griffin, gen mgr & progmg dir; Tony Richards, gen mgr & opns dir; Anna Quast, mktg dir & prom dir; Mike Mayfield, engrg dir & chief of engrg; Stu Steinmetz, chief of engrg & sls.

Ferguson

*KCFV(FM)— Apr 17, 1972: 89.5 mhz; 100 w. 159 ft. TL: N38 46 07 W90 17 16. Stereo. 3400 Pershall Rd., St. Louis 63135-1499. Phone: (314) 513-4472. Phone: (314) 513-4478. Fax: (314) 513-4217. E-mail: dkirby@fv.stlcc.edu. Web Site: www.stlcc.edu/fv/kcfv. Licensee: St. Louis Community College District. Dow, Lohnes & Albertson. Format: Alternative. News: 2 hrs wkly. Target aud: General. Spec prog: Jazz 4 hrs, Black 4 hrs, country 4 hrs, hard rock 4 hrs wkly. ◆ Dianna L. Kirby, gen mgr; Tim Croskey, chief of engrg.

Festus

KJFF(AM)— May 10, 1951: 1400 khz; 1 kw-U. TL: N38 13 56 W90 23 50. Box 368 63028. Phone: (636) 937-7642. Fax: (636) 937-3636. Web Site: www.kjff.com. Licensee: KREI Inc. Group owner: Shepherd Group (acq 2-1-89; $230,000; 2-1-89). Network: ABC. Format: News/talk. News staff: 4; News: 30 hrs wkly. Target aud: General. ◆ David Shepherd, pres; Dick Womack, gen mgr; Kirk Mooney, stn mgr & sls dir; Hal Neisler, progmg dir & news dir; Kevin Brooks, chief of engrg.

*KTBJ(FM)— 1998: 89.3 mhz; 25 kw. Ant 371 ft. TL: N38 09 16 W90 02 07. Stereo. 6022 S. Lindbergh Blvd., Suite 101, St. Louis 63123. Phone: (314) 892-9893. Fax: (314) 892-9527. E-mail: ktbj@csnradio.com. Web Site: www.csnradio.com. Licensee: CSN International (group owner; acq 6-17-98; $100,000). Format: Christian talk/music. ◆ Scott Parker, stn mgr.

Florissant

KFTK(FM)— Apr 15, 1977: 97.1 mhz; 100 kw. 560 ft. TL: N38 46 45 W90 43 43. Stereo. 800 St. Louis Union St., The Powerhouse, St. Louis 63103. Phone: (314) 231-9710. Fax: (314) 621-3000. Licensee: Emmis Radio License LLC. Group owner: Emmis Communications Corp. (acq 9-26-2000; grpsl). Rep: McGavren Guild. Format: Talk. ◆ John Beck, sr VP, gen mgr & gen mgr.

Fredericktown

KYLS(AM)— June 29, 1963: 1450 khz; 1 kw-U. TL: N37 35 00 W90 17 31. 540 Maple Valley Dr., Farmington 63640-1481. Phone: (573) 701-9590. Fax: (573) 701-9696. Web Site: www.froggy96.com. Licensee: Dockins Communications Inc. (acq 3-11-97). Format: Oldies. News: 8 hrs wkly. Target aud: 35-65. ◆ Fred M. Dockins Sr., pres & gen mgr.

Fulton

KFAL(AM)— Nov 14, 1950: 900 khz; 1 kw-D, 121 w-N. TL: N38 51 58 W91 57 15. 1805 Westminster, Jefferson City 65251. Phone: (573) 875-1099. Fax: (573) 642-3343. E-mail: kfal@socket.net. Web Site: www.kfal.com. Licensee: Zimmer Radio of Mid-Missouri Inc. Group owner: Zimmer Radio Group (acq 11-19-99; grpsl). Network: Network: Motor Racing Net, ABC Daytime Direction. Format: Traditional country. News staff: one; News: 3 hrs wkly. Target aud: 35 plus. Spec prog: Other 6 hrs wkly. ◆ Jerry Zimmer, CEO; John Zimmer, chmn; Don Zimmer, pres; Bob Steinberg, CFO; Jeremiah Washington, gen mgr; Peg Dzicek, stn mgr; Tony Richards, opns VP; Andy Tutin, gen sls mgr; Anna Quast, prom VP; Justin Dean, progmg dir; Mike Mayfield, chief of engrg.

Missouri

KKCA(FM)—Co-owned with KFAL(AM). 1970: 100.5 mhz; 6 kw. 300 ft. TL: N38 51 58 W91 57 15. Stereo. Network: Network: Network: ABC, Westwood One, Jones Radio Networks. Format: Oldies. News staff: one; News: 2 hrs wkly. Target aud: 25-54.

Gainesville

KMAC(FM)— Mar 17, 1994: 99.7 mhz; 50 kw. Ant 492 ft. TL: N36 36 06 W92 25 48. Stereo. Box 6610, 100 Bluebird St., Harrison, AR 72601. Phone: (870) 743-1157. Fax: (870) 743-1168. E-mail: kmac997@hotmail.com. Licensee: Pearson Broadcasting of Gainesville Inc. Group owner: Pearson Broadcasting (acq 12-19-94; $150,000; 2-13-95). Format: Hot adult contemp. Target aud: General. ◆ Dave Fransen, gen mgr.

Gallatin

KGOZ(FM)— June 1994: 101.7 mhz; 15 kw. Ant 423 ft. TL: N39 53 14 W93 43 24. Stereo. Box 217, 804 Main, Trenton 64683. Phone: (660) 359-2727. Fax: (660) 359-4126. E-mail: kttnamfm@grm.net. Web Site: www.parbroadcastgroup.com. Licensee: PAR Broadcasting Co. Inc. (acq 1-3-94; $11,571. for CP; FTR: 1-24-94). Network: Jones Radio Networks. Rep: Rgnl Reps. Reddy, Begley & McCormick. Format: Hot country. News: 2 hrs wkly. Target aud: 14-50. ◆ John Ausberger, pres; John Anthony, gen mgr.

Garden City

KCJK(FM)— January 2001: 105.1 mhz; 69 kw. 1,145 ft. TL: N39 05 26 W94 28 18. Stereo. 5800 Foxridge Dr., Suite 600, Mission, KS 66202. Phone: (913) 514-3000. Fax: (913) 514-3002. Web Site: www.1051jackfm.com. Licensee: 105.1FM LLC. Group owner: Susquehanna Radio Corp. Format: Hot adult contemp. News: 10.5 hrs wkly. Target aud: 25-44. ◆ Pat Gibbs, gen sls mgr; Todd Foxx, prom dir; Mike O'Reilly, progmg dir.

Gladstone

KGGN(AM)— Nov 18, 1996: 890 khz; 1 kw-D, DA. TL: N39 20 03 W94 34 01. (CP: 960 w-D, DA). 1734 E. 63rd St., Suite 600, Kansas City 64110. Phone: (816) 333-0092. Fax: (816) 363-8120. E-mail: kggnproduction@aol.com. Web Site: www.kggnam.com. Licensee: Mortenson Broadcasting Co. (group owner; acq 12-24-96; $450,000). Format: Gospel. ◆ Dorris Newman, gen mgr.

Gordonville

KCGQ-FM—Licensed to Gordonville. See Cape Girardeau

Halfway

KYOO-FM— April 1995: 99.1 mhz; 25 kw. 328 ft. TL: N37 45 41 W93 15 42. 205 N. Pike Ave., Bolivar 65613-1550. Phone: (417) 326-5259. Phone: (417) 326-5257. Fax: (417) 326-5900. E-mail: kyooradio@aol.com. Web Site: www.todayshits.com. Licensee: KYOO Communications. Network: ABC. Format: Adult contemp. News staff: one; News: 5 hrs wkly. Target aud: 10-72. ◆ Ann Paris, VP; Stephen Paris, pres & gen mgr.

Hannibal

KGRC(FM)— Nov 28, 1968: 92.9 mhz; 100 kw. 489 ft. TL: N39 43 45 W91 24 15. (CP: Ant 502 ft. TL: N39 43 48 W91 24 19). Stereo. Lincoln Douglas Bldg., 329 Main St., Quincy, IL 62301. Phone: (217) 224-4102. Fax: (217) 224-4133. E-mail: jbates@staradio.com. Web Site: www.real929.com. Licensee: STARadio Corp. (group owner; acq 12-2-98; $2.1 million with KZZK(FM) New London). Network: Westwood One. Rep: Katz Radio. Pepper & Corazzini. Format: Hot adult contemp. News staff: one; News: one hr wkly. Target aud: 18-49; women. ◆ Howard Doss, pres; Michael J. Moyers, VP & gen mgr; Joe Bates, progmg dir & chief of engrg.

KHMO(AM)— April 1941: 1070 khz; 5 kw-D, 1 kw-N, DA-3. TL: N39 37 43 W91 22 34. Box 711 63401. Phone: (573) 221-3450. Fax: (573) 221-5331. E-mail: kickfm@bicbroadcasting.com. Licensee: Bick Broadcasting. (acq 8-1-85; $1.35 million; 6-17-85). Rep: McGavren Guild. Eugene T. Smith. Format: News/talk, sports. News staff: 2; News: 22 hrs wkly. ◆ Ed Foxall, gen mgr & gen sls mgr.

*KJIR(FM)— April 2000: 91.7 mhz; 5.1 kw. Ant 554 ft. TL: N39 43 48 W91 24 19. Stereo. Believers Broadcasting Corp., 220 N. 6th St., Quincy, IL 62301. Phone: (217) 221-9410. Fax: (217) 228-0966.

E-mail: kjir@motion.net. Licensee: Believers Broadcasting Corp. Format: Southern gospel. News: 7.5 hrs wkly. Target aud: Christian; 30-70. ◆ I. Carl Geisendorfer, gen mgr.

Harrisonville

KCFX(FM)— July 19, 1974: 101.1 mhz; 97 kw. Ant 1,099 ft. TL: N39 01 20 W94 30 49. Stereo. 6th Fl., 5800 Foxridge Dr., Mission, KS 66202. Phone: (913) 514-3000. Fax: (913) 514-3004. Web Site: www.101thefox.net. Licensee: Susquehanna Kansas City Partnership. Group owner: Susquehanna Radio Corp. (acq 7-14-00; grpsl). Format: Classic rock. Target aud: 25-54; baby boomers. ◆ Dave Alpert, gen mgr.

Hayti

KCRV(AM)—See Caruthersville

KCRV-FM—See Caruthersville

High Point

*KMCV(FM)— 2001: 89.9 mhz; 18 kw vert. Ant 325 ft. TL: N38 35 48 W92 32 17. 3732 W. Truman Blvd., Jefferson City 65109. Phone: (573) 893-8990. Fax: (573) 893-8991. E-mail: kmcv@bottradionetwork.com. Web Site: www.bottradionetwork.com. Licensee: Community Broadcasting Inc. Group owner: Bott Radio Network (acq 2-7-01; $1.25 million. with KSCV(FM) Springfield). Format: Relg. ◆ Richard Bott II, exec VP.

Hollister

KBCV(AM)— 2004: 1570 khz; 5 kw-D, 3 kw-N, DA-2. TL: N36 36 52 W93 12 49 (D), N36 36 51 W93 12 50 (N). 10550 Barkley, Suite 108, Overland Park, KS 66212. Phone: (913) 642-7600. Fax: (913) 642-1319. Licensee: Bott Communications Inc. Group owner: Bott Radio Network. Format: Relg. ◆ Eben Fowler, gen mgr.

Houston

KBTC(AM)—Listing follows KUNQ(FM).

KUNQ(FM)— May 1965: 99.3 mhz; 30 kw. Ant 604 ft. TL: N37 05 32 W92 03 10. (CP: 33 kw). Stereo. Box 230, 17647 Hwy. B 65483. Phone: (417) 967-3353. Fax: (417) 967-2281. E-mail: kunq@kunq.net. Web Site: www.kunq.net. Licensee: Metropolitan Radio Group Inc. (group owner; acq 6-22-00; $150,000. with co-located AM). Network: ABC Information & Entertainment. Fisher, Wayland, Cooper, Leader & Zaragoza. Format: Classic country. News staff: one; News: 12 hrs wkly. Target aud: 25-69; blue collar. Spec prog: Farm 2 hrs, gospel 10 hrs wkly. ◆ Beatrice Hall, stn mgr; Lea Ann Hall, sls dir & gen sls mgr; Marilou Candela, mus dir; Michael Dickens, chief of engrg.

KBTC(AM)—Co-owned with KUNQ(FM). June 28, 1962: 1250 khz; 1 kw-D, 51 w-N. TL: N37 19 45 W91 53 55. Format: Country.

Independence

KCTE(AM)— 1947: 1510 khz; 10 kw-D, DA. TL: N39 04 14 W94 26 58. 6721 W. 121 St., Overland Park 66209. Phone: (913) 344-1500. Fax: (913) 344-1599. Web Site: www.1510.com. Licensee: Union Broadcasting Inc. (acq 8-19-98; $925,000). Network: ABC. Format: Sports. ◆ Chad Boeger, gen mgr.

Ironton

KYLS-FM— Jan 6, 1984: 95.9 mhz; 3.2 kw. 922 ft. TL: N37 34 23 W90 41 35. Stereo. 540 S. Maple Valley Dr., Farmington 63640. Phone: (573) 701-9590. Fax: (573) 701-9696. E-mail: freddockins@froggy96.com. Web Site: www.froggy96.com. Licensee: Dockins Communications Inc. (acq 1-29-97). Format: Country. News staff: 2; News: 8 hrs wkly. Target aud: 18-54. ◆ Fred M. Dockins Sr., pres & opns mgr; Sheila Dockins, gen sls mgr; Jenny Solomon, prom dir; Tom Calvin, news dir.

Jackson

KUGT(AM)— March 1972: 1170 khz; 250 w-D. TL: N37 22 54 W89 39 07. 901 S. Kings Hwy., Cape Giradeau 63702. Phone: (573) 339-7000. Fax: (573) 651-4100. Licensee: W. Russell Withers Jr. (acq 4-20-2005; $150,000). Network: Network: USA, Salem Radio Network.

Format: Relg, adult contemp. Target aud: General. Spec prog: Parenting and family talk. ◆ Ed Foxall, gen mgr; Rick Lambert, gen mgr.

KYRX(FM)—(Marble Hill). December 1999: 97.3 mhz; 3.6 kw. Ant 426 ft. TL: N37 22 49 W90 04 49. 901 S. Kings Hwy., Cape Girardean 63702. Phone: (573) 339-7000. Fax: (573) 651-4100. Licensee: Dana R. Withers. Format: Oldies. ◆ Rick Lambert, gen mgr.

Jefferson City

KBBM(FM)—Listing follows KLIK(AM).

*KJLU(FM)— August 1973: 88.9 mhz; 29.5 kw. 510 ft. TL: N38 27 29 W92 13 32. Stereo. 1004 E. Dunklin St. 65102-0029. Phone: (573) 681-5301. Fax: (573) 681-5299. E-mail: info@kjlu.com. Web Site: www.lincolnu.edu/~kjlu/. Licensee: Board of Curators of Lincoln University. Network: ABC FM Connection. Format: Jazz, Urban Contemporary, Blues, Gospel, R&B, Reggae. News staff: one; News: 5 hrs wkly. Target aud: 18-54. Spec prog: Pub affrs, gospel, blues, reggae, oldies. ◆ Michael P. Downey, gen mgr.

KJMO(FM)— 2000: 104.1 mhz; 6 kw. Ant 312 ft. TL: N38 34 45 W92 14 02. 3605 Country Club Dr. 65109. Phone: (573) 893-5100. Fax: (573) 893-8330. Web Site: www.kjmo.com. Licensee: Cumulus Licensing LLC. Group owner: Cumulus Media Inc. (acq 4-26-2004; grpsl). Rep: Katz Radio. Format: Oldies. ◆ Lewis W. Dickey Jr., pres; Jack Lawson, opns VP; Scott Boltz, mktg mgr.

KLIK(AM)— January 1937: 1240 khz; 1 kw-U. TL: N38 33 50 W92 11 21. 3605 Country Club Dr. 65109. Phone: (573) 893-5100. Fax: (573) 893-8330. Web Site: www.klik1240.com. Licensee: Cumulus Licensing LLC. Group owner: Cumulus Media Inc. (acq 4-26-2004; grpsl). Network: ABC Information & Entertainment. Format: News/talk. News staff: 4; News: 39 hrs wkly. Target aud: 35 plus; mid to upper income-well informed. ◆ Lew Dickey, pres; Scott Boltz, gen mgr & mktg mgr.

KBBM(FM)—Co-owned with KLIK(AM). 1974: 100.1 mhz; 33 kw. 600 ft. TL: N38 31 25 W92 24 25. Stereo. Web Site: www.buzz.fm. Format: Active rock. News staff: 2. Target aud: 18-34.

KTXY(FM)—Listing follows KWOS.

KWOS(AM)— February 1954: 950 khz; 5 kw-D, 500 w-N, DA-N. TL: N38 31 13 W92 10 42. 3109 S. 10 Mile Dr. 65109. Phone: (573) 893-7857. Fax: (573) 893-4137. Licensee: Zimmer Radio of Mid-Missouri Inc. Group owner: Zimmer Radio Group (acq 11-19-99; grpsl). Format: News/talk. Spec prog: Farm 12 hrs wkly. ◆ James Zimm, gen mgr; Tony Richards, opns mgr; Stu Steinmetz, gen sls mgr; John Marsh, progmg dir & news dir; Steve Morse, chief of engrg.

KTXY(FM)—Co-owned with KWOS. Dec 1, 1969: 106.9 mhz; 100 kw. 1,250 ft. TL: N38 38 16 W92 29 34. Stereo. 3215 LeMone Industrial, Suite 200, Columbia 65201. Phone: (573) 875-1099. Fax: (573) 875-2439. E-mail: rmeyer@zrgmail.com. Web Site: www.y107.com. Format: Hot adult contemp. ◆ Rob Meyer, progmg dir; Shelley Tucker, gen mgr & news dir; Mike Mayfield, chief of engrg.

Joplin

KIXQ(FM)— November 1974: 102.5 mhz; 100 kw. 410 ft. TL: N37 04 43 W94 32 26. Stereo. 2702 E. 32nd 64804. Phone: (417) 624-1025. Fax: (417) 781-6842. Web Site: www.kix1025.com. Licensee: Zimco Inc. Group owner: Zimmer Radio Group (acq 6-30-97; grpsl). Format: Contemp country. News staff: one; News: 2 hrs wkly. Target aud: 18-49. Spec prog: Class 3 hrs wkly. ◆ John Zimmer, exec VP; Larry Boyd, gen mgr; Jason Knight, opns mgr.

*KOBC(FM)— Mar 17, 1969: 90.7 mhz; 60 kw. 500 ft. TL: N37 03 11 W94 23 17. Stereo. 1111 N. Main St. 64801. Secondary address: 2711 Peace Church 64801. Phone: (417) 781-6401. Fax: (417) 782-1841. E-mail: kobc@kobc.org. Web Site: www.kobc.org. Licensee: Ozark Christian College. Format: Adult Christian contemp. Target aud: 25-45. ◆ Rob Kime, gen mgr; T.C. Andrews, sls dir & gen sls mgr; Lisa Davis, progmg dir & mus dir; Lisa Satterfield, news dir; Mitch Piercy, chief of engrg.

KOCR(AM)—Co-owned with KOBC(FM). Nov 21, 1948: 1310 khz; 5 kw-D, 1 kw-N, DA-2. TL: N37 07 03 W94 32 41. (Acq 1-22-97;

Stations in the U.S.
Missouri

Developers & Brokers of Radio Properties
contact American Media Services at our suite:
Philadelphia Marriott Downtown
215-625-2900
843-972-2200
americanmediaservices.com
Charleston, SC
Dallas, TX · Chicago, IL · Austin, TX
American Media Services, LLC

$150,000). Network: UPI. Format: Inspirational, praise. News staff: one. Target aud: 45 plus. ♦ Rob Kime, progmg dir.

KQYX(AM)— 1927: 1450 khz; 1 kw-U. TL: N37 04 43 W94 32 26. 2510 W. 20th St. 64804-0216. Phone: (417) 781-1313. Fax: (417) 781-1316. Licensee: FFD Holdings I Inc. Group owner: Petracom Media L.L.C. (acq 12-20-2004; grpsl). Borsari & Paxson. Format: News/talk. Target aud: 18-39. ♦ Steve Smith, opns mgr; Matt Kruger, progmg dir.

KSYN(FM)— Dec 19, 1960: 92.5 mhz; 100 kw. 430 ft. TL: N37 04 10 W94 32 49. Stereo. 2702 E. 32nd 64804. Phone: (417) 624-1025. Fax: (417) 781-6842. Web Site: www.ksyn925.com. Licensee: Zimco Inc. Group owner: Zimmer Radio Group (acq 6-30-97; grpsl). Format: CHR. Target aud: 18-39. ♦ Larry Boyd, gen mgr; Jason Knight, opns mgr.

KWAS(AM)— June 1, 1946: 1230 khz; 1 kw-U. TL: N37 04 48 W94 33 10. 3001 W. 13th St. 64801. Phone: (417) 624-1230. Fax: (417) 626-7111. Licensee: New Life Evangelistic Center Inc. (acq 8-10-98; $730,000 with KKLL(AM) Webb City). Format: MOR, contemp Christian. News staff: one; News: 2 hrs wkly. Target aud: General. Spec prog: Webb City High School sports.

***KXMS(FM)**— Apr 5, 1986: 88.7 mhz; 10 kw. 185 ft. TL: N37 05 57 W94 27 46. Stereo. Missouri Southern State Univ., 3950 E. Newman 64801-1595. Phone: (417) 625-9356. Fax: (417) 625-9742. E-mail: kxms@mssc.edu. Web Site: www.kxms.org. Licensee: Board of Governors— Missouri Southern State College Format: Joplin's fine art stn. Spec prog: Big band 2 hrs wkly. ♦ Jeffrey Skibbe, gen mgr.

WMBH(AM)— May 25, 1962: 1560 khz; 10 kw-D, DA. TL: N37 04 10 W94 32 49. 2510 W. 20th St. 64804. Phone: (417) 781-1313. Fax: (417) 781-1316. Licensee: Hardman Broadcasting Inc. Group owner: Petracom Media L.L.C. (acq 6-3-2005; $1). Format: Sports. Target aud: 25 plus. ♦ James Hardman, pres.

Kansas City

KBEQ-FM— November 1960: 104.3 mhz; 100 kw. 987 ft. TL: N39 04 59 W94 28 49. Stereo. 4717 Grand Ave., Suite 600 64112. Phone: (816) 753-4000. Fax: (816) 753-4046. Web Site: www.youngcountryq104.com. Licensee: Infinity Radio Holdings Inc. Group owner: Infinity Broadcasting Corp. (acq 12-14-00; grpsl). Rep: Allied Radio Partners. Koteen & Naftalin. Format: Country. News staff: one; News: 6 hrs wkly. Target aud: 18-54; women. ♦ Herndon Hasty, gen mgr.

KCCV(AM)—See Overland Park, KS

KCFX(AM)—See Harrisonville

KCMO(AM)— March 1922: 710 khz; 10 kw-D, 5 kw-N, DA-2. TL: N39 19 08 W94 29 48. Stereo. 5800 Foxridge Dr., Suite 600, Mission, KS 66202. Phone: (913) 514-3000. Fax: (913) 514-3007. Web Site: www.710kcmo.com. Licensee: Susquehanna Kansas City Partnership. Group owner: Susquehanna Radio Corp. (acq 7-14-2000; grpsl). Rep: MG Susquehanna. Cohn & Marks. Format: Talk. News staff: 3; News: 30 hrs wkly. Target aud: 35-64. Spec prog: Pub affrs one hrs wkly. ♦ David Kennedy, CEO; Nancy Vaeth Du-Broff, pres; Dave Alpert, VP & mktg mgr.

KCMO-FM— May 4, 1948: 94.9 mhz; 100 kw. Ant 1,120 ft. TL: N39 05 26 W94 28 18. Stereo. Phone: (913) 514-3000. Fax: (913) 514-3003. Format: Greatest Hits of the 60's & 70's. News staff: one; News: 2 hrs wkly. Target aud: 25-54.

KCNW(AM)—See Fairway, KS

KCSP(AM)— Feb 16, 1922: 610 khz; 5 kw-U. TL: N38 59 03 W94 37 40. Stereo. 4935 Belinder Rd., Westwood, KS 66205. Phone: (913) 677-8998. Fax: (913) 677-8061. Web Site: www.610sports.com. Licensee: Entercom Kansas City License L.L.C. Group owner: Entercom Communications Corp. (acq 10-17-97; grpsl). Network: Sporting News Radio Network, Premiere Action. Rep: D & R Radio. Format: Country. News staff: News progmg 8 hrs wkly Target aud: 25-54; general. ♦ Cindy Schloss, CEO; Michael Keck, stn mgr; Bob Olson, opns dir; Tom Tilley, gen sls mgr; Neal Jones, progmg dir; West McShea, progmg dir & progmg mgr; Scott Parks, news dir; Ananda Sallman, prom.

KCTE(AM)—See Independence

***KCUR-FM**— October 1957: 89.3 mhz; 100 kw. Ant 820 ft. TL: N39 04 59 W94 28 49. Stereo. 4825 Troost, Suite 202 64110. Phone: (816) 235-1551. Fax: (816) 235-2864. E-mail: kcur@umkc.edu. Web Site: www.kcur.org. Licensee: Curators of the University of Missouri. Group owner: The Curators of the University of Missouri Network: Network: NPR, PRI. Format: Pub affrs, news. News staff: 3; News: 50 hrs wkly. Target aud: General; educated. Spec prog: Sp 2 hrs wkly. ♦ Patricia Deal Cahill, gen mgr; Parker Van Hecke, dev dir; Bill Anderson, progmg VP; Robert Moore, mus dir; Frank Morris, news dir; Michael Douthat, engrg VP & chief of engrg.

KCZZ(AM)—See Mission, KS

KEXS(AM)—See Excelsior Springs

***KKFI(FM)**— Feb 28, 1988: 90.1 mhz; 100 kw. 503 ft. TL: N39 05 05 W94 28 47. Stereo. Box 32250 64171-2250. Secondary address: 900 1/2 Westport Rd. 64111. Phone: (816) 931-3122. Phone: (816) 931-5534. Fax: (816) 931-7870. E-mail: kkfi901@aol.com. Web Site: www.kkfi.org. Licensee: Mid-Coast Radio Project Inc. Format: News, talk, Sp. News: 10 hrs wkly. Target aud: General; women & minorities. Spec prog: Jazz 10 hrs, blues 9 hrs, Sp 16 hrs, Sp 4 hrs, American Indian 2 hrs wkly. ♦ Josh Powers, gen mgr.

***KLJC(FM)**— Aug 9, 1970: 88.5 mhz; 100 kw. 745 ft. TL: N39 04 24 W94 29 06. Stereo. c/o Calvary Bible College, 15800 Calvary Rd. 64147-1341. Phone: (816) 331-8700. Fax: (816) 331-3497. E-mail: kljc@kljc.org. Web Site: www.kljc.org. Licensee: Calvary Bible College. Network: Moody. Format: Var/div. Target aud: 25-54. ♦ Dr. Elwood Chipchase, pres & gen mgr; Bud Jones, stn mgr.

KMBZ(AM)— 1921: 980 khz; 5 kw-U, DA-N. TL: N39 02 17 W94 36 55. 4935 Belinder Rd., Westwood, KS 66205. Phone: (913) 677-8998. Fax: (913) 677-8901. Web Site: www.kmbz.com. Licensee: Entercom Kansas City News License L.L.C. Group owner: Entercom Communications Corp. (acq 3-6-97; grpsl). Network: ABC Information & Entertainment. Format: News radio. ♦ Michael Keck, gen mgr; Rich Deutsch, gen sls mgr; Neil Larrimore, progmg dir; Scott Parks, news dir; Mike Cooney, chief of engrg.

KYYS(FM)— Co-owned with KMBZ(AM). October 1962: 99.7 mhz; 100 kw. 1,010 ft. TL: N39 05 01 W94 30 57. Stereo. Web Site: www.kyys.com. Licensee: Entercom Kansas City License L.L.C. Format: Rock. ♦ Cindy Schloss, gen mgr; Carrie Brockleman, gen sls mgr; Greg Bergen, progmg dir.

KMXV(FM)— Mar 3, 1958: 93.3 mhz; 100 kw. 1,066 ft. TL: N39 00 57 W94 30 57. Stereo. 508 Westport Rd., Suite 202, Kansasn City 64111. Phone: (816) 756-5698. Fax: (816) 531-6547. Web Site: www.mix93.com. Licensee: Infinity Radio Inc. Group owner: Infinity Broadcasting Corp. (acq 11-13-98; grpsl). Format: CHR. News staff: one. Target aud: 18-49; women. ♦ Herndon Hasty, gen mgr & mktg mgr.

KPHN(AM)— Sept 1, 1971: 1190 khz; 5 kw-D, 250 w-N, DA-N. TL: N39 03 49 W94 30 37. Stereo. 1212 Baltimore 64105. Phone: (816) 421-1900. Fax: (816) 471-1320. E-mail: mark.t.ballard@abc.com. Web Site: www.radiodisney.com. Licensee: Radio Disney Group LLC. Group owner: ABC Inc. (acq 7-19-02; $3.8 million). Network: Radio Disney. Format: Children. ♦ Mark Ballard, gen mgr & chief of opns.

KPRS(FM)—Listing follows KPRT(AM).

KPRT(AM)— 1950: 1590 khz; 1 kw-D, 47 w-N. TL: N39 04 05 W94 32 10. 11131 Colorado Ave. 64137. Phone: (816) 763-2040. Fax: (816) 966-1055. Licensee: Carter Broadcast Group Inc. (group owner). Rep: McGavren Guild. Bryan Cave. Format: Gospel. ♦ Cheryl Douglas, chmn; Michael Carter, pres & gen mgr; Maureen Furlong, CFO; Sam Weaver, opns dir; Audrey Herbert, natl sls mgr; Vic Dyson, sls dir & rgnl sls mgr; Rich McCauley, mktg dir, prom mgr & news dir; Fred Bell, progmg dir; Debbie Rutledge, mus dir; Brooke Callowich, pub affrs dir; Mark Leaver, chief of engrg.

KPRS(FM)— Co-owned with KPRT(AM). 1963: 103.3 mhz; 100 kw. 994 ft. TL: N39 00 57 W94 30 24. Stereo. E-mail: 103@kprs.com. Web Site: www.kprs.com. Network: ABC FM Connection. Format: Urban contemp. News: one hr wkly. Target aud: 25-54; mid-upper income. ♦ Mildred Carter, CEO; Andre Carson, opns mgr; Victor Dyson, sls dir; Gail Horman, natl sls mgr; Rich McCauley, prom dir; Myron Fears, progmg dir.

KQRC-FM—(Leavenworth).KS 1962: 98.9 mhz; 100 kw. 990 ft. TL: N39 04 14 W94 54 39. Stereo. 4935 Belinder Rd., Westwood, KS 66206. Phone: (913) 677-8998. Fax: (913) 677-7510. Web Site: www.989therock.com. Licensee: Entercom Kansas City License LLC. Group owner: Entercom Communications Corp. (acq 7-14-00; grpsl). Crowell & Moring. Format: AOR. Target aud: 18-34; above average education & income; upscale professionals. ♦ Robert Zuroweste, gen mgr.

KRBZ(FM)— Jan 1, 1959: 96.5 mhz; 99 kw. 984 ft. TL: N39 00 57 W94 30 24. Stereo. 4935 Belinder Rd., West Wood 66205. Phone: (913) 677-8998. Fax: (913) 677-7520. Web Site: www.965thebuzz.com. Licensee: Entercom Kansas City License L.L.C. Group owner: Entercom Communications Corp. (acq 7-14-00; grpsl). Wiley, Rein & Fielding. Format: Rock/AOR. Target aud: 25 plus; adults with above-average disposable income. ♦ Cindy Schloss, gen mgr.

KSRC(FM)— Mar 5, 1961: 102.1 mhz; 100 kw. Ant 1,118 ft. TL: N39 05 26 W94 28 18. 508 Westport Rd., Suite 202 64111. Phone: (816) 561-9102. Fax: (816) 531-6547. Web Site: www.star102.net. Licensee: Infinity Radio Inc. Group owner: Infinity Broadcasting Corp. (acq 11-13-98; grpsl). Format: Hot adult contemp. ♦ Chris Taylor, gen mgr; Neal Dunker, prom dir.

KUDL(FM)—See Kansas City, KS

WHB(AM)— June 10, 1936: 810 khz; 50 kw-D, 5 kw-N, DA-N. TL: N39 18 21 W94 34 30. 6721 W. 121st St., Overland Park, KS 66209. Phone: (913) 344-1500. Fax: (913) 469-8488. Web Site: www.810whb.com. Licensee: Union Broadcasting Inc. (acq 11-23-99; $8 million). Format: Sports talk. News staff: 2; News: 19 hrs wkly. Target aud: 25 plus; farm families. Spec prog: Sp 2 hrs wkly. ♦ Chad Boeger, gen mgr; Nick McCabe, opns dir.

Kennett

***KAUF(FM)**— June 1998: 89.9 mhz; 1 kw. 164 ft. TL: N36 14 32 W90 03 54. Box 3206, American Family Radio, Tupelo, MS 38803. Phone: (662) 844-8888. Fax: (662) 842-6791. Web Site: www.afr.net. Licensee: American Family Association. Group owner: American Family Radio Format: Inspirational Christian. ♦ Marvin Sanders, gen mgr.

KBOA(AM)— 1963: 1540 khz; 1 kw-D. TL: N36 15 11 W90 02 56. Box 509 63857. Phone: (573) 888-4616. Fax: (573) 888-4890. Licensee: Pollack Broadcasting Co. (group owner; acq 9-25-98; $450,000 with KBOA-FM Piggott, AR). Network: ABC Information & Entertainment. Format: Music of Your Life. Spec prog: Farm 5 hrs wkly. ♦ Perry Jones, gen mgr.

KOTC(AM)— July 19, 1947: 830 khz; 10 kw-D. TL: N36 13 29 W90 04 31. Box 271 63857. Secondary address: 700 N. Bypass 63857. Phone: (573) 888-8881. Fax: (573) 888-8878. E-mail: kotc@sheltonbbs.com. Licensee: Eagle Bluff Enterprises (acq 9-18-96; $190,000). Format: Country gold, contemp country. News staff: one. Target aud: 28-55. ♦ Steven Fuchs, pres; Randy Kanci, gen mgr & gen sls mgr; Missy Odum, progmg dir; Charles Isabell, news dir; Palmer Johnson, chief of engrg.

Missouri

KXOQ(FM)—Co-owned with KOTC(AM). Dec 13, 1995: 104.3 mhz; 6 kw. 328 ft. TL: N36 21 01 W90 02 43. Phone: (573) 888-9878. Format: Oldies.

Kimberling City

KOMC-FM— 1992: 100.1 mhz; 36 kw. Ant 577 ft. TL: N36 31 58 W93 19 43. Stereo. 202 Courtney St., Branson 65616. Phone: (417) 334-6003. Fax: (417) 334-7141. E-mail: krzk@krzk.com. Web Site: www.komc.com. Licensee: Turtle Broadcasting Co. L.P. Group owner: Orr & Earls Broadcasting Inc. (acq 6-27-97; $1,064,919). Network: Network: ABC, CBS. Format: Adult standards, big band. News staff: 2; News: 11 hrs wkly. Target aud: 45 plus; Branson & local tourists. ♦Charles Earls, pres; Scottie Earls, gen mgr & chief of opns; Steve Willoughby, stn mgr.

Kirksville

*KHGN(FM)— Oct 6, 1997: 90.7 mhz; 32.5 kw. 325 ft. TL: N40 13 46 W92 32 38. Stereo. Box 500 63501. Secondary address: RR5, Box 14AB 63501. Phone: (660) 665-0466. Fax: (660) 665-7304. E-mail: khgn@kvmo.net. Web Site: www.khgn.org. Licensee: Care Broadcasting Inc. Network: Moody. Format: Relg. Target aud: 30 plus; general. ♦Dennis Phelps, pres; Gary A. Schilt, sr VP & gen mgr; Tom Lloyd, chief of engrg.

KIRX(AM)— Oct 17, 1947: 1450 khz; 1 kw-U. TL: N40 12 24 W92 34 31. Box 130, 1308 N. Baltimore 63501. Phone: (660) 665-3781. Fax: (660) 665-0711. E-mail: kirx@calleone.net. Web Site: www.1450kirx.com. Licensee: KIRX Inc. (acq 10-1-85; $1.3 million with co-located FM; 8-12-85). Network: ABC Daytime Direction. Format: Oldies. News staff: 2; News: 40 hrs wkly. Target aud: 25-54; general. Spec prog: Farm 10 hrs wkly. ♦David L. Nelson, pres; Steven D. Lloyd, exec VP, gen mgr & gen sls mgr.

KRXL(FM)— Co-owned with KIRX(AM). September 1967: 94.5 mhz; 100 kw. 1,010 ft. TL: N40 13 32 W92 00 54. (CP: 90.4 kw). Stereo. Phone: (816) 627-8439. E-mail: radiopark@cableone.net. Web Site: www.945thex.com. Network: ABC. Format: Classic rock. News: 2 hrs wkly. Target aud: 25-54.

*KKTR(FM)— 2002: 89.7 mhz; 1 kw. Ant 197 ft. TL: N40 10 40 W92 34 40. 409 Jesse Hall, Columbia 65211-1310. Phone: (573) 882-3431. Fax: (573) 882-2636. Web Site: www.kbia.org. Licensee: Truman State University. Format: News, class, talk. ♦Mike Dunn, gen mgr.

KLTE(FM)— May 20, 1991: 107.9 mhz; 100 kw. 715 ft. TL: N39 57 23 W92 58 29. 3 Crown Dr., Suite 100 63501. Phone: (660) 627-5583. Fax: (660) 626-8900. E-mail: klte@bottradionetwork.com. Web Site: www.bottradionetwork.com. Licensee: Bott Communications Inc. Group owner: Bott Radio Network Network: USA. Format: Christian. Target aud: 35 plus. ♦Dick Bott Sr., CEO & pres; Richard Bott II, chmn; Tom Holdeman, CFO; Judy Lene, gen mgr.

*KTRM(FM)— Feb 10, 1998: 88.7 mhz; 1 kw. Ant 197 ft. TL: N40 10 40 W92 34 40. Div. Language & Literature SUB, Truman State Univ. 63501. Phone: (660) 349-0076. E-mail: ktrmtheedge@hotmail.com. Web Site: ktrm.truman.edu. Licensee: Truman State University. Format: Alternative. News: 3 hrs wkly.

KTUF(FM)— Feb 14, 1983: 93.7 mhz; 50 kw. 492 ft. TL: N40 13 38 W92 36 35. Stereo. Box 130 63501. Secondary address: 1308 N. Baltimore Rd. 63501. Phone: (660) 627-5883. Fax: (660) 665-0711. E-mail: ktuf@cableone.net. Web Site: www.937ktuf.com. Licensee: KIRX Inc. Network: ABC. Format: Country. News staff: 2; News: 40 hrs wkly. Target aud: 18-44. ♦David L. Nelson, pres; Steven D. Lloyd, exec VP & gen mgr; Duncan Miller, opns mgr.

Knob Noster

*KCVQ(FM)— July 1998: 89.7 mhz; 5 kw. 230 ft. TL: N38 52 10 W93 32 58. Stereo. Box 800, c/o Spirit FM Radio, Camdenton 65020. Phone: (573) 346-3200. Fax: (573) 346-1010. E-mail: email@spiritfm.org. Web Site: www.spiritfm.org. Licensee: Lake Area Educational Broadcasting Foundation. Format: Christian, div. Target aud: 25-45. ♦Alice McDermott, CFO; James J. McDermott, pres & gen mgr.

KXKX(FM)— June 24, 1983: 105.7 mhz; 40 kw. 502 ft. TL: N38 46 28 W93 37 34. Stereo. 2209 S. Limit, Sedalia 65301. Phone: (660) 826-1050. Fax: (660) 827-5072. E-mail: info@kxkx.com. Web Site: www.kxkx.com. Licensee: Bick Broadcasting Co. (acq 7-19-89; $185,000).

8-7-89). Network: ABC Information & Entertainment. Format: Hot Country. News staff: one; News: 5 hrs wkly. Target aud: 25-54. ♦Dennis Polk, gen mgr.

La Monte

KPOW-FM— Nov 18, 1998: 97.7 mhz; 100 kw. Ant 981 ft. TL: N39 03 10 W93 16 01. Stereo. 301 S. Ohio Ave., Sedalia 65301-4431. Phone: (660) 826-5005. Phone: (660) 829-9700. Fax: (660) 826-5557. Web Site: www.power97.net. Licensee: Sedalia Investment Group L.L.C. Network: CNN Radio. Format: Classic rock. News staff: one; News: 2 hrs wkly. Target aud: 25-54. Spec prog: Blues 6 hrs wkly. ♦James Mathewson, pres; Adam B. Fischer, VP; Dianne M. Simon, gen mgr; Bill Barrick, opns mgr & prom mgr.

Lake Ozark

KQUL(FM)— May 9, 1994: 102.7 mhz; 6 kw. 328 ft. TL: N38 02 06 W92 34 31. 160 Hwy. 42, Kaiser 65047. Phone: (573) 348-1958. Fax: (573) 348-1923. Licensee: Benne Broadcasting of Lake Ozark Inc. (acq 5-20-98; $800,000). Format: Oldies. Target aud: 35-60. ♦Mike Clayton, opns mgr; Kelly Thomas, gen sls mgr.

Lamar

KHST(FM)— May 1, 1992: 101.7 mhz; 22 kw. Ant 328 ft. TL: N37 25 27 W94 16 11. Stereo. Box 383, Pittsburg, KS 66762. Secondary address: 412 Locust St., Pittsburg, KS 66762. Phone: (620) 232-5993. Fax: (620) 232-5550. Licensee: Innovative Broadcasting Corp. (group owner; acq 9-22-98; $330,000). Format: New rock. ♦Lance Sayler, pres; Rob Strand, gen mgr; Mike Snow, opns mgr.

Lebanon

KBNN(AM)— Oct 20, 1973: 750 khz; 5 kw-D. TL: N37 41 10 W92 41 39. Box 1112, 18553 Gentry Rd. 65536. Phone: (417) 532-9111. Fax: (417) 588-4191. E-mail: kjel@regionalradio.com. Licensee: Ozark Broadcasting Inc. Group owner: Shepherd Group (acq 7-83; $450,000 with co-located FM; 7-4-83). Network: ABC Information & Entertainment. Format: Talk. News staff: 5; News: 35 hrs wkly. Target aud: 35-64; middle America. Spec prog: News, farm 8 hrs wkly. ♦Mike Edwards, gen mgr; Michael Sommer, gen sls mgr; Warren McDonald, opns mgr & progmg dir; Patty Burns, news dir; Kelly Nelson, chief of engrg.

KJEL(FM)— Co-owned with KBNN(AM). Oct 20, 1973: 103.7 mhz; 100 kw. 984 ft. TL: N37 49 10 W92 44 51. Stereo. Web Site: www.regionalradio.com. Format: Country. News staff: 5; News: 45 hrs wkly. Target aud: 25-65; affluent, business oriented.

KCLQ(FM)—Listing follows KLWT(AM).

KLWT(AM)— July 4, 1948: 1230 khz; 1 kw-U. TL: N37 40 40 W92 41 16. 18785 Finch Rd. 65536. Phone: (417) 532-2962. Fax: (417) 532-5184. E-mail: klwt@klwt1230.com. Web Site: www.klwt1230.com. Licensee: Pearson Broadcasting of Lebanon Inc. Format: Country, news/talk, sports. News staff: 3; News: 10 hrs wkly. Target aud: 30 plus; adults. ♦Max H. Pearson, pres; Dan Caldwell, gen mgr; Kit Caldwell, opns dir; Brian McClendon, rgnl sls mgr; Betty Bishop, news dir.

*KTTK(FM)— 1992: 90.7 mhz; 11 kw. Ant 476 ft. TL: N37 37 58 W92 45 22. Box 1232 65536. Phone: (417) 588-1435. Fax: (417) 532-3055. Licensee: Lebanon Educational Broadcasting Foundation. Network: USA. Format: Christian. Spec prog: Southern gospel 80 hrs, gospel 7 hrs wkly. ♦Max Rhoades, gen mgr.

Lee's Summit

KZPL(FM)— 1998: 97.3 mhz; 55 kw. Ant 1,171 ft. TL: N39 05 26 W94 28 18. 6721 W. 121st, Leawood, KS 66209. Phone: (913) 344-1500. Fax: (913) 344-1599. Web Site: www.973theplanet.com. Licensee: Union First Broadcasting LLC. (acq 12-11-03; $10 million). Format: AAA. ♦Chad Boeger, gen mgr; Nick McCabe, opns dir.

Lexington

KLEX(AM)— Apr 19, 1956: 1570 khz; 250 w-D, 58 w-N. TL: N39 11 14 W93 50 03. 111 W. Main St., Richmond 64085. Phone: (816) 470-9925. Fax: (816) 470-8925. Web Site: www.bottradionetwork.com. Licensee: Bott Communications Inc. Group owner: Bott Radio Network

Directory of Radio

(acq 1994; with KAYX(FM) Richmond). Network: USA. Format: Christian talk. ♦Richard P. Bott, pres; Richard P. Bott II, exec VP.

KMJK(FM)— Sept 11, 1969: 107.3 mhz; 100 kw. 1,184 ft. TL: N39 02 15 W93 55 48. Stereo. Blue Ridge Towers, 4240 Blue Ridge Blvd., Suite 820, Kansas City 64133. Phone: (816) 353-7600. Fax: (816) 353-2300. Web Site: www.k107fm.com. Licensee: Cumulus KC Licensing Corp. Group owner: Cumulus Media Inc. (acq 11-26-03; $25 million. with KCHZ(FM) Ottawa, KS). Format: Urban. News staff: one; News: 5 hrs wkly. Target aud: 25-54. ♦Lewis W. Dickey Jr., CEO; Mike Payne, gen mgr.

Liberty

KCXL(AM)— Feb 14, 1967: 1140 khz; 500 w-D, 5 w-N. TL: N39 14 18 W94 23 59. 310 S. La Frenz 64068. Phone: (816) 792-1140. Phone: (816) 792-8258. Fax: (816) 792-8258. E-mail: kcxl@kcxl.com. Web Site: www.kcxl.com. Licensee: Alpine Broadcasting Corp. FTR: (4-2-84). Network: Jones Radio Networks. Reddy, Begley & McCormick. Format: Talk, variety, MOR. Target aud: 25-54; baby boomers. Spec prog: News 4 hrs, Sp 5 hrs, relg 3 hrs, health 12 hrs wkly. ♦Peter E. Schartel, pres & progmg dir; Vern Windsor, opns mgr; Jonne Santoli, rgnl sls mgr; Ed Treese, chief of engrg.

*KWJC(FM)— Apr 14, 1974: 91.9 mhz; 240 w. 166 ft. TL: N39 14 52 W94 24 47. Stereo. 500 College Hill, Box 1063 64068. Phone: (816) 415-7594. Fax: (816) 415-5027. E-mail: wirtht@william.jewell.edu. Web Site: www.jewel91-9fm.com. Licensee: William Jewell College. Format: CHR, modern rock, class. News: 5 hrs wkly. Target aud: 12-34; men & women. Spec prog: Class 10 hrs, Christian 10 hrs wkly. ♦Dr. Todd Wirth, gen mgr, stn mgr, chief of opns & progmg dir.

WDAF-FM— Nov 9, 1979: 106.5 mhz; 100 kw. 981 ft. TL: N39 04 23 W94 29 06. Stereo. 4935 Belinder Rd., Westwood, KS 66205. Phone: (913) 677-8998. Fax: (913) 677-8061. Web Site: www.wdaf.com. Licensee: Entercom Kansas City License LLC. Group owner: Entercom Communications Corp. (acq 7-14-00; grpsl). Rep: D & R Radio. Format: Smooth jazz. Target aud: 18-34. ♦West McChay, gen mgr & opns mgr.

Louisiana

KJFM(FM)— Sept 4, 1984: 102.1 mhz; 1.85 kw. 387 ft. TL: N39 26 29 W91 02 19. Stereo. Box 438 63353. Secondary address: 615 Georgia St. 63353. Phone: (573) 754-5102. Fax: (573) 754-5544. E-mail: kjfmradio@yahoo.com. Licensee: Foxfire Communications Inc. Network: CBS Radio. Format: Country. News: 27 hrs wkly. Target aud: 25-54. ♦Thom T. Sanders, pres; Gordon Sanders, opns.

Lutesville

KMHM(FM)— Aug 4, 1995: 104.1 mhz; 2.5 kw. 508 ft. TL: N37 22 40 W89 56 04. Box 266E, Hwy. B, Marble Hill 63764. Phone: (573) 238-1041. Fax: (573) 238-0104. E-mail: kmhm1041@clas.net. Web Site: www.kmhm.net. Licensee: Southern Gospelality LLC. Network: Salem Radio Network. Format: Christian. News staff: one; News: 14 hrs wkly. Target aud: 30-55; Christians and family-oriented listeners. ♦Harold L. Lawder, CEO; Doug Apple, gen mgr & gen sls mgr; Joy Duprey, stn mgr & progmg mgr; Carolyn Cremeens, mus dir; Joe Bellis, chief of engrg.

Macon

KIRK(FM)— 1998: 99.9 mhz; 12.5 kw. 462 ft. TL: N39 36 02 W92 34 24. Box 619, Moberly 65270. Secondary address: 300 W. Reed St., Moberly 65270. Phone: (660) 263-6999. Fax: (660) 263-2300. Web Site: regionalradio.com. Licensee: KIRK L.L.C. Group owner: Shepherd Group Format: Adult contemp. ♦David Shepherd, gen mgr.

KLTI(AM)— Jan 30, 1966: 1560 khz; 1 kw-D, 44 w-N. TL: N39 42 34 W92 27 50. 32968 US Hwy. 63 S. 63552. Phone: (660) 385-1560. Phone: (660) 258-3383. Fax: (660) 385-7090. Fax: (660) 258-7307. E-mail: klti@kltiradio.com. Web Site: www.kltiradio.com. Licensee: Chirillo Electronics Inc. Group owner: Best Broadcast Group. Format: Country. Target aud: 25-44. ♦Dale A. Palmer, gen mgr.

Madison

WGNU(AM)—See Saint Louis

Stations in the U.S. — Missouri

Malden

KLSC(FM)—Listing follows KMAL(AM).

KMAL(AM)— Sept 15, 1954: 1470 khz; 1 kw-D. TL: N36 33 08 W89 58 42. Box 69, Sikeston 63801-0069. Secondary address: 519 Greer Ave., Sikeston 63801. Phone: (573) 471-1400. Fax: (573) 471-1402. Licensee: MRR License LLC. Group owner: MAX Media L.L.C. (acq 3-29-2004); grpsl). Format: News/talk. News staff: 3. Target aud: 35 plus. ◆ Bill Powers, gen mgr; Brenda Woodall, gen sls mgr; Tyler Morrison, progmg dir & news dir; Charley Lampe, chief of engrg.

KLSC(FM)—Co-owned with KMAL(AM). Nov 23, 1979: 92.9 mhz; 23.5 kw. 174 ft. TL: N36 33 08 W89 58 42. Stereo. Format: Hot adult contemp. News staff: 2; News: 30 hrs wkly. Target aud: General. ◆ Bill Powers, progmg dir.

Malta Bend

KRLI(FM)— Oct 28, 1996: 103.9 mhz; 3.4 kw. Ant 879 ft. TL: N39 21 59 W93 24 12. Stereo. 615 Cherokee, Marshall 65340. Phone: (660) 831-1234. Fax: (660) 831-1290. E-mail: sb@global.net. Web Site: krli.com. Licensee: Kanza Inc. Format: Jazz, big band, oldies. News staff: 2; News: 6 hrs wkly. Target aud: 45 plus; baby boomers. ◆ Lynn Hammond, exec VP; Miles Carter, CEO, pres & gen mgr.

Mansfield

KTRI-FM— 1978: 95.9 mhz; 6 kw. Ant 312 ft. TL: N37 02 18 W92 40 29. Stereo. 1569 N. Central St., Monett 65708. Phone: (417) 235-6041. Fax: (417) 235-6388. Web site: www.talonbroadcasting.com. Licensee: KTRI Radio Inc. (group owner; (acq 4-2000). Format: Adult contemp. ◆ Duane Gandy, gen mgr.

Marble Hill

KYRX(FM)—Licensed to Marble Hill. See Jackson

Marshall

KMMO-FM— December 1968: 102.9 mhz; 100 kw. 380 ft. TL: N39 08 03 W93 13 19. Stereo. Box 128, Hwy. 65 N. 65340. Phone: (660) 886-7422. Fax: (660) 886-6291. Licensee: Missouri Valley Broadcasting Inc. (acq 11-19-84; with co-located AM; 12-10-84). Network: CBS. Format: Country. Target aud: General. Spec prog: Farm 6 hrs wkly. ◆ Mike Phillips, pres & progmg dir; John Wilson, gen mgr; Peter Hollabaugh, gen sls mgr.

KMMO(AM)— May 29, 1949: 1300 khz; 1 kw-D, 68 w-N. TL: N39 08 03 W93 13 19.

***KMVC(FM)**— Nov 1, 1968: 91.7 mhz; 100 w vert. 51 ft. TL: N39 06 31 W93 11 29. (CP: 93.1 mhz, 16 w). Stereo. Missouri Valley College, 500 E. College St. 65340. Phone: (660) 831-4193. Fax: (660) 886-9818. E-mail: kmvc@moval.edu. Licensee: Missouri Valley College. Format: Alternative, rhythm and blues. News: 3 hrs wkly. Target aud: 17-26; pre-, current & post-college age. Spec prog: Black 10 hrs, progsv 10 hrs, relg 16 hrs, classic rock 4 hrs, hip hop 10 hrs, urban 10 hrs wkly. ◆ Brent Foster, gen mgr; Josh Branch, stn mgr.

Marshfield

KKLH(FM)— June 1982: 104.7 mhz; 34 kw. Ant 594 ft. TL: N37 12 21 W92 54 20. Stereo. 319 B-East Battlefield, Springfield 65807. Phone: (417) 886-5677. Fax: (417) 886-2155. E-mail: info@kklh.fm. Web Site: www.kklh.fm. Licensee: MW SpringMo Inc. Group owner: The Mid-West Family Broadcast Group (acq 1996; $1.8 million). Rep: McGavren Guild. Format: Classic rock. Target aud: 25-45. ◆ Rick McCoy, pres & gen mgr; Jeff Couch, opns mgr; Malcolm Hurriede, gen sls mgr; Keith Abercrombie, rgnl sls mgr; Tim Smith, prom dir; John Kimmons, progmg VP & progmg mgr.

KMRF(AM)— Nov 1, 1969: 1510 khz; 250 w-D. TL: N37 20 55 W92 54 28. (CP: 1 kw). 3208 State Hwy 00 65706-2438. Secondary address: Box 693 65706. Phone: (417) 468-6188. Phone: (417) 468-5999. Fax: (417) 859-859-2916. Licensee: New Life Evangelistic Center Inc. (acq 4-4-94). Network: USA. Format: Southern gospel. News staff: one; News: 6 hrs wkly. Target aud: General. ◆ Fred Kinsey, gen mgr; Terrell Coleman, stn mgr.

KNLM(FM)—Co-owned with KMRF(AM).Not on air, target date: unknown: 91.9 mhz; 3 kw. 210 ft. TL: N37 19 09 W92 57 43. Format: Contemp Christian. Target aud: General.

Maryville

KNIM(AM)— 1953: 1580 khz; 500 w-D, 7 w-N. TL: N40 23 31 W94 58 04. Box 278 64468. Secondary address: 1618 S. Main 64468. Phone: (660) 582-2151. Fax: (660) 582-3211. E-mail: knim@knimmaryville.com. Web Site: knimmaryville.com. Licensee: Nodaway Broadcasting Corp. (acq 5-14-2003; $50,000. for 10% of stock with co-located FM). Network: AP Radio. Rep: Keystone (unwired net). Format: News, sports. News staff: one. Target aud: 25-54. Spec prog: Farm 5 hrs wkly. ◆ Joyce Cronin, pres; Jim Cronin, exec VP & gen mgr.

KNIM-FM— September 1972: 97.1 mhz; 21.5 kw. Ant 354 ft. TL: N40 23 31 W94 58 04. Stereo. Web Site: www.knimmaryville.com. Format: Classic rock. News staff: one; News: 25 hrs wkly.

***KXCV(FM)**— 1971: 90.5 mhz; 100 kw. 500 ft. TL: N40 21 36 W94 53 00. Stereo. Wells Hall, 800 University Dr. 64468. Phone: (660) 562-1163. Phone: (660) 562-1164. Fax: (660) 562-1832. Web Site: www.kxcv.org. Licensee: Northwest Missouri State University. Network: NPR, PRI. Format: News, class, jazz. News staff: 2; News: 39 hrs wkly. Target aud: General. ◆ Dean L. Hubbard, pres; Patty Holley, opns mgr & mus dir; Gayle Hull, dev mgr & mktg dir; John Coffey, prom mgr; Sharon Cross Bonnett, gen mgr & progmg dir; Marcia Fish, progmg mgr; KIRK WAYMAN, news dir; Charles Maley, engrg dir.

Memphis

KMEM-FM— Mar 29, 1982: 100.5 mhz; 25 kw. 298 ft. TL: N40 29 59 W92 09 58. Stereo. Box 121 63555. Secondary address: 650 N. Clay 63555. Phone: (660) 465-7225/465-2715. Fax: (660) 465-2626. E-mail: mdenney@kmemfm.com. Web Site: www.kmemfm.com. Licensee: Boyer Broadcasting Co. Inc. (acq 2-14-01; $202,000). Network: ABC Information & Entertainment. Format: Country. News: 15 hrs wkly. Target aud: General; adult audience 30+. Spec prog: Farm 8 hrs, relg 4 hrs wkly. ◆ Mark McVey, pres; Karen McVey, VP & gen mgr; Mark Denney, gen mgr.

Mexico

***KJAB-FM**— Oct 9, 1985: 88.3 mhz; 6 w. Ant 128 ft. TL: N39 10 24 W91 53 22. (CP: 4.8 kw vert, ant 272 ft. TL: N39 06 13 W91 53 35). Stereo. 621 W. Monroe 65265. Phone: (573) 581-8606. Fax: (573) 581-9655. E-mail: kjab@kjab.com. Web Site: www.kjab.com. Licensee: Mexico Educational Broadcasting Foundation. Network: USA. Format: Southern gospel. News staff: one; News: 2 hrs wkly. Target aud: General. Spec prog: Gospel 20 hrs, relg 20 hrs wkly. ◆ Kevin Weber, pres, gen mgr & opns mgr.

KWWR(FM)— Dec 14, 1966: 95.7 mhz; 100 kw. Ant 1,181 ft. TL: N39 15 39 W92 08 06. Stereo. Box 475 65265-0475. Secondary address: 1705 E. Liberty St. 65265-0475. Phone: (573) 581-5500. Fax: (573) 581-1801. E-mail: kwwr@country96.com. Licensee: KXEO Radio Inc. (acq 2-4-91; with co-located AM; 2-18-91). Network: Network: CNN Radio, Westwood One. Format: Country. Target aud: 25-54. Spec prog: Farm 4 hrs wkly. ◆ Anne Johnson, pres; Gary Leonard, gen mgr; John Caran, mktg dir; Greg Holman, progmg dir.

KXEO(AM)—Co-owned with KWWR(FM). Dec 3, 1948: 1340 khz; 1 kw-U. TL: N39 10 01 W91 51 44. Phone: (573) 581-2340. Network: CNN Radio, Westwood One. Format: Adult contemp. News: 4 hrs wkly. Target aud: 25-54.

Miner

KBHI(FM)—Licensed to Miner. See Sikeston

Moberly

***KBKC(FM)**— 2004: 90.1 mhz; 250 w. Ant 256 ft. TL: N39 24 39 W92 26 46. Covenant Network, 3515 Hampton Ave., St. Louis 63139. Phone: (314) 752-7000. Web Site: www.covenantnet.net. Licensee: Covenant Network (acq 3-30-2004; $112,500. with WHOJ(FM) Terre Haute, IN). Format: Christian. ◆ Tony Holman, gen mgr.

KRES(FM)—Listing follows KWIX(AM).

KWIX(AM)— June 1950: 1230 khz; 1 kw-U. TL: N39 24 11 W92 25 57. Box 619 65270. Secondary address: 300 W. Reed 65270. Phone: (660) 263-1500. Fax: (660) 269-8811. Web Site: www.regionalradio.com. Licensee: KWIX Inc. Group owner: Shepherd Group Network: CBS. Format: Talk. News staff: 4; News: 30 hrs wkly. Target aud: General. ◆ David Shepherd, pres & gen mgr; Howard Miedler, gen sls mgr; Ken Kujawa, progmg dir; Stephanie Ross, mus dir; Brad Boyer, news dir; Montie Barcus, chief of engrg.

KRES(FM)—Co-owned with KWIX(AM). October 1966: 104.7 mhz; 100 kw. 1,025 ft. TL: N39 27 53 W92 42 07. Stereo. Box 430 65270. Phone: (660) 263-1600. Network: ABC Information & Entertainment. Format: Modern country, farm.

KZZT(FM)— Apr 10, 1987: 105.5 mhz; 25 kw. 328 ft. TL: N39 24 54 W92 24 36. (CP: 50 kw). Stereo. Box 128, Rt. 4, Jct. Hwy. 63/EE 65270. Secondary address: 107 S. Main St., Brookfield 65270. Phone: (660) 263-9390. Phone: (660) 263-1055. Fax: (660) 263-8800. E-mail: kzzt@bestbroadcastgroup.com. Web Site: oldiesradio.com. Licensee: FM 105 Inc. Group owner: Best Broadcast Group (acq 7-9-97; $200,000. for 43%). Network: ABC. Bryan Cave. Format: Oldies. News: 5 hrs wkly. Target aud: 25-54; men & women with spendable income. ◆ Phil Chirillo, pres; Dale A. Palmer, gen mgr.

Monett

KKBL(FM)—Listing follows KRMO(AM).

KRMO(AM)—(Cassville). August 1950: 990 khz; 2.5 kw-D, 47 w-N. TL: N36 56 15 W93 55 30. 1569 N. Central 65708. Phone: (417) 235-6041. Fax: (417) 235-6388. Web site: www.krmokkbl.com. Licensee: Eagle Broadcasting Inc. (acq 8-4-03; $650,000. with KKBL(FM) Monett). Network: ABC Information & Entertainment. Format: Country, div, news. News staff: one; News: 10 hrs wkly. Target aud: 35 plus; business professionals, farmers, elderly. Spec prog: Farm 10 hrs, gospel 2 hrs wkly. ◆ Dale D. Gandy, pres; Janet Gandy, stn mgr; Lance Mettlach, gen sls mgr; Sue Ann Merritt, chief of engrg.

KKBL(FM)—Co-owned with KRMO(AM). December 1977: 95.9 mhz; 6 kw. 269 ft. TL: N36 56 15 W93 55 30. Stereo. Format: CHR. News staff: one; News: 4 hrs wkly. Target aud: General; young, adults, families. Spec prog: Children 2 hrs wkly.

Monroe City

KWBZ(FM)— July 4, 1981: 107.5 mhz; 10 kw. Ant 328 ft. TL: N39 35 12 W91 47 57. Stereo. 3702 Palmayra Rd., Hannibal 63401. Phone: (573) 221-4000. Fax: (573) 221 1142. E-mail: thebreeze@socket.net. Licensee: WPW Broadcasting Inc. (acq 8-17-2000). Format: Soft adult classic rock. Spec prog: Gospel 4 hrs wkly. ◆ Phil Alexander, gen mgr.

Montgomery City

KMCR(FM)— Aug 15, 1977: 103.9 mhz; 3 kw. 300 ft. TL: N38 59 12 W91 30 48. Stereo. 205 E. Norman St. 63361. Phone: (573) 564-2275. Fax: (573) 564-8036. E-mail: kmcr@socket.net. Web Site: www.bestbroadcastgroup.com. Licensee: Broadcast Management Inc. Group owner: Best Broadcast Group (acq 6-22-2005; $450,000). Network: ABC Information & Entertainment. Format: Hot adult contemp.

Missouri

News staff: one; News: 3 hrs wkly. Target aud: 25-60; male/female. Spec prog: Farm 2 hrs, relg 2 hrs wkly. ♦Dale A. Palmer, VP & gen mgr.

Mount Vernon

KZRQ-FM— July 29, 1993: 106.7 mhz; 25 kw. 328 ft. TL: N37 09 16 W93 36 58. 2330 W. Grand St., Springfield 65781. Phone: (417) 873-2000. Fax: (417) 873-2025. Web Site: www.2rocks.com. Licensee: Journal Broadcast Corp. Group owner: Journal Communications Inc. (acq 11-26-2003; $5 million. with KSGF-FM Ash Grove). Format: Rock. ♦Rex Hansen, gen mgr.

Mountain Grove

KELE(AM)— Nov 16, 1954: 1360 khz; 1 kw-D, 60 w-N. TL: N37 08 07 W92 14 59. 800 N. Hubbard 65711. Phone: (417) 926-4650. Fax: (417) 926-7604. Licensee: Quorum Radio Partners Inc. (group owner; (acq 8-8-2002; grpsl). Network: USA. Format: Christian, talk, relg, country. News staff: one; News: 10 hrs wkly. Target aud: Christian. ♦Todd Fowler, CEO; Jason Wert, gen mgr, opns mgr & progmg dir; Rick Jesse, chief of engrg.

KELE-FM— Jan 1, 1977: 92.5 mhz; 3 kw. 299 ft. TL: N37 08 07 W92 14 59. Stereo. Format: Real country. News staff: one; News: 8 hrs wkly. Target aud: 24-59; general. Spec prog: Relg 3 hrs wkly.

Mountain View

KUPH(FM)— July 31, 1998: 96.9 mhz; 50 kw. 420 ft. TL: N36 59 29 W91 47 41. Stereo. 6962 U.S. Hwy. 60 W. 65548. Phone: (417) 934-1000. Phone: (417) 934-0969. Fax: (417) 934-2565. E-mail: ed@thefox969.com. Web Site: www.thefox969.com. Licensee: Central Ozark Radio Network Inc. (acq 8-21-98; $196,500). Format: Hot adult contemp. News: 2 hrs wkly. Target aud: 25-54; upscale, mature individuals. ♦Ed Martin, stn mgr; Tom Marhefka, CEO, pres, gen mgr & opns mgr.

Naylor

KZMA(FM)—Not on air, target date: unknown: 99.9 mhz; 6 kw. Ant 328 ft. TL: N36 35 51 W90 36 51. 6120 Waldo Church Rd., Metropolis, IL 62960. Phone: (618) 564-2171. Fax: (618) 564-3202. Licensee: Daniel S. Stratemeyer (acq 6-1-2003; $30,000. for CP). Shaw Pittman LLP. ♦Daniel S. Stratemeyer, gen mgr.

Neosho

KBTN(AM)— Feb 1, 1954: 1420 khz; 1 kw-D, 500 w-N, DA-N. TL: N36 50 52 W94 19 12. Box K, 216 W. Spring 64850. Phone: (417) 451-1420. Fax: (417) 451-2526. Licensee: FFD Holdings I Inc. Group owner: Petracom Media L.L.C. (acq 12-20-2004; grpsl). Format: Country, news. News staff: 2; News: 14 hrs wkly. Target aud: 18-54. Spec prog: Farm 6 hrs wkly. ♦Kyle Thomas, gen mgr & opns mgr; Gail Johnson, gen sls mgr; Monica Blain, progmg mgr; David Horrath, news dir; Wilbur Blankenship, chief of engrg.

KBTN-FM— 1995: 99.7 mhz; 4.2 kw. 393 ft. TL: N36 46 05 W94 19 52. 2510 W. 20th St, Joplin 64804. Phone: (417) 781-1313. Format: Country. News staff: 2; News: 9 hrs wkly. Target aud: 18 plus. ♦Chris Stevens, progmg dir; Jerry Tibbets, chief of engrg.

*****KNEO(FM)**— October 1986: 91.7 mhz; 2.75 kw. 374 ft. TL: N36 52 49 W94 26 59. 10827 E. Hwy. 86 64850. Phone: (417) 451-5636. Fax: (417) 451-1891. E-mail: cqr@kneo.org. Web Site: www.kneo.org. Licensee: Sky High Broadcasting Inc. (acq 6-19-00). Network: Network: USA, Moody. Format: Southern gospel. News staff: 3; News: 10 hrs wkly. Target aud: 21-50; rural people & older shut-ins. ♦Mark Taylor, pres & gen mgr.

Nevada

KNEM(AM)— 1949: 1240 khz; 500 w-U. TL: N37 51 37 W94 22 54. Box 447, 414 E. Walnut. 64772. Phone: (417) 667-3113. Fax: (417) 667-9797. E-mail: mharbit@knemknmo.com. Web Site: www.knemknmo.com. Licensee: Harbit Communications Inc. (acq 12-5-97; $475,000 with co-located FM). Network: ABC Daytime Direction. Format: Country. News staff: one; News: 30 hrs wkly. Target aud: General. Spec prog: Farm one hr, Christian 5 hrs wkly. ♦Mike Harbit, pres, gen mgr & gen sls mgr; Jeanne Radspinner, opns mgr; Christina Davis, progmg dir; Russ Warren, news dir; Lloyd Collins, chief of engrg.

KNMO(FM)—Co-owned with KNEM(AM). Sept 10, 1984: 97.5 mhz; 6 kw. Ant 281 ft. TL: N37 52 45 W94 20 15. Stereo. Web Site: www.knemknmo.com.

New Bloomfield

*****KNLG(FM)**— July 20, 1997: 90.3 mhz; 150 w. 216 ft. TL: N38 42 16 W92 05 20. Stereo. c/o KNLJ(TV) Box 2525 65603. Phone: (573) 896-5105. Fax: (573) 896-4376. Web Site: www.heresshelpnet.org. Licensee: New Life Evangelistic Center Inc. Format: Southern gospel. News: 9 hrs wkly. Target aud: General. ♦Rev. Larry Rice, pres & gen mgr.

New London

KZZK(FM)— April 1996: 105.9 mhz; 10 kw. 515 ft. TL: N39 43 45 W91 24 15. Stereo. 329 Main St., Quincy, IL 62301. Phone: (217) 224-4102. Phone: (800) 900-1059. Fax: (217) 224-4133. E-mail: kzzk@staradio.com. Web Site: www.kzzk.com. Licensee: STARadio Corp. (group owner; acq 12-2-98; $2.1 million with KGRC(FM) Hannibal). Format: Adult alternative, classic rock. News: 2 hrs wkly. Target aud: 18-49; skews male. ♦Howard Doss, pres; Michael J. Moyers, gen mgr.

New Madrid

KTMO(FM)—Licensed to New Madrid. See Portageville

Nixa

KGBX-FM—Licensed to Nixa. See Springfield

North Kansas City

WDAF-FM—See Liberty

Osage Beach

KRMS(AM)— December 1952: 1150 khz; 1 kw-D, 55 w-N. TL: N38 07 29 W92 40 39. Box 225, Hwy. 54 65065. Phone: (573) 348-2772. Fax: (573) 348-2779. Licensee: Viper Communications Inc. Group owner: Viper Communications Broadcast Group (acq 11-97; $500,000. with co-located FM). Network: CBS. Format: News/talk. ♦Ken Kuenzie, pres & chief of engrg; Dennis Klautzer, VP, sls dir & progmg dir; Paul Hannigan, news dir.

KRMS-FM— Apr 12, 1964: 93.5 mhz; 39 kw. 551 ft. TL: N38 07 29 W92 40 39. Stereo. Format: AOR, classic rock.

Osceola

*****KCVJ(FM)**— June 29, 1990: 100.3 mhz; 6 kw. Ant 282 ft. TL: N38 03 43 W93 33 24. Box 800, c/o Spirit FM Radio, Camdenton 65020. Phone: (573) 346-3200. Fax: (573) 346-1010. E-mail: email@spiritfm.org. Web Site: www.spiritfm.org. Licensee: Lake Area Educational Broadcasting Foundation (acq 1999; $70,000). Format: Div, Christian. Target aud: 25-45. ♦Alice McDermott, CFO; James McDermott, pres & gen mgr.

Otterville

*****KCVK(FM)**— 2001: 107.7 mhz; 2.7 kw. Ant 499 ft. TL: N38 39 21 W92 54 27. Stereo. Box 800, % Spirit FM Radio, Camdenton 65020. Phone: (573) 346-3200. Fax: (573) 346 1010. E-mail: email@spirit.org. Web Site: www.spiritfm.org. Licensee: Lake Area Educational Broadcasting Foundation (acq 8-15-01; at least $450,000. including two-year noncompete agreement). Format: Christian, div. ♦Alice McDermott, CFO; James McDermott, pres & gen mgr.

Overland

*****KRHS(FM)**— Nov 7, 1977: 90.1 mhz; 10 w. 60 ft. TL: N38 42 38 W90 21 22. 9100 St. Charles Rock Rd., St. Louis 63114. Phone: (314) 429-7111. Fax: (314) 429-6725. Licensee: Ritenour Consolidated School District. Format: Educ. Target aud: General. ♦Jane Bannester, gen mgr.

Owensville

KXMO-FM— Jan 1, 2001: 95.3 mhz; 37 kw. 564 ft. TL: N38 08 06 W91 23 59. Box 4584, Springfield 65808. Phone: (417) 883-9180.

Directory of Radio

Licensee: KDAA-KMOZ LLC (acq 8-23-01; $357,655). Format: Oldies. Target aud: 35-64; Male & female. ♦John B. Mahaffey, chmn; Robert B. Mahaffey, pres; Alan Risener, gen mgr.

Ozark

KOMG(FM)— 1995: 92.9 mhz; 50 kw. Ant 492 ft. TL: N36 58 26 W93 25 37. Stereo. 319 E. Battlefield, Suite B, Springfield 65807. Phone: (417) 886-5677. Fax: (417) 886-2155. E-mail: info@basscountry.fm. Web Site: www.basscountry.fm. Licensee: MW Springmo Inc. Group owner: The Mid-West Family Broadcast Group (acq 12-15-99). Rep: McGavren Guild. Format: Classic country. Target aud: 30-50. ♦Rick McCoy, pres & gen mgr; Jeff Couch, opns mgr; Malcolm Hukriede, gen sls mgr; Keith Abercrombie, rgnl sls mgr; John Kimmons, progmg dir; Rick Moore, prom.

Palmyra

KICK-FM— Sept 1, 1981: 97.9 mhz; 50 kw. 348 ft. TL: N39 45 25 W91 29 57. Stereo. Box 711, Hannibal 63401-0711. Phone: (573) 221-3450. Fax: (573) 221-5331. Web Site: www.979kickfm.com. Licensee: Bick Broadcasting Co. Rep: McGavren Guild. Format: Country. News staff: 2. Target aud: 25-54; mainstream adults. ♦Ed Foxall, gen mgr.

Park Hills

*****KBGM(FM)**— 2001: 91.1 mhz; 8 kw. Ant 620 ft. TL: N37 48 04 W90 33 51. Box 3206, American Family Radio, Tupelo, MS 38803. Phone: (662) 844-8888, EXT. 204. Fax: (662) 842-6791. Web Site: www.afr.net. Licensee: American Family Association. Group owner: American Family Radio Format: Inspirational Christian. ♦Marvin Sanders, gen mgr.

KFMO(AM)— July 1947: 1240 khz; 1 kw-U. TL: N37 51 10 W90 31 13. Box 36 63601. Secondary address: 804 St. Joe Dr. 63601. Phone: (573) 431-2000. Fax: (573) 431-0850. E-mail: radio@b104fm.com. Web Site: www.kfmo.com. Licensee: MKS Broadcasting Inc. (acq 3-16-92; 4-6-92). Network: Westwood One. Format: Sports, news/talk loc information. Target aud: 25-54; females. ♦M.L. Steinmetz III, pres; Larry D. Joseph, VP & gen mgr; Kelly Valle, gen sls mgr; Greg Camp, progmg dir; Gilbert Collins, news dir.

Parkville

*****KGSP(FM)**— April 1972: 90.3 mhz; 100 w. 140 ft. TL: N39 11 24 W94 40 49. Stereo. Box 2, 8700 N.W. River Park Dr. 64152. Phone: (816) 741-2000. Fax: (816) 741-4911. Web Site: www.park.com. Licensee: Board of Trustees of Park College. Format: Alternative, var. News: 6 hrs wkly. Target aud: General; college students. Spec prog: Jazz 14 hrs, gospel 3 hrs, blues 12 hrs wkly. ♦Steve Youngblood, gen mgr.

Perryville

KBDZ(FM)— Jan 30, 1990: 93.1 mhz; 1.6 kw. ant 623 ft. TL: N37 38 56 W89 56 21. Stereo. Box 344, 122 Perry Plaza 63775. Secondary address: Box 428, Radio Hill, St. Genevieve 63670. Phone: (573) 883-2980. Phone: (573) 547-6780. Fax: (573) 883-2866. Fax: (573) 547-8005. E-mail: news@suntimenews.com. Web Site: www.suntimesnews.com. Licensee: Donze Communications Inc. Format: Hot country, news. News staff: 3; News: 5 hrs wkly. Target aud: 25-54. Spec prog: Sports 5 hrs, relg 5 hrs, farm 2 hrs wkly. ♦Bob Scott, gen sls mgr & progmg dir; Don Pritchard, news dir; Elmo L. Donze, pres, gen mgr & chief of engrg.

Piedmont

KPWB(AM)— May 16, 1966: 1140 khz; 1 kw-D. TL: N37 08 29 W90 42 11. 235 Business HH 63957. Phone: (573) 223-4218. Fax: (573) 223-2351. Licensee: Hunt Broadcasting Group Inc. (acq 2-28-2003; $100,000. with co-located FM). Network: USA. Format: Gospel. Target aud: 18 plus; Christians. ♦Fred Dockins Sr., pres; Charles Mikel, mus dir; Wanda Emert, gen mgr, mktg dir, progmg dir & news dir.

KPWB-FM— Sept 5, 1985: 104.9 mhz; 3 kw. 300 ft. TL: N37 07 54 W90 41 28. Stereo. Network: USA. Format: Country. Target aud: General. ♦Wanda Emert, opns mgr, gen sls mgr, mktg mgr, prom mgr & progmg mgr; Raymond Hodo, chief of engrg.

Stations in the U.S. — Missouri

Pleasant Hope

KTOZ-FM— May 1, 1993: 95.5 mhz; 50 kw. 497 ft. TL: N37 25 32 W93 16 38. 1856 S. Glenstone, Springfield 65804. Phone: (417) 890-5555. Fax: (417) 890-5050. E-mail: alice955@alice955.com. Web Site: www.alice955.com. Licensee: Clear Channel Broadcasting Licenses Inc. Group owner: Clear Channel Communications Inc. (acq 10-10-00; grpsl). Format: Modern adult contemp. Target aud: 18-34; young adults, 60/40 female/male split. ♦Mary Fleenor, gen mgr; Paul Kelley, opns dir.

Point Lookout

*****KCOZ(FM)**— January 1995: 91.7 mhz; 200 w. 151 ft. TL: N36 36 40 W93 14 29. Stereo. College of the Ozarks 65726. Phone: (417) 334-6411. Fax: (417) 335-2618. Licensee: College of the Ozarks. Network: Network: PRI, NPR. Format: News/talk, jazz, new age, blues. Target aud: Older & educated. Spec prog: Folk 10 hrs, new age 10 hrs wkly. ♦Ini Offong, opns VP, news dir & pub affrs dir; Courtney Hutton, progmg VP & mus dir; Jae Jones, gen mgr & chief of engrg.

*****KSMS-FM**— Feb 12, 1962: 90.5 mhz; 8.5 kw. 768 ft. TL: N36 33 44 W93 15 35. Missouri State Univ., 901 S. National Ave., Springfield 65804. Phone: (417) 836-5878. Fax: (417) 836-5889. E-mail: ksmu@smsu.edu. Web Site: www.ksmu.org. Licensee: Board of Governors, Southwest Missouri State University (acq 6-21-93; 7-19-93). Ernest Sanchez. Format: NPR News & Classical Music. Target aud: 25-54. ♦Tammy Wiley, gen mgr & stn mgr.

Poplar Bluff

KAHR(FM)— Mar 3, 1985: 96.7 mhz; 6 kw. 328 ft. TL: N36 45 59 W90 28 52. Stereo. 932 County Rd. 448 63901. Phone: (573) 686-3700. Fax: (573) 686-1713. Web Site: www.foxradionetwork.com. Licensee: Eagle Bluff Enterprises. (acq 8-3-93; $350,000; 8-30-93). Format: Hot adult contemp. Target aud: 25-54; listeners living in the middle-class strata. ♦Steven C. Fuchs, gen mgr.

KJEZ(FM)— Aug 20, 1977: 95.5 mhz; 100 kw. 860 ft. TL: N36 50 50 W90 19 52. Stereo. 1015 West Pine St. 63901. Phone: (573) 785-0881. Fax: (573) 785-0646. Web Site: www.kjez.zrgmil.com. Licensee: MRR License LLC. Group owner: MAX Media L.L.C. (acq 3-29-2004; grpsl). Network: Westwood One. Format: Classic rock and roll. News: 10 hrs wkly. Target aud: 18-49; general. ♦John Rice, gen mgr.

KKLR(FM)—Listing follows KWOC(AM).

KLID(AM)— May 22, 1961: 1340 khz; 1 kw-U. TL: N36 46 03 W90 22 11. KLID Bldg., 102 N. 11th St. 63901. Phone: (573) 686-1600. Fax: (573) 785-9844. Licensee: Browning Skidmore Broadcasting Inc. (acq 5-21-93; 6-14-93). Format: Oldies, talk, sports. News: 15 hrs wkly. Target aud: 18-54; upper class, professionals. Spec prog: Relg 2 hrs, Black 2 hrs wkly. ♦Chris Browning, pres; Dolores Skidmore, gen mgr, dev mgr & progmg dir; Alverna Skidmore, sls dir & pub affrs dir; Palmer Johnson, chief of engrg.

KLUE(FM)— Jan 1, 1995: 103.5 mhz; 50 kw. 492 ft. TL: N36 53 56 W90 18 27. 6120 Waldo Church Rd., Metropolis, IL 62960. Phone: (618) 564-2171. Fax: (618) 564-3202. Licensee: Benjamin Stratemeyer (acq 5-1-02; $800,000). Fisher, Wayland, Cooper, Leader & Zaragoza. Format: Div. ♦Sam Stratemeyer, gen mgr.

*****KLUH(FM)**— Oct 8, 1988: 90.3 mhz; 25 kw. 300 ft. TL: N36 43 07 W90 23 48. Box 1313 63902-1313. Phone: (573) 686-1663. Fax: (573) 686-7703. Web Site: www.unity903.org. Licensee: Word of Victory Outreach Center Inc. (acq 4-5-95; 7-10-95). Format: Relg. Target aud: General. ♦David Craig, gen mgr.

*****KOKS(FM)**— Oct 2, 1988: 89.5 mhz; 100 kw. 423 ft. TL: N36 48 40 W90 27 50. Box 280 63902. Phone: (573) 686-5080. Fax: (573) 686-5544. E-mail: koksradio@mycitycable.com. Web Site: www.koksradio.org. Licensee: Calvary Educational Broadcasting Foundation. Format: Christian, gospel, relg. News: 14 hrs wkly. Target aud: General. ♦Don Stewart, gen mgr; Nina Stewart, stn mgr & progmg dir; Ben Stewart, mus dir; Charles Lampley, chief of engrg.

KPPL(FM)— 2003: 92.5 mhz; 25 kw. Ant 328 ft. TL: N36 50 59 W90 22 20. Stereo. 932 County Rd. 448 63901. Phone: (573) 686-3700. Fax: (573) 686-1713. Licensee: George S. Flinn Jr. Format: Country. ♦Steven Fuchs, gen mgr.

KWOC(AM)— May 10, 1938: 930 khz; 5 kw-D, 500 w-N, DA-N. TL: N36 43 15 W90 22 04. Box 130 63902. Phone: (573) 785-0881. Fax: (573) 785-0646. Web Site: www.kwoc.com. Licensee: MRR License LLC. Group owner: MAX Media L.L.C. (acq 3-29-2004; grpsl). Network: ABC Daytime Direction. Format: News/talk. News staff: 2; News: 5 hrs wkly. Target aud: 25-54; adults with middle to upper income. ♦John Rice, gen mgr; Katie Wylie, sls dir & gen sls mgr; Rick Carl, progmg dir & news dir; Charlie Lampe, chief of engrg.

KKLR(FM)—Co-owned with KWOC(AM). 1952: 94.5 mhz; 100 kw. 807 ft. TL: N36 43 18 W90 22 10. Stereo. Web Site: www.kklr.com. Format: Country. Target aud: 18-49. ♦Galen Stevens, progmg dir & mus dir.

Portageville

KMIS(AM)— Sept 1, 1960: 1050 khz; 1 kw-D, 87 w-N. TL: N36 25 30 W89 41 39. Box 509, Kennett 63857. Fax: (573) 888-4616. E-mail: ktme@il.net. Licensee: Pollack Broadcasting Co. (group owner; acq 5-7-2001; with KTMO(FM) New Madrid). Network: ABC Information & Entertainment. Format: News, sports. News staff: one. Target aud: General. Spec prog: Relg gospel 5 hrs wkly. ♦Bill Pollack, pres; Monte Lyons, opns mgr, prom dir & progmg dir; Perry Jones, gen mgr, sls dir & gen sls mgr; Bill Page, news dir; P.J. Johnson, chief of engrg.

KTMO(FM)—Co-owned with KMIS(AM). Jan 31, 1976: 106.5 mhz; 50 kw. 469 ft. TL: N36 25 30 W89 41 39. Stereo. Phone: (573) 888-4616. Network: ABC. Format: Country. News staff: one. Target aud: 18-49 adults; males.

Potosi

KHZR(FM)— Apr 17, 1997: 97.7 mhz; 9.4 kw. Ant 528 ft. TL: N37 52 51 W90 47 01. 13358 Manchester Rd., Suite 100, Des Peres 63131. Phone: (314) 909-8569. Fax: (314) 835-9739. E-mail: info@joyfmonline.org. Web Site: www.joyfmonline.org. Licensee: Four Him Enterprises L.L.C. (acq 11-2-2000; $1.2 million). Format: Contemp Christian. ♦Sandi Brown, gen mgr.

*****KNLP(FM)**— April 1998: 89.7 mhz; 2.3 kw. 262 ft. TL: N37 55 42 W90 46 02. New Life Evangelistic Center, 1411 Locust St., St. Louis 63103. Phone: (314) 436-2424. Phone: (573) 438-1473. Fax: (314) 436-2434. E-mail: larryr@hereshelpnet.org. Web Site: www.hereshelpnet.org. Licensee: New Life Evangelistic Center Inc. Format: Adult contemp, gospel, talk. ♦Larry Rice, gen mgr.

KYRO(AM)— Feb 22, 1959: 1280 khz; 500 w-D. TL: N37 58 28 W90 45 44. Stereo. Hwy. 21 N. 63664. Phone: (573) 438-2136. Fax: (573) 438-3108. E-mail: news@kyro.com. Web Site: www.kyro.com. Licensee: KYRO Inc. (acq 5-12-2005; $145,000). Network: ABC Daytime Direction. Cohn & Marks. Format: Country, news. News staff: one; News: 12 hrs wkly. Target aud: 25 plus; general. ♦Debra S. Porter, VP; James T. Porter, pres & gen mgr. Co-owned TV: KTVI-TV affil

Republic

KADI-FM— June 18, 1990: 99.5 mhz; 6 kw. 328 ft. TL: N37 09 54 W93 23 44. Stereo. 5431 W. Sunshine, Springfield 65619. Phone: (417) 831-0995. Fax: (417) 831-4026. Web Site: www.kadi.com. Licensee: Vision Communications Inc. (acq 7-10-2000; $550,000). Format: Adult contemp Christian mus. News: 8 hrs wkly. Target aud: General; adults in their mid 30s. ♦R.C. Aner, gen mgr.

Richmond

KAYX(FM)— Aug 1, 1990: 92.5 mhz; 6 kw. 500 ft. TL: N39 14 52 W93 58 16. Stereo. 111 W. Main St. 64085. Phone: (816) 470-9925. Fax: (816) 470-8925. E-mail: kayx@bottradionetwork.com. Web Site: www.bottradionetwork.com. Licensee: Bott Communications, Inc. Group owner: Bott Radio Network (acq 1996). Format: Christian talk & info. ♦Richard P. Bott Sr., pres; Richard P. Bott II, VP; Evan Fowler, stn mgr.

Rolla

KDAA(FM)— Nov 20, 1964: 97.5 mhz; 6 kw. 292 ft. TL: N37 57 50 W91 45 54. Stereo. Box 588 65402. Phone: (573) 364-9211. Fax: (573) 364-9216. Licensee: KDAA-KMOZ LLC. Group owner: Mahaffey Enterprises Inc. (acq 9-28-01; $418,000. assumption of debt for 50% with co-located AM). Network: Network: Westwood One, Jones Radio Networks. Format: Adult contemp. Target aud: 18-44. ♦Alan Risener, gen mgr; Bob Moore, mus dir & chief of engrg.

KMOZ(AM)—Co-owned with KDAA(FM). Aug 19, 1960: 1590 khz; 1 kw-D, 88 w-N. TL: N37 56 41 W91 48 40. Format: Country. Target aud: 50 plus; mature adults.

*****KMNR(FM)**— 1974: 89.7 mhz; 450 w. 230 ft. TL: N37 57 12 W91 46 29. Univ. of Missouri, 113 University Ctr. W. 65409-1440. Phone: (573) 341-4272. Phone: (573) 341-4273. Fax: (573) 341-6021. E-mail: kmnr@umr.edu. Web Site: web.umr.edu/~kmnr/. Licensee: Curators of the University of Missouri. (group owner) Network: AP Radio. Format: Div, educ. Target aud: 18-25; college community. Spec prog: Jazz 3 hrs wkly. ♦Fred Goss, gen mgr; Matt Rogers, stn mgr.

KTTR(AM)— Sept 30, 1947: 1490 khz; 1 kw-U. TL: N37 56 42 W91 44 46. Box 727 65402. Phone: (573) 364-2525. Fax: (573) 364-5161. Licensee: KTTR-KZNN Inc. Group owner: Mahaffey Enterprises Inc. (acq 6-1-84; with co-located FM; 4-16-84). Network: ABC Information & Entertainment. Format: News/talk, sports. News staff: one. Target aud: General. ♦John Mahaffey, chmn & pres; Robert B. Mahaffey, pres, gen mgr & stn mgr; Sue Corey, gen sls mgr; Rob Fell, progmg dir; Lee Buhr, news dir; Bob Moore, chief of engrg.

KZNN(FM)—Co-owned with KTTR(AM). Feb 12, 1973: 105.3 mhz; 100 kw. 631 ft. TL: N37 52 39 W91 44 45. Stereo. Network: ABC. Format: Modern country.

*****KUMR(FM)**— January 1964: 88.5 mhz; 100 kw. 480 ft. TL: N37 47 56 W91 43 28. Stereo. G-6 Library, 1870 Miner Cir. 65409-0130. Phone: (573) 341-4386. Fax: (573) 341-4889. E-mail: kumr@umr.edu. Web Site: www.kumr.org. Licensee: The Curators of the University of Missouri. (group owner) Network: NPR. Fisher, Wayland, Cooper, Leader & Zaragoza. Format: Class, div, news. News staff: one; News: 35 hrs wkly. Target aud: General. Spec prog: Bluegrass 5 hrs, jazz 3 hrs, folk 5 hrs wkly. ♦Jim Sigler, gen mgr; Karen Roberts, sls VP; Louise Morgan, mktg mgr; John Francis, progmg dir; Charles Knapp, chief of engrg. Co-owned TV: *KOMU-TV affil.

Saint Charles

*****KCLC(FM)**— October 1968: 89.1 mhz; 35 kw. 257 ft. TL: N38 47 12 W90 29 49. Stereo. 209 S. Kings Hwy. 63301. Phone: (636) 949-4890. Phone: (636) 949-4891. Fax: (636) 949-4111. Web Site: www.lindenwood.edu/kclc. Licensee: Lindenwood University. Network: ABC Daytime Direction. Format: Jazz, CHR. News: 12 hrs wkly. Target aud: 18-34; young adults. Spec prog: Bluegrass 12 hrs, progsv rock 12 hrs, gospel 9 hrs, contemp Christian 7 hrs wkly. ♦Dennis C. Spellmann, pres; Richard Reighard, opns mgr; Ralph Brancato, chief of engrg.

KFTK(FM)—See Florissant

KHOJ(AM)— Apr 13, 1958: . Stn currently dark 1460 khz; 5 kw-D, 500 w-N, DA-2. TL: N38 47 56 W90 25 12. Covenant Network, 3515 Hampton Ave., St. Louis 63139. Phone: (314) 752-7000. E-mail:

office@covenantnet.net. Web Site: www.covenantnet.net. Licensee: Covenant Network (acq 5-13-2005; $730,000). ♦Tony Holman, gen mgr.

Saint James

KTTR-FM— 1994: 99.7 mhz; 12 kw. 472 ft. TL: N37 56 41 W91 42 23. Stereo. Secondary address: 1505 Soest Rd., Rolla 65808. Phone: (573) 364-2525. Fax: (573) 364-5161. Licensee: KTTR-KZNN Inc. Group owner: Mahaffey Enterprises Inc. Network: ABC Information & Entertainment. Format: News/talk. News staff: one; News: 20 hrs wkly. Target aud: 25-54. ♦John B. Mahaffey, chmn; Robert B. Mahaffey, pres; Joe Munsell, gen mgr.

Saint Joseph

KFEQ(AM)— Feb 16, 1926: 680 khz; 5 kw-U, DA-2. TL: N39 49 43 W94 48 20. Box 8550 64508. Secondary address: 4104 Country Ln. 64506. Phone: (816) 233-8881. Fax: (816) 279-8280. E-mail: garyexline @eagleradio.net. Web Site: www.stjoeradio.com. Licensee: Eagle Communications Inc. Group owner: Eagle Communications Group (acq 3-20-69; grpsl; FTR: 4-8-91). Network: ABC. Rep: Katz Radio. Wiley, Rein & Fielding. Format: News/talk, Sports. News staff: 4; News: 50 hrs wkly. Target aud: 18 plus; adults. Spec prog: Farm 20 hrs wkly. ♦Gary Shorman, CEO; Gary Exline, VP & gen mgr; Kevin Wagner, opns dir.

KGNM(AM)— November 1955: 1270 khz; 1 kw-D, DA. TL: N39 44 39 W94 47 16. 2414 S. Leonard Rd. 64503. Phone: (816) 233-2577. Fax: (816) 233-2374. E-mail: kgnm@stjoelive.com. Web Site: kgnmradio.com. Licensee: Orama Inc. (acq 6-80; $400,000; 6-30-80). Network: USA. Format: Adult contemp, Christian music. Target aud: 30-55; conservative. ♦Rory Pullen, pres; Greg Glauser, VP; Chris Meikel, gen mgr; Marci Meikel, progmg dir.

KKJO(FM)—Listing follows KSFT(AM).

KSFT(AM)— June 1, 1946: 1550 khz; 5 kw-U, DA-N. TL: N39 42 23 W94 44 36. Box 8550 64508. Secondary address: 4104 Country Ln. 64506. Phone: (816) 233-8881. Fax: (816) 279-8280. Web Site: www.stjoeradio.com. Licensee: Eagle Communications Inc. Group owner: Eagle Communications Group (acq 3-1-99; $4 million. with co-located FM). Wiley, Rein & Fielding. Format: Oldies. News: 5 hrs wkly. Target aud: 45-64. ♦Gary Sherman, CEO; Mark Vail, COO & gen mgr; Gary Shorman, pres; Kevin Wagner, opns dir & progmg dir; Nick Kunels, sls dir & gen sls mgr; Teresa Hetz, prom mgr; Barry Birr, news dir; Jack W. Thouvenell, engrg dir & chief of engrg.

KKJO(FM)—Co-owned with KSFT(AM). Sept 1, 1962: 105.5 mhz; 100 kw. Ant 981 ft. TL: N39 42 35 W95 02 33. Stereo. Web Site: www.stjoeradio.com. Format: Adult contemp. News staff: 2; News: 2 hrs wkly. Target aud: 18-49.

***KSRD(FM)**— 2004: 91.9 mhz; 10 kw. Ant 492 ft. TL: N39 42 35 W95 02 33. 1212 Faran St. 64501. Phone: (816) 279-8877. Fax: (816) 233-5777. Licensee: Horizon Christian Fellowship (acq 8-26-2004; $10,600). Format: Christian. ♦Jim Long, gen mgr.

Saint Louis

KATZ(AM)— Jan 3, 1955: 1600 khz; 5 kw-U, DA-N. TL: N38 39 19 W90 07 53. 1001 Highlands Plaza Dr. W., Suite 100 63110. Phone: (314) 333-8000. Fax: (314) 333-8311. Web Site: www.gospel1600.com. Licensee: Citicasters Licenses L.P. Group owner: Clear Channel Communications Inc. (acq 5-4-99; grpsl). Network: American Urban. Format: Gospel. ♦Lee Clear, VP & gen mgr; Chuck Atkins, opns VP; Pierre Troupe, gen sls mgr; Calvin King, progmg dir & engrg dir.

***KDHX(FM)**— Oct 14, 1987: 88.1 mhz; 42.4 kw. 1,314 ft. TL: N38 25 01 W90 25 59. Stereo. 3504 Magnolia 63118. Phone: (314) 664-3955. Fax: (314) 664-1020. Web Site: www.kdhx.org. Licensee: Double Helix Corp. Network: PRI. Format: Div. News staff: one; News: 18 hrs wkly. Target aud: General. Spec prog: Country 10 hrs, jazz 12 hrs, Sp 4 hrs, folk 10 hrs, bluegrass 8 hrs, new age 6 hrs, blues 12 hrs, pub affrs 5 hrs, African mus 2 hrs wkly. ♦Beverly Hacker, gen mgr & stn mgr.

KEZK-FM— September 1968: 102.5 mhz; 100 kw. 400 ft. TL: N38 36 47 W90 20 09. Stereo. 3100 Market St., St. Louis 63103. Phone: (314) 531-0000. Fax: (314) 969-7638. Web Site: www.kezk.com. Licensee: Infinity Radio Holdings Inc. Group owner: Infinity Broadcasting Corp. (acq 11-13-98; grpsl). Format: Soft adult contemp. Target aud: 25-54; high average household income. ♦Beth Davis, gen mgr.

KFNS(AM)—See Wood River, IL

KFUO(AM)—See Clayton

KHOJ(AM)—See Saint Charles

KIHT(FM)— Dec 22, 1959: 96.3 mhz; 100 kw. 650 ft. TL: N38 36 47 W90 20 09. (CP: 80 kw, ant 1,027 ft.). Stereo. 800 Saint Louis Union Stn., The Powerhouse 63103. Phone: (314) 621-4106. Fax: (314) 621-3000. Web Site: www.k-hits.com. Licensee: Emmis Radio License LLC. Group owner: Emmis Communications Corp. (acq 9-26-2000; grpsl). Rep: Allied Radio Partners. Format: Classic hits. Target aud: 25-54. ♦John Beck, sr VP.

KJFF(AM)—See Festus

KJSL(AM)— Sept 19, 1938: 630 khz; 5 kw-U, DA-2. TL: N38 40 18 W90 06 52. KJSL(AM), 10845 Olive Blvd., Suite 160 63141. Phone: (314) 878-3600. Fax: (314) 656-3608. E-mail: mflora@crawfordbroadcasting.com. Web Site: www.kjslradio.com. Licensee: WMUZ Radio Inc. Group owner: Crawford Broadcasting Co. (acq 1994; $1.57 million). Format: Christian, talk. Target aud: 30-60. ♦Don Crawford Jr., gen mgr; Micle Flora, stn mgr & gen sls mgr.

KLOU(FM)— November 1962: 103.3 mhz; 100 kw. 920 ft. TL: N38 31 47 W90 17 58. Stereo. 10001 Highlands Dr. 63110. Phone: (314) 333-8000. Fax: (314) 333-8300. Web Site: klou.com. Licensee: Citicasters Licenses L.P. Group owner: Clear Channel Communications Inc. (acq 5-4-99; grpsl). News staff: one. Target aud: 25-54. ♦Lee Clear, VP & gen mgr; Mike Wheeler, opns dir.

KMOX(AM)— Dec 24, 1925: 1120 khz; 50 kw-U. TL: N38 43 20 W90 03 16. Stereo. One Memorial Dr., St. Louis 63102-2498. Phone: (314) 621-2345. Fax: (314) 444-1860 (SALES). E-mail: kmox@kmox.com. Web Site: www.kmox.com. Licensee: Infinity Broadcasting East Inc. Group owner: Infinity Broadcasting Corp. (acq 11-13-98; grpsl). Network: CBS. Leventhal, Senter & Lerman. Format: News/talk, info, sports. News staff: 16; News: 60 hrs wkly. Target aud: 25 plus. Spec prog: Jazz 4 hrs, relg one hr wkly.

KSD(FM)— November 1954: 93.7 mhz; 100 kw. 859 ft. TL: N38 34 05 W90 19 55. Stereo. 10001 Highlands Dr. 63110. Phone: (314) 333-8000. Fax: (314) 333-8300. Web Site: www.allnewbull.com. Licensee: Citicasters Licenses L.P. Group owner: Clear Channel Communications Inc. (acq 5-4-99; grpsl). Format: Country. News staff: one. Target aud: 25-54. ♦Lee Clear, sr VP & VP; Mike Wheeler, opns dir.

KSHE(FM)—See Crestwood

KSIV(AM)—See Clayton

***KSIV-FM**— Apr 13, 1950: 91.5 mhz; 12.5 kw. Ant 400 ft. TL: N38 37 10 W90 14 12. 1750 S. Brentwood Blvd., Suite 811 63144. Phone: (314) 961-1320. Fax: (314) 961-7562. Web Site: www.bottradionetwork.com. Licensee: Community Broadcasting Inc. Group owner: Bott Radio Network (acq 1996; $1.625 million). Format: Christian info, relg. ♦Richard P. Bott, pres & VP; Michael McHardy, gen mgr; Joy Elder, sls dir & mktg dir.

KSLG(AM)— 1927: 1380 khz; 5 kw-D, 1 kw-N, DA-3. TL: N38 31 27 W90 14 17. 520 N. Skinker 63130. Phone: (314) 969-1380. Fax: (314) 367-8647. Web Site: www.kslgam.com. Licensee: Simmons-Austin, LS LLC. Group owner: Simmons Media Group (acq 7-29-2004; $2.05 million). Network: Sporting News Radio Network. Format: Sports. News: 168 hrs wkly. Target aud: 25-54; men and women. ♦Dave Green, gen mgr & gen sls mgr.

KSLZ(FM)— Sept 28, 1972: 107.7 mhz; 100 kw. 1,027 ft. TL: N38 34 24 W90 19 30. Stereo. 10001 Highlands Dr. 63110. Phone: (314) 333-8000. Fax: (314) 333-8300. Web Site: www.z1077.com. Licensee: Citicasters Licenses L.P. Group owner: Clear Channel Communications Inc. (acq 5-4-99; grpsl). Format: Contemp hit/Top-40. ♦Lee Clear, VP & gen mgr; Mike Wheeler, opns mgr.

KSTL(AM)— 1948: 690 khz; 1 kw-D, 18 w-N. TL: N38 37 01 W90 10 17. 10845 Olive Blvd., Suite 160, Creve Coeur 63141. Phone: (314) 878-3600. Phone: (618) 874-5785. Fax: (314) 656-3608. E-mail: dholmes@crawfordbroadcasting.com. Licensee: WMUZ Radio Inc. Group owner: Crawford Broadcasting Co. (acq 1994). Bryan Cave. Format: Gospel. ♦Donald Crawford, pres; Deborah E. Holmes, stn mgr.

KTRS(AM)— Feb 14, 1922: 550 khz; 5 kw-U, DA-N. TL: N38 39 45 W90 07 43. Stereo. 638 West Port Plaza 63146. Phone: (314) 453-5500. Fax: (314) 453-9704. Web Site: www.ktrs.com. Licensee: KTRS-AM License L.L.C. (acq 1997). Network: ABC. Rep: McGavren Guild. Bryan Cave. Format: News/talk, sports. News staff: 4. Target aud: 35-64. ♦Tim Dorsey, pres & gen mgr; Greg Unger, stn mgr.

***KWMU(FM)**— June 2, 1972: 90.7 mhz; 97 kw. 981 ft. TL: N38 34 50 W90 19 45. (CP: 100 kw, ant 1,000 ft.). Stereo. Univ. of Missouri-St. Louis, 8001 Natural Bridge Rd. 63121. Phone: (314) 516-5968. Fax: (314) 516-5993. E-mail: kwmu@kwmu.org. Web Site: www.kwmu.org. Licensee: The Curators of the University of Missouri. (group owner) Network: Network: NPR, PRI. Shaw Pittman. Format: News info. News staff: 5; News: 40 hrs wkly. Target aud: 27-45; upscale. ♦Patricia Wente, gen mgr; Shelly Korley, stn mgr; Shelley Korley, dev dir; Mike Schrand, progmg dir.

KXEN(AM)— May 10, 1951: 1010 khz; 50 kw-D, 500 w-n, DA-2. TL: N38 45 46 W90 03 35. Box 8085, Granite City, IL 62040. Phone: (314) 436-6550. Fax: (618) 797-2293. Web Site: www.kxen1010.com. Licensee: BDJ Radio Enterprises LLC (acq 7-2-02). Format: Relg. ♦Dirk L. Hallemeier, gen mgr.

KYKY(FM)— 1960: 98.1 mhz; 90 kw. 1,027 ft. TL: N38 34 24 W90 19 30. Stereo. 3100 Market St., St. Louis 63103. Phone: (314) 531-0000. Fax: (314) 531-9855. Web Site: www.y98.com. Licensee: Infinity Radio Holdings Inc. Group owner: Infinity Broadcasting Corp. (acq 11-13-98; grpsl). Network: Westwood One. Format: Hot adult contemp. Target aud: 25-54. ♦Beth Davis, gen mgr.

WARH(FM)—(Granite City).IL Nov 24, 1965: 106.5 mhz; 90 kw. Ant 1,027 ft. TL: N38 34 24 W90 19 30. Stereo. 11647 Olive Blvd., St. Louis 63141. Phone: (314) 983-6000. Fax: (314) 994-9447. Web Site: www.wssm.com. Licensee: Bonneville Holding Co. Group owner: Bonneville International Corp. (acq 9-26-2000; grpsl). Format: Smooth jazz. ♦Bruce Reese, CEO & pres; Bob Johnson, CFO; John Kijowski, VP & gen mgr; Mike Jennewein, sls dir; Ben Granger, gen sls mgr & natl sls mgr; Angie Perino, prom dir; David Myers, progmg dir; Amanda Koeppe, pub affrs dir; Marshall Rice, chief of engrg.

WEW(AM)— Apr 26, 1921: 770 khz; 1 kw-D. TL: N38 37 17 W90 04 36. 2740 Hampton Ave. 63139. Secondary address: 21700 Northwestern Hwy, Tower 14, Ste 1190, Southfield, MI 48075. Phone: (314) 781-9397. Phone: (314) 969-7700. Fax: (314) 781-8545. E-mail: wewradio@oal.com. Web Site: www.wewradio.com. Licensee: Birach Broadcasting Corp. (group owner; acq 1-6-2004; $1.35 million). Network: Network: CBS Radio, CNN Radio. Format: Ethnic. Target aud: 35-64; Mature audience/older. Spec prog: Ger 2 hrs, Pol 2 hrs wkly. ♦Sima Birach, CEO, pres & gen mgr; Rich Vannoy, opns mgr.

WGNU(AM)—(Granite City).IL Dec 1, 1961: 920 khz; 450 w-D, 500 w-N, DA-2. TL: N38 45 33 W90 03 00. 265 Union Blvd., Suite 1301, St. Louis 63108-1262. Phone: (314) 454-6660. Fax: (314) 454-6609. E-mail: gm@wgnu.net. Web Site: www.wgnu.net. Licensee: Norman Broadcasting Co. (acq 2004). Network: Network: ABC News/Talk, ABC Information & Entertainment. Miller & Miller. Format: Talk. News staff: one; News: 2 hrs wkly. Target aud: 25-54; active, educated adults. Spec prog: German 2 hrs, Bosnian 2 hrs wkly. ♦Esther Wright, gen mgr; Joan Goceman, opns dir; Brian Boyland, gen sls mgr; Charles Geer, progmg dir & news dir.

WIL(AM)— Feb 9, 1922: 1430 khz; 5 kw-U, DA-2. TL: N38 32 09 W90 11 26. 11647 Olive St. 63141. Phone: (314) 983-6000. Fax: (314) 994-9421. Web Site: www.legends1430.com. Licensee: Bonneville Holding Co. Group owner: Bonneville International Corp. (acq 9-26-2000; grpsl). Network: Westwood One. Rep: Allied Radio Partners. Format: Country. News staff: one. Target aud: 35 plus; affluent, mature baby boomers. ♦Eric Hellum, gen mgr; Keith Kraus, gen sls mgr; Greg Mozingo, progmg dir; Monica Adams, news dir; Marshall Rice, chief of engrg.

WILI-FM— June 16, 1975: 98.3 mhz; 1.05 kw. 525 ft. TL: N41 41 00 W72 13 01. Stereo. Web Site: www.wili.com. Network: Superadio. Format: CHR. News staff: one; News: 6 hrs wkly. Target aud: 22-44; college students, young married couples, young families.

WILL-FM— Sept 1, 1941: 90.9 mhz; 105 kw. 850 ft. TL: N40 06 52 W88 13 27. Stereo. Network: Network: NPR, PRI. Format: Class. News: 2 hrs wkly. Target aud: 35-70. ♦Jake Schumacher, progmg dir. Co-owned TV: *WILL-TV affil

Stations in the U.S.   Missouri

Developers & Brokers of Radio Properties

contact American Media Services at our suite:
Philadelphia Marriott Downtown
215-625-2900
843-972-2200
americanmediaservices.com
Charleston, SC
Dallas, TX · Chicago, Il · Austin, TX

American Media Services, LLC

WIL-FM— July 15, 1962: 92.3 mhz; 99 kw. 984 ft. TL: N38 28 56 W90 23 53. Stereo. Web Site: www.wil92.com. Rep: Allied Radio Partners. Format: Contemp country.

WRDA(FM)—See Jerseyville, IL

Saint Robert

KFLW(FM)— Mar 22, 1994: 98.9 mhz; 6 kw. 328 ft. TL: N37 52 41 W92 01 05. 250 Marshall Dr., St. Robert 65584-8600. Phone: (573) 336-5359. Fax: (573) 336-7619. E-mail: toquinn@kflw99.com. Web Site: kflw99.com. Licensee: Ozark Media (acq 2-19-02; $575,000). Format: Solid rock. News: 3 hrs wkly. Target aud: 25-55. ♦ Dalton Wright, pres; Tracey O'Quinn, gen mgr.

Sainte Genevieve

KPNT(FM)— March 1967: 105.7 mhz; 100 kw. Ant 1,374 ft. TL: N38 13 10 W90 35 44. Stereo. 800 St. Louis Union Stn., The Power House, St. Louis 63103. Phone: (314) 231-1057. Fax: (314) 621-3000. Web Site: www.1057thepoint.com. Licensee: Emmis Radio License LLC. Group owner: Emmis Communications Corp. Network: ABC. Format: New rock alternative. Target aud: 18-34. ♦ John Beck, gen mgr; Tommy Mathern, natl sls mgr & progmg dir; Sam Caputa, chief of engrg.

KSGM(AM)—See Chester, IL

Salem

*KCVX(FM)— February 2004: 91.7 mhz; 40kw. Ant 210 ft. TL: N37 39 53 W91 32 00. Stereo. Box 800, % Spirit FM Radio, Camdenton 65020-0800. Phone: (573) 346-3200. Fax: (573) 346-1010. E-mail: email@spiritfm.org. Web Site: www.spiritfm.org. Licensee: Lake Area Educational Broadcasting Foundation (acq 12-20-02; $35,000. for CP). Format: Div, Christian. Target aud: 25-45; primarily females, married with children. ♦ James J. McDermott, pres; Alice McDermott, gen mgr.

KKID(FM)— January 1971: 92.9 mhz; 21 kw. Ant 361 ft. TL: N37 43 45 W91 28 23. Stereo. 1415 Forum Dr., Rolla 65401-2508. Phone: (573) 364-4433. Fax: (573) 364-8385. Web Site: www.kkid929fm. Licensee: Ultra-Sonic Broadcast Stations Inc. Network: USA. Format: Classic country. News staff: one; News: 20 hrs wkly. Target aud: 30-49. ♦ David Wheeler, pres & gen mgr.

KSMO(AM)— November 1953: 1340 khz; 1 kw-U. TL: N37 37 36 W91 32 09. 800 S. Main 65560. Phone: (573) 729-6117. Fax: (573) 729-7337. E-mail: ksmoradio@ksmoradio.com. Web Site: www.ksmoradio.com. Licensee: KSMO Enterprises. (acq 11-84). Network: AP Network News. Booth, Freret, Imlay & Tepper. Format: Country, news/talk, sports. News staff: one; News: 40 hrs wkly. Target aud: General; middle class. Spec prog: Farm 18 hrs wkly. ♦ Stanley M. Podorski, pres & gen mgr.

Savannah

KSJQ(FM)— September 1991: 92.7 mhz; 50 kw. 492 ft. TL: N39 58 34 W94 58 37. Stereo. Box 8550, St. Joseph 64508. Secondary address: 4104 Country Ln., St. Joseph 64506. Phone: (816) 233-8881. Fax: (816) 279-8280. Web Site: stjoeradio.com. Licensee: Eagle Communications Inc. Group owner: Eagle Communications Group (acq 1993; $450,000; FTR: 9-13-93). Rep: Katz Radio. Wiley, Rein & Fielding. Format: Country. News staff: 2; News: 3 hrs wkly. ♦ Gary Shorman, CEO & pres; Mark Vail, COO & VP; Gary Exline, VP & gen mgr; Kevin Wagner, opns dir; Nick Kunels, sls dir; Teresa Hetz, prom mgr; Brent Harmon, progmg dir; Barry Birr, news dir; Jay Thouvenell, engrg dir.

Scott City

KGKS(FM)— 1998: 93.9 mhz; 5.4 kw. 344 ft. TL: N37 22 07 W89 35 34. Box 1610, 324 Broadway, Cape Girardeau 63701. Phone: (573) 335-8291. Fax: (573) 335-4806. E-mail: kiss@zrgmail.com. Web Site: www.kiss939.com. Licensee: MRR License LLC. Group owner: MAX Media L.L.C. (acq 3-29-2004; grpsl). Format: Adult contemp. ♦ Carla Liebl, gen mgr; Whitney Thomas, progmg dir.

Sedalia

KDRO(AM)— Sept 13, 1939: 1490 khz; 1 kw-U. TL: N38 40 35 W93 15 18. 301 S. Ohio 65301-4431. Phone: (660) 826-5005. Phone: (660) 440-1490. E-mail: 1490@kdro.com. Web Site: www.kdro.com. Licensee: Mathewson Broadcasting Co. (acq 4-16-90; $300,000; 5-7-90). Network: CBS. Format: Country. News staff: 2; News: 11 hrs wkly. Target aud: General. Spec prog: Farm 6 hrs, Black one hr, relg 3 hrs wkly. ♦ James Mathewson, pres; Adam B. Fischer, VP; Dianne M. Simon, gen mgr; Bill Barrick, opns mgr.

KSDL(FM)—Listing follows KSIS(AM).

KSIS(AM)— Feb 18, 1954: 1050 khz; 1 kw-D, 86 w-N. TL: N38 43 52 W93 13 32. Stereo. Box 1056 65302-1056. Secondary address: 2209 S. Limit 65301. Phone: (660) 826-1050. Fax: (660) 827-5072. E-mail: ksis@bickbroadcasting.com. Licensee: Bick Broadcasting Co. (acq 1-1-87). Network: ABC Information & Entertainment. Format: News/talk. News staff: 2. Target aud: 25-54. ♦ Dennis Polk, gen mgr, gen sls mgr & chief of engrg; Doug Sokolowski, progmg dir; Frank Powell, news dir.

KSDL(FM)—Co-owned with KSIS(AM). May 11, 1964: 92.1 mhz; 3 kw. 280 ft. TL: N38 43 52 W93 13 32. Stereo. Phone: (660) 826-9210. E-mail: radio92@ksdl.com. Format: Adult contemp. News staff: 2. Target aud: 12-40; women. ♦ Paul Aberli, mus dir.

Seligman

KIGL(FM)— Aug 1, 1986: 93.3 mhz; 100 kw. Ant 492 ft. TL: N36 28 03 W94 10 25. Stereo. Box 8190, Fayetteville, AR 72703. Secondary address: 4209 Frontage Rd., Fayetteville, AR 72703. Phone: (479) 973-9339. Fax: (479) 582-5302. Web Site: www.933theeagle.com. Licensee: Capstar TX L.P. Group owner: Clear Channel Communications Inc. (acq 8-30-00; grpsl). Network: USA. Format: Classic rock. News staff: one; News: 7 hrs wkly. Target aud: 35 plus; mature, upscale professionals. ♦ Tony Beriegee, gen mgr.

Shell Knob

KQMO(FM)— July 16, 1999: 97.7 mhz; 2.1 kw. 558 ft. TL: N36 44 54 W93 39 32. Stereo. 126 S. Jefferson St., Aurora 65605. Phone: (417) 678-0416. Fax: (417) 678-4111. Web Site: www.talonbroadcasting.com. Licensee: Falcon Broadcasting Inc. (acq 8-19-2005; $417,500). Network: USA. Format: Sp. ♦ Dewayn Gandy, gen mgr.

Sikeston

KBHI(FM)—(Miner). 2001: 107.1 mhz; 3.7 kw. Ant 420 ft. TL: N36 56 33 W89 41 47. 125 S. Kingshighway 63801. Phone: (573) 471-2000. Fax: (573) 471-8525. Licensee: Dana R. Withers. Format: Rock/AOR. ♦ Rick Lambert, gen mgr.

KBXB(FM)—Listing follows KRHW(AM).

KRHW(AM)— Mar 17, 1966: 1520 khz; 5 kw-D, 1.6 kw-N, DA-3. TL: N36 49 25 W89 35 45. Box 907, 125 S. Kings Hwy. 63801. Phone: (573) 471-2000. Fax: (573) 471-8525. Licensee: Withers Broadcasting Co. of Southeast Missouri LLC. Group owner: Withers Broadcasting Co. (acq 4-96; with co-located FM). Format: Country, relg. Target aud: 45 plus. Spec prog: Farm 6 hrs wkly. ♦ Rick Lambert, gen mgr; Joe Bill Davis, rgnl sls mgr; Kidd Manning, progmg dir; John Steeke, news dir; Smokey King, chief of engrg.

KBXB(FM)—Co-owned with KRHW(AM). Sept 12, 1968: 97.9 mhz; 50 kw. 469 ft. TL: N36 59 52 W89 38 52. Stereo. Target aud: 18-49. ♦ Joe Bill Davis, rgnl sls mgr & progmg dir.

KSIM(AM)— July 17, 1948: 1400 khz; 1 kw-U. TL: N36 52 12 W89 36 32. 519 Greer Ave. 63801. Phone: (573) 471-1400. Fax: (573) 471-1402. Web Site: www.ksim.com. Licensee: MRR License LLC. Group owner: MAX Media L.L.C. (acq 3-29-2004; grpsl). Network: ABC Information & Entertainment. Format: News/talk. Target aud: 25-54. Spec prog: Loc sports, news, Paul Harvey, farm 12 hrs wkly. ♦ Bill Powers, gen mgr, opns mgr & news dir.

South West City

KLTK(AM)— Mar 2, 1977: 1140 khz; 250 w-D. TL: N36 30 28 W94 36 34. 113 E. New Hope Rd., Rogers, AR 72758. Phone: (479) 633-0790. Fax: (479) 631-9711. Licensee: KERM Inc. (group owner; acq 3-15-02; $350,000. with co-located FM). Dow, Lohnes & Albertson. Format: Sports, talk. Target aud: 25-54; rural, agricultural. ♦ Diane Womack, gen sls mgr; Kermit Womack, pres, pres, gen mgr & progmg dir; Eric Morris, chief of engrg.

KURM-FM—Co-owned with KLTK(AM). October 1989: 100.3 mhz; 3 kw. 328 ft. TL: N36 30 28 W94 36 35. Web Site: www.kwmg.com. Network: Network: Westwood One, CBS. Dow, Lohnes & Albertson. Format: News/talk. ♦ Eric Morris, engrg VP.

Sparta

KSPW(FM)— Mar 1, 1989: 96.5 mhz; 3.2 kw. 453 ft. TL: N37 05 17 W93 10 34. (CP: 50 kw, ant 492 ft. TL: N35 56 23 W93 17 15). Stereo. Box 2180, Springfield 65801. Secondary address: 2330 W. Grand St., Springfield 65802. Phone: (417) 865-6614. Fax: (417) 865-9643. Web Site: www.power965jams.com. Licensee: Journal Broadcast Corp. Group owner: Journal Communications Inc. (acq 6-11-99; grpsl). Rep: Christal. Format: CHR. News staff: 6. Target aud: 18-34; young active adults. ♦ Steven Smith, CEO & chmn; Doug Kiel, pres; Carl Gardner, exec VP; Rex Hansen, gen mgr, gen sls mgr & natl sls mgr; Brad Kirk Hansen, opns mgr; Dawn McClain, prom dir; Chris Cannon, progmg dir; David Rahmoeller, chief of engrg.

Springfield

KADI(AM)— July 29, 1949: 1340 khz; 1 kw-U. TL: N37 12 30 W93 17 32. 5431 W. Sunshine St., Brookline Station 65619. Phone: (417) 831-0995. Fax: (417) 831-4026. Web Site: www.kadi.com. Licensee: Vision Communications Inc. (acq 5-26-2005; $375,000). Format: Talk. ♦ R.C. Amer, gen mgr.

KGBX-FM—Listing follows KGMY(AM).

KGMY(AM)— Oct 31, 1926: 1400 khz; 1 kw-U. TL: N37 11 46 W93 19 21. Stereo. 1856 S. Glenstone 65804. Phone: (417) 890-5555. Fax: (417) 890-5050. Web Site: www.mycountry.com. Licensee: Clear Channel Broadcasting Licenses Inc. Group owner: Clear Channel Communications Inc. (acq 10-10-00; grpsl). Format: Sports. Target aud: 35 plus; affluent, educated white-collar skewing 35 plus year olds. ♦ Mary Flennor, gen mgr & stn mgr; Paul Kelley, opns dir; Mary Fleenor, sls VP; Raylene Lee, prom dir; Rick Masters, progmg dir; Shawn Baker, engrg mgr.

KGBX-FM—Co-owned with KGMY(AM). December 1989: 105.9 mhz; 38 kw. 558 ft. TL: N37 25 16 W93 24 06. Stereo. Format: Adult contemp. News staff: one; News: 5 hrs wkly. Target aud: 25-54; educated, high income, women.

KLFJ(AM)— Nov 1, 1974: 1550 khz; 5 kw-D, 28 w-N. TL: N37 11 45 W93 19 07. 610 W. College 65806. Phone: (417) 831-1550. Licensee: 127 Inc. (acq 6-99; $432,500). Format: Info, news. ♦ R. R. Johnson, gen mgr.

KLPW(AM)—See Union

*KSCV(FM)— October 1995: 90.1 mhz; 9 kw. Ant 492 ft. TL: N37 17 41 W93 09 10. (CP: 9 kw, ant 492 ft. TL: N37 17 41 W93 09 10). Stereo. 1111 S. Glenstone Ave., Suite 3-102 65804. Phone: (417) 864-0901. Fax: (417) 862-7263. E-mail: pschneider@bottradionetwork.com. Web Site: bottradionetwork.com. Licensee: Community Broadcasting

Missouri
Directory of Radio

Inc. Group owner: Bott Radio Network (acq 2-7-01; 1.25 million. with KMCV(FM) High Point). Format: Christian, talk. Target aud: 35-54 plus; women 60%, men 40%. ♦ Paul Schneider, gen mgr.

KSGF(AM)— 1926: 1260 khz; 5 kw-U, DA-N. TL: N37 15 51 W93 19 04. Stereo. Box 2180 65801. Secondary address: 2330 W. Grand 65802. Phone: (417) 865-6614. Fax: (417) 865-9643. Licensee: Journal Broadcast Corp. Group owner: Journal Communications Inc. (acq 6-11-99; grpsl). Network: ABC Daytime Direction. Rep: Christal. Format: News/talk. News staff: 4; News: 30 hrs wkly. Target aud: 35-54. Spec prog: Farm 5 hrs wkly. ♦ Steven Smith, CEO & chmn; Doug Kiel, pres; Carl Gardner, exec VP; Rex Hansen, VP, gen mgr, gen sls mgr & natl sls mgr; Brad Kirk, opns mgr; Kris Addison, prom dir & mus dir; David Hayes, progmg dir; Morris James, news dir; David Rahmoeller, chief of engrg.

KTTS-FM—Co-owned with KSGF(AM). Aug1948: 94.7 mhz; 100 kw. 1,125 ft. TL: N37 13 26 W93 14 33. Stereo. 2330 W. Grand 65802. Web Site: www.ktts.com. Dow, Lohnes & Albertson. Format: Country. News staff: 4; News: 5 hrs wkly. Target aud: 25-54; adults. ♦ Brad Kirk, mus dir; Curly Clark, asst music dir & pub affrs dir.

*KSMU(FM)— May 7, 1974: 91.1 mhz; 40 kw. 403 ft. TL: N37 10 14 W93 19 25. Stereo. Missouri State Univ., 901 S. National Ave. 65804-0089. Phone: (417) 836-5878. Fax: (417) 836-5889. E-mail: ksmu@smsu.edu. Web Site: www.ksmu.org. Licensee: Board of Governors, Southwest Missouri State University Network: NPR. Ernest Sanchez. Format: NPR News & Classical Music. News staff: one; News: 54 hrs wkly. Target aud: 25-54. Spec prog: Jazz 10 hrs wkly. ♦ Tammy Wiley, gen mgr.

KTOZ(AM)— 1972: 1060 khz; 500 w-D. TL: N37 11 29 W93 19 45. Stereo. 610 W. College. 65806. Phone: (417) 832-1060. Fax: (417) 864-4111. E-mail: ktozam@pcis.net. Web Site: www.ktozam.com. Licensee: T.E.N. USA Inc. (acq 6-7-94; $35,000;. FTR: 7-4-94). Format: Big band, nostalgia, MOR. Target aud: General. Spec prog: Jazz 12 hrs, blues 4 hrs, 50s mus 4 hrs wkly. ♦ James Cooper, VP; William H. Thomas, chmn, pres & gen mgr; Jim Cooper, progmg dir.

KTXR(FM)— June 12, 1962: 101.3 mhz; 97.8 kw. Ant 1,488 ft. TL: N37 11 41 W92 56 07. 3000 E. Chestnut Expwy. 65802. Secondary address: Box 3925 65802. Phone: (417) 862-3751. Fax: (417) 869-7675. E-mail: manager@radiospringfield.com. Web Site: www.radiospringfield.com. Licensee: Stereo Broadcasting Inc. Group owner: Meyer Communications Inc. Format: Contemp easy lstng. News staff: one; News: 2 hrs wkly. Target aud: 35 plus; female. ♦ Kenneth E. Meyer, pres & gen mgr; Gene Brown, gen sls mgr; Tom Ladd, opns dir, opns mgr & progmg dir; Dale Blankenship, chief of engrg.

*KWFC(FM)— Apr 17, 1985: 89.1 mhz; 100 kw. 1,122 ft. TL: N37 12 06 W92 56 33. Stereo. Box 8000 65801-8900. Secondary address: 2316 N. Benton 65801. Phone: (417) 869-0891. Fax: (417) 866-7525. E-mail: info@kwfc.org. Web Site: www.kwfc.org. Licensee: Baptist Bible College Inc. Network: USA. Format: Relg, Christian. News staff: one; News: 17 hrs wkly. Target aud: General; conservative, church-oriented. ♦ Gary Longstaff, gen mgr; Kyle Dowden, progmg dir; Brady Shoemaker, news dir.

*KWND(FM)— July 12, 1993: 88.3 mhz; 12 kw. 328 ft. TL: N37 10 30 W93 02 35. Stereo. 2550-100 S. Campbell 65807. Phone: (417) 889-0883. Fax: (417) 886-8656. Web Site: www.88.3thewind.com. Licensee: The Radio Training Network. (acq 7-95). Format: Adult contemp, Christian. Target aud: 25-49. Spec prog: Gospel 3 hrs wkly. ♦ Ben Birdsong, gen mgr.

KWTO(AM)— Dec 25, 1933: 560 khz; 5 kw-U, DA-N. TL: N37 08 08 W93 16 36. Box 3793 65808. Secondary address: 3000 E. Chestnut Expwy. 65808. Phone: (417) 862-5600. Fax: (417) 869-7675. E-mail: manager@radiospringfield.com. Web Site: www.radiospringfield.com. Licensee: KWTO Inc. Group owner: Meyer Communications Inc. (acq 3-20-95; $1.88 million with co-located FM; 6-19-95). Network: ABC Information & Entertainment. Format: Sports, news/talk. News: one hr wkly. Target aud: 25-55; male. Spec prog: Farm 20 hrs, relg one hr wkly. ♦ Kenneth E. Meyer, pres, gen mgr & gen sls mgr; Bonnie Bell, dev mgr; Tom Ladd, opns mgr & progmg dir; Dale Blankenship, chief of engrg.

KWTO-FM— Nov 23, 1967: 98.7 mhz; 100 kw. 600 ft. TL: N37 04 06 W93 18 31. Stereo. Web Site: www.radiospringfield.com. Format: Sports, talk. Target aud: 25-45; male dominant middle class.

KXUS(FM)— Apr 17, 1969: 97.3 mhz; 100 kw. 479 ft. TL: N37 14 23 W93 17 05. (CP: Ant 987 ft. TL: N37 11 10 W93 01 23). Stereo. 1856 S. Glenstone Ave. 65804. Phone: (417) 890-5555. Fax: (417) 823-8506. E-mail: us97@us97.com. Web Site: www.us97.com. Licensee: Clear Channel Broadcasting Licenses Inc. Group owner: Clear Channel Communications Inc. (acq 10-10-00; grpsl). Format: Classic rock. News staff: one; News: 5 hrs wkly. Target aud: 25-54; males -75%. ♦ Mary Fleenor, gen mgr & sls dir; Paul Kelley, opns dir; Raylene Lee, prom dir & prom mgr; Tony Metteo, progmg dir; Mark McClain, mus dir; Shawn Baker, chief of engrg.

Steelville

KNSX(FM)— September 1985: 93.3 mhz; 8.5 kw. 1,168 ft. TL: N38 06 16 W91 02 30. 3418 Douglas Rd., Florissant 63034. Phone: (314) 921-9330. E-mail: 93x@knsx.com. Web Site: www.knsx.com. Licensee: Twenty-One Sound Communications Inc. Format: Alternative. ♦ Ruth Choate, gen mgr.

Stockton

KRWP(FM)— Jan 20, 1999: 107.7 mhz; 11.7 kw. Ant 479 ft. TL: N37 31 24 W93 52 40. Box 1020, 126 S. Jefferson 65605. Secondary address: 1225 South Hwy. 39 65785. Phone: (417) 276-5253. Fax: (417) 276-2255. Licensee: Cumulus Licensing LLC. Group owner: Cumulus Media Inc. (acq 4-27-2004; $825,000). Network: Jones Radio Networks. Fletcher, Heald & Hildreth. Format: Classic country. News: 16 hrs wkly. Target aud: 25-54; male and female. Spec prog: Local news, weather, Chief's football, farm 8 hrs wkly. ♦ Lance Beamer, gen mgr.

Sullivan

KTUI(AM)— Feb 14, 1966: 1560 khz; 1 kw-D. TL: N38 11 42 W91 11 12. Box 99 63080-0099. Phone: (573) 468-5101. Fax: (573) 468-5884. Web Site: www.ktui.com. Licensee: Fidelity Broadcasting Inc. (acq 10-23-97; $497,000 with co-located FM). Network: UPI. Format: News/talk. News staff: one. Target aud: General. ♦ John C. Rice, gen mgr & gen sls mgr; Sam Scott, progmg dir & news dir.

KTUI-FM— 1981: 100.9 mhz; 3 kw. 276 ft. TL: N38 11 42 W91 11 12. Stereo. Web Site: www.ktui.com. Network: UPI. Format: Country, sports. Target aud: General. ♦ John Rice, opns dir.

Sunrise Beach

*KCRL(FM)— Sept 1, 1998: 90.3 mhz; 4.5 kw. 197 ft. TL: N38 14 11 W92 46 03. Community Broadcasting, 10550 Barkley Attn: Richard Bott II, Overland Park, KS 66212. Secondary address: 30690 Gray Eagle Rd., Gravois Mills 65037. Phone: (573) 372-1903. Fax: (573) 372-3801. E-mail: kcrl@bottradionetwork.com. Web Site: www.bottradionetwork.net. Licensee: Community Broadcasting Inc. Group owner: Bott Radio Network Network: USA. Format: Christian talk. ♦ Richard P. Bott, pres; Richard P. Bott II, exec VP; Terrie Kobolt, gen mgr; Sherry Gaut, sls dir & mktg dir.

Tarkio

*KRSS(FM)— Aug 22, 1977: 93.5 mhz; 11 kw. 489 ft. TL: N40 31 11 W95 11 03. 23979 Hwy. 136 64491. Phone: (660) 736-4321. Fax: (660) 736-5789. Web Site: www.calvarychapel.com/krss. Licensee: CSN International (group owner). Format: Christian. Target aud: General. ♦ Mick Miller, gen mgr.

Thayer

KALM(AM)— Dec 11, 1953: 1290 khz; 1 kw-D, 56 w-N. TL: N36 32 58 W91 33 05. Box 15, N. Hwy. 63 65791. Phone: (417) 264-7211. Phone: (417) 264-7063. Fax: (417) 264-7212. E-mail: kkountry@kkountry.com. Web Site: www.kkountry.com. Licensee: Ozark Radio Network Inc. Network: ABC Daytime Direction. Rep: Keystone (unwired net). Richard Hayes. Format: News/talk. News staff: one; News: 70 hrs wkly. Target aud: 18 plus; farmers, ranchers, rural families. ♦ Shawn N. Marhefka, pres; Robert Eckman, gen mgr; Jerry Elam, progmg dir.

KAMS(FM)—See Mammoth Spring, AR

KSAR(FM)—Not on air, target date: unknown: 92.3 mhz; 50 kw. 426 ft. TL: N36 21 58 W91 28 35. Box 458, Salem, AR 72576. Secondary address: 352 Hwy. 62/412, Salem, AR 72576. Phone: (870) 895-2665. Fax: (870) 895-4088. E-mail: hometownradio@centurytel.net. Web Site: www.yourhometownstations.com. Licensee: Bragg Broadcasting Corp. Network: ABC Information & Entertainment. Format: Country, news, sports. Target aud: 25-54. Spec prog: Farm 4 hrs wkly. ♦ James Bragg, gen mgr.

Trenton

KTTN-FM— Sept 15, 1978: 92.3 mhz; 18.5 kw. Ant 380 ft. TL: N40 05 00 W93 33 30. Stereo. Box 307 64683. Secondary address: 804 Main St. 64683. Phone: (660) 359-2261. Fax: (660) 359-4126. E-mail: kttnamfm@gm.net. Web Site: www.kttn.com. Licensee: Luehrs Broadcasting Co. (acq 8-1-92). Network: AP Radio. Rgnl Reps Reddy, Begley & McCormick. Format: Country, news, sports. News staff: 2; News: 15 hrs wkly. Target aud: General. Spec prog: Gospel 6 hrs wkly. ♦ John Ausberger, pres; John Anthony, gen mgr.

KTTN(AM)— Apr 17, 1955: 1600 khz; 500 w-D, 35 w-N. TL: N40 05 00 W93 33 30. Stereo. Network: Network: AP Radio, Jones Radio Networks. Reddy, Begley & McCormick. Format: Adult contemp. News: 8 hrs wkly. Target aud: 35 plus; general.

Troy

KFNS-FM— Nov 29, 1993: 100.7 mhz; 6 kw. 328 ft. TL: N39 03 13 W90 59 47. 8045 Big Bend Blvd., Suite 200, St. Louis 63119. Phone: (314) 962-0590 (main #). Fax: (314) 962-7576. E-mail: kfns@kfns.com. Web Site: www.kfns.com. Licensee: Big Stick Two LLC. Group owner: Big League Broadcasting LLC (acq 7-13-2004); grpsl). Format: Sports radio. ♦ Mike Phares, gen mgr.

Union

KLPW(AM)— Aug 18, 1954: 1220 khz; 1 kw-D, 126 w-N. TL: N38 28 57 W91 02 39. Box 623, Washington 63090. Phone: (636) 583-5155. Phone: (636) 239-3355. Fax: (636) 583-1644. E-mail: klpwam@klpw.com. Web Site: www.klpwam.com. Licensee: Broadcast Properties Inc. (acq 1999; grpsl). Network: ABC Information & Entertainment. Format: All talk. News staff: 2; News: 40 hrs wkly. Target aud: 25-54; male. Spec prog: Relg 6 hrs wkly. ♦ Tim McDonald, gen mgr & gen sls mgr; Ray Heller, opns dir & pub affrs dir; Dee Coppeans, sls dir; Diana Stanley, prom dir; Greg Marshall, progmg dir; John Covington, news dir; Tom Lyons, chief of engrg.

KLPW-FM— Aug 1, 1966: 101.7 mhz; 3.3 kw horiz. Ant 341 ft. TL: N38 28 57 W91 02 39. Stereo. Box 623, Washington 63090. Secondary address: 6531 Hwy. BB, Washington 63090. Phone: (636) 583-5155. Phone: (636) 239-3355. Fax: (636) 583-1644. Web Site: www.klpwfm.com. Licensee: Marathon Media Group L.L.C. (acq 1999; grpsl). Format: Country. News staff: 2; News: 16.5 hrs wkly. Target aud: 18-49. ♦ Tim McDonald, gen mgr; Steve Leslie, mus dir.

Van Buren

*KBIY(FM)— 2001: 91.3 mhz; 100 kw. Ant 492 ft. TL: N37 06 25 W90 59 30. New Life Evangelistic Center Inc., 1411 Locust St., St. Louis 63103. Phone: (314) 436-2424. Fax: (314) 436-2434. E-mail: larryr@hereshelpnet.org. Web Site: www.hereshelpnet.org. Licensee: New Life Evangelistic Center Inc. Format: Adult contemp, gospel, loc pub affrs-news. ♦ Larry Rice, pres & gen mgr.

Vandalia

KKAC(FM)—Not on air, target date: unknown: 104.3 mhz; 6 kw. 292 ft. TL: N39 19 00 W91 28 22. 400 S. Lindell St. 63382. Phone: (573) 594-6000. Fax: (314) 594-2100. E-mail: kkacfm@vandaliamo.net. Web site: www.actioncountry.com. Licensee: Twenty-One Sound Communications Inc. Format: Country.

Versailles

KTKS(FM)— June 16, 1989: 95.1 mhz; 12.5 kw. Ant 462 ft. TL: N38 24 32 W92 45 42. Stereo. Box 409 65084. Secondary address: 16875 Hwy 52, Barnett 65011. Phone: (573) 378-5669. Fax: (573) 378-6640. E-mail: jay@lakeradio.net. Web site: lakeradio.com. Licensee: Twin Lakes Communications Inc. Network: CNN Radio. Fletcher, Heald & Hildreth. Format: Country. News staff: one; News: 23 hrs wkly. Target aud: 25-54; loc rural audience & transient tourist population. Spec prog: Farm 2 hrs, relg 3 hrs wkly. ♦ Douglas A. Fisher, chmn; James D. Fisher, pres & gen mgr; Sheryl Lehman, gen sls mgr; J.T. Gerlt, progmg dir.

Developers & Brokers of Radio Properties

contact American Media Services
at our suite:
Philadelphia Marriott Downtown
215-625-2900
843-972-2200
americanmediaservices.com
Charleston, SC
Dallas, TX · Chicago, Il · Austin, TX

American Media Services, LLC

Vienna

*KNLN(FM)—Not on air, target date: unknown: 90.9 mhz; 10 kw. 328 ft. TL: N38 11 27 W92 07 22. New Life Evangelistic Center Inc., 1411 Locust St., St. Louis 63103. Phone: (314) 421-3020. Fax: (314) 436-2434. E-mail: larry@hereshelpnet.org. Web Site: www.hereshelpnet.org. Licensee: New Life Evangelistic Center Inc. Format: Relg. ♦ Larry Rice, gen mgr.

Warrensburg

KOKO(AM)— December 1953: 1450 khz; 1 kw-U. TL: N38 46 32 W93 43 12. Box 398 64093. Phone: (660) 747-9191. Fax: (660) 747-5611. Web Site: www.koko.com. Licensee: D & H Media L.L.C. (acq 10-3-01; $435,000). Network: ABC. Format: Oldies, Sports. News staff: one; News: 20 hrs wkly. Target aud: 25-54; educated-mainly female & sports enthusiasts. Spec prog: Farm 4 hrs, relg 6 hrs wkly. ♦ Vance Delozier, pres; Larry Rice, gen mgr; Marion Woods, gen mgr; Greg Hassler, opns mgr.

*KTBG(FM)— Apr 1, 1962: 90.9 mhz; 100 kw. 400 ft. TL: N38 55 54 W93 49 06. Stereo. Wood 11 64093. Phone: (660) 543-4130. Fax: (660) 543-8863. Web Site: www.ktbg.fm. Licensee: Central Missouri State University Board of Regents. Network: Network: NPR, PRI. Format: AAA. Target aud: General. ♦ Donald Peterson, gen mgr.

Warrenton

KFAV(FM)—Listing follows KWRE(AM).

KWRE(AM)— Mar 9, 1949: 730 khz; 1 kw-D, 120 w-N. TL: N38 49 20 W91 08 15. Box 220 63383. Phone: (636) 456-3311. Fax: (636) 456-8767. E-mail: kwrekfav@socket.net. Web Site: www.kwre.com. Licensee: Kaspar Broadcasting Co. Group owner: Kaspar Broadcasting Group. Format: Traditional country. Target aud: 35 plus. Spec prog: Farm 10 hrs wkly. ♦ Mike Thomas, opns dir, mus dir & news dir; Mark Becker, gen sls mgr; V.J. Kaspar, pres, gen mgr & chief of engrg.

KFAV(FM)—Co-owned with KWRE(AM). November 1991: 99.9 mhz; 10.5 kw. 512 ft. TL: N38 50 20 W91 02 40. Fax: (636) 978-4710. Web Site: www.kfav.com. Format: Today's hot country. Target aud: 20-49; general.

Warsaw

KAYQ(FM)— Mar 10, 1980: 97.1 mhz; 6 kw. Ant 239 ft. TL: N38 17 19 W93 18 32. Stereo. Box 1420 65355. Secondary address: Truman Hills Mall, Suite 6 Phone: (660) 438-7343. Fax: (660) 438-7159. E-mail: glenna@thelake.fm. Web Site: www.thelake.fm. Licensee: Valkyrie Broadcasting Co. Inc. Network: AP Radio. Format: Classic country. News staff: one; News: 5 hrs wkly. ♦ Jim McCollum, pres; Joey Anderson, gen mgr & chief of opns; Glenna Thrasher, prom mgr.

Washington

*KGNV(FM)— Dec 25, 1990: 89.9 mhz; 1 kw. 213 ft. TL: N38 35 49 W91 06 17. Box 187 63090. Phone: (636) 239-0400. Fax: (636) 293-4448. Web Site: goodnewsvoice.org. Licensee: Missouri River Christian Broadcasting Inc. Network: Network: Network: Moody, Salem Radio Network, Premiere Focus. Format: Christian, MOR, news/talk. News: 14 hrs wkly. Target aud: 35-55; inquisitive, conservative, liberal, philosophical, young & old. Spec prog: Class 5 hrs, children 6 hrs, teen 5 hrs wkly. ♦ James Goggan, pres & gen mgr.

KLPW-FM—See Union

KSLQ-FM—Listing follows KWMO(AM).

KWMO(AM)— Oct 19, 1985: 1350 khz; 500 w-D, 84 w-N, DA-1. TL: N38 34 44 W90 59 57. 511 W. 5th St. 63090. Phone: (636) 239-5432. Fax: (636) 239-0364. Licensee: Computraffic Inc. (acq 2-13-98; $200,000). Network: USA. Format: Oldies. Target aud: 35-54. ♦ Waldo Zimarskie, gen mgr, opns mgr, gen sls mgr, chief of engrg & chief of engrg.

KSLQ-FM—Co-owned with KWMO(AM). Nov 21, 1989: 104.5 mhz; 3 kw. 328 ft. TL: N38 36 03 W90 56 04. Stereo. Licensee: Y2K Inc. (acq 6-24-98; $1.1 million). Network: USA. Format: Hot adult contemp. Target aud: 25-54.

Waynesville

KFBD-FM—Listing follows KOZQ(AM).

KJPW(AM)— Apr 3, 1962: 1390 khz; 5 kw-D, 67 w-N. TL: N37 49 09 W92 09 06. Box D 65583-0480. Secondary address: 313 Old Rte 66, St. Robert 65583-0480. Phone: (573) 336-4913. Phone: (573) 336-4450. Fax: (573) 336-2222. E-mail: kjcountry@webound.com. Licensee: Ozark Broadcasting Inc. Group owner: Shepherd Group (acq 10-1-2003; $735,000. with co-located FM). Network: NBC. Cohn & Marks. Format: Talk radio. News staff: one; News: 14 hrs wkly. Target aud: General. Spec prog: Relg 3 hrs wkly. ♦ David Shepherd, pres; Mike Edwards, exec VP & gen mgr; Gary Knehans, stn mgr & prom mgr; Jim Anthony, gen sls mgr; Warren McDonald, progmg dir; Warren Goforth, news dir; Bob Moore, chief of engrg.

KJPW-FM— May 2, 1968: 102.3 mhz; 2.65 kw. 492 ft. TL: N37 49 09 W92 09 06. Stereo. Format: Adult contemp. News staff: one; News: 14 hrs wkly. Target aud: General.

KOZQ(AM)— May 9, 1968: 1270 khz; 500 w-D. TL: N37 49 42 W92 10 27. Box 4371 65583. Phone: (573) 336-3133. Fax: (573) 336-1228. Licensee: Viper Communications Inc. (acq 6-14-2005; $450,000 with co-located FM). Network: USA. Format: News/talk. Target aud: 40 plus. ♦ John Rice, gen mgr; Alan Holcomb, opns mgr, gen sls mgr & asst music dir; Sam Scott, progmg dir.

KFBD-FM—Co-owned with KOZQ(AM). Dec 9, 1964: 97.9 mhz; 3 kw. 259 ft. TL: N37 49 42 W92 10 27. Stereo. Format: Classic rock. ♦ Woody Schuler, progmg dir.

Webb City

KJMK(FM)— Sept 10, 1985: 93.9 mhz; 48 kw. 505 ft. TL: N37 14 34 W94 30 21. Stereo. 2702 E. 32nd, Joplin 64804. Phone: (417) 624-1025. Fax: (417) 781-6842. Web Site: www.magic939.com. Licensee: Zimco Inc. Group owner: Zimmer Radio Group (acq 6-17-97; grpsl). Network: ABC Information & Entertainment. Format: Adult contemp. Target aud: 25-54. ♦ Larry Boyd, gen mgr; Jason Knight, opns mgr.

KKLL(AM)— Mar 10, 1984: 1100 khz; 5 kw-D. TL: N37 06 23 W94 16 50. Box 1153, Joplin 64802. Secondary address: 3001 W. 13th, Joplin 64802. Phone: (417) 781-1100. Phone: (417) 624-1230. Fax: (417) 626-7111. Licensee: New Life Evangelistic Center Inc. (acq 8-10-98; $730,000 with KWAS(AM) Joplin). Format: Christian. ♦ Larry Rice, gen mgr.

KXDG(FM)— Sept 1, 1988: 97.9 mhz; 6 kw. 400 ft. TL: N37 06 11 W94 24 11. Stereo. 2702 E. 32nd St., Joplin 64804. Phone: (417) 624-1310. Fax: (417) 781-6842. Web Site: www.bigdog979.com. Licensee: Zimco Inc. Group owner: Zimmer Radio Group (acq 6-17-97; grpsl). Network: USA. Format: Classic rock. Target aud: General. ♦ Larry Boyd, gen mgr; Jason Knight, opns mgr.

West Plains

KKDY(FM)— Mar 31, 1984: 102.5 mhz; 50 kw. 485 ft. TL: N36 41 22 W91 53 45. Stereo. 983 E. Hwy. 160 65775. Phone: (417) 256-1025. Fax: (417) 256-2208. E-mail: hotcountrykdy@kkdy.com. Web Site: www.kkdy.com. Licensee: Central Ozark Radio Network Inc. (acq 8-1-94). Network: CNN Radio. Haley, Bader & Potts. Format: Hot country. News staff: 2; News: 10 hrs wkly. Target aud: 18-49. Spec prog: Contemp Christian 3 hrs wkly. ♦ Tom Marhefka, pres & gen mgr; Bob Eckman, opns VP; Chuck Boone, opns dir & progmg dir; Jonathan Bergman, sls dir & gen sls mgr; Bobby Helm, news dir; Bill Martin, chief of engrg.

*KSMW(FM)—Not on air, target date: unknown: 90.9 mhz; 350 w. Ant 387 ft. TL: N36 45 00 W91 49 40. Missouri State Univ., 901 S. National Ave., Springfield 65804-0089. Phone: (417) 836-5878. Fax: (417) 836-5889. E-mail: ksmu@smsu.edu. Web Site: www.ksmu.org. Licensee: Board of Governors, Southwest Missouri State University. Format: Class, news. ♦ Tammy Wiley, gen mgr.

KSPQ(FM)—Listing follows KWPM(AM).

KWPM(AM)— 1947: 1450 khz; 1 kw-U. TL: N36 44 28 W91 50 01. 983 U.S. Hwy. 160 E. 65775. Phone: (417) 256-3131. Phone: (417) 256-5976. Fax: (417) 256-2208. Web Site: www.ozarkradionetwork.com. Licensee: Missouri Ozarks Radio Network. (acq 1996). Network: ABC Daytime Direction. Format: News/talk. News staff: 4. Target aud: 25-54. ♦ Gerry Elan, gen mgr & progmg dir; Tom Marheska, opns dir; Jonathan Bergman, gen sls mgr; Bobby Helm, news dir; Bill Martin, chief of engrg.

KSPQ(FM)—Co-owned with KWPM(AM). 1951: 93.9 mhz; 100 kw. 650 ft. TL: N37 00 12 W91 54 24. Stereo. Phone: (417) 256-2322. Format: Classic rock. Target aud: 45-65 plus. ♦ Jonathan Bergman, natl sls mgr; Mike Crase, progmg dir.

Wheeling

KULH(FM)— May 3, 1999: 105.9 mhz; 6 kw. 328 ft. TL: N39 54 25 W93 20 28. 802 Calhoun St., Chillicothe 64601. Phone: (660) 646-2255. Fax: (660) 646-2242. E-mail: contactus@1059thewave.com. Web Site: www.1059thewave.com. Licensee: Resources Management Unlimited, Inc. (acq 3-28-01; $350,000). Network: USA. Reddy, Begley & McCormick. Format: Christian, adult contemp. Target aud: General. ♦ Ean Leppin, gen mgr.

Willard

KOSP(FM)— Aug 15, 1992: 105.1 mhz; 50 kw. 492 ft. TL: N37 01 01 W93 30 31. Stereo. 319-B E. Battlefield, Springfield 65807. Phone: (417) 886-5677. Fax: (417) 886-2155. E-mail: info@kosp.fm. Web Site: www.kosp.fm. Licensee: MW SpringMo Inc. Group owner: The Mid-West Family Broadcast Group Rep: McGavren Guild. Shaw Pittman. Format: Oldies. Target aud: 35-64; baby boomers. ♦ Rick McCoy, pres & gen mgr; Jeff Couch, opns mgr; Malcolm Hukriede, gen sls mgr; Keith Abercrombie, rgnl sls mgr; Asha Martin, prom mgr; Mike Roberts, progmg mgr.

Willow Springs

KUKU(AM)— Oct 1957: 1330 khz; 1 kw-D, 52 w-N. TL: N36 58 47 W91 59 29. 6962 US Hwy. 60, Mountain View 65548. Phone: (417) 469-2500. Fax: (417) 934-2565. Licensee: Missouri Ozarks Radio Network. (acq 1996). Network: ABC. Format: News/talk.

KUKU-FM— June 15, 1985: 100.3 mhz; 50 kw. 492 ft. TL: N37 03 49 W92 01 39. Stereo. Format: Oldies. News staff: 2; News: 27 hrs wkly. Target aud: 29 plus. ♦ Gary Taylor, progmg dir.

Windsor

KWKJ(FM)— Feb 21, 2002: 98.5 mhz; 2.3 kw. Ant 535 ft. TL: N38 35 37 W93 31 26. Stereo. Box 398, Warrensburg 64093. Phone: (660) 747-9191. Phone: (660) 747-3883. Fax: (660) 747-5611. Web Site: www.kwkj.com. Licensee: D & H Media LLC (acq 7-26-00; $47,500. for CP). Format: CHR. News staff: one; News: 1 hr wkly. Target aud: Students; Central MO State Univ. Students and like age group. ♦ Vance DeLozier, pres; Greg Hassler, VP; Marion Woods, gen mgr.

Montana

Alberton

KRQS(FM)—Not on air, target date: unknown: 105.5 mhz; 1.1 kw. Ant 787 ft. TL: N47 02 05 W114 41 11. Box 4106, Missoula 59806. Phone: (406) 728-5000. Fax: (406) 721-3020. Licensee: Fisher Radio Regional Group Inc. ♦ Chad Parrish, gen mgr.

Anaconda

KANA(AM)— Aug 1947: 580 khz; 1 kw-D, 197 w-N. TL: N46 07 50 W112 55 07. 105 Main St. 59711. Phone: (406) 563-8011. Fax: (406) 563-8259. Licensee: Jimmy Ray Carroll. Group owner: Jimmy Ray Carroll Stns (acq 10-9-01; grpsl). Format: Oldies. ♦ Kerrie Ross, gen mgr; Dave Michaels, progmg dir.

KGLM-FM— Jan 18, 1974: 97.7 mhz; 210 w. Ant 941 ft. TL: N46 06 07 W112 56 59. Stereo. 105 Main St. 59711. Phone: (406) 563-8011. Fax: (406) 563-8259. E-mail: kkglm@montana.com. Licensee: Jimmy Ray Carroll. Group owner: Jimmy Ray Carroll Stns (acq 10-9-01; grpsl). Format: Hot A/C. News staff: one; News: 4 hrs wkly. Target aud: 18 plus. ♦ Jim Carroll, pres; Kerrie Ross, gen mgr; Dave Michaels, progmg dir; John Mullen, pub affrs dir; Ron Huckeby, engrg VP.

Arlee

*KJFT(FM)—Not on air, target date: unknown: 90.3 mhz; 110 w. Ant 1,938 ft. TL: N47 01 04 W114 00 49. CSN International, 3232 W. MacArthur Blvd., Santa Ana, CA 92704. Phone: (714) 825-9463. Fax: (714) 825-9660. Web Site: www.csnradio.com. Licensee: CSN International (group owner). ♦ Jeffrey W. Smith, VP.

Baker

KATQ-FM—See Plentywood

KFLN(AM)— July 14, 1964: 960 khz; 5 kw-D, 91 w-N. TL: N46 22 31 W104 16 25. Box 790, 3600 Hwy. 7 59313. Phone: (406) 778-3371. Fax: (406) 778-3373. E-mail: kfln@midrivers.com. Licensee: Newell Broadcasting Corp. (acq 3-1-84; $870,000; 3-5-84). Network: ABC. Format: C&W. Spec prog: Farm 10 hrs wkly. ♦ Russ Newell, pres, gen mgr & progmg dir; Devin Bannister, gen sls mgr; Darrin Nutt, news dir; Tony Cuesta, chief of engrg.

KJJM(FM)—Co-owned with KFLN(AM). May 26, 2001: 100.5 mhz; 6 kw. Ant 108 ft. TL: N46 22 31 W104 16 25. Stereo. Format: Classic rock.

Belgrade

KCMM(FM)—Listing follows KGVW(AM).

KGVW(AM)— Feb 1, 1959: 640 khz; 10 kw-D, 1 kw-N, DA-2. TL: N45 46 15 W111 13 26. 2050 Amsterdam Rd. 59714. Phone: (406) 388-4281. Fax: (406) 388-1700. Licensee: Gallatin Valley Witness Inc. (acq 1996). Network: USA. Format: Relg, news/talk. News staff: one; News: 16 hrs wkly. Target aud: 35-64; business people, farmers & housewives. ♦ Bryan Brucks, sr VP, dev VP & adv dir; Mark Brashear, pres, gen mgr, opns mgr, gen sls mgr & adv VP; C.J. Swoboda, progmg dir; Dale Heidner, chief of engrg.

KCMM(FM)—Co-owned with KGVW(AM).Not on air, target date: unknown: 99.1 mhz; 6 kw. 200 ft.

KISN(FM)— Nov 1, 1963: 96.7 mhz; 8.6 kw. Ant 748 ft. TL: N45 40 24 W110 52 02. 125 W. Mendenhall, Suite 1, Bozeman 59715. Phone: (406) 586-2343. Fax: (406) 587-2202. Web Site: www.allhit967.com. Licensee: Capstar TX L.P. Group owner: Clear Channel Communications Inc. (acq 2-21-01; grpsl). Format: Hot adult contemp. Target aud: 25-54; women. ♦ Dave Cowan, gen mgr & progmg dir; Erik O'Connor, progmg dir.

*KQLU(FM)—Not on air, target date: unknown: 90.9 mhz; 2.35 kw vert. Ant 623 ft. TL: N45 57 25 W111 22 11. 5700 West Oaks Blvd., Rocklin, CA 95765. Phone: (916) 251-1600. Fax: (916) 251-1650. Web Site: www.air1.com. Licensee: Educational Media Foundation. Network: Air 1. ♦ Richard Jenkins, pres.

Big Sky

KBZM(FM)— July 31, 1998: 104.7 mhz; 5 kw. Ant 3,336 ft. TL: N45 16 41 W111 26 57. 102 S. 19th, Suite 5, Bozeman 59715. Phone: (406) 582-1045. Fax: (406) 582-0388. Licensee: Orion Media LLC (acq 10-29-03; $400,000). Format: Classic hits. Target aud: Adults; 25-54. ♦ Jeff Balding, gen mgr; Susan Balding, gen sls mgr; Colter Langan, progmg dir.

KSCY(FM)—Not on air, target date: unknown: 96.3 mhz; 175 w. Ant 3,326 ft. TL: N45 16 41 W111 26 57. Box 161268 59716. Phone: (406) 581-4818. Licensee: Radick Construction Inc. ♦ John Radick, VP.

Billings

KBBB(FM)— Dec 6, 1987: 103.7 mhz; 100 kw. 480 ft. TL: N45 46 00 W108 27 27. Stereo. Box 1276 59103. Phone: (406) 248-7827. Fax: (406) 252-9577. Web Site: www.bee104.com. Licensee: Capstar TX L.P. Group owner: Clear Channel Communications Inc. (acq 4-13-01; grpsl). Network: ABC Information & Entertainment. Rep: Tacher. Reddy, Begley & McCormick. Format: Adult contemp. Target aud: 25-54; general. ♦ Dennis Koffman, gen mgr; Roy Brown, opns dir, prom VP & progmg dir; Dick Jones, chief of engrg.

KBLG(AM)—Listing follows KRKX(FM).

*KBLW(FM)— August 2002: 90.1 mhz; 250 w vert. Ant 331 ft. TL: N45 45 51 W108 27 18. Stereo. Box 2426, Havre 59501. Secondary address: 317 First St., Havre 59501. Phone: (406) 265-5845. Fax: (406) 265-8860. E-mail: ynop@ynopradio.org. Web Site: www.ynopradio.org. Licensee: Hi-Line Radio Fellowship Inc. (acq 8-7-02). Format: Inspirational. Target aud: General; those looking for Christian inspirational music & progmg. ♦ Ed Matter, gen mgr; Brenda Boyum, opns mgr; Roger Lonnquist, dev dir; Brian Jackson, progmg dir.

KBUL(AM)— Mar 20, 1951: 970 khz; 5 kw-U, DA-N. TL: N45 44 35 W108 32 37. Stereo. Box 1276 59103. Secondary address: 27 N. 27th St., 23rd Fl. 59103. Phone: (406) 248-7827. Fax: (406) 252-9577. E-mail: denniscoffman@clearchannel.com. Licensee: Capstar TX L.P. Group owner: Clear Channel Communications Inc. (acq 4-13-01; grpsl). Network: ABC Information & Entertainment. Rep: Christal. Format: News. News staff: one; News: 2 hrs wkly. Target aud: 25-54. ♦ Dennis Coffman, pres & gen mgr; Roy Brown, sls dir & gen sls mgr; Tommy Braaten, progmg dir & mus dir; Dick Jones, chief of engrg.

KCTR-FM—Co-owned with KBUL(AM). Aug 14, 1979: 102.9 mhz; 100 kw. 500 ft. TL: N45 45 59 W108 27 19. Stereo. Format: Country. ♦ Erik Bowen, progmg dir.

*KEMC(FM)— Apr 25, 1973: 91.7 mhz; 100 kw. 520 ft. TL: N45 39 51 W108 34 14. Stereo. 1500 N. 30th St. 59101-0298. Phone: (406) 657-2941. Fax: (406) 657-2977. E-mail: mail@yellowstonepublicradio.org. Web Site: www.yellowstonepublicradio.org. Licensee: Montana State University/Billings. Network: Network: NPR, AP Radio. Format: News, class, jazz. News staff: one; News: 24 hrs wkly. Target aud: General. Spec prog: Folk 5 hrs wkly. ♦ Marvin Granger, gen mgr.

KGHL(AM)— June 8, 1928: 790 khz; 5 kw-U, DA-N. TL: N45 43 34 W108 36 35. Stereo. 222 N. 32nd St. 59101. Phone: (406) 238-1000. Fax: (406) 238-1038. Licensee: New Northwest Broadcasters LLC (group owner; acq 8-10-99; grpsl). Network: CBS. Rep: Allied Radio Partners. Dow, Lohnes & Albertson. Format: Country. News staff: one; News: 4 hrs wkly. Target aud: 25-54. ♦ Pete Benedetti, CEO; Tommy Ehrman, gen mgr; Dave Tester, sls dir; Jeff Howell, progmg dir; Mike Powers, chief of engrg.

KGHL-FM— August 1978: 98.5 mhz; 85 kw. 370 ft. TL: N45 45 51 W108 27 18. Stereo. Format: Continuous country. Target aud: 18-54. ♦ Karen Gallagher, progmg dir.

KKBR(FM)— Dec 17, 1963: 97.1 mhz; 28 kw. 325 ft. TL: N45 45 51 W108 27 18. Stereo. Box 1276 59103. Phone: (406) 248-7827. Fax: (406) 252-9577. Web Site: www.kbear.com. Licensee: Clear Channel Broadcasting Licenses Inc. Group owner: Clear Channel Communications Inc. (acq 4-13-01; grpsl). Format: Oldies. ♦ Dennis Koffman, gen mgr; Keith Todd, progmg dir.

*KLMT(FM)— Dec 18, 2002: 89.3 mhz; 1 kw vert. Ant 335 ft. TL: N45 45 41 W108 27 19. Western Inspirational Broadcasters Inc., 6363 Hwy. 50 E., Carson City, NV 89701. Phone: (775) 883-5647. Licensee: Western Inspirational Broadcasters Inc. Format: Contemp Christian.

News staff: 5; News: 7 hrs wkly. Spec prog: Children 2 hrs wkly. ♦ Paul Lierman, stn mgr; Tim Weidemann, opns mgr.

*KLRV(FM)— 2005: 90.9 mhz; 7.5 kw vert. Ant 593 ft. TL: N45 45 54 W108 27 19. 5700 West Oaks Blvd., Rocklin, CA 95765. Phone: (916) 251-1600. Fax: (916) 251-1650. Web Site: www.klove.com. Licensee: Educational Media Foundation. (acq 12-8-2004; $100,000. for CP with CP for KLWC(FM) Casper, WY). Network: K-Love. Format: Christian. ♦ Lloyd Parker, gen mgr.

KMZK(AM)— Sept 8, 1946: 1240 khz; 1 kw-U. TL: N45 45 26 W108 32 08. Box 31038, 636 Haugen St. 59102. Phone: (406) 245-3121. Fax: (406) 245-0822. E-mail: www.genmgr@kmzk.com. Web Site: www.kmzk.com. Licensee: Elenbaas Media Inc. (acq 1-8-98; $115,000). Format: Contemp hit, urban contemp. Target aud: 18-44; young & energetic high school & college students & young adults. ♦ Herm Elenbaas, pres.

KQBL(FM)— December 1998: 105.1 mhz; 6 kw. 233 ft. TL: N45 45 57 W108 27 17. 222 N. 32nd St., 10th Floor 59101. Phone: (406) 238-1000. Fax: (406) 238-1038. Web Site: www.1051theend.com. Licensee: New Northwest Broadcasters LLC (group owner; (acq 10-26-99; grpsl). Target aud: 25-54. ♦ Pete Benedetti, CEO; Tommy Ehrman, gen mgr; Tom Oakes, opns mgr; Dean Alexander, sls dir; Ray Edwards, progmg VP; Casey Paul, mus dir; Mike Powers, chief of engrg.

KRKX(FM)— July 1989: 94.1 mhz; 100 kw. 590 ft. TL: N45 32 25 W108 38 31. Stereo. 2075 Central Ave. 59102. Phone: (406) 652-8400. Fax: (406) 652-4899. Web Site: www.krkx.com. Licensee: Fisher Broadcasting Inc. Group owner: Fisher Broadcasting Company (acq 12-28-94; grpsl, including co-located AM; FTR: 2-20-95). Format: Classic rock. Target aud: 25-54; affluent. ♦ Mark Byford, gen mgr; Terry Keys, opns mgr; Augie Aga, gen sls mgr.

KBLG(AM)—Co-owned with KRKX(FM). Sept 25, 1955: 910 khz; 1 kw-D, 63 w-N. TL: N45 45 10 W108 30 57. Web Site: www.kblg.com. Network: Network: CBS, ABC News/Talk. Format: News/talk, sports. News staff: one; News: 46 hrs wkly. Target aud: 35-64; upscale executives. ♦ Debbie Sundberg, gen mgr.

KRZN(FM)— 1998: 96.3 mhz; 100 kw. 695 ft. TL: N45 45 37 W108 27 09. 2075 Central Ave. 59102. Phone: (406) 652-8400. Fax: (406) 652-4899. Web Site: www.thezone963.com. Licensee: Fisher Radio Regional Group Inc. Group owner: Fisher Broadcasting Company. Format: New rock. ♦ Dan Reese, gen mgr & stn mgr.

KURL(AM)— Oct 15, 1959: 730 khz; 5 kw-D, 236 w-N. TL: N45 45 29 W108 29 53. Box 31038 59107. Secondary address: 636 Haugen 59107. Phone: (406) 245-3121. Fax: (406) 245-0822. E-mail: genmgr@kurlradio.com. Web Site: www.kurlradio.com. Licensee: Elenbaas Media Inc. (acq 11-14-94; $300,000; 1-2-95). Network: Network: USA, AP Radio. Format: Relg, syndicated talk. Target aud: 35-64. ♦ Herm Elenbaas, pres & gen mgr.

KYYA(FM)— Apr 5, 1969: 93.3 mhz; 100 kw. 700 ft. TL: N45 45 37 W108 27 09. Stereo. 2075 Central Ave. 59102. Phone: (406) 652-8400. Fax: (406) 652-4899. Web Site: www.y93.9.com. Licensee: Fisher Broadcasting Inc. Group owner: Fisher Broadcasting Company (acq 5-1-95; grpsl; FTR: 2-20-95). Rep: Allied Radio Partners. Format: Hot adult contemp. News staff: one; News: 2 hrs wkly. Target aud: 18-49; women. Spec prog: Casey Kasems Hot-20. ♦ Larry Roberts, chmn & pres; Debbie Sundberg, gen mgr, gen sls mgr, natl sls mgr & rgnl sls mgr; Ted Brown, progmg dir; Michael Lyon, news dir; Bruce Faulkner, chief of engrg.

KZRV(FM)— 2001: 107.5 mhz;; 100 kw. Ant 984 ft. TL: N45 44 29 W108 08 19. 222 N. 32nd St. 59101. Phone: (406) 238-1000. Fax: (406) 238-1038. Licensee: New Northwest Broadcasters LLC (group owner; acq 10-26-99). Format: Hot adult contemp. Target aud: 25-54. ♦ Pete Benedetti, CEO; Dave Tester, gen mgr.

Bozeman

*KBMC(FM)— October 1991: 102.1 mhz; 20.5 kw. 728 ft. TL: N45 38 18 W111 16 05. Stereo. 1500 N. 30th St., Billings 59101-0298. Phone: (406) 657-2941. Fax: (406) 657-2977. Licensee: Montana State University/Billings. (acq 3-29-91; 4-15-91). Format: Class, jazz, news. ♦ Marvin F. Granger, gen mgr; Randall Rocks, chief of engrg.

KBOZ(AM)— Dec 19, 1975: 1090 khz; 5 kw-U, DA-N. TL: N45 36 58 W111 05 16. Box 20 59718. Secondary address: 5445 Johnson Rd.

Stations in the U.S. Montana

59715. Phone: (406) 587-9999. Fax: (406) 587-5855. Licensee: Reier Broadcasting Co. Inc. (group owner; acq 10-18-96; grpsl). Network: Network: CBS, ABC Information & Entertainment, Jones Radio Networks. Format: Talk. Target aud: 25-64. ♦ Bill Reier, gen mgr & opns mgr; Eric Reier, gen sls mgr; Brian Bennett, progmg dir; Les Clay, news dir; Dick Jones, chief of engrg.

KOBB-FM—Co-owned with KBOZ(AM). Nov 1, 1980: 93.7 mhz; 100 kw. 245 ft. TL: N45 41 35 W110 58 50. Stereo. Format: Oldies. Target aud: 25-54. ♦ Tuck Reier, opns dir; Dave Visscher, progmg dir.

KBOZ-FM—Listing follows KOBB(AM).

*KGLT(FM)— December 1963: 91.9 mhz; 2 kw. 365 ft. TL: N45 41 35 W110 59 00. Stereo. Montana State Univ., Rm. 324 59717. Phone: (406) 994-3001. Fax: (406) 994-1987. Licensee: Montana State University. Format: Div, educ, alternative. Target aud: General. Spec prog: Black one hr, class 11 hrs, folk 12 hrs wkly. ♦ Philip Charles, gen mgr; Jim Kehoe, mus dir; John Campbell, chief of engrg; Ron Craig Head, mktg.

KMMS(AM)— Oct 15, 1939: 1450 khz; 1 kw-U. TL: N45 39 33 W111 03 22. 125 W. Mendenhall 59715. Phone: (406) 586-2343. Fax: (406) 587-2202. Web Site: www.mooseradio.com. Licensee: Capstar TX L.P. Group owner: Clear Channel Communications Inc. (acq 2-21-01; grpsl). Network: ABC. Rep: Clear Channel. Hogan & Hartson. Format: News/talk, sports. News: one hr wkly. Target aud: 35-64. ♦ Lowery Mays, chmn; Randy Michaels, pres; Dave Cowan, gen mgr; Kay Ruh, sls dir, gen sls mgr & natl sls mgr; Sylvia Drain, rgnl sls mgr; Mary Atkins, prom dir & prom mgr; George Carter, progmg dir; John Russell, news dir; Ron Huckaby, chief of engrg.

KMMS-FM— Aug 14, 1986: 95.1 mhz; 94 kw. 781 ft. TL: N45 40 24 W110 52 02. Rep: McGavren Guild. Format: AAA. ♦ Michelle Wolfe, progmg dir.

KOBB(AM)— May 22, 1950: 1230 kHz; 1 kw-U, DA-2. TL: N45 42 02 W111 02 49. Box 20 59718. Secondary address: 5445 Johnson Rd. 59718. Phone: (406) 587-9999. Fax: (406) 587-5855. E-mail: reier@bigsky.net. Licensee: Reier Broadcasting Co. Inc. (group owner; (acq 2-19-93; $125,000;. FTR: 5-17-93). Network: ABC. Tacher. Reddy, Begley & McCormick. Format: Adult Standards. News: 15 hrs wkly. Target aud: 30 plus; affluent adults. ♦ William Reier Sr., pres & gen mgr; Eric Reier, gen sls mgr; Diane Stovall, progmg dir; Dick Jones, chief of engrg.

KBOZ-FM—Co-owned with KOBB(AM). 1983: 99.9 mhz; 100 kw. 338 ft. TL: N45 41 34 W110 58 57. Format: Hot country. ♦ Terry Michaels, progmg dir; Diane Stovall, chief of engrg.

KOZB(FM)—See Livingston

*KRFR(FM)—Not on air, target date: unknown: 89.3 mhz; 7 kw vert. Ant 679 ft. TL: N45 57 25 W111 22 11. 5700 West Oaks Blvd., Rocklin, CA 95765. Phone: (916) 251-1600. Fax: (916) 251-1650. Licensee: Educational Media Foundation. ♦ Lloyd Parker, gen mgr.

KZMY(FM)— 2004: 103.5 mhz; 100 kw. Ant 948 ft. TL: N45 57 25 W111 22 11. 125 W. Mendenhall St., Suite 102 59715. Phone: (406) 556-0123. Fax: (406) 587-2202. E-mail: kzmy@hotmail.com. Web Site: my1035.com. Licensee: Capstar TX L.P. Group owner: Clear Channel Communications Inc. (acq 2-27-2004); $1.4 million. for CP). Format: Adult contemp. ♦ Nick Shannon, gen mgr & progmg dir.

Butte

KAAR(FM)— Nov 1, 1988: 92.5 mhz; 4.5 kw. 1,840 ft. TL: N46 00 29 W112 26 30. 750 Dewey Blvd., Suite 1 59701. Secondary address: Box 3788 59702. Phone: (406) 494-1030. Fax: (406) 494-6020. Licensee: Fisher Radio Regional Group Inc. Group owner: Fisher Broadcasting Company (acq 12-28-94; grpsl; FTR: 2-20-95). Rep: McGavren Guild. Format: Country. News: 8 hrs wkly. Target aud: General. ♦ Chris Ackerman, gen mgr; Jeff Gray, opns dir; Rene Wimberley, sls dir; Tom O'Neill, news dir & pub affrs dir.

*KAPC(FM)— 1999: 91.3 mhz; 880 w. 1,893 ft. TL: N46 00 29 W112 26 30. c/o KUFM(FM), Univ. of Montana, Missoula 59812. Phone: (406) 243-4931. Fax: (406) 243-3299. Web Site: www.kufm.org. Licensee: University of Montana. Format: Jazz, classical, news. News: 2 hrs wkly. ♦ William Marcus, gen mgr.

KBOW(AM)— Feb 14, 1947: 550 khz; 5 kw-D, 1 kw-N, DA-N. TL: N45 58 30 W112 34 18. Box 3389 59702. Secondary address: 660 Dewey Blvd. 59702. Phone: (406) 494-7777. Fax: (406) 494-5534. E-mail: bbi@inpch.com. Licensee: Butte Broadcasting Inc. (acq 1-13-94; $550,000 with co-located FM; 1-31-94). Network: CBS. Haley, Bader & Potts. Format: Sports. Target aud: 25 plus; general. Spec prog: Farm 5 hrs, relg 2 hrs wkly. ♦ Fran Workman, opns mgr & progmg dir; Ron Davis, pres, gen mgr & gen sls mgr; Mike Beckworth, prom dir; Paul Panisko, progmg dir; Pat Schulte, news dir; Chuck Beardslee, engrg VP.

KOPR(FM)—Co-owned with KBOW(AM). Oct 26, 1972: 94.1 mhz; 100 kw. 1,840 ft. TL: N46 00 23 W112 26 28. (CP: 58.4 kw). Stereo. (Acq 4-1-94). Format: 80's & more. News staff: 2; News: 5 hrs wkly. Target aud: 25-45; women. ♦ Fran Workman, pub affrs dir.

*KFRD(FM)— 2003: 88.3 mhz; 650 w. Ant 1,729 ft. TL: N46 00 27 W112 26 30. Family Stations Inc., 4135 Northgate Blvd., Suite 1, Sacramento, CA 95834. Phone: (510) 568-6200. Fax: (510) 568-6190. Licensee: Family Stations Inc. (group owner). Format: Relg. ♦ Harold Camping, gen mgr.

KMBR(FM)—Listing follows KXTL(AM).

*KMSM-FM— 1975: 106.9 mhz; 500 w. 93 ft. TL: N46 00 43 W112 33 23. Stereo. Student Union Bldg, Montana Tech. 59701. Phone: (406) 496-4601. E-mail: kmsm@mtech.edu. Web Site: www.mtech.edu/kmsm. Licensee: Associated Students of Montana Tech. Pepper & Corazzini. Format: Educ, div, alternative. News: 2 hrs wkly. Target aud: General; very diversified group. Spec prog: Jazz 5 hrs, relg 3 hrs, class 2 hrs wkly. ♦ Wendy Dyer, gen mgr; Ben Carter, stn mgr.

KXTL(AM)— 1927: 1370 khz; 5 kw-U. TL: N46 09 37 W112 37 54. Stereo. Box 3788 59702. Secondary address: 750 Dewey Blvd., Suite 1 59702. Phone: (406) 494-4442. Fax: (406) 494-6020. Web Site: www.kxtl.com. Licensee: Fisher Radio Regional Group Inc. Group owner: Fisher Broadcasting Company (acq 12-28-94; grpsl, including co-located FM; FTR: 2-20-95). Rep: McGavren Guild. Format: Hits of the 50s, 60s & 70s. News: 14 hrs wkly. Target aud: 25-54. Spec prog: Relg one hr wkly. ♦ Chris Ackerman, gen mgr & gen sls mgr; Jeff Gray, opns mgr, progmg dir & news dir; Roger Bennett, chief of engrg.

KMBR(FM)—Co-owned with KXTL(AM). Feb 7, 1980: 95.5 mhz; 50 kw. 1,820 ft. TL: N46 00 29 W112 26 30. Stereo. Phone: (406) 494-5895. Web Site: www.955kmbr.com. Rep: McGavren Guild. Format: Classic rock.

Cascade

KIKF(AM)— January 2002: 104.9 mhz; 94 kw. Ant 2,037 ft. TL: N47 09 34 W111 00 39. Box 3129, Great Falls 59403. Phone: (406) 761-2800. Fax: (406) 727-7218. E-mail: tjlee@mykikfm.com. Web Site: www.mykikfm.com. Licensee: Fisher Radio Regional Group Inc. Group owner: Fisher Broadcasting Company (acq 3-12-01). Format: Country. ♦ Terry Strickland, gen mgr.

Chinook

KRYK(FM)—Licensed to Chinook. See Havre

Colstrip

KMCJ(FM)— August 2001: 99.5 mhz; 100 kw. Ant 800 ft. TL: N46 10 32 W106 24 21. Stereo. Box 2426, Havre 59501. Secondary address: 317 First St., Havre 59501. Phone: (406) 265-5845. Fax: (406) 265-8860. E-mail: ynop@ynopradio.org. Web Site: www.ynopradio.org. Licensee: Hi-Line Radio Fellowship Inc. (acq 4-13-01; $52,000. for CP). Format: Christian Inspirational. Target aud: General:; those looking for alternative progmg. ♦ Ed Matter, gen mgr; Brenda Boyum, opns mgr; Roger Lonnquist, dev dir; Brian Jackson, progmg dir.

Columbia Falls

KKMT(FM)— Nov 17, 1998: 95.9 mhz; 50 kw. 285 ft. TL: N48 27 35 W114 20 25. Box 5409, 2432 Hwy. 2 E., Kalispell 59903-5409. Phone: (406) 755-8700. Fax: (406) 755-8770. E-mail: kkmt@beebroadcasting.com. Web Site: www.beebroadcasting.com. Licensee: Bee Broadcasting Inc. (group owner; acq 12-31-97; $337,500). Format: Soft rock. ♦ Mark Wagner, gen mgr.

Conrad

KTZZ(FM)— July 1, 1997: 93.7 mhz; 100 kw. 558 ft. TL: N47 49 13 W111 47 56. Box 1239, Great Falls 59403. Secondary address: 3313 15th St. N.E., Black Eagle 59414. Phone: (406) 761-1310. Fax: (406) 454-3775. Licensee: Jeannine M. Mason. Format: Classic rock. News staff: one; News: 5 hrs wkly. Target aud: 25-54; general. ♦ Laurie Vosberg, adv dir; Steven Dow, pres & chief of engrg.

Deer Lodge

KBCK(AM)— 1963: 1400 khz; 1 kw-U. TL: N46 24 26 W112 43 08. 105 Main St., Anaconda 59711. Phone: (406) 563-8011. Fax: (406) 563-8259. Licensee: Jimmy Ray Carroll. Group owner: Jimmy Ray Carroll Stns (acq 10-9-01; grpsl). Format: Real country. Target aud: 18 plus. Spec prog: Farm 2 hrs wkly. ♦ Jimmy Ray Carroll, pres; Kerrie Ross, gen mgr; Dave Michaels, progmg dir.

KQRV(FM)— July 4, 1997: 96.9 mhz; 20 kw. Ant 984 ft. TL: N46 06 03 W112 57 00. 7956 Eastside Rd. 59722-8799. Phone: (406) 846-1100. Fax: (406) 846-1100. E-mail: river@3riversdbs.net. Licensee: Robert Cummings Toole. Format: Country, full service. ♦ Robert Cummings Toole, gen mgr; Karen Toole, gen sls mgr.

Dillon

KBEV-FM—Listing follows KDBM(AM).

KDBM(AM)— Jan 1, 1957: 1490 khz; 1 kw-U. TL: N45 14 13 W112 38 32. 610 N. Montana St. 59725. Phone: (406) 683-2800. Phone: (406) 683-6171. Fax: (406) 683-9480. Licensee: Dead-Air Broadcasting Co. Inc. (acq 3-6-98; $330,000 with co-located FM). Network: ABC Information & Entertainment. Format: Country. ♦ Jo Ann Juliano, pres; Kathy Wise, gen mgr; Kasey Briggs, sls dir; John Schuyler, progmg dir & news dir; Ron Huckaby, chief of engrg.

KBEV-FM—Co-owned with KDBM(AM). August 1972: 98.3 mhz; 10.5 kw. 495 ft. TL: N45 14 22 W112 40 03. Stereo. Format: Contemp hit.

*KDWG(FM)—Not on air, target date: unknown: 90.9 mhz; 850 w. -236 ft. TL: N45 12 33 W112 38 14. Univ. of Montana, Western, Campus Box 52, 710 S. Atlantic St. 59725. Phone: (406) 683-7156. Licensee: Western Montana College University of Montana. Format: Mainstream, educ, rock. ♦ Cory Craden, mus dir.

Dutton

KVVR(FM)— Aug 7, 2001: 97.9 mhz; 100 kw. Ant 715 ft. TL: N47 36 52 W111 20 51. Box 3309, Great Falls 59403. Phone: (406) 761-7600. Fax: (406) 761-5511. Licensee: CCR-Great Falls IV LLC. Group owner: Cherry Creek Radio LLC (acq 12-19-2003; grpsl). Format: Adult contemp. ♦ Ron Korb, gen mgr.

East Helena

KHKR-FM— Apr 13, 1989: 104.1 mhz; 5 kw. Ant 653 ft. TL: N46 46 11 W112 01 25. Stereo. 110 Broadway St., Helena 59601. Phone: (406) 442-4490. Fax: (406) 447-7356. Web Site: www.khkr.com. Licensee: CCR-Helena IV LLC. Group owner: Cherry Creek Radio LLC (acq 12-19-2003; grpsl). Format: Hot country. Target aud: 25-54. ♦ Dewey Bruce, gen mgr.

Montana

KKGR(AM)— May 26, 1988: 680 kHz; 5 kw-D. TL: N46 33 58 W111 54 12. 1400 11th Ave., Helena 59601. Phone: (406) 443-5237. Phone: (406) 442-7595. Licensee: KKGR Inc. (acq 3-16-99). Format: Oldies. ♦Jim Schaffer, gen mgr; Ron Davidson, gen mgr.

East Missoula

KLCY(AM)—Licensed to East Missoula. See Missoula

Florence

KDTR(FM)— 2005: 103.3 mhz; 1.95 kw. Ant 2,083 ft. TL: N46 48 06 W113 58 22. 2425 W. Central Ave., Suite 203, Missoula 59801. Phone: (406) 721-6800. Fax: (406) 329-1850. Web Site: www.trail1033.com. Licensee: Spanish Peaks Broadcasting Inc. Format: Triple A. ♦Dave Cowan, gen mgr; Robert Chase, progmg dir.

Forsyth

KIKC(AM)— Oct 10, 1975: 1250 kHz; 5 kw-D. TL: N46 15 30 W106 41 21. Box 1140 59327. Secondary address: 210 Front St. 59327. Phone: (406) 346-2711. Fax: (406) 346-2712. E-mail: kikc@rangeweb.net. Web Site: klkcamfm.com. Licensee: Miles City, Forsyth Broadcasting Inc. (acq 1996; grpsl). Rep: Interep. Allied Radio Partners Format: CHR, oldies. Target aud: 18-35; general. ♦Stephen Marks, pres; Dick Haugen, VP, gen mgr & adv mgr.

KIKC-FM— September 1980: 101.3 mhz; 100 kw. 1,010 ft. TL: N46 10 32 W106 24 21. Stereo. Web Site: klkcamfm.com. Network: Network: Westwood One, CNN Radio. Rep: Allied Radio Partners. Format: Country. News: 4 hrs wkly. Target aud: 18 plus; general. ♦Steve Marks, CEO.

Fort Belknap Agency

***KGVA(FM)**— October 1996: 88.1 mhz; 95 kw. 797 ft. TL: N48 11 18 W108 42 36. Box 159, Harlem 59526. Phone: (406) 353-4656. Fax: (406) 353-2898. Licensee: Fort Belknap College. Network: NPR. Format: Eclectic, news/talk. Target aud: General. Spec prog: American Indian 15 hrs wkly. ♦Will Gray Jr., gen mgr.

Glasgow

KLAN(FM)— Mar 1, 1983: 93.5 mhz; 3 kw. 300 ft. TL: N48 05 42 W106 37 08. Stereo. Box 671 59230. Phone: (406) 228-9336. Fax: (406) 228-9338. E-mail: kltz@kltz.com. Web Site: www.kltz.com. Licensee: Glasgow Broadcasting Corp. Format: Adult contemp. ♦Shirley Trang, gen mgr; Tim Philips, progmg dir; Stan Ozark, news dir.

KLTZ(AM)— Aug 14, 1954: 1240 kHz; 1 kw-U. TL: N48 13 09 W106 38 54. Box 671 59230. Phone: (406) 228-9336. Fax: (406) 228-9338. E-mail: kltz@kltz.com. Web Site: www.kltz.com. Licensee: Glasgow Broadcasting Inc. Network: ABC Information & Entertainment. Format: C&W. Target aud: 25 plus. ♦Shirley Trang, gen mgr; Tim Phillips, progmg dir; Stan Ozark, news dir.

Glendive

KDZN(FM)— Dec 21, 1969: 96.5 mhz; 100 kw. 400 ft. TL: N47 05 15 W104 48 04. Stereo. 210 S. Douglas 59330. Phone: (406) 377-3377. Fax: (406) 365-2181. Licensee: Magic Air Communications Co. Format: Country. News: 4 hrs wkly. Target aud: 25-54. ♦Steven Marks, pres; Paul Sturlaugson, gen mgr; Marcy Copp, progmg dir.

KGLE(AM)— Aug 22, 1962: 590 kHz; 1 kw-D. TL: N47 05 50 W104 47 09. Box 931, 86 Seven Mile Dr. 59330. Phone: (406) 377-3331. Fax: (406) 377-3332. E-mail: kgle@midrivers.com. Licensee: Friends of Christian Radio Inc. (acq 1-12-93; $90,000; 2-1-93). Network: Moody. Format: Relg, farm. Target aud: 35-64; general. ♦Tom Fatzinger, pres; Jim McBride, gen mgr.

KXGN(AM)— Sept 23, 1948: 1400 kHz; 1 kw-U. TL: N47 05 40 W104 42 50. 210 S. Douglas 59330. Phone: (406) 377-3377. Fax: (406) 365-2181. E-mail: kxgnkdzn@midrivers.com. Web Site: www.glendivebroadcasting.com. Licensee: Glendive Broadcasting Corp. Network: ABC Information & Entertainment. Format: Adult contemp, oldies. News staff: one; News: 6 hrs wkly. Spec prog: Derry Brownfield 5 hrs, farm 2 hrs wkly. ♦Stephen Marks, pres; Paul Strulaugson, exec VP; Paul Sturlaugson, gen mgr. Co-owned TV: KXGN-TV affil

Great Falls

KAAK(FM)—Listing follows KXGF(AM).

***KAFH(FM)**—Not on air, target date: unknown: 91.5 mhz; 250 w. Ant 249 ft. TL: N47 32 23 W111 17 06. Drawer 2440, Tupelo, MS 38803. Phone: (662) 844-8888. Fax: (662) 842-6791. Licensee: American Family Association. ♦Marvin Sanders, gen mgr.

KEIN(AM)— July 1922: 1310 kHz; 5 kw-D, 1 kw-N. TL: N47 31 20 W111 23 18. Box 1239 59403. Secondary address: 3313 15th St. N.E., Black Eagle 59414. Phone: (406) 761-1310. Fax: (406) 454-3775. Licensee: Munson Radio Inc. (acq 7-1-97). Format: Adult standards. News staff: one; News: 5 hrs wkly. Target aud: 35 plus. ♦Laurie Vosberg, adv dir; Steven Dow, pres & chief of engrg.

***KFRW(FM)**—Not on air, target date: unknown: 91.9 mhz; 50 kw. Ant 466 ft. TL: N47 49 13 W111 47 56. 136 E.S. Temple, Suite 1630, Salt Lake City, UT 84111. Phone: (801) 359-3147. Fax: (801) 359-8112. Web Site: www.familyradio.com. Licensee: Family Stations Inc. ♦Harold Camping, gen mgr.

***KGFA(FM)**—Not on air, target date: unknown: 90.7 mhz; 250 w. Ant 249 ft. TL: N47 32 23 W111 17 06. Drawer 3206, Tupelo, MS 38803. Phone: (662) 844-8888. Fax: (662) 842-6791. Licensee: American Family Association. ♦Marvin Sanders, gen mgr.

***KGFC(FM)**— 1996: 88.9 mhz; 6 kw. Ant 243 ft. TL: N47 27 53 W111 21 24. Stereo. Box 2426, Havre 59501. Phone: (406) 265-5845. Fax: (406) 265-8860. E-mail: ynop@ynopradio.org. Web Site: www.ynopradio.org. Licensee: Hi-Line Radio Fellowship Inc. Format: Christian Inspirational. Target aud: General; those looking for inspirational Christian music & progmg. ♦Ed Matter, gen mgr; Brenda Boyum, opns mgr; Roger Lonnquist, dev dir; Brian Jackson, progmg dir.

***KGPR(FM)**— April 1984: 89.9 mhz; 9.5 kw. 295 ft. TL: N47 32 23 W111 17 06. Stereo. Box 3343 59403. Secondary address: Box 6010, 2100 16th Ave. S. 59406-6010. Phone: (406) 268-3739. Fax: (406) 268-3736. E-mail: kgpr@msugf.edu. Licensee: Great Falls Public Radio Association. Network: Network: PRI, NPR. Format: Class, educ, news, world mus. News: 44 hrs wkly. Target aud: General. ♦Joseph Duffy, pres; Bill Tacke, VP; Craig Peritz, stn mgr; Karola Brockway, dev dir; Doug Wendt, progmg dir; Pat Long, mus dir; Mike Dalton, news dir & pub affrs dir; Jim Van Cleave, chief of engrg.

KINX(FM)— Feb 4, 2002: 107.3 mhz; 94 kw. Ant 2,037 ft. TL: N47 09 34 W111 00 39. Box 3129 59403. Phone: (406) 761-2800. Fax: (406) 727-7218. E-mail: mail@x107.com. Web Site: www.x107.com. Licensee: Fisher Radio Regional Group Inc. Group owner: Fisher Broadcasting Company. Format: Active rock. ♦Terry Strickland, gen mgr.

KLFM(FM)— Feb 14, 1982: 92.9 mhz; 98 kw. 410 ft. TL: N47 32 19 W111 15 41. Box 3309 59403. Secondary address: 20 3rd St. N. 59403. Phone: (406) 761-7600. Fax: (406) 761-5511. Licensee: CCR-Great Falls IV LLC. Group owner: Cherry Creek Radio LLC (acq 12-19-2003; grpsl). Rep: Allied Radio Partners. Format: Good time oldies. Target aud: 25-54. ♦Ron Korb, gen mgr & gen sls mgr.

KLSK(FM)— 2003: 100.3 mhz; 100 kw. Ant 495 ft. TL: N47 15 57 W111 08 39. 6080 Mt. Moriah, Memphis, TN 38115. Phone: (901) 375-9324. Fax: (901) 375-0041. Licensee: Flinn Broadcasting Corp. Format: Hip-hop-rap. ♦Karen Wheatley, gen mgr.

KMON(AM)— May 30, 1947: 560 kHz; 5 kw-U, DA-N. TL: N47 25 29 W111 17 20. Stereo. Box 3309, 20 3rd St. N., Suite 231 59401. Phone: (406) 761-7600. Fax: (406) 761-5511. E-mail: 560@kmon.com. Web Site: www.kmon.com. Licensee: CCR-Great Falls IV LLC. Group owner: Cherry Creek Radio LLC (acq 12-19-2003; grpsl). Network: ABC Information & Entertainment. Rep: Allied Radio Partners. Pepper & Corazzini. Format: Country, farm. News staff: one; News: 20 hrs wkly. Target aud: 35-64. Spec prog: Sports 5 hrs wkly. ♦Ron Korb, gen mgr; Melissa Horton, gen sls mgr; Skip Walters, progmg dir & news dir; Ken Eklund, chief of engrg.

KMON-FM— Oct 1, 1972: 94.5 mhz; 98 kw. 495 ft. TL: N47 32 19 W111 15 41. Stereo. Web Site: www.kmonfm.com. Format: Hot country. News staff: one; News: 5 hrs wkly. Target aud: 25-54. ♦Ron Korb, sls dir & gen sls mgr; Scott Hershey, progmg dir.

KQDI(AM)— 1955: 1450 kHz; 1 kw-U. TL: N47 31 26 W111 18 04. 1300 Central Ave. W. 59404. Phone: (406) 761-2800. Fax: (406) 727-7218. Licensee: Fisher Radio Regional Group Inc. Group owner: Fisher Broadcasting Company (acq 9-27-95; with co-located FM). Rep: Christal. Format: News/talk. Target aud: 25-54. ♦Terry Strickland, gen mgr; Dave France, opns mgr & progmg dir; Anna Palagi, gen sls mgr; Pam Bennett, mus dir; Joe Bower, chief of engrg.

KQDI-FM— Dec 31, 1963: 106.1 mhz; 100 kw. 276 ft. TL: N47 31 57 W111 16 41. Stereo. Box 3129 Format: Classic rock, AOR. Target aud: 18-49.

KXGF(AM)— 1987: 1400 kHz; 1 kw-U. TL: N47 27 56 W111 20 22. Box 3129 59403. Secondary address: 1300 Central Ave. W. 59403. Phone: (406) 761-2800. Fax: (406) 727-7218. Licensee: Fisher Radio Regional Group Inc. Group owner: Fisher Broadcasting Company (acq 12-28-94; grpsl, including co-located FM; FTR: 2-20-95). Rep: McGavren Guild. Format: MOR. Target aud: 35-64. Spec prog: Farm 2 hrs wkly. ♦Larry Roberts, pres; Terry Strickland, gen mgr; Dave France, opns mgr & sls dir; Kim Landers, gen sls mgr; Tammie Toren, progmg dir; Joe Bower, chief of engrg.

KAAK(FM)— Co-owned with KXGF(AM). June 19, 1972: 98.9 mhz; 100 kw. 500 ft. TL: N47 32 08 W111 17 02. Stereo. Format: Adult contemp. Target aud: 25-44. ♦Tonya Jorgensen, gen sls mgr.

Hamilton

KBAZ(FM)—Listing follows KLYQ(AM).

KLYQ(AM)— Feb 3, 1961: 1240 kHz; 1 kw-U. TL: N46 15 22 W114 09 45. Box 660, 217 N. 3rd St., Suite L 59840. Phone: (406) 363-3010. Fax: (406) 363-6436. E-mail: contact@klyq.com. Web Site: www.klyq.com. Licensee: Capstar TX L.P. Group owner: Clear Channel Communications Inc. (acq 2-21-01; grpsl). Network: ABC Information & Entertainment. Format: News/talk. News staff: one; News: 25 hrs wkly. Target aud: 25-54; adults. ♦Gene Peterson, gen mgr; Jim Coulter, sls dir; Steve Fullerton, opns dir, progmg dir & news dir; Mike Daniels, chief of engrg.

KBAZ(FM)— Co-owned with KLYQ(AM). Feb 11, 1969: 96.3 mhz; 85 kw. Ant 2,066 ft. TL: N46 48 08 W113 58 21. Stereo. 400 Ryman, Missoula 59801. Web Site: www.kluq.com. Format: Alternative rock. ♦Denny Bedard, opns dir; Jim Coulter, gen sls mgr.

***KMZO(FM)**—Not on air, target date: unknown: 90.3 mhz; 725 w. Ant 331 ft. TL: N46 13 46 W114 14 01. Faith Communications Corp., 2201 S. 6th St., Las Vegas, NV 89104. Phone: (702) 731-5452. Fax: (702) 731-1992. E-mail: info@sosradio.net. Web Site: www.sosnetwork.org. Licensee: Faith Communications Corp. Format: Contemp Christian.

***KUFN(FM)**— October 1998: 91.9 mhz; 850 w. 499 ft. TL: N46 13 46 W114 14 01. c/o KUFM(FM), Univ. of Montana, Missoula 59812. Phone: (406) 243-4931. Fax: (406) 243-3299. Web Site: www.kurn.org. Licensee: The University of Montana. Format: Jazz, classical, news, eclectic. News: 2 hrs wkly. ♦William Marcus, gen mgr; Daniel Plante, stn mgr.

KXDR(FM)— July 16, 1999: 98.7 mhz; 100 kw. 417 ft. TL: N46 30 36 W113 58 45. 1600 North Ave. W., Suite 101, Missoula 59801. Phone: (406) 728-5000. Fax: (406) 721-3020. Web Site: www.starfm.net. Licensee: Fisher Radio Regional Group Inc. Group owner: Fisher Broadcasting Company Format: Hot adult contemp. ♦Larry Roberts, pres; Chad Parrish, gen mgr; Bill McPherson, gen sls mgr; Cary Nicklay, natl sls mgr; Shawn Wilde, progmg dir; Vern Argo, chief of engrg.

Hardin

KHDN(AM)— Dec 28, 1962: 1230 kHz; 1 kw-U. TL: N45 42 55 W107 35 59. Box 230 59034. Phone: (406) 665-2828. Fax: (406) 665-2131. Web Site: www.bigskyradio.net. Licensee: Sun Mountain Inc. (acq 11-30-2000). Network: Jones Radio Networks. Format: Adult standards/news. News: 2 hrs wkly. Target aud: 25-54. ♦Richard Solberg, pres & gen mgr.

KMHK(FM)— 1975: 95.5 mhz; 100 kw. 984 ft. TL: N45 44 29 W108 08 19. Stereo. Box 1276, Billings 59103. Phone: (406) 248-7827. Fax: (406) 252-9577. Web Site: www.kmhk.com. Licensee: Clear Channel Broadcasting Licenses Inc. Group owner: Clear Channel Communications Inc. (acq 4-13-01; grpsl). Format: Rock. Target aud: 18-34; general. ♦Dennis Koffman, gen mgr; Jay Branden, mktg dir & progmg dir.

Havre

*KNMC(FM)— February 1979: 90.1 mhz; 10 w. 56 ft. TL: N48 32 30 W109 41 06. (CP: 375 w, ant -112 ft. TL: N48 32 31 W109 41 17). Stereo. c/o KEMC, 1500 University Dr., Billings 59101-0298. Phone: (406) 657-2941. Fax: (406) 657-2977. Licensee: Montana State University-Northern. Format: Class, jazz. Spec prog: Class 10 hrs wkly. ♦Marvin Granger, gen mgr; Lois Bent, progmg dir.

KOJM(AM)— Oct 31, 1947: 610 khz; 1 kw-U, DA-2. TL: N48 34 48 W109 38 54. 2210 31st St. N. 59501. Phone: (406) 265-7841. Fax: (406) 265-8855. E-mail: nmb@nmbi.com. Web Site: www.nmbi.com. Licensee: New Media Broadcasters Inc. (group owner; (acq 12-30-2002); grpsl). Network: ABC Information & Entertainment. Cohn & Marks. Format: Adult contemp, news/talk. News staff: 2; News: 20 wkly. Target aud: 30-64; boomer generation. Spec prog: Agriculture 4 hrs wkly. ♦C. David Leeds, pres & natl sls mgr; Jon Anderson, progmg dir; Krystal Spring, news dir; Bruce Faulkner, chief of engrg.

KPQX(FM)— Mar 8, 1975: 92.5 mhz; 100 kw. Ant 1,788 ft. TL: N48 10 55 W109 41 01. Stereo. 2210 31st St. N. 59501. Phone: (406) 265-7841. Fax: (406) 265-8855. E-mail: nmb@nmbi.com. Web Site: www.nmbi.com. Licensee: New Media Broadcasters Inc. (acq 12-30-2002); grpsl). Network: ABC. Cohn & Marks. Format: Country. News staff: 2; News: 20 hrs wkly. Target aud: 19-49. Spec prog: Farm 10 hrs wkly. ♦C. David Leeds, pres & natl sls mgr; Jon Anderson, progmg dir; Krystal Spring, news dir; Bruce Faulkner, chief of engrg.

KRYK(FM)— (Chinook). Nov 19, 1983: 101.3 mhz; 100 kw. Ant 688 ft. TL: N48 33 29 W109 17 50. Stereo. 2210 31st St. N. 59501. Phone: (406) 265-7841. Fax: (406) 265-8855. E-mail: nmb@nmbi.com. Web Site: www.nmbi.com. Licensee: New Media Broadcasters Inc. (group owner; acq 12-30-2002). Network: ABC. Cohn & Marks. Format: Hot adult contemp. News staff: 2; News: 5 hrs wkly. Target aud: 18-49. ♦C. David Leeds, pres & natl sls mgr; Jon Anderson, progmg dir; Krystal Spring, news dir; Bruce Faulkner, engrg dir.

*KXEI(FM)— July 28, 1983: 95.1 mhz; 98 kw. Ant 1,699 ft. TL: N48 10 42 W109 41 21. Stereo. Box 2426 59501. Secondary address: 317 First St. 59501. Phone: (406) 265-5845. Fax: (406) 265-8860. E-mail: ynop@ynopradio.org. Web Site: www.ynopradio.org. Licensee: Hi-Line Radio Fellowship Inc. Network: Moody. Cohn & Marks. Format: Christian Inspirational. Target aud: General; those looking for Christian inspirational music & progmg. Spec prog: C&W one hr, farm one hr wkly. ♦Ed Matter, gen mgr; Brenda Boyum, opns mgr; Roger Lonnquist, dev dir; Brian Jackson, progmg dir.

Helena

KBLL(AM)— September 1937: 1240 khz; 1 kw-U. TL: N46 35 24 W112 00 59. 110 Broadway St. 59601. Secondary address: Box 4111 59604. Phone: (406) 442-4490. Fax: (406) 442-6161. Licensee: CCR-Helena IV LLC. Group owner: Cherry Creek Radio LLC (acq 6-30-2004; $2.8 million. with co-located FM). Dow, Lohnes & Albertson. Format: News/talk. Target aud: 29-54; high buying power. ♦Dewey Bruce, gen mgr; Chris McCarthy, gen sls mgr; Stan Evans, progmg dir; Cato Butler, news dir; Ken Eklund, chief of engrg.

KBLL-FM— August 1979: 99.5 mhz; 30 kw. 790 ft. TL: N46 46 12 W112 01 22. Stereo. Format: Country. ♦Kurt Kittelson, progmg dir.

KCAP(AM)— October 1949: 1340 khz; 1 kw-U. TL: N46 36 43 W112 03 13. 110 Broadway St. 59601. Secondary address: Box 4111 59604. Phone: (406) 442-4490. Fax: (406) 442-7356. Web Site: www.kcap.com. Licensee: CCR-Helena IV LLC. Group owner: Cherry Creek Radio LLC (acq 12-19-2003; grpsl). Network: Network: CBS, Moody. Format: News/talk. Target aud: 25-54. ♦Dewey Bruce, gen mgr; Chris McCarthy, gen sls mgr; Stan Evans, progmg dir; Cato Butler, news dir; Ken Eklund, chief of engrg.

KZMT(FM)— Co-owned with KCAP(AM). 1975: 101.1 mhz; 95 kw. 1,899 ft. TL: N46 44 52 W112 19 47. Stereo. Web Site: www.kzmt.com. Format: Classic rock. Target aud: 18-54; upscale, entrepreneurial, adults.

*KHLV(FM)— Not on air, target date: unknown: 90.1 mhz; 1.8 kw vert. Ant 725 ft. TL: N46 46 12 W112 01 22. Stereo. 5700 W. Oaks Blvd., Rocklin, CA 95765. Phone: (916) 251-1600. Fax: (916) 251-1650. E-mail: klove@klove.com. Web Site: www.klove.com. Licensee: Educational Media Foundation. Group owner: EMF Broadcasting. Network: K-Love. Shaw Pittman. Format: Contemp Christian. News staff: 3. Target aud: 25-44; Judeo Christian, female. ♦Richard Jenkins, pres; Mike Novak, VP & progmg dir; Lloyd Parker, gen mgr; Ed Lenane, opns dir & news dir; Keith Whipple, dev dir; Eric Allen, natl sls mgr; Ted Gillette, rgnl sls mgr; Chris Joyce, prom dir; David Pierce, progmg mgr; Jon Rivers, mus dir; Sam Wallington, engrg dir.

KMTX(AM)— Nov 1, 1976: 950 khz; 5 kw-U, DA-N. TL: N46 40 28 W112 01 05. Stereo. Box 1183 59624. Secondary address: 516 Fuller 59601. Phone: (406) 442-0400. Fax: (406) 442-0491. Licensee: KMTX LLC. Network: AP Radio. Format: Nostalgia, adult contemp. ♦James O'Connell, pres; Kevin Skaalure, gen mgr.

KMTX-FM— Jan 19, 1985: 105.3 mhz; 86.9 kw. 1,878 ft. TL: N46 44 52 W112 19 47. (CP: 100 kw, ant 1,954 ft.). Stereo. Phone: (406) 443-1053. Network: ABC. Format: Adult contemp.

KUFM(FM)— See Missoula

*KUHM(FM)— 2000: 91.7 mhz; 910 w. Ant 761 ft. TL: N46 46 11 W112 01 22. PARTV Bldg., Univ. of Montana, Missoula 59812. Phone: (406) 243-4931. Phone: (800) 325-1565. Fax: (406) 243-3299. Licensee: The University of Montana. Format: Jazz, classical, news. News staff: 2. ♦William Marcus, gen mgr.

*KVCM(FM)— Aug 2, 1993: 103.1 mhz; 30 kw. Ant 679 ft. TL: N46 46 11 W112 01 25. Stereo. Box 2426, 317 First St., Havre 59501. Phone: (406) 265-5845. Fax: (406) 265-8860. E-mail: ynop@ynopradio.org. Web Site: www.ynopradio.org. Licensee: Hi-Line Radio Fellowship Inc. Network: ABC. Format: Christian Inspirational. Target aud: General:; those looking for inspirational Christian music & progmg. ♦Ed Matter, gen mgr; Brenda Boyum, opns mgr; Roger Lonnquist, stn mgr & dev dir; Brian Jackson, progmg dir.

Kalispell

KALS(FM)— November 1974: 97.1 mhz; 26 kw. 2,488 ft. TL: N48 00 48 W114 21 55. Stereo. Box 9710 59904-2710. Phone: (406) 752-5257. Fax: (406) 752-3416. Web Site: www.kals.com. Licensee: Kalispell Christian Radio Fellowship Inc. (acq 11-26-01; $700,000). Format: Christian, adult contemp. Spec prog: Class one hr wkly. ♦Brad Rauch, gen mgr.

KBBZ(FM)— Sept 12, 1983: 98.5 mhz; 58 kw. 2,378 ft. TL: N48 30 42 W114 22 14. (CP: 60 kw, ant 2,313 ft.). Stereo. Box 5409 59903-5409. Phone: (406) 755-8700. Fax: (406) 755-8770. E-mail: kbbz@beebroadcasting.com. Web Site: www.beebroadcasting.com. Licensee: Bee Broadcasting Inc. (group owner; acq 6-12-83; $315,000; 9-26-83). Format: Adult classic, contemp rock. ♦Benny Bee, pres; Mark Wagner, gen mgr; Benny Bee Jr., opns mgr; James Paulson, gen sls mgr; Barry Bennet, progmg dir.

KDBR(FM)— November 1993: 106.3 mhz; 30 kw. 413 ft. TL: N48 10 34 N114 20 53. Box 5409 59903. Phone: (406) 257-5327. Phone: (406) 755-8700. Fax: (406) 755-8770. E-mail: kdbr@beebroadcasting.com. Web Site: www.beebroadcasting.com. Licensee: Bee Broadcasting Inc. (group owner) Format: Country. ♦Benny Bee, pres; Mark Wagner, gen mgr; James Paulson, gen sls mgr; John Michaels, progmg dir.

KGEZ(AM)— Mar 24, 1927: 600 khz; 5 kw-D, 1 kw-N, DA-2. TL: N48 09 40 W114 16 51. Box 169 59903. Phone: (406) 752-2600. Fax: (406) 257-0459. Web Site: www.z600.com. Licensee: Skyline Broadcasters Inc. (acq 12-2-99). Network: CBS. Format: Sports, talk. Target aud: 25-60. ♦John Stokes, gen mgr & gen sls mgr & prom dir; Tony Mulligan, chief of engrg.

*KLKM(FM)— Not on air, target date: unknown: 88.7 mhz; 100 kw. Ant 400 ft. TL: N48 10 34 W114 20 53. 5700 West Oaks Blvd., Rocklin, CA 95765. Phone: (916) 251-1600. Fax: (916) 251-1650. Licensee: Educational Media Foundation. (acq 1-11-2005; $95,000. for CP). ♦Lloyd Parker, gen mgr.

KOFI(AM)— Nov 11, 1955: 1180 khz; 50 kw-D, 10 kw-N, DA-N. TL: N48 11 52 W114 15 03. Stereo. Box 608 59903. Secondary address: 317 First Ave. E. 59901. Phone: (406) 755-6690. Fax: (406) 752-5078. E-mail: kofi@kofi.radio.com. Web Site: www.kofi.com. Licensee: KOFI Inc. (acq 9-11-90; $750,000. with co-located FM; FTR: 10-1-90). Network: Network: ABC, CNN Radio. Rep: Tacher. Reddy, Begley & McCormick. Format: CHR, oldies, news/talk. News staff: 2; News: 35 hrs wkly. Target aud: 25-54. ♦Dave Rae, gen mgr.

KZMN(FM)— Co-owned with KOFI(AM). June 10, 1988: 103.9 mhz; 100 kw horiz, 55 kw vert. 571 ft. TL: N48 05 39 W114 16 11. Stereo. Web Site: www.kzmn.com. Network: CNN Radio. Format: Classic rock. News: 3 hrs wkly. Target aud: 18-49. ♦Dave Rae, pres; Mike Jorgensen, VP.

KQRK(FM)— See Ronan

*KSPL(FM)— February 1997: 90.9 mhz; 250 w. 2,529 ft. TL: N48 30 22 W114 20 49. c/o KMBI-FM, 5408 S. Freya, Spokane, WA 99223. Phone: (509) 448-2555. Fax: (509) 448-6855. E-mail: kmbi@moody.edu. Web Site: www.moody.edu. Licensee: Moody Bible Institute of Chicago. Group owner: The Moody Bible Institute of Chicago Format: Relg. Target aud: 35-54; Christian men & women. ♦Richard Monteith, gen mgr & progmg mgr; Scott Richardson, chief of engrg.

*KUKL(FM)— October 1998: 89.9 mhz; 850 w. 443 ft. TL: N48 10 34 W114 20 53. c/o KUFM(FM), Univ. of Montana, Missoula 59812. Phone: (406) 243-4931. Fax: (406) 243-3299. Fax: (800) 325-1565. Licensee: University of Montana. Format: Jazz, classical, news, eclectic. News: 2 hrs wkly. ♦William Marcus, gen mgr.

Laurel

KBSR(AM)— September 1979: 1490 khz; 1 kw-U. TL: N45 39 11 W108 45 09. Box 248 59044. Phone: (406) 651-5277. Fax: (406) 665-2131. Web Site: www.bigskyradio.net. Licensee: Sun Mountain Inc. (acq 11-30-2000). Network: Jones Radio Networks. Format: Adult contemp, radio theatre. Target aud: 35 plus; professional, business people. ♦Richard Solberg, pres.

KRSQ(FM)— June 9, 1994: 101.9 mhz; 100 kw. Ant 367 ft. TL: N45 45 48 W108 27 20. 222 North 32nd St., 10th Floor, Billings 59101. Phone: (406) 238-1000. Fax: (406) 238-1038. Web Site: www.hot1019.com. Licensee: New Northwest Broadcasters LLC (group owner; acq 8-10-99; grpsl). Network: ABC. Rep: Allied Radio Partners. Dow, Lohnes & Albertson. Format: CHR. Target aud: 18-49. ♦Pete Benedetti, CEO; Tommy Ehrman, gen mgr; Tom Oakes, opns mgr; Dean Alexander, sls dir; Ray Edwards, progmg VP; Kyle McCoy, progmg dir; Willie Tyler, mus dir; Mike Powers, chief of engrg.

Lewistown

KLCM(FM)— Listing follows KXLO(AM).

*KLEU(FM)— Oct 21, 2003: 91.1 mhz; 4 kw. Ant 1,879 ft. TL: N47 10 46 W109 32 05. Box 2426, Havre 59501-2426. Phone: (406) 265-5845. Fax: (406) 265-8860. Web Site: www.ynopradio.org. Licensee: Hi-Line Radio Fellowship Inc. acq 12-10-2003; $20,000. for CP). Format: Christian Inspirational. ♦Ed Matter, gen mgr; Brenda Boyum, opns mgr; Roger Lonnquist, dev dir; Brian Jackson, progmg dir.

KXLO(AM)— 1947: 1230 khz; 1 kw-U. TL: N47 04 13 W109 24 26. Box 620 95457. Secondary address: 620 N.E. Main St. 95457. Phone: (406) 538-3441. Fax: (406) 538-3495. E-mail: kxlo@lewistown.net. Web Site: www.kxlo-klcm.com. Licensee: KXLO Broadcast Inc. (acq 4-16-73). Network: Network: CBS, ABC Information & Entertainment. Format: Classic rock. Target aud: General. Spec prog: Farm. ♦Fred Lark, pres & gen mgr; Bethany Brezinski, stn mgr & gen sls mgr; Joe Zeller, opns mgr; Perry Brezinski, progmg dir.

Montana

KLCM(FM)—Co-owned with KXLO(AM). April 1975: 95.9 mhz; 3 kw. 205 ft. TL: N47 04 13 W109 24 26. Stereo. Web Site: www.kxlo-klcm.com. Licensee: Montana Broadcast Communications Inc. Format: Country. Target aud: 18-54.

Libby

KLCB(AM)— Dec 23, 1950: 1230 khz; 1 kw-U. TL: N48 22 14 W115 32 19. Box 730, 251 W. Cedar St. 59923. Phone: (406) 293-6234. Fax: (406) 293-6235. Licensee: Lincoln County Broadcasters Inc. (acq 12-66). Network: ABC. Format: Country. News: 13 hrs wkly. Target aud: 25-54. ♦ Duane J. Williams, VP & gen mgr.

KTNY(FM)—Co-owned with KLCB(AM). Apr 5, 1986: 101.7 mhz; 3 kw. -1,029 ft. TL: N48 22 14 W115 32 19. Stereo. Network: ABC. Format: MOR, adult contemp, oldies. News staff: one; News: 16 hrs wkly. Target aud: 35-54. ♦ Duane J. Williams, CEO.

Livingston

KOZB(FM)— December 1977: 97.5 mhz; 100 kw. 265 ft. TL: N45 39 26 W110 48 22. (CP: Ant 790 ft.). Stereo. Box 20, 5445 Johnson Rd., Bozeman 59718. Phone: (406) 587-9999. Fax: (406) 586-5858. Fax: (406) 587-5855. E-mail: reier@bigsky.net. Licensee: Reier Broadcasting Co. Inc. (group owner; acq 10-18-96; grpsl). Format: Rock alternative. News staff: 2. Target aud: 18-44. ♦ Bill Reier, gen mgr.

KPRK(AM)— Jan 10, 1947: 1340 khz; 1 kw-U. TL: N45 40 21 W110 32 21. Box1340, Hwy. 10 E. 59047. Phone: (406) 222-2841. Phone: (406) 222-1340. Fax: (406) 222-1341. E-mail: kprkam@mooseradio.com. Licensee: Capstar TX L.P. Group owner: Clear Channel Communications Inc. (acq 2-21-01; grpsl). Network: Network: ABC Information & Entertainment, AP Radio. Format: Classic hits. News: 15 hrs wkly. Target aud: 25-64; general. Spec prog: Oldies 5 hrs, big band 4 hrs, sports wkly. ♦ Dave Cowan, gen mgr; Courtney Lehman, stn mgr; Kaye Rugh, gen sls mgr; Gary Weiss, news dir; Ron Huckeby, chief of engrg.

KXLB(AM)—Co-owned with KPRK(AM).Not on air, target date: unknown: 100.7 mhz; 94 kw. 813 ft. TL: N45 40 24 W110 52 02. Format: Country.

Lockwood

KYLW(AM)— 2005: 1450 khz; 1 kw-U. TL: N45 48 37 W108 25 38. 9045 Hobble Creek, Billings 59101. Phone: (406) 665-2828. Fax: (406) 665-2131. Web site: www.bigskyradio.net. Licensee: Sun Mountain Inc. (acq 7-7-2005; $26,000 for CP). ♦ Richard Solberg, pres & gen mgr.

*KYWH(FM)—Not on air, target date: unknown: 88.9 mhz; 750 w. Ant 1,017 ft. TL: N45 32 20 W108 38 07. CSN International, 3232 W. MacArthur Blvd., Santa Ana, CA 92704. Phone: (714) 825-9663. Fax: (714) 825-9661. Licensee: CSN International (group owner).

Malta

KLTZ(AM)—See Glasgow

KMMR(FM)— Sept 9, 1980: 100.1 mhz; 2.25 kw. 377 ft. TL: N48 15 17 W107 49 18. Stereo. Box 1073, 140 S. 2nd Ave. E. 59538. Phone: (406) 654-2472. Fax: (406) 654-2506. Licensee: KMMR Radio Inc. (acq 5-95; $160,000). Network: ABC Information & Entertainment. Format: Country, MOR. News staff: one; News: 3 hrs wkly. Target aud: 18-65; general, rural. ♦ Gregory A. Kielb, pres, gen mgr, gen sls mgr, news dir & engrg VP; Claudette Kielb, opns VP & prom VP; Joyce Robinson, opns dir & mus dir; Roxie Cummings, adv mgr & asst music dir; Valene Kielb, prom dir, adv dir & progmg dir; Dan Sisco, engrg dir & chief of engrg.

Miles City

KATL(AM)— Sept 4, 1941: 770 khz; 10 kw-D, 1 kw-N, DA-N. TL: N46 23 46 W105 46 44. Box 700 59301. Secondary address: 818 Main St. 59301. Phone: (406) 234-7700. Fax: (406) 234-7783. E-mail: katlradio@katlradio.com. Web site: www.katlradio.com. Licensee: Star Printing Co. Network: Network: Westwood One, ABC. Cohn & Marks. Format: Adult contemp. News staff: one; News: 17 hrs wkly. Target aud: 25-54; Adults. ♦ John Sullivan, pres; Donald L. Richard, gen mgr, progmg dir & chief of engrg; Albert Homme, gen sls mgr.

*KECC(FM)— Nov 17, 1988: 90.7 mhz; 500 w. 502 ft. TL: N46 23 22 W105 45 22. Stereo. M.S.U. Billings, 1500 University Dr., Billings 59101-0298. Phone: (406) 657-2941. Fax: (406) 657-2977. Web Site: www.yellowstonepublicradio.org. Licensee: Montana State University-Billings. Network: Network: NPR, PRI. Format: Div. News: 39 hrs wkly. Target aud: General. ♦ Marvin Granger, stn mgr.

KIKC-FM—See Forsyth

KKRY(FM)— Nov 8, 1984: 92.3 mhz; 100 kw. Ant 984 ft. TL: N46 24 04 W105 39 06. Stereo. Box 1426 59301. Secondary address: 508 Main St., Rm. 200 53901. Phone: (406) 234-5626. Fax: (406) 232-7000. E-mail: studio@hotcountry925.com. Web Site: www.hotcountry925.com. Licensee: Senger Broadcasting Corp. (acq 6-17-97; $200,000 with co-located AM). Format: Country. News staff: one; News: 3 hrs wkly. Target aud: 18-54; programmed for general audience appeal. Spec prog: Farm one hr wkly. ♦ Kevin J. Senger, gen mgr; Kevin Senger, opns mgr & gen sls mgr; Karla Ellison, progmg dir; C.W. Wilcox, news dir; Tony Questa, chief of engrg.

KMTA(AM)—Co-owned with KKRY(FM). October 1986: 1050 khz; 10 kw-D, 136 w-N. TL: N46 24 04 W105 39 06. Web Site: www.1050kmta.com. Format: Classic rock. News staff: one; News: 6 hrs wkly. Target aud: 25-54. ♦ Kevin J. Senger, chmn.

Missoula

*KBGA(FM)— Aug 24, 1996: 89.9 mhz; 1 kw. -262 ft. TL: N46 52 56 W113 59 08. Univ. Center, Univ. of Montana 59812. Phone: (406) 243-6758. Fax: (406) 243-6428. E-mail: kbga@selway.umt.edu. Web Site: www.kbga.org. Licensee: The University of Montana. Format: Alternative, rock and roll, educ. ♦ Carly Dandrea, gen mgr.

KGGL(FM)—Listing follows KGRZ(AM).

KGRZ(AM)— 1947: 1450 khz; 1 kw-U. TL: N46 52 36 W114 00 47. (CP: TL: N46 52 39 W114 02 36). Box 4106 59806. Secondary address: 1600 N. Ave. W. 59801. Phone: (406) 728-1450. Fax: (406) 721-3020. Licensee: Fisher Radio Regional Group Inc. Group owner: Fisher Broadcasting Company (acq 3-1-95; grpsl, including co-located FM; FTR: 2-20-95). Rep: McGavren Guild. Fisher, Wayland, Cooper, Leader & Zaragoza L.L.P. Format: Sports, talk. Target aud: 25-54; male, sports orientated. ♦ Larry Roberts, pres; Chad Parrish, gen mgr; Bill McPherson, rgnl sls mgr; Scott Richards, progmg dir & news dir; Vern Argo, chief of engrg.

KGGL(FM)—Co-owned with KGRZ(AM). Apr 29, 1977: 93.3 mhz; 43 kw. 2,440 ft. TL: N47 02 24 W113 59 00. Stereo. Phone: (406) 728-9399. Format: Country. Target aud: 25-54.

KGVO(AM)— Jan 18, 1931: 1290 khz; 5 kw-U, DA-N. TL: N46 49 47 W114 04 45. Box 5417 59806. Secondary address: 3250 S. Reserve, Suite 200 59801. Phone: (406) 728-9300. Fax: (406) 542-2329. Licensee: Capstar TX L.P. Group owner: Clear Channel Communications Inc. (acq 4-12-01). Network: CBS. Format: News/talk. Target aud: General. ♦ Denny Bedard, stn mgr & opns mgr; Gene Peterson, CEO, pres, CFO & gen sls mgr.

KKNS-FM— July 2005: 105.9 mhz; 1.84 kw. Ant 2,083 ft. TL: N46 48 06 W113 58 22. 2425 W. Central Ave., Suite 203 59801. Phone: (406) 721-6800. Fax: (406) 329-1850. Licensee: Spanish Peaks Broadcasting Inc. Format: News/progressive talk. ♦ Dave Cowan, gen mgr.

KLCY(AM)—(East Missoula). June 27, 1959: 930 khz; 5 kw-D, 1 kw-N, DA-N. TL: N46 51 57 W114 04 57. 3250 S00. Reserve, Suite 200 59801. Phone: (406) 728-9300. Fax: (406) 542-2329. Web Site: www.klcy930.com. Licensee: Capstar TX L.P. Group owner: Clear Channel Communications Inc. (acq 2-21-01; grpsl). Cohn & Marks. Format: Oldies. Target aud: 35-54; adult spenders. ♦ Gene Peterson, gen mgr; Jim Colter, gen sls mgr; Julie Vacca, progmg dir; Steve Fullerton, progmg dir; Bill Schwanke, news dir; Todd Clark, chief of engrg.

KYSS-FM—Co-owned with KLCY(AM). May 11, 1969: 94.9 mhz; 62 kw horiz, 12.5 kw vert. 2,381 ft. TL: N47 01 57 W113 59 30. Stereo. Web site: www.kyssfm.com. Network: ABC Information & Entertainment. Format: Hot country. ♦ Tom Anthony, progmg dir.

KMSO(FM)— Feb 9, 1985: 102.5 mhz; 21 kw. Ant 1,748 ft. TL: N46 48 30 W113 58 38. Stereo. Box 309 59806-0309. Secondary address: 725 Strand Ave. 59801. Phone: (406) 542-1025. Fax: (406) 721-1036. E-mail: info@kmso.com. Web site: www.moclub.com. Licensee: Sheila Callahan & Friends Inc. Network: AP Radio. Tacher, Portland Keller & Heckman. Format: Hot adult contemp. News: 6 hrs wkly. Target aud: 25-54; upscale professional, well-educated mgmt level. Spec prog: Relg one hr wkly. ♦ Sheila Callahan, gen mgr; Diana Helms, gen sls mgr; Dale Desmond, progmg dir.

*KMZL(FM)— 1998: 91.1 mhz; 1 kw. 2,040 ft. TL: N46 48 09 W113 58 21. 2201 S. 6th St., Las Vegas, NV 89104. Phone: (800) 804-5452. E-mail: info@sosradio.net. Licensee: Faith Communications Corp. Cohn & Marks. Format: Adult contemp Christian. Target aud: 25-44. ♦ Jack French, CEO; Brad Staley, gen mgr & opns VP.

*KUFM(FM)— Jan 31, 1965: 89.1 mhz; 17 kw. 2,510 ft. TL: N47 02 24 W113 59 00. (CP: 32 kw, ant 2,473 ft. TL: N47 01 58 W113 59 29). Univ. of Montana 59812. Phone: (406) 243-4931. Fax: (406) 243-3299. Web Site: www.mtpr.org. Licensee: University of Montana. Network: NPR. Format: Class, jazz, pub radio. News staff: 2. ♦ William Marcus, gen mgr & stn mgr.

KYLT(AM)— July 15, 1955: 1340 khz; 1 kw-U. TL: N46 52 56 W113 59 08. Box 4106, 1600 North Ave. W. 59806. Phone: (406) 728-5000. Fax: (406) 721-3020. Licensee: Fisher Radio Regional Group Inc. Group owner: Fisher Broadcasting Company (acq 11-20-96; $3.9 million. with co-located FM). Format: Oldies. Target aud: 35-55. ♦ Chad Parrish, gen mgr; Bill McPherson, gen sls mgr; Mark Morris, natl sls mgr & progmg dir; Scott Richards, news dir; Vern Argo, chief of engrg.

KZOQ-FM—Co-owned with KYLT(AM). July 29, 1974: 100.1 mhz; 13.5 kw. Ant 2,102 ft. TL: N46 48 09 W113 58 21. Stereo. Format: Classic rock. Target aud: 25-54. ♦ Lily Konda, progmg dir.

Park City

*KBIL(FM)—Not on air, target date: unknown: 89.7 mhz; 540 w. Ant 1,066 ft. TL: N45 32 24 W108 38 34. 5700 W. Oaks Blvd., Rocklin, CA 95765. Phone: (916) 251-1600. Fax: (916) 251-1650. E-mail: klove@klove.com. Web Site: www.klove.com. Licensee: Educational Media Foundation. Group owner: EMF Broadcasting (acq 10-2-2003; grpsl). Network: K-Love. Shaw Pittman. Format: Contemp Christian. News staff: 3. Target aud: 25-44; Judeo Christian female. ♦ Richard Jenkins, pres; Mike Novak, VP & progmg dir; Lloyd Parker, gen mgr; Ed Lenane, opns dir & news dir; Keith Whipple, dev dir; Eric Allen, natl sls mgr; Chris Joyce, prom dir; David Pierce, progmg mgr; Jon Rivers, mus dir; Sam Wallington, engrg dir.

Pinesdale

KBQQ(FM)— 2003: 106.7 mhz; 13 kw. Ant 2,089 ft. TL: N46 48 09 W113 58 19. Fisher Radio Regional Group Inc., 1600 North Ave., Missoula 59801. Phone: (406) 728-5000. Fax: (406) 721-3020. Licensee: Fisher Radio Regional Group Inc. Group owner: Fisher Broadcasting Company (acq 2-4-03). Format: Oldies. ♦ Larry Roberts, pres; Chad Parrish, gen mgr; Bill McPherson, gen sls mgr; Cary Nicklay, natl sls mgr; Mark Morris, progmg dir; Vern Argo, engrg dir.

Plains

*KPLG(FM)— 1998: 91.5 mhz; 470 w. 4,041 ft. TL: N47 22 21 W114 51 31. Stereo. Box 2426, Havre 59501. Phone: (406) 265-5845. Fax: (406) 265-8860. E-mail: ynop@ynopradio.org. Web Site: www.ynopradio.org. Licensee: Hi Line Radio Fellowship Inc. Format: Religious. Target aud: General; those who are looking for Christian progmg. ♦ Ed Matter, gen mgr; Brenda Boyum, opns mgr; Roger Lonnquist, dev dir; Brian Jackson, progmg dir.

Plentywood

KATQ(AM)— Sept 14, 1979: 1070 khz; 5 kw-D. TL: N48 46 03 W104 32 45. 112 E. 3rd Ave. 59254. Phone: (406) 765-1480. Fax: (406) 765-2357. E-mail: katq@airtimeisp.net. Licensee: Radio International-KATQ Broadcast Association Inc. (acq 1-13-92; $5,000 with co-located FM; 2-10-92). Network: ABC Information & Entertainment. Format: Country. Target aud: 18-54. Spec prog: Top-40, farm 5 hrs, relg 6 hrs wkly. ♦ Marvel Hellegaard, pres; Casandra Syme, gen mgr, stn mgr, sls dir & gen sls mgr; Grant Lindsay, opns dir & engrg dir; Bruce Lapke, mus dir & news dir; Art Gehnert, chief of engrg.

KATQ-FM— June 1, 1962: 100.1 mhz; 3 kw. 34 ft. TL: N48 47 06 W104 32 00. Stereo.

Stations in the U.S. Nebraska

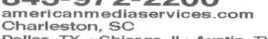

Developers & Brokers of Radio Properties

contact American Media Services at our suite:
Philadelphia Marriott Downtown
215-625-2900
843-972-2200
americanmediaservices.com
Charleston, SC
Dallas, TX • Chicago, Il • Austin, TX
American Media Services, LLC

Polson

KERR(AM)— Mar 22, 1976: 750 khz; 50 kw-D, 1 kw-N, DA-N. TL: N47 38 34 W114 07 25. 581 N. Reservoir Rd. 59860. Phone: (406) 883-5255. Fax: (406) 883-4441. Web Site: www.750kerr.com. Licensee: Anderson Radio Broadcasting Inc. (group owner; acq 9-22-2003; grpsl). Network: ABC Information & Entertainment. Format: Country. Target aud: General. ♦ Dennis Anderson, pres, gen mgr & gen sls mgr; Tony Mulligan, chief of engrg.

Pryor

*KPGB(FM)—Not on air, target date: unknown: 88.3 mhz; Box 24 59066. Phone: (406) 255-0994. Licensee: Faith Baptist Church. Format: Gospel. ♦ Ronnie Henderson, gen mgr.

Red Lodge

KMXE-FM— Jan 24, 1994: 99.3 mhz; 30 kw. 1,210 ft. TL: N45 11 15 W109 14 46. Stereo. Box 1678 59068. Phone: (406) 446-1199. Fax: (406) 446-9178. E-mail: fm99mtn@starband.net. Licensee: Silver Rock Communications Inc. (acq 7-19-89; $30,000;. FTR: 8-7-89). Format: Class rock. News staff: one; News: one hr wkly. Target aud: 25-49; upwardly mobile. ♦ Jeffrey S. Oliphant, exec VP, opns mgr & news dir; Leslie Brent-Oliphant, pres & gen mgr.

Ronan

KQRK(FM)— Oct 4, 1981: 92.3 mhz; 60 kw. 3,500 ft. TL: N47 46 25 W114 16 04. Stereo. 581 N. Reservoir Rd., Polson 59860. Phone: (406) 883-5255. Fax: (406) 883-4441. Web Site: www.750kerr.com. Licensee: Anderson Radio Broadcasting Inc. (group owner; acq 9-22-2003; grpsl). Format: Adult contemp. Target aud: 25-49. ♦ A.L. Anderson, pres; Dennis Anderson, gen mgr.

Scobey

KCGM(FM)— June 21, 1971: 95.7 mhz; 52 kw. Ant 660 ft. TL: N48 48 03 W105 21 00. Stereo. Box 220, 20 Main St. 59263. Phone: (406) 487-2293. Fax: (406) 487-5922. Licensee: Prairie Communications Inc. Network: USA. Taylor Brown Format: Country. News staff: 2; News: 8 hrs wkly. Spec prog: Farm 6 hrs wkly. ♦ Clifford Hagfeldt, CEO; Dixie Halverson, gen mgr.

Shelby

KSEN(AM)— Aug 11, 1947: 1150 khz; 5 kw-U, DA-2. TL: N48 28 54 W111 53 03. 830 Oilfield Ave. 59474. Phone: (406) 434-5241. Fax: (406) 434-2122. E-mail: ksen@shelby.mt.us. Licensee: Capstar TX L.P. Group owner: Clear Channel Communications Inc. (acq 2-21-01; grpsl). Network: ABC Information & Entertainment. Rep: Allied Radio Partners. Format: Golden oldies. News staff: one; News: 15 hrs wkly. Target aud: 25-59. Spec prog: Farm 8 hrs wkly. ♦ Lowrey Maya, CEO & pres; Julie Martin, gen mgr, gen sls mgr & progmg dir; Jim Sargent, opns dir, opns mgr & progmg dir; Mark Daniels, news dir; Anne James, pub affrs dir; Tony Mulligan, chief of engrg.

KZIN-FM—Co-owned with KSEN(AM). Dec 9, 1978: 96.7 mhz; 100 kw. Ant 551 ft. TL: N48 19 42 W112 02 03. Stereo. Format: C&W. News staff: one; News: 6 hrs wkly. Target aud: 18-49. ♦ Anne Weins, progmg dir.

Sidney

KGCX(FM)— June 1, 2004: 93.1 mhz; 55 kw. Ant 499 ft. TL: N47 45 02 W104 18 22. Stereo. 213 2nd Ave. S.W. 59270. Phone: (406) 433-5429. Fax: (406) 433-5430. E-mail: kgcxeagle@midrivers.com. Web Site: eagle93fm.com. Licensee: Sidney Community Broadcasting Corp. (acq 7-30-2002; $10,000. for CP). Network: ABC. Format: Classic rock. News: 15 hrs wkly. ♦ Stephen A. Marks, pres; Mitch Miller, gen mgr; Melissa Quilling, gen sls mgr.

KTHC(FM)— December 1996: 95.1 mhz; 100 kw. 718 ft. TL: N48 02 52 W103 59 01. Stereo. 120 E. Main 59270. Secondary address: Box 2048, Williston, ND 58802. Phone: (406) 433-5090. Phone: (701) 572-5371. Fax: (406) 433-5095. Fax: (701) 572-7511. E-mail: power95@midrivers.com. Licensee: CCR-Williston IV LLC. Group owner: Cherry Creek Radio LLC (acq 12-19-2003; grpsl). Format: Adult contemp. Target aud: General. ♦ Larry Timpe, VP & gen mgr.

Stevensville

KKVU(FM)— July 16, 2005: 104.5 mhz; 14.15 kw. Ant 2,083 ft. TL: N46 48 06 W113 58 22. 2425 W. Central Ave., Suite 203, Missoula 59801. Phone: (406) 721-6800. Fax: (406) 329-1850. Licensee: Spanish Peaks Broadcasting Inc. Format: Adult contemp. ♦ Dave Cowan, gen mgr.

Superior

KLTC-FM— October 1999: 107.5 mhz; 2 kw. -1,443 ft. TL: N47 12 23 W114 55 55. Stereo. 3250 Reserve St., Suite 200, Missoula 59801. Phone: (406) 822-1075. Fax: (406) 542-2329. Web Site: www.kltcfm.com. Licensee: Clear Channel Broadcasting Licenses Inc. Group owner: Clear Channel Communications Inc. (acq 8-7-02; $900,000). Format: C&W. ♦ Gene Peterson, gen mgr.

West Yellowstone

KEZQ(FM)— June 1, 1996: . Stn currently dark 92.9 mhz; 46 kw. Ant 2,732 ft. TL: N44 33 41 W111 26 32. 670 West Broadway NO OPERATIONAL, Idaho Falls, ID 83401. Phone: (888) 505-5397. Fax: (208) 726-5459. Licensee: Chaparral Broadcasting Inc. Group owner: Chaparral Communications (acq 7-30-2004; grpsl). Format: Oldies. ♦ Scott Parker, gen mgr.

KWYS(AM)—Co-owned with KEZQ(FM). Dec 20, 1967: 920 khz; 1 kw-D. TL: N44 38 56 W111 05 50. Phone: (406) 646-7361. Network: CNN Radio. Format: Classic rock.

Whitefish

KJJR(AM)— Feb 14, 1979: 880 khz; 10 kw-D, 500 w-N. TL: N48 23 44 W114 19 11. (CP: 1 kw-N, DA-N). Box 5409, Kalispell 59903. Phone: (406) 755-8700. Fax: (406) 755-8770. E-mail: KJJR@beebroadcasting.com. Web Site: WWW.beebroadcasting.com. Licensee: Bee Broadcasting Inc. (group owner) Format: News/talk. ♦ Benny Bee, pres; Mark Wagner, gen mgr.

KWOL-FM—Not on air, target date: unknown: 105.1 mhz; 1.6 kw. Ant 2,253 ft. TL: N48 30 42 W114 22 16. Metropolitan Tower #1014, 1942 Westlake Ave., Seattle, WA 98101. Licensee: Cathleen R. Bee dba Rose Communications. ♦ Cathleen R. Bee, gen mgr.

Whitehall

*KAIB(FM)—Not on air, target date: unknown: 89.7 mhz; 18 kw. Ant 1,850 ft. TL: N46 00 25 W112 26 29. Colorado Christian University, 180 S. Garrison St., Lakewood, CO 80226. Phone: (303) 963-3352. Licensee: Colorado Christian University.

Wolf Point

KVCK(AM)— Sept 1, 1957: 1450 khz; 1 kw-U. TL: N48 05 18 W105 39 22. 324 Main St. 59201. Phone: (406) 653-1900. Phone: (406) 653-1902. Fax: (406) 653-1909. E-mail: kvck@nemontel.net. Licensee: Wolf Town Wireless Inc. (acq 8-31-92; $120,000 with co-located FM; 11-16-92). Format: Memories-Unforgettable Favorites. News: 15 hrs wkly. Target aud: General. Spec prog: Farm 6 hrs wkly.

KVCK-FM— Sept 1, 1981: 92.7 mhz; 860 w. 508 ft. TL: N48 11 09 W105 40 08. Stereo. Network: ABC Information & Entertainment. Format: Country. ♦ Arline Robenberg, gen mgr.

Nebraska

Ainsworth

KBRB(AM)— Feb 6, 1968: 1400 khz; 1 kw-U. TL: N42 33 16 W99 49 52. Box 285, 122 E. 2nd St. 69210. Phone: (402) 387-1400. Fax: (402) 387-2624. E-mail: kbrb@sscg.net. Licensee: K.B.R. Broadcasting Co. Network: ABC Daytime Direction. Bryan Cave. Format: C&W, MOR. News: 30 hrs wkly. Target aud: General. ♦ Lorris C. Rice, pres & gen mgr; Angie Von Heeder, prom VP; Cody Goochey, progmg dir; Randy Brudigan, chief of engrg.

KBRB-FM— May 30, 1983: 92.7 mhz; 4.5 kw. 331 ft. TL: N42 33 16 W99 49 52.

Albion

KUSO(FM)— May 10, 2000: 92.7 mhz; 50 kw. 492 ft. TL: N41 49 50 W97 41 12. Box 747, Norfolk 68702-0747. Secondary address: 214 N. 7th St., Norfolk 68701. Phone: (402) 371-0100. Fax: (402) 371-0050. E-mail: us92@us92.com. Web Site: www.us92.com. Licensee: Flood Communications L.L.C. (acq 4-27-99; $50,000). Reddy, Begley & McCormick. Format: Full service, country. News staff: one; News: 3 hrs wkly. Target aud: General. Spec prog: Farm 10 hrs wkly. ♦ Michael J. Flood, pres & gen mgr; Dave Amick, opns dir; Angela Richard, gen sls mgr; Brian Masters, progmg dir; Tammy Partch, news dir.

Alliance

KAAQ(FM)—Listing follows KCOW(AM).

KCOW(AM)— Feb 15, 1949: 1400 khz; 1 kw-U. TL: N42 06 26 W102 53 15. Box 600 69301. Secondary address: 1210 W. 10th 69301. Phone: (308) 762-1400. Fax: (308) 762-7804. E-mail: kcow@bbc.net. Web Site: www.doubleqcountry.com. Licensee: Eagle Communications Inc. Group owner: Eagle Communications Group (acq 1965). Network: ABC. Howard Anderson, Allied Radio Partners. Format: Oldies, news/talk. News staff: 2; News: 22 hrs wkly. Target aud: 25-54. Spec prog: Farm 18 hrs wkly. ♦ Gary Shorman, pres; Mark Vail, VP; Mike Garwood, gen mgr.

KAAQ(FM)—Co-owned with KCOW(AM). Sept 30, 1985: 105.9 mhz; 100 kw. Ant 705 ft. TL: N41 50 29 W103 05 07. Stereo. Web Site: www.doubleqcountry.com. Network: ABC. Howard Anderson Format: Country. News staff: 2; News: 15 hrs wkly. Target aud: 18-54. Spec prog: Farm 4 hrs wkly. ♦ Mark Vail, opns VP.

KPNY(FM)— 1978: 102.1 mhz; 100 kw. 521 ft. TL: N42 07 01 W103 07 09. Stereo. Box 245 69301. Secondary address: 2106 1st Ave., Scottsbluff 69361. Phone: (308) 635-1996. Fax: (308) 635-1984. E-mail: kpnyfm@scottsbluff.net. Web Site: www.kpnyfm.com. Licensee: Halstead Communications Inc. (acq 1988). Format: Hot adult contemp. News staff: 5; News: 5 hrs wkly. Target aud: 18-35. ♦ Leon Halstead, pres; Lee Hall, gen mgr.

KQSK(FM)—(Chadron). Sept 15, 1979: 97.5 mhz; 100 kw. Ant 840 ft. TL: N42 38 06 W103 06 12. Stereo. Box 600 69301. Secondary address: 1210 W. 10th 69301. Phone: (308) 762-1400. Fax: (308) 762-7804. E-mail: kcow@bbc.net. Web Site: www.doubleqcountry.com. Licensee: Eagle Communications Inc. Group owner: Eagle Communications Group (acq 6-13-91; $125,000;. FTR: 7-1-91). Network: ABC. Howard Anderson. Format: Country. News staff: 2; News: 15 hrs wkly. Target aud: 18-54. Spec prog: Farm 4 hrs wkly. ♦ Mike Garwood, gen mgr; John Howard, stn mgr; Michael Gilesinger, opns mgr; John Howard, gen sls mgr; John Axtell, news dir; Paul Montoya, chief of engrg.

*KTNE-FM— May 1990: 91.1 mhz; 92.3 kw. 1,325 ft. TL: N41 50 24 W103 03 18. Stereo. Box 83111, Lincoln 68501. Secondary address: 1800 N. 33rd St., Lincoln 68583. Phone: (402) 472-3611. Fax: (402) 472-2403. Fax: (402) 472-1785. Web Site: www.npm.org. Licensee: Nebraska Educational Telecommunications Commission. Network: Network: PRI, NPR. Dow, Lohnes & Albertson. Format: Class, news.

Broadcasting & Cable Yearbook 2006

Nebraska

Target aud: 35 plus; general. ◆ Rod Bates, gen mgr; Jeff Smith, opns mgr; Michael Winkle, gen sls mgr; Nancy Finken, progmg dir; Martin Wells, news dir.

Auburn

KNCY-FM— Sept 18, 1981: 103.1 mhz; 14 kw. Ant 436 ft. TL: N40 57 W95 45 38. Box 278, 814 Central Ave., Nebraska City 68410. Phone: (402) 873-3348. Fax: (402) 873-7882. Licensee: Arbor Day Broadcasting Inc. (acq 12-30-02) $600,000. with KNCY(AM) Nebraska City). Network: ABC. Format: Country, news. News staff: 2; News: 30 hrs wkly. ◆ Scott Kooistra, VP & gen mgr; Doug Jennings, progmg dir.

Aurora

KRGY(FM)— Mar 1, 1980: 97.3 mhz; 50 kw. 354 ft. TL: N40 52 44 W98 05 36. Stereo. 3205 W. North Front St. 68802. Secondary address: Box 4907 68802. Phone: (308) 381-1430. Fax: (308) 382-6701. E-mail: krgi@krgi.com. Web Site: www.krgi.com. Licensee: Legacy Communications LLC (group owner; acq 5-17-2004; grpsl). Network: ABC. Format: Classic hit country. News staff: 2; News: 2 hrs wkly. Target aud: 18-49. ◆ Lyle Nelson, gen mgr; Jim Davis, opns mgr.

KROA(FM)—See Grand Island

Bassett

***KMNE-FM**— June 1991: 90.3 mhz; 92.3 kw. 1,292 ft. TL: N42 20 05 W99 29 01. Stereo. Box 83111, Lincoln 68501. Secondary address: 1800 N. 33rd St., Lincoln 68583. Phone: (402) 472-3611. Fax: (402) 472-2403. E-mail: npm@unl.edu. Web Site: www.npm.org. Licensee: Nebraska Educational Telecommunications Commission. Network: Network: NPR, PRI. Format: Class, news/talk, edu. Target aud: General. ◆ Ray Dilley, gen mgr.

Beatrice

KTGL(FM)—Licensed to Beatrice. See Lincoln

KWBE(AM)— June 12, 1949: 1450 khz; 1000 W. TL: N40 15 49 W96 46 27. Box 10, 200 Sherman St. 68310. Phone: (402) 228-5923. Fax: (402) 228-3704. E-mail: kwbe@broadcasthouse.com. Web Site: www.kwbe.com. Licensee: Nebraska Broadcasting LLC. Group owner: Triad Broadcasting Co. LLC (acq 5-00; grpsl). Network: Network: CBS, Westwood One, ABC Information & Entertainment. Howard Anderson. Format: Adult contemp, news/talk. News staff: one; News: 25 hrs wkly. Target aud: 24-54; mature, affluent adults. Spec prog: Farm 14 hrs wkly. ◆ David Benjamin, CEO; Charlie Brogan, gen mgr & gen sls mgr; Jay Stalder, gen mgr & progmg dir; Doug Kennedy, news dir; Dave Neidfeldt, pub affrs dir.

Bellevue

KOZN(AM)— June 1999: 1620 khz; 10 kw-D, 1 kw-N. TL: N41 16 12 W95 47 10. 5011 Capitol Ave., Omaha 68132. Phone: (402) 342-2000. Fax: (402) 827-5293. Web Site: www.1620thezone.com. Licensee: Waitt Omaha LLC. Group owner: Waitt Radio Inc. (acq 1-7-2002; grpsl). Rep: Katz Radio. Pepper & Corazzini. Format: Sports. ◆ Mike Delich, pres; Mike Payne, gen mgr; Mark Todd, opns mgr.

KYDZ(AM)— Mar 19, 1987: 1180 khz; 25 kw-D, 1 kw-N, DA-2. TL: N41 16 12 W95 47 10. Stereo. 5011 Capitol Ave., Omaha 68132. Phone: (402) 342-2000. Fax: (402) 342-5874. Web Site: www.radiodisney.com. Licensee: Waitt Omaha LLC. (group owner; (acq 1-7-2002; grpsl). Network: Radio Disney. Rep: Katz Radio. Format: Children. Target aud: 0-12; Children. ◆ Michael Delich, pres; Michael Payne, exec VP; Ken Fearnow, gen mgr; Mark Todd, opns mgr; Bill Ryan, sls dir; Neil Nelkin, prom VP & progmg dir; Terry Leahy, news dir; Darwin Stinton, chief of engrg.

Bennington

KHUS(FM)— June 10, 1991: 93.3 mhz; 6 kw. 350 ft. TL: N41 22 57 W96 07 57. Stereo. 5010 Underwood Ave., Omaha 68132. Phone: (402) 561-2000. Fax: (402) 556-8937. E-mail: michellematthews @clearchannel.com. Web Site: www.krrk.com. Licensee: Capstar TX L.P. Group owner: Clear Channel Communications Inc. (acq 8-30-00; grpsl). Format: Hard rock. ◆ Donna Baker, gen mgr & engrg mgr; Rhonda Gerrard, gen sls mgr; Michelle Matthews, progmg dir.

Blair

KBLR-FM— Sept 10, 2002: 97.3 mhz; 25 kw. Ant 302 ft. TL: N41 38 21 W96 12 31. 5011 Capitol, Omaha 68132. Phone: (402) 342-2000. Fax: (402) 342-5874. Web Site: www.hot1077.com. Licensee: Waitt Omaha LLC. (group owner; (acq 1-7-2002; grpsl). Format: Black, urban contemp, rhythm and blues. ◆ Mary Quass, CEO & pres; Ken Fearnow, VP & gen mgr; Mark Todd, progmg VP.

***KDCV-FM**— Oct 1, 1972: 91.1 mhz; 10 w. 60 ft. TL: N41 33 07 W96 09 20. Stereo. 2848 College Dr. 68008. Phone: (402) 426-7322. Fax: (402) 426-7382. E-mail: kdcv@acad2.dana.edu. Web Site: www.huntel.net/kdcv. Licensee: Dana College. Format: Var/div. Target aud: 25-54 community; 18-34 college community. ◆ Vern Wirka, gen mgr.

Bridgeport

KOLT-FM— 2001: 101.3 mhz; 100 kw. Ant 1,112 ft. TL: N41 50 23 W103 49 36. Box 532, Scottsbluff 69361-0532. Phone: (308) 632-5667. Fax: (308) 436-7296. Licensee: Tracy Broadcasting Corp. (group owner). Format: Country. ◆ Michael Tracy, pres; Larry Swikard, gen mgr & gen sls mgr; Krista Sarchett, prom dir; Jeff McKenzie, progmg dir; Pat Leach, engrg dir & chief of engrg.

Broken Bow

KBBN-FM—Listing follows KCNI(AM).

KCNI(AM)— Sept 28, 1949: 1280 khz; 1 kw-D. TL: N41 24 31 W99 40 28. Box 409, W. Hwy., 2 Calaway Rd. 68822. Phone: (308) 872-5881. Fax: (308) 872-3284. Licensee: Custer County Broadcasting Co. Format: C&W. News staff: one; News: 24 hrs wkly. Target aud: General; rural audience of all ages with focus on 25-65. Spec prog: Farm & country mus specials. ◆ David Birnie, VP, gen mgr, opns dir & sls dir; Brent Apperson, progmg dir; Dale Sell, news dir & pub affrs dir; Val Lane, chief of engrg.

KBBN-FM—Co-owned with KCNI(AM). June 15, 1982: 98.3 mhz; 25 kw. Ant 312 ft. TL: N41 23 49 W99 37 02. Stereo. Format: Classic rock. News staff: one; News: 10 hrs wkly. Target aud: 24-45; baby boomers & on either edge of age breakdown.

Central City

KZEN(FM)— July 22, 1985: 100.3 mhz; 100 kw. 1,854 ft. TL: N41 32 28 W97 40 45. Stereo. 1418 25th St., Columbus 68601. Phone: (402) 564-2866. Fax: (402) 564-2867. Licensee: Three Eagles of Columbus Inc. Group owner: Three Eagles Communications (acq 9-5-97; grpsl). Network: Network: ABC, AP Radio. Rep: Interep. Format: Country. News staff: 2; News: 18 hrs wkly. Target aud: 25-54; rgnl, rural & small town audience. Spec prog: Relg 5 hrs, farm 20 hrs wkly. ◆ Rolland Johnson, CEO; Gary Buchanan, pres; Cindy Harris, CFO; Greg Wells, gen mgr; Dean Johnson, opns dir & mus dir.

Chadron

***KCNE-FM**— Aug 29, 1991: 91.9 mhz; 8.4 kw. 338 ft. TL: N42 48 47 W103 00 22. Stereo. Secondary address: 1800 N. 33rd St., Lincoln 68503. Phone: (402) 472-3611. Fax: (402) 472-1785. E-mail: npm@unl.edu. Web Site: www.npm.org. Licensee: Nebraska Educational Telecommunications Commission. Network: Network: PRI, NPR. Format: Class, news. Target aud: General. ◆ Ray Dilley, gen mgr.

KCSR(AM)— May 9, 1954: 610 khz; 1 kw-D, 118 w-N. TL: N42 49 56 W103 01 00. Stereo. 226 Bordeaux 69337. Phone: (308) 432-5545. Phone: (308) 432-2233. Fax: (308) 432-5601. E-mail: kcsr@chadrad.com. Web Site: www.chadrad.com. Licensee: Chadrad Communications Inc. (acq 8-30-91; $150,000). Network: Network: ABC Information & Entertainment, AP Radio. Fletcher, Heald & Hildreth. Format: Country, farm. News staff: 2. News: 20 hrs wkly. Target aud: 25-54; people in the ranch, farm & agricultural industry. Spec prog: Farm 6 hrs wkly. ◆ Dennis A. Brown, pres; Kathi Brown, gen sls mgr; J.J. Archer, progmg dir; Joe Lowery, mus dir; Brian Taylor, asst music dir & chief of engrg; Chris Faukhauser, news dir; Duanne Ekwall, pub affrs dir.

KQSK(FM)—Licensed to Chadron. See Alliance

Columbus

KJSK(AM)— Apr 28, 1948: 900 khz; 1 kw-D, 66 w-N. TL: N41 26 12 W97 23 47. 1418 25th St. 68601. Phone: (402) 564-9101. Fax: (402) 564-1999. E-mail: kjskkdjs@megavision.com. Web Site: www.kjsk.com. Licensee: Three Eagles of Columbus Inc. Group owner: Three Eagles Communications (acq 8-23-01; $2.7 million. with co-located FM including five-year noncompete agreement). Format: News/talk, farm. News staff: one. Target aud: General. Spec prog: Pol 4 hrs, Sp 6 hrs, relg 20 hrs wkly. ◆ Dean Johnson, opns mgr & progmg dir; Greg Wells, gen mgr & gen sls mgr; Denise Kollath, prom dir; Bob Cook, engrg dir & chief of engrg.

KLIR(FM)—Co-owned with KJSK(AM). August 1964: 101.1 mhz; 100 kw. 760 ft. TL: N41 16 55 W97 24 30. Stereo. Phone: (402) 564-9101. E-mail: klirnet@megavision.com. Web Site: www.klir.net. Format: Adult contemp. News staff: one. Target aud: General. Spec prog: Oldies 12 hrs wkly. ◆ Cec Hottory, sls dir; Dave Rinehart, opns mgr, prom dir & progmg dir; Bobbie Freeborn, mus dir.

KKOT(FM)—Listing follows KTTT(AM).

***KTLX(FM)**— July 1974: 91.9 mhz; 100 w. 78 ft. TL: N41 26 26 W97 21 14. c/o Trinity Lutheran Church, 2200 25th St. 68601. Phone: (402) 564-8548. Fax: (402) 562-6003. E-mail: ktlx@megavision.com. Licensee: TLC Educational Corp. Format: Educ, relg. ◆ Gary Spuit, pres; Russ Rote, gen mgr.

KTTT(AM)— Dec 2, 1962: 1510 khz; 500 w-D. TL: N41 27 14 W97 24 20. 1418 25th St. 68601. Phone: (402) 564-2866. Fax: (402) 564-2867. Licensee: Three Eagles Communications Inc. (group owner; acq 1996). Network: ABC Information & Entertainment. Rep: McGavren Guild. Format: Talk. News staff: one; News: 10 hrs wkly. Target aud: 25-65. Spec prog: Polka, farm 5 hrs, Ger 5 hrs, Pol 5 hrs wkly. ◆ Rolland Johnson, CEO; Gary Buchanan, pres; Cindy Harris, CFO; Greg Wells, gen mgr; Dean Johnson, opns dir; Melissa Sanford, sls dir; Jim Dolezel, progmg dir; Bob Cook, chief of engrg.

KKOT(FM)—Co-owned with KTTT(AM). Nov 25, 1969: 93.5 mhz; 100 kw. 981 ft. TL: N41 32 28 W97 40 45. Stereo. Network: ABC Information & Entertainment. Rep: McGavren Guild. Format: Classic Rock. News staff: 2; News: 15 hrs wkly. Target aud: 18-49; young families. Spec prog: Farm 8 hrs wkly. ◆ Gary Buchanan, COO & opns dir; Dean Johnson, progmg dir.

Cozad

KAMI(AM)—Listing follows KCVN(FM).

***KCVN(FM)**— Aug 4, 1983: 104.5 mhz; 100 kw. Ant 360 ft. TL: N40 46 35 W100 01 47. Stereo. 100 N. 56th St., Suite 400, Lincoln 68504. Phone: (402) 465-8850. Fax: (402) 465-8852. E-mail: kcvn@bottradionetwork.com. Web Site: www.bottradionetwork.com /station_cozad/cozad_home.asp. Licensee: Community Broadcasting Inc. Group owner: Bott Radio Network (acq 7-9-2004; $365,000. with co-located AM). Format: Christian teaching and talk. Target aud: 25-54; adults. ◆ Tom Millett, gen mgr.

KAMI(AM)—Co-owned with KCVN(FM). November 1965: 1580 khz; 1 kw-D, 17 w-N. TL: N40 50 18 W99 56 20.

Crete

***KDNE(FM)**— Aug 30, 1993: 91.9 mhz; 200 w. 66 ft. TL: N40 37 16 W96 57 04. Stereo. 1014 Boswell Ave. 68333. Phone: (402) 826-8611. Fax: (402) 826-8600. E-mail: kdne@doane.edu. Licensee: Doane College Board of Trustees. Format: Progsv. Target aud: General; males & females between the ages of 12 to 34. ◆ Fred Brown, pres; Lee Thomas, gen mgr; Jennifer Gustafson, stn mgr.

KIBZ(FM)— Aug 20, 1976: 104.1 mhz; 50 kw. 613 ft. TL: N40 31 06 W96 46 07. Stereo. 4630 Antelope Creek Rd., Suite 200, Lincoln 68506. Phone: (402) 826-4393. Fax: (402) 483-9138. Web Site: www.kibz.com. Licensee: Capstar TX L.P. Group owner: Clear Channel Communications Inc. (acq 8-30-00; grpsl). Format: New rock. News staff: one. Target aud: 18-34. ◆ Julie Gade, stn mgr; Charlie Thomas, progmg dir.

Nebraska

Crookston

*KINI(FM)— January 1978: 96.1 mhz; 90 kw. Ant 499 ft. TL: N43 07 50 W100 54 02. Stereo. Box 419, 100 S. Main, St. Francis, SD 57572. Phone: (605) 747-2291. Fax: (605) 747-5791. E-mail: kinifm@gwtc.net. Web Site: www.gwtc.net/~kinifm. Licensee: Rosebud Educational Society Inc. (acq 1-78). Format: Adult contemp, rock, native American. News staff: one; News: 12 hrs wkly. Target aud: General; Indian & white. Spec prog: American Indian 15 hrs, gospel 6 hrs, relg 6 hrs wkly. ♦Fr. John Hatcher, pres; Marcy VanWinkle, exec VP; Bernard Whiting Jr., gen mgr.

Dakota City

KTFJ(AM)— 1991: 1250 khz; 500 w-D, 700 w-N, DA-2. TL: N42 26 33 W96 15 41. 1521 Buchanan Ave., Sioux City, IA 51106. Phone: (712) 252-4621. Web Site: www.worldwidebibleradio.com. Licensee: Donald A. Swanson. Network: USA. Format: Gospel. ♦Donald A. Swanson, pres & gen mgr.

Fairbury

KGMT(AM)— June 13, 1960: 1310 khz; 500 w-D, 97 w-N. TL: N40 06 58 W97 09 05. 414 4th St. 68352. Phone: (402) 729-3382. Fax: (402) 729-3446. E-mail: kutt@diodecom.net. Licensee: Siebert Communications Inc. (acq 8-1-84). Network: ABC Daytime Direction. Rep: Farmakis. Shaw Pittman. Format: Oldies, news. News: one. Target aud: 25-52. Spec prog: Farm 18 hrs wkly. ♦Rick Siebert, pres; Randy Bauer, gen mgr.

KUTT(FM)— Co-owned with KGMT(AM). December 1983: 99.5 mhz; 100 kw. 692 ft. TL: N40 10 57 W96 58 33. Stereo. Network: ABC. Format: Hot country. ♦Randy Bauer, stn mgr & progmg mgr.

Falls City

KLZA(FM)— July 7, 1998: 101.3 mhz; 6 kw. 328 ft. TL: N40 06 54 W95 39 06. (CP: 25 kw). Box 101 68355. Phone: (402) 245-6010. Fax: (402) 245-6040. E-mail: sunny1013fm@hotmail.com. Licensee: KNZA Inc. (group owner) Network: UPI. Format: Soft rock. ♦Mike Gilmore, stn mgr; Robert Hilton, opns mgr; Mike Slocum, chief of engrg.

KTNC(AM)— Aug 3, 1957: 1230 khz; 500 w-D, 1 kw-N. TL: N40 03 57 W95 36 55. 1602 Stone St. 68355. Phone: (402) 245-2453. Fax: (402) 245-5862. E-mail: ktnc@sentco.net. Licensee: C.R. Communications Inc. (acq 8-1-81; $270,000 7-13-81). Network: ABC Information & Entertainment. Howard Anderson. Format: Oldies. News staff: one; News: 23 hrs wkly. Target aud: 25 plus; farmers, businessmen, employees, retirees. Spec prog: Christian mus one hr wkly. ♦Charles A. Radatz, pres & gen mgr.

Fremont

KFMT(FM)—Listing follows KHUB(AM).

KHUB(AM)— December 1939: 1340 khz; 500 w-D, 1 kw-N. TL: N41 25 58 W96 27 16. 118 E. Fifth St. 68025. Phone: (402) 721-1340. Fax: (402) 721-5023. Licensee: JCM Broadcasting Co. LLC. Group owner: Waitt Radio Inc. (acq 1-7-02; grpsl). Network: ABC Information & Entertainment. Format: News/talk. News staff: one; News: 25 hrs wkly. Target aud: 35 plus; mature adults. Spec prog: Farm 6 hrs wkly. ♦Del Meyer, gen mgr, dev dir & progmg dir; Chris Walz, opns mgr, progmg dir & chief of engrg; Barry Reker, gen sls mgr; Jessica Meistrell, news dir.

KFMT(FM)— Co-owned with KHUB(AM). July 1972: 105.5 mhz; 1.2 kw. 450 ft. TL: N41 24 40 W96 31 53. Stereo. Web Site: www.kfmt.com. Format: Oldies, classic rock. Target aud: 25-54.

Gering

KMOR(FM)—See Scottsbluff

KOZY-FM— August 1996: 103.9 mhz; 7 kw. 102 ft. TL: N41 51 50 W103 42 20. Box 1263, Scottsbluff 69363-1263. Phone: (308) 632-5667. Fax: (308) 635-1905. E-mail: kmor@tracybroadcasting.com. Web Site: www.tracybroadcasting.com. Licensee: Tracy Broadcasting Corp. (group owner). Format: Soft rock. News staff: 2. Target aud: 25-54; general. ♦Larry Swikard, gen mgr.

Gordon

KSDZ(FM)— May 19, 1979: 95.5 mhz; 60 kw. 310 ft. TL: N42 47 56 W102 15 40. Stereo. Box 390, W. Hwy. 20 69343. Phone: (308) 282-2500. Fax: (308) 282-0061. Licensee: DJ Broadcasting Inc. (acq 12-26-91; 1-13-92). Network: ABC. Format: C&W, oldies. ♦Jim Lambley, pres.

Grand Island

*KLNB(FM)— 2005: 88.3 mhz; 1.7 kw. Ant 147 ft. TL: N40 54 50 W98 23 52. Educational Media Foundation, 5700 W. Oaks Blvd., Rocklin, CA 95765. Phone: (916) 251-1600. Fax: (916) 251-1650. E-mail: klove@klove.com. Web Site: www.klove.com. Licensee: Educational Media Foundation. Group owner: EMF Broadcasting (acq 3-11-2003; grpsl). Network: K-Love. Shaw Pittman. Format: Contemp Christian. News staff: 3. Target aud: 25-44; Judeo Christian, female. ♦Richard Jenkins, pres; Mike Novak, VP; Lloyd Parker, gen mgr; Ed Lenane, opns dir; Keith Whipple, dev dir.

KMMJ(AM)— November 1925: 750 khz; 10 kw-U, DA-1. TL: N41 08 05 W97 59 38. 3205 W. North Front St. 68802. Secondary address: Box 4907 68802. Phone: (308) 382-2800. Phone: (308) 381-1430. Fax: (308) 382-6701. E-mail: krgi@krgi.com. Web Site: www.krgi.com. Licensee: Legacy Communications LLC (group owner; acq 5-17-2004; grpsl). Rep: McGavren Guild, Howard Anderson. Format: var/div. Target aud: General. ♦Lyle Nelson, gen mgr; Jim Davis, progmg dir.

*KNFA(FM)—Not on air, target date: unknown: 90.7 mhz; 250 w. Ant 161 ft. TL: N40 54 50 W98 23 52. Box 2440, Tupelo, MS 38803-2440. Phone: (662) 844-8888. Fax: (662) 842-6791. Web Site: www.afr.net. Licensee: American Family Association. (acq 6-21-2005). ♦Donald Wildmon, chmn; Marvin Sanders, gen mgr.

KRGI(AM)— Apr 1, 1953: 1430 khz; 5 kw-D, 1 kw-N, DA-N. TL: N40 62 26 W98 16 24. Box 4907 68802-4907. Secondary address: 3205 W. N. Front St. 68803. Phone: (308) 381-1430. Fax: (308) 382-6701. E-mail: krgi@krgi.com. Licensee: Legacy Communications LLC. (group owner; acq 5-17-2004; grpsl). Network: ABC Information & Entertainment. Rep: Christal. Fletcher, Heald & Hildreth. Format: Adult contemp, news/talk. Target aud: 25-54. ♦Alan Usher, gen mgr & gen sls mgr; Chris Loghry, opns dir & progmg dir; Rob Fossberg, news dir; Chuck Walker, chief of engrg.

KRGI-FM— Oct 30, 1975: 96.5 mhz; 100 kw. 416 ft. TL: N40 51 53 W98 23 47. Stereo. Network: ABC. Format: Hot C&W.

*KROA(FM)— Aug 11, 1967: 95.7 mhz; 100 kw. 460 ft. TL: N40 47 11 W98 22 00. Stereo. Box 495, Doniphan 68832. Phone: (402) 845-6595. Fax: (402) 845-6597. E-mail: kroafm@kroa.org. Web Site: www.kroa.org. Licensee: Mission Nebraska Inc. (acq 11-25-2003; $1.5 million). Network: Moody. Format: Adult contemp Christian. ♦Dr. James Eckman, pres; Gordon Wheeler, stn mgr; Taryn Julane, mus dir.

KSYZ-FM— November 1982: 107.7 mhz; 100 kw. 899 ft. TL: N40 51 53 W98 23 47. (CP: TL: N40 42 07 W98 35 20). Stereo. 3532 W. Captial Ave. 68803. Phone: (308) 381-1077. Fax: (308) 384-8900. E-mail: ksyzprod@waittradio.com. Web Site: www.ksyz.com. Licensee: Neuhoff Broadcasting-Grand Island Inc. (acq 8-5-99; $5.9 million). Format: Adult contemp. Target aud: 25-49; adults. ♦Dan Zabka, gen mgr; Jim Cartwright, opns mgr.

Hastings

*KCNT(FM)— Feb 22, 1971: 88.1 mhz; 2 kw. 182 ft. TL: N40 34 52 W98 19 58. Box 1024 68902. Phone: (402) 461-2580. Fax: (402) 461-2507. E-mail: jbrooks@ccneb.edu. Web Site: www.cccneb.edu /programs/mart/kent/index.html. Licensee: Central Community College. Format: CHR, educ. ♦John L. Brooks, gen mgr.

*KFKX(FM)— Aug 30, 1997: 90.1 mhz; 1 kw vert. 292 ft. TL: N40 38 56 W98 23 01. Stereo. 710 Turner Hastings College 68901. Phone: (402) 461-7367. Fax: (402) 461-7442. E-mail: kfkx@hastings.edu. Licensee: Hastings College. Booth, Freret, Imlay & Tepper. Format: Div, AOR. News: 7 hrs wkly. Target aud: General. Spec prog: Jazz 3 hrs, relg 3 hrs, urban contemp 8 hrs wkly. ♦Phillip Dudley, pres; Sharon Behl Brooks, gen mgr; Meg Bernt, stn mgr; Bart Jones, opns dir.

KHAS(AM)— Sept 30, 1940: 1230 khz; 1 kw-U. TL: N40 34 40 W98 24 17. Box 726 68902. Secondary address: 500 East J St. 68901. Phone: (402) 462-5101. Fax: (402) 461-3866. E-mail: khas@gtmc.net. Web Site: hastingslink.com. Licensee: KHAS Broadcasting Inc. (acq 7-1-93; $200,000; 6-28-93). Network: CBS. Howard Anderson Miller & Neely. Format: Adult contemp. News staff: one; News: 20 hrs wkly. Target aud: 35 plus; general. Spec prog: Farm 2 hrs, class 2 hrs wkly. ♦Wayne Specht, pres & gen mgr; Jim Stevens, stn mgr, prom VP, progmg VP & progmg dir; Mike Smithson, news dir.

*KHNE-FM— June 1990: 89.1 mhz; 64.3 kw. 328 ft. TL: N40 46 17 W98 05 22. Stereo. Box 83111, Lincoln 68501. Secondary address: 1800 N. 33rd St., Lincoln 68583. Phone: (402) 472-3611. Fax: (402) 472-2403. Licensee: Nebraska Educational Telecommunications Commission. Network: Network: PRI, NPR. Dow, Lohnes & Albertson. Format: Class, news. Target aud: General. ♦Ray Dilley, gen mgr; Nancy Finken, progmg dir; Susan Dinsmore, progmg dir; Martin Wells, news dir.

KICS(AM)— Apr 15, 1964: 1550 khz; 500 w-D. TL: N40 34 09 W98 21 57. 500 E. J St. 68901-7113. Phone: (402) 462-5101. Fax: (402) 461-3866. E-mail: khas@gtmc.not. Web Site: www.khasradio.com. Licensee: KHAS Broadcasting Inc. (acq 8-6-98; $110,000). Network: ESPN Radio. Howard Anderson Miller & Miller. Format: ESPN sports. News staff: one; News: 12 hrs wkly. Target aud: 18-54; males. ♦Wayne Specht, pres & gen mgr; Jim Stevens, stn mgr.

KLIQ(FM)— 2001: 94.5 mhz; 97.7 kw. Ant 948 ft. TL: N40 36 08 W98 50 21. 906 W. 2nd St., Suite 68901. Phone: (402) 461-4922. Fax: (402) 461-4950. E-mail: dbrock@waittradio.com. Web Site: www.kliqfm.com. Licensee: WMMP LLC. Group owner: Waitt Radio Inc. (acq 1-7-02; grpsl). Pepper & Corazzini. Format: Adult contemp. Target aud: 25-54. Spec prog: News & special community interest. ♦David Brock, gen mgr & stn mgr; Theresa Parr, gen sls mgr; Cody Hanson, progmg dir.

*KNHA(FM)—Not on air, target date: unknown: 90.9 mhz; 500 w. Ant 148 ft. TL: N40 38 56 W98 23 01. Drawer 2440, Tupelo, MS 38803. Phone: (662) 844-8888. Fax: (662) 842-6791. Web Site: www.afr.net. Licensee: American Family Association. ♦Marvin Sanders, gen mgr.

KROR(FM)— February 1965: 101.5 mhz; 100 kw. Ant 1,004 ft. TL: N40 39 28 W98 52 04. Stereo. 3532 W. Capital Ave., Grand Island 68803. Phone: (308) 381-1077. Fax: (308) 384-8900. E-mail: ksyzprod@waittradio.com. Web Site: www.rock1015.com. Licensee: Eternal Broadcasting LLC. (acq 11-20-00; $750,000). Format: Classic rock. Target aud: 25-54. ♦Dan Zabka, gen mgr; Jim Cartwright, opns mgr.

Holdrege

KMTY(FM)—Listing follows KUVR(AM).

KUVR(AM)— Oct 20, 1956: 1380 khz; 500 w-D. TL: N40 26 26 W99 23 58. Box 465 68949. Phone: (308) 995-4020. Fax: (308) 995-2202. Licensee: Waitt Radio Inc. (group owner; acq 1-7-02; grpsl). Network: ABC Information & Entertainment. Borsari & Paxson. Format: Oldies. Target aud: 35-54. Spec prog: Farm 5 hrs, big band 5 hrs, contemp gospel 5 hrs wkly. ♦Mike Delich, pres; John McDonald, gen mgr, progmg dir & news dir; Jim Conner, gen sls mgr; Randy Issler, mus dir; Val Lane, chief of engrg.

KMTY(FM)—Co-owned with KUVR(AM). October 1970: 97.7 mhz; 55 kw. 262 ft. TL: N40 26 19 W99 23 59. Stereo. Network: ABC. Format: Hot adult contemp. Target aud: 20-45.

Hubbard

***KAYA(FM)**— 1998: 91.3 mhz; 5.1 kw. Ant 377 ft. TL: N42 21 10 W96 31 32. Box 3206, Sioux City, MS 38803. Secondary address: 1211 Tri-View, Sioux City, IA 51103. Phone: (662) 844-8888. Phone: (712) 255-9191. Fax: (662) 842-6791. Fax: (712) 255-3177. E-mail: comments@afr.net. Web Site: www.afr.net. Licensee: American Family Association. Group owner: American Family Radio Format: Christian inspirational, relg. ♦Marvin Sanders, gen mgr.

Imperial

KADL(FM)— 2003: 102.9 mhz; 300 w. Ant 223 ft. TL: N40 30 45 W101 38 39. Box 333, McCook 69001. Phone: (308) 345-5400. Fax: (308) 345-4720. Licensee: Imperial Media Association (acq 10-17-01). Format: Oldies. ♦David M. Stout, gen mgr.

Kearney

KGFW(AM)— 1927: 1340 khz; 1 kw-U. TL: N40 40 05 W99 04 52. Box 666 68848. Secondary address: 2223 Central Ave. 68847. Phone: (308) 237-2131. Fax: (308) 237-0312. E-mail: mail@kgfw.com. Web Site: www.kgfw.com. Licensee: WMMP LLC. Group owner: Waitt Radio Inc. (acq 1-7-02; grpsl). Network: Westwood One. Rep: Christal. Format: News/talk. News staff: 2; News: 25 hrs wkly. Target aud: 25 plus; adults in central Nebraska. Spec prog: Farm 8 hrs, sports 10 hrs wkly. ♦Norman Waitt Jr, chmn; Mary Quess, pres; John McDonald, gen mgr.

KQKY(FM)—Co-owned with KGFW(AM). October 1979: 105.9 mhz; 97.6 kw. Ant 1,204 ft. TL: N40 36 08 W98 50 21. Stereo. Phone: (308) 236-6464. Web Site: www.kqky.com. Rep: Christal. Format: Top-40. Target aud: 18-49.

KKPR-FM—Listing follows KXPN(AM).

***KLPR(FM)**— Mar 8, 1968: 91.3 mhz; 1 kw. 100 ft. TL: N40 42 30 W99 05 45. Stereo. Univ. of Nebraska at Kearney 68849. Phone: (308) 865-8217. Phone: (308) 865-8216. Fax: (308) 865-8217. Licensee: University of Nebraska at Kearney. Format: Jazz, new age, AOR. Spec prog: Class 18 hrs wkly. ♦Roy Hyatte, gen mgr.

KRNY(FM)— 1987: 102.3 mhz; 77.1 kw. Ant 1,086 ft. TL: N40 36 08 W98 50 21. Stereo. Box 669 68848. Secondary address: 2223 Central Ave. 68847. Phone: (308) 237-2131. Phone: (308) 236-8600. Fax: (308) 237-0312. E-mail: mail@krny.com. Web Site: www.krny.com. Licensee: WMMP LLC. Group owner: Waitt Radio Inc. (acq 1-7-02; grpsl). Haley, Bader & Potts. Format: Hot country. News: 2 hrs wkly. Target aud: 25 plus. ♦John McDonald, gen mgr; Dirk Christensen, opns mgr.

KXPN(AM)— Dec 5, 1956: 1460 khz; 5 kw-D, 56 w-N. TL: N40 42 45 W99 10 15. Box 130 68848. Secondary address: 403 E. 25th St. 68848. Phone: (308) 236-9900. Fax: (308) 234-6781. E-mail: espn1460@charter.net. Web Site: www.kkpr.com. Licensee: Platte River Radio Inc. (acq 1-1-94; $750,000. with co-located FM; FTR: 12-13-93). Network: ESPN Radio. Format: Sports. News staff: one; News: 2 hrs wkly. Target aud: 25-54; men. ♦David Oldfather, pres; Craig Eckert, exec VP & gen mgr; Dan Beck, opns mgr; Johnnie McCann, sls dir; Mike Cahill, news dir.

KKPR-FM—Co-owned with KXPN(AM). Nov 1, 1962: 98.9 mhz; 100 kw. Ant 700 ft. TL: N40 48 53 W98 46 12. Stereo. E-mail: generalmanager@kkpr.com. Web Site: www.kkpr.com. Format: Oldies. News staff: one; News: 3 hrs wkly. Target aud: 35-64. ♦Dan Beck, chief of opns; Johnnie McCann, gen sls mgr.

Kimball

KBFZ(FM)— 1999: 100.1 mhz; 6 kw. 295 ft. TL: N41 11 36 W103 31 47. Stereo. Box 532, Scottsbluff 69363-0532. Phone: (308) 632-5667. Fax: (308) 635-1905. Web Site: tracybroadcasting.com. Licensee: Tracy Broadcasting Corp. (group owner). Network: AP Radio. Format: Oldies. News staff: 2. ♦Michael Tracy, pres; Larry Swikard, gen mgr.

KIMB(AM)— 1958: 1260 khz; 1 kw-D, 500 w-N. TL: N41 15 42 W103 40 06. 3205 W. North Front St., Grand Island 68803. Phone: (308) 381-1430. Fax: (308) 382-6701. Web Site: www.krgi.com. Licensee: Legacy Communications LLC. (group owner; (acq 5-17-2004; grpsl). Format: Country. Target aud: General. ♦Alan Usher, VP & gen mgr.

Lexington

***KLNE-FM**— May 4, 1990: 88.7 mhz; 43.8 kw. 938 ft. TL: N40 23 05 W99 27 30. Stereo. Box 83111, Lincoln 68501. Secondary address: 1800 N. 33rd St., Lincoln 68583. Phone: (402) 472-3611. Fax: (402) 472-2403. Web Site: www.ntrn.org. Licensee: Nebraska Educational Telecommunications Commission. Network: Network: PRI, NPR. Dow, Lohnes & Albertson. Format: Class, news & info. Target aud: 25 plus; general. ♦Ray Dilley, gen mgr.

KRVN(AM)— Feb 1, 1951: 880 khz; 50 kw-U, DA-N. TL: N40 31 03 W99 23 20. Box 880, 1007 Plum Creek Pkwy. 68850-0880. Phone: (308) 324-2371. Fax: (308) 324-5786. E-mail: krvnam@krvn.com. Web Site: www.krvn.com. Licensee: Nebraska Rural Radio Assn. (group owner) (acq 2-1-51). Network: ABC Information & Entertainment. Rep: Katz Radio. Garvey Schubert & Barer. Format: C&W, news, farm. News staff: 4; News: 30 hrs wkly. Target aud: General; Nebraska farm/ranch families & consumers. Spec prog: Relg 12 hrs, country 8 hrs wkly. ♦Eric Brown, gen mgr; Ed Bennett, opns mgr; Dennis Waddle, gen sls mgr; Pam Snyder, prom dir; Stafford Thompson, progmg dir; Frank Snyder, news dir; Vern Killion, engrg dir.

KRVN-FM— Nov 1, 1962: 93.1 mhz; 100 kw. 320 ft. TL: N40 41 50 W99 47 17. Stereo. Web Site: www.krvnfm.com. Network: Westwood One. Rep: Katz Radio. Format: News, new country. News staff: one; News: 30 hrs wkly. Contemp young adults. Spec prog: Farm 10 hrs wkly.

Lincoln

KBBK(FM)—Listing follows KLIN(AM).

KFOR(AM)—Listing follows KFRX(FM).

KFRX(FM)— May 2, 1965: 102.7 mhz; 100 kw. 500 ft. TL: N40 49 12 W96 39 29. (CP: TL: N45 46 51 W96 22 52). Stereo. 3800 Cornhusker Hwy. 68504-1533. Phone: (402) 466-1234. Fax: (402) 467-4095. E-mail: kfrx@threeeagles.com. Web Site: www.kfrxfm.com. Licensee: Three Eagles Communications Inc. Group owner: Three Eagles Communications (acq 1996; $5.3 million with co-located AM). Network: ABC FM Connection. Rep: McGavren Guild. Tierney & Swift. Format: CHR. Target aud: 18-49; women. ♦Roland Johnson, CEO; Gary Buchanan, COO; Cindy Harris, CFO; Jerry Hinrikus, gen mgr; Peg Schoen, stn mgr & sls dir; Coby Mach, opns mgr; Diane Wells, sls dir; Vicki Marker, prom dir; Ryan Sampson, progmg dir; Adam Michaels, mus dir; Bob Cook, chief of engrg; Roger Dodson, sls.

***KLCV(FM)**— 1996: 88.5 mhz; 4.7 kw vert. 315 ft. TL: N40 55 49 W96 32 42. KLCV Radio, 100 N. 56th St., Suite 110 68504. Secondary address: Bott Radio Network, 10550 Barkley, Suite 108, Overland Park, KS 68504. Phone: (402) 465-8850. Phone: (913) 642-7770. Fax: (402) 465-8852. Fax: (913) 642-1319. E-mail: klcv1@juno.com. Licensee: Community Broadcasting Inc. Format: Christian talk. Target aud: 25 plus; Christian families. ♦Richard Bott Sr., pres; Tom Millett, gen mgr.

KLIN(AM)— August 1947: 1400 khz; 1 kw-U. TL: N40 50 54 W96 40 29. 4343 O St. 68510. Phone: (402) 475-4567. Fax: (402) 479-1411. Licensee: Monterey Licenses LLC. Group owner: Triad Broadcasting Co. LLC (acq 3-31-00; grpsl). Network: Network: CBS, ABC News/Talk. Format: News/talk. News staff: 4; News: 80 hrs wkly. Target aud: 35-64; upper income, business owner, educated with high disposable income. ♦David Benjamin, pres; Mark Halverson, gen mgr; John Bishop, progmg dir; Greg Jackson, news dir & pub affrs dir; Bill Frost, chief of engrg.

KBBK(FM)—Co-owned with KLIN(AM). Sept 1, 1968: 107.3 mhz; 100 kw. 551 ft. TL: N40 43 38 W96 36 49. Stereo. Web Site: www.b1073.com. Format: Adult contemp. Target aud: 25-54; middle-to-upper income, households, in-office & in-store lstng. ♦T. Pat Miller, progmg dir.

KLMS(AM)—Listing follows KRKR(FM).

KLMY(FM)— Feb 23, 1973: 106.3 mhz; 3 kw. 213 ft. TL: N40 48 48 W96 42 25. (CP: 50 kw, ant 190 ft.). Stereo. 4630 Antelope Creek Rd., Suite 200 68506. Phone: (402) 484-8000. Fax: (402) 483-9138. E-mail: sonny@my1063.com. Web Site: www.my1063.com. Licensee: Capstar TX L.P. Group owner: Clear Channel Communications Inc. (acq 8-30-00; grpsl). Format: AOR/current rock. News: one hr wkly. Target aud: 35-64. ♦Julie Gade, gen mgr; Michelle Hay, gen sls mgr; Sonny Valentine, progmg dir; Tim Cawley, news dir; Dave Agnew, chief of engrg.

KLNC(FM)— 1992: 105.3 mhz; 3 kw. Ant 328 ft. TL: N40 49 12 W96 39 29. 4343 O St. 68510. Phone: (402) 475-4567. Fax: (402) 479-1411. Licensee: Monterey Licenses LLC. Group owner: Triad Broadcasting Co. LLC (acq 3-31-2000; grpsl). Format: Oldies. ♦David Benjamin, CEO; Mark Halverson, VP & gen mgr; J. Pat Miller, opns mgr; Ami Graham, gen sls mgr; E.J. Marshall, progmg dir; Steve Looney, chief of engrg.

KLTQ(FM)— June 22, 1958: 101.9 mhz; 100 kw. 1,132 ft. TL: N40 47 09 W96 23 07. Stereo. 5011 Capitol Ave., Omaha 68132. Phone: (402) 342-2000. Fax: (402) 827-5293. Web Site: www.literock1019.com. Licensee: Waitt Omaha LLC. (group owner; (acq 1-7-2002; grpsl). Rep: Katz Radio. Pepper & Corazzini. Format: Light rock. Target aud: 25-54; general. ♦Ken Fearnow, VP.

KRKR(FM)— Mar 6, 1975: 95.1 mhz; 50 kw. 287 ft. TL: N40 58 49 W96 41 45. Stereo. 3800 Cornhusker Hwy. 68504. Phone: (402) 466-1234. Fax: (402) 467-4095. Web Site: www.95rocklincoln.com. Licensee: Three Eagles Communications Co. Group owner: Three Eagles Communications (acq 1996; grpsl). Tierney & Swift. Format: Classic rock. News staff: one; News: 2 hrs wkly. Target aud: 25-54. ♦Roland Johnson, CEO; Gary Buchanan, COO; Cindy Harris, CFO; Jerry Hinrikus, gen mgr & stn mgr; Coby Mach, opns mgr; Joy Patton, sls dir; Vicki Marker, prom dir; Scott Kaye, progmg dir; Dale Johnson, news dir; Bob Cook, chief of engrg.

KLMS(AM)—Co-owned with KRKR(FM). October 1949: 1480 khz; 5 kw-D, 1 kw-N, DA-2. TL: N40 47 47 W96 34 56. Stereo. Web Site: www.espn1480.com. Format: Sports. ♦Bill Doleman, progmg dir.

***KRNU(FM)**— Feb 23, 1970: 90.3 mhz; 100 w. 180 ft. TL: N40 49 11 W96 42 11. Stereo. 147 Anderson Hall, Univ. of Nebraska 68588-0466. Phone: (402) 472-3054. Fax: (402) 472-8403. E-mail: krnu@unl.edu. Web Site: www.krnu.unl.edu. Licensee: University of Nebraska. Network: ABC. Dow, Lohnes & Albertson. Format: Alternative. News: 10 hrs wkly. Spec prog: Black 2 hrs, blues 2 hrs, folk 2 hrs, gospel 2hrs, Jazz 2 hrs, Sp 2 hrs, sports 2 hrs wkly. ♦Rick Alloway, gen mgr, opns mgr, gen sls mgr & progmg dir; Trina Creighton, news dir; Vance Payne, chief of engrg. Co-owned TV: *KUON-TV affil.

KTGL(FM)—(Beatrice). Nov 26, 1962: 92.9 mhz; 100 kw. 809 ft. TL: N40 31 06 W96 46 07. Stereo. 4630 Antelope Creek Rd., Suite 200 68506. Phone: (402) 484-8000. Phone: (402) 489-9291. Fax: (402) 489-9607. E-mail: juliegade@clearchannel.com. Web Site: www.ktgl.com. Licensee: Capstar TX L.P. Group owner: Clear Channel Communications Inc. (acq 8-30-00; grpsl). Format: Classic rock. News staff: one; News: 3 hrs wkly. Target aud: 18-49. ♦Julie Gade, gen mgr; Julie Broman, sls dir; Joe Skare, progmg dir; Tim Cawley, news dir; Eric Taylor, pub affrs dir; Mike Elliott, chief of engrg.

***KUCV(FM)**— Jan 1, 1968: 91.1 mhz; 19.5 kw horiz, 100 kw vert. Ant 689 ft. TL: N40 31 06 W96 46 06. Stereo. Box 83111 68501. Phone: (402) 472-3611. Fax: (402) 472-2403. Web Site: www.nprn.org. Licensee: Nebraska Educational Telecommunications Commission. (acq 8-88). Network: Network: NPR, PRI. Format: Classical, news. News staff: 3; News: 30 hrs wkly. Target aud: General. Spec prog: Jazz 5 hrs, blues 1 hr, world 1 hr, folk 1 hr wkly. ♦Ray Dilley, gen mgr.

KZKX(FM)—See Seward

***KZUM(FM)**— 1978: 89.3 mhz; 1.5 kw. 174 ft. TL: N40 48 47 W96 42 24. Stereo. 941 O St., Suite 1025 68508-3608. Phone: (402) 474-5086. Fax: (402) 474-5091. E-mail: kzumradio@aol.com. Web Site: www.kzum.org. Licensee: Sunrise Communications Inc. Format: Div, jazz, urban contemp. News: 11 hrs wkly. Target aud: General; the unserved & underserved population. Spec prog: Sp 4 hrs, rock/progsv 15 hrs, new age 8 hrs, blues 13 hrs, folk 8 hrs, gospel 3 hrs wkly. ♦Steve Alvis, gen mgr; Dennis Suoboda, dev dir; Dennis Svoboda, dev dir; Jeff Gilbreath, prom dir; Craig Lowe, progmg dir.

McCook

KBRL(AM)— Sept 26, 1947: 1300 khz; 5 kw-D, DA. TL: N40 11 31 W100 39 06. Box 333 69001. Secondary address: 1811 W. O St. 699001. Phone: (308) 345-5400. Fax: (308) 345-4720. E-mail: dave@kicx.net. Web Site: www.kicx.net. Licensee: McCook Radio Group L.L.C. (group owner; acq 3-9-99). Format: Oldies, full service.

Stations in the U.S.   Nebraska

Developers & Brokers of Radio Properties — contact American Media Services at our suite: Philadelphia Marriott Downtown 215-625-2900 843-972-2200 americanmediaservices.com Charleston, SC Dallas, TX · Chicago, Il · Austin, TX American Media Services, LLC

Target aud: 35-64. ♦ David Stout, pres & gen mgr; Connie Stout, gen sls mgr & adv dir; Rich Barnett, news dir; Ron Fritz, chief of engrg.

KICX-FM—Co-owned with KBRL(AM). Jan 31, 1979: 96.1 mhz; 55 kw. 318 ft. TL: N40 10 19 W100 41 05. Stereo. Web Site: www.kicx.net. Format: Adult contemp. News staff: one. Target aud: 25-64. ♦ Connie Stout, sls VP.

KIOD(FM)— May 1, 1981: 105.3 mhz; 100 kw. 591 ft. TL: N40 11 27 W100 48 29. Stereo. Box 939 69001. Secondary address: 106 W. 8th St. 69001. Phone: (308) 345-1981. Fax: (308) 345-7202. E-mail: jay@coyote105.com. Web Site: www.coyote105.com. Licensee: Austin McCook L.L.C. (acq 4-22-96; $470,000; 1-13-92). Larry D. Perry. Format: Hot country. News staff: one; News: 5 hrs wkly. Target aud: 25-54. Spec prog: Sports 10 hrs, farm 6 hrs wkly. ♦ Jay D. Austin, pres, gen mgr, gen sls mgr & news dir; Jesse Stevens, opns VP, progmg dir & progmg mgr; Derek Beck, mus dir.

KNAX(AM)—Not on air, target date: unknown: 700 khz; 250 w-U, DA-N. TL: N40 16 00 W100 34 09. Box 333 69001. Phone: (308) 345-5400. Fax: (308) 345-4720. Licensee: McCook Radio Group L.L.C. (group owner). ♦ David Stout, gen mgr & opns mgr; Connie Stout, gen sls mgr; Rich Barnett, news dir.

***KNGN(AM)**— June 23, 1961: 1360 khz; 1 kw-D. TL: N40 11 45 W100 41 57. R.R. 3, Box 1360 69001-9510. Phone: (308) 345-2006. Fax: (308) 345-2052. E-mail: goodnews@mccooknet.com. Web Site: www.christianlink.com/kngn. Licensee: Kansas Nebraska Good News Broadcasting Corp. (acq 9-5-01). Format: Relg. News: 7 hrs wkly. Target aud: 35 plus; family oriented. ♦ Paul Warneke, pres; Mike Nielsen, gen mgr.

KRKU(FM)—Not on air, target date: unknown: 98.5 mhz; 55 kw. 361 ft. TL: N40 10 19 W100 41 05. Box 333 69001. Secondary address: 1811 W. O St. 69001. Phone: (308) 345-5400. Fax: (308) 345-4720. E-mail: dave@kicx.net. Web Site: www.kicx.net. Licensee: McCook Radio Group L.L.C. (group owner; acq 9-8-00). Format: Classic rock. Target aud: 18-54. ♦ David Stout, gen mgr & opns mgr; Connie Stout, gen sls mgr; Rich Barnett, news dir.

KSWN(FM)— Sept 17, 1998: 93.9 mhz; 50 kw. Ant 492 ft. TL: N40 11 27 W100 48 29. Stereo. Box 939, 106 W. 8th St. 69001-0218. Phone: (308) 345-1100. Fax: (308) 345-7202. E-mail: jay@coyote105.com. Web Site: www.theprairie.net. Licensee: Austin McCook L.L.C. Network: CBS. Larry D. Perry. Format: News/talk, sports, adult contemp. News staff: one; News: 18 hrs wkly. Target aud: 25-54. Spec prog: Sports 10 hrs, farm 6 hrs wkly. ♦ Jay D. Austin, pres & gen mgr; Eileen G. Austin, opns VP; Jay Austin, gen sls mgr; Jesse Stevens, progmg mgr.

Merriman

***KRNE-FM**— Aug 29, 1991: 91.5 mhz; 92 kw. 964 ft. TL: N42 40 38 W101 42 36. Stereo. Box 83111, Lincoln 68501. Phone: (402) 472-3611. Fax: (402) 472-2403. Web site: www.nprn.org. Licensee: Nebraska Educational Telecommunications Commission. Network: Network: NPR, PRI. Format: Class, news. Target aud: General. ♦ Ray Dilley, gen mgr.

Milford

KFGE(FM)— 1996: 98.1 mhz; 100 kw. 981 ft. TL: N40 51 52 W97 16 14. 4343 O St., Lincoln 68510. Phone: (402) 475-4567. Fax: (402) 479-1411. Licensee: Monterey Licenses LLC. Group owner: Triad Broadcasting Co. LLC (acq 3-31-00; grpsl). Format: Country. ♦ David Benjamin, CEO; Mark Halverson, VP & gen mgr; J. Pat Miller, opns mgr; Ami Graham, gen mgr; Steve Albertson, progmg dir; Steve Looney, chief of engrg.

Mitchell

***KOSJ(FM)**—Not on air, target date: unknown: 89.5 mhz; 100 kw. Ant 454 ft. TL: N41 45 35 W102 58 12. CSN International, 3232 W. MacArthur Blvd., Santa Ana, CA 92704. Phone: (714) 825-9663. Fax: (714) 825-9660. Web Site: www.csnradio.com. Licensee: CSN International (group owner). ♦ Jeffrey W. Smith, VP.

Nebraska City

KBBX-FM— Feb 1, 1995: 97.7 mhz; 100 kw. 981 ft. TL: N40 53 31 W96 09 10. 11128 John Galt Blvd., Suite 192, Omaha 68137. Phone: (402) 592-5300. Fax: (402) 592-6605. Licensee: Journal Broadcast Corp. Group owner: Journal Broadcast Group Inc. (acq 12-6-96; $5 million). Network: ABC. Rosenman & Colin. Format: Sp. Target aud: 25-54. ♦ Steve Wexler, gen mgr; Tom Land, opns dir; Jim Timm, gen sls mgr; RosAnna Salcido, mktg mgr; Kurt Owens, progmg dir; Bill Jensen, news dir.

KNCY(AM)— June 29, 1959: 1600 khz; 500 w-D, 31 w-N, DA-2. TL: N40 40 27 W95 53 08. Box 278, 814 Central Ave. 68410. Phone: (402) 873-3348. Fax: (402) 873-7882. E-mail: kncy@kncycountry.com. Web Site: www.kncycountry.com. Licensee: Arbor Day Broadcasting Inc. (acq 12-30-02; $600,000. with KNCY-FM Auburn). Network: Westwood One. Format: Country. News staff: 2; News: 21 hrs wkly. Target aud: 18-80; local residents, farmers, business owners, workers, students. Spec prog: Farm 3 hrs, sports 6 hrs wkly. ♦ Mike Overton, exec VP, gen mgr & gen sls mgr; Doug Jennings, progmg dir; Tammy Partsch, news dir; George Blessing, chief of engrg.

Norfolk

KEXL(FM)—Listing follows WJAG(AM).

KNEN(FM)— Apr 6, 1979: 94.7 mhz; 100 kw. Ant 531 ft. TL: N41 55 16 W97 36 20. Stereo. Box 937 68702. Secondary address: 300 Madison Ave. 68701. Phone: (402) 379-3300. Fax: (402) 379-3008. E-mail: knen@waittradio.com. Licensee: Central Radio Inc. Network: ABC Information & Entertainment. Format: Adult contemp. News staff: 2; News: 15 hrs wkly. Target aud: 25-54; young to middle-aged. Spec prog: Farm 10 hrs wkly. ♦ Neil Lipetzky, gen mgr; Steve Farlee, gen sls mgr; Kevin Rahfelat, progmg dir; William Seifert, news dir.

***KPNO(FM)**— Sept 23, 1992: 90.9 mhz; 50 kw. 351 ft. TL: N42 06 16 W97 20 11. Stereo. 109 S. 2nd St. 68701-5327. Phone: (402) 379-3677. Fax: (402) 379-3662. E-mail: kpno@conpoint.com. Web Site: www.kpno.org. Licensee: The Praise Network Inc. Network: Moody, USA. Format: Relg, inspirational. News: 14 hrs wkly. Target aud: 25-54; family-oriented adults. ♦ Herb Roszhart Jr., CEO; Jon Shipman, gen mgr.

***KXNE-FM**— May 29, 1990: 89.3 mhz; 42.3 kw. 984 ft. TL: N42 14 15 W97 16 41. Box 83111, Lincoln 68501. Secondary address: 1800 N. 33rd St., Lincoln 68583. Phone: (402) 472-3611. Fax: (402) 472-2403. Web Site: www.nprn.org. Licensee: Nebraska Educational Telecommunications Commission. Network: Network: PRI, NPR. Format: Class. Target aud: General. ♦ Ray Dilley, gen mgr.

WJAG(AM)— July 27, 1922: 780 khz; 1 kw-U (L-WBBM). TL: N42 01 54 W97 29 47. Stereo. Box 789 68702. Secondary address: 309 Braasch Ave. 68701. Phone: (402) 371-0780. Fax: (402) 371-6303. E-mail: wjagkexl@wjag.com. Web Site: www.wjag.com. Licensee: WJAG Inc. Network: CNN Radio. Fletcher, Heald & Hildreth. Format: News/talk. News staff: 2; News: 10 hrs wkly. Target aud: 35-64; info-oriented. ♦ Jerry Huse, pres; Robert G. Thomas, VP & gen mgr; Jeffrey Steffen, opns mgr & progmg dir; Brad Hughes, sls dir, gen sls mgr, mktg dir & prom dir; Todd Michaels, mus dir; Jim Curry, news dir; J. Alan Johnson, pub affrs dir.

KEXL(FM)—Co-owned with WJAG(AM). Aug 1, 1971: 106.7 mhz; 100 kw. 1,027 ft. TL: N41 55 59 W97 40 49. Stereo. E-mail: wjagkexl@kexl. Web Site: www.kexl.com. Format: Adult contemp. News staff: 2; News: 6 hrs wkly. Target aud: 18-49; full service FM adults. ♦ Todd Michaels, mus dir.

North Platte

KELN(FM)—Listing follows KOOQ(AM).

***KJLT(AM)**— July 1, 1957: 970 khz; 5 kw-D, 55 w-N. TL: N41 09 30 W100 52 36. (CP: TL: N41 09 36 W100 52 42). Box 709 69103. Secondary address: 201 S. Bailey 69103. Phone: (308) 532-5515. E-mail: kjlt@kjlt.org. Web Site: www.kjlt.org. Licensee: Tri-State Broadcasting Assn. Inc. (acq 7-1-57). Network: USA. Format: Christian educ. Target aud: General; families. Spec prog: Sp one hr wkly. ♦ John L. Townsend, pres, gen mgr & progmg dir; Gary Hofer, chief of engrg.

KJLT-FM— Sept 24, 1979: 94.9 mhz; 100 kw. 652 ft. TL: N40 59 49 W100 52 47. Stereo. Web Site: www.kjlt.org. (Acq 3-22-90; $85,000; 4-16-90). Format: Inspirational, gospel. Target aud: General; young adults.

KODY(AM)— July 5, 1930: 1240 khz; 1 kw-U. TL: N41 09 14 W100 46 23. 305 E. Fourth St. 69101. Phone: (308) 532-3344. Fax: (308) 534-6651. Web Site: www.kodyradio.com. Licensee: JCM Broadcasting Co. LLC. Group owner: Waitt Radio Inc. (acq 1-7-02; grpsl). Network: Network: CBS, Moody, Westwood One. Rep: Howard Anderson, Katz Radio. Format: News/talk. Target aud: 25 plus; middle to upper income. ♦ Norm Waitt, pres; Rob Mandeville, gen mgr; Rob Mandeville, gen sls mgr; George Keltz, news dir; Tony Lama, opns mgr, progmg dir & chief of engrg.

KXNP(FM)—Co-owned with KODY(AM). June 7, 1982: 103.5 mhz; 100 kw. 479 ft. TL: N41 12 49 W100 43 48. Stereo. Web Site: www.kx104.com. Network: Jones Radio Networks. Format: Contemp country.

KOOQ(AM)— January 1966: 1410 khz; 5 kw-D, 1 kw-N, DA-N. TL: N41 10 30 W100 45 07. Box 248 69103. Secondary address: 1301 E. 4th St. 69103. Phone: (308) 532-1120. Fax: (308) 532-0458. E-mail: chuck.schwartz@eagleradio.net. Web Site: oldiesradio.com. Licensee: Eagle Communications Inc. Group owner: Eagle Communications Group. Network: Jones Radio Networks. Rep: Allied Radio Partners. Format: Oldies. News staff: one; News: 8 hrs wkly. Target aud: 30-55; baby boomers. ♦ Chuck Schwartz, gen mgr; Gary Shorman, pres & gen sls mgr.

KELN(FM)—Co-owned with KOOQ(AM). February 1979: 97.1 mhz; 100 kw. 458 ft. TL: N41 14 20 W100 41 43. Stereo. Web Site: mix97one.com. Network: Westwood One. Format: Adult contemp. News staff: one; News: one hr wkly. Target aud: 25-40; Young adults.

***KPNE-FM**— July 1, 1991: 91.7 mhz; 16.5 kw horiz, 81 kw vert. 59 ft. TL: N41 01 21 W101 09 13. Stereo. Box 83111, Lincoln 68501. Secondary address: 1800 N. 33rd St., Lincoln 68583. Phone: (402) 472-3611. Fax: (402) 472-2403. Web Site: www.nprn.org. Licensee: Nebraska Educational Telecommunications Commission. Network: Network: PRI, NPR. Format: Class, news. ♦ Rod Bates, gen mgr; Jeff Smith, opns mgr; Michael Winkle, gen sls mgr; Nancy Finkea, progmg dir; Martin Wells, news dir.

Ogallala

KMCX(FM)— 1975: 106.5 mhz; 100 kw. 300 ft. TL: N41 08 02 W101 41 42. Stereo. Box 509, 113 W. 4th St. 69153. Phone: (308) 284-3633. Fax: (308) 284-3517. Web Site: www.4koga.com. Licensee: Capstar TX L.P. Group owner: Clear Channel Communications Inc. (acq 8-30-2000; grpsl). Network: ABC Daytime Direction. Format: Country. News staff: one; News: 10 hrs wkly. Target aud: 25-54; general. Spec prog: Farm 2 hrs wkly. ♦ Katrina Twomey, gen mgr; Corey Andersen, opns dir; John Brandt, gen sls mgr; Dave Geho, chief of engrg.

KOGA(AM)— Jan 23, 1955: 930 khz; 5 kw-U, DA-2. TL: N41 08 32 W101 42 48. Stereo. Box 509 69153. Secondary address: 113 W. 4th St. 69153. Phone: (308) 284-3633. Fax: (308) 284-3517. E-mail: thelake@lakemac.net. Web Site: www.4koga.com. Licensee: Capstar TX L.P. Group owner: Clear Channel Communications Inc. (acq 8-30-00; grpsl). Network: ABC Information & Entertainment. Fletcher, Heald & Hildreth. Format: Oldies. Spec prog: Farm 10 hrs wkly. ♦ Katrina Twomby, gen mgr; Corey Anderson, opns mgr; John Brandt, sls dir; Tracey Knapp, progmg mgr; Greg Holl, news dir; Dave Geho, chief of engrg.

KOGA-FM— November 1978: 99.7 mhz; 100 kw. 805 ft. TL: N41 03 50 W101 20 16. Stereo. Web Site: 997thelake.com. Format: Adult rock.

Omaha

KCRO(AM)— March 1922: 660 khz; 1 kw-D, 54 w-N. TL: N41 18 47 W96 00 36. 11717 Burt St, Suite 2 68154. Phone: (402) 422-1600. Phone: (402) 422-1601. Fax: (402) 422-1602. E-mail: kcro@kcro.com. Web Site: www.kcro.com. Licensee: Salem Media of Illinois LLC. (acq 6-30-2005; $3.1 million). Network: USA. Gardner, Carton & Douglas. Format: Christian talk. Target aud: 25-54. ♦Richard Chapin, VP.

KEFM(FM)— Oct 21, 1983: 96.1 mhz; 100 kw. Ant 1,414 ft. TL: N41 04 14 W96 13 33. Stereo. 5010 Underwood Avenue 68132. Phone: (402) 561-2000. Fax: (402) 558-3036. Web Site: www.961kefm.com. Licensee: Clear Channel Broadcasting Licenses Inc. (acq 10-9-2003; $10.5 million). Rep: McGavren Guild. Format: Adult contemp. News staff: one; News: one hr wkly. Target aud: 25-54; women. Spec prog: Backgracks 2 hrs wkly. ♦Donna Baker, gen mgr.

KEZO-FM—Listing follows KOMJ(AM).

KFAB(AM)— 1924: 1110 khz; 50 kw-U, DA-N. TL: N41 07 11 W96 00 06. Stereo. 5010 Underwood Ave. 68132. Phone: (402) 561-2000. Fax: (402) 556-8937. Web Site: www.kfab.org. Licensee: Capstar TX L.P. Group owner: Clear Channel Communications Inc. (acq 8-30-00; grpsl). Network: ABC. Rep: Christal. Format: News/talk. News staff: 3; News: 6 hrs wkly. Target aud: 35-64. Spec prog: Farm 5 hrs wkly. ♦Donna Baker, gen mgr; Jim Steel, opns mgr; Rhonda Gerrard, gen sls mgr; Kevin Simonson, prom dir; Gary Sadlemyer, progmg dir; Tom Stanton, news dir; Steve George, chief of engrg.

KGOR(FM)—Co-owned with KFAB(AM). 1959: 99.9 mhz; 110 kw. Ant 1,214 ft. TL: N41 18 29 W96 01 36. Stereo. Web Site: www.kgor.com. Format: Oldies. Target aud: 35-54. ♦Todd McCarty, sls dir; Drew Bentley, progmg dir.

***KGBI-FM**— May 17, 1966: 100.7 mhz; 100 kw. Ant 1,161 ft. TL: N41 03 10 W96 11 35. Stereo. 831 Pine St. 68108. Phone: (402) 449-2900. Fax: (402) 449-2825. E-mail: kgbi@thebridge.fm. Web Site: www.thebridge.fm. Licensee: Pennsylvania Media Associates Inc. (acq 12-23-2004; $8 million). Format: Contemp Christian. News staff: one; News: 28 hrs wkly. Target aud: 25-54; conservative, Evangelical. ♦Tom Somerville, gen mgr; Mark Michaels, progmg dir; Tom Fifer, news dir; Bob Drake, chief of engrg.

KHLP(AM)— Mar 2, 1957: 1420 khz; 1 kw-D, 330 w-N, DA-2. TL: N41 11 59 W95 54 34. 11128 John Galt Blvd., Suite 192 68137. Phone: (402) 592-5300. Fax: (402) 592-6605. E-mail: owens@journalbroadcastgroup.com. Licensee: Journal Broadcast Corp. Group owner: Journal Broadcast Group Inc. (acq 1-98; $5.475 million. with co-located FM). Network: ABC Daytime Direction. Rep: D & R Radio. Format: Talk. Target aud: 25-54. ♦Steve Wexler, gen mgr; Jim Timm, gen sls mgr; Tom Land, opns mgr & progmg dir; Bill Jensen, news dir; John Gaeta, chief of engrg.

KSRZ(FM)—Co-owned with KHLP(AM). May 12, 1972: 104.5 mhz; 100 kw. 1,040 ft. TL: N41 18 25 W96 01 37. Stereo. Format: Hot adult contemp. ♦Jill Butler, stn mgr & gen sls mgr; Larkin Cavanaugh, prom dir; Darla Thomas, progmg dir; Dave Swan, mus dir.

***KIOS-FM**— September 1969: 91.5 mhz; 55 kw. 554 ft. TL: N41 17 15 W95 59 37. Stereo. 3230 Burt St. 68131. Phone: (402) 557-2777. Fax: (402) 557-2559. E-mail: edward.mcgrath@ops.org. Web Site: www.kios.org. Licensee: Douglas County School District 001. Network: Network: NPR, PRI. Cohn & Marks. Format: Class, educ, news & jazz. Spec prog: Black 2 hrs, jazz 10 hrs wkly. ♦Wilson W. Perry, stn mgr; Edward McGrath, dev dir & sls dir.

KKAR(AM)— March 1925: 1290 khz; 5 kw-U, DA-N. TL: N41 11 20 W96 00 21. 5011 Capitol Ave. 68132. Phone: (402) 342-2000. Fax: (402) 342-5874. Web Site: www.1290kkar.com. Licensee: Waitt Omaha LLC. (group owner; (acq 1-7-2002; grpsl). Rep: Katz Radio. Format: News/talk. Target aud: General. ♦Ken Fearnow, gen mgr; Mark Todd, opns mgr; Sandy Johnston, gen sls mgr; Tanya Parker, prom dir; Billy Shears, progmg dir; Terry Leahy, pres & news dir; Darwin Stinton, chief of engrg.

KKCD(FM)— Aug 11, 1990: 105.9 mhz; 50 kw. 479 ft. TL: N41 18 16 W96 01 41. 11128 John Galt Blvd., Suite 192 68137-2321. Phone: (402) 592-5300. Fax: (402) 331-1348. Web Site: www.classicrock1059.com. Licensee: Journal Broadcast Corp. Group owner: Journal Broadcast Group Inc. (acq 2-95; $3.55 million; 3-13-95). Network: AP Network News. Leventhal, Senter & Lerman. Format: Classic Rock. News staff: one; News: 10 hrs wkly. Target aud: 25-54. Spec prog: Jazz 4 hrs, blues one hr, reggae one hr wkly. ♦Steve F. Wexler, VP & gen mgr; Tom Land, opns dir; Mike Stodden, gen sls mgr; Kurt Owens, progmg dir; Bill Jensen, news dir; John Gaeta, chief of engrg.

KOMJ(AM)— March 1942: 1490 khz; 1 kw-U. TL: N41 14 06 W95 57 57. Stereo. 11128 John Galt Blvd., Suite 192 68137. Phone: (402) 592-5300. Fax: (402) 592-9434. Licensee: Journal Broadcast Corp. Group owner: Journal Broadcast Group Inc. (acq 11-29-94; $9 million. with co-located FM; FTR: 1-16-95). Format: Adult standards. News staff: one. Target aud: 18-49. ♦Steve Wezler, gen mgr; Tom Land, opns dir & opns mgr; Kathy Hedstrom, gen sls mgr; Heath Hedstrom, prom dir & prom mgr; Kurt Owens, progmg dir; Bill Jensen, news dir; John Gaeta, chief of engrg.

KEZO-FM—Co-owned with KOMJ(AM). May 15, 1961: 92.3 mhz; 100 kw. 1,250 ft. TL: N41 18 40 W96 01 37. Stereo. Format: Rock/AOR. ♦James Barton, prom dir; Lester St. James, progmg dir.

KQCH(FM)—Listing follows KXSP(AM).

***KVNO(FM)**— Aug 27, 1972: 90.7 mhz; 8.9 kw. Ant 646 ft. TL: N41 18 25 W96 01 37. Stereo. Engineering 200, 60th & Dodge 68182. Phone: (402) 559-5866. Fax: (402) 554-2440. Web Site: www.kvno.org. Licensee: University of Nebraska Board of Regents. Format: Class. News staff: one; News: 2.5 hrs wkly. Target aud: General. ♦Debra Aliano, gen mgr; Joe Toppi, opns mgr; Marzia Puccioni, mktg mgr; Mike Hagstrom, progmg dir; Kristi Enyart, mus dir; Cheril Lewis, news dir & pub affrs dir; Frank Vacek, engrg mgr & chief of engrg.

***KVSS(FM)**— Jan 9, 1999: 88.9 mhz; 1 kw. 380 ft. TL: N41 18 40 W96 01 37. Secondary address: 5829 N. 60th St. 68104. Phone: (402) 571-0200. Fax: (402) 571-0833. E-mail: kvss@kvss.com. Web Site: www.kvss.com. Licensee: VSS Catholic Communications Inc. (acq 7-7-99). Format: Catholic, Christian. Target aud: General. ♦Jim Taphorn, pres & CFO; Mike Delich, VP; Jim Carroll, gen mgr; D. Ann Yeoman, opns mgr; Vicki Sempek, dev dir; Mary Beth Jorgensen, gen sls mgr; Bruce McGregor, progmg dir; T. Scott Marr, news dir; Chuck Ramold, chief of engrg.

KXSP(AM)— Apr 2, 1923: 590 khz; 5 kw-U. TL: N41 19 00 W95 59 52. Stereo. 11128 John Gault Blvd. 68137. Phone: (402) 592-5300. Fax: (402) 331-1348. Licensee: Journal Broadcast Corp. Group owner: Journal Broadcast Group Inc. (acq 10-26-98 with co-located FM). Rep: Allied Radio Partners. Format: Sports. News staff: 4. Target aud: General. ♦Steve Wexler, gen mgr; Jim Timm, gen sls mgr; Tom Land, opns mgr & progmg dir; Bill Jensen, news dir; John Gaeta, chief of engrg.

KQCH(FM)—Co-owned with KXSP(AM). 1959: 94.1 mhz; 100 kw. 508 ft. TL: N41 18 47 W96 00 36. Stereo. Format: Rhythm-based contemp. Target aud: 25-54. ♦Jill Butler, gen sls mgr; Larkin Cavanaugh, gen mgr & prom dir; Erik Johnson, progmg dir.

O'Neill

KBRX(AM)— November 1955: 1350 khz; 1 kw-D, 44 W-N. TL: N42 27 34 W98 39 23. Box 150 68763. Secondary address: 251 N. Jefferson Phone: (402) 336-1612. Fax: (402) 336-3585. E-mail: Gil@kbrx,com. Web Site: www.kbrx.com. Licensee: Ranchland Broadcasting Co. Inc. (acq 7-1-61). Network: ABC Information & Entertainment. Bryan Cave. Format: Oldies. News staff: one; News: 25 hrs wkly. Target aud: 25-65. Spec prog: Farm 12 hrs, Ger 6 hrs wkly. ♦Gilbert L. Poese, pres; Scott Poese, gen mgr.

KBRX-FM— December 1973: 102.9 mhz; 100 kw. Ant 500 ft. TL: N42 26 06 W98 33 39. Stereo. Box 150, 251 N. Jefferson 68763. Phone: (402) 336-1612. Fax: (402) 336-3585. E-mail: gil@kbrx.com. Web Site: www.kbrx.com. Licensee: Ranchland Broadcasting Co. Inc. Network: ABC Information & Entertainment. Bryan Cave . Format: Country. News staff: one. Target aud: 25-60. ♦Gil Poese, pres; Scott Poese, gen mgr; Pat Poese, sls VP.

Orchard

***KGRD(FM)**— June 14, 1987: 105.3 mhz; 100 kw. 502 ft. TL: N42 20 45 W98 25 05. Stereo. 128 S. 4th St., O'Neill 68763-1814. Phone: (402) 336-3886. Fax: (402) 336-3833. E-mail: kgrd@kgrd.org. Web Site: www.kgrd.org. Licensee: The Praise Network Inc. (acq 10-16-91). Network: Salem Radio Network. Format: Christian, Inspirational. News: 10 hrs wkly. Target aud: 35-54. ♦Lloyd Mintzmeyer, pres; Todd Gunnarson, gen mgr & stn mgr; Gene Henes, mus dir.

Ord

KNLV(AM)— July 15, 1965: 1060 khz; 1 kw-D. TL: N41 34 16 W98 55 29. 205 S. 16th St. 68862. Phone: (308) 728-3263. Fax: (308) 728-3264. E-mail: knlv@yahoo.com. Licensee: Sandhills Advertising Corp. (acq 6-1-74). Network: ABC Daytime Direction. Rep: Howard Anderson. Target aud: 18-54. Spec prog: Farm 8 hrs, Pol/Czeck/Bohemian 5 hrs wkly. ♦Johnnie James, gen mgr & progmg dir; Jeannie Niehart, gen sls mgr; Johnnie James, news dir; Randy Brannigan, chief of engrg.

KNLV-FM— July 10, 1981: 103.9 mhz; 3.85 kw. 379 ft. TL: N41 34 16 W98 55 29. Stereo. ♦Johnnie James, stn mgr.

Plattsmouth

KCTY-FM— July 1993: 106.9 mhz; 6 kw. Ant 328 ft. TL: N41 01 35 W95 54 00. Stereo. 5011 Capitol Ave., Omaha 68132. Phone: (402) 342-2000. Fax: (402) 342-5874. Web Site: www.1069thecity.com. Licensee: Waitt Omaha LLC. Network: ABC. Rep: Katz Radio. Pepper & Corazzini. Format: Alternative. Spec prog: Jazz 4 hrs, Sp 2 hrs wkly. ♦Mike Delich, pres; Mike Payne, gen mgr; Lori Storz, stn mgr.

KOIL(AM)— Oct 26, 1970: 1020 khz; 1 kw-D. TL: N41 01 35 W95 54 00. 5011 Capital Ave., Omaha 68132. Phone: (402) 342-2000. Fax: (402) 342-5874. E-mail: kfearnow@waittradio.com. Licensee: Waitt Omaha LLC. (group owner; (acq 1-17-2001; $750,000). Format: News, classic and traditional country. News staff: one. Target aud: 35-64. Spec prog: Sports, talk, polka 1 hr, farm. ♦Mike Delich, pres; Ken Fearnow, gen mgr; Mark Todd, opns mgr; Sandy Johnston, gen sls mgr; Julie Hansen, prom dir; Neil Nelkin, progmg dir; Terry Leahy, news dir; Darwin Stinton, chief of engrg.

Ralston

***KMLV(FM)**— July 21, 2001: 88.1 mhz; 3.7 kw vert. Ant 794 ft. TL: N41 18 40 W96 01 37. Stereo. 5700 W. Oak Blvd., Rocklin, CA 95765. Phone: (916) 251-1600. Fax: (916) 251-1650. E-mail: klove@klove.com. Web Site: www.klove.com. Licensee: Educational Media Foundation. Group owner: EMF Broadcasting. Network: K-Love. Shaw Pittman. Format: Contemp Christian music. News staff: 3. Target aud: 25-44; Judeo Christian, female. ♦Richard Jenkins, pres; Mike Novak, VP & progmg dir; Lloyd Parker, gen mgr; Ed Lenane, opns dir & news dir; Keith Whipple, dev dir; Eric Allen, natl sls mgr; John D. Burkholder, rgnl sls mgr; Chris Joyce, prom dir; David Pierce, progmg mgr; Jon Rivers, mus dir; Sam Wallington, engrg dir.

Ravenna

KKJK(FM)—Not on air, target date: unknown: 103.1 mhz; 100 kw. Ant 567 ft. TL: N40 48 57 W98 46 18. 9330 Old Southwick Pass, Alpharetta, GA 30022. Phone: (404) 909-0660. Licensee: Community Radio Inc. ♦Donald Wilks, pres & gen mgr.

Scottsbluff

***KKSB(FM)**—Not on air, target date: unknown: 89.1 mhz; 100 kw. Ant 249 ft. TL: N41 55 06 W103 51 49. 188 S. Bellevue, Suite 222, Memphis, TN 38104. Phone: (901) 726-8970. Licensee: Broadcasting for the Challenged Inc. ♦George S. Flinn Jr., pres.

***KLJV(FM)**— Feb 20, 2003: 88.3 mhz; 390 w. Ant 259 ft. TL: N41 56 24 W103 39 20. Stereo. 5700 W. Oaks Blvd., Rocklin, CA 95765. Phone: (916) 251-1600. Fax: (916) 251-1650. E-mail: klove@klove.com. Web Site: www.klove.com. Licensee: Educational Media Foundation. Group owner: EMF Broadcasting. Network: K-Love. Shaw Pittman. Format: Contemp Christian. News staff: 3. Target aud: 25-44. ♦Richard Jenkins, pres; Mike Novak, VP & progmg dir; Lloyd Parker, gen mgr; Ed Lenane, opns dir & news dir; Keith Whipple, dev dir; Eric Allen, natl sls mgr; Roger Chapman, rgnl sls mgr; Chris Joyce, prom dir; David Pierce, progmg mgr; Jon Rivers, mus dir; Sam Wallington, engrg dir.

KMOR(FM)— Aug 4, 1978: 92.9 mhz; 100 kw. 1,023 ft. TL: N41 50 23 W103 49 36. Stereo. Box 532 69361. Phone: (308) 632-5667. Fax: (308) 635-1905. E-mail: KMOR@tracybroadcasting.com. Web Site: tracybroadcasting.com. Licensee: Tracy Corp. Group owner: Tracy

Stations in the U.S.   Nevada

Developers & Brokers of Radio Properties

contact American Media Services at our suite: Philadelphia Marriott Downtown
215-625-2900
843-972-2200
americanmediaservices.com
Charleston, SC
Dallas, TX • Chicago, Il • Austin, TX
American Media Services, LLC

Broadcasting Corp. Art Moore. Format: Classic rock. News staff: 2; News: 7 hrs wkly. Target aud: 18-55. ♦ Michael Tracy, pres; Larry Swikard, gen mgr & stn mgr.

KNEB(AM)— Jan 1, 1948: 960 khz; 5 kw-D, 350 w-N, DA-2. TL: N41 47 30 W103 38 29. Box 239 69363-0239. Phone: (308) 632-7121. Fax: (308) 635-1079. E-mail: kneb@actcom.net. Web Site: www.kneb.com. Licensee: Nebraska Rural Radio Association. Group owner: Nebraska Rural Radio Assn. (acq 8-1-84). Network: ABC Information & Entertainment. Format: C&W, news/talk. News staff: 2. Target aud: 18 plus. Spec prog: Farm 18 hrs, Sp 5 hrs wkly. ♦ Dale Hanson, pres; Barbara Martinson, gen sls mgr & rgnl sls mgr; Dennis Ernest, progmg dir; Marty Martinson, gen mgr, natl sls mgr & news dir.

KNEB-FM— Dec 25, 1960: 94.1 mhz; 100 kw. 680 ft. TL: N41 42 04 W103 40 49. Stereo. Format: Farm, C&W.

KOAQ(AM)—See Terrytown

KOLT(AM)— Feb 15, 1930: 1320 khz; 5 kw-D, 1 kw-N, DA-N. TL: N41 51 37 W103 41 53. Box 660 69363. Phone: (308) 635-1320. Fax: (308) 635-1905. Web Site: www.tracybroadcasting.com. Licensee: Tracy Corp. Group owner: Tracy Broadcasting Corp. (acq 2-25-92; $37,000;. FTR: 3-23-92). Network: ABC. Michael Glaser. Format: Talk. Target aud: 39 plus. Spec prog: Farm 10 hrs wkly. ♦ Michael Tracy, pres; Larry Swikard, gen mgr, stn mgr & gen sls mgr; Jeff McKenzie, progmg dir.

Seward

KZKX(FM)— Nov 12, 1976: 96.9 mhz; 100 kw. 610 ft. TL: N41 07 26 W96 50 03. Stereo. 4630 Antelope Creek Rd., Suite 200, Lincoln 68506. Phone: (402) 484-8000. Fax: (402) 489-9989. Web Site: www.kzkx.com. Licensee: Capstar TX L.P. Group owner: Clear Channel Communications Inc. (acq 8-30-00; grpsl). Network: ABC Daytime Direction. Rep: D & R Radio. Gammon & Grange. Format: Country. Target aud: 25-54. ♦ Julie Gade, gen mgr; Julie Broman, gen sls mgr & news dir; Brian Jennings, progmg dir; Dave Agnew, chief of engrg.

Sidney

KSID(AM)— June 2, 1952: 1340 khz; 1 kw-U. TL: N41 07 50 W102 58 15. Box 37, Legion Park 69162. Phone: (308) 254-5803. Fax: (308) 254-5901. Licensee: KSID Radio Inc. (acq 1962). Network: ABC Information & Entertainment. Format: Country. Target aud: General. Spec prog: Farm 5 hrs wkly. ♦ Elizabeth Young, pres; Susan Ernest, gen mgr; Lana Butts, opns mgr & gen sls mgr; Marge Elliott, progmg dir; Jason Lockwood, news dir; Dennis Brothers, engrg mgr & chief of engrg.

KSID-FM— Sept 13, 1974: 98.7 mhz; 62 kw. 368 ft. TL: N41 11 03 W103 11 37. Stereo. Format: Adult contemp.

South Sioux City

KSFT-FM— 1997: 107.1 mhz; 1.55 kw. 328 ft. TL: N42 29 00 W96 35 34. Stereo. Box 3009, Sioux City, IA 51102. Secondary address: 1113 Nebraska St., Sioux City, IA 51102. Phone: (712) 258-6740. Fax: (712) 252-2430. Licensee: AMFM Radio Licenses LLC. Group owner: Clear Channel Communications Inc. (acq 10-1-2002; grpsl). Network: Westwood One. Rep: Christal. Format: Soft rock. News staff: one; News: one hr wkly. Target aud: 25-54. ♦ Rick Schorg, gen mgr & gen sls mgr.

Superior

KRFS(AM)— Mar 17, 1959: 1600 khz; 500 w-D. TL: N40 01 30 W98 04 38. Rte. 2, Box 149 68978. Phone: (402) 879-3207. Fax: (402) 879-4741. Licensee: CK Broadcasting Inc. (acq 1-4-02; $150,000. with co-located FM). Network: ABC Daytime Direction. Format: Adult standards. News: 11 hrs wkly. Target aud: 25-55; general. Spec prog: Farm 5 hrs, gospel 3 hrs, relg 3 hrs wkly. ♦ Cory Kopsa, gen mgr, sls VP, gen sls mgr, prom mgr, progmg dir & news dir; Marvin Hoffman, chief of engrg.

KRFS-FM— Feb 25, 1977: 103.9 mhz; 2 kw. 220 ft. TL: N40 01 30 W98 04 38. (CP: TL: N40 06 20 W98 06 20). Stereo. Network: ABC Daytime Direction. Format: Country.

Terrytown

KCMI(FM)— Mar 1, 1981: 96.9 mhz; 100 kw. 692 ft. TL: N41 42 08 W103 41 00. Stereo. Box 1888, 209 E. 15th, Scottsbluff 69363-1888. Phone: (308) 632-5264. Fax: (308) 635-0104. E-mail: cmi@prairieweb.com. Web Site: www.kcmi.cc. Licensee: Christian Media Inc. Network: USA. Format: Relg. News: 12 hrs wkly. Target aud: 25 plus. Spec prog: Class 4 hrs wkly. ♦ Glenn A. Hascall, gen mgr; Todd Rasnic, gen sls mgr & progmg dir.

KOAQ(AM)— June 15, 1961: 690 khz; 1 kw-D, 64 w-N, DA-1. TL: N41 50 02 W103 39 20. Stereo. Box 1263, Scottsbluff 69361. Phone: (308) 635-1320. Fax: (308) 635-1905. Web Site: www.tracybroadcasting.com. Licensee: Tracy Broadcasting Corp. (group owner; acq 12-86; $164,000;. FTR: 11-10-86). Network: Jones Radio Networks. Michael Glaser. Format: Oldies. News staff: 2; News: 21 hrs wkly. Target aud: 25-54; Baby Boomers. Spec prog: Farm 5 hrs wkly. ♦ Michael Tracy, pres; Larry Swikard, gen mgr & gen sls mgr; Krista Sarchet, prom mgr; Jeff McKenzie, progmg dir; Bob Hinze, chief of engrg.

Valentine

KVSH(AM)— Mar 6, 1961: 940 khz; 5 kw-D, 20 w-N. TL: N42 51 54 W100 31 07. 126 W. 3rd St. 69201. Phone: (402) 376-2400. Fax: (402) 376-2402. Licensee: Heart City Radio Corp. (acq 6-90; $235,000; 6-4-90). Network: ABC Information & Entertainment. Fletcher, Heald & Hildreth. Format: Country. News staff: one; News: 24 hrs wkly. Target aud: 35-60; general. ♦ Dave Otradovsky, pres; Zach Dean, gen sls mgr; Mike Burge, progmg dir, news dir & chief of engrg.

Wayne

KTCH(AM)— Mar 18, 1968: 1590 khz; 2.5 kw-D, 33.4 w-N, DA-2. TL: N42 14 03 W97 03 19. Box 413, W. Hwy. 35 68787. Phone: (402) 375-3700. Fax: (402) 375-5402. E-mail: ktch@ktch.com. Web Site: www.ktch.com. Licensee: Waitt Radio Inc. (group owner; acq 3-8-00; $900,000. with co-located FM and loc mktg agreement with KNEN(FM) Norfolk). Network: ABC Daytime Direction. Rep: Howard Anderson. Format: Country. News staff: one; News: 15 hrs wkly. Target aud: 30-64. Spec prog: Farm 20 hrs wkly. ♦ Jerry Haack, gen mgr; Mick Kemp, gen sls mgr; Dan Baddorf, progmg dir; Scott Gannon, news dir; Tim Geuntz, chief of engrg.

KTCH-FM— Oct 19, 1975: 104.9 mhz; 25,000 kw. 300 ft. TL: N42 14 03 W97 03 19. Stereo. Web Site: www.ktch.com. Format: Oldies. Target aud: General.

*KWSC(FM)— Oct 13, 1971: 91.9 mhz; 350 w. 96 ft. TL: N42 14 30 W97 00 48. 1111 Main St. 68787. Phone: (402) 375-7536. Phone: (402) 375-7426. E-mail: k92radio@hotmail.com. Web Site: www.wsc.edu/k92. Licensee: Wayne State College. Network: Westwood One. Format: AOR, alternative. Target aud: 18 plus. Spec prog: Black 4 hrs, jazz 2 hrs, heavy metal 2 hrs, blues 2 hrs wkly.

West Point

KTIC(AM)— Mar 17, 1985: 840 khz; 5 kw-D. TL: N41 47 06 W96 40 39. Box 84, 1011 N. Lincoln St. 68788-0084. Phone: (402) 372-5423. Fax: (402) 372-5425. E-mail: ktickwpn@kwpnfm.com. Web Site: www.kticam.com. Licensee: Nebraska Rural Radio Association. Group owner: Nebraska Rural Radio Association (acq 8-1-97; $1.5 million with co-located FM). Network: ABC. Rep: Katz Radio. Neb. Pub. Format: Farm market news, country. News staff: one; News: 20 hrs wkly. Target aud: General; farmers, ranchers, stockmen and all involved in agri-business. ♦ Charlie Brogan, gen mgr, stn mgr & progmg dir; Denny Waddle, sls dir & gen sls mgr; Judy Mauch, gen sls mgr; Richard Sterling, mus dir; Bob Flittie, news dir; Vern Killion, chief of engrg.

KWPN-FM—Co-owned with KTIC(AM). Aug 1, 1988: 107.9 mhz; 50 kw. 318 ft. TL: N41 47 06 W96 40 39. Stereo. Web Site: www.kwpnfm.com. (Acq 1997.). Network: ABC. Format: Adult contemp, loc news, sports. News staff: one; News: 12 hrs wkly. Target aud: 25-49; general audience, adults. Spec prog: Farm 10 hrs wkly. ♦ Richard Sterling, progmg dir.

Wilber

*KFLV(FM)— Mar 1, 2001: 89.9 mhz; 8.8 kw. Ant 351 ft. TL: N40 30 33 W96 50 41. Stereo. 5700 W. Oaks Blvd., Rocklin, CA 95765. Phone: (916) 251-1600. Fax: (916) 251-1650. E-mail: klove@klove.com. Web Site: www.klove.com. Licensee: Educational Media Foundation. Group owner: EMF Broadcasting. Network: K-Love. Shaw Pittman. Format: Contemp Christian music. News staff: 3. Target aud: 25-44; Judeo-Christian, female. ♦ Richard Jenkins, pres; Mike Novak, VP & progmg dir; Lloyd Parker, gen mgr; Ed Lenane, opns dir & news dir; Keith Whipple, dev dir; Eric Allen, natl sls mgr; John D. Burkholder, rgnl sls mgr; Chris Joyce, prom dir & prom mgr; David Pierce, progmg mgr & mus dir; Jon Rivers, mus dir; Sam Wallington, engrg dir.

Winnebago

KSUX(FM)— June 1, 1990: 105.7 mhz; 50 kw. 463 ft. TL: N42 20 33 W96 31 13. Stereo. 2000 Indian Hills Dr., Sioux City, IA 51104. Phone: (712) 239-2100. Fax: (712) 239-3346. Web Site: www.ksux.com. Licensee: Powell Broadcasting Co. (acq 1996; $3.8 million. with KSCJ(AM) Sioux City, IA). Rep: Allied Radio Partners. Format: Country. News staff: 2. Target aud: 25-54; female average to above average income, secondary male. ♦ Dennis Ballock, gen mgr; Randy Renshaw, gen mgr & news dir; Dave Grosenhelder, gen sls mgr; Justin Barker, prom mgr; Bob Rounds, progmg dir; Tony Michaels, mus dir; Stan Culley, chief of engrg.

York

KAWL(AM)— September 1954: 1370 khz; 500 w-D, 176 w-N. TL: N40 50 30 W97 35 16. 1309 Rd. 11 68467. Phone: (402) 362-4433. Fax: (402) 362-6501. E-mail: kawl@alltel.net. Web Site: www.oldiesradioonline.com. Licensee: MWB Broadcasting LLC (acq 12-3-2004; $1 million. with co-located FM). Network: ABC. Rep: Interep. Format: Oldies, talk. News staff: one; News: 10 hrs wkly. Target aud: 20 plus; general. Spec prog: Farm 7 hrs, women 3 hrs wkly. ♦ Mark Jensen, gen mgr; Stephanie Wellmen, opns mgr; Bob Bedient, news dir; Tami Peterson, chief of engrg & sls.

KTMX(FM)—Co-owned with KAWL(AM). Sept 1, 1970: 104.9 mhz; 25 kw. 974 ft. TL: N40 45 07 W97 27 04. Stereo. Web Site: hitsandfavorites.com. Network: ABC. Rep: McGavren Guild. Format: Adult contemp. News staff: one; News: 3 hrs wkly. Target aud: 25-54; general.

Nevada

Amargosa Valley

KPKK(FM)— 2003: 101.1 mhz; 51 kw horiz. Ant -49 ft. TL: N36 38 33 W116 23 53. Sky Media L.L.C., 980 N. Michigan Ave., Chicago, IL 60611. Phone: (312) 204-9900. Fax: (312) 587-9466. Licensee: Sky Media L.L.C. (acq 11-20-2002; $5.1 million. for CP). ♦ Bruce Buzil, gen mgr.

Boulder City

KSTJ(FM)—Licensed to Boulder City. See Las Vegas

Carlin

KHIX(FM)— March 2001: 96.7 mhz; 33 kw. Ant 1,597 ft. TL: N40 55 18 W115 50 58. 1250 Lamoille Hwy., # 944, Elko 89801. Phone: (775) 777-1196. Fax: (775) 777-9587. E-mail: ken@mix96.fm. Web Site: www.mix96.fm. Licensee: Ruby Radio Corp. (group owner; acq

Broadcasting & Cable Yearbook 2006

Nevada

6-15-2003; $475,000. for CP). David Tillotson. Format: Adult hit radio (contemp). ♦Alene Sutherland, VP; Ken Sutherland, stn mgr.

Carson City

KBUL-FM— Nov 30, 1984: 98.1 mhz; 72.5 kw. 2,273 ft. TL: N39 15 32 W119 42 06. (CP: Ant 2,286 ft.). Stereo. 595 E. Plumb Ln., Reno 89502-3773. Phone: (775) 789-6700. Fax: (775) 789-6767. Web Site: www.kbul.com. Licensee: Citadel Broadcasting Co. Group owner: Citadel Broadcasting Corp. (acq 5-29-92). Format: C&W. News staff: one; News: 4 hrs wkly. Target aud: 25-54. ♦Dana Johnson, gen mgr.

*KNIS(FM)— Oct 15, 1989: 91.3 mhz; 67 kw. 2,165 ft. TL: N39 15 30 W119 42 36. Stereo. Western Inspirational Broadcasters, Inc., 6363 Hwy. 50 E. 89701. Phone: (775) 883-5647. Licensee: Western Inspirational Broadcasters Inc. (acq 10-15-89). Format: Contemp Christian, educ, talk. News: 16 hrs wkly. Target aud: 24-44. ♦Tom Hess, gen mgr; Tim Weiddemann, opns mgr.

KPTL(AM)— May 14, 1955: 1300 khz; 5 kw-D, 500 w-N, DA-N. TL: N39 09 59 W119 43 37. 1960 Idaho 89701. Phone: (775) 884-8000. Fax: (775) 882-3961. Licensee: The Evans Broadcast Co. Inc. (acq 4-28-2004; $700,000). Network: CBS Radio. Shainis & Peltzman. Format: Talk. Target aud: 35-54. ♦Jerry Evans, gen mgr, progmg dir & progmg.

KZTQ(FM)—Licensed to Carson City. See Reno

Dayton

KTHX-FM—Licensed to Dayton. See Reno

Elko

KELK(AM)— Dec 7, 1948: 1240 khz; 1 kw-U. TL: N40 50 37 W115 44 58. Box 5566, 1800 Idaho St. 89802. Phone: (775) 738-1240. Fax: (775) 753-5556. Web Site: elkoradio.com. Licensee: Elko Broadcasting Co. (acq 11-1-74). Network: ABC Information & Entertainment. Format: Full service, adult contemp. News staff: news progmg 25 hrs wkly News: one;. Target aud: 25-54; upscale, family oriented, white collar workforce. ♦Paul G. Gardner, pres & gen mgr.

KLKO(FM)—Co-owned with KELK(AM). May 1982: 93.7 mhz; 4.5 kw. Ant 1,538 ft. TL: N40 55 20 W115 50 56. Stereo. Web Site: elkoradio.com. Format: Rock. News staff: one; News: 20 hrs wkly.

*KNCC(FM)— 1992: 91.5 mhz; 50 w. 741 ft. TL: N40 49 16 W115 42 04. Great Basin College, 1500 College Pkwy. 89801. Phone: (775) 753-2181. Fax: (775) 738-8771. E-mail: carl@gbcnv.edu. Licensee: Great Basin College. Format: Class, big band, educ, jazz, news. Spec prog: Public radio. ♦Carl Diekhans, gen mgr.

KOYT(FM)—Not on air, target date: unknown: 94.5 mhz; 90 kw. Ant 1,604 ft. TL: N40 55 43 W115 50 33. College Creek Broadcasting Inc., 980 N. Michigan Ave., Suite 1875, Chicago, IL 60611. Phone: (312) 204-9900. Licensee: College Creek Broadcasting Inc. ♦Neal J. Robinson, pres.

KRJC(FM)— October 1981: 95.3 mhz; 25 kw. Ant 774 ft. TL: N40 54 35 W115 49 05. Stereo. 1250 Lamoille Hwy., Suite 1045 89801-1626. Phone: (775) 738-9895. Fax: (775) 753-8085. E-mail: krjc@krjc.com. Web Site: www.krjc.com. Licensee: Holiday Broadcasting of Elko. Group owner: Carlson Communications International. Network: Network: UPI, CNN Radio. Format: Hot country. News staff: one; News: 4 hrs wkly. Target aud: 25-54; above median income & education averages. ♦Ralph J. Carlson, pres; Jennifer Ford, gen sls mgr; Tammy Stewart, gen mgr & rgnl sls mgr; John Hunt, progmg dir; Mike Allen, news dir.

KTSN(AM)— November 1996: 1340 khz; 1 kw-D. TL: N40 52 08 W115 43 09. 1250 Lamoille Hwy., Suite 1045 89801. Phone: (775) 738-9895. Fax: (775) 753-8085. Web Site: www.ktsn1340.com. Licensee: Humboldt Broadcasting LLC. Group owner: Carlson Communications International. Format: Talk, sports, news. ♦Tammy Stewart, gen mgr; Jennifer Ford, gen sls mgr; Josh Ellison, progmg dir; Kenneth Meyer, chief of engrg.

Ely

KCLS(FM)—Listing follows KELY(AM).

KDSS(FM)— Dec 22, 1984: 92.7 mhz; 14 kw. Ant 941 ft. TL: N39 14 46 W114 55 39. Stereo. 501 Aultman, Suite 208 89301. Phone: (775) 289-6474. Fax: (775) 289-6531. E-mail: kdss@wpis.net. Licensee: Coates Broadcasting Inc. (acq 5-1-96; $180,000). Network: Jones Radio Networks. Irwin, Campbell & Tannenwald, P.C. Format: C & W. News: 10 hrs wkly. Target aud: 18-64; older demographics, new & classic C&W listeners. Spec prog: Nashville News, fishing, outdoor. ♦Pat Coates, pres; Samantha Coates, VP; James Lee, sls VP; Jim Liebsack, chief of engrg.

KELY(AM)— July 8, 1950: 1230 khz; 1 kw-U. TL: N39 15 45 W114 51 46. 23941 W. Patton Rd., Wittmann 85361-8505. Phone: (775) 289-2077. Fax: (775) 289-4857. E-mail: illusion@webcave.net. Web Site: www.elyrocks.com. Licensee: Ruby Radio Corp. (group owner; acq 3-15-2004; $178,000. with co-located FM). Format: Oldies. Target aud: 40 plus. Spec prog: Swap shop 3 hrs, radio bingo 5 hrs wkly. ♦Ken Sutherland, pres, gen mgr & gen sls mgr; Shawn Denavon, progmg dir; Fred Gilles, chief of engrg.

KCLS(FM)—Co-owned with KELY(AM). Nov 1, 1986: 101.7 mhz; 480 w. 804 ft. TL: N39 14 46 W114 55 39. Stereo. Web Site: www.elyrocks.com. Format: Adult contemp.

Fallon

KHWG(AM)—Not on air, target date: unknown: 750 khz; 10 kw-D, 280 w-N, 10 kw-CH. TL: N39 28 57 W118 45 36. 250 W. Nopah Vista Dr., Pahrump 89060. Phone: (775) 751-9709. Licensee: Media Enterprises Inc. (acq 1-8-2003). ♦Keily Miller, pres & gen mgr.

KRNG(FM)— July 4, 1997: 101.3 mhz; 1.65 kw. 2,207 ft. TL: N39 42 30 W119 10 16. Stereo. Box 490, Wadsworth 89442. Secondary address: 360 Pyramid St., Wadsworth 89442. Phone: (775) 575-7777. Fax: (775) 575-7737. E-mail: email@renegaderadio.org. Web Site: www.renegaderadio.org. Licensee: Sierra Nevada Christian Music Association Inc. Format: Christian. Target aud: 12-35; Youth, young adults, families. Spec prog: Rap, AOR, alternative. ♦Rev. Karry Crites, pres & stn mgr; William E. Bauer PhD., opns VP; Cary Crites, dev VP.

KVLV(AM)— May 9, 1957: 980 khz; 5 kw-D. TL: N39 29 47 W118 48 50. 1155 Gummow Dr. 89406. Phone: (775) 423-2243. Phone: (775) 423-5858. Fax: (775) 423-8889. E-mail: kvlv@phonewave.net. Licensee: Lahontan Valley Broadcasting LLC. Network: ABC. Format: C&W. News: 10 hrs wkly. Target aud: 25 plus. ♦Mike McGinness, gen mgr.

KVLV-FM— Nov 26, 1966: 99.3 mhz; 3.7 kw. 250 ft. TL: N39 29 47 W118 48 50. Stereo. Network: AP Radio. Format: Adult contemp. News: 10 hrs wkly.

Gardnerville-Minden

KCMY(FM)— Sept 19, 1985: 99.1 mhz; 25 kw. Ant -817 ft. TL: N38 57 35 W119 50 36. Stereo. 1960 Idaho St/, Carson City 89701. Phone: (775) 884-8000. Fax: (775) 882-3961. E-mail: prod@kptlradio.com. Licensee: Jerry Evans (acq 11-28-2003; $850,000). Shainis & Peltzman. Format: Country. News staff: 2; News: 8 hrs wkly. Target aud: 25-54; btfl people. ♦Jerry Evans, CEO, gen mgr & stn mgr.

Hawthorne

*KQMC(FM)—Not on air, target date: unknown: 90.1 mhz; 1.3 kw. Ant 3,677 ft. TL: N38 47 04 W118 49 59. American Educational Broadcasting Inc., 3185 S. Highland Dr. #13, Las Vegas 89109. Phone: (702) 731-5588. Fax: (702) 731-5851. Licensee: American Educational Broadcasting Inc.

Henderson

KDOX(AM)— May 1956: 1280 khz; 5 kw-D, 28 w-N. TL: N36 03 13 W114 58 30. 740 North Eastern Ave., Ste. 100-A, Las Vegas 89101. Phone: (702) 732-1664. Fax: (702) 732-3060. Licensee: S & R Broadcasting Inc. (acq 10-16-90; $600,000; 11-5-90). Rep: Lotus Entravision Reps LLC. Rosenman & Colin L.L.P. Format: Sp. Target aud: General; Hispanic, above-average income, high home ownership. ♦Paul Ruttan, pres; Scott Gentry, gen mgr; Ellen Walker, gen sls mgr; Roberto Ibarra, progmg dir; Warren Brown, chief of engrg.

KKJJ(FM)— Nov 28, 1982: 100.5 mhz; 100 kw. 1,105 ft. TL: N36 00 28 W115 00 20. Stereo. 6655 W. Sahara Ave., Suite C 216, Las Vegas 89146. Phone: (702) 889-5100. Fax: (702) 257-2936. Web Site: www.litelasvegas.com. Licensee: Infinity Radio Inc. Group owner: Infinity Broadcasting Corp. (acq 11-13-98; grpsl). Format: Adult contemp. News staff: one; News: 10 hrs wkly. Target aud: 25-49. ♦Mel Karmazin, CEO; John Sykes, pres; Tom Humm, VP, gen mgr & gen sls mgr; Lorene Malis, natl sls mgr; Terry Massie, mktg dir & prom dir; Craig Powers, progmg dir; Eric Chase, mus dir; Herb Perry, pub affrs dir; Tracy Teagarden, chief of engrg.

KMXB(FM)— Feb 10, 1970: 94.1 mhz; 100 kw. 1,210 ft. TL: N36 00 26 W115 00 24. Stereo. 6655 W. Sahara, Suite C 216, Las Vegas 89146. Phone: (702) 889-5100. Fax: (702) 257-2936. E-mail: charese@mix941.fm. Web Site: www.mix941.fm. Licensee: Infinity Radio Inc. Group owner: Infinity Broadcasting Corp. (acq 11-13-98; grpsl). Network: CBS Radio. Leventhal, Senter & Lerman. Format: Modern adult contemp. News staff: one. Target aud: 18-49; female. ♦John Sykes, CEO & chmn; John Fullam, COO & pres; Jacques Tortoli, CFO; Tom Humm, VP & gen mgr; Lorene Malis, natl sls mgr; Lori Heeren, rgnl sls mgr; Jennifer Monteith, mktg dir & prom dir; Charese Fruge, progmg dir; Justin Chase, asst music dir; Tracy Teagarden, chief of engrg.

KWNR(FM)— July 18, 1972: 95.5 mhz; 92 kw. 1,161 ft. TL: N36 00 31 W115 00 22. 1130 E. Desert Inn Rd., Las Vegas 89109. Phone: (702) 732-7753. Fax: (702) 733-0433. Web Site: www.kwnr.com. Licensee: Citicasters Licenses L.P. Group owner: Clear Channel Communications Inc. (acq 1999; grpsl). Hogan & Hartson. Format: Country. Target aud: 18-54. ♦Kelly Kibler, gen mgr; Jeff Mitchell, natl sls mgr; Bill Lubitz, prom dir; Brooks O'Brien, progmg dir; Mitch Kelly, news dir; Miguel Randtree, engrg dir.

Incline Village

KRNO(FM)—Licensed to Incline Village. See Reno

Indian Springs

KRGT(FM)— Nov 22, 2002: 99.3 mhz; 31 kw. Ant 2,263 ft. TL: N36 19 28 W115 33 58. 6767 W. Tropicana Ave., Suite 102, Las Vegas 89103. Phone: (702) 284-6400. Fax: (702) 284-6403. Licensee: Univision Radio License Corp. Group owner: Univision Radio (acq 9-22-2003; grpsl). Format: Sp. ♦Dana Demerjian, gen mgr.

Jackpot

*KBSJ(FM)—Not on air, target date: unknown: 91.3 mhz; 3.7 kw. 2,463 ft. Idaho State Board of Education, 1910 University Dr., Boise, ID 83725. Phone: (208) 426-3663. Fax: (208) 344-6631. Licensee: Idaho State Board of Education. Format: Classical jazz.

Las Vegas

KBAD(AM)— June 1953: 920 khz; 5 kw-D, 500 w-N, DA-2. TL: N36 11 25 W115 10 35. 8755 W. Flamingo Rd. 89147-8667. Phone: (702) 876-1460. Fax: (702) 876-6685. Web Site: www.komp.com. Licensee: Lotus Broadcasting Corp. (acq 11-4-92; $1.42 million with co-located FM; 11-23-92). Network: ABC Information & Entertainment. Format: Sports. Target aud: 18 plus; men. ♦Tony Bonnici, gen mgr; John Hanson, progmg dir.

KXPT(FM)—Co-owned with KBAD(AM). Nov 29, 1961: 97.1 mhz; 50 kw. 1,950 ft. TL: N35 56 44 W115 02 31. (CP: 24 kw). Stereo. Web Site: www.point97.com. Network: ABC FM Connection. Format: Classic hits. Target aud: 35-49. ♦John Griffin, opns mgr & progmg dir.

KBTB(AM)—Not on air, target date: unknown: 670 khz; 10 kw-D, 600 w-N, DA-2. TL: N36 22 48 W115 20 39. Kemp Communications Inc., 3800 Howard Hughes Pkwy., 17th Fl. 89109. Phone: (702) 385-6000. Licensee: Kemp Communications Inc. ♦Will Kemp, pres & gen mgr.

*KCEP(FM)— October 1973: 88.1 mhz; 10 kw. -39 ft. TL: N36 10 51 W115 08 43. (CP: 10 kw, ant 1,079 ft.). Stereo. 330 W. Washington St. 89106. Phone: (702) 648-4218. Phone: (702) 648-0104. Fax: (702) 647-0803. Web Site: www.power88lu.com. Licensee: Economic Opportunity Board of Clark County. Format: Black, urban contemp, rhythm & blues. News: 5 hrs wkly. Target aud: 12-55; African-Americans. Spec prog: Gospel 19 hrs, Jazz 12 hrs wkly. ♦Lee Winston, gen mgr; William Thompson, progmg dir; Warren Brown, engrg VP.

*KCNV(FM)— Mar 24, 1980: 89.5 mhz; 98 kw. Ant 1,532 ft. TL: N35 56 50 W115 03 01. Stereo. 1289 S. Torrey Pines 89146. Phone: (702) 258-9895. Fax: (702) 258-5646. E-mail: info@knpr.org. Web Site: www.knpr.org. Licensee: Nevada Public Radio Corp. Dow, Lohnes & Albertson. Format: Classical. Target aud: 35-54. ♦Lamar Marchese, CEO, pres & gen mgr; Louis Castle, chmn; Kathleen Hechinger, CFO;

Stations in the U.S. — Nevada

Developers & Brokers of Radio Properties
contact American Media Services at our suite: Philadelphia Marriott Downtown
215-625-2900
843-972-2200
americanmediaservices.com
Charleston, SC
Dallas, TX · Chicago, IL · Austin, TX
American Media Services, LLC

Phil Burger, opns dir; Valerie Freshwater, dev dir; Florence Rogers, progmg dir; John Clare, mus dir; Jay Bartos, pub affrs dir; Warren Brown, chief of engrg.

KDOX(AM)—See Henderson

KDWN(AM)— Apr 7, 1975: 720 khz; 50 kw-U, DA-N. TL: N36 04 22 W114 58 20. Box 760, . 89125. Secondary address: # 1 Main St. 89101. Phone: (702) 385-7212. Fax: (702) 385-7990. E-mail: kdwn@kdwn.com. Web Site: www.kdwn.com. Licensee: Radio Nevada Inc. Network: AP Radio. Rep: Roslin. Format: News/talk. Target aud: 35 plus; middle & upper middle class. ♦A.J. Williams, CEO, chmn & pres; C.B. Benezra, gen mgr; Donna Lee, mktg dir. Co-owned TV: KAIL-TV affil.

KENO(AM)— 1940: 1460 khz; 5 kw-D, 1 kw-N, DA-N. TL: N36 06 16 W115 12 16. (CP: 30 kw-D. TL: N36 12 44 W115 09 43). 8755 W. Flamingo Rd. 89147-8667. Phone: (702) 876-1460. Fax: (702) 876-6685. Web Site: www.foxsportsradio1460.com. Licensee: Lotus Broadcasting Corp. (group owner; acq 6-1-65). Rep: Christal. Format: Sports. Target aud: 18 plus. ♦Tony Bonnici, gen mgr; John Hanson, progmg dir.

KOMP(FM)—Co-owned with KENO(AM). Sept 1, 1966: 92.3 mhz; 100 kw. 1,520 ft. TL: N35 56 50 W115 03 01. (CP: 22.9 kw, ant 3,844 ft.). Stereo. Format: AOR. ♦John Griffin, progmg dir.

KISF(FM)— March 1989: 103.5 mhz; 100 kw. Ant 1,158 ft. TL: N36 00 29 W115 00 20. 6767 W. Tropicana Ave., Suite 102 89103. Phone: (702) 284-6400. Fax: (702) 284-6403. Web Site: kisf.netmio.com. Licensee: HBC License Corp. Group owner: Univision Radio (acq 9-22-2003; grpsl). Format: Rgnl Mexican. ♦Dana Demerjian, gen mgr.

KKLZ(FM)— Jan 26, 1984: 96.3 mhz; 100 kw. 1,170 ft. TL: N36 00 29 W115 00 20. Stereo. 1455 E. Tropican, Suite 800 89119. Phone: (702) 739-9600. Fax: (702) 736-8447. Web Site: www.kklz.net. Licensee: Beasley Broadcasting of NV LLC. Group owner: Beasley Broadcast Group Inc. (acq 2-1-2001; grpsl). Format: Classic rock. News staff: one. Target aud: 25-44; baby boomers. ♦Harry Williams, gen mgr; Tom Davis, gen sls mgr; Steve Marchese, progmg dir; Dan Lea, mus dir; Dennis Mitchell, news dir; Joe Sands, chief of engrg.

KKVV(AM)— May 1, 1990: 1060 khz; 5 kw-D, 43 w-N. TL: N36 09 22 W115 15 24. 3185 S. Highland Dr., Suite 13 89109. Phone: (702) 731-5588. Phone: (702) 650-5588. Fax: (702) 731-5851. E-mail: kkvv@kkvv.com. Web Site: www.kkvv.com. Licensee: Las Vegas Broadcasters Inc. (acq 11-8-93; $17,000; 11-29-93). Network: Network: USA, Salem Radio Network. Format: Relg, talk, adult contemp, christian, Sp. Target aud: General; General. Spec prog: Sp christian 20 hrs wkly. ♦Carl J. Auel, pres & dev dir; Jane A. Filler, VP; Fred Hodges, gen mgr.

KLAV(AM)— June 1947: 1230 khz; 1 kw-U. TL: N36 11 20 W115 08 40. 1810 Weldon 89104. Phone: (702) 796-1234. Fax: (702) 796-7433. E-mail: klavradio@aol.com. Web Site: www.klav1230am.com. Licensee: AIM Broadcasting-Las Vegas L.L.C. (acq 8-6-2004; $3.2 million). Haley, Bader & Potts. Format: Talk, info, sports. Target aud: 25-54. Spec prog: Relg 3 hrs, Indian one hr, Hawaiian 4 hrs, Arabic 7 hrs, Filipino 5 hrs, Hebrew one hr wkly. ♦Lisa Lupo, VP & gen mgr; Peggy Merrill, stn mgr; Jon Lindquist, opns mgr.

KLSQ(AM)—See Whitney

KLUC-FM— 1956: 98.5 mhz; 100 kw. 1,191 ft. TL: N36 00 29 W115 00 20. Stereo. 6655 W. Sahara Ave., Suite D208 89146. Phone: (702) 253-9800. Fax: (702) 889-7373. Web Site: www.kluc.com. Licensee: Infinity Radio Inc. Group owner: Infinity Broadcasting Corp. (acq 12-14-00; grpsl). Format: CHR/top-40. News staff: one. Target aud: 18-34. ♦Marty Basch, gen mgr; Frank Feder, gen sls mgr; Cat Thomas, progmg dir; Tracy Teagarden, chief of engrg.

KSFN(AM)—Co-owned with KLUC-FM. 1956: 1140 khz; 10 kw-D, 2.5 kw-N, DA-N. TL: N36 16 03 W115 02 41. Web Site: www.hottalk1140.com.

Format: Talk. ♦Raina Weathers, gen sls mgr; Jave Patterson, prom dir & progmg dir; Steve Diamond, news dir; Mike Weaver, chief of engrg.

***KNPR(FM)**—Not on air, target date: unknown: 88.9 mhz; 24.7 kw. Ant 3,680 ft. TL: N35 58 02 W115 30 06. 1289 S. Torrey Pines Dr. 89146. Phone: (702) 258-9895. Fax: (702) 258-5646. E-mail: info@knpr.org. Web Site: www.knpr.org. Licensee: Nevada Public Radio Corp. Network: Network: NPR, PRI. Format: All news and info. ♦Lamar Marchese, pres & gen mgr.

KNUU(AM)—(Paradise). Feb 21, 1962: 970 khz; 5 kw-D, 500 w-N, DA-2. TL: N36 04 23 W115 15 05. 1455 E. Tropicana Ave., Suite 550 89119. Phone: (702) 735-8644. Fax: (702) 735-8184. Fax: (702) 734-4755. E-mail: knewsradio@hotmail.com. Web Site: www.knews970.com. Licensee: Nevada Media Group Inc. (acq 7-31-98). Network: Network: Wall Street, ABC, CNN Radio. Format: News/talk. News staff: 8; News: 154 hrs wkly. Target aud: 35 plus. ♦Ron Cohen, pres; Cindy K. Johnson, gen mgr.

KQOL-FM— Sept 1, 1977: 93.1 mhz; 25 w. 3,724 ft. TL: N35 58 02 W115 36 06. Stereo. 1130 E. Dessert Inn 89109. Phone: (702) 732-7753. Fax: (702) 732-4890. Web Site: www.kqol.com. Licensee: Citicasters Licenses L.P. Group owner: Clear Channel Communications Inc. (acq 1999). Hogan & Hartson. Format: Oldies. Target aud: 35-64; upscale, well educated with disposable income. ♦Kelly Kibler, gen mgr; Marty Thompson, opns dir & progmg dir; Jason Courtemanche, natl sls mgr; David Himmel, mktg dir; Rik McNeil, mus dir; Joe McCarthy, news dir; Tree Lee, chief of engrg.

KQRT(FM)— 1993: 105.1 mhz; 50 kw. 1,614 ft. TL: N36 19 46 W115 21 49. Stereo. 500 Pilot Rd., Suite D89119 89119. Phone: (702) 597-3070. Fax: (702) 507-1081. Licensee: Entravision Holdings LLC. Group owner: Entravision Communications Corp. (acq 3-14-2000; grpsl). Rep: Lotus Entravision Reps LLC. Format: Sp, CHR. Target aud: Spanish; young. ♦Walter Ulloa, CEO & pres; Chris Roman, gen mgr; Kathy Koch, stn mgr & gen sls mgr; Kerina Barzena, prom dir. Co-owned TV: KINC(TV)

KRLV(AM)— 1947: 1340 khz; 1 kw-U. TL: N36 09 22 W115 15 24. 5010 S. Spencer St. 89119. Phone: (702) 736-3145. Fax: (702) 740-8196. E-mail: generalmanager@krlv.net. Web Site: www.krlv.net. Licensee: Continental Radio Broadcasting Acquisition LLC (D.I.P.) (acq 7-13-2004). Cohn & Marks, LLP. Format: Sp, news, sports. News staff: 3; News: 12 hrs wkly. Target aud: 25-54. ♦Patrice Donley, gen mgr & sls; Rod Stowell, opns mgr.

KSHP(AM)—(North Las Vegas). 1954: 1400 khz; 1 kw-U. TL: N36 12 52 W115 09 18. Stereo. 2400 S. Jones, Suite 3 89146. Phone: (702) 221-1200. Fax: (702) 221-2285. Licensee: Las Vegas Radio Co. Group owner: McNaughton-Jakle Stations (acq 9-20-96; $600,000). Format: Radio shopping, sports. ♦K. Richard Jakle, pres; Brett Grant, VP, gen mgr, gen sls mgr & progmg dir; Joe Sands, chief of engrg.

KSNE-FM— Aug 18, 1987: 106.5 mhz; 100 kw. 1,155 ft. TL: N36 00 30 W115 00 20. Stereo. 1130 E. Dessert Inn Rd. 89109. Phone: (702) 732-7753. Fax: (702) 732-4890. Licensee: Citicasters Licenses L.P. Group owner: Clear Channel Communications Inc. (acq 1999; grpsl). Hogan & Hartson. Format: Soft adult contemp. News: 4 hrs wkly. Target aud: 25-54; emphasis on women. Spec prog: Relg one hr, pub affrs one hr wkly. ♦Kelly Kibler, gen mgr; Tom Chase, opns mgr & progmg dir; Jason Courtemanche, natl sls mgr; Karolyn Knight, prom dir; John Berry, mus dir; Joe McCarthy, news dir; Tree Lee, engrg dir & chief of engrg.

***KSOS(FM)**— July 18, 1972: 90.5 mhz; 100 kw. 1,269 ft. TL: N36 00 29 W115 00 20. Stereo. 2201 S. 6th St. 89104. Phone: (702) 731-5452. Phone: (800) 804-5452. Fax: (702) 731-1992. E-mail: info@sosradio.net. Web Site: www.sosradio.net. Licensee: Faith Communications Corp. (acq 12-31-71). Cohn & Marks. Format: Relg, adult contemp. News: 5 hrs wkly. Target aud: 25-44; young families. ♦Brad Staley, VP, gen mgr & opns mgr.

KSTJ(FM)—(Boulder City). Sept 1, 1982: 102.7 mhz; 96 kw. Ant 1,978 ft. TL: N35 56 46 W115 02 34. Stereo. 1455 E. Tropicana Ave., Suite

800 89119. Phone: (702) 730-0300. Fax: (702) 736-8447. Web Site: www.star1027fm.com. Licensee: KJUL License LLC. Group owner: Beasley Broadcast Group Inc. (acq 9-6-2000; grpsl). Format: Music of the 80s. News: one hr wkly. Target aud: 25-54. ♦Harry Williams, CEO; Allen Shaw, exec VP; Tom Davis, gen sls mgr; Mike O'Brien, progmg dir; Joe Sands, chief of engrg.

***KUNV(FM)**— Apr 21, 1981: 91.5 mhz; 15 kw. 1,100 ft. TL: N36 00 28 W115 00 20. Stereo. Univ. of Nevada, 1515 E. Tropicana Ave., Suite 240 89119. Phone: (702) 798-9169. Fax: (702) 895-3877. Web Site: www.kunv.univ.org. Licensee: University of Nevada Board of Regents. Format: Var/div. Target aud: General. Spec prog: Sp 5 hrs, electronic 2 hrs, community affrs 4 hrs, Ger one hr wkly. ♦David Reese, gen mgr; Gig Brown, progmg dir; Joe Sands, chief of engrg.

***KVKL(FM)**—Not on air, target date: unknown: 91.1 mhz; 1.6 kw vert. Ant 994 ft. TL: N35 37 37 W115 16 11. 3185 S. Highland Dr., Suite 13 89108. Phone: (702) 731-5588. Licensee: Southern Nevada Educational Broadcasters. ♦Carl J. Auel, pres.

KWID(FM)— Mar 22, 1963: 101.9 mhz; 100 kw. Ant 1,181 ft. TL: N36 00 28 W115 00 20. Stereo. 1130 E. Desert Inn Rd. 89109. Phone: (702) 732-7753. Fax: (702) 732-4890. Licensee: Citicasters Licenses L.P. Group owner: Clear Channel Communications Inc. (acq 1999; grpsl). Hogan & Hartson. Format: Contemporary hit. Target aud: 25-49. ♦Kelly Kibler, gen mgr; Tom Chase, opns dir; Terry King, gen sls mgr; Jason Courtemasche, natl sls mgr; Joe McCarthy, news dir; Tree Lee, engrg dir & chief of engrg.

KWWN(AM)—Not on air, target date: unknown: 1100 khz; 20 kw-D, 1 kw-N, DA-2. TL: N36 12 45 W115 09 45. 8755 W. Flamingo Rd. 89147-8667. Phone: (702) 876-1460. Fax: (702) 876-6685. Licensee: Lotus Broadcasting Corp. ♦Tony Bonnici, gen mgr.

Laughlin

KVGS(FM)— 1991: 107.9 mhz; 98 kw. Ant 1,984 ft. TL: N35 39 07 W114 18 42. 2725 E. Desert Inn Rd, Suite 180, Las Vegas 89121. Phone: (702) 784-4000. Phone: (928) 704-4540. Fax: (702) 784-4040. Web Site: www.v108fm.com. Licensee: Desert Sky Media LLC (acq 11-24-99). Network: ABC. Format: Urban contemp. Target aud: 25-54; adults. ♦Frank Woodbeck, gen mgr; Jodie Dames, gen sls mgr; Craig Knight, prom dir; Tony Rankin, progmg dir; Amy Stone, mus dir; Al Kirsckner, engrg VP & chief of engrg; Joe Sands, chief of engrg; Rick Fulkerson, chief of engrg.

Logandale

KADD(FM)— September 1997: 93.5 mhz; 82 kw horiz. Ant 2,148 ft. TL: N36 38 07 W114 07 18. Box 67, Santa Clara, CA 95052. Secondary address: 1955 S. Casino Dr., Santa Clara 89029. Phone: (520) 855-1051. Fax: (928) 855-7996. Web Site: www.maddog.net. Licensee: M&M Broadcasting LLC (acq 5-10-01; $150,000). Format: Hot adult contemp. ♦Chris Rolando, gen mgr.

Lund

***KWPR(FM)**— September 2000: 88.7 mhz; 3 kw. 905 ft. TL: N38 49 48 W115 17 38. Nevada Public Radio, 1289 S. Torrey Pines Dr., Las Vegas 89146. Phone: (702) 258-9895. Fax: (702) 258-5646. Web Site: www.nevadapublicradio.org. Licensee: Nevada Public Radio Corp. Format: Div, news. ♦Lamar Marchese, gen mgr.

Mesquite

***KAIZ(FM)**— 2005: 91.1 mhz; 400 w. Ant 827 ft. TL: N36 53 51 W114 17 10. Stereo. 5700 W. Oaks Blvd., Rocklin, CA 95765. Phone: (916) 251-1600. Fax: (916) 251-1650. E-mail: info@air1.com. Web Site: www.air1.com. Licensee: Educational Media Foundation. Group owner: EMF Broadcasting. Network: Air 1. Shaw Pittman. Format: Contemp Christian. News staff: 3. Target aud: 18-35; Judeo-Christian, female. ♦Richard Jenkins, pres; Mike Novak, VP & progmg dir; Lloyd Parker, gen mgr; Keith Whipple, dev dir; Eric Allen, natl sls mgr; Dan Beek,

Nevada

rgnl sls mgr; Chris Joyce, prom dir; Bryan O'Neal, progmg mgr; Liz Morton, mus dir; Ed Lenane, news dir; Sam Wallington, engrg dir.

*KEKL(FM)— 2005: 88.5 mhz; 20.5 kw. Ant 489 ft. TL: N36 41 00 W114 30 48. Southern Nevada Educational Broadcasters, 3185 S. Highland St., Suite 13, Las Vegas 89109-1029. Phone: (702) 731-5588. Licensee: Southern Nevada Educational Broadcasters. ♦ Carl J. Auel, gen mgr.

KVEG(FM)— July 23, 2001: 97.5 mhz; 100 kw. Ant 981 ft. TL: N36 34 52 W114 35 59. 3999 Las Vegas Blvd. S., Suite K, Las Vegas 89119. Phone: (702) 736-6161. Fax: (702) 736-2986. E-mail: mail@kvegas.com. Web Site: www.kvegas.com. Licensee: Kemp Broadcasting Inc. Koerner & Olender, P.C. Format: CHR/rhythmic. Target aud: 25-39. ♦ Gary Cox, gen mgr.

Moapa Valley

KWLY(FM)— July 1, 2001: 104.7 mhz; 100 kw. Ant 604 ft. TL: N36 41 00 W114 30 48. Summit American Inc., 5000 W. Oakey, Las Vegas 89146. Phone: (702) 258-0039. Fax: (702) 258-6536. Licensee: Summit American Inc. KMZ Rosenman. Format: Adult contemp, country. Target aud: 25-54. ♦ Scott Gentry, gen mgr.

North Las Vegas

KJUL(FM)— April 1989: 104.3 mhz; 24.5 kw. 3,700 ft. TL: N35 58 02 W115 30 06. Stereo. 1455 E. Tropicana Ave., Suite 800, Las Vegas 89119. Phone: (702) 730-0300. Fax: (702) 736-8447. Web Site: www.kjul.com. Licensee: KJUL License LLC. Group owner: Beasley Broadcast Group Inc. (acq 1-31-2001; grpsl). Format: Adult standards. News: one hr wkly. Target aud: 35-64. ♦ Allen Shaw, CEO; Harry Williams, gen mgr; Tom Davis, sls dir & gen sls mgr; Patti Mills, natl sls mgr; Kevin Miskimmons, rgnl sls mgr; David Allen, progmg dir; Joe Sands, chief of engrg.

KSFN(AM)— Licensed to North Las Vegas. See Las Vegas

KSHP(AM)— Licensed to North Las Vegas. See Las Vegas

KXNT(AM)— 1986: 840 khz; 50 kw-D, 25 kw-N, DA-2. TL: N36 23 53 W114 54 57. Stereo. 6655 W. Sahara Ave., Suite D208, Las Vegas 89146. Phone: (702) 364-8400. Fax: (702) 889-7384. Web Site: www.kxnt.com. Licensee: Infinity Radio Inc. Group owner: Infinity Broadcasting Corp. (acq 11-13-98; grpsl). Network: CBS Radio. Baraff, Koerner & Olender. Format: News/talk. Target aud: 35-64; upscale adults. ♦ Tom Humm, gen mgr; Frank Feder, sls VP; Nicki Amsden, sls dir; Jeff Burkett, mktg dir; Jack Landreth, progmg dir; Tracy Teagarden, engrg dir & chief of engrg.

Pahrump

KNYE(FM)— Nov 19, 2001: 95.1 mhz; 6 kw. Ant -92 ft. TL: N36 11 52 W116 02 08. 1230 Dutch Ford Rd. 89048. Phone: (775) 537-6100. Fax: (775) 537-6574. E-mail: knye@knye.com. Web Site: www.knye.com. Licensee: Pahrump Radio Inc. (acq 2-14-01). Format: Oldies. ♦ Art Bell, pres, gen mgr & chief of engrg.

KXTE(FM)— 1989: 107.5 mhz; 24.5 kw. 3,715 ft. TL: N35 58 02 W115 30 06. Stereo. 6655 W. Sahara Ave., Suite C-202, Las Vegas 89146. Phone: (702) 257-1075. Fax: (702) 889-7575. Web Site: www.xtremeradio.fm. Licensee: Infinity Radio Inc. Group owner: Infinity Broadcasting Corp. (acq 11-13-98; grpsl). Format: Talk, alternative. Target aud: 18-49. ♦ Marty Basch, gen mgr; Marc Isquith, gen sls mgr; Chris Ripley, mus dir.

Panaca

*KLNR(FM)— May 1989: 91.7 mhz; 100 w. Ant 3,424 ft. TL: N37 50 38 W114 34 40. 1289 S. Torrey Pines Dr., Las Vegas 89146. Phone: (702) 258-9895. Fax: (702) 258-5646. Licensee: Nevada Public Radio Corp. Network: NPR. Format: All news. ♦ Lamar Marchese, gen mgr.

Paradise

KNUU(AM)— Licensed to Paradise. See Las Vegas

Pioche

KBZB(FM)— 2002: . Stn currently dark 98.9 mhz; 5 kw. Ant 3,375 ft. TL: N37 53 44 W114 34 41. (CP: 100 kw, ant 1,958 ft. TL: N37 27 40 W114 27 55). Box 692 89043. Phone: (775) 962-5681. Licensee: 3 Point Media - Nevada LLC. (acq 1-26-2004; $1.96 million). Format: Div, talk.

Reno

KBZZ(AM)—See Sparks

KDOT(FM)— Oct 12, 1966: 104.5 mhz; 25 kw. 2,929 ft. TL: N39 18 48 W119 52 59. Stereo. Box 9870, 2900 Sutro St. 89512. Phone: (775) 329-9261. Fax: (775) 323-1450. E-mail: javet@kdot.com. Web Site: www.kdot.com. Licensee: Lotus Radio Corp. Group owner: Lotus Communications Corp. (acq 3-30-93; $600,000. with KIRS(AM) Sun Valley; FTR: 4-19-93). Rep: D & R Radio. Format: Active rock. News staff: one; News: 3 hrs wkly. Target aud: 18-49; young active adults that like today's lifestyle. ♦ Dane Wilt, gen mgr; Marc Isquith, gen sls mgr; Derek Sante, prom dir; Jack Landreth, progmg dir.

KPLY(AM)—Co-owned with KDOT(FM). Oct 25, 1928: 630 khz; 5 kw-D, 1 kw-N, DA-N. TL: N39 34 25 W119 50 48. E-mail: espnradio630@aol.com. (Acq 1995; $325,000). Format: Sports. Target aud: 25-54. ♦ Dane Wilt, VP; Ken Allen, progmg mgr.

KHIT(AM)— Jan 29, 1955: 1450 khz; 1 kw-U. TL: N39 33 26 W119 47 47. Box 9870, 2900 Sutro St. 89512. Phone: (775) 329-9261. Fax: (775) 323-1450. E-mail: kena@kozzradio.com. Licensee: Lotus Radio Corp. Group owner: Lotus Communications Corp. (acq 9-67). Rep: D & R Radio. Format: Big band. News staff: one; News: 2 hrs wkly. Target aud: 25-49. ♦ Dane Wilt, gen mgr; Jim McClain, opns mgr; Raina Weathers, gen sls mgr; Ken Allen, prom dir & progmg dir; Steve Diamond, news dir; Mike Weaver, chief of engrg.

KOZZ-FM—Co-owned with KHIT(AM). September 1969: 105.7 mhz; 75 kw. 2,120 ft. TL: N39 15 34 W119 42 21. Stereo. Web Site: www.kozzradio.com. (Acq 1-1-78). Format: Classic rock. ♦ Bill Shriftman, CFO; Dawn Keeble, gen sls mgr; Rick Carter, prom mgr & progmg dir.

*KIHM(FM)— Jan 1, 1984: 920 khz; 4.6 kw-D, 850 w-N. TL: N39 30 41 W119 42 51. 3550 Berron Way, Suite 3B 89511. Phone: (775) 828-4228. Fax: (775) 823-5444. Web Site: www.kihmradio.org. Licensee: IHR Educational Broadcasting (group owner; acq 8-24-2000). Format: Catholic. ♦ Doug Pearson, stn mgr.

KJFK(AM)— Listing follows KRNO(FM).

KKOH(AM)— Oct 13, 1970: 780 khz; 50 kw-U, DA-N. TL: N39 40 41 W119 48 06. 595 E. Plumb Ln. 89502. Phone: (775) 789-6700. Fax: (775) 789-6767. E-mail: dan.mason@citcomm.com. Web Site: www.kkoh.com. Licensee: Citadel Broadcasting Co. Group owner: Citadel Broadcasting Corp. (acq 5-18-92; $12.5 million;. grpsl; FTR: 6-8-92). Network: ABC Information & Entertainment. Rep: McGavren Guild. Format: News/talk. News staff: 4; News: 28 hrs wkly. Target aud: 35-64. Spec prog: Sports, Sp 2 hrs wkly. ♦ Farid Suleman, CEO & pres; Dana Johnson, gen mgr; Andrew Perini, gen sls mgr & chief of engrg; Dan Mason, progmg dir.

KLCA(FM)—(Tahoe City).CA Apr 5, 1985: 96.5 mhz; 4 kw. 2,965 ft. TL: N39 18 47 W119 52 59. Stereo. 300 E. 2nd St., Suite 1410 89501. Phone: (775) 829-1964. Fax: (775) 825-3183. Web Site: www.alice965.com. Licensee: Americom Broadcasting. Group owner: Americom (acq 1996; $1.225 million). Format: Modern hits. News: 3 hrs wkly. Target aud: 18-34. Spec prog: Metal shop 2 hrs wkly. ♦ Daniel Cook, gen mgr.

KNEV(FM)— Dec 25, 1953: 95.5 mhz; 60 kw. 2,280 ft. TL: N39 15 34 W119 42 16. Stereo. 595 E. Plumb 89502. Phone: (775) 789-6700. Fax: (775) 789-6767. Web Site: www.magic95.com. Licensee: Citadel Broadcasting Co. Group owner: Citadel Broadcasting Corp. (acq 4-13-93; $500,000;. FTR: 5-3-93). Network: ABC Information & Entertainment. Format: Hot adult contemp. Target aud: General. Spec prog: Jazz 2 hrs, relg one hr, pub affrs one hr wkly. ♦ Dana Johnson, gen mgr.

KNIS(FM)—See Carson City

KODS(FM)—(Carnelian Bay).CA 1970: 103.7 mhz; 6.3 kw. 2,985 ft. TL: N39 18 16 W119 53 00. Stereo. 300 E. 2nd St., Suite1410 89501. Phone: (775) 829-1964. Fax: (775) 825-3183. Web Site: www.river1037.com. Licensee: Americom Broadcasting. (acq 1996). Rep: CBS Radio. Format: Hits of the 60s & 70s. ♦ Tom Quinn, gen mgr; Daniel Cook, gen mgr; Lisa Brown, gen sls mgr; Laurie Adamson, progmg dir; Bob Garrison, news dir & pub affrs dir; Steve Weber, chief of engrg.

KRNO(FM)—(Incline Village). July 1974: 106.9 mhz; 35 kw. Ant 2,988 ft. TL: N39 18 38 W119 53 01. Stereo. 300 E. 2nd St., 14th Floor 89501. Phone: (775) 829-1964. Fax: (775) 825-3183. Licensee: Americom Las Vegas L.P. Group owner: Americom (acq 4-16-98; grpsl). Rep: Allied Radio Partners. Shaw Pittman. Format: Soft rock, soft adult contemp. News staff: one; News: 18 hrs wkly. Target aud: 25-54; women. ♦ Daniel Cook, gen mgr; Eric Bowlin, gen sls mgr; Dan Fritz, progmg dir; Wanda Schiwart, news dir; Steve Weber, chief of engrg.

KJFK(AM)—Co-owned with KRNO(FM). Oct 30, 1963: 1230 khz; 1 kw-U. TL: N39 30 42 W119 42 48. Format: Progressive talk. Target aud: 35 plus. ♦ Heather Forcier, gen sls mgr; Dan Fritz, progmg dir.

KRNV-FM— Aug 12, 1986: 102.1 mhz; 11 kw. Ant 492 ft. TL: N39 35 03 W119 47 52. 300 S. Wells Ave., Suite 12 89502. Phone: (775) 333-1017. Fax: (775) 333-9046. Web Site: www.entravision.com.Network progmg Licensee: Entravision Holdings LLC. Group owner: Entravision Communications Corp. (acq 3-14-00; grpsl). Format: Sp. Target aud: 18-49; adults.Philip Wilkinson, COO; Walter F. Ulloa, CEO & chmn; Jeff Liberman, pres; John DeLorenzo, CFO & exec VP; Michael G. Rowles, sr VP; Larry Safir, VP; Viola Cody, gen mgr, sls dir, gen sls mgr & rgnl sls mgr; Michelle Ferreia, mktg VP; Jill Bridgman, mktg dir & prom dir; Manuel Sepulveda, prom VP & mus dir; Edwardo Rios, prom dir; Haz Montana, progmg dir & progmg; Glenn Graves, chief of engrg; Mike Weaver, chief of engrg

KRZQ-FM—See Sparks

KTHX-FM—(Dayton). June 10, 1983: 100.1 mhz; 12.2 kw. Ant 2,162 ft. TL: N39 15 34 W119 42 21. Stereo. 300 E Second St., 14th Fl. 89501. Phone: (775) 333-0123. Fax: (775) 322-7361. Web Site: www.kthxfm.com. Licensee: NM Licensing LLC. Group owner: NextMedia Group L.L.C. (acq 11-26-01; grpsl). Network: ABC. Leventhal, Senter & Lerman. Format: AAA. News: 2 hrs wkly. Target aud: 18-49; upscale, high income & educated. ♦ Skip Weiler, pres; April Clark, gen mgr.

*KUNR(FM)— Oct 7, 1963: 88.7 mhz; 20 kw. 2,169 ft. TL: N39 15 34 W119 42 16. Stereo. Mail Stop 294, Univ. of Nevada 89557. Phone: (775) 327-5867. Fax: (775) 784-1381. Web Site: www.kunr.org. Licensee: University of Nevada Board of Regents. Network: Network: NPR, PRI. Format: News, jazz, class music. Target aud: General. Spec prog: Folk 2 hrs, ethnic 9 hrs wkly. ♦ Steven Zink, exec VP; Bobbi Lazzarone, stn mgr; Terry Joy, opns dir; Kate Grey, sls dir & news dir; James Shannon, chief of engrg.

KURK(FM)— November 1994: 92.9 mhz; 48 kw. Ant 502 ft. TL: N39 35 03 W119 48 06. c/o KKOH(AM) and KNEV(FM), 595 East Plumb Ln. 89502. Phone: (775) 789-6700. Fax: (775) 789-6767. Licensee: NM Licensing LLC. Group owner: NextMedia Group L.L.C. (acq 12-15-2003; $4.25 million). Format: Classic rock and roll. ♦ Dana Johnson, gen mgr.

KXEQ(AM)— July 1946: 1340 khz; 1 kw-U. TL: N39 32 22 W119 46 53. 225 Linden St. 89502. Phone: (775) 827-1111. Phone: (775) 827-1313. Fax: (775) 827-2082. Licensee: Azteca Broadcasting Corp. (group owner; acq 10-16-91; $30,000; 11-4-91). Network: AP Radio. Format: Sp. ♦ Juan Morales, gen mgr & progmg dir.

KXTO(AM)— 1991: 1550 khz; 2.5 kw-D, 94 w-N. TL: N39 34 39 W119 50 52. 1085 E. 2nd St., Suite 2 89502. Phone: (775) 348-5850. Web Site: www.kxto.com. Licensee: First Broadcasting of Nevada Inc. Format: Sp, relg. News: 10 hrs wkly. Target aud: Hispanics. ♦ Yolanda Amaya, gen mgr.

KZTQ(FM)—(Carson City). June 27, 1972: 97.3 mhz; 87 kw. 2,112 ft. TL: N39 15 21 W119 42 37. Stereo. 300 E. 2nd St., 14th Fl. 89501. Phone: (775) 829-1964. Fax: (775) 825-3183. Licensee: Americom Las Vegas L.P. Group owner: Americom (acq 4-27-98; grpsl). Rep: Allied Radio Partners. Format: CHR. News staff: one; News: 2 hrs wkly. Target aud: 18-34; women. ♦ Daniel Cook, gen mgr; Steve Webber, chief of engrg.

Smith

KSVL(FM)— 1999: 92.3 mhz; 490 w. Ant 2,073 ft. TL: N38 41 06 W119 11 04. Box 123 89430. Phone: (775) 465-2200. Licensee: Donegal Enterprises. Format: Class. ♦ Wayne Donegal, gen mgr.

Stations in the U.S. — New Hampshire

Developers & Brokers of Radio Properties — contact American Media Services at our suite: Philadelphia Marriott Downtown 215-625-2900 · 843-972-2200 · americanmediaservices.com · Charleston, SC · Dallas, TX · Chicago, IL · Austin, TX — American Media Services, LLC

Sparks

KBDB(AM)— 2002: 1400 khz; 600 w-U. TL: N39 34 10 W119 45 03. 188 S. Bellevue, Suite 222, Memphis, TN 38104. Secondary address: 160 E. Plumb Ln., Reno 89502. Phone: (775) 689-3679. Fax: (775) 689-3680. E-mail: lymapps@aol.com. Web Site: www.kbdbradio.com. Licensee: George S. Flinn Jr. Format: Big Band, Talk. ♦George S. Flinn Jr., gen mgr.

KBZZ(AM)— Aug 9, 1960: 1270 khz; 5 kw-U, DA-2. TL: N39 32 03 W119 39 44. 300 E. 2nd St., 14th Fl., Reno 89501-1500. Phone: (775) 829-1964. Fax: (775) 825-3183. Licensee: Americom Las Vegas L.P. Group owner: Americom (acq 1996; grpsl). Network: Network: CBS, Westwood One. Rep: Allied Radio Partners. Format: Sports & info, news/talk. Target aud: 25-54; primarily men who are interested in sports. ♦Tom Quinn, pres; Daniel Cook, gen mgr; Dan Fritz, gen sls mgr & progmg dir; Heather Forcier, gen sls mgr; Steve Webber, chief of engrg.

KJZS(FM)— 1993: 92.1 mhz; 440 w. 804 ft. TL: N39 32 03 W119 39 44. 300 E. Second St. 14 th Fl., Reno 89501. Phone: (775) 333-0123. Web Site: www.smoothjazzreno.com. Licensee: NM Licensing LLC. Group owner: NextMedia Group L.L.C. (acq 11-26-01; grpsl). Latham & Watkins. Format: Jazz, adult Contempo. ♦Robert Dees, gen mgr & progmg dir.

*KLRH(FM)—Not on air, target date: unknown: 88.3 mhz; 1.78 kw. Ant 2,886 ft. TL: N39 45 38 W119 27 59. 5700 W. Oaks Blvd., Rocklin, CA 95765. Phone: (916) 251-1600. Fax: (916) 251-1650. E-mail: klove@klove.com. Web Site: www.klove.com. Licensee: Educational Media Foundation. Group owner: EMF Broadcasting. Network: K-Love. Shaw Pittman. Format: Contemp Christian. News staff: 3. Target aud: 25-44; Judeo Christian female. ♦Richard Jenkins, pres; Mike Novak, VP & progmg dir; Lloyd Parker, gen mgr; Ed Lenane, opns dir & news dir; Keith Whipple, dev dir; Eric Allen, natl sls mgr; Chris Joyce, prom dir; David Pierce, progmg mgr; Jon Rivers, mus dir; Sam Wallington, engrg dir.

KRZQ-FM— July 1, 1983: 100.9 mhz; 2.9 kw. 203 ft. TL: N39 22 04 W119 47 07. Stereo. 300E. 2nd St. 14th Floor, Reno 89015. Phone: (775) 333-0123. Fax: (775) 333-0110. Licensee: NM Licensing LLC. Group owner: NextMedia Group L.L.C. (acq 11-26-01; grpsl). Network: ABC. Leibowitz & Associates. Format: Alternative rock, talk. Target aud: 18-54; general. ♦Skip Weller, pres; April Clark, gen mgr; Jeremy Smith, progmg dir; Matt Bates, mus dir; Robert Barfoot, chief of engrg.

Sun Valley

KQLO(AM)— 1946: 1590 khz; 5 kw-D, 67 w-N. TL: N39 24 57 W119 42 51. 101 Locust St., Reno 89501-1012. Phone: (775) 322-0847. Fax: ((775) 322-0927. E-mail: business@kqlo.com. Web Site: www.kqlo.com. Licensee: Universal Broadcasting Inc. (acq 12-22-2003; $140,000). Rep: Caballero, Interep. Format: Sp contemp. Target aud: General. ♦Lee Chavez, gen mgr & natl sls mgr; Lourdes Rincon, system mgr.

KUUB(FM)— 1999: 94.5 mhz; 12 kw. Ant 459 ft. TL: N39 35 02 W119 47 53. (CP: 50 kw). 2900 Sutro St., Reno 89512. Phone: (775) 329-9261. Fax: (775) 323-1450. Web Site: www.945themountain.com. Licensee: Lotus Radio Corp. Group owner: Lotus Communications Corp. Format: Country. ♦Dane Wilt, gen mgr.

KWNZ(AM)— 2002: 93.7 mhz; 3.6 kw. Ant 423 ft. TL: N39 35 02 W119 47 54. 595 E. Plumb Ln., Reno 89502. Phone: (775) 789-6700. Fax: (775) 789-6767. E-mail: angel.garcia@citcomm.com. Web Site: wild937.com. Licensee: Flinn Broadcasting Corp. Format: CHR. ♦Dana Johnson, gen mgr.

Tonopah

KHWK(FM)— July 29, 1982: . Stn currently dark 92.7 mhz; 290 w. Ant 971 ft. TL: N38 04 22 W117 13 16. Stereo. Box 1669 89049. Phone: (775) 482-5724. Licensee: Donald W. Kaminiski Jr. (acq 3-16-92; $240,000);. FTR: 4-6-92). ♦Don Kaminski, CEO & gen mgr.

*KTPH(FM)— October 1988: 91.7 mhz; 100 w. 1,433 ft. TL: N38 03 07 W117 13 30. 1289 S. Torrey Pines Dr., Las Vegas 89146. Phone: (702) 258-9895. Fax: (702) 258-5646. Licensee: Nevada Public Radio Corp. Network: NPR. Format: Class, news. ♦Lamar Marchese, pres & gen mgr.

Wendover

KVUW(FM)—Not on air, target date: unknown: 102.3 mhz; 3 kw. Ant 26 ft. TL: N40 44 30 W114 02 10. 218 N. Wolcott St., Casper, WY 82601. Phone: (307) 265-1984. Licensee: Laramie Mountain Broadcasting LLC. (group owner). (acq 4-18-2005; $750,000. with CP for KHIH(FM) Laramie, WY).

Whitney

KLSQ(AM)— Aug 15, 1986: 870 khz; 5 kw-D, 430 w-N, DA-N. TL: N35 58 35 W114 57 03. Stereo. 6767 W. Tropicana, Ste. 102, Las Vegas 89103. Phone: (702) 284-6400. Fax: (702) 284-6403. Web Site: www.netmio.com. Licensee: HBC-Las Vegas Inc. Group owner: Univision Radio (acq 9-22-2003; grpsl). Format: Sp. Target aud: 35 plus. ♦Dana Demerjian, gen mgr; Cristina Valarezo, gen sls mgr; Jose Elias Cruz, progmg dir; Oscar Mahi, news dir; Eric Martell, chief of engrg.

Winchester

KBET(AM)—Not on air, target date: June 30, 2005:. Stn currently dark 790 khz; 1 kw-D, 300 w-N, DA-2. TL: N36 05 27 W115 00 59. Box 1450, St. George, UT 84771-1450. Secondary address: 210 North 1000 East, Box 1450, St. George, UT 84771-1450. Phone: 435-628-1000. Fax: 435-628-6636. E-mail: legacy1@infowest.com. Licensee: AM Radio 790 Inc. Group owner: Diamond Broadcasting Corp. (acq 12-6-04). Network: CNN Radio. Dan J. Alpert. Format: Adult Standards. ♦E. Morgan Skinner Jr., CEO & pres.

Winnemucca

KWNA(AM)— Jan 28, 1955: 1400 khz; 1 kw-U. TL: N40 57 23 W117 42 48. Box 1400 89446. Secondary address: 5130 E. Weikel Dr. 89446. Phone: (775) 623-5203. Fax: (775) 625-1011. Web Site: www.kwnaradio.com. Licensee: Sheen Broadcasting Co. (acq 9-15-81; $200,000; 9-28-81). Network: ABC Information & Entertainment. Art Moore, Gardner, Carton & Douglas. Format: Oldies. News staff: one; News: 12 hrs wkly. Target aud: General. Spec prog: Farm 2 hrs wkly. ♦Joyce Sheen, news dir; Torrey Sheen, gen mgr, gen sls mgr, progmg dir & chief of engrg.

KWNA-FM— Apr 3, 1982: 92.7 mhz; 60 w. 2,120 ft. TL: N41 00 40 W117 45 59. (CP: 140 w). Stereo. Format: C&W.

New Hampshire

Bedford

WMLL(FM)— June 1996: 96.5 mhz; 730 w. Ant 935 ft. TL: N42 59 02 W71 35 22. 500 Commercial St., Manchester 03101. Phone: (603) 669-7979. Fax: (603) 669-4641. Web Site: www.965themill.com. Licensee: Saga Communications of New England LLC. Group owner: Saga Communications Inc. (acq 9-29-97; $3.3 million). Rep: Katz Radio. Format: Classic rock. Target aud: 35-54; baby boomers. ♦Edward Christian, CEO; Raymond R. Garon, pres; Samuel Bush, CFO; J.C. Haze, opns dir & progmg dir.

Belmont

WNHW(FM)— May 8, 1994: 93.3 mhz; 300 w. Ant 1,020 ft. TL: N43 23 52 W71 33 03. Stereo. Box 1923, Concord 03302-1923. Secondary address: 11 Kimball Dr., Suite 114, Hooksett 03106. Phone: (603) 225-1160. Fax: (603) 224-7280. Web Site: www.933thewolf.com. Licensee: Nassau Broadcasting III L.L.C. Group owner: Nassau Broadcasting Partners L.P. (acq 10-1-2004; $8 million. with WJYY(FM) Concord). Format: Country. ♦Brit Johnson, gen mgr; Dawn Parris, gen sls mgr; Matt Forrest, progmg dir; Steve Ordinetz, engrg mgr & chief of engrg.

Berlin

WMOU(AM)— 1947: 1230 khz; 1 kw-U. TL: N44 27 32 W71 10 16. Box 489, 297 Pleasant St. 03570. Phone: (603) 752-1230. Fax: (603) 752-3117. E-mail: wmou@ncia.net. Licensee: Barry P. Lunderville (acq 11-7-03; $75,000). Network: Westwood One. Format: Adult standards. News staff: one; News: 6 hrs wkly. Target aud: 25-54; local residents of northern New Hampshire. Spec prog: Fr 3 hrs, talk 2 hrs, swap shop 3 hrs wkly. ♦Barry Lunderville, pres & progmg dir; Bob Barbin, opns dir; Randy Frank, gen sls mgr; Brian Lunderville, chief of engrg.

Campton

WLKC(FM)— 1997: 105.7 mhz; 125 w. Ant 2,001 ft. TL: N43 57 32 W71 33 23. Stereo. 288 S. River Rd., Bedford 03110. Phone: (603) 669-1250. Fax: (603) 528-1638. E-mail: nebco231@hotmail.com. Licensee: Devon Broadcasting Co. Inc. (acq 3-5-99; $300,000). Format: AAA. Target aud: 25-54. ♦Steve Young, gen mgr; Dana Marshall, progmg dir; Lou Muise, chief of engrg.

Claremont

WHDQ(FM)—Listing follows WTSV(AM).

WTSV(AM)— 1948: 1230 khz; 1 kw-U. TL: N43 22 15 W72 19 42. Box 1230, Rt. 12 & 103 03743. Phone: (603) 542-7735. Fax: (603) 542-8721. E-mail: espnthescore@aol.com. Web Site: www.scoreradio.com. Licensee: Nassau Broadcasting III L.L.C. Group owner: Nassau Broadcasting Partners L.P. (acq 8-2-2004; grpsl). Network: ABC Information & Entertainment. Roslin. Rini & Coran. Format: Sports. Target aud: 35 plus. ♦Jeffrey Shapiro, pres; Wally Caswell, gen mgr & gen sls mgr; Heath Cole, prom dir & progmg dir; Neil Langer, chief of engrg.

WHDQ(FM)—Co-owned with WTSV(AM). 1948: 106.1 mhz; 9.51 kw. 1,068 ft. TL: N43 23 48 W72 18 01. Stereo. E-mail: info@q106rock.com. Web site: www.whdq.com. Format: Adult rock and roll. ♦Cliff McNaughton, sls VP.

Concord

*WEVO(FM)— Aug 4, 1981: 89.1 mhz; 50 kw. Ant 385 ft. TL: N43 12 53 W71 34 28. Stereo. 207 N. Main St. 03301. Phone: (603) 228-8910. Fax: (603) 224-6052. E-mail: admin@nhpr.org. Web Site: www.nhpr.org. Licensee: New Hampshire Public Radio Inc. Network: Network: NPR, PRI. Garvey, Schubert & Barer. Format: News/talk. News staff: 9; News: 42 hrs wkly. Target aud: 25-54; well educated adults. Spec prog: Folk 3 hrs wkly. ♦Elizabeth Gardella, pres; Mark Handley, gen mgr; Sean Gillery, dev dir; Mark Bevis, news dir; John Huntley, engrg dir.

WJYY(FM)— Sept 15, 1983: 105.5 mhz; 1.55 kw. 456 ft. TL: N43 16 46 W71 30 15. Stereo. Box 1923 03302-1923. Secondary address: 7 Perley St. 03301. Phone: (603) 228-9036. Phone: (603) 485-8104. Fax: (603) 224-7280. Web Site: www.wjyy.com. Licensee: Nassau Broadcasting III L.L.C. Group owner: Nassau Broadcasting Partners L.P. (acq 10-1-2004; $8 million. with WNHW(FM) Belmont). Format: CHR. News staff: one; News: 6 hrs wkly. Target aud: 25-54. ♦Brit Johnson, gen mgr; Dawn Parris, gen sls mgr; Andy Subbiondo, natl sls mgr; A.J. Dukette, progmg dir; Steve Ordinetz, news dir & engrg mgr.

WKXL(AM)— June 15, 1946:: 1450 khz; 1 kw-U. TL: N43 11 39 W71 33 17. 37 Redington Rd. 03301. Phone: (603) 225-5521 Office. Phone: (603) 224-1450 Studio. Fax: (603) 224-6404. E-mail: info@wkxl1450.com. Web Site: www.wkxl1450.com. Licensee: New Hampshire Family Radio LLC (acq 12-16-2004;: $800,000). Network: ABC. Format: News/talk. News staff: 2; News: 30 hrs wkly. Target aud: 35 plus; adults in Concord, Hillsboro, Manchester & contiguous towns. ♦Dick Pistey, gen mgr; Gardner Hill, opns mgr.

New Hampshire

WNNH(FM)—See Henniker

***WSPS(FM)**— 1974: 90.5 mhz; 200 w. 110 ft. TL: N43 11 37 W71 34 29. St. Paul's School, 325 Pleasant St. 03301. Phone: (603) 228-4810. Phone: (603) 229-4600. Fax: (603) 229-4891. E-mail: wsps@sps.edu. Web Site: www.wsps.sps.edu. Licensee: St. Paul's School. Drinker Biddle & Reath. Format: Div. Target aud: General. ♦ David Harvey, gen mgr.

WTPL(FM)—(Hillsboro). Oct 1, 1989:: 107.7 mhz; 580 w. 738 ft. TL: N43 09 00 W71 47 56. Stereo. 501 South St., Bow 03304. Phone: (603) 545-0777. Fax: (603) 545-0781. Web Site: www.wtplfm.com. Licensee: Great Eastern Radio LLC (acq 6-3-2004; $1.5 million). Network: Network: CBS Radio, ESPN Radio. Format: News/talk, sports. News staff: 2; News: 50 hrs wkly. Target aud: 35 plus; adult audience in Merrimack & Hillsborough counties. ♦ Mike Johnson, gen mgr.

***WVNH(FM)**— Mar 7, 1999: 91.1 mhz; 650 w vert. 331 ft. TL: N43 23 54 W71 25 24. Box 40 03302. Phone: (603) 227-0911. E-mail: info@wvnh.org. Web Site: www.wvnh.org. Licensee: New Hampshire Gospel Radio Inc. Format: Christian. ♦ Peter Stohrer, gen mgr; Cheryl Eggert, stn mgr.

WWHK(FM)— Mar 7, 1972:: 102.3 mhz; 3 kw. Ant 285 ft. TL: N43 13 00 W71 34 34. Stereo. 11 Kimbell Dr., Suite 114, Hooksett 03106. Phone: (603) 225-1160. Fax: (603) 225-8935. Licensee: Capitol Broadcasting Corp. Inc. Group owner: Vox Radio Group L.P. (acq 8-12-99). Format: Classic rock. Target aud: 25-54; adult audience in Merrimack county - south central NH. ♦ Brid Johnson, gen mgr.

Conway

WBNC(AM)—Listing follows WVMJ(FM).

WMWV(FM)— June 23, 1967: 93.5 mhz; 3 kw. 420 ft. TL: N43 56 48 W71 08 24. Stereo. Box 2008 03818. Phone: (603) 356-8870. Fax: (603) 356-8875. E-mail: office@wmwv.com. Web Site: www.wmwv.com. Licensee: Mt. Washington Radio & Gramophone L.L.C. (group owner; acq 9-27-01; grpsl). Rep: Roslin. Format: AAA. ♦ Ronald Frizzell, gen mgr; Charles Osgood, opns VP & chief of engrg; Greg Mosston, gen sls mgr.

WVMJ(FM)— Oct 23, 1995: 104.5 mhz; 3 kw. 328 ft. TL: N43 55 34 71 05 46. Stereo. Box 2008 03818. Secondary address: Settlers' Green Rt. 16, N. Conway 03860. Phone: (603) 356-8870. Fax: (603) 356-8875. Web Site: www.conwaymagic.com. Licensee: Mt. Washington Radio & Gramophone L.L.C. (group owner; acq 10-15-01; grpsl). Format: Adult contemp. ♦ Ron Frizzell, gen mgr; Charles Osgood, opns mgr & chief of engrg; Greg Frizzell, gen sls mgr; Cooper Fox, progmg mgr; Dean Luttrell, news dir.

WBNC(AM)—Co-owned with WVMJ(FM). Dec 21, 1955: 1050 khz; 1 kw-D, 63 w-N. TL: N43 58 48 W71 06 36. Web Site: www.conwaymagic.com. ♦ Greg Frizzell, sls dir.

Derry

WDER(AM)— October 1983: 1320 khz; 10 kw-D, 1 kw-N, DA-2. TL: N42 51 59 W71 17 14. Box 465, 8 Lawrence Rd. 03038-6465. Phone: (603) 437-9337. Phone: (603) 434-9302. Fax: (603) 434-1035. Web Site: www.lifechangingradio.com. Licensee: Blount Communications Inc. of NH. Group owner: Blount Communications Group (acq 9-5-00; $793,000). Network: Salem Radio Network. Format: Talk, relg. ♦ William Blount, pres; David Young, VP & gen mgr; Emanuel DaCunha, stn mgr; Steve Sobozenski, opns mgr.

Dover

WOKQ(FM)— August 1970: 97.5 mhz; 50 kw. 492 ft. TL: N43 13 26 W70 58 18. Stereo. Box 576 03821-0576. Secondary address: 292 Middle Rd. 03820-4901. Phone: (603) 749-9750. Fax: (603) 749-1459. Web Site: www.wokq.com. Licensee: Citadel Broadcasting Co. Group owner: Citadel Broadcasting Corp. (acq 9-1-99; grpsl). Network: CNN Radio. Rep: Christal. Paul, Hastings, Janofsky & Walker. Format: Country. News staff: 2. Target aud: 25-54; general. ♦ Farid Suleman, CEO; Judy Ellis, pres; Martin Lessard, gen mgr; Mark Ericson, opns mgr; Bill Elliott, progmg dir.

WTSN(AM)— August 1956: 1270 khz; 5 kw-U, DA-2. TL: N43 11 01 W70 51 14. Box 400, 101 Back Rd. 03821-0400. Phone: (603) 742-1270. Fax: (603) 742-0448. Licensee: Garrison City Broadcasting Inc. (acq 3-18-83). Network: ABC Information & Entertainment. Rep: Roslin. Format: News/talk, sports. News staff: 3. Target aud: 25-54; very affluent. ♦ Bob Demers, CEO; Rick Bean, gen mgr.

Durham

***WUNH(FM)**— July 15, 1963: 91.3 mhz; 3 kw. 300 ft. TL: N43 09 23 W70 56 26. Stereo. Memorial Union Bldg., Univ. of New Hampshire 03824. Phone: (603) 862-2541. Phone: (603) 862-2087. Fax: (603) 862-2543. E-mail: gm@wunh.unh.edu. Web Site: www.wunh.unh.edu. Licensee: University of New Hampshire. Network: AP Radio. Format: Progsv. News: 7 hrs wkly. Target aud: Diverse. Spec prog: Black 4 hrs, blues 3 hrs, jazz 5 hrs, Pol 2 hrs, folk 4 hrs, celtic 2 hrs wkly. ♦ Josh Cilley, gen mgr; Alexandra Buchalski, opns dir; Abbie Crocker, prom dir; Augie Ciotti, progmg dir; Greg Falla, mus dir; John Bosselman, news dir; Peter Geremia, chief of engrg.

Exeter

WERZ(FM)—Listing follows WGIP(AM).

WGIP(AM)— June 4, 1966: 1540 khz; 5 kw-D. TL: N42 59 23 W70 56 14. 815 Lafayette Rd., Portsmouth 03801. Phone: (603) 436-7300. Fax: (603) 430-9415. Licensee: Capstar TX L.P. Group owner: Clear Channel Communications Inc. (acq 8-30-00; grpsl). Rep: McGavren Guild. Format: News/talk, sports. ♦ Robert Greer, gen mgr; Dan Pierce, opns mgr & progmg dir; Judy Figliulo, gen sls mgr; Jennifer McElreavy, prom dir; Kelly Brown, news dir; Roger Wood, news dir; Ken Neeman, chief of engrg.

WERZ(FM)—Co-owned with WGIP(AM). Sept 21, 1972: 107.1 mhz; 5.2 kw. 351 ft. TL: N43 01 38 W70 52 51. Web Site: www.werz.com. Format: Top-40. ♦ Michael O'Donnell, progmg dir.

***WPEA(FM)**— 1964: 90.5 mhz; 115 w. 170 ft. TL: N42 58 44 W70 57 00. Stereo. Phillips Exeter Academy, 20 Main St. 03833-2460. Phone: (603) 777-4414. Fax: (603) 777-4384. E-mail: WPEA@exeter.edu. Licensee: Trustees of Phillips Exeter Academy. Format: Var. Target aud: General; students.

Farmington

WMEX(FM)— July 9, 1999: 106.5 mhz; 2.9 kw. Ant 486 ft. TL: N43 24 01 W71 09 27. Stereo. 1 Wakefield St., Suite 302, Rochester 03867-1913. Phone: (603) 335-6600. Fax: (603) 299-0325. E-mail: oldies1065@aol.com. Web Site: wmexfm.com. Licensee: Wimmex LLC. Cohn & Marks. Format: Oldies. Target aud: 25 plus. ♦ Dennis Jackson, CEO; Gary James, VP & gen mgr; Gene Vallee, gen sls mgr; Ron Malone, chief of engrg.

Franklin

WFTN(AM)— Oct 30, 1966: 1240 khz; 1 kw-U. TL: N43 27 16 W71 38 33. Box 941, 110 Babbitt Rd. 03235. Phone: (603) 934-2500. Fax: (603) 934-2933. E-mail: onair@mix941fm.com. Web Site: www.mix941fm.com. Licensee: Northeast Communications Corp. (group owner; acq 9-30-74). Network: ABC Information & Entertainment. Format: Mus of your life. ♦ Jeff Fisher, pres, gen mgr & stn mgr; Fred Caruso, opns mgr & progmg dir; Jeff Levitan, gen sls mgr; Rick Ganley, prom dir; Gary Ford, mus dir; Amy Bates, news dir.

WFTN-FM— Apr 10, 1987: 94.1 mhz; 6 kw. 328 ft. TL: N43 28 23 W71 36 20. Stereo. Web Site: www.mix941fm.com. Format: Adult contemp.

Gorham

***WEVC(FM)**— May 1995: 107.1 mhz; 6 kw. 157 ft. TL: N44 27 32 W71 10 16. Stereo. 207 N. Main St., Concord 03301. Phone: (603) 228-8910. Fax: (603) 224-6052. E-mail: admin@nhpr.org. Web Site: www.nhpr.org. Licensee: New Hampshire Public Radio Inc. Network: CNN Radio. Format: News/talk. News staff: 9; News: 42 hrs wkly. Target aud: 25-54. Spec prog: Folk 3 hrs wkly. ♦ Elizabeth Gardella, pres & gen mgr; Scott McPherson, opns dir & progmg dir; Sean Gillery, dev dir; Mike Arnold, progmg dir; Mark Bevis, news dir; John Huntley, engrg dir.

Hampton

WSAK(FM)— August 1992: 102.1 mhz; 3 kw. 328 ft. TL: N42 53 51 W70 53 02. Stereo. Box 576, Dover 03821-0576. Secondary address: 292 Middle Rd., Dover 03820-4901. Phone: (603) 749-9750. Fax: (603) 749-1459. E-mail: shark.mail@citcomm.com. Web Site: www.shark1053.com. Licensee: Citadel Broadcasting Co. Group owner: Citadel Broadcasting Corp. (acq 7-7-99; grpsl). Network: CNN Radio, AP Radio. Rep: McGavren Guild. Wiley, Rein & Fielding. Format: Classic rock. News staff: 2. Target aud: 25-49. ♦ Farid Suleman, CEO; Judy Ellis, pres; Marty Lessard, gen mgr; Mark Ericson, opns mgr; Ken Hoffman, gen sls mgr; Bill Elliott, progmg dir.

Hanover

WDCR(AM)— Mar 4, 1958: 1340 khz; 1 kw-U. TL: N43 41 59 W72 16 47. Box 957 03755. Phone: (603) 646-3313. Phone: (603) 643-7625. Fax: (603) 643-7655. Licensee: Trustees of Dartmouth College. Rep: New England. Format: Div, Black, progsv. News: 4 hrs wkly. Target aud: General. Spec prog: Class 8 hrs, jazz 6 hrs, reggae 9 hrs, metal 3 hrs wkly. ♦ Kekane Yuen, gen mgr & gen sls mgr; Pam Cortland, progmg dir; Nikhil Gore, news dir; Lynn Lee, chief of engrg.

WFRD(FM)—Co-owned with WDCR(AM). Feb 19, 1976: 99.3 mhz; 3.4 kw. 285 ft. TL: N43 39 14 W72 17 43. Stereo. Format: AOR. Target aud: 18-45. ♦ Evelyn Flint, progmg dir.

***WEVH(FM)**— October 1993: 91.3 mhz; 150 w. 1,240 ft. TL: N43 42 30 W72 09 16. 207 N. Main St., Concord 03301. Phone: (603) 228-8910. Fax: (603) 224-6052. Web Site: www.nhpr.org. Licensee: New Hampshire Public Radio Inc. Network: Network: NPR, PRI. Garvey, Schubert & Barer. Format: News/talk. News staff: 9; News: 42 hrs wkly. Target aud: 25-54. Spec prog: Folk 3 hrs wkly. ♦ Elizabeth Gardella, pres & gen mgr; Sean Gillery, dev dir.

WGXL(FM)—Listing follows WTSL(AM).

WQTH(AM)—Not on air, target date: unknown:. Stn currently dark 720 khz; 50 kw-D, 500 w-N, DA-2. TL: N43 39 26 W72 14 36. Box 2295, New London 03257. Phone: (603) 448-0500. Fax: (603) 448-6601. Licensee: KOOR Communications Inc. (group owner) Format: Talk, news/talk. ♦ Robert L. Vinikoor, gen mgr.

WTSL(AM)— October 1950: 1400 khz; 1 kw-U. TL: N43 41 03 W72 17 46. 31 Hanover, Suite 4, Lebanon 03766. Phone: (603) 448-1400. Fax: (603) 448-1755. Licensee: Capstar TX L.P. Group owner: Clear Channel Communications Inc. (acq 1-1-01; with co-located FM). Network: Network: CBS, ABC Information & Entertainment. David Tillotson. Format: News/talk, sports. News staff: 2; News: 25 hrs wkly. Target aud: 35 plus. ♦ Christopher Olsen, gen mgr; Tim Plant, gen mgr; Michael Barrett, opns mgr, progmg dir & news dir; Gary Laperle, chief of engrg.

WGXL(FM)—Co-owned with WTSL(AM). Jan 12, 1987: 92.3 mhz; 6 kw. 326 ft. TL: N43 39 17 W72 17 41. Stereo. Format: Hot adult contemp. Target aud: 25-49.

WXXK(FM)—See Lebanon

Haverhill

WYKR-FM— Feb 19, 1990: 101.3 mhz; 3 kw. 39 ft. TL: N44 06 49 W71 58 54. Stereo. Box 675, Rt. 302, Wells River, VT 05081. Secondary address: Box 1013, Woodsville 03785. Phone: (802) 757-2773. Fax: (802) 757-2774. E-mail: wykr@kingcon.com. Web Site: www.wykr.com. Licensee: Puffer Broadcasting Inc. Network: Network: Network: Westwood One, NBC, Jones Radio Networks. Rep: Roslin. Fisher, Wayland, Cooper, Leader & Zaragoza. Format: Country. Target aud: 25 plus. ♦ Stephen J. Puffer, pres, gen mgr, gen sls mgr, adv mgr & progmg dir; Teresa Puffer, opns mgr; Don Smith, chief of engrg.

Henniker

***WNEC-FM**— Feb 9, 1971: 91.7 mhz; 120 w. -210 ft. TL: N43 10 34 W71 49 22. New England College, 28 Bridge St. 03242. Phone: (603) 428-2278. Phone: (603) 428-6393. Fax: (603) 428-7230. E-mail: A.Metzegen@nec.edu. Licensee: New England College. Network: Network: ABC FM Connection, ABC Information & Entertainment. Format: Progsv, adult contemp, Black, jazz, new age, urban contemp. News: one hr wkly. Target aud: 18-25; college students. Spec prog: Blues 4 hrs, country 3 hrs, American Indian 18 hrs, folk 18 hrs, farm 4 hrs wkly. ♦ Ambrose Metzegen, CEO; Chris Collord, progmg VP; Kristen Westhoven, mus dir; Dale Carlow, engrg VP.

WNNH(FM)— Nov 17, 1989: 99.1 mhz; 6 kw. 712 ft. TL: N43 09 17 W71 47 44. Stereo. 11 Kimball Dr., Unit 114, Hooksett 03106. Phone:

Stations in the U.S. — New Hampshire

Developers & Brokers of Radio Properties

contact American Media Services at our suite: Philadelphia Marriott Downtown 215-625-2900
843-972-2200
americanmediaservices.com
Charleston, SC
Dallas, TX · Chicago, Il · Austin, TX
American Media Services, LLC

(603) 225-1160. Fax: (603) 225-5938. E-mail: oldies99@wnnh.com. Web Site: www.wnnh.com. Licensee: Nassau Broadcasting III L.L.C. Group owner: Nassau Broadcasting Partners L.P. (acq 3-16-2004; grpsl). Rep: McGavren Guild. Verner, Liipfert, Bernhard, McPherson & Hand. Format: Oldies. News staff: 2; News: 20 hrs wkly. Target aud: 25-54; mass appeal. ♦ Scott Brady, gen mgr; Andy Mack, opns mgr, progmg dir & progmg mgr; Ken Cail, news dir.

Hillsboro

WTPL(FM)—Licensed to Hillsboro. See Concord

Hinsdale

WYRY(FM)—Licensed to Hinsdale. See Keene

Jackson

WEVJ(FM)— 8/02: 99.5 mhz; 4.7 kw. Ant 171 ft. TL: N44 10 30 W71 10 07. New Hampshire Public Radio, 207 N. Main St., Concord 03301-5003. Phone: (603) 228-8910. Fax: (603) 224-6052. E-mail: admin@nhpr.org. Web Site: www.nhpr.org. Licensee: New Hampshire Public Radio. Garvey,Schubert & Barer. Format: News/talk. News staff: 9. ♦ Mark Handley, pres & gen mgr; Scott McPherson, opns dir; Sean Gillery, dev dir; Mike Arnold, progmg dir; Mark Bevis, news dir; John Huntley, engrg dir.

Jaffrey

WXNH(AM)—Not on air, target date: unknown: 540 khz; 250 w-D, 330 w-N, DA-2. TL: N42 50 55 W71 57 53. 17 Knightsbridge Ct., Nanuet, NY 10954. Phone: (845) 356-9613. Licensee: Steven Wendell. ♦ Steven Wendell, gen mgr.

Keene

***WEVN(FM)**— April 1994: 90.7 mhz; 1.5 kw. 938 ft. c/o Radio Stn WEVO(FM), 207 N. Main St., Concord 03301. Phone: (603) 228-8910. Fax: (603) 224-6052. E-mail: admin@nhpr.org. Web Site: www.nhpr.org. Licensee: New Hampshire Public Radio Inc. Network: Network: NPR, PRI. Garvey, Schubert & Barer. Format: News/talk. News staff: 9; News: 42 hrs wkly. Target aud: 25-54. Spec prog: Folk 3 hrs wkly. ♦ Elizabeth Gardella, pres & gen mgr; Scott McPherson, opns dir; Sean Gillery, dev dir; Michael Arnold, progmg dir; Mark Bevis, news dir; John Huntley, engrg dir.

WINQ(FM)—Winchester

WKBK(AM)— June 2, 1927: 1290 khz; 5 kw-U, DA-1. TL: N42 56 56 W72 18 22. Box 466 03431. Secondary address: 69 Stanhope Ave. 03431. Phone: (603) 352-9230. Fax: (603) 357-3926. Licensee: Saga Communications of New England LLC. Group owner: Saga Communications Inc. (acq 5-1-02; grpsl). Network: CBS. Rep: McGavren Guild. Format: News, talk. Target aud: 25 plus. ♦ Bruce Lyons, gen mgr; Stephen Hamel, opns dir; Vicky Lenahan, prom dir; Dan Mitchell, progmg dir; Paul Scheuring, news dir; Ira Wilner, chief of engrg.

WKNE(FM)—Co-owned with WKBK(AM). May 1964: 103.7 mhz; 12.2 kw. 991 ft. TL: N43 02 00 W72 22 04. Stereo. Format: Adultcontemp, top-40. Target aud: 18-49.

***WKNH(FM)**— November 1975: 91.3 mhz; 274 w. 79 ft. TL: N42 55 29 W72 16 42. (CP: 91.7 mhz, 192 w, ant 363 ft.). Stereo. Keene State College, 229 Main St. 03435-2704. Phone: (603) 358-2420. Phone: (603) 358-2421. Fax: (603) 358-2417. E-mail: wknhinfo@aol.com. Web Site: www.jumblue.com/wknh/. Licensee: Board of Trustees University System of New Hampshire. Format: Progsv. News staff: 2; News: 3 hrs wkly. Target aud: General. Spec prog: Class 4 hrs, folk 6 hrs, jazz 3 hrs, blues 3 hrs, rap 4 hrs, new age 4 hrs, reggae 3 hrs, Christian 3 hrs, metal 4 hrs, experimental 3 hrs wkly. ♦ James McCluskey, gen mgr.

WYRY(FM)—(Hinsdale). June 30, 1987: 104.9 mhz; 1.55 kw. 456 ft. TL: N42 46 33 W72 27 19. (CP: 725 w, ant 669 ft.). Stereo. 30 Warwick Rd., Suite 10, Winchester 03470. Phone: (603) 239-8200. Fax: (603) 239-6203. Web Site: www.wyry.com. Licensee: Tri-Valley Broadcasting Corp. (acq 8-86). Network: Jones Radio Networks. Reddy, Begley & McCormick. Format: Country. News staff: 3; News: 10 hrs wkly. Target aud: 25-49; upscale adults & business decision makers. ♦ Brian McCormick, VP & gen mgr; Sean Patrick, sls VP & progmg dir; Dan Guy, chief of engrg.

WZBK(AM)— May 1959: 1220 khz; 1 kw-U. TL: N42 55 50 W72 17 56. 69 Stanhope Ave. 03431. Phone: (603) 352-9230. Fax: (603) 357-3926. Licensee: Saga Communications of New Hampshire LLC. Group owner: Saga Communications Inc. (acq 7-1-02; $2.63 million. with WOQL(FM) Winchester). Booth, Freret, Imlay & Tepper P. Format: Standards. Target aud: 25-54; general. ♦ Bruce Lyons, stn mgr & prom VP; Susan Wells, gen sls mgr; Steve Hamill, progmg dir & chief of engrg; Paul Schering, news dir; Ira Wilner, chief of engrg.

Laconia

WEMJ(AM)—Listing follows WLNH-FM.

WEZS(AM)— Aug 22, 1922: 1350 khz; 5 kw-D, 112 w-N. TL: N43 30 27 W71 31 00. 277 Union Ave. 03246. Phone: (603) 524-6288. Fax: (603) 528-1638. E-mail: info@wezs.com. Web Site: www.wezs.com. Licensee: Gary W. Hammond. (acq 3-17-94; 6-6-94). Network: USA. Format: Easy lstng, smooth jazz. Target aud: 45 plus. ♦ Gary W. Hammond, gen mgr.

WLNH-FM— Nov 22, 1965: 98.3 mhz; 3.8 kw. 413 ft. TL: N43 35 46 W71 29 55. Box 7326, Village West Bldg. 1, Gilford 03247. Phone: (603) 524-1323. Fax: (603) 528-5185. E-mail: info@wlnh.com. Web Site: www.wlnh.com. Licensee: Nassau Broadcasting III L.L.C. Group owner: Nassau Broadcasting Partners L.P. (acq 4-7-2004; grpsl). Rosenman & Colin L.L.P. Format: Hot adult contemp. Target aud: 25-54. ♦ Molly King, prom dir; Chris Ialuna, progmg dir.

WEMJ(AM)—Co-owned with WLNH-FM. Apr 9, 1961: 1490 khz; 1 kw-U. TL: N43 32 29 W71 27 45. Network: CBS. Rep: D & R Radio. Format: Talk.

Lancaster

WXXS(FM)— 1998: 102.3 mhz; 1.5 kw. 964 ft. TL: N44 23 39 W71 39 20. Stereo. Box 896, Littleton 03561. Secondary address: 195 Main St. 03584. Phone: (603) 444-4102. Fax: (603) 788-3536. E-mail: kiss102@together.net. Licensee: Barry P. Lunderville. Network: CBS. Format: Contemp hit/top-40. ♦ Barry P. Lunderville, gen mgr; Brian Lunderville, opns mgr; Barry Lunderville, progmg dir.

Lebanon

WGXL(FM)—See Hanover

WHDQ(FM)—See Claremont

WUVR(AM)— 2004: 1490 khz; 640 w-U. TL: N43 39 12 W72 14 16. Box 2295, New London 03257. Phone: (603) 448-0500. Fax: (603) 448-6601. E-mail: bob@wntk.com. Web Site: www.wntk.com. Licensee: KOOR Communications Inc. Format: News/talk. ♦ Robert Vinikoor, gen mgr, gen sls mgr & progmg dir; Dave Shurtleff, news dir; Russ McCallister, chief of engrg.

***WVFA(FM)**— Feb 6, 2004: 90.5 mhz; 7 w. Ant 695 ft. TL: N43 37 17 W72 10 30. Box 126, Hartford, VT 05047-0126. Secondary address: 48 Wescott Rd., Enfield 03748. Phone: (802) 295-9683. Fax: (802) 295-9683. E-mail: vtpreacher@aol.com. Licensee: Green Mountain Educational Fellowship Inc. Format: Inspirational, educ, relg. News: 11 hrs wkly. Target aud: 25-49; primary. ♦ William A. Wittik, pres, CFO & gen mgr; Betsy Murray, opns mgr; Elmer Murray, opns mgr.

WXXK(FM)— Dec 18, 1990: 100.5 mhz; 22 kw. 325 ft. TL: N43 37 17 W72 10 30. 31 Hanover St., Suite 4 03766. Phone: (603) 448-1400. Fax: (603) 448-1755. Web Site: www.kixx.com. Licensee: Clear Channel Radio Licenses, Inc. Group owner: Clear Channel Communications Inc. (acq 11-27-00; grpsl). Network: Network: Westwood One, CNN Radio. Format: Country. News staff: 3; News: 20 hrs wkly. Target aud: 25-54. ♦ Cheryl Frisch, CFO & dev VP; Robert Frisch, gen mgr; Kenny Michaels, opns mgr & prom dir; Matt Cross, sls dir; Michael Barrett, progmg dir & news dir.

Lisbon

WLTN-FM—Licensed to Lisbon. See Littleton

Littleton

WLTN(AM)— Oct 10, 1963: 1400 khz; 1 kw-U. TL: N44 18 47 W71 46 08. 15 Main St. 03561. Phone: (603) 444-3911. Fax: (603) 444-7186. E-mail: oldies1400@adelphia.net. Licensee: Barry P. Lunderville L.L.C. (acq 2-18-2005; with WLTN-FM Lisbon). Network: ABC Information & Entertainment. Rep: New England. Format: Oldies, Red Sox. News staff: one; News: 40 hrs wkly. Target aud: 21-65. ♦ Barry Lunderville, gen mgr; Christina Brooks, gen sls mgr; Phil Rivera, progmg dir; Jim Clothey, news dir; Brian Lunderville, chief of engrg.

WLTN-FM— Sept 1, 1991: 96.7 mhz; 6 kw. 295 ft. TL: N44 13 11 W71 52 07. Stereo. E-mail: mix967@adelphia.net. Network: Westwood One. Format: Bright adult contemp. News staff: one; News: 7 hrs wkly. Target aud: 25-54.

WMTK(FM)— Feb 23, 1985: 106.3 mhz; 390 w. 1,256 ft. TL: N44 21 14 W71 44 23. Stereo. Box 106 03561-0106. Phone: (603) 444-5106. Fax: (603) 444-1205. E-mail: thenotch@kington.net. Licensee: Vermont Broadcast Associates Inc. (acq 8-00; $250,000). Bryan Cave. Format: Classic hits. News staff: one. Target aud: 30-50; slightly more males, active lifestyles. ♦ Bruce James, gen mgr & progmg dir; Steve Nichols, gen sls mgr; Todd Wellington, news dir; Don Smith, chief of engrg.

Madbury

WWNH(AM)— May 20, 1989: 1340 khz; 1 kw-U. TL: N43 10 22 W70 55 00. Box 69, Dover 03821. Secondary address: 284 Rt. 155, Dover 03821. Phone: (603) 742-8575. Fax: (603) 743-6444. E-mail: info@loveradio.net. Web Site: www.loveradio.net. Licensee: Harvest Broadcasting. Network: USA. Format: MOR. News: 3 hrs wkly. Target aud: General; 29 plus. Spec prog: Family 24 hrs wkly. ♦ Patti Smith, CEO, gen mgr, stn mgr & gen sls mgr; Ernie Jenkins, chief of opns, progmg dir & news dir; Steve Donnell, engrg dir & chief of engrg.

Manchester

WFEA(AM)— Mar 8, 1932: 1370 khz; 5 kw-U, DA-2. TL: N42 54 26 W71 27 45. 500 Commercial St. 03101. Phone: (603) 669-5777. Fax: (603) 669-4641. Licensee: Saga Communications of New England LLC. Group owner: Saga Communications Inc. (acq 6-2-92; grpsl, including co-located FM). Katz. Smithwick & Belendiuk. Format: Adult standards. Target aud: 50 plus; "Modern Maturity" market. Spec prog: Fr 3 hrs, Sp 2 hrs wkly. ♦ Raymond R. Garron, gen mgr.

WZID(FM)—Co-owned with WFEA(AM). 1948: 95.7 mhz; 14.5 kw. 930 ft. TL: N42 59 02 W71 35 22. E-mail: radionh@com. Web Site: www.wzid.com. Format: Adult contemp. Target aud: 25-54.

WGIR(AM)— October 1941: 610 khz; 5 kw-D, 1 kw-N, DA-2. TL: N43 00 57 W71 28 48. Box 610 03105. Phone: (603) 625-6915. Fax: (603) 625-9255. Web Site: www.wgiram.com. Licensee: Capstar TX L.P. Group owner: Clear Channel Communications Inc. (acq 8-30-00; grpsl). Format: News/talk, sports. News staff: 2; News: 38 hrs wkly. Target aud: 35-54. ♦ Joseph Graham, gen mgr; Jon Erdhal, opns mgr; Dorie Dawkins, gen sls mgr & natl sls mgr; Paul Hanson, rgnl sls mgr; Sara Anderson, prom dir; Dan Pierce, progmg dir; Angela Anderson, news dir; Ken Neenam, chief of engrg.

WGIR-FM— June 5, 1963: 101.1 mhz; 11.5 kw. Ant 1,027 ft. TL: N42 58 54 W71 35 21. Stereo. 195 McGregor St., Suite 810 03105. Web Site: www.rock101fm.com. Format: AOR. ♦ Jason Russell, progmg dir.

Broadcasting & Cable Yearbook 2006

New Hampshire

WKBR(AM)— Oct 1, 1946: 1250 khz; 5 kw-U, DA-2. TL: N43 00 40 W71 30 19. 922 Elm St., Suite 301 03101. Phone: (603) 669-1250. Fax: (603) 647-1260. E-mail: newstalk1250@aol.com. Web Site: www.wkbram.com. Licensee: Devon Broadcasting Co. Inc. Group owner: Northeast Broadcasting Company Inc. (acq 7-22-97; $145,000). Format: Newtalk, Sports. Target aud: 25 plus. Spec prog: Greek 8 hrs wkly. ♦ Steve Young, gen mgr; Jerri Stanford, stn mgr; Charles Dent, gen sls mgr; Dana Marshall, progmg dir; Ron Travers, news dir; Lou Muse, chief of engrg.

*****WLMW(FM)**— September 1997: 90.7 mhz; 15 w. 869 ft. TL: N42 58 59 W71 35 25. Box 366, Auburn 03032. Secondary address: 134 Hollis Rd., Amherst 03031. Phone: (603) 483-8950. Fax: (603) 483-8908. Licensee: Knowledge For Life. Format: Christian family radio. ♦ Jim Phelan, gen mgr.

WOKQ(FM)—See Dover

Meredith

WWHQ(FM)— Nov 16, 1988: 101.5 mhz; 6 kw. Ant 328 ft. TL: N43 35 46 W71 29 55. Stereo. Box 7326, Gilford 03247. Phone: (603) 524-1323. Fax: (603) 528-5185. Web Site: www.big1015.com. Licensee: Nassau Broadcasting III L.L.C. Group owner: Nassau Broadcasting Partners L.P. (acq 4-7-2004; grpsl). Format: Classic rock. ♦ Louis Mercatanti, pres; Dominic Biello, opns dir; Rob Fulmer, gen mgr & gen sls mgr.

Moultonborough

WSCY(FM)— May 31, 1993: 106.9 mhz; 130 w. 2,096 ft. TL: N43 46 09 W71 18 52. Stereo. Box 99, Franklin 03235. Phone: (603) 253-8080. Fax: (603) 934-2933. Web Site: www.mix941fm.com. Licensee: Northeast Communications Corp. (group owner; acq 5-4-93; $399,072; 5-24-93). Format: Hot country. ♦ Jeff Fisher, pres & stn mgr; Amy Bates, sls VP & news dir; Jeff Levitan, opns mgr & gen sls mgr; Gene Terwilliger, chief of engrg.

Mt. Washington

WHOM(FM)— July 9, 1958: 94.9 mhz; 48 kw. 3,760 ft. TL: N44 16 13 W71 18 13. (CP: Ant 46 ft.). Stereo. 1 City Center, Portland, ME 04101. Phone: (207) 773-0200. Fax: (207) 774-8707. E-mail: whom@whom949.com. Web Site: www.whom949.com. Licensee: Citadel Broadcasting Co. Group owner: Citadel Broadcasting Corp. (acq 7-7-99; grpsl). Rep: Christal. Format: Light rock, adult contemp. Target aud: 35-64; professionals with active lifestyles. ♦ Mike Sambrook, gen mgr; Barbara Cole, gen sls mgr; Tim Moore, progmg dir.

Nashua

*****WEVS(FM)**— 2005: 88.3 mhz; 3.5 kw horiz, 5 kw vert. Ant 69 ft. TL: N42 45 00 W71 28 47. 207 N. Main St., Concord 03301-5003. Phone: (603) 228-8910. Fax: (603) 224-6052. Web Site: www.nhpr.org. Licensee: New Hampshire Public Radio Inc. Network: NPR. Format: News/talk. ♦ Elizabeth Gardella, gen mgr; Sean Gillery, dev dir; Michael Arnold, progmg dir; Mark Bevis, news dir; John Huntley, chief of engrg.

WFNQ(FM)— Oct 19, 1987: 106.3 mhz; 3 kw. 100 ft. TL: N42 44 07 W71 23 37. (CP: 950 w, ant 541 ft.). Stereo. 11 Kimball Dr., Suite 114, Hooksett 03106. Phone: (603) 889-1063. Fax: (603) 882-0688. Web Site: www.wjyy.com. Licensee: Nassau Broadcasting III L.L.C. Group owner: Nassau Broadcasting Partners L.P. (acq 3-16-2004; grpsl). Rep: Allied Radio Partners. Cole, Raywid & Braverman. Format: Hot adult contemp. News staff: one; News: 5 hrs wkly. Target aud: 18-49. ♦ Louis F. Mercatanti, pres; Steve Garsh, gen mgr; Andy Mack, opns dir; Phyllis Knight, gen sls mgr; Sarah Sullivan, progmg dir; Dirk Nadon, chief of engrg.

WSMN(AM)— Mar 9, 1958: 1590 khz; 5 kw-U, DA-1. TL: N42 44 40 W71 29 52. 502 W. Hollis St. 03062. Phone: (603) 882-1590. Fax: (603) 889-6736. E-mail: wsmn1590@aol.com. Licensee: Absolute Broadcasting LLC (acq 8-19-2005; $250,000). Rep: New England. Format: Sports, news/talk. News staff: 2; News: 21 hrs wkly. Target aud: General. Spec prog: Fr 3 hrs, Pol one hr wkly. ♦ Tom O'Brien, exec VP & gen mgr.

WSNH(AM)— 1991: 900 khz; 920 w-D. TL: N42 45 34 W71 28 37. One Indian Head Plaza, Box 900, 5th Fl 03061-0900. Phone: (603) 880-9001. Phone: (603) 883-9900. Fax: (603) 577-8682. E-mail: info@wsnh900am.com. Web Site: www.espn900.com. Licensee: Absolute Broadcasting LLC (acq 8-19-2005; $925,000). Network: ESPN Radio.

Format: Sports. Target aud: 35 plus. ♦ Jerry DiGrezio, gen mgr; Marty Terrell, gen sls mgr; John Kosian, progmg dir & chief of engrg.

New London

WNTK-FM— Nov 30, 1992: 99.7 mhz; 620 w. 712 ft. TL: N43 26 52 W72 02 04. Box 2295, 25 Newport Rd. 03257. Secondary address: 103 Hanover St., Lebanon 03766. Phone: (603) 448-0500. Fax: (603) 448-6601. Web Site: www.wntk.com. Licensee: Koor Communications Inc. (group owner) Network: ABC News/Talk. Shaw Pittman. Format: Talk/news. News staff: 2. Target aud: 24-54. ♦ Robert L. Vinikoor, CEO, gen mgr & progmg dir; Sheila E. Vinikoor, pres; Dave Shurtleff, news dir; Russ McCallister, chief of engrg.

*****WSCS(FM)**— February 1996: 90.9 mhz; 63 w horiz, 250 w vert. 297 ft. TL: N43 24 41 W71 58 33. Colby-Sawyer College, 100 Main St. 03257. Phone: (603) 526-3493. Fax: (603) 526-3452. E-mail: wscs@colby-sawyer.edu. Web Site: www.colby-sawyer.edu/wscs. Licensee: Colby-Sawyer College. Format: Educ. ♦ Sean Joncas, stn mgr.

Newport

WNTK(AM)— Aug 11, 1960: 1010 khz; 10 kw-D, 37 w-N. TL: N43 21 52 W72 10 47. Box 2295, New London 03257. Phone: (603) 448-0500. Fax: (603) 448-6601. E-mail: bob@wntk.com. Web Site: www.wntk.com. Licensee: KOOR Communications. (group owner; acq 8-88; $250,000; 8-29-88). Network: ABC News/Talk. Shaw Pittman. Format: Classic country/Americanna. Target aud: 25-54; informed adults. ♦ Robert L. Vinikoor, pres & gen mgr; Robert Vinikoor, progmg dir & chief of engrg.

WVRR(FM)— 1971: 101.7 mhz; 260 w. Ant 1,115 ft. TL: N43 23 45 W72 17 40. Stereo. 31 Hanover St., Suite 4, Lebanon 03766-1312. Phone: (603) 448-1400. Fax: (603) 448-5231. Web Site: www.wvrrfm.com. Licensee: Capstar TX L.P. Group owner: Clear Channel Communications Inc. (acq 11-28-00). Network: Westwood One. Format: Rock. News staff: one. Target aud: 25-54. ♦ Tim Plante, gen mgr.

North Conway

WPKQ(FM)— October 1952: 103.7 mhz; 21.5 kw horiz, 16.5 kw vert. 3,874 ft. TL: N44 16 14 W71 18 15. Stereo. P.O. Box 576, Dover 03821-0576. Phone: (603) 749-9750. Fax: (603) 749-6589. E-mail: mail@wokq.com. Web Site: www.wokq.com. Licensee: Citadel Broadcasting Co. Group owner: Citadel Broadcasting Corp. (acq 7-7-99; grpsl). Network: Network: CNN Radio, AP Radio. Rep: Christal. Wiley, Rein & Fielding. Format: Country. News staff: 2. Target aud: 25-54; New England residents. ♦ Farid Suleman, CEO; Judy Ellis, pres; Mark Ericson, gen mgr & opns mgr; Martin Lessard, gen mgr; Ken Hoffman, gen sls mgr; Mark Jennings, progmg dir.

Peterborough

WFEX(FM)— June 1971: 92.1 mhz; 180 w. Ant 1,332 ft. TL: N42 51 42 W71 52 46. Stereo. 25 Exchange St., Lynn, MA 01901. Secondary address: 307 Elm St., Milford 03055. Phone: (781) 595-6200. Phone: (603) 672-4105. Fax: (781) 595-3810. Fax: (603) 672-4114. E-mail: fnxradio@fnxradio.com. Web Site: www.fnxradio.com. Licensee: FNX Broadcasting of New Hampshire LLC. Group owner: Phoenix Media Communications Group (acq 11-29-99). Rubin, Winston, Dierks, Harris, & Cooke. Format: Alternative rock. News staff: 2; News: 11 hrs wkly. Target aud: Adults 18-33; young, educated white collar professionals with extremely active lifestyles. Spec prog: Gay talk 2 hrs, jazz 6 hrs wkly. ♦ Stephen Mindich, CEO; H. Barry Morris, pres; Brad Mindich, exec VP; Andy Kingston, gen mgr; Joe Charves, gen sls mgr; Max Polkoff, progmg dir; Chris Hall, chief of engrg.

Plymouth

*****WPCR-FM**— Sept 29, 1974: 91.7 mhz; 215 w. 95 ft. TL: N43 45 25 W71 38 59. WPCR HUB, Plymouth State College, 17 High St. 03264-1594. Phone: (603) 535-2242 (office). Phone: (603) 536-5000 (univ. switchboard). Fax: (603) 535-2783. E-mail: genmgr@wpcr.plymouth.edu. Web Site: wpcr.plymouth.edu. Licensee: Plymouth State College. Network: AP Radio. Format: AOR, progsv. Target aud: 15-35; college students & those interested in progressive alternative music. Spec prog: Class 3 hrs, jazz 3 hrs, reggae 3 hrs, blues 3 hrs, comedy 3 hrs wkly.

WPNH(AM)— Nov 10, 1965: 1300 khz; 5 kw-D, DA-D. TL: N43 46 32 W71 42 20. Box 99, Franklin 03235. Secondary address: 110 Babbitt Rd., Franklin 03235. Phone: (603) 536-2500. Phone: (603) 536-2501. Fax: (603) 934-2933. Licensee: Northeast Communications Corp.

(group owner; acq 2-9-99; with co-located FM). Reddy, Begley & McCormick. Format: Big band. Target aud: 35 plus. Spec prog: Breakfast with the bands 6 hrs wkly. ♦ Jeff Fisher, gen mgr; Fred Caruso, opns mgr & progmg dir; Jess Levitan, gen sls mgr; Amy Bates, news dir.

WPNH-FM— Oct 1, 1975: 100.1 mhz; 2.35 kw. 364 ft. TL: N43 45 47 W71 38 59. (CP: 4.9 kw, ant 358 ft.). Stereo. Web Site: www.wpnhfm.com. Format: Alternative. ♦ Rick Ganley, progmg dir.

Portsmouth

WERZ(FM)—See Exeter

WGIP(AM)—See Exeter

WHEB(FM)— Jan 14, 1964: 100.3 mhz; 50 kw. 459 ft. TL: N43 03 11 W70 46 04. (CP: Ant 446 ft. TL: N43 03 05 W70 46 09). Stereo. 815 Lafayette Rd. 03801. Phone: (603) 436-7300. Fax: (603) 430-9415. Web Site: www.wheb.com. Licensee: Capstar TX L.P. Group owner: Clear Channel Communications Inc. (acq 8-30-00; grpsl). Network: UPI. Format: Rock and roll. Target aud: 18-49. ♦ Robert Greer, gen mgr; Christopher Garrett, opns mgr, progmg dir & mus dir; Christine Sieks, gen sls mgr; Kelly Brown, news dir; Kenneth Neelan, chief of engrg.

WMYF(AM)—Co-owned with WHEB(FM). Dec 5, 1960: 1380 khz; 1 kw-U, DA-N. TL: N43 03 48 W70 47 09. Format: Music of your life. Target aud: 25-54. ♦ Judy Figliulo, gen sls mgr; Michael O'Donnell, progmg dir.

Rochester

WGIN(AM)—Listing follows WQSO(FM).

WQSO(FM)— Oct 21, 1979: 96.7 mhz; 3 kw. 328 ft. TL: N43 17 14 W70 56 49. (CP: 5.8 kw, ant 98 ft. TL: N43 23 40 W71 02 22). Stereo. 815 Lafayette Rd., Portsmouth 03801. Phone: (603) 436-7300. Fax: (603) 430-9415. Licensee: Capstar TX L.P. Group owner: Clear Channel Communications Inc. (acq 8-30-00; grpsl). Wiley, Rein & Fielding. Format: Oldies. News staff: 3; News: 12 hrs wkly. Target aud: 25-54. ♦ Robert Greer, gen mgr.

WGIN(AM)—Co-owned with WQSO(FM). 1947: 930 khz; 5 kw-U, DA-N. TL: N43 17 13 W70 56 55. Format: News/talk, sports. Target aud: 25-64; decision-makers, heads of businesses, households. ♦ Dan Pierce, progmg dir; Kelly Brown, news dir; Roger Wood, news dir.

Salem

WCEC(AM)— Jan 10, 1977: 1110 khz; 5 kw-D, DA-D. TL: N42 45 42 W71 16 13. 462 Merrimack St., Methuen, MA 01844. Phone: (978) 686-9966. Phone: (978) 975-1110. Fax: (978) 687-1180. Web Site: www.wnnw.com. Licensee: Costa-Eagle Radio Ventures L.P. (group owner; acq 1996). Rep: Roslin. Bryan Cave. Format: Sp, talk and info. Target aud: Sp speaking. ♦ Pat Costa, CEO & gen mgr; Louis Reyes, opns mgr.

Somersworth

WBYY(FM)— Jan 25, 1995: 98.7 mhz; 6 kw. 315 ft. TL: N43 14 12 W70 53 47. Box 400, 101 Back Rd., Dover 03820-0400. Phone: (603) 742-0987. Fax: (603) 742-0448. Licensee: Garrison City Broadcasting Inc. Format: Adult contemp. News staff: 2. Target aud: 25-54. ♦ Bob Demers, CEO; Rick Bean, gen mgr; Mike Pomp, news dir; Mark Ward, chief of engrg.

Walpole

WCFR-FM— November 2000: 96.3 mhz; 320 w. Ant 407 ft. TL: N43 08 14 W72 25 59. 106 N. Main St., West Lebanon 03784. Phone: (603) 298-0332. Fax: (603) 298-7554. E-mail: info@bestoldies104.com. Web Site: www.bestoldies104.com. Licensee: Nassau Broadcasting III L.L.C. Group owner: Nassau Broadcasting Partners L.P. (acq 8-13-2004; grpsl). Format: Oldies. ♦ Camille Losapio, gen mgr.

Winchester

WINQ(FM)— Oct 15, 1991: 98.7 mhz; 6 kw. Ant 328 ft. TL: N42 49 56 W72 23 34. Stereo. 69 Stanhope Ave., Keene 03431. Phone: (603)

Stations in the U.S.   New Jersey

Developers & Brokers of Radio Properties

contact American Media Services at our suite:
Philadelphia Marriott Downtown
215-625-2900
843-972-2200
americanmediaservices.com
Charleston, SC
Dallas, TX • Chicago, Il • Austin, TX

American Media Services, LLC

352-9230. Fax: (603) 357-3926. Web Site: www.cool987.com. Licensee: Saga Communications of New Hampshire LLC. Group owner: Saga Communications Inc. (acq 7-1-2002; $2.63 million. with WZBK(AM) Keene). Network: Network: ABC, Jones Radio Networks. Booth, Freret, Imlay & Tepper. Format: Country. News staff: 4; News: 8 hrs wkly. Target aud: 25-54. ♦Bruce Lyons, gen mgr.

WZBK(AM)—See Keene

Wolfeboro

WASR(AM)— April 1970: 1420 khz; 5 kw-D, 137 w-N. TL: N43 35 31 W71 13 12. Box 900 03894-0900. Secondary address: 73 Varney Rd. 03894-0900. Phone: (603) 569-1420. Fax: (603) 569-1900. E-mail: wkrp@metrocast.net. Web Site: www.wasr.net. Licensee: Winnipesaukee Network Inc. (acq 3-31-2004; $350,000). Network: ABC Information & Entertainment. Format: Adult contemp, news. News staff: 4; News: 35 hrs wkly. Target aud: 25-54. ♦Grant P. Hatch, pres; Gary Hammond, engrg dir.

WLKZ(FM)— Feb 1, 1985: 104.9 mhz; 570 w, 1,053 ft. TL: N43 32 44 W71 22 45. Stereo. 21 Meadowbrook Ln., Suite 15, Gilford 03249. Phone: (603) 524-0105. Fax: (603) 293-0699. E-mail: wlkz@metroczst.net. Web Site: www.wlkz.com. Licensee: Nassau Broadcasting III L.L.C. Group owner: Nassau Broadcasting Partners L.P. (acq 3-16-2004; grpsl). Rep: McGavren Guild. Haley, Bader & Potts. Format: Oldies. News staff: 0; News: 5 hrs wkly. Target aud: 25-54; baby boomers. Spec prog: Dick Clark/The Beatle Years/Lil Walters Time Machine. ♦Louis F. Mercatanti, pres; Jim Cande, sr VP; Rob Fulmer, gen mgr; Pat Kelly, opns dir & progmg dir; Ron Piro, gen mgr & gen sls mgr; Dirk Nadon, chief of engrg.

New Jersey

Andover

WOF(AM)— Oct 8, 1946: 1000 khz; 1 kw-D, 250 w-N, DA-D (L-KQSL). TL: N35 48 31 W121 43 28. (CP: 5 kw-U). Stereo. 12 Coulter Pl. 07821. Fax: (908) 219-0182. Licensee: General Broadcasting Corp. (group owner; (acq 7-20-69; $255,000. with co-located FM; FTR: 2-12-83). Network: ABC Information & Entertainment. Format: MOR, C&W. Spec prog: Sp 3 hrs wkly. ♦Edgar Adcock, gen mgr.

Asbury Park

WADB(AM)— 1926: 1310 khz; 2.5 kw-D, 1 kw-N, DA-2. TL: N40 13 47 W74 05 27. 2401 Rt. 66, Ocean 07712. Phone: (732) 897-8282. Fax: (732) 897-8283. Licensee: Millennium Shore License Holdco LLC. Group owner: Millennium Radio Group LLC (acq 6-11-02; grpsl). Format: Adult standards. ♦Bill Saurer, gen mgr; Lou Russo, progmg dir; Jay Pierce, chief of engrg; John Surno, sls.

WJLK-FM—Co-owned with WADB(AM). Nov 20, 1947: 94.3 mhz; 1.3 kw. Ant 499 ft. TL: N40 13 45 W74 05 24. Stereo. Web Site: www.getthepoint.com. Format: Hot adult contemp. ♦Lou Russo, opns mgr & progmg dir; Debbie Mazzella, mus dir.

WHTG(AM)—See Eatontown

*****WYGG(FM)**—Not on air, target date: unknown: 88.1 mhz; 100 w. 33 ft. TL: N40 13 01 W74 00 35. Minority Business & Housing Development, Inc., 1480 New York Ave., Brooklyn, NY 11210. Phone: (718) 434-7250. Fax: (718) 434-4899. Web Site: www.radiobonnenouvelle.com. Licensee: Evangelical Crusade of Fishers of Men Inc. ♦Samuel Nicolas, gen mgr.

Atlantic City

WAJM(FM)— 1997: 88.9 mhz; 150 w vert. 102 ft. TL: N39 21 54 W74 28 31. Atlantic City High School, 1400 N. Albany Ave. 08401.

Secondary address: 1809 Pacific Ave. 08402. Phone: (609) 343-7300. Licensee: Atlantic City Board of Education. Format: Div. ♦Mark Mangel, gen mgr.

WAYV(FM)— April 1961: 95.1 mhz; 50 kw. Ant 331 ft. TL: N39 22 51 W74 27 04. Stereo. 8025 Black Horse Pike, Suite 100-102, West Atlantic City 08232. Phone: (609) 484-8444. Fax: (609) 646-6331. E-mail: gfequity@aol.com. Web Site: www.951wayv.com. Licensee: Equity Communications L.P. (group owner; (acq 6-21-96; $3.1 million). Network: Westwood One. Rep: Katz Radio. Latham & Watkins. Format: Hot adult contemp. Target aud: 18-49; adults. ♦Gary Fisher, sr VP, VP & gen mgr; Keith Fader, sls dir; Paul Kelly, progmg dir.

WFPG-FM—Listing follows WKXW(AM).

WJSE(FM)—(Petersburg). August 1991: 102.7 mhz; 3.3 kw. Ant 295 ft. TL: N39 12 18 W74 39 33. Stereo. 550 New Rd., Somers Point 08244. Phone: (609) 927-5713. Fax: (609) 927-5712. E-mail: alp@wjse.com. Web Site: www.wjse.com. Licensee: Parinello Enterprises Inc. (acq 10-19-94; $355,684; 11-28-94). Format: Alternative rock. News staff: 12. Target aud: 18-44; upscale young adults. ♦Al Parinello, CEO, gen mgr & gen sls mgr; Lou Romanini, opns VP & opns mgr; Brian Finkelstein, sls dir & adv dir; Scott Reilly, prom dir.

WKXW(AM)— 1940: 1450 khz; 1 kw-U. TL: N39 22 42 W74 26 53. 950 Tilton Rd., Suite 200, Northfield 08225. Phone: (609) 645-9797. Fax: (609) 272-9228. E-mail: harry.hurley@citcomm.com. Web Site: www.literock969.com. Licensee: Millennium Atlantic City License Holdco LLC. Group owner: Millennium Radio Group LLC (acq 5-11-01; grpsl). Network: CBS. Format: Talk. News staff: one; News: 24 hrs wkly. Target aud: 25 plus; the population of South Jersey. ♦Dan Sullivan, gen mgr; Mike Ruble, gen sls mgr; Jennifer Doughton, prom dir; Eric Johnson, progmg dir; Tom McNally, chief of engrg.

WFPG-FM—Co-owned with WKXW(AM). September 1962: 96.9 mhz; 50 kw. 400 ft. TL: N39 22 42 W74 26 53. Stereo. Web Site: www.literock969.com. Format: Light rock, soft adult contemp. News staff: one. Target aud: 25-54. ♦Gary Guida, progmg dir.

WMGM(FM)— June 14, 1961: 103.7 mhz; 50 kw. 400 ft. TL: N39 23 38 W74 30 34. Stereo. 1601 New Rd., Linwood 08221. Phone: (609) 653-1400. Fax: (609) 601-0450. E-mail: wmgm1037@aol.com. Web Site: www.theshark1037.com. Licensee: Access.1 New Jersey License Co. Group owner: Access.1 Communications Corp. (acq 11-17-2003; grpsl). Rep: McGavren Guild. Format: Classic rock. Target aud: 25-54. ♦Chesley Maddox-Dorsey, pres; John Ford, gen mgr; Nick Giorno, progmg dir; Sydney L. Small, chmn & news dir; Dan Merlo, chief of engrg.

WMID(AM)— May 30, 1947: 1340 khz; 890 w-U. TL: N39 22 35 W74 27 08. Margate Communications, 8025 Black Horse Pike, Suite 100, Pleasantville 08232-2959. Phone: (609) 484-8444 EXT 317. Fax: (609) 646-6331. Web Site: classicoldieswmid.com. Licensee: Equity Communications L.P. (group owner; (acq 3-29-2002; grpsl). Rep: Katz Radio. Latham & Watkins. Format: Classic oldies. Target aud: 35-64; adults. ♦Gary Fisher, VP & gen mgr; Keith Fader, sls dir; Rob Garcia, progmg dir.

*****WNJN-FM**— September 1996: 89.7 mhz; 25 w horiz, 6 kw vert. Ant 272 ft. TL: N39 27 40 W74 41 06. Box 777, Trenton 08625-0777. Phone: (609) 777-5036. Fax: (609) 777-5217. Web Site: www.njn.net. Licensee: New Jersey Public Broadcasting Authority. Network: Network: NPR, PRI. Schwartz, Woods & Miller. Format: News/talk. Target aud: General. ♦Elizabeth G. Christopherson, CEO; Bill Jobes, gen mgr; Pharoah Cranston, opns mgr.

WOND(AM)—See Pleasantville

WPUR(FM)— June 1998: 107.3 mhz; 13.5 kw. Ant 449 ft. TL: N39 21 40 W74 25 05. 950 Tilton Rd., Suite 200, Northfield 08225. Phone: (609) 645-9797. Fax: (609) 272-9224. Web Site: www.catcountry1073.com. Licensee: Millennium Atlantic City License Holdco LLC. Group owner: Millennium Radio Group LLC (acq 5-11-01; grpsl). Rep: McGavren Guild. Format: Country. Target aud: 25-54. ♦Dan Sullivan, gen mgr;

Joe Kelly, opns dir & progmg dir; John DeLucia, sls dir; Mike Ruble, gen sls mgr; Hank Weisbecher, news dir; Tom McNally, chief of engrg.

WZBZ(FM)—See Pleasantville

Avalon

WILW(FM)— Mar 29, 1976: 94.3 mhz; 3 kw. 300 ft. TL: N39 07 48 W74 47 20. Stereo. 3208 Pacific Ave., Wildwood 08260. Licensee: Coastal Broadcasting Systems Inc. (acq 3-5-98; $470,000). Format: Oldies. ♦Bill Huff, gen mgr.

Beach Haven West

*****WVBH(FM)**— 2003: 88.3 mhz; 1 w horiz, 100 w vert. Ant 426 ft. TL: N39 42 56 W74 17 32. Box 7679, Newark, DE 19719-7679. Phone: (302) 731-7270. Fax: (302) 738-3090. Licensee: Priority Radio Inc. (group owner; (acq 11-14-2003; $400,000). Format: Christian. ♦Steve Hare, gen mgr.

Belvidere

WWYY(FM)— Oct 15, 1992: 107.1 mhz; 1.2 kw. Ant 718 ft. TL: N40 56 53 W75 09 38. 22 S. 6th St., Stroudsburg, PA 18360. Phone: (570) 421-2100. Fax: (570) 421-2040. Licensee: Nassau Broadcasting Holdings Inc. Group owner: Nassau Broadcasting Partners L.P. (acq 2-25-03; grpsl). Network: ABC. Format: Lite music. Target aud: 20 plus. ♦Maureen Barth, gen mgr.

Berlin

*****WNJS-FM**— Aug 21, 1992: 88.1 mhz; 1 w horiz, 20 w vert. Ant 781 ft. TL: N39 43 41 W74 50 39. (CP: 1 w horiz, 250 w vert). Box 777, Trenton 08625-0777. Phone: (609) 777-5036. Fax: (609) 777-5217. Web Site: www.njn.net. Licensee: New Jersey Public Broadcasting Authority (acq 3-6-91; FTR: 3-25-91). Network: Network: NPR, PRI. Schwartz, Woods & Miller. Format: News/talk. Target aud: General. ♦Elizabeth G. Christopherson, CEO; Bill Jobes, gen mgr; Pharoah Cranston, opns mgr; Larry Orfaly, progmg dir; Bill Schorbus, engrg dir.

Blackwood

*****WDBK(FM)**— June 7, 1979: 91.5 mhz; 100 w. 87 ft. TL: N39 47 06 W75 02 19. Box 200 08012. Phone: (856) 227-7200, EXT. 4441. Fax: (856) 374-4912. Licensee: Camden County College. Format: Top-40, rap. ♦Joe Hekman, gen mgr; Mike Ryan, stn mgr.

Blairstown

WHCY(FM)— Oct 21, 1973: 106.3 mhz; 340 w. 859 ft. TL: N41 02 51 W74 58 22. Stereo. 45 Mitchell Ave., Franklin 07416. Phone: (973) 827-2525. Fax: (973) 827-2135. E-mail: vincethomas@clearchannel.com. Web Site: www.max1063.com. Licensee: Capstar TX L.P. Group owner: Clear Channel Communications Inc. (acq 2-13-01). Rep: Katz Radio. Format: Hot adult contemp. Target aud: 25-54; baby boomers. Spec prog: Relg one hr wkly. ♦John Hogan, CEO, pres & CFO; Andrew Rosen, VP; Bob Dunphy, gen mgr; Vince Thomas, opns mgr; Rob Ryan, progmg dir.

Brick Township

*****WBGD(FM)**— June 1975: 91.9 mhz; 150 w. 72 ft. TL: N40 06 17 W74 07 34. Stereo. Brick Memorial High School, 2001 Lanes Mill Rd. 08724. Phone: (732) 785-3090. Phone: (732) 785-3173. Fax: (732) 836-9246. Licensee: Brick Township Board of Educ. Format: Var. Target aud: General. ♦Fran Bristol, gen mgr.

Bridgeton

*****WNJB(FM)**— 1998: 89.3 mhz; 1 w horiz, 2.5 kw vert. Ant 220 ft. TL: N39 27 35 W75 09 28. Box 777, Trenton 08625-0777. Phone: (609) 777-5036. Fax: (609) 777-5217. Web Site: www.njn.net. Licensee: New Jersey Public Broadcasting Authority. Network: Network: NPR,

Broadcasting & Cable Yearbook 2006

New Jersey   **Directory of Radio**

PRI. Schwartz, Woods & Miller. Format: News/talk. Target aud: General. ♦ Elizabeth G. Christopherson, CEO; Bill Jobes, gen mgr; Pharoah Cranston, opns mgr; Susan Sands, adv mgr; Larry Orfaly, progmg dir; Bill Schorbus, engrg dir.

WSNJ(AM)— August 1937: 1240 khz; 1 kw-U. TL: N39 27 40 W75 12 21. 1771 S. Burlington Rd. 08302. Phone: (856) 451-2930. Fax: (856) 453-9440. E-mail: information@wsnjam.com. Web Site: wsnjam.com. Licensee: Quinn Broadcasting Inc. (acq 2-18-2004; $550,000). Wiley, Rein & Fielding. Format: Var. News staff: one; News: 10 hrs wkly. Target aud: 25 plus. Spec prog: Big band, MOR, news/talk, farm 10 hrs wkly. ♦ James F. Quinn, pres & exec VP; Toni Coogan, CFO; Greg Hennis, gen mgr; Fred Sharkey, gen sls mgr & progmg dir; John Casey, mus dir; Richard Arsenault, chief of engrg.

Bridgewater

WWTR(AM)— Dec 23, 1971: 1170 khz; 243 w-D, DA. TL: N40 33 30 W74 35 52. Box 1250, Morristown 07929. Phone: (973) 538-1250. Fax: (973) 538-3060. Licensee: The Sentinel Publishing Co. Group owner: Greater Media Inc. (acq 7-12-01; grpsl). Format: Oldies. Target aud: General. Spec prog: Pol 3 hrs wkly. ♦ Dan Finn, exec VP; John Ryan, gen mgr; Chris Edwards, opns mgr, progmg VP & progmg dir; Jim Donnelly, gen sls mgr; Chris DeMeo, news dir; Michael Ferriola, engrg dir.

Brigantine

*WWFP(FM)—Not on air, target date: unknown: 90.5 mhz; 1.31 kw vert. Ant 108 ft. TL: N39 29 30 W74 26 07. CSN International, 3232 W. MacArthur Blvd., Santa Ana, CA 92704. Phone: (714) 825-9673. Fax: (714) 825-9660. Licensee: CSN International (group owner).

Camden

WEMG(AM)— September 1925: 1310 khz; 1 kw-D, 250 w-N. TL: N39 57 28 W75 06 54. 1341 N. Delaware Ave., Suite 509, Philadelphia, PA 19125. Phone: (215) 426-1900. Fax: (215) 426-1550. Licensee: Mega Communications of Camden Licensee L.L.C. Group owner: Mega Communications Inc. (acq 11-20-98). Format: Tropical Hispanic. ♦ Kevin Jones, gen mgr.

*WKDN-FM— July 23, 1968: 106.9 mhz; 38 kw. 600 ft. TL: N39 54 33 W75 06 00. Stereo. 2906 Mt. Ephraim Ave. 08104. Phone: (215) 922-0282. Licensee: Family Stations Inc. (group owner; acq 7-23-68). Dow, Lohnes & Albertson. Format: Relg. Target aud: General; families. Spec prog: Class 2 hrs wkly. ♦ Rich Archut, gen mgr.

WTMR(AM)— Nov 1, 1948: 800 khz; 5 kw-D, 500 w-N. TL: N39 54 33 W75 06 00. 2775 Mt. Ephraim Ave. 08104. Phone: (856) 962-8000. Fax: (856) 962-8004. Licensee: KAAY License L.P. Group owner: Beasley Broadcast Group (acq 9-4-98; $8 million). Format: Relg. ♦ Louise Bessler, gen mgr & gen sls mgr; Mike Roberts, progmg dir.

Canton

WJKS(FM)— Jan 15, 1972: 101.7 mhz; 3 kw. 263 ft. TL: N39 25 51 W75 20 13. First Federal Plaza Bldg., 704 Kings St., Suite 604, Wilmington, DE 19801. Phone: (302) 622-8895. Fax: (302) 622-8678. E-mail: tonyq@wjks1017.com. Web Site: www.wjks1017.com. Licensee: QC Communication Inc. (acq 3-17-97; $1.8 million. with WFAI(AM) Salem). Network: ABC Information & Entertainment. Format: Urban Contemporary. Target aud: 18-44. ♦ Mel Brittingham, opns dir; Maria Sylvanus, gen sls mgr; Tony Quartarone, gen mgr & progmg dir; Jeff DePaulo, chief of engrg.

Cape May

WAIV(FM)— June 3, 1967: 102.3 mhz; 3.2 kw. Ant 292 ft. TL: N39 00 33 W74 52 13. Stereo. 8025 Black Horse Pike, Suite 100-102, West Atlantic City 08232. Phone: (609) 484-8444. Fax: (609) 646-6331. E-mail: gfequity@aol.com. Web Site: 951wayv.com. Licensee: Equity Communications L.P. (group owner; (acq 3-29-2002; grpsl); Network: Westwood One. Rep: Katz Radio. Latham & Watkins. Format: Hot adult contemp. Target aud: 18-49; adults. ♦ Gary Fisher, sr VP, VP & gen mgr; Keith Fader, sls dir; Paul Kelly, progmg dir.

*WWCJ(FM)— September 1999: 89.1 mhz; 15 kw. Ant 308 ft. TL: N39 02 58 W74 51 14. Box B, Trenton 08690. Phone: (609) 587-8989. Fax: (609) 586-4533. Web Site: www.wwfm.org. Licensee: Mercer County Community College. Format: Classical. ♦ Jeffery R. Sekerka, gen mgr.

Cape May Court House

WGBZ(FM)— Sept 5, 1985: 105.5 mhz; 3.3 kw. Ant 295 ft. TL: N39 07 32 W74 49 26. Stereo. 8025 Black Horse Pike, Suite 100-102, West Atlantic City 08232. Phone: (609) 484-8444. Fax: (609) 646-6331. E-mail: gfequity@aol.com. Web Site: 993thebuzz.com. Licensee: Equity Communications L.P. (group owner; acq 5-31-2002; grpsl). Network: Westwood One. Rep: Katz Radio. Latham & Watkins. Format: CHR. Target aud: 18-49; adults. ♦ Gary Fisher, sr VP, VP & gen mgr; Keith Fader, sls dir; Rob Garcia, progmg dir.

*WJPG(FM)— 2004: 88.1 mhz; 550 w vert. Ant 213 ft. TL: N39 07 32 W74 49 27. Joy Communications Inc., Box 603, Woodbine 08270-0603. Phone: (609) 861-3700. Fax: (609) 861-3730. Licensee: Maranatha Ministries. Format: Christian. ♦ Kenneth Manri, gen mgr.

*WNJZ(FM)— August 1999: 90.3 mhz; 6 kw. Ant 236 ft. TL: N39 06 18 W74 48 06. Box 777, Trenton 08625-0777. Phone: (609) 777-5036. Fax: (609) 777-5217. Web Site: www.njn.net. Licensee: New Jersey Public Broadcasting Authority. Network: Network: NPR, PRI. Format: News/talk. ♦ Elizabeth G. Christopherson, CEO; Bill Jobes, gen mgr; Pharoah Cranston, opns mgr.

Cherry Hill

*WSJI(FM)— Jan 7, 1985: 89.5 mhz; 50 w horiz, 2 kw vert. 171 ft. TL: N39 51 33 W74 57 00. Box 895 08003. Phone: (856) 596-8950. E-mail: info@wsji.org. Web Site: www.wsji.org. Licensee: Broadcast Learning Center Inc. (acq 11-25-86; $175,000;. FTR: 10-27-86). Network: UPI. Format: Educ, relg, inspirational mus. Target aud: General. Spec prog: Arts 10 hrs wkly. ♦ Tom Moffit Sr., pres; William Fentor, CFO; Tom Moffit Jr., gen mgr; Gary Fizzana, stn mgr.

Delaware Township

*WDVR(FM)— Feb 19, 1990: 89.7 mhz; 4.8 kw. Ant 302 ft. TL: N40 30 37 W74 57 29. Stereo. Box 191, Rt. 604, Sergeantsville 08557-0191. Phone: (609) 397-1620. Fax: (609) 397-5991. Web Site: www.wdvrfm.org. Licensee: Penn-Jersey Educational Radio Corp. Network: ABC. Schwartz, Woods & Miller. Format: Div. News: 2 hrs wkly. Target aud: 30 plus. Spec prog: Folk 6 hrs, relg 6 hrs, jazz 11 hrs, oldies 13 hrs, bluegrass 6 hrs, wkly. ♦ Frank W. Napurano, pres & gen mgr; Grinny Lee, prom dir; Frank Napurano, progmg dir; Carlo Van Dyke, mus dir.

Dover

WDHA-FM— Feb 22, 1961: 105.5 mhz; 3 kw. 564 ft. TL: N40 51 19 W74 30 42. Stereo. 55 Horsehill Rd., Cedar Knolls 07927. Phone: (973) 538-1250. Phone: (973) 455-1055. Fax: (973) 538-3060. E-mail: rock@wdhafm.com. Web Site: www.wdhafm.com. Licensee: The Sentinel Publishing Co. Group owner: Greater Media Inc. (acq 7-6-01; grpsl). Rep: Katz Radio. Pepper & Corazzini. Format: Album oriented rock. Target aud: 18-49. ♦ John Ryan, stn mgr; Jim Donnelly, gen sls mgr; Pete Forester, natl sls mgr; Ellen Anapolle Paola, rgnl sls mgr.

Dover Township

*WWNJ(FM)— December 1991: 91.1 mhz; 50 w horiz, 50 kw vert. Ant 151 ft. TL: N39 58 07 W74 04 19. Stereo. Box B, Trenton 08690. Phone: (609) 587-8989. Fax: (609) 586-4533. Web Site: www.wwfm.org. Licensee: Mercer County Community College Board of Trustees. (acq 11-4-91). Network: PRI. Format: Classical. Target aud: General. ♦ Jeffery R. Sekerka, gen mgr & dev mgr.

East Orange

*WFMU(FM)— 1958: 91.1 mhz; 1.25 kw. 360 ft. TL: N40 47 15 W74 04 19. (CP: Ant 505 ft. TL: N40 47 19 W74 15 20). Stereo. Box 2011, Jersey City 07303. Phone: (201) 521-1416. Fax: (201) 521-1286. E-mail: wfmu@wfmu.org. Web Site: www.wfmu.org. Licensee: Auricle Communications. Format: Div, free-form. Target aud: General. Spec prog: International 15 hrs wkly. ♦ Ken Freedman, gen mgr; Brian Turner, progmg dir; John Fogarazzo, chief of engrg.

Eatontown

WHTG(AM)— Nov 1, 1957: 1410 khz; 500 w-D, 126 w-N. TL: N40 16 10 W74 04 19. 2355 W. Bango Ave., Neptune 07753. Phone: (732) 774-4755. Fax: (732) 774-4974. Licensee: Press Communications L.L.C. (group owner; acq 11-4-00; $15 million. with co-located FM). Rep: Christal. Format: Great gold. Target aud: 35 plus; general. Spec prog: Baseball 20 hrs, football 3 hrs, basketball 6 hrs wkly. ♦ Robert McAllan, CEO & pres; Richard T. Morena, CFO; John Dziuba, gen mgr; Cindy Brennan, stn mgr; John Kaszuba, gen sls mgr; Mathew Schwenker, natl sls mgr & prom mgr; Jack Aponte, progmg dir & mus dir; Mike Heilman, chief of engrg.

WHTG-FM— Oct 11, 1961: 106.3 mhz; 1.1 kw. Ant 528 ft. TL: N40 16 41 W74 04 51. Stereo. E-mail: g1063@g1063.com. Web Site: www.g1063.com. Leventhal, Senter & Lerman. Format: Alternative rock, modern adult contemp. Target aud: 18-34. ♦ John Kaszuba, opns dir & rgnl sls mgr; Michael Gavin, progmg mgr; Brian Phillips, mus dir.

Egg Harbor City

WSJO(FM)— Sept 23, 1971: 104.9 mhz; 10 kw. Ant 508 ft. TL: N39 32 49 W74 38 19. Stereo. 109 Walters Ave., Trenton 08638. Phone: (609) 771-8181. Fax: (609) 406-7956. Fax: (609) 771-0581. Web Site: www.sojo1049.com. Licensee: Millennium Egg Harbor License Holdco LLC. Group owner: Nassau Broadcasting Partners L.P. (acq 11-23-2004; $14 million). Network: AP Radio. Format: Hot adult contemp. Target aud: 35 plus. Spec prog: Relg 4 hrs wkly.

Egg Harbor Township

*WXGN(FM)— 2000: 90.5 mhz; 500 w vert. Ant 82 ft. TL: N39 16 46 W74 34 34. Box 810, Ocean City 08226-0810. Phone: (609) 391-9050. Web Site: wxgn.com. Licensee: Joy Broadcasting Inc. Format: Contemp Christian. ♦ Bob Green, gen mgr.

Elizabeth

WJDM(AM)— Mar 11, 1970: 1530 khz; 1 kw-D. TL: N40 38 56 W74 14 32. 407 N. Broad St. 07208. Phone: (908) 352-3400. Fax: (908) 352-4268. Web Site: www.puertadepaz.com. Licensee: Multicultural Radio Broadcasting Licensee LLC. Group owner: Multicultural Radio Broadcasting Inc. (acq 2-4-2004; grpsl). Format: Sp. ♦ Richard Dirocco, gen mgr; Didier Ugalde, stn mgr.

Ewing

WIMG(AM)—Licensed to Ewing. See Trenton

Flemington

WCHR(AM)— Jan 5, 1998: 1040 khz; 4.7 kw-D, 1 kw-N, DA-2. TL: N40 30 18 W74 58 37. (CP: 15 kw-D, 2.5 kw-N, 7.5 kw-CH, DA-3). 119 Locktown Rd. 08822. Phone: (215) 493-4252. Fax: (215) 321-5583. Web Site: wchram.com. Licensee: Nassau Broadcasting II L.L.C. Group owner: Nassau Broadcasting Partners L.P. (acq 2-15-02; grpsl). Format: Relg. Target aud: General; Religious adults. ♦ Chuck Zulker, stn mgr, opns mgr & sls dir.

*WCVH(FM)— April 1974: 90.5 mhz; 78 w. 449 ft. TL: N40 33 25 W74 54 18. Stereo. Rt. 31 08822. Phone: (908) 782-9595. Fax: (908) 284-7109. Licensee: Hunterdon Central Board of Education. Format: Div. Spec prog: Class 10 hrs, talk 2 hrs wkly. ♦ David R. Kelber, gen mgr; Joanna Lynch, opns dir; John Anastasio, chief of engrg.

Florence

WIFI(AM)— 1985: 1460 khz; 5 kw-D, DA. TL: N40 04 53 W74 47 41. 2025 Burllington-Columbus Rd., Burlington 08016. Phone: (609) 499-4800. Fax: (609) 499-4905. Licensee: Real Life Broadcasting. Network: USA. Format: News/talk, oldies. Spec prog: Relg 12 hrs wkly. ♦ Ron Graban, gen mgr; Mark Vanness, engrg dir.

Franklin

WSUS(FM)— Feb 28, 1965: 102.3 mhz; 590 w. 745 ft. TL: N41 08 37 W74 32 21. Stereo. 45 Mitchell Ave. 07416. Phone: (973) 827-2525. Fax: (973) 827-2135. E-mail: wsus1023@aol.com. Web Site: www.wsus1023.com. Licensee: Clear Channel Broadcasting Licenses Inc. Group owner: Clear Channel Communications Inc. (acq 2-15-01; grpsl). Rep: Katz Radio. Format: Adult contemp, news. News staff: 2; News: 10 hrs wkly. Target aud: 25-54; women. ♦ John Hogan, CEO, pres & CFO; Andy Rosen, VP; Bob Dunphy, gen mgr; Vince Thomas, stn mgr & opns mgr.

Stations in the U.S. — New Jersey

Developers & Brokers of Radio Properties

contact American Media Services at our suite: Philadelphia Marriott Downtown 215-625-2900
843-972-2200
americanmediaservices.com
Charleston, SC
Dallas, TX · Chicago, Il · Austin, TX

American Media Services, LLC

Freehold Township

*WRDR(FM)— Feb 20, 1997: 89.7 mhz; 10 w horiz, 2 kw vert. 170 ft. TL: N40 11 19 W74 15 01. Stereo. 6550 Rt. 9 S., Howell 07731. Phone: (732) 901-9953. Fax: (732) 901-0356. Web Site: www.bridgefm.org. Licensee: Bridgelight LLC (acq 1-31-03; $875,000). Format: Christian. News staff: one. Target aud: 25-62. Spec prog: Relg 6 hrs wkly. ♦Chris McCarrick, gen mgr; Don Gates, progmg dir.

Glassboro

*WGLS-FM— January 1964: 89.7 mhz; 750 w. 489 ft. TL: N39 41 41 W75 17 55. Stereo. Rowan Univ., 201 Mullica Hill Rd. 08028-1701. Phone: (856) 863-9457. Fax: (856) 256-4704. E-mail: wgls@rowan.edu. Web Site: http://wgls.rowan.edu. Licensee: Rowan University. Network: ABC. Format: Div, educ. Target aud: 18-45; general. Spec prog: Black 10 hrs wkly. ♦Frank Hogan, gen mgr; Kristin Davis, news dir; Libby Watts, pub affrs dir.

Hackensack

WWDJ(AM)— 1921: 970 khz; 5 kw-U, DA-2. TL: N40 54 40 W40 01 42. 777 Terrace Ave, 6th floor, Hasbrouck Heights 07604-3100. Phone: (201) 298-9700. Web Site: www.wwdj.com. Licensee: Salem Media Corp. Group owner: Salem Communications Corp. (acq 8-3-94). Format: Relg. Target aud: 25-44. ♦Edward Atsinger, pres; Joe D. Davis, VP; Carl J. Miller, gen mgr.

Hackettstown

*WNTI(FM)— Dec 5, 1957: 91.9 mhz; 5.6 kw. 510 ft. TL: N40 51 07 W74 52 35. Stereo. 400 Jefferson St. 07840. Phone: (908) 852-4545. Phone: (908) 979-4355. Fax: (908) 852-8515. Web Site: www.wnti.org. Licensee: Centenary College. Network: PRI. Format: Free form. News: 2 hrs wkly. Target aud: 15 plus. Spec prog: Big band 4 hrs, blues 11 hrs, heavy metal 6 hrs, reggae 3 hrs, oldies 3 hrs, jazz 9 hrs, relg 4 hrs wkly. ♦Paul Massen, gen mgr.

WRNJ(AM)— 1996: 1510 khz; 900 w-D, 230 w-N, DA-N. TL: N40 50 47 W74 48 16 (D), N40 48 55 W74 49 38 (N). 100 Rte. 46 W. 07840. Phone: (908) 850-1000. Fax: (908) 850-0001. Web Site: www.oldies1510.com. Licensee: WRNJ Radio Inc. Network: ABC Information & Entertainment. Shaw Pittman. Format: News/talk, oldies. News staff: 3; News: 10 hrs wkly. Target aud: 25-50 plus; upwardly mobile. Spec prog: Talk 10 hrs wkly. ♦Norman Worth, pres & gen mgr; Russ Long, opns dir; Dan Hollis, gen sls mgr & news dir; Chuck Reiger, progmg dir; Larry Tighe, chief of engrg.

Hammonton

WGYM(AM)— May 11, 1961: 1580 khz; 1 kw-D, 7 w-N. TL: N39 37 33 W74 47 44. 1601 New Rd., Linwood 08221. Phone: (609) 653-1400. Fax: (609) 927-7014. Licensee: Access.1 New Jersey License Co. LLC. Group owner: Access.1 Communications Corp. (acq 11-17-2003; grpsl). Network: Westwood One, ABC Information & Entertainment. Format: News/talk. ♦Sydney L. Small, chmn; Chesley Maddox-Dorsey, pres; John Ford, gen mgr; John De Lucia, gen sls mgr; Stuart Abrams, progmg dir; Dan Merlo, chief of engrg.

Hazlet

*WFJS(FM)— May 24, 1979: 89.3 mhz; 100 w. Ant 260 ft. TL: N40 25 37 W74 11 40. Stereo. 505 Thornall St., Suite 306, Edison 08837. Phone: (732) 516-1030. Fax: (732) 516-9399. E-mail: info@dhoomfm.com. Licensee: WVRM Inc. (acq 3-28-2001; $175,000. for stock). Format: European Indian music, news/talk. Target aud: General. Spec prog: Black 12 hrs, gospel 12 hrs, relg 5 hrs, Pol 2 hrs wkly. ♦Stephan Liadjg, pres; Alka Agrawal, gen mgr.

Jersey City

WSNR(AM)— December 1948: 620 khz; 3 kw-D, 7.6 kw-N, DA-2. TL: N40 47 53 W74 06 24. (CP: 8.5 kw-D, 5 kw-N, DA-2. TL: N40 50 52 W74 20 22). Stereo. 475 Park Ave. S., New York, NY 10016-6901. Phone: (847) 509-1661. Fax: (646) 424-2232. Fax: (847) 509-7750. Web Site: www.sportingnews.com. Licensee: Rose City Radio Corp. (group owner; acq 3-23-01; grpsl). Network: CBS. Format: multicultural. Target aud: General. ♦Clancy Woods, pres, gen mgr & progmg dir; Colleen Mamzella, chief of engrg.

WWRU(AM)— Dec 8, 1995: 1660 khz; 10 kw-U, DA-2. TL: N40 49 13 W74 04 09 (D), N40 49 13 W74 04 09 (N). (CP: TL: N40 49 13 W74 04 04 (D), N40 49 13 W74 04 09 (N). 449 Broadway, 5th Fl., New York, NY 10013. Phone: (212) 966-8700. Fax: (212) 966-9580. Licensee: Multicultural Radio Broadcasting Licensee LLC. Group owner: Multicultural Radio Broadcasting Inc. (acq 2-4-2004; grpsl). Format: Korean. ♦Gene Heinemeyer, gen mgr.

Lakewood

WOBM(AM)— Nov 20, 1970: 1160 khz; 5 kw-D, 8.9 kw-N, DA-2. TL: N40 08 09 W74 13 48. Box 927, Toms River 08754. Phone: (732) 269-0927. Fax: (732) 269-9292. Licensee: Millennium Shore License Holdco LLC. Group owner: Millennium Radio Group LLC (acq 5-14-02; grpsl). Network: AP Radio. Rep: Katz Radio. Blair, Joyce & Silva. Format: Oldies, Big Band, talk. News staff: 5; News: 14 hrs wkly. Target aud: 45 plus; educated. Spec prog: Talk 12 hrs wkly. ♦Bill Saurer, gen mgr; Tom Hesslein, gen sls mgr; Steve Ardolina, progmg dir; Tom Mongelli, news dir; Jay Pierce, chief of engrg.

WOBM-FM—See Toms River

Lawrenceville

*WRRC(FM)— Sept 23, 1989: 107.7 mhz; 17 w. 36 ft. TL: N40 16 44 W74 44 15. Stereo. Rider Univ., Bart Luedeke Ctr., 2083 Lawrenceville Rd. 08648. Phone: (609) 896-5369. Fax: (609) 219-4729. Licensee: Rider University Board of Trustees. Format: Var. News staff: 3; News: 4 hrs wkly. Target aud: 16-21; high school & college students. Spec prog: Black 10 hrs, heavy metal 10 hrs wkly. ♦Nicole DeMaria, gen mgr.

Lincroft

*WBJB-FM— Jan 13, 1975: 90.5 mhz; 11 kw. 135 ft. TL: N40 19 19 W74 07 57. Stereo. Brookdale Community College, 765 Newman Springs Rd. 07738. Phone: (732) 224-2490. Phone: (732) 224-2252. Fax: (732) 224-2494. E-mail: comments@wbjb.org. Web Site: www.90.5thenight.org. Licensee: Board of Trustees of Brookdale Community College. Network: NPR. Erwin, Campbell & Tannenwald. Format: AAA, news. News: 16 hrs wkly. Target aud: 18-54; general. Spec prog: Haitian 3 hrs, pub affrs 5 hrs, bluegrass 3 hrs, Sp 4 hrs, blues 4 hrs wkly. ♦Tom Brennan, stn mgr; Russ Boris, mus dir; Robin Shannon, pub affrs dir; George Marshall, chief of engrg.

Long Branch

WWZY(FM)— June 1, 1960: 107.1 mhz; 4.7 kw. Ant 371 ft. TL: N40 18 17 W73 59 08. Stereo. 2355 W. Bangs Ave., Neptune 07753. Phone: (732) 774-4755. Fax: (732) 774-4974. Web Site: www.107thebreeze.com. Licensee: Press Communications LLC (group owner; acq 6-18-2003; $20 million). Format: Soft adult contemp. ♦Frank Calderaro, gen mgr; John Kaszuba, gen sls mgr; Mike Gavin, progmg dir; Mike Heilman, chief of engrg.

Madison

*WMNJ(FM)— Sept 15, 1980: 88.9 mhz; 8 w. 75 ft. TL: N40 45 30 W74 25 48. Stereo. Drew Univ., 36 Madison Ave. 07940. Phone: (973) 408-4753. Phone: (973) 408-3000 (univ.). Fax: (973) 408-3939. Licensee: Drew University (acq 9-25-89). Format: Alternative, AOR. News: 28 hrs wkly. Spec prog: Black 6 hrs, class 2 hrs, jazz 2 hrs, relg 2 hrs, blues 4 hrs, show tunes 6 hrs wkly. ♦Jay Clawson, pres & gen mgr.

Mahwah

*WRPR(FM)— July 15, 1980: 90.3 mhz; 100 w. 30 ft. TL: N41 04 51 W74 10 34. Stereo. 505 Ramapo Valley Rd. 07430. Phone: (201) 825-7449. Fax: (201) 327-9030. Licensee: Ramapo College of New Jersey. Format: College contemp. News staff: 4; News: 10 hrs wkly. Target aud: 18-24; college students. Spec prog: Pub affrs 12 hrs wkly. ♦Evan Brown, gen mgr; Andrew Bernstein, progmg dir; Sarah Tucci, mus dir & news dir.

Manahawkin

WCHR-FM— 2002: 105.7 mhz; 13 kw. Ant 459 ft. TL: N39 42 56 W74 17 32. 2401 Rt. 66, Ocean 07712. Phone: (732) 897-8282. Phone: (732) 818-9303 (business). Fax: (732) 897-8283. Fax: (732) 818-9304. Web Site: www.1057thehawkfm.com. Licensee: Millennium Shore License Holdco LLC. Group owner: Millennium Radio Group LLC (acq 3-15-2004; $12 million). Format: Classic rock. ♦Bill Saurer, gen mgr; Russ DelCore, gen sls mgr; Phil LoCascio, progmg dir; Tom Monzeli, news dir; Jay Pierce, engrg dir.

WJRZ-FM— July 4, 1976: 100.1 mhz; 3 kw. Ant 499 ft. TL: N39 47 53 W74 12 12. Stereo. Box 1000, 1001 Beach Ave. 08050. Secondary address: Box 100, 22 W. Water St., Toms River 08754. Phone: (609) 597-1100. Phone: (732) 349-1100. Fax: (609) 597-4400. Fax: (732) 505-8700. Web Site: www.oldies100fm.com. Licensee: Jersey Shore Broadcasting Corp. Group owner: Greater Media Inc. (acq 7-19-02). Network: AP Radio. Rep: Christal. Format: Oldies. News staff: one; News: 4 hrs wkly. Target aud: 18-54. ♦Dan Finn, exec VP & VP; Mike Kazala, gen mgr & stn mgr; Jeff Rafter, opns mgr & progmg dir; Andria Iridoy, gen sls mgr; Peter Iridoy, prom dir; Bill Clanton Sr., chief of engrg.

*WNJM(FM)— August 1999: 89.9 mhz; 1 w horiz, 200 w vert. Ant 259 ft. TL: N39 41 57 W74 14 05. Box 777, Trenton 08625-0777. Phone: (609) 777-5036. Fax: (609) 777-5217. Web Site: www.njn.net. Licensee: New Jersey Public Broadcasting Authority. Network: Network: NPR, PRI. Format: News/talk. ♦Elizabeth G. Christopherson, CEO; Bill Jobes, gen mgr; Pharoah Cranston, opns mgr.

*WYRS(FM)— Mar 27, 1995: 90.7 mhz; 1 w horiz, 500 w vert. Ant 289 ft. TL: N39 41 57 W74 14 05. Stereo. Box 730 08050. Secondary address: 113 Lighthouse Dr. Phone: (609) 978-1678. Fax: (609) 597-4146. E-mail: info@wyrs.org. Web Site: www.wyrs.org. Licensee: WYRS Broadcasting (acq 2-18-2005; $1). Network: AP Radio. Format: Christian, educ, relg. Target aud: General. ♦Bob Wick, CEO, gen mgr & chief of engrg.

Margate City

WTTH(FM)— Nov 19, 1991: 96.1 mhz; 2.8 kw. Ant 400 ft. TL: N39 21 02 W74 26 55. Stereo. 8025 Black Horse Pike, Suite 100-102, West Atlantic City 08232. Phone: (609) 484-8444. Fax: (609) 646-6331. E-mail: gfequity@aol.com. Web Site: www.hitsandoldies.com. Licensee: Equity Communications L.P. (group owner; acq 5-30-2003; grpsl). Network: Westwood One. Rep: Katz Radio. Laitham & Watkins. Format: Urban adult contemp. Target aud: 18-49; adults. Spec prog: Gospel 5 hrs, relg one hr wkly. ♦Gary Fisher, sr VP, VP & gen mgr; Keith Fader, sls dir; Rob Garcia, progmg dir.

Medford Lakes

*WVBV(FM)—Not on air, target date: unknown: 90.5 mhz; 2.5 kw. Ant 295 ft. TL: N39 48 26 W74 35 24. Hope Christian Church of Marlton Inc., 55 E. Main St., Marlton 08053. Phone: (856) 983-1662. Fax: (856) 983-1814. Licensee: Hope Christian Church of Marlton Inc. Format: Christian/talk. ♦William C. Luebkemann Jr., pres & gen mgr.

Millville

WIXM(FM)— Feb 2, 1962: 97.3 mhz; 50 kw. Ant 466 ft. TL: N39 19 15 W74 46 17. Stereo. 950 Tilton Rd., Suite 200, Northfield 08225. Phone: (609) 771-8181. Fax: (609) 926-5907. Web Site: www.nj1015.com. Licensee: Millennium Atlantic City II License Holdco LLC. Group owner: Millennium Radio Group LLC (acq 12-21-2001; grpsl). Format: Talk. Target aud: 25-54. ♦Dan Sullivan, gen mgr.

WMVB(AM)— December 1953: 1440 khz; 1 kw-D, 65 w-N, DA-2. TL: N39 25 19 W75 01 14. 415 N. High St. 08332. Phone: (856) 327-8800. Fax: (856) 327-0408. E-mail: greg@wmvb.net. Web Site: www.wmvb.net. Licensee: Quinn Broadcasting Inc (acq 4-26-2000; $500,000). Format: Var. News staff: 4. Target aud: 25-54; general public. Spec prog: Sp 2 hrs, gospel 8 hrs, children 3 hrs wkly. ♦James F. Quinn, pres; Toni Coogan, CFO; Greg Hennis, gen mgr; Fred Shankey, prom dir & progmg dir; Richard Arsenault, engrg dir & chief of engrg.

Morristown

***WJSV(FM)**— Feb 22, 1971: 90.5 mhz; 124 w. 17 ft. TL: N40 50 10 W74 29 16. Stereo. WJSV c/o Morristown High School, 50 Early St. 07960. Phone: (973) 292-2168. Fax: (973) 539-5573. Web Site: www.morristown.com/wjsv. Licensee: Morris School District Board of Education. Format: AOR, progsv. News staff: one; News: 3 hrs wkly. Target aud: General. Spec prog: News/talk 3 hrs, sports 3 hrs wkly. ♦Norman Wallerstein, gen mgr; Conor McGee, stn mgr; Lee Tylee, adv mgr.

WMTR(AM)— Dec 12, 1948: 1250 khz; 5 kw-D, 7 kw-N, DA-2. TL: N40 48 45 W74 27 36. Stereo. Box 1250 07962-1250. Phone: (973) 538-1250. Fax: (973) 538-3060. Web Site: www.wmtram.com. Licensee: The Sentinel Publishing Co. Group owner: Greater Media Inc. (acq 7-6-01; grpsl). Pepper & Corazzini. Format: Oldies. Target aud: 35 plus. Spec prog: Community connection 5 hrs wkly. ♦Dan Finn, exec VP; Chris Edwards, opns mgr, mktg dir & progmg mgr; Jim Donnelly, gen sls mgr; John Ryan, gen mgr & natl sls mgr.

Mount Holly

WWJZ(AM)— November 1992: 640 khz; 50 kw-D, 950 w-N, DA-2. TL: N40 05 28 W74 50 30. 500 Office Center Dr., Fort Washington, PA 19034. Phone: (215) 591-0100. Fax: (215) 591-4527. Web Site: www.radiodisney.com. Licensee: Radio Disney Group LLC. Group owner: ABC Inc. (acq 12-30-99). Format: Top-40. Target aud: 45 plus. ♦Ralph Cosenza, gen mgr.

New Brunswick

WCTC(AM)— Dec 12, 1946: 1450 khz; 1 kw-U. TL: N40 29 32 W74 25 11. Stereo. Box 100, Broadcast Ctr. 08903. Secondary address: 78 Veronica Ave., Somerset 08873. Phone: (732) 249-2600. Fax: (732) 249-9010. Licensee: Raritan Valley Broadcasting Co. Group owner: Greater Media Inc. (acq 5-1-57). Network: ABC Information & Entertainment. Format: News/talk. News staff: 6; News: 15 hrs wkly. Target aud: 35-54. Spec prog: Rutgers Univ. & high school sports. ♦Dan Finn, VP; Frank Calderaro, gen mgr; John Ford, gen mgr & stn mgr; Bruce Johnson, opns mgr, progmg dir & news dir; Jack Cahill, gen sls mgr; Dave Kirby, prom dir; Keith Smeal, chief of engrg.

***WRSU-FM**— April 1974: 88.7 mhz; 1.4 kw. 150 ft. TL: N40 28 00 W74 26 15. Stereo. 126 College Ave. 08903. Phone: (732) 932-7800. Fax: (732) 932-1768. E-mail: wrsu@wrsu.rutgers.sdu. Web Site: www.wrsu.rutgers.edu. Licensee: Board of Governors Rutgers University. Format: Var/div. News: 6 hrs wkly. Target aud: 15-30; college students, div group of young adults. ♦Dan Strafford, gen mgr; Tim Espar, stn mgr.

Newark

***WBGO(FM)**— Feb 7, 1948: 88.3 mhz; 10 kw. 431 ft. TL: N40 44 11 W74 10 15. 54 Park Pl. 07102. Phone: (973) 624-8880. Fax: (973) 824-8888. E-mail: jazz88@wbgo.org. Web Site: www.wbgo.org. Licensee: Newark Public Radio Inc. (acq 12-77). Network: Network: NPR, AP Radio. Dow, Lohnes & Albertson. Format: Jazz. News staff: 3; News: 5 hrs wkly. Target aud: General. ♦Oliver Quinn, chmn; Cephas Bowles, gen mgr; Arajua Backman, gen sls mgr & rgnl sls mgr; Grey Johnson, mktg mgr; Thurston Briscoe, progmg dir; Doug Doyle, news dir; Brian McCabe, chief of engrg.

WCAA(FM)— August 1992: 105.9 mhz; 2.4 kw. 722 ft. TL: N40 45 04 W73 58 25. 485 Madison Ave., New York, NY 10022. Phone: (212) 310-6000. Fax: (212) 888-3694. E-mail: latinomix@univisonradio.com. Web Site: www.latinomixfm.com. Licensee: WADO-AM License Corp. ("WADO"). Group owner: Univision Radio (acq 9-22-2003; grpsl). Format: Sp, tropical. ♦Stephanie McNamara, gen mgr; Danny Cruz, progmg dir.

***WFME(FM)**— 1959: 94.7 mhz; 38 kw. 570 ft. TL: N40 47 18 W74 15 19. Stereo. 289 Mt. Pleasant Ave., West Orange 07052. Phone: (973) 736-3600. Phone: (212) 736-3600. Fax: (973) 736-4832. E-mail: WFME@wfme.net. Web Site: www.familyradio.com. Licensee: Family Stations Inc. (group owner; acq 3-10-66). Network: Family Radio. Format: Christian educ. Target aud: General. ♦Harold Camping, pres & gen mgr; Charles Menut, stn mgr & chief of engrg; George Robson, pub affrs dir.

WHTZ(FM)— June 1, 1961: 100.3 mhz; 7.8 kw. 1,220 ft. TL: N40 44 54 W73 59 10. 36th Fl., 101 Hudson St., Jersey City 07302. Phone: (212) 239-2300. Fax: (212) 239-2308. E-mail: z100radio@aol.com. Web Site: www.z100.com. Licensee: AMFM Radio Licenses L.L.C. Group owner: Clear Channel Communications Inc. (acq 8-30-00; grpsl). Rep: Christal. Format: Top 40. ♦Andy Rosen, exec VP & gen mgr; Bob McCuin, gen sls mgr; Tom Poleman, progmg dir; Josh Hadden, chief of engrg.

WNSW(AM)— 1947: 1430 khz; 5 kw-U, DA-N. TL: N40 42 32 W74 14 31. Stereo. 449 Broadway 2nd Fl., New York, NY 10013. Phone: (212) 966-1059. Fax: (212) 966-9580. E-mail: geneh@mrbi.net. Licensee: Multicultural Radio Broadcasting Licensee LLC. Group owner: Multicultural Radio Broadcasting Inc. (acq 1-30-98; grpsl). Rep: Katz Radio. Hopkins & Sutter. Format: Multicultural, gospel, American popular standards. Target aud: 25-54. ♦Gene Heinemeyer, gen mgr & progmg dir; Harold Chou, chief of engrg.

Newton

WNNJ(AM)— Dec 15, 1953: 1360 khz; 2 kw-D, 320 w-N, DA-2. TL: N41 02 22 W74 44 19. 45 Mitchell Ave., Franklin 07416. Phone: (973) 827-2525. Fax: (973) 827-2135. Web Site: www.oldies1360.com. Licensee: Clear Channel Broadcasting Licenses Inc. Group owner: Clear Channel Communications Inc. (acq 1-31-2001; grpsl). Network: Westwood One. Rep: Katz Radio. Format: Oldies. News staff: one; News: 5 hrs wkly. Target aud: 35 plus; mature adults with high incomes. Spec prog: Relg one hr, pub affrs one hr wkly. ♦John Hogan, CEO, pres & CFO; Randy Michaels, chmn; Andy Rosen, VP; Bob Dunphy, gen mgr; Vince Thomas, stn mgr, opns dir & opns mgr.

WNNJ-FM— Oct 15, 1961: 103.7 mhz; 2.3 kw. 892 ft. TL: N41 11 33 W74 45 13. Stereo. Web Site: wnnj.com. Format: Classic rock. News staff: 2. Target aud: 18-49; upscale, young families with teenage children. ♦Matthew Jeff, mus dir; Judi Edwards, pub affrs dir.

North Cape May

WDOX(FM)— 1993: 106.7 mhz; 3 kw. 200 ft. TL: N38 57 32 W74 55 23. 3155 Rt. 9, Reo Grande 08242. Phone: (609) 463-9369. Phone: (609) 522-1987. Web Site: www.wdox.com. Licensee: WBES LLC (acq 11-1-2004; $700,000). Network: Network: USA, Moody. Format: Modern rock, alternative. Spec prog: Class 3 hrs wkly. ♦Bob Maschio, gen mgr.

Oakland

WVNJ(AM)— Dec 13, 1993: 1160 khz; 20 kw-D, 2.5 kw-N, DA-2. TL: N41 03 26 W74 15 00. Stereo. 1086 Teaneck Rd., Suite 4F, Teaneck 07666. Phone: (201) 837-0400. Fax: (201) 837-9664. E-mail: wvnj1160am@aol.com. Web Site: www.wvnj.com. Licensee: Universal Broadcasting of New York Inc. (group owner; acq 3-24-94; $12,050,000. with WTHE(AM) Mineola, NY; FTR: 6-20-94) Format: Adult standards, talk. News staff: one; News: 8 hrs wkly. Target aud: 35-64; upscale. Spec prog: Health related. ♦Miriam Warshaw, pres; Howard Warshaw, sr VP; Dr. Abe Warshaw, gen mgr; David Margalotti, opns dir & progmg dir; Pete Bucky, mus dir & news dir.

Ocean Acres

WBBO(FM)— 1992: 98.5 mhz; 6 kw. Ant 328 ft. TL: N39 45 06 W74 15 39. 703 Millcreek Rd., Manahawkin 08050. Secondary address: Rt. 35 & 66, Ocean 08050. Phone: (609) 597-6700. Fax: (609) 597-0639. E-mail: g1063@g1063.com. Web Site: www.g1063.com. Licensee: Press Communications LLC. Group owner: Millennium Radio Group LLC (acq 8-9-2004; $17 million). Format: Alternative rock, modern adult contemp. News staff: one; News: one hr wkly. Target aud: 25-55; women. ♦Frank Calderaro, gen mgr; John Kaszuba, gen sls mgr; Mike Gravin, progmg dir; Mike Heilman, chief of engrg.

Ocean City

WIBG(AM)— October 1992: 1020 khz; 1.9 kw-D, 680 w-CH. TL: N39 13 45 W74 40 54. Traders Lane Professional Complex, 3328 Simpson Ave. 08226. Phone: (609) 398-1020. Fax: (609) 398-3736. E-mail: wibg@wibg.com. Web Site: www.wibg.com. Licensee: Enrico S. Brancadora. (acq 12-1-92; $140,000; 12-21-92). Format: Adult contemp, Christian, praise & worship. News staff: one; News: one hr wkly. Target aud: 25-45; young urban-suburban professional. ♦Tom Sappie, opns mgr; Nancy Zimmerman, sls dir & gen sls mgr; Nancy Manno, prom mgr.

WKOE(FM)— Oct 1, 1972: 106.3 mhz; 3 kw. Ant 308 ft. TL: N34 13 40 W74 40 57. Stereo. 950 Tilton Rd., Northfield 08225. Phone: (609) 645-9797. Fax: (609) 272-9224. Licensee: Press Communications LLC. (acq 1-28-2005; $3.16 million). Rep: McGavren Guild. News staff: one. Target aud: 18-49. ♦Dan Sullivan, gen mgr; Michael Ruble, sls dir; Jennifer Doughten, prom mgr; Eric Scott, progmg dir & news dir; Tom McNally, engrg dir.

***WRTQ(FM)**— Sept 27, 1994: 91.3 mhz; 82 w horiz, 10.5 kw vert. 384 ft. TL: N39 19 15 W74 46 17. Annenberg Hall (011-00), 2020 N. 13th St., Philadelphia, PA 19122-6080. Phone: (215) 204-8405. Fax: (215) 204-7027. E-mail: comments@wrti.org. Web Site: www.wrti.org. Licensee: Temple University of the Commonwealth System of Higher Education. Network: Network: NPR, AP Radio. Format: Jazz, class. News staff: one; News: 15 hrs wkly. Target aud: 30-65. ♦Jack Moore, progmg dir; Jeff DePolo, chief of engrg.

WTKU(FM)— April 1983: 98.3 mhz; 3 kw. 300 ft. TL: N34 12 18 W74 39 33. (CP: Ant 328 ft.). Stereo. 1601 New Rd., Linwood 08221. Phone: (609) 601-1100. Fax: (609) 601-0450. Licensee: Access.1 New Jersey License Co. Group owner: Access.1 Communications Corp. (acq 11-17-2003; grpsl). Format: Hits of the 60s & 70s. News: 5 hrs wkly. Target aud: 25-54. ♦Chesley Maddox-Dorsey, pres; John Ford, gen mgr; Anne Newman, opns dir; John De Lucia, gen sls mgr; David Allen Pratt, progmg dir; Sydney L. Small, chmn & news dir; Dan Merlo, chief of engrg.

Parsippany-Troy Hills

WXMC(AM)— Jan 13, 1973: 1310 khz; 1 kw-D, 100 w-N, DA. TL: N40 51 51 W74 21 06. (CP: 360 w-N). Box 160, TCB, West Orange 07052. Secondary address: 204E 23 St, NYC, NY 10010. Phone: (212) 575-5561. Fax: (973) 575-5637. E-mail: hoyestudia@hotmail.com. Licensee: James Chladek Chladek Broadcast Group (acq 1-15-93; $200,000;. FTR: 2-8-93). KMZ Roseman. Format: Tropical, romantic Sp mus, regl. News staff: one; News: 4 hrs wkly. Target aud: 25 plus; young upper middle class business professionals. Spec prog: Mexican one hr wkly. ♦James Chladek, CEO & gen mgr; Edwin Blas, stn mgr & chief of engrg; Otto Gust, chief of opns.

Paterson

WPAT(AM)— May 3, 1941: 930 khz; 5 kw-U, DA-2. TL: N40 50 59 W74 10 59. Stereo. 449 Broadway, New York, NY 10013. Phone: (212) 966-1059. Fax: (212) 966-9580. Licensee: WPAT Licensee LLC. Group owner: Multicultural Radio Broadcasting Inc. (acq 7-22-98). Format: Multilingual, sports in Sp. ♦Gene Heinemeyer, gen mgr; Harold Chou, chief of engrg.

WPAT-FM— Mar 29, 1957: 93.1 mhz; 5.3 kw. 1,420 ft. TL: N40 42 43 W74 00 49. (CP: 21.88 kw, ant 338 ft.). Stereo. 26 W. 56th St., New York, NY 10019. Phone: (212) 541-9200. Fax: (212) 246-9239. Licensee: WPAT Licensing Inc. Group owner: Spanish Broadcasting System Inc. (acq 1996; $83.5 million). Format: Sp adult contemp. ♦Raul Alarcon Jr., CEO & pres; Raul Alarcon Sr., chmn; Jose A. Garcia, CFO.

Pemberton

***WBZC(FM)**— Jan 24, 1995: 88.9 mhz; 120 w-horiz, 2.5 kw-vert. 195 ft. TL: N39 50 34 W74 32 40. Stereo. Burlington County College, County Rt. 530 08068. Phone: (609) 894-9311, EXT. 7223. Phone: (609) 894-9311. Fax: (609) 894-9440. Licensee: Burlington County College. Bechtel & Cole. Format: Rock & Blues. News: 4 hrs wkly. Target aud: 18-35. Spec prog: Folk 4 hrs, jazz 4 hrs, bluegrass 4 hrs, reggae 4 hrs, Jewish 4 hrs wkly. ♦Dr. Robert C. Messina Jr., pres; Rich Pokrass, gen mgr; Bonnie Hart, stn mgr.

Pennsauken

WRNB(FM)— 1946: 107.9 mhz; 780 w. Ant 905 ft. TL: N39 57 09 W75 10 05. Stereo. 1000 River Rd., Suite 400, Conshohocken, PA 19428-2437. Phone: (610) 276-1100. Fax: (610) 279-1139. Licensee:

Stations in the U.S. — New Jersey

Radio One Licenses LLC. Group owner: Radio One Inc. (acq 2-2-2004; $35 million). Format: Urban contemp. ◆Chester Schofield, gen mgr.

Petersburg

WJSE(FM)—Licensed to Petersburg. See Atlantic City

Piscataway

*****WVPH(FM)**— May 1976: 90.3 mhz; 200 w. 7 ft. TL: N40 32 45 W74 28 25. 100 Behmer Rd. 08854-4173. Phone: (732) 981-0153. Fax: (732) 981-1985. E-mail: wvph@pway.org. Licensee: Board of Education Piscataway High School. Format: Educ, progsv, talk. ◆Dawne Dionisio, gen mgr.

Pleasantville

WMGM(FM)—See Atlantic City

WOND(AM)— July 1950: 1400 khz; 1 kw-U. TL: N39 23 26 W74 30 47. 1601 New Rd., Linwood 08221. Phone: (609) 653-1400. Fax: (609) 927-7014. Licensee: Access.1 New Jersey License Co. Group owner: Access.1 Communications Corp. (acq 11-17-2003; grpsl). Network: Network: Westwood One, ABC Information & Entertainment. Rep: McGavren Guild. Format: News/talk. ◆Sydney L. Small, chmn; Chesley Maddox-Dorsey, pres; John Ford, gen mgr; Stuart Abrams, opns VP; John De Lucia, gen sls mgr; Kathi Bauder, natl sls mgr; Dan Merlo, chief of engrg.

WUSS(AM)— Jan 1, 1955: 1490 khz; 290 w-U. TL: N39 23 24 W74 30 45. 1601 New Rd., Linwood 08221. Phone: (609) 601-1100. Fax: (609) 601-0450. Licensee: Access.1 New Jersey License Co. Group owner: Access.1 Communications Corp. (acq 11-17-2003; grpsl). Network: Sporting News Radio Network. Rep: McGavren Guild. Format: Oldies. Target aud: 18-48. ◆Sydney L. Small, chmn; Chesley Maddox-Dorsey, pres; John Ford, gen mgr; David Allen, progmg dir.

WZBZ(FM)— 1974: 99.3 mhz; 3 kw. Ant 328 ft. TL: N39 22 35 W74 27 08. Stereo. Equity Communications L.P., 8025 Black Horse Pike, Suite 100-102, West Atlantic City 08232. Phone: (609) 484-8444. Fax: (609) 646-6331. E-mail: gfequity@aol.com. Web site: 993thebuzz.com. Licensee: Equity Communications L.P. (group owner; acq 5-31-2002; grpsl). Network: Westwood One. Rep: Katz Radio. Lathmam & Watkins. Format: CHR. Target aud: 18-49; adults. ◆Gary Fisher, sr VP & gen mgr; Keith Fader, sls dir; Rob Garcia, progmg dir.

Point Pleasant

WRAT(FM)— Oct 4, 1968: 95.9 mhz; 4 kw. Ant 293 ft. TL: N40 10 17 W74 01 39. Stereo. 1731 Main St., South Belmar 07719-3051. Phone: (732) 681-3800. Fax: (732) 681-5995. Web site: www.wrat.com. Licensee: The Sentinel Publishing Co. Group owner: Greater Media Inc. (acq 7-6-01; grpsl). Rep: Katz Radio. Format: Rock. Target aud: 21-44; men 25-54. ◆Dan Finn, VP & gen mgr; Mike Kazala, stn mgr; Carl Craft, opns mgr & progmg dir; Larry Tendrick, gen sls mgr; William Clanton Sr., chief of engrg.

Pomona

*****WLFR(FM)**— Oct 16, 1984: 91.7 mhz; 1.35 kw. 135 ft. TL: N39 28 45 W74 32 23. (CP: 900 w). Stereo. Stockton State College, Jim Leeds Rd. 08240. Phone: (609) 652-4506. Fax: (609) 652-4550. Licensee: Stockton State College Format: Alternative, var/rock. News: one hr wkly. Target aud: General. Spec prog: Folk 3 hrs, class 4 hrs, jazz 10 hrs wkly. ◆Greg Adamo, gen mgr.

Pompton Lakes

WGHT(AM)— Oct 3, 1964: 1500 khz; 1 kw-D, DA-D. TL: N40 58 51 W74 17 06. Box 316, 1878 Lincoln Ave. 07442. Secondary address: Box 4015, Wayne 07474. Phone: (973) 839-1500. Fax: (973) 839-2400. Web Site: www.ghtradio.com. Licensee: Mariana Broadcasting Inc. (acq 7-8-93; 8-23-93). Network: AP Radio. Format: Oldies, talk. News staff: 3; News: 10 hrs wkly. Target aud: 25-54; general. Spec prog: Relg 2 hrs, polka one hr, loc sports 2 hrs wkly. ◆John Silliman, pres, gen mgr & stn mgr; Tom Niven, opns VP; Cindy Wear, gen sls mgr, prom VP & progmg dir; Debra Valentine, news dir.

Port Republic

*****WXXY-FM**— 2003: 88.7 mhz; 760 w vert. Ant 131 ft. TL: N39 35 34 W74 26 15. 465 Rt. 9 S., Little Egg Harbor 08087. Phone: (609) 347-0088. E-mail: comments@wxxy.fm. Web Site: www.wxxy.fm. Licensee: In His Name Broadcasting Inc. (acq 10-23-01). Format: Gospel.

Princeton

WHWH(AM)— Sept 7, 1963: 1350 khz; 5 kw-U, DA-2. TL: N40 22 00 W74 44 38. 619 Alexander Rd. 08540. Phone: (609) 419-0300. Fax: (609) 419-0143. E-mail: epalladino@nassaubroadcasting.com. Web Site: www.moneytalk1350.com. Licensee: Multicultural Radio Broadcasting Licensee LLC. Group owner: Multicultural Radio Broadcasting Inc. (acq 5-24-2002; grpsl). Network: Network: Wall Street, ABC Information & Entertainment. Rep: Katz Radio. Booth, Freret, Imlay & Tepper P. Format: News/talk. News staff: 4; News: 36 hrs wkly. Target aud: 35 plus. Spec prog: Princeton University football & basketball, Trenton Thunder baseball. ◆Lou Mercatani, pres; Peter D. Tonks, CFO; Michelle Stevens, exec VP & gen mgr; Josh Gertzog, VP, gen mgr, sls dir & pub affrs dir; Ed Palladino, opns dir.

WPRB(FM)— October 1955: 103.3 mhz; 14 kw. 731 ft. TL: N40 17 00 W74 41 20. Box 342 08542. Secondary address: Box 108 08542. Phone: (609) 258-3655. Phone: (609) 258-3656. Fax: (609) 258-1806. E-mail: wprb@princeton.edu. Web Site: www.wprb.com. Licensee: Princeton Broadcasting Service Inc. Format: Class, jazz, progsv. Target aud: 13-60. Spec prog: Asian Indian 6 hrs wkly. ◆Spencer Salazer, gen mgr.

WTHK(FM)—See Trenton

WTTM(AM)— May 1999: 1680 khz; 10 kw-D, 1 kw-N. TL: N40 22 00 W74 44 38. (CP: COL Lindenwold. TL: N39 52 13 W75 01 38). 456 Middlesex Ave., Metuchen 08840. Phone: (732) 452-9533. Fax: (732) 452-9537. Web Site: www.ebcmusic.com. Licensee: Multicultural Radio Broadcasting Licensee LLC. Group owner: Multicultural Radio Broadcasting Inc. (acq 5-24-2002; grpsl). Format: South Asian ethnic. ◆Alka Agrawal, gen mgr.

Princeton Junction

*****WWPH(FM)**— November 1975: 107.9 mhz; 10 w. 36 ft. TL: N40 18 20 W74 37 16. West Windsor-Plainsboro High School, 346 Clarksville Rd. 08550-1518. Phone: (609) 716-5050. Phone: (609) 897-7360. Fax: (609) 716-5092. Fax: (609) 936-9226. E-mail: wwph@wwprsd.mercernet.net. Web Site: www.wwph1079.com. Licensee: West Windsor Plainsboro Regional Board of Education. Format: Var. Target aud: 14-30; West Windsor & Plainsboro residents interested in their community. ◆Glenn Allison, gen mgr.

Salem

WFAI(AM)—Licensed to Salem. See Wilmington DE

WJKS(FM)—See Canton

South Belmar

WRAT(FM)—See Point Pleasant

South Orange

*****WSOU(FM)**— Apr 14, 1948: 89.5 mhz; 2.4 kw. 370 ft. TL: N40 44 44 W74 14 50. Stereo. 400 S. Orange Ave. 07079. Phone: (973) 313-6110. Fax: (973) 275-2001. E-mail: wsou@shu.edu. Web Site: www.wsou.net. Licensee: Seton Hall University. Booth, Freret, Imlay & Tepper. Format: Morden rock. News: 7 hrs wkly. Target aud: 18-34. Spec prog: Sp one hr, Pol 2 hrs, Black 2 hrs, Ethnic 10 hrs, sports 10 hrs wkly. ◆Mark Maben, gen mgr; Frank Scafidi, chief of engrg.

Stirling

WKMB(AM)— February 1972: 1070 khz; 250 w-D. TL: N40 40 35 W74 28 36. 120 W. 7th, Suite 201, Plainfield 07060. Phone: (908) 822-1515. Fax: (908) 822-1927. E-mail: mprayer@harvestradio.com. Web Site: www.harvestradio.net. Licensee: World Harvest Communications Inc. (acq 1-15-03). Format: Christian. ◆Gary Kirkwood Sr., CEO & pres; Melissa Prayer, gen mgr; Robert Hunt, opns mgr.

Sussex

*****WNJP(FM)**— 1998: 88.5 mhz; 450 w. Ant 636 ft. TL: N41 08 37 W74 32 18. Box 777, Trenton 08625-0777. Phone: (609) 777-5036. Fax: (609) 777-5217. Web Site: www.njn.net. Licensee: New Jersey Public Broadcasting Authority. Network: Network: NPR, PRI. Schwartz, Woods & Miller. Format: News/talk. Target aud: General. ◆Elizabeth G. Christopherson, CEO; Bill Jobes, gen mgr; Pharoah Cranston, opns mgr.

Teaneck

*****WFDU(FM)**— Aug 30, 1971: 89.1 mhz; 550 w. 550 ft. TL: N40 57 39 W73 55 23. Stereo. 1000 River Rd. 07666. Phone: (201) 692-2806. Fax: (201) 692-2807. E-mail: barrys@fdu.edu. Web Site: www.wfdu.fm. Licensee: Fairleigh Dickinson University. Schwartz, Woods & Miller. Format: Americana, blues, gospel. News: 3 hrs wkly. Target aud: General. Spec prog: Progsv, folk 18 hrs, jazz 3 hrs, Sp 3 hrs, bluegrass 18 hrs, news/talk 6 hrs wkly. ◆Carl J. Kraus, gen mgr; Barry Sheffield, opns mgr.

Toms River

WOBM-FM— Mar 1, 1968: 92.7 mhz; 1.4 kw. 485 ft. TL: N39 52 30 W74 09 52. Stereo. Box 927 08754. Phone: (732) 269-0927. Fax: (732) 269-9292. Fax: (732) 269-8831. E-mail: wobm@wobm.com. Web site: www.wobm.com. Licensee: Millennium Shore Holdco LLC. Group owner: Millennium Radio Group LLC (acq 5-14-02; grpsl). William D. Silva. Format: Adult contemp. ◆William Saurer, gen mgr; Russ Del Core, gen sls mgr; Colin Coogan, prom dir & progmg dir; Tom Mongelli, news dir.

Trenton

WBUD(AM)— Jan 20, 1947: 1260 khz; 5 kw-D, 2.5 kw-N, DA-2. TL: N40 15 56 W74 45 27. Box 5698 08638. Secondary address: 109 Walters Ave. 08638. Phone: (609) 771-8181. Phone: (800) 678-9599. Fax: (609) 406-7956. Licensee: Millennium Central New Jersey License Holdco LLC. Group owner: Millennium Radio Group LLC (acq 12-21-01; grpsl). Rep: Christal. Irwin, Campbell, Crowe & Tannenwald. Format: MOR. News: 20 hrs wkly. Target aud: 35 plus. ◆Jim Donahoe, CEO; Andy Santoro, VP & gen mgr; Ray Handel, mktg dir; Lorenzo Caldara, adv dir; Eric Johnson, progmg dir; Eric Scott, news dir; Ray Fodge, engrg dir.

WKXW-FM—Co-owned with WBUD(AM). Aug 27, 1962: 101.5 mhz; 15.5 kw. Ant 902 ft. TL: N40 16 58 W74 41 11. Stereo. Web Site: www.nj1015.com. Rep: Christal. Format: Talk. News staff: 15; News: 75 hrs wkly. Target aud: General; New Jersey residents. ◆Eric Johnson, progmg dir.

WIMG(AM)—(Ewing). 1923: 1300 khz; 5 kw-D, 2.5 kw-N, DA-2. TL: N40 17 16 W74 52 23. Box 9078 08650. Secondary address: 1842 S. Broad St. 08610. Phone: (609) 695-1300. Fax: (609) 278-1588. E-mail: wimg1300@aol.com. Web Site: www.wimg1300.com. Licensee: Morris Broadcasting Co. of New Jersey Inc. (acq 12-3-93; 12-20-93). Network: Network: American Urban, NBC. Rep: Williams Radio Sales. Booth, Freret, Imlay & Tepper. Format: Urban adult contemp, gospel. News staff: News progmg 17 hrs wkly Target aud: 25-54. ◆Johnny Morris, CEO; Louise E. Morris, chmn; Michael Morris, pres; Maggie Guzzardo, exec VP & gen mgr; Felicia Brannon, opns VP; Pamela Pruitt, dev VP.

Broadcasting & Cable Yearbook 2006

New Jersey

WNJT-FM— May 20, 1991: 88.1 mhz; 110 w. Ant 689 ft. TL: N40 16 58 W74 41 11. Box 777 08625-0777. Phone: (609) 777-5036. Fax: (609) 777-5217. E-mail: pcrast@njn.org. Web Site: www.njn.net. Licensee: New Jersey Public Broadcasting Authority. Network: Network: NPR, PRI. Schwartz, Woods & Miller. Format: News/talk. Target aud: General. ♦Elizabeth G. Christopherson, CEO; Bill Jobes, gen mgr; Pharoah Cranston, opns mgr; Andre Butts, progmg dir.

WPHY(AM)— Apr 11, 1941: 920 khz; 1.4 kw-D, 1 kw-N, DA-2. TL: N40 15 19 W74 51 44. Stereo. 619 Alexander Rd., Princeton 08540-6003. Phone: (609) 924-1515. Fax: (609) 419-0147. Web Site: www.920espn.com. Licensee: Nassau Broadcasting II L.L.C. (group owner; acq 4-25-2002; with co-located FM). Network: ESPN Radio. Cohn & Marks. Format: Sports. ♦Josh Gertzog, sls dir; Tony Henry, prom dir; Tripp Rogers, gen mgr & progmg dir; Tim Anderson, news dir; Tony Gervasi, chief of engrg.

WPST(FM)— Co-owned with WPHY(AM). Aug 7, 1965: 94.5 mhz; 50 kw. Ant 492 ft. TL: N40 11 22 W74 50 47. Stereo. 619 Alexander Rd., Princeton 08540-6003. Phone: (609) 924-1515. Fax: (609) 419-0143. Web Site: www.wpst.com. Format: CHR. ♦Jim Spector, progmg dir; Randy Ellis, mus dir.

WTHK(FM)— Jan 19, 1949: 97.5 mhz; 50 kw. Ant 470 ft. TL: N40 14 05 W74 46 02. Stereo. 619 Alexander Rd., 3rd Floor, Princeton 08540. Phone: (609) 419-0300. Fax: (609) 419-0143. Web Site: www.975thehawk.com. Licensee: Nassau Broadcasting II L.L.C. Booth, Freret, Imlay & Tepper. Format: Classic rock. Target aud: 18-49. ♦Louis F. Mercatanti, CEO & chmn; Peter D. Tonks, CFO; Don Dalesio, exec VP; Michelle Stevens, VP & gen mgr; Dave McKay, opns dir & opns mgr; Josh Gertzog, sls dir.

*WTSR(FM)— September 1966: 91.3 mhz; 1.5 kw. 35 ft. TL: N40 16 17 W74 46 55. Stereo. The College of New Jersey, WTSR(FM), Box 7718, Ewing 08628-7718. Phone: (609) 771-3200. Phone: (609) 771-2554. Fax: (609) 637-5113. Web Site: www.wtsr.org. Licensee: The College of New Jersey Radio System. Network: UPI. Format: Progsv, alternative. News: 15 hrs wkly. Target aud: 13-40; people who listen to div mus formats. Spec prog: Gospel 6 hrs, pub affrs 8 hrs, folk 4 hrs, jazz 4 hrs, oldies 6 hrs wkly. ♦Megan Becky Baglivio, stn mgr.

*WWFM(FM)— Sept 6, 1982: 89.1 mhz; 1.15 kw. Ant 292 ft. TL: N40 15 30 W74 38 59. Stereo. Box B 08690. Phone: (609) 587-8989. Fax: (609) 586-4533. Web Site: www.wwfm.org. Licensee: Mercer County Community College Board of Trustees. Network: PRI. Format: Classical. Target aud: General. ♦Jeffery R. Sekerka, gen mgr & dev mgr.

Tuckerton

WBHX(FM)— 1999: 99.7 mhz; 5.3 kw. Ant 108 ft. TL: N39 33 41 W74 14 27. 703 Millcreek Rd., Manahawkin 08050. Phone: (609) 597-9497. Fax: (609) 597-0639. E-mail: 997thebreeze@997thebreeze.com. Web Site: www.997 thebreeze.com. Licensee: Press Communications L.L.C. (group owner; acq 9-18-02; $1.15 million). Format: Lite rock. ♦John Dziuba, gen mgr; Cindy Brennan, stn mgr.

Union Township

*WKNJ-FM— January 1980: 90.3 mhz; 8.7 w. 88 ft. TL: N40 40 35 W74 14 02. Stereo. Kean Univ., J 101 Hutchinson Hall, 1000 Morris Ave., Union 07083. Phone: (908) 737-3949. Fax: (908) 282-9793. E-mail: wknjfm@yahoo.com. Web Site: www. kean.edu/~cahss/acad_dept /comm/wknj/index/html. Licensee: Kean University. Format: New mus. Spec prog: Black 2 hrs, jazz 8 hrs, new age 8 hrs wkly. ♦Scott McHugh, gen mgr; Cathleen Londino, stn mgr.

Upper Montclair

*WMSC(FM)— Dec 9, 1974: 90.3 mhz; 10 w. 672 ft. TL: N40 51 53 W74 12 03. Stereo. Student Ctr. Annex, Montclair State College 07043. Phone: (973) 655-4257. Phone: (973) 655-4256. Fax: (973) 655-7433. Web Site: www.montclair.edu/org/wmsc. Licensee: Montclair State University. Format: Alternative. News: 5 hrs wkly. Target aud: Under 35. Spec prog: Black 4 hrs, gospel 3 hrs, jazz 2 hrs, Sp 2 hrs, sports 3 hrs wkly. ♦Johan Naranjo, gen mgr; Troy Pauuk, opns dir; Jacklyn Pedraza, prom dir; D.J. Haze, progmg dir; Shannon Billera, mus dir; Kruten Anderson, pub affrs dir.

Villas

WCZT(FM)— February 1992: 98.7 mhz; 3 kw. 292 ft. TL: N39 00 33 W74 52 13. 3208 Pacific Ave., Wildwoodk 08260. Phone: (609) 522-1987. Fax: (609) 522-3666. E-mail: wahls@987thecoast.com. Web Site: www.987thecoast.com. Licensee: WZK LLC (acq 5-21-01; $1.4 million. for stock). Format: Adult contemp. ♦Bob Maschio, gen mgr; Ed Rosenfeld, gen sls mgr; Scott Wahl, stn mgr & news dir; Ray Bradley, chief of engrg.

Vineland

WMIZ(AM)—Listing follows WVLT(FM).

WVLT(FM)— October 1968: 92.1 mhz; 3 kw. 328 ft. TL: N39 29 53 W75 04 31. Stereo. Box 689, 638 E. Landis Ave. 08360. Phone: (856) 692-8888. Fax: (856) 696-2568. Licensee: Clear Communications Inc. (acq 8-1-86; $400,000; 5-12-86). Network: ABC. Format: Adult contemp. Target aud: 25-54; baby boomers.

WMIZ(AM)— Co-owned with WVLT(FM). Aug 19, 1959: 1270 khz; 500 w-D, 350 w-N, DA-2. TL: N39 29 53 W75 04 31. (CP: 360 w-D, 210 w-N). Format: Sp. Target aud: Hispanic.

Washington Township

WNJC(AM)— July 29, 1946: 1360 khz; 5 kw-D, 800 w-N, DA-2. TL: N39 47 23 W75 06 11. 1374 Hwy. 41-47, Sewell 08080. Phone: (856) 227-1360. Fax: (856) 232-9093. Web Site: www.wnjc1360.com. Licensee: Forsyth Broadcasting Inc. (acq 1995; $161,000). Bechtel & Cole. Format: Talk, progsv, gospel. News staff: 3; News: 20 hrs wkly. Target aud: 30 plus; 52% women, upper income. Spec prog: Relg 6 hrs wkly. ♦John Forsythe, pres; Joan Venditti, gen mgr & progmg dir.

Wayne

*WPSC-FM— Nov 1, 1988: 88.7 mhz; 200 w. Ant 259 ft. TL: N40 59 46 W74 16 51. Stereo. Hobart Hall, 300 Pompton Rd. 07470. Phone: (973) 720-3319. Fax: (973) 720-2454. E-mail: wpsc887fm@wpunj.edu. Web Site: wpunj.edu/coac/communication/wpsc.htm. Licensee: William Paterson University of New Jersey. (acq 7-90; $1; 7-16-90). Network: Network: USA, ABC. Format: Alternative. Target aud: 18-35; independent thinking. Spec prog: Punk 3 hrs, hip hop 18 hrs, metal 18 hrs, classic rock 12 hrs, jazz 12 hrs wkly. ♦Ron Stotyn, gen mgr.

West Long Branch

*WMCX(FM)— May 2, 1974: 88.9 mhz; 1 kw. 118 ft. TL: N40 16 44 W74 00 26. Stereo. Monmouth Univ., Cedar & Norwood Ave. 07764. Phone: (732) 571-3482. Fax: (732) 263-5145. E-mail: wmcxradio@monmouth.edu. Web Site: www.monmouth.com. Licensee: Monmouth University. Network: AP Radio. Format: MOR. News: 2.5 hrs wkly. Target aud: 18-25; college students, recent grads, young adults. Spec prog: Sports 11 hrs, jazz 3 hrs, gospel 6 hrs wkly. ♦Frank Della Femina, gen mgr.

Wildwood

WCMC(AM)— Nov 25, 1951: 1230 khz; 1 kw-U. TL: N39 00 09 W74 48 46. 8025 Black Horse Pike, Suite 100-102, West Atlantic City 08232. Phone: (609) 484-8444 x317. Fax: (609) 646-6331. E-mail: gfequity@aol.com. Licensee: Equity Communications L.P. (group owner; (acq 11-4-97; $7.1 million. with co-located FM). Network: ABC. Rep: Katz Radio. Laitham & Watkins. Format: Adult standards. Target aud: Adults 35-64. ♦Gary Fisher, pres, VP & gen mgr; Keith Fader, sls dir & gen sls mgr; Jim MacMillan, progmg dir.

WZXL(FM)— Co-owned with WCMC(AM). Dec 17, 1959: 100.7 mhz; 38 kw. Ant 331 ft. TL: N39 07 28 W74 45 56. Stereo. 8025 Black Horse Pike, Suite 100-102, West Atlantic City 08232. Fax: (609) 646-6331. Web Site: www.wzxl.com. Network: Westwood One. Rep: Katz Radio. Laitham & Watkins. Format: Classic rock. Target aud: Adults 18-49. ♦Steve Raymond, progmg dir.

Wildwood Crest

WDTH(FM)— Aug 15, 1993: 93.1 mhz; 4.2 kw. Ant 216 ft. TL: N39 00 33 W74 52 13. Stereo. 8025 Black Horse Pike, Suite 100-102, West Atlantic City 08232. Phone: (609) 484-8444. Fax: (609) 646-6331. E-mail: gfequity@aol.com. Web Site: www.hitsandoldies.com. Licensee: Equity Communications L.P. (group owner; (acq 5-30-2003; grpsl). Network: Westwood One. Rep: Katz Radio. Laitham & Watkins. Format: Urban adult contemp. Target aud: 18-49; adults. Spec prog: . ♦Gary Fisher, sr VP, VP & gen mgr; Keith Fader, sls dir; Rob Fader, progmg dir.

Woodbine

*WJPH(FM)— Feb 16, 1999: 89.9 mhz; 1 kw. Ant 105 ft. TL: N39 16 51 W74 51 11. Box 603 08270-0603. Phone: (609) 861-3700. E-mail: letters@praise899.org. Web Site: www.praise899.org. Licensee: Maranatha Ministries/Joy Communications Inc. Booth, Freret, Imlay & Tepper. Format: Praise & worship. News: 10 hrs wkly. Target aud: 25-54; women. Spec prog: Gospel one hr wkly. ♦Kenneth Manri, pres.

Zarephath

WAWZ(FM)— Aug 22, 1954: 99.1 mhz; 28 kw. Ant 656 ft. TL: N40 36 41 W74 34 12. Stereo. Box 9058 08890. Phone: (732) 469-0991. Fax: (732) 469-2115. E-mail: info@star991fm.com. Web Site: www.star991fm.com. Licensee: Pillar of Fire Inc. (group owner) Format: Adult contemp, Christian. Target aud: 25-54. ♦Stacey Austin, prom dir; Ed Abels, adv dir; Johnny Stone, progmg dir; Ron Habegger, engrg dir & chief of engrg.

New Mexico

Alamo Community

*KABR(AM)— August 1983: 1500 khz; 1 kw-D. TL: N34 25 01 W107 30 04. Box 907, Magdalena 87825. Phone: (505) 854-2632. Phone: (505) 854-2641. Fax: (505) 854-2545. Web Site: www.alamo.bia.edu. Licensee: Alamo Navajo Community School. Format: Ethnic. Target aud: General; Native Americans, loc ranchers, tourists, teachers & health professionals. Spec prog: American Indian 10 hrs wkly. ♦James Apachito, pres; Sarah Apache, gen mgr & stn mgr.

Alamogordo

KINN(AM)— June 10, 1957: 1270 khz; 1 kw-D, 500 w-N. TL: N32 53 13 W105 57 04. Stereo. Box 1848 88311. Phone: (505) 434-1414. Fax: (505) 434-2213. Licensee: Burt Broadcasting Inc. (group owner; acq 4-1-01; with co-located FM). Network: ABC Information & Entertainment. Baraff, Koerner & Olender. Format: News/talk. News: 22 hrs wkly. Target aud: 24-50; military & civil service personnel employed in high-tech jobs. ♦William F. Burt, pres & gen mgr; Lori Swinford, gen sls mgr; James White, progmg dir & news dir; Ken Bass, engrg dir.

KZZX(FM)—Co-owned with KINN(AM). 1979: 105.5 mhz; 6 kw. 157 ft. TL: N32 53 13 W105 57 04. (CP: 105.3 mhz, 2.23 kw, ant 524 ft.). Stereo. Format: Country. News: 22 hrs wkly. Target aud: 20-55.

KKBO(FM)—Not on air, target date: unknown: 107.9 mhz; 6 kw. Ant 328 ft. TL: N33 01 42 W105 56 49. Box 1848 88311. Phone: (505) 434-1414. Licensee: Burt Broadcasting Inc. (group owner; acq 10-29-2003; $93,000. for CP). ♦William F. Burt, gen mgr.

KNMZ(FM)— 1997: 103.7 mhz; 47 kw. 1,338 ft. TL: N33 10 45 W105 53 53. Box 2710 88311. Secondary address: Cuba Ave. & Canyon Rd. 88310. Phone: (505) 437-1505. Fax: (505) 437-5566. E-mail: alamogordo@snmradio.com. Web Site: www.snmradio.com. Licensee: Linda S. Bloom, trustee for Runnels Broadcasting System LLC. Group owner: Runnels Broadcasting System L.L.C. (acq 9-19-2002; grpsl). Format: Classic rock. ♦Philip Runnels, gen mgr; Sherry Runnels, gen mgr.

KRSY(AM)— June 28, 1950: 1230 khz; 1 kw-U. TL: N32 53 46 W105 56 42. Box 2710, Cuba Ave. & Canyon Rd. 88311. Phone: (505) 437-1505. Phone: (505) 437-1230. Fax: (505) 437-5566. Web Site: www.snmradio.com. Licensee: Linda S. Bloom, trustee for Runnels Broadcasting System LLC. Group owner: Runnels Broadcasting System L.L.C. (acq 9-19-2002; grpsl). Jones, Waldo, Holbrook & McDonough; Barry Wood. Format: Talk, sports. News staff: 2; News: 10 hrs wkly. Target aud: 25-54; active adults, community-oriented. Spec prog: Big band 6 hrs, farm one hr, gospel 8 hrs, relg 4 hrs wkly. ♦Phil Reynolds, gen mgr; Les Hanks, gen sls mgr; Kelly Lynch, progmg dir; Jim Huff, chief of engrg.

KRSY-FM— Jan 17, 1987: 92.7 mhz; 3 kw. 192 ft. TL: N32 98 15 W105 59 21. (CP: 103.7 mhz, 50.2 kw, ant 1,338 ft. TL: N33 10 45 W105 53 53). Stereo. Phone: (505) 437-1063. Web Site: www.snmradio.com. Format: Hot country. News staff: 2; News: 2 hrs wkly. Target aud: 18-34; active adults, young adults. ♦Les Henke, natl sls mgr; Kelly Lynch, progmg mgr; Jim Huff, engrg dir.

Developers & Brokers of Radio Properties
contact American Media Services
at our suite:
Philadelphia Marriott Downtown
215-625-2900
843-972-2200
americanmediaservices.com
Charleston, SC
Dallas, TX - Chicago, Il - Austin, TX
American Media Services, LLC

***KUPR(FM)**— Oct 14, 2000: 91.7 mhz; 100 w. Ant 1,683 ft. TL: N32 49 47 W105 53 10. Stereo. 1510 N. White Sands Blvd. 88310. Secondary address: 3001 N. Florida Ave. 88310. Phone: (505) 437-0917. Fax: (505) 434-6060. E-mail: kupr@yahoo.com. Licensee: Southern New Mexico Radio Foundation. Wood, Maines & Brown. Format: Sp, country Gospel. News: 4 hrs wkly. Target aud: 25-60; adults. ♦Bob Flotte, pres; Will Sims, VP; T.J. Curry, opns dir; Mark Swalley, progmg.

KYEE(FM)— July 21, 1980: 94.3 mhz; 3 kw. -492 ft. TL: N32 56 42 W105 56 47. Stereo. Box 1848 88310. Phone: (505) 434-1414. Fax: (505) 434-2213. E-mail: 94key@totacc.com. Web Site: www.sos.state.nm.us/radio.htm. Licensee: Burt Broadcasting Inc. (group owner; acq 11-88; $230,000;. FTR: 12-19-88). Format: CHR. Target aud: 18-44; young adults. ♦Donnie L. Burt, VP; William F. Burt, pres & gen mgr; Lori Swinford, gen sls mgr & adv dir.

Albuquerque

KABQ(AM)— 1947: 1350 khz; 5 kw-D, 500 w-N, DA-N. TL: N35 06 02 W106 40 34. 5411 Jefferson N.E. 87109. Phone: (505) 338-7400. Fax: (505) 830-6599. Licensee: Clear Channel Broadcasting Licenses. Group owner: Clear Channel Communications Inc. (acq 3-01-00; grpsl). Rep: Lotus Entravision Reps LLC. Format: Sports. Target aud: General. ♦Chuck Hammond, CEO & pres; Barry Shainman, gen sls mgr; Bill May, progmg dir & news dir; Michael Creager, chief of engrg.

KAJZ(FM)—See Rio Rancho

KALY(AM)—(Los Ranchos de Albuquerque). 1982: 1240 khz; 1 kw-U. TL: N35 12 06 W106 35 56. Stereo. 2505 6th St. N.W. 87102. Phone: (505) 244-1100. Fax: (505) 244-0612. Web Site: www.radiodisney.com. Licensee: Radio Disney Group LLC. Group owner: ABC Inc. (acq 2-21-03; $650,000). Format: Children. Target aud: 25-49. ♦Doris Budris, gen mgr.

***KANW(FM)**— October 1950: 89.1 mhz; 20 kw. 4,152 ft. TL: N35 12 44 W106 26 57. Stereo. 2020 Coal Ave. S.E. 87106. Phone: (505) 242-7163. Phone: (505) 242-7848. Licensee: Board of Education of the City of Albuquerque. Network: Network: NPR, PRI. Format: Sp. ♦Michael Brasher, gen mgr.

KBQI(FM)— Apr 27, 1979: 107.9 mhz; 22.5 kw. 4,130 ft. TL: N35 12 43 W106 26 57. Stereo. 2700 San Pedro Dr. N.E. 87110. Phone: (505) 830-6400. Fax: (505) 830-6543. Licensee: Citicasters Licenses L.P. Group owner: Clear Channel Communications Inc. (acq 9-28-99; grpsl). Format: Country. Target aud: 18-49. ♦Chuck Hammond, gen mgr; Bill May, chief of opns & progmg dir; Bruce Pollock, gen sls mgr; Skip Isley, prom dir; Nick Manhattan, progmg dir.

KBZU(FM)— November 1954: 96.3 mhz; 20 kw. 4,110 ft. TL: N35 12 44 W106 26 58. Stereo. 500 4th St. N.W., 5th Fl. 87102. Phone: (505) 767-6700. Fax: (505) 767-6767. Licensee: Citadel Broadcasting Co. Group owner: Citadel Broadcasting Corp. (acq 1996; $5.725 million. with KTBL(AM) Los Ranchos de Albuquerque). Rep: McGavren Guild. Kaye, Scholer, Fierman, Hays & Handler. Format: Classic rock. News: 2 hrs wkly. Upscale affluent professionals. ♦Scott Souhrada, opns dir; Tim Gannon, gen sls mgr & natl sls mgr; Slade Carlson, mktg dir, prom dir & prom mgr; John Richards, progmg dir; Paul Bailey, mus dir; Art Ortega, pub affrs dir; Bill Harris, engrg dir.

KDAZ(AM)— 1959: 730 khz; 1 kw-D, 76 w-N, DA-2. TL: N35 00 31 W106 42 52. Box 4338 87196. Secondary address: 5010 4th St. N.W. 87107. Phone: (505) 345-7373. Fax: (505) 345-5669. E-mail: kdaz@kdaz.org. Web Site: www.kdaz.org. Licensee: Pan American Broadcasting Inc. (acq 11-17-2003). Network: USA. Gammon & Grange. Format: Variety. Target aud: 25-54; three cultures-Indian, Hispanic, Anglo. ♦Belarmint Gonzalez, CEO, chmn & pres; Vickie Archiveque, CFO; Annette Garcia, VP & gen mgr; Jim Sandell, progmg dir.

KDEF(AM)— September 1953: 1150 khz; 5 kw-D, 500 w-N, DA-2. TL: N35 12 06 W106 35 54. 10424 Edith N.E. 87113. Phone: (505) 888-1150. Fax: (505) 899-1977. Licensee: RAMH Corp. (acq 7-95; $125,000). Format: Sports. Target aud: General. ♦Henry Tafoya, gen mgr.

KDRF(FM)— Apr 20, 1988: 103.3 mhz; 22 kw. 4,069 ft. TL: N35 12 50 W106 27 00. Stereo. Citadel Southwest, 500 4th St. N.W., 5th Fl. 87102. Phone: (505) 767-6700. Fax: (505) 767-6767. E-mail: ktzo@citcomm.com. Web Site: www.103.3thezone.com. Licensee: Citadel Broadcasting Co. Group owner: Citadel Broadcasting Corp. (acq 1996; $5 million). Rep: Christal. Format: Adult alternative. Target aud: 18-49. ♦Linda Rosenberg, gen sls mgr.

***KFLQ(FM)**— Feb 20, 1983: 91.5 mhz; 22.5 kw. 4,060 ft. TL: N35 12 51 W106 27 02. Stereo. 3801 Eubank N.E. 87111. Phone: (505) 296-9100. Fax: (505) 296-6262. E-mail: flrradio@flc.org. Web Site: www.flc.org/flc/kflq. Licensee: Family Life Broadcasting System. Group owner: Family Life Communications Inc. (acq 1982). Network: Network: Moody, USA. Format: Inspirational, praise & worship. News: 3 hrs wkly. Target aud: 35-54; female. Spec prog: Sp 3 hrs wkly. ♦Randy Carlson, pres; Dan Rosecrans, stn mgr.

KJFA(FM)— October 1994: 101.3 mhz; 3.7 kw. Ant 420 ft. TL: N35 04 06 W106 46 46. 8009 Marble N.E. 87110. Phone: (505) 260-4400. Fax: (505) 262-9211. Web Site: www.netmio.com. Licensee: Univision Radio License Corp. Group owner: Univision Radio (acq 9-22-2003; grpsl). Format: Mexican rgnl. Target aud: 35-54. ♦Chuck Morgan, gen mgr; Jim Ray, gen mgr.

KKIM(AM)— Apr 15, 1972: 1000 khz; 10 kw-D. TL: N35 10 14 W106 37 51. Box 30925 87190-0925. Secondary address: 4125 Carlisle Blvd. N.E. 87107-4806. Phone: (505) 878-0980. Fax: (505) 878-0098. Licensee: AGM-Nevada L.L.C. Group owner: American General Media (acq 12-22-97; grpsl). Format: Christian, talk. Target aud: 25-54. Spec prog: Black 2 hrs wkly. ♦Scott Hutton, gen mgr.

KKJY(AM)— Feb 22, 1971: 1550 khz; 5 kw-D, 20 w-N. TL: N35 06 02 W106 40 34. 307 Los Ranchos Rd. N.W. 87107. Phone: (505) 899-5029. Fax: (505) 899-6865. Web Site: www.joyam.com. Licensee: Vanguard Media L.L.C. (acq 1-21-2000; $112,000). Format: Adult standards. News: 5 hrs wkly. Target aud: 35-64; Mature upscale adults. ♦Don Davis, CEO, pres & gen mgr; Josie Bunch, stn mgr; Crystal Felice, rgnl sls mgr & mktg mgr; Berit Koltveit, progmg dir.

KKOB(AM)— Apr 5, 1922: 770 khz; 50 kw-U, DA-N. TL: N35 12 09 W106 36 41. 500 4th St. N.W. 87102. Phone: (505) 767-6700. Fax: (505) 767-6767. E-mail: kkobam@citcomm.com. Web Site: www.770kkob.com. Licensee: Citadel Broadcasting Co. Group owner: Citadel Broadcasting Corp. (acq 3-15-94; $7.8 million. with co-located FM; FTR: 4-11-94). Network: ABC Information & Entertainment. Rep: McGavren Guild. Haley, Bader & Potts. Format: News/talk. ♦Milt McConnell, gen mgr & stn mgr; Pat Frisch, opns mgr; Tim Gannon, gen sls mgr; Alison Atwood, prom dir; Kris Abrams, progmg dir; Alex Cuellar, news dir; Bill Harris, chief of engrg.

KKOB-FM— Aug 1, 1967: 93.3 mhz; 21.5 kw. 4,150 ft. TL: N35 12 42 W106 26 59. Stereo. Format: Adult contemp. ♦Milt McConnell, gen mgr; Kris Abrans, opns dir & opns mgr; Tim Gannon, sls VP & rgnl sls mgr; Mark Anderson, mktg dir; Kris Abrams, progmg dir.

***KLYT(FM)**— Sept 11, 1976: 88.3 mhz; 4.1 kw. Ant 4,244 ft. TL: N35 12 49 W106 27 01. Stereo. 4001 Osunda Rd. N.E. 87109. Phone: (505) 344-9146. Fax: (505) 344-9193. Web Site: www.m88.org. Licensee: Connection Communications Association Inc. (acq 11-30-2000). Format: Contemp Christian hits. ♦Chip Lusko, VP & gen mgr; Kenny Grebe, gen sls mgr.

KMGA(FM)—Listing follows KTBL(AM).

KNML(AM)— Mar 28, 1928: 610 khz; 5 kw-U, DA-N. TL: N35 01 56 W106 39 48. 500 4th St. N.W., 5th Flr. 87102. Phone: (505) 767-6700. Fax: (505) 767-6767. E-mail: knml@citcomm.com. Web Site: www.610thesportsanimal.com. Licensee: Citadel Broadcasting Co. Group owner: Citadel Broadcasting Corp. (acq 3-23-00; swap with KSVA(AM) Albuquerque). Format: All sports. Target aud: 25-54. ♦Milt McConnell, gen mgr; Pat Frisch, opns dir.

KPEK(FM)— December 1974: 100.3 mhz; 22.5 kw. 4,110 ft. TL: N35 12 51 W106 27 02. Stereo. 5411 Jefferson N.E., Suite A100 87109. Phone: (505) 830-6400. Fax: (505) 830-6506. Web Site: www.1003thepeak.com. Licensee: Citicasters Licenses L.P. Group owner: Clear Channel Communications Inc. (acq 9-28-99; grpsl). Rep: Allied Radio Partners. Format: Modern adult contemp. Target aud: 25-54; adults, high income professional and technical. ♦Chuck Hammond, gen mgr; Bill May, chief of opns.

KRKE(AM)— May 14, 1956: 1600 khz; 10 kw-D, 128 w-N. TL: N35 10 14 W106 37 51. 14018 Bonito Svenos N.W. 87107. Phone: (505) 269-8463. Fax: (505) 345-6891. E-mail: kbtkpd@thuntek.net. Licensee: Vanguard Media LLC (acq 12-15-2004; $650,000). Network: CNN Radio. Rep: Christal. Format: Oldies. Target aud: 30-50. ♦Bruce Pollack, gen mgr; Doris Budris, prom dir; Dave Scott, progmg dir.

KRST(FM)— Sept 15, 1965: 92.3 mhz; 22.5 kw. 4,110 ft. TL: N35 12 55 W106 27 02. Stereo. 5th Fl., 500 4th St. N.W. 87102. Phone: (505) 767-6700. Fax: (505) 767-6767. Licensee: Citadel Broadcasting Co. Group owner: Citadel Broadcasting Corp. (acq 9-30-96; grpsl). Format: Hot new country. ♦Milt McConnell, gen mgr; John Richards, opns mgr; Joe Biondi, gen sls mgr & natl sls mgr; Brian Gutierrez, prom dir; Scott Southrada, progmg dir; Paul Bailey, mus dir & asst music dir; Art Ortega, pub affrs dir; Bill Harris, engrg dir & chief of engrg.

KRZY(AM)— June 1956: 1450 khz; 1 kw-U. TL: N35 06 26 W106 35 20. (CP: 1090 khz, 50 kw-LS, DA-2). Stereo. 3451 Candelaria Rd. N.E. 87107. Phone: (505) 342-4141. Fax: (505) 344-8714. E-mail: mwilder@entravision.com. Web Site: www.entravision.com. Licensee: Entravision Holdings LLC. Group owner: Entravision Communications Corp. (acq 3-14-00; grpsl). Format: Sp/rgnl Mexican. ♦Jeff Liberman, pres; Margarita Wilder, gen mgr & gen sls mgr; Fernando del Valle, prom mgr; Manuel Sepulveda, progmg dir.

KSVA(AM)— Mar 28, 1928: 920 khz; 1 kw-D, 130 w-N. TL: N35 07 56 W106 37 18. Box 2378, Corrales 87048. Phone: (505) 890-0800. Phone: (866) 578-2920. Fax: (505) 890-0808. E-mail: ksva@lobo.net. Web Site: www.lifetalk.net. Licensee: Lifetalk Broadcasting Association. (acq 04-07-00; swap with KNML(AM) Albuquerque). Network: AP Radio. Format: Inspirational Christian. News: 2 hrs wkly. Target aud: 35 plus; Christians. Spec prog: Sp 4 hrs wkly. ♦Phil Folett, CEO; Ricardo Barratta, stn mgr; Clare Gallimore, dev dir; Jeremy Woodruff, progmg dir; Elvin Vence, chief of engrg.

KTBL(AM)—(Los Ranchos de Albuquerque). Dec 16, 1987: 1050 khz; 1 kw-D, 500 w-N, DA-1. TL: N34 58 46 W106 44 13. 500 4th St. N.W. 87102. Phone: (505) 767-6700. Fax: (505) 767-6767. Web Site: www.1050kbull.com. Licensee: Citadel Broadcasting Co. Group owner: Citadel Broadcasting Corp. (acq 6-28-96; $5.725 million. with KBZU(FM) Albuquerque). Format: News/talk. Target aud: 25-54. ♦Milt McConnell, gen mgr; Blake Mendenhall, rgnl sls mgr; Glenn Herbert, mktg dir & prom dir; Pat Frisch, opns dir & progmg dir; Art Ortega, pub affrs dir; Bill Harris, chief of engrg.

KMGA(FM)—Co-owned with KTBL(AM). Nov 11, 1963: 99.5 mhz; 19.5 kw. 4,134 ft. TL: N35 12 44 W106 26 58. Stereo. E-mail: kmga@citconm.com. Web Site: www.99.5magicfm.com. Rep: McGavren Guild. Format: Light contemp. Target aud: 25-54; upscale, business professionals & families. ♦Kim Gannon, gen sls mgr; Kris Abrams, progmg dir.

***KUNM(FM)**— Oct 17, 1966: 89.9 mhz; 13.6 kw. 4,070 ft. TL: N35 12 44 W106 26 57. Stereo. MSC06 3520, Univ. of New Mexico 87131-0001. Phone: (505) 277-4806. Fax: (505) 277-8004. E-mail: kunm@kunm.org. Web Site: www.kunm.org. Licensee: Regents of the University of New Mexico. Network: Network: NPR, PRI. Dow, Lohnes & Albertson. Format: Div, news/talk. News staff: 3; News: 50 hrs wkly. Target aud: 25-54; those who enjoy NPR and diverse community-produced programs. Spec prog: Class 12 hrs, Sp 9 hrs, Indian 9 hrs, folk 5 hrs, reggae 3 hrs wkly. ♦Richard Towne, gen mgr; Mary Bokuniewicz, dev dir.

KXKS(AM)— Dec 16, 1969: . Stn currently dark 1190 khz; 10 kw-D. TL: N35 03 04 W106 38 34. Stereo. Wilkins Communications Network Inc., Box 444, Spartanburg, SC 29304. Phone: (864) 585-1885. Fax:

Broadcasting & Cable Yearbook 2006

D-335

New Mexico

(864) 597-0687. Licensee: Wild West Radio Corp. (group owner; (acq 10-20-2004; $775,000). ♦ Robert L. Wilkins, pres.

KZRR(FM)— June 25, 1961: 94.1 mhz; 100 kw. 4,130 ft. TL: N35 12 44 W106 26 58. Stereo. 2700 San Pedro N.E. 87110. Phone: (505) 830-6400. Fax: (505) 830-6543. Web Site: www.94rock.com. Licensee: Clear Channel Broadcasting Licenses Inc. Group owner: Clear Channel Communications Inc. (acq 9-28-99; grpsl). Network: Westwood One. Format: AOR. ♦ Chuck Hammond, gen mgr; Bill May, chief of opns.

Angel Fire

KKIT(FM)— Jan 15, 1990: 99.1 mhz; 5.74 kw. 1,377 ft. TL: N36 22 33 W105 14 12. Stereo. Box 1914, Taos 87571. Secondary address: 1128-A Paseo del Pueblo Sur, Taos, ID 87571. Phone: (505) 758-4491. Phone: (877) 737-KKIT. Fax: (505) 758-4452. E-mail: daniel@kkit.com. Web Site: www.kkit.com. Licensee: DMC Broadcasting Inc. (acq 3-19-2003; $645,000. with KXMT(FM) Taos). Haley, Bader & Potts. Format: Classic rock. News staff: one; News: 7 hrs wkly. Target aud: Adults 25-54; middle-, upper-income residents & tourists. Spec prog: Jazz 4 hrs, relg 8 hrs wkly. ♦ Darin Cordova, pres & gen mgr.

Armijo

KNKT(FM)— Dec 17, 1991: 107.1 mhz; 50 kw. 304 ft. TL: N35 03 15 W106 51 31. (CP: 60 kw, 2,365 ft.). Stereo. 4001 Osuna Rd. N.E., Albuquerque 87109. Secondary address: Box 95707, Albuquerque 87109. Phone: (505) 344-9146. Fax: (505) 344-9193. E-mail: knkt@calvaryabq.org. Web Site: www.calvaryabq.org. Licensee: Calvary Chapel of Albuquerque Inc. (acq 9-29-94; $800,000 with KDEF(AM) Albuquerque; 11-21-94). Format: Praise, worship, Bible teaching. News: 4 hrs wkly. Target aud: 25-54. ♦ Chip Lusko, gen mgr; Kenny Grebe, gen sls mgr.

Artesia

KSVP(AM)— Nov 14, 1946: 990 khz; 1 kw-D, 250 w-N. TL: N32 49 29 W104 23 59. 317 W. Quay 88210. Phone: (505) 746-2751. Fax: (505) 748-3748. E-mail: info@ksvpradio.com. Web Site: www.ksvpradio.com. Licensee: Pecos Valley Broadcasting Co. (acq 1993; $150,000 with co-located FM; 9-13-93). Network: CBS. Cohn & Marks. Format: Talk. News staff: one; News: 18 hrs wkly. Target aud: General. ♦ Gene Dow, gen mgr, gen sls mgr & chief of engrg.

KTZA(FM)—Co-owned with KSVP(AM). May 9, 1969: 92.9 mhz; 100 kw. 1,089 ft. TL: N32 47 39 W104 12 27. Stereo. 121 S. Canal St., Suite C, Carlsbad 88220. E-mail: info@kz93.com. Web Site: www.kz93.com. Network: ABC. Format: Country. News: 3 hrs wkly. Target aud: 25-54. ♦ Gene Dow, VP.

Aztec

KCQL(AM)— Sept 4, 1959: 1340 khz; 1 kw-U. TL: N36 49 17 W107 59 58. Stereo. Box 6030, Farmington 87499. Phone: (505) 325-1716. Fax: (505) 325-6797. Web Site: www.foxsports1340.com. Licensee: Capstar TX L.P. Group owner: Clear Channel Communications Inc. (acq 8-30-00; grpsl). Format: Sports. News: 14 hrs wkly. Target aud: 18-54. Spec prog: Sp 6 hrs wkly. ♦ Bill Kruger, gen mgr; Dan Kelley, opns dir.

KWYK-FM— Jan 2, 1978: 94.9 mhz; 100 kw. Ant 433 ft. TL: N32 47 39 W104 12 27. Stereo. 1515 W. Main, Farmington 87401. Phone: (505) 325-1996. Fax: (505) 327-2019. Licensee: Basin Broadcasting Co. Format: Adult contemp. News: 15 hrs wkly. Target aud: 25-54; mainstream population. Spec prog: Jazz 3 hrs wkly. ♦ Jim Gober, gen mgr; Kevin Taylor, progmg dir; Jim Burk, chief of engrg.

Bayard

KNFT(AM)— July 4, 1968: 950 khz; 5 kw-D. TL: N32 46 51 W108 11 58. Box 1320, Silver City 88062. Secondary address: 5 Racetrack Rd., Silver City 88061. Phone: (505) 388-1958. Fax: (505) 388-5000. Web Site: www.gilanet.com. Licensee: Linda S. Bloom, trustee for Runnels Broadcasting System LLC. Group owner: Runnels Broadcasting System L.L.C. (acq 9-19-2002; grpsl). Format: Talk, sports. ♦ Matthew Runnell, pres, gen mgr, gen sls mgr & progmg dir; Rita Niccum, chief of engrg.

KNFT-FM— June 15, 1981: 102.9 mhz; 3 kw. 135 ft. TL: N32 50 40 W108 14 18. (CP: 29.14 kw, ant 491 ft.). Web Site: www.gilanet.com. Format: C&W.

Belen

KARS(AM)— Oct 7, 1961: 860 khz; 1.3 kw-D, 186 w-N. TL: N34 41 43 W106 46 13. Stereo. Box 860, 208 N. 2nd St. 87002. Phone: (505) 864-3024. Fax: (505) 864-2719. Licensee: AGM-Nevada L.L.C. Group owner: American General Media (acq 12-22-97; grpsl). Network: ABC Information & Entertainment. Rep: Lotus Entravision Reps LLC. Format: Country. News staff: one; News: 30 hrs wkly. Target aud: 25 plus. Spec prog: Relg. ♦ Scott Hutton, gen mgr; Ron Ortega, stn mgr & gen sls mgr; Ron Travis, mus dir & news dir; Bob Picknell, chief of engrg.

KLVO(FM)—Co-owned with KARS(AM). 1982: 97.7 mhz; 100 kw. 859 ft. TL: N34 47 55 W106 48 59. Stereo. 4125 Carlisle NE, Albuquerque 87107. Phone: (505) 878-0980. Fax: (505) 878-0098. Web Site: www.agmradio.com. Licensee: AGM-Nevada L.L.C. Format: Sp.

*****KVLK(FM)**— 2004: 90.9 mhz; 46 kw. Ant 1,899 ft. TL: N34 04 17 W106 57 45. 5700 W. Oaks Blvd., Rocklin 95765. Phone: (916) 251-1600. Phone: (800) 525-5683. Fax: (916) 251-1650. Web Site: www.klove.com. Licensee: Educational Media Foundation. Group owner: EMF Broadcasting. Format: Christian. ♦ Richard Jenkins, pres.

Bloomfield

KKFG(FM)— 1988: 104.5 mhz; 100 kw. 1,086 ft. TL: N36 38 33 W107 46 54. Stereo. 200 E. Broadway, Farmington 87401. Phone: (505) 325-1716. Fax: (505) 325-6797. Web Site: www.kool1045.com. Licensee: Capstar TX L.P. Group owner: Clear Channel Communications Inc. (acq 8-30-00; grpsl). Format: Oldies. ♦ Bill Kruger, gen mgr.

Bosque Farms

*****KQLV(FM)**— Nov 16, 2001: 105.5 mhz; 22 kw. Ant 745 ft. TL: N34 47 55 W106 48 59. Stereo. 5700 W. Oaks Blvd., Rocklin, CA 95765. Phone: (916) 251-1600. Fax: (916) 251-1650. E-mail: klove@klove.com. Web Site: www.klove.com. Licensee: Educational Media Foundation. Group owner: EMF Broadcasting. Network: K-Love. Shaw Pittman. Format: Contemp Christian mus. News staff: 3. Target aud: 25-44; Judeo-Christian, female. ♦ Richard Jenkins, pres; Mike Novak, VP & progmg dir; Lloyd Parker, gen mgr; Ed Lenane, opns dir & news dir; Keith Whipple, dev dir; Eric Allen, natl sls mgr; Russ Lloyd, rgnl sls mgr; Chris Joyce, prom dir & prom mgr; David Pierce, progmg mgr & mus dir; Jon Rivers, mus dir; Sam Wallington, engrg dir.

KTEG(FM)— July 1, 1987: 104.7 mhz; 100 kw. 1,822 ft. TL: N34 47 55 W106 48 59. (CP: Ant 843 ft. TL: N34 46 12 W106 51 42). Stereo. 5411 Jefferson N.E., Suite A100, Albuquerque 87109. Phone: (505) 830-6400. Fax: (505) 830-6506. Web Site: www.1047edgeradio.com. Licensee: Clear Channel Broadcasting Licenses Inc. group owner: Clear Channel Communication Inc. Format: Alternative. ♦ Bill May, pres & chief of opns; Chuck Hammond, gen mgr.

Cannon AFB

*****KKCJ(FM)**—Not on air, target date: unknown: 90.7 mhz; 10 kw. Ant 341 ft. TL: N34 38 04 W103 33 25. CSN International, 3232 W. MacArthur Blvd., Santa Ana, CA 92704. Phone: (714) 825-9663. Fax: (714) 825-9661. Licensee: CSN International (group owner).

Carlsbad

KAMQ(AM)— June 10, 1938: 1240 khz; 1 kw-U. TL: N32 23 43 W104 14 48. Box 1538 88220. Secondary address: 1609 Radio Blvd. 88220. Phone: (505) 887-5323. Fax: (505) 887-7000. Fax: (505) 887-7000. Licensee: KAMQ Inc. (acq 1-21-76). Format: Adult contemp, Christian. ♦ Don Hughes, gen mgr & gen sls mgr; Reginald James, progmg dir; Frank Nymeyer, chief of engrg.

KCDY(FM)—Co-owned with KAMQ(AM). July 1989: 104.1 mhz; 100 kw. 676 ft. TL: N32 34 22 W104 05 32. Box 1538 88220. Secondary address: 1609 Radio Blvd. Phone: (505) 887-7563. Fax: (505) 887-7000. Format: Adult contemp. ♦ Steve Sparks, progmg dir & progmg mgr.

KATK(AM)— May 17, 1950: 740 khz; 1 kw-D, 500 w-N. TL: N32 27 02 W104 12 47. 1609 Radio Blvd. 88220. Phone: (505) 887-7563. Fax: (505) 887-7000. E-mail: katk@pccnm.com. Web Site: www.katkradio.com. Licensee: Stubbs Broadcasting Co. Inc. (acq 3-31-00; $475,000 with co-located FM). Network: ABC Information & Entertainment. Reddy, Begley & McCormick. Format: Adult standards. News: 70 hrs wkly. Target aud: 50 plus; bilingual Hispanics. Spec prog: Gospel 2 hrs wkly. ♦ Don Hughes, gen mgr & gen sls mgr; Reginald James, progmg dir; Frank Nymeyer, chief of engrg.

KATK-FM— Sept 15, 1966: 92.1 mhz; 3 kw. 190 ft. TL: N32 27 02 W104 12 47. Stereo. Web Site: www.katkradio.com. Format: Country. News: 70 hrs wkly. Target aud: 18-54. Spec prog: Hispanic.

KCCC(AM)— July 1, 1966: 930 khz; 1 kw-D, 60 w-N. TL: N32 24 20 W104 11 21. 930 N. Canal 88220. Phone: (505) 887-5521. Fax: (505) 885-5481. Licensee: Compass Enterprises Inc. (acq 8-14-95). Format: Oldies. ♦ Nick Jenkins, pres, gen sls mgr & prom dir; Michelle McCutcheon, opns mgr & progmg dir; Phil Tozier, news dir; Frank Nymeyer, engrg mgr & chief of engrg.

KPZE-FM— 2000: 106.1 mhz; 39 kw. Ant 558 ft. TL: N32 34 22 W104 05 32. Box 1320, Silver City 88062. Secondary address: 5 Racetrack Rd., Silver City 88061. Phone: (505) 388-1958. Fax: (505) 388-5000. Licensee: Linda S. Bloom, trustee for Runnels Broadcasting System LLC. Group owner: Runnels Broadcasting System L.L.C. (acq 9-19-2002; grpsl). Format: Contemp Hispanic. ♦ Matt Runnels, gen mgr.

Chama

KZRM(FM)— Oct 8, 1999: 95.9 mhz; 1 kw. Ant 312 ft. TL: N36 53 58 W106 36 07. Box 307 87520. Phone: (505) 756-1617. Fax: (505) 756-1317. Web Site: www.kzrmradio.com. Licensee: Lance Broadcasting LLC (acq 5-3-2004; $220,000). Format: Classic rock. ♦ Gwen Williams, gen mgr.

Clayton

KLMX(AM)— Nov 10, 1949: 1450 khz; 1 kw-U. TL: N36 26 39 W103 11 24. Box 547, Union County Fairgrounds 88415. Phone: (505) 374-2555. Fax: (505) 374-2557. Licensee: Johnson County Broadcasters Inc. (acq 11-10-78). Format: Country. Spec prog: Sp 2 hrs wkly. ♦ Avis Green Tucker, pres; Jim McCollum, VP; Janet Dillon, gen mgr & gen sls mgr; Paula V. Maestas-Ballew, progmg dir & news dir; Henry Walker, chief of engrg.

Cloudcroft

*****KHII(FM)**— 2004: 88.9 mhz; 100 w. Ant 1,187 ft. TL: N32 59 48 W105 42 38. Stereo. 1510 N. White Sands Blvd., Alamogordo 88310. Phone: (505) 437-0917. Fax: (505) 434-6060. Licensee: Southern New Mexico Radio Foundation. Format: All Gospel music formats. ♦ Bob Flotte, pres; Will Sims, VP.

KNMB(FM)—Not on air, target date: unknown: 96.7 mhz; 25 kw. 2,880 ft. Box 2010, Ruidoso Downs 88346. Phone: (505) 258-9922. Fax: (505) 258-2363. Licensee: MTD Inc. (group owner) Format: Class. ♦ Tim Keithley, gen mgr.

Clovis

*****KAQF(FM)**— March 1998: 91.1 mhz; 1 kw. 174 ft. TL: N34 24 05 W103 12 12. Box 3206, American Family Radio, Tupelo, MS 38803. Phone: (662) 844-8888. Fax: (662) 842-6791. Licensee: American Family Association. Group owner: American Family Radio Format: Inspirational Christian. ♦ Marvin Sanders, gen mgr.

KCLV(AM)— February 1953: 1240 khz; 1 kw-U. TL: N34 22 40 W103 12 17. Box 1907 88102-1907. Secondary address: 2112 Thornton 88101. Phone: (505) 763-4401. Fax: (505) 769-2564. Licensee: Zia Broadcasting Co. (acq 7-1-71). Format: ESPN sports. ♦ Lonnie D. Allsup, pres; Randy Moore, gen sls mgr; Roy N. Teeters, gen mgr, prom mgr, progmg dir & news dir; Gary Jackson, chief of engrg.

KCLV-FM— Jan 8, 1970: 99.1 mhz; 74.2 kw. 230 ft. TL: N34 23 18 W103 11 07. Stereo. (Acq 11-12-81). Network: ABC Information & Entertainment. Format: Country. Target aud: 18-49. ♦ Randolph Moore, sls VP.

KICA(AM)— 1933: 980 khz; 50 kw-D, 188 w-N, DA-D. TL: N34 20 55 W102 57 18. 1000 Sycamore St. 88101. Phone: (505) 762-6200. Fax: (505) 762-8800. Web Site: www.kkyckiva@plateau.net. Licensee: Broadcast Entertainment Corp. (group owner; acq 10-27-99; grpsl). Network: USA. Shaw Pittman. Format: Talk. Target aud: 30 plus. Spec prog: Farm 5 hrs, high school sports 4 hrs wkly. ♦ Rick Keefer, CEO, engrg & chief of engrg; Joe Daniels, opns dir, progmg dir & news dir; Ron Pierson, pres & gen sls mgr.

Stations in the U.S. — New Mexico

*KKCC(FM)—Not on air, target date: unknown: 90.3 mhz; 30 kw. Ant 115 ft. TL: N34 14 34 W103 15 30. 6080 Mount Moriah Ext., Memphis, TN 38115. Phone: (901) 375-9324. Licensee: Broadcasting for the Challenged Inc. ♦ George S. Flinn Jr., pres.

KKYC(FM)— 1993: 102.3 mhz; 25 kw horiz. Ant 177 ft. TL: N34 24 31 W103 11 15. (CP: 100 kw, ant 485 ft. TL: N34 29 36 W103 23 46). 1000 Sycamore St. 88101. Phone: (505) 762-6200. Fax: (505) 762-8800. E-mail: kica-kkyc@plateautel.com. Licensee: Broadcast Entertainment Corp. Format: Country. News staff: one; News: 2 hrs wkly. Target aud: 25-54. ♦ Rick Keefer, CEO, gen mgr & chief of engrg; Joe Daniels, opns dir & progmg dir; Ron Pierson, pres, gen mgr & gen sls mgr; Frank Sherman, news dir; Bev Kuhnly, pub affrs dir.

KRMQ-FM— 2003: 101.5 mhz; 100 kw. Ant 453 ft. TL: N34 15 08 W103 14 21. Mount Rushmore Broadcasting Inc., 218 N. Wolcott St., Casper, WY 82601. Phone: (307) 265-1984. Licensee: Mount Rushmore Broadcasting Inc. (group owner). ♦ Jan Charles Gray, pres & gen mgr.

KSMX(FM)— November 1982: 107.5 mhz; 100 kw. 550 ft. TL: N34 11 34 W103 16 44. Stereo. 208 E. Grand Ave. 88101. Secondary address: 42437 U.S. 70, Portales 88130. Phone: (505) 763-4649. Fax: (505) 359-0724. E-mail: bettermix@bettermix.com. Web Site: www.bettermix.com. Licensee: Rooney Moon Broadcasting Inc. (group owner; acq 7-15-02; grpsl). Format: Hot adult contemp. ♦ Duffy Moon, opns dir & mktg VP; Steve Rooney, pres, gen mgr, sls VP & progmg dir; Jeff Lynn, news dir; Jeff Burmeister, chief of engrg.

KTQM-FM—Listing follows KWKA(AM).

KWKA(AM)— 1971: 680 khz; 500 w-U, DA-1. TL: N34 21 48 W103 13 05. Box 869 88102. Secondary address: 710 Curry Rd. K 88101. Phone: (505) 762-4411. Fax: (505) 769-0197. Licensee: Curry County Broadcasting Inc. (acq 10-24-80; $650,000; with co-located FM; 11-10-80). Network: Jones Radio Networks. Rgnl Reps. Fletcher, Heald & Hildreth. Format: Oldies. News staff: one; News: 3 hrs wkly. Target aud: 25 plus; baby boomers. ♦ C. Hewel Jones, pres & gen mgr; Robert D. Coker, VP, stn mgr & natl sls mgr.

KTQM-FM—Co-owned with KWKA(AM). Mar 1, 1963: 99.9 mhz; 100 kw. 360 ft. TL: N34 21 48 W103 13 05. Stereo. Network: Network: ABC, ESPN Radio. Format: Adult contemp. News: 3 hrs wkly. Target aud: 18-49; young affluent.

Corrales

KKNS(AM)— July 15, 1985: 1310 khz; 5 kw-D, 500 w-N, DA-N. TL: N35 12 00 W106 35 59. Stereo. 1100 Rhode Island N.E., Suite B, Albuquerque 87110. Phone: (505) 255-5015. Fax: (505) 262-4792. E-mail: dustin@kkns.com. Licensee: Simmons-Austin, LS LLC. Group owner: Simmons Media Group (acq 4-4-2001; grpsl). Format: News, talk. Target aud: 45 plus. ♦ Dustin Drew, gen mgr.

KSYU(FM)— Apr 27, 1996: 95.1 mhz; 3 kw. -531 ft. TL: N35 14 42 W106 36 18. 2700 San Pedro Dr. N.E., Albuquerque 87110. Phone: (505) 830-6400. Fax: (505) 830-6543. Licensee: Clear Channel Broadcasting Licenses Inc. Group owner: Clear Channel Communications Inc. (acq 9-28-99). Format: Adult contemp. ♦ Bill May, gen mgr; Chuck Hammond, gen mgr; Craig Hulsebos, progmg dir; Dave Dart, progmg dir.

Deming

KDEM(FM)—Listing follows KOTS(AM).

KOTS(AM)— Mar 10, 1954: 1230 khz; 1 kw-U. TL: N32 15 05 W107 45 28. Box 470, 1700 S. Gold 88031. Phone: (505) 546-9342. E-mail: radio@demingradio.com. Web Site: www.demingradio.com. Licensee: Luna County Broadcasting Co. (acq 3-14-90). Network: Westwood One. Format: Country. News staff: one; News: 13 hrs wkly. Target aud: General. Spec prog: Farm 5 hrs, Sp 8 hrs wkly. ♦ Candie G. Sweetser, stn mgr.

*KZPI(FM)— Mar 25, 1996: 91.7 mhz; 600 w. 62 ft. TL: N32 15 31 W107 46 45. Box 252, Paulino Bernal Evangelism, McAllen, TX 78505. Phone: (956) 686-6382. Fax: (956) 686-2999. Licensee: Paulino Bernal Evangelism. (acq 2-13-98; $45,000). Format: Christian, relg, Sp. Target aud: General. ♦ Paulino Bernal, pres.

Dulce

*KCIE(FM)— Dec 3, 1990: 90.5 mhz; 100 kw. 1,535 ft. TL: N36 59 00 W106 58 12. Box 603, A.I.E. Bldg., Narrow Gauge Rd. 87528. Phone: (505) 759-3681. Phone: (505) 759-3023. Fax: (505) 759-9140. Licensee: Jicarilla Apache Tribe. Format: Div. News staff: one; News: 2 hrs wkly. Target aud: General. ♦ Lisa Vigil-Gomez, stn mgr; Romaine Wood, progmg dir; Kathy James, mus dir; William Vicenti, chief of engrg.

Espanola

KDCE(AM)— 1963: 950 khz; 4.2 kw-D, 90 w-N. TL: N36 00 08 W106 03 59. 403 W. Pueblo Dr. 87532. Phone: (505) 753-2201. Fax: (505) 753-8685. E-mail: kdce@espanola.com. Web Site: www.kdce.net. Licensee: Richard L. Garcia Broadcasting Inc. (acq 11-29-82; $625,000; 11-8-82). Format: Sp. ♦ Casey Gallegos, gen mgr; Richard Garcia, pres & gen sls mgr; Ray Casias, progmg dir; Ken Bass, chief of engrg.

KYBR(FM)—Co-owned with KDCE(AM). July 6, 1981: 92.9 mhz; 3 kw. -249 ft. TL: N36 00 08 W106 03 59. (CP: 50 kw, ant 203 ft.). Web Site: www.kdce.net. Licensee: Rio Chama Broadcasting Co. (acq 1995; $50,000). Format: Rgnl Mexican. ♦ Efrem Galindo, progmg dir.

Eunice

KEJL(FM)— 1996: 100.9 mhz; 50 kw. Ant 295 ft. TL: N32 28 10 W103 09 36. Stereo. Box 5967, Hobbs 88240. Secondary address: 1423 W. Bender, Hobbs 888240. Phone: (505) 393-6000. Fax: (505) 397-6088. E-mail: kejltheeagle@hotmail.com. Licensee: FiveStar Enterprises L.C. (acq 1999; $20,000). Format: Classic rock. ♦ Larry Philpot, gen mgr; Al Lobeck, gen sls mgr.

Farmington

KDAG(FM)— Sept 1, 1969: 96.9 mhz; 100 kw. 1,010 ft. TL: N36 39 49 W108 12 55. Stereo. 200 E. Broadway 87401. Phone: (505) 325-1716. Fax: (505) 325-6797. Web Site: www.bigdog969.com. Licensee: Capstar TX L.P. Group owner: Clear Channel Communications Inc. (acq 8-30-00; grpsl). Network: Westwood One. Fisher, Wayland, Cooper, Leader & Zaragoza. Format: Classic rock. Target aud: 18-49. ♦ Bill Kruger, gen mgr.

KENN(AM)— November 1951: 1390 khz; 5 kw-D, 1.3 kw-N, DA-N. TL: N36 42 27 W108 08 50. 212 W. Apache 87401. Phone: (505) 325-3541. Fax: (505) 327-5796. Licensee: Winton Road Broadcasting Co. LLC (group owner; acq 5-3-01; grpsl). Network: ABC Information & Entertainment. Pepper & Corazzini. Format: News/talk, sports. Target aud: 25-54; upper middle class. ♦ Sara Olsen, gen mgr.

KRWN(FM)—Co-owned with KENN(AM). 1974: 92.9 mhz; 30 kw. 430 ft. TL: N36 41 45 W108 13 23. (CP: 62 kw, ant 394 ft.). Stereo. Phone: (505) 327-4449. Web Site: www.krwn.com. Format: Classic rock. Target aud: 18-49. ♦ Leslie Granger, progmg dir.

KISZ-FM—See Cortez, CO

KNDN(AM)— Aug 1, 1957: 960 khz; 5 kw-D, 163 w-N. TL: N36 43 48 W108 13 47. 1515 W. Main 87401. Phone: (505) 325-1996. Fax: (505) 327-2019. Licensee: Basin Broadcasting Co. Format: Navajo Indian. Target aud: General; Navajo Indian reservation; all Navajo language. ♦ Jim Gober, gen mgr; Kerwin Gober, opns mgr; George Werito, progmg dir & news dir; Jim Burt, chief of engrg.

*KNMI(FM)— Mar 18, 1980: 88.9 mhz; 6.22 kw. 360 ft. TL: N36 40 16 W108 13 54. Stereo. Box 1230, 2103 W. Main St. 87401. Phone: (505) 325-0255. Fax: (505) 325-9035. E-mail: email@verticalraid.org. Web Site: www.verticalradio.org. Licensee: Navajo Missions Inc. Network:

USA. Format: Christian, talk, CHR hits. News: 9 hrs wkly. Target aud: 24-40; general. ♦ Johnny Curry, gen mgr.

KPCL(FM)— Dec 14, 1988: 95.7 mhz; 100 kw. 394 ft. TL: N36 41 44 W108 13 11. Stereo. Box 232 87499. Secondary address: 1105 W. Apache 87401. Phone: (505) 327-7202. Fax: (505) 327-2163. E-mail: kpcl@kpcl.org. Web Site: www.kpcl.org. Licensee: Voice Ministries of Farmington Inc. Network: Moody. Format: Christian contemp. News staff: one; News: 3 hrs wkly. Target aud: General; relg audience. Spec prog: Class one hr, Navajo 7 hrs wkly. ♦ Fareed W. Ayoub, pres.

KRZE(AM)— July 1, 1958: 1280 khz; 5 kw-D. TL: N36 49 03 W108 05 47. Radio Fiesta, 204 E. Broadway 87401. Phone: (505) 327-5287. Fax: (505) 327-5289. Licensee: J. Thomas Development of New Mexico Inc. (acq 12-18-91; with co-located FM). Shaw Pittman. Format: Sp var. ♦ Jeff Thomas, pres; Rogelio Esparva, gen mgr.

*KSJE(FM)— November 1990: 90.9 mhz; 15 kw. 390 ft. TL: N36 41 52 W108 13 14. Stereo. 4601 College Blvd. 87402. Phone: (505) 566-3517. Fax: (505) 566-3385. Web Site: www.ksje.com. Licensee: San Juan College. Format: Class. News: 15 hrs wkly. Target aud: 25-65. Spec prog: Jazz 15 hrs, folk 15 hrs wkly. ♦ Carol Spenser, pres; Ray Francis, gen mgr; Constance Gotsch, progmg dir; Jim Burt, chief of engrg.

KTRA-FM— Feb 19, 1987: 102.1 mhz; 100 kw. 1,033 ft. TL: N36 48 52 W107 53 32. Stereo. 200 E. Broadway 87401. Phone: (505) 325-1716. Fax: (505) 325-6797. Web Site: www.102ktra.com. Licensee: Clear Channel Radio Licenses Inc. Group owner: Clear Channel Communications Inc. (acq 8-30-00; grpsl). Network: ABC. Format: Classic Country. News: 8 hrs wkly. Target aud: 25-54. ♦ Dave Schaefer, progmg dir.

*KUSW(FM)—Not on air, target date: unknown: 89.7 mhz; 500 w vert. Ant 600 ft. TL: N36 40 16 W108 13 54. Box 737, Ignacio, CO 81137-0737. Phone: (970) 563-0255. Web Site: www.ksut.org. Licensee: KUTE Inc. ♦ Eddie Box Jr., pres; Beth Warren, gen mgr.

KWYK-FM—See Aztec

Fruitland

*KTGW(FM)—Not on air, target date: unknown: 91.7 mhz; 20 kw. 308 ft. TL: N36 41 44 W108 13 11. Attn: Fareed W. Ayoub, Box 232, Farmington 87499. Secondary address: 1105 W. Apache St., Farmington 87401. Phone: (505) 327-7202. Fax: (515) 327-2163. E-mail: kpcl@kpcl.org. Web Site: www.kpcl.org. Licensee: Native American Christian Voice Inc. Southmayd & MIller. Format: Christian-talk. ♦ Fareed W. Ayoub, pres; Annette Ayoub, exec VP.

Gallup

KFMQ(FM)— 1996: 106.1 mhz; 26 kw. 185 ft. TL: N35 32 27 W108 44 32. c/o KGLX(FM), 1632 S. 2nd St. 87301. Phone: (505) 863-9391. Fax: (505) 863-9393. Licensee: Clear Channel Broadcasting Licenses Inc. (Group owner: Clear Channel Communications Inc. (acq 4-17-97). Format: Rock. ♦ Mary Ann Armijo, gen mgr & gen sls mgr; Ted Foster, opns mgr; Blas Saucedo, progmg dir.

KGAK(AM)— Feb 9, 1945: 1330 khz; 5 kw-D, 1 kw-N, DA-N. TL: N35 32 34 W108 44 11. 401 E. Coal Ave. 87301. Phone: (505) 863-4444. Fax: (505) 722-7381. Licensee: KRJG Inc. (acq 6-30-98; $102,600). Network: CBS. Rep: Savalli, Gillis. Format: Navajo, Indian. Target aud: 30-55. ♦ Jim Gober, CEO & gen mgr; Jim Burt, gen sls mgr & chief of engrg; Leaudro Jodie, progmg dir.

*KGLP(FM)— Sept 1, 1992: 91.7 mhz; 160 w. Ant 1,145 ft. TL: N35 36 13 W108 40 45. Stereo. Univ. of New Mexico, 200 College Rd. 87301. Phone: (505) 863-7626. Fax: (505) 863-7532. Fax: (505) 863-7633. Web Site: www.kglp.org. Licensee: Gallup Public Radio. Network: NPR. Format: News, div, public stn. News: 40 hrs wkly. Target aud: General; adult professional, academic, business community.

New Mexico

Spec prog: Sp 10 hrs, American Indian 10 hrs, class 8 hrs, bluegrass 12 hrs, folk 10 hrs wkly. ♦Frank Bosler, gen mgr & opns dir; Tom Funk, mus dir.

KGLX(FM)— Mar 1, 1989: 99.1 mhz; 51 kw. 1,249 ft. TL: N35 36 18 W108 41 11. Stereo. 1632 S. 2nd St., AZ 87301. Phone: (505) 863-9391. Fax: (505) 863-9393. Licensee: Clear Channel Broadcasting Licenses Inc. Group owner: Clear Channel Communications Inc. (acq 8-18-00; grpsl). Bechtel & Cole. Format: Country. News staff: 2; News: 14 hrs wkly. Target aud: 25-54. Spec prog: American Indian 3 hrs wkly. ♦Mary Ann Armijo, gen mgr & adv dir; Sylvester Paquin, sls dir; Ted Foster, opns mgr & progmg dir.

KKNM(FM)—Not on air, target date: unknown: 88.1 mhz; 30 kw. Ant -13 ft. TL: N35 30 01 W108 44 06. 188 S. Bellevue, Suite 222, Memphis, TN 38104. Phone: (901) 726-8970. Licensee: Broadcasting for the Challenged Inc. ♦George S. Flinn Jr., pres.

KKOR(FM)—Listing follows KYVA(AM).

*KLLU(FM)—Not on air, target date: unknown: 88.9 mhz; 900 w. Ant 1,184 ft. TL: N35 36 22 W108 41 26. 5700 West Oaks Blvd., Rocklin, CA 95765. Phone: (916) 251-1600. Fax: (916) 251-1650. Licensee: Educational Media Foundation. ♦Richard Jenkins, pres.

KXXI(FM)— Aug 15, 1975: 93.7 mhz; 62 kw. 161 ft. TL: N35 36 22 W108 41 26. Stereo. Box 420 87301. Secondary address: 300 W. Aztec, Suite 200 Phone: (505) 863-6851. Fax: (505) 863-2429. E-mail: mm1@cia-g.com. Web Site: www.gallupradio.com. Licensee: Millennium Media Inc. (acq 6-7-94). Network: ABC. Fletcher, Heald & Hildreth. Format: Classic rock. Target aud: 25-44. ♦George Malti, CEO; Sammy Chioda, pres & stn mgr; Thomas Devlin, sls dir; Brian Smith, progmg mgr; John McBreen, news dir; Keith Desautels, chief of engrg.

KYVA(AM)— July 15, 1959: 1230 khz; 1 kw-U. TL: N35 32 02 W108 42 22. Stereo. Box 420 87305. Phone: (505) 863-6851. Fax: (505) 863-2429. Licensee: Millennium Media Inc. (acq 3-77). Network: ABC. Format: Country. News staff: one; News: 12 hrs wkly. Target aud: 35-54; mature, with buying power. ♦George Malti, pres; Sammy Chioda, exec VP & gen mgr; Tom Devlin, sls dir; Brian Smith, prom dir & progmg dir; John McBreen, news dir; Keith DeSautels, chief of engrg.

KKOR(FM)—Co-owned with KYVA(AM). Oct 6, 1974: 94.5 mhz; 100 kw. 1,388 ft. TL: N35 28 03 W108 14 25. Stereo. Phone: (505) 863-5567. Web Site: www.gallupradio.com. Format: Adult contemp. News staff: one. Target aud: 25-44; young families with buying power.

Grants

KDSK(FM)— June 1, 1997: 92.7 mhz; 1.7 kw. Ant 230 ft. TL: N35 07 09 W107 54 08. (CP: 26 kw, ant 171 ft). Stereo. 733 Roosevelt 87020. Phone: (505) 285-5598. Fax: (505) 285-5575. Licensee: KD Radio Inc. (acq 11-16-00; with KMIN(AM) Grants). Format: Oldies. Target aud: 30-50; earning boom. ♦Derek Underhill, pres.

*KLGQ(FM)—Not on air, target date: unknown: 90.3 mhz; 1 kw. Ant 2,713 ft. TL: N35 15 08 W107 35 45. 5700 West Oaks Blvd., Rocklin, CA 95765. Phone: (916) 251-1600. Fax: (916) 251-1650. Licensee: Educational Media Foundation. Network: K-Love. ♦Lloyd Parker, gen mgr.

KMIN(AM)— Sept 1, 1956: 980 khz; 1 kw-D, 250 kw-N. TL: N35 09 05 W107 52 31. 733 Roosevelt 87020. Phone: (505) 285-5598. Fax: (505) 285-5575. E-mail: info@kmin980.com. Web Site: www.kmin980.com. Licensee: KD Radio Inc. (acq 1-2-01; $145,000. with KDSK(FM) Grants). Format: Oldies. Target aud: 25-54; active, working adults. Spec prog: Spanish. ♦Derek Underhill, pres & opns mgr; Bernie Bustos Jr., gen mgr; Sue Loudner, news dir.

KYVA-FM— Aug 7, 1997: 103.7 mhz; 100 kw. 1,299 ft. TL: N35 28 03 W108 14 25. Box 420, Gallup 87305. Phone: (505) 863-6851. Fax: (505) 863-2429. E-mail: mm1@cia-g.com. Web Site: www.gallupradio.com. Licensee: Millennium Media Inc. (acq 6-98). Network: ABC. Format: Oldies. News staff: one; News: 12 hrs wkly. Target aud: 25+. 0. Spec prog: American Indian 10 hrs, Sp 4 hrs wkly. ♦George M. Malti, CEO & pub affrs dir; Sammy Chioda, pres; Thomas Devlin, sls dir; John McBreen, news dir; Keith Desautels, chief of engrg.

Hatch

KVLC(FM)— Apr 1, 1994: 101.1 mhz; 100 kw. 1,033 ft. TL: N32 41 35 W107 04 06. Stereo. 105 E. Idaho, Suite B, Las Cruces 88005. Phone: (505) 527-1111. Fax: (505) 527-1100. E-mail: kvlc@zianet.com. Web Site: www.101gold.com. Licensee: Radio Property Development Inc. (acq 5-5-98). Network: Jones Radio Networks. Format: Good time oldies. News staff: one; News: 3 hrs wkly. Target aud: 25-54. Spec prog: Bi-lingual Sp/English 6 hrs wkly. ♦Allen Moore, opns mgr & progmg dir; Linda Woodward, gen mgr & sls dir; Brandon Hettinger, news dir & pub affrs dir; Gil Edwards, chief of engrg.

Hobbs

KHOB(AM)— Aug 7, 1954: 1390 khz; 5 kw-D, 500 w-N, DA-N. TL: N32 44 21 W103 10 48. 3301, N. Bensing Rd. 88240. Phone: (505) 392-9292. Fax: (505) 392-7579. Licensee: American Asset Management Inc. (acq 2-28-90; $255,000; 3-19-90). Format: Oldies. News staff: 2; News: 48 hrs wkly. Target aud: General; adult. ♦Harmon Hann, gen mgr; Pat Hann, progmg dir.

KIXN(FM)— Feb 1, 1996: 102.9 mhz; 100 kw. Ant 518 ft. TL: N32 43 26 W103 34 34. Stereo. 619 N.Turner St. 88240. Phone: (505) 397-4969. Fax: (505) 393-4310. E-mail: paul@1radiosquare.com. Web Site: www.1radiosquare.com. Licensee: Noalmark Broadcasting Corp. (group owner; acq 1995; $53,000. for CP). Jones, Waldo, Holbrook & McDonough. Format: Country. News staff: one; News: 5 hrs wkly. Target aud: Adults 18-49. ♦William C. Nolan, CEO & pres; Edwin Alderson, exec VP; Paul J. Starr, VP & gen mgr; Harry Harlan, sls dir & adv dir; Will Rooney, mus dir; Dawn Morgan, news dir; Ken Bass, engrg dir.

KLMA(FM)— November 1993: 96.5 mhz; 13 kw. Ant 459 ft. TL: N32 46 08 W103 07 00. Box 457, 108 S. Willow 88240. Phone: (505) 391-9650. Fax: (505) 397-9373. Web Site: www.klmaradio.com. Licensee: Ojeda Broadcasting Inc. Group owner: Ojeda Broadcasting Inc. Mullin, Rhyne, Emmons & Topel. Format: Sp. Target aud: Hispanic. ♦Hermilo Ojeda, CEO, gen mgr, gen sls mgr, mktg mgr & prom mgr; Pearl Ojeda, pres.

KPER(FM)— August 1965: 95.7 mhz; 36 kw. Ant 255 ft. TL: N32 43 28 W103 09 03. Stereo. Box 5967 88241-5967. Secondary address: 1423 W. Bender St. 88240. Phone: (505) 393-1551. Fax: (505) 397-6088. E-mail: kper@wtaccess.com. Web Site: www.hobbsradio.com. Licensee: Noalmark Broadcasting Corp. (group owner; acq 1-99). Format: Country. Target aud: 25-54. ♦Al Lobeck, gen mgr & gen sls mgr; Conrad Dean, news dir; Ken Bass, chief of engrg.

KYKK(AM)— July 17, 1971: 1110 khz; 5 kw-D. TL: N32 48 59 W103 13 56. Box 5967 88241. Secondary address: 1423 W. Bender Blvd. 88240. Phone: (505) 393-1551. Fax: (505) 397-6088. E-mail: kykk@hobbsradio.com. Web Site: www.hobbsradio.com. Licensee: Noalmark Broadcasting Corp. (group owner; acq 8-7-77). Network: ABC Information & Entertainment. Format: News/talk, sports. News staff: one; News: 10 hrs wkly. Target aud: 25-54; men & women. ♦William Nolan, pres; Al Lobeck, gen mgr, gen sls mgr & adv VP; Harry Harlan, progmg dir; Dawn Morgan, news dir; Ken Bass, chief of engrg.

KZOR(FM)—Co-owned with KYKK(AM). March 1975: 94.1 mhz; 100 kw. 400 ft. TL: N32 48 59 W103 13 56. Stereo. Web Site: www.1radiosquare.com. Format: Hot adult contemp. Target aud: 18-44; female. ♦William Nolan, CEO; Paul J. Starr, opns VP, sls VP & mktg VP; Bill Rediker, prom VP; Harry Harlan, progmg VP.

Hurley

KWNM(FM)— 2002: 105.5 mhz; 23 kw. Ant 1,063 ft. TL: N32 50 40 W108 14 19. Stereo. 2700 Hwy. 180 E., Silver City 88061. Phone: (505) 534-1055. Fax: (505) 534-1400. E-mail: theranch@signalpeak.net. Web Site: realcountryonline.com. Licensee: James S. Bumpous dba Yellow Dog Radio. Format: Country. News: 5 hrs wkly. Target aud: 25-54. Spec prog: Su AM relg progmg. ♦Keven McCauley, gen mgr; Misty Bock, progmg.

Jal

KPZA-FM— Nov 1, 1998: 103.7 mhz; 100 kw. Ant 371 ft. TL: N32 25 53 W103 09 08. c/o KIXN(FM)-KYKK(AM)-KZOR(FM), 619 N. Turner St., Hobbs 88240. Phone: (505) 397-4969. Fax: (505) 393-4310. E-mail: paul@1radiosquare.com. Web Site: www.1radiosquare.com. Licensee: Noalmark Broadcasting Corp. (group owner; acq 5-29-98; $10,000. for CP). Format: Sp. News staff: one; News: 5 hrs wkly.

Target aud: Hispanic. ♦William C. Nolan, CEO & pres; Edwin Alderson, sr VP; Paul J. Starr, gen mgr & opns VP; Gerald Sanchez, stn mgr; Harry Harlan, sls dir & adv dir.

Kirtland

KAZX(FM)— 1999: 102.9 mhz; 100 kw. Ant 1,007 ft. TL: N36 48 57 W107 53 32. 200 E. Broadway, Farmington 87401. Phone: (505) 325-1716. Fax: (505) 325-6797. Web Site: www.star1029.com. Licensee: Capstar TX L.P. Group owner: Clear Channel Communications Inc. (acq 12-19-00; $1.26 million). Format: CHR. ♦Bill Kruger, gen mgr.

La Luz

KRSY-FM—Licensed to La Luz. See Alamogordo

Las Cruces

KGRT-FM— Sept 8, 1966: 103.9 mhz; 3 kw. 151 ft. TL: N32 18 33 W106 49 24. Stereo. Box 968 88004. Secondary address: 1355 E. California St. 88001. Phone: (505) 525-9298. Fax: (505) 525-9419. E-mail: radiolc@kgrt.com. Web Site: www.kgrt.com. Licensee: Sunrise Broadcasting Inc. (acq 12-30-88; with co-located AM; FTR: 12-19-88). Format: Country. News staff: 2; News: 2 hrs wkly. Target aud: 25-54. ♦Allen Lumeyer, VP & gen mgr.

KSNM(AM)—Co-owned with KGRT-FM. Dec 15, 1955: 570 khz; 5 kw-D, 155 w-N. TL: N32 18 33 W106 49 24. Web Site: www.ksnm570.am. Network: ABC Daytime Direction. Format: MOR. News staff: 2; News: 4 hrs wkly. Target aud: 25 plus.

KHQT(FM)— Dec 12, 1974: 103.1 mhz; 3 kw. -111 ft. TL: N32 18 21 W106 46 43. Stereo. Box 968 88004. Secondary address: 1355 E. California 88001. Phone: (505) 525-9298. Fax: (505) 525-9419. E-mail: radiolc@kgrt.com. Web Site: www.hot103.fm. Licensee: Richardson Commercial Corp. (acq 8-6-01; $1,650,000. with KKVS(FM) Truth or Consequences). Fletcher, Heald & Hildreth. Format: CHR. News staff: 2; News: one hr wkly. Target aud: 18-34; general. ♦Allen Lumeyer, VP & gen mgr; Ernesto Garcia, opns mgr.

KKVS(FM)—See Truth or Consequences

*KMBN(FM)— 2000: 89.7 mhz; 500 w. Ant 171 ft. TL: N32 16 41 W106 54 39. Box 16691 88004. Phone: (505) 521-8053. E-mail: kmbn@moody.edu. Web Site: www.kmbn.org. Licensee: Moody Bible Institute of Chicago. Group owner: The Moody Bible Institute of Chicago Format: Christian. ♦John Powell, gen mgr.

KMVR(FM)—See Mesilla Park

KOBE(AM)— April 1947: 1450 khz; 1 kw-U. TL: N32 18 07 W106 48 08. Drawer 1838 88004. Secondary address: 1832 W. Amador 88005. Phone: (505) 526-2496. Fax: (505) 523-3918. E-mail: kmvr-kobe@totacc.com. Licensee: Edwards Media Ltd. Co. (acq 3-8-96; $700,000; with KMVR(FM) Mesilla Park). Network: CBS, ABC News/Talk. Format: News/talk, sports. News staff: one; News: 25 hrs wkly. Target aud: 25 plus. ♦Larry Edwards, pres & gen mgr; Amanda Diana, opns VP & progmg dir; Edmundo Refendez, gen sls mgr; Gino Aragon, news dir; Gil Edwards, chief of engrg.

KROL(FM)— May 1994: 99.5 mhz; 100 kw. 1,023 ft. TL: N32 31 33 W107 12 21. Stereo. 277 E. Amador, Suite 305 88001. Phone: (505) 523-2511. Fax: (505) 523-2212. Web Site: www.krolradio.com. Licensee: Rio Grande Christian Broadcasting Corp. (acq 12-95). James L. Oyster. Format: Contemp Christian. Target aud: 25-54. ♦Arnold McClatchey, pres & gen mgr; Joe M. Olivas, rgnl sls mgr; Gil Edwards, chief of engrg.

*KRUC(FM)— March 1998: 88.9 mhz; 500 w. 197 ft. TL: N32 16 41 W106 54 39. 5120 Prince Edward Ave., El Paso, TX 79924. Phone: (915) 544-9192. Web Site: www.wrn-rcm.org. Licensee: World Radio Network Inc. (group owner) Format: Sp relg.

*KRUX(FM)— Sept 20, 1989: 91.5 mhz; 1 kw. -194 ft. TL: N32 17 03 W106 45 00. Box 30004, Corbett Ctr. 88003. Phone: (505) 646-4640. E-mail: infor@krux.fm. Web Site: www.quadphonic.com. Licensee: Board of Regents New Mexico State University. Format: Var. News staff: one; News: 2 hrs wkly. Target aud: General. ♦Michael Edenfield, gen mgr.

Stations in the U.S. New Mexico

KRWG(FM)— Oct 3, 1964: 90.7 mhz; 100 kw. 350 ft. TL: N32 15 24 W106 58 34. Stereo. Box 3000 88003. Phone: (505) 646-4525. Fax: (505) 646-1974. E-mail: krwgfm@nmsu.edu. Web Site: krwgfm.org. Licensee: Regents of New Mexico State University. Network: Network: NPR, PRI. Wiley, Rein & Fielding. Format: Class, jazz, news, SP. News staff: 2; News: 39 hrs wkly. Target aud: 18-60. Spec prog: Sp 10 hrs, bluegrass/folk 8 hrs wkly. ♦Colin Gromatzky, gen mgr; Carrie Hamblen, chief of opns; L. Ford Ballard, dev dir; Robert Nosbisch, news dir. Co-owned TV: *KRWG-TV affil

Las Vegas

KBAC(FM)— Nov 10, 1989: 98.1 mhz; 97 kw. 1,037 ft. TL: N35 22 20 W105 22 02. Stereo. 1401 Maclovia St., Suite E, Santa Fe 87505. Phone: (505) 989-3338. Fax: (505) 989-3881. E-mail: irag@kbac.com. Web Site: www.kbac.com. Licensee: Clear Channel Broadcasting Licenses Inc. Group owner: Clear Channel Communications Inc. (acq 8-18-00). Format: AAA, new adult contemp. News: 2 hrs wkly. Target aud: 35-44; female, affluent, hip, baby boomers. Spec prog: World 3 hrs, blues 2 hrs, swing one hr, soul 2 hrs wkly. ♦Ira Gordon, gen mgr & progmg dir; John Reid, rgnl sls mgr; Dana Olsen, prom dir & pub affrs dir; John Chidesder, chief of engrg.

*****KEDP(FM)**— September 1968: . Stn currently dark 91.1 mhz; 72 w. Ant -215 ft. TL: N35 35 46 W105 13 18. New Mexico Highlands Univ., Media Arts Dept. 87701. Phone: (505) 454-3588. Fax: (505) 454-3109. Web Site: www.nmhu.edu/non-academic/radiokedp. Licensee: Board of Regents, New Mexico Highlands University. ♦Drake Bingham, gen mgr.

KFUN(AM)— Dec 25, 1941: 1230 khz; 1 kw-U. TL: N35 35 48 W105 12 21. Box 700 87701. Phone: (505) 425-6766. Fax: (505) 425-6767. E-mail: jpbaca1946@yahoo.com. Licensee: Meadows Media LLC. (acq 4-19-91; $400). Network: ABC Information & Entertainment. Format: Sp, C&W. Target aud: General. ♦Joseph Baca Jr., pres, gen mgr, gen sls mgr, news dir & sls.

KLVF(FM)—Co-owned with KFUN(AM). June 19, 1973: 100.7 mhz; 10 kw. -77 ft. TL: N33 35 48 W105 12 21. Stereo. Format: Adult contemp. Target aud: 17-40.

KMDZ(FM)— 2000: 96.7 mhz; 4 kw. 381 ft. Sangre de Cristo Broadcasting Co., 304 S. Grand 88701. Phone: (505) 425-3555. Fax: (505) 425-3557. E-mail: mattmartinez@kmx.com. Licensee: Sangre de Cristo Broadcasting Co. Format: Classic rock. ♦Matt Martinez, gen mgr.

KNMX(AM)— Oct 1, 1980: 540 khz; 5 kw-D, DA. TL: N35 34 25 W105 10 17. 304 S. Grand Ave. 87701. Phone: (505) 425-3555. Fax: (505) 425-3557. Licensee: Sangre de Cristo Broadcasting Co. (acq 9-26-96; $235,000). Rep: Caballero. Format: Sp, news/talk. News staff: one; News: 15 hrs wkly. Target aud: 25-55; Hispanic, Anglo. ♦Amos Johnson, prom dir; Matt C. Martinez, pres, gen mgr & progmg dir; John Chichester, chief of engrg.

Lordsburg

KPSA-FM— July 4, 1986: 97.7 mhz; 250 w. Ant -134 ft. TL: N32 20 57 W108 42 18. Stereo. Box 2710, Alamogordo 88310. Phone: (505) 437-1505. Fax: (505) 388-5000. Licensee: Linda S. Bloom, trustee for Runnels Broadcasting System LLC. Group owner: Runnels Broadcasting System L.L.C. (acq 9-19-2002; grpsl). Format: Rock.

Los Alamos

KABG(FM)— June 1956: 98.5 mhz; 100 kw. 1,781 ft. TL: N35 53 08 W106 23 14. (CP: 100 kw, ant 1,906 ft.). Stereo. Box 30925, Albuquerque 87190. Phone: (505) 878-0980. Fax: (505) 878-0098. Web Site: www.bigoldies.net. Licensee: AGM-Nevada L.L.C. Format: Oldies. Target aud: 25-54; affluent, upscale male professionals. ♦Scott Hutton, gen mgr & progmg dir.

KQBA(FM)— Mar 1, 1998: 107.5 mhz; 100 kw. 298 ft. TL: N36 01 34 W105 48 18. 2502C Camino Entrada, Santa Fe 87505. Phone: (505) 471-1067. Fax: (505) 473-2667. Licensee: Hutton Media L.L.C. (acq 9-14-00; $1 million). Format: Latin music, Sp, rock. Target aud: 18-49; male. ♦Scott Hutton, gen mgr.

KRSN(AM)— Dec 9, 1949: 1490 khz; 1 kw-U. TL: N35 53 46 W106 17 21. 145 Central Park Square 87544. Phone: (505) 661-2490. Phone: (505) 662-1999. Fax: (505) 661-2476. E-mail: krsn@losalamos.com. Web Site: krsn.losalamos.com. Licensee: Real Radio L.L.C. (acq 1997). Network: Network: CBS, Westwood One. Format: News/talk, sports. News staff: one; News: 25 hrs wkly. Target aud: 35 plus; well educated, affluent. Spec prog: Big Band 8 hrs, jazz 2 hrs wkly. ♦Mark M. Bentley, CEO & gen mgr; Jason Pierotti, chief of opns.

KZNM(FM)— Mar 19, 1987: 106.7 mhz; 15.5 kw. 1,948 ft. TL: N35 47 15 W106 31 35. Stereo. 4125 Carlisle N.E., Santa Fe 87107. Phone: (505) 878-0980. Fax: (505) 878-0098. Web Site: www.1067radiosol.com. Licensee: A.G.M.-Nevada L.L.C. Group owner: American General Media (acq 8-9-00; grpsl). Format: Sp var. News: 7 hrs wkly. Target aud: 25-54; mainstream audience with all socio-economic cells represented. ♦Scott Hutton, gen mgr.

Los Lunas

KAGM(FM)— January 1995: 106.3 mhz; 100 kw. 656 ft. TL: N34 48 51 W106 50 29. Stereo. 4125 Carlisle Blvd. N.E., Albuquerque 87107-4806. Phone: (505) 878-0980. Fax: (505) 878-0098. Web Site: www.wild106.net. Licensee: AGM-Nevada L.L.C. Group owner: American General Media (acq 12-22-97; grpsl). Format: Rhythmic CHR. Target aud: 18-49. Spec prog: Club mix 18 hrs wkly. ♦Scott Hutton, gen mgr; Eileen Munroe, prom dir; D.J. Lopez, mus dir.

KIOT(FM)— July 6, 1981: 102.5 mhz; 20 kw. Ant 4,159 ft. TL: N35 12 55 W106 27 02. Stereo. 8009 Marble Ave. N.E., Albuquerque 87110-7942. Phone: (505) 262-1142. Fax: (505) 262-9211. Web Site: www.coyote1025.netnio.com. Licensee: HBC License Corp. Group owner: Univision Radio (acq 9-22-2003; grpsl). Jones, Waldo, Holbrook & McDonough. Format: Classic rock. News staff: one. Target aud: 25-49; hip adults who like diversity & have disposable income. Spec prog: Gospel 4 hrs wkly. ♦Pete Manriger, gen mgr.

Los Ranchos de Albuquerque

KALY(AM)—Licensed to Los Ranchos de Albuquerque. See Albuquerque

KTBL(AM)—Licensed to Los Ranchos de Albuquerque. See Albuquerque

Lovington

KLEA(AM)— Dec 25, 1952: 630 khz; 500 w-D, 69 w-N. TL: N32 56 30 W103 19 12. Box 877, Country Club Rd. 88260. Phone: (505) 396-2244. Fax: (505) 396-3355. E-mail: klea@leaconet.com. Web Site: www.107oldies.com. Licensee: Lea County Broadcasting Co. Format: Soft hits. Target aud: 25-54. Spec prog: Relg 3 hrs wkly. ♦Keith Kelly, progmg dir; Susan Coe, gen mgr, gen sls mgr & news dir; Rita Niccum, chief of engrg.

KLEA-FM— October 1965: 101.7 mhz; 25 kw. 280 ft. TL: N32 56 30 W103 19 12. Stereo. Web Site: www.107oldies.com. Format: Oldies. ♦Susan Coe, exec VP.

Maljamar

*****KMTH(FM)**— Feb 14, 1985: 98.7 mhz; 100 kw. Ant 710 ft. TL: N32 54 55 W103 46 31. Stereo. Eastern New Mexico Univ., 52 Broadcast Ctr., Portales 88130. Phone: (505) 562-2112. Fax: (505) 562-2590. Web Site: www.kenw.org. Licensee: Eastern New Mexico University. Network: Network: NPR, PRI. Dow, Lohnes & Albertson. Format: Class, btfl mus, news. News staff: one; News: 41 hrs wkly. Target aud: General. ♦Steven G. Gamble, pres; K. Paul Jones, VP; Duane W. Ryan, gen mgr; Shannon Hearn, opns dir; Virginia McReynolds, dev dir & mktg dir; James Lee, news dir; Jeff Burmeister, engrg dir; Bob Scott, engrg dir.

KWMW(FM)— Jan 17, 1990: 105.1 mhz; 100 kw. 917 ft. TL: N32 52 40 W103 41 13. Box 2010, Ruinuso 88346. Secondary address: 916 Ave. D, Levington 88260. Phone: (505) 396-0499. Fax: (505) 396-8349. E-mail: kruikwmw@trailnet.com. Web Site: www.w105country.com. Licensee: M.T.D. Inc. Group owner: MTD Inc. Format: Country. ♦Tim Keithley, gen mgr.

Mentmore

*****KPKJ(FM)**—Not on air, target date: unknown: 88.5 mhz; 1.3 kw. Ant 491 ft. TL: N35 33 36 W109 06 30. 4002 N. 3300 E., Twin Falls, ID 83301. Phone: (208) 734-6633. Fax: (208) 736-1958. Web Site: www.csnradio.com. Licensee: CSN International. ♦Michael Kestler, pres.

Mesilla Park

KMVR(FM)— June 1, 1974: 104.9 mhz; 3 kw. -32 ft. TL: N32 18 07 W106 48 08. Stereo. Drawer 1838, Las Cruces 88005. Secondary address: 1832 W. Amador, Las Cruces 88004. Phone: (505) 526-2496. Fax: (505) 523-3918. E-mail: kmvr-kobe@totacc.com. Licensee: Edwards Media Ltd. Co. (acq 3-8-96). Format: Hot adult contemp. Target aud: 18-54. ♦Larry Edwards, CEO, gen mgr, gen sls mgr & progmg dir; Gil Edwards, chief of engrg.

Mesquite

*****KELP-FM**— February 2004: 89.3 mhz; 680 w. Ant 66 ft. TL: N32 09 42 W106 42 03. Stereo. 6900 Commerce, El Paso, TX 79915. Phone: (915) 779-0016. Fax: (915) 779-6641. E-mail: info@kelpradio.com. Licensee: Sky High Broadcasting Inc. (acq 3-28-02). Network: Salem Radio Network. Format: Christian. Target aud: 25-55 plus. ♦Arniold McClatchey, pres.

Milan

KQNM(AM)— Sept 1, 1989: 1100 khz; 250 w-D, 20 w-N. TL: N35 05 51 W107 52 19. 809 Wellesly N.E., Albuqueque 87106. Phone: (505) 285-5598 Station. Phone: (505) 261-0130 Office. Fax: (505) 285-5575. Licensee: Cibola Radio Co. (acq 7-12-99; $29,800). Format: News/talk. Target aud: 25-54; upscale men. ♦Don Davis, pres; Derek Underhill, gen mgr.

*****KXXQ(FM)**— June 1991: . Stn currently dark 100.7 mhz; 100 kw. Ant 1,361 ft. TL: N35 28 07 W108 14 24. Stereo. Box 180, Tahoma, CA 96142. Phone: (530) 584-5700. Fax: (530) 584-5705. Web Site: www.ihradio.org. Licensee: IHR Educational Broadcasting. (acq 5-31-2005; $450,000). ♦Douglas M. Sherman, pres.

Pecos

KLBU(FM)— Aug 1, 2001: 102.9 mhz; 3.7 kw horiz. Ant 686 ft. TL: N35 39 06 W105 33 15. Stereo. 551C Cordova Rd., Santa Fe 87505. Phone: (505) 984-1029. Fax: (505) 984-0880. Web Site: www.blu1029.com. Licensee: Blu Media LLC (acq 2-19-2004; $1.15 million). Wood, Maines & Brown, Chartered. Format: Modern adult contemp.

KWRP(FM)— 2004: 101.5 mhz; 25 kw. Ant 279 ft. TL: N35 32 50 W105 45 54. Box 1863, Santa Fe, TX 87504. Phone: (505) 438-7007. Fax: (505) 438-7007. Web Site: www.kwrp-radio.com. Licensee: James S. Bumpous (acq 3-9-2004; grpsl). Format: Var. ♦James S. Bumpous, gen mgr.

Portales

*****KENW-FM**— Oct 1, 1968: 89.5 mhz; 100 kw. Ant 185 ft. TL: N34 10 27 W103 21 03. Stereo. Eastern New Mexico Univ., 52 Broadcast Ctr. 88130. Phone: (505) 562-2112. Fax: (505) 562-2590. Web Site: www.kenw.org. Licensee: Eastern New Mexico University. Network: Network: NPR, PRI. Format: Btfl mus, class, news/talk. News staff: one; News: 41 hrs wkly. Target aud: General. ♦Steven G. Gamble, pres; K. Paul Jones, VP; Duane W. Ryan, gen mgr; Shannon Hearn,

New Mexico Directory of Radio

opns dir; Virginia McReynolds, dev dir & mktg dir; James Lee, news dir; Jeff Burmeister, engrg dir; Bob Scott, engrg mgr. Co-owned TV: *KENW-TV affil

KSEL(AM)— February 1950: 1450 khz; 1 kw-U. TL: N34 11 51 W103 19 24. 42437 US 70 88130. Phone: (505) 359-4649. Fax: (505) 359-0724. Licensee: Rooney Moon Broadcasting Inc. (group owner; acq 7-15-02; grpsl). Network: CNN Radio. Format: News/talk. News: 168 hrs wkly. Target aud: 35+. ♦Duffy Moon, opns mgr & prom dir; Steve Rooney, pres, gen mgr, sls dir & progmg dir; Jeff Burmeister, chief of engrg.

KSEL-FM— March 1980: 95.3 mhz; 6 kw. Ant 298 ft. TL: N34 11 51 W103 19 24. Stereo. Network: CNN Radio. Garvey, Schubert & Barer. Format: Country. Target aud: 18-54. Spec prog: Farm 4 hrs wkly.

Ramah

***KTDB(FM)—** Apr 24, 1972: 89.7 mhz; 15 kw. 300 ft. TL: N34 57 59 W108 25 31. (CP: Ant 288 ft.). Box 40, B.I.A. Rt. 125, Pine Hill 87357. Phone: (505) 775-3215. Fax: (505) 775-3551. Web Site: www.rnsbinc.com. Licensee: Ramah Navajo School Board Inc. Network: NPR. Format: C&W, cultural info, educ. Target aud: General; Native American. Spec prog: Navajo. ♦Barbara Maria, gen mgr & prom mgr; Irene Beaver, progmg dir; Martha Pino, news dir; Bernard J. Bustos, chief of engrg.

Raton

KBKZ(FM)— Dec 20, 2001: 96.5 mhz; 5.4 kw. Ant 968 ft. TL: N36 59 33 W104 28 24. 100 Fisher Dr., Trinidad, CO 81082. Phone: (719) 846-3355. Fax: (719) 846-4711. Licensee: Phillips Broadcasting Co. Inc. Group owner: Phillips Broadcasting Inc. Format: Country. ♦David Phillips, gen mgr.

KRTN(AM)— 1948: 1490 khz; 1 kw-U. TL: N36 53 10 W104 26 35. Box 638, 1128 State St. 87740. Phone: (505) 445-3652. Fax: (505) 445-2911. E-mail: krtn@raton.com. Licensee: Enchanted Air Inc. (acq 5-31-2005; $750,000 with co-located FM). Format: Adult contemp. Target aud: General. ♦Jim Roper, stn mgr & prom mgr; Bill Donati, progmg dir & mus dir; Flo Roper, progmg dir; Jim Veltri, chief of engrg.

KRTN-FM— April 1982: 93.9 mhz; 26 kw. Ant 1,446 ft. TL: N36 40 59 W104 24 50. Stereo. Format: Oldies.

Red River

***KRDR(FM)—** 2002: 90.1 mhz; 3.2 kw vert. Ant 718 ft. TL: N36 41 25 W105 33 43. Box 788, Questa 87556. Phone: (505) 586-1919. Fax: (505) 586-2332. E-mail: krdr@newmex.com. Web Site: www.krdr.com. Licensee: Red River Radio Inc. Format: Classic rock, oldies. ♦Lynn Nolen, stn mgr & progmg dir; Mike Nolen, gen mgr & chief of engrg.

Reserve

KLBZ(FM)— 2005: 104.5 mhz; 500 w. Ant -751 ft. TL: N33 42 35 W108 45 56. Box 41497, Mesa, AZ 85274. Phone: (505) 533-6100. Fax: (505) 533-6103. Web Site: www.klbz.com. Licensee: New Star Broadcasting LLC (acq 12-18-2002; $80,000). Format: Talk, news. ♦Karey Barbee, pres & gen mgr.

Rio Rancho

KAJZ(FM)— Nov 2, 1984: 101.7 mhz; 3.2 kw. 99 ft. TL: N35 11 35 W106 28 15. 8009 Marble Ave., Albuquerque 87110. Phone: (505) 262-1142. Fax: (505) 262-9211. Licensee: Univision Radio License Corp. Group owner: Univision Radio (acq 9-22-2003; grpsl). Rep: Christal. Format: New adult contemp/smooth jazz. ♦Jim Ray, gen mgr.

Roswell

KBCQ(FM)— Oct 15, 1977: 97.1 mhz; 100 kw. 300 ft. TL: N33 24 05 W104 22 45. Stereo. Box 670 88202. Phone: (505) 622-6450. Fax: (505) 622-9041. E-mail: kbcq@roswellradio.org. Web Site: www.roswellradio.org. Licensee: Roswell Radio Inc. Group owner: Roswell Radio Inc./Quay Broadcasters Inc. (acq 11-2000; grpsl). Network: ABC. Fletcher, Heald & Hildreth. Format: CHR. News staff: one. Target aud: 18-49. ♦John Dunn, CEO & exec VP; J.P. Law, stn mgr; Ron Stevens, opns mgr; Kathy Romero, rgnl sls mgr; Gary Babcock, engrg VP.

KBIM(AM)— May 1953: 910 khz; 5 kw-D, 500 w-N, DA-N. TL: N33 26 26 W104 31 35. Box 1953 88202. Secondary address: 1301 N. Main 88201. Phone: (505) 623-9100. Fax: (505) 623-4775. E-mail: kbim@dfn.com. Web Site: kbim-roswell.com. Licensee: King Broadcasting Co. Inc. Network: ABC. Dow, Lohnes & Albertson. Format: News/talk. News: 16 hrs wkly. Target aud: 25-54; upscale male & active working female. ♦Betty King, chmn & gen sls mgr; John King, pres, gen mgr, natl sls mgr, rgnl sls mgr, progmg dir & progmg mgr; Michael Liles, opns dir & chief of engrg.

KBIM-FM— June 1959: 94.9 mhz; 100 kw. 1,880 ft. TL: N33 03 20 W103 49 12. Stereo. Web Site: kbim-roswell.com. Network: ABC Information & Entertainment. Dow, Lohnes & Albertson. Format: Adult contemp. News: 16 hrs wkly. Target aud: 25-54. ♦Betty King, sls dir & progmg dir; John King, CEO & gen sls mgr.

KCRX(AM)— Mar 15, 1927: 1430 khz; 5 kw-D, 1 kw-N, DA-N. TL: N33 26 11 W104 36 18. Box 2052 88202-2052. Secondary address: 200 W. 1st St. 88202-2052. Phone: (505) 622-1432. Fax: (505) 622-1432. Licensee: Rosendo Casarez Jr. Network: Network: CBS, Westwood One. Format: Oldies. News staff: one. Target aud: 35 plus. ♦Rosendo Casarez Jr., pres & opns dir.

KEND(FM)— May 30, 1990: 106.5 mhz; 52 kw. 135 ft. TL: N33 23 05 W104 43 22. Stereo. Box 388 88202-0388. Phone: (505) 625-2098. Fax: (505) 622-3877. Web Site: www.themix1065.com. Licensee: Burkbery Communications Group Inc. (acq 9-5-01; $450,000). Format: AOR. News: 6 hrs wkly. Target aud: 18-34; upscale adults. Spec prog: Farm one hr wkly. ♦Roxy Burkfield, gen mgr.

KINF(AM)— Dec 20, 1965: 1020 khz; 50 kw-U, DA-2. TL: N33 27 53 W104 29 58. Box 670 88202. Secondary address: 5206 W. 2nd. 88201. Phone: (505) 622-6450. Fax: (505) 622-9041. E-mail: kinf@roswellradio.org. Web Site: roswellradio.org. Licensee: JCE Licenses L.L.C. Group owner: James Crystal Inc. (acq 2000; $2.5 million). Network: Network: Network: CBS, Westwood One, ABC Information & Entertainment. Cohn & Marks. Format: News/talk, adult contemp, Sp, religious. News staff: 2; News: 5 hrs wkly. Target aud: 25-54; adult professionals. Spec prog: Relg 15 hrs wkly. ♦Jim Hilliard Jr., pres; John Dunn, gen mgr & gen sls mgr; Brenda McCasland, prom dir; Ron Stevens, progmg dir; Gary Babcock, mus dir & chief of engrg; Chris Johnson, news dir.

KMOU(FM)— August 1992: 104.7 mhz; 100 kw. Ant 328 ft. TL: N33 24 49 W104 22 49. Stereo. Box 670 88202-0670. Secondary address: 5206 W. 2nd St. 88203. Phone: (505) 625-6450. Fax: (505) 622-9041. E-mail: kmou@roswellradio.org. Web Site: www.,roswellradio.org. Licensee: Roswell Radio Inc. Group owner: Roswell Radio Inc./Quay Broadcasters Inc. (acq 11-22-2000; $750,000). Network: Network: Westwood One, ABC. Fletcher, Heald & Hildreth. Format: Country. News staff: 2; News: 12 hrs wkly. ♦John M. Dunn, CEO & gen mgr; Tracy Nelson, stn mgr; Kathy Romero, rgnl sls mgr; J.R. Law, progmg dir; Chris Johnson, news dir; Gary Babcock, engrg VP.

KPSA(AM)— May 1947: 1230 khz; 1 kw-U. TL: N33 25 00 W104 30 40. Box 670 88201. Secondary address: 5206 W. 2nd St. 88201. Phone: (505) 622-0290. Fax: (505) 622-9041. E-mail: kpsa@roswellradio.org. Web Site: www.roswellradio.org. Licensee: Roswell Radio Inc. Group owner: Roswell Radio Inc./Quay Broadcasters Inc. (acq 2-28-03). Network: ABC. Format: Contemporary Latin. Target aud: 35-75. Spec prog: Talk 15 hrs wkly. ♦John M. Dunn, pres; Gabe Mendez, gen mgr & progmg dir; J.R. Law, gen mgr; Penny Dunn, gen sls mgr.

KRDD(AM)— 1963: 1320 khz; 1 kw-D. TL: N33 24 14 W104 28 12. Box 1615, 170 Redbridge Rd. 88201. Phone: (505) 623-8111. Fax: (505) 623-8111. Web Site: www.countrigirl@aol.com. Licensee: Media Mining Group LLC (acq 5-11-2004). Format: Sp. ♦Carlos Espinoza, pres, gen mgr & prom mgr; Monica Cardeas, gen sls mgr; Ramiro Vasquez, progmg dir.

***KRLU(FM)—**Not on air, target date: unknown: 90.1 mhz; 2 kw vert. Ant 394 ft. TL: N33 21 47 W104 38 11. 5700 W. Oaks Blvd., Rocklin, CA 95765. Phone: (916) 251-1600. Fax: (916) 251-1650. E-mail: klove@klove.com. Web Site: www.klove.com. Licensee: Educational Media Foundation. Group owner: EMF Broadcasting. Shaw Pittman. Format: Contemp Christian. News staff: 3. Target aud: 25-44; Judeo Christian, female. ♦Richard Jenkins, pres; Mike Novak, VP & progmg dir; Lloyd Parker, gen mgr; Ed Lenane, opns dir & news dir; Keith Whipple, dev dir; Eric Allen, natl sls mgr; Russ Lloyd, rgnl sls mgr; Chris Joyce, prom dir; David Pierce, progmg mgr; Jon Rivers, mus dir; Sam Wallington, engrg dir.

***KRSR(FM)—**Not on air, target date: unknown: 89.1 mhz; 100 kw vert. Ant 79 ft. TL: N33 29 12 W104 29 48. 6080 Mount Moriah Ext., Memphis, TN 38115. Phone: (901) 375-9324. Licensee: Broadcasting for the Challenged Inc. ♦George S. Flinn Jr., pres.

KSFX(FM)— Mar 15, 1991: 100.5 mhz; 100 kw. 122 ft. TL: N33 28 54 W104 39 12. Box 670 88201. Secondary address: 5206 W. 2nd St. 88201. Phone: (505) 622-6450. Fax: (505) 622-9041. E-mail: ksfx@roswellradio.org. Web Site: roswellradio.org. Licensee: Roswell Radio Inc. Group owner: Roswell Radio Inc./Quay Broadcasters Inc. (acq 11-2000; grpsl). Fletcher, Hearld & Hildreth. Format: Classic rock, AOR. News staff: 2; News: 12 hrs wkly. Target aud: 25-49; mainstream upscale. ♦John Dunn, CEO & sls dir; John M. Dunn, CEO & gen mgr; Gary Babock, exec VP & engrg VP; J.R. Law, stn mgr & sls dir; Bob Taylor, opns mgr, progmg dir, progmg mgr & mus dir; Kathy Romero, rgnl sls mgr; Steve Roberts, adv mgr; Chris Johnson, news dir; Tracy Nelson, pub affrs dir; Gary Babcock, engrg VP & chief of engrg.

***KWFL(FM)—** Dec 21, 1989: 99.5 mhz; 6.1 kw. Ant 459 ft. TL: N33 21 47 W104 38 11. Stereo. Box 2684 88202. Phone: (800) 776-1050. Fax: (505) 296-6262. E-mail: flrradio@flc.org. Web Site: www.flc.org/flr/kwfl. Licensee: Family Life Broadcasting System. Group owner: Family Life Communications Inc. (acq 3-24-2004; $1). Network: Moody. Format: Relg. Target aud: Christian community. ♦Randy L. Carlson, pres; Dan Rosecrans, gen mgr.

Ruidoso

KBUY(AM)— November 1959: 1360 khz; 5 kw-D, 199 w-N. TL: N33 19 35 W105 40 02. Box 39 88355. Secondary address: 1096 Mechen Dr., Suite G3 88345. Phone: (505) 258-2222. Fax: (505) 258-2224. E-mail: kwesradio@kwes.net. Web Site: www.kwes.net. Licensee: Walton Stations New Mexico Inc. Group owner: Walton Stations (acq 10-22-82; $475,000 with co-located FM; 11-15-82). Network: Network: Westwood One, CNN Radio. Cohn & Marks. Format: Oldies. News staff: one; News: 14 hrs wkly. Target aud: 38 plus; 25-54 females. Spec prog: Sp 4 hrs wkly. ♦Layle Snead, progmg dir; Steve Swayze, chief of engrg.

KWES(FM)—Co-owned with KBUY(AM). 1982: 93.5 mhz; 25 kw. 58 ft. TL: N33 23 12 W105 40 14. Stereo. Web Site: www.kwes.net. Network: Westwood One. Format: C&W. News staff: one; News: 17 hrs wkly. Target aud: 18-54. ♦Harold Oakes, stn mgr; Steve Swayze, mus dir.

KIDX(FM)— 2000: 101.5 mhz; 920 w. Ant 2,850 ft. TL: N33 24 14 W105 46 56. Box 2010 88346. Phone: (505) 258-9922. Fax: (505) 258-2363. Web Site: www.kidx-thekid.com. Licensee: MTD Inc. (group owner) Format: Classic rock. ♦Tim Keithley, gen mgr.

Ruidoso Downs

KRUI(AM)— April 1984: 1490 khz; 1 kw-U. TL: N33 19 17 W105 35 24. 1086 Mechem Dr., Ruidoso 88345. Phone: (505) 258-9922. Fax: (505) 258-2363. E-mail: krui@ruidoso.net. Web Site: www.ruidoso.net/krui. Licensee: MTD Inc. (group owner; acq 12-88; $20,000; 12-19-88). Network: Network: Westwood One, ABC Information & Entertainment. Format: News, talk, sports. News: 14 hrs wkly. ♦Tim Keithley, gen mgr.

Santa Clara

KNUW(FM)— 1996: 95.3 mhz; 7.7 kw. 1,548 ft. TL: N32 51 47 W108 14 28. 106 S. Bullard St., Silver City 88061. Phone: (505) 534-8700. Phone: (505) 534-8701. Fax: (505) 534-8702. E-mail: knuw@zianet.com. Licensee: Mel-Mike Enterprise, Inc. Format: Sp. Target aud: General; Hispanic. ♦George H. Mesa, pres, gen mgr, opns VP, sls VP & progmg VP; Ken Bass, engrg VP.

Santa Fe

KABQ-FM— Nov 24, 1983: 104.1 mhz; 100 kw. 1,876 ft. TL: N35 46 50 W106 31 35. Stereo. 2700 San Pedro N.E., Albuquerque 87110. Phone: (505) 830-6400. Fax: (505) 830-6543. Web Site: www.eagle104.com. Licensee: Citicasters Licenses L.P. Group owner: Clear Channel Communications Inc. (acq 9-28-99; grpsl). Daniel Brenner. Format: World classic rock. News staff: one. Target aud: 25-54. ♦Chuck Hammond, VP & gen mgr; Bill May, chief of opns.

KBOM(FM)—Listing follows KTRC(AM).

KHFM(FM)— Aug 15, 1965: 95.5 mhz; 19 kw. 1,850 ft. TL: N35 53 08 W106 23 14. Stereo. 4125 Carlisle N. E., Albuquerque 87107. Phone:

Stations in the U.S. New Mexico

(505) 878-0980. Fax: (505) 878-0098. Web Site: www.agmradio.com. Licensee: AGM-Nevada L.L.C. Format: Class. Target aud: 18-49. ♦ Kip Allen, progmg dir.

KKOB Exp Stn— 1986: 770 khz; 230 w-U. TL: N35 40 56 W105 58 21. 500 4th St. N.W., Suite 500, Albuquerque 87102. Phone: (505) 767-6700. Fax: (505) 767-6767. Web Site: www.770kkob.com. Licensee: Citadel Broadcasting Co. Rep: McGavren Guild. Format: MOR. ♦ Milt McConnell, gen mgr & stn mgr; Dennis Logsdon, rgnl sls mgr; Glen Hebert, mktg dir & prom dir; Pat Frisch, opns mgr & progmg dir; Art Ortega, pub affrs dir; Mike Langner, chief of engrg.

KKRG(FM)— Sept 28, 1985: 105.1 mhz; 100 kw. 1,937 ft. TL: N35 47 15 W106 31 35. Stereo. 8009 Marble NE, Albuquerque 87110-7901. Phone: (505) 260-4400. Fax: (505) 262-9211. Licensee: Univision Radio License Corp. Group owner: Univision Radio (acq 9-22-2003; grpsl). Network: ABC. Rep: Allied Radio Partners. Format: Classic country. ♦ Chuck Morgan, gen mgr.

KKSS(FM)— March 1969: 97.3 mhz; 94 kw. 1,876 ft. TL: N35 46 50 W106 31 55. (CP: 100 kw, ant 1,631 ft.). Stereo. 8009 Marble N.E., Albuquerque 87110. Phone: (505) 262-1142. Fax: (505) 262-9211. Web Site: www.kiss973.com. Licensee: HBC License Corp. Group owner: Univision Radio (acq 9-22-2003; grpsl). Rep: D & R Radio. Format: CHR. Target aud: 18-34; Hispanic females. ♦ Chuck Morgan, gen mgr.

KRZY-FM— Nov 2, 1983: 105.9 mhz; 100 kw. Ant 1,919 ft. TL: N35 46 49 W106 31 34. Stereo. 2725 Broadbent Pkwy. N.E., Suite F, Albuquerque 87107. Phone: (505) 342-4141. Fax: (505) 344-8714. Licensee: Entravision Holdings LLC. Group owner: Entravision Communications Corp. (acq 3-14-2000; grpsl). Rep: Caballero. Leventhal, Senter & Lerman. Format: Sp. Target aud: 18-34. ♦ Margarita Wilder, gen mgr.

***KSFR(FM)—** Mar 16, 1990: 90.7 mhz; 3 kw. 199 ft. TL: N35 40 41 W105 59 29. Stereo. 6401 Richards Ave. 87508. Phone: (505) 428-1319. Fax: (505) 428-1237. E-mail: info@ksfr. Web Site: ksfr.org. Licensee: Santa Fe Community College. Format: Class, news/talk, jazz. News staff: one; News: 14 hrs wkly. Target aud: General. Spec prog: American Indian 4 hrs, Sp 4 hrs wkly. ♦ Dr. John McLaughlin, pres; Dallas Dearmin, stn mgr; Mickey Browne, opns dir; Christine Lord, sls VP; John P. Greenspan, progmg dir; William Dupuy, news dir; John Chiddester, chief of engrg.

KSWV(AM)— June 1966: 810 khz; 5 kw-D. TL: N35 39 17 W106 00 05. Box 1088, 102 Taos St. 87504. Phone: (505) 989-7441. Fax: (505) 989-7607. Licensee: La Voz Broadcasting Co. (acq 12-20-90; $150,000). Rep: Katz Hispanic. Format: Sp loc info & mus. Target aud: 25-54. ♦ Celina V. Gonzales, pres; Anthony Gonzales, gen mgr; John Chidester, progmg dir & chief of engrg.

KTRC(AM)— 1935: 1260 khz; 5 kw-D, 1 kw-N. TL: N35 40 36 W105 58 21. 2502 C Camino Entrada 87505. Phone: (505) 471-1067. Fax: (505) 473-2667. Licensee: A.G.M.-Nevada L.L.C. Group owner: American General Media (acq 8-9-00; grpsl). Network: ABC. Jones, Waldo, Holbrook & McDonough. Format: Sports. News staff: one; News: 14 hrs wkly. Target aud: 35-64; involved affluent adults. ♦ Scott Hutton, gen mgr.

KBOM(FM)— Co-owned with KTRC(AM).Not on air, target date: unknown: 94.7 mhz; 35 kw. 2,916 ft. TL: N36 14 50 W105 39 15. (CP: 100 kw, ant 981 ft.). (Acq 1996; $96,250.). Format: Dance.

KVSF(AM)— Feb 20, 1947: 1400 khz; 1 kw-U. TL: N35 41 16 W105 56 04. 2502 Camino Entrada, Suite C 87505. Phone: (505) 471-1067. Fax: (505) 473-2667. Licensee: A.G.M.-Nevada L.L.C. Group owner: American General Media (acq 8-9-00; grpsl). Format: Nostalgia. ♦ Russ Withers, pres; Scott Hutton, gen mgr; Gene Thompson, gen sls mgr & pub affrs dir; Susan Olivares, gen sls mgr; Eileen Munroe, prom dir; Dave Anderson, chief of engrg.

Santa Rosa

KIVA(FM)— 2001: 95.9 mhz; 1.5 kw. Ant 118 ft. TL: N34 56 47 W104 39 10. HC 69 Box 78 88435. Secondary address: 2818 Historic Rt. 66 88435. Phone: (505) 472-5777. Fax: (505) 472-5777. Licensee: KNXX Inc. Format: Adult contemp, country, Sp. ♦ Joseph Esquibel, gen mgr.

***KNLK(FM)—** 2004: 91.9 mhz; 100 w. Ant -26 ft. TL: N34 57 20 W104 40 53. 2020 Coal Ave. S.E., Albuquerque 87106. Phone: (505) 242-7163. Licensee: Board of Education of the City of Albuquerque, NM. Format: Sp. ♦ Michael Brasher, gen mgr.

KSSR(AM)— Nov 2, 1960: 1340 khz; 1 kw-U. TL: N34 56 40 W104 39 00. HC 69 Box 78 88435. Secondary address: 2818 Historic Rt. 66 88435. Phone: (505) 472-5777. Fax: (505) 472-5777. Licensee: J. Michael Esquibel. (acq 1989; $50,000). Network: Westwood One. Format: Adult contemp, country, Sp. News staff: one; News: 16 hrs wkly. Target aud: General; 85% Hispanic, plus largely transient motorists. ♦ Joseph Esquibel, gen mgr.

Silver City

KSCQ(FM)— Nov 28, 1989: 92.9 mhz; 11.5 kw. 1,023 ft. TL: N32 50 40 W108 14 18. Stereo. Box 2577 88062. Secondary address: 1560 N. Corbin St. 88061. Phone: (505) 388-4116. Fax: (505) 388-1759. E-mail: kscqfm@gilanet.com. Web Site: kscqfm.com. Licensee: The Q Inc. (acq 8-2-2004; $325,000). Format: Hot adult contemp, classic rock, oldies. News: 3 hrs wkly. Target aud: 25-55; baby boomers, generation X. ♦ Michael Rowse, pres, news dir & pub affrs dir; Bob Cosgrove, chief of engrg.

Socorro

KMXQ(FM)— Jan 22, 1995: 92.9 mhz; 6 kw. -177 ft. TL: N34 02 43 W106 54 21. Box 699 87801. Secondary address: 834 Hwy. 60 W. 87801. Phone: (505) 835-1286. Fax: (505) 835-2015. E-mail: kmxq@sdc.org. Licensee: Lakeshore Media L.L.C. (acq 10-29-2002; $450,000). Format: Country. Target aud: 12 plus. Spec prog: Farm 2 hrs, talk one hr wkly. ♦ Virgil Vigil, gen mgr, gen sls mgr, mktg mgr & prom dir; John Gonzales, prom mgr, progmg VP & engrg dir.

***KNMA(FM)—** Not on air, target date: unknown: 88.1 mhz; 7 kw vert. Ant 1,900 ft. TL: N32 49 49 W105 53 25. CSN International, 4002 N. 3300 E., Twin Falls, ID 83301. Phone: (208) 734-6633. Fax: (208) 736-1958. Licensee: CSN International. ♦ Michael Kestler, pres.

***KQRI(FM)—** Not on air, target date: unknown: 89.5 mhz; 100 kw. Ant 325 ft. TL: N34 16 37 W106 54 08. 5700 W. Oaks Blvd., Rocklin, CA 95765. Phone: (916) 251-1600. Fax: (916) 251-1650. Licensee: Educational Media Foundation. Group owner: EMF Broadcasting. ♦ Lloyd Parker, gen mgr.

Taos

KKTC(FM)— Not on air, target date: unknown: 95.9 mhz; 4 kw. Ant -630 ft. TL: N36 23 22 W105 35 09. Box 1914 87571. Phone: (505) 758-4491. Fax: (505) 758-4452. Licensee: DMC Broadcasting Inc. ♦ Darren Cordova, gen mgr.

KTAO(FM)— January 1978: 101.9 mhz; 1.05 kw. 2,824 ft. TL: N36 14 48 W105 39 15. Stereo. Box 1844, 192 Blueberry Hill Rd. 87571. Phone: (505) 758-5826. Fax: (505) 758-8430. Web Site: www.ktao.com. Licensee: Taos Communications Corp. (acq 1-78). Brown, Nietert & Kaufman. Format: AAA. News staff: 2; News: 7 hrs wkly. Target aud: 25-49; educated, responsive, upwardly mobile. Spec prog: Jazz 5 hrs, world beat 5 hrs wkly. ♦ Brad Hockmeyer, CEO, pres & progmg dir; Mitch Miller, opns dir; Paddy Mac, mus dir; Sara Allen, chief of engrg.

KVOT(AM)— Not on air, target date: unknown: 1340 khz; 1 kw-U. TL: N36 23 22 W105 35 09. 403 W. Pueblo Rd., Espanola 87532. Phone: (505) 753-2201. Licensee: Richard L. Garcia and Darren Cordova. ♦ Darren Cordova, gen mgr.

KXMT(FM)— Dec 1, 2000: 99.1 mhz; 60 kw. Ant 2,135 ft. TL: N36 51 32 W106 00 28. Box 1914 87571. Secondary address: 1128-A Paseo del Pueblo Sur 87571. Phone: (505) 758-4491. Fax: (505) 758-4452. Web Site: www.kxmt.com. Licensee: DMC Broadcasting Inc. (acq 3-19-2003; $645,000. with KKIT(FM) Angel Fire). Format: Mexican rgnl. ♦ Darren Cordova, pres & gen mgr.

Tatum

KTUM(FM)— 2003: 107.1 mhz; 100 kw. Ant 918 ft. TL: N32 52 50 W103 41 01. Box 2010, Ruidoso Downs 88346. Phone: (505) 258-9922. Fax: (505) 258-2363. Licensee: MTD Inc. (group owner) Format: Classic rock. ♦ Tim Keithley, gen mgr.

Thoreau

KXTC(FM)— Oct 21, 1991: 99.9 mhz; 100 kw. Ant 1,210 ft. TL: N35 36 13 W108 40 45. Stereo. 1632 S. 2nd St., Gallup 87301-5836. Phone: (505) 722-4442. Fax: (505) 722-7745. Licensee: Clear Channel Broadcasting Licenses Inc. (acq 9-7-2000). Borsari & Paxson. Format: Top 40 hits. News staff: 2; News: 2 hrs wkly. Target aud: 18-44; Women. Spec prog: American Indian one hr, Sp 8 hrs wkly. ♦ MaryAnn Armijo, gen mgr.

Truth or Consequences

KCHS(AM)— September 1944: 1400 khz; 1 kw-U. TL: N33 08 26 W107 13 55. 1747 E. 3rd, Box 351 87901. Phone: (505) 894-2400. Fax: (505) 894-3998. E-mail: gpkohs@zianet.com. Web Site: www.gpkmedia.com. Licensee: Myrna Baird-Kohs dba GPK Media LLC (acq 6-18-92). Network: AP Radio. Format: Country, news, oldies. News staff: 3. Target aud: General; area residents & visitors at lake. Spec prog: Sp 12 hrs wkly. ♦ Myrna Kohs, gen mgr, gen sls mgr & mus dir; Patrick Kohs, pres, prom VP, progmg dir & news dir; Gil Edwards, pub affrs dir & chief of engrg.

KKVS(FM)— Nov 1, 1984: 98.7 mhz; 100 kw. 2,644 ft. TL: N32 58 15 W107 13 26. Stereo. Box 968, Las Cruces 88004. Secondary address: 1355 E. California St., Las Cruces 88001. Phone: (505) 525-9298. Fax: (505) 525-9419. E-mail: radiolc@kgrt.com. Web Site: www.vista.fm. Licensee: Richardson Commercial Corp. (acq 8-6-01; $1,650,000). Fletcher, Heald & Hildreth. Format: Rgnl Mexican. News staff: 2; News: 2 hrs wkly. Target aud: 25-54; Hispanic. ♦ Allen Lumeyer, VP & gen mgr; Ernesto Garcia, opns mgr.

Tse Bonito

KHAC(AM)— Mar 21, 1967: 880 khz; 10 kw-D, 430 w-N. TL: N35 38 41 W109 01 13. Box 9090, Hwy. 264, Window Rock, AZ 86515. Phone: (505) 371-5587. Fax: (505) 371-5588. E-mail: wim@westernindian.net. Web Site: www.westernindian.org. Licensee: Western Indian Ministries. (group owner) Format: Christian, CHR, Navajo. Indian. ♦ Lenora A. Brown, gen mgr; Bill Vadasy, mus dir; Bruce Kinde, engrg mgr.

Tucumcari

KQAY-FM— Listing follows KTNM(AM).

KTNM(AM)— 1941: 1400 khz; 1 kw-U. TL: N35 10 15 W103 42 25. Box 668, 902 S. Date St. 88401. Phone: (505) 461-0522. Phone: (505) 461-1400. Fax: (505) 461-0092. E-mail: ktnmkqay@yahoo.com. Web Site: www.tucumcari.ws. Licensee: Quay Broadcasters Inc. Group owner: Roswell Radio Inc./Quay Broadcasters Inc. (acq 1-10-03; with co-located FM). Network: ABC. Cohn & Marks. Format: C&W. Target aud: General. Spec prog: Sp 18 hrs wkly. ♦ Diane Paris, gen mgr, gen sls mgr, prom mgr & news dir; Greg Carnefix, progmg dir.

KQAY-FM— Co-owned with KTNM(AM). Jan 19, 1968: 92.7 mhz; 3 kw. 64 ft. TL: N35 10 15 W103 42 25. Stereo. Web Site: www.tucumari.was. Format: Adult contemp.

New Mexico • Directory of Radio

White Rock

KSFQ(FM)— 1991: 101.1 mhz; 600 w. Ant 1,863 ft. TL: N35 53 09 W106 23 16. (CP: 2.5 kw). Stereo. 1401 Maclovia, Suite E, Santa Fe 87505. Phone: (505) 989-3338. Fax: (505) 989-3881. E-mail: john@majhor.com. Web Site: www.mix100radio.com. Licensee: Clear Channel Broadcasting Licenses Inc. (acq 9-1-2000). Network: Westwood One. Rep: Roslin. Fisher, Wayland, Cooper, Leader & Zaragoza. Format: Urban oldies. News: 7 hrs wkly. Target aud: 25-54. ♦ Bill Rogan, opns dir; Steve Rossler, gen sls mgr; John Majhor, progmg mgr; Margie Jaramillo, pub affrs dir; Don Davis, engrg dir.

Zuni

*KSHI(FM)— Apr 6, 1978: 90.9 mhz; 100 w. Ant -249 ft. TL: N35 05 18 W108 47 22. Stereo. Box 339 87327. Phone: (505) 782-4144. Fax: (505) 782-5069. Licensee: Zuni Communications Authority. Format: Educ. Target aud: 18-34; primarily Indian. Spec prog: Indian 20 hrs wkly. ♦ Duane Chimoni, gen mgr.

New York

Albany

WAMC(AM)— 1934: 1400 khz; 1 kw-U. TL: N42 41 21 W73 47 37. Box 66600 12206. Secondary address: 318 Central Ave. 12206. Phone: (518) 465-5233. Fax: (518) 432-6974. Web Site: www.wamc.org. Licensee: WAMC. Group owner: WAMC/Northeast Public Radio (acq 4-24-03; $500,000). Format: News/talk. ♦ Alan S. Chartock, CEO.

*WAMC-FM— Oct 1, 1958: 90.3 mhz; 10 kw. Ant 1,970 ft. TL: N42 38 14 W73 10 07. Stereo. Box 66600, 318 Central Ave. 12206. Phone: (518) 465-5233. Phone: (800) 323-9262. Fax: (518) 432-6974. E-mail: mail@wamc.org. Web Site: www.wamc.org. Licensee: WAMC. Group owner: WAMC/Northeast Public Radio (acq 7-1-82). Network: Network: NPR, PRI. Dow, Lohnes & Albertson. Format: News, talk. News staff: 5; News: 48 hrs wkly. Target aud: General. Spec prog: Jazz 18 hrs, folk 7 hrs. ♦ Alan S. Chartock, CEO; Dona Frank, chmn & sls dir.

*WCDB(FM)— Mar 1, 1978: 90.9 mhz; 100 w. 222 ft. TL: N42 41 16 W73 49 19. Stereo. Campus Ctr. 316, 1400 Washington Ave. 12222. Phone: (518) 442-5234. Phone: (518) 442-5262. Fax: (518) 442-4366. Web Site: www.wcdb.albany.edu. Licensee: State University of New York. Format: Div, AOR, urban contemp. News: 15 hrs wkly. Target aud: 15-55; students & surrounding community. Spec prog: Gospel 3 hrs, Sp 3 hrs, dance 3 hrs, jazz 10 hrs, metal 10 hrs wkly. ♦ Ed Horn, mus dir; Jeff Harfield, chief of engrg.

WDCD(AM)— May 1948: 1540 khz; 50 kw-U, DA-1. TL: N42 44 01 W73 51 49. 4243 Albany St. 12212. Phone: (518) 862-1540. Fax: (518) 862-1545. Web Site: www.crawfordbroadcasting.com. Licensee: Kimtron Inc. Group owner: Crawford Broadcasting Co. (acq 1995; $700,000). Target aud: 30-54; educated, conservative, committed religious. ♦ Donald B. Crawford, pres; Robert Hammond, gen mgr; Mark Shuttleworth, prom dir & progmg dir.

WDDY(AM)— June 14, 1924: 1460 khz; 5 kw-U, DA-N. TL: N42 37 21 W73 48 09. 52 Corporate Cir., Suite K 12203. Phone: (518) 464-1311. Fax: (518) 464-4185. Web Site: www.radiodisney.com. Licensee: Radio Disney Group LLC. Group owner: ABC Inc. (acq 2-12-02; $2 million). Network: ABC. Rep: Katz Radio. Format: Family & children programs. News staff: one. Target aud: 25-54; general. ♦ Rob Thomson, gen mgr; Diane Frank, prom mgr.

WGNA-FM— December 1973: 107.7 mhz; 12.5 kw. 984 ft. TL: N42 38 18 W73 59 51. 800 New Loudon Rd., Suite 4200, Latham 12110. Phone: (518) 782-1474. Fax: (518) 782-1486. E-mail: wgna1077@aol.com. Web Site: www.wgna.com. Licensee: Regent Licensee of Mansfield Inc. Group owner: Regent Communications Inc. (acq 8-24-2001; grpsl). Latham & Watkins. Format: Country. ♦ Robert Ausfeld, gen mgr; John Hirsh, stn mgr.

WGY(AM)— See Schenectady

WHAZ(AM)— See Troy

WHRL(FM)— Sept 1, 1966: 103.1 mhz; 6 kw. 328 ft. TL: N42 39 46 W73 40 37. Stereo. One Washington Sq. 12205. Phone: (518) 452-4800. Fax: (518) 452-4855. Web Site: www.whrl.com. Licensee: Clear Channel Radio License Inc. Group owner: Clear Channel Communications Inc. (acq 8-5-98; grpsl). Rep: Clear Channel. Format: Alternative. Target aud: 21-54; upscale arrivers. ♦ Dennis Lamme, exec VP & gen mgr; John Cooper, stn mgr; Lisa Biello, opns dir, progmg dir & mus dir; Kristen Delaney, sls dir; Melissa Keegan, natl sls mgr; Selena Dutcher, mktg dir & prom dir; Chuck Custer, news dir; Rebecca Harrington, pub affrs dir; Dave Abdoo, chief of engrg.

WKLI-FM— 1972: 100.9 mhz; 6 kw. Ant 298 ft. TL: N42 43 54 W73 52 56. Stereo. 6 Johnson Rd., Latham 12110. Phone: (518) 786-6600. Fax: (518) 786-6610. Web Site: www.albanymagic.com. Licensee: 6 Johnson Road Licenses Inc. Group owner: Pamal Broadcasting Ltd. (acq 10-9-2001). Format: Adult standards. Target aud: 25-54; upscale women. ♦ Stacy Rogers, gen mgr.

WOFX(AM)— See Troy

WPYX(FM)— Sept 16, 1980: 106.5 mhz; 15.3 kw. 902 ft. TL: N42 38 09 W74 00 05. Stereo. One Washington Sq. 12205. Phone: (518) 452-4800. Fax: (518) 452-4855. Web Site: www.pyx106.com. Licensee: Capstar TX L.P. Group owner: Clear Channel Communications Inc. (acq 8-30-00; grpsl). Format: Classic rock. Target aud: 25-54. ♦ Dennis Lamme, VP & gen mgr; John Cooper, opns dir.

WROW(AM)— Sept 30, 1947: 590 khz; 5 kw-D, 1 kw-N, DA-2. TL: N42 34 25 W73 47 12. 6 Johnson Rd., Lathan 12110. Phone: (518) 786-6600. Fax: (518) 786-6610. Web Site: www.wrow.com. Licensee: 6 Johnson Road Licenses Inc. Group owner: Pamal Broadcasting Ltd. (acq 10-19-01; grpsl). Network: CBS. Rep: Allied Radio Partners. Format: News/talk. News: 8 hrs wkly. Target aud: 35 plus; affluent, educated, white collar, upwardly mobile, homeowners. Spec prog: Gospel 3 hrs wkly. ♦ Jim Morrell, pres; Mike Morgan, opns VP; Stacy Rogers, gen mgr & gen sls mgr; Paul Vandenburg, progmg VP; Mike Carey, news dir; Dave Abdoo, chief of engrg.

WYJB(FM)— Co-owned with WROW(AM). October 1966: 95.5 mhz; 12 kw. 1,020 ft. TL: N42 38 11 W74 00 00. Stereo. Web Site: www.b95.com. Format: Soft adult contemp. Target aud: 25-54. ♦ Amy Smith, prom dir; Mike Morgan, opns dir & progmg VP; Chris Holmberg, mus dir.

WTMM(AM)— See Rensselaer

WTRY-FM— See Rotterdam

Albion

*WJCA(FM)— Dec 27, 2001: 102.1 mhz; 3.7 kw. Ant 423 ft. TL: N43 11 19 W78 08 53. Box 110 14411. Secondary address: 111 N. Main St., Elmira 14901. Phone: (585) 589-7963. Fax: (585) 589-7956. E-mail: wjca@csnradio.com. Licensee: CSN International (group owner; acq 4-19-99). Format: Christian. ♦ Lorenzo Galletti, gen mgr; Gina Galletti, opns VP.

Alfred

*WALF(FM)— 1971: 89.7 mhz; 200 w. 73 ft. TL: N42 15 17 W77 47 13. Stereo. 1 Saxon Dr 14802. Phone: (607) 871-2287. Web Site: www.walfradio.org. Licensee: Alfred University. Network: Network: NPR, ABC Information & Entertainment. Format: Div. ♦ Kelly Donohoe, stn mgr.

*WETD(FM)— Mar 19, 1973: 90.7 mhz; 360 w. 282 ft. TL: N42 15 37 W77 47 51. Stereo. WETD Studios, Alfred State College, 10 Upper Campus Dr. 14802. Phone: (607) 587-2907. E-mail: wetd@alfredstate.edu. Web Site: www.alfredstate.edu/wetd. Licensee: State University of New York. Format: Rock/AOR. ♦ Maria Terrigino, gen mgr.

WZKZ(FM)— Feb 28, 1999: 101.9 mhz; 1.3 kw. 699 ft. TL: N42 12 20 W77 48 46. 3012 Eastside Ave., Wellsville 14895. Phone: (585) 593-9553; (607) 733-5626. Fax: (585) 593-9554. E-mail: wzkz@wzkzradio.com. Web Site: www.wzkzradio.com. Licensee: Pembrook Pines Elmira Ltd. Group owner: Pembrook Pines Media Group. Network: Jones Radio Networks. Rep: Interep. Format: Country. News staff: 2; News: 10 hrs wkly. Target aud: 18-54. ♦ Robert Pfuntner, CEO; Rod Biehler, gen mgr; Bob Weigand, opns mgr & news dir; Jim Davison, progmg.

Altamont

WZMR(FM)— June 26, 1968: 104.9 mhz; 570 w. Ant 1,050 ft. TL: N42 37 00 W74 00 45. 6 Johnson Rd., Lathan 12110. Phone: (518) 786-6600. Fax: (518) 786-6610. Web Site: www.froggy107.com. Licensee: 6 Johnson Road Licenses Inc. Group owner: Pamal Broadcasting Ltd. (acq 10-19-2001; grpsl). Network: ABC. Format: Country. Target aud: 45 plus. ♦ Stacy Rogers, gen mgr.

Amherst

WUFO(AM)— 1948: 1080 khz; 1 kw-D. TL: N42 56 46 W78 49 43. 89 LaSalle Ave., Buffalo 14214. Phone: (716) 834-1080. Fax: (716) 837-1438. E-mail: wufo1080am@aol.com. Web Site: www.wufoam.com. Licensee: Sheridan Broadcasting. (acq 3-1-72). Network: American Urban. Format: Gospel. News: 5 hrs wkly. Target aud: 25-54; Black adults, relg foundation, strong work ethics. Spec prog: Talk. ♦ Ron Davenport, pres; Alan Lincoln, gen mgr; Carol M. Salter, stn mgr, opns mgr & progmg dir.

Amsterdam

WBKK(FM)— Aug 1, 1975: 97.7 mhz; 790 w. 623 ft. TL: N42 59 05 W74 10 49. (CP: 1.6 kw). Stereo. 2nd Fl., 108 Erie Blvd., Schenectady 12305. Phone: (518) 388-9255. Fax: (518) 374-6851. Web Site: www.wbkk.com. Licensee: GEM Co. (acq 10-3-94; $400,000 with co-located AM; 10-24-94). Rep: Christal. Format: Class. Target aud: 18-45; general. ♦ Michael Schaus, gen mgr & stn mgr.

WCSS(AM)— Apr 8, 1948: 1490 khz; 1 kw-U. TL: N42 57 40 W74 10 35. 135 Guy Park Ave., Suite 1 12010. Phone: (518) 843-2500. Fax: (518) 842-0315. E-mail: wcss@verizon.net. Licensee: IZ Communications Corp. (acq 9-13-99; $188,000). Network: Network: Jones Radio Networks, USA. Format: News/talk, Music of Your Life. News staff: one; News: 20 hrs wkly. Target aud: 25 plus; adults interested in loc, community info & mus. Spec prog: Local progmg & talk 12 hrs wkly. ♦ Joseph Isabel, pres; Sam Zurlo, gen mgr.

WVTL(AM)— Aug 16, 1961: 1570 khz; 1 kw-D, 207 w-N. TL: N42 54 38 W74 13 04. 5816 State Hwy. 30 12010. Phone: (518) 843-9284. Fax: (518) 843-5225. Web Site: www.1570wvtl.com. Licensee: Roser Communications Network Inc. (acq 10-21-94; $400,000. with WBUG-FM Fort Plain; FTR: 12-5-94). Format: News, talk, sports. News staff: 2; News: 10 hrs wkly. Target aud: 25 plus. ♦ Ken Roser Jr., gen mgr; J.P. Marks, stn mgr; Roxanne Roser, gen sls mgr.

Arcade

*WCOF(FM)— 2005: 89.5 mhz; 1 kw. Ant 593 ft. TL: N42 27 41 W78 18 26. Box 506, Bath 14819. Phone: (607) 776-4151. Fax: (607) 776-6929. E-mail: mail@fln.org. Web Site: www.fln.org. Licensee: Family Life Ministries Inc. Group owner: Family Life Network. Format: Contemp Christian. News staff: 7; News: 14 hrs wkly1. Target aud: 25-55; general. ♦ Dick Snavely, CFO; Rick Snavely, pres & gen mgr.

Argyle

*WNGN(FM)— August 1994: 91.9 mhz; 240 w. 571 ft. TL: N43 13 33 W73 26 34. Box 36 King Rd., Buskirk 12028. Phone: (518) 686-0975. Fax: (518) 686-0975. E-mail: wngn@wngn.net. Licensee: Northeast Gospel Broadcasting Inc. (acq 3-17-93; 4-5-93). Network: Moody. Format: Christian, inspirational. News: one hr wkly. Target aud: 35-54; general. ♦ Brian Larson, pres.

Arlington

WRRB(FM)— December 1989: 96.9 mhz; 3 kw. 1,010 ft. TL: N41 43 11 W73 59 45. (CP: 310 w). Stereo. Box 416, Poughkeepsie 12602. Secondary address: 2 Pendell Rd., Poughkeepsie 12602. Phone: (845) 471- 1500. Fax: (845) 454-1204. Web Site: www.cumulus.com. Licensee: Cumulus Licensing Corp. Group owner: Cumulus Media Inc. (acq 1-23-02; grpsl). Fisher, Wayland, Cooper, Leader & Zaragoza. Format: Progsv adult rock. News: 5 hrs wkly. Target aud: 25-54; upscale professionals. ♦ Chuck Benfer, gen mgr.

Attica

WLOF(FM)— Nov 9, 1977: 101.7 mhz; 3 kw. Ant 295 ft. TL: N42 50 51 W78 21 01. Stereo. 6325 Sheridan Dr., Williamsville 14221. Phone: (716) 839-6117. Fax: (716) 839-0400. Web Site: www.wlof.net. Licensee: Holy Family Communications Inc. Group owner: Holy Family Communications acq 12-20-99; $655,000). Format: Relg. Target aud: 25-54; blue collar, housewives. ♦ Jim Wright, gen mgr.

Stations in the U.S.   New York

Developers & Brokers of Radio Properties
contact American Media Services at our suite: Philadelphia Marriott Downtown
215-625-2900
843-972-2200
americanmediaservices.com
Charleston, SC
Dallas, TX · Chicago, Il · Austin, TX

American Media Services, LLC

Auburn

WAUB(AM)— Dec 24, 1959: 1590 khz; 500 w-D, 1 kw-N, DA-2. TL: N42 54 34 W76 36 09. 5998 Experimental Blvd., Geneva 13021. Phone: (315) 258-0937. Fax: (315) 258-9248. E-mail: tbaker@flradiogroup.com. Web Site: www.fingerlakes1.com. Licensee: Auburn Broadcasting Inc. Group owner: Finger Lakes Radio Group (acq 7-2-97; $70,000 plus additonal consideration). Network: CBS. James L. Oyster. Format: Talk radio. Target aud: General. ♦Alan Bishop, pres; Kelly Bailey, gen sls mgr; Ted Baker, news dir.

*****WDWN(FM)**— Oct 31, 1972: 89.1 mhz; 3 kw. 102 ft. TL: N42 56 40 W76 32 33. Stereo. 197 Franklin St. 13021. Phone: (315) 255-1743, EXT. 2282. Phone: (315) 253-0449. Fax: (315) 255-2690. Web Site: www.wdwn.fm. Licensee: Cayuga County Community College. (acq 10-72). Format: AOR. Target aud: 18-25; high school & college students, young adults. ♦Dennis Golladay, pres; Steven Keeler, gen mgr; Stephen Roder, chief of engrg.

WPHR(FM)— May 20, 1949: 106.9 mhz; 14 kw. 941 ft. TL: N42 48 05 W76 26 14. Stereo. 500 Plum St., Suite 100, Syracuse 13243. Phone: (315) 472-9797. Fax: (315) 473-0049. Licensee: Clear Channel Broadcasting Licenses Inc. Group owner: Clear Channel Communications Inc. (acq 3-24-2000). Format: Urban Contemp. Target aud: 25-54; educated, up-scale, high income, mobile, family oriented. ♦Merrill B. Charles, pres; Joel Delmonico, gen mgr; Laura Kaplan, prom dir; Butch Charles, progmg dir; Kenny Dees, mus dir; John Paul, news dir.

WWLF(AM)— Jan 26, 1927: 1340 khz; 1 kw-U. TL: N42 57 05 W76 35 05. 401 W. Kirkpatrick St., Syracuse 13204. Phone: (315) 472-0222. Fax: (315) 478-7745. Web Site: www.radiodisney.com. Licensee: WOLF Radio Inc. (group owner; acq 6-26-98; $103,000). Network: Radio Disney. Format: Children. ♦Craig Fox, pres & gen mgr; Larry Goldberg, gen sls mgr & chief of engrg; Melissa Burnett, prom mgr.

Avon

WYSL(AM)— Jan 23, 1987: 1040 khz; 2.5 kw-D, 500 w-N, DA-2. TL: N42 51 16 W77 42 39. Stereo. Box 236 14414-0236. Secondary address: 5620 S. Lima Rd. 14414. Phone: (585) 346-3000. Fax: (585) 346-0450. E-mail: info@wysl1040.com. Web Site: www.wysl1040.com. Licensee: Radio Livingston Ltd. Network: CNN Radio. Format: News/sports. News staff: 3; News: 160 hrs wkly. Target aud: 35 plus; general. Spec prog: Relg 4 hrs wkly. ♦Robert Savage, CEO; Robert C. Savage, pres; Judith Day, CFO & exec VP; J.C. Delass, gen mgr & stn mgr; Bob D'Angelo, opns dir.

Babylon

WBAB(FM)— Aug 27, 1958: 102.3 mhz; 3 kw. 268 ft. TL: N40 47 58 W73 20 08. Stereo. 555 Sunrise Hwy., West Babylon 11704-6009. Phone: (631) 587-1023. Fax: (631) 587-1282. E-mail: wbab@wbab.com. Web Site: wbab.com. Licensee: CXR Holdings L.L.C. Group owner: Cox Broadcasting (acq 5-22-98; grpsl). Rep: Christal. Format: AOR. News staff: one; News: 2 hrs wkly. Target aud: 25-54; men. ♦Kim Guthrie, gen mgr.

WNYG(AM)— Jan 1, 1958: 1440 khz; 1 kw-D, 38 w-N. TL: N40 42 32 W73 21 53. 404 Rt. 109, West Babylon 11704. Phone: (631) 321-9640. Fax: (631) 422-5992. E-mail: spiritny@verizon.net. Web Site: www.wnygspiritofny.com. Licensee: Multicultural Radio Broadcasting Licensee LLC. Group owner: Multicultural Radio Broadcasting Inc. (acq 6-14-00; $850,000). Format: Contemp Christian. News staff: one; News: 3 hrs wkly. Target aud: 25-64. ♦Doug Edwards, pres & progmg dir; Phyllis Rose, gen mgr.

Baldwinsville

*****WBXL(FM)**— Jan 29, 1975: 90.5 mhz; 175 w. 207 ft. TL: N43 09 47 W76 18 47. Stereo. Baker High School, 29 E. Oneida St. 13027. Phone: (315) 638-6010. Phone: (315) 638-6000. Licensee: Baldwinsville Central School District. Format: CHR. Family of school district students. ♦Peter Hunn, gen mgr.

WSEN(AM)— Feb 25, 1959: 1050 khz; 2.5 kw-D, DA. TL: N43 10 46 W76 20 19. Stereo. Box 1050 13027. Secondary address: 8456 Smoky Hollow Rd. 13027. Phone: (315) 635-3971. Fax: (315) 635-3490. Web Site: www.wfbl.com. Licensee: Buckley Broadcasting of New York LLC. Group owner: Buckley Broadcasting Corp. (acq 8-20-80; $700,000. with co-located FM; FTR: 8-11-80). Network: CBS. Rep: McGavren Guild. Format: Talk. Target aud: 35 plus; well-educated professionals with disposable income. ♦Richard Buckley, pres; Doug Fleniken, VP & gen mgr; Judith Kelly, gen sls mgr; John Carucci, prom mgr; Jim Tate, progmg dir; Al Jenner, chief of engrg.

WSEN-FM— Nov 10, 1967: 92.1 mhz; 25 kw. 300 ft. TL: N43 10 46 W76 20 19. Stereo. E-mail: webmaster@wsenfm.com. Web Site: www.wsenfm.com. Format: Oldies. Target aud: 25-54; well-educated professionals with disposable income. ♦John Carucci, prom dir; Gary Dunes, progmg dir.

Ballston Spa

WKKF(FM)— May 27, 1968: 102.3 mhz; 4.1 kw. 386 ft. TL: N42 52 44 W73 51 47. Stereo. 1 Washington Sq., Albany 12205. Phone: (518) 452-4800. Fax: (518) 452-4885. Web Site: www.wkkf.com. Licensee: Clear Channel Radio Licenses Inc. Group owner: Clear Channel Communications Inc. (acq 3-6-97). Rep: Clear Channel. Wilmer, Cutler & Pickering. Format: Contemp hit. Target aud: 18-34; upscale, hip women. ♦Dennis Lamme, pres, exec VP & gen mgr; John Cooper, stn mgr; Rob Dawes, opns dir.

Batavia

WBTA(AM)— Feb 6, 1941: 1490 khz; 500 w-D, 1 kw-N. TL: N42 58 37 W78 11 12. (CP: 1 kw-U. TL: N42 58 35 W78 11 12). 113 Main St. 14020. Phone: (585) 344-1490. Fax: (585) 344-1441. E-mail: debbie@wbta1490.com. Web Site: www.wbta1490.com. Licensee: HPL Communications Inc. (acq 11-24-2003; $275,000). Network: ABC Information & Entertainment. Format: News/talk, soft rock. Target aud: Older, upscale audience. Spec prog: Farm 10 hrs, sports 9 hrs wkly. ♦Daniel C. Fischer, pres; Daniel Fischer, gen mgr; Lorne Way, gen sls mgr; Joe Condidorio, prom dir & news dir.

*****WGCC-FM**— Nov 13, 1985: 90.7 mhz; 880 w. 164 ft. TL: N43 01 03 W78 08 18. Stereo. One College Rd. 14020. Phone: (585) 343-0055, EXT. 6284. Phone: (585) 343-9422. Fax: (585) 345-6806. E-mail: cmplatt@genesee.edu. Web Site: wgcc-fm.com. Licensee: Genesee Community College Board of Trustees. Format: Serious rock, rock/AOR, modern rock, classic rock. News staff: one; News: 5 hrs wkly. Target aud: 13-30; high school & college youth. Spec prog: .Heavy metal, alternative, oldies ♦Chuck Platt, pres; Melody Nardone, stn mgr.

Bath

WABH(AM)— Nov 2, 1962: 1380 khz; 500 w-D. TL: N42 20 11 W77 17 34. (CP: 5 kw-D, 350 w-N). Box 72, E. Washington St. Ext. 14810. Phone: (607) 776-3326. Fax: (607) 776-6161. E-mail: wvinsales@stny.rr.com. Web Site: www.wvinradio.com. Licensee: Pembrook Pines Mass Media Inc. Group owner: Pembrook Pines Media Group (acq 4-13-90; with co-located FM; FTR: 5-7-90). Network: CBS. Format: Oldies. Target aud: General. Spec prog: Farm one hr wkly. ♦Bill Fleishman, gen mgr.

WVIN-FM—Co-owned with WABH(AM). Oct 10, 1971: 98.3 mhz; 3 kw. 351 ft. TL: N42 19 06 W77 21 27. (CP: 2.75 kw, ant 341 ft.). Stereo. Web Site: www.wvinradio.com. Format: Soft adult contemp. Spec prog: Jazz 2 hrs wkly.

*****WCIK(FM)**— Aug 29, 1983: 103.1 mhz; 790 w. Ant 532 ft. TL: N42 20 07 W77 27 27. Stereo. Box 506, 7634 Campbell Creek Rd. 14810. Phone: (607) 776-4151. Fax: (607) 776-6929. E-mail: mail@fln.org. Web Site: www.fln.org. Licensee: Family Life Ministries Inc. Group owner: Family Life Network. Network: Salem Radio Network. Format: Christian contemp. News staff: 7; News: 14 hrs wkly. Target aud: 25-55; general. ♦Dick Snavely, CFO & VP; Rick Snavely, pres & gen mgr.

Bay Shore

WBZO(FM)— February 1993: 103.1 mhz; 3 kw. 285 ft. TL: N40 45 04 W73 12 52. Stereo. 234 Airport Plaza Blvd., Farmington 11735. Phone: (631) 770-4200. Fax: (631) 770-0101. Web Site: www.b103.com. Licensee: WCMB Broadcasting L.P. Group owner: Barnstable Broadcasting Inc. (acq 3-6-97; $12.45 million). Rep: D & R Radio. Verner, Liipfert, Bernhard, McPherson & Hand. Format: Oldies. News staff: one; News: 25 hrs wkly. Target aud: General. ♦Dave Widmer, gen mgr; Bill Wise, progmg dir; Michael Glaser, chief of engrg.

Beacon

WBNR(AM)— Dec 17, 1959: 1260 khz; 1 kw-D, 500 w-N, DA-2. TL: N41 29 32 W73 58 43. Stereo. Box 310 12508. Secondary address: 715 Rt. 52 12508. Phone: (845) 831-8000. Fax: (845) 838-2109. Web Site: www.thesoundofthevalley.com. Licensee: 6 Johnson Road Licenses Inc. Group owner: Pamal Broadcasting Ltd. (acq 10-19-2001; grpsl). Network: ABC. Format: Stardust. News staff: 2; News: 2 hrs wkly. Target aud: 35 plus. Spec prog: Relg 5 hrs wkly. ♦James Morrell, CEO; Fred Bennett, exec VP & stn mgr.

WGNY-FM—See Newburgh

WSPK(FM)—See Poughkeepsie

Big Flats

WENI-FM— April 1989: 97.7 mhz; 1.30 kw. Ant 482 ft. TL: N42 09 43 W77 02 15. Box 1047, Corning 14830. Secondary address: 2309 Davis Rd., Corning 14830. Phone: (607) 962-4646. Fax: (607) 962-1138. Licensee: Group A Licensee LLC. Group owner: Route 81 Radio LLC (acq 10-31-2003; grpsl). Network: ABC. Rep: Roslin. Format: Oldies. Target aud: 25-54. ♦Bob Eolin, gen mgr, natl sls mgr & progmg dir; Richard Burton, rgnl sls mgr; Dee Eolin, news dir & pub affrs dir; Jim Appleton, chief of engrg.

Binghamton

WAAL(FM)—Listing follows WYOS(AM).

WENE(AM)—See Endicott

*****WHRW(FM)**— Mar 1, 1966: 90.5 mhz; 1.45 kw. -47 ft. TL: N42 05 24 W75 58 05. Stereo. Box 2000, Univ. Union, Binghamton Univ. 13902-6000. Phone: (607) 777-2137. Fax: (607) 777-6501. E-mail: whrwfm@binghamton.edu. Web Site: www.whrwfm.org. Licensee: State University of New York. Format: Var/div. News: 5 hrs wkly. Target aud: General. Spec prog: It 3 hrs, Jazz 9 hrs, Pol 3 hrs, Relg 6 hrs, Sp 9 hrs wkly. ♦Sam Smith, gen mgr; Brian Napolitano, chief of engrg.

WHWK(FM)—Listing follows WNBF(AM).

*****WIFF(FM)**— 1995: 90.1 mhz; 100 w. Ant 686 ft. TL: N42 03 10 W75 42 07. 111 N. Main St., Elmira 14901. Phone: (607) 732-2484. Fax: (607) 732-8704. E-mail: wiff@csnradio.com. Web Site: www.csnradio.com. Licensee: CSN International (group owner; acq 5-30-2003; $67,000). Format: Christian adult contemp. News staff: 2; News: 8 hrs wkly. Target aud: General. ♦Lorenzo Galletti, gen mgr.

WINR(AM)— 1946: 680 khz; 5 kw-D, 500 w-N, DA-2. TL: N42 06 53 W75 51 16. 320 N. Jensen Rd., Vestal 13850-2111. Phone: (607) 785-3131. Fax: (607) 584-5900. Licensee: AMFM Radio Licenses LLC. Group owner: Clear Channel Communications Inc. (acq 2-13-2001; $1 million). Network: CBS. Rep: Savalli, Fisher, Wayland, Cooper, Leader & Zaragoza. Format: MOR, news/talk. News staff: one; News: 10 hrs wkly. Target aud: 35 plus. ♦Tom Barney, gen mgr; Doug Mosher, opns mgr.

WNBF(AM)— 1928: 1290 khz; 5 kw-U, DA-2. TL: N42 03 31 W75 57 14. Box 414 13902. Phone: (607) 772-8400. Fax: (607) 772-9806. Web Site: www.wnbf.com. Licensee: Citadel Broadcasting Co. Group

New York

owner: Citadel Broadcasting Corp. (acq 6-9-99; grpsl). Format: News/talk. Target aud: 35-64. ♦ Roger Neal, progmg dir; Bernie Fionte, news dir; Larry Hodge, chief of engrg.

WHWK(FM)— Co-owned with WNBF(AM). September 1956: 98.1 mhz; 10 kw. 960 ft. TL: N42 03 34 W75 57 06. Stereo. Web Site: www.whwk.com. Format: Country. Target aud: 25-54. ♦ Ed Walker, progmg dir.

*WSKG-FM— Oct 22, 1975: 89.3 mhz; 10.2 kw. 942 ft. TL: N42 03 22 W75 56 39. Stereo. Box 3000 13902. Phone: (607) 729-0100. Fax: (607) 729-7328. Fax: (607) 231-0996. E-mail: wskg_mail@wskg.pbs.org. Web Site: www.wskg.com. Licensee: WSKG Public Telecommunications Council. Network: Network: NPR, PRI. Dow, Lohnes & Albertson. Format: Class, news. News staff: one; News: 33 hrs wkly. Target aud: General. Spec prog: Jazz, folk 5 hrs wkly. ♦ Gary Reinbolt, CEO & gen mgr; Gregory Keeler, opns dir; Linda Cohen, prom dir; William Snyder, mus dir; Mike Pufky, engrg dir & chief of engrg. Co-owned TV: *WSKG-TV affil.

*WSQX-FM— Jan 17, 1995: 91.5 mhz; 3.5 kw. 380 ft. TL: N42 07 54 W75 55 56. Stereo. Box 3000 13902. Phone: (607) 729-0100. Fax: (607) 729-7328. Web Site: www.wskg.com. Licensee: WSKG Public Telecommunications Council. Network: Network: NPR, PRI. Dow, Lohnes & Albertson. Format: Jazz, news. Target aud: General. Spec prog: Talk 10 hrs wkly. ♦ Gary Reinbolt, CEO & pres; Suzanne Miller-Cormier, sr VP; Gregory Keeler, opns VP; Mike Pufky, prom mgr. Co-owned TV: *WSKG-TV affil

WYOS(AM)— June 1947: 1360 khz; 5 kw-D, 500 w-N, DA-2. TL: N42 04 03 W75 54 20. 59 Court St. 13901. Secondary address: Box 414 13902. Phone: (607) 772-8850. Fax: (607) 772-9806. Web Site: www.wyos.com. Licensee: Citadel Broadcasting Co. Group owner: Citadel Broadcasting Corp. (acq 6-9-99; grpsl). Rep: McGavren Guild. Format: Mus of your Life. News staff: one; News: 3 hrs wkly. Target aud: 40 plus. Spec prog: Pol 3 hrs, Irish 2 hrs, Polka 4 hrs, relg 3 hrs, Czech one hr wkly. ♦ Roger Neal, gen sls mgr & progmg dir.

WAAL(FM)— Co-owned with WYOS(AM). March 1954: 99.1 mhz; 8.7 kw. Ant 954 ft. TL: N42 03 31 W75 57 06. Stereo. Web Site: www.waal.com. Format: Classic rock. News staff: one; News: 2 hrs wkly. Target aud: 18-49; CHR/rock listeners. ♦ Don Morgan, progmg dir.

Blue Mountain Lake

*WXLH(FM)— November 1992: 91.3 mhz; 78 w. 1,729 ft. TL: N43 52 18 W74 24 02. St. Lawrence Univ., North Country Public Radio, Canton 13617. Phone: (315) 229-5356. Fax: (315) 229-5373. Web Site: www.ncpr.org. Licensee: St. Lawrence University. Donald E. Martin. Format: Eclectic public radio. News staff: 2; News: 35 hrs wkly. Target aud: General. Spec prog: Gospel, jazz, class, folk, pub affrs. ♦ Ellen Rocco, gen mgr; Sandra Demarest, dev dir.

Boonville

WBRV(AM)— June 22, 1955: 900 khz; 1 kw-D, 52 w-N. TL: N43 30 47 W75 21 46. 7606 State St., Lowville 13367. Phone: (315) 942-4311. Phone: (315) 376-7500. Fax: (315) 376-8549. Web Site: www.themoose.net. Licensee: Flack Broadcasting Group L.L.C. Network: USA. Shaw Pittman. Format: Country. News: 18 hrs wkly. Target aud: General. ♦ Sara Flack, sr VP; William Flack, pres, gen mgr & progmg dir; Brian Best, news dir.

WBRV-FM— Jan 31, 1989: 101.3 mhz; 5.5 kw. 348 ft. TL: N43 26 53 W75 20 48. Stereo. Web Site: www.themoose.net. News: 10 hrs wkly. Target aud: General. Spec prog: Farm 3 hrs, relg 3 hrs wkly.

Brentwood

*WXBA(FM)— June 21, 1975: 88.1 mhz; 180 w. 90 ft. TL: N40 46 19 W73 15 19. Stereo. Ross High School, First & 5th Aves. 11717. Phone: (631) 434-2581. Phone: (631) 434-2582. Fax: (631) 273-6572. E-mail: wxba@88x.net. Web Site: www.88x.net. Licensee: Brentwood Public School District. Format: Educ, CHR. News staff: 6; News: 3 hrs wkly. Target aud: 18-54; general. Spec prog: Black 5 hrs wkly. ♦ Les Black, gen mgr; Jaimie Ottone, stn mgr; Charles Vollmer, progmg dir; Sam Nassetta, mus dir; Danny Mahr, asst music dir; Paul Bryant, news dir; Ashley Tanner, pub affrs dir; Rick Hollwedel, chief of engrg.

Brewster

WPUT(AM)—Licensed to Brewster. See Patterson

Briarcliff Manor

WXPK(FM)— Apr 8, 1960: 107.1 mhz; 890 w. 590 ft. TL: N41 04 49 W73 48 26. Stereo. 56 Lafayette Ave., White Plains 10603. Phone: (845) 838-6000. Fax: (848) 838-2109. Web Site: www.1071thepeak.com. Licensee: 6 Johnson Road Licenses Inc. Group owner: Nassau Broadcasting Partners L.P. (acq 11-5-2004; $18.4 million). Hogan & Hartson. Format: AAA. News staff: one. Target aud: 18-44; upscale, young, suburban. ♦ Peter Murtino, stn mgr.

Bridgehampton

WBAZ(FM)— 1996: 102.5 mhz; 4.8 kw. 367 ft. TL: N40 53 58 W72 23 06. Stereo. Box 7162, Amagansett 11930. Secondary address: 249 Montauk Hwy., Amagansett 11930. Phone: (631) 267-7800. Fax: (631) 267-1018. E-mail: info@wbaz.com. Web Site: www.wbaz.com. Licensee: AAA Licensing LLC. Group owner: AAA Entertainment L.L.C. (acq 8-22-2000; $2.75 million. with WBEA(FM) Southold). Rep: Allied Radio Partners. Pepper & Corazinni. Format: Soft adult contemp. Target aud: 25-44; adults with active lifestyles. Spec prog: News, sports. ♦ Malcolm A. Kahn, pres & gen mgr; Laura Marie, prom dir & chief of engrg; John Lynch, mus dir.

Bridgeport

WTKW(FM)— Nov 9, 1992: 99.5 mhz; 3 kw. 318 ft. TL: N43 09 07 W75 56 05. (CP: 2.85 kw). Stereo. 235 Walton St., Syracuse 13202. Phone: (315) 472-9111. Fax: (315) 472-1888. E-mail: geninfo@classicrock.com. Web Site: www.classicrock.com. Licensee: Galaxy Communications LP. (group owner; acq 4-6-00; grpsl). Network: Network: ABC, AP Radio. Rep: Allied Radio Partners. James L. Oyster. Format: Classic rock. News staff: one; News: 3 hrs wkly. Target aud: 25-54 plus; stable, peak-earning adults. ♦ Ed Levine, pres; Joy Putnam, CFO; Ed Levine, gen mgr.

Brighton

WZNE(FM)— November 1996: 94.1 mhz; 6 kw. 318 ft. TL: N43 08 07 W77 35 07. (CP: 1.8 kw, ant 407 ft.). Stereo. 1700 HSBC Plaza, Rochester 14604. Phone: (585) 399-5700. Fax: (585) 399-5750. Web Site: www.thezone941.com. Licensee: Infinity Radio Inc. Group owner: Infinity Broadcasting Corp. (acq 6-5-98; grpsl). Network: CNN Radio. Format: Alternative. Target aud: Men 18-34; Affluent fans of Alternative Rock music. ♦ Kevin Murphy, gen mgr.

Brockport

WASB(AM)— Feb 15, 1970: 1590 khz; 1 kw-U, DA-2. TL: N43 11 44 W77 57 05. 6675 4th Section Rd. 14420. Phone: (585) 637-7040. Web Site: www.fountain-of-truth.com. Licensee: David L. Wolfe (acq 1-15-91; $27,500; 1-28-91). Format: Christian. Target aud: All ages; rural audience, western Rochester & suburbs. ♦ Daniel Wolfe, gen mgr & stn mgr.

*WBSU(FM)— Jan 14, 1981: 89.1 mhz; 7.33 kw. 160 ft. TL: N43 12 45 W77 57 17. Stereo. Seymour Union 14420. Phone: (585) 395-2580. Fax: (585) 395-5334. E-mail: wkozires@brockport.edu. Web Site: www.891thepoint.com. Licensee: State University of New York. Network: AP Radio. Format: CHR, AOR, alternative. News: 4 hrs wkly. Target aud: 17-34; college & young professional. Spec prog: Black one hr, pub affrs 8 hrs wkly. ♦ Dr. Paul Yu, pres; Warren Kozireski, gen mgr; Dean King, chief of engrg.

WMJQ(FM)— 1999: 104.9 mhz; 6 kw. Ant 328 ft. TL: N43 09 51 W77 47 02. Canandaigua Broadcasting Inc., 3568 Lenox Rd., Geneva 14456. Phone: (315) 781-7000. Fax: (315) 781-7700. Web Site: www.klove.com. Licensee: Canandaigua Broadcasting Inc. (acq 3-10-99). Network: K-Love. Format: Contemp Christian. ♦ George W. Kimble, pres.

Brooklyn

WKRB(FM)—Licensed to Brooklyn. See New York

WNYE(FM)—See New York

Brookville

*WCWP(FM)— April 1965: 88.1 mhz; 100 w. 190 ft. TL: N40 49 00 W73 35 49. Stereo. Long Island Univ., C.W. Post Campus. 11548. Phone: (516) 299-2683. Phone: (516) 299-2626. Fax: (516) 299-2767. E-mail: wcwp@cwpost.liu.edu. Web Site: www.liu.edu/wcwp. Licensee: Long Island University. (acq 8-90; 8-13-90). Network: NPR. Format: News, jazz, AOR. News staff: one; News: 15 hrs wkly. Target aud: General. Spec prog: Relg 4 hrs, Sp one hr, pub affrs 5 hrs, sports 3 hrs, classic rock 2 hrs wkly. ♦ Dan Cox, gen mgr; Joe Manfredi, opns dir; Jan Robin, mktg mgr; Joe Sallo, progmg mgr; Lauren Shallash, mus dir.

Buffalo

WBBF(AM)—Listing follows WHTT-FM.

WBEN(AM)— Sept 8, 1930: 930 khz; 5 kw-U, DA-N. TL: N42 58 42 W78 57 27. 500 Corporate Pkwy., Suite 200, Amherst 14226. Phone: (716) 843-0600. Fax: (716) 832-2872. Web Site: www.wben.com. Licensee: Entercom Buffalo License L.L.C. Group owner: Entercom Communications Corp. (acq 1999). Network: CBS. Rep: D & R Radio. Format: News/talk, sports. News staff: 10; News: 20 hrs wkly. Target aud: 35-64; general. Spec prog: Buffalo Bills football. ♦ L. Greene, gen mgr; Brian Meany, sls dir; Mike Krupa, natl sls mgr; Cheryl Klocke, prom mgr; Tim Wenger, progmg dir; John Zach, news dir; Kevin Keenan, pub affrs dir; Dennis Kavanaugh, engrg VP.

WTSS(FM)— Co-owned with WBEN(AM). Nov 11, 1946: 102.5 mhz; 110 kw. 1,340 ft. TL: N42 39 33 W78 37 33. Stereo. Web Site: www.star1025.com. Rep: D & R Radio. Format: CHR, adult contemp. Target aud: 18-49. ♦ Dave Gillen, progmg dir.

*WBFO(FM)— Jan 7, 1959: 88.7 mhz; 24 kw. 240 ft. TL: N43 00 13 W78 45 54. (CP: 50 kw, ant 256 ft.). Stereo. 3435 Main St., 205 Allen Hall 14214. Phone: (716) 829-2880. Phone: (716) 829-6000. Fax: (716) 829-2277. E-mail: mail@wbfo.org. Web Site: www.wbfo.org. Licensee: State University of New York. Network: NPR. Format: Jazz, news. News staff: 2; News: 50 hrs wkly. Target aud: General; educated professionals. Spec prog: Blues 8 hrs, bluegrass 3 hrs, class one hr, Pol 3 hrs wkly. ♦ Carole Smith Petro, VP & gen mgr; Matthew Katafiaz, gen mgr; Mark Wozniak, opns mgr; Joan Wilson, dev dir.

WBLK(FM)—See Depew

*WBNY(FM)— 1982: 91.3 mhz; 100 w. TL: N42 55 59 W78 52 59. Campbell Student Union, 1300 Elmwood 14222. Phone: (716) 878-5104. Phone: (716) 878-3080. Fax: (716) 878-6600. E-mail: wbny@hotmail.com. Web site: www.wbny.org. Licensee: State University of New York. Format: New mus, alternative rock. News: 6 hrs wkly. Target aud: 18-25; college student. Spec prog: Black 12 hrs, jazz 3 hrs, reggae 3 hrs, heavy metal 3 hrs, folk 3 hrs wkly. ♦ Dan Organ, gen mgr & mus dir.

WBUF(FM)— 1947: 92.9 mhz; 93 kw. Ant 580 ft. TL: N42 38 12 W78 42 58. Stereo. 14 Lafayette Sq., Suite 1300 14203. Phone: (716) 852-9292. Fax: (716) 852-9290. Web site: www.wbuf.com. Licensee: Infinity Radio Inc. Group owner: Infinity Broadcasting Corp. (acq 12-14-2000; grpsl). Network: Network: CBS Radio, CNN Radio. Rep: Christal. Format: Talk. Target aud: 18-34; men. ♦ Jeff Silver, sr VP & gen mgr; Scott McCandless, gen sls mgr; Mike Krupa, natl sls mgr.

WDCX(FM)— February 1963: 99.5 mhz; 115 kw. 640 ft. TL: N42 38 07 W78 46 05. (CP: 17 kw, ant 430 ft.). Stereo. 625 Delaware Ave. 14202. Phone: (716) 883-3010. Fax: (716) 883-3606. E-mail: wdcxinfo@crawfordbroadcasting.com. Web Site: www.crawfordbroadcasting.com. Licensee: Kimtron Inc. Group owner: Crawford Broadcasting Co. Format: Christian & relg talk. Target aud: General. ♦ Donald B. Crawford, pres; Nevin W. Larson, gen mgr.

WECK(AM)—See Cheektowaga

WEDG(FM)— 1947: 103.3 mhz; 49 kw. 340 ft. TL: N42 55 33 W78 50 28. Stereo. 50 James E. Casey Dr. 14206. Phone: (716) 881-4555. Fax: (716) 884-2931. Web Site: www.wedg.com. Licensee: Citadel Broadcasting Co. Group owner: Citadel Broadcasting Corp. (acq 2-23-00; grpsl). Shaw Pittman. Format: Alternative rock. Target aud: 18-34; alternative rock listeners.

*WFBF(FM)— 1989: 89.9 mhz; 16 kw. Ant 295 ft. TL: N42 41 19 W78 45 15. 918 Chesapeake Ave., Annapolis, MD 21403. Phone: (716)

Stations in the U.S.   New York

312-0911. Fax: (410) 268-0931. Web Site: www.familyradio.com. Licensee: Family Stations Inc. (group owner) Format: Christian, educ. ♦Harold Camping, pres.

WGR(AM)— May 22, 1922: 550 khz; 5 kw-U, DA-2. TL: N42 46 04 W78 50 39. Stereo. 500 Corporate Pkwy., Amherst 14226. Phone: (716) 843-0600. Fax: (716) 832-3080. Fax: (803) 0550 (studio). E-mail: studio@wgr55.com. Web Site: www.wgr55.com. Licensee: Entercom Buffalo License LLC. Group owner: Entercom Communications Corp. (acq 12-13-99; grpsl). Network: ABC Information & Entertainment. Fisher, Wayland, Cooper, Leader & Zaragoza L.L.P. Format: Sports. News staff: 15; News: 168 hrs wkly. Target aud: 25-54. ♦Greg Ried, VP & gen mgr; Andy Roth, progmg dir & chief of engrg.

WGRF(FM)— Sept 14, 1959: 96.9 mhz; 24 kw. 712 ft. TL: N42 57 14 W78 52 37. Stereo. 50 James E. Casey Dr. 14206. Phone: (716) 881-4555. Fax: (716) 882-ufax. Web Site: www.97rock.com. Licensee: Citadel Broadcasting Co. Group owner: Citadel Broadcasting Corp. (acq 2-23-00; grpsl). Fisher, Wayland, Cooper, Leader & Zaragoza. Format: Classic rock. Target aud: 25-49; classic rock listeners. ♦John Hager, opns mgr.

WHTT-FM— Oct 3, 1954: 104.1 mhz; 50 kw. 500 ft. TL: N42 49 50 W78 47 54. Stereo. 50 James E. Casey Dr. 14206. Phone: (716) 881-4555. Fax: (716) 884-2931. Web Site: www.whtt.com. Licensee: Citadel Broadcasting Co. Group owner: Citadel Broadcasting Corp. (acq 2-23-2000; grpsl). Format: Oldies. ♦Kevin Legrett, gen mgr; Chet Osadchey, gen sls mgr; Joe Siragusa, progmg dir; Chris Klein, news dir; Al Marranca, pub affrs dir & chief of engrg.

WBBF(AM)—Co-owned with WHTT-FM. September 1947: 1120 khz; 1 kw-D. TL: N42 49 50 W78 47 54. 225 Delaware, Suite 1 A 14202. Phone: (716) 848-1120. Fax: (716) 848-9518. E-mail: totallygospel@adelphia.net. Web Site: www.totallygospel.net. Format: Gospel. ♦Michael Brummer, gen mgr; John Young, opns; Natalie Hutchen, opns.

WJYE(FM)— Nov 11, 1966: 96.1 mhz; 47.1 kw. 505 ft. TL: N42 53 10 W78 52 25. Stereo. 14 Lafayette Sq., Suite 1200 14203. Phone: (716) 856-3550. Fax: (716) 852-0537. Web Site: www.wjye.com. Licensee: Infinity Radio Inc. Group owner: Infinity Broadcasting Corp. (acq 12-14-00; grpsl). Rep: Christal. Format: Adult contemp. News staff: one; News: 23 hrs wkly. Target aud: 25-54. Spec prog: Pub affrs 2 hrs wkly. ♦Jeff Silver, sr VP & VP; Joe Chille, opns mgr; Bob Courtney, gen sls mgr.

***WNED(AM)**— Oct 14, 1924: 970 khz; 5 kw-U, DA-1. TL: N42 44 41 W78 00 00. Box 1263 14240. Secondary address: 140 Lower Terr. 14202. Phone: (716) 845-7000. Fax: (716) 845-7043. Web Site: www.wned.org. Licensee: Western New York Public Broadcasting Assoc. (acq 8-14-76). Network: Network: PRI, NPR. Format: News/talk. News staff: 8. Target aud: 35 plus. Spec prog: Pub affrs. ♦Donald K. Boswell, pres; Richard J. Daly, stn mgr; Cynthia Dwyer, dev VP; Jim Dimino, sls VP; Gwen Mysiak, prom dir; Al Wallack, progmg dir; Jon Herrington, engrg VP.

WNED-FM— June 6, 1960: 94.5 mhz; 105 kw. 710 ft. TL: N42 38 13 W78 46 05. Stereo. Web Site: www.wned.org. Network: PRI. Schwartz, Woods & Miller. Format: Class. ♦Peter Goldsmith, progmg dir. Co-owned TV: *WNED-TV affil

WWKB(AM)— 1925: 1520 khz; 50 kw-U, DA-1. TL: N42 46 10 W78 50 34. 500 Corporate Pkwy. 14226. Phone: (716) 843-0600. Fax: (716) 832-3323. Licensee: Entercom Buffalo License LLC. Group owner: Entercom Communications Corp. (acq 12-13-99; grpsl). Network: ABC. Rep: D & R Radio. Format: Oldies. News staff: 4; News: 20 hrs wkly. Target aud: 25-54. ♦Gregory Reed, gen mgr & prom mgr.

WWWS(AM)— 1934: 1400 khz; 1 kw-U. TL: N42 55 33 W78 50 28. 500 Corporate Pkwy. 14226. Phone: (716) 843-0600. Fax: (716) 843-3323. Licensee: Entercom Buffalo License LLC. Group owner: Entercom Communications Corp. (acq 12-13-99; grpsl). Rep: Katz Radio. Format: Urban contemp. Target aud: 35-54.

WYRK(FM)— Nov 14, 1962: 106.5 mhz; 50 kw. 390 ft. TL: N42 53 10 W78 52 25. Stereo. 14 Lafayette Sq., Suite 1200 14203. Phone: (716) 852-7444. Fax: (716) 852-5683. Web Site: www.wyrk.com. Licensee: Infinity Radio Inc. Group owner: Infinity Broadcasting Corp. (acq 6-98; grpsl). Rep: Katz Radio. Format: Country. Target aud: 25-54; adults. ♦Jeff Silver, sr VP & VP; Mark Plimpton, gen sls mgr; Mike Krupa, natl sls mgr; Sue Durwald, prom dir; John Paul, progmg dir.

Calverton-Roanoke

WDRE(FM)— 1998: 105.3 mhz; 1 kw. Ant 492 ft. TL: N40 51 18 W72 46 12. (CP: 660 w, ant 607 ft). 1103 Stewart Ave., Garden City 11530. Phone: (516) 222-1103. Fax: (516) 222-1391. Web Site: www.party105.com. Licensee: Jarad Broadcasting Co. of Calverton Inc. Group owner: The Morey Organization Inc. (acq 10-2-98). Rep: Christal. Format: Dance, top-40. ♦Howard Frank, VP & gen mgr; John Acero, gen sls mgr; Jon Daniels, prom dir.

Canajoharie

***WCAN(FM)**— October 1988: 93.3 mhz; 6 kw. 268 ft. TL: N42 53 46 W74 35 45. Stereo. Box 66600, 318 Central Ave., Albany 12206-6600. Phone: (518) 465-5233. Phone: (800) 323-9262. Fax: (518) 432-6974. E-mail: mail@wamc.org. Web Site: www.wamc.org. Licensee: WAMC. Group owner: WAMC/Northeast Public Radio Network: Network: PRI, NPR. Dow, Lohnes & Albertson. Format: News, talk. News: 48 hrs wkly. Target aud: General. Spec prog: Jazz 17 hrs, folk 7 hrs. ♦Alan Chartock, CEO; Dona Chartock, dev dir.

Canandaigua

WCGR(AM)— Apr 5, 1961: 1550 khz; 250 w-D. TL: N42 52 52 W77 15 02. 3568 Lenox Rd., Geneva 14456. Phone: (315) 781-7000. Fax: (315) 781-7000. Licensee: Canandaigua Broadcasting Inc. (acq 12-93; with co-located FM; FTR: 1-3-94). Network: ABC Information & Entertainment. James L. Oyster. Format: News/talk, middle of the road. News staff: one; News: 10 hrs wkly. Target aud: General. ♦George Kimble, pres; Alan Bishop, gen mgr.

***WCIY(FM)**— Dec 14, 1992: 88.9 mhz; 500 w. Ant 1,043 ft. TL: N42 44 51 W77 25 24. Stereo. Box 506, Bath 14810. Secondary address: 7634 Campbell Creek Rd., Bath Phone: (607) 776-4151. Fax: (607) 776-6929. E-mail: mail@fln.org. Web Site: www.fln.org. Licensee: Family Life Ministries Inc. Group owner: Family Life Network Format: Contemp Christian. News staff: 7; News: 14 hrs wkly. Target aud: 30-54. ♦Rick Snavely, pres, pres, CFO, VP & gen mgr.

WISY(FM)— July 16, 1974: 102.3 mhz; 3.4 kw. 282 ft. TL: N42 51 47 W77 19 22. 207 Midtown Plaza, Rochester 14604. Phone: (585) 454-3942. Fax: (585) 454-5081. E-mail: wisy.wfxfproductions@clearchannel.com. Web Site: www.radiosunny.com. Licensee: Citicasters Licenses L.P. Group owner: Clear Channel Communications Inc. (acq 5-4-99; grpsl). Format: Soft adult contemp. News: 3 hrs wkly. Target aud: 25-54. ♦Karen Carey, gen mgr; David Lefrois, progmg dir.

WRSB(AM)— Apr 5, 1997: 1310 khz; 1 kw-U, DA-2. TL: N42 53 20 W77 19 09. 6675 Fourth Section Rd., Brockport 14420. Phone: (585) 637-7040. Licensee: David Wolfe. (acq 3-10-99). Network: ABC. Format: Christian. Target aud: Everyone; all ages. ♦Dr. David Wolfe, gen mgr.

Canton

WNCQ-FM— July 1984: 102.9 mhz; 23.5 kw. Ant 338 ft. TL: N44 32 10 W75 05 46. Stereo. 1 Bridge Plaza, Suite 204, Ogdensburg 13669. Phone: (315) 393-1220. Fax: (315) 393-3974. E-mail: john@q1029.com. Web Site: www.q1029.com. Licensee: Radio Power Inc. Group owner: Martz Communications Group (acq 9-28-99). Eugene T. Smith. Format: Hot country. Target aud: 25-54; adults. ♦John Winter, gen mgr.

WRCD(FM)— Jan 1, 1997: 101.5 mhz; 2.4 kw. 364 ft. TL: N44 32 01 W75 05 50. Stereo. Box 210, Massena 13662. Phone: (315) 769-3333. Fax: (315) 769-3299. E-mail: studio@1015thefox.com. Web Site: www.1015thefox.com. Licensee: Radio Power Inc. Group owner: Martz Communications Group (acq 6-16-99). Eugene T. Smith. Format: Rock. News staff: 2; News: 7 hrs wkly. Target aud: 30-50; country fans. ♦Mike Boldt, gen mgr; Drew Scott, progmg dir.

***WSLU(FM)**— December 1964: 89.5 mhz; 40.3 kw. 299 ft. TL: N44 32 01 W75 05 50. St. Lawrence Univ. 13617. Phone: (315) 229-5356. Fax: (315) 229-5373. Web Site: www.ncpr.org. Licensee: St. Lawrence University. Network: Network: NPR, PRI. Donald E. Martin. Format: Eclectic public radio. News staff: 2; News: 35 hrs wkly. Target aud: General. Spec prog: Gospel, jazz, class, folk, pub affrs, Black. ♦Ellen Rocco, gen mgr; Sandra Demarest, dev dir; Jacqueline Sauter, progmg dir; Martha Foley, news dir; Robert G. Sauter, chief of engrg.

Cape Vincent

WBDR(FM)— Apr 21, 1997: 102.7 mhz; 6 kw. 328 ft. TL: N44 06 58 W76 20 21. 199 Wealtha Ave., Watertown 13601. Phone: (315) 782-0103. Fax: (315) 782-0312. Licensee: Border International Broadcasting Inc. Group owner: Clancy-Mance Communications (acq 10-15-98; $50,000). Rep: Roslin. Format: CHR. ♦David Mance, CEO, pres & gen mgr; Todd Dalessandro, opns VP; Dick Whelan, rgnl sls mgr.

***WMHI(FM)**— Oct 1, 1990: 94.7 mhz; 3 kw. 284 ft. TL: N44 02 42 W76 15 37. Stereo. 4044 Makyes Rd., Syracuse 13215. Phone: (315) 469-5051. E-mail: marshillnetwork@marshillnetwork.org. Web Site: www.marshillnetwork.org. Licensee: Mars Hill Broadcasting Co. Inc. dba Mars Hill Network. (group owner) Network: Network: Moody, USA. Wiley, Rein & Fielding. Format: Relg, Christian. News: 6 hrs wkly. Target aud: General; Christian families. ♦Clayton Roberts, pres; Roderick Tidd, VP; Wayne Taylor, gen mgr.

Carthage

WTOJ(FM)— Nov 1, 1984: 103.1 mhz; 6 kw. 500 ft. TL: N43 57 16 W75 43 45. Stereo. 199 Wealtha Ave., Watertown 13601. Phone: (315) 782-1240. Fax: (315) 782-0312. Licensee: Clancy-Mance Communications Inc. (group owner; acq 6-20-88; grpsl; 6-20-88). Rep: Roslin. Format: Adult contemp. Target aud: 25-54. ♦David W. Mance, pres & gen mgr; Joseph Brosk, stn mgr; Todd Dalesantro, opns dir.

Catskill

WCKL(AM)— Feb 6, 1970: 560 khz; 1 kw-D, DA. TL: N42 12 00 W73 50 07. 1156 Rt. 23 12414. Phone: (212) 234-1695. Fax: (212) 234-7129. Licensee: Black United Fund of New York Inc. (acq 6-10-2003; $100,000). Format: Talk. ♦Kermit Eady, pres.

WCTW(FM)— September 1990: 98.5 mhz; 2.1 kw. Ant 393 ft. TL: N42 12 00 W73 50 07. (CP: 4.7 kw). Stereo. 20 Tucker Drive, Poughkepsie 12534. Phone: (845) 471-2300. Fax: (845) 471-2683. Web Site: www.985litefm.com. Licensee: Clear Channel Broadcasting Licenses Inc. Group owner: Clear Channel Communications Inc. (acq 1-17-2002; grpsl). Network: Westwood One. Format: Bright adult contemp. News staff: one; News: 2 hrs wkly. Target aud: 25-44; female. ♦Bob Dunphy, gen mgr & gen sls mgr; Wade Lott, sls dir; Jeanette Relyea, natl sls mgr; Doug MacLeod, mktg dir; Bill Williams, prom dir & progmg dir; Cameron Hendrix, news dir; Bill Draper, chief of engrg.

Cazenovia

***WITC(FM)**— April 1978: 88.9 mhz; 129 w. 33 ft. TL: N42 55 53 W75 51 15. Cazenovia College, 22 Sullivan St. 13035. Phone: (315) 655-7154. Licensee: Cazenovia College. Format: Alternative. News: 3 hrs wkly. Target aud: 15-35; college & young area residents. Spec prog: News/talk 3 hrs, div 10 hrs wkly. ♦Roger Benn, gen mgr.

Center Moriches

WLVG(FM)— Mar 3, 1997: 96.1 mhz; 2.65 kw. Ant 499 ft. TL: N40 51 08 W72 45 55. 3241 Rt. 112, Bldg. #7, Medford 11763. Phone: (631) 451-1039. Fax: (631) 451-0891. Web Site: www.wrcn.com. Licensee: IW Limited Liability Co. Group owner: Barnstable Broadcasting Inc.

Broadcasting & Cable Yearbook 2006

New York

acq 1-13-2004; $3.75 million). Format: Adult contemp. ♦Steve Hobbs, gen mgr; Stefan Rybak, gen sls mgr; Wendy Summers, prom dir; Bob Anderson, chief of engrg.

Champlain

WCHP(AM)— Aug 20, 1985: 760 khz; 35 kw-D, DA. TL: N44 56 44 W73 25 48. Box 888, 137 Rapids Rd. 12919. Phone: (518) 298-2800. Fax: (518) 298-2604. E-mail: wchp@wchp.com. Web Site: www.wchp.com. Licensee: Champlain Radio Inc. (acq 1-31-91; 2-18-91). Format: Relg, talk. Target aud: 25 plus. Spec prog: Fr, Sp. ♦Robert A. Jones, VP; Teri Billiter, gen mgr; Tonya Billiter, opns dir; Brandi Lloyd, progmg dir.

Chateaugay

WYUL(FM)— Apr 15, 1997: 94.7 mhz; 1.9 kw. 2,081 ft. TL: N44 41 43 W73 53 00. Stereo. 86 Porter Rd., Malone 12953. Phone: (518) 483-1100. Fax: (518) 483-1382. Licensee: Cartier Communications Inc. Group owner: Martz Communications Group Smithwick & Belendiuk. Format: CHR. ♦Timothy D. Martz, CEO, pres & CFO; Michael T. Boldt, gen mgr; Kim Scott, sls dir; Drew Scott, progmg dir.

Cheektowaga

WECK(AM)— August 1956: 1230 khz; 1 kw-U. TL: N42 55 27 W78 46 41. 14 Lafayette Sq., Suite 1200, Buffalo 14203. Phone: (716) 856-3550. Fax: (716) 852-0537. Web Site: www.weckradio.com. Licensee: Infinity Radio Inc. Group owner: Infinity Broadcasting Corp. (acq 6-98; grpsl). Network: Westwood One. Rep: Christal. Format: MOR. Target aud: 35-64. Spec prog: Pol 2 hrs wkly. ♦Jeff Silver, sr VP; Joe Chille, opns mgr.

Chenango Bridge

WWYL(FM)— July 1, 1996: 104.1 mhz; 3.1 kw. 462 ft. TL: N42 08 20 W75 52 24. Box 414, Binghamton 13902. Phone: (607) 772-8400. Fax: (607) 772-9806. Web Site: www.wild104fm.com. Licensee: Citadel Broadcasting Co. Group owner: Citadel Broadcasting Corp. (acq 6-9-99; grpsl). Format: CHR. ♦Mary Beth Walsh, gen mgr; Tim Skinner, prom dir; K.J. Bryant, progmg dir.

Cherry Valley

WJIV(FM)— 1949: 101.9 mhz; 11.5 kw. 1,027 ft. TL: N42 47 36 W74 41 41. Stereo. Box 507 13320. Secondary address: 1668 Country Hwy. 50 13320. Phone: (607) 264-3062. Fax: (518) 437-1251. Fax: (607) 264-8277. Licensee: Christian Broadcasting System Ltd. (group owner; acq 6-5-00; $1.3 million). Bechtel & Cole. Format: Relg, talk. Target aud: 25-54. ♦John Yinger, pres.

Clifton Park

WPTR(FM)— November 1985: 96.7 mhz; 4.7 kw. 328 ft. TL: N42 52 44 W73 51 47. Stereo. 4243 Albany St., Albany 12212. Phone: (518) 862-1540. Fax: (518) 862-1545. Web Site: www.crawfordbroadcasting.com. Licensee: Kimtron Inc. Group owner: Crawford Broadcasting Co. (acq 1996; $820,000). Format: Big band, oldies. Target aud: 30-64; financially capable. ♦Donald B. Crawford, pres; Robert Hammond, gen mgr & stn mgr; Mark Shuttleworth, progmg dir; David Groth, chief of engrg.

Clinton

*****WHCL-FM**— Feb 18, 1963: 88.7 mhz; 270 w. 97 ft. TL: N43 03 04 W75 24 24. Stereo. Hamilton College, 198 College Hill Rd. 13323. Phone: (315) 859-4200. E-mail: mngrwhcl@hamilton.edu. Web Site: www.whcl.org. Licensee: The Trustees of Hamilton College. Format: Div, progsv, AOR. Target aud: General. Spec prog: Class 9 hrs, jazz 9 hrs, relg 2 hrs. ♦Alan Clark, gen mgr.

Clyde

*****WCOV-FM**— Dec 5, 1995: 93.7 mhz; 3.8 kw. Ant 328 ft. TL: N42 59 38 W76 51 59. Box 506, Bath 14810. Secondary address: 7634 Campbell Creek Rd., Bath 14810. Phone: (607) 776-4151. Fax: (607) 776-6929. E-mail: mail@fln.org. Web Site: www.fln.org. Licensee: Family Life Ministries Inc. Group owner: Family Life Network (acq 10-3-00). Network: Salem Radio Network. Format: Contemp Christian. News staff: 7.; News: 14 hrs wkly. ♦Dick Snavely, CFO; Rick Snavely, pres & gen mgr.

Cobleskill

WQBJ(FM)— Sept 1, 1986: 103.5 mhz; 50 kw. 492 ft. TL: N42 58 21 W74 29 30. Stereo. 800 New Louden Rd., Suite 4200, Latham 12110. Phone: (518) 785-9800. Fax: (518) 785-0122. Web Site: www.wqbk.com. Licensee: Regent Licensee of Mansfield Inc. Group owner: Regent Communications Inc. (acq 8-7-00; grpsl). Haley, Bader & Potts. Format: Rock/AOR. Target aud: 18-49; general. ♦Robert Ausfeld, gen mgr; Glen Stacey, prom dir; Chili Walker, progmg dir; Bob O'Neal, chief of engrg.

WSDE(AM)— July 1, 1981: 1190 khz; 1 kw-D. TL: N42 41 26 W74 26 40. Box 608 12043. Phone: (518) 234-3400. Fax: (518) 234-4567. Web Site: www.wsde1190.com. Licensee: Viva Communications Group LLC (acq 4-26-2004; $120,000). Format: Personality talk. Target aud: General. ♦Floyld Hamilton, opns mgr.

Copenhagen

WBDI(FM)— 1994: 106.7 mhz; 1.7 kw. 1,191 ft. TL: N43 52 47 W75 43 11. 199 Wealthea Ave., Watertown 13601. Phone: (315) 782-0103. Fax: (315) 782-0312. Licensee: Force Communications Inc. Group owner: Clancy-Mance Communications (acq 1-6-97; $608,203). Rep: Roslin. Format: CHR. ♦David W. Mance, pres & gen mgr; Todd Dalesandro, opns mgr; Dick Whelan, rgnl sls mgr.

Corinth

WFFG-FM— June 26, 1967: 107.1 mhz; 2.85 kw. Ant 482 ft. TL: N43 14 40 W73 46 18. Stereo. 89 Everts Ave., Queensbury 12804. Phone: (518) 793-7733. Fax: (518) 793-0838. Web Site: www.froggy107.com. Licensee: 6 Johnson Road Licenses Inc. Group owner: Pamal Broadcasting Ltd. (acq 4-1-2004; grpsl). Format: Country. News staff: one; News: 2 hrs wkly. Target aud: 18-54. ♦Clay Ashworth, gen mgr.

Corning

WCBA(AM)— November 1948: 1350 khz; 2 kw-D. TL: N42 07 01 W77 02 25. Box 1047 14830. Phone: (607) 962-4646. Fax: (607) 962-1138. Licensee: Group A Licensee LLC. Group owner: Route 81 Radio LLC (acq 10-31-2003; grpsl). Network: Westwood One. Rep: Roslin. Format: MOR, btfl mus, big band. Target aud: 50 plus. ♦Dee Eolin, opns mgr, news dir & pub affrs dir; Richard Burton, gen sls mgr & rgnl sls mgr; Robert Eolin, gen mgr & natl sls mgr; Jim Appleton, chief of engrg.

WGMM(FM)—Co-owned with WCBA(AM). February 1989: 98.7 mhz; 2 kw. Ant 393 ft. TL: N42 09 38 W77 02 19. Stereo. Network: ABC. Rep: McGavren Guild. Format: Adult contemp.

*****WCEB(FM)**— 1979: 91.9 mhz; 10 w. 1,784 ft. TL: N42 07 10 W77 05 02. Corning Community College, One Academic Dr. 14830. Phone: (607) 962-9360. Fax: (607) 962-9456. E-mail: wceb919@hotmail.com. Licensee: Corning Community College. Format: AOR. Target aud: Students; CCC and surrounding community. Spec prog: Oldies 6 hrs wkly. ♦Sarah Meyers, pres, gen mgr, stn mgr & adv VP; Cassandra Gryzbowski, gen mgr; Yuri Charlanow, opns dir.

WENI(AM)— November 1949: 1450 khz; 1 kw-D, 930 w-N. TL: N42 06 59 W77 02 24. 21 E. Market St. 14830. Phone: (607) 962-4646. Fax: (607) 962-1138. Licensee: Group A Licensee LLC. Group owner: Route 81 Radio LLC (acq 10-31-2003; grpsl). Network: USA. Rep: McGavren Guild. Format: News/talk. Target aud: 25-64. ♦Paul Lyle, gen mgr.

WNKI(FM)— May 1947: 106.1 mhz; 40 kw. 532 ft. TL: N42 09 43 W77 02 15. Stereo. 2205 College Ave., Elmira 14903. Phone: (607) 732-4400. Fax: (607) 732-7774. Web Site: www.wink106.com. Licensee: Chemung County Radio Inc. Group owner: Backyard Broadcasting LLC (acq 12-1-02; grpsl). Rep: Christal. Format: Adult contemp, CHR. News staff: one; News: one hr wkly. Target aud: 25-54; women. ♦Kevin White, gen mgr; Maggie Paige, news dir.

*****WSQE(FM)**— 1995: 91.1 mhz; 3.6 kw. Ant 653 ft. TL: N42 06 20 W76 52 17. Box 3000, Binghamton 13902. Phone: (607) 729-0100. Web Site: www.wskg.com. Licensee: WSKG Public Telecommunications Council. Network: Network: Network: NPR, PRI, AP Radio. Dow, Lohnes & Albertson. Format: Class, news. News staff: ; News: 33 hrs wkly. Target aud: General. Spec prog: Jazz, folk 5 hrs wkly. ♦Gary Reinbolt, CEO & gen mgr.

Cornwall

WWLE(AM)— Nov 22, 1969: 1170 khz; 1 kw-D, DA. TL: N41 26 24 W74 04 25. Box 2130, Newburgh 12550. Phone: (845) 569-7010. Fax: (845) 562-1348. Licensee: 1170 Broadcast Radio Inc. (acq 1-1-00; $100,000). Network: USA. Gammon & Grange. Format: News/talk. Spec prog: Farm one hr wkly. ♦Charles Stewart, gen mgr.

Cortland

WIII(FM)—Listing follows WKRT(AM).

WKRT(AM)— Nov 15, 1947: 920 khz; 1 kw-D, 500 w-N, DA-N. TL: N42 33 22 W76 09 17. 277 Tompkins St. 13045. Phone: (607) 756-2828. Fax: (607) 756-2953. E-mail: wiii.wkrt@citcamm.com. Web Site: www.wkrt.com. Licensee: Citadel Broadcasting Co. Group owner: Citadel Broadcasting Corp. (acq 2-23-00; grpsl). Network: ABC Information & Entertainment. Rep: McGavren Guild. Leventhal, Senter & Lerman. Format: News/talk. News staff: one; News: 20 hrs wkly. Target aud: 30-60; general. ♦Todd Mallinson, gen mgr; Margaret Tollner, gen sls mgr; Tony DeFranco, opns mgr & progmg dir; Dave Edwards, engrg mgr & chief of engrg.

WIII(FM)—Co-owned with WKRT(AM). Nov 15, 1947: 99.9 mhz; 24 kw. 710 ft. TL: N42 33 22 W76 09 17. Stereo. 605 W. State St., Suite 2, Ithaca 14850. E-mail: i100@wiii.com. Web Site: www.wiii.com. Format: Classic rock. News staff: one; News: one hr wkly. Target aud: 25-54; men. ♦Tony DeFranco, opns mgr.

*****WSUC-FM**— Nov 17, 1976: 90.5 mhz; 241 w. -110 ft. TL: N42 35 53 W76 11 13. Stereo. State Univ. of New York, Brockway Hall, Graham Ave. 13045. Phone: (607) 753-2936. Fax: (607) 753-2807. Licensee: State University of New York. Network: AP Radio. Format: Var/div, rock. Target aud: 12-50. ♦Peter Johams, gen mgr.

Dannemora

*****WKVJ(FM)**— 2005: 89.7 mhz; 4.4 kw. Ant 1,096 ft. TL: N44 34 24 W73 40 31. Stereo. American Educational Broadcasting Inc., 3185 S. Highland Dr., Suite 13, Las Vegas, NV 89109. Secondary address: Box 888, Studio, Champlain 12919. Phone: (518) 298-8200. Fax: (518) 298-2604. Licensee: American Educational Broadcasting Inc. Fletcher, Heald & Hildreth. Format: Christian. ♦Carl J. Auel, pres; Teri Billiter, gen mgr.

Dansville

WDNY-FM— March 1990: 93.9 mhz; 570 w. 741 ft. TL: N42 30 45 W77 38 07. Stereo. 129 Main St. 14437. Phone: (585) 335-9369. Fax: (585) 335-9677. E-mail: wdny@frontiernet.net. Licensee: Miller Media Inc. Network: CBS Radio. Format: Adult contemp. News staff: one; News: 8 hrs wkly. Target aud: 25-54. Spec prog: Relg one hr, big band 3 hrs, sports 4 hrs wkly. ♦Dorothy Hotchkiss, gen mgr & gen sls mgr; Mark Miller, opns mgr & progmg dir; Terry Van, news dir.

WDNY(AM)— Oct 20, 1978: 1400 khz; 1 kw-U. TL: N42 32 19 W77 40 57. (Acq 4-13-92; $290,000; 5-4-92). Format: Mus of your Life. News staff: one; News: 8 hrs wkly.

Delhi

WDHI(FM)— Mar 16, 1992: 100.3 mhz; 770 w. 643 ft. TL: N42 22 40 W74 50 23. Stereo. 34 Chestnut St., Oneonta 13820. Phone: (607) 432-1030. Fax: (607) 432-6909. Licensee: Double O Central New York Corp. (group owner; (acq 10-22-2004; grpsl). Network: USA. Rep: Savalli. Format: CHR. ♦George Wells, gen mgr.

Depew

WBLK(FM)— December 1964: 93.7 mhz; 47 kw. 505 ft. TL: N42 53 10 W78 52 25. Stereo. Rand Bldg., 14 Lafayette Sq., Buffalo 14203. Phone: (716) 852-9393. Fax: (716) 852-9390. Web Site: www.wblk.com. Licensee: Infinity Radio Inc. Group owner: Infinity Broadcasting Corp. (acq 2000; grpsl). Network: CBS Radio. Rep: Katz Radio. Format: Urban contemp. Target aud: General. ♦Jeff Silver, sr VP & VP; Mike Krupa, gen sls mgr.

Deposit

WIYN(FM)— Jan 16, 1991: 94.7 mhz; 770 w. Ant 642 ft. TL: N42 01 43 W75 28 25. Stereo. 34 Chestnut St., Oneonta 13820. Phone: (607)

Stations in the U.S. New York

432-1030. Fax: (607) 432-6909. Licensee: Double O Central New York Corp. (group owner; (acq 10-22-2004); grpsl). Format: Oldies. Target aud: 28-55. ◆George Wells, gen mgr.

DeRuyter

WWDG(FM)— 1948: 105.1 mhz; 42 kw. 541 ft. TL: N42 46 58 W75 50 28. Stereo. 500 Plum St., Suite 100, Syracuse 13204. Phone: (315) 472-9797. Fax: (315) 472-0049. Licensee: Clear Channel Broadcasting Licenses Inc. Group owner: Clear Channel Communications Inc. (acq 3-12-01; $5 million). Format: Modern rock. Target aud: 18-40; general. ◆Joel Delmonico, gen mgr.

Dewitt

WVOA(AM)—Not on air, target date: unknown: 720 khz; 2.5 kw-D, 390 w-N, DA-N. TL: N43 03 30 W76 10 01 (D), N42 56 02 W76 06 59 (N). 4853 Manor Hill Dr., Syracuse 13215-1336. Phone: (315) 468-0908. Licensee: Cram Communications LLC. ◆Craig Fox, gen mgr.

Dundee

WFLR(AM)— Oct 1, 1956: 1570 khz; 5 kw-D, 442 w-N. TL: N42 32 40 W76 59 35. 30 Main St. 14837. Phone: (607) 243-7158. Phone: (607) 243-7070. Fax: (607) 243-7662. E-mail: wflr@linkny.com. Web Site: www.linkny.com/wflr. Licensee: Finger Lakes Radio Group Inc. Group owner: Finger Lakes Radio Group (acq 12-11-03; $600,000. with co-located FM). Network: Motor Racing Net. Format: Country, news/talk. News staff: one; News: 40 hrs wkly. Target aud: 25-55. Spec prog: Relg 5 hrs wkly. ◆Dick Evans, gen mgr; Mark Feiock, prom dir.

WFLR-FM— Aug 20, 1968: 95.9 mhz; 780 w. 600 ft. TL: N42 32 40 W76 59 35. Stereo. Format: Adult contemp, news/talk. News: 35 hrs wkly. Target aud: 21-55.

Dunkirk

WDOE(AM)— Dec 24, 1949: 1410 khz; 1 kw-D, 500 w-N, DA-N. TL: N42 27 51 W79 21 21. Stereo. Box 209, Willow Rd. 14048. Phone: (716) 366-1410. Phone: (716) 366-8580. Fax: (716) 366-1416. Licensee: Chadwick Bay Broadcasting Corp. (acq 2-26-2001); with WBKX(FM) Fredonia). Network: ABC. Format: Oldies, news/talk. News staff: News progmg 12 hrs wkly Target aud: 45-65. Spec prog: Pol 6 hrs, Sp 2 hrs wkly. ◆John Bulmer, pres; Chuck Telford, gen mgr.

East Aurora

WLKK(FM)—See Wethersfield Township

East Hampton

WHBE(FM)— Mar 1, 1993: 96.7 mhz; 4.3 kw. Ant 383 ft. TL: N40 59 37 W72 10 19. Box 7162, Amagansett 11930. Secondary address: 249 Montauk Hwy., Amagansett 11930. Phone: (631) 267-7800. Fax: (631) 267-1018. Licensee: AAA Licensing LLC. Group owner: AAA Entertainment L.L.C. (acq 5-31-2000; grpsl). Network: CNN Radio. Format: News/talk. Target aud: 24-54; upscale Hamptons residents and NYC second homeowners. ◆Brian Cosgrove, opns mgr.

East Patchogue

WALK(AM)—Licensed to East Patchogue. See Patchogue

East Syracuse

WSIV(AM)—Licensed to East Syracuse. See Syracuse

Ellenville

WFKP(FM)—Listing follows WRWD(AM).

WRWD(AM)— December 1964: 1370 khz; 5 kw-D. TL: N41 44 19 W74 23 48. 20 Tucker Dr., Poughkeepsie 12603. Secondary address: 22 N. Main St. 12428. Phone: (845) 471-2300. Fax: (845) 471-2683. Web Site: www.wrwdfm.com. Licensee: Clear Channel Broadcasting Licenses Inc. Group owner: Clear Channel Communications Inc. (acq 7-14-2000); grpsl). Network: Jones Radio Networks. Rep: Christal. Format: Big band, MOR, relg. Target aud: 30-64. ◆Lowry Mays, pres; Bob Dunphy, gen mgr; Reggie Osterhoudt, opns dir; Wade Lott, sls dir; Frank Curcio, gen sls mgr; Jeanette Relyea, natl sls mgr; Doug MacLeod, mktg dir; Joe Daily, progmg dir; Michelle Taylor, progmg dir; Bill Draper, chief of engrg.

WFKP(FM)—Co-owned with WRWD(AM). August 1970: 99.3 mhz; 115 w. Ant 1,630 ft. TL: N41 41 06 W74 21 23. Stereo. Web Site: www.933litefm.com. Wiley, Rein & Fielding. News staff: one. Target aud: 18-34; general. ◆Rick Knight, mus dir; Cameron Hendrix, pub affrs dir; Gwen Ceruti, pub affrs dir.

Elmira

***WCIH(FM)**— July 31, 1989: 90.3 mhz; 4 kw. Ant 526 ft. TL: N41 53 39 W76 51 32. Stereo. Box 506, Bath 14810. Secondary address: 7634 Campbell Creek Rd., Bath 14810. Phone: (607) 776-4151. Fax: (607) 776-6929. E-mail: mail@fln.org. Web Site: www.fln.org. Licensee: Family Life Ministries Inc. Group owner: Family Life Network Network: Salem Radio Network. Format: Contemp Christian. News staff: 7; News: 14 hrs wkly. Target aud: 25-59; general Christian public. ◆Rick Snavely, pres; Dick Snavely, CFO, VP & gen mgr.

***WECW(FM)**— Jan 19, 1959: 107.7 mhz; 6 w. -312 ft. TL: N42 05 52 W76 48 53. Stereo. Elmira College, One Park Pl. 14901. Phone: (607) 735-1885. E-mail: wecw@elmira.edu. Licensee: Elmira College. Network: ABC FM Connection. Format: Classic rock, Top-40. Target aud: 18-30.

WEHH(AM)—See Elmira Heights-Horseheads

WELM(AM)— April 1947: 1410 khz; 5 kw-D, 1 kw-N, DA-N. TL: N42 07 11 W76 48 37. Stereo. 1705 Lake St. 14901. Phone: (607) 733-5626. Phone: (607) 732-1400. Fax: (607) 733-5627. E-mail: ppinesmedia1@stny.rr.com. Licensee: Pembrook Pines Elmira Ltd. Group owner: Pembrook Pines Media Group (acq 10-1-77). Network: CBS. Bechtel & Cole. Format: Sports. News staff: one; News: 10 hrs wkly. Target aud: 25-54. Spec prog: Relg one hr wkly. ◆Robert J. Pfuntner, CEO, pres & gen mgr; Gary Knight, opns dir; David Crum, gen sls mgr & adv mgr; Patrick Leiby, mktg dir; Bob Michaels, progmg dir; Brian Stoll, mus dir; Mike Jacobs, news dir; Nancy Nicastro, pub affrs dir.

WLVY(FM)—Co-owned with WELM(AM). Aug 1, 1966: 94.3 mhz; 800 w. Ant 745 ft. TL: N42 07 51 W76 47 26. Stereo. E-mail: airstaff@wlvy94rock.com. Web Site: www.wlvy94rock.com. Network: Westwood One. Rep: Allied Radio Partners. Pembrook Pines Format: CHR, hot adult contemp, Top 40s. News staff: one; News: 5 hrs wkly. Target aud: 18-36; young vibrant adults. ◆Dave Crum, sls dir & adv dir; Sue Schneck, mktg dir; Bob Smith, prom dir; Mike Strobel, progmg dir; Jim Reed, engrg dir; Mark Saia, engrg mgr.

WENY(AM)— 1939: 1230 khz; 1 kw-U. TL: N42 04 30 W76 46 55. Box 1047, Corning 14830. Phone: (607) 962-4646. Fax: (607) 962-1138. Web Site: www.theradioworks.com. Licensee: Group A Licensee LLC. Group owner: Route 81 Radio LLC (acq 12-31-2003; grpsl). Rep: McGavren Guild. Format: News/talk. Target aud: 30 plus. ◆Bob Eolin, gen mgr; Dee Eolin, news dir; Jim Appleton, chief of engrg.

WENY-FM— Aug 15, 1965: 92.7 mhz; 700 w. Ant 561 ft. TL: N42 01 55 W76 47 02. Stereo. Network: ABC. Format: Adult contemp.

WNKI(FM)—See Corning

WPGI(FM)—See Horseheads

WWLZ(AM)—See Horseheads

Elmira Heights-Horseheads

WEHH(AM)— July 4, 1956: 1600 khz; 5 kw-D, 170 w-N, DA-2. TL: N42 07 11 W76 48 37. 1705 Lake St., Elmira 14901. Phone: (607) 733-5626. Phone: (607) 732-1400. Fax: (607) 733-5627. E-mail: ppinesmedial@sty.rr.com. Licensee: Pembrook Pines Elmira Ltd. Group owner: Pembrook Pines Media (acq 5-19-99). Rep: Allied Radio Partners. Format: Adult classics. News: 2 hrs wkly. Target aud: 45 plus; upscale adults. ◆Robert J. Pfuntner, CEO & gen mgr; Sue Schneck, opns VP.

Endicott

WENE(AM)— September 1947: 1430 khz; 5 kw-U, DA-N. TL: N42 04 56 W76 01 53. Stereo. 320 N. Jensen Rd., Vestal 13850-2111. Phone: (607) 785-3351. Fax: (607) 584-5900. E-mail: info@1430theteam.com. Web Site: www.1430theteam.com. Licensee: Clear Channel Broadcasting Licenses Inc. Group owner: Clear Channel Communications Inc. (acq 4-14-00; grpsl). Network: Westwood One. Rep: McGavren Guild. Proskauer, Rose, Goetz & Mendelsohn, L. Format: Talk, sports. News staff: 2; News: 28 hrs wkly. Target aud: 35 plus. ◆Tom Barney, gen mgr.

WMRV-FM—Co-owned with WENE. 1969: 105.7 mhz; 35 kw. 570 ft. TL: N42 08 20 W75 59 58. Stereo. Web Site: www.1430theteam.com. Format: CHR. Target aud: 18-34.

Endwell

WBBI(FM)— 1998: 107.5 mhz; 1.1 kw. Ant 544 ft. TL: N42 08 17 W75 59 59. 320 North Jensen Rd., Vestal 13850. Phone: (607) 584-5800. Fax: (607) 584-5900. Licensee: Clear Channel Broadcasting Licenses Inc. Group owner: Clear Channel Communications Inc. (acq 4-14-00; grpsl). Format: Classic rock. ◆Joanna Alay, gen mgr.

Essex

WCPV(FM)— Oct 1, 1994: 101.3 mhz; 1 kw. 797 ft. TL: N44 24 12 W73 26 02. 1500 Hegeman Ave., Colchester, VT 05446. Phone: (802) 654-9300. Fax: (802) 655-0478. Web Site: www.champrocks.com. Licensee: Capstar TX L.P. Group owner: Clear Channel Communications Inc. (acq 8-30-00; grpsl). Format: Classic rock. ◆Karen Marshall, gen mgr; Steve Cormier, opns mgr; John Hill, sls dir.

Fairport

WFKL(FM)— 1993: 93.3 mhz; 4.4 kw. Ant 384 ft. TL: N43 10 37 W77 28 39. Stereo. Entercom Rochester LLC, 70 Commercial St., Rochester 14614-1010. Phone: (585) 423-2900. Fax: (585) 325-5139. Web Site: www.93bbf.com. Licensee: Entercom Rochester Inc. Group owner: Entercom Communications Corp. (acq 4-23-98; grpsl). Rep: Katz Radio. Akin, Gump, Strauss, Hauer & Feld. Format: Oldies. News staff: one. Target aud: 25-54; upscale. ◆Michael Doyle, gen mgr; Dave Symonds, opns mgr; Mike Pallini, gen sls mgr; Mike Rockwell, natl sls mgr; Mike Johnson, rgnl sls mgr; Christine Neenan, prom dir; Dave Simmons, progmg dir; Steve Hausmann, news dir; Joe Fleming, chief of engrg.

Fenner

***WXXE(FM)**— Dec 21, 1998: 90.5 mhz; 7 w. 413 ft. TL: N42 58 12 W75 47 12. 826 Euclid Ave., Syracuse 13210. Phone: (315) 426-0850. Fax: (315) 701-0303. E-mail: info@wxxe.org. Web Site: www.wxxe.org. Licensee: Syracuse Community Radio Inc. Format: Var. ◆Dana Bonn, pres & opns mgr; Danny Danhauser, gen mgr; Dale Gowin, progmg dir; Mark Hughson, mus dir.

Fort Plain

WBUG-FM— Mar 1, 1990: 101.1 mhz; 1.25 kw. 718 ft. TL: N42 52 44 W74 47 07. Stereo. 185 Genesee St., Suite 1601, Utica 13501. Phone: (315) 734-9245. Fax: (315) 624-9245. Licensee: Roser Communications Network Inc. (acq 10-21-94; $400,000. with WVTL(AM)

New York   Directory of Radio

Amsterdam; FTR: 12-5-94). Network: ABC. Format: C&W. News staff: 2; News: 10 hrs wkly. Target aud: 25 plus. ♦Ken Roser Jr., gen mgr; Roxanne Roser, gen sls mgr.

Frankfort

WKLL(FM)—Licensed to Frankfort. See Utica

Fredonia

WBKX(FM)— April 1989: 96.5 mhz; 1.4 kw. Ant 686 ft. TL: N42 22 02 W79 23 12. Stereo. Box 209, 4561 Willow Rd., Dunkirk 14048. Phone: (716) 366-8580. Phone: (716) 366-1410. Fax: (716) 366-1416. Licensee: Chadwick Bay Broadcasting Corp. (acq 2-26-2001; with WDOE(AM) Dunkirk). Network: ABC. Format: Adult Contemporary. News: 12 hrs wkly. Target aud: 25-54. ♦John Bulmer, pres; Chuck Telford, gen mgr; David Rowley, news dir.

*WCVF-FM— July 6, 1978: 88.9 mhz; 130 w. 125 ft. TL: N42 27 08 W79 20 14. Stereo. 115 McEwen Hall, State Univ. of New York 14063. Phone: (716) 673-3420. Phone: (716) 673-3520. Fax: (716) 673-3427. Web Site: www.fredoniaradio.com. Licensee: State University of New York. Format: Div, progsv. News: 15 hrs wkly. Target aud: 18-20; campus & community of Fredonia. Spec prog: Black 8 hrs, reggae 3 hrs, It 3 hrs, folk 3 hrs, Latin 10 hrs wkly. ♦Michelle Ostowski, pres & gen mgr.

Freeport

WGBB(AM)— August 1924: 1240 khz; 1 kw-U. TL: N40 38 44 W73 34 38. 1850 Lausdown Ave., 404 Rte 109, W. Babylon 11704. Phone: (516) 623-1240. Fax: (516) 623-1240. E-mail: support@am1240wgbb.com. Web Site: www.am1240wgbb.com. Licensee: WGBB-AM Inc. Group owner: Cox Broadbasting (acq 5-22-98; grpsl). Format: Var. Target aud: 25-65. Spec prog: Relg 6 hrs, Sp 2 hrs wkly. ♦Jeff Lo, opns mgr.

Friendship

*WCID(FM)— 1989: 89.1 mhz; 7 kw. Ant 492 ft. TL: N42 07 07 W78 10 43. Stereo. Box 506, 7634 Campbell Creek Rd., Bath 14810. Phone: (607) 776-4151. Fax: (607) 776-6929. E-mail: mail@fln.org. Web Site: www.fln.org. Licensee: Family Life Ministries Inc. Group owner: Family Life Network Network: Salem Radio Network. Format: Christian, contemporary. News staff: 7; News: 14 hrs wkly. Target aud: 25-55; general. Spec prog: Inspirational. ♦Dick Snavely, pres; Rick Snavely, gen mgr.

Fulton

WAMF(AM)— Aug 19, 1949: 1300 khz; 1 kw-D. TL: N43 17 41 W76 26 35. Stereo. 174 Lakeshore Road 13069. Phone: (315) 593-1300. Fax: (315) 598-5158. E-mail: wamf1300@alltel.net. Web Site: realcountryonline.com. Licensee: Donald H. Derosa (acq 8-6-2002; $300,000). Network: ABC. Format: Country. Target aud: 35 plus; hometown listeners, county coverage. Spec prog: It 2 hrs, Pol 5 hrs wkly. ♦Don Derosa, gen mgr.

WBBS(FM)— Aug 1, 1961: 104.7 mhz; 50 kw. 310 ft. TL: N43 12 53 W76 23 44. (CP: Ant 479 ft.). Stereo. 500 Plum St., Suite 100, Bridgewater Pl., Syracuse 13204. Phone: (315) 448-1047. Fax: (315) 474-7879. Web Site: www.b1047.net. Licensee: Citicasters Licenses L.P. Group owner: Clear Channel Communications Inc. (acq 5-4-99; grpsl). Format: Country. ♦Joel DelMonico, gen mgr.

Garden City

*WHPC(FM)— Oct 12, 1972: 90.3 mhz; 500 w. Ant 213 ft. TL: N40 43 47 W73 35 33. Stereo. Nassau Community College,, One Education Dr. 11530-6793. Phone: (516) 572-7835. Phone: (516) 572-7438. Fax: (516) 572-7831. Web Site: www.sunynassau.edu. Licensee: Nassau Community College Board of Trustees. Format: Div, educ, adult contemp. News staff: 2; News: 5 hrs wkly. Target aud: 20-65; general. Spec prog: Pol one hr, Irish 3 hrs, classic rock 2 hrs, rock 2 hrs, progsv 4 hrs, new age one hr, big band 4 hrs, country 2 hrs, Italian 2 hrs, jazz 5 hrs, Sp one hr wkly. ♦Sean Fanelli, CEO; Jack Ostling, exec VP; Dr. John P. McGovern, gen mgr; John McGovern, opns dir; Jim Green, opns mgr & progmg dir.

WZAA(FM)— 1988: 92.7 mhz; 2 kw. Ant 521 ft. TL: N40 45 26 W73 42 52. Stereo. 485 Madison Ave., New York 10022. Phone: (212) 310-6000. Fax: (212) 310-6095. Licensee: HBC License Corp. Group owner: Univision Radio (acq 12-4-2003; $60 million). Format: Sp contemp. ♦McHenry T. Tichenor Jr., pres; Stephanie McNamara, gen mgr.

Geneseo

*WGSU(FM)— Feb 18, 1963: 89.3 mhz; 1.8 kw. 11 ft. TL: N42 47 51 W77 49 13. Stereo. Dept. of Communication, State Univ. College, One College Cir. 14454. Phone: (585) 245-5229. Fax: (585) 245-5240. E-mail: pruszyns@geneseo.edu. Web Site: www.geneseo.edu~/wgsu. Licensee: State University of New York. Format: News, alternative. News: 7 hrs wkly. Target aud: 12-55; college, immediate community. ♦Chris Pruszynski, gen mgr.

Geneva

*WEOS(FM)— Mar 30, 1971: 89.7 mhz; 4 kw. 312 ft. TL: N42 51 27 W76 59 21. Stereo. 300 Pulteney St. 14456. Secondary address: 113 Hamilton St. 14456. Phone: (315) 781-3456. Phone: (315) 781-3897. Fax: (315) 781-3916. E-mail: weos@hws.edu. Web Site: www.weos.org. Licensee: The Colleges of the Seneca. Network: Network: NPR, PRI. Format: Jazz, progsv, news/talk. News staff: one; News: 40 hrs wkly. Target aud: 18-plus. Spec prog: AAA 12 hrs, world 10 hrs, metal 6 hrs, gospel 3 hrs, reggae 3 hrs wkly. ♦Mark Gearan, pres; Michael R. Black, gen mgr; Elizabeth Kenney, opns dir; Greg Cotterill, dev dir; Emily Schmerbeck, prom dir; Liz Kenny, progmg dir.

WFLK(FM)— 1974: 101.7 mhz; 5.4 kw. Ant 125 ft. TL: N42 51 34 W77 00 29. Stereo. Box 1017 14456. Phone: (315) 781-1101. Fax: (315) 781-6666. E-mail: k1017@fltg.net. Web Site: www.k1017.com. Licensee: MB Communications Inc. (acq 1993). Henry Crawford. Format: Super hit country. News staff: 2; News: 10 hrs wkly. Target aud: 25-49. ♦Russ Kimble, pres & stn mgr; John Thomas, opns mgr & pub affrs dir; Lori Rose, dev mgr; Mary Ann Hurlburt, gen sls mgr; Tom Gallagher, prom dir & progmg dir.

WGVA(AM)— 1947: 1240 khz; 1 kw-U. TL: N42 51 37 W77 00 59. 3568 Lenox Rd. 14456. Phone: (315) 781-1240. Fax: (315) 781-7700. Licensee: Geneva Broadcasting Inc. (acq 9-27-96). Network: ABC Information & Entertainment. James L. Oyster. Format: News/talk. News staff: one; News: 10 hrs wkly. Target aud: General. ♦George Kimble, pres; Alan Bishop, exec VP & gen mgr.

WNYR-FM—See Waterloo

Glens Falls

WCQL(FM)—Listing follows WWSC(AM).

WENU-FM—See Hudson Falls

WFFG-FM—See Corinth

*WGFR(FM)— January 1977: 92.7 mhz; 13 w. 49 ft. TL: N43 18 44 W73 38 58. Adirondack Community College, 640 Bay Rd., Queensbury 12804-1498. Phone: (518) 743-2311. Fax: (518) 745-1433. Web Site: www.wgfr.org. Licensee: Board of Trustees of Adirondack Community College. Format: Progsv, AAA, loud rock. Target aud: 12-20. ♦Kevin Ankeny, gen mgr; Brian Young, progmg dir.

*WLJH(FM)— 2001: 90.9 mhz; 360 w. Ant 663 ft. TL: N43 19 55 W73 20 20. Box 777, Lake Katrine 12449. Phone: (845) 336-6199. Fax: (845) 336-7205. Web Site: www.soundoflife.org. Licensee: Sound of Life Inc. Format: Christian. ♦Tom Zahradnik, gen mgr.

WMML(AM)— May 28, 1959: 1230 khz; 1 kw-U. TL: N43 19 43 W73 38 58. 89 Everts Ave., Queensbury 12804. Phone: (518) 793-7733. Fax: (518) 793-0838. Licensee: 6 Johnson Road Licenses Inc. Group owner: Pamal Broadcasting Ltd. (acq 4-1-2004; grpsl). Network: ESPN Radio. Format: Sports. News staff: one; News: 6 hrs wkly. Target aud: 18-54 plus. Spec prog: Relg 3 hrs wkly. ♦James Morrell, pres; Clay Ashworthy, gen mgr; Bob Vojnar, opns mgr.

WWSC(AM)— Dec 18, 1946: 1450 khz; 1 kw-U. TL: N43 18 59 W73 37 23. 128 Glen St. 12801. Phone: (518) 761-9890. Fax: (518) 761-9893. Web Site: www.radiowins.com. Licensee: Entertronics Inc. Broadcasting. (acq 1999; with co-located FM). Network: ABC Information & Entertainment. Format: MOR, news/talk, sports. News staff: one; News: 88 hrs wkly. Target aud: 30 plus; people who want full service radio, news, info, mus, talk. Spec prog: Big band, oldies. ♦David Covey, pres & gen mgr; William H. Walker III, VP; Robin Covey, opns dir; Gary Gifford, opns mgr; Paul Van Amburgh, gen sls mgr; Pete Cloutier, prom dir; Dan Miner, progmg dir; Jim Scott, news dir; Kevin Smith, chief of engrg.

WCQL(FM)—Co-owned with WWSC(AM). September 1967: 95.9 mhz; 410 w. Ant 863 ft. TL: N43 18 17 W73 45 07. Stereo. Web Site: www.radiowins.com. Format: Classic rock. Target aud: 18-49. ♦Paul Van Amburgh, sls dir & progmg mgr.

Gloversville

WENT(AM)— July 1, 1944: 1340 khz; 1 kw-U. TL: N43 01 30 W74 21 10. Box 831, 138 Harrison St. Ext. 12078. Phone: (518) 725-7175. Fax: (518) 725-7177. E-mail: went@capital.net. Web Site: www.am1340went.com. Licensee: Whitney Radio Broadcasting Inc. (acq 12-15-86; $700,000; 11-3-86). Network: Network: CNN Radio, ESPN Radio. Format: Full service, adult contemp. News staff: 2; News: 14 hrs wkly. Target aud: 30 plus. Spec prog: Talk one hr wkly. ♦Jack Scott, pres & gen mgr; Jon W. Clark, VP; Shirley V. Clark, stn mgr.

WFNY(AM)— 3/2003: 1440 khz; 800 w-D, 500 w-N, DA-2. TL: N43 01 57 W74 21 02. 101 S. Main St. 12078. Phone: (518) 725-1108. Licensee: Michael A. Sleezer. Format: Hits past & present. ♦Michael A. Sleezer, gen mgr.

Gouverneur

WGIX-FM— Dec 5, 1967: 95.3 mhz; 3 kw. 220 ft. TL: N44 19 47 W75 27 20. (CP: 5 kw, ant 328 ft. TL: N44 20 20 W75 24 01). Stereo. 2315 Knox St., Ogdensburg 13669. Phone: (315) 393-1100. Fax: (315) 393-6673. Web Site: www.coololdies.us. Licensee: Clancy-Mance Communications North Inc. Group owner: Clancy-Mance Communications (acq 7-10-03; grpsl). Format: Oldies. News staff: 3; News: 7 hrs wkly. Target aud: 35-54. ♦David Mance, pres & gen mgr; Dallas Sutton, sls dir; Nate Townsend, progmg dir; Roger Ousterhaust, chief of engrg.

Grand Gorge

*WGKR(FM)— November 1997: 105.3 mhz; 60 w. 1,342 ft. TL: N42 23 58 W74 35 27. Box 777, Lake Katrine 12449. Secondary address: 199 Tuytenbridge Rd., Lake Katrine 12449. Phone: (845) 336-6199. Fax: (845) 336-7205. E-mail: email@soundoflife.org. Web Site: www.soundoflife.org. Licensee: Sound of Life Inc. Format: Contemp Christian. ♦Tom Zahradnik, gen mgr.

Greece

*WGMC(FM)— Nov 11, 1973: 90.1 mhz; 15 kw. Ant 138 ft. TL: N43 14 40 W77 41 36. Stereo. Box 300, North Greece 14515. Secondary address: Apollo Bldg., 750 Maiden Ln., Rochester 14615. Phone: (585) 966-2660. Fax: (585) 621-8692. Web Site: www.jazz901.org. Licensee: Greece Central School District. Dow, Lohnes & Albertson. Format: Jazz. Target aud: 25-50; upscale, educated, mus lovers. Spec prog: Pol 2 hrs, Sp 10 hrs, Lithuanian one hr, Turkish one hr, blues 3 hrs wkly. ♦Jack Mindy, opns mgr; Rob Linton, stn mgr & opns mgr.

Hamilton

*WRCU-FM— Mar 22, 1970: 90.1 mhz; 1.9 kw. 155 ft. TL: N42 48 38 W75 31 58. Stereo. Colgate Univ. 13346. Phone: (315) 228-7104. Fax: (315) 228-7028. Licensee: Colgate University. Format: Progsv, div, jazz. Spec prog: Jazz 12 hrs, class 4 hrs, Black 10 hrs wkly. ♦Matt Pysher, gen mgr; Andy Jackson, progmg mgr.

Hampton Bays

WLIR-FM— Nov 20, 1980: 107.1 mhz; 6 kw. Ant 279 ft. TL: N40 52 10 W72 34 37. Stereo. 1103 Stewart Ave., Garden City 11530. Phone: (516) 222-1103. Fax: (516) 222-1391. Web Site: www.box1071.com. Licensee: Jarad Broadcasting Co. of Hampton Bays LLC Group owner: The Morey Organization Inc. (acq 12-23-03; $2 million). Rep: Roslin. Format: Alternative. ♦Howard Frank, VP & gen mgr.

Hempstead

WHLI(AM)— July 22, 1947: 1100 khz; 10 kw-D, DA. TL: N40 41 06 W73 36 38. 234 Airport Plaza Blvd., #5, Farmingdale 11735-3938. Phone: (631) 770-4200. Fax: (631) 770-0090. Web Site: www.whli.com. Licensee: Long Island Broadcasting Inc. Group owner: Barnstable Broadcasting Inc. (acq 12-15-84; $5 million with co-located FM;

Stations in the U.S. — New York

Developers & Brokers of Radio Properties — contact American Media Services at our suite: Philadelphia Marriott Downtown 215-625-2900 · 843-972-2200 · americanmediaservices.com · Charleston, SC · Dallas, TX · Chicago, Il · Austin, TX — American Media Services, LLC

9-24-84). Rep: D & R Radio. Format: Adult standards. News staff: one; News: 2 hrs wkly. Target aud: 35-64; adults. Spec prog: Black one hr wkly. ♦Dave Widmer, gen mgr; Janine Kelly, gen sls mgr; Wendy Morra, prom dir; Dean Anthony, progmg VP & progmg dir; Frank Brinka, news dir; John Bennett, engrg dir.

WKJY(FM)—Co-owned with WHLI(AM). July 22, 1947: 98.3 mhz; 3 kw. 328 ft. TL: N40 41 08 W73 36 37. Stereo. Web Site: www.whli.com. Rep: D & R Radio. Format: Adult contemp. News staff: one. Target aud: 25-54. Spec prog: Black one hr wkly. ♦Bill George, progmg dir.

***WRHU(FM)**— June 9, 1959: 88.7 mhz; 470 w. 200 ft. TL: N40 43 03 W73 36 12. Stereo. Rm. 127, 111 Hofstra Univ. 11549-1110. Phone: (516) 463-5667. Fax: (516) 463-5668. E-mail: mail@wrhu.org. Web Site: www.wrhu.org. Licensee: Hofstra University. Dow, Lohnes & Albertson. Format: Div. News: 11 hrs wkly. Target aud: General. Spec prog: Radio theatre one hr, C&W 2 hrs, Irish 5 hrs, pub affrs 4 hrs, rhythm & blues 2 hrs, lt 4 hrs, Pol 3 hrs, classical, jazz 20 hrs wkly. ♦Bruce Avery, gen mgr; Andrew Falzon, stn mgr; Joel Meyer, opns mgr; Meghan Attreed, prom dir; Dustin Gervais, progmg dir.

Henderson

WOTT(FM)— 1991: 100.7 mhz; 3 kw. 328 ft. TL: N43 49 13 W76 05 29. (CP: 6 kw). 199 Wealtha Ave., Watertown 13601. Phone: (315) 782-1240. Fax: (315) 782-0132. Web Site: www.realrock1007.com. Licensee: Jefferson Broadcasting Inc. Rep: Roslin. Format: Active rock. ♦David Mance, pres; Glenn Curry, gen mgr; Todd Dalesandro, opns mgr; Vickie Fenn, sls dir; Johnny Keegan, progmg dir; Kenny Ruhland, engrg dir.

Henrietta

***WITR(FM)**— Mar 7, 1975: 89.7 mhz; 910 w. 154 ft. TL: N43 05 08 W77 40 05. Stereo. 32 Lomb Memorial Dr., Rochester 14623. Phone: (585) 475-2000. Phone: (585) 475-2271. Fax: (585) 475-4988. Licensee: Rochester Institute of Technology. Format: Modern music. Target aud: General. Spec prog: Reggae 5 hrs, jazz 8 hrs, contemp Christian rock 10 hrs, gospel 8 hrs, industrial 2 hrs, comedy 2 hrs, world beat 2 hrs wkly. ♦Mark Zuriga, gen mgr; Justin Ricci, prom dir; Steve Montario, progmg dir.

Herkimer

WNRS(AM)— October 1956: 1420 khz; 1 kw-D. TL: N43 03 40 W75 01 44. Box 927, 381 Otsego St., Ilion 13357. Phone: (315) 866-9200. Fax: (315) 866-6906. E-mail: wxur@hotmail.com. Licensee: Arjuna Broadcasting Corp. (acq 10-23-96). Rep: Savalli. Cohn & Marks. Format: Sports. News staff: one. Target aud: 18 plus; men. ♦Mindy Barstein, pres & gen mgr; Tom Davenport, opns VP; Tim Barstein, sls VP; Jenna Davenport, prom VP; Chris Miller, progmg dir & news dir; Anthony Falvo, chief of engrg.

WXUR(FM)—Co-owned with WNRS(AM). Apr 28, 1979: 92.7 mhz; 6 kw. 299 ft. TL: N43 03 50 W75 01 44. Stereo. Network: Westwood One. Format: Oldies. News staff: one. Target aud: 35-64; adults. ♦Tim Barstein, dev VP; Jenna Davenport, mktg mgr; Chris Miller, progmg VP; Tony Falvo, engrg VP.

***WVHC(FM)**— October 1993: 91.5 mhz; 350 w vert. -115 ft. Stereo. Reservoir Rd. 13350. Phone: (315) 866-0300, EXT. 354. Fax: (315) 866-7253. Licensee: Herkimer County Community College. Format: Jazz. News: 5 hrs wkly. Target aud: General; residents of southern Herkimer county & college community. ♦Michael Giudice, stn mgr; Cari Knight, progmg dir.

Highland

WRWD-FM— Oct 3, 1989: 107.3 mhz; 330 w. Ant 968 ft. TL: N41 41 58 W74 00 11. Stereo. 20 Tucker Dr., Poughkeepsie 12603. Phone: (845) 454-2800. Fax: (845) 471-0793. E-mail: wrwd@hvi.net. Web Site: www.wrwdcountry1073.com. Licensee: AMFM Radio Licenses LLC. Group owner: Clear Channel Communications Inc. (acq 12-10-97;

$7.5 million. with WBWZ(FM) New Paltz). Gammon & Grange. Format: C&W. Target aud: 18 plus. Spec prog: Farm one hr wkly. ♦Bob Dunphy, gen mgr.

Homer

WXHC(FM)— 1991: 101.5 mhz; 1.3 kw. 489 ft. TL: N42 41 12 W76 11 54. Stereo. Box 386, 12 S. Main St. 13077. Phone: (607) 749-9942. Fax: (607) 749-2374. E-mail: johneves@wxhc.com. Web Site: www.wxhc.com. Licensee: John Eves. Rep: Roslin. Cole, Raywid & Braverman. Format: Oldies. News staff: one; News: 10 hrs wkly. Target aud: 25-54. Spec prog: Bluegrass 2 hrs, relg 1 hr, farm 1 hr wkly. ♦John Eves, pres; Bruce Eves, exec VP; Patricia Eves, VP; Sonny King, opns VP.

Honeoye Falls

WFXF(FM)— 1948: 95.1 mhz; 50 kw. Ant 479 ft. TL: N43 02 01 W77 25 18. Stereo. 207 Midtown Plaza, Rochester 14604. Phone: (585) 246-0440. Fax: (585) 454-5081. Licensee: Citicasters Licenses Inc. (NEW). Group owner: Clear Channel Communications Inc. (acq 1999; grpsl). Format: Modern rock, AOR. News: one hr wkly. Target aud: 18-44. Spec prog: Rgnl news one hr wkly. ♦Karen Kary, gen mgr.

Hoosick Falls

WZEC(FM)— July 4, 1991: 97.5 mhz; 450 w. 1,115 ft. TL: N42 51 47 W73 13 56. (CP: 880 w, ant 702 ft.). 409 Main St., Bennington, VT 05201. Phone: (802) 442-5446. Fax: (802) 442-1531. E-mail: wzec@sover.net. Web Site: www.voxradio.com. Licensee: Capital Media Corp. Group owner: Vox Radio Group L.P. (acq 5-31-2005; $1.1 million). Format: Modern adult contemp. Target aud: 25-65. ♦Doug Tweedy, stn mgr; Jason Costello, prom mgr; Ken Barlow, progmg VP; Ed Garcia, progmg dir.

Hornell

WCKR(FM)—Listing follows WLEA(AM).

WHHO(AM)— 1949: 1320 khz; 5 kw-D. TL: N42 17 32 W77 40 27. Box 726, 1484 Beech St. 14843. Phone: (607) 324-2000. Phone: (607) 324-2002. Fax: (607) 324-2001. E-mail: devin@wkpq.com. Web Site: www.wkpq.com. Licensee: Bilbat Radio Inc. (acq 6-10-83; $450,000 with co-located FM; 5-30-83). Format: Talk. News staff: one; News: 14 hrs wkly. Target aud: 25-54. Spec prog: Farm. ♦William H. Berry, CFO; Bob Lee, gen sls mgr; Susan Macool, progmg dir; Mickey Slansburgs, mus dir; Johnathan Mark, news dir; Ralph Van, chief of engrg.

WKPQ(FM)— Co-owned with WHHO(AM). 1946: 105.3 mhz; 50 kw. 530 ft. TL: N42 17 32 W77 40 27. Stereo. E-mail: bilbat@wkpq.com. Web Site: www.wkpq.com. Format: Hot adult comtemp. News staff: one; News: 7 hrs wkly. Target aud: 18-54; females.

WLEA(AM)— September 1951: 1480 khz; 2.5 kw-D. TL: N42 17 15 W77 38 47. 5942 Ashbaugh Hill Rd. 14843. Phone: (607) 324-1480. Fax: (607) 324-5415. Web Site: www.wckr.com. Licensee: PMJ Communications Inc. (acq 10-18-90; $538,000 with co-located FM; 11-19-90). Network: ABC Information & Entertainment. Format: Oldies, news/talk. News staff: 2; News: 16 hrs wkly. Target aud: 35 plus. ♦Tom Booth, gen mgr; Bill Dubensky, news dir.

WCKR(FM)—Co-owned with WLEA(AM). June 1981: 92.1 mhz; 1.25 kw. 512 ft. TL: N42 20 38 W77 37 36. Stereo. E-mail: radione@infoblvd.net. Web Site: www.wckr.com. Network: USA. Format: Country. News: 11 hrs wkly. Target aud: 21 plus.

***WSQA(FM)**— 2000: 88.7 mhz; 4.5 kw. Ant 495 ft. TL: N42 16 02 W77 37 55. Box 3000, Binghamton 13902. Phone: (607) 729-0100. Fax: (607) 729-7328. Web Site: www.wskg.com. Licensee: WSKG Public Telecommunications Council. Format: Jazz, news. ♦Susan Miller-Cormien, sr VP; Gary Reinbolt, gen mgr.

Horseheads

WEHH(AM)—See Elmira Heights-Horseheads

WLNL(AM)— May 7, 1967: 1000 khz; 5 kw-D. TL: N42 09 14 W76 50 47. 3134 Lake Rd. 14845. Phone: (607) 737-9208. Fax: (607) 737-9210. Web Site: www.wlnlradio.com. Licensee: Trinity Media Ltd. (acq 1-21-92; $256,000;. FTR: 11-11-91). Network: USA. Format: Relg. News: 5 min per hr. Target aud: 25-54; Christian families, women/mothers who work at home. Spec prog: Country/bluegrass one hr wkly. ♦James Pierce, pres & gen mgr.

WPGI(FM)—Listing follows WWLZ(AM).

WWLZ(AM)— April 1966: 820 khz; 5 kw-D, 1 kw-N, DA-2. TL: N42 09 14 W76 50 47. 2205 College Ave., Elmira 14903. Phone: (607) 732-4400. Fax: (607) 732-7774. Licensee: Chemung County Radio Inc. Group owner: Backyard Broadcasting LLC (acq 12-1-2002; grpsl). Network: ABC Information & Entertainment. Format: News/talk. Target aud: 25-54; baby boomers. ♦Kevin White, gen mgr; Jim Poteat, prom mgr & progmg dir.

WPGI(FM)—Co-owned with WWLZ(AM). July 4, 1970: 100.9 mhz; 3 kw. 245 ft. TL: N42 12 00 W76 51 30. Stereo. Format: Country. Target aud: General.

Houghton

***WJSL(FM)**— Jan 18, 1979: 90.3 mhz; 6 kw. 216 ft. TL: N42 22 39 W78 10 45. Stereo. Box 30021, Rochester 14603. Phone: (585) 325-7500. E-mail: newsroom@wxxi.org. Web Site: www.wxxi.org. Licensee: WXXI Public Broadcasting Council. Format: Class. Target aud: 18-36; college. Spec prog: Class 5 hrs wkly. ♦Norm Silverstein, CEO & pres; Sue Rogers, VP.

Hudson

WHUC(AM)— 1947: 1230 khz; 1 kw-U. TL: N42 15 13 W73 45 45. 20 Tucker Dr., Poughkeepsie 12603. Secondary address: 5620 Rt. 96 12534. Phone: (518) 828-5006. Fax: (518) 828-1080. Licensee: Clear Channel Broadcasting Licenses Inc. Group owner: Clear Channel Communications Inc. (acq 1-17-2002; grpsl). Network: Jones Radio Networks. Format: Adult standards. News staff: one; News: 4 hrs wkly. Target aud: 35 plus; loc people in Columbia & Greene counties. ♦Bob Dunphy, gen mgr.

WZCR(FM)—Co-owned with WHUC(AM). Jan 20, 1969: 93.5 mhz; 3 kw. Ant -15 ft. TL: N42 15 13 W73 45 45. Stereo. Network: Westwood One. Format: Oldies. News: 3 hrs wkly. Target aud: General; adults 35-54.

***WHVP(FM)**— May 1998: 91.1 mhz; 362 w vert. 991 ft. TL: N42 17 52 W73 53 57. Stereo. Box 777, Lake Katrine 12449. Phone: (845) 336-6199. Fax: (845) 336-7205. E-mail: email@soundoflife.org. Web Site: www.soundoflife.org. Licensee: Sound of Life Inc. Format: Christian. ♦Tom Zahradnik, gen mgr.

Hudson Falls

WENU-FM— Sept 19, 1983: 101.7 mhz; 4.6 kw. 180 ft. TL: N43 22 40 W73 39 56. Stereo. 89 Everts Ave., Queensbury 12804. Phone: (518) 793-7733. Fax: (518) 793-0838. Licensee: 6 Johnson Road Licenses Inc. Group owner: Pamal Broadcasting Ltd. (acq 4-1-2004; grpsl). Format: Adult Standards. News staff: one. Target aud: 35-64. ♦Clay Ashworth, gen mgr; Mike Morgan, opns mgr; Rolly Merrill, gen sls mgr.

Huntington

WGSM(AM)— Sept 1, 1951: . Stn currently dark 740 khz; 25 kw-D, 43 w-N, DA-2. TL: N40 51 04 W73 26 16. (CP: 20 kw-D, 50 w-N, DA-2). Stereo. 100-25 Queens Blvd., Suite 1CC, Forest Hills 11375. Phone: (718) 335-3333. Licensee: Win Radio Broadcasting Corp. (acq 6-17-2005; $2.2 million). ♦Richard S. Yoon, pres & gen mgr.

Broadcasting & Cable Yearbook 2006

Hyde Park

WCZX(FM)— Aug 18, 1970: 97.7 mhz; 300 w. 1,030 ft. TL: N41 43 11 W73 59 45. Stereo. Box 416, 2 Pendell Rd., Poughkeepsie 12602. Phone: (845) 471-1500. E-mail: randyturner@mix97fm.com. Web Site: www.mix97fm.com. Licensee: Cumulus Licensing Corp. Group owner: Cumulus Media Inc. (acq 1-23-02; grpsl). Rep: Katz Radio. Format: Adult contemp. News staff: one; News: 10 hrs wkly. Target aud: 25-54. ♦John Dickie, CEO; Lew Dickie, pres; Chuck Benfer, gen mgr.

WHVW(AM)— July 4, 1963: 950 khz; 500 w-D, 57 w-N. TL: N41 44 46 W73 54 46. 316 Main St., Poughkeepsie 12601-3123. Phone: (845) 471-9500. Fax: (845) 452-8696. E-mail: whvw@hui.net. Web Site: www.whvw.org,.com,.net. Licensee: Joseph-Paul Ferraro. (acq 3-9-92; $350,000; 3-30-92). Format: Oldies. Target aud: 25-54. Spec prog: Ger one hr, It one hr, Irish one hr wkly. ♦J.P. Ferraro, pres.

Irondequoit

WKGS(FM)— March 1992: 106.7 mhz; 3.5 kw. 627 ft. TL: N43 11 27 W77 37 11. Stereo. 207 Midtown Plaza, Rochester 14604. Phone: (585) 232-8870. Fax: (585) 454-5081. Fax: (585) 262-2334. E-mail: wkgs@eznet.net. Web Site: www.kiss1067.com. Licensee: Citicasters Licenses L.P. Group owner: Clear Channel Communications Inc. (acq 1999; grpsl). Format: CHR. Target aud: 18-34. ♦Ken Spitzer, VP & gen mgr; Jeff Oar, gen sls mgr; Erick Anderson, progmg dir; Marilee Terran, progmg dir.

Islip

WLIE(AM)— 1960: 540 khz; 2.5 kw-D, 220 w-N, DA-2. TL: N40 45 06 W73 12 50. Stereo. 2137 Deer Park Ave., Deer Park 11729. Phone: (631) 243-5400. Fax: (631) 243-5444. E-mail: Info@wlie.com. Web Site: www.wlie.com. Licensee: Stuart Henry (acq 12-4-2003). . Network: Network: USA, Jones Radio Networks. Thompson, Hine L.L.P. Format: Talk radio. News: 10 hrs wkly. Target aud: 45 plus. Spec prog: Relg 3 hrs wkly. ♦Stuart Henry, pres & gen mgr; Matt Taylor, opns dir.

Ithaca

WHCU(AM)— Jan 23, 1923: 870 khz; 5 kw-D, 1 kw-N, DA-N. TL: N42 21 49 W76 36 20. 1751 Hanshaw Rd. 14850. Phone: (607) 257-6400. Fax: (607) 257-6497. Licensee: Saga Communications of New England LLC. (acq 5-31-2005; grpsl). Network: Network: Network: CBS, Westwood One, AP Radio. Rep: Christal. Richard Carr. Format: News/talk, sports. News staff: 3; News: 40 hrs wkly. Target aud: 25-64. ♦Edward K. Christian, pres; Susan Johnston, gen mgr; Chris Allinger, opns dir; Connie Fairfax-Ozmun, mktg dir; Geoff Dunn, progmg dir & news dir.

WYXL(FM)—Co-owned with WHCU(AM). Sept 1, 1947: 97.3 mhz; 26 kw. 879 ft. TL: N42 27 54 W76 22 23. Stereo. Format: Adult contemp. Target aud: 25-54. ♦Kevin English, progmg dir.

***WICB(FM)**— Jan 14, 1947: 91.7 mhz; 5.5 kw. 105 ft. TL: N42 25 07 W76 29 39. Stereo. Ithaca College, 118 Park Hall 14850. Phone: (607) 274-1040. Fax: (607) 274-1061. E-mail: wicb@ithaca.edu. Web Site: www.wicb.org. Licensee: Ithaca College. Network: ABC. Format: Modern rock, urban contemp, jazz. News: 6 hrs wkly. Target aud: 18-34; young audience with taste for innovative mus. Spec prog: Jazz 13 hrs, folk 2 hrs, blues 2 hrs, reggae 2 hrs, world beat 2 hrs wkly. ♦Christopher Wheatley, gen mgr.

WIII(FM)—See Cortland

WNYY(AM)— April 1956: 1470 khz; 5 kw-D, 1 kw-N, DA-N. TL: N42 23 32 W76 28 29. 1751 Hanshaw Rd. 14850. Phone: (607) 257-6400. Fax: (607) 257-6497. Licensee: Saga Communications of New England LLC. (acq 5-31-2005; grpsl). Network: Westwood One. Rep: Christal. Format: Progressive talk. News staff: 3. Target aud: 35-54. ♦Edward K. Christian, pres; Susan Johnston, gen mgr; Chris Allinger, opns dir; Connie Fairfax-Ozmun, mktg dir; Geoff Dunn, progmg dir & news dir.

WQNY(FM)—Co-owned with WNYY(AM). 1948: 103.7 mhz; 15.5 kw. Ant 879 ft. TL: N42 23 13 W76 40 10. Stereo. Richard Carr. Format: Country. News staff: 3. Target aud: 25-54. ♦Chris Allinger, progmg dir.

***WSQG-FM**— 1988: 90.9 mhz; 5 kw. 294 ft. TL: N42 34 55 W76 33 22. Stereo. Box 3000, Binghamton 13902. Phone: (607) 729-0100. Fax: (607) 729-7328. Web Site: www.wskg.com. Licensee: WSKG Public Telecommunications Council. Network: Network: NPR, PRI. Dow, Lohnes & Albertson. Format: Class, news. News staff: one; News: 33 hrs wkly. Target aud: General. Spec prog: Jazz 7 hrs, folk/bluegrass 5 hrs wkly. ♦Gary Reinbolt, CEO & gen mgr.

WVBR-FM— June 7, 1958: 93.5 mhz; 3 kw. 250 ft. TL: N42 25 42 W76 26 57. Stereo. 957-B Mitchell St. 14850. Phone: (607) 273-4000. Fax: (607) 273-4069. E-mail: radio@wvbr.com. Web Site: www.wvbr.com. Licensee: Cornell Radio Guild Inc. Network: Westwood One. Format: Full service, AOR. News: 10 hrs wkly. Target aud: 18-49; highly educated listeners. Spec prog: Oldies 5 hrs, heavy metal 6 hrs, folk 8 hrs,blues 5 hrs, Latin 5 hrs wkly. ♦Matt Todaro, gen mgr; Dan Zarrow, opns VP; Dave Kheel, dev VP; Bob Fletcher, natl sls mgr; Joslin Madreperl, prom dir; Chris Bianchi, progmg dir.

Jamestown

***WCOT(FM)**— Dec 14, 1992: 90.9 mhz; 12 kw. Ant 653 ft. TL: N42 00 06 W79 03 19. Stereo. Box 506, 7634 Campbell Creek Rd., Bath 14810. Phone: (607) 776-4151. Fax: (607) 776-6929. E-mail: mail@fln.org. Web Site: www.fln.org. Licensee: Family Life Ministries Inc. Group owner: Family Life Network Format: Contemp Christian. News staff: 7; News: 14 hrs wkly. Target aud: 30-54. ♦Rick Snavely, pres, VP & gen mgr.

WHUG(FM)—Listing follows WKSN(AM).

WJTN(AM)— December 1924: 1240 khz; 500 w-D, 1 kw-N. TL: N42 06 18 W79 15 28. Box 1139 14702-1139. Secondary address: 2 Orchard Rd. W.E. 14701. Phone: (716) 487-1151. Fax: (716) 664-9326. E-mail: wjtn@wjtn.com. Web Site: www.wjtn.com. Licensee: Media One Group LLC (acq 8-30-2002; $5.05 million. with co-located FM). Network: Network: Westwood One, ABC Information & Entertainment. Rep: Rgnl Reps. Format: News, talk, sports. News staff: 3; News: 16 hrs wkly. Target aud: 35 plus; adults seeking full service progmg. Spec prog: It one hr, Sp one hr, Swedish one hr, farm one hr wkly. ♦Merrill Rosen, gen mgr; Nick Keefe, opns mgr, prom dir & progmg dir; Larry Sazacki, sls dir; Wayne Goff, chief of engrg.

WWSE(FM)—Co-owned with WJTN(AM). October 1947: 93.3 mhz; 26.5 kw. 643 ft. TL: N42 05 06 W79 17 23. Stereo. Phone: (716) 664-9393. E-mail: wwsefm@wwsefm.com. Web Site: wwsefm.com. Format: Adult contemp. News staff: 3; News: 7 hrs wkly. Target aud: 12554; female. ♦Cheryl Akin, sls VP; Nick Keefe, mus dir; Brian Papalia, asst music dir.

WKSN(AM)— Jan 26, 1948: 1340 khz; 500 w-D, 1 kw-N. TL: N42 05 46 W79 14 48. Box 1199, 202 Front St. 14701. Phone: (716) 664-2313. Fax: (716) 488-1471. E-mail: jadmin@wksn.com. Web Site: www.wksn.com. Licensee: Media One Group II LLC. Group owner: Vox Radio Group L.P. (acq 5-31-2005; grpsl). Rep: Savalli. Format: Music of your life. News staff: 2; News: 3 hrs wkly. Spec prog: Relg 2 hrs, Swedish one hr wkly. ♦Daniel C. Fischer, VP & gen mgr; Guy Ditonto, gen sls mgr; Tom Marshall, progmg mgr; Joel Keefer, news dir; Burton O. Waterman, chief of engrg.

WHUG(FM)—Co-owned with WKSN(AM). Feb 1, 1965: 101.9 mhz; 3.3 kw. 298 ft. TL: N42 07 55 W79 13 09. Stereo. E-mail: jadmin@whug.com. Web Site: www.whug.com. Format: Country. News staff: 2; News: 2 hrs wkly.

***WNJA(FM)**— 1991: 89.7 mhz; 6 kw. 754 ft. TL: N42 02 48 W79 05 26. Box 1263, Buffalo 14240. Secondary address: 140 Lower Terr., Buffalo 14202-1263. Phone: (716) 845-7000. Fax: (716) 845-7043. Web Site: www.wned.org. Licensee: Western New York Public Broadcasting Association. Schwartz, Woods & Miller. Format: Class. Target aud: 35 plus. ♦Donald K. Boswell, CEO, pres & gen mgr; Michael Sutton, CFO; Richard Daly, sr VP; Peter Goldsmith, progmg dir.

***WUBJ(FM)**— July 11, 1994: 88.1 mhz; 265 w. Ant 558 ft. TL: N42 05 06 W79 17 23. c/o Radio Stn. WBFO(FM), 3435 Main St., 205 Allen Hall, Buffalo 14214-3003. Phone: (716) 829-6000. Fax: (716) 829-2277. E-mail: mail@wbfo.org. Web Site: www.wbfo.org. Licensee: State University of New York. Network: NPR. Format: Jazz, news. News staff: 2; News: news progrmg 50 hrs wkly. Target aud: General; educated professional. Spec prog: Blues 8 hrs, bluegrass music 3 hrs, Pol 3 hrs wkly. ♦Carole Smith Petro, VP & gen mgr; Matthew Katafiaz, gen mgr; Mark Wozniak, opns mgr; Joan Wilson, dev dir.

Jeffersonville

WDNB(FM)— Nov 15, 1999: . Stn currently dark 102.1 mhz; 2.2 kw. Ant 535 ft. TL: N41 44 30 W74 51 23. Stereo. 575 Grove St., Honesdale, PA 18431. Phone: (570) 253-1616. Fax: (570) 253-6297. E-mail: brian@infocow.net. Web Site: www.infocow.net. Licensee: Bold Gold Media Group L.P. (group owner; (acq 5-23-2005; grpsl). Schwartz, Woods & Miller. Format: Country. Target aud: 25 plus; male & female general high school education plus. ♦George Schmitt, opns VP; Brian Walker, gen sls mgr; John Emerson, news dir.

***WJFF(FM)**— Feb 12, 1990: 90.5 mhz; 3.7 kw. 629 ft. TL: N41 48 58 W74 47 15. Stereo. Box 546, 4765 State Rt. 52 12748. Phone: (845) 482-4141. Fax: (845) 482-WJFF. E-mail: wjff@catskill.net. Web Site: www.wjffradio.org. Licensee: Radio Catskill. Network: Network: NPR, PRI. Haley, Bader & Potts. Format: News/talk,eclectic. News: 39 hrs wkly. Target aud: 16-60; general. Spec prog: Folk 10 hrs, jazz 10 hrs wkly. ♦Bill Duncan, pres; Christine Aherne, stn mgr.

WPDA(FM)— January 1993: 106.1 mhz; 1.6 kw. 627 ft. TL: N41 48 57 W74 45 42. Stereo. Box 416, Poughkeepsie 12602. Phone: (845) 471-1500. Fax: (845) 454-1204. Web Site: www.wpda.com. Licensee: Cumulus Licensing Corp. Group owner: Cumulus Media Inc. (acq 1-23-02; grpsl). Rep: Katz Radio. Format: Main stream rock. ♦Charles Benfer, gen mgr.

Johnson City

WLTB(FM)— Sept 3, 1972: 101.7 mhz; 1.25 kw. Ant 699 ft. TL: N42 03 45 W75 56 37. Stereo. Box 7, Vestal 13851. Secondary address: 1808 Vestal Pkwy. E., Vestal 13851. Phone: (607) 748-9131. Fax: (607) 748-0061. Web Site: www.magic1017fm.com. Licensee: GM Broadcasting Inc. (acq 9-2-97; $176,000. with co-located AM). Format: Adult contemp. Target aud: 18-49; emphasis on females. ♦Steve Gilinsky, gen mgr.

Johnstown

WENT(AM)—See Gloversville

WIZR(AM)— 1964: 930 khz; 1 kw-D. TL: N42 59 54 W74 21 31. Stereo. 135 Guy Park Ave., Amsterdam 12010. Phone: (518) 762-4631. Fax: (518) 762-0105. Licensee: 6 Johnson Road Licenses Inc. Group owner: Pamal Broadcasting Ltd. (acq 10-19-2001; grpsl). Fisher, Wayland, Cooper, Leader & Zaragoza L.L.P. Format: Adult Contemp. News staff: 1; News: 6 hrs wkly. Target aud: 25-54. Spec prog: It one hr, Pol one hr, Sp one hr wkly. ♦Joey Caruso, gen mgr.

Kingston

***WAMK(FM)**— March 1988: 90.9 mhz; 940 w. 1,486 ft. TL: N42 04 35 W74 06 26. Stereo. Box 66600, 318 Central Ave., Albany 12206-6600. Phone: (518) 465-5233. Phone: (800) 323-9262. Fax: (518) 432-6974. E-mail: mail@wamc.org. Web Site: www.wamc.org. Licensee: WAMC. Group owner: WAMC/Northeast Public Radio Network: Network: PRI, NPR. Dow, Lohnes & Albertson. Format: News/talk. News: 77 hrs wkly. Target aud: General. Spec prog: Jazz 13 hrs, folk 7 hrs. ♦Alan Chartock, CEO, chmn & pres; David Galletly, VP & progmg dir; Selma Kaplan, VP & news dir.

WDST(FM)—See Woodstock

***WFGB(FM)**— January 1985: 89.7 mhz; 3.1 kw. 1,486 ft. TL: N42 04 35 W74 06 26. Stereo. Box 777, Lake Katrine 12449. Phone: (845) 336-6199. Fax: (845) 336-7205. E-mail: email@soundoflife.org. Web Site: www.soundoflife.org. Licensee: Sound of Life Inc. Format: Christian. News: 3 hrs wkly. Target aud: General. ♦Tom Michaels, gen mgr.

***WFRH(FM)**— Sept 1993: 91.7 mhz; 950 w. 272 ft. TL: N41 59 04 W74 02 56. 918 Chesapeake Ave., Annapolis 21403. Phone: (845) 336-0234. Fax: (410) 268-0931. Web Site: www.familyradio.com. Licensee: Family Stations Inc. (group owner) Format: Relg. ♦Harold Camping, pres & gen mgr; Dan Elmendorf, stn mgr.

WGHQ(AM)— Mar 4, 1956: 920 khz; 5 kw-D, 262 w-N, DA-1. TL: N41 53 09 W73 58 15. 20 Tuckee Drive, Poughkeepsie 12603. Phone: (845) 471-2300. Fax: (845) 471-2683. Licensee: AMFM Radio Licenses LLC. Group owner: Clear Channel Communications Inc. (acq 12-6-2000; grpsl). Format: News/talk. News staff: one. Target aud: 30 plus. Spec prog: Relg 3 hrs wkly. ♦Bob Dunphy, gen mgr; Jim Brady, sls dir; Linda Bradley, sls dir; Frank Curcio, gen sls mgr.

Stations in the U.S. — New York

Developers & Brokers of Radio Properties
contact American Media Services at our suite:
Philadelphia Marriott Downtown
215-625-2900
843-972-2200
americanmediaservices.com
Charleston, SC
Dallas, TX · Chicago, Il · Austin, TX
American Media Services, LLC

WJGK(AM)—Not on air, target date: unknown: 1200 khz; 2 kw-D, 400 w-N, DA-2. TL: N41 53 09 W73 58 15. Box 2307, Newburgh 12550. Phone: (845) 561-2131. Fax: (845) 561-2138. Licensee: Sunrise Broadcasting Corp. Group owner: Sunrise Broadcasting Corp. Format: Var. ♦Joerg Klebe, pres.

WKNY(AM)— Aug 1, 1939: 1490 khz; 1 kw-U. TL: N41 56 11 W74 00 30. 718 Broadway 12401. Secondary address: Box 1398 12402. Phone: (845) 331-1490. Fax: (845) 331-9569. E-mail: wknynews@pendellrd.com. Licensee: Cumulus Licensing Corp. Group owner: Cumulus Media Inc. (acq 1-23-02; grpsl). Network: CBS. Rep: Katz Radio. Format: Adult contemp. News staff: 2; News: 26 hrs wkly. Target aud: 25-54; 60% female. Spec prog: Ger one hr, Pol one hr, Irish one hr wkly. ♦Chuck Benfer, gen mgr; Warren Lawrence, progmg dir.

WKXP(FM)— Dec 13, 1965: 94.3 mhz; 1.1 w. 554 ft. TL: N41 53 44 W73 59 32. Stereo. Box 416, Poughkeepsie 12602-0416. Secondary address: 2 Pendell Rd., Poughkeepsie 12602. Phone: (845) 471-1500. Fax: (845) 454-1204. E-mail: newsroom@pendelled.com. Web Site: www.kicks943.com. Licensee: Cumulus Licensing Corp. Group owner: Cumulus Media Inc. (acq 2-3-2004; $3.5 million). Format: Country. Target aud: 18-49; women. ♦Charles Benfer, gen mgr; Victor Goodman, sls VP; Frank Curcio, gen sls mgr; Rob Vanderbeck, rgnl sls mgr; Courtney Hoppe, prom dir; Randy Turner, progmg dir; Brian Jones, news dir; Beth Christy, pub affrs dir; Dave Groth, chief of engrg.

Lake George

WCKM-FM— Apr 21, 1994: 98.5 mhz; 6 kw. 1,289 ft. TL: N43 25 12 W73 45 37. Stereo. 128 Glen St., Glens Falls 12801-4432. Phone: (518) 761-9890. Fax: (518) 761-9893. E-mail: staffmail@radiowins.com. Web Site: www.radiowins.com. Licensee: Entertronics Inc. Network: ABC. Joseph E. Dunne III. Format: Hits of the 60s, 70s & 80s. News staff: one; News: 7 hrs wkly. Target aud: 25-54; upscale baby boomers. Spec prog: Interviews. ♦David L. Covey, CEO & gen mgr; William Walker, exec VP; Robin G. Covey, opns dir; Paul VanAmburgh, gen sls mgr.

Lake Luzerne

WBAR-FM— June 30, 1992: 94.7 mhz; 300 w. 892 ft. TL: N43 17 22 W73 44 35. Stereo. 30 Park Ave., Cohoes 12047-3330. Phone: (518) 237-1330. Fax: (518) 235-4468. E-mail: info@whaz.com. Web Site: www.whaz.com. Licensee: Capital Media Corp. (group owner; acq 10-1-92; 11-9-92). Format: Bible teaching & preaching. Target aud: 25-75. ♦Paul F. Lotters, pres, gen mgr & progmg mgr; Steven L. Klob, opns dir, dev dir, sls dir, prom dir & adv dir; Rex P. Gregory, mus dir, news dir & pub affrs dir; John W. Shafer, chief of engrg.

Lake Placid

WIRD(AM)— Nov 21, 1961: 920 khz; 5 kw-D, 250 w-N. TL: N44 15 36 W74 01 22. Box 211, Saranac Lake 12983. Phone: (518) 891-1544. Fax: (518) 891-1545. Licensee: Radio Lake Placid Inc. Group owner: Mountain Communications (acq 1-10-2005). Network: CBS. Tierney & Swift. Format: ESPN radio. News staff: 2; News: 20 hrs wkly. Target aud: 25-54; working blue collar/college educated.

WLPW(FM)—Co-owned with WIRD(AM). October 1979: 105.5 mhz; 3 kw. -236 ft. TL: N44 15 36 W74 01 22. Stereo. Format: Classic rock.

Lake Ronkonkoma

***WSHR(FM)**— January 1966: 91.9 mhz; 2.8 kw. 141 ft. TL: N40 50 00 W73 06 01. Stereo. Sachem North High School, 212 Smith Rd. 11779. Phone: (631) 471-1472. Phone: (631) 471-1400. Fax: (631) 471-1491. Licensee: Board of Education Sachem Central School District at Holbrook. (acq 1967). Format: Var. Target aud: General. ♦Stuart Harris, gen mgr; Isaic Ramaswamy, stn mgr.

Lake Success

WKTU(FM)—Licensed to Lake Success. See New York

Lakewood

WKZA(FM)— Mar 2001: 106.9 mhz; 5.2 kw. 715 ft. TL: N41 57 31 W79 16 11. 106 W. T/hird St., Suite 106, Jamestown 14701. Phone: (716) 487-1106. Fax: (716) 488-2169. Web Site: www.1069kissfm.com. Licensee: Cross Country Communications LLC. Format: Top-40 hits. ♦John Newman, gen mgr.

Lancaster

WXRL(AM)— 1964: 1300 khz; 5 kw-D, 2.5 kw-N, DA-2. TL: N42 52 58 W78 37 54. Box 170, 5426 William St. 14086. Phone: (716) 681-1313. Fax: (716) 681-7172. Web Site: www.wxrl.com. Licensee: Dome Broadcasting Inc. (acq 11-1-70). Network: CNN Radio. Smithwick & Belendiuk. Format: Country. Target aud: 35 plus; Mature men & women 35 and older. Spec prog: Relg 5 hrs, gospel 2 hrs, German 1 hr, Polish 8 hrs wkly. ♦Louis A. Schriver, pres & gen mgr; Joan C. Schriver, exec VP & progmg dir; Lori Arumygam, dev dir; Louis E. Schriver, gen sls mgr & progmg mgr; Linda Sukennik, prom dir & prom mgr; Lynn Carol Supparits, opns dir, opns mgr & mus dir.

Liberty

***WGWR(FM)**— November 1997: 88.1 mhz; 60 w. 561 ft. TL: N41 48 55 W74 45 48. Box 777, Lake Katrine 12449. Phone: (845) 336-6199. Fax: (845) 336-7205. E-mail: wmial@soundoflife.org. Web Site: www.soundoflife.org. Licensee: Sound of Life Inc. Format: Christian. ♦Tom Michaels, gen mgr.

WVOS(AM)— 1947: 1240 khz; 1 kw-U. TL: N41 46 54 W74 43 49. Box 150 12754. Secondary address: Old Rt. 17, Ferndale 12734. Phone: (914) 292-5533. Fax: (914) 292-5534. E-mail: wvosfm@catskill.net. Licensee: Watermark Broadcasting LLC. (acq 8-19-2005; $1.7 million. with co-located FM Network: Network: ABC, Jones Radio Networks. Fisher, Wayland, Cooper, Leader & Zaragoza. Format: Country. News staff: one; News: 17 hrs wkly. Target aud: 25-54. ♦Eugene H. Blabey, gen mgr; Mike Sakell, opns dir & chief of engrg; Debbie Segall, mus dir; Nicholai Busko, news dir.

WVOS-FM— December 1964: 95.9 mhz; 6 kw. 328 ft. TL: N41 45 09 W74 43 01. Network: ABC. Format: Adult contemp. News staff: 2. Target aud: 25-54. ♦Debbie Segall, asst music dir.

Little Falls

WIXT(AM)— June 10, 1952: 1230 khz; 1 kw-U. TL: N43 02 33 W74 51 31. 239 Genesee St., Suite 500, Utica 13501-3407. Phone: (315) 797-0803. Fax: (315) 797-7813. Web Site: www.starsradionetwork.com. Licensee: Capstar TX L.P. Group owner: Clear Channel Communications Inc. (acq 4-16-2001; $500,000). Richard Hayes. Format: Sports. News staff: one; News: 16 hrs wkly. Target aud: 25-54. Spec prog: Farm one hr, relg one hr wkly. ♦Brian Delaney, gen mgr.

WSKU(FM)— Jan 3, 1991: 105.5 mhz; 2.3 kw. 152 ft. TL: N42 59 27 W74 55 06. Stereo. 239 Genesee St., Suite 500, Utica 13501. Phone: (315) 797-0803. Fax: (315) 797-7813. Web Site: www.cnykiss.com. Licensee: Capstar TX L.P. Group owner: Clear Channel Communications Inc. (acq 4-16-2001; $2.15 million. with WSKS(FM) Whitesboro). Rep: Roslin. Richard Hayes. Format: CHR, rhythmic. News staff: one; News: one hr wkly. Target aud: 25-54. ♦Brian Delany, gen mgr; Stephen Lawrence, opns mgr.

Lockport

WLVL(AM)— May 8, 1947: 1340 khz; 1 kw-U. TL: N43 10 30 W78 42 39. Box 477 14094. Secondary address: 320 Michigan St. 14094. Phone: (716) 433-5944. Fax: (716) 433-6588. E-mail: wlvl@wlvl.com. Web Site: www.wlvl.com. Licensee: Culver Communications Inc. (acq 9-81; $600,000; 10-5-81). Network: Network: Westwood One, ABC Information & Entertainment. Format: News/talk, sports, music. Target aud: 25-64; adult Lockport area citizens. Spec prog: Farm one hr, lt 2 hrs, Pol one hr, relg 3 hrs, 70s album rock 5 hrs, oldies 5 hrs wkly. ♦Richard C. Greene, pres & gen mgr.

Loudonville

***WVCR-FM**— Apr 26, 1963: 88.3 mhz; 2.8 kw. Ant 840 ft. TL: N42 38 13 W74 00 05. Stereo. 515 Loudon Rd. 12211-1462. Phone: (518) 782-6751. Fax: (518) 782-6498. Fax: (518) 782-6751. Web Site: www.wvcr.com. Licensee: Siena College. Format: CHR/pop. Target aud: 12-34; female. Spec prog: Pol 3 hrs, Sp 3 hrs, gospel 3 hrs, Irish 3 hrs, reggae 3 hrs wkly. ♦Neerav Patel, gen mgr; Christopher Elsesser, opns mgr.

Lowville

WLLG(FM)— Apr 1, 1987: 99.3 mhz; 1 kw. 561 ft. TL: N43 45 12 W75 33 50. Stereo. 7606 N. State St. 13367. Phone: (315) 376-7500. Fax: (315) 376-8549. E-mail: sales@themoose.net. Web Site: www.themoose.net. Licensee: The Flack Broadcasting Group L.L.C. Network: USA. Shaw Pittman. Format: Country, news. News staff: one; News: 18 hrs wkly. Target aud: General. Spec prog: Farm 3 hrs, relg 2 hrs wkly. ♦William Flack, pres, gen mgr & progmg dir; Brian Best, news dir; Ken Ruhlend, chief of engrg.

Malone

WICY(AM)— Nov 4, 1946: 1490 khz; 1 kw-U. TL: N44 50 46 W74 16 07. 86 Porter Rd. 12953. Phone: (518) 483-1100. Fax: (518) 483-1382. Web Site: www.oldiesradioonline.com. Licensee: Cartier Communications Inc. Group owner: Martz Communications Group (acq 6-30-97; $761,000 with co-located FM). Rep: Rgnl Reps. Arter & Hadden. Format: Oldies. News staff: 2; News: 15 hrs wkly. Target aud: 25-54. Spec prog: Farm one hr wkly. ♦Michael Boldt, gen mgr & gen sls mgr.

WVNV(FM)—Co-owned with WICY(AM). May 1, 1993: 96.5 mhz; 2.4 kw. 361 ft. TL: N44 49 37 W74 22 46. Stereo. Web Site: www.country965.com. Format: Country. News staff: 2; News: 2 hrs wkly. Target aud: 18-54. ♦Drew Scott, progmg dir.

***WMHQ(FM)**— 12/03/2003: 90.1 mhz; 3 kw. Ant 325 ft. TL: N44 49 48 W74 22 35. Stereo. 4044 Makyes Rd., Syracuse 13215. Phone: (315) 469-5051. E-mail: mhn@marshillnetwork.org. Web Site: www.marshillnetwork.org. Licensee: Mars Hill Broadcasting Co. Inc. Network: Network: Moody, Salem Radio Network. Wiley, Rein & Fielding. Format: Christian, regl. Target aud: General; Christian families. ♦Clayton Roberts, pres; Michael Gettman, VP; Wayne Taylor, gen mgr.

***WSLO(FM)**— February 1989: 90.9 mhz; 200 w. 354 ft. TL: N44 49 46 W74 22 31. St. Lawrence Univ., Canton 13617. Phone: (315) 229-5356. Fax: (315) 229-5373. E-mail: radio@ncpr.org. Web Site: www.ncpr.org. Licensee: St. Lawrence University. Donald E. Martin. Format: Eclectic public radio. News staff: 2; News: 35 hrs wkly. Target aud: General. ♦Ellen Rocco, gen mgr; Shelly Pike, opns mgr & chief of opns; Sandra Demarest, dev dir.

Manlius

WAQX-FM— Aug 23, 1978: 95.7 mhz; 25 kw. 300 ft. TL: N43 00 25 W76 05 38. Stereo. 1064 James St., Syracuse 13203. Phone: (315) 472-0200. Fax: (315) 472-1146. Web Site: www.95x.com. Licensee: Citadel Broadcasting Co. Group owner: Citadel Broadcasting Corp. (acq 4-26-01; grpsl). Network: ABC. Rep: D & R Radio. Shaw Pittman. Format: AOR. News: 3 hrs wkly. Target aud: 19-49; male. Spec prog: Pub service one hr wkly. ♦Farid Suleman, CEO & chmn; Tom Mitchell, opns dir & opns mgr; Dave Edwards, chief of engrg.

Massena

WMSA(AM)— Oct 12, 1945: 1340 khz; 1 kw-U. TL: N44 54 14 W74 53 01. Box 210, 2155 State Rt. 420 13662. Phone: (315) 769-3594. Fax: (315) 769-3299. E-mail: info@1340wmsa.com. Web Site: www.1340wmsa.com. Licensee: Seaway Broadcasting Inc. Group owner: Martz Communications Group (acq 5-6-99; $545,000). Network:

New York

ABC Information & Entertainment. Rep: Allied Radio Partners. Format: Adult contemp. News staff: one; News: 16 hrs wkly. Target aud: 18 plus. ◆Mike Boldt, gen mgr.

WYBG(AM)— Aug 18, 1958: 1050 khz; 1 kw-D, 500 w-N. TL: N44 53 42 W74 56 05. Box 298, 24 Andrews St. 13662. Phone: (315) 764-0554. Fax: (315) 764-0118. E-mail: wybgradio@slic.com. Web Site: www.wybg1050.com. Licensee: Wade Communications Inc. (acq 8-15-88; $450,000; 8-15-88). Network: USA. Format: News/talk. News staff: 2; News: 14 hrs wkly. Target aud: 25-65; baby boomers & seniors. Spec prog: American Indian, children, farm, folk. ◆Curran Wade, pres & gen mgr; Dorothy Wade, VP.

Mechanicville

WABT(FM)— Jan 4, 1993: 104.5 mhz; 5 kw. Ant 351 ft. TL: N42 52 44 W73 51 47. Stereo. 800 New Loudon Rd., Suite 4200, Latham 12110. Phone: (518) 785-9800. Fax: (518) 785-0122. Web Site: www.1045thebuzz.com. Licensee: Regent Licensee of Mansfield Inc. Group owner: Regent Communications Inc. (acq 8-24-01; grpsl). Format: Hits of the 80s. ◆John Hirsch, stn mgr.

WABY(AM)— Oct 19, 1981: 1160 khz; 5 kw-D, 570 w-N. TL: N42 55 12 W73 42 08. 100 Saratoga Village Blvd., Malta 12020. Phone: (518) 899-3000. Fax: (518) 889-3057. E-mail: moonradioam@aol.com. Licensee: The Anastos Media Group Inc. Group owner: Anastos Media Group Inc. (acq 12-7-00; $280,000). Network: ABC. Format: Big band. News staff: one; News: 50 hrs wkly. Target aud: 40 plus; adults, male & female. ◆Scott Collins, pres & gen mgr; John Meaney, opns mgr, progmg dir, progmg mgr & news dir.

Mexico

WVOA-FM— 1997: 103.9 mhz; 3 kw. 292 ft. TL: N43 28 36 W76 16 44. Renard Communications Corp., 401 W. Kirkpatrick St., Syracuse 13204. Phone: (315) 472-0222. Fax: (315) 478-7745. E-mail: wvoaradio@msn.com. Licensee: Renard Communications Corp. (acq 3-13-97; $3,000. for CP). Format: Relg. Spec prog: Ger 2 hrs, It 2 hrs, Pol 4 hrs , Sp 15 hrs wkly. ◆Sam Furco, gen mgr.

Middletown

WALL(AM)— Aug 6, 1942: 1340 khz; 1 kw-U. TL: N41 27 25 W74 26 24. Box 416, Poughkeepsie 12602. Secondary address: 2 Pendel Rd., Poughkeepsie 12602. Phone: (845) 471-1500. Fax: (845)-454-1204. E-mail: weoknews.@bestweb.net. Web Site: www.cumulus.com. Licensee: Cumulus Licensing Corp. Group owner: Cumulus Media Inc. (acq 1-23-02; grpsl). Hogan & Hartson. Format: Sp. News staff: 2; News: 30 hrs wkly. Target aud: 35-64; educated, upscale families. ◆Victor Goodman, gen sls mgr; Nick Robbins, progmg dir; Beth Christie, pub affrs dir.

WRRV(FM)— Co-owned with WALL(AM). Nov 11, 1966: 92.7 mhz; 3 kw. 300 ft. TL: N41 27 21 W74 26 22. Stereo. Web Site: www.cumulus.com. Format: Alternative ROCK. News staff: one; News: 3 hrs wkly. Target aud: 18-44; younger, mobile, upscale families. Spec prog: New mus 2 hrs wkly. ◆Mike Harris, pres; Bill Palmeri, gen mgr; Greg O'Brien, progmg dir; Andrew Boris, mus dir.

*****WOSR(FM)**— Feb 3, 1992: 91.7 mhz; 1.8 kw. 630 ft. TL: N41 36 04 W74 33 13. Stereo. Box 66600, Albany 12206-6600. Secondary address: 318 Central Ave. 12206-6600. Phone: (518) 465-5233. Phone: (800) 323-9262. Fax: (518) 432-6974. E-mail: mail@wamc.org. Web Site: www.wamc.org. Licensee: WAMC. Group owner: WAMC/Northeast Public Radio Network: Network: NPR, PRI. Dow, Lohnes & Albertson. Format: News, talk. News: 77 hrs wkly. Target aud: General. Spec prog: Folk 7 hrs, jazz 13 hrs wkly. ◆Alan Chartock, CEO, chmn & pres; David Galletly, VP & progmg dir; Selma Kaplan, VP & news dir.

Mineola

WTHE(AM)— Jan 1, 1964: 1520 khz; 1 kw-D. TL: N40 44 45 W73 37 29. 260 E. Second St. 11501. Phone: (516) 742-1520. Fax: (516) 742-2878. E-mail: nygospelradio@aol.com. Web Site: www.the1520am.com. Licensee: Universal Broadcasting of New York Inc. (group owner; acq 7-10-69; $235,000). Format: Relg, Black gospel. Target aud: General. Spec prog: Ger one hr, polka one hr, Guyanese 2 hrs, Haitian one hr, Scandanavian one hr, Sp 10 hrs, Greek 5 hrs wkly. ◆Howard Warshaw, CEO, exec VP & gen mgr; Miriam Warshaw, pres; Abe Warshaw, sr VP & VP; Howard Warshaw Sr., VP; Darren Greggs, opns VP.

Minetto

WKRH(FM)— October 1996: 106.5 mhz; 5.1 kw. 328 ft. TL: N43 25 45 W76 32 14. 235 Walton St., Syracuse 13202-1351. Phone: (315) 343-1440. Phone: (315) 472-9111. Fax: (315) 472-1888. E-mail: generalinfo@krock.com. Web Site: www.krock.com. Licensee: Galaxy Communications L.P. Format: Modern rock. ◆Ed Levine, pres; Joy Putnam, CFO.

Monroe

*****WLJP(FM)**— May 1991: 89.3 mhz; 200 w. 1,023 ft. TL: N41 22 38 W74 07 55. (CP: Ant 1,038 ft.). Stereo. Box 777, Lake Katrine 12449. Phone: (845) 336-6199. Fax: (845) 336-7205. E-mail: email@soundoflife.org. Web Site: www.soundoflife.org. Licensee: Sound of Life Inc. Format: Contemp Christian. Target aud: General. ◆Tom Michaels, gen mgr; Robert Conti, progmg mgr.

Montauk

WMOS(FM)— Feb 19, 1993: 104.7 mhz; 6 kw. 328 ft. TL: N41 01 57 W71 58 31. Stereo. 7 Governor Winthrop Blvd., New London 06320. Phone: (866) 441-9653. Fax: (860) 444-7970. Licensee: Citadel Broadcasting Co. Group owner: Citadel Broadcasting Corp. (acq 4-3-03). Format: Classic rock. News staff: one. Target aud: 25-45; upscale Hamptons, at-work & New York City 2nd homeowners. ◆Kevin O'Connor, opns dir; Steve Ardolina, opns dir; Julie Johnson, progmg dir.

*****WPKM(FM)**— 2004: 88.7 mhz; 8 w horiz, 2.7 kw vert. Ant 226 ft. TL: N41 01 53 W71 58 32. 244 University Ave., Bridgeport, CT 06604. Phone: (203) 331-9756. E-mail: wpkn@wpkn.org. Web Site: www.wpkn.org. Licensee: WPKN Inc. Format: Div. ◆Harry Minot, gen mgr.

Monticello

WJUX(FM)— Nov 1, 1994: 99.7 mhz; 6 kw. 328 ft. TL: N41 39 24 W74 43 40. Stereo. 6550 Rt. 9 S., Howell 07731. Phone: (732) 901-9953. Fax: (732) 901-0356. Web Site: www.bridgefm.com. Licensee: Bridgelight LLC (acq 11-13-03). Koteen & Naftalin. Format: Relg. Target aud: 35-54. ◆Eugene Blabey, stn mgr.

WSUL(FM)— Apr 16, 1977: 98.3 mhz; 2.2 kw. 535 ft. TL: N41 39 38 W74 41 14. Stereo. Box 98.3, 198 Bridgeville Rd. 12701. Phone: (845) 794-9898. Phone: (845) 794-0242. Fax: (845) 794-0125. E-mail: office@wsul.com. Web Site: www.wsul.com. Licensee: Watermark Communications LLC (acq 3-17-2005; $2.5 million). Wilkinson Barker Knauer. Format: Hot Adult Contemp. News staff: 2. Target aud: 25-54. ◆Helena Manzione, gen mgr; Shannon Marie Holland, opns mgr.

WVOS-FM—See Liberty

Montour Falls

WNGZ(FM)— June 1973: 104.9 mhz; 1 kw. 480 ft. TL: N42 15 05 W76 52 53. Stereo. 2205 College Ave., Elmira 14903. Phone: (607) 732-4400. Fax: (607) 732-7774. Licensee: Chemung County Radio Inc. Group owner: Backyard Broadcasting LLC (acq 12-1-02; grpsl). Format: Classic rock. News staff: one. Target aud: 20-49; baby boomers, young adults. ◆Kevin White, gen sls mgr; Joe Monroe, progmg dir.

Morristown

WYSX(FM)— Noverber 1998: 96.7 mhz; 17 kw. Ant 354 ft. TL: N44 34 43 W75 30 51. Stereo. One Bridge Plaza, Suite 204, Ogdensburg 13669. Phone: (315) 393-1220. Fax: (315) 393-3974. E-mail: john@yesfm.com. Web Site: www.yesfm.com. Licensee: Waters Communications Inc. Group owner: Martz Communications Group (acq 3-5-99; $285,000. with WPAC(FM) Ogdensburg). Format: CHR. Target aud: 18-34. ◆Tim Martz, pres; John Winter, gen mgr.

Mount Hope

*****WXHD(FM)**— September 1994: 90.1 mhz; 1.1 kw. 600 ft. TL: N41 25 36 W74 34 54. Stereo. Box 2011, Jersey City, NJ 07303-2011. Secondary address: 4th Floor, 43 Montgomery St., Jersey City, NJ 07302. Phone: (201) 521-1416. Fax: (201) 521-1286. Web Site: www.wfmu.org. Licensee: Auricle Communications. (acq 6-97). Haley, Bader & Potts. Format: Div, free form. Target aud: General. ◆Ken Freedman, pres & gen mgr.

Mount Kisco

WFAF(FM)— Jan 15, 1964: 106.3 mhz; 1.4 kw. Ant 440 ft. TL: N41 11 56 W73 41 37. Stereo. Box 416, Poughkeepsie 12602-0416. Secondary address: 2 Pendell Rd., Poughkeepsie 12602. Phone: (845) 471-1500. Fax: (845) 454-1204. E-mail: newsroom@pendelled.com. Web Site: www.wpdh.com. Licensee: Cumulus Licensing Corp. Group owner: Cumulus Media Inc. (acq 1-23-2002; grpsl). Format: Classic rock. ◆Charles Benfer, gen mgr.

WVIP(AM)— Oct 27, 1957: 1310 khz; 5 kw-D, 33 w-N, DA-2. TL: N41 11 37 W73 44 22. 1310 Radio Cir. 10549. Phone: (914) 244-1187. Fax: (973) 881-8324. Web Site: www.radiovision.net. Licensee: Radio Vision Cristiana Management Corp. (acq 6-10-02; $1.36 million). Koteen & Naftalin. Format: Sp Christian. News staff: 3. Target aud: General. ◆Milton Donato, stn mgr.

Nanuet

WRCR(AM)—See Spring Valley

New City

WRKL(AM)— July 4, 1964: 910 khz; 1 kw-D, 800 w-N, DA-2. TL: N41 10 52 W74 02 53. 1551 Rt. 202, Pomona 10970. Phone: (845) 354-2000. Fax: (845) 354-4796. E-mail: wrkl@polskieradio.com. Web Site: www.polskieradio.com. Licensee: Polnet Communications Ltd. (group owner; acq 3-19-99). Wiley, Rein and Fielding. Format: Polish language. News staff: one; News: 50 hrs wkly. Target aud: 18-54; Polish language audience. ◆Kent D. Gustafson, CEO & gen mgr; Walter Kotaba, pres; Grzegorz Sliwecki, opns mgr.

New Paltz

WBWZ(FM)— Nov 19, 1992: 93.3 mhz; 350 w. 1,328 ft. TL: N41 41 58 W74 00 11. 20 Tucker Dr., Poughkeepsie 12603. Phone: (845) 471-2300. Fax: (845) 471-2683. Web Site: www.star933fm.com. Licensee: AMFM Radio Licenses LLC. Group owner: Clear Channel Communications (acq 12-22-2000; with WRWD-FM Highland). Format: Adult contemp, 70s, 80's, 90's. News staff: one; News: 7 hrs wkly. Target aud: 25-54; baby boomers. ◆Bob Dunphy, gen mgr.

New Rochelle

WRTN(FM)—Listing follows WVOX(AM).

WVOX(AM)— 1950: 1460 khz; 500 w-D. TL: N40 55 42 W73 46 30. One Broadcast Forum 10801. Phone: (914) 636-1460. Fax: (914) 636-2900. Web Site: www.wvox.com. Licensee: Hudson-Westchester Radio Inc. (acq 5-1-68). Koteen & Naftalin. Format: MOR, news/talk. News staff: one; News: 50 hrs wkly. Target aud: 24 plus; community minded. Spec prog: Black one hr, gospel one hr, relg 3 hrs wkly. ◆William O'Shaughnessy, CEO & pres; Cindy Gallagher, CFO & exec VP; Nancy Curry, VP; Don Stevens, opns mgr; Matthew O'Shaughnessy, dev dir; Judy Fremont, sls VP & gen sls mgr; David O'Shaughnessy, progmg VP; Richard Littlejohn, mus dir; Larry Goldstin, news dir.

WRTN(FM)— Co-owned with WVOX(AM). 1953: 93.5 mhz; 3 kw. 325 ft. TL: N40 57 45 W73 50 32. Stereo. Web Site: www.wrtn.com. Format: Adult standards. News staff: one; News: 14 hrs wkly. Target aud: 25-60; adults. ◆William O'Shaughnessy, chmn; Don Stevens, stn mgr; Richard LittleJohn, sls VP & progmg dir.

New York

WABC(AM)— Oct 7, 1921: 770 khz; 50 kw-U. TL: N40 52 50 W74 04 12. 17th Fl., 2 Penn Plaza 10121. Phone: (212) 613-3800. Fax: (212) 613-3823. Web Site: www.wabcradio.com. Licensee: WABC-AM Radio Inc. Network: Network: ABC Information & Entertainment, ABC News/Talk. Rep: Interep. Format: Talk. ◆Mitch Dolan, pres & gen mgr; Tim McCarthy, stn mgr & sls dir; Fred Bennett, gen sls mgr; Russ King, prom dir & pub affrs dir; Phil Boyce, progmg dir; Kevin Plumb, chief of engrg.

WPLJ(FM)— Co-owned with WABC(AM). Jan 18, 1960: 95.5 mhz; 6.7 kw. 1,335 ft. TL: N40 44 54 W73 59 10. Stereo. 17th Fl., 2 Penn Plaza 10121. Phone: (212) 613-8900. Fax: (212) 613-8956. Fax: (212) 613-8950. E-mail: writeus@Plj.com. Web Site: www.plj.com. Licensee: WPLJ-FM Radio Inc. (acq 6-27-86). Rep: Interep. Format: Hot adult contemp. News: 5 hrs wkly. Target aud: 18-54; females. ◆Steven W. Borneman, stn mgr & gen sls mgr; Tom Cuddy, opns VP; Theresa

Angela, prom dir; Scott Shannon, progmg dir; Tony Mascaro, mus dir; Patty Steele, news dir; Kevin Plumb, engrg dir. Co-owned TV: WABC-TV affil.

WADO(AM)— Mar 12, 1934: 1280 khz; 5 kw-U, DA-1. TL: N40 49 35 W74 04 35. (CP: 50 kw-D, 5 kw-N, DA-1). 485 Madison Ave., 3rd Flr. 10022. Phone: (212) 310-6000. Fax: (212) 888-3694. Licensee: Wado-Am License Corp. Group owner: Univision Radio (acq 9-22-2003; grpsl). Rep: Katz Hispanic. Format: Sp, news/talk, sports. News staff: 13; News: 50 hrs wkly. Target aud: 25-54; Hispanics in the NY metropolitan area. ♦Stephanie McNamara, gen mgr.

WAXQ(FM)— Dec 1, 1956: 104.3 mhz; 6 kw. 1,361 ft. TL: N40 44 54 W73 59 10. Stereo. 1180 Ave. of the Americas 10036. Phone: (212) 575-1043. Fax: (212) 302-7814. Web Site: www.q1043.com. Licensee: AMFM Radio Licenses LLC. Group owner: Clear Channel Communications Inc. (acq 8-30-2000; grpsl). Fleischman & Walsh. Format: Classic rock. News staff: one; News: 2 hrs wkly. ♦Andy Rosen, gen mgr; Tony Hammel, gen sls mgr; Bob Buchmann, progmg dir; Eric Wellman, mus dir; Henry Behring, chief of engrg.

***WBAI(FM)**— January 1960: 99.5 mhz; 5.4 kw horiz, 3.9 kw vert. 1,220 ft. TL: N40 44 54 W73 59 10. Stereo. 120 Wall St., 10th Fl. 10005. Phone: (212) 209-2800. Phone: (212) 209-2800. Fax: (212) 747-1698. Web Site: www.wbai.org. Licensee: Pacifica Foundation. Group owner: Pacifica Foundation Inc. dba Pacifica Radio (acq 1-9-60). Format: Div, educ, news/talk. News staff: 2; News: 5 hrs wkly. Target aud: General; NY metropolitan area. Spec prog: American Indian one hr, Black 10 hrs, class 5 hrs, folk 2 hrs, jazz 5 hrs, Sp 3 hrs wkly. ♦Don Rojas, gen mgr; Denise Haynes, dev dir.

WBBR(AM)— Feb 13, 1991: 1130 khz; 50 kw-U, DA-N. TL: N40 48 39 W74 02 24. 731 Lexington Ave. 10022. Phone: (212) 318-2000. Fax: (917) 369-5000. Web Site: www.bloomberg.com. Licensee: Bloomberg Communications Inc. (acq 11-4-92; $13.58 million; 11-23-92). Format: Business news.

WBLS(FM)—Listing follows WLIB(AM).

WCBS(AM)— 1924: 880 khz; 50 kw-U. TL: N40 51 35 W73 47 09. 524 W. 57th St., 9th Fl. 10019. Phone: (212) 975-4321. Fax: (212) 975-4674. Web Site: www.wcbs880.com. Licensee: Infinity Broadcasting East Inc. Group owner: Infinity Broadcasting Corp. (acq 11-13-98; grpsl). Network: CBS. Format: News. Target aud: 25-54. ♦Chad Brown, VP & gen mgr; Matt Timothy, gen sls mgr; Mary Butler, natl sls mgr; Manny Severin, mktg dir, prom dir & adv dir; Cry Quimby, progmg dir; Tim Scheld, news dir; Mark Olkowski, chief of engrg.

WCBS-FM— 1941: 101.1 mhz; 6.8 kw. 1,353 ft. TL: N40 44 54 W73 59 10. 1515 Broadway 10036. Phone: (212) 258-6000. Fax: (212) 846-5188. Web Site: www.wcbsfm.com. Format: Oldies. ♦Chad Brown, VP & gen mgr; Ezio Torres, gen sls mgr; Joe McCoy, progmg dir.

WEPN(AM)— Aug 28, 1922: 1050 khz; 50 kw-U. TL: N40 48 26 W74 04 11. Stereo. 2 Penn Plaza, 17th Fl. 10121. Phone: (212) 613-3800. Fax: (212) 613-3861. Web Site: www.1050espnradio.com. Licensee: New York AM Radio LLC. Group owner: ABC Inc. (acq 2-28-03; $78 million). Network: ESPN Radio. Format: Sports, talk. News staff: 2. Target aud: Men 25-54. ♦Tim McCarthy, pres & gen mgr.

WFAN(AM)— 1930: 660 khz; 50 kw-U. TL: N40 51 35 W73 47 09. Stereo. Kaufman-Astoria Studios, 34-12 36th St., Astoria 11106. Phone: (718) 706-7690. Fax: (718) 361-1059. Web Site: www.wfan.com. Licensee: Infinity Broadcasting East Inc. Group owner: Infinity Broadcasting Corp. (acq 2-25-92; $70 milliori;. FTR: 4-92). Network: CBS. Rep: Infinity Radio Sales. Format: Sports, talk. News staff: 34. Target aud: 25-54; sports fans. ♦Lee Davis, gen mgr; Mark Chernoff, progmg dir; Mike Fagan, gen sls mgr & news dir.

***WFUV(FM)**— July 1947: 90.7 mhz; 50 kw. 492 ft. TL: N40 51 44 W73 53 00. Stereo. Fordham University, Bronx 10458. Phone: (718) 817-4550. Fax: (718) 365-9815. Fax: (718) 817-5595. E-mail: thefolks@wfuv.org. Web Site: www.wfuv.org. Licensee: Fordham University, Executive Committee, Board of Trustees. Network: Network: NPR, PRI. Renouf & Polivy. Format: AAA, div. News staff: 2; News: 8 hrs wkly. Target aud: 25 plus; intelligent & sophisticated mus listeners. Spec prog: Irish 10 hrs wkly. ♦Joseph McShane, pres; John Hollwitz, VP; Ralph M. Jennings, gen mgr; George Evans, opns dir; John Platt, mktg dir; Janeen Shalteman, prom dir; Chuck Singleton, progmg dir; Rita Houston, mus dir; Julianne Welby, news dir; George Bodarky, pub affrs dir.

***WHCR-FM**— February 1985: 90.3 mhz; 10 w. 266 ft. TL: N40 49 09 W73 56 59. City College of New York, 138th & Convent Ave., Nac Building, Room 1515 10031. Phone: (212) 650-7481. Fax: (212) 650-7480. E-mail: info@whcr.org. Web Site: www.whcr.org. Licensee: City College of New York. Format: Jazz, Sp, Black. News: 70 hrs wkly. Target aud: Community of Harlem. ♦Angela Harden, gen mgr.

WHTZ(FM)—See Newark, NJ

WINS(AM)— 1924: 1010 khz; 50 kw-U, DA-1. TL: N40 48 16 W74 06 25. (CP: TL: N40 48 39 W74 02 24). 888 7th Ave. 10106. Phone: (212) 315-7000. Fax: (212) 315-7015. Web Site: www.1010wins.com. Licensee: Infinity Broadcasting East Inc. Group owner: Infinity Broadcasting Corp. Network: ABC Information & Entertainment. Leventhal. Senter & Lerman. Format: News. News staff: 50; News: 168 hrs wkly. Target aud: General. ♦Joel Hollander, CEO; Jacques Tortoroli, CFO; Greg Janoff, gen mgr; Mike Felicetti, gen sls mgr; Mark Mason, progmg dir; Ben Mevorach, news dir; Mark Olkowski, engrg dir & engrg mgr. Co-owned TV: WCBS-TV affil.

***WKCR-FM**— October 1941: 89.9 mhz; 1 kw. 849 ft. TL: N40 42 43 W74 00 49. (CP: 630 w, ant 1,419 ft.). Stereo. 2920 Broadway mailcode 2612 10027. Phone: (212) 854-9920. Fax: (212) 854-9296. Web Site: www.wkcr.org. Licensee: Trustees of Columbia University. Format: Var/div, class, jazz. News: 3 hrs wkly. Target aud: General. Spec prog: Country 6 hrs, news/sports 6 hrs, international 8 hrs, Sp 10 hrs, Black 12 hrs wkly. ♦Matt Herman, stn mgr.

WKDM(AM)— 1927: 1380 khz; 5 kw-U, DA-1. TL: N40 49 13 W74 04 09. (CP: 5 kw-D, 13 kw-N, DA-2). 2nd Fl., 449 Broadway 10013. Phone: (212) 966-1059. Fax: (212) 966-9580. Licensee: Multicultural Radio Broadcasting Licensee LLC. Group owner: Multicultural Radio Broadcasting Inc. (acq 6-30-03; $37 million). Format: Multicultural. Spec prog: Community service. ♦Arthur Liu, pres; Gene Heinemeyer, gen mgr.

***WKRB(FM)**—(Brooklyn). May 28, 1978: 90.9 mhz; 10 w. 136 ft. TL: N40 34 36 W73 56 04. Stereo. Kingsborough Community College, 2001 Oriental Blvd., Brooklyn 11235. Phone: (718) 368-5817. Fax: (718) 368-4776. Licensee: Kingsborough Community College. Format: Div, CHR. Target aud: General; young adults. ♦Leon Goldstein, pres.

WKTU(FM)—(Lake Success). 1940: 103.5 mhz; 5.4 kw. 1,417 ft. TL: N40 42 43 W74 00 49. Stereo. 16th Fl., 525 Washington Blvd., Jersey City, NJ 07310. Phone: (201) 420-3700. Fax: (201) 420-3770. Web Site: www.ktu.com. Licensee: AMFM Radio Licenses LLC. Group owner: Clear Channel Communications Inc. (acq 8-30-00; grpsl). Rep: D & R Radio. Leventhal, Senter & Lerman. Format: CHR. News staff: one. Target aud: 18-54. ♦Andy Rosen, gen mgr.

WLIB(AM)— 1942: 1190 khz; 10 kw-D, 30 kw-N, DA. TL: N40 47 48 W74 06 06. 3 Park Ave. 10016. Phone: (212) 447-1000. Fax: (212) 447-5193. E-mail: info@wlib.com. Web Site: www.wlib.com. Licensee: Urban Radio I L.L.C. Group owner: Inner City Broadcasting (acq 7-72). Rep: McGavren Guild. Format: Black news/talk, Caribbean news, info & mus. ♦Pierre M. Sutton, chmn; Kernie Anderson, stn mgr; Raul Lahee, sls dir; Bob Rie Jefferson, prom dir; Cynthia Smith, progmg dir; Rich Lamotter, mus dir; Bill Stallman, chief of engrg.

WBLS(FM)—Co-owned with WLIB(AM). Sept 15, 1965: 107.5 mhz; 5.4 kw horiz, 3.8 kw vert. 1,220 ft. TL: N40 44 54 W73 59 10. E-mail: kernieanderson@wbls.com. Web Site: www.wbls.com. Network: ABC. Format: Black, urban contemp. Target aud: 25-54; upscale, urban. ♦Pierre M. Sutton, CEO; Kernie Anderson, gen mgr; Vinny Brown, progmg dir; Bill Stallman, engrg dir.

WLTW(FM)— Jan 26, 1961: 106.7 mhz; 5.4 kw horiz, 7.8 kw vert. 1,220 ft. TL: N40 44 54 W73 59 10. Stereo. 1133 Ave. of the Americas, 34th Floor 10036. Phone: (212) 603-4600. Fax: (212) 603-4602. Web Site: www.1067litefm.com. Licensee: AMFM Radio Licenses LLC. Group owner: Clear Channel Communications Inc. (acq 8-30-2000; grpsl). Network: AP Radio. Rep: Katz Radio. Latham & Watkins. Format: Adult contemp. ♦Andrew Rosen, gen mgr; Steve Chessare, gen sls mgr; Bridget Sullivan, prom dir; Jim Ryan, progmg dir.

WMCA(AM)— 1925: 570 khz; 5 kw-U, DA-1. TL: N40 45 10 W74 06 15. (CP: 50 kw-D, 30 kw-N). 777 Terrace Ave., 6th floor, Hasbrouck Heights, NJ 07604-3100. Phone: (201) 298-5700. Fax: (201) 298-5757. E-mail: office@wmca.com. Licensee: Salem Media of New York LLC. Group owner: Salem Communications (acq 9-15-89; $13 million; 8-14-89). Format: Relg, talk. News: 5 hrs wkly. Target aud: General. Spec prog: Jewish 9 hrs wkly. ♦Edward G. Atsinger III, pres; Joe D. Davis, VP; Dave Armstrong, gen mgr.

WNEW(FM)— August 1958: 102.7 mhz; 7.8 kw. 1,220 ft. TL: N40 44 54 W73 59 10. (CP: 1.2 kw, ant 462 ft.). Stereo. 888 7th Ave., 9th Fl. 10106. Phone: (212) 489-1027. Fax: (212) 489-1263. Web Site: www.mix1027fm.com. Licensee: Infinity Broadcasting East Inc. Group owner: Infinity Broadcasting Corp. (acq 12-89; grpsl; FTR: 12-11-89). Network: Westwood One. Format: Music, gossip, talk. ♦Maire Mason, VP & gen mgr; Mark Olkowski, chief of engrg.

***WNYC(AM)**— July 8, 1924: 820 khz; 10 kw-D, 1 kw-N, DA. TL: N40 45 10 W74 06 15. One Centre St. 10007. Phone: (212) 669-7800. Fax: (212) 669-8986. Web Site: www.wnyc.org. Licensee: WNYC Radio Broadcasting Foundation (acq 10-3-96; $20 million. with co-located FM). Network: Network: PRI, NPR. Format: News/talk, info. Target aud: General. Spec prog: Big band 2 hrs, spoken word 3 hrs wkly. ♦Laura Walker, CEO & pres; Mitchell Heskel, CFO; Phil Redo, opns VP; Peter Wilderotter, dev VP; Ellen Reynolds, dev dir; Dean Cappello, progmg VP & progmg dir.

WNYC-FM— Sept 21, 1943: 93.9 mhz; 5.4 kw. 1,418 ft. TL: N40 42 43 W74 00 49. Stereo. Web Site: www.wnyc.com. Format: News, class. News: 35 hrs wkly. Spec prog: Drama & literature 5 hrs, jazz 4 hrs wkly. ♦Phil Redo, mktg VP & mus dir.

***WNYE(FM)**— November 1938: 91.5 mhz; 18 kw. Ant 430 ft. TL: N40 41 21 W73 58 37. 112 Tillary St. 11201. Phone: (718) 250-5800. Fax: (718) 855-8863. E-mail: wnyemail@wyne.org. Web Site: www.wyne.org. Licensee: New York City Dept. of Info Technology & Telecommunications. Network: Network: NPR, PRI. Arnold & Porter. Format: Educ. Target aud: General. ♦Terence M. O'Driscoll, gen mgr; Chang Kim, chief of engrg. Co-owned TV: WNYE-TV affil

***WNYU-FM**— May 3, 1973: 89.1 mhz; 8.3 kw. 256 ft. TL: N40 51 26 W73 54 48. Stereo. 11th Fl., 721 Broadway 10003. Phone: (212) 998-1660. Fax: (212) 998-1652. Web Site: www.wnyu.org. Licensee: New York University. Network: ABC. Format: AOR. News: 4 hrs wkly. Spec prog: Dance mus 13 hrs, Black 5 hrs, reggae 2 hrs, Sp 2 hrs, oldies 3 hrs wkly. ♦Gabriel Mousesyan, gen mgr.

WOR(AM)— Feb 22, 1922: 710 khz; 50 kw-U, DA-1. TL: N40 47 30 W74 05 38. 111 Broadway 10008. Secondary address: 166 West Putnam Ave., Greenwich, CT 06830. Phone: (212) 642-4500. Fax: (212) 642-4486. Web Site: www.wor710.com. Licensee: Buckley Broadcasting/WOR LLC. Group owner: Buckley Broadcasting Corp. (acq 12-89; $25.1 million;. FTR: 12-11-89). Network: ABC Information & Entertainment. Rep: McGavren Guild. Format: Info, news/talk. News staff: 5; News: 4 hrs wkly. Target aud: 35-64. Spec prog: Relg 4 hrs wkly. ♦Rick Buckley, pres; Joseph Bilotta, exec VP; Bob Bruno, VP & gen mgr; Eloise Maroney, opns dir & opns mgr.

WQCD(FM)— 1945: 101.9 mhz; 6.2 kw. Ant 1,355 ft. TL: N40 44 54 W73 59 10. Stereo. 7th Fl., 395 Hudson St. 10014. Phone: (212) 352-1019. Fax: (212) 929-8559. E-mail: cd1019@cd1019.com. Web Site: www.cd1019.com. Licensee: Emmis Radio License LLC. Group owner: Emmis Communications Corp. (acq 3-26-98; grpsl). Rep: McGavren Guild. News staff: one; News: 4 hrs wkly. Target aud: 25-54. Spec prog: Jazz 2 hrs wkly. ♦Barry Mayo, gen mgr; John Mullen, opns mgr.

New York

WQEW(AM)—Listing follows WQXR-FM.

WQHT(FM)— 1940: 97.1 mhz; 6.7 kw. Ant 1,338 ft. TL: N40 44 54 W73 59 10. Stereo. 395 Hudson St., 7th Floor 10014. Phone: (212) 229-9797. Fax: (212) 929-8559. Web Site: www.hot97.com. Licensee: Emmis License Corp. of New York. Group owner: Emmis Communications Corp. Rep: Allied Radio Partners. Format: CHR. Target aud: General. ♦ Barry Mayo, gen mgr; Matt Ross, sls VP.

WQXR-FM— Nov 8, 1939: 96.3 mhz; 6 kw, 1,361 ft. TL: N40 44 54 W73 59 10. Stereo. 122 5th Ave., 3rd Fl. 10011. Phone: (212) 633-7600. Phone: (212) 633-7650. Fax: (212) 633-7666. Licensee: The New York Times Electronic Media Co. Group owner: The New York Times Co. (acq 2-1-44). Format: Class. ♦ Tom Bartunek, pres & gen mgr; Hester Furman, mus dir.

WQEW(AM)— Co-owned with WQXR-FM. Dec 3, 1936: 1560 khz; 50 kw-U, DA-2. TL: N40 42 59 W73 55 04. c/o WABC(AM), 2 Penn Plaza, 17th Fl. 10121. Phone: (212) 760-1560. Fax: (212) 947-1340. Web Site: www.wabcradio.com. Koteen & Naftalin. Format: Children. Target aud: 25-64; educated & affluent. ♦ Tim McCarthy, gen mgr.

WRKS(FM)— 1941: 98.7 mhz; 6 kw. 1, 361ft. TL: N40 44 54 W73 59 10. Stereo. 395 Hudson St., 7th Floor 10014. Phone: (212) 242-9870. Fax: (212) 929-8559. E-mail: 987kissfm@987kissfm.com. Web Site: www.987kissfm.com. Licensee: Emmis Radio License Corp. of New York. Group owner: Emmis Communications Corp. (acq 10-26-94; $68 million;. FTR: 12-5-94). Rep: D & R Radio. Format: Rhythm and blues, classic soul. News staff: 2. ♦ Barry Mayo, gen mgr.

*WSIA(FM)—(Staten Island). Aug 31, 1981: 88.9 mhz; 10 w. 650 ft. TL: N40 35 51 W74 06 53. Stereo. 2800 Victory Blvd., Staten Island 10314. Phone: (718) 982-3050. Fax: (718) 982-3052. Web Site: www.wsia.fm. Licensee: College of Staten Island. Format: Alternative rock. Target aud: General. ♦ Scott Saloway, gen mgr & prom dir.

WSKQ-FM— 1950: 97.9 mhz; 7.6 kw horiz, 5.4 kw vert. 1,220 ft. TL: N40 44 54 W73 59 10. Stereo. 26 W. 56th St. 10019. Phone: (212) 541-9200. Fax: (212) 541-9408. Web site: www.lamega.com. Licensee: WSKQ Licensing Inc. Group owner: Spanish Broadcasting System Inc. (acq 2-1-89; $55 million). Rep: Caballero, McGavren Guild. Format: Sp, tropical salsa. Target aud: 18-49; Hispanic. ♦ Raul Alarcon Jr., CEO & pres; Raul Alarcon Sr., chmn; Joseph A. Garcia, CFO.

WSNR(AM)—See Jersey City, NJ

WWPR-FM— Dec 14, 1953: 105.1 mhz; 6 kw, 1,362 ft. TL: N40 44 54 W73 59 10. Stereo. 18th Fl., 1120 Ave. of Americas 10036-6798. Phone: (212) 704-1051. Fax: (212) 398-3299. Web Site: www.power1051fm.com. Licensee: AMFM Radio Licenses LLC. Group owner: Clear Channel Communications Inc. (acq 8-30-00; grpsl). Wilkinson Barker Knauer. Format: Urban contemp. News staff: one. Target aud: 25-54. ♦ Andrew Rosen, gen mgr.

WWRL(AM)— Aug 26, 1926: 1600 khz; 5 kw-U, DA-2. TL: N40 47 44 W74 03 18. 333 7th Ave. 14th 10003. Phone: (212) 631-0800. Fax: (212) 239-7203. Web Site: www.wwrl1600.com. Licensee: Access. 1 New York License Co. LLC. Group owner: Access.1 Communications Corp. (acq 9-28-89; $1.98 million;. FTR: 10-16-89). Network: American Urban. Rubin, Winston, Diercks, Harris & Cooke. Format: Soul. Target aud: 24-54; African-American. ♦ Adriane Gaines, pres & gen mgr; Rennie Bishop, progmg dir.

*WWRV(AM)— May 1, 1972: 1330 khz; 5 kw-U, DA-1. TL: N40 32 45 W74 12 11. Box 2908, Radiovision Christiana Mgmt., 419 Broadway, Paterson, NJ 07501. Phone: (973) 881-8700. Fax: (973) 881-8324. Web Site: www.radiovision.net. Licensee: Radio Vision Christiana Management Corp. (acq 6-30-89; $13 million; 5-15-89). Format: Relg, Sp, Christian. News staff: one. Target aud: General. ♦ Rev. Milton Donato, pres & gen mgr; Julio Carbrera, stn mgr; Jose Lastra, chief of opns.

WXRK(FM)— 1951: 92.3 mhz; 6 kw. 1,220 ft. TL: N40 44 54 W73 59 10. Stereo. 40 W. 57th St., 14th Fl. 10019. Phone: (212) 314-9230. Fax: (212) 314-9282. E-mail: wxrk923@aol.com. Web Site: www.krockradio.com. Licensee: Infinity Broadcasting East Inc. Group owner: Infinity Broadcasting Corp. Network: ABC. Rep: CBS Radio. Format: Alternative, rock. ♦ Tom Chiusano, VP & gen mgr; Alan Leinwand, sls VP; Mike Peer, mus dir; Richard Herby, engrg mgr.

WZRC(AM)— 1925: 1480 khz; 5 kw-U, DA-2. TL: N40 50 42 W74 01 12. 449 Broadway, 2nd Fl 10013. Phone: (212) 965-1480. Fax: (212) 965-8917. Licensee: Multicultural Radio Broadcasting Licensee LLC. Group owner: Multicultural Radio Broadcasting Inc. (acq 1-30-98; grpsl). Rep: Caballero. Format: Cantonese. Target aud: 12-34. ♦ Tony Wong, gen mgr.

Newark

WACK(AM)— Oct 19, 1957: 1420 khz; 5 kw-D, 500 w-N, DA-2. TL: N43 01 08 W77 04 41. Box 1420, 187 Vienna Rd. 14513. Phone: (315) 331-1420. Fax: (315) 331-7101. E-mail: 1420wack@rochester.rr.com. Web Site: www.1420wack.com. Licensee: Waynco Radio Inc. Group owner: Pembrook Pines Media Group (acq 3-11-2005; $600,000). Network: Network: Network: CNN Radio, Motor Racing Net, Westwood One. Baraff, Koerner & Olender. Format: News/talk, sports. News staff: one; News: 30 hrs wkly. Target aud: 25-54; active, affluent, upscale audience. Spec prog: Farm 5 hrs wkly. ♦ John Tinkner, pres; John Tickner, gen mgr; John Derleth, rgnl sls mgr; Dennis Federico, progmg dir; Dick Reeves, sls; Ralph Vanderlinden, engr.

Newburgh

WBNR(AM)—See Beacon

WGNY(AM)— Feb 25, 1933: 1220 khz; 5 kw-D, DA. TL: N41 29 57 W74 03 54. (CP: 5 kw-D, 180 w-N, DA-1. TL: N41 31 53 W74 06 48). Box 2307 12550. Secondary address: 661 Little Britain Rd., New Windsor 12553. Phone: (845) 561-2131. Phone: (845) 561-2132. Fax: (845) 561-2138. Web Site: www.wgny.net. Licensee: Sunrise Broadcasting Corp. Group owner: Sunrise Broadcasting Corp. (acq 8-90; $10,000. with co-located FM; FTR: 8-20-90). Rosenman & Colin L.L.P. Format: Oldies. Target aud: General. Spec prog: Relg 4 hrs, Sp one hr wkly. ♦ Joerg Klebe, pres; Robert A. DeFelice, gen mgr; Robert Maines, opns VP, opns dir & chief of engrg; Janice Valentino, sls dir; Chris Cordani, news dir & pub affrs dir.

WGNY-FM— Oct 29, 1966: 103.1 mhz; 6 kw. 275 ft. TL: N41 28 22 W74 08 22. Stereo. Web Site: www.wgnyfm.com. Format: Hot adult contemp.

Newport Village

WBGK(FM)— 2001: 99.7 mhz; 1.4 kw. Ant 676 ft. TL: N43 08 28 W75 01 49. 185 Genesee St., Suite 1601, Utica 13501. Phone: (315) 734-9245. Fax: (315) 624-9245. Web Site: www.bugcountry.com. Licensee: Roser Communications Network Inc. (acq 3-20-01; $575,000). Format: Country. ♦ Ken Roser, gen mgr.

Niagara Falls

WHLD(AM)— May 20, 1940: 1270 khz; 5 kw-D, 1 kw-N, DA-2. TL: N42 44 41 W78 53 13. 225 Delaware Ave., Buffalo 14202. Phone: (716) 855-1270. Fax: (716) 855-4681. Licensee: Citadel Broadcasting Co. Group owner: Citadel Broadcasting Corp. Format: Ethnic, relg, talk. Target aud: 35 plus. Spec prog: Sp 19 hrs, Black 2 hrs, Pol 17 hrs, Ukranian one hr wkly. ♦ Michael Brummer, gen mgr & stn mgr.

WJJL(AM)— Dec 21, 1947: 1440 khz; 1 kw-D, 55 w-N. TL: N43 04 43 W79 00 40. 920 Union Rd., West Seneca 14224. Secondary address: 6929 Williams Rd. 14304. Phone: (716) 674-9555. Fax: (716) 674-0400. E-mail: wjjl@buffalo.com. Web Site: www.wjjl.com. Licensee: M.J. Phillips Communications Inc. (acq 10-20-92; $600,000;. FTR: 11-23-92). Leonard S. Joyce. Format: Old time rock & roll. News staff: one; News: 3 hrs wkly. Target aud: 25-54; baby boomers. Spec prog: Black 2 hrs, It 4 hrs, news/talk 5 hrs wkly, gospel one hr wky, Pol 2 hrs wkly. ♦ Earl Morgan, chmn; John Phillips, pres; Dennis Westberg, CFO; Mark Phillips, CEO & opns VP; M.J. Phillips, opns dir.

WJYE(FM)—See Buffalo

WKSE(FM)— Jan 1, 1946: 98.5 mhz; 46 kw. 420 ft. TL: N43 00 18 W78 59 35. Stereo. 500 Corporate Pkwy., Suite 200, Amherst 14226. Phone: (716) 843-0600. Fax: (716) 843-0250. Fax: (716) 644-9fax. E-mail: Info@kiss985.com. Web Site: www.kiss985.com. Licensee: Entercom Buffalo License LLC. Group owner: Entercom Communications Corp. (acq 12-13-99; grpsl). Network: ABC. Rep: D & R Radio. Mullin, Rhyne, Emmons & Topel. Format: CHR. News staff: 3. Target aud: 12-49. ♦ Larry Robb, gen mgr; Jimmy Steele, progmg dir.

North Creek

*WXLG(FM)— 1995: 89.9 mhz; 200 w. 1,994 ft. TL: N43 40 22 W74 02 58. St. Lawrence Univ., North Country Public Radio, Canton 13617.

Phone: (315) 229-5356. Fax: (315) 229-5373. Web Site: www.ncpr.org. Licensee: St. Lawrence University. Donald E. Martin. Format: Eclectic public radio. News staff: 2; News: 35 hrs wkly. Target aud: General. ♦ Ellen Rocco, gen mgr; Shelly Pike, chief of opns; Sandra Demarest, dev dir; Jacqueline Sauter, progmg dir.

North Syracuse

WKRL-FM—Listing follows WTLA(AM).

WTLA(AM)— Aug 1, 1959: 1200 khz; 1 kw-U, DA-N. TL: N43 09 06 W76 07 58. 235 Walton, Syracuse 13202. Phone: (315) 472-1200. Fax: (315) 472-1888. Licensee: Galaxy Communications LLC. Group owner: Galaxy Communications LP (acq 4-6-00; grpsl). Network: Jones Radio Networks. Rep: Allied Radio Partners. James L. Oyster. Format: Music of your life. News staff: one; News: 2 hrs wkly. Target aud: 35-64; white collar executives. Spec prog: Ger 2 hrs, Pol 2 hrs, relg 2 hrs wkly. ♦ Ed Levine, pres & gen mgr; Joy Putnam, CFO; Lisa Morrow, sls VP; Mimi Griswald, progmg VP; Tim Backer, chief of engrg.

WKRL-FM— Co-owned with WTLA(AM). March 1972: 100.9 mhz; 6 kw. 164 ft. TL: N43 09 06 W76 07 58. Stereo. Web Site: www.krock.com. Network: ABC. Format: Modern rock. Target aud: 18-34; upscale, educated. ♦ Scott Petibone, progmg dir.

Norwich

WBKT(FM)— June 1, 1997: 95.3 mhz; 470 w. Ant 841 ft. TL: N42 26 08 W75 30 47. 34 Chestnut St., Oneonta 13820. Phone: (607) 334-2218. Phone: (607) 432-1030. Fax: (607) 334-9867. Licensee: Double O Central New York Corp. (group owner; acq 10-22-2004; grpsl). Network: ABC. Format: Country. News staff: 2. Target aud: 25-54; general. ♦ Bill Covert, chief of engrg.

WCHN(AM)— January 1953: 970 khz; 1 kw-D. TL: N42 30 24 W75 29 29. 43 Hale St. 13815. Phone: (607) 334-2218. Fax: (607) 334-9867. Licensee: Double O Central New York Corp. (group owner; (acq 10-22-2004; grpsl). Network: ABC. Format: Stardust memories. News: 20 hrs wkly. Target aud: 35-65; mature. ♦ James V. Johnson, gen mgr; Skip Barlow, progmg dir; James Sargent, news dir.

WKXZ(FM)— Co-owned with WCHN(AM). 1961: 93.9 mhz; 26 kw. 680 ft. TL: N42 32 52 W75 27 07. Stereo. Network: ABC. Format: Hot adult contemp. News: 10 hrs wkly. Target aud: 25-54; growing families.

Norwood

WVLF(FM)— 2001: 96.1 mhz; 25 kw. Ant 328 ft. TL: N44 54 11 W74 53 02. Box 210, Massena 13662. Phone: (315) 769-3333. Fax: (315) 769-3299. E-mail: frank@valley961.com. Web Site: www.valley961.com. Licensee: Seaway Broadcasting Inc. Group owner: Martz Communications Group (acq 9-15-2000). Format: Yesterday's favorites, today's hits. ♦ Michael Bolt, gen mgr.

Noyack

*WSUF(FM)— Sept 15, 1996: 89.9 mhz; 12 kw. 357 ft. TL: N41 06 35 W72 22 05. Stereo. 5151 Park Ave., Fairfield, CT 06825. Secondary address: 533 College Rd., Seldon 11784. Phone: (203) 365-6604. Fax: (203) 371-7991. E-mail: lombardi@wshu.org. Web Site: www.wshu.org. Licensee: Sacred Heart University Inc. Network: NPR, PRI. Mullin, Rhyne, Emmons & Topel. Format: News/talk. News staff: 4; News: 45 hrs wkly. Target aud: General. Spec prog: Folk 5 hrs, new age 6 hrs wkly. ♦ George Lombardi, gen mgr; Barbara Bashar, opns mgr; Gillian Anderson, dev dir.

Nyack

*WNYK(FM)— May 5, 1982: 88.7 mhz; 10 w. 55 ft. TL: N41 04 59 W73 55 45. Stereo. Nyack College, One South Blvd. 10960. Phone: (845) 358-1828. Phone: (845) 358-1710. Fax: (845) 348-8838. E-mail: wnyk@nyack.edu. Web Site: www.nyackonline.org. Licensee: Nyack College. Format: Positive alternative, Christian. Target aud: 18-35; 60%/40% -F/M, well educated. Spec prog: Black 6 hrs, relg 2 hrs wkly.

Ogdensburg

WBDB(FM)—Listing follows WSLB(AM).

WPAC(FM)— June 1998: 98.7 mhz; 3 kw. Ant 92 ft. TL: N44 43 41 W75 26 36. 1 Bridge Plaza, Suite 204 13369. Phone: (315) 393-1220. Fax: (315) 393-3974. E-mail: john@qlo29.com. Web Site: par987.com. Licensee: Waters Communications Inc. Group owner: Martz Communications Group (acq 3-5-99; $285,000. with WYSX(FM) Morristown). Format: Super hits of the 60s and 70s. News staff: one. ♦ Tim Martz, pres; John Winter, gen mgr.

WSLB(AM)— 1940: 1400 khz; 1 kw-U. TL: N44 42 21 W75 27 55. Box 239 13669. Secondary address: 2315 Knox St. 13669. Phone: (315) 393-1100. Fax: (315) 393-6673. Web Site: www.talk1400.com. Licensee: Clancy-Mance Communications North Inc. Group owner: Clancy-Mancy Communications (acq 7-10-03; grpsl). Fisher, Wayland, Cooper, Leader & Zaragoza L.L.P. Format: Talk. Target aud: 25-49; community connected, active, mature, responsible & responsive. ♦ David Mance, pres & gen mgr; Dallas Sutton, sls dir; Nate Townsend, gen sls mgr & progmg dir.

WBDB(FM)—Co-owned with WSLB(AM). July 1981: 92.7 mhz; 3 kw. 310 ft. TL: N44 42 21 W75 27 55. Stereo. Web Site: www.pac93.com. Format: CHR. Target aud: 18-34; young, educated, active, oriented to recreation, travel & self development. ♦ David Mance, pres.

Olean

WHDL(AM)— February 1929: 1450 khz; 1 kw-U. TL: N42 04 39 W78 28 32. 3163 New State Rt. 417 14760. Phone: (716) 372-0161. Fax: (716) 372-0164. Web Site: www.whdlradio.com. Licensee: Arrow Communication of N.Y. Inc. Group owner: Backyard Broadcasting LLC (acq 12-1-2002; grpsl). Rgnl Reps: Wiley, Rein & Fielding. Format: Oldies. News staff: 2; News: 6 hrs wkly. Target aud: 25-54. ♦ John J. Morton, gen mgr; Mark Thomson, progmg dir.

WPIG(FM)—Co-owned with WHDL(AM). Feb 1, 1949: 95.7 mhz; 43 kw. 740 ft. TL: N42 02 08 W78 26 47. Stereo. Web Site: www.wpig.com. Network: ABC. Format: Contemp country.

WMXO(FM)—Listing follows WOEN(AM).

WOEN(AM)— May 20, 1957: 1360 khz; 1 kw-D, 30 w-N. TL: N42 06 24 W78 23 28. 231 N. Union St. 14760. Phone: (716) 375-1015. Fax: (716) 375-7705. E-mail: traffic@mix101.com. Web Site: www.mix101.com. Licensee: Pembrook Pines Inc. Group owner: Vox Radio Group L.P. (acq 2-22-2005; $950,000. with co-located FM). Network: Network: CBS, Westwood One. Rep: Dome. Format: MOR. News staff: one. Target aud: 45-65. ♦ Robert J. Pfuntner, pres; John R. Sirianni, gen mgr; Michael McAdam, progmg dir; Ralph Vanderlinden, chief of engrg.

WMXO(FM)—Co-owned with WOEN(AM). Nov 1, 1978: 101.5 mhz; 1.55 kw. 405 ft. TL: N42 06 24 W78 23 28. Stereo. Network: Network: CBS, Westwood One. Format: Adult contemp. Target aud: 18-49.

***WOLN(FM)**— March 1993: 91.3 mhz; 115 w. Ant 656 ft. TL: N42 02 08 W78 26 47. c/o WBFO(FM), 3435 Main St., 205 Allen Hall, Buffalo 14214. Phone: (716) 829-2880. Fax: (716) 829-2277. E-mail: mail@wbfo.org. Web Site: www.wbfo.org. Licensee: State University of New York. Network: NPR. Format: News, jazz. News staff: 2; News: 50 hrs wkly. Target aud: General; educated professionals. Spec prog: Blues 8 hrs, bluegrass music 3 hrs, Pol 3 hrs wkly. ♦ Carole Smith Petro, VP; Carole Smith Petro PhD., gen mgr; Mark Wozniak, opns mgr; Joan Wilson, dev dir.

Olivebridge

***WFSO(FM)**— Dec 27, 1996: 88.3 mhz; 100 w vert. 69 ft. TL: N41 54 30 W74 14 46. 314 Acorn Hill Rd. 12461. Phone: (845) 657-5723. Licensee: Christian Media Associates Inc. Format: Relg. ♦ Clarence Elmendorf, stn mgr.

Oneida

WMCR(AM)— Sept 26, 1956: 1600 khz; 1 kw-D, 20 w-N. TL: N43 05 04 W75 41 35. 237 Genesee St. 13421. Phone: (315) 363-6050. Fax: (315) 363-9149. Licensee: Warren Broadcasting Co. Inc. (acq 1-1-69). Format: Adult contemp, current CD's, oldies. Target aud: General. ♦ Joel Meltzer, gen mgr, opns mgr & progmg dir.

WMCR-FM— September 1972: 106.3 mhz; 390 w. 718 ft. TL: N43 02 48 W75 39 58.

Oneonta

WDOS(AM)— Dec 1, 1947: 730 khz; 1 kw-D. TL: N42 27 29 W75 00 20. 850 Main St. 13820. Phone: (607) 432-1500. Fax: (607) 432-8952. Web Site: www.wdos.com. Licensee: Ultimate Broadcasting Network Inc. (acq 3-2-92; with co-located FM). Network: ABC Information & Entertainment. Haley, Bader & Potts. Format: Country. Target aud: General; adult. Spec prog: Big band 7 hrs, nostalgia 2 hrs, relg 7 hrs wkly. ♦ Janet Laytham, exec VP, gen mgr & progmg dir.

WSRK(FM)—Co-owned with WDOS(AM). Jan 26, 1970: 103.9 mhz; 850 w. 520 ft. TL: N42 25 33 W75 02 47. (CP: 2.05 kw). Stereo. Web Site: www.wsrk.com. Format: Adult contemp. News: 5 hrs wkly. Target aud: 25-54; adult males & females. Spec prog: Class 2 hrs wkly.

***WONY(FM)**— 1975: 90.9 mhz; 177 w. -72 ft. TL: N42 28 02 W75 03 40. Stereo. Alumni Hall, SUCO Campus 13820. Phone: (607) 436-2712. Fax: (607) 436-2713. Licensee: State University of New York. Format: Educ, div. Target aud: General. Spec prog: Black 3 hrs, class 3 hrs, jazz 6 hrs, Broadway 3 hrs, rock/metal 3 hrs, hardcore 3 hrs wkly.

***WRHO(FM)**— Jan 1, 1970: 89.7 mhz; 150 w. 150 ft. TL: N42 27 24 W75 04 28. Stereo. Hartwick College, Dewar Hall 13820. Phone: (607) 431-4555. Fax: (607) 431-4556. Fax: (607) 431-4064. Licensee: Hartwick College. Network: AP Radio. Format: AOR, classic rock, progsv. News: 4 hrs wkly. Target aud: General; teenagers, college students & young adults. Spec prog: Folk 5 hrs, jazz 4 hrs, Sp 2 hrs, world beat 2 hrs, children's 2 hrs wkly. ♦ Brian Knox, gen mgr.

***WSQC-FM**— 1992: 91.7 mhz; 570 w horiz, 2.3 kw vert. 528 ft. TL: N42 25 27 W75 02 33. Box 3000, Binghamton 13902. Phone: (607) 729-0100. Fax: (607) 729-7328. Web Site: www.wskg.com. Licensee: WSKG Public Telecommunications Council. Network: Network: NPR, PRI. Dow, Lohnes & Albertson. Format: Class, news. News staff: one; News: 33 hrs wkly. Target aud: General. Spec prog: Jazz, folk 5 hrs wkly. ♦ Gary V. Reinbolt, CEO, pres & gen mgr; Linda Cohen, sls VP; Robert Armstrong, mktg VP & progmg dir; Bill Snyder, mus dir.

WZOZ(FM)— Nov 28, 1972: 103.1 mhz; 2 kw. 360 ft. TL: N42 25 28 W75 04 36. 34 Chestnut St. 13820-2466. Phone: (607) 432-1030. Fax: (607) 432-2130. E-mail: banjoradio@stny.rr.com. Licensee: Double O Central New York Corp. (group owner; (acq 10-22-2004); grpsl). Format: 80s hits. News staff: 2; News: 8 hrs wkly. Target aud: 25-54. Spec prog: Jazz 2 hrs, blues 2 hrs, oldies 2 hrs wkly. ♦ George Wells, gen mgr.

Ossining

***WDFH(FM)**— July 15, 1995: 90.3 mhz; 200 w. -33 ft. TL: N41 09 59 W73 51 22. Stereo. 21 Brookside Ln., Dobbs Ferry 10522. Phone: (914) 674-0900. Web Site: www.wdfh.org. Licensee: Westchester Council for Public Broadcasting Inc. Carter, Ledyard & Milburn. Format: Alternative, rock/AOR, news. Target aud: 18-39. Spec prog: Pub affrs 20 hrs wkly. ♦ Marc Sophos, chmn & pres.

***WOSS(FM)**— Feb 22, 1972: 91.1 mhz; 10 w. 100 ft. TL: N41 09 36 W73 51 38. (CP: 91.9 mhz, 16.42 w, ant 69 ft.). Stereo. 190 Croton Ave. 10562. Secondary address: 29 S. Highland Ave. 10562. Phone: (914) 762-5760 x370. Licensee: Board of Education Union Free School District 1. Format: Top-40, educ, urban contemp. News staff: 3. Target aud: General. Spec prog: Black 2 hrs, jazz 2 hrs, rock 2 hrs, news 7 hrs, news/talk 3 hrs wkly. ♦ Sebastion Bernal, VP; Martin McDonald, stn mgr; William Lloyd Leslie, pres, gen mgr & chief of opns.

Oswego

WAMF(AM)—See Fulton

WBBS(FM)—See Fulton

***WNYO(FM)**— 1993: 88.9 mhz; 100 w. 10 ft. TL: N43 27 07 W76 32 40. State Univ. of NY, 9B Hewitt Union 13126. Phone: (315) 312-2101. Fax: (315) 312-3542. E-mail: wnyo@oswego.edu. Web Site: www.oswego.edu/~wnyo. Licensee: State University of New York. Format: Div, rock, urban contemp. Target aud: 13-34. Spec prog: Sp 6 hrs, news/talk 4 hrs wkly. ♦ Jenny Lickey, gen mgr & progmg dir.

WOLF-FM— July 1990: 96.7 mhz; 3 kw. 328 ft. TL: N43 29 12 W76 23 10. Stereo. 401 W. Kirkpatrick St., Syracuse 13204. Phone: (315) 472-0222. Fax: (315) 478-7745. E-mail: wolfamfm@aol.com. Licensee: WOLF Radio Inc. (group owner; acq 8-4-97; $65,000). Network: Radio Disney. Rgnl Reps James L. Oyster. Format: Children's Radio Disney. Target aud: 12 & under. ♦ Karen Hurt, sls dir; Sam Furco, gen mgr, opns mgr, gen sls mgr & progmg mgr.

***WRVO(FM)**— Jan 6, 1969: 89.9 mhz; 24 kw. Ant 430 ft. TL: N43 25 14 W76 32 39. (CP: 50 kw, ant 440 ft). Stereo. 7060 State Rt. 104 13126. Phone: (315) 312-3690. Fax: (315) 312-3174. E-mail: wrvo@wrvo.fm. Web Site: www.wrvo.fm. Licensee: State University of New York. Network: NPR. Format: News/talk, old time radio. News staff: 4; News: 140 hrs wkly. Target aud: 25-55. ♦ John E. Krauss, gen mgr; Fred Vigeant, opns dir; Thomas Herbert, dev dir.

WSGO(AM)— 1960: 1440 khz; 1 kw-D, 42 w-N. TL: N43 24 56 W76 28 00. 235 Walton Street, Syracuse 13202. Phone: (315) 472-9111. Fax: (315) 472-1888. Licensee: Galaxy Communications LLC. Group owner: Galaxy Communications LP (acq 4-6-00; grpsl). Network: Jones Radio Networks. Format: Big band, nostalgia. News: one hr wkly. Target aud: 40 plus; retired & mobile. Spec prog: Ger 2 hrs, Pol 2 hrs wkly. ♦ Ed Levine, pres & gen mgr; Joy Putnam, CFO; Lisa Morrow, sls VP & gen sls mgr; Mimi Griswold, progmg VP; Tim Backer, chief of engrg.

WTKV(FM)—Co-owned with WSGO(AM). Mar 15, 1973: 105.5 mhz; 3 kw. 450 ft. TL: N43 24 56 W76 27 54. Stereo. Web Site: www.classicrock.com. Rep: Allied Radio Partners. Format: Classic rock. News staff: one; News: 2 hrs wkly. Target aud: 25-54. Spec prog: Folk 3 hrs, blues one hr wkly. ♦ Sheila Parkes, prom dir; Mimi Griswold, progmg dir.

Owego

WEBO(AM)— July 27, 1957: 1330 khz; 5 kw-D, 50 w-N. TL: N42 06 19 W76 16 22. 212 Main St. 13827. Phone: (607) 687-9605. Fax: (607) 687-4184. Licensee: Tioga Media Inc. (acq 6-30-00; $1). Network: USA. Rep: D & R Radio. Baraff, Koerner & Olender. Format: News, talk. News staff: 2. Target aud: 35 plus. Spec prog: NASCAR racing 16 hrs, relg 6 hrs wkly. ♦ Terry Coleman, gen mgr.

Palmyra

WZXV(FM)— May 1993: 99.7 mhz; 2.8 kw. 485 ft. TL: N43 02 00 W77 25 17. Box 25099, Farmington 14425. Secondary address: 1777 Rt. 332, Farmington 14425. Phone: (315) 597-9574; (585) 398-3569. Fax: (585) 398-3250. E-mail: wzxv@ccfingerlake.org. Web Site: www.wzxv.org. Licensee: Calvary Chapel of the Finger Lakes Inc. (acq 8-2-95; $70,000). Format: Christian worship, Bible teaching. ♦ Jeff Gallatin, gen mgr.

Patchogue

WALK(AM)—(East Patchogue). May 20, 1952: 1370 khz; 500 w-D, 102 w-N. TL: N40 45 14 W72 59 14. Box 230 11772. Phone: (631) 475-5200. Fax: (631) 475-9016. Web Site: www.1370walk.com. Licensee: AMFM Radio Licenses LLC. Group owner: Clear Channel Communications Inc. (acq 8-30-00; grpsl). Format: Bib band, oldies. News: 15 hrs wkly. Target aud: 50 plus. ♦ Andy Rosen, VP & gen mgr;

New York

Jim Condron, gen sls mgr; Linda Healy, mktg dir; Bill Terry, prom dir; Rob Miller, progmg dir; John Lorentz, chief of engrg.

WALK-FM— December 1952: 97.5 mhz; 39 kw. 544 ft. TL: N40 50 41 W73 02 01. Stereo. Web Site: walkradio.com. Format: Adult contemp. Target aud: 25-54. Spec prog: Hits of the 70s, love songs.

WBLI(FM)— Dec 1, 1958: 106.1 mhz; 49 kw horiz, 47 kw vert. 499 ft. TL: N40 50 32 W73 02 23. Stereo. 555 Sunrise Hwy., W. Babylon 11704. Phone: (631) 669-9254. Fax: (631) 376-0812. E-mail: wbli@wbli.com. Web Site: www.wbli.com. Licensee: CXR Holdings L.L.C. Group owner: Cox Broadcasting (acq 5-22-98; grpsl). Network: AP Radio. Rep: Christal. Format: CHR. News staff: one; News: 5 hrs wkly. Target aud: 18-34; women. ♦Austin Vali, VP & gen mgr; Nancy Cambino, opns mgr; Suzanne Riccio, pub affrs dir.

WLIM(AM)— Dec 1, 1951: 1580 khz; 10 kw-D, 37 w-N, DA-N. TL: N40 47 45 W72 59 32. (CP: 1 kw-D, 500 w-N, DA-N). Stereo. 1551 Rt. 202, Pomona 10970. Secondary address: 41 Pennsylvania Ave, Medford 11763. Phone: (631) 475-1580. Phone: (845) 354-2000. Fax: (631) 475-1523. Fax: (845) 354-4796. E-mail: wlim@polskieradio.com. Web Site: www.polskieradio.com. Licensee: Polnet Communications Ltd. (group owner; acq 6-1-01; $850,000. including five-year noncompete agreement). Network: Network: ABC Daytime Direction, ABC Information & Entertainment. Wiley, Rein and Fielding. Format: Pol language. News: 20 hrs wkly. Target aud: 18-54; Polish language audience. Spec prog: Class 7 hrs, It 4 hrs, gospel 2 hrs, jazz 4 hrs, Irish one hr, international one hr wkly. ♦Kent Gustafson, CEO; Walter Kotaba, pres; Tomasz Sliwicka, stn mgr & opns mgr; Grzegorz Sciwecki, opns mgr.

Patterson

WDBY(FM)— Jan 17, 1982: 105.5 mhz; 1.5 kw. 460 ft. TL: N41 31 18 W73 38 06. Stereo. 1004 Federal Rd., Brookfield, CT 06804. Phone: (203) 775-1212. Fax: (203) 775-6452. Web Site: www.y105radio.com. Licensee: Cumulus Licensing Corp. Licensee: Cumulus Media Inc. (acq 1-23-2002; grpsl). Network: Westwood One. Haley, Bader & Potts. Format: Hits of the 80s & 90s. News staff: 2; News: 4 hrs wkly. Target aud: 25-54. ♦Robert Mordente, gen mgr; Tim Sheehan, opns mgr; Cathy Moore, gen sls mgr; Keith Salant, progmg dir; Robert Smith, news dir; Peter Partenio, chief of engrg.

WPUT(AM)— Co-owned with WDBY(FM). July 3, 1958: 1510 khz; 1 kw-D. TL: N41 24 34 W73 37 29. Network: ESPN Radio. Format: Sports.

Pattersonville

*****WPGL(FM)**— Aug 15, 1994: 90.7 mhz; 30 w. 653 ft. TL: N42 51 00 W74 03 58. Stereo. Box 777, Lake Katrine 12449. Secondary address: 199 Tuytenbridge Rd., Lake Katrine 12449. Phone: (845) 336-6199. Fax: (845) 336-7205. E-mail: email@soundoflife.org. Web Site: www.soundoflife.org. Licensee: Sound of Life Inc. Format: Christian. News: 3 hrs wkly. Target aud: General. ♦Tom Michaels, gen mgr.

Paul Smiths

*****WPSA(FM)**— Jan 10, 1973: 98.3 mhz; 10 w. -7 ft. TL: N44 26 04 W74 15 04. Co-ordinator of Student Activities, Paul Smiths College, Rts. 86 & 30 12970. Phone: (518) 327-6401. Fax: (518) 327-6369. Licensee: Paul Smiths College of Arts & Sciences. Format: Educ, pub affrs, MOR.

Pawling

WDBY(FM)—See Patterson

Peekskill

WHUD(FM)—Listing follows WLNA(AM).

WLNA(AM)— 1948: 1420 khz; 5 kw-D, 1 kw-N, DA-2. TL: N41 18 31 W73 55 00. Box 310, Beacon 12508. Secondary address: 715 Rt. 82, Beacon 12508. Phone: (914) 838-6000. Fax: (914) 838-2109. Web Site: www.hvnet.com. Licensee: 6 Johnson Road Licenses Inc. Group owner: Pamal Broadcasting Ltd. (acq 10-19-2001; grpsl). Network: ABC. Format: Sports, Adult standards. News staff: 2; News: 40 hrs wkly. Target aud: 35 plus. ♦James Morrell, pres; Jake Russell, exec VP; Fred Bennett, gen mgr; Steve Petrone, opns VP; Bob Outer, gen sls mgr; Tom Michaels, progmg VP; Rich Flaaherty, news dir; Paul Thurst, chief of engrg.

WHUD(FM)—Co-owned with WLNA(AM). Oct 24, 1958: 100.7 mhz; 50 kw. 500 ft. TL: N41 20 18 W73 53 41. Network: ABC. Format: Adult contemp. Target aud: Upscale adults. Spec prog: Oldies 5 hrs wkly. ♦Maggie Carbaugh, gen sls mgr; Jay Pugliese, natl sls mgr; Marie Martelli, prom mgr; Steve Petrone, opns mgr & progmg mgr.

Penn Yan

WYLF(AM)— 1988: 850 khz; 1 kw-D, 47 w-N. TL: N42 39 41 W77 07 14. 100 Main St. 14527. Phone: (315) 536-0850. Fax: (315) 536-3299. Fax: (315) 781-6666. E-mail: wylf@linkny.com. Licensee: M.B. Communications. (acq 10-88). Henry E. Crawford. Format: Adult standards. News staff: 2. Target aud: 35 plus. ♦Russ Kimble, pres, gen mgr & stn mgr; Don Radigan, opns mgr; Mary Ann Hurlburt, gen sls mgr.

Peru

*****WXLU(FM)**— 1991: 88.3 mhz; 200 w. 1,109 ft. TL: N44 34 26 W73 40 29. N. Country Public Radio, St. Lawrence Univ., Canton 13617. Phone: (315) 229-5356. E-mail: radio@mcpr.org. Web Site: www.ncpr.org. Licensee: St. Lawrence University. Donald E. Martin. Format: Eclectic public radio. News staff: 2; News: 35 hrs wkly. Target aud: General. ♦Ellen Rocco, gen mgr.

Phoenix

WZUN(FM)— May 22, 1995: 102.1 mhz; 6 kw. 220 ft. TL: N43 06 03 W76 16 56. 235 Walton St., Syracuse 13202. Phone: (315) 472-9111. Fax: (315) 472-1888. Web Site: www.thesunnyspot.com. Licensee: Galaxy Communications L.P. (group owner; acq 12-15-00; $3.75 million). Network: Network: ABC, American Urban. Format: Adult contemp. Target aud: 25-54; general. ♦Ed Levine, pres & gen mgr; Joy Putnam, CFO.

Plainview

*****WPOB-FM**— September 1973: 88.5 mhz; 125 w. 150 ft. TL: N40 46 53 W73 27 36. (CP: Ant 259 ft. TL: N40 47 48 W73 27 44). 50 Kennedy Dr. 11803-4098. Phone: (516) 937-6373. Fax: (516) 937-6384. Licensee: Plainview-Old Bethpage Central School District. Format: Educ, AOR. Target aud: General. ♦Adam Weinstock, gen mgr; Joel Genero, opns dir.

Plattsburgh

WBTZ(FM)— Feb 3, 1960: 99.9 mhz; 100 kw. 984 ft. TL: N44 46 13 W73 36 47. Stereo. 255 S. Champlain St., Burlington, VT 05402. Phone: (802) 860-2465. Fax: (802) 860-1818. E-mail: mailbag@99thebuzz.com. Web Site: www.99thebuzz.com. Licensee: Plattsburgh Broadcasting Corp. Format: Alternative rock. ♦Jenny McCann, gen mgr; Matt Grasso, progmg dir.

WCEL(FM)— Jan 14, 1991: 91.9 mhz; 380 w. 852 ft. TL: N44 46 27 W73 36 48. Stereo. Box 666000, Albany 12206. Secondary address: 318 Central Ave., Albany 12206. Phone: (518) 465-5233. Phone: (800) 323-9262. Fax: (518) 432-6974. E-mail: mail@wamc.org. Web Site: www.wamc.org. Licensee: WAMC. Group owner: WAMC/Northeast Public Radio (acq 1996; $160,000). Network: Network: PRI, NPR. Dow, Lohnes & Albertson. Format: News, talk. News: 77 hrs wkly. Target aud: General. Spec prog: Folk 7 hrs, jazz 13 hrs wkly. ♦Alan Chartock, CEO, chmn & pres; David Galletly, VP & progmg dir; Selma Kaplan, VP.

WEAV(AM)— Feb 3, 1935: 960 khz; 5 kw-U, DA-2. TL: N44 34 27 W73 26 54. 1500 Hegeman Ave., Colchester, VT 05446. Phone: (802) 655-0093. Fax: (802) 655-0478. Web Site: www.wxzofm.com. Licensee: Clear Channel Broadcasting Licenses Inc. Group owner: Clear Channel Communications Inc. (acq 9-25-01). Format: Hot talk, sports. Target aud: General. ♦Karen Marshall, gen mgr; Steve Cormier, opns mgr.

WIRY(AM)— Jan 30, 1950: 1340 khz; 1 kw-U. TL: N44 41 49 W73 28 40. 301 Cornelia St. 12901. Phone: (518) 563-1340. Fax: (518) 563-1343. E-mail: wiry@wiry.com. Web Site: www.wiry.com. Licensee: Hometown Radio Inc. (acq 2-1-95; $175,000; 2-27-95). Network: Westwood One. Rep: Roslin. Format: Adult contemp. News staff: 2; News: 11 hrs wkly. Target aud: 18 plus. ♦Dan Santa, exec VP; William D. Santa, pres & gen mgr.

WKOL(FM)— Aug 22, 1994: 105.1 mhz; 23.5 kw. 338 ft. TL: N44 31 31 W73 31 07. Box 4489, Burlington, VT 05406. Secondary address: 70 Joy Dr., South Burlington, VT 05403. Phone: (802) 658-1230. Fax: (802) 862-0786. E-mail: kool105@hallradio.com. Web Site: www.wkol.com. Licensee: Hall Communications Inc. (group owner; acq 6-13-95; $1.1 million). Rep: D & R Radio. Fletcher, Heald & Hildreth. Format: Oldies. Target aud: 25-54. ♦Bonnie Rowbotham, chmn; Arthur Rowbotham, pres; Richard P. Reed, exec VP; Bill Baldwin, sr VP; Dan Dubonnet, gen mgr; Steve Pelkey, opns dir.

*****WQKE(FM)**— April 1979: 93.9 mhz; 10 w. 156 ft. TL: N44 41 40 W73 28 00. Stereo. Angell College Ctr., State Univ. of NY 12901. Phone: (518) 564-2727. Phone: (518) 564-3694. Fax: (518) 564-3994. Fax: (518) 564-3205. Web Site: www.goecities.com/wqke2000. Licensee: State University of N.Y. Format: College alternative. Target aud: 18-24. Spec prog: Heavy metal 10 hrs, classic rock 12 hrs, Black 9 hrs, relg 3 hrs wkly. ♦Phil Czterwastek, opns dir; Andy Martinez, mus dir.

WTWK(AM)— January 1998: 1070 khz; 5 kw-D. TL: N44 36 14 W73 27 18. Box 712, St. Albans, VT 05478. Phone: (802) 524-2133. Fax: (802) 527-1450. Licensee: Champlain Communications Corp. Group owner: Northeast Broadcasting Company Inc. (acq 1-11-02; $150,000). Format: News/talk. ♦Bob Rowe, gen mgr.

Port Henry

WVTK(FM)— Sept 5, 1982: 92.1 mhz; 18 kw. 10 ft. TL: N44 01 38 W73 28 54. Stereo. Box 1093, Burlington, VT 05402. Phone: (802) 655-0093. Fax: (802) 655-0478. Web Site: www.vermontskiss.com. Licensee: Capstar TX L.P. Group owner: Clear Channel Communications Inc. (acq 12-22-00; grpsl). Rep: New England. Mullin, Rhyne, Emmons & Topel. Format: Contemporary hit/ top 40. News: one hr wkly. Target aud: 25-54. ♦Karen Marshall, gen mgr.

Port Jervis

WDLC(AM)— July 4, 1953: 1490 khz; 1 kw-U. TL: N41 21 49 W74 40 41. 18 Neversink Dr. 12771. Phone: (845) 856-5185. Licensee: PJ Radio L.L.C. (acq 2-7-2005; $4 million. with co-located FM). Format: Oldies. ♦James Morley, gen mgr.

WTSX(FM)—Co-owned with WDLC(AM). Oct 30, 1970: 96.7 mhz; 3 kw. 300 ft. TL: N41 22 24 W74 43 49. Stereo. Web Site: www.fox967fm.com. News staff: 2. Target aud: 25-54.

*****WRPJ(FM)**— October 1992: 88.9 mhz; 500 w. 590 ft. TL: N41 25 36 W74 34 45. Stereo. Box 777, Lake Katrine 12449. Secondary address: 199 Tuytenbridge Rd., Lake Katrine 12449. Phone: (845) 336-6199. Phone: (800) 724-8518. Fax: (845) 336-7205. E-mail: email@soundoflife.org. Web Site: www.soundoflife.org. Licensee: Sound of Life Inc. Format: Christian. Target aud: General. ♦Tom Michaels, gen mgr.

Potsdam

*****WAIH(FM)**— Sept 10, 1998: 90.3 mhz; 100 w. -16 ft. TL: N44 39 43 W74 58 26. Student Union, 9050 Barrington Dr. 13676. Phone: (315) 267-4888. Fax: (315) 267-2798. E-mail: waih@potsdam.com. Web Site: www2.potsdam.edu/waih. Licensee: State University of New York. Format: Music, talk. ♦Alex Neumann, gen mgr.

WPDM(AM)— Apr 30, 1955: 1470 khz; 1 kw-D. TL: N44 38 38 W75 03 32. Box 348 13676. Phone: (315) 265-5510. Fax: (315) 265-4040. E-mail: hits@slic.com. Licensee: St. Lawrence Radio Inc. Network: ABC Information & Entertainment. Cohn & Marks. Format: Adult contemp. News staff: one; News: 5 hrs wkly. Target aud: 25 plus; div audience. ♦Jane A. Kyle, pres; William Solomon, VP & gen mgr; Derry Loucks, gen sls mgr; Justin James, mus dir; Scott Dosztan, news dir; Dan Simmons, chief of engrg.

WSNN(FM)—Co-owned with WPDM(AM). Oct 15, 1968: 99.3 mhz; 3 kw. 155 ft. TL: N44 38 38 W75 03 32. Web Site: www.99hits.com. Cohn & Marks. News staff: one; News: 5 hrs wkly. Target aud: 25-54. ♦Derry Loucks, stn mgr; Justin Gonyea, mus dir.

*****WTSC-FM**— Nov 3, 1963: 91.1 mhz; 700 w. 155 ft. TL: N44 39 45 W75 00 07. Stereo. Clarkson University, Box 8743 13699. Phone: (315) 268-7658. E-mail: radio@clarkson.edu. Web Site: http://radio.clarkson.edu. Licensee: Clarkson University. Format: Alternative. ♦Michael Forte, gen mgr; Lyle Santzi, stn mgr.

Stations in the U.S.   New York

Developers & Brokers of Radio Properties

contact American Media Services at our suite:
Philadelphia Marriott Downtown
215-625-2900
843-972-2200
americanmediaservices.com
Charleston, SC
Dallas, TX · Chicago, Il · Austin, TX

American Media Services, LLC

Poughkeepsie

WEOK(AM)— October 1949: 1390 khz; 5 kw-D, DA. TL: N41 43 14 W73 54 29. Box 416 12602-0416. Secondary address: 2 Penvell Rd. 12602-0416. Phone: (845) 471-1500. Fax: (845) 454-1204. Web Site: www.cumulus.com. Licensee: Cumulus Licensing Corp. Group owner: Cumulus Media Inc. (acq 1-23-2002). Network: ABC Daytime Direction. Format: Sp. News staff: 3. Target aud: 35 plus. Spec prog: Farm 2 hrs, Pol one hr, relg 2 hrs, talk 5 hrs, Sinatra 2 hrs wkly. ◆Charles Benfer, pres; Nick Robbins, opns dir & prom dir; Victor Goodman, gen sls mgr.

WPDH(FM)—Co-owned with WEOK(AM). December 1962: 101.5 mhz; 4.5 kw. Ant 1,540 ft. TL: N41 43 09 W73 59 47. Stereo. Web Site: www.wpdh.com. Format: Classic rock. Spec prog: Blues deluxe, flashback 4 hrs wkly. ◆Nick Robbins, opns mgr; Greg O'Brien, progmg dir & mus dir.

WKIP(AM)— June 1940: 1450 khz; 1 kw-U, DA-D. TL: N41 42 18 W73 53 16. 20 Tucker Dr. 12603-1644. Phone: (845) 471-2300. Fax: (845) 471-2683. Licensee: Clear Channel Broadcasting Licenses Inc. Group owner: Clear Channel Communications Inc. (acq 7-12-2000; grpsl). Network: Jones Radio Networks. Rep: Christal. Format: Big band, MOR. News staff: one; News: 2 hrs wkly. Target aud: 35-64. ◆Bob Dunphy, gen mgr & gen sls mgr; Reggie Osterloudt, opns mgr; Jeanette Relyea, natl sls mgr; Doug MacLeod, mktg dir; Michelle Taylor, prom dir; Joe Daily, progmg dir; Cameron Hendrix, news dir; Bill Draper, engrg mgr.

WRNQ(FM)—Co-owned with WKIP(AM). June 30, 1989: 92.1 mhz; 2.15 kw. Ant 384 ft. TL: N41 40 36 W73 49 14. Stereo. Web Site: www.921litefm.com. News staff: one; News: 20 hrs wkly. Target aud: 35-54; primary market is women. ◆Reggie Osterhoudt, opns dir & prom dir; Wade Lott, sls dir; Doug MacLeod, mktg dir; Rick Knight, mus dir; Bill Draper, chief of engrg.

WPKF(FM)— 1996: 96.1 mhz; 3 kw. Ant 171 ft. TL: N41 44 46 W73 54 46. 20 Tucker Dr. 12603. Phone: (845) 471-2300. Fax: (845) 471-2683. Web Site: www.kissfmjams.com. Licensee: Clear Channel Broadcasting Licenses Inc. Group owner: Clear Channel Communications Inc. (acq 7-14-2000; grpsl). Rep: Clear Channel, Katz Radio. Format: Rhythmic CHR. ◆Bob Dunphy, gen mgr; Reggie Osterhoudt, opns dir; Wade Lott, sls dir; Jeanette Relyea, natl sls mgr; Doug MacLeod, mktg dir; Michelle Taylor, prom dir; Jimi Jamm, progmg dir; Cameron Hendrix, news dir; Bill Draper, chief of engrg.

*****WRHV(FM)**— Sept 5, 1990: 88.7 mhz; 230 w. 1,289 ft. TL: N41 43 09 W73 59 47. Box 17, Schenectady 12301. Secondary address: 17 Fern Ave., Schenectady 12306. Phone: (518) 357-1700. Fax: (518) 357-1709. E-mail: email@wmht.org. Web Site: www.wmht.org. Licensee: WMHT Educational Telecommunications. Network: PRI. Schwartz, Woods & Miller. Format: Class. Target aud: 35-54; class mus lovers. Spec prog: Jazz 2 hrs, ethnic one hr wkly. ◆Deborah Onslow, pres; Dave Nicosia, chief of engrg.

WSPK(FM)— Dec 7, 1947: 104.7 mhz; 7.4 kw. 1,260 ft. TL: N41 29 19 W73 56 52. Stereo. 715 Rt. 52 12508. Phone: (845) 838-8600. Fax: (845) 838-2109. Web Site: www.k104online.com. Licensee: 6 Johnson Road Licenses Inc. Group owner: Pamal Broadcasting Ltd. (acq 10-19-2001; grpsl). Network: Network: Westwood One, ABC. Rep: Katz Radio. Format: CHR. News staff: one. Target aud: 18-49. ◆James Morrell, CEO; Fred Bennett, VP & natl sls mgr.

*****WVKR-FM**— 1976: 91.3 mhz; 3.7 kw. 820 ft. TL: N41 38 25 W74 01 16. Stereo. Box 726, Vassar College 12604. Phone: (845) 437-5475. Phone: (845) 437-7010. Fax: (845) 437-7656. Licensee: Vassar College. Format: Div. News staff: 4; News: 5 hrs wkly. Target aud: General. Spec prog: Class 3 hrs, folk 5 hrs, Pol 5 hrs, Sp 3 hrs, techno 8 hrs, metal 3 hrs, new age 6 hrs wkly. ◆Halimah Marcus, gen mgr & stn mgr; Caitlin Buckley, stn mgr & news mgr; Nat Sandler, progmg dir.

Pulaski

WSCP(AM)—See Sandy Creek-Pulaski

WSCP-FM— January 1987: 101.7 mhz; 2.5 kw. 364. TL: N43 36 32 W75 58 23. 5090 U.S. Rt. 11 13142. Phone: (315) 298-3185. Phone: (315) 298-6500. Fax: (315) 298-6181. Licensee: Galaxy Communications L.P. (group owner; acq 7-17-01; $400,000. with WSCP(AM) Sandy Creek-Pulaski). Format: Classic country. ◆Ed Levine, gen mgr; Gary Dennis, mus dir.

Queensbury

WNYQ(FM)— October 1996: 105.7 mhz; 1.57 kw. Ant 1,273 ft. TL: N43 25 12 W73 45 39. (CP: COL Malta. 4.8 kw, ant 367 ft. TL: N42 52 44 W73 51 47). 89 Everts Ave. 12804. Phone: (518) 793-7733. Fax: (518) 793-0838. Licensee: Vox New York L.L.C. Group owner: Vox Radio Group L.P. (acq 8-16-00; grpsl). Format: Hot adult contemp. Target aud: 18-54; general. ◆Clay Ashworth, gen mgr.

Ravena

WRCZ(FM)— 1991: 94.5 mhz; 3 kw. 328 ft. TL: N42 33 23 W73 52 05. 11 Dennis Terr., Schenectady 12303. Phone: (518) 456-6101. Fax: (518) 456-6377. Web Site: www.94rock.net. Licensee: DOT Communications Inc. Group owner: Galaxy Communications L.P. (acq 2-8-02; $2.5 million. with WHTR(AM) Albany). Network: Network: ABC, Westwood One. Rep: Williams Radio Sales. Format: Class rock. Target aud: 18-44. ◆Shew Schantz, opns dir & opns mgr.

Remsen

WADR(AM)— Dec 12, 1966: 1480 khz; 5 kw-D, 50 w-N. TL: N43 19 31 W75 10 29. Stereo. 239 Genesee St., Suite 500, Utica 13501. Phone: (315) 797-0803. Fax: (315) 797-7813. Web Site: www.starsradionetwork.com. Licensee: Clear Channel Broadcasting Licenses Inc. Group owner: Clear Channel Communications Inc. (acq 8-5-98; grpsl). Network: Westwood One. Rep: Christal. Latham & Watkins. Format: Sports. News: 3 hrs wkly. Target aud: 35 plus; 60% female, 40% male. ◆Brian Delaney, gen mgr; Gene Conte, progmg dir; Joe Petro, chief of engrg.

WOKR(FM)—Co-owned with WADR(AM). Dec 1, 1982: 93.5 mhz; 1.15 kw. Ant 748 ft. TL: N43 20 44 W75 15 00. Stereo. Web Site: www.warmfm.com. Network: ABC. Format: Lite adult contemp. News: one hr wkly. Target aud: 25-54. ◆Stew Schantz, opns mgr; Jack Moran, progmg mgr.

Rensselaer

WQBK-FM—Listing follows WTMM(AM).

WTMM(AM)— Dec 3, 1961: 1300 khz; 5 kw-U, DA-2. TL: N42 35 23 W73 44 37. 800 New Loudon Rd., Latham 12110. Phone: (518) 785-9800. Fax: (518) 462-0784. Web Site: www.wtmm.com. Licensee: Regent Licensee of Mansfield Inc. Group owner: Regent Communications Inc. (acq 2000; grpsl). Format: Sports. Target aud: 35 plus. Spec prog: Auto repair one hr, money mgmt 3 hrs, real estate one hr wkly. ◆Bob Ausfeld, exec VP; John Hirsch, stn mgr; Bill Brindle, opns dir; Buzz Brindle, progmg dir; Bob O'Neal, chief of engrg.

WQBK(FM)—Co-owned with WTMM(AM). Dec 1, 1972: 103.9 mhz; 3 kw. 300 ft. TL: N42 35 06 W73 46 29. (CP: 6 kw). Stereo. Web Site: www.wtmm.com. Format: Alternative. News: 4 hrs wkly. Target aud: 18-49. Spec prog: Jazz 2 hrs wkly. ◆Jim Clifford, sls dir; Chili Walker, progmg dir.

Riverhead

WFTU(AM)— Aug 8, 1963: 1570 khz; 1 kw-D, 500 w-N, DA-2. TL: N40 54 48 W72 39 16. Five Towns College, 305 N. Service Rd., Dix Hills 11746. Phone: (631) 424-7000. Web Site: www.wftu.net. Licensee: Five Towns College (acq 5-24-01; $80,000). Format: College radio. ◆David Cohen, stn mgr.

WRCN-FM— Aug 14, 1962: 103.9 mhz; 1.5 kw. 466 ft. TL: N40 51 07 W72 45 55. Stereo. 3241 Rt 112, Bldg. 7, Medford 11763. Phone: (631) 451-1039. Fax: (631) 451-0891. Fax: (631) 451-0896. Web Site: www.wrcn.com. Licensee: IW L.L.C. Group owner: Barnstable Broadcasting Inc. (acq 10-1-97; grpsl). Rep: Katz Radio. Haley, Bader & Potts. Format: Classic hits, rock. Target aud: 18-49. ◆Mike Kaneb, pres; Steve Hobbs, stn mgr; Stefan Rybak, gen sls mgr; David Musser, prom dir.

WRIV(AM)— June 1955: 1390 khz; 1 kw-D, 64 w-N. TL: N40 55 22 W72 38 52. Box 1390 11901. Secondary address: 40 W. Main St. 11901. Phone: (631) 727-1390. Fax: (631) 369-WRIV (9748). Web Site: www.wrivonline.com. Licensee: Crystal Coast Communications. (acq 10-87). Network: ABC Information & Entertainment. Rep: Savalli. Format: Adult standards. News staff: one; News: 14 hrs wkly. Target aud: 35-64. Spec prog: Farm 8 hrs, Pol 4 hrs wkly. ◆Bruce Tria, gen mgr.

Rochester

WBEE-FM— February 1961: 92.5 mhz; 50 kw. 500 ft. TL: N43 10 37 W77 28 39. Stereo. 70 Commercial St. 14614-1010. Phone: (585) 423-2900. Fax: (585) 325-5139. Fax: (585) 423-2947. Web Site: www.wbee.com. Licensee: Entercom Rochester License LLC. Group owner: Entercom Communications Corp. (acq 4-23-98; grpsl). Network: Westwood One. Format: Country. News staff: one; News: 4 hrs wkly. Target aud: 25-54. ◆Michael Doyle, gen mgr; Dave Symonds, opns mgr & chief of engrg; Sue Munn, gen sls mgr; Billy Kidd, progmg dir; Steve Hausmann, news dir; Joe Fleming, chief of engrg.

WROC(AM)—Co-owned with WBEE-FM. 1947: 950 khz; 1 kw-U, DA-2. TL: N43 06 25 W77 35 51. Format: News/talk. News staff: one; News: 3 hrs wkly. Target aud: 35 plus; high income empty-nesters. ◆Joe Fleming, gen sls mgr & chief of engrg; Jim White, progmg mgr; Steve Hausmann, VP & news dir.

*****WBER(FM)**— 1974: 90.5 mhz; 2.5 kw. 417 ft. TL: N43 02 00 W77 25 11. (CP: 50 kw). Stereo. 2596 Baird Rd., Penfield 14526-2333. Phone: (585) 419-8190. Fax: (585) 419-8191. E-mail: wber@monroe.edu. Web Site: http://wber.monroe.edu. Licensee: Monroe B.O.C.E.S #1. Format: Alternative. Target aud: 12-24; male & female. ◆Bret Apthorpe, gen mgr; Joey Guisto, stn mgr & progmg dir; Shaun Dulen, mus dir; Scott Ballou, chief of engrg.

WBZA(FM)— 1939: 98.9 mhz; 50 kw. 560 ft. TL: N43 10 14 W77 40 23. Stereo. Entercom Rochester LLC, 70 Commercial St. 14614-1010. Phone: (585) 423-2900. Fax: (585) 325-5139. Fax: (585) 423-2947. Web Site: www.rochesterbuzz.com. Licensee: Entercom Rochester Inc. Group owner: Entercom Communications Corp. (acq 4-23-98; grpsl). Network: Westwood One. Rep: Katz Radio. Akin, Gump, Strauss, Hauer & Feld. Format: Classic Hits. News staff: one. Target aud: 25-54; upscale. ◆Mike Johnson, VP; Michael Doyle, gen mgr; Dave Symonds, opns mgr.

WCMF-FM— June 9, 1960: 96.5 mhz; 50 kw. 457 ft. TL: N43 08 07 W77 35 02. Stereo. 1700 HSBC Plaza 14604. Phone: (585) 399-5700. Fax: (585) 399-5750. Web Site: www.wcmf.com. Licensee: Infinity Radio Inc. Group owner: Infinity Broadcasting Corp. (acq 11-13-98; grpsl). Format: AOR. News staff: one; News: 10 hrs wkly. ◆Kevin Murphy, gen mgr.

WDKX(FM)— Apr 6, 1974: 103.9 mhz; 800 w. 540 ft. TL: N43 09 17 W77 36 16. Stereo. 683 E. Main St. 14605. Phone: (585) 262-2050. Fax: (585) 262-2626. Web Site: www.wdkx.com. Licensee: Monroe County Broadcasting Co. Ltd. (acq 9-19-02). Rep: Allied Radio Partners. Format: Urban contemp. News staff: 2; News: 6 hrs wkly. Target aud: General. Spec prog: Jazz 4 hrs, gospel 7 hrs wkly. ◆Andrew A. Langston, CEO & gen mgr; Andre Langston, pres & opns dir; Marietta Avery, CFO; Camilla Maas, sr VP; Gloria M. Langston, stn mgr.

WFXF(FM)—See Honeoye Falls

WHAM(AM)— July 11, 1922: 1180 khz; 50 kw-U. TL: N43 04 55 W77 43 30. Stereo. Box 40400, Euclid Bldg., 207 Midtown Plaza 14604. Phone: (585) 454-4884. Fax: (585) 454-5081. Web Site: www.wham1180.com. Licensee: Citicasters Licenses L.P. Group owner:

Broadcasting & Cable Yearbook 2006

D-357

New York

Clear Channel Communications Inc. (acq 3-7-97; grpsl). Network: CBS. Format: News/talk. News staff: 6. Target aud: 35 plus. ♦ Jeff Howlett, gen mgr & stn mgr.

WVOR-FM— Co-owned with WHAM(AM). 1962: 100.5 mhz; 50 kw. 480 ft. TL: N43 02 00 W77 25 17. Stereo. Phone: (585) 454-3942. Web Site: www.mixrochester.com. Format: Adult contemp. News staff: one. Target aud: 25-54. ♦ Ken Spitzer, stn mgr; Karen Kelly, gen sls mgr; Danyelle Dodge, prom dir; Dave LeFrois, progmg dir & mus dir; Randy Gorbman, news dir; Diane DeNiro, pub affrs dir.

WHIC(AM)— Sept 11, 1925: 1460 khz; 5 kw-U, DA-N. TL: N43 06 34 W77 34 20. Box 25433 14625. Secondary address: 2 Cambridge Pl., 1840 Winton Rd. S. 14618. Phone: (585) 271-0530. Fax: (585) 271-0530. Licensee: Holy Family Communications (group owner; acq 7-1-2003; $300,000). Format: Catholic. ♦ James N. Wright, pres; Jack Palvino, gen mgr.

WHTK(AM)— Nov 22, 1947: 1280 khz; 5 kw-U, DA-N. TL: N43 05 54 W77 35 00. 207 Midtown Plaza 14604. Phone: (585) 454-4884. Fax: (585) 262-2334. Web Site: www.whtk.com. Licensee: Citicasters Licenses L.P. Group owner: Clear Channel Communications Inc. (acq 5-4-99; grpsl). Rep: McGavren Guild. Format: Talk. Target aud: 25-54; men. ♦ Jeff Howlett, gen mgr & progmg dir; Scott Gordon, gen sls mgr.

*****WIRQ(FM)**— January 1960: 104.7 mhz; 10 w. 485 ft. TL: N43 12 59 W77 35 46. Stereo. 260 Cooper Rd. 14617. Phone: (585) 336-3065. Phone: (716) 336-3066. Fax: (589) 336-2929. Licensee: Board of Education West, Irondequoit Central School District. Format: Progsv, alternative. News: one hr wkly. Target aud: 13-45. Spec prog: Top-35 countdown 3 hrs, Progressive Pioneers 3 hrs, techno 3 hrs wkly. ♦ Hannah Jacobs, gen mgr.

WJZR(FM)— Jan 22, 1993: 105.9 mhz; 3 kw. 180 ft. TL: N43 09 35 W77 34 44. Stereo. Fedder Industrial Park, 1237 E. Main St. 14609. Phone: (585) 288-5020. Licensee: North Coast Radio Inc. Network: AP Radio. Cohn & Marks. Format: Blues, jazz. News: 14 hrs wkly. Target aud: 25 plus. Spec prog: News review one hr wkly. ♦ Lee Rust, pres & stn mgr; Barry Vee, gen sls mgr.

WLGZ(AM)— February 1947: 990 khz; 5 kw-D, 2.5 kw-N, DA-2. TL: N43 13 54 W77 52 00. 2494 Browncroft Blvd. 14625. Phone: (585) 264-1027. Fax: (585) 264-1165. Web Site: www.crawfordbroadcasting.com. Licensee: Kimtron Inc. Group owner: Crawford Broadcasting Co. (acq 6-5-97; $650,000). Format: Adult standards. ♦ Robert Harmmond, gen mgr; Scott Ensign, opns mgr.

WPXY-FM— Sept 14, 1959: 97.9 mhz; 50 kw. 456 ft. TL: N43 08 08 W77 35 02. Stereo. 1700 HSBC Plaza. 14604. Phone: (585) 399-5700. Fax: (585) 399-5750. Web Site: www.98pxy.com. Licensee: Infinity Radio Inc. Group owner: Infinity Broadcasting Corp. (acq 11-13-98; grpsl). Format: CHR. ♦ Ray Noone, gen mgr; Barbara Williams, gen sls mgr; Mike Danger, progmg dir.

WRMM-FM— Nov 14, 1966: 101.3 mhz; 27 kw. 640 ft. TL: N43 10 14 W77 40 23. Stereo. Secondary address: 1700 HSBC Plaza 14604. Phone: (585) 399-5700. Fax: (585) 399-5750. Web Site: www.warmradio.com. Licensee: Infinity Radio Inc. Group owner: Infinity Broadcasting Corp. (acq 11-13-98; grpsl). Format: Adult contemp. Target aud: 25-54; baby boomers. ♦ Kevin Murphy, gen mgr.

*****WRUR-FM**— Mar 6, 1966: 88.5 mhz; 3 kw. 348 ft. TL: N43 09 23 W77 36 31. Stereo. CPU Box 277356, Univ. of Rochester 14627-7356. Phone: (585) 275-6400. Phone: (585) 275-7400. Fax: (585) 273-1357. E-mail: jlapin@wrur.org. Web Site: www.wrur.org. Licensee: University of Rochester Broadcasting Corp. Format: Div. News: 4 hrs wkly. Target aud: General. Spec prog: Jazz, gospel 3 hrs, relg one hr, world 10 hrs, folk 2 hrs, Sp 6 hrs, techno 5 hrs, death metal 8 hrs, industrial 3 hrs wkly. ♦ Jared Lapin, gen mgr; Paul Szymanski, opns mgr; James Lamara, progmg dir.

*****WXXI(AM)**— 1936: 1370 khz; 5 kw-U, DA-N. TL: N43 06 01 W77 34 23. 280 State St. 14614. Phone: (585) 325-7500. Fax: (585) 258-0339. Web Site: www.wxxi.org. Licensee: WXXI Public Broadcasting Council. Network: NPR. Schwartz, Woods & Miller. Format: News/talk, blues. ♦ Norm Silverstein, pres & gen mgr.

WXXI-FM— December 1974: 91.5 mhz; 45 kw. 400 ft. TL: N43 08 07 W77 35 03. Stereo. Web Site: www.wxxi.org. Network: PRI. Format: Class. ♦ Julia Figueras, mus dir. Co-owned TV: *WXXI-TV affil.

WYSL(AM)— See Avon

Rome

WFRG-FM—See Utica

WODZ-FM— August 1968: 96.1 mhz; 7.4 kw. 600 ft. TL: N43 02 14 W75 26 40. Stereo. 9418 State Rt.49, Marcy 13403. Phone: (315) 768-9500. Fax: (315) 736-0720. Web Site: www.wodz.com. Licensee: Regent License of Utica/Rome Inc. Group owner: Regent Communications Inc. (acq 11-5-99; grpsl). Format: Oldies. ♦ Mary Jo Beach, gen mgr.

WRNY(AM)— Oct 12, 1959: 1350 khz; 500 w-D, 60 w-N. TL: N43 12 18 W75 29 08. 239 Genesee St., Suite 500, Utica 13501. Phone: (315) 797-0803. Fax: (315) 797-7813. Licensee: Clear Channel Broadcasting Licenses Inc. Group owner: Clear Channel Communications Inc. (acq 8-5-98; grpsl). Baraff, Koerner & Olender. Format: Sports. News staff: one. Target aud: 25 plus. Spec prog: Black 3 hrs wkly. ♦ Brian Deleney, gen mgr; Chuck Hebbard, gen sls mgr; Gene Conte, progmg dir; Joe Petro, chief of engrg.

WUMX(FM)— Co-owned with WRNY(AM). May 1, 1983: 102.5 mhz; 27 kw. 649 ft. TL: N43 02 14 W75 26 40. Stereo. Web Site: www.1025kiss.com. Format: Country. News staff: one. Target aud: 18-49. Spec prog: Pub affrs one hr wkly. ♦ Chris Spiwak, natl sls mgr & prom dir; Stew Schantz, progmg dir; Joe Petro, engrg mgr & chief of engrg.

WRUN(AM)—See Utica

WYFY(AM)— September 1946: 1450 khz; 1 kw-U. TL: N43 12 18 W75 28 48. Bible Broadcasting Network, 11530 Carmel Commons Blvd., Charlotte, NC 28226. Phone: (704) 523-5555. Fax: (704) 522-1967. Web Site: www.bbnradio.org. Licensee: Bible Broadcasting Network Inc. Group owner: Bible Broadcasting Network (acq 5-7-99; $50,000). Format: Relg. ♦ Jason Padgett, stn mgr.

Rosendale

*****WFNP(FM)**— Sept 5, 1990: 88.7 mhz; 230 w. 1,289 ft. TL: N41 43 09 W73 59 47. Stereo. SUB Rm. 413, State Univ. of New York, New Paltz 12561. Phone: (845) 257-3084. Fax: (845) 257-3099. Web Site: www.wfnp.org. Licensee: State University of New York, Albany. Network: Network: ABC, AP Radio. Dow, Lohnes & Albertson. Format: Progsv, urban contemp. News: 3 hrs wkly. Target aud: General; demographic-specific programs. Spec prog: Black 14 hrs, jazz 4 hrs, Sp 3 hrs, news/talk 5 hrs, metal 7 hrs wkly. ♦ William Clark, opns dir & opns mgr.

Rotterdam

WTRY-FM— Dec 15, 1986: 98.3 mhz; 6 kw. 318 ft. TL: N42 44 43 W74 04 10. Stereo. 1203 Troy Schenectady Rd., Suite 201, Latham 12110. Phone: (518) 452-4800. Fax: (518) 452-4855. Web Site: www.wtry.com. Licensee: Capstar TX L.P. Group owner: Clear Channel Communications Inc. (acq 8-30-00; grpsl). Rep: McGavren Guild. Format: Oldies. News staff: one; News: 20 hrs wkly. Target aud: 35-54. ♦ Dennis Lamme, exec VP & gen mgr; John Cooper, stn mgr; Kristen Delaney, sls dir; Jeanmarie Manning, gen sls mgr.

Rouses Point

*****WKYJ(FM)**—Not on air, target date: unknown: 88.7 mhz; 3.4 kw. Ant 148 ft. TL: N44 56 44 W73 25 48. 3185 S. Highland Dr., Suite 13, Las Vegas, NV 89109. Phone: (702) 731-5588. Licensee: American Educational Broadcasting Inc. ♦ Carl J. Auel, pres.

Sag Harbor

WLNG(FM)— Apr 13, 1969: 92.1 mhz; 5.3 kw. 350 ft. TL: N40 58 19 W72 20 54. Box 2000 11963. Phone: (631) 725-2300. Fax: (631) 725-5897. E-mail: info@wlng.com. Web Site: www.wlng.com. Licensee: Mainstreet Broadcasting Co. Format: Oldies, Top-40. ♦ Paul Sidney, pres & gen mgr.

Saint Bonaventure

*****WSBU(FM)**— Apr 13, 1975: 88.3 mhz; 165 w. Ant -256 ft. TL: N42 04 45 W78 29 07. Stereo. Box O, Rm. 210, Reilly Ctr. 14778. Phone: (716) 375-2307. Fax: (716) 375-2583. E-mail: webmaster@wsbu.net. Web Site: www.wsbu.net. Licensee: St. Bonaventure University. Format: AOR. News: 10 hrs wkly. Target aud: General; primarily students. ♦ Dr. Robert Wickenheiser, pres; Joe O'Neil, stn mgr.

Salamanca

WGGO(AM)— June 18, 1957: 1590 khz; 5 kw-D. TL: N42 10 24 W78 41 07. Box 62 14779. Phone: (716) 945-1590. Fax: (716) 945-1515. E-mail: wgrt983@direcway.com. Licensee: Catt Communications, Inc. (acq 10-14-92; $550,000 with co-located FM; 11-23-92). Network: ABC Information & Entertainment. Format: Adult contemp, oldies. Target aud: General. Spec prog: Country 5 hrs, Pol one hr wkly. ♦ Michael Washington, pres, gen mgr & progmg dir; Sue Washington, VP, gen sls mgr & mus dir; Scott Douglas, news dir; Russ Ehman, chief of engrg.

WQRT(FM)— Co-owned with WGGO(AM). Oct 15, 1988: 98.3 mhz; 1.6 kw. 430 ft. TL: N42 06 32 W78 36 28. Stereo. E-mail: wqrt983@direcway.net. Network: ABC Information & Entertainment. Format: Classic rock. ♦ Mary Washington, VP.

Sandy Creek-Pulaski

WSCP(AM)— Aug 8, 1974: 1070 khz; 2.5 kw-D. TL: N43 36 19 W76 07 48. Box 640, 5090 U.S. Rt. 11, Pulaski 13142-0640. Phone: (315) 298-3185. Phone: (315) 298-6500. Fax: (315) 298-6181. Web Site: www.wscp.net. Licensee: Galaxy Communications L.P. (group owner; acq 7-17-01; $400,000. with WSCP-FM Pulaski). Network: Jones Radio Networks. Format: Country. News staff: one; News: one hr wkly. Target aud: 35+. ♦ Rick Jordan, progmg dir.

Saranac Lake

WNBZ(AM)— Sept 11, 1927: 1240 khz; 1 kw-U. TL: N44 18 58 W74 07 08. Box 211 12983. Secondary address: Colony Ct. Ext. 12983. Phone: (518) 891-1544. Phone: (518) 891-3636. Fax: (518) 891-1545. E-mail: mail@wnbz.com. Web Site: www.wnbz.com. Licensee: Saranac Lake Radio L.L.C. Group owner: Mountain Communications (acq 6-1-98; $397,500. with co-located FM). Network: ABC Information & Entertainment. Rep: New England. Irwin, Campbell, Crowe & Tannenwald. Format: Adult contemp. News staff: one; News: 36 hrs wkly. Target aud: 35 plus; loc community. ♦ Ted Morgan, pres & gen mgr; John Gagnon, opns mgr & progmg dir; James Williams, gen sls mgr; Chris Knight, news dir; Crystal Tatro, pub affrs dir; Chris Brescia, chief of engrg.

WYZY(FM)— Co-owned with WNBZ(AM). July 12, 1989: 106.3 mhz; 50 kw. Ant 394 ft. TL: N44 20 28 W74 07 43. Stereo. Web Site: www.wnbz.com. Rep: New England. Format: Adult contemp. News staff: 2; News: 10 hrs wkly. Target aud: 18-49; adults. ♦ Crystal Tatro, opns mgr.

*****WSLL(FM)**— July 1, 1989: 89.5 mhz; 200 w. 355 ft. TL: N44 20 28 W74 07 43. St. Lawrence Univ., Canton 13617. Phone: (315) 229-5356. Fax: (315) 229-5373. Web Site: www.ncpr.org. Licensee: St. Lawrence University. Format: Eclectic public radio. Target aud: General. ♦ Ellen Rocco, stn mgr; Sandra Demarest, dev dir.

Saratoga Springs

*****WSPN(FM)**— Sept 9, 1974: 91.1 mhz; 253 w. 98 ft. TL: N43 05 55 W73 47 10. Stereo. Skidmore College 12866. Phone: (518) 580-5783. Licensee: Skidmore College. Network: AP Radio. Format: Blues, progsv, jazz. Target aud: All ages. Spec prog: Folk 3 hrs, Pol 3 hrs, Sp 3 hrs, blues 9 hrs, world mus 3 hrs wkly. ♦ Mike Clifford, gen mgr.

*****WSSK(FM)**— 2001: 89.7 mhz; 50 w. Ant 430 ft. TL: N43 11 35 W73 45 25. Box 777, Lake Katrine 12449. Phone: (845) 336-6199. Fax: (845) 336-7205. Web Site: www.soundoflife.org. Licensee: Sound of Life Inc. Format: Contemp Christian. ♦ Tom Michaels, gen mgr.

WUAM(AM)— Mar 23, 1964: 900 khz; 250 w-U. TL: N43 04 24 W73 48 07. 100 Saratoga Blvd., Sutie 21, Malta 12020. Phone: (518) 899-3000. Fax: (518) 899-3057. E-mail: moonradioam@aol.com. Web Site: www.sta1013.com. Licensee: Anastos Media Group Inc. (group owner; acq 9-99; $100,000). Network: USA. Gammon & Grange. Format: Big band. News staff: 2; News: 20 hrs wkly. Target aud: 25-54. Spec prog: Farm one hr wkly. ♦ Scott Collins, gen mgr; John H. Meaney, stn mgr & opns dir.

Saugerties

WBPM(FM)— 1999: 92.9 mhz; 6 kw. Ant 289 ft. TL: N41 59 20 W74 01 08. 20 Tucker Dr., Poughkeepsie 12603. Phone: (845) 471-2300. Fax: (845) 471-2683. Web Site: www.cool929fm.com. Licensee: Clear Channel Broadcasting Licenses Inc. Group owner: Clear Channel

Broadcasting & Cable Yearbook 2006

Stations in the U.S.   New York

Communications Inc. (acq 7-14-2000; grpsl). Format: Oldies. News: 7 hrs wkly. Target aud: 25-54. ♦Bob Dunphy, gen mgr.

Schenectady

WGY(AM)— February 1922: 810 khz; 50 kw. TL: N42 47 37 W74 00 36. One Washington Sq., Albany 12205. Phone: (518) 452-4800. Fax: (518) 452-4855. Web Site: www.wgy.com. Licensee: Clear Channel Radio License Inc. Group owner: Clear Channel Communications Inc. (acq 8-5-98; grpsl). Network: ABC. Rep: Clear Channel. Format: News/talk. News staff: 12; News: 23 hrs wkly. Target aud: 25-54; college graduate, married, homeowner. ♦Dennis Lamme, VP & gen mgr; Greg Foster, opns dir, opns mgr & progmg dir; Kristen Delaney, sls dir & gen sls mgr; Melissa Keegan, natl sls mgr; Jill Manti, mktg mgr & prom dir; Chuck Custer, news dir; Rebecca Harrington, pub affrs dir; Dave Abdoo, chief of engrg.

WRVE(FM)—Co-owned with WGY(AM). April 1940: 99.5 mhz; 14.5 kw. 925 ft. TL: N42 38 13 W73 59 48. Stereo. Web Site: www.wrve.com. Format: Adult contemp, classic rock. News staff: one; News: 3 hrs wkly. Target aud: 25-54. ♦Dennis Lamme, exec VP & rgnl sls mgr; Randy McCarten, opns mgr & progmg dir.

***WMHT-FM**— June 8, 1972: 89.1 mhz; 11 kw. 930 ft. TL: N42 38 13 W74 00 06. Stereo. Box 17 12301. Secondary address: 17 Fern Ave. 12306. Phone: (518) 357-1700. Fax: (518) 357-1709. E-mail: email@wmht.org. Web Site: www.wmht.org. Licensee: WMHT Educational Telecommunications. Format: Class. Spec prog: Jazz one hr wkly. ♦Deborah Onslow, gen mgr; Dave Nicosia, chief of engrg. Co-owned TV: *WMHT(TV) affil.

WOFX(AM)—See Troy

***WRUC(FM)**— May 9, 1975: 89.7 mhz; 100 w. -88 ft. TL: N42 49 04 W73 55 45. Stereo. Union College 12308. Phone: (518) 388-6151. Phone: (518) 388-6154. Fax: (518) 388-6790. Licensee: Trustees of Union College. Network: AP Radio. Format: Alternative. Target aud: 18 plus; general. Spec prog: It one hr, Sp 3 hrs, jazz 15 hrs, sports 4 hrs wkly.

WTRY-FM—See Rotterdam

WVKZ(AM)— Apr 15, 1942: 1240 khz; 1 kw-U. TL: N42 48 37 W73 59 04. 100 Saratoga Village Blvd., Ste. 21, Malta 12020. Phone: (518) 899-3000. Fax: (518) 899-3057. E-mail: talk1240@aol.com. Licensee: The Anastos Media Group Inc. Group owner: Anastos Media Group Inc. (acq 4-10-2000; $137,500). Format: Real oldies. News staff: one. Target aud: 25-54; men. ♦Ernie Anastos, chmn; Scott Collins, pres & gen mgr; John H. Meaney, opns mgr.

Schoharie

WMYY(FM)— 1990: 97.3 mhz; 810 w. 886 ft. TL: N42 37 51 W74 16 01. Stereo. 30 Park Ave., Cohoes 12047-3330. Phone: (518) 237-1330. Fax: (518) 235-4468. E-mail: info@whaz.com. Web Site: www.whaz.com. Licensee: Capital Media Corp. (group owner; acq 2-14-92; 2-17-92). Format: Adult Christian. Target aud: 25-75; young to old. Spec prog: Gospel, relg. ♦Paul F. Lotters, pres & gen mgr; Steven L. Klob, opns dir, dev dir, sls dir, mktg dir, prom dir & adv dir; Rex P. Gregory, progmg dir, news dir & pub affrs dir; John W. Shafer, chief of engrg.

Schuyler Falls

***WAVX(FM)**— 2004: 90.9 mhz; 2.7 kw. Ant 1,073 ft. TL: N44 34 24 W73 40 31. Box 8310, Essex, VT 05451-8310. Phone: (802) 878-8885. Fax: (802) 879-6835. E-mail: cmi.radio@verizon.net. Web Site: www.wavx.net. Licensee: Christian Ministries Inc. Format: Christian. ♦Mark Kinsley, pres; Richard McClary, gen mgr.

Scotia

WEGQ(FM)— December 1981: 93.7 mhz; 1.25 kw. Ant 705 ft. TL: N42 51 24 W74 04 03. 11 Dennis Terr., Schenectady 12303. Phone: (518) 456-6101. Fax: (518) 456-6377. Web Site: www.neweagle.net. Licensee:

Galaxy Communications L.P. (group owner; acq 2-20-2002; $2.4 million). Format: Modern rock. ♦Ed Levine, CEO & pres; Joy Putnam, CFO; Lisa Morrow, VP; Chris Holmberg, opns mgr.

Seneca Falls

WLLW(FM)—Listing follows WSFW(AM).

WSFW(AM)— Oct 1, 1968: 1110 khz; 1 kw-D. TL: N42 54 55 W76 46 28. 3568 Lenox Rd., Geneva 14456. Phone: (315) 781-7000. Fax: (315) 781-7700. E-mail: wnyr@flare.net. Licensee: Auburn Broadcasting Inc. Group owner: Finger Lakes Radio Group (acq 3-2-01; with co-located FM). Rep: Rgnl Reps. Borsari & Paxson. Format: Talk. News staff: one; News: 24 hrs wkly. Target aud: 25-54. Spec prog: Irish 2 hrs, It 2 hrs, jazz one hr, oldies 3 hrs, Pol 2 hrs wkly. ♦Allan Bishop, gen mgr.

WLLW(FM)—Co-owned with WSFW(AM). Nov 1, 1968: 99.3 mhz; 5 kw. Ant 358 ft. TL: N42 59 38 W76 51 59. Stereo. Format: Classic Rock. ♦Ken Paradise, progmg dir.

Sidney

WCDO(AM)— 1983: 1490 khz; 1 kw-U. TL: N42 19 24 W75 22 57. 75 Main St. 13838. Phone: (607) 563-3588. Phone: (607) 563-3589. Fax: (607) 563-7805. Licensee: CDO Broadcasting Inc. Group owner: Clancy-Mance Communications (acq 3-8-86; $180,000 with co-located FM; 1-13-86). Format: Adult contemp. Target aud: 25-54. ♦Craig Harris, gen mgr; Jim Tomeo, progmg dir.

WCDO-FM— May 1982: 100.9 mhz; 970 w. 577 ft. TL: N42 17 33 W75 22 03. (CP: 1.88 kw). Format: Adult contemp, oldies. Target aud: 25-54. ♦Craig Stevens, gen mgr & gen sls mgr; Greg Davie, sls dir.

Smithtown

***WFRS(FM)**— Oct 17, 1988: 88.9 mhz; 1.5 kw horiz, 1.45 kw vert. 453 ft. TL: N40 48 27 W73 10 48. Stereo. 3200 Expressway Dr. S., Islandia 11749. Phone: (631) 234-4151. Web Site: www.familyradio.com. Licensee: Family Stations Inc. (group owner; acq 9-27-83). Network: Family Radio. Format: Nondenominational Christian educ. News: 5 hrs wkly. Target aud: General.

WMJC(FM)— May 21, 1957: 94.3 mhz; 2.6 kw. Ant 315 ft. TL: N40 48 08 W73 17 12. Stereo. The Island 94.3, 234 Airport Plaza, Suite 5, Farmingdale 11735. Phone: (631) 770-4200. Fax: (631) 770-0101. Web Site: www.island943.com. Licensee: IW L.L.C. Group owner: Barnstable Broadcasting Inc. (acq 10-1-97; grpsl). Network: AP Radio. Format: Hot adult contemp. News staff: one; News: 2 hrs wkly. Target aud: 25-54; men & women. ♦Al Kaneb, CEO & natl sls mgr; Dave Widmer, gen mgr.

Sodus

WUUF(FM)— 1991: 103.5 mhz; 6 kw. 243 ft. TL: N43 16 05 W77 09 40. Box 1420, Newark 14513. Phone: (315) 331-9667. Fax: (315) 331-7101. E-mail: bigdogfm@rochester.rr.com. Web Site: www.bigdog1035.com. Licensee: Waynco Radio (acq 8-90; $10,000;. FTR: 8-13-90). Network: Network: Motor Racing Net, Westwood One. Format: Country. News staff: one; News: one hr wkly. Target aud: 25-45. ♦Robert Pfutner, pres; John Tickner, VP & gen mgr; Jim Hill, opns dir.

South Bristol Township

WNVE(FM)— Jan 22, 1996: 107.3 mhz; 650 w. Ant 994 ft. TL: N42 44 47 W77 25 35. 207 Midtown Plaza, Rochester 14604. Phone: (585) 232-8870. Fax: (585) 454-5081. Licensee: Citicasters Licenses L.P. Group owner: Clear Channel Communications Inc. (acq 1999; grpsl). Format: Rhythmic oldies. ♦Ken Spitzer, VP; Debbie Johnston, gen mgr; Laurie Zsedely, natl sls mgr; Debbie Richards, prom dir.

South Glens Falls

WENU(AM)— September 1988: 1410 khz; 1 kw-D, 126 w-N. TL: N43 16 07 W73 40 14. 89 Everts Ave., Queensbury 12804. Phone: (518) 793-7733. Fax: (518) 793-0838. Licensee: 6 Johnson Road Licenses Inc. Group owner: Pamal Broadcasting Ltd. (acq 4-1-2004; grpsl). Network: Westwood One. Format: Contemporary. News staff: one. Target aud: 35 plus. ♦James Morrell, pres; Mike Morgan, opns mgr.

Southampton

WEHM(FM)— July 21, 2003: 92.9 mhz; 2.75 kw. Ant 489 ft. TL: N40 58 11 W72 20 49. Box 7162, Amagansett 11930. Secondary address: 249 Montauk Hwy., Amagansett 11930. Phone: (631) 267-7800. Fax: (631) 267-1018. E-mail: info@wehm.com. Web Site: www.wehm.com. Licensee: AAA Licensing LLC. Group owner: AAA Entertainment L.L.C. (acq 4-30-2003). Format: Progsv adult rock.

WHFM(FM)— October 1971: 95.3 mhz; 5 kw. 354 ft. TL: N40 56 05 W72 23 15. Stereo. Box 674, Center Moriches 11934. Phone: (631) 587-1023. Fax: (631) 283-9506. Web Site: www.wbab.com. Licensee: CXR Holdings L.L.C. Group owner: Cox Broadcasting (acq 5-22-98; grpsl). Rep: Christal. Format: Adult contemp, rock/AOR. Target aud: 25-49; upscale. ♦Kim Guthrie, VP; Tim Guthrie, gen mgr; Todd Dinetz, gen sls mgr; Vinny DiMarco, natl sls mgr; John Olsen, progmg dir; Matthew Connor, chief of engrg.

***WLIU(FM)**— Mar 3, 1979: 88.3 mhz; 5.9 kw horiz, 25 kw vert. 217 ft. TL: N40 53 17 W72 26 43. (CP: 16 kw, ant 748 ft.) TL: N40 51 18 W72 46 12). Stereo. WPBX/LIU, 239 Montauk Hwy. 11968. Phone: (631) 591-7000. Web Site: www.wliu.org. Licensee: Long Island University. Network: Network: PRI, NPR. Lawrence Bernstein. Format: Jazz. News staff: one; News: 34 hrs wkly. Target aud: 34-55; upscale, educ, public radio listeners. Spec prog: Pub affrs one hr wkly. ♦Dr. Wallace Smith, gen mgr.

***WRLI-FM**— July 1999: 91.3 mhz; 10 kw. 312 ft. TL: N40 56 05 W72 23 15. 1049 Asylum Ave., Hartford, CT 06015. Phone: (860) 278-5310. Fax: (860) 244-9624. E-mail: info@wnpr.org. Web Site: www.cptv.org. Licensee: Connecticut Public Television & Radio. Network: Network: NPR, PRI. Format: Class, NPR news. ♦Jerry Franklin, CEO & pres; Kim Grehn, gen mgr.

Southold

WBEA(FM)— July 3, 1985: 101.7 mhz; 6 kw. Ant 283 ft. TL: N40 52 10 W72 34 37. Stereo. Box 7162, Amagansett 11930. Phone: (631) 267-7800. Fax: (631) 267-1018. Web Site: www.1017blaze.com. Licensee: AAA Licensing LLC. Group owner: AAA Entertainment L.L.C. (acq 8-22-2000; $2.75 million. with WBAZ(FM) Bridgehampton). Network: Westwood One. Rep: Allied Radio Partners. Haley, Bader & Potts. Format: Hip hop. Target aud: 25-54; adults with active lifestyles. Spec prog: Health talk, financial news, CNN news. ♦Bonnie Gomes, gen mgr & gen sls mgr.

Southport

WOKN(FM)— Sept 15, 1993: 99.5 mhz; 1.25 kw. 485 ft. TL: N42 07 49 W76 47 23. 1705 Lake St., Elmira 14901. Phone: (607) 733-5626. Fax: (607) 733-4040. Fax: (607) 733-5627. E-mail: airstaff@wlvy94rock.com. Web Site: www.wlvy94rock.com. Licensee: Pembrook Pines Elmira Ltd. Group owner: Pembrook Pines Media Group. Network: Jones Radio Networks. Bechtel & Cole. Format: Country. News staff: one; News: 2 hrs wkly. Target aud: 18-49; female. ♦Robert J. Pfuntner, CEO & pres; Nancy E. Nicastro, gen mgr; Donna VanDeBogart, opns mgr.

Spencer

***WCII(FM)**— Oct 1, 1989: 88.5 mhz; 17 kw. 590 ft. TL: N42 00 50 W76 15 53. Stereo. Box 506, 7634 Campbell Creek Rd., Bath 14810. Phone: (607) 776-4151. Fax: (607) 776-6929. E-mail: mail@fln.org. Web Site: www.fln.org. Licensee: Family Life Ministries Inc. Group owner: Family Life Network Network: Salem Radio Network. Format:

New York

Christian, inspirational, educ. News staff: 7; News: 14 hrs wkly. Target aud: 25-55; general public. Spec prog: News 14 hrs wkly. ◆Rick Snavely, pres, VP & gen mgr.

Spring Valley

WRCR(AM)— Sept 15, 1977: 1300 khz; 500 w-D, 83 w-N, DA-2. TL: N41 05 48 W74 00 18. Nanuet Mall, 75 W. Rt. 59, Ste. 2126, Nanuet 10954. Phone: (845) 624-1313. Fax: (845) 624-1639. E-mail: mail@wrcr.com. Web Site: www.wrcr.com. Licensee: Alexander Broadcasting Inc. (acq 4-14-2000; $270,000). Network: USA. Format: Adult contemp, news. News staff: 2; News: 18 hrs wkly. Target aud: 25-54; upscale. ◆Alexander Medakovic, pres; Alexander Metakovic, gen mgr.

Springville

WSPQ(AM)— Apr 20, 1986: 1330 khz; 1 kw-U, DA-2. TL: N42 29 53 W78 41 10. 51 Franklin St. 14141. Phone: (716) 592-9500. Fax: (716) 592-9522. Licensee: Hawk Communications Ltd. (acq 1996). Network: Network: CNN Radio, ESPN Radio, Motor Racing Net. Format: Var/Diverse, adult contemp, country, sports. News staff: one; News: 10 hrs wkly. Target aud: 25-54. Spec prog: Farm 5 hrs, relg 2 hrs wkly. ◆Kevin Bower, gen mgr.

Staten Island

WSIA(FM)—Licensed to Staten Island. See New York

Stillwater

WQAR(FM)— Oct 3, 1988: 101.3 mhz; 2.9 kw. 470 ft. TL: N43 00 42 W73 41 01. Stereo. 100 Saratoga Blvd., Ste. 21, Malta 12020. Phone: (518) 899-3000. Phone: (518) 899-1013. Fax: (518) 899-3057. E-mail: star1013fm@aol.com. Web Site: www.star1013.com. Licensee: Anastos Media Group Inc. (group owner; acq 9-4-98; $900,000). Rep: Allied Radio Partners. Shaw Pittman. Format: Adult contemp. News staff: one; News: 6 hrs wkly. Target aud: 25-54; upscale. Spec prog: Saratoga Forum one hr. ◆Ernie Anastos, chmn; J. Scott Collins, pres & gen mgr; John Meaney, opns mgr; Fran Dingeman, sls dir.

Stony Brook

*WUSB(FM)— June 27, 1977: 90.1 mhz; 3.6 kw. 531 ft. TL: N40 50 32 W73 02 23. Stereo. Union Building, University at Stony Brook 11794-3263. Phone: (631) 632-6501. Fax: (631) 632-7182. E-mail: info@wusb.org. Web Site: www.wusb.org. Licensee: State University of New York. Dow, Lohnes & Albertson. Format: News/talk, diversified, progsv. News: 20 hrs wkly. Target aud: 18-49; progsv & musically adventurous. Spec prog: Black 12 hrs, Pol one hr, Sp 3 hrs, Chinese one hr, Korean one hr, class 14 hrs, folk 15 hrs, jazz 20 hrs, blues 10 hrs wkly. ◆Norman L. Prusslin, gen mgr; Marko Srdanovic, opns dir.

Sylvan Beach

WBGJ(FM)— April 1999: 100.3 mhz; 6 kw. Ant 328 ft. TL: N43 14 46 W75 46 25. 401 W. Kirkpatrick St., Syracuse 13204. Phone: (315) 472-0222. Fax: (315) 478-7745. Licensee: WOLF Radio Inc. (group owner; acq 2-28-02; $350,000). Format: Var. ◆Sam Furco, gen mgr.

Syosset

*WKWZ(FM)— July 24, 1973: 88.5 mhz; 125 w. 90 ft. TL: N40 49 48 W73 28 57. (CP: Ant 259 ft.). 70 Southwoods Rd. 11791. Phone: (516) 364-5745. Phone: (516) 364-5746. Fax: (516) 364-5737. Licensee: Syosset Central School District. Format: Div. Spec prog: C&W 6 hrs, class 6 hrs, jazz 12 hrs wkly. ◆Jack B. DeMasi, gen mgr; Chris Hoffman, stn mgr; Roy Dippel, chief of engrg.

Syracuse

*WAER(FM)— Apr 1, 1947: 88.3 mhz; 50 kw. Ant 276 ft. TL: N43 02 01 W76 07 53. Stereo. 795 Olsrom Ave. 13244-2110. Phone: (315) 443-4021. Fax: (315) 443-2148. E-mail: waer@waer.org. Web Site: www.waer.org. Licensee: Syracuse University. Network: NPR. Arter & Hadden. Format: Jazz, sports, news. News staff: 3; News: 20 hrs wkly. Target aud: 25-49. Spec prog: Gospel 3 hrs, blues 3 hrs, world mus 4 hrs, new age 3 hrs wkly. ◆Joe Lee, gen mgr; Ron Ockert, progmg dir & progmg mgr; Eric Cohen, mus dir.

WAMF(AM)—See Fulton

WAQX-FM—See Manlius

WBBS(FM)—See Fulton

*WCNY-FM— Dec 4, 1971: 91.3 mhz; 18.6 kw. 740 ft. TL: N42 56 42 W76 01 28. Stereo. Box 2400 13220-2400. Secondary address: 506 Old Liverpool Rd., Liverpool 13088. Phone: (315) 453-2424. Fax: (315) 451-8824. E-mail: wcny-online@wcny.org. Web Site: www.wcny.org. Licensee: Public Broadcasting Council of Central New York. Network: NPR. Dow, Lohnes & Albertson. Format: Class. Target aud: General. Spec prog: Bluegrass 3 hrs, jazz 7 hrs wkly. ◆Michael A. Fields, CEO & pres; Colleen Edwards, CFO; Peter Hirsch, mktg dir; David Valesky, prom dir; Don Dolloff, progmg dir; John Duffy, chief of engrg. Co-owned TV: *WCNY-TV affil

WFBL(AM)— Feb 4, 1922: 1390 khz; 5 kw-U, DA-N. TL: N43 05 30 W76 05 19. Box 1050, Baldwinsville 13027. Phone: (315) 635-3971. Fax: (315) 635-3490. Web Site: www.wfbl.com. Licensee: Buckley Broadcasting of New York LLC. Group owner: Buckley Broadcasting Corp. (acq 11-10-03; $1.2 million). Format: Talk. ◆Doug Fleniken, stn mgr; Chris Tetta, opns mgr.

WHEN(AM)— Apr 14, 1941: 620 khz; 5 kw-D, 1 kw-N, DA-N. TL: N43 05 35 W76 11 19. Stereo. 500 Plum St., Suite 100 13204. Phone: (315) 472-9797. Fax: (315) 472-1904. Web Site: www.sportsradio620.com. Licensee: Clear Channel Broadcasting Licenses Inc. Group owner: Clear Channel Communications Inc. (acq 1999). Network: ABC Information & Entertainment. Format: Sports. Spec prog: Syracuse Chiefs, Buffalo Bills, Syracuse Crunch. ◆Joel Delmonico, gen mgr.

WWHT(FM)—Co-owned with WHEN(AM). Sept 1, 1958: 107.9 mhz; 50 kw. 490 ft. TL: N42 57 21 W76 06 36. Stereo. Web Site: www.hot1079.com. Format: CHR.

*WJPZ-FM— Jan 30, 1985: 89.1 mhz; 100 w. 120 ft. TL: N43 02 01 W76 07 53. Stereo. 316 Waverly Ave. 13210. Phone: (315) 443-4689. Phone: (315) 443-2106. Fax: (315) 443-4379. Web Site: www.z89.com. Licensee: WJPZ Radio Inc. Gardner, Carton & Douglas. Format: CHR. Target aud: 12-34; women & teenagers. Spec prog: Black 12 hrs, pub service 13 hrs wkly. ◆Geoff Herbert, gen mgr; Scott Purdy, opns VP; Louise Vazquez, dev VP; Joan Kump, prom dir; David McKinley, progmg dir.

WKRL-FM—See North Syracuse

WLTI(FM)— Apr 8, 1996: 105.9 mhz; 4 kw. 200 ft. TL: N43 05 23 W76 09 10. Stereo. 1064 James St. 13203. Phone: (315) 472-0200. Fax: (315) 478-5625. Web Site: www.lite1059.com. Licensee: Citadel Broadcasting Co. Group owner: Citadel Broadcasting Corp. (acq 2000; grpsl). Network: CBS Radio. Format: Soft adult contemp. Target aud: 25-54; general. ◆Tom Mitchell, opns dir; Dave Allen, progmg dir & progmg mgr.

*WMHR(FM)— Mar 9, 1969: 102.9 mhz; 20 kw. 780 ft. TL: N42 58 00 W76 12 01. Stereo. 4044 Makyes Rd. 13215. Phone: (315) 469-5051. E-mail: marshillnetwork@marshillnetwork.org. Web Site: www.marshillnetwork.org. Licensee: Mars Hill Broadcasting Co. Inc. dba Mars Hill Network. (group owner) Network: Moody, Salem Radio Network. Wiley, Rein & Fielding. Format: Christian. News: 6 hrs wkly. Target aud: General; Christian families. Spec prog: Children 11 hrs wkly. ◆Clayton Roberts, pres; Ronald C. Westcott, CFO; Michael Gettman, VP; Wayne Taylor, gen mgr.

WNSS(AM)—Listing follows WNTQ(FM).

WNTQ(FM)— 1956: 93.1 mhz; 97 kw. 659 ft. TL: N42 56 47 W76 01 32. Stereo. 1064 James St. 13203. Phone: (315) 472-0200. Fax: (315) 478-5625. Web Site: www.93q.com. Licensee: Citadel Broadcasting Co. Group owner: Citadel Broadcasting Corp. (acq 4-26-01; grpsl). Rep: McGavren Guild. Format: CHR. Target aud: 25-54; women. ◆Darren Smith, gen mgr; Laura Serway, sls dir; Janice Cole, prom dir; Tom Mitchell, opns mgr & progmg dir; Phil Spevak, news dir; Dave Edwards, chief of engrg.

WNSS(AM)— Co-owned with WNTQ(FM). 1946: 1260 khz; 5 kw-U, DA-2. TL: N43 09 10 W76 11 35. Web Site: www.espnradio1260.com. Network: ESPN Radio. Format: Sports/Talk. Target aud: 25-54; men. ◆Jim Tully, natl sls mgr & progmg dir.

WOLF(AM)— Apr 27, 1940: 1490 khz; 620 w-D, 750 w-N, DA-D. TL: N43 03 30 W76 10 00. (CP: 1510 khz. TL: N42 57 42 W76 06 13). Stereo. 401 W. Kirkpatrick 13204. Phone: (315) 472-0222. Fax: (315) 478-7745. E-mail: wolfam/fm@aol.com. Web Site: www.radiodisney.com. Licensee: WOLF Radio Inc. (group owner; acq 10-5-82). Network: Radio Disney. James L. Oyster. Format: Children. ◆Sam Furco, gen mgr & opns dir.

*WRVD(FM)— June 1, 1999: 90.3 mhz; 280 w. Ant 43 ft. TL: N43 02 27 W76 08 22. Stereo. c/o WRVO(FM), Lanigan Hall, State Univ. College, Oswego 13126. Phone: (315) 312-3690. Fax: (315) 312-3174. E-mail: wrvd@wrvo.fm. Web Site: www.wrvo.fm. Licensee: State University of New York. Network: NPR. Format: News/talk, old time radio. News staff: 4; News: 140 hrs wkly. Target aud: 35-54. ◆John E. Krauss, gen mgr; Fred Vigeant, opns dir; Thomas Herbert, dev dir.

WSEN(AM)—See Baldwinsville

WSIV(AM)—(East Syracuse). Dec 6, 1955: 1540 khz; 1 kw-D. TL: N43 05 40 W76 02 00. (CP: 1.5 kw-D, 57 w-N). 7095 Myers Rd., East Syracuse 13057. Phone: (315) 656-2231. Phone: (315) 956-2250. Fax: (315) 656-2259. E-mail: wvoaradio@msn.com. Licensee: CRAM Communications L.L.C. (acq 1-6-97; $900,000. with WVOA(FM) DeRuyter). Format: Christian, relg, Black gospel, music. Spec prog: Black 20 hrs, Gospel music. ◆Sam Furco, CEO; James Wall, gen mgr; Suzanne Anderson, stn mgr; Allen Elson, opns mgr.

WSYR(AM)— 1922: 570 khz; 5 kw-U, DA-2. TL: N42 59 13 W76 09 09. Stereo. Bridgewater Pl., 500 Plum St. 13204. Phone: (315) 472-9797. Fax: (315) 472-1904. Web Site: www.sybercuse.com. Licensee: Clear Channel Broadcasting Licenses Inc. Group owner: Clear Channel Communications Inc. Network: PRI. Format: Full service, news/talk. News: 35 hrs wkly. Target aud: 25-54. ◆Joel Delmonico, gen mgr.

WYYY(FM)—Co-owned with WSYR(AM). 1946: 94.5 mhz; 100 kw. 650 ft. TL: N42 56 40 W76 07 08. Stereo. Web Site: www.sybercuse.com. Format: Adult contemp.

WTLA(AM)—See North Syracuse

WWDG(FM)—See DeRuyter

Ticonderoga

*WANC(FM)— Sept 6, 1982: 103.9 mhz; 1.55 kw. 380 ft. TL: N43 49 55 W73 24 28. Stereo. Box 66600, 318 Central Ave., Albany 12206-6600. Phone: (518) 465-5233. Phone: (800) 323-9262. Fax: (518) 432-6974. E-mail: mail@wamc.org. Web Site: www.wamc.org. Licensee: WAMC. Group owner: WAMC/Northeast Public Radio (acq 8-90; $400,000; 8-13-90). Network: Network: NPR, PRI. Dow, Lohnes & Albertson. Format: News, Talk. Target aud: General. Spec prog: Folk 6 hrs, jazz 17 hrs wkly. ◆Alan Chartock, chmn.

WIPS(AM)— July 1955: 1250 khz; 1 kw-D. TL: N43 51 16 W73 23 24. PO Box 600, Crown Point 12928-0600. Phone: (518) 597-9477. Phone: (518) 597-3201. Fax: (518) 597-9479. E-mail: info@wipsradio.com. Web Site: www.wipsradio.com. Licensee: BisiBlue L.L.C. (acq 3-17-2004; $93,000). Network: ABC Information & Entertainment. Format: Oldies. News staff: one; News: 24 hrs wkly. Target aud: 25-54. Spec prog: Farm 6 hrs wkly. ◆Gregg Trask, pres & gen mgr; Patricia Knapp, chmn & CFO.

Troy

WFLY(FM)— August 1948: 92.3 mhz; 17 kw. 850 ft. TL: N42 38 16 W73 59 55. 6 Johnson Rd., Latham 12210. Phone: (518) 786-6600. Fax: (518) 786-6610. Licensee: 6 Johnson Road Licenses Inc. Group owner: Pamal Broadcasting Ltd. (acq 10-19-2001; grpsl). Network: ABC. Rep: Allied Radio Partners. Format: CHR. News staff: one; News: 5 hrs wkly. Target aud: 18-49. ◆Dan Austin, gen mgr; Suzette Anthony, gen sls mgr.

WGNA-FM—See Albany

WHAZ(AM)— August 1922: 1330 khz; 1 kw-U. TL: N42 46 35 W73 41 10. 30 Park Ave., Cohoes 12047-3330. Phone: (518) 237-1330. Fax: (518) 235-4468. Web Site: www.whaz.com. Licensee: Capital Media Corp. (group owner; acq 9-24-87). Format: Adult Christian. Target aud: 25-75; young to old. Spec prog: Gospel, rel. ◆Paul F. Lotters, pres & gen mgr; Steven L. Klob, opns dir & dev dir.

WOFX(AM)— Apr 15, 1940: 980 khz; 5 kw-U, DA-N. TL: N42 46 56 W73 50 07. River Hill Ctr., 1203 Troy Schenectady Rd., Suite 201, Latham 12110. Phone: (518) 452-4800. Fax: (518) 785-0122. Web

Stations in the U.S. New York

Site: www.wofx.com. Licensee: Capstar TX L.P. Group owner: Clear Channel Communications Inc. (acq 8-30-00; grpsl). Rep: Clear Channel. Format: Sports talk. Target aud: 18-49. ♦ Dennis Lamme, exec VP, gen mgr & chief of engrg; Greg Foster, opns mgr.

WPYX(FM)—See Albany

***WRPI(FM)**— Nov 1, 1957: 91.5 mhz; 10 kw. 450 ft. TL: N42 41 14 W73 42 22. Stereo. One WRPI Plaza 12180. Phone: (518) 276-6248. Fax: (518) 276-2360. Web Site: www.wrpi.org. Licensee: Rensselaer Polytechnic Institute. Format: Div. News: 5 hrs wkly. Target aud: General; open minded, educated listeners. Spec prog: Black 8 hrs, country 2 hrs, Indian 2 hrs, Greek 2 hrs, women's mus 2 hrs, Chinese 2 hrs, African one hr, folk 2 hrs wkly. ♦ John Corbett, pres; Colin Fredericks, gen mgr.

Trumansburg

WPIE(AM)— Jan 15, 1990: 1160 khz; 5 kw-D, 31 w-N, DA-2. TL: N42 32 42 W76 42 39. 1705 Lake St., Elmira 14901. Phone: (607) 733-5626. Fax: (607) 733-5627. E-mail: ppinesmedia1@stny.rr.com. Licensee: Pembrook Pines Ithaca Ltd. Group owner: Pembrook Pines Media Group (acq 3-3-93; $150,000;. FTR: 3-22-93). Bechtel & Cole. Format: Sports. News staff: one; News: 18 hrs wkly. Target aud: 25-54; mature, upscale adults. ♦ Ericka Scott, opns dir; Robert J. Pfuntner, pres, gen mgr & dev dir.

Tupper Lake

WRGR(FM)— Feb 29, 1980: 102.3 mhz; 150 w. 1,446 ft. TL: N44 09 35 W74 28 34. Stereo. Box 211, Saranac Lake 12983-0211. Phone: (518) 891-1544. Fax: (518) 891-1545. E-mail: sales@wnbz.com. Web Site: www.wnbz.com. Licensee: Radio Lake Placid Inc. Group owner: Mountain Communications (acq 2003; grpsl). Network: ABC. Format: Classic rock, adult contemp. News staff: 2; News: 2 hrs wkly. Target aud: 25-54; men. Spec prog: Relg one hr, big band 2 hrs wkly. ♦ Ted Morgan, pres & gen mgr; Susan Harington, gen sls mgr.

Utica

WFRG-FM— Oct 10, 1948: 104.3 mhz; 100 kw. Ant 500 ft. TL: N43 03 27 W75 25 04. Stereo. 9418 River Rd., Marcy 13403. Phone: (315) 768-9500. Fax: (315) 736-3311. Web Site: www.bigfrog104.com. Licensee: Regent Licensee of Utica/Rome Inc. (acq 11-5-99; grpsl). Format: Country. Target aud: 25-54. ♦ Mary Jo Beach, gen mgr.

WIBX(AM)— Dec 5, 1925: 950 khz; 5 kw-U, DA-1. TL: N43 06 16 W75 20 20. 8280 Clark Mills Rd., Whitesboro 13492. Phone: (315) 768-9500. Fax: (315) 736-0720. Web Site: www.wibx950.com. Licensee: Regent Licensee of Utica/Rome Inc. Group owner: Regent Communications Inc. (acq 2-11-00; grpsl). Network: CBS. Format: News/talk, sports. News staff: 5. Target aud: 35-64; middle to upper income adults. Spec prog: Pol 3 hrs, farm 14 hrs wkly. ♦ Tom Jacobson, gen mgr & opns dir.

WLZW(FM)—Co-owned with WIBX(AM). Jan 1, 1972: 98.7 mhz; 25 kw. 660 ft. TL: N43 08 39 W75 10 45. Stereo. Web Site: www.wibx950.com. Format: Lite adult contemp. News staff: 6. Target aud: 25-54; middle to upper income & educ levels. ♦ Peter Naughton, progmg dir.

WIXT(AM)—See Little Falls

WKLL(FM)—(Frankfort). Feb 12, 1990: 94.9 mhz; 50 kw. 276 ft. TL: N43 03 26 W75 07 24. (CP: 34 kw, ant 567 ft.). 39 Kellogg Rd., New Hartford 13413. Phone: (315) 797-1330. Fax: (315) 738-1073. Web Site: www.krock.com. Licensee: Galaxy Communications L.P. Group owner: Route 81 Radio LLC (acq 4-6-2000; grpsl). Network: ABC. Rep: D & R Radio. Format: Modern rock. ♦ Mike Ninnie, gen mgr.

***WKVU(FM)**— July 11, 1994: 100.7 mhz; 1.2 w. 551 ft. TL: N43 09 12 W75 09 32. 1017 Higby Rd., New Hartford 13413. Phone: (315) 793-1007. Fax: (315) 793-1044. Web Site: www.klove.com. Licensee: Educational Media Foundation. Group owner: EMF Broadcasting (acq 6-7-01; $1.25 million). Network: K-Love. Format: Christian music. Target aud: 25-45. ♦ Bob Cain, chief of opns.

WOUR(FM)—Listing follows WUTQ(AM).

***WPNR-FM**— November 1977: 90.7 mhz; 450 w. 30 ft. TL: N43 05 35 W75 16 21. Stereo. c/o Utica College, 1600 Burstone Rd. 13502. Phone: (315) 792-3069. Phone: (315) 792-3066. Fax: (315) 792-3292. Licensee: Utica College. (acq 9-12-96). Format: Div, urban contemp, AOR. Spec prog: Class 10 hrs, jazz 14 hrs, reggae 5 hrs wkly. ♦ Todd Hutton, pres.

WRCK(FM)—Listing follows WTLB(AM).

WRNY(AM)—See Rome

WRUN(AM)— Apr 24, 1948: 1150 khz; 5 kw-D, 1 kw-N, DA-2. TL: N43 10 31 W75 21 03. 318 Central Ave., Albany 12206. Phone: (518) 465-5233. Fax: (518) 432-6974. Web Site: www.wamc.org. Licensee: WAMC. Group owner: Regent Communications Inc. (acq 7-6-2005; $275,000). Format: News/talk. ♦ Alan S. Chartock, CEO.

***WRVN(FM)**— Jun 4, 1986: 91.9 mhz; 1.9 kw. Ant -62 ft. TL: N43 08 31 W75 13 36. Stereo. 7060 State Rt. 104, Oswego 13126. Phone: (315) 312-3690. Fax: (315) 312-3174. E-mail: wrvn@wrvo.fm. Web Site: www.wrvo.fm. Licensee: State University of New York. Network: Network: NPR, PRI. Format: News/talk, old time radio. News staff: 3; News: 140 hrs wkly. ♦ John E. Krauss, gen mgr; Fred Vigeant, opns dir; Thomas Herbert, dev dir; Chris Ulanowski, news dir; Jeff Windsor, chief of engrg.

WTLB(AM)— 1946: 1310 khz; 5 kw-D, 500 w-N, DA-2. TL: N43 03 24 W75 16 42. Box 398, Washington Mills 13479-0398. Phone: (315) 797-1330. Fax: (315) 738-1073. Licensee: Galaxy Communications L.P. Group owner: Route 81 Radio LLC (acq 4-6-2000; grpsl). Network: Network: ABC Daytime Direction, ABC News/Talk. Format: Btfl mus, MOR. News: one hr wkly. Target aud: 55 plus. ♦ Ed Levine, pres; Ken Karaszkiewicz, CFO; Larry Brown, gen mgr; Mimi Griswold, progmg VP; Dave Doughty, chief of engrg.

WRCK(FM)—Co-owned with WTLB(AM). Apr 23, 1962: 107.3 mhz; 50 kw. 499 ft. TL: N43 08 40 W75 10 32. Stereo. Web Site: www.wrck.com. Format: Classic rock. ♦ Marsha Dionne, gen sls mgr; Mimi Griswold, mus dir.

WUMX(FM)—See Rome

***WUNY(FM)**— Oct 30, 1985: 89.5 mhz; 6.3 kw. 777 ft. TL: N43 08 38 W75 10 40. Stereo. Box 2400, 506 Old Liverpool Rd., Syracuse 13220-2400. Phone: (315) 453-2424. Fax: (315) 451-8824. E-mail: wcny—online@wcny.org. Web Site: www.wcny.org. Licensee: Public Broadcasting Council of Central New York. Network: NPR. Haley, Bader & Potts. Format: Class. Target aud: General. Spec prog: Bluegrass 3 hrs, jazz 7 hrs wkly. ♦ Michael Fields, CEO & pres; Colleen Edwards, CFO; Peter Hirsch, mktg dir; David Valesky, prom dir.

WUTQ(AM)— Jan 29, 1962: 1550 khz; 1 kw-D. TL: N43 06 48 W75 15 25. Stereo. Mayro Bldg., 239 Genesee St. 13501. Phone: (315) 797-0803. Fax: (315) 797-7813. Licensee: Clear Channel Radio License Inc. Group owner: Clear Channel Communications Inc. (acq 8-5-98; grpsl). Network: Westwood One. Rep: Christal. Latham & Watkins. Format: Sports. Target aud: 35 plus; 60% female, 40% male. Spec prog: It 2 hrs, Pol 4 hrs wkly. ♦ Brian Delaney, gen mgr; Gene Conte, progmg dir; Jack Moran, news dir; Joe Petro, chief of engrg.

WOUR(FM)—Co-owned with WUTQ(AM). June 1967: 96.9 mhz; 16 kw. 790 ft. TL: N43 08 46 W75 10 40. Stereo. Web Site: www.wour.com. Format: Rock/AOR. Target aud: 25-49; adults. ♦ Jerry Kraus, prom mgr; Stew Schantz, progmg dir & mus dir.

Valhalla

***WARY(FM)**— Oct 3, 1973: 88.1 mhz; 171 w. 403 ft. TL: N41 04 13 W73 47 25. 75 Grasslands Rd. 10595. Phone: (914) 606-6752. Phone: (914) 606-6753. Fax: (914) 606-6260. E-mail: radprime1@aol.com. Licensee: Westchester Community College. Garvey, Schubert & Barer. Format: AOR. Target aud: 12-24. Spec prog: Pub service 10 hrs wkly. ♦ Radames Ocasio, gen mgr.

Vestal

WMXW(FM)— June 2, 1989: 103.3 mhz; 6 kw. 1,014 ft. TL: N42 03 22 W75 56 39. (CP: 592 w). Stereo. 320 N. Jensen Rd. 13850-2111. Phone: (607) 785-3131. Fax: (607) 584-5900. Licensee: Clear Channel Broadcasting Licenses Inc. Group owner: Clear Channel Communications Inc. (acq 9-00; grpsl). Rep: Katz Radio. Format: Spectrum adult contemp. News staff: one. Target aud: 25-54. ♦ Dave Lozzi, progmg dir & news dir.

Voorheesville

WAJZ(FM)— May 24, 1991: 96.3 mhz; 6 kw. 1,118 ft. TL: N42 37 01 W74 00 46. Stereo. 6 Johnson Rd., Latham 12110. Phone: (518) 786-6600. Fax: (518) 786-6620. Fax: (518) 786-6610. Web Site: www.jamz963.com. Licensee: 6 Johnson Road Licenses Inc. Group owner: Pamal Broadcasting Ltd. (acq 10-19-2001; grpsl). Network: ABC Information & Entertainment. Format: Urban contemp. News staff: 2; News: 3 hrs wkly. Target aud: 18-54; upscale urban. Spec prog: Relg one hr wkly. ♦ Dan Austin, gen mgr; Suzette Anthony, sls VP.

Walton

WDLA(AM)— May 30, 1951: 1270 khz; 5 kw-D, 100 w-N. TL: N42 08 08 W75 04 52. Box 58, Rt. 206 13856. Phone: (607) 865-4321. Licensee: Double O Central New York Corp. (group owner; (acq 10-22-2004; grpsl). Network: Network: UPI, Jones Radio Networks. Rep: Savalli. Format: Music of your life. Target aud: 28-55; general. Spec prog: Farm 2 hrs wkly. ♦ Jim Johnson, gen mgr; Skip Barlow, progmg dir.

WDLA-FM— Nov 16, 1973: 92.1 mhz; 690 w. 656 ft. TL: N42 08 10 W75 04 48.

Warrensburg

WKBE(FM)— 1990: 100.3 mhz; 1.45 kw. 1,312 ft. TL: N43 25 12 W73 45 39. 6 Johnson Rd., Latham 12110. Phone: (518) 786-6600. Fax: (518) 786-6610. Licensee: 6 Johnson Road Licenses Inc. Group owner: Pamal Broadcasting Ltd. (acq 10-9-2001). Format: CHR. News staff: one; News: 10 hrs wkly. Target aud: 18-34; women. ♦ Dan Austin, gen mgr.

Warsaw

WCJW(AM)— May 16, 1973: 1140 khz; 2.5 kw-D, DA. TL: N42 43 35 W78 06 47. Box 251, 3258 Merchant Rd. 14569. Phone: (585) 786-8131. Fax: (585) 786-2241. E-mail: wcjw@wcjw.com. Web Site: www.wcjw.com. Licensee: Lloyd Lane Inc. (acq 9-1-84). Network: USA. Format: Country. News staff: one; News: 20 hrs wkly. Target aud: 25-54; adults. Spec prog: Farm 11 hrs wkly. ♦ Lloyd Lane, pres & gen mgr.

***WCOU(FM)**— Dec 14, 1992: 88.3 mhz; 11 kw. Ant 535 ft. TL: N42 49 36 W78 12 25. Stereo. Box 506, Bath 14810. Secondary address: 7634 Campbell Creek Rd., Bath 14810. Phone: (607) 776-4151. Fax: (607) 776-6929. E-mail: mail@fln.org. Web Site: www.fln.org. Licensee: Family Life Ministries Inc. Group owner: Family Life Network Format: Contemp Christian. News staff: 7; News: 14 hrs wkly. Target aud: 30-54; general. ♦ Rick Snavely, pres, VP & gen mgr.

Broadcasting & Cable Yearbook 2006

New York

Warwick

WTBQ(AM)— July 24, 1969: 1110 khz; 500 w-D (non-directional). TL: N41 16 51 W74 21 46. 62 N. Main St., Florida 10921. Phone: (845) 651-1110. Fax: (845) 651-1025. E-mail: am1110@magiccarpet.com. Web Site: www.wtbq.com. Licensee: FST Broadcasting Corp. (acq 7-94; $150,000). Network: ABC. Format: Oldies, talk. News: 10 hrs wkly. Target aud: 24-55; affluent Orange County-New York City commuters. Spec prog: Folk, Pol, relg, farm. ◆Frank Truatt, pres & gen mgr; Frank Lowell, opns mgr; Rob McLean, gen sls mgr; Rich Ball, progmg dir.

Waterloo

WNYR-FM— Apr 19, 1989: 98.5 mhz; 3.2 kw. 446 ft. TL: N42 48 22 W76 50 47. Stereo. 3568 Lenox Rd., Geneva 14456. Phone: (315) 781-7000. Fax: (315) 781-7700. Web Site: www.fingerlakes.com. Licensee: Lake Country Broadcasting. James L. Oyster. Format: Adult contemp. News staff: one; News: 5 hrs wkly. Target aud: 25-54. ◆George Kimble, pres; Alan Bishop, VP & gen mgr; Mike Smith, opns mgr.

Watertown

WATN(AM)— Feb 3, 1941: 1240 khz; 1 kw-U. TL: N43 58 49 W75 56 12. 199 Wealtha Ave. 13601. Phone: (315) 782-1240. Fax: (315) 782-0312. Licensee: Clancy-Mance Communications, Inc. (group owner; acq 6-20-88; grpsl; 6-20-88). Network: ABC Information & Entertainment. Rep: Roslin. Format: Talk. ◆David W. Mance, pres & gen mgr; Todd Dalesandro, opns dir.

WCIZ-FM—Listing follows WTNY(AM).

WFRY-FM—Listing follows WNER(AM).

*WJNY(FM)— July 24, 1986: 90.9 mhz; 7.09 kw. 449 ft. TL: N43 51 44 W75 43 40. Stereo. Box 2400, Syracuse 13220-2400. Secondary address: 506 Old Liverpool Pl., Syracuse 13220. Phone: (315) 453-2424. Fax: (315) 451-8824. E-mail: wcny-online@wcny.org. Web Site: www.wcny.org. Licensee: Public Broadcasting Council of Central New York Inc. Network: NPR. Haley, Bader & Potts. Format: Class. Spec prog: Bluegrass 3 hrs, jazz 5 hrs wkly. ◆Michael Fields, CEO; Peter Hirsch, mktg dir.

WNER(AM)— Nov 2, 1959: 1410 khz; 3.5 kw-D, 58 w-N. TL: N43 56 47 W75 56 52. 134 Mullin St. 13601. Phone: (315) 788-0790. Fax: (315) 788-4379. Licensee: Regent Licensee of Watertown Inc. Group owner: Regent Communications Inc. (acq 11-5-99; grpsl). Network: ESPN Radio. Format: Sports. Target aud: 35-64. ◆Don Wagner, pres & CFO; Lance Thomas, progmg dir.

WFRY-FM—Co-owned with WNER(AM). Nov 22, 1968: 97.5 mhz; 100 kw. 285 ft. TL: N43 57 23 W75 50 45. Stereo. Web Site: www.froggy97.com. Format: Country. ◆Matt Raisman, progmg dir.

*WRVJ(FM)— July 1, 1989: 91.7 mhz; 1.6 kw. Ant 443 ft. TL: N43 51 44 W75 43 40. Stereo. 7060 State Rt. 104, Oswego 13126. Phone: (315) 312-3690. Fax: (315) 312-3174. E-mail: wrvo@wrvo.fm. Web Site: www.wrvj.fm. Licensee: State University of New York. Network: Network: NPR, PRI. Format: News/talk, old time radio. News staff: 3; News: 140 hrs wkly. Target aud: 25-55. ◆John E. Krauss, gen mgr; Fred Vigeant, opns dir; Thomas Herbert, dev dir; Chris Ulanowski, news dir; Jeff Windsor, chief of engrg.

*WSLJ(FM)— 1992: 88.9 mhz; 200 w. 454 ft. TL: N43 57 23 W75 50 28. St. Lawrence Univ., Canton 13617. Phone: (315) 229-5356. Fax: (315) 229-5373. Web site: www.ncpr.org. Licensee: St. Lawrence University. Donald E. Martin. Format: Eclectic public radio. News staff: 2; News: 35 hrs wkly. Target aud: General. ◆Ellen Rocco, gen mgr; Shelly Pike, chief of opns; Sandra Demarest, dev dir.

WTNY(AM)— Apr 29, 1941: 790 khz; 1 kw-U, DA-N. TL: N43 56 44 W75 56 54. Stereo. 134 Mullin St. 13601. Phone: (315) 788-0790. Fax: (315) 788-4379. Web site: www.production@790wtny.com. Licensee: Regent Licensee of Watertown Inc. Group owner: Regent Communications Inc. (acq 11-5-99; grpsl). Network: CBS. Dow, Lohnes & Albertson. Format: News. News staff: 3; News: 20 hrs wkly. Target aud: 25 plus. Spec prog: Farm 3 hrs wkly. ◆Don Wagner, CFO & pres; Lance Thomas, progmg dir.

WCIZ-FM—Co-owned with WTNY(AM). Aug 25, 1986: 93.3 mhz; 6 kw. 328 ft. TL: N43 57 23 W75 50 45. Stereo. Web Site: www.production@790wtny.com. Format: Classic hits. News staff: 3; News: 2 hrs wkly. Target aud: 35-54.

*WWJS(FM)— June 26, 2000: 90.1 mhz; 1 kw. 499 ft. TL: N43 57 15 W75 43 45. Stereo. 210 Court St. 13601. Phone: (315) 786-9957. Fax: (315) 779-9671. Web Site: wwjsfm.net. Licensee: Liberty Communications Family B/G. Colby M. May. Format: Educ, Christian. ◆Karleen Savidge, pres; David Collins, VP; Charles Savidge, gen mgr; Tony Gullo, opns mgr.

Watkins Glen

WNGZ(FM)—See Montour Falls

WTYX(AM)— June 22, 1968: 1490 khz; 400 w-U. TL: N42 21 11 W76 52 13. 2205 College Ave., Elmira 14903. Phone: (607) 732-4400. Fax: (607) 732-7774. Licensee: Chemung County Radio Inc. Group owner: Backyard Broadcasting LLC (acq 12-1-2002; grpsl). Rep: D & R Radio. Format: Country. Target aud: 20-49; baby boomers. ◆Kevin White, gen mgr.

Waverly

WATS(AM)—See Sayre, PA

WAVR(FM)— October 1974: 102.1 mhz; 1.5 kw. Ant 400 ft. TL: N42 03 48 W76 31 28. Stereo. 204 Desmond St., Sayre, PA 18840. Phone: (570) 888-7745. Fax: (570) 888-9005. Web Site: www.thechoiceradio.com. Licensee: Wats Broadcasting Inc. (acq 10-28-86). Network: UPI. Format: Adult contemp. Target aud: 25-54; upscale bedroom community. ◆Charles C. Carver, pres & gen mgr; Meade T. Murtland, stn mgr.

Webster

*WFRW(FM)— October 1988: 88.1 mhz; 8.5 kw. 337 ft. TL: N43 04 18 W77 05 35. Stereo. 918 Chesapeake Ave., Annapolis 21403. Phone: (315) 331-7482. Fax: (410) 268-0931. Web Site: www.familyradio.com. Licensee: Family Stations Inc. (group owner) Format: Relg, educ. News: 4 hrs wkly. Target aud: General. Spec prog: Class 2 hrs wkly. ◆Harold Camping, pres & gen mgr.

*WMHN(FM)— Feb 29, 1988: 89.3 mhz; 1 kw. 75 ft. TL: N43 13 45 W77 26 52. Stereo. 4044 Makyes Rd., Syracuse 13215. Phone: (315) 469-5051. E-mail: marshillnetwork@marshillnetwork.org. Web Site: www.marshillnetwork.org. Licensee: Mars Hill Broadcasting Co. Inc. (group owner) Network: Network: Moody, Salem Radio Network. Wiley, Rein & Fielding. Format: Christian. News: 13 hrs wkly. Target aud: 35-65; Christian families. Spec prog: Children 11 hrs wkly. ◆Clayton Roberts, pres; Michael Gettman, VP; Wayne Taylor, gen mgr & opns mgr.

WRCI(FM)— Feb 15, 1993: 102.7 mhz; 6 kw. Ant 328 ft. TL: N43 10 14 W77 40 23. 2494 Browncroft Blvd., Rochester 14625. Phone: (585) 264-1027. Fax: (585) 264-1165. Web Site: www.wrcifm.com. Licensee: Kimtron Inc. Group owner: Crawford Broadcasting Co. (acq 11-25-92; $950,000;. FTR: 12-21-92). Format: Christian, talk. ◆Robert Hammond, gen mgr; Scott Ensign, opns mgr; Mark Shuttleworth, progmg dir; Brian Cunningham, chief of engrg.

Wellsville

WJQZ(FM)—Listing follows WLSV(AM).

WLSV(AM)— Oct 31, 1955: 790 khz; 1 kw-D, 41 w-N. TL: N42 04 37 W77 55 47. 82 Railroad Ave. 14895. Phone: (585) 593-6070. Fax: (585) 593-6212. E-mail: oldiesz103@yahoo.com. Licensee: DBM Communications Inc. (acq 8-21-98; $850,000 with co-located FM). Baraff, Koerner & Olender. Format: Country. Target aud: General. ◆Richard Mangels, pres; Bob Mangels, news dir.

WJQZ(FM)—Co-owned with WLSV(AM). Feb 3, 1986: 103.5 mhz; 3 kw. 466 ft. TL: N42 09 26 W77 55 26. Stereo. Format: Oldies. Target aud: 25-54. ◆Robert Mangels, progmg dir.

Westhampton

WBON-FM— Nov 18, 1993: 98.5 mhz; 3 kw. Ant 328 ft. TL: N40 51 18 W72 46 12. (CP: 950 w, ant 525 ft). Stereo. 3075 Vets Hwy., Ronkonkoma 11779. Phone: (631) 648-2500. Fax: (631) 648-2550.

Web Site: www.985thebone.com. Licensee: Jarad Broadcasting Co. of Westhampton Inc. Group owner: The Morey Organization Inc. Rep: Christal. Format: Classic rock. Target aud: 25-54. ◆John Carraciolo, pres & chief of engrg.

Westhampton Beach

WRCN-FM—See Riverhead

Westport

WCLX(FM)— January 1995: 102.9 mhz; 6 kw. Ant 312 ft. TL: N44 13 15 W73 24 41. Stereo. Westport Broadcasting, 19 Boas Ln., Wilton, CT 06897-1031. Phone: (203) 762-9425. Fax: (509) 752-4105. E-mail: dj@broadcast.net. Web Site: www.wclxfm.com. Licensee: Westport Broadcasting. Cohn & Marks. Format: Progressive rock. Target aud: 25-54. ◆Dennis Jackson, CEO; Russ Kinsley, gen mgr; Diane Desmond, progmg dir.

Wethersfield Township

WLKK(FM)— 1948: 107.7 mhz; 19.5 kw. Ant 800 ft. TL: N42 37 23 W78 17 16. Stereo. 500 Corporate Pkwy., Suite 200, Buffalo 14226. Phone: (716) 843-0600. Fax: (716) 832-3323. Web Site: www.1077thelake.com. Licensee: Entercom Buffalo License LLC. Group owner: Entercom Communications Corp. (acq 5-5-2004; $9 million). Network: Westwood One. Format: Progsv, classic rock. Target aud: 25-54; adults. ◆Greg Ried, gen mgr; Jeff Surdej, prom mgr; Hank Dole, progmg dir.

White Plains

WFAS(AM)— Aug 11, 1932: 1230 khz; 1 kw-U. TL: N41 01 32 W73 49 39. 365 Secor Rd., Hartsdale 10530. Phone: (914) 693-2400. Fax: (914) 693-0000. Web Site: www.wfasam.com. Licensee: Cumulus Licensing Corp. Group owner: Cumulus Media Inc. (acq 1-23-02; grpsl). Network: AP Radio. Rep: McGavren Guild. Format: MOR. News staff: 2; News: 5 hrs wkly. Target aud: General. Spec prog: Sports progmg 8 hrs wkly. ◆Rod Colarco, gen mgr; Dave Ashton, opns mgr; Bob Barnum, progmg dir.

WFAS-FM— Sept 1, 1947: 103.9 mhz; 600 w. 669 ft. TL: N41 01 32 W73 49 39. Stereo. E-mail: music@wfasfm.com. Web Site: www.wfasfm.com. Format: Adult contemp. News: one hr wkly. Target aud: 25-54. ◆Robert Bongiardino, gen sls mgr; Misty Wien, prom dir; Dave Ashton, progmg dir; Pam Puso, news dir; Joan Franzino, pub affrs dir.

WXPK(FM)—See Briarcliff Manor

Whitehall

WNYV(FM)— July 14, 1990: 94.1 mhz; 3 kw. 328 ft. TL: N43 28 37 W73 26 56. Stereo. Box 141 12887. Secondary address: Box 568, East Poultney, VT 05741. Phone: (802) 287-9031. Licensee: Pine Tree Broadcasting. Rep: Commercial Media Sales. Format: Adult contemp, country, oldies. News staff: one; News: 3 hrs wkly. Target aud: 25-55; active community oriented, working professional & families. Spec prog: Big band 3 hrs, pub affrs 5 hrs, relg 2 hrs, Pol one hr wkly. ◆Michael Leech, pres; Judith E. Leech, VP & gen mgr.

Whitesboro

WSKS(FM)— 1994: 97.9 mhz; 1.5 kw. 669 ft. TL: N43 02 14 W75 26 40. 239 Genesee St., Suite 500, Utica 13501. Phone: (315) 797-0803. Fax: (315) 797-7813. E-mail: stewschantz@clearchannel.com. Licensee: Clear Channel Broadcasting Licenses Inc. Group owner: Clear Channel Communications Inc. (acq 3-12-01; $2.15 million. with WSKU(FM) Little Falls). Format: CHR, rhythmic. ◆Brian Delaney, gen mgr; Stew Schantz, opns mgr; Jim Hartnett, sls dir; Ken Morrison, prom dir.

Willsboro

WXZO(FM)— 1997:: 96.7 mhz; 1 kw. 797 ft. TL: N44 24 12 W73 26 02. Box 1093, Burlington 05403. Phone: (866) 696-7967. Web Site: www.wxzofm.com. Licensee: Capstar TX L.P. Group owner: Clear Channel Communications Inc. (acq 8-30-00; grpsl). Format: Talk. ◆Karen Marshall, gen mgr; Steve Cormier, opns dir.

Windham

WRIP(FM)— Aug 5, 1999: 97.9 mhz; 580 w. Ant 1,056 ft. TL: N42 17 06 W74 15 52. Stereo. 134 South St., P.O. Box 979 12496-0979. Phone: (518) 734-4747. Fax: (413) 375-4711. E-mail: wrip@mhcable.com. Web Site: www.wripfm.com. Licensee: Rip Radio LLC. Network: AP Network News. Cohn & Marks. Format: Adult contemp, full service, Christian contemp. Target aud: 25 plus; mass appeal. Spec prog: Jazz 3 hrs, Christian contemp 2 hrs wkly. ♦Dennis Jackson, CEO; Guy Patrick Garraghan, VP & gen mgr; Jay Fink, gen sls mgr & mus dir.

Woodside

WWRL(AM)—See New York

Woodstock

WDST(FM)— Apr 29, 1980: 100.1 mhz; 2.9 kw. 308 ft. TL: N41 59 04 W74 02 56. Stereo. Box 367 12498. Secondary address: 293 Tinker St. 12498. Phone: (845) 679-7266. Fax: (845) 679-5395. E-mail: live@wdst.com. Web Site: www.wdst.com. Licensee: CHET-5 Broadcasting L.P. (acq 2-12-93; $1.65 million with WKNY(AM) Kingston; 3-8-93). Network: CBS Radio. Rep: Christal. Shaw Pittman. Format: Progsv adult rock. News staff: one; News: 5 hrs wkly. Target aud: 24-55; upscale professionals. ♦Gary H. Chetkof, chmn & pres; Ike Phillips, exec VP, sr VP & adv VP; Phil Howort, gen mgr; Greg Gattine, progmg dir.

Wurtsboro

WZAD(FM)— Sept 1, 1990: 97.3 mhz; 620 w. 718 ft. TL: N41 36 04 W74 33 17. Stereo. Box 416, 2 Pendell Rd., Poughkeepsie 12602. Phone: (845) 471-1500. Fax: (845) 454-1204. E-mail: randyturner@mix97fm.com. Web Site: www.mix97fm.com. Licensee: Cumulus Licensing Corp. Group owner: Cumulus Media Inc. (acq 1-23-02; grpsl). Akin, Gump, Strauss, Hauer & Feld. Format: Oldies. News staff: one; News: 5 hrs wkly. Target aud: 25-54; upscale, educated. ♦Lew Dickie, pres; Chuck Benfer, gen mgr.

Yonkers

WRTN(FM)—See New Rochelle

Youngstown

WTOR(AM)— May 6, 1998: 770 khz; 9 kw-D. TL: N43 13 05 W78 56 53. 904 Center St., Lewiston 14092-1737. Phone: (716) 754-9514. Fax: (716) 754-9515. Licensee: Birach Broadcasting Corp. (group owner; acq 1996; $409,000 less land cost for CP). Format: International mus. Target aud: Ethnic; Serbian, Lithuanian, Sp, Pol, Macedonian. ♦Sima Birach, CEO, gen mgr & opns mgr.

North Carolina

Aberdeen

WEEB(AM)—See Southern Pines

WKQB(FM)—See Southern Pines

WQNX(AM)— January 1982: 1350 khz; 2.5 kw-D, 28 w-N, DA-2. TL: N35 07 20 W79 24 57. Box 1350 28315. Phone: (910) 944-1350. Fax: (910) 944-8182. E-mail: qtalk@pinehurst.net. Web Site: www.wqnxtalk.com. Licensee: Golf Capital Broadcasting Inc. (acq 1987; $128,000; 4-20-87). Format: News/talk. ♦T.O. Calcutt, gen mgr; N.M. Calcutt, gen sls mgr.

Ahoskie

*WBKU(FM)— 2002: 91.7 mhz; 87 kw. Ant 430 ft. TL: N36 05 45 W77 12 30. Drawer 3206, Tupelo, MS 38803. Phone: (662) 844-8888. Fax: (662) 842-6791. Licensee: American Family Association. Group owner: American Family Radio Format: Christian. ♦Marvin Sanders, gen mgr.

WQDK(FM)— Sept 2, 1968: 99.3 mhz; 3 kw. 300 ft. TL: N36 16 46 W77 01 59. Stereo. 332 Highway 42 W. 27910. Phone: (252) 332-7993. Fax: (252) 332-6887. Licensee: Max Radio of the Carolinas Licenses LLC. Group owner: MAX Media L.L.C. (acq 11-12-2002; grpsl). Format: Country. Spec prog: Farm 7 hrs wkly. ♦Don Upchurch, gen mgr & opns mgr.

WRCS(AM)— Apr 25, 1948: 970 khz; 1 kw-D. TL: N36 16 46 W77 01 59. 443 North Carolina Hwy 42 W 27910. Phone: (252) 332-3101. Fax: (252) 332-3103. E-mail: wrcs@gate811.net. Licensee: WRCS-AM 970 Inc. (acq 6-14-02). Format: Gospel. ♦J. C. Watford, gen mgr, opns mgr, gen sls mgr & news dir; Willie Jones, progmg dir; Willie Jones, mus dir.

Albemarle

WPZS(FM)— February 1958: 100.9 mhz; 3 kw. Ant 200 ft. TL: N35 22 40 W80 11 38. (CP: COL Indian Trail. 6 kw, ant 328 ft. TL: N35 07 29 W80 43 30). Stereo. 2303 W. Morehead St., Charlotte 28208. Phone: (704) 358-0211. Fax: (704) 358-3752. Licensee: Radio One of North Carolina LLC. (group owner; acq 11-12-2004; $11.5 million). Format: Inspirational. ♦Debbie Kwei, gen mgr.

WSPC(AM)— July 1947: 1010 khz; 1 kw-D, 64 w-N. TL: N35 22 40 W80 11 38. Box 550 28002. Secondary address: 1234 Magnolia St. 28802. Phone: (704) 983-1580. Fax: (704) 983-1436. E-mail: wspc@c&c.net. Web Site: 1010wspc.com. Licensee: Stanly Communications Inc. (acq 2-5-2004; $600,000. with WZKY(AM) Albemarle). Brooks, Pierce, McLendon, Humphrey & Leonard. Format: News/talk. News staff: one. Target aud: General. ♦Bill Norman, sls VP; Matt Smith, gen mgr, opns VP & news dir.

WZKY(AM)— July 9, 1956: 1580 khz; 1 kw-D, 12 w-N. TL: N35 21 38 W80 10 39. Stereo. Box 550, 1234 Magnolia St. 28002-0550. Phone: (704) 983-1580. Fax: (704) 983-1436. Web Site: www.1010wspc.com. Licensee: Stanly Communications Inc. (acq 2-5-2004; $600,000. with WSPC(AM) Albemarle). Format: Oldies. Target aud: 30 plus. ♦Susi Norman, sr VP & adv dir; Bob Brpwn, stn mgr; John Caudle, opns dir; Matt Smith, opns mgr & news dir; William Norman Jr., gen mgr, gen sls mgr & mktg dir; Larry Schropp, engrg dir.

Asheboro

WKRR(FM)— November 1948: 92.3 mhz; 100 kw. 1,275 ft. TL: N35 22 40 W80 11 38. Stereo. Box 36070, Greensboro 27406. Phone: (336) 274-8042. Fax: (336) 274-1629. Web Site: www.rock92.com. Licensee: Dick Broadcasting Co. Inc. of Tennessee (acq 4-84). Format: Classic rock. Target aud: 18-49. ♦Allen Dick, CEO, chmn & pres; David Henderlight, CFO; Bruce Wheeler, VP, gen mgr & progmg VP; James Kerr, opns mgr & natl sls mgr; Jennifer Hart, gen sls mgr; Neil Matson, mktg mgr; Dave Ailcen, prom mgr; Doug McKnight, progmg dir & mus dir; Chris Demm, news dir; Tom Caldwell, chief of engrg.

WKXR(AM)— May 24, 1947: 1260 khz; 5 kw-D, 500 w-N, DA-2. TL: N35 43 26 W79 48 21. 1119 Eastview Dr. 27203. Phone: (336) 625-2187/ 625-1260. E-mail: wkxr@atomic.net. Web Site: www.wkxr.com. Licensee: Randolph Broadcasting Inc. (acq 8-4-86; $500,000; 7-7-86). Network: AP Network News, Jones Radio Networks. Format: Country. News: 8 hrs wkly. Target aud: 18 plus. Spec prog: Farm one hr, gospel 10 hrs wkly. ♦Edward F. Swicegood II, pres & gen mgr; Ted Swicegood, opns mgr; Larry Reed, gen sls mgr & progmg dir; Larry Reid, mktg dir & chief of engrg.

*WTJY(FM)— June 30, 1999: 89.5 mhz; 10 kw. 544 ft. TL: N35 36 55 W79 53 28. Box 25775, Winston-Salem 27114. Phone: (336) 788-9959. Fax: (336) 788-7199. E-mail: joyfm@bellsouth.net. Web Site: www.joyfm.org. Licensee: Positive Alternative Radio Inc. Group owner: Baker Family Stations (Positive Radio Group) Booth, Freret, Imlay & Tepper. Format: Southern gospel. ♦Rodney Baucom, gen mgr.

Asheville

*WCQS(FM)— 1975: 88.1 mhz; 1.6 kw. 1,168 ft. TL: N35 35 23 W82 40 26. Stereo. 73 Broadway 28801. Phone: (828) 253-6875. Fax: (828) 253-6700. Web Site: www.wcqs.org. Licensee: Western N.C. Public Radio Inc. (acq 1984). Network: Network: NPR, PRI. Cohn & Marks. Format: Class, jazz, news. News staff: one; News: 35 hrs wkly. Target aud: 25 plus. Spec prog: Folk 9 hrs wkly. ♦Ed Subkis, gen mgr; Margaret Marchur, sls dir; Barbara Sayer, progmg dir; David Hurand, news dir; Richard J. Kowal, news dir; Tom Spaight, chief of engrg.

WFGW(AM)—See Black Mountain

WISE(AM)— 1939: 1310 khz; 5 kw-D, 1 kw-N, DA-N. TL: N35 37 09 W82 34 21. Stereo. Saga Communications of NC, 90 Lookout Rd. 28804. Phone: (828) 253-1310. Fax: (828) 253-5619. Licensee: Asheville Radio Partners LLC (acq 5-1-02; $1.7 million). Network: ABC. Format: Sports. News staff: one; News: 15 hrs wkly. Target aud: 35 plus; mature upscale audience. ♦Randy Cable, VP; Chris Hoffman, prom dir; Jeremy Debrull, progmg dir; Tim Nesse, engrg VP.

WKSF(FM)—Listing follows WWNC(AM).

*WLFA(FM)— 1975: 91.3 mhz; 440 w. 3,340 ft. TL: N35 36 02 W82 39 07. 2420 Wade Hampton Blvd., Greenville, SC 29615. Phone: (800) 849-8930. Phone: (828) 254-9532. Fax: (864) 292-8428. Web Site: www.hisradio.com. Licensee: Asheville Educational Association Inc. Format: Contemp Christian mus. ♦Jim Campbell, pres; Alan Henderson, gen mgr; Ted McCall, chief of engrg.

WMIT(FM)—See Black Mountain

WMYI(FM)—See Greenville, SC

WSKY(AM)— Apr 11, 1947: 1230 khz; 1 kw-U. TL: N35 35 43 W82 33 57. 40 Westgate Pkwy., Suite F 28806. Phone: (828) 251-2000. Fax: (828) 251-2135. Web Site: www.willkinsradio.com. Licensee: Wilkins Communications Network Inc. (group owner; acq 1996). Network: CBS. Format: Gospel. Target aud: 25-54. Spec prog: Gospel 6 hrs wkly. ♦Ruthie Spears, gen mgr; Chris Campbell, progmg dir.

WWNC(AM)— Feb 22, 1927: 570 khz; 5 kw-U, DA-N. TL: N35 35 49 W82 36 20. Box 6447 28806. Phone: (828) 253-3835. Fax: (828) 255-7850. Web Site: www.wwnc.com. Licensee: Capstar TX L.P. Group owner: Clear Channel Communications Inc. (acq 8-30-00; grpsl). Network: Motor Racing Net, ABC Information & Entertainment. Rep: McGavren Guild. Format: News/talk. News staff: 3; News: 30 hrs wkly. Target aud: 25-54. Spec prog: Farm one hr, gospel 3 hrs, relg 3 hrs wkly. ♦Diane Augram, gen mgr; Shaunna Conner, prom dir & prom mgr; Jim Edwards, progmg dir; Bill McClement, news dir; Lemont Bryant, chief of engrg.

WKSF(FM)—Co-owned with WWNC(AM). August 1947: 99.9 mhz; 53 kw. 2,672 ft. TL: N35 25 32 W82 45 25. Stereo. Web Site: www.99kisscountry.com. Format: Country. News: 3 hrs wkly. Target aud: 25-44. ♦Andy Woods, mus dir.

Atlantic

WTKF(FM)— May 1992: 107.3 mhz; 7 kw. Ant 607 ft. TL: N34 53 01 W76 30 21. Box 70, Newport 28570-0070. Secondary address: 5447 Hwy. 70, Morehead City 28557. Phone: (252) 247-6343. Phone: (800) 818-2255. Fax: (252) 247-7343. Web Site: www.wtkf107.com. Licensee: Atlantic Ridge Telecasters Inc. (acq 11-30-94; $430,000; 1-16-95). Network: Network: Network: Westwood One, Motor Racing Net, USA. Format: News/talk, sports. Target aud: 25 plus; educated, informed. ♦Lockwood Phillips, CEO; Ben Ball, gen mgr; Shane Willis, opns mgr.

Atlantic Beach

*WBJD(FM)— 1999: 91.5 mhz; 50 kw. Ant 384 ft. TL: N34 45 34 W76 51 16. c/o WTEB(FM), 800 College Ct., New Bern 28562. Phone:

North Carolina

(252) 638-3434. Fax: (252) 638-3538. Web Site: www.publicradioeast.org. Licensee: Craven Community College. Format: News & Ideas. ♦ Kathleen Beal, gen mgr.

Aurora

WSTK(FM)—Not on air, target date: unknown: 104.5 mhz; 4.2 kw. Ant 393 ft. TL: N35 18 09 W76 34 00. 702 Hartness Rd., Statesville 28677. Phone: (704) 878-9004. Licensee: Media East LLC (acq 1-15-2003). ♦ Ronald Benfield, pres & gen mgr.

Banner Elk

WZJS(FM)— Aug 5, 1989: 100.7 mhz; 6 kw. 758 ft. TL: N36 10 34 W81 50 05. 738 Blowing Rock Rd., Boone 28607. Phone: (828) 264-2411. Fax: (828) 264-2412. Web site: www.mix1023fm.com. Licensee: Aisling Broadcasting of Banner Elk LLC (group owner; acq 12-1-2003; $2.2 million. with WATA(AM) Boone). Network: Motor Racing Net. Format: Contemp Christian. News staff: one; News: 14 hrs wkly. Target aud: 18-44. Spec prog: Gospel one hr, bluegrass 3 hrs wkly. ♦ Jonathan Hoffman, CEO & sr VP; Andy Glass, opns dir.

Bath

*****WZPE(FM)**— 2005: 90.1 mhz; 675 w. Ant 128 ft. TL: N35 28 32 W76 48 44. Box 828, Wake Forest 27588. Phone: (919) 556-5178. Fax: (919) 556-9273. Web site: www.wcpe.org. Licensee: Educational Information Corp. Format: Classic. ♦ Deborah S. Proctor, gen mgr.

Bayboro

WNBB(FM)— 2001: 97.9 mhz; 14.5 kw. Ant 433 ft. TL: N35 00 02 W76 49 58. Stereo. 233 Middle St., Suite 107B, New Bern 28562. Phone: (252) 638-8500. Fax: (252) 638-8597. E-mail: mail@bear979.com. Web Site: www.bear979.com. Licensee: Coastal Carolina Radio LLC (acq 11-25-2003; $800,000). Network: ABC. Format: Classic country. Target aud: 35-64; adults. ♦ Dann Miller, gen mgr.

Beaufort

*****WXBE(FM)**— 2005: 88.5 mhz; 1 kw. Ant 180 ft. TL: N34 43 26 W55 43 18. Drawer 2440, Tupelo, MS 38801. Phone: (662) 844-8888. Fax: (662) 842-6791. Web Site: www.afr.net. Licensee: American Family Association. Group owner: American Family Radio. Format: Christian. ♦ Marvin Sanders, gen mgr.

Beech Mountain

WECR-FM— 1996: 102.3 mhz; 130 w. 1,948 ft. TL: N36 11 03 W81 52 48. 738 Blowing Rock Rd., Boone 28607. Phone: (828) 264-2411. Fax: (828) 264-2412. E-mail: info@werc1023.com. Web Site: www.mix1023.com. Licensee: Aisling Broadcasting of Banner Elk LLC (group owner; acq 4-1-2004; grpsl). Network: CBS Radio. Format: Light adult contemp. News staff: one; News: 2 hrs wkly. Target aud: 25-54. Spec prog: North Carolina Univ. football, basketball, jazz. ♦ Jonathan Hoffman, CEO & gen mgr.

Belhaven

WQZL(FM)— Oct 15, 1980: 101.1 mhz; 31 kw. Ant 607 ft. TL: N35 18 18 W76 45 45. Stereo. 500 Newbridge St., Jacksonville 28540. Phone: (910) 522-4141. Fax: (910) 455-0330. Web Site: www.wqsl.com. Licensee: NM Licensing LLC. Group owner: NextMedia Group L.L.C. (acq 11-26-2001; grpsl). Network: ABC Daytime Direction. Format: R&B. News: 3 hrs wkly. Target aud: 35-54; baby boomers. ♦ Brad Blake, gen mgr.

Belmont

WCGC(AM)— Dec 11, 1954: 1270 khz; 5 kw-D, 500 w-N, DA-2. TL: N35 15 05 W81 03 26. Stereo. Box 1360, 6021 W. Wilkinson Blvd. 28012. Phone: (704) 825-2812. Fax: (704) 825-2127. E-mail: wcgc1270am@yahoo.com. Licensee: WHVN Inc. Group owner: GHB Radio Group (acq 4-17-98; $250,000). Network: Westwood One. Format: Relg,talk. News staff: 2; News: 8 hrs wkly. Target aud: General. Spec prog: Sports. ♦ Tom Gentry, pres & gen mgr; Chris Preslar, opns dir, progmg dir, mus dir, news dir & pub affrs dir; Larry Hess, gen sls mgr, prom mgr & adv mgr; Stu Albert, chief of engrg.

Benson

WPYB(AM)— Sept 1, 1961: 1130 khz; 1 kw-D. TL: N35 21 40 W78 34 45. Box 215 27504. Phone: (919) 894-1130. Fax: (919) 894-1530. E-mail: wpbyb@surrealnet.net. Web Site: www.wpyb.org. Licensee: Benson-Dunn Broadcasting Inc. (acq 5-1-96; $250,000). Format: Country,bluegrass, gospel. Target aud: General. ♦ Jasper L. Tart, pres & gen mgr; Mable Sue Tart, exec VP.

Biltmore Forest

WOXL-FM— 2002: 96.5 mhz; 1.85 kw. Ant 1,171 ft. TL: N35 35 23 W82 40 26. 90 Lookout Rd., Asheville 28804. Phone: (828) 259-9695. Fax: (828) 253-5619. Web Site: www.965woxl.com. Licensee: Saga Communications of North Carolina LLC. (acq 7-7-2005; $8 million). Format: Oldies. ♦ Larry Williams, gen mgr.

Black Mountain

WFGW(AM)— May 27, 1962: 1010 khz; 50 kw-D, 500 w-N, 19 kw-CH, DA-3. TL: N35 36 19 W82 21 00. Box 159, 1330 U.S. Hwy. 70 28711. Phone: (828) 669-8477. Fax: (828) 669-6983. E-mail: thankyou@brb.org. Web Site: www.wfgw.org. Licensee: Blue Ridge Broadcasting Corp. Network: AP Radio. Fisher, Wayland, Cooper, Leader & Zaragoza L.L.P. Format: Southern gospel, talk. News: 1 hrs wkly. Spec prog: Black 1 hrs wkly. ♦ Billy Graham, chmn; David Bruce, pres; Jim Kirkland, gen mgr; Miranda Curtis, dev mgr; Carol Davis, progmg dir; Mike Dwinell, engr.

WMIT(FM)— Co-owned with WFGW(AM). June 1, 1942: 106.9 mhz; 35 kw. Ant 3,109 ft. TL: N35 44 06 W82 17 11. Stereo. Web Site: www.wmit.org. (Acq 1963). Format: Contemp Christian music & teaching. News: one hr wkly. Spec prog: Children 2.5 hrs wkly. ♦ Matt Stockman, mus dir.

WZNN(AM)— Feb 26, 1966: 1350 khz; 1 kw-D, 74 w-N. TL: N35 37 19 W82 19 02. 22 S. Pack Sq. 28711. Phone: (828) 251-1352. Fax: (828) 251-1336. Web Site: www.action1350.com. Licensee: Zybek Media Group LLC (acq 12-6-2004; $375,000). Network: Network: CNN Radio, Jones Radio Networks, Westwood One. Format: News/talk, sports. News staff: one; News: 15 hrs wkly. Target aud: General. ♦ Beth Howerton, pres; Truett Yarborough, gen mgr.

Blowing Rock

WXIT(AM)— 1983: 1200 khz; 10 kw-D, 7 kw-CH. TL: N36 09 17 W81 39 41. 643G Greenway Business Park, Boone 28605. Phone: (828) 265-1023. Fax: (828) 264-8902. E-mail: wxit@newstalk1200.com. Licensee: Aisling Broadcasting of Banner Elk LLC (group owner; acq 2-10-2004; grpsl). Network: CBS. Format: News/talk. Target aud: 25-60; professionals. Spec prog: Relg 8 hrs, big band 4 hrs wkly. ♦ Donna Hoffman, VP; Jonathan Hoffman, gen mgr; Bill Fisher, opns mgr.

Boiling Springs

*****WGWG(FM)**— Jan 22, 1974: 88.3 mhz; 50 kw. 302 ft. TL: N35 13 52 W81 42 57. Stereo. Box 876, 106 Emily Ln. 28017. Phone: (704) 406-3525. Fax: (704) 434-4338. E-mail: info@wgwg.org. Web Site: www.wgwg.org. Licensee: Gardner-Webb University. Format: Triple A. News: one hr wkly. Target aud: General. Spec prog: Gospel 15 hrs wkly. ♦ Frank Campbell, pres; Dan McClellan, stn mgr; Matt Webber, gen mgr & opns mgr.

Boone

*****WASU-FM**— May 18, 1972: 90.5 mhz; 220 w. 57 ft. TL: N36 12 48 W81 41 10. Stereo. Appalachian State Univ., Wey Hall 28608. Phone: (828) 262-3170. Phone: (828) 262-2543. Licensee: Appalachian State University. Network: Westwood One. Format: New rock, AOR, jazz. Target aud: 18-30; college students & area residents. Spec prog: Urban contemp 6 hrs, blues 2 hrs, Christian rock 3 hrs, country 8 hrs wkly. ♦ Carl Tyrie, gen mgr.

WATA(AM)— September 1950: 1450 khz; 1 kw-U. TL: N36 12 59 W81 42 06. Stereo. 738 Blowing Rock Rd. 28607. Phone: (828) 264-2411. Fax: (828) 264-2412. E-mail: wata@boone.net. Licensee: Aisling Broadcasting of Banner Elk LLC (group owner; acq 12-1-2003; $2.2 million. with WZJS(FM) Banner Elk). Network: ABC. Format: Local newstalk. News staff: one; News: 4 hrs wkly. Target aud: 25-54. Spec prog: Gospel 5 hrs, Paul Harvey 2.5 hrs.,Watauga High sports wkly. ♦ Jonathan Hoffman, CEO & gen mgr; Andy Glass, opns mgr.

Directory of Radio

Brevard

WGCR(AM)— Sept 16, 1985: 720 khz; 10 kw-D. TL: N35 15 10 W82 40 28. Stereo. 3400New Hendersonville Hwy., Pisgah Forest 28768. Phone: (828) 884-9427. Fax: (828) 883-9427. Web Site: www.wgcr.net. Licensee: Anchor Baptist Broadcasting Association. (acq 2-87). Network: USA. Format: Relg, news. Target aud: General. Spec prog: Gospel. ♦ Randy C. Barton, pres, gen mgr & gen sls mgr; Shanna Barton, prom mgr & progmg dir; Shamma Barton, news dir; Lamar Owen, chief of engrg.

WSQL(AM)— July 6, 1950: 1240 khz; 1 kw-U. TL: N35 13 23 W82 42 20. Box 1240 28712. Secondary address: 1319 Wilson Rd., Pisgah Forest 28768. Phone: (828) 877-5252. Fax: (828) 877-5253. Licensee: A & L Broadcasting Inc. (acq 3-14-97; $110,000). Network: CBS. Format: Talk, adult contemp, MOR. Target aud: General. Spec prog: Jazz 10 hrs, gospel 8 hrs, relg 4 hrs wkly. ♦ Allen Reese, gen mgr, opns mgr & gen sls mgr; Leah Reese, progmg dir.

Bryson City

WBHN(AM)— Oct 1, 1967: 1590 khz; 500 w-D, 37 w-N. TL: N35 25 41 W83 26 18. Box 1309 28713. Phone: (828) 488-2682. Fax: (828) 488-3594. E-mail: wbhn@dnet.net. Licensee: Starcast South Inc. Group owner: Starcast Systems Inc. (acq 10-84; $355,000; 10-15-84). Network: ABC Information & Entertainment. Format: Oldies. ♦ Jack Mullen Jr., pres; Rob Henline, gen mgr, gen sls mgr & mus dir; J.B. Jacobs, chief of engrg.

Buie's Creek

*****WCCE(FM)**— Oct 7, 1974: 90.1 mhz; 3 kw. 105 ft. TL: N35 24 36 W78 44 21. Stereo. Box 1030, Science Bldg., Campbell Univ. 27506. Phone: (910) 893-1745. Fax: (910) 893-1746. E-mail: wcce@mailcenter.campbell.edu. Web Site: www.wccefm.org. Licensee: Campbell University. Format: Smooth jazz, soft rock, relg. News: 10 hrs wkly. Target aud: General. Spec prog: Bluegrass 3 hrs, big band 4 hrs wkly. ♦ Travis Autry, gen mgr; Carolyn Bowden, opns mgr.

Burgaw

WKXB(FM)— Dec 13, 1964: 99.9 mhz; 100 kw. Ant 774 ft. TL: N34 14 37 W78 07 24. Stereo. 122 Cinema Dr., Wilmington 28403. Phone: (910) 772-6300. Fax: (910) 772-6310. Web Site: www.b999fm.com. Licensee: NM Licensing LLC. (group owner) (acq 12-20-2004; grpsl). Rep: McGavren Guild. Format: Oldies. News staff: one; News: 3 hrs wkly. Target aud: 25-54. ♦ Steven Dinetz, pres; Paul Knight, VP & gen mgr; Barbara Raybourne, gen sls mgr; Missy Andrus, prom dir; Stanley B., progmg dir; Suzanne Jalot, news dir.

WVBS(AM)— June 21, 1963: 1470 khz; 1 kw-D, 93 w-N. TL: N34 32 05 W77 54 31. (CP: TL: N34 31 22 W77 54 17). Box 914, Bible Baptist Church, 2190 Hwy. 117 S. 28425. Phone: (910) 259-5718. E-mail: oldtimer@intrstar.net. Licensee: Grace Christian School. (acq 12-23-94; 2-27-95). Format: Christian. ♦ Carl Gibbs, gen mgr; Dick Jones, stn mgr.

Burlington

WPCM(AM)— September 1941: 920 khz; 5 kw-D, 55 w-N. TL: N36 05 50 W79 29 03. Box 1119 27215. Secondary address: 1109 Tower Dr. 27215. Phone: (336) 584-0126. Fax: (336) 584-6333. Licensee: Carolina Radio Group Inc. Group owner: Curtis Media Group (acq 3-1-90). Format: Oldies and beach. Target aud: 25 plus; upscale. ♦ Bill Whitley, gen mgr.

WZTK(FM)—Co-owned with WPCM(AM). December 1946: 101.1 mhz; 100 kw. Ant 1,191 ft. TL: N35 56 31 W79 26 33. Stereo. Fax: (336) 854-1039. Web Site: www.fmtalk1011.com. Format: Talk. Target aud: 25-54. Spec prog: Bluegrass 3 hrs wkly. ♦ Bryon Tucker, progmg dir.

WRSN(FM)— 1946: 93.9 mhz; 100 kw. 1,269 ft. TL: N35 52 16 W79 09 38. Stereo. 3100 Smoketree Ct., Suite 700, Raleigh 27604-1052. Phone: (919) 877-0939. Fax: (919) 876-2929. Licensee: Capstar TX L.P. Group owner: Clear Channel Communications Inc. (acq 8-30-00; grpsl). Format: Adult contemp. Target aud: 25-49; men. ♦ Jon Robbins, CFO & opns dir; Ken Spitzer, gen mgr; Tammy O'Dell, VP & sls dir; Jinnie Forsythe, gen sls mgr & rgnl sls mgr; Jessica Hayes, prom dir; Brian Taylor, progmg dir; Fred Pace, chief of engrg.

Broadcasting & Cable Yearbook 2006

Stations in the U.S. — North Carolina

Developers & Brokers of Radio Properties — contact American Media Services at our suite: Philadelphia Marriott Downtown 215-625-2900 / 843-972-2200 / americanmediaservices.com / Charleston, SC / Dallas, TX · Chicago, Il · Austin, TX — American Media Services, LLC

Burlington-Graham

WBAG(AM)— 1946: 1150 khz; 1 kw-D, 48 w-N. TL: N36 06 48 W79 27 00. Box 2450 27216. Secondary address: 1745 Burch Bridge Rd. 27217. Phone: (336) 226-1150. Fax: (336) 226-1180. Licensee: Gray Broadcasting LLC (acq 10-27-98; $150,000). Format: Adult standards/talk. News staff: 2; News: 25 hrs wkly. Target aud: 25-54; general. Spec prog: Relg 5 hrs wkly. ♦Joe Gray, gen mgr; Harry Myers, opns mgr & progmg dir; Bill Huff, gen sls mgr; Tim Walker, chief of engrg.

WSML(AM)—See Graham

Burnsville

WKYK(AM)— May 28, 1967: 940 khz; 5 kw-D, 250 w-N, DA-N. TL: N35 55 32 W82 16 20. Stereo. Box 744, Mark Group Bldg. 28714. Secondary address: 749 Sawmill Road 28714. Phone: (828) 682-3510. Phone: (828) 682-3798. Fax: (828) 682-6227. Fax: (828) 682-0998. E-mail: 940@wkyk.com. Web Site: www.wkyk.com. Licensee: Mark Media Inc. (acq 4-10-69). Network: ABC. Format: Real country. News staff: one; News: 10 hrs wkly. Target aud: 18-55. Spec prog: Gospel 12 hrs wkly. ♦J. Ardell Sink, CEO & pres; Remelle Sink, exec VP; Michael Sink, VP, gen mgr & chief of engrg; Holly S. Hall, opns mgr & mktg dir; Mary Marsh, prom dir; Steve Murphy, news dir & pub affrs dir.

Buxton

***WBUX(FM)**— 1999: 90.5 mhz; 5.9 kw. Ant 154 ft. TL: N35 16 01 W75 32 38. 120 Friday Center Dr., Chapel Hill 27517-9495. Phone: (919) 966-5454. Fax: (919) 966-5955. E-mail: wunc@wunc.org. Web Site: www.wunc.org. Licensee: Board of Trustees/University of North Carolina at Chapel Hill. Network: Network: Network: NPR, PRI, CBC Radio One. Format: News & Info. News staff: 7; News: 124 hrs wkly. Spec prog: Folk 20 hrs wkly.

WHDX(FM)—Not on air, target date: unknown: 99.9 mhz; 50 kw. Ant 164 ft. TL: N35 14 44 W75 32 02. 1400 12th St. N., Suite 5, Arlington, VA 22209-3666. Phone: (703) 527-1434. E-mail: radiobuxton@yahoo.com. Licensee: David Wilson. ♦David Wilson, gen mgr.

WHDZ(FM)—Not on air, target date: unknown: 101.5 mhz; 50 kw. Ant 164 ft. TL: N35 14 44 W75 32 02. 1400 12th St. N., Suite 5, Arlington, VA 22209-3666. Phone: (703) 527-1434. E-mail: radiobuxton@yahoo.com. Licensee: David Wilson. ♦David Wilson, gen mgr.

Calabash

WYNA(FM)— June 1964: 104.9 mhz; 15 kw. Ant 338 ft. TL: N33 49 19 W78 46 18. Stereo. 3926 Wesley St., Suite 301, Myrtle Beach, SC 29578. Phone: (843) 903-9962. Fax: (843) 903-1797. E-mail: staff@cool1049.com. Web Site: www.cool1049.com. Licensee: Coastline Communications of Carolina Inc. (acq 1-14-99; $1.1 million). Format: Hot adult contemp. Target aud: 25-49; adult females. ♦Jerome Bresson, pres; Will Isaacs, gen mgr.

Camp Lejeune

WSME(AM)— Sept 8, 1980: . Stn currently dark 1120 khz; 6 kw-D, 4.2 kw-CH. TL: N34 43 03 W77 16 57. 337 E. Centre St., Jacksonville 28540. Secondary address: 333 Center St. 28546. Phone: (910) 355-9763. Fax: (910) 355-9763. Licensee: CTC Media Group Inc. (group owner). Format: Country. ♦Edwin Lee Afflerbach, VP.

Canton

WLZR(AM)— July 12, 1954: 970 khz; 5 kw-D. TL: N35 31 58 W82 51 58. 90 Lookout, Asheville 28804. Phone: (828) 259-9695. Fax: (828) 253-5619. Licensee: Saga Communications of North Carolina LLC. Group owner: Saga Communications Inc. (acq 3-11-2003). Miller & Fields, P.C. Format: Oldies of the 50s, 60s & 70s. Target aud: 28-50. Spec prog: Relg 7 hrs wkly. ♦Ed Christian, pres; Randy Cable, gen mgr.

WPTL(AM)— Aug 3, 1963: 920 khz; 500 w-D, 38 w-N. TL: N35 31 15 W82 48 24. Box 909, 133 Pisgah Dr. 28716. Phone: (828) 648-3576. Phone: (828) 648-3577. Fax: (828) 648-3577. E-mail: admin@wptlradio.com. Web Site: www.wptlradio.com. Licensee: Skycountry Broadcasting Inc. (acq 3-1-78). Network: Network: AP Radio, Jones Radio Networks. Format: C&W, relg. News: 8 hrs wkly. Target aud: 25 plus; adult family. ♦Linda Reck, VP & stn mgr; William Reck, pres & gen mgr.

Carolina Beach

WMYT(AM)— July 1, 1989: 1180 khz; 10 kw-D, DA. TL: N34 09 03 W78 04 48. Box 957, Wilmington 28402-0957. Phone: (910) 763-2452. Fax: (910) 763-6578. E-mail: familyradio@familyradio.to. Web Site: www.familyradio.to. Licensee: Family Radio Network Inc. (group owner; acq 3-2-01; $100,000. with WDVV(FM) Wilmington). Format: Relg, Sp. Target aud: General. ♦Jim Stephens, gen mgr.

WUIN(FM)— October 1996: 106.7 mhz; 5.6 kw. Ant 341 ft. TL: N34 03 02 W77 57 20. 122 Cinema Dr., Wilmington 28403. Phone: (910) 772-6300. Web Site: www.carolinapenguin.com. Licensee: Ocean Broadcasting II LLC (acq 7-3-2003; $1.5 million. with WMFD(AM) Wilmington). Format: Triple A. ♦Dennis Deason, gen mgr; Mark Keefe, progmg dir.

Chadbourn

WVOE(AM)— Apr 23, 1962: 1590 khz; 1 kw-D. TL: N34 21 05 W78 50 38. 1528 Old 74 Hwy. W. 28431. Phone: (910) 654-5621. Fax: (910) 654-4385. E-mail: wvoe@weblink.net. Licensee: Ebony Enterprises Inc. Format: Urban contemp, r & b, jazz, gospel. Target aud: General; white & blue collar workers, housewives, students, sr citizens. ♦Willie J. Walls, pres; Willie J. Walls, gen mgr; Willie J. Walls, stn mgr.

Chapel Hill

WCHL(AM)— Jan 25, 1953: 1360 khz; 5 kw-D, 1 kw-N, DA-N. TL: N35 56 18 W79 01 36. Stereo. 88 VilCom Cir., Suite 100 27514. Phone: (919) 933-4165. Fax: (919) 968-3748. E-mail: cdixon@wchl1360.com. Web Site: www.wchl1360.com. Licensee: Vilcom Interactive Media LLC (acq 8-5-2004; $775,000). Network: Network: ABC, CBS Radio, Jones Radio Networks. Format: News/talk. News staff: 3; News: 25 hrs wkly. Target aud: 25-54; educated adults with high median incomes. ♦Christy Jones Taylor, VP & gen mgr; Christy Dixon, stn mgr; Ron Stutts, progmg dir.

WDCG(FM)—See Durham

WLLQ(AM)— December 1973: 1530 khz; 10 kw-D, DA. TL: N35 58 07 W79 00 10. Estuardo Valdemar Rodriguez and Leonor Rodriguez Stns, 1010 Vermont Ave. N.W., Suite 100, Washington, DC 20005. Phone: (202) 638-1959. Fax: (202) 393-7464. Licensee: Estuardo Valdemar Rodriguez and Leonor Rodriguez. Group owner: WRTP Radio Network (acq 12-13-2004; grpsl). Format: Sp. ♦Estuardo Valdemar Rodriguez, gen mgr.

WRSN(FM)—See Burlington

***WUNC(FM)**— Nov 3, 1952: 91.5 mhz; 100 kw. Ant 1,361 ft. TL: N35 51 59 W79 10 00. 120 Friday Center Dr. 27517-9495. Phone: (919) 966-5454. Fax: (919) 966-5955. E-mail: wunc@wunc.org. Web Site: www.wunc.org. Licensee: University of North Carolina at Chapel Hill. Network: Network: Network: NPR, PRI, CBC Radio One. Brooks, Pierce, McLendon, Humphrey & Leonard, LLP. Format: News & info. News staff: 7; News: 124 hrs wkly. Target aud: 25-54; highly educated, pro-active in the community, concerned about local issues. Spec prog: Folk 20 hrs wkly. ♦Joan Siefert Rose, gen mgr; Kevin Wolf, opns mgr; Regina Yeager, dev dir; Fred Wasser, progmg mgr; Emily Hanford, news dir; John Francioni, engrg dir & chief of engrg.

***WXYC(FM)**— Mar 18, 1977: 89.3 mhz; 400 w. 280 ft. TL: N35 54 15 W79 02 50. Stereo. Ch5210, Carolina Union 27599. Phone: (919) 962-7768. Phone: (919) 962-8989 (request line). E-mail: wxyc@unc.edu. Web Site: www.wxyc.org. Licensee: Student Educational Broadcasting Inc. Format: Div. News: 3 hrs wkly. Target aud: General. ♦Jason Perlmutter, stn mgr.

Charlotte

WBT(AM)— Apr 10, 1922: 1110 khz; 50 kw-U, DA-N. TL: N35 07 56 W80 53 23. Stereo. One Julian Price Pl. 28208. Phone: (704) 374-3500. Fax: (704) 374-3889. Web Site: www.wbt.com. Licensee: Jefferson-Pilot Communications Co. (group owner; acq 9-45). Network: CBS. Format: News/talk. News staff: 5; News: 20 hrs wkly. Target aud: 35-54; men. ♦David Stoneciper, CEO; Terry stone, pres; Rick Jackson, sr VP & gen mgr; Lisa Gergely, gen mgr; Terry Mace, dev VP; Larry Rideaux, natl sls mgr; Matt Dubois, prom mgr; Bill White, progmg dir; Marshall Adams, news dir; Jerry Dowd, chief of engrg.

WCGC(AM)—See Belmont

***WFAE(FM)**— June 29, 1981: 90.7 mhz; 100 kw. 760 ft. TL: N35 15 06 W80 41 12. Stereo. 8801 J.M. Keynes Dr., Suite 91 28262-8485. Phone: (704) 549-9323. Fax: (704) 547-8851. E-mail: wfae@wfae.org. Web Site: www.wfae.org. Licensee: University Radio Foundation Inc. (acq 4-12-93). Network: Network: NPR, PRI. Garvey, Schubert & Barer. Format: News/talk. News staff: 4; News: 42 hrs wkly. Target aud: 35-49; professionals. ♦Roger Sarow, gen mgr; Tena Simmons, opns dir; Barbara Vermeire, dev dir; Catherine Little, dev dir & sls dir; Renee Ballos, prom dir & pub affrs dir; Paul Stribling, progmg dir; Mark Rumsey, news dir; Jobie Sprinkle, engrg dir.

WFNA(AM)— Dec 1, 2003: 1660 khz; 10 kw-D, 1 kw-N. TL: N35 14 57 W80 51 41. 1520 South Blvd., Suite 300 28203. Phone: (704) 342-2644. Fax: (704) 727-8985. Licensee: Infinity Radio Holdings Inc. Group owner: Infinity Broadcasting Corp. Network: Sporting News Radio Network. Rep: D & R Radio, Katz Radio. Leventhal, Senter & Leman. Format: Sports. ♦Bill Schoening, gen mgr; O.J. Stout, opns mgr.

WFNZ(AM)— 1941: 610 khz; 5 kw-D, 1 kw-N, DA-2. TL: N35 17 53 W80 53 40. 1520 South Blvd # 300 28203. Phone: (704) 319-9369. Fax: (704) 319-3934. Licensee: Infinity Radio Holdings Inc. Group owner: Infinity Broadcasting Corp. (acq 11-13-98; grpsl). Format: Sports. Target aud: 18 plus; male, sports oriented. ♦William Schoening, gen mgr; D.J. Stout, opns mgr & progmg dir; Scott Vandivier, gen sls mgr; Chele Fassig, prom dir; Eric Lakey, chief of engrg.

WNKS(FM)—Co-owned with WFNZ(AM). July 21, 1962: 95.1 mhz; 100 kw, 1,542 ft. TL: N35 21 44 W81 09 19. Stereo. 4015 Stuart Andrew Blvd. 28217. Phone: (704) 331-9510. Fax: (704) 344-8656. Web Site: www.kiss951.com. Format: CHR. ♦John Renolds, opns mgr; Rob Whitehead, gen sls mgr; Chad Fitzsimmons, mktg mgr & prom mgr.

WGFY(AM)— Jan 18, 1955: 1480 khz; 5 kw-U, DA-2. TL: N35 17 05 W80 52 34. 1100 S Troyn St., Suite 210 28203. Phone: (704) 377-2223. Fax: (704) 373-2245. Web Site: www.radiodisney.com. Licensee: Radio Disney Group LLC. Group owner: ABC Inc. (acq 8-22-00; grpsl). Fisher, Wayland, Cooper, Leader & Zaragoza. Format: Children, Radio Disney. News staff: 6; News: 25 hrs wkly. Target aud: Under 12; kids, mothers, families. Spec prog: Children pop top 40. ♦Jon Pendleton, gen mgr & rgnl sls mgr; Kevin Campbell, pub affrs dir; Clay Steely, engrg VP.

WGSP(AM)— Aug 23, 1958: 1310 khz; 5 kw-D. TL: N35 15 23 W80 51 52. 3719 Latrobe Dr., Suite 860 28211. Phone: (704) 442-7277. Fax: (704) 442-9518. Licensee: Norsan Consulting and Management Inc. (acq 12-13-2004; $2 million). Network: Network: ABC Information & Entertainment, ABC Daytime Direction. Format: Hispanic music. ♦Norberto Sanchez, pres.

WHVN(AM)— 1958: 1240 khz; 1 kw-U, DA-1. TL: N35 12 00 W80 48 39. 5732 N. Tryon St. 28213. Phone: (704) 596-4900. Fax: (704) 596-6939. E-mail: bboonewhvn@bellsouth.net. Licensee: WHVN Inc. Group owner: GHB Radio Group (acq 7-11-83). Network: ABC Information & Entertainment. Reddy, Begley & McCormick. Format: Relg. Target aud: 35 plus; Christian. ♦George Buck, pres; Tom Gentry, gen mgr, sls VP, mktg VP, prom VP & adv VP; Buddy Boone, progmg mgr; Brant Hart, pub affrs dir; Steward Albert, chief of engrg.

Broadcasting & Cable Yearbook 2006

North Carolina

WKQC(FM)— 1972: 104.7 mhz; 96 kw. Ant 1,210 ft. TL: N35 15 06 W80 41 12. Stereo. 4015 Stuart Andrew Blvd. 28217. Phone: (704) 372-1104. Fax: (704) 523-1047. Web Site: www.star1047.com. Licensee: Infinity Radio Holdings Inc. Group owner: Infinity Broadcasting Corp. (acq 11-13-98; grpsl). Leventhal, Senter & Lerman. Format: Hits of the 70s & 80s. News staff: 2. Target aud: 25-54. ♦Keith Cornwell, gen mgr; John Reynolds, prom mgr.

WOGR(AM)— May 7, 1964: 1540 khz; 2.5 kw-D, DA. TL: N35 13 45 W80 58 32. (CP: TL: N35 16 26 W80 51 50). Box 16408, 1501 N. I-85 Service Rd. 28216. Secondary address: Box 16408 28297. Phone: (704) 393-1540. Phone: (704) 393-1588. Fax: (704) 393-1527. E-mail: cynthia@wordnet.org. Web Site: wordnet.org. Licensee: Victory Christian Center Inc. (acq 7-27-88). Network: Salem Radio Network. Gardner, Carton & Douglas. Format: Relg. Target aud: General. ♦Robyn Gool, pres; Wayne Hammond, gen mgr; James Sims, opns mgr; Cynthia Neely, gen sls mgr, prom dir & pub affrs dir; Eleasah Hammond, mus dir.

WPEG(FM)—See Concord

WSOC-FM— 1947: 103.7 mhz; 100 kw. 1,040 ft. TL: N35 15 41 W80 43 38. (CP: Ant 1,059 ft.). Stereo. 1520 South Blvd, Suite 300 28203. Phone: (704) 522-1103. Fax: (704) 523-2104. Web Site: www.wsocfm.com. Licensee: Infinity Radio Holdings Inc. Group owner: Infinity Broadcasting Corp. (acq 11-13-98; grpsl). Leventhal, Senter & Lerman. Format: Country. Target aud: 25-54. ♦Bill Schoening, VP & gen mgr; Barry Roach, natl sls mgr; Billy Grooms, rgnl sls mgr; Chele Fassig, prom dir; Jeff Roper, progmg dir; Rick McCracken, mus dir; Frank Laseter, pub affrs dir; Eric Lakey, chief of engrg.

*WYFQ(AM)— Oct 14, 1933: 930 khz; 5 kw-D, 1 kw-N, DA-N. TL: N35 16 00 W80 54 05. 11530 Carmel Commons Blvd. 28226. Secondary address: 2004 Walkup Ave., Monroe 28110. Phone: (704) 523-5555. Fax: (704) 291-7807. E-mail: wyfq@bbnradio.org. Licensee: Bible Broadcasting Network Inc. (group owner; acq 2-6-92; $475,000; 2-24-92). Format: Traditional Christian. News: 3 hrs wkly. Target aud: General. ♦Dan Austin, gen mgr & stn mgr; John Woolery, progmg dir; Ron Muffley, engrg dir.

Cherry Point

WANG(AM)—See Havelock

WSSM(FM)—See Havelock

Cherryville

WCSL(AM)— June 28, 1967: 1590 khz; 1 kw-D, 42 w-N. TL: N35 22 28 W81 24 23. 1366 Startown Rd., Lincolnton 28092. Phone: (704) 735-8071. Fax: (704) 732-9567. Licensee: HRN Broadcasting Inc. (acq 4-14-2004; $500,000. with WLON(AM) Lincolnton). Network: Westwood One. Format: Oldies, sports. Target aud: General. Spec prog: Loc sports 3 hrs wkly. ♦Mark Boyd, pres; Lanny Ford, gen mgr, sls dir, gen sls mgr & adv dir; Milton Biggerstaff, mus dir; Larry Seagle, news dir; Tim Biggerstaff, progmg dir & pub affrs dir; Larry Schropp, chief of engrg.

China Grove

WRNA(AM)— Nov 17, 1980: 1140 khz; 1 kw-D, 250 w-CH, DA-D. TL: N35 34 20 W80 35 21. Box 8146, Kannapolis 28083. Secondary address: 633 Patterson St. 28023. Phone: (704) 857-1101. Fax: (704) 857-0680. E-mail: info@fordbroadcasting.com. Web Site: www.fordbroadcasting.com. Licensee: South Rowan Broadcasting Co. Group owner: Ford Broadcasting Inc. Network: USA. Format: Southern gospel. Target aud: General. ♦Carl Ford, pres, gen mgr, stn mgr, gen sls mgr & progmg mgr; Taylor Ford, exec VP; Angela Ford, sr VP.

Claremont

WCXN(AM)— Sept 5, 1985: 1170 khz; 10 kw-D. TL: N35 43 34 W81 08 52. 1812 Davie Ave, Statesville 28677. Phone: (828) 459-9803. Fax: (828) 459-9805. E-mail: metroradio@carolina.rr.com. Licensee: Davidson Media Carolinas Stations LLC. Group owner: Davidson Media Group LLC (acq 5-10-2004; grpsl). Network: USA. Format: Sp. Target aud: General. ♦Peter W. Davidson, pres; Russ Jones, gen mgr & progmg dir; Larry Schropp, chief of engrg.

Clayton

WHPY(AM)— 1974: 1590 khz; 5 kw-D, DA. TL: N35 38 49 W78 30 21. Box 535, Fellowship Baptist Church, 911 W. Main St. 27520. Phone: (919) 553-6774. Fax: (919) 359-0016. E-mail: whpy@dockpoint.net. Licensee: Fellowship Baptist Church Inc. dba Fellowship Christian Academy. (acq 8-4-97). Format: Christian. ♦Charles Ennis, pres; Keith Holland, gen mgr & stn mgr.

Clinton

WCLN(AM)— Sept 27, 1975: 1170 khz; 5 kw-D. TL: N35 01 21 W78 20 58. Box 28, 118 E. Main St. 28328. Phone: (910) 592-8949. Fax: (910) 592-3732. Web Site: www.oldies1170.com. Licensee: Broadcasting Good News Inc. Format: Oldies, beach. Spec prog: Community, gospel 8 hrs wkly. ♦George Wilson, pres; Pat Dixon, gen mgr.

WCLN-FM— June 11, 1967: 107.3 mhz; 13 kw. 453 ft. TL: N35 02 14 W78 29 56. Stereo. 996 Helen St., Fayetteville 28303. Phone: (910) 864-5028. Fax: (910) 864-6270. E-mail: wcln@christian107.com. Web Site: www.christian107.com. Licensee: Christian Listening Network Inc. (acq 7-94). Format: Contemp Christian, inspirational. ♦George Wilson, pres; Linda Miller, gen mgr & sls dir; Dan DeBruler, prom dir; Steve Turley, progmg dir & progmg mgr; Van Clough, chief of engrg.

WRRZ(AM)— Apr 5, 1947: 880 khz; 1 kw-D. TL: N34 58 40 W78 18 15. Box 378 28329. Phone: (910) 592-2165. Fax: (910) 592-8556. E-mail: wrrzradio@webtv.net. Licensee: Sanchez Broadcasting Corp. (acq 10-14-2004). Brooks, Pierce, McLendon, Humphrey & Leonard. Format: Sp. Target aud: 25 plus. Spec prog: Black 5 hrs, relg 6 hrs, Sp 5 hrs wkly. ♦Victor Sanchez, pres; Martha Sanchez, gen mgr.

Columbia

WERX-FM— Mar 14, 1983: 102.5 mhz; 64 kw. 689 ft. TL: N36 05 00 W76 36 00. Stereo. Box 1418, Nags Head 27959. Secondary address: 2422 S. Wrightsville Ave., Nags Head 27959. Phone: (252) 441-1024. Fax: (252) 441-2109. Web Site: www.1025theshark.com. Licensee: East Carolina Radio of Elizabeth City Inc. Group owner: East Carolina Radio Group. Network: UPI. Format: Oldies. Target aud: 18-49; moderate to high income, mobile professionals & families with children. Spec prog: Flashback, in concert, off the record, BBC classic tracks. ♦Rick Loesch, pres & gen mgr; Tom Charity, opns mgr; Chris Ling, gen sls mgr.

WRSF(FM)—Licensed to Columbia. See Elizabeth City

Concord

WEGO(AM)— Mar 5, 1943: 1410 khz; 1 kw-D, 182 w-N. TL: N35 24 29 W80 36 41. Box 126 28026. Phone: (704) 788-9346. Fax: (704) 720-9346. Licensee: GHB of Waxhaw Inc. Group owner: GHB Radio Group (acq 10-28-2002; $450,000. with WSVM(AM) Valdese). Format: Timeless Classics. ♦Bob Brown, gen mgr.

WPEG(FM)— June 15, 1962: 97.9 mhz; 95 kw. 1,608 ft. TL: N35 21 44 W81 09 19. Stereo. 1520 South Blvd., Suite 300, Charlotte 28203. Phone: (704) 342-2644. Fax: (704) 227-8979. Web Site: www.power98fm.com. Licensee: Infinity Radio Holdings Inc. Group owner: Infinity Broadcasting Corp. (acq 11-13-98; grpsl). Network: Westwood One. Rep: Katz Radio. Format: Urban contemp. News staff: one; News: 20 hrs wkly. Target aud: 12 plus; Black. Spec prog: Gospel 6 hrs, mix show 8 hrs wkly. ♦Bill Schoening, gen mgr; Terri Avery, opns mgr.

Cullowhee

*WWCU(FM)— Jan 15, 1977: 90.5 mhz; 760 w. -771 ft. TL: N35 18 40 W83 10 34. Stereo. Box 2728, Western Carolina Univ. 28723. Secondary address: WCU-Moore Bldg., Suite 18 28723. Phone: (828) 227-7454. Phone: (828) 227-7173 (request line). Fax: (828) 227-7099. E-mail: info@wwcufm.com. Web Site: www.wwcufm.com. Licensee: Western Carolina University. Network: ABC. Format: Adult contemp; rock; sports;. Target aud: 25-54; univ students & faculty, general public. ♦Will Candler, gen mgr; Matt Sprinkler, opns dir.

Dallas

*WSGE(FM)— Oct 27, 1980: 91.7 mhz; 3 kw. Ant 134 ft. TL: N35 18 28 W81 11 31. Stereo. Ray Craig Classroom Bldg., 201 Hwy. 321 S. 28034-1499. Phone: (704) 922-4286. Fax: (704) 922-4294. Fax: (704) 922-2347. E-mail: jpowell@gaston.ccnc.us. Web Site: www.wsge.org. Licensee: Gaston College Board of Trustees. Format: AAA, Variety. News: 5 hrs wkly. Target aud: General. ♦Pat Skinner, pres; Stephanie Michael-Pickett, gen mgr; Sarah Trexler, stn mgr.

WZRH(AM)— Jan 1, 1963: 960 khz; 1 kw-D, 500 w-N, DA-N. TL: N35 18 03 W81 10 13. Box 477 28034. Secondary address: 407 Robinson Clemmer Rd. 28034. Phone: (704) 922-3411. Phone: (704) 922-5960. Fax: (704) 922-6998. E-mail: manager@wzrh.com. Web Site: www.wzrh.com. Licensee: Truth Broadcasting Corp. (group owner; acq 6-30-2004; $775,000). Smithwick & Belendiuk. Format: Talk. News: 10 hrs wkly. Target aud: Male 25-59; college educ, income 50K. ♦Stuart Epperson, pres & natl sls mgr.

Davidson

*WDAV(FM)— Sept 1, 1973: 89.9 mhz; 100 kw. 807 ft. TL: N35 26 55 W80 50 24. Stereo. Box 7178 28035-7178. Secondary address: 423 N. Main St. 28036. Phone: (704) 894-8900. Fax: (704) 894-2997. E-mail: wdav@davidson.edu. Web Site: www.wdav.org. Licensee: Trustees of Davidson College. Network: Network: PRI, NPR. Fletcher, Heald & Hildrreth. Format: Class. News: 2 hrs wkly. Target aud: General. ♦F. Kim Hodgson, gen mgr; Jill McGuire, dev dir; Luann Ritsema, mktg dir & prom dir; Frank Dominguez, progmg dir; Ted Weiner, mus dir; Larry Schropp, chief of engrg.

Dobson

WYZD(AM)— Oct 10, 1978: 1560 khz; 1 kw-D. TL: N36 23 36 W80 44 05. Box 797, 131 1/2 Atkin St. 27017. Phone: (336) 356-1560. Licensee: Gospel Broadcasting Inc. (acq 5-3-02). Format: Gospel. ♦Ricky Cothren, gen mgr.

Dunn

WCKB(AM)— Dec 7, 1946: 780 khz; 7 kw-D, 1 w-N. TL: N35 17 00 W78 35 49. Box 789 28335. Secondary address: 17336 US 421 S. 28334. Phone: (910) 892-3133. Fax: (910) 892-3135. E-mail: wckb@wckb780.com. Web Site: www.wckb780.com. Licensee: N.C. Central Broadcasters Inc. (acq 9-15-89; $216,000; 10-2-89). Format: Southern gospel, religious. News: 6 hrs wkly. Target aud: 25 plus; Christian, family-oriented with regional interests. Spec prog: Buy-sell-trade 9 hrs wkly. ♦Charles Fowler, pres; Ronald Tart, gen mgr, gen sls mgr, natl sls mgr, rgnl sls mgr, prom mgr & adv dir; Margie Hughes, progmg dir; Neal Wood, asst music dir; Lottie Squires, pub affrs dir; Bill Lambert, chief of engrg.

WRCQ(FM)— May 17, 1971: 103.5 mhz; 48 kw. 502 ft. TL: N35 03 09 W78 38 54. Stereo. Box 35297, Fayetteville 28303-0297. Secondary address: 1009 Drayton Rd., Fayetteville 28303. Phone: (910) 864-5222. Fax: (910) 864-3065. Web Site: www.rock103rocks.com. Licensee: Cumulus Licensing Corp. Group owner: Cumulus Media Inc. (acq 3-12-01; grpsl). Network: ABC. Borsari & Paxson. Format: Rock/AOR. News staff: one; News: one hr wkly. Target aud: 18-49. ♦Tom Haymond, gen mgr.

Durham

WDCG(FM)— Feb 28, 1948: 105.1 mhz; 100 kw. 1,141 ft. TL: N35 52 20 W79 09 29. Stereo. 3100 Smoketree Ct., Suite 700, Raleigh 27604. Phone: (919) 871-1051. Fax: (919) 876-2929. Web Site: www.g105.com. Licensee: Capstar TX L.P. Group owner: Clear Channel Communications Inc. (acq 8-30-00; grpsl). Network: ABC. Format: Contemporary Hit. Target aud: 18-49. ♦Ken Spitzer, gen mgr; Jon Robbins, opns dir; Tammy O'Dell, sls dir; Myron Bethea, gen sls mgr; Jessica Hayes, prom dir; Rick Schmidt, progmg dir; Dan McLeod, pub affrs dir; Fred Pace, chief of engrg.

WDNC(AM)— Apr 9, 1934: 620 khz; 5 kw-D, 1 kw-N, DA-2. TL: N36 02 10 W78 58 07. 407 Blackwell St. 27701. Phone: (919) 687-6580. Fax: (919) 688-0180. E-mail: dncprod@curtismedia.com. Web Site: www.dncradio.com. Licensee: Durham Herald Co. Inc. (Group owner: Curtis Media Group (acq 12-30-86). Network: ABC. Rep: McGavren Guild. Format: News/talk, sports. News staff: 3; News: 17 hrs wkly. Target aud: 35-64. ♦Don Curtis, pres; Jeremy Thompson, stn mgr & opns mgr; Beth Przestrzlski, sls dir; Paul Michels, chief of opns & progmg dir; Eddie Harrell, chief of engrg.

WDUR(AM)— 1947: 1490 khz; 1 kw-U. TL: N35 58 03 W78 53 18. 3100 Smoketree Ct., Suite 700, Raleigh 27604. Phone: (919) 878-1500. Fax: (919) 876-8578. Web Site: www.wdur.com. Licensee: Triangle Sports Broadcasters LLC Group owner: Clear Channel Communications Inc. (acq 6-28-2005; $1.13 million). grpsl). Rep:

Stations in the U.S.   North Carolina

Developers & Brokers of Radio Properties
contact American Media Services at our suite:
Philadelphia Marriott Downtown
215-625-2900
843-972-2200
americanmediaservices.com
Charleston, SC
Dallas, TX • Chicago, Il • Austin, TX
American Media Services, LLC

Clear Channel. Wilmer, Cutler & Pickering. Format: Black Gospel. News: 0. Target aud: 35-54; 35-54. ♦Ken Spitzer, gen mgr; Jon Robbins, opns dir.

WFXC(FM)— May 15, 1971: 107.1 mhz; 2.6 kw. Ant 502 ft. TL: N35 58 41 W78 48 59. 8001-101 Creedmoor Rd., Raleigh 27613. Phone: (919) 848-9736. Fax: (919) 863-4859. Web Site: www.foxyhits.com. Licensee: Radio One Licenses LLC. Group owner: Radio One Inc. (acq 11-8-2001; grpsl). Format: Urban contemp. News staff: one; News: 5 hrs wkly. Target aud: 25-54; African American. Spec prog: Gospel 4 hrs wkly. ♦Gary Weiss, gen mgr; Cy Young, opns VP.

*WNCU(FM)— August 1995: 90.7 mhz; 50 kw. 433 ft. TL: N36 03 33 W78 57 14. Stereo. 1801 Fayetteville St., Box 19875 27707. Phone: (919) 560-9628. Fax: (919) 560-5283. E-mail: ethorpe@wpo.nccu.edu. Web Site: www.wncu.org. Licensee: North Carolina Central University. Network: Network: NPR, PRI. Format: Jazz, news/talk, info. News staff: one; News: 33 hrs wkly. Target aud: 25-54; middle class/middle age. Spec prog: Black, gospel. ♦Edith Thorpe, gen mgr, mktg VP, prom VP, adv VP & progmg VP; Chris Whitfield, opns mgr; Uchenna Johnson, dev dir & sls dir; B.H. Hudson, mus dir; Kimberley Pierce, news dir & pub affrs dir; Jim Davis, engrg mgr.

WRSN(FM)—Burlington

WSRC(AM)— Oct 14, 1954: 1410 khz; 5 kw-D, 290 w-N, DA-2. TL: N36 01 44 W78 51 00. 3202 Guess Rd. 27705-2647. Phone: (919) 477-7999. Fax: (919) 477-9811. Licensee: Durham Christian Radio Inc. Group owner: Willis Broadcasting Corp. (acq 6-2-87). Format: Relg. News staff: one. Target aud: 35-54. ♦L.E. Willis Sr., pres; Anthony Lee, gen mgr & gen sls mgr; Shelia Chislom, opns VP & sls dir; Harold Jackson, progmg dir; Roger King, mus dir; Steve Saterfield, news dir; Jermaine White, pub affrs dir.

WTIK(AM)— 1945: 1310 khz; 5 kw-D, 1 kw-N, DA-2. TL: N36 01 30 W78 54 08. 1812 Davie Ave., Statesville 28677. Phone: (919) 220-3226. Fax: (919) 220-0006. Licensee: Davidson Media Carolinas Stations LLC. Group owner: Davidson Media Group LLC (acq 5-10-2004; grpsl). Network: Moody. Format: Black gospel, Christian teaching. News staff: 2. Target aud: 24-54. ♦Peter W. Davidson, pres; Larry Cobb, stn mgr & gen sls mgr; Chuck Harris, opns mgr.

*WXDU(FM)— November 1983: 88.7 mhz; 1.18 kw. 103 ft. TL: N36 02 08 W79 04 48. Stereo. Box 90689, Duke Station 27708. Phone: (919) 684-2957. Fax: (919) 684-3260. E-mail: wxdu@duke.edu. Web Site: www.wxdu.org. Licensee: Duke University. Format: Diversified. Target aud: General. Spec prog: Jazz 18 hrs, urban sound & hip hop 12 hrs wkly. ♦Jim Davis, chief of engrg.

Eden

WCLW(AM)— Aug 16, 1970: 1130 khz; 1 kw-D. TL: N36 31 21 W79 45 55. 116 S. Franklin St., Reidsville 27320. Phone: (336) 634-1774. Web Site: www.carolinabaptistcollege.com/radio.html. Licensee: Dr. Jerry L. Carter dba Reidsville Baptist Church. (acq 6-26-98; $150,000). Format: Gospel. Target aud: 25-49. ♦Dean Lundy, gen mgr, opns mgr & progmg mgr.

WGBT(FM)— Mar 20, 1949: 94.5 mhz; 100 kw. 981 ft. TL: N36 20 48 W79 54 30. Stereo. 2-B Pai park, Greensboro 27409. Secondary address: Box 3018, Winston Salem 27102. Phone: (336) 822-2000. Fax: (336) 887-0104. Licensee: Clear Channel Broadcasting Licenses Inc. Group owner: Clear Channel Communications Inc. (acq 1996; grpsl). Rep: Clear Channel. Format: Urban. ♦Bill Dotson, gen mgr; Chris Rollins, progmg dir.

WLOE(AM)— Dec 20, 1946: 1490 khz; 1 kw-U. TL: N36 30 21 W79 46 18. Box 279, Mayodan 27027. Phone: (336) 427-9696; (336) 627-9563. Fax: (336) 548-4636. E-mail: info@wloewmyn.com. Web Site: www.wloewmyn.com. Licensee: Mayo Broadcasting Corp. (acq 6-90; $100,000; 6-4-90). Network: Salem Radio Network, USA. Format: Info, talk, relg. News staff: one; News: 30 hrs wkly. Target aud: 25 plus; general. ♦Richard D. Hall, pres; Mike Moore, gen mgr; Annette Moore, stn mgr.

Edenton

WBXB(FM)— June 18, 1976: 100.1 mhz; 50 kw. 302 ft. TL: N36 07 11 W76 35 29. Stereo. Box 765 27932. Secondary address: 1900 Paradise Rd. 27932. Phone: (252) 482-8680. Fax: (252) 482-4260. Licensee: Willis Family Broadcasting Inc. (group owner; acq 3-4-92; grpsl; 3-23-92). Network: American Urban. Format: Gospel. News: 8 hrs wkly. Target aud: General. ♦Bishop L.E. Willis Sr., pres; Toina Willis, gen mgr.

WZBO(AM)— November 1955: 1260 khz; 1 kw-D, 34 kw-N. TL: N36 05 00 W76 36 00. Box 950 27932. Phone: (252) 482-2104. Fax: (252) 482-5591. Web Site: www.ecri.net. Licensee: East Carolina Radio of Elizabeth City Inc. Group owner: East Carolina Radio Group (acq 3-12-90; $400,000. with co-located FM; FTR: 4-2-90). Network: UPI. Tharrington, Smith & Hargrove. Format: Adult standard. Target aud: 35 plus; Edenton residents, business owners, professionals, NASCAR fans, community service groups. Spec prog: Sports. ♦Rick Loesch, pres, gen mgr, stn mgr & opns mgr.

Elizabeth City

WCNC(AM)— September 1939: 1240 khz; 1 kw-U. TL: N36 18 38 W76 13 56. Box 1246 27906-1246. Secondary address: 911 Parsonage St. Ext. 27909. Phone: (252) 335-4379. Fax: (252) 338-5275. E-mail: swalker@ecri.net. Web Site: ecri.net. Licensee: East Carolina Radio of Elizabeth City Inc. Group owner: East Carolina Radio Group (acq 10-29-98; $230,000). Network: Network: AP Radio, Westwood One. Format: Adult standards. News staff: one; News: 22 hrs wkly. Target aud: 35 plus. Spec prog: Gospel 7 hrs wkly. ♦Rick Loesh, pres; Tom Charity, opns mgr & gen sls mgr; Sam Walker, progmg dir & progmg mgr.

WGAI(AM)— Nov 2, 1947: 560 khz; 1 kw-D, 500 w-N, DA-2. TL: N36 20 16 W76 14 49. Stereo. Box 1897, Kill Devil Hills 27948. Phone: (252) 335-4371. Phone: (252) 480-4655. Fax: (252) 441-8063. Licensee: Max Radio of the Carolinas Licenses LLC. Group owner: MAX Media L.L.C. (acq 11-12-2002; grpsl). Network: CNN Radio. Format: News/talk, sports. News staff: 3; News: 30 hrs wkly. Target aud: General. Spec prog: Relg 4 hrs, farm 7 hrs, Black 4 hrs, relg 4 hrs wkly. ♦Mike Smith, gen mgr.

*WGPS(FM)— February 2003: 88.3 mhz; 50 kw. Ant 446 ft. TL: N36 18 40 W76 17 34. 905 Halstead Blvd., Suite 29 27909. Phone: (252) 334-1883. Fax: (252) 333-1459. E-mail: wgpsradio@earthlink.net. Web Site: www.wgpsradio.com. Licensee: CSN International (group owner). Format: Christian teaching, praise & worship music. ♦Jeff Ozanne, gen mgr; Darla Ozanne, progmg dir.

WKJX(FM)— Aug 21, 1984: 96.7 mhz; 50 kw. Ant 407 ft. TL: N36 12 10 W75 52 23. Stereo. Box 1246 27906. Secondary address: 911 Parsonage St. E. 27906. Phone: (252) 338-0196. Fax: (252) 338-5275. E-mail: swalker@ecri.net. Web Site: www.ecri.net. Licensee: East Carolina Radio of Elizabeth City Inc. Group owner: East Carolina Radio Group (acq 5-21-98; $475,000). T-N. Format: Soft adult contemp. News staff: one; News: 1 hr wkly. Target aud: 18-55. ♦Rick Loesch, pres; Tom Charity, gen mgr & opns mgr; Sam Walker, progmg dir.

WRSF(FM)—(Columbia). June 13, 1983: 105.7 mhz; 100 kw. 613 ft. TL: N35 53 18 W76 13 50. (CP: Ant 987 ft.). Stereo. Box 1418, Nags Head 27959. Secondary address: 2422 S. Wrightsville Ave., Nags Head 27959. Phone: (252) 441-1024. Fax: (252) 441-2109. Web Site: www.ecri.net. Licensee: East Carolina Radio of Elizabeth City Inc. Group owner: East Carolina Radio Group (acq 1996). Format: Country. News staff: one; News: 5 hrs wkly. Target aud: 18-54; young & mid-range adults. ♦Tom Charity, opns mgr; Chris Ling, gen sls mgr & natl sls mgr.

*WRVS-FM— Mar 18, 1986: 89.9 mhz; 41 kw. 280 ft. TL: N36 16 55 W76 12 44. Stereo. 1704 Weeksville Rd., Campus Box 800, Williams Hall 27909. Phone: (252) 335-3515. Fax: (252) 335-3745. Licensee: Elizabeth City State University. Network: NPR. Format: Urban contemp, var/div, pub affrs. News staff: one; News: 5 hrs wkly. Target aud: 18-24; young adult, college. Spec prog: Jazz 19 hrs, Black 15 hrs, gospel 19 hrs wkly. ♦Mickey L. Burnim, CEO; Talbert Gray, gen mgr.

Elizabethtown

WBLA(AM)— Aug 3, 1956: 1440 khz; 5 kw-D, 189 w-N. TL: N34 37 38 W78 37 23. Box 458, 512 Peanut Rd. 28337. Phone: (910) 862-3184. Phone: (910) 862-2000. Fax: (910) 872-0100. E-mail: wgqr1057@carolina.net. Web Site: www.wgqr1057.com. Licensee: Sound Business of Elizabethtown Inc. (acq 4-29-98; $525,000 with co-located FM). Format: Oldies, beach. News: 5 hrs wkly. Target aud: 25-54. Spec prog: Black gospel/relg 8 hrs wkly. ♦Bruce Dickerson, VP; Lee Hauser, pres & gen mgr; Al Radlein, progmg dir; Buddy Wommack, chief of engrg.

WGQR(FM)—Co-owned with WBLA(AM). December 1989: 105.7 mhz; 6 kw. Ant 387 ft. TL: N34 37 38 W78 37 23. Stereo. Web Site: www.wgqr1057.com. Format: Oldies, beach. News: 6 hrs wkly.

Elkin

WIFM-FM— 1949: 100.9 mhz; 600 w. 709 ft. TL: N36 11 33 W80 50 59. Box 1038 28621. Secondary address: 813 N. Bridge St. 28621. Phone: (336) 835-2511. Fax: (336) 835-5248. E-mail: wifm@wifmradio.com. Web Site: www.wifmradio.com. Licensee: Yadkin Valley Broadcasting Corp. (acq 1-12-2004; $1.15 million). Network: ABC. Format: Classic hits/Today's hits, Adult contemp. News staff: one. Target aud: 25-45. ♦Gary York, pres; Paula Rice, gen mgr & gen sls mgr; Jerry Laws, progmg dir; Stony Owens, engrg mgr.

Elon

*WSOE(FM)— November 1978: 89.3 mhz; 500 w. 104 ft. TL: N36 06 25 W79 30 22. Stereo. Campus Box 6000 27244. Phone: (336) 584-9763. Phone: (336) 278-7510. Fax: (336) 278-7298. E-mail: wsoe@elon.edu. Web Site: www.elon.edu/wsoe. Licensee: Elon University. Format: Diversified. ♦Jon Chuk, gen mgr; Greg Piel, progmg dir & progmg.

Erwin

*WUAW(FM)— May 11, 1990: 88.3 mhz; 3 kw. 191 ft. TL: N35 20 15 W78 39 49. Stereo. Triton High School, 215 Maynard Lake Rd. 28339. Phone: (910) 897-8070. Fax: (910) 897-3148. E-mail: wuaw883fm@gaggle.net. Web Site: www.wuaw.homestead.com. Licensee: Central Carolina Community College. Format: Variety/Diverse (urban, contemp hits/top-40, rock, alternative). News: 7 hrs wkly. Spec prog: Black, country & rock. ♦Dr. Marvin Joyner, pres; Ron McLamb, gen mgr & progmg dir; Dr. Jim Davis, chief of engrg.

Fair Bluff

WODR(FM)— 2003: 105.3 mhz; 11 kw. Ant 492 ft. TL: N34 17 01 W78 48 09. 6100 Fairview Rd., Suite 650, Charlotte 28210. Phone: (704) 643-4148. Licensee: The Padner Group LLC (acq 12-4-2003; $1.25 million). Format: Oldies.

WZFB(AM)— July 1988: . Stn currently dark 1480 khz; 1 kw-D, 48 w-N. TL: N34 19 23 W79 00 07. Box 1038, Whiteville 28439. Phone: (910) 642-8214. Licensee: Good Samaritan Broadcasting of Pioche Inc. (acq 3-11-2004; $125,000). ♦Pat Guinn, gen mgr.

Fairmont

WFMO(AM)— July 13, 1953: 860 khz; 1 kw-D. TL: N34 31 03 W79 06 19. Box 668, Hwy 41 N. 28340. Phone: (910) 628-6781. Fax: (910) 628-6648. Licensee: Pro Media Inc. Group owner: Clark-Pittman Group (acq 12-31-86; $600,000 with co-located FM; 11-10-86). Format: Black, gospel, relg. Target aud: 25-54. Spec prog: Farm 5 hrs wkly. ♦James C. Clark, pres, gen mgr, stn mgr & gen sls mgr.

WSTS(FM)— August 1975: 100.9 mhz; 50 kw. Ant 489 ft. TL: N34 16 17 W78 56 24. Stereo. Box 668 28340. Phone: (910) 628-6781. Fax:

(910) 628-6648. E-mail: wstf@carolina.net. Licensee: Davidson Media Station WSTS Licensee LLC. (acq 8-8-2005). Format: Southern gospel. ♦James Clark, gen mgr.

Fairview

WPEK(AM)— July 4, 1997: 880 khz; 1.1 kw-D, DA. TL: N35 32 52 W82 28 16. 1318 Patton Ave., Suite B, Asheville 28816. Phone: (828) 255-1906. Fax: (828) 255-7850. Web Site: www880ThePEK. Licensee: Clear Channel Broadcasting Licenses Inc. Group owner: Clear Channel Communications Inc. (acq 3-21-01; grpsl). Network: CBS. Format: Talk. Target aud: 25-64; generally upscale adults. ♦Ken Salyer, gen mgr.

Farmville

WGHB(AM)— Dec 12, 1959: 1250 khz; 5 kw-D, 2.5 kw-N, DA-2. TL: N35 36 17 W77 34 29. Box 3333, Hwy. 121 N., Greenville 27836. Phone: (252) 317-1250. Web Site: www.pirateradio1250.com. Licensee: Pirate Media Group LLC (acq 11-25-03; $650,000). Network: USA. Format: Talk, sports. News: 8 hrs wkly. Target aud: 25-54. ♦Troy Dreyfus, gen mgr.

WWNK(FM)— Mar 24, 1974: 94.3 mhz; 1.95 kw. 407 ft. TL: N35 36 25 W77 28 05. Stereo. 211 Commerce St., Suite C, Greenville 27835. Phone: (252) 756-9898. Fax: (252) 355-2234. Licensee: ABG North Carolina LLC. Group owner: Archway Broadcasting Group (acq 2-27-2003; $3 million. with WLGT(FM) Washington). Cole, Raywid & Braverman. Format: Country. News: 3 hrs wkly. Target aud: 25-54. ♦Bill Baailey, gen mgr & chief of engrg.

Fayetteville

WAZZ(AM)— 1947: 1490 khz; 1 kw-U. TL: N35 03 45 W78 54 30. 508 Person St. 28301. Phone: (910) 486-2055. Phone: (910) 484-1490. Fax: (910) 323-5635. Licensee: WFLB License L.P. Group owner: Beasley Broadcast Group (acq 1996; $228,635). Network: Westwood One. Rep: D & R Radio. Format: MOR. News staff: one; News: 14 hrs wkly. Target aud: 35-64. Spec prog: Atlanta Braves baseball, Charlotte Hornets basketball, auto racing. ♦George G. Beasley, CEO & gen mgr; Danny Highsmith, sr VP; Mac Edwards, VP; Curt Nunnery, opns mgr, sls dir & gen sls mgr; Bryan Kusilka, natl sls mgr; Van Clough, chief of engrg.

WFAY(AM)— 1947: 1230 khz; 1 kw-U. TL: N35 04 15 W78 52 45. 346 Wagoner Dr. 28303. Phone: (910) 222-3776. Fax: (910) 860-3329. E-mail: wfay@espnradio1230.com. Web Site: www.espnradio1230.com. Licensee: Colonial Radio Group Inc. (acq 1996; $175,000). Network: ABC Information & Entertainment. Format: Sports. Target aud: 25-54; upscale, educated, business people. ♦Jeffrey M. Andrulonis, CEO & gen mgr; Cheryl Roberts, stn mgr.

WFLB(FM)—See Laurinburg

WFNC(AM)— 1940: 640 khz; 10 kw-D, 1 kw-N. TL: N35 04 46 W78 55 58. 1009 Drayton Rd. 28303. Phone: (910) 864-5222. Fax: (910) 864-6208. Web Site: www.cumulus.com. Licensee: Cumulus Licensing Corp. Group owner: Cumulus Media Inc. (acq 3-12-01; grpsl). Network: CBS. Format: News/talk. News staff: 4; News: 20 hrs wkly. Target aud: 35 plus. ♦Tom Haymond, gen mgr & stn mgr; Perry Stone, opns dir; Alan Buffalo, gen sls mgr; Flo Knight, prom dir; Laura Chais-Price, progmg dir, news dir & pub affrs dir; Gail Galbreath, engrg dir.

WQSM(FM)—Co-owned with WFNC(AM). 1947: 98.1 mhz; 100 kw. 830 ft. TL: N35 04 46 W78 55 58. Stereo. Web Site: www.cumulus.com. Format: CHR. Target aud: General. ♦Chris Chaos, progmg dir.

***WFSS(FM)**— Dec 7, 1977: 91.9 mhz; 100 kw. 440 ft. TL: N35 04 22 W78 53 27. Stereo. 1200 Murchison Rd. 28301. Phone: (910) 672-1381. Fax: (910) 672-1964. E-mail: wfss@uncfsu.edu. Web Site: wfss.org. Licensee: Fayetteville State University Board of Trustees. Network: Network: NPR, PRI. Format: Jazz, news. News staff: one; News: 38 hrs wkly. Target aud: 18 plus; general. Spec prog: Reggae 3 hrs, gospel 4 hrs, American Indian 3 hrs, African rhythms 3 hrs, class 3 hrs, folk 3 hrs wkly. ♦Joseph C. Ross, gen mgr; Phyllis Washington, dev dir, mktg dir & prom dir; Janet G. Wright, progmg dir; Jimmy Miller, mus dir; Kathy Klaus, news dir; Eric Lanc, chief of engrg.

WIDU(AM)— Jan 20, 1958: 1600 khz; 5 kw-D, 147 w-N, DA-2. TL: N35 02 58 W78 51 33. Box 2247 28302. Secondary address: 1338 Bragg Blvd. 28301. Phone: (910) 483-6111. Phone: (910) 486-9438. Fax: (910) 483-6601. E-mail: slofton3@aol.com. Licensee: Charles W. Cookman (acq 1-17-89). Format: Black, gospel, news/talk. ♦Wes Cookman, pres; Sandra Lofton, gen mgr; Robert Smith, opns mgr; Val Holiday, progmg dir.

WZFX(FM)—(Whiteville). Feb 21, 1962: 99.1 mhz; 100 kw. 1,000 ft. TL: N34 44 05 W78 47 25. Stereo. Box 710 28302. Phone: (910) 486-4991. Fax: (910) 486-6720. Web Site: www.fox99.com. Licensee: WDAS License L.P. Group owner: Beasley Broadcast Group (acq 5-8-97; $11.5 million). Network: ABC Information & Entertainment. Rep: McGavren Guild. Format: Urban contemp. Target aud: 18-49. ♦George G. Beasley, CEO; Daniel Highsmith, VP & gen mgr; Mac Edwards, opns VP; Walter Sturdivant, sls VP; Tila Comstock, gen sls mgr; Bryan Kusilka, natl sls mgr; Jeff Anderson, progmg mgr; Van Clough, chief of engrg.

Fletcher

WQNQ(FM)— Feb 5, 1991: 104.3 mhz; 470 w. Ant 1,145 ft. TL: N35 31 39 W82 29 49. Stereo. 13 Summerlin Rd., Asheville 28806. Phone: (828) 257-2700. Fax: (828) 281-3299. Licensee: Clear Channel Broadcasting Licenses Inc. Group owner: Clear Channel Communications Inc. (acq 3-21-2001; grpsl). Reddy, Begley & McCormick. Format: 80s, 90s & now. News staff: 2; News: 10 hrs wkly. Target aud: 25-54. Spec prog: Relg 2 hrs, news/talk 5 hrs wkly. ♦Ken Falyer, gen mgr.

Forest City

WTPT(FM)— Sept 10, 1947: 93.3 mhz; 93 kw. Ant 2,030 ft. TL: N35 16 19 W82 14 00. Stereo. Box 5200, Greenville, SC 29606. Secondary address: 225 S. Pleasantburg Dr., Suite B-3, Greenville, SC 29607. Phone: (864) 242-0101. Fax: (864) 271-5029. Web Site: www.newrock933.com. Licensee: Upstate Broadcasting LLC. Group owner: Barnstable Broadcasting Inc. (acq 8-15-00; grpsl). Format: Active rock. ♦John Shea, pres & gen mgr; Mark Hemdrix, opns mgr; Tom Hoyt, sls dir; Hugh Mcpherson, gen sls mgr; Sandy Smith, natl sls mgr; Bob Ross, prom dir; Mark Hendrix, progmg dir; Smack Taylor, mus dir; Paige Pirtle, news dir & pub affrs dir; Blake Lanford, engrg mgr.

WWOL(AM)— Sept 10, 1947: 780 khz; 10 kw-D. TL: N35 21 02 W81 54 04. 1381 W. Main St. 28043. Phone: (828) 245-0078. Fax: (828) 245-8528. E-mail: wwol@rfci.net. Licensee: Holly Springs Baptist Church. (acq 3-1-90; $150,000; 3-19-90). Network: USA. Format: Southern gospel, relg. News staff: 3. Target aud: General. Spec prog: Our community forum, NC family policy issues. ♦Wade H. Huntley, pres & stn mgr; Ray Davis, chief of opns, progmg dir & pub affrs dir; Terri Frashier, sls dir, gen sls mgr & mktg dir.

Franklin

***WFQS(FM)**— Mar 31, 1989: 91.3 mhz; 265 w. 2,304 ft. TL: N35 10 24 W83 34 52. Stereo. 73 Broadway, Asheville 28801. Phone: (828) 253-6875. Fax: (828) 253-6700. Web Site: www.wcqs.org. Licensee: Western N.C. Public Radio Inc. Network: Network: NPR, PRI. Cohn & Marks. Format: Class, jazz, news. News staff: one; News: 35 hrs wkly. Target aud: 25 plus. Spec prog: Folk 9 hrs wkly. ♦Edward Subkis, gen mgr; Margaret Marchuk, sls dir; Barbara Sayer, progmg dir; Richard J. Kowal, mus dir; David Hurand, news dir; Terry Spaight, chief of engrg.

WFSC(AM)— May 5, 1957: 1050 khz; 1 kw-D. TL: N35 12 42 W83 22 07. Box 470 28744. Secondary address: 180 Radio Hill Rd. 28734. Phone: (828) 524-4418. Phone: (828) 524-5395. Fax: (828) 524-2788. E-mail: moore@gacaradio.com. Web Site: www.1050wfsc.com. Licensee: Sutton Radiocasting Corp. Group owner: Georgia-Carolina Radiocasting Companies (acq 12-14-2001; grpsl). Network: Network: CBS, ABC. Dan J. Alpert. Format: MOR. News staff: one; News: 12 hrs wkly. Target aud: 35+. ♦Douglas M. Sutton Jr., pres; Patrick Moore, VP & gen mgr; Chad Dorsette, news dir; Tim Stephens, chief of engrg.

WNCC-FM—Co-owned with WFSC(AM). Sept 1, 1965: 96.7 mhz; 6 kw. 204 ft. TL: N35 12 42 W83 22 07. Stereo. Web Site: www.967wncc.com. Network: ABC. Format: Country. News staff: one; News: 6 hrs wkly. Target aud: 25+.

WPFJ(AM)— May 24, 1979: 1480 khz; 5 kw-D, 13 w-N. TL: N35 10 58 W83 21 27. Stereo. 185 Franklin Plaza 28744. Phone: (828) 369-5033. Fax: (828) 369-3197. E-mail: thedove@wpfj.com. Web Site: www.wpfj.com. Licensee: Drake Enterprises Ltd. (acq 2-16-94; $250,000; 3-28-94). Network: Salem Radio Network. Format: Relg. News: 12 hrs wkly. Target aud: 25-54. ♦Jeremy Duke, stn mgr; Morris Stamey, rgnl sls mgr; Brenda Wooten, prom mgr; Randy Raby, progmg dir.

Fuquay-Varina

WNNL(FM)— Dec 1, 1980: 103.9 mhz; 7.9 kw. 577 ft. TL: N35 35 47 W78 45 18. Stereo. 8001-101 Creedmoor Rd., Raleigh 27613. Phone: (919) 848-9736. Fax: (919) 848-4724. E-mail: mmarinaro@radio-one.com. Web Site: www.thelight1039.com. Licensee: Radio One Licenses LLC. Group owner: Radio One Inc. (acq 11-8-01; grpsl). Network: ABC. Rep: Christal. Format: Inspirational, gospel. News: 20 hrs wkly. Target aud: 25-54; educated, upper income, professionals. ♦Gary Weiss, gen mgr; Cy Young, opns dir; Kim Gattis, sls dir; Jodi Luke, natl sls mgr; Steven Walker, gen sls mgr & prom dir; Jerry Smith, progmg dir.

Garner

WRTG(AM)— Aug 11, 1969: 1000 khz; 1 kw-D. TL: N35 43 50 W78 36 12. Estuardo Valdemar Rodriguez and Leonor Rodriguez Stns, 1010 Vermont Ave. N.W., Suite 100, Washington, DC 20005. Phone: (202) 638-1959. Fax: (202) 393-7464. Licensee: Estuardo Valdemar Rodriguez and Leonor Rodriguez. Group owner: WRTP Radio Network (acq 12-13-2004; grpsl). Network: USA. Format: Mexican rgnl. ♦Estuardo Valdemar Rodriguez, gen mgr.

Gaston

WTRG(FM)— Nov 28, 1988: 97.9 mhz; 1.35 kw. Ant 488 ft. TL: N36 27 38 W77 33 52. Stereo. 3 East 1st St., Roanoke Rapids 27870. Phone: (252) 538-9790. Fax: (252) 538-0378. Licensee: First Media Radio LLC. (group owner; (acq 7-22-2003; grpsl). Format: Urban adult contemp. News: 2 hrs wkly. Target aud: 21-54. ♦Al Haskins, gen mgr; Les Atkins, opns dir.

Gastonia

WBAV-FM— September 1947: 101.9 mhz; 99 kw. Ant 987 ft. TL: N35 13 56 W81 16 35. Stereo. 1520 South Blvd., Suite 300, Charlotte 28203. Phone: (704) 342-2644. Fax: (704) 227-8985. Web Site: www.v1019.com. Licensee: Infinity Radio Holdings Inc. Group owner: Infinity Broadcasting Corp. (acq 11-13-98; grpsl). Network: ABC FM Connection. Rep: Christal. Leventhal, Senter & Leman. Format: Adult contemp. News staff: one; News: 20 hrs wkly. Target aud: 25-54; black adults. Spec prog: Gospel 6 hrs, mixed shows 8 hrs wkly. ♦Bill Schoening, gen mgr; Terri Avery, opns mgr.

WGAS(AM)—See South Gastonia

WGNC(AM)— March 1939: 1450 khz; 1 kw-U. TL: N35 16 32 W81 12 04. 1416 Shelby Hwy., Cherryville 28021. Phone: (704) 868-8222. Fax: (704) 435-1217. E-mail: netoldies@aol.com. Web Site: superstations.net. Licensee: KTC Broadcasting Inc. (acq 10-3-89; $125,000;. FTR: 10-23-89). Format: Oldies, sports, beach. News staff: one; News: 5 hrs wkly. Target aud: 18-49. ♦Calvin R. Hastings, pres, gen mgr & gen sls mgr; Terresa Hastings, VP; Harold Watson, sls dir & adv dir; Lori Deitz, prom mgr; Mike Slade, progmg dir; Andy Foster, mus dir; Anna McGinnis, news dir & pub affrs dir; Larry Schropp, chief of engrg.

WLTC(AM)— Mar 8, 1948: 1370 khz; 5 kw-D. TL: N35 15 40 W81 08 45. Box 11584, Rock Hill, SC 29731. Phone: (803) 329-2760. Fax: (803) 329-3317. E-mail: fneely@rejoiceradio.com. Web Site: www.RejoiceRadio.com. Licensee: Frank Neely. Group owner: Neely Enterprises (acq 4-1-98). Network: USA. Smithwick & Belendiuk. Format: Christian. Target aud: 30 plus. ♦Emma Neely, VP; Frank Neely, gen mgr & stn mgr; Frankie Hemphill, stn mgr.

WZRH(AM)—See Dallas

Goldsboro

WFMC(AM)— Nov 11, 1951: 730 khz; 1 kw-D, 98 w-N. TL: N35 22 25 W78 00 41. Stereo. 914 W. Grantham St. 27530. Phone: (919) 734-4211. Fax: (919) 736-3876. Licensee: New Age Communications Inc. Group owner: Curtis Media Group (acq 6-95; $300,000). Format: Black gospel, relg. News staff: one; News: 10 hrs wkly. Target aud: 18 plus. ♦Donald W. Curtis, pres; Tony Denton, gen mgr; Jeff Davis, opns dir; Bryan Rouse, sls dir; Mike Wilson, progmg dir; Eddie Harreil, chief of engrg.

WGBR(AM)— 1939: 1150 khz; 5 kw-D, 800 w-N, DA-2. TL: N35 22 26 W78 00 42. Stereo. 2581 U.S. Hwy. 70 W. 27530. Phone: (919) 736-1150. Fax: (919) 736-3876. Licensee: New Age Communications L.P. Group owner: Curtis Media Group (acq 2-15-89; $2.2 million with co-located FM; 3-6-89). Network: CNN Radio. Format: News/talk. News staff: one; News: 11 hrs wkly. Target aud: 25 plus. ♦Donald W.

Stations in the U.S.   North Carolina

Developers & Brokers of Radio Properties

contact American Media Services at our suite:
Philadelphia Marriott Downtown
215-625-2900
843-972-2200
americanmediaservices.com
Charleston, SC
Dallas, TX · Chicago, Il · Austin, TX
American Media Services, LLC

Curtis, pres; Tony Denton, gen mgr; Bryan Rouse, gen sls mgr; Wayne Alley, progmg dir; Thomas Vick, news dir; Kari DelaCruz, chief of engrg.

WYMY(FM)—Co-owned with WGBR(AM). 1946: 96.9 mhz; 100 kw. 1,056 ft. TL: N35 23 52 W78 08 07. Stereo. 3012 Highwoods Blvd., Raleigh 27604. Phone: (919) 790-9392. Format: Mexican, Sp. News: 2 hrs wkly. Target aud: 25-54. ♦ Jon Bloom, gen mgr.

WKIX(FM)— Feb 2, 1972: 102.3 mhz; 2.1 kw. Ant 561 ft. TL: N35 23 54 W78 00 38. Stereo. 2581 U.S. Hwy. 70 W. 27530. Phone: (919) 934-3630. Phone: (919) 736-1699. Fax: (919) 736-3876. Web Site: www.yourfavoritecountry.com. Licensee: New Age Communications Inc. Group owner: Curtis Media Group (acq 7-1-96; $550,000). Format: Country. News staff: one. Target aud: 25-54. Spec prog: Gospel 4 hrs wkly. ♦ Don Curtis, pres; Tony Denton, gen mgr; Kari DelaCruz, opns mgr.

WRSV(FM)—See Rocky Mount

Graham

WBAG(AM)—See Burlington-Graham

WSML(AM)— Dec 2, 1967: 1200 khz; 10 kw-D, 1 kw-N, DA-N. TL: N36 08 01 W79 28 14. 875 W. 5th St., Winston Salem 27101. Phone: (336) 227-4254. Fax: (336) 227-4254. Licensee: Infinity Radio Inc. Group owner: Infinity Broadcasting Corp. (acq 8-7-00; grpsl). Network: ABC Information & Entertainment. Miller & Fields,P.C. Format: News/talk. Spec prog: Black 18 hrs wkly. ♦ Tom Hamilton, gen mgr & gen sls mgr; Larry Ingold, progmg dir; George Newman, chief of engrg.

Granite Falls

WYCV(AM)— Feb 22, 1963: 900 khz; 2.5 kw-D, 251 w-N. TL: N35 47 10 W81 25 00. Box 486, 398 South Main St. 28630. Phone: (828) 396-3361. Phone: (828) 396-3362. Fax: (828) 396-9193. E-mail: wycvradio@charter.net. Web Site: www.gospel9.com. Licensee: Freedom Broadcasting Corp. Group owner: Marvin L. Sizemore (acq 4-29-92). Network: Network: USA, AP Radio. Smithwick & Belendiuk. Format: Relg, southern gospel. News staff: 5; News 2 hrs wkly. Target aud: 3-100. Spec prog: Gospel. ♦ Marvin Sizemore, pres; Buddy Sizemore, gen mgr & stn mgr; Ann Martin, gen sls mgr & sls; Clyde Smith, mus dir & sls; Teresa S. Sizemore, asst music dir; Ted Fuller, chief of engrg & engr.

Greensboro

WCOG(AM)— May 22, 1948: 1320 khz; 5 kw-U, DA-2. TL: N36 09 01 W79 54 48. 4405 Providence Ln., Suite D, Winston-Salem 27106. Phone: (336) 759-0363. Fax: (336) 759-0366. E-mail: truthradio@trial.rr.com. Licensee: Truth Broadcasting Corp. (acq 4-29-99; $500,000). Format: Radio Disney. Target aud: General. ♦ Stuart Epperson Jr., pres & gen mgr.

WEAL(AM)—Listing follows WQMG-FM.

WJMH(FM)—See Reidsville

WKEW(AM)— Feb 16, 1942: 1400 khz; 1 kw-U. TL: N36 04 00 W79 47 49. 4405 Providence Ln., #A, Winston Salem 27106-3226. Phone: (336) 288-5044. Fax: (336) 286-7060. Licensee: Truth Broadcasting Corp. (group owner; acq 8-9-00; $800,000). Network: ABC Information & Entertainment. Format: Gospel. Target aud: 35 plus. Spec prog: Black 10 hrs wkly. ♦ Stuart Epperson, gen mgr.

WMAG(FM)—See High Point

WMQX-FM—(Winston-Salem). April 1947: 93.1 mhz; 100 kw. 1,050 ft. TL: N36 16 33 W79 56 27. Stereo. 7819 National Service Rd., Suite 401 27409. Phone: (336) 605-5200. Fax: (336) 605-5221. Web Site: www.oldies93.com. Licensee: Entercom Greensboro License LLC.

Group owner: Entercom Communications Corp. (acq 12-13-99; grpsl). Network: CBS. Rep: McGavren Guild. Format: Oldies. Target aud: 35-54; baby boomers who grew up with 60s rock and roll. ♦ Brent Millar, gen mgr; Lisa Powell, sls dir & gen sls mgr; Jim Faires, gen sls mgr; Randy Bliss, progmg dir; Larry Allen, chief of engrg.

*WNAA(FM)— 1979: 90.1 mhz; 10 kw. 467 ft. TL: N36 04 58 W79 46 08. Stereo. North Carolina A&T State Univ., Price Hall, Suite 200 27411-1135. Phone: (336) 334-7936. Fax: (336) 334-7960. E-mail: wnaafm@ncat.edu. Web Site: wnaalive.ncat.edu. Licensee: North Carolina Agricultural & Technical State University. Format: Gospel, black, jazz. News: 7 hrs wkly. Target aud: 35-45; general. Spec prog: Blues 3 hrs, reggae 7 hrs, oldies 5 hrs wkly. ♦ Tony Welborne, gen mgr, chief of opns & dev dir; Cherie Lofton, progmg dir; Mamie Johnson, pub affrs dir; Larry Allen, chief of engrg.

WPET(AM)— 1954: 950 khz; 500 w-D. TL: N36 02 16 W79 47 42. 7819 National Service Rd., Ste. 401 27409-9401. Secondary address: 221 W. Meadowview Rd. 27406. Phone: (336) 275-9738. Fax: (336) 387-7206. Web Site: www.wpetam950.com. Licensee: Entercom Greensboro License LLC. Group owner: Entercom Communications Corp. (acq 1-28-2002; $20.5 million. with co-located FM). Format: Southern gospel. Target aud: 25-54.

WSMW(FM)—Co-owned with WPET(AM). Jan 9, 1958: 98.7 mhz; 100 kw. 1,000 ft. TL: N36 02 16 W79 47 42. Stereo. Phone: (910) 275-9895. Web Site: www.987thezone.com. Format: Adult contemporary. Target aud: 18-49. ♦ Leigh Sobel, prom mgr; Brant Millar, mus dir.

WPOL(AM)—(Winston-Salem). Mar 25, 1937: 1340 khz; 1 kw-U. TL: N36 04 26 W80 15 19. 4405 Providence Ln., Winston-Salem 27106. Phone: (336) 759-0363. Fax: (336) 759-0366. Web Site: www.830wtru.com. Licensee: Truth Broadcasting Corp. (acq 5-10-2000). Format: Relg, gospel. News: one hr wkly. Relg. ♦ Stuart Epperson Jr., pres & gen mgr; Forrest Ritchey, opns mgr.

*WQFS(FM)— January 1970: 90.9 mhz; 1.9 kw. 200 ft. TL: N36 05 39 W79 53 21. Stereo. Box 17714, Founders Halls, 5800 W. Friendly Ave. 27410. Phone: (336) 316-2352. Phone: (336) 316-2444. Web Site: www.gilford.edu. Licensee: Guilford College Board of Trustees. Format: Free-form. News staff: one; News: 4 hrs wkly. Target aud: 15-50. Spec prog: Class 3 hrs, Black 20 hrs, bluegrass 3 hrs, folk 6 hrs, hardcore 4 hrs, jazz 3 hrs, relg 1 hr, blues 2 hrs, hardcore 2 hrs wkly. ♦ Erin Kauffman, gen mgr.

WQMG-FM— July 8, 1962: 97.1 mhz; 100 kw. 1,289 ft. TL: N36 05 09 W79 45 38. (CP: TL: N35 56 43 W79 51 44). Stereo. 7819 National Service Rd., Suite 401 27409. Phone: (336) 605-5200. Fax: (336) 605-0138. Web Site: www.wqmg.com. Licensee: Entercom Greensboro License LLC. Group owner: Entercom Communications Corp. (acq 12-13-99; grpsl). Network: ABC. Rep: McGavren Guild. Format: Smooth rhythm and blues, classic soul. News staff: one. Target aud: 18-49; Black. ♦ Brant Millar, gen mgr; Lisa Powell, sls dir; Linda Greenwood, prom dir; A.C. Stow, progmg mgr; Larry Allen, chief of engrg.

WEAL(AM)—Co-owned with WQMG-FM. Oct 5, 1962: 1510 khz; 1 kw-D, 250 w-CH. TL: N36 03 42 W79 47 35. Fax: (336) 605-0138. Rep: McGavren Guild. Format: Gospel. Target aud: 25-54; North Carolina A&T State Univ. ♦ Joseph Level, progmg dir.

*WUAG(FM)— July 20, 1964: 103.1 mhz; 18.1 w. 230 ft. TL: N36 03 51 W79 48 37. (CP: Ant 259 ft.). Stereo. Taylor Bldg., Univ. of North Carolina at Greensboro 27412. Phone: (336) 334-5450. E-mail: wuag@uncg.edu. Web Site: www.uncg.edu/wua. Licensee: University of North Carolina at Greensboro Board of Trustees. Format: Progsv rock, div, jazz. News staff: one; News: 2 hrs wkly. Target aud: 12-40; high school & college students. Spec prog: Sp 2 hrs, hip hop 6 hrs, world music 2 hrs, bluegrass 2 hrs, and blues 4 hrs wkly. ♦ Jack Bonney, gen mgr.

WWBG(AM)— 1998: 1470 khz; 3.5 kw-D, 5 kw-N, DA-2. TL: N36 12 46 W79 54 46. Box 12876, Winston-Salem 27117. Phone: (336) 784-9004. Fax: (336) 784-8337. Licensee: Davidson Media Station WWBG Licensee LLC. (acq 3-25-2005; swap with WTOB(AM)

Winston-Salem for WDRU(AM) Wake Forest). Rep: Salem. Format: Mexican rgnl. ♦ Stuart W. Epperson, gen mgr.

Greenville

WNCT(AM)— 1940: 1070 khz; 10 kw-U, DA-N. TL: N35 36 14 W77 25 29. 2929 Radio Station Rd. 27834. Phone: (252) 757-0011. Fax: (252) 757-0286. Web Site: www.lafavorita.com. Licensee: Beasley Broadcasting of Coastal North Carolina. (acq 1996). Network: Network: CBS, ABC. Format: Talk, spanish. Target aud: General. Spec prog: Farm 10 hrs wkly. ♦ Brad Hood, gen mgr & stn mgr.

WNCT-FM— Dec 22, 1963: 107.9 mhz; 100 kw. 1,800 ft. TL: N35 21 55 W77 23 38. Stereo. Web Site: www.oldies1079.com. Network: ABC Information & Entertainment. Format: Oldies. ♦ Jerry Wayne, progmg dir. Co-owned TV: WNCT-TV affil.

WRSV(FM)—See Rocky Mount

*WZMB(FM)— Feb 2, 1982: 91.3 mhz; 282 w. 134 ft. TL: N35 36 01 W77 21 53. Stereo. Mendenhall Student Ctr., East Carolina Univ. 27834. Phone: (252) 328-4751. Phone: (252) 328-4752. Fax: (252) 328-4773. Web Site: www.wzmb.ecu.edu. Licensee: East Carolina University Media Board. (acq 2-82). Network: ABC. Format: Alternative rock. News: 12 hrs wkly. Target aud: 18-24; univ students. Spec prog: Reggae 7 hrs, jazz 4 hrs, blues 3 hrs, contemp Christian 3 hrs, metal 9 hrs, others 9 hrs wkly.

Grifton

WXNR(FM)— Sept 11, 1989: 99.5 mhz; 16.5 kw. 830 ft. TL: N35 12 07 W77 11 15. Stereo. 207 Glenbernie Dr., New Bern 28560. Phone: (252) 633-1500. Fax: (252) 633-6546. Web Site: www.wxnr.com. Licensee: WXNR License L.P. Rep: D & R Radio. Format: New rock. Target aud: 18-34. ♦ Bruce Simel, gen mgr; Joe Peters, sls dir; Wilbur Vitols, gen sls mgr; Jeff Sanders, progmg dir; Richard Banks, chief of engrg.

Hamlet

WJSG(FM)— Aug 25, 1991: 104.3 mhz; 2.5 kw. 489 ft. TL: N34 48 44 W79 43 38. 180 Airport Rd., Rockingham 28379. Phone: (910) 895-3787. Fax: (910) 895-8811. E-mail: g104fm@104fm.com. Web Site: www.g104fm.com. Licensee: Jackson Broadcasting Co. Format: Christian country. ♦ Sherrell Jackson, gen mgr & progmg dir; Jerry Stout, news dir.

WKDX(AM)— June 30, 1957: 1250 khz; 1 kw-D. TL: N34 53 06 W79 40 50. Box 827 28345. Phone: (910) 582-1997. Fax: (910) 582-1920. Web Site: www.wkdx.net. Licensee: The McLaurin Group (acq 5-19-00). Format: Christian contemp gospel. ♦ Howard McLaurin Jr., pres & gen mgr.

Harkers Island

WLGP(FM)— Aug 1, 1996: 100.3 mhz; 100 kw. 485 ft. TL: N34 48 18 W76 54 21. Stereo. 2278 Wortham Ln., Grovetown, GA 30813. Phone: (706) 309-9670. Fax: (706) 309-9669. E-mail: ctbarinowski@gnnradio.org. Web Site: www.gnnradio.org. Licensee: Barinowski Investment Co., a Georgia L.P. Group owner: Good News Network. Format: Christian. ♦ C.T. Barinowski, pres.

Harrisburg

WQNC(FM)— 1995: 92.7 mhz; 6 kw. 328 ft. TL: N35 16 20 W80 45 54. 2303 W. Morehead St., Charlotte 28208. Phone: (704) 358-0211. Fax: (704) 358-3752. Licensee: Radio One of North Carolina LLC. Group owner: Radio One Inc. (acq 11-8-01; grpsl). Rep: McGavren Guild. Format: R&B. Target aud: Adults 25-54. ♦ Debbie Kwei, gen mgr; Michael Taylor, gen sls mgr; Latoya Whitt, mktg dir & prom dir; Phil Woods, chief of engrg.

Broadcasting & Cable Yearbook 2006

Hatteras

WWOC(FM)— May 1999: 94.5 mhz; 91 kw. 981 ft. TL: N35 29 10 W75 59 58. Stereo. 104 Radio Rd., Powells Point 27966. Phone: (252) 925-9450. Fax: (252) 491-2939. Licensee: Max Radio of the Carolinas Licenses LLC. Group owner: MAX Media L.L.C. (acq 11-12-2002; grpsl). Network: Jones Radio Networks. Format: Hot country. News staff: 2. ♦Kay Haller, opns mgr; Scott Fortenberry, chief of engrg.

WYND-FM— March 1995: 97.1 mhz; 48 kw. 558 ft. TL: N35 27 48 W76 02 07. Stereo. Box 367, Wanchese 27981. Secondary address: 637 Harbor Rd., Wanchese 27981. Phone: (252) 475-1888. Fax: (252) 475-1881. E-mail: obxradio@beachlink.com. Licensee: Convergent Broadcasting Outer Banks LLC. Group owner: Convergent Broadcasting LLC (acq 11-7-02; with WZPR(FM) Nags Head). Richard Hayes. Format: Adult contemp. ♦Bruce A. Biette, pres; Tom Pierce, gen mgr; Hunt Thomas, opns dir & progmg dir.

Havelock

WANG(AM)— June 16, 1962: 1330 khz; 1 kw-D. TL: N34 55 24 W76 56 37. 331 B.W. Main St. 28532. Phone: (252) 447-3333. Fax: (252) 447-2997. Licensee: NM Licensing LLC. Group owner: NextMedia Group L.L.C. (acq 11-26-2001; grpsl). Format: Adult standards. Target aud: 35 plus; active lifestyle, early militaary retirees, relocated retirees. ♦Steven Dinetz, pres; Dale Powers, gen mgr; Don Brown, chief of engrg.

WSSM(FM)—Co-owned with WANG(AM). Nov 12, 1971: 105.1 mhz; 18.5 kw. 384 ft. TL: N34 45 06 W76 52 57. (CP: 25 kw). Stereo. Format: Adult standards. ♦Bruce Reese, CEO & pres; Bob Johnson, CFO; John Kijowski, VP & gen mgr.

Henderson

WCBQ(AM)—See Oxford

WHNC(AM)— June 20, 1945: 890 khz; 1 kw-D. TL: N36 21 04 W78 22 35. PO Box 1005, One Broadcast Ctr., 601 Henderson St., Oxford 27565. Phone: (919) 693-3540. Phone: (919) 693-1340. Fax: (919) 693-9054. Licensee: The Paradise Network (TPN) of North Carolina Inc. (acq 4-30-01; $650,000. with WCBQ(AM) Oxford). Rep: Keystone (unwired net). T-N. Format: Black gospel. News staff: one; News: 7 hrs wkly. Target aud: 18 plus. ♦Alvin Augustis Jones, chmn; Nathaniel Smith, stn mgr; Jim Davis, engrg mgr; Ronald Smith, sls dir & chief of engrg.

WIZS(AM)— May 1, 1955: 1450 khz; 1 kw-U. TL: N36 19 31 W78 24 36. Box 192, Studio & Transmitter Bldg., 535 Radio Ln. 27536. Phone: (252) 492-3001. Fax: (252) 492-3002. E-mail: wizs@vance.net. Web Site: hendersonnews.com. Licensee: Rose Farm and Rentals Inc. (acq 6-1-89; $265,000; 6-19-89). Format: Country. News staff: one; News: 6 hrs wkly. Target aud: 25 plus; fans of top 60 country music. ♦John D. Rose III, pres, news dir & chief of engrg; John C. Rose, sls dir; Martha Pelaquin, opns mgr & mus dir; Bill Dinicola, pub affrs dir.

WYFL(FM)— 1948: 92.5 mhz; 100 kw. Ant 1,020 ft. TL: N36 13 23 W78 12 07. Stereo. 203 Capcom Ave., Suite 102-D, Wake Forest 27587. Secondary address: 120 E. Belle St. 27536. Phone: (919) 562-3198. E-mail: wyfl@bbnradio.org. Web Site: www.bbnradio.org. Licensee: Bible Broadcasting Network Inc. (group owner; acq 10-3-81; $335,000; 9-14-81). Format: Relg. Target aud: General. ♦Bryant Nelson, gen mgr & news dir.

Hendersonville

WHKP(AM)— Oct 24, 1946: 1450 khz; 1 kw-U. TL: N35 20 20 W82 27 20. Box 2470, 1450 7th Ave. E. 28793. Phone: (828) 693-9061. Fax: (828) 696-9329. E-mail: 1450@whkp.com. Web Site: www.whkp.com. Licensee: Radio Hendersonville Inc. (acq 6-4-86). Network: ABC Information & Entertainment. Brooks, Pierce, McLendon, Humphrey & Leonard. Format: Var, adult contemp music, talk. Target aud: 25 plus; middle to upper income. Spec prog: Var 18 hrs wkly. ♦Art Cooley, pres, gen mgr & prom VP; Richard Rhodes, sls VP; Al Hope, progmg dir; Larry Freeman, news dir; Norman Lyda, chief of engrg.

WMYI(FM)—Licensed to Hendersonville. See Greenville SC

WTZQ(AM)— Dec 25, 1964: 1600 khz; 1 kw-D, 12 w-N. TL: N35 18 53 W82 25 58. 418 Duncun Road, Flat Rock 28731. Phone: (828) 692-1600. Phone: (828) 697-1506. Fax: (828) 697-1416. E-mail: 1600@wtzq.com. Web Site: www.wtzq.com. Licensee: Houston Broadcasting Inc. (acq 2-11-02; $750,000). Network: ABC. Format: Adult standards. News staff: one; News: 15 hrs wkly. Target aud: 35 plus; mature upscale audiences. Spec prog: Gospel 4 hrs wkly. ♦Randy Houston, pres, gen mgr & gen sls mgr; Glenn Trent, opns dir, progmg dir & news dir; Mark Warwick, sls dir & adv dir; Susan Houston, VP & prom dir; Michael Sink, chief of engrg.

Hertford

WFMZ(FM)— December 1997: 104.9 mhz; 50 kw. Ant 492 ft. TL: N36 10 45 W76 21 12. Box 1447, Elizabeth City 27906. Phone: (252) 338-7729. Fax: (252) 338-9611. Web Site: classichits1049.com. Licensee: Convergent Broadcasting of Hertford LLC. Group owner: Convergent Broadcasting LLC (acq 5-14-2004; $2.1 million). Network: USA. Format: Classic hits. Target aud: 25-54. ♦Bruce Biette, pres; Dave Hinson, VP.

Hickory

WAIZ(AM)— Dec 5, 1948: 630 khz; 1 kw-D, 57 w-N. TL: N35 43 07 W81 18 36. Box 938 28603. Secondary address: Box 430, Newton 28658. Phone: (828) 322-9472. Fax: (828) 464-9662. E-mail: totalradio@aol.com. Licensee: Newton-Conover Communications Inc. (acq 10-5-94; $225,000). Network: ABC. Format: Oldiies. Target aud: 25 plus. ♦Dave Lingafelt, pres & gen mgr; Jim Turner, gen sls mgr; Al Mainess, news dir.

***WFHE(FM)**— Aug 31, 1995: 90.3 mhz; 150 w. 804 ft. TL: N35 39 27 W81 24 23. c/o WFAE(FM), 8801 J.M. Keynes Dr., Suite 91, Charlotte 28262-8485. Phone: (704) 549-9323. Fax: (704) 547-8851. E-mail: wfae@wfae.org. Web Site: www.wfae.org. Licensee: University Radio Foundation Inc. Format: NPR/PRI Affiliate. ♦Roger Sarow, pres & gen mgr; Debra Peterson, CFO; Barbara Vermeire, dev dir; Catherine Little, dev dir; Paul Stribling, mktg dir & progmg dir; Renee Rallos, prom dir & pub affrs dir; Tena Simmons, opns dir & mus dir; Mark Rumsey, news dir; Jobie Sprinkle, engrg dir.

WHKY(AM)— June 10, 1940: 1290 khz; 50 kw-D, 1 kw-N, DA-2. TL: N35 43 35 W81 18 02. Box 1059, 526 Main Ave. S.E. 28603. Phone: (828) 322-5115. Fax: (828) 322-8256. E-mail: whky@whky.com. Web Site: www.whky.com. Licensee: Long Communications LLC (acq 12-31-01; with WHKY-TV Hickory). Network: ABC Daytime Direction. Hardy & Carey. Format: News/talk. News staff: 3; News: 50 hrs wkly. Target aud: 35-54. ♦Thomas E. Long, gen mgr; Jeff Long, stn mgr. Co-owned TV: WHKY-TV affil.

WLYT(FM)— Jan 20, 1959: 102.9 mhz; 31 kw. 1,545 ft. TL: N35 24 26 W81 07 47. Stereo. 801 Wood Ridge Center Dr., Charlotte 28217. Phone: (704) 714-9444. Fax: (704) 372-3208. Web Site: www.wlyt.com. Licensee: Capstar TX L.P. Group owner: Clear Channel Communications Inc. (acq 8-30-00; grpsl). Format: Adult contemp. Target aud: 25-54. ♦Morgan Johannon, gen mgr; Nick Allen, opns mgr; Kim Kyle, sls dir; Tom Hunt, sls dir; Amanda Knepp, mktg dir; Anthony Testa, prom dir; Jeff Kent, progmg dir; Linda Silver, news dir; Alan Lane, chief of engrg; Ben Birnitzer, chief of engrg.

***WPIR(FM)**— Dec 3, 1985: 88.1 mhz; 10 kw. 300 ft. TL: N35 43 34 W81 08 52. Stereo. Box 909, Claremont 28610. Secondary address: 3289 WCXN Radio Rd., Claremont 28610. Phone: (828) 459-2772. Fax: (828) 459-9805. Licensee: Positive Alternative Radio Inc. Group owner: Baker Family Stations Format: Southern gospel, educ. ♦Rodney Baucom, gen mgr.

WXRC(FM)— Dec 7, 1962: 95.7 mhz; 100 kw. 1,276 ft. TL: N35 42 32 W81 31 32. Stereo. 1515 Mocking Bird Lane., Suite 910, Charlotte 28208 - 28209. Phone: (704) 527-0957. Fax: (704) 527-2720. E-mail: totalradio@aol.com. Web Site: 957theride.com. Licensee: Pacific Broadcasting Group Inc. (acq 10-5-94; $3.05 million; 10-17-94). Format: AOR. Target aud: 18-49. ♦Dave Lingafelt, pres & gen mgr; Jim Turner, natl sls mgr; Nancy Golden, rgnl sls mgr; Peggy Barrett, prom dir; Ron Bowen, progmg dir; Karol Lowery, pub affrs dir; Larry Schropp, chief of engrg.

WYCV(AM)—See Granite Falls

High Point

WGOS(AM)— July 1947: 1070 khz; 1 kw-D. TL: N35 54 58 W80 01 00. 6223 Old Mendenhall Rd. 27263-7624. Phone: (336) 434-5024. Fax: (336) 434-6018. E-mail: wgosradio@triad.rr.com. Web Site: www.wgos.net. Licensee: Ritchy Broadcasting Co. Inc. (acq 8-6-79). Format: Loc talk, Sp. News: 2 hrs wkly. Target aud: General. Spec prog: Loc college sports 10 hrs wkly. ♦Lynn Ritchy, gen mgr & gen sls mgr; Max Parrish, stn mgr & chief of engrg; Simon Ritchy, pres & progmg dir; D.W. Long, mus dir.

***WHPE-FM**— November 1947: 95.5 mhz; 100 kw. 440 ft. TL: N35 55 10 W80 01 47. Stereo. 1714 Tower Ave. 27260. Phone: (336) 889-9473. Fax: (336) 889-9773. E-mail: whpe@rrnradio.org. Web Site: www.rrnradio.org. Licensee: Bible Broadcasting Network. (acq 10-74). Network: USA. Format: Relg. ♦Lowell Davey, pres; Dan Austin, gen mgr.

WJMH(FM)—See Reidsville

WMAG(FM)— 1946: 99.5 mhz; 100 kw. 1,500 ft. TL: N35 52 13 W79 50 25. Stereo. 2 B PAI Park, Greensboro 27409. Phone: (336) 822-2000. Fax: (336) 887-0104. Web Site: www.wmagradio.com. Licensee: Capstar TX L.P. Group owner: Clear Channel Communications Inc. (acq 8-30-00; grpsl). Format: Adult contemp. Target aud: 25-54. ♦Cheryl Salamone, VP; Scott Keith, opns mgr; Shannon Sopina, prom dir; Ed Skurka, news dir.

WMFR(AM)— Oct 15, 1935: 1230 khz; 1 kw-U. TL: N35 57 20 W80 00 22. 875 W. 5th St., Winston Salem 27101-2505. Phone: (336) 777-3900. Fax: (336) 885-3299. Web Site: www.wmfr.com. Licensee: Infinity Radio Inc. Group owner: Infinity Broadcasting Corp. Network: ABC Information & Entertainment. Format: News/talk. ♦Tom Hamilton, VP; Marty Holbrook, mktg dir & progmg dir; Bob Costner, news dir; Robert La Fore, chief of engrg.

WVBZ(FM)— June 1953: 100.3 mhz; 100 kw. 1,049 ft. TL: N35 58 09 W79 49 29. Stereo. 2-B PAI Park, Greensboro 27409. Phone: (336) 822-2000. Fax: (336) 887-0104. Web Site: www.buzzitrocks.com. Licensee: Capstar TX L.P. Group owner: Clear Channel Communications Inc. (acq 8-30-00; grpsl). Format: Rock. Target aud: 25-54. ♦Bill Dotson, gen mgr; Paul Franklin, sls dir; Tim Fattafield, progmg dir.

WYSR(AM)— June 1953: 1590 khz; 1.4 kw-D, 14 w-N. TL: N35 59 04 W80 04 08. 808 English Rd., Suite 101 27262. Phone: (336) 883-8852. Fax: (336) 882-1594. E-mail: wysr@northstate.net. Licensee: Eastern Broadcasting Group Inc. (group owner; acq 2-7-03; $416,646). Format: Talk, sports. Target aud: General. ♦Michael J. Sbuttoni, pres; Carrie Armstrong, gen mgr; L.A. Batchelor, opns dir & opns mgr.

Highlands

WHLC(FM)— July 1993: 104.5 mhz; 460 w. Ant 1,158 ft. TL: N35 03 40 W83 11 05. Stereo. Box 1889 28741. Secondary address: 2420 Hwy. 64 E. 28741. Phone: (828) 526-1045. Fax: (828) 526-4900. E-mail: whlc@dnet.net. Web Site: www.whlc.com. Licensee: Charisma Radio Corp. Format: Easy lstng. Target aud: 35 plus. ♦Charles B. Cooper, pres & gen mgr; Steve Day, opns mgr.

Hope Mills

WCCG(FM)— July 1997: 104.5 mhz; 6 kw. 305 ft. TL: N34 56 34 W78 51 41. 115 Gillespie St., Fayetteville 28301. Phone: (910) 484-4932. Fax: (910) 485-5192. Web Site: www.hot1045fm.com. Licensee: James E. Carson. Format: Oldies. ♦James Carson, gen mgr.

Jacksonville

WILT(FM)— Apr 28, 1965: 98.7 mhz; 100 kw. 1,015 ft. TL: N34 29 38 W77 29 18. Stereo. P.O. Drawer 1126 28540-1126. Phone: (910) 455-5300. Fax: (910) 455-3112. Web Site: www.wkoo987.com. Licensee: NM Licensing LLC. Group owner: NextMedia Group L.L.C. (acq 11-26-2001; grpsl). Wilmer, Cutler & Pickering. Format: Oldies. News staff: one; News: 3 hrs wkly. Target aud: 25-54; middle to upper-income adults. ♦Brad Blake, gen mgr; Stephaine Gladwell, gen mgr & sls dir; Brian Bell, progmg dir; Don Brown, chief of engrg.

WJCV(AM)— Oct 10, 1968: 1290 khz; 1 kw-D. TL: N35 45 51 W77 23 18. Box 1216 28541. Phone: (910) 347-6141. Fax: (910) 347-1290. Licensee: Down East Broadcasting Co. Inc. (acq 1996). Network: USA. Format: Southern gospel, Christian, MOR, light contemp. Target aud: 25-54; general. ♦Melvin Bland, stn mgr, opns mgr & progmg dir; Michael Bland, pres, gen mgr, sls dir & adv mgr; Don Brown, chief of engrg.

***WJKA(FM)**—Not on air, target date: unknown: 90.1 mhz; 20 kw vert. Ant 305 ft. TL: N34 31 31 W77 35 27. Box 2440, Tupelo, MS

38803-2440. Phone: (662) 844-8888. Fax: (662) 842-6791. Web Site: www.afr.net. Licensee: American Family Association. ◆Marvin Sanders, gen mgr.

WJNC(AM)— Oct 16, 1945: 1240 khz; 1 kw-U. TL: N34 44 56 W77 24 51. Box 70, Newport 28570. Phone: (910) 455-7222. Fax: (252) 247-7343. Licensee: Heritage Broadcasting LLC (acq 8-10-01; $358,500). Network: Westwood One. Hogan & Hartson. Format: News/talk, sports. Target aud: 18-45 plus. ◆Ben Ball, gen mgr; Dave Gremoske, chief of engrg.

WQSL(FM)— November 1993: 92.3 mhz; 22.5 kw. Ant 725 ft. TL: N34 31 10 W77 26 52. 1361 Colony Dr., New Bern 28562. Phone: (252) 639-7900. Fax: (252) 639-7979. Web Site: thebeatnc.com. Licensee: NM Licensing LLC. Group owner: NextMedia Group L.L.C. (acq 11-26-01; grpsl). Format: CHR rhythm. ◆Paul Kingman, gen mgr.

WSRP(AM)— June 21, 1954: 910 khz; 5 kw-U, DA-N. TL: N34 47 31 W77 29 40. Stereo. 907 Lejeune Blvd. 28540. Phone: (910) 455-2202. Fax: (910) 355-2203. Licensee: Eastern Broadcasting Inc. (acq 9-21-2000). Format: Hispanic bcstg. ◆Henry Gonzalez, stn mgr.

WXQR(FM)— Mar 14, 1966: 105.5 mhz; 19 kw. 794 ft. TL: N34 31 10 W77 26 52. Stereo. 1361 Colony Dr., New Bern 28562. Phone: (252) 639-7979. Fax: (910) 455-0330. Licensee: NM Licensing LLC. Group owner: NextMedia Group L.L.C. (acq 11-26-01; grpsl). Network: ABC. Format: AOR. ◆Paul Kingman, gen mgr & stn mgr.

Jefferson

WMMY(FM)— October 1999: 106.1 mhz; 10.5 kw. Ant 508 ft. TL: N36 19 53 W81 35 17. 738 Blowing Rock Rd., Boone 28607. Phone: (828) 264-2411. Fax: (828) 264-2412. Web Site: www.mix1023fm.com. Licensee: Aisling Broadcasting of Banner Elk LLC (group owner; acq 4-13-2004; $1.58 million). Format: Country. ◆Jonathan Hoffman, CEO.

Kannapolis

WRFX-FM— October 1964: 99.7 mhz; 100 kw. 1,044 ft. TL: N35 33 45 W80 42 40. (CP: 84 kw, ant 1,056 ft.). Stereo. 801 Wood Ridge Center Dr., Charlotte 28217. Phone: (704) 714-9444. Fax: (704) 371-3238. Web Site: www.wrfx.com. Licensee: Capstar TX L.P. Group owner: Clear Channel Communications Inc. (acq 8-30-00; grpsl). Format: Classic rock, AOR. Target aud: 25-54; male. Spec prog: Talk 3 hrs wkly. ◆Morgan Bohannon, gen mgr; Nick Allen, opns mgr; Kim Kyle, sls dir; Amanda Knepp, mktg dir; Jeff Kent, progmg dir; Linda Silver, news dir; Ben Brinitzer, chief of engrg.

WRKB(AM)— Dec 11, 1960: 1460 khz; 500 w-D, 194 w-N. TL: N35 29 14 W80 36 18. Box 8146 28083. Phone: (704) 938-1460. Phone: (704) 857-1101. Fax: (704) 857-0680. Web Site: www.fordbroadcasting.com. Licensee: Ford Broadcasting Inc. (group owner; acq 1994). Network: USA. Smithwick & Belendiuk. Format: Southern gospel. ◆Carl Ford, pres, gen mgr & opns mgr; Taylor Ford, exec VP; Angela Ford, sr VP.

Kernersville

WTRU(AM)— Aug 16, 1970: 830 khz; 50 kw-D, 10 kw-N, DA-2. TL: N36 11 58 W80 12 25. 4405 Providence Ln., Suite D, Winston-Salem 27106. Phone: (336) 759-0363. Fax: (336) 759-0366. E-mail: info@830wtru.com. Web Site: www.830wtru.com. Licensee: Truth Broadcasting Corp. (group owner; (acq 7-20-2000; $3.5 million with WGTK(AM) Louisville, KY). Format: News, Christian. News: 24 hrs wkly. Target aud: General. ◆Stuart Epperson Jr., gen mgr; David Albright, progmg dir, news dir & news dir; Allan Boar, engrg dir.

Kill Devil Hills

WCXL(FM)— January 1993: 104.1 mhz; 100 kw. 981 ft. TL: N36 07 42 W75 49 39. Stereo. Box 1897 27948. Phone: (252) 480-4655. Fax: (252) 441-4827. Web Site: www.beach104.com. Licensee: Max Radio of the Carolinas Licenses LLC. Group owner: MAX Media L.L.C. (acq 11-12-2002; grpsl). Format: Adult contemp. News staff: 2. Target aud: 18-54. Spec prog: Farm 2 hrs wkly. ◆Mike Smith, gen mgr; Bob Davis, gen sls mgr & rgnl sls mgr.

King

WKTE(AM)— Dec 4, 1963: 1090 khz; 1 kw-D. TL: N36 17 48 W80 22 18. Stereo. Box 465, Wkte Dr. 27021. Phone: (336) 983-3111. Fax: (336) 368-1090. Web Site: www.wktelogo.com. Licensee: Booth-Newsom Broadcasting Inc. (acq 3-1-86; $105,000; 1-6-86). Format: Gospel. Spec prog: Farm 2 hrs wkly. ◆P.W. Booth, pres; Rodney Booth, gen mgr; Lee Daniels, progmg dir; Deon Stoker, chief of engrg.

Kings Mountain

WKMT(AM)— Mar 12, 1953: 1220 khz; 1 kw-D, 106 w-N. TL: N35 15 59 W81 19 23. Stereo. Box 1220 28086. Secondary address: 2100 Cleveland Ave. 28086. Phone: (704) 739-1220. Fax: (704) 739-4900. Web Site: www.1060radio.com. Licensee: Geddings & Phillips Broadcasting Corp. (acq 6-17-2004). Format: Talk. ◆Kevin L. Geddings, pres.

Kinston

WELS(AM)— September 1950: 1010 khz; 1 kw-D, 75 w-N. TL: N35 15 45 W77 37 35. (CP: N35 17 02 W77 39 55). Box 3384 28502. Secondary address: 313 N. Queen St. 28501. Phone: (252) 523-5151. Fax: (252) 523-9357. E-mail: wels1029@yahoo.com. Licensee: Willis Broadcasting. (acq 1-13-95; 2-27-95). Rep: Clayton-Davis. Format: Gospel. Target aud: 25-54; middle income. ◆Anthony Gonzales, gen mgr.

WELS-FM— Nov 21, 1990: 102.9 mhz; 3 kw. 295 ft. TL: N35 17 03 W77 39 53. Network: ABC. Target aud: General; middle to upper income, married, working, college grads. Spec prog: East Carolina Univ. sports, Kinston Indians baseball.

***WKNS(FM)**— Mar 26, 1977: 90.3 mhz; 20 kw. 312 ft. TL: N35 25 01 W77 48 57. Stereo. c/o WTEB(FM), 800 College Ct., New Bern 28562. Phone: (252) 638-3434. Fax: (252) 638-3538. Web Site: www.publicradioeast.org. Licensee: Craven Community College. (acq 1-18-95; 6-19-95). Format: Class mus, news. Spec prog: Jazz 6 hrs wkly. ◆Kathleen Beal, gen mgr; Charles Wethington, opns mgr; Lynn McCoy, dev dir & dev mgr; Tomothy Kimble, progmg dir; Sefton Wiggs, mus dir; George Olsen, news dir; J. Howard Jones, chief of engrg.

WLNR(AM)— May 1954: 1230 khz; 1 kw-U. TL: N35 15 31 W77 36 33. 1223 W. New Bern Rd. 28504-4713. Phone: (252) 522-4501. Fax: (252) 522-4501. Licensee: Estuardo Valdemar Rodriguez & Leonor Rodriguez. Group owner: Estuardo Valdemar Rodriguez and Leonor Rodriguez Stns (acq 1-2004; $315,000). Format: Sp. ◆Wallace Bullock, gen mgr.

WRNS-FM— Oct 12, 1968: 95.1 mhz; 100 kw. 1,499 ft. TL: N35 06 18 W77 20 15. Stereo. 2030 Banks School Rd. 28504. Phone: (252) 522-4141. Phone: (252) 523-9292. Fax: (252) 523-4877. E-mail: mail@wrns.com. Web Site: www.wrns.com. Licensee: NM Licensing LLC. Group owner: NextMedia Group L.L.C. (acq 11-26-01; grpsl). Network: ABC. Wilmer, Cutler & Pickering. Format: Country. News staff: one. Target aud: 25-54. Spec prog: NASCAR racing 6 hrs wkly.Steven Dinetz, CEO; Jeff Dinetz, COO; Carl Hirsch, chmn; Skip Weller, pres; Sean Stover, CFO; Jackie Graham, VP; Dale Powers, gen mgr; Brad Blale, sls dir; Paul Kingman, gen sls mgr; Barbara Ball, natl sls mgr; Liz Hynes, mktg dir, prom dir & news dir; Mike Farley, progmg dir; Boomer Lee, mus dir; Sally Barnades, pub affrs dir; Mark Stennett, engrg VP; Don Brown, chief of engrg

WRNS(AM)— Feb 28, 1937: 960 khz; 5 kw-D, 1 kw-N, DA-N. TL: N35 16 59 W77 39 01. Format: Relg. Target aud: 25-64.

WWNF(FM)— Sept 15, 1976: 97.7 mhz; 3 kw. Ant 249 ft. TL: N35 15 31 W77 36 33. Stereo. 1307 S. Glenburnie Rd., New Bern 28562. Phone: (252) 672-5900. Fax: (252) 637-6872. Web Site: www.sunnybeachfm.com. Licensee: New Age Communications Inc. Group owner: Curtis Media Group (acq 8-3-2004; $875,000). Network: Westwood One. Pepper & Corazzini. Format: Beach & oldies. Target aud: 25 plus; general. ◆Rodney Rainey, gen mgr.

Laurinburg

WEWO(AM)— Sept 1, 1947: 1460 khz; 5 kw-U, DA-2. TL: N34 47 00 W79 30 40. Box 788 28353. Phone: (910) 276-1460. Fax: (910) 276-9787. E-mail: wewo1460@aol.com. Licensee: Service Media Inc. (acq 5-27-98; $150,000). Format: Gospel. Target aud: 25-54. ◆Charles E. Robinson, gen mgr.

WFLB(FM)— May 1, 1951: 96.5 mhz; 100 kw. 1,043 ft. TL: N34 46 50 W79 02 45. Stereo. 508 Person St., Fayetteville 28301. Phone: (910) 486-0965. Fax: (910) 323-5635. Licensee: Beasley FM Acquisition Corp. Group owner: Beasley Broadcast Group (acq 7-31-96; $4.2 million. with co-owned AM). Format: Oldies. News staff: 16; News: 3 hrs wkly. Target aud: 35-64; affluent men & women in their peak earning years. Spec prog: University of North Carolina football & basketball. ◆George Beasley, pres; Danny Highsmith, sr VP & gen mgr; Mac Edwards, VP & opns VP; Walter Sturdivant, sls VP; Angela Godwin, gen sls mgr; Bryan Kusilka, natl sls mgr; Larry Smith, progmg dir; Van Clough, chief of engrg.

WLNC(AM)— Jan 2, 1962: 1300 khz; 500 w-D. TL: N34 47 00 W79 26 22. Box 1748 28353. Secondary address: 1300 Lila Dr. 28352. Phone: (910) 276-1300. E-mail: wlncradio@carolina.net. Web Site: www.wlncradio@carolina.com. Licensee: Fox Broadcasting Inc. (acq 2-1-90; $325,000). Format: Adult contemp. Target aud: General. Spec prog: Gospel 4 hrs wkly. ◆Fred Fox, gen mgr.

Leaksville

WGBT(FM)—See Eden

WLOE(AM)—See Eden

Leland

WAAV(AM)—Licensed to Leland. See Wilmington

WKXS-FM—Licensed to Leland. See Wilmington

Lenoir

WJRI(AM)— Mar 15, 1947: 1340 khz; 1 kw-U. TL: N35 53 47 W81 33 57. 827 Fairview Dr. 28645. Secondary address: Box 1678 28645. Phone: (828) 754-5361. Fax: (828) 757-3300. Licensee: Foothills Radio Group LLC (group owner; acq 11-28-01). Format: News/talk. News staff: one; News: 14 hrs wkly. Target aud: 20-45. ◆William M. McClatchey Jr., pres; Patty Guthrie, gen mgr & sls VP; Davy Crockett, opns VP, progmg dir & pub affrs dir; Beth McCorkle, mktg dir; Rob Eastwood, news dir; Stoney Owen, chief of engrg.

WKGX(AM)— Feb 13, 1969: 1080 khz; 5 kw-D. TL: N35 54 38 W81 33 35. Stereo. 827 Fairview Dr., . 28645. Phone: (828) 754-5361. Fax: (828) 757-3300. E-mail: wxgx@twave.net. Licensee: Foothills Radio Group LLC (group owner; acq 11-28-01). Format: Country, bluegrass. News staff: one; News: 6 hrs wkly. Target aud: 24-55; older, mature wise spenders. Spec prog: Trading post show 16 hrs wkly. ◆Patty Guthrie, gen mgr.

WKVS(FM)— Sept 27, 1993: 103.3 mhz; 740 w. 670 ft. TL: N35 58 31 W81 33 05. Box 1678, 808 Harper Ave. 28645. Phone: (828) 758-1033. Fax: (828) 757-3300. Licensee: Foothills Radio Group LLC (group owner; acq 11-28-01). Format: Hot new country. Target aud: 18-54. ◆William M. McClatchey Jr., pres; Patty Guthrie, gen mgr & sls dir; Beth McCorkle, mktg dir; Davy Crockett, progmg dir & pub affrs dir; Rob Eastwood, news dir; Stonie Owen, engrg dir.

Lewisville

WSGH(AM)— 1986: 1040 khz; 10 kw-D, DA. TL: N36 08 06 W80 30 14. (CP: 10 kw-D, 182 w-N). 1812 Davie Ave., Statesville 28677.

North Carolina

Phone: (336) 759-0524. Fax: (336) 759-9327. Web Site: www.radiolamovidita.com. Licensee: Davidson Media Carolinas Stations LLC. Group owner: Davidson Media Group LLC (acq 5-10-2004; grpsl). Network: USA. Format: Sp. Target aud: 17-28. ♦ Marco Antonio Saucedo, pres; Lucy Saucedo, VP; Samuel Saucedo, gen mgr.

Lexington

WLXN(AM)— Sept 22, 1946: 1440 khz; 5 kw-D, 1 kw-N, DA-N. TL: N35 50 22 W80 14 02. 200 Radio Dr. 27292. Secondary address: 2107 Chester Ridge Dr., Suite 102, High Point 27262. Phone: (336) 248-2716. Fax: (336) 248-2800. Web Site: www.wlxn.com. Licensee: Davidson County Broadcasting Co. Inc. Format: News/talk, sports. News staff: one; News: 30 hrs wkly. Target aud: 35 plus; those interested in news & sports. ♦ Greeley N. Hilton Jr., pres; Tom Collins, opns VP & chief of opns; Willie Edwards, prom dir; Bob Mahoney, news dir; Hal McGee, engrg dir.

WTHZ(FM)— Co-owned with WLXN(AM). Aug 24, 1949: 94.1 mhz; 100 kw. 1,014 ft. TL: N35 55 02 W80 17 37. Stereo. Web Site: www.hitz94.com. T-N. Format: 80's hits, 90's hits. News staff: one; News: 1 hr wkly. Target aud: General; 25-49. ♦ Greeley N. Hilton Jr., exec VP; Ann Thomas, progmg dir; Hal McGee, chief of engrg.

Lillington

*****WLLN(AM)**— Feb 12, 1979: 1370 khz; 5 kw-D, 49 w-N, DA-2. TL: N35 23 16 W78 48 22. Box 969 27546. Secondary address: 910 E. McNeil St. 27546. Phone: (910) 893-2811. Fax: (910) 893-2811. Web Site: www.radiolagrande.net. Licensee: Estuardo Valdemar Rodriguez (acq 9-21-99; $145,000). Format: Latin music. Target aud: General. ♦ Estuardo Rodriguez, chmn & gen mgr; Leonor Rodriguez, pres; Orlando Henao Henao, stn mgr, sls dir & mus dir.

Lincolnton

WLON(AM)— Aug 28, 1953: 1050 khz; 1 kw-D, 231 w-N. TL: N35 29 28 W81 16 03. Box 430, 1366 Startown Rd. 28093. Secondary address: 1500 E. Main St. 28092. Phone: (704) 735-8071. Fax: (704) 732-9067. E-mail: info@hrnb.com. Licensee: HRN Broadcasting Inc. (acq 4-14-2004; $500,000. with WCSL(AM) Cherryville). Network: Westwood One. Format: Oldies, sports. Target aud: 25 plus. Spec prog: Gospel 5 hrs wkly. ♦ Mark . Boyd, pres; Lanny Ford, gen mgr; Milton Baker, opns mgr.

Lockwoods Folly Town

*****WGHW(FM)**— Not on air, target date: unknown: 88.1 mhz; 2.9 kw vert. Ant 311 ft. TL: N34 03 48 W78 05 32. Box 159, Rural Hall 27045. Phone: (605) 868-0525. Licensee: Church Planters of America (acq 5-18-2005). Fletcher, Heald & Hildreth. ♦ Danny Hawkins, pres & gen mgr.

Louisburg

WKXU(FM)—Listing follows WYRN(AM).

WYRN(AM)— Sept 12, 1958: 1480 khz; 500 w-D. TL: N36 06 46 W78 16 50. Box 463 27549. Phone: (919) 496-3155. Fax: (919) 496-5864. Web Site: www.country102.com. Licensee: New Century Media Group LLC. Group owner: Curtis Media Group (acq 6-1-2003; $2.8 million. with co-located FM). Format: Country, talk. News staff: one; News: 20 hrs wkly. Target aud: Adults 25-54. Spec prog: Black. ♦ William M. McClatchey Jr., pres, gen mgr, opns mgr, dev mgr & gen sls mgr; Mollie B. Evans, prom mgr & news dir; Charlie M. Evans Jr., mus dir; Kristen Gillian, pub affrs dir; Bill Lambert, engrg mgr.

WKXU(FM)—Co-owned with WYRN(AM). Dec 5, 1989: 102.5 mhz; 6 kw. 328 ft. TL: N36 07 12 W78 22 48. Stereo. Web Site: www.country102.com. News: 6 hrs wkly. Spec prog: News, birthday celebration, country exchange, sports.

Lumberton

WAGR(AM)— Nov 27, 1954: 1340 khz; 1 kw-U. TL: N34 35 58 W79 00 33. 145 Rowan St. A-3, Fayetteville 28301. Secondary address: 1498 Alamac Rd. 28301. Phone: (910)486-9438. Fax: (910) 671-1812. E-mail: wcookman@aol.com. Licensee: WAGR Broadcasting Inc. (acq 6-30-98; $50,000). License and equipment only Williams Format: Gospel. News: 4 hrs wkly. Target aud: 25-54. ♦ Charles W. Cookman, pres; Sandra Lofton, gen mgr; Val Halliday, opns mgr & progmg dir.

WFNC-FM— July 19, 1964: 102.3 mhz; 6 kw. 267 ft. TL: N34 35 58 W79 00 33. Stereo. Box 35297, Fayetteville 28303. Secondary address: 1009 Drayton Rd., Fayetteville 28303. Phone: (910) 864-5222. Fax: (910) 864-3065. Web Site: www.cumulus.com. Licensee: Cumulus Licensing Corp. Group owner: Cumulus Media Inc. (acq 3-12-01; grpsl). Format: News/talk. Target aud: 18-54. ♦ Laura Gavis-Price, progmg dir & mus dir; Tom Haymond, gen mgr & chief of engrg.

WKML(FM)— Dec 1, 1960: 95.7 mhz; 100 kw. 1,064 ft. TL: N34 46 56 W79 04 42. Stereo. Box 2563, Fayetteville 28302. Secondary address: 508 Person St., Fayetteville 28301. Phone: (910) 483-9565. Fax: (910) 483-6008. Licensee: Beasley Broadcasting of Eastern North Carolina Inc. Group owner: Beasley Broadcast Group (acq 1981). Network: ABC Information & Entertainment. Rep: D & R Radio. Brooks, Pierce, McLendon, Humphrey & Leonard. Format: C&W. News staff: one; News: 5 hrs wkly. Target aud: 25-54. ♦ George G. Beasley, pres; J. Daniel Highsmith, opns mgr; Mac Edwards, opns VP; Angela Godwin, gen sls mgr; Bryan Kusilka, natl sls mgr; Paul Johnson, progmg dir; Van Clough, chief of engrg.

Manteo

WOBX-FM— 2001: 98.1 mhz; 50 kw. Ant 295 ft. TL: N35 51 52 W75 39 01. Box 1418, Nags Head 27959. Secondary address: 2422 S. Wrightsville Rd., Nags Head 27959. Phone: (252) 441-1024. Fax: (252) 441-2109. E-mail: wobx@ecri.net. Web Site: www.wobx.net. Licensee: East Carolina Radio of Elizabeth City Inc. Format: Active rock. ♦ L.F. Loesch, gen mgr; Chris Ling, gen sls mgr.

*****WUND-FM**— 2004: 88.9 mhz; 50 kw horiz, 47 kw vert. Ant 1,371 ft. TL: N35 54 00 W76 20 45. 120 Friday Center Dr., Chapel Hill 27517-9495. Phone: (919) 966-5454. Fax: (919) 966-5955. E-mail: wunc@wunc.org. Web Site: www.wunc.org. Licensee: Board of Trustees of the University of North Carolina at Chapel Hill. Network: Network: NPR, PRI. Format: News & info. News staff: 7; News: 124 hrs wkly. Spec prog: Folk 20 hrs wkly. ♦ Joan Siefert Rose, gen mgr.

*****WURI(FM)**— 1999: 90.9 mhz; 3.9 kw. Ant 187 ft. TL: N35 54 28 W75 40 26. 120 Friday Center Dr., Chapel Hill 27517-9495. Phone: (919) 966-5454. Fax: (919) 966-5955. E-mail: wunc@wunc.org. Web Site: www.wunc.org. Licensee: Board of Trustees/University of North Carolina at Chapel Hill. Network: Network: Network: CBC Radio One, NPR, PRI. Format: News & Info. Spec prog: Folk 20 hrs wkly.

WVOD(FM)— Mar 28, 1986: 99.1 mhz; 50 kw. 491 ft. TL: N35 50 44 W75 38 50. Stereo. 637 Harbor Rd., Wanchese 27981. Phone: (252) 475-1888. Fax: (252) 475-1881. Web Site: www.wvod.com. Licensee: Convergent Broadcasting Licensee LLC. Group owner: Convergent Broadcasting LLC (acq 12-16-2002; $1 million). Format: AAA. News staff: one. Target aud: 25-49. Spec prog: Class 6 hrs, blues 2 hrs, reggae 2 hrs wkly. ♦ Bruce A. Biette, pres; Tom Pierce, gen mgr; Hunt Thomas, opns dir; Matt Cooper, progmg dir; Tad Abbey, mus dir; John Kerner, chief of engrg.

Marion

WBRM(AM)— May 9, 1949: 1250 khz; 5 kw-D, 62 w-N. TL: N35 40 59 W82 02 08. 147 N. Garden St. 28752. Phone: (828) 652-9500. Web Site: wbrm@wnclink.com.6 pm-6 am Westwood One Mainstream Country Licensee: WBRM Inc. (acq 12-1-88; $450,000). Format: Country. News staff: one; News: 9 hrs wkly. Target aud: 25-55; young adult to mature. Spec prog: Gospel 5 hrs, relg 7 hrs wkly. ♦ Annette Bryant, CEO & pres; Kevin Estes, opns mgr.

Mars Hill

*****WYQS(FM)**— 1974: 90.5 khz; 250 w. 230 ft. TL: N35 49 30 W82 33 00. Stereo. 73 Broadway, Asheville 28801. Phone: (828) 689-1407. Fax: (828) 689-1106. Licensee: Western North Carolina Public Radio Inc. (acq 8-26-2004; $177,000). Format: Var. News staff: 3; News: 7 hrs wkly. Target aud: 14-30; college students & college community. Spec prog: Jazz 7 hrs, class 7 hrs, new age 6 hrs, Christian music 15 hrs wkly.

Marshall

WHBK(AM)— Sept 20, 1956: 1460 khz; 500 w-D, 139 w-N. TL: N35 48 01 W82 40 34. 1055 Skyway Dr. 28753. Phone: (828) 649-3914. Fax: (828) 649-2869. Licensee: Southern Broadcasting Inc. (acq 10-22-91; $145,000). Format: Southern gospel. Spec prog: Farm 3 hrs wkly. ♦ Bruce Philips, pres; Ricky Seay, gen mgr.

Mayodan

WMYN(AM)— July 15, 1957: 1420 khz; 1 kw-D, 70 w-N. TL: N36 24 58 W79 59 29. Box 279 27027. Phone: (336) 427-9696. Fax: (336) 548-4636. E-mail: info@wloewmyn.com. Web Site: www.wloewmyn.com. Licensee: Mayo Broadcasting Corp. (acq 1982; $110,000). Network: Network: Salem Radio Network, USA. Format: Info, talk, relg. News staff: one; News: 30 hrs wkly. Target aud: 25 plus; general. ♦ Richard D. Hall, pres; Mike Moore, gen mgr; Annette Moore, stn mgr.

Mebane

WGSB(AM)— Dec 7, 1973: 1060 khz; 1 kw-D, DA. TL: N36 03 28 W79 16 36. Estuardo Valdemar Rodriguez and Leonor Rodriguez Stns, 1010 Vermont Ave. N.W., Suite 100, Washington, DC 20005. Phone: (202) 638-1959. Fax: (202) 393-7464. Licensee: Estuardo Valdemar Rodriguez and Leonor Rodriguez. Group owner: WRTP Radio Network (acq 12-13-2004; grpsl). Format: Sp. ♦ Estuardo Valdemar Rodriguez, gen mgr.

Mint Hill

WNOW(AM)— Aug 1, 1987: 1030 khz; 10 kw-D, DA. TL: N35 08 30 W80 36 05. Box 19448, Charlotte 28219. Secondary address: 4201-J Stewart Andrew Blvd., Matthews 28217. Phone: (704) 665-9355. Fax: (208) 545-9888. Licensee: Davidson Media Carolinas Stations LLC. Group owner: Davidson Media Group LLC (acq 5-10-2004; grpsl). Format: Mexican regional. ♦ Peter W. Davidson, pres; Russ Douglass Jones, gen mgr, gen sls mgr & progmg dir; Aura Gavilan, prom mgr; Winston Hawkins, chief of engrg.

Mocksville

WDSL(AM)— October 1964: 1520 khz; 5 kw-D, 1 kw-CH. TL: N35 52 50 W80 32 26. Box 1520 27028. Secondary address: 125 W. Deport St. 27028. Phone: (336) 751-9375. E-mail: wdslradio@mailcity.com. Licensee: Davie Broadcasting Inc. (acq 10-26-90; $52,000; 11-19-90). Format: Country, bluegrass, gospel. Target aud: 25-80; general.

Monroe

WDEX(AM)— December 1983: 1430 khz; 2.5 kw-U, DA-2. TL: N34 59 04 W80 36 14. Box 8146, Kannapolis 28083. Secondary address: Weddington Rd. 28110. Phone: (704) 857-1101. Fax: (704) 857-0680. Web Site: fordbroadcasting.com. Licensee: Ford Broadcasting Inc. (acq 11-2-99). Network: USA. Smithwick & Belendiuk. Format: Southern gospel. Target aud: 25-55. ♦ Carl Ford, pres & gen mgr.

WIXE(AM)— May 3, 1968: 1190 khz; 5 kw-D, 2 kw-CH. TL: N34 57 41 W80 32 40. Stereo. Box 1007 28111. Secondary address: 1700 Buena Vista Dr. 28112. Phone: (704) 289-2525. Fax: (704) 289-1416. E-mail: wixeradio@carolina.rr.com. Web Site: www.wixe.com. Licensee: Monroe Broadcasting Co. (acq 5-2-00; $800,000). Yelverton. Format: C&W, gospel, talk. News: 8 hrs wkly. Target aud: 18-55. Spec prog: Beach & oldies 5 hrs wkly. ♦ Archie Morgan, pres & gen mgr.

WXNC(AM)— July 1947: 1060 khz; 4 kw-D. TL: N34 58 45 W80 30 48. Stereo. 4801 E. Independence Blvd., Suite 803, Charlotte 28212. Phone: (704) 537-9322. Fax: (704) 537-9735. E-mail: cheri@geddings.com. Web Site: www.1060radio.com. Licensee: Norsan Consulting and Management Inc. (acq 8-3-2005; $1.15 million). Network: CNN Radio. Format: Talk. News staff: one; News: 5 hrs wkly. ♦ Norberto Sanchez, pres; Kris Phillips, CFO; Cheri Moore, gen mgr.

Mooresville

WHIP(AM)— 1950: 1350 khz; 1 kw-D, 670 w-N. TL: N35 36 04 W80 48 51. Box 600, 2432 Statesville Hwy. 28115. Phone: (704) 664-9447. Fax: (704) 664-5551. Licensee: Mooresville Media Inc. (acq 8-76). Network: USA. Format: Oldies. News: 13 hrs wkly. Target aud: 25-45. Spec prog: Black 6 hrs, relg 6 hrs wkly. ♦ Glenn Hamrick, pres; Martha Hamrick, VP; Norman Tindal, sls VP & gen sls mgr; Harrill Hamrick, chief of engrg.

Morehead City

*****WOTJ(FM)**— Dec 12, 1988: 90.7 mhz; 24 kw. 466 ft. TL: N34 46 41 W76 52 42. Stereo. 520 Roberts Rd., Newport 28570. Phone: (252) 223-4600/223-6088. Fax: (252) 223-2201. Web Site: www.fbnradio.com.

Stations in the U.S. — North Carolina

Developers & Brokers of Radio Properties

contact American Media Services at our suite:
Philadelphia Marriott Downtown
215-625-2900
843-972-2200
americanmediaservices.com
Charleston, SC
Dallas, TX · Chicago, Il · Austin, TX

American Media Services, LLC

Licensee: Grace Christian School. Network: USA. Format: Relg. News: 8 hrs wkly. Target aud: General; family. ◆ Michael D. Ebron, gen mgr.

WRHT(FM)— Dec 20, 1972: 96.3 mhz; 100 kw. 492 ft. TL: N34 44 18 W76 48 40. Stereo. 1307 S. Glenburnie Rd., New Bern 28562. Phone: (252) 672-5900. Fax: (252) 637-6872. E-mail: thehotfm@thehotfm.com. Web Site: www.thehotfm.com. Licensee: ABG North Carolina LLC. Group owner: Archway Broadcasting Group (acq 1-9-03; grpsl). Rep: Allied Radio Partners. Format: CHR. News staff: one; News: 7 hrs wkly. Target aud: 18-49; young active adults & military personnel. ◆ Bill Bailey, gen mgr.

Morganton

WCIS(AM)— Mar 1, 1988: 760 khz; 3.5 kw-D. TL: N35 47 40 W81 43 12. Stereo. Box 1806 28680-1806. Secondary address: 1399 Bost Rd. 28655. Phone: (828) 433-9247. Fax: (828) 433-1498. E-mail: powerhouse76@aol.com. Licensee: W.F.M. Inc. (acq 10-1-93; $65,000). Network: USA. Format: Southern gospel. ◆ John L. Whisnant Sr., pres; Jeff Whisnant, VP; John L. Whisnant Jr., gen mgr; Jeffrey K. Whisnant, opns mgr.

WMNC(AM)— Sept 23, 1947: 1430 khz; 5 kw-D, 1 kw-N, DA-N. TL: N35 45 09 W81 43 03. Box 969 28680-0969. Secondary address: 1103 N. Green St. 28655. Phone: (828) 437-0521. Phone: (828) 437-0009. Fax: (828) 433-8855. E-mail: wmnc@wmnc.net. Web Site: www.wmnc.com. Licensee: Cooper Broadcasting Co. (acq 9-23-47). Format: Class country. Spec prog: Farm 2 hrs wkly.

WMNC-FM— Aug 3, 1963: 92.1 mhz; 6 kw. 327 ft. TL: N35 45 09 W81 43 19. Stereo. Web Site: www.wmnc.com. Format: Hot new country.

WSVM(AM)— See Valdese

Mount Airy

WPAQ(AM)— February 1948: 740 khz; 10 kw-D, 1 kw-CH. TL: N36 32 04 W80 35 48. Box 907 27030. Phone: (336) 786-6111. Fax: (336) 789-7792. Licensee: Ralph D. Epperson. Format: Country, bluegrass, big band. News staff: one; News: 13 hrs wkly. Target aud: 25-64. Spec prog: Farm one hr, community affrs one hr, old time string mus 15 hrs wkly. ◆ Ralph D. Epperson, gen mgr; Kelly D. Epperson, stn mgr; Kathy Edmonds, gen sls mgr; Susan Carroll, prom mgr; Bernie Wise, news dir; John Mullins, chief of engrg.

WSYD(AM)— Oct 4, 1951: 1300 khz; 5 kw-D, 1 kw-N, DA-N. TL: N36 30 12 W80 35 35. 115 City View Dr. 27030. Phone: (336) 786-2147. Fax: (336) 789-9858. Licensee: Granite City Broadcasters Inc. (acq 1996). Format: Pure country. News staff: one; News: 8 hrs wkly. Target aud: General. ◆ Kelly D. Epperson, pres & gen mgr; Deborah Cochran, progmg dir; Bernie Wise, news dir; John Mullins, chief of engrg.

Mount Olive

WDJS(AM)— Dec 27, 1961: 1430 khz; 1 kw-D. TL: N35 12 16 W78 03 06. Box 479 28365. Secondary address: 990 N. Center St., Ext. 28365. Phone: (919) 658-9751. Fax: (919) 658-4894. Licensee: The Mount Olive Broadcasting Co. Format: Relg, Christian. Spec prog: Black 5 hrs, gospel 5 hrs, Sp 5 hrs wkly. ◆ Ann W. Mayo, CEO & gen mgr; Nancy West, progmg dir.

Moyock

WCDG(FM)— Oct 17, 1974: 92.1 mhz; 18 kw. Ant 384 ft. TL: N36 41 39 W76 02 57. Stereo. 1003 Norfolk Sq., Norfolk, VA 23502-4948. Phone: (757) 466-0009. Fax: (757) 466-7043. Web Site: www.921thebeat.com. Licensee: Clear Channel Broadcasting Licenses Inc. Group owner: Clear Channel Communications Inc. Format: Oldies. Target aud: 18-34; males 18-49. ◆ Lowery Mays, CEO; Reggie Jordan, gen mgr; Eric Mychaels, opns mgr; Terry Ratliff, gen sls mgr; Bob Rischitelli, natl sls mgr; Toni B. Jones, prom dir; Greg Gabriel, chief of engrg.

Murfreesboro

WDLZ(FM)— Listing follows WWDR(AM).

WWDR(AM)— Mar 20, 1965: 1080 khz; 930 w-D. TL: N36 26 24 W77 08 10. Box 38, 1714 W. Main St. 27855. Phone: (252) 398-4111. Fax: (252) 398-3581. Licensee: First Media Radio LLC (group owner; acq 1-7-03; grpsl). Network: Moody. Format: Team radio. Spec prog: Farm 10 hrs wkly. ◆ Amy Davis, gen mgr & gen sls mgr; Frank Knapper, prom mgr & progmg dir.

WDLZ(FM)— Co-owned with WWDR(AM). Oct 11, 1970: 98.3 mhz; 3 kw. Ant 328 ft. TL: N36 26 24 W77 08 10. Stereo. Format: Soft rock.

Murphy

WCNG(AM)— Listing follows WCVP(AM).

WCVP(AM)— Oct 12, 1958: 600 khz; 1 kw-D, 20 w-N. TL: N35 04 00 W83 59 58. Box 280 28906. Phone: (828) 837-2151. Phone: (828) 837-2152. Licensee: Cherokee Broadcasting Co. Format: MOR, news, gospel. Target aud: All ages. Spec prog: Farm 3 hrs, class 20 hrs, C&W 12 hrs wkly. ◆ Dennis Blakemore, pres, gen sls mgr, prom mgr & chief of engrg; Jane Blakemore, gen mgr & progmg dir; Skip Ballard, mus dir.

WCNG(FM)— Co-owned with WCVP(AM). Oct 23, 1990: 102.7 mhz; 3 kw. 426 ft. TL: N35 04 00 W83 59 58. (CP: Ant 236 ft.). Stereo. Format: Soft rock. ◆ Dennis Blakemore, pres.

WKRK(AM)— Aug 8, 1958: 1320 khz; 5 kw-D, 62 w-N. TL: N35 06 42 W84 00 31. 427 Hill Street 28906. Phone: (828) 837-1320. Fax: (828) 837-8610. Web Site: www.1320am.com. Licensee: Radford Communications Inc. (acq 1995; $250,000). Network: Westwood One. Rep: Keystone (unwired net). Format: C&W, news/talk, relg. News: 7 hrs wkly. Target aud: 25-54. Spec prog: Pub affrs 3 hrs wkly. ◆ Tim Radford, CEO, pres, gen mgr, opns mgr & progmg mgr; Ab Radford, VP & gen sls mgr; Emma Ramsey, mktg mgr & adv mgr; Suzanne Crawford, prom dir; Vic Stiles, chief of engrg.

Nags Head

WZPR(FM)— Apr 4, 1990: 92.3 mhz; 18.5 kw. 384 ft. TL: N35 50 49 W75 38 19. Stereo. 637 Harbor Rd., Wanchese 27981. Phone: (252) 475-1888. Fax: (252) 475-1881. Licensee: Convergent Broadcasting Outer Banks LLC. Group owner: Convergent Broadcasting LLC (acq 11-7-02; with WYND-FM Hatteras). Network: Motor Racing Net. Format: CHR. News staff: one. Target aud: 25-54. ◆ Hunt Thomas, opns mgr; Tom Pierce, mktg mgr.

Nashville

WZAX(FM)— February 1997: 99.7 mhz; 6 kw. 328 ft. TL: N35 57 01 W77 57 26. 12717 East N.C 97, Rocky Mount 27803. Phone: (252) 442-8092. Fax: (252) 977-6664. Licensee: First Media Radio LLC (group owner; acq 7-22-03; grpsl). Format: Adult Contemp. ◆ Alex Kolobielski, pres; Mike Binkley, gen mgr; David Perkins, opns mgr & progmg mgr; Chris Hordy, sls dir & adv mgr; Karen Bullock, prom dir.

New Bern

***WAAE(FM)**— 1997: 91.9 mhz; 1 kw. 164 ft. TL: N35 09 17 W77 02 00. Box 2440, Tupelo, MS 38803. Phone: (662) 844-8888. Fax: (662) 840-3187. Web Site: www.afr.net. Licensee: American Family Association. Group owner: American Family Radio Format: Lite contemp, praise, talk. ◆ Marvin Sanders, gen mgr; Joey Moody, chief of engrg.

WIKS(FM)— August 1977: 101.9 mhz; 100 kw. 1,020 ft. TL: N35 12 07 W77 11 15. Stereo. 207 Glenburnie Dr. 28560. Phone: (252) 633-1500. Fax: (252) 633-6546. Web Site: kiss102.com. Licensee: Beasley FM Acquisition Corp. Rep: D & R Radio. Format: Urban adult contemp. Spec prog: Gospel 4 hrs, jazz 2 hrs wkly. ◆ Bruce Beasley, pres; Bruce Simel, VP & gen mgr.

WNOS(AM)— Apr 23, 1942: 1450 khz; 1 kw-U. TL: N35 06 03 W77 04 33. 116 S. Business Plaza 28562. Phone: (252) 638-8888. Fax: (252) 636-5848. Licensee: CTC Media Group Inc. (group owner; acq 7-1-00; $65,000). Format: Big band, adult standards. Target aud: 45 plus; mature, retired & semi-retired adults. Spec prog: Jazz 12 hrs wkly. ◆ Lee Afflerbach, pres; Mike Afflerbach, gen mgr.

WSFL-FM— July 20, 1968: 106.5 mhz; 100 kw. 915 ft. TL: N35 02 27 W77 21 11. Stereo. 207 Glenburnie Dr. 28560. Phone: (252) 633-1500. Fax: (252) 633-6546. Web Site: www.wsfl.com. Licensee: W & B Media Inc. Group owner: Beasley Broadcast Group (acq 7-10-91; $500,000 with co-located AM; 7-29-91). Rep: D & R Radio. Format: Classic rock, AOR. Target aud: 18-54. ◆ Bruce Simel, gen mgr; Jeff Sanders, opns dir; Alan Wells, prom dir; Mike Carson, mus dir; Richard Banks, engrg dir.

***WTEB(FM)**— June 4, 1984: 89.3 mhz; 100 kw. 522 ft. TL: N35 06 32 W77 06 10. Stereo. 800 College Ct. 28562. Phone: (252) 638-3434. Fax: (252) 638-3538. Web Site: www.publicradioeast.org. Licensee: Board of Trustees, Craven Community College. Network: Network: NPR, PRI. Format: Class, news & info. News: 44 hrs wkly. Target aud: 35 plus; highly educated professionals. Spec prog: Jazz 4 hrs wkly. ◆ Kathleen Beal, gen mgr; Charles Wethington, opns mgr; Glen Lynn, dev dir; Tim Kimble, progmg dir; J. Howard Jones, chief of engrg.

WWNB(AM)— July 5, 1953: 1490 khz; 1 kw-U. TL: N35 07 59 W77 03 56. 116 S. Business Plaza 28562. Phone: (252) 633-1490. Fax: (252) 636-5848. E-mail: wwnb1490@coastalnet.com. Licensee: CTC Media Group Inc. (group owner; acq 11-15-90; $75,000). Network: Network: UPI, USA. Jimmy Young. Format: All talk, black gospel. Target aud: 25-54; general. ◆ Mike Afflerbach, gen mgr; John Rawson, gen sls mgr.

***WZNB(FM)**— Not on air, target date: unknown: 88.5 mhz; 300 w. Ant 121 ft. TL: N35 06 32 W77 06 10. Public Radio East, 800 College Ct. 28562. Phone: (252) 638-3434. Fax: (252) 638-3538. Web Site: www.publicradioeast.org. Licensee: Craven Community College. Format: News, public radio, contemp. ◆ Kathleen Beal, gen mgr; Charles Wethington, opns mgr; Glen Lynn, dev dir; Tim Kimble, progmg dir; J. Howard Jones, chief of engrg.

New Hope

WAUG(AM)— July 20, 1987: 750 khz; 500 w-D. TL: N35 47 28 W78 37 10. Stereo. 1315 Oakwood Ave., Raleigh 27610. Phone: (919) 516-4750. E-mail: waug@st-aug.edu. Licensee: Saint Augustine's College. Network: American Urban. Format: Relg, news/talk, gospel. Target aud: 18 plus; Black adults. ◆ Dr. Diane Suber, pres; Alan Riggs, gen mgr & stn mgr; Frank Butler, opns mgr; John Hardee, chief of engrg.

Newland

WECR(AM)— Aug 14, 1978: 1130 khz; 1 kw-D. TL: N36 04 39 W81 54 59. 1281 Newland Hwy. 28657. Phone: (828) 733-0188. Fax: (828) 733-0189. Licensee: Aisling Broadcasting of Banner Elk LLC (group owner; acq 2-10-2004; grpsl). Format: Country. Target aud: 25-54; middle class, blue collar. Spec prog: Gospel 10 hrs, relg 5 hrs, bluegrass 2 hrs wkly, Avery High Sports, NASCAR. ◆ Jonathan Hoffman, gen mgr.

Newport

WMGV(FM)— Sept 4, 1983: 103.3 mhz; 100 kw. 980 ft. TL: N34 45 06 W76 52 57. 207 Glenburnie Dr., New Bern 28560. Phone: (252) 633-1500. Fax: (252) 633-0718. Web Site: www.v1033.com. Licensee: WMGV License L.P. Group owner: Beasley Broadcast Group Inc. (acq 2-3-2000; grpsl). Rep: D & R Radio. Pepper & Corazzini. Format: Soft rock. Target aud: 18-54. ◆ Bruce Simel, gen mgr; B.K. Kirkland, progmg dir.

Broadcasting & Cable Yearbook 2006

North Carolina / Directory of Radio

Newton

WNNC(AM)— June 18, 1948: 1230 khz; 1 kw-U. TL: N35 40 20 W81 14 12. Stereo. Box 430 28658. Phone: (828) 464-4041. Fax: (828) 464-9662. E-mail: totalradio@aol.com. Licensee: Newton-Conover Communications Inc. (acq 8-76). Network: ABC Information & Entertainment. Format: Adult contemp. News staff: one. Target aud: 25-49. Spec prog: Black 2 hrs, jazz 3 hrs wkly. ♦Dave Lingafelt, pres, gen mgr & chief of engrg; Jim Turner, gen sls mgr; Al Mainess, news dir.

Norlina

WJIJ(FM)— January 2001: 94.3 mhz; 6 kw. Ant 328 ft. TL: N36 29 46 W78 11 14. 5 W. Hargett St., Suite 801, Raleigh 27607. Phone: (919) 899-6778. Fax: (919) 899-6779. Web Site: www.csnradio.com. Licensee: CSN International (group owner; acq 12-18-98). Format: Religious. ♦Jim Walker, gen mgr.

*WZRN(FM)—Not on air, target date: unknown: 90.5 mhz; 2.3 kw. Ant 298 ft. TL: N36 29 38 W78 11 23. 230-B Roanoke Ave., Roanoke Rapids 27870. Phone: (252) 537-9999. Fax: (252) 537-3333. Web Site: www.wzru.org. Licensee: Roanoke Valley Communications Inc. Format: Talk, class, news. ♦George Campbell, pres; Bryan Lewis, gen mgr.

North Wilkesboro

WKBC(AM)— June 1947: 800 khz; 1 kw-D, 308 w-N. TL: N36 11 18 W81 08 07. Box 938, 400 C St. 28659. Phone: (336) 667-2221. Fax: (336) 667-3677. E-mail: bbrownwkbc@aol.com. Licensee: Wilkes Broadcasting Co. Inc. (acq 1-24-03); with co-located FM). Format: Country. ♦Robert Brown, pres & gen mgr; Ed Racey, news dir.

WKBC-FM— July 1962: 97.3 mhz; 100 kw. 1,350 ft. TL: N36 04 34 W81 07 44. (CP: 100 kw horiz, 92 kw vert, ant 1,332 ft. TL: N36 04 34 W81 07 43). Stereo. Format: CHR.

Oak Island

WSFM(FM)— July 2000: 98.3 mhz; 18.5 kw. 380 ft. TL: N33 57 40 W78 01 37. 25 N. Kerr Ave., Suite C, Wilmington 28405. Phone: (910) 791-3088. Fax: (910) 791-0112. Web Site: www.983channelz.com. Licensee: NM Licensing LLC. Group owner: NextMedia Group L.L.C. (acq 12-20-2004; grpsl). Format: CHR.

Ocean Isle Beach

WLQB(FM)— 1999: 93.5 mhz; 6 kw. Ant 328 ft. TL: N33 55 37 W78 23 48. 4841 Hwy. 17 Bypass S., Myrtle Beach, SC 29577. Phone: (843) 293-0107. Fax: (843) 293-1717. Licensee: Qantum of Myrtle Beach License Co. LLC. Group owner: Qantum Communications Corp. (acq 7-2-2003; grpsl). Format: Country. ♦Michael Meeks, gen mgr; Serap Jackson, opns mgr & progmg mgr.

Oriental

WWHA(FM)— Mar 18, 1993: 94.1 mhz; 11 kw. 485 ft. TL: N35 00 02 W76 49 58. Stereo. 1307 S. Glenburnie Rd., New Bern 28562. Phone: (252) 672-5900. Fax: (252) 637-6872. Web Site: www.eagle64fm.com. Licensee: ABG North Carolina LLC. Group owner: Archway Broadcasting Group (acq 1-9-2003; grpsl). Pepper & Corazzini. Format: Country. Target aud: 25 plus; adults with disposable incomes. ♦Bill Bailey, gen mgr.

Oxford

WCBQ(AM)— June 9, 1949: 1340 khz; 1 kw-U. TL: N36 18 27 W78 34 37. Stereo. PO Box 1005, One Broadcast Ctr., 601 Henderson St. 27565. Phone: (919) 693-3540. Phone: (919) 693-1340. Fax: (919) 693-9054. E-mail: wcbgwhne@gloryroad.net. Licensee: The Paradise Network (TPN) of North Carolina Inc. (acq 4-30-01; $650,000. with WHNC(AM) Henderson). Network: UPI. T-N. Format: Black gospel. News: 10 hrs wkly. Target aud: General. Spec prog: Farm, professional & college sports, news/talk. ♦Dr. Alvin Augustus Jones, gen mgr & chief of engrg; Jim Davis, engrg mgr.

Pinehurst

*WBFY(FM)— September 2003: 90.3 mhz; 3.5 kw vert. Ant 328 ft. TL: N35 09 13 W79 34 16. Drawer 2440, Tupelo, MS 38803. Phone: (662) 844-8888. Fax: (662) 840-3187. Web Site: www.afr.net. Licensee: American Family Association. Group owner: American Family Radio Format: Christian. ♦Marvin Sanders, gen mgr.

WEEB(AM)—See Southern Pines

WIOZ(AM)— Mar 25, 1980: 550 khz; 1 kw-D, 260 w-N, DA-2. TL: N35 09 04 W79 28 40. 200 Short Rd., Southern Pines 28387. Phone: (910) 692-2107. Fax: (910) 692-6849. Licensee: Muirfield Broadcasting Inc. (group owner; acq 12-28-83). Format: Adult standards. News staff: one; News: 5 hrs wkly. Target aud: General. ♦Walker Morris, pres; Tiffany Hewitt, gen mgr & gen sls mgr; Rich Rushforth, opns mgr.

WKQB(FM)—See Southern Pines

Pinetops

WPWZ(FM)— Dec 2, 1996: 95.5 mhz; 12.5 kw. 459 ft. TL: N35 56 45 W77 39 37. Stereo. 12714 East NC 97, Rocky Mount 27803. Phone: (252) 442-8092. Fax: (252) 977-6664. Licensee: First Media Radio LLC (group owner; acq 12-3-2003; grpsl). Format: Adult urban. News staff: one. Target aud: 24-54. ♦Alex Kolobielski, pres; Mike Binkley, gen mgr; David Perkins, opns mgr.

Plymouth

WPNC-FM— December 1979: 95.9 mhz; 2.6 kw. 350 ft. TL: N35 50 48 W76 45 22. Stereo. 930 Hwy. 32 S. 27962. Phone: (252) 793-9995. Fax: (252) 793-4673. E-mail: magic959production@yahoo.com. Web Site: www.gomagic959.com. Licensee: Durlyn Broadcasting Inc. (acq 1996). Format: Adult contemp. ♦Bill Benjamin, CEO & gen mgr; W.B. Cox Jr., VP; Alex Rains, opns mgr.

Raeford

WMFA(AM)— Apr 25, 1963: 1400 khz; 1 kw-U. TL: N35 58 43 W79 12 32. 1085 E. Central Ave. 28376. Phone: (910) 875-6225. Phone: (910) 875-6477. Fax: (910) 875-3220. E-mail: wmfa1400@yahoo.com. Licensee: W & V Broadcasting Enterprises Inc. (acq 6-2-93; $12,000; 6-21-93). Format: Gospel. Target aud: General. Spec prog: Sp 6 hrs wkly. ♦William Hollingsworth, CEO & pres; Vera Hollingsworth, CFO; Jeremy Hollingsworth, gen mgr & opns mgr.

*WRAE(FM)—Not on air, target date: unknown: 88.7 mhz; 4 kw vert. Ant 194 ft. TL: N34 54 55 W79 07 32. Box 2440, Tupelo, MS 38803. Phone: (662) 844-8888. Fax: (662) 842-6791. Web Site: www.afr.net. Licensee: American Family Association. ♦Marvin Sanders, gen mgr.

Raleigh

WBBB(AM)— 1947: 96.1 mhz; 100 kw. 985 ft. TL: N35 41 07 W78 43 14. Stereo. 3012 High Woods Blvd., Suite 200 27604. Phone: (919) 876-6464. Fax: (919) 790-8893. Web Site: www.96rockonline.com. Licensee: Carolina Media Group Inc. Group owner: Curtis Media Group (acq 1996; $16 million). Format: Active Rock. Target aud: 18-34; male. ♦Don Curtis, pres; Mike Hartel, gen mgr; Jay Naclis, progmg dir & progmg mgr; Eddie Harrel, chief of engrg.

WCLY(AM)— Aug 15, 1962: 1550 khz; 1 kw-D, 7 w-N. TL: N35 45 37 W78 39 27. 3012 Highwoods Blvd., Suite 200 27604. Phone: (919) 954-1550. Fax: (919) 954-1556. Web Site: www.1550wcly.com. Licensee: Triangle Broadcast Associates LLC. (acq 4-5-99). Format: Relg. Target aud: 25-65; primarily Black. ♦Thomas Hill, gen mgr.

*WCPE(FM)— July 17, 1978: 89.7 mhz; 96.7 kw. Ant 1,178 ft. TL: N35 56 25 W78 28 45. Stereo. Box 897, Wake Forest 27588. Phone: (919) 556-5178. Fax: (919) 556-9273. E-mail: wcpe@wcpe.org. Web Site: theclassicalstation.org.Galaxy 5, transponder 7, 5.58/6.12 mhz Licensee: Educational Information Corp. Brooks, Pierce, McLendon, Humphrey & Leonard. Format: Classical. Target aud: 35 plus; class mus listeners. Spec prog: Sacred music, Opera. ♦Deborah S. Proctor, CEO, pres & gen mgr; Rae C. Weaver, dev dir.

WDCG(FM)—See Durham

WDNZ(AM)— Dec 1, 1981: 570 khz; 500 w-D, 54 w-N. TL: N35 45 37 W78 39 27. 3012 Highwoods Blvd. 27604. Phone: (919) 855-9383. Fax: (919) 790-6654. Web Site: www.wdnc.com. Licensee: Triangle Broadcast Associates LLC. Group owner: Curtis Media Group (acq 6-1-99). Network: CBS. Format: News/talk. ♦Bill Whitley, gen mgr; Beth Przestrzlski, sls mgr; Peter Richon, progmg dir.

*WKNC-FM— 1966: 88.1 mhz; 3 kw. 259 ft. TL: N35 47 15 W78 40 14. Stereo. Box 8607, North Carolina State Univ. Mail Ctr. 27695-8607. Phone: (919) 515-2401. Fax: (919) 515-2400. Fax: (919) 213-2353. Web Site: www.wknc.org. Licensee: North Carolina State University. Format: Rock, alternative. News: 5 hrs wkly. Target aud: 16-50; high school & college students of all demographics. Spec prog: Progsv/new wave 12 hrs, Christian rock 4 hrs, reggae 5 hr, Black 10 hrs wkly. ♦Jamie Proctor, gen mgr; Will Patnaud, chief of engrg.

WPJL(AM)— March 1939: 1240 khz; 1 kw-U. TL: N35 46 25 W78 37 09. Stereo. Box 27946, 515 Bart St. 27611. Phone: (919) 834-6401. Licensee: WPJL Inc. (acq 7-86; $600,000; 4-21-86). Network: USA. Format: Full-time Christian. News: 10 hrs wkly. Target aud: 25-54; Evangelical Christian community of greater Raleigh area. Spec prog: Black gospel. ♦William C. Suttles, pres & gen mgr; LaRue Porter, opns mgr; Jon Hardee, chief of engrg.

WPTF(AM)— Sept 22, 1924: 680 khz; 50 kw-U, DA-N. TL: N35 47 38 W78 45 41. Stereo. 3012 Highwoods Blvd., Suite 200 27604. Phone: (919) 876-0674. Fax: (919) 790-8369. Web Site: www.wptf.com. Licensee: First State Communications, Inc. Network: CBS. Rep: McGavren Guild. Format: News/talk. News: 20 hrs wkly. Target aud: 35-64. Spec prog: Farm 10 hrs wkly. ♦Al Bunch, gen mgr; Kevin Miller, progmg dir.

WQDR(FM)—Co-owned with WPTF(AM). August 1949: 94.7 mhz; 96 kw. 1,679 ft. TL: N35 40 35 W78 32 09. Stereo. Phone: (919) 876-6464. Fax: (919) 790-8893. Web Site: www.wqdr.net. Network: ABC Information & Entertainment. Format: Modern country. News staff: one; News: 2 hrs wkly. Target aud: 25-54. Spec prog: NASCAR racing, bluegrass. ♦Trip Savery, gen sls mgr; Marty Young, prom dir; Lisa McKay, progmg dir.

WQOK(FM)—(South Boston).VA Oct 1, 1960: 97.5 mhz; 100 kw. 981 ft. TL: N36 20 52 W78 40 00. Stereo. 8001-101 Creedmoor, Rd. 27613. Phone: (919) 848-9736. Fax: (919) 848-4724. E-mail: mmarinaro@radio-one.com. Web Site: www.k975.com. Licensee: Radio One Licenses LLC. Group owner: Radio One Inc. (acq 11-8-01; grpsl). Network: ABC. Rep: Christal. Format: Urban contemp. News staff: one; News: 20 hrs wkly. Target aud: 25-54; upwardly mobile with discretionary income. Spec prog: Gospel 9 hrs wkly. ♦Gary Weiss, gen mgr; Cy Young, opns dir & progmg dir; Saundra Lemaster, sls dir & gen sls mgr; Jodi Luke, natl sls mgr.

WRAL(FM)— 1947: 101.5 mhz; 96 kw. 1,820 ft. TL: N35 40 35 W78 32 09. Stereo. Box 10100 27605. Secondary address: 711 Hillsborough St. 27603. Phone: (919) 890-6101. Fax: (919) 890-6146. E-mail: mixonline@wralfm.com. Web Site: www.wralfm.com. Licensee: Capitol Broadcasting Co. Inc. (group owner; acq 1946). Rep: Katz Radio. Holland & Knight. Format: Adult contemp. News: 7 hrs wkly news progmg. Target aud: 25-54. Spec prog: Public Affafirs Block - 6:30-8:00am Sundays. ♦Jim Goodmon, pres; Dan McGrath, CFO; Ardie Gregory, VP & gen mgr; Joe Formicola, opns dir; Robert Wallace, gen sls mgr; Mark Turak, natl sls mgr; Karen Cates, mktg dir. Co-owned TV: WRAL-TV affil.

WRBZ(AM)— 1947: 850 khz; 10 kw-D, 5 kw-N, DA-N. TL: N35 48 04 W78 48 51. Stereo. 5000 Falls of Neuse Rd., Suite 308 27609. Phone: (919) 875-9100. Fax: (919) 875-9080. E-mail: brianm@850thebuzz.com. Web Site: www.850thebuzz.com. Licensee: NC Sportsnet LLC (acq 1-28-2005). Network: Westwood One. Rep: McGavren Guild. Format: Sports, talk/news. News: 5 hrs wkly. Target aud: 25-54. ♦Brian Maloney, gen mgr; Stephanie Wetzel, prom mgr; Adam Gold, progmg dir.

WRDU(FM)—(Wilson). Mar 1, 1961: 106.1 mhz; 100 kw. Ant 1,364 ft. TL: N35 45 36 W78 11 04. Stereo. 3100 Smoketree Ct., Suite 700 27604. Phone: (919) 876-1061. Fax: (919) 876-2929. Web Site: www.1061rdu.com. Licensee: Clear Channel Communications Group owner: Clear Channel Communications Inc. (acq 8-30-00; grpsl). Fisher, Wayland, Cooper, Leader & Zaragoza. Format: Classic rock. News staff: one; News: 3 hrs wkly. Target aud: 18-49. ♦Ken Spitzer, gen mgr; Jon Robbins, opns dir; Tammy O'Dell, sls dir; Jinnie Forsythe, gen sls mgr; Jessica Hayes, prom dir; Jimmy Tidwell, progmg dir; Dan McLeod, pub affrs dir; Fred Pace, chief of engrg.

WRSN(FM)—See Burlington

WRTG(AM)—See Garner

WRVA-FM—(Rocky Mount). November 1947: 100.7 mhz; 100 kw. Ant 1,968 ft. TL: N35 49 53 W78 08 50. Stereo. 3100 Smoketree Ct., Suite 700 27604. Phone: (919) 878-1500. Fax: (919) 876-8578. Web Site: www.oldies1007.com. Licensee: Capstar TX L.P. Group owner: Clear Channel Communications Inc. (acq 8-30-2000; grpsl). Network: ABC.

Broadcasting & Cable Yearbook 2006

Stations in the U.S. — North Carolina

Developers & Brokers of Radio Properties — contact American Media Services at our suite: Philadelphia Marriott Downtown 215-625-2900 / 843-972-2200 / americanmediaservices.com / Charleston, SC / Dallas, TX · Chicago, Il · Austin, TX — American Media Services, LLC

Fisher, Wayland, Cooper, Leader & Zaragoza. Target aud: 25-54; upscale adults. ♦ Ken Spitzer, gen mgr; Jon Robbins, opns dir; Myron Bethea, sls dir & gen sls mgr; Tammy O'Dell, sls dir; Jessica Hayes, prom dir; Fred Pace, engrg VP & chief of engrg.

*WSHA(FM)— Nov 18, 1968: 88.9 mhz; 50 kw. Ant 456 ft. TL: N35 45 05 W78 36 01. Stereo. 118 E. South St. 27601. Phone: (919) 546-8432. Phone: (919) 546-8430. Fax: (919) 546-8315. E-mail: wsha@shawu.edu. Web Site: www.wshafm.org. Licensee: Shaw University. Network: NPR. Format: Jazz. News: 13.5 hrs wkly. Target aud: 25-55; high income, well educated. Spec prog: Sp 3 hrs, African 3 hrs, Caribbean 4 hrs, world mus 4 hrs, blues 8 hrs, gospel 20 hrs wkly. ♦ Dr. Clarence G. Newsone, pres; Dr. Emeka Emekauwa, gen mgr; Michael Rochelle, dev dir; Rashad Muhaimin, progmg dir; Jim Davis, chief of engrg.

WWMY(FM)— 2000: 102.9 mhz; 1.7 kw. Ant 620 ft. TL: N35 47 38 W78 45 41. 3012 Highwoods Blvd., Suite 201 27604. Phone: (919) 790-6961. Fax: (919) 790-8369. Web Site: www.star80.com. Licensee: WWND LLC. Group owner: Curtis Media Group (acq 10-2-98; $495,000 for stock). Format: 80s hits. ♦ Mike Hartel, gen mgr.

Red Springs

WTEL(AM)— June 15, 1970: 1160 khz; 5 kw-D, 250 w-N. TL: N35 50 19 W79 10 36. Box 711 28377. Phone: (910) 843-5946. Fax: (910) 843-8694. Licensee: WDAS License L.P. Group owner: Beasley Broadcast Group Inc. (acq 6-12-97; $1.2 million. with WUKS(FM) Saint Pauls). Format: Southern gospel, Black gospel. News staff: 2. Target aud: 24-54. Spec prog: Farm 5 hrs wkly. ♦ Danny Highsmith, gen mgr; Towanna Locklear, gen sls mgr; Deanna Hodges, prom mgr; Garrette Davis, progmg dir; Gilbert Baez, news dir; Van Clough, chief of engrg.

Reidsville

WJMH(FM)— Sept 6, 1948: 102.1 mhz; 100 kw. 1,203 ft. TL: N36 16 33 W79 56 27. Stereo. 7819 National Service Rd., Suite 401, Greensboro 27409. Phone: (336) 605-5200. Fax: (336) 605-5219. Web Site: www.102jaimz.com. Licensee: Entercom Greensboro License LLC. Group owner: Entercom Communications Corp. (acq 12-13-99; grpsl). Network: ABC Information & Entertainment. Rep: McGavren Guild. Format: Urban, Hip-Hop. Target aud: 16-35; 65% Black, 35% white. ♦ Brent Miller, gen mgr; Erin Casey, gen sls mgr; Nancy Tate, prom dir; Brian Douglas, progmg dir; Larry Allen, chief of engrg.

WREV(AM)— 1948: 1220 khz; 1 kw-D. TL: N36 23 19 W79 38 51. 1010 Vermont Ave. N.W., Suite 100, Washington, DC 20005. Phone: (202) 638-1959. Fax: (202) 393-7464. Licensee: Estuardo Valdemar Rodriguez and Leonor Rodriguez. Group owner: Estuardo Valdemar Rodriguez and Leonor Rodriguez Stns (acq 8-5-2004; $125,000). Format: Sp music. ♦ Estuardo Valdemar Rodriguez, gen mgr.

Roanoke Rapids

WCBT(AM)— November 1940: 1230 khz; 1 kw-U. TL: N36 26 45 W77 39 51. Box 910, 3 E. First St., Weldon 27890. Phone: (252) 538-4184. Fax: (252) 538-0378. E-mail: haskinsal@yahoo.com. Web Site: www.wcbt1230.com. Licensee: First Media Radio LLC (group owner; acq 7-22-03; grpsl). Format: Old country. ♦ Al Haskin, gen mgr; John Green, opns mgr; Allen Garrett, progmg dir; Frank White, chief of engrg.

*WPGT(FM)— January 2001: 91.1 mhz; 2 kw. Ant 69 ft. TL: N36 28 08 W77 39 02. Winchester Stn., 905 Halstead Blvd., Elizabeth City 27909. Phone: (252) 334-1883. Fax: (252) 333-1459. E-mail: wpgt@csnradio.com. Licensee: CSN International (group owner; (acq 5-5-2000; $20,000. for CP). Format: Christian. News: one hr wkly. ♦ Jeff Ozanne, gen mgr; Darla Ozanne, progmg dir.

WPTM(FM)— 1973: 102.3 mhz; 6 kw. 300 ft. TL: N36 30 12 W77 44 47. (CP: 5.4 kw, ant 344 ft.). Stereo. Box 910 27870. Secondary address: 3 E. 4th St., Weldon 27890. Phone: (252) 536-3115. Fax: (252) 538-0378. E-mail: amyhmoran@yahoo.com. Web Site: www.wptm1023.com. Licensee: First Media Radio LLC (group owner;

acq 7-22-03; grpsl). Network: ABC Information & Entertainment. Format: Country. News staff: 3; News: 14 hrs wkly. Target aud: 25-54; females with spendable income, decision-makers. Spec prog: Farm15 hrs, relg 3 hrs wkly. ♦ Al Haskins, gen mgr.

*WRTP(FM)— July 4, 1994: 88.5 mhz; 35 kw. Ant 413 ft. TL: N36 27 38 W77 33 52. (CP: 24 kw, ant 479 ft). Stereo. 3013 Guess Rd., Durham 27705. Phone: (919) 477-7222. Fax: (919) 477-4424. E-mail: wrtp@goodnews.org. Web Site: www.hisradiowrtp.com. Licensee: Radio Training Network Inc. (acq 4-29-2005; swap for WZRU(FM) Roanoke Rapids). Network: Salem Radio Network. Rep: Salem. Format: Contemp Christian music. News: 14 hrs wkly. Target aud: 25-54; Christian. ♦ Mark G. Parker, CEO, gen mgr & progmg dir; James Campbell, pres; Randy Jordan, sls dir.

WTRG(FM)—See Gaston

*WZRU(FM)— Dec 8, 1972: 90.1 mhz; 760 w. Ant 174 ft. TL: N36 26 13 W77 38 12. (CP: 11 kw, ant 505 ft. TL: N36 14 39 W77 34 40). Stereo. 232 Roanoke Ave. 27870-1916. Phone: (252) 308-0885. Fax: (252) 537-3333. E-mail: wzru@schoollink.net. Web Site: www.wzru.org. Licensee: Roanoke Valley Communications Inc. (acq 5-6-2005; swap for WRTP(FM) Roanoke Rapids). Network: NPR. Arter & Hadden. Format: Adult contemp. News staff: 2; News: 30 hrs wkly. Target aud: 35 plus; community oriented, above-average education. Spec prog: Gospel 6 hrs, jazz 6 hrs, folk 5 hrs, oldies 4 hrs, new age 10 hrs, big band 4 hrs wkly. ♦ Brian Lewis, gen mgr.

Robbins

WLHC(FM)— June 2, 2003: 103.1 mhz; 6 kw. Ant 328 ft. TL: N35 26 33 W79 26 37. Box 1087, Angier 27501. Secondary address: 102 S. Steele St., Suite 301 27330. Phone: (919) 775-1031. Fax: (919) 775-1397. Licensee: Woolstone Corp. Network: ABC. Format: Lifestyle. Spec prog: Folk 3 hrs, jazz 15 hrs, Christian, 7 hrs, bluegrss 3 hr, big band 4 hrs, news/talk 10 hrs wkly. ♦ Alan Button, pres; Norm Allen, gen mgr; Peggy Kilgore, opns mgr; Scott Evans, sls dir.

Robbinsville

WCVP-FM— 1987: 95.9 mhz; 60 w. 2,008 ft. TL: N35 15 28 W83 47 44. Box 756, 129 N. By-Pass 28771. Phone: (828) 479-8080. Phone: (828) 479-2296. Fax: (828) 479-2296. Licensee: Cherokee Broadcasting Co. Format: C&W. Target aud: General. ♦ Dennis G. Blakemore, pres, gen mgr, gen sls mgr, prom mgr, progmg dir & chief of engrg; Penny Wade, pub affrs dir.

Rockingham

WAYN(AM)— September 1946: 900 khz; 1 kw-U, DA-2. TL: N34 55 30 W79 44 35. Box 519 28380. Secondary address: 1223 Rockingham Rd. 28380. Phone: (910) 895-4041. Fax: (910) 895-4993. Licensee: WAYN Inc. (acq 5-10-01). Cohn & Marks. Format: Adult contemp, info. News: 20 hrs wkly. Target aud: 25-49; event-conscious adults. ♦ William F. Futterer, pres, gen mgr & gen sls mgr; Jim Smith, progmg dir & news dir; Mary Futterer Morgan, mus dir; Gene Shaw, chief of engrg.

WLWL(AM)— Oct 27, 1969: 770 khz; 5 kw-D. TL: N34 55 30 W79 47 11. Box 1536 28380. Secondary address: 275 River Rd. 28379. Phone: (910) 997-2526. Fax: (910) 997-2527. E-mail: wlwl@77bibwaves.com. Web Site: www.77bigwaves.com. Licensee: Sandhills Broadcasting Co. Inc. Network: UPI. Format: Beach, oldies. Target aud: 25-60. ♦ Keith Davis, gen mgr & opns mgr; Jeff Ballard, progmg dir.

*WRSH(FM)— May 1973: 91.1 mhz; 10 w. 60 ft. TL: N34 57 03 W79 42 56. (CP: 339.7 w, ant 161 ft.). Box 1748 28380. Secondary address: Richmond Sr. High School, 838 N. US Hwy. 1 28379. Phone: (910) 997-9812. Fax: (910) 997-9816. Licensee: Richmond County Board of Education. Format: Educ. ♦ Kim Newton, gen mgr.

Rocky Mount

WDWG(FM)—Listing follows WRMT(AM).

WEED(AM)— Sept 10, 1933: 1390 khz; 5 kw-D, 30 w-N. TL: N35 57 43 W77 49 35. Box 2666, 115 N. Church St. 27802. Secondary address: 115 N. Church St. 27802. Phone: (252) 937-6111. Fax: (252) 443-5977. Web Site: www.coul92jams.com. Licensee: Northstar Broadcasting Corp. (acq 7-22-03; with co-located FM). Network: Network: ABC, Premiere Focus. Format: Relg, news, talk. News staff: one; News: 14 hrs wkly. Target aud: Males; 18+. ♦ Sarah M. Johnson, pres; Charles Johnson II, VP & gen mgr; Derrick Alston, progmg dir; Theresa Alston, news dir.

WRSV(FM)—Co-owned with WEED(AM). 1949: 92.1 mhz; 2.35 kw. 531 ft. TL: N35 48 40 W77 44 33. Stereo. Phone: (252) 937-7400. Web Site: www.soul92jams.com. Format: Urban contemp. News: 3 hrs wkly. Target aud: General; African American consumers of all age groups. ♦ Ernestine Neal, gen mgr; Sharon Macon, natl sls mgr.

WFXK(FM)—See Tarboro

WRMT(AM)— Dec 15, 1958: 1490 khz; 1 kw-U. TL: N35 55 57 W77 49 49. Stereo. Box 4005, 12714 E. NC#97 27803-0005. Phone: (252) 442-8092. Fax: (252) 977-6664. E-mail: wsay@rockymountnc.com. Licensee: First Media Radio LLC (group owner; acq 1-7-03; grpsl). Network: UPI. Format: Sports. Target aud: 30 plus. ♦ R. Gordon Finney, pres; Amy M. Davis, gen mgr; Amy Davis, sls dir & adv dir.

WDWG(FM)—Co-owned with WRMT(AM). Dec 18, 1989: 98.5 mhz; 16 kw. 417 ft. TL: N35 54 43 W77 50 06. Format: Country. Target aud: 18 plus.

*WRQM(FM)— April 1, 1996: 90.9 mhz; 6 kw. Ant 626 ft. TL: N35 48 40 W77 44 33. 120 Friday Ctr Dr., CB-0915, Chapel Hill 27517-9495. Phone: (919) 966-5454. Fax: (919) 966-5955. E-mail: wunc@unc.edu. Web Site: www.wunc.org. Licensee: The Board of Trustees of the University of NC at Chapel Hill (acq 5-99). Network: Network: Network: NPR, PRI, CBC Radio One. Format: News & Info. News staff: 7; News: 124 hrs wkly. Target aud: 35 plus; educated, successful, community active.

WRVA-FM—Licensed to Rocky Mount. See Raleigh

Rose Hill

WEGG(AM)— 1971: 710 khz; 250 w-D. TL: N34 51 48 W78 02 16. Box 608 28458. Secondary address: 3228 U.S. Hwy. 117 28458. Phone: (910) 289-2031. Fax: (910) 289-2032. Licensee: Conner Media Corp. Network: ABC Information & Entertainment. Rep: Keystone (unwired net). Format: Gospel/relg, Black. Spec prog: Farm 9 hrs, bluegrass gospel 10 hrs wkly. ♦ Suzanne Wilson, gen mgr, opns mgr, progmg dir & news dir; Don Brown, chief of engrg.

WZUP(FM)— January 1993: 104.7 mhz; 2.8 kw. Ant 256 ft. TL: N34 55 41 W78 03 22. 907 Lejeune Blvd., Jacksonville 28540. Phone: (910) 455-2202. Fax: (910) 355-2203. Licensee: Conner Media Corp. Format: Sp. ♦ Rodney Rainey, gen mgr.

Roxboro

WKRX(FM)—Listing follows WRXO.

WRXO(AM)— 1949: 1430 khz; 1 kw-D, 65 w-N. TL: N36 22 04 W78 59 58. Box 1176, 2070 Hurdle Mills Rd. 27573. Phone: (336) 599-0266. Fax: (336) 599-9411. E-mail: radiod@aol.com. Licensee: Roxboro Broadcasting Co. (acq 5-8-92). Network: ABC. Format: Edmundson & Edmundson. Format: Oldies-Stardust. News staff: one; News: 7 hrs wkly. Target aud: 18-49. Spec prog: Black 4 hrs, farm 5 hrs, Southern gospel 5 hrs wkly. ♦ David Bradsher, pres, gen mgr, gen sls mgr, adv mgr & progmg dir; Ralph Shaw, news dir; Conrad Kimbrough, chief of engrg.

North Carolina

WKRX(FM)— Co-owned with WRXO. 1958: 96.7 mhz; 3 kw. 300 ft. TL: N36 22 04 W78 59 58. Stereo. Network: ABC. Edmundson & Edmundson. Format: Country. News staff: one; News: 7 hrs wkly. Target aud: 18-49. ♦David Bradsher, mktg dir, prom VP & adv VP; Don Carroll, progmg dir.

Rutherfordton

WCAB(AM)— Oct 19, 1966: 590 khz; 1 kw-D, 228 w-N. TL: N35 23 35 W81 55 23. Box 511, 191 Whiteside Rd. 28139. Phone: (828) 287-3356. Fax: (828) 287-7182. E-mail: wcab@blueridge.net. Web Site: www.wcab59.com. Licensee: Isothermal Broadcasting Corp. (acq 8-1-84; 7-16-84). Network: ABC Information & Entertainment. Format: Country, news/talk, sports. News: 25 hrs wkly. Target aud: 25 plus; adult consumers. ♦James H. Bishop, pres & gen mgr; Van Austin, progmg dir.

Saint Pauls

WUKS(FM)— Oct 16, 1994: 107.7 mhz; 6 kw. 328 ft. TL: N34 46 59 W79 07 11. Box 710, 508 Person St., Fayetteville 28302. Phone: (910) 486-4114. Fax: (910) 486-2124. Web Site: www.kiss1077.com. Licensee: WDAS License L.P. Group owner: Beasley Broadcast Group (acq 6-12-97; $1.2 million. with WTEL(AM) Red Springs). Format: Urban adult contemp. George Beasley, chmn; Bruce Beasley, pres; Caroline Beasley, CFO; Brian Beasley, exec VP; Daniel Highsmith, VP & gen mgr; Mac Edwards, opns VP; Walter Sturdivant, sls VP; Tila Comstock, gen sls mgr; Bryan Kusilka, natl sls mgr; Taylor Morgan, prom dir & mus dir; Garrett Davis, progmg dir & progmg mgr; Val Jones, pub affrs dir; Dave Cooke, engrg dir; Van Clough, chief of engrg

Salisbury

WEND(FM)— Mar 16, 1946: 106.5 mhz; 100 kw. 1,003 ft. TL: N35 44 11 W80 38 52. (CP: 84 kw, ant 1,046 ft.). Stereo. 801 E. Moorehead St., Suite 200, Charlotte 28202-2729. Phone: (704) 376-1065. Fax: (704) 334-9525. Web Site: www.1065.com. Licensee: Capstar TX L.P. Group owner: Clear Channel Communications Inc. (acq 3-12-01). Rep: McGavren Guild. Format: New rock, modern, alternative. Target aud: 18-34. ♦Jack Daniel, progmg dir; Liz Luke, pub affrs dir; Rob Caskey, chief of engrg.

*****WOGR-FM**— November 1996: 93.3 mhz; 10 w. 180 ft. TL: N35 40 03 W80 28 13. Box 16408, Charlotte 28297. Phone: (704) 630-1075. Fax: (704) 393-1527. Web Site: www.wordnet.org. Licensee: Victory Christian Center Inc. Format: Christian contemp gospel. ♦Robyn Gool, pres; Cynthia Neely, gen mgr, sls dir, prom VP & pub affrs dir.

WSAT(AM)— June 1947: 1280 khz; 1 kw-U, DA-N. TL: N35 40 30 W80 30 30. 1525 Jake Alexander Blvd. 28145. Phone: (704) 633-0621. Fax: (704) 636-2955. E-mail: buddy@WSAT1280.com. Licensee: Cap Communications Inc. (acq 6-28-02). Network: Network: Motor Racing Net, ABC Information & Entertainment. Format: Adult standards. Target aud: 25-64; people that can afford high ticket items. ♦Charles Poole, pres; Bubby Poole, mus dir; Ted Fuller, chief of engrg.

WSTP(AM)— Jan 1, 1939: 1490 khz; 1 kw-U. TL: N35 41 12 W80 30 15. Stereo. Box 4157 28145-4157. Secondary address: 1105 Statesville Blvd. 28144. Phone: (704) 636-3811. Fax: (704) 637-1490. E-mail: newsradio1490@yahoo.com. Web Site: www.1490wstp.com. Licensee: Rowan Media INC. (acq 12-31-01). Network: Network: CNN Radio, Premiere Focus, Westwood One. Format: News/talk. News: 24 hrs wkly. Target aud: 25-59. Spec prog: Reunion Su Am 5 hrs wkly. ♦Timothy H. Coates, pres; Mike Mangan, VP, gen mgr, gen sls mgr & natl sls mgr; Joni Duggins, rgnl sls mgr; Mark Brown, news dir; Hal McGee, chief of engrg.

Sanford

*****WDCC(FM)**— 1971: 90.5 mhz; 3 kw. 148 ft. TL: N35 28 19 W79 08 36. 1105 Kelly Dr. 27330. Phone: (919) 718-7257. Fax: (919) 718-7429. E-mail: bfreeman@gw.ccarolina.cc.nc.us. Web Site: www.wdccfm.com. Licensee: Central Carolina Community College. Format: Rock, college, progsv, jazz, alternative. ♦Bill Freeman, gen mgr, progmg VP & mus dir.

WFJA(FM)— Listing follows WWGP.

WWGP(AM)— 1946: 1050 khz; 1 kw-D, 161 w-N. TL: N35 26 28 W79 12 54. Box 3457 27331. Phone: (919) 775-3525. Fax: (919) 775-4503.

Licensee: Richard K. Feindel. (acq 1-13-94; $190,000 with co-located FM; 2-7-94). Network: ABC Information & Entertainment. Format: Country, Sp. News staff: one; News: 7 hrs wklyone. Target aud: 18-54. Spec prog: Farm 7 hrs wkly. ♦Richard K. Feindel, pres & gen mgr; Pete Saunders, gen sls mgr; Dori Marshall, progmg dir; Margaret Murchison, news dir; Jim Vest, chief of engrg.

WFJA(FM)— Co-owned with WWGP. 1950: 105.5 mhz; 2.25 kw. 377 ft. TL: N35 26 28 W79 12 54. Stereo. 2201 Jefferson Davis Hwy. 27330. Format: Oldies. News staff: 2. Target aud: 25-54. ♦Pete Saunders, adv VP.

WXKL(AM)— Oct 2, 1952: 1290 khz; 1 kw-D, 44 w-N. TL: N35 27 01 W79 09 30. Box 1290, 705 Wall St. 27330-5919. Phone: (919) 774-1290. Phone: (919) 774-1080. Fax: (919) 774-1118. Licensee: Thomas Broadcasting Inc. (acq 7-8-2003). Network: NBC. Format: Gospel. News: 6 hrs wkly. Target aud: 25 plus; general. ♦James Thomas, pres & gen mgr.

Scotland Neck

WYAL(AM)— Apr 3, 1960: 1280 khz; 5 kw-D. TL: N36 08 03 W77 25 53. Box 425 27874. Phone: (252) 826-3114. Licensee: Sky City Communications Inc. (acq 1-31-97; $100,000). Format: Gospel. Spec prog: Farm 2 hrs wkly. ♦Frank Knapper, gen mgr.

Selma

WTSB(AM)— Aug 4, 1964: 1090 khz; 9 kw-D, 1.7 kw-CH. TL: N35 36 57 W78 24 33. 3505 Durham Dr., Suite 111, Raleigh 27603. Phone: (919) 329-9810. Fax: (919) 329-9803. Web Site: www.trianglesportstalk.com. Licensee: Triangle Sports Broadcasters LLC (acq 8-6-2004; $1.5 million). Format: Sports. Target aud: 18-45; general. Spec prog: Sp 5 hrs, Black 6 hrs wkly. ♦Brian Mishkin, stn mgr & progmg dir.

Semora

WKVE(FM)— Mar 1, 1996: 106.7 mhz; 6 kw. 328 ft. TL: N36 29 24 W79 00 36. Phone: (843) 267-0036. Fax: (843) 399-9031. Web Site: www.klove.com. Licensee: Southern Entertainment Corp. Network: K-Love. Format: Christian Contemp. ♦Kurt Reeder, stn mgr.

Shallotte

WBNU(FM)— Oct 31, 1977: 103.7 mhz; 25 kw. 328 ft. TL: N33 59 55 W78 22 25. 122 Cinema Dr., Wilmington 28403. Web Site: www.937thebone.com. Licensee: Sea-Comm Inc. (group owner; acq 11-26-03; with WLTT(FM) Shallotte). Network: Jones Radio Networks. Format: Class rock. News staff: one; News: 7 hrs wkly. Target aud: 25-54; upscale female. ♦Paul Knight, gen mgr & stn mgr.

WLTT(FM)— Sept 20, 1986: 106.3 mhz; 6 kw. 328 ft. TL: N34 02 50 W78 16 12. Stereo. Box 1550 28459. Secondary address: 122 Cinema Dr., Wilmington 28403. Phone: (910) 772-6300. Fax: (910) 772-6310. E-mail: wltt1037@atmc.net. Web Site: www.thebigtalker1063fm.com. Licensee: Sea-Comm Inc. (group owner; acq 11-26-03; with WBNU(FM) Shallotte). Format: News/talk info. Target aud: 25 plus; mature professionals. Spec prog: Beach mus 6 hrs wkly. ♦Paul Knight, gen mgr; Jonathan Knight, opns mgr; Max Deutsch, gen sls mgr; Suzanne Jalot, news dir; Buddy Womack, chief of engrg.

WVCB(AM)— June 11, 1964: 1410 khz; 500 w-D. TL: N33 58 20 W78 23 02. Box 314 28459. Secondary address: 4640 Main St. 28459. Phone: (910) 754-4512. Fax: (910) 754-3461. E-mail: wvcb@atmc.net. Licensee: John G. Worrell. (acq 3-1-84; $30,000; 1-30-84). Format: Relg, gospel. Target aud: General. ♦John Worrell, gen mgr; Rhonda Worrell, stn mgr & opns mgr.

Shelby

WADA(AM)— July 9, 1958: 1390 khz; 1 kw-D, 500 w-N, DA-N. TL: N35 19 28 W81 32 00. Stereo. 205 S. Washington St., Suite 1 28150. Secondary address: Box 2266 28151-2266. Phone: (704) 482-1390. Fax: (704) 481-9007. E-mail: wada.2@juno.com. Web Site: classiccountry1390.com. Licensee: Edwin Keith Johnson. (acq 7-29-99; $80,000). Network: ABC. Format: Country. Target aud: 25-54; middle and older. ♦Keith Johnson, pres; Joe Martin, stn mgr & opns mgr; Andy Johnson, gen sls mgr.

WBT(AM)— See Charlotte

Directory of Radio

WIBT(FM)— 1948: 96.1 mhz; 100 kw. 1,738 ft. TL: N35 21 44 W81 09 19. Stereo. 801 E. Morehead St. #200, Charlotte 28202. Phone: (704) 338-9600. Fax: (704) 334-9525. Web Site: www.magic96.com. Licensee: Clear Channel Broadcasting Licenses Inc. Group owner: Clear Channel Communications Inc. (acq 10-18-2000). Rep: McGavren Guild. Format: Hits of the 60s & 70s. News staff: one; News: 4 hrs wkly. Target aud: 25-54. ♦Morgan Bohannon, gen mgr; Graves Upchurch, gen sls mgr; Nick Allen, progmg dir; Linda Silver, news dir; Ben Brinitzer, chief of engrg.

WOHS(AM)— Aug 21, 1946: 730 khz; 1 kw-D, 168 w-N. TL: N35 17 27 W81 34 05. Stereo. 1511 W. Dixon Blvd, Box 1590 28151. Phone: (704) 482-4510. Phone: (704) 487-6313. Fax: (704) 482-4680. E-mail: thebossradio@bellsouth.net. Web Site: www.theboss.us. Licensee: KTC Broadcasting Inc. (acq 11-23-93; $150,000). Network: ABC. T-N. Format: Beach, Oldies, Sports. News staff: 2. Target aud: General. ♦Calvin R. Hastings, pres & gen mgr.

Siler City

WNCA(AM)— Aug 19, 1952: 1570 khz; 1 kw-D, 290 w-N. TL: N35 43 40 W79 29 18. Box 429, 17890 Hwy. 64 W. 27344. Phone: (919) 742-2135. Fax: (919) 663-2843. Licensee: Chatham Broadcasting Co. Inc. of Siler City. (acq 3-1-62). Smithwick & Belendiuk. Format: Loc prgmg, Sp, News/talk, adult contemp, christian, sports. News staff: 2; News: 30 hrs wkly. Target aud: 25-55; rural, agri-oriented, blue-collar, growing spanish community. Spec prog: Gospel 15, relg 12 hrs, loc sports 6 hrs, Sp 25 hrs wkly. ♦Barry Hayes, pres, gen mgr, news dir & engrg mgr; Dacia Hayes, dev VP; Renee Kennedy, opns VP, sls VP & sls dir.

Smithfield

WMPM(AM)— 1950: 1270 khz; 5 kw-D. TL: N35 31 33 W78 20 01. Box 240, 1270 Buffalo Rd. 27577. Phone: (919) 934-2434. Phone: (919) 989-7161. Fax: (919) 989-6388. E-mail: Info@1270wmpm.com. Web Site: www.1270wmpm.com. Licensee: Carolina Broadcasting Service Inc. (acq 12-1-58). Network: CBS. Format: Country, bluegrass, gospel. Target aud: 30 plus; general. Spec prog: Farm 2 hrs, relg 8 hrs, news/talk 12 hrs wkly. ♦Carl E. Lamm, gen mgr, adv mgr & progmg dir; Larry D. Barnes, stn mgr & pub affrs dir; Mickey Lamm, news dir; Bill Lambert, chief of engrg.

WTSB(AM)—See Selma

Snow Hill

*****WAGO(FM)**— July 1, 1998: 88.7 mhz; 17 kw. 310 ft. TL: N35 30 07 W77 36 22. Stereo. Box 1895, Goldsboro 27533. Phone: (252) 747-8887. Fax: (252) 747-7888. E-mail: wago@gomixradio.org. Web Site: www.gomixradio.org. Licensee: Pathway Christian Academy. Network: Network: Moody, Salem Radio Network. Steve Yelverton. Format: Christian. News staff: one; News: 14 hrs wkly. Target aud: General. ♦Dr. T.D. Worthington, pres & gen mgr; Ashley Worthington, prom dir; Keith Aycock, progmg dir; Tim Sutton, mus dir; Paul Matthews, chief of engrg.

South Gastonia

*****WGAS(AM)**— Aug 14, 1959: 1420 khz; 500 w-D. TL: N35 12 53 W81 10 31. Box 16408, Charlotte 28297. Phone: (704) 865-9427. Fax: (704) 393-1527. E-mail: wayne@wordnet.org. Web Site: www.wordnet.org. Licensee: Victory Christian Center Inc. Format: Christian. Target aud: General. ♦Robyn Gool, pres; Wayne Hammond, stn mgr; James Sims, opns mgr; Cynthia Neely, sls dir, prom mgr & pub affrs dir; Eleasah Hammond, mus dir.

Southern Pines

WEEB(AM)— Nov 15, 1947: 990 khz; 10 kw-D, 500 w-N. TL: N35 11 37 W79 24 42. Box 1855, Midland Rd. 28388. Phone: (910) 692-7440. Fax: (910) 692-7372. Web Site: www.weeb990.com. Licensee: Pinehurst Broadcasting Corp. (acq 8-31-91; $275,000; 6-10-91). Network: ABC Information & Entertainment. Maupin, Taylor, Ellis & Adams. Format: News/talk. News staff: 3; News: 26 hrs wkly. Target aud: 25 plus; business professionals, CEOs, retirees. Spec prog: High school & college sports, gospel 6 hrs wkly. ♦Rich McCarthy, opns mgr; Steve Adams, CFO, VP, gen mgr & progmg dir.

WIOZ-FM— 1995: 102.5 mhz; 3.4 kw. 436 ft. TL: N35 09 04 W79 28 40. 200 Short Rd. 28387. Phone: (910) 692-2107. Fax: (910) 692-6849. Web Site: www.star1025fm.com. Licensee: Meridian Communications L.L.C. Group owner: Muirfield Broadcasting Inc. (acq

Broadcasting & Cable Yearbook 2006

Stations in the U.S. — North Carolina

6-17-97; $316,500). Format: Adult contemp. ◆ Walker Morris, pres; Tiffany Hewitt, gen mgr; Rich Rushforth, opns mgr.

WKQB(FM)— Aug 14, 1973: 106.9 mhz; 50 kw. Ant 492 ft. TL: N35 09 04 W79 28 40. Stereo. 1009 Drayton Rd., Fayetteville 28303. Phone: (910) 864-5222. Fax: (910) 864-3065. Web Site: kix1069fm.com. Licensee: Cumulus Licensing Corp. Group owner: Cumulus Media Inc. (acq 3-12-01; $6.15 million). Format: Country. News staff: 2; News: 18 hrs wkly. Target aud: 35 plus. ◆ Tom Haymond, gen mgr; Perry Stone, opns mgr.

Southern Shores

WFMI(FM)— 2003: 100.9 mhz; 39 kw. Ant 485 ft. TL: N36 12 10 W75 52 23. 4801 Columbus St., Suite 202, Virginia Beach, VA 23462. Phone: (757) 490-9364. Fax: (757) 490-2524. E-mail: rejoice@rejoice100point9.com. Web Site: www.rejoice100point9.com. Licensee: Communications Systems Inc. Format: Gospel, talk. ◆ Mike Chandler, gen mgr; Vickie Bright, stn mgr.

Southport

WAZO(FM)— Apr 15, 1978: 107.5 mhz; 32 kw. 594 ft. TL: N34 03 02 W77 57 20. Stereo. 122 Cinema Dr., Wilmington 28403. Phone: (910) 772-6300. Fax: (910) 772-6310. Licensee: NM Licensing LLC. (group owner) (acq 12-20-2004; grpsl). Rep: McGavren Guild. Format: New Rock. News staff: one; News: one hr wkly. Target aud: 18-49; young, upwardly mobile professionals. ◆ Steven Dinetz, pres; Paul Knight, VP, gen mgr & chief of engrg; Barbara Raybourne, gen sls mgr; Mike Kennedy, progmg dir; Suzanne Jalot, news dir.

Sparta

WCOK(AM)— April 1967: 1060 khz; 800 w-D. TL: N36 28 55 W81 05 35. Box 578 28675. Phone: (336) 372-8231. Fax: (336) 372-5863. E-mail: luke@ls.net. Licensee: Mountain Empire Broadcasting Inc. (acq 10-1-99). Format: C&W, relg. Target aud: General. ◆ Andy Wright, pres & gen mgr; Jos Reynoso, gen mgr.

Spindale

WGMA(AM)— October 1982: 1520 khz; 500 w-D. TL: N35 21 00 W81 56 18. Box 805, 301 W. Main St. 28160. Phone: (828) 287-5151. Phone: (828) 287-5150. Fax: 1-828-287-0081. E-mail: wgma1520@juno.com. Licensee: Moonglow Broadcasting Inc. (acq 5-16-03). Smithwick & Belendiuk. Format: Southern gospel. News staff: one; News: one hr wkly. Target aud: 30-50; adults. ◆ Barbara Martin, exec VP; Dean Long, gen mgr; Thomas Freemann, sls VP; Dr. Billy D. Martin, natl sls mgr; Neil Murray, mus dir; Ted Fuller, chief of engrg.

*****WNCW(FM)**— Oct 13, 1989: 88.7 mhz; 17 kw. 3,054 ft. TL: N35 44 05 W82 17 10. Stereo. Box 804 28160. Phone: (828) 287-8000. Fax: (828) 287-8012. E-mail: info@wncw.org. Web Site: www.wncw.org. Licensee: Isothermal Community College. Network: Network: PRI, NPR. Schwartz, Woods & Miller. Format: AAA, news. News staff: one; News: 31 hrs wkly. Target aud: 35-49; anyone interested in diverse info & culture. Spec prog: Blues 4 hrs, jazz 5 hrs, folk 12 hrs, drama 3 hrs, gospel 2 hrs wkly. ◆ David Gordon, gen mgr & opns mgr; Kate Barkschat, dev mgr, gen sls mgr & prom mgr; Kim Clark, progmg dir; Martin Anderson, mus dir; Dennis Jones, chief of engrg.

Spring Lake

WCIE(AM)— May 22, 1963: 1450 khz; 1 kw-U. TL: N35 11 00 W78 57 45. 5418 Yadkin Road, Fayetteville 28303. Phone: (910) 222-1450. Fax: (910) 223-1451. E-mail: radiolatina1450@earthlink.net. Web Site: www.radiolatina1450.com. Licensee: WCIE-AM Inc. (acq 4-20-01). Format: Spanish/news. Target aud: 12-65; Male & Female/Hispanic orintated culture. ◆ Teo Rodriguez, gen mgr.

*****WZRI(FM)**— 2005: 89.3 mhz; 2 kw vert. Ant 179 ft. TL: N35 10 14 W78 57 44. Stereo. 5700 W. Oaks Blvd., Rocklin, CA 95765. Phone: (916) 251-1600. Fax: (916) 251-1650. E-mail: info@air1.com. Web Site: www.air1.com. Licensee: Educational Media Foundation. Group owner: EMF Broadcasting (acq 11-12-2002). Network: Air 1. Shaw Pittman. Format: Contemp Christian. News staff: 3. Target aud: 18-35; Judeo-Christian, female. ◆ Richard Jenkins, pres; Mike Novak, VP & progmg dir; Lloyd Parker, gen mgr; Keith Whipple, dev dir; Eric Allen, natl sls mgr; Kurt Reeder, rgnl sls mgr; Chris Joyce, prom dir; Bryan O'Neal, progmg dir; Liz Morton, mus dir; Sam Wallington, engrg dir.

Spruce Pine

WTOE(AM)— Dec 24, 1955: 1470 khz; 5 kw-D, 100 w-N. TL: N35 54 24 W82 06 21. Box 607, Mark Group Bldg., 749 Sawmill Rd., Burnsville 28714. Secondary address: 749 Sawmill Road, Burnsville 28714. Phone: (828) 765-7441. Fax: (828) 682-6227. E-mail: 1470@wtoe.com. Web Site: www.wtoe.com. Licensee: Mountain Valley Media Inc. (acq 9-27-91; $140,000). Network: ABC. Format: Soft Oldies. News staff: one; News: 10 hrs wkly. Target aud: 25 plus. Spec prog: Relg 8 hrs wkly. ◆ Remelle K. Sink, CEO & pres; J. Ardell Sink, exec VP; Michael Sink, VP, gen mgr & chief of engrg; Holly Hall, opns mgr & mktg dir; Mary Marsh, prom dir; Dennis Renfro, adv dir; Steve Murphy, news dir & pub affrs dir.

Statesville

WAME(AM)— Oct 7, 1957: 550 khz; 500 w-D. TL: N35 47 43 W80 51 17. 212 Signal Hill Dr. 28625. Phone: (704) 872-0550. Fax: (704) 872-0551. E-mail: wame@statesville.net. Licensee: Statesville Family Radio Corp. Group owner: GHB Radio Group (acq 4-22-86; $210,000; 3-31-86). Network: USA. Format: Adult standards. News: 2 hrs wkly. Target aud: 35-64. Spec prog: Loc & pro sports, gospel 5 hrs wkly.

WFMX(FM)— May 3, 1947: 105.7 mhz; 100 kw. Ant 1,517 ft. TL: N35 49 55 W80 42 13. Stereo. 1117 Radio Rd. 28677. Phone: (704) 872-6345. Fax: (704) 873-6921. E-mail: 1057@wfmx.com. Web Site: www.wfmx.com. Licensee: Mercury Broadcasting Co. Inc. (group owner; acq 3-12-01). Network: ABC Daytime Direction. Format: C&W. News: 5 hrs wkly. Target aud: 25-54; adults, mid-to-upper-income. ◆ Greg Ryan, gen mgr & sls dir; Dave Kester, progmg dir & news dir; Matthew Cockerham, chief of engrg.

WKKT(FM)— Mar 16, 1961: 96.9 mhz; 100 kw. 1,550 ft. TL: N35 31 57 W80 47 47. Stereo. 801 Wood Ridge Center Dr., Charlotte 28217. Phone: (704) 714-9444. Fax: (704) 332-8805. Web Site: www.wkktfm.com. Licensee: Capstar TX L.P. Group owner: Clear Channel Communications Inc. (acq 8-30-00; grpsl). Format: Country. Target aud: 25-54; middle to upper income adults. ◆ Morgan Bohannon, gen mgr; Bruce Logan, opns mgr; Robin Colfax, natl sls mgr & rgnl sls mgr; Valerie Gladden, prom dir; John Roberts, progmg dir & news dir; Linda Silver, news dir; Ben Brinitzer, chief of engrg.

WSIC(AM)— May 3, 1947: 1400 khz; 1 kw-U. TL: N35 48 09 W80 53 30. Stereo. 1117 Radio Rd. 28677. Phone: (704) 872-6345. Fax: (704) 873-6921. Web Site: www.1400wsic.com. Licensee: Capstar TX L.P. Group owner: Clear Channel Communications Inc. (acq 8-30-00; grpsl). Rep: Rgnl Reps. T-N. Format: Sports, news. News staff: one; News: 21 hrs wkly. Target aud: 35 plus; upscale. ◆ Greg Sauthared, gen mgr; Dave Michaels, opns mgr & mus dir.

Swanquarter

*****WHYC(FM)**— Mar 8, 1981: 88.5 mhz; 3 kw. 293 ft. TL: N35 26 29 W76 13 09. Stereo. Box 155-A, 204 72 US 264, Swan Quarter 27885. Phone: (252) 926-7201. Fax: (252) 926-1557. Licensee: Hyde County Board of Education. Format: Var. Target aud: General; eastern North Carolina population.

Sylva

WRGC(AM)— Nov 8, 1957: 680 khz; 1 kw-D, 250 w-N, DA-N. TL: N35 23 35 W83 11 38. Box 1044, 1846 Skyland Dr. 28779. Phone: (828) 586-2221. Fax: (828) 586-6834. E-mail: sutton@gacaradio.com. Web Site: www.wrgc.com. Licensee: Georgia-Carolina Radiocasting Co. LLC. Group owner: Sutton Radiocasting Companies (acq 1-17-2002; $450,000). Network: ABC. Dan J. Alpert. Format: Adult contemp. News staff: one; News: 14 hrs wkly. Target aud: General. ◆ Tom Stanwood, COO; Douglas M. Sutton Jr., pres; Terry Carter, CFO & VP; Charlie Bauder, news dir; Tim Stephens, engrg dir & chief of engrg.

Tabor City

WTAB(AM)— July 1, 1954: 1370 khz; 5 kw-D, 109 w-N. TL: N34 09 00 W78 51 40. Box 127 28463. Secondary address: 210 Avon St. 28463. Phone: (910) 653-2131. Fax: (910) 653-5146. E-mail: wtab@wtabradio.com. Web Site: www.wtabradio.com. Licensee: WTAB Inc. (acq 7-1-95; $175,000). Format: Southern gospel, country. News: 7 hrs wkly. Target aud: General. Spec prog: Swap shop, farm 12 hrs wkly. ◆ Bonnie Miller, exec VP; Jack Miller, pres, gen mgr & sls VP; Bobby Pait, mus dir; Bob Gause, chief of engrg.

Tarboro

WCPS(AM)— January 1947: 760 khz; 1 kw-D. TL: N35 55 40 W77 34 15. Box 1202 27886. Phone: (252) 824-7878. Fax: (252) 824-7818. Licensee: Johnson Broadcast Ventures Ltd. (acq 5-6-00; $100,000). Format: Gospel. Target aud: General. ◆ Jimmy Johnson, pres & gen mgr.

WFXK(FM)— September 1952: 104.3 mhz; 100 kw. 987 ft. TL: N35 48 40 W77 44 33. 8001-101 Creedmoor Rd., Raleigh 27613. Phone: (919) 848-9736. Fax: (919) 848-4724. E-mail: mmarinaro@radio-one.com. Web Site: www.foxyhits.com. Licensee: Radio One Licenses LLC. Group owner: Radio One Inc. (acq 11-8-01; grpsl). Network: ABC Daytime Direction. Format: Adult contemp, urban. News staff: one; News: 3 hrs wkly. Target aud: 25-54. Spec prog: Gospel 3 hrs, jazz 4 hrs wkly. ◆ Gary Weiss, gen mgr; Cy Young, opns dir & progmg dir; Kim Gattis, sls dir; Jodi Luke, natl sls mgr; Bruce Farmer, prom dir; Jodi Berri, mus dir; Jim Davis, chief of engrg.

Taylorsville

WACB(AM)— May 2, 1964: 860 khz; 1 kw-D. TL: N35 55 57 W81 10 19. 133 E. Main Ave. 28681. Phone: (828) 632-4621. Fax: (828) 632-9081. Licensee: Apple City Broadcasting Co. Inc. (acq 9-24-93; $70,239; 10-11-93). Format: Modern country, oldies. News staff: 2; News: 4 hrs wkly. Target aud: General. Spec prog: Gospel 12 hrs wkly. ◆ Norris Keever, pres; Mary Alice Brown, VP; Joyce Brown, gen sls mgr; Lisa McLain, prom dir; Lonnie Carrigan, mus dir; Pete Ray, asst music dir; Roger Brown, CEO, exec VP, gen mgr, opns dir, news dir & pub affrs dir; Jeff Watts, chief of engrg.

WTLK(AM)— June 17, 1962: 1570 khz; 1 kw-D, 248 w-N. TL: N35 55 45 W81 09 44. 133 E. Main Ave. 28681. Phone: (828) 632-4621. Fax: (828) 632-9081. Licensee: Apple City Broadcasting Co. Inc. (acq 6-95; $225,000). Network: Moody. Format: Gospel. ◆ Norris Keever, pres; Mary Alice Brown, exec VP & mus dir; Roger Brown, CEO, gen mgr & opns dir; Joyce Brown, gen sls mgr; Lisa McLain, prom dir; Jeff Watts, chief of engrg.

Thomasville

WBLO(AM)— September 1947: 790 khz; 2.5 kw-D, 26 w-N. TL: N35 57 41 W80 02 13. Box 5663, High Point 27262. Secondary address: 1607 Country Club Dr., High Point 27262. Phone: (336) 887-0983. Fax: (336) 887-3055. Web Site: www.wist983.com. Licensee: GHB Radio Inc. Group owner: GHB Radio Group (acq 4-3-2001; $350,000). Reddy, Begley & McCormick. Format: Adult standards. Target aud: 35+; older, mature audience. ◆ George H. Buck Jr., pres; Stan Thomas, gen mgr, prom VP & prom dir; Wes Jones, opns mgr; Susan Childress, gen sls mgr, prom VP & prom mgr; Ed Kasovic, chief of engrg.

WIST(FM)— April 1949: 98.3 mhz; 1.68 kw. Ant 429 ft. TL: N35 57 41 W80 02 13. Stereo. Box 5663, 1607 Country Club Dr., High Point 27262. Phone: (336) 887-0983. Fax: (336) 887-3055. Web Site: www.wist983.com. Licensee: WEAM Quality Radio Corp. Group owner: GHB Radio Group (acq 1997; $925,000). Format: Oldies, adult standards. Target aud: 35 plus. ◆ George H. Buck Jr., pres; Stan Thomas, gen mgr & prom dir; Wes Jones, opns mgr; Susan Childress, gen sls mgr & prom dir; Bud Bushardt, mus dir; Ed Kasovic, chief of engrg.

North Carolina

Topsail Beach

WWTB(FM)— Sept 12, 1993: 103.9 mhz; 21.5 kw. 328 ft. TL: N34 29 38 W77 29 18. Stereo. 122 Cinema Dr., Wilmington 28403. Phone: (910) 772-6300. Fax: (910) 771-6310. Web Site: www.thebigtalker1063fm.com. Licensee: Sea-Comm Inc. (group owner; acq 1-15-2004; $2.3 million). Gardner, Carton & Douglas. Format: Talk, news. News: 6 hrs wkly. Target aud: 35 plus; baby boomers, upper income & affluent retirees. ♦ Paul Knight, gen mgr.

Troy

WJRM(AM)— Dec 8, 1961: 1390 khz; 1 kw-D. TL: N35 21 43 W79 51 38. Box 706 27371. Phone: (910) 576-1390. Fax: (910) 576-1393. E-mail: wjrm@carolina.net. Licensee: Family Worship Ministries Inc. (acq 6-10-02; $115,000). Format: Christian gospel. ♦ Harold Pope, pres & gen mgr; Jeffrey Pope, opns mgr & gen sls mgr.

Tryon

WJFJ(AM)— Oct 1, 1954: 1160 khz; 10 kw-D, 500 w-N, DA-N. TL: N35 14 07 W82 14 27. Box 279, Courthouse St., Columbus 28772. Phone: (828) 894-5858. Fax: (828) 894-2957. E-mail: wjfjradio@wjfjradio.com. Web Site: www.wjfjradio.com. Licensee: Columbus Broadcast Corp. Inc. (acq 1996; $265,000). Network: USA. Format: Christian. News staff: one; News: 25 hrs wkly. Target aud: 25 plus; middle-to-upper income. ♦ John Owens, gen mgr & opns mgr.

Valdese

WSVM(AM)— Oct 6, 1961: 1490 khz; 1 kw-U. TL: N35 44 03 W81 34 04. Box 99, 1117 S. Praley St. 28690. Phone: (828) 874-0000. Fax: (828) 874-2123. E-mail: radio@1490wsvm.com. Web Site: www.1490wsvm.com. Licensee: GHB of Waxhaw Inc. Group owner: GHB Radio Group (acq 10-28-2002; $450,000. with WEGO(AM) Concord). Network: ABC. Format: Oldies. News: 4 hrs wkly. Target aud: 25-64. Spec prog: Gospel 4 hrs, sports 15 hrs wkly. ♦ Jerry Clegg, gen mgr.

Wadesboro

WADE(AM)— July 23, 1947: 1340 khz; 1 kw-U. TL: N34 57 01 W80 03 23. One Radio St. 28170. Phone: (704) 695-1060. Fax: (704) 695-1495. Licensee: Inspirational Deliverance Center Inc. (acq 6-8-93; $27,500; 6-28-93). Format: Adult contemp Christian. Spec prog: Farm one hr wkly. ♦ Myra Davis, stn mgr.

*WYFQ-FM— 1994: 93.5 mhz; 8.7 kw. 554 ft. TL: N35 02 57 W80 18 38. Stereo. 2004 Walkup Ave., Monroe 28110. Phone: (704) 523-5555. Fax: (704) 522-1967. Web Site: www.bbnradio.net. Licensee: Bible Broadcasting Network Inc. (group owner; acq 1996; $2,425,000). Smithwick & Belendiuk. Format: Relg. Target aud: 18-55. ♦ Lowell L. Davey, CEO & pres; Hank Crull, stn mgr; Richard Johnson, opns mgr.

Wake Forest

WDRU(AM)— Sept 1, 1989: 1030 khz; 50 kw-D, DA. TL: N36 10 43 W78 45 30. Stereo. 1812 Davie Ave., Statesville 28677. Phone: (919) 781-1030. Phone: (919) 220-3226. Fax: (919) 220-0006. Web Site: www.830wtru.com. Licensee: Truth Broadcasting Corp. Group owner: Davidson Media Group LLC (acq 5-2-2005; swap for WWBG(AM) Greensboro and WTOB(AM) Winston-Salem). Format: Christian. Target aud: 25-54; middle-class families. ♦ Stuart W. Epperson Jr., pres; Larry Cobb, gen mgr; Chuck Harris, progmg dir; Winston Hawkins, chief of engrg.

Wallace

WZKB(FM)— July 20, 1972: 94.3 mhz; 3.3 kw. 300 ft. TL: N34 45 29 W78 00 00. Stereo. Box 520 28466. Phone: (910) 285-4900. Fax: (910) 285-6166. Web Site: www.christian107.com. Licensee: Christian Listening Network Inc. (acq 12-15-2003; $425,000). Network: Salem Radio Network. Rep: Salem. Putbrese, Huntsaker & Trent. Format: Christian contemp. News: 11 hrs wkly. Target aud: 25-44; women. Spec prog: Southern gospel 3 hrs wkly. ♦ George E. Wilson, pres & gen mgr; Dan DeBruler, stn mgr; Joni Beck, gen sls mgr; Steve Turley, progmg dir.

Wanchese

WOBR-FM—Listing follows WOBX(AM).

WOBX(AM)— May 29, 1970: 1530 khz; 1 kw-D, DA. TL: N35 51 52 W75 39 01. Box 340 27981. Secondary address: 3855 Mill Landing Rd., Hwy. 345 27981. Phone: (252) 473-5402. Fax: (252) 473-5838. E-mail: obcr@beachhlink.com. Licensee: East Carolina Radio Inc. Group owner: East Carolina Radio Group (acq 8-82; $110,000;. FTR: 8-9-82). Format: Relg, gospel. Target aud: Christian. ♦ Elmo Daniels, pres; Jim Mills, chief of engrg.

WOBR-FM—Co-owned with WOBX(AM). June 1, 1973: 95.3 mhz; 25 kw. 324 ft. TL: N35 51 53 W75 39 01. (CP: TL: N35 51 52 W75 39 01). Stereo. Box 400, 2046 Hwy. 345 S. 27981. Phone: (252) 473-3434. Fax: (252) 473-1584. Network: ABC. Format: Alternative rock. News staff: one. Target aud: 25-54; upscale, affluent baby boomers. Spec prog: Jazz 3 hrs wkly. ♦ Elmo Daniels, pres; Randy Gil, opns mgr; Jim Mills, chief of engrg.

Warrenton

WARR(AM)— 1970: 1520 khz; 5 kw-D, 1 kw-CH. TL: N36 24 18 W78 08 09. 109 N. Maine St. 27589. Phone: (252) 257-5557/257-9277. Fax: (252) 257-5988. Web Site: www.warr1520am.com. Licensee: Quad Divisions Inc. dba Darensburg Broadcasting (acq 7-1-02). Format: Rhythm and blues, jazz, reggae. News: 5 hrs wkly. Target aud: 25-56. ♦ Logan Darensburg, pres & gen mgr; Ann Alston, stn mgr & prom dir.

Washington

WDLX(AM)— Mar 3, 1942: 930 khz; 5 kw-D, 1 kw-N, DA-N. TL: N35 31 34 W77 04 43. Box 1707 27889. Secondary address: 1813 US Hwy 17 S., Chocwinity 27817. Phone: (252) 946-2162. Fax: (252) 946-0330. Licensee: Pirate Media Group LLC Group owner: NextMedia Group L.L.C. (acq 6-27-2005; $400,000). Network: ABC Information & Entertainment. Format: Talk. Target aud: 35 plus. ♦ Paul Kingman, gen mgr.

WERO(FM)— Jan 20, 1961: 93.3 mhz; 100 kw. Ant 1,781 ft. TL: N35 21 55 W77 23 38. Stereo. Box 1707 27889. Phone: (252) 946-2162. Fax: (252) 946-0330. Web Site: www.bob933.com. Licensee: NM Licensing LLC (acq 11-26-2001; grpsl). Network: ABC FM Connection. Format: Hot adult contemp. News staff: one; News: 12 hrs wkly. Target aud: 25-54. ♦ Paul Kingman, gen mgr.

WLGT(FM)— December 1988: 98.3 mhz; 1.3 kw. Ant 490 ft. TL: N35 29 14 W77 02 42. Stereo. 211 Commerce St., Suite C, Greenville 27858-5030. Phone: (252) 756-9898. Phone: (252) 830-0943. Fax: (252) 355-2234. Web Site: www.983litefm.com. Licensee: ABG North Carolina LLC. Group owner: Archway Broadcasting Group (acq 2-27-2003; $3 million. with WWNK(FM) Farmville). Format: Adult contemp. Target aud: 25-54; upscale, affluent audience. ♦ Bill Bailey, gen mgr; Jeff Davis, opns mgr.

Waxhaw

WNMX-FM— Mar 1, 1995: 106.1 mhz; 32 kw. 365 ft. TL: N34 53 01 W80 47 37. Stereo. 5732 N. Tryon St., Charlotte 28213. Phone: (704) 596-4900. Fax: (704) 599-1061. Web Site: www.mix106.net. Licensee: GHB of Waxhaw Inc. Group owner: GHB Radio Group (acq 6-95; $325,000). Network: ABC. Reddy, Begley & McCormick. Format: Adult Standards. News: 7 hrs wkly. Target aud: 45 plus; general. ♦ George H. Buck Jr., pres; Tom Gentry, gen mgr; Brant Hart, opns dir; Bob Wood, gen sls mgr & prom dir; Ken Conrad, pub affrs dir; Stu Albert, chief of engrg.

Waynesville

WMXF(AM)— August 1947: 1400 khz; 1 kw-U. TL: N35 30 14 W82 58 25. Box 6447, Asheville 28816. Secondary address: 54 Main St. 28786. Phone: (828) 456-8661. Fax: (828) 255-7850. Licensee: Clear Channel Broadcasting Licenses Inc. Group owner: Clear Channel Communications Inc. (acq 3-21-01; grpsl). Rep: Keystone (unwired net). Format: Music of your life. News staff: one. Target aud: General. Spec prog: Relg 3 hrs wkly. ♦ Diane Ougran, gen mgr; Paul McNeal, opns dir.

WQNS(FM)— Co-owned with WMXF(AM). October 1979: 104.9 mhz; 245 w. 1,581 ft. TL: N35 34 07 W82 54 27. Stereo. Web Site: www.rock1049.com. Format: Classic rock. Target aud: General. ♦ Dennis Deason, gen sls mgr; Shaunna Connee, prom dir; B.J. Nichols, adv dir; Lamont Bryant, engrg dir.

Weldon

WSMY(AM)— 1957: 1400 khz; 1 kw-U. TL: N36 24 43 W77 37 06. Box 910, Roanoke Rapids 27870. Phone: (252) 536-0209. Fax: (252) 538-0378. E-mail: info@wsmy1400.com. Web Site: www.wsmy1400.com. Licensee: First Media Radio LLC (group owner; acq 7-22-03; grpsl). Network: ABC Information & Entertainment. Format: Urban, relg. Target aud: 18 plus; affluent adults. ♦ Al Haskins, gen mgr; John Green, stn mgr; Allen Garrett, opns mgr.

Wendell-Zebulon

WETC(AM)— June 16, 1959: 540 khz; 5 kw-D, 500 w-N, DA-2. TL: N35 52 06 W78 25 56. (CP: 8 kw-D). Box 536., Wendell 27591. Phone: (919) 269-0089. Licensee: Prieto Broadcasting Inc. (acq 4-13-2004; $1.8 million). Format: Sp. Spec prog: Sp, farm 5 hrs wkly. ♦ Limo Cruz, stn mgr.

West Jefferson

WKSK(AM)— May 27, 1959: 580 khz; 5 kw-D, 34 w-N. TL: N36 24 39 W81 29 46. Stereo. 240 Radio Rd. 28694. Phone: (336) 246-6001. E-mail: wksk@skybest.com. Web Site: www.580wksk.com. Licensee: Caddell Broadcasting, Inc. (acq 8-1-78). Format: C&W. News staff: one; News: 16 hrs wkly. Target aud: General. Spec prog: Farm 3 hrs, gospel 5 hrs, Sp one hr wkly. ♦ Jan Caddell, pres & gen mgr; Graham Caddell, opns mgr.

Whiteville

WENC(AM)— July 14, 1946: 1220 khz; 5 kw-D, 152 w-N. TL: N34 18 30 W78 43 00. 108 Radio Station Rd. 28472. Phone: (910) 642-2133. Fax: (910) 642-5981. Licensee: DHA Communications. (acq 1-5-94; $135,000;. FTR: 1-17-94). Format: Urban contemp, gospel, blues. News staff: one; News: 10 hrs wkly. Target aud: 25-54; women. Spec prog: Farm 5 hrs, relg 4 hrs, talk 5 hrs wkly. ♦ Jesse Lee Godwin, gen mgr.

WTXY(AM)— Jan 1, 1976: 1540 khz; 1 kw-D. TL: N34 19 23 W78 42 47. Box 1038, 501 W. Virgil St. 28472. Phone: (910) 642-8214. Phone: (910) 642-8215. Fax: (910) 640-1540. E-mail: wtxy@weblink.net. Web Site: www.whitevillnc.com. Licensee: Stanley Broadcasting System Inc. (acq 2-2-87; $80,000; 12-22-86). Network: Network: Network: Westwood One, Motor Racing Net, ABC Information & Entertainment. Format: News/talk. News staff: 2; News: 84 hrs wkly. Target aud: General. Spec prog: Farm 2 hrs, relg 10 hrs wkly. ♦ Thomas V. Stanley Jr., pres, gen mgr, prom mgr & progmg VP; John H. Stanley, exec VP & mktg dir; Linda Shaver, opns mgr & progmg mgr; Buddy Wommack, chief of opns & chief of engrg; Thomas V Stanley Jr., gen sls mgr; Bill Jackson, rgnl sls mgr; John Scott, progmg dir & asst music dir; Tom Stanley, mktg VP, mus dir, news dir & pub affrs dir.

WZFX(FM)—Licensed to Whiteville. See Fayetteville

Wilkesboro

*WSIF(FM)— Apr 6, 1977: 90.9 mhz; 1 kw. Ant -171 ft. TL: N36 08 12 W81 11 02. Stereo. Box 120 28697. Secondary address: Collegiate Dr. 28697. Phone: (336) 838-6179. Phone: (336) 838-6222. E-mail: al.delachica@wilkescc.edu. Web Site: (336) 838-6282. Licensee: Wilkes Community College. Format: Classic rock, div, progsv. Target aud: 18-44. ♦ Dr. Gordon G. Burns Jr., pres; Al de Lachica, gen mgr.

WWWC(AM)— Jan 26, 1970: 1240 khz; 1 kw-U. TL: N36 09 00 W81 09 42. Box 580 28697. Secondary address: 413 Wilkesboro Blvd. 28697. Phone: (336) 838-1241/838-9992. Fax: (336) 838-9040. E-mail: onair@12403wc.com. Web Site: www.12403wc.com. Licensee: Foothills Media Inc. (acq 1994). Network: USA. Format: Southern gospel. Target aud: General. ♦ Alan G. Combs, pres, gen mgr, gen sls mgr, prom dir & chief of engrg; John Wishon, VP & progmg dir.

Williamston

WIAM(AM)— March 1951: 900 khz; 1 kw-D, 258 w-N. TL: N35 51 27 W77 02 34. Box 590 27892. Phone: (252) 792-4161. Fax: (252) 809-0039. E-mail: wiam@lifelineradio.com. Web Site: www.lifelineradio.com. Licensee: Lifeline Ministries Inc. (acq 6-18-90; 7-9-90). Format: Relg, gospel. Target aud: General. ♦ Johnny Bryant, pres, gen mgr & progmg dir.

WRHD(FM)— Aug 1, 1962: 103.7 mhz; 100 kw. 981 ft. TL: N35 53 47 W76 58 58. Stereo. 408 W. Arlington Blvd., Suite 101-C, Greenville

Stations in the U.S.   North Carolina

27834. Phone: (252) 355-1037. Fax: (252) 355-2234. Web Site: www.thehotfm.com. Licensee: ABG North Carolina LLC. Group owner: Archway Broadcasting Group (acq 1-9-03; grpsl). Rep: Allied Radio Partners. Davis Wright Tremaine P.C. Format: Contemp hit/Top-40. Target aud: 18-49; young adults. ♦Rodney Rainey, gen mgr & mktg dir; Jeff Davis, opns mgr, progmg dir & news dir; Tori Gray, gen sls mgr; Rob LeBron, chief of engrg.

Wilmington

WAAV(AM)—(Leland). Dec 20, 1957: 980 khz; 5 kw-U, DA-N. TL: N34 14 54 W78 00 09. 3233 Burnt Mill Rd. 28403-2654. Phone: (910) 763-9977. Fax: (910) 762-0456. Web Site: www.cumulus.com. Licensee: Cumulus Licensing Corp. Group owner: Cumulus Media L.L.C. (acq 7-2-97; $1.6 million with co-located FM). Network: ABC News/Talk. Rep: McGavren Guild. Format: News/talk. Target aud: 35 plus. ♦Jim Principi, gen mgr; Perry Stone, opns mgr; Jennifer McLean, gen sls mgr; Dave Carroll, mktg dir & prom dir; Mike Farow, progmg dir; Mark Ward, pub affrs dir; Tim Nelson, chief of engrg.

WKXS-FM—Co-owned with WAAV(AM). Dec 10, 1994: 94.1 mhz; 3 kw. 328 ft. TL: N34 09 03 W78 04 48. (CP: 5.5 kw). Format: Urban contemp. ♦Ken Johnson, progmg dir.

*****WDVV(FM)**— 1999: 89.7 mhz; 6 kw. Ant 144 ft. TL: N34 09 03 W78 04 46. Stereo. Box 957 28402. Phone: (910) 763-2452. Fax: (910) 763-6578. E-mail: familyradio@familyradio.to. Web Site: www.familyradio.to. Licensee: Family Radio Network Inc. (group owner; acq 2-16-01; $100,000. with WMYT(AM) Carolina Beach). Network: USA. Format: Christian praise & worship. ♦Jim Stephens, gen mgr; Buddy Womack, chief of opns.

WGNI(FM)— Mar 1, 1970: 102.7 mhz; 100 kw. 981 ft. TL: N34 03 00 W78 04 56. Stereo. 3233 Burnt Mill Rd. 28403-2654. Phone: (910) 763-9977. Fax: (910) 762-0456. Web Site: www.cumulus.com. Licensee: Cumulus Licensing Corp. Group owner: Cumulus Media Inc. Rep: McGavren Guild. Format: Hot Adult Contemp. News staff: two. ♦Jim Principi, gen mgr; Perry Stone, opns dir; Jennifer McLean, gen sls mgr; David Carroll, prom dir & adv dir; Mike Farrow, progmg dir; Tim Nelson, chief of engrg.

*****WHQR(FM)**— Apr 24, 1984: 91.3 mhz; 100 kw. Ant 1,141 ft. TL: N34 07 53 W78 11 17. Stereo. 254 N. Front St., Wilminton 28401. Phone: (910) 343-1640. Fax: (910) 251-8693. E-mail: whqr@whqr.org. Web Site: www.whqr.org. Licensee: Friends of Public Radio Inc. Network: NPR, PRI. Jane McClanahan Schwartz, Woods & Miller. Format: Class, news, jazz. News: 63 hrs wkly. Target aud: 35 plus. Spec prog: Jazz 15 hrs, folk one hr, reggae 3 hrs, flamenco one hr, Latino one hr wkly. ♦John Jordan, opns; Susan G. Dankel, gen mgr; George Scheibner, opns mgr; Ann Berry, prom mgr; David Srebnik, mus dir; John McHarry, chief of engrg.

WKXB(FM)—See Burgaw

WLSG(AM)— Dec 24, 1946: 1340 khz; 1 kw-U. TL: N34 12 35 W77 56 53. 201 N. Front St., Suite 805 28401. Secondary address: Box 957 28402. Phone: (910) 763-2452. Fax: (910) 763-6578. E-mail: familyradio@familyradio.to. Web Site: www.familyradio.to. Licensee: Family Radio Network Inc. (group owner; acq 6-30-00; $75,000). Network: Network: Salem Radio Network, USA. Format: Southern gospel, relg. Target aud: 30 plus. ♦Jim Stephens, gen mgr.

WMFD(AM)—Listing follows WRQR(FM).

WMNX(FM)— Feb 24, 1970: 97.3 mhz; 100 kw. 602 ft. TL: N34 16 34 W78 09 09. (CP: Ant 977 ft. TL: N34 03 00 W78 04 56). Stereo. 3233 Burnt Mill Dr. 28403-2654. Phone: (910) 763-9977. Fax: (910) 762-0456. Web Site: www.coast973.com. Licensee: Cumulus Licensing Corp. Group owner: Cumulus Media Inc. (acq 3-12-01; grpsl). Rep: McGavren Guild. Format: Urban contemp. News staff: one. Target aud: 18-49; general. ♦Jim Principi, gen mgr; Perry Stone, opns dir.

WRQR(FM)— February 1994: 104.5 mhz; 4.5 kw. 377 ft. TL: N34 16 15 W77 57 23. 25 N. Kerr Ave., Suite C 28405. Phone: (910) 791-3088. Fax: (910) 791-0112. Web Site: www.wrqr.com. Licensee: NM Licensing LLC. (acq 12-20-2004; grpsl). Format: AOR. Target aud: 25-54. ♦Bea Raybourne, pres & gen mgr; Christine Martinez, opns mgr, progmg dir & progmg mgr; Gayle Brown, gen sls mgr; Missy Andrus, prom mgr; Doug Carlisle, news dir; Roger Brace, chief of engrg.

WMFD(AM)—Co-owned with WRQR(FM). Apr 15, 1935: 630 khz; 1 kw-U, DA-2. TL: N34 13 31 W77 59 17. Stereo. Web Site: www.wmfd.com. Network: CBS. Format: Sports. News staff: one; News: 3 hrs wkly. Target aud: 30 plus; upscale audience. ♦JIm Clark, progmg dir.

WVBS(AM)—See Burgaw

WWIL(AM)— Aug 25, 1963: 1490 khz; 1 kw-U. TL: N34 13 52 W77 57 18. Box 957 28402-0957. Phone: (910) 763-2452. Fax: (910) 763-6578. E-mail: familyradio@familyradio.to. Web Site: www.familyradio.to. Licensee: Family Radio Network Inc. (group owner; acq 10-28-92; $35,000; 11-23-92). Network: USA. Format: Black gospel "the light". Target aud: 25-49. ♦Jim Stephens, gen mgr; Pastor James Utley, stn mgr & mktg mgr.

WWIL-FM— December 1995: 90.5 mhz; 1 kw horiz, 20 kw vert. 328 ft. TL: N34 10 52 W78 02 33. (Acq 6-95; 1-9-95). Network: USA. Format: Adult contemp, Christian. Target aud: 25-54.

WWQQ-FM— Mar 31, 1969: 101.3 mhz; 50 kw. 525 ft. TL: N34 13 31 W77 59 17. (CP: 40 kw, ant 544 ft.). Stereo. 3233 Burnt Mill Rd. 28403-2654. Phone: (910) 763-9977. Fax: (910) 762-0456. Web Site: www.cumulus.com. Licensee: Cumulus Licensing Corp. Group owner: Cumulus Media L.L.C. (acq 7-3-97; Network: ABC Daytime Direction. Rep: McGavren Guild. Format: Today's Country. News staff: one. Target aud: 25-54. ♦Jim Principi, gen mgr; Perry Stone, opns mgr; Robin Batson, natl sls mgr; Dave Carroll, mktg dir & prom dir; Paul Johnson, progmg mgr; Tim Nelson, chief of engrg.

Wilson

*****WAJC(FM)**— May 1990: 90.5 mhz; 3.8 kw. 100 ft. TL: N35 47 48 W78 18 31. 5. W. Hargett St., Suite 801, Raleigh 27601-1348. Phone: (919) 899-6778. Fax: (919) 899-6779. Licensee: CSN International (group owner; acq 6-23-2000; $150,000). Format: Christian. ♦Jim Walker, gen mgr; Alan Riggs, opns mgr & progmg mgr; Mickel Pruden, chief of engrg.

WGTM(AM)— July 18, 1937: 590 khz; 5 kw-U, DA-2. TL: N35 43 04 W78 03 33. 4002 Hwy. 42 W. 27895. Phone: (252) 243-2188. Fax: (252) 237-8813. Licensee: Celestine L. Willis. Group owner: Willis Broadcasting Corp. (acq 12-15-89; $375,000; 3-3-86). Format: Gospel. ♦Celestine L. Willis, gen mgr; Raymond Grant, progmg dir.

WLLY(AM)— 1961: 1350 khz; 1 kw-D, 79 w-N. TL: N35 43 24 W77 55 16. WLLY Radio Station, Box 637, 210 Beacon St. W. 27894-0637. Phone: (252) 237-5171. Fax: (252) 237-5172. Licensee: Estuardo Valdemar Rodriguez and Leonor Rodriguez, joint tenants. Group owner: Estuardo Valdemar Rodriguez and Leonor Rodriguez Stns (acq 10-11-2002; $255,000). Network: USA. Format: Southern Gospel. Target aud: General. ♦Wallace Bullock, gen mgr, opns mgr, gen sls mgr, prom mgr & progmg dir.

WRDU(FM)—Licensed to Wilson. See Raleigh

WVOT(AM)— June 1948: 1420 khz; 1 kw-D, 500 w-N, DA-N. TL: N35 44 08 W77 53 02. 103 N. Jackson St. 27893. Phone: (252) 243-5157. Phone: (252) 243-1420. Fax: (252) 291-5000. E-mail: wvot@bbnp.com. Licensee: Kingdom Expansion Corp. (acq 1-18-01; $100,000). Format: Christian, sports. News: 25 hrs wkly. Target aud: 25-55. ♦M.K. Smith, pres; Joyce Farmer, gen mgr & stn mgr.

Windsor

WBTE(AM)— 1969: 990 khz; 1 kw-D. TL: N35 58 00 W76 56 54. 645 Church St., Suite 400, Norfolk 23510. Phone: (757) 622-4600. Fax: (757) 624-6515. Licensee: 99 Broadcasting Corp. Group owner: Willis Broadcasting Corp. Format: Contemp gospel, relg.

WURB(FM)—Co-owned with WBTE(AM). 1980: 97.7 mhz; 3 kw. 300 ft. TL: N36 04 06 W76 58 35.

WNBR-FM— Dec 5, 1988: 98.9 mhz; 6 kw. 350 ft. TL: N35 54 25 W77 00 32. Box 590, Williamston 27892. Secondary address: 1012 East Blvd., Williamston 27892. Phone: (252) 792-4161. Fax: (252) 809-0039. E-mail: wdrp@lifelineradio.com. Web Site: www.lifelineradio.com. Licensee: Eure Communications Inc. (group owner), (acq 5-17-2004; $1.07 million). Format: Southern gospel. ♦Johnny Bryant, gen mgr, gen sls mgr & progmg dir; Doug Ferris, chief of engrg.

Wingate

*****WRCM(FM)**— June 14, 1993: 91.9 mhz; 17.7 kw. 515 ft. TL: N35 03 33 W80 40 14. Stereo. Box 17069, Charlotte 28227. Secondary address: 1092 Radio Drive, Indian Trail 28079. Phone: (704) 821-9293. Phone: (704) 570-9200. Fax: (704) 821-9285. E-mail: newlife91.9@wrcm.org. Web Site: www.wrcm.org. Licensee: Columbia Bible College Broadcasting Co. Network: Salem Radio Network. Format: Adult contemp, Christian. Target aud: 25-44; female. ♦Joe Paulo, gen mgr; Elizabeth Poplin, prom dir & adv dir; Dwayne Harrison, progmg dir; Joyce Younts, pub affrs dir; Dave Morrison, chief of engrg.

Winston-Salem

WAAA(AM)— Oct 28, 1950: 980 khz; 1 kw-D, 69.3 w-N. TL: N36 09 15 W80 16 34. Box 11197 27116-1197. Phone: (336) 971-7852. Licensee: Media Broadcasting Corp. (acq 9-1-56). Format: Urban, gospel. ♦Ms. Mutter D. Evans, pres & gen mgr.

WBFJ(AM)— Oct 1, 1960: 1550 khz; 1 kw-D, DA. TL: N36 06 33 W80 14 47. Stereo. 1249 Trade St. 27101. Phone: (336) 721-1560. Fax: (336) 777-1032. Web Site: www.wbfj.org. Licensee: Word of Life Broadcasting Inc. (acq 6-29-83). Network: USA. Format: Christian, talk, educational. Target aud: 29-54; general. ♦Philip T. Watson, pres & gen sls mgr; John Hill, progmg dir; Wally Decker, gen mgr & mus dir; Larry Schropp, chief of engrg.

*****WBFJ-FM**— Sept 1, 1994: 89.3 mhz; 2.5 kw. 423 ft. TL: N36 05 56 W80 15 00. 1249 Trade St. 27101. Phone: (336) 721-1560. Phone: (336) 777-1893. Fax: (336) 777-1032. E-mail: wbfj@netunlimited.net. Web Site: www.wbfj.org. Licensee: Triad Family Network Inc. Network: USA. Format: Contemp Christian mus. Target aud: 25-49. ♦Kurt Myers, prom mgr; Wally Decker, gen mgr, gen sls mgr & progmg dir; Verne Hill, news dir; Larry Shropp, chief of engrg.

*****WFDD-FM**— Mar 13, 1961: 88.5 mhz; 60 kw. 345 ft. TL: N35 58 12 W80 12 54. (CP: TL: N35 55 15 W80 17 37). Stereo. Box 8850 27109. Secondary address: 56 Wake Forest Rd. 27109. Phone: (336) 758-8850. Fax: (336) 758-5193. E-mail: wfdd@wfu.edu. Web Site: www.wfdd.org. Licensee: Trustees of Wake Forest University. Network: PRI, NPR. Public Radio Adv. Alliance Fletcher, Heald & Hildreth. Format: Class, news. News staff: 3; News: 29 hrs wkly. Target aud: General; educated/public radio. Spec prog: Jazz 16 hrs wkly. ♦Jay Banks, stn mgr; Linda Word, dev dir; Denise Franklin, news dir.

WKTE(AM)—See King

WKZL(FM)— 1972: 107.5 mhz; 100 kw. 994 ft. TL: N36 16 33 W79 56 27. Stereo. 192 E. Lewis St., Greensboro 27406-1459. Phone: (336) 274-8042. Fax: (336) 274-1629. Web Site: www.1075kzl.com. Licensee: Dick Broadcasting Co. Inc. of Tennessee (acq 11-23-92; $6.5 million. with WGFX(FM) Gallatin, TN; FTR: 12-14-92). Kaye, Scholer, Fierman, Hays & Handler. Format: Contemp hit/Top-40. Target aud: 25-49; women. ♦Allen Dick, CEO, chmn & pres; David Henderlight, CFO; Bruce Wheeler, VP & gen mgr; James Kerr, opns mgr & natl sls mgr; Jennifer Hart, gen sls mgr; Jeff McHugh, progmg dir; Marcia Gan, mus dir; Tom Caldwell, chief of engrg.

WMAG(FM)—See High Point

North Carolina   **Directory of Radio**

WMQX-FM—Licensed to Winston-Salem. See Greensboro

WPIP(AM)— June 1, 1995: 880 khz; 900 w-D. TL: N36 06 33 W80 14 47. 4135 Thomasville Rd. 27107. Phone: (336) 785-0527. Fax: (336) 785-0529. Web Site: www.wpipbereanradio.org. Licensee: Berean Baptist Church. (acq 5-95; $80,000; 5-8-95). Network: USA. Format: Conservative Christian. ♦ Dr. Ron Baity, gen mgr; Jeff Baity, chief of opns.

WPOL(AM)—Licensed to Winston-Salem. See Greensboro

WSJS(AM)— Apr 17, 1930: 600 khz; 5 kw-D, 5 kw-N, DA-2. TL: N36 07 00 W80 21 26. Stereo. 875 W. 5th St. 27101. Phone: (336) 727-8826. Fax: (336) 777-3915. Web Site: www.wsjs.com. Licensee: Infinity Radio Inc. Group owner: Infinity Broadcasting Corp. (acq 8-7-00; grpsl). Network: Wall Street. Rep: Clear Channel. Format: News/talk. Target aud: 25-64. ♦ Tom Hamilton, gen mgr & gen sls mgr; Marty Holbrook, prom dir; Mike Fenely, progmg dir; Bob Costner, news dir; Robert Lafore, chief of engrg.

WSMX(AM)— October 1964: 1500 khz; 1 kw-D, DA. TL: N36 06 34 W80 12 42. 1225 E. 5th St., Suite 104 27101. Phone: (336) 725-2190. Fax: (336) 724-6368. E-mail: watsonwsmx@aol.com. Licensee: Gospel Media Inc. (acq 6-82). Format: Gospel, community affrs. News: 12 hrs wkly. Target aud: 30-50 plus; blue collar, minorities, church members. Spec prog: Country 3 hrs wkly. ♦ Joe Watson, pres & gen mgr; Robin M. Watson, VP & chief of engrg.

***WSNC(FM)**— 1982: 90.5 mhz; 125 w. 92 ft. TL: N36 05 36 W80 13 53. (CP: 10 kw, ant 194 ft. TL: N36 05 24 W80 13 20). Stereo. Campus Box 19281, Hall-Patterson, 601 M.L.K. Jr. Dr. 27110. Phone: (336) 750-2433. Fax: (336) 750-2329. Licensee: Winston-Salem State University. Format: Adult contemp, jazz, relg. Target aud: 12-70; African-Americans. Spec prog: Class 4 hrs wkly. ♦ Dr. Brian Blount, CEO; Donald Baker, gen mgr; Monica Melton, progmg dir & mus dir; Baxter Griffin, chief of engrg.

WTOB(AM)— Apr 22, 1947: 1380 khz; 5 kw-D, 2.5 kw-N, DA-2. TL: N36 08 53 W80 19 11. Stereo. 4405 Providence Ln. 27106. Phone: (336) 759-0363. Fax: (336) 759-0366. Licensee: Davidson Media Station WTOB Licensee LLC. (acq 3-25-2005; swap with WWBG(AM) Greensboro for WDRU(AM) Wake Forest). Smithwick & Belendiuk. Format: Sp. Target aud: 35 plus; affluent audience. ♦ Forrest Ritchey, opns mgr; Stuart Epperson Jr., gen mgr & gen sls mgr.

WTQR(FM)— Dec 1, 1947: 104.1 mhz; 100 kw. 1,420 ft. TL: N36 22 28 W80 22 31. Stereo. 2-B PAI Park, Greensboro 27409. Phone: (336) 822-2000. Fax: (336) 887-0104. Web Site: www.wtqr.com. Licensee: Clear Channel Radio Licenses Inc. Group owner: Clear Channel Communications Inc. (acq 1996; grpsl). Format: Country. Target aud: 25-54. Spec prog: NASCAR, bluegrass 2 hrs wkly. ♦ Sheryl Solomone, gen mgr.

WVBZ(FM)—See High Point

***WXRI(FM)**— May 17, 1997: 91.3 mhz; 50 kw. 216 ft. TL: N36 08 06 W80 22 32. Box 25775 27114. Phone: (336) 699-8036. Phone: (336) 788-1155. Fax: (336) 788-7199. E-mail: joyfm@bellsouth.net. Web Site: www.joyfm.org. Licensee: Positive Alternative Radio Inc. Group owner: Baker Family Stations (Positive Radio Group) (acq 5-21-92). Booth, Freret, Imlay & Tepper. Format: Southern gospel. ♦ Vernon H. Baker, pres; Edward A. Baker, VP; Rodney Baucom, gen mgr & stn mgr; Sam Stutts, mktg mgr; Dean Lilly, chief of engrg.

Winterville

WECU(AM)—Not on air, target date: unknown: 1570 khz; 3.8 kw-D, 200 w-N. TL: N35 32 06 W77 25 06. Box 401, Clarksville, MD 21029. Phone: (410) 964-5700. Phone: (252) 633-1490 (station). Licensee: CTC Media Group. Group owner: CTC Media Group Inc. ♦ Edwin Lee Afflerbach, pres; Mike Afflerbach, stn mgr.

Wrightsville Beach

WBNE(FM)— Nov 27, 2000: 93.7 mhz; 6 kw. 328 ft. TL: N34 18 04 W77 48 07. 122 Cinema Dr., Wilmington 28403. Phone: (910) 772-6300. Fax: (910) 772-6310. Web Site: www.937thebone.com. Licensee: Sea-Comm Inc. (group owner; acq 6-30-00; $1.2 million. for CP). Format: Classic rock. ♦ Paul Knight, gen mgr; Max Deutsch, gen sls mgr; Bud Stone, progmg mgr; Suzanne Jalot, news dir.

Yanceyville

WYNC(AM)— Nov 9, 1979: 1540 khz; 2.5 kw-D. TL: N36 24 52 W79 20 06. Box 670 27379. Secondary address: 545 Firetower Rd. 27379. Phone: (336) 694-7343. Fax: (336) 694-7514. Licensee: Semora Broadcasting Inc. (acq 12-9-91; $102,041; 1-6-92). Network: Westwood One. Format: Gospel. Target aud: General; rural Caswell county & Danville, VA. Spec prog: Gospel 16 hrs wkly. ♦ George Thaxton, gen mgr, stn mgr & chief of engrg.

North Dakota

Arthur

KVMI(FM)— April 1994: 103.9 mhz; 25 kw. Ant 328 ft. TL: N47 07 20 W97 19 29. 314 Dale Ave., Moorhead, MN 56560. Phone: (701) 866-0799. Fax: (218) 287-8274. Licensee: Vision Media Inc. (acq 2-25-2000). Network: Westwood One. Format: Hot adult contemp. ♦ Jim Babbitt, gen mgr.

Belcourt

***KEYA(FM)**— October 1975: 88.5 mhz; 19 kw. 263 ft. TL: N48 50 37 W99 45 02. Stereo. Box 190, Media Bldg., Hospital Rd. 58316. Phone: (701) 477-5686. Phone: (701) 477-3527. Fax: (701) 477-3252. E-mail: keya@utma.com. Web Site: www.keya.utma.com. Licensee: KEYA Inc. Network: Network: NPR, PRI. Steptoe & Johnson. Format: C&W, oldies, rock/AOR. News: 2 hrs wkly. Target aud: General; members of the Turtle Mountain Band of Chippewa Indians. Spec prog: American Indian 6 hrs, relg 10 hrs, old-time fiddle mus 4 hrs, Chippewa 3 hrs wkly. ♦ Kimberly Thomas, gen mgr; William Morin, adv dir; Jarle Kvale, progmg dir; Janice Keplin, chief of engrg.

Beulah

KHOL(FM)— Oct 5, 1978: 1410 khz; 1 kw-D, 180 w-N. TL: N47 17 15 W101 45 46. 850 County Rd. 21 58523. Phone: (701) 873-2215. Fax: (701) 873-2363. E-mail: kholam@westriv.com. Licensee: KHOL 1410 AM Radio Inc. Network: ABC Information & Entertainment. Format: Adult contemp. News staff: one; News: 14 hrs wkly. Target aud: 24-65; general. ♦ Marlene Knaup, gen mgr.

Bismarck

KACL(FM)— Apr 22, 1997: 98.7 mhz; 100 kw. 1,092 ft. TL: N46 35 23 W100 48 02. Box 1377, 1830 N. 11th St. 58501. Phone: (701) 250-6602. Fax: (701) 250-6632. Web Site: www.cumulus.com. Licensee: Cumulus Licensing Corp. Group owner: Cumulus Media Inc. (acq 5-11-98; grpsl). Format: Oldies. ♦ Rod Murthum, gen mgr; Debbie Boechler, gen sls mgr; Bob Beck, progmg dir; Matt Murphy, news dir; Dennis Wilson, chief of engrg.

***KBFR(FM)**— June 2003: 91.9 mhz; 1 kw. Ant 194 ft. TL: N46 49 38 W100 46 28. Family Stations Inc., 4135 Northgate Blvd., Suite 1, Sacramento, CA 95834. Phone: (510) 568-6200. Web Site: www.familyradio.com. Licensee: Family Stations Inc. (group owner). Format: Relg. ♦ Harold Camping, gen mgr.

***KBMK(FM)**—Not on air, target date: unknown: 88.3 mhz; 100 kw vert. Ant 482 ft. TL: N46 47 06 W100 34 35. Broadcasting for the Challenged Inc., 188 S. Bellevue, Suite 222, Memphis, TN 38104. Phone: (901) 516-8970. Licensee: Broadcasting for the Challenged Inc. ♦ George S. Flinn Jr., gen mgr.

KBMR(AM)— Aug 15, 1958: 1130 khz; 50 kw-D, DA. TL: N46 50 04 W100 31 19. (CP: 10 kw-D). Stereo. 3500 E. Rosser Ave. 58501. Phone: (701) 255-1234. Fax: (701) 222-1131. Licensee: Clear Channel Broadcasting Licenses Inc. Group owner: Clear Channel Communications Inc. (acq 2-13-2004;. grpsl). Rep: McGavren Guild. Borsari & Paxson. Format: C&W. Target aud: 25 plus. Spec prog: Farm 4 hrs wkly. ♦ Bob Denver, gen mgr; Terry Fleck, gen sls mgr; Charlie Williams, progmg dir; Jeff Alexander, news dir; Bcyan Funk, chief of engrg.

KBYZ(FM)— Listing follows KLXX(AM).

***KCND(FM)**— Sept 1, 1981: 90.5 mhz; 50 kw. 1,216 ft. TL: N46 35 23 W100 48 02. Stereo. 207 N 5th St., Fargo 58102. Phone: (701) 224-1700. Fax: (701) 224-0555. E-mail: program@pol.org. Web Site: www.prairiepublic.org. Licensee: Prairie Public Broadcasting Inc.

Network: Network: PRI, NPR. Format: Class, jazz, news. News staff: 2; News: 40 hrs wkly. Target aud: General. Spec prog: American Indian 2 hrs, folk 6 hrs, blues 2 hrs wkly. ♦ Bill Thomas, gen mgr & stn mgr; Duane Lee, opns mgr; David Thompson, news dir. Co-owned TV: *KBME-TV affil.

KFYR(AM)— 1925: 550 khz; 5 kw-U, DA-N. TL: N46 51 12 W100 32 37. Stereo. Box 1658 58502. Secondary address: 210 N. Fourth St. 58502. Phone: (701) 255-8147. Fax: (701) 255-8155. E-mail: frontdesk@kfyr.com. Web Site: www.kfyr.com. Licensee: Citicasters Licenses L.P. Group owner: Clear Channel Communications Inc. (acq 5-4-99; grpsl). Network: ABC Information & Entertainment. Format: Adult contemp, news/talk, sports. ♦ Syd Stewart, gen mgr & gen sls mgr.

KYYY(FM)—Co-owned with KFYR(AM). Aug 15, 1966: 92.9 mhz; 100 kw. 1,180 ft. TL: N46 36 19 W100 48 30. Stereo. 206 N. 4th St. 58501. Phone: (701) 224-9393. Fax: (701) 255-8293. Web Site: www.kfyr.com. Format: Hot adult contemp. ♦ Todd Mitchell, opns dir.

KKCT(FM)— 1994: 97.5 mhz; 100 kw. 324 ft. TL: N46 35 25 W100 47 47. Box 1377, 1830 N. 11th St. 58501. Phone: (701) 250-6602. Fax: (701) 250-6632. Web Site: www.cumulus.com. Licensee: Cumulus Licensing Corp. Group owner: Cumulus Media Inc. (acq 5-11-98; grpsl). Format: Country. ♦ Rod Murthum, gen mgr; Debbie Boechler, gen sls mgr; Dan Edwards, progmg dir; Matt Murphy, news dir; Dennis Wilson, chief of engrg.

KLXX(AM)—(Bismarck-Mandan). 1925: 1270 khz; 1 kw-D, 250 w-N. TL: N46 48 37 W100 50 10. Box 1377 58502. Phone: (701) 663-6411. Phone: (701) 250-6602. Fax: (701) 663-8790. Fax: (701) 250-6632. Licensee: Cumulus Licensing Corp. Group owner: Cumulus Media Inc. (acq 5-11-98; grpsl). Format: adult standards. News staff: one. Spec prog: Sports 6 hrs wkly. ♦ Rod Knodez, gen mgr; Phillip Duchscher, gen sls mgr; Larry Slabik, progmg dir; Dennis Wilson, chief of engrg.

***KNRI(FM)**—Not on air, target date: unknown: 89.7 mhz; 250 w. Ant 157 ft. TL: N46 51 00 W100 46 11. 5700 West Oaks Blvd., Rocklin, CA 95765. Phone: (916) 251-1600. Fax: (916) 251-1650. E-mail: info@air1.com. Web Site: www.air1.com. Licensee: Educational Media Foundation. Group owner: EMF Broadcasting. Network: Air 1. Shaw Pittman. Format: Contemp Christian. News staff: 3. Target aud: 18-35; Judeo Christian female. ♦ Richard Jenkins, pres; Mike Novak, VP & progmg dir; Lloyd Parker, mgr; Keith Whipple, dev dir; Eric Allen, gen sls mgr; John D. Burkholder, rgnl sls mgr; Chris Joyce, prom dir; Bryan O'Neal, progmg dir; Liz Morton, mus dir; Ed Lenane, news dir; Sam Wallington, engrg dir.

KQDY(FM)— Sept 13, 1968: 94.5 mhz; 100 kw. 1,117 ft. TL: N46 51 31 W100 41 38. Stereo. Box 2156 56502-2156. Secondary address: 3500 E. Rosser 58501. Phone: (701) 255-1234. Fax: (701) 222-1131. Web Site: www.kqdy.com. Licensee: Clear Channel Broadcasting Licenses Inc. Group owner: Clear Channel Communications Inc. (acq 2-13-2004; grpsl). Format: Contemp country. News: 4 hrs wkly. Target aud: 18-49. ♦ Bob Denver, gen mgr.

KSSS(FM)— Aug 1, 1994: 101.5 mhz; 100 kw. 987 ft. TL: N46 56 31 W100 41 38. 3500 E. Rosser Ave. 58501. Phone: (701) 255-1234. Fax: (701) 222-1131. Web Site: www.1015arockandrockstation.com. Licensee: Clear Channel Broadcasting Licenses Inc. Group owner: Clear Channel Communications Inc. (acq 2-13-2004; grpsl). Format: AOR. ♦ Bob Denver, gen mgr; Terry Flack, gen sls mgr; Rick Anthony, progmg dir; Jeff Alexander, news dir; Brian Funk, engrg dir.

KXMR(AM)— Mar 20, 1999: 710 khz; 50 kw-D, 4 kw-N, DA-3. TL: N46 50 04 W100 31 19 (D), N46 40 08 W100 46 33 (N). 3500 E. Rosser Ave. 58501. Phone: (701) 255-1234. Fax: (701) 222-1131. Licensee: Clear Channel Broadcasting Licenses Inc. Group owner: Clear Channel Communications Inc. (acq 12-10-03). Format: News/talk. ♦ Bob Denver, gen mgr.

Bismarck-Mandan

KLXX(AM)—Licensed to Bismarck-Mandan. See Bismarck

Bottineau

KBTO(FM)— Nov 9, 1980: 101.9 mhz; 52 kw. 492 ft. TL: N48 51 10 W100 20 01. Stereo. 1120 Highway 5 west 58318. Phone: (701) 228-5151. Fax: (701) 228-2483. E-mail: sunnyradio@hotmail.com. Licensee: Programmers Broadcasting Inc. (acq 1-2-2002; $595,000).

Stations in the U.S. — North Dakota

Format: Country. ♦ John Kircher, pres; Jay Davis, gen mgr & chief of engrg; Jean Schempp, opns mgr; Rick Gustafson, gen sls mgr; Dylan Connor, mus dir.

Bowman

KPOK(AM)— Aug 9, 1980: 1340 khz; 1 kw-U. TL: N46 10 48 W103 22 12. Box 829, 11 1/2 N. Main 58623. Phone: (701) 523-3883. Fax: (701) 523-3885. Licensee: Tri-State Communications Inc. Network: Westwood One. Format: Country. News staff: one; News: 14 hrs wkly. Target aud: 25-54. Spec prog: Farm 2 hrs wkly. ♦ Larry Kemnitz, pres; Richard Peterson, VP; Brian Fischer, gen mgr.

Burlington

KWGO(FM)— 2005: 102.9 mhz; 100 kw. Ant 512 ft. TL: N48 03 04 W101 20 23. Box 28, Bottineau 58318-0028. Phone: (701) 228-5151. Fax: (701) 228-2483. Licensee: Programmers Broadcasting Inc. Fletcher, Heald & Hildreth. ♦ John Kircher, pres.

Carrington

KDAK(AM)— Oct 16, 1961: 1600 khz; 500 w-D, 90 w-N. TL: N47 25 43 W99 05 03. Box 50 58421. Secondary address: Box1170, Jamestown 58402. Phone: (701) 652-3151. Fax: (701) 652-2916. E-mail: kdakam@daktel.com. Licensee: Two Rivers Broadcasting Inc. Group owner: Robert Ingstad Broadcast Properties (acq 7-1-94). Format: C&W. Target aud: 30 plus. ♦ Robert J. Ingstad, pres; Scott Lane, gen mgr & stn mgr.

KYNU(FM)— Co-owned with KDAK(AM). 1997: 98.3 mhz; 100 kw. 866 ft. TL: N47 05 38 W99 02 11. Stereo. Box 1170, Jamestown 58402. Phone: (701) 252-1400. Fax: (701) 252-1402. Format: Country. ♦ Dave Reed, gen mgr.

Cavalier

KAOC(FM)— Sept 29, 1998: 105.1 mhz; 44 kw. 512 ft. TL: N48 37 44 W98 00 35. 1420 3rd St., Langdon 58249. Phone: (701) 256-1067. Fax: (701) 256-1051. E-mail: kndk1080@utma.com. Licensee: Simmons Broadcasting Inc. (group owner; acq 9-7-2004; $1). Format: Hot country. ♦ Bob Simmons, gen mgr; Jen Taylor, opns mgr.

Devils Lake

KDLR(AM)— Jan 25, 1925: 1240 khz; 1 kw-U. TL: N48 06 42 W98 50 43. Box 190, 400 12th Ave. 58301. Phone: (701) 662-2161. Fax: (701) 662-2222. E-mail: kdlrkdvl@stellarnet.com. Web Site: lrradioworks.com. Licensee: Double Z Broadcasting Inc. Group owner: Lake Region Radio Works (acq 1-1-2003; $820,000. with KDVL(FM) Devils Lake). Format: Country, news. Target aud: 25 plus; general. Spec prog: Minnesota Twins baseball, Vikings football. ♦ Curt Teigen, pres & gen mgr; Roger Metens, sls dir; Eric Arndt, news dir.

KDVL(FM)— Jan 1, 1967: 102.5 mhz; 100 kw. 471 ft. TL: N47 59 16 W98 55 59. Stereo. Box 190 58301. Secondary address: 400 12th Ave. 58301. Phone: (701) 662-2161. Fax: (701) 662-2222. Fax: (701) 662-7564. E-mail: kdlrkdvl@stellarnet.com. Web Site: lrradioworks.com. Licensee: Double Z Broadcasting Inc. Group owner: Lake Region Radio Works (acq 1-1-2003; $820,000. with KDLR(AM) Devils Lake). Format: Oldies. News staff: one. Target aud: 18-54. ♦ Curt Teigen, pres & gen mgr; Roger Mertens, sls dir; Bob Gunderson, progmg dir; Eric Arndt, news dir.

KQZZ(FM)— August 1996: 96.7 mhz; 45 kw. 512 ft. TL: N47 58 46 W99 03 16. 318 W. Walnut St. 58301. Phone: (701) 662-7563. Fax: (701) 662-7564. Web Site: lrradioworks.com. Licensee: Two Rivers Broadcasting Inc. Group owner: Lake Region Radio Works (acq 3-11-99; $250,000). Shaw Pittman. Format: AOR. ♦ Curt Teigen, gen mgr & stn mgr.

KZZY(FM)— March 1984: 103.5 mhz; 100 kw. 433 ft. TL: N47 59 28 W98 56 57. Stereo. 318 W. Walnut St. 58301. Phone: (701) 662-7563. Fax: (701) 662-7564. E-mail: kzzyfm@stellarnet.com. Web Site: www.zzcountry.com. Licensee: Double Z Broadcasting Inc. Group owner: Lake Region Radio Works (acq 4-11-90). Network: ABC Information & Entertainment. Format: C&W. News staff: one. ♦ Curt Teigen, gen mgr, opns mgr & chief of engrg; Roger Mertens, gen sls mgr; Rob Hendricks, progmg dir.

Dickinson

KCAD(FM)— Nov 20, 1996: 99.1 mhz; 100 kw. Ant 794 ft. TL: N46 56 09 W102 43 55. 11291 39th St. SW 58601-9206. Phone: (701) 227-1876. Fax: (701) 483-1959. Licensee: Clear Channel Broadcasting Licenses Inc. Group owner: Clear Channel Communications Inc. (acq 9-1-00; grpsl). Network: ABC. Format: Hot country. Target aud: 16-50; general. ♦ George Smith, gen mgr & gen sls mgr; Chad Barta, progmg dir & news dir.

KLTC(AM)— Co-owned with KCAD(FM). July 4, 1978: 1460 khz; 5 kw-U, DA-N. TL: N46 50 54 W102 49 49. Rep: Hyett/Ramsland. Format: C&W. Target aud: General.

KDIX(AM)— 1947: 1230 khz; 1 kw-U. TL: N46 53 44 W102 47 06. 119 Second Ave. W. 58601. Phone: (701) 225-5133. Phone: (800) 934-1230. Fax: (701) 225-4136. Licensee: Starrdak Inc. (acq 4-1-93). Network: CBS. Format: Adult contemp, oldies. News staff: 8; News: 6 hrs wkly. Target aud: 35-60. Spec prog: College sports. ♦ Lee Leiss, chmn & gen mgr; Rod Kleinjan, opns dir.

*****KDPR(FM)**— Oct 12, 1987: 89.9 mhz; 12.5 kw. 488 ft. TL: N46 43 34 W102 54 56. Stereo. 1814 N. 15th St., Bismarck 58501. Phone: (701) 241-6900. Fax: (701) 239-7650. E-mail: program@prairiepublic.org. Web Site: www.prairiepublic.org. Licensee: Prairie Public Broadcasting Inc. Network: Network: PRI, NPR. Format: Class, jazz, news. News staff: 2; News: 40 hrs wkly. Target aud: General. Spec prog: American Indian 2 hrs, folk 6 hrs wkly. ♦ Bill Thomas, gen mgr; Duane Lee, opns mgr; Dave Thompson, news dir.

KZRX(FM)— Aug 15, 1983: 92.1 mhz; 10.5 kw. Ant 492 ft. TL: N46 56 09 W102 43 55. Stereo. 11291 39 St. SW 58601. Phone: (701) 227-1876. Fax: (701) 483-1959. Web Site: www.z92fm.net. Licensee: Clear Channel Broadcasting Licenses Inc. Group owner: Clear Channel Communications Inc. (acq 9-1-00; grpsl). Rep: Hyett/Ramsland. Format: Classic rock. News staff: one. Target aud: 18-45. ♦ George Smith, gen mgr; Don Reisenauer, gen sls mgr; Chad Barta, progmg dir; Kim Kramer, news dir; Brian Funk, chief of engrg.

Fargo

*****KDSU(FM)**— Jan 17, 1966: 91.9 mhz; 100 kw. 991 ft. TL: N47 00 48 W97 11 37. Stereo. Box 3240 58108. Phone: (701) 241-6900. Fax: (701) 231-8899. Web Site: www.prairiepublic.org. Licensee: North Dakota State University. Network: Network: NPR, PRI. Format: Var/div. News staff: 3; News: 45 hrs wkly. Target aud: 24 plus; general. ♦ John Harris, CEO; Bill Thomas, gen mgr; Nancy Wood, dev dir.

*****KFBN(FM)**— Dec 8, 1997: 88.7 mhz; 30 kw horiz, 100 kw vert. 869 ft. TL: N47 00 48 W97 11 37. Box 107 58107. Phone: (701) 298-8877. Licensee: Fargo Baptist Church. Format: Mus, world news/rgnl weather, bible instruction. ♦ T.C. Scheving, pres & gen mgr.

KFGO(AM)— Mar 14, 1948: 790 khz; 5 kw-U, DA-N. TL: N46 04 05 W96 48 05. Stereo. 1020 S. 25th St. 58103. Phone: (701) 237-5346. Fax: (701) 235-4042. Web Site: www.kfgo.com. Licensee: Capstar TX L.P. Group owner: Clear Channel Communications Inc. (acq 11-9-00; grpsl). Network: ABC Information & Entertainment. Rep: CBS Radio. Format: Talk. Target aud: General. Spec prog: Farm 20 hrs, natl sports 20 hrs wkly. ♦ Tank McNamara, progmg dir.

KKBX(FM)— Co-owned with KFGO(AM). Feb 23, 1984: 101.9 mhz; 93 kw. Ant 1,000 ft. TL: N47 00 37 W97 11 40. Stereo. Web Site: www.kfgo.com. Format: Country.

*****KFNW(AM)**— (West Fargo). Oct 28, 1955: 1200 khz; 10 kw-D, 1 kw-N, DA-N. TL: N46 48 06 W96 52 57. 5702 52nd Ave. S. 58104. Secondary address: 5702 52nd Ave. S. 58104. Phone: (701) 282-5910. Fax: (701) 282-5781. E-mail: kfnw@kfnw.org. Web Site: www.kfnw.org. Licensee: Northwestern College. Group owner: Northwestern College & Radio. Format: Relg. News staff: one; News: 6 hrs wkly. Target aud: 25-54. ♦ Gary D. Herr, stn mgr; Phil Kvamme, progmg dir; Gary Ellingson, chief of engrg.

KFNW-FM— Mar 12, 1965: 97.9 mhz; 100 kw. 1,000 ft. TL: N46 48 07 W96 52 58. Stereo. Format: Christian contemp. Target aud: 25-54.

KPFX(FM)— Jan 4, 1993: 107.9 mhz; 100 kw. Ant 713 ft. TL: N46 32 41 W96 37 33. Stereo. Box 9919 58106. Secondary address: 2720 Seventh Ave. S. 58103. Phone: (701) 237-4500. Phone: (701) 237-4949. Fax: (701) 237-5400. Web Site: www.1079thfox.com. Licensee: Monterey Licenses LLC. Group owner: Triad Broadcasting Co. LLC (acq 8-18-99; grpsl). Rep: Christal. Shaw Pittman. Format: Classic rock. Target aud: 25-49; skews male. ♦ Nancy Odney, gen mgr; John Austin, opns mgr; Michael Brooks, gen sls mgr.

KQWB-FM— (Moorhead).MN November 1966: 98.7 mhz; 100 kw. 460 ft. TL: N46 45 35 W96 36 26. Stereo. Box 9919 58106-9919. Secondary address: 2720 7th Ave. S. 58103. Phone: (701) 237-4500. Phone: (701) 234-9898. Fax: (701) 235-9082. E-mail: studio@q98.com. Web Site: www.q98.com. Licensee: Monterey Licenses LLC. Group owner: Triad Broadcasting Co. LLC (acq 10-99; grpsl). Rep: Christal. Shaw Pittman. Format: Active rock. Target aud: 18-49; men. ♦ Nancy Odney, VP & gen mgr; John Austin, opns dir; Anne Phibian, opns mgr.

KVOX(AM)—See Moorhead, MN

KVOX-FM—See Moorhead, MN

WDAY(AM)— May 22, 1922: 970 khz; 5 kw-U, DA-N. TL: N46 52 43 W96 53 05. Stereo. Box 2466 58108. Secondary address: 301 S. 8th St. 58103. Phone: (701) 237-6500. Fax: (701) 241-5373. E-mail: jsunday@wday.com. Web Site: www.wday.com. Licensee: Forum Communications Co. Inc. (group owner) Network: ABC Information & Entertainment. Rep: Christal. Format: News/talk, farm, sports. News staff: 3; News: 35 hrs wkly. Target aud: 35-64. ♦ William Marcil Sr., CEO & pres; Jack Sunday, progmg dir; Mike Tanner, news dir.

WDAY-FM— 1965: 93.7 mhz; 100 kw. 1,040 ft. TL: N47 00 43 W97 11 58. Stereo. 1020 25th St. S. 58103. Phone: (701) 237-5346. Fax: (701) 235-4042. E-mail: dickvoight@clearchannel.com. Licensee: Capstar TX L.P. Group owner: Clear Channel Communications Inc. (acq 10-30-00; grpsl). Rep: Christal. Format: Top-40. Target aud: 18-49. ♦ Dick Voight, gen mgr.

Fort Totten

*****KABU(FM)**— Mar 15, 1999: 90.7 mhz; 6 kw. 328 ft. TL: N47 59 28 W98 56 57. Box 7 58335. Secondary address: KABU Radio Station, 7889 Hwy. 57, St. Michaels 58370. Phone: (701) 766-1995. Fax: (701) 766-4774. E-mail: kabu@stellarnet.com. Licensee: Dakota Circle Tipi Inc. Format: Educ, community, mus. Target aud: General; community on Spirit Lake Nation & surrounding areas to reach all age groups. Spec prog: American Indian 19 hrs, children 12 hrs, gospel 7 hrs, community & school 5 hrs wkly. ♦ Mark Blackcloud, gen mgr & stn mgr.

Four Bears

*****KMHA(FM)**— March 1984: 91.3 mhz; 100 kw. 380 ft. TL: N47 44 23 W102 43 24. Stereo. 601 Lodge Rd., Newtown 58763. Phone: (701) 627-3333/627-4306. Fax: (701) 627-3376. E-mail: kmha_fm@restel.net. Licensee: Fort Berthold Communications Enterprise. Format: Div. News staff: one. Target aud: Ranchers, farmers, Native Americans. Spec prog: American Indian-Mandan/Hidatsa/Arikara 4 hrs, country 8 hrs, farm one hr wkly. ♦ Rose Crow Flies High, gen mgr; Clarence Sun, opns mgr.

Grafton

KAUJ(FM)—Listing follows KXPO(AM).

North Dakota

KXPO(AM)— July 12, 1958: 1340 khz; 1 kw-U. TL: N48 23 53 W97 26 56. 856 12th St. W. 58237. Phone: (701) 352-0431. Fax: (701) 352-0436. Licensee: KGPC Co. (acq 12-12-72). Network: ABC. Sam Miller. Format: Country. News staff: 2; News: 15 hrs wkly. Target aud: 30-70. Spec prog: Farm 18 hrs, gospel 5 hrs, relg 4 hrs wkly. ◆Del Nygard, pres; Brian James, gen mgr & progmg dir; Todd Ingstad, adv mgr; Don Brintmall, chief of engrg.

KAUJ(FM)—Co-owned with KXPO(AM). Sept 17, 1984: 100.9 mhz; 3 kw. 125 ft. TL: N48 23 53 W97 26 56. E-mail: kzzpo@polarcomm.com. Format: Oldies radio. News staff: one; News: 2 hrs wkly. Target aud: 18-60.

Grand Forks

KCNN(AM)—See East Grand Forks, MN

*KFJM(FM)— Mar 6, 1995: 90.7 mhz; 2.4 kw. 154 ft. TL: N47 55 55 W97 04 26. Box 8117 58202-8117. Phone: (701) 777-2577. Licensee: University of North Dakota. Network: Network: NPR, PRI. Format: AAA, jazz. News staff: 2; News: 15 hrs wkly. Target aud: 25-44; well-educated. Spec prog: Blues 3 hrs wkly. ◆Michael Olson, gen mgr, opns mgr & dev dir.

KJKJ(FM)— Aug 1, 1985: 107.5 mhz; 100 kw. 500 ft. TL: N48 07 24 W97 04 20. Stereo. Box 13598 58206-3598. Secondary address: 505 University Ave. 58203. Phone: (701) 746-1417. Fax: (701) 746-1410. E-mail: patmclean@clearchannel.com. Web Site: www.kjkj.com. Licensee: Citicasters Licenses L.P. Group owner: Clear Channel Communications Inc. (acq 10-26-99; grpsl). Format: AOR. News: 5 hrs wkly. Target aud: 18-49. ◆Jeff Hoberg, gen mgr; Pat McLean, stn mgr; Laura Hammack, gen sls mgr.

KKXL(AM)— 1941: 1440 khz; 1 kw-D, 500 w-N. TL: N47 57 52 W97 01 46. Stereo. Box 13598 58208-3598. Secondary address: 505 University Ave. 58203. Phone: (701) 746-1417. Phone: (701) 775-0575. Fax: (701) 746-1410. Web Site: www.1440kkxl.com. Licensee: Citicasters Licenses L.P. Group owner: Clear Channel Communications Inc. (acq 10-26-99; grpsl). Network: Jones Radio Networks. Format: Adult standards, news, mus of the 40s, 50s & 60s. News staff: one; News: 10 hrs wkly. Target aud: 25-54; farm community. ◆Pat McLean, gen mgr.

KKXL-FM— March 1975: 92.9 mhz; 63 kw. 385 ft. TL: N47 57 52 W97 01 46. Stereo. Web Site: www.xl93.com. Format: CHR. Target aud: 18-34.

KNOX(AM)— Sept 7, 1947: 1310 khz; 5 kw-U, DA-N. TL: N47 50 39 W97 01 30. Box 13638, Old Belmont Rd. S. 58208-3638. Phone: (701) 775-4611. Fax: (701) 772-0540. Web Site: www.leightonbroadcasting.com. Licensee: Leighton Enterprises Inc. (group owner; acq 10-23-96; $1.1 million with co-located FM). Network: ABC Information & Entertainment. Rep: Katz Radio. Format: Farm, news/talk. News staff: 3; News: 80 hrs wkly. Target aud: 35 plus. ◆Lynn Hodgson, gen mgr & stn mgr.

KNOX-FM— Feb 4, 1967: 94.7 mhz; 100 kw. 325 ft. TL: N48 00 20 W97 04 18. Stereo. Network: Network: ABC, ABC FM Connection. Format: Country. Target aud: 18-45.

KQHT(FM)—(Crookston).MN March 1986: 96.1 mhz; 100 kw. 413 ft. TL: N47 50 43 W96 50 22. Stereo. 505 University Ave. 58203. Phone: (701) 746-1417. Fax: (701) 746-1410. Web Site: www.961thefox.com. Licensee: Citicasters Licenses L.P. Group owner: Clear Channel Communications Inc. (acq 10-26-99; grpsl). Hyett/Ramsland. Format: World class rock. Target aud: 18-49. ◆Pat McLean, gen mgr & gen sls mgr; Dave Schroeder, chief of engrg.

*KUND-FM— May 30, 1976: 89.3 mhz; 38 kw. 215 ft. TL: N47 55 55 W97 04 26. Stereo. Box 8117 58202. Phone: (701) 777-2577. Licensee: University of North Dakota. Format: Class. Spec prog: New age 5 hrs wkly. ◆Gary Olson, stn mgr.

*KWTL(AM)— Oct 22, 1923: 1370 khz; 1 k-D, 250 w-N. TL: N47 55 55 W97 04 26. Box 88, Casselton 58012. Phone: (701) 347-5441. Licensee: Real Presence Radio (acq 10-26-2004; $317,400). Format: Christian. ◆Steve W. Loegering, pres.

KYCK(FM)—See Crookston, MN

Harvey

KHND(AM)— July 21, 1981: 1470 khz; 1 kw-D, 160 w-N. TL: N47 45 23 W99 55 06. Box 6 58341. Secondary address: 718 Lincoln Ave. 58341. Phone: (701) 324-4848. Fax: (701) 324-2043. E-mail: khndsj@gondtc.com. Web Site: khnd1470.com. Licensee: Three Way Broadcasting Inc. (acq 1-16-03). Network: ABC. Format: Adult contemp. Target aud: 12 -85. Spec prog: Big band 3 hrs, polka 3 hrs, talk show 8 hrs wkly. ◆Rick Jensen, VP; Sheila Jensen, pres, gen mgr, stn mgr & gen sls mgr.

Harwood

KDJZ(FM)— 2001: 100.7 mhz; 25 kw. Ant 328 ft. TL: N47 08 43 W96 58 18. Phone: (800)350-5390. Fax: (707) 528-9246. Licensee: Educational Media Foundation. Group owner: EMF Broadcasting (acq 1-8-2004; $750,000). Network: K-Love. Format: Christian. ◆John Burkholder, gen mgr.

Hettinger

KNDC(AM)— Mar 1, 1954: 1490 khz; 1 kw-U. TL: N46 01 11 W102 41 33. Box 151, 505 2nd Ave. S. 58639. Phone: (701) 567-2421. Phone: (701) 567-2889. Fax: (701) 567-4636. E-mail: kndc1490@ndsupernet.com. Web Site: www.knde.com. Licensee: Schweitzer Media Inc. (acq 5-19-99). Network: ABC Information & Entertainment. Format: C&W. News: 24 hrs wkly. Target aud: 24-52; rural residents. Spec prog: Farm. ◆Mike Schweitzer, pres; Nolan Dix, gen mgr, progmg dir & mus dir.

Hope

KDAM(FM)— 2002: 104.7 mhz; 100 kw. Ant 702 ft. TL: N47 03 15 W97 24 44. 1020 25th St. S., Fargo 58103. Phone: (701) 237-5346. Fax: (701) 235-4042. E-mail: dickvoight@clearchannel.com. Licensee: Clear Channel Broadcasting Licenses Inc. Group owner: Clear Channel Communications Inc. (acq 5-24-01; $800,000. for CP). Format: AOR. ◆Richard Voight, gen mgr; Mike Kapel, opns mgr; Eric Grande, progmg dir; Paul Jurgens, news dir; Al Murray, chief of engrg.

Jamestown

*KLJA(FM)—Not on air, target date: unknown: 88.9 mhz; 1.8 kw vert. Ant 144 ft. TL: N46 55 27 W98 46 19. 5700 West Oaks Blvd., Rocklin, CA 95765. Phone: (916) 251-1600. Fax: (916) 251-1650. Licensee: Educational Media Foundation. ◆Richard Jenkins, pres.

*KPRJ(FM)— 1993: 91.5 mhz; 18.5 kw. 354 ft. TL: N46 46 36 W98 31 20. 207 N 5th St., Fargo 58102. Phone: (701) 241-6900. Fax: (701) 224-0555. E-mail: bthomas@prairiepublic.org. Web Site: www.prairiepublic.org. Licensee: Prairie Public Broadcasting Inc. Network: Network: NPR, PRI. Format: Class, jazz, news. News staff: 3. Target aud: General. Spec prog: American Indian 2 hrs, folk 6 hrs wkly. ◆John Harris, pres; Bill Thomas, gen mgr & stn mgr; Duane Lee, opns mgr; Nancy Wood, dev dir; Marie Luceo, prom dir; David Thompson, news dir.

KQDJ(AM)— Aug 12, 1954: 1400 khz; 1 kw-U. TL: N46 53 37 W98 41 20. Box 1170 58401. Secondary address: 203 1/2 First Ave. S. 58402. Phone: (701) 252-1400. Fax: (701) 252-1402. E-mail: bigdog@daktel.com. Licensee: Two Rivers Broadcasting Inc. Group owner: Robert Ingstad Broadcast Properties (acq 1994; $600,000). Network: CBS. Format: News/talk, sports, adult standards. Spec prog: Farm 6 hrs wkly. ◆Dave Reed, gen mgr.

KXGT(FM)—Co-owned with KQDJ(AM). Aug 25, 1984: 95.5 mhz; 100 kw. 398 ft. TL: N46 51 52 W98 40 11. Stereo. Network: ABC. Format: Oldies.

KSJB(AM)— 1937: 600 khz; 5 kw-U, DA-1. TL: N46 49 03 W98 42 34. Box 5180 58402-1840. Secondary address: 2400 8th Ave. S. W. 58402-1840. Phone: (701) 252-3570. Fax: (701) 252-1277. Web Site: www.ksjbam.com. Licensee: Chesterman Communications Inc. (acq 8-20-90; $850,000 with co-located FM; 9-10-90). Network: ABC Information & Entertainment. Format: Classic country. News staff: one; News: 13 hrs wkly. Target aud: 25 plus. Spec prog: Farm 12 hrs wkly. ◆Patrick Pfeiffer, gen mgr; Patrick Pfeiffer, gen sls mgr, mktg mgr & prom mgr.

KSJZ(FM)—Co-owned with KSJB(AM). 1968: 93.3 mhz; 57 kw. 256 ft. TL: N46 49 03 W98 42 34. Stereo. Web Site: www.ksjbam.com. Format: Adult hit radio. Target aud: 28-52; 60% male, 40% female.

Kindred

KFAB-FM— June 6, 1986: 92.7 mhz; 25 kw. Ant 328 ft. TL: N49 36 38 W96 41 03. Stereo. 1020 25th St. S., Fargo 58103-5421. Phone: (701) 232-9207. Fax: (701) 235-4042. Web Site: www.kool927.com. Licensee: Capstar TX L.P. Group owner: Clear Channel Communications Inc. (acq 10-30-00; grpsl). Fletcher, Heald & Hildreth. Format: Oldies. News: one hr wkly. Target aud: 18-49. ◆Dick Voight, gen mgr.

Langdon

KNDK(AM)— June 27, 1967: 1080 khz; 1 kw-D. TL: N48 46 25 W98 21 50. Box 9, Rt. 5 58249. Phone: (701) 256-1080. Fax: (701) 256-1081. E-mail: kndk1080@utma.com. Licensee: KNDK Inc. (group owner; acq 12-1-87). Network: CBS. Haley, Bader & Potts. Format: News/talk, country. News staff: 3; News: 42 hrs wkly. Target aud: 25 plus. Spec prog: Farm 12 hrs, relg 4 hrs wkly. ◆Bob Simmons, pres, gen mgr, gen sls mgr, progmg dir & chief of engrg.

KNDK-FM— Jan 15, 1992: 95.7 mhz; 6 kw. 328 ft. TL: N48 45 18 W98 21 38. (Acq 11-20-91; $90,000; 12-16-91). Format: Hot adult contemp.

Lincoln

*KCJL(FM)—Not on air, target date: unknown: 88.5 mhz; 80 kw vert. Ant 423 ft. TL: N46 44 09 W102 06 26. CSN International, 3232 W. MacArthur Blvd., Santa Ana, CA 92704. Phone: (714) 825-9663. Fax: (714) 825-9661. Web Site: csn.com. Licensee: CSN International (group owner). Format: Relg. ◆Mike Kestler, pres; Jeffrey W. Smith, VP; Mike Stocklin, opns dir.

*KVLQ(FM)—Not on air, target date: unknown: 89.1 mhz; 540 w. Ant 951 ft. TL: N46 35 24 W100 47 46. 5700 West Oaks Blvd., Rocklin, CA 95765. Phone: (916) 251-1600. Fax: (916) 251-1650. E-mail: klove@klove.com. Web Site: www.klove.com. Licensee: Educational Media Foundation. Group owner: EMF Broadcasting. Network: K-Love. Shaw Pittman. Format: Contemp Christian. News staff: 3. Target aud: 25-44; Judeo Christian, female. ◆Richard Jenkins, pres; Mike Novak, VP; Lloyd Parker, gen mgr; Keith Whipple, dev dir.

Lisbon

KQLX(AM)— November 1984: 890 khz; 1 kw-D. TL: N46 26 43 W97 39 07. Stereo. Box 1008, 1206 S. Main 58054. Phone: (701) 683-5287. Fax: (701) 683-9029. E-mail: kqlx@kqlx.com. Web Site: www.kqlx.com. Licensee: Loomis Broadcasting Inc. Format: News/talk. News staff: one; News: 5 hrs wkly. Target aud: 18-65; farmers. Spec prog: Farm 18 hrs, Gospel 6 hrs wkly. ◆Terry Loomis, pres; Rita Loomis, VP; Bruce Dougherty, gen mgr.

KQLX-FM— Oct 24, 1986: 106.1 mhz; 50 kw. 249 ft. TL: N46 26 43 W97 39 07. Stereo. Web Site: www.kqlx.com. Licensee: Sheyenne Valley Broadcasting Inc. Network: CNN Radio. Format: Country music. News staff: news progmg 5 hrs wkly News: one;. Target aud: 18-54; general.

Mandan

KLXX(AM)—See Bismarck

KNDR(FM)— June 21, 1977: 104.7 mhz; 100 kw. 852 ft. TL: N46 35 11 W100 48 20. Stereo. Box 516 58554. Secondary address: 1400 NE 3rd Str. 58554. Phone: (701) 663-2345. Fax: (701) 663-2347. E-mail: kndr@midconetwork.com. Web Site: www.kndr.fm. Licensee: Central Dakota Enterprise Inc. Network: Moody. Format: Christian. Target aud: 35-54; women and famlies (with children). ◆La Rue Goetz, chmn; Arvid Morken, VP; Brad Bales, gen mgr.

Mayville

KMAV(AM)— Oct 20, 1967: 1520 khz; 2.5 kw-D. TL: N47 29 45 W97 21 03. Box 216 58257. Phone: (701) 786-2335. Fax: (701) 786-2268. E-mail: sports@kmavradio.com. Web Site: www.kmav.com. Licensee: R & J Broadcasting. (acq 7-7-93; $200,000 with co-located FM; 8-2-93). Network: ABC. Format: Country. News staff: one; News: 15 hrs wkly. Target aud: 25-55. Spec prog: Area high school and Mayville State Univ. sports, Minnesota Twins baseball. ◆Jim Birkemeyer, pres & sls dir; Rich Haraldson, exec VP; Dan Keating, gen mgr, adv mgr & progmg dir; Eric Michaels, prom dir; Mary Keating, news dir.

Stations in the U.S. Ohio

KMAV-FM— Jan 10, 1977: 105.5 mhz; 25 kw. 328 ft. TL: N47 29 45 W97 21 03. Stereo. Web Site: kmav.com.

Minot

KCJB(AM)— September 1950: 910 khz; 5 kw-D, 1 kw-N, DA-2. TL: N40 11 57 W101 17 37. Box 10, 3425 S. Broadway 58702. Phone: (701) 852-0361. Fax: (701) 852-1953. Licensee: Clear Channel Broadcasting Licenses Inc. Group owner: Clear Channel Communications Inc. (acq 1-12-00; grpsl). Network: CBS. Fisher, Wayland, Cooper, Leader & Zaragoza L.L.P. Format: Full service, country. Target aud: 25 plus. Spec prog: Loc sports, various loc talk segments, farm 4 hrs wkly. ♦Rick Stensby, gen mgr.

KYYX(FM)—Co-owned with KCJB(AM). Nov 15, 1966: 97.1 mhz; 100 kw. 984 ft. TL: N48 03 02 W101 20 29. Stereo. News staff: one; News: 6 hrs wkly. Target aud: 18-49; young families. Co-owned TV: KXMC-TV affil.

KHRT(AM)— Nov 17, 1957: 1320 khz; 2.5 kw-D, 310 w-N. TL: N48 11 48 W101 14 30. Box 1210 58702. Secondary address: 3600 County Rd. 195 S. 58702. Phone: (701) 852-3789. Fax: (701) 852-8498. E-mail: khrt@srt.com. Licensee: Faith Broadcasting Inc. (acq 9-1-82; $188,248;. FTR: 8-30-82). Format: Relg, news/talk, Southern gospel. News staff: one; News: 10 hrs wkly. Target aud: 25-54; large families, loyal, upper-income professionals. Spec prog: Farm one hr wkly. ♦Richard Leavitt, pres, gen mgr, gen sls mgr & progmg dir; Roy Leavitt, stn mgr; Johas Nelson, mus dir; John Kennedy, news dir; John McCann, chief of engrg.

KHRT-FM— 1992: 106.9 mhz; 26 kw. Ant 344 ft. TL: N48 09 48 W101 17 55. Format: Contemp Christian. ♦Johas Nelson, progmg dir.

KIZZ(FM)— Sept 7, 1968: 93.7 mhz; 98 kw. 571 ft. TL: N48 12 56 W101 19 05. Stereo. Box 10 58702. Secondary address: 101 S. Main St. 58702. Phone: (701) 852-2494. Fax: (701) 852-1390. E-mail: kizz@srt.com. Licensee: Clear Channel Broadcasting Licenses Inc. Group owner: Clear Channel Communications Inc. (acq 9-1-00; grpsl). Format: Adult contemp. News staff: one; News: 3 hrs wkly. Target aud: 25-54. ♦Allison Bostow, opns mgr & progmg dir; Rick Stensby, gen mgr & gen sls mgr; Don May, news dir; Brian Funk, chief of engrg.

*KMPR(FM)— Nov 23, 1983: 88.9 mhz; 100 kw. 930 ft. TL: N48 03 03 W101 23 24. (CP: 50 kw). Stereo. 1814 N. 15th St., Bismarck 58501. Phone: (701) 224-1700. Fax: (701) 224-0555. E-mail: program@pol.org. Licensee: Prairie Public Broadcasting Inc. Network: Network: PRI, NPR. Format: Class, news, jazz. News staff: 2; News: 40 hrs wkly. Target aud: General. Spec prog: American Indian 2 hrs, folk 6 hrs wkly. ♦Bill Thomas, gen mgr; Duane Lee, opns mgr; Jack Anderson, dev dir; Marie Lucero, prom dir; David Thompson, news dir. Co-owned TV: *KSRE(TV) affil.

KMXA-FM— April 1984: 99.9 mhz; 100 kw. 500 ft. TL: N48 10 57 W101 31 57. Stereo. 1000 20th Ave. S.W. 58701. Phone: (701) 852-2494. Fax: (701) 852-1390. E-mail: allisonbostow@clearchannel.com. Web Site: www.mix999fm.com. Licensee: Clear Channel Broadcasting Licenses Inc. Group owner: Clear Channel Communications Inc. (acq 1-12-00; grpsl). Format: Hot adult contemp. News: 4 hrs wkly. Target aud: 25-54; adult upper middle class with teens at home. ♦Rick Stensby, gen mgr & stn mgr; Allison Bostow, opns mgr.

KRRZ(AM)— Oct 28, 1929: 1390 khz; 5 kw-D, 1 kw-N. TL: N48 12 45 W101 14 30. Stereo. Box 10, 101 S. Main 58702. Phone: (701) 852-4646. Fax: (701) 852-1390. Licensee: Clear Channel Broadcasting Licenses Inc. Group owner: Clear Channel Communications Inc. (acq 9-1-00; grpsl). Rep: Roslin. Format: Oldies. Target aud: 25-54. Spec prog: Sports. ♦Allison Bostow, progmg dir.

KZPR(FM)—Co-owned with KRRZ(AM). July 8, 1985: 105.3 mhz; 100 kw. 579 ft. TL: N48 03 13 W101 26 03. Stereo. Format: Classic rock. News: 4 hrs wkly. Spec prog: Farm 4 hrs wkly. ♦Allison Bostow, adv dir.

Oakes

KDDR(AM)— July 31, 1959: 1220 khz; 1 kw-D, 327 w-N. TL: N46 07 23 W98 05 21. 412 Main Ave. 58474. Phone: (701) 742-2187. Fax: (701) 742-2009. E-mail: kddr@drtel.net. Licensee: Sioux Valley Broadcasting Co. Group owner: Robert Ingstad Broadcast Properties (acq 2-1-93; $85,000;. FTR: 2-22-93). Network: ABC Information & Entertainment. Fletcher, Heald & Hildreth. Format: Country, news. Target aud: 28-59; farm/agriculture. Spec prog: Farm 15 hrs, relg 3 hrs wkly. ♦Tim Ost, gen mgr; Terry James, progmg dir.

Rugby

KZZJ(AM)— Aug 21, 1961: 1450 khz; 1 kw-U. TL: N48 21 14 W99 59 31. 230 Hwy. 2 S.E. 58368. Phone: (701) 776-5254. Fax: (701) 776-6154. E-mail: kzzj@kzzj.com. Web Site: www.kzzj.com. Licensee: Rugby Broadcasters Inc. (acq 7-6-89; $10,000;. FTR: 7-24-89). Format: Modern country, farm. News staff: one. Target aud: 25-65. ♦Lila Brossart, gen mgr; Jay Schmalz, opns mgr & mus dir; Cheryl Holm, gen sls mgr & chief of engrg; Bruce Allen, news dir.

Tioga

KTGO(AM)— Feb 27, 1966: 1090 khz; 1 kw-D. TL: N48 23 30 W102 56 12. Box 457 58852. Secondary address: 301 S.E. 2nd St. 58852. Phone: (701) 664-3322. Phone: (701) 664-3432. Fax: (701) 664-3322. E-mail: ktgo@wccray.com. Licensee: Tioga Broadcasting Corp. Network: CBS. Format: Country, Christian, talk. Target aud: 18-55. Spec prog: Gospel 11 hrs wkly. ♦David Guttormson, pres, gen mgr, stn mgr, gen sls mgr, prom mgr, progmg dir & news dir; Bernie Arcand, chief of engrg.

Valley City

KOVC(AM)— Oct 19, 1936: 1490 khz; 1 kw-U. TL: N46 54 48 W98 01 02. 136 Central Ave. N. 58072. Phone: (701) 845-1490. Fax: (701) 845-1245. Licensee: Sioux Valley Broadcasting Co. Group owner: Robert Ingstad Broadcast Properties. Network: ABC Information & Entertainment. Format: Country, news, sports. News: 7 hrs wkly. Target aud: 25 plus. ♦Tim Ost, gen mgr; Dave Reed, opns mgr; Ron Lee, prom dir, progmg dir & mus dir; Kerry Johnson, adv mgr; Ryan Cunningham, news dir; Don Brintnall, engrg mgr & chief of engrg.

KQDJ-FM—Co-owned with KOVC(AM). Aug 1, 1983: 101.1 mhz; 12 kw. 1,000 ft. TL: N46 54 24 W97 58 20. Format: news/talk, sports info, adult standards. Target aud: 25-54. ♦Dave Reed, progmg mgr.

Velva

KTZU(FM)— 2005: 94.9 mhz; 100 kw. Ant 512 ft. TL: N48 03 04 W101 20 23. Box 28, Bottineau 58318-0028. Phone: (701) 228-5151. Fax: (701) 228-2483. Licensee: Programmers Broadcasting Inc. Fletcher, Heald & Hildreth. ♦John Kircher, pres.

Wahpeton

KBMW(AM)—(Breckenridge).MN Aug 28, 1948: 1450 khz; 1 kw-U. TL: N46 16 41 W96 35 19. 605 Dakota Ave. 58075. Phone: (701) 642-8747. Fax: (701) 642-9501. E-mail: studio@kbmwam.com. Licensee: Monterey Licenses LLC. Group owner: Triad Broadcasting Co. LLC (acq 1-31-03; $1.2 million). Network: ABC Information & Entertainment. Format: Country. News staff: one; News: 18 hrs wkly. Target aud: 25-54; general. ♦Bill Dadlow, stn mgr.

KEGK(FM)— May 21, 1989: 106.9 mhz; 42 kw. Ant 535 ft. TL: N46 32 41 W96 37 33. Stereo. Box 1115 58074. Secondary address: 605 Dakota Ave. 58075. Phone: (701) 642-8747. Phone: (701) 237-4500. Fax: (701) 642-9501. Web Site: www.eagle1069.com. Licensee: Guderian Broadcasting Inc. (acq 7-17-2002). Rep: Midwest Radio. Quest Marketing. Format: Oldies. News staff: one; News: 5 hrs wkly. Target aud: 25-54. ♦Nancy Odney, gen mgr; John Austin, opns mgr & gen sls mgr; Michael Brooks, sls dir; Tim Murphy, adv mgr & progmg dir.

Walhalla

KYTZ(FM)— Sept 1, 1998: 106.7 mhz; 16 kw. Ant 836 ft. TL: N48 38 38 W97 58 46. 1420 3rd St., Langdon 58249. Phone: (701) 256-1067. Fax: (701) 256-1051. E-mail: kndk1080@vtma.com. Licensee: Simmons Broadcasting Inc. (acq 9-7-2004). Format: Hot adult contemp. ♦Bob Simmons, gen mgr; Jen Taylor, opns mgr.

West Fargo

KFNW(AM)—Licensed to West Fargo. See Fargo

KQWB(AM)— Sept 1, 2000: 1660 khz; 10 kw-D, 1 kw-N. TL: N46 58 33 W96 35 02. Stereo. 2720 7th Ave. S., Fargo 58103. Phone: (701) 237-4500. Fax: (701) 235-9082. Web Site: www.123fargo.com. Licensee: Monterey Licenses LLC. Group owner: Triad Broadcasting Co. LLC (acq 8-18-99; grpsl). Network: Westwood One. Rep: Christal. Fisher, Wayland, Cooper, Leader & Zaragoza. Format: Talk/personality. Target aud: 35 plus. ♦David Benjamin, pres; Tom Douglas, CFO; Nancy Odney, gen mgr; Anne Phibian, opns mgr; John Austin, progmg dir.

Williston

KDSR(FM)— Feb 28, 1985: 101.1 mhz; 98 kw. 800 ft. TL: N48 03 30 W104 00 00. Stereo. 910 E. Broadway 58801. Phone: (701) 572-4478. Fax: (701) 572-1419. E-mail: kdsr@dia.net. Licensee: Williston Community Broadcasting Corp. dba KDSR(FM) (acq 6-28-02). Network: CNN Radio. Booth, Freret, Imlay & Tepper. Format: Country. News: 7 hrs wkly. Target aud: 18-84; city, farm, ranch & rural. ♦Stephen A. Marks, pres; Mitch Miller, gen mgr; Danita Bloom, progmg dir; Guy Evans, chief of engrg & opns.

KEYZ(AM)— 1948: 660 khz; 5 kw-U, DA-2. TL: N48 14 20 W103 39 01. Stereo. Box 2048 58802-2048. Secondary address: 410 E. 6th 58801. Phone: (701) 572-5371. Fax: (701) 572-7511. Licensee: CCR-Williston IV LLC. Group owner: Cherry Creek Radio LLC (acq 12-19-2003; grpsl). Network: ABC Information & Entertainment. Format: Country, news/talk. News staff: one. Target aud: 25-54. Spec prog: Relg 5 hrs wkly. ♦Larry Timpe, gen mgr; Lyla Semenko, natl sls mgr; Jeff Nelson, progmg dir; Scott Haugen, mus dir; Earl Gross, news dir, pub affrs dir & chief of engrg.

KYYZ(FM)—Co-owned with KEYZ(AM). Dec 1, 1979: 96.1 mhz; 100 kw. 873 ft. TL: N48 02 52 W103 59 01. Stereo. Format: Hot country. News staff: one. Target aud: 25-54. ♦Sean Archer, progmg dir.

*KPPR(FM)— Nov 20, 1986: 89.5 mhz; 10.5 kw. 492 ft. TL: N48 08 30 W103 53 34. Stereo. 207 N 5th St., Fargo 58102. Phone: (701) 224-1700. Phone: (800) 359-5566. Fax: (701) 224-0555. E-mail: program@pol.org. Web Site: www.prairiepublic.org. Licensee: Prairie Public Broadcasting. Network: Network: PRI, NPR. Format: Jazz, class, news. News staff: 2; News: 40 hrs wkly. Target aud: General. Spec prog: American Indian 2 hrs, folk 6 hrs wkly. ♦John Harris, pres; Bill Thomas, stn mgr; Nancy Wood, dev dir; Marie Lucero, prom dir; Dave Thompson, news dir. Co-owned TV: KWSE(TV) affil

Wimbledon

KRVX(FM)—Not on air, target date: unknown: 103.1 mhz; 99 kw. Ant 472 ft. TL: N46 56 21 W98 18 30. Box 907, Valley City 58072. Phone: (701) 845-1490. Fax: (701) 845-1245. Licensee: James River Broadcasting Inc.

Ohio

Ada

*WONB(FM)— Oct 18, 1991: 94.9 mhz; 3 kw. 328 ft. TL: N40 45 58 W83 50 14. Stereo. Freed Ctr. 45810. Phone: (419) 772-1194. Phone: (419) 772-1195. Fax: (419) 772-2794. E-mail: wonb@onu.edu. Web Site: www.onu.edu/wonb. Licensee: Ohio Northern University. Format:

Broadcasting & Cable Yearbook 2006

Ohio

CHR. News: 8 hrs wkly. Target aud: 18-49; general. Spec prog: Relg one hr, blues 6 hrs, gospel 3 hrs, smooth jazz 12 hrs wkly. ◆ Dr. Kendall Baker, pres; John Green, CFO; G. Richard Gainey, gen mgr; Josh Reams, progmg mgr; Kristin Stoner, mus dir.

Akron

WAKR(AM)— Oct 16, 1940: 1590 khz; 5 kw-U, DA-N. TL: N41 01 14 W81 30 20. 1795 W. Market St. 44313. Phone: (330) 869-9800. Fax: (330) 864-6799. Fax: (330) 864-9750. Web Site: www.wakr.net. Licensee: Rubber City Radio Group Inc. (group owner; acq 10-6-93; $9.3 million. with co-located FM; FTR: 10-25-93). Network: ABC Information & Entertainment. Rep: Christal. Verner, Liipfert, Bernhard, McPherson & Hand. Format: MOR/full service, news. News staff: 7; News: 40 hrs wkly. Target aud: 35 plus. ◆ Henry Zelman, CFO; Mark Biviano, exec VP & sls VP; Nick Anthony, sr VP; Thomas Mandel, CEO, pres & gen mgr; Kevin Mason, opns dir; Dominic Rizzo, gen sls mgr; Joyce Lagios, mktg dir & mktg mgr; Ed Esposito, progmg dir & news dir; Al Hruska, chief of engrg.

WONE-FM—Co-owned with WAKR(AM). October 1947: 97.5 mhz; 12 kw. 900 ft. TL: N41 03 57 W81 34 59. Stereo. Web Site: www.wone.net. Format: Rock. Target aud: 18-49. ◆ Brett Russell, prom mgr; T.K. O'Grady, progmg dir.

WAKS(FM)—Listing follows WTOU(AM).

***WAPS(FM)**— Oct 4, 1955: 91.3 mhz; 800 w. Ant 151 ft. TL: N41 03 18 W81 31 35. Stereo. 65 Steiner Ave. 44301. Phone: (330) 761-3099. Fax: (330) 761-3240. Web Site: www.913thesummit.com. Licensee: Board of Education, Akron City School District. Format: AAA, div. Target aud: 25-54; college educated adults. Spec prog: Ger 2 hrs, It 2 hrs, Hungarian one hr, Slovenian 2 hrs, Latin 2 hrs wkly. ◆ Tommy Bruno, gen mgr; Andrew James, opns dir; Ryan Humbert, gen sls mgr.

WARF(AM): 1926: 1350 khz; 5 kw-U, DA-1. TL: N41 10 05 W81 30 45. 1867 W. Market St. 44313. Phone: (330) 836-4700. Fax: (330) 836-5321. Web Site: www.espn1350.com. Licensee: Capstar TX L.P. Group owner: Clear Channel Communications Inc. (acq 2000; grpsl). Network: ABC Information & Entertainment. Format: Sports. ◆ Belinda Holland, gen mgr.

WCUE(AM)—See Cuyahoga Falls

WHLO(AM)— October 1944: 640 khz; 5 kw-D, 500 w-N, DA-2. TL: N41 04 47 W81 38 45. Stereo. 7755 Freedom Ave., N. Canton 44720. Phone: (330) 836-4700. Fax: (330) 836-5321. Licensee: Clear Channel Broadcasting Licenses Inc. Group owner: Clear Channel Communications Inc. (acq 11-16-01; $4.5 million). Format: News/talk. ◆ Don Lankford, gen mgr.

WJMP(AM)—See Kent

WNIR(FM)—See Kent

WQMX(FM)—(Medina). 1960: 94.9 mhz; 16.2 kw. 880 ft. TL: N40 04 58 W81 38 00. Stereo. 1795 W. Market St. 44313. Phone: (330) 869-9800. Fax: (330) 864-6799. E-mail: kmason@wqmx.com. Web Site: wqmx.com. Licensee: Rubber City Radio Group Inc. (group owner; acq 7-21-88). Rep: Christal. Verner, Liipfert, Bernhard, McPherson & Hand. Format: Country. Target aud: 25-54; upwardly mobile adults. ◆ Henry Zelman, CFO; Mark Biviano, exec VP; Nick Anthony, sr VP; Thomas Mandel, CEO, pres & gen mgr; Kenn Mason, progmg dir; Paul Christopher, sls.

***WZIP(FM)**— Dec 10, 1962: 88.1 mhz; 7.5 kw. 827 ft. TL: N41 04 58 W81 38 00. Stereo. 302 E. Buchtel Ave. 44325-1004. Phone: (330) 972-7105. Fax: (330) 972-5521. E-mail: wzip@uakron.edu. Web Site: www.wzip.fm. Licensee: University of Akron. Network: AP Network News. Format: CHR, AOR. Target aud: 18-34. Spec prog: Polka 4 hrs, pub affrs 11 hrs, sports talk 3 hrs wkly. ◆ Thomas G. Beck, gen mgr; Blake Thompson, chief of engrg.

Alliance

WDPN(AM)—Listing follows WZKL(FM).

***WRMU(FM)**— Oct 17, 1970: 91.1 mhz; 2.8 kw. 190 ft. TL: N40 54 16 W81 06 45. Stereo. Mount Union College, 1972 Clark Ave. 44601. Phone: (330) 823-2414. Phone: (330) 823-3777. Fax: (330) 829-4913. E-mail: wrmu@muc.edu. Web Site: www.muc.edu/wrmu. Licensee: Mount Union College. Format: Smooth jazz, Rock/AOR, oldies. Spec prog: Gospel 2 hrs wkly, news/talk 5 hrs wkly. ◆ Dr. Jack Ewing, pres; Mark A. Bergmann, gen mgr; William Weisinger, chief of engrg.

WZKL(FM)— April 1947: 92.5 mhz; 50 kw. 500 ft. TL: N40 47 24 W81 06 26. Stereo. Box 2356 44601. Secondary address: 392 Smyth Ave. 44601. Phone: (330) 450-9250. Fax: (330) 821-0379. E-mail: radiosales@alliancelink.com. Web Site: www.q92radio.com. Licensee: D.A. Peterson Inc. Network: ABC Information & Entertainment. Format: Hot adult contemp. News staff: 2; News: 4 hrs wkly. Target aud: 25-54. ◆ Don Peterson III, gen mgr; Mark O'Brian, sls dir; Mark O'Brien, gen sls mgr; John Stewart, progmg VP & progmg dir; Clint M, news dir; Steve Hundt, engrg dir & chief of engrg.

WDPN(AM)—Co-owned with WZKL(FM). Sept 2, 1953: 1310 khz; 1 kw-D, 500 w-N, DA-2. TL: N40 55 34 W81 07 41. Network: ABC Information & Entertainment. Format: Unforgettable favorites. News staff: 2; News: 21 hrs wkly. Target aud: 35-64. Spec prog: Relg 4 hrs wkly. ◆ Doug Lane, progmg dir; Rex Coombs, progmg dir.

Archbold

***WBCY(FM)**— Dec 1, 1992: 89.5 mhz; 20 kw. 328 ft. TL: N41 30 33 W84 17 50. c/o WBCL(FM), 1025 W. Rudisill Blvd., Fort Wayne, IN 46807. Phone: (260) 745-0576. Fax: (260) 456-2913. Web Site: www.wbcl.org. Licensee: Taylor University Broadcasting Inc. (acq 6-24-92). Format: Contemp Christian. ◆ Char Binkley, gen mgr; Craig Albrecht, opns mgr; Janelle Becker, prom dir; Scott Tusleff, progmg dir & progmg mgr.

WMTR-FM— Mar 1968: 96.1 mhz; 3.8 kw. Ant 400 ft. TL: N41 33 29 W84 11 08. Stereo. 303 1/2 N. Defiance St. 43502. Phone: (419) 445-9050. Fax: (419) 445-3531. E-mail: wmtr@adelphia.net. Web Site: www.961wmtr.com. Licensee: Nobco Inc. Network: Westwood One. Rep: Rgnl Reps. Hogan & Hartson. Format: Adult top-40. News staff: one; News: 8 hrs wkly. Target aud: 25-54. ◆ Max E. Smith Sr., pres; Max E. Smith Jr., gen mgr; Mark Knapp, mus dir Larry Christy, news dir.

Ashland

WNCO(AM)— 1949: 1340 khz; 1 kw-U. TL: N40 50 25 W82 21 18. Box 327, 2435 Mansfield Rd. 44805. Phone: (419) 289-2605. Phone: (419) 526-5825. Fax: (419) 289-0304. Web Site: www.theohioradio.com. Licensee: Capstar TX L.P. Group owner: Clear Channel Communications Inc. (acq 2-12-01; grpsl). Rep: Rgnl Reps. Arent, Fox, Kintner, Plotkin & Kahn. Format: Stardust, MOR, big band. News staff: 2; News: 20 hrs wkly. Target aud: 35 plus. Spec prog: Farm 3 hrs wkly. ◆ Diana Coon, gen mgr.

WNCO-FM— May 1947: 101.3 mhz; 50 kw. 500 ft. TL: N40 50 25 W82 21 18. Stereo. Format: Country. News staff: 3; News: 14 hrs wkly. Target aud: 25 plus. ◆ Dean Stampfli, opns dir & mktg dir; Martin Larsen, sls dir; Darla Stampfli, prom mgr & pub affrs dir.

***WRDL(FM)**— Aug 24, 1967: 88.9 mhz; 3 kw. 171 ft. TL: N40 51 41 W82 19 11. Stereo. 401 College Ave. 44805. Phone: (419) 289-5678. Phone: (419) 289-5311. Fax: (419) 289-5329. Licensee: Ashland University. Format: Rock, educ. News: 7 hrs wkly. Target aud: 18-35; general. Spec prog: Christian contemp 7 hrs, jazz 5 hrs, oldies 4 hrs wkly. ◆ Dr. G. William Benz, pres; Tom Griffiths, gen mgr & chief of engrg.

Ashtabula

WFUN(AM)— November 1937: 970 khz; 5 kw-D, 1 kw-N, DA-2. TL: N41 48 52 W80 46 45. Box 738 44005. Secondary address: 3226 Jefferson Rd. 44004. Phone: (440) 993-2126. Fax: (440) 992-2658. E-mail: danschulte@clearchannel.com. Web Site: www.wfunam97.com. Licensee: Clear Channel Broadcasting Licenses Inc. Group owner: Clear Channel Communications Inc. (acq 7-11-00; grpsl). Network: ABC. Format: News, talk, sports. News staff: 2; News: 20 hrs wkly. Target aud: General; Socially conscious, community-oriented listeners. ◆ Dennis Brockman, pres & opns dir; Dana Schulte, VP & sls VP; Erin Edison, gen mgr & mktg dir; Michelle Baird, sls dir; Cindy Steiner, prom mgr; Kathy Davis, news dir; John Riccio, chief of engrg.

WREO-FM—Co-owned with WFUN(AM). 1949: 97.1 mhz; 50 kw. 500 ft. TL: N41 48 58 W80 46 52. Stereo. E-mail: star97@star97.com. Web Site: www.star97.com. Format: Adult contemp. Target aud: 25-54; professionals. ◆ Dennis O'Brien, opns dir; Carrie Ellison, prom dir; Mark Allen, progmg dir.

WYBL(FM)— 2005: 98.3 mhz; 5.3 kw. Ant 344 ft. TL: N41 50 23 W80 44 36. Box 738 44005. Phone: (440) 993-2126. Fax: (440) 992-2658. Web Site: www.983thebull.com. Licensee: Clear Channel Broadcasting Licenses Inc. Group owner: Clear Channel Communications Inc. (acq 8-30-2002; $525,000. for CP). Format: News. ◆ Dana Schulte, gen mgr.

WZOO-FM—See Edgewood

Athens

WATH(AM)— Oct 25, 1950: 970 khz; 1 kw-D, 160 w-N. TL: N39 20 40 W82 06 21. Stereo. Box 210 45701. Secondary address: 300 Columbus Rd. 45701. Phone: (740) 593-6651. Phone: (740) 593-7982 (News). Fax: (740) 594-3488. E-mail: palmerd@wxtq.com. Web Site: www.wxtq.com. Licensee: WATH Inc. (acq 10-7-2003; with co-located FM). Network: CBS. Rgnl Reps: Pepper & Corazzini. Format: MOR, news/talk,sports. News staff: 3; News: 20 hrs wkly. Target aud: 45 plus. Spec prog: Big band 15 hrs wkly. ◆ David W. Palmer, pres & gen mgr; Robert E. Lambert, VP.

WXTQ(FM)—Co-owned with WATH(AM). Sept 16, 1964: 105.5 mhz; 6 kw. 312 ft. TL: N39 21 18 W82 05 32. Stereo. Web Site: www.wxtq.com. Format: Hot adult contemp. News: 5 hrs wkly. Target aud: 18-34.

WJKW(FM)— Sept 1, 1998: 95.9 mhz; 6 kw. 199 ft. TL: N39 22 37 W81 57 46. 3809 Maple Ave., Castalia 44824. Phone: (740) 592-9879. Fax: (740) 592-9952. E-mail: wjkw@cfbroadcast.net. Licensee: Christian Faith Broadcast Inc. Group owner: Christian Faith Broadcasting Inc. Joseph E. Dunne III. Format: Adult contemp, Christian. Target aud: 25-44. ◆ Rusty Yost, gen mgr; Kevin Ingle, stn mgr.

***WOUB(AM)**— Sept 14, 1957: 1340 khz; 500 w-D, 1 kw-N. TL: N39 19 45 W82 05 29. Stereo. 9 S. College St. 45701. Phone: (740) 593-4554. Fax: (740) 593-0240. Licensee: Ohio University. Network: Network: NPR, PRI. Format: News/talk, progsv. Spec prog: Black 8 hrs wkly. ◆ Carolyn Lewis, gen mgr; David Wiseman, opns VP & engrg VP; Steve Skidmore, opns dir; Scott Martin, opns mgr; Doug Partusch, dev dir, sls dir, mktg dir, prom dir & adv dir; Olivea Oldham, prom mgr & adv mgr; Bryan Gibson, progmg dir & progmg mgr; Tim Myers, progmg dir; Tim Sharp, news dir; DAve Riley, engrg dir.

WOUB-FM— Dec 13, 1949: 91.3 mhz; 50 kw. 500 ft. TL: N39 18 50 W82 08 54. Stereo. Format: Adult contemp. ◆ Rusty Smith, progmg mgr; Jan Sole, asst music dir; Mark Hellenberg, asst music dir. Co-owned TV: *WOUB-TV affil.

Bainbridge

***WKHR(FM)**— May 6, 1977: 91.5 mhz; 1.1 kw. 269 ft. TL: N41 23 42 W81 18 25. (CP: 100 w). Stereo. Kenston High School, 17425 Snyder Rd., Chagrin Falls 44023. Phone: (440) 543-9646. Fax: (440) 543-9012. Web Site: www.wkhr.org. Licensee: Kenston Local School District. Format: Big band. Target aud: 55 plus; well established, mature. ◆ Scott McVay, gen mgr; Chris Kofron, stn mgr, opns dir & dev dir.

Barnesville

WBNV(FM)— July 1, 1991: 93.5 mhz; 6 kw. 489 ft. TL: N39 54 10 W81 12 37. Stereo. Box 338, 4988 Skyline Dr., Cambridge 43725. Secondary address: Box 293, 175 E. Main St. 43713-0293. Phone: (740) 484-4430. Phone: (740) 425-9268. Fax: (740) 432-1991. Licensee: W. Grant Hafley. Network: USA. Rep: Rgnl Reps. Format: Soft adult contemp. News: 15 hrs wkly. Target aud: 25-54. ◆ W. Grant Hafley, gen mgr; David L. Wilson, opns mgr.

Batavia

***WOBO(FM)**— July 30, 1981: 88.7 mhz; 15.5 kw. 428 ft. TL: N39 03 43 W84 05 50. Stereo. Box 338, Owensville 45160. Phone: (513) 724-3939/724-2969. Fax: (513) 724-6042. Licensee: Educational Community Radio Inc. Format: Var/div. Target aud: 35 plus. Spec prog: Ger 5 hrs, Scottish 2 hrs, Pol 3 hrs wkly. ◆ Mel Reifan, gen mgr.

Beach City

***WOFN(FM)**— Sept 27, 2000: 88.7 mhz; 3.3 kw horiz, 21 kw vert. Ant 358 ft. TL: N40 35 41 W81 34 39. Box 1924, Tulsa, OK 74101. Secondary address: 4916 Spruce Hill Dr., Suite 400, Canton 44617. Phone: (330) 244-9151. Phone: (918) 455-5693. Fax: (330) 244-0153.

Stations in the U.S. — Ohio

Developers & Brokers of Radio Properties
contact American Media Services at our suite: Philadelphia Marriott Downtown
215-625-2900
843-972-2200
americanmediaservices.com
Charleston, SC
Dallas, TX · Chicago, Il · Austin, TX
American Media Services, LLC

E-mail: mail@oasisnetwork.org. Web Site: www.oasisnetwork.org. Licensee: Creative Educational Media Corp. Inc. Format: Positive easy gospel, relg, talk. Target aud: General. ♦David Ingles, pres; Bobbie Cook, gen mgr.

Beavercreek

WXEG(FM)— June 18, 1972: 103.9 mhz; 1.15 kw. 522 ft. TL: N39 44 12 W84 09 25. Stereo. 101 Pine St., Dayton 45402. Phone: (937) 224-1137. Fax: (937) 224-3667. Web Site: www.wxeg.com. Licensee: Citicasters Licenses L.P. Group owner: Clear Channel Communications Inc. (acq 1999; grpsl). Format: Alternative rock. News staff: one. Target aud: 18-34. ♦Karrie Sudbrack, gen mgr.

Bellaire

WOMP(AM)— Dec 2, 1947: 1290 khz; 1 kw-D, 33 w-N. TL: N40 02 09 W80 46 16. Box 448, Rt. 214, 56325 High Ridge Rd. 43906. Phone: (740) 676-5661. Fax: (740) 676-2742. Licensee: Keymarket Licenses LLC. Group owner: Keymarket Communications LLC (acq 1-15-93; $575,000. with co-located FM; FTR: 1-25-93). Network: CNN Radio. Rep: Rgnl Reps. Fleischman & Walsh L. Format: News/talk. News staff: 2; News: 20 hrs wkly. Target aud: 35 plus; affluent, educated adults. Spec prog: Pol 2 hrs, Czech 2 hrs wkly. ♦Gerald Getz, pres; John Crawford, gen mgr.

WOMP-FM— 1947: 100.5 mhz; 48 kw. 518 ft. TL: N40 02 09 W80 46 16. Stereo. Fax: (740) 671-4487. Web Site: www.wompfm.com. Format: CHR. News staff: one. Target aud: 18-44; educated adults.

Bellefontaine

WBLL(AM)— 1951: 1390 khz; 500 w-D, 81 w-N. TL: N40 22 05 W83 44 02. 1501 Rd. 235 43311-9506. Phone: (937) 592-1045. Fax: (937) 592-3299. E-mail: cwilkinson@wbll.com. Web Site: www.wbll.com. Licensee: V-Teck Communications Inc. (acq 12-2-87; grpsl; 10-19-87). Network: ABC. Rep: Rgnl Reps. Format: News/talk, sports. News staff: 2; News: 126 hrs wkly. Target aud: General. Spec prog: Relg 6 hrs wkly. ♦Lou Vito, pres; Amie Huffman, gen mgr & adv dir; Chad Wilkinson, opns mgr & pub affrs dir; Sheryl Godwin, dev dir; Jo Ann Rans, gen sls mgr; Ken Keller, prom dir; Bill Tipple, news dir; Bill Bowin, chief of engrg.

WPKO-FM— Co-owned with WBLL(AM). July 15, 1969: 98.3 mhz; 1.75 kw. Ant 430 ft. TL: N40 22 05 W83 44 02. Stereo. E-mail: lvito@wpko.com. Web Site: www.wpko.com. Format: Adult contemp. News staff: 2. Target aud: 12 plus. ♦Vaughn Miller, mktg dir & mktg mgr; Chad Wilkinson, mus dir; Louie Vito, asst music dir; Bill Bowin, engrg dir.

Bellevue

WOHF(FM)— Apr 4, 1973: 92.1 mhz; 3.7 kw. 108 ft. TL: N41 16 26 W82 50 25. Stereo. 905 W. State St., Fremont 43420. Phone: (419) 332-8218. Fax: (419) 333-8226. Licensee: BAS Broadcasting Inc. (acq 10-1-03; $550,000). Network: CNN Radio. Format: Classic rock. News staff: one; News: 5 hrs wkly. Target aud: 18-49; upscale. ♦Jim Lorenzen, pres.

Belpre

*****WCVV(FM)—** 1986: 89.5 mhz; 4.4 kw. Ant 384 ft. TL: N39 19 27 W81 37 33. Stereo. Box 405 45714. Phone: (740) 423-5895. Fax: (740) 423-9951. Licensee: Belpre Educ. Broadcasting Foundation. Format: Christian, news. Target aud: General. ♦Clay Sloan, gen mgr & stn mgr; Ralph Matheny, chief of engrg.

*****WLKP(FM)—** May 1991: 91.9 mhz; 4.5 kw. Ant 325 ft. TL: N39 20 46 W81 29 55. 5700 West Oaks Blvd., Rocklin, CA 95765. Phone: (916) 251-1600. Fax: (916) 251-1650. Web Site: www.klove.com. Licensee: Educational Media Foundation. (acq 3-31-2005; $700,000. with WLKV(FM) Ripley, WV). Network: K-Love. Format: Christian.

WNUS(FM)— Sept 12, 1981: 107.1 mhz; 4.7 kw. 370 ft. TL: N39 18 36 W81 35 49. Stereo. Box 5559, Vienna, WV 26105. Secondary address: 6006 Grand Central Ave., Vienna, WV 26105. Phone: (304) 295-9441. Phone: (740) 423-9687. Fax: (304) 295-4389. E-mail: roadcrew@wnus.com. Web Site: www.wnus.com. Licensee: Clear Channel Broadcasting Licenses Inc. Group owner: Clear Channel Communications Inc. (acq 4-17-01; grpsl). Rep: Clear Channel. Format: Country. News staff: 2; News: 2 hrs wkly. Target aud: 18 plus. ♦Chuck Poet, gen mgr.

Berea

*****WBWC(FM)—** Mar 2, 1958: 88.3 mhz; 4 kw. Ant 256 ft. TL: N41 25 05 W81 54 03. Stereo. 275 Eastland Rd. 44017. Phone: (440) 826-2145. Fax: (440) 826-3426. E-mail: jtaranto@bw.edu. Web Site: www.wbwc.com. Licensee: Baldwin-Wallace College. Network: AP Radio. Format: Modern rock. Target aud: 12-25; alternative mus listeners. ♦Allen Thompson, opns dir.

Bowling Green

*****WBGU(FM)—** November 1951: 88.1 mhz; 450 w. 178 ft. TL: N41 22 33 W83 38 34. Dept. of Telecommunications, 322 W. Hall, Bowling Green State Univ. 43403. Phone: (419) 372-8657. Phone: (419) 372-2138. Fax: (419) 372-9449. Web Site: www.wbgufm.com. Licensee: Bowling Green State University. Format: Div, jazz, Black. News: 7 hrs wkly. Target aud: General. Spec prog: Country 4 hrs, class 3 hrs, folk 4 hrs, Sp 4 hrs wkly. ♦Kyle Gephardt, gen mgr; Jim Davis, chief of engrg. Co-owned TV: *WBGU-TV affil.

WJYM(AM)— December 1964: 730 khz; 1 kw-D, 359 w-N, DA-2. TL: N41 31 57 W83 33 55. 8919 World Ministry Ave., Baton Rouge, KY 70810. Phone: (225) 768-3202. Fax: (225) 768-3729. Licensee: Family Worship Center Church Inc. (group owner; acq 12-15-99). Network: USA. Format: Relg. News: 3 hrs wkly. Target aud: 25-49.

WRQN(FM)— June 1964: 93.5 mhz; 4.1 kw. 397 ft. TL: N41 27 28 W83 39 33. 3225 Arlington Ave., Toledo 43614. Phone: (419) 725-5700. Fax: (419) 389-5172. Web Site: www.935wrqn.com. Licensee: Cumulus Licensing Corp. Group owner: Cumulus Media Inc. (acq 9-11-97; grpsl). Format: Oldies. Target aud: 25-54. Spec prog: Pub service one hr wkly. ♦Brian Olson, gen mgr & stn mgr; Ron Finn, opns mgr & progmg dir.

Bryan

WBNO-FM— June 30, 1966: 100.9 mhz; 6 kw. Ant 299 ft. TL: N41 28 44 W84 34 50. 12810 State Rd. 34 43506-8809. Phone: (419) 636-3175. Fax: (419) 636-4570. E-mail: jbo1520@wbno-wqct.com. Licensee: Impact Radio LLC. (acq 8-1-2002; grpsl). Network: ABC. Reddy, Begley & McCormick. Format: Classic hits. News staff: one; News: 27 hrs wkly. Target aud: General; loc oriented. ♦Dennis Rumsey, pres & gen mgr.

WQCT(AM)— Co-owned with WBNO-FM. December 1962: 1520 khz; 500 w-D, 5 w-N, 250 w-CH. TL: N41 28 43 W84 34 49. (group owner; . Network: ABC Music Radio. Regional Reps Format: Nostalgia. News staff: one; News: 3 hrs wkly. Target aud: 40 plus; general. Spec prog: Professional, collegiate, & loc sports.

*****WGBE(FM)—** 1996: 90.9 mhz; 850 w. 387 ft. TL: N41 28 30 W84 35 14. 1270 S. Detroit Ave., Toledo 43614. Phone: (419) 380-4600. Fax: (419) 380-4710. E-mail: firstname-lastname@wgte.pbs.org. Web Site: www.wgte.org. Licensee: The Public Broadcasting Foundation of Northwest Ohio. Network: NPR, PRI. Schwartz, Woods & Miller. Format: Class, pub affrs, news. News: 23 hrs wkly. Target aud: General. Spec prog: Jazz 16 hrs wkly. ♦Marlon P. Kiser, CEO, pres & gen mgr; George Jones, chmn; Chris Peiffer, opns mgr; Ross Pfeiffer, dev dir.

Buchtel

WAIS(AM)— Dec 3, 1984: 770 khz; 1 kw-D. TL: N39 25 56 W82 12 02. 15751 U.S. Rt. 33 S., Nelsonville 45764. Phone: (740) 753-4094.

Fax: (740) 753-4965. E-mail: wseo33@sbcglobal.net. Licensee: Nelsonville TV Cable Inc. Network: ABC. Frank Jazzo. Format: News, talk, classic country. News staff: 3; News: 21 hrs wkly. Target aud: 35 plus. Spec prog: Farm 5 hrs, gospel 3 hrs wkly. ♦Eugene Edwards, pres & gen mgr; Sharon Elliott, stn mgr.

Bucyrus

WBCO(AM)— Dec 22, 1962: 1540 khz; 500 w-D, DA. TL: N40 45 47 W82 56 05. Box 1140, 403 East Rensselaer St. 44820-1140. Phone: (419) 562-2222. Fax: (419) 562-0520. Licensee: Franklin Communications Inc. Group owner: Saga Communications Inc. (acq 12-1-2003; $2.2 million. with co-located FM). Network: CBS. Rep: Rgnl Reps. Format: Oldies. News staff: 2; News: 25 hrs wkly. Target aud: 30-60. Spec prog: Farm 4 hrs, relg 4 hrs wkly. ♦Debbi Gifford, gen mgr, stn mgr, sls dir & prom dir; Dave Jones, gen sls mgr; Jim Radke, progmg dir, news dir & pub affrs dir; Bill Bowin, chief of engrg.

WQEL(FM)— Co-owned with WBCO(AM). Sept 5, 1964: 92.7 mhz; 3 kw. 300 ft. TL: N40 45 45 W82 55 50. Network: CBS. Rep: Rgnl Reps. Format: Classic rock, sports. News staff: 2; News: 10 hrs wkly. Target aud: 25-54. ♦Will Beard, progmg dir.

Byesville

WILE-FM— Oct 29, 1994: 97.7 mhz; 1.8 kw. 413 ft. TL: N40 02 24 W81 38 50. Box 338, Cambridge 43725. Secondary address: 4988 Skyline Dr., Cambridge 43725. Phone: (740) 432-5605. Fax: (740) 432-1991. Web Site: www.yourradioplace.com. Licensee: AVC Communications Inc. (group owner; acq 7-13-00). Format: Adult standard. ♦Joel Losego, gen mgr; W. Grant Hafley, CEO & gen mgr; Dave Wilson, opns dir; Bill Cassler, progmg dir.

Cadiz

WCDK(FM)— Aug 28, 1985: 106.3 mhz; 6 kw. 360 ft. TL: N40 15 14 W80 50 35. Stereo. 2307 Pennsylvania Ave., Weirton, WV 26062. Phone: (304) 723-1444. Fax: (304) 723-1688. E-mail: wcdk@weir.net. Web Site: www.106.3theriver.com. Licensee: Priority Communications Ohio LLC. Group owner: Priority Communications (acq 12-98; $475,000 with WEIR(AM) Weirton, WV). Network: Jones Radio Networks. Rep: Dome. Pepper & Corazzini. Format: Classic hits. News staff: one; News: 5 hrs wkly. Target aud: 25-54; general. Spec prog: OSU football, Cleveland Browns football, high school football. ♦Jay M. Philippone, pres & gen mgr; Jude Sheets, opns mgr; Judy Vavrek, stn mgr & sls dir.

Caldwell

WWKC(FM)— July 1, 1989: 104.9 mhz; 3 kw. 300 ft. TL: N39 48 47 W81 56 38. Box 338, Cambridge 43725. Secondary address: Box 19 43724. Phone: (740) 432-5605. Fax: (740) 432-1991. Web Site: www.yourradioplace.com. Licensee: W. Grant Hafley. (acq 8-23-89; $15,000; 9-18-89). Rep: Rgnl Reps. Format: Country. Target aud: 25-54. ♦W. Grant Hafley, gen mgr; David L. Wilson, opns mgr.

Cambridge

WCMJ(FM)— Listing follows WILE(AM).

WILE(AM)— Apr 9, 1948: 1270 khz; 1 kw-D. TL: N40 02 24 W81 38 50. Box 338, 4988 Skyline Dr. 43725. Phone: (740) 432-5605. Fax: (740) 432-1991. Web Site: www.yourradioplace.com. Licensee: AVC Communications Inc. (group owner; acq 5-5-83). Network: Network: AP Radio, ESPN Radio. Rgnl Reps. Format: News, sports. Target aud: 25-54. ♦Grant Hafley, gen mgr.

WCMJ(FM)— Co-owned with WILE(AM). October 1964: 96.7 mhz; 2.3 kw. 367 ft. TL: N40 02 24 W81 38 50. Stereo. Web Site: www.yourradioplace.com. Format: Adult contemp. News: 2. Target aud: 18-49.

*****WOUC-FM—** May 11, 1987: 89.1 mhz; 5 kw. 500 ft. TL: N40 05 32 W81 17 19. Stereo. 9 S. College St., Athens 45701. Phone: (740)

Ohio

593-4554. Fax: (740) 593-0240. Web Site: www.woub.org. Licensee: Ohio University. Network: Network: PRI, NPR. Format: News/talk. ♦ Carolyn Lewis, gen mgr; David Wiseman, opns VP; Steve Skidmore, opns dir; Scott Martin, opns mgr; Doug Partusch, dev dir. Co-owned TV: *WOUC-TV affil

Campbell

WGFT(AM)—Licensed to Campbell. See Youngstown

WHOT-FM—See Youngstown

Canton

WCER(AM)— 1947: 900 khz; 500 w-D, 78 w-N. TL: N40 49 17 W81 25 34. Stereo. 4537 22nd St. N.W. 44708. Phone: (330) 478-6655. Fax: (330) 478-6651. E-mail: wcerradio@neo.rr.com. Web Site: www.wcer.us. Licensee: Melodynamic Broadcasting Corp. (acq 7-11-91; $85,000;. FTR: 7-29-91). Network: UPI. Format: Christian, news/talk, sports. Spec prog: Farm 6 hrs, gospel 11 hrs, relg 5 hrs wkly. ♦ Jack Ambrozic, gen mgr; John Amrhein, progmg dir.

WDPN(AM)—See Alliance

WHBC(AM)— Mar 9, 1925: 1480 khz; 5 kw-U, DA-2. TL: N40 43 15 W81 26 28. Stereo. Box 9917 44711. Phone: (330) 456-7166. Fax: (330) 456-7199. Web Site: www.whbc.com. Licensee: NM Licensing LLC. Group owner: NextMedia Group L.L.C. (acq 11-26-01; grpsl). Network: ABC Information & Entertainment. Rep: Christal. Cohn & Marks. Format: Full service, oldies. Target aud: 25 plus. Spec prog: Farm one hr wkly. ♦ Richard Bossler, gen mgr.

WHBC-FM— Feb 2, 1948: 94.1 mhz; 50 kw. 500 ft. TL: N40 53 53 W81 19 07. Stereo. Web Site: www.mix941.com. Format: Adult contemp. Target aud: 25-54. ♦ Terry Simmons, progmg dir.

WILB(AM)— Aug 11, 1946: 1060 khz; 5 kw-D, DA. TL: N40 50 04 W81 25 46. 4365 Fulton Dr. N.W. 44718. Phone: (330) 966-2903. Fax: (330) 966-3177. Web Site: www.livingbreadradio.com. Licensee: Living Bread Radio Inc. (acq 7-1-2004; $300,000). Format: Catholic talk. ♦ Barbara Gaskell, pres; Kate Sell, stn mgr; Dan Clark, opns mgr.

WINW(AM)— Apr 14, 1966: 1520 khz; 1 kw-D, DA. TL: N40 50 41 W81 21 02. 237 W. Tuscarawas 44705. Phone: (330) 453-1520. Fax: (330) 454-3030. E-mail: christfirst@joy1520.com. Web Site: www.joy1520am.com. Licensee: Pinebrook Corp. (acq 9-27-96; $75,000). Rep: Rgnl Reps. Format: Gospel. Target aud: 35-54; professionals. ♦ Patrick Barb, pres; Curtis Perry, gen mgr.

WKDD(FM)— Nov 19, 1961: 98.1 mhz; 50 kw. Ant 344 ft. TL: N40 57 10 W81 19 20. Stereo. 1867 W. Market St., Akron 44313. Phone: (330) 836-4700. Fax: (330) 836-5321. Web Site: www.wkdd.com. Licensee: Citicasters Licenses L.P. Group owner: Clear Channel Communications Inc. (acq 12-22-2000; grpsl). Format: Hot adult contemp. ♦ Dan Lankford, gen mgr; Becky Clark, gen sls mgr; Keith Kennedy, progmg dir; Tom Duresky, news dir; Don Kreiger, chief of engrg.

WRQK(FM)— Mar 1, 1961: 106.9 mhz; 27.5 kw. Ant 340 ft. TL: N40 49 17 W81 25 34. Stereo. Box 7579 44705. Secondary address: 4111 Martindale Rd. N.E. 44705. Phone: (330) 492-5630. Fax: (330) 492-5633. E-mail: wrqk@wrqk.com. Web Site: www.wrqk.com. Licensee: Cumulus Licensing Corp. Group owner: Cumulus Media Inc. (acq 3-15-00; grpsl). Format: Mainstream rock. News: 1 hrs wkly. Target aud: 18-49; emphasis on men. ♦ Clyde Bass, gen mgr; Pam Allen, rgnl sls mgr; Tim Roberts, opns mgr & progmg dir.

WZKL(FM)—See Alliance

Castalia

WGGN(FM)— January 1975: 97.7 mhz; 1.25 kw. 660 ft. TL: N41 23 48 W82 47 31. Stereo. 3809 Maple Ave. 44824. Secondary address: P. O. Box 247 44824. Phone: (419) 684-5311. Fax: (419) 684-5378. E-mail: fm977@cfbroadcast.net. Licensee: Christian Faith Broadcasting Inc. (group owner). Network: USA. Format: Adult contemp Christian. Target aud: 25-49; general. ♦ Shelby Gillam, pres; Rusty Yost, gen mgr & chief of engrg; Jeff Ferback, gen sls mgr; Dave Yost, prom dir & progmg dir.

Cedarville

*****WCDR-FM**— Dec 1, 1962: 90.3 mhz; 30 kw. 354 ft. TL: N39 45 46 W83 53 05. Stereo. Box 601 45314-0601. Phone: (937) 766-7815. Fax: (937) 766-7927. E-mail: info@thepath.fm. Web Site: www.thepath.fm. Licensee: The Cedarville University. Network: Network: Network: AP Radio, CNN Radio, Moody. Format: Relg, full service. News staff: one; News: 16 hrs wkly. Target aud: 35-54. Spec prog: Black 2 hrs wkly. ♦ William Brown, pres; Martin Clark, VP; Paul Gathany, gen mgr; Keith Hamer, opns mgr; John Davis, dev dir & mktg dir; Eric Johnson, progmg dir; John Tocknell, chief of engrg.

Celina

WCSM(AM)— Sept 11, 1963: 1350 khz; 500 w-D, 11 w-N, DA-1. TL: N40 32 17 W84 35 20. Box 492, Meyers & Schunck Rds. 45822. Phone: (419) 586-5134. Fax: (419) 586-3814. E-mail: wcsm@bright.net. Web Site: www.wcsmradio.com. Licensee: Hayco Broadcasting Inc. (acq 1977). Network: ABC Daytime Direction. News staff: one; News: 20 hrs wkly. Target aud: 18-49. ♦ John H. Coe, pres & gen mgr; Sue Heiser, gen sls mgr; Jim Hyatt, progmg dir & mus dir; Kevin Sandler, news dir & chief of engrg.

WCSM-FM— 1968: 96.7 mhz; 3 kw. 328 ft. TL: N40 33 08 W84 30 46. Network: Network: ABC, Jones Radio Networks. Format: Sports.

WKKI(FM)— Dec 18, 1960: 94.3 mhz; 2.2 kw. 448 ft. TL: N40 33 08 W84 30 46. 126 W. Fayette St. 45822. Phone: (419) 586-7715. Fax: (419) 586-1074. E-mail: k94@bright.net. Web Site: www.wkki.net. Licensee: The Sonshine Communications Corp. (acq 5-26-2004; $370,000. for stock). Network: Network: CNN Radio, Westwood One. Rep: Roslin, Rgnl Reps. Format: Adult contemp. Target aud: 25-54. Spec prog: Contemp Christian 2 hrs wkly. ♦ Paul Schmitmeyer, pres, pres & gen mgr; Hilany Dickey, stn mgr; Dan Dietz, chief of opns; Brian Mathews, progmg dir.

Centerville

*****WCWT-FM**— Sept 20, 1971: 101.5 mhz; 10 w. 110 ft. TL: N39 37 39 W84 09 57. (CP: Ant 194 ft.). 500 E. Franklin 45459. Phone: (937) 439-3558. Phone: (937) 439-3557. Fax: (937) 439-3574. E-mail: wcwt@centerville.k12.oh.us. Licensee: Centerville City Board of Education. Format: Classic rock. Target aud: General. ♦ Bob Romond, gen mgr & progmg dir.

Chillicothe

WBEX(AM)— September 1947: 1490 khz; 1 kw-U. TL: N39 19 56 W82 59 50. Box 94 45601. Secondary address: 45 W.Main St. 45601. Phone: (740) 773-3000. Fax: (740) 774-4494. E-mail: newsroom@wkkj.com. Web Site: www.wbex.com. Licensee: Citicasters Licenses L.P. Group owner: Clear Channel Communications Inc. (acq 1999; grpsl). Network: Network: CBS, Westwood One. Rep: Katz Radio. Format: News/talk, full service. News staff: 3; News: 10 hrs wkly. Target aud: 30-50. ♦ Dan Latham, VP & gen mgr; Tracy Taylor, sls dir; Dan Ramey, progmg dir.

WCHI(AM)— Oct 1, 1951: 1350 khz; 1 kw-D, 28 w-N. TL: N39 19 13 W82 57 03. Box 94, 45 W. Main St. 45601. Phone: (740) 775-1350. Phone: (740) 773-3000. Fax: (740) 774-4494. Web Site: www.wchiam.com. Licensee: Clear Channel Broadcasting Licenses Inc. Group owner: Clear Channel Communications Inc. (acq 10-19-99; $4 million. with co-located FM). Network: ABC. Rep: Katz Radio. Format: Nostalgia. News staff: 2. Target aud: 25-65. ♦ Dan Latham, gen mgr; Bob Neal, opns mgr; Tracy Taylor, sls dir.

WKKJ(FM)— Co-owned with WCHI(AM). Dec 22, 1978: 94.3 mhz; 25 kw. 266 ft. TL: N39 19 52 W82 59 49. Stereo. Web Site: www.wkkj.com. Network: ABC. Format: Country. News staff: 3; News: 14 hrs wkly. ♦ Dan Latham, VP; Mike Smith, news dir.

WLZT(FM)— July 1, 1961: 93.3 mhz; 50 kw. 335 ft. TL: N39 19 52 W82 59 49. Stereo. 2323 W. Fifth Ave., Columbus 43204. Phone: (614) 486-6101. Fax: (614) 487-2537. E-mail: pegbuehrle@clearchannel.com. Web Site: www.933litefm.com. Licensee: Clear Channel Broadcasting Licenses Inc. Group owner: Clear Channel Communications Inc. (acq 4-11-03). Network: ABC. Format: Adult contemp. News staff: 3. Target aud: 24-54. ♦ Tom Thon, gen mgr; Peg Buehrle, gen sls mgr; Steve Cherry, progmg dir.

*****WOHC(FM)**— May 1, 1992: 90.1 mhz; 2 kw. 393 ft. TL: N39 20 45 W83 11 15. Stereo. Box 601, Cedarville 45314. Phone: (937) 766-7815. Fax: (937) 766-7927. E-mail: info@thepath.fm. Web Site:

Directory of Radio

thepath.fm. Licensee: The Cedarville University. Network: Network: AP Radio, CNN Radio, Moody. Cohen & Berfield. Format: Relg, full service. News staff: one; News: 16 hrs wkly. Target aud: 35-54; information-oriented Christians and/or church members. Spec prog: Black 2 hrs wkly. ♦ Paul Gathany, gen mgr; John Davis, dev dir; Eric Johnson, progmg dir; Chad Bresson, news dir; John Tocknell, chief of engrg.

*****WOUH-FM**— October 1992: 91.9 mhz; 750 w. 649 ft. TL: N39 19 46 W82 48 08. Stereo. 9 S. College St., Athens 45701. Phone: (740) 593-4554. Fax: (740) 593-0240. Licensee: Ohio University. Format: News, class, jazz. Spec prog: Pub affrs. ♦ Carolyn Lewis, gen mgr; David Wiseman, opns VP & engrg dir; Steve Skidmore, opns dir; Scott Martin, opns mgr; Doug Partusch, dev dir, gen sls mgr & mktg dir; Olivea Oldham, prom mgr & adv mgr; Tim Myers, progmg dir; Rusty Smith, progmg mgr; Tim Sharp, news dir.

*****WVXC(FM)**— Jan 15, 1988: 89.3 mhz; 2.5 kw. Ant 351 ft. TL: N39 20 45 W83 11 15. Stereo. c/o WVXU(FM), 1223 Central Pkwy., Cincinnati 45214. Phone: (513) 352-9170. Fax: (513) 241-8456. E-mail: wvxu@cinradio.org. Web Site: www.wvxu.org. Licensee: Cincinnati Classical Public Radio Inc. (acq 8-22-2005; grpsl). Network: Network: PRI, NPR. Baker & Hostetler LLP. Format: News and info. ♦ Richard Eiswerth, gen mgr.

Cincinnati

WAKW(FM)— Nov 21, 1961: 93.3 mhz; 50 kw. 500 ft. TL: N39 12 22 W84 33 23. Stereo. Box 24G, 6275 Collegevue Pl. 45224. Phone: (513) 542-9393. Fax: (513) 542-9333. E-mail: wakw@eos.net. Web Site: www.wakw.com. Licensee: Pillar of Fire Inc. (group owner) Network: Moody. Format: Full service Christian radio, Adult contemp. News staff: one. Target aud: General; families. ♦ Gerald Croucher, gen mgr & stn mgr; Alexa Workman, stn mgr; Beverly Fenton, opns dir; Daryl Pierce, progmg dir & mus dir; Rob Lewis, progmg dir.

WCIN(AM)— October 1953: 1480 khz; 5 kw-D, 500 w-N, DA-1. TL: N39 09 19 W84 30 03. (CP: 114 w). 3540 Reading Rd. 45229. Phone: (513) 281-7180. Fax: (513) 281-6125. E-mail: thepulseofthecity@hotmail.com. Web Site: www.1480wcin.com. Licensee: J4 Broadcasting of Cincinnati Inc., debtor-in-possession. (acq 9-23-98). Format: Urban oldies & black talk. Target aud: 25-64; affluent, upscale, $50,000 plus income. ♦ John Thomas, CEO & progmg mgr; John C. Thomas, pres & gen mgr.

WCKY(AM)— Sept 16, 1929: 1530 khz; 50 kw-U, DA-N, (LSS-Sacramento, CA). TL: N39 03 55 W84 36 27. 8044 Montgomery Rd., Suite 650 45236. Phone: (513) 686-8300. Fax: (513) 333-4269. Web Site: www.wcky.com. Licensee: Jacor Broadcasting Corp. Group owner: Clear Channel Communications Inc. Network: CBS. Format: Talk. Target aud: 35 plus; special focus on ages 35-64. ♦ Darryl Parks, opns dir.

WCVG(AM)—See Covington, KY

WDBZ(AM)— 1927: 1230 khz; 1 kw-U. TL: N39 06 27 W84 30 09. 705 Central Ave., Suite 200 45202. Phone: (513) 679-6000. Fax: (513) 948-1985. E-mail: rporter@radio-one.com. Web Site: www.1230thebuzz.com. Licensee: Blue Chip Communications Inc. (acq 4-2-01). Rep: Christal. Format: Talk. News staff: one. Target aud: 25-54. ♦ Rick Porter, VP & gen mgr; Lincoln Ware, opns mgr & progmg dir; Josh Guttman, gen sls mgr & natl sls mgr.

WEBN(FM)—Listing follows WLW(AM).

WGRR(FM)—See Hamilton

*****WGUC(FM)**— Sept 21, 1960: 90.9 mhz; 15 kw. Ant 960 ft. TL: N39 07 27 W84 31 18. Stereo. 1223 Central Pkwy. 45214. Phone: (513) 241-8282. Fax: (513) 241-8456. Web Site: www.wguc.org. Licensee: Cincinnati Classical Public Radio Inc. (acq 2-14-02). Network: NPR. Format: Class. News: 10 hrs wkly. Target aud: 35 plus; well-educated. ♦ Richard Eiswerth, CEO & gen mgr; Bruce Ellis, opns dir; Sherri Mancini, dev dir.

WIZF(FM)—See Erlanger, KY

*****WJVS(FM)**— Apr 7, 1976: 88.3 mhz; 175 w. 105 ft. TL: N39 17 21 W84 24 52. Stereo. 3254 E. Kemper Rd. 45241. Phone: (513) 771-8810. Fax: (513) 771-4928. Licensee: Great Oaks Institute of Technical and Career Development. (acq 1976). Format: Adult contemp. ♦ Dave Angeline, gen mgr & progmg dir.

Broadcasting & Cable Yearbook 2006

Stations in the U.S. Ohio

Developers & Brokers of Radio Properties
contact American Media Services
at our suite:
Philadelphia Marriott Downtown
215-625-2900
843-972-2200
americanmediaservices.com
Charleston, SC
Dallas, TX · Chicago, Il · Austin, TX
American Media Services, LLC

WKRC(AM)— 1922: 550 khz; 5 kw-D, 1 kw-N, DA-2. TL: N39 00 29 W84 26 39. 1111 St. Gregory 45202. Phone: (513) 241-1550. Fax: (513) 241-9834. Licensee: Jacor Broadcasting Corp. Group owner: Clear Channel Communications Inc. (acq 5-4-99; grpsl). Network: Network: Westwood One, CBS. Hogan & Hartson. Format: Talk. Target aud: 35-64; adult, affluent, conservative. ♦Mike Kenney, VP & gen mgr; Darryl Parks, opns dir; Sharon McCormick, gen sls mgr; Mike Finney, natl sls mgr; Sherry Rowland, prom dir; Tony Bender, opns mgr & progmg dir; Craig Kopp, news dir; Paul Jellison, engrg dir.

WOFX-FM—Co-owned with WKRC(AM). Aug 19, 1964: 92.5 mhz; 16 kw. Ant 866 ft. TL: N39 06 59 W84 30 07. Phone: (513) 621-9326. Web Site: www.wofx.com. Format: Classic rock. Target aud: 25-54. ♦Chuck Fredrick, VP & gen mgr; Scott Reinhart, opns dir; Lisa Thal, sls dir; Lu Semona, gen sls mgr; Jennifer McElroy, prom mgr; Joel Barnhill, adv mgr; Tony Tolliver, progmg dir. Co-owned TV: WKRC-TV affil.

WKRQ(FM)— 1947: 101.9 mhz; 16 kw. 876 ft. TL: N39 06 58 W84 30 05. Stereo. 2060 Reading Rd., Cincinatti 45202. Phone: (513) 699-5102. Fax: (513) 699-5000. Web Site: www.wkrq.com. Licensee: Infinity Radio Inc. Group owner: Infinity Broadcasting Corp. (acq 11-13-98; grpsl). Rep: Katz Radio. Format: Hot adult contemp. ♦Jim Bryant, VP & gen mgr; Bryson Lair, sls dir & prom dir; Patti Marshall, progmg dir; Brian Douglas, mus dir.

WLW(AM)— Mar 22, 1922: 700 khz; 50 kw-U. TL: N39 21 11 W84 19 30. 1111 St. Gregory St. 45202. Phone: (513) 241-9597. Phone: (513) 621-9326. Fax: (513) 241-5427. Licensee: Jacor Broadcasting Corp. Group owner: Clear Channel Communications Inc. (acq 4-99; grpsl). Network: ABC Daytime Direction. Format: Full service, adult contemp, news/talk. ♦Mike Kenney, VP & gen mgr.

WEBN(FM)—Co-owned with WLW(AM). Aug 27, 1967: 102.7 mhz; 16.6 kw. 876 ft. TL: N39 07 31 W84 29 57. Stereo. (Acq 2-86; $8 million;. FTR: 2-17-86). Format: AOR. ♦Alene Grevey, VP & gen mgr; Scott Reinhart, opns dir; Chuck Fredrick, gen sls mgr; Jennifer McElroy, prom mgr; Michael Walter, progmg dir; Bob Garrett, mus dir; Rick Bird, news dir; Cameron Adkins, engrg mgr.

WMOJ(FM)—See Fairfield

WRRM(FM)— Oct 1, 1959: 98.5 mhz; 17.5 kw. 807 ft. TL: N39 07 19 W84 32 52. Stereo. 895 Centeral Ave., Suite 900 45202. Phone: (513) 241-9898. Fax: (513) 749-3398. Fax: (513) 241-6689. Web Site: www.warm98.com. Licensee: WRRM Lico Inc. Group owner: Susquehanna Radio Corp. (acq 1-72). Format: Adult contemp. ♦TJ Holland, opns dir.

WSAI(AM)— June 7, 1923: 1360 khz; 5 kw-U, DA-N. TL: N39 14 51 W84 31 52. 5th Fl., 1111 St. Gregory St. 45202. Phone: (513) 421-9724. Fax: (513) 665-9700. Web Site: www.1360homer.com. Licensee: Clear Channel Broadcasting Inc. Group owner: Clear Channel Communications Inc. (acq 4-29-99; grpsl). Wiley, Rein & Fielding. Format: Sports. Target aud: 25-54; males. ♦Mike Kenney, gen mgr; Darryl Parks, opns mgr & progmg VP; Mike Jamison, sls dir; Holly Nesser, mktg dir; Vince Marotta, prom dir; Ted Ryan, engrg dir.

WTSJ(AM)— 1947: 1050 khz; 1 kw-D, 278 w-N. TL: N39 04 50 W84 31 18. 635 W. 7th St., Suite 400 45203. Phone: (513) 579-1050. Fax: (513) 421-0821. E-mail: 1050am@wtsj.com. Web Site: www.wtsj.com. Licensee: Caron Broadcasting Inc. Group owner: Salem Communications Corp. (acq 7-97; grpsl). Network: Salem Radio Network. Format: Relg, talk. News: 10 hrs wkly. Target aud: 24-54; family oriented young adults. Spec prog: Gospel 15 hrs, Sp 3 hrs wkly. ♦Edward G. Atsinger III, CEO; Stuart W. Epperson, chmn; Errol Dengler, VP; Dan Craig, gen mgr.

WUBE-FM— July 20, 1949: 105.1 mhz; 14 kw. 920 ft. TL: N39 07 31 W84 29 57. Stereo. 2060 Reading Rd. 45202. Phone: (513) 699-5105. Fax: (513-) 699-5000. Web Site: www.b105.com. Licensee: Infinity Radio Inc. Group owner: Infinity Broadcasting Corp. (acq 2000; grpsl). Format: Country. ♦Jim Bryant, gen mgr; Christine Mello, gen sls mgr; Duke Hamilton, mus dir; Marty Thompson, progmg dir & mus dir.

WVMX(FM)— 1955: 94.1 mhz; 32 kw. 600 ft. TL: N39 06 18 W84 33 24. Stereo. 8044 Montomery Rd., Suite 650 45236. Phone: (513) 686-8300. Fax: (513) 421-3299. Web Site: www.mixcincinnati.com. Licensee: Citicasters Licenses L.P. Group owner: Clear Channel Communications Inc. (acq 5-4-99; grpsl). Koteen & Naftalin. Format: Adult contemp. News staff: one. Target aud: 25-54. ♦Bobby Dayer, gen mgr & progmg dir; Mike Kenney, gen mgr.

***WVXU(FM)**— Oct 1, 1971: 91.7 mhz; 26.1 kw. Ant 683 ft. TL: N39 07 31 W84 29 57. Stereo. 1223 Central Pkwy. 45214. Phone: (513) 352-9170. Fax: (513) 241-8456. E-mail: wvxu@cinradio.org. Web Site: www.wvxu.org. Licensee: Cincinnati Classical Public Radio Inc. (acq 8-22-2005; grpsl). Network: Network: PRI, NPR. Baker & Hostetler LLP. Format: News and info. ♦Cathy Beltz-Williams, CFO; Richard Eiswerth, gen mgr; Sherri Mancini, dev VP; Chris Phelps, mktg VP; Robin Gehl, progmg VP; Maryanne Zeleznik, news dir & pub affrs dir; Don Danko, engrg VP.

WYGY(FM)—See Lebanon

Circleville

WAZU(FM)— Oct 1, 1965: 107.1 mhz; 3 kw. 328 ft. TL: N39 39 52 W82 51 04. 10th Floor, 280 Plaza N. High St., Columbus 43215. Secondary address: 219 S. Court St. 43215. Phone: (614) 233-9208. Fax: (614) 677-0083. Licensee: Infinity Radio Inc. Group owner: Infinity Broadcasting Corp. (acq 7-23-98; grpsl). Rep: Allied Radio Partners. Format: Active rock. Target aud: 18-34. ♦Valerie Brooks, gen mgr & stn mgr; Ross Wagner, gen sls mgr; Joe Sttow, progmg dir.

Cleveland

WABQ(AM)— 1947: 1540 khz; 1 kw-D. TL: N41 30 10 W81 37 57. 8000 Euclid Ave. 44103. Phone: (216) 231-8005. Fax: (216) 231-9803. E-mail: wabq1540@sbcglobal.net. Licensee: WABQ Inc. (acq 5-3-2002; $3 million). Format: Relg, gospel. Target aud: 25-64; adult African-American church-going audience. Spec prog: Gospel. ♦Dale Edwards, pres & gen mgr; Almira Byrd, exec VP; Danelle Caldwell, opns mgr, progmg mgr & mus dir.

***WCPN(FM)**— Sept 8, 1984: 90.3 mhz; 50 kw. 500 ft. TL: N41 22 18 W81 42 48. Stereo. 3100 Chester Ave., Suite 300 44114. Phone: (216) 432-3700. Fax: (216) 432-3681. Web Site: www.wcpn.org. Licensee: Ideastream (acq 2-27-01). Network: Network: PRI, NPR. Schwartz, Woods & Miller. Format: News, jazz. News staff: 16; News: 50 hrs wkly. Target aud: General. Spec prog: Ger one hr, Hungarian one hr, Lithuanian one hr, Pol one hr, Slovak one hr wkly. ♦Jerry Wareham, CEO & CFO; Dr. Jeanette Brown, chmn; Keith Turner, opns dir & opns mgr; Maureen Paschke, dev VP & dev dir; David Kanzeg, progmg dir.

***WCRF(FM)**— Nov 23, 1958: 103.3 mhz; 25.5 kw. Ant 660 ft. TL: N41 17 48 W81 39 27. Stereo. 9756 Barr Rd. 44141. Phone: (440) 526-1111. Fax: (440) 526-1319. E-mail: wcrf@moody.edu. Web Site: wcrfradio.org. Licensee: Moody Bible Institute of Chicago. (group owner) Southmayd & Miller. Format: Inspirational. Target aud: 25-55. ♦Dr. Michael Easley, pres; Dick Lee, stn mgr & opns mgr; Gary Bittner, mus dir.

***WCSB(FM)**— May 10, 1976: 89.3 mhz; 1 kw. 190 ft. TL: N41 30 12 W81 40 30. Stereo. Cleveland State Univ., Rhodes Tower 44115. Phone: (216) 687-3523. Web Site: www.wcsb.org. Licensee: Cleveland State University. Format: Alternative, commerical. News: 7 hrs wkly. Target aud: General. Spec prog: Black 20 hrs, Ger one hr, jazz 12 hrs, Sp 12 hrs, foreign/ethnic 8 hrs wkly. ♦Tommy Fox, gen mgr; Mike Hughes, dev dir.

WDOK(FM)— Apr 30, 1950: 102.1 mhz; 12 kw. 1,004 ft. TL: N41 23 02 W81 42 06. Stereo. One Radio Ln. 44114. Phone: (216) 696-0123. Fax: (216) 363-7189. Web Site: www.wdok.com. Licensee: Infinity Radio Inc. Group owner: Infinity Broadcasting Corp. (acq 2000; grpsl). Format: Soft rock. Target aud: 25-54; general. ♦Chris Maduri, gen mgr.

WENZ(FM)— July 14, 1959: 107.9 mhz; 70 kw. 750 ft. TL: N41 28 03 W81 17 25. Stereo. 2510 Saint Clair Ave. 44114. Phone: (216) 579-1111. Fax: (216) 575-9141. E-mail: dbevins@radio-one.com. Licensee: Radio One Licenses LLC. Group owner: Radio One Inc. (acq 11-8-01; grpsl). Rep: McGavren Guild. Format: Urban contemp. News staff: one. Target aud: 18-34. ♦David Bevins, gen mgr; Kim Johnson, progmg dir; Rick Bennett, chief of engrg.

WERE(AM)— July 6, 1949: 1300 khz; 5 kw-U, DA-1. TL: N41 20 28 W81 44 29. 2510 St. Claire Ave. NE 44114. Phone: (216) 579-1111. Fax: (216) 575-9141. E-mail: dbevins@radio-one.com. Web Site: www.1300were.com. Licensee: Radio One Licenses LLC. Group owner: Radio One Inc. (acq 11-8-01; grpsl). Rep: McGavren Guild. Format: News/talk, sports. News staff: 4; News: 30 hrs wkly. Spec prog: Black 6 hrs, It one hr, Pol 2 hrs, relg 2 hrs, Slovak one hr, Czech one hr wkly. ♦David Bevins, gen mgr; Kim Johnson, opns mgr, gen sls mgr, prom mgr & mus dir.

WFHM-FM— Apr 1, 1960: 95.5 mhz; 31 kw. 620 ft. TL: N41 26 32 W81 29 28. Stereo. 4 Summit Park Dr., Suite 150, Independence 44131. Phone: (216) 901-0921. Fax: (216) 901-1104. E-mail: office@whkradio.com. Web Site: www.whkradio.com. Licensee: SCA License Corp. Group owner: Salem Communications Corp. (acq 12-22-00; grpsl). Rep: Salem. Format: Christian, adult contemp. News: one hr wkly. Target aud: 25-54; female. ♦Edward Atsinger, pres; Errol Dengler, gen mgr & opns VP; Joe Prokop, gen sls mgr; Sue Wilson, progmg dir.

WGAR-FM— July 1948: 99.5 mhz; 50 kw. 500 ft. TL: N41 22 18 W81 43 04. Stereo. 6200 Oak Tree Blvd., 4th Floor, Independence 44131-2510. Phone: (216) 520-2600. Fax: (216) 524-2600. Web Site: www.wgar.com. Licensee: Citicasters Licenses L.P. Group owner: Clear Channel Communications Inc. (acq 5-4-99; grpsl). Network: AP Radio. Rep: Christal. Format: Contemp country. News staff: 2. Target aud: 25-54. ♦Jim Meltzer, gen mgr; Bob Butts, gen sls mgr; Meg Stevens, progmg dir; Chuck Collier, mus dir; R.C. Bauer, news dir.

WHK(AM)— July 28, 1921: 1420 khz; 5 kw-U, DA-N. TL: N41 21 30 W81 40 03. 4 Summit Park Dr., Suite 150, Independence 44131. Phone: (216) 901-0921. Fax: (216) 901-5517. E-mail: office@whkradio.com. Web Site: www.whkradio.com. Licensee: Caron Broadcasting Inc. (acq 9-1-2004; $10 million). Network: Salem Radio Network. Hogan & Hartson. Format: Conservative talk. Target aud: 25-54; male & female. ♦Michael Luczak, progmg dir.

WHKW(AM)— December 1930: 1220 khz; 50 kw-U, DA-1. TL: N41 18 26 W81 41 21. Stereo. 4 Summit Park Dr., Suite 150 44131. Phone: (216) 901-0921. Fax: (216) 901-5517. Web Site: www.whkwradio.com. Licensee: Caron Broadcasting Inc. Group owner: Salem Communications Corp. (acq 8-24-2000; grpsl). Format: Christian talk. ♦Errol Dengler, gen mgr.

WJMO(AM)—See Cleveland Heights

WKNR(AM)— 1926: 850 khz; 10 kw-D, 5 kw-N, DA-2. TL: N41 19 00 W81 43 51. (CP: 50 kw-D). Stereo. 9446 Broadview Rd. 44147-2397. Phone: (440) 838-8585. Fax: (440) 838-1546. E-mail: slegerski@sportstalk850.com. Web Site: sportstalkcleveland.com. Licensee: Caron Broadcasting Inc. Group owner: Salem Communications Corp. (acq 8-7-00;; grpsl). Format: Sports/talk. Target aud: 25-54; male sports fans. ♦Dave Urbach, stn mgr; Larry Gawthrop, sls dir.

WMJI(FM)— Dec 6, 1948: 105.7 mhz; 27 kw. 900 ft. TL: N41 23 09 W81 41 23. (CP: 15.5 kw, ant 1,020 ft.). Stereo. 6200 Oak Tree Blvd., 4th Fl. 44131-2510. Phone: (216) 520-2600. Fax: (216) 524-3200. Web Site: www.wmji.com. Licensee: Citicasters Licenses L.P. Group owner: Clear Channel Communications Inc. (acq 5-4-99; grpsl). Network: AP Radio. Rep: Christal. Format: Oldies. News staff: 4; News: 5 hrs wkly. Target aud: 25-54. ♦Jim Meltzer, gen mgr; Kevin Metheny, opns dir; David Popovich, opns mgr; Sophie Fry, gen sls mgr.

WMMS(FM)— Nov 11, 1948: 100.7 mhz; 34 kw. 600 ft. TL: N41 21 30 W81 40 03. Stereo. 6200 Oak Tree Blvd., Fourth Floor 44131. Phone: (216) 520-2600. Fax: (216) 901-8166. E-mail: buzzard@wmms.com. Web Site: www.wmms.com. Licensee: Citicasters Licenses L.P. Group owner: Clear Channel Communications Inc. (acq 1999; grpsl). Format:

Broadcasting & Cable Yearbook 2006

D-387

Ohio Directory of Radio

Rock. Target aud: 18-34. ♦Bo Matthews, opns mgr & mktg dir; Jacky Purje, gen sls mgr & prom dir; Jim Meltzer, gen mgr & gen sls mgr; David Popovich, progmg dir.

WMVX(FM)—Listing follows WTAM(AM).

WNCX(FM)— Oct 23, 1948: 98.5 mhz; 16 kw. 960 ft. TL: N41 20 28 W81 44 29. Stereo. 1041 Huron Rd. 44115. Phone: (216) 861-0100. Fax: (216) 696-0385. E-mail: wncx@wncx.com. Web Site: www.wncx.com. Licensee: Infinity Radio License Inc. Group owner: Infinity Broadcasting Corp. Network: ABC. Leventhal, Senter & Lerman, PLLC. Format: Classic rock. Target aud: 18-54; men. ♦Tom Herschel, VP & gen mgr; Linda Rodriguez, gen sls mgr; George Cohn, natl sls mgr; Marshall Goudy, mktg dir, prom dir & progmg dir.

WQAL(FM)— 1948: 104.1 mhz; 11 kw. 1,060 ft. TL: N41 22 45 W81 43 12. Stereo. 1 Radio Lane 44114. Phone: (216) 696-0123. Fax: (216) 363-7199. Web Site: www.q104.com. Licensee: Infinity Radio Inc. Group owner: Infinity Broadcasting Corp. (acq 12-14-00; grpsl). Wiley, Rein & Fielding. Format: Hot adult contemp. News staff: one. Target aud: 25-49; women. ♦Chris Maduri, gen mgr.

***WRUW-FM**— Feb 26, 1967: 91.1 mhz; 15 kw. 292 ft. TL: N41 31 14 W81 35 03. (CP: 14.5 kw, ant 276 ft.). Stereo. 11220 Bellflower Rd. 44106. Phone: (216) 368-2207. Phone: (216) 368-2208. Fax: (216) 368-5414. E-mail: gm@wruw.org. Web Site: www.wruw.org. Licensee: Case Western Reserve University. Format: Free-form. Target aud: General; Cleveland & CWRU community. Spec prog: Folk/Celtic Blues 18 hrs, Indie rock 16 hrs, Jazz 11 hrs, metal 10 hrs, pub affrs 8 hrs, reggae 7 hrs wkly. ♦Micah Waldstein, gen mgr; Peter McCall, stn mgr; James Eastman, opns mgr; Steve Hanley, chief of opns; Mike Hammer, dev dir.

WTAM(AM)— 1923: 1100 khz; 50 kw-U. TL: N41 16 50 W81 37 22. 6200 Oak Tree Blvd., 4th Fl. 44131-2510. Phone: (216) 520-2600. Fax: (216) 901-8152 (progmg). Web Site: www.wtam.com. Licensee: Clear Channel Broadcasting Inc. Group owner: Clear Channel Communications Inc. (acq 5-4-99; grpsl). Network: ABC Information & Entertainment. Hogan & Hartson. Format: News/talk, sports. News staff: 14; News: 25 hrs wkly. Target aud: 25-54. ♦Jim Meltzer, VP & gen mgr; Kevin Metheny, opns mgr; Gary Mincer, sls dir; Dave Ianni, gen sls mgr; Gaye Ramstrom, natl sls mgr; Jeff Zukauckas, prom dir; Ray Davis, progmg dir; R.C. Bauer, news dir; Cheryl Zivich, pub affrs dir; Dave Szucs, chief of engrg.

WMVX(FM)—Co-owned with WTAM(AM). May 4, 1960: 106.5 mhz; 11.3 kw. 1,036 ft. TL: N41 22 45 W81 43 12. Stereo. Fax: (216) 520-3008. Web Site: www.wmvx.com. Format: Adult contemp. ♦Jim Meltzer, stn mgr; Bill Kiessel, gen sls mgr; Todd Flennen, prom dir; Dave Popovich, progmg mgr; Jay Hudson, mus dir; Mike Camarato, chief of engrg.

WWMK(AM)— Apr 3, 1950: 1260 khz; 10 kw-D, 5 kw-N. TL: N41 17 10 W81 38 34. Stereo. 175 Kenmar Industrial Pkwy., Broadview Heights 44147. Phone: (440) 746-1010. Fax: (440) 746-1720. Web Site: www.radiodisney.com. Licensee: Radio Disney Group LLC. Group owner: ABC Inc. (acq 8-26-98; $3.9 million). Network: USA. Haley, Bader & Potts. Format: Children, CHR. Target aud: 3-12, women 21-44; children & families. ♦John Gucan, gen mgr; Jen Buza, gen sls mgr & prom dir; Jeniffer Hansen, rgnl sls mgr & mktg dir.

WXTM(FM)—See Cleveland Heights

WZAK(FM)— May 26, 1963: 93.1 mhz; 27.5 kw. 620 ft. TL: N41 16 50 W81 37 22. Stereo. 2510 St. Clair Ave. 44114. Phone: (216) 579-1111. Fax: (216) 771-4164. E-mail: dbevins@radio-one.com. Web Site: www.931wzak.com. Licensee: Radio One Licenses LLC. Group owner: Radio One Inc. (acq 11-8-01; grpsl). Rep: D & R Radio. Paul, Hastings, Janofsky & Walker. Format: Urban contemp. News staff: one. Target aud: 18-49; Black adults. ♦David Bevins, gen mgr; Kim Johnson, opns mgr & mus dir; Larry Gawthrop, gen sls mgr.

Cleveland Heights

WJMO(AM)— 1947: 1490 khz; 1 kw-U. TL: N41 30 48 W81 36 05. 2510 St. Clair Ave., Cleveland 44114. Phone: (216) 579-1111. Fax: (216) 771-4164. E-mail: dbevins@radio-one.com. Licensee: Radio One Licenses LLC. Group owner: Radio One Inc. (acq 8-7-00; grpsl). Network: ABC FM Connection. Arent, Fox, Kintner, Plotkin & Kahn. Format: Gospel. News staff: 2; News: 4 hrs wkly. Target aud: 25-54; Black adults. ♦Cathy Hughes, CEO; Dave Bevins, gen mgr; Kim Johnson, stn mgr.

WXTM(FM)— Nov 23, 1960: 92.3 mhz; 40 kw. 548 ft. TL: N41 30 01 W81 33 59. Stereo. 1041 Huron Rd., Cleveland 44115. Phone: (216) 861-0100. Fax: (216) 696-3710. Web Site: www.923xtreme.com. Licensee: Infinity Radio Inc. Group owner: Infinity Broadcasting Corp. (acq 12-14-00; grpsl). Network: ABC. Leventhal, Senter & Lerman, PLLC. Format: Alternative Rock. Target aud: 18-34; mass appeal, young adults. ♦Tom Herschel, VP; Tom Hershel, gen mgr; Jeff Miller, gen sls mgr; George Cohn, natl sls mgr & progmg dir; Marshall Goudy, mktg dir & prom dir.

Clyde

***WHVT(FM)**— December 1986: 90.5 mhz; 370 w. 170 ft. TL: N41 17 45 W82 58 26. (CP: 2.6 kw, ant 154 ft.). Box 273 43410. Phone: (419) 547-8254. Fax: (419) 547-7195. Web Site: www.whvtfm.com. Licensee: Clyde Educ. Broadcasting Foundation. Format: Educ, relg. ♦James Lewis, pres & gen mgr.

WMJK(FM)— July 16, 1981: 100.9 mhz; 3 kw. 134 ft. TL: N41 26 28 W82 41 14. Stereo. 1640 Cleveland Rd., Sandusky 44870-4357. Phone: (419) 625-3380. Fax: (419) 625-1348. E-mail: tomlewis@clearchannel.com. Web Site: www.wmjkradio.com. Licensee: Citicasters Licenses L.P. Group owner: Clear Channel Communications Inc. (acq 5-4-99; grpsl). Network: ABC. Rep: Katz Radio. Rgnl Reps. Format: Class. News staff: 2; News: 4 hrs wkly. Target aud: 35-64; adults. ♦Lisa J. Rich, gen mgr; Randy Hugg, opns mgr & progmg dir; Todd Lewis, gen sls mgr; Steve Shoffner, news dir; Gary Homza, chief of engrg.

WOHF(FM)—See Bellevue

Coal Grove

WBVB(FM)— Feb 1, 1990: 97.1 mhz; 3 kw. 472 ft. TL: N38 25 27 W82 32 04. Box 2288, Huntington, WV 25724. Secondary address: 134 4th Ave. 25701. Phone: (304) 525-7788. Fax: (304) 525-6281. Fax: (304) 525-7861 (Sales). E-mail: info@B97fm.com. Web Site: www.B97fm.com. Licensee: Capstar TX L.P. Group owner: Clear Channel Communications Inc. (acq 8-30-00; grpsl). Format: Oldies. Target aud: 18-34. Spec prog: Winston Cup racing. ♦Judy Jennings, gen mgr; Gloria Ward, sls dir; Mark Wood, progmg dir.

Columbus

WBNS(AM)— 1922: 1460 khz; 5 kw-D, 1 kw-N, DA-N. TL: N39 57 06 W82 54 23. 605 S. Front St. 43215. Phone: (614) 460-3850. Fax: (614) 460-3757. Web Site: www.1460thefan.com. Licensee: RadiOhio Inc. Group owner: Dispatch Broadcast Group (acq 1933). Network: ESPN Radio. Rep: McGavren Guild. Format: Sports. Target aud: Men 25-54. ♦Dave VanStone, gen mgr; Tom Bunyard, sls dir; Mike Kearney, gen sls mgr; Lori Sompres, natl sls mgr; Dan Zampillo, progmg dir; Steve Clawson, chief of engrg.

WBNS-FM— June 1959: 97.1 mhz; 26 kw. 660 ft. TL: N39 58 16 W83 01 40. (CP: 20.5 kw, ant 800 ft.). Stereo. Web Site: www.971moremusic.com. Format: Adult contemp. Target aud: Adults 25-54. ♦Dave VanStone, VP & gen sls mgr; Randy Parker, gen sls mgr; Jeff Ballentine, progmg dir. Co-owned TV: WBNS-TV affil.

WBZX(FM)— Apr 26, 1962: 99.7 mhz; 20 kw. 784 ft. TL: N39 58 16 W83 01 40. Stereo. 1458 Dublin Rd. 43215. Phone: (614) 481-7800. Fax: (614) 481-8070. E-mail: mail@wbzx.com. Web Site: www.wbzx.com. Licensee: North American Broadcasting Co. Inc. (group owner) Rep: D & R Radio. Format: Rock. News staff: 5. Target aud: 18-49. ♦Matthew Mnich, CEO & pres; Norma J. Mnich, chmn; Mark E. Jividen, VP & gen mgr; Tom Simkins, sls VP & sls dir; Jim Pontius, gen sls mgr; Greg Moebius, prom dir; Hal Fish, progmg dir; Ronni Hunter, mus dir; Mark Nuce, news dir & pub affrs dir; Bill Bowin, engrg mgr.

WMNI(AM)—Co-owned with WBZX(FM). Apr 26, 1958: 920 khz; 1 kw-D, 500 w-N, DA-2. TL: N39 53 32 W83 02 51. Stereo. E-mail: mail@wmni.com. Web Site: www.wmni.com. Format: Adult standards. News staff: 5; News: 20 hrs wkly. Target aud: 35 plus. Spec prog: Farm 2 hrs, relg 2 hrs wkly. ♦Steve Cantrell, progmg dir.

***WCBE(FM)**— Sept 26, 1956: 90.5 mhz; 11 kw. 531 ft. TL: N39 57 48 W83 00 17. 540 Jack Gibbs Blvd. 43215. Phone: (614) 365-5555. Fax: (614) 365-5060. E-mail: wcbe@wcbe.org. Web Site: www.wcbe.org. Licensee: Board of Education, City School District of Columbus, Ohio. Network: Network: NPR, PRI. Ernest Sanchez. Format: Var, news. News staff: 3; News: 37 hrs wkly. Spec prog: Jazz 4 hrs, blues 3 hrs, Celtic 4 hrs wkly. ♦Michael A. J. Randolph, gen mgr; Dan Mushalko, opns dir; Katie Bundy, dev dir; Maggie Brennan, mus dir; Richelle Antczak, opns mgr & pub affrs dir.

WCKX(FM)— February 1996: 107.5 mhz; 1.9 kw. 413 ft. TL: N39 57 46 W82 59 46. 1500 W. 3rd Ave., Suite 300 43212. Phone: (614) 487-1444. Fax: (614) 487-5862. Web Site: www.power1075.com. Licensee: Blue Chip Broadcasting Licenses Ltd. Group owner: Radio One Inc. (acq 4-30-01; grpsl). Network: ABC. Rep: D & R Radio. Format: Adult urban contemp. News: one hr wkly. ♦Jeff Wilson, gen mgr.

WCOL-FM— 1947: 92.3 mhz; 22 kw. 754 ft. TL: N39 58 16 W83 01 40. Stereo. 1301 Dublin Rd. 43215. Phone: (614) 486-6101. Fax: (614) 487-2554. Web Site: www.wcol.com. Licensee: Citicasters Licenses L.P. Group owner: Clear Channel Communications Inc. (acq 5-4-99; grpsl). Format: Country. News staff: one. Target aud: 18-49. ♦Tom Thon, gen mgr & opns mgr; Eric Feucht, gen sls mgr; John Crenshaw, progmg dir; Dave Isaacs, news dir; Greg Savoldi, chief of engrg.

WTPG(AM)— 1922: 1230 khz; 1 kw-U. TL: N39 56 31 W83 01 20. Stereo. Web Site: www.1230thezone.com. Format: Talk. Target aud: 35 plus; general. ♦Jeff Rehl, gen sls mgr; Steve Konrad, progmg dir; Dave Isaacs, news dir.

***WHKC(FM)**—Not on air, target date: unknown: 91.5 mhz; 340 w. Ant 938 ft. TL: N39 56 14 W83 01 16. 1630 Strathshire Hall Pl., Powell 43065. Phone: (614) 433-0433. Licensee: Christian Broadcasting Services Inc. ♦Robert G. Casagrande, pres & gen mgr.

WJYD(FM)—See London

WLVQ(FM)— Apr 1, 1959: 96.3 mhz; 40 kw. 550 ft. TL: N39 58 16 W83 01 40. Stereo. 10th Fl., 280 Plaza N. High St. 43215. Phone: (614) 227-9696. Fax: (614) 461-1059. Web Site: www.qfm96.com. Licensee: Infinity Radio Inc. Group owner:Infinity Broadcasting Corp. (acq 11-13-98; grpsl). Format: Classic Rock. Target aud: 25-54. ♦Valerie Brooks, VP & gen mgr; David Cooper, opns mgr & prom mgr; Ross Wagner, gen sls mgr; Dave Redelberger, mktg dir & prom mgr.

WNCI(FM)— July 1961: 97.9 mhz; 175 kw. 560 ft. TL: N39 58 10 W83 00 10. Stereo. 6172 Busch Blvd., Suite 2000 43229. Phone: (614) 486-6101. Fax: (614) 487-3553. Web Site: www.wnci.com. Licensee: Citicasters Licenses L.P. Group owner: Clear Channel Communications Inc. (acq 1999; grpsl). Rep: Allied Radio Partners. Holland & Knight. Format: Adult contemp. News staff: one; News: 4 hrs wkly. Target aud: 18-49. ♦Tom Thon, gen mgr.

***WOSU(AM)**— Apr 24, 1922: 820 khz; 5 kw-D, 790 w-N (L-WBAP Ft. Worth, Tex.). TL: N40 01 44 W82 03 22. (CP: 1 kw-N). 2400 Olentangy River Rd. 43210. Phone: (614) 292-9678. Fax: (614) 292-0513. Web Site: www.wosu.org. Licensee: Ohio State University. Network: Network: NPR, PRI. Dow, Lohnes & Albertson. Format: Pub affrs, news/talk. News staff: 9; News: 114 hrs wkly. Target aud: 35 plus; general. Spec prog: Black one hr, bluegrass 12 hrs wkly. ♦Thomas Rieland, gen mgr; Tim Eby, stn mgr.

WOSU-FM— Dec 13, 1949: 89.7 mhz; 13.3 kw. 938 ft. TL: N39 56 16 W83 01 16. Stereo. Web Site: www.wosu.org. Network: PRI. Format: Class music. Target aud: 25 plus. Co-owned TV: *WOSU-TV affil.

WRFD(AM)—(Columbus-Worthington). Sept 27, 1947: 880 khz; 23 kw-D. TL: N39 56 31 W83 01 20. 8101 N. High St., Suite 360 43235-1406. Phone: (614) 885-0880. Fax: (614) 885-6322. E-mail: mail@wrfd.com. Web Site: www.wrfd.com. Licensee: Salem Media of Ohio Inc. Group owner: Salem Communications Corp. (acq 2-1-82; $1.8 million; 12-21-81). Rep: Christal, Salem. Format: Relg, farm. News staff: 2; News: 12 hrs wkly. Target aud: 30-60; conservatives, Christians, farmers. ♦Edward Atsinger III, pres; Errol Dengler, VP; Dan Craig, gen mgr & gen sls mgr; Anne Rea, opns mgr; Bill Montgomery, rgnl sls mgr; Mark Bohack, prom dir, progmg dir & engrg dir.

WSNY(FM)— Aug 12, 1982: 94.7 mhz; 22 kw. 753 ft. TL: N39 58 16 W83 01 40. Stereo. 4401 Carriage Hill Ln. 43220. Phone: (614) 451-2191. Fax: (614) 451-1831. Web Site: www.sunny95.com. Licensee: Franklin Communications Inc. Group owner: Saga Communications Inc. (acq 9-86). Rep: Christal, Katz Radio. Format: Adult contemp. News staff: one; News: 3 hrs wkly. Target aud: 25-64; women, upscale families. ♦Alan Goodman, pres, VP & gen mgr; Chuck Knight, opns dir; Chris Forgy, sls dir & news dir; Katie Cyr, gen sls mgr & natl sls mgr; Michelle Hurley, mktg dir.

Stations in the U.S.   Ohio

Developers & Brokers of Radio Properties
contact American Media Services at our suite:
Philadelphia Marriott Downtown
215-625-2900
843-972-2200
americanmediaservices.com
Charleston, SC
Dallas, TX · Chicago, Il · Austin, TX
American Media Services, LLC

WTVN(AM)— 1924: 610 khz; 5 kw-U, DA-N. TL: N39 52 26 W82 58 36. 2323 W. 5th Ave., Suite 200 43204. Phone: (614) 486-6101. Fax: (614) 487-2559. E-mail: tomthorn@clearchannel.com. Web Site: www.610wtvn.com. Licensee: Citicasters Licenses L.P. Group owner: Clear Channel Communications Inc. (acq 1999; grpsl). Network: ABC Information & Entertainment. Koteen & Naftalin. Format: Talk. Target aud: 25-54; leaning male. ♦Tom Thon, VP; Jeff Rehl, gen sls mgr; Steve Konrad, progmg dir.

*****WUFM(FM)**— Mar 22, 1996: 88.7 mhz; 5 kw. Ant 774 ft. TL: N39 56 16 W83 01 16. Stereo. Box 1887, Westerville 43086-1887. Secondary address: 116 County Line Rd., Westerville 43082. Phone: (614) 839-7100. Fax: (614) 839-1329. E-mail: radiou@radiou.com. Web Site: www.radiou.com.GE-1 (ku) Licensee: Spirit Communications Inc. (acq 9-27-96; $95,000). Gammon & Grange. Format: Contemporary hit/top-40, rock, progressive. Target aud: 12-24; Male. ♦John P. Shumate Sr., pres; Kathy Shumate, VP; Michael Buckingham, gen mgr; Cole Drake, prom dir; Nikki Canter, mus dir.

WVKO(AM)— Nov 21, 1951: 1580 khz; 1 kw-D, 250 w-N, DA-2. TL: N40 02 50 W83 03 44. 513 E. Rich St., Suite 335 43215. Phone: (614) 469-1930. Fax: (614) 224-6208. Web Site: www.1580thelight.com. Licensee: Stop 26 Riverbend Licenses LLC (acq 12-30-02). Rep: McGavren Guild. Format: Gospel. ♦Bill Cusack, gen mgr.

WVKO-FM—(Johnstown). June 16, 1975: 103.1 mhz; 3 kw. 444 ft. TL: N40 13 44 W82 39 32. Stereo. 513 E. Rich St. 43215. Phone: (614) 469-1930. Fax: (614) 224-6208. Licensee: Stop 26 Riverbend Licenses LLC. Rep: D & R Radio. Format: Sp/Mexicana. Target aud: 18-54; upscale, professional; homeowners with disposable incomes. Spec prog: Jazz 10 hrs, relg 13 hrs, reggae 5 hrs wkly. ♦Bill Cusack, gen mgr; Scott Wooten, gen mgr & opns mgr.

Columbus Grove

WLWD(FM)— 2003: 93.9 mhz; 14 kw. Ant 436 ft. TL: N40 57 21 W84 07 59. Box 1128, Lima 45802-1128. Phone: (419) 223-2060. Fax: (419) 229-3888. E-mail: phil@wild939.com. Web Site: www.wild939.com. Licensee: Clear Channel Broadcasting Licenses Inc. Group owner: Clear Channel Communications Inc. (acq 8-10-2000). Format: CHR. News: one hr wkly. ♦Bill Gentry, sr VP; Art Versnick, VP; Phil Austin, opns mgr; Aaron Matthews, progmg dir; Mark Gierhart, chief of engrg.

Columbus-Worthington

WRFD(AM)—Licensed to Columbus-Worthington. See Columbus

Conneaut

*****WGOJ(FM)**— Apr 5, 1964: 105.5 mhz; 6 kw. 295 ft. TL: N41 51 42 W80 31 01. Stereo. Box 725 44030. Secondary address: 236 State St. 44030. Phone: (440) 599-7252. Phone: (440) 593-1127. Fax: (440) 593-4761. E-mail: wgoj@suite224.net. Licensee: Developing Radio LLC (acq 1-28-2004; $750,000). Network: Bible Bcstg Net. Format: Christian. Target aud: General. ♦Dr. Roger P. Hogle, gen mgr; Robert Jackson, stn mgr & progmg dir; Jonathon Pulaski, pub affrs dir; Floyd Huston, chief of engrg.

WWOW(AM)— Oct 25, 1959: 1360 khz; 5 kw-D, 35 w-N. TL: N41 55 32 W80 32 32. 229 Broad St. 44030. Phone: (440) 593-2233. Fax: (440) 593-6885. E-mail: developingradio@aol.com. Web Site: www.newsradio1360.net. Licensee: Developing Radio LLC (acq 11-14-2003; $270,000). Format: News. News staff: one; News: 15 hrs wkly. Target aud: 34-59. Spec prog: Farm one hr wkly. ♦Larry Weiss, gen mgr & progmg dir; Pat Williams, news dir.

Cortland

WKTX(AM)— Apr 1, 1985: 830 khz; 1 kw-D. TL: N41 24 56 W80 43 49. 11906 Madison Ave., Lakewood 44107. Phone: (216) 221-0330. Fax: (216) 221-3638. Licensee: Miklos Kossanyi, Maria Kossanyi (acq 10-91). Network: USA. Format: Variety, ethnic, polka. Target aud: 35 plus; homeowners. Spec prog: Slovenian 2 hrs, Greek 2 hrs, Pol one hr, German 5 hrs wkly. ♦Miklos Kossanyi, pres; Maria Kossanyi, VP; Jim Georgiades, opns dir & chief of opns; Jack Cory, progmg dir.

Coshocton

*****WOSE(FM)**— 1996: 91.1 mhz; 6 kw. Ant 321 ft. TL: N40 20 30 W81 57 56. Stereo. 2400 Olentangy River Rd., Columbus 43210. Phone: (614) 292-9678. Fax: (614) 292-0513. E-mail: radio@wosu.org. Web Site: www.wosu.org. Licensee: The Ohio State University. Network: PRI, NPR. Dow, Lohnes & Albertson. Format: Class, news/talk. ♦Thomas Rieland, gen mgr; Tim Elby, stn mgr; Mary Alice Akins, opns mgr; Susan Johnson Lyons, progmg dir.

WTNS(AM)— Nov 9, 1947: 1560 khz; 1 kw-D. TL: N40 16 30 W81 49 37. 114 N. 6th St. 43812. Phone: (740) 622-1560. Fax: (740) 622-7940. Licensee: Coshocton Broadcasting Co. (group owner; acq 9-86; $560,653; 9-22-86). Format: Country. ♦Bruce Wallace, pres & gen mgr; Tom Thompson, gen sls mgr; Mike Bechtol, mus dir; Ken Smailes, news dir; Jay Drummond, chief of engrg.

WTNS-FM— Apr 25, 1968: 99.3 mhz; 1.2 kw. 440 ft. TL: N40 16 30 W81 49 37. Format: Adult contemp.

Covington

WPTW(AM)—See Piqua

Crestline

WYKL(FM)—Licensed to Crestline. See Mansfield

Crooksville

WYBZ(FM)— Oct 26, 1990: 107.3 mhz; 3 kw. 328 ft. TL: N39 47 23 W82 05 39. (CP: Ant 302 ft.). Stereo. Box 669, 2895 A Maysville Pike, Zanesville 43702-0669. Phone: (740) 453-6004. Fax: (740) 453-5865. E-mail: wybz@rrohio.com. Web Site: www.wybz.com. Licensee: Y Bridge Broadcasting Inc. (acq 12-26-90; $60,000; 1-14-91). Network: CNN Radio. Smithwick & Belendiuk. Format: Oldies. News staff: one; News: 9 hrs wkly. Target aud: 25-55. ♦Michael Jaye, opns mgr & prom mgr; Monica Martinelli, sls VP; Rick Sabine, pres, gen mgr, gen sls mgr & progmg dir; Mark Hines, chief of engrg.

Cuyahoga Falls

WAKS(FM)—See Akron

*****WCUE(AM)**— 1950: 1150 khz; 5 kw-U, DA-2. TL: N41 12 05 W81 31 25. 13 Fairlane Dr., Joliet, IL 60435. Secondary address: 4075 Bellaire Ln., Peninsula 44264. Phone: (815) 725-1331. Phone: (330) 920-1150. Web Site: www.familyradio.com. Licensee: Family Stations Inc. (group owner; acq 10-22-86). Network: UPI. Dow, Lohnes & Albertson. Format: Relg. News: 4 hrs wkly. Target aud: 25 plus; Christians. Spec prog: Class 2 hrs wkly. ♦Harold Camping, pres & gen mgr.

WQAL(FM)—See Cleveland

Dayton

WDAO(AM)— Mar 1, 1955: 1210 khz; 1 kw-D. TL: N39 43 36 W84 12 23. 1012 West 3rd St. 45407. Phone: (937) 222-9326. Fax: (937) 461-6100. E-mail: wdaoamizo@aol.com. Licensee: Johnson Communications Inc. (acq 1-88; $725,000; 1-18-88). Rep: Christal. Format: Rhythm and blues. ♦Jim Johnson, VP & gen mgr; Sotia Carr, gen sls mgr; Jim Johnston, mus dir.

WDPR(FM)—See West Carrollton

*****WDPS(FM)**— 1976: 89.5 mhz; 6 kw. 198 ft. TL: N39 45 28 W84 11 36. 441 River Corridor Dr. 45402. Phone: (937) 542-7182. Fax: (937) 542-6714. Licensee: Dayton Public Schools. (acq 1976). Format: Jazz, AAA. News: 2 hrs wkly. Spec prog: Celtic 2 hrs, folk 2 hrs, pub affrs 2 hrs, blues 6 hrs, world mus 3 hrs, educ 2 hrs wkly. ♦Michael Reisz, gen mgr, mus dir & news dir; Jennifer Bryant, opns VP & asst music dir; Tom Nornhold, chief of engrg.

WFCJ(FM)—See Miamisburg

WGTZ(FM)—See Eaton

WHIO(AM)— Feb 9, 1935: 1290 khz; 5 kw-U, DA-N. TL: N39 40 41 W84 07 53. Box 1206 45401. Secondary address: 1414 Wilmington Ave. 45420. Phone: (937) 259-2111. Fax: (937) 259-2168. Fax: (937) 259-2024. Licensee: CXR Holdings L.L.C. Group owner: Cox Broadcasting Rep: D & R Radio. Dow, Lohnes & Albertson. Format: Full service, news/talk. News staff: 4; News: 30 hrs wkly. Target aud: 35-54. Spec prog: Relg 2 hrs wkly. ♦Donna Hall, VP & gen mgr; Lisa Allan, gen sls mgr; Marc Herbst, natl sls mgr; Kathy Eagle-Norris, rgnl sls mgr; Vicky Forrest, mktg dir; Tracey Slife, prom mgr; Larry Hansgen, progmg dir; Jim Barrett, news dir & pub affrs dir; Ron Gaier, chief of engrg. Co-owned TV: WHIO-TV affil.

WHKO(FM)—Co-owned with WHIO(AM). 1946: 99.1 mhz; 50 kw. 1,066 ft. TL: N39 44 02 W84 14 52. Stereo. Rep: Christal. Format: Country. ♦Nick Roberts, opns mgr, progmg dir & mus dir. Co-owned TV: WHIO-TV affil.

WING(AM)— May 24, 1921: 1410 khz; 5 kw-U, DA-N. TL: N39 40 56 W84 09 33. 717 E. David Rd. 45429. Phone: (937) 294-5858. Fax: (937) 297-5233. Web Site: www.wingam.com. Licensee: Blue Chip Broadcasting Licenses Ltd. Group owner: Radio One Inc. (acq 8-7-01; grpsl). Network: CBS, Westwood One. Rep: McGavren Guild. Format: News/talk, sports. Target aud: 25-54; well educated. Spec prog: Pittsburgh Steelers football, Ohio State football & basketball, loc sports talk. ♦Don Griffin, VP & gen mgr.

WLQT(FM)—See Kettering

WMMX(FM)— September 1964: 107.7 mhz; 50 kw. 420 ft. TL: N39 43 36 W84 12 23. Stereo. 101 Pine St. 45402. Phone: (937) 224-1137. Fax: (937) 224-7655. Web Site: www.wmmx.com. Licensee: Citicasters Licenses L.P. Group owner: Clear Channel Communications Inc. (acq 1999; grpsl). Format: Adult contemp. Target aud: 25-54. ♦Karrie Sudbrack, gen mgr; Jeff Stevens, opns mgr & progmg dir; Tony Tilford, opns mgr; Nick Gnau, gen sls mgr.

WONE(AM)— Mar 20, 1949: 980 khz; 5 kw-U, DA-N. TL: N39 40 03 W84 10 01. Stereo. 101 Pine St. 45402. Phone: (937) 224-1137. Fax: (937) 224-3667. Web Site: www.wone.com. Licensee: Citicasters Licenses L.P. Group owner: Clear Channel Communications Inc. (acq 5-4-99; grpsl). Network: ABC Information & Entertainment. Format: Sports. News staff: 3; News: 18 hrs wkly. Target aud: 35-64. ♦Rick Porter, VP; Mary Fleenor, opns mgr.

*****WQRP(FM)**— 1976: 89.5 mhz; 6 kw. 270 ft. TL: N39 45 26 W84 12 24. Stereo. 915 East Central Ave., West Carrollton 45449. Phone: (937) 865-5900. Fax: (937) 865-0041. E-mail: radio@praise895.com. Web Site: praise895.com. Licensee: WQRP Family Radio Inc. (acq 5-1-00). Format: Contemporary Christian. Target aud: 25-45. Spec prog: Ger 3 hrs, Hungarian 3 hrs wkly. ♦Joe Laber, gen mgr; Rex Wood, pres & dev dir.

WTUE(FM)— 1959: 104.7 mhz; 50 kw. 499 ft. TL: N39 43 19 W84 12 36. Stereo. 101 Pine St. 45402. Phone: (937) 224-1137. Fax: (937) 224-3667. E-mail: wtue@wtue.com. Web Site: www.wtue.com. Licensee: Citicasters Licenses L.P. Group owner: Clear Channel Communications Inc. Format: AOR. News staff: one; News: 2 hrs wkly. Target aud: 18-49. ♦Karrie Sudbrack, gen mgr; Tony Tilford, opns mgr; Mike Finney, gen sls mgr; Erin Mober, prom dir; John Beaulieu, mus dir.

*****WUDR(FM)**—Not on air, target date: unknown: 98.1 mhz; 13 w. Ant 59 ft. TL: N39 48 57 W84 11 33. University of Dayton, 300 College Park 45469-1679. Phone: (937) 229-3058. Web Site: www.udayton.edu. Licensee: University of Dayton. Format: Var. ♦Greg Hansberry, gen mgr.

*****WWSU(FM)**— Apr 4, 1977: 106.9 mhz; 10 w. 150 ft. TL: N39 46 57 W84 03 43. Stereo. Wright State University 45435. Phone: (937) 775-5554. Phone: (937) 775-5555. Fax: (937) 873-5553. Licensee: Wright State University. Format: Various/diverse. Target aud: 15-26;

Broadcasting & Cable Yearbook 2006

D-389

Ohio

college & high school students. Spec prog: Black 12 hrs, relg 11 hrs, gospel 3 hrs, jazz 3 hrs, Sp 3 hrs wkly. ♦ Rod Hissong, gen mgr; Matt Hughes, progmg dir; Annie Hall, news dir.

De Graff

WDEQ-FM— Sept 1, 1967: 103.3 mhz; 10 w. 23 ft. TL: N40 18 48 W83 55 06. 2096 County Rd. 24 S. 43318. Phone: (937) 585-5981. Fax: (937) 585-4599. Web Site: www.riverside.k12.oh.us. Licensee: Riverside Local Board of Education. Format: Educ. ♦ Jennifer Thompson, gen mgr.

Defiance

WDFM(FM)— June 25, 1985: 98.1 mhz; 50 kw. 500 ft. TL: N41 17 28 W84 32 17. Stereo. 118 Clinton St. 43512. Phone: (419) 782-9336. Fax: (419) 784-0306. Web Site: www.981mix.com. Licensee: Citicasters Licenses L.P. Group owner: Clear Channel Communications Inc. (acq 5-4-99; grpsl). Network: CNN Radio. Rep: Katz Radio, MediaGroup West. Fletcher, Heald & Hildreth. Format: Adult contemp. News staff: one; News: 7 hrs wkly. Target aud: 25-54. Spec prog: Relg 3 hrs wkly. ♦ Rick Small, pres & opns dir; Bob McLimans, gen mgr; Russ Ryder, progmg dir.

***WGDE(FM)**— Mar 14, 1999: 91.9 mhz; 6 kw. 305 ft. TL: N41 17 41 W84 23 24. 1270 S. Detroit, Toledo 43614. Phone: (419) 380-4600. Fax: (419) 380-4710. Web Site: www.wgte.org. Licensee: Public Broadcast Foundation of NW Ohio. Schwartz, Woods & Miller. Format: Class, pub affrs, news. News: 23 hrs wkly. Target aud: General. Spec prog: Jazz 16 hrs, new age 4 hrs wkly. ♦ George Jones, chmn; Marlon P. Kiser, CEO, pres & gen mgr.

WONW(AM)— 1949: 1280 khz; 1 kw-D, 500 w-N, DA-N. TL: N41 16 44 W84 23 50. 2110 Radio Dr. 43512. Secondary address: 709 N. Perry St., Napoleon 43545. Phone: (419) 782-8126. Fax: (419) 784-4154. E-mail: bobmclimans@clearchannel.com. Web Site: www.wonw1280.com. Licensee: Clear Channel Broadcasting Licenses Inc. Group owner: Clear Channel Communications Inc. (acq 11-5-99; grpsl). Network: CNN Radio. Rep: Katz Radio. Format: Oldies. News staff: one. Target aud: General. Spec prog: Rush Limbaugh. ♦ Robert E. McLimans, VP & gen mgr; Rick Small, opns dir & opns mgr; John Schuette, gen sls mgr; Rusty Hoops, progmg dir.

WZOM(FM)— Aug 25, 1989: 105.7 mhz; 6 kw. 347 ft. TL: N41 13 23 W84 22 36. Stereo. 2110 Radio Dr. 43512. Secondary address: 709 N. Perry St., Napoleon 43512. Phone: (419) 782-8126. Fax: (419) 784-4154. E-mail: billmurphy@clearchannel.com. Web Site: www.1057thebull.com. Licensee: Clear Channel Broadcasting Licenses Inc. Group owner: Clear Channel Communications Inc. (acq 1-1-00; grpsl). Rep: Katz Radio. Rgnl Reps. Format: Country. News staff: one; News: 4 hrs wkly. Target aud: 25-54. Spec prog: Relg 6 hrs wkly. ♦ Robert E. McLimans, sr VP, VP & gen mgr; Rick Small, opns dir; Bill Murphy, progmg dir.

Delaware

***WJJE(FM)**— 2005: 89.1 mhz; 6 kw vert. Ant 328 ft. TL: N40 24 01 W82 46 43. Drawer 2440, Tupelo, MS 38803. Phone: (662) 844-8888. Fax: (662) 842-6791. Licensee: American Family Association. Group owner: American Family Radio (acq 12-15-2003; $10. for CP). Format: Relg. ♦ Marvin Sanders, gen mgr.

WODB(FM)— June 21, 1991: 107.9 mhz; 6 kw. 285 ft. TL: N40 17 57 W83 02 45. Stereo. 4401 Carriage Hill Ln., Columbus 43202. Phone: (614) 451-2191. Fax: (614) 451-1831. Web Site: www.oldies1079fm.com. Licensee: Franklin Communications Inc. Group owner: Saga Communications Inc. (acq 12-30-02; $9 million). Rep: Allied Radio Partners. Format: Oldies. News staff: one; News: 10 hrs wkly. Target aud: 25-44. ♦ Alan Goodman, pres, gen mgr & gen mgr.

***WSLN(FM)**— Apr 28, 1952: 98.7 mhz; 100 w. 105 ft. TL: N40 17 46 W84 22 36. Stereo. Ohio Wesleyan Univ., 61 S. Sandusky St. 43015. Phone: (740) 369-4431. Fax: (740) 368-3649. Licensee: The Trustees of Ohio Wesleyan University. Network: ABC FM Connection. Format: Progsv rock, Black, jazz.

WXOL(AM)— Jan 18, 1961: 1550 khz; 500 w-D, 29 w-N, DA-2. TL: N40 17 56 W83 02 46. 501 Bowtown Rd. 43015. Phone: (740) 368-9357. Fax: (740) 369-9463. Licensee: The Fifteen Fifty Corp. (acq 10-19-2001). Format: Adult contemp. ♦ Mark Litton, gen mgr & stn mgr.

Delhi Hills

***WJYC(FM)**— July 1998: 90.1 mhz; 16 kw. Ant 371 ft. TL: N39 12 28 W84 49 17. Educational Media Foundation, 5700 W. Oaks Blvd., Rocklin, CA 95765. Phone: (916) 251-1600. Fax: (916) 251-1650. E-mail: info@air1.com. Web Site: www.air1.com. Licensee: Educational Media Foundation. Group owner: EMF Broadcasting (acq 10-2-03; grpsl). Network: Air 1. Shaw Pittman. Format: Contemp Christian. Target aud: 18-35; Judeo Christian, female. ♦ Richard Jenkins, pres; Mike Novak, VP; Lloyd Parker, gen mgr; Keith Whipple, dev dir.

Delphos

***WBIE(FM)**— 2001: 91.5 mhz; 5.5 kw. Ant 321 ft. TL: N40 56 48 W84 15 24. Box 158, Upper Sandusky 43351. Phone: (419) 294-2900. Fax: (419) 294-1786. Licensee: Kayser Broadcast Ministries Inc. Group owner: American Family Radio (acq 4-7-2005; $1.5 million. with WAUI(FM) Shelby). Format: Inspirational Christian. ♦ Daniel L. Kayser, gen mgr.

WDOH(FM)— Dec 16, 1972: 107.1 mhz; 3.3 kw. Ant 298 ft. TL: N40 49 55 W84 21 11. Stereo. 1301 N. Cable Rd., Lima 45805. Phone: (419) 331-1600. Fax: (419) 228-5085. Web Site: www.wdoh.com. Licensee: Maverick Media of Lima Licensee LLC (acq 11-15-2004; $1.15 million). Network: CBS. Fletcher, Heald & Hildreth. Format: Lite rock. News staff: one; News: 7 hrs wkly. Target aud: 25 plus. Spec prog: Farm 8 hrs wkly. ♦ Gary S. Rozynek, pres; David P. Roach, gen mgr; Deb Klaus, opns dir; Matt Childers, gen sls mgr; Justin Kage, prom dir & mus dir.

Delta

WRWK(FM)— September 1994: 106.5 mhz; 3 kw. 328 ft. TL: N41 35 13 W83 54 11. 3225 Arlington Ave., Toledo 43614. Phone: (419) 725-5700. Fax: (419) 389-5172. Licensee: Cumulus Licensing Corp. Group owner: Cumulus Media Inc. (acq 11-18-99; $4,925,000). Format: Alternative. Target aud: 18-34; male. ♦ Kathy Stinehour, gen mgr; Tim Roberts, opns mgr; Larry Scott, gen sls mgr; Chris Ammel, progmg dir.

Dover

WJER-FM—Licensed to Dover. See Dover-New Philadelphia

Dover-New Philadelphia

WJER-FM—(Dover). Aug 29, 1968: 101.7 mhz; 3 kw. 280 ft. TL: N40 33 50 W81 31 05. Stereo. 646 Blvd., Dover 44622. Phone: (330) 343-7755. Fax: (330) 364-4538. Web Site: www.wjer.com. Licensee: Clear Channel Broadcasting Licenses Inc. Group owner: Clear Channel Communications Inc. (acq 5-30-03; $4.3 million. with WJER(AM) Dover-New Philadelphia). Rep: Rgnl Reps. Format: Adult contemp. Spec prog: Farm 2 hrs wkly. ♦ Dan Pitzo, VP & gen sls mgr; Bob Scanlon, gen mgr; Steve Kelly, progmg dir; Jennifer Clark, news dir.

WJER(AM)— Feb 10, 1950: 1450 khz; 1 kw-U. TL: N40 30 46 W81 27 24. Format: Oldies.

East Liverpool

WOGF(FM)—Listing follows WOHI(AM).

WOHI(AM)— Dec 1, 1949: 1490 khz; 1 kw-U. TL: N40 37 47 W80 36 09. (CP: 660 w-U). Box 2050, 15655 St. Rt. 170 43920. Phone: (330) 385-1490. Fax: (330) 385-2339. Licensee: Keymarket Licenses LLC. Group owner: Keymarket Communications LLC (acq 2000; grpsl). Network: Jones Radio Networks. Rep: Rgnl Reps. Format: MOR. Target aud: General. Spec prog: Big band 4 hrs, gospel one hr wkly. ♦ Gerald Getz, pres; Bob Simpson, opns mgr; Ron Aughinbaugh, gen mgr & gen sls mgr; Jim Martin, prom mgr & progmg dir.

WOGF(FM)—Co-owned with WOHI(AM). Apr 15, 1959: 104.3 mhz; 50 kw. 330 ft. TL: N40 37 48 W80 36 10. (CP: Ant 492 ft.). Stereo. 15655 State Rt. 170 43920. Format: Country. Target aud: 25-54. ♦ Frank Bell, prom mgr & progmg VP; Steve Kline, progmg dir; Bob Simpson, news dir.

Eaton

WEDI(AM)— January 1979: 1130 khz; 250 w-D, DA. TL: N39 44 55 W84 35 02. 486 W. Second St., Xenia 45385. Phone: (937) 372-3531.

Fax: (937) 372-3508. E-mail: jmullins@myclassiccountry.com. Web Site: www.myclassiccountry.com. Licensee: Town and Country Broadcasting Inc. Rep: Rgnl Reps. Format: Country, agriculture news. News staff: 2; News: 6 hrs wkly. Target aud: 35-64; adults. ♦ Joe Mullins, pres & gen mgr; Roy Hatfield, progmg dir.

WGTZ(FM)— Nov 28, 1960: 92.9 mhz; 31.6 kw. 600 ft. TL: N39 50 10 W84 24 16. Stereo. 717 E. David Rd., Dayton 45429. Phone: (937) 294-5858. Fax: (937) 297-5233. Web Site: www.wgtz93.com. Licensee: Blue Chip Broadcasting Licenses Ltd. Group owner: Radio One Inc. (acq 4-30-01; grpsl). Format: CHR. Target aud: 18-49; contemp middle America. ♦ Don Griffin, VP & gen mgr.

Edgewood

WZOO-FM— Jan 23, 1989: 102.5 mhz; 5.8 kw. 328 ft. TL: N41 49 44 W80 49 28. Stereo. 102 Zoo, Box 768, Ashtabula 44004. Secondary address: 3226 Jefferson Rd., Ashtabula 44004. Phone: (440) 993-2126. E-mail: danaschulte@clearchannel.com. Web Site: www.102zoo.com. Licensee: Clear Channel Broadcasting Licenses Inc. Group owner: Clear Channel Communications Inc. (acq 7-11-00; grpsl). Miller & Miller. Format: Hot adult contemp. News staff: 3. Target aud: General. ♦ Dana Schulte, VP & gen mgr; Dennis O'Brien, opns dir.

Elyria

WEOL(AM)— October 1948: 930 khz; 1 kw-U, DA-2. TL: N41 16 10 W82 00 21. Box 4006, 4th Fl., 538 Broad St. 44036. Phone: (440) 322-3761. Fax: (440) 284-3189. Licensee: Elyria-Lorain Broadcasting Co. (group owner) Network: ABC Information & Entertainment. Rep: McGavren Guild. Rgnl Reps. Putbrese, Hunsaker & Trent. Format: News/talk, sports. News staff: 4. Target aud: 35 plus. Spec prog: Sp 2 hrs wkly. ♦ Gary L. Kneisley, pres & gen mgr.

WNWV(FM)—Co-owned with WEOL(AM). October 1948: 107.3 mhz; 20 kw. Ant 781 ft. TL: N41 16 10 W82 00 16. Stereo. Web Site: www.wnwv.com. Format: Smooth jazz. News: 4 hrs wkly. Target aud: 21 plus; upscale.

Englewood

WDKF(FM)— Dec 15, 1993: 94.5 mhz; 6 kw. 328 ft. TL: N39 57 17 W84 18 25. 101 Pine St., Dayton 45402. Phone: (937) 224-1137. Fax: (937) 224-3667. Web Site: www.945kissfm.com. Licensee: Citicasters Licenses L.P. Group owner: Clear Channel Communications Inc. (acq 5-4-99; grpsl). Format: Top 40. Target aud: 18-34. ♦ Kerri Sudbrack, gen mgr.

Fairborn

WGNZ(AM)— Sept 1, 1968: 1110 khz; 2.5 kw-D, 1.7 kw-CH, DA. TL: N39 41 15 W83 57 55. Box 1100, Dayton 45405-0879. Phone: (937) 454-9000. Fax: (937) 454-1980. E-mail: wgnz@good-news.org. Web Site: www.wgnz.com. Licensee: L & D Broadcasters Inc. (acq 11-16-01). Network: USA. Miller & Miller, P.C. Format: Relg. Target aud: General; listeners who like family radio. ♦ Norman Livingston, pres & gen mgr; Tim Livingston, stn mgr.

WXEG(FM)—See Beavercreek

Fairfield

WCNW(AM)— Feb 14, 1964: 1560 khz; 5 kw-D, DA. TL: N39 20 20 W84 31 30. 8686 Michael Ln. 45014. Phone: (513) 829-7700. Licensee: Vernon R. Baldwin Inc. (group owner; acq 6-11-84; $700,000; 3-19-84). Format: Southern gospel. ♦ Vernon R. Baldwin, pres, CFO & gen mgr; Mark Mitchell, stn mgr.

WMOJ(FM)— 1925: 94.9 mhz; 10.5 kw. 1,056 ft. TL: N39 12 01 W84 31 22. Stereo. 895 Central Ave., Ste. 900, Cincinnati 45202. Phone: (513) 241-9898. Fax: (513) 241-6689. E-mail: kmitchell@cincyradio.com. Web Site: www.mojo949.com. Licensee: WVAE LICO, Inc. Group owner: Susquehanna Radio Corp. (acq 4-23-97; grpsl). Akin, Gump, Strauss, Hauer & Feld. Format: Jammin oldies. News staff: one; News: 4 hrs wkly. Target aud: 25-44. ♦ Gary Lewis, gen mgr; Kyle Simpson, gen sls mgr & chief of engrg; T.J. Holland, prom mgr & progmg dir.

Findlay

WBVI(FM)—See Fostoria

Stations in the U.S. Ohio

Developers & Brokers of Radio Properties

contact American Media Services at our suite:
Philadelphia Marriott Downtown
215-625-2900
843-972-2200
americanmediaservices.com
Charleston, SC
Dallas, TX · Chicago, Il · Austin, TX
American Media Services, LLC

WFIN(AM)— Dec 15, 1941: 1330 khz; 1 kw-D, 79 w-N. TL: N41 00 36 W83 38 04. Stereo. Box 1507 45840-1507. Secondary address: 551 Lake Cascades Pkwy. 45840. Phone: (419) 422-4545. Fax: (419) 422-6736. E-mail: wfin@wfin.com. Web Site: www.wfin.com. Licensee: Blanchard River Broadcasting Co. Group owner: Findlay Publishing Co. (acq 1949). Network: ABC Information & Entertainment. Rgnl Reps. Format: Local news/talk. News staff: 2. Target aud: 45 plus. Spec prog: Farm 7 hrs, sports 12 hrs wkly. ♦ Edwin L. Heminger, chmn; Kurt P. Kah, pres; Robert L. Gordon, CFO; David P. Glass, VP; Sandy Kozlevcar, gen mgr & gen sls mgr; Kurt F. Heminger, opns dir; John Marshall, progmg dir; Tom Sheldon, news dir; Dennis Rund, chief of engrg.

WKXA-FM—Co-owned with WFIN(AM). 1948: 100.5 mhz; 20 kw. 440 ft. TL: N40 55 00 W83 35 45. Stereo. E-mail: wkxa@wkxa.com. Web Site: www.wkxa.com. Format: Adult contemp, alternative. News staff: 2. Target aud: 25-54. ♦ Meg Stevens, mus dir.

*WLFC(FM)— Nov 1, 1973: 88.3 mhz; 155 w. 66 ft. TL: N41 03 11 W83 39 13. Stereo. 1000 N. Main St. 45840. Phone: (419) 424-6921. Licensee: University of Findlay. Network: UPI. Format: Rock/AOR. News: 3 hrs wkly. Target aud: 18-40. Spec prog: Class 3 hrs, folk 3 hrs, relg 3 hrs, Sp 3 hrs wkly. ♦ Nick Meyers, gen mgr.

WPFX-FM—See North Baltimore

*WTKC(FM)—Not on air, target date: unknown: 89.7 mhz; 125 w. Ant 30 ft. TL: N41 02 43 W83 39 02. Box 1212 45839-1212. Phone: (419) 423-3285. Licensee: Church of the Living God Ministries.

Fort Shawnee

WZRX-FM— 1991: 107.5 mhz; 3 kw. 328 ft. TL: N40 40 04 W84 01 41. Box 1128, 667 W. Market St., Lima 45802. Secondary address: 667 W. Market St., Lima 45801. Phone: (419) 223-2060. Fax: (419) 229-3888. E-mail: comments@wzrx.com. Web Site: www.x1075fm.com. Licensee: Jacor Broadcasting Corp. Group owner: Clear Channel Communications Inc. (acq 5-4-99; grpsl). Rep: Clear Channel. Format: Oldies, rock/AOR. News: one hr wkly. Target aud: 18-49; male dominated. ♦ Art Versnick, pres & gen mgr; Phil Austin, opns mgr; Eric Michaels, progmg dir.

Fostoria

WBVI(FM)—Listing follows WFOB(AM).

WFOB(AM)— Dec 9, 1952: 1430 khz; 1 kw-U, DA-2. TL: N41 06 11 W83 24 00. (CP: TL: N41 06 06 W83 23 59). Stereo. Box 1157 44830. Secondary address: Box 1624, Findlay 45840. Phone: (419) 435-5666. Phone: (419) 422-9284. Fax: (419) 435-6611. E-mail: wfob1430@aol.com. Web Site: www.wfob.com. Licensee: TCB Holdings Inc. c/o Roppe Corp. (acq 11-24-97; with co-located FM). Network: CBS. Rep: Rgnl Reps. Baker & Hostetler. Format: Adult contemp, talk. Target aud: General. Spec prog: Sp 3 hrs wkly. ♦ Greg Peiffer, pres, gen mgr & adv mgr.

WBVI(FM)— Co-owned with WFOB(AM). 1946: 96.7 mhz; 3 kw. 330 ft. TL: N41 06 01 W83 28 41. (CP: Ant 298 ft. TL: N41 06 00 W83 28 32). Stereo. Web Site: www.wbvi.com. Network: Westwood One. News staff: one. Target aud: 25-54.

Fredericktown

WXXR(FM)— Sept 14, 1987: 98.3 mhz; 1.8 kw. Ant 423 ft. TL: N40 34 27 W82 30 27. Stereo. 2435 Mansfield Rd., Ashland 44805. Phone: (419) 289-2605. Fax: (419) 289-0304. E-mail: info@kissmidohio.com. Web Site: www.kissmidohio.com. Licensee: Capstar TX L.P. Group owner: Clear Channel Communications Inc. (acq 2-12-2001; grpsl). Format: Classic rock. ♦ Diana Coon, gen mgr; Joe Rinehart, stn mgr.

Fremont

WFRO-FM— Dec 15, 1946: 99.1 mhz; 20 kw. 195 ft. TL: N41 20 58 W83 07 10. 905 W. State St. 43420. Phone: (419) 332-8218. Fax: (419) 333-8226. Web Site: www.hitsandfavorites.com. Licensee: BAS Broadcasting Inc. (acq 6-28-02; $1.3 million). Network: ABC. Format: Adult contemp, top-40. News staff: 2; News: 5 hrs wkly. Target aud: 25-54; adults. ♦ Jim Lorensen, pres; Tom Klein, CEO & gen mgr; Dave Campbell, opns mgr.

Gahanna

*WCVO(FM)— Oct 13, 1972: 104.9 mhz; 6 kw. 298 ft. TL: N40 04 16 W82 48 35. Stereo. Box 783, 4400 Reynoldsburg-New Albany Rd., New Albany 43054. Phone: (614) 855-9171. Fax: (614) 855-9280. E-mail: theriver@104theriver.org. Web Site: www.wcvo.org. Licensee: Christian Voice of Central Ohio Inc. Network: USA. Format: Christian, Adult Contempo. News: 15 hrs wkly. Target aud: 25-54; Christian, politically aware, female, middle aged professionals. ♦ Dan Baughman, pres, gen mgr & stn mgr; Tate Luck, opns mgr; Mike Russell, mus dir.

Galion

WFXN-FM— Nov 8, 1974: 102.3 mhz; 3.5 kw. Ant 430 ft. TL: N40 45 26 W82 47 23. 2435 Mansfield Rd., Ashland 44805. Phone: (419) 289-2605. Fax: (419) 289-0304. E-mail: info@foxclassicrock.com. Web Site: www.foxclassicrock.com. Licensee: Capstar TX L.P. Group owner: Clear Channel Communications Inc. (acq 2-12-2001; grpsl). Format: Classic rock. ♦ Diana Coon, gen mgr; Jeff Schendel, progmg dir.

Gallipolis

WJEH(AM)— June 19, 1950: 990 khz; 1 kw-D, 16 w-N, 250 w-CH. TL: N38 48 20 W82 13 23. Stereo. 117 Portsmouth Rd. 45631. Phone: (740) 446-3543. Fax: (740) 446-3001. Licensee: Legend Communications of Ohio LLC. (acq 8-21-98; $1.45 million with co-located FM). Rep: Rgnl Reps. Dean George Hill. Format: Mus memories. News staff: one; News: 10 hrs wkly. Target aud: 35 plus. ♦ John Pelletier, gen mgr; Steve Reinhardt, progmg dir; Bob Triplett, news dir & chief of engrg.

WRYV(FM)—Co-owned with WJEH(AM). Dec 15, 1961: 101.5 mhz; 50 kw. 500 ft. TL: N38 48 19 W82 13 36. Stereo. Web Site: www.1015theriver.net. Format: Classic hits. Target aud: 24-49.

Gambier

*WKCO(FM)— 1975: 91.9 mhz; 266 w. 190 ft. TL: N40 22 25 W82 23 45. Stereo. Box 312, Kenyon College 43022. Phone: (740) 427-5411. E-mail: wkco@kenyon.edu. Licensee: Kenyon College. Format: Var. News: 8 hrs wkly. Target aud: 18-25; college population. ♦ Alex Matlack, gen mgr.

Geneva

WKKY(FM)— Nov 2, 1987: 104.7 mhz; 6 kw. 328 ft. TL: N41 47 30 W81 05 31. Stereo. 95 W. Main St. 44041. Phone: (440) 466-9559. Fax: (440) 466-3138. E-mail: wkky@wkky.com. Web Site: www.wkky.com. Licensee: Music Express Broadcasting Corp. of Northeast Ohio. (acq 3-15-90; $441,965; 4-2-90). Network: ABC. Rep: Rgnl Reps. Format: Country. News: 6 hrs wkly. Target aud: 25-54. Spec prog: Pub affrs 2 hrs wkly. ♦ Warren Jones, pres; Gary Hayes, gen mgr.

Georgetown

WAXZ(FM)— Apr 19, 1976: 97.7 mhz; 1.6 kw. 390 ft. TL: N38 52 03 W83 48 44. Stereo. 8354 Fryer Rd. 45121. Phone: (937) 378-6151. Fax: (937) 377-2200. E-mail: info@977waxz.com. Web Site: www.977waxz.com. Licensee: First Broadcasting Capital Partners LLC. Group owner: First Broadcasting Investment Partners LLC (acq 3-17-2004; $4.06 million. with WAOL(FM) Ripley). Network: ABC Information & Entertainment. Format: Modern country. Spec prog: Farm 10 hrs wkly. ♦ Heather Frye, gen mgr.

Gibsonburg

WIMX(FM)— Jan 24, 1989: 95.7 mhz; 3.5 kw. 433 ft. TL: N41 28 19 W83 25 05. Stereo. 5744 Southwyck Blvd., # 200, Toledo 43614. Phone: (419) 868-7914. Fax: (419) 868-8765. Web Site: www.mix957.fm. Licensee: Urban Radio Licenses LLC. (acq 5-13-2005; $2 million). Format: Urban contemp. News staff: one. Target aud: 20-40. Spec prog: Mexican 8 hrs wkly. ♦ Jeffrey Hedgeman, gen mgr; Barbara Hubley, opns mgr.

Granville

*WDUB(FM)— Feb 7, 1962: 91.1 mhz; 100 w. 171 ft. TL: N40 04 16 W82 31 24. Stereo. Slayter Hall, Denison Univ. 43023. Phone: (740) 587-3008. Phone: (740) 587-6382. Fax: (740) 587-8364. Web Site: listen.to/wdub. Licensee: Denison University. Network: Network: UPI, USA. Format: Progsv, classic rock, free-form. News staff: 3. Target aud: General; college students, faculty & loc residents. Spec prog: Black 9 hrs, reggae 2 hrs, Sp 2 hrs, Swedish 2 hrs wkly. ♦ Ben Berry, gen mgr & opns mgr.

Greenfield

WVNU(FM)— May 1, 1994: 97.5 mhz; 3.2 kw. 305 ft. TL: N39 24 01 W83 26 48. Box 329, 321 Jefferson St. 45123. Phone: (937) 981-5050. Fax: (937) 981-2107. E-mail: wvnu@bright.net. Web Site: wvnu.com. Licensee: Southern Ohio Broadcasting Inc. (acq 1-12-94; $35,227; 2-7-94). Network: Network: Jones Radio Networks, CNN Radio. Pepper & Corazzini. Format: Lite adult contemp. Target aud: 24-54. ♦ Patrick Hays, pres & gen mgr; Tom Archibald, VP; Nelson Hunter, progmg dir.

Greenville

*WDPG(FM)— February 1994: 89.9 mhz; 50 kw. 403 ft. TL: N40 08 49 W84 36 36. 126 N. Main St., Dayton 45402. Phone: (937) 496-3850. Fax: (937) 496-3852. E-mail: dpr@dpr.org. Web Site: www.dpr.org. Licensee: Dayton Public Radio Inc. Format: Class, fine arts. ♦ Georgie Woessner, gen mgr; Charles Wendelken-Wilson, mus dir.

WDSJ(FM)— Oct 26, 1990: 106.5 mhz; 50 kw. 482 ft. TL: N40 08 49 W84 36 36. Stereo. 101 Pine St., Dayton 45402-2925. Phone: (937) 224-1137. Fax: (937) 224-3667. Web Site: www.daytonjazz.com. Licensee: Citicasters Licenses L.P. Group owner: Clear Channel Communications (acq 5-4-99; grpsl). Network: Jones Radio Networks. Reddy, Begley & McCormick. Format: Jazz. Target aud: 25-54. ♦ Karrie Sudbrack, gen mgr.

Grove City

WWCD(FM)— Aug 21, 1990: 101.1 mhz; 6 kw. 328 ft. TL: N39 48 50 W83 03 19. Stereo. 503 S. Front St., Suite 101, Columbus 43215. Phone: (614) 221-9923. Fax: (614) 227-0021. E-mail: wcbmaster@cd101.com. Web Site: www.cd101.com. Licensee: Fun With Radio LLC (acq 8-16-01). Drinker Biddle & Reath. Format: Alternative rock. Target aud: 21-40; well educated, upscale professionals with discretionary income. Spec prog: Jazz 3 hrs, acoustic 2 hrs, mix show 2 hrs wkly. ♦ Roger Vaughan, pres & gen mgr; Randy Malloy, opns dir.

Hamilton

WGRR(FM)— Apr 15, 1961: 103.5 mhz; 19.3 kw. 790 ft. TL: N39 16 24 W84 31 37. Stereo. 2060 Reading Rd., Cincinnati 45202. Phone: (513) 699-5103. Fax: (513) 699-5000. Web Site: www.wgrr.com. Licensee: Infinity Radio Inc. Group owner: Infinity Broadcasting Corp. (acq 11-13-98; grpsl). Format: Oldies. News staff: one. Target aud: 35-54. ♦ Jim Bryant, gen mgr; Tim Closson, opns mgr; Stefan Schellhas, gen sls mgr.

*WHSS(FM)— May 12, 1975: 89.5 mhz; 190 w. 282 ft. TL: N39 25 51 W84 37 40. Hamilton High School, 1165 Eaton Rd. 45013. Phone: (513) 887-4832. Phone: (513) 887-4818. Fax: (513) 887-4804. Licensee: Hamilton City Schools Board of Education. Format: Rock,

Ohio
Directory of Radio

educ. News staff: one; News: 3 hrs wkly. Target aud: 12 plus; general. Spec prog: Heavy metal one hr, dance/hip hop one hr, alternative one hr, pub affrs 5 hrs, gospel 2 hrs wkly. ◆ David P. Spurrier, gen mgr & progmg dir; Robert Wilson, chief of engrg.

WMOH(AM)— Aug 15, 1944: 1450 khz; 1 kw-U. TL: N39 24 10 W84 31 54. Stereo. 2081 Fairgrove Ave. 45011. Phone: (513) 863-1111. Fax: (513) 863-6856. E-mail: kertradel@wmoh.com. Web Site: www.wmoh.com. Licensee: Vernon R. Baldwin Inc. (group owner; acq 1-7-03; $950,000). Network: Network: CNN Radio, ESPN Radio, Sporting News Radio Network. Rep: Rgnl Reps. Format: ESPN sports. News staff: one; News: 25 hrs wkly. Target aud: 35-64; adults above medium income. Spec prog: Professional, collegiate & loc sports, motor racing net, Ohio State football, Miami University pre-game shows. ◆ Kert Radel, gen mgr, opns dir, opns mgr & gen sls mgr; Bill Douglas, progmg dir.

Harrison

WNLT(FM)— Sept 1, 1991: 104.3 mhz; 3 kw. 328 ft. TL: N39 15 02 W84 50 10. 8686 Michael Ln., Fairfield 45014. Phone: (513) 829-7700. Licensee: Vernon R. Baldwin Inc. (group owner) Network: K-Love. Format: Adult contemp Christian mus. ◆ Marci Baldwin, VP; Vernon R. Baldwin, pres & gen mgr; Mark Mitchell, stn mgr; Glenn Moore, progmg dir.

Heath

WHTH(AM)— Oct 16, 1970: 790 khz; 1 kw-D, DA-1. TL: N40 03 05 W82 28 08. Box 1057, 1000 N. 40th St., Newark 43058-1057. Phone: (740) 522-8171. Fax: (740) 522-8174. E-mail: sales@wnko.com. Web Site: www.wnko.com. Licensee: Runnymede Corp. (acq 10-15-98; $100,000 for stock with WNKO(FM) Newark). Format: Talk radio. Target aud: 35-54. ◆ Charles Franks, pres; J. Thomas Swank, gen mgr; John Franks, opns VP.

WNKO(FM)—See Newark

Hicksville

WFGA(FM)— 2002: 106.7 mhz; 2.85 kw. Ant 482 ft. TL: N41 19 16 W84 43 12. 450 N. Grand Staff Dr., Auburn, IN 46706. Phone: (260) 920-3602. Fax: (260) 920-3604. Web Site: ilovefroggy.com. Licensee: Fallen Timber Communications, LLC (acq 6-28-2000; $512,000). Format: Var. ◆ Tony Richards, gen mgr.

Hilliard

WFJX(FM)— Feb 6, 1991: 105.7 mhz; 2.4 kw. 522 ft. TL: N39 58 10 W83 00 10. Stereo. 2323 W. 5th Ave., Suite 200, Columbus 43229. Phone: (614) 486-6101. Fax: (614) 487-3575. Web Site: www.1057thefox.com. Licensee: Citicasters Licenses L.P. Group owner: Clear Channel Communications Inc. (acq 1999; grpsl). Network: ABC. Format: Classic Rock. News staff: one. Target aud: 18-34. ◆ Tom Thon, gen mgr; Rob O'Boyle, gen sls mgr & prom dir; J.P. Hastings, progmg dir; Clint Buckingham, mus dir; Dave Isaacs, news dir; Greg Savoldi, chief of engrg. Co-owned TV: WHOK-TV affil

Hillsboro

WSRW(AM)— July 15, 1956: 1590 khz; 500 w-D. TL: N39 09 58 W83 36 25. Box 9, 5675 State Rt. 247 45133. Phone: (937) 393-1590. Fax: (937) 393-1611. E-mail: wsrw@clearchannel.com. Web Site: www.wsrwam.com. Licensee: Clear Channel Broadcasting Licenses Inc. Group owner: Clear Channel Communcations Inc. (acq 10-26-99; $2.5 million with WSRW-FM Hillsboro). Network: AP Radio. Rep: Katz Radio. Format: Music of your life. News: 3 hrs wkly. Target aud: 35-54; general. ◆ Dan Latham, sr VP & gen mgr; Joe Fisher, stn mgr; John Barney, sls dir & gen sls mgr; Damon Haught, progmg dir; Paul Levo, chief of engrg.

WSRW-FM— 1962: 106.7 mhz; 50 kw. 300 ft. TL: N39 09 58 W83 36 25. Stereo. Box 9, 5675 St., Rt. 247 45133. Phone: (937) 393-1590. Fax: (937) 393-1611. Web Site: www.wsrw.com. Licensee: Clear Channel Broadcasting Licenses Inc. Group owner: Clear Channel Communications Inc. (acq 10-26-99; $2.5 million with WSRW(AM) Hillsboro). Network: ABC. Rep: Katz Radio. Format: Country. News staff: one; News: 8 hrs wkly. Target aud: General. ◆ Dan Latham, gen mgr; Kim Scaggs, opns mgr.

Holland

WPOS-FM— Sept 1, 1966: 102.3 mhz; 6 kw. 312 ft. TL: N41 37 32 W83 42 41. Stereo. Box 457 43528. Secondary address: 7112 Angola Rd. 43528. Phone: (419) 865-5551. Fax: (419) 862-0112. E-mail: radio@wposfm.com. Web Site: www.wposfm.com. Licensee: Maumee Valley Broadcasting Association. (acq 8-1-65). Wiley, Rein & Fielding. Format: Christian. News: 10 hrs wkly. Spec prog: Gospel 20 hrs wkly. ◆ Rick Waldron, gen mgr.

Hubbard

WRBP(FM)— Aug 16, 1993: 101.9 mhz; 3 kw. 328 ft. TL: N41 05 29 W30 30 05. 34 Federal Plaza W., Youngstown 44503. Phone: (330) 744-5115. Fax: (330) 744-2221. Licensee: Stop 26 Riverbend Licenses LLC. Format: Adult urban contemp, classic rock, oldies. Target aud: 25-54; general. Spec prog: Black, news/talk, jazz 12 hrs, relg 6 hrs, Sp 2 hrs wkly. ◆ Percy Squire, CEO; Frank Halfacre, chmn; Bill Cusack, gen mgr; Linda Penny, gen mgr & stn mgr; Charles Rhodes, gen sls mgr; Madaline Halfacre, progmg dir; Kenneth King, news dir; Savannah Thomas, pub affrs dir; Del King, engrg dir; Charlie Ring, chief of engrg.

Huron

WKFM(FM)— Apr 1, 1996: 96.1 mhz; 3.4 kw. 436 ft. TL: N41 18 05 W82 29 16. Stereo. 10327 Milan Rd., US Rte. 250, Milan 44846. Phone: (419) 609-5961. Fax: (419) 609-2679. E-mail: k96@wkfm.com. Web Site: www.wkfm.com. Licensee: Elyria-Lorain Broadcasting Co. (group owner; acq 7-1-96; $450,000). Network: Westwood One. Putbrese, Hunsaker & Trent. Format: Country. News staff: one; News: 1 hr wjky. Target aud: General. ◆ Gary Kneisley, pres & gen mgr; Tim Kelly, opns mgr; Shelly Luipold, gen sls mgr.

Ironton

WBKS(FM)— July 1, 1973: 107.1 mhz; 3 kw. 125 ft. TL: N38 32 22 W82 40 17. (CP: Ant 285 ft.). Box 2288, Huntington, WV 25724. Phone: (304) 525-7788. Fax: (304) 525-3299. E-mail: kiss107fm@clearchannel.com. Web Site: www.1071kiss.com. Licensee: Capstar TX L.P. Group owner: Clear Channel Communications Inc. (acq 8-30-00; grpsl). Format: Hot CHR. News: 3 hrs wkly. Target aud: 35 plus; affluent, middle-aged. Spec prog: Relg 2 hrs wkly. ◆ Judy Jennings, gen mgr; Matt Tweel, gen sls mgr; Jim Davis, progmg mgr; Gary Miller, mus dir; Bill Cornwell, news dir; Scott Hensley, chief of engrg.

WIRO(AM)— September 1951: 1230 khz; 1 kw-U. TL: N38 32 22 W82 40 17. Box 2288, Huntington, WV 25724. Phone: (304) 525-7788. Fax: (304) 525-6281. E-mail: paulswann@clearchannel.com. Web Site: www.800wvhu.com. Licensee: Capstar TX Limited Partnership Group owner: Clear Channel Communications Inc. (acq 8-7-00; grpsl). Rep: Keystone (unwired net), Rgnl Reps. Format: News/talk. News: 5 hrs wkly. Target aud: 21-49. Spec prog: Relg 7 hrs wkly. ◆ Judy Jennings, gen mgr; Matt Tweel, gen sls mgr; Paul Swann, progmg dir & chief of engrg.

*WOUL-FM— Oct 12, 1987: 89.1 mhz; 50 kw. 400 ft. TL: N38 31 23 W82 39 20. Stereo. 9 S. College St., Athens 45701. Phone: (740) 593-4554. Fax: (740) 593-0240. Licensee: Ohio University. Network: Network: PRI, NPR. Format: News/talk. ◆ David Wiseman, VP & opns VP; Carolyn Lewis, gen sls mgr; Steve Skidmore, opns dir; Scott Martin, opns mgr; Doug Partusch, dev dir.

Jackson

WCJO(FM)— 1971: 97.7 mhz; 3 kw. 300 ft. TL: N39 01 45 W82 35 51. Box 667 45640. Secondary address: 295 E. Main St. 45640. Phone: (740) 286-3023. Fax: (740) 286-6679. E-mail: rburtrand@jcbiradio.com. Licensee: Jackson County Broadcasting Inc. (group owner; acq 4-22-93; $260,000; 5-10-93). Network: Westwood One. Fletcher, Heald & Hildreth. Format: Hot country. News staff: one; News: 8 hrs wkly. Target aud: General; current-country music lovers. ◆ Jerry Mossbarger, gen mgr; Bill Forthofer, gen sls mgr; John Pelletier, progmg mgr.

Jefferson

*WCVJ(FM)— 1978: 90.9 mhz; 5.5 kw. 372 ft. TL: N41 37 48 W80 45 46. (CP: 1.85 kw, ant 643 ft.). Stereo. 4422 Lenox New Lyme Rd. 44047. Phone: (440) 294-3854. Fax: (440) 294-3855. E-mail: wcvj@suite224.org. Web Site: www.wcvj.org. Licensee: Agape School Inc. Format: Christian educ. ◆ Myron J. Hubler, pres; Sarah Hubler, gen mgr.

Johnstown

WVKO-FM—Licensed to Johnstown. See Columbus

Kent

WJMP(AM)— March 1964: 1520 khz; 1 kw-D, DA. TL: N41 09 35 W81 18 19. Box 2170, Akron 44309-2170. Secondary address: 2449 S.R. 59 44240. Phone: (330) 673-2323. Fax: (330) 673-0301. Licensee: Media-Com Inc. (acq 1971). Format: MOR. Target aud: 18 plus. ◆ Richard M. Klaus, pres; William Klaus, stn mgr; Robert Klaus, sls VP; Jim Midock, news dir; Bob Sassman, chief of engrg.

WNIR(FM)—Co-owned with WJMP(AM). Feb 19, 1962: 100.1 mhz; 4.2 kw. Ant 394 ft. TL: N41 06 28 W81 21 19. Wombel, Carlyle, Sandridge & Rice. Format: Talk. Target aud: General.

*WKSU-FM— 1950: 89.7 mhz; 14.5 kw. Ant 909 ft. TL: N41 04 58 W81 38 02. Stereo. Box 5190 44242-0001. Secondary address: 1613 E. Summit St. 44242-0001. Phone: (330) 672-3114. Fax: (330) 672-4107. E-mail: letters@wksu.org. Web Site: www.wksu.org. Licensee: Kent State University. Network: Network: PRI, NPR, AP Radio. Dow, Lohnes & Albertson. Format: Class, news. News staff: 5; News: 35 hrs wkly. Target aud: 35-65; college grad, professional & upper income. Spec prog: Folk 12 hrs wkly. ◆ Allen E. Bartholet, gen mgr; Deborah Frazier, gen mgr; N. Vincent Duffy, opns dir & progmg dir; Abbe Turner, dev dir; Ronald Bartlebaugh, engrg dir.

Kenton

WKTN(FM)— June 20, 1963: 95.3 mhz; 3 kw. 270 ft. TL: N40 38 41 W83 33 59. Stereo. 112 N. Detroit St. 43326. Phone: (419) 675-2355. Fax: (419) 673-1096. E-mail: wktn@kenton.com. Web Site: www.wktn.com. Licensee: Radio General Ltd. (acq 5-12-77). Arent, Fox, Kintner, Plotkin & Kahn. Format: Adult contemp. News staff: one; News: 10 hrs wkly. Target aud: 25-54. Spec prog: Farm 2 hrs wkly. ◆ Keith P. Gensheimer, pres & gen mgr; Quentin White, gen sls mgr.

Kettering

*WKET(FM)— May 5, 1975: 98.3 mhz; 10 w. 150 ft. TL: N39 41 46 W84 09 43. 3301 Shroyer Rd., Dayton 45419. Phone: (937) 296-7669. Fax: (937) 297-7435. Licensee: Kettering City School District. Format: Educ, classic rock, AOR. Target aud: 13-18; high school students. ◆ Karl Bremer, gen mgr & stn mgr.

WLQT(FM)— Feb 20, 1962: 99.9 mhz; 50 kw. 500 ft. TL: N39 44 07 W84 10 10. Stereo. 101 Pine St., Dayton 45402. Phone: (937) 224-1137. Fax: (937) 224-3667. E-mail: theboss@wlqt.com. Web Site: www.wlqt.com. Licensee: Citicasters Licenses L.P. Group owner: Clear Channel Communications Inc. (acq 1999; grpsl). Format: Adult contemp. Target aud: 35-64; persons 35-64. ◆ Karrie Sudbrack, gen mgr; Jeff Stevens, opns mgr; Tony Tilford, opns mgr; Nick Gnau, gen sls mgr; Sandy Collins, progmg dir; Chris Collins, news dir; Jeff Bennett, chief of engrg.

WQRP(FM)—See Dayton

Lancaster

*WFCO(FM)— August 1988: 90.9 mhz; 200 w. 223 ft. TL: N39 40 49 W82 35 51. Stereo. 201 S. Broad St., Studio 301 43130. Phone: (740) 654-8556. Fax: (740) 654-8581. E-mail: jtburcham@wfcofm.com. Web Site: wfcofm.com. Licensee: Lancaster Educational Broadcasting Foundation. Network: Network: Bible Bcstg Net, Moody. Format: Btfl mus, Christian, news. News: one hr wkly. Target aud: 30 plus; Christian audience & those interested in community events. Spec prog: Live coverage of sports & community events. ◆ Robert Rauch, gen mgr; Steve Rauch, stn mgr; J.T. Burcham, opns dir.

WHOK(FM)— December 1958: 95.5 mhz; 50 kw. 492 ft. TL: N39 40 32 W82 40 34. Stereo. 10th Fl., 280 Plaza N. High St., Columbus 43215. Phone: (614) 225-9465. Fax: (614) 677-0116. Licensee: Infinity Radio Holdings Inc. Group owner: Infinity Broadcasting Corp. (acq 11-18-98; grpsl). Format: Country legends. News: 2 hrs wkly. Target aud: 25-54. ◆ Valerie Brooks, gen mgr; Dave Cooper, opns dir; Jill McCarron, gen sls mgr; Katie Rychener, prom dir; George Wolf, progmg dir.

WJZA(FM)— Oct 7, 1989: 103.5 mhz; 4 kw. 435 ft. TL: N39 51 52 W82 38 19. Stereo. 4401 Carriage Hill Ln., Columbus 43220. Phone: (614) 451-2191. Fax: (614) 451-1831. Web Site: www.wjza.com.

Broadcasting & Cable Yearbook 2006

Stations in the U.S. Ohio

Developers & Brokers of Radio Properties
contact American Media Services at our suite:
Philadelphia Marriott Downtown
215-625-2900
843-972-2200
americanmediaservices.com
Charleston, SC
Dallas, TX · Chicago, Il · Austin, TX
American Media Services, LLC

Licensee: Franklin Communications Inc. Group owner: Saga Communications Inc. (acq 10-1-2003; $13 million). Format: Smooth jazz. News: 2 hrs wkly. Target aud: 25-54. Spec prog: New age 2 hrs wkly. ♦Alan Goodman, gen mgr.

WLOH(AM)— October 1948: 1320 khz; 1 kw-D, 28 w-N. TL: N39 44 21 W82 37 48. 724 So. Columbus St. 43130. Phone: (740) 653-4373. Fax: (740) 653-0702. E-mail: wloh@greenapple.com. Web Site: www.wloh.net. Licensee: Frontier Broadcasting LLC No. 3 (acq 2-13-01; $325,000). Rep: D & R Radio. Covington & Burling. Format: Talk radio. News staff: 2; News: 24 hrs wkly. Target aud: General; Fairfield, Franklin & surrounding county residents. Spec prog: Cleveland Cavaliers, Cincinnati Reds, farm one hr wkly. ♦Bart Johnson, CEO; Mark Bonah, gen mgr; Mark Bonach, opns mgr; Michael O'Riley, gen sls mgr.

Lebanon

WYGY(FM)— May 26, 1958: 96.5 mhz; 19.5 kw. 810 ft. TL: N39 21 11 W84 19 30. Stereo. c/o Radio Cincinnati, 895 Central Ave., Suite 900, Cincinnati 45202. Phone: (513) 241-9898. Fax: (513) 241-6689. Web Site: www.965thestar.com. Licensee: WVAE Lico Inc. Group owner: Susquehanna Radio Corp. (acq 9-30-02; $45 million). Rep: Christal. Format: Country. Target aud: 18-34. ♦Dan Swensson, gen mgr & progmg dir.

Lima

WFGF(FM)— 1985: 93.1 mhz; 3 kw. 328 ft. TL: N40 45 47 W84 10 59. 1301 N. Cable Rd. 45805. Secondary address: Box 1487 45802. Phone: (419) 331-1600. Fax: (419) 222-3755. E-mail: polly@froggy93.com. Web Site: www.froggy93.com. Licensee: Maverick Media of Lima License LLC. Group owner: Maverick Media LLC (acq 12-4-2003; grpsl). Format: Country. Target aud: 25-54; young, affluent. Spec prog: Nascar Nextel Races. ♦Gary Rozynek, pres & prom dir; Dave Roach, gen mgr & mus dir; Bill McAdams, stn mgr; Stacy McAdams, prom dir; Brandy Rader, engrg dir.

*****WGLE(FM)—** Dec 2, 1981: 90.7 mhz; 50 kw. 420 ft. TL: N40 39 15 W84 06 36. Stereo. 1270 S. Detroit Ave., Toledo 43614. Phone: (419) 380-4600. Fax: (419) 380-4710. Web Site: www.wgte.org. Licensee: The Public Broadcasting Foundation of Northwest Ohio. Network: Network: PRI, NPR. Format: Class, NPR, News, Public Affairs. News: 23 hrs wkly. Target aud: General. Spec prog: Jazz 16 hrs, new age/eclectic 4 hrs wkly. ♦Marlon P. Kiser, CEO, pres & gen mgr; George Jones, chmn; Chris Peiffer, opns mgr; Ross Pfeiffer, dev dir. Co-owned TV: *WGTE-TV affil.

WIMA(AM)— Dec 5, 1948: 1150 khz; 1 kw-U, DA-2. TL: N40 40 47 W84 06 34. Box 1128 45802. Secondary address: 667 W. Market St. 45801. Phone: (419) 223-2060. Fax: (419) 229-3888. E-mail: comments@1150wima.com. Web Site: www.1150wima.com. Licensee: Jacor Broadcasting Corp. Group owner: Clear Channel Communications Inc. (acq 5-4-99; grpsl). Network: ABC Information & Entertainment. Rep: Clear Channel. Format: News/talk, sports. News staff: 2; News: 20 hrs wkly. Target aud: 35 plus. Spec prog: Farm 3 hrs wkly. ♦Art Versnick, VP & gen mgr; Phil Austin, opns mgr; Jennifer Cartwright, sls dir; Jack Wheelbarger, natl sls mgr; Dave Woodward, progmg dir; Jeff Gunter, news dir; Mark Gierhart, chief of engrg.

WLJM(AM)— Aug 22, 1963: 940 khz; 250 w-D, DA-2. TL: N40 43 21 W84 05 04. Stereo. 1301 N. Cable Rd. 45805. Phone: (419) 331-1600. Fax: (419) 222-5085. Web Site: www.940jamz.com. Licensee: Maverick Media of Lima License LLC. Group owner: Maverick Media LLC (acq 12-4-2003; grpsl). Rep: Christal, Rgnl Reps. Format: Urban contemp. News staff: 2; News: 20 hrs wkly. Target aud: 35-54; affluent, community involved. Spec prog: Jazz 2 hrs, relg 11 hrs wkly. ♦Gary S. Rozynek, pres; Mark Mackey, gen mgr & stn mgr; Bill McAdams, opns mgr.

*****WTGN(FM)—** Sept 27, 1966: 97.7 mhz; 6 kw. 300 ft. TL: N40 45 26 W84 08 12. Stereo. 1600 Elida Rd. 45805. Phone: (419) 227-2525. Fax: (419) 222-5438. E-mail: info@wtgn.org. Web Site: www.wtgn.org. Licensee: Associated Christian Broadcasters Inc. Format: Christian. ♦Wesley Lytle, pres; Scott Young, gen mgr.

WUZZ-FM— Nov 25, 1970: 104.9 mhz; 3 kw. 260 ft. TL: N40 43 21 W84 05 04. (CP: Ant 286 ft.). Stereo. 1301 N. Cable Rd. 45805. Phone: (419) 331-1600. Phone: (419) 331-1049 (request line). Fax: (419) 222-3755. E-mail: bill@1049wuzz.com. Web Site: www.wuzz104.com. Licensee: Maverick Media of Lima License LLC. Group owner: Maverick Media LLC (acq 12-4-2003; grpsl). Network: ABC. Rep: Christal. Format: Classic rock. Target aud: 25-54; affluent, community involved. ♦Dave Roach, gen mgr; Matt Childers, gen sls mgr; Bill Rice, progmg dir.

*****WYSM(FM)—** 2001: 89.3 mhz; 3 kw. Ant 220 ft. TL: N40 39 15 W84 06 36. 5115 Glendale Ave., Toledo 43614. Phone: (419) 389-0893. Fax: (419) 381-0731. E-mail: yesfm@yeshome.com. Web Site: www.yeshome.com. Licensee: Side by Side Inc. Network: Salem Radio Network. Format: Christian. ♦J. Todd Hostetler, gen mgr.

WZOQ(FM)—See Wapakoneta

Logan

WLGN(AM)— December 1967: 1510 khz; 1 kw-D, 250 w-CH. TL: N39 31 47 W82 23 10. Stereo. Box 429, One Radio Ln. 43138. Phone: (740) 385-2151. Fax: (740) 385-4022. E-mail: wlgn@magicohio.com. Licensee: Edward A. Baker. (acq 12-6-2004; $675,000. with co-located FM). Rep: Rgnl Reps. Format: Country. News staff: one; News: 10 hrs wkly. Target aud: 18-54. ♦Roger L. Hinerman, gen mgr; Judy Davis, gen sls mgr; Kevin Reed, mus dir; Steve Carmean, chief of engrg.

WLGN-FM— Dec 10, 1965: 98.3 mhz; 3 kw. 240 ft. TL: N39 31 47 W82 23 10. Stereo. News staff: one; News: 25 hrs wkly. ♦Roger L. Hinerman, CEO.

London

WJYD(FM)— 1965: 106.3 mhz; 6 kw. 328 ft. TL: N39 53 05 W83 25 23. Stereo. 1500 W. 3rd Ave., Suite 300, Columbus 43212. Phone: (614) 487-1444. Fax: (614) 487-5862. Web Site: www.joy106.com. Licensee: Blue Chip Broadcasting Licenses Ltd. Group owner: Radio One Inc. (acq 4-30-01; grpsl). Network: ABC. Rep: D & R Radio. Format: Gospel. News staff: 3. Target aud: 18-34. Spec prog: Gospel 10 hrs wkly. ♦Jeff Wilson, gen mgr.

Lorain

WCLV(FM)— July 1975: 104.9 mhz; 6 kw. Ant 328 ft. TL: N41 28 32 W81 59 24. Stereo. 26501 Renaissance Pkwy., Cleveland 44128. Phone: (216) 464-0900. Fax: (216) 464-2206. E-mail: wclv@wclv.com. Web Site: www.wclv.com. Licensee: Radio Seaway Inc. (acq 11-1-01). Rep: D & R Radio, Interep. Hogan & Hartson. Format: Classical. News staff: one; News: 5 hrs wkly. Target aud: 35-64; high-income, college graduates & professionals. Spec prog: Jazz 5 hrs, financial news one hr wkly. ♦Robert D. Conrad, CEO & pres; Richard G. Marschner, CFO, exec VP & gen mgr; Jenny Northern, stn mgr & gen sls mgr; John Simna, opns mgr; Bill O'Connell, progmg mgr.

WDLW(AM)— December 1969: 1380 khz; 500 w-D, 67 w-N. TL: N41 25 48 W82 09 07. 45624 State Rt. 20, Oberlin 44074. Phone: (440) 775-1380. Fax: (440) 774-1336. Licensee: WDLW Radio Inc. (acq 2-14-02; $250,000). News staff: 3; News: 10 hrs wkly. Target aud: 35-64. ♦Doug Wilber, pres & gen mgr; Lorie Wilber, VP; Terry Coffee, progmg dir.

*****WNZN(FM)—** 1992: 89.1 mhz; 2.2 kw. 374 ft. TL: N41 18 34 W82 26 31. 9712 State Rd. 113, Berlin Heights 44814. Phone: (419) 588-3700. E-mail: tony10491@adelphia.net. Licensee: Spanish Cultural Network. Format: Sp. ♦Milton Velazquez, gen mgr & progmg mgr.

Loudonville

WXXF(FM)—Licensed to Loudonville. See Wooster

Manchester

WAGX(FM)— 1992: 101.3 mhz; 3 kw. 299 ft. TL: N38 40 58 W83 39 45. 9503 Mason-Lewis Rd., Maysville, KY 41056. Phone: (606) 564-8474. Fax: (606) 564-8384. Licensee: Jewell Schaeffer Broadcasting Inc. Format: Oldies, adult contemp, classic rock. Target aud: 25-54; upscale adults. ♦James P. Wagner, CEO; James P. Wagner, gen mgr.

Mansfield

WMAN(AM)— Dec 4, 1939: 1400 khz; 1 kw-U. TL: N40 46 13 W82 32 36. Box 8 44901. Secondary address: 1400 Radio Ln. 44906. Phone: (419) 529-2516. Licensee: Capstar TX L.P. Group owner: Clear Channel Communications Inc. (acq 8-7-00; grpsl). Network: Network: Network: CBS, Westwood One, ABC Information & Entertainment. Format: News/talk, sports. News staff: 3; News: 30 hrs wkly. Target aud: 35 plus; upscale, active mgmt/exec. Spec prog: Black one hr wkly. ♦Diana Coon, gen mgr; Margie Tasseff, gen sls mgr; Rusty Cates, progmg dir; Jeff Swank, news dir; Ron Allen, chief of engrg.

WYHT(FM)—Co-owned with WMAN(AM). Oct 18, 1962: 105.3 mhz; 50 kw. 370 ft. TL: N40 46 09 W82 32 23. (CP: 17.5 kw, ant 217 ft.). Stereo. Format: Hot adult contemp. ♦Eric Hanson, progmg dir.

WNCO-FM—See Ashland

*****WOSV(FM)—** June 27, 1989: 91.7 mhz; 750 w. 450 ft. TL: N40 42 33 W82 29 11. Stereo. 2400 Olentangy River Rd., Columbus 43210. Phone: (614) 292-9678. Fax: (614) 292-0513. Web Site: www.wosu.org. Licensee: The Ohio State University. Network: Network: PRI, NPR. Dow, Lohnes & Albertson. Format: Classical, NPR News. News: 28 hrs wkly. Target aud: 35 plus. ♦Thomas Rieland, gen mgr; Tim Eby, stn mgr; Kevin Petrilla, opns mgr.

WRGM(AM)—See Ontario

*****WVMC-FM—** March 1979: 90.7 mhz; 170 w. 100 ft. TL: N40 43 19 W82 31 52. 500 Logan Rd. 44907. Phone: (419) 756-5651 ext 227. Fax: (419) 756-7470. Web Site: wvmcfm.com. Licensee: Mansfield Christian School. Format: MOR, inspirational, Christian, CHR. Target aud: 18-34; middle income adults, mostly female. ♦Todd Stach, gen mgr.

WVNO-FM— Aug 11, 1962: 106.1 mhz; 40 kw. 545 ft. TL: N40 45 50 W82 37 04. Stereo. 2900 Park Ave. W. 44906. Phone: (419) 529-5900. Fax: (419) 529-2319. Web Site: www.wvno.com. Licensee: Johnny Appleseed Broadcasting Co. Rgnl Reps Format: Adult contemp. News staff: 5; News: 10 hrs wkly. Target aud: 25-54; female. ♦Gunther S. Meisse, pres & gen mgr; Jim Holmes, opns mgr.

*****WYKL(FM)—**(Crestline). Dec 10, 1990: 98.7 mhz; 1.8 kw. Ant 418 ft. TL: N40 46 08 W82 46 03. Stereo. EMF Broadcasting, 5700 West Oaks Blvd., Rocklin, CA 95765. Phone: (916) 251-1600. Fax: (916) 251-1650. E-mail: klove@klove.com. Web Site: www.klove.com. Licensee: Educational Media Foundation. Group owner: EMF Broadcasting (acq 12-18-03; $900,000). Network: K-Love. Shaw Pittman. Format: Contemp Christian. Target aud: 25-44; Judeo Christian female. ♦Richard Jenkins, pres; Mike Novak, VP & progmg dir; Lloyd Parker, gen mgr; Ed Lenane, opns dir & news dir; Keith Whipple, dev dir; Eric Allen, natl sls mgr; Amu Bawnann, rgnl sls mgr; Chris Joyce, prom dir; David Pierce, progmg mgr; Jon Rivers, mus dir; Sam Wallington, engrg dir.

Mariemont

WKFS(FM)—See Milford

Marietta

*****WCMO(FM)—** Oct 1, 1960: 98.5 mhz; 40 w. 105 ft. TL: N39 25 07 W81 26 32. Marietta College, 215 5th St. 45750. Phone: (740) 376-4802. Phone: (740) 376-4800. Fax: (740) 376-4807. Web Site: www.wmrtfm.com. Licensee: Marietta College. Format: AOR. ♦Marilee Morrow, gen mgr & progmg dir.

Ohio

WLTP(AM)— May 8, 1996: 910 khz; 5 kw-D, 61 w-N, DA-2. TL: N39 26 07 W81 28 01. Stereo. 6006 Grand Central Ave., Vienna, WV 26105. Phone: (304) 295-6070. Fax: (304) 295-4389. Web Site: www.wltp.com. Licensee: Clear Channel Broadcasting Licenses Inc. Group owner: Clear Channel Communications Inc. (acq 9-4-02). Network: Network: Network: CBS, Westwood One, AP Radio. Format: New, talk. News staff: one; News: 8 hrs wkly. Target aud: 18-54; males. ♦Chuck Poet, gen mgr.

WMOA(AM)— Sept 8, 1946: 1490 khz; 1 kw-U. TL: N39 25 07 W81 28 34. 925 Lancaster St. 45750. Phone: (740) 373-1490. Fax: (740) 373-1717. E-mail: dcastelli@wmoa1490.com. Web Site: www.mariettaonline.com. Licensee: Jawco Inc. (acq 7-11-97; $659,000. with WJAW(FM) McConnelsville). Network: ABC Information & Entertainment. Pepper & Corazzini. Format: Adult contemp, news, sports. News staff: 2; News: 5 hrs wkly. Target aud: 35 plus; mature, middle-class to affluent. Spec prog: Farm one hr, relg one hr, sports 15 hrs wkly. ♦John A. Wharff III, pres, gen mgr & gen sls mgr; Dan Castelli, mus dir.

***WMRT(FM)**— Nov 13, 1975: 88.3 mhz; 9.2 kw. 205 ft. TL: N39 25 07 W81 26 32. Stereo. Marietta College 45750. Phone: (740) 376-4800. Fax: (740) 376-4807. Web Site: www.wmrtfm.com. Licensee: Marietta College. Format: Class, news/talk, jazz. ♦Marilee Morrow, gen mgr.

WRVB(FM)— Dec 1, 1964: 102.1 mhz; 25 kw. 400 ft. TL: N39 25 07 W81 28 34. Stereo. 6006 Grand Central Ave., Box 5559, Vienna, WV 26105. Phone: (304) 295-6070. Fax: (304) 295-4389. Web Site: www.102theriver.com. Licensee: Clear Channel Broadcasting Licenses Inc. Group owner: Clear Channel Communications Inc. (acq 4-17-01; grpsl). Format: CHR. Target aud: 25-54; general. ♦Chuck Poet, gen mgr.

WXIL(FM)—See Parkersburg, WV

Marion

WDIF(FM)— Feb 27, 1975: 94.3 mhz; 3 kw. 300 ft. TL: N40 36 27 W83 14 14. Stereo. 1330 N. Main St. 43302. Phone: (740) 383-1131. Fax: (740) 387-8349. Web Site: www.wdif.com. Licensee: Citicasters Licenses L.P. Group owner: Clear Channel Communications Inc. (acq 1999; grpsl). Rep: Rgnl Reps. Format: CHR. Target aud: 25-54; upscale adult females. ♦Diane Glassmeyer, gen mgr; Audra Meadows, prom dir; Mike Mitchell, adv dir; Scott Shawver, opns mgr & mus dir.

WMRN(AM)— Dec 23, 1940: 1490 khz; 1 kw-U. TL: N40 36 54 W83 07 54. 1330 N. Main St. 43302. Phone: (740) 383-1131. Fax: (740) 387-3697. Web Site: www.wmrn.com. Licensee: Citicasters Licenses L.P. Group owner: Clear Channel Communications Inc. (acq 1999; grpsl). Format: Oldies, news/talk. Spec prog: Farm 5 hrs wkly. ♦Diane Glassmeyer, gen mgr.

WMRN-FM— April 1953: 106.9 mhz; 25 kw. 340 ft. TL: N40 36 54 W83 07 54. (CP: Ant 358 ft. TL: N40 36 50 W83 07 47). Stereo. Web Site: www.buckeyecountry107.com. Network: Westwood One. Format: Buckeye country.

***WOSB(FM)**— Apr 14, 1998: 91.1 mhz; 2.5 kw horiz, 6.8 kw vert. 285 ft. TL: N40 41 06 W83 15 24. 2400 Olentangy River Rd., Columbus 43210. Phone: (614) 292-9678. Fax: (614) 292-0513. Web Site: www.wosu.org. Licensee: The Ohio State University. Network: NPR. Format: Classical, News. ♦Thomas Rieland, gen mgr.

Marysville

WUCO(AM)— Dec 1, 1983: 1270 khz; 500 w-U, DA-2. TL: N40 14 46 W83 19 50. 107 N. Main St. 43040. Phone: (937) 642-1270. Fax: (937) 644-1617. E-mail: wuco@urec.net. Web Site: www.ontheradio.net /radiostations/wucoam.aspx. Licensee: Frontier Broadcasting LLC (acq 11-1-98; $270,000). Network: ABC. Format: Country, news/talk, sports. News staff: one; News: 10 hrs wkly. Target aud: 25-54. Spec prog: Farm 10 hrs wkly. ♦Bart Johnson, pres; Rick Wilson, stn mgr; Amy Day, gen sls mgr & progmg dir.

Massillon

WTIG(AM)— Aug 1, 1957: 990 khz; 250 w-D, 119-N, DA-2. TL: N40 49 56 W81 33 40. Box 608 44648. Secondary address: 3580 Karen Ave. N.W. 44647. Phone: (330) 837-9900. Fax: (330) 837-9844. E-mail: espn@espn990.com. Web Site: www.espn990.com. Licensee: WTIG Inc. (acq 1991; 8-12-85). Format: Sports. Target aud: 25-54;

male. Spec prog: Local church services. ♦Donovan Resh, VP, opns dir, chief of opns & progmg dir; Ray Jeske, pres & gen mgr.

Maumee

***WYSZ(FM)**— Nov 14, 1992: 89.3 mhz; 6.3 kw. 321 ft. TL: N41 38 55 W83 42 22. Stereo. 5115 Glendale Ave., Toledo 43614. Phone: (419) 389-0893. Fax: (419) 381-0731. Licensee: Side By Side Inc. Network: Salem Radio Network. Gammon & Grange. Format: Christian, CHR/Rock. Target aud: 15-25. ♦J. Todd Hostetler, gen mgr; Janet Yonke, dev dir & progmg dir.

McArthur

WYRO(FM)— 1994: 98.7 mhz; 6 kw. 328 ft. TL: N39 08 59 W82 35 36. Box 667, Jackson 45640. Secondary address: 295 E. Main St., Jackson 45640. Phone: (740) 286-3023. Fax: (740) 286-6679. E-mail: jmossbarger@jcbiradio.com. Licensee: Davis Broadcasting Media Inc. (acq 4-26-99). Network: Westwood One. Keystone (unwired net), Rgnl Reps. Format: Classic rock. News staff: one. Target aud: 18-65. ♦Jerry Mossbarger, gen mgr; Bill Forthoter, gen sls mgr; John Pelletier, progmg mgr.

McConnelsville

WJAW-FM— October 1992: 100.9 mhz; 930 w. 577 ft. TL: N39 33 24 W81 51 06. Stereo. Box 547, 3733 Monasterly Rd. 43756. Phone: (740) 373-1490. Fax: (740) 373-1717. Licensee: JAW Co. Inc. (acq 6-25-97; $659,300. with WMOA(AM) Marietta). Network: ABC. Format: Sports. News staff: 4. Target aud: 35 plus. ♦John Wharff III, pres, sr VP & gen mgr.

Medina

WQMX(FM)—Licensed to Medina. See Akron

Miamisburg

WFCJ(FM)— Jan 7, 1961: 93.7 mhz; 50 kw. Ant 492 ft. TL: N39 39 35 W84 18 53. Stereo. Box 93,7, Dayton 45449-0999. Secondary address: 7333 Manning Rd. 45342. Phone: (937) 866-2471. Fax: (937) 866-2062. E-mail: inspiration@wfcj.com. Web Site: www.wfcj.com. Licensee: Miami Valley Christian Broadcasting Association Inc. Network: Network: USA, Salem Radio Network. Miller & Neely. Format: Relg, Christian. News: 10 hrs wkly. Target aud: 35-64; Evangelical Christians. Spec prog: Black 4 hrs, children 2 hrs wkly. ♦Bud Schindler, pres; Clair D. Miller, VP & gen mgr.

Middleport

WYVK(FM)—Licensed to Middleport. See Middleport-Pomeroy

Middleport-Pomeroy

WMPO(AM)— Aug 28, 1959: 1390 khz; 5 kw-D, 120 w-N. TL: N39 00 35 W82 04 14. Box 71, 39520 Bradbury Rd., Middleport 45760. Phone: (740) 992-6485. Fax: (740) 992-6486. Licensee: Positive Radio Group Inc. of Ohio. Group owner: Baker Family Stations (acq 1999; $492,000 with WYVK(FM) Middleport). Network: ABC Information & Entertainment. Rep: Rgnl Reps. Format: Sports. Target aud: 35 plus. Spec prog: Relg 6 hrs, farm one hr, gospel 18 hrs wkly. ♦Kevin Nott, pres, gen mgr & progmg dir.

WYVK(FM)— Co-owned with WMPO(AM). Aug 27, 1973: 92.1 mhz; 4.7 kw. 113 ft. TL: N39 03 30 W82 02 31. Stereo. Format: Top 40. News: 3 hrs wkly. Target aud: 25-54. ♦Kevin Nott, mus dir.

Middletown

WPFB(AM)— Sept 1, 1947: 910 khz; 1 kw-D, 100 w-N. TL: N39 30 57 W84 21 05. 4505 Central Ave. 45044. Phone: (513) 422-3625. Fax: (513) 424-9732. Web Site: www.wpfb.com. Licensee: Radio Station WPFB Inc. Group owner: WPAY/WPFB Inc. Rep: Roslin. Format: Talk. News staff: 2; News: 26 hrs wkly. Target aud: 25-55; baby boomers. Spec prog: Radio Movie of the Week 2 hrs wkly. ♦Douglas L. Braden, pres & gen mgr.

WPFB-FM— July 1, 1959: 105.9 mhz; 34 kw. 590 ft. TL: N39 30 57 W84 21 05. Stereo. Web Site: www.therebel1059.com. Format: Country. Target aud: 25-54.

Milford

WKFS(FM)— Aug 1, 1969: 107.1 mhz; 3 kw. 299 ft. TL: N39 06 16 W84 20 10. (CP: 6 kw). Stereo. 1906 Highland ve., Cincinnati 45219. Phone: (513) 686-8300. Web Site: www.kiss107fm.com. Licensee: Jacor Broadcasting Corp. Group owner: Clear Channel Communications Inc. (acq 5-4-99; grpsl). Verner, Liipfert, Bernhard, McPherson & Hand. Format: Top 40. ♦Mike Kenney, gen mgr; Chuck Fredrick, opns mgr & chief of opns.

Millersburg

WKLM(FM)— 1988: 95.3 mhz; 3 kw. 328 ft. TL: N40 29 07 W81 50 40. Stereo. 7409 White Hill Ln. 44654. Phone: (330) 674-1953. Fax: (330) 674-9556. Licensee: Coshocton Broadcasting Co. (group owner; acq 7-10-90; $490,000; 8-6-90). Network: ABC. Format: Adult contemp. News staff: one; News: 12 hrs wkly. Target aud: General. Spec prog: Loc sports. ♦Bruce Wallace, pres & gen mgr; Tom Thompson, gen sls mgr; Mark Lonsinger, progmg dir.

***WVML(FM)**— June 2004: 90.5 mhz; 4.8 kw. Ant 367 ft. TL: N40 36 08 W81 44 32. WCRF Radio, 9756 Barr Rd., Cleveland 44141. Phone: (440) 526-1111. Fax: (440) 526-1319. E-mail: wcrf@moody.edu. Web Site: wcrfradio.org. Licensee: The Moody Bible Institute of Chicago (group owner). Format: Inspirational. ♦Dr. Michael Easley, pres; Dick Lee, prog mgr; Phil Villareal, progmg dir; Doug Hainer, chief of engrg.

Montpelier

WLZZ(FM)— 1991: 104.5 mhz; 3 kw. Ant 328 ft. TL: N41 30 54 W84 39 43. 209 W. Main St. 43543. Phone: (419) 485-5530. Phone: (800) 788-1045. Fax: (419) 485-5539. E-mail: wlzz@wlzzradio.com. Licensee: Lake Cities Broadcasting Corp. Network: ABC Information & Entertainment. Format: Country. News staff: one; News: 12 hrs wkly. Target aud: 25-54. ♦Tom Andrews, CEO, chrmn & pres; William Kerner, exec VP & gen mgr.

Morrow

***WLMH(FM)**— 1970: 89.1 mhz; 100 w. 200 ft. TL: N39 20 51 W84 08 13. 3001 E. US. 22nd & 3rd 45152. Phone: (513) 899-3884. Fax: (513) 899-4912. Licensee: Little Miami Local Schools. Format: Educ, oldies, classic rock. ♦Wayne Lyke, opns mgr.

Mount Gilead

WVXG(FM)— March 1994: 95.1 mhz; 6 kw. Ant 328 ft. TL: N40 35 15 W82 48 20. Stereo. Box 102, Powell 43065. Phone: (740) 549-7002. Licensee: ICS Holdings Sub 1 Inc. (acq 12-17-2003; $384,588). ♦Mark Litton, gen mgr.

Mount Vernon

WMVO(AM)— Nov 26, 1953: 1300 khz; 500 w-D, DA. TL: N40 24 17 W82 26 23. 17421 Coshocton Rd., Box 348 43050. Phone: (740) 397-1000. Fax: (740) 392-9300. Web Site: www.wmvo.com. Licensee: Capstar TX L.P. Group owner: Clear Channel Communications Inc. (acq 2-12-01; grpsl). Network: ABC. Rep: Rgnl Reps. Format: Var, news/talk. Spec prog: Relg 7 hrs wkly. ♦Diana Coon, gen mgr & mktg mgr; Michael Hayes, opns mgr & news dir.

WQIO(FM)— Co-owned with WMVO(AM). May 26, 1951: 93.7 mhz; 37 kw. 565 ft. TL: N40 24 18 W82 26 20. Stereo. E-mail: info@ohioradio.com. Web Site: www.wqiofm.com. Format: Adult contemp. News staff: one. Target aud: 35-54. Spec prog: Hit mus 4 hrs, gospel 2 hrs wkly.

***WNZR(FM)**— May 1, 1986: 90.9 mhz; 100 w. 193 ft. TL: N40 22 14 W82 28 05. Stereo. 800 Martinsburg Rd. 43050. Phone: (740) 392-9090. Fax: (740) 392-9155. E-mail: wnzr@mvnu.edu. Web Site: www.mvnu.edu/wnzr. Licensee: Mt. Vernon Nazarene University. Shaw Pittman. Format: Christian adult contemp. News: 5 hrs wkly. Target aud: 25-54; Christian adults.

Napoleon

WNDH(FM)— June 1972: 103.1 mhz; 3.3 kw. 300 ft. TL: N41 18 00 W84 09 22. Stereo. 709 N. Perry St. 43545. Phone: (419) 592-8060. Fax: (419) 592-1085. E-mail: wndh@clearchannel.com. Web Site: www.wndh1031.com. Licensee: Clear Channel Broadcasting Licenses Inc. Group owner: Clear Channel Communications Inc. (acq 1-1-00; grpsl). Network: CBS. Rgnl Reps Format: Adult contemp. News staff:

Stations in the U.S. — Ohio

Developers & Brokers of Radio Properties
contact American Media Services at our suite:
Philadelphia Marriott Downtown
215-625-2900
843-972-2200
americanmediaservices.com
Charleston, SC
Dallas, TX · Chicago, Il · Austin, TX
American Media Services, LLC

one. Target aud: General. Spec prog: Ger Polka 2 hrs wkly. ♦Robert E. McLimans, sr VP, VP & gen mgr; Rick Small, opns dir; John Schuette, gen sls mgr.

Nelsonville

WSEO(FM)— September 1990: 107.7 mhz; 3 kw. 328 ft. TL: N39 27 38 W82 13 09. Stereo. 15751 U.S. Rt. 33 S. 45764. Phone: (740) 753-2154. Phone: (740) 753-4094. Fax: (740) 753-4965. E-mail: wseo33@sbcglobal.net. Licensee: Nelsonville TV Cable Inc. Format: Contemp country. News staff: 3; News: 15 hrs wkly. Target aud: 25-49. Spec prog: Farm. ♦Eugene R. Edwards, pres & gen mgr; Nick Brooks, mus dir.

New Boston

WIOI(AM)— Sept 2, 1959: 1010 khz; 1 kw-D, 22 w-N. TL: N38 43 48 W82 57 10. Box 1233, Portsmouth 45662. Phone: (606) 932-4796. Fax: (606) 932-4796. E-mail: chip@wioiradio.com. Web Site: wioiradio.com. Licensee: Maillet Media Inc. (acq 1996). Format: Adult standards. ♦Charles Maillet Jr., gen mgr.

New Concord

*WMCO(FM)— Jan 28, 1961: 90.7 mhz; 1.3 kw. 84 ft. TL: N39 59 46 W81 43 18. Stereo. Caldwell Hall, 163 Stormont St. 43762. Phone: (740) 826-8375. Fax: (740) 826-8357. E-mail: wmco@muskingum.edu. Web Site: www.muskingum.edu/~wmco. Licensee: Muskingum College. Format: Div, educ, progsv. News: 10 hrs wkly. Target aud: General. Spec prog: Class 4 hrs, jazz 10 hrs, relg 2 hrs wkly. ♦Jeffrey D. Harman, gen mgr; Kim Fox, stn mgr; James Rose, progmg dir; Jessica Allen, mus dir.

New Lexington

WWJM(FM)— May 1, 1978: 105.9 mhz; 1.7 kw. 627 ft. TL: N39 46 37 W82 09 54. Stereo. 210 S. Jackson St. 43764. Secondary address: 247 Market St., Zanesville 43701. Phone: (740) 342-1988. Fax: (740) 342-1036. E-mail: wwjm@aol.com. Web Site: wwjm.com. Licensee: Perry County Broadcasting Co. Network: Network: Westwood One, ABC News/Talk. Format: Adult contemp. News staff: one; News: 2 hrs wkly. Target aud: 18-54; young to middle-aged. ♦Charles Edwards, chmn, pres & gen mgr.

New Philadelphia

WJER(AM)—See Dover-New Philadelphia

*WKRJ(FM)— July 12, 1994: 91.5 mhz; 2 kw. 240 ft. TL: N40 33 50 W81 31 05. c/o WKSU-FM, 1613 E. Summit St., Kent 44242-0001. Phone: (330) 672-3114. Fax: (330) 672-4107. Web Site: www.wksu.org. Licensee: Kent State University. Network: Network: NPR, PRI. Dow, Lohnes & Albertson. Format: News, class. News staff: 5; News: 35 hrs wkly. Target aud: 35-65; college grad, professional & upper income. ♦Allen E. Bartholet, gen mgr; Patricia Gerber, dev dir; Robert Burford, mktg dir & prom dir; Eric Nuzum, progmg dir; David Roden, mus dir; Vincent Duffy, news dir; Ronald Bartlebaugh, engrg dir.

WNPQ(FM)— Feb 2, 1969: 95.9 mhz; 3 kw. 400 ft. TL: N40 35 51 W81 29 32. Stereo. 3969 Convenience Cir. N.W., Suite 205, Canton 44718. Phone: (330) 492-9590. Fax: (330) 492-3702. Web Site: www.wnpqfm.com. Licensee: Tuscarawas Broadcasting Co. Network: CBS Radio. Format: Christian contemp. Target aud: 18-49; family oriented. Spec prog: Black 4 hrs, southern gospel 4 hrs wkly. ♦James Natoli Jr., pres; Garry Meeks, gen mgr; Tom Bishop, gen sls mgr.

WTUZ(FM)—(Uhrichsville). May 1, 1990: 99.9 mhz; 5.3 kw. 348 ft. TL: N40 26 19 W81 26 01. Stereo. 2424 E. High Ave. 44663. Phone: (330) 339-2222. Fax: (330) 339-5930. E-mail: info@wtuz.com. Web Site: www.wtuz.com. Licensee: WTUZ Radio Inc. Smithwick & Belendiuk. Format: Country. News staff: 2; News: 7 hrs wkly. Target aud: General. Spec prog: Farm one hr, relg one hr wkly. ♦Edward A. Schumacher,

pres & gen mgr; Melanie Osborn, gen sls mgr; Pat Smith, prom dir; Greg Morrison, progmg dir; Brad Shupe, news dir; John Demuth, chief of engrg.

Newark

WCLT(AM)— Jan 4, 1949: 1430 khz; 500 w-D, 48 w-N. TL: N40 02 02 W82 24 08. Box 5150 43058-5150. Secondary address: 674 Jacksontown Rd. S.E., Heath 43056. Phone: (740) 345-4004. Fax: (740) 345-5775. E-mail: wclt@wclt.com. Web Site: www.wclt.com. Licensee: WCLT Radio Inc. (acq 1-1-58). Network: AP Network News. Format: News/talk. News staff: 2; News: 12 hrs wkly. Target aud: General. ♦Robert H. Pricer, CEO; Douglas C. Pricer, pres & gen mgr.

WCLT-FM— Aug 7, 1947: 100.3 mhz; 50 kw. 390 ft. TL: N40 02 02 W82 24 08. Stereo. Format: Country. Target aud: 25-54.

WHTH(AM)—See Heath

WNKO(FM)— Dec 8, 1972: 101.7 mhz; 3 kw. Ant 298 ft. TL: N39 59 38 W82 30 13. Stereo. Box 1057, 1000 N. 40th St. 43058-1057. Phone: (740) 522-8171. Fax: (740) 522-8174. E-mail: sales@wnko.com. Web Site: www.wnko.com. Licensee: Runnymede Corp. (acq 10-15-98; $100,000 for stock with WHTH(AM) Heath). Format: Oldies. News staff: 2. Target aud: 25-54. ♦Charles Franks, pres; Tom Swank, gen mgr; John Franks, opns VP.

Niles

WBBG(FM)— May 15, 1988: 106.1 mhz; 3 kw. 328 ft. TL: N41 15 52 W80 45 35. 7461 South Ave., Youngstown 44512. Phone: (330) 965-0057. Fax: (330) 729-9991. E-mail: billkelly@clearchannel.com. Web Site: www.wbbgfm.com. Licensee: Citicasters Licenses L.P. Group owner: Clear Channel Communications Inc. (acq 5-4-99; grpsl). Cohn & Marks. Format: Oldies. Target aud: 18-49. ♦Bill Kelly, gen mgr; Dan Rivers, opns mgr; Jeff Kelly, progmg dir; John Nagy, news dir; Jim Hartzler, chief of engrg.

WRTK(AM)— Nov 1, 1963: 1540 khz; 500 w-D, DA. TL: N41 07 56 W80 45 40. Box 1194, Youngstown 44501. Phone: (330) 740-0154. Web Site: www.wrtk.net. Licensee: D & E Communications of Ohio Inc. (acq 6-1-01; $300,000. with WPAO(AM) Farrell, PA). Format: Urban contemp. Spec prog: It one hr, Pol one hr wkly. ♦Dominic Baragona, gen mgr; Jay Curtis, opns mgr; Robert Hotchkiss, gen sls mgr & rgnl sls mgr; Chris Patrick, progmg dir.

North Baltimore

WPFX-FM— July 30, 1990: 107.7 mhz; 3 kw. 328 ft. TL: N41 07 04 W83 32 38. Stereo. Box 108, Findlay 45839. Secondary address: 1624 Tiffin Ave., Findlay 45840. Phone: (419) 425-1077. Fax: (419) 422-2954. Web Site: www.1077thefox.com. Licensee: Citicasters Licenses L.P. Group owner: Clear Channel Communications Inc. (acq 5-4-99; grpsl). Miller & Miller. Format: Classic rock. Target aud: General. ♦Kim Fields, gen mgr.

North Kingsville

WFXJ-FM— Apr 8, 2002: 107.5 mhz; 6 kw. Ant 328 ft. TL: N41 54 10 W80 39 36. Box 738, Ashtabula 44005. Secondary address: 3226 Jefferson Rd., Ashtabula 44004. Phone: (440) 998-1075. Fax: (440) 992-2658. E-mail: danaaschulte@ckearchannel.com. Web Site: www.theforx1075.com. Licensee: Clear Channel Broadcasting Licenses Inc. Group owner: Clear Channel Communications Inc. (acq 7-11-00; grpsl). Format: Classic rock. Target aud: 18-54; males. ♦Dana Schulte, VP & gen mgr; Dennis O'Brien, opns dir; Michelle Baird, sls dir; Erin Edison, mktg dir; Cindy Steiner, prom dir; Ron Fantone, progmg mgr; John Riccio, chief of engrg.

North Ridgeville

WJTB(AM)— Sept 16, 1984: 1040 khz; 5 kw-D. TL: N41 22 37 W82 00 27. 105 Lake Ave., Elyria 44035. Phone: (440) 327-1844. Fax: (440) 322-8942. E-mail: wjtb1040am@aol.com. Licensee: Taylor

Broadcasting Co. Network: UPI. Format: Urban contemp, gospel. ♦James Taylor, pres & gen mgr; Henry Dunn, opns mgr.

Norwalk

WLKR(AM)— Mar 18, 1968: 1510 khz; 500 w-D, DA. TL: N41 16 45 W82 39 23. 10327 Milan Rd., U.S. Rt. 250, Milan 44846. Phone: (419) 609-5961. Fax: (419) 609-2679. E-mail: wikr@acc.com. Web Site: www.wlkrradio.com.yes Licensee: Elyria-Lorain Broadcasting Co. (group owner; acq 4-9-02; with co-located FM). Network: Westwood One. Format: Oldies. News staff: one; News: 2 hrs wkly. Target aud: 40 plus. ♦Bill Hatheway, gen sls mgr; Shelly Luipold, rgnl sls mgr; Tim Kelly, stn mgr & progmg mgr; Scott Truxell, news dir; Ken Wilde, chief of engrg.

WLKR-FM— Sept 17, 1962: 95.3 mhz; 3 kw. 300 ft. TL: N41 16 49 W82 39 27. Stereo. yes Network: ABC Information & Entertainment. Format: MOR, adult contemp. News staff: one; News: 3 hrs wkly. Target aud: General; residents of Huron & Erie counties. Spec prog: Farm 3 hrs wkly. ♦Tim Kelly, mus dir; Carol Walters, pub affrs dir.

*WNRK(FM)— 2004: 90.7 mhz; 4 kw. Ant 407 ft. TL: N41 10 50 W82 23 21. c/o WKSU-FM, Box 5190, Kent 44242-0001. Secondary address: 1613 E. Summit St. 44242-0001. Phone: (330) 672-3114. Fax: (330) 672-4107. Web Site: www.wksu.org. Licensee: Kent State University. Network: Network: AP Radio, NPR, PRI. Dow, Lohnes & Albertson. Format: Classical, news. ♦Allen E. Bartholet, gen mgr; Deborah Frazier, gen mgr; N. Vincent Duffy, opns dir & progmg dir; Abbe Turner, dev dir; Ronald Bartlebaugh, engrg dir.

Oak Harbor

WJZE(FM)— August 1993: 97.3 mhz; 1.6 kw. 407 ft. TL: N41 29 17 W83 19 25. Stereo. 110 Ottawa St., Toledo 43602. Phone: (419) 255-6600. Fax: (419) 255-6600. Licensee: Urban Radio Licenses LLC. (acq 5-3-2005; $2.6 million). Smithwick & Belendiuk. Format: Active rock. News staff: one. Target aud: 25-64; general, upscale. Spec prog: Saturday nite Root Hoot blues show. ♦Clyde Roberts, gen mgr.

Oberlin

*WOBC-FM— November 1951: 91.5 mhz; 440 w. 124 ft. TL: N41 17 39 W82 13 26. (CP: 88.3 mhz, 3.5 kw). Stereo. Wilder Hall, 135 W. Lorain St. 44074. Phone: (440) 775-8107. Phone: (440) 775-8139. Fax: (440) 775-6678. Web Site: www.wobc.org. Licensee: Oberlin College Student Network Inc. Format: Div, educ. News: 5 hrs wkly. Target aud: General. Spec prog: Folk 12 hrs, Fr one hr, jazz 15 hrs, electronic 20 hrs wkly. ♦Dean Bein, stn mgr; Evan Smith, opns mgr & dev dir.

WOBL(AM)— Dec 24, 1971: 1320 khz; 1 kw-U, DA-2. TL: N41 16 05 W82 12 40. Box 277, 45624 Rt. 20 E. 44074. Phone: (440) 774-1320. Fax: (440) 774-1336. E-mail: woblwdlw@earthlink.net. Licensee: WOBL Inc. Reddy, Begley & McCormick, LLP. Format: Country Gold. News staff: 3; News: 14 hrs wkly. Target aud: 35-55. Spec prog: Farm 5 hrs, relg one hr wkly. ♦Doug Wilber, gen mgr; Terry Coffee, progmg dir & progmg mgr.

Ontario

WRGM(AM)— July 17, 1987: 1440 khz; 1 kw-D, DA. TL: N40 46 05 W82 37 04. Stereo. 2900 Park Ave. W., Mansfield 44906. Phone: (419) 529-5900. Fax: (419) 529-2319. Web Site: www.wrgm.com. Licensee: GSM Media Corp. Network: Network: ESPN Radio, Westwood One NBC Radio. Rep: Rgnl Reps. Format: Sports. News staff: 5; News: 10 hrs wkly. Target aud: 25 plus. Spec prog: High school football & basketball, NASCAR races. ♦Gunther Meisse, pres & gen mgr.

Ottawa

WBUK(FM)— Feb 4, 1977: 106.3 mhz; 1.4 kw. 489 ft. TL: N40 57 21 W83 54 42. Stereo. 1624 Tiffin Ave., Findlay 45840. Phone: (419) 425-1077. Fax: (419) 422-2954. Web Site: www.wbuk.com. Licensee:

Ohio
Directory of Radio

Citicasters Licenses L.P. Group owner: Clear Channel Communications Inc. (acq 1999; grpsl). Format: Oldies. News staff: one; News: 3 hrs wkly. Target aud: 18-49; affluent, upscale adults. Spec prog: Farm 5 hrs, sports 2 hrs, MOR 4 hrs wkly. ◆ Kim Fields, gen mgr.

Oxford

WMUB(FM)— 1950: 88.5 mhz; 24.5 kw. 499 ft. TL: N39 33 26 W84 47 35. Stereo. Williams Hall, Miami Univ. 45056. Phone: (513) 529-5885. Fax: (513) 529-6048. E-mail: wmub@wmub.org. Web Site: www.wmub.org. Licensee: President & Trustees of Miami University. Network: Network: NPR, PRI. Baker & Hostetler. Format: News/Talk/Jazz/Eclectic. News staff: 2; News: 42 hrs wkly. Target aud: General. Spec prog: Folk 5 hrs wkly. ◆ Cleve Callison, gen mgr; John E. Hingsbergen, progmg dir; Darrel Gray, news dir; Kim Keen, chief of engrg.

WOXY(FM)— Dec 24, 1959: 97.7 mhz; 3 kw. 255 ft. TL: N39 28 44 W84 45 51. (CP: Ant 321 ft.). Stereo. 5120 College Corner Pike 45056. Phone: (937) 378-6151. Fax: (513) 377-2200. Licensee: First Broadcasting Capital Partners LLC. Group owner: First Broadcasting Investment Partners LLC (acq 3-17-2004; $5.64 million). Fletcher, Heald & Hildreth. Format: Alternative. Target aud: 18-34. ◆ Heather Frye, gen mgr.

Painesville

WBKC(AM)— Apr 25, 1956: 1460 khz; 1 kw-D, 500 w-N, DA-2. TL: N41 44 20 W81 14 09. One Radio Pl. 44077. Phone: (440) 951-1460. Fax: (440) 352-8194. Fax: (440) 357-7701. E-mail: wbkc@wbkc.com. Web Site: www.wbkc.com. Licensee: Radio Advantage One LLC (acq 12-15-2004; $450,000). Format: News/talk, classical music. News staff: 3; News: 40 hrs wkly. Target aud: 35 plus. Spec prog: Cleveland Indians, Ohio State Buckeyes. ◆ Dale Edwards, pres; Clarence Bucaro, gen mgr.

Parma

WCCD(AM)— Jan 9, 1973: 1000 khz; 500 w-D, DA. TL: N41 19 11 W81 46 07. 4 Summit Park Dr., Suite 150, Independence 44131. Phone: (216) 901-0921, EXT. 205. Fax: (216) 901-1104. Licensee: Caron Broadcasting, Inc. Group owner: Salem Communications Corp. (acq 4-20-2005; $2.1 million). Network: Salem Radio Network. Format: Relg, talk. Target aud: 25-54. Spec prog: Black 3 hrs, Greek 2 hrs, Ukrainian one hr wkly. ◆ Errol Dengler, gen mgr.

Paulding

WKSD(FM)— Aug 14, 1989: 99.7 mhz; 3 kw. 328 ft. TL: N41 03 32 W84 35 30. Box 487, Van Wert 45891. Phone: (419) 238-1220. Fax: (419) 238-2578. Licensee: First Family Broadcasting Inc. (acq 1-3-95; $225,000; with WERT(AM) Van Wert; 3-6-95). Rep: Rgnl Reps. Format: Hot Adult Contemp. ◆ Chris Roberts, pres, gen mgr, progmg dir, news dir & chief of engrg; Mona Kennedy, gen sls mgr.

Piketon

WXZQ(FM)— December 1997: 100.1 mhz; 6 kw. 328 ft. TL: N39 05 53 W82 57 20. Stereo. Box 820 45661. Phone: (740) 947-0059. Fax: (740) 947-4600. Licensee: Piketon Communications. Format: Current hit radio. Target aud: 18-49. ◆ Gerald E. Davis, gen mgr; Tim Hughes, progmg dir.

Piqua

WDPT(FM)— Nov 30, 1960: 95.7 mhz; 50 kw. 476 ft. TL: N40 13 02 W84 17 35. Stereo. 1414 Wilmington Ave., Dayton 45420. Phone: (937) 259-2111. Fax: (937) 259-2328. Web Site: daytonspoints.com. Licensee: CXR Holdings L.L.C. Group owner: Cox Broadcasting (acq 1998; grpsl). Format: Hits of the 80s. Target aud: 25-54. ◆ Donna Hall, gen mgr; Nick Roberts, opns mgr; Marc Herbst, gen sls mgr; Jason Michaels, mus dir.

WPTW(AM)— November 1947: 1570 khz; 250 w-U. TL: N40 08 14 W84 16 00. Stereo. 1625 Covington Ave. 45356. Phone: (937) 773-3513. Fax: (937) 773-4345. E-mail: wptwnews@1570wptw.com. Web Site: www.1570wptw.com. Licensee: Frontier Broadcasting L.L.C. #2 (acq 5-28-99; $75,000). Network: CBS. Rep: Rgnl Reps. Miller & Fields. Format: Oldies. News staff: one; News: 8 hrs wkly. Target aud: 35 plus. Spec prog: Farm 6 hrs, sports sports 8 hrs wkly,. ◆ Bart Johnson, pres; Joe Neues, gen mgr.

Pleasant City

WBIK(FM)— 2002: 92.1 mhz; 6 kw. Ant 169 ft. TL: N40 01 37 W81 33 09. 4988 Skyline Dr., Cambridge 43725. Phone: (740) 432-5605. Fax: (740) 432-1991. Web Site: wbik.com. Licensee: David L. Wilson (acq 8-1-00). Format: Classic rock. ◆ David L. Wilson, gen mgr.

Pomeroy

WMPO(AM)—See Middleport-Pomeroy

Port Clinton

WXKR(FM)— Oct 4, 1961: 94.5 mhz; 30 kw. 640 ft. TL: N41 29 51 W83 16 12. Stereo. 3225 Arlington Ave., Toledo 43614. Secondary address: 2965 Pickle Rd., Oregon 43616. Phone: (419) 385-2507. Fax: (419) 385-2902. Web Site: www.wxkr.com. Licensee: Cumulus Licensing Corp. Group owner: Cumulus Media L.L.C. (acq 12-18-97; $5 million cash). Network: ABC. Fletcher, Heald & Hildreth. Format: Classic Rock. News staff: one; News: one hr wkly. Target aud: 25-49. Spec prog: Sp one hr wkly. ◆ Kathy Stinehour, gen mgr; Tim Roberts, opns dir; Beth Gleason, gen sls mgr; Ryan Young, prom dir; Andi McKay, progmg dir; Dave Waters, news dir; Kevin Hawley, engrg dir.

Portsmouth

WNXT(AM)— Aug 30, 1951: 1260 khz; 5 kw-D, 1 kw-N, DA-2. TL: N38 48 38 W82 59 21. Box 1228, Masonic Temple Bldg., 602 Chillicothe St. 45662. Phone: (740) 353-1161. Fax: (740) 353-8080. E-mail: wnxtradio@yahoo.com. Web Site: www.wnxt.cc. Licensee: Hometown Broadcasting of Portsmouth Inc. (acq 5-96; $477,500. with co-located FM). Network: ABC Information & Entertainment. Rep: Rgnl Reps. Pepper & Corazzini. Format: Classic country, news. News staff: one; News: 35 hrs wkly. Target aud: 24-60; office workers. Spec prog: Rush Limbaugh. ◆ Phillip Bruce Leslie, pres; Steve Hayes, exec VP; Rick Mayne, gen mgr & gen sls mgr; Sam McKibbin, news dir; Tyrone Henry, chief of engrg.

WNXT-FM— Sept 15, 1965: 99.3 mhz; 2.55 kw. 512 ft. TL: N38 43 20 W83 00 05. Stereo. Web Site: www.wnxt.cc. Format: Adult contemp. News staff: one; News: one hr wkly. Target aud: 18-34. ◆ Rick Mayne, stn mgr; Chris Smith, progmg mgr.

WOHP(FM)— Feb 18, 1992: 88.3 mhz; 1 kw. 643 ft. TL: N38 43 20 W83 00 05. Box 601, 251 N. Main St., Cedarville 45314. Phone: (937) 766-7815. Fax: (937) 766-7927. Web Site: www.thepath.fm. Licensee: The Cedarville University. Cohen & Berfield. Format: Relg, full-service. News staff: one; News: 16 hrs wkly. Target aud: 35-54; church oriented audience. Spec prog: Black 2 hrs wkly. ◆ William Brown, pres; Paul Gathany, gen mgr; Keith Hamer, opns mgr.

WOSP(FM)— May 25, 1993: 91.5 mhz; 110 w. 1,207 ft. TL: N38 45 42 W83 03 41. Stereo. 2400 Olentangy River Rd., Columbus 43210. Phone: (614) 292-9678. Fax: (614) 292-0513. Web Site: www.wosu.org. Licensee: The Ohio State University. Network: Network: PRI, NPR, AP Radio. Dow, Lohnes & Albertson. Format: Classical. Target aud: 35 plus. ◆ Thomas Rieland, gen mgr; Tim Eby, stn mgr; Kevin Petrilla, opns mgr. Co-owned TV: *WPBO-TV affil.

WPAY(AM)— Apr 15, 1935: 1400 khz; 800 w-U. TL: N38 43 22 W83 00 05. 1009 Gallia St. 45662-4140. Phone: (740) 353-5176. Fax: (740) 353-1715. E-mail: comments@f1400wpay.com. Web Site: www.1400wpay.com. Licensee: WPAY Inc. Group owner: WPAY/WPFB Inc. (acq 2-1-57). Network: CBS. Format: Talk. Target aud: 18-65; young, affluent & upwardly mobile adults. Spec prog: Gospel 6 hrs wkly. ◆ Douglas Braden, pres; Frank Lewis, gen mgr; Lorenzo Bentley, news dir.

WPAY-FM— June 15, 1948: 104.1 mhz; 100 kw. 1,000 ft. TL: N38 43 20 W83 00 05. Stereo. Web Site: www.104wpay.com. Network: CBS. Format: Country.

WZZZ(FM)— January 2003: 107.5 mhz; 2.6 kw. Ant 495 ft. TL: N38 43 22 W82 59 56. Stereo. Box 1228 45662. Secondary address: 602 Chillicothe St. 45662. Phone: (740) 353-1161. Fax: (740) 353-3191. E-mail: wnxtradio@yahoo.com. Web Site: www.1075thebreeze.com. Licensee: Hometown Broadcasting of Portsmouth 2 Inc (acq 6-28-02). Rgnl Reps Smithwick & Bellendiuk. P.C. Format: Classic rock. News staff: one; News: .25 hrs wkly. Target aud: 25-54; working class and progessional adults. ◆ Rick Mayne, gen mgr; Steve Hayes, opns dir; Mistie Cook, news dir; Tyrone Henry, chief of engrg.

Proctorville

*WMEJ(FM)— Jan 25, 1986: 91.9 mhz; 3.5 kw. 220 ft. TL: N38 27 14 W82 25 05. Stereo. Box 7575, Huntington, WV 25777. Phone: (740) 867-5333. Licensee: Maranatha Broadcasting Inc. Format: Easy lstng Christian mus. Target aud: General. ◆ Paul S. Warren, pres; Tim Jenkins, gen mgr.

Reading

*WMKV(FM)— 1995: 89.3 mhz; 41 kw. 236 ft. TL: N39 13 23 W84 25 56. Stereo. 11100 Springfield Pike, Cincinnati 45246. Phone: (513) 782-2427. Fax: (513) 782-2720. Web Site: www.wmkvfm.org. Licensee: Lifesphere. Format: Nostalgia. Target aud: 50 plus. ◆ Alan Bayowski, gen mgr & stn mgr.

Richwood

WJZK(FM)— Nov 30, 1995: 104.3 mhz; 3.4 kw. 436 ft. TL: N40 21 52 W83 15 34. 4401 Carriage Hill Ln., Columbus 43220. Phone: (614) 451-2191. Fax: (614) 451-1831. Licensee: Franklin Communications Inc. Group owner: Saga Communications Inc. (acq 10-1-2003; $13 million. with WJZA(FM) Lancaster). Format: Smooth jazz. Target aud: 25-54. Spec prog: New age 2 hrs wkly. ◆ Alan Goodman, gen mgr.

Ripley

WAOL(FM)— 1993: 99.5 mhz; 3 kw. 328 ft. TL: N38 45 14 W83 50 24. 8354 Fryer Rd., Georgetown 45121. Phone: (937) 378-6151. Fax: (937) 377-2200. Web Site: www.classiccountry995.com. Licensee: First Broadcasting Capital Partners LLC. Group owner: First Broadcasting Investment Partners LLC (acq 3-17-2004; $4.06 million. with WAXZ(FM) Georgetown). Format: Classic country. ◆ Heather Frye, gen mgr.

Rossford

WDMN(AM)— Nov 28, 1966: 1520 khz; 500 w-D, 400 w-N, DA-2. TL: N41 30 32 W83 33 07. 1520 S. Reynolds Rd., Maumee 43537. Phone: (419) 725-9366/725-1520. Fax: (419) 725-2600. Web Site: www.toledo1520am.com. Licensee: Cornerstone Church Inc. (acq 5-20-98; $200,000). Network: American Urban. Rep: Roslin. Rgnl Reps. Format: Contemp Christian. Target aud: 25-59; older established audience. Spec prog: Relg (church ministry). ◆ Robert Pitts, gen mgr.

Rushville

*WLRY(FM)— December 1998: 88.5 mhz; 1 kw vert. Ant 138 ft. TL: N39 46 43 W82 25 25. (CP: 900 w, ant 298 ft). Box 220, Arcangel Broadcasting Foundation 43150. Phone: (740) 536-0885. Fax: (740) 536-1885. E-mail: wlry@wlry.org. Web Site: www.wlry.org. Licensee: Arcangel Broadcasting Foundation. Network: USA. Format: Regl, Christian, talk. News: 40 hrs wkly. Target aud: 15-55; youth & adult mentors. Spec prog: Issues talk 16 hrs wkly. ◆ Richard Finke, gen mgr.

Saint Mary's

WKKI(FM)—See Celina

WMLX(FM)— 1998: 103.3 mhz; 950 w. 823 ft. TL: N40 38 03 W84 12 29. Box 1128, Lima 45802. Secondary address: 667 W. Market St., Lima 45801. Phone: (419) 223-2060. Fax: (419) 229-3888. E-mail: comments@wmlx.com. Web Site: www.1075thebreeze.com. Licensee: Clear Channel Radio Licenses, Inc. Group owner: Clear Channel Communications Inc. (acq 5-4-99; grpsl). Format: Hits of the 80s & 90s, adult contemp. News: 2 hrs wkly. Target aud: 18-49; women. ◆ Bill Gentry, sr VP & opns mgr; Art Versnick, VP & gen mgr; Phil Austin, opns mgr; Jennifer Cartwright, sls dir; Jack Wheelbarger, natl sls mgr; Tom Francis, rgnl sls mgr; Kathy Hague, progmg dir; Mark Gierhart, engrg dir.

WZOQ(FM)—See Wapakoneta

Salem

WQXK(FM)—Listing follows WSOM(AM).

WSOM(AM)— June 2, 1965: 600 khz; 1 kw-D, 45 w-N, DA-2. TL: N40 49 47 W80 55 54. 4040 Simon Rd, Youngstown 44512. Phone: (330) 783-1000. Fax: (330) 783-0060. Web Site: www.600wsom.com. Licensee: Cumulus Licensing Corp. Group owner: Cumulus Media Inc. (acq 3-15-00; grpsl). Rep: Allied Radio Partners. Kaye, Scholer,

Stations in the U.S. — Ohio

Developers & Brokers of Radio Properties

contact American Media Services at our suite:
Philadelphia Marriott Downtown
215-625-2900
843-972-2200
americanmediaservices.com
Charleston, SC
Dallas, TX • Chicago, Il • Austin, TX

American Media Services, LLC

Fierman, Hays & Handler. Format: Nostalgia. Target aud: 35 plus. Spec prog: Farm 2 hrs wkly. ♦ Lou Dickey, CEO; Donna Palowitz, gen sls mgr; Tim Roberts, progmg dir; Wes Boyd, chief of engrg.

WQXK(FM)—Co-owned with WSOM(AM). Nov 25, 1958: 105.1 mhz; 88 kw. Ant 430 ft. TL: N40 53 06 W80 49 50. (CP: N40 53 08 W80 49 55). Stereo. Web Site: www.q105country.com. Format: Country. Target aud: 25-54. ♦ Dave Steele, progmg dir.

Sandusky

WCPZ(FM)— Aug 15, 1959: 102.7 mhz; 50 kw. 141 ft. TL: N41 26 29 W82 41 12. Stereo. 1640 Cleveland Rd. 44870. Phone: (419) 625-1010. Fax: (419) 625-1348. Web Site: www.wcpz.com. Licensee: Citicasters Licenses L.P. Group owner: Clear Channel Communications Inc. (acq 5-4-99; grpsl). Format: Hot AC. News: 2 hrs wkly. Target aud: 18-54. ♦ Lisa Rice, gen mgr & gen sls mgr; Randi Hugg, opns mgr; Paul Mize, progmg dir; Nick Paolano, mus dir; Steve Schoffner, news dir; Gary Homza, chief of engrg.

WLEC(AM)—Co-owned with WCPZ(FM). Dec 7, 1947: 1450 khz; 1 kw-U. TL: N41 26 29 W82 41 10. Phone: (419) 626-2000. Web Site: www.wlec.com. Network: CBS. Rgnl Reps. Format: American music classics. News: 2 hrs wkly. Target aud: 35 plus. ♦ Mark Fogg, progmg dir; Steve Shoffner, news dir.

WGGN(FM)—See Castalia

*WVMS(FM)— December 1993: 89.5 mhz; 2.12 kw horiz, 5.36 kw vert. Ant 69 ft. TL: N41 26 29 W82 48 20. c/o Radio Stn WCRF(FM), 9756 Barr Rd., Cleveland 44141. Phone: (440) 526-1111. Fax: (440) 526-1319. E-mail: wcrf@moody.edu. Web Site: wcrfradio.org. Licensee: The Moody Bible Institute of Chicago. Format: Inspirational, relg, Christian. ♦ Richard Lee, stn mgr; Gary Bittner, mus dir; Doug Hainer, chief of engrg.

Shadyside

WVKF(FM)— Sept 1, 1990: 95.7 mhz; 6.8 kw horiz, 6.67 kw vert. Ant 626 ft. TL: N40 03 41 W80 45 09. Clear Channel Communications, 1015 Main St., Wheeling, WV 26003-2709. Phone: (304) 232-1170. Fax: (304) 234-0067. Web Site: www.wvkffm.com. Licensee: Capstar TX L.P. Group owner: Clear Channel Communications Inc. (acq 2-26-2004; $930,000). Rep: Christal. Format: CHR. ♦ Scott Miller, gen mgr; Mike Allodi, gen sls mgr; Jim Elliott, progmg dir.

Shelby

*WAUI(FM)— November 1998: 88.3 mhz; 900 w. Ant 138 ft. TL: N40 55 14 W82 38 51. Box 3206 American Family Radio, Tupelo, MS 38803. Phone: (662) 844-8888. Fax: (662) 842-6791. Web Site: www.afr.net. Licensee: Kayser Broadcast Ministries Inc. Group owner: American Family Radio (acq 4-7-2005; $1.5 million. with WBIE(FM) Delphos). Format: Inspirational Christian. ♦ Marvin Sanders, gen mgr.

WSWR(FM)— Dec 1, 1981: 100.1 mhz; 3 kw. 300 ft. TL: N40 56 42 W82 39 42. Stereo. 100 E. River Center Blvd., 9th Fl., Covington 41011. Phone: (859) 292-0030. Fax: (859) 292-0352. Web Site: www.regentcomm.com. Licensee: Regent Licensee of Mansfield Inc. Group owner: Regent Communications Inc. (acq 12-19-97; grpsl). Format: Oldies. Spec prog: Farm 12 hrs wkly. ♦ Diana Coon, gen mgr.

Sidney

WMVR-FM— 1965: 105.5 mhz; 3 kw. Ant 155 ft. TL: N40 18 04 W84 12 21. Stereo. 2929 W. Russell Rd. 45365. Phone: (937) 498-1055. Fax: (937) 498-2277. E-mail: hits@hits1055.com. Licensee: Dean Miller Broadcasting Corp. (acq 6-10-2004). Rep: Rgnl Reps. Format: Adult contemp. ♦ Dean Miller, pres; Brad Smith, gen mgr & mus dir; Debby McNeely, prom dir.

South Vienna

*WVSO(FM)—Not on air, target date: unknown: 88.3 mhz; 700 w vert. Ant 298 ft. TL: N39 56 12 W83 36 25. Box 2440, Tupelo, MS 38803-2440. Phone: (662) 844-8888. Fax: (662) 842-6791. Licensee: American Family Association. (acq 6-20-2005). ♦ Donald E. Wildmon, chmn; Marvin Sanders, gen mgr.

South Webster

WSNA(FM)— 1996: 94.9 mhz; 3 kw. Ant 328 ft. TL: N38 45 39 W82 43 17. Box 478, Wheelersburg 45694. Secondary address: Box 506, Chillicothe 45601. Phone: (740) 574-9497. Fax: (740) 574-6895. Licensee: IM-Media Broadcasting Inc. (acq 11-5-2003). Format: Classic rock. News staff: one.

South Zanesville

*WCVZ(FM)— Jan 5, 1983: 92.7 mhz; 16 kw. 304 ft. TL: N39 56 55 W81 57 48. (CP: Ant 407 ft.). Stereo. 2477 E. Pike 43701-4626. Secondary address: Box 3208, Zanesville 43701. Phone: (740) 455-3181. Fax: (740) 455-6195. E-mail: joyfm@927joyfm.com. Web Site: www.927joyfm.com. Licensee: Christian Voice of Central Ohio Inc. Network: USA. Format: Relg, talk, adult contemp. News: 10 hrs wkly. Target aud: General; young children 5-10 to senior citizens. ♦ Dan Baughman, pres & gen mgr; Tate Luck, opns mgr; Michael James, progmg dir; Mike Russell, mus dir.

Spencerville

*WBCJ(FM)— Sept 1, 1997: 88.1 mhz; 2.6 kw. 492 ft. TL: N40 42 41 W84 23 01. 1025 W. Rudisill Blvd., Fort Wayne, IN 46807. Phone: (260) 745-0576. Fax: (260) 745-2001. E-mail: wbcl@wbcl.org. Web Site: www.wbcl.org. Licensee: Taylor University Broadcasting Inc. Format: Contemp Christian. ♦ Craig Albrecht, opns mgr; Janelle Becker, prom dir.

Springfield

WDHT(FM)— August 1958: 102.9 mhz; 50 kw. 492 ft. TL: N39 57 11 W83 52 07. Stereo. 717 E. David Rd., Dayton 45429. Phone: (937) 294-5858. Fax: (937) 297-5233. Web Site: www.hot1029.com. Licensee: Blue Chip Broadcasting Licenses Ltd. Group owner: Radio One Inc. (acq 4-30-01; grpsl). Format: Mainstream Urban. Target aud: General. ♦ Don Griffin, gen mgr; J.D. Kunes, opns mgr & progmg dir; Keith Wright, gen sls mgr; Tom Nornhold, chief of engrg.

*WEEC(FM)— Dec 15, 1961: 100.7 mhz; 50 kw. 469 ft. TL: N39 57 42 W83 52 05. Stereo. 2265 Troy Rd. 45504. Phone: (937) 399-7837. Fax: (937) 399-7802. E-mail: info@weec.org. Web Site: www.weec.org. Licensee: World Evangelistic Enterprise Corp. Network: Network: Network: USA, Moody, AP Radio. Miller & Neely. Format: Relg, Christian. News staff: one; News: 16 hrs wkly. Target aud: 40 plus; general. Spec prog: Black one hr, farm one hr wkly. ♦ Duane Helman, pres; Newell Moore, VP; Tracy Figley, CEO & gen mgr.

WIZE(AM)— Nov 1, 1940: 1340 khz; 1 kw-U. TL: N39 56 33 W83 47 15. 101 Pine St., Dayton 45402. Phone: (937) 224-1137. Fax: (937) 224-3667. E-mail: tonytilford@clearchannel.com. Web Site: www.wize.com. Licensee: Citicasters Licenses L.P. Group owner: Clear Channel Communications Inc. (acq 5-4-99; grpsl). Network: ABC Information & Entertainment. Rgnl Reps. Haley, Bader & Potts. Format: Sports. News staff: one; News: 14 hrs wkly. Target aud: 25 plus; upper income, businesses, offices. ♦ Karrie Sudbrack, gen mgr; Tony Tilford, progmg dir; Jeff Bennett, chief of engrg.

WULM(AM)— 1947: 1600 khz; 1 kw-D, 34 w-N. TL: N39 57 11 W83 52 07. 1529 Miracle Mile Rd. 45503. Phone: (937) 390-1693. Fax: (937) 399-8767. E-mail: webmaster@1600wuim.net. Web Site: www.1600wulm.net. Licensee: Urban Light Ministries Inc. (acq 4-9-02; $250,000). Network: Network: CNN Radio, Westwood One. Rep: Rgnl Reps. Haley, Bader & Potts. Format: Oldies. News staff: 2. Target aud: 34-54. Spec prog: Gospel. ♦ Eli Williams, CEO & pres; Judy Williams, CFO; Robert Pitsch, gen mgr; Marco Simmons, stn mgr.

*WUSO(FM)— Feb 20, 1966: 89.1 mhz; 10 w. 1,109 ft. TL: N39 56 09 W83 48 43. Box 720, Wittenberg Univ. 45501. Phone: (937) 327-7026. Fax: (937) 327-6340. Licensee: Wittenberg University. Format: Progsv, rock. Target aud: General; liberal arts students & residents of Springfield, OH. Spec prog: Jazz 6 hrs, class 3 hrs, blues 3 hrs, urban contemp 9 hrs wkly. ♦ Jason Williams, gen mgr.

Steubenville

*WBJV(FM)— 2002: 88.9 mhz; 125 w. Ant 256 ft. TL: N40 21 56 W80 43 36. Drawer 3206, Tupelo, MS 38803. Phone: (662) 844-8888. Fax: (662) 842-6791. Licensee: American Family Association. Group owner: American Family Radio. Format: Christian. ♦ Marvin Sanders, gen mgr.

WDIG(AM)— Sept 25, 1973: 950 khz; 1 kw-D, DA. TL: N40 26 49 W80 34 06. 4039 Sunset Blvd. 43952. Phone: (740) 264-1760. Fax: (740) 264-5035. Licensee: World Witness For Christ Ministries Inc. Network: American Urban. Format: Urban, oldies. Target aud: 25-54; general. ♦ Roy Dawkins, CEO; Del King, gen mgr & engrg VP.

WKWK-FM—See Wheeling, WV

WSTV(AM)— Nov 4, 1940: 1340 khz; 1 kw-U. TL: N40 26 49 W80 34 06. Box 1340 43952. Secondary address: 320 Market St. 43952. Phone: (740) 283-4747. Fax: (740) 283-3655. E-mail: wstv@wstv.com. Web Site: www.wstv.com. Licensee: Keymarket Licences LLC. Group owner: Keymarket Communications LLC (acq 3-20-00; grpsl). Network: Westwood One. Rep: Rgnl Reps. Fleischman & Walsh L. Format: News/talk. News staff: 2; News: 5 hrs wkly. Target aud: 35 plus. Spec prog: Po 2 hrs, Czech 2 hrs wkly. ♦ Gerald Getz, pres; Jim Seemiller, gen mgr; Joyce Nicholson, opns mgr, progmg mgr & pub affrs dir; Frank Bell, progmg VP; Marjie De Fede, news dir; Greg Harper, chief of engrg.

WOGH(FM)—Co-owned with WSTV(AM). May 1, 1947: 103.5 mhz; 19.5 kw. Ant 810 ft. TL: N40 20 33 W80 37 14. Stereo. Web Site: www.froggyland.com. Format: Country. Target aud: 25-54. ♦ Stu Schroeder, prom mgr; Scott Feist, progmg dir & mus dir.

Streetsboro

*WSTB(FM)— September 1973: 88.9 mhz; 1 kw. 125 ft. TL: N41 14 02 W81 19 29. 1900 Annalane Dr. 44241. Phone: (330) 626-4906. Fax: (330) 626-4906. E-mail: wstbfm@wstbfm.com. Web Site: www.rock889.com. Licensee: Streetsboro City Schools. Format: Modern rock. News staff: one; News: 4 hrs wkly. Target aud: 16-34. ♦ Robert L. Long, gen mgr; Adam Oliver, opns mgr.

Struthers

*WKTL(FM)— Sept 6, 1965: 90.7 mhz; 15 kw. 23 ft. TL: N41 03 06 W80 35 56. Stereo. Struthers High School, 111 Euclid Ave. 44471. Phone: (330) 755-1435. Fax: (330) 755-4525. Licensee: Struthers Board of Education. Format: Adult contemp, classic rock. Spec prog: Hungarian one hr, Lithuanian one hr, Irish one hr, Greek one hr, Sp one hr, Ukranian one hr, Pol 14 hrs wkly. ♦ Tom Krestal, gen mgr; Jim Hartzler, chief of engrg.

Swanton

WJUC(FM)—Licensed to Swanton. See Toledo

Sylvania

WWWM-FM— Nov 29, 1968: 105.5 mhz; 2.15 kw. Ant 390 ft. TL: N41 38 48 W83 36 22. (CP: 2.7 kw). Stereo. 3225 Arlington Ave., Toledo 43614. Secondary address: 2965 Pickle Rd., Oregon 43616. Phone: (419) 385-2507. Fax: (419) 385-2902. Web Site: www.star105toledo.com. Licensee: Cumulus Licensing Corp. Group owner: Cumulus Media L.L.C. (acq 9-11-97; $10 million with WLQR(AM) Toledo). Rep: D & R Radio. Format: Hot Adult Contemp. Target aud: 25-54. ♦ Clyde Roberts, exec VP; Kathy Stinehour, gen mgr; Carolyn Smithers, sls dir

Ohio   Directory of Radio

& adv dir; Lyn Casye, prom dir & news dir; Ryan Young, prom dir; Steve Mars, progmg dir; Kevin Howley, chief of engrg.

Thompson

WKSV(FM)— June 1997: 89.1 mhz; 50 kw. 489 ft. TL: N41 41 29 W81 02 49. Stereo. c/o WKSU-FM, Box 5190, 1613 E. Summit St., Kent 44242-0001. Phone: (330) 672-3114. Fax: (330) 672-4107. Web Site: www.wksu.org. Licensee: Kent State University. Network: Network: NPR, PRI, AP Radio. Dow, Lohnes & Albertson. Format: Class, news. News staff: 5; News: 35 hrs wkly. Target aud: 35-65; college grad, professional & upper income. ◆ Allen E. Bartholet, gen mgr; Deborah Frazier, gen mgr; N. Vincent Duffy, opns dir, prom dir, progmg dir & news dir; Abbe Turner, dev dir; Ronald Bartlebaugh, engrg dir.

Tiffin

WCKY-FM—Listing follows WTTF(AM).

WHEI(FM)— Sept 13, 1972: 88.9 mhz; 100 w. 59 ft. TL: N41 06 59 W83 10 03. Founder's Hall, 310 E. Market St., Heidelberg College 44883. Phone: (419) 448-2283. Phone: (419) 448-2282. Fax: (419) 448-2124. E-mail: whei@heidelberg.edu. Licensee: Heidelberg College. Format: Progsv. ◆ Dr. Gary Dickerson, gen mgr.

WTTF(AM)— Dec 19, 1959: 1600 khz; 500 w-D, 20 w-N, DA-1. TL: N41 07 32 W83 13 45. 122 S. Washington St. 44883. Phone: (419) 447-2212. Fax: (419) 447-1709. Web site: www.wttf.com. Licensee: Citicasters Licenses L.P. Group owner: Clear Channel Communications Inc. (acq 5-4-99; grpsl). Network: ABC Information & Entertainment. Miller & Miller, P.C. Format: Adult contemp, oldies. News staff: 2; News: 18 hrs wkly. Target aud: General. Spec prog: Farm 3 hrs wkly. ◆ Kim Field, gen mgr; Jim Bickel, progmg dir; Greg Salbolda, chief of engrg.

WCKY-FM—Co-owned with WTTF(AM). July 11, 1963: 103.7 mhz; 50 kw. 492 ft. TL: N41 08 20 W83 14 45. Stereo. Web Site: www.1037wcky.com. Format: Country.

Toledo

WCWA(AM)— Apr 10, 1938: 1230 khz; 1 kw-U. TL: N41 38 13 W83 33 52. 125 S. Superior 43602. Phone: (419) 244-8321. Fax: (419) 244-7631. E-mail: wcwa@clearchannel.com. Web site: www.wcwa.com. Licensee: Jacor Broadcasting Corp. Group owner: Clear Channel Communications Inc. (acq 1999; grpsl). Rep: Clear Channel. Hogan & Hartson. Format: News/talk. Target aud: 25-54; male. Spec prog: Ger one hr, Pol one hr, relg 3 hrs, sports 15 hrs wkly. ◆ John Hogan, CEO; Andy Stuart, VP & gen mgr; Jack Jolly, gen sls mgr; Kellie Holeman, sls dir & mktg dir; Al Brandy Law, prom mgr & progmg dir.

WIOT(FM)—Co-owned with WCWA(AM). October 1949: 104.7 mhz; 50 kw. 540 ft. TL: N41 40 23 W83 25 31. Stereo. Web Site: www.wiot.com. (Acq 1997). Format: Rock/AOR. Spec prog: Progsv rock 2 hrs, metal 2 hrs wkly. ◆ Brian Kohler, gen sls mgr; Don Grosselin, progmg dir.

WGTE-FM— May 2, 1976: 91.3 mhz; 13.5 kw. 949 ft. TL: N41 39 27 W83 25 55. Stereo. 1270 S. Detroit Ave. 43614. Phone: (419) 380-4600. Fax: (419) 380-4710. Web site: www.wgte.org. Licensee: The Public Broadcasting Foundation of Northwest Ohio. Network: Network: NPR, PRI. Schwartz, Woods & Miller. Format: Class, NPR, News, Public Affairs. News: 23 hrs wkly. Target aud: General. Spec prog: Jazz 16 hrs, new age 4 hrs wkly. ◆ Marlon P. Kiser, CEO, pres & gen mgr; George Jones, chmn; Chris Peiffer, opns mgr; Ross Pfieffer, dev dir. Co-owned TV: *WGTE-TV affil.

WJUC(FM)—(Swanton). Feb 27, 1997: 107.3 mhz; 3 kw. 328 ft. TL: N41 38 30 W83 54 03. Box 351450 43635-1450. Secondary address: 5902 Southwyck Blvd. 43614. Phone: (419) 861-9582. Fax: (419) 861-2866. E-mail: wcharleswelch@aol.com. Licensee: Welch Communications Inc. Rep: Allied Radio Partners. Interep J. Richard Carr. Format: Urban, rhythm & blues. Target aud: 18-54; African Americans 70%, others 30%. Spec prog: Blues, gospel. ◆ W. Charles Welch, CEO, chmn, pres & gen mgr.

WJYM(AM)—See Bowling Green

WKKO(FM)—Listing follows WTOD(AM).

WLQR(AM)— October 1954: 1470 khz; 1 kw-U, DA-2. TL: N41 37 55 W83 28 45. 3225 Arlington Ave. 43614. Phone: (419) 385-2507. Fax: (419) 385-2902. Licensee: Cumulus Licensing Corp. Group owner: Cumulus Media L.L.C. (acq 9-11-97; $10 million with WWWM-FM Sylvania). Format: Sports. Target aud: 25-54. ◆ Kathy Stinehour, gen mgr.

WOTL(FM)— Mar 24, 1988: 90.3 mhz; 700 w. 377 ft. TL: N41 38 48 W83 36 22. Stereo. 13 Fairlane Dr., Joliet, IL 60435. Secondary address: 716 N. Westwood Ave. 43607. Phone: (815) 725-1331. Web Site: www.familyradio.com. Licensee: Family Stations Inc. (group owner) Format: Relg. Target aud: General. ◆ Harold Camping, pres; John Rorvik, gen mgr.

WRVF(FM)—Listing follows WSPD(AM).

WSPD(AM)— Apr 15, 1921: 1370 khz; 5 kw-U, DA-N. TL: N41 36 03 W83 32 11. Stereo. 125 S. Superior St. 43602. Phone: (419) 244-8321. Fax: (419) 244-7631. Web Site: www.wspd.com. Licensee: Citicasters Licenses L.P. Group owner: Clear Channel Communications Inc. (acq 5-4-99; grpsl). Network: ABC Information & Entertainment. Rgnl Reps. Hogan & Hartson. Format: News/talk. Target aud: 25-54; mostly males. Spec prog: Relg 5 hrs, farm 3 hrs wkly. ◆ Andy Stuart, VP; Jack Jolly, gen sls mgr & rgnl sls mgr; Kellie Holeman, sls dir & natl sls mgr; A.T. Simen, prom dir & prom mgr; Al Brady Law, progmg dir.

WRVF(FM)—Co-owned with WSPD(AM). Aug 11, 1946: 101.5 mhz; 19.1 kw. 810 ft. TL: N41 41 00 W83 24 29. Stereo. Web Site: www.wrvf.com. Rep: Clear Channel. Format: Adult contemp. Target aud: 25-54; mostly female. Spec prog: Jazz 6 hrs wkly. ◆ Maureen DeTange, gen sls mgr; Don Gosselin, progmg dir.

WTOD(AM)— June 16, 1946: 1560 khz; 5 kw-D, DA. TL: N41 36 59 W83 37 22. 3225 Arlington Ave. 43614. Phone: (419) 725-5700. Fax: (419) 385-2902. Web site: www.am1560wtod.com. Licensee: Cumulus Licensing Corp. Group owner: Cumulus Media Inc. (acq 9-11-97; grpsl). Network: ABC Information & Entertainment. Format: Contemp country. News staff: one; News: 3 hrs wkly. Target aud: 25-54; adults. Spec prog: Pol 4 hrs wkly. ◆ Kathy Stinehour, gen mgr; Gary Shores, progmg dir; London Mitchell, news dir; Kevin Hawley, chief of engrg.

WKKO(FM)—Co-owned with WTOD(AM). Dec 7, 1956: 99.9 mhz; 50 kw. 499 ft. TL: N41 40 05 W83 27 01. (CP: 6.8 kw, ant 180 ft. TL: N41 37 00 W83 37 19). Stereo. Web Site: www.k100country.com. Network: ABC. ◆ Gary Outlaw, mus dir.

WVKS(FM)— Oct 14, 1957: 92.5 mhz; 50 kw. 480 ft. TL: N41 31 55 W83 35 37. Stereo. 125 S. Superior 43602. Phone: (419) 244-8321. Fax: (419) 244-7631. Web site: www.925kissfm.com. Licensee: Citicasters Licenses L.P. Group owner: Clear Channel Communications Inc. (acq 5-15-99; grpsl). Rep: Clear Channel. Hogan & Hartson. Format: CHR. News staff: one; News: one hr wkly. Target aud: 18-49; educated, employed adults, mostly females. ◆ Andrew Stuart, gen mgr; Bill Michaels, opns dir & progmg dir; Kellie Holeman, sls dir; Amy Jo Simon, prom dir.

WWWM-FM—See Sylvania

WXTS-FM— February 1975: 88.3 mhz; 1 kw. 125 ft. TL: N41 40 07 W83 33 15. Stereo. 2400 Collingwood Blvd. 43620. Phone: (419) 244-6875. Fax: (419) 249-8248. Licensee: Toledo Board of Education. Format: Jazz. Target aud: 28-55. Spec prog: Blues 5 hrs wkly. ◆ John Kuschell, gen mgr.

WXUT(FM)— Nov 4, 1990: 88.3 mhz; 100 w horiz. 190 ft. TL: N41 39 26 W83 36 57. Stereo. Student Union, 2801 W. Bancroft St. 43606. Phone: (419) 530-4172. Phone: (419) 530-4455. Fax: (419) 530-2210. E-mail: wxut@wxut.com. Web site: www.wxut.com. Licensee: University of Toledo. Format: Alternative. News: 4 hrs wkly. Target aud: General. Spec prog: Black 8 hrs, heavy metal 4 hrs, R&B 2 hrs, poetry one hr, women 2 hrs, gay 2 hrs wkly. ◆ Terrance Teagarden, gen mgr; Chad Mikant, stn mgr; Eric Toth, stn mgr.

Troy

WDPT(FM)—See Piqua

WOKL(FM)— 1991: 96.9 mhz; 3 kw. Ant 315 ft. TL: N40 01 41 W84 11 28. Stereo. 5700 W. Oaks Blvd., Rocklin, CA 95765. Phone: (916) 251-1600. Fax: (916) 251-1650. E-mail: klove@klove.com. Web Site: www.klove.com. Licensee: Educational Media Foundation. Group owner: EMF Broadcasting (acq 7-17-03; $1.2 million). Network: K-Love. Shaw Pittman. Format: Contemp Christian. News staff: 3. Target aud: 25-44; Judeo Christian, female. ◆ Richard Jenkins, pres; Mike Novak, VP; Lloyd Parker, gen mgr; Ed Lenane, opns dir & news dir; Keith Whipple, dev dir; Eric Allen, natl sls mgr; Amy Baumann, rgnl sls mgr; Chris Joyce, prom dir; Mike Novak, progmg dir; David Pierce, progmg mgr; Jon Rivers, mus dir; Sam Wallington, engrg dir.

Uhrichsville

WBTC(AM)— Dec 13, 1963: 1540 khz; 250 w-D, 5 w-N. TL: N40 25 26 W81 21 47. 125 Johnson Dr. 44683. Phone: (740) 922-2700. Fax: (740) 922-2702. E-mail: jim@wbtcam.com. Licensee: Tuscarawas Broadcasting Co. Network: CBS. Rep: Rgnl Reps. Format: News/talk, sports. Target aud: 30-55. Spec prog: Relg 2 hrs wkly. ◆ James Natoli Jr., pres, stn mgr & gen sls mgr; J.R. Richards, progmg dir.

WTUZ(FM)—Licensed to Uhrichsville. See New Philadelphia

Union City

WTGR(FM)— Dec 31, 1994: . Stn currently dark 97.5 mhz; 6 kw. Ant 328 ft. TL: N40 11 32 W84 47 58. Box 176, Greenville 45331. Secondary address: 514 Martin St., Greenville 45331. Phone: (937) 548-5085. Fax: (937) 548-5089. Web site: www.wtgr.com. Licensee: Positive Radio Group Inc. of Ohio. Group owner: Baker Family Stations. Network: CNN Radio. Format: Country. News staff: one; News: one hr wkly. Target aud: 25-54; 25-49 female. ◆ Vernon H. Baker, CEO; Edward A. Baker, VP; Chris Clift, stn mgr.

University Heights

WJCU(FM)— May 13, 1969: 88.7 mhz; 850 w. 321 ft. TL: N41 29 24 W81 31 54. Stereo. John Carroll Univ., 20700 N. Park Blvd., Cleveland 44118. Phone: (216) 397-4437. Phone: (216) 397-4438. Fax: (216) 397-4439. E-mail: wjcu@jcu.edu. Web site: www.wjcu.org. Licensee: John Carroll University. Network: AP Radio. Format: Div, modern, progsv. News: one hr wkly. Target aud: General. Spec prog: It 2 hrs, folk 2 hrs, Pol 2 hrs, Lithuanian 2 hrs, Hungarian 3 hrs, Armenian 2 hrs, Celtic 2 hrs wkly. ◆ Dave Reese, gen mgr; Matt Taylor, stn mgr.

Upper Arlington

WXMG(FM)— May 25, 1989: 98.9 mhz; 3 kw. 328 ft. TL: N39 58 16 W83 01 40. (CP: 2.6 kw, ant 505 ft.). Stereo. 1500 W. 3rd Ave., Suite 300, Columbus 43212. Phone: (614) 487-1444. Fax: (614) 487-5862. Web Site: www.wxmg.fm.com. Licensee: Blue Chip Broadcasting Licenses Ltd. Group owner: Radio One Inc. (acq 4-30-01; grpsl). Rep: Christal. Fisher, Wayland, Cooper, Leader & Zaragoza. Format: Soul/rhythm and blues. News staff: one. Target aud: 25-54; upscale, educated, active & responsive. ◆ Jeff Wilson, gen mgr.

Upper Sandusky

WXML(FM)— Dec 26, 1992: 90.1 mhz; 3 kw. 328 ft. TL: N40 50 10 W83 14 11. Stereo. Box 158, 1800 E. Wyandot Ave. 43351. Phone: (419) 294-2900. Fax: (419) 294-1786. E-mail: wxmlradio@udata.com. Web Site: www.wxml.cc. Licensee: Kayser Broadcast Ministries Inc. Verner, Llipfert, Bernhard, McPherson & Hand. Format: Relg. News: 8 hrs wkly. Target aud: General. ◆ Daniel L. Kayser, CEO, pres, CFO & gen mgr; Richard Johnson, VP; Terry Snyder, progmg dir.

WYNT(FM)— Oct 1, 1986: 95.9 mhz; 3 kw. 299 ft. TL: N40 49 30 W83 15 06. Stereo. 1330 No. Main St., Marion 43302. Phone: (877) 472-3464. Fax: (740) 387-3697. Licensee: Clear Channel Broadcasting Licenses Inc. Group owner: Clear Channel Communications Inc. (acq 4-2-02; $825,000). Format: Adult contemp, country crossover. Target aud: 27 plus; general. Spec prog: Farm 3 hrs wkly. ◆ Forest Whitehead, pres; Diane Glass Meyer, gen mgr; Scott Shawver, progmg dir; Ben Pailor, news dir.

Urbana

WKSW(FM)— Aug 1, 1965: 101.7 mhz; 3.2 kw. 407 ft. TL: N40 02 57 W83 46 06. Stereo. 2963 Derr Rd., Springfield 45503. Phone: (937) 399-5300. Fax: (937) 399-3661. E-mail: email@kisscountry.com. Web Site: www.kisscountry.com. Licensee: Blue Chip Broadcasting Licenses Ltd. Group owner: Radio One Inc. (acq 4-30-01; grpsl). Format: Country. Target aud: 25-54; above-average income, blue-collar. ◆ Cathy Hughes, CEO; Mary Catherine Sneed, COO; Alfred Liggens, pres; Scott Royster, CFO; Don Griffin, gen mgr; Roger C. Mackall, stn mgr;

Stations in the U.S. Ohio

Developers & Brokers of Radio Properties
contact American Media Services at our suite:
Philadelphia Marriott Downtown
215-625-2900
843-972-2200
americanmediaservices.com
Charleston, SC
Dallas, TX · Chicago, Il · Austin, TX
American Media Services, LLC

J.D. Kunes, opns dir; Andy Lawrence, prom mgr; Lee Riley, progmg dir; Chris Daniels, news dir; Brian Kelly, pub affrs dir; Gene Simmons, chief of engrg.

Van Wert

WBYR(FM)— Oct 1, 1962: 98.9 mhz; 50 kw. 450 ft. TL: N40 53 33 W84 31 40. Stereo. 1005 Production Rd., Fort Wayne, IN 46808. Phone: (260) 471-5100. Fax: (260) 471-5224. Web Site: www.989thebear.com. Licensee: Pathfinder Communications Corp. Group owner: Federated Media (acq 1996; $5.85 million). Format: Active rock. Target aud: 18-49; men. ♦ Jim Allgeier, gen mgr.

WERT(AM)— Nov 27, 1958: 1220 khz; 250 w-U. TL: N40 52 19 W84 33 15. Box 487 45891. Phone: (419) 238-1220. Fax: (419) 238-2578. E-mail: wireless@wcoil.com. Web Site: www.vanwert.com. Licensee: Richard Ford. (acq 1-03-95; $225,000 with WKSD-FM Paulding; 11-7-94). Network: ABC. Rep: Rgnl Reps. Format: Adult standard. News staff: 2; News: 30 hrs wkly. Target aud: 35 plus; spendable income. Spec prog: Gospel 3 hrs, Sp one hr wkly. ♦ Chris Roberts, pres & gen mgr.

Wapakoneta

WZOQ(FM)— July 1, 1964: 92.1 mhz; 3 kw. 320 ft. TL: N40 39 20 W84 06 54. Stereo. Box 1487, Lima 45802. Secondary address: 1301 N. Cable Rd., Lima 45805. Phone: (419) 331-1600. Phone: (419) 222-4487. Fax: (419) 222-3755. E-mail: justin@92zoo.com. Web Site: www.92zoo.com. Licensee: Maverick Media of Lima License LLC. Group owner: Maverick Media LLC (acq 12-4-2003; grpsl). Rep: Christal. Rgnl Reps. Format: CHR. News staff: one; News: 6 hrs wkly. Target aud: 18-49; young, affluent women. ♦ Gary S. Rozynek, pres; Dave Roach, gen mgr; Justin Kase, stn mgr; Matt Childers, gen sls mgr.

Warren

WANR(AM)— Apr 7, 1971: 1570 khz; 500 w-D, 116 w-N, DA-1. TL: N41 12 22 W80 50 29. 124 N Park Ave., Suite 10 44481. Phone: (330) 394-7700. Fax: (330) 394-7701. Licensee: Beacon Broadcasting Inc. (group owner; (acq 9-7-2005); grpsl). Network: Network: UPI, Westwood One. Format: News/talk info. News staff: one; News: 20 hrs wkly. Target aud: 25-49; adult men. ♦ Bill Henry, CFO; Michael Arch, gen mgr.

WHKZ(AM)— Nov 11, 1941: 1440 khz; 5 kw-U, DA-2. TL: N41 09 52 W80 50 47. 4 Summit Park Dr., Suite 150, Independence 44131. Phone: (216) 901-0921. Fax: (216) 901-5517. Web Site: www.whkwradio.com. Licensee: SCA License Corp. Group owner: Salem Communications Corp. (acq 1-19-2001; $675,000). Rep: Salem. Format: Christian talk. ♦ Errol Dengler, gen mgr.

Washington Court House

WCHO(AM)— February 1952: 1250 khz; 500 w-D. TL: N39 32 59 W83 27 10. 1535 N. North St. 43160. Phone: (740) 335-0941. Fax: (740) 335-6869. Web Site: www.wchoam.com. Licensee: Citicasters Licenses L.P. Group owner: Clear Channel Communications Inc. (acq 5-4-99; grpsl). Network: ABC. Rep: Katz Radio. Format: MOR. News: 18 hrs wkly. Spec prog: Farm 5 hrs wkly. ♦ Dan Latham, sr VP & gen mgr; Kim Skaggs, opns VP; Tracy Taylor, sls dir; John Barney, gen sls mgr; Carl Staffan, mus dir & news dir; Todd Jellison, engrg mgr.

WCHO-FM— December 1968: 105.5 mhz; 3 kw. 300 ft. TL: N39 32 59 W83 27 10. Web Site: www.wcho.com. Network: ABC. Format: Country.

Wauseon

WMTR-FM—See Archbold

WNKL(FM)— 2003: 96.9 mhz; 5 kw. Ant 358 ft. TL: N41 36 03 W83 54 27. Box 351630, Toledo 43635. Secondary address: 1510 Reynolds Rd., Maumee 43537. Phone: (419) 725-9366. Fax: (419) 725-2600. E-mail: info@q969.fm. Licensee: Cornerstone Church Inc. (acq 8-31-2000). Format: Rhythmic CHR. ♦ Brandon Brandon, gen mgr & progmg dir; Alan Colwell, chief of engrg.

*WYSA(FM)— 1996: 88.5 mhz; 25 kw. 292 ft. TL: N41 33 29 W84 11 08. 5115 Glendale Ave., Toledo 43614. Phone: (419) 389-0893. Fax: (419) 381-0731. Web Site: www.yeshome.com. Licensee: Side by Side Inc. Network: Salem Radio Network. Format: Christian, CHR, rock/AOR. Target aud: 15-25. ♦ Jim Oedy, pres; J. Todd Hostetler, gen mgr; Jeff Howe, opns dir.

Waverly

WXIC(AM)— 1954: 660 khz; 1 kw-D. TL: N39 07 50 W83 00 46. Box 227, 6655 St. Rt. 220 W. 45690. Phone: (740) 947-2166. Fax: (740) 947-4600. E-mail: wxic@zoomnet.net. Web Site: wxic.com. Licensee: Crystal Communications Corp. (acq 7-1-79). Network: ABC Information & Entertainment. Rep: Keystone (unwired net). Format: Southern gospel mus. Target aud: Gospel mus lovers. ♦ Gerald E. Davis, pres, gen mgr & chief of engrg; Rick Schweinburg, opns mgr; Brad Lambert, sls dir & adv mgr; Rick Schweinsburg, prom mgr; Rick Schweinburgh, progmg mgr.

WXIZ(FM)—Co-owned with WXIC(AM). March 1971: 100.9 mhz; 920 w. 500 ft. TL: N39 13 17 W82 59 33. Stereo. Web Site: www.wxiz.com. Format: Country. News staff: one; News: 10 hrs wkly. Target aud: 25-50. ♦ Gerald E. Davis, stn mgr; Brad Lambert, gen sls mgr; Tim Hughes, opns mgr, prom mgr, progmg mgr, mus dir & news dir.

Wellston

WKOV-FM—Listing follows WYPC(AM).

WYPC(AM)— 1953: 1330 khz; 500 w-D, 50 w-N. TL: N39 06 22 W82 34 44. Box 667, 295 E. Main, Jackson 45640. Phone: (740) 286-3023. Fax: (740) 286-6679. Licensee: Jackson County Broadcasting Inc. (group owner; acq 9-14-70). Network: Westwood One. Format: Adult Standards. News staff: one; News: 8 hrs wkly. Target aud: 50 plus. ♦ Jerry Mossbarger, gen mgr.

WKOV-FM—Co-owned with WYPC(AM). July 17, 1971: 96.7 mhz; 16.5 kw. 430 ft. TL: N39 01 45 W82 35 51. Stereo. Fletcher, Heald & Hildreth. Format: Hot adult contemp. News staff: one; News: 21 hrs wkly. Target aud: 20-55.

West Carrollton

*WDPR(FM)— Apr 9, 1977: 88.1 mhz; 600 w. Ant 781 ft. TL: N39 43 16 W84 15 00. Stereo. 126 N. Main St., Dayton 45402. Phone: (937) 496-3850. Fax: (937) 496-3852. E-mail: gmw@dpr.org. Web Site: www.dpr.org. Licensee: Dayton Public Radio Inc. (acq 4-28-98). Network: USA. Format: Class. Target aud: 24-50. ♦ Georganne M. Woessner, gen mgr; Larry Coressel, opns dir & progmg dir; Charles Wendelken-Wilson, mus dir; Gene Simmons, chief of engrg.

WROU-FM— Nov 25, 1991: 92.1 mhz; 890 w. Ant 597 ft. TL: N39 43 15 W84 15 39. 717 E. David Rd., Dayton 45429. Phone: (937) 294-5858. Fax: (937) 297-5233. Web Site: www.wrou.com. Licensee: Radio One of Dayton Licenses LLC. Group owner: Radio One Inc. (acq 7-17-2003; $6.7 million). Network: ABC. Format: Urban contemp. Target aud: 25-54. ♦ Don Griffin, gen mgr.

West Chester

*WLHS(FM)— Sept 3, 1976: 89.9 mhz; 100 w. 338 ft. TL: N39 19 10 W84 22 04. 6840 Lakota Ln., Liberty Township 45044-9578. Phone: (513) 759-4163. Fax: (513) 759-4165. Licensee: Lakota School District. Format: Educ, rock/AOR. Target aud: General; div, open minded crowd. ♦ Mark Hattersley, stn mgr; R.C. Anderson, opns dir; Corey Wyatt, sls dir; Danny Hall, mus dir; Matt Townsley, mus dir; Brandon Enright, asst music dir.

West Union

WRAC(FM)— Dec 15, 1981: 103.1 mhz; 3.3 kw. 426 ft. TL: N38 51 25 W83 36 38. Stereo. Box 103, 114 Manchester St. 45693. Phone: (937) 544-9722. Fax: (937) 544-5523. E-mail: c103country@yahoo.com. Licensee: DreamCatcher Communications Inc. (group owner; acq 9-21-81; $4,820;. FTR: 10-12-81). Rep: Rgnl Reps. Format: Country, gospel. Target aud: General. Spec prog: Farm 10 hrs wkly. ♦ Donald Bowles, pres & gen mgr; Venita Bowles, VP; Ted Foster, stn mgr & progmg dir; Brad Rolfe, mus dir & news dir.

*WVXW(FM)— 1990: 89.5 mhz; 3.2 kw. Ant 330 ft. TL: N38 51 36 W83 36 42. Stereo. c/o WVXU(FM), 1223 Central Pkwy., Cincinnati 45214. Phone: (513) 352-9170. Fax: (513) 241-8456. E-mail: wvxu@cinradio.org. Web Site: www.wvxu.org. Licensee: Cincinnati Classical Public Radio Inc. (acq 8-22-2005; grpsl). Network: NPR. Baker & Hostetler LLP. Format: News and info. ♦ Richard Eiswerth, gen mgr; George Zahn, opns dir.

Westerville

*WOBN(FM)— Oct 8, 1958: 101.5 mhz; 28 w. 40 ft. TL: N40 07 28 W82 56 15. Stereo. Otterbein College, Cowan Hall 43081. Phone: (614) 823-1725. Phone: (614) 823-1557. Fax: (614) 823-1998. Web Site: www.wobn.net. Licensee: Otterbein College. Format: Rock, alternative rock, progsv. Target aud: General; Westerville & Otterbein College community. Spec prog: Black 2 hrs, jazz one hr, relg 4 hrs, heavy metal 2 hrs wkly. ♦ Alicia Payne, gen mgr.

WTDA(FM)— 1998: 103.9 mhz; 6 kw. 328 ft. TL: N40 09 33 W82 55 21. Stereo. 1458 Dublin Rd., Columbus 43215. Phone: (614) 481-7800. Fax: (614) 481-8070. E-mail: mail@edfm.com. Web Site: www.tedfm.com. Licensee: North American Broadcasting Co. Inc. (group owner; (acq 1999; $5 million). Rep: D & R Radio. Hogan & Hartson. Format: Classic hits. Target aud: 25-54. ♦ Matthew Mnich, CEO & pres; Norma J. Mnich, chmn; Mark E. Jividen, VP & gen mgr.

Wilberforce

*WCSU-FM— Dec 15, 1962: 88.9 mhz; 1 kw. 150 ft. TL: N39 42 57 W83 54 27. Stereo. Box 1004 45384-1004. Phone: (937) 376-6371. Fax: (937) 376-6436. Licensee: Central State University. Format: Gospel, urban contemp, jazz. Target aud: 12-49; African-Americans. ♦ J.C. Logan, gen mgr; Tony Chappel, mus dir.

Willard

WLRD(FM)— January 2000: 96.9 mhz; 6 kw. Ant 328 ft. TL: N40 57 36 W82 37 16. 3809 Maple Ave., Castalia 44824. Phone: (419) 684-5311. Fax: (419) 684-5378. Licensee: Christian Faith Broadcast Inc. Group owner: Christian Faith Broadcasting Inc. Format: Southern gospel. Target aud: 25-54. ♦ Rusty Yost, gen mgr.

Willoughby-Eastlake

WELW(AM)— Jan 25, 1965: 1330 khz; 500 w-D. TL: N41 38 56 W81 25 19. Box 1330, Willoughby 44096. Phone: (440) 946-1330. Fax: (440) 953-0320. E-mail: email@welw.com. Web Site: www.welw.com. Licensee: Spirit Broadcasting Corp. (acq 9-11-90; 10-1-90). Format: Oldies, sports. Target aud: 35 plus; community adults. Spec prog: German 1; Italian 1; Polish 1; Polka 15 hrs wkly. ♦ Ray Somich, pres & gen mgr; Tony Petkovsek, exec VP; Ron Somich, VP; Van Lane, gen sls mgr.

Wilmington

WKFI(AM)— Dec 5, 1964: 1090 khz; 1 kw-D, DA. TL: N39 26 12 W83 51 21. 200 R. Gordon Dr. 45177. Phone: (937) 382-1608. Phone: (937) 382-1023. Fax: (937) 382-1665. Licensee: Vernon R. Baldwin Inc. (group owner; acq 4-22-03; $1.2 million. with co-located FM). Network: Network: PRI, ABC Information & Entertainment. Cohn & Marks. Format: Gospel. Target aud: General. Spec prog: Big band 5 hrs wkly. ♦ Rick Johnston, gen mgr & gen sls mgr.

Broadcasting & Cable Yearbook 2006

Ohio

Directory of Radio

WKLN(FM)—Co-owned with WKFI(AM). 1974: 102.3 mhz; 3 kw. 300 ft. TL: N39 21 54 W83 46 08. Stereo. Phone: (937) 382-1023. Network: ABC Information & Entertainment. Format: Country.

Wooster

***WCWS(FM)**— April 1968: 90.9 mhz; 1.05 kw. 230 ft. TL: N40 48 34 W81 56 18. Stereo. Box 3177, Wishart Hall, College of Wooster 44691. Phone: (330) 263-2240. Fax: (330) 263-2690. E-mail: wcws@wooster.edu. Web Site: www.wooster.edu/wcws. Licensee: The College of Wooster. Network: AP Radio. Format: Div, CHR, rock/AOR. News: 10 hrs wkly. Target aud: General; college students & people of the surrounding area. Spec prog: Urban contemp 3 hrs, heavy metal 4 hrs, reggae 3 hrs, Indian 2 hrs wkly. ♦ Rachel Grinnan, gen mgr; Drew Glassroth, progmg dir; Danny Kavka, mus dir.

WKRW(FM)— Mar 29, 1993: 89.3 mhz; 2.1 kw. 318 ft. TL: N40 46 28 W81 55 05. Stereo. Box 5190, 1613 E. Summit St., Kent 44242-0001. Phone: (330) 672-3114. Fax: (330) 672-4107. Web Site: www.wksu.org. Licensee: Kent State University. Network: Network: NPR, PRI. Dow, Lohnes & Albertson. Format: Class, in-depth news. News staff: 5; News: 35 hrs wkly. Target aud: 35-65; college grad, professional & upper income. Spec prog: Folk 12 hrs wkly. ♦ Allen E. Perry, gen mgr; Patricia Gerber, dev dir.

WKVX(AM)—Listing follows WQKT(FM).

WQKT(FM)— 1947: 104.5 mhz; 52 kw. Ant 330 ft. TL: N40 47 31 W81 54 17. Stereo. Box 39 44691. Secondary address: 186 S. Hillcrest Dr. 44691. Phone: (330) 264-5122. Fax: (330) 264-3571. E-mail: wqkt@aol.com. Web Site: www.wqkt.com. Licensee: WWST Corp. L.L.C. Network: ABC. Rgnl Reps Format: C&W, sports. ♦ Ken Nemeth, gen mgr.

WKVX(AM)— Co-owned with WQKT(FM). 1947: 960 khz; 1 kw-D, 32 w-N. TL: N40 47 31 W81 54 17. Stereo. Web Site: www.wkvx.com. Group owner: Dix Communications Network: Network: ABC, AP Radio. Rep: Rgnl Reps. Format: Oldies.

WXXF(FM)—(Loudonville). March 1990: 107.7 mhz; 6 kw. Ant 328 ft. TL: N40 36 58 W82 05 34. Stereo. 2435 Mansfield Rd., Ashland 44805. Phone: (419) 289-2605. Fax: (419) 289-0304. E-mail: info@kissmidohio.com. Web Site: www.kissmidohio.com. Licensee: Capstar TX L.P. Group owner: Clear Channel Communications Inc. (acq 2-12-2001; grpsl). Format: Classic rock. ♦ Diana Coon, gen mgr; Joe Rinehart, stn mgr.

Xenia

WBZI(AM)— Nov 11, 1963: 1500 khz; 500 w-D. TL: N39 42 48 W83 54 48. 486 W. Second St. 45385. Phone: (937) 372-3531. Fax: (937) 372-3508. E-mail: myclassiccountry@myclassiccountry.com. Web Site: www.wbzi.com. Licensee: Town & Country Broadcasting Inc. (acq 10-4-95; $140,000). Format: Classic country. News staff: one; News: 14 hrs wkly. Target aud: 25-64; upper income, married, homeowners. Spec prog: Gospel 6 hrs, farm 5 hrs wkly. ♦ Joe Mullins, gen mgr.

WGNZ(AM)—See Fairborn

WZLR(FM)— Mar 3, 1967: 95.3 mhz; 6 kw. 300 ft. TL: N39 37 54 W83 53 49. Stereo. 1414 Wilmington Ave., Dayton 45420. Phone: (937) 259-2111. Fax: (937) 259-2328. Web Site: daytonspoint.com. Licensee: CXR Holdings L.L.C. Group owner: Cox Broadcasting (acq 1998; grpsl). Rep: Christal. Dow, Lohnes & Albertson. Format: Classic rock. Target aud: 25-54. ♦ Donna Hall, VP & gen mgr; Marc Herbst, gen sls mgr; Jason Michaels, progmg dir & mus dir.

Yellow Springs

WYSO(FM)— Feb 8, 1958: 91.3 mhz; 37 kw. 410 ft. TL: N39 45 46 W83 53 05. Stereo. 800 Livermore St. 45387. Phone: (937) 767-6420. Fax: (937) 769-1382. E-mail: wyso@wyso.org. Web Site: www.wyso.org. Licensee: Antioch University. Network: Network: PRI, NPR. Garvey, Schubert & Barer. Format: News/talk, Americana, AAA. News staff: 2; News: 77 hrs wkly. Target aud: 25-54; college educated, professional, mid-upper income. Spec prog: Folk 2 hrs, jazz 12 hrs, blues 4 hrs, new age 4 hrs, Celtic/British Isles 3 hrs,bluegrass 6 hrs wkly. ♦ Glenn Watts, CFO; Paul Maassen, gen mgr; Yana Davis, dev dir; Tim Tattan, progmg dir.

Youngstown

WAKZ(FM)—(Sharpsville).PA Dec 28, 1976: 95.9 mhz; 3 kw. Ant 328 ft. TL: N41 13 05 W80 33 43. Stereo. 7461 South Ave., Boardman 44512. Phone: (330) 965-0057. Fax: (330) 729-9991. Web Site: www.959kiss.com. Licensee: Citicasters Licenses L.P. Group owner: Clear Channel Communications Inc. (acq 1-15-2004; grpsl). Format: CHR. ♦ Bill Kelly, gen mgr; Cornell Bogdon, gen sls mgr & rgnl sls mgr; John Thomas, prom dir & prom mgr; Jerry Mac, progmg mgr; Jim Hartzler, chief of engrg.

WASN(AM)— May 9, 1976: 1500 khz; 500 w-D, 250 w-CH, DA. TL: N41 06 26 W80 34 57. 12th Fl., 34 Federal Plaza W. 44503. Phone: (330) 744-5115. Fax: (330) 744-4020. Licensee: Stop 26 Riverbend Licenses LLC (acq 1995; $250,000). Format: Relg, Black, talk. News: 4 hrs wkly. Target aud: General; families. ♦ Percy Squire, pres; Linda Penny, gen mgr; Charles Rhodes, gen sls mgr; Kenneth King, news dir.

WBBG(FM)—See Niles

WBBW(AM)— Feb 20, 1949: 1240 khz; 1 kw-U. TL: N41 04 50 W80 38 54. 4040 Simon Rd. 44512. Phone: (330) 783-1000. Fax: (330) 783-0060. Web Site: www.cumulus.com. Licensee: Cumulus Licensing Corp. Group owner: Cumulus Media Inc. (acq 3-15-00; grpsl). Network: Westwood One. Rep: Allied Radio Partners. Format: Sports. Target aud: General. ♦ Larry Weiss, gen mgr; Lee B. Jolly, prom mgr; Pat Mulrooney, progmg mgr; Wesley Boyd, chief of engrg.

WHOT-FM—Co-owned with WBBW(AM). November 1959: 101.1 mhz; 24 kw. Ant 711 ft. TL: N41 03 28 W80 38 24. (CP: 25 kw, ant 694 ft.). Stereo. Web Site: www.cumulus.com. Putbrese, Hunsaker & Trent. Format: CHR. Target aud: 18-54. ♦ Kelley McGrath, gen sls mgr; Angie Capaldi, natl sls mgr; Lee B. Jolly, prom dir; Mike Thomas, mus dir; Pat Mulrooney, progmg dir & news dir.

WGFT(AM)—(Campbell). Oct 16, 1955: 1330 khz; 500 w-D, 1 kw-N, DA-2. TL: N40 58 30 W80 35 15. 34 Federal Plaza W., 12th Fl. 44503. Phone: (330) 744-5115. Fax: (330) 744-2221. Licensee: Stop 26 Riverbend Licenses LLC (acq 12-30-02). Format: Gospel talk radio. Target aud: General; family. ♦ Frank Halfacre, chmn; Percy Squire, CEO & pres; Linda Penny, gen mgr.

WHKZ(AM)—See Warren

WKBN(AM)— 1926: 570 khz; 5 kw-U, DA-N. TL: N40 59 07 W80 36 02. Box 9248 44513. Secondary address: 7461 South Ave., Boardman 44512. Phone: (330) 965-0057. Fax: (330) 965-8277. Licensee: Citicasters Licenses L.P. Group owner: Clear Channel Communications Inc. (acq 1-22-99; $11 million. with co-located FM). Network: Network: ABC, CBS. Format: News/talk, sports. Spec prog: Polka 2 hrs, Croation 2 hrs wkly. ♦ Bill Kelly, VP & gen sls mgr; Dan Rivers, progmg dir.

WMXY(FM)— Co-owned with WKBN(AM). Aug 26, 1947: 98.9 mhz; 4.5 kw. 1,370 ft. TL: N41 03 24 W80 38 44. Stereo. Format: Adult contemp.

WLOA(AM)—(Farrell).PA Oct 3, 1954: 1470 khz; 1 kw-D, 500 w-N, DA-N. TL: N41 11 58 W80 31 22. 6325 Sheridan Dr., Williamsville, NY 14221. Phone: (716) 839-6117. Fax: (716) 839-0400. E-mail: info@holyfamily.ws. Web Site: www.holyfamily.ws. Licensee: Holy Family Communications (group owner; acq 12-11-2002; $350,000. $100,000 of which was paid in a tax-relief donation). Format: Catholic. ♦ James Wright, gen mgr.

WNCD(FM)—Listing follows WNIO(AM).

WNIO(AM)— Sept 7, 1939: 1390 khz; 9.5 kw-D, 4.8 kw-N, DA-N. TL: N41 07 17 W80 42 05 (day), N40 59 11 W80 35 54 (night). Stereo. 7461 South Ave. 44512. Phone: (330) 965-0057. Fax: (330) 965-8277. Web Site: www.wnio.com. Licensee: Citicasters Licenses L.P. Group owner: Clear Channel Communications Inc. (acq 1-15-2004; grpsl). Rep: Allied Radio Partners. Format: Nostalgia. News staff: 2; News: 3 hrs wkly. Target aud: General. Spec prog: It 3 hrs wkly. ♦ Bill Kelly, gen mgr & gen sls mgr; Dan Rivers, adv dir.

WNCD(FM)— Co-owned with WNIO(AM). June 1959: 93.3 mhz; 50 kw. 280 ft. TL: N41 04 50 W80 38 54. Stereo. Box 9248 445123. Web Site: www.wnio.com. Format: Oldies. Target aud: 25-54. ♦ Thomas John, prom dir; Dan Rivers, progmg dir.

WRTK(AM)—See Niles

WYSU(FM)— September 1969: 88.5 mhz; 50 kw. 499 ft. TL: N41 03 28 W80 38 42. Stereo. Youngstown State University, One University Plaza 44555. Phone: (330) 941-3363. Fax: (330) 941-1501. E-mail: sexton@wysu.org. Web Site: www.wysu.org. Licensee: Youngstown State University. Network: Network: PRI, NPR. Bakeer & Hostetler. Format: Class, news. News: 48 hrs wkly. Target aud: General. Spec prog: Folk 3 hrs wkly. ♦ Gary Sexton, gen mgr; David Linscher, opns mgr & progmg dir; Michele Grant, dev dir; William C. Panko, chief of engrg.

WYTN(FM)— May 1991: 91.7 mhz; 3 kw. 299 ft. TL: N41 03 28 W80 38 42. Stereo. 13 Fairlane Dr., Joliet, IL 60435. Secondary address: 3930 Sunset Blvd. 60435. Phone: (815) 725-1331. Web Site: www.familyradio.com. Licensee: Family Stations Inc. (group owner) Network: UPI. Dow, Lohnes & Albertson. Format: Relg. Target aud: 25 plus; Christians. Spec prog: Class 2 hrs wkly. ♦ Harold Camping, pres; John Rorvik, gen mgr.

Zanesville

WHIZ(AM)— July 8, 1924: 1240 khz; 1 kw-U. TL: N39 55 42 W81 59 06. 629 Downard Rd. 43701. Phone: (740) 452-5431. Fax: (740) 452-6553. Web Site: www.whizamfmtv.com. Licensee: Southeastern Ohio Broadcasting System Inc. (acq 6-47). Rep: Roslin, Rgnl Reps. Format: Adult standards, news/talk. News staff: 10; News: 30 hrs wkly. Target aud: 25-54; general. Spec prog: Farm progmg 2 hrs wkly. ♦ N.J. Littick, chmn; Henry Littick, pres; Van Vannelli, VP; Jay Benson, stn mgr, sls dir & adv dir; Brian Wagner, opns dir, mktg dir & progmg dir; George Hiotis, news dir; Ken Cash, chief of engrg.

WHIZ-FM— Dec 16, 1961: 102.5 mhz; 50 kw. 490 ft. TL: N39 55 42 W81 59 06. Stereo. Web Site: www.whizamfmtv.com. Format: Adult contemp. News: 12 hrs wkly. Target aud: 25 plus; general. Spec prog: Relg one hr, sports 3 hrs wkly. ♦ Jeff Ball, mus dir. Co-owned TV: WHIZ-TV affil.

WJIC(FM)— 2000: 91.7 mhz; 6 kw. 276 ft. TL: N40 04 16 W82 11 30. c/o VCY/America, 3434 W. Kilbourn Ave., Milwaukee, WI 53208. Secondary address: 9152 Gratiot Rd., Newark 43055. Fax: (800) 729-9829. Web Site: www.wcyamerica.org. Licensee: VCY/America Inc. (group owner; acq 10-31-01; $64,000. for CP). Network: USA. Format: Relg. ♦ Vic Eliason, gen mgr.

WOUZ(FM)— Nov 1, 1993: 90.1 mhz; 3 kw. 279 ft. TL: N39 48 50 W81 57 21. Stereo. 9 S. College St., Athens 45701. Phone: (740) 593-4554. Fax: (740) 593-0240. E-mail: woub@woub.org. Web Site: www.ohio.edu. Licensee: Ohio University. Format: Class, jazz, news. ♦ Carolyn Lewis, gen mgr; Doug Partusch, dev dir.

WYBZ(FM)—See Crooksville

Oklahoma

Ada

KADA(AM)— September 1934: 1230 khz; 1 kw-U. TL: N34 47 06 W96 40 44. Box 609 74821. Secondary address: 1019 N. Broadway 74820. Phone: (580) 332-1212. Fax: (580) 332-0128. Licensee: The Chickasaw Nation. Format: Sports. Target aud: 25-54. Spec prog: Gospel 5 hrs wkly. ♦ Roger Harris, gen mgr, dev mgr & adv mgr.

KADA-FM— 1979: 99.3 mhz; 5.5 kw. 299 ft. TL: N34 42 31 W96 44 24. Stereo. (acq 7-88). Format: Country. ♦ Roger Harris, mktg mgr.

KEOR(AM)—See Atoka

KQUJ(FM)—Not on air, target date: unknown: 88.7 mhz; 31 kw. Ant 239 ft. TL: N34 46 32 W96 35 15. The Sister Sherry Lynn Foundation Inc., 1101 North 81 Hwy., Marlow 73055. Phone: (580) 658-9292. Fax: (580) 658-2561. E-mail: kfxi@texhoma.net. Licensee: The Sister Sherry Lynn Foundation Inc. Group owner: American Family Radio. (acq 9-27-2004). Southmayd & Miller. Format: Southern gospel. ♦ Sherry Austin, pres; Ken Austin, gen mgr; Ron Harris, opns mgr; Bill Mashall, progmg dir; James Wilson, engr.

KTGS(FM)— January 1999: 89.9 mhz; 300 w. Ant 246 ft. TL: N34 46 31 W96 41 44. Box 1343 74821. Phone: (580) 332-0902. Fax: (580)

Stations in the U.S. — Oklahoma

Developers & Brokers of Radio Properties — contact American Media Services at our suite: Philadelphia Marriott Downtown 215-625-2900. 843-972-2200. americanmediaservices.com. Charleston, SC. Dallas, TX · Chicago, IL · Austin, TX. American Media Services, LLC

456-7488. E-mail: email@thegospelstation.com. Web Site: www.thegospelstation.com. Licensee: South Central Oklahoma Christian Broadcasting Inc. Format: Southern gospel. ♦Randall Christy, pres & gen mgr; Rick Cody, opns mgr; Danny Allen, chief of engrg.

Altus

KEYB(FM)— Dec 25, 1988: 107.9 mhz; 50 kw. Ant 492 ft. TL: N34 46 15 W99 32 20. Stereo. Box 1077 73522. Secondary address: 808 N. Main 73521. Phone: (580) 482-1555. Fax: (580) 482-8353. E-mail: keyb@keyb.net. Web Site: www.keyb.net. Licensee: Altus FM Inc. (acq 2-5-91; FTR: 12-31-90). Network: Jones Radio Networks, AP Network News. Shaw Pittman. Format: Country. News staff: one; News: 3 hrs wkly. Target aud: 25-54. Spec prog: Farm 2 hrs wkly. ♦Gayle Ledbetter, CEO; Jerry T. Butler, gen mgr, opns mgr & progmg VP; Larry Sisco, engrg dir.

*KKVO(FM)— 1985: 90.9 mhz; 400 w. Ant 121 ft. TL: N34 42 44 W99 19 03. Stereo. 5700 West Oaks Blvd., Rocklin, CA 95765. Phone: (916) 251-1600. Fax: (916) 251-1650. Web Site: www.klove.com. Licensee: Educational Media Foundation. (acq 6-6-2005; $150,000). Network: K-Love. Format: Relg, educ. ♦Lloyd Parker, gen mgr.

*KOCU(FM)— July 2002: 90.1 mhz; 5 kw. Ant 85 ft. TL: N34 40 14 W99 20 13. 2800 W. Gore, Lawton 73505. Phone: (580) 581-2425. Fax: (580) 581-5571. E-mail: kccu@cameron.edu. Web Site: www.kccu.org. Licensee: Cameron University. Network: NPR. Format: News, classical. ♦Mark Norman, gen mgr; Michael V. Leal, progmg dir.

KRKZ(FM)—Listing follows KWHW(AM).

KWHW(AM)— Apr 2, 1947: 1450 khz; 1 kw-U. TL: N34 37 35 W99 20 10. Box 577 73522. Secondary address: 212 W. Cypress 73522. Phone: (580) 482-1450. Fax: (580) 482-3420. E-mail: 1450@kwhw.com. Web Site: www.kwhw.com. Licensee: Monarch Broadcasting Inc. (group owner; acq 12-12-03; grpsl). Network: ABC Information & Entertainment. Format: C&W, news/talk, agriculture info. Spec prog: Sp 16 hrs wkly. ♦Jimmy Young, gen mgr & gen sls mgr.

KRKZ(FM)—Co-owned with KWHW(AM). Apr 1, 1974: 93.5 mhz; 45 kw. 528 ft. TL: N34 37 35 W99 20 10. Stereo. E-mail: 935@krkz.com. Web Site: www.krkz.com. Format: Classic rock.

Alva

KALV(AM)— Oct 18, 1956: 1430 khz; 500 w-U, DA-2. TL: N36 49 06 W98 38 38. Stereo. Box 53, Rt. 1 73717. Phone: (580) 327-1430. Fax: (580) 327-1433. Licensee: MM&K of Alva Inc. (acq 8-30-94; $165,000; 9-19-94). Network: ABC Information & Entertainment. Format: Oldies. News staff: one; News: 8 hrs wkly. Target aud: 45-70; loc residents. ♦Randy Mitchel, pres & gen mgr.

KNID(FM)—Licensed to Alva. See Enid

KPAK(FM)—Not on air, target date: unknown: 97.5 mhz; 50 kw. Ant 492 ft. TL: N37 01 27 W98 41 22. 188 S. Bellevue Blvd., Suite 222, Memphis, TN 38104. Phone: (901) 516-8970 (office). Phone: (901) 375-9324 (station). Licensee: George S. Flinn Jr. ♦George Flinn Jr., pres.

KTTL(FM)— 2001: 105.7 mhz; 50 kw. Ant 492 ft. TL: N36 47 06 W98 33 01. R.R. 1 Box 53 73717. Phone: (580) 327-1430. Fax: (580) 327-1433. Licensee: Women, Handicapped Americans and Minorities for Better Broadcasting Inc. Format: Adult contemp. ♦Randy Mitchel, pres & gen mgr; Craig Killman, progmg mgr.

Anadarko

KVSP(FM)— September 1981: 103.5 mhz; 100 kw. Ant 1,968 ft. TL: N35 15 04 W98 36 53. Box 1360 73005. Secondary address: 115 W. Broadway 73005. Phone: (405) 247-6682. Fax: (405) 247-1051. Licensee: Perry Broadcasting of Southwest Oklahoma Inc. Group owner: Perry Publishing & Broadcasting Co. (acq 11-22-2002; grpsl). Network: ABC. Format: Urban. Target aud: 18 plus. ♦Kevin Perry, gen mgr; Russell M. Perry, chief of opns.

Ardmore

KACO(FM)— Jan 1, 1989: 98.5 mhz; 14 kw. 330 ft. TL: N34 10 56 W97 05 01. Stereo. Box 1487 73402. Secondary address: 115 W. Broadway, Suite 501 73401. Phone: (580) 226-9850. Fax: (580) 226-5113. E-mail: klcm@cableone.net. Web Site: oldiesradio.com. Licensee: A.M. & P.M. Communications L.L.C. (acq 1-5-98; $475,000). Network: ABC. Cordon & Kelly. Format: Oldies, rock and roll. Target aud: 25-54. ♦Bill Countrymen, VP; Steve Spain, gen mgr; Rob Carter, opns mgr & sls dir; Ron Ricord, progmg mgr.

KKAJ-FM— June 24, 1974: 95.7 mhz; 100 kw. Ant 449 ft. TL: N34 05 56 W97 10 54. Stereo. 1205 Northglen 73401. Phone: (580) 226-0421. Fax: (580) 226-0464. E-mail: webmaster@kkaj.com. Web Site: www.kkaj.com. Licensee: NM Licensing LLC (acq 11-14-2002; grpsl). Network: ABC Daytime Direction. Format: Country. News staff: one; News: 25 hrs wkly. Target aud: 18-54. ♦David Smith, VP & gen mgr; Dave Hilton, opns mgr; David MacMullen, sls dir.

KVSO(AM)—Co-owned with KKAJ-FM. September 1935: 1240 khz; 1 kw-U. TL: N34 10 54 W97 08 48. Stereo. E-mail: webmaster@kvso.com. Web Site: www.kvso.com. Group owner: NextMedia Group L.L.C. Network: ABC. Rep: Christal. Format: Sports. News staff: one; News: 4 hrs wkly. Target aud: 25 plus.

*KLCU(FM)— June 19, 1998: 90.3 mhz; 25 kw. 213 ft. TL: N34 12 10 W97 09 12. c/o KCCU(FM), Admin. Bldg., 2800 W. Gore Blvd., Lawton 73505. Phone: (580) 581-2425. Phone: (580) 581-2474. Fax: (580) 581-5571. E-mail: kccu@cameron.edu. Web Site: www.kccu.org. Licensee: Cameron University. Network: Network: NPR, PRI. Format: Classical/National Public Radio. ♦Mark Norman, gen mgr; Terry Anderson, dev dir & dev dir; Michael V. Leal, progmg dir.

*KQPD(FM)— 2003: 91.1 mhz; 250 w. Ant 167 ft. TL: N34 11 01 W97 07 23. Drawer 2440, Tupelo, MS 38803. Phone: (662) 844-8888. Fax: (662) 842-6791. Licensee: American Family Association. Group owner: American Family Radio. Format: Christian. ♦Marvin Sanders, gen mgr.

KYNZ(FM)—See Lone Grove

Atoka

KEOR(AM)— Jan 29, 1968: 1110 khz; 5 kw-D, DA. TL: N34 25 08 W96 11 24. Box 810, Hwy. 75 N. 74525. Phone: (580) 889-3392. Phone: (580) 889-6300. Fax: (580) 889-9308. E-mail: gospelradio@yahoo.com. Licensee: First Broadcasting Capital Partners LLC. Group owner: First Broadcasting Investment Partners LLC (acq 6-16-03; $350,000). Network: ABC Information & Entertainment. Format: Relg. Target aud: General. ♦Don L. Turner, pres; Ricky Chase, gen mgr & stn mgr; John Clemmetsen, progmg dir; Chris Hoopes, mus dir & chief of engrg.

KHKC-FM— June 15, 1984: 102.1 mhz; 3.3 kw. Ant 449 ft. TL: N34 25 08 W96 11 24. Stereo. Box 810 74525. Secondary address: Hwy. 75 N. 74525. Phone: (580) 889-3392. Phone: (580) 889-6300. Fax: (580) 889-9308. Licensee: Keystone Broadcasting Corp. (acq 10-23-2001; with co-located AM). Network: ABC Information & Entertainment. Format: Country. ♦Ricky Chase, gen mgr & progmg dir.

KKNG-FM—See Newcastle

Bartlesville

KRIG-FM—(Nowata). 1965: 104.9 mhz; 15 kw. 419 ft. TL: N36 44 35 W95 45 17. Stereo. Box 1100 74005. Secondary address: 1200 S.E. Frank Phillips Blvd. 74003. Phone: (918) 336-1001. Phone: (918) 336-1400. Fax: (918) 336-6939. E-mail: radio@bartlesvilleradio.com. Web Site: www.bartlesvilleradio.com. Licensee: KCD Enterprises Inc. (group owner; acq 6-26-98; $775,000). Network: ABC. Rgnl Reps Lauren A. Colby. Format: Country. News: 20 hrs wkly. Target aud: 35-65; mature buyers. Spec prog: Gospel 4 hrs wkly. ♦Kevin Potter, pres & gen mgr; Charlie Taraboletti, opns mgr; Dorea Potter, prom mgr.

KWON(AM)— April 1942: 1400 khz; 1 kw-U. TL: N36 45 53 W95 57 35. Stereo. Box 1100 74005. Secondary address: 1200 S.E. Frank Phillips Blvd. 74003. Phone: (918) 336-1001. Phone: (918) 336-1400. Fax: (918) 336-6939. E-mail: radio@bartlesvilleradio.com. Web Site: www.bartlesvilleradio.com. Licensee: KCD Enterprises Inc. (group owner; acq 2-1-97; $625,000 with co-located FM). Network: CBS. Rgnl Reps Lauren A. Colby. Format: News/talk. News staff: 2; News: 25 hrs wkly. Target aud: 25-54; general. Spec prog: Relg 5 hrs wkly. ♦Charlie Taraboletti, opns mgr, opns mgr, progmg dir, news dir, engrg dir & engrg mgr; Kevin Potter, pres, stn mgr, sls dir & gen sls mgr; Dorea Potter, prom dir.

KYFM(FM)—Co-owned with KWON(AM). Nov 6, 1961: 100.1 mhz; 25 kw. Ant 695 ft. TL: N36 37 42 W96 11 26. Stereo. Web Site: www.bartlesvilleradio.com. Network: ABC. Rgnl Reps Lauren A. Colby. Format: Adult contemp. News: 15 hrs wkly. Target aud: 25-49. Spec prog: Gospel 4 hrs wkly.

*KWRI(FM)—Not on air, target date: unknown: 89.1 mhz; 100 kw vert. Ant 626 ft. TL: N36 42 13 W95 30 57. 5700 W. Oaks Blvd., Rocklin, CA 95765. Phone: (916) 251-1600. Fax: (916) 251-1650. E-mail: info@air1.com. Web Site: www.air1.com. Licensee: Educational Media Foundation. Group owner: EMF Broadcasting. Network: Air 1. Shaw Pittman. Format: Contemp Christian. News staff: 3. Target aud: 18-35; Judeo-Christian, female. ♦Richard Jenkins, pres; Mike Novak, VP; Keith Whipple, dev dir; Chris Joyce, prom dir.

Bethany

WWLS-FM—Licensed to Bethany. See Oklahoma City

Bixby

KJMM(FM)— November 1994: 105.3 mhz; 10 kw. 879 ft. TL: N35 51 41 W95 46 03. 7030 S. Yale, Suite 302, Tulsa 74136. Phone: (405) 427-5877. Fax: (918) 494-9683. Web Site: www.1053kjamz.com. Licensee: KJMM Inc. Group owner: Perry Publishing & Broadcasting Co. (acq 1-95). Network: Network: ABC, American Urban, Westwood One. Meyer, Faller, Weisman & Rosenberg. Format: Urban. News staff: one; News: 10 hrs wkly. Target aud: General. ♦Russell Perry, CEO; Kevin Perry, chmn; Bryan K. Robinson, gen mgr; Terry Monday, progmg VP.

Blackwell

KLOR-FM—See Ponca City

KOKB(AM)— October 1952: 1580 khz; 1 kw-D, 49 w-N. TL: N36 48 35 W97 15 50. Box 2509, Ponca City 74602. Secondary address: 122 N. Third St., Ponca City 74602. Phone: (580) 765-2485. Fax: (580) 767-1103. E-mail: kokb@eteamradio.com. Web Site: www.eteamradio.com. Licensee: Team Radio LLC (group owner; acq 10-18-96; $90,000). Network: ABC Information & Entertainment. Format: Talk, sports. News: 30 hrs wkly. Target aud: 35-75; adult, upper-middle income. Spec prog: Gospel 11 hrs wkly. ♦Bill Coleman, pres, gen mgr & stn mgr.

Bristow

KREK(FM)— Nov 14, 1978: 104.9 mhz; 5 kw. 351 ft. TL: N35 47 11 W96 27 35. Stereo. Box 1280 74010. Phone: (918) 367-5501. Licensee: Big Chief Broadcasting Co. of Bristow Inc. Network: ABC Information & Entertainment. Format: C&W. Target aud: 18-49. ♦Clifford W. Smith, pres & gen mgr.

Broken Arrow

KIZS(FM)— Dec 23, 1970: 92.1 mhz; 27 kw. 656 ft. TL: N36 06 38 W96 01 57. Stereo. 2625 S. Memorial, Tulsa 74129. Phone: (918) 388-5100. Fax: (918) 665-0555. Web Site: www.kissfmtulsa.com.

Broadcasting & Cable Yearbook 2006

Oklahoma

Licensee: Clear Channel Broadcasting Licenses Inc. Group owner: Clear Channel Communications Inc. Rep: Clear Channel. Format: CHR. Target aud: 18-34; women. ◆ Michael Oppenheimer, gen mgr; Don Cristi, opns mgr.

*KNYD(FM)— Aug 19, 1986: 90.5 mhz; 100 kw. 1,638 ft. TL: N36 01 15 W95 40 32. Stereo. Box 1924, Tulsa 74101. Secondary address: 11719 S. 129th East Ave. 74011. Phone: (918) 455-5693. Fax: (918) 455-3059. E-mail: mail@oasisnetwork.org. Web Site: www.oasisnetwork.org. Licensee: Creative Educational Media Inc. (acq 1985). Format: Positive easy gospel, relg, talk. Target aud: General. ◆ David Ingles, pres & gen mgr.

Broken Bow

KKBI(FM)— January 1983: 106.1 mhz; 17 kw. 817 ft. TL: N34 14 45 W94 46 58. Stereo. Box 1016 74728-1016. Phone: (580) 584-3388. Fax: (580) 584-3341. E-mail: kkbi@pine-net.com. Licensee: J.D.C. Radio Inc. (acq 1-27-98; $800,000). Network: Network: ABC Information & Entertainment, Jones Radio Networks. Putbrese, Hunsaker & Trent. Format: Country. News staff: one; News: 5 hrs wkly. Target aud: 24-55. Spec prog: Farm 5 hrs, gospel 4 hrs wkly. ◆ Homer Coleman, pres; David Smulyan, exec VP & gen mgr; Rod Kennedy, progmg dir & mus dir.

Byng

KYKC(FM)— Sept 17, 1992: 100.1 mhz; 50 kw. 492 ft. TL: N34 43 43 W96 42 45. (CP: 12.87 kw, ant 459 ft.). 121 S. Constant, Ada 74820. Phone: (580) 436-6351. Fax: (580) 436-3388. E-mail: kykc@cableone.net. Web Site: www.kykc.net. Licensee: The Chickasaw Nation. (acq 1-14-2005; $900,000). Format: Country. Target aud: 12 plus; across the board. ◆ Dexter Pruitt, exec VP; Mike Hall, gen mgr; Kay Hall, gen sls mgr; David Wayne, progmg mgr.

Cache

*KARU(FM)— 2005: 88.9 mhz; 440 w vert. Ant 259 ft. TL: N34 38 10 W98 41 32. Stereo. 5700 W. Oaks Blvd., Rocklin, CA 95765. Phone: (916) 251-1600. Fax: (916) 251-1650. E-mail: info@air1.com. Web Site: www.air1.com. Licensee: Educational Media Foundation. Group owner: EMF Broadcasting. Network: Air 1. Shaw Pittman. Format: Contemp Christian. News staff: 3. Target aud: 18-35; Judeo-Christian, female. ◆ Richard Jenkins, pres; Mike Novak, VP & progmg dir; Lloyd Parker, gen mgr; Keith Whipple, dev dir; Eric Allen, natl sls mgr; Ron Moore, rgnl sls mgr; Chris Joyce, prom dir; Bryan O'Neal, progmg mgr; Liz Morton, mus dir; Ed Leane, news dir; Sam Wallington, engrg dir.

Carnegie

*KJCC(FM)— 2005: 89.5 mhz; 350 w vert. Ant 194 ft. TL: N35 06 59 W98 28 26. CSN International, 3232 W. MacArthur Blvd., Santa Ana, CA 92704. Phone: (714) 825-9663. Fax: (714) 825-9660. Web Site: www.csnintl.com. Licensee: CSN International (group owner). Format: Christian praise & worship, Bible teaching. ◆ Mike Stocklin, gen mgr.

Chelsea

KTFR(FM)— March 1, 2001: 100.7 mhz; 6 kw. 328 ft. TL: N36 30 12 W95 26 29. 2448 E. 81st St., Suite 4500, Tulsa 74137. Phone: (918) 492-2660. Fax: (918) 492-8840. E-mail: kxoj@kxoj.com. Web Site: www.kxoj.com. Licensee: Michael P. Stephens. Group owner: Adonai Radio Group (acq 2-17-95; FTR: 5-15-95). Format: Contemp Christian. ◆ Mike Stephens, pres; David Stephens, gen mgr; Bob Thornton, progmg dir.

Chickasha

*KSSX(FM)—Not on air, target date: unknown: 90.5 mhz; 1.3 kw. Ant 305 ft. TL: N35 00 43 W97 56 07. 1101 N. 81 Hwy., Marlow 73055. Phone: (580) 658-9292. Fax: (580) 658-2561. Licensee: Sister Sherry Lynn Foundation Inc. ◆ Sherry Austin, pres.

KWCO-FM— Nov 4, 1966: 105.5 mhz; 3.3 kw. 443 ft. TL: N35 00 38 W97 55 54. Stereo. Phone: (405) 224-1560. Fax: (405) 224-2890. Web Site: www.ktuz.com. Licensee: Kenny Communications Inc. (acq 1-1-2004; $114,400). Network: Jones Radio Networks. Format: Classic rock. News: 10 hrs wkly. Target aud: 18-54; Spanish persons. ◆ Matthew Mollman, gen mgr; Keith Michaels, progmg dir; George Plummer, news dir; Christopher Hoops, chief of engrg.

Claremore

*KRSC-FM— Aug 4, 1980: 91.3 mhz; 2.2 kw. 364 ft. TL: N36 19 06 W95 38 18. Stereo. Rogers State University., 1701 W. Will Rogers Blvd. 74017-3252. Phone: (918) 343-7670. Phone: (918) 343-7659. Fax: (918) 343-7952. E-mail: alambert@vsu.edu. Web Site: www.rsu.edu. Licensee: Board of Regents of the University of Oklahoma. Format: AAA, Alternative, new pop. Target aud: General; college & community, young & older adults. Spec prog: Folk 5 hrs, gospel 4 hrs, jazz 5 hrs, progsv 12 hrs, blues 6 hrs, country 5 hrs wkly. ◆ Alan Lambert, gen mgr & stn mgr; Dr. David Nelson, opns mgr. Co-owned TV: *KRSC-TV affil.

KRVT(AM)— Jan 17, 1958: 1270 khz; 1 kw-U, DA-N. TL: N36 17 59 W95 37 16. Box 702588, Tulsa 74170. Phone: (918) 496-7700. Fax: (918) 746-7615. E-mail: river@krvt.net. Web Site: www.krvt.com. Licensee: Reunion Broadcasting L.L.C. (group owner; acq 2-25-2000). Network: CNN Radio. Hardy, Carey & Chautin. Format: Oldies. News: 4 hrs wkly. Target aud: 35 plus; upscale adults. ◆ D. Stanley Tacker, pres & gen mgr.

Clinton

KCLI(AM)— Apr 15, 1949: 1320 khz; 1 kw-D, 108 w-N. TL: N35 29 00 W98 58 54. 700 Frisco 73601. Phone: (580) 323-5254. Fax: (580) 323-0717. E-mail: sales@wrightradio.com. Web Site: www.kcli.com. Licensee: Wright Broadcasting Systems Inc. Group owner: Wright Broadcasting Systems (acq 9-13-00; $25,000). Network: ABC Daytime Direction. Fletcher, Heald & Hildreth. Format: News/talk. Target aud: General. ◆ Harold Wright, gen mgr.

KQMX(FM)— Apr 9, 1978: 95.5 mhz; 40 kw. 492 ft. TL: N35 27 04 W98 58 19. Stereo. Box 587, Weatherford 73096. Phone: (580) 323-5254. Fax: (580) 772-1590. E-mail: sales@wrightradio.com. Web Site: kqmx.com. Licensee: Wright Broadcasting Systems Inc. Group owner: Wright Broadcasting Systems (acq 1996; $300,000). Format: Adult contemp. News: 8 hrs wkly. Target aud: 18-54; upwardly mobile adults. ◆ Harold Wright, CEO, pres & gen mgr; Todd Brunner, opns mgr; Rob Grogan, progmg dir.

*KYCU(FM)— September 2002: 89.1 mhz; 40 kw. Ant 633 ft. TL: N35 26 40 W98 59 22. c/o KCCU(FM), 2800 W. Gore Blvd., Lawton 73505. Phone: (580) 581-2472. Fax: (580) 581-5571. Licensee: Cameron University. Format: News, classical. ◆ Mark Norman, gen mgr.

Coalgate

KKFC(FM)— Dec 7, 2001: 105.5 mhz; 20 kw. Ant 364 ft. TL: N34 41 43 W96 23 17. 1188 North Hills Centre, Ada 74820. Phone: (580) 332-2211. Fax: (580) 436-1629. E-mail: kkfc@kkfcradio.com. Web Site: www.kkfcradio.com. Licensee: Woodstone Broadcasting Inc. (acq 10-9-01). Network: Network: AP Radio, Jones Radio Networks. Smithwick & Belendink. Format: Classic country. Target aud: 25+. ◆ Rick Woodward, pres & gen mgr; Howard Stone, VP; Sam Jackson, progmg dir.

Collinsville

KTBT(FM)— June 25, 1996: 101.5 mhz; 6.2 kw. 656 ft. TL: N36 20 02 W95 47 08. 2625 S. Memorial, Tulsa 74129. Phone: (918) 388-5100. Fax: (918) 665-0555. Web Site: www.1015thebeat.com. Licensee: Clear Channel Broadcasting Licenses Inc. Group owner: Clear Channel Communications Inc. (acq 10-6-97; $1.9 million). Format: Hip hop. Target aud: 18-34; general. ◆ John Hogan, CEO; Bill Richards, sr VP; Michael Oppenheimer, gen mgr & stn mgr; Don Cristi, opns mgr.

Comanche

KDDQ(FM)— Apr 1, 1982: 105.3 mhz; 6 kw. Ant 298 ft. TL: N34 26 12 W97 54 47. Stereo. Box 1808, Duncan 73534. Phone: (580) 255-1350. Fax: (580) 470-9993. Licensee: Perry Broadcasting of Southwest Oklahoma Inc. Group owner: Perry Publishing & Broadcasting Co. (acq 1-9-2003; grpsl). Format: Classic rock. News staff: one; News: 4 hrs wkly. Target aud: 25-54; females with mid-level income. Spec prog: Gospel 2 hrs wkly. ◆ Kevin Perry, gen mgr; Joy Chapman, sls dir & prom dir; Mike Hoffman, chief of engrg.

Cordell

KCDL(FM)— Sept 1, 1988: 99.3 mhz; 10.5 kw. 505 ft. TL: N35 26 49 W98 59 17. 700 Frisco, Clinton 73601. Phone: (580) 323-9900. Fax: (580) 323-0717. E-mail: sales@wrightradio.com. Web Site: kcdl.com.

Licensee: Wright Broadcasting Systems Inc. Group owner: Wright Broadcasting Systems (acq 8-30-99; $350,000). Network: Network: ABC, CNN Radio. Format: Classic rock. Target aud: General. ◆ Harold Wright, CEO & pres; Todd Brunner, gen mgr & opns dir; Rob Grogan, progmg dir.

Coweta

*KDIM(FM)—Not on air, target date: unknown: 88.1 mhz; 100 kw vert. Ant 466 ft. TL: N35 34 08 W95 47 59. Box 1924, Tulsa 74101. Phone: (918) 455-5693. E-mail: mailpraise881@oasisnetwork.org. Web Site: www.oasisnetwork.org. Licensee: Creative Educational Media Corp. Inc. Format: Christian. ◆ David Ingles, pres & gen mgr.

Del City

KOCY(AM)— November 1946: 1560 khz; 1 kw-D, 250 w-N, DA-2. TL: N35 26 26 W97 29 24 (D), N35 26 27 W97 29 24 (N). 5101 S. Shields, Oklahoma City 73129. Phone: (405) 616-5500. Fax: (405) 616-5551. Licensee: Oklahoma Land Co. L.L.C. Group owner: Tyler Media Broadcasting Corp. (acq 12-15-2003; $250,000). Network: Radio Disney. Format: Children. News staff: one; News: 8 hrs wkly. Target aud: 18 plus. Spec prog: Loc sports. ◆ Skip Stow, gen mgr.

Dickson

KTRX(FM)— June 2001: 92.7 mhz; 5.5 kw. Ant 341 ft. TL: N34 06 56 W97 00 06. Stereo. 1205 Northglen, Ardmore 73402. Phone: (580) 226-0421. Fax: (580) 226-0464. E-mail: webmaster@texomarocks.com. Web Site: www.texomarocks.com. Licensee: NM Licensing LLC. Group owner: NextMedia Group L.L.C. (acq 11-14-02; grpsl). Network: Jones Radio Networks. Format: Classic rock. News staff: 1; News: 25 hrs wkly. Target aud: 25-54; men. ◆ Dave Smith, VP & gen mgr; Dave Hilton, opns mgr & progmg dir; David MacMullen, sls dir.

Duncan

KKEN(FM)—Listing follows KPNS(AM).

KPNS(AM)— Oct 31, 1947: 1350 khz; 250 w-D, 100 w-N. TL: N34 40 43 W97 58 05. Stereo. 1701 Pine St., W. 73533. Phone: (580) 255-1350. Fax: (580) 470-9993. Licensee: Perry Broadcasting of Southwest Oklahoma Inc. Group owner: Perry Publishing & Broadcasting Co. (acq 11-22-02; grpsl). Network: ABC Information & Entertainment. Format: Sports talk. News staff: one; News: 20 hrs wkly. Target aud: General. ◆ Peggy Richardson, gen mgr; Kristin Rei, opns mgr; Joy Chatman, gen sls mgr & adv dir; Terry Monday, progmg VP & progmg dir.

KKEN(FM)—Co-owned with KPNS(AM). Dec 31, 1975: 102.3 mhz; 3 kw. 207 ft. TL: N34 40 43 W97 58 05. Stereo. Network: ABC Information & Entertainment. Format: Country. Target aud: 25-54. ◆ Pam Peck, rgnl sls mgr.

Durant

*KAYC(FM)— 2000: 91.1 mhz; 403 w. Ant 210 ft. TL: N34 01 17 W96 28 18. Box 3206, American Family Radio, Tupelo, MS 38803. Phone: (662) 844-8888. Fax: (662) 842-6791. Web Site: www.afr.net. Licensee: American Family Association. Group owner: American Family Radio. Format: Inspirational Christian. ◆ Marvin Sanders, gen mgr.

KLAK(FM)— Jan 6, 1984: 97.5 mhz; 45 kw. 513 ft. TL: N33 47 14 W96 33 00. Stereo. 101 E. Main St., Suite 255, Denison, TX 75020. Phone: (903) 463-6800. Fax: (903) 463-9816. E-mail: jason@klake.com. Web Site: www.klake.com. Licensee: NM Licensing LLC. Group owner: NextMedia Group L.L.C. (acq 11-26-01; grpsl). Network: ABC. Format: Adult contemp. News staff: one; News: 7 hrs wkly. Target aud: 18-54; people who like personality adult contemp. ◆ Steven Dinitz, CEO; Carl Hirsch, chmn; Bill Harrison, pres, VP & gen mgr; Sean Stover, CFO; David MacMullen, stn mgr & sls dir; Jason Taylor, opns mgr & progmg dir; Anne Oliver, prom dir; Tiffany Reynolds, news dir; Vince Richardson, chief of engrg.

KLBC(FM)—Listing follows KSEO(AM).

KSEO(AM)— May 1947: 750 khz; 250 w-D. TL: N34 00 07 W96 25 19. Box 190 74702. Phone: (580) 924-3100. Fax: (580) 920-1426. Web Site: www.klbc.com.yes Licensee: Texoma Broadcasting Inc. (acq 5-28-99; with co-located FM). Format: Adult contemp, golden

Stations in the U.S. — Oklahoma

oldies. News staff: one; News: 3 hrs wkly. Target aud: Adults; 18-54. ♦ Bob McKenzie, opns dir & progmg dir; Todd Tidwell, pres, gen mgr & gen sls mgr; J.B. Conley, prom dir; Ron Eudaly, pub affrs dir.

KLBC(FM)—Co-owned with KSEO(AM). November 1958: 107.1 mhz; 6 kw. 365 ft. TL: N34 00 07 W96 25 19. Stereo. 1418 N. 1st Ave. 74701. E-mail: klbcradio@netcommander.com. Web Site: www.klbcfm.com.yes Format: Country. News staff: one; News: 20 hrs wkly. Target aud: General.

*KSSU(FM)— Feb 1, 1972: 91.9 mhz; 1.5 kw. 341 ft. TL: N34 00 45 W96 19 45. Stereo. 1405 N. 4th St., PMB 4129 74701-0609. Phone: (580) 745-2000. E-mail: kssu@sosu.edu. Web Site: www.sosu.edu/kssu. Licensee: Southeastern Oklahoma State University. Format: CHR. News: 3 hrs wkly. Target aud: 18-25; college, high school students & area residents. ♦ Dr. John Hendricks, exec VP & gen mgr.

Edmond

*KCSC(FM)— April 1966: 90.1 mhz; 100 kw. Ant 840 ft. TL: N35 34 24 W97 29 08. Stereo. Univ. of Central Okla., 100 N. University Dr. 73034-5209. Phone: (405) 974-3333. Fax: (405) 974-3844. E-mail: kcscfm@kcscfm.com. Web Site: www.kcscfm.com. Licensee: University of Central Oklahoma. Network: PRI. Format: Class. News: 5 hrs wkly. Target aud: 35 plus; educated, affluent. ♦ Bradford Ferguson, gen mgr; Kent Anderson, opns mgr & progmg dir; Susan Reger, dev dir.

KKWD(FM)—Licensed to Edmond. See Oklahoma City

*KOKF(FM)— September 1977: 90.9 mhz; 100 kw. 480 ft. TL: N35 33 59 W97 28 28. Stereo. Box 22000, Oklahoma City 73123. Secondary address: 7700 N. Council Rd., Oklahoma City 73123. Phone: (405) 773-2291. Fax: (405) 773-2244. E-mail: info@kokf.com. Web Site: www.kokf.com. Licensee: RDM Broadcasting Enterprises. (acq 10-85). Format: Christian hit radio. Target aud: 18-34; generation X, twenty something. Spec prog: Talk 5 hrs, party mix 5 hrs, rap 3 hrs, on the edge 12 hrs wkly. ♦ Greg Griffin, opns mgr & dev dir; Ron Dryden, pres & gen sls mgr; Rachael Decker, prom mgr; Brandon Rohbar, progmg VP & progmg dir.

El Reno

KZUE(AM)— Sept 9, 1962: 1460 khz; 500 w-D. TL: N35 30 30 W97 54 00. 2715 S. Radio Rd. 73036. Phone: (405) 262-1460. Fax: (405) 262-1886. Licensee: La Tremenda Inc. (acq 12-8-93; $40,000; 1-3-94). Network: ABC Information & Entertainment. Rep: Keystone (unwired net). Format: Sp. Spec prog: Farm 7 hrs, Indian one hr wkly. ♦ Nancy Galvan, gen mgr.

Elk City

KADS(AM)— October 1932: 1240 khz; 1 kw-U. TL: N35 22 51 W99 24 25. Box 945 73648. Phone: (580) 225-9696. Fax: (580) 225-9699. E-mail: bbrewerkeco@cableone.net. Web Site: kecofm.com. Licensee: Paragon Communications Inc. (group owner; acq 6-15-01; $15,000). Network: Network: ABC Information & Entertainment, ESPN Radio. Format: Sports. News staff: one. ♦ Blake Brewer, gen mgr.

KECO(FM)— July 20, 1982: 96.5 mhz; 100 kw. 500 ft. TL: N35 24 22 W99 29 54. Stereo. Box 945 73648. Secondary address: 220 S. Pioneer Rd. 73648. Phone: (580) 225-9696. Fax: (580) 225-9699. E-mail: bbrewerkeco@cableone.net. Web Site: www.kecofm.com. Licensee: Paragon Communications Inc. (group owner; acq 4-22-98; $100,000. for 72% with KXOO(FM) Elk City). Bryan Cave. Format: Country. News staff: one; News: 2.5 hrs wkly. Target aud: General. ♦ Blake Brewer, pres, gen mgr & gen sls mgr; Connie Legrand, opns mgr.

KTIJ(FM)— July 15, 2000: 98.5 mhz; 100 kw. 1,089 ft. TL: N34 58 39 W99 24 35. Box 311, 1515 N. Broadway, Hobart 73651. Phone: (580) 726-5656. Fax: (580) 726-2222. E-mail: thezone@itlnet.net. Licensee: Fuchs Radio LLC. Format: CHR/pop. ♦ Chad Fox, gen mgr; Shelly Fox, VP & opns mgr.

KXOO(FM)— April 1995: 94.3 mhz; 12 kw. 469 ft. TL: N35 24 22 W99 29 54. Stereo. Box 945 73648. Phone: (580) 225-9696. Fax: (580) 225-9699. Licensee: Paragon Communications Inc. (group owner; acq 4-22-98; $100,000. for 72% with KECO(FM) Elk City). Format: Contemp christian. News staff: one; News: 2 hrs wkly. ♦ Blake Brewer, pres & gen mgr; Guy Baker, chief of engrg.

Enid

KCRC(AM)— 1926: 1390 khz; 1 kw-U, DA-1. TL: N36 25 11 W97 52 28. Box 952 73702. Secondary address: 316 E. Willow 73701. Phone: (580) 237-1390. Fax: (580) 242-1390. E-mail: ctbradio@yahoo.com. Licensee: Chisholm Trail Holding Co. Inc. (acq 6-1-83; $1.38 million;. FTR: 6-20-83). Network: Jones Radio Networks. Rep: Savalli. Format: ESPN. News staff: one; News: 2 hrs wkly. Target aud: General. Spec prog: Polka one hr, talk 5 hrs wkly. ♦ Hiram Champlin, pres & gen mgr; Ricky Roggow, opns mgr & mus dir; Sandy Daniels, gen sls mgr; Barbara Keller, prom mgr; Chad McKee, progmg dir; Geoff Haxton, news dir & pub affrs dir; G.B. Bonham, chief of engrg.

KQOB(FM)—Co-owned with KCRC(AM). May 1, 1967: 96.9 mhz; 97.5 kw horiz, 100 kw vert. Ant 1,450 ft. TL: N35 58 50 W97 41 42. Stereo. Licensee: Champlin Broadcasting Inc. Format: Soft adult contemp. Target aud: 18-54.

KFXY(AM)— January 2004: 1640 khz; 10 kw-D, 1 kw-N. TL: N36 25 14 W97 52 28. Box 952 73702. Secondary address: 316 E. Willow 73701. Phone: (580) 237-1390. Fax: (580) 242-1390. E-mail: hchamplin@knid.com. Licensee: Chisholm Trail Broadcasting Co. Format: Sports. ♦ Hiram Champlin, gen mgr; Ricky Roggow, opns mgr; Sandy Daniels, gen sls mgr; Chad McKee, progmg dir.

KGWA(AM)— 1950: 960 khz; 1 kw-U, DA-1. TL: N36 26 13 W97 55 16. Box 3128 73702. Secondary address: 1710 W. Willow Rd., Suite 300 73703. Phone: (580) 234-4230. Fax: (580) 234-2971. E-mail: radio@kofm.com. Web Site: www.kofm.com. Licensee: Williams Broadcasting LLC. (acq 9-10-99; with co-located FM). Network: ABC. Putbrese, Hunsaker & Trent. Format: News/talk. News staff: 2; News: 15 hrs wkly. Target aud: 35 plus. Spec prog: Farm 3 hrs wkly. ♦ Kyle Williams, pres & gen mgr; Cheryl Myatt, gen sls mgr; J. Curtis Huckleberry, progmg dir & news dir.

KOFM(FM)—Co-owned with KGWA(AM). March 1982: 103.1 mhz; 25 kw. 298 ft. TL: N36 26 14 W97 55 15. Stereo. Phone: (580) 234-6371. E-mail: kwilliams@kofm.com. Format: Country. News staff: one; News: one hr wkly.

*KKRD(FM)— Oct 1, 1986: 91.1 mhz; 300 w. Ant 297 ft. TL: N36 23 48 W97 52 38. Stereo. 5700 West Oaks Blvd., Rocklin, CA 95765. Phone: (916) 251-1600. Fax: (916) 251-1650. E-mail: info@air1.com. Web Site: www.air1.com. Licensee: Educational Media Foundation. (acq 10-15-2004; $102,500). Network: Network: Air 1, Moody. Format: Relg. ♦ Richard Jenkins, pres.

KNID(FM)—(Alva). Feb 1, 1981: 99.7 mhz; 100 kw. 850 ft. TL: N36 35 41 W98 15 38. Stereo. Box 952 73702. Secondary address: 316 E. Willow Rd. 73701. Phone: (580) 237-1390. Fax: (580) 242-1390. E-mail: hchamplin@knid.com. Licensee: Chisholm Trail Holding Co. Inc. Network: ABC. Format: Country. News staff: one; News: 2 hrs wkly. Target aud: 25-49. ♦ Hiram Champlin, pres & gen mgr; Ricky Roggow, opns mgr & progmg dir; Sandy Daniels, gen sls mgr; G.B. Bonham, chief of engrg.

Eufaula

KTNT(FM)— June 15, 1967: 102.5 mhz; 25 kw. 150 ft. TL: N35 22 25 W95 34 00. Box 956 74432. Phone: (918) 689-3663. Fax: (918) 689-5451. E-mail: egp@lakewebs.net. Web Site: www.kfoxradio.com. Licensee: K95.5 Inc. (group owner; acq 9-24-98; $400,000). Format: C&W. Spec prog: Gospel 3 hrs, bluegrass 3 hrs, relg 5 hrs wkly. ♦ William H. Payne, pres; Dan Storrs, gen mgr; Edwin Branstetter, stn mgr, opns mgr & progmg dir; JoAnne Matthews, gen sls mgr; William Payne, mus dir.

Frederick

*KSYE(FM)— July 1992: 91.5 mhz; 100 kw. 390 ft. TL: N34 21 52 W98 50 04. Stereo. Box 582, 400 E. Gladstone Ave. 73542. Phone: (817) 792-3800. Fax: (580) 335-5900. E-mail: info@ksye.org. Web Site: www.kcbi.org. Licensee: Criswell College. (group owner) Network: USA. Format: Inspirational. Target aud: General. ♦ Dr. Royce Laycock, chmn; Dr. Jerry Johnson, pres; Ronald L. Harris, CEO, exec VP & gen mgr; Doug Price, opns VP; James Nance, dev VP; John McLain, progmg dir.

KTAT(AM)— 1948: 1570 khz; 250 w-D. TL: N34 23 30 W99 01 51. Box 1088 73542. Secondary address: 207 W. Grand Ave. 73542. Phone: (580) 335-5923. Fax: (580) 335-7659. Licensee: Tomar Broadcasting Co. Inc. (acq 12-18-90; $60,000 with co-located FM; 1-7-91). Network: ABC Information & Entertainment. Format: Adult standards, Sp. Spec prog: Farm 2 hrs wkly. ♦ Brent Morey, gen mgr & gen sls mgr.

KYBE(FM)— Aug 15, 1982: 95.9 mhz; 6 kw. Ant 249 ft. TL: N34 23 30 W99 01 51. Stereo. Box 1088 73542. Phone: (580) 335-5923. Fax: (580) 335-7659. Web Site: www.coyotenews.com. Licensee: Fort Worth Media Group G.P. LLC. (acq 7-21-2005; $325,000). Format: Country.

Glenpool

KTSO(FM)— May 24, 1976: 94.1 mhz; 100 kw. Ant 691 ft. TL: N36 07 52 W96 04 13. 5810 E. Skelly Dr., Suite 801, Tulsa 74135. Phone: (918) 665-3131. Fax: (918) 663-6622. E-mail: production@softoldies.com. Web Site: www.softoldiesonline.com. Licensee: Shamrock Communications Inc. (group owner; acq 1996; $1.8 million). Format: Soft Oldies. News staff: one; News: 35 hrs wkly. Target aud: 35-64. ♦ J. Michael Demarco, gen mgr; William Lynett, CEO & opns mgr.

Goodwell

*KPSU(FM)— September 1977: 91.7 mhz; 380 w. 121 ft. TL: N36 35 41 W101 38 10. Stereo. Box 430 73939. Phone: (580) 349-2414. Fax: (580) 349-2302. Web Site: www.opsu.edu. Licensee: Panhandle State University. Format: Div. Target aud: College age. ♦ Dr. David Bryant, pres; Russell Guthrie, gen mgr.

Grandfield

*KWKL(FM)— Sept 19, 2003: 89.9 mhz; 11 kw vert. Ant 499 ft. TL: N34 16 19 W98 25 30. Stereo. 5700 W. Oaks Blvd., Rocklin, CA 95765. Phone: (916) 251-1600. Fax: (916) 251-1650. E-mail: klove@klove.com. Web Site: www.klove.com. Licensee: Educational Media Foundation. Group owner: EMF Broadcasting. Network: K-Love. Shaw Pittman. Format: Contemp Christian. News staff: 3. Target aud: 25-44; Judeo Christian, female. ♦ Richard Jenkins, pres; Mike Novak, VP & progmg dir; Lloyd Parker, gen mgr; Ed Lenane, opns dir & news dir; Keith Whipple, dev dir; Eric Allen, natl sls mgr; Russ Lloyd, rgnl sls mgr; Chris Joyce, prom dir; David Pierce, progmg mgr; Jon Rivers, mus dir; Sam Wallington, engrg dir.

Grove

KGVE(FM)— Dec 12, 1980: 99.3 mhz; 15 kw. 312 ft. TL: N36 36 49 W94 45 53. Stereo. Box 451749, One W. Third 74345. Phone: (918) 786-2211. Fax: (918) 786-2284. Licensee: Caleb Corp. (acq 4-1-92; 3-16-92). Network: ABC. Format: C&W. News staff: one. Target aud: General. ♦ Janell Hestand, VP, opns dir & progmg dir; Larry Hestand, pres, dev dir & prom dir.

*KWXC(FM)—Not on air, target date: unknown: 88.9 mhz; 6 kw vert. Ant 266 ft. TL: N36 35 42 W94 38 05. 69601 E. 290 Rd. 74344. Phone: (918) 854-3523. Licensee: Grove Broadcasting Inc.

Oklahoma   Directory of Radio

Guthrie

KMFS(AM)— Nov 16, 1955: 1490 khz; 1 kw-U. TL: N35 52 56 W97 23 34. Family Worship Center Church Inc., 8919 World Ministry Ave., Baton Rouge, LA 70810. Phone: (225) 768-8300. Fax: (225) 768-3729. Licensee: Family Worship Center Church Inc. (group owner; acq 9-27-2002; $150,000). Network: Network: ABC, AP Radio. Format: Relg. ♦ John Santiago, gen mgr.

Guymon

KGYN(AM)— Dec 12, 1948: 1210 khz; 10 kw-U, DA-N. TL: N36 40 34 W101 22 58. Box 130 73942. Phone: (580) 338-1210. Phone: (800) 227-1210. Fax: (580) 338-8255. E-mail: kgyn@ptsi.net. Web Site: www.kgynam1210.com. Licensee: Telns Broadcasting Co. Inc. (acq 9-5-86; $400,000; 8-4-86). Network: ABC Information & Entertainment. Format: Country. News staff: one; News: 12 hrs wkly. Target aud: 25-65; broad based listenership. Spec prog: Relg 8 hrs, Sp 8 hrs wkly. ♦ Ed Smith, pres; Jim Smith, gen mgr; Lindsey Smith, stn mgr; Richard Ryther, opns mgr; Curt Edenbourough, gen sls mgr & progmg dir.

KKBS(FM)— Dec 25, 1983: 92.7 mhz; 11.5 kw. 485 ft. TL: N36 42 43 W101 27 27. Stereo. Box 1756, 2143 Hwy. 64 N. 73942. Phone: (580) 338-5493. Fax: (580) 338-0717. E-mail: kkbs@kkbs.com. Web Site: www.kkbs.com. Licensee: MLS Communications Inc. (acq 8-7-90; 8-27-90). Format: Adult rock. News staff: 2; News: 17 hrs wkly. Target aud: 24-66; working people, 2 income families, farmers. Spec prog: Financial markets 5 hrs wkly. ♦ Marsha Strong, pres & gen mgr; Ramey Cozart, opns mgr.

Healdton

KICM(FM)— October 1978: 97.7 mhz; 25 kw. Ant 328 ft. TL: N34 21 00 W97 27 35. Stereo. Box 1487, Ardmore 73402. Phone: (580) 226-5105. Fax: (580) 226-5113. Web Site: www.kicm.com. Licensee: Keystone Broadcasting Corp. (acq 5-31-2005; $1.2 million). Format: Country. Target aud: 21-49. Spec prog: Relg 6 hrs wkly. ♦ Bill Countrymen, gen mgr.

Heavener

KPRV-FM— Oct 1, 1989: 92.5 mhz; 1.55 kw. 640 ft. TL: N34 53 54 W94 34 30. Stereo. Box 368, Poteau 74953. Phone: (918) 647-3221. Fax: (918) 647-5092. E-mail: lbilly@clnk.com. Web Site: www.kprvradio.com. Licensee: LeRoy Billy. Network: ABC. Format: Country. News: 24 hrs wkly. Target aud: 24-54. Spec prog: Gospel 12 hrs wkly. ♦ David Billy, progmg dir; LeRoy Billy, VP, gen mgr, gen sls mgr & mus dir; Larry Johnson, chief of engrg.

Henryetta

*KVAZ(FM)— Dec 26, 1985: 91.5 mhz; 250 w. Ant 178 ft. TL: N35 21 56 W96 00 34. The Gospel Station Network, Box 1343, Ada 74821. Phone: (580) 332-0902. Fax: (580) 456-7488. Web Site: www.thegospelstation.com. Licensee: South Central Oklahoma Broadcasting Inc. (acq 7-1-2005; $25,000). Format: Southern gospel. ♦ Randall Christy, pres & gen mgr.

KXBL(FM)— Dec 20, 1966: 99.5 mhz; 100 kw. 984 ft. TL: N35 50 02 W96 07 28. Stereo. 4590 E. 29th, Tulsa 74114. Phone: (918) 743-7814. Fax: (918) 743-7613. Web Site: bigcountry995.com. Licensee: Journal Broadcast Corp. Group owner: Journal Communications Inc. (acq 6-11-99; grpsl). Koteen & Naftalin. Format: Young country. Target aud: 18-34. ♦ Carl Gardner, pres; Ron Kurtis, CFO; Randy Bush, gen mgr; Ric Hampton, opns mgr, mus dir & chief of engrg.

Hobart

KQTZ(FM)— May 28, 1979: 105.9 mhz; 100 kw. 1,020 ft. TL: N34 52 15 W99 17 36. Stereo. Box 577, Altus 73522. Phone: (580) 482-1450. Fax: (580) 482-3420. Web Site: www.kq106.com. Licensee: Monarch Broadcasting Inc. (group owner; acq 12-12-03; grpsl). Format: Hot adult contemp. Target aud: General; contemp adults during the day, rockers at night. ♦ Matthew L. Ward, pres & gen mgr; Dean Minnick, chief of opns & sls dir; Dick Fontana, progmg dir; Cameron Dole, mus dir.

KTJS(AM)— June 21, 1947: 1420 khz; 1 kw-D, 360 w-N. TL: N35 02 57 W99 05 48. Box 311, 1515 N. Broadway 73651. Phone: (580) 726-5656. Fax: (580) 726-2222. E-mail: thezone@itlnet.net. Licensee: Fuchs Broadcasting Co. (acq 11-24-98; $182,000). Network: ABC Information & Entertainment. Format: Country, news/talk. News: 19 hrs wkly. Target aud: 30 plus; agri-related businessmen. Spec prog: Relg 15 hrs wkly. ♦ Chad Fox, pres, gen mgr, progmg dir & mus dir.

Holdenville

KTLS-FM— Nov 30, 1991: 106.5 mhz; 25 kw. 328 ft. TL: N34 54 50 W96 31 20. 1188 North Hills Centre, Ada 74820. Phone: (580) 332-2211. Fax: (580) 436-1629. E-mail: ktls@ktlsradio.com. Web Site: www.ktlsradio.com. Licensee: Woodstone Broadcasting Inc. (acq 10-9-01). Network: Jones Radio Networks. Smithwick & Belendink. Format: Hot adult contemp. News staff: one. Target aud: 25-54. ♦ Howard Stone, sr VP; Rick Woodward, pres, gen mgr & opns dir; Craig Stone, progmg dir.

KWSH(AM)—See Wewoka

Hollis

KKRE(FM)— 2005: 92.5 mhz; 6 kw. Ant 328 ft. TL: N34 36 34 W99 50 57. Box 1077, Altus 73522. Phone: (580) 482-1555. Fax: (580) 482-8353. Licensee: Altus FM Inc. ♦ Scott Wilmes, VP.

Hugo

KIHN(AM)— October 1948: 1340 khz; 1 kw-U. TL: N34 00 15 W95 29 20. Box 430, Hwy. 70 E. 74743. Phone: (580) 326-6411. Fax: (580) 326-7921. E-mail: kihn@1starnet.com. Licensee: Little Dixie Broadcasting Co. Format: Var, news. News staff: one; News: 20 hrs wkly. Target aud: General. Spec prog: Gospel music 5 hrs, children one hr, farm one hr wkly. ♦ Leeta M. Henson, pres & gen mgr.

KITX(FM)— June 1983: 95.5 mhz; 50 kw. 492 ft. TL: N33 54 56 W95 28 00. Stereo. 1600 W. Jackson 74743. Secondary address: 3605 N.E. loop 286, Paris, TX 74743. Phone: (580) 326-2555. Phone: (903) 784-6952. Fax: (580) 326-2623. E-mail: k955@k955.com. Web Site: www.k955.com. Licensee: K95.5 Inc. (group owner; acq 10-95; $400,000). Format: Country, news. News staff: one; News: 22 hrs wkly. Target aud: General. Spec prog: Farm 2 hrs, gospel 3 hrs wkly. ♦ Joe Ann Matthews, adv mgr & sls; Will Payne, gen mgr, progmg dir, mus dir & chief of engrg.

Idabel

KBEL-FM— Oct 1, 1973: 96.7 mhz; 25 kw. Ant 300 ft. TL: N33 52 54 W94 49 10. Stereo. Box 418 74745. Secondary address: 813 Lincoln Rd. 74745. Phone: (580) 286-6642. Phone: (877) 329-8280. Fax: (580) 286-6643. E-mail: kbel967@yahoo.com. Web Site: www.kbelcountry.com. Licensee: Box Broadcasting Corp. (acq 9-1-99; with co-located AM). Format: Country. Target aud: 25 plus; country audience. Spec prog: tball. ♦ Donald R. Box, chmn; Paul W. Box, CEO, pres & gen mgr; Kelly P. Kirkland, opns dir.

KBEL(AM)— June 3, 1948: 1240 khz; 1 kw-U. TL: N33 52 54 W94 49 10. Format: Sports talk. News: 30 hrs wkly. Target aud: 18 plus; men.

KKBI(FM)—See Broken Bow

KQIB(FM)— Aug 1, 1999: 102.9 mhz; 6 kw. Ant 318 ft. TL: N33 59 57 W94 47 29. 617 S. Park Dr., Broken Bow 74728. Phone: (580) 584-3388. Fax: (580) 584-3341. E-mail: kkbi@pine-net.com. Licensee: JDC Radio Inc. (acq 9-2-98). Network: ABC. Putbrese, Hunsaker & Trent. Format: Hot adult contemp. News staff: one; News: 5 hrs wkly. Target aud: 25-44. ♦ Homer Coleman, pres; David Smulyan, gen mgr & gen sls mgr; Rod Kennedy, natl sls mgr & progmg dir.

*KXRT(FM)— 2003: 90.9 mhz; 500 w. Ant 210 ft. TL: N33 53 33 W94 49 26. Drawer 2440, Tupelo, MS 38801. Phone: (662) 844-8888. Fax: (662) 842-6791. Licensee: American Family Association. Group owner: American Family Radio (acq 1-31-01). Format: Christian. ♦ Marvin Sanders, gen mgr.

Ketchum

*KOSN(FM)— May 26, 1989: 107.5 mhz; 100 kw. Ant 981 ft. TL: N36 46 13 W95 27 07. Stereo. Oklahoma State University, 302 PM Bldg., Stillwater 74078. Phone: (405) 744-6352. Fax: (405) 744-9970. Web Site: www.kosu.org. Licensee: PRC Tulsa I-LLC (acq 1-13-2005; $4 million). Network: NPR. Format: Class, educ, news. News staff: 2; News: 18 hrs wkly. Target aud: General. Spec prog: American Indian one hr wkly. ♦ Craig Beeby, gen mgr; Debbie Coston, dev dir; Ted Riley, progmg dir; Carrie Hulsey, news dir; Dan Schroeder, chief of engrg.

Kingfisher

KINB(FM)— 2000: 105.3 mhz; 800 w. Ant 840 ft. TL: N35 43 38 W97 52 30. 4045 N.W. 64th St., Suite 600, Oklahoma City 73116. Phone: (405) 848-0100. Fax: (405) 843-5288. Licensee: Citadel Broadcasting Co. Group owner: Citadel Broadcasting Corp. (acq 9-30-2002; $3.1 million). Format: Sp. ♦ Larry Bastida, gen mgr; Steve English, stn mgr; Luis Medina, opns mgr.

Lahoma

KXLS(FM)— Nov 1, 1995: 95.7 mhz; 9.6 kw. Ant 502 ft. TL: N36 25 14 W98 01 12. Box 952, Enid 73702. Secondary address: 316 E. Willow Rd., Enid 73701. Phone: (580) 237-1390. Fax: (580) 242-1390. E-mail: hchamplin@knid.com. Licensee: Chisholm Trail Broadcasting Co. (acq 11-1-99; $525,000). Network: ABC. Format: Adult contemp. News staff: one; News: 2 hrs wkly. Target aud: 30-60; female. ♦ Hiram Champlin, gen mgr; Ricky Roggow, gen mgr, opns mgr & progmg dir; Sandy Daniels, gen sls mgr; Geoff Haxton, news dir; G.B. Bonham, chief of engrg.

Langston

*KALU(FM)— Mar 3, 1975: 89.3 mhz; 150 w. Ant 200 ft. TL: N35 56 36 W97 15 32. c/o Gen. Mgr., Sanford Hall, Langston Univ. 73050. Phone: (405) 466-2924. Phone: (405) 466-3342. Fax: (405) 466-2921. E-mail: mfjackson@lunet.edu. Web Site: www.lunet.edu. Licensee: Langston University. Format: Jazz, relg, urban contemp. ♦ Michael Jay Jackson, gen mgr.

Lawton

KBZQ(FM)— May 1, 1992: 99.5 mhz; 16 kw. 338 ft. TL: N34 35 14 W98 32 55. Stereo. Box 6888, 1006 N.W. 47th St., Suite B 73506-6888. Phone: (580) 357-9950. Fax: (580) 357-9995. E-mail: kbzq@sbcglobal.net. Licensee: William R. Fritsch Jr. Arter & Hadden. Format: Adult contemp. News: one hr wkly. Target aud: 25-54; baby boomers, upscale white collar workers. Spec prog: Jazz 4 hrs, Hits of the 70s 5 hrs, Sp 4 hrs wkly. ♦ Chuck Pettigrew, opns dir, opns mgr & progmg dir; Rick Fritsch, gen mgr & sls dir.

*KCCU(FM)— July 13, 1989: 89.3 mhz; 2 kw. Ant 463 ft. TL: N34 37 26 W98 16 15. Stereo. Admin. Bldg., 2800 W. Gore Blvd. 73505. Phone: (580) 581-2472. Phone: (580) 581-2474. Fax: (580) 581-5571. E-mail: markn@cameron.edu. Web Site: www.kccu.org. Licensee: Cameron University. Network: Network: NPR, PRI. Format: News, classical. News staff: 5; News: 40 hrs wkly. Target aud: General. Spec prog: Jazz. ♦ Mark Norman, gen mgr.

KJMZ(FM)—Listing follows KKRX(AM).

*KJRF(FM)— Jan 1, 2001: 91.1 mhz; 10 kw. Ant 413 ft. TL: N34 41 22 W98 07 34. The Christian Center Inc., 2405 S.W. Lee Blvd. 73505. Phone: (580) 357-4498. Fax: (580) 357-1818. E-mail: jesusman@sirinet.net. Web Site: www.thechristian-center.org. Licensee: The Christian Center Inc. Format: Christian. ♦ Reverend Paul Craig, pres; Randy Muirhead, stn mgr, chief of opns & progmg dir; Allan Hampton, engrg dir.

KKRX(AM)— May 27, 1956: 1050 khz; 250 w-D, DA. TL: N34 35 27 W98 21 10. 1525 S.E. Flowermound Rd. 73501. Phone: (580) 355-1050. Fax: (580) 355-1056. Web Site: www.kjmz.com. Licensee: Perry Broadcasting of Lawton Inc. Group owner: Perry Publishing & Broadcasting. (acq 1-31-97; $486,000. with co-located FM). Rep: D & R Radio. Format: Gospel. Spec prog: Ger one hr wkly. ♦ Joy Chapman, gen mgr, opns mgr & gen sls mgr; Michelle Campbell, news dir; Shawn Bailey, chief of engrg.

KJMZ(FM)—Co-owned with KKRX(AM). Oct 23, 1970: 98.1 mhz; 100 kw. 202 ft. TL: N34 35 27 W98 21 10. Stereo. Web Site: www.kjmz.com. Eugene T. Smith. Format: Urban contemp. ♦ Day Lorrezz, progmg dir.

KLAW(FM)— Jan 1, 1965: 101.3 mhz; 100 kw. Ant 584 ft. TL: N34 32 59 W98 32 21. Stereo. 626 D Ave. S.W. 73501. Phone: (580) 581-3600. Fax: (580) 357-2880. E-mail: klaw@clearchannel.com. Web Site: www.klaw.com. Licensee: Capstar TX L.P. Group owner: Clear Channel Communications Inc. (acq 8-30-00; grpsl). Wiley, Rein & Fielding. Format: Country. News staff: one; News: 4 hrs wkly. Target

Stations in the U.S. — Oklahoma

Developers & Brokers of Radio Properties — contact American Media Services at our suite: Philadelphia Marriott Downtown 215-625-2900 / 843-972-2200 / americanmediaservices.com / Charleston, SC / Dallas, TX · Chicago, Il · Austin, TX — American Media Services, LLC

aud: 25-54; adults. ♦Kim Dodds, gen mgr; David Crawford, opns mgr; JoAnne Taylor, gen sls mgr; Helen Cox-Chedester, prom dir.

KMGZ(FM)— Nov 1, 1982: 95.3 mhz; 14 kw. 312 ft. TL: N34 34 36 W98 28 30. Stereo. 1421 Great Plains Blvd., Suite C 73505-2843. Phone: (580) 536-9530. Fax: (580) 536-3299. E-mail: gm@kmgz.com. Web Site: www.kmgz.com. Licensee: Broadco of Texas Inc. (acq 3-9-92; trade and joint venture agreement for KMGZ(FM); 4-6-92). Format: CHR. News: one hr wkly. Target aud: 18-49. ♦Chuck Morgan, pres & gen mgr; Jane O'Malley, gen sls mgr; Albert Young, progmg mgr.

*KVRS(FM)— December 1989: 90.3 mhz; 1 kw vert. Ant 187 ft. TL: N34 37 32 W98 31 43. Stereo. 11 Winding Creek Rd. 73505-9642. Phone: (580) 536-8886. Fax: (580) 536-8891. E-mail: kvvs@kvvsfm.com. Licensee: American Family Association. Group owner: American Family Radio (acq 4-29-2004; $10). Network: American Family Radio. Format: Christian, relg. News: 14 hrs wkly. Target aud: General. ♦Dan Meir, stn mgr & engrg VP.

KVRW(FM)— Mar 13, 1992: 107.3 mhz; 50 kw. 492 ft. TL: N34 36 27 W98 16 26. Stereo. 626 S.W. D Avenue 73501. Phone: (580) 581-3600. Fax: (580) 357-2880. E-mail: oldies@oldies107.com. Web Site: www.oldies107.com. Licensee: Citicasters Licenses L.P. (acq 11-8-2004; $1.6 million). Network: ABC. Format: Oldies. News: one hr wkly. Target aud: 25-54. ♦Kim Dodds, CEO & gen mgr.

KXCA(AM)— May 1, 1941: 1380 khz; 1 kw-U, DA-2. TL: N34 35 24 W98 21 44. 1525 SE Flower Mound 73501. Phone: (580) 355-1050. Fax: (580) 355-1056. E-mail: trevor1380@hotmail.com. Web Site: www.1380theticket.com. Licensee: Perry Broadcasting of Southwest Oklahoma Inc. Group owner: Perry Publishing & Broadcasting Co. (acq 11-22-2002; grpsl). Rep: Roslin. Format: Sports, talk. Target aud: 35 plus. ♦Joy Chapman, gen mgr & gen sls mgr; Trevor Myers, progmg dir.

KZCD(FM)— June 8, 1987: 94.1 mhz; 18 kw. 524 ft. TL: N34 34 24 W98 28 40. Stereo. 626 S.W. D Ave. 73501. Phone: (580) 581-3600. Fax: (580) 357-2880. E-mail: z94@clearchannel.com. Web Site: www.z94.com. Licensee: Capstar TX L.P. Group owner: Clear Channel Communications Inc. (acq 8-30-00; grpsl). Wiley, Rein & Fielding. Format: Rock. News staff: one; News: 2 hrs wkly. Target aud: 18-49; males. ♦Kim Dodds, gen mgr; JoAnne Taylor, gen sls mgr; Helen Cox-Chedester, prom dir; Dan Brown, progmg dir; Scott Maingi, engrg dir.

Lindsay

KBLP(FM)— Oct 1, 1988: 105.1 mhz; 850 w. 564 ft. TL: N34 54 01 W97 33 56. Stereo. 204 S. Main 73052. Phone: (405) 756-4438. Fax: (405) 756-2040. Web Site: www.kblpsports.com. Licensee: South Central Oklahoma Broadcasting & Advertising Corp. Format: Country. News staff: 2; News: 21 hrs wkly. Target aud: 21-65; working consumers. ♦Charlie Jones, pres & gen mgr.

Locust Grove

KEMX(FM)— Feb 14, 1991: 94.5 mhz; 2.3 kw. 367 ft. TL: N36 15 05 W95 13 21. Stereo. 2448 E. 81st St., Suite 4500, Tulsa 74137. Phone: (918) 492-2660. Fax: (918) 492-8840. E-mail: kxoj@kxoj.com. Web Site: www.kxoj.com. Licensee: KXOJ Inc. Group owner: Adonai Radio Group (acq 4-29-92; grpsl). Network: UPI. Format: Contemp Christian music. Target aud: 18-35; young married or single Christians. ♦Mike Stephens, pres; Joy Stephens, VP; David Stephens, gen mgr & adv dir; Bob Thornton, progmg dir.

Lone Grove

KYNZ(FM)— May 25, 1988: 107.1 mhz; 24.5 kw. Ant 335 ft. TL: N34 17 52 W97 09 12. Stereo. 1205 Northglen, Ardmore 73401. Secondary address: Next Media, 1205 Northglen, Ardmore 73401. Phone: (580) 226-0421. Fax: (580) 226-0464. E-mail: webmaster@kynz.com. Web Site: www.kynz.com. Licensee: NM Licensing LLC. Group owner: NextMedia Group L.L.C. (acq 11-14-02;. grpsl). Rep: Christal. Format: Hot adult contemp. News staff: one; News: 25 hrs wkly. Target aud:

18-54. ♦David Smith, pres, VP, gen mgr & stn mgr; Dave Hilton, opns dir; David MacMullen, sls dir & natl sls mgr; Steve Bart, progmg dir.

Madill

KMAD(AM)— May 20, 1962: 1550 khz; 250 w-D. TL: N34 06 24 W96 46 30. Box 576, 6/10 Mile N. on Hwy. 199 73446. Phone: (580) 795-2345. Fax: (580) 795-5623. Licensee: Robert S. Sullins (acq 3-20-98). Network: Network: ABC Information & Entertainment, Jones Radio Networks. Format: Classic hit country. News: 12 hrs wkly. Target aud: General. Spec prog: Farm 2 hrs wkly. ♦Jay Lindley, gen mgr.

Mangum

*KHIM(FM)— 1998: 97.7 mhz; 1.5 kw. 138 ft. TL: N34 52 27 W99 30 01. 509 N. Main, Altus 73521. Phone: (580) 482-9797. Fax: (580) 379-9201. E-mail: info@97khim.com. Licensee: Ray Broadcasting Inc. (acq 12-22-2003; $320,000. with KJCM(FM) Snyder). Format: Classic rock. ♦Terri Kamphaus, gen mgr.

Marlow

KFXI(FM)— August 1987: 92.1 mhz; 100 kw. Ant 390 ft. TL: N34 42 35 W98 03 00. Stereo. 1101 Hwy. 81 N. 73055. Phone: (580) 658-9292. Fax: (580) 658-2561. E-mail: kfxi@texhoma.net. Licensee: DFWU Inc. (group owner). Southmayd & Miller. Format: Country. Target aud: 25-55. Spec prog: Gospel 8 hrs wkly. ♦K.D. Austin, gen mgr; Amy Helton, opns mgr; Sherry Lynn, gen sls mgr; Bill Marshall, progmg dir.

McAlester

*KBCW(FM)— 1999: 91.9 mhz; 700 w. Ant 446 ft. TL: N34 59 13 W95 42 10. Stereo. Univ. of Central Oklahoma, 100 N. University Dr., Edmond 73034-5209. Phone: (405) 974-3333. Phone: (877) 359-3334. Fax: (405) 974-3844. E-mail: kcscfm@kcscfm.com. Web Site: www.kcscfm.com. Licensee: The University of Central Oklahoma. Network: PRI. Format: Class. News staff: one; News: 5 hrs wkly. Target aud: 35 plus; educ, affluent. ♦Bradford Ferguson, gen mgr; Kent Anderson, opns mgr & progmg dir; Barbara Hendrickson, news dir; Preston Walker, chief of engrg.

KMCO(FM)—Listing follows KNED(AM).

KNED(AM)— Mar 14, 1950: 1150 khz; 1 kw-D, 500 w-N, DA-N. TL: N34 56 12 W95 43 59. Stereo. Box 1068 74502-1068. Secondary address: 1801 E. Gene Stipe Blvd. 74501. Phone: (918) 423-1460. Fax: (918) 423-7119. E-mail: kmcokned@mcalesterradio.com. Web Site: mcalesterradio.com. Licensee: Southeastern Oklahoma Radio LLC. (group owner; (acq 1-18-2005; $222,223). Network: ABC Information & Entertainment. Shaw Pittman. Format: C&W Classic. Target aud: 45 plus. ♦Lee Anderson, gen mgr & stn mgr; Sheila Turnbow, gen sls mgr.

KMCO(FM)—Co-owned with KNED(AM). November 1965: 101.3 mhz; 100 kw. 494 ft. TL: N34 59 13 W95 42 10. Stereo. Phone: (918) 426-1050. (Acq 1-18-2005; $766,666). Shaw Pittman. Format: C&W. Target aud: 18-45.

KTMC(AM)— Mar 3, 1946: 1400 khz; 1 kw-U. TL: N34 57 00 W95 45 00. Box 1068 74502. Secondary address: 1801 E. Gene Stipe 74502. Phone: (918) 426-1050. Fax: (918) 423-7119. E-mail: kmconed@mclesteradio.com. Web Site: mcalesterradio.com. Licensee: Southeastern Oklahoma Radio LLC. (acq 1-18-2005; $444,445 with co-located FM). Network: Network: ABC, AP Radio. Shaw Pittman. Format: Oldies. News: 2 hrs wkly. Target aud: 50 plus; older, middle-aged, mature & retired adults. Spec prog: Gospel 5 hrs wkly. ♦Lee Anderson, gen mgr & stn mgr; Sheila Turnbow, gen sls mgr.

KTMC-FM— June 24, 1987: 105.1 mhz; 1.6 kw. 454 ft. TL: N34 59 13 W95 42 10. Stereo. Format: Classic rock. Target aud: 34-50.

Miami

KGLC(FM)—Listing follows KVIS(AM).

KVIS(AM)— February 1948: 910 khz; 1 kw-U, DA-1. TL: N36 53 27 W94 47 00. Box 1555, 8400 S. Hwy. 137 74355. Phone: (918) 542-1818. Phone: (918) 542-7175. Fax: (918) 542-1819. Licensee: Eagle Broadcasting Inc. (acq 2-15-91; with co-located FM; 3-11-91). Latham & Watkins. Format: Southern Gospel. News staff: one; News: 9 hrs wkly. Target aud: Christian/family. ♦Gordon Chirillo, pres; Robert Suman, gen mgr, gen sls mgr & progmg dir; Shanda Daugherty, prom dir & prom mgr; Kimberley Barnes, news dir; Rusty Wynn, chief of engrg.

KGLC(FM)—Co-owned with KVIS(AM). December 1975: 100.9 mhz; 3.6 kw. 273 ft. TL: N36 53 27 W94 47 01. Stereo. Network: USA. Format: Christian, inspirational. Target aud: 25-44.

Midwest City

KEBC(AM)—Licensed to Midwest City. See Oklahoma City

KTLV(AM)— April 1973: 1220 khz; 250 w-D, DA. TL: N35 23 50 W97 27 04. 3336 S.E. 67th St., Oklahoma City 73135. Phone: (405) 672-1220. Phone: (405) 672-3886. Fax: (405) 672-5858. E-mail: ktlv1220@aol.com. Web Site: www.ktlv1220.com. Licensee: First Choice Broadcasting Inc. (acq 6-19-92). Format: Gospel, Christian. Target aud: 24 plus. Spec prog: Sp 4 hrs wkly. ♦Howard D. Williams, pres; Dale Williams, gen mgr & progmg dir.

Moore

*KMSI(FM)— Mar 26, 1991: 88.1 mhz; 30 kw vert. 597 ft. TL: N35 12 07 W97 35 18. Stereo. Box 1924, Tulsa 74101. Secondary address: 120 S.W. 4th St. 73160. Phone: (405) 794-5674; (918) 455-5693. Fax: (405) 794-5112. E-mail: mail@oasisnetwork.org. Web Site: www.oasisnetwork.org. Licensee: Creative Educational Media Corp. Inc. Format: Christian. Target aud: General. ♦David Ingles, pres; Cherri Willis, gen mgr; David Warren, progmg dir; Hal Smith, chief of engrg.

WWLS(AM)— Sept 26, 1922: 640 khz; 1 kw-U, DA-N. TL: N35 17 21 W97 30 08. 4045 N.W. 64th St., Suite 600, Oklahoma 73116. Phone: (405) 848-0100. Fax: (405) 848-5288. Web Site: www.thesportsanimal.com. Licensee: Citadel Broadcasting Co. Group owner: Citadel Broadcasting Corp. (acq 10-28-99; grpsl). Format: Sports. ♦Larry Bastida, gen mgr; Chris Baker, opns mgr.

Muskogee

KBIX(AM)— May 1, 1936: 1490 khz; 450 w-U. TL: N35 46 56 W95 22 37. 215 State, Suite 910 74401. Phone: (918) 682-9700. Fax: (918) 682-6775. Licensee: KMMY Inc. Group owner: Adonai Radio Group (acq 12-11-2002; $1 million. with KCXR(FM) Taft). Format: Sports. ♦David Stephens, gen mgr.

KCXR(FM)—See Taft

KHTT(FM)— February 1972: 106.9 mhz; 100 kw. 1,005 ft. TL: N35 51 41 W95 46 03. Stereo. 7030 S. Yale Ave., Suite 711, Tulsa 74136. Phone: (918) 492-2020. Fax: (918) 496-2681. E-mail: pbryson@rendabroadcasting.com. Web Site: www.khits.com. Licensee: Renda Broadcasting Corp. Group owner: Renda Broadcasting Corp.-Renda Radio Inc. (acq 4-15-93; $1.6 million; 5-3-93). Network: ABC FM Connection. Format: Hot contemp hits. News: 5 hrs wkly. Target aud: 18-34; young adults. ♦Tony Renda, pres; Tod Tucker, opns mgr & progmg dir; Pat Bryson, gen sls mgr; Frank Canoli, prom dir.

KMMY(FM)— Jan 19, 1984: 97.1 mhz; 100 kw. 1,274 ft. TL: N35 17 05 W95 25 26. Stereo. 2448 E. 81 St, Suite 5500, Tulsa 74137. Phone: (918) 492-2660. Fax: (918) 492-8840. Licensee: KMMY Inc.

(acq 9-15-93; $500,000;. FTR: 10-11-93). Format: Country. Target aud: 21-49; middle, upper-middle class. Spec prog: Farm 5 hrs wkly. ♦David Stephens, gen mgr.

Newcastle

KKNG-FM— Apr 15, 1971: 93.3 mhz; 100 kw. 797 ft. TL: N35 11 28 W97 35 49. Stereo. 5101 S. Shields Blvd., Oklahoma City 73129. Phone: (405) 616-5500. Fax: (405) 616-5505. E-mail: info@kkng.com. Web Site: www.kkng.com. Licensee: Tyler Broadcasting Corp. Group owner: Tyler Media Broadcasting Corp. (acq 10-95; $441,000). Network: ABC. Rep: Katz Radio. Format: Classic country. Target aud: 25-54. Spec prog: Oldies 12 hrs, gospel 8 hrs wkly. ♦Kevin Young, progmg dir; Skip Stow, gen mgr, opns mgr & news dir; Randy Mullinax, chief of engrg.

Norman

***KGOU(FM)**— Sept 25, 1970: 106.3 mhz; 3 kw. 300 ft. TL: N35 17 22 W97 21 30. Stereo. Kaufman Hall, Rm. 339, University of Oklahoma 73019. Phone: (405) 325-3388. Fax: (405) 325-7129. E-mail: manager@kgou.org. Web Site: www.kgou.org. Licensee: University of Oklahoma. Network: NPR. Dow, Lohnes & Albertson. Format: News/talk, jazz. News staff: one; News: 82 hrs wkly. Target aud: 25-54; general. Spec prog: Blues 8 hrs, new age 4 hrs wkly. ♦Karen Holp, gen mgr; Jennifer Smith, opns mgr; Jolly Brown, dev dir; Jim Johnson, progmg dir; Scott Gurian, news dir; David White, chief of engrg.

KREF(AM)— November 1949: 1400 khz; 1 kw-U. TL: N35 13 04 W97 24 37. 2020 E. Alameda 73071. Phone: (405) 321-1400. Fax: (405) 321-6820. E-mail: kref@telepath.com. Web Site: www.kref.com. Licensee: Fox Broadcasting, Inc. (acq 1-9-98; $300,000). Reed, Smith, Shaw & McClay. Format: Sports. News staff: one. Target aud: 25-54; middle, upper class adults. ♦John Fox, pres; Mike Holt, gen mgr, chief of opns & gen sls mgr.

***KSSO(FM)**—Not on air, target date: unknown: 89.3 mhz; 4.5 kw. Ant 164 ft. TL: N35 13 04 W97 24 37. 1101 N. 81 Hwy., Marlow 73055. Phone: (580) 658-9292. Fax: (580) 658-2561. Licensee: The Sister Sherry Lynn Foundation Inc. ♦Sherry Austin, pres.

Nowata

KRIG-FM—Licensed to Nowata. See Bartlesville

Okarche

KTUZ-FM— September 1968: 106.7 mhz; 13 kw. Ant 958 ft. TL: N35 36 49 W97 52 19. Stereo. 5101 S. Shields Blvd., Oklahoma City 73129. Phone: (405) 616-9900. Fax: (405) 616-0328. Web Site: www.ktuz.com. Licensee: Tyler Broadcasting Corp. Group owner: Tyler Media Broadcasting Corp. (acq 1-27-98; $100,000. with co-located AM). Network: ABC. Format: Sp. News: 16 hrs wkly. Target aud: 18-65. ♦Skip Stow, gen mgr.

Oklahoma City

KATT-FM— Oct 17, 1960: 100.5 mhz; 97 kw. 1,191 ft. TL: N35 35 22 W97 29 03. Stereo. 4045 N.W. 64th, Suite 600 73116. Phone: (405) 848-0100. Fax: (405) 843-5288. E-mail: todd.griffin@citcomm.com. Web Site: www.katt.com. Licensee: Citadel Broadcasting Co. Group owner: Citadel Broadcasting Corp. (acq 10-28-99; grpsl). Format: AOR. ♦Larry Bastida, gen mgr; Tricia York, gen sls mgr; Chad Lunsford, prom mgr; Chris Baker, progmg dir.

KEBC(AM)—(Midwest City). 1922: 1340 khz; 1 kw-U. TL: N35 29 58 W97 30 33. Stereo. 50 Penn Pl., Suite 1000 73105. Phone: (405) 840-5271. Fax: (405) 840-5808. E-mail: derricknance@clearchannel.com. Licensee: Clear Channel Broadcasting Licenses, Inc. (acq 6-10-2002). Rep: McGavren Guild. Kaye, Scholer, Fierman, Hays & Handler L.L.P. Format: News/talk. News staff: one; News: 3 hrs wkly. Target aud: 25-54. ♦Bill Hurley, gen mgr; Derrick Nance, gen sls mgr; Ken Post, progmg dir.

KHBZ-FM— June 6, 1967: 94.7 mhz; 98 kw. 1,387 ft. TL: N35 32 58 W97 29 50. Stereo. Box 1000 73101. Phone: (405) 840-5271. Fax: (405) 842-1315. Licensee: Clear Channel Broadcasting Licenses, Inc. Group owner: Clear Channel Communications Inc. (acq 1-94; $7.5 million). Format: Alt rock. News staff: one. Target aud: 25-54. ♦Jimmy Barreda, VP & progmg dir.

KJYO(FM)—Listing follows KTOK.

KKWD(FM)—(Edmond). June 28, 1962: 97.9 mhz; 6 kw. 315 ft. TL: N35 34 11 W97 30 01. Stereo. 4045 N.W. 64, Suite 600 73116. Phone: (405) 848-0100. Fax: (405) 843-5288. Web Site: www.wild979.com. Licensee: Citadel Broadcasting Co. Group owner: Citadel Broadcasting Corp. (acq 10-28-99; grpsl). Birch, Horton, Bittner & Cherot. Format: Urban Hits. News: 3 hrs wkly. Target aud: 35-49 & 25-34; young, professional. Spec prog: Relg 2 hrs wkly. ♦Larry Bastida, pres & gen mgr; Chris Baker, stn mgr.

KMGL(FM)— Nov 25, 1965: 104.1 mhz; 100 kw. 1,425 ft. TL: N35 32 58 W97 29 18. Stereo. Box 14818 73113. Secondary address: 400 E. Britton Rd. 73113. Phone: (405) 478-5104. Fax: (405) 478-0448. E-mail: vance@magic104.com. Web Site: www.magic104.com. Licensee: Renda Broadcasting. (group owner; acq 4-88). Format: Adult contemp. ♦Vance Harrison, gen mgr; Harold Patterson, gen sls mgr; Jeff Couch, progmg dir; Dennis Orcutt, chief of engrg.

KOKC(AM)— Dec 24, 1922: 1520 khz; 50 kw-U, DA-N. TL: N35 20 00 W97 30 16. Stereo. Box 14818 73113. Secondary address: 400 E. Britton Rd. 73113. Phone: (405) 794-4000. Fax: (405) 793-0514. Web Site: www.komaradio.com. Licensee: Renda Broadcasting Corp. of Nevada. Group owner: Renda Broadcasting Corp. (acq 6-30-98; grpsl). Network: CBS. Rep: CBS Radio. Format: News/talk. Target aud: 25-54. ♦Vance Harrison Jr., gen mgr; Jim Williston, gen sls mgr; Garth Maier, progmg dir; Dennis Orcutt, chief of engrg.

KOMA(FM)— 1964: 92.5 mhz; 98 kw. 984 ft. TL: N35 32 52 W97 29 29. Stereo. 400 E. Britton Rd. 73114. Phone: (405) 478-5104. Web Site: www.komaradio.com. Licensee: Renda Broadcasting Corp. of Nevada. Group owner: Renda Broadcasting Corp. (acq 6-30-98; grpsl). Rep: Allied Radio Partners. Format: Oldies. Target aud: 25-54. ♦Vance Harrison Jr., gen mgr.

KQCV(AM)— 1948: 800 khz; 2.5 kw-D, 500 w-N, DA. TL: N35 24 45 W97 40 26. 1919 N. Broadway Ave. 73103. Phone: (405) 521-0800. Phone: (405) 521-1414. Fax: (405) 521-1391. Web Site: www.bottradionetwork.com. Licensee: Bott Broadcasting Co. Group owner: Bott Radio Network (acq 1-76). Format: Christian info, news. Target aud: 25-54; family oriented. ♦Richard P. Bott, pres; Richard Bott II, VP; Paul Sublett, gen mgr; Eben Fowler, opns dir.

KRMP(AM)— 1946: 1140 khz; 1 kw-D. TL: N35 23 14 W97 29 56. 1528 N.E. 23rd St. 73111. Phone: (405) 427-5877. Fax: (405) 424-6708. Web Site: www.kvsp.com. Licensee: Perry Broadcasting Co. Inc. Group owner: Perry Publishing & Broadcasting Co. (acq 3-3-93; $375,000;. FTR: 3-22-93). Format: Urban contemp. ♦Russell Perry, CEO; Kevin Perry, gen mgr, gen sls mgr & adv mgr; Terry Monday, opns mgr & progmg dir; George Chambers, chief of engrg.

KROU(FM)—See Spencer

KRXO(FM)— Aug 7, 1987: 107.7 mhz; 99 kw. 991 ft. TL: N35 32 58 W97 29 18. Stereo. Box 14818 73113. Secondary address: 400 E. Britton Rd. 73113. Phone: (405) 478-5104. Fax: (405) 478-0448. E-mail: bwiley@krxo.com. Web Site: www.krxo.com. Licensee: Renda Broadcasting Corp of Nevada. Group owner: Renda Broadcasting Corp. Format: Classic rock. ♦Vance Harrison, gen mgr; Buddy Wiley, progmg dir; Steve Bennett, news dir.

KTLR(AM)— 1946: 890 khz; 1 kw-D. TL: N35 33 59 W97 28 28. 5101 S. Shields Blvd. 73129. Phone: (405) 616-5500. Fax: (405) 616-5505. Web Site: www.ktlr.com. Licensee: Tyler Broadcasting Corp. Group owner: Tyler Media Broadcasting Corp. (acq 1999; $40,000). Rep: Christal. Format: Community/talk. Target aud: 10-80. Spec prog: Sp 3 hrs wkly. ♦Skip Stow, gen mgr; Mike Miller, stn mgr, opns mgr, gen sls mgr & chief of engrg; Cody Sparks, progmg dir.

KTOK(AM)— Jan 29, 1927: 1000 khz; 5 kw-U, DA-2. TL: N35 21 29 W97 27 48. Box 1000 73101. Secondary address: 10th Fl., 50 Penn Place 73101. Phone: (405) 840-5271. Fax: (405) 842-1315. Web Site: www.ktok.com. Licensee: Clear Channel Broadcasting Licences, Inc. (group owner; acq 8-5-92). Network: ABC Information & Entertainment. Rep: Clear Channel. Format: News/talk. ♦Mike McCarville, CEO & progmg dir.

KJYO(FM)—Co-owned with KTOK. Apr 9, 1961: 102.7 mhz; 98 kw. 900 ft. TL: N35 32 52 W97 29 29. (CP: Ant 984 ft.). Stereo. Web Site: www.kj103fm.com. Licensee: Clear Channel Broadcasting Licenses, Inc. Network: ABC Information & Entertainment. Format: CHR. ♦Mike McCoy, progmg dir.

KTST(FM)— Mar 16, 1962: 101.9 mhz; 100 kw. 1,390 ft. TL: N35 32 58 W97 29 50. Stereo. 50 Penn Place / Ste 1000 73118. Phone: (405) 858-1400. Fax: (405) 858-1106. E-mail: tomtravis@clearchannel.com. Web Site: www.thetwister.com. Licensee: Clear Channel Broadcasting Licenses, Inc. (group owner; acq 1996; grpsl). Format: Country. News staff: one. Target aud: 18-49. ♦Bill Hurley, gen mgr; Tom Travis, opns dir & progmg dir.

KXXY-FM— October 1964: 96.1 mhz; 100 kw. 1,167 ft. TL: N35 32 58 W97 29 18. (CP: Ant 256 ft.). Stereo. Box 1000 73101. Phone: (405) 840-5271. Fax: (405) 842-1315. Licensee: Clear Channel Broadcasting Licenses Inc. Group owner: Clear Channel Communications Inc. (acq 1996; grpsl). Format: Country. ♦Bill Reed, gen mgr & progmg dir.

KYIS(FM)— June 1969: 98.9 mhz; 100 kw. 1,108 ft. TL: N35 33 36 W97 29 07. Stereo. 4045 N.W. 64th St., Suite 600 73116. Phone: (405) 848-0100. Fax: (405) 843-5288. E-mail: equest@kyis.com. Web Site: www.kyis.com. Licensee: Citadel Broadcasting Co. Group owner: Citadel Broadcasting Corp. (acq 10-28-99; grpsl). Network: AP Radio. Format: Hot adult contemp. News staff: one. Target aud: 25-54; female. ♦Larry Bastida, gen mgr; Tricia York, gen sls mgr; Don Sweeney, prom dir; Ray Kalusa, progmg dir.

***KYLV(FM)**— Nov 3, 1980: 88.9 mhz; 4.3 kw. 502 ft. TL: N35 36 48 W97 28 29. Stereo. 2351 Sunset Blvd., Suite 170-218, Rocklin, CA 95765. Phone: (916) 434-8400. Fax: (916) 251-1650. E-mail: klove@klove.com. Web Site: www.klove.com. Licensee: Educational Media Foundation. Group owner: EMF Broadcasting (acq 11-9-98; $1.2 million). Network: K-Love. Shaw Pittman. Format: Contemp Christian. News staff: 3. Target aud: 25-44; Judeo-Christian female. Spec prog: Black 3 hrs, relg 2 hrs, gospel 4 hrs, pub affrs 4 hrs wkly. ♦Richard Jenkins, pres; Mike Novak, VP; Lloyd Parker, gen mgr; Chris Joyce, prom dir & prom mgr.

WKY(AM)— January 1920: 930 khz; 5 kw-U, DA-N. TL: N35 33 43 W97 30 27. Stereo. 4045 NW 64th, Ste 600, Oklahoma City 73116. Phone: (405) 848-0100. Fax: (405) 843-5288. Web Site: www.supertalk930wky.com. Licensee: Citadel Broadcasting Co. Group owner: Citadel Broadcasting Corp. (acq 1-31-03; $7.7 million). Wiley, Rein & Fielding. Format: News/talk. Target aud: 25-54. ♦Mike Beckner, gen sls mgr; Debbie Schaer, natl sls mgr; L.J. Smith, progmg dir; Jerry Bohnen, news dir; Jay Perkey, chief of engrg.

WWLS-FM—(Bethany). Oct 29, 1965: 104.9 mhz; 3 kw. 299 ft. TL: N35 29 58 W97 37 08. 4045 Northwest 64th St., Suite 600 73116. Phone: (405) 848-0100. Fax: (405) 843-5288. Web Site: www.thesportsanimal.com. Licensee: Citadel Broadcasting Co. Group owner: Citadel Broadcasting Corp. (acq 10-28-99; grpsl). Network: USA. Format: Sports. Target aud: 25-54. Spec prog: Relg. ♦Larry Bastida, gen mgr; Jay Davis, gen sls mgr; Chad Lunsford, prom dir; Dax Barry Jr., news dir.

Okmulgee

KOKL(AM)— October 1937: 1240 khz; 1 kw-U. TL: N35 36 31 W95 58 19. 100 E. 7th St., Suite 100 74447. Phone: (918) 756-3646. Fax: (918) 756-1800. E-mail: kokl@aol.com. Licensee: Regency Radio Inc. (acq 2-22-94; 3-21-94). Network: ABC. Format: Oldies. News staff: one; News: 16 hrs wkly. Target aud: 25 plus; mid to upper income. Spec prog: Tulsa Univ. sports 10 hrs. ♦James R. Brewer, pres; Paul Brown, gen mgr.

Owasso

KQLL-FM— Oct 1, 1981: 106.1 mhz; 100 kw. 1,315 ft. TL: N36 31 36 W95 39 12. Stereo. 2625 South Memorial, Tulsa 74129. Phone: (918) 388-5100. Fax: (918) 665-0555. Web Site: www.kooltulsa.com. Licensee: Clear Channel Broadcasting Licenses Inc. Group owner: Clear Channel Communications Inc. (acq 1997; grpsl). Format: Oldies. Target aud: Adults 35-64. ♦Michael Oppenheimer, gen mgr; Don Cristi, opns mgr.

Pauls Valley

KVLH(AM)— December 1947: . Stn currently dark 1470 khz; 890 w-D, 35 w-N, DA-2. TL: N34 42 15 W97 15 19. DFWU Inc., 1101 N. 81 Hwy., Marlow 73055. Phone: (580) 658-9292. Fax: (580) 658-2561. Licensee: DFWU Inc. (group owner; acq 1-27-00; $25,000). Southmayd & Miller. Format: Oldies. ♦Sherry Lynn, pres; K.D. Austin, gen mgr.

Pawhuska

KBVL(FM)— 1997: 103.9 mhz; 3 kw. 328 ft. TL: N36 44 56 W96 17 51. 2245 S.E. Washington Blvd., St. A1/2, Box 3546, Bartleaville

Stations in the U.S. Oklahoma

74006. Phone: (918) 333-8550. Fax: (918) 333-8553. Web Site: www.kbvl.com. Licensee: Kurtis Media LLC (acq 12-18-2003; $213,500). Format: Top-40. ♦ Jack Borgen, gen mgr.

KPGM(AM)— Oct 19, 1963: 1500 khz; 500 w-D. TL: N36 45 42 W96 11 58. Box 1526 74056. Phone: (918) 287-1145. Fax: (918) 287-1473. Licensee: Potter Radio LLC (acq 5-31-2005; $100,000). Format: Gospel. ♦ Kevin Potter, pres & gen mgr; Charlie Taraboletti, progmg dir.

Perry

KOKP(AM)— July 6, 1986: 1020 khz; 400 w-D, 250 w-N, DA-2. TL: N36 15 35 W97 13 01. Box 2509, Ponca City 74602. Phone: (580) 765-2485. Fax: (580) 767-1103. Licensee: Team Radio L.L.C. (group owner; (acq 7-14-98; $308,000. with co-located FM). Booth, Freret, Imlay & Tepper P. Format: Sports. Target aud: 24 plus; agriculture-related country. ♦ John Singer, pres & gen mgr; Bill Coleman, stn mgr & gen sls mgr; Danny Diamond, progmg dir.

KOSB(FM)— Co-owned with KOKP(AM). Nov 24, 1988: 105.1 mhz; 6 kw. Ant 328 ft. TL: N36 14 15 W97 21 59. Stereo. Network: Westwood One. Format: All 70s. News staff: one. Target aud: 25-55.

Pocola

*KKRI(FM)— June 11, 2002: 88.1 mhz; 26 kw vert. Ant 420 ft. TL: N35 09 02 W94 13 48. Stereo. 5700 W. Oaks Blvd., Rocklin, CA 95765. Phone: (916) 251-1600. Fax: (916) 251-1650. E-mail: info@air1.com. Web Site: www.air1.com. Licensee: Educational Media Foundation. Group owner: EMF Broadcasting. Network: Air 1. Shaw Pittman Format: Contemp Christian. News staff: 3. Target aud: 18-35; Judeo-Christian, female. ♦ Jeff Cooke, chmn; Richard Jenkins, pres; Thomas R. Mason, exec VP.

Ponca City

KIXR(FM)— June 1984: 104.7 mhz; 25 kw. Ant 292 ft. TL: N36 47 21 W97 02 53. Stereo. Box 2631 74602. Secondary address: 3924 Santa Fe Rd. 74602. Phone: (580) 765-5491. Fax: (580) 762-8329. E-mail: kixr@kixr.com. Web Site: www.kixr.com. Licensee: Mur-Thom Broadcasting Inc. (acq 8-10-94; $80,000; 9-12-94). Network: Westwood One. Format: Community radio. News: 4 hrs wkly. Target aud: 24-55; core audience of females between the ages of 24-45. Spec prog: Native American 3 hrs wkly. ♦ Carol Murphy, pres; Gordon Thompson, gen mgr & progmg dir; Dave Foster, chief of engrg.

*KJTH(FM)— 2004: 89.7 mhz; 100 kw. Ant 1,007 ft. TL: N36 35 42 W97 34 38. Box 14 74602. Secondary address: 6600 W. Hwy. 60 74601. Phone: (580) 767-1400. Fax: (580) 765-1700. E-mail: mail@klvv.com. Web Site: www.thehousefm.com. Licensee: The Love Station Inc. Format: Christian music. Target aud: 25-45; young Christian adults. ♦ Doyle Brewer, CEO, pres & gen mgr; Janelle Keith, prom dir; Shaun Michaels, progmg dir.

KLOR-FM— December 1965: 99.3 mhz; 3 kw. 300 ft. TL: N36 46 59 W97 04 15. Stereo. 122 N. 3rd St. 74601. Phone: (580) 762-9930. Fax: (580) 767-1103. E-mail: billc@eteamradio.com. Web Site: www.eteamradio.com. Licensee: Team Radio L.L.C. (group owner; acq 3-18-99). Network: Network: Westwood One, Jones Radio Networks. Format: Classic rock, oldies. News staff: one; News: 75 hrs wkly. Target aud: 18-55. ♦ Bill Coleman, pres & gen mgr; Darrel Dye, gen sls mgr; Jerry Vaughn, progmg dir.

*KLVV(FM)— December 1992: 88.7 mhz; 11.5 kw. 479 ft. TL: N36 41 25 W97 10 20. Stereo. Box 14 74602. Secondary address: 6600 W. Hwy. 60 74601. Phone: (580) 767-1400. Fax: (580) 765-1700. E-mail: mail@klvv.com. Web Site: www.klvv.com; www.mychristianfm.com. Licensee: The Love Station Inc. Format: Inspirational music, Christian teaching. Target aud: 25-45; young Christian adults. ♦ Doyle Brewer, CEO, pres & gen mgr; Tony Weir, progmg.

KOKB(AM)—See Blackwell

KPNC-FM— June 5, 1979: 100.9 mhz; 6 kw. 285 ft. TL: N36 39 56 W97 04 20. Stereo. Box 2509, 1000 Oakland Rd. 74602. Phone: (580) 765-2485. Phone: (580) 767-1101. Fax: (580) 767-1103. E-mail: billc@eteamradio.com. Web Site: www.eteamradio.com. Licensee: Team Radio L.L.C. (group owner; acq 7-20-90). Network: ABC Information & Entertainment. Format: Country. News: 20 hrs wkly. Target aud: 25-54; working middle class. Spec prog: Farm 5 hrs wkly. ♦ Bill Coleman, chmn, VP & gen mgr; Darrel Dye, sls dir & gen sls mgr; Jerry Vaughn, progmg dir.

WBBZ(AM)— 1927: 1230 khz; 1 kw-U. TL: N36 41 46 W97 03 07. Stereo. Box 588, 1601 E. Oklahoma 74602. Phone: (580) 765-6607. Fax: (580) 765-6611. E-mail: wbbz@poncacity.net. Web Site: www.wbbz.com. Licensee: Ponca City Publishing Co. (acq 1949). Format: Classic favorites. News: one; News: 12 hrs wkly. Target aud: 35 plus. Spec prog: Class 5 hrs, relg 5 hrs, big band 3 hrs wkly. ♦ Phil Turney, gen mgr, stn mgr, gen sls mgr & news dir; Randy Bishop, pub affrs dir; Tom Muchmore, CEO & chief of engrg.

Poteau

*KARG(FM)— June 1998: 91.7 mhz; 3.25 kw. 1,866 ft. TL: N35 04 17 W94 40 47. Box 3206, American Family Radio, Tupelo, MS 38803. Phone: (662) 844-8888, EXT. 204. Fax: (662) 842-6791. Web Site: www.afr.net. Licensee: American Family Association. Group owner: American Family Radio Format: Inspirational Christian. ♦ Marvin Sanders, gen mgr.

KOMS(FM)— Oct 18, 1969: 107.3 mhz; 100 kw. 1,810 ft. TL: N34 57 50 W94 22 34. Stereo. 4608 Radio Tower Rd., Van Buren, AR 72956. Phone: (501) 479-3422. Fax: (479) 474-2649. E-mail: jpmorgan@hotmail.com. Web Site: www.bigcountry1073.com. Licensee: Cumulus Licensing Corp. Group owner: Cumulus Media Inc. (acq 5-17-99; $950,000). Network: CNN Radio. Format: Class country. News staff: News progmg 60 hrs wkly Target aud: 25-54; but we gather in all from 12 plus. ♦ Smitty O'Loughlin, gen mgr; J.P. Morgan, opns mgr; Michael Hauser, progmg dir; Cindi Cover, sls; Jim McMormick, sls; Don Jones, engr.

KPRV(AM)— Nov 25, 1953: 1280 khz; 1 kw-D. TL: N35 01 08 W94 39 22. Box 1331, Rt. 1 74953. Phone: (918) 647-3221. Fax: (918) 647-5092. E-mail: lbilly@clnk.com. Web Site: www.kprvradio.com. Licensee: LeRoy Billy. Network: ABC. Robert Allen. Format: Classic Rock/Adult Contemporary. News: 24 hrs wkly. Target aud: 24-54. Spec prog: Gospel 12 hrs wkly. ♦ Joann Billy, gen mgr; LeRoy Billy, gen sls mgr; David Billy, progmg dir & pub affrs dir; Larry Johnson, chief of engrg.

KZBB(FM)— 1967: 97.9 mhz; 100 kw. 2,000 ft. TL: N35 04 19 W94 40 46. 311 Lexington Ave., Fort Smith, AR 72901. Phone: (479) 782-8888. Fax: (479) 782-0366. E-mail: b98@kzbb.com. Web Site: www.kzbb.com. Licensee: Capstar TX L.P. Group owner: Clear Channel Communications Inc. (acq 8-30-00; grpsl). Format: CHR. News: one hr wkly. Target aud: 18-49; upscale. Spec prog: Black 2 hrs, jazz 2 hrs, relg one hr wkly. ♦ Paul Swint, gen mgr; Lee Matthews, opns mgr & progmg mgr; Daren Bobb, news dir & prom.

Pryor

KMUR(AM)— July 3, 1950: 1570 khz; 1 kw-D. TL: N36 18 04 W95 19 29. Box 702588, Tulsa 74170. Phone: (918) 496-7700. Fax: (918) 746-7615. E-mail: KMUR@1570country.com. Web Site: www.1570country.com. Licensee: Reunion Broadcasting L.L.C. (group owner; (acq 11-23-2003; $75,000). Network: CNN Radio. Hardy, Carey & Chautin. Format: Country. News staff: one; News: 10 hrs wkly. Target aud: 25 plus. ♦ Stan Tacker, gen mgr; Terri Tacker, gen sls mgr.

KMYZ-FM— July 3, 1969: 104.5 mhz; 78 kw. 1,250 ft. TL: N36 18 04 W95 19 29. Stereo. 5810 E. Skelly Dr., Suite 801, Tulsa 74135. Phone: (918) 665-3131. Fax: (918) 663-6622. Web Site: www.edgetulsa.com. Licensee: Shamrock Communications Inc. (group owner; acq 4-14-84). Format: Alternative rock. ♦ William Lynett, CEO; J. Michael Demarco, gen mgr.

Roland

KREU(FM)— Dec 29, 1995: 92.3 mhz; 740 w. 932 ft. TL: N35 31 22 W94 23 32. 605 N. Greenwood, Fort Smith, AR 72901. Phone: (479) 785-2527. Fax: (501) 782-9127. Licensee: Star 92 Co. (acq 6-13-2003; $10,000). Format: Spanish. ♦ Gary Keifer, gen mgr; Fred Baker Jr., opns mgr & gen sls mgr.

Sallisaw

KKBD(FM)— May 18, 1972: 95.9 mhz; 30 kw. 600 ft. TL: N35 24 29 W94 41 13. Stereo. 311 Lexington ve., Fort Smith, AR 72901. Phone: (479) 782-8888. E-mail: info@bigdog959.com. Web Site: www.bigdog959.com. Licensee: Clear Channel Radio Licenses, Inc. Group owner: Clear Channel Communiations Inc. (acq 8-30-00; grpsl). Format: Classic Rock. Target aud: 25-49; adults. ♦ Paul Swint, gen mgr.

KKUZ(AM)— Sept 16, 1968: . Stn currently dark 1560 khz; 250 w-D. TL: N35 26 34 W94 46 33. 7th Fl., 532 Garrison Ave., Fort Smith, AR 72901-2522. Licensee: Teddy Bear Communications Inc. ♦ Ted Hite Sr., gen mgr.

Sand Springs

KRTQ(FM)— June 1989: 102.3 mhz; 1.7 kw. Ant 436 ft. TL: N36 09 40 W95 53 06. 7136 S. Yale, Suite 500, Tulsa 74136. Phone: (918) 493-3434. Fax: (918) 493-2376. E-mail: chris.kelly@cox.com. Web Site: www.rock1023.com. Licensee: CXR Holdings L.L.C. Group owner: Cox Broadcasting (acq 3-16-99; $3.5 million). Format: Rock/AOR. Target aud: 25-54; general. ♦ Dan Lawrie, gen mgr; Chris Kelly, progmg dir; Wayne Smith, opns mgr & chief of engrg.

KTFX(AM)— July 22, 1961: 1340 khz; 500 w-D, 1 kw-N. TL: N36 09 40 W96 03 10. (CP: TL: N36 07 58 W96 05 36). 8886 W. 21st St. 74063. Phone: (918) 245-0254. Fax: (918) 245-0255. Licensee: K95.5 Inc. (group owner; acq 8-28-98; $750,000 with co-located FM). Format: Christian contemp. News: one hr wkly. Target aud: 18-54; general. Spec prog: Sp 12 hrs wkly. ♦ Gail C. Payne, pres & gen mgr.

Sapulpa

KXOJ-FM—Listing follows KYAL(AM).

KYAL(AM)— June 15, 1962: 1550 khz; 2.5 kw-D, 47 w-N, DA-1. TL: N36 01 08 W96 05 55. Stereo. Cityplex Towers, 2448 E. 81st St., Tulsa 74137-4272. Phone: (918) 492-2660. Fax: (918) 492-8840. Licensee: KXOJ Inc. Group owner: Adonai Radio Group (acq 5-2-73). Format: Sports. Target aud: 35 plus. ♦ David Stephens, pres, gen mgr, opns mgr, sls dir & mktg dir.

KXOJ-FM— Co-owned with KYAL(AM). Feb 22, 1977: 100.9 mhz; 5 kw. 360 ft. TL: N36 03 38 W96 06 03. Stereo. E-mail: mail@kxoj.com. Web Site: www.kxoj.com. Format: Contemp Christian mus. ♦ Mike Stephens, CEO; David Stephens, stn mgr, opns dir, dev dir & adv dir.

Seminole

KIRC(FM)— Nov 1, 1978: 105.9 mhz; 4.4 kw. 384 ft. TL: N35 18 28 W96 45 18. Stereo. 2 E. Main St., Shawnee 74801-6906. Phone: (405) 878-1803. Phone: (405) 382-0105. Fax: (405) 878-0162. E-mail: kirc1059@aol.com. Licensee: One Ten Broadcast Group Inc. (group owner; acq 9-6-91). Format: Country. News staff: 9; News: 2 hrs wkly. Target aud: 12-55; general. Spec prog: Area tribes one hr wkly. ♦ Linda Jones, pres & VP; Dennis Burton, gen mgr; David Beerley, gen sls mgr & progmg dir; Hal Smith, chief of engrg.

KTLS-FM—See Holdenville

KWSH(AM)—See Wewoka

*KXTH(FM)— October 2003: 89.1 mhz; 2.3 kw vert. Ant 387 ft. TL: N35 12 53 W96 44 26. Box 14, Ponca City 74602-0014. Secondary

Oklahoma

address: 6600 W. Hwy. 60, Ponca City 74601. Phone: (580) 767-1400. Fax: (580) 765-1700. E-mail: mail@klvv.com. Web Site: www.thehousefm.com. Licensee: The Love Station Inc. (acq 9-16-03). Format: Adult contemp, Christian. Target aud: 25-45; young Christian adults. ◆ Doyle Brewer, CEO, pres & gen mgr; Janelle Keith, prom; Tony Weir, progmg.

Shawnee

KGFF(AM)— Dec 10, 1930: 1450 khz; 1 kw-U. TL: N35 21 39 W96 53 41. Box 9 74802. Secondary address: 1570 S. Gordon Cooper Drive 74801. Phone: (405) 273-4390. Fax: (405) 273-4530. Web Site: www.kgff.com. Licensee: Citizen Band Potawatomi Indian Tribe of Oklahoma Inc. (acq 11-10-98; $155,000). Format: Adult standards. News staff: one; News: 20 hrs wkly. General. Spec prog: school, University of Oklahoma, Oklahoma Baptist University, St. Gregory's University, relg 4 hrs wkly. ◆ Michael Askins, gen mgr & opns dir.

KQCV-FM— Apr 13, 1998: 95.1 mhz; 100 kw. 1,004 ft. TL: N35 15 47 W96 22 43. 1919 N. Broadway, Oklahoma City 73103. Phone: (405) 521-0800. Fax: (405) 521-1391. Web Site: bottradionetwork.com. Licensee: Community Broadcasting Inc. Group owner: Bott Radio Network Format: Christian info & teaching. ◆ Paul Sublett, gen mgr; Jerry McCall, opns mgr.

Snyder

*****KJCM(FM)**— 2000: 100.3 mhz; 18 kw. Ant 384 ft. TL: N34 38 02 W99 05 03. 509 N. Main St., Altus 73521. Phone: (580) 482-9797. Fax: (580) 397-9201. Licensee: Ray Broadcasting Inc. (acq 12-22-2003; $320,000. with KHIM(FM) Mangum). Format: Adult contemp. ◆ Bat Masterson, gen mgr.

Spencer

*****KROU(FM)**— Jan 28, 1993: 105.7 mhz; 4 kw. 328 ft. TL: N35 35 22 W97 29 03. 780 Van Vleet Oval, Norman 73019. Phone: (405) 325-3388. Fax: (405) 325-7129. E-mail: manager@kgou.org. Web Site: www.kgou.org. Licensee: University of Oklahoma. Network: NPR. Dow, Lohnes & Albertson. Format: News/talk, jazz. News staff: one; News: 82 hrs wkly. Target aud: 25-54; general. Spec prog: Blues 8 hrs, new age 4 hrs wkly. ◆ Karen Holp, gen mgr; Jim Johnson, progmg dir.

Sperry

KMUS(AM)— July 3, 1948: 1380 khz; 7 kw-D, 250 w-N, DA-2. TL: N36 15 59 W95 58 15. 8321 E. 61st St., Tulsa 74145. Phone: (918) 250-8484. Fax: (918) 250-6464. Web Site: www.radiodisney.com. Licensee: Radio Disney Group LLC. Group owner: ABC Inc. (acq 2-28-2003; $1.5 million). Format: Contemp hit. ◆ Stan Tacker, gen mgr; Terri Tacker, gen sls mgr; Jason Walker, progmg dir.

Stigler

*****KTKL(FM)**— 2003: 88.5 mhz; 1 w horiz, 22 kw vert. Ant 643 ft vert. TL: N35 08 30 W95 21 20. Stereo. 5700 W. Oaks Blvd., Rocklin, CA 95765. Phone: (916) 251-1600. Fax: (916) 251-1650. E-mail: klove@klove.com. Web Site: www.klove.com. Licensee: Educational Media Foundation. Group owner: EMF Broadcasting. Network: K-Love. Shaw Pittman. Format: Christian contemp. News staff: 3. Target aud: 25-44; Judeo Christian, female. ◆ Richard Jenkins, pres; Mike Novak, VP; Lloyd Parker, gen mgr.

Stillwater

KGFY(FM)— Feb 6, 1967: 105.5 mhz; 4.9 kw. Ant 361 ft. TL: N36 10 31 W97 00 51. Stereo. 408 E. Thomas Rd. 74075. Phone: (405) 372-6000. Fax: (405) 372-6969. Licensee: Stillwater Broadcasting LLC. Group owner: Mahaffey Enterprises Inc. (acq 9-28-2001). Network: ABC Information & Entertainment. Fletcher, Heald & Hildreth. Format: Country. News staff: 2; News: 5 hrs wkly. Target aud: 25-54; young, college community & upscale educated people. Spec prog: Contemp Christian 4 hrs wkly. ◆ David Webb, gen mgr.

*****KOSU(FM)**— Dec 29, 1955: 91.7 mhz; 100 kw. Ant 1,010 ft. TL: N36 06 33 W97 11 43. Stereo. Oklahoma State Univ., 303 P.M. Bldg. 74078. Phone: (405) 744-6352. Fax: (405) 744-9970. Web Site: www.kosu.org. Licensee: Oklahoma State University. Network: NPR. Format: Class, educ, news. News staff: 2; News: 48 hrs wkly. Target aud: General. Spec prog: American Indian one hr wkly. ◆ Craig Beeby, gen mgr; Debbie Coston, dev dir.

KSPI(AM)— June 1, 1947: 780 khz; 250 w-D. TL: N36 04 56 W97 03 13. Stereo. Box 1269 74076. Secondary address: 408 E. Thomas Rd. 74076. Phone: (405) 372-7800. Fax: (405) 372-6969. E-mail: stillwaterradio@provalue.net. Licensee: Stillwater Broadcasting LLC. Group owner: Mahaffey Enterprises Inc. (acq 7-21-97; $650,000 with co-located FM). Network: ESPN Radio. Format: News/talk, sports. News staff: one; News: 12 hrs wkly. Target aud: 30 plus. Spec prog: News, sports, features. ◆ John Mahaffey, pres; David Webb, gen mgr & sls VP; Gil Stuart, progmg mgr; Bill Van Ness, news dir.

KSPI-FM— Nov 1, 1947: 93.7 mhz; 16 kw. 886 ft. TL: N36 06 31 W97 11 46. Stereo. Format: Adult contemp. News staff: 2; News: 11 hrs wkly. Target aud: 24 plus. ◆ Diane Keenom, opns mgr & mus dir; David Webb, gen sls mgr; Gil Stuart, prom dir & progmg dir; Bill Vanness, news dir & pub affrs dir.

KVRO(FM)— Apr 12, 1997: 98.1 mhz; 6 kw. Ant 328 ft. TL: N36 13 10 W97 09 47. Stereo. Box 1269 74076-1269. Secondary address: 408 E. Thomas 74075. Phone: (405) 372-6000. Fax: (405) 372-6969. E-mail: stillwaterradio@coxinet.net. Licensee: Stillwater Broadcasting LLC. Group owner: Mahaffey Enterprises Inc. (acq 9-28-2001). Network: ABC. Fletcher, Heald & Hildreth. Format: Oldies. News staff: 2; News: 24 hrs wkly. Target aud: 25-54. Spec prog: Crossroads/ Blues Showw/Chad Weaver - 7pm-9pm. ◆ David Webb, gen mgr; Gil Stuart, opns mgr; Bill Van Ness, news dir.

Stuart

*****KLRB(FM)**— July 25, 2003: 89.3 mhz; 3 kw vert. Ant 272 ft. TL: N34 54 57 W96 08 10. Box 145, 2.2 mi W of Stuart, 1/2 mi N 74570. Phone: (918) 697-4019. Fax: (580) 892-3941. Licensee: Lighthouse of Prayer Inc. Format: Country. ◆ Walter Kuhlman, pres; Stephen Burke, gen mgr & stn mgr.

Sulphur

*****KFXT(FM)**— 2000: 90.7 mhz; 7 kw. Ant 298 ft. TL: N34 32 57 W96 58 34. Sister Sherry Lynn Foundation Inc., 1101 N. 81 Hwy., Marlow 73055. Phone: (580) 658-9292. Fax: (580) 658-2561. Licensee: Sister Sherry Lynn Foundation Inc. Southmayd & Miller. Format: Gospel.

KIXO(FM)— Nov 11, 1979: 106.1 mhz; 2.65 kw. Ant 499 ft. TL: N34 39 03 W96 59 24. Stereo. 1101 Hwy. 81 N., Marlow 73055. Phone: (580) 658-9292. Fax: (580) 658-2561. Licensee: DFWU Inc. (group owner; acq 10-1-90). Southmayd & Miller. Format: Country. News: 5 hrs wkly. Target aud: 25-52. ◆ Ken Austin, gen mgr; Sherry Lynn, gen sls mgr; Bill Marshall, progmg dir; Amy Helton, chief of engrg.

Taft

KCXR(FM)— Mar 20, 1990: 100.3 mhz; 6 kw. Ant 380 ft. TL: N35 48 42 W95 34 12. Stereo. 2448 E. 81st, Suite 5500, Tulsa 74137. Phone: (918) 492-2660. Fax: (918) 492-8840. Licensee: KXOJ Inc. (group owner; (acq 12-11-2002; $1 million. with KBIX(AM) Mukogee). Format: Christian Rock. News staff: one; News: 14 hrs wkly. Target aud: 25-54. Spec prog: Farm one hr wkly. ◆ Michael P. Stephens, pres; David Stevens, gen mgr.

Tahlequah

KEOK(FM)— Listing follows KTLQ(AM).

KTLQ(AM)— August 1957: 1350 khz; 1 kw-D, 61 w-N. TL: N35 53 43 W94 57 12. Stereo. 517 S. Muskogee 74465. Phone: (918) 456-2511. Fax: (918) 456-3231. E-mail: okctry@fullnet.net. Web Site: www.tahlequah.com/okcountry. Licensee: Payne 5 Communications LLC (acq 11-24-2003; $1.15 million. with co-located FM). Network: Westwood One. Format: Sports, Southern Gospel. News staff: one; News: 6 hrs wkly. Target aud: 25-54. ◆ Ralph Lynch, gen mgr; Mitchell Johnson, progmg VP; C.H. Jackson, news dir; Mick Reed, pub affrs dir; Eric Morris, engrg mgr.

KEOK(FM)— Co-owned with KTLQ(AM). Aug 20, 1966: 101.7 mhz; 6.6 kw. 295 ft. TL: N35 53 43 W94 57 12. Stereo. Web Site: www.tahlequah.com/okcountry. Format: Country, sports. News staff: one; News: 4 hrs wkly. Target aud: 25-60.

Tishomingo

*****KAZC(FM)**— Sept 29, 1998: 88.3 mhz; 5.5 kw. Ant 922 ft. TL: N34 21 34 W96 33 34. Box 1343, Ada 74821. Phone: (580) 371-2235.

Phone: (580) 332-0902. Fax: (580) 456-7488. E-mail: email@thegospelstation.com. Web Site: www.thegospelstation.com. Licensee: South Central Oklahoma Christian Broadcasting Inc. Format: Southern gospel. ◆ Randall Christy, pres; Rick Cody, gen mgr & opns mgr.

Tonkawa

*****KAYE-FM**— June 1, 1976: 90.7 mhz; 1.2 kw. 67 ft. TL: N36 40 42 W97 17 50. Stereo. Central Hall 306, 1220 E. Grand 74653. Phone: (580) 628-6446. Phone: (580) 628-6200. Fax: (580) 628-6209. E-mail: kaye@north-ok.edu. Web Site: www.north-ok.edu. Licensee: Northern Oklahoma College. Format: Top 40. News: 6 hrs wkly. Target aud: 13-25. ◆ Dr. Joe Kinzer, pres.

Tulsa

KAKC(AM)— July 15, 1938: 1300 khz; 5 kw-D, 1 kw-N, DA-2. TL: N35 59 40 W95 51 27. 2625 S. Memorial 74129. Phone: (918) 388-5100. Fax: (918) 665-0555. Web Site: 1300kakc.com. Licensee: Clear Channel Broadcasting Licenses Inc. (group owner; (acq 8-5-92). Rep: Clear Channel. Format: Business talk. Target aud: 35-64. ◆ M. Oppenheimer, gen mgr; Garry Weaver, prom dir.

KMOD-FM— Co-owned with KAKC(AM). Oct 10, 1959: 97.5 mhz; 100 kw. 1,800 ft. TL: N36 11 46 W96 05 53. Stereo. Web Site: www.kmod.com. Rep: Clayton-Davis. Format: AOR. Target aud: 25-49; men.

KBEZ(FM)— March 1964: 92.9 mhz; 100 kw. 1,319 ft. TL: N36 11 26 W96 05 50. Stereo. 7030 S. Yale Ave., Suite 711 74136. Phone: (918) 496-9336. Fax: (918) 496-1937. E-mail: jobs@kbez.com. Web Site: www.kbez.com. Licensee: Renda Broadcasting Corp. (group owner; acq 6-8-90; FTR: 6-25-90). Format: Adult contemp. Target aud: 25-54. Spec prog: Big band 5 hrs wkly. ◆ Pat Bryson, VP & gen mgr; Keith Marlow, opns mgr & progmg dir; Richard Harley, chief of engrg; Sammy Carrillo, pub affrs dir & prom.

KCFO(AM)— 1946: 970 khz; 2.5 kw-D, 1 kw-N, DA-2. TL: N36 11 46 W96 02 22. 3737 S. 37th W. Ave. 74107. Phone: (918) 445-1186. Phone: (918) 622-0970. Fax: (918) 622-0985. Web Site: www.kcfo.com. Licensee: Friendship Broadcasting L.P. (acq 8-1-90; $953,000; 7-2-90). Network: USA. Format: Relg, talk, sports. News: 3 hrs wkly. Target aud: 25-54; women. ◆ Ray Clatworthy, pres; Kenneth Staley, gen mgr.

KFAQ(AM)— Jan 23, 1925: 1170 khz; 50 kw-U, DA-N. TL: N36 08 49 W95 48 27. Stereo. 4590 E. 29th 74114. Phone: (918) 743-7814. Fax: (918) 743-7613. Web Site: www.kfaq.com. Licensee: Journal Broadcast Corp. Group owner: Journal Broadcast Group Inc. (acq 6-11-99; grpsl). Network: CBS. Rep: Clear Channel. Dow, Lohnes & Albertson. Format: News/talk. News staff: 3; News: 24 hrs wkly. Target aud: 35 plus. Spec prog: Farm 5 hrs, gospel 2 hrs wkly. ◆ Carl Gardner, pres; Ron Kurtis, CFO; Jay Werth, gen mgr; Moon Mullins, opns mgr & mus dir; Randy Bush, gen sls mgr; Claudette Rogers, prom dir; Michael DelGiorno, progmg dir; Brian Gann, news dir; Ray Klotz, engrg dir.

KVOO-FM— Co-owned with KFAQ(AM). Nov 16, 1973: 98.5 mhz; 100 kw. 1,229 ft. TL: N36 11 26 W96 05 50. Web Site: www.kvoo.com. Format: Today's country. Target aud: 25-54.

KGTO(AM)— 1946: 1050 khz; 1 kw-D. TL: N36 09 40 W96 03 10. 7030 S. Yale, Suite 302 74136. Phone: (918) 494-9886. Fax: (918) 494-9683. Licensee: KJMM Inc. Group owner: Perry Publishing & Broadcasting Co. (acq 3-30-01; $455,000). Network: Westwood One. Rep: Allied Radio Partners. Format: Urban Contemp. News staff: one; News: 3 hrs wkly. Target aud: 35-54. ◆ Bryan K. Robinson, gen mgr.

KJSR(FM)— Nov 1, 1966: 103.3 mhz; 100 kw. Ant 1,279 ft. TL: N36 01 10 W95 39 24. Stereo. 7136 S. Yale, Suite 500 74136. Phone: (918) 493-3434. Fax: (918) 493-5383. Web Site: www.star103fm.com. Licensee: CXR Holdings L.L.C. Group owner: Cox Broadcasting (acq 3-28-97; grpsl). Format: Classic rock/classic hits. News staff: one. Target aud: 25-44. Spec prog: Pub affrs 2 hrs wkly. ◆ Dan Lawrie, gen mgr; Steve Hunter, opns mgr.

KRAV(FM)— Nov 21, 1962: 96.5 mhz; 100 kw. Ant 137 ft. TL: N36 11 46 W96 05 53. Stereo. 7136 S. Yale, Suite 500 74136. Phone: (918) 491-9696. Fax: (918) 493-5385. Web Site: www.mix96tulsa.com. Licensee: CXR Holdings L.L.C. Group owner: Cox Broadcasting (acq 11-21-96; $5.5 million. with co-located AM). Format: Hot adult contemp. Target aud: 25-54; 30% men, 70% women. ◆ Robert Neil, pres; Marc Morgan, exec VP; Dan Lawrie, VP; Dan Lawrie, gen mgr.

Stations in the U.S.   Oregon

KRMG(AM)— Dec 31, 1949: 740 khz; 50 kw-D, 25 kw-N, DA-2. TL: N36 04 50 W96 17 09. Stereo. 7136 S. Yale 74136. Phone: (918) 493-7400. Fax: (918) 493-2376. Web Site: www.krmg.com. Licensee: CXR Holdings L.L.C. Group owner: Cox Broadcasting (acq 3-28-97; grpsl). Network: ABC Information & Entertainment. Format: News/talk. News staff: 7. Target aud: 25-54; those interested in news, info & issue oriented talk. ♦ Chuck Browning, gen mgr; Steve Laswell, gen sls mgr; Drew Anderssen, progmg dir.

KWEN(FM)—Co-owned with KRMG(AM). 1961: 95.5 mhz; 96 kw. 1,328 ft. TL: N36 11 46 W95 05 53. Stereo. Web Site: www.krmg.com. Format: Contemp country. News staff: one. Target aud: 25-54; country life group. ♦ Jim Vidler, gen sls mgr; Gerry McCracken, progmg dir.

KRVT(AM)—See Claremore

KTBZ(AM)— Jan 22, 1934: 1430 khz; 5 kw-U, DA-N. TL: N36 14 10 W95 56 50. 2625 S. Memorial Dr. 74129-2600. Phone: (918) 388-5100. Fax: (918) 665-0555. Web Site: www.1430thebuzz.com. Licensee: Clear Channel Broadcasting Licenses Inc. Group owner: Clear Channel Communications Inc. (acq 1997; grpsl). Format: Sports. Target aud: 25-49. ♦ Michael Oppenheimer, gen mgr.

KTFX(AM)—See Sand Springs

***KWGS(FM)**— Oct 19, 1947: 89.5 mhz; 50 kw. Ant 1,067 ft. TL: N36 01 15 W95 40 32. Stereo. 600 S. College 74104. Phone: (918) 631-2577. Fax: (918) 631-3695. E-mail: answers@kwgs.org. Web Site: www.kwgs.org. Licensee: The University of Tulsa. Network: Network: NPR, PRI. John D. Pellegrin. Format: News & info/public radio. News: 84 hrs wkly. Target aud: General. ♦ Frank Christel, sr VP; Richard Fisher, gen mgr; P. Casey Morgan, dev dir; Brad Newman, chief of engrg; Michelle McKee, opns.

***KWTU(FM)**— Oct 15, 2004: 88.7 mhz; 5 kw. Ant 1,066 ft. TL: N36 01 15 W95 40 32. The University of Tulsa, 600 S. College 74104. Phone: (918) 631-2577. Licensee: The University of Tulsa. Format: Classical. ♦ Rich Fisher, gen mgr; Michelle McKee, opns mgr.

KYAL(AM)—See Sapulpa

Vinita

KGND(AM)—Listing follows KITO-FM.

KITO-FM— Apr 9, 1981: 96.1 mhz; 50 kw. 492 ft. TL: N36 34 56 W95 01 35. Stereo. Box 961 74301. Secondary address: 402 N. Wilson St. 74301. Phone: (918) 256-2255. Phone: (918) 542-9824. Fax: (918) 256-2633. Licensee: Mid America Ag Network Inc. (acq 9-1-2005; $900,000 with co-located AM). Format: Country. News: 28 hrs wkly. Target aud: General; traditional country music fans. ♦ Leona Boyd, gen mgr & gen sls mgr; Dave Boyd, progmg dir; Troy Langham, chief of engrg.

KGND(AM)—Co-owned with KITO-FM. Dec 7, 1954: 1470 khz; 500 w-D, 88 w-N. TL: N36 38 44 W95 07 35. Format: Country. Target aud: 30-50. ♦ David Boyd, gen mgr.

Wagoner

KXTD(AM)— Mar 1, 1966: 1530 khz; 5 kw-D, DA. TL: N35 58 30 W95 29 30. Stereo. 5807 S. Garnett, Suite F, Tulsa 74146. Phone: (918) 254-7556. Fax: (918) 252-0036. E-mail: maria@quebuenaok.com. Web Site: www.quebuenaok.com. Licensee: Gaytan-Galvan Limited Liability Co. (acq 1-31-97). Format: Sp. ♦ Maria Gaytan, gen mgr.

Warner

KTFX-FM— March 1995: 102.1 mhz; 6 kw. 276 ft. TL: N35 34 39 W95 12 36. Stereo. 401 W. Broadway, Muskogee 74401. Phone: (918) 684-1021. Fax: (918) 686-6159. E-mail: ktfx@k955.com. Web Site: www.country1021.com. Licensee: K95.5 Inc (group owner) Format:

Country. News staff: one; News: 21 hrs wkly. Target aud: General. ♦ William H. Payne, CEO & pres; Dan Storrs, gen mgr & gen sls mgr; Katey Sherrick, progmg dir.

Watonga

KIMY(FM)— Dec 12, 1987: 93.9 mhz; 3 kw. Ant 328 ft. TL: N35 54 17 W98 23 09. (CP: 4.2 kw, ant 394 ft. TL: N35 50 27 W98 19 09). Stereo. Box 1343, Ada 74821. Phone: (580) 332-0902. Fax: (580) 456-7488. Web Site: www.thegospelstation.com. Licensee: South Central Oklahoma Broadcasting Inc. (acq 3-11-2004; $163,000). Format: Southern gospel. News staff: one; News: 4 hrs wkly. Target aud: 25-54; general. Spec prog: Farm one hr, gospel 4 hrs, news/talk 7 hrs wkly. ♦ Randall Christy, pres; Ronald W. Gabe, gen mgr.

Weatherford

***KAYM(FM)**— 2000: 90.5 mhz; 1 kw. Ant 282 ft. TL: N35 29 47 W98 44 11. Box 3206, American Family Radio, Tupelo, MS 38803. Phone: (662) 844-8888, EXT. 204. Fax: (662) 842-6791. E-mail: comments@afr.net. Web Site: www.afr.net. Licensee: American Family Association. Group owner: American Family Radio Format: Inspirational Christian. ♦ Marvin Sanders, gen mgr.

KWEY(AM)— June 1, 1970: 1590 khz; 1 kw-D, DA. TL: N35 33 33 W98 43 11. Box 587, Hwy. 54 N. 73096. Phone: (580) 772-5939. Fax: (580) 772-1590. Licensee: Wright Broadcasting Systems Inc. (acq 7-17-91; $407,435 with co-located FM; 8-5-91). Network: ABC Information & Entertainment. Putbrese, Hunsaker & Trent. Format: C&W. News staff: one; News: 14 hrs wkly. Target aud: 25 plus; full service station. ♦ G. Harold Wright, CEO; Rene' Strong, sls dir; Todd Brunner, opns mgr & progmg dir; Ray Michaels, engrg dir.

KWEY-FM— Aug 18, 1977: 97.3 mhz; 70 kw. 385 ft. TL: N35 33 02 W98 43 59.

Wewoka

KSLE(FM)—Listing follows KWSH(AM).

KWSH(AM)— July 1951: 1260 khz; 1 kw-U, DA-N. TL: N35 10 10 W96 32 30. 2 E. Main, Shawnee 74801. Phone: (405) 382-1260. Phone: (405) 378-1803. Fax: (405) 257-2011. Fax: (405) 382-0128. E-mail: kwsh@earthlink.net. Licensee: One Ten Broadcast Group Inc. (group owner; acq 4-1-99; $400,000. with co-located FM). Network: ABC Information & Entertainment. Format: Country. Target aud: 21-61. Spec prog: American Indian one hr wkly. ♦ Dennis Burton, stn mgr; Garry Walker, opns mgr & progmg dir; Linda Jones, pres, gen mgr, sls dir, prom mgr & adv mgr; Hal Smith, chief of engrg.

KSLE(FM)—Co-owned with KWSH(AM). October 1997: 104.7 mhz; 6 kw. 328 ft. TL: N35 04 51 W96 35 03. Format: Oldies. ♦ Linda Jones, prom dir.

Wilburton

KESC(FM)— Nov 1, 2002: 103.7 mhz; 100 kw. Ant 607 ft. TL: N34 59 13 W95 42 10. Stereo. Box 1068, McAlester 74502. Phone: (918) 423-1460. Fax: (918) 465-3622. Licensee: KESC Enterprises LLC (group owner) (acq 1-18-2005; $766,666). Network: AP Radio. Shaw Pittman. Format: Adult contemp. Target aud: 25-54. ♦ Lee Anderson, gen mgr; Todd Minchall, stn mgr.

Woodward

KAZY(FM)— 2001: 95.9 mhz; 6 kw. Ant 328 ft. TL: N36 24 40 W99 21 05. 1222-10th St., Suite 111, TX 73801. Phone: (580) 256-0959. Fax: (580) 256-4959. Licensee: Shaffer Communications Group. Format: Alternative. ♦ Robert Fisher, gen mgr.

***KJOV(FM)**— 1998: 90.7 mhz; 4 kw. 400 ft. TL: N36 24 08 W99 25 47. Box 991, Meade, KS 67854. Secondary address: 922 Webster

73802. Phone: (620) 873-2991. Fax: (620) 873-2755. Licensee: Christian Community Radio. Format: Contemp Christian. ♦ Lawrence Powell, gen mgr.

KMZE(FM)— Oct 15, 1989: 92.1 mhz; 2.15 kw. 1,099 ft. TL: N36 16 06 W99 26 56. Stereo. Box D, 2728 Williams Ave. 73801. Phone: (580) 256-3692. Fax: (580) 256-3825. Licensee: FM 92 Broadcasters Inc. (acq 8-17-89; FTR: 9-5-89). Network: Jones Radio Networks. Format: Adult contemp. News staff: one. Target aud: 25-54. ♦ Mike Mitchel, CEO & chmn; Kevin Grice, gen mgr.

KSIW(AM)— September 1947: 1450 khz; 1 kw-U. TL: N36 25 42 W99 24 10. Box 1600 73802. Secondary address: 1922 22nd St. 73801. Phone: (580) 256-1450. Fax: (580) 254-9102. Licensee: Classic Communications Inc. (acq 6-13-2005). Network: ABC Information & Entertainment. Format: Oldies. News staff: one. Target aud: 40 plus. Spec prog: Farm & relg. ♦ Sherre House, pres, gen mgr & gen sls mgr; Sam Piel, progmg dir.

KWFX(FM)—Co-owned with KSIW(AM). Nov 1, 1974: 93.5 mhz; 3 kw. Ant 151 ft. TL: N36 25 42 W99 24 10. (CP: 106.3 mhz, 100 kw, ant 868 ft. TL: N36 22 31 W99 28 32). Stereo. Phone: (580) 256-0935. (Acq 4-30-96). Format: Country, talk. Target aud: 25-45; affluent, predominantly females.

KWDQ(FM)— Jan 9, 1990: 102.3 mhz; 2.35 kw. 355 ft. TL: N36 24 02 W99 25 44. 1922 22nd St. 73801. Phone: (580) 254-9103. Fax: (580) 254-9102. Licensee: Classic Communications Inc. (acq 3-20-92). Format: Classic rock. ♦ Sherre House, CEO & gen mgr.

KWOX(FM)— Dec 16, 1983: 101.1 mhz; 100 kw. 1,204 ft. TL: N36 16 06 W99 26 56. Stereo. K-101 Center, 2728 Williams Ave. 73801. Phone: (580) 256-4101. Phone: (580) 256-4101. Fax: (580) 256-3825. E-mail: k101@k101online.com. Web Site: k101online.com. Licensee: Omni Communications Corp. Network: Network: Network: Westwood One, CBS, ABC Information & Entertainment. Womble, Carlyle, Sandridge & Rice. Format: Country. News staff: 2; News: 5 hrs wkly. Target aud: General. Spec prog: Farm 10 hrs wkly. ♦ J. Douglas Williams, CEO, chmn, pres & gen mgr; Justin Stephenson, CFO; Brooke Williams, VP; Shawn Tiemann, news dir; Patrick Macek, prom. Co-owned TV: KOMI-TV affil.

Oregon

Albany

KGAL(AM)—See Lebanon

KHPE(FM)— Jan 12, 1969: 107.9 mhz; 100 kw. 1,160 ft. TL: N44 38 46 W123 16 11. Stereo. Box 278, 34545 Hwy. 20 97321. Phone: (541) 926-2233. Fax: (541) 926-3925. Web Site: www.khpeonline.com. Licensee: Integrity Media Inc. Gammon & Grange. Format: Contemp Christian. ♦ Bill Zipp, gen mgr, sls dir & gen sls mgr; Jeff McMahon, opns mgr & progmg dir; John Kenneke, chief of engrg.

KWIL(AM)—Co-owned with KHPE(FM). Jan 14, 1941: 790 khz; 1 kw-U, DA-2. TL: N44 37 54 W123 00 57. (Acq 7-1-57). Format: Christian. ♦ Jeff McMahon, progmg mgr.

KRKT-FM—Listing follows KTHH(AM).

KSHO(AM)—See Lebanon

KTHH(AM)— 1959: 990 khz; 250 w-D. TL: N44 35 43 W123 07 54. 2840 Marion St. S.E. 97322. Phone: (541) 926-8628. Fax: (541) 928-1261. Licensee: Citicasters Licenses L.P. Group owner: Clear Channel Communications Inc. (acq 5-4-99; grpsl). Network: ABC Information & Entertainment. Rep: Tacher. Fisher, Wayland, Cooper, Leader & Zaragoza L.L.P. Format: Classic country. News staff: one; News: 10 hrs wkly. Target aud: 25-54. ♦ Robert Dove, gen mgr & gen sls mgr; Scott Schuler, adv dir.

Oregon

KRKT-FM—Co-owned with KTHH(AM). June 1978: 99.9 mhz; 100 kw. Ant 1,069 ft. TL: N44 38 46 W123 16 11. Stereo. Web Site: www.krktcountry.com. Format: Country. ♦Scott Schuler, progmg dir.

Altamont

KRAT(FM)—Licensed to Altamont. See Klamath Falls

Ashland

KCMX-FM—Listing follows KTMT(AM).

KIFS(FM)— Nov 25, 1996; 107.5 mhz; 5.8 kw. Ant 1,374 ft. TL: N42 17 54 W122 44 53. 3624 Avion Dr., Medford 97504. Phone: (541) 858-5423. Fax: (541) 857-0326. Web Site: www.107kiss.com. Licensee: Citicasters Licenses L.P. Group owner: Clear Channel Communications Inc. (acq 5-1-99; grpsl). Rep: Tacher. Format: Contemp hit. Target aud: 18-49. ♦Bill Nielsen, gen mgr.

KSJK(AM)—See Talent

*KSMF(FM)— Nov 7, 1987: 89.1 mhz; 2.3 kw. 1,340 ft. TL: N42 17 54 W122 44 59. Stereo. 1250 Siskiyou Blvd. 97520. Phone: (541) 552-6301. Fax: 9541) 552-8565. Web Site: www.jeffnet.org. Licensee: The State of Oregon, acting by and through the State Board of Higher Education. Network: Network: NPR, PRI. Ernest Sanchez. Format: Jazz, AAA, news. News staff: one; News: 45 hrs wkly. Target aud: General. Spec prog: Blues 6 hrs, folk 3 hrs, pub affrs 7 hrs wkly. ♦Ronald Kramer, CEO; Mitchell Christian, CFO; Bryon Lambert, opns dir; Jessica Robinson, engrg dir.

*KSOR(FM)— April 1969: 90.1 mhz; 38 kw. 2,657 ft. TL: N42 41 30 W123 13 44. Stereo. Southern Oregon University, 1250 Siskiyou Blvd. 97520. Phone: (541) 552-6301. Fax: (541) 552-8565. Web Site: www.jeffnet.org. Licensee: The State of Oregon, acting by and through the State Board of Higher Education. Network: Network: PRI, NPR. Ernest Sanchez. Format: Class, news. News staff: one; News: 35 hrs wkly. Target aud: General. Spec prog: Pub affrs 7 hrs wkly. ♦Ronald Kramer, CEO.

*KSRG(FM)— 1995: 88.3 mhz; 230 w. 410 ft. TL: N42 17 52 W122 44 58. Southern Oregon Univ., 1250 Siskiyou Blvd. 97520. Phone: (541) 552-6301. Fax: (541) 552-8565. Web Site: www.jeffnet.org. Licensee: The State of Oregon, acting by and through the State Board of Higher Education, for the benefit of Southern Oregon State University. Network: Network: NPR, PRI. Ernest Sanchez. Format: Div, classical. News staff: one; News: 35 hrs wkly. Target aud: General. ♦Ronald Kramer, CEO & gen mgr.

KTMT(AM)— 1946: 580 khz; 1 kw-U, DA-N. TL: N42 09 46 W122 38 51. 1438 Rossanley Dr., Medford 97501. Phone: (541) 779-1550. Fax: (541) 776-2360. Web Site: www.espnam580.com. Licensee: Mapleton Communications LLC (group owner; acq 10-26-01; grpsl). Network: ABC. Dow, Lohnes & Albertson. Format: Sports. ♦Ron Hren, gen mgr; Alan Vezzani, sls dir; Devin Harpole, mktg dir & prom dir; Bill Jacobs, progmg dir; Chris Canter, news dir & pub affrs dir; Jim Sute, chief of engrg.

KCMX-FM—Co-owned with KTMT(AM). July 20, 1978: 101.9 mhz; 31.5 kw, 1,457 ft. TL: N42 17 54 W122 44 53. (CP: 31.62 kw, ant 1,426 ft.). Stereo. Web Site: www.lite102.com. Network: ABC. Format: Adult contemp. News staff: one. Target aud: 25-54. ♦Grant Tressel, progmg dir & mus dir; Bill Jacobs, news dir; Cindy Long, engrg dir.

Astoria

KAST(AM)— 1922: 1370 khz; 1 kw-U, DA-N. TL: N46 10 30 W123 50 50. 1006 W. Marine Dr. 97103. Phone: (503) 325-2911. Fax: (503) 325-5570. Licensee: New Northwest Broadcasters LLC (group owner; acq 10-26-99; grpsl). Network: ABC Information & Entertainment. Format: News/talk, sports. News: 50 hrs wkly. Target aud: 35 plus. ♦Paul Mitchell, gen mgr.

KAST-FM— May 10, 1981: 92.9 mhz; 99 kw. Ant 541 ft. TL: N46 10 54 W123 48 19. Stereo. 6400 S.E. Lake Rd., Suite 350, Portland 97222. Phone: (503) 786-0600. Phone: (503) 325-2911. Fax: (503) 786-1551. Web Site: www.kastradio.com. Licensee: Salem Media of Oregon Inc. (acq 12-1-2004). Format: Adult contemp. Target aud: 18-49. ♦Dennis Hayes, gen mgr.

KKEE(AM)— 1950: 1230 khz; 1 kw-U. TL: N46 11 15 W123 49 30. 1006 W. Marine Dr. 97103-5826. Phone: (503) 325-2911. Fax: (503) 325-5570. E-mail: kastam@newnw.com. Web Site: www.yourcommunityradio.com. Licensee: New Northwest Broadcasters LLC (group owner; acq 8-24-99; grpsl). Network: CBS. Format: ESPN. News staff: one; News: 7 hrs wkly. Target aud: 25-54; diverse. ♦Paul Mitchell, gen mgr.

*KLOY(FM)—Not on air, target date: unknown: 88.7 mhz; 250 w. Ant 1,053 ft. TL: N46 15 46 W123 53 09. 5700 W. Oaks Blvd., Rocklin, CA 95765. Phone: (916) 251-1600. Fax: (916) 251-1650. Licensee: Educational Media Foundation. Group owner: EMF Broadcasting (acq 2-2-2004). ♦Lloyd Parker, gen mgr.

*KMUN(FM)— Feb 2, 1982: 91.9 mhz; 3 kw. 1,060 ft. TL: N46 15 46 W123 53 09. Stereo. Box 269 97103. Secondary address: 1445 Exchange St. 97103. Phone: (503) 325-0010. Fax: (503) 325-3956. E-mail: kmun@kmun.org. Web Site: www.kmun.org. Licensee: Tillicum Foundation. Network: NPR. Haley, Bader & Potts. Format: Eclectic. News staff: one; News: 12 hrs wkly. Target aud: General. Spec prog: Folk 18 hrs, children's 6 hrs, Sp 3 hrs, American Indian 2 hrs, Black 2 hrs wkly. ♦Ray Merritt, pres; David Hammock, gen mgr; Stephanie Stern, dev dir.

*KORM(FM)—Not on air, target date: unknown: 90.5 mhz; 48 w vert. Ant 469 ft. TL: N46 10 56 W123 48 09. Box 3333, McAllen, TX 78502. Phone: (956) 787-9788. Fax: (956) 787-9783. Licensee: World Radio Network Inc. (group owner). Format: Sp language/evangelical. ♦Dr. William Haney, gen mgr.

*KWYA(FM)— 2001: 89.7 mhz; 200 w. Ant 1,027 ft. TL: N46 15 46 W123 53 09. c/o KZOE, 3609 Columbia Heights Rd., Longview 98632. Phone: (360) 577-5433. E-mail: office@wayfm.com. Web Site: kwyq.wayfm.com. Licensee: WAY-FM Media Group Inc. (group owner; acq 8-1-03; $135,000. with KWYQ(FM) Longview, WA). Format: Inspirational Christian. ♦Danny Houle, gen mgr & stn mgr.

Baker City

*KANL(FM)— 2005: 90.7 mhz; 250 w. Ant 653 ft. TL: N44 45 58 W117 52 54. Box 3206, Tupelo, MS 38803. Phone: (662) 844-8888. Web Site: www.afr.net. Licensee: American Family Association. Group owner: American Family Radio. Format: Christian. ♦Marvin Sanders, gen mgr.

KBKR(AM)— 1939: 1490 khz; 1 kw-U. TL: N44 47 18 W117 48 35. Box 907, 2510 E. Cove Ave., La Grande 97850. Phone: (541) 963-4121. Phone: (541) 963-4122. Fax: (541) 963-3117. E-mail: supertalk@eoni.com. Licensee: Pacific Empire Radio Corp. (group owner; acq 7-19-2004; grpsl). Network: Network: Westwood One, ABC Information & Entertainment. Rep: McGavren Guild. McGavren Guild. Format: News/talk. News staff: one; News: 25 hrs wkly. Target aud: 25-54. Spec prog: Farm 2 hrs wkly. ♦Mark Bolland, pres; Linda Ashlock, gen mgr & stn mgr; John Russell, progmg dir.

KKBC-FM—Co-owned with KBKR(AM). Feb 1, 1981: 95.3 mhz; 6 kw. -200 ft. TL: N44 47 18 W117 48 35. (CP: 25 kw). Stereo. Phone: (541) 532-4431. E-mail: theboomer@eoni.com. Format: Oldies. News staff: one; News: 6 hrs wkly. Target aud: 25-54.

KCMB-FM—June 26, 1988: 104.7 mhz; 100 kw. 1,747 ft. TL: N45 07 26 W117 46 48. Stereo. 1009-C Adams Ave., La Grande 97850. Secondary address: 2950 Church St. 97814. Phone: (541) 523-3400. Fax: (541) 523-5481. Licensee: Oregon Trail Radio Inc. Group owner: Capps Broadcast Group. Network: ABC. Rep: Tacher. Format: Country. Target aud: 25-54. ♦Randy McKone, gen mgr.

*KDJC(FM)— 2005: 88.1 mhz; 100 w. Ant 1,185 ft. TL: N44 44 20 W117 44 45. CSN International, 3232 W. MacArthur Blvd., Santa Ana, CA 92704. Phone: (714) 825-9663. Fax: (714) 825-9660. Web Site: www.csnintl.com. Licensee: CSN International. (group owner).

*KOBK(FM)—Not on air, target date: unknown: 91.5 mhz; 30 w. Ant 1,814 ft. TL: N44 35 57 W117 46 58. Oregon Public Broadcasting, 7140 S.W. Macadam Ave., Portland 97219. Phone: (503) 244-9900. Licensee: Oregon Public Broadcasting. ♦Jack Galmiche, gen mgr.

Bandon

KBDN(FM)— October 1996: 96.5 mhz; 1.5 kw. 1,296 ft. TL: N42 57 27 W124 16 13. 320 Central Ave., Suite 519, Coos Bay 97420. Phone: (541) 267-2121. Fax: (541) 267-5229. Licensee: Bicoastal CB LLC.

Directory of Radio

Group owner: Bicoastal Media L.L.C. (acq 10-16-2003; grpsl). Rep: Tacher. Format: Classic rock and roll. Target aud: 35-54. ♦John Pundt, gen mgr; Mike O'Brien, opns mgr & chief of opns.

Banks

KVMX(FM)— June 1990: 107.5 mhz; 35 kw. Ant 1,443 ft. TL: N45 58 W122 43 59. 2040 S.W. First Ave., Portland 97201. Phone: (503) 497-1075. Fax: (503) 222-2047. E-mail: mix1075webmaster @mix1075portland.com. Web Site: www.mix1075portland.com. Licensee: Infinity Radio Inc. Group owner: Infinity Broadcasting Corp. (acq 11-13-98; grpsl). Network: Westwood One. Format: Eighties, adult contemp. Target aud: 25-49; adult. ♦Mark Walen, gen mgr.

Bay City

KIXT(FM)—Not on air, target date: unknown: 96.3 mhz; 430 w. Ant 1,197 ft. TL: N45 27 59 W123 55 11. 1600 Gray Lynn Dr., Walla Walla, WA 99362. Phone: (509) 527-1000. Fax: (509) 529-5534. Licensee: Alexandra Communications Inc. (acq 6-14-2005; $150,000 for CP). ♦Tom Hodgins, pres & gen mgr.

Beaverton

KKCW(FM)— February 1984: 103.3 mhz; 100 kw. 1,654 ft. TL: N45 31 22 W122 45 12. Stereo. 4949 S.W. MacAdam Ave., Portland 97239. Phone: (503) 222-5103. Fax: (503) 222-0030. Web Site: www.k103.com. Licensee: Citicasters Licenses L.P. Group owner: Clear Channel Communications Inc. (acq 5-4-99; grpsl). Rep: D & R Radio. Format: Adult contemp. News staff: 3. Target aud: 25-54. ♦Mary Lou Gunn, gen mgr; Tony Coles, opns mgr.

Bend

KBND(AM)— 1938: 1110 khz; 10 kw-D, 5 kw-N, DA-N. TL: N44 06 25 W121 14 39. Box 5037 97708. Secondary address: 711 N.E. Butler Market Rd. 97701. Phone: (541) 382-5263. Fax: (541) 388-0456. E-mail: kbnd@kbnd.com. Web Site: www.kbnd.com. Licensee: Combined Communications. (group owner; acq 4-27-90). Network: CBS. Rep: McGavren Guild. Dow, Lohnes & Albertson. Format: Sports. News staff: 2. Target aud: 35-64; upscale, professionals. ♦Mike Chaney, gen mgr & gen sls mgr; Frank Bonacquispi, progmg dir.

KLRR(FM)—Co-owned with KBND(AM). June 17, 1985: 101.7 mhz; 27.5 kw. 985 ft. TL: N44 04 41 W121 19 57. Stereo. Web Site: www.kbnd.com. Format: Rock adult contemp. Target aud: 25-54; upscale, professional women & men. Spec prog: Jazz 5 hrs wkly. ♦Doug Danolo, progmg dir.

KICE(AM)— Feb 4, 1960: 940 khz; 10 kw-D, 60 w-N, DA-2. TL: N44 04 50 W121 16 51. 969 SW Colorado Ave. 97702. Phone: (541) 388-3300. Fax: (541) 388-3303. Licensee: GCC Bend LLC. (group owner; (acq 1999). Network: ABC. Format: Sports. News staff: one; News: 2 hrs wkly. Target aud: 35 plus. ♦Della Pizzati, gen mgr; Rob Walker, opns dir; Brian Canady, sls dir; Matt Green, engrg dir.

KXIX(FM)—Co-owned with KICE(AM). December 1974: 94.1 mhz; 100 kw. 1,028 ft. TL: N44 04 41 W121 19 57. Stereo. E-mail: clark@x94.com. Web Site: www.power94.com. (Acq 2000.) Format: CHR. Target aud: 18-49. ♦John Gross, pres; Brian Canady, gen sls mgr; Jim Gross, natl sls mgr & chief of engrg; Mike Flanagan, progmg dir; R. L. Garrigus, news dir.

*KLBR(FM)—Not on air, target date: unknown: 88.1 mhz; 5 kw. Ant 850 ft. TL: N44 02 49 W121 31 50. 4000 E. 30th Ave., Eugene 97405-0640. Phone: (541) 463-6000. Fax: (541) 463-6046. Web Site: www.klcc.org. Licensee: Lane Community College. ♦Steve Barton, gen mgr.

KMGX(FM)— July 4, 1973: 100.7 mhz; 50 kw horiz, 20 kw vert. Ant 518 ft. TL: N44 04 40 W121 19 49. Stereo. 969 S.W. Colorado 97709. Phone: (541) 388-3300. Fax: (541) 388-3303. E-mail: dhorner@bendradiogroup.com. Web Site: www.magic100fm.com. Licensee: GCC Bend LLC. (group owner). Network: ABC Information & Entertainment. Allied Radio Partners. Format: Adult contemp. Target aud: 25 plus; middle to upper income consumers. ♦John Gross, pres; Dana Horner, gen mgr; Marie McCallister, progmg dir.

KMTK(FM)— 2000: 99.7 mhz; 26 kw. Ant 682 ft. TL: N44 04 39 W121 19 57. 711 N.E. Butler Market Rd. 97701. Phone: (541) 382-5263. Fax: (541) 388-0456. E-mail: country@mountain997.com. Web Site: www.mountain997.com. Licensee: Combined Communications Inc.

Stations in the U.S.   Oregon

Developers & Brokers of Radio Properties
contact American Media Services at our suite:
Philadelphia Marriott Downtown
215-625-2900
843-972-2200
americanmediaservices.com
Charleston, SC
Dallas, TX · Chicago, Il · Austin, TX
American Media Services, LLC

Group owner: Combined Communications Format: Country. ♦ Chuck Chackel, CEO & pres; Mike Cheney, gen mgr.

KNLR(FM)— Dec 31, 1984: 97.5 mhz; 97 kw. Ant 536 ft. TL: N44 04 38 W121 19 49. Stereo. Box 7408 97708. Phone: (541) 389-8873. Fax: (541) 389-5291. E-mail: info@knlr.com. Web Site: www.knlr.com. Licensee: Terry A. Cowan. Network: USA. Format: Christian. ♦ Terry A. Cowan, gen mgr.

*KOAB-FM— 1994: 91.3 mhz; 25 kw. 604 ft. TL: N44 04 41 W121 19 57. 7140 S.W. Macadam, Portland 97219. Phone: (503) 293-1905. Fax: (503) 293-1919. Web Site: www.opb.org. Licensee: Oregon Public Broadcasting. (acq 9-20-93; grpsl; 10-11-93). Network: NPR. Format: News, info music. News staff: news progmg 146 hrs wkly News: 5;. ♦ Jack Galmiche, COO, exec VP & gen mgr. Co-owned TV: *KOAB-TV affil.

KQAK(FM)— Sept 5, 1986: 105.7 mhz; 40 kw. Ant 592 ft. TL: N44 04 40 W121 19 48. Stereo. 854 N.E. 4th St. 97701. Phone: (541) 383-3825. Fax: (541) 383-3403. Licensee: Horizon Broadcasting Group L.L.C. (group owner; acq 2000; $3.45 million). Rep: Tacher. Format: Rock and roll oldies. Target aud: 25-54; baby boomers, upscale adults. ♦ Keith Shipman, pres & gen mgr; Brian Canady, stn mgr; Larry Wilson, opns mgr; Bruce Cannon, progmg dir; Paul Valle, news dir.

KTWS(FM)— Dec 21, 1990: 98.3 mhz; 5.2 kw. Ant 731 ft. TL: N44 04 39 W121 19 57. Stereo. Box 5037 97701. Secondary address: 711 N.E. Butler Market Rd. 97701. Phone: (541) 382-5263. Fax: (541) 388-0456. E-mail: thetwins@thetwins.com. Web Site: www.thetwins.com. Licensee: Combined Communications, Inc. (group owner; acq 9-1-96). Rep: McGavren Guild. Format: Classic rock. Target aud: 25-54. ♦ Chuck Chackel, pres; Mike Cheney, gen mgr.

*KVLB(FM)— 2003: 90.5 mhz; 500 w. Ant 564 ft. TL: N44 04 40 W121 19 48. 2351 Sunset Blvd., Suite 170-218, Rocklin, CA 95765. Phone: (916) 251-1600. Fax: (916) 251-1650. E-mail: klove@klove.com. Web Site: www.klove.com. Licensee: Educational Media Foundation. Group owner: EMF Broadcasting (acq 3-11-03; grpsl). Network: K-Love. Shaw Pittman. Format: Contemp Christian. News staff: 3. Target aud: 25-44; Judeo Christian, female. ♦ Richard Jenkins, pres; Mike Novak, VP; Lloyd Parker, gen mgr.

Bonanza

KYSF(FM)— 1999: 102.9 mhz; 460 w. Ant 2,106 ft. TL: N42 05 48 W121 37 57. Box 339, Klamath Falls 97601. Phone: (541) 882-8833. Fax: (541) 882-8836. Web Site: www.kiss102fm.com. Licensee: New Northwest Broadcasters LLC (group owner; acq 10-20-98; grpsl). Format: Adult contemp. ♦ Pete Benedetti, CEO & pres; Greg Dourian, gen mgr.

Brookings

*KMWR(FM)— Oct 31, 2002: 90.7 mhz; 100 w. Ant 1,233 ft. TL: N42 07 23 W124 17 56. Box 492727, Redding, CA 96049-2727. Phone: (530) 222-4455. Fax: (530) 222-4484. E-mail: info@kvip.org. Web Site: www.kvip.org. Licensee: Pacific Cascade Communications Corp. Format: Inspirational, Christian. News staff: 2. ♦ David L. Morrow, VP; Steve Hafen, gen mgr; Steve Alexander, stn mgr.

KURY(AM)— May 2, 1958: 910 khz; 1 kw-D, 37 w-N. TL: N42 04 32 W124 18 52. Box 1029, 605 Railroad W97415. Phone: (541) 469-2111. Phone: (541) 469-2112. Fax: (541) 469-6397. E-mail: kury@charbernet.com. Licensee: Eureka Broadcasting Co. Inc. (acq 4-19-2005; $775,000. with co-located FM). Network: Jones Radio Networks. Format: Oldies, country classic. Target aud: General. ♦ Hugo Papstein, pres; Rick Wafler, gen sls mgr; Kevin Bane, progmg dir; Vern Garvin, gen mgr, engrg & chief of engrg.

KURY-FM— May 1977: 95.3 mhz; 8.7 kw. 1,164 ft. TL: N42 07 23 W124 17 56. Stereo. E-mail: kury@charterinternet.com. Format: Adult contemp. News staff: one; News: 11 hrs wkly. ♦ Vern R. Garvin, stn mgr; Rick Waffler, gen sls mgr; Rich Moore, adv mgr; Kevin Bane, progmg mgr.

Brownsville

KEHK(FM)— Apr 1, 1991: 102.3 mhz; 100 kw horiz, 43 kw vert. 918 ft. TL: N44 00 08 W123 06 50. Stereo. Box 1200 Executive Pkwy., Suite 440, Eugene 97405. Secondary address: 4222 Commerce St., Eugene 97402. Phone: (541) 485-5846. Fax: (541) 485-0969. Web Site: www.starfm.com. Licensee: Cumulus Licensing Corp. Group owner: Cumulus Media Inc. (acq 8-24-00; grpsl). Rep: McGavren Guild. Format: Classic rock hits. News staff: one; News: 2 hrs wkly. Target aud: 25-54. ♦ Bill Bradley, pres.

Burns

KQHC(FM)—Listing follows KZZR(AM).

KZZR(AM)— Sept 28, 1957: 1230 khz; 1 kw-U. TL: N43 33 49 W119 03 22. Box 877, Fairgrounds Rd. 97720. Phone: (541) 573-2055. Fax: (541) 573-5223. Licensee: SS Radio LLC (acq 11-3-94; FTR: 3-28-94). Network: ABC Information & Entertainment. Rep: Tacher. Format: Contemp country, news, talk. News staff: one; News: 30 hrs wkly. Target aud: 18-55. Spec prog: Farm 6 hrs wkly. ♦ Leslie Ann Carson, gen mgr; Stan Swol, pres & gen mgr; Randy Parks, progmg dir.

KQHC(FM)— Co-owned with KZZR(AM). Sept 1, 1997: 92.7 mhz; 750 w. 905 ft. TL: N43 34 22 W119 07 50. Stereo. E-mail: kzzr_amkqhc_fm @centurytel.net. Network: Jones Radio Networks. Rep: Tacher. Format: Classic hits. ♦ Stan Swol, CEO.

Cannon Beach

KCBZ(FM)— 1997: 96.5 mhz; 950 w. Ant 302 ft. TL: N45 57 08 W123 56 14. Calcomm Stations Oregon LLC, 615 Broadway, Seaside 97138. Phone: (503) 738-8668. Fax: (503) 738-8778. E-mail: calbrady@pacbell.net. Web Site: www.kcbzfm.com. Licensee: Calcomm Stations Oregon LLC (acq 12-7-2004; $240,000). Format: Hot adult contemp. ♦ Cal Brady, gen mgr.

Canyon City

KJDY-FM— Dec 13, 1996: 94.5 mhz; 51 kw. Ant 1,364 ft. TL: N44 17 50 W119 02 09. Stereo. Box 399, 413 N.W. Bridge St., John Day 97845. Phone: (541) 575-1185. Fax: (541) 575-2313. Licensee: Blue Mountain Broadcasting Co. Inc. Network: ABC. Format: Country. Target aud: 25-54. ♦ Phil Gray, gen mgr.

Cave Junction

KCNA(FM)— Apr 30, 1985: 102.7 mhz; 100 kw. 1,976 ft. TL: N42 15 30 W123 39 38. (CP: 50.7 kw). 511 Rossanley Dr., Medford 97501. Phone: (541) 772-0322. Fax: (541) 772-4233. E-mail: jim@opusradio.com. Web Site: www.kcnafm.com. Licensee: Opus Broadcasting Systems Inc. (group owner; acq 12-94). Format: Classic hits. ♦ Henry Flock, pres; Dean Flock, gen mgr.

Cherryville

*KLVP(FM)— 1997: 88.7 mhz; 3.7 kw. 1,568 ft. TL: N45 19 57 W121 42 57. Stereo. 2351 Sunset Blvd., Suite 170-218, Rocklin, CA 95765. Phone: (916) 251-1600. Fax: (916) 251-1650. E-mail: klove@klove.com. Web Site: www.klove.com. Licensee: Educational Media Foundation. Group owner: EMF Broadcasting. Network: K-Love. Shaw Pittman. Format: Contemp Christian. News staff: 3. Target aud: 25-44; Judeo-Christian, female. ♦ Richard Jenkins, pres; Mike Novak, VP; Lloyd Parker, gen mgr.

Condon

KHAL(FM)— Not on air, target date: unknown: 93.5 mhz; 100 kw. Ant 945 ft. TL: N45 15 29 W120 17 11. NT Radio LLC, 750 N. Saint Paul, 10th Fl., Dallas, TX 75201. Phone: (214) 855-5582. Fax: (214) 855-5145. Licensee: NT Radio LLC. ♦ Ronald Unkefer, gen mgr.

Coos Bay

KDCQ(FM)— May 24, 1995: 93.5 mhz; 6 kw. 512 ft. TL: N43 22 00 W124 12 54. Stereo. 3505 S.E. Ocean Blvd. 97423. Phone: (541) 269-0935. Fax: (541) 267-9376. E-mail: oldies@kdcq.com. Web Site: www.kdcq.com. Licensee: Bay Cities Building Co. Inc. Network: ABC. Rep: Tacher. Format: Oldies. News: 5 hrs wkly. Target aud: 35-54; baby boomers. ♦ Bruce Latta, pres; Stephanie Kilmer, gen mgr & opns mgr.

KHSN(AM)— Mar 15, 1928: 1230 khz; 1 kw-U. TL: N43 22 11 W124 12 54. 320 Central, Suite 519 97420. Phone: (541) 267-2121. Fax: (541) 267-5229. Licensee: W7 Broadcasting LLC (acq 8-7-03). Network: ABC Information & Entertainment. Allied Radio Partners. Format: ESPN radio. News: 14 hrs wkly. Target aud: 35- plus. ♦ Laura Peck, gen mgr; Mike O'Brien, opns mgr.

*KJCH(FM)—Not on air, target date: unknown: 90.9 mhz; 25 kw. Ant 1,476 ft. TL: N42 57 32 W124 16 23. CSN International, 3232 W. MacArthur Blvd., Santa Ana, CA 92704-6916. Phone: (714) 979-0706. Fax: (714) 825-9660. Licensee: CSN International (group owner). Format: Relg.

KMHS(AM)— Dec 7, 1956: 1420 khz; 1 kw-D. TL: N43 21 45 W124 11 33. 10th & Ingersoll 97420. Phone: (541) 267-1451. Phone: (541) 267-1420. Fax: (541) 269-0161. E-mail: stevew@coosbay.k12.or.us. Web Site: www.marshfield.coos-bay.k12.or.us/kmhs/index.htm. Licensee: Coos Bay School District No. 9. (acq 7-22-97; $8,505 donation). Format: Var. ♦ Steve Walker, gen mgr.

KOOS(FM)—See North Bend

*KSBA(FM)— Nov 4, 1988: 88.5 mhz; 2.2 kw. 532 ft. TL: N43 23 26 W124 04 46. Stereo. 1250 Siskiyou Blvd., Ashland 97520. Phone: (541) 552-6301. Fax: (541) 552-8565. Web Site: www.jeffnet.org. Licensee: The State of Oregon, acting by and through the State Board of Higher Education. Network: Network: NPR, PRI. Ernest Sanchez. Format: Jazz, news, AAA. News staff: one; News: 45 hrs wkly. Target aud: General. Spec prog: Blues 6 hrs, folk 3 hrs, pub affrs 7 hrs wkly. ♦ Ronald Kramer, CEO & gen mgr.

KYSJ(FM)— Nov 1, 1979: 106.5 mhz; 4 kw. 544 ft. TL: N43 21 15 W124 14 31. Stereo. 580 Kingwood Ave. 97420. Phone: (541) 269-2022. Fax: (541) 267-0114. E-mail: kysj@lighthouseradio.com. Web Site: www.lighthouseradio.com. Licensee: Lighthouse Radio Group. (acq 10-25-93; $64,400; 11-8-93). Format: Christian. ♦ Joshua Tanner, progmg dir; Rick Stevens, gen mgr & opns.

KYTT-FM— November 1978: 98.7 mhz; 31 kw. 551 ft. TL: N43 23 26 W124 07 46. (CP: 12.8 kw, ant 962 ft.). Stereo. 580 Kingwood 97420. Phone: (541) 269-2022. Fax: (541) 267-0114. Web Site: www.lighthouseradio.com. Licensee: Lighthouse Radio Group. (acq 3-1-89). Format: Contemp Christian. News: 8 hrs wkly. ♦ Rick Stevens, gen mgr & opns mgr.

Coquille

KSHR-FM—Listing follows KWRO(AM).

KWRO(AM)— Feb 1, 1949: 630 khz; 5 kw-D. TL: N43 10 17 W124 11 54. Box 250 97423. Secondary address: 1270 W. 13th 97423. Phone: (541) 396-2141. Fax: (541) 396-2143. E-mail: connie@crbradio.com. Web Site: www.kwro.com. Licensee: Bicoastal CB LLC. Group owner: Bicoastal Media L.L.C. (acq 10-16-2003; grpsl). Rep: McGavren Guild. Format: News/talk. ♦ Connie Williamson, gen mgr & prom dir; Connie Willanson, gen sls mgr; Mikel Chavez, opns mgr & progmg dir; Matt Jarvis, news dir.

Broadcasting & Cable Yearbook 2006

Oregon

KSHR-FM—Co-owned with KWRO(AM). Nov 1, 1981: 97.3 mhz; 61 kw. 856 ft. TL: N43 14 51 W124 06 46. Stereo. Web Site: www.crbradio.com. Format: Hot country. ♦Mikel Chavez, opns dir & progmg mgr.

Corvallis

*KBVR(FM)— Oct 26, 1965: 88.7 mhz; 340 w. -80. TL: N44 33 50 W123 16 30. Stereo. Oregon State Univ., M.U. East, Snell Hall, Rm. 210 97331-1618. Phone: (541) 737-2008. Fax: (541) 737-4545. Licensee: State Board of Higher Education. Format: Jazz, urban contemp, alternative rock. Target aud: 15-45; general. Spec prog: Class 4 hrs, Sp 4 hrs, folk 4 hrs wkly. ♦Ian Rose, stn mgr.

KEJO(AM)— August 1955: 1240 khz; 1 kw-U. TL: N44 35 44 W123 14 54. 2840 Marion St. S.E., Albany 97321-3978. Phone: (541) 926-8628. Fax: (541) 928-1261. Web Site: www.kejoam.com. Licensee: Citicasters Licenses L.P. Group owner: Clear Channel Communications Inc. (acq 8-24-99; $2.3 million. with co-located FM). Network: ABC Information & Entertainment. Rep: Tacher. Reddy, Begley & McCormick. Format: Talk. Target aud: 40 plus. ♦Gary Grossman, gen mgr; Glenn Nobel, opns mgr, opns mgr, prom mgr & mus dir; Robert Dove, gen sls mgr.

KFLY(FM)—Co-owned with KEJO(AM). Oct 1, 1966: 101.5 mhz; 28 kw. 98 ft. TL: N44 35 44 W123 14 54. Stereo. 1345 Olive St., Box1120 97440. Phone: (541) 485-1120. Fax: (541) 484-5769. Web Site: www.kflyfm.com. Network: ABC FM Connection. Format: Hot adult contemp. Target aud: 25-49; general.

KGAL(AM)—See Lebanon

KLOO(AM)— Aug 23, 1947: 1340 khz; 1 kw-U. TL: N44 33 25 W123 16 22. 2840 Marion St. S.E., Albany 97322. Phone: (541) 926-8628. Fax: (541) 928-1261. Web Site: www.news1340.com. Licensee: Citicasters Licenses L.P. Group owner: Clear Channel Communications Inc. (acq 5-4-99; grpsl). Rep: Tacher. Format: News/talk, sports. News staff: one; News: 83 hrs wkly. Target aud: 35-54. ♦Robert Dove, gen mgr; Larry Rogers, gen sls mgr; Rick Rogers, news dir; Robin O'Kelley, chief of engrg.

KLOO-FM— January 1973: 106.1 mhz; 100 kw. 1,140 ft. TL: N44 38 45 W123 16 13. Stereo. Web Site: www.kloo.com. Format: Classic rock. News: 15 hrs wkly. Target aud: 18-54.

*KOAC(AM)— Dec 7, 1922: 550 khz; 5 kw-U, DA-2. TL: N44 38 12 W123 11 33. 7140 S. W. Macadam Ave. 97219. Phone: (503) 293-1905. Phone: (541) 737-5332. Fax: (503) 293-1919. Licensee: Oregon Public Broadcasting. (acq 9-20-93; grpsl; 10-11-93). Network: Network: PRI, NPR. Format: News/talk. News staff: 5; News: 40 hrs wkly. Target aud: 25-54; college educated with an interest in news & mus. Spec prog: Jazz 12 hrs wkly. ♦Lynne Clendenin, opns mgr; Roger Dominigues, chief of engrg. Co-owned TV: *KOAC-TV affil

KSHO(AM)—See Lebanon

Cottage Grove

KCGR(FM)— Mar 21, 1994: 100.5 mhz; 6 kw. 115 ft. TL: N43 44 41 W123 05 29. 321 Main St. 97424. Phone: (541) 942-2468. Fax: (541) 942-5797. Licensee: Thornton Pfleger Inc. Rep: Tacher. Format: Adult contemp, light rock, Mexican music. News: 6 hrs wkly. Target aud: 25-49. ♦Diane O'Renick, gen mgr; Paul Schwartzberg, news dir.

KNND(AM)— August 1953: 1400 khz; 950 w-U. TL: N43 45 43 W123 04 42. 321 Main St. 97424. Phone: (541) 942-2468. Fax: (541) 942-5797. E-mail: paul@knnd.com. Licensee: Schwartzberg Communications Inc. (acq 5-2-2005; $300,000). Network: AP Radio. Rep: Tacher. Dow, Lohnes & Albertson. Format: Country. News/talk. News staff: one; News: 40 hrs wkly. Target aud: General. Spec prog: Relg 3 hrs wkly. ♦Clif Wilson, progmg dir; Paul Schwartzberg, pres, gen mgr & news dir.

Creswell

KUJZ(FM)— Sept 1, 1983: 95.3 mhz; 625 kw. 1,207 ft. TL: N44 00 04 W123 06 45. Stereo. 200 Executive Pkwy., Suite 440, Eugene 97405. Phone: (541) 485-5846. Fax: (541) 485-0969. Web Site: www.953moose.com. Licensee: Cumulus Licensing Corp. Group owner: Cumulus Media Inc. (acq 2-29-00;; grpsl). Rep: Christal. Format: Country. Target aud: 18-34. Spec prog: Blues 2 hrs, women 2 hrs, Grateful Dead 2 hrs, Veterans of Foreign Wars 1 hr, loc musicians 1 hr wkly. ♦B.J. O'Brien, gen mgr.

Dallas

KWIP(AM)—Licensed to Dallas. See Salem

Eagle Point

KZZE(FM)— March 1995: 106.3 mhz; 900 w. 1,591 ft. TL: N42 21 13 W122 47 05. 3624 Avion Dr., Medford 97504. Phone: (541) 857-0340. Fax: (541) 857-0326. Web Site: www.kzze.com. Licensee: Citicasters Licenses L.P. Group owner: Clear Channel Communications Inc. (acq 5-1-99; grpsl). Rep: Tacher. Format: Rock/AOR. News staff: one; News: one hr wkly. Target aud: 18-49; rock listeners. ♦Bill Nielsen, pres & gen mgr.

Elgin

KRJT(FM)—Not on air, target date: unknown: 105.9 mhz; 160 w. Ant 1,916 ft. TL: N45 26 26 W117 53 31. 403 C St., Lewiston, ID 83501. Phone: (208) 743-4560. Fax: (208) 798-0110. Licensee: Pacific Empire Radio Corp. ♦Mike Bolland, pres.

Enterprise

KWVR(AM)— June 1, 1960: 1340 khz; 1 kw-U. TL: N45 26 14 W117 17 30. 220 W. Main St. 97828-1244. Phone: (541) 426-4577. Fax: (541) 426-4578. Licensee: Wallowa Valley Radio Broadcasting Corp. (acq 9-1-84; grpsl; 7-2-84). Network: ABC. Rep: Allied Radio Partners. Format: News/talk. Target aud: General. Spec prog: Farm 4 hrs wkly. ♦Dave Nelson, gen mgr, stn mgr & progmg dir.

KWVR-FM— 1986: 92.1 mhz; 6 kw. Ant -689 ft. TL: N45 19 19 W117 13 18. Stereo. Network: Network: ABC, Jones Radio Networks. Format: Country.

Eugene

KDUK-FM—(Florence). Nov 21, 1983: 104.7 mhz; 63 kw. 2,326 ft. TL: N44 17 35 W123 32 15. Stereo. Box 1120. Secondary address: 1345 Olive St. 977400. Phone: (541) 485-1120. Fax: (541) 484-5769. Web Site: www.kduk.com. Licensee: Capstar TX L.P. Group owner: Clear Channel Communications Inc. (acq 12-1-00; grpsl). Format: CHR/Top-40. ♦Robert Dove, gen mgr.

KKNU(FM)—(Springfield-Eugene). Dec 18, 1958: 93.1 mhz; 100 kw horiz, 43 kw vert. 1,299 ft. TL: N44 00 04 W123 06 45. Stereo. 925 Country Club Rd., Suite 200 97401. Phone: (541) 484-9400. Fax: (541) 344-9424. Web Site: www.kknu.com. Licensee: McKenzie River Broadcasting Co. Inc. Group owner: McKenzie River Broadcasting Group (acq 11-17-92; $1.01 million. with KEED(AM) Eugene; FTR: 12-14-92). Rep: D & R Radio. Holland & Knight. Format: New country. Target aud: 25-49; country life group. ♦John Tilson, pres & gen mgr; Dave Wiles, gen sls mgr; Jim Davis, progmg dir.

KKNX(AM)— 1992: 840 khz; 1 kw-D, 220 w-N. TL: N44 05 48 W123 04 18. Stereo. 945 Garfield St. 97402. Phone: (541) 342-1012. Fax: (541) 342-6201. E-mail: john@radio84.com. Web Site: www.radio84.com. Licensee: John S. Mielke, Susan J. Mielke. (acq 7-18-96; $150,000). Network: AP Radio. Rep: Tacher. Tacher & Co. Format: Oldies. News staff: one; News: 7 hrs wkly. Target aud: 25-64; general. Spec prog: Black 3 hrs wkly. ♦John S. Mielke, pres; John S. Mielke, gen mgr.

*KLCC(FM)— Feb 17, 1967: 89.7 mhz; 81 kw horiz, 54 kw vert. Ant 1,161 ft. TL: N44 00 05 W123 06 48. Stereo. 4000 E. 30th Ave. 97405-0640. Phone: (541) 463-6000. Fax: (541) 463-6046. E-mail: klcc@lanecc.edu. Web Site: www.klcc.org. Licensee: Lane Community College. Network: NPR. Arter & Hadden. Format: News/talk, adult contemp. News staff: one; News: 60 hrs wkly. Target aud: 25-54. Spec prog: Sp 5 hrs, folk 12 hrs, Black 3 hrs, blues 4 hrs, world 3 hrs, electronic 6 hrs wkly. ♦Steve Barton, gen mgr; Paula Chan Carpenter, dev dir; Don Hein, progmg dir; Tripp Sommer, news dir.

KLZS(AM)— Sept 7, 1954: 1450 khz; 1 kw-U. TL: N44 04 54 W123 06 34. 925 Country Club Rd., Suite 200 97401. Phone: (541) 343-4100. Fax: (541) 343-0448. Licensee: Churchill Communications LLC Group owner: McKenzie River Broadcasting Group (acq 11-3-2004; $87,500). Network: CNN Radio. Format: Progsv talk. News staff: 2; News: 30 hrs wky. Target aud: 25-54.

Directory of Radio

KMGE(FM)— Oct 10, 1965: 94.5 mhz; 49 kw horiz, 21 kw vert. Ant 1,299 ft. TL: N44 00 04 W123 06 45. Stereo. 925 Country Club Rd., Suite 200 97401. Phone: (541) 484-9400. Fax: (541) 344-9424. Web Site: www.kmge.com. Licensee: McKenzie River Broadcasting Co. Inc. (acq 3-87; $950,000;. FTR: 9-29-86). Format: Adult contemp. Target aud: 18-49. ♦John Tilson, pres.

KNRQ-FM—Listing follows KUGN(AM).

KODZ(FM)—Listing follows KPNW(AM).

KOPT(AM)— Sept 19, 1947: 1600 khz; 5 kw-D, 1 kw-N, DA-N. TL: N44 03 05 W123 03 48. 895 Country Club Rd., Suite A200 97401. Phone: (541) 343-4100. Fax: (541) 343-0448. Licensee: Churchill Communications I LLC. (acq 3-16-2005; $225,000). Format: Progressive talk.

KORE(AM)—See Springfield-Eugene

KPNW(AM)— July 22, 1968: 1120 khz; 50 kw-U, DA-1. TL: N43 57 24 W123 02 10. Box 1120 97440. Secondary address: 1345 Olive St. 97440. Phone: (541) 485-1120. Fax: (541) 484-5769. Web Site: www.kpnw.com. Licensee: Capstar TX L.P. Group owner: Clear Channel Communications Inc. (acq 12-1-00; grpsl). Network: ABC Information & Entertainment. Format: News/talk. News staff: 2. Target aud: 25 plus; upper income, conservative. Spec prog: Sports. ♦Robert Dove, gen mgr; Lee Chabre, progmg dir.

KODZ(FM)—Co-owned with KPNW(AM). November 1968: 99.1 mhz; 100 kw. 1,945 ft. TL: N44 06 56 W122 59 56. Stereo. Format: Oldies. Target aud: 25-54; working women. ♦Robert Dove, sls dir; Paul Walker, progmg dir.

KRVM(AM)— Nov 9, 1949: 1280 khz; 5 kw-D, 1 kw-N, DA-N. TL: N44 04 47 W123 04 12. Stereo. P.M.B. 237, 1574 Cobug Rd. 97401. Phone: (541) 687-3370. Fax: (541) 687-3573. Web Site: www.krvm.org. Licensee: Lane County School District 4J. (acq 1-10-97). Rep: McGavren Guild. Format: Talk, sports. ♦Carl Sundberg, gen mgr, gen sls mgr & chief of engrg.

KRVM-FM— Dec 8, 1947: 91.9 mhz; 1.9 kw. -36 ft. TL: N44 03 44 W123 06 17. (CP: 1.12 kw, ant 98 ft.). Stereo. Phone: (541) 687-3147. Web Site: www.krvm.org. Licensee: School District 4 J Lane County. Network: NPR. Format: AAA, AOR, blues. News: 3 hrs wkly. Target aud: General. Spec prog: Black 2 hrs, country one hr, folk 3 hrs wkly.

KSCR(AM)— June 12, 1962: 1320 khz; 1 kw-D, 40 w-N. TL: N44 05 25 W123 03 43. 1200 Executive Pkwy., Suite 440 97401. Phone: (541) 485-5846. Fax: (541) 485-0969. Licensee: Cumulus Licensing Corp. Group owner: Cumulus Media Inc. (acq 2-29-00; grpsl). Network: ESPN Radio. Rep: Christal. Format: ESPN sports. Target aud: 18-44; general. ♦Steve Ries, gen mgr.

KUGN(AM)— July 4, 1946: 590 khz; 5 kw-D, 5 kw-N, DA-N. TL: N44 05 48 W123 04 18. Stereo. 1200 Executive Pkwy., Suite 440 97405. Phone: (541) 284-8500. Fax: (541) 284-8500. Web Site: www.kugn.com. Licensee: Cumulus Licensing Corp. Group owner: Cumulus Media Inc. (acq 6-15-00; grpsl). Network: CBS. Dow, Lohnes & Albertson. Format: News/talk. News staff: 6; News: 28 hrs wkly. Target aud: 30-65; general. ♦Bill Bradley, gen mgr; Troy Murphy, gen sls mgr; Wendy Wintrode, prom dir; Jerry Allen, progmg dir; Rick Little, news dir; Cory Schruth, chief of engrg.

KNRQ-FM—Co-owned with KUGN(AM). Dec 26, 1958: 97.9 mhz; 100 kw. 1,230 ft. TL: N44 00 08 W123 06 50. Stereo. Web Site: www.nrq.com. Format: Alternative. ♦Chris Crowley, progmg dir.

*KWAX(FM)— Apr 4, 1951: 91.1 mhz; 21.5 kw horiz, 12.5 kw vert. 1,214 ft. TL: N44 00 04 W123 06 45. Stereo. Agate Hall, Univ. of Oregon 97403. Phone: (541) 345-0800. Web Site: www.kwax.com. Licensee: State Board of Higher Education. Akin, Gump, Strauss, Hauer & Feld. Format: Class. News: 7 hrs wkly. Target aud: 35 plus. ♦Paul C. Bjornstad, gen mgr; Rocky Lammana, opns mgr.

*KWVA(FM)— May 27, 1993: 88.1 mhz; 500 w. -56 ft. TL: N44 00 07 W123 06 53. Box 3157, ERB Memorial Union, Univ. of Oregon 97403. Secondary address: Univ. of Oregon, EMU, Suite M-112 97403. Phone: (541) 346-4091. Fax: (541) 346-0648. E-mail: kwva@gladstone.uoregon.edu. Web Site: gladstone.uoregon.edu/~kwva. Licensee: Associated Students of University of Oregon. (acq 6-29-92; 7-20-92). Format: Div, progsv, urban contemp. News: 12 hrs wkly. Target aud: 3-30; college, alternative, underrepresented, varying educ

Broadcasting & Cable Yearbook 2006

Stations in the U.S. — Oregon

levels & music lover. Spec prog: Asian 4 hrs, Black 4 hrs, jazz 6 hrs, country 3 hrs, Japanese 2 hrs, Sp 6 hrs wkly. ♦Charlotte Nisser, gen mgr, opns dir & dev dir; Michael Zarkesh, prom dir; Anna Jensen, progmg dir.

KZEL-FM— Apr 22, 1962: 96.1 mhz; 100 kw. 1,093 ft. TL: N44 00 04 W123 06 45. Stereo. Box 23410 97402. Phone: (541) 485-5846. Fax: (541) 485-0969. Web Site: www.96kzel.com/main. Licensee: Cumulus Licensing Corp. Group owner: Cumulus Media Inc. (acq 2-29-00; grpsl). Rep: Christal. Format: Classic Rock. Target aud: 18-44. ♦Steve Ries, gen mgr; Russ Davidson, opns mgr.

Florence

KCST(AM)— May 5, 1985: 1250 khz; 1 kw-D, 68 w-N. TL: N44 00 18 W124 05 37. Box 20000 97439. Secondary address: Radio Center Bldg., 4480 Hwy. 101 N. 97439. Phone: (541) 997-9136. Fax: (541) 997-9165. E-mail: radioway@kcst.com. Web Site: www.kcst.com. Licensee: Coast Broadcasting Co. Inc. (acq 12-18-97). Format: Music of your life. Target aud: 55+. ♦John Thompson, gen mgr.

KCST-FM— October 1992: 106.9 mhz; 2.3 kw. 508 ft. TL: N43 57 19 124 04 26. Stereo. Box 20,000 97439. Secondary address: 4480 Hwy 101 N., Radio Centre Bldg. 97439. Phone: (541) 997-9136. Fax: (541) 997-9165. E-mail: radiowaves@kcst.com. Web Site: www.kcst.com. Network: ABC. Tacher Company Format: Adult contemp, country, oldies. Target aud: 35+.

KDUK-FM—Licensed to Florence. See Eugene

*KLFO(FM)— Aug 16, 1999: 88.1 mhz; 300 w. 508 ft. TL: N43 57 23 W124 04 26. Stereo. Lane Community College, 4000 E. 30th Ave., Eugene 97405. Phone: (541) 463-6000. Fax: (541) 463-6046. Web Site: www.klcc.org. Licensee: Lane Community College. Format: Var/div, jazz, news. ♦Steve Barton, gen mgr & stn mgr; Paula Chan Carpenter, dev dir; Don Hein, progmg dir; Chris Heck, chief of engrg.

*KWVZ(FM)— 2001: 91.5 mhz; 150 w. Ant 558 ft. TL: N43 57 19 W124 04 26. c/o KWAX(FM), 75 Centennial Loop, Eugene 97401. Phone: (541) 345-0800. Licensee: Oregon State Board of Higher Education. Format: Classical. ♦Paul C. Bjornstad, gen mgr.

Garibaldi

KDEP(FM)— 2001: 105.5 mhz; 320 w. Ant 1,181 ft. TL: N45 27 59 W123 55 11. 1550 N. Main, Tillamook 97141. Phone: (503) 842-3888. Fax: (503) 842-5640. E-mail: coast105@earthlink.net. Web Site: www.kdepfm.com. Licensee: Royal Communications of Oregon (acq 5-17-2004); $112,500). Format: Soft rock. ♦Thomas Hodgins, gen mgr.

Gleneden Beach

KSHL(FM)— December 1992: 97.5 mhz; 17 kw. 843 ft. TL: N44 45 22 W124 02 57. Stereo. Box 1180, 131 N.E. 15th St., Newport 97365. Phone: (541) 265-6477. Fax: (541) 265-6478. E-mail: news@ksh.com. Web Site: www.kshl.com. Licensee: Stephanie Linn. McGavren Guild Format: Modern country. News: 2 hrs wkly. Target aud: 25-55; general. ♦Dick Linn, gen mgr & opns mgr; Stephanie Linn, pres & gen sls mgr.

Gold Beach

KGBR(FM)— December 1984: 92.7 mhz; 265 w. 1,030 ft. TL: N42 23 50 W124 21 50. (CP: 42.06 kw, ant 2,700 ft. TL: N42 23 44 W124 21 47). Box 787, BetGar Bldg., 29795 Ellensburg Ave. 97444. Phone: (541) 247-7211. Phone: (541) 247-7418. Fax: (541) 247-4155. E-mail: info@kgbr.com. Web Site: www.ontheradio.net/radiostations/kgbrfm.aspx. Licensee: St. Marie Communications Inc. (acq 3-87; $60,000; 11-16-87). Rep: Tacher. Fisher, Wayland, Cooper, Leader & Zaragoza. Format: Adult contemp. News staff: 2. News: 4 hrs wkly. Target aud: 25-54. ♦Dale L. St. Marie, gen mgr.

Gold Hill

KRWQ(FM)— Aug 11, 1980: 100.3 mhz; 30 kw. 970 ft. TL: N42 27 07 W123 03 20. Stereo. 3624 Avion Dr., Medford 97504. Phone: (541) 772-4170. Fax: (541) 858-5416. Web Site: www.krwq.com. Licensee: Citicasters Licenses L.P. Group owner: Clear Channel Communications Inc. (acq 1999; grpsl). Rep: Tacher. Format: Contemp country. News staff: 2. Target aud: 18-54. ♦Bill Nielsen, gen mgr.

Grants Pass

*KAGI(AM)— Dec 16, 1939: 930 khz; 5 kw-D, 123 w-N. TL: N42 25 24 W123 20 04. 1250 Siskiyou Blvd., Ashland 97520. Phone: (541) 552-6301. Fax: (541) 552-8565. Web Site: www.jeffnet.org. Licensee: The State of Oregon, acting by and through the State Board of Higher Education, for the benefit of Southern Oregon University. (acq 7-11-91; FTR: 7-29-91). Network: Network: PRI, NPR. Ernest Sanchez. Format: News, info. Spec prog: Sp 6 hrs wkly. ♦Mitchell Christian, CFO; Bryon Lambert, opns dir; Paul Westhelle, dev dir & mktg dir; Ronald Kramer, CEO, gen mgr & progmg dir; Eric Alan, mus dir; Darin Ransom, engrg dir.

KAJO(AM)— Aug 15, 1957: 1270 khz; 10 kw-D, 48 w-N. TL: N42 26 16 W123 21 27. Stereo. 888 Rogue River Hwy. 97526. Phone: (541) 476-6608. Fax: (541) 476-4018. E-mail: kajo@kajo.com. Web Site: www.kajo.com. Licensee: Grants Pass Broadcasting Corp. Format: Adult standards, news/talk. News staff: 2; News: 22 hrs wkly. Target aud: 35 plus. Spec prog: Gospel one hr, relg 8 hrs wkly. ♦Jim Wilson, pres; Carl Wilson, sr VP, gen mgr, opns dir & mktg dir; Matt Wilson, VP, gen sls mgr & adv dir; Don Monette, prom dir & progmg dir; Charles Wright, mus dir; Mike Carmichael, chief of engrg.

*KAPK(FM)— April 1998: 91.1 mhz; 250 w. 13 ft. TL: N42 27 44 W123 18 33. Box 3206, American Family Radio, Tupelo, MS 38803. Phone: (662) 844-8888. Fax: (662) 842-6791. Web Site: www.afr.net. Licensee: American Family Association. Group owner: American Family Radio Format: Inspirational Christian. ♦Marvin Sanders, gen mgr.

KROG(FM)— Oct 2, 1981: 96.9 mhz; 25 kw. 2,058 ft. TL: N42 22 56 W123 16 29. (CP: 74 kw). Stereo. 511 Rossanley Dr., Medford 97501. Phone: (541) 772-0322. Fax: (541) 772-4233. E-mail: krogstudio@yahoo.com. Web Site: www.97therogue.com. Licensee: Opus Broadcasting Systems Inc. (group owner; acq 3-6-91; $63,634. with KRTA(AM) Medford; FTR: 7-29-91). Rep: Tacher. Format: Alternative. News staff: one. Target aud: 25-54; affluent middle America. ♦Dean Flock, gen mgr & stn mgr; Dave Hatton, opns dir.

Gresham

*KMHD(FM)— January 1984: 89.1 mhz; 7.9 kw. Ant 1,433 ft. TL: N45 30 58 W122 43 59. Stereo. 26000 S.E. Stark St. 97030. Phone: (503) 661-8900. Phone: (503) 491-7233. Fax: (503) 491-6999. Web Site: www.kmhd.org. Licensee: Mt. Hood Community College. Network: NPR. Garvey, Schubert & Barer. Format: Jazz/blues. News: 5 hrs wkly. Target aud: 35-65; music lovers. Spec prog: Blues 15 hrs, news 5 hrs wkly. ♦Doug Sweet, gen mgr; Calvin Walker, dev dir; Greg Gomez, mus dir.

KMUZ(AM)—Licensed to Gresham. See Portland

Harbeck-Fruitdale

KLDR(FM)— May 3, 1991: 98.3 mhz; 185 w. 2,096 ft. TL: N42 22 56 W123 16 29. Stereo. 888 Rogue River Hwy., Grants Pass 97527. Phone: (541) 474-7292. Fax: (541) 474-7300. Web Site: www.kldr.com. Licensee: Grants Pass Broadcasting Corp. Format: Adult contemp. News staff: one; News: 10 hrs wkly. Target aud: 25-54; Middle Age demo- actually a wide range in listeners. ♦Jim Wilson, pres; Carl Wilson, gen mgr; Matt Wilson, gen sls mgr; Jason Allen, progmg dir.

Hermiston

KOHU(AM)— Feb 6, 1956: 1360 khz; 4.3 kw-D, 500 w-N, DA-N. TL: N45 51 57 W119 18 45. Box 145, 80404 Cooney Ln. 97838. Phone: (541) 567-6500. Fax: (541) 567-6068. Licensee: Westend Radio L.L.C. (acq 4-16-97; with co-located FM). Network: ABC. Rep: Farmakis. Target. Format: C&W. News staff: one; News: 10 hrs wkly. Target aud: General; two county loc audience. Spec prog: Sp 6 hrs wkly. ♦Angela Pursel, gen mgr, stn mgr, sls VP & gen sls mgr; Ron Hughes, pres & gen mgr; Jeff Walker, opns dir, prom dir & progmg dir; Adam Russell, news dir; Richard Wilson, engrg dir.

KQFM(FM)—Co-owned with KOHU(AM). Sept 18, 1978: 100.5 mhz; 5.3 kw. Ant 298 ft. TL: N45 51 57 W119 18 38. Stereo. Network: ABC. Format: Pure gold, adult contemp. News staff: one; News: 5 hrs wkly. Target aud: 25-54. ♦Ron Hughes, gen mgr & prom VP; Jeff Walker, mus dir.

Hillsboro

KUIK(AM)— 1954: 1360 khz; 5 kw-U, DA-N. TL: N45 29 13 W122 54 31. Box 566 97123. Secondary address: 3355 N.E. Cornell Rd. 97124. Phone: (503) 640-1360. Fax: (503) 640-6108. E-mail: dave@kuik.com. Web Site: www.kuik.com. Licensee: Dolphin Communications Inc. (group owner; (acq 8-1-78). Network: ABC Daytime Direction. David Tillotson. Format: News/talk, sports, Sp. News staff: one; News: 24 hrs wkly. Target aud: 25-54; Seekers of locally produced unique programming. Spec prog: Relg 2 hrs, Sp 21 hrs wkly. ♦Don McCoun, pres & gen mgr; Donna McCoun, sr VP; Paul Warren, opns mgr.

Hood River

KCGB(FM)—Listing follows KIHR(AM).

KIHR(AM)— Oct 17, 1950: 1340 khz; 1 kw-U. TL: N45 42 07 W121 32 10. Box 360 97031. Secondary address: 1190 22nd St. 97031. Phone: (541) 386-1511. Fax: (541) 386-7155. Web Site: www.kihrk105.com. Licensee: Columbia Gorge Broadcasters Inc. (group owner; acq 4-1-67). Rep: Tacher. Fisher, Wayland, Cooper, Leader & Zaragoza L.L.P. Format: C&W. News staff: 3; News: 12 hrs wkly. Target aud: 25-54. ♦Gary Grossman, pres, gen mgr & stn mgr; Rick Cavagnaro, sls VP & sls dir; Jeff Skye, mus dir; Mark Bailey, news dir; Jim Keightley, engrg dir & chief of engrg.

*KQHR(FM)— January 2002: 90.1 mhz; 44 w. Ant 1,105 ft. TL: N45 43 20 W121 26 16. 515 N.E. 15th Ave., Portland 97323. Phone: (503) 916-5828. Fax: (503) 916-2642. E-mail: musicinfo@allclassical.org. Web Site: www.allclassical.org. Licensee: KBPS Public Radio Foundation. Format: Class. News: 5 hrs wkly. ♦Suzanne White, gen mgr.

John Day

KJDY(AM)— Dec 13, 1963: 1400 khz; 1 kw-U. TL: N44 25 17 W118 57 09. 413 N.W. Bridge St-., . 97845. Phone: (541) 575-1400. Fax: (541) 575-2313. E-mail: kjdy@centurytel.net. Licensee: Blue Mountain Broadcasting Co. (acq 11-87; $150,000; 11-9-87). Network: ABC Information & Entertainment. J. Dominic Monahan. Format: C&W. News staff: one. ♦Phil Gray, gen mgr; Patricia Webb, gen sls mgr; J. Kelly Carlson, engrg VP & chief of engrg.

Jordan Valley

*KIDH(FM)— 2005: 90.9 mhz; 21.5 kw vert. Ant 2,161 ft. TL: N43 00 26 W116 42 23. Stereo. 5700 W. Oaks Blvd., Rocklin, CA 95765. Phone: (916) 251-1600. Fax: (916) 251-1650. E-mail: info@air1.com. Web Site: www.air1.com. Licensee: Educational Media Foundation. Group owner: EMF Broadcasting. Network: Air 1. Shaw Pittman. Format: Contemp Christian. News staff: 3. Target aud: 18-35; Judeo-Christian, female. ♦Richard Jenkins, pres; Mike Novak, VP; Lloyd Parker, gen mgr.

Broadcasting & Cable Yearbook 2006

Junction City

***KPIJ(FM)**—Not on air, target date: unknown: 88.5 mhz; 630 w. Ant 2,312 ft. TL: N44 16 48 W123 34 57. CSN International, 3232 W. MacArthur Blvd., Santa Ana, CA 92704. Phone: (714) 825-9663. Fax: (714) 825-9660. Licensee: CSN International. ♦Mike Stocklin, gen mgr.

KXOR(AM)— 1998: 660 khz; 10 kw-D, 75 w-N. TL: N44 12 36 W123 10 56. 895 Country Club Rd., Suite A200, Eugene 97401. Phone: (541) 343-4100. Fax: (541) 343-0448. Web Site: www.lax660.com. Licensee: Churchill Communications LLC. Group owner: Pamplin Broadcasting (acq 1-14-2005; $550,000). Format: Sp. Target aud: 35+. ♦Bob Bosche, gen mgr; Phil Polter, gen sls mgr.

Keizer

KYKN(AM)— 1951: 1430 khz; 5 kw-U. TL: N44 55 36 W122 57 19. Box 1430, Salem 97308. Secondary address: 4205 Cherry Ave. N.E. 97303. Phone: (503) 390-3014. Fax: (503) 390-3728. E-mail: mfrith@kykn.com. Web Site: www.kykn.com. Licensee: Willamette Broadcasting Co. Inc. (acq 10-27-01). Network: CNN Radio. Allied Radio Partners. Format: News/talk. News staff: 3; News: 46 hrs wkly. Target aud: 25-64; $40-60K income, homeowners, white collar. Spec prog: Portland Trailblazers, University of Oregon, gospel 6 hrs wkly. ♦Michael Frith, pres, gen mgr & gen sls mgr.

Klamath Falls

KAGO(AM)— July 19, 1923: 1150 khz; 5 kw-D, 1 kw-N, DA-N. TL: N42 12 56 W121 47 51. Box 339 97601. Phone: (541) 882-2551. Fax: (541) 882-8836. Licensee: New Northwest Broadcasters LLC (group owner; acq 3-16-99; $1.6 million. with co-located FM). Network: Network: CBS, ABC News/Talk. Rep: Allied Radio Partners. Dan Alpert. Format: News/talk. News staff: 2; News: 25 hrs wkly. Target aud: 35-65; upscale, professional. Spec prog: Farm 3 hrs, Sp 5 hrs wkly. ♦Gregory J. Dourian, gen mgr & gen sls mgr.

KAGO-FM— Oct 15, 1973: 99.5 mhz; 60 kw. 360 ft. TL: N42 12 56 W121 47 56. (CP: 100 kw, ant 994 ft. TL: N42 13 08 W121 48 56). Stereo. Network: CBS. Format: Classic rock. ♦Rob Siems, prom dir; Vivian Dickey, pub affrs dir.

KFEG(FM)— 2002: 104.7 mhz; 51 kw. Ant 645 ft. TL: N42 13 24 W121 49 02. Box 938 97601. Phone: (541) 850-5242. Fax: (541) 884-2845. E-mail: sales@theeagle1047.fm. Web Site: www.theeagle1047.fm. Licensee: Cove Road Publishing LLC (acq 3-1-01). Format: Classic rock. Target aud: 25-54. ♦Bill Ifft, pres & gen mgr.

KFLS(AM)— 1946: 1450 khz; 1 kw-U. TL: N42 12 19 W121 46 04. Stereo. Box 1450, 1338 Oregon Ave. 97601. Phone: (541) 882-4656. Fax: (541) 884-2845. Web Site: www.klamathradio.com. Licensee: Wynne Enterprises LLC (group owner; acq 1-1-71). Network: ABC. Tacher. Format: News/talk, sports. Target aud: 35 plus. ♦Robert Wynne, CEO, chmn, pres, gen mgr & gen sls mgr.

KKRB(FM)—Co-owned with KFLS(AM). Apr 1, 1983: 106.9 mhz; 100 kw. 1,200 ft. TL: N42 13 26 W121 49 02. Stereo. Format: Adult contemp, top 40.

KKJX(AM)— September 1955: 960 khz; 5 kw-U. TL: N42 09 42 W121 39 01. Box 339 97601. Secondary address: 4509 S. 6th St., Suite 201 97601. Phone: (541) 882-8833. Fax: (541) 882-8836. Licensee: New Northwest Broadcasters LLC (group owner; acq 10-20-98; grpsl). Network: ABC Daytime Direction. Rep: Allied Radio Partners. Format: Sports. News staff: one; News: 3 hrs wkly. Target aud: 25-54; mature with spendable income. Spec prog: Farm one hr wkly. ♦Brent Phillipy, stn mgr; Rob Siems, opns mgr & progmg dir; Greg Dourian, sls dir & adv dir; Jamie Jackson, news dir; Scott Noland, pub affrs dir; James Boyd, chief of engrg.

KLAD-FM—Co-owned with KKJX(AM). July 19, 1974: 92.5 mhz; 63 kw. 2,188 ft. TL: N42 05 51 W121 37 58. E-mail: rodeoradio@aol.com. Network: ABC. Allied Radio Partners. Dow, Lohnes & Albertson. Format: Country. ♦Michael O'Shea, CEO; Ivan Braiker, pres; Tricia Houston, CFO; Scott Allen, VP; Rob Siems, opns dir & mus dir.

***KKLJ(FM)**— Mar 14, 2003: 88.9 mhz; 32 w. Ant 2,132 ft. TL: N42 03 54 W121 58 14. Stereo. 5700 W. Oaks Blvd., Rocklin, CA 95765. Phone: (916) 251-1600. Fax: (916) 251-1650. E-mail: klove@klove.com. Web Site: www.klove.com. Licensee: Educational Media Foundation. Group owner: EMF Broadcasting. Network: K-Love. Shaw Pittman. Format: Contemp Christian. News staff: 3. Target aud: 25-44; Judeo Christian, female. ♦Richard Jenkins, pres; Mike Novak, VP; Lloyd Parker, gen mgr; Ed Lenane, opns dir.

***KLMF(FM)**— 2002: 88.5 mhz; 95 w. Ant 2,162 ft. TL: N42 05 50 W121 37 59. Jefferson Public Radio, 1250 Siskiyou Blvd., Ashland 97520. Phone: (541) 552-6301. Web Site: www.jeffnet.org. Licensee: The State of Oregon, acting by and through the State Board of Higher Education, for the benefit of Southern Oregon University. Network: Network: NPR, PRI. Ernest Sanchez. Format: Class, news. News staff: one; News: 35 hrs wkly. ♦Mitchell Christian, CFO; Ronald Kramer, CEO & gen mgr; Bryon Lambert, opns dir; Paul Westhelle, dev dir.

KRAT(FM)—(Altamont). 1991: 97.7 mhz; 22 kw. Ant 1,712 ft. TL: N42 10 06 W122 09 06. Stereo. Box 235 97601. Phone: (541) 884-8167. Fax: (541) 884-8226. Web Site: www.krat.com. Licensee: George J. Wade. Format: Oldies.

***KSKF(FM)**— Nov 10, 1989: 90.9 mhz; 2 kw. 2,253 ft. TL: N42 05 50 W121 37 59. Stereo. 1250 Siskiyou Blvd., Ashland 97520. Phone: (541) 552-6301. Fax: (541) 552-8565. Web Site: ww.jeffnet.org. Licensee: The State of Oregon, acting by and through the State Board of Higher Education. Network: Network: NPR, PRI. Ernest Sanchez. Format: AAA, jazz, news. News staff: one; News: 45 hrs wkly. Target aud: General. Spec prog: Blues 6 hrs, folk 3 hrs, pub affrs 7 hrs wkly. ♦Mitchell Christian, CFO; Ronald Kramer, CEO & gen mgr; Bryon Lambert, opns dir; Paul Westhelle, dev dir; Jessica Robinson, news dir.

***KTEC(FM)**— Dec 19, 1950: 89.5 mhz; 250 w. 184 ft. TL: N42 12 59 W121 47 57. (CP: Ant 597 ft. TL: N42 13 26 W121 49 02). Stereo. Oregon Institute of Technology, Box 2009, 3201 Campus Dr. 97601. Phone: (541) 885-1840. Phone: (541) 885-1841. Fax: (541) 885-1857. E-mail: ktec@oit.edu. Web Site: www.oit.edu/-ktec. Licensee: Oregon State Board of Higher Education. Format: Freeform (diversified). News staff: one; News: 5 hrs wkly. Target aud: 15 plus; eclectic, free thinking, progsv individuals. Spec prog: American Indian one hr, Black 3 hrs, folk 3 hrs, Sp 3 hrs, world mus 6 hrs, electronic 9 hrs wkly. ♦Carola Roufs, gen mgr; Jake Byron, progmg mgr; Len Simpson, mus dir.

La Grande

***KEOL(FM)**— October 1973: 91.7 mhz; 310 w. -750 ft. TL: N45 19 16 W118 05 26. Stereo. One Univ. Blvd. 97850. Phone: (541) 962-3698. Web Site: www.eou.edu/. Licensee: Oregon State Board of Higher Education. Format: CHR, div, progsv. Target aud: 14-25; college students & loc youth. Spec prog: Black 12 hrs, class 4 hrs, jazz 6 hrs, reggae 7 hrs wkly. ♦Dave McDermot, stn mgr.

KLBM(AM)— 1938: 1450 khz; 1 kw-U. TL: N45 19 45 W118 04 00. Box 907, 2510 E. Cove Ave. 97850. Phone: (541) 963-4121. Phone: (541) 963-4122. Fax: (541) 963-3117. E-mail: supertalk@eoni.com. Licensee: Pacific Empire Radio Corp. (group owner; acq 7-19-2004; grpsl). Network: Network: Westwood One, ABC. McGavren Guild Denise Moline, P.C. Format: News/talk. News staff: one; News: 25 hrs wkly. Target aud: 25-54. Spec prog: Farm 2 hrs. ♦Mark Bolland, pres; Linda Ashlock, gen mgr; John Russell, progmg dir.

KUBQ(FM)—Co-owned with KLBM(AM). Aug 15, 1977: 98.7 mhz; 2.25 kw. 1,942 ft. TL: N45 26 26 W117 53 31. Stereo. E-mail: q98@eoni.com. Rep: McGavren Guild. Format: Classic rock. News staff: one; News: 6 hrs wkly. Target aud: 18-49. ♦Marie Madison, progmg dir.

***KTVR-FM**— 2004: 90.3 mhz; 400 w. Ant 2,519 ft. TL: N45 18 33 W117 43 54. 7140 S.W. Macadam Ave., Portland 97219. Phone: (503) 293-1905. Fax: (503) 293-1919. Web Site: www.opb.org. Licensee: Oregon Public Broadcasting. Format: News, info music. News staff: 5; News: 146 hrs wkly. ♦Jack Galmiche, COO & exec VP.

KWRL(FM)— Sept 27, 1988: 99.9 mhz; 60 kw. 377 ft. TL: N45 12 59 W118 00 00. Stereo. 1009 Adams Ave., Suite C 97850. Phone: (541) 963-7911. Fax: (541) 963-5090. E-mail: 999@eoni.com. Licensee: KSRV Inc. Group owner: Capps Broadcast Group (acq 12-14-98; $800,000). Network: Network: ABC, Jones Radio Networks. Rep: Tacher. Tacher. Format: Adult contemp. Target aud: 18-49; general. ♦Dave Capps, pres; Randy McKone, gen mgr.

La Pine

***KKLP(FM)**— 2005: 90.1 mhz; 2.5 kw vert. Ant 131 ft. TL: N43 34 50 W121 34 13. Stereo. 5700 W. Oaks Blvd., Rocklin, CA 95765. Phone: (916) 251-1600. Fax: (916) 2511650. E-mail: klove@klove.com. Web Site: www.kove.com. Licensee: Educational Media Foundation. Group owner: EMF Broadcasting. Network: K-Love. Shaw Pittman. Format: Contemp Christian. News staff: 3. Target aud: 25-44; Judeo Christian, female. ♦Richard Jenkins, pres; Mike Novak, VP; Lloyd Parker, gen mgr; Ed Lenane, opns dir.

Lake Oswego

KDZR(AM)—Licensed to Lake Oswego. See Portland

KKSL(AM)—Licensed to Lake Oswego. See Portland

KLTH(FM)— Aug 1, 1977: 106.7 mhz; 100 kw. 1,443 ft. TL: N45 30 58 W122 43 59. Stereo. 222 S.W. Columbia, Suite 350, Portland 97201. Phone: (503) 223-0300. Fax: (503) 223-6542. Fax: (503) 223-6795. E-mail: reachus@literock1067.com. Web Site: www.literock1067.com. Licensee: Infinity Radio of Portland Inc. Group owner: Infinity Broadcasting Corp. (acq 11-13-98; grpsl). Leventhal, Senter & Lerman. Format: Adult Contemp. News staff: one. Target aud: 35-54; 55% women, 45% men. ♦Michael Jordan, CEO; Mel Karmazin, chmn; Mark Walen, gen mgr; Maureen Pulicella, gen sls mgr; Rob Bertrand, prom dir; Chris Miller, progmg dir; Diana Jordan, news dir.

Lakeview

KLCR(FM)— 2003: 95.3 mhz; 780 w. Ant 1,378 ft. TL: N42 12 40 W120 19 35. 613 S. G St. 97630-1829. Phone: (541) 947-3325. Licensee: Woodrow Michael Warren. Group owner: Woodrow Michael Warren Stns. Format: Classic rock. ♦Mike Warren, gen mgr.

***KOAP(FM)**— 2000: 88.7 mhz; 170 w. Ant -590 ft. TL: N42 10 42 W120 21 19. Oregon Public Broadcasting, 7140 S.W. Macadam Ave., Portland 97219. Phone: (503) 293-1905. Licensee: Oregon Public Broadcasting. Format: News, jazz, class, world beat. ♦Jack Galmiche, gen mgr.

KQIK(AM)— Dec 5, 1956: 1230 khz; 1 kw-U. TL: N42 12 30 W120 21 39. Stereo. 17968 Hwy. 395 97630. Phone: (541) 947-3351. Fax: (541) 947-3375. E-mail: kqikradio@hotmail.com. Licensee: Crystal Clear Broadcasting Co. Inc. (acq 12-10-2003; $118,000. with co-located FM). Network: Network: ABC Daytime Direction, Jones Radio Networks. Rep: Tacher. Format: Country. News staff: one; News: 2 hrs wkly. Target aud: General. Spec prog: Relg 2 hrs wkly. ♦Tommie Dodd, CEO & chmn; Tommie S. Dodd, pres & gen mgr.

KQIK-FM— 1987: 93.5 mhz; 1 kw. Ant 951 ft. TL: N42 12 18 W120 19 39. Stereo. Format: Adult contemp. Target aud: General.

Lebanon

KGAL(AM)— Aug 5, 1995: 1580 khz; 1 kw-U, DA-1. TL: N44 34 30 W122 55 15. 36991 KGAL Dr. 97355. Phone: (541) 451-5425. Fax: (541) 451-5429. E-mail: charlie@kgal.com. Web Site: www.kgal.com. Licensee: EADS Broadcasting Corp. Network: Network: Network: Network: Network: CBS, Westwood One, Salem Radio Network, Sporting News Radio Network, ABC. Rep: McGavren Guild. Crowell & Moring. Format: News, Talk, Sports. News staff: 4; News: 25 hrs wkly. Target aud: 25-54; active listeners. ♦Richard B. Eads, pres; Florence R. Eads, CFO; Charlie Eads, exec VP & gen mgr; Jim Willhight, opns mgr; Shelly Garrett, gen sls mgr.

***KGRI(FM)**—Not on air, target date: unknown: 88.1 mhz; 1 w horiz, 170 w vert. 2,473 ft vert. TL: N44 28 59 W122 34 55. Stereo. 5700 W. Oaks Blvd., Rocklin, CA 95765. Phone: (916) 251-1600. Fax: (916) 251-1650. E-mail: info@air1.com. Web Site: www.air1.com. Licensee: Educational Media Foundation. Group owner: EMF Broadcasting. Network: Air 1. Shaw Pittman. Format: Contemp Christian. News staff: 3. Target aud: 18-35; Judeo-Christian, female. ♦Richard Jenkins, pres; Mike Novak, VP; Lloyd Parker, gen mgr.

KSHO(AM)— 1950: 920 khz; 1 kw-U, DA-1. TL: N44 34 30 W122 55 15. 36991 KGAL Dr. 97355. Phone: (541) 451-5425. Fax: (541) 451-5429. E-mail: kgal@kgal.com. Web Site: www.ksho.net. Licensee: Eads Broadcasting Corp. (acq 10-1-81; $425,000; 10-5-81). Network: Jones Radio Networks. Rep: McGavren Guild. Crowell & Moring. Format: MOR, adult standards. News staff: 4; News: 7 hrs wkly. Target

Broadcasting & Cable Yearbook 2006

D-414

Stations in the U.S. Oregon

Developers & Brokers of Radio Properties

contact American Media Services at our suite:
Philadelphia Marriott Downtown
215-625-2900
843-972-2200
americanmediaservices.com
Charleston, SC
Dallas, TX · Chicago, Il · Austin, TX

American Media Services, LLC

aud: 35 plus; mature adults with money & leisure. ♦ Richard B. Eads, pres; Florence R. Eads, CFO; Charlie Eads, exec VP & gen mgr; Jim Willhight, opns mgr; Shelly Garrett, gen sls mgr.

KXPC(FM)— Apr 8, 1974: 103.7 mhz; 100 kw. 1,099 ft. TL: N44 30 17 W122 57 20. Stereo. 1207 9th Ave. S.E., Albany 97322. Phone: (541) 928-1926. Fax: (541) 791-1054. E-mail: kxpc@kxpc.com. Web Site: www.kxpc.com. Licensee: Portland Broadcasting L.L.C. (acq 4-11-01; $4.1 million). Rep: McGavren Guild. Format: Country. News: 2 hrs wkly. Target aud: 18-54. ♦ Rich Coleman, gen mgr.

Lincoln City

KBCH(AM)—Listing follows KCRF-FM.

KCRF-FM— Nov 1, 1981: 96.7 mhz; 19.5 kw. Ant 872 ft. TL: N44 45 22 W124 02 57. Stereo. Box 1430, Newport 97365. Phone: (541) 265-2266. Fax: (541) 265-6397. E-mail: info@kcrffm.com. Web Site: kcrffm.com. Licensee: Pacific West Broadcasting Inc. (group owner; acq 1-15-00; grpsl). Network: Network: AP Network News, Jones Radio Networks. Tacher Format: Classic rock. News staff: 2; News: 2 hrs wkly. ♦ David Miller, pres & gen mgr.

KBCH(AM)—Co-owned with KCRF-FM. May 27, 1955: 1400 khz; 1 kw-U. TL: N44 59 27 W123 58 45. E-mail: info@kbcham.com. Web Site: kbcham.com. Network: ABC Information & Entertainment. Rep: Tacher. Format: MOR, full service. News staff: 2; News: 4 hrs wkly.

Malin

*KBUG(FM)— 2000: 100.9 mhz; 750 w. Ant 899 ft. TL: N42 05 48 W121 37 57. Stereo. Box 111, Klamath Falls 97601. Phone: (541) 883-6331. Fax: (541) 884-8226. Web Site: www.christiancountrynetwork.com. Licensee: Malin Christian Church, Inc. (acq 7-1-99; $3,000). Format: Christian country.

McMinnville

KLYC(AM)— June 18, 1949: 1260 khz; 1 kw-U, DA-N. TL: N45 13 19 W123 10 21. Box 1099 97128. Secondary address: 1975 Colvin Ct. 97128. Phone: (503) 472-1260. Fax: (503) 472-3243. E-mail: klyc@viclink.com. Licensee: Bohnsack Strategies Inc. (acq 10-2-90; $120,000; 10-22-90). Network: CNN Radio. Format: Adult contemp, oldies. Target aud: 25-54. Spec prog: Sp 8 hrs wkly. ♦ Larry Bohnsack, pres & gen mgr.

*KSLC(FM)— Jan 17, 1972: 90.3 mhz; 320 w. -46 ft. TL: N45 12 06 W123 11 52. Stereo. Unit DD, 900 S.E. Baker St. 97128. Phone: (503) 434-2550. Phone: (503) 434-2666. Fax: (503) 434-2665. Web Site: www.linfield.edu/kslc. Licensee: Linfield College. Format: Alternative rock. News: 3 hrs wkly. Target aud: 12-25; young people looking for new mus. Spec prog: Black 2 hrs, heavy metal 7 hrs wkly, relg 2 hrs wkly. ♦ Julie Kanago, gen mgr; Dave McAdams, opns dir; Zach Bowden, dev VP.

Medford

KBOY-FM— February 1958: 95.7 mhz; 100 kw. 935 ft. TL: N42 27 07 W23 03 20. (CP: 60 kw, ant 751 ft.). Stereo. 1438 Rossanley Dr. 97501. Phone: (541) 779-1550. Fax: (541) 776-2360. E-mail: cbaker@radiomedford.com. Web site: www.957kboy.com. Licensee: Mapleton Communications LLC (group owner; acq 10-26-01; grpsl). Format: Classic rock. News: One. ♦ Ron Hren, gen mgr.

KCMX(AM)—(Phoenix). Apr 7, 1962: 880 khz; 1 kw-U. TL: N42 18 36 W122 48 41. 1438 Rossanley Dr. 97501. Phone: (541) 779-1550. Fax: (541) 776-2360. Web Site: www.kcmxam.com. Licensee: Mapleton Communications LLC (group owner; acq 10-26-01; grpsl). Rep: Allied Radio Partners. Art Moore. Format: Talk, news. News staff: one. Target aud: 18 plus. ♦ Ed Hardy, pres; Ron Hren, gen mgr; Alan Vezzani, sls dir; Devin Harpole, mktg dir & prom dir; Bill Jacobs, progmg dir; Chris Canter, news dir & pub affrs dir; Jim Sute, chief of engrg.

KTMT-FM—Co-owned with KCMX(AM). Oct 15, 1970: 93.7 mhz; 31 kw. 7,580 ft. TL: N42 04 55 W122 43 07. Stereo. Web Site: www.beat93.com. Dow, Lohnes & Albertson. Format: Adult CHR. News staff: one; News: 3 hrs wkly. Target aud: 18-49. ♦ Casey Baker, mktg dir, prom dir & mus dir; Matt Roberts, progmg dir.

KCMX-FM—See Ashland

KCNA(FM)—See Cave Junction

*KDOV(FM)— Aug 1, 1995: 91.7 mhz; 26 kw. -364 ft. TL: N42 20 13 W122 51 44. 1236 Disk Drive St. E. 97501. Phone: (541) 776-5368. Fax: (541) 776-0618. E-mail: kdov@kdov.net. Web Site: www.kdov.net. Licensee: UCB USA Inc. (acq 1-16-2004; $750,000). Network: Salem Radio Network. Edmundson & Edmundson. Format: Relg, news/talk. News staff: one; News: 5 hrs wkly. Target aud: 25-54; women. ♦ Perry A. Atkinson, pres; Dallas Rhoden, VP; Perry Atkinson, gen mgr; Pat Daly, opns mgr.

*KEZX(FM)— May 31, 1954: 730 khz; 1 kw-D, 74 w-N. TL: N42 18 36 W122 48 41. Stereo. 625 E. Jackson St., Suite B #377 97501. Phone: (541) 621-7266. Fax: (541) 772-4233. E-mail: ladybugsho @ladybugshows.com. Licensee: Opus Broadcasting Systems Inc. (group owner; acq 12-17-03; $70,000). Format: Easy Listening, jazz. News staff: 3. ♦ Dean Flock, gen mgr.

KLDZ(FM)— Aug 19, 1991: 103.5 mhz; 100 kw. Ant 479 ft. TL: N42 17 13 W123 00 15. Stereo. 3624 Avion Dr. 97504. Phone: (541) 774-1324. Fax: (541) 857-0326. Web Site: www.kool103.net. Licensee: Citicasters Licenses L.P. Group owner: Clear Channel Communications Inc. (acq 5-1-99; grpsl). Rep: Tacher. Format: Oldies. Target aud: 25 plus. ♦ Bill Nielsen, gen mgr.

KMED(AM)— 1922: 1440 khz; 5 kw-D, 1 kw-N. TL: N42 18 36 W122 48 41. 3624 Avion Dr. 97504. Phone: (541) 773-1440. Fax: (541) 857-0326. E-mail: news@kmed.com. Web Site: www.kmed.com. Licensee: Citicasters Licenses L.P. Group owner: Clear Channel Communications Inc. (acq 5-1-99; grpsl). Network: Network: Westwood One, CBS. Rep: Tacher. Format: News/talk. News staff: 3; News: 14 hrs wkly. Target aud: 35 plus. ♦ Bill Nielsen, gen mgr; Bill Meyer, stn mgr.

KRTA(AM)— October 1947: 610 khz; 5 kw-U, DA-2. TL: N42 23 15 W122 46 11. Stereo. 511 Rossanley Dr. 97501. Phone: (541) 772-0322. Fax: (541) 772-4233. E-mail: brian@opusradio.com. Licensee: Opus Broadcasting Systems Inc. (group owner; acq 7-9-91; $63,634. with KROG(FM) Grants Pass; FTR: 7-29-91). Rep: Tacher. Leibowitz & Spencer. Format: Sp. News: 9 hrs wkly. Target aud: 12 plus; Hispanic. Spec prog: Southern Oregon A's, North Medford & Oregon State football & basketball, Portland Trailblazers. ♦ Dean Flock, CEO & gen mgr; Brian Fraser, gen sls mgr; Oscar Bonilla, opns mgr & progmg dir.

KTMT(AM)—See Ashland

Milton-Freewater

KHTO(FM)— Sept 10, 1992: 97.9 mhz; 20 kw. Ant 1,322 ft. TL: N45 47 51 W118 06 54. Stereo. Box 4814, Tri-Cities, WA 99302. Secondary address: 2621 W. A St., Pasco, WA 99301. Phone: (509) 547-9791. Fax: (509) 547-8509. Fax: (417) 873-2000. Web Site: www.ok95radio.com. Licensee: Alexandra Communications Inc. Group owner: Clear Channel Communications Inc. (acq 4-11-2005). Tacher Format: Top 40. News staff: one; News: 6 hrs wkly. Target aud: General. ♦ Eric Van Winkle, gen mgr.

*KLRF(FM)— Jan 1, 1999: 88.5 mhz; 5 kw. 1,302 ft. TL: N45 47 16 W118 10 31. Box 209, Venore, TN 37885. Secondary address: 1390 W. Poplar St., Suite 201, Wallawalla, WA 99362. Phone: (509) 524-0885; (423) 884-2800. Fax: (509) 524-0884; (423) 884-2802. E-mail: office@lifetalk.net. Web Site: www.lifetalk.net. Licensee: Lifetalk Broadcasting Association. Format: Relg, Christian. ♦ Grant McPherson, gen mgr.

Milwaukie

KZNY(AM)— February 1988: 1010 khz; 4.5 kw-D. TL: N45 29 03 W122 24 40. Stereo. 5110 S.E. Stark St., Suite C, Portland 97415. Phone: (503) 227-2156. Fax: (503) 234-5583. Licensee: Bustos Media of Oregon License LLC. Group owner: Bustos Media Holdings (acq 11-19-2003; $1 million). Format: Sp. ♦ Spencer French, VP & gen mgr; Tom Oberg, gen sls mgr; Henry Cualio, progmg dir.

Molalla

KRSK(FM)—Licensed to Molalla. See Portland

Monmouth

KSND(FM)— Mar 23, 1995: 95.1 mhz; 1 kw. Ant 1,565 ft. TL: N44 53 19 W123 36 26. Stereo. 285 Liberty St. N.E., #340, Salem 97301. Phone: (503) 763-9951. Fax: (503) 763-2676. E-mail: ernie@ksnd.com. Web Site: www.ksnd.com. Licensee: Radio Beam LLC (acq 6-7-02; $400,000). Tacher Wiley, Rein & Fielding. Format: Adult contemp. News staff: one; News: 5 hrs wkly. Target aud: 25-54. ♦ Ernie Hopseker, pres, gen mgr & gen mgr; Patrick Garcia, gen sls mgr; Carl Widing, progmg dir; Art Bobrowitz, pub affrs dir.

Myrtle Point

*KOOZ(FM)— Aug 1, 1996: 94.1 mhz; 1 kw. Ant 1,456 ft. TL: N42 57 32 W124 16 23. Jefferson Public Radio, 1250 Siskiyou Blvd., Ashland 97520. Phone: (541) 552-6301. Web Site: www.jeffnet.org. Licensee: JPR Foundation Inc. (acq 4-19-02; $83,700. with KTBR(AM) Roseburg). Network: NPR, PRI. Ernest Sanchez. Format: Class, news. News staff: one; News: 35 hrs wkly. ♦ Mitchell Christian, CFO; Ronald Kramer, CEO & gen mgr; Bryon Lambert, opns dir; Paul Westhelle, dev dir.

Newport

KCUP(AM)—See Toledo

*KLCO(FM)— Sept 11, 1990: 90.5 mhz; 3.2 kw. 256 ft. TL: N44 45 22 W124 02 57. Stereo. 4000 E. 30th Ave., Eugene 97405-0640. Phone: (541) 463-6000. Fax: (541) 463-6046. E-mail: klcc@lanecc.edu. Web Site: www.klcc.org. Licensee: Lane Community College. Network: NPR. Format: Jazz, div, news. News staff: one; News: 60 hrs wkly. Target aud: 25-54. Spec prog: Sp 5 hrs, Black 3 hrs, folk 12 hrs, blues 4 hrs, world 3 hrs, electronic 6 hrs wkly. ♦ Jerry Moskus, pres; Steve Barton, gen mgr.

KNCU(FM)— June 2000: 92.7 mhz; 3.8 kw. 840 ft. TL: N44 45 22 W124 02 57. Stereo. Box 1430 97365. Phone: (541) 265-2266. Fax: (541) 265-6397. E-mail: info@u92fm.com. Web Site: www.u92fm.com. Licensee: Pacific West Broadcasting Inc. (group owner; acq 10-27-00; grpsl). Tacher. Format: Country. News staff: one; News: 2 hrs wkly. Target aud: 24-54; adults. ♦ David J. Miller, pres & gen mgr.

KNPT(AM)— June 28, 1948: 1310 khz; 5 kw-D, 1 kw-N, DA-N. TL: N44 37 40 W123 59 15. Box 1430, 906 S.W. Alder St. 97365. Phone: (541) 265-2266. Fax: (541) 265-6397. E-mail: info@kuptam.com. Web Site: knptam.com. Licensee: Yaquina Bay Communications Inc. (acq 1-96). Network: ABC Information & Entertainment. Tacher. Format: News/talk, sports. News staff: 2; News: 21 hrs wkly. Target aud: 34 plus. Spec prog: Relg 2 hrs wkly. ♦ David J. Miller, pres & gen mgr; Vern Morris, gen sls mgr; Johnny Randolph, progmg dir; Howard Wright, mus dir; Bill Hall, news dir.

KYTE(FM)—Co-owned with KNPT(AM). Oct 25, 1976: 102.7 mhz; 66 kw. 881 ft. TL: N44 45 22 W124 02 57. Stereo. Fax: (541) 265-6397. E-mail: info@kytefm.com. Network: ABC Information & Entertainment. Format: Adult contemp. News staff: 2; News: 4 hrs wkly. Target aud: 24-49.

*KYOR(FM)—Not on air, target date: unknown: 88.9 mhz; 35 w. Ant 899 ft. TL: N44 45 23 W124 02 59. c/o Radio Station KUFR(FM), 136 E. S. Temple, Suite 1630, Salt Lake City, UT 84111. Phone: (801)

Oregon

359-3147. Fax: (801) 359-8112. Web Site: www.familyradio.com. Licensee: Family Stations Inc. ♦ Harold Camping, gen mgr.

North Bend

KACW(FM)— October 1990: 107.3 mhz; 51 kw. Ant 692 ft. TL: N43 12 18 W124 18 07. Stereo. Box 180, Coos Bay 97420. Secondary address: 320 Central Ave., Suite 519, Coos Bay 97420. Phone: (541) 267-2121. Fax: (541) 267-5229. Licensee: Bicoastal CB L.L.C. Group owner: Bicoastal Media L.L.C. (acq 8-22-03; grpsl). Tacher Format: Adult contemp. News: 14 hrs wkly. Target aud: 18-45. ♦ Kenneth R. Dennis, pres; John Pundt, gen mgr.

KBBR(AM)— Co-owned with KACW(FM). December 1950: 1340 khz; 1 kw-U. TL: N43 25 52 W124 12 23. Network: Network: Network: CBS Radio, Jones Radio Networks, Westwood One. Rep: Katz Radio, Tacher. Format: News/talk. News: 40 hrs wkly. Target aud: 25-54.

KOOS(FM)— Dec 10, 1979: 94.9 mhz; 89 kw. Ant 626 ft. TL: N43 12 18 W124 18 07. Stereo. 320 Central Ave., Suite 519, Coos Bay 97420. Phone: (541) 267-2121. Fax: (541) 267-5229. Web Site: www.southcoastradio.com. Licensee: Bicoastal CB L.L.C. Group owner: Bicoastal Media L.L.C. (acq 8-22-03; grpsl). Network: ABC. Rep: Tacher. Format: Classic hits. News: 8 hrs wkly. Target aud: 25-54. ♦ Kenneth R. Dennis, pres; John Pundt, gen mgr & rgnl sls mgr; Mike O.Brien, opns mgr.

North Powder

*****KEFS(FM)**—Not on air, target date: unknown: 89.5 mhz; 120 w. Ant 1,787 ft. TL: N45 07 26 W117 46 48. CSN International, 4002 N. 3300 E., Twin Falls, ID 83301. Phone: (208) 734-6633. Fax: (208) 736-1958. Web Site: www.csnradio.com. Licensee: CSN International. ♦ Mike Kestler, pres.

Nyssa

KARO(FM)— 1997: 98.7 mhz; 100 kw. 968 ft. TL: N43 24 09 W116 54 09. Box 1600, Napa, ID 83653. Phone: (208) 322-3437. Fax: (208) 322-3438. Licensee: Educational Media Foundation (acq 2-25-03; $1 million). Format: Christian contemp. ♦ Steve Sumner, gen mgr.

Oakridge

*****KAVE(FM)**— Oct 22, 1990: 92.1 mhz; 580 w. -817 ft. TL: N43 44 34 W122 26 03. Oakridge High School, 47997 W. First St. 97463. Phone: (541) 782-2231. Fax: (541) 782-4692. E-mail: kave921@hotmail.com. Web Site: www.geocities.com/kave921. Licensee: School District #76. Format: CHR. Target aud: General. ♦ Debbie Gillespie, gen mgr & chief of opns; Abbie Pierce, prom dir; Aaron Stone, progmg dir.

*****KMKR(FM)**—Not on air, target date: unknown: 88.5 mhz; 400 w. Ant -1,286 ft. TL: N43 44 27 W122 26 50. Lane County School District 4J, 200 N. Monroe St., Eugene 97402. Phone: (541) 687-3123. Fax: (541) 687-3573. Web Site: www.krvm.org. Licensee: Lane County School District 4J. ♦ George Russell, gen mgr; Carl Sundbert, stn mgr; Ken Martin, progmg dir; Carl Sundberg, chief of engrg.

Ontario

KSRV(AM)— Nov 23, 1946: 1380 khz; 5 kw-D, 1 kw-N, DA-N. TL: N44 02 45 W116 58 24. Box 129, 1725 N. Oregon St. 97914. Phone: (541) 889-8651. Fax: (541) 889-8733. E-mail: ksrv@ksrv.com. Web Site: www.ksrv.com. Licensee: FM Idaho Co. LLC (acq 9-9-2004; $2.5 million. with co-located FM). Network: ABC Information & Entertainment. Dow, Lohnes & Albertson. Format: News/talk. News staff: one; News: 15 hrs wkly. Target aud: 25 plus. Spec prog: Farm 15 hrs wkly. ♦ Mark Maier, gen mgr; Bill Sauer, sls dir; Kimber Lundy, prom dir; Carl Follick, progmg dir & news dir.

KSRV-FM— July 4, 1977: 96.1 mhz; 100 kw. 450 ft. TL: N44 01 50 W117 04 36. Stereo. Web Site: www.ksrv.com. ♦ Dave Adams, progmg dir.

Oregon City

KGDD(AM)— July 4, 1947: 1520 khz; 50 kw-D, 10 kw-N, DA-2. TL: N45 24 44 W122 34 37. 0700 S.W. Bancroft St., Portland 97239. Phone: (503) 223-1441. Fax: (503) 223-6909. Licensee: Bustos Media of Oregon License LLC. Group owner: Bustos Media Holdings (acq 11-17-2003; $2.8 million). Rep: D & R Radio. Format: Sp. News staff: one. ♦ David Field, pres; Allan Davis, opns mgr.

KGON(FM)—See Portland

Pendleton

*****KRBM(FM)**— Apr 18, 1970: 90.9 mhz; 25 kw. 587 ft. TL: N45 35 21 W118 59 53. Stereo. 7140 S.W. Macadam Ave., Portland 97219. Phone: (503) 293-1905. Phone: (1-888) 293-1982. Fax: (503) 293-1919. Web Site: www.opb.org. Licensee: Oregon Public Broadcasting. (acq 9-20-93; grpsl; 10-11-93). Network: Network: PRI, NPR. Format: News, info music. News staff: 5; News: 146 hrs wkly. Target aud: Teens to adults. ♦ Jack Galmiche, COO, exec VP & VP.

KTIX(AM)— 1941: 1240 khz; 1 kw-U. TL: N45 39 49 W118 47 19. Stereo. 2003 NW 56th Dr. 97801. Phone: (541) 278-2500. Fax: (541) 276-1480. Licensee: KSRV Inc. Group owner: Capps Broadcast Group (acq 5-14-98; $1.2 million. with co-located FM). Network: Network: ESPN Radio, ABC Information & Entertainment. Rep: McGavren Guild. Format: Sports. News staff: one. Target aud: 25-54; upscale adults. ♦ Randy McKone, pres & stn mgr; J.J. Ford, opns mgr; John Thomas, prom mgr & progmg dir.

KWHT(FM)— Co-owned with KTIX(AM). May 1, 1984: 103.5 mhz; 100 kw. 720 ft. TL: N45 47 51 W118 22 17. Stereo. Network: ABC. Format: Country. News: 2 hrs wkly. Target aud: 25-54; adults. ♦ Randy McKone, CEO; Matthew Richards, progmg dir; J.J. Ford, engrg VP.

KUMA(AM)— Aug 25, 1955: 1290 khz; 5 kw-U, DA-N. TL: N45 40 25 W118 44 48. 2003 N.W. 56th Dr. 97801. Phone: (541) 276-1511. Fax: (541) 276-1480. Licensee: Round-Up Radio Inc. Group owner: Capps Broadcast Group (acq 7-1-93; $340,000. with co-located FM; FTR: 7-26-93). Tacher. Format: Talk, news. News staff: one; News: 20 hrs wkly. Target aud: 25 plus; adults. Spec prog: Farm 10 hrs wkly. ♦ Dave Capps, pres; Randy McKone, VP & gen mgr; J.J. Ford, opns dir & opns mgr; Butch Thurman, news dir.

KUMA-FM— Oct 1, 1978: 107.7 mhz; 50 kw. 171 ft. TL: N42 35 19 W118 59 45. (CP: 100 kw, ant 1,128 ft.). Stereo. Network: ABC. Format: Adult contemp. Target aud: 18 plus. ♦ J.J. Ford, opns mgr & progmg mgr.

Phoenix

KAKT(FM)— 1991: 105.1 mhz; 52 kw. 545 ft. TL: N42 25 41 W123 00 04. 1438 Rossanley Dr., Medford 97501. Phone: (541) 779-1550. Fax: (541) 776-2360. Web Site: www.kat105.com. Licensee: Mapleton Communications LLC (group owner; acq 10-26-01; grpsl). Format: Country. News staff: one. Target aud: 25-49; female. ♦ Ron Hren, gen mgr; Casey Baker, opns mgr & prom mgr; Matt Roberts, progmg dir.

*****KAPL(AM)**— Jan 2, 1977: 1300 khz; 20 kw-U, DA-N. TL: N42 17 44 W122 48 15. Box 1090, Jacksonville 97530. Phone: (541) 899-5275. Fax: (541) 899-8068. E-mail: kapl@applegatefellowship.org. Web Site: www.applegatefellowship.org. Licensee: Applegate Media Inc. (acq 10-24-91). Format: News/talk, Christian. Target aud: 25-54. ♦ Chris Thompson, gen mgr & opns mgr.

KCMX(AM)—Licensed to Phoenix. See Medford

Pine Grove

*****KPFR(FM)**— 2005: 89.5 mhz; 7 kw vert. Ant 1,673 ft. TL: N45 19 58 W121 42 48. Family Stations Inc., 4135 Northgate Blvd., Suite 1, Sacramento, CA 95834. Phone: (510) 568-6200. Fax: (510) 568-6190. Web Site: familyradio.com. Licensee: Family Stations Inc. (group owner; acq 9-9-2002). Format: Christian.

Portland

KBMS(AM)—See Vancouver, WA

KBNP(AM)— 1949: 1410 khz; 5 kw-D, 250 w-N. TL: N45 28 24 W122 39 36. 278 S.W. Arthur St. 97201. Phone: (503) 223-6769. Fax: (503) 223-4305. E-mail: kbnp@kbnp.com. Web Site: www.kbnp.com. Licensee: 2nd Amendment Foundation. (acq 8-8-90; $320,000; 8-27-90). Davis Wright Tremaine. Format: Business news & info, financial. News staff: 2; News: 163 hrs wkly. Target aud: General; corporations & individuals concerned with how-to's of making & keeping money. Spec prog: People w/disabilities, computer shows, home improvement. ♦ Keith P. Lyons, gen mgr.

*****KBOO(FM)**— June 1968: 90.7 mhz; 25.5 kw. 1,266 ft. TL: N45 29 20 W122 41 40. Stereo. 20 S.E. 8th Ave. 97214. Phone: (503) 231-8032. Fax: (503) 231-7145. E-mail: program@kboo.org. Web Site: www.kboo.fm. Licensee: KBOO Foundation. (acq 8-5-75). Haley, Bader & Potts. Format: Div. News staff: 2; News: 5 hrs wkly. Target aud: General. Spec prog: Sp 10 hrs, Indian one hr, ethnic 4 hrs, African/reggae 10 hrs wkly. ♦ Denise Kowalczyk, gen mgr & stn mgr; Gene Bradley, gen mgr & prom mgr; Justin Miller, adv mgr; Chris Merrick, progmg dir; John Mackey, mus dir & chief of engrg.

*****KBPS(AM)**— Mar 23, 1923: 1450 khz; 1 kw-U. TL: N45 31 38 W122 29 03. 515 N.E. 15th Ave. 97232. Phone: (503) 916-5830. Fax: (503) 916-2642. E-mail: music.info@allclassical.org. Web Site: www.allclassical.org. Licensee: School District No. 1 Multnomah County, OR. Format: Children programs. News: one hr wkly. Spec prog: Sp one hr wkly. ♦ Sally Lewis, dev dir & mktg dir.

*****KBPS-FM**— August 1983: 89.9 mhz; 8.7 kw. Ant 964 ft. TL: N45 30 58 W122 43 59. Stereo. 515 N.E. 15th Ave. 97232. Phone: (503) 916-5828. Fax: (503) 916-2642. Web Site: www.allclassical.org. Licensee: KBPS Public Radio Foundation (acq 12-15-2003; $5.5 million). Network: PRI. Garvey, Schubert & Barer. Format: Class. News: 5 hrs wkly. ♦ Sarah Shelley, gen mgr; Sally Lewis, dev dir.

*****KBVM(FM)**— Dec 8, 1989: 88.3 mhz; 1.85 kw, 1,434 ft. TL: N45 29 23 W122 41 47. (CP: Ant 1,404 ft.). Stereo. Box 5888 97228-5888. Secondary address: 5000 N. Willamette, N. 44 97203. Phone: (503) 285-5200. Fax: (503) 285-3322. Web Site: www.kbvm.com. Licensee: Catholic Broadcasting NW Inc. Format: Relg. Target aud: General; anyone desiring Christian mus, inspiration, Catholic prayer & evangelism. Spec prog: Sp 14 hrs wkly. ♦ Steven J. Moffitt, CEO & gen mgr; Mark Andreas, progmg dir.

KCMD(AM)— Oct 18, 1925: 970 khz; 5 kw-D, DA-N. TL: N45 30 56 W122 43 56. Stereo. 222 S.W. Columbia 97201. Phone: (503) 223-0300. Fax: (503) 497-2314. Licensee: Infinity Radio Inc. Group owner: Infinity Broadcasting Corp. (acq 11-13-98; grpsl). Format: Country, class. Target aud: 35 plus. ♦ Dave McDonald, gen mgr; Mark Whaler, gen sls mgr.

KUFO-FM—Co-owned with KCMD(AM). May 1, 1977: 101.1 mhz; 100 kw. 1,640 ft. TL: N45 30 58 W122 43 59. Stereo. 20040 S.W. 1st Ave. 97201. Web Site: www.kufo.com. Format: AOR.

KDZR(AM)— (Lake Oswego). 1998: 1640 khz; 10 kw-D, 1 kw-N. TL: N45 27 14 W122 32 47. 3030 S.W. Moody, Suite 210 97201. Phone: (503) 228-4322. Fax: (503) 228-4325. Web Site: www.radiodisney.com. Licensee: Radio Disney Group LLC. Group owner: ABC Inc. (acq 2-03; $3.8 million. with KKSL(AM) Lake Oswego). Network: Radio Disney. Format: Children. ♦ Jean-Paul Colaco, pres & gen mgr; Pamela Herrold, stn mgr.

KEX(AM)— Dec 24, 1926: 1190 khz; 50 kw-U, DA-N. TL: N45 25 20 W122 33 57. 4949 S.W. Macadam Ave. 97201. Phone: (503) 225-1190. Fax: (503) 227-5873. Web Site: www.1190kex.com. Licensee: Citicasters Licenses L.P. Group owner: Clear Channel Communications Inc. Network: ABC Information & Entertainment. Hogan & Hartson. Format: News, talk. News: 25 hrs wkly. Target aud: 25-54; general. Spec prog: Portland Trailblazers basketball. ♦ Ron Saito, pres & gen mgr; Mike Dirkx, opns dir & progmg dir; dave Milner, sls dir & gen sls mgr; Mike Lulich, natl sls mgr; Scott Thompson, mktg VP & mktg dir; Teri Rodrigues, prom mgr; Brad Ford, news dir; Shane Ruark, chief of engrg.

KKRZ(FM)—Co-owned with KEX(AM). May 1946: 100.3 mhz; 95 kw. 1,433 ft. TL: N45 31 22 W122 45 07. Stereo. Phone: (503) 226-0100. Fax: (503) 295-9281. Web Site: www.2100portland.com. Format: Contemp hit. Target aud: 18-49. ♦ Jen Dalton, prom mgr; Michael Hayes, progmg dir; Shane Raurk, news dir.

KFXX(AM)— Jan 17, 1925: 1080 khz; 50 kw-D, 10 kw-N, DA-2. TL: N45 33 26 W122 29 08. Stereo. 2000 S.W. First Ave., Suite 300 97201. Phone: (503) 228-4393. Fax: (503) 227-3938. E-mail: comments@koth.com. Web Site: www.kotk.com. Licensee: Entercom Portland License LLC. Group owner: Entercom Communications Corp. (acq 12-18-2003; $44 million. with co-located FM). Format: Talk/personality. Target aud: 25-54. Spec prog: Portland Pilots basketball, Portland Forest Dragons football, Washington Huskies football. ♦ Ron Carter,

Stations in the U.S. — Oregon

CFO & gen mgr; Trey Yant, gen sls mgr; Rick Boeker, prom dir; Bruce Agler, progmg dir; Dave Paul, news dir; Michael Everhart, engrg mgr.

KWJJ-FM—Co-owned with KFXX(AM). 1968: 99.5 mhz; 50 kw. 1,266 ft. TL: N45 29 20 W122 41 40. Stereo. Web Site: www.kwjj.com. Format: Country. Target aud: 25-54. ♦Ken Boesen, progmg dir; Craig Lockwood, mus dir; Michael Everhart, engrg VP.

KGON(FM)— December 1967: 92.3 mhz; 100 kw. 920 ft. TL: N45 20 23 W122 41 47. Stereo. 0700 S.W. Bancroft 97239. Phone: (503) 223-1441. Fax: (503) 223-6909. E-mail: jhutchinson@entercom.com. Web Site: www.kgon.com. Licensee: Entercom Portland License LLC. Group owner: Entercom Communications Corp. (acq 8-1-95; grpsl). Rep: D & R Radio. Format: Classic rock. News staff: 3; News: one hr wkly. ♦David Field, pres; Jack Hutchinson, sr VP & VP; Erin Hubert, gen mgr; Dick Loughney, stn mgr & chief of engrg; Keevin Wagner, gen mgr & prom dir; Clark Ryan, progmg dir.

KINK(FM)— Dec 24, 1968: 101.9 mhz; 100 kw. 1,673 ft. TL: N45 31 21 W122 44 46. Stereo. 1501 S.W. Jefferson St. 97201. Phone: (503) 517-6000. Fax: (503) 517-6100. E-mail: lwarren@kink.fm. Web Site: www.kink.fm. Licensee: Infinity Radio Inc. Group owner: Infinity Broadcasting Corp. (acq 11-13-98; grpsl). Network: AP Radio. Rep: Major Market Broadcasters Ltd. Format: AAA. News staff: 2; News: 3 hrs wkly. Target aud: 25-54; primary, secondary. ♦Stan Mak, gen mgr; Maureen Pulicella, gen sls mgr; Candace Gonzales, mktg dir; Dennis Constantine, progmg dir; Sheila Hamilton, news dir; Leana Warren, pub affrs dir.

KKCW(FM)—See Beaverton

KKPZ(AM)— Nov 12, 1923: 1330 khz; 5 kw-U, DA-1. TL: N45 27 13 W122 32 45. 4700 S. W. Macadam Ave., Suite 102 97239. Phone: (503) 242-1950. Fax: (503) 242-0155. E-mail: info@kkpz.com. Web Site: www.kkpz.com. Licensee: KPHP Radio Inc. Group owner: Crawford Broadcasting Co. (acq 1995; $2 million). Format: Christian, talk. Target aud: 34-54. ♦Donald Crawford Sr., pres; Don Crawford Jr., gen mgr; James Autry, stn mgr; Phil Bethune, opns dir; John White, chief of engrg.

KKSL(AM)—(Lake Oswego). June 1948: 1290 khz; 5 kw-U, DA-N. TL: N45 28 27 W122 39 33. 4700 S.W. Macadam Ave., Suite 102 97239. Secondary address: 3030 SW Moody, Suite 210 97201. Phone: (503) 242-1950. Fax: (503) 242-0155. E-mail: info@kksl1290.com. Web Site: www.kksl1290.com. Licensee: Radio Disney Group LLC. Group owner: ABC Inc. (acq 1-2-03; $3.8 million. with KDZR(AM) Lake Oswego). Format: Christian, talk. Target aud: 25-54. Spec prog: Gospel 15 hrs wkly. ♦Pamela Herrold, stn mgr; Phil Bethune, opns mgr.

KLTH(FM)—See Lake Oswego

***KLVP(AM)**—(Tigard). June 28, 1993: 1040 khz; 2.2 kw-D, 200 w-N. TL: N45 28 24 W122 39 36. Stereo. 5700 West Oak Blvd., Rocklin, CA 95765. Phone: (916) 251-1600. Fax: (916) 251-1650. E-mail: klove@klove.com. Web Site: www.klove.com. Licensee: Educational Media Foundation Inc. Group owner: EMF Broadcasting (acq 4-25-90; $45,000;. FTR: 5-14-90). Network: K-Love. Shaw Pittman. Format: Contemp Christian. News staff: 3. Target aud: 25-44; female (Judeo-Christian). ♦Richard Jenkins, pres; Mike Novak, VP; Lloyd Parker, gen mgr; Ed Lenane, opns dir.

KMUZ(AM)—(Gresham). Sept 28, 1956: 1230 khz; 1 kw-U. TL: N45 29 35 W122 24 40. Stereo. 5110 S.E. Stark St., WA 97215. Phone: (503) 227-2156. Phone: (360) 835-3400. Fax: (360) 835-7593. E-mail: sfrench@bustosmedia.com. Web Site: www.bustosmedia.com. Licensee: Bustos Media of Oregon License LLC. Group owner: Bustos Media Holdings (acq 7-15-2003; $1.13 million). Format: Sp. News: 3 hrs wkly. Target aud: 12-54; lower to upper middle income. Spec prog: News 3 hrs, relg one hr wkly. ♦Amador S. Bustos, pres; Spencer French, VP & gen mgr; Tom Trullinger, stn mgr.

KNRK(FM)—(Camas).WA Nov 1, 1992: 94.7 mhz; 6.3 kw. Ant 1,322 ft. TL: N45 29 20 W122 41 40. Stereo. 0700 S.W. Bancroft 97239. Phone: (503) 223-1441. Fax: (503) 223-6909. Web Site: www.knrk.com.

Licensee: Entercom Portland License L.L.C. Group owner: Entercom Communications Corp. Format: Alternative rock. News staff: one. Target aud: 25-54. ♦David Field, pres; Jack Hutchison, exec VP; Mark Hamilton, stn mgr & progmg dir; Greg Spencer, gen sls mgr; Linda Smith, natl sls mgr; Steve Forsyth, natl sls mgr; Karin Shipley, mktg dir; Mike Turner, news dir & pub affrs dir; Gary Hilliard, engrg dir.

***KOPB-FM**— 1962: 91.5 mhz; 70 kw horiz, 21 kw vert. 1,558 ft. TL: N45 31 22 W122 45 07. Stereo. 7140 S.W. Macadam Ave. 97219. Phone: (503) 293-1905. Fax: (503) 293-1919. E-mail: opbnews@opb.org. Web Site: www.opb.org. Licensee: Oregon Public Broadcasting. (acq 9-20-93; grpsl; 10-11-93). Network: Network: NPR, PRI. Format: News, info music. News staff: 5; News: 146 hrs wkly. Target aud: 34-54. ♦Jack Galmiche, COO, exec VP, dev VP & news dir; Virginia Breen, VP. Co-owned TV: *KOPB-TV affil.

KPDQ-FM— 1961: 93.7 mhz; 97 kw. 1,269 ft. TL: N45 29 20 W122 41 40. Stereo. 6400 S.E. Lake Rd. 97222. Phone: (503) 786-0600. Fax: (503) 786-1551. Web Site: www.kpdq.com. Licensee: Salem Media of Oregon Inc. Group owner: Salem Communications Corp. (acq 8-86; grpsl; FTR: 7-28-86). Format: Christian talk. Target aud: 25-54; listeners of Christian talk progmg. ♦Dennis Hayes, gen mgr; David Schulte, opns dir, opns mgr, progmg dir & progmg mgr; Damon Balch, gen sls mgr; Georgene Rice, news dir; Don Perkins, chief of engrg.

KPDQ(AM)— July 30, 1947: 800 khz; 1 kw-D, 500 w-N. TL: N45 28 45 W122 44 55. Web Site: www.kpdq.com. Format: Conservative talk, Christian. Target aud: 18-54; listeners of talk.

KPOJ(AM)— Mar 25, 1922: 620 khz; 25 kw-D, 10 kw-N, DA-2. TL: N45 25 20 W122 33 57. 4949 S.W. Macadam 97201. Phone: (503) 323-6400. Fax: (503) 323-6664. E-mail: deaveosporne@clearchannel.com. Web Site: www.620ktlk.com. Licensee: Citicasters Licenses L.P. Group owner: Clear Channel Communications Inc. (acq 1999; grpsl). Network: ABC. Format: News/talk. Target aud: 25-54. ♦Ron Saito, gen mgr; Mike Dirkx, opns mgr.

***KRRC(FM)**— May 1958: 97.9 mhz; 8 w. Ant 13 ft. TL: N45 28 51 W122 37 50. Reed College, 3203 S.E. Woodstock 97202. Phone: (503) 771-1112. Fax: (503) 777-7769. Licensee: The Reed Institute. (acq 1959). Format: Div. Target aud: 17-21; Reed College student body. Spec prog: Black 10 hrs, class 4 hrs, country 2 hrs, Fr 2 hrs, jazz 10 hrs, Sp 2 hrs wkly. ♦Nicholas Wright, gen mgr; Kristin Holmberg, opns dir & mus dir.

KRSK(FM)—(Molalla). July 3, 1970: 105.1 mhz; 21 kw. Ant 1,542 ft. TL: N45 31 21 W122 44 45. Stereo. 0700 S.W. Bancroft St. 97239. Phone: (503) 223-1441. Fax: (503) 223-6909. Web Site: www.thebuzz1051.com. Licensee: Entercom Portland License L.L.C. Group owner: Entercom Communications Corp. (acq 4-23-98; grpsl). Network: ABC Information & Entertainment. Format: Top 40. ♦Erin Hubert, gen mgr.

KUPL-FM— 1948: 98.7 mhz; 37 kw. 1,443 ft. TL: N45 30 58 W122 43 59. Stereo. 222 S.W. Columbia, Suite 350 97201. Phone: (503) 223-0300. Fax: (503) 223-6995. E-mail: laura.klein@infinitybroadcasting.com. Web Site: www.kupl.com. Licensee: Radio Systems of Miami Inc. Group owner: Infinity Broadcasting Corp. (acq 11-13-98; grpsl). Network: AP Radio. Leventhal, Senter & Lerman. Format: Country. News staff: one. Target aud: 25-54. ♦Mel Karmazin, chmn; Dan Mason, pres; Mark Walen, gen mgr; Lee Rogers, opns mgr; Tom Hunter, prom mgr; Cary Rolfe, progmg dir.

KXJM(FM)—Listing follows KXL(AM).

KXL(AM)— 1926: 750 khz; 50 kw-D, 20 kw-N, DA-2. TL: N45 24 05 W122 26 47. 0234 S.W. Bancroft 97201. Phone: (503) 243-7595. Fax: (503) 417-7662. Web Site: www.kxl.com. Licensee: Rose City Radio Corp. (group owner; acq 11-30-98; $55 million. with co-located FM). Network: Network: CBS, ABC News/Talk. Rep: McGavren Guild. Format: News/talk. Target aud: 25-54. ♦Rose City Radio, CFO; Tim McNamara, gen mgr; James Derby, opns mgr; Bill Ashenden, gen sls mgr.

KXJM(FM)—Co-owned with KXL(AM). June 18, 1965: 95.5 mhz; 100 kw. 990 ft. TL: N45 29 23 W122 41 47. Stereo. Web Site: www.jamminfm.com. Format: CHR. ♦Tim McNamara, gen sls mgr; Mark Adams, progmg dir.

KXMG(AM)— July 4, 1954: 1150 khz; 5 kw-D, 47 w-N, DA-1. TL: N45 38 34 W122 36 49. 5110 S.E. Stark 97215. Phone: (503) 234-5550. Fax: (503) 234-5583. E-mail: sfrench@bustosmedia.com. Web Site: www.bustosmedia.com. Licensee: Bustos Media of Oregon License LLC. Group owner: Bustos Media Holdings (acq 11-18-2003; $1.25 million). Rep: Interep. Format: Sp contemp. Target aud: 25-54; general. Spec prog: Black one hr, Scandinavian one hr, URDU Hindi one hr, It one hr wkly. ♦Spencer French, gen mgr; Tom Oberg, gen sls mgr; Chitra Gade, chief of engrg.

KYCH-FM— Apr 1, 1980: 97.1 mhz; 100 kw. Amt 1,266 ft. TL: N45 29 20 W122 41 40. Stereo. 0700 S.W. Bancroft St. 97239. Phone: (503) 223-1441. Fax: (503) 223-6909. E-mail: cryan@entercom.com. Web Site: www.charliefm.com. Licensee: Entercom Portland License L.L.C. Group owner: Entercom (acq 4-23-98; grpsl). Rep: Christal. Format: Adult contemp hits. Target aud: 25-54. ♦David Field, pres; Jack Hutchinson, exec VP; Dick Loughney, gen sls mgr; Clark Ryan, progmg dir; Keevin Wagner, prom dir & news dir; Gary Hilliard, chief of engrg.

Prineville

KLTW-FM—Listing follows KRCO(AM).

KRCO(AM)— Feb 1, 1950: 690 khz; 1 kw-D, 77 w-N. TL: N44 20 30 W120 54 10. Box 690 97754. Secondary address: 854 N.E. 4th St., Bend 97701. Phone: (541) 447-6770. Fax: (541) 383-3403 (sales). Licensee: Horizon Broadcasting Group L.L.C (group owner; acq 3-2-00; grpsl). Network: ABC. Rep: Tacher. Format: Classic country. Target aud: 35-64. Spec prog: Hispanic 4 hrs wkly. ♦Keith Shipman, pres & gen mgr; Larry Wilson, opns mgr; Dave Clemens, progmg dir; Paul Valle, news dir.

KLTW-FM—Co-owned with KRCO(AM). Apr 8, 1981: 95.1 mhz; 100 kw. Ant 472 ft. TL: N44 18 32 W120 55 47. Stereo. Phone: (541) 383-3825. Rep: Tacher. Format: Soft adult contemp. Target aud: 25-54; adults.

Rainier

KJNI(FM)—Not on air, target date: unknown: 98.3 mhz; 1.6 kw. Ant 640 ft. TL: N46 10 59 W122 57 29. PMB333, 1 Blackfield Dr., Tiburon, CA 94920. Phone: (415) 789-5035. Licensee: Bicoastal Longview LLC. ♦Kevin P. Mostyn, VP.

Redmond

***KKJA(FM)**—Not on air, target date: unknown: 89.9 mhz; 750 w. Ant 2,217 ft. TL: N44 26 17 W120 57 14. CSN International, 4002 N. 3300 E., Twin Falls, ID 83301. Phone: (208) 734-6633. Licensee: CSN International. ♦Michael Kestler, pres.

KLRR(FM)—Licensed to Redmond. See Bend

KRDM(AM)— June 2004: 1240 khz; 750 w-U. TL: N44 17 18 W121 11 02. Box 1309 97756. Secondary address: 1514 S.W. Highland Ave. 97756. Phone: (541) 548-7621. Fax: (541) 504-8145. E-mail: krdm@krdm.net. Web Site: www.krdm.net. Licensee: Sage-Com Inc. Network: ABC. Format: News/talk. News staff: one; News: 6 hrs wkly. Target aud: General; Redmond residents. ♦Bud Hutchinson, pres & gen mgr; Sam KirKaldie, sr VP; Bob Smith, opns mgr.

KSJJ(FM)— Feb 4, 1981: 102.9 mhz; 100 kw. 885 ft. TL: N44 10 25 W121 16 29. Stereo. 969 S.W. Colorado, Bend 97702. Secondary address: 1500 N.E. Butler Market Rd., Bend 97702. Phone: (541) 388-3300. Fax: (541)389-7885. Web Site: www.ksjj.com. Licensee: GCC Bend LLC. (group owner; (acq 1999; grpsl). Network: ABC

Oregon

Information & Entertainment. Arent, Fox, Kintner, Plotkin & Kahn. Format: Country. News staff: one; News: 8 hrs wkly. Target aud: 25-54. ♦Dana Horner, stn mgr & sls dir.

KWRX(FM)— 2002: 88.5 mhz; 250 w. Ant 2,198 ft. TL: N44 26 14 W120 57 12. (CP: 720 w). Agate Hall, Univ. of Oregon 97403. Phone: (541) 345-0800. E-mail: kwax@qwest.net. Web Site: www.kwax.com. Licensee: State Board of Higher Education for the University of Oregon. Format: Classical. ♦Paul C. Bjornstad, gen mgr.

Reedsport

KDUN(AM)— June 2, 1961: 1030 khz; 10 kw-D, 630 w-N. TL: N43 44 17 W124 04 30. Box 168 97467. Phone: (541) 271-1030. Fax: (541) 271-2598. Web Site: www.kdun.com. Licensee: Pamplin Broadcasting-Oregon Inc. Group owner: Pamplin Broadcasting (acq 10-29-99). Rep: Allied Radio Partners. Format: Real Country. News staff: one. Target aud: 25 plus. ♦Mark Ail, gen mgr.

KJMX(FM)— 1993: 99.5 mhz; 11 kw. Ant 400 ft. TL: N43 40 40 W124 06 36. Box180, Coos Bay 97467. Phone: (541) 267-2121. Fax: (541) 267-5229. Web Site: www.southcoastradio.com. Licensee: Bicoastal CB LLC. Group owner: Bicoastal Media L.L.C. (acq 10-16-2003; grpsl). Format: Adult contemp. News staff: one; News: 2 hrs wkly. Target aud: 20-50; general. ♦John Pundt, gen mgr; Mike O'Brien, opns mgr.

*KLFR(FM)— 1999: 89.1 mhz; 1 kw. 400 ft. TL: N43 43 21 W124 05 40. 4000 E. 30th Ave., Eugene 97405-0640. Phone: (541) 463-6000. Fax: (541) 463-6046. E-mail: klcc@lanecc.edu. Web Site: www.klcc.org. Licensee: Lane Community College (acq 1-5-01; $32,500. for CP). Format: News/talk, adult contemp. ♦Steve Barton, gen mgr; Paula Chan Carpenter, dev dir; Gayle Chisholm, prom mgr; Don Heim, progmg dir.

KSYD(FM)— March 1990: 92.1 mhz; 2.78 kw. 335 ft. TL: N43 43 21 W124 05 20. PMB 237, 1574 Coburg Rd., Eugene 97401. Phone: (541) 687-3370. Fax: (541) 687-3573. Licensee: School District 4J Lane County. Format: AAA. Target aud: 12-40. ♦Carl Sundberg, gen mgr & chief of engrg; Bobbie Cirel, dev dir & gen sls mgr; Raymond Scully, progmg dir.

Rockaway Beach

*KLON(FM)—Not on air, target date: unknown: 90.3 mhz; 1.8 kw vert. Ant 342 ft. TL: N45 36 18 W123 55 30. EMF Broadcasting, 5700 W. Oaks Blvd., Rocklin, CA 95765. Phone: (916) 251-1600. Fax: (916) 251-1650. E-mail: klove@klove.com. Web Site: www.klove.com. Licensee: Educational Media Foundation. Group owner: EMF Broadcasting. Network: K-Love. Shaw Pittman. Format: Contemp Christian. News staff: 3. Target aud: 25-44; Judeo Christian, female. ♦Richard Jenkins, pres; Mike Novak, VP; Lloyd Parker, gen mgr; Ed Lenane, opns dir; Chris Joyce, prom dir.

Rogue River

KRRM(FM)— October 1994: 94.7 mhz; 130 w. 2,043 ft. TL: N42 26 44 W123 12 56. 225 Rogue River Hwy., Grants Pass 97527. Phone: (541) 479-6497. Fax: (541) 479-5726. E-mail: krrm@krrm.com. Web Site: www.krrm.com. Licensee: Shirley M. Bell. Format: Classic country. Target aud: 35 plus. ♦Herb Bell, gen mgr, opns dir & progmg mgr; Shirley Bell, opns dir & sls dir.

Roseburg

*KMPQ(FM)— Nov 24, 2004: 88.1 mhz; 950 w. Ant 351 ft. TL: N43 12 22 W123 21 50. 4000 E. 30th Ave., Eugene 97405-0640. Phone: (541) 463-6000. Fax: (541) 463-6046. E-mail: klcc@lanecc.edu. Web Site: www.klcc.org. Licensee: Lane Community College. Network: NPR. Format: News/talk, adult contemp. ♦Steve Barton, gen mgr; Paula Carpenter, dev dir; Don Hein, progmg dir.

KQEN(AM)— Sept 19, 1950: 1240 khz; 1 kw-U. TL: N43 11 44 W123 21 33. Cox 5180 97470. Secondary address: 1445 W. Harvard Ave. 97470. Phone: (541) 672-6641. Fax: (541) 673-7598. Web Site: www.am1240kqen.com. Licensee: Brooke Communications Inc. (group owner; acq 5-1-86; $173,000). Network: Network: ABC Information & Entertainment, ESPN Radio. Rep: Tacher. Haley, Bader & Potts. Format: News/ talk, sports. News staff: 2; News: 4 hrs wkly. Target aud: 35 plus; general. Spec prog: Sports. ♦Patrick A. Markham, pres; Mike Carter, opns mgr; Brian Prawitz, news dir.

KRNR(AM)— August 1935: 1490 khz; 1 kw-U. TL: N43 13 39 W123 20 42. 1445 W. Harvard Ave. 97470. Phone: (541) 672-6641. Phone: (541) 673-5551. Fax: (541) 673-7598. Licensee: Brooke Communications Inc. (acq 1-14-2005). Network: CBS. Rep: Allied Radio Partners. Format: Country, news/talk. Target aud: 25 plus. ♦Patrick A. Markham, pres; Mike Carter, gen mgr, progmg dir & mus dir; Dave Hansen, gen sls mgr; Wayne B. Hoobler, chief of engrg.

KRSB-FM— Oct 1, 1970: 103.1 mhz; 2.75 kw. 308 ft. TL: N43 12 24 W123 21 47. (CP: 25.5 kw, ant 676 ft. TL: N43 13 59 W123 19 22). Stereo. 1445 W. Harvard Ave. 97470. Phone: (541) 672-6641. Fax: (541) 673-7598. E-mail: country@bciradio.com. Web Site: www.bestcountry103.com. Licensee: Brooke Communications Inc. (group owner; acq 4-30-89). Rep: Tacher. Haley, Bader & Potts. Format: Contemp country. News staff: 2; News: 15 hrs wkly. Target aud: 25-54. ♦Patrick A. Markham, pres & gen mgr; Mike Carter, chief of opns.

*KSRS(FM)— December 1990: 91.5 mhz; 2 kw. 305 ft. TL: N43 12 24 W123 21 47. Stereo. 1250 Siskiyou Blvd., Ashland 97520. Phone: (541) 552-6301. Fax: (541) 552-8565. Web Site: www.jeffnet.org. Licensee: The State of Oregon, Acting By and Through the State Board of Higher Education, for the benefit of Southern Oregon University. Network: Network: NPR, PRI. Ernest Sanchez. Format: Class, news. News staff: one; News: 35 hrs wkly. Target aud: General. ♦Ronald Kramer, CEO & gen mgr; Bryon Lambert, opns dir; Paul Westhelle, dev dir.

*KTBR(AM)— November 1955: 950 khz; 1 kw-D, 20 w-N. TL: N43 10 08 W123 22 28. Jefferson Public Radio, Southern Oregon University, 1250 Siskiyou Blvd., Ashland 97520. Phone: (541) 552-6301. Web Site: www.jeffnet.org. Licensee: JPR Foundation Inc. (acq 4-19-02; $83,700. with KOOZ(FM) Myrtle Point). Network: Network: NPR, PRI. Ernest Sanchez. Format: News info. News staff: one. Target aud: General. ♦Mitchell Christian, CFO; Ronald Kramer, CEO & gen mgr; Bryon Lambert, opns dir; Paul Westhelle, dev dir.

Saint Helens

KOHI(AM)— Mar 2, 1960: 1600 khz; 1 kw-D, 12 w-N. TL: N45 51 18 W122 49 29. (CP: TL: N45 51 15 W122 49 11). Box 398 97051. Phone: (503) 397-1600. Fax: (503) 397-1601. Web Site: www.1600kohi.com. Licensee: Volcano Broadcasting. (acq 5-21-82; $150,000; 6-14-82). Network: UPI. Rep: Keystone (unwired net), Tacher. Format: Country, news/talk. News staff: one; News: 7 hrs wkly. Target aud: 35 plus. ♦Kenneth E. Karge, pres; Forrest W. Smith, VP & gen mgr.

Salem

*KAJC(FM)—Not on air, target date: unknown: 90.1 mhz; 560 w. Ant 128 ft. TL: N44 45 33 W123 13 34. CSN International, 3232 W. MacArthur Blvd., Santa Ana, CA 92704. Phone: (714) 875-9663. Fax: (714) 825-9660. Web Site: www.kajcfm.org. Licensee: CSN International (group owner). Format: Relg. ♦Mike Kestler, pres; Jeffrey W. Smith, VP; Mike Stocklin, opns dir.

KBZY(AM)— May 1957: 1490 khz; 1 kw-U. TL: N44 57 03 W123 02 43. 4340 Commercial St. S.E. 97302-3914. Phone: (503) 362-1490. Fax: (503) 362-6545. Web Site: www.kbzy.com. Licensee: Capital Broadcasting Inc. (acq 6-15-82; $365,000; 7-5-82). Network: ABC Information & Entertainment. Rep: Tacher. Tacher Format: Local svc oldies. Target aud: 25-54. ♦Roy Dittman, pres & gen mgr; Terry Sol, progmg dir.

KCCS(AM)— Dec 12, 1961: 1220 khz; 1 kw-D, 171 w-N. TL: N44 58 57 W123 00 17. Box 1430 97308. Phone: (503) 364-1000. Phone: (503) 585-1220. Fax: (503) 364-1022. E-mail: info@kccs.org. Web Site: www.1220thevoice.com. Licensee: KCCS LLC (acq 4-15-2004; $500,000). Network: USA. Reddy, Begley & McCormick. Format: Christian Family Radio. News: 14 hrs wkly. Target aud: 25-54; family. ♦Christina Evans, gen mgr; Phil Swearingin, opns mgr.

KGAL(AM)—Lebanon

KSHO(AM)—Lebanon

KSLM(AM)— 1934: 1390 khz; 5 kw-D, 1 kw-N. TL: N44 56 32 W123 04 17. (CP: 690 w-N. TL: N44 59 43 W123 04 15). 0700 S.W. Bancroft St., Portland 97239. Phone: (503) 223-1441. Fax: (503) 223-6909. Web Site: www.max910.com. Licensee: Entercom Portland License LLC. Group owner: Entercom Communications Corp. (acq 10-22-98; $605,000). Allied Radio Partners. Format: Sports/talk. Target aud: 25-54. ♦David Field, pres; Jack Hutchison, exec VP.

Directory of Radio

*KWBX(FM)— Apr 1, 2002: 90.3 mhz; 135 w vert. Ant 46 ft. TL: N44 52 57 W122 57 34. Stereo. Western Baptist College, 5000 Deer Park Dr. S.E. 97301. Phone: (503) 375-7195. Fax: (503) 375-7196. E-mail: kwbx@corban.edu. Web Site: www.wbc.edu/radio. Licensee: Western Baptist College. Reddy, Begley & McCormick. Format: Christian hit music, positive alternative. Target aud: 25-44; young adults. ♦Dr. Reno Hoff, pres; Bryce Bernard, sr VP; Steve Hunt, gen mgr; Mike Allegre, stn mgr; Ron Martens, chief of engrg.

KWIP(AM)—(Dallas). Apr 15, 1955: 880 khz; 5 kw-D, 1 kw-N. TL: N44 55 45 W123 17 22. Stereo. 1405 E. Ellendale, Dallas 97338. Phone: (503) 623-0245. Fax: (503) 623-6733. Web Site: www.kwip.com. Licensee: Jupiter Communications Corp. (acq 6-10-91; $21,000; 7-1-91). Format: Rgnl Mexican. Target aud: 18-54; families & blue collar workers. Spec prog: Talk 5 hrs wkly. ♦Diana Burns, gen mgr.

KYKN(AM)—See Keizer

Scappoose

KFIS(FM)— May 1986: 104.1 mhz; 6.9 kw. Ant 1,266 ft. TL: N45 29 20 W122 41 40. 6400 S.E. Lake Rd., Suite 350, Portland 97222. Phone: (503) 786-0600. Fax: (503) 786-1551. Web Site: www.1041thefish.com. Licensee: Caron Broadcasting Inc. Group owner: Salem Communications Corp. (acq 9-20-2001; $35.8 million). Gardner, Carton & Douglas. Format: Christian. Target aud: General. ♦Dennis Hayes, gen mgr; David Schult, opns mgr; Leslie Pfau, mktg mgr; Dave Arthur, progmg dir.

Seaside

KCRX-FM— 1998: 102.3 mhz; 25 kw. Ant 328 ft. TL: N45 57 08 W123 56 14. 1006 W. Marine St., Astoria 97103. Phone: (503) 325-2911. Fax: (503) 325-5570. E-mail: kcrx@nnbradio.com. Web Site: www.kcrx1023.com. Licensee: New Northwest Broadcasters LLC (group owner; acq 8-24-99; grpsl). Format: Classic rock. ♦Paul Mitchell, gen mgr; Tom Freel, opns mgr; Bob Castle, progmg dir.

KCYS(FM)— Nov 26, 1996: 98.1 mhz; 6 kw. 174 ft. TL: N45 54 35 W123 56 07. Stereo. Box 1258, Astoria 97103. Phone: (503) 717-9643. Fax: (503) 717-9578. Licensee: Dave's Broadcasting Co. (acq 6-23-2005; for 66.66% of stock). Tacher. Format: Country. Target aud: 35-44; working moms with kids, some college. ♦Dave Heick, gen mgr, gen sls mgr, progmg dir & chief of engrg; Dennis Brodigan, news dir.

KSWB(AM)— July 12, 1968: 840 khz; 1 kw-D, 500 w-N. TL: N45 58 55 W123 55 02. 1006 W. Marine Dr., Astoria 97103. Phone: (503) 325-2911. Fax: (503) 325-5570. Licensee: Cannon Beach Radio (acq 3-10-2000). Format: Oldies. ♦Jim Servino, gen mgr.

Selma

*KJKL(FM)— 2003: 88.7 mhz; 9 kw vert. Ant 1,916 ft. TL: N42 15 29 W123 39 32. 5700 W. Oaks Blvd., Rocklin, CA 95765. Phone: (916) 251-1600. Fax: (916) 251-1650. E-mail: klove@klove.com. Web Site: www.klove.com. Licensee: Educational Media Foundation. Group owner: EMF Broadcasting. Network: K-Love. Shaw Pittman. Format: Contemp Christian. News staff: 3. Target aud: 25-44; Judeo Christian, female. ♦Richard Jenkins, pres; Mike Novak, VP & progmg dir; Lloyd Parker, gen mgr; Ed Lenane, opns dir.

Sisters

KWPK-FM— 2001: 104.1 mhz; 34 kw. Ant 590 ft. TL: N44 04 40 W121 19 49. 854 N.E. 4th St., Bend 97701. Phone: (541) 383-3825. Fax: (541) 383-3403. Licensee: Thunderegg Wireless L.L.C. (acq 1-14-99; $160,000). Rep: Tacher. Format: Hot adult contemp. Target aud: 18-49. ♦Lance Anderson, pres; Brian Canady, stn mgr; Larry Wilson, progmg dir; Paul Valle, news dir; Jennifer Calderazzo, sls.

Springfield

*KQFE(FM)— Mar 7, 1989: 88.9 mhz; 2 kw. 418 ft. TL: N44 02 01 W123 00 25. 1029 Olympic St. 97477-3221. Phone: (541) 726-9156. Phone: (800) 835-4810. Web Site: www.familyradio.com. Licensee: Family Stations Inc. (group owner) Network: Family Radio. Format: Relg. Target aud: 30 plus; older relg. ♦Harold Camping, gen mgr; Carmen Brambora, opns mgr.

KSCR(AM)—See Eugene

Stations in the U.S. — Oregon

Developers & Brokers of Radio Properties
contact American Media Services at our suite:
Philadelphia Marriott Downtown
215-625-2900
843-972-2200
americanmediaservices.com
Charleston, SC
Dallas, TX · Chicago, Il · Austin, TX
American Media Services, LLC

Springfield-Eugene

KKNU(FM)—Licensed to Springfield-Eugene. See Eugene

KORE(AM)— September 1927: 1050 khz; 5 kw-D, 149 w-N. TL: N44 04 07 W123 01 45. 2080 Laura St. 97477-2197. Phone: (541) 747-5673. E-mail: kore@kore1050am.com. Licensee: Support Christian Broadcasting Inc. (acq 8-87). Network: USA. Format: Christian. Target aud: 18 plus. ♦ Larry Knight, gen mgr.

KPNW(AM)—See Eugene

KSCR(AM)—See Eugene

KUGN(AM)—See Eugene

Stanfield

KLKY(FM)—Not on air, target date: unknown: 96.1 mhz; 8.5 kw. Ant 1,178 ft. TL: N45 29 12 W119 25 52. 1600 Gray Lynn Dr., Walla Walla, WA 99362. Phone: (509) 527-1000. Fax: (509) 529-5534. Licensee: Alexandra Communications Inc. ♦ Tom Hodgins, gen mgr.

Stayton

KCKX(AM)— June 1, 1987: 1460 khz; 1 kw-D, 15 w-N. TL: N44 48 10 W122 44 03. 1665 James St., Woodburn 97071. Phone: (503) 981-9400. Phone: (503) 769-1460. Fax: (503) 981-3561. E-mail: don@cowboy-country.com. Licensee: Sanlee Broadcasting Corp. (acq 1-21-98; $130,000). Network: ABC. Allied Radio Partners. Format: Classic country/western. News: 3 hrs wkly. Target aud: 25 plus; stable, mature adults with above average income. Spec prog: Portland Trailblazers basketball, Forest Dragons arena football, high school sports, farm 15 hrs wkly. ♦ Donald Coss, pres & exec VP.

Sutherlin

KAVJ(FM)— 1999: 101.1 mhz; 3.6 kw. Ant 859 ft. TL: N43 22 19 W123 21 15. 1445 W. Harvard Ave., Roseburg 97470. Phone: (541) 672-6641. Fax: (541) 673-7598. E-mail: collfm@bciradio.com. Web Site: www.cool101fm.com. Licensee: Brooke Communications Inc. (group owner; acq 12-16-02; $650,000). Format: Oldies. News staff: one; News: 24 hrs wkly. Target aud: 25-54; 60% female, 40% male. Spec prog: Black one hr, Jazz 2 hrs wkly. ♦ Pat Markham, pres & gen mgr; Mike Carter, opns dir & progmg dir; Dave Hansen, gen sls mgr.

Sweet Home

KFIR(AM)— Aug 7, 1968: 720 khz; 1 kw-D, 184 w-N. TL: N44 24 52 W122 44 22. Box 720, 28041 Pleasant Valley Rd. 97386. Phone: (541) 367-5115. Fax: (541) 367-5233. Licensee: Shae Enterprises Inc. (acq 6-1-97). Network: ABC Information & Entertainment. Allied Broadcast Partners. Format: Traditional country. Target aud: 25 plus. ♦ Bob Ratter, gen mgr.

***KLVU(FM)**— Sept 20, 1989: 107.1 mhz; 9 kw. 2,476 ft. TL: N44 28 59 W122 34 55. Stereo. 5700 W. Oaks Blvd., Rocklin, CA 95765. Phone: (916) 251-1600. Fax: (916) 251-1650. E-mail: klove@klove.com. Web Site: www.klove.com. Licensee: Educational Media Foundation. Group owner: EMF Broadcasting (acq 3-12-97; $4 million). Network: K-Love. Shaw Pittman. Format: Contemp Christian. News staff: 3. Target aud: 25-44; Judeo-Christian female. ♦ Richard Jenkins, pres; Mike Novak, VP; Lloyd Parker, gen mgr; Ed Lenane, opns dir; Keith Whipple, dev dir.

Talent

***KSJK(AM)**— October 1960: 1230 khz; 1 kw-U. TL: N42 13 27 W122 44 33. Southern Oregon State College, 1250 Siskiyou Blvd., Ashland 97520. Phone: (541) 552-6301. Web Site: www.jeffnet.org. Licensee: The State of Oregon, acting by and through the State Board of Higher Education. for the benefit of Southern Oregon University. (acq 7-28-89). Network: Network: PRI, NPR. Ernest Sanchez. Format: News, info. Target aud: General. Spec prog: Talk 6 hrs wkly. ♦ Mitchell Christian, CFO; Ronald Kramer, CEO & gen mgr; Bryon Lambert, opns dir; Paul Westhelle, dev dir.

The Dalles

KACI(AM)— June 1955: 1300 khz; 1 kw-D, 13 w-N. TL: N45 34 54 W121 07 53. 502 Washington St. 97058-8003. Phone: (541) 296-2211. Fax: (541) 296-2213. Licensee: Columbia Gorge Broadcasters Inc. (group owner; acq 4-1-98; $390,000 with co-located FM). Network: Network: ABC Information & Entertainment, Jones Radio Networks. Rep: Tacher. Fisher, Wayland, Cooper, Leader & Zaragoza L.L.P. Format: News/talk. News staff: one; News: 14 hrs wkly. Target aud: 25-54. Spec prog: Relg one hr, home improvement 3 hrs, financial talk 6 hrs, computer talk 3 hrs, farm one hr, gardening one hr, pub affrs one hr wkly. ♦ Gary M. Grossman, CEO, pres, gen mgr, stn mgr & gen sls mgr; Greg LeBlanc, opns dir; Rick Cavagnaro, sls dir; Greg LaBlanc, news dir.

KACI-FM— Feb 1, 1985: 97.7 mhz; 5 kw. 890 ft. TL: N45 38 56 W121 16 20. Stereo. Format: Oldies. ♦ Paulette LaRoque, chief of opns; Brian Thompson, progmg mgr.

KMCQ(FM)— Nov 28, 1968: 104.5 mhz; 100 kw. Ant 1,998 ft. TL: N45 42 44 W121 06 50. Stereo. Box 104, 719 E. 2nd St. 97058. Phone: (541) 298-5116. Phone: (541) 298-5117. Fax: (541) 298-5119. E-mail: q104@q104radio.com. Web Site: www.q104radio.com. Licensee: Mid Columbia Broadcasting Inc. (acq 1983; 12-31-84). Network: CNN Radio. Rep: McGavren Guild. FCC Attorney Dominic Monahan, Luvaas Cobb, Eugene, Or. Format: Adult contemp. News staff: one; News: 7 hrs wkly. Target aud: Females 25-49; mothers & family friendly. Spec prog: Blues 4 hrs, teen show 3 hrs wkly. ♦ Frank Diegmann, pres; John Huffman, VP & gen mgr; Linda Griswold, sls dir & gen sls mgr; Paula Fairclo, opns dir & progmg dir.

KMSW(FM)— Oct 1, 2002: 92.7 mhz; 3.4 kw. Ant 892 ft. TL: N45 38 56 W121 16 20. Stereo. 502 Washington St. 97058-8003. Phone: (541) 296-2211. Fax: (541) 296-2213. Web Site: www.gorgeradio.com. Licensee: M.S.W. Communications L.L.C. Tacher Format: Classic rock. Target aud: 25-54. ♦ Gary Grossman, pres & gen mgr; Rick Cavagnaro, sls dir.

KODL(AM)— Oct 12, 1940: 1440 khz; 5 kw-D, 1 kw-N, DA-N. TL: N45 35 31 W121 11 57. Box 1488 97058. Secondary address: 404 E. 2nd St. 97058. Phone: (541) 296-2101. Fax: (541) 296-3766. E-mail: web-master@kodi.net. Web Site: www.kodl.com. Licensee: Larson-Wynn Inc. (acq 9-1-74). Rep: Tacher. Format: Adult standard. Spec prog: Farm 4 hrs, Sp 2 hrs wkly. ♦ Al Wynn, pres & gen mgr; Marcia Wynn, opns dir.

Tigard

KLVP(AM)—Licensed to Tigard. See Portland

Tillamook

***KAIK(FM)**—Not on air, target date: unknown: 88.5 mhz; 60 w vert. Ant 1,276 ft. TL: N45 27 59 W123 55 11. EMF Broadcasting, 5700 W. Oaks Blvd., Rocklin, CA 95765. Phone: (916) 251-1600. Fax: (916) 251-1650. E-mail: info@air1.com. Web Site: www.air1.com. Licensee: Educational Media Foundation. Group owner: EMF Broadcasting. Network: Air 1. Shaw Pittman. Format: Contemp Christian. News staff: 3. Target aud: 18-35; Judeo Christian female. ♦ Richard Jenkins, pres; Mike Novak, VP; Lloyd Parker, gen mgr.

KMBD(AM)— August 1947: 1590 khz; 5 kw-D, 1 kw-N, DA-N. TL: N45 27 24 W123 52 36. Box 40 97141. Secondary address: 170 W. 3rd St. 97141. Phone: (503) 842-4422. Fax: (503) 842-2755. E-mail: comments@ktil-kmbd.com. Web Site: www.ktil-kmbd.com. Licensee: Oregon Eagle Inc. (acq 12-29-86; $250,000; grpsl; 10-26-86). Network: ABC Information & Entertainment. Format: News/talk, sports. ♦ Van Moe, pres & gen mgr.

***KTCB(FM)**— Aug 25, 2004: 89.5 mhz; 380 w. Ant 1,151 ft. TL: N45 27 59 W123 55 11. Stereo. Box 269, Astoria 97103. Phone: (503) 325-0010. Fax: (503) 325-3956. E-mail: kmun@kmun.org. Web Site: www.kmun.org. Licensee: Tillicum Foundation (acq 1-23-2003; swap for KTMK(FM) Tillamook). Network: NPR. Garvey, Schubert & Barer. Format: Public/Eclectic. News: 35 hrs wkly. ♦ David Hammock, gen mgr; Arlene Layton, dev dir; Elizabeth Grant, progmg dir; Joanne Rideout, news dir.

KTIL-FM— October 1998: 94.1 mhz; 1.8 kw. 1,171 ft. TL: N45 27 59 W123 55 11. Stereo. Box 40,, 170 3rd St. 97141. Phone: (503) 842-4422. Fax: (503) 842-2755. E-mail: comments@ktil-kmbol.com. Web Site: www.ktil-kmbol.com. Licensee: Oregon Eagle Inc. (acq 2-4-99). Format: MOR, Music of your life. Target aud: General. ♦ Van Moe, pres & gen mgr.

***KTMK(FM)**— 2005: 91.1 mhz; 140 w. Ant 1,168 ft. TL: N45 27 59 W123 55 11. Oregon Public Broadcasting, 7140 S.W. Macadam Ave., Portland 97219-3099. Phone: (503) 244-9900. Phone: (503) 244-1905. Fax: (503) 293-1919. Web Site: www.opb.org. Licensee: Oregon Public Broadcasting (acq 1-16-2003; swap for KTCB(FM) Tillamook). ♦ Maynard Orme, gen mgr.

Toledo

KCUP(AM)— Sept 26, 1960: 1230 khz; 1 kw-U. TL: N44 37 47 W123 56 35. Box 456, 145 N. Coast Hwy., Newport 97365. Phone: (541) 265-5000. Fax: (541) 265-9576. Licensee: Agpal Broadcasting Inc. (acq 3-14-90; grpsl; FTR: 4-2-90). Network: ABC Daytime Direction. Rep: McGavren Guild. Haley, Bader & Potts. Format: Oldies. Target aud: 25-54. ♦ Cheryl Harle, gen mgr; Ed Kowas, gen sls mgr.

KPPT-FM—Co-owned with KCUP(AM). December 1980: 100.7 mhz; 3 kw. 430 ft. TL: N48 38 40 W124 00 52. Stereo. Format: Classic rock. ♦ Cheryl Harle, VP.

Tri City

KKMX(FM)— June 1, 1993: 104.3 mhz; 5.6 kw. 1,384 ft. TL: N43 00 13 W123 21 26. Stereo. 1445 W. Harvard Ave., Roseburg 97470. Phone: (541) 672-6641. Fax: (541) 673-7598. E-mail: kissfm@bciradio.com. Web Site: www.1045kiss.com. Licensee: Brooke Communications Inc. (group owner; acq 11-21-96). Rep: Tacher. Garvey, Schubert & Barer. Format: Adult contemp. News staff: one; News: 2 hrs wkly. Target aud: 25-54; general. ♦ Pat Markham, CEO, pres & gen mgr; Mike Carter, opns dir.

Troutdale

KPAM(AM)— 1997: 860 khz; 50 kw-D, 5 w-N. TL: N45 33 24 W122 29 08. 888 SW Fifth Ave., Suite 790, Portland 97204. Phone: (503) 223-4321. Fax: (503) 294-0074. E-mail: email@kpam.com. Web Site: www.kpam.com. Licensee: Pamplin Broadcasting-Oregon Inc. Group owner: Pamplin Broadcasting (acq 12-29-97; $652,500 for 87% of stock). Network: ABC. Rep: Tacher. The Tacher Co., Inc. Format: News/talk. News staff: 11; News: 35.4 hrs wkly. Target aud: 35-54; adults. Spec prog: Wall St. Journal. ♦ Paul Clithero, gen mgr; Mark Ail, opns dir; Margaret Evans, sls dir & gen sls mgr; Jeanne Winters, natl sls mgr; Misty Osko, prom mgr; Bill Gallagher, progmg dir & news dir; Paul Duckworth, progmg dir; Dave Bischoff, chief of engrg.

Umatilla

KLWJ(AM)— June 1980: 1090 khz; 2.5 kw-D. TL: N45 52 46 W119 20 37. 80898 Powerline Rd. 97882. Phone: (541) 567-2102. Fax: (541) 567-2103. E-mail: klwjradio@hotmail.com. Licensee: Umatilla Broadcasting Inc. Network: USA. Format: Relg, news/talk, contemp Christian mus. News staff: one. Target aud: General. Spec prog: Farm one hr, Sp one hr wkly. ♦ Darrell Marlow, pres; John Marlow, VP, gen mgr & opns mgr.

Oregon

Veneta

KEUG(FM)— 1998: 105.5 mhz; 2.8 kw. Ant 994 ft. TL: N44 00 11 W123 06 48. 925 Country Club Rd., Suite 200, Eugene 97401. Phone: (541) 484-9400. Fax: (541) 344-9424. Licensee: McKenzie River Broadcasting Co. Inc. Group owner: McKenzie River Broadcasting Group (acq 1-28-2004; $1.02 million). Rep: D & R Radio. Holland & Knight. Format: Adult contemp, cllassic hits. ◆ John Tilson, pres & gen mgr; Dave Wiles, gen sls mgr; Jeff Baird, progmg dir.

Waldport

KORC(AM)— July 1, 1988: 820 khz; 1000 w-D, 15 w-N. TL: N44 26 05 W124 01 20. Box 1419 97394. Phone: (541) 563-5100. Fax: (541) 563-5116. Web Site: www.am320korc.com. Licensee: Larry D. and Margaret E. Profitt, a General Partnership (acq 10-7-2003; $185,000). Network: ABC FM Connection. Format: Easy lstng. ◆ Larry Profitt, gen mgr.

Warm Springs

KWLZ-FM— Jan 18, 1986: 96.5 mhz; 100 kw. Ant 1,092 ft. TL: N44 50 24 W121 13 56. Stereo. 854 N.E. 4th St., Bend 97701. Phone: (541) 383-3825. Fax: (541) 383-3403. Licensee: Horizon Broadcasting Group L.L.C. (group owner; acq 3-2-2000; grpsl). Rep: Tacher. Format: Active rock. Target aud: 18-49. ◆ Keith Shipman, pres & gen mgr; Larry Wilson, opns mgr.

***KWSO(FM)**— Sept 22, 1986: 91.9 mhz; 3.3 kw. 203 ft. TL: N44 50 24 W121 13 56. Stereo. Box 489, Warehouse 1, Holiday St. 97761. Phone: (541) 553-1968. Phone: (541) 553-1969. Fax: (541) 553-3348. E-mail: kwso@wstribes.org. Licensee: Confederated Tribes of Warm Springs. Format: Div, Native American, adult contemp. Target aud: General. ◆ Sue Matters, gen mgr, opns mgr & mus dir; Mike Villalobos, stn mgr; Wayne Gilbert, progmg dir; Duncan Brunoe, news dir.

Welches

***KZRI(FM)**— May 10, 2001: 90.3 mhz; 280 w. Ant 1,568 ft. TL: N45 19 57 W121 42 57. Stereo. 5700 W. Oaks Blvd., Rocklin, CA 95765. Phone: (916) 251-1600. Fax: (916) 251-1650. E-mail: info@air1.com. Web Site: www.air1.com. Licensee: Educational Media Foundation. Group owner: EMF Broadcasting. Network: Air 1. Shaw Pittman. Format: Contemp Christian. News staff: 3. Target aud: 18-35; Judeo-Christian, female. ◆ Richard Jenkins, pres; Mike Novak, VP; Lloyd Parker, gen mgr.

West Klamath

KRAM(AM)— Dec 1, 1987: 1070 khz; 1 kw-D. TL: N42 10 38 W121 46 25. Box 1270, Klamath Falls 97601. Phone: (541) 884-8074. Fax: (541) 884-8226. Licensee: Sandra Ann Falk. (acq 12-16-96). Format: Nostalgia. Target aud: 55 plus. ◆ Sandra Falk, CEO.

Weston

KMMG(FM)— 1997: 101.9 mhz; 13.5 kw. Ant 958 ft. TL: N45 47 41 W118 10 06. Stereo. Box 2888, Yakima, WA 98907. Secondary address: 706 Butterfield Rd., Yakima, WA 98901. Phone: (509) 457-1000. Fax: (509) 452-0541. Licensee: Bustos Media of Eastern Washington License LLC. (group owner; acq 11-18-2004; grpsl). Rep: Tacher. Tacher Format: Spanish. News staff: one; News: one hr wkly. Target aud: 25-54; Hispanic. ◆ Bob Berry, gen mgr; Keith Teske, opns dir.

Winchester

***KLOV(FM)**— August 1997: 89.3 mhz; 3.8 kw. Ant 420 ft. TL: N43 14 06 W123 19 20. Stereo. 5700 W. Oaks Blvd., Rocklin, CA 95765. Phone: (916) 251-1600. Fax: (916) 251-1650. E-mail: klove@klove.com. Web Site: www.klove.com. Licensee: Educational Media Foundation. Group owner: EMF Broadcasting. Network: K-Love. Shaw Pittman. Format: Contemp Christian mus. News staff: 3. Target aud: 25-44; Judeo-Christian, female. ◆ Richard Jenkins, pres; Mike Novak, VP; Lloyd Parker, gen mgr; Ed Lenane, opns dir.

Winston

KGRV(AM)— Feb 12, 1984: 700 khz; 25 kw-D, 500 w-N. TL: N43 03 26 W123 23 48. Box 1598 97496. Secondary address: 196 S.E. Main St. 97496. Phone: (541) 679-8185. Fax: (541) 679-6456. E-mail: info@kgru700.net. Web Site: www.kgru700.net. Licensee: Pacific Cascade Communications Corp. (acq 4-15-85). Network: Moody. Format: Christian, regl, inspirational music. News: 10 hrs wkly. Target aud: 25-54. Spec prog: Southern gospel 3 hrs wkly. ◆ David Morrow, pres & exec VP; Phil Morrow, gen mgr.

Woodburn

KWBY(AM)— July 10, 1964: 940 khz; 10 k-D, 500 w-N. TL: N45 10 37 W122 50 58. 1665 James St. 97071. Phone: (503) 981-9400. Fax: (503) 981-3561. E-mail: doncradio@fiesta.com. Web Site: www.lapantcra940.com. Licensee: Donald D. Coss. (acq 10-18-91; $300,000; 11-4-91). Format: Sp (regional Mexican). News staff: one; News: 35 hrs wkly. Target aud: 18-49; larger-than-average Hispanic families. Spec prog: Relg 5 hrs, gospel 3 hrs wkly. ◆ Donald Coss, pres; Dorecia Luse, gen mgr & opns dir; Natasha Holstein, mktg VP & prom VP; Gilberto Galvan, progmg dir.

Pennsylvania

Allentown

WAEB(AM)— 1949: 790 khz; 1 kw-U, DA-2. TL: N40 37 05 W75 26 58 (day), N40 39 37 W75 30 50 (night). (CP: 3.8 kw-D, 1.5 kw-N, DA-2. TL (night): N40 39 33 W75 30 48). 1541 Alta Dr., Suite 400, Whitehall 18052. Phone: (610) 434-1742. Phone: (610) 434–3808 (News). Fax: (610) 434-6288. Web Site: www.waeb.com. Licensee: Capstar TX L.P. Group owner: Clear Channel Communications Inc. (acq 8-30-00; grpsl). Network: CBS. Format: News/talk. Target aud: 35-64. ◆ Chris Taylor, gen mgr; Pat Gremling, gen sls mgr; Leanne Costelli, rgnl sls mgr; Laura St. James, progmg dir.

WAEB-FM— June 30, 1961: 104.1 mhz; 50 kw. 500 ft. TL: N40 43 13 W75 35 44. (CP: 19.4 kw, ant 164 ft.). Stereo. Web Site: www.b104.com. Format: CHR. Target aud: 18-44. ◆ Diane Lee, gen sls mgr & prom dir; Craig Stevens, progmg dir.

***WDIY(FM)**— Jan 8, 1995: 88.1 mhz; 100 w vert. 843 ft. TL: N40 33 54 W75 26 26. 301 Broadway, Bethlehem 18015. Phone: (610) 694-8100. Fax: (610) 954-9474. E-mail: info@wdiyfm.org. Web Site: www.wdiy.org. Licensee: Lehigh Valley Community Broadcasters Association Board of Directors Inc. Network: NPR. Schwartz, Woods & Miller. Format: News, class, pub affrs. News: 30 hrs wkly. Target aud: General. Spec prog: Folk 12 hrs, jazz 10 hrs, Sp 3 hrs, Asian-Indian one hr, Arabic one hr, Jewish one hr wkly. ◆ Bill Dautremont-Smith, pres & sls dir; Rick Weaver, VP; Burr Beard, stn mgr; Sharon Ettinger, dev dir.

WHOL(AM)— Sept 12, 1948: 1600 khz; 500 w-D, 100 w-N, DA-2. TL: N40 35 33 W75 28 42. 1125 Colorado St. 18103. Phone: (610) 434-4801. Licensee: Matthew P. Braccili (acq 11-25-2003; $940,000). Network: Network: USA, Radio Unica. Rep: Salem. Format: Contemp Spanish topical top 40. Target aud: 18-65. ◆ Matthew Braccili, stn mgr.

***WJCS(FM)**— Feb 29, 1996: 89.3 mhz; 125 w vert. 804 ft. TL: N40 33 54 W75 26 26. Box 8900 18105-8900. Secondary address: 300 E. Rock Rd., Suite 205 18103. Phone: (610) 434-1742. Fax: (610) 797-6922. E-mail: wjcs@wjcs.org. Web Site: www.wjcs.org. Licensee: Beacon Broadcasting Corp. Network: Moody. Format: Educ, relg, news/talk, Christian. Target aud: General. ◆ Frank Ginther, stn mgr; Kim Bretzik, gen sls mgr & chief of engrg; Paula Divello, prom dir; Craig Stevens, progmg dir.

WKAP(AM)— May 24, 1923: 1470 khz; 5 kw-U, DA-N. TL: N40 38 10 W75 29 06. Stereo. 1541 Alta Dr., Suite 400, Whitehall 18052. Phone: (610) 434-1742. Fax: (610) 434-6288. Web Site: www.1470wkap.com. Licensee: Capstar TX L.P. Group owner: Clear Channel Communications Inc. (acq 8-30-00; grpsl). Network: ABC Information & Entertainment. Rep: D & R Radio. Format: Nostalgia, oldies. Target aud: 25-54. Spec prog: Pol 3 hrs wkly. ◆ John Piccirillo, gen mgr.

WLEV(FM)— July 1947: 100.7 mhz; 11 kw. 1,073 ft. TL: N40 33 54 W75 26 26. Stereo. Box 25096, Lehigh Valley 18002. Secondary address: 2158 Avenue C, Suite 100, Bethlehem 18017. Phone: (610) 266-7600. Fax: (610) 231-0400. Licensee: Citadel Broadcasting Co. Group owner: Citadel Broadcasting Corp. (acq 9-5-97; $23 million). Rep: Christal, Katz Radio. Format: Adult contemp. ◆ Wayne Leland, pres; John Fraunfelter, gen mgr; Shelly Easton, opns mgr & progmg dir; Elizabeth Pembleton, sls dir.

***WMUH(FM)**— Feb 6, 1966: 91.7 mhz; 500 w. -3 ft. TL: N40 35 52 W75 30 38. Stereo. Muhlenberg College, 2400 Chew St. 18104. Phone: (484) 664-3456. Fax: (484) 664-3539. E-mail: wmuh@muhlenberg.edu. Web Site: www.muhlenberg.edu/wmuh. Licensee: Muhlenberg College. Network: NPR. Format: Div. Target aud: General. Spec prog: Sp 4 hrs, Arabic 2 hrs, Ger 2 hrs, It 2 hrs, Pol 2 hrs wkly. ◆ Joe A. Swanson, gen mgr; Emily Skrzat, stn mgr; Rich Gensiak, progmg dir.

WTKZ(AM)— September 1948: 1320 khz; 5 kw-D, 1 kw-N, DA-2. TL: N40 37 40 W75 29 09. 107 Paxinosa Rd. W., Easton 18040. Phone: (610) 258-6155. Fax: (610) 253-3384. Licensee: Nassau Broadcasting II L.L.C. Group owner: Mega Communications Inc. (acq 2-14-2005; $500,000). Network: ESPN Radio. Format: Sports. ◆ Rick Musselman, gen mgr.

WYNS(AM)—(Lehighton). Apr 12, 1962: 1160 khz; 4 kw-D, 1 kw-N, DA-2. TL: N40 49 03 W75 41 31. Stereo. 107 Paxinosa Rd. W., Easton 18040-1344. Phone: (610) 377-1160. Fax: (610) 253-3384. Licensee: Nassau Broadcasting II LLC (acq 4-25-2003; $375,000). Network: ESPN Radio. Format: Country. ◆ Rick Musselman, gen mgr.

WZZO(FM)—See Bethlehem

Altoona

WALY(FM)—(Bellwood). Mar 28, 1970: 103.9 mhz; 3 kw. 984 ft. TL: N40 34 04 W79 26 26. Stereo. One Forever Dr., Hollidaysburg 16648-3029. Phone: (814) 944-2221. Fax: (814) 943-2754. E-mail: rog@waly1039.com. Web Site: www.waly1039.com. Licensee: Forever Broadcasting LLC. Group owner: Forever Broadcasting (acq 7-16-97; grpsl). Network: AP Radio. Rep: Katz Radio. Dome. Format: Oldies. Target aud: 35-64; earlier boomers, socially & financially active. ◆ Carol B. Logan, pres; Dave Davies, gen mgr; Bobbi Castelluci, gen sls mgr.

WFBG(AM)— Oct 30, 1924: 1290 khz; 5 kw-D, 1 kw-N, DA-N. TL: N40 27 20 W78 23 50. Stereo. One Forever Dr., Hollidaysburg 16648. Phone: (814) 941-9800. Phone: (814) 944-1290. Fax: (814) 943-2754. Fax: (814) 941-7198. Web Site: www.wfbg.com. Licensee: Forever of PA L.L.C. Group owner: Forever Broadcasting (acq 12-24-90; $2.1 million. with co-located FM; FTR: 1-14-91). Rep: Christal. Format: Adult standards. News staff: 2; News: 2 hrs wkly. Target aud: 25-54. ◆ Dave Davies, gen mgr.

WFGY(FM)—Co-owned with WFBG(AM). Oct 17, 1960: 98.1 mhz; 30 kw. 1,020 ft. TL: N40 34 01 W78 26 31. (CP: Ant 941 ft.). Stereo. Web Site: www.froggyradio.com. Network: CBS. Format: Contemp country. News staff: one. Target aud: 25-64.

WRKY-FM—See Hollidaysburg

WRTA(AM)— June 12, 1946: 1240 khz; 1 kw-U. TL: N40 30 26 W78 25 15. 1417-19 12th Ave. 16603. Phone: (814) 943-6112. Fax: (814) 944-9782. E-mail: contactus@wrta.com. Web Site: www.wrta.com. Licensee: Handsome Brothers Inc. (acq 1-9-2004; $500,000). Network: Network: Westwood One, ABC Information & Entertainment, ABC News/Talk. Marv Roslin Pepper & Corazzini. Format: News/talk. News staff: 2; News: 15 hrs wkly. Target aud: 25 plus; middle/upper income, college educated, professional. Spec prog: Sports play-by-play/loc college & high schools. ◆ David Barger, pres; David R. Wolf, gen mgr & gen sls mgr; Ken Maguda, stn mgr, opns mgr, rgnl sls mgr & progmg dir; Dave Weaver, news dir; Bob Taylor, chief of engrg.

WVAM(AM)— July 1948: 1430 khz; 5 kw-D, 1 kw-N, DA-N. TL: N40 29 42 W78 24 06. One Forever Dr., Hollidaysburg 16648. Phone: (814) 941-9800. Fax: (814) 943-2754. Web Site: www.wvamam.com. Licensee: Forever Broadcasting LLC. Group owner: Forever Broadcasting (acq 12-12-2003; $2.1 million. with co-located FM). Network: ESPN Radio. Rep: Allied Radio Partners. Format: Sports. Target aud: 25 plus; white collar professionals. Spec prog: Pol one hr wkly. ◆ Dave Davies, gen mgr; Rich DeLeo, progmg dir; Troy Barnhart, chief of engrg.

WWOT(FM)—Co-owned with WVAM(AM). July 1976: 100.1 mhz; 3 kw. Ant 981 ft. TL: N40 29 42 W78 24 06. Stereo. Web Site: www.hot100radio.com. Format: CHR. ◆ Jonathan Reed, progmg dir; Mark Haze, news dir.

Pennsylvania

Stations in the U.S.

Developers & Brokers of Radio Properties
contact American Media Services at our suite:
Philadelphia Marriott Downtown
215-625-2900
843-972-2200
americanmediaservices.com
Charleston, SC
Dallas, TX · Chicago, Il · Austin, TX
American Media Services, LLC

Ambridge

WMBA(AM)— May 1957: 1460 khz; 500 w-U, DA-2. TL: N40 35 08 W80 12 11. 1316 7th Ave., Beaver Falls 15010. Phone: (724) 846-4100. Fax: (724) 843-7771. E-mail: 1230@wbvp-wmba.com. Web Site: www.wbvp-wmba.com. Licensee: Iorio Broadcasting Inc. (acq 5-23-00; $325,000). Format: Talk, sports. News staff: one; News: 10 hrs wkly. Target aud: 35+. Spec prog: Polka review 2 hrs, auction radio 5 hrs, one hr, oldies 3 hrs, Polish 2 hrs wkly. ◆ Frank Iorio, pres; Mark Peterson, gen mgr; John Nuzzo, progmg dir.

Annville-Cleona

WWSM(AM)— Aug 4, 1968: 1510 khz; 5 kw-D, DA. TL: N40 17 44 W76 27 46. 621 Cumberland St., Suite 4, Lebanon 17042. Phone: (717) 272-1510. Fax: (717) 272-7074. Web Site: www.wwsm.us. Licensee: Patrick H. Sickafus. (acq 10-14-93; $1; 11-1-93). Network: USA. Format: Classic western. Target aud: 34 plus. Spec prog: Polka 2 hrs, bluegrass 3 hrs, gospel music 3 hrs wkly. ◆ Patrick H. Sickafus, pres; Gary Gruver, gen mgr.

Apollo

WAVL(AM)— Dec 13, 1947: 910 khz; 5 kw-D, DA. TL: N40 35 01 W79 31 34. 120 Beale Rd., Sarver 16055. Phone: (724) 295-2000. Fax: (724) 295-9009. Web Site: www.praise910.com. Licensee: Evangel Heights Assembly of God (acq 5-16-01; $400,000). Network: USA. Format: Contemp Christian. News: 2 hrs wkly. ◆ John P. Kuert, pres; Paul Barton, gen mgr; Jeff Bogaczyk, opns dir.

Avis

WQBR(FM)— Aug 11, 1989: 99.9 mhz; 900 w. 823 ft. TL: N41 13 42 W77 22 21. Stereo. Box 999, McElhattan 17748. Secondary address: 330 McElhattan Dr., McElhattan 17748. Phone: (570) 769-2327. Fax: (570) 769-7746. E-mail: bear@cub.kcnet.org. Web Site: www.bear999.com. Licensee: Maximum Impact Communications Inc. (acq 9-9-93; $270,000; 10-4-93). Network: Jones Radio Networks. Format: Country / Americana. News staff: one; News: 2 hrs wkly. Target aud: 18-34. ◆ Karyn O'Brien Stratton, pres, gen mgr, opns mgr & progmg mgr; Dave Stratton, gen sls mgr, mktg dir, prom mgr, adv mgr & news dir; Mark Schlesinger, prom mgr; Whiteall Ferriola, engrg mgr.

Avoca

WFEZ(FM)— Apr 2, 1976: 103.1 mhz; 6 kw. Ant 72 ft. TL: N41 18 20 W75 45 38. Stereo. 305 Hwy. 315, Pittstown 18640. Phone: (570) 883-9850. Fax: (570) 883-9851. E-mail: jimr@102themountain.com. Web Site: www.102themountain.com. Licensee: Entercom Wilkes-Barre Scranton LLC. Group owner: Entercom Communications Corp. (acq 12-13-99; grpsl). Format: Adult contemp. Target aud: 18-54; general. ◆ Jim Rising, opns mgr; Andy Zapotek, gen sls mgr.

Beaver Falls

WAMO-FM—Licensed to Beaver Falls. See Pittsburgh

WBVP(AM)— May 25, 1948: 1230 khz; 1 kw-U. TL: N40 44 16 W80 17 47. Box 719, 1316 7th Ave. 15010. Phone: (724) 846-4100. Phone: (412) 761-6600. Fax: (724) 843-7771. E-mail: 1230@wbvp-wmba.com. Web Site: www.wbvp-wmba.com. Licensee: Iorio Broadcasting Inc. (acq 1996). Network: Network: ABC Information & Entertainment, ABC News/Talk. Format: Full service, News, Talk, Sports. News staff: 2. Target aud: 35 plus. Spec prog: Black 6 hrs, relg 6 hrs, It one hr, Pol one hr wkly. ◆ Frank Iorio, pres & gen mgr; Mark Peterson, stn mgr; John Nuzzo, opns mgr.

*****WGEV(FM)**— Nov 15, 1965: 88.3 mhz; 15 w. 240 ft. TL: N40 46 21 W80 18 33. Geneva College 15010. Phone: (724) 847-6678. Fax: (724) 847-6675. Web Site: www.geneva.edu. Licensee: Geneva College Board of Trustees. Network: ABC Information & Entertainment. Format: Christian contemp hit. News: 2 hrs wkly. Target aud: 14-24; college plus surrounding community. ◆ Pete Croisant, gen mgr; Todd Hughes, chief of opns.

*****WITX(FM)**— June 19, 1986: 90.9 mhz; 100 w. 167 ft. TL: N40 47 05 W80 20 36. Box 928, 3700 High St. Ext. 15010. Phone: (724) 846-8738. Licensee: Beaver Falls Educational Broadcasting Foundation. Format: Relg. ◆ Rev. Kenneth Manypenny, pres.

Beaver Springs

WLZS(FM)— Feb 21, 1993: 106.1 mhz; 175 w. Ant 1,312 ft. TL: N40 42 04 W77 12 50. Stereo. Box 209, Mexico 17056. Secondary address: Box 146 17812. Phone: (717) 436-2135. Fax: (717) 436-8155. Licensee: Starview Media Inc. (acq 1996; $235,000). Format: Oldies. News staff: one; News: 2 hrs wkly. Target aud: 25-54. ◆ Curt Dreibelbis, gen mgr.

Bedford

WAYC(FM)— Dec 22, 1966: 100.9 mhz; 190 w. ant 1,279 ft. TL: N40 00 46 W78 33 12. Stereo. Box 1 15522. Secondary address: 134 E. Pitt St., 2nd Fl. 15522. Phone: (814) 623-1000. Fax: (814) 623-9692. E-mail: cesscomm@earthlink.net. Web Site: www.hitsandfavorites.com. Licensee: Cessna Communications Inc. (group owner; acq 3-22-93; $350,000. with WBFD(AM) Bedford; FTR: 3-29-93). Network: ABC. Commercial Media Sales. G S B Law. Format: Adult contemp. News staff: one. Target aud: 18-49; general. ◆ Jay B. Cessna, pres; John H. Cessna, VP & gen mgr; Chris Collins, opns mgr.

WBFD(AM)— July 2, 1955: 1310 khz; 2.5 kw-D, 85 w-N. TL: N40 02 37 W78 30 11. Box one. 15522. Secondary address: 2nd Fl., 134 E. Pitt St. 15522. Phone: (814) 623-5131. Fax: (814) 623-9692. E-mail: cesscom@earthlink.net. Licensee: Cessna Communications Inc. (group owner; acq 3-22-93; $350,000 with WAYC(FM) Bedford; 3-29-93). Network: Network: USA, ABC. Commercial Media Sales. Format: Oldies, news/talk. News staff: one. Target aud: 30 plus; general. ◆ Jay B. Cessna, pres; John H. Cessna, VP & gen mgr.

WBVE(FM)—Co-owned with WBFD(AM). Aug 15, 1988: 107.5 mhz; 370 w. 1,309 ft. TL: N40 00 46 W78 33 12. Stereo. Network: Westwood One. Format: Classic rock. News staff: one. Target aud: 25-54.

WHJB(FM)— Aug 5, 1974: 1600 kw-D, 28 w-N. TL: N40 00 45 W78 29 54. Box 672 15522. Secondary address: 134 E. Pitt St., 2nd Fl. 15522. Phone: (814) 624-0016. Fax: (814) 623-9692. E-mail: johnwhjb@earthlink.net. Licensee: John H. Cessna. (acq 1-1-99; $29,000). Network: Salem Radio Network. G S B Law. Format: Relg. Target aud: 35 plus. ◆ John H. Cessna, gen mgr.

*****WUFR(FM)**—Not on air, target date: unknown: 91.1 mhz; 470 w vert. Ant 1,145 ft. TL: N40 17 40 W78 34 25. Family Stations Inc., 4135 Northgate Blvd., Suite 1, Sacramento, CA 95834-1226. Phone: (916) 641-8191. Fax: (916) 641-8238. Licensee: Family Stations Inc.

Bellefonte

WBLF(AM)— Aug 1, 1958: 970 khz; 1 kw-D, 61 w-N. TL: N40 54 12 W77 46 06. 160 Clearview Ave., State College 16893. Phone: (814) 238-5085. Fax: (814) 238-8993. Web Site: www.wrscwblf.com. Licensee: Magnum Broadcasting Inc. (group owner; (acq 8-10-2005; $150,000). . Format: News, sports, talk. Spec prog: Relg 2 hrs wkly. ◆ Michael M. Stapleford, pres; Joe Trimarchi, gen mgr; Jason Miller, opns VP.

WTLR(FM)—See State College

WZWW(FM)—Licensed to Bellefonte. See State College

Bellwood

WALY(FM)—Licensed to Bellwood. See Altoona

Benton

WGGI(FM)— Oct 4, 1985: 95.9 mhz; 6 kw. 328 ft. TL: N41 10 16 W76 24 37. 305 Hwy. 315, Box 729, Pittston 18640. Phone: (570) 883-9850. Fax: (570) 883-9851. E-mail: feedback@froggy101.com. Web Site: www.froggy101.com. Licensee: Entercom Scranton Wilkes-Barre License LLC. Group owner: Entercom Communications Corp. (acq 12-13-99; grpsl). Format: Country. Target aud: 25-54. ◆ John Burkavage, VP; Jim Rising, opns mgr.

Berwick

WFBS(AM)— Aug 1, 1957: 1280 khz; 1 kw-D, 175 w-N. TL: N41 04 36 W76 15 32. 114 N. Market St. 18603. Phone: (570) 752-8012. Fax: (570) 752-1131. E-mail: way750am@aol.com. Licensee: FBS Wireless Corp. (acq 3-18-00; $32,500; 5-20-91). Network: ABC Information & Entertainment. Format: Oldies. ◆ JoAnn Germers Hausen, VP; Kevin Fennessy, gen mgr.

WKAB(FM)— Feb 14, 1992: 103.5 mhz; 4.1 kw. 387 ft. TL: N41 05 11 W76 16 41. 212 Pine St. 18603. Phone: (570) 759-3570. Fax: (570) 759-3438. E-mail: wkab@bwkip.com. Web Site: www.wkab.net. Licensee: 4M Broadcasting. (acq 6-8-92; $350,000; 6-29-92). Format: Classic hits. Target aud: 25-54; females at work, 18-39 men on weekends. ◆ Jan Banko, gen mgr & stn mgr.

Bethlehem

WGPA(AM)— Feb 14, 1946: 1100 khz; 250 w-D. TL: N40 37 27 W75 21 19. 528 N. New St. 18018. Phone: (610) 866-8074. Fax: (610) 866-9381. E-mail: joetimmer@jollyjoetimmer.com. Web Site: www.regiononline.com/joetimmer. Licensee: Joseph Timmer dba Timmer Broadcasting Co. (acq 6-19-92; $100,000; 7-13-92). Network: USA. Format: Var, news/talk. News staff: one; News: 2 hrs wkly. Target aud: General. Spec prog: Ger 2 hrs, polka 12 hrs, Sp 4 hrs wkly. ◆ Joe Timmer, pres & gen mgr; Mark Staller, opns dir.

*****WLVR(FM)**— May 3, 1973: 91.3 mhz; 185 w. 60 ft. TL: N40 36 22 W75 22 42. Stereo. Lehigh Univ., 29 Trembley Dr. 18015-3066. Phone: (610) 758-4187. Fax: (610) 758-4186. Licensee: Lehigh University. Format: Var. News: 10 hrs wkly. Target aud: General. Spec prog: Black 12 hrs, class 8 hrs, reggae 6 hrs, jazz 12 hrs wkly. ◆ Aimee Van House, gen mgr; Killian O'Conner, progmg dir.

WZZO(FM)— Feb 14, 1946: 95.1 mhz; 30 kw. 631 ft. TL: N40 37 13 W75 17 37. Stereo. 1541 Alta Dr., Suite 400, Whitehall 18052. Phone: (610) 434-1742. Fax: (610) 434-6288. E-mail: webmaster@wzzo.com. Web Site: www.wzzo.com. Licensee: Capstar TX L.P. Group owner: Clear Channel Communications Inc. (acq 8-30-00; grpsl). Rep: Katz Radio. Format: AOR. ◆ Tom Barney, gen mgr; Pat Gremling, gen sls mgr.

Blairsville

WLCY(FM)— Apr 15, 1985: 106.3 mhz; 2.4 kw. Ant 363 ft. TL: N40 31 10 W79 13 26. Stereo. 400 Unity St., Suite 200, Latrobe 15650. Phone: (724) 537-3338. Fax: (724) 539-9798. Web Site: www.1063luckyfm.com. Licensee: The St. Pier Group LLC. Group owner: Renda Broadcasting Corp. (acq 6-22-2004; $900,000). Network: Jones Radio Networks. Dome. Format: Adult contemp. News staff: 2; News: 2 hrs wkly. Target aud: 25-54. ◆ John Longo, gen mgr; Tony Michaels, stn mgr.

Bloomsburg

*****WBUQ(FM)**— Sept 16, 1986: 91.1 mhz; 600 w. 500 ft. TL: N41 00 29 W76 26 51. Stereo. Bloomsburg Univ., 400 E. Second St.,, 1250 McCormick Center for Human Services 17815. Phone: (570) 389-4686. Fax: (570) 389-2718. E-mail: wbuq@bloomu.edu. Web Site: www.wbuqfm.com. Licensee: Bloomsburg University of Pennsylvania. Format: Alternative, rock/AOR. News staff: one; News: 2 hrs wkly. Target aud: General; college & area high school students. Spec prog: Talk 10 hrs, urban 10 hrs, specialty 15 hrs, folk 2 hrs, gospel 2 hrs, jazz 2 hrs wkly. ◆ Krystal Mueller, gen mgr; Courtney Kelley, progmg dir.

WFYY(FM)— September 1956: 106.5 mhz; 36.5 kw. 570 ft. TL: N40 59 42 W76 29 51. Stereo. Box 90, Selinsgrove 17870. Secondary

Pennsylvania

address: 246 W. Main St. 17815. Phone: (570) 374-5711. Fax: (570) 784-1004. E-mail: sales@wfyyradio.com. Web Site: www.wfyyradio.com. Licensee: MMP License LLC. Group owner: MAX Media L.L.C. (acq 10-17-03; grpsl). Network: Westwood One. Dome. Format: Adult contemp. Target aud: 18-49. ♦ John A. Trinder, pres; Scott Richards, VP & gen mgr; Dawn Marie, opns dir; Greg Adair, gen sls mgr; Ted Koppen, chief of engrg.

WHLM(AM)— Sept 26, 1947: 930 khz; 1 kw-D, 23 w-N. TL: N41 01 00 W76 27 44. Box One, 105 W. Main St., 2nd FL. 17815-3329. Phone: (570) 784-1200. Fax: (570) 784-6060. E-mail: whlmam@aol.com. Web Site: www.whlm.com. Licensee: Columbia Broadcasting Co. (acq 9-5-01; $45,000). Network: CBS Radio. Borsari & Paxson. Format: Var/div. News staff: one; News: 15 hrs wkly. Target aud: 25-54. Spec prog: Farm one hr, relg 2 hrs wkly. ♦ Joseph Reilly, pres & gen mgr; Larry Hopper, gen sls mgr.

Boalsburg

WBUS(FM)— Apr 13, 1998: 93.7 mhz; 33 kw. 1,361 ft. TL: N40 45 08 W77 45 16. Stereo. 160 Clearview Ave., State College 16603. Phone: (814) 237-9370. Fax: (814) 237-9371. Web Site: www.wbus.net. Licensee: 2510 Licenses LLC. (group owner; (acq 2-16-2005; grpsl). Schwartz, Woods & Miller. Format: Classic hits, classic rock. Target aud: 25-54. ♦ Joe Trimarchi, VP & gen mgr; Jason Miller, opns mgr.

Boyertown

WBYN(FM)— Oct 31, 1960: 107.5 mhz; 30 kw. Ant 610 ft. TL: N40 24 15 W75 39 09. Stereo. 280 Mill St. 19512. Phone: (610) 369-7777. Fax: (610) 369-7780. E-mail: promotions@1075alive.com. Web Site: www.1075alive.com. Licensee: WDAC Radio Co. (acq 11-5-91; $3 million; 12-2-91). Jones, Waldo, Holbrook & McDonough. Format: Christian praise & worship, Christian talk. Target aud: 25-54; Evangelical Christians, families. ♦ Richard Crawford, pres; John White, gen mgr.

Braddock

WRRK(FM)— June 1959: 96.9 mhz; 44.7 kw. Ant 530 ft. TL: N40 24 42 W79 55 53. Stereo. 650 Smithfield St., Suite 2200, Pittsburgh 15222. Phone: (412) 316-3342. Fax: (412) 316-3388. E-mail: 97@rrk.com. Web Site: www.rrk.com. Licensee: WPNT Associates. Network: ABC. Dow, Lohnes & Albertson. Format: Classic rock. ♦ Greg Frischling, gen mgr; Chris Kohan, gen sls mgr; Vicki Wolfe, prom dir; John Robertson, progmg dir; Amy Crago, news dir; Paul Carroll, chief of engrg.

WURP(AM)— June 1947: 1550 khz; 1 kw-D, 4 w-N. TL: N40 24 47 W79 51 13. 4736 Penn Ave., Pittsburgh 15224. Phone: (412) 942-0076. Web Site: www.theedge1550.com. Licensee: Urban Radio of Pennsylvania L.L.C. Group owner: Inner City Broadcasting (acq 5-24-00; $1.5 million. for 55% of both WHAT(AM) Philadelphia and WURP(AM) Braddock) Network: American Urban. Format: Talk. News staff: one; News: 6 hrs wkly. Target aud: 25-54. ♦ Coddy Anderson, chmn & dev dir; Chris Squire, gen mgr; Shelia Corley, stn mgr.

Bradford

WBRR(FM)—Listing follows WESB(AM).

WESB(AM)— April 1947: 1490 khz; 1 kw-U. TL: N41 27 54 W78 37 01. Box 545, 1490 St. Francis Dr. 16701. Phone: (814) 368-4141. Fax: (814) 368-3180. E-mail: 1490@wesb.com. Web Site: www.wesb.com. Licensee: Radio Station WESB Inc. Network: CNN Radio. Rep: Dome. Baraff, Koerner & Olender. Format: Adult contemp. News staff: 2. Target aud: 25-54. ♦ Donald J. Fredeen, pres & gen mgr; Frank Williams, opns dir; Peggy Austin, sls dir; Christine Brookins, prom dir; Jason Fredeen, progmg dir; Bruce Fyfe, mus dir; Mandi Wilton, news dir.

WBRR(FM)—Co-owned with WESB(AM). Dec 1, 1987: 100.1 mhz; 1.65 kw. 525 ft. TL: N41 58 12 W78 42 03. Stereo. Web Site: www.wesb.com. (Acq 10-87; $21,000; 10-12-87). Format: Oldies. Target aud: 25-54.

Bristol

*****WLBS(FM)**— April 1998: 91.7 mhz; 100 w vert. 68 ft. TL: N40 09 33 W74 51 24. Box 2012, Warminster 18974. Phone: (215) 674-8002. Fax: (215) 674-4586. E-mail: info@wrdv.org. Web Site: www.wrdv.org. Licensee: Bux-Mont Educational Radio Association. Format: Big band, oldies. ♦ Charles W. Loughary, chmn; Todd H. Allen, gen mgr.

Brookville

WMKX(FM)— Aug 22, 1981: 105.5 mhz; 16 kw. Ant 418 ft. TL: N41 07 21 W79 03 51. Stereo. 51 Pickering St. 15825. Phone: (814) 849-8100. Fax: (814) 849-4585. E-mail: megarock@alltel.net. Licensee: Strattan Broadcasting Inc. Format: Classic rock. News staff: one; News: 5 hrs wkly. Target aud: 25-54; general. Spec prog: Jazz 3 hrs, rock classics 6 hrs, oldies 8 hrs wkly. ♦ Jim Farley, pres & gen mgr; Nathan Sharp, gen sls mgr.

WYTR(FM)— Jan 17, 2000: 103.3 mhz; 10.5 kw. 508 ft. TL: N41 04 04 W79 04 59. 904 N. Main St., Punxsutawney 15767. Secondary address: Renda Radio Inc., Broadcast Plaza, Pittsburgh 15767. Phone: (814) 938-6000. Fax: (814) 938-4237. E-mail: rendaradio@adelphia.net. Licensee: Renda Radio Inc. Group owner: Renda Broadcasting Corp. Network: ABC. Latham & Watkins. Format: Oldies. News staff: one; News: 2 hrs wkly. Target aud: 35-54; adults. ♦ Anthony F. Renda, pres; Alan Serena, exec VP; Doug Metheney, gen mgr; Jennifer Black, gen sls mgr; Lou Jordan, progmg dir; Larry McGuire, news dir; Phil Lenz, engrg dir; Martine Palmer, chief of engrg.

Brownsville

WASP(AM)— Aug 3, 1968: 1130 khz; 5 kw-D, DA. TL: N40 02 33 W79 54 20. 123 Blaine Rd. 15417. Phone: (724) 938-2000. Fax: (724) 938-7824. E-mail: pickleonline@yahoo.com. Licensee: Keymarket Licenses LLC. Group owner: Keymarket Communications LLC (acq 8-31-99; $2.875 million. with WPKL(FM) Uniontown). Network: USA. Format: Oldies. Target aud: 35-64. ♦ Gerald Getz, pres; Andrew Powaski, gen mgr.

Burgettstown

WOGH(FM)—Listing follows WSTV(AM).

Burnham

WVNW(FM)— August 1994: 96.7 mhz; 450 w. 850 ft. TL: N40 35 10 W77 41 40. Box 911, One Juniata St., Lewistown 17044. Phone: (717) 242-1493. Fax: (717) 242-3764. E-mail: traffic@star967.com. Licensee: WVNW Inc. (acq 2-1-94; 4-25-94). Format: Hot country. Target aud: 25-54. ♦ Tom Sheeder, progmg dir.

Butler

WBUT(AM)— Mar 14, 1949: 1050 khz; 500 w-D, 65 w-N. TL: N40 53 51 W79 53 22. Box 1645, 112 Hollywood Dr., Suite 203 16001. Phone: (724) 287-5778. Fax: (724) 282-9188. Fax: (724) 283-2005. Web Site: www.wbut.com. Licensee: Butler County Radio Network Inc. (group owner; (acq 5-19-98; grpsl). Rep: Dome. Format: Oldies. Target aud: General. ♦ Bob Tupp, progmg dir; Victoria Hinterberger, gen mgr & progmg dir.

WLER-FM—Co-owned with WBUT(AM). Mar 14, 1949: 97.7 mhz; 2.3 kw. 374 ft. TL: N40 53 51 W79 53 22. Stereo. Web Site: www.wler.com. Network: Westwood One. Format: All hits. ♦ Victoria Hinterberger, stn mgr.

WISR(AM)— Sept 26, 1941: 680 khz; 250 w-D, 50 w-N. TL: N40 52 39 W79 54 09. 112 Hollywood Dr., Suite 203 16003-0151. Phone: (724) 283-1500. Fax: (724) 283-3005. Licensee: Butler County Radio Network Inc. (group owner; (acq 5-19-98; grpsl). Network: CBS. Commercial Media Sales. Format: News/talk, sports. News staff: 3; News: 28 hrs wkly. Target aud: 25 plus. Spec prog: Relg 6 hrs wlky. ♦ Ronald Brandon, CEO; Daniel Vernon, CFO; Vicki Hinterberger, gen mgr.

California

*****WCAL(FM)**— September 1973: 91.9 mhz; 3 kw. 160 ft. TL: N40 02 57 W79 54 01. Stereo. California Univ. of PA, 428 Hickory St. 15419. Phone: (724) 938-3000. Phone: (724) 938-4330. Fax: (724) 938-5959. E-mail: wheeler@cup.edu. Licensee: The Student Association Inc. (acq 6-3-78). Network: Westwood One. Format: Active rock. News: 5 hrs wkly. Target aud: 18-25; students at California Univ. Spec prog: Contemp Christian 6 hrs, urban contemp 12 hrs, rap 4 hrs, alternative 6 hrs, metal 5 hrs wkly. ♦ J.R. Wheeler, opns mgr; Richie Wirdzek, progmg dir; Ben Slazek, mus dir; Crystal Rupp, news dir; Rich Filchuk, chief of engrg.

Directory of Radio

Cambridge Springs

WXXO(FM)— July 14, 1997: 104.5 mhz; 2.65 kw. 502 ft. TL: N41 42 17 W80 09 53. Stereo. 1411 Liberty St., Franklin 16323. Phone: (814) 432-2188. Fax: (814) 437-9372. E-mail: radio@zoominternet.com. Web Site: www.mykissfm.com. Licensee: Forever Broadcasting LLC. Group owner: Forever Broadcasting (acq 7-21-00; grpsl). Format: Hot AC. Target aud: 25-54. ♦ Carol Logan, pres; Terry Deitz, gen mgr; Joe Elan, gen sls mgr; Todd Adkins, opns mgr & progmg dir.

Canonsburg

WWCS(AM)— Nov 28, 1957: 540 khz; 7.5 kw-D, 500 w-N, DA-2. TL: N40 17 22 W80 11 07. (CP: 5 kw-D, 500 w-N, DA-2). 38 Angerer Rd. 15317. Phone: (724) 745-5400. Fax: (724) 745-8790. Web Site: www.radiodisney.com. Licensee: Birach Broadcasting Corp. (acq 5-28-92; $475,000;. FTR: 6-22-92). Format: Children. Target aud: Educated adults, ethnic groups, open minded. ♦ Sima Birach Sr., gen mgr.

Canton

WHGL-FM— Aug 30, 1978: 100.3 mhz; 3.9 kw. 846 ft. TL: N41 44 32 W76 50 08. Stereo. Box 100, 170 Redington Ave., Troy 16947. Phone: (570) 297-0100. Fax: (570) 297-3193. E-mail: wiggle100@sosbbs.com. Web Site: www.wiggle100.com. Licensee: Cantroair Communications Inc. (acq 1-7-99; $560,000 for 85% of stock with WTZN(AM) Troy). Network: ABC. Format: Country. News staff: one. Target aud: 25-54. ♦ Bob Gisler, VP; Mike Powers, pres & gen mgr; Georgia Pepper, prom mgr.

WTZN(AM)—See Troy

Carbondale

WCDL(AM)— January 1950: 1440 khz; 5 kw-D. TL: N41 33 28 W75 29 11. 1 N. Main St., Suite 1440 18704. Phone: (570) 282-1440. Fax: (570) 282-1435. Licensee: Group B Licensee LLC. Group owner: Route 81 Radio LLC (acq 12-2-2003; grpsl). ♦ Ed Histed, gen mgr.

*****WCIG(FM)**—Not on air, target date: unknown: 91.3 mhz; 300 w. Ant 551 ft. TL: N41 45 27 W75 26 28. Box 506, Bath, NY 14810. Phone: (607) 776-4151. Fax: (607) 776-6929. E-mail: mail@fln.org. Web Site: www.fln.org. Licensee: Family Life Ministries Inc. Format: Christian. ♦ Dick Snavely, CFO & gen mgr.

WNAK-FM— 1965: 94.3 mhz; 1.1 kw. Ant 770 ft. TL: N41 32 37 W75 27 44. Stereo. 84 S. Prospect St., Nanticoke 18634. Phone: (570) 735-0730. Fax: (570) 735-4844. Licensee: Group B Licensee LLC. Group owner: Route 81 Radio LLC (acq 12-2-2003; grpsl). Network: CBS Radio. Format: MOR, btfl music, nostalgia. ♦ Margie McQuillin, stn mgr.

Carlisle

WCAT-FM— 1959: 102.3 mhz; 3 kw. Ant 328 ft. TL: N40 17 23 W77 08 10. Stereo. Box 450, Hershey 17033. Secondary address: 1703 Walnut Bottom Rd. 17013. Phone: (610) 266-7600. Phone: (508) 752-1045. Fax: (717) 258-4638. Web Site: www.red1023.com. Licensee: Citadel Broadcasting Co. Group owner: Citadel Broadcasting Corp. (acq 1999; $4.5 million. with WHYL(AM) Carlisle). Network: CNN Radio. Format: Country. Target aud: 25-54. ♦ Cindy Miller, gen mgr; John Fraunfelter, opns mgr; Jay Hunter, prom dir; Will Robinson, progmg dir.

*****WDCV-FM**— January 1972: 88.3 mhz; 450 w. 150 ft. TL: N40 12 09 W77 11 46. Stereo. Box 1773, Dickinson College, Student Activities Office 17013-2896. Phone: (717) 245-1444. Fax: (717) 245-1899. E-mail: webmaster@dickinson.edu. Web Site: www.the-freq.com. Licensee: Board of Trustees Dickinson College. Format: Div. News staff: 5; News: 5 hrs wkly. Spec prog: Jazz 6 hrs, Ger one hr, Sp one hr, funk/rap 15 hrs, Russian one hr, politics one hr, blues 6 hrs wkly. ♦ Nick Stamos, gen mgr.

WHYL(AM)— 1948: 960 khz; 5 kw-D, 22 w-N. TL: N40 11 34 W77 10 28. 1703 Walnut Bottom Rd. 17013. Phone: (717) 249-1717. Fax: (717) 258-4638. Web Site: www.whylradio.com. Licensee: Group B Licensee LLC. Group owner: Route 81 Radio LLC (acq 12-2-2003; grpsl). Rep: McGavren Guild. Format: News/talk. News staff: one. Target aud: 45 plus; older, mature adults. Spec prog: Polka 2 hrs.

Stations in the U.S.   Pennsylvania

Developers & Brokers of Radio Properties — contact American Media Services at our suite: Philadelphia Marriott Downtown 215-625-2900. 843-972-2200. americanmediaservices.com. Charleston, SC. Dallas, TX · Chicago, Il · Austin, TX. American Media Services, LLC

♦Lloyd Roach, CEO; Gavin Stief, COO; Bruce Collier, gen mgr & gen sls mgr; Cindy Miller, stn mgr; Ruth O'Brien, progmg dir; John Domen, news dir.

WIOO(AM)— July 8, 1965: 1000 khz; 1 kw-D. TL: N40 09 30 W77 11 49. 180 York Rd. 17013. Phone: (717) 243-1200. Fax: (717) 243-1277. E-mail: wioo@pa.net. Web Site: www.wioo.com. Licensee: Harold Swidler. Network: ABC Information & Entertainment. Format: Classic country. News staff: 2; News: 15 hrs wkly. Target aud: 21 plus. Spec prog: Relg 5 hrs wkly. ♦Harold Swidler, pres; Florence Fisher, gen mgr & opns mgr.

Carnegie

WZUM(AM)— July 1962: 1590 khz; 1 kw-D, DA. TL: N40 25 40 W80 05 09. (CP: 5 kw-D). Box 27, Monroeville 15146. Phone: (412) 460-4000. Fax: (412) 460-0317. Licensee: Starboard Media Foundation Inc. (acq 7-25-2005; $435,000). Lauren A. Colby. Format: Var, news, info. Target aud: General. Spec prog: Ethnic 2 hrs wkly. ♦Mike Horvath, gen mgr.

Cashtown

*****WFKJ(AM)**— Dec 7, 1988: 890 khz; 1 kw-D. TL: N39 52 59 W77 20 43. Box 115 17310. Secondary address: 3425 Chambersburg Rd., Biglerville 17307. Phone: (717) 337-1607. Phone: (717) 337-1635. Fax: (717) 334-8914. E-mail: jil@wordbroadcast.org. Web Site: www.wordbroadcast.org. Licensee: Jesus is Lord Ministries International. Network: Moody. Format: Relg. Target aud: General. Spec prog: Country 4 hrs, children 12 hrs wkly. ♦Fred Bream, prom mgr, prom mgr, progmg dir, mus dir & pub affrs dir; Rev. Michael H. Yeager, pres, gen mgr, gen sls mgr & news dir; Larry Angle, chief of engrg.

Central City

WCCL(FM)— Oct 19, 1972: 101.7 mhz; 725 w. 643 ft. TL: N40 06 42 W78 51 33. Stereo. Cool 101.7, 2447 Bedford St., Suite 101, Johnstown 15904. Phone: (814) 266-9458. Fax: (814) 266-9212. Web Site: www.cool101online.com. Licensee: 2510 Licenses LLC. (group owner; (acq 2-16-2005); grpsl). Format: Oldies. News staff: 4. Target aud: 25-54. Spec prog: Relg 4 hrs wkly. ♦Nick Ferrara, gen mgr.

Chambersburg

WCHA(AM)— Aug 11, 1946: 800 khz; 1 kw-D, 196 w-N. TL: N39 55 41 W77 41 44. Stereo. 25 Penncraft Ave. 17201. Phone: (717) 263-0813. Fax: (717) 263-9649. E-mail: mix95@mix95.com. Licensee: MLB-Hagerstown-Chambersburg IV LLC. (acq 7-20-2005; grpsl). Network: ABC. Latham Watkins. Format: News/talk. News staff: one. Target aud: 25-54. Spec prog: Relg 8 hrs, gospel 2 hrs wkly. ♦Rich Bateman, gen mgr; Craig Stevens, opns mgr & gen sls mgr; Rick Alexander, chief of opns & progmg mgr; Tammy Heckman, prom mgr.

WIKZ(FM)—Co-owned with WCHA(AM). Apr 15, 1948: 95.1 mhz; 50 kw horiz, 42 kw vert. 449 ft. TL: N39 55 41 W77 41 44. Stereo. Web Site: www.mix95.com. Format: Adult contemp. News staff: one. Target aud: 25-44. ♦Lisa Harding, prom mgr; Rick Alexander, opns mgr & mus dir; J.P. McCartney, asst music dir; Jeff Baker, engrg mgr.

WHGT(AM)— 1956: . Stn currently dark 1590 khz; 5 kw-D, 1 kw-N, DA-N. TL: N39 54 15 W77 39 45. M. Belmont VerStandig Inc., 4850 Connecticut Ave. N.W., Suite 103, Washington, DC 20008. Phone: (202) 244-1422. Fax: (202) 362-4149. Licensee: M. Belmont Verstandig Inc. (acq 1993; $1.6 million. with WSRT(FM) Mercersburg; FTR: 9-6-93). ♦John VerStandig, CEO.

*****WZXQ(FM)**— 2005: 88.3 mhz; 110 w vert. Ant 1,155 ft. TL: N39 57 40 W77 28 32. Box 186, Sellersville 18960. Phone: (215) 721-2141. Fax: (215) 721-9811. E-mail: wordfm@wordfm.org. Web Site: www.wordfm.org. Licensee: Four Rivers Community Broadcasting Corp. Format: Adult contemp, Christian, relg. ♦David Baker, VP; Charles W. Loughery, gen mgr.

Charleroi

WFGI(AM)— 1947: 940 khz; 250 w-D, 5 w-N, U. TL: N40 07 24 W79 53 45. 123 Blaine Rd., Brownsville 15417. Phone: (724) 938-2000. Fax: (724) 938-7824. Licensee: Keymarket Licenses LLC. Group owner: Keymarket Communications LLC (acq 12-15-99; $3.5 million. with co-located FM). Baraff, Koerner & Olender. Format: Country. News staff: one; News: 8 hrs wkly. Target aud: General; Mon Valley area. Spec prog: Croation one hr, Pol 2 hrs wkly. ♦David Zynkhamm, gen sls mgr; Terry Hunt, progmg dir.

WOGI(FM)—Co-owned with WFGI(AM). July 10, 1967: 98.3 mhz; 6 kw. 300 ft. TL: N40 07 24 W79 53 45. Stereo. 100 Ryan Ct., Suite 98, Pittsburgh 15205. Phone: (412) 279-5400. Fax: (412) 279-5500. Web Site: www.froggyland.com. Target aud: 18-49. ♦G. Getz, gen sls mgr; Mark Lindow, progmg dir; Scott Tavares, mus dir.

Chester

*****WDNR(FM)**— Apr 22, 1977: 89.5 mhz; 10 w. 117 ft. TL: N39 51 42 W75 21 20. Stereo. Widener University,, Box 1000,, One University Pl. 19013. Phone: (610) 499-4439. Phone: (610) 499-4000. Fax: (610) 499-4531. E-mail: wdnr895@mail.widener.edu. Web Site: www.wdnr.com. Licensee: Widener University. Format: Free-form. Target aud: 16-30; high school & college age population. Spec prog: Jazz 2 hrs, blues 2 hrs, oldies 2 hrs, children 2 hrs wkly. ♦Art Kalemkarian, gen mgr; Sean Sheenan, opns dir; Drena Gwin, progmg dir & mus dir; John Blazek, chief of engrg.

WPWA(AM)— October 1947: 1590 khz; 3.2 kw-D, 1 kw-N, DA-N. TL: N39 52 39 W75 27 22. Stereo. 12 Kent Rd., Aston 19014. Phone: (610) 358-1400. Fax: (610) 358-1845. Web Site: www.wpwa.net. Licensee: Mount Ocean Media L.L.C. (acq 8-20-01; $675,000). Booth, Freret, Imlay & Tepper P. Format: Gospel, Christian, relg. News: 20 hrs wkly. Target aud: 25-64; affluent, mature adults. ♦Steve Skalish, gen mgr.

WVCH(AM)— Apr 4, 1948: 740 khz; 1 kw-D. TL: N39 52 38 W75 24 24. (CP: 50 kw-D, 450 w-N; DA-1). Box 157, Blue Bell 19477-0102. Secondary address: 308 Dutton Mill Rd., Brookhaven 19015. Phone: (610) 872-8861. Fax: (610) 279-9002. E-mail: wvch@juno.com. Web Site: www.wvch.com. Licensee: WVCH Communications Inc. (acq 10-74). Network: Network: Moody, USA. Wiley, Rein & Fielding. Format: Relg, Christian. Target aud: General. ♦Thomas H. Moffit, pres; Tom Moffit Jr., sr VP; William Fenton, VP; Tom Harvey, gen mgr.

Clarendon

WKNB(FM)— Aug 31, 1995: 104.3 mhz; 4.7 kw. 371 ft. TL: N41 47 21 W79 08 29. Stereo. Box 824, 310 Second Ave., Warren 16365. Phone: (814) 723-1310. Fax: (814) 723-3356. E-mail: info@kibcoradio.com. Web Site: www.kibcoradio.com. Licensee: Kinzua Broadcasting Co. Inc. (acq 2-95). Network: AP Radio. Commercial Media Sales Borsari & Paxson. Format: Country. News staff: one. Target aud: 18-45. ♦W. LeRoy Schneck, pres & gen mgr; David Whipple, gen sls mgr; Dale Bliss, prom dir & sls; Mark Silvis, progmg mgr; Robert Seiden, news dir.

Clarion

WCCR(FM)—Listing follows WWCH(AM).

*****WCUC-FM**— April 1977: 91.7 mhz; 3.2 kw. Ant 318 ft. TL: N41 12 35 W79 22 39. Stereo. G55 Becker Hall, Clarion Univ. of Pa. 16214. Phone: (814) 393-2514. Phone: (814) 393-2245. Fax: (814) 393-2186. E-mail: wadams@clarion.edu. Licensee: Clarion University of Pennsylvania. (acq 6-76). Format: Top 40. Spec prog: Black 6 hrs, country 6 hrs, jazz 3 hrs, new wave 9 hrs wkly. ♦William Adams, gen mgr.

WWCH(AM)— June 12, 1960: 1300 khz; 1 kw-D, 36 w-N. TL: N41 10 34 W79 20 22. Box 688 16214. Phone: (814) 226-4500. Fax: (814) 226-5898. E-mail: wccrwwch@apelphia.net. Web Site: www.insideclarioncounty.com. Licensee: Clarion County Broadcasting Corp. Network: AP Radio. Rep: Dome.

Frederick Polner. Format: Classic country/news/talk. News staff: one; News: 8 hrs wkly. Target aud: 25-54. Spec prog: Pub affrs, relg 8 hrs wkly. ♦William S. Hearst, pres & gen mgr.

WCCR(FM)—Co-owned with WWCH(AM). June 28, 1985: 92.7 mhz; 3 kw. 400 ft. TL: N41 14 41 W79 15 42. Stereo. Web Site: www.insideclarioncountry.com. Format: Adult contemp. News staff: one; News: 8 hrs wkly. Target aud: 25-54.

Clearfield

WCPA(AM)— 1947: 900 khz; 2.5 kw-D, 500 w-N, DA-2. TL: N41 02 32 W78 26 54. 110 Healy Ave. 16830. Phone: (814) 765-5541. Fax: (814) 765-6333. Web Site: www.besthitsbestvariety.com. Licensee: Clearfield Broadcasters Inc. Network: ABC Information & Entertainment. Rep: Dome. Format: Oldies. Target aud: 35 plus. ♦Bob Day, gen sls mgr & progmg dir.

WQYX(FM)—Co-owned with WCPA(AM). July 12, 1967: 93.1 mhz; 3.0 kw. 95 ft. TL: N41 04 32 W78 26 54. Stereo. Web Site: www.besthitsbestvariety.com. Baraff, Koerner & Olender. Format: Hot adult contemp. Target aud: 18-44.

Coatesville

WCOJ(AM)— Nov 29, 1949: 1420 khz; 5 kw-U, DA-N. TL: N40 01 21 W75 48 53. 17 W. Gay St., Lower Atrium, West Chester 19380-3090. Phone: (610) 701-9300. Fax: (610) 701-9412. E-mail: wcoj@wcoj.com. Web Site: www.wcoj.com. Licensee: Group A Licensee LLC. Group owner: Route 81 Radio LLC (acq 2-10-2004). Network: CBS. Booth, Freret & Imlay. Format: News/talk. News staff: 3; News: 14 hrs wkly. Target aud: 35-64. Spec prog: Relg 8 hrs, children 2 hrs, farm 2 hrs, gospel 2 hrs wkly. ♦Lloyd B. Roach, pres & gen mgr; Lloyd Roach, opns dir; Michelle Witkowski, opns mgr; Steve Bryant, progmg dir; Robert Henson, news dir; Jeffrey Depolo, chief of engrg.

Columbia

WVZN(AM)— 1957: 1580 khz; 500 w-D, 5 w-N. TL: N40 00 53 W76 28 13. 244 N. Queen St., Lancaster 17603. Phone: (717) 394-7644. Phone: (888) 299-1580. Fax: (717) 291-9183. E-mail: dwights@sabvi.com. Licensee: Esfuerzo de Union Cristiana (acq 11-16-01; $165,000). Network: Network: Westwood One, Radio Unica. Format: News/talk. News: 21 hrs wkly. Target aud: 35 plus; vision-impaired. ♦Dennis Steiner, gen mgr; Dwight Smith, stn mgr & progmg mgr.

Connellsville

WPNT(AM)— Apr 23, 1947: 1340 khz; 1 kw-U. TL: N40 01 27 W79 36 35. 123 Blaine Rd., Brownsville 15417. Phone: (724) 938-2000. Fax: (724) 938-7824. E-mail: pickieonline@yahoo.com. Licensee: Keymarket Licenses LLC Group owner: Keymarket Communications LLC (acq 1-17-01; $475,000. with WPKL(FM) Uniontown). Network: ABC Information & Entertainment. Format: Oldies. Target aud: 25-64. ♦Gerald Getz, pres; Andrew Ponaski, gen mgr.

Cooperstown

WUUZ(FM)— 2002: 107.7 mhz; 4.5 kw. Ant 377 ft. TL: N41 29 23 W79 44 07. Forever Broadcasting LLC, One Forever Dr., Holidaysburg 16648. Phone: (814) 941-9800. Licensee: Forever Broadcasting LLC. Group owner: Forever Broadcasting (acq 7-5-01; $342,000. for CP). Format: Classic hits. ♦Terry Deitz, gen mgr.

Corry

WWCB(AM)— Apr 2, 1955: 1370 khz; 1 kw-D, 500 w-N, DA-N. TL: N41 56 10 W79 39 20. Box 4, 418 N. Center 16407. Phone: (814) 664-8694. Fax: (814) 664-8695. E-mail: power1370@yahoo.com. Web Site: www.power1370.com. Licensee: Corry Communications Corp. (acq 1-22-89; $140,000; 1-15-90). Network: Network: Motor Racing Net, Westwood One, CBS. Format: Adult contemp,

Pennsylvania

classic rock, sports. Target aud: General. ♦William Hammond III, pres; Kevin Thomas, stn mgr & progmg dir; Debbie Swanson, gen sls mgr.

Coudersport

WFRM(AM)— May 1953: 600 khz; 1 kw-D, 46 w-N. TL: N41 45 11 W78 00 03. 9 S. Main St. 16915. Phone: (814) 274-8600. Phone: (814) 642-9396. Fax: (814) 274-0760. E-mail: gmiller@wfrm.net; radio@wfrm.net. Web Site: www.wfrm.net. Licensee: Farm & Home Broadcasting Co. Group owner: Allegheny Mountain Network Stations Network: ABC. Rep: Dome. Borsari & Paxson. Format: Hit country, strong loc news/talk. Target aud: General. Spec prog: Farm 2 hrs wkly. ♦Gerri Miller, gen sls mgr, prom mgr & progmg mgr.

WFRM-FM— Sept 18, 1985: 96.7 mhz; 1.45 kw. 666 ft. TL: N41 45 11 W78 00 03. Stereo. Web Site: www.wfrm.net. Format: Adult contemp. News: 9 hrs wkly.

Covington

WDKC(FM)— 1994: 101.5 mhz; 1.9 kw. Ant 594 ft. TL: N41 43 25 W77 02 46. Stereo. Box 101.5, Mansfield 16933. Secondary address: 8767 Rt. 414, Liberty 16930. Phone: (570) 662-9000. Fax: (570) 324-1015. E-mail: kc101@sosbbs.com. Licensee: Mid-Atlantic Broadcasting Inc. (acq 4-95; $105,000). Format: Country. News staff: one; News: 3 hrs wkly. Target aud: 25-54; 70% female. Spec prog: Bluegrass one hr wkly. ♦Kevin Thomas, CEO & pres; Thomas Gluszczak, chmn; Kevin Gluszczak, gen mgr.

Cresson

WBXQ(FM)— November 1981: 94.3 mhz; 350 w. 958 ft. TL: N40 27 55 W78 31 17. 4000 5th Ave., Altoona 16602. Phone: (814) 944-9320. Fax: (814) 944-9350. Web Site: www.wbxq.com. Licensee: Sounds Good Inc. Network: ABC FM Connection. Format: Classic rock. News staff: one; News: 7 hrs wkly. Target aud: 18-54; males. ♦Diane Boslet, gen mgr & stn mgr.

Curwensville

WOKW(FM)— Aug 1, 1989: 102.9 mhz; 350 w. Ant 945 ft. TL: N41 04 29 W78 31 58. Stereo. Box 589, Clearfield 16830. Secondary address: 712 River Rd., Clearfield 16830. Phone: (814) 765-4955. Fax: (814) 765-7038. E-mail: news@wokw.com. Web Site: www.wokw.com. Licensee: Raymack Broadcasting Co. Inc. Southmayd & Miller. Format: Adult contemp. News staff: one; News: 14 hrs wkly. Target aud: 21-54. Spec prog: Oldies 2 hrs wkly. ♦Mark E. Harley, pres; Yvonne Lehman, exec VP; Mark Harley, gen mgr.

Dallas

WSJR(FM)— May 29, 1989: 93.7 mhz; 750 w. 679 ft. TL: N41 15 43 W75 58 04. (CP: 1.45 kw). Stereo. 600 Baltimore Dr., Wilkes-Barre 18702. Phone: (570) 824-9000. Fax: (570) 820-0520. Web Site: www.jr937.us. Licensee: Citadel Broadcasting Co. Group owner: Citadel Broadcasting Corp. (acq 2-4-98; grpsl). Network: CBS. Rep: Roslin. Format: Rock. News staff: one; News: 3 hrs wkly. Target aud: 25-54. Spec prog: Community affrs one hr wkly. ♦Taylor Walet, gen mgr; Jim Dorman, opns mgr.

Danville

*****WPGM(AM)**— June 1963: 1570 khz; 2.5 kw-D. TL: N40 59 10 W76 37 37. 8 E. Market St. 17821. Phone: (570) 275-1570. Fax: (570) 275-4071. Web Site: www.wpgm.info. Licensee: Montrose Broadcasting Corp. (group owner; acq 1-6-64). Format: Relg, btfl mus. Target aud: General; families. ♦George Vacca, gen sls mgr & progmg dir.

WPGM-FM— Sept 6, 1968: 96.7 mhz; 340 w. 760 ft. TL: N40 59 16 W76 32 51. Stereo. Web Site: www.wpgm.info.

Doylestown

WISP(AM)— 1948: 1570 khz; 5 kw-D, 900 w-N, DA-2. TL: N40 19 34 W75 09 40. (CP: 950 w-N). Box 798 18901. Secondary address: 40 Rickerts Rd., Doylestown 18901. Phone: (215) 345-1570. Fax: (215) 345-1946. E-mail: 1570am@holyspiritradio.org. Web Site: www.holyspiritradio.org. Licensee: Holy Spirit Radio Foundation Inc. (acq 1999; $1,023,750). Cohn and Marks. Format: Relg. News: 14 hrs wkly. Target aud: General. ♦Dale W. Meier, CEO & gen mgr.

DuBois

WCED(AM)— February 1941: 1420 khz; 5 kw-D, 500 w-N, DA-N. TL: N41 08 31 W78 48 07. 51 W. Long Ave. 15801. Phone: (814) 375-5260. Phone: (814) 371-6100. Fax: (814) 375-5262. Licensee: WCED Radio LLC. Group owner: Priority Communications acq 11-28-2003; $150,000). Format: Oldies. ♦Jay Philippone, gen mgr.

WDBA(FM)— Nov 12, 1975: 107.3 mhz; 50 kw. 499 ft. TL: N41 11 28 W78 41 27. Stereo. 28 W. Scribner Ave. 15801. Phone: (814) 371-1330. Fax: (814) 375-5650. E-mail: wdba@wdba.com. Web Site: www.wdba.com. Licensee: DuBois Area Brdcst Co. Inc. (acq 10-6-93; $360,000; 10-25-93). Network: Salem Radio Network. Reddy, Begley & McCormick. Format: Inspirational, Christian. News: 6 hrs wkly. Target aud: 25-54; married women, household heads. Spec prog: Children 2 hrs wkly. ♦Daniel Brownlee, pres; Dan Kennard, gen mgr & progmg mgr; Gerald Meloon, opns dir & opns mgr; Barry Winter, gen sls mgr.

WOWQ(FM)— 1948: 102.1 mhz; 28 kw. Ant 663 ft. TL: N41 02 43 W78 42 11. Stereo. 801 E. DuBois Ave. 15801. Phone: (814) 371-6100. Fax: (814) 371-7724. E-mail: q102@adelphia.net. Web Site: www.q102radio.fm. Licensee: First Media Radio LLC (group owner; acq 4-10-02; $4.2 million. with WCED(AM) DuBois). Format: Country. News staff: one; News: 10 hrs wkly. Target aud: 18 plus. ♦Alex Kolobielski, CEO, chmn & pres; F. "Moose" Rosana, gen mgr.

Dunmore

WBHD(FM)—(Olyphant). 1991: 95.7 mhz; 300 w, 1,010 ft. TL: N41 26 10 W75 43 45. 600 Baltmore Dr., Wilkes-Barre 18702. Phone: (570) 824-9000. Fax: (570) 820-0520. Web Site: www.bearrocks.com. Licensee: Citadel Broadcasting Co. Group owner: Citadel Broadcasting Corp. (acq 1999; $950,000). Format: CHR. Target aud: 18-49; men, sports fans. Spec prog: Talk. ♦Taylor Walet, gen mgr.

East Stroudsburg

*****WESS(FM)**— Mar 10, 1971: 90.3 mhz; 1.37 kw. -165 ft. TL: N40 59 55 W75 10 21. Stereo. McGarry Communications Ctr., East Stroudsburg Univ. 18301. Phone: (570) 422-3512. Fax: (570) 422-3777. E-mail: wess@esu.edu. Web Site: www.esu.edu/wess. Licensee: East Stroudsburg University Board of Trustees/Student Activities Association. (acq 3-79). Format: Div, alternative, sports. Spec prog: Class 4 hrs, educ 7 hrs, jazz 6 hrs, news/talk 6 hrs,oldies 8 hrs wkly. ♦Jillian Kane, stn mgr & prom dir; Jennifer Haney, prom dir; Nicholas Frey, news dir.

Easton

WCTO(FM)— 1948: 96.1 mhz; 50 kw. 500 ft. TL: N40 35 55 W75 25 12. Stereo. Box 25096, Lehigh Valley 18002-5096. Secondary address: 2158 Avenue C, Bethlehem 18017. Phone: (610) 266-7600. Fax: (610) 231-0400. Web Site: www.catcountry96.fm. Licensee: Citadel Broadcasting Co. Group owner: Citadel Broadcasting Corp. Rep: Christal, Katz Radio. Format: Country. ♦John Fraunfelter, gen mgr; Shelly Easton, opns mgr; Elizabeth Penbleton, sls dir.

WEEX(AM)— May 1956: 1230 khz; 840 w-D, 1 kw-N, DA-D. TL: N40 42 30 W75 13 00. 107 Paxinosa Rd. W. 18040-1344. Phone: (610) 258-6155. Fax: (610) 253-3384. Licensee: Nassau Broadcasting II LLC. Group owner: Nassau Broadcasting Partners L.P. (acq 1-31-01; grpsl). Network: ESPN Radio. Format: Sports. ♦Rick Musselman, gen mgr & gen sls mgr; Tom Fallon, progmg dir.

WODE-FM—Co-owned with WEEX(AM). June 1950: 99.9 mhz; 50 kw. 449 ft. TL: N40 42 30 W75 13 00. Stereo. Format: Classic hits. ♦Bill Sheridan, progmg dir.

WEST(AM)— Feb 17, 1936: 1400 khz; 1 kw-U. TL: N40 40 23 W75 12 30. Stereo. 436 Northampton St. 18042. Phone: (610) 250-9557. Fax: (610) 250-9675. E-mail: infor@am1400west.net. Web Site: www.am1400west.net. Licensee: Maranatha Broadcasting Co. Inc. Rep: McGavren Guild. Fleischman & Walsh L. Format: MOR. News staff: 2; News: 20 hrs wkly. Target aud: General. ♦Richard Dean, pres; David Hinson, gen mgr; John Richetta, sls dir & progmg mgr; Pamela Richetta, prom mgr; Terry Rich, news dir; Bob Kratz, chief of engrg.

WJRH(FM)— March 1953: 104.9 mhz; 8 w. 23 ft. TL: N40 41 53 W75 12 30. (CP: 100 w). Stereo. Box 9473, Hogg Hall, Lafayette College 18042. Phone: (610) 330-5316. Fax: (610) 250-5318. Web Site: www.lafayette.edu. Licensee: Lafayette College. Format: Var. News staff: 3; News: 6 hrs wkly. Target aud: General; college students &

community. Spec prog: Jazz 9 hrs, reggae 6 hrs, metal 6 hrs, Sp 6 hrs, classic rock 4 hrs wkly. ♦Sergey Tosninski, gen mgr; Brian Hertz, progmg dir; Fred Lott, chief of engrg.

Ebensburg

WRDD(AM)— May 25, 1961: 1580 khz; 1 kw-D. TL: N40 29 33 W78 42 54. Stereo. Box 1095, Northern Cambria 15714. Secondary address: 104 S. Center St. 15931. Fax: (814) 471-0282. Licensee: Vernal Enterprises Inc. (group owner; acq 3-19-97; $20,000. with WNCC(AM) Northern Cambria). Network: USA. Format: Oldies. News: 4 hrs wkly. Target aud: General; church goers. ♦Denny Pompa, pres; Larry Schrecongost, gen mgr.

WWGE(AM)—See Loretto

WYOT(FM)— July 15, 1962: 99.1 mhz; 50 kw. Ant 499 ft. TL: N40 24 41 W78 46 29. Stereo. 109 Plaza Dr., Suite 2, Johnstown 15905. Phone: (814) 255-4186. Fax: (814) 255-6145. Web Site: www.hot99radio.com. Licensee: Forever Broadcasting LLC. (group owner; acq 5-1-2005; $2.73 million. with WRKW(FM) Johnstown). Format: Contemporary hit. ♦Verla Price, gen mgr; Vicki Lichtenfels, gen sls mgr; Mitch Edwards, progmg dir; Rick Shepard, news dir; Jim Boxler, chief of engrg.

Edinboro

*****WFSE(FM)**— Apr 3, 1979: 88.9 mhz; 3 kw. 312 ft. TL: N41 52 41 W80 10 40. Stereo. Edinboro Univ. of Pa., Faculty Annex 110 16444. Phone: (814) 732-2641. Phone: (814) 732-2889 (request line). E-mail: dumbluck77@hotmail.com. Licensee: Edinboro University. Format: Alternative, modern rock. News: 18 hrs wkly. Target aud: 18-25; college students with community interest. Spec prog: Football & basketball, Black 15 hrs, relg 4 hrs, loc news 3 hrs, swing 2 hrs wkly. ♦Dr. Frank Pogue, CEO; Terrence Warburton, chmn; Chris Volack, gen mgr; Richard Smith, dev dir.

WXTA(FM)— Oct 15, 1988: 97.9 mhz; 10 kw. 505 ft. TL: N41 57 57 W80 06 40. Stereo. 471 Robison Rd., Erie 16509. Phone: (814) 864-4835. Fax: (814) 868-1876. Web Site: www.country98wxta.com. Licensee: Citadel Broadcasting Co. Group owner: Citadel Broadcasting Corp. (acq 5-12-2004; grpsl). Rep: Katz Radio. Format: Country. Target aud: 18-54. ♦Farid Suleman, CEO; Gary Spurgeon, gen mgr.

Elizabethtown

WMHX(FM)—(Hershey). Apr 30, 1964: 106.7 mhz; 14 kw. Ant 928 ft. TL: N40 10 16 W76 35 50. Stereo. 919 Buckingham Blvd. 17022. Phone: (717) 367-7700. Fax: (717) 367-0239. Web Site: www.mix1067fm.com. Licensee: Citadel Broadcasting Co. Group owner: Citadel Broadcasting Corp. (acq 5-29-97; grpsl). Rep: Allied Radio Partners. Fleischman & Walsh. Format: Adult contemp. ♦Bob Adams, gen mgr; Steve Gallagher, opns mgr; Jay Hunter, prom dir.

WPDC(AM)— May 1958: 1600 khz; 500 w-D, 79 w-N. TL: N40 10 16 W76 35 50. 1051 Dairy Lane 17022. Phone: (717) 367-1600. Licensee: JVJ Communications Inc. (acq 10-1-84; $125,000; 10-15-84). Network: ESPN Radio. Format: Sports. News: 10 hrs wkly. Target aud: 25-54; men. ♦Vincent Grande, pres & gen mgr; Bill Wilson, opns VP; Sam Conrad, opns dir.

*****WWEC(FM)**— Aug 25, 1990: 88.3 mhz; 100 w. 373 ft. TL: N40 08 83 W76 35 38. Stereo. Elizabethtown College, One Alpha Dr. 17022-2298. Phone: (717) 361-1413. Phone: (717) 361-1589. Fax: (717) 361-1180. E-mail: wwec@etown.edu. Web Site: www.etown.edu. Licensee: Elizabethtown College. Format: Progressive, Alternative. News: 6 hrs wkly. Target aud: General; college students, high school, churches, community. ♦Dr. Randyll K. Yoder, gen mgr; John Treese, stn mgr; Sara Robinson, dev dir; Adam Steiner, mktg dir; Kate Norton, prom dir.

Elizabethville

WYGL-FM— Dec 7, 1989: 100.5 mhz; 1.2 kw. 515 ft. TL: N40 37 24 W76 49 54. Stereo. Box 90, Selinsgrove 17870. Phone: (570) 374-8819. Fax: (570) 374-7444. E-mail: bigcountryrequest@hotmail.com. Web Site: www.bigcountrynow.com. Licensee: MMP License LLC. Group owner: MAX Media L.L.C. (acq 10-17-03; grpsl). Network: USA. Kaye, Scholer, Fierman, Hays & Handler. Format: Contemp country. News staff: one; News: 8 hrs wkly. Target aud: 25-54. ♦John A. Trinder, pres; Scott Richards, VP & gen mgr; Greg Adair, gen sls mgr; Ted Koppen, chief of engrg.

Stations in the U.S. — Pennsylvania

Developers & Brokers of Radio Properties

contact American Media Services at our suite:
Philadelphia Marriott Downtown
215-625-2900
843-972-2200
americanmediaservices.com
Charleston, SC
Dallas, TX • Chicago, Il • Austin, TX

American Media Services, LLC

Ellwood City

WKPL(FM)— July 4, 1968: 92.1 mhz; 2.5 kw. Ant 512 ft. TL: N40 46 09 W80 16 56. Stereo. 349 Beaver St., Beaver 15009. Phone: (724) 728-6955. Fax: (724) 728-6955. Licensee: Keymarket Licenses LLC. Group owner: Keymarket Communications LLC (acq 6-30-2004; grpsl). Format: Oldies.

Emporium

WLEM(AM)— Mar 2, 1958: 1250 khz; 2.5 kw-D, 30 w-N. TL: N41 30 22 W78 13 26. 145 E. 4th 15834. Phone: (814) 486-3712. Fax: (814) 486-1772. Licensee: Priority Communications Inc. Network: Westwood One. Rep: Commercial Media Sales. Pepper & Corazzini. Format: Country. News staff: one; News: 3 hrs wkly. Target aud: 25-65. ♦ J. Philippone, pres & gen mgr; Gary Mitchell, opns mgr & progmg dir.

WQKY(FM)—Co-owned with WLEM(AM). May 20, 1985: 98.9 mhz; 2 kw. 548 ft. TL: N41 29 32 W78 15 19. Stereo. Format: Adult contemp.

Ephrata

WIOV-FM— Nov 9, 1962: 105.1 mhz; 25 kw. 702 ft. TL: N40 10 30 W76 09 31. Stereo. 44 Bethany Rd. 17522-2416. Phone: (717) 738-1191. Fax: (717) 738-1661. E-mail: dick.raymond@citcomm.com. Web Site: www.wiov.com. Licensee: Citadel Broadcasting Co. Group owner: Citadel Broadcasting Corp. (acq 5-12-2004; grpsl). Network: ABC Information & Entertainment. Rep: McGavren Guild. Format: Country. ♦ Mitch Carroll, gen sls mgr; Dick Raymond, progmg dir.

*WRTL(FM)— 2000: 90.7 mhz; 1 w horiz, 850 w vert. Ant 869 ft. TL: N40 19 22 W76 11 52. Temple University Public Radio, c/o WRTI(FM), Annenberg Hall, 2020 N. 13th St., Philadelphia 19122. Phone: (215) 204-8405. Fax: (215) 204-4870. Web site: www.wrtl.org. Licensee: Temple University of The Commonwealth System of Higher Education. Format: Public radio. ♦ Dave Conant, gen mgr.

Erie

*WEFR(FM)— January 1992: 88.1 mhz; 630 w. 430 ft. TL: N41 57 59 W80 06 40. Stereo. 4135 Northgate Blvd., Sacramento, CA 95834-1226. Phone: (916) 641-8191. Fax: (916) 641-8238. Fax: (510) 568-6190. E-mail: info@familyradio.org. Web Site: www.familyradio.com. Licensee: Family Stations Inc. (group owner) Network: UPI. Format: Relg. Target aud: General. ♦ Harold Camping, pres; John Rorvik, opns mgr.

*WERG(FM)— Dec 1, 1972: 90.5 mhz; 2.75 kw. Ant 374 ft. TL: N42 02 34 W80 03 57. Stereo. Gannon Univ., University Sq. 16541. Phone: (814) 871-5841. Fax: (814) 871-7302. E-mail: comedian13@hotmail.com. Web Site: www.wergfm.com. Licensee: Gannon University. Network: UPI. Format: Var/div. News staff: 4; News: 5 hrs wkly. Target aud: 12-30. Spec prog: It 3 hrs, Pol 3 hrs, Sp 3 hrs, gospel 3 hrs, reggae 4 hrs wkly. ♦ Evan O'Polka, gen mgr; Maggie Bausin, prom dir; Lacey Johnson, progmg dir & chief of engrg.

WFGO(FM)— Sept 1, 1993: 94.7 mhz; 1.7 kw. 613 ft. TL: N42 02 31 W80 03 57. 1 Boston Store Place 16501. Phone: (814) 461-1000. Phone: (814) 874-0011. Fax: (814) 874-0011. Web Site: www.froggy947.com. Licensee: NM Licensing LLC. Group owner: NextMedia Group L.L.C. (acq 11-26-01; grpsl). Format: Oldies. Target aud: 25-54. ♦ Rick Rambaldo, gen mgr.

WFNN(AM)— 1947: 1330 khz; 5 kw-U, DA-2. TL: N42 03 18 W80 02 24. One Boston Store Place 16501. Phone: (814) 461-1000. Fax: (814) 874-0011. Fax: (814) 455-6000. Web Site: www.sportsradio1330.com. Licensee: NM Licensing LLC. Group owner: NextMedia Group L.L.C. (acq 11-26-01; grpsl). Network: ABC Information & Entertainment. Rep: Katz Radio. Format: All sports. ♦ Rick Rambaldo, gen mgr.

WJET(AM)— 1951: 1400 khz; 1 kw. TL: N42 07 28 W80 03 54. 1 Boston Store Pl. 16501. Phone: (814) 461-1000. Phone: (814) 874-0011. Fax: (814) 874-0011. Fax: (814) 416-6655. E-mail: jet1400@jet1400.com. Web Site: www.jetradio1400.com. Licensee: NM Licensing LLC. Group owner: NextMedia Group L.L.C. (acq

11-26-01; grpsl). Kaye, Scholer, Fierman, Hays & Handler L.L.P. Format: News/talk. News staff: one. Target aud: 35 plus; middle to upper middle income, business owners, upscale. ♦ Rick Rambaldo, gen mgr & stn mgr.

*WMCE(FM)— Feb 2, 1989: 88.5 mhz; 750 w. Ant 499 ft. TL: N42 05 25 W79 56 37. Stereo. 501 E. 38th St. 16546. Phone: (814) 824-2260. Phone: (814) 824-2261. Fax: (814) 824-2590. E-mail: wshannon@mercyhurst.edu. Web Site: www.mercyhurst.edu. Licensee: Mercyhurst College. Network: AP Radio. Gammon & Grange. Format: Class. News: 6 hrs wkly. Target aud: General; Adults 45+. Spec prog: Pol 3 hrs, Ger 4 hrs, Sp 3 hrs, jazz 4 hrs wkly. ♦ William T. Shannon, gen mgr.

WPSE(AM)— Apr 21, 1935: 1450 khz; 1 kw-U. TL: N42 08 11 W80 02 25. Penn State-Behrend, Station R. 16563-1450. Phone: (814) 898-6495. Phone: (814) 898-6491. Licensee: Board of Trustees, Pennsylvania State University. (acq 12-23-89). Network: Network: CBS, Westwood One. Format: Business news, sports. Target aud: General. ♦ Ron Slomski, gen mgr.

WQHZ(FM)— Oct 15, 1951: 102.3 mhz; 1.7 kw. Ant 613 ft. TL: N42 02 25 W80 04 08. Stereo. 471 Robison Rd. 16509. Phone: (814) 868-5355. Fax: (814) 868-1876. Web Site: www.z1023online.com. Licensee: Citadel Broadcasting Co. Group owner: Citadel Broadcasting Corp. (acq 5-12-2004; grpsl). Rep: Katz Radio. Format: Classic rock. Target aud: 30-55; Adults. ♦ Farid Suleman, CEO; Gary Spurgeon, gen mgr & natl sls mgr.

*WQLN-FM— Jan 7, 1973: 91.3 mhz; 35 kw. 500 ft. TL: N42 02 35 W80 03 59. Stereo. 8425 Peach St. 16509. Phone: (814) 864-3001. Fax: (814) 864-4077. E-mail: dmiller@wqin.org. Web Site: www.wqln.org. Licensee: Public Broadcasting of Northwest Pennsylvania Inc. Network: Network: NPR, PRI. Dow, Lohnes & Albertson. Format: Classical; news; jazz. News staff: one. News: 24 hrs wkly. Target aud: General. Spec prog: Sp one hr, pub affrs 5 hrs, new age 2 hrs, call-in show 3 hrs wkly. ♦ Dwight Miller, pres & gen mgr; Tracy B. Ferrior, VP; Tom Pysz, opns mgr & progmg dir; Kim Young, news dir. Co-owned TV: *WQLN(TV) affil.

WRIE(AM)— 1941: 1260 khz; 5 kw-U, DA-2. TL: N42 03 18 W80 02 24. 471 Robison Rd. W. 16509. Phone: (814) 868-5355. Fax: (814) 868-1876. Licensee: Citadel Broadcasting Co. Group owner: Citadel Broadcasting Corp. (acq 5-12-2004; grpsl). Rep: Katz Radio. Format: Music of Your Life, big band. Target aud: 45 plus; general. Spec prog: Pol 1 hr wkly. ♦ Farid Suleman, CEO; Judy Ellis, COO; Gary Spurgeon, gen mgr & gen sls mgr; Marcia Diehl, opns mgr; Donna Palowitz, sls dir; Tina Achhammer, prom dir; Ron Arlen, progmg dir; Heather Rose, mus dir; Dave Benson, news dir; Rick Pogson, chief of engrg.

WXKC(FM)—Co-owned with WRIE(AM). 1949: 99.9 mhz; 50 kw. 492 ft. TL: N42 05 24 W79 57 12. Stereo. Web Site: www.classy100.com. Format: Adult contemp. News staff: one. Target aud: Adults; 35-64.

WRKT(FM)—See North East

WRTS(FM)— May 1, 1969: 103.7 mhz; 50 kw. Ant 499 ft. TL: N42 05 25 W79 56 37. Stereo. 1 Boston Store Pl. 16501. Phone: (814) 461-1000. Fax: (814) 455-6000. E-mail: star104@star104.com. Web Site: www.star104.com. Licensee: NM Licensing LLC. Group owner: NextMedia Group L.L.C. (acq 11-26-01; grpsl). Fletcher, Heald & Hildreth. Format: Top 40. News staff: one; News: one hr wkly. Target aud: 25-54. Spec prog: PSA one hr wkly. ♦ Richard Rambaldo, pres & gen mgr.

WYNE(AM)—See North East

Everett

WSKE(FM)—Listing follows WZSK(AM).

WZSK(AM)— Mar 15, 1963: 1040 khz; 10 kw-D. TL: N40 00 26 W78 21 44. Box 133 15537-0133. Phone: (814) 652-2600. Fax: (814) 652-9347. E-mail: wzsk@penn.com. Licensee: New Millennium

Communications Group Inc. (acq 9-27-01; with co-located FM). Network: Network: Westwood One, ABC Information & Entertainment. Dome. Fletcher, Heald & Hildreth. Format: News/talk. News: 10 hrs wkly. Target aud: 25-54. ♦ John C. Imler, gen mgr & progmg dir; Shane S. Imler, pres & adv dir; Bob Resconsin, chief of engrg.

WSKE(FM)—Co-owned with WZSK(AM). Mar 15, 1988: 104.3 mhz; 820 w. Ant 886 ft. TL: N40 00 11 W78 23 58. Stereo. Format: Country. News: 7 hrs wkly. Target aud: 25-54.

Fairless Hills

WKXW-FM—See Trenton, NJ

Fairview

WUSE(FM)— October 2001: 93.9 mhz; 3 kw. Ant 469 ft. TL: N41 57 59 W80 06 40. One Boston Store Pl., Erie 16501. Phone: (814) 461-1000. Fax: (814) 461-1500. E-mail: us939@us939.com. Web Site: www.us939.com. Licensee: NM Licensing LLC. Group owner: NextMedia Group L.L.C. (acq 11-26-01; grpsl). Format: Country. ♦ Richard Rambaldo, pres & gen mgr.

Farrell

WAKZ(FM)—See Youngstown, OH

WLOA(AM)—Licensed to Farrell. See Youngstown OH

Folsom

*WRSD(FM)— Jan 5, 1983: 94.9 mhz; 1.4 kw. 20 ft. TL: N39 53 12 W75 20 01. Ridley School District Admin. Bldg., 901 Morton Ave., Ste. 100 19033. Phone: (610) 534-1900. Fax: (610) 534-2335. Licensee: Ridley School District. Format: Div, adult contemp. ♦ Ann Brutch, gen mgr & progmg dir.

Forest City

WQFN(FM)— 2000: 100.1 mhz; 750 w. 935 ft. TL: N41 35 35 W75 25 56. 149 Penn Ave., Scranton 18503. Phone: (570) 346-6555. Fax: (570) 346-6038. E-mail: oldies@oldiesfm.com. Web Site: www.oldiesfm.com. Licensee: The Scranton Times L.P. Group owner: Shamrock Communications Inc. (acq 3-23-00). Format: Oldies. Target aud: 35-64; adults. ♦ William R. Lynett, CEO; Jim Loftus, gen mgr.

Franklin

*WAWN(FM)— 1998: 89.5 mhz; 1 kw. 315 ft. TL: N41 23 39 W49 46 20. Box 3206, Tupelo, MS 38803. Phone: (662) 844-8888. Fax: (662) 842-6791. E-mail: comments@afr.net. Web Site: www.afr.net. Licensee: American Family Association. Group owner: American Family Radio Format: Christian, inspirational. ♦ Marvin Sanders, gen mgr.

WFRA(AM)— Apr 13, 1958: 1450 khz; 1 kw-U. TL: N41 23 27 W79 48 43. Box 908, 1411 Liberty St. 16323. Phone: (814) 432-2189. Fax: (814) 437-9372. Licensee: Forever Broadcasting LLC. Group owner: Forever Broadcasting (acq 7-20-00; grpsl). Reddy, Begley & McCormick. Format: MOR, news, sports. News staff: one; News: 12 hrs wkly. Target aud: 45 plus. ♦ Carol Logan, pres; Terry Deitz, gen mgr; Tim Snyder, progmg dir & news dir; Lynn Deppen, engrg VP & chief of engrg.

WOXX(FM)—Co-owned with WFRA(AM). Mar 5, 1971: 99.3 mhz; 7.3 kw. 600 ft. TL: N41 26 16 W79 55 29. Stereo. Format: Hot adult contemp. News: 4 hrs wkly. Target aud: 18-44. ♦ Tim Snyder, prom dir.

Galeton

*WCOG-FM— 1996: 100.7 mhz; 7.7 kw. Ant 492 ft. TL: N41 39 36 W77 38 02. Box 506, Bath, NY 14810. Secondary address: 7634 Campbell Creek Rd., Bath, NY 14810. Phone: (607) 776-4151. Fax:

Broadcasting & Cable Yearbook 2006

Pennsylvania

(607) 776-6929. E-mail: mail@fln.org. Web Site: www.fln.org. Licensee: Family Life Ministries Inc. Group owner: Family Life Network (acq 10-1-96; $20,130). Network: Salem Radio Network. Format: Contemp Christian. News staff: 7; News: 14 hrs wkly. Target aud: 25-55; general. ♦ Dick Snavely, pres & CFO; Rick Snavely, chmn, VP, gen mgr & stn mgr.

Gettysburg

WGET(AM)— Aug 27, 1950: 1320 khz; 1 kw-D, 500 w-N, DA-2. TL: N39 50 30 W77 13 25. Box 3179, 1560 Fairfield Rd. 17325. Phone: (717) 334-3101. Fax: (717) 334-5822. Web Site: www.wget.com. Licensee: Times and News Publishing Co. Network: CBS. Hogan & Hartson. Format: Adult contemp, news, sports. News staff: 3; News: 40 hrs wkly. Target aud: 35-64; mainstream mature adults. ♦ Philip Jones, CEO; Cindy Ford, pres; Dave Jackson, opns mgr & mus dir; John C. Martin, gen sls mgr; Kim Alexander, news dir; Scott Steffan, engrg mgr & chief of engrg.

WGTY(FM)—Co-owned with WGET(AM). July 5, 1962: 107.7 mhz; 16 kw. 829 ft. TL: N39 51 23 W76 56 57. Stereo. Web Site: www.wgty.com. Format: Country. News: 2 hrs wkly. Target aud: 25-54. ♦ Cindy Ford, gen mgr, opns mgr & progmg dir; Casey Lee Summers, mktg mgr & pub affrs dir; Lisa Sneddin, prom mgr; Brad Austin, mus dir; John LeMay, chief of engrg.

***WZBT(FM)**— Oct 23, 1976: 91.1 mhz; 180 w. 380 ft. TL: N39 50 15 W77 14 09. Gettysburg College, Box 435 17325. Secondary address: 300 N. Washington St. 17325. Phone: (717) 337-6000. Fax: (717) 337-6666. E-mail: wzbtexec@gettysburg.edu. Web Site: www.gettesburg.edu/~wzbt/. Licensee: Gettysburg College. Format: Progsv. Target aud: General. Spec prog: Class 3 hrs, folk 6 hrs, jazz 4 hrs, Sp 4 hrs, gospel one hr wkly. ♦ Ryan Gottschall, stn mgr; Laura Benincasa, progmg dir.

Glen Mills

***WZZE(FM)**— May 20, 1975: 97.3 mhz; 18 w. 180 ft. TL: N39 55 15 W75 29 58. (CP: Ant 184 ft.). Box 5001, Concordville 19331. Secondary address: Glen Mills Schools, Glen Mills Rd. 19342. Phone: (610) 459-8100, ext: 307. Phone: (610) 459-4829. E-mail: msmith@glenmillerschools.org. Licensee: Glen Mills Schools. (acq 2-28-84). Network: ABC. Format: CHR. ♦ C.D. Ferrainola, pres; Mark Smith, opns mgr.

Grantham

***WVMM(FM)**— Sept 29, 1989: 90.7 mhz; 100 w. 300 ft. TL: N40 09 34 W76 59 00. Stereo. Messiah College, One College Ave., Box 3050 17027. Phone: (717) 691-6081. Fax: (717) 796-5353. E-mail: earke@messiah.edu. Web Site: www.messiah.edu/wvmm. Licensee: Messiah College. Network: PRI. Format: Contemp Christian. Target aud: General. Spec prog: Jazz 4, bluegrass 2 hrs, gospel 2 hrs, hip hop 4 hrs wkly. ♦ Edward T. Arke, gen mgr; Sheryl Ezbiansky, chief of engrg & opns.

Greencastle

WQCM(FM)— May 6, 1967: 94.3 mhz; 3.5 kw. 430 ft. TL: N39 47 29 W77 40 30. Stereo. 25 Penncraft Ave., Chambersburg 17201. Phone: (717) 263-0813. Fax: (717) 263-9649. E-mail: rbateman@damebroadcasting.net. Web Site: www.wqcmfm.com. Licensee: MLB-Hagerstown-Chambersburg IV LLC. (group owner; (acq 7-20-2005); grpsl). Latham & Watkins. Format: Classic rock. News staff: one. Target aud: 25-44. ♦ Rich Bateman, gen mgr; Tammy Heckman, prom dir; Mike Holder, progmg dir.

Greensburg

WJJJ(FM)— July 8, 1968: 107.1 mhz; 2.85 kw. Ant 482 ft. TL: N40 15 54 W79 20 25. Stereo. 960 Penn Ave., Suite 200, Pittsburgh 15222. Phone: (412) 471-2181. Fax: (412) 391-3559. Web Site: www.wamo.com. Licensee: MCL/MCM-Inc. (group owner). Format: Urban contemp. News staff: one; News: one hr wkly. ♦ Ronald Davenport Jr., pres & gen mgr.

Greenville

WEXC(FM)— July 1965: 107.1 mhz; 3 kw. Ant 328 ft. TL: N41 22 50 W80 24 48. Stereo. 64 Clinton St. 16125. Secondary address: 6578 Summers Rd., Windsor, OH 44099. Phone: (724) 588-8000. Fax: (724) 588-2470. Licensee: Beacon Broadcasting Inc. (group owner; (acq 9-7-2005); grpsl). Format: Positive rock. News staff: one. Target aud: 34-55. ♦ Bill Henry, gen mgr.

WGRP(AM)— Sept 19, 1959: 940 khz; 1 kw-D, 2 w-N, DA-2. TL: N41 23 10 W80 24 35. Box 846, Meadville 16335. Phone: (814) 337-8440. Fax: (814) 333-2562. E-mail: wmvl@zoominternet.net. Licensee: WGRP Radio Inc. (acq 9-7-2005); grpsl). Hogan & Hartson. Format: Adult contemp. Target aud: 30-64 persons. ♦ Joseph M. Vilkie, pres & gen mgr.

***WTGP(FM)**— Sept 3, 1971: 88.1 mhz; 1.1 kw. 6 ft. TL: N41 24 51 W80 24 50. Stereo. Thiel College, 75 College Ave. 16125. Secondary address: 57 Irvine Dr. 16125. Phone: (724) 589-2210. Phone: (724) 589-2171. Fax: (724) 589-2010. Fax: (724) 589-2730. E-mail: dwest@pathway.net. Web Site: www.thiel.edu/studentlife/student_org/wtgp. Licensee: Thiel College. Format: Div, progsv. Target aud: 18-23; Thiel college students, faculty & staff. Spec prog: Relg one hr wkly. ♦ Ang Baker, progmg dir.

Grove City

***WSAJ-FM**— September 1968: 91.1 mhz; 3 kw. 125 ft. TL: N41 09 20 W80 04 47. Stereo. Grove City College, 100 Campus Dr. 16127. Phone: (724) 458-2077. Fax: (724) 458-2329. E-mail: wsaj@gcc.edu. Licensee: Grove City College. Format: Class. News staff: one. Target aud: General; listeners who are generally unfamiliar with class mus & arts. ♦ Darren Morton, gen mgr & stn mgr.

WSAJ(AM)— April 1920: 1340 khz; 100 w-U. TL: N41 09 30 W80 11 30. ♦ Darren Morton, stn mgr.

WWGY(FM)— Sept 10, 1962: 95.1 mhz; 19 kw. Ant 805 ft. TL: N41 15 08 W80 21 28. Stereo. 219 Savannah Gardner Rd., New Castle 16101. Phone: (724) 346-5070. Fax: (724) 346-5075. E-mail: webmaster@foreverradio.com. Web Site: fforeverradio.com. Licensee: Forever Broadcasting LLC. Group owner: Forever Broadcasting (acq 2-23-2004; $2.28 million). Format: Country. News staff: one; News: 2 hrs wkly. Target aud: 18-34. ♦ Scott D. Cohagan, gen mgr; John Thomas, progmg dir.

Hanover

WHVR(AM)— Jan 9, 1949: 1280 khz; 5 kw-D, 500 w-N, DA-2. TL: N39 49 11 W77 00 25. Box 234 17331. Secondary address: 275 Radio Rd. Phone: (717) 637-3831. Fax: (717) 637-9006. Licensee: Radio Hanover Inc. Network: UPI. Format: Classic country. ♦ Joan McAnall, gen mgr; Rick McCauslin, gen sls mgr; Deanna Forney, news dir; Daryll Harcock, chief of engrg.

WYCR(FM)—Co-owned with WHVR(AM). Dec 22, 1962: 98.5 mhz; 10.5 kw. Ant 928 ft. TL: N39 51 30 W76 56 52. Stereo. E-mail: info@thepeak.com. Web Site: www.thepeak985.com. Format: Classic hits.

Harrisburg

WHKF(FM)—Listing follows WTKT(AM).

WHP(AM)— 1924: 580 khz; 5 kw-U, DA-N. TL: N40 18 11 W76 57 07. Stereo. 600 Corporate Circle 17110. Phone: (717) 540-8800. Fax: (717) 541-0094. Fax: (717) 540-9268. Web Site: www.whp580.com. Licensee: Clear Channel Radio License Inc. Group owner: Clear Channel Communications Inc. (acq 8-5-98); grpsl). Network: Network: Network: Westwood One, ABC Information & Entertainment, ABC News/Talk. Format: News/talk. News staff: 4. Target aud: 35-64. ♦ Ron Roy, gen sls mgr & natl sls mgr.

WRVV(FM)—Co-owned with WHP(AM). 1946: 97.3 mhz; 17 kw. 840 ft. TL: N40 20 44 W76 52 09. Stereo. Web Site: www.wrvv.com. Format: Rock, adult contemp. Target aud: 25-54.

***WITF-FM**— Apr 1, 1971: 89.5 mhz; 5.9 kw. Ant 1,361 ft. TL: N40 20 45 W76 52 06. Stereo. Box 2954 17105. Secondary address: 1982 Locust Ln. 17109. Phone: (717) 236-6000. Fax: (717) 232-7612. E-mail: info@witf.org. Web Site: www.witf.org. Licensee: WITF Inc. Network: Network: NPR, PRI. Dow, Lohnes & Albertson. Format: Class, news/talk. News staff: 3; News: 43 hrs wkly. ♦ Kathleen Pavelko, pres; Mitzi Trostle, gen mgr & stn mgr. Co-owned TV: *WITF-TV affil.

WKBO(AM)— 1922: 1230 khz; 48 kw-U. TL: N40 16 52 W76 52 06. 600 Corporate Cir. 17110-9787. Phone: (717) 540-8800. Fax: (717) 540-8814. E-mail: fortress1230am@oneheartministries.com. Web Site: www.oneheartministries.com. Licensee: Clear Channel Broadcasting Licenses Inc. Group owner: Clear Channel Communications Inc. (acq 8-5-98; grpsl). Rep: Salem. Format: Contemp Christian. News staff: 6; News: 168 hrs wkly. Target aud: 35-54; well educated, upscale professionals. Spec prog: Pop standards, Music of Your Life. ♦ Pete Hamel, gen mgr, stn mgr & gen sls mgr.

WNNK-FM—Listing follows WTCY(AM).

WRBT(FM)— Sept 30, 1962: 94.9 mhz; 25 kw. 699 ft. TL: N40 18 57 W76 57 02. Stereo. 600 Corporate Cir. 17110. Phone: (717) 671-9949. Fax: (717) 540-8814. Web Site: www.bobradio.com. Licensee: Clear Channel Radio License Inc. Group owner: Clear Channel Communications Inc. (acq 8-5-98; grpsl). Rep: Christal. Latham & Watkins. Format: Hot country. News staff: one. Target aud: 25-54. ♦ Ronald Roy, gen mgr. Co-owned TV: WHP-TV.

WSJW(FM)—See Starview

WTCY(AM)— May 28, 1945: 1400 khz; 1 kw-U. TL: N40 14 58 W76 52 03. 2300 Vartan Way 17110-9720. Phone: (717) 238-1041. Fax: (717) 234-4842. Web Site: www.cumulus.com. Licensee: Cumulus Licensing Corp. Group owner: Cumulus Media Inc. (acq 11-28-00; grpsl). Format: Urban adult contemp. News staff: 2; News: 2 hrs wkly. Target aud: 25-54. Spec prog: Gospel, sportscasting for Harrisburg Heat. ♦ Ron Vioavinannell, mktg mgr.

WNNK-FM—Co-owned with WTCY(AM). 1962: 104.1 mhz; 22.5 kw. 725 ft. TL: N40 18 59 W76 57 04. Stereo. Web Site: www.cumulus.com. Format: CHR. News staff: 2; News: 15 hrs wkly.

WTKT(AM)— February 1948: 1460 khz; 2.4 kw-D, 4.2 kw-N, DA-N. TL: N40 18 32 W76 56 13. 600 Corporate Cir. 17110. Phone: (717) 540-8800. Fax: (717) 540-8814. Web Site: www.1460theticket.com. Licensee: Clear Channel Radio License Inc. Group owner: Clear Channel Communications Inc. (acq 8-5-98; grpsl). Rep: Clear Channel. Fisher, Wayland, Cooper, Leader & Zaragoza L.L.P. Format: Oldies, sports. News staff: 4; News: 30 hrs wkly. Target aud: General. Spec prog: Gospel 2 hrs, pub service 2 hrs wkly. ♦ Ken Austin, progmg dir.

WHKF(FM)—Co-owned with WTKT(AM). July 1965: 99.3 mhz; 6 kw. 328 ft. TL: N40 15 44 W76 54 37. Stereo. Web Site: www.wwklfm.com. Target aud: 35-54. ♦ Doug Baker, gen sls mgr; Kraig Nace, prom mgr; Peter MacArthur, news dir; Tom Presite, chief of engrg.

***WXPH(FM)**— 1995: 88.1 mhz; 540 w. Ant 105 ft. TL: N40 15 44 W76 53 11. 3025 Walnut St., Philadelphia 19104. Phone: (215) 898-6677. Fax: (215) 898-0707. E-mail: wxpndesk@xpn.org. Web Site: www.xpn.org. Licensee: The Trustees of University of Pennsylvania. (acq 12-18-92; $5,000; 1-18-93). Format: Adult alternative. News staff: one; News: one hr wkly. ♦ Roger LaMay, gen mgr; Quyen Shanahan, dev VP.

Havertown

***WHHS(FM)**— Dec 6, 1949: 107.9 mhz; 14 w. Ant 161 ft. TL: N39 58 59 W75 18 10. Stereo. 200 Mill Rd. 19083. Phone: (610) 446-7111. Fax: (610) 853-5952. E-mail: whhsnewsdirector@yahoo.com. Web Site: www.whhs.org. Licensee: School District of Haverford Township. Format: Div. Target aud: General. ♦ Kevin Moran, gen mgr & opns dir.

Hawley

***WBYH(FM)**— December 2000: 89.1 mhz; 200 w. 525 ft. TL: N41 24 43 W75 09 51. Box 186, Sellersville 18960. Phone: (215) 721-2141. Fax: (215) 721-9811. E-mail: wordfm@wordfm.org. Web Site: www.wordfm.com. Licensee: Four Rivers Communications Broadcasting Co. Schwartz, Woods & Miller. Format: Contemp Christian. ♦ David Baker, gen mgr.

WYCY(FM)— Sept 13, 1993: 105.3 mhz; 2.9 kw. 479 ft. TL: N41 35 01 W75 10 30. 575 Grove St., Honesdale 18431. Phone: (570) 253-1616. Fax: (570) 253-6297. E-mail: rhm@infocow.net. Web Site: www.infocow.net. Licensee: Bold Gold Media Group L.P. (group owner; (acq 5-23-2005); grpsl). Format: Oldies. News staff: one; News: 5 hrs wkly. Target aud: 25-55. ♦ Robert Mermell, CEO & gen mgr; Brian Wilken, gen sls mgr; George Schmitt, progmg mgr.

Stations in the U.S.   Pennsylvania

Developers & Brokers of Radio Properties
contact American Media Services at our suite:
Philadelphia Marriott Downtown
215-625-2900
843-972-2200
americanmediaservices.com
Charleston, SC
Dallas, TX · Chicago, Il · Austin, TX
American Media Services, LLC

Hazleton

WAZL(AM)— Dec 19, 1932: 1490 khz; 1 kw-U. TL: N40 56 24 W75 58 04. 8 W. Broad St. 18201. Phone: (570) 455-1490. Fax: (570) 501-1112. E-mail: patwazl@nni.com. Licensee: Group B Licensee LLC. Group owner: Route 81 Radio LLC (acq 12-2-2003; grpsl). Format: Oldies. News staff: 5; News: 1.5 hrs wkly. Target aud: 18-64. ♦Patrick Ward, gen mgr; Rich Savillo, gen sls mgr; Rocky Brown, progmg dir.

WBSX(FM)— 1949: 97.9 mhz; 19.5 kw. Ant 728 ft. TL: N41 04 55 W75 56 55. (CP: 6.3 kw, ant 1,335 ft. TL: N41 10 56 W75 52 22). Stereo. 600 Baltimore Dr., Wilkes-Barre 18702. Phone: (570) 824-9000. Fax: (570) 820-0520. Web Site: www.979x.com. Licensee: Citadel Broadcasting Co. Group owner: Citadel Broadcasting Corp. (acq 5-29-97; grpsl). Network: Network: ABC, Moody. Pepper & Corazzini. Format: Active rock. Target aud: 18-34. ♦Taylor Walet, gen mgr; Jules Riley, opns mgr; Bill Palmeri, gen sls mgr & mktg mgr; Chris Lloyd, progmg dir; Phil Galasso, chief of engrg.

Hershey

WMHX(FM)—Licensed to Hershey. See Elizabethtown

Hollidaysburg

WKMC(AM)—See Roaring Spring

WRKY-FM— Dec 1, 1978: 104.9 mhz; 280 w. Ant 1,417 ft. TL: N40 29 15 W78 21 09. Stereo. One Forever Dr., Hollidaysburg 16648. Phone: (814) 941-9800. Fax: (814) 943-2754. E-mail: xman@rocky1049.com. Web Site: www.rocky1049.com. Licensee: Forever of PA L.L.C. Group owner: Forever Broadcasting (acq 2-18-97; $2 million. with WKMC(AM) Roaring Spring). Rep: Roslin. Format: Rock, adult contemp. Target aud: 25-54; adults with significant income. ♦Carol B. Logan, pres; David Davies, gen mgr.

Homer City

WCCS(AM)— Oct 25, 1983: 1160 khz; 10 kw-D, 1 kw-N, DA-1. TL: N40 34 18 W79 10 12. Stereo. Box 1020, Indiana 15701. Secondary address: 840 Philadelphia St., Suite 100, Indiana 15701. Phone: (724) 479-1160. Phone: (724) 465-4700. Fax: (724) 479-3500. E-mail: mbertig@rendabroadcasting.com. Web Site: www.1160.com. Licensee: The St. Pier Group LLC. Group owner: Renda Broadcasting Corp. (acq 10-4-2002; $650,000). Network: ABC. Dome & Associates Format: Adult contemp. News staff: 2; News: 14 hrs wkly. Target aud: 25-49. Spec prog: Pol 3 hrs, oldies 9 hrs wkly. ♦Tony Renda Sr., CEO & pres; Mark A. Bertig, gen mgr; Alan Serena, opns VP; Jack Benedict, opns dir; Ron Nocco, news dir.

Honesdale

WDNH-FM—Listing follows WPSN(AM).

WPSN(AM)— September 1972: 1590 khz; 2.5 kw-D. TL: N41 33 13 W75 15 18. 575 Grove St. 18431. Phone: (570) 253-1616. Fax: (570) 253-6297. Web Site: www.infocow.net. Licensee: Bold Gold Media Group L.P. (group owner; (acq 5-23-2005; grpsl). Network: USA. Rep: Dome. Schwartz, Woods & Miller. Format: Real country. Target aud: General. ♦George Schmitt, progmg mgr; John Emerson, news dir.

WDNH-FM—Co-owned with WPSN(AM). Oct 12, 1981: 95.3 mhz; 3 kw. 256 ft. TL: N41 34 23 W75 11 30. Stereo. Phone: (570) 253-9595. Web Site: www.wdnh.com. Network: USA. Format: Hot adult contemp. News staff: one; News: 6 hrs wkly. Target aud: 25-54. ♦George Schmitt, progmg dir.

*****WZZH(FM)**—Not on air, target date: unknown: 90.9 mhz; 200 w. Ant 912 ft. TL: N41 35 35 W75 25 56. Box 186, Sellersville 18960-0186. Phone: (215) 721-2141. Fax: (215) 721-9811. E-mail: wordfm@wordfm.org. Web Site: www.wordfm.org. Licensee: Four Rivers Community Broadcasting Corp. ♦Charles W. Loughery, pres.

Hughesville

WRKK(AM)— Aug 4, 1985: 1200 khz; 10 kw-D, 250 w-N, DA-2. TL: N41 12 43 W76 44 56. 1559 W. 4th St., Williamsport 17701. Phone: (570) 327-1400. Fax: (570) 327-8156. Web Site: www.wrak.com. Licensee: Clear Channel Broadcasting License Inc. Group owner: Clear Channel Communications Inc. (acq 8-5-98; grpsl). Network: Network: ABC, Westwood One. Format: News/talk. News staff: one. Target aud: 35 plus. ♦James Dabney, gen mgr; Ken Sawyer, opns dir & progmg dir.

Huntingdon

WHUN(AM)— Mar 2, 1947: 1150 khz; 5 kw-D, 36 w-N. TL: N40 27 18 W77 58 50. RD4 Box 160A, Huntington 16652. Phone: (814) 542-8648. Fax: (814) 643-9625. Licensee: Megahertz Licenses LLC. Group owner: Forever Broadcasting (acq 3-13-2002; $875,000. with WXOT(FM) Mount Union). Network: Motor Racing Net. Commercial Media Sales Inc. Format: Country. News staff: one; News: 15 hrs wkly. Target aud: 25 plus; general. Spec prog: Relg 2 hrs wkly. ♦Kristin Cantrell, gen mgr.

*****WKVR-FM**— March 1978: 92.3 mhz; 10 w. -376 ft. TL: N40 30 00 W78 00 52. Stereo. Juniata College 16652. Phone: (814) 643-5031. Phone: (814) 641-3341. Fax: (814) 643-4477. Licensee: Juniata College Board of Trustees. Network: ABC Information & Entertainment. Format: Classic rock, progsv, AOR. News: 8 hrs wkly. Target aud: 18-25; college students. Spec prog: CHR 15 hrs, jazz 3 hrs, Black 10 hrs, contemp Christian 3 hrs, reggae 3 hrs wkly. ♦Chad Herzog, gen mgr; J. Andrew Scott, prom dir.

WLAK(FM)— Sept 12, 1967: 103.5 mhz; 160 w. 1,427 ft. TL: N40 29 51 W78 08 00. Stereo. Box 667, Lewistown 17044. Secondary address: 12 East Market St., 2nd Floor, Lewistown 17044. Phone: (717) 248-6757. Fax: (717) 248-6759. E-mail: merfradio@acsworld.net. Web Site: www.merfradio.com. Licensee: First Media Radio LLC (group owner; acq 3-28-01; grpsl). Format: Adult contemp. Target aud: 18-44. ♦Peter Herman, gen mgr; Jeff Stevens, opns dir & progmg dir; Mary Lee Shaffer, news dir.

WWLY(FM)— Mar 30, 1992: 106.3 mhz; 6 kw. 154 ft. TL: N40 29 11 W77 59 35. Stereo. R.R. Box 160-A, Fairgrounds Rd. 16652. Phone: (814) 643-9620. Phone: (814) 643-1063. Fax: (814) 643-9625. E-mail: webmaster@waly1039.com. Web Site: www.waly1039.com. Licensee: Megahertz Licenses LLC. Group owner: Forever Broadcasting (acq 3-13-02; $620,000). Network: Jones Radio Networks. Rep: Dome. Mullin, Rhyne, Emmons & Topel. Format: Oldies. News staff: one. Target aud: 25-54; women, above average educ, income & status. ♦Kristen Cantrell, gen mgr.

Indiana

WCCS(AM)—See Homer City

WDAD(AM)— Nov 4, 1945: 1450 khz; 1 kw-U. TL: N40 37 01 W79 07 55. 840 Philadelphia St., Suite 100 15701. Phone: (724) 465-4700. Fax: (724) 349-6842. Web Site: www.wdadradio.com. Licensee: The St. Pier Group. Group owner: Renda Broadcasting Corp. (acq 2-13-2004; $3.25 million). Network: CBS. Rep: Dome. Pepper & Corazzini. Format: Good time oldies. News staff: one. Target aud: 35 plus. Spec prog: Relg 2 hrs wkly. ♦Mark Bertig, gen mgr; Tony Renda Sr., pres & gen mgr.

WQMU(FM)— Co-owned with WDAD(AM). Aug 14, 1968: 92.5 mhz; 3 kw. 108 ft. TL: N40 38 17 W79 08 47. Stereo. Web Site: www.wqmuradio.com. Dome Format: Adult hits. Target aud: 21-41.

*****WIUP-FM**— October 1969: 90.1 mhz; 1.6 kw. 88 ft. TL: N40 36 57 W79 09 40. Stereo. Indiana Univ. of Pa., 121 Davis Hall 15705. Phone: (724) 357-9487. Licensee: Indiana University of Pennsylvania. Format: Div. News: 11 hrs wkly. Target aud: General. Spec prog: Black 14 hrs, class 15 hrs, folk 4 hrs, gospel one hr, jazz 15 hrs, new age 4 hrs, radio drama one hr wkly. ♦James Rogers, gen mgr. Co-owned TV: *WIUP-TV affil.

Irwin

WKHB(AM)—Licensed to Irwin. See Pittsburgh

Jackson Township

*****WRTY(FM)**— Aug 23, 1991: 91.1 mhz; 3.5 kw. 862 ft. TL: N41 02 40 W75 22 45. Stereo. 1509 Cecel B. Moore Ave., 3rd Fl., Philadelphia 19121. Phone: (215) 204-8405. Fax: (215) 204-7027. E-mail: comments@wrti.org. Web Site: www.wrti.org. Licensee: Temple University of The Commonwealth System of Higher Education. Network: NPR. Format: Jazz, class. News staff: one; News: 15 hrs wkly. Target aud: 30-65. ♦Dave Conant, gen mgr.

Jeannette

WKFB(AM)— Jan 28, 1974: 770 khz; 750 w-D, 750 w-CH. TL: N40 17 20 W79 42 04. Box 990, Greensburg 15601-0990. Secondary address: 1918 Lincoln Hwy., North Versailles 15137. Phone: (412) 823-7000. Licensee: Broadcast Communications Inc. (group owner; acq 4-98). Format: Var. ♦Ashley R. Stevens, VP; Robert M. Stevens, pres & gen mgr.

Jenkintown

WPPZ-FM— Nov 1, 1960: 103.9 mhz; 340 w. Ant 1,000 ft. TL: N40 02 26 W75 14 20. 100 River Rd., Suite 400, Conshohocken 19428. Fax: (610) 276-1139. Licensee: Radio One Licenses LLC. Group owner: Radio One Inc. (acq 11-8-2001; grpsl). Dickstein Shapiro Morin & Oshinsky. Format: Urban, hip hop. Target aud: 18-34. ♦Lynn Bruder, gen mgr.

Jersey Shore

WJSA(AM)— July 10, 1979: 1600 khz; 1 kw-D, 20 w-N. TL: N41 13 32 W77 16 01. 262 Allegheny St., Suite 4 17740-1442. Phone: (570) 398-7200. Fax: (570) 398-7201. E-mail: am@wjsaradio.com. Web Site: www.wjsaradio.com. Licensee: Covenant Broadcasting Co. Network: Salem Radio Network. Gammon & Grange. Format: Relg. News staff: one; News: 14 hrs wkly. Target aud: General. Spec prog: Class one hr, southern gospel 2 hrs wkly. ♦John K. Hogg Jr., CEO, gen mgr & chief of engrg; Jerry G. Frear Jr., gen sls mgr; Justin S. Hogg, mus dir; Liz Brady, news dir.

WJSA-FM— Nov 1, 1984: 96.3 mhz; 4.4 kw. 777 ft. TL: N41 13 28 W77 22 48. Stereo. E-mail: fm@wjsaradio.com. Web Site: www.wjsaradio.com. News staff: one; News: 14 hrs wkly.

Johnsonburg

WJNG(FM)— July 1998: 100.5 mhz; 1.3 kw. 666 ft. TL: N41 23 11 W78 41 32. 517 Market St. 15845. Phone: (814) 965-2921. Fax: (814) 965-2921. Licensee: Strattan Broadcasting Inc. Format: Classic rock. ♦James W. Farley, gen mgr; Kevin Heinrick, opns mgr & progmg dir; Nathan Sharpe, gen sls mgr.

WKBI-FM—See Saint Marys

Johnstown

WCRO(AM)— September 1947: 1230 khz; 1 kw-U. TL: N40 19 55 W78 54 46. 222 Central Ave. 15904. Phone: (814) 533-5533. Fax: (814) 533-5698. Licensee: Greater Johnstown School District. (acq 1-11-99; $75,000). Format: Adult standards. News: 35 hrs wkly. Target aud: 45 - 64; Fastest growing and most financially secure demographically. ♦Ed Scherloch, stn mgr; Ed Sherlock, pres & opns mgr.

WFGI-FM—Listing follows WNTJ(AM).

*****WFRJ(FM)**— June 6, 1986: 88.9 mhz; 900 w. 1,063 ft. TL: N40 22 15 W78 59 02. 13 Fair Lane Dr., Suite 5, Jolette, IL 60435. Phone: (814) 322-3144. Web Site: www.familyradio.com. Licensee: Family Stations

Broadcasting & Cable Yearbook 2006
D-427

Pennsylvania

Inc. (group owner) Format: Conservative Christian. News: 6 hrs wkly. Target aud: General; every age group. ♦Harold Camping, pres; Gary Johnson, opns mgr.

WKYE(FM)—Listing follows WPRR(AM).

WNTJ(AM)— April 1925: 850 khz; 10 kw-U, DA-1. TL: N40 10 54 W78 53 20. 109 Plaza Dr. 15905. Phone: (814) 255-4186. Fax: (814) 255-6145. Licensee: Forever Broadcasting LLC. Group owner: Forever Broadcasting (acq 9-9-97; grpsl). Rep: McGavren Guild, Dome. Format: Country. Target aud: 25 plus. Spec prog: Sports 20 hrs, Pol 5 hrs wkly. ♦Carol Logan, pres; Verla Price, gen mgr & gen sls mgr; Mike Stevens, progmg dir; Rick Shepard, news dir; Jim Boxler, chief of engrg.

WFGI-FM—Co-owned with WNTJ(AM). Aug 1949: 95.5 mhz; 57 kw. Ant 1,060 ft. TL: N40 22 18 W78 58 57. Stereo. 109 Plaza Dr., Suite 2 15905. Web Site: www.key95.com. Format: Adult contemp. Target aud: 25-54. ♦Jack Michaels, progmg dir; Brian Wolfe, mus dir.

WPRR(AM)— August 1946: 1490 khz; 1 kw-U. TL: N40 19 25 W78 53 49. Box 370, Cover Hill 15907-0370. Phone: (814) 535-8554. Fax: (814) 535-8557. E-mail: mt965@mountain96-5.com. Licensee: Forever Broadcasting LLC. Group owner: Forever Broadcasting (acq 1-30-2004; $9.13 million. with co-located FM). Network: Westwood One. Rep: Clear Channel. Latham & Watkins. Format: News/talk. News staff: one; News: 15 hrs wkly. Target aud: General. ♦Ron Kight, gen mgr; John Piccirillo, gen sls mgr & natl sls mgr; Carey Togh, prom mgr; Steve Walker, opns mgr & progmg dir; Lara Mosby, mus dir; Bill Cody, news dir & pub affrs dir.

WKYE(FM)—Co-owned with WPRR(AM). Aug 14, 1973: 96.5 mhz; 50 kw. Ant 489 ft. TL: N40 19 45 W78 53 54. Stereo. Web Site: www.mountain96-5.com. Format: New country. News staff: one; News: one hr wkly. Target aud: 12-54. ♦Steve Walker, opns dir; John Piccirillo, sls dir; Tom Benson, progmg VP.

*WQEJ(FM)— 1997: 89.7 mhz; 3.3 kw. Ant 1,036 ft. TL: N40 22 17 W78 58 58. c/o WQED-FM, 4802 5th Ave., Pittsburgh 15213. Phone: (412) 622-1436. Fax: (412) 622-7073. Fax: (412) 622-1488. E-mail: radio@wqej.org. Web Site: www.wqed.org. Licensee: WQED Pittsburgh. Format: Class. ♦George L. Miles Jr., CEO & pres.

WRKW(FM)— Sept 1, 1974: 92.1 mhz; 580 w. Ant 1,043 ft. TL: N40 22 15 W78 59 02. Stereo. 109 Plaza Dr., Suite 2 15905. Phone: (814) 255-4186. Fax: (814) 255-6145. Web Site: www.rocky92.com. Licensee: Forever Broadcasting LLC. (group owner; (acq 5-1-2005; $2.73 million. with WYOT(FM) Ebensburg). Format: Rock. ♦Verla Price, gen mgr; Tina Perry, gen sls mgr; Mike Stevens, progmg dir; Rick Shepard, news dir.

WYOT(FM)—See Ebensburg

Kane

WLMI(FM)— Sept 17, 1984: 103.9 mhz; 3 kw. 300 ft. TL: N41 39 34 W78 48 42. Stereo. Box 868 16735. Secondary address: 27 Fraley St. 16735. Phone: (814) 837-9711. Fax: (814) 837-6154. E-mail: wlmifm@penn.com. Web Site: www.wlmifm.com. Licensee: Beech Tree Broadcasting Co. (acq 12-2-92; $245,000; 12-21-92). Network: ABC. Dome, Commercial Media Sales Garvey, Schubert, Barer. Format: Country. News staff: one; News: 12 hrs wkly. Target aud: 25-49; families. Spec prog: Polka one hr, bluegrass one hr wkly. ♦Charles W. Crouse, pres & gen mgr; Ginny Crouse, VP.

*WPSB(FM)— 1995: 90.1 mhz; 17 kw. 761 ft. TL: N41 37 04 W78 48 14. Stereo. c/o WPSU(FM)/WPSB(FM), Wagner Annex, University Park 16802. Phone: (814) 865-9778. Fax: (814) 865-3145. E-mail: wpsu@wpsu.edu. Web Site: wpsu.psu.edu. Licensee: The Pennsylvania State University. Format: Class, div. News staff: one; News: 35 hrs wkly. Upscale educated adults. Spec prog: Folk 10 hrs, jazz 3 hrs, blues 2 hrs wkly. ♦Ted Krichels, gen mgr; Greg Petersen, stn mgr.

Kittanning

WTYM(AM)— 1948: 1380 khz; 1 kw-D, 28 w-N. TL: N40 47 19 W79 32 05. Box 14A, R.D. 7 16201. Phone: (724) 543-1380. Fax: (724) 543-1140. E-mail: wtym@alltel.net. Web Site: www.wtym.8m.com. Licensee: Vernal Enterprises Inc. (group owner; acq 7-22-92; $85,000; FTR: 6-15-92). Haley, Bader & Potts. Format: Oldies, sports. Target aud: 20-55. Spec prog: Relg 4 hrs wkly. ♦Larry L. Schrecongost, pres, gen mgr & opns mgr; Nancy W. Schrecongost, VP; John DeFeo, gen sls mgr & chief of engrg.

Lancaster

WDAC(FM)— Dec 13, 1959: 94.5 mhz; 19 kw. 810 ft. TL: N39 53 46 W76 14 22. Stereo. Box 3022 17604. Secondary address: for UPS, Fed-Ex only:, 683 Lancaster Pike, New Providence 17560. Phone: (717) 284-4123. Fax: (717) 284-2300. Web Site: www.wdac.com. Licensee: WDAC Radio Co. Network: Network: Moody, Salem Radio Network. Wiley, Rein & Fielding. Format: Christian, talk. News staff: one; News: 8 hrs wkly. Target aud: 25-49; Evangelical Christians, families. Spec prog: Farm 4 hrs wkly. ♦Paul R. Hollinger, CEO; Richard Crawford, pres; Doug Myer, gen mgr; Mike Stike, opns mgr; John E. Eby, progmg dir.

*WFNM(FM)— May 1973: 89.1 mhz; 100 w. 150 ft. TL: N40 02 43 W76 19 14. Stereo. Box 3220, Franklin and Marshall College 17604-3003. Phone: (717) 291-4098. Fax: (717) 358-4437. Web Site: wfnm.fandm.edu. Licensee: Franklin and Marshall College. Format: Var/div. News: 4 hrs wkly. Target aud: 13-35. Spec prog: Black 6 hrs, sports talk 2 hrs, class 2 hrs, jazz 8 hrs wkly.

*WJTL(FM)— Aug 27, 1984: 90.3 mhz; 4.7 kw. Ant 198 ft. TL: N40 04 13 W76 17 19. (CP: 11.8 kw, ant 495 ft.). Stereo. Box 1614 17608. Phone: (717) 392-3690. Fax: (717) 390-2892. E-mail: contact@wjtl.com. Web Site: www.wjtl.com. Licensee: Creative Ministries Inc. (acq 11-30-90; $500,000; 12-31-90). Network: USA. Fisher, Wayland, Cooper, Leader & Zaragoza. Format: Contemp Christian. ♦Fred McNaughton, stn mgr.

WLAN(AM)— Aug 9, 1946: 1390 khz; 5 kw-D, 1 kw-N, DA-2. TL: N40 03 12 W76 20 26. Stereo. 252 N. Queen St. 17603. Phone: (717) 295-9700. Fax: (717) 295-7329. E-mail: webmaster@1390wlan.com. Web Site: www.1390wlan.com. Licensee: Clear Channel Radio Licenses Inc. Group owner: Clear Channel Communications Inc. (acq 1996; $7 million with co-located FM). Network: ABC. Rep: Clear Channel. Format: Adult standards. News staff: 3; News: 9 hrs wkly. Target aud: 35-64. ♦Dick Taylor, gen mgr & gen sls mgr.

WLAN-FM— January 1948: 96.9 mhz; 50 kw. 500 ft. TL: N40 02 52 W76 27 25. Stereo. E-mail: webmaster@fm97.com. Web Site: www.fm97.com. Rep: Clear Channel. Format: Adult contemp, Top-40. News staff: news progmg 9 hrs wkly News: 3;. Target aud: 18-54. Spec prog: Penn State sports.

*WLCH(FM)— Sept 14, 1987: 91.3 mhz; 160 w. 135 ft. TL: N40 04 13 W76 17 19. 30 N. Ann St., 1st Fl 17602. Phone: (717) 295-7996. Fax: (717) 295-7759. E-mail: radiocenter@aol.com. Licensee: Spanish American Civic Association for Equality Inc. Format: Sp, educ, div. Target aud: General; Hispanics. ♦Mayra Guevar, CEO & pres; Carlos Groupera, exec VP & mktg mgr; Enid Vazquez, gen mgr.

WLPA(AM)— 1922: 1490 khz; 600 w-U. TL: N40 03 38 W76 18 59. Stereo. Box 4368 17604. Secondary address: 1996 Auction Rd., Manheim 17545. Phone: (717) 653-0800. Phone: (800) 222-1013. Fax: (717) 653-0122. Licensee: Hall Communications Inc. (group owner; (acq 2-13-77). Network: Sporting News Radio Network. Fletcher, Heald & Hildreth. Format: Sports. News: 8 hrs wkly. Target aud: 25-54; men. ♦Bonnie H.M. Rowbotham, chmn; Arthur J. Rowbotham, pres; William S. Baldwin, sr VP & gen mgr.

WROZ(FM)—Co-owned with WLPA(AM). 1944: 101.3 mhz; 50 kw. 1,289 ft. TL: N40 02 04 W76 37 08. Stereo. E-mail: wroz@hallradio.com. Web Site: www.roseradio.com. Format: Soft adult contemp. News staff: one. Target aud: 25-54; women. ♦Tom Shannon, progmg dir; Michael C. Anthony, mus dir; Valerie Baldwin, news dir.

Lansdale

WNPV(AM)— Oct 17, 1960: 1440 khz; 2.5 kw-D, 500 w-N, DA-2. TL: N40 14 18 W75 19 00. Box 1440, 1210 Snyder Rd. 19446. Phone: (215) 855-8211. Fax: (215) 368-0180. Web Site: www.wnpv1440.com. Licensee: WNPV Inc. (acq 10-1-80). Network: Network: Westwood One, Motor Racing Net. Format: News/talk. News staff: 2; News: 20 hrs wkly. Target aud: 30 plus. Spec prog: Big band 3 hrs, relg 5 hrs, sports 6 hrs wkly. ♦John G. Skibbe, pres; Phillip N. Hunt, VP & gen mgr; Randy Brock, news dir.

Directory of Radio

Lansford

WLSH(AM)— Dec 24, 1952: 1410 khz; 5 kw-D, DA. TL: N40 50 40 W75 50 37. 2147 Market St. 18232. Phone: (570) 645-3123. Fax: (570) 645-2159. E-mail: wmgh@ptdprolog.net. Web Site: www.wmgh.com. Licensee: J-Systems Franchising Corp. (group owner; acq 1-89; $300,000;. FTR: 1-16-89). Network: Westwood One. Format: MOR. Target aud: 35-64; Mature adults. Spec prog: Big Band 4 hrs, Oldies 3 hrs wkly. ♦Harold G. Fulmer, III, CEO, chmn & pres; Christopher G. Fulmer, VP; Bill Lakatas, gen mgr.

Laporte

WCOZ(FM)— August 1998: 103.9 mhz; 6 kw. Ant 276 ft. TL: N41 26 06 W76 28 28. Stereo. Box 230, 201 Bernice Rd., Suite 2, Dushore 18614. Phone: (570) 928-7200. Fax: (570) 928-2100. E-mail: contact_us@cozy.com. Web Site: www.cozyradio.com. Licensee: Smith and Fitzgerald, Partnership (acq 5-7-01). Format: Adult contemp. News: 4 hrs wkly. Target aud: 25-54; adults. ♦Ben Smith, gen mgr & progmg VP; Cindi McCarty, adv mgr; Kevin Fitzgerald, engrg VP.

Latrobe

WCNS(AM)— Aug 11, 1956: 1480 khz; 500 w-D, 1 kw-N, DA-N. TL: N40 16 12 W79 23 13. 400 Unity St., Suite 200 15650. Phone: (724) 537-3338. Fax: (724) 539-9798. E-mail: info@wcnsradio.com. Web Site: www.1480wcns.com. Licensee: Longo Media Group. (acq 1-89). Network: Westwood One. Format: Oldies, sports. News staff: 3; News: 15 hrs wkly. Target aud: 25-54; general. Spec prog: Relg 2 hrs wkly. ♦John Longo, pres; Greg Zahornacky, stn mgr; Dow Carnahan, opns mgr & progmg dir.

WQTW(AM)— 1952: 1570 khz; 1 kw-D, 220 w-N. TL: N40 18 07 W79 21 26. Box 208, George St. 15650. Phone: (724) 532-1778. Fax: (724) 532-1779. Licensee: L. Stanley Wall. (acq 4-84; $66,000; 4-23-84). Format: Hot adult contemp. ♦L. Stanley Wall, pres & gen mgr.

Lebanon

WADV(AM)— July 4, 1976: 940 khz; 1 kw-D, 5 w-N. TL: N40 22 22 W76 21 53. Stereo. 720 E Kercher Ave. 17046. Phone: (717) 273-2611. Fax: (717) 273-7293. Licensee: WADV Radio Inc. (acq 12-4-01). Network: Moody. Format: Southern & bluegrass gospel, country. News staff: one; News: 18 hrs wkly. Target aud: 25 plus; loyal, exclusive. ♦Jennifer Taylor Kochel, pres; Earl Kochel, gen mgr; Pearl Kochel, gen mgr; Julie Kochel, opns VP.

WLBR(AM)— Nov 13, 1946: 1270 khz; 5 kw-D, 1 kw-N, DA-2. TL: N40 21 35 W76 27 30. 440 Rebecca St. 17042. Phone: (717) 272-7651. Fax: (717) 274-0161. Licensee: Lebanon Broadcasting Co. Network: ABC Information & Entertainment. Rep: Roslin. Dome Shaw Pittman. Format: News/talk. News staff: 2. Target aud: 25-64. ♦Lester P. Etter, pres; Mickey Santora, gen sls mgr; Robert D. Etter, VP, gen mgr & progmg dir; Greg Lyons, mus dir; Gordon Weise, news dir; Glenn Waybright, chief of engrg.

WQIC(FM)—Co-owned with WLBR(AM). January 1948: 100.1 mhz; 3 kw. 267 ft. TL: N40 21 37 W76 27 31. Stereo. Format: Adult contemp. Target aud: 25-54. ♦Steve Todd, progmg dir; Mike Ebersole, mus dir.

WWSM(AM)—See Annville-Cleona

Lehighton

WYNS(AM)—Licensed to Lehighton. See Allentown

Levittown-Fairless Hills

WBCB(AM)— Dec 8, 1957: 1490 khz; 1 kw-U. TL: N40 10 08 W74 57 08. 200 Magnolia Dr., Levittown 19054. Phone: (215) 949-1490. Fax: (215) 949-3671. Web Site: www.wbcb1490.com. Licensee: Progressive Broadcasting Co. (acq 11-13-92; $550,000; 11-30-92). Network: USA. Format: Community radio. Target aud: 18 plus; varied programming appeals to different age groups. Spec prog: Sports. ♦Pasquale T. Deon Sr., pres; Merrill Reese, VP & gen mgr; Erica Darragh, opns mgr; Lee Alexander, sls dir & gen sls mgr; Paul Baroli, progmg dir.

Lewisburg

WCXR(FM)— Oct 18, 1990: 103.7 mhz; 3 kw. 418 ft. TL: N40 56 07 W76 52 45. (CP: 103.7 mhz, 1.35 kw, ant 715 ft.). Stereo. 1685 Four

Stations in the U.S. — Pennsylvania

Mile Dr., Williamsport 17740. Phone: (570) 323-8200. Fax: (570) 327-9138. E-mail: dfarr54@aol.com. Licensee: South Williamsport SabreCom Inc. Group owner: Backyard Broadcasting LLC (acq 12-1-02; grpsl). Network: ABC. Rep: Christal. Format: Classic rock. News staff: one. Target aud: 25-54. ◆ Barry Drake, pres; Robin Smith, CFO; Dan Farr, gen mgr.

*WGRC(FM)— Apr 22, 1988: 91.3 mhz; 3 kw. Ant 321 ft. TL: N40 56 40 W76 52 45. Stereo. 101 Armory Blvd. 17837-9504. Phone: (570) 523-1190. Fax: (570) 523-1114. E-mail: email@wgrc.com. Web Site: www.wgrc.com. Licensee: Salt and Light Media Ministries Inc. Network: Salem Radio Network. Miller & Neely. Format: Christian, adult contemp. News staff: 3; News: 16 hrs wkly. Target aud: 25-54; young to middle-aged adult. ◆ Larry Weidman, gen mgr; Jim Diehl, progmg dir; Jenna Lunt, news dir; Lamar Smith, chief of engrg.

*WVBU-FM— October 1965: 90.5 mhz; 500 w. -120 ft. TL: N40 57 18 W76 52 46. (CP: 225 w, ant 66 ft.). Stereo. Box C-3956, Bucknell Univ., 701 Moore Ave. 17837. Phone: (570) 577-2000. Phone: (570) 577-3824. Fax: (570) 577-1174. E-mail: wvbu@bucknell.edu. Web Site: www.orgs.bucknell.edu/wvbu. Licensee: Bucknell University. Format: Modern Rock. News: 7 hrs wkly. Target aud: 18-23; college students. Spec prog: Jazz 3 hrs, dance/club 6 hrs, prison request 2 hrs, modern/new age one hr wkly.

Lewistown

WCHX(FM)— July 1, 1987: 105.5 mhz; 3 kw. 817 ft. TL: N40 39 43 W77 34 28. (CP: 465 w, ant 816 ft.). Stereo. Box 911 17044. Secondary address: 114 N. Logan Blvd., Burnham 17009. Phone: (717) 242-1493. Fax: (717) 242-3764. Licensee: Mifflin County Communications Inc. Network: ABC Information & Entertainment. Wilkinson Barker Knauer. Format: Classic rock. News staff: one; News: 10 hrs wkly. Target aud: 25-54; mature, affluent, middle & upper class adults. ◆ Anna Hain, pres & stn mgr; Maria Stringfellow, opns mgr, sls dir & gen sls mgr; Eric Lane, progmg dir.

WIEZ(AM)— June 1, 1941: 670 khz; 5.4 kw-D. TL: N40 36 30 W77 34 45. Box 667 17044. Secondary address: 12 E. Market St. 2nd Floor 17044. Phone: (717) 248-6757. Fax: (717) 248-6759. E-mail: wiez@meradio.com. Licensee: First Media Radio LLC (group owner; acq 3-28-01; grpsl). Network: ABC Information & Entertainment. Rep: Dome. Format: News, info. News staff: 2; News: 12 hrs wkly. Target aud: 45 plus; adults who control the area's disposable income. ◆ Pete Herman, gen mgr; Jeff Stevens, opns mgr; Mary Lee Schaeffer, news dir.

*WJRC(FM)— July 1996: 90.9 mhz; 100 w. 1,128 ft. TL: N40 34 58 W77 29 48. Stereo. 101 Armory Blvd., Lewisburg 17837-0279. Phone: (570) 523-1190. Fax: (570) 523-1114. E-mail: email@wgrc.com. Web Site: www.wgrc.com. Licensee: Salt and Light Media Ministries Inc. Network: Salem Radio Network. Miller & Neely. Format: Contemp Christian. News staff: 3; News: 9 hrs wkly. Target aud: 25-54. ◆ Larry Weidman, gen mgr; Jenna Lunt, news dir; Lamar Smith, chief of engrg.

WKVA(AM)— Dec 4, 1949: 920 khz; 1 kw-D, 500 w-N, DA-N. TL: N40 34 45 W77 34 18. Box 911 17044. Secondary address: 114 N. Logan Blvd., Burnham 17009. Phone: (717) 242-1055. Phone: (717) 242-1495. Fax: (717) 242-3764. E-mail: wkva@oldies920.com. Web Site: www.oldies920.com. Licensee: Mifflin County Communications Inc. (acq 2-18-98; $277,692). Putbrese, Hunsaker & Trent, P. Format: Oldies. News staff: 2; News: 31 hrs wkly. Target aud: 25-54; blue collar mix of agricultural & industrial adults. ◆ Anna A. Hain, pres.

WMRF-FM— Oct 1, 1964: 95.7 mhz; 3.9 kw. 407 ft. TL: N40 36 30 W77 34 45. Stereo. 12 E. Market St., 2nd Floor 17044. Phone: (717) 248-6757. Fax: (717) 248-6759. E-mail: merfradio@acsworld.net. Web Site: www.merfradio.com. Licensee: First Media Radio LLC (group owner; acq 5-14-01; grpsl). Format: Hot adult contemp. News staff: 2; News: 8 hrs wkly. Target aud: 18-44. ◆ Peter Herman, gen mgr; Jeff Stevens, opns dir, progmg dir & progmg mgr; Mary Lee Sheaffer, news dir.

Lincoln University

*WWLU(FM)— Aug 1, 1975: 88.7 mhz; 10 w. 100 ft. Box 179, Lincoln Univ. 19352. Phone: (610) 932-1876. Fax: (9610) 932-1095. Licensee: Lincoln University. Format: Urban contemp, hip hop.

Linesville

WMVL(FM)— May 4, 1970: 101.7 mhz; 1.4 kw. Ant 554 ft. TL: N41 42 38 W80 16 29. Stereo. Box 846, Meadville 16335. Secondary address: 16271Conneaut Lake Rd., Ste 102, Meadville 16335. Phone: (814) 337-8440. Fax: (814) 333-2562. E-mail: wmvl@zoominternet.net. Licensee: Vilkie Communications Inc. (acq 4-1-2003; $330,000). Network: ABC. Regional Reps, CLE, OH Hogan & Hartson. Format: Oldies. News: 8 hrs wkly. Target aud: 29 plus. ◆ Eugene Vilkie, VP; Joseph M. Vilkie, pres & gen mgr; Chuck Stopp, progmg dir; Dave Hanahan, sls; Dave Voisin, sls; Jim Jewell, sls.

Lock Haven

WBPZ(AM)— Feb 20, 1947: 1230 khz; 1 kw-U. TL: N41 08 03 W77 28 09. Box 420 17745. Secondary address: 21 E. Main St. 17745. Phone: (570) 748-4038. Fax: (570) 748-0092. Licensee: Lipez Broadcasting Corp. (acq 3-27-86). Rep: Keystone (unwired net), Dome. Format: Oldies. News staff: one; News: 10 hrs wkly. Target aud: General. Spec prog: Loc sports. ◆ John Lipez, pres & gen mgr; John Lupez, gen sls mgr; Randy Dorey, progmg dir; Bill Daney, mus dir; Mark Sohmer, news dir; Dennis Sherman, chief of engrg.

WSNU(FM)— Co-owned with WBPZ(AM). September 1965: 92.1 mhz; 3 kw. 255 ft. TL: N41 08 49 W77 29 16. (CP: Ant 328 ft.). Stereo. Format: Adult contemp. News staff: one; News: 6 hrs wkly. Target aud: 21-48.

Loretto

WWGE(AM)— Dec 7, 1963: 1400 khz; 1 kw-U. TL: N40 30 12 W78 38 10. Box 88, Ebensburg 15931. Secondary address: 104 S. Center St., Suite 401, Ebensburg 15931. Phone: (814) 255-9943. Fax: (814) 255-3343. Web Site: www.edge1400.com. Licensee: Pennsylvania Radiowerks LLC (acq 10-15-98; $100,000). Network: Jones Radio Networks. Format: News/talk, sports. ◆ Rev. Michael H. Yeager, pres; Jennifer Strelnik, gen mgr.

Mansfield

WNBQ(FM)— June 1999: 92.3 mhz; 800 w. 643 ft. TL: N41 53 53 W77 05 38. Box 98, Wellsboro 16901. Secondary address: R.R. 7, Rt. 6 Box 198-B, Wellsboro 16901. Phone: (570) 724-1490. Fax: (570) 724-6971. E-mail: wnbt@ptb.net. Web Site: www.wnbt.net. Licensee: Farm & Home Broadcasting Co. Group owner: Allegheny Mountain Network Stations Network: Westwood One. Dome & Assoc. . Borsari & Paxson Format: Bright adult contemporary. ◆ Cary Simpson, pres; Al Harer, gen mgr.

*WNTE(FM)— Sept 15, 1968: 89.5 mhz; 115 w. -320. TL: N41 48 22 W77 04 27. Box 84, South Hall, Mansfield Univ. 16933. Phone: (570) 662-4653. Fax: (570) 662-4654. Web Site: mustuweb.mnsfld.edu. Licensee: Mansfield University (acq 9-15-78). Format: AOR, Top-40. Target aud: 17-25; college students/community. Spec prog: Black 5 hrs, jazz 2 hrs wkly.

Markleysburg

*WLOG(FM)— 2002: . Stn currently dark 89.1 mhz; 100 w vert. Ant 328 ft. TL: N39 43 32 W79 28 53. Box 5459, Twin Falls, ID 83301. Phone: (208) 733-3551. Fax: (208) 733-3548. Licensee: Edgewater Broadcasting Inc. (acq 5-27-2005; $10,000). ◆ Clark Parrish, pres.

Martinsburg

WJSM(AM)— Feb 27, 1968: 1110 khz; 1 kw-D. TL: N40 18 14 W78 15 59. Box 87, Rt. 2 16662. Phone: (814) 793-2188. Fax: (814) 793-9727. Licensee: Martinsburg Broadcasting Inc. (acq 10-1-89). Harold McCombs. Format: Relg, news, talk. Target aud: General. Spec prog: Farm one hr wkly. ◆ Deborah J. Walters, opns mgr; Larry S. Walters, pres, gen mgr & progmg dir; Bill Reed, news dir.

WJSM-FM— Apr 19, 1965: 92.7 mhz; 640 w. 964 ft. TL: N40 17 37 W78 15 38. Network: USA. Format: Relg, news/talk, gospel.

WKMC(AM)—See Roaring Spring

Masontown

*WRIJ(FM)— November 1990: 106.9 mhz; 3 kw. 328 ft. TL: N39 47 15 W79 59 20. Stereo. Box 540, 34 Springs Rd., Grantsville, MD 21536. Phone: (301) 895-3292. Fax: (301) 895-3293. E-mail: hesalive@hesalive.net. Web Site: www.hesalive.net. Licensee: He's Alive Inc. (group owner) Network: USA. Format: Gospel, Christian, relg, adult contemp. Target aud: 18-35. ◆ Dewayne Johnson, pres.

*WYFU(FM)— 2003: 88.5 mhz; 16 kw vert. Ant 328 ft. TL: N39 47 15 W79 59 20. Bible Broadcasting Network, 11530 Carmel Commons Blvd., Charlotte, NC 28226. Phone: (704) 523-5555. Fax: (704) 522-1967. E-mail: bbn@bbnradio.org. Web Site: www.bbnradio.org. Licensee: Bible Broadcasting Network Inc. Group owner: Bible Broadcasting Network (acq 2-12-99; $250,000). Format: Christian. ◆ Richard Johnson, gen mgr.

McConnellsburg

WEEO-FM— 1997: 103.7 mhz; 135 w. 1,555 ft. TL: N39 55 25 W77 57 20. 37 South Main St., Suite 103, Chambersburg 17201. Phone: (717) 709-0800. Phone: (717) 709-0801. Fax: (717) 709-0802. Web Site: revolution1037.net. Licensee: Allegheny Mountain Network. Group owner: Allegheny Mountain Network Stations (acq 10-95; $18,000). Dome Borsari & Paxson. Format: Modern Rock. ◆ John F. Simpson, CEO & pres.

WFYL(FM)— December 1976: 1530 khz; 1 kw-D, 250 w-CH. TL: N39 55 50 W77 58 58. (CP: COL King of Prussia. 1180 khz; 510 w-D. TL: N40 04 47 W75 19 50). 37 S. Main St., Suite 103, Chambersburg 17201. Phone: (941) 225-0061. Fax: (941) 255-0061. Licensee: Langer Broadcasting Group L.L.C. (group owner). Format: Talk. ◆ Helen Lenza, gen mgr.

*WWCF(FM)—Not on air, target date: unknown: 88.7 mhz; 100 w. Ant -10 ft. TL: N39 53 46 W78 02 19. 611 Longview Rd. 17233-9740. Phone: (717) 485-5526. Licensee: Morris Broadcasting & Communications Inc. Format: Children. ◆ Linda F. Morris, pres; Glenn Morris, gen mgr.

McKean

WQHZ(FM)—See Erie

McKeesport

WEDO(AM)— 1947: 810 khz; 1 kw-D. TL: N40 21 52 W79 48 49. 1985 Lincoln Way, White Oak 15131. Phone: (412) 664-4431. Fax: (412) 664-1236. Web Site: www.am81wedo.com. Licensee: 810 Inc. (acq 5-72). Format: Talk, health, var. Target aud: 25-54. Spec prog: Relg one hr, Slovenian one hr, Hungarian one hr, Slovak one hr, Greek one hr, Croation one hr, Serbian one hr, Bulgarian one hr, It one hr, Lithuanian one hr, Pol one hr, Sp one hr wkly. ◆ Judith Baron, pres; John James, VP & gen mgr; Ron Zosak, opns dir.

WPTT(AM)— April 1947: 1360 khz; 5 kw-D, 1 kw-N, DA-N. TL: N40 24 30 W79 55 40. 3rd Fl., 900 Parish St., Pittsburgh 15220. Phone: (412) 875-9500. Fax: (412) 875-9474. Web Site: www.1360wptt.com. Licensee: Renda Broadcasting Corp. of Nevada. (acq 9-10-97). Network: ABC. Rep: McGavren Guild. Format: News/talk. News: 15 hrs wkly. Target aud: 25-54. Spec prog: Oldies 9 hrs, polka 2 hrs wkly. ◆ Tony Renda Sr., CEO; Tony Renda Jr., gen mgr.

Pennsylvania   Directory of Radio

Meadville

WARC(FM)— Feb 3, 1963: 90.3 mhz; 150 w. 86 ft. TL: N41 38 55 W80 08 45. (CP: 340 w, ant 75 ft.). Stereo. Box C, Allegheny College, 520 N. Main St. 16335. Phone: (814) 332-5275 (studio). Phone: (814) 332-3376. Web Site: www.warcallegheny.org. Licensee: Allegheny College. Format: Alternative, div. Spec prog: Black 8 hrs, class 10 hrs, jazz 4 hrs wkly. ♦Phil Denman, gen mgr.

WGYY(FM)—Listing follows WMGW(AM).

WMGW(AM)— 1947: 1490 khz; 1 kw-U. TL: N41 37 53 W80 10 37. Box 397, Downtown Mall 16335. Phone: (814) 724-1111. Fax: (814) 333-9628. Web Site: www.radio@zoominternet.net. Licensee: Forever Broadcasting LLC. Group owner: Forever Broadcasting (acq 7-20-00; grpsl). Network: ABC Information & Entertainment. Format: News/talk, sports, info. Target aud: 25-54. ♦Terry Dietz, gen mgr & gen sls mgr; Dave Galentine, progmg dir.

WGYY(FM)—Co-owned with WMGW(AM). 1947: 100.3 mhz; 20 kw. 587 ft. TL: N41 37 53 W80 10 37. Stereo. Web Site: www.radio@zoominternet.net. Network: Network: ABC Daytime Direction, ABC Information & Entertainment. Format: Country.

WVME(FM)— 2002: 91.9 mhz; 4.4 kw. Ant 308 ft. TL: N41 37 50 W80 10 38. WCRF Radio, 9756 Barr Rd., Cleveland, OH 44141. Phone: (440) 526-1111. Fax: (440) 526-1319. Web Site: wcrfradio.org. Licensee: The Moody Bible Institute of Chicago. (group owner) Network: Salem Radio Network. Format: Christian, religious. ♦Dick Lee, gen mgr; Phil Villareal, progmg dir.

Mechanicsburg

WTPA(FM)— Nov 1, 1978: 93.5 mhz; 1.25 kw. 718 ft. TL: N40 10 38 W76 52 38. Stereo. Cumulus Media, 2300 Vartan Way, Harrisburg 17110-9720. Phone: (717) 238-1041. Fax: (717) 234-4842. Web Site: www.935WTPA.com. Licensee: Cumulus Licensing Corp. Group owner: Cumulus Media Inc. (acq 2000; grpsl). Wilkinson Barker Knauer. Format: Active rock. Target aud: 18-49. ♦Ron Giovaniello, stn mgr; John O'Dea, opns VP; Karen Richards, sls VP; John Butler, gen sls mgr; Diane Sohanuch, prom dir; Chris James, progmg dir; Dave Supplee, chief of engrg.

Media

WPHI-FM— November 1982: 100.3 mhz; 35 kw. Ant 600 ft. TL: N39 58 29 W75 25 22. (CP: 17 kw, ant 863 ft. TL: N40 02 36 W75 14 33). Stereo. 1000 River Rd., Suite 400, Conshohocken 19428-2437. Phone: (610) 276-1100. Fax: (610) 276-1139. E-mail: cschofield@radio.one.com. Web Site: www.1003thebeaatphilly.com. Licensee: Radio One Licenses LLC. Group owner: Radio One Inc. (acq 11-8-2001; grpsl). Format: Rhythm and blues. News staff: one. Target aud: 18-44; savvy suburban educated professional. ♦Chester Schofield, gen mgr; Helen Little, opns mgr & chief of engrg.

Mercer

WLLF(FM)— January 1985: 96.7 mhz; 1.4 kw. Ant 485 ft. TL: N41 18 43 W80 16 39. Stereo. 4040 Simon Rd., Youngstown, OH 44512. Phone: (724) 346-4113. Fax: (330) 783-0060. E-mail: jbilo@theradiocenter. Web Site: www.cumulus.com. Licensee: Cumulus Licensing Corp. Group owner: Cumulus Media Inc. (acq 3-15-00; grpsl). Network: Jones Radio Networks. Format: Soft rock. ♦Clyde Bass, gen mgr; Joe Bilo, natl sls mgr & news dir; Bob Popa, progmg dir; Wes Boyd, chief of engrg.

WWIZ(FM)— October 1972: 103.9 mhz; 3 kw. 300 ft. TL: N41 12 10 W80 21 30. Stereo. 4040 Simon Rd., Youngstown, OH 44512. Phone: (330) 783-1000. Fax: (330) 783-0060. Web Site: www.realrock104.com. Licensee: Cumulus Licensing Corp. Group owner: Cumulus Media Inc. (acq 3-15-00; grpsl). Rep: Allied Radio Partners. Format: Active rock. Target aud: 25-54. ♦Clyde Bass, gen mgr.

Mercersburg

WPPT(FM)— Mar 23, 1976: 92.1 mhz; 3.3 kw. 295 ft. TL: N39 48 34 W77 48 22. (CP: 2.7 kw, ant 465 ft.). Stereo. Box 788, 10960 John Wayne Dr., Greencastle 17225. Phone: (717) 597-9200. Fax: (717) 597-9210. E-mail: webmaster@wayz.com. Web Site: www.star921fm.com. Licensee: M. Belmont VerStandig Inc. Group owner: VerStandig Broadcasting (acq 10-1-93; $1.6 million. with WCBG(AM) Chambersburg; FTR: 9-6-93). Network: ABC Daytime Direction. Leventhal, Senter &

Lerman. Format: Rock adult contemp, news/talk. News staff: one; News: 6 hrs wkly. Target aud: 25-54; double income households. ♦Dottie Hedglin, gen mgr.

Mexico

WJUN(AM)— Sept 8, 1955: 1220 khz; 1 kw-D, 46 w-N. TL: N40 32 06 W77 20 26. Box 209, Old Rt. 22 E. 17056. Phone: (717) 436-2135. Fax: (717) 436-8155. Licensee: Starview Media Inc. (acq 11-16-89; grpsl; 12-19-88). Format: Sports. Target aud: 25-54. Spec prog: Gospel 3 hrs, relg 6 hrs wkly. ♦Douglas George, pres; Curt Dreibelbis, gen mgr & gen sls mgr; Dan Roland, news dir; John Hess, chief of engrg.

WJUN-FM— July 4, 1989: 92.5 mhz; 440 w. Ant 1,181 ft. TL: N40 34 58 W77 29 48. Stereo. Format: Country. ♦Mel Thomas, progmg dir.

Meyersdale

WQZS(FM)— 1992: 93.3 mhz; 630 w. 964 ft. TL: N39 47 49 W79 10 05. 128 Hunsrick Rd. 15552. Phone: (814) 634-9111. Fax: (814) 634-0882. E-mail: helenwahl27@hotmail.com. Licensee: Roger Wahl. Format: Oldies. News staff: one. Target aud: 25-60; females 60%, males 40%. Spec prog: Gospel 5 hrs wkly. ♦Helen E. Wahl, gen mgr & progmg dir; Jessy Chabol, gen sls mgr.

Middletown

WMSS(FM)— Sept 7, 1978: 91.1 mhz; 1.35 w. -69 ft. TL: N40 11 52 W76 43 30. Stereo. 214 Race St. 17057. Phone: (717) 948-9136. E-mail: sales@wmssfm.com. Web Site: www.wmssfm.com. Licensee: Middletown Area School District. Format: Adult contemp, progsv, educ. News: one hr wkly. Target aud: General. Spec prog: Sports 5 hrs, relg 10 hrs wkly. ♦John Wilsbach, gen mgr; Maureen Denis, opns dir; Steve Leedy, opns mgr.

WZXM(FM)—Not on air, target date: unknown: 88.7 mhz; 3.1 kw. Ant 485 ft. TL: N40 04 29 W76 48 02. Box 186, Sellersville 18960. Phone: (215) 721-2141. Fax: (215) 721-9811. E-mail: wordfm@wordfm.org. Web Site: www.wordfm.org. Licensee: Four Rivers Community Broadcasting Corp. Format: Contemp Christian. ♦Charles Loughery, pres; Charlie Loughery, gen mgr; Dave Baker, VP & stn mgr.

Mifflinburg

WWBE(FM)— 1975: 98.3 mhz; 1.4 kw. 482 ft. TL: N40 53 27 W76 59 54. Stereo. Rd. 1, Box 90, Selinsgrove 17870-0090. Secondary address: Rt. 204 & State School Rd., Selinsgrove 17870-0090. Phone: (570) 374-8819. Fax: (570) 374-7444. E-mail: bigcountryrequest@hotmail.com. Web Site: www.bigcountrynow.com. Licensee: MMP License LLC. Group owner: MAX Media L.L.C. (acq 10-17-03; grpsl). Network: Network: Westwood One, Jones Radio Networks. Rep: Dome. Format: Country. News staff: one; News: 2 hrs wkly. Target aud: 25-54. Spec prog: Gospel 2 hrs wkly. ♦Scott Richards, gen mgr; Dawn Marie, opns mgr & progmg dir; Greg Adair, gen sls mgr; Ted Koopen, chief of engrg.

Mifflintown

WQJU(FM)— Oct 15, 1985: 107.1 mhz; 370 w. Ant 1,302 ft. TL: N40 34 20 W77 30 51. 2020 Cato Ave., State College 16801. Phone: (814) 237-9857. E-mail: mail@cpci.org. Licensee: Central Pennsylvania Christian Institute. (acq 1-22-93; $132,500; 2-15-93). Network: Network: Moody, USA. Format: Christian. News staff: one; News: 8 hrs wkly. Target aud: 30-55; adults, family oriented. ♦Mark Van Ouse, gen mgr & stn mgr.

Mill Hall

WVRT(FM)— Aug 20, 1979: 97.7 mhz; 6 kw. Ant 295 ft. TL: N41 13 14 W77 16 39. Stereo. 1559 W. 4th St., Williamsport 17701. Phone: (570) 327-1400. Fax: (570) 327-8156. E-mail: kcote@clearchannel.com. Web Site: www.variety977.com. Licensee: Clear Channel Radio Licenses, Inc. Group owner: Clear Channel Communications Inc. (acq 3-12-01; $1.5 million). Rep: Christal. Format: Hot adult contemp. Target aud: 18-49. ♦Karen Cote, gen sls mgr & adv mgr; Tom Scott, progmg dir; Mike Myer, engrg dir.

Millersburg

WQLV(FM)— Feb 24, 1992: 98.9 mhz; 780 w. 895 ft. TL: N40 30 18 W77 07 03. Stereo. 234 Union St. 17061. Phone: (717) 692-2193. Fax: (717) 692-2080. E-mail: wqlv@love99.com. Web Site: www.love99.com. Licensee: Hepco Communications Inc. Format: Soft adult contemp. News: 4 hrs wkly. Target aud: 25-60. Spec prog: High school sports 6 hrs wkly. ♦James F. Hepler, pres & gen mgr.

Millersville

WIXQ(FM)— 1978: 91.7 mhz; 129 w. 69 ft. TL: N39 59 53 W76 21 20. Box 1002, Millersville Univ. 17551. Phone: (717) 872-3518. Phone: (717) 871-2317. Fax: (717) 872-3383. E-mail: comments@wixg.com. Web Site: www.wixq.com. Licensee: Millersville University. Format: Progsv, Black, Diversified. News: one hr wkly. Target aud: 18-24; college students. Spec prog: Jazz 2 hrs wkly. ♦Greg Park, stn mgr; Paul Galvin, prom dir; Steve Entrekin, progmg dir.

Millvale

WAMO(AM)—Licensed to Millvale. See Pittsburgh

Milton

WMLP(AM)— Oct 27, 1955: 1380 khz; 1 kw-D, 18 w-N. TL: N40 59 52 W76 52 17. Box 334 17847. Secondary address: 8811 Westbranch Hwy., Lewisburg 17837. Phone: (570) 568-1380. Fax: (570) 568-1300. E-mail: valley@wvly.com. Web Site: www.wvly.com. Licensee: Milton-Lewisburg Broadcasting Inc. (acq 6-1-94; $900,000 with co-located FM; 6-6-94). Rep: Dome. Commercial Media Sales. Format: Talk. News staff: one; News: 11 hrs wkly. Target aud: 25-54. ♦Donald C. Steese, VP, gen mgr, opns VP & progmg VP; John H. Yingling, pres, stn mgr, gen sls mgr & news dir; John Callahan, pub affrs dir; Joe Portelli, chief of engrg.

WVLY-FM—Co-owned with WMLP(AM). Oct 1, 1967: 100.9 mhz; 1.3 kw. Ant 715 ft. TL: N40 57 12 W76 45 05. Stereo. Web Site: www.wvly.com. Format: Adult contemp. Target aud: 25-54; medium to upper income college grads. Spec prog: Jazz 3 hrs wkly. ♦John H. Yingling, adv mgr.

Monroeville

WPGR(AM)— Sept 27, 1964: 1510 khz; 1 kw-D, DA. TL: N40 26 03 W79 46 54. 960 Penn Ave., Suite 200, Pittsburgh 15222. Secondary address: Sheridan Broadcasting Co., 960 Penn Ave., Pittsburgh 15222. Phone: (412) 471-2181. Fax: (412) 391-3559. E-mail: mdouglass@sbcol.com. Web Site: www.wamo.com. Licensee: MCL/MCM-Inc. (group owner; acq 9-28-01; $625,000). Format: Urban gospel. Target aud: 25-54; middle class & higher income households. Spec prog: Relg 6 hrs wkly. ♦Ronald Davenport Jr., chmn & pres; Michael Douglass, gen mgr.

Montrose

WPEL(AM)— May 30, 1953: 1250 khz; 1 kw-D. TL: N41 51 16 W75 51 50. Box 248, 9 Locust St. 18801. Phone: (570) 278-2811. Fax: (570) 278-1442. E-mail: mail@wpel.org. Licensee: Montrose Broadcasting Corp. (group owner) Network: AP Network News. Gammon & Grange. Format: Relg. News: 7 hrs wkly. Target aud: General; families. Spec prog: Class one hr, farm one hr wkly. ♦Larry Souder, pres & gen mgr; Lloyd Sheldon, opns mgr; LaVerne Sollick, prom mgr; Robert Brigham, chief of engrg.

WPEL-FM— June 5, 1961: 96.5 mhz; 57 kw. 459 ft. TL: N41 51 16 W75 51 50. Stereo. Web Site: www.mail@wpel.org. Network: Moody. Format: btfl mus. News: 12 hrs wkly. Target aud: General.

Mount Carmel

WSPI(FM)— March 1993: 99.7 mhz; 790 w. 646 ft. TL: N40 49 09 W76 27 45. 612 N. Shamokin St., Shamokin 17872. Phone: (570) 644-0700. Fax: (570) 644-2232. E-mail: mail@litefm.us. Web Site: www.litefm.us. Licensee: H & P Communications Ltd. (acq 12-28-92; $124,000;. FTR: 1-25-93). Format: Adult contemp. Target aud: 25-65. ♦Gene Picarella, CEO & gen mgr; Jesse James, stn mgr, gen sls mgr, rgnl sls mgr, mktg dir & chief of engrg; Rick Brody, progmg dir.

Broadcasting & Cable Yearbook 2006

Developers & Brokers of Radio Properties

contact American Media Services
at our suite:
Philadelphia Marriott Downtown
215-625-2900
843-972-2200
americanmediaservices.com
Charleston, SC
Dallas, TX · Chicago, Il · Austin, TX

American Media Services, LLC

Mount Pocono

WPLY(AM)— Apr 8, 1981: 960 khz; 1 kw-D, 24 w-N, DA-2. TL: N41 04 41 W75 23 33. 22 S. 6th St., Stroudsburg 18360. Phone: (570) 421-2100. Fax: (570) 421-2040. Licensee: Nassau Broadcasting II LLC. Group owner: Nassau Broadcasting Partners L.P. (acq 6-28-2000). Format: Oldies. ♦ Rick Musselman, gen mgr.

Mount Union

WXOT(FM)— May 24, 1989: 99.5 mhz; 300 w. Ant 1,440 ft. TL: N40 24 53 W77 54 13. Stereo. R.R. 4, Box 160 A, Huntington 16526. Phone: (814) 643-9620. Fax: (814) 643-9625. Web Site: www.hot100radio.com. Licensee: Megahertz Licenses LLC. Group owner: Forever Broadcasting (acq 3-13-2002; $875,000. with WHUN(AM) Huntingdon). Commercial Media Sales. Format: CHR. Target aud: 25-54; community-minded adults. ♦ Dave Davies, gen mgr.

Mountain Top

WBHT(FM)— September 1992: 97.1 mhz; 500 w. 1,102 ft. TL: N41 10 57 W75 52 19. 600 Baltimore Dr., Wilkes-Barre 18702. Phone: (570) 824-9000. Fax: (570) 820-0520. Web Site: www.97bht.com. Licensee: Citadel Broadcasting Co. Group owner: Citadel Broadcasting Co. (acq 10-23-98; grpsl). Cohn & Marks. Format: CHR. Target aud: 18-34. ♦ Taylor Walet, gen mgr; Jules Riley, opns mgr; Mark McKay, progmg dir; Bill Palmeri, sls; Mike Jarvie, sls.

Muncy

WBZD-FM—Licensed to Muncy. See Williamsport

Murrysville

***WRWJ(FM)**— July 1994: 88.1 mhz; 250 w. 243 ft. TL: N40 28 51 W79 43 26. Box 540, 34 Springs Rd., Grantsville, MD 21536-0540. Phone: (301) 895-3292. Fax: (301) 895-3293. E-mail: hesalive@hesalive.net. Web Site: www.hesalive.net. Licensee: He's Alive Inc. Network: USA. Format: Gospel, Christian, relg, adult contemp. Target aud: 18-35. ♦ Dewayne Johnson, pres.

Nanticoke

WNAK(AM)— February 1947: 730 khz; 1 kw-D, 38 w-N. TL: N41 13 10 W75 59 28. Stereo. 84 S. Prospect St. 18634. Phone: (570) 735-0730. Fax: (570) 735-4844. Licensee: Group B Licensee LLC. Group owner: Route 81 Radio LLC (acq 12-2-2003; $475,000). Rep: Katz Radio. Format: MOR, btfl mus, nostalgia. Target aud: 35 plus. Spec prog: Relg 8 hrs wkly. ♦ Lloyd B. Roach, pres; Margie McQuillin, stn mgr.

WQFM(FM)— Oct 31, 1973: 92.1 mhz; 280 w. 1,056 ft. TL: N41 10 59 W75 52 31. Stereo. 149 Penn Ave., Scranton 18503. Phone: (570) 346-6555. Fax: (570) 346-6038. E-mail: oldies@oldiesfm.com. Web Site: www.oldiesfm.com. Licensee: The Scranton Times L.P. Group owner: Shamrock Communications Inc. (acq 8-10-94). Rep: Roslin. Format: Oldies. News staff: one; News: 5 hrs wkly. Target aud: 25-54. Spec prog: Pol 3 hrs wkly. ♦ William R. Lynett, CEO; Jim Loftus, gen mgr.

***WSFX(FM)**— Oct 25, 1987: 89.1 mhz; 100 w. 50 ft. TL: N41 11 42 W75 59 28. Stereo. Luzerne County Community College, Prospect St. & Middle Rd. 18634. Phone: (570) 740-0632. Fax: (570) 740-0605. Licensee: Luzerne County Community College. Format: Div. Target aud: 16-25; college age alternative mus audience. ♦ Ron Reino, gen mgr.

Nanty Glo

***WLGY(FM)**—Not on air, target date: unknown: 90.7 mhz; 750 w vert. Ant 551 ft. TL: N40 30 20 W78 48 12. Box 2440, Tupelo, MS 38803-2440. Phone: (662) 844-8888. Fax: (662) 842-6791. Licensee: American Family Association. ♦ Marvin Sanders, gen mgr.

New Berlin

***WBGM(FM)**— September 1996: 88.1 mhz; 550 w. 417 ft. TL: N40 53 27 W76 59 54. 8 E. Market St., Danville 17821. Phone: (570) 275-1570. Fax: (570) 275-4071. E-mail: info@wpgm.org. Licensee: Montrose Broadcasting Corp. (group owner) Format: Relg, Christian. ♦ George Vacca, gen mgr; Deanna Force, mus dir.

New Castle

WJST(AM)— Oct 23, 1938: 1280 khz; 4.9 kw-D, 1 kw-N, DA-N. TL: N40 57 14 W80 19 05. 219 Savannah Gardner Rd. 16101-5546. Phone: (724) 346-5070. Fax: (724) 654-3101. Licensee: Forever Broadcasting LLC. Group owner: Forever Broadcasting (acq 6-30-2004; grpsl). Network: ABC. Rep: Dome, Rgnl Reps. Format: Oldies. Target aud: 30 plus. Spec prog: Black one hr, class one hr wkly. ♦ Scott D. Cohagan, gen mgr.

WKST(AM)— Aug 25, 1968: 1200 khz; 5 kw-D, 1 kw-N, DA-N. TL: N40 56 22 W80 23 38. 219 Savanah Gardner Rd. 16101. Phone: (724) 346-5070. Fax: (724) 654-3101. Web Site: www.wkst.com. Licensee: Forever Broadcasting LLC. Group owner: Forever Broadcasting (acq 6-30-2004; grpsl). Commercial Media Sales. Format: Nesw/talk, sports. News staff: 2; News: 7 hrs wkly. Target aud: 34 plus. Spec prog: Ger one hr, Pol one hr, Greek one hr wkly. ♦ Scott D. Cohagan, gen mgr; Ken Hlebovy, progmg dir; Wade Sutton, news dir.

***WVMN(FM)**— Nov 22, 1995: 90.1 mhz; 2 kw. Ant 236 ft. TL: N41 00 47 W80 17 36. c/o Radio Stn WCRF(FM), 9756 Barr Rd., Cleveland, OH 44141. Phone: (440) 526-1111. Fax: (440) 526-1319. E-mail: wcrf@moody.edu. Web Site: wcrf.mbn.org. Licensee: Moody Bible Institute of Chicago. (group owner) Network: Salem Radio Network. Format: Inspirational. Target aud: 25-55. ♦ Richard Lee, gen mgr & stn mgr.

New Kensington

WGBN(AM)— October 1940: 1150 khz; 1 kw-D, 70 w-N, DA-1. TL: N40 34 24 W79 46 58. 560 7th St. 15068. Phone: (724) 337-3588. Fax: (724) 337-1318. Licensee: Pentecostal Temple Development Corp. (acq 11-3-92; 11-23-92). Network: USA. Rep: Dome. Fletcher, Heald & Hildreth. Format: Gospel. News staff: one; News: 19 hrs wkly. Target aud: 30 plus; older, upscale. Spec prog: Pol 3 hrs, It 2 hrs, Irish 2 hrs, relg 2 hrs wkly. ♦ Lauren Mann, gen mgr; Stacy Taylor, asst music dir; Del King, chief of engrg.

WPGB(FM)—See Pittsburgh

WZPT(FM)— Aug 17, 1967: 100.7 mhz; 17 kw. Ant 850 ft. TL: N40 29 43 W80 00 18. Stereo. 651 Holiday Dr., Foster Plaza Five, Pittsburgh 15220. Phone: (412) 920-9400. Fax: (412) 920-9444. Web Site: www.1007.com. Licensee: Infinity Radio Holdings Inc. Group owner: Infinity Broadcasting Corp. (acq 6-8-98; grpsl). Network: ABC FM Connection. Format: Hot adult contemp. Target aud: 18-49. ♦ Joel Hollander, pres; Scott Herman, exec VP; Keith Clark, sr VP, opns VP, progmg VP & progmg dir; Don Oylear, VP & gen mgr; Keith Belden, sls dir & natl sls mgr; Ronda Zegarelli, gen sls mgr; Susie Barker, prom mgr; Jonny Hortwell, mus dir; Kerri Griffith, news dir & pub affrs dir; Chris Hudak, chief of engrg.

New Wilmington

***WWNW(FM)**— Jan 31, 1968: 88.9 mhz; 200 w. Ant 75 ft. TL: N41 06 42 W80 20 02. Stereo. Box 89, Westminster College 16172. Phone: (724) 946-7242. Fax: (724) 946-7070. E-mail: barnerdl@westminster.edu. Licensee: Westminster College Board of Trustees. Network: ABC. Format: Hot adult contemp. News: 3 hrs wkly. Target aud: 18-35; college students & staff. Spec prog: Relg 3 hrs wkly. ♦ Dr. David Barner, chmn; R. Thomas Williamson, pres; Dr. David L. Barner, gen mgr; Charles Chirozzi, chief of engrg.

Norristown

WNAP(AM)— Aug 6, 1946: 1110 khz; 4.8 kw-D, DA. TL: N40 08 05 W75 18 48. 2311 Old Arch Rd. 19401. Secondary address: Box 11, Philadelphia 19128. Phone: (610) 272-7600. Fax: (610) 272-5793. E-mail: wnap@nni.com. Licensee: George H. Buck. Group owner: GHB Radio Group (acq 12-15-87; $725,000; 4-2-84). Format: Black gospel. Target aud: General. ♦ Charles Grundy, gen sls mgr; Fred Blain, gen mgr & progmg dir; Dave McCrork, chief of engrg.

North East

WRKT(FM)— Mar 29, 1970: 100.9 mhz; 4.2 kw. 252 ft. TL: N42 11 51 W79 45 10. Stereo. Boston Store Pl., Erie 16501. Phone: (814) 461-1000. Fax: (814) 461-1500. E-mail: rocket101@rocket101.com. Licensee: Next Media Group owner: NextMedia Group L.L.C. (acq 11-26-01; grpsl). Fletcher, Heald & Hildreth. Format: Classic rock. News staff: one; News: one hr wkly. Target aud: 25-54. Spec prog: Loc bands one hr wkly. ♦ Richard Rambaldo, gen mgr; Michael Malpiedi, gen sls mgr.

WYNE(AM)— Nov 24, 1966: 1530 khz; 1 kw-D, 250 w-CH, DA-1. TL: N42 12 05 W79 51 43. 501 E. 38th St., Erie 16546. Phone: (814) 824-2261. Fax: (814) 824-2590. Web Site: www.mercyhurst.edu. Licensee: Mercyhurst College (acq 2-18-2005; $110,000). Format: Classical. Target aud: 25-54; men & women. ♦ William T. Shannon, gen mgr.

Northern Cambria

WHPA(FM)— 1999: 93.5 mhz; 1.3 kw. 499 ft. TL: N40 36 10 W78 42 57. Box 1095 15714. Phone: (814) 472-4060. Fax: (814) 472-9370. E-mail: whpa@forspeed.net. Licensee: Vernal Enterprises Inc. (group owner). Format: Oldies 50s & 60s. ♦ Larry Schrengost, gen mgr.

WNCC(AM)— Oct 15, 1950: . Stn currently dark 950 khz; 500 w-D. TL: N40 40 47 W78 44 26. Box 1095 15714. Phone: (814) 472-4060. Fax: (814) 948-0950. E-mail: wncc@forspeed.net. Licensee: Vernal Enterprises Inc. (group owner; (acq 3-19-97; $20,000. with WRDD(AM) Ebensburg). Format: Adult contemp, oldies. News staff: one; News: 6 hrs wkly. Target aud: 35 plus; females & males in the 35 plus age range. ♦ Larry Schrengost, gen mgr.

WPCL(FM)— Sept 30, 1991: 97.3 mhz; 6 kw. 610 ft. TL: N40 38 26 W78 47 45. Stereo. Box 540, 34 Spring Rd., Grantsville, MD 21536. Phone: (301) 895-3292. Fax: (301) 895-3293. E-mail: hesalive@hesalive.net. Web Site: www.hesalive.com. Licensee: He's Alive Inc. (group owner; acq 3-18-97; $105,000). Network: USA. Rep: Commercial Media Sales. Format: Christian, relg. Target aud: 18-35. ♦ Dewayne Johnson, pres; Monte Palmer, stn mgr.

Northumberland

WEGH(FM)— Aug 22, 1994: 107.3 mhz; 900 w. Ant 843 ft. TL: N40 47 10 W76 41 49. Stereo. Box 1070, Sunbury 17801. Secondary address: RD#2 County Line Rd., Selinsgrove 17870. Phone: (570) 286-5838. Phone: (570) 743-1841. Fax: (570) 743-7837. Fax: (570) 743-1605. E-mail: eagle107@eagle107.com. Web Site: www.eagle107.com. Licensee: Sunbury Broadcasting Corp. Rep: Roslin. Dome. Format: Classic Hits. News staff: 4; News: one hr wkly. Target aud: 25-54. ♦ Roger S Haddon Jr., CEO; Roger S. Haddon Jr., pres; Kevin Herr, opns mgr; Gayle Fedder, gen sls mgr & mktg mgr; Rob Senter, progmg dir & mus dir; Kelli Tyler, prom.

Oil City

WGYI(FM)—Listing follows WOYL(AM).

WKQW(AM)— Dec 1, 1986: 1120 khz; 1 kw-D. TL: N41 23 45 W79 39 53. 222 Seneca St. 16301. Phone: (814) 676-8254. Fax: (814) 677-4272. Web Site: www.kqw.com. Licensee: Clarion County Broadcasting Corp. (acq 2-25-2005; $540,000. with co-located FM). Format: 70s oldies, talk, adult contemp. Target aud: 25-54.

WKQW-FM— September 1992: 96.3 mhz; 6 kw. 328 ft. TL: N41 23 45 W79 39 53. Stereo. Web Site: www.kqw.com.

WOYL(AM)— Feb 14, 1946: 1340 khz; 1 kw-U, DA-D. TL: N41 25 04 W79 42 53. Box 908, 1411 Liberty St., Franklin 16323. Phone: (814) 676-5744. Fax: (814) 437-9372. Licensee: Forever Broadcasting LLC. Group owner: Forever Broadcasting (acq 7-20-00; grpsl). Rep: Dome, Keystone (unwired net). Format: MOR, news/talk. News staff: one. ♦Terry Deitz, gen mgr; Joe Elan, sls dir & gen sls mgr; Todd Adkins, progmg dir; Paul Joseph, news dir.

WGYI(FM)—Co-owned with WOYL(AM). May 1, 1957: 98.5 mhz; 20 kw. 299 ft. TL: N41 25 04 W79 72 53. Stereo. Format: America's Best Country.

Oliver

WOGG(FM)— June 11, 1993: 94.9 mhz; 1.65 kw. Ant 1,233 ft. TL: N39 52 11 W79 38 22. Stereo. 123 Blaine Rd., Brownsville 15417. Phone: (724) 938-2000. Fax: (724) 938-7824. E-mail: jtrunzo@zoominternet.net. Web Site: foggyland.com. Licensee: Keymarket Licenses LLC. Group owner: Keymarket Communications LLC (acq 8-31-99; $2.875 million. with WASP(AM) Brownsville). Network: ABC Information & Entertainment. Format: Country. News staff: one. Target aud: 25-54. ♦Andrew Powaski, gen mgr, opns mgr & gen sls mgr; Jeffrey Trunzo, chief of engrg.

Olyphant

WBHD(FM)—Licensed to Olyphant. See Dunmore

WQOR(AM)— July 20, 1987: 750 khz; 1.6 kw-D. TL: N41 28 34 W75 29 41. 6325 Sheridan Dr., Williamsville, NY 14221. Phone: (716) 839-6117. Fax: (716) 839-0400. Web Site: www.holyfamily.ws. Licensee: Holy Family Communications (group owner; acq 3-24-2003; $170,000). Format: Catholic radio. ♦James Wright, pres.

Palmyra

WWKL(FM)— Sept 22, 1959: 92.1 mhz; 3.3 kw. 300 ft. TL: N40 19 35 W76 36 33. Stereo. Cumulus Media-WNNK FM-WTCY AM, 2300 Vartan Way, Harrisburg 17110-9720. Phone: (717) 238-1041. Fax: (717) 234-4842. Web Site: www.hot92.com. Licensee: Cumulus Licensing Corp. Group owner: Cumulus Media Inc. (acq 11-28-00; grpsl). Network: ABC Information & Entertainment. Wilkinson Barker Knauer. Format: CHR/ rhythmic. Target aud: 25-54. Spec prog: Relg 6 hrs, Sp 14 hrs, Hershey Bears hockey, Hershey Wildcats soccer wkly. ♦Ron Giovanniello, gen mgr; Karen Richards, sls dir; Todd Matthews, gen sls mgr; John O'Dea, progmg dir; Amy Warner, mus dir; Dave Supplee, chief of engrg.

Patton

WBRX(FM)— 1991: 94.7 mhz; 1.05 kw. 551 ft. TL: N40 42 03 W78 37 26. 1417 12th Ave, Altoona 16601. Phone: (814) 944-9344. Fax: (814) 944-9350. Web Site: www.wbrx.com. Licensee: Sherlock Broadcasting Inc. (acq 3-95; $450,000; 6-26-95). Network: ABC FM Connection. Format: Classic rock. Target aud: 35-65. ♦Diane Boslet, gen mgr.

Pen Argyl

***WWPJ(FM)**— 2001: 89.5 mhz; 1 w horiz, 40 w vert. Ant 1,125 ft. TL: N40 53 03 W75 15 43. Mercer County Community College, 1200 Old Trenton Rd., Trenton, NJ 08690. Phone: (609) 587-8989. Licensee: Mercer County Community College. Format: Classical. ♦Jeffery Sekerka, gen mgr.

Philadelphia

KYW(AM)— 1921: 1060 khz; 50 kw-U, DA-1. TL: N40 06 12 W75 14 56. Stereo. 101 S. Independence Mall E. 19106. Phone: (215) 238-4700. Fax: (215) 238-4505. Web Site: www.kyw1060.com. Licensee: Infinity Broadcasting East Inc. Group owner: Infinity Broadcasting Corp. Network: Network: ABC, CBS. Rep: Infinity Radio Sales. Leventhal Senter & Lerman. Format: News. News staff: 33; News: 168 hrs wkly. Target aud: 25-54; adults. ♦David Yadgaroff, VP & gen mgr; Karen Gilligan, gen sls mgr; Michael Berkowitz, natl sls mgr; Rich Iovanisci, rgnl sls mgr; Rob Kaloustian, rgnl sls mgr; Kyle Ruffin, mktg dir; Steve Butler, progmg dir & news dir; Tracey Russell, news dir; Jan Kowalczyk, chief of engrg. Co-owned TV: KYW-TV affil.

WBEB(FM)— May 13, 1963: 101.1 mhz; 14 kw. 941 ft. TL: N40 02 21 W75 14 13. Stereo. 10 Presidential Blvd., Bala Cynwyd 19004. Phone: (610) 667-8400. Fax: (610) 667-6795. Web Site: www.b101radio.com. Licensee: WEAZ-FM Radio Inc. (acq 5-63). Rep: McGavren Guild. Borsari & Paxson. Format: Adult contemp. Target aud: 25-54. ♦Jerry Lee, CEO & pres; David L. Kurtz, chmn & CFO; Blaise Howard, VP & gen mgr; William F. Boone, stn mgr; Dave Giordano, sls dir, natl sls mgr & natl sls mgr; Agnes Fuller, rgnl sls mgr; Emily Elfenbein, mktg dir & pub affrs dir; Bonnie Hoffman, prom mgr; Chris Conley, progmg dir; Chris Sarris, engrg dir.

WBEN-FM— Mar 1, 1949: 95.7 mhz; 50 kw. 500 ft. TL: N40 03 33 W75 14 20. Stereo. One Bala Plaza, Suite 424, Bala Cynwyd 19004. Phone: (610) 771-0933. Fax: (610) 771-9690. E-mail: gdefrancesco@greaterphila.com. Web Site: www.mix957online.com. Licensee: Greater Philadelphia Radio Group. Group owner: Greater Media Inc. (acq 5-29-97; $41.8 million). Rep: CMBS. Shaw Pittman. Format: Hot Adult Contemp. News: 3 hrs wkly. Target aud: 25-54; professional, upscale executives. ♦Rick Feinblatt, VP & gen mgr; Larry Paulauski, chief of engrg.

WDAS(AM)— 1923: 1480 khz; 5 kw-D, 1 kw-N, DA-2. TL: N39 59 53 W75 12 43. 23 W. City Ave., Bala Cynwyd 19004. Phone: (610) 617-8500. Fax: (610) 617-8501. Web Site: www.wdasam.com. Licensee: AMFM Radio Licenses LLC. Group owner: Clear Channel Communications Inc. (acq 8-30-00; grpsl). Network: American Urban. Format: Black gospel, relg, talk. ♦Joseph Tamburro, gen mgr, gen sls mgr & progmg dir.

WDAS-FM— 1959: 105.3 mhz; 3.3 kw. 870 ft. TL: N40 02 30 W75 14 24. (CP: 16.3 kw). Stereo. Web Site: www.wdas.fm.com. Format: Black adult contemp. Target aud: 25-54.

WFIL(AM)— 1922: 560 khz; 5 kw-U, DA-2. TL: N40 05 42 W75 16 38. Stereo. 117 Ridge Pike, Lafayette Hill 19444. Phone: (610) 941-9560. Fax: (610) 828-8879. E-mail: wfil@wfil.com. Web Site: www.wfil.com. Licensee: Pennsylvania Media Associates Inc. Group owner: Salem Communications Corp. (acq 11-1-93; $4 million). Network: Salem Radio Network. Rep: Salem. Borsari & Paxson. Format: Relg, Christian, talk. News: 2 hrs wkly. Target aud: 35-64; parents & grandparents. ♦Russ Whitnah, VP & gen mgr; Kevin Manna, opns dir; David Handler, gen sls mgr; Carol Healey, rgnl sls mgr; Mark Daniels, mktg mgr & progmg mgr; Fred Moore, chief of engrg; Rene Tetro, chief of engrg.

WHAT(AM)— 1925: 1340 khz; 1 kw-U. TL: N40 00 06 W75 12 35. 2471 N. 54 St., Suite 220 19131. Phone: (215) 482-0956. Fax: (215) 581-5185. E-mail: gmwhat1340am@aol.com. Licensee: Urban Radio I L.L.C. Group owner: Inner City Broadcasting (acq 2-2-99). Format: Talk, urban,. Target aud: 25-54. Spec prog: Gospel 12 hrs wkly. ♦Pierre Sutton, CEO; Charles Warfield, pres; Bill Cooper, CFO; Christopher Squire, VP & gen mgr.

***WHYY-FM**— 1954: 90.9 mhz; 13.5 kw. 920 ft. TL: N40 02 30 W75 14 24. Stereo. 150 N. 6th St., Independence Mall West 19106. Phone: (215) 351-1200. Phone: (215) 351-9204. Fax: (215) 351-3352. E-mail: talkback@whyy.org. Web Site: www.whyy.org. Licensee: WHYY Inc. Network: Network: NPR, PRI. Schwartz, Woods & Miller. Format: News, info. News staff: 7; News: 35 hrs wkly. Target aud: 35-49. Spec prog: Opera 4 hrs, folk 4 hrs, jazz 4 hrs wkly. ♦William J. Marrazzo, pres; Paul Gluck, gen mgr.

WIOQ(FM)— 1941: 102.1 mhz; 27 kw. 669 ft. TL: N40 02 40 W75 14 30. Stereo. One Bala Plaza, Suite 243, Bala Cynwyd 19004. Phone: (610) 667-8100. Fax: (610) 668-4657. Web Site: www.q102philly.com. Licensee: AMFM Radio Licenses LLC. Group owner: Clear Channel Communications Inc. (acq 8-30-00; grpsl). Format: CHR. Target aud: 18-34; females & teens. Spec prog: Pub affrs. ♦Rich Lewis, VP & gen mgr; Cassandra Banko, gen sls mgr; Lisa Acchione, mktg dir; Jeff Jordan, prom dir; Brian Bridgman, progmg dir; Marian Newsome, mus dir; Wendy McClure, pub affrs dir; Michael Guidotti, chief of engrg.

WIP(AM)— Mar 16, 1922: 610 khz; 5 kw-U, DA-1. TL: N39 51 56 W75 06 43. 441 N. 5th St. 19123. Phone: (215) 922-5000. Fax: (215) 922-2364. Licensee: Infinity Broadcasting Corp. of Philadelphia. Group owner: Infinity Broadcasting Corp. (acq 8-12-93; FTR: 8-30-93). Network: Westwood One. Rep: CBS Radio. Format: Sports, talk. ♦Cecil R. Forster Jr., VP & gen mgr; Cecil Foster, stn mgr; Tom Bigby, progmg mgr.

WYSP(FM)—Co-owned with WIP(AM). August 1971: 94.1 mhz; 16 kw. 900 ft. TL: N40 02 30 W75 14 24. Stereo. 101 S. Independence Mall E. 19106. Phone: (215) 625-9460. Fax: (215) 625-6555. Web Site: www.94wysp.com. Licensee: Infinity Broadcasting East Inc. (acq 11-1-81; grpsl; FTR: 9-28-81). Network: Westwood One. Rep: CBS Radio. Format: Rock. ♦Peter Kleiner, VP & gen mgr; Tim Sabean, VP; Gil Edwards, progmg dir.

WJJZ(FM)— Nov 11, 1959: 106.1 mhz; 22 kw. 740 ft. TL: N40 04 58 W75 10 54. Stereo. 440 Domino Ln. 19128. Phone: (215) 508-1200. Fax: (215) 509-1083. Web Site: www.wjjz.com. Licensee: AMFM Radio Licenses LLC. Group owner: Clear Channel Communications Inc. (acq 8-30-2000; grpsl). Rep: Christal. Latham & Watkins. Format: Smooth jazz. Target aud: 25-54. ♦Richard Lewis, gen mgr; Cassandra Banko, sls dir; Michael Tozzi, progmg dir; Charles Benner, chief of engrg.

***WKDU(FM)**— 1970: 91.7 mhz; 110 w. 155 ft. TL: N39 57 36 W75 11 27. Stereo. 3210 Chestnut St. 19104. Phone: (215) 895-5920. Phone: (215) 895-5917. Fax: (215) 895-1050. Web Site: www.wkdu.org. Licensee: Drexel University. Format: Progsv, alternative rock, free format. Target aud: General. Spec prog: International 12 hrs, rhythm & blues 3 hrs, gospel 4 hrs, Israeli 3 hrs, new age 2 hrs, metal 4 hrs, Black 8 hrs wkly. ♦Evan Caposerri, gen mgr; Casey Ross, progmg dir; Ryan McIntyre, pub affrs dir; Jim Cavanaugh, chief of engrg.

WMGK(FM)—Listing follows WPEN(AM).

WMMR(FM)— Apr 20, 1942: 93.3 mhz; 18 kw. 827 ft. TL: N39 57 09 W75 10 05. Stereo. One Bala Plaza, Suite 424, Bala Cynwyd 19004. Phone: (610) 771-0933. Fax: (610) 771-9710. Web Site: www.wmmr.com. Licensee: Greater Philadelphia Radio Inc. Group owner: Greater Media Inc. (acq 7-23-97; grpsl). Network: Westwood One. Rep: McGavren Guild. Format: Main stream rock. News staff: one; News: 5 hrs wkly. Target aud: 25-54; suburban rockers. ♦Richard D. Feinblatt, sr VP; John Fullam, gen mgr; Paul Blake, gen sls mgr; Scott Segelbeum, mktg dir; Bill Weston, progmg dir; Ken Zipeto, mus dir; Larry Paulauski, chief of engrg.

WNTP(AM)— 1923: 990 khz; 50 kw-D, 10 kw-N, DA-2. TL: N40 05 43 W75 16 37. Stereo. 117 Ridge Pike, Lafayette Hill 19444. Phone: (610) 940-0990. Fax: (610) 828-8879. E-mail: wntp@wntp.com. Web Site: www.wntp.com. Licensee: Pennsylvania Media Associates Inc. Group owner: Salem Communications Corp. (acq 1994; $3.5 million. grpsl). Network: Salem Radio Network. Borsari & Paxson. Format: News/talk. News: one hr wkly. Target aud: 18-49; young adults & parents. Spec prog: Sports, Sp. ♦Russ Whitnah, VP & gen mgr; Kevin Manna, opns mgr; David Handler, gen sls mgr; Carol Healey, rgnl sls mgr; Julie Carmichael, mktg dir; Mark Daniels, mktg mgr & progmg mgr; Fred Moore, chief of engrg.

WNWR(AM)— July 11, 1947: 1540 khz; 50 kw-D, DA. TL: N40 02 46 W74 14 15. 200 Monument Rd., Suite 6, Bala Cynwyd 19004. Phone: (610) 664-6780. Fax: (610) 664-8529. Web Site: www.wnwr.com. Licensee: Global Radio L.L.C. (acq 6-95; $1.4 million). Rep: Roslin. Taylor, Thiemann & Aitken. Format: Var/div, ethnic multicultural. Target aud: 25-54. ♦Jim Weitzman, pres; Sam Speiser, gen mgr & stn mgr; Shawn Laughlin, opns mgr.

WOGL(FM)—Listing follows WPHT(AM).

***WPEB(FM)**— May 15, 1981: 88.1 mhz; 1 w. Ant 49 ft. TL: N39 57 33 W75 12 13. 4134 Lancaster Ave., 3rd Fl. 19104. Phone: (215) 387-6155. E-mail: volta@phillyinc.org. Web Site: www.radiovolta.org. Licensee: West Philadelphia Educational Broadcasting Foundation. Format: Div. Target aud: General.

WPEN(AM)— April 1929: 950 khz; 5 kw-U, DA-N. TL: N39 58 28 W75 16 30. Stereo. One Bala Plaza, Suite 339, Bala Cynwyd 19004. Phone: (610) 667-8500. Fax: (610) 664-9610. E-mail: bcraig@greaterphila.com. Web Site: www.wpen.com. Licensee: Greater Philadelphia Radio Inc. Group owner: Greater Media Inc. (acq 1-6-75). Format: Adult standards, big band, nostalgia. News staff: 4. Target aud: 35 plus. ♦Richard D. Feinblatt, sr VP & gen mgr; Richard D. Fernblatt, gen sls mgr; Bob Craig, progmg dir & progmg mgr; Vicky Kramer, prom dir & pub affrs dir; Larry Paulausky, chief of engrg.

WMGK(FM)—Co-owned with WPEN(AM). 1942: 102.9 mhz; 8.5 kw. 1,140 ft. TL: N40 02 21 W75 14 13. (CP: 8.9 kw, ant 1,148 ft.). Stereo. One Bala Plaza Suite 429, Cynwyd 19004. E-mail: programdirector@wmgk.com. Web Site: www.wmgk.com. Rep: McGavren Guild. Format: Classic hits. Target aud: 25-54; women. ♦Don Braun, sls dir; Ed McCusker, gen sls mgr; Buzz Knight, progmg dir.

WPHE(AM)—See Phoenixville

Developers & Brokers of Radio Properties
contact American Media Services at our suite: Philadelphia Marriott Downtown 215-625-2900
843-972-2200
americanmediaservices.com
Charleston, SC
Dallas, TX · Chicago, Il · Austin, TX
American Media Services, LLC

WPHT(AM)— 1922: 1210 khz; 50 kw-U. TL: N39 58 46 W74 59 13. 10 Monument Rd., Bala Cynwyd 19004. Phone: (610) 668-5839. Fax: (610) 667-1904. E-mail: talkradio1210@cbs.com. Web Site: www.thebigtalker1210.com. Licensee: Infinity Broadcasting East Inc. Group owner: Infinity Broadcasting Corp. (acq 8-58). Network: Network: CBS, Westwood One. Rep: CBS Radio. Format: Talk. Target aud: 25-64; adults. ♦Sil Scaglione, gen mgr; Mike Baldini, sls VP; Carrie Hartman, mktg dir; Grace Blazer, prom mgr; Walter Koss, prom mgr; Dave Skalish, chief of engrg.

WOGL(FM)—Co-owned with WPHT(AM). May 16, 1944: 98.1 mhz; 12.5 kw. 1,000 ft. TL: N40 02 31 W75 14 11. Stereo. Phone: (610) 668-5900. Web Site: www.wogl.com. Leventhal, Senter & Lerman. Format: Oldies. News staff: one; News: 1.25 hrs wkly. Target aud: 25-54. ♦John Sykes, chmn; John Fullam, pres; Brian Nagy, gen sls mgr; Anthony Fuscaldo, natl sls mgr; Cindy Webster, mktg dir; Dennis Winslow, progmg dir; Tommy McCarthy, mus dir; Jan Kowakczyk, engrg dir.

WRDW-FM— 1957: 96.5 mhz; 17 kw. 866 ft. TL: N40 02 21 W75 14 13. Stereo. 555 City Line Ave., Ste. 330, Bala Cynwyd 19004. Phone: (610) 667-9000. Fax: (610) 667-2972. Web Site: www.wired965.com. Licensee: WDAS License L.P. Group owner: Beasley Broadcast Group (acq 3-11-97). Network: Network: Network: Wall Street, ABC Daytime Direction, ABC Information & Entertainment. Rep: D & R Radio. Fisher, Wayland, Cooper, Leader & Zaragoza. Format: CHR. Target aud: 18 plus; general. ♦Bruce Beasley, CEO, chmn, pres & progmg dir; Lynn Bruder, gen mgr; Don Melnyk, chief of engrg.

***WRTI(FM)**— July 9, 1953: 90.1 mhz; 12.5 kw. 1,010 ft. TL: N40 02 21 W75 14 13. Stereo. 1509 Cecil B. Moore Blvd., 3rd Fl. 19121. Phone: (215) 204-8405. Fax: (215) 204-4870. E-mail: comments@wrti.org. Web Site: www.wrti.org. Licensee: Temple University of The Commonwealth System of Higher Education. Network: Network: NPR, PRI. Format: Class, jazz. News staff: one; News: 15 hrs wkly. Target aud: 30-65. ♦David S. Conant, CEO & gen mgr; Vic Scarpato, CFO; Tobias Poole, opns dir; William P. Johnson, dev dir & dev mgr; Rick Torpey, natl sls mgr & mktg mgr; Lorna Nixon, prom dir; Jack Moore, progmg dir; Windsor Johnston, news dir; Jeff DePolo, chief of engrg.

WSNI(FM)— February 1965: 104.5 mhz; 12.5 kw. 1,008 ft. TL: N40 02 30 W75 14 24. Stereo. One Bala Plaza, Suite 243, Bala Cynwyd 19004. Phone: (610) 668-0750. Fax: (610) 668-8253. Web Site: www.sunny1045.com. Licensee: AMFM Radio Licenses LLC. Group owner: Clear Channel Communications Inc. (acq 8-30-00; grpsl). Format: Hot adult contemp. News staff: one. Target aud: 25-54. ♦L. Lowry Mays, CEO; Richard Lewis, VP & mktg mgr; Cassanda Banko, sls VP; Wes Franks, gen sls mgr; Lisa Acchione, mktg dir; Faith Cook, prom dir & prom; Shelvia Williams, prom mgr; Brian Check, progmg dir; Tom Cook, mus dir; Jennifer Ryan, news dir & pub affrs dir; Michael Guidotti, chief of engrg.

WTMR(AM)—See Camden, NJ

WURD(AM)— July 23, 1958: 900 khz; 1 kw-D, 105 w-N, DA-2. TL: N39 55 02 W75 13 18. 1341 N. Delaware Ave., Suite 300 19125. Phone: (215) 425-7875. Fax: (215) 634-6003. Licensee: Levas Communications LLC Group owner: Levas Communications LLC (acq 4-30-2003;. $4.25 million). Network: CNN Radio. Rep: McGavren Guild. Womble, Carlyle, Sandridge & Rice. Format: Urban talk. Spec prog: Gospel 9 hrs, It 3 hrs wkly. ♦Art Camiolo, pres; Cody Anderson, gen mgr; Steve Ballard, opns dir; Bill Anderson, progmg dir.

WUSL(FM)— 1961: 98.9 mhz; 18 kw. 830 ft. TL: N40 02 31 W75 14 11. Stereo. 440 Domino Ln. 19128. Phone: (215) 483-8900. Fax: (215) 483-5930. Web Site: www.power99.com. Licensee: Clear Channel Radio Licenses, Inc. Group owner: Clear Channel Communications Inc. (acq 8-30-00; grpsl). Latham & Watkins. Format: Urban contemp. News staff: 2; News: 4 hrs wkly. Target aud: 18-49. Spec prog: Gospel 4 hrs wkly. ♦Richard Lewis, VP; Jay Sterin, opns dir; Laurindo Muniz, gen sls mgr; Marie Tolson, prom dir; Glenn Cooper, mus dir; Loraine Ballard-Morrill, news dir; Charles Benner, chief of engrg.

WWDB(AM)— 1925: 860 khz; 10 kw-D, DA. TL: N40 09 15 W75 22 10. (CP: 500 w-N, DA-2). 555 City Line Ave., Suite 330, Bala Cynwyd 19004. Phone: (610) 822-1321. Phone: (610) 822-1320. Fax: (610) 667-5978. Web Site: www.wwdbam.com. Licensee: Beasley Broadcasting of Eastern Pennsylvania Inc. Group owner: Beasley Broadcast Group (acq 9-9-86; $2.4 million;. FTR: 8-11-86). Rep: Caballero. Format: Talk. Target aud: 18-49. ♦Bruce Gilbert, gen mgr; Tim Halloran, opns mgr.

***WXPN(FM)**— April 1957: 88.5 mhz; 5 kw. 918 ft. TL: N40 02 36 W75 14 33. Stereo. 3025 Walnut St. 19104. Phone: (215) 898-6677. Fax: (215) 898-0707. E-mail: wxpndesk@xpnonline.net. Web Site: www.xpn.org. Licensee: Trustees of the University of Pennsylvania. Network: Network: PRI, NPR. Levanthol Senter & Lerman. Format: Adult alternative. News: 3 hrs wkly. Target aud: 25-54; educated. Spec prog: Children 5 hrs, folk 5 hrs wkly. ♦Quyen Shanahan, dev VP & mktg dir; Jay Ricci, sls VP; Tom Mara, gen sls mgr; Debby Seitz, prom mgr; Bruce Warren, progmg dir; Ann Reed, mus dir; Bob Bumbera, news dir; Jay Goldman, engrg dir.

WXTU(FM)— September 1958: 92.5 mhz; 15.5 kw. 900 ft. TL: N40 02 21 W75 14 13. Stereo. 555 City Line Ave., Suite 330, Bala Cynwyd 19004. Phone: (610) 667-9000. Fax: (610) 667-1355. Web Site: www.925xtu.com. Licensee: Beasley Broadcasting of Eastern Pennsylvania Inc. Group owner: Beasley Broadcast Group (acq 7-83; $6 million;. FTR: 7-11-83). Format: Contemp country. ♦Bruce Beasley, VP; Natalie Conner, gen mgr; Mark Vizza, mktg dir; Joe Ceccola, prom dir & prom mgr; Chuck Tisa, progmg dir; Don Melnyk, chief of engrg.

Philipsburg

WPHB(AM)— June 1, 1956: 1260 khz; 5 kw-D, 34 w-N. TL: N40 53 39 W78 11 51. 1884 Port Matilda Hwy., Radio Park 16866. Phone: (814) 342-2300. Fax: (814) 342-WPHB/9742. E-mail: wphb@wphbradio.com. Web Site: www.wphbradio.com. Licensee: Magnum Broadcasting Inc. (acq 11-24-2004; $2,022,527 with co-located FM). Network: CNN Radio. Dome & Assoc Haley, Bader, Potts. Format: Classic country & news/talk, sports. Target aud: Men & women; generally 25+. Spec prog: Bluegrass 4 hrs, polka 6 hrs, Gospel 6 hrs, big band 5 hrs wkly. ♦Michael M. Stapleford, pres; Laura Shore Mack, gen mgr; Cliff Mack, chief of opns; Marian Kovach, gen sls mgr; Jason Torrance, prom dir; C.J. Daniels, progmg dir; Sherry Flick, pub affrs dir; Joe Portelli, chief of engrg.

WUBZ-FM—Co-owned with WPHB(AM). March 1989: 105.9 mhz; 710 w. Ant 951 ft. TL: N40 47 34 W78 10 29. Stereo. Phone: (814) 342-6900. E-mail: buzz@buzzfm.com. Web Site: www.buzzfm.com. Format: Modern rock/alternative. News: 2.5 hrs wkly. Target aud: 18-49; men & women. ♦Austin Davis, progmg dir.

Phoenixville

WPHE(AM)— Aug 23, 1978: 690 khz; 1 kw-D, DA. TL: N40 08 08 W75 33 37. Box 46327, Philadelphia 19160. Secondary address: 321 W. Sedgley Ave., Philadelphia 19140. Phone: (215) 291-7532. Fax: (215) 739-1337. E-mail: rs@radiosalvation.com. Web Site: www.radiosalvation.com. Licensee: Salvation Broadcasting Co. (acq 12-1-88). Rep: Caballero. Format: Sp, relg, div. Spec prog: Por 3 hrs wkly. ♦Sarrial Salva, pres; Mr. Sarrial Salva, gen mgr; Isabel Salva, sls dir; Juan Izquierdo, progmg dir; Juan Pydeck, chief of engrg.

Pittsburgh

KDKA(AM)— Nov 2, 1920: 1020 khz; 50 kw-U. TL: N40 33 33 W79 57 11. Stereo. One Gateway Ctr. 15222. Phone: (412) 575-2200. Fax: (412) 575-2845. Web Site: www.kdkaradio.com. Licensee: Infinity Broadcasting East Inc. Group owner: Infinity Broadcasting Corp. Format: News/talk. News: 9 hrs wkly. Target aud: 25-54. ♦Michael J. Young, VP & gen mgr; Scott Schutt, gen sls mgr; Gleyn Ward, natl sls mgr; Jeff Hathhorn, mktg dir; Greg Jena, prom dir; Steve Hansen, progmg dir & news dir; Vic Pasquarelli, engrg dir.

KQV(AM)— Nov 19, 1919: 1410 khz; 5 kw-U, DA-2. TL: N40 31 17 W80 00 34. Centre City Tower, 650 Smithfield St. 15222. Phone: (412) 562-5900. Phone: (412) 562-5960. Fax: (412) 562-5936. Fax: (412) 563-5603. Web Site: www.kqv.com. Licensee: Calvary Inc. (acq 12-1-82; $1.75 million; 1-3-83). Network: Network: Wall Street, AP Radio. Format: News. News staff: 18; News: 168 hrs wkly. Target aud: 35 plus; affluent, info-oriented adults. Spec prog: NFL football (regular season, playoffs & Superbowl), Notre Dame football, Duquesne University men's basketball. ♦Robert W. Dickey Sr., pres & gen mgr; Erik F. Selby, chief of opns.

WAMO(AM)—(Millvale). Aug 1, 1948: 860 khz; 1 kw-D, 830 w-N, DA-2. TL: N40 29 27 W79 58 55. 960 Penn Ave., Suite 200 15222. Phone: (412) 471-2181. Fax: (412) 391-3559. Web Site: www.wamo.com. Licensee: Sheridan Broadcasting Corp. (acq 3-1-73). Network: American Urban. Rep: D & R Radio. Format: Urban contemp, oldies.Ronald Davenport Jr., chmn, pres & gen mgr; Kathy Gersha, opns VP; LaTonya Washington, gen sls mgr & natl sls mgr; Stephen Bates, gen sls mgr & natl sls mgr; Heidi Huck, mktg mgr; Harriet Jackson, prom dir; George Cook, progmg dir; Ron Atkins, progmg dir; Tracey Lee, progmg mgr, mus dir & mus dir; Tene Croom, news dir & pub affrs dir; Bob Sharkey, chief of engrg

WAMO-FM—(Beaver Falls). 1960: 106.7 mhz; 37 kw. Ant 554 ft. TL: N40 37 11 W80 05 36. Stereo. 960 Penn Ave., Suite 200 15222. Phone: (412) 456-4064. Fax: (412) 391-3559. E-mail: rdavenportjr@sbcol.com. Web Site: www.wamo.com. Licensee: MCL/MCM-Inc. (group owner). Format: Urban contemp. ♦Ronald Davenport Jr., chmn & pres; Michael Douglass, gen mgr; Heidi Huck, mktg dir; George Cook, progmg dir.

WBGG(AM)— 1932: 970 khz; 5 kw-U, DA-2. TL: N40 30 30 W80 00 30. 200 Fleet St. 15220. Phone: (412) 937-1441. Fax: (412) 937-0323. E-mail: feedback@970theburgh.com. Web Site: www.970theburgh.com. Licensee: AMFM Radio Licenses L.L.C. Group owner: Clear Channel Communications Inc. (acq 8-30-00; grpsl). Network: ABC Daytime Direction. Format: Talk, Sports. News staff: one. ♦John Rohn, gen mgr; Mark Turley, gen sls mgr; Milanna Miljenodic, natl sls mgr; Allison Hilliard, prom mgr; Greg Gillispie, progmg dir.

WWSW-FM—Co-owned with WBGG(AM). 1940: 94.5 mhz; 50 kw. 810 ft. TL: N40 27 48 W80 00 18. Stereo. Web Site: www.970theburgh.com. ♦Missy Gawaldo, gen sls mgr.

WDSY-FM— September 1962: 107.9 mhz; 17.5 kw. Ant 827 ft. TL: N40 28 20 W79 59 41. Stereo. Foster Five, 651 Holiday Dr. 15220. Phone: (412) 920-9400. Fax: (412) 920-9449. Web Site: www.y108.com. Licensee: Infinity Radio Holdings Inc. Group owner: Infinity Broadcasting Corp. (acq 12-14-00; grpsl). Network: Westwood One. Rep: Katz Radio. Leventhal, Senter & Lerman, P.L.L.C. Format: Country. Target aud: 25-54; general. ♦Joel Hollander, pres; Jacques Tortoroli, CFO; Scott Herman, exec VP; Don Oyleaar, VP; Don Oylear, gen mgr; Keith Clark, opns VP & opns dir; Christine Fallon-McKenna, gen sls mgr & news dir; Keith Belden, natl sls mgr; Norm Slemanda, rgnl sls mgr; Michael Young, mktg mgr & chief of engrg; Jane O'Malia, prom dir; Stoney Richards, mus dir.

***WDUQ(FM)**— Dec 15, 1949: 90.5 mhz; 25 kw. 480 ft. TL: N40 25 52 W80 00 26. Stereo. 600 Forbes Ave. 15282-0001. Phone: (412) 396-6030. Fax: (412) 396-5061. E-mail: info@wduq.org. Web Site: www.wduq.org. Licensee: Duquesne University. Network: Network: NPR, PRI. Rep: Interep. Cohn & Marks. Format: Jazz, news, pub affairs, NPR. News staff: 5; News: 47 hrs wkly. Educated, moderately affluent. ♦Scott Hanley, gen mgr; Helen Wigger, opns dir; Fred Serrino, dev dir; Mary Lloyd, sls dir; Cynthia Ference-Kelly, mktg dir & prom dir; Shaunna Morrison, mus dir; Kevin Gavin, news dir; Chuck Leavens, engrg dir.

WDVE(FM)— May 10, 1962: 102.5 mhz; 55 kw. 820 ft. TL: N40 29 38 W80 01 09. Stereo. 200 Fleet St., 4th Fl. 15220. Phone: (412) 937-1441. Fax: (412) 937-0323. Web Site: www.dve.com. Licensee: Capstar TX L.P. Group owner: Clear Channel Communications Inc. (acq 8-00; grpsl). Rep: Christal. Format: News, all talk. News staff: one. Target aud: 25-54. ♦Missy Gawaldo, gen sls mgr.

WEAE(AM)— May 1922: 1250 khz; 5 kw-U, DA-N. TL: N40 23 50 W79 57 43. 400 Ardmore Blvd. 15221. Phone: (412) 731-1250. Fax: (412) 244-4596. Fax: (412) 244-4409. Web Site: www.ESPNradio1250.com. Licensee: Sports Radio Group LLC. Group owner: ABC Inc. (acq 4-26-99; $5 million). Network: ESPN Radio. Rep: ABC Radio Sales. Format: Sports, talk. Target aud: General; men 25-54. Spec prog: Penn State University football & basketball. ♦Jessamy Tang, pres;

Dennis Begley, gen mgr; David Waugaman, natl sls mgr; Bryan Engel, prom mgr; John Lund, progmg dir; Joe DeStio, news dir; Thad Mazur, engrg mgr.

WEDO(AM)—See McKeesport

WJAS(AM)— Oct 19, 1921: 1320 khz; 5 kw-U, DA-N. TL: N40 25 11 W79 54 38. 900 Parish St. 15220. Phone: (412) 875-4800. Phone: (412) 875-9500. Fax: (412) 875-9570. Web Site: www.1320wjas.com. Licensee: Renda Broadcasting Corp. (group owner; acq 7-16-85; $700,000; 12-17-84). Format: Big band, nostalgia, MOR. Target aud: 35 plus; older, upscale. Spec prog: Big band jump, Frank Sinatra 2 hrs wkly. ♦Anthony F. Renda, pres; Lawrence Weiss, gen mgr; David Pavlic, gen sls mgr; Chris Shovlin, prom dir; Mike McGann, progmg dir; Phil Lenz, chief of engrg.

WSHH(FM)—Co-owned with WJAS(AM). Mar 8, 1948: 99.7 mhz; 10.5 kw. 928 ft. TL: N40 27 47 W80 00 17. Stereo. Fax: (412) 875-9474. Web Site: www.wshh.com. (Acq 11-83; $2.7 million; 11-14-83). Format: Soft adult contemp. News staff: one. Target aud: 25-54; white collar, upscale office workers, professionals, managers. Spec prog: Pub affrs one hr wkly. ♦Susan Kelly, gen sls mgr; Ron Antill, progmg dir; Allan Freed, pub affrs dir.

WKHB(AM)—(Irwin). Oct 28, 1934: 620 khz; 5.5 kw-D, 50 w-N. TL: N40 17 20 W79 42 04. 1918 Lincoln Hwy., North Versailles 15137. Phone: (412) 823-7000. Licensee: Broadcast Communications Inc. (group owner; acq 10-9-96; $300,000). Format: Var. News staff: one; News: 19 hrs wkly. Target aud: Adults. Spec prog: Talk, Pol 2 hrs, alternative health 14 hrs wkly. ♦Ashley R. Stevens, VP; Robert M. Stevens, pres & gen mgr; Barry Banker, stn mgr.

WKST-FM— Aug 8, 1960: 96.1 mhz; 44 kw. 522 ft. TL: N40 23 49 W79 57 43. Stereo. 200 Fleet St., 4th Fl. 15220. Phone: (412) 937-1441. Fax: (412) 937-0323. Web Site: www.kissfm961.com. Licensee: Capstar TX L.P. Group owner: Clear Channel Communications Inc. (acq 8-30-00; grpsl). Format: CHR. ♦Missy Gawaldo, gen sls mgr.

WLTJ(FM)— Apr 4, 1942: 92.9 mhz; 47 kw. 890 ft. TL: N40 29 38 W80 01 09. 650 Smith Field St., Suite 2200 15222. Phone: (412) 316-3342. Fax: (412) 316-3388. E-mail: info@wltj.com. Web Site: www.wltj.com. Licensee: WPNT Inc. (acq 4-84; $3 million;. FTR: 3-19-84). Rep: McGavren Guild. Format: Lite rock. Target aud: 25-54; affluent, professional, working public. ♦Saul Frischling, pres; Greg Frischling, gen mgr; Chris Kohan, gen sls mgr; Vicki Wolfe, prom dir; Chuck Stevens, progmg dir; Amy Crago, news dir; Paul Carroll, chief of engrg.

WORD-FM— 1948: 101.5 mhz; 48 kw. 505 ft. TL: N40 29 02 W79 59 34. Stereo. Seven Parkway Ctr., Suite 625 15220. Phone: (412) 937-1500. Fax: (412) 937-1576. E-mail: word@wordfm.com. Web Site: www.wordfm.com. Licensee: Pennsylvania Media Associates Inc. Group owner: Salem Communications Corp. Format: Christian. Target aud: 25-49. ♦Chuck Gratner, CEO & gen mgr; Randy Dietterich, chmn & chief of engrg; Kenny Woods, opns mgr & progmg dir; Smitty Boros, gen sls mgr; Shaun Pierce, news dir.

WPIT(AM)—Co-owned with WORD-FM. 1947: 730 khz; 5 kw-D. TL: N40 29 02 W79 59 34. Web Site: www.wpitam.com. (Acq 12-2-92; $6.5 million;. FTR: 12-21-92). Format: Christian.

WPGB(FM)— Feb 4, 1963: 104.7 mhz; 13 kw. Ant 827 ft. TL: N40 28 20 W79 59 41. Stereo. 200 Fleet, 4th Fl. 15220. Phone: (412) 937-1441. Fax: (412) 937-0323. Web Site: www.1047thebeat.com. Licensee: Capstar TX L.P. Group owner: Clear Channel Communications Inc. (acq 8-30-00; grpsl). Format: News, all talk. News staff: one; News: 5 hrs wkly. Target aud: 18-34; white collar workers. ♦Missy Gawaldo, gen sls mgr & chief of engrg.

***WPTS-FM**— Aug 26, 1984: 92.1 mhz; 16 w. 462 ft. TL: N40 26 39 W79 57 12. Stereo. Univ. of Pittsburgh, 411 William Pitt Union 15260. Phone: (412) 648-7990. Fax: (412) 648-7988. E-mail: wpts@pitt.edu. Web Site: www.wpts.pitt.edu. Licensee: University of Pittsburgh. (acq 8-26-84). Format: Eclectic, contemp, progsv. News staff: 3; News: 10 hrs wkly. Target aud: General. ♦Gregory Weston, gen mgr.

***WQED-FM**— Jan 25, 1973: 89.3 mhz; 43 kw. Ant 500 ft. TL: N40 26 46 W79 57 51. Stereo. 4802 5th Ave. 15213. Phone: (412) 622-1300. Fax: (412) 622-1488. E-mail: radio@wqed.org. Web Site: www.wqed.org. Licensee: WQED Multimedia. Network: Network: NPR, PRI. Schwartz, Woods & Miller. Format: Class. News: one hr wkly. Target aud: General; hip, young, educated, fun-loving, class mus listeners. Spec prog: Arts one hr, new age one hr wkly. ♦George L. Miles Jr., pres; B.J. Leber, sr VP, stn mgr & prom VP; Michelle Pagano Heck, gen mgr; Ted Sohier, opns mgr; Lilli Mosco, dev VP & dev mgr; Rick Vaccarielli, sls dir; Karen Colbert, mktg dir; Gigi Saladna, prom mgr & progmg dir; George Hazimanois, adv dir; Paul Byers, chief of engrg. Co-owned TV: *WQED(TV) affil.

***WRCT(FM)**— April 1974: 88.3 mhz; 1.75 kw. 53 ft. TL: N40 26 39 W79 56 37. Stereo. One WRCT Plaza, 5000 Forbes Ave. 15213. Phone: (412) 621-0728. Phone: (412) 621-9728. Fax: (412) 268-6549. E-mail: info@wrct.org. Web Site: www.wrct.org. Licensee: Carnegie Mellon Student Government Corp. Putbrese, Hunsaker & Trent. Format: Div, educ. News: 10 hrs wkly. Target aud: General. Spec prog: Black 12 hrs, class 3 hrs, country 3 hrs, folk 3 hrs, experimental 12 hrs, jazz 18 hrs wkly. ♦Matt Siko, gen mgr; Pauline Law, progmg dir.

WRKZ(FM)— July 19, 1948: 93.7 mhz; 41 kw. Ant 550 ft. TL: N40 26 28 W80 01 32. Stereo. 651 Holiday Dr., Suite 310, Foster Plaza Bldg 5 15220. Phone: (412) 920-9400. Fax: (412) 920-9444. Web Site: www.937bzz.com. Licensee: Infinity Radio Holdings Inc. Group owner: Infinity Broadcasting Corp. (acq 11-13-98; grpsl). Target aud: 18-49; adults. ♦Joel Hollander, pres; Jacques Tortoroli, CFO; Scott Herman, exec VP; Michael Young, VP & gen mgr; Keith Clark, opns VP; Norm Slemenda, gen sls mgr; Brandon Davis, prom dir; Ryan Mill, mus dir; Shelley Duffy, news dir & pub affrs dir; Chris Hudak, chief of engrg.

WRRK(FM)—See Braddock

WURP(AM)—See Braddock

WWCS(AM)—See Canonsburg

WWNL(AM)— 1947: 1080 khz; 50 kw-D, DA. TL: N40 36 17 W79 57 37. 5316 Rt. 8, Unit 3N, Gibsonia 15044. Phone: (724) 443-4844. Fax: (724) 443-4847. Licensee: Steel City Radio Inc. Group owner: Wilkins Communications Network Inc. (acq 6-14-01). Format: Christian talk. ♦Bumper Morgan, gen mgr.

WXDX-FM— 1960: 105.9 mhz; 72 kw. 440 ft. TL: N40 29 27 W79 58 55. Stereo. 200 Fleet St. 15220. Phone: (412) 937-1441. Fax: (412) 937-0323. Web Site: www.wxdx.com. Licensee: Capstar TX L.P. Group owner: Clear Channel Communications Inc. (acq 8-30-00; grpsl). Rep: Christal. Format: Alternative. Target aud: 18-34. ♦Missy Gawaldo, gen sls mgr.

***WYEP-FM**— Apr 30, 1974: 91.3 mhz; 18.2 kw. 265 ft. TL: N40 24 42 W79 55 33. Stereo. 2313 E. Carson St. 15203. Phone: (412) 381-9131. Phone: (412) 381-9900. Fax: (412) 381-9126. E-mail: info@wyep.org. Web Site: www.wyep.org. Licensee: Pittsburgh Community Broadcasting Corp. Network: Network: PRI, NPR. Format: AAA. Target aud: 25-49; socially, politically & culturally aware & active; well-educated. Spec prog: Folk 9 hrs, blues 7 hrs, bluegrass 4 hrs, soul 3 hrs, celtic 2 hrs wkly. ♦Blaine Lucas, chmn; Sean Sebastian, pres; Lee Ferraro, gen mgr; Tony Pirollo, sls dir; Rosemary Welsch, progmg dir.

WZUM(AM)—See Carnegie

Pittston

WDMT(FM)— November 1983: 102.3 mhz; 5.8 kw. Ant 72 ft. TL: N41 18 20 W75 45 38. Stereo. 305 Hwy. 315 18640. Phone: (570) 883-9850. Fax: (570) 883-9851. Web Site: www.102themountain.com. Licensee: Entercom Wilkes-Barre Scranton LLC. Group owner: Entercom Communications Corp. (acq 12-13-99; grpsl). Network: Jones Radio Networks. Rep: D & R Radio. Format: AAA. Target aud: 35-64; female. Spec prog: Philadelphia Eagles, Penn State football. ♦John Burkavage, gen mgr; Jim Rising, stn mgr; Andy Zapotek, gen sls mgr; Michael Ignatz, prom dir; Jerry Padden, progmg dir; Elizabeth Masich, mus dir; Lamar Smith, chief of engrg.

WITK(AM)— June 21, 1953: 1550 khz; 10 kw-D, 500 w-N, DA-2. TL: N41 20 45 W75 47 08. 1049 N. Sekol Rd., Scranton 18504. Phone: (570) 344-1221. Fax: (570) 344-0996. Web Site: www.wick-am.com. Licensee: Robert C. Cordaro Inc. Group owner: Citadel Communications Corp. (acq 1996; $275,000). Network: ABC News/Talk. Rep: Savalli. Format: Oldies. ♦Jules Reilly, gen mgr & opns mgr; Jack Williams, gen sls mgr; Greg Foster, progmg dir; Paula Deignan, news dir; Dave Schmidt, chief of engrg.

Plains

WYCK(AM)— 1923: 1340 khz; 810 w-U. TL: N41 15 01 W75 49 32. 1049 N. Sekol Rd., Scranton 18504. Phone: (570) 344-1221. Phone: (570) 655-6660. Fax: (570) 344-0996. Fax: (570) 300-1996. Web Site: www.wick-am.com. Licensee: L.B. Radio Corp. Network: ABC. Holland & Knight. Format: Oldies. News staff: one; News: 8 hrs progmg wkly. Target aud: Adults 35-64; adults who love original hits of top 40 era. Spec prog: Relg 3 hrs wkly, Polish 3 hrs wkly. ♦Ed Kerber, opns mgr; Phil Bullwinkel, gen sls mgr.

Pleasant Gap

WQWK(FM)— 1997: 98.7 mhz; 2.2 kw. Ant 551 ft. TL: N40 55 58 W77 45 40. 2551 Park Center Blvd., State College 16801. Phone: (814) 237-9800. Fax: (814) 237-2477. Web Site: www.foreverradio.com. Licensee: Forever Broadcasting L.L.C. Group owner: Forever Broadcasting (acq 1-27-99). Format: Oldies. ♦Carol Logan, pres; Don A. Bedell, gen mgr; Nick Ferrara, opns mgr; Scott Cohagan, gen sls mgr; Doug Herendeen, progmg dir; Robert Taylor, chief of engrg.

Pocono Pines

WPZX(FM)— 2000: 105.9 mhz; 6 kw. Ant 328 ft. TL: N41 05 06 W75 38 09. 149 Penn Ave., Scranton 18503. Phone: (570) 346-6555. Fax: (570) 346-6038. Web Site: www.rock107.com. Licensee: The Scranton Times L.P. Group owner: Shamrock Communications Inc. (acq 9-8-00). Format: Classic rock. ♦William R. Lynett, CEO; Jim Loftus, COO & gen mgr; Tim Durkin, sls dir; Jenny Arndt, natl sls mgr; Mark Hoover, prom dir; Eric Logan, mus dir; Ruth Miller, news dir; Kevin Fitzgerald, chief of engrg.

Port Allegany

WHKS(FM)— 1990: 94.9 mhz; 1.15 w. Ant 758 ft. TL: N41 48 36 W78 23 10. Stereo. 42 N. Main St. 16743. Secondary address: 59 Lent Hollow Rd., Coudersport 16915. Phone: (814) 642-7004. Phone: (814) 274-5368. Fax: (814) 642-9491. Licensee: L-Com Inc. Network: Network: Jones Radio Networks, AP Radio. Rep: Dome. Commercial Media Sales. Format: Adult contemp. News: 2 hrs wkly. Target aud: 25-54; general. Spec prog: Relg 2 hrs wkly. ♦David F. Lent, pres, gen mgr, opns dir, opns mgr, gen sls mgr, adv mgr, progmg mgr & news dir; Joe Taylor, gen sls mgr & mktg mgr; Pat Kostur, chief of engrg.

Port Matilda

WKVB(FM)— Oct 17, 1994: 107.9 mhz; 450 w. 1,174 ft. TL: N40 55 11 W77 58 28. 160 Clearview Ave., State College 16803. Phone: (814) 238-5085. Fax: (814) 238-8993. E-mail: hot1079@statecollege.com. Web Site: www.hot107fm.com. Licensee: 2510 Licenses LLC. (group owner; (acq 2-16-2005; grpsl). Format: CHR, hip-hop. ♦Dave Bricker, CFO; Joe Trimarchi, gen mgr; Jason Miller, opns dir & progmg dir; Diana Albright, gen sls mgr & adv dir; Mike Martin, mktg dir & prom dir; Dave Shannon, news dir; Matt Lightner, chief of engrg.

Portage

WLKJ(FM)— Nov 15, 1990: 105.7 mhz; 3 kw. Ant 321 ft. TL: N40 22 59 W78 39 31. Stereo. 109 Plaza Dr., Suite 2, Johnstown 15905. Phone: (814) 255-4186. Fax: (814) 255-6145. Licensee: Forever Broadcasting LLC. Group owner: Forever Broadcasting. Format: Classic hits. News: 10 hrs wkly. Target aud: 18-54; middle to upper income. ♦Carol Logan, pres; Verla Price, gen mgr; Mike Stevens, progmg dir; Jim Baxler, chief of engrg.

Pottstown

WPAZ(AM)— Oct 1, 1951: 1370 khz; 1 kw-D. TL: N40 16 35 W75 37 44. 224 Maugers Mill Rd. 19464. Phone: (610) 326-4000. Phone: (610) 326-6832. Fax: (610) 326-7984. Web Site: www.1370wpaz.com. Licensee: Faye Scott. Group owner: Great Scott Broadcasting Network: ABC Daytime Direction. Format: News/talk. News staff: 2; News: 8 hrs wkly. Target aud: 25 plus; most affluent people. Spec prog: Pol one hr, relg 12 hrs wkly. ♦Faye Scott, pres; Mike LiCata, gen mgr & sls VP; Jay Warren, progmg dir; Paul Fanelli, news dir; Terry Dalton, chief of engrg.

WRFY-FM—See Reading

Pottsville

WAVT-FM—Listing follows WPPA(AM).

WPAM(AM)— 1946: . Stn currently dark 1450 khz; 1 kw-U. TL: N40 41 27 W76 11 39. 145 Lawtons Hill 17901. Phone: (570) 622-1450. Fax: (570) 622-4690. E-mail: phoenix1450@verizon.net. Licensee:

Developers & Brokers of Radio Properties

contact American Media Services at our suite: Philadelphia Marriott Downtown 215-625-2900
843-972-2200
americanmediaservices.com
Charleston, SC
Dallas, TX · Chicago, Il · Austin, TX

American Media Services, LLC

Curran Communications Inc. (acq 1-76). Blair, Joyce & Silva. Format: Oldies. Target aud: 25-54; active, upwardly mobile adults. ◆James J. Curran, pres; Caitlyn Curran, VP; Robert Murray, gen mgr & gen sls mgr; Ric Kull, progmg dir.

WPPA(AM)— May 9, 1946: 1360 khz; 5 kw-D, 500 w-N, DA-2. TL: N40 41 56 W76 11 43. Box 540, 212 S. Centre St. 17901. Phone: (570) 622-1360. Fax: (570) 622-2822. Web Site: www.wpparadio.com. Licensee: Pottsville Broadcasting Co. Inc. Network: CBS. Format: Adult contemp. News staff: 2; News: 14 hrs wkly. Target aud: 25-54. ◆Argie D. Tidmore, pres, gen mgr & chief of engrg; Les Blankenhorn, opns mgr, progmg dir & progmg mgr; William Tidmore, gen sls mgr & adv mgr; Mike Kimmel, news dir; Deb Daugherty, pub affrs dir.

WAVT-FM—Co-owned with WPPA(AM). Nov 20, 1948: 101.9 mhz; 50 kw. 540 ft. TL: N40 49 50 W76 12 32. Stereo. Web Site: www.t102radio.com. Format: CHR. ◆James A. Bowman, stn mgr, gen sls mgr & adv mgr; Chad Gerber, progmg dir.

Punxsutawney

WECZ(AM)— Mar 18, 1953: 1540 khz; 5 kw-D, 1 kw-CH. TL: N40 57 36 W79 00 08. 904 N. Main St. 15767. Phone: (814) 938-6000. Fax: (814) 938-4237. Licensee: Renda Radio Inc. (group owner; acq 6-1-81; $512,000; 5-11-81). Network: Network: Westwood One, ABC Information & Entertainment. Latham & Watkins. Format: News, talk. News staff: 2; News: 10 hrs wkly. Target aud: 45 plus. Spec prog: Pol 3 hrs wkly. ◆Anthony F. Renda, pres; Doug Metherey, gen mgr & stn mgr; Jennifer Black, gen sls mgr; Marty Palmer, engrg dir.

WPXZ-FM—Co-owned with WECZ(AM). Dec 12, 1973: 104.1 mhz; 3 kw. 300 ft. TL: N40 57 36 W79 00 08. Stereo. E-mail: rendaradio@adelphia.net. Network: ABC. Format: Adult contemp. Target aud: 35-64. ◆Larry McGuire, mus dir.

Radnor Township

***WYBF(FM)**— August 1991: 89.1 mhz; 700 w. 223 ft. TL: N40 03 22 W75 22 30. Widener Ctr., 610 King of Prussia Rd., Radnor 19087-3698. Phone: (610) 902-8457. Fax: (610) 902-8285. Licensee: Cabrini College. Format: Div, contemp hit, news/talk. ◆Dr. Jerry Zurek, chmn; Krista Mazzeo, gen mgr.

Reading

WBYN(FM)—See Boyertown

WEEU(AM)— 1931: 830 khz; 20 kw-D, 6 kw-N, DA-2. TL: N40 30 54 W76 07 24. Stereo. 34 N. 4th St. 19601-3996. Phone: (610) 376-7335. Fax: (610) 376-7756. Web Site: www.weeu.com. Licensee: WEEU Broadcasting Co. (acq 12-46). Network: ABC Information & Entertainment. Rep: McGavren Guild. Cohn & Marks. Format: Full service, talk, news, sports. News staff: 2; News: 6 hrs wkly. Target aud: 30 plus; mature. Spec prog: Farm 2 hrs, folk one hr, Ger 2 hrs wkly. ◆James C. Flippin, pres; Dave Kline, gen mgr & stn mgr.

WIOV(AM)—Sept 1, 1946: 1240 khz; 1 kw-U. TL: N40 19 28 W75 56 31. 44 Bethany Rd., Ephrata 17522-2416. Phone: (717) 738-1191. Fax: (717) 738-1661. E-mail: widv@ptd.net. Web Site: www.espn1240.com. Licensee: Citadel Broadcasting Co. Group owner: Citadel Broadcasting Corp. (acq 5-12-2004; grpsl). Network: ESPN Radio. Format: Sports. Target aud: 35-54; Male. ◆Mitch Carroll, VP, gen mgr, gen sls mgr & natl sls mgr; Jim Rudley, opns mgr; Brenda Perkins, natl sls mgr; Crissy Wall, rgnl sls mgr & adv mgr; CJ Taylor, prom dir; Susie Summer, prom mgr; Bob Moody, progmg VP; Dick Raymond, progmg dir; Steve Haage, progmg mgr.

WRAW(AM)— September 1922: 1340 khz; 1 kw-U. TL: N40 19 27 W75 55 10. Stereo. 1265 Perkiomen Ave. 19602. Phone: (610) 376-7173. Phone: (610) 376-6671. Fax: (610) 376-1270. Web Site: www.1340wraw.com. Licensee: Clear Channel Radio Licenses Inc. Group owner: Clear Channel Communications Inc. (acq 1996; grpsl). Network: CBS. Rep: Allied Radio Partners. Arent, Fox, Kintner, Plotkin & Kahn. Format: Music for your life. News staff: 2. Target aud: 45 plus.

Spec prog: Class one hr, Pol 3 hrs, Sp 3 hrs, big band 5 hrs, gospel one hr, relg one hr wkly. ◆Chris Taylor, gen mgr; Bob Minnich, progmg dir; Stefanie Wood, news dir & chief of engrg.

WRFY-FM—Co-owned with WRAW(AM). Sept 23, 1962: 102.5 mhz; 19 kw. 807 ft. TL: N40 19 19 W75 53 41. Stereo. Web Site: www.y102.com. Format: CHR. Target aud: 18-49. ◆Al Burke, progmg mgr; Jason Mitchell, mus dir.

***WXAC(FM)**— 1967: 91.3 mhz; 200 w. 33 ft. TL: N40 22 08 W75 54 37. Stereo. 1621 N. 13th St. 19612-5234. Phone: (610) 921-7545. Fax: (610) 921-7685. E-mail: wxac@albright.edu. Licensee: Albright College. Format: Progsv, Jazz, AOR, Sp. Target aud: General; Albright college community & Reading area. Spec prog: Sp 40 hrs wkly. ◆Mindy Cohen, stn mgr.

Red Lion

WGLD(AM)— Oct 22, 1950: 1440 khz; 1 kw-D, 56 w-N. TL: N39 54 17 W76 34 49. 140 E. Market St., York 17401. Phone: (717) 852-2305. Fax: (717) 246-1717. Licensee: Susquehanna License Co. LLC. (acq 5-11-2005; $280,000). Format: Relg. ◆David E. Kennedy, pres; Bill Fenton, gen mgr; John Peeling, stn mgr; Lisa Dissinger, opns mgr.

WSOX(FM)— October 1960: 96.1 mhz; 13.5 kw. Ant 951 ft. TL: N39 54 16 W76 34 48. Stereo. Box 910, York 17402. Phone: (717) 764-1155. Fax: (717) 755-3714. Web Site: www.oldies961.com. Licensee: Susquehanna License Co. LLC. Group owner: Susquehanna Radio Corp. (acq 8-1-2003; $23 million). Format: Oldies. ◆Tom Ranker, VP & gen mgr; Dave Anthony, progmg dir; Scott Steffan, chief of engrg.

Renovo

WZYY(FM)— Sept 19, 1996: 106.9 mhz; 800 w. Ant 876 ft. TL: N41 14 15 W77 45 02. Box 426, Warren 16365. Secondary address: 240 11th St. 17764. Phone: (570) 923-9106. Fax: (570) 923-3291. Licensee: Magnum Broadcasting Inc. (acq 7-21-2004; $200,000). Format: Hot adult contemp. ◆Michael M. Stapleford, pres.

Reynoldsville

WDSN(FM)— Feb 14, 1990: 106.5 mhz; 6 kw. 328 ft. TL: N41 08 41 W78 52 41. Stereo. 51 W. Long Ave., Dubois 15801. Phone: (814) 375-5260. Fax: (814) 375-5262. Web Site: www.sunny1065.fm. Licensee: Priority Communications. (acq 11-6-90; $275,000; 11-26-90). Network: Jones Radio Networks. Commerical Media Sales Pepper & Corazzini. Format: Adult contemp. News staff: one; News: 18 hrs wkly. Target aud: 25-54. ◆Jay M. Philippone, pres & gen mgr; Beth Walters, opns dir; Kevin Brown, sls dir; Lori Lewis, stn mgr, opns mgr & progmg dir; Lindsay Schoening, news dir; Al Lockwood, pub affrs dir.

Ridgebury

WREQ(FM)— 1991: 96.9 mhz; 3.6 kw. Ant 430 ft. TL: N41 55 43 W76 46 58. 111 N. Main St., Elmira, NY 14901. Phone: (607) 732-2484. Fax: (607) 732-8704. E-mail: wreq@csnradio.com. Web Site: q969online.com. Licensee: CSN International (group owner; acq 6-14-2001; $300,000). Reddy, Begley & McCormick. Format: Edu, contemp Christian mus, modern praise & worship. News: 4 hrs wkly. Target aud: 25-44; women with families (small children), heads of households. ◆Chuck Smith, pres; Lorenzo Galletti, gen mgr & stn mgr; Mike Stocklin, gen mgr; Doug Wakil, progmg mgr & mus dir; Gina Galletti, mus dir; Nora Cooper, asst music dir.

Ridgway

WKBI(AM)—See Saint Marys

WKBI-FM—See Saint Marys

Riverside

WLGL(FM)— Oct 25, 1990: 92.3 mhz; 440 w. 833 ft. TL: N40 57 30 W76 42 53. Stereo. Box 90, Rt. 204, State School Rd,, Selinsgrove 17870. Phone: (570) 374-8819. Fax: (570) 374-7444. Licensee: MMP License LLC. Group owner: MAX Media L.L.C. (acq 10-17-03; grpsl). Network: Network: Jones Radio Networks, CNN Radio. Dome & Associates. Kaye, Scholer, Fierman, Hays & Handler. Format: Contemp hot country. News staff: one; News: 5 hrs wkly. Target aud: 25-54. ◆Scott Richards, gen mgr; Dawn Marie, opns dir & news dir; Greg Adair, gen sls mgr & mktg dir; Shelly Marx, prom dir & mus dir; Ted Koppen, chief of engrg.

Roaring Spring

WKMC(AM)— May 1, 1955: 1370 khz; 5 kw-D, 38 w-N, DA-2. TL: N40 19 26 W78 23 40. Stereo. 1345 S. Main St. 16673. Phone: (814) 224-7501. Fax: (814) 224-7504. E-mail: wkmc@cove.net. Web Site: www.wkmcam.com. Licensee: Allegheny Mountain Network. Group owner: Allegheny Mountain Network Stations. Format: Adult standard. Target aud: 45 plus; mature, loyal listeners. ◆Cary Simpson, pres; Mike Martin, gen mgr, mktg dir, prom dir, progmg dir & news dir; Robert Lynn, chief of engrg.

WRKY-FM—See Hollidaysburg

Russell

WQFX-FM— Nov 11, 1984: 103.1 mhz; 2.5 kw. 351 ft. TL: N41 57 48 W79 09 42. Stereo. Box 1199, Jamestown, NY 14702-1199. Phone: (716) 664-2313. Fax: (716) 488-1471. E-mail: jadmin@wksn.com. Licensee: Media One Group II LLC. (acq 5-31-2005; grpsl). Rep: Dome. Fisher, Wayland, Cooper, Leader & Zaragoza. Format: Classic rock. Target aud: 25-54. ◆Joyce Marshall, gen mgr; Joel Keefer, rgnl sls mgr.

Saegertown

WHUZ(FM)— Jan 19, 1979: 94.3 mhz; 3 kw. 298 ft. TL: N41 42 23 W80 10 09. Stereo. Box 397, Meadville 16335. Phone: (814) 724-1111. Fax: (814) 333-9628. Licensee: Forever Broadcasting LLC. Group owner: Forever Broadcasting (acq 7-20-00; grpsl). Format: Classic hits. ◆Terry Deitz, gen mgr.

Saint Marys

WDDH(FM)— Apr 22, 1986: 97.5 mhz; 23 kw. 705 ft. TL: N41 37 04 W78 48 14. (CP: 19.5 kw, ant 800 ft.). Stereo. 14902 Bootjack Rd., Ridgway 15853. Phone: (814) 772-9700. Fax: (814) 772-9750. E-mail: brm@houndcountry.com. Web Site: www.houndcountry.com. Licensee: Intrepid Broadcasting Inc. (acq 3-25-2004; $1.25 million). Network: Network: Westwood One, Jones Radio Networks, ABC. Rep: Rgnl Reps. Dome & Associates Format: Country. Target aud: 25-54. ◆Michael Stapleford, CEO; Bryan Mallette, gen mgr; John Allen, opns mgr; Peter Butler, rgnl sls mgr.

WKBI(AM)— July 23, 1950: 1400 khz; 1 kw-U. TL: N41 24 56 W78 33 56. Box 466, 137 Melody Rd. 15857. Phone: (814) 834-2821. Phone: (814) 834-2822. Fax: (814) 834-4319. E-mail: b94@wkbi.net. Web Site: www.wkbi.net. Licensee: Elk-Cameron Broadcasting Co. Group owner: Allegheny Mountain Network Stations Network: Westwood One. Rep: Dome. Borsari & Paxson. Format: Adult contemp, oldies, sports. News staff: one; News: 10 hrs wkly. Target aud: 35-55. ◆Cary H. Simpson, pres; Ted Simpson, gen mgr; Erik Lane, opns dir & pub affrs dir; Nancy Bowser, prom mgr; Phil Leslie, news dir; Robert Lynn, chief of engrg.

WKBI-FM— August 1966: 93.9 mhz; 2.35 kw. 800 ft. TL: N41 23 11 W78 41 32. Stereo. Web Site: www.wkbi.net. Network: Network: Westwood One, Jones Radio Networks. Target aud: General; young adults. Spec prog: Relg 2 hrs wkly.

Pennsylvania

Salladasburg

WBYL(FM)— 1989:: 95.5 mhz; 3.9 kw. 239 ft. TL: N41 14 00 W77 12 09. Stereo. 1559 W. 4th St., Williamsport 17701. Phone: (570) 327-1400. Fax: (570) 327-8156. Web Site: www.billcountry.com. Licensee: Clear Channel Radio License Inc. Group owner: Clear Channel Communications Inc. (acq 8-5-98; grpsl). Network: ABC Information & Entertainment. Format: Country. News staff: one; News: 4 hrs wkly. Target aud: 35 plus. ♦James Dabney, gen mgr; Joe Daniels, gen sls mgr; Gary Chrisman, prom dir; Ken Sawyer, opns dir & progmg mgr; Kathy Thomas, news dir; Jerry Maiolo, engrg. dir.

Sayre

WATS(AM)— June 1950: 960 khz; 5 kw-D. TL: N41 59 48 W76 30 03. 204 Desmond St. 18840. Phone: (570) 888-7745. Fax: (570) 888-9005. E-mail: wats.wavr@cqservices.com. Licensee: WATS Broadcasting Inc. (acq 10-17-86). Network: UPI. Format: Adult contemp. Target aud: 25-54. Spec prog: Farm one hr wkly. ♦Charles C. Carver Jr., VP, gen mgr & news dir; Meade T. Murtland, stn mgr; Meade Murtland, rgnl sls mgr; Joel Clawson, progmg dir; Lawrence Brown, chief of engrg.

WAVR(FM)—See Waverly, NY

Schnecksville

*****WXLV(FM)**— Sept 23, 1983: 90.3 mhz; 670 w. 177 ft. TL: N40 39 52 W75 36 40. (CP: 420 w, ant 230 ft.). Stereo. 4525 Education Park Dr. 18078. Phone: (610) 799-4141. Fax: (610) 799-1571. E-mail: wxlv@hotmail.com. Web Site: www.wxlvfm.com. Licensee: Lehigh Carbon Community College. Format: Div. alternative. Spec prog: Class 13 hrs, jazz 6 hrs, Pol 6 hrs, blues 4 hrs, new wave 6 hrs wkly. ♦Tony Peiffer, gen mgr & chief of opns.

Scottdale

WLSW(FM)— Dec 21, 1971: 103.9 mhz; 325 w. 780 ft. TL: N40 00 51 W79 31 01. Stereo. Box 763, Connellsville 15425. Phone: (724) 628-2800. Fax: (724) 628-7380. Web Site: www.wlsw.com. Licensee: Wall Broadcasting. Network: Westwood One. Format: Hot adult contemp, oldies. Target aud: 25-54; general. ♦L. Stanley Wall, pres; Chris Molton, gen mgr, gen sls mgr & chief of engrg; Debbie Larson, progmg dir.

Scranton

WARM(AM)— 1940: 590 khz; 5 kw-U, DA-2. TL: N41 28 44 W75 52 51. 600 Baltimore Dr., Wilkes Barre 18702. Phone: (570) 824-9000. Fax: (570) 820-0520. E-mail: warm.webmaster@citcomm.com. Web Site: www.590warm.com. Licensee: Citadel Broadcasting Co. Group owner: Citadel Broadcasting Corp. (acq 7-1-97; grpsl). Format: News/talk, sports. News staff: 7; News: 30 hrs wkly. Target aud: 35 plus. Spec prog: Phillies baseball, Penn State football, Eagles football. ♦Jules Reilly, opns mgr; Camille LoSapio, sls dir; Jack Williams, rgnl sls mgr; Greg Foster, progmg dir; Paula Deignan, news dir; Dave Schmidt, chief of engrg.

WBAX(AM)—See Wilkes-Barre

WBZU(AM)— Jan 12, 1925: 910 khz; 1 kw-D, 500 w-N. TL: N41 22 56 W75 41 51. 305 Hwy. 315, Pittston 18640. Phone: (570) 883-9850. Fax: (570) 883-0832. Web Site: www.wilknewsradio.com. Licensee: Entercom Scranton Wilkes-Barre License LLC. Group owner: Entercom Communications Corp. (acq 12-16-99; grpsl). Network: ABC Information & Entertainment. Rep: D & R Radio. Format: News/talk. News staff: 6; News: 25 hrs wkly. Target aud: 25-54; affluent, educated. Spec prog: Relg one hr wkly. ♦John Burkavage, gen mgr; Jim Rising, opns dir; Andy Zapotell, gen sls mgr; Bob DeMono, natl sls mgr; Liz Masich, prom mgr; Nancy Kman, progmg dir; Joe Thomas, news dir; Lamar Smith, chief of engrg.

WGGY(FM)—Co-owned with WBZU(AM). Dec 25, 1948: 101.3 mhz; 7 kw. 1,110 ft. TL: N41 25 38 W75 44 53. Stereo. 305 Hwy. 315, Pittston 18640. Phone: (570) 883-1111. Fax: (570) 883-1360. Web Site: www.froggy101.com. Network: CBS. Format: Country. ♦John Burkavage, VP & gen mgr; Jim Rising, opns dir; Andy Zapotek, gen sls mgr; Bob De Mono, natl sls mgr; Elizabeth Masieh, mktg dir; Cheryl Willis, prom mgr; Mike Krinik, progmg dir; Jaymie Gordon, mus dir; Kelly Green, mus dir; Laman Smith, chief of engrg.

WEJL(AM)— Nov 29, 1922: 630 khz; 500 w-D, 32 w-N. TL: N41 24 35 W75 40 41. 149 Penn Ave. 18503. Phone: (570) 346-6555. Fax: (570) 346-6038. Web Site: www.wejl-wbax.com. Licensee: The Scranton Times LP. Group owner: Shamrock Communications Inc. (acq 1922). Network: ABC Information & Entertainment. Format: Sports. ♦William R. Lynett, CEO; Jim Loftus, COO & gen mgr; Tim Durkin, sls dir; Jenny Arndt, natl sls mgr; Mark Hoover, mktg dir; Michael Neff, progmg dir; Ruth Miller, news dir; Kevin Fitzgerald, chief of engrg.

WEZX(FM)—Co-owned with WEJL(AM). Nov 1, 1967: 106.9 mhz; 1.45 kw. 617 ft. TL: N41 20 52 W75 39 03. Stereo. Fax: (570) 346-6038. (Acq 1967). Format: Classic rock. ♦Mark Hoover, prom mgr; Kevin Fritzgerald, engrg dir.

WICK(AM)— Apr 17, 1954: 1400 khz; 1 kw-U. TL: N41 25 05 W75 39 43. Stereo. 1049 N. Sekol Rd. 18504. Phone: (570) 344-1221. Fax: (570) 344-0996. Web Site: www.wick-am.com. Licensee: Lancom Inc. (acq 9-11-78). Network: ABC. Holland & Knight. Format: Oldies. News staff: one; News: 8 hrs of wkly. Target aud: 35-64; adults who love original hits of Top 40 Era. Spec prog: Relg 3 hrs, Pol 3 hrs wkly. ♦Ed Kerber, opns mgr; Phil Bunkwell, gen sls mgr.

WWDL-FM—Co-owned with WICK(AM). Nov 26, 1964: 104.9 mhz; 270 w. 1,092 ft. TL: N41 26 06 W75 43 35. Stereo. Phone: (570) 344-1221. Fax: (570) 344-0996. Web Site: www.wwdl.com. Licensee: Lane Broadcasting Corp. Holland & Knight. Format: Adult contemp. News staff: one. Target aud: 25-54; men & women. ♦Ed Kerber, prom dir.

WILK(AM)—See Wilkes-Barre

WITK(AM)—See Pittston

WKRZ(FM)—See Wilkes-Barre

WMGS(FM)—See Wilkes-Barre

*****WUSR(FM)**— Feb 27, 1993: 99.5 mhz; 300 w. 1,014 ft. TL: N41 26 09 W75 43 33. Stereo. Univ. of Scranton, St. Thomas Hall, 800 Linden St. 18510. Phone: (570) 941-7648. Fax: (570) 941-4628. E-mail: wusr@scranton.edu. Web Site: www.scranton.edu/wusr. Licensee: University of Scranton. Format: Alternative, jazz, rock/AOR, Urban contemp, blues. Target aud: General. Spec prog: Class 5 hrs, relg 4 hrs, loud rock 8 hrs, urban contemp 6 hrs, Latin 10 hrs wkly, polka, talk, showtunes, world music, reggae, Celtic. ♦Ken Sandrowicz, gen mgr; Margo Christiansen, stn mgr.

*****WVIA-FM**— Apr 23, 1973: 89.9 mhz; 5 kw. 1,250 ft. TL: N41 10 55 W75 52 17. Stereo. 100 Wvia Way, Pittston 18640-6197. Phone: (570) 655-2808. Phone: (570) 826-6144. Fax: (570) 655-1180. E-mail: webadmin@wvia.org. Web Site: www.wvia.org. Licensee: N.E. Pa. Educational TV Association. Network: NPR, PRI. Format: Class, jazz, news. News staff: 31 hrs wkly. ♦A. William Kelly, CEO & pres; Chris Norton, VP; Mollie Worrell, dev VP; George Graham, mus dir; Joseph Glynn, engrg VP. Co-owned TV: *WVIA-TV affil.

*****WVMW-FM**— September 1974: 91.7 mhz; 2 kw. Ant -285 ft. TL: N41 25 57 W75 38 06. Stereo. Marywood University, 2300 Adams Ave. 18509. Phone: (570) 348-6202. Fax: (570) 961-4769. E-mail: mengoni@marywood.edu. Web Site: www.vmfm917.com. Licensee: Marywood College. Format: Alternative. News staff: 2; News: 7 hrs wkly. Target aud: 15-25; young adults. Spec prog: Black 2 hrs, class 7 hrs, jazz 10 hrs wkly. ♦Earnest Mengoni, stn mgr; George Graham, chief of engrg.

WYCK(AM)—See Plains

Selinsgrove

*****WQSU(FM)**— September 1967: 88.9 mhz; 12 kw. 620 ft. TL: N40 57 06 W75 45 03. Stereo. Susquehanna Univ., 514 University Ave. 17870. Phone: (570) 372-4030. Fax: (570) 372-2757. E-mail: augustin@susqu.edu. Web Site: www.wqsu.com. Licensee: Susquehanna University. Network: AP Radio. Format: Modern rock. News: 7 hrs wkly. Target aud: 18-34. Spec prog: Classic country 6 hrs, sports 4 hrs, bluegrass 7 hrs wkly. ♦Larry D. Augustine, gen mgr; Harry Bingaman, chief of engrg.

WYGL(AM)— Jan 16, 1967: 1240 khz; 1 kw-U. TL: N40 48 59 W76 52 13. Box 90, Rt. 204 & State School Rd. 17870. Phone: (570) 374-1155. Fax: (570) 374-8819. Web Site: www.bigcountrynow.com. Licensee: MMP License LLC. Group owner: MAX Media L.L.C. (acq 10-17-03; grpsl). Network: USA. Kaye, Scholer, Fierman, Hays & Handler L.L.P. Format: Contemp hot country. News staff: one; News: 8 hrs wkly. Target aud: 18 plus. ♦John A. Trinder, pres; Scott Richards, VP & gen mgr; Dawn Marie, opns dir; Greg Adair, gen sls mgr; Shelly Marks, prom dir & asst music dir; Lisa Richards, mus dir; Nat O'Brien, news dir; Ted Koppen, chief of engrg.

Sellersville

*****WBYO(FM)**— March 1991: 88.9 mhz; 900 w. Ant 436 ft. TL: N40 23 02 W75 21 02. Stereo. Box 186 18960. Phone: (215) 721-2141. Fax: (215) 721-9811. E-mail: wordfm@wordfm.org. Web Site: www.wordfm.org. Licensee: Four Rivers Community Broadcasting Corp. Schwartz, Woods & Miller. Format: Adult contemp, Christian, religious. News staff: one; News: 10 hrs wkly. Target aud: General. Spec prog: Country gospel 2 hrs, gospel bluegrass 2 hrs wkly. ♦Charles W. Loughery, pres, gen mgr, engrg mgr & chief of engrg; Nancy K. Loughery, CFO; David Baker, VP & stn mgr; Kristine McClain, progmg mgr.

Shamokin

WBLJ-FM— 1968: 95.3 mhz; 1.25 kw. 505 ft. TL: N40 45 36 W76 32 19. Stereo. Box 3638, Williamsport 17701-3638. Phone: (570) 327-1400. Fax: (570) 327-8156. E-mail: bill@billcountry.com. Web Site: www.billcountry.com. Licensee: Clear Channel Broadcasting Licenses Inc. Group owner: Clear Channel Communications Inc. (acq 10-4-01; $800,000. with co-located AM). Format: Country. ♦Jim Dabney, gen mgr; Joe Daniels, gen sls mgr; Gary Chrisman, prom dir; Ken Sawyer, progmg dir; Kathy Thomas, news dir.

WISL(AM)— January 1948: . Stn currently dark 1480 khz; 1 kw-U, DA-N. TL: N40 45 53 W76 31 18. 550 California Rd., Unit 11, Quakertown 18951. Phone: (215) 536-6648. Licensee: Basic Licensing Inc. (acq 11-18-2002). ♦David C. Gorman, pres, CFO & gen mgr; Kurt Gorman, exec VP.

Sharon

WPIC(AM)— Oct 25, 1938: 790 khz; 1 kw-D, 51 w-N. TL: N41 13 10 W80 28 25. 220 Pine Hollow, Hermitage, OH 16148. Phone: (330) 783-1000. Fax: (330) 783-0060. Web Site: www.cumulus.com. Licensee: Cumulus Licensing Corp. Group owner: Cumulus Media Inc. (acq 3-15-00; grpsl). Network: ABC Information & Entertainment. Rep: Allied Radio Partners. Format: Nostalgia. News staff: 2; News: 22 hrs wkly. Target aud: 35 plus. Spec prog: Pol 6 hr, It 2 hrs, relg 2 hrs, infomercials 12 hrs wkly. ♦Don Kidwell, exec VP; Larry Weiss, gen mgr; Pam Black, sls dir; Sheri Foffit, gen sls mgr & natl sls mgr; Bob Popa, progmg dir; Joe Biro, news dir; Charles Ring, chief of engrg.

WYFM(FM)—Co-owned with WPIC(AM). Oct 25, 1947: 102.9 mhz; 44 kw. Ant 455 ft. TL: N41 13 10 W80 28 25. Stereo. 4040 Simon Rd., Youngstown 44512. Web Site: www.cumulus.com. Network: Westwood One. Format: Classic hits, classic rock. Target aud: 25-54. ♦Kelly McGrath, sls dir; Lee Jolly, prom mgr; Malinda Michaels, prom mgr; Scott Kennedy, progmg dir; Lynn Davis, news dir.

Sharpsville

WAKZ(FM)—Licensed to Sharpsville. See Youngstown OH

Shippensburg

WEEO(AM)— Dec 5, 1961: 1480 khz; 460 w-D, 9 w-N. TL: N40 04 30 W77 32 09. 37 S. Main St., Chambersburg 17201. Phone: (717) 709-0801. Fax: (717) 709-0802. Licensee: Allegheny Mountain Network. Format: Adult contemp. Target aud: 30 plus. ♦Cary Simpson, pres; Matthew J. Becker, prom dir & prom mgr.

*****WSYC-FM**— February 1975: 88.7 mhz; 100 w. 155 ft. TL: N40 03 32 W77 31 20. (CP: TL: N40 04 30 W77 31 15). Stereo. Shippensburg Univ., Cumberland Union Bldg., Shippenburg 17257. Phone: (717) 532-6006. Fax: (717) 477-4024. Web Site: www.wsyc.org. Licensee: Shippensburg University. Network: Westwood One. Format: AOR. News staff: 7; News: 3 hrs wkly. Target aud: 16-25; college & area high school students. Spec prog: Black 9 hrs, class 2 hrs, jazz 3 hrs, blues 2 hrs, wkly. ♦Melanie Warfel, gen mgr; Phil Smith, opns dir; Becke Arline, sls dir.

Shiremanstown

WWII(AM)— June 1987: 720 khz; 2 kw-D. TL: N40 11 28 W76 57 09. Stereo. 8 W. Main St. 17011. Phone: (717) 731-9944. Fax: (717) 761-0665. E-mail: therock@igateway.com. Web Site: www.720therock.com.

Stations in the U.S.   **Pennsylvania**

Developers & Brokers of Radio Properties — contact American Media Services at our suite: Philadelphia Marriott Downtown 215-625-2900 • 843-972-2200 • americanmediaservices.com • Charleston, SC • Dallas, TX • Chicago, Il • Austin, TX — American Media Services, LLC

Licensee: Hensley Broadcasting. Format: Christian. News: 2 hrs wkly. Target aud: 25 plus; Christian. Spec prog: Gospel 2 hrs, polka 7 hrs, Indian one hr, blues 4 hrs wkly. ♦ Dean Lebo, gen mgr; Joe Green, sls dir & progmg dir; Tom Sullivan, progmg dir.

Slippery Rock

*WRSK(FM)— Sept 20, 1991: 88.1 mhz; 100 w. 79 ft. TL: N41 03 43 W80 02 35. Stereo. Box C-211, Univ. Union 16057. Phone: (724) 738-2655. Phone: (724) 738-2931. Fax: (724) 738-2754. Web Site: www.wrsk.org. Licensee: Slippery Rock University. Network: ABC. Format: Classic rock, progsv, var/div. News staff: one; News: 14 hrs wkly. Target aud: 18-24; on & off campus students. Spec prog: Relg one hr, campus info one hr, sports one hr wkly. ♦ Jay Hunsicker, gen mgr; Carly Dobbins-Bucklad, stn mgr; Erin McConahy, sls dir; Laura Cooper, prom VP; Vinny Karpuska, progmg dir; Bob Kitzinger, mus dir; Anthony Skariot, asst music dir; Kaleena Zohoranacky, news dir & pub affrs dir; Werner Ullrich, chief of engrg.

Smethport

WQRM(FM)— January 1990: 106.3 mhz; 1.2 kw. 731 ft. TL: N41 48 36 W78 23 10. Stereo. 211 W. Main St. 16749. Phone: (814) 887-1977. Phone: (814) 887-2425. Fax: (814) 887-5178. E-mail: wqrm@usachoice.net. Licensee: Farm & Home Broadcasting Co. Group owner: Allegheny Mountain Network Stations Rep: Dome. Format: Adult contemp, news. News: one hr wkly. Target aud: 18-54; 60% females & 40% males. Spec prog: Relig 2 hrs wkly, Sports 3 hrs wkly. ♦ Cary Simpson, pres; Rose Bishop, gen mgr.

Somerset

WBHV(AM)— June 15, 1981: 1330 khz; 5 kw-D, 35 w-N, DA-1. TL: N39 59 33 W79 05 41. 2447 Bedford St., Johnstown 15904-2522. Phone: (814) 266-9458. Fax: (814) 266-9212. Licensee: 2510 Licenses LLC. (group owner; (acq 2-16-2005; grpsl). Network: Westwood One, Motor Racing Net. Booth, Freret, Imlay & Tepper P. Format: News/talk. News: 7 hrs wkly. Target aud: 35-64. Spec prog: Sports 12 hrs wkly. ♦ Al Dame, gen mgr; Jeannie Feathers, gen sls mgr; Brad Lorence, progmg dir.

WLKH(FM)—Listing follows WNTW(AM).

WNTW(AM)— Jan 15, 1951: 990 khz; 10 kw-D, 75 w-N, DA-1. TL: N40 01 31 W79 05 42. 109 Plaza Dr. Suite 2, Johnstown 15501-1212. Phone: (814) 255-4186. Fax: (814) 255-6145. Licensee: Forever Broadcasting LLC. Group owner: Forever Broadcasting (acq 9-9-97; grpsl). Network: ABC Information & Entertainment. Format: Country. News staff: one; News: 8 hrs wkly. Target aud: 35-55. ♦ Carol Logan, pres; Verla Price, gen mgr & gen sls mgr; Mike Stevens, progmg dir; Rick Sheppard, news dir & pub affrs dir; Jim Boxler, chief of engrg.

WLKH(FM)—Co-owned with WNTW(AM). June 15, 1966: 97.7 mhz; 3.5 kw. Ant 430 ft. TL: N40 01 31 W79 05 42. 109 Plaza Dr., Johnstown 15905. Web Site: www.wuzz105.com. Format: Classic hits. Target aud: 25-54. ♦ Mike Stevens, mus dir.

South Waverly

WPHD(FM)— 2003: 96.1 mhz; 920 w. Ant 612 ft. TL: N41 58 04 W76 40 02. 734 Chemung St., Horseheads, NY 14845. Secondary address: 495 Court St., 2nd Fl., Binghamton 13904. Phone: (607) 795-0795. Phone: (607) 772-1005. Fax: (607) 795-1095. Fax: (607) 772-2945. E-mail: geoequinox@aol.com. Licensee: Fitzgerald and Hawras Partnership (acq 3-22-01). Rep: Katz Radio. Format: Oldies. Target aud: 35-64; adults. ♦ George Harris, gen mgr; Stephen Shimer, opns mgr; Kevin Fitzgerald, chief of engrg.

South Williamsport

WZXR(FM)— June 1, 1968: 99.3 mhz; 6 kw. 1,237 ft. TL: N41 12 42 W76 57 16. Stereo. 1685 Four Mile Dr., Williamsport 17740. Phone: (570) 323-8200. Fax: (570) 323-5075. Web Site: www.wzxr.com. Licensee: South Williamsport SabreCom Inc. Group owner: Backyard Broadcasting LLC (acq 12-1-02; grpsl). Network: ABC. Format: AOR, classic rock. News staff: one; News: 7 hrs wkly. Target aud: 25-54. ♦ Barry Drake, pres; Robin Smith, CFO; Dan Farr, gen mgr; Bob Pawlikowski, sls dir; Ted Minier, progmg dir; John Finn, news dir; Tom Atkins, chief of engrg.

Starview

WSJW(FM)— Nov 22, 1971: 92.7 mhz; 700 w. Ant 954 ft. TL: N40 04 32 W76 48 03. Stereo. Box 4368, Lancaster 17604. Secondary address: 1996 Auction Rd., Manheim 17545. Phone: (717) 653-0800. Phone: (800) 222-1013. Fax: (717) 653-0122. E-mail: bbaldwin@halradio.com. Web Site: smoothjazz927.com. Licensee: Hall Communications Inc. (group owner: acq 1-16-96; $2.3 million). Rep: D & R Radio. Fletcher, Heald & Hildreth. Format: Smooth jazz. Target aud: 25-54. ♦ Bonnie H. Rowbotham, chmn; Arthur J. Rowbotham, pres; Bill Baldwin, sr VP & gen mgr; Tom Shannon, opns mgr; Fran Martin, prom dir.

State College

WBLF(AM)—See Bellefonte

WGMR(FM)—See Tyrone

WJHT(FM)—Listing follows WMAJ(AM).

*WKPS(FM)— 1995: 90.7 mhz; 100 w. 85 ft. TL: N40 47 58 W77 52 11. James Bldg., 125 Hub-Robeson Ctr. 16802. Phone: (814) 865-7983. Phone: (814) 865-9577. Fax: (814) 865-2751. E-mail: lion-officers@psu.edu. Web Site: www.lion-radio.org. Licensee: Board of Trustees of Pennsylvania State University. Format: Var. News: 4 hrs wkly. Target aud: University students. Spec prog: Jazz 11 hrs, Sp 8 hrs wkly. ♦ Scott DeBourke, VP; Mike Fecht, stn mgr; Don Hausmann, opns dir.

WLTS(FM)— Oct 23, 1991: 94.5 mhz; 940 w. 581 ft. TL: N40 54 04 W77 50 20. Stereo. 2551 Park Center Blvd. 16801. Phone: (814) 237-9800. Fax: (814) 237-2477. Licensee: Forever of PA LLC. Group owner: Forever Broadcasting (acq 1996). Rep: Christal. Format: Lite, Easy favorites. ♦ Carol Logan, pres; Don A. Bedell, gen mgr; Nick Ferrara, opns mgr; Bill Edmiston, gen sls mgr; Scott Cohagan, gen sls mgr; Doug Herendeen, progmg dir; Bob Taylor, chief of engrg.

WMAJ(AM)— 1945: 1450 khz; 1 kw-U. TL: N40 48 32 W77 50 28. 2551 Park Center Blvd. 16801. Phone: (814) 237-9800. Fax: (814) 237-2477. Web Site: www.pennlive.com. Licensee: Forever Broadcasting LLC. Group owner: Forever Broadcasting (acq 3-10-98; $2.9 million. with co-located FM). Network: CBS. Rep: Christal. Format: Sports. News staff: 2; News: 49 hrs wkly. Target aud: 30 plus; college educated, upscale. ♦ Carol Logan, pres; Don A. Bedell, gen mgr; Nick Ferrara, opns mgr; Scott Cohagan, gen sls mgr; Patrick Boland, news dir; Bob Taylor, chief of engrg.

WJHT(FM)—Co-owned with WMAJ(AM). 1965: 103.1 mhz; 3 kw. -55 ft. TL: N40 48 32 W77 50 28. Stereo. Web Site: www.Beaver103.com. Format: CHR. News staff: one. Target aud: 18-34; college-aged youth, young adults. ♦ Keith Allen, progmg dir; Lynn Deppen, engrg VP.

WOWY(FM)—Listing follows WRSC(AM).

*WPSU(FM)— Dec 6, 1953: 91.5 mhz; 1.7 kw. 1,197 ft. TL: N40 48 32 W77 50 28. Stereo. Wagner Annex, University Park 16802. Phone: (814) 865-9778. Fax: (814) 865-3145. E-mail: wpsu@psu.edu. Web Site: www.wpsu.org. Licensee: Pennsylvania State University. Network: NPR. Format: News, class, folk, jazz. News staff: one; News: 35 hrs wkly. Target aud: General; upscale, educated adults. Spec prog: Folk 11 hrs, jazz 3 hrs, blues 2 hrs wkly. ♦ Ted Krichels, gen mgr; Greg Petersen, stn mgr; Steve Shipman, opns dir; Joy Vincent Killian, dev dir; Ashear Barr, sls dir; Bill Hiergeist, rgnl sls dir; Sam Komlenic, rgnl sls mgr; Carol Wonsavage, mktg mgr; Kristine Allen, progmg dir; Cindi Deutschman-Ruiz, news dir; Carl Fisher, chief of engrg.

WRSC(AM)— May 29, 1961: 1390 khz; 2 kw-D, 1 kw-N, DA-N. TL: N40 48 50 W77 53 30. 160 Clearview Ave. 16803. Phone: (814) 238-5085. Fax: (814) 238-8993. Licensee: 2510 Licenses LLC. (group owner; (acq 2-16-2005); grpsl). Network: ABC Information & Entertainment. Rep: McGavren Guild. Dome. Latham & Watkins. Format: News/talk. News staff: 2; News: 10 hrs wkly. Target aud: 35 plus. Spec prog: Class 3 hrs wkly. ♦ Rob Schmidt, gen mgr; Diana Albright, gen sls mgr; Dave Shannon, progmg mgr; Keith Fledderman, news dir.

WOWY(FM)—Co-owned with WRSC(AM). April 1965: 97.1 mhz; 3 kw. Ant 403 ft. TL: N40 48 27 W77 56 29. Stereo. Format: Rock/AOR. Target aud: 18-49. ♦ Dave Shannon, adv mgr; Jason Miller, progmg dir.

*WRXV(FM)— June 18, 2004: 89.1 mhz; 1 w horiz, 4.4 kw vert. Ant 1,099 ft. TL: N40 43 56 W78 19 33. 925 Houserville Rd. 16801. Phone: (814) 867-1922. Fax: (814) 867-1922. E-mail: info@revfm.net. Web Site: www.revfm.net. Licensee: Invisible Allies Ministries. Format: Contemp Christian. ♦ Michael Schomer, gen mgr; Erik Lane, stn mgr.

*WTLR(FM)— Jan 1, 1978: 89.9 mhz; 25 kw. Ant 584 ft. TL: N40 53 32 W77 51 49. Stereo. 2020 Cato Ave. 16801. Phone: (814) 237-9857. E-mail: mail@cpci.org. Licensee: Central Pennsylvania Christian Institute Inc. Format: Christian. News staff: one; News: 9 hrs wkly. Target aud: 30-55; Adults, family oriented. ♦ Mark Van Ouse, gen mgr.

*WXFR(FM)—Not on air, target date: unknown: 88.3 mhz; 1.8 kw vert. Ant 544 ft. TL: N40 54 07 W77 50 11. Family Stations Inc., 4135 Northgate Blvd., Suite 1, Sacramento, CA 95834. Phone: (916) 641-8191. E-mail: info@familyradio.org. Web Site: www.familyradio.com. Licensee: Family Stations Inc.

WZWW(FM)—(Bellefonte). Sept 15, 1986: 95.3 mhz; 933 w. 577 ft. TL: N40 53 32 W77 51 49. (CP: 794 w, ant 636 ft.). Stereo. 863 Benner Pike, Suite 200 16801. Phone: (814) 231-0953. Fax: (814) 231-0950. E-mail: nancy@3wz.com. Web Site: www.3wz.com. Licensee: First Media Radio LLC (group owner; acq 8-28-00). Network: CNN Radio. Rep: Allied Radio Partners. Commercial Media Sales. Format: Adult contemp. News staff: 2; News: 7 hrs wkly. Target aud: 25-54; upscale families. Spec prog: Sports 3 hrs wkly. ♦ Alex Kolobielski, pres; Mike McGough, gen mgr; Dave Kurten, gen sls mgr & progmg dir; Steve Jones, mus dir.

Stroudsburg

*WBYX(FM)— Oct. 1, 1999: 88.7 mhz; 1 w horiz, 4 kw vert. Ant 794 ft. TL: N41 02 40 W75 22 45. Stereo. Box 186, Sellersville 18960. Phone: (215) 721-2141. Fax: (215) 721-9811. E-mail: wordfm@wordfm.org. Web Site: www.wordfm.com. Licensee: Four Rivers Community Broadcasting Corp. Schwartz, Woods & Miller. Format: Adult contemp, Christian, religious. Target aud: 25-45. Spec prog: Bluegrass Gospel;. ♦ Nancy Loughery, CFO; David W. Baker, VP; Charles W. Loughery, gen mgr; Kristine McClain, progmg dir.

WSBG(FM)—Listing follows WVPO(AM).

WVPO(AM)— 1947: 840 khz; 250 w-D. TL: N40 58 26 W75 11 43. 22 S. 6th St. 18360. Phone: (570) 421-2100. Fax: (570) 421-2040. Licensee: Nassau Broadcasting II L.L.C. Group owner: Nassau Broadcasting Partners L.P. (acq 2-15-02; grpsl). Format: Adult standards. Target aud: 35 plus. ♦ Peter Tonks, CFO; Rick Musselman, gen mgr; Michele Stevens, progmg VP; Rod Bauman, progmg dir; Bob Matthews, news dir; Tony Gervasi, engrg VP; George Guilda, engrg mgr.

WSBG(FM)—Co-owned with WVPO(AM). Oct 1, 1964: 93.5 mhz; 550 w. 764 ft. TL: N40 56 56 W57 09 29. Stereo. Format: Hot adult contemp, rock & hip. Target aud: 18-49. Spec prog: Modern rock 3 hrs wkly.

Broadcasting & Cable Yearbook 2006
D-437

Pennsylvania   Directory of Radio

Summerdale

WJAZ(FM)— Jan 10, 1991: 91.7 mhz; 140 w. 683 ft. TL: N40 18 16 W76 55 53. Stereo. 100 Annenberg Hall (011-00), 1509 Cecil B. Moore Ave., 2nd Fl., Philadelphia 19122. Phone: (215) 204-8405. Fax: (215) 204-7027. E-mail: comments@wrti.org. Web Site: www.wrti.org. Licensee: Temple University of the Commonwealth System of Higher Education (acq 12-88; $5,000;. FTR: 12-5-88). Format: Classical, jazz. News staff: one; News: 15 hrs wkly. Target aud: 30-65. ♦Dave Conant, CEO & gen mgr; Bill Johnson, pres; Vic Scarpato, CFO; Tobias Poole, opns dir; William P. Johnson, dev dir; Rick Torpey, gen sls mgr & mktg mgr; Lorna Nixon, prom dir; Jack Moore, progmg dir; Windsor Johnson, news dir; Jeff DePolo, chief of engrg.

Sunbury

WKOK(AM)— 1933: 1070 khz; 10 kw-D, 1 kw-N, DA-N. TL: N40 52 46 W76 49 18. Box 1070 17801. Secondary address: R.D. 2, County Line Rd., Selinsgrove 17870. Phone: (570) 286-5838. Phone: (570) 743-1841. Fax: (570) 743-7837. Fax: (570) 743-1605. E-mail: wkok@wkok.com. Web Site: www.wkok.com. Licensee: Sunbury Broadcasting Corp. (acq 5-33). Network: Network: Network: CBS, ESPN Radio, AP Radio. Rep: Roslin. Dome. Wilkinson Barker Knauer. Format: News/talk, sports. News staff: 4; News: 168 hrs wkly. Target aud: 35-64. ♦Roger Haddon Jr., CEO, pres & gen mgr; Kevin Herr, opns mgr & news dir; Gayle Fedder, gen sls mgr & mktg mgr; Mark Lawrence, progmg dir.

WQKX(FM)—Co-owned with WKOK(AM). Sept 15, 1948: 94.1 mhz; 16 kw. 879 ft. TL: N40 47 07 W76 41 51. Stereo. E-mail: wqkx@wqkx.com. Web Site: www.wqkx.com. Format: CHR. News staff: 4; News: 7 hrs wkly. Target aud: 25-54. ♦Drew Kelly, progmg dir; Rob Senter, mus dir.

Susquehanna

WCDW(FM)— March 1995: 100.5 mhz; 1.35 kw. Ant 692 ft. TL: N42 03 10 W75 42 07. Stereo. 495 Court St., 2nd Floor, Binghamton 13904. Phone: (607) 772-1005. Fax: (607) 772-2945. E-mail: coololdies@aol.com. Web Site: www.coololdies.com. Licensee: Equinox Broadcasting Corp. Rep: Katz Radio. Format: Oldies. Target aud: 35-64. Spec prog: Polish 5 hrs wkly. ♦George Harris, CEO & pres; Tom Shiptenko, stn mgr; Stephen Shimer, opns VP.

WKGB-FM— Feb 11, 1989: 92.5 mhz; 6 kw. 709 ft. TL: N42 03 10 W75 42 07. (CP: 1.3 kw). Stereo. 320 N. Jensen Rd., Vestal, NY 13850. Phone: (607) 584-5800. Fax: (607) 584-5900. Web Site: www.925kgb.com. Licensee: Clear Channel Broadcasting Licenses Inc. Group owner: Clear Channel Communications Inc. (acq 4-14-2000; grpsl). Rep: D & R Radio. Carr, Morris & Graeff. Format: AOR, classic rock. News: one hr wkly. Target aud: 25-49; baby boomers who grew up with rock and roll of the 60s & 70s. Spec prog: Jazz 2 hrs, farm one hr wkly. ♦Tom Burney, gen mgr; Jim Free, opns mgr & progmg dir; Michele Page, sls dir; Tom Barney, mktg mgr; Tim Boland, mus dir; Jon Scaptura, engrg dir.

Swarthmore

*WSRN-FM— Dec 31, 1939: 91.5 mhz; 110 w. 140 ft. TL: N39 54 18 W75 21 16. Stereo. Swarthmore College, 500 College Ave. 19081. Phone: (610) 328-8336. Phone: (610) 328-8335. Web Site: wsrn.swarthmore.edu. Licensee: Swarthmore College. Format: Div. ♦Alex Flurie, gen mgr.

Sweet Valley

*WRGN(FM)— Oct 15, 1984: 88.1 mhz; 500 w. 239 ft. TL: N41 17 54 W76 07 28. (CP: Ant 302 ft.). 2457 State Rt. 118, Hunlock Creek 18621. Phone: (570) 477-3688. Fax: (570) 477-2310. E-mail: wrgn@epix.net. Web Site: www.wrgn.com. Licensee: Gospel Media Institute Inc. Format: Relg. ♦Burl F. Updyke, pres, gen mgr, gen sls mgr & chief of engrg; Shirley J. Updyke, prom dir & progmg dir.

Tafton

*WPGP(FM)— 2002: 88.3 mhz; 580 w. Ant 968 ft. TL: N41 35 36 W75 25 56. The Sound of Life, Box 777, Lake Katrine, NY 12449. Phone: (845) 336-6199. Fax: (845) 336-7205. E-mail: email@soundoflife.org. Web Site: soundoflife.org. Licensee: Sound of Life Inc. (acq 3-10-00). Format: Contemp Christian. ♦Tom Zahradnik, gen mgr.

Tamaqua

WMGH-FM— June 14, 1965: 105.5 mhz; 1.4 kw. 485 ft. TL: N40 47 14 W76 01 59. Stereo. Box D, Lansford 18232. Phone: (570) 668-2992. Phone: (570) 645-2105. Fax: (570) 645-2159. E-mail: wmgh@ptdprolog.net. Web Site: www.wmgh.com. Licensee: J-Systems Franchising Corp. (group owner; acq 2-28-87; $300,000;. FTR: 12-15-86). Network: Westwood One. Format: Adult contemp. Target aud: 25-54; primary women, secondary adults. Spec prog: Oldies 14 hrs, polka 3 hrs wkly. ♦Harold G. Fulmer III, pres; Christopher G. Fulmer, VP & gen sls mgr; Bill Lakatas, gen mgr & progmg dir; James Greech, gen sls mgr; Mark Marek, news dir; Joe Manjack, chief of engrg.

Tarentum

WZPT(FM)—See New Kensington

Telford

*WBMR(FM)— June 1967: 91.7 mhz; 115 w. Ant 249 ft. TL: N40 18 15 W75 17 39. 300 E. Rock Rd., Allentown 18103. Phone: (610) 797-4530. Fax: (610) 791-3000. Licensee: United Ministries. (acq 8-30-2002). Format: Relg.

Tioga

WMTT(FM)— May 23, 1991: 94.7 mhz; 820 w. 895 ft. TL: N41 54 36 W77 00 40. (CP: 12 kw). Stereo. 734 Chemung St., Horseheads, NY 14845. Secondary address: 495 Court St., 2nd Fl, Binghamton, NY 13904. Phone: (607) 795-0795. Phone: (607) 772-1005. Fax: (607) 795-1095. Fax: (607) 772-2945. E-mail: themetrocks@aol.com. Web Site: www.95themet.com. Licensee: Europa Communications Inc. (acq 5-22-92). Rep: Katz Radio. Format: Classic rock, AOR. News: 2 hrs wkly. Target aud: 25-49. ♦Kevin Fitzgerald, CEO & VP; George Harris, gen mgr & opns dir; Robert Smith, stn mgr; Stephen Shimer, opns mgr.

Titusville

WTIV(AM)— Nov 27, 1955: 1230 khz; 1 kw-U. TL: N41 37 00 W79 41 34. Box 606 16354. Secondary address: WTIV Bldg., 150 W. Central Ave. 16354. Phone: (814) 827-3651. Fax: (814) 827-1679. Web Site: www.foreverradio.com. Licensee: Forever Broadcasting LLC. Group owner: Forever Broadcasting (acq 7-20-00; grpsl). Reddy, Begley & McCormick. Format: MOR, Unforgettable Music. News: 13 hrs wkly. Target aud: 22-54; mixed. ♦Thomas J. Sauber, gen mgr; Tim Snyder, opns dir; Laurie Vogan, gen sls mgr; Dave English, progmg dir; Robert H. Sauber, chief of engrg.

Tobyhanna

WKRF(FM)— Jan 15, 1993: 107.9 mhz; 5.7 kw. 564 ft. TL: N41 07 04 W75 22 43. Stereo. 305 Hwy. 315, Pittston 18640. Phone: (570) 839-5858. Fax: (570) 883-9851. Web Site: www.wkrf.com. Licensee: Entercom Wilkes-Barre Scranton LLC. Group owner: Entercom Communications Corp. (acq 5-11-00). Network: Jones Radio Networks. Format: Top-40. News staff: one; News: one hr wkly. Target aud: 25-54. ♦John Burkavage, gen mgr; Jim Rising, stn mgr & opns mgr; Andy Zapotek, gen sls mgr; Bob Demono, natl sls mgr; Michael Ignatz, prom dir; Jerry Padden, progmg dir; Elizabeth Masich, mus dir; Lamar Smith, chief of engrg.

Towanda

WTTC(AM)— 1959: 1550 khz; 500 w-D. TL: N41 45 55 W76 29 10. 204 Desmond St., Sayre 18840. Phone: (570) 888-7745. Fax: (570) 888-9005. Licensee: WATS Broadcasting Inc. (acq 5-1-96; $175,000 for stock with co-located FM). Network: Motor Racing Net. Format: Oldies. Target aud: General. ♦Charles C Carver Jr., pres; Charles C. Carver Jr., gen mgr; Meade T. Murtland, stn mgr.

WTTC-FM— November 1959: 95.3 mhz; 3 kw. 125 ft. TL: N41 45 55 W76 29 10. ♦Joel Clawson, adv dir.

Trout Run

*WCIT(FM)— 2001: 90.1 mhz; 350 w. Ant 295 ft. TL: N41 27 26 W77 06 55. Box 506, Bath, NY 14810. Secondary address: 7634 Campbell Creek Rd., Bath, NY 14810. Phone: (607) 776-4151. Fax: (607) 776-6929. E-mail: mail@fln.org. Web Site: www.fln.org. Licensee: Family Life Ministries Inc. Group owner: Family Life Network Network:

Salem Radio Network. Format: Contemp Christian. News staff: 7; News: 14 hrs wkly. ♦Rick Snavely, pres & gen mgr; Dick Snavely, CFO; Roger Settje, prom mgr; John Owens, progmg dir; Bruce Barrows, mus dir; Ed Spencer, news dir; Jim Travis, chief of engrg.

Troy

WHGL-FM—See Canton

WTZN(AM)— Mar 3, 1982: 1310 khz; 1 kw-D, 72 w-N. TL: N41 46 51 W76 49 09. Box 100, 170 Redington Ave. 16947. Phone: (570) 297-0100. Fax: (570) 297-3193. E-mail: whgl@ptd.net. Web Site: www.wtzn.com. Licensee: Cantroair Communications Inc. (acq 1-7-99; $560,000 for 85% of stock with WHGL-FM Canton). Format: All sports. Target aud: 25-54. ♦Bob Gisler, VP & gen sls mgr; Georgia Pepper, prom mgr; Mike Powers, pres, gen mgr & progmg dir; Michael Dean, mus dir; Kevin Smith, chief of engrg.

Tunkhannock

WBZR(FM)—Listing follows WEMR(AM).

WEMR(AM)— June 13, 1986: 1460 khz; 5 kw-D, 1.25 kw-N, DA-2. TL: N41 33 46 W75 58 11. Box 230, Dushore 18614. Phone: (570) 928-7200. Fax: (570) 928-2100. Licensee: GEOS Communications (acq 1-30-2004); $515,000. with co-located FM). Format: Adult contemp. ♦Ben Smith, gen mgr.

WBZR(FM)—Co-owned with WEMR(AM). Oct 10, 1990: 107.7 mhz; 490 w. Ant 1,138 ft. TL: N41 30 45 W76 04 16. Stereo. Format: Adult contemp.

Tyrone

WGMR(FM)—Listing follows WTRN(AM).

WTRN(AM)— Jan 12, 1955: 1340 khz; 1 kw-U. TL: N40 39 48 W78 15 24. Box 247 16686. Secondary address: Washington Ave. & 1st St. 16686. Phone: (814) 684-3200. Fax: (814) 684-1220. E-mail: amnnet@aol.com. Web Site: www.wtrn.net. Licensee: Allegheny Mountain Network Stations. (group owner) Network: Jones Radio Networks. Rep: Dome. Borsari & Paxson. Format: Adult contemp. News: 16 hrs wkly. Target aud: General; total community targeted. Spec prog: Relg 4 hrs wkly. ♦Cary H. Simpson, pres.

WGMR(FM)—Co-owned with WTRN(AM). Aug 15, 1961: 101.1 mhz; 8.5 kw. 1,171 ft. TL: N40 55 10 W77 58 28. Stereo. 2351 Commercial Blvd., State College 16801. Phone: (814) 238-0717. Fax: (814) 234-3533. Web Site: www.revolution101.com. Dome. Format: CHR. Target aud: 18-49.

Union City

WCTL(FM)— Apr 23, 1967: 106.3 mhz; 3.4 kw. 430 ft. TL: N42 00 04 W79 52 33. Stereo. 10912 Peach St., Waterford 16441-9151. Phone: (814) 796-6000. Fax: (814) 796-3200. E-mail: wctl@wctl.org. Web Site: www.wctl.org. Licensee: Inspiration Time Inc. (acq 3-72). Network: USA. Rep: Salem. Wiley, Rein & Fielding. Format: Adult contemp, christian. News staff: one; News: 2.5 hrs wkly. Target aud: 25-54; Christian families. Spec prog: Children one hr wkly. ♦Ed Mattson, pres; Adam Frase, progmg dir & mus dir; Ron Raymond, gen mgr & progmg dir.

Uniontown

WMBS(AM)— July 15, 1937: 590 khz; 1 kw-U, DA-N. TL: N39 51 35 W79 44 44. 44 S. Mt. Vernon Ave. 15401. Phone: (724) 438-3900. Fax: (724) 438-2406. E-mail: bmroziak@wmbs590.com. Web Site: www.wmbs590.com. Licensee: Fayette Broadcasting Corp. Network: Jones Radio Networks. Format: Var/div. News staff: one; News: 24 hrs wkly. Target aud: 25 plus; General. Spec prog: Talk shows, traditional country 4 hrs, polka 3 hrs wkly. ♦Bob Pritts, pres; Brian Mroziak, gen mgr; Doreen Minafee, opns VP; Sandy Tracy, sls VP; Michael Pasqua, gen sls mgr; Jim Morgan, news dir; Timothy Schwer, pub affrs dir; Larry Campbell, chief of engrg.

WPKL(FM)— Dec 20, 1968: 99.3 mhz; 3 kw. Ant 300 ft. TL: N39 53 09 W79 46 29. Stereo. 123 Blaine Rd., Brownsville 15417. Phone: (724) 938-2000. Fax: (724) 938-7842. E-mail: picklejar@zoominternet.net. Web Site: oldiesradioonline.com. Licensee: Keymarket Licenses LLC Group owner: Keymarket Communications LLC (acq 1-17-2001;

Stations in the U.S. Pennsylvania

Developers & Brokers of Radio Properties — contact American Media Services at our suite: Philadelphia Marriott Downtown 215-625-2900 • 843-972-2200 • americanmediaservices.com • Charleston, SC • Dallas, TX • Chicago, Il • Austin, TX — American Media Services, LLC

$475,000. with WPNT(AM) Connellsville). Network: ABC Information & Entertainment. Rep: Dome. Format: Oldies. Target aud: 25 plus. ♦Gerald Getz, pres; Andrew Powaski, gen mgr, sls dir, gen sls mgr & progmg dir.

University Park

WOWY(FM)—Licensed to University Park. See State College

Upton

WPPT(FM)—See Mercersburg

Villanova

***WXVU(FM)**— August 1991: 89.1 mhz; 710 w. 223 ft. TL: N40 03 22 W75 22 30. (CP: 100 w vert, ant 279 ft. TL: N40 01 58 W75 20 15). Villanova Univeristy, 210 Dougherty Hall, 800 Lancaster Ave. 19085-1699. Phone: (610) 519-7200. Fax: (610) 519-7956. Web Site: wxvu.villanova.edu. Licensee: Villanova University. Format: Hip hop. Target aud: 15-25; youngsters. Spec prog: Black 10 hrs, relg 2 hrs wkly. ♦Brian Golden, gen mgr; Laysan Unger, progmg dir; Kristin Lavin, mus dir; Greg Ebbecke, pub affrs dir.

Warminster

***WRDV(FM)**— Sept 6, 1976: 89.3 mhz; 1 kw horiz, 100 w vert. 118 ft. TL: N40 12 19 W75 06 27. Stereo. Box 2012 18974. Secondary address: 126 S. York Rd., Hatboro 19040. Phone: (215) 674-8002. Fax: (215) 674-4586. Web Site: wrdv.org. Licensee: Bux-Mont Educational Radio Associates. (acq 3-80). Format: Big band, oldies, relg, adult standards. News: 2 hrs wkly. Target aud: General. Spec prog: C&W 4 hrs, blues 3 hrs, folk 4 hrs, new age 3 hrs, jazz 3 hrs wkly. ♦Charles W. Loughary, pres; Todd H. Allen, gen mgr & progmg dir.

Warren

WNAE(AM)— Dec 31, 1946: 1310 khz; 5 kw-D, 94 w-N. TL: N41 48 50 W79 10 04. Box 824 16365. Secondary address: 310 2nd Ave. 16365. Phone: (814) 723-1310. Fax: (814) 723-3356. E-mail: info@kibcoradio.com. Web Site: www.kibcoradio.com. Licensee: Kinzua Broadcasting Co. (acq 1974). Format: Adult contemp. News staff: one; News: 21 hrs wkly. Target aud: General. ♦David Whipple, VP & gen sls mgr; Denny Haight Jr., VP & engr; W. LeRoy Schneck, pres & gen mgr; Karen White, opns mgr; Dale Bliss, prom dir & sls; Mark Silvis, progmg dir; Robert Seiden, news dir.

WRRN(FM)—Co-owned with WNAE(AM). March 1948: 92.3 mhz; 50 kw. 410 ft. TL: N41 48 50 W79 10 04. Stereo. Web Site: www.kibcoradio.com. (acq 1946). Format: Oldies.

Warwick

***WZZD(FM)**— December 2000: 88.1 mhz; 180 w vert. 587 ft. TL: N40 07 45 W75 52 43. Stereo. Box 186, Sellersville 18960. Phone: (215) 721-2141. Fax: (215) 721-9811. E-mail: wordfm@wordfm.org. Web Site: www.wordfm.org. Licensee: Four Rivers Community Broadcasting Corp. Format: Contemp Christian. Spec prog: Bluegrass/gospel 3 hrs wkly. ♦David Baker, gen mgr; Charles W. Loughery, stn mgr.

Washington

WJPA(AM)— Feb 1, 1941: 1450 khz; 1 kw-U. TL: N40 11 23 W80 14 02. 98 S. Main St. 15301. Phone: (724) 222-2110. Fax: (724) 228-2299. E-mail: email@wjpa.com. Web Site: www.wjpa.com. Licensee: Washington Broadcasting Co. Format: Oldies. News staff: 2; News: 6 hrs wkly. ♦Michael S. Siegel, pres & gen mgr; Bob Gregg, opns dir, chief of opns & gen sls mgr; Dale Allen, prom mgr; Pete Povich, progmg dir; Margie Konstantinou, mus dir; Jim Jefferson, news dir.

WJPA-FM— Sept 26, 1964: 95.3 mhz; 2.15 kw. 390 ft. TL: N40 11 23 W80 14 02. (CP: 4.2 kw). Web Site: www.jwpa.com.

WKZV(AM)— August 1968: 1110 khz; 1 kw-D, DA. TL: N40 13 16 W80 14 34. 80 E. Chestnut St. 15301. Phone: (724) 228-6678. Fax: (724) 228-6678. Licensee: My-Key Broadcasting Inc. (acq 11-9-92; $100,000; 11-30-92). Rep: Dome. Format: Country. Target aud: 35 plus. Spec prog: Pol 3 hrs, polka 2 hrs, Croatian one hr, gospel one hr, racing one hr, relg one hr wkly. ♦Helen C. Supinski, pres; Michael Panjuscek, VP, gen mgr & progmg dir.

***WNJR(FM)**— Nov 26, 1972: 91.7 mhz; 950 w. Ant 112 ft. TL: N40 10 13 W80 14 43. Stereo. 60 S. Lincoln St. 15301. Phone: (724) 503-1001 x3025 (gen mgr). Phone: (724) 223-6039 (studio). Fax: (724) 223-5271. E-mail: wnjr@washjeff.edu. Web Site: www.wasjeff.edu. Licensee: Washington and Jefferson College. News: 4 hrs wkly. Target aud: All ages; college students, staff, community, alumni. ♦Rob Valella, gen mgr; Steve Capone Jr., stn mgr; Ryan Ray, sls dir; Christine Briski, prom dir; Megan McCauley, mus dir; Alex Hines, news dir; Cliff Bryson, chief of engrg.

Waynesboro

WCBG(AM)— Aug 19, 1953: 1380 khz; 1 kw-D. TL: N39 44 20 W77 36 10. Box 788, Greencastle 17225. Secondary address: 10960 John Wayne Dr., Greencastle 17225. Phone: (717) 597-9200. Fax: (717) 597-9210. Licensee: HJV L.P. Group owner: VerStandig Broadcasting (acq 1-6-97; $1,068,699. with co-located FM). Format: Contemp country. Target aud: 25-54. ♦Marge Martin, gen mgr & gen sls mgr; Don Brake, progmg dir.

WFYN(FM)—Co-owned with WCBG(AM). Feb 3, 1959: 101.5 mhz; 50 kw horiz, 48 kw vert. 230 ft. TL: N39 49 44 W77 33 10. Stereo. Format: Rock. ♦Marge Martin, mktg mgr; Don Blake, progmg dir.

Waynesburg

WANB-FM— Apr 21, 1978: 103.1 mhz; 970 w. Ant 617 ft. TL: N39 52 12 W80 08 01. Stereo. 369 Tower Rd. 15370. Phone: (724) 627-5555. Fax: (724) 627-4021. Licensee: Broadcast Communications Inc. (group owner; (acq 4-1-2002; with co-located AM). Rep: Dome. Format: Country. Target aud: 20 plus. ♦Judy E. Rastoka, gen mgr; Doug Wilson, progmg dir; Rick Williams, chief of engrg.

WXXP(AM)—Co-owned with WANB-FM. Sept 27, 1956: 1580 khz; 1 kw-D. TL: N39 52 11 W80 08 02.

***WCYJ-FM**— July 6, 1979: 88.7 mhz; 18 w. -33 ft. TL: N39 53 59 W80 11 07. Waynesburg College, 51 W. College St. 15370. Phone: (724) 627-8191. Fax: (724) 627-4757. E-mail: wcyjgm@hotmail.com. Web Site: www.waynesburg.edu. Licensee: Waynesburg College. (acq 7-3-79). Format: Adult contemp. News staff: one. Target aud: 18-25; college & high school students. Spec prog: Oldies 3 hrs, country 3 hrs, Christian 3 hrs, R&B 3 hrs, classic rock 3 hrs wkly. ♦Brad Baker, gen mgr; Mark Perry, stn mgr; Nick Daniels, opns dir.

Wellsboro

WNBT(AM)— May 13, 1955: 1490 khz; 1 kw-U. TL: N41 44 41 W77 17 35. Box 98 16901. Secondary address: 198-B RR 7 16901. Phone: (570) 724-1490. Phone: (570) 662-7100. Fax: (570) 724-6971. E-mail: wnbt@ynt.net. Web Site: www.wnbt.net. Licensee: Farm & Home Broadcasting Co. Group owner: Allegheny Mountain Network Stations Network: Network: Westwood One, ABC Information & Entertainment. Rep: Dome. Borsari & Paxson. Format: Adult standards. News staff: one; News: 10 hrs wkly. Target aud: 45+. ♦Cary Simpson, pres.

WNBT-FM— July 2, 1969: 104.5 mhz; 50 kw. 380 ft. TL: N41 44 17 W77 21 50. Stereo. Web Site: www.wnbt.net. Network: Network: Westwood One, ABC Information & Entertainment. Format: CHR, popular music, adult contemp. News staff: one; News: 2 hrs wkly. Target aud: 18-55.

West Chester

WCHE(AM)— Oct 4, 1963: 1520 khz; 250 w-D. TL: N39 58 06 W75 37 59. 105 W. Gay St. 19380. Phone: (610) 692-3131. Fax: (610) 692-3133. E-mail: wcheam@aol.com. Licensee: Chester County Radio Inc. (acq 7-11-97; $230,000). Network: Network: USA, Westwood One. Pepper & Corazzini. Format: News/talk, Adult Standard, Soft Rock & Folk. News staff: one; News: 20 hrs wkly. Target aud: 24-64; upscale. Spec prog: Relg 8 hrs, country 2 hrs wkly. ♦David S. Shur, pres, sls dir, progmg dir & news dir; Jay Shur, gen mgr, opns mgr, chief of opns, prom dir & pub affrs dir.

WCOJ(AM)—See Coatesville

***WCUR(FM)**— 1999: 91.7 mhz; 100 w. Ant 108 ft. TL: N39 57 02 W75 35 58. West Chester University, Sykes Union Bldg. 19383. Phone: (610) 436-2414. Fax: (610) 436-2477. E-mail: wcur@yahoo.com. Web Site: www.wcur.fm. Licensee: Student Services Inc. Format: Diversified.

West Hazleton

WKZN(AM)— 1982: 1300 khz; 5 kw-D, 500 w-N, DA-2. TL: N40 56 26 W76 00 07. Box 729, 305 Hwy. 315, Pittstown 18640. Phone: (570) 883-9850. Fax: (570) 883-0832. Web Site: www.wilknewsradio.com. Licensee: Entercom Scranton Wilkes-Barre License LLC. Group owner: Entercom Communications Corp. (acq 12-13-99; grpsl). Network: ABC Information & Entertainment. Rep: D & R Radio. Format: News/talk. News staff: 6; News: 25 hrs wkly. Target aud: General; affluent, educated. Spec prog: Relg one hr wkly. ♦John Burkavage, gen mgr; Jim Rising, opns dir; Andy Zapotek, sls mgr; Bob DeMond, natl sls mgr; Casey Consagra, prom mgr; Nancy Kman, progmg dir; Joe Thomas, news dir; Lamar Smith, chief of engrg.

Whitneyville

WLIH(FM)— Mar 15, 1987: 107.1 mhz; 3.3 kw. Ant 298 ft. TL: N41 46 13 W77 12 08. Stereo. Box 97, 2352 Charleston Rd., Wellsboro 16901. Phone: (570) 724-4272. Fax: (570) 724-2302. E-mail: wlih107@quik.com. Web Site: www.wlih.com. Licensee: Good Christian Radio Broadcasting Inc. Network: Family Radio. Format: Relg, Christian, news. News: 28 hrs wkly. Target aud: General; serving the Christian community of the county. ♦Robert Makin, pres; Carol Makin, gen mgr.

Wilkes-Barre

WARM(AM)—See Scranton

WBAX(AM)— May 1, 1922: 1240 khz; 1 kw-U. TL: N41 15 13 W75 54 25. 149 Penn Ave., Scranton 18503. Phone: (570) 346-6555. Fax: (570) 346-6038. Web Site: www.wejl-wbax.com. Licensee: The Scranton Times L.P. Format: Sports. News staff: one; News: 5 hrs wkly. Target aud: 18 + men. Spec prog: sports. ♦William R. Lynett, CEO; Jim Loftus, COO & gen mgr; Tim Durkin, sls dir; Jerry Arndt, natl sls mgr; Mark Hoover, mktg dir & prom mgr; Michael Neff, progmg dir; Ruth Miller, news dir; Kevin Fitzgerald, engrg dir.

WBZU(AM)—See Scranton

***WCLH(FM)**— Feb 6, 1972: 90.7 mhz; 175 w. 1,020 ft. TL: N41 10 58 W75 52 21. Stereo. Wilkes Univ., Darte Center for the Performing Arts, South St. & S. River St., Wilkes Barre 18766. Phone: (570) 408-5907. Phone: (570) 408-4567. Fax: (570) 408-5908. E-mail: wclh@wilkes.edu. Web Site: www.wclh.net. Licensee: Wilkes University. Network: AP Network News. Format: Div, educ, progsv new mus. News: 10 hrs wkly. Target aud: 12-44. Spec prog: Heavy metal 18 hrs, classic rock 9 hrs, jazz 3 hrs, Ger 3 hrs, Sp 3 hrs wkly. ♦Dr. Tom Baldino, CEO; Renee Loftus, gen mgr; Dr. Mark Stine, opns VP.

WEJL(AM)—See Scranton

WGGY(FM)—See Scranton

WICK(AM)—See Scranton

WILK(AM)— Feb 13, 1947: 980 khz; 5 kw-D, 1 kw-N, DA-N. TL: N41 13 42 W75 56 53. Stereo. 305 Hwy. 315, Pittston 18640. Phone: (570) 883-9850. Fax: (570) 883-9851. E-mail: feedback@thewilknetwork.com.

Broadcasting & Cable Yearbook 2006

Pennsylvania

Web Site: www.wilknetwork.com. Licensee: Entercom Scranton Wilkes-Barre License LLC. Group owner: Entercom Communications Corp. (acq 12-13-99; grpsl). Network: ABC Information & Entertainment. Format: News/talk. Target aud: 15-54. Spec prog: Relg one hr wkly. ♦ Joseph Fields, pres; John Burkavage, gen mgr; Jim Rising, opns dir & opns mgr; Ryan Flynn, gen sls mgr; Nancy Kman, progmg dir.

WITK(AM)—See Pittston

WKRZ(FM)— 1947: 98.5 mhz; 8.7 kw. 1,171 ft. TL: N41 11 56 W75 49 06. Stereo. 305 Hwy. 315, Box 729, Pittston 18640. Phone: (570) 883-9850. Fax: (570) 883-9851. Web Site: www.wkrz.com. Licensee: Entercom Scranton Wilkes-Barre License LLC. Group owner: Entercom Communications Corp. (acq 12-13-99; grpsl). Format: CHR. Target aud: 19-54; women. ♦ John Burkavage, gen mgr; Jim Rising, opns mgr; Ryan Flynn, gen sls mgr & sls; Tias Schuster, progmg dir; Elizabeth Masich, mus dir; Lamar Smith, chief of engrg.

WMGS(FM)— 1946: 92.9 mhz; 5.3 kw. Ant 1,384 ft. TL: N41 10 58 W75 52 26. Stereo. 600 Baltimore Dr. 18702. Phone: (570) 824-9000. Fax: (570) 820-0520. Licensee: Citadel Broadcasting Co. Group owner: Citadel Broadcasting Corp. (acq 7-1-97; grpsl). Format: Soft rock. News staff: one; News: 2 hrs wkly. Target aud: 25-54; adult women. Spec prog: Farm one hr, relg 3 hrs wkly. ♦ Taylor Walet, gen mgr.

WNAK(AM)—See Nanticoke

*WRKC(FM)— Sept 18, 1968: 88.5 mhz; 440 w. -470 ft. TL: N41 14 57 W75 52 26. Stereo. King's College, 133 N. River St. 18711. Phone: (570) 208-5821. Phone: (570) 208-5931. Fax: (570) 825-9049. Licensee: King's College. Format: Jazz, AOR, reading for the blind. Target aud: General; people who need wide-ranging svcs. ♦ Pete Phillips, gen mgr.

WWDL-FM—See Scranton

Wilkinsburg

WPYT(AM)— Aug 25, 1960: 660 khz; 260 w-D. TL: N40 24 47 W79 51 14. 4736 Penn Ave., Pittsburgh 15224. Phone: (412) 661-6001. Fax: (412) 661-7195. Licensee: Langer Broadcasting Group L.L.C. (group owner; acq 5-22-98). Reddy, Begley & McCormick. Format: Talk. ♦ Ed Dehart, gen sls mgr; Stephen Zelenko, gen mgr, gen mgr & progmg dir.

Williamsport

WBZD-FM—(Muncy). Aug 11, 1983: 93.3 mhz; 1.7 kw. Ant 1,220 ft. TL: N41 12 42 W76 57 16. Stereo. 1685 Four Mile Dr. 17701. Phone: (570) 323-8200. Fax: (570) 323-5075. E-mail: bobpawlikowski@byradio.com. Web Site: www.wbzd.com. Licensee: South Williamsport SaberCom Inc. Group owner: Backyard Broadcasting LLC (acq 12-1-02; grpsl). Network: ABC FM Connection. Rep: Christal. Format: Oldies. News staff: one; News: 3 hrs wkly. Target aud: 18-54; adult oriented, mass appeal. ♦ Barry Drake, pres; Robin Smith, CFO; Dan Farr, gen mgr; Bob Pawlikowski, gen sls mgr; Ted Minier, progmg dir; Brian Hill, chief of engrg & engr.

*WCRG(FM)— Feb 20, 2002: 90.7 mhz; 3 kw. Ant -216 ft. TL: N41 13 50 W77 08 59. Stereo. 101 Armory Blvd., Lewisburg 17837. Phone: (570) 523-1190. Fax: (570) 523-1114. E-mail: email@wgrc.com. Web Site: www.wgrc.com. Licensee: Salt & Light Media Ministries Inc. Miller & Neely. Format: Contemp Christian. News staff: 3; News: 12 hrs wkly. Target aud: 25-54. ♦ Larry Weidman, gen mgr; Lamar Smith, chief of engrg.

WILQ(FM)— July 31, 1949: 105.1 mhz; 9.2 kw. Ant 1,135 ft. TL: N41 11 43 W76 58 18. Stereo. 1685 Four Mile Dr. 17701. Phone: (570) 323-8200. Fax: (570) 323-5075. E-mail: dougd@wilq.com. Web Site: www.wilq.com. Licensee: South Williamsport SaberCom Inc. Group owner: Backyard Broadcasting LLC (acq 12-1-02; grpsl). Network: ABC Information & Entertainment. Format: Country. News staff: one; News: 7 hrs wkly. Target aud: 25 plus; adults in a 10 county area. ♦ Barry Drake, pres; Robin Smith, CFO; Dan Farr, gen mgr; Doug Dodge, gen sls mgr; Ted Minier, progmg dir; John Finn, news dir.

WKSB(FM)— Listing follows WRAK(AM).

WLYC(AM)— June 1951: 1050 khz; 1 kw-D, 36 w-N. TL: N41 15 44 W77 01 59. 101 Phillips Park Dr., So. Williamsport 17702-7063. Phone: (570) 327-1300. Fax: (570) 327-1331. E-mail: wlyc1050@yahoo.com.

Web Site: www.sports1050.com. Licensee: Sentry Communications License LLC (acq 7-19-2005; $75,000). Network: Network: ESPN Radio, Westwood One. . Miller and Neely, PC. Format: Sports. News: Sports news only. Target aud: 25-54; male. ♦ James R. McKowne, gen mgr; Jeffrey Andruionis, opns mgr; Christy Andruionis, sls.

*WPTC(FM)— Sept 3, 1980: 88.1 mhz; 494 w. -101 ft. TL: N41 14 11 W77 01 26. Stereo. One College Ave. 17701. Phone: (570) 326-3761, EXT. 7548. Fax: (570) 320-2423. E-mail: wptc@pct.edu. Web Site: www.pct.edu/wptc. Licensee: Pennsylvania College of Technology. (acq 3-14-90). Format: Jazz, modern rock. News: 2 hrs wkly. Target aud: 18-24; college students. Spec prog: Sports 2 hrs, dance 10 hrs, metal 5 hrs wkly. ♦ Davie Gilmour, pres; Brad Nason, gen mgr.

WRAK(AM)— Apr 10, 1930: 1400 khz; 1 kw-U. TL: N41 14 22 W77 02 27. Box 3638, 1559 W. 4th St. 17701. Phone: (570) 327-1400. Fax: (570) 327-8156. E-mail: wrak@wrak.com. Web Site: www.wrak.com. Licensee: Clear Channel Radio License Inc. Group owner: Clear Channel Communications Inc. (acq 8-5-98; grpsl). Network: Network: Westwood One, ABC Information & Entertainment. Format: News/talk, sports. News staff: one; News: 3 hrs wkly. Target aud: 35 plus. ♦ James Dabney, gen mgr & gen sls mgr; Tom Scott, mktg dir; Ken Sawyer, progmg dir.

WKSB(FM)— Co-owned with WRAK(AM). Apr 1, 1948: 102.7 mhz; 53 kw. 1,270 ft. TL: N41 11 21 W76 58 53. Stereo. E-mail: wksb@wksb.com. Web Site: www.wksb.com. Format: Adult contemp. News staff: one. Target aud: 25-54. ♦ Russell Davidson, opns dir; Tom Scott, progmg dir; Tom Turner, asst music dir; Mark Lawrence, pub affrs dir; Dan Milliken, engrg dir.

*WRLC(FM)— Apr 5, 1976: 91.7 mhz; 740 w. -298 ft. TL: N41 14 42 W76 59 50. Stereo. Mass Communication Dept., Lycoming College, 700 College Place 17701. Phone: (570) 321-4060. Fax: (570) 321-4372. E-mail: koehn@lycoming.edu. Web Site: www.lycoming.edu. Licensee: Lycoming College. (acq 1-76). Format: Div, progsv, urban contemp. News: 15 hrs wkly. Target aud: General; Lycoming College & its surrounding communities. Spec prog: Class one hr, gospel 6 hrs, pub affrs 2 hrs, Christian rock 3 hrs, jazz 8 hrs, blues 3 hrs wkly. ♦ Steve Koehn, gen mgr.

WRVH(FM)— Aug 16, 1989: 107.9 mhz; 360 w. 1,289 ft. TL: N41 12 39 W76 57 17. Stereo. 1685 Four Mile Dr. 17701. Phone: (570) 323-8200. Fax: (570) 327-9138. Licensee: South Williamsport SabreCom Inc. Group owner: Backyard Broadcasting LLC (acq 12-1-02; grpsl). Network: ABC. Rep: Christal. Bechtel & Cole. Format: Soft adult contemp. News staff: one; News: one hr wkly. Target aud: 35 plus. ♦ Dan Farr, gen mgr.

WVRT(FM)—See Mill Hall

*WVYA(FM)— 2003: 89.7 mhz; 3.3 kw. Ant -16 ft. TL: N41 14 54 W77 01 52. Stereo. 100 Wvia Way, Pittston 18640-6197. Phone: (570) 655-2808. Fax: (570) 655-1180. E-mail: wvianews@epix.net. Web Site: www.wvia.org. Licensee: Northeastern Pennsylvania Educational TV Association. Network: NPR. Dow, Lohnes & Albertson. Format: Class, jazz, news. News staff: one; News: 30 hrs wkly. Target aud: Upscale, mature audience. ♦ A. William Kelly, CEO & gen mgr; A William Kelly, pres; Chris Norton, VP; Larry Vojtko, progmg mgr.

WWPA(AM)— May 22, 1949: 1340 khz; 1 kw-U. TL: N41 13 45 W77 00 45. 1685 Four Mile Dr. 17701. Phone: (570) 323-8200. Fax: (570) 327-9138. Licensee: South Williamsport SabreCom Inc. Group owner: Backyard Broadcasting LLC (acq 12-1-02; grpsl). Network: CSN. Rep: Christal. Format: News/talk. News staff: one; News: 168 hrs wkly. Target aud: 35 plus. Spec prog: Sports. ♦ Barry Drake, pres; Robin Smith, CFO; Dan Farr, gen mgr.

WZXR(FM)—See South Williamsport

Wyomissing

*WYTL(FM)— 2005: 91.7 mhz; 10 w horiz, 320 w vert. Ant 840 ft. TL: W40 19 22 W76 11 52. Box 186, Sellersville 18960. Phone: (215) 721-2141. Fax: (215) 721-9811. Web Site: www.wordfm.org. Licensee: Four Rivers Community Broadcasting Corp. Format: Aduct contemp Christian. ♦ David Baker, gen mgr.

York

WARM-FM—Listing follows WSBA(AM).

Directory of Radio

WOYK(AM)— March 1932: 1350 khz; 5 kw-D, 1 kw-N, DA-N. TL: N39 56 00 W76 49 06. Box 20249 17402. Phone: (717) 840-0355. Fax: (717) 840-0355. E-mail: radioman@blazenet.net. Web Site: sportsradioespn1350.com. Licensee: WOYK Inc. (acq 12-87). Network: Motor Racing Net, ESPN Radio. Format: Sports. Target aud: 25-64; men. ♦ Douglas George, pres; Vincent Grande, gen mgr; Sam Conrad, opns dir.

WQXA(AM)— 1948: 1250 khz; 1 kw-D. TL: N39 59 56 W76 41 43. Stereo. 919 Buckingham Blvd., Elizabethtown 17022. Phone: (717) 757-9402. Fax: (717) 367-9322. Licensee: Steel City Radio Inc. Group owner: Citadel Broadcasting Corp. (acq 8-23-2005; $250,000). Rep: D & R Radio. Format: Real country. News: 10 hrs wkly. Target aud: 35 plus. Spec prog: High school football & basketball, Philadelphia Phillies. ♦ Nancy Tulli, gen mgr; Tim Michaels, stn mgr & gen sls mgr; Richard Hill, engrg VP.

WQXA-FM— 1948: 105.7 mhz; 25 kw. Ant 705 ft. TL: N39 59 56 W76 41 43. Stereo. 919 Buckingham Blvd., Elizabethtown 17022. Phone: (717) 367-7700. Fax: (717) 367-0239. Web Site: www.1057thex.com. Licensee: Citadel Broadcasting Co. (acq 5-29-97; grpsl). Format: Active rock. Target aud: 18-49. ♦ Cindy Miller, sls dir & gen sls mgr; Claudine DeLorenzo, progmg mgr.

WSBA(AM)— Sept 1, 1942: 910 khz; 5 kw-D, 1 kw-N, DA-2. TL: N39 59 53 W76 44 42. Box 910 17402-0910. Secondary address: 5989 Susquehanna Plaza Dr. 17406. Phone: (717) 764-1155. Fax: (717) 252-4708. Web Site: www.wsba910.com. Licensee: WSBA Lico Inc. Group owner: Susquehanna Radio Corp. Format: News/talk. News staff: 5. Spec prog: Black 3 hrs, farm 4 hrs wkly. ♦ Tom Rawker, gen mgr; Bob Popa, prom mgr & chief of engrg; Jim Horn, progmg dir.

WARM-FM—Co-owned with WSBA(AM). Sept 1, 1962: 103.3 mhz; 6.4 kw. 1,305 ft. TL: N40 01 38 W76 36 08. Stereo. Web Site: www.warm103.com. Format: Adult contemp. ♦ Tom Ranker, VP & stn mgr; Tina Heim, gen sls mgr; Bob Hurbert, prom mgr; Kelly West, progmg dir.

WSJW(FM)—See Starview

*WVYC(FM)— Nov 18, 1976: 99.7 mhz; 370 w. 97 ft. TL: N39 56 49 W76 43 47. (CP: 99.7 mhz). Stereo. York College of Pennsylvania, Country Club Rd. 17405-7199. Phone: (717) 815-1932. Phone: (717) 815-1311. E-mail: tgibson@ycp.edu. Web Site: www.ycp.edu/wvyc. Licensee: York College of Pennsylvania. Format: Educ, progsv, rock. News staff: one; News: 3 hrs wkly. Target aud: 14-24; new mus lovers. Spec prog: Class 8 hrs, jazz 8 hrs, Sp one hr wkly. ♦ Kevin Peterson, gen mgr.

York-Hanover

WYCR(FM)—Licensed to York-Hanover. See Hanover

Youngsville

*WTMV(FM)— Jan 19, 1999: 88.5 mhz; 100 w. -335 ft. TL: N41 51 01 W79 18 41. Stereo. 409 E. Main St. 16371. Phone: (814) 563-4510. Fax: (814) 563-4903. E-mail: wtmv@westpa.net. Web Site: www.wtmv.com. Licensee: Living Word of Faith Christian Outreach. Network: American Family Radio. Format: Christian. Target aud: 21 plus; Christians of all ages. Spec prog: Children 10 hrs, class 2.5 hrs wkly. ♦ Rev. Patricia A. Baker, VP & mus dir; Rev. William E. Baker, pres & gen mgr.

Rhode Island

Block Island

WCRI(FM)— June 13, 1994: 95.9 mhz; 6 kw. 174 ft. TL: N41 10 21 W71 33 52. Stereo. 19 Railroad Ave, Westerly 02891. Phone: (401) 596-6795. Fax: (401) 596-6782. E-mail: mail@classical959.com. Web Site: www.classical959.com. Licensee: Charles River Broadcasting WCRI License Corp. (acq 7-16-99). Format: Class. Target aud: General. Spec prog: New age 4 hrs, folk 4 hrs, big band 4 hrs, relg 2 hrs wkly. ♦ William Campbell, CEO; Mark Halliday, gen mgr; Michael Abranson, stn mgr.

WJZS(FM)— Oct 3, 1988: 99.3 mhz; 6 kw. Ant 256 ft. TL: N41 10 28 W71 24 20. Stereo. Box 367, Newport 02480. Phone: (401) 846-1540. Fax: (401) 846-1598. E-mail: fm993@wadk.com. Web Site: www.wadk.com. Licensee: Astro Tele-Communications Corp. (acq 8-24-99). Shaw

Stations in the U.S. Rhode Island

Developers & Brokers of Radio Properties — contact American Media Services at our suite: Philadelphia Marriott Downtown 215-625-2900 / 843-972-2200 / americanmediaservices.com / Charleston, SC / Dallas, TX · Chicago, IL · Austin, TX — American Media Services, LLC

Pittman. Format: Jazz/swing. Target aud: 30-50; total community. ♦William C. Lancaster, gen mgr; Lynn Abrams, gen sls mgr; Steve Bianchi, progmg dir; Robert Sullivan, news dir; Kate Jennings, pub affrs dir & prom; Maurice B. Polayes, chief of engrg.

Bristol

*WQRI(FM)— April 1989: 88.3 mhz; 100 w. 75 ft. TL: N41 38 49 W91 15 34. One Old Ferry Rd., Campus Program 02809. Phone: (401) 254-3283. Phone: (401) 254-3282. Fax: (401) 254-3355. Licensee: Roger Williams University. Format: AOR. ♦Becky Riopel, gen mgr.

Coventry

*WCVY(FM)— Oct 19, 1978: 91.5 mhz; 200 w. 36 ft. TL: N41 41 10 W71 35 37. Stereo. 40 Reservoir Rd. 02816-6404. Phone: (401) 822-9499. Fax: (401) 822-9492. Licensee: Coventry Public Schools. Format: Top-40. Target aud: 12-30. Spec prog: Sports 2 hrs wkly. ♦Jason Murry, stn mgr.

East Greenwich

WARV(AM)—See Warwick

Greenville

WALE(AM)—Licensed to Greenville. See Providence

Hope Valley

WCNX(AM)— Oct 7, 1985: 1180 khz; 1.8 kw-D. TL: N41 31 36 W71 44 35. Stereo. 19 Railroad Ave., Westerly 02891. Phone: (401) 596-6795. Fax: (401) 596-6782. Web Site: realcountryonline.com. Licensee: Charles River Broadcasting WJJF License Corp. (acq 1-10-2003; $585,500). Network: USA. Smithwick & Belendiuk. Format: Country, loc news. ♦William Campbell, pres; Mike Abramson, gen mgr & chief of engrg; Larry Milesky, gen sls mgr.

Kingston

*WRIU(FM)— Feb 16, 1964: 90.3 mhz; 3.44 kw. 415 ft. TL: N41 29 52 W71 31 42. Stereo. 326 Memorial Union 02881. Phone: (401) 874-4949. Fax: (401) 874-4349. Web Site: www.wriu.org. Licensee: University of Rhode Island. Format: Div, rock. Target aud: Diverse. Spec prog: Folk 15 hrs, gospel 5 hrs, heavy metal 6 hrs, blues 3 hrs, reggae 7 hrs, Sp 3 hrs wkly. ♦James Proctor, gen mgr.

Middletown

WKKB(FM)— Oct 6, 1978: 100.3 mhz; 1.55 kw. Ant 656 ft. TL: N41 35 48 W71 11 24. Stereo. 1185 N. Main St., Providence 02904. Phone: (401) 331-1003. Fax: (401) 521-5077. E-mail: marcklowan@supermaxfm.com. Web Site: latina 1003.com. Licensee: Davidson Media Rhode Island Stations LLC. Group owner: Citadel Broadcasting Corp. (acq 1-24-2005; $7.5 million. with WAKX(FM) Narragansett Pier). Format: Sp tropical. News staff: one; News: 7 hrs wkly. Target aud: 12+; Latino Americans 1st & 2nd generation. ♦Craig Rapoza, gen mgr; Cesar Salas, gen sls mgr; Enrique Ortaga, progmg VP; Juan Gonzalez, progmg dir.

Narragansett Pier

WAKX(FM)— July 15, 1990: 102.7 mhz; 1.95 kw. Ant 226 ft. TL: N41 25 27 W71 28 38. Stereo. 1185 N. Main St., Providence 02904. Phone: (401) 273-1027. Fax: (401) 521-5077. Licensee: Davidson Media Rhode Island Stations LLC. Group owner: Citadel Communications Corp. (acq 1-24-2005; $7.5 million. with WKKB(FM) Middletown). Format: Portuguese, Brazilian, Cape Verdean. News staff: one; News: news progmg 7 hrs wkly. Target aud: Americans 12+; Portuguese, Brazilian, Cape Verdean. ♦Craig Rapoza, gen mgr; Eduardo Rodriques, gen sls mgr; Enrique Ortaga, progmg VP; Beta Marques, progmg dir; Eduardo Fernandos, news dir.

Newport

WADK(AM)— Nov 6, 1948: 1540 khz; 1 kw-D, 3 w-N. TL: N41 30 13 W71 18 43. Box 367 02840. Phone: (401) 846-1540. Fax: (401) 846-1598. E-mail: blancaster@wadk.com. Web Site: www.wadk.com. Licensee: Astro Tele-Communications Corp. (acq 8-24-99). Network: ABC Information & Entertainment. Shaw Pittman. Format: News/talk/sports. News staff: 2. Target aud: 25-54. Spec prog: Jazz 4 hrs wkly. ♦William Lancaster, gen mgr; Lynn Abrams, gen sls mgr; Bobb Angel, progmg dir; Robert Sullivan, news dir; Art Berluti, pub affrs dir; Maurice B. Polayes, chief of engrg.

Pawtucket

WDDZ(AM)— Feb 12, 1950: 550 khz; 1 kw-D, 500 w-N, DA-N. TL: N41 54 20 W71 23 56. Stereo. 203 Concord St., Suite 453 02860. Phone: (401) 722-0839. Fax: (401) 722-1459. Licensee: Radio Disney Group LLC. Group owner: ABC Inc. (acq 5-29-2001; $2.05 million). Network: Radio Disney. Format: Children. ♦Jamie Reese, stn mgr; AAlisa Capaldi, prom dir.

Portsmouth

*WJHD(FM)— Apr 3, 1972: 90.7 mhz; 360 w. 80 ft. TL: N41 36 06 W71 16 20. Portsmouth Abbey School, Cory's Ln. 02871. Phone: (401) 683-2000. Fax: (401) 683-5888. Licensee: The Order of St. Benedict. Format: Div. Spec prog: Opera, rock. ♦Edmund Adams, gen mgr.

Providence

WALE(AM)—(Greenville). 1948: 990 khz; 50 kw-D, 5 kw-N, DA-2. TL: N41 57 18 W71 35 39. 1185 N. Main St., Greenville 02904. Phone: (401) 521-0990. Fax: (401) 521-5077. Web Site: info@poder1110.com. Licensee: Cumbre Communications Corp., debtor in possession (acq 8-10-2004). Format: Sp. Target aud: . ♦Jaime Aguayo, pres; Manolo Pazos, gen mgr; Craig Rapoza, opns mgr; Richard Aybar, progmg dir & news dir.

WBRU(FM)— Feb 21, 1966: 95.5 mhz; 20 kw. 440 ft. TL: N41 49 40 W71 22 09. (CP: 50 kw, ant 492 ft. TL: N41 48 28 W71 28 12). Stereo. 88 Benevolent St. 02906. Phone: (401) 272-9550. Fax: (401) 272-9278. E-mail: wbru@wbru.com. Web Site: www.wbru.com. Licensee: Brown Broadcasting Service Inc. Format: Alternative Urban contemp. News: 3 hrs wkly. Target aud: 18-34; highly educated professionals. Spec prog: Black 20 hrs, jazz 18 hrs wkly. ♦Reva Gaur, prom dir.

WCTK(FM)—Listing follows WNBH(AM).

*WDOM(FM)— Mar 15, 1966: 91.3 mhz; 125 w. 130 ft. TL: N41 50 39 W71 26 14. Stereo. Providence College 02918. Phone: (401) 865-2460. Fax: (401) 865-2822. E-mail: wdom@studentweb.providence.edu. Web Site: www.listen.to/wdom. Licensee: Providence College. Format: College alternative. News: one hr wkly. Target aud: General; college students & professionals. Spec prog: Urban contemp 16 hrs, metal 6 hrs, country 2 hrs, classic rock 3 hrs, sports 2 hrs wkly. ♦Brian Wall, opns dir, mktg dir & progmg dir; Carlin Corrigan, prom dir; Dan Devine, mus dir; Jaclyn Schede, asst music dir; Scott Seseske, gen mgr, dev dir & pub affrs dir.

*WELH(FM)— September 1994: 88.1 mhz; 150 w. 98 ft. TL: N41 51 30 W71 19 04. 216 Hope St. 02906. Phone: (401) 421-8100. Fax: (401) 751-7674. Web Site: www.wheelerschool.org. Licensee: The Wheeler School. Fletcher, Heald & Hildreth. Format: Div, jazz, Sp. Target aud: General. ♦Dave Schiano, gen mgr.

WHJJ(AM)— Sept 6, 1922: 920 khz; 5 kw-U, DA-1. TL: N41 46 53 W71 19 55. 75 Oxford St. 02905. Phone: (401) 781-9979. Fax: (401) 781-9329. Web Site: www.920whjj.com. Licensee: Capstar TX L.P. Group owner: Clear Channel Communications Inc. (acq 8-30-00; grpsl). Network: CBS. Rep: Clear Channel. Wilkinson, Barker, Knauer & Quinn. Format: News/talk. Target aud: 35-64. ♦Jim Corwin, gen mgr; Kevin Hickey, sls dir; Bill George, progmg dir.

WHJY(FM)—Co-owned with WHJJ(AM). Mar 14, 1966: 94.1 mhz; 50 kw. 546 ft. TL: N41 49 40 W71 22 09. Stereo. Web Site: www.whjy.com. Format: AOR. Target aud: 18-34; adults. ♦Scott Laudani, progmg dir.

WLKW(AM)—(West Warwick). Aug 12, 1986: 1450 khz; 1 kw-U. TL: N41 41 38 W71 31 26. 75 Oxford St. 02905. Phone: (401) 467-4366. Fax: (401) 941-2795. E-mail: twall@hallradio.com. Licensee: Hall Communications Inc. (group owner; acq 6-4-01; $410,000). Rep: D & R Radio. Fletcher, Heald and Hildreth. Format: Adult Standards. News staff: one. Target aud: 35-64. Spec prog: Pol 2 hrs wkly. ♦Bonnie Rowbotham, CEO; Arthur Rowbotham, pres; Tom Wall, gen mgr; Rick Everett, opns mgr.

WNBH(AM)—(New Bedford).MA May 21, 1921: 1340 khz; 1 kw-U. TL: N41 37 21 W70 55 07. 888 Purchase St., New Bedford, MA 02740. Phone: (508) 979-8003. Phone: (401) 467-4366. Fax: (508) 979-8009. E-mail: twall@hallradio.com. Licensee: Hall Communications Inc. (group owner; acq 10-1-66). Network: Westwood One. Rep: D & R Radio. Fletcher, Heald & Hildreth. Format: Btfl mus. News: 3 hrs wkly. Target aud: 35-64. Spec prog: Pol 2 hrs wkly. ♦Bonnie H. Rowbotham, chmn; Arthur J. Rowbotham, pres; Tom Wall, gen mgr & sls dir.

WCTK(FM)—Co-owned with WNBH(AM). Dec 9, 1946: 98.1 mhz; 47.3 kw. 508 ft. TL: N41 37 21 W70 55 07. Stereo. 75 Oxford St. 02905. Phone: (401) 467-4366. Fax: (401) 941-2795. E-mail: mail@wctk.com. Web Site: www.wctk.com. Rep: D & R Radio. Fletcher, Heald & Hildreth. Format: Country. Target aud: 25-54.

WPMZ(AM)— Apr 15, 1947: 1110 khz; 5 kw-D. TL: N41 49 40 W71 22 09. 1270 Mineral Spring Ave., North Providence 02904. Phone: (401) 726-8413. Fax: (401) 726-8649. E-mail: wpmz@aol.com. Licensee: Videomundo Broadcasting Co. L.L.C. (acq 1-27-98; $900,000). Format: Sp. Target aud: General. ♦Dilson Mendez, pres; Tony Mendez, gen mgr; Johanna Petrarca, sls dir; Zoilo Garcia, progmg dir.

WPRO(AM)— Oct 16, 1931: 630 khz; 5 kw-U, DA-N. TL: N41 46 28 W71 19 23. 1502 Wampanoag Tr., East Providence 02915. Phone: (401) 433-4200. Fax: (401) 433-5967. Web Site: www.630wpro.com. Licensee: Citadel Broadcasting Co. Group owner: Citadel Broadcasting Corp. (acq 5-29-97; grpsl). Network: ABC Information & Entertainment. Rep: McGavren Guild. Format: News/talk, sports. ♦Andrea Scott, gen sls mgr.

WPRO-FM— April 1949: 92.3 mhz; 39 kw. 550 ft. TL: N41 48 18 W71 28 24. (CP: 45.4 kw, ant 489 ft.). Stereo. Web Site: www.92wpro.com. Format: CHR. ♦Steve Maully, rgnl sls mgr; Tony Brisco, progmg dir.

WRIB(AM)— June 16, 1946: 1220 khz; 1 kw-D, 166 w-N. TL: N41 49 15 W71 23 07. 200 Water St., East Providence 02914. Phone: (401) 434-0406. Fax: (401) 434-0409. Licensee: Carter Broadcasting Corp. (acq 12-24-86; $378,841; 9-15-86). Format: Relg, Sp. Spec prog: It 5 hrs, Portugese 3 hrs, Armenian one hr wkly. ♦John Pierce, gen mgr.

WRNI(AM)— April 1948: 1290 khz; 5 kw-U, DA-2. TL: N41 51 21 W71 26 41. 890 Commonwealth Ave., Boston, MA 02215. Secondary address: One Union Station 02093. Phone: (401) 351-2800. Fax: (401) 351-0246. E-mail: info@wrni.org. Web Site: www.wrni.org. Licensee: WRNI Foundation (acq 7-1-98). Network: Network: NPR, PRI. Rep: Rgnl Reps. Format: News/talk. News staff: 8; News: 80 hrs wkly. Target aud: 25-54; intelligent adults interested in news & politics. ♦Jane Christo, gen mgr; Anna Kosof, stn mgr; Jerry Feusterman, dev dir; Corey Lewis, sls. dir; Mike Steffon, mktg dir; George Boosey, progmg dir; Sam Fleming, news dir; Jeffrey Hutton, engrg dir; Michael LeClair, chief of engrg.

WSKO(AM)— June 2, 1922: 790 khz; 5 kw-U, DA-N. TL: N41 50 03 W71 21 56. Stereo. 1502 Wampanoag Tr., East Providence 02915. Phone: (401) 433-4200. Fax: (401) 433-5967. Web Site: www.790thescore.com. Licensee: Citadel Broadcasting Co. Group owner: Citadel Broadcasting Corp. (acq 5-29-97; grpsl). Rep: McGavren Guild. Format: All sports. Target aud: 25-64; upper class, affluent, college educated. ♦Ron St. Pierre, VP; Chris Gardiner, gen mgr; Steve Maully, rgnl sls mgr & prom mgr; Kristen Chudy, prom mgr; Tony Brisco, progmg dir.

Rhode Island

WWLI(FM)—Co-owned with WSKO(AM). July 11, 1948: 105.1 mhz; 50 kw. 500 ft. TL: N41 48 22 W71 28 12. Stereo. Web Site: www.lite105.com. Format: Adult contemp. Target aud: 25-54; mid to upper income professionals, general appeal format.

WSNE-FM—See Taunton, MA

WWBB(FM)— June 7, 1968: 101.5 mhz; 13.5 kw horiz, 12 kw vert. 951 ft. TL: N41 52 13 W71 17 47. Stereo. 75 Oxford St., 3rd Fl. 02905. Phone: (401) 781-9979. Fax: (401) 781-9329. Web Site: www.b101.com. Licensee: Clear Channel Radio Licenses Inc. Group owner: Clear Channel Communications Inc. Format: Big hits. Target aud: 35-54; indispensable & powerful adults. ♦Jim Corwin, gen mgr; Michelle Maker, mktg dir & pub affrs dir; Steve Lariviere, chief of engrg.

Smithfield

*WJMF(FM)— Aug 1, 1974: 88.7 mhz; 225 w. 130 ft. TL: N41 55 13 W71 32 26. Stereo. Box 6, Bryant College, 1150 Douglas Pike 02917. Phone: (401) 232-6044. Phone: (401) 232-6160. Fax: (401) 232-6748. Web Site: www.wjmf887.com. Licensee: Bryant College of Business Administration. Format: Urban, alternative. News staff: one; News: 12 hrs wkly. Target aud: 16-30; from teenagers to young executives. Spec prog: Folk 4 hrs, gospel 2 hrs, relg 2 hrs wkly. ♦Bryan Adams, gen mgr.

Wakefield-Peacedale

WSKO-FM— June 1995: 99.7 mhz; 2.3 kw. 535 ft. TL: N41 25 31 W71 34 59. 1502 Wampanoag Trail, East Providence 02915. Phone: (401) 433-4200. Fax: (401) 437-3297. Web Site: www.790thescore.com. Licensee: Citadel Broadcasting Co. Group owner: Citadel Broadcasting Corp. (acq 8-6-97; $8.5 million. with WKKB(FM) Middletown). Network: Westwood One. Wiley, Rein & Fielding. Format: Sports. ♦Barbara Haynes, gen mgr; Duffy Egan, chief of engrg.

Warwick

WARV(AM)— Aug 12, 1959: 1590 khz; 5 kw-U, DA-2. TL: N41 43 40 W71 27 46. 19 Luther Ave. 02886. Phone: (401) 737-0700. Fax: (401) 737-1604. E-mail: warv@aol.com. Web Site: www.warv.net. Licensee: Blount Communications Inc. Group owner: Blount Communications Group (acq 7-7-78). Network: Salem Radio Network. Format: Relg. Target aud: 25-54; Adults. Spec prog: Black 2 hrs wkly. ♦Deborah C. Blount, exec VP; David O. Young, VP; William A. Blount, pres & gen mgr; Kevin Linegan, opns mgr.

West Warwick

WLKW(AM)—Licensed to West Warwick. See Providence

Westerly

*WBLQ(FM)— Dec 8, 1997: 88.1 mhz; 100 w. 66 ft. TL: N41 21 16 W71 46 12. Stereo. Southern Rhode Island Public Radio, 244 Post Rd. 02891. Phone: (401) 322-9091. Fax: (401) 322-1645. Web Site: www.wblqfm.org. Licensee: Southern Rhode Island Public Radio Broadcasting Inc. Format: Full service. News staff: one; News: 1 hr wkly. ♦Chris Di Paola, pres & gen mgr; Vito Di Paola, exec VP; Dade Nunez, opns mgr.

WEEI-FM— Oct 17, 1967: 103.7 mhz; 37 kw. 570 ft. TL: N41 34 22 W71 37 55. Stereo. 150 Chestnut St., Providence 02903. Phone: (401) 751-9334. Fax: (401) 351-8109. Web Site: www.fnxradio.com. Licensee: Entercom Providence License LLC. Group owner: Entercom Communications Corp. (acq 6-15-2004; $14.5 million). Network: Westwood One. Format: Sports, talk. News staff: one. Target aud: 25-49. ♦David J. Field, CEO; Joseph M. Field, chmn & VP; Joseph Harrington, stn mgr; Rod Morrison, prom dir & prom mgr.

WXNI(AM)— July 1949: 1230 khz; 1 kw-U. TL: N41 21 57 W71 50 11. 890 Commonwealth Ave., Boston, MA 02215. Secondary address: One Union Station, Providence 02903. Phone: (401) 351-2800. Fax: (401) 351-0246. E-mail: info@wrni.org. Web Site: www.wrni.org. Licensee: WRNI Foundation (acq 3-26-99). Network: Network: NPR, PRI. Format: News, talk. News: 80 hrs wkly. Target aud: 25-54; intelligent adults interested in news & politics. Spec prog: Sp 5 hrs wkly. ♦Jane Christo, gen mgr; Anna Kosof, stn mgr; Corey Lewis, sls dir; Mike Steffon, mktg dir; George Boosey, progmg dir; Sam Fleming, news dir; Jeffrey Hutton, engrg dir; Michael Le Clair, chief of engrg.

Wickford

WKKB(FM)—See Middletown

Woonsocket

WNRI(AM)— Nov 28, 1954: 1380 khz; 2.5 kw-D, 16 w-N. TL: N42 00 58 W71 29 30. Stereo. 786 Diamond Hill Rd. 02895. Phone: (401) 769-6925. Fax: (401) 762-0442. E-mail: rogerwnri@prodigy.net. Web Site: www.wnri.com. Licensee: Bouchard Broadcasting Inc. (group owner; (acq 10-20-2004; $900,000). Network: USA. Format: News/talk. Target aud: 35 plus. Spec prog: Fr 4 hrs, Pol 2 hrs, Por 2 hrs wkly. ♦Roger Bouchard, gen mgr & progmg dir; Jeff Gamache, opns mgr; Sue Pouliot, gen sls mgr.

WOON(AM)— Nov 11, 1946: 1240 khz; 1 kw-U. TL: N41 59 35 W71 30 33. (CP: TL: N41 59 34 W71 30 20). One Social St. 02895-3136. Phone: (401) 766-1240. Fax: (401) 769-8232. E-mail: email@onworldwide.com. Web Site: www.onworldwide.com. Licensee: O-N Radio Inc. (acq 10-19-99). Network: CBS. Format: News/talk. Target aud: 35 plus. Spec prog: Fr one hr, Pol 3 hrs, Black one hr, gospel one hr wkly. ♦Dave Richards, gen mgr.

WWKX(FM)— July 1, 1949: 106.3 mhz; 1.5 kw. 518 ft. TL: N41 59 43 W71 26 54. (CP: Ant 520 ft.). Stereo. 1502 Wampanoaq Tr., East Providence 02915. Phone: (401) 433-4200. Fax: (401) 433-5967. E-mail: hot1063@hot1063.com. Web Site: www.hot1063.com. Licensee: Citadel Broadcasting Co. Group owner: Citadel Communications Corp. (acq 1-24-2005; $16.5 million. with WAKX(FM) Narragansett Pier). Network: Westwood One. Christal. Format: Rhythm/dance, CHR. Target aud: 18-49. ♦Barbara Haynes, gen mgr; Duffy Egan, chief of engrg.

South Carolina

Abbeville

WABV(AM)— March 1956: . Stn currently dark 1590 khz; 1 kw-D, 27 w-N. TL: N34 09 03 W82 23 34. Box 280, Jasper, GA 30143. Licensee: Mark Hellinger (acq 4-14-97). ♦Mark Hellinger, pres & gen mgr.

WZLA-FM— Jan 1, 1990: 92.9 mhz; 6 kw. Ant 243 ft. TL: N34 11 13 W82 19 28. Stereo. Box 548 29620. Secondary address: 112 N. Main St. 29620. Phone: (864) 366-5785. Fax: (864) 366-9391. E-mail: z93@wctel.net. Licensee: Shelley Reid. Network: ABC. Fletcher, Heald & Hildreth. Format: Oldies. Target aud: 25-65. Spec prog: Gospel 8 hrs wkly. ♦Oscar H. Reid Jr., stn mgr & gen sls mgr; Shelley Reid, pres, gen mgr, opns dir, progmg dir & chief of engrg.

Aiken

WGOR(FM)—See New Ellenton

WKSP(FM)— Sept 17, 1966: 96.3 mhz; 17.5 kw. Ant 846 ft. TL: N33 41 06 W81 55 36. 2743 Perimeter Pkwy., Augusta, GA 30909. Phone: (706) 396-6000. Fax: (706) 396-6010. Web Site: www.kiss963.com. Licensee: Capstar TX L.P. Group owner: Clear Channel Communications Inc. (acq 12-19-00; grpsl). Format: Rhythm and blues, oldies. ♦Barry Kaye, gen mgr.

WKXC-FM— August 1966: 99.5 mhz; 22.5 kw. 728 ft. TL: N33 38 44 W21 55 40. Stereo. 4051 Jimmie Dyess Pky, Augusta 30908. Phone: (706) 396-7000. Fax: (706) 396-7100. Web Site: www.kicks99.com. Licensee: WGAC License LLC. Group owner: Beasley Broadcast Group Inc. (acq 4-2-2001; $12 million. with WSLT(FM) Clearwater). Format: Country. ♦Coni E. Sansom, gen mgr.

*WLJK(FM)— 1990: 89.1 mhz; 10 kw. 1,374 ft. TL: N33 24 18 W81 50 15. 1101 George Rogers Blvd., Columbia 29201. Phone: (803) 737-3420. Fax: (803) 737-3552. E-mail: gasque@scetv.org. Web Site: www.scern.org. Licensee: South Carolina Educational TV Commission. Network: Network: NPR, PRI. Dow, Lohnes & Albertson. Format: Talk, NPR news. ♦Moss Bresnahan, pres; Paul Zweimiller, VP & stn mgr; Tom Holloway, dev dir.

Directory of Radio

Allendale

WDOG(AM)— Jan 1, 1966: 1460 khz; 1 kw-D. TL: N33 01 22 W81 19 58. 2447 Agusta Hwy. 29810. Phone: (803) 584-3500. Fax: (240) 358-7473. Licensee: Good Radio Broadcasting Inc. Network: ABC Information & Entertainment. Format: C&W, Black. ♦H. Carl Gooding, pres, gen mgr, gen sls mgr & chief of engrg; Rick Gooding, prom mgr & progmg dir; Lisa Gooding, news dir.

WDOG-FM— Aug 29, 1983: 93.5 mhz; 3 kw. 300 ft. TL: N33 01 22 W81 19 58. Stereo.

Anderson

WAIM(AM)— April 1935: 1230 khz; 1 kw-U. TL: N34 31 52 W82 36 50. 2203 Old Williamston Rd. 29621. Phone: (864) 226-1511. Phone: (864) 225-1230. Fax: (864) 226-1513. E-mail: waimrd@carol.net. Licensee: Palmetto Broadcasting Corp FTR: 10-19-92) Format: News/talk. Target aud: 25-64. ♦Rick Driver, gen mgr, gen sls mgr & progmg dir.

WANS(AM)— June 1, 1949: 1280 khz; 5 kw-D, 1 kw-N, DA-N. TL: N34 32 17 W82 41 28. 141 Powell Rd. 29625. Phone: (864) 224-9267. Fax: (864) 224-8841. Web Site: www.wans1280am.com. Licensee: FM 103 Inc. (acq 10-28-96). Format: Gospel. ♦Ray Morris, gen mgr.

WJMZ-FM— Aug 1, 1963: 107.3 mhz; 100 kw. 1,008 ft. TL: N34 42 06 W82 36 20. Stereo. 220 N. Main St., Suite 402, Greenville 29601. Phone: (864) 235-1073. Fax: (864) 370-3403. Web Site: www.1073jamz.com. Licensee: CXR Holdings L.L.C. Group owner: Cox Communications Inc. (acq 2-1-2001; grpsl). Format: Urban contemp. ♦Steve Sinicropi, VP & gen mgr; Bob Grossmall, gen sls mgr; Cathy Tabor, natl sls mgr; Laurie Madden, mktg dir & prom mgr; Doug Davis, mus dir; K.J. Bland, asst music dir; Ed Bailey, news dir; Lemont Bryant, chief of engrg.

WROQ(FM)— 1947: 101.1 mhz; 100 kw. 994 ft. TL: N34 38 51 W82 16 13. Stereo. Box 5200, Greenville 29607. Phone: (864) 242-0101. Fax: (864) 271-5029. Web Site: www.wroq.com. Licensee: OBC Broadcasting Inc. Group owner: Barnstable Broadcasting Inc. (acq 8-7-00; grpsl). Format: Classic rock. Target aud: 25-54; baby boomers. ♦John Shea, pres & gen mgr; Mark Hendrix, opns dir & progmg dir; Tom Hoyt, sls dir; Bob Dellert, gen sls mgr; Sandy Smith, natl sls mgr; Bob Ross, prom dir; J.D. Stone, mus dir; Anitra Lively, news dir & pub affrs dir; Blake Lanford, engrg mgr.

WTBI(AM)—See Pickens

Andrews

WGTN-FM—Licensed to Andrews. See Georgetown

Atlantic Beach

WMIR(AM)— Oct 1, 1997: 1200 khz; 690 w-D. TL: N33 50 10 W78 51 08. 4337 Big Barn Dr., Little River 29566. Phone: (843) 399-2653. Fax: (843) 399-2659. E-mail: reggiedyson@juno.com. Licensee: Atlantic Beach Radio Inc. (acq 1-31-97). Format: Relg. Target aud: 25-65; southern gospel listeners. ♦Dr. Gardner Altman, pres; Reggie Dyson, CEO & gen mgr.

WSEA(FM)— 1998: 100.3 mhz; 12 kw. Ant 476 ft. TL: N33 47 03 W78 52 44. 11640 Hwy. 17 Bypass S., Murrells Inlet 29576-9332. Phone: (843) 651-7869. Fax: (843) 651-3197. Web Site: www.hot100fm.com. Licensee: Cumulus Licensing Corp. Group owner: Cumulus Media Inc. (acq 7-16-98; $1.3 million). Format: CHR. ♦Bill Hazen, gen mgr.

Bamberg

WWBD(FM)—Licensed to Bamberg. See Bamberg-Denmark

Bamberg-Denmark

WVCD(AM)— June 23, 1957: 790 khz; 1 kw-D, 100 w-N. TL: N33 18 50 W81 04 43. Box 678, Denmark 29042. Phone: (803) 703-7002. Fax: (803) 703-7022. Licensee: Voorhees College (acq 1-29-03; $112,500). Format: Relg. Spec prog: Farm one hr wkly. ♦Annette Gantt, gen mgr.

WWBD(FM)—(Bamberg). May 1967: 95.7 mhz; 6 kw. 308 ft. TL: N33 18 50 W81 04 43. Stereo. 200 Regional Pkwy., Bldg. C, Suite 200, Bamberg 29118. Phone: (803) 536-1710. Fax: (803) 531-1089. E-mail:

Stations in the U.S.　　　　South Carolina

Developers & Brokers of Radio Properties

contact American Media Services at our suite: Philadelphia Marriott Downtown 215-625-2900
843-972-2200
americanmediaservices.com
Charleston, SC
Dallas, TX · Chicago, Il · Austin, TX

American Media Services, LLC

advertising@bd957.com. Web Site: www.baddog957.com. Licensee: Miller Communications Inc. (group owner; acq 7-31-2003; $850,000). Format: Rock & roll classics. ♦Harold T. Miller Jr., pres.

Barnwell

WBAW-FM— Aug 31, 1966: 99.1 mhz; 25 kw. 328 ft. TL: N33 13 25 W81 21 35. Stereo. Box 685, 173 Jackson St. 29812. Phone: (803) 541-9989. Fax: (803) 541-6215. Licensee: Bullie Broadcasting Corp. (acq 2-5-99; $475,000). Format: Gospel. Target aud: General. ♦Tony Moye, gen mgr & chief of opns; Barry Wall, progmg dir.

Batesburg

WBLR(AM)— May 10, 1956: 1430 khz; 5 kw-D, 142 w-N. TL: N33 54 58 W81 31 42. 2278 Wortham Lane, Grovetown, GA 30813. Phone: (706) 309-9609. Fax: (706) 309-9669. E-mail: ctbarinowski@comcast.net. Licensee: Barinowski Investment Co., a Georgia L.P. Group owner: Good News Network. (acq 8-18-98). Format: Sp. Target aud: General. ♦C. T. Barinowski, pres & gen mgr.

WZMJ(FM)— Aug 5, 1965: 93.1 mhz; 2.1 kw. Ant 561 ft. TL: N33 54 02 W81 24 25. Stereo. 1900 Pineview Rd., Columbia 29209. Phone: (803) 695-8600. Fax: (803) 695-8605. E-mail: mhanisch@innercity.sc.com. Licensee: Urban Radio II L.L.C. Group owner: Inner City Broadcasting (acq 5-30-2003; $11.1 million. with WHXT(FM) Orangeburg). Network: ESPN Radio, Jones Radio Networks. Format: Sports. ♦Steve Patterson, gen mgr; Scott Norton, gen sls mgr; Dave Stewart, progmg dir & chief of engrg.

Beaufort

***WAGP(FM)**— Oct 10, 1987: 88.7 mhz; 6 kw. 302 ft. TL: N32 24 05 W80 44 21. Stereo. Box 119 29901. Secondary address: 4 Grober Hill Rd., Suite C 29901. Phone: (843) 525-1859. Fax: (843) 522-3691. E-mail: waagp@islc.net. Web Site: www.wagp.net. Licensee: The Christian Broadcasting Corp. of Beaufort. Network: Moody. Format: Relg. News: 20 hrs wkly. Target aud: General; evangelical Christians. ♦Carl J. Broggi, pres; Richard Forschner, gen mgr.

WGZO(FM)—See Parris Island

***WJWJ-FM**— Aug 1, 1980: 89.9 mhz; 47 kw, 1,100 ft. TL: N32 42 44 W80 40 49. 1101 George Rogers Blvd., Columbia 29201. Phone: (803) 737-3420. Fax: (803) 737-3552. E-mail: gasque@scetv.org. Web Site: www.etvradio.org. Licensee: South Carolina Educational TV. Network: NPR. Format: News info. News: 25 hrs wkly. Target aud: General. ♦Moss Brenahan, pres & gen mgr; Tom Fowler, VP; Paul Zweimiller, stn mgr.

WVGB(AM)— 1959: 1490 khz; 1 kw-U. TL: N32 26 08 W80 41 54. Box 1477, 806 Monson St. 29901. Phone: (843) 524-4700. Phone: (843) 524-9742. Fax: (843) 524-1329. E-mail: vgbradio@earthlink.net. Licensee: Vivian Broadcasting Inc. (acq 1-21-83). Network: American Urban. Format: Relg, gospel. Target aud: 18-65; African American. Spec prog: Community progmg, sports. ♦William A. Galloway, pres; Vivian M. Galloway, gen mgr, opns VP & sls VP; Darryl Jamison, stn mgr, rgnl sls mgr & adv dir; Derrick Moon, progmg dir; Martin Foglia, chief of engrg.

WYKZ(FM)— Aug 8, 1962: 98.7 mhz; 100 kw, 1,001 ft. TL: N32 19 50 W80 56 19. Stereo. 245 Alfred St., Savannah, GA 31408. Phone: (912) 964-7794. Fax: (912) 964-9414. Licensee: Capstar TX L.P. Group owner: Clear Channel Communications Inc. (acq 8-30-00; grpsl). Wiley, Rein & Fielding. Format: Light adult contemp. News staff: one; News: 3 hrs wkly. Target aud: 25-54; female. Spec prog: Oldies 5 hrs wkly. ♦Alene Grevey, sr VP; Jeffrey A. Storey, VP & gen mgr; Brad Kelly, opns mgr; Sheryl Collison, sls dir; Tara Friedman, prom mgr; Mark Robertson, progmg mgr; Marty Foglia, chief of engrg.

Belton

***WEPC(FM)**— May 1994: 88.5 mhz; 50 kw. 298 ft. TL: N34 23 43 W82 29 49. TFC Radio Network, Box 780, Toccoa Falls, GA 30598. Phone: (706) 282-6030. Fax: (706) 282-6090. E-mail: tfcrn@tfc.edu. Web Site: www.myfavoritestation.net. Licensee: Toccoa Falls College. Format: Christian, MOR, educ. ♦Dr. Wayne Gardner, CEO; David Cornelius, gen mgr; Bryan Race, stn mgr.

WLUA(AM)— October 1956: . Stn currently dark 1390 khz; 1 kw-D, 17 w-N. TL: N34 35 19 W82 32 17. Box 646 29627. Phone: (864) 338-7742. Fax: (864) 338-7743. Licensee: Robert Earl Bryson (acq 4-2-97; $4,000). Format: Christian. Target aud: General. Spec prog: Black gospel 8 hrs wkly. ♦Robert Earl Bryson, gen mgr.

Belvedere

***WAFJ(FM)**— August 1994: 88.3 mhz; 4.5 kw. 1,387 ft. TL: N33 24 29 W81 50 36. Stereo. 102 LeCompte Ave., N. Augusta 29841. Phone: (803) 819-3125. Fax: (803) 819-3129. Web Site: www.wafj.com. Licensee: Radio Training Network Inc. (acq 1994; $291,000). Format: Contemp Christian. News staff: one. ♦Brian Dickert, gen mgr; Jeremy Daley, progmg dir & mus dir; Cleve Walker, news dir.

Bennettsville

WBSC(AM)— June 1947: 1550 khz; 10 kw-D, 5 kw-N, DA-N. TL: N34 40 52 W79 42 04. Box 1275, 226 Radio Rd. 29512-1275. Phone: (843) 479-7121. Fax: (843) 479- 4474. E-mail: wbsc@aol.com. Web Site: www.wbsc1550.com. Licensee: D. Mitch Broadcasting Inc. (acq 4-95). Rep: Dora-Clayton. Format: Oldies, gospel. Spec prog: Black 15 hrs wkly. ♦Dwight Johnson, CEO, pres, VP, gen mgr & sls VP; Richard Gehm, chief of opns, progmg mgr & chief of engrg.

Bishopville

WAGS(AM)— Feb 24, 1954: 1380 khz; 1 kw-D. TL: N34 12 35 W80 13 34. 142 Wags Dr. 29010. Phone: (803) 484-5415. Licensee: Beaver Communications (acq 11-01-99; $27,500). Network: USA. Format: Country. News: 6 hrs wkly. Target aud: 25-55 plus. Spec prog: Live remotes-parades, civic events, festivals 2 hrs, relg 7 hrs wkly. ♦James D. Jenkins, gen mgr & chief of opns.

WSIM(FM)— October 1992: 93.7 mhz; 5 kw. Ant 358 ft. TL: N34 07 10 W80 08 49. (CP: COL Lamar. 2.8 kw, ant 485 ft. TL: N34 12 12 W79 51 52). 51 Commerce St., Sumter 29151. Phone: (803) 775-2321. Fax: (803) 773-4856. Web Site: www.miller.fm/oldschool. Licensee: Miller Communications Inc. (group owner; (acq 11-14-2000; grpsl). Network: ABC. Smithwick & Belendiuk. Format: Oldies solid gold. News staff: one. Target aud: 35-64; adults. ♦Harold T. Miller Jr., CEO & pres; Theresa Miller, VP & gen mgr; Dave Baker, opns VP & opns mgr.

Blackville

WIIZ(FM)— April 1996: 97.9 mhz; 50 kw. 433 ft. TL: N33 06 52 W81 23 13. 8968 Marlboro Ave., Barnwell 29812. Phone: (843) 259-9797. Fax: (803) 541-9700. Licensee: NicWild Communications Inc. (acq 10-9-96; $340,000). Format: Urban contemp. ♦Bobby Nichols, gen mgr & progmg dir.

Bluffton

WGZR(FM)— June 22, 1988: 106.9 mhz; 100 kw. 800 ft. TL: N32 13 36 W80 50 53. Stereo. One St. Augustine Pl., Hilton Head Island 29928. Phone: (843) 785-9569. Fax: (843) 842-3369. E-mail: gator1069@adventureradio.fm. Web Site: www.gator1069.com. Licensee: Monterey Licenses LLC. Group owner: Triad Broadcasting Co. LLC (acq 8-8-00; grpsl). Rep: Christal. Format: Country. News staff: 2. Target aud: 18-49; hip, Gen Xers, particularly ages 22-40. ♦Robert Leonard, gen mgr.

Blythwood

WBAJ(AM)— 1999: 890 khz; 50 kw-D, 8.5 kw-CH. TL: N34 06 31 W81 04 28. 241-A Riverchase Way, Lexington 29072. Phone: (803) 794-9673. E-mail: radio@wbaj.net. Web Site: www.wbaj.net. Licensee: Family First. (acq 8-29-98; $60,000). Format: Christian. ♦Linda de Romanett, pres & gen mgr.

Bowman

WSPX(FM)— October 1997: 94.5 mhz; 3.5 kw. Ant 434 ft. TL: N33 19 13 W80 43 52. Box 1445, Orangeburg 29116. Secondary address: 1236 Five Chop Rd., Orangeburg 29115. Phone: (803) 539-9450. Fax: (803) 539-9458. E-mail: email@wfmv.com. Web Site: wspx@sc.rr.com. Licensee: Glory Communications Inc. (group owner; acq 4-19-01; $400,000). Format: Gospel. ♦Alex Snipes Jr., gen mgr.

Branchville

WGFG(FM)— Dec 13,1993: 105.1 mhz; 6 kw. Ant 328 ft. TL: N33 16 30 W80 50 08. 200 Regional Pkwy., Bldg. C, Suite 200, Orangeburg 29118. Phone: (803) 536-1710. Fax: (803) 531-1089. E-mail: mail@miller.fm. Web Site: www.miller.fm. Licensee: Miller Communications Inc. (group owner; acq 4-30-03; $1.25 million. with WQKI-FM Orangeburg). Network: ABC. Format: Oldies. Target aud: 25-64; baby boomers. ♦Harold Miller Jr., pres; Theresa Miller, gen mgr; Russ T. Fender, opns mgr.

Briarcliff Acres

WQSD(FM)— Apr 5, 1975: 107.1 mhz; 50 kw. Ant 492 ft. TL: N33 56 14 W78 57 53. Stereo. Box 16000, Surfside Beach 29578. Secondary address: 4841 Hwy. 17 by-pass South, Myrtle Beach 29577. Phone: (843) 293-0107. Fax: (843) 293-1717. Web Site: www.thesound1071.com. Licensee: Qantum of Myrtle Beach License Co. LLC. Group owner: Qantum Communications Corp. (acq 7-2-2003; grpsl). Format: Classic Rock. ♦Jimmy Feuger, gen mgr.

Bucksport

WGTR(FM)— June 1, 1993: 107.9 mhz; 20 kw. Ant 784 ft. TL: N33 35 45 W79 03 11. 4841 Hwy.17 by-pass South, Myrtle Beach 29577. Phone: (843) 293-0107. Fax: (843) 293-1717. Web Site: www.gator1079.com. Licensee: Qantum of Myrtle Beach License Co. LLC. Group owner: Qantum Communications Corp. (acq 7-2-2003; grpsl). Format: Country. Spec prog: Motor racing 8 hrs wkly. ♦Jimmy Feuger, gen mgr.

Camden

WCAM(AM)— July 23, 1948: 1590 khz; 1 kw-D, 27 w-N. TL: N34 13 36 W80 40 45. Stereo. Box 753 29020. Secondary address: 5 The Commons Ward Rd., Lugoff 29078. Phone: (803) 438-9002. Fax: (803) 408-2288. Web Site: www.kol1027.com. Licensee: Kershaw Radio Corp. (acq 8-87; $75,000; 5-5-86). Network: ABC Information & Entertainment. Format: Nostalgia, adult standards. Target aud: 45 plus. ♦Chris Johnson, gen mgr; Bill Rogers, progmg dir.

WPUB-FM—Co-owned with WCAM(AM). December 1974: 102.7 mhz; 3.3 kw. 299 ft. TL: N34 13 31 W80 40 44. Stereo. Web Site: www.kol1027.com. Format: Oldies. Target aud: 25-55

WQIS(AM)— Dec 10, 1970: 1130 khz; 1 kw-D, 7 w-N. TL: N34 15 32 W80 34 47. Box 127 29020-0127. Secondary address: 1709-1711 Lynhurst Dr. 29020. Phone: (803) 432-8717. E-mail: wqis@sports1130.com. Web Site: www.sports1130.com. Licensee: Jeff Andrulonis Group owner: GHB Radio Group (acq 10-13-2004; $200,000). Format: Sports. ♦Jeffrey M. Andrulonis, gen mgr.

Cayce

WGCV(AM)— Aug 22, 1958: 620 khz; 2.5 kw-D, 126 w-N. TL: N33 57 34 W81 02 28. 2440 Millwood Ave., Colombia 29205. Phone: (803) 748-9620. Fax: (803) 799-1620. E-mail: wgcvproduction@wgcv.net. Web Site: www.wgcv.net. Licensee: Glory Communications Inc. (group owner; acq 10-8-99). Network: American Urban. Format: Gospel.

News staff: one. Target aud: 34-65; Black adults. ♦Alex Snipe, pres & gen mgr; Rev. Isaac Heyward, stn mgr & prom dir; Tezra Haire, gen sls mgr; Tony Green, progmg dir.

WLTY(FM)—Licensed to Cayce. See Columbia

***WYFV(FM)**— Oct 10, 1990: 88.7 mhz; 150 w. 141 ft. TL: N33 55 22 W81 04 42. 6150 Cannons Campground Rd., Cowpens 290330. Phone: (864) 487-5836. Fax: (864) 487-5836. E-mail: wyfu@bbnradio.org. Web Site: bbnradio.org. Licensee: Bible Broadcasting Network Inc. (group owner; acq 6-26-90; 7-23-90). Format: Relg, bible preaching & teaching. News: 10 hrs wkly. Target aud: General.

Charleston

WALC(FM)— Apr 4, 1990: 100.5 mhz; 17.5 kw. Ant 394 ft. TL: N32 49 20 W79 58 45. Stereo. 950 Houston Northcutt Blvd., Ste. 201, Mt. Pleasant 29464. Phone: (843) 884-2534. Fax: (843) 884-1218. Web Site: www.thedrive100.com. Licensee: Citicasters Licenses L.P. Group owner: Clear Channel Communications Inc. (acq 5-4-99; grpsl). Rep: Katz Radio. Format: Adult contemp. ♦Alene Grevey, gen mgr.

WAVF(FM)—See Hanahan

WEZL(FM)— Oct 3, 1970: 103.5 mhz; 100 kw. Ant 659 ft. TL: N32 49 04 W79 50 08. (CP: Ant 987 ft.). Stereo. 950 Houston Northcutt Blvd., Mount Pleasant 29464. Phone: (843) 884-2534. Fax: (843) 884-1218. Web Site: www.wezlfm.com. Licensee: Citicasters Licenses L.P. Group owner: Clear Channel Communications Inc. (acq 5-4-99; grpsl). Format: C&W. News staff: one; News: 3 to 4 hrs wkly. ♦Paul Smith, gen mgr; Lee Mathews, progmg mgr; Teri Hegel, mus dir & sls; Willie Bennett, news dir & engr.

***WFCH(FM)**— December 1986: 88.5 mhz; 29.6 kw. 305 ft. TL: N32 49 04 W79 50 08. Box 1505, Mount Pleasant 29465. Phone: (843) 881-9450. Phone: (510) 568-6200. Fax: (510) 568-6190. E-mail: famradio@familyradio.com. Web Site: www.familyradio.com. Licensee: Family Stations Inc. (group owner) Network: Family Radio. Format: Relg. ♦Harold Camping, gen mgr; Joe Papp, chief of engrg.

WLTQ(AM)— 1947: 730 khz; 1 kw-D, 100 w-N. TL: N32 46 22 W80 00 58. 950 Houston North Cutt Blvd., Suite 201, Mount Pleasant 29464. Phone: (843) 884-2534. Fax: (843) 884-1218. Licensee: Citicasters Licenses L.P. Group owner: Clear Channel Communications Inc. (acq 5-4-99; grpsl). Format: Standards. ♦Alene Grevey, gen mgr & gen sls mgr; Greg Alan, prom mgr & progmg dir; Willie Bennett, chief of engrg.

WQNT(AM)— 1948: 1450 khz; 1 kw-U. TL: N32 48 15 W79 57 43. 60 Markfield Dr., Suite 4 29407. Phone: (843) 763-6631. Fax: (843) 766-1239. E-mail: wqnt@kirkmanbroadcasting.com. Licensee: Kirkman Broadcasting Inc. (group owner; acq 1995). Network: CNN Radio. Brian Madden & Assoc. Format: News. News: 24 hrs news prog wkly. Target aud: 25-54; Adults. Spec prog: Relg one hr wkly. ♦Gil Kirkman, pres; Stew Williams, opns mgr & progmg dir; Robby Robinson, gen sls mgr; John Dixon, news dir; Wally Momeier, chief of engrg.

WQSC(AM)— 1946: 1340 khz; 1 kw-U. TL: N32 49 07 W79 57 43. 60 Markfield Dr., Suite 4 29407. Phone: (843) 763-6631. Fax: (843) 766-1239. E-mail: wqsc@berkeleyelectric.net. Licensee: Kirkman Broadcasting Inc. (group owner; acq 11-1-94). Network: Westwood One. Format: Talk. News staff: 1; News: 5 hrs wkly. Target aud: 25-54; Male. Spec prog: Relg 1 hr wkly. ♦Gil Kirkman, pres; Robby Robinson, gen mgr & gen sls mgr; Stew Williams, opns mgr; John Dixon, news dir; Wally Momeier, chief of engrg.

***WSCI(FM)**— 1973: 89.3 mhz; 97 kw. 540 ft. TL: N32 47 44 W79 50 27. Stereo. 1101 George Rogers Blvd., Columbia 29201. Phone: (803) 737-3420. Fax: (803) 737-3552. E-mail: gasque@scetv.org. Web Site: www.etvradio.org. Licensee: South Carolina Educational TV Commission. Network: Network: NPR, PRI. Format: Class, jazz, news. News staff: 2. Spec prog: Black 5 hrs wkly. ♦Moss Bresnahan, pres; Tom Fowler, sr VP; Paul Zweimiller, stn mgr & engrg mgr; Tom Holloway, sls dir; John Gasque, progmg dir; Hap Griffin, engrg VP.

WSSX-FM— 1945: 95.1 mhz; 100 kw. 361 ft. TL: N32 49 20 W79 58 45. (CP: Ant 1,000 ft.). Stereo. 4230 Faber Place Dr., Ste. 100, No. Charleston 99405. Phone: (843) 277-1200. Fax: (843) 277-1212. Web Site: www.95fx.com. Licensee: Citadel Broadcasting Co. Group owner: Citadel Broadcasting Corp. (acq 6-9-99; grpsl). Network: Westwood One. Format: Adult contemp, Top-40. News staff: one. Target aud: 18-34. ♦Paul O'Mailey, gen mgr.

WSUY(FM)— Apr 1, 1948: 96.9 mhz; 100 kw. 1,750 ft. TL: N32 55 28 W79 41 58. Stereo. 4230 Faber Place Drive, Suite 100, North Charleston 29405. Phone: (843) 277-1200. Fax: (843) 277-1212. Web Site: www.sunny969.com. Licensee: Citadel Broadcasting Co. Group owner: Citadel Broadcasting Corp. Rep: McGavren Guild. Format: Soft rock. ♦Paul O'Malley, gen mgr; Bocky Gilleath, gen sls mgr; Eric Chaney, progmg dir; J.T. Tucker, chief of engrg.

WTMA(AM)— 1939: 1250 khz; 5 kw-D, 1 kw-N, DA-N. TL: N32 49 20 W79 58 45. 4230 Faber Place Dr., Suite 100, N. Charleston 29405. Phone: (843) 277-1200. Fax: (843) 227-1212. Web Site: www.wtma.com. Licensee: Citadel Broadcasting Co. Group owner: Citadel Broadcasting Corp. (acq 6-9-99; grpsl). Network: Network: CBS, Westwood One. Format: News/talk. News: 5 hrs wkly. Target aud: 25-54. ♦Paul O'Malley, gen mgr; Terrence Bryant, opns dir.

WXLY(FM)—See North Charleston

WXTC(AM)— May 14, 1930: 1390 khz; 5 kw-U, DA-N. TL: N32 49 26 W80 00 06. Stereo. 4230 Faber Place Dr. Suite 100, North Charleston 29405-6512. Phone: (843) 308-9300. Fax: (843) 566-1222. Web Site: www.wtma.com. Licensee: Citadel Broadcasting Co. Group owner: Citadel Broadcasting Corp. (acq 6-9-99; grpsl). Rep: McGavren Guild. Haley, Bader & Potts. Format: Black gospel. News staff: one. Target aud: 25-54. ♦Paul O'Malley, gen mgr; Terry Base, stn mgr.

WYBB(FM)—See Folly Beach

WZJY(AM)—See Mt. Pleasant

Cheraw

WCRE(AM)— July 1953: 1420 khz; 1 kw-D, 97 w-N. TL: N34 41 12 W79 53 42. Box 160 29520. Phone: (843) 537-7887. Fax: (843) 537-7307. Web Site: www.wcreradio.com. Licensee: Pee Dee Broadcasting LLC (acq 1-28-2004; $50,000). Format: Adult contemp, oldies. News: 12 hrs wkly. Target aud: 25 plus. Spec prog: Black 5 hrs wkly. ♦Jane Pigg, pres; Mike Orr, gen mgr & prom dir; Susan Gilmour, news dir; Dave Raley, chief of engrg.

WJMX-FM— July 17, 1979: 103.3 mhz; 44 kw. 525 ft. TL: N34 30 19 W79 54 15. (CP: 50 kw, ant 492 ft.). Stereo. 181 E. Evans St., Suite 311, Florence 29501. Phone: (843) 667-9569. Fax: (843) 673-7390. Web Site: www.wjmx.com. Licensee: Qantum of Florence License Co. LLC. Group owner: Qantum Communications Corp. (acq 7-2-2003; grpsl). Rep: McGavren Guild. Format: CHR. Target aud: 18-34. ♦Jonathan Brewster, gen mgr & stn mgr; Gary Downes, opns dir; Craig Dallariva, gen sls mgr & engrg dir.

Chester

WBT-FM— Aug 30, 1969: 99.3 mhz; 7.6 kw. 603 ft. TL: N34 47 29 W81 16 01. Stereo. One Julian Price Pl., Charlotte, NC 28208. Phone: (704) 374-3500. Fax: (704) 338-3062. Web Site: www.wbt.com. Licensee: Jefferson-Pilot Communications Co. (group owner; acq 1995; $1.5 million). Format: News/talk. News staff: 7; News: 6 hrs wkly. Target aud: 25-54; information, sports seekers. Spec prog: Gospel 6 hrs wkly. ♦Rick Jackson, VP & gen mgr; Tom Jackson, opns dir; Terry Mace, dev VP. Co-owned TV: WBTV-TV affil

WGCD(AM)— July 19, 1948: 1490 khz; l kw-U. TL: N34 41 54 W81 12 06. Box 11584, Rock Hill 29731. Phone: (803) 329-2760. Fax: (803) 329-3317. Web Site: www.rejoynetwork.com. Licensee: Frank Neely. Group owner: Neely Enterprises (acq 5-7-97; $65,000). Format: Gospel. ♦Frank K. Neeley, gen mgr; Frankie Hemphill, stn mgr.

Chesterfield

***WRFE(FM)**—Not on air, target date: unknown: 89.3 mhz; 2 kw. Ant 184 ft. TL: N34 44 07 W80 05 21. Box 371177, Cayey, PR 00737. Phone: (787) 263-1367. Fax: (787) 263-1367. Licensee: Christian Educational Association. ♦Aurio Chaparro, pres & gen mgr.

WVSZ(FM)— 1993: 107.3 mhz; 3 kw. 328 ft. TL: N34 43 12 W80 05 45. Box 307, Rock Hill 29731. Phone: (843) 286-1071. Phone: (843) 623-3299. Fax: (803) 324-2860. E-mail: almiller@wrhi.com. Web Site: www.wrhi.com. Licensee: Our Three Sons Broadcasting L.L.P. (group owner; acq 2-28-97; $142,500). Format: Country. ♦Allan M. Miller, gen mgr; Steven Stone, opns mgr.

Clearwater

WSLT(FM)— April 1987: 98.3 mhz; 2.8 kw. 484 ft. TL: N33 28 07 W81 52 26. Stereo. 4051 Jimmie Dyess Pky., Augusta 30908. Phone: (706) 396-7000. Fax: (706) 396-7100. Web Site: www.wslt.com. Licensee: WGAC License LLC. Group owner: Beasley Broadcast Group Inc. (acq 4-2-2001; $12 million. with WKXC-FM Aiken). Format: Soft adult contemp. ♦Coni E. Sansom, gen mgr.

Clemson

WAHT(AM)— July 27, 1969: 1560 khz; 1 kw-D, 500 w-CH. TL: N34 42 04 W82 49 30. Box 1560, 202 Lawrence Rd. 29631. Phone: (864) 654-1560. Fax: (864) 654-3300. E-mail: waht@wahtam.com. Web Site: www.wahtam.com. Licensee: Golden Corners Broadcasting Inc. (acq 9-28-89; $100,000; 10-16-89). Format: Oldies. News staff: one; News: 35 hrs wkly. Target aud: 35-58; older yuppies. ♦George W. Clement, pres & gen mgr; Faye Clement, VP; Jeff Bright, stn mgr, gen sls mgr, progmg dir & chief of engrg.

WCCP-FM—Co-owned with WAHT(AM). Apr 8, 1993: 104.9 mhz; 6 kw. 302 ft. TL: N34 38 11 W82 42 26. Stereo. Phone: (864) 654-4004. E-mail: info@wccpfm.com. Web Site: www.wccpfm.com. Network: Network: CBS, Sporting News Radio Network. Format: Sports. Target aud: 25-50. ♦George Clement, CEO; Aly Darby, stn mgr & progmg dir; Barry Clement, opns VP, opns mgr & prom dir; Pam Ponder, gen sls mgr.

***WSBF-FM**— Mar 16, 1961: 88.1 mhz; 3 kw. 200 ft. TL: N34 40 42 W82 49 15. Stereo. Clemson University, 210 Hendrix Student Ctr. 29634. Phone: (864) 656-4010. Fax: (864) 656-4011. E-mail: program@wsbf.net. Web Site: www.wsbf.net. Licensee: Clemson University Board of Trustees. Network: Westwood One. Format: Progsv. Target aud: 16-25.

Clinton

WPCC(AM)— Sept 11, 1957: 1410 khz; 1 kw-D, 100 w-N. TL: N34 26 42 W81 53 24. Box 1455, 1766 Hwy. 72 W. 29325. Phone: (864) 833-1410. Fax: (864) 833-2467. E-mail: wpcc@charter.net. Licensee: Laurens County Communications Inc. (acq 12-83; $90,000; 12-5-83). Format: Sports. News staff: one; News: 1 wkly. Target aud: General. ♦A. Cruickshanks, pres; Rhonda Cruickshanks, opns mgr, gen sls mgr & mktg dir; Chris Burgin, progmg dir & news dir; Wyatt Mattison, chief of engrg.

Columbia

WARQ(FM)— Feb 6, 1971: 93.5 mhz; 2.8 kw. 443 ft. TL: N34 02 00 W80 58 56. Stereo. Box 9127 29290. Secondary address: 1900 Pineview Rd. 29290. Phone: (803) 695-8600. Fax: (803) 695-8605. Web Site: www.warq.com. Licensee: Urban Radio II L.L.C. Group owner: Inner City Broadcasting (acq 8-7-2000; grpsl). Network: Network: ABC, Westwood One. Format: Rock. News staff: one; News: 5 hrs wkly. Target aud: 18-49. ♦Steve Patterson, gen mgr; Scott Norton, gen sls mgr; Jamie Muldrow, prom dir; Dave Stewart, progmg dir.

WCEO(AM)— Jan 1, 1994: 840 khz; 50 kw-D, DA. TL: N34 12 42 W80 50 05. Stereo. 108 Columbia N.E. Dr., Suite F 29223. Secondary address: 6734 Runnymede Dr., Sparks, NV 89436. Phone: (803) 419-7366. Fax: (803) 419-7363. E-mail: wceoradio@bellsouth.net. Licensee: Eastern Broadcasting Group Inc. (group owner; (acq 7-1-2002). Tom McCoy. Format: Sp. ♦Dr. M. J. Sbuttoni, pres; Ken Allen, opns mgr; Bob Simpkins, gen sls mgr; Teri Allen, prom dir; Tom McCoy, COO, gen mgr, stn mgr, rgnl sls mgr, progmg dir & progmg mgr; Ed Shiflett, engrg dir.

WCOS(AM)— 1939: 1400 khz; 1 kw-U. TL: N34 00 18 W81 00 43. 316 Greystone Blvd. 29210-8007. Phone: (803) 343-1100. Fax: (803) 798-5255. Licensee: Capstar TX L.P. Group owner: Clear Channel Communications Inc. (acq 9-1-00; grpsl). Rep: Clear Channel. Format: Sports. Target aud: Men 25-54. ♦Bobby Martin, gen mgr; Tim McFalls, gen mgr; Gary Barboza, opns mgr & progmg dir; Gary Frakes, prom dir; Gary Robinson, engrg dir.

WCOS-FM— March 1951: 97.5 mhz; 100 kw. 981 ft. TL: N34 08 23 W81 03 22. Stereo. Web Site: www.wcosfm.com. Format: Country. News staff: one. Target aud: 25-54. ♦Margret Wallace, sls dir & gen sls mgr; Susan Brown, prom mgr; Ron Brooks, progmg dir & news dir; Glen Garrett, mus dir; Gary Robinson, chief of engrg.

Stations in the U.S. — South Carolina

Developers & Brokers of Radio Properties

contact American Media Services at our suite: Philadelphia Marriott Downtown 215-625-2900
843-972-2200
americanmediaservices.com
Charleston, SC
Dallas, TX · Chicago, Il · Austin, TX

American Media Services, LLC

WISW(AM)— June 30, 1954: 1320 khz; 5 kw-D, 2.5 kw-N, DA-N. TL: N34 00 16 W81 04 15. 1801 Charleston Hwy., Cayce 29033. Phone: (803) 796-7600. Fax: (803) 796-5502. Licensee: Citadel Broadcasting Co. Group owner: Citadel Broadcasting Corp. Rep: Christal. Reddy, Begley & McCormick. Format: Talk Radio. News staff: 5; News: 168 hrs wkly. Target aud: 35-64. Spec prog: Sports. ♦ William L. McElveen, pres & gen mgr; Tim Miller, opns mgr; Bill MacAvine, gen sls mgr; Al Conner, progmg dir; Ray Allen, news dir; Ed Noyes, engrg dir.

WOMG(FM)—Co-owned with WISW(AM). Apr 15, 1989: 103.1 mhz; 3 kw. 300 ft. TL: N34 03 05 W81 00 07. (CP: 6 kw, ant 308 ft.). Stereo. Format: Oldies. Target aud: 25-54. ♦ Ray Allen, prom dir; Al Conner, news dir.

*WLTR(FM)— July 1, 1976: 91.3 mhz; 96 kw. 761 ft. TL: N34 07 07 W80 56 12. Stereo. 1101 George Rogers Blvd. 29201. Phone: (803) 737-3420. Fax: (803) 737-3552. E-mail: gasque@scetv.org. Web Site: www.etvradio.org. Licensee: South Carolina Educ. TV Commission. Network: Network: NPR, PRI. Dow, Lohnes & Albertson. Format: Classical, NPR news. ♦ Moss Bresnahan, pres & VP; Paul Zweimiller, pres & stn mgr; Tom Fowler, sr VP; Tom Holloway, dev dir.

WLTY(FM)—(Cayce). July 11, 1974: 96.7 mhz; 3.3 kw. 443 ft. TL: N34 00 04 W81 02 05. Stereo. 316 Greystone Blvd. 29250. Phone: (803) 343-1100. Fax: (803) 779-9727. Web Site: www.lite967.com. Licensee: Capstar TX L.P. Group owner: Clear Channel Communications Inc. (acq 8-30-00; grpsl). Rep: Clear Channel. Format: Light Adult Contemp. News: 6 hrs wkly. Target aud: 25-44; professionals & young adults. ♦ Bob Huntley, gen mgr.

WMFX(FM)—(Saint Andrews). Jan 23, 1985: 102.3 mhz; 6 kw. 322 ft. TL: N34 05 55 W81 04 48. Stereo. Box 9127 29290-0127. Secondary address: 1900 Pineview Rd. 29209. Phone: (803) 695-8600. Fax: (803) 695-8605. E-mail: mhanisch@innercity.sc.com. Web Site: www.fox102.com. Licensee: Urban Radio II L.L.C. Group owner: Inner City Broadcasting (acq 8-7-2000; grpsl). Format: Classic rock, AOR. News staff: one; News: one hr wkly. Target aud: 18-49. ♦ Maggie Hanisch, gen mgr; Scott Norton, gen sls mgr; Jamie Bowman, prom dir; Dave Stewart, progmg dir.

*WMHK(FM)— Aug 30, 1976: 89.7 mhz; 100 kw. 1,398 ft. TL: N34 05 49 W80 45 51. (CP: Ant 1,397 ft.). Stereo. Box 3122 29230. Phone: (803) 754-5400. Fax: (803) 714-0849. E-mail: wmhk@wmhk.com. Web Site: www.wmhk.com. Licensee: Columbia Bible College Broadcasting Co. Format: Relg. Target aud: 25-49. ♦ Jim Marshall, gen mgr.

WNOK(FM)— July 15, 1959: 104.7 mhz; 100 kw. 1,014 ft. TL: N34 09 06 W80 54 36. (CP: 96 kw, ant 1,033 ft. TL: N34 09 03 W80 54 36). Stereo. 316 Greystone Blvd 29210. Phone: (803) 343-1080. Fax: (803) 256-1968. Web Site: www.wnok.com. Licensee: Capstar TX L.P. Group owner: Clear Channel Communications Inc. (acq 8-30-00; grpsl). Format: CHR. Target aud: 18-34; landed gentry. ♦ Bob Hentley, gen mgr.

WOIC(AM)— Jan 1, 1947: 1230 khz; 1 kw-U, DA-N. TL: N33 59 34 W81 02 45. Box 9127 29290. Phone: (803) 776-1013. Fax: (803) 695-8605. Web Site: www.espn1230am.com. Licensee: Urban Radio II L.L.C. Group owner: Inner City Broadcasting (acq 8-7-2000; grpsl). Network: ESPN Radio. Rep: D & R Radio. Format: Sports. News: 3 hrs wkly. Target aud: 25-54; Male. ♦ Steve Patterson, gen mgr; Mike Love, opns dir & progmg dir; Al King, sls dir; Bert Smith, chief of engrg.

WQXL(AM)— June 15, 1945: 1470 khz; 5 kw-D, 138 w-N. TL: N34 01 44 W81 02 23. Box 3277 29230-3277. Phone: (803) 742-1470. Fax: (803) 252-2158. E-mail: wqxl1470@aol.com. Licensee: Metro Communications Inc. (acq 7-3-89). Network: USA. Format: Christian, relg, praise & worship. Target aud: 25-49. ♦ John Lastinger, pres; Karen Watkins, stn mgr, sls dir, mktg dir, adv dir & progmg mgr; Olin Jenkins, opns mgr, news dir & pub affrs dir; M. Fayne Anderson, engrg dir.

WTCB(FM)—See Orangeburg

*WUSC-FM— Jan 17, 1977: 90.5 mhz; 2.5 kw. 233 ft. TL: N34 00 02 W81 01 19. (CP: Ant 253 ft.). Stereo. Drawer B, Univ. of South Carolina, 1400 Greene St. 29208. Phone: (803) 777-5468. Fax: (803) 777-6482. Web Site: wusc.sc.edu. Licensee: University of South Carolina. Format: Var. News staff: one; News: 3 hrs wkly. Target aud: General; alternative generation. ♦ Will Belenger, stn mgr.

WVOC(AM)— July 10, 1930: 560 khz; 5 kw-U, DA-N. TL: N34 02 00 W81 08 32. Stereo. 316 Greystone Blvd. 29210-8007. Phone: (803) 343-1100. Fax: (803) 256-1968. Web Site: www.wvoc.com. Licensee: Capstar TX L.P. Group owner: Clear Channel Communications Inc. (acq 8-30-00; grpsl). Network: CNN Radio. Rep: Allied Radio Partners. Format: News/talk, sports. News staff: 2; News: 40 hrs wkly. Target aud: 35-64. ♦ Tim McFalls, gen mgr.

WXBT(FM)—(West Columbia). Aug 5, 1975: 100.1 mhz; 5.9 kw. 331 ft. TL: N34 04 08 W81 04 16. Stereo. 316 Greystone Blvd. 29210. Phone: (803) 343-1100. Fax: (803) 252-9267. Licensee: Capstar TX L.P. Group owner: Clear Channel Communications Inc. (acq 8-30-00; grpsl). Network: CBS. Format: Rhythm and blues, urban contemp. News staff: one; News: 17 hrs wkly. Target aud: 35 plus; mature adults. ♦ Bryan Anthony, progmg dir & chief of engrg; Tim McFalls, gen mgr & news dir.

Conway

*WHMC-FM— Sept 15, 1985: 90.1 mhz; 30 kw. 706 ft. TL: N33 57 05 W79 06 31. 1101 George Rogers Blvd., Columbia 29201. Phone: (803) 737-3420. Fax: (803) 737-3552. E-mail: gasque@scetv.org. Web Site: www.etvradio.org. Licensee: South Carolina Educational Television Commission. Network: Network: NPR, PRI. Format: Classical, NPR news. ♦ Moss Bresnahan, pres; Paul Zweimiller, VP & stn mgr.

WIQB(AM)— Feb 23, 1977: 1050 khz; 5 kw-D, 473 w-N, DA-2. TL: N33 50 56 W79 05 03. Stereo. 11640 Hwy. 17 Bypass, Murrells Inlet 29576. Phone: (843) 651-7869. Fax: (843) 397-3197. Licensee: Cumulus Licensing Corp. Group owner: Cumulus Media Inc. (acq 12-29-97; grpsl). Gardner, Carton & Douglas. Format: Sports. News staff: one. Target aud: 50 plus; affluent retirees. ♦ Ron Raybourne, gen mgr; Dave Solomon, progmg dir; Robert Kesler, news dir; Buddy Womack, chief of engrg.

WJXY-FM—Co-owned with WIQB(AM). October 1990: 93.9 mhz; 3.7 kw. 420 ft. TL: N33 50 07 W78 52 06. Stereo. Network: ABC. Format: Sports. News: 2 hrs wkly. Target aud: 18-34. ♦ Lou Dickey, pres & opns dir; Dave Solomon, adv dir & pub affrs dir; Lisa Van Horn, pub affrs dir.

WPJS(AM)— August 1945: 1330 khz; 5 kw-D, 500 w-N, DA-N. TL: N33 50 57 W79 04 11. Box 961 29528. Phone: (843) 248-9040. Fax: (843) 248-6365. Licensee: WPJS Broadcasters Inc. Format: Black gospel. Target aud: 12 plus. ♦ P.J. Parrish, gen mgr.

Cross Hill

WHZQ(FM)— September 1999: 94.1 mhz; 3.6 kw. Ant 417 ft. TL: N34 12 16 W81 54 37. 637 E. Durst Ave., Greenwood 29649. Phone: (864) 223-8553. Fax: (864) 943-0314. Web Site: www.941thebull.com. Licensee: Pro-Com Communications LLC (acq 11-25-2003; $475,000). Format: Country. ♦ Carl Pundt, gen mgr.

Darlington

WDAR-FM— December 1965: 105.5 mhz; 4.1 kw. 400 ft. TL: N34 18 58 W79 53 17. (CP: 17 kw). Stereo. Box 103000, Florence 29501. Secondary address: 181 E. Evans St., Suite 311, Florence 29506. Phone: (843) 667-4600. Fax: (843) 673-7390. E-mail: production@rootsc.com. Licensee: Qantum of Florence License Co. LLC. Group owner: Qantum Communications Corp. (acq 7-2-2003); grpsl). Format: Easy lstng. ♦ Jonathan Brewster, gen mgr; Craig Dallariviva, gen sls mgr; Scott Gorman, progmg dir; Thoma Lesieur, news dir; Doug Carter, chief of engrg.

WPFM(AM)—Co-owned with WDAR-FM. 1955: 1350 khz; 1 kw-D. TL: N34 18 58 W79 53 17. Format: Black gospel. Target aud: 25 plus.

Dillon

WDSC(AM)— May 22, 1946: 800 khz; 1 kw-D, 382 w-N. TL: N34 22 11 W79 24 08. Box 103000, Florence 29501. Secondary address: 181 E. Evans St., Florence 29506. Phone: (843) 667-4600. Fax: (843) 673-7390. Licensee: Qantum of Florence License Co. LLC. Group owner: Qantum Communications Corp. (acq 7-2-2003); grpsl). Format: Gospel. Target aud: General. ♦ Jonathan Brewster, gen mgr & gen sls mgr.

WEGX(FM)—Co-owned with WDSC(AM). Feb 16, 1954: 92.9 mhz; 100 kw. 1,801 ft. TL: N34 21 53 W79 19 49. Stereo. Box 103000, Florence 29501. Format: Gospel. Spec prog: Jazz one hr wkly. ♦ Randy Wilcox, progmg dir.

*WWHW(FM)—Not on air, target date: unknown: 91.1 mhz; 135 w. Ant 308 ft. TL: N34 30 18 W79 54 18. CSN International, 3232 W. MacArthur Blvd., Santa Ana, CA 92704-6916. Phone: (714) 825-9663. Fax: (714) 825-9660. Web Site: www.csnintl.com. Licensee: CSN International (group owner).

Dorchester Terrace-Brentwood

WTMZ(AM)—Licensed to Dorchester Terrace-Brentwood. See North Charleston

Easley

WELP(AM)— Mar 4, 1951: 1360 khz; 5 kw-D, 36 w-N. TL: N34 50 20 W82 38 24. 100 Cross Hill Rd. 29640. Phone: (864) 855-9300. Fax: (864) 855-8444. Web Site: www.welp.com. Licensee: Upstate Radio Inc. Group owner: Wilkins Communications Network Inc. (acq 1999; $150,000). Format: Religious. News staff: 2; News: 22 hrs wkly. Target aud: 12-24; children & their families. ♦ Robert Wilkins, VP; Greg Garrett, gen mgr & mus dir; Doyce Rogers, gen sls mgr; Ted McCall, chief of engrg.

WOLI(FM)— 1964: 103.9 mhz; 3 kw. 328 ft. TL: N34 50 21 W82 31 37. Stereo. 25 Garlington Rd., Greenville 29615. Phone: (864) 271-9200. Fax: (864) 242-1567. Web Site: thewalkonline.com. Licensee: Entercom Greenville License LLC. Group owner: Entercom Communications Corp. (acq 12-13-99; grpsl). Format: Christian. ♦ Mark Yearout, gen sls mgr; Tom Durney, gen mgr & prom dir; Jerry Massey, engr.

Elloree

WORG(FM)—Licensed to Elloree. See Elloree-Santee

Elloree-Santee

WORG(FM)—(Elloree). May 1988: 100.3 mhz; 25 kw. 328 ft. TL: N33 21 42 W80 41 05. Stereo. 1675 Chestnut St., Orangeburg 29115. Phone: (803) 516-8400. Fax: (803) 516-0704. E-mail: worg@worg.com. Web Site: www.worg.com. Licensee: Garris Communications Inc. (acq 7-95). Format: Adult contemp. Target aud: 25-54. ♦ Marion R. Garris, pres & gen mgr.

Florence

WDSC(AM)—See Dillon

WEGX(FM)—See Dillon

WJMX(AM)— July 13, 1947: 970 khz; 5 kw-D, 3 kw-N, DA-N. TL: N34 13 47 W79 48 07. Stereo. Box 103000 29501. Secondary address: Florence Bus. & Tech. Ctr., 181 E. Evans St., Ste. 311 29506. Phone: (843) 667-4600. Fax: (843) 673-7390. Web Site: www.wjmx.com. Licensee: Qantum of Florence License Co. LLC. Group owner: Qantum Communications Corp. (acq 7-2-03; grpsl). Network: CBS. Rep: McGavren Guild. Format: Talk. News staff: one; News: 49 hrs wkly. Target aud: 25-54. Spec prog: Big band 3 hrs wkly. ♦ Jonathan Brewster, gen mgr; Craig Dalla Riva, stn mgr; Randy Wilcox, opns mgr; T.J. Phillips, progmg dir; Mark Ness, chief of engrg.

South Carolina

WJMX-FM—See Cheraw

***WLPG(FM)**— May 15, 1993: 91.7 mhz; 10 kw horiz, 9.2 kw vert. 492 ft. TL: N34 07 45 W79 50 06. 2278 Wortham Ln., Augusta, GA 30802. Phone: (706) 309-9610. Fax: (706) 309-9669. E-mail: ctbarinowski@comcast.net. Web Site: www.gnnradio.org. Licensee: Augusta Radio Fellowship Institute Inc. Format: Christian. News: 12 hrs wkly. ♦Clarence Barinowski, gen mgr.

WOLS(AM)— Nov 18, 1937: 1230 khz; 1 kw-U. TL: N34 13 48 W79 44 49. 338 E. McIver Rd. 29506. Phone: (843) 665-1230. Fax: (843) 665-8786. E-mail: jjones1990@sc.rr.com. Licensee: WOLS Broadcasting Corp. Group owner: GHB Radio Group (acq 9-13-88). Network: ABC. Jim D. Jones Format: Sports/talk. News staff: one; News: 4 hrs wkly. Target aud: 21-101; within a 30 mile radius. Spec prog: Farm one hr, gospel 4 hrs, jazz 4 hrs, talk 16 hrs wkly. ♦Geo. H. Buck Jr., pres; Jeffrey Andrew Lonas, gen mgr.

WYNN(AM)— Nov 5, 1958: 540 khz; 250 w-U. TL: N34 13 05 W79 48 22. 2014 N. Irby St. 29501. Phone: (843) 661-5000. Fax: (843) 661-0888. Licensee: Cumulus Licensing Corp. Group owner: Cumulus Media Inc. (acq 12-17-98; with co-located FM). Network: American Urban. Scott Johnson. Format: Black gospel, blues, Black classics. News staff: one; News: 12 hrs wkly. Target aud: 35 plus; Black. Spec prog: Jazz. ♦Matt Scurry, opns mgr; Rick Howze, gen sls mgr; Ollie Williams, progmg dir; Daniel Tindal, asst music dir.

WYNN-FM— Oct 1, 1964: 106.3 mhz; 1.1 kw. 507 ft. TL: N34 14 03 W79 46 52. (CP: 1.7 kw). Stereo. Format: Urban contemp. News staff: one; News: one hr wkly. Target aud: 12-34. ♦Gerald McSwain, progmg dir.

Folly Beach

WYBB(FM)— July 4, 1988: 98.1 mhz; 50 kw. 500 ft. TL: N32 39 57 W80 03 11. Stereo. 59 Windermere Blvd., Charleston 29407. Phone: (843) 769-4799. Fax: (843) 769-4797. Web Site: www.98xonline.com. Licensee: L.M. Communications of South Carolina Inc. Group owner: L.M. Communications Inc. (acq 5-17-88). Network: ABC. Leventhal, Senter & Lerman. Format: New rock. News: 28 hrs wkly. Target aud: 25-49; men. ♦Lynn Martin, pres; Charlie Cohn, gen mgr; Mike Allen, opns dir.

Forest Acres

WWNQ(FM)— 2005: 94.3 mhz; 2.55 kw. Ant 446 ft. TL: N34 00 04 W81 02 05. Double O Radio Corp., 1010 Jervais St., Columbia 29201. Phone: (212) 486-4446. E-mail: live@countrylegends94.3. Web Site: www.countrylegends943.com. Licensee: Double O South Carolina Corp. (acq 9-10-2004; $4.73 million. for CP). Format: Country. ♦Robert Sherman, sr VP; Margaret Wallace, gen mgr.

Fountain Inn

WFIS(AM)— October 1956: 1600 khz; 1 kw-D, 29 w-N. TL: N34 42 28 W82 13 40. Box 156 29644. Secondary address: 1318 N. Main St. 29644. Phone: (864) 963-5991. Fax: (864) 963-5992. E-mail: wfis16@aol.com. Licensee: Golden Strip Broadcasting Inc. (acq 2-19-99; $195,000 for stock). Network: Network: Network: Westwood One, Jones Radio Networks, ABC. Rep: Rgnl Reps. Format: Talk, sports. News staff: one; News: 3 hrs wkly. Target aud: 25-49; working adults. Spec prog: Gospel 4, Black 4 hrs, Christian 3 hrs wkly. ♦Joseph E. LaStringer, gen mgr.

Gaffney

WAGI-FM— 1959: 105.3 mhz; 100 kw. 1,190 ft. TL: N35 25 05 W81 46 32. Stereo. Box 1210 29342. Secondary address: 340 Providence Rd. 29341. Phone: (864) 489-9066. Fax: (864) 489-9069. E-mail: feedback@wagifm.com. Web Site: www.wagifm.com. Licensee: Gaffney Broadcasting Inc. (acq 8-2-2005; with co-located AM). Network: CNN Radio. Format: Contemp country, gospel, talk. News staff: one; News: 6 hrs wkly. Target aud: 18-54. Spec prog: Clemson Univ. sports, loc sports, talk 10 hrs wkly. ♦Ronald Owenby, pres & gen mgr; Dennis Fowler, stn mgr & news dir; Ernie Payne, Jr., gen sls mgr; Randy Catoe, mus dir.

WEAC(AM)—Co-owned with WAGI-FM. Sept 28, 1962: 1500 khz; 1 kw-D, 500 w-N. TL: N35 05 18 W81 38 40. Format: News/talk, Black. News: 2 hrs wkly. Target aud: 18-54.

WFGN(AM)— 1948: 1180 khz; 2.5 kw-D. TL: N35 02 59 W81 38 42. 470 Leadmine Rd. 29342. Phone: (864) 489-9430. Fax: (864) 489-9440. Licensee: Hope Broadcasting Inc. (acq 8-7-90; $160,000; 8-27-90). Format: Relg. ♦Eddie Leroy Bridges Jr., pres; Ed Ridges, gen mgr; Charles Montgomery, opns mgr; Rev. Eula Miller, gen sls mgr.

***WYFG(FM)**— Oct 12, 1982: 91.1 mhz; 100 kw. 574 ft. TL: N35 06 57 W81 46 42. Stereo. 6150 Cannons Campground Rd., Suite A, Cowpens 29330. Phone: (864) 487-5836. Fax: (864) 487-5836. Licensee: Bible Broadcasting Network Inc. (group owner) Network: USA. Format: Relg. News staff: one. Target aud: General. ♦Lowell Davey, pres; Stan Schenkel, gen mgr.

Garden City

WWXM(FM)— Sept 25, 1971: 97.7 mhz; 100 kw. Ant 718 ft. TL: N33 35 45 W79 03 11. Stereo. 4841 Hwy. 17 By-pass S., Myrtle Beach 29577. Phone: (843) 293-0107. Fax: (843) 293-1717. Web Site: www.977online.com. Licensee: Qantum of Myrtle Beach License Co. LLC. Group owner: Qantum Communications Corp. (acq 7-2-2003; grpsl). Fletcher, Heald & Hildreth. Format: CHR. News staff: one; News: 2 hrs wkly. Target aud: 18-49. ♦Jimmy Feuger, gen mgr.

Georgetown

WGTN(AM)— July 1, 1949: 1400 khz; 1 kw-U. TL: N33 24 15 W79 19 36. Stereo. Box 1400 29442. Phone: (843) 546-1400. Fax: (843) 527-2337. Web Site: www.gtnradio.com. Licensee: RJ Stalvey. (Dec 2000 Network: NBC. Format: News/talk. News staff: one; News: 12 hrs wkly. Target aud: 25-54; upscale adult; bus, professional and technical. ♦Rod Stalvey, gen mgr.

WGTN-FM—(Andrews). Aug 19, 1985: 100.7 mhz; 3.1 kw. Ant 446 ft. TL: N33 24 03 W79 27 30. Stereo. 3926 Wesley St., Suite 301, Myrtle Beach 29578. Phone: (843) 903-9962. Fax: (843) 903-1797. E-mail: staff@cool1049.com. Web Site: www.cool1049.com. Licensee: Coastline Communications of Carolina Inc. (acq 10-12-00; $800,000). Format: Hot adult contemp. Spec prog: Gospel 5 hrs, relg 2 hrs wkly. ♦Will Isaacs, gen mgr; Jerome Bresson, news dir.

WLMC(AM)— March 1962: 1470 khz; 1 kw-D. TL: N33 22 15 W79 16 39. Stereo. 129 King St. 29442. Phone: (843) 546-8863. Fax: (843) 546-6821. E-mail: wradio@sc.rr.com. Licensee: Cumberland A & A Corp. (acq 2-10-2003; $200,000). Network: ABC. Format: Gospel, Christian, inspirational. Target aud: 25 plus; African-Americans. Spec prog: Talk 4 hrs wkly. ♦Reggie Dyson, CEO, sls VP, adv VP & mus dir.

WSYN(FM)— May 1, 1973: 106.5 mhz; 50 kw. 530 ft. TL: N33 26 20 W79 08 11. Stereo. 11640 Hwy. 17 By-pass S., Murrells Inlet 29576. Phone: (843) 651-7869. Fax: (843) 651-3197. Web Site: www.sunny1065.net. Licensee: Cumulus Licensing Corp. Group owner: Cumulus Media Inc. (acq 1-27-98). Format: Oldies. ♦Bill Hazen, gen mgr.

WWGS(AM)—Not on air, target date: unknown: 1580 khz; 20 kw-D, 5 kw-N, DA-2. TL: N33 23 25 W79 27 34. Box 1400 29442. Phone: (843) 546-2337. E-mail: stalvey@aol.com. Licensee: R.J. Stalvey. ♦R.J. Stalvey, gen mgr.

WXJY(FM)— Sept 1, 1990: 93.7 mhz; 6 kw. 328 ft. TL: N33 16 09 W79 17 49. Stereo. 3535 Piedmont Rd., Bldg. 14, 14th Fl., Atlanta, GA 30305. Phone: (404) 949-0700. Fax: (404) 949-0740. Web Site: www.cumulus.com. Licensee: Cumulus Licensing Corp. Group owner: Cumulus Media Inc. (acq 12-29-97; grpsl). Network: ABC News/Talk. Format: Sports. News: 4 hrs wkly. Target aud: 25-49; career-oriented, college-educated adults.

Goose Creek

WSCC-FM— May 19, 1983: 94.3 mhz; 25 kw. Ant 328 ft. TL: N32 49 04 W79 50 08. Stereo. 950 Houston Northcutt Blvd., Mt. Pleasant 29464. Phone: (843) 744-6007. Fax: (843) 884-1218. Web Site: www.newsradio943.com. Licensee: Clear Channel Broadcasting Licenses Inc. Group owner: Clear Channel Communications Inc. (acq 7-29-2003). Network: ABC. Rep: McGavren Guild. Format: Talk. Target aud: 35 plus. ♦Paul Smith, gen mgr; Willy Bennett, chief of engrg.

Gray Court

WSSL-FM—Licensed to Gray Court. See Greenville

Directory of Radio

Greenville

WCSZ(AM)—(Sans Souci). May 26, 1966: 1070 khz; 50 kw-D, 1.5 kw-N, DA-3. TL: N34 55 05 W82 27 21. Stereo. 200 N. Hwy. 25 Bypass 29617. Phone: (864) 294-1071. Fax: (864) 246-8695. Web Site: rejoice1070.com. Licensee: WHYZ Radio L.P. (acq 1996; $200,000 for foreclosure). Network: Network: Westwood One, American Urban. Format: Inspirational gospel. News: 10 hrs wkly. Target aud: 25-54; $50,000 plus houshold income, college educated, 60% male, 40% female. ♦Glenn Cherry, CEO; Jerry Young, gen mgr & stn mgr; Stanley Toole, progmg.

***WEPR(FM)**— Sept 3, 1972: 90.1 mhz; 85 kw. 1,184 ft. TL: N34 56 26 W82 24 38. Stereo. 1101 George Rogers Blvd., Columbia 29201. Phone: (803) 737-3420. Fax: (803) 737-3552. E-mail: gasque@scetv.org. Web Site: www.etvradio.org. Licensee: South Carolina Educ. TV Commission. Network: Network: NPR, PRI. Dow, Lohnes & Albertson. Format: Classical, NPR news. ♦Moss Bresnahan, pres; Tom Fowler, sr VP & prom dir; Paul Zweimiller, stn mgr & engrg mgr; Tom Holloway, dev dir & sls dir; John Gasque, progmg dir; Hap Griffin, engrg VP.

WESC-FM— March 1948: 92.5 mhz; 100 kw. 2,000 ft. TL: N35 08 16 W82 36 31. Stereo. Box 100 29602. Secondary address: 7 N. Laurens St., Suite 700 29601. Phone: (864) 242-4660. Fax: (864) 242-8813. Web Site: www.wescfm.com. Licensee: Clear Channel Broadcasting Licenses Inc. Group owner: Clear Channel Communications Inc. (acq 1998; grpsl). Format: Country. ♦Bill McMartin, gen mgr; Bob Hooper, sls dir; Sandra Dill, mktg VP; Vicky Sexton, prom VP; Scott Johnson, progmg dir; John Landrum, mus dir; Roger Davis, news dir; Jim Graham, chief of engrg.

WFBC-FM—Listing follows WYRD(AM).

WGVL(AM)— 1950: 1440 khz; 5 kw-U, DA-N. TL: N34 52 06 W82 28 04. Box 100 29602. Secondary address: Bank of America, 7 N. Laurens St. 29601. Phone: (864) 242-1005. Fax: (864) 271-9775. Fax: (864) 233-7827. Web Site: www.clearchannel.com. Licensee: Capstar TX L.P. Group owner: Clear Channel Communications Inc. (acq 8-30-00; grpsl). Network: Network: Network: USA, Westwood One, ABC. Rep: McGavren Guild. Fisher, Wayland, Cooper, Leader & Zaragoza L.L.P. Format: Hispanic. News staff: 2; News: 4 hrs wkly. Target aud: 25-54. ♦Bill McMartin, gen mgr & gen sls mgr; Bruce Logan, progmg dir.

WSSL-FM—Co-owned with WGVL(AM). November 1960: 100.5 mhz; 100 kw. 1,240 ft. TL: N34 34 19 W82 06 41. Fax: (864) 271-9775. Format: Country.

WLFJ(AM)— March 1947: 660 khz; 50 kw-D, 10 kw-CH. TL: N34 53 10 W82 28 03. 2420 Wade Hampton Blvd. 29615. Phone: (864) 292-6040. Fax: (864) 292-8428. E-mail: wlfj@wlfj.com. Web Site: www.hisradio.com. Licensee: Clear Channel Broadcasting Licenses Inc. Group owner: Clear Channel Communications Inc. (acq 1998; grpsl). Format: Contemp Christian. Target aud: 25-54. ♦Allen Henderson, gen mgr.

***WLFJ-FM**— May 1983: 89.3 mhz; 41 kw. 1,100 ft. TL: N34 56 26 W82 24 44. Stereo. 2420 Wade Hampton Blvd. 29615. Phone: (864) 292-6040. Phone: (864) 292-5683. Fax: (864) 292-8428. E-mail: wlfj@wlfj.com. Web Site: www.hisradio.com. Licensee: Radio Training Network Inc. (acq 8-31-89). Format: Contemp Christian. News: 9 hrs wkly. Target aud: 18-49. ♦Allen Henderson, gen mgr; Rob Dempsey, progmg dir; Ted McCall, chief of engrg.

WMUU(AM)— Sept 15, 1949: 1260 khz; 5 kw-D, 29 w-N. TL: N34 53 16 W82 23 27. 920 Wade Hampton Blvd. 29609. Phone: (864) 242-6240. Fax: (864) 370-3829. E-mail: generalmanaager@wmuu.com. Web Site: www.WMUU Inc. (acq 3-27-75). Fletcher, Heald & Hildreth. Format: Relg. Target aud: 35 plus. ♦Paul Wright, gen mgr; Jeff Gainous, prom mgr; Brigette Barrett, progmg dir; Charles Koelsch, mus dir; Joe Norris, chief of engrg.

WMUU-FM— Aug 15, 1960: 94.5 mhz; 100 kw. 1,200 ft. TL: N34 56 29 W82 24 41. Stereo. Web Site: www.wmuu.com. Format: Btfl mus. Target aud: 35 plus. Spec prog: Class 14 hrs, relg 20 hrs wkly. ♦Jeff Gainous, prom dir; Brigette Barrett, progmg mgr; Joe Norris, engrg dir.

WMYI(FM)—(Hendersonville).NC Apr 15, 1958: 102.5 mhz; 20 kw. 1,778 ft. TL: N35 13 22 W82 32 57. Stereo. 7 N. Laurens St., Suite 700 29601-2744. Phone: (864) 235-1025. Fax: (864) 242-2536. Web Site: www.wmyi.com. Licensee: Clear Channel Radio Licenses, Inc.

Broadcasting & Cable Yearbook 2006

Stations in the U.S.   South Carolina

Group owner: Clear Channel Communications Inc. (acq 8-30-00; grpsl). Format: Adult contemp. News staff: one. ◆Bill McMartin, gen mgr.

WPCI(AM)— Feb 8, 1954: 1490 khz; 1 kw-U. TL: N34 51 38 W82 24 31. 840 N. Hwy. 25 Bypass 29617. Phone: (864) 834-3193, EXT. 35. Phone: (864) 836-3551. Licensee: Hunter Broadcast Group. (acq 12-88; $15,000; 2-20-89). Format: Rhythm oldies. ◆Randy Mathena, pres & gen mgr.

*****WTBI-FM**— June 1991: 91.7 mhz; 3 kw. 328 ft. TL: N34 49 43 W82 26 59. 3931 White Horse Rd. 29611. Phone: (864) 295-2145. Fax: (864) 295-6313. E-mail: wtbi@tabernacleministries.org. Web Site: www.tabernacleministries.org. Licensee: Tabernacle Baptist Bible College. Format: Relg mus, educ, gospel. Target aud: General. ◆Charles Garrett, Sr., gen mgr.

WYRD(AM)— May 1933: 1330 khz; 5 kw-U, DA-N. TL: N34 51 18 W82 25 24. 501 Rutherford St. 29609. Phone: (864) 271-9200. Fax: (864) 242-1567. Web Site: www.newsradioword.com. Licensee: Entercom Greenville License LLC. Group owner: Entercom Communications Corp. (acq 12-13-99; grpsl). Network: Network: CBS, ABC. Rep: Allied Radio Partners. Format: News/talk. News staff: 3; News: 50 hrs wkly. Target aud: 30-64. Spec prog: Univ. of South Carolina football & basketball, Atlanta Falcons football, relg 5 hrs wkly. ◆Tom Durney, gen mgr & gen sls mgr; Peter Phiele, progmg dir.

WFBC-FM—Co-owned with WYRD(AM). March 1947: 93.7 mhz; 100 kw. 1,850 ft. TL: N35 06 40 W82 36 17. Stereo. Web Site: www.wfbcfm.com. Rep: Allied Radio Partners. Format: Adult contemp. News staff: 4; News: one hr wkly. Target aud: 35-64. Spec prog: Alternative 2 hrs wkly. ◆Robin Smith, CFO; Jim Kirkland, opns dir; Nikki Knight, progmg dir; Jerry Massey, engrg dir.

Greenwood

WCRS(AM)— Sept 1, 1941: 1450 khz; 1 kw-U. TL: N34 12 34 W82 09 05. 637 E. Durst Ave. 29649. Phone: (864) 223-1450. Fax: (864) 943-0314. Web Site: www.wcrs.com. Licensee: Pro-Com Communications LLC (acq 11-25-03; $310,000). Network: CBS. Format: Adult Standards, news/talk. News staff: 2; News: 20 hrs wkly. Target aud: 25 plus; middle & upper income adults. ◆Mike Hatfield, opns mgr.

WCZZ(AM)— June 20, 1973: 1090 khz; 5 kw-D, 2.25 kw-CH. TL: N34 09 46 W82 11 41. Stereo. 210 Montague Ave. 29649. Phone: (864) 223-4300. Phone: (864) 223-9689. Fax: (864) 223-4096. E-mail: sunny@sunny103-5.com. Licensee: Broomfield Broadcasting LLC (acq 7-28-2005; $1.03 million. with co-located FM). Network: Westwood One. Wiley, Rein & Fielding. Format: Cruzin' oldies. News: 12 hrs wkly. Target aud: 25-65. ◆John Broomfield, pres; Kathleen Prusator, exec VP, mktg VP & prom VP; Rick Prusator, gen mgr & sls VP; Dave Feller, progmg dir.

WZSN(FM)—Co-owned with WCZZ(AM). March 1989: 103.5 mhz; 25 kw. 328 ft. TL: N34 09 46 W82 11 41. Stereo. Network: Westwood One. Format: Adult contemp. Target aud: 25-54.

Greer

WCKI(AM)— Mar 3, 1955: 1300 khz; 1 kw-D. TL: N34 55 39 W82 15 42. Box 170022, Spartanburg 29301. Phone: (864) 877-8458. Phone: (864) 877-8459. Fax: (864) 877-8500. Licensee: Mediatrix SC Inc. (acq 10-13-2004; $280,000). Format: Christian, talk radio. News: one hr wkly. Target aud: 25-54; working people who spend money. ◆Mike Brannen, pres; Gary Powery, stn mgr.

WOLT(FM)— January 1993: 103.3 mhz; 2.7 kw. 495 ft. TL: N34 59 13 W82 09 56. 25 Garlington Rd., Greenville 29615. Phone: (864) 271-9200. Fax: (864) 242-1567. Web Site: thewalkonline.com. Licensee: Entercom Greenville License LLC. Group owner: Entercom Communications Corp. (acq 12-13-99; grpsl). Network: CBS. Format: Christian. ◆Jerry Massey, gen mgr & engr; Mark Yearout, sls.

WPJM(AM)— June 15, 1949: 800 khz; 1 kw-D, 438 w-N. TL: N34 56 59 W82 14 43. 305 N. Tryon St. 29651. Phone: (864) 877-1112. Phone: (864) 877-1821. Fax: (864) 877-0342. Licensee: Full Gospel WPJM 800 AM Radio Inc. (acq 11-28-97; $200,000). Format: Gospel. Target aud: General. ◆Bobby Cohen, pres & gen mgr; J.B. Adams, progmg dir.

Hampton

WBHC-FM— September 1970: 92.1 mhz; 6 kw. 328 ft. TL: N32 50 38 W81 07 31. Stereo. Box 666 29924. Secondary address: 1816 Savannah Hwy. 29924. Phone: (803) 943-2831. Fax: (803) 943-5450. Licensee: Bocock Communications LLC (acq 5-27-2004; $375,000. with co-located AM). Format: Country. Spec prog: Relg 11 hrs wkly. ◆Carrie Michaels, opns mgr & adv dir; John Bocock, pres & gen sls mgr.

WHGS(AM)—Co-owned with WBHC-FM. September 1957: . Stn currently dark 1270 khz; 1 kw-D. TL: N32 50 39 W81 07 28. NOT OPERATIONAL

Hanahan

WAVF(FM)— Mar 11, 1985: 96.1 mhz; 538 w. 1,443 ft. TL: N32 49 04 W79 50 08. Stereo. 2294 Clements Ferry Rd., Charleston 29492-7729. Phone: (843) 972-1100. Fax: (843) 972-1200. Web Site: www.96wave.com. Licensee: Apex Broadcasting Inc. (group owner; acq 12-5-01; $6 million). . Rep: Christal. Format: Rock alternative. ◆Dean Pearce, CEO, pres & gen mgr; John Anthony, opns VP.

Hardeeville

WLVH(FM)— Aug 30, 1992: 101.1 mhz; 50 kw. 476 ft. TL: N32 05 48 W81 19 17. Stereo. 245 Alfred St., Savannah, GA 31408. Phone: (912) 964-7794. Fax: (912) 964-9414. E-mail: garyyoung@clearchannel.com. Web Site: www.love1011.com. Licensee: Capstar TX L.P. Group owner: Clear Channel Communications Inc. (acq 8-30-00; grpsl). Network: ABC. Format: Adult urban contemp. News: one hr wkly. Target aud: 25-54; affluent Black adults. ◆Jeff Storey, gen mgr & sls; Sheryl Collison, sls.

Hartsville

WBZF(FM)—Listing follows WHSC(AM).

WHSC(AM)— Oct 1, 1946: 1450 khz; 1 kw-U. TL: N34 21 15 W80 04 20. 2014 N. Irby St., Florence 29501. Phone: (843) 661-5000. Fax: (843) 661-0888. Web Site: www.cumulus.com. Licensee: Cumulus Licensing Corp. Group owner: Cumulus Media Inc. (acq 4-20-98; 700,000 with co-located FM). Network: ABC Information & Entertainment. Reddy, Begley & McCormick. Format: CHR. News: 12 hrs wkly. Target aud: 19-49; those with buying power. Spec prog: Farm 3 hrs, gospel 3 hrs, relg 6 hrs, big band 3 hrs, oldies 6 hrs wkly. ◆Dave McWhorter, gen mgr; Steve Crumbley, opns mgr; Rick Howze, gen sls mgr; Buzz Bowman, progmg dir; Gale Gilbraith, chief of engrg.

WBZF(FM)—Co-owned with WHSC(AM). Nov 19, 1992: 98.5 mhz; 6 kw. 328 ft. TL: N34 21 16 W80 04 06. Web Site: www.cumulus.com. Format: Black, relg.

WJDJ(AM)— Dec 4, 1972: 1490 khz; 1 kw-U. TL: N34 21 47 W80 04 28. 142 Wags Dr., Bishopville 29010. Phone: (803) 484-5415. Licensee: Beaver Communications (acq 4-26-02). Network: USA. Format: Country, bluegrass, gospel. Target aud: 28 & up; Adults 28 & up. ◆James D. Jenkins, pres & gen mgr.

Hemingway

*****WLGI(FM)**— July 1, 1984: 90.9 mhz; 50 kw. 505 ft. TL: N33 43 09 W79 19 50. Stereo. 1272 Williams Hill Rd. 29554. Phone: (843) 558-9544. Phone: (843) 558-9100. Fax: (843) 558-5778. Licensee: Louis G. Gregory Baha'i Institute. Reddy, Begley & McCormick. Format: Gospel, Black, urban contemp. Target aud: General. Spec prog: Jazz.

Hilton Head Island

WFXH(AM)— Feb 14, 1983: 1130 khz; 1 kw-D, 500 w-N, DA-N. TL: N32 12 01 W80 43 27. Stereo. One Saint Augustine Pl. 29928. Phone: (843) 785-9569. Fax: (843) 842-3369. Licensee: Monterey Licenses LLC. Group owner: Triad Broadcasting Co. LLC (acq 7-18-00; grpsl). Format: Talk, sports. News staff: one; News: 5 hrs wkly. Target aud: 35 plus. ◆Bob Noonan, opns mgr; Mike Baxter, gen sls mgr; D.J. Conrad, progmg dir.

WFXH-FM— July 14, 1973: 106.1 mhz; 10.5 kw. 794 ft. TL: N32 19 50 W80 56 19. (CP: 25 kw, ant 594 ft.). Stereo. E-mail: email@106.1thefox.com. Web Site: www.106.1thefox.com. Rep: Christal. Format: AOR. News staff: 2. Target aud: 18-49; more male than female.

WWVV(FM)—(Ridgeland). July 15, 1986: 104.9 mhz; 3 kw. 300 ft. TL: N32 26 10 W80 55 23. (CP: 16 kw, ant 410 ft.). Stereo. One Saint Augustine Pl. 29928. Phone: (843) 785-9569. Fax: (843) 842-3369. E-mail: wave1049@adventureradio.fm. Web Site: www.wave1049.com. Licensee: Monterey Licenses LLC. Group owner: Triad Broadcasting Co. LLC (acq 7-18-00; grpsl). Format: Modern adult contemp. News staff: 2. Target aud: 18-49; general persons. ◆Robert Leonard, gen mgr.

Holly Hill

WJBS(AM)— Dec 1, 1972: 1440 khz; 1 kw-D, 98 w-N. TL: N33 20 23 W80 26 18. Box 1087, Bunch Ford Rd. 29059. Phone: (803) 496-5352. Fax: (803) 496-2526. E-mail: wjds1440am@internetx.netx.net. Licensee: Eugene Schoebinger. (acq 7-1-85). Format: Gospel. Spec prog: Black 17 hrs, fishing/hunting 2 hrs, farm 2 hrs wkly. ◆Harry Govan, gen mgr, gen sls mgr & prom mgr; Robert Small, prom dir; Pastor Michael Aiken, progmg dir; Robert Small, mus dir; Robert Small, pub affrs dir.

Hollywood

WXST(FM)— July 15, 1988: 99.7 mhz; 70 kw. Ant 781 ft. TL: N32 49 04 W79 50 08. Stereo. 2294 Clements Ferry Rd., Charleston 29492-7729. Phone: (843) 972-1100. Fax: (843) 972-1200. Web Site: www.star997.com. Licensee: Apex Broadcasting Inc. (group owner; acq 11-20-01). Network: Jones Radio Networks. Garvey Schubert Barer. Format: Adult urban contemp. Target aud: 25-54; urban professional. ◆Dean Pearce, CEO, pres & gen mgr; John Anthony, opns mgr; Carl Wine, gen sls mgr & prom dir; Walt Rosen, sls.

Homeland Park

WRIX(AM)— Sept 1, 1986: 1020 khz; 10 kw-D. TL: N34 28 14 W82 38 03. 102 E. Shockley Ferry Rd., Anderson 29624. Phone: (864) 224-6733. Fax: (864) 224-0260. Licensee: AM 1020 Inc. (acq 10-28-99). Format: Relg. Spec prog: Black 7 hrs wkly. ◆Karen Small, pres; Michael Branch, gen mgr; Paul Lindsey, mus dir.

Honea Path

WRIX-FM— June 10, 1977: 103.1 mhz; 6 kw. 392 ft. TL: N34 23 43 W82 29 49. Stereo. 102 E. Shockley Ferry Rd., Anderson 29624. Phone: (864) 224-9749. Fax: (864) 224-0260. Licensee: FM 103 Inc. (acq 10-28-99). Network: ABC. Format: News/talk. Spec prog: Talk 20 hrs wkly. ◆Karen Small, gen mgr.

Irmo

WWNU(FM)— May 23, 1987: 92.1 mhz; 15 kw. Ant 427 ft. TL: N34 04 55 W81 07 36. Stereo. Drawer 1, Johnston 29832. Secondary address: 121 B N. Main St. 29138. Phone: (803) 275-4444. Fax: (803) 275-3185. Licensee: Double O South Carolina Corp. (acq 11-1-2004; $4.7 million). Format: Oldies. News: 7 hrs wkly. Target aud: 25-54; upper middle class. ◆Mike Casey, gen mgr; Frank Davis, opns dir & sls VP; Jay West, prom mgr & progmg mgr.

South Carolina / Directory of Radio

Johnsonville

WPDT(FM)— May 1995: 105.1 mhz; 2.95 kw. Ant 472 ft. TL: N33 54 36 W79 40 09. 109 N. McAllister St., Lake City 29560. Phone: (843) 374-5255. Fax: (843) 374-5256. E-mail: wpdt@ftc-i.net. Web Site: www.wfmv.com. Licensee: Glory Communications Inc. (group owner; acq 5-20-02). Format: Urban inspiration. ♦ Alex Snipes Jr., gen mgr; Tersa Haire, sls dir; Tony Gee, progmg VP.

Johnston

WJES(AM)— June 12, 1961: 1190 khz; 1 kw-D. TL: N33 50 18 W81 49 48. (CP: COL Saluda. 350 w-D, 350 w-CH. TL: N33 57 27 W81 47 34). Drawer I 29832. Secondary address: 102 Slide Hill Rd. 29832. Phone: (803) 275-4444. Fax: (803) 275-3185. Licensee: Edgefield-Saluda Radio Co. Inc. Network: ABC Daytime Direction. Rep: Keystone (unwired net). Format: Oldies. ♦ Mike Casey, pres & gen mgr; Andy Moore, chief of engrg.

WKSX(FM)— Co-owned with WJES(AM). Aug 26, 1985: 92.7 mhz; 3 kw. 268 ft. TL: N33 42 11 W79 49 08. (CP: 1.79 kw, ant 577 ft.). Stereo. (Acq 4-85; $3,586; 4-8-85).

Kershaw

WKSC(AM)— Dec 21, 1961: 1300 khz; 500 w-D. TL: N34 33 30 W80 33 34. Box 516, 203 E. Hilton St. 29067. Phone: (803) 475-8585. Fax: (803) 475-2230. E-mail: wksc1300@onlineexpress.net. Web Site: www.wkscradio.com. Licensee: Kershaw Broadcasting Corp. (acq 7-23-03). Format: Oldies. Target aud: 25-54. ♦ John Griffin, pres; Denise Robinson, stn mgr.

Kiawah Island

WCOO(FM)— Dec 7, 1969: 105.5 mhz; 50 kw. Ant 436 ft. TL: N32 39 57 W80 03 11. Stereo. c/o WYBB(FM), 59 Windermere Blvd., Charleston 29407. Phone: (843) 769-4799. Fax: (843) 769-4797. Web Site: www.thebridgeat1055.com. Licensee: L.M. Communications II of South Carolina Inc. Group owner: L.M. Communications Inc. (acq 3-30-95; 6-26-95). Network: ABC. Leventhal Senter & Lerman. Format: Rhythmic oldies. Target aud: 25-54; general. ♦ Lynn Martin, pres; Charlie Cohn, gen mgr; Mike Allen, opns mgr.

Kingstree

WDKD(AM)— July 1949: 1310 khz; 5 kw-D, 67 w-N. TL: N33 42 11 W79 49 08. 51 Commerce St., Sumter 29150. Phone: (803) 775-2321. Fax: (803) 773-4856. Licensee: Miller Communications Inc. (group owner; acq 12-18-2001; $1,415,456. assumption of debt with co-located FM). Network: ABC. Format: Oldies. Target aud: 35 plus. ♦ Harold T. Miller Jr., CEO; Harold T. Miller, Jr., pres; Theresa Miller, VP & gen mgr; Dave Baker, opns VP & progmg VP; John Mcleod, pub affrs dir.

WWKT-FM— Co-owned with WDKD(AM). May 28, 1966: 99.3 mhz; 19 kw. Ant 377 ft. TL: N33 47 51 W80 07 04. Stereo. Smithwick & Belendiuk. Format: Urban oldies. News staff: one; News: 14 hrs wkly. ♦ Johnny Green, progmg dir.

WGSS(FM)— 1998: 94.1 mhz; 6 kw. 328 ft. TL: N33 43 32 W79 58 19. (CP: 6 kw). Box 103000, BTC-311, 181 E. Evans St., Florence 29506. Phone: (843) 667-4600. Phone: (843) 665-0970. Fax: (843) 673-7390. Licensee: Qantum of Florence License Co. LLC. Group owner: Qantum Communications Corp. (acq 7-2-2003; grpsl). Format: Gospel. Target aud: 25-54; urban & caucasian. ♦ Jonathan Brewster, gen mgr; Craig Dalla Riva, stn mgr.

Ladson

WJNI(FM)— June 15, 1998: 106.3 mhz; 6 kw. 328 ft. TL: N32 55 42 W80 06 13. Stereo. 5081 Rivers Ave., North Charleston 29418. Phone: (843) 554-1063. Fax: (843) 554-1088. E-mail: traffic@jabarcommunications.com. Web Site: jabarcommunications.com. Licensee: Thomas B. Daniels. Group owner: Jabar Communications. Format: Urban contemp, inspirational. ♦ Michael Baynard, gen mgr.

*****WKCL(FM)**— Jan 11, 1982: 91.5 mhz; 100 kw. 305 ft. TL: N33 00 24 W80 05 17. Stereo. 526 College Park Rd. 29456. Phone: (843) 553-5420. Fax: (843) 553-0636. E-mail: wkcl@msn.com. Web Site: www.wkclradio.com. Licensee: Chapel of the Holy Spirit and Holy Spirit Bible College. Format: Contemp MOR, southern gospel. Target aud: General; baby boomers. ♦ Carl L. Wiggins Sr., pres & gen mgr.

Lake City

WHYM(AM)— Oct 9, 1953: 1260 khz; 5 kw-D, 55 w-N. TL: N33 51 42 W79 44 15. Box 1177, . 29560. Secondary address: 925 E. Main St. 29560. Phone: (843) 665-1230. Licensee: GHB of Lake City Inc. (group owner; acq 5-28-92; $35,000;. FTR: 6-15-92). Network: ABC. Jim D.Jones Format: Country. News staff: one; News: 5 hrs wkly. Target aud: 35 plus. Spec prog: Loc news. ♦ Jeff Andrew Lonis, gen mgr.

WWFN-FM— May 11, 1977: 100.1 mhz; 3.3 kw. 433 ft. TL: N33 51 42 W79 44 15. Stereo. 2014 N. Irby St., Florence 29501. Phone: (843) 661-5000. Fax: (843) 661-0888. Licensee: Cumulus Licensing Corp. Group owner: Cumulus Media Inc. (acq 3-12-2001; $850,000). Format: Sports. Target aud: 25-54. ♦ Rick House, gen mgr.

Lancaster

WAGL(AM)— Aug 7, 1962: 1560 khz; 50 kw-D, DA. TL: N34 49 53 W80 52 08. Stereo. Box 28, 101 S. Woodland Dr. 29720. Phone: (803) 283-8431. Fax: (803) 286-4702. E-mail: waglradio@infoave.net. Web Site: www.waglradio.com. Licensee: Palmetto Broadcasting System Inc. Format: Gospel, oldies. ♦ B.L. Phillips Jr., pres, gen mgr, gen sls mgr, progmg dir, news dir & chief of engrg.

WRHM(FM)— July 27, 1964: 107.1 mhz; 3.3 kw. 436 ft. TL: N34 48 05 W80 47 51. Stereo. Box 307, Rock Hill 29731. Secondary address: 142 N. Confederate Ave., Rock Hill 29730. Phone: (803) 286-1071. Fax: (803) 324-2860. E-mail: almiller@wrhi.com. Web Site: fm107.com. Licensee: Our Three Sons Broadcasting L.L.P. (acq 10-1-87). Network: ABC. Format: Country, news, sports. Target aud: 25-54. ♦ Allan M. Miller, gen mgr; Steven Stone, opns mgr.

Latta

WCMG(FM)— Sept 18, 1970: 94.3 mhz; 10.5 kw. 502 ft. TL: N34 11 14 W79 31 23. Stereo. 2014 N. Irby St., Florence 29501. Phone: (843) 661-5000. Fax: (843) 661-0888. E-mail: mattscurry@cumulus.com. Web Site: www.cumulus.com. Licensee: Cumulus Licensing Corp. Group owner: Cumulus Media Inc. (acq 6-99; $525,000). Network: USA. Smithwick & Belendiuk. Format: Ault urban contemp. News staff: one; News: 8 hrs wkly. Target aud: 21-54; African-American. ♦ Matt Scurry, opns mgr; Bill Brooks, gen sls mgr & sls; Ernie Frierson, progmg dir; Gail Gilbreath, chief of engrg.

Laurens

WLBG(AM)— Mar 1, 1947: 860 khz; 1 kw-D, 12 w-N. TL: N34 30 13 W82 01 06. Box 1289, 315 Hillcrest 29360. Phone: (864) 984-3544. Fax: (864) 984-3545. E-mail: mail@wlbg.com. Licensee: Southeastern Broadcast Associates Inc. (acq 8-5-83). Pepper & Corazzini. Format: Var. News: 4 hrs wkly. Target aud: 30 plus; Black. ♦ Emil J. Finley, pres; Michael C. Johnson, dev VP.

Leesville

WBLR(AM)—See Batesburg

Lexington

WLXC(FM)— Aug 31, 1994: 98.5 mhz; 6 kw. 328 ft. TL: N33 52 42 W81 12 59. Box 5106, Columbia 29250. Secondary address: 1801 Charleston Hwy., Suite J, Cayce 29033. Phone: (803) 796-9975. Fax: (803) 796-5502. E-mail: doug.william@citcomm.com. Web Site: www.kiss985fm.com. Licensee: Citadel Broadcasting Co. Group owner: Citadel Broadcasting Corp. (acq 5-30-00; grpsl). Fletcher, Heald & Hildreth. Format: Urban contemp. News staff: one; News: one hr wkly. Target aud: 25-54; upward, mobile, higher income. Spec prog: Beach, boogie & blues. ♦ William McElveen, gen mgr.

WQVA(AM)— 1983: 1170 khz; 10 kw-D. TL: N33 58 17 W81 16 43. Box 537, Irmo 29063. Phone: (803) 407-5223. Fax: (803) 407-6160. Licensee: Peregon Communications Inc. Group owner: Levas Communications LLC (acq 4-28-2005; $575,000). Format: Sp. ♦ Sergio Perez, gen mgr & stn mgr.

Loris

WLSC(AM)— August 1958: 1240 khz; 1 kw-U. TL: N34 02 41 W78 53 39. Box 578 29569. Phone: (843) 756-1183. Licensee: JARC Broadcasting Inc. (acq 8-15-88). Rep: Keystone (unwired net). Format: Full service. Target aud: 21-54. ♦ Jerry Jenrette, gen mgr.

WVCO(FM)— Nov 19, 1993: 94.9 mhz; 11 kw. Ant 489 ft. TL: N33 59 39 W78 46 16. 9644 N. Kings Hwy., Myrtle Beach 29577. Phone: (843) 445-9491. Fax: (843) 445-9490. Web Site: www.949thesurf.com. Licensee: Carolina Beach Music Broadcasting Corp. (acq 6-18-03; $2.2 million). Format: beach and boogie. News: 2 hrs wkly. Target aud: 25-45. ♦ Earl P. Taylor, exec VP, VP & gen mgr; Selene Graham, sr VP.

Manning

WCSQ(FM)— Apr 16, 1973: 92.5 mhz; 100 kw. 1,207 ft. TL: N33 32 05 W79 59 15. Stereo. 2294 Clements Ferry Rd., Charleston 29492-7729. Phone: (843) 972-1100. Fax: (843) 972-1200. Web Site: www.coast925.com. Licensee: Apex Broadcasting Inc. (group owner; acq 10-17-01; $3 million). Format: Adult contemp. ♦ Dean Pearce, CEO, pres, gen mgr & stn mgr; John Anthony, opns VP; Carl Wine, prom dir; Bruce Roberts, chief of engrg; Walt Rosen, sls.

WYMB(AM)— July 15, 1957: 920 khz; 2.3 kw-D, 1 kw-N. TL: N33 41 22 W80 16 16. (CP: 920 khz; 2.3 kw-D, 1 kw-N, DA-N. TL: N33 41 22 W80 16 16). 2014 N. Irby St., Florence 29501. Phone: (843) 661-5000. Fax: (843) 661-0888. Licensee: Cumulus Licensing Corp. Group owner: Cumulus Media Inc. (acq 3-24-99; with co-located FM). Rep: McGavren Guild. Format: Country. Target aud: General. ♦ Ron Ray Bourne, gen mgr; Matt Scurry, opns mgr & progmg dir; Vicki Gathings, sls dir; Marva Mays, pub affrs dir; Gail Gilbreath, chief of engrg.

Marion

WHLZ(FM)— August 1991: 100.5 mhz; 21.5 kw. 354 ft. TL: N34 19 36 W79 32 35. 2014 N. Irby St., Florence 29501. Phone: (843) 661-5000. Fax: (843) 661-0888. E-mail: ernie.frieson@cumulus.com. Web Site: www.cumulus.com. Licensee: Cumulus Licensing Corp. Group owner: Cumulus Media Inc. (acq 3-24-99; $3.8 million. with WMXT(FM) Pamplico). Format: Country. ♦ Matt Scurry, opns mgr & progmg dir; Gail Gilbreath, chief of engrg & engr; Bill Brooks, sls.

Mauldin

WBZT-FM— Apr 28, 1965: 96.7 mhz; 700 w. Ant 964 ft. TL: N34 55 16 W82 24 05. Stereo. Box 100, Greenville 29602. Secondary address: 7 N. Laurens St., Suite 700, Greenville 29601. Phone: (864) 242-1005. Fax: (864) 242-8813. E-mail: craigdebolt@clearchannel.com. Web Site: www.thebuzzardjustrocks.con. Licensee: Clear Channel Broadcasting Licenses Inc. Group owner: Clear Channel Communications Inc. (acq 12-22-00). Network: ABC Information & Entertainment. Format: Mainstream rock. Target aud: 18-49; males. ♦ Marc Chase, exec VP; Bruce Logan, VP; Bill McMartin, gen mgr; Craig Debolt, stn mgr; Scott Johnson, opns mgr.

McClellanville

WAZS-FM— Dec 1, 1994: 98.9 mhz; 50 kw. Ant 492 ft. TL: N33 11 20 W79 33 25. Stereo. 5081 Rivers Ave., North Charleston 29406. Phone: (843) 554-1063. Fax: (843) 554-1088. E-mail: traffic@jabarcommunications.com. Web Site: www.jabarcommunications.com. Licensee: 98.9 Inc. Group owner: Jabar Communications (acq 1-5-2001). Format: Rgnl Mexican. Target aud: 25-54; upscale profesionals, yuppies. ♦ Michael Baynard, gen mgr & opns mgr.

Moncks Corner

WQTK(AM)— December 1963: 950 khz; 10 kw-D, 6 kw-N, DA-2. TL: N33 12 20 W80 03 54. 60 Markfield Dr., Suite 4, Charleston 29407. Secondary address: 337 E. Main St. 29461. Phone: (843) 763-6611. Fax: (843) 766-1239. Licensee: Kirkman Broadcasting Inc. (group owner; acq 11-29-00; $150,000). Brian Madden. Format: Sports. Target aud: 25-54; male. ♦ Gil Kirkman, pres; John Dixon, gen mgr & news dir; Stew Williams, opns mgr; Robby Robinson, gen sls mgr; Wally Momeier, chief of engrg.

Mt. Pleasant

WRFQ(FM)— June 1, 1985: 104.5 mhz; 28 kw. Ant 656 ft. TL: N32 47 15 W79 51 00. Stereo. 950 Houston Northcutt Blvd. 29464. Phone: (843) 884-2534. Fax: (843) 884-6096. E-mail: michaelblaze @clearchannel.com. Web Site: q1045.com. Licensee: Citicasters

Broadcasting & Cable Yearbook 2006

Stations in the U.S.   South Carolina

Developers & Brokers of Radio Properties
contact American Media Services at our suite:
Philadelphia Marriott Downtown
215-625-2900
843-972-2200
americanmediaservices.com
Charleston, SC
Dallas, TX · Chicago, Il · Austin, TX
American Media Services, LLC

Licenses L.P. Group owner: Clear Channel Communications Inc. (acq 5-4-99; grpsl). Rep: Allied Radio Partners. Format: Classic rock. Target aud: 25-54; adults, men. ◆ Paul Smith, VP & mktg mgr; Lee Matthews, opns mgr; Tom Bustard, sls dir; Kevin Harbison, progmg dir.

WZJY(AM)— May 21, 1982: 1480 khz; 1 kw-D, 44 w-N. TL: N32 48 59 W79 50 18. Box 6196, North Charleston 29405-0196. Secondary address: 2045 Spalding Dr., North Charleston 29405-0196. Phone: (843) 529-1185. Fax: (843) 974-6002. Licensee: Levas Charleston Communications Inc. Group owner: Levas Communications LLC (acq 7-23-2003; $380,000). Format: Relg. News staff: one; News: 28 hrs wkly. Target aud: General. Spec prog: Gospel. ◆ Edwin Wright, gen mgr, gen sls mgr, prom prod dir & pub affrs dir; Matt Homer, stn mgr; Al Finley, progmg dir & mus dir; Joe Papp, chief of engrg.

Mullins

WJAY(AM)— June 1, 1949: 1280 khz; 5 kw-D, 270 w-N. TL: N34 11 30 W79 18 55. Box 1020, U.S. Hwy. 76, Marion 29571. Phone: (843) 423-1140. Fax: (843) 423-2829. Web Site: www.wjay.com. Licensee: The Greater Highway Church of Christ. Format: Gospel. News: 8 hrs wkly. Target aud: General. Spec prog: Farm 10 hrs wkly. ◆ Curtis Campbell, pres, gen mgr, progmg dir & chief of engrg; Raymond Davis, mus dir.

Murrell's Inlet

*WMBJ(FM)— 1997: 88.3 mhz; 1.8 kw vert. Ant 331 ft. TL: N33 26 35 W79 08 21. 2420 Wade Hampton Blvd., Greenville 29615. Phone: (864) 292-6040. Fax: (864) 292-8428. Web Site: www.hisradio.com. Licensee: Radio Training Network Inc. (acq 7-20-99; $5,000 cash). Format: Talk, Christian, educ. ◆ Allen Henderson, gen mgr.

WYEZ(FM)— Apr 7, 1991: 94.5 mhz; 25 kw. Ant 328 ft. TL: N33 33 13 W79 13 14. Stereo. Box 2830, Myrtle Beach 29578. Secondary address: 3926 Wesley St., Suite 301 29579. Phone: (843) 903-9962. Fax: (843) 903-1797. Web Site: www.wezv.com. Licensee: Fidelity Broadcasting Corp. (acq 11-30-2000; $1 million). Network: Network: CBS, Wall Street. Format: Easy lstng. News staff: one; News: 40 hrs wkly. Target aud: 35 plus. ◆ Matt Sedota, gen mgr; Bob Gauss, engrg dir.

Myrtle Beach

WKZQ-FM— July 3, 1969: 101.7 mhz; 50 kw. 601 ft. TL: N33 56 14 W78 57 53. Stereo. 1116 Ocala St. 29577. Phone: (843) 448-1041. Fax: (843) 626-5988. Web Site: www.wkzq.net. Licensee: NM Licensing LLC. Group owner: NextMedia Group L.L.C. (acq 11-26-01; grpsl). Format: Rock. Target aud: 18-34. ◆ Steven Dinetz, CEO; Jeff Dinetz, COO; Carl Hirsch, chmn; Skip Weller, pres; Barry Brown, gen mgr; Art Greene, sls dir; Stephanie Nix, prom mgr; Brian Rickman, progmg dir; Paul Matthews, chief of engrg.

WMYB(FM)— Jan 11, 1965: 92.1 mhz; 94 kw. Ant 863 ft. TL: N33 35 27 W79 02 55. Stereo. 1116 Ocala St. 29577. Phone: (843) 448-1041. Fax: (843) 626-5988. Web Site: www.wmybstar92.net. Licensee: NM Licensing LLC. Group owner: NextMedia Group L.L.C. (acq 11-26-01; grpsl). Cohn & Marks. Format: Adult contemporary. Target aud: 18 plus; adults. ◆ Steven Dinetz, CEO; Jeff Dinetz, COO; Carl Hirsch, chmn; Skip Weller, pres; Barry Brown, gen mgr; Art Greene, sls dir; Kim Johnson, sls dir; Stephanie Nix, prom dir; Bill Catcher, progmg dir; Paul Matthews, chief of engrg.

WQJM(AM)— Apr 24, 1965: 1450 khz; 5 kw-D, DA. TL: N33 42 20 W78 58 23. 1116 Ocala St. 29577. Phone: (843) 448-1041. Fax: (843) 626-5988. Web Site: www.wqjm.net. Licensee: NM Licensing LLC. Group owner: NextMedia Group LLC (acq 11-26-01; grpsl). Format: News/talk. Target aud: 25-60. ◆ Steven Dinetz, CEO; Jeff Dinetz, COO; Carl Hirsch, chmn; Skip Weller, pres; Barry Brown, gen mgr; Art Greene, sls dir; Stephani E. Nix, prom dir; Dave Priest, progmg dir; Paul Matthews, chief of engrg.

WYAV(FM)— July 1964: 104.1 mhz; 100 kw. Ant 981 ft. TL: N33 35 27 W79 02 55. Stereo. 1116 Ocala St. 29577. Phone: (843) 448-1041. Fax: (843) 626-5988. Web Site: www.wave104.net. Licensee: NM

Licensing LLC. Group owner: NextMedia Group L.L.C. (acq 11-26-01; grpsl). Format: Classic rock. Target aud: 18-49. ◆ Steven Dinetz, CEO; Jeff Dinetz, COO; Carl Hirsch, chmn; Skip Weller, pres; Barry Brown, gen mgr; Art Greene, sls dir; Kim Johnson, sls dir; Stephanie Nix, prom dir; Brian Rickman, progmg dir; Paul Matthews, chief of engrg.

New Ellenton

WGOR(FM)— December 1989: 102.7 mhz; 4.3 kw. Ant 387 ft. TL: N33 30 49 W81 38 03. Box 221045, Augusta 30917. Phone: (706) 396-7000. Fax: (706) 396-7100. Web Site: www.oldies107.com. Licensee: WGAC License LLC. Group owner: Beasley Broadcast Group (acq 12-22-94; $700,000;. FTR: 2-13-95). Format: Oldies. News: 7 hrs wkly. Target aud: 25-55. ◆ Kent Dunn, gen mgr; T. Gentry, opns dir.

Newberry

WKDK(AM)— October 1946: 1240 khz; 1 kw-U. TL: N34 17 30 W81 37 15. Box 753, 3000 Hazel St. 29108. Phone: (803) 276-2957. Fax: (803) 276-3337. E-mail: jcoggins@wkdk.com. Web Site: www.wkdk.com. Licensee: Newberry Broadcasting Co. (acq 1951). Network: ABC Information & Entertainment. Dora-Clayton. Format: Adult contemp, oldies. Target aud: General. ◆ James P. Coggins, VP & gen mgr; Heather Hawkins, opns mgr.

WKMG(AM)— May 22, 1968: 1520 khz; 1 kw-D. TL: N34 15 12 W81 35 44. 1840 Glenn St. Extention 29108. Phone: (803) 405-0111. Fax: (803) 276-5677. Licensee: Cornell Blakely (acq 3-20-01; $10,000). Format: Hispanic. Spec prog: Relg 2 hrs, gospel 3 hrs, Sp 10 hrs wkly. ◆ Cornell Blakely, gen mgr.

North Augusta

WKZK(AM)— May 9, 1962: 1600 khz; 500 w-D. TL: N34 09 03 W82 23 34. Box 1454, Augusta, GA 30903. Secondary address: 2 Milledge Rd., Augusta, GA 30904. Phone: (706) 738-0044. Fax: (706) 481-8442. E-mail: wkzk@juno.com. Licensee: Gospel Radio Inc. (acq 9-22-83; $190,000; 10-10-83). Network: American Urban. Rep: Dora-Clayton. Format: Black gospel, relg. Target aud: Black adults. ◆ Robbie Hunnicutt, pres; Garfield Turner, gen mgr & progmg dir.

WPCH(AM)—Licensed to North Augusta. See Augusta GA

WTHB(AM)—See Augusta, GA

North Charleston

WTMZ(AM)—(Dorchester Terrace-Brentwood). Nov 17, 1960: 910 khz; 500 w-U, DA-N. TL: N34 09 03 W82 23 34. 4230 Faber Place Dr., Suite 100, N. Charleston 29405. Phone: (843) 277-1200. Fax: (843) 277-1212. Web Site: www.wtma.com. Licensee: Kirkman Broadcasting Inc. Group owner: Citadel Broadcasting Corp. (acq 1-5-2005; $500,000). Format: Sports. ◆ Paul O'Maury, gen mgr; Katie Guido, mktg dir; Judy Herold, news dir; Justin Tucker, chief of engrg.

WXLY(FM)— July 17, 1962: 102.5 mhz; 100 kw. Ant 659 ft. TL: N32 49 04 W79 50 09. Stereo. 950 Houston Northcutt Blvd., 2nd Fl., Mt. Pleasant 29464. Phone: (843) 884-2534. Fax: (843) 884-6096. E-mail: lisacooper@clearchannel.com. Web Site: www.wxly.com. Licensee: Citicasters Licenses L.P. Group owner: Clear Channel Communications Inc. (acq 5-4-99; grpsl). Format: Oldies. News staff: 2. Target aud: 25-54. ◆ Paul Smith, VP, gen mgr & mktg mgr; Lee Matthews, opns mgr; Tom Bustard, sls dir; Michelle Kelly, gen sls mgr; Willie Bennett, chief of engrg.

*WYFH(FM)— July 7, 1984: 90.7 mhz; 50 kw. 492 ft. TL: N32 58 23 W80 13 54. Stereo. 10870 Dorchester Rd., Summerville 29485. Phone: (843) 875-9095. Web Site: www.bbnradio.org. Licensee: Bible Broadcasting Network Inc. (group owner) Network: Bible Bcstg Net. Format: Relg, Christian. ◆ Dave Phillps, pres.

North Myrtle Beach

WEZV(FM)— Aug 15, 1972: 105.9 mhz; 17 kw. Ant 360 ft. TL: N33 49 19 W78 46 18. Stereo. Box 2830, Myrtle Beach 29578. Secondary address: 3926 Wesley St., Suite 301, Myrtle Beach 29579. Phone: (843) 903-9962. Fax: (843) 903-1797. Web Site: www.wezv.com. Licensee: Fidelity Broadcasting Corp. (acq 4-1-2000; $2.6 million. with WNMB(AM) North Myrtle Beach). Format: Easy lstng. Target aud: 35 plus. ◆ Matt Sedota, gen mgr & gen sls mgr.

*WKVC(FM)— Sept 9, 1997: 88.9 mhz; 100 kw vert. 587 ft. TL: N34 05 46 W78 28 28. 4337 Big Barn Dr., Little River 29566. Phone: (843) 399-9649. Fax: (843) 399-9031. E-mail: kreeder@klove.com. Web Site: www.klove.com. Licensee: Educational Media Foundation. Group owner: EMF Broadcasting (acq 5-11-00; $1.2 million). Network: K-Love. Format: Relg. Target aud: 25-65; contemp Christian. ◆ Richard Jenkins, CEO & pres; Kurt Reeder, gen mgr.

WNMB(AM)— Apr 1, 1983: 900 khz; 500 w-U, DA-2. TL: N33 49 26 W78 45 59. 429 Pine Ave. 29582. Phone: (843) 249-6662. Fax: (843) 249-7823. Licensee: Norman Communications NMB Inc. (acq 6-4-2004; $250,000). Format: Relg. ◆ Bill Norman, gen mgr.

Orangeburg

WHXT(FM)— September 1973: 103.9 mhz; 3 kw. 299 ft. TL: N33 26 23 W80 49 11. (CP: 9.2 kw, ant 531 ft.). Stereo. 1900 Pineview Rd., Columbia 29209. Phone: (803) 695-8680. Phone: (803) 376-1039. Fax: (803) 695-8605. E-mail: mhanisch@innercity.sc.com. Web Site: www.hot1039fm.com. Licensee: Urban Radio II L.L.C. Group owner: Inner City Broadcasting (acq 5-30-2003; $11.1 million. with WZMJ(FM) Batesburg). Format: Urban contemp. ◆ Steve Patterson, gen mgr.

WPJK(AM)— Nov 3, 1958: 1580 khz; 1 kw-D. TL: N33 28 43 W80 52 46. 175 Cannon Bridge Rd. 29115. Phone: (803) 534-4848. Fax: (803) 534-0888. Licensee: Radio Orangeburg Partnership. (acq 6-86). Network: USA. Format: Relg, urban contemp, gospel. ◆ Bose Gowdy, pres & gen mgr; Rev. Pinckney Palmer Jr., opns mgr.

WQKI-FM— Oct 10, 1987: 102.9 mhz; 2.7 kw. Ant 492 ft. TL: N33 27 55 W80 56 44. Stereo. 200 Regional Pkwy., Bldg. C, Suite 200 29118. Phone: (803) 536-1710. Fax: (803) 531-1089. E-mail: mail@miller.fm. Web Site: miller.fm. Licensee: Miller Communications Inc. (group owner; acq 4-30-03; $1.25 million. with WGFG(FM) Branchville). Network: ABC. Format: Classic rock. News staff: one; News: 10 hrs wkly. Target aud: 25-54. Spec prog: Relg 6 hrs wkly. ◆ Harold Miller Jr., pres; Russ T. Fender, opns mgr & progmg dir; Sonny Pagan, sls VP; Theresa Miller, gen mgr & gen sls mgr; Dave Baker, progmg VP; Dave Dalesky, engrg VP & chief of engrg.

*WSSB-FM— Mar 15, 1985: 90.3 mhz; 90 kw. 225 ft. TL: N33 29 55 W80 50 30. Stereo. Box 7619, Nance B-114 29117. Phone: (803) 536-8196. Fax: (803) 533-3652. Web Site: www.scsu.edu. Licensee: South Carolina State University. Network: Network: American Urban, NPR. Format: Urban contemp, gospel, jazz. News staff: one; News: 7 hrs wkly. Target aud: 8-65. Spec prog: Jazz 10 hrs, reggae 4 hrs, blues 2 hrs, rap 4 hrs wkly. ◆ Marion White, progmg dir & mus dir; Milton E. McKissick, gen mgr & news dir; Ken Durst, chief of engrg.

WTCB(FM)— July 6, 1967: 106.7 mhz; 100 kw. 787 ft. TL: N33 46 52 W80 55 14. Stereo. Box 5106, Columbia 29250. Secondary address: 1801 Charleston Hwy., Suite J, Cayce 29033. Phone: (803) 796-7600. Fax: (803) 796-9291. Web Site: www.b106fm.com. Licensee: Citadel Broadcasting Co. Group owner: Citadel Broadcasting Corp. (acq 5-30-00; grpsl). Rep: Christal. Format: Adult contemp. Target aud: 25-54; affluent, upscale young adults. ◆ William L. McElveen, pres & gen mgr; Brent Johns, opns mgr.

Pageland

WRML(FM)— Feb 22, 1975: 102.3 mhz; 3 kw. Ant 280 ft. TL: N34 45 53 W80 15 43. Stereo. 120 N. Pearl St. 29728. Phone: (843) 672-7839. Fax: (843) 672-1023. E-mail: wrml1023@wrml1023.com. Web Site: www.wrml1023.com. Licensee: Robert Broadcasting Inc. (acq 12-18-98).

Broadcasting & Cable Yearbook 2006

South Carolina

Format: Southern gospel. Spec prog: Black 2 hrs, relg 5 hrs wkly. ♦ John Griffin, pres; Wayne Haas, gen mgr; Angela Rollins, opns mgr; Johnny Knight, progmg dir & sls; Larry Schroop, engr.

Pamplico

WMXT(FM)— Nov 1, 1990: 102.1 mhz; 50 kw. 500 ft. TL: N34 04 56 W79 37 19. Stereo. 2014 N. Irby St., Florence 29501-1504. Phone: (843) 661-5000. Fax: (843) 661-0888. E-mail: buzz.bowman@cumulus.com. Web Site: www.cumulus.com. Licensee: Cumulus Licensing Corp. Group owner: Cumulus Media Inc. (acq 3-24-99; $3.8 million. with WHLZ(FM) Marion). Network: ABC FM Connection. Fletcher, Heald & Hildreth. Format: Classic Rock. News staff: 2; News: 3 hrs wkly. Target aud: 25-54. Spec prog: Beach mus 5 hrs wkly. ♦ Matt Scurry, opns mgr; Buzz Bowman, prom dir & progmg dir; Gail Gilbreath, chief of engrg; Bill Brooks, sls.

Parris Island

WGZO(FM)— July 1985: 103.1 mhz; 17.5 kw. 328 ft. TL: N32 26 10 W80 55 23. Stereo. One St. Augustine Pl., Hilton Head 29928. Phone: (843) 785-9569. Fax: (843) 842-3369. Web Site: www.1031thedrive.com. Licensee: Zip Communications Inc. (acq 7-10-01; $100,000). Rep: Christal. Format: Classic hits of the 80s. News staff: 2. Target aud: 12-34; young, hip, trendy adults. ♦ Robert Leonard, gen mgr.

Pawley's Island

WDAI(FM)— Oct 2, 1993: 98.5 mhz; 6.1 kw. Ant 666 ft. TL: N33 35 27 W79 02 55. Stereo. 11640 Highway 17 Bypass, Murrells Inlet 29576. Phone: (843) 651-7869. Fax: (843) 651-3197. Web Site: www.985kissfm.net. Licensee: Cumulus Licensing Corp. Group owner: Cumulus Media Inc. (acq 1-27-98). Network: Westwood One. Format: Urban contemporary. News staff: one; News: 6 hrs wkly. Target aud: 25-54. ♦ Bill Hazen, gen mgr.

Pickens

WTBI(AM)— Aug 3, 1967: 1540 khz; 10 kw-D. TL: N34 51 37 W82 43 25. 3931 White Horse, Greenville 29611. Phone: (864) 295-2145. Fax: (864) 295-6313. E-mail: wtbi@tabernacleministries.org. Web Site: www.tabernacleministries.org. Licensee: Tabernacle Bible College. (acq 11-83; $150,000; 1-30-84). Network: USA. Format: Christian. Target aud: All ages. ♦ Dr. Melvin Aiken, pres; Charles Garrett Sr., stn mgr, opns mgr & gen sls mgr; John Watts, progmg dir.

Port Royal

WLOW(FM)— February 1988: 107.9 mhz; 24 kw. Ant 725 ft. TL: N32 13 36 W80 50 53. One St. Augustine Pl., Hilton Head Island 29928. Phone: (843) 785-9569. Fax: (843) 842-3369. E-mail: wlow1079@adventureradio.fm. Web Site: www.wlow.com. Licensee: Monterey Licenses LLC. Group owner: Triad Broadcasting Co. LLC (acq 7-18-00; grpsl). Rep: Christal. Format: Adult standards, nostalgia, big band. Target aud: 45 plus; active, affluent, older. ♦ David Benjamin, CEO; Mike Buxser, VP & gen mgr; John Ihrig, news dir; Brett Wiggins, pub affrs dir; C.B. Gaffney, chief of engrg.

Ravenel

WMGL(FM)— February 1986: 101.7 mhz; 3 kw. 482 ft. TL: N32 46 44 W80 10 37. (CP: 6.5 kw, ant 689 ft. TL: N32 38 59 W80 19 00). Stereo. 4230 Faber Place Dr., Suite 100, North Charleston 29405. Phone: (843) 277-1200. Fax: (843) 277-1212. Web Site: www.magic1017.com. Licensee: Citadel Broadcasting Co. Group owner: Citadel Broadcasting Corp. (acq 6-9-99; grpsl). Cole, Raywid & Braverman. Format: New adult contemp. News staff: 2; News: 6 hrs wkly. Target aud: 25-54; upscale adults. ♦ Paul O'Malley, gen mgr.

Richburg

***WRBK(FM)**— 1998: 90.3 mhz; 7.5 kw horiz, 7.3 kw vert. Ant 538 ft. TL: N34 41 46 W81 01 23. Stereo. Box 15, Chester 29706. Phone: (803) 581-9030. Fax: (803) 581-9932. Licensee: Richburg Educational Broadcasters Inc. Format: Beach mus, oldies. Target aud: 30-60; middle aged adults who like beach flavored oldies. ♦ Jeff Sigmon, pres & gen mgr.

Ridgeland

WNFO(AM)— 1964: 1430 khz; 1 kw-D, 880 w-N. TL: N32 28 07 W81 00 15. (CP: COL: Sun City-Hilton Head, 213 w-D. TL: N32 21 24 W80 55 23). Box 6567, Hilton Head Island 29938. Phone: (843) 785-5769. Fax: (843) 785-8139. Licensee: Walter M. Czura (acq 7-9-91; $22,500;. FTR: 7-29-91). Format: Hispanic. Target aud: General; incoming visitors to South Carolina. Spec prog: Catholic. ♦ Walter M. Czura, pres & gen mgr.

WWVV(FM)—Licensed to Ridgeland. See Hilton Head Island

Ridgeville

WPAL-FM— September 1968: 100.9 mhz; 25 kw. Ant 328 ft. TL: N33 04 16 W80 21 31. Stereo. 2045 Spaulding Dr., North Charleston 29406. Phone: (843) 974-6001. Fax: (843) 974-6002. Licensee: Gresham Communications Inc. (acq 12-12-93; $150,000;. FTR: 12-20-93). Gardner, Carton & Douglas. Format: Urban adult contemp. ♦ Judith Aidoo, gen mgr.

Rock Hill

WAGL(AM)—See Lancaster

WAVO(AM)— May 18, 1948: 1150 khz; 1 kw-D, 57 w-N. TL: N34 57 02 W81 00 16. Box 1024 29731. Secondary address: 400 Pineview Rd. 29731. Phone: (803) 327-1150. Phone: (704) 596-4900. Fax: (704) 596-6939. E-mail: bboonewhvn@bellsouth.net. Licensee: WHVN Inc. Group owner: GHB Radio Group (acq 2-4-92; $115,000; 2-24-92). Network: Network: Moody, USA. Reddy, Begley & McCormick. Format: Relg, talk. News staff: one; News: 15 hrs wkly. Target aud: 25-54; career-oriented. Spec prog: College football & baseball. ♦ Tom Gentry, gen mgr, stn mgr & gen sls mgr; Buddy Boone, progmg dir; Brant Hart, mus dir & pub affrs dir; Stu Albert, chief of engrg.

WBT-FM—See Chester

WBZK(AM)—See York

***WNSC-FM**— Jan 3, 1978: 88.9 mhz; 100 kw. 600 ft. TL: N34 50 24 W81 01 07. Stereo. 1101 George Rogers Blvd., Columbia 29201. Phone: (803) 737-3420. Fax: (803) 737-3552. E-mail: gasque@scetv.org. Web Site: www.etvradio.org. Licensee: South Carolina Educational Television Commission. Network: NPR. Format: Jazz. ♦ Moss Bresnahan, pres; Paul Zweimiller, stn mgr; Tom Holloway, dev dir.

WRHI(AM)— Dec 14, 1944: 1340 khz; 1 kw-U. TL: N34 54 51 W81 00 42. Box 307 29731. Secondary address: 142 N. Confederate Ave. 29730. Phone: (803) 324-1340. Fax: (803) 324-2860. E-mail: newsroom@cetlink.net. Web Site: www.WRHI.com. Licensee: Our Three Sons Broadcasting L.L.P. (group owner; acq 10-1-84). Network: ABC. Format: News/talk, sports. News staff: 2; News: 14 hrs wkly. Target aud: 30 plus. Spec prog: Gospel 5 hrs wkly. ♦ Allan M. Miller, gen mgr; Steven Stone, opns mgr.

Saint Andrews

WMFX(FM)—Licensed to Saint Andrews. See Columbia

Saint George

WNKT(FM)— Jan 5, 1971: 107.5 mhz; 100 kw. 984 ft. TL: N33 05 11 W80 22 33. Stereo. 4230 Faber Place Dr., Suite 100, N. Charleston 29405. Phone: (843) 277-1200. Fax: (843) 277-1212. Web Site: www.catcountry1075.com. Licensee: Citadel Broadcasting Co. Group owner: Citadel Broadcasting Corp. (acq 6-9-99; grpsl). Rep: McGavren Guild. Format: Country. News: one hr wkly. Target aud: 25-54. ♦ Paul O'Malley, gen mgr; Bob McNeill, progmg dir; Justin Tucker, chief of engrg.

WQIZ(AM)— Aug 23, 1962: 810 khz; 5 kw-D. TL: N33 08 51 W80 33 47. 173 Radio Rd. 29477. Phone: (904) 859-0980. Licensee: Radio Properties LLC (acq 6-12-2003; $200,000). Format: Catholic. ♦ Paul Danese, gen mgr.

Saint Matthews

WIGL(FM)— 1990: 93.9 mhz; 1.75 kw. Ant 607 ft. TL: N33 45 46 W80 49 23. 200 Regional Pkwy., Bldg. C, Suite 200, Orangeburg 29118. Phone: (803) 534-2777. Fax: (803) 531-1089. Licensee: Miller Communications Inc. (acq 6-30-2003; $900,000 with co-located AM). Format: Hot adult contemp. ♦ Theresa Miller, gen mgr.

Directory of Radio

WQKI(AM)— Aug 15, 1975: 710 khz; 1 kw-D, DA. TL: N33 37 04 W80 46 50. 4305 Columbia Rd., Orangeburg 29118-1268. Phone: (803) 536-4300. Licensee: Grace Baptist Church of Orangeburg (group owner; (acq 8-23-2005; $235,000). Format: Gospel. ♦ Gene G. Soult, gen mgr.

Saint Stephen

WTUA(FM)— May 1990: 106.1 mhz; 3 kw. 328 ft. TL: N33 29 36 W79 53 21. Box 1240 29479. Secondary address: 4013 Burns Dr. 29479. Phone: (843) 567-2091. Fax: (843) 567-3088. E-mail: wtuaradio@direcway.com. Licensee: Praise Communications Inc. (acq 1-27-2005). Format: Gospel. News staff: one; News: 5 hrs wkly. Target aud: 20-65; African American. ♦ Lynette L. Nelson, gen mgr.

Sans Souci

WCSZ(AM)—Licensed to Sans Souci. See Greenville

Scranton

WWRK(FM)— 1991: 102.9 mhz; 2.9 kw. 466 ft. TL: N34 00 39 W79 45 24. Box 103000, Florence 29501. Phone: (843) 667-4600. Phone: (843) 667-0970. Fax: (843) 673-7390. Licensee: Qantum of Florence License Co. LLC. Group owner: Qantum Communications Corp. (acq 7-2-2003; grpsl). Format: Rock. ♦ Jonathan Brewster, gen mgr.

Seneca

WHZT(FM)— June 6, 1953: 98.1 mhz; 100 kw. 1,004 ft. TL: N34 41 14 W82 59 12. Stereo. 220 N. Main St., Suite 402, Greenville 26901. Phone: (864) 232-9810. Fax: (864) 370-3403. Web Site: www.hot981.com. Licensee: CXR Holdings L.L.C. Group owner: Cox Communications Inc. (acq 2-1-2001; grpsl). Network: Network: Westwood One, CBS. Dickstein Shapiro Morin & Oshinsky. Format: CHR. News staff: 2; News: 18 hrs wkly. Target aud: 25-54; affluent adults. ♦ Steve Sinicropi, VP & gen mgr; Rob Grossman, gen sls mgr; Cathy Tabor, natl sls mgr; Laurie Madden, mktg VP, prom dir & news dir; Murph Dawg, mus dir; Lemont Bryant, chief of engrg.

WSNW(AM)— June 1, 1949: 1150 khz; 1 kw-D, 58 w-N. TL: N34 41 11 W82 59 17. Box 1251 29679. Secondary address: 103 Ram Cat Alley 29678. Phone: (864) 882-9769. Fax: (864) 886-0082. E-mail: allgood@gacaradio.com. Web Site: www.wsnwradio.com. Licensee: Tugart Properties LLC. Group owner: Georgia-Carolina Radiocasting Companies (acq 9-28-2001). Network: Network: ABC, CBS Radio. Dan J. Alpert. Format: MOR, local news. News staff: one; News: 12 hrs wkly. Target aud: Adults 35 plus. ♦ Art Sutton, pres; Terry Carter, VP; George Allgood, stn mgr.

Simpsonville

WFIS(AM)—See Fountain Inn

WGVC(FM)— July 10, 1989: 106.3 mhz; 25 kw. Ant 328 ft. TL: N34 50 33 W82 09 59. Stereo. 225 S. Pleasantburg Dr., Suite B3, Greenville 29607. Phone: (864) 242-0101. Fax: (864) 271-5029. Web Site: www.oldies1063fm.com. Licensee: Simpsonville Broadcasting LLC. Group owner: Barnstable Broadcasting Inc. (acq 4-8-02; $4 million). Format: Oldies. News staff: 4; News: 2 hrs wkly. Target aud: 25-54; early 20s to 40 plus, goers, doers, buyers. ♦ John Shea, pres & stn mgr; Mark Hendrix, opns mgr.

Socastee

WRNN(FM)— 1997: 99.5 mhz; 14.5 kw. 430 ft. TL: N33 49 30 W78 51 47. 1116 Ocala St., Myrtle Beach 29577. Phone: (843) 448-1041. Fax: (843) 626-5988. Web Site: www.wrnn.net. Licensee: NM Licensing LLC. Group owner: NextMedia Group L.L.C. (acq 11-26-01; grpsl). Format: Talk. ♦ Steven Dinetz, CEO; Jeff Dinetz, COO; Carl Hirsch, chmn; Skip Weller, pres; Barry Brown, gen mgr; Art Greene, sls dir; Stephanie Nix, prom dir; Dave Priest, progmg dir; Paul Matthews, chief of engrg.

South Congaree

WFMV(FM)— 1993: 95.3 mhz; 6 kw. 328 ft. TL: N33 53 58 W81 13 29. Box 2355, West Columbia 29171. Secondary address: 2440 Millwood Ave., Columbia 29205. Phone: (803) 939-9530. Fax: (803) 939-9469. E-mail: email@wfmv.com. Web Site: www.wfmv.com. Licensee: Glory Communications. Group owner: Glory Communications Inc.

Stations in the U.S. — South Carolina

Developers & Brokers of Radio Properties — contact American Media Services at our suite: Philadelphia Marriott Downtown 215-625-2900 / 843-972-2200 / americanmediaservices.com / Charleston, SC / Dallas, TX · Chicago, Il · Austin, TX — American Media Services, LLC

Format: Urban inspirational. Target aud: Primary : adult 25-54; secondary: Women 25-54. ◆Alex Snipe Jr., gen mgr; Tezra Haire, gen sls mgr.

Spartanburg

WASC(AM)— Jan 15, 1968: 1530 khz; 1 kw-D, 250 w-CH. TL: N34 56 58 W81 57 33. Box 5686 29304. Secondary address: 840 Wofford St. 29304. Phone: (864) 585-1530. Fax: (864) 573-7790. Licensee: New South Broadcasting Corp. (acq 2-9-76). Format: Black, Urban Gold. ◆Sam E. Floyd, pres; K. Joseph Sessoms, VP & chief of engrg; K. Joseph Sessmos, gen mgr.

WORD(AM)— Feb 17, 1930: 950 khz; 5 kw-U, DA-N. TL: N34 58 53 W81 59 14. 25 Garlington Rd., Greenville 29615. Phone: (864) 271-9200. Fax: (800) 967-9329. Fax: (864) 242-1567. Web Site: www.newsradioword.com. Licensee: Entercom Greenville License L.L.C. Group owner: Entercom Communications Corp. (acq 12-13-99; grpsl). Network: Network: CBS, Motor Racing Net. Rep: Allied Radio Partners. Format: News/talk. News staff: 4; News: 45 hrs wkly. Target aud: 35-64. Spec prog: Atlanta Braves baseball, Wofford College football & basketball, Spartanburg H.S. football, NASCAR, relg 4 hrs wkly. ◆David J. Field, CEO; Steve Fisher, CFO; Tom Durney, gen mgr; Jim Kirkland, opns mgr; Jerry Stevens, gen sls mgr; Kelli Gowan, prom dir; Ken Beck, progmg VP; Peter Thiele, progmg dir & news dir; Jerry Massey, engrg dir.

WSPA(AM)— Sept 1, 1940: 910 khz; 3.6 kw-D, 960 w-N. TL: N35 01 10 W84 20 00 36. 6665 Pottery Rd. 29303. Phone: (864) 271-9200. Fax: (864) 241-4225. Web Site: www.newstalkword.com. Licensee: Entercom Greenville License LLC. Group owner: Entercom Communications Corp. (acq 12-13-99; grpsl). Network: Network: CBS, ABC. Rep: Allied Radio Partners. Format: News/talk, sports. News staff: 4; News: 50 hrs wkly. Target aud: 35-64. Spec prog: Atlanta Falcons football, Univ. of South Carolina football and basketball, relg 5 hrs, sports 12 hrs wkly. ◆Barry Drake, pres; Jimmy Vineyard, gen mgr; Jim Kirkland, opns mgr; Tom Durney, gen sls mgr; Kelly Cowen, prom dir; Peter Phiele, progmg dir; Lisa Rollins, news dir; Jerry Massey, chief of engrg.

WSPA-FM— Aug 29, 1946: 98.9 mhz; 100 kw. 1,910 ft. TL: N35 10 12 W82 17 27. Stereo. 501 Rutherford St., Grenville 29609. Phone: (864) 271-9200. Fax: (864) 370-1473. Web Site: www.lightrock989.com. Format: Light adult contemp. News: one hr wkly. Spec prog: Relg 3 hrs, jazz 6 hrs, 70s oldies 10 hrs wkly. ◆Jerry Stevens, gen sls mgr; David Patella, natl sls mgr; Michael McKeel, progmg dir.

WSPG(AM)— Sept 1, 1952: 1400 khz; 1 kw. TL: N34 58 26 W81 55 37. Box 193 29304. Secondary address: 340 Garner Rd. 29303. Phone: (864) 573-1400. Fax: (864) 573-8699. E-mail: info@spartanburg1400.com. Licensee: Fulmer Broadcasting Corp. (acq 12-30-2003; $300,000). Format: News/talk, sports. Target aud: Adult male 25-54. ◆Matthew Y. Fulmer, pres; J. Dwayne Corn, gen mgr; Jan Scruggs, progmg dir & progmg.

Summerton

WLJI(FM)— 1997: 98.3 mhz; 6 kw. 328 ft. TL: N33 42 58 W80 20 44. Box 1348, Sumter 29151. Phone: (803) 774-5512. Fax: (803) 774-5534. Licensee: Glory Communications Inc. (group owner; acq 4-1-97). Format: Urban inspirational. Target aud: Adults 25-54. ◆Alex Snipe Jr., gen mgr; Tony Jamison, opns mgr; Tezra Haire, gen sls mgr.

Summerville

WAZS(AM)— June 7, 1963: 980 khz; 1 kw-D, 131 w-N. TL: N33 01 57 W80 12 00. 5081 Rivers Ave., North Charleston 29406. Phone: (843) 554-1063. Fax: (843) 554-1088. E-mail: traffic@jaborcommunications.com. Web Site: jabarcommunications.com. Licensee: Thomas B. Daniels. Group owner: Jabar Communications (acq 9-1-2000). Format: Jazz. ◆Michael Baynard, gen mgr.

WWWZ(FM)— May 10, 1974: 93.3 mhz; 50 kw. 492 ft. TL: N33 06 54 W79 54 25. 4230 Faber Place Drive, Suite 100, North Charleston 29405. Phone: (843) 277-1200. Fax: (843) 277-1212. Web Site: www.z93jams.com. Licensee: Citadel Broadcasting Co. Group owner:

Citadel Broadcasting Corp. (acq 6-9-99; grpsl). Format: Urban contemp. ◆Paul O'Malley, gen mgr; Star Israel, gen sls mgr; Terry Base, progmg dir; Judy Herold, news dir; Justin Tucker, chief of engrg.

Sumter

WDXY(AM)— May 23, 1960: 1240 khz; 1 kw-U. TL: N33 54 16 W80 19 25. Box 1269 29151. Secondary address: 51 Commerce St. 29150. Phone: (803) 775-2321. Fax: (803) 773-4856. Web Site: www.newsstalk1240.am. Licensee: Miller Communications Inc. (group owner; acq 1-2-2001; grpsl). Rep: Rgnl Reps. Smith & Belendiuk. Format: News, talk. News staff: one; News: 6 hrs wkly. Target aud: 35 plus. ◆Harold T. Miller, CEO & pres; Theresa Miller, VP & gen mgr; Dave Baker, opns VP.

WICI(FM)— June 21, 1995: 94.7 mhz; 3 kw. 479 ft. TL: N33 51 55 W80 17 09. Box 1269 29151. Secondary address: 51 Commerce St. 29150. Phone: (803) 773-1859. Fax: (803) 773-4856. E-mail: Tmiller55@aol.com. Web Site: www.mix947.fm. Licensee: Miller Communications Inc. (group owner; acq 9-27-01). Network: American Urban. Smithwick & Belendiuk. Format: Hits of the 80s, 90s & now. News staff: one. Adults 25 to 49 & secondary females 25-54. ◆Harold T. Miller, Jr., CEO & pres; Dave Baker, opns VP & sls dir; Theresa Miller, chmn, VP, gen mgr & gen sls mgr.

WQMC(AM)— Mar 16, 1940: 1290 khz; 1 kw-U, DA-N. TL: N33 55 16 W80 16 59. Richardson-Johnson Learning Resc. Ctr., 100 W. College St. 29150-3599. Phone: (803) 775-1290. Phone: (803) 775-6262. Fax: (803) 773-3687. Fax: (803) 775-2580. Licensee: Morris College. Format: Gospel, talk, christian. News staff: one; News: 4 hrs wkly. Target aud: General; working adults & retirees. Spec prog: Farm 2 hrs, class 15 hrs wkly. ◆Janet Clayton, gen mgr; Fred Brown, progmg dir; Willete Stocker, mus dir.

***WRJA-FM**— Aug 25, 1975: 88.1 mhz; 98 kw. 1,000 ft. TL: N33 52 32 W80 16 14. Stereo. 1101 George Rogers Blvd., Columbia 29201. Phone: (803) 737-3404. Phone: (803) 737-3420. Fax: (803) 737-3552. E-mail: gasque@scetv.org. Web Site: www.etvradio.org. Licensee: South Carolina Educational TV Commission. Network: Network: NPR, PRI. Format: News/talk, jazz. ◆Moss Bresnahan, pres; Tom Fower, sr VP; Paul Zweimiller, stn mgr & chief of engrg; Tom Holloway, sls dir; John Gasque, progmg dir.

WSSC(AM)— Apr 27, 1953: 1340 khz; 1 kw-U. TL: N33 55 45 W80 19 29. 201 Oswego Rd. 29150. Phone: (803) 469-0288. Fax: (803) 469-0297. Web Site: www.sumterbaptisttemple.org. Licensee: Sumpter Baptist Temple. (acq 2-28-94; $157,500; 5-2-94). Format: Christian radio. Target aud: 25-54. ◆Eddie Richardson, pres & gen mgr.

WWDM(FM)— 1961: 101.3 mhz; 100 kw. 1,322 ft. TL: N33 52 52 W80 16 14. Stereo. 1900 Pineview Rd., Columbia 29209. Phone: (803) 695-8600. Fax: (803) 695-8605. E-mail: mhanisch@innercity.sc.com. Web Site: www.thebigdm.com. Licensee: Urban Radio II L.L.C. Group owner: Inner City Broadcasting (acq 8-7-2000; grpsl). Network: Network: ABC, Westwood One. Rep: D & R Radio. Format: Urban contemp. News staff: one; News: 6 hrs wkly. Target aud: 18-49. ◆Maggie Hanisch, gen mgr; Mike Love, opns dir & progmg dir; Scott Norton, gen sls mgr; Susan Morningstar, VP & prom dir.

Surfside Beach

WYAK-FM— Apr 4, 1977: 103.1 mhz; 12.5 kw. 325 ft. TL: N33 34 32 W79 02 29. (CP: 11.5 kw, ant 485 ft. TL: N33 43 22 W79 03 43). Stereo. 11640 Hwy. 17 Bypass, Murrells Inlet 29576. Phone: (843) 651-7869. Fax: (843) 651-3197. Web Site: www.cumulus.com. Licensee: Cumulus Licensing Corp. Group owner: Cumulus Media Inc. (acq 12-6-00; swap of WYAK-FM for WQSL(FM) & WXQR(FM) Jacksonville, NC). Network: Westwood One. Fisher, Wayland, Cooper, Leader & Zaragoza. Format: Country. News staff: one; News: 4 hrs wkly. Target aud: 25-54; adults & families of loc towns & tourists. ◆John Sheftic, gen mgr.

Union

WBCU(AM)— Aug 27, 1949: 1460 khz; 1 kw-U, DA-N. TL: N34 43 10 W81 39 44. 210 E. Main 29379. Phone: (864) 427-2411. Phone: (864) 427-2412. Fax: (864) 429-2975. E-mail: cwoodson@gacaradio.com. Web Site: www.wbcuradio.com. Licensee: Union-Carolina Broadcasting Co. Inc. (acq 3-2-99). Network: ABC. Dan J. Alpert. Format: Country standards, loc news. News staff: 2; News: 24 hrs wkly. Target aud: 30 plus; working class adult buyers. Spec prog: Sports 10 hrs, news/talk 10 hrs wkly. ◆Douglas M. Sutton Jr., CEO & pres; James C. Woodson, chmn, VP & gen mgr; Daniel Prince, opns mgr; Adam Wright, gen sls mgr; Erin Wade, news dir; Tim Stephens, chief of engrg.

Walhalla

WGOG(FM)— Sept 1, 1991: 96.3 mhz; 6 kw. Ant 302 ft. TL: N34 51 33 W83 03 31. Stereo. Box 10 29691. Secondary address: 2058 Westminster Hwy. 29691. Phone: (864) 638-3616. Fax: (864) 638-6810. E-mail: wgog@wgog.com. Web Site: www.wgog.com. Licensee: Appalachian Broadcasting Co. Inc. (acq 10-16-2001; with co-located AM). Network: ABC. Dan J. Alpert. Format: Country. News staff: one; News: 15 hrs wkly. Target aud: 25-54. ◆Douglas M. Sutton Jr., pres; M. Terry Carter, VP; Gary Butts, gen mgr; Doug Stephens, opns mgr; Kris Butts, progmg dir; Dick Mangrum, news dir.

WWOF(AM)— Co-owned with WGOG(FM). Apr 15, 1959: 1000 khz; 1 kw-D. TL: N34 44 29 W83 04 18. E-mail: wgog@wgog.com. Licensee: Tugart Properties LLC. Group owner: Georgia-Carolina Radiocasting Companies Network: ABC. Dan J. Alpert. Format: Oldies, talk. News staff: one; News: 6 hrs wkly. Target aud: 25-64; emphasis on women.

Walterboro

WALD(AM)— August 1947: . Stn currently dark 1080 khz; 2.5 kw-D. TL: N32 52 52 W80 41 24. (CP: TL: N32 52 56 W80 41 13). 111 Reece Park Ln., Tallahassee, FL 32301-2852. Phone: (850) 942-1806. Licensee: Jacquelyn Collier Pembroke (acq 5-28-02; with WBGC(AM) Chipley, FL). Format: Gospel, rhythm and blues. ◆Jacquelyn Collier Pembroke, gen mgr.

WALI(FM)— Dec 13, 1991: 93.7 mhz; 6 kw. 345 ft. TL: N32 49 54 W80 43 30. 724 S. Jefferies Blvd. 29488. Phone: (843) 549-1543. Fax: (843) 549-2711. Licensee: Hess Communications L.L.C. (acq 1996; $285,000). Network: ABC Information & Entertainment. Rgnl Reps. Format: Country, sports. News: 3 hrs wkly. Target aud: General. Spec prog: Gospel 5 hrs wkly. ◆Karl Hess, pres, gen mgr, opns VP, mus dir & chief of engrg; Thomas Heirs, sls dir & adv dir; Belinda Pierpaoli, progmg dir, asst music dir & pub affrs dir; Samantha Hess, mus dir.

Wedgefield

WIBZ(FM)— Mar 1, 1985: 95.5 mhz; 4.4 kw. Ant 387 ft. TL: N33 56 56 W80 23 34. Stereo. Box 1269, Sumter 29151. Secondary address: 51 Commerce St., Sumter 29150. Phone: (803) 773-1859. Fax: (803) 773-4856. Licensee: Miller Communicatins Inc. (group owner; acq 11-14-00; grpsl). Network: ABC. Smithwick & Belendiuk. Format: Solid gold. News staff: one. Target aud: 18-49. ◆Harold T. Miller, CEO & pres; Dave Baker, opns VP; Theresa Miller, VP & gen sls mgr.

West Columbia

WGCV(AM)—See Cayce

WLTY(FM)—See Columbia

WXBT(FM)—Licensed to West Columbia. See Columbia

Williston

WAAW(FM)— Aug 12, 1994: 94.7 mhz; 2.11 kw. 561 ft. TL: N33 28 33 W81 32 57. Stereo. 2166 Park Ave S.E., Aiken 29801. Phone: (803) 641-6499. Fax: (803) 641-8844. E-mail: frank@rejoiceradio.com.

South Carolina

Licensee: Frank Neely. Group owner: Neely Enterprises (acq 7-9-02; $700,000). Format: Gospel music. ♦ Larry Adamson, stn mgr.

Woodruff

WDRF(AM)— July 7, 1967: 1510 khz; 1 kw-D, 250 w-CH. TL: N34 45 22 W82 03 18. Box 547 29388. Phone: (864) 476-7184. Fax: (864) 476-0474. Licensee: B&B Media Inc. (acq 8-10-99). Format: Relg. ♦ T.C. Lewis, gen mgr.

York

WBZK(AM)— Apr 19, 1956: 980 khz; 3.15 kw-D, 291 w-N, DA-2. TL: N34 59 50 W81 15 09. 1812 Davie Ave., Statesville, NC 28677. Secondary address: 4201-J Stuart Andrew Blvd., Charlotte, NC 28217. Phone: (704) 665-9355. Fax: (208) 545-9888. E-mail: metroradio @carolina.rr.com. Web Site: www.wbzk.com. Licensee: Davidson Media Carolinas Stations LLC. Group owner: Davidson Media Group LLC (acq 5-10-2004; grpsl). Network: ABC. Format: Spanish, Christian. News: 6 hrs wkly. Target aud: 22-54. Spec prog: Chinese 10 hrs, Greek 10 hrs wkly. ♦ Peter W. Davidson, pres; Russ Jones, gen mgr; Robert Freeze, opns dir; Humberto Martinez, progmg dir; Winston Hawkins, chief of engrg.

South Dakota

Aberdeen

KBFO(FM)— Feb 20, 1999: 106.7 mhz; 100 kw. 338 ft. TL: N45 27 57 W98 20 08. Box 1930 57401. Secondary address: 3980 Dakota St. S. 57401. Phone: (605) 225-1560. Fax: (605) 225-8290. Licensee: Aberdeen Radio Ranch Inc. Group owner: Clear Channel Communications Inc. (acq 10-22-2004; grpsl). Jones Satellite Audio. Format: Hot adult contemp. Target aud: 18-35. ♦ DaLime LeGrand, gen mgr; Rob Feller, gen sls mgr; Doug Pitts, progmg mgr.

KGIM(AM)— September 1933: 1420 khz; 1 kw-D, 232 w-N. TL: N45 29 07 W98 29 46. 13541 386th Ave. 57401. Phone: (605) 229-3632. Fax: (605) 229-4849. Licensee: Aberdeen Radio Ranch Inc. Group owner: Robert Ingstad Broadcast Properties (acq 11-19-2004; grpsl). Fisher, Wayland, Cooper, Leader & Zaragoza L.L.P. Format: Country, news, sports. News staff: 10 hrs wkly Target aud: 25 plus; general. Spec prog: Weather, farm 12 hrs wkly. ♦ Robert Ingstad, pres; Brian Lundquist, gen mgr.

KKAA(AM)— Sept 12, 1974: 1560 khz; 10 kw-D, 5 kw-N, DA-2. TL: N45 25 05 W98 28 36. Family Stations Inc., 4135 Northgate Blvd., Suite 1, Sacramento, CA 95834. Phone: (916) 641-8191. Licensee: Family Stations Inc. Group owner: Clear Channel Communications Inc. (acq 10-22-2004; $75,000. with KQKD(AM) Redfield). Network: ABC, CBS Radio. Format: Relg. ♦ Harold Camping, pres.

KLRJ(FM)— September 1979: 94.9 mhz; 100 kw. Ant 446 ft. TL: N45 27 57 W98 20 08. Stereo. 5700 West Oaks Blvd., Rocklin, CA 95765. Phone: (916) 251-1600. Fax: (916) 251-1650. Web Site: www.klove.com. Licensee: Educational Media Foundation. (acq 11-30-2004; $200,000). Network: K-Love. Format: Christian music. ♦ Richard Jenkins, pres.

KSDN(AM)— Apr 16, 1947: 930 khz; 5 kw-D, 1 kw-N, DA-2. TL: N45 25 29 W98 31 03. Box 1930 57402. Secondary address: 3980 S. Dakota St. 57402. Phone: (605) 225-1560. Fax: (605) 225-8290. Web Site: www.ksdnaberdeen.com. Licensee: Aberdeen Radio Ranch Inc. Group owner: Clear Channel Communications Inc. (acq 10-22-2004; grpsl). Network: ABC. Format: News, sports. News staff: one; News: 15 hrs wkly. Target aud: 25-54. Spec prog: Farm 15 hrs wkly. ♦ Ron Feller, gen sls mgr; Doug Pitts, progmg dir.

KSDN-FM— Nov 18, 1979: 94.1 mhz; 100 kw. 440 ft. TL: N45 25 27 W98 31 00. Stereo. Web Site: www.ksdnaberdeen.com. Format: Classic rock.

Belle Fourche

KBFS(AM)— July 22, 1959: 1450 khz; 1 kw-U. TL: N44 40 02 W103 51 22. Box 787 57717. Phone: (605) 892-2571. Fax: (605) 892-2573. E-mail: kbfs@mato.com. Web Site: www.kbfs.com. Licensee: Ultimate Caps Inc. (acq 3-17-94; $95,000; 6-20-83). Network: Network: Network: Network: Jones Radio Networks, ESPN Radio, Motor Racing Net, CBS Radio, Westwood One. Colorado Avalanche, Colorado Rockies Format: Country, sports, news, talk. News: 20 hrs wkly. Target aud: 25-54; farmers, ranchers, sports fans. Spec prog: Farm 20 hrs, relg 2 hrs wkly. ♦ Cynthia A. Grimmelmann, pres; Karl Grimmelmann, exec VP, gen mgr & opns mgr.

KFMH(FM)—Not on air, target date: unknown: 102.1 mhz; 7 kw. Ant -12 ft. TL: N44 39 48 W103 51 26. Bad Lands Broadcasting Co. Inc., 288 S. River Rd., Bedford, NH 03110. Phone: (603) 668-6400. Fax: (603) 668-6470. Licensee: Bad Lands Broadcasting Co. Inc. Group owner: Kona Coast Radio LLC (acq 9-6-2005; $915,000). ♦ Steven A. Silberberg, pres.

KZZI(FM)— Sept 22, 1995: 95.9 mhz; 18 kw. 1,817 ft. TL: N44 19 36 W103 50 10. Stereo. 2827 E. Colorado Blvd., Spearfish 57783. Phone: (605) 642-85747. Fax: (605) 642-7849. Web Site: www.kzcountry.com. Licensee: Western South Dakota Broadcasting L.L.C. (acq 1999; $79,006). Rep: Katz Radio. Format: Country. Target aud: 18-54. ♦ Steve Duffy, gen mgr; Ted Peiffer, gen sls mgr.

Brookings

KBRK(AM)— July 28, 1955: 1430 khz; 1 kw-D, 100 w-N. TL: N44 18 13 W96 46 10. (CP: TL: N44 18 12 W96 46 01). 227 22nd Ave. S. 57006. Phone: (605) 692-1430. Fax: (605) 692-6434. Web Site: www.brookingsradio.com. Licensee: Three Eagles Communications Co. Group owner: Three Eagles Communications Format: Traditional radio today. Spec prog: Farm 9 hrs wkly. ♦ Cami Powers, gen mgr.

KBRK-FM— Aug 10, 1968: 93.7 mhz; 36 kw. 571 ft. TL: N44 20 22 W96 09 16. 227 22nd Ave. S. 57006. Phone: (605) 692-1430. Fax: (605) 692-4441. Web Site: www.b937.com. Licensee: Three Eagles of Huron Inc. Network: Westwood One. Format: Adult contemp. Target aud: 20-45. ♦ Cami Powers, gen mgr.

***KESD(FM)**— July 1967: 88.3 mhz; 50 kw. 623 ft. TL: N44 20 10 W97 13 41. Stereo. Box 2218B Pugsely Ctr. 57007. Phone: (605) 688-4191. Fax: (605) 677-5010. E-mail: sdpr@sdpb.org. Web Site: www.sdpb.org. Licensee: South Dakota Board of Directors for Educational Telecommunications. Network: Network: NPR, PRI. Format: News, class. Target aud: 35-65; upscale, higher educated & arts-oriented. ♦ Julie Andersen, pres; Terry Harris, gen mgr & stn mgr; Terry Spencer, dev dir. Co-owned TV: *KESD-TV affil.

KJJQ(AM)—(Volga). May 6, 1981: 910 khz; 500 w-U. TL: N44 15 01 W96 57 22. 111 Main Ave. 57006. Phone: (605) 692-9125. Fax: (605) 692-6434. E-mail: info@depotradio.com. Web Site: www.depotradio.com. Licensee: Three Eagles of Joliet Inc. Group owner: Three Eagles Communications (acq 6-18-2004; grpsl). FTR: . Network: Network: Westwood One, ABC Information & Entertainment. Rep: Allied Radio Partners. Pepper & Corazzini. Format: News. News staff: one; News: 20 hrs wkly. Target aud: 30-60; general. ♦ Tom Coughlin, gen mgr; Scott Kwas, opns mgr; Bryan Waltz, progmg dir, pub affrs dir & engrg mgr; Perry Miller, news dir; John Brendall, engrg mgr & chief of engrg.

KKQQ(FM)— Co-owned with KJJQ(AM). Apr 15, 1984: 102.3 mhz; 25 kw. 234 ft. TL: N44 15 01 W96 57 22. (CP: Ant 243 ft.). Stereo. Web Site: www.depotradio.com. Format: Country. Target aud: 18-49.

***KSDJ(FM)**— 1993: 90.7 mhz; 1 kw. 148 ft. TL: N44 19 01 W96 47 02. Stereo. Box 2815, Rm. 069-D 57007-2815. Phone: (605) 688-5559. E-mail: newrock907ksdj@hotmail.com. Web Site: www.907ksdj.com. Licensee: South Dakota State University. (group owner) Format: Alternative. News staff: one; News: 5 hrs wkly. Target aud: 17-22; college students. Spec prog: Black 8 hrs, jazz 2 hrs wkly. ♦ Peggy Gordon-Miller, pres; Jay Buchholz, gen mgr.

Canton

KYBB(FM)— 1996: 102.7 mhz; 50 kw. 485 ft. TL: N43 28 48 W96 41 05. 5100 S. Tennis Ln., Sioux Falls 57108. Phone: (605) 339-9999. Fax: (605) 339-2735. Web Site: www.61027.com. Licensee: Southern Minnesota Broadcasting Co. Group owner: Cumulus Media Inc. (acq 3-29-2004; grpsl). Format: Classic rock. Target aud: 25-49; men. ♦ Don Jacobs, gen mgr; Scott Maguire, opns dir.

Clear Lake

KDBX(FM)— 1999: 107.1 mhz; 15 kw. 430 ft. TL: N44 52 36 W96 52 28. 227 22nd Ave. S., Brookings 57006. Phone: (605) 692-9125. Fax: (605) 692-6434. Web Site: www.brookingsradio.com. Licensee: Three Eagles of Joliet, Inc. Group owner: Waitt Radio Group (acq 8-6-2004). Format: Classic rock. ♦ Cami Powers, gen mgr.

Directory of Radio

Custer

KAWK(FM)—Listing follows KFCR(AM).

KFCR(AM)— May 1, 1988: 1490 khz; 830 w-U. TL: N43 43 03 W103 35 00. Box 804 57730. Secondary address: 145 Mount Rushmore Rd. 57730. Phone: (605) 673-5327. Phone: (605) 673-5094. Fax: (605) 673-3079. Licensee: Mount Rushmore Broadcasting Inc. (group owner; (acq 5-6-92; FTR: 5-25-92). Format: Adult contemp.

Deadwood

KDSJ(AM)— July 2, 1947: 980 khz; 5 kw-D, 1 kw-N, DA-N. TL: N44 22 57 W103 39 44. Box 567 57732. Phone: (605) 578-1826. Fax: (605) 578-1827. Web Site: www.kdsj980.com. Licensee: Goldrush Broadcasting. (acq 7-1-82). Network: ABC Information & Entertainment. Format: Top-40, oldies, news, sports. Target aud: 25-50. ♦ Al Decker, pres & gen mgr.

KSQY(FM)— Sept 4, 1982: 95.1 mhz; 100 kw. 1,707 ft. TL: N44 19 49 W103 50 10. Stereo. Box 1680, Rapid City 57709. Secondary address: 306 E. St. Joe, Rapid City 57709. Phone: (605) 343-0888. Fax: (605) 342-3075. Web Site: www.951ksky.com. Licensee: Haugo Broadcasting Inc. (group owner) Rep: Midwest Radio. Midwest Radio. Format: Triple A. News: 2 hrs wkly. Target aud: 18-49; young, active adults within a 5 state region. ♦ Houston Haugo, CEO & pres; Chris Haugo, exec VP & gen mgr.

Dell Rapids

KSQB-FM— Oct 2, 1998: 95.7 mhz; 25 kw. 328 ft. TL: N43 45 48 W96 48 27. Stereo. 3205 S. Meadow Pky., Sioux Falls 57105. Phone: (605) 335-6896. Fax: (605) 332-3730. E-mail: rob@fellerbroadcast.com. Licensee: Feller Broadcasting LLC. (acq 10-29-2004; grpsl). Rep: Rgnl Reps. Format: Classic hits. Target aud: 20-40; young, active adults with spending ability. ♦ Rob Feller, pres; Mark Nelson, opns mgr.

Faith

KPSD(FM)— June 1, 1989: 97.1 mhz; 100 kw. 1,525 ft. TL: N45 03 14 W102 15 47. Box 5000, Vermillion 57069. Secondary address: 555 N. Dakota St. 57069. Phone: (605) 677-5861. Fax: (605) 677-5010. E-mail: sdpr@sdpb.org. Web Site: www.sdpb.org. Licensee: South Dakota Board of Directors for Educational Telecommunications. Network: NPR. Format: Class, jazz, news. ♦ Julie Andersen, pres; Terry Harris, gen mgr; Terry Spencer, dev dir; Carol Robertson, prom dir; Matt Weesner, progmg mgr; Stacey Decker, chief of engrg.

Flandreau

KWSF(FM)— October 2000: 107.9 mhz; 21 kw. Ant 761 ft. TL: N43 57 56 W96 49 11. Stereo. 3205 S. Meadow Pkwy., Sioux Falls 57105. Phone: (605) 335-6896. Fax: (605) 332-3730. E-mail: rob@fellerbroadcast.com. Licensee: Feller Broadcasting LLC. (acq 10-29-2004; grpsl). Rep: Rgnl Reps. Format: Country hits. Target aud: 24-54 adults; upbeat country music listeners. ♦ Rob Feller, pres; Mark Nelson, opns mgr.

Freeman

***KVCF(FM)**— 2002: 90.5 mhz; 9 kw. Ant 807 ft. TL: N43 29 22 W97 26 33. 3434 W. Kilbourn Ave., Milwaukee, WI 53208-3313. Phone: (414) 935-3000. Fax: (414) 935-3015. Licensee: VCY America Inc. Format: Relg, Christian. ♦ Vic Eliason, gen mgr.

Gregory

***KVCX(FM)**— May 8, 1982: 101.5 mhz; 100 kw. 640 ft. TL: N43 07 41 W99 26 10. Stereo. 3434 W. Kilbourn Ave., Milwaukee, WI 53208. Phone: (414) 935-3000. Fax: (414) 935-3015. E-mail: kvcx@vcyamerica.org. Web Site: www.vcyamerica.org. Licensee: VCY/America Inc. (group owner; acq 4-87). Network: Network: USA, Moody. Format: Relg, Christian. ♦ Dr. Randall Melchert, pres; Vic Eliason, VP & gen mgr; Jim Schneider, progmg dir & pub affrs dir; Tom Schlueter, mus dir; Gordon Morris, news dir; Andrew Eliason, chief of engrg.

Hot Springs

KZMX(AM)— July 4, 1958: 580 khz; 2.3 kw-D, 310 w-N. TL: N43 27 24 W103 28 34. Box 611 57747. Secondary address: North Wind Cave Rd. 57747. Phone: (605) 745-3637. Fax: (605) 745-3517.

Stations in the U.S. South Dakota

E-mail: themorningshow@email.com. Licensee: Mount Rushmore Broadcasting Inc. (group owner; (acq 5-20-93; $45,000. with co-located FM; FTR: 6-14-93). Network: ABC Information & Entertainment. Format: Real country. Spec prog: Farm 6 hrs wkly. ♦ Gary Baker, gen mgr, gen sls mgr & progmg dir.

KZMX-FM— Feb 10, 1981: 96.7 mhz; 1.4 kw. Ant 440 ft. TL: N43 26 34 W103 27 27. Stereo. Format: Real country.

Huron

KIJV(AM)— July 1, 1947: 1340 khz; 1 kw-U. TL: N44 20 46 W98 12 34. 1726 Dakota Ave. S. 57350. Phone: (605) 352-8621. Fax: (605) 352-8622. Licensee: Dakota Communications Ltd. (group owner; acq 3-11-2004; $400,000. with co-located FM). Format: Oldies, talk, sports. News staff: one. Target aud: 35 plus. ♦ Duane D. Butt, pres; John Speeney, gen mgr & gen sls mgr; Matt Price, progmg dir; Curt Coleman, news dir.

KZNC(FM)—Co-owned with KIJV(AM). Nov 1, 1972: 99.1 mhz; 3 kw. 184 ft. TL: N44 20 46 W98 12 34. (CP: 91 kw, ant 804 ft. TL: N44 05 47 W98 37 09). Stereo. Format: Hot country. Target aud: 25-54.

KOKK(AM)— Jan 13, 1976: 1210 khz; 5 kw-D, 1 kw-N, DA-2. TL: N44 21 44 W98 09 09. Box 931 57350. Secondary address: 1835 Dakota Ave. 57350. Phone: (605) 352-1933. Fax: (605) 352-0911. E-mail: traffic@kokk.com. Web Site: www.kokk.com. Licensee: Dakota Communications Ltd. (group owner). Network: ABC Information & Entertainment. Format: Country, agriculture, info. News staff: one; News: 20 hrs wkly. Target aud: 25 plus. ♦ Linda Marcus, gen mgr & gen sls mgr; Jeff Duffy, chief of opns & progmg dir; Sarah Klick, mus dir; Mike Rudd, news dir; Dick Schultz, chief of engrg.

KZKK(FM)—Co-owned with KOKK(AM). 1993: 105.1 mhz; 6 kw. 154 ft. TL: N44 21 44 W98 09 09. Web Site: www.kokk.com. Format: Adult contemp. News staff: one.

Lemmon

KBJM(AM)— Apr 1, 1966: 1400 khz; 1 kw-U. TL: N45 55 05 W102 11 55. Box 540 57638. Secondary address: 500 First Ave. E. 57638. Phone: (605) 374-5747. Fax: (605) 374-5332. E-mail: kbjm@kbjm.com. Web Site: www.kbjm.com. Licensee: Media Associates Inc. (acq 1-17-91; $108,240; 2-4-91). Rep: Keystone (unwired net). Format: C&W, oldies, farm. News: 30 hrs wkly. Target aud: General. ♦ Mike Schweitzer, pres, gen mgr & gen sls mgr; James Schwab, progmg dir.

Little Eagle

*****KLND(FM)**— June 25, 1997: 89.5 mhz; 100 kw. Ant 679 ft. TL: N45 44 54 W100 48 30. Stereo. HC61 Box 1, Hwy. 63 S., McLaughlin 57642. Phone: (605) 823-4661. Fax: (605) 823-4660. E-mail: klnd@westriv.com. Web Site: www.klnd.org. Licensee: Seventh Generation Media Services Inc. Morrison & Foerster. Format: Var. News staff: one; News: 5 hrs wkly. Target aud: General; tribal people on the Standing Rock & Cheyenne River Nations. Spec prog: Gospel 3 hrs, children 4 hrs, Sp one hr, elders 2 hrs, news/talk 5 hrs wkly. ♦ Jana Shields Gipp, chmn; Beau Fontenalla, gen mgr & stn mgr.

Lowry

KMLO(FM)— 1996: 100.7 mhz; 100 kw. 587 ft. TL: N45 16 26 W99 58 21. c/o KMLO-FM, 214 W. Pleasant Dr., Pierre 57501. Phone: (605) 224-8686. Fax: (605) 224-8984. E-mail: drgprod1@amfmradio.biz. Licensee: James River Broadcasting Inc. Group owner: Robert Ingstad Broadcast Properties. Format: Country. ♦ Robert Inqstad, pres; Mark A. Swendsen, gen mgr.

*****KQSD-FM**— 1994: 91.9 mhz; 100 kw. 725 ft. TL: N45 16 34 W99 59 03. Box 5000, Vermillion 57069. Secondary address: 555 N. Dakota St. 57069. Phone: (605) 677-5861. Fax: (605) 677-5010. Web Site: www.sdpb.org. Licensee: South Dakota Board of Directors for Educational Telecommunications. Format: Class, news, pub affrs, jazz.

Madison

KJAM(AM)— Dec 3, 1959: 1390 khz; 500 w-D, 62 w-N. TL: N44 00 37 W97 10 18. 101 S. Egan Ave. 57042. Phone: (605) 256-4515. Fax: (605) 256-6477. Web Site: www.kjamradio.com. Licensee: Three Eagles of Brookings Inc. Group owner: Three Eagles Communications (acq 12-8-99; $1.2 million. with co-located FM). Format: C&W, news/talk. News staff: 13; News: 12 hrs wkly. Target aud: 21 plus. Spec prog: National agriculture talk program 11 hrs wkly. ♦ Gary Buchanan, pres; Lorin Larsen, gen mgr & dev dir; Jim Hockett, gen sls mgr; Peg Nordling, progmg dir; Sue Bergheim, news dir; Bob Cook, chief of engrg.

KJAM-FM— Dec 17, 1967: 103.1 mhz; 33 kw. 305 ft. TL: N43 59 08 W97 07 41. Stereo. E-mail: manager@kjamradio.com. Web Site: www.kjamradio.com. Format: Country, news. News staff: 2; News: 20 hrs wkly. Target aud: 21 plus.

Martin

*****KZSD-FM**— July 3, 1991: 102.5 mhz; 100 kw. 754 ft. TL: N43 26 06 W101 33 14. Box 5000, Vermillion 57069. Secondary address: 555 N. Dakota St. 57069. Phone: (605) 677-5861. Fax: (605) 677-5010. E-mail: sdpr@sdpb.org. Web Site: www.sdpb.org. Licensee: South Dakota Board of Directors for Educational Telecommunications. Format: Class, jazz, folk, news. ♦ Terry Harris, gen mgr.

Milbank

KCGN-FM—(Ortonville).MN Sept 23, 1983: 101.5 mhz; 98 kw. Ant 1,000 ft. TL: N45 22 29 W97 02 20. Stereo. Box 247, Osakis, MN 56360. Phone: (320) 859-3000. Fax: (320) 859-3010. Web Site: www.praisefm.org. Licensee: Praise Broadcasting Inc. (acq 10-24-2003). Format: Praise & worship, adult contemp Christian. Target aud: 25-44; middle-aged women. ♦ David McIver, gen mgr.

KKSD(FM)— Feb 4, 1991: 104.3 mhz; 100 kw. 981 ft. TL: N45 10 31 W96 59 15. Stereo. 3 E. Kemp Ave., Suite 300, Watertown 57201. Phone: (605) 882-1480. Fax: (605) 886-2121. Web Site: www.ksdr.com. Licensee: Three Eagles of Joliet Inc. Group owner: Three Eagles Communications (acq 6-18-2004; grpsl). Network: ABC Information & Entertainment. Format: Oldies. Target aud: 25-54. Spec prog: Sports 5 hrs wkly. ♦ Nancy Linneman, gen mgr.

KMSD(AM)— Mar 20, 1975: 1510 khz; 5 kw-D. TL: N45 11 42 W96 38 18. PO Box 1005 57252. Phone: (605) 432-5516. Fax: (605) 432-4231. E-mail: kmsd@tnics.com. Licensee: Big Stone Broadcasting Inc. Group owner: Robert Ingstad Broadcast Properties (acq 10-15-99; grpsl). Network: ABC Information & Entertainment. Format: News/talk, oldies. Target aud: General. Spec prog: Farm 6 hrs wkly. ♦ Jeff Kurtz, gen mgr.

Mitchell

KMIT(FM)— Mar 10, 1975: 105.9 mhz; 100 kw. 549 ft. TL: N43 41 25 W98 00 27. Stereo. Box 520 57301. Secondary address: 501 S. Ohlman Phone: (605) 996-9667. Fax: (605) 996-0013. E-mail: kmit@kmit.com. Web Site: www.kmit.com. Licensee: Saga Communications of South Dakota LLC. Group owner: Saga Communications Inc. (acq 5-1-01; $4.05 million. with KUQL(FM) Wessington Springs). Network: ABC Information & Entertainment. Format: Modern country. News staff: 2. Target aud: 18-54. Spec prog: Farm 18 hrs wkly. ♦ Tim Smith, gen mgr; Nikki Frederickson, gen sls mgr; Lisa Youngstrom, prom mgr; Joel VanDover, progmg dir; John Cyr, chief of engrg.

KORN(AM)— 1947: 1490 khz; 1 kw-U. TL: N43 42 14 W97 59 57. Box 921 57301. Secondary address: 319 N. Main 57301. Phone: (605) 996-1490. Fax: (605) 996-6680. E-mail: kornnews@waittradio.com. Licensee: Sorenson Broadcasting Corp. (group owner; acq 7-1-97; $1.2 million with co-located FM). Network: Network: Westwood One, ABC. Format: Talk, news/talk, sports. News staff: one; News: 15 hrs wkly. Target aud: 35 plus; mature adults. Spec prog: Farm 10 hrs wkly. ♦ Dean Sorenson, pres; John Koons, gen mgr; Sherri Porter, gen sls mgr; Clayton Mick, progmg dir; J.P. Skelly, news dir.

KQRN(FM)—Co-owned with KORN(AM). Aug 17, 1980: 107.3 mhz; 100 kw. 450 ft. TL: N43 41 46 W98 03 35. Stereo. Fax: (605) 996-6680. Web Site: q107radio.com. Format: Adult Contemp, CHR. News staff: one; News: 4 hrs wkly. Target aud: 10-49; adult female. ♦ Steve Morgan, progmg dir.

Mobridge

KOLY(AM)— Aug 10, 1956: 1300 khz; 5 kw-D, 111 w-N. TL: N45 32 07 W100 20 45. Box 400, 118 E. 3rd St. 57601. Phone: (605) 845-3654. Fax: (605) 845-5094. Licensee: James River Broadcasting Co. Group owner: Robert Ingstad Broadcast Properties (acq 7-8-97; $890,742 with co-located FM). Network: ABC Information & Entertainment. Format: Pop standards. News staff: one; News: 21 hrs wkly. Target aud: General. Spec prog: Farm, American Indian. ♦ Dawn Konold, gen mgr; Mark Swenden, gen sls mgr; John Schreier, progmg dir & news dir; Rolland Cory, chief of engrg.

KOLY-FM— Oct 1, 1973: 99.5 mhz; 56 kw. 560 ft. TL: N45 31 50 W100 20 30. (CP: 100 kw, ant 361 ft. TL: N45 32 07 W100 20 45). Stereo. Format: Adult contemp. ♦ Cindy Dafnis, opns mgr.

Pierpont

*****KDSD-FM**— Apr 1, 1984: 90.9 mhz; 70 kw. 1,057 ft. TL: N45 29 55 W97 40 35. Stereo. Box 5000, Vermillion 57069. Secondary address: 555 N. Dakota St., Vermillion 57069. Phone: (605) 677-5861. Fax: (605) 677-5010. E-mail: sdpr@sdpb.org. Web Site: www.sdpb.org. Licensee: South Dakota Board of Directors for Educational Telecommunications. Network: Network: PRI, NPR. Format: News, class, jazz. ♦ Terry Harris, gen mgr; Terry Spencer, dev dir.

Pierre

KCCR(AM)— Feb 4, 1959: 1240 khz; 1 kw-U. TL: N44 21 02 W100 19 08. Phone: (605) 224-1240. Fax: (605) 224-0095. Licensee: Sorenson Broadcasting Corp. (acq 3-1-72). Network: CBS. Format: Oldies, news/talk. News staff: 2; News: 24 hrs wkly. Target aud: 35 plus; well-educated, upper income, politically aware business people, retirees, housewives. ♦ Dean Sorenson, pres; Steve White, gen mgr; Tanya Martin, gen sls mgr; Dan Myer, progmg dir.

KLXS-FM—Co-owned with KCCR(AM). Apr 15, 1981: 95.3 mhz; 49 kw. 299 ft. TL: N44 22 15 W100 24 17. Stereo. Phone: (605) 224-7381. Network: Westwood One. Format: Adult contemp. Target aud: 18-34; 55% female, 45% male.

KGFX(AM)— 1927: 1060 khz; 10 kw-D, 1 kw-N, DA-2. TL: N44 17 12 W100 20 18. Box 1197, 214 W. Pleasant Dr. 57501. Phone: (605) 224-8686. Fax: (605) 224-8984. Licensee: James River Broadcasting. Group owner: Robert Ingstad Broadcast Properties (acq 11-15-68). Network: ABC Information & Entertainment. Shaw Pittman. Format: Country, farm. News staff: one; News: 20 hrs wkly. Target aud: 25-54. ♦ Robert E. Ingstad, pres; Mark A. Swendsen, gen mgr & gen sls mgr; Paul Rollie, progmg dir.

KGFX-FM— Jan 4, 1982: 92.7 mhz; 3 kw. 245 ft. TL: N44 22 15 W100 24 17. Stereo. Licensee: Robert E. Ingstad Properties. Format: Adult contemp. Target aud: 25-49.

KSQP(AM)—Not on air, target date: unknown: 1450 khz; 1 kw-U. TL: N44 25 54 W100 30 49. 207 E. Capitol Ave., Ste. 412 57501. Phone: (605) 224-4999. Licensee: Patriot Radio of South Dakota Inc. Network: ABC. Format: Talk. ♦ Lee O. Axdahl, pres & gen mgr.

*****KVFL(FM)**—Not on air, target date: unknown: 89.1 mhz; 400 w vert. Ant 371 ft. TL: N44 25 33 W100 21 28. 3434 W. Kilbourn Ave., Milwaukee, WI 53208-3313. Phone: (414) 935-3000. Fax: (414) 935-3015. E-mail: vcy@vcyamerica.org. Web Site: www.vcyamerica.org. Licensee: VCY America Inc. ♦ Vic Eliason, VP & gen mgr.

Broadcasting & Cable Yearbook 2006

South Dakota

Pine Ridge

KVAR(FM)—Not on air, target date: unknown: 93.7 mhz; 13.5 kw. Ant 453 ft. TL: N42 49 38 W102 39 30. 19801 Huntsville-Brownferry Rd., Tanner, AL 35671. Phone: (256) 345-2478. Licensee: Alleycat Communications. ♦ Richard W. Dabney, gen mgr.

Rapid City

***KASD(FM)**—Not on air, target date: unknown: 90.3 mhz; 250 w. Ant 390 ft. TL: N44 01 19 W103 15 35. Drawer 2440, Tupelo, MS 38803. Phone: (662) 844-8888. Fax: (662) 842-6791. Web Site: www.afr.net. Licensee: American Family Association. ♦ Marvin Sanders, gen mgr.

KBHB(AM)—See Sturgis

*KBHE-FM— 1984: 89.3 mhz; 9.8 kw. 410 ft. TL: N44 03 09 W103 14 38. Stereo. 703 Kansas City, Suite 107 57701. Phone: (605) 394-3363. E-mail: sdpr@sdpb.org. Web Site: www.sdpb.org. Licensee: South Dakota Board of Educational Telecommunications. Network: Network: PRI, NPR. Format: Classical Jazz. Spec prog: Sioux one hr wkly. ♦ Terry Harris, gen mgr.

KFXS(FM)— Apr 11, 1977: 100.3 mhz; 100 kw. 450 ft. TL: N44 04 14 W103 15 01. Stereo. Box 2480 57709. Secondary address: 660 Flormann St., Suite 100 57709. Phone: (605) 343-6161. Fax: (605) 343-9012. E-mail: request@foxradio.com. Web Site: www.foxradio.com. Licensee: Monterey Licenses L.L.C. Group owner: Triad Broadcasting Co. LLC (acq 11-19-99; grpsl). Shaw Pittman. Format: Classic rock. News staff: one; News: 3 hrs wkly. Target aud: 25-54. ♦ Lia Green, gen mgr; Charlie O'Douglas, opns mgr.

KIMM(AM)— Mar 16, 1962: 1150 khz; 5 kw-D, 500 w-N, DA-N. TL: N44 04 35 W103 08 49. Box 2480 57709. Phone: (605) 343-6161. Fax: (605) 343-9012. Licensee: KIMM Radio Inc. (acq 1-7-98; $150,000). Network: ABC Information & Entertainment. Rep: Christal. Format: Classic country. Target aud: 35-64. Spec prog: Colorado Rockies baseball, farm one hr wkly. ♦ Matthew Ward, pres; Ron Hansen, gen mgr; Gary Peterson, chief of opns & chief of engrg; Michael Goodroad, sls dir; Gail Hanson, gen sls mgr; Wayne Janke, progmg mgr, news dir & pub affrs dir.

KIQK(FM)—Listing follows KTOQ(AM).

KKLS(AM)— June 7, 1959: 920 khz; 5 kw-D, 100-N, DA-2. TL: N44 03 43 W103 10 29. Stereo. Box 2480, 660 Flormann St. 57709-2480. Phone: (605) 343-6161. Fax: (605) 343-9012. Licensee: Monterey Licenses LLC. Group owner: Triad Broadcasting Co. LLC (acq 11-19-99; grpsl). Network: Westwood One. Rep: Christal. Shaw Pittman. Format: Oldies. Target aud: 35-64. ♦ Lia Green, gen mgr; Charlie O'Douglas, opns mgr; Michael Goodroad, gen sls mgr; Scott McCormick, progmg dir; Gary Peterson, chief of engrg.

KKMK(FM)— Co-owned with KKLS(AM). 1971: 93.9 mhz; 100 kw. 650 ft. TL: N44 02 48 W103 14 46. Stereo. E-mail: kkmk@rapidnet.comm. Format: Adult contemp. Target aud: 25-54. ♦ Michael Goodroad, sls dir; Gail Hanson, natl sls mgr; Charlie O'Douglas, progmg dir; Brian Lintz, mus dir & asst music dir.

KLMP(FM)— Oct 1, 1968: 97.9 mhz; 100 kw horiz. 390 ft. TL: N44 02 46 W103 14 41. Stereo. Box 168 57709-0168. Secondary address: 1853 Fountain Plaza Dr. 57702. Phone: (605) 342-6822. Fax: (605) 342-0854. E-mail: klmp@klmp.com. Web Site: www.klmp.com. Licensee: Bethesda Christian Broadcasting Inc. Group owner: Bethesda Christian Broadcasting (acq 6-25-96; $350,000). Network: USA. Format: Inspirational programs. Target aud: 35 plus; general. ♦ Tom Schoenstedt, gen mgr; Joe Meunch, progmg dir; Joe Standish, mus dir; Tracey Krsnak, chief of engrg.

KOTA(AM)— November 1936: 1380 khz; 5 kw-U, DA-N. TL: N44 02 00 W103 11 15. Stereo. Box 1760, 518 St. Joe 57709-1760. Phone: (605) 342-2000. Fax: (605) 342-7305. E-mail: kotaradio@rapidnet.com. Web Site: www.kotaradio.rapidnet.com. Licensee: Duhamel Broadcasting Enterprises. (group owner; acq 5-54). Network: CBS. Shaw Pittman. Format: News/talk. News staff: 2; News: 10 hrs wkly. Target aud: 35 plus. ♦ William F. Duhamel, pres; Ted Peiffer, stn mgr. Co-owned TV: KOTA-TV affil

KOUT(FM)— 1993: 98.7 mhz; 100 kw. 515 ft. TL: N44 01 50 W103 15 34. Box 2480 57709-2480. Secondary address: 660 Flormann St., Suite 100 57701. Phone: (605) 343-6161 (605) 343-9012. Web Site: www.katcountry.com. Licensee: Monterey Licenses LLC. Group owner: Triad Broadcasting Co. LLC (acq 11-19-99; grpsl). Shaw Pittman. Format: Country. ♦ Lia Green, gen mgr; Charlie O'Douglas, opns mgr.

*KQFR(FM)— 2005: 89.9 mhz; 2.3 kw. Ant 1,843 ft. TL: N44 19 42 W103 50 03. Family Stations Inc., 4135 Northgate Blvd., Suite 1, Sacramento, CA 95834. Phone: (510) 568-6200. Phone: (916) 641-8191. Fax: (510) 568-6190. Fax: (916) 641-8238. E-mail: famradio@familyradio.com. Web Site: www.familyradio.com. Licensee: Family Stations Inc. (group owner). Format: Relg. ♦ Harold Camping, pres; Peggy L. Renscher, gen mgr; John Rorvik, opns mgr & rgnl sls mgr; Joe Papp, chief of engrg.

KQRQ(FM)— October 2002: 92.3 mhz; 86 kw. Ant 581 ft. TL: N44 04 07 W103 15 02. Box 1760 57709. Phone: (605) 342-2000. Fax: (605) 721-5732. Web Site: www.q923.com. Licensee: New Generation Broadcasting LLC. Rep: Katz Radio. Format: Classic hits. ♦ Ted Peiffer, gen mgr; Lil Anderson, gen sls mgr.

KRCS(FM)—See Sturgis

KTOQ(AM)— Sept 26, 1953: 1340 khz; 1 kw-U. TL: N44 04 06 W103 10 11. Box 1680, 306 1/2 E. St. Joseph St. 57709. Phone: (605) 343-0888. Fax: (605) 342-3075. Licensee: Haugo Braodcasting Inc. (group owner; acq 11-20-98; $1.97 million with co-located FM). Rep: McGavren Guild. Booth, Freret, Imlay & Tepper. Format: Talk. News staff: 2; News: 3 hrs wkly. Target aud: 35 plus; upscale. Spec prog: Farm 2 hrs wkly. ♦ Houston Haugo, CEO & pres; Christian Haugo, VP & gen mgr; Georgia McGaa, gen sls mgr; Brad Anderson, news dir; Rose Jeffert, pub affrs dir; Tracy Krsnak, chief of engrg.

KIQK(FM)— Co-owned with KTOQ(AM). Jan 7, 1992: 104.1 mhz; 100 kw. 515 ft. TL: N44 01 50 W103 15 34. Stereo. Phone: (605) 341-5425. Format: Country. News staff: one; News: 3 hrs wkly. Target aud: 25-54. ♦ Cory Ward, prom dir.

*KTPT(FM)— Feb 17, 2005: 88.3 mhz; 63 kw. Ant 1,712 ft. TL: N44 19 42 W103 50 03. 1853 Fountain Plaza Dr. 57702. Phone: (605) 342-6822. Fax: (605) 342-0854. Web Site: www.883thepoint.com. Licensee: Bethesda Christian Broadcasting Inc. Format: Contemp Christian. ♦ Mark Pluimer, pres & gen mgr.

*KWRC(FM)—Not on air, target date: unknown: 90.9 mhz; 875 w. Ant 1,116 ft. TL: N43 44 43 W103 28 52. 4002 N. 3300 E., Twin Falls, ID 83301. Phone: (208) 734-6633. Fax: (208) 736-1958. Web Site: www.csnradio.com. Licensee: CSN International. ♦ Michael Kestler, VP.

KZLK(FM)— 2001: 106.3 mhz; 92 kw. Ant 695 ft. TL: N44 04 07 W103 15 02. Box 1760 57709. Phone: (605) 342-2000. Fax: (605) 721-5732. E-mail: gm@star1063.com. Web Site: www.star1063.com. Licensee: Steven E. Duffy. Rep: Katz Radio. Shaw Pittman. Format: Adult contemp. Target aud: Women 25-54. ♦ Ted Peiffer, gen mgr; Lil Anderson, gen sls mgr.

Redfield

KGIM-FM— Apr 7, 1991: 103.7 mhz; 100 kw. Ant 564 ft. TL: N45 12 52 W98 40 54. Stereo. 13541 386th Ave., Aberdeen 57401. Phone: (605) 229-3632. Fax: (605) 229-4849. Licensee: Aberdeen Radio Ranch. (acq 11-19-2004; grpsl). Format: Country. News staff: one. Target aud: 25-49. ♦ Robert Ingstad, pres.

KNBZ(FM)— 1999: 97.7 mhz; 62 kw. Ant 190 ft. TL: N44 54 30 W98 19 40. 133541 386 Ave., Aberdeen 57401. Phone: (605) 229-3632. Fax: (605) 229-4849. Web site: www.kool977.com. Licensee: Aberdeen Radio Ranch Inc. Group owner: Robert Ingstad Broadcast Properties. (acq 11-19-2004; grpsl). Format: Adult contemp. ♦ Robert Ingstad, pres; Brian Lundquist, gen mgr.

KQKD(AM)— December 1962: 1380 khz; 500 w-D, 140 w-N, DA-2. TL: N44 53 53 W98 30 23. Family Stations Inc., 4135 Northgate Blvd., Suite 1, Sacramento, CA 95834. Phone: (916) 641-8191. Licensee: Family Stations Inc. Group owner: Robert Ingstad Broadcast Properties (acq 10-22-2004; $75,000. with KKAA(AM) Aberdeen). Format: Relg. ♦ Harold Camping, pres.

Reliance

KPLO-FM— January 1986: 94.5 mhz; 95 kw. 1,000 ft. TL: N43 57 55 W99 36 11. Stereo. 214 W. Pleasant Dr., Pierre 57325. Phone: (605) 734-4000. Phone: (605) 224-8686. Fax: (605) 224-8984. E-mail: drgprod1@amfmradio.biz. Licensee: James River Broadcasting Co. Group owner: Robert Ingstad Broadcast Properties (acq 8-21-98; $98,000). Format: Country. Target aud: 25-54. Spec prog: Farm 5 hrs wkly. ♦ Mark Swendsen, gen mgr.

*KTSD-FM— 1984: 91.1 mhz; 100 kw. 1,480 ft. TL: N43 57 55 W99 35 56. Stereo. Box 5000, Vermillion 57069. Secondary address: 555 N. Dakota St., Vermillion 57069. Phone: (605) 677-5861. Fax: (605) 677-5010. E-mail: sdpr@sdpb.org. Web Site: www.sdpb.org. Licensee: S.D. Board of Educational Telecommunications. Network: Network: PRI, NPR. Format: Class, jazz , news. Spec prog: Sioux one hr wkly. ♦ Terry Harris, gen mgr.

Saint Francis

KINI(FM)—See Crookston, NE

Salem

KIKN-FM— Nov 4, 1993: 100.5 mhz; 100 kw. 981 ft. TL: N43 29 18 W97 26 34. Stereo. 5100 S. Tennis Ln., Sioux Falls 57108. Phone: (605) 361-0300. Fax: (605) 361-5410. Licensee: Southern Minnesota Broadcasting Co. Group owner: Cumulus Media Inc. (acq 4-1-2004; grpsl). Format: New country. News staff: one. Target aud: 18-49. ♦ Lew Dickey, pres; Don Jacobs, gen mgr.

Sioux Falls

*KAUR(FM)— Oct 9, 1972: 89.1 mhz; 680 w. 184 ft. TL: N43 31 37 W96 44 18. Stereo. Box 751, KAUR-FM, Augustana College 57197. Secondary address: 2001 S. Summit Ave. 57197. Phone: (605) 274-0770. Fax: (605) 336-5465. Web Site: www.kaur.com. Licensee: Augustana College Association. Network: ABC FM Connection. Format: Rock, jazz, alternative. Target aud: General. Spec prog: Folk 2 hrs, world mus 6 hrs, blues 3 hrs wkly. ♦ Chuck Carlson, gen mgr.

*KCFS(FM)— July 1985: 94.5 mhz; 2.35 kw. 190 ft. TL: N43 31 57 W96 44 20. Sioux Falls College, 1101 W. 22nd St. 57105. Phone: (605) 331-6691. Fax: (605) 331-6615. E-mail: kcfs@thecoo.edu. Web Site: www.usiouxfalls.edu/campus/radio/index.html. Licensee: University of Sioux Falls. Format: Div. Spec prog: Urban 6 hrs wkly. ♦ Jesse Logterman, gen mgr; Chris Stafford, stn mgr; Jason Peiser, progmg dir.

*KCSD(FM)— July 1, 1985: 90.9 mhz; 2.35 kw. 190 ft. TL: N43 31 57 W96 44 20. Stereo. 1101 W. 22nd St. 57105. Phone: (605) 331-6691. Fax: (605) 331-6692. E-mail: sdpr@sdpb.org. Web Site: www.sdpb.org. Licensee: University of Sioux Falls. Network: NPR. Format: Class. News staff: one; News: 44 hrs wkly. Target aud: 25 plus; educated males & females. Spec prog: Folk 5 hrs, jazz 10 hrs wkly. ♦ Janice Davis, stn mgr.

KDLO-FM—See Watertown

KELO-FM— July 11, 1965: 92.5 mhz; 100 kw. Ant 1,820 ft. TL: N43 31 07 W96 32 05. Stereo. 500 S. Phillips 57104. Phone: (605) 331-5350. Fax: (605) 336-0415. Licensee: Backyard Broadcasting South Dakota Licensee LLC (acq 4-2005; grpsl). Leventhal, Senter & Lerman. Format: Light adult contemp. Spec prog: Jazz 6 hrs wkly. ♦ Barry Drake, pres; Craig Hodgson, gen mgr.

KELO(AM)— 1937: 1320 khz; 5 kw-U, DA-N. TL: N43 29 17 W96 38 14. Stereo. Group owner: Midcontinent Media Inc. Network: AP Radio. Format: News/talk, weather. News staff: 6. Target aud: 25-54.

KKLS-FM—Listing follows KXRB(AM).

KMXC(FM)—Listing follows KSOO(AM).

*KNWC(AM)— March 1961: 1270 khz; 2.5 kw-U, DA-2. TL: N43 29 19 W96 47 08. 26908 S. Tallgrass 57108-8107. Phone: (605) 339-1270. Fax: (605) 339-1271. E-mail: knwc@knwc.org. Web Site: www.knwc.org. Licensee: Northwestern College. Group owner: Northwestern College & Radio (acq 1961). Bryan Cave. Format: Relg, news. News staff: one; News: 24 hrs wkly. Target aud: 35-54. ♦ David Martin, opns dir; Jeff Rupp, gen mgr & progmg dir.

KNWC-FM— Mar 28, 1969: 96.5 mhz; 100 kw. 1,600 ft. TL: N43 31 07 W96 32 05. Stereo. Web Site: www.knwc.org. Bryan Cave. Format: Christian. News staff: one; News: 24 hrs wkly. Target aud: 20-54. ♦ Tim Unsinn, prom dir & progmg dir.

Broadcasting & Cable Yearbook 2006

South Dakota

KRRO(FM)— May 6, 1969: 103.7 mhz; 38 kw. Ant 394 ft. TL: N43 27 28 W96 40 14. Stereo. 500 S. Phillips 57104. Phone: (605) 331-5350. Fax: (605) 336-0415. Web Site: www.krro.com. Licensee: Backyard Broadcasting South Dakota Licensee LLC. (acq 4-2005; grpsl). Network: CBS. Shaw Pittman. Format: Classic rock, AOR. News staff: 2; News: 12 hrs wkly. Target aud: 25-49; young adults, family-rearing age with disposable income. ♦ Barry Drake, pres; Craig Hodgson, gen mgr.

KWSN(AM)—Co-owned with KRRO(FM). May 6, 1948: 1230 khz; 1 kw-U. TL: N43 33 31 W96 46 10. Web Site: www.kwsn.com. Group owner: Midcontinent Media Inc. . Network: ESPN Radio. Rep: Katz Radio. Format: All sports. News staff: 2; News: 27 hrs wkly. Target aud: 25-54; adults with disposable income, business leaders.

*KRSD(FM)— May 11, 1985: 88.1 mhz; 2 kw. 183 ft. TL: N43 31 37 W96 44 18. Stereo. Box 737, Augustana College 57197. Phone: (605) 335-6666. Phone: (800) 228-7123. Fax: (605) 335-1259. E-mail: mail@mpr.org. Web Site: www.mpr.org. Licensee: Minnesota Public Radio. Network: Network: NPR, PRI. Format: Class, news. News staff: one. Target aud: General. ♦ William H. Kling, pres; Michael Olsen, gen mgr; Mike Edgerly, news dir; Vince Fuhs, chief of engrg.

*KSFS(FM)—Not on air, target date: unknown: 90.1 mhz; 1 kw. Ant 118 ft. TL: N43 33 31 W96 49 10. Box 2440, Tupelo, MS 38803-2440. Phone: (662) 844-8888. Fax: (662) 842-6791. Web Site: www.afr.net. Licensee: American Family Association. ♦ Marvin Sanders, gen mgr.

KSOO(AM)— 1926: 1140 khz; 10 kw-D, 5 kw-N, DA-N. TL: N43 28 47 W96 41 04. 2600 S. Spring Ave. 57105. Phone: (605) 339-1140. Fax: (605) 339-2735. Web Site: www.ksoo.com. Licensee: Southern Minnesota Broadcasting Co. Group owner: Cumulus Media Inc. (acq 3-29-2004); grpsl). Network: ABC Information & Entertainment. Rep: Christal. Format: News/talk, sports. Target aud: 35-54. ♦ Lew Dickey, pres & gen mgr; Don Jacobs, stn mgr; Brad Peterson, progmg dir; Gene Hetland, news dir; Mike Langford, chief of engrg.

KMXC(FM)—Co-owned with KSOO(AM). Oct 1, 1973: 97.3 mhz; 60 kw. 221 ft. TL: N43 35 48 W96 38 20. Stereo. Web Site: www.mix97-3.com. Network: ABC FM Connection. Format: Adult contemp, CHR. Target aud: 25-44; females. ♦ Scott Maguire, progmg dir.

KSQB(AM)— June 13, 1970: 1520 khz; 500 w-D. TL: N43 33 28 W96 47 46. 3205 S. Meadow Pkwy. 57105. Phone: (605) 335-6896. Fax: (605) 332-3730. E-mail: rob@fellerbroadcast.com. Licensee: Feller Broadcasting. (acq 10-29-2004; grpsl). Network: Westwood One. Rep: Rgnl Reps. Law Offices of Richard J. Hayes. Format: Adult standards. News: 7 hrs wkly. Target aud: General; 35-65. Spec prog: Gospel 4 hrs wkly. ♦ Rob Feller, pres; Mark Nelson, opns dir.

KSQB-FM—See Dell Rapids

KTWB(FM)— May 5, 1990: 101.9 mhz; 34 kw. 580 ft. TL: N43 45 11 W96 53 22. Stereo. 500 S. Phillips Ave. 57104. Phone: (605) 331-5350. Fax: (605) 336-0415. E-mail: ktwb@mmi.net. Web Site: www.ktwb.com. Licensee: Backyard Broadcasting South Dakota Licensee LLC. Group owner: Midcontinent Media Inc. (acq 4-2005; grpsl). Richard Hayes. Format: Country. News staff: one; News: 10 hrs wkly. Target aud: 25-44. ♦ Barry Drake, pres; Craig Hodgson, gen mgr.

KWSF(FM)—See Flandreau

KXRB(AM)— February 1969: 1000 khz; 10 kw-D, DA. TL: N43 29 13 W96 35 48. 5100 S. Tennis Ln 57108. Phone: (605) 361-0300. Fax: (605) 361-5410. Licensee: Southern Minnesota Broadcasting Co. Group owner: Cumulus Media Inc. (acq 3-29-2004; grpsl). Network: CNN Radio. Rep: Christal. Format: Country, farm. News staff: one; News: 5 hrs wkly. Target aud: 25-54. ♦ Lew Dickey, pres; Don Jacobs, gen mgr; Joe Morrison, progmg dir & mus dir; Jerry Dohmen, news dir; Mike Langford, progmg dir & chief of engrg.

KKLS-FM—Co-owned with KXRB(AM). March 1975: 104.7 mhz; 100 kw. 860 ft. TL: N43 43 46 W97 05 10. Stereo. Format: Contemp hit. Target aud: 18-49. ♦ Andy Erickson, progmg dir & progmg mgr.

Sisseton

KBWS-FM— Dec 28, 1983: 102.9 mhz; 100 kw. 496 ft. TL: N45 36 52 W97 24 51. Stereo. 509 Veterans Ave. 57262. Phone: (605) 698-3471. Fax: (605) 698-3330. E-mail: kbws@tnics.com. Web Site: www.phcountry.com. Licensee: Pheasant Country Broadcasting Inc. Group owner: Robert Ingstad Broadcast Properties. Format: Country. Target aud: General. ♦ Robert Ingstead, pres; Jeff Kurtz, gen mgr; Randy Peterson, rgnl sls mgr; John Seiber, progmg dir & news dir; Terry Heitman, pub affrs dir; Don Brittnal, chief of engrg.

Spearfish

*KBHU-FM— Oct 18, 1974: 89.1 mhz; 100 w. 55 ft. TL: N44 29 48 W103 52 13. Stereo. Unit 9003, 1200 University St. 57799. Phone: (605) 642-6011. Phone: (605) 642-6265. Fax: (605) 642-6762. E-mail: kbhufm@hotmail.com. Web Site: www.kbhufm.com. Licensee: Black Hills State University. Network: Westwood One. Format: Alternative. News: 3 hrs wkly. Target aud: 12-35. ♦ Dave Diamond, CEO; Thomas O. Flickemna, pres; Cody Oliver, gen mgr; Stephen Webb, stn mgr; Cody Holliwell, dev dir.

KDDX(FM)— July 19, 1985: 101.1 mhz; 100 kw. 1,604 ft. TL: N44 19 40 W103 50 14. (CP: Ant 1,817 ft. TL: N44 19 36 W103 50 12). Stereo. 2827 E. Colorado Blvd. 57783. Phone: (605) 642-5747. Fax: (605) 642-7849. Web Site: www.xrock.fm. Licensee: Duhamel Broadcasting Enterprises. (group owner; acq 3-16-92; $525,000; 3-30-92). Format: Active rock. News staff: one; News: 3 hrs wkly. Target aud: 18-49. ♦ Ted Peiffer, gen mgr & gen sls mgr; Jim Kallas, progmg dir; Tom Collins, news dir.

KSLT(FM)— Feb 17, 1984: 107.3 mhz; 100 kw. 1,702 ft. TL: N44 19 36 W103 50 12. Stereo. Box 168, Rapid City 57709. Secondary address: 1853 Fountain Plaza Dr. Phone: (605) 342-6822. Fax: (605) 342-0854. E-mail: kslt@kslt.com. Web Site: www.kslt.com. Licensee: Bethesda Christian Broadcasting Inc. Network: USA. Format: Contemp Christian. News: 9 hrs wkly. Target aud: 25-49; affluent, educated, 60% female, 40% male. Spec prog: Focus on the Family 5 hrs, Insight for living 3 hrs, family news in focus one hr, Revival time one hr wkly. ♦ Mark Pluimer, pres; Mark Plumer, gen mgr; John Derrek, rgnl sls mgr; Jon Anderson, progmg dir; Joe Standish, mus dir; Tracey Krsnak, chief of engrg.

Sturgis

KBHB(AM)— Sept 27, 1962: 810 khz; 21 kw-D. TL: N44 25 23 W103 25 38. Box 99, Hwy. 79 N. 57785. Phone: (605) 347-4455. Fax: (605) 347-5120. Licensee: Monterey Licenses LLC. Group owner: Triad Broadcasting Co. LLC (acq 8-18-99; grpsl). Network: ABC. Format: Farm. News staff: one; News: 17 hrs wkly. Target aud: 35 plus. Spec prog: American Indian one hr, gospel 3 hrs wkly. ♦ Dean Kinney, gen mgr & gen sls mgr; Toni Kinney, opns dir; Gary Matthews, progmg dir; Gary Maki, news dir; Gary Peterson, chief of engrg.

KRCS(FM)—Co-owned with KBHB(AM). Dec 5, 1972: 93.1 mhz; 100 kw. 1,059 ft. TL: N44 19 58 W103 32 20. Stereo. Box 2480, Rapid City 57709. Phone: (605) 343-6161. Fax: (605) 343-9012. Web Site: www.hot931.com. Format: Continuous hit radio. ♦ Lia Green, gen mgr; Charlie O'Douglas, opns mgr; Leah Green, sls dir & gen sls mgr; Chad Bower, progmg dir; D. Ray Knight, news dir; Gary Peterson, chief of engrg.

Vermillion

*KAOR(FM)— September 1986: 91.1 mhz; 120 w. 107 ft. TL: N42 47 01 W96 55 26. Stereo. Contemporary Media & Journalism, 414 E. Clark 57069-2390. Phone: (605) 677-5477. Fax: (605) 677-4250. E-mail: kaor@usd.edu. Web Site: www.usd.edu/kaor. Licensee: The University of South Dakota. Cohn & Marks. Format: AOR, CHR, progsv. News: 2 hrs wkly. Target aud: 16-30; college age students & faculty. Spec prog: American Indian 2 hrs wkly. ♦ Ramon Chavez, chmn; Kent Osborne, gen mgr; Don Harris, chief of engrg.

*KUSD(FM)— Oct 1, 1967: 89.7 mhz; 50 kw horiz, 21.5 kw vert. 518 ft. TL: N43 03 00 W96 47 12. (CP: 32 kw, ant 663 ft.). Stereo. Box 5000 57069. Secondary address: 555 N. Dakota St. 57069. Phone: (605) 677-5861. Fax: (605) 677-5010. E-mail: sdpr@sdpb.org. Web Site: www.sdpb.org. Licensee: South Dakota Board of Directors/Educational Telecommunications. Network: Network: NPR, PRI. Format: Class, news & pub affrs, jazz. Spec prog: Sioux one hr wkly. ♦ Julie Anderson, pres; Terry Harris, gen mgr; Terry Spencer, dev dir. Co-owned TV: *KUSD-TV affil.

KVHT(FM)— Nov 16, 1967: 106.3 mhz; 50 kw. 390 ft. TL: N42 59 45 W96 49 25. Stereo. Box 718, Yankton 57078. Secondary address: 210 W. 3rd St., Yankton 57078. Phone: (605) 665-2600. Fax: (605) 665-8875. E-mail: mix106@kvht.com. Web Site: www.kvht.com. Licensee: Culhane Communications Inc. (acq 5-6-93; $340,000 with co-located AM; 5-24-93). Network: ABC Information & Entertainment. Shaw Pittman. Format: Adult contemp. News staff: one; News: 42 hrs wkly. Target aud: 18 plus. ♦ Kevin Culhane, gen mgr; Julie Auch, gen sls mgr & chief of engrg; Randy Eichelburg, opns mgr & progmg dir; Lee Rettig, news dir.

Volga

KJJQ(AM)—Licensed to Volga. See Brookings

KKQQ(FM)—Licensed to Volga. See Brookings

Watertown

KDLO-FM— Mar 1, 1968: 96.9 mhz; 100 kw. 1,571 ft. TL: N44 57 57 W97 35 22. Stereo. 921 9th Ave. S. 57201. Phone: (605) 886-8444. Fax: (605) 886-9306. E-mail: kwatprod@iw.net. Licensee: Three Eagles of Joliet Inc. Group owner: Three Eagles Communications (acq 6-18-2004); grpsl). Network: USA. Format: C&W. News staff: one. Target aud: 25-54. ♦ Dean Johnson, gen mgr; Bruce Erlandson, opns mgr.

KIXX(FM)—Listing follows KWAT(AM).

*KJBB(FM)— August 2000: 89.1 mhz; 200 w vert. Ant 20 ft. TL: N44 53 57 W97 06 18. 501 E. Kemp Ave. 57201. Phone: (605) 884-0156. E-mail: kjbbradio89-1fm@dailypost.com. Web Site: http://www.dailypost.com/kjbb89.1fm/. Licensee: Church Planters of America (acq 5-29-2003). Format: Educational. ♦ Ms. Sheila Hawkins, VP; Danny Hawkins, gen mgr.

KSDR(AM)— Apr 16, 1961: 1480 khz; 1 kw-D, 53 w-N. TL: N44 55 58 W97 06 19. Box 1480, 3 E. Kemp, Suite 300 57201. Phone: (605) 886-5747. Phone: (605) 882-1480. Fax: (605) 886-2121. Licensee: Three Eagles of Brookings Inc. Group owner: Three Eagles Communications (acq 6-19-00; $3.25 million. with co-located FM). Network: ABC Information & Entertainment. Tierney & Swift. Format: Talk. News staff: 3; News: 15 hrs wkly. Target aud: 25-54. ♦ Gary Buchanan, pres; Judy Ring, gen sls mgr; Heather Lentz, prom dir; Randy Grimes, progmg dir; John Wiik, mus dir; Shari Wirkus, news dir; Bob Koch, chief of engrg.

KSDR-FM— Mar 10, 1992: 92.9 mhz; 97 kw. 977 ft. TL: N45 10 31 W96 59 15. Stereo. Format: C&W. News staff: one; News: 12 hrs wkly. Target aud: General; rgnl country stn with wide var of ages. Spec prog: Farm 8 hrs, sports 8 hrs wkly.

KWAT(AM)— Mar 8, 1940: 950 khz; 1 kw-U, DA-N. TL: N44 52 12 W97 06 49. Box 950 57201. Secondary address: 921 9th Ave S. E. 57201. Phone: (605) 886-8444. Fax: (605) 886-9306. E-mail: radionews@home.com. Licensee: Three Eagles of Joliet Inc. Group owner: Three Eagles Communications (acq 6-18-2004; grpsl). Network: CBS. Format: MOR, news, farm. Target aud: 35 plus. ♦ Gary Buchanan, pres; Dean Johnson, VP, gen mgr & gen sls mgr; Bruce Erlandson, opns mgr; Mike Blakenship, mus dir; David Law, news dir.

KIXX(FM)—Co-owned with KWAT(AM). Sept 29, 1968: 96.1 mhz; 97 kw. 977 ft. TL: N45 10 31 W96 59 15. Stereo. Phone: (605) 886-9696. Network: ABC Daytime Direction. Format: Adult contemp. Target aud: 25-54. ♦ Curt Crawford, progmg dir.

Broadcasting & Cable Yearbook 2006

South Dakota

Wessington Springs

KJRV(FM)—Not on air, target date: unknown: 93.3 mhz; 100 kw. Ant 758 ft. TL: N44 11 39 W98 19 05. 711 Wells Ave., Pierre 57501. Phone: (605) 224-5434. Licensee: Alpena Broadcasting Co. ♦ Duane Butt, gen mgr.

KUQL(FM)— 1999: 98.3 mhz; 100 kw. Ant 899 ft. TL: N43 45 28 W98 24 39. Box 520, Mitchell 57301. Secondary address: 501 S. Ohlman, Mitchell 57301. Phone: (605) 996-9667. Phone: (605) 996-1100. Fax: (605) 996-0013. Web Site: www.kool98.com. Licensee: Saga Communications of South Dakota LLC. Group owner: Saga Communications Inc. (acq 5-1-01; $4.05 million. with KMIT(FM) Mitchell). Format: Oldies. ♦ Tim Smith, gen mgr; Nikki Frederickson, gen sls mgr; Kory Hartman, progmg dir; John Cyr, chief of engrg.

Winner

KWYR(AM)— Sept 27, 1957: 1260 khz; 5 kw-D, 146 w-N. TL: N43 22 57 W99 54 38. Stereo. 346 Main St. 57580. Secondary address: Box 491 57580. Phone: (605) 842-3333. Fax: (605) 842-3875. E-mail: 937radio@gwtc.net. Web Site: www.kwyr.com. Licensee: Midwest Radio Corp. (acq 11-23-58). Network: ABC Information & Entertainment. Format: Country. News staff: one; News: 14 hrs wkly. Target aud: 25-60. ♦ John Driscoll, VP; Scott Schramm, pres & gen mgr.

KWYR-FM— Nov 25, 1971: 93.7 mhz; 100 kw. 560 ft. TL: N43 17 46 W99 52 02. Stereo. Phone: (605) 842-3693. Web Site: www.kwyr.com. Network: Jones Radio Networks. Format: Adult contemp, CHR. Target aud: 18-45. ♦ John Driscoll, gen sls mgr & engrg dir.

Yankton

KKYA(FM)—Listing follows KYNT(AM).

KYNT(AM)— Mar 15, 1955: 1450 khz; 1 kw-U. TL: N42 53 30 W97 25 10. Box 628 57078. Secondary address: 202 W. 2ndn St. 57078. Phone: (605) 665-7892. Fax: (605) 665-0818. E-mail: kynt1450@yahoo.com. Licensee: Sorenson Broadcasting Corp. (group owner; acq 7-1-73). Network: Network: Westwood One, ABC Music Radio. Rep: Katz Radio. Format: Adult contemp. News staff: 2; News: 25 hrs wkly. Target aud: General. Spec prog: Farm 5 hrs, polka one hr, Pol one hr wkly. ♦ Dean Sorenson, pres; Bill Holst, gen mgr; Dave Lesher, opns mgr; Dave Bradbury, prom mgr.

KKYA(FM)—Co-owned with KYNT(AM). May 25, 1982: 93.1 mhz; 100 kw. 469 ft. TL: N42 43 49 W97 24 13. Stereo. E-mail: kk93fm@hotmail.com. Cindy Weiland Format: Country. News staff: 2; News: 1.5 hrs wkly.

WNAX(AM)— November 1922: 570 khz; 5 kw-U, DA-N. TL: N42 54 47 W97 18 58. 1609 E. Hwy. 50 57078. Phone: (605) 665-7442. Fax: (605) 665-8788. E-mail: wnax@wnax.com. Web Site: www.wnax.com. Licensee: Saga Communications Inc. (acq 1996). Network: Network: CBS, ABC Information & Entertainment. Rep: Katz Radio. Smithwick & Belendiuk. Format: News/talk, farm. News staff: 5; News: 23 hrs wkly. Target aud: 25 plus; farmers & agri-businesses. Spec prog: Relg 16 hrs, sports 10 hrs, weather 15 hrs, farm news 35 hrs wkly. ♦ Edward Christian, pres; Les Tuttle, gen mgr; Jerry Oster, opns mgr & news dir; Jim Reimler, progmg mgr & mus dir; John Cyr, chief of engrg.

WNAX-FM— Aug 9, 1973: 104.1 mhz; 97 kw. 981 ft. TL: N42 38 24 W97 03 21. Stereo. Web Site: www.wnax.com. Format: Country. News staff: one; News: 3 hrs wkly. Target aud: 25-54. ♦ Edward Christian, CEO; Drew Wilson, gen sls mgr & progmg mgr.

Tennessee

Alamo

WCTA(AM)— October 1983: 810 khz; 250 w-D, DA. TL: N35 47 59 W89 07 20. 114 S. Johnson St. 38001. Phone: (731) 696-2781. Fax: (731) 696-5006. E-mail: billy@wcta810.com. Web Site: www.wcta810.com. Licensee: Billy H. Williams. (acq 5-1-96; $119,933). Format: News, talk. Target aud: 30 plus. Spec prog: Relg 9 hrs wkly. ♦ Billy H. Williams, pres & gen mgr; Billy Williams, progmg mgr; Dave Hacker, chief of engrg.

WWGM(FM)—Aug 10, 1989: 93.1 mhz; 25 kw. 443 ft. TL: N35 43 31 W89 03 25. Stereo. 25 Stonebrook Pl., Suite 322, Jackson 38305. Phone: (731) 855-9334. Fax: (731) 855-1600. Web Site: www.gracebroadcasting.com. Licensee: Grace Broadcasting Services Inc. (acq 8-18-97; $800,000). Miller & Miller. Format: Southern gospel, relg. News staff: one; News: 3 hrs wkly. Target aud: 24-54; upscale women. ♦ Lacy Ennis, stn mgr & sls VP; Phillip Chambers, prom dir.

Alcoa

WBCR(AM)— Aug 25, 1957: 1470 khz; 1 kw-D. TL: N35 47 47 W83 56 17. Box 130 37701. Secondary address: 118 Defoe Cir. 37701. Phone: (865) 984-1470. Fax: (865) 983-0890. E-mail: truthradioam1470@yahoo.com. Licensee: Blount County Broadcasting Co. (acq 2-20-96). Format: News/talk. News staff: local news/ talk 10 hrs wkly News: one;. Target aud: 35+. ♦ Harry Grothjahn, gen mgr.

***WYLV(FM)**— Feb 14, 1993: 89.1 mhz; 4.5 kw. 994 ft. TL: N36 00 13 W83 56 35. Stereo. 1621 E. Magnolia Ave., Knoxville 37917. Phone: (865) 521-8910. Fax: (865) 521-8923. E-mail: love89@aol.com. Web Site: www.love89.org. Licensee: Foothills Broadcasting Inc. Format: Contemp Christian. ♦ David Wells, gen mgr & opns mgr; Marisa Lykins, prom dir; Jonathan Unthank, progmg dir; Dan Klug, chief of engrg.

Algood

WATX(AM)— Oct 5, 1981: 1590 khz; 1 kw-D, 500 w-N. TL: N36 11 02 W85 25 03. 259 S. Willow Ave., Cookeville 38501. Phone: (931) 528-6064. Fax: (931)520-1590. E-mail: billpenn@jwcbroadcasting.com. Licensee: JWC Broadcasting (group owner; acq 8-3-01). Network: Salem Radio Network. Format: Christian. News staff: 2; News: 34 hrs wkly. Target aud: General. Spec prog: Gospel. ♦ Lisa Bush, gen mgr.

Ardmore

WSLV(AM)— September 1968: 1110 khz; 2.5 kw-D. TL: N34 59 35 W86 51 22. Box 96, 25995 Stateline Rd. 38449. Phone: (931) 427-2178. Fax: (931) 427-2179. E-mail: wslv@ardmore.net. Web Site: www.wslvam.com. Licensee: B&E Broadcasting Inc. (acq 1-13-89; $85,000; 1-30-89). Format: New country, classic country, Southern gospel. Target aud: 25 plus; country & Christian listeners. ♦ Ernie Ashworth, pres; Becky Parker, gen mgr & stn mgr.

Ashland City

WQSV(AM)— July 14, 1982: 790 khz; 500 w-U. TL: N36 17 08 W87 04 58. Box 619, 208 1/2 N. Main St. 37015. Phone: (615) 792-6789. Fax: (615) 792-7795. E-mail: wqsvam790radio@aol.com. Web Site: www.wqsvradio@bellsouth.net. Licensee: Sycamore Valley Broadcasting Inc. (acq 12-20-91; $55,000; 1-13-92). Network: ABC Daytime Direction. Format: Christian country. Target aud: General. ♦ Richard Albright, CEO, gen mgr & stn mgr.

Athens

WJSQ(FM)—Listing follows WLAR(AM).

WLAR(AM)— May 15, 1946: 1450 khz; 1 kw-U. TL: N35 26 44 W84 36 43. 2110 Oxnard Rd. 37303. Phone: (423) 745-1000. Fax: (423) 745-2000. Web Site: www.1017wlar.com. Licensee: James C. Sliger. (acq 4-18-83; $200,000; 5-9-83). Format: Contemp country. Spec prog: Farm 2 hrs wkly. ♦ James Sigler, gen mgr & gen sls mgr.

WJSQ(FM)—Co-owned with WLAR(AM). Dec 1, 1979: 101.7 mhz; 7.5 kw. 528 ft. TL: N35 31 19 W84 27 29. Stereo. Web Site: www.1017wlar.com. Format: Country.

WYXI(AM)— Oct 5, 1966: 1390 khz; 2.5 kw-D, 62 w-N. TL: N35 26 48 W84 34 19. Box 1390, 112 E. Madison Ave. 37371-1390. Phone: (423) 746-1390. Fax: (432) 745-4439. E-mail: wyxi@bellsouth.net. Web Site: www.wyxi.com. Licensee: Cornerstone Broadcasting Inc. (acq 9-11-86; $75,000; 7-21-86). Network: Network: ABC Information & Entertainment, CBS Radio, Westwood One. Rgnl Reps Format: Talk. News staff: one; News: 10 hrs wkly. Target aud: 25-64; mature middle class. Spec prog: Black one hr, relg 8 hrs wkly. ♦ Mark Lefler, pres & stn mgr; Bob Ketchersid, VP, opns dir & progmg dir; Roger Pickett, stn mgr.

Directory of Radio

Atwood

WTKB-FM— 1992: 93.7 mhz; 6 kw. Ant 328 ft. TL: N35 57 25 W88 41 44. (CP: 15 kw, ant 325 ft). Box 500, 302 W. Eaton St., Trenton 38382. Phone: (731) 686-9852. Fax: (731) 855-1600. E-mail: wtkbwtne@bellsouth.nct. Licensee: Thunderbolt Broadcasting Services Inc. Group owner: Thunderbolt Broadcasting Co./Gibson County Broadcasting (acq 1-7-2005; grpsl). Format: Christian music. ♦ Sherry L. Vaughn, stn mgr; Randy Gardner, sls dir; Steve Hilton, progmg dir; Robin Cude, news dir; David Hacker, chief of engrg.

Bartlett

WMFS(FM)— May 1994: 92.9 mhz; 6 kw. 328 ft. TL: N35 10 20 W89 56 40. 1960 Union Ave., Memphis 38104-4031. Phone: (901) 726-0555. Fax: (901) 725-5101. Web Site: 93xmemphis.com. Licensee: Infinity Broadcasting Corp. of Illinois. Group owner: Infinity Broadcasting Corp. (acq 7-25-01; $7.2 million). Rep: Interep. Leventhal, Senter & Lerman. Format: Alternative. News: one hr wkly. Target aud: 18-49; Adults. ♦ Terry Wood, pres, sr VP & gen mgr.

WMPS(AM)—Licensed to Bartlett. See Memphis

Baxter

WBXE(FM)— October 1995: 93.7 mhz; 25 kw. 328 ft. TL: N36 18 53 W85 32 00. 259 S. Willow Ave., Cookeville 38501. Phone: (931) 528-6064. Fax: (931) 520-1590. Web Site: www.brock937.com. Licensee: JWC Broadcasting (group owner; acq 8-29-01). Network: Westwood One. Rep: Allied Radio Partners. Format: Rock, classic rock. News staff: one. Target aud: 18-45; Men 25 plus. ♦ Jim Stapleton, gen mgr.

Belle Meade

WNFN(FM)— 1998: 106.7 mhz; 1.1 kw. 774 ft. TL: N36 08 27 W86 51 56. 10 Music Circle E., Nashville 37203. Phone: (615) 321-1067. Fax: (615) 321-5771. E-mail: danielle.haese@cumulus.com. Web Site: www.cumulus.com. Licensee: Cumulus Licensing Corp. Group owner: Cumulus Media Inc. (acq 2-12-2002; grpsl). Format: Sports. ♦ Michael Dickey, gen mgr; Derick Corbett, progmg dir; Dan Goodman, chief of engrg; Dave Elliott, sls.

Bells

WNWS(AM)—See Brownsville

Benton

WBIN(AM)— May 18, 1977: 1540 khz; 1 kw-D, 2 w-N, 500 w-CH. TL: N35 11 15 W84 38 13. (CP: 1 kw-D, 4 w-N, 500 w-CH. TL: N35 10 50 W84 38 34). 108 Lifestyle Way 37307. Phone: (423) 338-2864. Fax: (423) 338-2865. E-mail: www.wbin@volfirst.net. Licensee: John A. Sines and L. Jane Sines, JTWROS (acq 12-29-99; $79,000). Format: Relg. Target aud: All ages; Includes baby boomers and seniors. ♦ Joy Croft, gen mgr & progmg dir.

WOCE(FM)— November 1996: 93.1 mhz; 5 kw. Ant 358 ft. TL: N35 05 40 W84 53 45. Stereo. Box 9170, Chattanooga 37412. Phone: (423) 485-8987. Fax: (423) 485-8946. Licensee: LB Radio of Chattanooga, LLC Format: Sp hits. Target aud: 25-54. Spec prog: Pub affrs 2 hrs, talk, Univ. of Tennessee sports, loc sports wkly.

***WTSE(FM)**— 2005: 91.1 mhz; 8.5 kw vert. Ant 466 ft. TL: N35 19 25 W84 17 54. Box 5459, Twin Falls, ID 83303. Phone: (208) 733-3551. Fax: (208) 733-3548. Licensee: Radio Assist Ministry Inc. (acq 9-13-2004; $1. for CP). Sciarrino & Associates. ♦ Clark Parrish, pres.

Berry Hill

WVOL(AM)— December 1951: 1470 khz; 5 kw-D, 1 kw-N, DA-2. TL: N36 12 01 W86 46 47. 1320 Brickchurch Pike, Nashville 37207. Phone: (615) 226-9510. Fax: (615) 226-0709. E-mail: wvol1470@aol.com. Web Site: www.wvol1470.com. Licensee: Heidelberg Broadcasting LLC. (acq 4-24-00). Format: Classic oldies, R&B. Target aud: 25-54; relg. Spec prog: Gospel 6 hrs wkly. ♦ John Heidelberg, chmn, pres, gen mgr & sls mgr; Roderick M. Heidelberg, opns mgr & progmg dir; Watt Harriston, chief of engrg.

Broadcasting & Cable Yearbook 2006

Tennessee

Blountville

WGOC(AM)— Sept 20, 1967: 640 khz; 10 kw-D, 810 w-N, DA-N. TL: N36 31 19 W81 25 25. Stereo. Box 8668, Gray 37615. Phone: (423) 477-1000. Fax: (423) 477-4747. Web Site: www.wgoc.com. Licensee: Citadel Broadcasting Co. Group owner: Citadel Broadcasting Corp. (acq 5-30-00; grpsl). Rep: Dora-Clayton. Format: Top Gun classic country/bluegrass. News staff: one; News: 12 hrs wkly. Target aud: 25-54; $35,000 household income, families of 3. Spec prog: Relg 16 hrs wkly. ♦Dave Hogan, pres & progmg dir; Don Raines, gen mgr; Jeff Hall, news dir; Al LeFevre, chief of engrg.

Bolivar

WBOL(AM)— Oct 19, 1962: 1560 khz; 250 w-D. TL: N35 15 30 W88 58 50. Box 191, 123 W. Market 38008. Phone: (731) 658-3633. Phone: (731) 658-3690. Fax: (731) 658-3408. E-mail: wojg@hcaol.com. Licensee: Shaw's Broadcasting Co. Format: Blues, light jazz, oldies. ♦Johnny W. Shaw, gen mgr; Dewayne Dickerson, gen sls mgr; Opal Shaw, progmg dir.

WOJG(FM)—Co-owned with WBOL(AM). June 1992: 94.7 mhz; 6 kw. 328 ft. TL: N35 16 39 W88 55 41. Licensee: Johnny W. Shaw & Opal J. Shaw. Format: Gospel. ♦Dwayne Dickerson, opns dir & sls dir; Dave Hacker, chief of engrg.

WMOD(FM)— Jan 27, 1975: 96.7 mhz; 3 kw. 300 ft. TL: N35 15 00 W88 53 28. Stereo. 100 E. Market St. 38008. Phone: (731) 658-4320. Fax: (731) 658-7328. E-mail: wmod@gointer.net. Licensee: WMOD Inc. (acq 6-17-97; $320,000). Network: ABC. Midsouth. Format: Country. News: 7 hrs wkly. Target aud: 25-55; males & females. ♦D. Richard Teubner, pres & gen mgr; Gail R. Teubner, opns mgr.

Brentwood

WNSR(AM)— Sept 4, 1985: 560 khz; 4.5 kw-D, 75 w-N, DA-2. TL: N35 54 32 W86 46 13. 435 37th Ave. N., Nashville 37209. Phone: (615) 844-1039. Fax: (615) 777-2284. E-mail: info@wnsr.com. Web Site: www.wnsr.com. Licensee: Southern Wabash Communications Middle Tennessee Inc. Group owner: Southern Wabash Communications Corp. (acq 11-25-97; $245,000). Format: Sports. Target aud: 18-54; men. ♦Ted Johnson, gen mgr.

Bristol

*****WHCB(FM)**— Aug 10, 1984: 91.5 mhz; 1.5 kw. Ant 2,326 ft. TL: N36 26 03 W82 08 03. Stereo. Box 2061 37621-2061. Secondary address: 340 Edgemont Ave., Suite 100 37620. Phone: (423) 878-6279. Fax: (423) 878-6520. E-mail: whcb@aecc.org. Web Site: www.whcbradio.org.yes Licensee: Appalachian Educational Communication Corp. Network: Moody, USA. Format: Talk, educ, Christian. News staff: one; News: 14 hrs wkly. Target aud: General. Spec prog: Class one hr, Appalachian culture 2 hrs, farm one hr, folk one hr, Sp one hr, Jewish one hr, black 9 hrs, children 10 hrs, gospel 15 hrs wkly.,. ♦Kenneth C. Hill, pres & gen mgr.

WIGN(AM)— Aug 18, 1962: 1550 khz; 5 kw-D. TL: N36 33 58 W82 09 30. Box 68 37621. Phone: (276) 591-5800. Fax: (276) 591-5278. Licensee: Sunshine Broadcasters Inc. (acq 8-4-2005; $245,000 for stock). Format: Southern gospel. News: 3 hrs wkly. Target aud: General. ♦Rick Mitchell, gen mgr.

WKPT(AM)—See Kingsport

WOPI(AM)— June 15, 1929: 1490 khz; 1 kw-U. TL: N36 35 45 W82 09 42. 222 Commerce St., Kingsport 37660. Secondary address: 288 Delaney St. 37620. Phone: (423) 764-5131. Fax: (423) 246-6261. Fax: (423) 247-9836. E-mail: davidw@wtfm.com. Web Site: www.wopi.com. Licensee: Holston Valley Broadcasting Corp. Group owner: Glenwood Communications Corp. (acq 5-16-96; $140,000; 5-7-90). Network: ABC Information & Entertainment. Rep: McGavren Guild. Cordon & Kelly. Format: Full Service, news, sports. News staff: 2. Target aud: 35 plus. Spec prog: Bluegrass & old time country 18 hrs wkly. ♦George

DeVault, pres; Bettte Lawson, CFO; David Widener, exec VP & gen mgr; Jason Mullins, opns dir & pub affrs dir.

WQUT(FM)—See Johnson City

WXBQ-FM— 1945: 96.9 mhz; 67 kw. 2,200 ft. TL: N36 25 59 W82 08 11. Stereo. Box 1389, VA 24203. Secondary address: 901 E. Valley Dr., VA 24201. Phone: (276) 669-8112. Fax: (276) 669-0541. Web Site: www.wxbq.com. Licensee: Bristol Broadcasting Inc. Group owner: Nininger Stations Network: ABC Information & Entertainment. Rep: McGavren Guild. Format: Country. Target aud: 25-54. ♦W.L. Nininger, pres; Pete Nininger, gen mgr; Winnie Quaintance, gen sls mgr; Roger Bowldin, prom dir & prom mgr; Bruce Clark, progmg dir; George Dixon, news dir; Chuck Lawson, chief of engrg.

Brownsville

WNWS(AM)— Oct 14, 1963: 1520 khz; 250 w-D. TL: N35 36 30 W89 14 40. Box 198, 42 S. Washington Ave. 38012. Phone: (901) 772-3700. Licensee: The Wireless Group Inc. (group owner; acq 4-80; $320,000. with co-located FM; FTR: 3-31-80). Network: ABC. Format: Sp. ♦Carlton Veirs, pres & gen mgr; Tanya Garcia, progmg dir.

WTBG(FM)—Co-owned with WNWS(AM). Nov 9, 1965: 95.3 mhz; 5 kw. 150 ft. TL: N35 36 30 W89 14 40. (CP: 6 kw, ant 328 ft.). Stereo. Network: ABC Information & Entertainment. Wyatt, Tarrant & Combs. Format: Country, news/talk. News staff: one. Target aud: 25-54. ♦Carlton Veirs, CEO; Kim Bishop, sls VP; Pam McCuan, progmg dir.

*****WQNN(FM)**—Not on air, target date: unknown: 88.3 mhz; 500 w. Ant 125 ft. TL: N35 35 33 W89 14 50. Broadcasting for the Challenged Inc., 188 S. Bellevue, Suite 222, Memphis 38104. Phone: (901) 375-9324. Fax: (901) 375-0041. Licensee: Broadcasting for the Challenged Inc. ♦George S. Flinn Jr., pres & gen mgr.

Bulls Gap

WBGQ(FM)— 2001: 100.7 mhz; 330 w. Ant 1,260 ft. TL: N36 22 48 W83 10 47. Stereo. Cherokee Broadcasting System, Box 519, Morristown 37815. Phone: (423) 235-4640. E-mail: www.wbgqfm@planetc.com. Web Site: wjdtfm@planetc.com. Licensee: S.J. Trent dba Cherokee Broadcasting System. Format: Adult contemp. Target aud: 18-54; female 65% & male 35%. ♦Clark Quillen, CEO & gen mgr; David Quillen, opns VP.

Calhoun

WCLE-FM— August 1993: 104.1 mhz; 2.3 kw. Ant 522 ft. TL: N35 15 59 W84 50 23. Stereo. Box 2695, Cleveland 33730. Secondary address: 1860 Executive Park, Suite E, Cleveland 37312. Phone: (423) 472-6700. Fax: (423) 476-4686. Licensee: Williams Communications Inc. (group owner; acq 8-8-02; $2.4 million. with WCLE(AM) Cleveland). Format: Adult contemp. News staff: one. Target aud: 25-54. ♦Paul Fink, gen mgr; Walt Williams III, gen mgr.

Camden

WFWL(AM)— Sept 18, 1956: 1220 khz; 250 w-D, 140 w-N. TL: N36 03 10 W88 05 15. Box 539, 117 Vicksburg Ave. 38320. Phone: (731) 584-7570. Phone: (731) 584-4444. Fax: (731) 584-7553. E-mail: reiddbell@morningcoffeebreak.com. Web Site: www.morningcoffeebreak.com. Licensee: Community Broadcasting Services Inc. (acq 4-30-98; $767,000 exercise of option with co-located FM). Network: ABC Information & Entertainment. Rep: Keystone (unwired net). Midsouth. Miller & Fields, P.C. Format: C&W. Target aud: 25-49; adult. Spec prog: Gospel 8 hrs wkly. ♦Stan Medlin, pres; Ron Lane, gen mgr, gen sls mgr & prom mgr; Jim Hart, progmg dir & news dir; Larry Nunnery, engrg mgr.

WRJB(FM)—Co-owned with WFWL. June 20, 1976: 98.3 mhz; 3 kw. 300 ft. TL: N36 03 25 W88 06 10. Stereo. Network: ABC Information & Entertainment. Format: Adult contemp. News: 4 hrs wkly. Target aud: 20-50. ♦Stan Medlin, pres & CFO; Charles Ennis, exec VP; Larry Nannery, engrg VP.

Carthage

WRKM(AM)— June 20, 1959: 1350 khz; 1 kw-D, 91 w-N. TL: N36 14 42 W85 56 44. Box 179 37030. Secondary address: 104 Z Country Ln. 37030. Phone: (615) 735-1350. Fax: (615) 735-0381. E-mail: am1350@smithcounty.com. Web Site: www.wucz-wrkm.com. Licensee: Wood Broadcasting Inc. (acq 11-1-87). Network: Sporting News Radio Network. Format: Sports. News staff: one; News: 2 hrs wkly. Target aud: 35 plus. ♦John Wood, pres, gen mgr & gen sls mgr; Dennis Banka, prom dir & progmg dir; Carl Campbell, chief of engrg.

WUCZ-FM—Co-owned with WRKM(AM). July 18, 1975: 104.1 mhz; 6 kw. 300 ft. TL: N36 18 43 W85 57 08. Stereo. E-mail: z104@smithcounty.com. Web Site: www.wucz-wrkm.com. Network: Westwood One. Format: Country. News staff: one; News: 2 hrs wkly. Target aud: 18-35. ♦John Wood, stn mgr & opns mgr.

Celina

WVFB(FM)— August 1994: 101.5 mhz; 6 kw. 328 ft. TL: N36 33 15 W85 36 39. Stereo. 341 Radio Station Rd., Tompkinsville, KY 42167. Phone: (270) 487-6119. Fax: (270) 487-8462. Licensee: Elizabeth Bernice Whittimore. (acq 5-5-93; $14,000; 5-24-93). Format: Country. News staff: news progmg 20 hrs wkly News: 2;. All age group. ♦Bernice Whittimore, gen mgr.

Centerville

WNKX(AM)— Nov 16, 1955: 1570 khz; 5 kw-D, 77 w-N. TL: N35 45 29 W87 27 35. Box 280 37033. Secondary address: 150 Hwy. 50 E. 37033. Phone: (931) 729-5191. Phone: (931) 729-9600. Fax: (931) 729-5467. E-mail: wnkx@countrykix96.com. Web Site: www.countrykix96.com. Licensee: Hickman County Broadcasting Co. Inc. (acq 5-7-97; $300,000 with co-located FM). Rep: Dora-Clayton. Midsouth. McCampbell & Young. Format: Talk, Christian, country. News staff: one; News: 10 hrs wkly. Target aud: 18-65; general. Spec prog: Farm one hr, gospel 5 hrs wkly. ♦Steve Turner, CEO, chmn, pres, gen mgr & sls dir; John Kimery, CFO; Wanda Turner, exec VP.

WNKX-FM— May 1974: 96.7 mhz; 6 kw. 300 ft. TL: N35 49 39 W87 34 02. Stereo. Web Site: www.countrykix96.com. McCampbell & Young. News staff: 3; News: 30 hrs wkly. Target aud: 6-80. ♦Mickey Bunn, opns mgr & asst music dir; Steve Turner, stn mgr & progmg mgr.

Chattanooga

WAWL-FM—See Red Bank

WDEF-FM— Sept 15, 1964: 92.3 mhz; 100 kw. 1,180 ft. TL: N35 08 06 W85 19 25. Stereo. Box 11008 37401. Secondary address: 2615 S. Broad St. 37408. Phone: (423) 321-6200. Fax: (423) 321-6264. Licensee: Bahakel Communications. (group owner; acq 1996; grpsl). Network: CBS. Format: Soft rock. News staff: one; News: 5 hrs wkly. Target aud: 25-54; upscale adults. ♦Gary Downs, gen mgr; Jeff Fontana, gen sls mgr; Danny Howard, progmg dir; James Howard, news dir; Ben Johnston, chief of engrg.

WDEF(AM)— Dec 31, 1940: 1370 khz; 5 kw-U, DA-N. TL: N35 02 25 W85 20 22. Format: News/talk, sports. News staff: one; News: 20 hrs wkly. Target aud: 25-64; males.

WDOD(AM)— Apr 13, 1925: 1310 khz; 5 kw-U, DA-N. TL: N35 04 54 W85 20 14. Box 1449 37401. Secondary address: 2615 Broad St. 37408. Phone: (423) 321-6200. Fax: (423) 321-6270. Licensee: WDOD of Chattanooga Inc. Group owner: Bahakel Communications (acq 6-62). Format: Big band, talk, btfl mus. News staff: 2; News: 10 hrs wkly. Target aud: 35 plus; empty nesters. ♦Gary Downs, gen mgr & gen sls mgr; Danny Howard, progmg VP.

WDOD-FM— February 1960: 96.5 mhz; 100 kw. 1,080 ft. TL: N35 09 39 W85 19 11. Stereo. Box 11008 37401. Network: ABC Information & Entertainment. Format: Adult rock. Target aud: 18-54; upscale, contemp adults. ♦Danny Howard, progmg dir.

Tennessee

*WDYN-FM— June 1, 1968: 89.7 mhz; 100 kw. 205 ft. TL: N35 10 17 W85 18 58. Stereo. 1815 Union Ave. 37404. Phone: (423) 493-4382. Phone: (423) 493-4383. Fax: (423) 493-4526. E-mail: wdyn@wdyn.com. Web Site: www.wdyn.com. Licensee: Tennessee Temple University. Format: Relg. News: 2 hrs wkly. Target aud: General; conservative Christians. ♦ Tommy L. Sneed, gen mgr & opns dir.

WFLI(AM)—See Lookout Mountain

WGOW(AM)— 1936: 1150 khz; 5 kw-D, 1 kw-N, DA-N. TL: N35 04 05 W85 20 04. Box 11202 37401. Secondary address: 821 Pineville Rd. 37405. Phone: (423) 756-6141. Fax: (423) 266-3629. Web Site: www.wgow.com. Licensee: Citadel Broadcasting Co. Group owner: Citadel Broadcasting Corp. (acq 5-30-00; grpsl). Rep: Christal, Reddy, Begley & McCormick. Format: News/talk. ♦ Dan Brown, pres, VP & gen mgr; Bill Lockhart, progmg dir.

WSKZ(FM)— Co-owned with WGOW(AM). November 1960: 106.5 mhz; 100 kw. 1,080 ft. TL: N35 09 42 W85 19 06. Stereo. Web Site: www.wskz.com. Format: Adult rock. ♦ Kelly McCoy, progmg dir.

WGOW-FM— (Soddy-Daisy). July 14, 1977: 102.3 mhz; 6 kw. 287 ft. TL: N35 11 45 W85 13 45. Stereo. Box 11202 37401. Secondary address: 821 Pineville Rd. 37405. Phone: (423) 756-6141. Fax: (423) 266-3629. Web Site: www.wgow.com. Licensee: Citadel Broadcasting Co. Group owner: Citadel Broadcasting Corp. (acq 5-30-00; grpsl). Format: News/talk. Target aud: 18-54; baby boomers. ♦ Dan Brown, gen mgr; Kennard Yamada, sls dir, sls dir & gen sls mgr; Bill Lockhart, progmg dir; Kevin West, news dir; Dave Fisher, chief of engrg.

WJOC(AM)— July 4, 1948: 1490 khz; 1 kw-U. TL: N35 03 07 W85 16 24. 805 Chickamauga Ave., Rossville, GA 30741. Phone: (706) 861-0800. Fax: (706) 861-2299. Web Site: www.wjoc.com. Licensee: Sara Margarett Fryar. (acq 8-11-97; $230,000). Network: USA. Format: Southern gospel, Christian mus. ♦ Trey Searcy, gen mgr, mus dir & news dir.

WJTT(FM)—See Red Bank

WLMR(AM)— 1961: 1450 khz; 1 kw-U. TL: N35 02 54 W85 16 26. 3809 Ringgold Rd. 37412. Phone: (423) 624-4200. Fax: (423) 624-4722. Web Site: www.wilkinsradio.com. Licensee: Grace Media Inc. Network: USA. Format: Contemp Christian, talk. Target aud: 25-54. ♦ Bob Wilkins, pres; LuAnn J. Wilkins, VP & prom VP; Mike King, stn mgr, progmg dir & news dir; Phil Patton, chief of engrg.

*WMBW(FM)— Aug 1, 1969: 88.9 mhz; 100 kw. 1,505 ft. TL: N34 57 43 W85 22 40. Stereo. Box 73026 37407. Phone: (423) 629-8900. Fax: (423) 629-0021. E-mail: wmbw@moody.edu. Web Site: www.wmbw.org. Licensee: Moody Bible Institute of Chicago. (group owner; acq 5-18-73). Network: Moody. Southmayd & Miller. Format: Educ, relg. News staff: one; News: 12 hrs wkly. Target aud: 25-54. Spec prog: Black one hr wkly. ♦ Dr. Joseph Stowell, pres; Leighton LeBoeuf, gen mgr & mktg dir; Andy Napier, prom dir, progmg dir & mus dir; Paul Martin, mus dir; David Morais, chief of engrg.

WMPZ(FM)— (Ringgold).GA Jan 1, 1995: 93.7 mhz; 3 kw. 328 ft. TL: N34 53 51 W85 10 25. 1305 Carter St. 37402. Phone: (423) 265-9494. Fax: (423) 266-2335. E-mail: jimii@brewerradio.com. Web Site: wmpz.com. Licensee: J.L. Brewer Broadcasting L.L.C. (acq 11-96). Network: ABC. Rep: D & R Radio. Format: Rhythm and blues, classic soul. Target aud: 25-54; adults. ♦ Jim Brewer II, pres, VP & gen mgr; Keith Landecker, opns mgr.

WNOO(AM)— June 1951: 1260 khz; 5 kw-D. TL: N35 03 08 W85 16 22. 1108 Hendricks St. 37406. Phone: (423) 698-8617. Fax: (423) 698-8796. Licensee: East Tennessee Radio Group III L.P. Group owner: Willis Broadcasting Corp. (acq 12-23-2004; $265,886). Format: Urban contemp. News staff: 4. Target aud: 25-54; mature Black adults & children. ♦ Charles Sanders, stn mgr.

WRXR-FM—See Rossville, GA

WSMC-FM—See Collegedale

*WUTC(FM)— March 1980: 88.1 mhz; 30 kw. 889 ft. TL: N35 12 28 W85 16 46. (CP: 30 kw). Stereo. 615 McCallie Ave. 37403. Phone: (423) 425-4756. Fax: (423) 425-2379. Web Site: www.wutc.org. Licensee: Board of Trustees of University of Tennessee. Network: NPR, PRI. Format: Jazz, blues , AAA. Target aud: General. ♦ John McCormack, gen mgr; Ken Dryden, dev dir & sls dir.

Church Hill

WEYE(FM)— (Surgoinsville). November 1990: 104.3 mhz; 4.1 kw. Ant 397 ft. TL: N36 32 05 W82 47 52. Stereo. Box 128 37642. Secondary address: 439 Richmond St. 37642. Phone: (423) 357-5601. Fax: (423) 357-3635. E-mail: w104@weye.us. Web Site: www.weye.us. Licensee: ASRadio LLC (acq 6-21-2005; $1.2 million). Network: USA. Rep: Rgnl Reps. Bryan Cave. Format: Southern gospel. Target aud: 25-54. ♦ Randall Seaver, stn mgr & progmg dir; Tony Cradic, gen sls mgr; Daryl Smith, chief of engrg.

WMCH(AM)— May 8, 1954: 1260 khz; 1 kw-D. TL: N36 31 15 W82 44 54. Box 128 37642. Phone: (423) 357-5601. Fax: (423) 357-3635. Web Site: www.weye.us. Licensee: Tri-City Radio L.L.C. (acq 10-11-01). Network: USA. Format: Gospel. Target aud: 25-54; Adult Audience. Spec prog: Farm programing 1hr wkly. ♦ Randall Seaver, gen mgr.

Clarksville

*WAPX-FM— Oct 1, 1984: 91.7 mhz; 3 kw. 160 ft. TL: N36 32 13 W87 21 24. Stereo. Box 4627, Austin Peay State Univ. 37044. Phone: (931) 221-7378. Fax: (931) 221-7265. Web Site: www.apsu.edu/comm_thea/student_activities/wapxfm.htm. Licensee: Austin Peay State University. Format: Consistently Diverse. News: 8 hrs wkly. Target aud: 18-34; college students & young professionals. Spec prog: Black 6 hrs, jazz 6 hrs wkly. ♦ Dr. David Michael von Palko, gen mgr.

*WAYQ(FM)— Oct 22, 2003: 88.3 mhz; 14 kw. Ant 745 ft. TL: N36 17 36 W87 18 21. 1012 McEwen Dr., Franklin 37067. Phone: (615) 261-9293. Fax: (615) 261-3967. Web Site: www.wayfm.com. Licensee: WAY-FM Media Group Inc. (group owner). Format: Christian hit radio. ♦ Matt Austin, gen mgr; B.J. O'Neil, gen sls mgr; Cliff Tredway, mus dir; Jeff Brown, news dir; Jim Turvaville, engrg dir.

WCTZ(AM)— Jan 24, 1980: 1550 khz; 2.5 kw-D, 250 w-N, DA-N. TL: N36 32 12 W87 22 24. Box 290099, Nashville 37217. Phone: (615) 645-1550. Fax: (615) 361-9873. E-mail: andreahutchison@cromwell.radio.com. Licensee: Bayard H. Walters. Group owner: The Cromwell Group Inc. (acq 10-17-91). Pepper & Corazzini. Format: Black gospel, talk. Target aud: 24-56; talk radio audience. ♦ Bayard Walters, pres; Bob Reich, sr VP & gen mgr; Jim Patrick, opns mgr.

WJZM(AM)— Oct 19, 1941: 1400 khz; 1 kw-U. TL: N36 30 57 W87 20 57. Box 648 37040. Secondary address: 925 Martin St. 37040. Phone: (931) 645-6414. Fax: (931) 551-8432. E-mail: 14jzm@wjzm.com. Web Site: www.wjzm.com. Licensee: Cumberland Radio Partners Inc. Format: News/talk, sports. News: 8 hrs wkly. Target aud: 25-60; blue collar, working women, businessmen. Spec prog: Relg. ♦ Hank Bonecutter, gen mgr, gen sls mgr & news dir; John Bastin, opns mgr; Ivan Davis, chief of engrg.

WKFN(AM)— Nov 12, 1954: 540 khz; 1 kw-D, 54.5 w-N. TL: N36 32 28 W87 19 33. 1640 Old Russelville Pike 37043. Phone: (931) 648-7720. Fax: (931) 648-7769. Licensee: Saga Communications of Tuckessee L.L.C. Group owner: Saga Communications Inc. (acq 2-1-2001; grpsl). Network: ABC Information & Entertainment. Format: Contemp Christian. News staff: 2; News: 36 hrs wkly. Target aud: 25-54. ♦ Susan Quesenberry, VP, gen mgr & prom mgr.

Cleveland

WALV(FM)—Listing follows WBAC(AM).

WBAC(AM)— June 18, 1945: 1340 khz; 1 kw-U. TL: N35 09 54 W84 51 13. 2640 Commerce Drive N.E. 37311. Phone: (423) 242-7656. Fax: (423) 472-5290. Web Site: www.wbacradio.com. Licensee: J.L. Brewer Broadcasting of Cleveland L.L.C. Group owner: Brewer Broadcasting Corp. (acq 6-2-98; $1.5 million with co-located FM). Network: ABC. Rep: D & R Radio. Format: News/talk. News staff: one; News: 16 hrs wkly. Target aud: 35-64. ♦ Jim Brewer Sr., pres; Jim Brewer II, VP; Don Schwartz, gen mgr; Mark Jacobus, gen sls mgr; Corky Whitlock, progmg dir; Mike Powers, news dir.

WALV(FM)— Co-owned with WBAC(AM). Feb 27, 1980: 95.3 mhz; 3.5 kw. 436 ft. TL: N35 09 54 W84 51 13. Stereo. Web Site: www.alive95.com. Rep: D & R Radio. Format: "Hot" adult contemp. News staff: one; News: .5 hrs wkly. Target aud: Adults; 18-49; 25-54. ♦ Duane Shannon, progmg dir; Ed Ramsey, mus dir & pub affrs dir.

WCLE(AM)— May 2, 1957: 1570 khz; 5 kw-D, 84 w-N. TL: N35 10 55 W84 50 55. Box 2695 37320. Phone: (423) 472-6700. Fax: (423) 476-4686. Licensee: Williams Communications Inc. (group owner; acq 8-8-02; $2.4 million. with WCLE-FM Calhoun). Greg Skall. Format: Gospel. Target aud: 25-54. Spec prog: Relg 6 hrs wkly. ♦ Walter Williams II, CEO.

WSMC-FM—See Collegedale

WUSY(FM)— Aug 1, 1961: 100.7 mhz; 100 kw. 1,191 ft. TL: N35 17 26 W85 17 10. Stereo. Box 8799, Chattanooga 37414. Secondary address: 7413 Old Lee Hwy., Chattanooga 37421. Phone: (423) 892-3333. Fax: (423) 899-7224. Fax: (423) 642-9329. Web Site: www.us101country.com. Licensee: Capstar TX L.P. Group owner: Clear Channel Communications Inc. (acq 8-7-00; grpsl). Format: Contemp country. ♦ Sammy George, gen mgr; Rhonda Rollins, gen sls mgr; Chris Van Dyke, progmg dir; Ed Buice, news dir; Andre Johnson, chief of engrg.

Clifton

WLVS-FM— 2002: 106.5 mhz; 3.8 kw. Ant 416 ft. TL: N35 28 41 W88 06 36. 624 Sam Philips St., Florence, AL 35630. Phone: (256) 764-8121. Fax: (256) 764-8169. Web Site: www.wxfl.com. Licensee: Gold Coast Broadcasting Co. (acq 8-3-00; $75,000. for 51% of CP). Format: Country. ♦ Nick Martin, gen mgr; Rocky Reich, sls dir; Gary Murdock, progmg mgr.

Clinton

*WDVX(FM)— November 1997: 89.9 mhz; 200 w. 1,960 ft. TL: N36 11 53 W84 13 51. Box 27568, Knoxville 37927. Phone: (865) 494-2020. Fax: (865) 494-3299. E-mail: mail@wdvx.com. Web Site: www.wdvx.com. Licensee: Cumberland Communities Communications Corp. Format: Americana mus. ♦ Tony Lawson, gen mgr.

*WYFC(FM)— July 4, 1966: 95.3 mhz; 540 w. 669 ft. TL: N36 04 21 W84 01 18. Stereo. 7901 Old Clinton Pike, Powell 37849. Phone: (865) 938-7843. Fax: (865) 938-7843. Web Site: www.bbnradio.com. Licensee: Bible Broadcasting Network Inc. (group owner; acq 8-18-89; $450,000; 9-5-89). Format: Traditional Christian. ♦ Lowell Davey, pres; Grant Bishop, stn mgr.

WYSH(AM)— November 1960: 1380 khz; 1 kw-D, 500 w-N, DA-N. TL: N36 06 48 W84 08 30. Stereo. Box 329, 111 Hillcrest Dr. 37717. Phone: (865) 457-1380. Fax: (865) 457-4440. E-mail: wysham@aol.com. Web Site: www.wyshradio.com. Licensee: Clinton Broadcasters Inc. (acq 6-10-91; 11-19-90). Network: AP Radio. Rep: Keystone (unwired net). Format: Classic country. News staff: one; News: 15 hrs wkly. Target aud: 25-54; families, blue collar to upper income. Spec prog: Relg 15 hrs wkly. ♦ Ronald C. Meredith Jr., pres, gen mgr & opns mgr.

Coalmont

WSGM(FM)— June 21, 1994: 104.7 mhz; 1 kw. 548 ft. TL: N35 20 22 W85 46 10. Stereo. Box 1269, Fire Tower Rd., Tracy City 37387. Phone: (931) 592-7777. Fax: (931) 592-7778. E-mail: wsgmfm@hotmail.com. Licensee: Cumberland Communication Corp. Donald E. Martin. Format: Div, relg, gospel. News: 30 hrs wkly. Target aud: General; interested in community affrs. ♦ Dr. Byron Harbolt, pres, exec VP & stn mgr; Sam Harbolt, sr VP; Geniveve Harbolt, VP; Tom Wiseman, chief of engrg.

Collegedale

*WSMC-FM— November 1961: 90.5 mhz; 100 kw. 554 ft. TL: N35 01 20 W85 04 32. (CP: 1,029 ft. TL: N35 15 20 W85 13 34). Stereo. Box 870 37315. Phone: (423) 236-2905. Fax: (423) 236-1905. Web Site: www.wsmc.org. Licensee: Southern Adventist University. Network: Network: PRI, NPR. Format: Class, news. Target aud: 25-54. ♦ Gordon Bietz, pres; David Brooks, gen mgr; Myrna Ott, opns dir & opns mgr.

Collierville

WCRV(AM)— Oct 1, 1966: 640 khz; 50 kw-D, 500 w-N, DA-N. TL: N34 59 35 W89 53 58. 555 Perkins Rd. Ext., Memphis 38117. Phone: (901) 763-4640. Fax: (901) 763-4920. Licensee: Bott Broadcasting. (group owner) Network: USA. Format: Christian info. Target aud: 25-54; family oriented. ♦ Richard P. Bott, pres; Richard Bott II, VP; Shirley Gossett, opns mgr; Sunny Caldwell, gen mgr & gen sls mgr; Byron Tyler, progmg dir.

Stations in the U.S.   Tennessee

Developers & Brokers of Radio Properties

contact American Media Services at our suite:
Philadelphia Marriott Downtown
215-625-2900
843-972-2200
americanmediaservices.com
Charleston, SC
Dallas, TX · Chicago, Il · Austin, TX

American Media Services, LLC

Collinwood

WMSR-FM— July 1991: 94.9 mhz; 7.7 kw. Ant 594 ft. TL: N35 01 46 W87 47 07. 122 W. Tombigbee, Florence, AL 35630. Phone: (256) 766-9436. Fax: (256) 760-9454. E-mail: thechief@star94.net. Web Site: www.star94.net. Licensee: Malkan Broadcasting L.P. Format: Top-40. News: 8 hrs wkly. ♦ Glen Powers, CEO & pres; Ann Southern, CFO; Sherrie Powers, gen mgr; Robin Mitchell, sls VP.

Colonial Heights

WPWT(AM)— Dec 31, 1984: 870 khz; 10 kw-D. TL: N36 27 40 W82 27 12. Box 2061, Bristol 37621. Secondary address: 340 Edgemont Ave., Suite 100, Bristol 3720. Phone: (423) 878-6279. Fax: (423) 878-6520. Web Site: www.powertalk870.com. Licensee: Appalachian Educational Communication Corp. Format: Conservative talk radio. News staff: one; News: 5 hrs wkly. Spec prog: Health Education one hr wkly. ♦ Kenneth C. Hill, gen mgr; Timothy Hill, sls VP; Barry Brickey, prom dir; Mathew Hill, progmg dir; Art Countiss, news dir; Bill Sutton, chief of engrg.

WRZK(FM)— Apr 4, 1997: 95.9 mhz; 7.4 kw. Ant 1,253 ft. TL: N36 31 36 W82 35 13. Stereo. 222 Commerce St., Kingsport 37660. Phone: (423) 246-9578. Fax: (423) 247-9836. E-mail: dmurray@wrzk.com. Web Site: www.wrzk.com. Licensee: Murray Communications. Network: ABC. Rep: McGavren Guild. Pepper & Corazzini. Format: Modern rock. News staff: 2. Target aud: 18-44; general. ♦ David Widener, exec VP & gen mgr; Scott Onksi, progmg dir.

Columbia

*WAYM(FM)— 1992: 88.7 mhz; 16.5 kw. 508 ft. TL: N35 49 27 W86 49 28. Stereo. 1012 McEwen Dr., Franklin 37067. Phone: (615) 261-9293. Fax: (615) 261-3967. E-mail: wayfm@wayfm.com. Web Site: www.wayfm.com. Licensee: WAY-FM Media Group Inc. (group owner; acq 3-13-91; FTR: 4-1-91). Format: Christian hit radio. Target aud: 12-34; females. ♦ Matt Austin, gen mgr.

WKOM(FM)—Listing follows WKRM(AM).

WKRM(AM)— Nov 25, 1946: 1340 khz; 1 kw-U. TL: N35 36 38 W87 03 22. Box 1377 38402. Secondary address: 315 W. 7th St. 38401. Phone: (931) 388-3636. Fax: (931) 381-1017. Licensee: Robert M. McKay III. (acq 12-26-89). Network: ABC. Format: Adult contemp. News staff: one; News: 8 hrs wkly. Target aud: 25-54. Spec prog: Relg 4 hrs wkly. ♦ Robert M. McKay III, pres & gen mgr.

WKOM(FM)—Co-owned with WKRM(AM). Jan 1, 1967: 101.7 mhz; 4.1 kw. 400 ft. TL: N35 37 04 W87 02 34. Stereo. (Acq 9-1-72). Network: Network: CBS, Motor Racing Net. Format: Pure Gold. News staff: one; News: 8 hrs wkly. Target aud: 30-50. ♦ Robert McKay III, CEO.

WMCP(AM)— Nov 12, 1956: 1280 khz; 5 kw-D, 500 w-N, DA-N. TL: N35 37 08 W86 58 52. Box 711 38402. Secondary address: 1st Farmer & Merchants Bank Bldg., 816 S. Garden, Suite 306 38401. Phone: (931) 388-3241. Fax: (931) 381-2510. Licensee: Maury County Boosters Corp. (acq 12-79). Network: ABC Information & Entertainment. Format: Country. News staff: one; News: 13 hrs wkly. Target aud: 18 plus. Spec prog: Farm 4 hrs weekly. ♦ Edna Williford, pres; Mack Shaw, VP & gen mgr.

WMRB(AM)— Aug 14, 1982: 910 khz; 500 w-D, 88 w-N. TL: N35 36 24 W87 01 30. 210 W. 8th St., Suite 5 38401. Phone: (931) 381-7100. Fax: (931) 381-0088. Web Site: www.wmrb910am.som. Licensee: Ogilvie Family Ministries Inc. (acq 7-3-97; $50,000). Rep: Dora-Clayton. Format: Gospel, Black, relg. Target aud: General; Christian families. ♦ Trent Ogilvie, gen mgr & opns mgr.

Cookeville

WGIC(FM)—Listing follows WHUB(AM).

WGSQ(FM)—Listing follows WPTN(AM).

*WHRS(FM)— Oct 1, 1996: 91.7 mhz; 500 w. 384 ft. TL: N36 08 34 W85 28 02. 630 Mainstream Dr., Nashville 37228-1204. Phone: (615) 760-2903. Fax: (615) 760-2904. E-mail: talkback@wpln.org. Web Site: www.wpln.org. Licensee: Nashville Public Radio. Format: Class, news. Spec prog: Bluegrass one hr, song writers one hr wkly. ♦ William Ivey, chmn; Robert Gordon, gen mgr.

WHUB(AM)— July 20, 1940: 1400 khz; 1 kw-U. TL: N36 10 25 W85 30 40. 698 S. Willow Ave. 38501. Phone: (931) 526-7144. Fax: (931) 528-8400. Licensee: Clear Channel Radio Licenses Inc. Group owner: Clear Channel Communications Inc. (acq 11-21-97; grpsl). Network: CBS. Format: Classic country, Southern gospel. News staff: one; News: 18 hrs wkly. Target aud: General. Spec prog: Sports 10 hrs, gospel 11 hrs wkly. ♦ Dave Thomas, gen mgr; Marty McFly, opns dir; Jim Stapleton, sls dir & natl sls mgr; Lehra Heidel, mktg dir; Lehar Heidel, prom dir; Jim Herrin, news dir; Mike Dinger, mus dir & chief of engrg.

WGIC(FM)—Co-owned with WHUB(AM). Mar 26, 1964: 98.5 mhz; 50 kw. 492 ft. TL: N36 08 34 W85 28 02. Stereo. E-mail: email@magic985.com. Web Site: www.magic985.com. Network: ABC. Rep: Clear Channel. Format: Hot adult Contemp. News staff: one; News: 8 hrs wkly. ♦ Marty McFly, progmg dir.

WPTN(AM)— July 10, 1962: 780 khz; 1 kw-D. TL: N36 09 30 W85 31 15. 698 S. Willow 38501. Phone: (931) 526-7144. Fax: (931) 528-8400. Licensee: Clear Channel Radio Licenses Inc. Group owner: Clear Channel Communications Inc. (acq 11-21-97; grpsl). Network: ABC Information & Entertainment. Rep: Clear Channel. Dow, Lohnes & Albertson. Format: News/talk, oldies. Target aud: General. ♦ David Roederer, gen mgr; Bruce Welker, sls VP; Lehra Mayfield, prom VP; Marty Selby, progmg VP; Jim Herrin, news dir; Dave Johnson, pub affrs dir.

WGSQ(FM)—Co-owned with WPTN(AM). Mar 8, 1963: 94.7 mhz; 100 kw. 1,319 ft. TL: N36 10 26 W85 20 37. Stereo. Format: Country. News staff: 2; News: 28 hrs wkly.

*WTTU(FM)— May 22, 1972: 88.5 mhz; 2.25 kw. 168 ft. TL: N36 10 26 W85 30 12. (CP: 2 kw horiz, ant 164 ft.). Stereo. Box 5113, University Ctr., Dixie Ave. 38505. Phone: (931) 372-3688. Fax: (931) 372-6225. E-mail: wttu_88.5@hotmail.com. Licensee: Tennessee Technological University. Format: Alternative. News staff: one; News: 2 hrs wkly. Target aud: 14-25. Spec prog: Jazz 3 hrs, metal 3 hrs, folk 3 hrs, hip-hop/rap 3 hrs, punk 3 hrs, techno 3 hrs, blues 3 hrs wkly.

*WWOG(FM)— 1994: 90.9 mhz; 40 kw. Ant 697 ft. TL: N36 11 05 W85 22 30. Box 1423, King of Kings Radio Network, Somerset, KY 42502. Phone: (606) 679-6300. Fax: (606) 679-1342. E-mail: david.carr@gte.net. Web Site: www.kingofkingsradio.net. Licensee: Somerset Educational Broadcasting Foundation. Format: Conservative, traditional relg, educ. ♦ S. David Carr, gen mgr; Carolyn Jones, progmg dir; Marvin Whittaker, chief of engrg.

Copperhill

WLSB(AM)— Dec 2, 1958: 1400 khz; 1 kw-U. TL: N34 58 04 W84 19 39. Box 430 37317. Phone: (423) 496-3311. Fax: (423) 496-2635. E-mail: wlsb@bellsouth.net. Web Site: www.wolfcreekbroadcasting.com. Licensee: Copper Basin Broadcasting Co., Inc. (acq 9-26-02). Format: Country, bluegrass. ♦ Rebecca St. John, stn mgr.

Covington

WKBL(AM)— Aug 16, 1954: 1250 khz; 800 w-D, 106 w-N. TL: N35 35 10 W89 38 35. 101 WKBL Dr. 38019. Phone: (901) 476-7129. Fax: (901) 476-7120. E-mail: q935@covingtones.com. Web Site: www.q935.com.

Licensee: Covington Broadcasting Inc. (acq 2-22-99; $600,000 with co-located FM). Network: Jones Radio Networks. Format: Classic country. News staff: one; News: 14 hrs wkly. Target aud: 21-55. Spec prog: Black 12 hrs wkly. ♦ Bob Lakey, CEO & pres; Jimmy Hicks, gen mgr.

WKBQ(FM)—Co-owned with WKBL(AM). Aug 31, 1965: 93.5 mhz; 6 kw. 328 ft. TL: N35 35 12 W89 38 21. Stereo. Web Site: www.q935.com. Network: Network: AP Radio, Jones Radio Networks. Format: Adult contemp. News staff: one; News: 14 hrs wkly.

Cowan

WZYX(AM)— Mar 10, 1957: 1440 khz; 5 kw-D, 100 w-N. TL: N35 09 39 W86 01 51. Stereo. 540 W. Cumberland St. 37318-0398. Phone: (931) 967-7471. Phone: (931) 967-7472. Fax: (931) 962-1440. Web Site: www.wzyxradio.com. Licensee: Tims Ford Broadcasting Co. Inc. (acq 4-26-2004). Network: Network: CNN Radio, Westwood One NBC Radio. Format: Country, oldies, talk. News staff: one; News: 15 hrs wkly. Target aud: 35-55; middle-of-the-road working people. Spec prog: Talk, gospel 10 hrs, farm 2 hrs, relg 12 hrs wkly. ♦ Jeff Pennington, VP; Mary Lou Garner, CEO, pres & stn mgr.

Crossville

WAEW(AM)— 1952: 1330 khz; 1 kw-D. TL: N35 56 59 W85 02 08. (CP: TL: N35 57 01 W85 02 09). 961 Miller Ave. 38555. Phone: (931) 484-5115. Phone: (931) 484-9014. Fax: (931) 456-1195. E-mail: waew@clearchannel.com. Web Site: www.waewradio.com. Licensee: Peg Broadcasting Crossville LLC (group owner; acq 10-1-2003; grpsl). Network: ABC Information & Entertainment. Format: Oldies. News staff: one; News: 4 hrs wkly. ♦ Jeff Shaw, gen mgr.

WCSV(AM)— June 15, 1968: 1490 khz; 1 kw-U. TL: N35 56 46 W85 02 13. (CP: TL: N35 57 01 W85 02 09). 961 Miller Ave. 38555. Phone: (931) 484-5115. Fax: (931) 456-1195. E-mail: wcsv@clearchannel.com. Licensee: Peg Broadcasting Crossville LLC (group owner; acq 10-1-2003; grpsl). Network: ABC. Format: Sports. ♦ Jeff Shaw, gen mgr.

*WMKW(FM)— November 1996: 89.3 mhz; 500 w. 1,395 ft. TL: N35 46 38 W84 58 34. 1920 E. 24th Street Pl., Chattanooga 37404. Secondary address: Box 73026, Chattanooga 37407. Phone: 423-629-8900. Fax: (423) 629-0021. Web Site: www.moody.edu. Licensee: The Moody Bible Institute of Chicago. Southmayd & Miller. Format: Educ, relg, news/talk. Target aud: General. Spec prog: Black 3 hrs wkly. ♦ Dr. Joseph Stowell, pres; Leighton LeBoeuf, gen mgr & mktg dir; Andy Napier, prom dir, progmg dir & film buyer; Paul Martin, mus dir; David Morais, chief of engrg.

WOWF(FM)— June 15, 1990: 102.5 mhz; 25 kw. 308 ft. TL: N36 01 22 W85 00 07. Stereo. 961 Miller Ave. 38555. Phone: (931) 707-1102. Fax: (931) 707-1220. E-mail: steve@pegbroadcasting.com. Web Site: www.1025wowcountry.com. Licensee: Peg Broadcasting Crossville LLC (group owner; acq 1-3-01; $2.5 million). Network: Jones Radio Networks. Rgnl Reps. Format: Country. News staff: 2; News: 10 hrs wkly. Target aud: 25 -54 adults; general. ♦ Jeffrey H. Shaw, gen mgr; Steve J. Sweeney, gen sls mgr; Jeffrey Shaw, mktg mgr & pub affrs dir; Gordon Stack, progmg dir & progmg mgr; Christy Lewis, news dir.

WPBX(FM)— May 12, 1967: 99.3 mhz; 6 kw. 259 ft. TL: N35 57 01 W85 02 09. Stereo. 961 Miller Ave. 38555. Phone: (931) 484-5115. Fax: (931) 707-1220. E-mail: steve@pegbroadcasting.com. Web Site: mix993.net. Licensee: Peg Broadcasting Crossville LLC (group owner; acq 10-1-2003; grpsl). Network: ABC. Rep: Clear Channel. Format: CHR. News staff: one. ♦ Jeffrey H. Shaw, gen mgr; Steve J. Sweeney, gen sls mgr; Jeffrey Shaw, mktg mgr; Gordon Stack, progmg dir & chief of engrg; Christy Lewis, news dir.

Dayton

WDNT(AM)— Dec 6, 1957: 1280 khz; 1 kw-D, 345 w-N. TL: N35 28 12 W85 02 15. 2640 Commerce Dr., N.E., Cleveland 37311. Phone: (423) 242-7656. Fax: (423) 472-5290. Web Site: www.wbacradio.com. Licensee: J.L. Brewer Broadcasting of Cleveland LLC. Group owner:

Broadcasting & Cable Yearbook 2006

D-459

Tennessee

Brewer Broadcasting Corp. (acq 7-1-2002; grpsl). Network: ABC. Rep: D & R Radio. Format: MOR. News staff: one; News: 26 hrs wkly. Target aud: 45 plus. ♦ James L. Brewer, pres; James L. Brewer II, VP; Don Schwartz, gen mgr; Mark Jacobus, gen sls mgr; Corky Whitlock, progmg dir; Mike Powers, news dir.

WDNT-FM— July 1, 1976: 104.9 mhz; 1.3 kw. Ant 712 ft. TL: N35 29 31 W85 02 59. Stereo. Web Site: www.oldies1049.com. Rep: D & R Radio. Format: Oldies. News: one hr wkly. Target aud: 35-64. ♦ Max Hackett, progmg dir.

Dickson

WDKN(AM)— Jan 1, 1955: 1260 khz; 5 kw-D. TL: N36 06 31 W87 22 14. 106 E. College St. 37055. Phone: (615) 446-4000. Phone: (615) 446-0752. Fax: (615) 446-9681. Web Site: www.wdkn.com. Licensee: Edmission & Eubank Communications Inc. (acq 6-15-87; $220,000;. FTR: 5-18-87). McCampbell & Young, P. Format: C&W, news/talk. News: 3 hrs wkly. Target aud: General. Spec prog: Relg 12 hrs wkly. ♦ Tommy Edmisson, pres; Oscar Eubank, VP; Leroy Kennell, gen mgr.

*WNRZ(FM)— Apr 7, 1997: 91.5 mhz; 8 kw. Ant 262 ft. TL: N36 00 36 W87 30 47. Stereo. 333 Murfreesboro Rd., Nashville 37210. Phone: (615) 248-1689. Fax: (615) 248-7786. Web Site: www.wnrz.com. Licensee: Trevecca Nazarene University Inc. Format: Christian, progsv contemp. Target aud: 14-28; Christians. ♦ Dr. Dan Boone, pres; Mark Myers, CFO; David Deese, gen mgr; Paul Eby, stn mgr; Dave Queen, opns dir.

WQZQ(FM)— Apr 27, 1964: 102.5 mhz; 37 kw. 500 ft. TL: N36 12 35 W87 20 16. Stereo. Box 150846, Nashville 37215. Phone: (615) 399-1029. Fax: (615) 436-7737. E-mail: programming@1025theparty.com. Web Site: www.1025theparty.com. Licensee: Montgomery Broadcasting. Group owner: The Cromwell Group Inc. (acq 1990). Pepper & Corazzini. Format: CHR. Target aud: 18-34; S. KY residents. ♦ Bayard H. Walters, pres; Bob Reich, stn mgr; Jim Patrick, opns mgr; Shaunna Conner, prom dir; Russell Schenek, progmg dir; Ted Randall, chief of engrg.

Dresden

WCDZ(FM)— Apr 10, 1992: 95.1 mhz; 21.5 kw. Ant 276 ft. TL: N36 15 50 W88 40 03. Box 318, 1410 N. Lindell St., Martin 38237. Phone: (731) 364-9595. Fax: (731) 587-5079. Web Site: www.wcmt.com. Licensee: Thunderbolt Broadcasting Co. Group owner: Thunderbolt Broadcasting Co./Gibson County Broadcasting (acq 1-28-94; $320,000;. FTR: 2-21-94). Womble, Carlyle, Sandridge & Rice. Format: Oldies. News staff: one; News: one hr wkly. Spec prog: Gospel one hs wkly. ♦ Paul Tinkle, CEO, pres & gen mgr; Cindy Prince, opns VP; Misty Menees, opns dir.

Dunlap

WSDQ(AM)— Nov 1, 1980: 1190 khz; 5 kw-D. TL: N35 21 41 W85 22 33. 16 Main St. N. 37327-6129. Phone: (423) 949-4114. Fax: (423) 949-5143. E-mail: wsdq@bledsoe.net. Licensee: Rodgson Inc. (acq 7-18-02; $165,000). Network: ABC Information & Entertainment. Format: Country, bluegrass. Spec prog: Gospel 7 hrs wkly. ♦ Charles Rodgers, pres; Earl Nunley, gen mgr.

Dyer

WLSQ-FM— Feb 1, 1995: 94.3 mhz; 6 kw. 328 ft. TL: N36 06 12 W89 07 45. Box 112, Humboldt 38343. Secondary address: 2603 Spangler Park Dr., Humboldt 38343. Phone: (731) 784-1053. Fax: (731) 784-4033. Licensee: F. Darrell Boyd/Boyd Enterprises Inc. Format: CHR. Target aud: 18-49. ♦ Darrell Boyd, gen mgr.

Dyersburg

WASL(FM)—Listing follows WTRO(AM).

*WKNQ(FM)— Oct 30, 1992: 90.7 mhz; 100 kw. 373 ft. TL: N36 06 00 W89 29 12. Stereo. Box 241880, Memphis 38124. Secondary address: 900 Getwell Rd., Memphis 38111. Phone: (901) 325-6544. Fax: (901) 325-6506. Web Site: www.wknofm.org. Licensee: Mid-South Public Communication Foundation. Network: Network: NPR, PRI. Schwartz, Woods & Miller. Format: News/talk. News staff: one; News: 76 hrs wkly. Target aud: 35 plus. ♦ Michael LaBonia, pres; Dan Campbell, gen mgr; Darel Snodgrass, opns mgr; Charles McLarty, dev dir. Co-owned TV: *WKNO-TV affil

WTRO(AM)— July 13, 1946: 1450 khz; 1 kw-U. TL: N36 03 02 W89 22 07. Box 100 38025. Secondary address: One Radio Rd. 38024. Phone: (731) 285-1450. Phone: (731) 285-1339. Fax: (731) 287-0100. Web Site: www.wasl.net. Licensee: Dr. Pepper/Pepsi Cola Bottling Co. of Dyersburg Inc. (acq 1991). Bryan Cave. Format: Oldies. ♦ Charles W. Maxey, exec VP, gen mgr & gen sls mgr; Steve James, progmg dir.

WASL(FM)—Co-owned with WTRO(AM). July 1, 1968: 100.1 mhz; 26 kw. Ant 676 ft. TL: N36 06 00 W89 29 12. Stereo. Web Site: www.wasl.net. Network: ABC. Format: Hot adult contemp. News: 5 hrs wkly. Target aud: 18-54.

East Ridge

WOGT(FM)— Nov 9, 1990: 107.9 mhz; 25 kw. Ant 328 ft. TL: N35 07 33 W85 17 25. Box 11202, Chattanooga 37401. Phone: (423) 756-6141. Fax: (423) 756-0292. Web Site: www.1079dukefm.com. Licensee: Citadel Broadcasting Co. Group owner: Citadel Broadcasting Corp. (acq 5-30-00; grpsl). Format: Country. ♦ Dan Brown, gen mgr.

Elizabethton

WBEJ(AM)— July 1946: 1240 khz; 1 kw-U. TL: N36 20 07 W82 13 03. 626 1/2 E. Elk Ave. 37643. Phone: (423) 542-2184. Fax: (423) 542-2185. E-mail: wbej@planetc.com. Web Site: www.wbej.com. Licensee: CB Radio Inc. (acq 9-24-82; $335,000; 10-18-82). Network: Westwood One. Format: Country. News staff: one; News: 3 hrs wkly. Target aud: 25-49. ♦ Don Crisp, pres; Cleo Reed, VP & gen mgr; David A. Miller, opns dir, dev dir & gen sls mgr.

WHHQ(AM)— Nov 11, 1964: . Stn currently dark 1520 khz; 1 kw-D, 500 w-CH. TL: N36 21 32 W82 13 53. Box 388, Elizabethtont 37644. Phone: (423) 543-6875. E-mail: whhq1520@hotmail.com. Licensee: Mediatrix SC Inc. Cordon & Kelly. ♦ Dennis J. Kelly, pres.

WTZR(FM)— May 17, 1968: 99.3 mhz; 3.6 kw. Ant 810 ft. TL: N36 24 07 W82 12 12. Stereo. Box 1389, Bristol, VA 24203. Secondary address: 901 E. Valley Dr., Bristol, VA 24201. Phone: (276) 669-8112. Fax: (276) 669-0541. Web Site: www.mix993.com. Licensee: Bristol Broadcasting Co. Group owner: Bristol Broadcasting Co. Inc. (acq 2-13-97; $3 million). Rep: Christal. Format: Alternative rock. Target aud: 18-49. ♦ W.L. Nininger, pres & gen mgr; Bruce Clark, stn mgr, prom dir & progmg dir; Winnie Quaintance, gen sls mgr; Chuck Lawson, chief of engrg.

*WUMC(FM)— 1999: 90.5 mhz; 500 w. -285 ft. TL: N36 17 58 W82 17 28. Box 9, Milligan College 37682. Phone: (423) 461-8464. Phone: (423) 461-8700. Licensee: Milligan College. Format: Contemp hits, contemp Christian music. ♦ Carrie Swanay, gen mgr.

Englewood

WENR(AM)— Apr 21, 1967: 1090 khz; 1 kw-D. TL: N35 25 35 W84 30 57. Box 676, Etowah 37331-0676. Phone: (423) 263-5555. Fax: (423) 263-2555. Licensee: Paul Wilson dba 1090 Radio, a Tennessee sole proprietorship (acq 10-2-98; $75,000). Format: Gospel. ♦ Carolyne Wilson, gen mgr.

Erwin

WEMB(AM)— May 17, 1956: 1420 khz; 5 kw-D. TL: N36 06 58 W82 26 49. Box 280, 101 Riverview Rd. 37650. Phone: (423) 743-6123. Phone: (423) 743-6124. Fax: (423) 743-6122. Licensee: WEMB Inc. (acq 4-1-61). Network: ABC Information & Entertainment. Format: Country, gospel, sports. Spec prog: Bluegrass 2 hrs, gospel 10 hrs wkly. ♦ Jim Crawford, pres & gen mgr; Charles W. Ray, opns mgr, progmg dir & chief of engrg; Kathy Thornberry, news dir.

WXIS(FM)—Co-owned with WEMB(AM). Nov 21, 1968: 103.9 mhz; 2.5 kw. 2,600 ft. TL: N36 08 15 W82 23 00. Stereo. Phone: (423) 743-7655. Network: ABC. Format: Rhythmic. Target aud: 12-44. ♦ Todd Ambrose, progmg dir.

Etowah

WCPH(AM)— 1955: 1220 khz; 1 kw-D, 109 w-N. TL: N35 19 15 W84 30 34. Box 676 37331. Phone: (423) 263-5555. Fax: (423) 263-2555. Licensee: Starr Mountain Broadcasting Co. (acq 3-18-97; $39,000). Format: News/talk, sports, easy listening mus. ♦ Carolyne Wilson, gen mgr.

WLLJ(FM)— 1977: 103.1 mhz; 50 kw. 492 ft. TL: N35 27 24 W84 40 43. Stereo. Box 9396, Chattanooga 37412. Secondary address: Box 212, McDonald 37353. Phone: (423) 892-1200. Fax: (423) 892-1633. E-mail: debbie@j103.com. Web Site: www.j103.com. Licensee: Friendship Broadcasting LLC. (acq 2-13-98). Network: Salem Radio Network. Format: Adult Contemp, Christian. News staff: one; News: 2 hrs wkly. Target aud: Female; 18-45. ♦ Bob Lubell, CEO & pres; Dave Skinner, CFO; Debbie Lubell, gen mgr & mktg dir; Elizabeth Gearu, chief of engrg.

Fairview

WPFD(AM)— May 28, 1982: 850 khz; 500 w-D. TL: N36 00 29 W87 08 38. 1074 Hwy. 96 N. 37062. Phone: (615) 799-8585. Fax: (615) 799-2999. Licensee: Robert Lee Martin, trustee. Format: Country. Target aud: 18-54. ♦ Sam Warden, pres; Chuck Hussey, gen mgr, mus dir & news dir; John Almon, chief of engrg.

Farragut

WMTY(AM)— Nov 10, 1988: 670 khz; 500 w-D. TL: N35 53 12 W84 14 48. Stereo. 517 Watts Rd., Knoxville 37922. Phone: (865) 671-7419. Fax: (865) 675-4859. Licensee: Horne Radio L.L.C. Group owner: Horne Radio Group (acq 1999; $275,000). Network: USA. Target aud: 25-54; upscale adults. ♦ Doug Horne, pres.

Fayetteville

WEKR(AM)— Oct 1, 1948: 1240 khz; 1 kw-U. TL: N35 09 28 W86 35 25. Box 656 37334. Secondary address: 7 Boonshill Rd. 37334. Phone: (931) 433-3545. Fax: (931) 438-0620. Licensee: Joseph D. Young, Wanda Young & Mary Elizabeth Miller. (acq 2-22-94; $194,000; 3-21-94). Network: Motor Racing Net. Format: Country, Southern gospel, sports, ESPN radio. News staff: one; News: 5 hrs wkly. Target aud: 25 plus; general. Spec prog: Farm one hr wkly. ♦ Joseph D. Young, CEO; Al Lawrence, stn mgr, chief of opns, gen sls mgr, progmg dir & pub affrs dir; Marie Caldwell, prom dir & adv mgr.

WYTM-FM— Mar 27, 1970: 105.5 mhz; 3 kw. 295 ft. TL: N35 07 37 W86 34 47. (CP: 2.25 kw, ant 495 ft.). Stereo. 76 Milano Rd. 37334. Phone: (931) 433-1531. Fax: (931) 433-4110. Licensee: Time Broadcasters Inc. Format: Country. ♦ Joseph D. Young, pres & gen mgr; Debbie Kawiecki, opns mgr.

Franklin

WAKM(AM)— Mar 18, 1953: 950 khz; 5 kw-D, 80 w-N. TL: N35 57 25 W86 50 03. (CP: 2.5 kw-D). 222 Mallory Station Rd. 37065. Phone: (615) 794-1594. Fax: (615) 794-1595. E-mail: wakm@worldnet.att.net. Licensee: Franklin Radio Associates Inc. (acq 10-1-82; $310,600; 10-18-82). Network: CNN Radio. Format: Country, news/talk. News staff: 2; News: 14 hrs wkly. Target aud: 24 plus; community interested adults. Spec prog: Relg 6 hrs, NASCAR racing 6 hrs wkly. ♦ James H. Hayes, CFO; Linda Jackson Carden, sls dir; Tom Lawrence, pres, gen mgr & gen sls mgr; Darrell Williams, progmg dir; Charles Dibrell, news dir; Jim Hayes, chief of engrg.

WHEW(AM)— Feb 1, 1969: 1380 khz; 2.8 kw-D, 500 w-N, DA-N. TL: N35 54 22 W86 54 21. 1811 Carters Creek Pike 37064. Phone: (615) 592-0595. E-mail: laley1330@aol.com. Licensee: SG Communications Inc. (acq 7-29-99; $208,398). Network: CNN en Espanol. Format: Spanish, sports, news/talk. News staff: one. Target aud: General; Hispanics. ♦ Paul Fink, gen mgr.

WRLT(FM)— Nov 16, 1961: 100.1 mhz; 3 kw. 1,134 ft. TL: N36 02 06 W86 50 54. Stereo. 1310 Clinton St., Suite 200, Nashville 37203. Phone: (615) 242-5600. Fax: (615) 523-2153. E-mail: comments@wrlt.com. Web Site: www.wrlt.com. Licensee: Tuned In Broadcasting Inc. (acq 1996). Network: ABC. Rep: Roslin. Shaw Pittman. Format: AAA. Target aud: 25-44. Spec prog: Jazz 2 hrs, new age 2 hrs, blues 2 hrs wkly. ♦ Lester Turner Jr., CEO, chmn & pres; Fred Buc, gen mgr; Laurel Creech, prom dir; David Hall, progmg dir.

Gallatin

WGFX(FM)— Dec 1, 1960: 104.5 mhz; 49 kw. 1,312 ft. TL: N36 16 05 W86 47 16. Stereo. 506 2nd Ave. S., Nashville 37210. Phone: (615) 244-9533. Fax: (615) 259-1271. Web Site: www.104thezone.com. Licensee: Citadel Broadcasting Co. Group owner: Citadel Broadcasting Corp. (acq 4-26-01; grpsl). Rep: Katz Radio. Kaye, Scholer, Fierman, Hays & Handler. Format: Sports/talk. Target aud: 18-49. ♦ Ken Bailey, gen mgr.

Stations in the U.S.

Tennessee

Developers & Brokers of Radio Properties
contact American Media Services at our suite:
Philadelphia Marriott Downtown
215-625-2900
843-972-2200
americanmediaservices.com
Charleston, SC
Dallas, TX · Chicago, Il · Austin, TX
American Media Services, LLC

WHIN(AM)— Aug 2, 1948: 1010 khz; 5 kw-D. TL: N36 26 00 W86 28 00. Stereo. Box 1685 37066. Phone: (615) 451-0450. Phone: (615) 451-0451. Fax: (615) 452-9446. E-mail: whinam@comcast.net. Licensee: WHIN Inc. (acq 10-84). Format: Country. News staff: one; News: 14 hrs wkly. Target aud: 25-54; upper middle to lower middle income. Spec prog: Black 2 hrs, farm 5 hrs wkly. ◆Jack Williams, pres & gen mgr.

WMRO(AM)— Feb 19, 1994: 1560 khz; 1 kw-D, 3 w-N. TL: N36 24 03 W86 27 03. Box 1445 37066. Phone: (615) 451-2131. Fax: (615) 452-0641. E-mail: wmroam@bellsouth.net. Licensee: Classic Broadcasting Inc. (acq 10-28-93; $40,000). Network: Network: Westwood One, CNN Radio. . Miller & Neeley. News staff: 2; News: 5 hrs wkly. Target aud: 25-65; middle to upper class adults. Spec prog: Religion 8 hrs wkly. ◆Scott Bailey, gen mgr.

*WVCP(FM)— Jan 4, 1979: 88.5 mhz; 1 kw. 390 ft. TL: N36 28 02 W86 28 35. Stereo. 1480 Nashville Pike, Suite 101, Ramer Bldg. 37066. Phone: (615) 230-3618. Fax: (615) 230-4803. E-mail: holly.nimmo@volstate.edu/wvcp. Web Site: www.volstate.edu. Licensee: Volunteer State Community College. Format: Black, CHR, adult contemp, oldies. News: 5 hrs wkly. Target aud: General. Spec prog: Black 8 hrs, metal 15 hrs, gospel 6 hrs, bluegrass 2 hrs wkly. ◆Dr. Warren R. Nichols, pres; Howard Espravnik, gen mgr; Holly Nimmo, opns dir.

WYXE(AM)— Nov 1, 1966: . Stn currently dark 1130 khz; 2.3 kw-D. TL: N36 24 38 W86 27 16. 506 Red River Rd. 37066. Phone: (615) 366-7366. Licensee: Jon Gary Enterprises Inc. (acq 3-31-2003). ◆Richard D. Deck Jr., gen mgr.

Gatlinburg

WSEV-FM— January 1983: 105.5 mhz; 650 w. 964 ft. TL: N35 42 13 W83 33 57. Stereo. 415 Middle Creek Rd., Sevierville 37862. Phone: (865) 525-1060. Fax: (865) 429-2601. E-mail: etrg@siviernct.com. Licensee: East Tennessee Radio Group L.P. (acq 3-22-2000); $1.45 million. with WSEV(AM) Sevierville). Network: CBS. Rep: Rgnl Reps. Format: Adult Contemporary. News staff: one. Target aud: 25-49; loc adults, tourists, C&W lovers. ◆Bill Burkett, stn mgr; Steve Hartford, progmg dir & news dir.

Germantown

WHBQ-FM— June 1994: 107.5 mhz; 3.9 kw. Ant 407 ft. TL: N35 10 30 W89 44 26. Stereo. 6080 Mt. Mariah Rd., Memphis 38115. Phone: (901) 375-9324. Fax: (901) 375-0041. Web Site: www.q1075.com. Licensee: Flinn Broadcasting Corp. (acq 1997; $4). Format: Top-40. ◆Donald Biggs, gen mgr.

WMBZ(FM)—Licensed to Germantown. See Memphis

WOWW(AM)—Licensed to Germantown. See Memphis

WPLX(AM)—Licensed to Germantown. See Memphis

Goodlettsville

WRQQ(FM)— Dec 3, 1999: 97.1 mhz; 43 kw. 518 ft. TL: N36 17 50 W86 45 11. 10 Music Cir. E., Nashville 37203. Phone: (615) 321-1067. Fax: (615) 321-5771. E-mail: danielle.haese@cumulus.com. Web Site: www.cumulus.com. Licensee: Cumulus Licensing Corp. Group owner: Cumulus Media Inc. (acq 2-12-02; grpsl). Format: Best of the 80s. ◆Michael Dickey, gen mgr; Don Boyd, gen sls mgr; Derick Corbett, progmg dir; Dan Goodman, chief of engrg.

Graysville

WAYB-FM— 1994: 95.7 mhz; 6 kw. Ant 328 ft. TL: N35 24 39 W85 07 54. Box 262550, Baton Rouge, LA 70826. Phone: (225) 768-3688. Web Site: www.jsm.org. Licensee: Family Worship Center Church Inc. (group owner; acq 5-20-02). Format: Christian. ◆David Whitelaw, gen mgr & chief of engrg; John Santiago, progmg dir.

Greeneville

WAEZ(FM)— 1956: 94.9 mhz; 100 kw. 1,090 ft. TL: N36 04 34 W82 41 28. Stereo. 901 E. Valley Dr., Bristol, VA 24201. Phone: (276) 669-8112. Fax: (276) 669-0541. Web Site: www.electric949.com. Licensee: Bristol Broadcasting Co. Inc. (group owner; acq 6-22-00). Rep: Rgnl Reps. Format: CHR. News staff: 2. Target aud: 25-49. Spec prog: Univ. of Tennessee football & basketball. ◆Pete Nininger, pres; Bill Hickey, opns mgr.

WGRV(AM)—Listing follows WIKQ(FM).

WIKQ(FM)—(Tusculum). February 1996: 103.1 mhz; 6 kw. -223 ft. TL: N36 07 40 W82 37 57. Box 278 37744. Secondary address: 1004 Arnold Rd. 37743. Phone: (423) 639-1831. Fax: (423) 638-1979. Licensee: Radio Greeneville Inc. (group owner; acq 6-22-00; $1.8 million. with WSMG(AM) Greeneville). Format: Country. News staff: one. Target aud: 25-55; middle to upper middle income. ◆Ron P. Metcalf, gen mgr; Ron P. Metcalfe, pres & opns VP; Brian Stayton, progmg dir; Nathan Humbard, mus dir; Bobby Rader, news dir; Ray C. Elliott, chief of engrg.

WGRV(AM)—Co-owned with WIKQ(FM). 1946: 1340 khz; 1 kw-U. TL: N36 10 10 W82 50 52. Phone: (423) 638-4147. Format: Modern country. News staff: 3. ◆Ron Metcalfe, prom mgr & progmg mgr.

WSMG(AM)— Dec 1, 1961: 1450 khz; 1 kw-U. TL: N36 10 30 W82 50 18. Box 278 37744. Secondary address: 10004 Arnold Rd. 37743. Phone: (423) 638-3188. Fax: (423) 638-1979. Licensee: Radio Greeneville Inc. (group owner; acq 6-22-00; $1.8 million with WIKQ(FM) Tusculum). Network: ABC Information & Entertainment. Format: Oldies. Target aud: General. ◆Ronnie Metcalfe, pres, gen mgr & opns mgr.

Harriman

WBZH(FM)— Jan 21, 1981: 92.7 mhz; 790 w. Ant 663 ft. TL: N35 55 41 W84 34 49. Stereo. Box 810, Crossville 38557. Phone: (931) 484-1057. Licensee: Southern Media Group Inc. (group owner; acq 5-23-03; grpsl). Format: Adult contemp. Target aud: 25-54. ◆Kirk Tollett, gen mgr, gen sls mgr, progmg dir & chief of engrg; Scott Humphrey, news dir.

Harrogate

*WLMU(FM)— Aug 5, 1987: 91.3 mhz; 190 w. 284 ft. TL: N36 35 10 W83 39 54. Stereo. Box 2025, Sigmon Communications Ctr., Hwy. 25 E. 37752. Phone: (423) 869-6315. Web Site: www.lmunet.edu/sigmon. Licensee: Lincoln Memorial University. Format: Adult contemp, oldies, Contemp hit/Top-40. Target aud: 25-54. ◆Dr. Nancy Moody, pres; Killian Heilsberg-McElrath, gen mgr & opns mgr.

WRWB(AM)— Nov 10, 1980: 740 khz; 1 kw-D. TL: N36 34 32 W83 39 37. 6965 Cumberland Gap Pkwy. 37752. Phone: (423) 869-6335. Fax: (423) 869-6435. E-mail: wrwb@usa.com. Licensee: Pine Hills of Tenn. Inc. (acq 7-86). Format: Talk. News staff: 4; News: 150 hrs wkly. Target aud: 34-65. ◆Tom Amis, gen mgr & opns mgr.

WXJB(FM)— Aug 15, 1991: 96.5 mhz; 6 kw. 325 ft. TL: N36 34 44 W83 34 42. Stereo. Box 719 37752. Secondary address: 2118 Cumberland Ave., Middlesboro, KY 40965. Phone: (423) 869-2266. Phone: (423) 248-0001. Fax: (606) 248-6397. E-mail: wxjbthebull@yahoo.com. Licensee: JBD Inc. (acq 5-1-01). Network: Network: Network: ABC Daytime Direction, ABC, CNN Radio. Rep: Rgnl Reps. Bechtel & Cole. Format: Country. News staff: 2; News: 25 hrs wkly. Target aud: 25-54; community-oriented adults. Spec prog: Farm 2 hrs, gospel 2 hrs, relg 2 hrs wkly. ◆Beulah Pursifull, pres; Bo Farmer, gen mgr, opns mgr & sls dir; David Manis, progmg dir; Rita Hansard, mus dir; Chuck Owens, engrg dir.

Hartsville

WTNK(AM)— Sept 1, 1966: 1090 khz; 1 kw-D. TL: N36 23 17 W86 09 55. (CP: 2 w-N). 165 Marlene St. 37074. Phone: (615) 374-2111.
Fax: (615) 374-3544. Licensee: G & L Aircasters Inc. (acq 2-14-03; $160,000). Rep: Keystone (unwired net). Format: Country & gospel on Sunday. News: 5 hrs wkly. Target aud: 35 plus. Spec prog: Local sports. ◆Gary Frank, CEO, pres, gen mgr, stn mgr & chief of opns; K. K. Wilson, sls dir, gen sls mgr & prom dir; Earl White, progmg dir; Jerry Richmond, news dir; Lisa Frank, COO, CFO, exec VP & pub affrs dir.

Henderson

*WFHU(FM)— May 22, 1967: 91.5 mhz; 10.5 kw. 300 ft. TL: N35 27 50 W88 41 10. Stereo. 158 E. Main St. 38340. Phone: (731) 989-6691. Phone: (731) 989-6749. E-mail: wfhc@fhu.edu. Web Site: www.fhu.edu/radio. Licensee: Freed-Hardeman University. Format: Jazz, classic rock, classical. News staff: one; News: 5 hrs wkly. Target aud: General; young adults to senior citizens. Spec prog: Class 10 hrs, gospel 9 hrs, jazz 45 hrs wkly. ◆Milton Sewell, pres; Ron Means, gen mgr.

WFKX(FM)— Feb 1, 1984: 95.7 mhz; 6 kw. 300 ft. TL: N35 29 52 W88 42 29. Stereo. 111 W. Main St., Jackson 38301. Phone: (731) 427-9616. Fax: (731) 424-2473. E-mail: cthomas@wwyn.fm. Web Site: wfkx.fm. Licensee: Thomas Radio LLC (group owner; acq 11-9-2001; grpsl). Network: ABC. Rep: Allied Radio Partners. Borsari & Paxson. Format: Urban contemp, Black. News: 5 hrs wkly. Target aud: 18-54; the general Black population & contemp women. Spec prog: Gospel 3 hrs wkly. ◆Billy Thomas, pres; Chip Thomas, gen mgr; Jim Smith, chief of engrg.

WHHM-FM— Nov 19, 1990: 107.7 mhz; 50 kw horiz, 49.07 kw vert. Ant 459 ft. TL: N35 27 23 W88 37 36. Stereo. 111 W. Main St., Jackson 38301. Phone: (731) 427-9616. Fax: (731) 424-2473. Web Site: www.star1077.fm. Licensee: Thomas Radio LLC (group owner; (acq 11-9-2001; grpsl). Network: ABC Daytime Direction. Rep: Allied Radio Partners. McFadden, Evans & Sill. Format: Var, adult contemp. News staff: one; News: 5 hrs wkly. Target aud: 25-54; adults. Spec prog: Gospel 10 hrs wkly. ◆Chip Thomas, gen mgr; Phil Hickerson, gen sls mgr; Shane Connor, opns mgr & progmg mgr; Jim Smith, chief of engrg.

Hendersonville

WQQK(FM)— Oct 16, 1970: 92.1 mhz; 3 kw. 462 ft. TL: N36 17 50 W86 45 11. Stereo. 10 Music Cir. E., Nashville 37203. Phone: (615) 321-1067. Fax: (615) 321-5771. E-mail: danielle.haese@cumulus.com. Web Site: www.cumulus.com. Licensee: Cumulus Licensing LLC. Group owner: Cumulus Media Inc. (acq 3-28-2002; grpsl). Network: ABC. Pepper & Corazzini. Format: Adult urban contemp. Target aud: 18-49; relg. Spec prog: Gospel 6 hrs wkly. ◆Michael Dickey, gen mgr; Don Boyd, gen sls mgr; Derrick Corbett, progmg dir; Dan Goodman, chief of engrg.

Henry

WMUF-FM— Apr 12, 1999: 104.7 mhz; 2.9 kw. Ant 476 ft. TL: N36 08 19 W88 15 52. Stereo. 110 India Rd., Paris 38242. Phone: (731) 644-9455. Fax: (731) 644-9970. E-mail: wmuf@bellsouth.net. Licensee: Benton-Weatherford Broadcasting Inc. of Tennessee (group owner). Network: ABC. Format: Country. Target aud: 25-54. ◆Gary Benton, pres & gen mgr; Janice Benton, opns VP.

Hohenwald

*WAUO(FM)— 1998: 90.7 mhz; 950 w. 233 ft. TL: N35 33 56 W87 33 27. Box 3206, American Family Radio, Tupelo, MS 38803. Phone: (662) 844-8888. Phone: (662) 844-8893 (call-in). Fax: (662) 842-6791. E-mail: comments@afr.net. Web Site: www.afr.net. Licensee: American Family Association. Group owner: American Family Radio Format: Relg. ◆Marvin Sanders, gen mgr.

WMLR(AM)— July 4, 1970: 1230 khz; 1 kw-U. TL: N35 31 22 W87 32 40. 184 Switzerland Rd. 38462. Phone: (931) 796-5966. Fax: (931) 796-7353. E-mail: harold@wmlr1230am.com. Licensee: Cochran Communication Corp. of Lewis County. (acq 6-4-99; $67,500).

Broadcasting & Cable Yearbook 2006

Tennessee

Network: ABC. Format: C&W. Spec prog: Gospel. ♦Harold Cochran, pres & gen mgr; Celeste Cochran, news dir.

Humboldt

WHMT(AM)— July 5, 1972: 1190 khz; 420 w-D. TL: N35 50 41 W88 54 08. Box 488, 2603 Spangler Park Dr. 38343. Phone: (731) 784-1190. Phone: (731) 784-1053. Fax: (731) 784-4033. Licensee: Boyd Enterprises Inc. (acq 3-84; 3-19-84). Format: Sports. Target aud: 18 plus. ♦F. Darrell Boyd Sr., pres & gen mgr; F. Darrell Boyd II, opns mgr; Scott Wyatt, gen sls mgr; Dave Hacker, chief of engrg.

WIRJ(AM)— Jan 20, 1949: 740 khz; 250 w-D, 50 w-N. TL: N35 48 52 W88 54 51. Box 740 38343-0740. Secondary address: 2606 East End Dr. 38343. Phone: (731) 784-5000. Fax: (731) 784-2533. Licensee: John F. Warmath. (acq 1996; $45,000). Format: Oldies, talk. ♦John F. Warmath, gen mgr.

WZDQ(FM)— Sept 1, 1964: 102.3 mhz; 6 kw. Ant 305 ft. TL: N35 45 45 W88 51 42. Stereo. 111 W. Main St., Jackcon 38301. Phone: (731) 427-9616. Fax: (731) 424-2473. Web Site: www.wzdq.fm. Licensee: Thomas Radio LLC. (group owner; (acq 11-9-2001; grpsl). Network: CNN Radio. Format: Rock. Target aud: 25-49; middle to upper class. ♦Chip Thomas, gen mgr; Marsha Hulsey, gen sls mgr; Shane Connor, opns mgr & prom dir.

Huntingdon

WDAP(AM)— Oct 21, 1975: 1530 khz; 1 kw-D. TL: N36 00 04 W88 26 02. 9662 H'way 77 38344. Phone: (731) 986-9746. Fax: (731) 986-9704. Licensee: Mark C. Johnson (acq 5-23-02). Format: 1530 Gold. News staff: 2. Target aud: General. ♦Mark C. Johnson, gen mgr; Sarah Dunning, gen sls mgr; Jay Jackson, news dir.

WVHR(FM)— November 1979: 100.9 mhz; 6 kw. 300 ft. TL: N35 57 05 W88 27 47. Stereo. 215 Baker Rd., Huntington 38344. Phone: (731) 986-0242. Fax: (731) 986-8557. E-mail: whhr@aeneas.net. Licensee: Milan Broadcasting Co. Inc. (acq 5-1-91; $150,000; 5-27-91). Format: Classic hit country. ♦Jerry Vandiver, gen mgr & sls dir; Michael Ray, opns dir, progmg dir & news dir; Dave Hacker, chief of engrg.

Jackson

*WAMP(FM)— 1995: 88.1 mhz; 750 w. 134 ft. TL: N35 39 38 W88 51 30. American Family Radio, Box 3206, Tupelo, MS 38803. Phone: (662) 844-8888. Phone: (662) 844-8893. Fax: (662) 842-6791. E-mail: comments@afr.net. Web Site: www.afr.net. Licensee: American Family Association. Group owner: American Family Radio Format: Christian. ♦Marvin Sanders, gen mgr.

WDXI(AM)— Oct 31, 1948: 1310 khz; 5 kw-D, 1 kw-N, DA-N. TL: N35 39 50 W88 49 20. Box 3845 38303-3845. Secondary address: 1 Radio Park Dr. 38305-4124. Phone: (731) 427-9611. Phone: (731) 424-1310. Fax: (731) 424-1321. Licensee: Gerald W. Hunt (acq 1-15-93; $480,000. with co-located FM; FTR: 2-8-93). Rep: D & R Radio. Format: Business news. News staff: one; News: 10 hrs wkly. Target aud: 25 plus. Spec prog: Farm 12 hrs, gospel 16 hrs, sports 16 hrs wkly. ♦Gerald W. Hunt, gen mgr & progmg mgr.

WMXX-FM—Co-owned with WDXI(AM). May 9, 1979: 103.1 mhz; 42 kw. Ant 538 ft. TL: N35 32 39 W88 47 18. Stereo. Format: Oldies. Target aud: 25-54.

WJAK(AM)— Nov 14, 1954: 1460 khz; 1 kw-D, 128 w-N. TL: N35 38 37 W88 46 24. 111 W. Main St. 38301. Phone: (731) 427-9616. Fax: (731) 427-9302. Licensee: Thomas Radio L.L.C. (group owner; (acq 7-21-2004; $318,000). Network: Network: Moody, USA. Rep: Rgnl Reps. Format: Urban Gospel. News: 14 hrs wkly. Target aud: 18-54; primarily Black Christian middle-class families with low to moderate income. ♦Chip Thomas, gen mgr.

*WKNP(FM)— Dec 17, 1990: 90.1 mhz; 17 kw. 528 ft. TL: N35 38 46 W88 49 57. Stereo. Box 241880, Memphis 38124. Secondary address: 900 Getwell Rd., Memphis 38111. Phone: (901) 325-6544. Fax: (901) 325-6506. Web Site: www.wknofm.org. Licensee: Mid-South Public Communications Foundation. Network: Network: NPR, PRI. Schwartz, Woods & Miller. Format: Class, news. News staff: one; News: 51 hrs wkly. Target aud: 35 plus. ♦Michael LaBonia, pres; Dan Campbell, gen mgr & stn mgr; Darel Snodgrass, opns mgr; Charles McLarty, dev dir. Co-owned TV: *WKNO-TV affil

WNWS-FM— August 1993: 101.5 mhz; 3 kw. 300 ft. TL: N35 38 59 W88 46 11. Stereo. 116 N. Church St., 4th Fl. 38301. Phone: (731) 423-8316. Fax: (731) 423-8304. E-mail: newstalk@wnws.com. Web Site: www.wnws.com. Licensee: Radiocorp of Jackson Inc. Group owner: The Wireless Group Inc. (acq 12-6-00; $925,000). Network: CBS. Format: News/talk. News staff: 2; News: 25 hrs wkly. Target aud: 25 plus; upscale adults. ♦Greg Wood, opns mgr; Larry Wood, gen mgr & progmg dir.

WTJS(AM)— 1931: 1390 khz; 5 kw-D, 1 kw-N, DA-N. TL: N35 38 50 W88 50 00. 122 Radio Rd. 38301. Phone: (731) 427-3316. Fax: (731) 427-4576. Licensee: Capstar TX L.P. Group owner: Clear Channel Communications Inc. (acq 8-30-00; grpsl). Network: ABC Information & Entertainment. Format: News/talk. News staff: 3; News: 30 hrs wkly. Target aud: 35 plus; general. ♦Roger Vestal, gen mgr; Dave Hacker, opns mgr & chief of engrg; Gina Langley, gen sls mgr; Todd Starnes, news dir.

WTNV(FM)—Co-owned with WTJS(AM). 1947: 104.1 mhz; 100 kw. 679 ft. TL: N35 38 46 W88 49 57. Stereo. Web Site: eagle104.net. Network: ABC Information & Entertainment. Format: Country. Target aud: 18-54. ♦Deb Smith, prom dir; Rusty Mac, news dir.

WYNU(FM)—See Milan

Jamestown

WCLC(AM)— Oct 28, 1957: 1260 khz; 1 kw-D. TL: N36 26 10 W84 55 42. Box 1509 38556. Phone: (931) 879-8188. Fax: (931) 879-1733. E-mail: wclc@twlakes.net. Licensee: Bible Believers Network Inc. Format: Bible believers network, relg. Spec prog: Farm 2 hrs, bluegrass 3 hrs wkly. ♦Jim Cody, gen mgr, gen sls mgr & progmg dir.

WCLC-FM— 1985: 105.1 mhz; 1.1 kw. 605 ft. TL: N36 26 31 W84 55 28. (CP: 2.85 kw, ant 476 ft.). Stereo. Format: Relg.

WDEB(AM)— Jan 12, 1968: 1500 khz; 1 kw-D, 500 w-CH. TL: N36 25 31 W84 56 32. Box 69 38556. Secondary address: 403 Livingston Ave. 38556. Phone: (931) 879-8164. Phone: (931) 879-9332. Fax: (931) 879-7437. E-mail: wdeb@multipro.com. Licensee: BAZ Broadcasting Inc. (acq 4-1-72). Network: ABC Information & Entertainment. Format: Country, relg. News staff: 7; News: 10 hrs wkly. Target aud: 18-54; household members who spend money in the marketplace. Spec prog: Farm 3 hrs wkly. ♦Jean Baz, VP & gen sls mgr; Gary Crocket, progmg dir; Kevin R. Baz, mus dir; N.A. Baz, pres, gen mgr, prom dir, adv dir & news dir; Gunther Muhsemann, chief of engrg.

WDEB-FM— Oct 10, 1972: 103.9 mhz; 1.6 kw. 450 ft. TL: N36 25 55 W84 56 33. Stereo. Format: Modern country, gospel. ♦Jean Baz, sls dir; N. A. Baz, rgnl sls mgr, mktg mgr & prom mgr.

Jasper

WWAM(AM)— Mar 2, 1987: 820 khz; 5 kw-D. TL: N35 04 23 W85 37 39. Stereo. Box 279 37347. Secondary address: 4896 Main St. 37347. Phone: (423) 942-1700. Phone: (423) 592-5588. Fax: (423) 942-1700. Licensee: Shelton Broadcasting System. Network: USA. Format: Gospel. Target aud: 25-49. Spec prog: Bluegrass one hr, acappella one hr wkly. ♦Rick Shelton, gen mgr.

Jefferson City

WJFC(AM)— Nov 1, 1961: 1480 khz; 500 w-D. TL: N36 06 15 W83 29 10. Box 430 37760. Phone: (865) 475-3825. Fax: (865) 475-3800. Licensee: Appalachian Educational Communication Corp. (acq 1-21-97; $150,000). Timothy K. Brady. Format: Country. News staff: one; News: 10 hrs wkly. Target aud: 25 plus; Jefferson, Grainger & Hamblen counties. Spec prog: Farm one hr, relg 4 hrs wkly. ♦Kenneth C. Hill, pres & gen mgr.

WNRX(FM)— Feb 1, 1976: 99.3 mhz; 3 kw. 654 ft. TL: N36 04 28 W83 34 56. 415 Middle Creek Rd., Sevierville 37862. Phone: (865) 453-2844. Fax: (865) 428-2601. Licensee: Citadel Broadcasting Inc. Group owner: Citadel Broadcasting Corp. (acq 7-20-2004; $1.65 million). Format: CHR. News staff: one; News: 17 hrs wkly. Spec prog: Gospel 4 hrs, relg 2 hrs wkly.

Jellico

WEKX(FM)— 1993: 102.7 mhz; 630 w. 1,008 ft. TL: N36 37 55 W84 08 31. 522 Main St., Williamsburg, KY 40769. Phone: (606) 549-1027.

Fax: (606) 549-5565. Licensee: Whitley Broadcasting Co. Inc. (group owner; acq 5-23-02; grpsl). Rgnl Reps. Format: Adult contemp. News: 5 hrs wkly. ♦David Estes, CEO, chmn, pres & gen mgr; Rick Campbell, stn mgr & opns mgr; Frank Folsom, gen sls mgr & chief of engrg; Kip Jervis, progmg dir.

WJJT(AM)— Feb 1, 1972: . Stn currently dark 1540 khz; 1 kw-D, 500 w-CH. TL: N36 34 13 W84 08 43. Box 210 37762. Phone: (423) 784-1540. Fax: (423) 784-5991. E-mail: wjjtam1540@aol.com. Licensee: Douglas Broadcasting Co. (acq 5-96; $100,000). Format: Gospel. ♦Betty Douglas, exec VP; Marvin Douglas, pres & gen mgr; Betty Douglas, stn mgr.

Johnson City

WETB(AM)— Oct 1, 1947: 790 khz; 5 kw-D, 72 w-N. TL: N36 19 43 W82 24 39. Box 4127 37602. Secondary address: 231 Brandonwood Dr. 37604. Phone: (423) 928-7131. Fax: (423) 928-8392. E-mail: webb@mounet.com. Licensee: Mountain Signals Inc. (acq 12-5-90; 12-31-90). Network: USA. Format: Gospel. News staff: one; News: 3 hrs wkly. Target aud: General. ♦Paul Gobble Jr., gen mgr & pres; Bob Morrison, stn mgr, opns mgr & progmg dir; Loretta Gouge, gen sls mgr.

*WETS(FM)— Feb 26, 1974: 89.5 mhz; 66 kw. 2,273 ft. TL: N36 26 02 W82 08 08. Stereo. c/o East Tennessee State University, Box 70630, Ellis Hall 37614-1709. Phone: (423) 439-6440. Phone: (423) 439-6441. Fax: (423) 439-6449. E-mail: winkler@xtn.net. Web Site: www.wets.org. Licensee: East Tennessee State University. Network: Network: NPR, PRI. Format: Class, folk, news/talk. News: 22 hrs wkly. Target aud: General. Spec prog: Blues 12 hrs, Sp one hr wkly. ♦Paul E. Stanton, pres; Wayne Winkler, gen mgr; Dan Hirschi, progmg dir; Jim Blalock, mus dir; Mitch Sandidge, chief of engrg.

WJCW(AM)— Dec 13, 1938: 910 khz; 5 kw-D, 1 kw-N, DA-N. TL: N36 24 37 W82 27 13. Box 8668, 162 Freehill, Gray 37615. Phone: (423) 477-1000. Fax: (423) 477-4747. E-mail: talk@preferred.com. Web Site: www.wjcw.com. Licensee: Citadel Broadcasting Co. Group owner: Citadel Broadcasting Corp. (acq 5-30-00; grpsl). Network: Network: CBS, ABC. Reddy, Begley & McCormick. Format: News/talk, sports. News staff: 2; News: 30 hrs wkly. Target aud: 25 plus. Spec prog: Relg 4 hrs wkly. ♦Don Raines, pres & gen mgr; Bob Gordon, opns mgr; Paul Overbay, sls dir & gen sls mgr; Debbie Caso, mktg dir & prom dir; Bill Meade, progmg dir; Leigh Hornsby, news dir & pub affrs dir; Al F. LeFevere, chief of engrg.

WQUT(FM)—Co-owned with WJCW(AM). Mar 1, 1948: 101.5 mhz; 100 kw. 1,500 ft. TL: N36 16 07 W82 20 21. Stereo. Phone: (423) 477-1015. E-mail: wqvt@preferred.com. Web Site: www.wqvt.com. Format: Classic rock. News staff: 2; News: 3 hrs wkly. Target aud: 18-49. ♦Randy Ross, gen sls mgr; Jeri George, prom dir; John Patrick, progmg dir.

WKTP(AM)—See Jonesborough

WTFM(FM)—See Kingsport

Jonesborough

WKTP(AM)— October 1958: 1590 khz; 5 kw-U, DA-2. TL: N36 19 54 W82 28 27. 222 Commerce St., Kingsport 37660. Phone: (423) 246-9578. Phone: (423) 926-9800. Fax: (423) 247-9836. Fax: (423) 246-6261. E-mail: davidw@wtfm.com. Web Site: www.wktpam.com. Licensee: Holston Valley Broadcasting Corp. Group owner: Glenwood Communications Corp. (acq 1-25-90; $90,000; 3-5-90). Network: ABC Information & Entertainment. Rep: McGavren Guild. Cordon & Kelly. Format: Full service, news, sports, adult standards. News staff: 2; News: 24 hrs wkly. Target aud: 35 plus. ♦George Devault, pres; N. David Widener, exec VP, gen mgr & stn mgr; Jason Mullins, chief of opns.

WTZR(FM)—See Elizabethton

Karns

WMYU(FM)— Jan 8, 1989: 93.1 mhz; 1.2 kw. 515 ft. TL: N35 58 59 W84 04 37. (CP: 2.4 kw, ant 512 ft. TL: N35 57 46 W84 01 23). 8419 Kingston Pike, Knoxville 37919. Phone: (865) 693-1020. Fax: (865) 693-8493. Web Site: www.thepoint931.com. Licensee: Journal Broadcast Corp. Group owner: Journal Communications Inc. (acq 5-19-97). Format: Adult Contemp. ♦Andy Laird, VP, progmg dir & engr; Chris Protzman, gen mgr; Bruce Patrick, progmg dir.

Developers & Brokers of Radio Properties

contact American Media Services at our suite:
Philadelphia Marriott Downtown
215-625-2900
843-972-2200
americanmediaservices.com
Charleston, SC
Dallas, TX · Chicago, Il · Austin, TX

American Media Services, LLC

Kingsport

*WCQR-FM— December 1996: 88.3 mhz; 1.2 kw. 2,132 ft. TL: N36 25 53 W82 08 16. Stereo. 2312 Oak St., Gray 37615-8039. Phone: (423) 477-5676. Fax: (423) 477-7060. E-mail: office@wcqr.org. Web Site: www.wcqr.org. Licensee: Positive Alternative Radio Inc. Group owner: Baker Family Stations/Positive Alternative Radio Inc. Network: Salem Radio Network. Booth, Freret, Imlay & Tepper. Format: Contemp Christian mus. Target aud: 25-54. ♦ Mike Perry, gen mgr.

*WCSK(FM)— Nov 5, 1984: 90.3 mhz; 195 w. 23 ft. TL: N36 31 37 W82 35 12. Stereo. 1800 Legion Dr. 37664. Phone: (423) 378-2150. Fax: (423) 378-2120. Web Site: www.kptk12.tn.us. Licensee: Kingsport Board of Education. Format: Educ, class, div.

WHGG(AM)— January 1997: 1090 khz; 10 kw-D. TL: N36 27 40 W82 27 12. Box 2061, Bristol 37621. Secondary address: 340 Edgemont Ave., Suite 100, Bristol 37620. Phone: (423) 878-6279. Fax: (423) 878-6520. Web Site: www.mighty1090.com. Licensee: Appalachian Educational Communication Corp. (acq 1995; $20,000). Format: Oldies. News staff: one; News: 10 hrs wkly. Target aud: 12-24. ♦ Kenneth C. Hill, pres & gen mgr; Matthew J. Hill, stn mgr.

WJCW(AM)—See Johnson City

WKIN(AM)— October 1951: 1320 khz; 5 kw-D, 500 w-N, DA-N. TL: N36 33 59 W82 33 22. Box 8668, Gray 37615. Secondary address: 162 Freehill Rd. 37615. Phone: (423) 477-1000. Fax: (423) 477-4747. E-mail: wjcwwkin@preferred.com. Web Site: www.wkin.com. Licensee: Citadel Broadcasting Co. Group owner: Citadel Broadcasting Corp. (acq 5-30-00; grpsl). Network: CBS Radio. Rep: McGavren Guild. Wiley, Rein & Fielding. Format: News/talk, sports. News staff: 2; News: 30 hrs wkly. Target aud: 25-54. ♦ Don Raines, gen mgr; Bob Gordon, opns mgr; Paul Overbay, gen sls mgr; Bob Lawrence, mktg dir & prom dir; Bill Meade, progmg dir; Jeff Hall, news dir; Al LeFevere, chief of engrg.

WKOS(FM)—Co-owned with WKIN(AM). Feb 21, 1970: 104.9 mhz; 2.75 kw. 492 ft. TL: N36 33 14 W82 27 00. Stereo. E-mail: oldies@preferred.com. Web Site: www.wkos.com. Network: Westwood One. Format: Oldies. Target aud: 25-54. ♦ Debbie Caso, gen sls mgr; Greg Price, natl sls mgr; Alan Austin, progmg dir; Bob Lawrence, pub affrs dir.

WKPT(AM)— July 14, 1940: 1400 khz; 1 kw-U. TL: N36 32 37 W82 31 21. 222 Commerce St. 37660. Phone: (423) 246-9578. Fax: (423) 247-9836. E-mail: gdv@wkpttv.com. Web Site: www.wkptam.com. Licensee: Holston Valley Broadcasting Corp. Group owner: Glenwood Communications Corp. (acq 6-1-66). Network: ABC Information & Entertainment. Cordon & Kelly. Format: News, sports, MOR. News staff: 2. Target aud: 35 plus. ♦ George Devault, pres; N. David Widener, exec VP & gen mgr; Jason Mullins, chief of opns, progmg dir & progmg mgr; Charles Aesque, gen sls mgr; Scott Onks, prom mgr; Duane Nelson, news dir.

WTFM(FM)—Co-owned with WKPT-TV. February 1948: 98.5 mhz; 74 kw. 2,241 ft. TL: N36 25 54 W82 08 15. Stereo. E-mail: davidw@wtfm.com. Web Site: www.wtfm.com. Network: ABC Information & Entertainment. Format: Adult contemp. News staff: 2. Target aud: 25-54. ♦ Tim Loy, sls VP & gen sls mgr; Elva Marie, prom mgr; Tiffany Hickman, prom mgr; Mark McKinney, progmg dir; Lyle Musser, chief of engrg. Co-owned TV: WKPT-TV affil

WQUT(FM)—Johnson City

Kingston

WBBX(AM)— July 1978: 1410 khz; 500 w-D. TL: N35 52 49 W84 30 56. Box 389 37763. Secondary address: 705 Greenwood St. 37763. Phone: (615) 376-6954. Licensee: Pilgrim Pathway Inc. (acq 6-30-92; $35,000; 7-27-92). Format: Gospel. Target aud: General. ♦ Grant Carter, pres.

*WKTS(FM)— August 2000: 90.1 mhz; 55 w vert. Ant 633 ft. TL: N35 45 57 W84 34 33. 331 Skyline View Ln. 37763. Phone: (865) 717-3335. E-mail: Charons@bellsouth.net. Web Site: www.wktsfm.com. Licensee: The Kingston Century Club Inc. Format: Adult contemp. News staff: one; News: 3 hrs wkly. Spec prog: Gospel 8 hrs wkly. ♦ Neil Scalf, pres; Charles R. Solomon, gen mgr & opns dir.

Kingston Springs

WFFI(FM)— Jan 15, 1993: 93.7 mhz; 1.15 kw. Ant 754 ft. TL: N36 08 10 W86 59 04. 402 BNA Dr., Suite 400, Nashville 37217. Phone: (615) 367-2210. Fax: (615) 367-0758. Web Site: www.94fmthefish.net. Licensee: Caron Broadcasting Inc. Group owner: Salem Communications Corp. (acq 12-18-02; $5.6 million. with WFFH(FM) Smyrna). Network: Salem Radio Network. Rep: Salem. Format: Contemp Christian. Target aud: 25-54; adults. ♦ Michael S. Miller, gen mgr; Kevin R. Anderson, gen sls mgr & rgnl sls mgr; Dick Marsh, prom dir; Vance Dillard, progmg dir; Kim Bindel, news dir.

Knoxville

WETR(AM)— July 5, 1995: 760 khz; 2.5 kw-D. TL: N36 02 34 W84 02 51. (CP: 2.4 kw). 1621 E. Magnolia Ave. 37917. Phone: (865) 525-1060. Fax: (865) 521-8923. Web Site: www.talkradio760.com. Licensee: Thomas H. Moffit Jr. (acq 1995). Network: USA. Format: News/talk. Target aud: 25-54; blue collar men & women. ♦ David Wells, gen mgr.

WIFA(AM)— Jan 21, 1941: 1240 khz; 1 kw-U. TL: N35 57 17 W83 57 04. Box 50840 37950. Secondary address: 818 N. Cedar Bluff Rd. 37923. Phone: (865) 531-2005. Fax: (865) 531-2006. Web Site: www.1240radio.com. Licensee: Progressive Media Inc. (acq 8-6-2004; $550,000). Format: Adult contemp Christian music and talk. ♦ Barry Culberson, pres; Brian Brooks, gen mgr.

WIMZ-FM— October 1949: 103.5 mhz; 100 kw. 1,723 ft. TL: N36 08 06 W83 43 29. Stereo. 1100 Sharps Ridge Rd. 37917. Phone: (865) 525-6000. Fax: (865) 525-2000. Web Site: www.wimz.com. Licensee: South Central Communications Corp. (group owner; acq 2-23-93; $3.5 million. with co-located AM; FTR: 3-15-93). Format: Classic rock. ♦ Terry Gillingham, VP & mktg mgr.

WITA(AM)— Sept 1, 1960: 1490 khz; 1 kw-U. TL: N35 58 11 W83 57 56. 7212 Kingston Pike 37919. Phone: (865) 588-2974. Phone: (865) 588-2975. E-mail: wita1490@aol.com. Web Site: www.wwcr.com. Licensee: RR Broadcast Group Inc. (group owner; acq 2-18-2005; $425,000). Format: Christian talk. Target aud: General. Spec prog: Black 8 hrs wkly. ♦ Rex D. Palmer, pres; Gail Scott, gen mgr; Greg McMahon, opns mgr.

WIVK-FM—Listing follows WNML(AM).

WJXB-FM— Apr 10, 1967: 97.5 mhz; 96 kw. 1,296 ft. TL: N36 00 36 W83 55 57. Stereo. 1100 Sharps Ridge Mem Park Dr. 37917. Phone: (865) 525-6000. Fax: (865) 656-3292. Web Site: www.b975.com. Licensee: South Central Communications Corp. (group owner). Format: Soft adult contemp. Target aud: 25-54; educated, above-average income. ♦ John D. Engelbrecht, chmn; Craig Jacobus, pres & gen mgr; Terry Gillingham, opns mgr; Jim Ridings, natl sls mgr; Deborah Cox, prom dir; Brad Jefferies, progmg dir.

*WKCS(FM)— December 1952: 91.1 mhz; 250 w. 73 ft. TL: N35 59 36 W83 55 24. Fulton High School, 2509 Broadway N.E. 37917. Phone: (865) 594-1259. E-mail: wkcsradio@hotmail.com. Licensee: Fulton High School. Format: Oldies. News: 3 hrs wkly. Target aud: 18 plus; University of Tennessee. ♦ Russell Mayes, gen mgr.

WKGN(AM)— Sept 28, 1947: 1340 khz; 1 kw-U. TL: N35 57 20 W83 58 14. Stereo. Box 10005 37919. Phone: (865) 546-7900. Fax: (865) 546-7965. Licensee: Triple S Enterprises Inc. (acq 11-26-91; $50,000; 12-16-91). Network: Westwood One. Rep: Roslin. Format: Urban contemp, gospel. Target aud: 18-34; young, mobile adults. Spec prog: Relg 5 hrs, medicine/health one hr wkly. ♦ Robert L. Stewart, pres & gen mgr; Thomas Henderson, progmg dir; Ed Martin, chief of engrg.

WKHT(FM)— November 1991: 104.5 mhz; 6 kw. 394 ft. TL: N36 00 36 W83 55 57. (CP: 2.3 kw, ant 528 ft.). 1533 Amhearst Rd. 37909. Phone: (865) 693-1020. Phone: (865) 824-1021. Fax: (865) 824-1880. Web Site: www.1045thebone.com. Licensee: Journal Broadcast Corp. (group owner; acq 3-4-98; $5.745 million. with WQBB(AM) Powell). Rep: Roslin. Format: Classic rock. Target aud: 35 plus; female. Spec prog: Pub affrs 2 hrs wkly. ♦ Chris Protzman, gen mgr; Rich Bailey, opns mgr; Eddy Roy, sls dir & news dir; Dodie Manalac, gen sls mgr; Russ Allen, progmg dir; Mark Lucas, chief of engrg.

WQBB(AM)—Co-owned with WKHT(FM). Aug 15, 1984: 1040 khz; 10 kw-D. TL: N36 02 34 W84 02 51. Stereo. Format: Talk, sports. ♦ Dan McKel, sls dir; Bruce Patrick, progmg dir.

WKVL(AM)— Jan 16, 1989: 850 khz; 50 kw-D, DA. TL: N36 04 12 W83 58 19. Stereo. 517 Watt Rd. 37922. Phone: (865) 675-4105. Fax: (865) 675-4859. Licensee: Horne Radio L.L.C. Group owner: Horne Radio Group (acq 10-15-99; grpsl). Format: Talk. Target aud: 25 plus; educated, informed adults. ♦ Brian Tatum, CEO & gen mgr.

WKXV(AM)— February 1953: 900 khz; 1 kw-D, 258 w-N. TL: N35 58 52 W83 59 15. 5106 Middlebrook Pike 37921. Phone: (865) 558-0900. Fax: (865) 588-5848. Licensee: Ratel Broadcasting Co. Inc. Format: Relg, Southern gospel. ♦ Ted L. Howe Sr., pres; Ted L. Howe Jr., gen mgr & gen sls mgr; Rick Whisman, news dir; Frank Folsom, chief of engrg.

WNFZ(FM)—See Oak Ridge

WNML(AM)— Mar 23, 1953: 990 khz; 10 kw-U, DA-N. TL: N36 02 33 W83 53 59. Stereo. WIVK711, Box 11167 37939. Secondary address: 4711 Old Kingston Pike 37919. Phone: (865) 588-6511. Fax: (865) 558-4218. Web Site: www.newstalk99.com. Licensee: Citadel Broadcasting Co. Group owner: Citadel Broadcasting Corp. (acq 4-26-2001; grpsl). Network: ABC Information & Entertainment. Format: News/talk, sports. News staff: 8; News: 28 hrs wkly. Target aud: 25-54. ♦ Farid Suleman, CEO; Donna Heffner, CFO; Ed Brantley, gen mgr & gen sls mgr; Mike Hammond, opns mgr; Charles Sells, sls dir; Lisa Rotton, natl sls mgr; Jack Lee Gillette, rgnl sls mgr; Steve Queisser, mktg dir; John Crooks, progmg dir; Tom Graham, news dir; Tim Berry, chief of engrg.

WIVK-FM—Co-owned with WNML(AM). Dec 16, 1965: 107.7 mhz; 91 kw. 2,053 ft. TL: N35 48 41 W83 40 10. Stereo. Fax: (423) 588-3725. Web Site: www.wivk.com. Format: C&W. ♦ John Crooks, progmg dir.

WNOX(FM)—(Oak Ridge). Apr 20, 1974: 100.3 mhz; 100 kw. Ant 2,001 ft. TL: N36 11 53 W84 13 51. Stereo. Box 11167 37939. Secondary address: 4711 Old Kingston Pike 37919. Phone: (865) 588-6511. Fax: (865) 588-3725. Web Site: www.wnoxnewstalk.com. Licensee: Oak Ridge FM Inc. Format: News/talk. ♦ Ed Brantley, VP & gen mgr; Mike Hammond, opns mgr; Jack Lee, gen sls mgr; Mickey Dearstone, mktg dir; John Crooks, progmg dir & news dir; Tim Berry, chief of engrg.

WNPZ(AM)— May 21, 1961: . Stn currently dark 1580 khz; 5 kw-D, 1 kw-CH. TL: N35 54 42 W83 53 33. Metropolitan Management Corp. of Tennessee, Box 639, Decatur, GA 30031. Phone: (404) 377-5531. Fax: (404) 377-6720. Licensee: Metropolitan Management Corp. of Tennessee (acq 5-10-02; $280,000). Format: Christian music. ♦ Randal A. Mangham, pres.

WNRX(FM)—See Jefferson City

WRJZ(AM)— Feb 12, 1927: 620 khz; 5 kw-U, DA-N. TL: N35 59 24 W83 50 15. Christian Media Ctr., 1621 E. Magnolia Ave. 37917. Phone: (865) 525-0620. Fax: (865) 521-8910. Licensee: Tennessee Media Associates. (acq 10-84). Network: USA, Moody. Rep: Salem. Format: Christian, talk. News: 5 hrs wkly. Target aud: 25-54; white collar men & woman. ♦ Thomas Moffitt Jr., pres; David Wells, gen mgr; Larry Richmond, opns mgr.

*WUOT(FM)— October 1949: 91.9 mhz; 100 kw. 1,580 ft. TL: N36 00 19 W83 56 23. Stereo. Univ. of Tennessee, 209 Communications Bldg. 37996-0322. Phone: (865) 974-5375. Fax: (865) 974-3941. E-mail:

Tennessee

wuot@utk.edu. Web Site: www.wuot.org. Licensee: University of Tennessee. Network: Network: PRI, NPR. Cohn & Marks. Format: Class, jazz, news. News staff: 2; News: 30 hrs wkly. Target aud: 35-54. ♦ Regina Dean, gen mgr.

*WUTK-FM— Jan 4, 1982: 90.3 mhz; 800 w. 23 ft. TL: N35 57 09 W83 55 34. Stereo. Univ. of Tenn., P-103 Andy Holt Tower 37996. Phone: (865) 974-2228. Phone: (865) 974-2229. Fax: (865) 974-2814. Web Site: www.wutkradio.com. Licensee: University of Tennessee. (acq 8-31-88). Format: New rock. Target aud: 18-24; students. ♦ Benny Smith, gen mgr.

WVLZ(AM)— June 1, 1988: 1180 khz; 10 kw-D, 2.6 kw-CH. TL: N35 58 48 W83 49 09. 802 S. Central Ave. 37902. Phone: (865) 546-4653. Fax: (865) 637-7133. Web Site: www.wvlz.com. Licensee: Kirkland Wireless Broadcasters Inc. (acq 3-25-02; $400,000. with WKCE(AM) Maryville). Format: Sports. Target aud: 30 plus; young, married with small children. ♦ John Hodge, gen mgr & stn mgr.

WWST(FM)—See Sevierville

WYFC(FM)—See Clinton

La Follette

WGLH(AM)— Sept 1, 1983: 960 khz; 1 kw-D. TL: N36 22 02 W84 08 50. Box 1530 37766. Phone: (423) 566-1000. Fax: (423) 457-5900. Fax: (865) 457-5900. Licensee: La Follette Broadcasters Inc. (acq 8-24-99; with co-located FM). Rep: Roslin. Format: Southern gospel. Target aud: General. ♦ Cliff Jennings, pres & gen mgr; Barbara Nuls, gen sls mgr.

WQLA-FM—Co-owned with WGLH(AM). Sept 1, 1982: 104.9 mhz; 1.1 kw. 499 ft. TL: N36 21 08 W84 05 20. (CP: 900 w). Stereo. E-mail: qq104@ccdogisland.net. Format: C&W, sports. Target aud: 18 plus. ♦ Barbara Nuls, gen sls mgr.

WLAF(AM)— May 17, 1953: 1450 khz; 1 kw-U. TL: N36 22 52 W84 07 32. Drawer 1409 37766. Secondary address: 210 N 5th St 37766. Phone: (423) 562-1450. Phone: (423) 562-3557. Fax: (423) 562-5764. E-mail: wlaf@campbellcounty.com. Licensee: Stair Co. Inc. (acq 12-15-88; $125,000; 1-16-89). Network: USA. Format: Gospel. News staff: one; News: 7 hrs wkly. Target aud: 12+ or 25+. Spec prog: Bluegrass 7 hrs wkly. ♦ Jim Stair, pres; Bill Waddell, VP, opns VP & dev VP.

La Vergne

WBUZ(FM)— May 1, 1962: 102.9 mhz; 100 kw. Ant 954 ft. TL: N35 48 01 W86 37 17. Stereo. 1824 Murfreesboro Rd., Nashville 37217. Phone: (615) 399-1029. Fax: (615) 399-1023. E-mail: programming @1029thebuzz.com. Web Site: www.1029thebuzz.com. Licensee: WYCQ Inc. Group owner: The Cromwell Group Inc. (acq 11-28-89). Format: New rock. Target aud: 18-34; residents in middle TN. Spec prog: Farm one hr wkly. ♦ Bayard Walters, pres; Bob Reich, stn mgr; Shauna Conner, prom dir; Russ Schenck, progmg dir; Jim Patrick, news dir; David Wilson, chief of engrg.

Lafayette

WEEN(AM)— Nov 3, 1958: 1460 khz; 1 kw-D, 138 w-N. TL: N36 32 06 W86 00 27. 231 Chaffin Rd. 37083. Phone: (615) 666-2169. Fax: (615) 666-8056. E-mail: wlct@nctc.com. Licensee: Lafayette Broadcasting Co. Inc. (acq 11-1-01). Network: Salem Radio Network. Format: Solid Gospel. Target aud: General; 25-54 year olds. Spec prog: Farm 5 hrs wkly. ♦ Ivan Davis, CEO & pres; Randall Swaffer, gen mgr, stn mgr & opns dir.

WLCT(FM)— July 1, 1995: 102.1 mhz; 6 kw. Ant 325 ft. TL: N36 32 06 W86 00 27. Stereo. 231 Chaffin Rd. 37083. Phone: (615) 666-2169. Fax: (615) 666-8056. E-mail: wlct@nctc.com. Licensee: Lafayette Broadcasting Co. Inc. Format: Country. Target aud: 20-60. ♦ Melinda White, gen mgr; Randy Swaffer, gen mgr & opns mgr; Jamie Dallas, mktg mgr, sls & mktg; Jamie DAllas, prom.

Lakeland

WMQM(AM)—Licensed to Lakeland. See Memphis

Lawrenceburg

*WAWI(FM)— 1999: 89.7 mhz; 6 kw. Ant 148 ft. TL: N35 16 04 W87 19 25. Box 3206, American Family Radio, Tupelo, MS 38803. Phone: (662) 844-8888. Fax: (662) 842-6791. E-mail: comments@afr.net. Web Site: www.afr.net. Licensee: American Family Association. Group owner: American Family Radio Format: Relg. ♦ Marvin Sanders, gen mgr.

WDXE(AM)— July 21, 1951: 1370 khz; 1 kw-D, 44 w-N. TL: N35 15 25 W87 18 24. 6 Public Square 38464. Phone: (931) 762-4411. Fax: (931) 762-4789. E-mail: wdxe@charter.net. Licensee: Lakewood Communications LLC (acq 9-11-02; $450,000. with co-located FM). Network: ABC Daytime Direction. Format: Classic country. ♦ Jack Cheatwood, gen mgr, stn mgr & news dir; Ron Fisher, gen sls mgr & progmg dir; Phillip Kemper, chief of engrg.

WDXE-FM— Aug 28, 1964: 106.7 mhz; 6 kw. Ant 292 ft. TL: N35 15 25 W87 18 24. Format: Adult contemp. ♦ Jack Cheatwood, gen mgr & progmg dir.

WLLX(FM)—Listing follows WWLX(AM).

WWLX(AM)— June 21, 1987: 590 khz; 600 w-D, 133 w-N. TL: N35 12 18 W87 19 39. Stereo. Box 156 38464. Secondary address: 1212 N. Locust Ave. 38464. Phone: (931) 762-6200. Fax: (931) 762-6200. E-mail: wwlx@bellsouth.net. Licensee: Roger W. Wright dba Prospect Communications. Network: ABC Information & Entertainment. Format: C&W. News staff: one; News: 10 hrs wkly. Target aud: General. Spec prog: Oldies R&R 8 hrs, old country 8 hrs wkly. ♦ Janet Wright, gen sls mgr & prom mgr; Dan Hollander, progmg dir; Michele Tankersley, news dir; Roger Wright, pres, gen mgr & chief of engrg.

WLLX(FM)—Co-owned with WWLX(AM). May 1991: 97.5 mhz; 2.3 kw. 535 ft. TL: N35 12 18 W87 19 39. Stereo. E-mail: wllxradio@lorettotel.net. Format: Country. News staff: one. Target aud: 25-54. ♦ Janet Wright, mktg mgr & adv mgr; Dan Hollander, mus dir; Roger Wright, pub affrs dir.

*WZXX(FM)— 2005: 88.5 mhz; 300 w. Ant 276 ft. TL: N35 15 18 W87 19 30. Box 5459, Twin Falls, ID 83303-5459. Phone: (208) 733-3551. Fax: (208) 733-3548. Web Site: www.radioassistministry.com. Licensee: Radio Assist Ministry Inc. (group owner). (acq 5-5-2005; $85,000). ♦ Clark Parrish, pres; Matt Austin, gen mgr.

Lebanon

WANT(FM)— Oct 1, 1993: 98.9 mhz; 5 kw. 320 ft. TL: N36 12 24 W86 16 02. Stereo. 510 Trousdale Ferry Pike 37087. Phone: (615) 449-3699. Fax: (615) 443-4235. Web Site: www.wantfm.com. Licensee: Bay-Pointe Broadcasting Co. Inc. Tierney & Swift. Format: Country. News staff: one. Target aud: General. ♦ Billy Goodman, opns mgr & news dir; M.J. Lucas, mus dir; Susan H. Bay, pres, gen mgr, progmg dir & pub affrs dir; Albert S. Jarratt Sr., chief of engrg.

WCKD(AM)— July 1, 2003: 1490 khz; 1 kw-U. TL: N36 11 42 W86 17 26. 1617 Lebonon Rd., Nashville 37210. Phone: (615) 889-1960. Licensee: WCKD Inc. Network: CNN Radio. Irwin, Campbell & Tannenbaum. Format: News/talk. ♦ William O. Barry, pres.

WCOR(AM)— Oct 5, 1949: 900 khz; 5 kw-D, 136 w-N. TL: N36 12 26 W86 16 03. Stereo. 510 Trousdale Ferry Pike 37087. Phone: (615) 444-0900. Fax: (615) 443-4235. Web Site: www.wantfm.com. Licensee: WCOR Inc. (acq 4-93; 3-15-93). Irwin, Campbell, & Tannewald. Format: Country. News staff: one. Target aud: General. ♦ Susan H. Bay, pres & gen mgr; Billy Goodman, news dir; Coleman Walker, pub affrs dir; Gary Brown, chief of engrg.

*WFMQ(FM)— Dec 15, 1966: 91.5 mhz; 500 w. 100 ft. TL: N36 12 13 W86 18 01. Stereo. One Cumberland Sq. 37087-3554. Phone: (615) 444-2562. Fax: (615) 444-2569. Licensee: Cumberland University. Format: Class, contemp urban rock. Spec prog: Jazz 4 hrs, Sp 3 hrs wkly.

WRVW(FM)— Aug 31, 1962: 107.5 mhz; 46 kw. Ant 1,342 ft. TL: N36 15 50 W86 47 39. Stereo. 55 Music Sq. W., Nashville 37203. Phone: (615) 664-2400. Fax: (615) 664-2434. E-mail: programming @1075theriver.com. Web Site: www.1075theriver.com. Licensee: Capstar TX L.P. Group owner: Clear Channel Communications Inc. (acq 8-30-00; grpsl). Network: ABC FM Connection. Format: CHR. News staff: one; News: 4 hrs wkly. Target aud: 18-49. ♦ Gene McKay, gen mgr; Keith Kaufman, opns mgr; Darren Smith, sls dir; Tom Schurr, mktg mgr; Temple Hancock, prom mgr; Rich Davis, progmg dir.

Lenoir City

WBLC(AM)— June 15, 1965: 1360 khz; 1 kw-D, 24 w-N. TL: N35 32 W84 17 45. Box 247 37771. Secondary address: 4787 Browder Hollow Rd. 37771. Phone: (865) 986-5332. Fax: (865) 986-5332. E-mail: wblc3abn@bellsouth.net. Licensee: Three Angels Broadcasting Network Inc. (acq 8-13-02; $55,000). Format: Christian, relg. Target aud: 35 plus. ♦ Jim Morris, gen mgr & stn mgr.

WKZX-FM—Listing follows WLIL(AM).

WLIL(AM)— May 30, 1950: 730 khz; 1 kw-D, 280 w-N. TL: N35 46 12 W84 16 47. Box 340, 406 E. Broadway 37771. Phone: (865) 986-7536. E-mail: wlilcountry@aol.com. Licensee: B.P. Broadcasters L.L.C. (acq 8-01-00; $1 million with co-located FM). Network: CNN Radio. Rep: Keystone (unwired net). Rgnl Reps. Format: Country oldies. News staff: one; News: 20 hrs wkly. Target aud: General; adults. Spec prog: Black one hr, farm one hr, gospel 18 hrs, American Indian one hr wkly. ♦ Dale Anthony, gen mgr; Glenn A. McNish Sr., stn mgr; Zollie Cantrell Jr., mktg mgr; Ronald McDonald, prom dir.

WKZX-FM—Co-owned with WLIL(AM). Sept 19, 1967: 93.5 mhz; 6 kw. 165 ft. TL: N35 46 12 W84 16 47. Fax: (865) 986-1716. E-mail: wkzx@aol.com. Format: Soft adult contemp. News staff: one; News: 20 hrs wkly. Target aud: General; Adults. ♦ Mark Herzog, progmg dir; Kevin Potter, chief of engrg.

Lewisburg

WAXO(AM)— Sept 1, 1980: 1220 khz; 1 kw-D. TL: N35 25 42 W86 46 22. 217 W. Commerce St. 37091. Phone: (931) 359-6641. Fax: (931) 270-9290. Web Site: www.waxo.com. Licensee: Marshall County Radio Corp. (acq 9-1-82; $250,000; 8-23-82). Network: USA. Format: Country. Spec prog: Gospel 12 hrs wkly. ♦ Bob Smartt, pres & gen mgr.

WJJM(AM)— May 15, 1947: 1490 khz; 1 kw-U. TL: N35 26 58 W86 46 55. Box 2025 37091. Secondary address: 344 E. Church St. 37091. Phone: (931) 359-4511. Fax: (931) 270-9556. E-mail: wjjm@wjjm.com. Web Site: www.wjjm.com. Licensee: WJJM Inc. (acq 3-26-2004; $230,000. with co-located FM). Rep: Keystone (unwired net). Fletcher, Heald & Hidreth. Format: Country. News staff: one; News: 1 hr wkly. Target aud: 25-65; manufacturing, business, family programming. ♦ Michelle W. Haislip, pres; Lisa Savage, gen mgr; Michelle W. Haislip, stn mgr & sls dir; Jeff Haislip, progmg mgr; Doug Hazelwood, mus dir; Tommy Allen, news dir; Don Roden, chief of engrg.

WJJM-FM— Feb 20, 1969: 94.3 mhz; 5.5 kw. Ant 115 ft. TL: N35 27 03 W86 46 57. Stereo. Web Site: www.wjjm.com. ♦ Doug Cheek, adv dir.

Lexington

WDXL(AM)— July 1954: 1490 khz; 1 kw-U. TL: N35 38 05 W88 23 34. Box 279 38351. Secondary address: 584 Smith Ave. 38351. Phone: (731) 968-3500. Phone: (731) 968-9990. Fax: (731) 968-0380. E-mail: wzlt@netease.net. Licensee: Lexington Broadcast Service Inc. (acq 1955). Network: Network: ABC Information & Entertainment, Jones Radio Networks. Format: Southern gospel. News staff: one; News: 10 hrs wkly. Target aud: 30 plus. Spec prog: Black 4 hrs, gospel 10 hrs wkly. ♦ Dan Hughes, gen mgr & gen sls mgr; Terry Rhodes, progmg dir.

WZLT(FM)—Co-owned with WDXL(AM). September 1964: 99.3 mhz; 5 kw. 150 ft. TL: N35 38 05 W88 23 34. Stereo. Phone: (731) 968-9990. E-mail: wzlt@netease.net. Format: Adult contemp. Target aud: General. ♦ Todd Buttrey, progmg dir.

*WIGH(FM)— Sept 30, 1995: 88.7 mhz; 15 kw. Ant 548 ft. TL: N35 42 12 W88 36 10. (CP: 14 kw, ant 538 ft. TL: N35 43 19 W88 36 07). Stereo. Box 3206, Tupelo, MS 38803. Secondary address: 107 Park Gate Dr., Tupelo, MS 38801. Phone: (662) 844-8888. Fax: (662) 842-6791. Licensee: American Family Association. Group owner: American Family Radio (acq 5-22-03; $20,000). Network: American Family Radio. Format: Christian. Target aud: Visually & physically impaired. ♦ Marvin Sanders, gen mgr.

Developers & Brokers of Radio Properties

contact American Media Services at our suite:
Philadelphia Marriott Downtown
215-625-2900
843-972-2200
americanmediaservices.com
Charleston, SC
Dallas, TX · Chicago, Il · Austin, TX

American Media Services, LLC

Livingston

WLIV(AM)— Nov 26, 1956: 920 khz; 1 kw-D. TL: N36 22 28 W85 18 20. Box 359, 1130 W. Main St. 38570. Phone: (931) 823-1226. Fax: (931) 823-6005. Licensee: Sunny Broadcasting G.P. (acq 1996; $100,000. with co-located FM). Network: CNN Radio. Rep: Keystone (unwired net). Format: Modern country. News staff: 2; News: 7 hrs wkly. Target aud: General. Spec prog: Farm 2 hrs, relg 15 hrs, gospel 18 hrs wkly. ♦Millard V. Oakley, pres; Joel Upton, gen mgr; Carolyn Peterman, stn mgr; Craig Cantrell, opns dir.

WLQK(FM)— December 1966: 95.9 mhz; 20 kw. 784 ft. TL: N36 11 36 W85 20 41. Stereo. 259 S. Willow Ave., Cookeville 38501. Phone: (931) 526-6064. Fax: (931) 520-1590. Web Site: www.literock959.com. Licensee: JWC Broadcasting (group owner; acq 12-18-98). Format: Soft rock. Target aud: General. ♦Jim Stapleton, gen mgr & stn mgr.

Lobelville

WFGZ(FM)— October 1974: 94.5 mhz; 22 kw. Ant 715 ft. TL: N35 45 56 W87 49 50. Stereo. 500 E. College, Dickson 37055. Phone: (888) 855-9394. Fax: (731) 855-1600. E-mail: info@gracebroadcasting.com. Web Site: www.gracebroadcasting.com. Licensee: Grace Broadcasting Services Inc. (acq 11-28-2003; $487,000). Format: Contemp Christian. News staff: one; News: 14 hrs wkly. Target aud: 18-54; mid to upper income adults with purchasing power. ♦Charles M. Ennis, pres; Lacy Ennis, gen mgr & opns mgr.

Lookout Mountain

WFLI(AM)— Feb 20, 1961: 1070 khz; 50 kw-D, 2.5 kw-N, DA-2. TL: N35 02 42 W85 21 44. 621 O' Grady Dr., Chattanooga 37419. Phone: (423) 821-3555. Fax: (423) 821-3557. E-mail: flipaul@aol.com. Licensee: WFLI Inc. Network: USA. Format: Relg. Target aud: 18-54. Spec prog: College football. ♦Ying Hua Benns, pres & gen mgr; Paul White, stn mgr & opns mgr.

Loretto

WJHX(AM)—See Lexington, AL

Loudon

WKVL-FM— May 20, 1991: 105.3 mhz; 6 kw. 328 ft. TL: N35 48 40 W84 16 02. Stereo. 517 Watt Rd., Knoxville 37922. Phone: (865) 675-4105. Fax: (865) 675-4859. E-mail: horneradio@nxs.net. Web Site: www.wkvl.com. Licensee: Horne Radio L.L.C. Group owner: Horne Radio Group (acq 8-29-01; grpsl). Network: CBS. Format: AAA. News: 3 hrs wkly. Target aud: 25-50; baby boomers. ♦Douglas A. Horne, pres; Jim Christensen, gen mgr; Shawn Nunally, gen sls mgr; Todd Ethridge, progmg dir; Brian Tatum, chief of engrg.

WLOD(AM)— Jan 1, 1983: 1140 khz; 1 kw-D. TL: N35 43 35 W84 20 49. 517 Watt Rd., Knoxville 37922. Phone: (865) 675-4105. Fax: (865) 675-4859. Licensee: Horne Radio LLC. Group owner: Horne Radio Group (acq 8-29-01; grpsl). Network: ABC. Format: News/Talk. News staff: one. Target aud: 35 plus. ♦Bill Tatum, gen mgr.

WNML-FM— Jan 5, 1989: 99.1 mhz; 6 kw. 328 ft. TL: N35 47 10 W84 17 24. Stereo. Box 11167, Knoxville 37939-1167. Secondary address: 4711 Old Kingston Pike, Knoxville 37919. Phone: (865) 588-6511. Fax: (865) 558-4217. Web Site: www.newstalk99.com. Licensee: Citadel Broadcasting Co. Group owner: Citadel Broadcasting Corp. (acq 8-2-00; grpsl). Network: Network: ABC, Westwood One. Rgnl Reps. Gardner, Carton & Douglas. Format: Sports. Target aud: 25-54. ♦Ed Brantley, gen mgr; Mike Hammond, opns mgr; Jack Lee, gen sls mgr; Mickey Dearstone, mktg dir; John Crooks, progmg dir; Tim Berry, chief of engrg.

Madison

WPLN(AM)—Licensed to Madison. See Nashville

WRLT(FM)—See Franklin

Madisonville

WRKQ(AM)— July 12, 1967: 1250 khz; 500 w-D, 86 w-N. TL: N35 30 29 W84 22 45. Box 489 37354. Phone: (423) 442-1446. Fax: (423) 440-9636. Web Site: www.wrkq.net. Licensee: Beverly Broadcasting Co. LLC (acq 5-4-2004; $40,000). Network: CBS Radio. Format: News/talk. News staff: one. Target aud: General. ♦Mike Beverly, pres & gen mgr.

WYGO(FM)— Nov 15, 1992: 99.5 mhz; 2.51 kw. 515 ft. TL: N35 30 20 W84 27 21. Stereo. Box 933, Athens 37371. Secondary address: 2110 Oxnard Rd., Athens 37303. Phone: (423) 337-0995. Phone: (423) 746-0995. Fax: (423) 745-2000. Licensee: Major Broadcasting Corp. Format: Music of 80s & 90s, hot adult contemp. Target aud: 18-54. ♦Randy Sliger, gen mgr.

Manchester

WFTZ(FM)— Nov 16, 1992: 101.5 mhz; 3 kw. 345 ft. TL: N35 23 51 W86 08 39. Stereo. Box 1015 37349. Secondary address: 1025 Hillsboro Blvd. 37349. Phone: (931) 723-1015. Phone: (931) 728-3458. Fax: (931) 723-1099. E-mail: kahuna@fantasyradio.com. Web Site: www.fantasyradio.com. Licensee: Phase Two Communications Inc. (acq 10-21-91). Network: ABC. Timothy K. Brady. Format: Adult contemp. News staff: one; News: 4 hrs wkly. Target aud: 25-45; white collar, educated. ♦Roger H. Dotson, CEO, pres, gen mgr, opns mgr & chief of engrg; Marsha T. Dotson, gen sls mgr; Amber Dotson, prom VP; Bill Priestly, progmg dir; Wayne D. Hudgens, news dir & pub affrs dir.

WMSR(AM)— Apr 7, 1957: 1320 khz; 5 kw-D, 79 w-N. TL: N35 28 03 W86 05 42. 1030 Oakdale St. 37355. Phone: (931) 728-3526. Phone: (931) 728-1320. Fax: (931) 728-3527. Web Site: www.wmsrthegroove.com. Licensee: Coffee County Broadcasting Inc. (acq 8-22-2005; $700,000). Format: Oldies, sports, talk. News staff: one; News: 21 hrs wkly. Target aud: General. Spec prog: High school sports, farm. ♦Scott Vaughn, gen mgr.

WWTN(FM)— June 20, 1962: 99.7 mhz; 100 kw. 2,033 ft. TL: N35 28 03 W86 05 42. Stereo. 10 Music Cir. E., Nashville 37203. Phone: (615) 321-1067. Fax: (615) 321-5771. Fax: (615) 871-6099. Web Site: www.997wtn.com. Licensee: Cumulus Licensing Corp. Group owner: Cumulus Media Inc. (acq 7-21-2003; $65 million. with WSM-FM Nashville). Network: Network: ABC, CBS Radio. Format: News/talk, sports. Target aud: 25-54; general. ♦Michael Dickey, gen mgr.

Martin

WCMT(AM)— June 8, 1957: 1410 khz; 700 w-D, 58 w-N. TL: N36 21 45 W88 50 56. Box 318, 1410 N. Lindell St. 38237. Phone: (731) 587-9526. Fax: (731) 587-5079. Licensee: Thunderbolt Broadcasting Co. Group owner: Thunderbolt Broadcasting Co./Gibson County Broadcasting (acq 3-1-80; FTR: 2-18-80). Network: Network: Westwood One, AP Radio. Womble, Carlyle, Sandridge & Rice. Format: News/talk, oldies. News: 10 hrs wkly. Target aud: 25-54; baby boomers. ♦Jimmy Smith, VP; Paul F. Tinkle, CEO, pres & gen mgr.

WCMT-FM— Sept 26, 1967: 101.3 mhz; 22 kw. Ant 308 ft. TL: N36 29 00 W88 57 10. Stereo. Web Site: www.wcmt.com/mix.htm. Womble, Carlyle, Sandridge & Rice. Format: Adult contemp mix. News: 25 hrs wkly.

***WUTM(FM)**— Sept 1, 1971: 90.3 mhz; 185 w. 250 ft. TL: N36 20 28 W88 51 39. Stereo. 220 Gooch Hall, Univ. of Tenn. at Martin 38238. Phone: (731) 881-7095. Fax: (731) 881-7550. E-mail: wutm@utm.edu. Web Site: www.utm.edu%7Ewutm/. Licensee: University of Tennessee. Format: CHR. Target aud: General; Univ. ♦Richard Robinson, gen mgr; Rodney Freed, stn mgr.

Maryville

WBCR(AM)—See Alcoa

###ized

WGAP(AM)— Aug 13, 1947: 1400 khz; 1 kw-U. TL: N35 45 41 W83 58 57. 517 Watt Rd. 37922. Phone: (865) 983-4310. Phone: (865) 983-4105. Fax: (865) 983-4314. Fax: (865) 675-4859. Licensee: Horne Radio LLC. Group owner: Horne Radio Group (acq 8-29-01; grpsl). Network: Motor Racing Net. Rep: Rgnl Reps. Pepper & Corazzini. Format: Country. News staff: one; News: 18 hrs wkly. Target aud: 25 plus; general. ♦Brian Tatum, gen mgr.

WKCE(AM)— 1989: 1120 khz; 500 w-D. TL: N35 45 08 W83 35 04. Stereo. 802 S. Central, Knoxville 37902. Phone: (865) 546-4653. Fax: (865) 637-7133. Web Site: www.wviz.com. Licensee: Kirkland Wireless Broadcasters Inc. (acq 3-25-02; $400,000. with WVLZ(AM) Knoxville). Format: Adult standards. ♦Doug Matthews, gen mgr.

WTXM(FM)— Feb 2, 1990: 95.7 mhz; 3 kw. 328 ft. TL: N35 49 53 W84 01 25. Stereo. 1100 Sharps Ridge Mem Park Dr., Knoxville 37917. Phone: (865) 525-6000. Fax: (865) 656-4386. Web Site: www.knoxoldies.com. Licensee: South Central Communications Corp. (group owner) Format: Oldies. ♦John D. Engelbrecht, CEO; Craig Jacobus, pres & gen mgr; Terry Gillingham, opns mgr; Randy Ross, sls dir & prom mgr; Brad Jeffries, progmg dir.

Maynardville

***WOEZ(FM)**— 2001: 88.3 mhz; 2.85 kw horiz. Ant 1,489 ft. TL: N36 00 13 W83 56 34. 1621 E. Magnolia Ave., Knoxville 37917. Phone: (865) 521-8910. Fax: (865) 521-8923. Licensee: Foothills Broadcasting Inc. Format: Btfl mus, jazz, big band. ♦David Wells, gen mgr.

McKenzie

***WAJJ(FM)**— 2002: 89.3 mhz; 1 kw. Ant 328 ft. TL: N36 06 55 W88 30 38. 1415 Island Ford Rd., Madisonville, KY 42431. Phone: (270) 825-3004. Fax: (270) 825-3005. Web Site: www.wsof.org. Licensee: Madisonville Christian School (acq 7-25-2005; $90,000). Format: Christian educ. ♦Gary Hall, gen mgr.

WHDM(AM)— Jan 29, 1954: 1440 khz; 500 w-D, 91 w-N. TL: N36 07 20 W88 31 31. 110 India Rd., Paris 38242. Phone: (731) 644-9455. Fax: (731) 644-9970. Licensee: WHDM Broadcasting Inc. (acq 1-4-2002; $69,000). Network: ABC. Format: Oldies. News staff: one; News: 4 hrs wkly. ♦Gary D. Benton, pres; Janice Benton, gen mgr & opns VP.

WWYN(FM)— Feb 11, 1963: 106.9 mhz; 100 kw. Ant 892 ft. TL: N35 54 06 W88 46 55. (CP: ant 886 ft. TL: N35 54 05 W88 46 51). Stereo. 111 W. Main St., Jackson 38301. Phone: (731) 427-9616. Fax: (731) 424-2773. E-mail: cthomas@wwyn.fm. Web Site: www.wwyn.fm. Licensee: Rainbow Media Inc. Group owner: Thomas Radio LLC (acq 11-9-2001). Format: Modern country. News staff: one; News: 4 hrs wkly. Target aud: 25-54; adults. ♦Chip Thomas, gen mgr; Shane Conner, progmg dir; Ellen Bennet, news dir; Jim Smith, chief of engrg.

McKinnon

WTPR-FM— 1992: 101.5 mhz; 790 w. 607 ft. TL: N36 24 39 W87 58 06. 206 N. Brewer St., Paris 38242. Phone: (731) 642-7100. Fax: (731) 642-9367.yes Licensee: WENK Broadcast Group Inc. (group owner; acq 1996; $200,000). Rgnl Reps. Verner, Liipfert, Bernhard, McPherson & Hand. Format: 60s & 70s Oldies. News staff: one; News: 12 hrs wkly. Target aud: 35-54. ♦Terry Hailey, gen mgr, progmg dir & engr.

McMinnville

WAKI(AM)— 1947: 1230 khz; 1 kw-U. TL: N35 41 42 W85 46 33. 100 Mullican St. 37110. Phone: (931) 473-6535. Fax: (931) 473-4149. E-mail: jeffbarnes@clearchannel.com. Licensee: Citicasters Licenses L.P. Group owner: Clear Channel Communications Inc. (acq 10-30-99; grpsl). Timothy K. Brady. Format: Sports, news, talk. News staff: one; News: 24 hrs wkly. Target aud: 25-54; general. Spec prog: Farm 2 hrs wkly. ♦Lowery Mays, pres; David Roederer, gen mgr; Bryan Kell, stn mgr; Marty McFly, chief of opns.

WBMC(AM)— May 1, 1955: 960 khz; 500 w-D. TL: N35 40 00 W85 46 00. Box 759 37110. Secondary address: 230 W. Colville St. 37110. Phone: (931) 473-2104. Fax: (931) 473-4149. Licensee: Citicasters Licenses L.P. Group owner: Clear Channel Communications Inc. (acq 10-14-99; grpsl). Network: ABC. Format: Country, Top-40, gospel. News staff: one; News: 10 hrs wkly. Target aud: General. Spec prog: Farm 5 hrs wkly. ♦Bryan Kell, gen mgr, stn mgr & gen sls mgr; Jeff Barnes, progmg dir; Jay Walker, news dir; Homer Wilson Jr., chief of engrg.

WTRZ-FM—Co-owned with WBMC(AM). Jan 23, 1964: 103.9 mhz; 5.3 kw. 130 ft. TL: N35 40 00 W85 46 00. Stereo. Phone: (931) 473-9253. Web Site: hotcountry104.com. Format: Hot country. Target aud: 18-40. ♦Bryan Kell, sls dir; Jeff Edwards, progmg dir.

***WCPI(FM)**— February 1997: 91.3 mhz; 1 kw vert. -85 ft. TL: N35 40 44 W85 46 01. Stereo. 110 S. Court Sq. 37110. Phone: (931) 506-9274. Fax: (931) 507-1005. Licensee: Warren County Education Foundation. Format: Educ. Target aud: 6 plus. ♦Dr. Norman Rone, pres; Gloria Grissom, stn mgr; Mary Cantrell, mktg dir; Richard Myers, chief of engrg.

Memphis

KJMS(FM)— Mar 10, 1965: 101.1 mhz; 100 kw. Ant 347 ft. TL: N35 08 01 W90 05 38. Stereo. 2650 Thousand Oaks Blvd., Suite 4100 38118. Phone: (901) 527-0101. Fax: (901) 259-6449. E-mail: jeffreyjones@clearchannel.com. Web Site: www.v10ll.com. Licensee: Clear Channel Broadcasting Licenses Inc. Group owner: Clear Channel Communications Inc. Network: ABC FM Connection. Format: Urban contemp. Target aud: 18-49. ♦Jeffrey Jones, gen sls mgr; Tim Davies, VP & mktg mgr; Franklin Gilbert Jr., prom dir & mus dir; Nate Bell, progmg dir; Alonso Pendleton, chief of engrg.

KSUD(AM)—See West Memphis, AR

KWAM(AM)— 1946: 990 khz; 10 kw-D, 450 w-N, DA-2. TL: N35 08 04 W90 05 38. 2650 Thousand Oaks Blvd., Suite 4100 38118. Phone: (901) 259-1300. Fax: (901) 259-6449. Licensee: Concord Media Group Inc. (acq 11-2-2000; $1 million). Format: Talk/news. Target aud: 25 plus; general. ♦Tim Davies, gen mgr; Jeffrey Jones, gen sls mgr; Leonard Blakely, progmg dir.

WBBP(AM)— Apr 11, 1964: 1480 khz; 5 kw-D, 100 w-N. TL: N35 03 18 W90 05 15. 369 GE Patterson Ave. 38126. Phone: (901) 278-7878. Fax: (901) 332-1707. Web Site: www.bbless.org. Licensee: Bountiful Blessings Inc. (acq 10-25-90; $462,000; 11-19-90). Format: Gospel. Target aud: 25-54; Listeners who enjoy a variety of gospel. ♦Bishop G.E. Patterson, pres & gen mgr.

WCRV(AM)—See Collierville

WDIA(AM)— June 7, 1947: 1070 khz; 50 kw-D, 5 kw-N, DA-2. TL: N35 16 05 W90 01 03. 2650 Thousand Oaks Blvd., Suite 4100 38118. Phone: (901) 529-4300. Phone: (901) 529-4300. Fax: (901) 529-9557. Web Site: www.am1070wdia.com. Licensee: Clear Channel Radio Licenses Inc. Group owner: Clear Channel Communications Inc. (acq 1996; grpsl). Network: ABC. Rep: McGavren Guild. Format: Black urban contemp. Target aud: 25-54; Black adults. Spec prog: Gospel. ♦Tim Davies, gen mgr; Jeffrey Jones, gen sls mgr; Franklin Gilbert Jr., prom dir; Bobby O'Jay, progmg dir; Alonzo Pendleton, chief of engrg.

WHRK(FM)—Co-owned with WDIA(AM). Jan 1, 1961: 97.1 mhz; 100 kw. Ant 530 ft. TL: N35 13 23 W90 02 33. Stereo. Phone: (901) 529-4397. Web Site: www.k97fm.com. Format: Urban contemp. Target aud: 18-49.

WEGR(FM)—Listing follows WREC(AM).

***WEVL(FM)**— May 1, 1976: 89.9 mhz; 9.3 kw. 374 ft. TL: N35 08 05 W89 45 38. Stereo. Box 40952 38174-0952. Secondary address: 518 S. Main St. 38103. Phone: (901) 528-0560. Phone: (901) 528-0561. E-mail: wevl@wevl.org. Web Site: www.wevl.org. Licensee: Southern Communication Volunteers Inc. Format: Var, educ, blues. News: 2 hrs wkly. Target aud: General. Spec prog: Jazz 15 hrs, C&W 15 hrs, Fr one hr, Irish 4 hrs, Indian subcontinent one hr wkly. ♦Dan Phillips, pres; Judy Dorsey, stn mgr, opns dir & dev dir.

WGKX(FM)— Jan 10, 1968: 105.9 mhz; 100 kw. Ant 993 ft. TL: N35 09 16 W89 49 20. Stereo. 5629 Murray Rd. 38119. Phone: (901) 682-1106. Fax: (901) 767-9531. Web Site: www.kix106.com. Licensee: Citadel Broadcasting Co. Group owner: Citadel Broadcasting Corp. (acq 3-23-2004; grpsl). Rep: Katz Radio. Kaye, Scholer, Fierman, Hays & Handler. Format: Country. News staff: 2; News: one hr wkly. Target aud: 25-54. ♦Dan Barron, sls dir & chief of engrg; Sheri Sawyer, gen mgr & sls dir; Penny Serpico, gen sls mgr & prom dir; Lance Tidwell, progmg dir.

WGSF(AM)— February 1984: 1030 khz; 50 kw-D, 1 kw-N, 10 kw-CH. TL: N35 10 59 W89 56 17. 3654 Park Ave. 38111. Phone: (901) 454-9948. Fax: (901) 454-1027. Licensee: Arlington Broadcasting Co. Inc. Network: Network: Westwood One, CBS. Format: Spanish. ♦Daniel Ybarra, gen mgr.

WHBQ(AM)— Mar 18, 1925: 560 khz; 5 kw-D, 1 kw-N, DA-2. TL: N35 15 12 W90 02 51. 6080 Mt. Moriah 38115. Phone: (901) 375-9324. Fax: (901) 375-4117. Web Site: www.sports56whbq.com. Licensee: Flinn Broadcasting Corp. (acq 10-1-88). Network: CBS. Format: Sports. News: 2 hrs wkly. Target aud: 18-54. ♦George S. Flinn, pres; Chris Coates, gen mgr; Eli Savoie, progmg dir & chief of engrg.

***WKNO-FM**— Mar 1, 1972: 91.1 mhz; 100 kw. 580 ft. TL: N35 09 17 W89 49 20. Stereo. Box 241880 38124. Secondary address: 900 Getwell Rd. 38111. Phone: (901) 325-6544. Fax: (901) 325-6506. Web Site: www.wknofm.org. Licensee: Mid-South Public Communications Foundation. Network: Network: NPR, PRI. Schwartz, Woods & Miller. Format: Class, news. News staff: one; News: 51 hrs wkly. Target aud: 35 plus. ♦Michael LaBonia, pres; Dan Campbell, gen mgr; Charles McCarty, dev dir. Co-owned TV: *WKNO-TV affil

WLOK(AM)— Mar 1, 1956: 1340 khz; 1 kw-U. TL: N35 07 01 W90 00 59. 363 S. 2nd St. 38103. Phone: (901) 527-9565. Fax: (901) 528-0335. Web Site: www.wlok.com. Licensee: Gilliam Communications Inc. (acq 1-12-77). Rep: McGavren Guild. Format: Gospel, talk. News staff: one. Target aud: 25-54. ♦H. A. Gillian Jr., gen mgr; Michael Anderson, gen sls mgr & natl sls mgr; Kim Harper, progmg dir; J.C. Floyd, news dir.

WMBZ(FM)—(Germantown). Apr 15, 1977: 94.1 mhz; 50 kw. Ant 472 ft. TL: N34 59 22 W89 51 45. Stereo. 5904 Ridgeway Ctr. Pkwy. 38120. Phone: (901) 767-0104. Fax: (901) 682-2804. Web Site: www.941thebuzz.com. Licensee: Entercom Memphis License LLC. Group owner: Entercom Communications Corp. (acq 12-13-99; grpsl). Format: Hot Adult Contemp. News staff: one; News: 2 hrs wkly. Target aud: 18-49; adults with discretionary income. ♦Mike Ginsburg, gen mgr; Jerry Dean, opns VP.

WMC(AM)— Jan 21, 1923: 790 khz; 5 kw-U, DA-N. TL: N35 10 09 W89 53 12. Stereo. 1960 Union Ave. 38104. Phone: (901) 726-0555. Fax: (901) 726-5847. Web Site: themighty790.com. Licensee: Infinity Radio Inc. Group owner: Infinity Broadcasting Corp. (acq 8-30-00; $75 million. with co-located FM). Rep: Interep. Format: Sports. News staff: one. Target aud: Men 25-54. ♦Terry Wood, sr VP, VP, gen mgr, gen mgr & opns mgr.

WMC-FM— May 22, 1947: 99.7 mhz; 300 kw. 970 ft. TL: N35 10 09 W89 53 12. Stereo. Fax: (901) 272-9618. Web Site: www.fm100memphis.com. Format: Adult contemp. Target aud: 25-54; adults.

WMCM(FM)—Co-owned with WRKD(AM). Apr 16, 1968: 103.3 mhz; 20.5 kw. 771 ft. TL: N44 07 35 W69 08 18. Stereo. Format: Country. News staff: one. Target aud: General. ♦D.J. McCoy, progmg dir.

WMCR-FM— September 1972: 106.3 mhz; 390 w. 718 ft. TL: N43 02 48 W75 39 58.

WMPS(AM)—(Bartlett). Aug 19, 1986: 1210 khz; 10 kw-D, 250 w-N, DA-2. TL: N35 18 27 W89 38 21. 6080 Mt. Moriah Rd. Ext. 38115. Phone: (901) 375-9324. Fax: (901) 375-0041. Licensee: Arlington Broadcasting Co. Inc. Format: Music of Your Life. Target aud: 25 plus. Spec prog: Relg progmg 7 hrs wkly. ♦Fred Flinn, pres; Shea Flinn, gen mgr.

WMQM(AM)—(Lakeland). Apr 27, 1955: 1600 khz; 50 kw-D, 35 w-N. TL: N35 10 34 W89 56 10. 3704 Whittier 38108. Secondary address: Sale Office, 1300 WWCR Ave., Nashville 37218. Phone: (901) 327-2500. Fax: (901) 327-2777. Web Site: www.wwcr.com. Licensee: WMQM Inc. Group owner: F.W. Robbert Broadcasting Co. Inc. Format: Relg. Target aud: General. ♦Fred P. Werstenberger, pres; George McClintock, gen mgr; David Brown, stn mgr; Adam Lock, opns mgr.

WOWW(AM)—(Germantown). October 1955: 1430 khz; 2.5 kw-U, DA-N. TL: N35 04 20 W89 51 40 (day); N35 12 50 W89 47 46 (night). (CP: 2.8 kw-U, DA-2. TL: N34 59 22 W89 51 45 (one-site)). 6080 Mt. Mariah Rd. Ext. 38115. Phone: (901) 375-9324. Fax: (901) 375-0041. Web Site: www.radiodisney.com. Licensee: Flinn Broadcasting Corp. (acq 9-22-93; $695,000; 10-11-93). Format: Radio disney. Target aud: 25-54. ♦George S. Flinn, pres; Lonnie Treadaway, gen mgr.

***WPLX(AM)**—(Germantown). April 1987: 1170 khz; 1 kw-D. TL: N35 01 28 W89 42 21. 5700 West Oak Blvd., Rocklin, CA 95765. Phone: (916) 251-1600. Fax: (916) 251-1650. E-mail: klove@klove.com. Web Site: www.klove.com. Licensee: Educational Media Foundation. Group owner: EMF Broadcasting (acq 10-20-00; grpsl). Network: K-Love. Shaw Pittman. Format: Contemp christian mus. News staff: 3. Target aud: 25-44; female (Judeo-Christian). ♦Richard Jenkins, pres; Mike Novak, VP; Ed Lenane, opns dir; Keith Whipple, dev dir.

***WQOX(FM)**— Apr 8, 1974: 88.5 mhz; 30 kw. 430 ft. TL: N35 09 17 W89 49 20. Stereo. Telecommunications Center, 2485 Union Ave. 38112. Phone: (901) 320-3460. Fax: (901) 454-7673. Web Site: www.wqoxmes/admin/avery/mes.com. Licensee: Board of Education Memphis City Schools. Format: Adult contemp, educ, pub affrs. News: 4 hrs wkly. Target aud: 12-54; Students, teachers, parents & admin staff. Spec prog: Sports 6 hrs, Black 5 hrs, folk 3 hrs, jazz/blues 10 hrs wkly. ♦Derek Wagner, gen mgr & opns mgr; Derek A. Wagner, opns mgr; Paul Gubala, progmg mgr & mus dir; Chris Malone, asst music dir & pub affrs dir; Sherman Austin, progmg dir & pub affrs dir; Joseph Chambers III, chief of engrg.

WREC(AM)— September 1922: 600 khz; 5 kw-U, DA-2. TL: N35 11 51 W90 00 31. 2650 Thousand Oaks Blvd., Suite 4100 38118. Phone: (901) 259-1300. Fax: (901) 259-6449. E-mail: srs103@rock103.com. Web Site: www.wrecradio.com. Licensee: Clear Channel Licenses Inc. Group owner: Clear Channel Communications Inc. (acq 1996; grpsl). Network: Network: Westwood One, ABC. Rep: Clear Channel. Format: News/talk, sports & info. News staff: 2; News: 5 hrs wkly. Target aud: 35 plus; upscale, professional, males 70%. Spec prog: Farm 3 hrs, relg 4 hrs wkly. ♦Lowry Mays, CEO; Mark Mays, chmn; Randy Michaels, pres; Herb Hill, CFO; Pete Ferrara, sr VP; Timothy P. Davies, gen mgr; Jackie Smith, opns mgr; Anne Sommer, gen sls mgr; Michelle Buckalew, mktg dir & prom mgr; Nate Lundy, progmg dir. Co-owned TV: WPTY-TV, WUMT(TV) affils

WEGR(FM)—Co-owned with WREC(AM). March 1967: 102.7 mhz; 100 kw. 970 ft. TL: N35 10 52 W89 49 56. Stereo. E-mail: rock103@aol.com. Web Site: www.rock103.com. Format: Classic rock. News staff: one; News: 15 hrs wkly. Target aud: 25-54; 25-34 core audience-70% male, 30% female. Spec prog: Rockline, flashback, blues show. ♦Ralph Salierno, gen sls mgr; Felicia Moore, prom mgr; Tim Spencer, opns mgr & progmg dir; Gary Condrey, chief of engrg. Co-owned TV: WPTY-TV, WLMT(TV) affils

WRVR-FM—Listing follows WWTQ(AM).

***WUMR(FM)**— August 1979: 91.7 mhz; 25 kw. 394 ft. TL: N35 09 17 W89 51 28. Stereo. Univ. of Memphis, 3745 Central Ave. 38152. Phone: (901) 678-3176. Phone: (901) 678-4843. Fax: (901) 678-4331. Licensee: The University of Memphis. (acq 1979). Schwartz, Woods & Miller. Format: Jazz, sports. News: 2 hrs wkly. Target aud: 18-49; upscale, college-educated. ♦Robert McDowell, gen mgr.

WWTQ(AM)— March 1925: 680 khz; 10 kw-D, 5 kw-N, DA-N. TL: N35 13 23 W90 02 33. Stereo. 5904 Ridgeway Ctr. Pkwy. 38120. Phone: (901) 767-0104. Fax: (901) 767-0582. Licensee: Entercom Memphis License LLC. Group owner: Entercom Communications Corp. (acq 12-13-99; grpsl). Format: Progressive talk. News staff: one; News: one hr wkly. Target aud: 35-64; adults. ♦Mike Ginsburg, gen mgr; Jerry Dean, opns dir, progmg dir & progmg mgr; Steve Mohammed, gen sls mgr; Jim Scott, prom mgr; Debby Hall, news dir; Mike Schwartz, chief of engrg.

WRVR-FM—Co-owned with WWTQ(AM). Sept 15, 1968: 104.5 mhz; 100 kw. 751 ft. TL: N35 09 17 W89 49 20. Stereo. E-mail: river104@wrvr.com. Web Site: www.wrvr.com. Format: Adult contemp. News staff: one; News: 2 hrs wkly. ♦Mike Ginsburg, VP; Gary Harkin, gen sls mgr; Jim Scott, prom dir.

WXMX(FM)—(Millington). Apr 12, 1960: 98.1 mhz; 100 kw. 1,240 ft. TL: N35 28 03 W90 11 27. (CP: Ant 768 ft.). Stereo. 5629 Murray Rd. 38119. Phone: (901) 682-1106. Fax: (901) 767-9531. Web Site: www.981themax.com. Licensee: Citadel Broadcasting Co. Group owner: Citadel Broadcasting Corp. (acq 3-23-2004; grpsl). Format: Classic hits, oldies. Target aud: 25-54; adults, upwardly mobile with above average income. ♦Timothy Martz, pres & gen mgr; Tony Yoken, gen mgr.

Stations in the U.S. Tennessee

Developers & Brokers of Radio Properties
contact American Media Services at our suite:
Philadelphia Marriott Downtown
215-625-2900
843-972-2200
americanmediaservices.com
Charleston, SC
Dallas, TX · Chicago, Il · Austin, TX
American Media Services, LLC

*WYPL(FM)— Apr 17, 1991: 89.3 mhz; 100 kw. Ant 1,253 ft. TL: N35 28 03 W90 11 27. Stereo. Memphis Public Library, 3030 Poplar Ave. 38111. Phone: (901) 415-2752. Fax: (901) 323-7902. Web Site: www.memphislibrary.org. Licensee: Memphis/Shelby County Public Library & Information Center. Reddy, Begley & McCormick. Format: News. News: 110 hrs wkly. Target aud: General. Spec prog: Sp one hr wkly. ♦ Tommy Warren, gen mgr.

Middleton

WYDL(FM)— 2001: 100.7 mhz; 25 kw. Ant 328 ft. TL: N35 00 13 W88 39 39. 102 N. Cass St., Suite D, Corinth, MS 38834. Phone: (662) 284-4611. Fax: (662) 284-9609. Web Site: www.wydl.com. Licensee: Flinn Broadcasting Corp. Format: CHR, top-40, adult contemp. ♦ Mike Brandt, gen mgr; Wendy Sherrod, gen sls mgr.

Milan

WYNU(FM)— Dec 12, 1964: 92.3 mhz; 100 kw. 991 ft. TL: N35 54 06 W88 46 55. Stereo. 122 Radio Rd., Jackson 38301. Phone: (731) 427-3316. Fax: (731) 427-4576. E-mail: steveburke@clearchannel.com. Web Site: www.rock923.net. Licensee: Capstar TX L.P. Group owner: Clear Channel Communications Inc. (acq 8-30-00; grpsl). Mullin, Rhyne, Emmons & Topel. Format: Classic rock. News staff: one; News: 5 hrs wkly. Target aud: 18-54; middle/upper income adults with disposable income & buying power. ♦ Roger Vestal, gen mgr; Dave Hacker, opns mgr; Gina Langley, gen sls mgr; Steve Burke, progmg dir.

Millington

WLRM(AM)— June 22, 1962: 1380 khz; 2.5 kw-D, 1 kw-N, DA-2. TL: N35 18 56 W89 55 23. 6655 Winchester Rd., Memphis 38115. Phone: (901) 454-4900. Licensee: CPT & T Radio Station Inc. (acq 12-28-2004; $400,000). Format: Inspirational love. ♦ Michelle Price, gen mgr.

WXMX(FM)—Licensed to Millington. See Memphis

Minor Hill

WEUZ(FM)— Sept 2, 1983: 92.1 mhz; 1.2 kw. 460 ft. TL: N35 07 18 W87 11 17. Stereo. 2609 Jordan Ln. N.W., Huntsville, AL 35806. Phone: (256) 837-9387. Fax: (256) 837-9404. E-mail: news@103weup.com. Web Site: www.103weup.com. Licensee: Broadcast One Inc. (acq 12-2-93; $310,000; 1-3-94). Network: ABC Information & Entertainment. Format: Urban contemp. ♦ Hundley Batts, pres & gen sls mgr; Steve Murry, stn mgr; Tony Jordan, mus dir & news dir; John Hain, chief of engrg.

Monterey

WKXD(FM)— Mar 3, 1986: 106.9 mhz; 23 kw. 735 ft. TL: N36 07 13 W85 14 44. Stereo. 259 S. Willow Ave., Cookeville 38501. Phone: (931) 528-6064. Fax: (931) 520-1590. Web Site: www.1069kicksfm.com. Licensee: JWC Broadcasting (group owner; acq 8-3-01). Network: ABC. Rep: Allied Radio Partners. Format: Rock. News staff: one; News: one hr wkly. Target aud: 18-49; young, adult & affluent audiences. ♦ Jim Stapleton, gen mgr.

WLIV-FM— Jan 8, 1997: 104.7 mhz; 1.25 kw. 712 ft. TL: N36 15 42 W85 16 35. Stereo. 1130 West Main St., Livingston 38570. Phone: (931) 823-1226. Fax: (931) 823-6005. Licensee: Sunny Broadcasting G.P. (acq 9-7-99). Network: Westwood One. Format: Country. News: 4 hrs wkly. Target aud: General. ♦ Millard V. Oakley, pres; Joel Upton, gen mgr; Carolyn Peterman, stn mgr; Craig Cantrell, opns dir.

Morristown

WCRK(AM)— October 1947: 1150 khz; 5 kw-D, 500 w-N, DA-N. TL: N36 14 11 W83 18 33. Box 220 37815-0220. Phone: (423) 586-9101. Fax: (423) 581-7756. E-mail: wcrk@lcs.net. Web Site: www.wcrk.com. Licensee: Radio Acquisition Corp. (acq 7-13-98; $250,000). Network: ABC. Rep: Rgnl Reps. Format: Adult contemp, oldies. News staff: one; News: 45 hrs wkly. Target aud: 25-54; slighty more female, average income $50,000 yearly. ♦ S. Herschel Lake, pres; Geraldine Lake, VP; Ed Dodson, gen mgr; Tim Crews, sls dir; Anisa Croxdale, progmg dir; Mike Rypel, news dir; Dan Trombley, engrg mgr & engr.

WJDT(FM)—See Rogersville

WMTN(AM)— Oct 19, 1957: 1300 khz; 5 kw-D, 100 w-N. TL: N36 12 15 W83 19 57. 510 W. Economy Rd. 37814. Phone: (423) 586-7993. Fax: (423) 581-4290. Licensee: Horne Radio LLC. Group owner: Horne Radio Group (acq 8-22-00; $1 million, with co-located FM). Network: USA. Format: Oldies. Target aud: 25-64; farmers & factory workers. ♦ William D. Buntin, gen mgr; Roddy Woods, stn mgr.

WMXK(FM)—Co-owned with WMTN(AM). May 31, 1964: 95.9 mhz; 1.1 kw. 771 ft. TL: N36 13 40 W83 19 58. (CP: 920 w, ant 817 ft.). Stereo. Format: Soft rock. News staff: one. Target aud: 18-54; middle to upper income.

Mount Pleasant

WXRQ(AM)— Dec 15, 1981: 1460 khz; 1 kw-D, 170 w-N. TL: N35 31 21 W87 11 34. Box 31, 209 Bond St. 38474. Phone: (931) 379-3119. Fax: (931) 379-3129. E-mail: gospel1460@yahoo.com. Licensee: New Life Broadcasting Inc. (acq 1-17-89; $75,000; 1-30-89). Network: USA. Format: Southern gospel. News staff: one; News: 7 hrs wkly. Target aud: General. Spec prog: Black 4 hrs wkly. ♦ Donald Paul, pres & gen mgr; Monty Gilliam, gen sls mgr; Eric Kennedy, progmg dir, mus dir & news dir.

Mountain City

WMCT(AM)— Dec 8, 1967: 1390 khz; 1 kw-D. TL: N36 29 23 W81 47 12. 1211 N. Church St. 37683. Phone: (423) 727-6701. Fax: (423) 727-9454. E-mail: wmct@tibonline.net. Web Site: www.wmct1390.com. Licensee: Johnson County Broadcasting Co. Network: ABC Information & Entertainment. Rep: Keystone (unwired net). Format: C&W, relg. Target aud: 25-50. ♦ Fran Atkinson, pres & gen mgr.

Munford

WMPW(FM)— 1948: 98.9 mhz; 40 kw. Ant 1,135 ft. TL: N35 28 03 W90 11 27. Stereo. 5629 Murray Rd., Memphis 38119. Phone: (901) 680-9898. Fax: (901) 767-9531. Web Site: www.power99memphis.com. Licensee: Citadel Broadcasting Co. Group owner: Citadel Broadcasting Corp. (acq 3-23-2004; grpsl). Rep: Katz Radio. Format: Urban adult contemp. Target aud: 24 plus. ♦ Sherri Sawyer, gen mgr; Dan Barron, sls dir; Amy Goodman, gen sls mgr; Keke Luv, progmg dir.

Murfreesboro

WCJK(FM)— Aug 10, 1963: 96.3 mhz; 52 kw. 1,286 ft. TL: N36 15 50 W86 47 38. Stereo. Box 40506, Nashville 37204. Secondary address: 504 Rosedale Ave., Nashville 37211. Phone: (615) 259-9696. Fax: (615) 259-4594. Web Site: www.963jackfm.com. Licensee: South Central Communications Corp. (group owner; (acq 2-4-94; $6 million; 3-28-94). Bryan Cave. Format: Adult contemp hits. News staff: one. Target aud: 25-54. ♦ John D. Engelbrecht, CEO; Craig Jacobus, pres; Robert Shirel, CFO; Dennis Gwiazdon, gen mgr; Melissa Fisher, prom dir; Randy Hill, progmg dir.

*WFCM-FM— September 1997: 91.7 mhz; 1 kw. 902 ft. TL: N35 43 52 W86 41 25. 1920 E. 24th Street Pl., Chattanooga 37404. Phone: (423) 629-8900. Fax: (423) 629-0021. E-mail: wfcm@moody.edu. Web Site: www.wfcm.org. Licensee: The Moody Bible Institute of Chicago. Network: Moody. Southmayd & Miller. Format: Educ, relg. News staff: one; News: 12 hrs wkly. Target aud: 25-54. ♦ Dr. Joseph Stowell, pres; Leighton LeBoeuf, gen mgr.

WGNS(AM)— Dec. 31, 1946: 1450 khz; 1 kw-U. TL: N35 50 26 W86 23 27. Stereo. 306 S. Church St. 37130-3732. Phone: (615) 893-5373. Fax: (615) 867-6397. E-mail: news@1450wgns.com. Web Site: www.1450wgns.com. Licensee: The Rutherford Group Inc. (acq 1984; FTR: 10-15-84). Network: ABC. Format: News/talk, sports. News: 80 hrs wkly. Target aud: 25 plus; active adults, "movers & shakers" in economic & educ groupings. Spec prog: Black 7 hrs, farm 3 hrs, relg 6 hrs wkly. ♦ Bart Walker, pres & gen mgr; Lee Ann Walker, VP; Scott Walker, sr VP & stn mgr; Melissa McCullough, opns mgr; Curt Miller, prom mgr & progmg dir; Gary Brown, chief of engrg. Co-owned TV: WETV-LP

WMGC(AM)— Nov 1, 1953: 810 khz; 5 kw-D, 6 w-N. TL: N35 50 14 W86 25 00. 435 37th Ave. N., Nashville 37209. Phone: (615) 844-1039. Licensee: Radio 810 Nashville Ltd. Group owner: Southern Wabash Communications Corp. (acq 7-10-01). Target aud: 18-54; adults. Spec prog: Relg 4 hrs wkly. ♦ Randolph Victor Bell, pres; Sally Dorgan Potts, exec VP; Martin Silva, gen mgr.

*WMOT-FM— Apr 9, 1969: 89.5 mhz; 1 kw. Ant 902 ft. TL: N35 43 52 W86 41 25. Stereo. Box 3, Middle Tennessee State Univ. 37132. Phone: (615) 898-2800. Phone: (615) 255-9071. Fax: (615) 898-2774. E-mail: wmot@mtsu.edu. Web Site: www.wmot.org. Licensee: Middle Tennessee State University. Network: Network: NPR, AP Radio. Format: Jazz. News staff: 2; News: 10 hrs wkly. Target aud: 24 plus; general. ♦ John L. High, gen mgr; John Egly, opns mgr; Keith Palmer, dev dir.

*WMTS-FM— 1996: 88.3 mhz; 680 w. Ant 138 ft. TL: N35 50 56 W86 21 11. Box 58, Middle Tenn. State Univ. 37132. Phone: (615) 898-5051. Phone: (615) 898-2636. Fax: (615) 898-5682. Web Site: www.wmtsradio.com. Licensee: Middle Tennessee State University. Format: Black, Sp, div. Target aud: 18-26; College age, diverse. Spec prog: Polka 2 hrs, electronic 10 hrs, jazz 4 hrs, funk 2 hrs wkly.

Nashville

WAMB(AM)— Apr 12, 1971: 1160 khz; 50 kw-D, 1 kw-N, DA-N. TL: N36 09 49 W86 42 55. Stereo. 1617 Lebanon Pike, Suite 100 37210. Phone: (615) 889-1960. Fax: (615) 902-9108. E-mail: wamb@bellsouth.net. Licensee: Great Southern Broadcasting Co. Inc. Network: CNN Radio. Rep: Roslin. Irwin, Campbell & Tannenwald. Format: MOR, nostalgia, talk, Sp. News: 20 hrs wkly. Target aud: General. Spec prog: Jazz 3 hrs, business news 6 hrs wkly. ♦ Will C. Baird Jr., VP; William O. Barry, pres & gen mgr; Harry P. Stephenson, gen sls mgr; Beth Lane, prom mgr; Michael D. Robbins, progmg dir.

WAMB-FM— Nov 26, 1990: 98.7 mhz; 75 w. 250 ft. TL: N36 09 49 W86 42 55. Stereo.

WCJK(FM)—See Murfreesboro

WENO(AM)— May 23, 1988: 760 khz; 1 kw-D. TL: N36 08 28 W86 45 23. Stereo. 333 Murfreesboro Rd. 37210. Phone: (615) 248-1689. Fax: (615) 248-7786. Web Site: www.weno.com. Licensee: WENO Inc. (acq 5-7-90; $300,000; 5-21-90). Network: AP Radio. Format: Christian, relg. News: 6 hrs wkly. Target aud: 25-54. ♦ Millard Reed, pres; Mark Myers, CFO; David Deese, gen mgr; Dave Queen, stn mgr; Tom Park, chief of engrg.

WNAZ-FM—Co-owned with WENO(AM). May 23, 1967: 89.1 mhz; 1.4 kw. Ant 200 ft. TL: N36 08 28 W86 45 23. Stereo. Web Site: www.wnaz.com. Licensee: Trevecca Nazarene University Inc. Format: Contemp Christian. News: 3 hrs wkly. Target aud: 30-60; white collar professionals & their families.

*WFSK(FM)— May 15, 1973: 88.1 mhz; 700 w. 6 ft. TL: N36 10 00 W86 48 17. Stereo. Fisk Univ., 1000 17th Ave. N. 37208-3051. Phone: (615) 329-8754. Fax: (615) 329-9305. E-mail: wdobbins@fisk.edu. Web Site: www.fisk.edu/wfsk. Licensee: Fisk University. Format: Jazz. News: 5 hrs wkly. Target aud: Jazz music; the smooth sounds of jazz. Spec prog: oldies 3 hrs, ladies nite 3 hrs, Spanish 15 hrs. ♦ Washington Dobbins, gen mgr; Michael Patterson, progmg dir; Chris Nochowicz, mus dir; Wayne Miller, chief of engrg.

WGFX(FM)—See Gallatin

WJXA(FM)— Apr 3, 1976: 92.9 mhz; 100 kw. 1,086 ft. TL: N36 07 14 W86 58 07. Stereo. Box 40506 37204-0506. Secondary address: 504 Rosedale Ave. 37211. Phone: (615) 259-9393. Phone: (615) 259-0929.

Fax: (615) 259-4594. Web Site: mix929.com. Licensee: South Central Communications Corp. (group owner) Bryan Cave. Format: Adult contemp. Target aud: 25-54. ♦John D. Engelbrecht, CEO; Craig Jacobus, pres; Robert L. Shirel, CFO; Dennis Gwiazdon, gen mgr; Becky Sweeney, sls dir; Neda Gayle, natl sls mgr; Katherine Salmon, prom dir & pub affrs dir; Barbara Bridges, progmg dir; Anna Marie Ritter, news dir; Don Haworth, chief of engrg.

WKDA(AM)— Dec 21, 2001: 1200 khz; 10 kw-D, 3.8 kw-CH. TL: N36 12 32 W86 52 21. (CP: 50 kw-D, 90 w-N, 3.8 kw-CH, DA-N). Stereo. 1617 Lebanon Rd. 37210. Phone: (615) 889-1960. Fax: (615) 902-9108. E-mail: wamb@bellsouth.net. Licensee: Radio Nashville Inc. (acq 12-4-01). Network: CNN Radio. Irwin, Campbell & Tannenwald. Format: Sp. ♦Will C. Baird Jr., VP; William O. Barry, pres & gen mgr; Harry P. Stephenson, gen sls mgr; Martin Silva, progmg dir; Gary M. Brown, chief of engrg.

WKDF(FM)— Jan 1, 1967: 103.3 mhz; 100 kw. 1,233 ft. TL: N36 02 08 W86 50 56. Stereo. Box 101604 37224-1604. Secondary address: 506 2nd ave. S. 07210. Phone: (615) 244-9533. Fax: (615) 259-1271. Web Site: www.1-3WKDF.com. Licensee: Citadel Broadcasting Co. Group owner: Citadel Broadcasting Corp. acq 4-26-01; grpsl). Format: Coutnry. Target aud: 18-34; general. ♦Steve Dickert, gen mgr; Cindy Francis, prom mgr; Dave Kelly, progmg dir; Eddy Foxx, mus dir; Cameron Adkins, chief of engrg.

WLAC(AM)— Nov 24, 1926: 1510 khz; 50 kw-U, DA-N. TL: N36 16 15 W86 45 24. 55 Music Sq. W. 37203. Phone: (615) 664-2400. Fax: (615) 664-2457. Web Site: www.1510wlac.com. Licensee: Capstar TX L.P. Group owner: Clear Channel Communications Inc. (acq 8-30-00; grpsl). Network: Network: Network: UPI, Wall Street, ABC. Haley, Bader & Potts. Format: News/talk, relg. News staff: 3; News: 18 hrs wly. Target aud: 35-64; professionals, business owners & managers. Spec prog: Black 20 hrs wkly. ♦Dave Alpert, pres; Keith Kaufman, opns dir & mktg dir; Darren Smith, sls dir; Temple Hancock, prom dir; Bruce Collins, progmg mgr; Mike Gideon, chief of engrg.

WNRQ(FM)—Co-owned with WLAC(AM). 1953: 105.9 mhz; 100 kw. 1,226 ft. TL: N30 02 08 W86 50 56. Stereo. Web Site: www.1059.com. Network: ABC FM Connection. Format: Adult contemp. News staff: one; News: 3 hrs wkly. Target aud: 25-54; upwardly mobile adults. Spec prog: Christian 6 hrs wkly. ♦David Alpert, gen mgr & mktg mgr; Keith Kaufman, opns mgr; Temple Hancock, prom mgr.

WMDB(AM)— Aug 15, 1983: 880 khz; 2.5 kw-D. TL: N36 12 43 W86 49 09. 3051 Stokers Ln. 37218. Phone: (615) 255-2876. Phone: (615) 254-8880. Fax: (615) 254-8228. Licensee: Davidson Media Station WMDB Licensee LLC. (acq 7-5-2005; $1.6 million). Format: Gumbo Black. Target aud: 18 plus; general. ♦Peter Davidson, pres; Dr. Morgan Babb, gen mgr; Michael Babb, opns mgr, progmg dir & news dir; Morgan Babb, gen sls mgr.

WNAH(AM)— Dec 24, 1949: 1360 khz; 1 kw-U. TL: N36 11 30 W86 46 26. 44 Music Sq. E. 37203. Phone: (615) 254-7611. Fax: (615) 467-8600. E-mail: mail@wnah.com. Web Site: www.wnah.com. Licensee: Hermitage Broadcasting Corp. Format: Southern gospel. News: 5 hrs wkly. Target aud: 21-50. ♦Van T. Irwin Jr., pres & gen mgr; Tony Cappuccilli, gen sls mgr; Bill Grist, prom mgr; Hoyt M. Carter Jr., progmg dir & chief of engrg; Bobby Lynn II, mus dir.

WNQM(AM)— July 1, 1948: 1300 khz; 50 kw-D, 5 kw-N, DA-N. TL: N36 12 30 W86 53 38. 1300 WWCR Ave. 37218. Phone: (615) 255-1300. Fax: (615) 255-1311. Web Site: www.wwcr.com. Licensee: WNQM Inc. Group owner: F.W. Robbert Broadcasting Co. Inc. (acq 1-83; $700,000; 12-19-83). Network: USA. Rep: Salem. Format: Relg, Sp. News: 2 hrs wkly. Target aud: General. Spec prog: Sp. ♦Fred P. Werstenberger, pres; George McClintock, gen mgr; Adam Lock, opns mgr.

WNSG(AM)— 1948:: 1240 khz; 1 kw-U. TL: N36 09 24 W86 46 15. Cummins Stn, 209 Tenth Ave. S. 37203. Phone: (615) 242-1411. Fax: (615) 242-3823. Licensee: Davidson Media Station WNSG Licensee LLC. (acq 6-6-2005; $2.7 million). Format: Urban gospel. Target aud: 25-54. Spec prog: Relg 2 hrs wkly. ♦Peter Davidson, pres & gen mgr; Clarence Kilcrease, gen mgr; Pat Hall-Easley, opns mgr; Brian Hogg, gen sls mgr; Vic Watkins, mus dir; Jay Shoemaker, chief of engrg.

WPLN(AM)—(Madison). Sept 14, 1958: 1430 khz; 5 kw-D, 1 kw-N, DA-N. TL: N36 16 19 W86 42 53. 15 kw-D, 1 kw-N, DA-N. Stereo. 630 Mainstream Dr. 37228. Phone: (615) 760-2903. Fax: (615) 760-2904. Web Site: www.wpln.org. Licensee: Nashville Public Radio (acq 2-15-02; $3 million). Tierney & Swift. Format: News/talk. Target aud: General. ♦Rob Gordon, pres & gen mgr.

***WPLN-FM**— Dec 17, 1962: 90.3 mhz; 80 kw. Ant 1,132 ft. TL: N36 02 08 W86 50 56. Stereo. 630 Mainstream Dr. 37228-1204. Phone: (615) 760-2903. Fax: (615) 760-2904. E-mail: talkback@wpln.org. Web Site: www.wpln.org. Licensee: Nashville Public Radio. Network: Network: NPR, PRI. Format: Class, cultural, news, bluegrass. Target aud: General. ♦Robert Gordon, gen mgr; Laura Landress, gen sls mgr; Henry Fennell, progmg dir; Will Griffin, mus dir; Anita Bugg, news dir; Tom Knox, chief of engrg.

WQQK(FM)—See Hendersonville

WQZQ(FM)—See Dickson

***WRVU(FM)**— Dec 3, 1971: 91.1 mhz; 14.5 kw. 457 ft. TL: N36 08 27 W86 51 56. Stereo. Box 9100-B, Vanderbilt Univ., 128 Sarratt Student Ctr. 37235. Phone: (615) 322-3691. Phone: (615) 322-7625. Fax: (615) 343-2582. Web Site: www.wrvu.org. Licensee: Vanderbilt Student Communications. Network: ABC. Format: Progsv rock, jazz, div. Target aud: General; div, adventurous individuals. ♦Jennifer Sexton, gen mgr; David Cash, progmg dir.

WSIX-FM— 1948: 97.9 mhz; 100 kw. 1,140 ft. TL: N36 02 49 W86 49 49. Stereo. 55 Music Sq. W. 37203. Phone: (615) 664-2400. Fax: (615) 664-2457. Licensee: Capstar TX L.P. Group owner: Clear Channel Communications Inc. (acq 8-30-00; grpsl). Format: Country. News staff: 2; News: one hr wkly. Target aud: 25-54. ♦David Alpert, gen mgr; Keith Kaufman, opns mgr, mktg dir & prom dir; Temple Hancock, prom dir; Mike Moore, progmg dir & pub affrs dir; Al Voecks, news dir; Mike Gideon, chief of engrg.

WSM(AM)— Oct 5, 1925: 650 khz; 50 kw-U. TL: N35 59 50 W86 47 32. Stereo. 2804 Opryland Dr. 37214. Phone: (615) 889-6595. Fax: (615) 458-2445. Web Site: www.wsmonline.com. Licensee: Gaylord Entertainment Co. (acq 11-14-00; grpsl). Network: ABC. Rep: Christal. Format: Country. News staff: 12; News: 11 hrs wkly. Target aud: 35 plus; high school graduates, married homeowners, income $25,000 plus. Spec prog: Farm 6 hrs, Grand Ole Opry 12 hrs wkly. ♦Chris Kulick, gen mgr; Bill Hutcherson, gen sls mgr & pub affrs dir.

WSM-FM— Nov 1, 1962: 95.5 mhz; 100 kw. Ant 1,279 ft. TL: N36 08 27 W86 51 56. Stereo. 10 Music Circle E. 37203. Phone: (615) 321-1067. Fax: (615) 321-5808. Web Site: www.955thewolf.com. Licensee: Cumulus Licensing LLC. Group owner: Cumulus Media Inc. (acq 7-21-2003; $65 million. with WWTN(FM) Manchester). Format: Country. Target aud: 25-54. ♦Michael Dickey, gen mgr.

WVOL(AM)—See Berry Hill

WYFN(AM)— Jan 7, 1927: 980 khz; 5 kw-U, DA-N. TL: N36 12 25 W86 40 25. Box 747, Madison 37116. Secondary address: 1940 Neely's Bend Rd., Madison 37115-3203. Phone: (804) 547-9421. Licensee: Bible Broadcasting Network. (group owner; acq 1-31-91; $600,000; 2-18-91). Network: ABC Information & Entertainment. Rep: McGavren Guild. Format: Relg. ♦Aaron Tuttle, gen mgr & stn mgr.

New Johnsonville

***WAYW(FM)**— 2001: 89.9 mhz; 3.1 kw. Ant 466 ft. TL: N35 56 17 W87 53 39. 1012 McEwen Dr., Franklin 37067. Phone: (615) 261-9293. Fax: (615) 261-3967. E-mail: waym@wayfm.com. Web Site: www.wayfm.com. Licensee: WAY-FM Media Group Inc. (group owner; acq 2-1-01). Format: Christian. ♦Matt Austin, stn mgr; Jim Turvaville, engrg dir.

Newport

WLIK(AM)— Apr 9, 1954: 1270 khz; 5 kw-D, 500 w-N, DA-N. TL: N35 57 49 W83 12 31. 640 W. Hwy. 25/70 37821. Phone: (423) 623-3095. Fax: (423) 623-3096. E-mail: wlik@planetc.com. Web Site: wlik.net. Licensee: WLIK Inc. Network: CNN Radio. Format: Oldies. Target aud: General. Spec prog: Relg 18 hrs wkly. ♦Dwight D. Wilkerson, pres, gen mgr & stn mgr; Angie Wilkerson, VP; Johnnie Swann, chief of opns.

WNPC(AM)— September 1978: 1060 khz; 1 kw-D. TL: N35 59 10 W83 10 46. 377 Graham St. 37821. Phone: (423) 623-8743. Phone: (423) 623-8744. Fax: (423) 623-0545. Licensee: Harris Broadcasting Inc. dba WNPC Inc. Network: ABC. Roberts & Eckard. Format: Country. Target aud: 25-49. ♦Dorothy Ann Harris, pres; Mona Sizemore, gen mgr; Brian Fredette, prom mgr & progmg dir.

WNPC-FM— February 1993: 92.9 mhz; 3.1 kw. 459 ft. TL: N35 57 27 W83 05 03. Stereo. ♦Jim Phillips, progmg VP.

Norris

WRMX-FM— April 2001: 106.7 mhz; 1.1 kw. 751 ft. TL: N36 07 12 W83 55 30. Stereo. Box 27100, Knoxville 37927-7100. Phone: (865) 525-6000. Fax: (865) 525-2000. Web Site: www.knoxoldies.com. Licensee: South Central Communications Corp. (group owner; acq 6-14-01; $2.5 million). Format: Oldies. Target aud: 35-64; mature adults with spendable income. ♦Craig Jacobus, pres; Terry Gillingham, VP & mktg mgr.

Oak Ridge

WATO(AM)— Feb 1, 1948: 1290 khz; 5 kw-D, 500 w-N, DA-2. TL: N36 03 02 W84 12 38. 517 Watt Rd., Knoxville 37922. Phone: (865) 482-1290. Phone: (865) 675-4105. Fax: (865) 675-4859. Licensee: Horne Radio LLC. Group owner: Horne Radio Group (acq 8-29-01; grpsl). Network: Westwood One. Format: Oldies. News staff: one. Target aud: 25-54. ♦Alex Carroll, sls dir & chief of engrg; Brian Tatum, stn mgr & progmg dir.

WNFZ(FM)— February 1967: 94.3 mhz; 2.5 kw. 515 ft. TL: N35 56 28 W84 09 28. Stereo. Box 27100, Knoxville 37927-7100. Secondary address: 1100 Sharps Ridge Rd., Knoxville 37917. Phone: (865) 525-6000. Fax: (865) 525-2000. Web Site: www.943extremradio.com. Licensee: John A. Pirkle. Format: Alternative. Target aud: General. ♦John W. Pirkle, CEO & chmn; Johnathan W. Pirkle, pres; Terry Gillingham, VP & gen mgr.

WNOX(FM)—Licensed to Oak Ridge. See Knoxville

Olive Hill

***WDNX(FM)**— Jan 10, 1975: 89.1 mhz; 100 kw. 249 ft. TL: N35 12 30 W88 03 46. Stereo. HHA Administration Bldg., 3575 Lonesome Pine Rd., Savannah 38372. Secondary address: WDNX Bldg., 3730 Lonesome Pine Rd., Savannah 38372. Phone: (731) 925-9236. Fax: (731) 925-4238. E-mail: sheriwdnx@yahoo.com. Web Site: www.lifetalk.net. Licensee: Rural Life Foundation. Format: Inspirational music, Christian teaching & inspiration. News staff: one; News: 5 hrs wkly. Target aud: General; families. Spec prog: Class 5 hrs, farm 1 hr wkly. ♦Charles Harris, chmn; Steven Dickman, pres, CFO, exec VP, stn mgr & dev mgr; Sheri Durbin, gen sls mgr, mktg mgr & pub affrs dir; Steve Dickman, chief of engrg.

Oliver Springs

WOKI(FM)— Sept 15, 1989: 98.7 mhz; 8 kw. Ant 571 ft. TL: N36 06 48 W84 03 44. Box 11167, Knoxville 37939. Secondary address: 4711 Old Kingston Pike, Knoxville 37919. Phone: (865) 588-6511. Fax: (865) 656-7487. Web Site: www.theriver987.com. Licensee: Citadel Broadcasting Co. Group owner: Citadel Broadcasting Corp. (acq 4-26-2001; grpsl). Rgnl Reps. Bryan Cave. Format: Rock. Target aud: 18 plus. ♦Mike Hammond, pres & opns mgr; Ed Brantley, VP & gen mgr; David Crouch, gen sls mgr; Shelby Deck, mktg dir.

Oneida

WBNT-FM—Listing follows WOCV(AM).

WOCV(AM)— Aug 1, 1959: 1310 khz; 1 kw-D. TL: N36 30 03 W84 29 24. Box 4370 37841. Secondary address: 1126 Buffalo Rd. 37841. Phone: (423) 569-8598. Phone: (423) 569-9268. Fax: (423) 569-5572. E-mail: wbnt@highland.net. Web Site: www.hive105.com. Licensee: Oneida Broadcasters Inc. (acq 5-1-69). Network: ABC. Format: Adult contemp, new country. News staff: 4; News: 15 hrs wkly. Target aud: 22-55; male & female. ♦George Guertin, pres; Hillard Mattie, gen mgr, gen sls mgr, prom mgr & progmg mgr; Paul C. Strunk, opns dir, sls dir, progmg dir & news dir; Darrel E. Smith, chief of engrg.

WBNT-FM—Co-owned with WOCV(AM). June 10, 1965: 105.5 mhz; 3 kw. Ant 285 ft. TL: N36 30 03 W84 29 24. Stereo. Web Site: www.hive105.com. Network: ABC. News staff: 4; News: 15 hrs wkly. Target aud: 16-56; male/female working class-retirees. ♦Hillard Mattie, stn mgr, dev mgr, adv mgr & progmg dir; Paul C. Strunk, opns mgr & mus dir.

Stations in the U.S.   Tennessee

Developers & Brokers of Radio Properties

contact American Media Services at our suite:
Philadelphia Marriott Downtown
215-625-2900
843-972-2200
americanmediaservices.com
Charleston, SC
Dallas, TX · Chicago, Il · Austin, TX
American Media Services, LLC

Paris

WAKQ(FM)—Listing follows WTPR(AM).

WLZK(FM)—Listing follows WMUF(AM).

WMUF(AM)— May 9, 1980: 1000 khz; 5 kw-D, DA. TL: N36 18 50 W88 17 33. 110 India Rd. 38242. Phone: (731) 644-9455. Fax: (731) 644-9970. E-mail: wmuf@bellsouth.net. Licensee: Benton-Weatherford Broadcasting Inc.of Tennessee (group owner; acq 4-1-85). Network: ABC. Format: Country. News staff: one; News: 3 hrs wkly. Target aud: 25-54; people with disposable income. Spec prog: Farm 2 hrs wkly. ♦Gary D. Benton, pres; Gary Benton, gen mgr.

WLZK(FM)—Co-owned with WMUF(AM). Nov 1, 1991: 94.1 mhz; 10.5 kw. 328 ft. TL: N36 18 50 W88 17 33. Stereo. E-mail: wlzk@bellsouth.net. (Acq 3-15-91; 4-8-91). Format: Adult contemp. News staff: one; News: 25 hrs wkly.

WTPR(AM)— May 7, 1947: 710 khz; 750 w-D. TL: N36 16 47 W88 20 32. Stereo. 206 N. Brewer St. 38242. Phone: (731) 644-9367. Fax: (731) 642-9367. E-mail: wtprkq105@charter.net. Licensee: WENK Broadcast Group Inc. (group owner; acq 10-28-89; 8-14-89). Network: ABC Information & Entertainment. Verner, Liipfert, Bernhard, McPherson & Hand. Format: Oldies. News staff: one; News: 12 hrs wkly. Target aud: 35-54. ♦Terry Hailey, pres, gen mgr & progmg dir; Brad Hosford, chief of engrg.

WAKQ(FM)—Co-owned with WTPR(AM). September 1967: 105.5 mhz; 3.7 kw. 419 ft. TL: N36 16 45 W88 20 31. Stereo. Format: CHR. Target aud: 12-34. ♦Terry Hailey, mus dir.

Parker's Crossroads

WBFG(FM)— 1999: 96.5 mhz; 6 kw. Ant 328 ft. TL: N35 45 33 W88 23 15. Box 279, Lexington 38351. Secondary address: 584 Smith Ave., Lexington 38351. Phone: (731) 968-9990. Fax: (731) 968-0380. E-mail: wbfg965@yahoo.com. Web Site: www.wbfg965.com. Licensee: Crossroads Broadcasting LLC. (acq 4-14-99). Network: ESPN Radio. Format: Sports. ♦Dan Hughes, gen mgr; Lori Becker, opns mgr.

Parsons

WKJQ(AM)— Oct 3, 1970: 1550 khz; 1 kw-D. TL: N35 39 26 W88 09 07. Box 576 38363. Secondary address: 109 Iron Hill Rd. 38363. Phone: (731) 847-3011. Fax: (731) 847-4600. Licensee: Clenney Broadcasting Corp. (acq 4-1-89). Robert S. Stone. Format: Relg. Target aud: General. ♦Ralph D. Clenney, pres & gen mgr.

WKJQ-FM— June 4, 1990: 97.3 mhz; 6 kw. 256 ft. TL: N35 39 39 W88 07 05. Stereo. Format: Country. Target aud: 25-54.

Pikeville

WUAT(AM)— Dec 19, 1972: 1110 khz; 250 w-D. TL: N35 36 18 W85 11 14. Box 128 37367. Secondary address: 101 N. Main 37367. Phone: (423) 447-2906. Fax: (423) 447-7309. Web Site: www.wuatradio.com. Licensee: Joyce V. Bownds. (acq 6-28-99; $1,500). Lukas, McGowan, Nace & Gutierrez. Format: Country, gospel, bluegrass. Spec prog: Farm 5 hrs, relg 15 hrs wkly. ♦Joyce Bownds, pres, gen mgr, gen sls mgr & progmg dir.

Portland

WQKR(AM)— July 15, 1980: 1270 khz; 1 kw-D, 59 w-N, DA-2. TL: N36 36 11 W86 32 01. 100 Main St., Suite 201 37148-1218. Phone: (615) 325-3250. Fax: (615) 325-0803. Licensee: Venture Broadcasting LLC (acq 8-8-2005; $50,000). Format: Oldies. Target aud: 25-54. ♦Floyd Howard Johnson, gen mgr.

Powell

WQBB(AM)—Licensed to Powell. See Knoxville

Pulaski

WKSR(AM)— May 6, 1947: 1420 khz; 1 kw-U, DA-N. TL: N35 12 04 W87 03 20. Box 738 38478. Secondary address: 104 S. Second St. 38478. Phone: (931) 363-2505. Fax: (931) 424-3157. Web Site: www.wksr.com. Licensee: Pulaski Broadcasting Inc. (acq 4-4-80; $481,300; 4-21-80). Network: ABC Information & Entertainment. Format: Oldies. Target aud: 25-54. ♦Ronnie Rose, gen mgr; Ed Carter, progmg dir.

WKSR-FM— Jan 12, 1970: 98.3 mhz; 3 kw. 453 ft. TL: N35 08 47 W87 05 28. Stereo. (Acq 1-1-84; $350,000; 12-19-83). Format: Country.

Red Bank

*****WAWL-FM**— Sept 12, 1980: 91.5 mhz; 11 kw. 951 ft. TL: N35 09 42 W85 19 06. Stereo. 4501 Amnicola Hwy., Chattanooga 37406. Phone: (423) 697-4470. Phone: (423) 697-4405. Fax: (423) 697-2596. Licensee: Chattanooga State Technical Community College. Format: Alternative, educ. News staff: one. Target aud: 18-34. ♦Dr. James L. Catanzaro, pres; Bob Riley, gen mgr & chief of engrg; Linda Miller, mktg VP; Patty Brown, prom VP; Sandy Smith, adv dir; Don Hixson, progmg dir; Jake Land, pub affrs dir.

WJTT(FM)— November 1972: 94.3 mhz; 2.8 kw. 331 ft. TL: N35 07 32 W85 17 23. Stereo. 1305 Carter St., Chattanooga 37402. Phone: (423) 265-9494. Fax: (423) 266-2335. Web Site: www.power94.com. Licensee: Brewer Broadcasting of Chattanooga Inc. (acq 12-26-93; $1.68 million). Rep: McGavren Guild. Format: Urban contemp. Target aud: 18-49. Spec prog: Jazz 2 hrs, relg 4 hrs wkly. ♦Jim L. Brewer Sr., pres; Jim L. Brewer II, VP, gen mgr & gen sls mgr; Brad Guagriri, natl sls mgr; Jay Holloway, prom mgr; Keith Landecker, progmg dir; Donna Harrison, news dir; Parks Hall, chief of engrg.

Ripley

*****WAUV(FM)**— 2000: 89.7 mhz; 5.3 kw. Ant 394 ft. TL: N35 46 31 W89 28 18. Box 3206, American Family Radio, Tupelo, MS 38803. Phone: (662) 844-8888. Fax: (662) 842-6791. E-mail: comments@afr.net. Web Site: www.afr.net. Licensee: American Family Association. Group owner: American Family Radio. Format: Relg. ♦Marvin Sanders, gen mgr.

WKVZ(FM)— Jan 1, 1993: 94.9 mhz; 6 kw. Ant 328 ft. TL: N35 48 28 W89 28 27. 102 N. 5th St., West Memphis, AR 72301. Fax: (916) 251-1650. E-mail: info@klove.com. Web Site: www.klove.com. Licensee: Educational Media Foundation. Group owner: EMF Broadcasting (acq 1-25-01; $450,000). Network: K-Love. Format: Contemp Christian. Target aud: 18-50. ♦Dick Jenkins, pres; Mike Novak, sr VP; Sam Wallington, engrg dir.

WTRB(AM)— Dec 11, 1954: 1570 khz; 1 kw-D, 50 w-N. TL: N35 43 46 W89 32 33. (CP: 28 kw-D, 534 w-N). Box 410, 372 S. Jefferson St. 38063. Phone: (731) 635-1570. Fax: (731) 635-9722. Licensee: West Tennessee Regional Broadcasting Inc. (group owner). (acq 11-16-2004; $265,000). Network: ABC Information & Entertainment. Rep: Keystone (unwired net). Format: C&W. Spec prog: Gospel 6 hrs wkly. ♦Phillip Ennis, pres; Don Paris, gen mgr & gen sls mgr.

Rockwood

WOFE(AM)— May 12, 1957: 580 khz; 1 kw-D, 49 w-N. TL: N35 49 40 W84 39 19. 2319 S. Roane St., Harriman 37748. Phone: (865) 590-0958. Fax: (865) 882-3291. E-mail: mike@faith580.com. Web Site: www.faith580.com. Licensee: Southern Media Group Inc. (group owner; acq 6-10-03; grpsl). Format: Southern gospel. Target aud: General. Spec prog: Black one hr wkly. ♦Kirk Tollett, gen mgr; Tony Perry, opns dir; Tracie Roberson, sls VP; Anthony Wick, progmg dir; Dudley Evans, progmg dir & news dir; Don Bible, chief of engrg.

WOFE-FM— July 9, 1991: 105.7 mhz; 930 w. Ant 836 ft. TL: N35 51 41 W84 43 11. Web Site: www.south1057.com. Format: Country. Target aud: 18-54.

Rogersville

WJDT(FM)— Dec 1, 1990: 106.5 mhz; 300 w. Ant 1,378 ft. TL: N36 22 51 W83 10 47. Stereo. Box 519, Morristown 37815-0519. Secondary address: N. Davy Crockett Pkwy., Morristown 37814. Phone: (423) 235-4640. Phone: (865) 993-3639. E-mail: www.wjdtfm@planetc.com. Web Site: www.wjdtfm.com. Licensee: C & S Broadcasting. Network: CNN Radio. Larry Perry. Format: Country. News: 6 hrs wkly. Target aud: 18-59; female 65%, male 35%. ♦Clark Quillen, pres; David C. Quillen, opns mgr.

WRGS(AM)— Aug 20, 1954: 1370 khz; 1 kw-D, 40 w-N. TL: N36 24 58 W82 59 04. 211 Burem Rd. 37857. Phone: (423) 272-3900. Fax: (423) 272-0328. E-mail: stationmanager@wrgsradio.com. Web Site: www.wrgsradio.com. Licensee: WRGS Inc. Network: USA. Format: Country. Target aud: General. ♦C. Philip Beal, pres; C. Philip Beale, gen mgr; Jay Phillips, opns mgr, progmg dir & progmg mgr; Craig Stapleton, gen sls mgr; Mavis Livingston, natl sls mgr; Jim Cox, rgnl sls mgr; Megan Collins, mktg dir & pub affrs dir; Chuck Windham, chief of engrg.

Saint Joseph

WJOR-FM— 1991: 101.5 mhz; 4 kw. 403 ft. TL: N35 00 42 W87 30 46. Box 374, 37 Old Jackson Hwys 38481. Phone: (931) 845-4172. Phone: (256) 757-9455. Fax: (931) 845-4172. Licensee: Urban Radio Licenses LLC. (acq 5-13-2005; grpsl). Format: Classic country, Southern gospel. ♦Rick Brown, gen mgr; Randy Paul, opns dir; Lance Knoll, gen sls mgr; Tony Fowler, prom dir; Jane Hoslan, adv dir & adv mgr; Lonnie Box, progmg dir; Sandi Summers, news dir; Craig Westbrook, chief of engrg.

Savannah

*****WAZD(FM)**— 2001: 88.1 mhz; 380 w. Ant 128 ft. TL: N35 12 58 W88 14 30. Box 3206, American Family Radio, Tupelo, MS 38803. Phone: (662) 844-8888. Fax: (662) 842-6791. E-mail: comments@afr.net. Web Site: www.afr.net. Licensee: American Family Association. Group owner: American Family Radio Format: Relg. ♦Marvin Sanders, gen mgr.

WKWX(FM)— June 23, 1980: 93.5 mhz; 25 kw. Ant 298 ft. TL: N35 17 08 W88 10 03. Stereo. Box 40 38372. Secondary address: 1714 Wayne Rd. 38372. Phone: (731) 925-9600. Fax: (731) 925-8828. Licensee: Melco Inc. (acq 12-19-02). Format: Country. ♦Melvin Carnal, pres & gen mgr; Jane Haggard, stn mgr; Jim Jerrolds, gen sls mgr; Dennis Brown, progmg dir, chief of engrg & chief of engrg.

WORM(AM)— June 29, 1956: 1010 khz; 250 w-D, 27 w-N. TL: N35 14 24 W88 14 29. Box 550 38372. Secondary address: 1207 Bowen Dr. 38372. Phone: (731) 925-4981. Phone: (731) 925-7102. Fax: (731) 925-4981. E-mail: thewormq105@excite.com. Licensee: Gerald W. Hunt. Format: Pure Gold. ♦Gerald W. Hunt, pres, gen mgr, gen sls mgr & chief of engrg; Dave Morgan, progmg dir; Randy Tucker, mus dir.

WORM-FM— Aug 25, 1966: 101.7 mhz; 3 kw. 175 ft. TL: N35 14 24 W88 14 29. Stereo. Format: Hot country.

Selmer

WDTM(AM)— Oct 31, 1967: 1150 khz; 1 kw-D. TL: N35 11 27 W88 35 21. 25 Stonebrook Pl., Suite G322, Jackson 38305. Phone: (731) 663-3931. Fax: (731) 663-9804. Licensee: Grace Broadcasting Services Inc. (acq 7-25-2005; $200,000 with co-located FM). Format: Contemp Christian. ♦Lacy Ennis, pres & gen mgr.

Broadcasting & Cable Yearbook 2006

Tennessee

WSIB(FM)—Co-owned with WDTM(AM). January 1990: 93.9 mhz; 6 kw. Ant 328 ft. TL: N35 11 27 W88 35 21. Stereo. Web Site: www.gracebroadcasting.com. Format: Inspirational gospel. Target aud: 20-45.

*****WSMM(FM)**—Not on air, target date: unknown: 90.5 mhz; 6 kw. Ant 236 ft. TL: N35 12 53 W88 32 44. 6080 Mt. Moriah Ext., Memphis 38115. Phone: (901) 375-9324. Licensee: Broadcasting for the Challenged Inc. ♦George S. Flinn Jr., pres & gen mgr.

WXOQ(FM)— June 15, 1986: 105.5 mhz; 6 kw. Ant 298 ft. TL: N35 13 11 W88 40 23. Stereo. Box 550, Savannah 38372. Secondary address: 1207 Bowen Dr., Savannah 38372. Phone: (731) 645-9880. Fax: (731) 925-4981. E-mail: thewormQ105@excite.com. Licensee: Gerald W. Hunt. (acq 6-28-94; $185,000; 7-11-94). Network: Westwood One. Format: Country. News staff: 2. Target aud: General. ♦Gerald W. Hunt, pres, gen mgr & chief of engrg; Dave Morgan, progmg dir; Randy Tucker, mus dir.

Sevierville

WSEV(AM)— Apr 23, 1955: 930 khz; 5 kw-D, 148 w-N. TL: N35 52 42 W83 33 18. Stereo. 415 Middle Creek Rd. 37862. Phone: (865) 453-2844. Fax: (865) 429-2601. Licensee: East Tennessee Radio Group L.P. (acq 3-22-2000; $1.45 million. with WSEV-FM Gatlinburg). Network: CBS. Rep: Rgnl Reps. Format: Adult contemp. News staff: one; News: 6 hrs wkly. Target aud: 25 plus. ♦Paul Sink, gen mgr & stn mgr; Bill Burkett, opns mgr; Steve Hartford, progmg dir & news dir.

WWST(FM)— Feb 3, 1961: 102.1 mhz; 15 kw. 1,979 ft. TL: N35 48 41 W83 40 08. Stereo. Journal Broadcast Group, 1533 Amhearst Rd., Knoxville 37909-1204. Phone: (865) 693-1020. Phone: (865) 824-1021. Fax: (865) 824-1880. Web Site: www.star1021fm.com. Licensee: Journal Broadcast Corp. Group owner: Journal Communications Inc. (acq 5-19-97). Network: ABC. Hogan & Hartson. Format: CHR. News: 4 hrs wkly. Target aud: 25-54. ♦Chris Protzman, gen mgr & natl sls mgr; Rich Bailey, opns dir, progmg dir & pub affrs dir; Dan McKee, rgnl sls mgr; Justin Buznedo, prom dir; Scott Bohannon, mus dir.

Sewanee

*****WUTS(FM)**— May 1972: 91.3 mhz; 200 w. 658 ft. TL: N35 12 20 W85 55 07. (CP: 88.5 mhz). Univ. of the South, 735 University Ave. 37383. Phone: (931) 598-1206. Phone: (931) 598-1112. Fax: (931) 598-1145. E-mail: wuts@sewanee.edu. Licensee: University of the South. Format: Div, progsv. Target aud: General; college students. Spec prog: Black 2 hrs, class 4 hrs, country 2 hrs, jazz 4 hrs, blues 3 hrs, reggae 5 hrs, new age 4 hrs, Fr 2 hrs, soul 2 hrs, musicals 2 hrs, bluegrass 2 hrs, punk/hardcore 2 hrs wkly. ♦John Lee, gen mgr; Austin Lacy, mus dir; Greg Banworth, chief of engrg.

Seymour

WJBZ-FM— Mar 31, 1991: 96.3 mhz; 3 kw. 328 ft. TL: N35 54 32 W83 40 59. Box 2526, Knoxville 37901. Phone: (865) 577-4885. Fax: (865) 579-4667. Web Site: www.praise963.com. Licensee: Seymour Communications. Format: Southern gospel. ♦Charlotte Mull, CEO; Doug Hutchison, pres & gen mgr; Mike Clark, opns mgr; Jamie Lewis, gen sls mgr & prom mgr; Tim Guinn, mus dir; Tim Berry, chief of engrg.

Shelbyville

*****WBIA(FM)**— 1999: 88.3 mhz; 250 w. Ant 46 ft. TL: N35 28 54 W86 27 28. Drawer 2440, Tupelo, MS 38803. Phone: (662) 844-8888. Fax: (662) 842-6791. Web Site: www.afr.net. Licensee: American Family Association. Group owner: American Family Radio Format: Christian. ♦Marvin Sanders, gen mgr; John Riley, progmg dir; Joey Moody, chief of engrg.

WLIJ(AM)— Dec 2, 1959: 1580 khz; 5 kw-D, 12 w-N. TL: N35 27 21 W86 27 09. Stereo. Box 7, 236 Woodland Dr. 37160. Phone: (931) 684-1514. Phone: (931) 684-1515. Fax: (931) 684-3956. Licensee: Hopkins-Hall Broadcasting Inc. (acq 7-19-90; $110,000; 8-6-90). Network: ABC. Haley, Bader & Potts. Format: Country, bluegrass, gospel. News staff: one; News: 14 hrs wkly. Target aud: General. Spec prog: Black one hr, farm 3 hrs, relg 11 hrs wkly. ♦Nadine Hopkins, pres & gen sls mgr; Jason H. Reed, progmg dir; Keith Cook, adv VP; Hal Ball, news dir; Paul Hopkins, progmg dir & chief of engrg.

WZNG(AM)—December 1946: 1400 khz; 1 kw-U. TL: N35 28 26 W86 26 45. Box 7 37162. Secondary address: 236 Woodland Dr. 37160. Phone: (931) 680-1214. Fax: (931) 684-3956. Licensee: Hopkins-Hall Broadcasting Inc. (acq 12-19-96; $250,000). Format: Talk America. Target aud: General; residents of the loc area. ♦Nadine Hopkins, pres; Paul Hopkins, sr VP; Rusty Reed, gen mgr & stn mgr.

Signal Mountain

WKXJ(FM)— Aug 29, 1994: 98.1 mhz; 1 kw. 794 ft. TL: N35 05 16 W85 21 47. 7413 Old Lee Hwy., Chattanooga 37421. Phone: (423) 892-3333. Fax: (423) 642-0097. E-mail: wkxj@clearchannel.com. Web Site: www.wkxj.com. Licensee: Capstar TX L.P. Group owner: Clear Channel Communications Inc. (acq 8-15-00; grpsl). Kaye, Scholer, Fierman, Hays & Handler. Format: CHR. News staff: one; News: 4 hrs wkly. Target aud: 35-54. ♦Sammy George, gen mgr; Kris Van Dyke, opns mgr & progmg dir; Rhonda Rollins, gen sls mgr.

Smithville

WJLE(AM)— Apr 11, 1964: 1480 khz; 1 kw-D, 34 w-N. TL: N35 55 31 W85 49 14. 2606 McMinnville Hwy. 37166-5071. Phone: (615) 597-4265. Fax: (615) 597-6025. E-mail: wjle@dtccom.net. Web Site: www.wjle.com. Licensee: Center Hill Broadcasting Corp. Network: ABC Information & Entertainment. Format: Country. News staff: one; News: 14 hrs wkly. Target aud: General. Spec prog: Gospel 15 hrs wkly. ♦W.E. Vanatta, pres & gen mgr; Dwayne Page, sls dir, progmg dir & news dir; Homer Wilson Jr., chief of engrg.

WJLE-FM— 1970: 101.7 mhz; 3 kw. 195 ft. TL: N35 55 31 W85 49 14. Web Site: www.wjle.com.

Smyrna

*****WFCM(AM)**— 1993: 710 khz; 250 w-D. TL: N35 58 31 W86 33 16. 1920 E. 24th Street Pl., Chattanooga 37404. Secondary address: 615 Potomac Pl. 37167. Phone: (423) 629-8900. Fax: (423) 629-0021. E-mail: wfcm@moody.edu. Web Site: www.wfcm.org. Licensee: The Moody Bible Institute of Chicago. (group owner; acq 5-16-97; $162,500). Network: Network: USA, Moody. Format: Educ, relg, news/talk. ♦Joseph Stowell, pres; Robert Neff, VP; Leighton LeBoeuf, gen mgr & stn mgr; Andy Napier, progmg dir; Paul Martine, mus dir.

WFFH(FM)— Oct 7, 1993: 94.1 mhz; 3.2 kw. Ant 305 ft. TL: N36 01 14 W86 38 18. Stereo. 402 BNA Dr., Suite 400, Nashville 37217. Phone: (615) 367-2210. Fax: (615) 367-0758. Web Site: www.94fmthefish.net. Licensee: Caron Broadcasting Inc. Group owner: Salem Communications Corp. (acq 12-18-02; $5.6 million. with WFFI(FM) Kingston Springs). Network: Salem Radio Network. Rep: Salem. Format: Contemp Christian. Target aud: 25-54; adults. ♦Michael S. Miller, gen mgr; Kevin R. Anderson, rgnl sls mgr; Dick Marsh, prom dir; Vance Dillard, progmg dir; Kim Bindel, news dir.

Soddy-Daisy

WGOW-FM—Licensed to Soddy-Daisy. See Chattanooga

WSDT(AM)— Feb 27, 1970: 1240 khz; 1 kw-U. TL: N35 16 16 W85 10 28. Willis Broadcasting Corp., 645 Church St., Suite 400, Norfolk, VA 23510. Phone: (757) 622-4600. Fax: (757) 624-6515. Licensee: Willis Broadcasting Corp. (group owner; acq 4-27-99; $65,000). ♦Levi E. Willis II, VP; Katrina Chase, gen mgr.

Somerville

WSTN(AM)— Nov 29, 1982: 1410 khz; 500 w-U, DA-2. TL: N35 14 31 W89 19 03. Family Worship Center Church Inc., 8919 World Ministry Ave., Baton Rouge, LA 70810. Phone: (225) 768-8300. Fax: (225) 769-2244. E-mail: info@jsm.org. Web Site: www.jsm.org. Licensee: Family Worship Center Church Inc. (group owner; acq 12-4-02). Format: Relg. ♦John Santiago, gen mgr & stn mgr.

South Fulton

WCMT-FM—Licensed to South Fulton. See Martin

South Pittsburg

WEPG(AM)— July 9, 1954: 910 khz; 5 kw-D, 95 w-N. TL: N35 00 57 W85 42 00. Box 8 37380. Secondary address: 105 N. Ash Ave. 37380. Phone: (423) 837-0747. Fax: (423) 837-2974. E-mail: wepgtv6@aol.com. Licensee: Stone/Collins Communications Inc. (acq 2-1-02). Format: Country. Target aud: 18-50; females. Spec prog: Gospel 10 hrs wkly. ♦Roger Spears, gen mgr; Glenda Frame, prom dir; Rogers Spears, gen sls mgr & progmg dir.

WMAX-FM— Nov 5, 1990: 97.3 mhz; 16 kw. 856 ft. TL: N34 58 21 W85 37 58. Stereo. Box 8799, Chattanooga 37414. Secondary address: 7413 Old Lee Hwy., Chattanooga 37414. Phone: (423) 892-3333. Fax: (423) 642-0096. Licensee: Capstar TX L.P. Group owner: Clear Channel Communications Inc. (acq 8-7-2000; grpsl). Format: Hip-Hop. News staff: 2; News: 20 hrs wkly. Target aud: 18-54. ♦Sammy George, gen mgr; Kris Van Dyke, opns mgr; Rhonda Rollins, gen sls mgr; Andre Johnson, engrg dir.

Sparta

WRKK-FM—Listing follows WSMT(AM).

WSMT(AM)— Apr 26, 1953: 1050 khz; 1 kw-D, 181 w-N. TL: N35 57 00 W85 28 50. 520 N. Spring St. 38583-1305. Phone: (931) 836-1055. Phone: (931) 836-2824. Fax: (931) 836-2320. Licensee: Clear Channel Broadcasting Licenses Inc. Group owner: Clear Channel Communications Inc. (acq 9-8-99; grpsl). Format: Southern gospel. News staff: one; News: 10 hrs wkly. Target aud: General. Spec prog: Relg 10 hrs wkly. ♦David Roederer, CEO & gen mgr.

WRKK-FM—Co-owned with WSMT(AM). Aug 2, 1964: 105.5 mhz; 1.05 kw. 46 ft. TL: N35 51 39 W85 26 40. Stereo. Web Site: rockdog1055.com. Format: Classic rock. News staff: one. Target aud: 18-34. ♦Don Howard, opns mgr.

WTZX(AM)— Nov 26, 1971: 860 khz; 1 kw-D, 9.9 w-N. TL: N35 55 20 W85 26 50. 520 N. Spring St. 38583-1305. Phone: (931) 836-1055. Fax: (931) 836-2320. Licensee: Clear Channel Broadcasting Licenses Inc. Group owner: Clear Channel Communications Inc. (acq 11-6-01; $85,000). Format: Oldies. News staff: one; News: 10 hrs wkly. Target aud: 35-54. ♦David Roederer, gen mgr; Don Howard, stn mgr, opns mgr, progmg dir & news dir; Bruce Walker, sls dir & gen sls mgr; Homer Wilson, chief of engrg.

Spencer

WKZP(FM)— Aug 1, 1993: 107.3 mhz; 2 kw. 508 ft. TL: N35 39 55 W85 31 19. 230 W. Colville St., Mc Minnville 37110. Phone: (931) 473-9253. Fax: (931) 473-4149. E-mail: bryankell@clearchannel.com. Web Site: www.kiss107radio.com. Licensee: Citicasters Licenses L.P. Group owner: Clear Channel Communications Inc. (acq 10-30-99; grpsl). Format: CHR. ♦Bryan Kell, gen mgr & sls; Jeff Edwards, progmg dir; Homer Wilson, chief of engrg.

*****WZYZ(FM)**— 2003: 90.1 mhz; 30 w. Ant 590 ft. TL: N35 44 03 W85 27 33. 120707 Beersheba Hwy., McMinnville 37110. Phone: (931) 946-7777. E-mail: questions@wzyz.org. Licensee: Church Faith Trinity Assemblies (acq 8-1-02). Format: Relg. ♦Daniel Lawson, gen mgr.

Spring City

WAYA(FM)—Listing follows WXQK(AM).

WXQK(AM)— July 12, 1979: 970 khz; 500 w-D. TL: N35 39 59 W84 52 44. 2640 Commerce Dr. N.E., Cleveland 37311. Phone: (423) 242-7656. Fax: (423) 472-5290. Web Site: www.wbacradio.com. Licensee: J.L. Brewer Broadcasting of Cleveland LLC. Group owner: Brewer Broadcasting Corp. (acq 7-1-02; grpsl). Network: ABC. Rep: D & R Radio. Format: News/talk. News staff: one; News: 16 hrs wkly. Target aud: 35-64. ♦James L. Brewer, pres; James L. Brewer II, VP; Don Schwartz, gen mgr; Mark Jacobus, gen sls mgr; Corky Whitlock, progmg dir; Mike Powers, news dir.

WAYA(FM)—Co-owned with WXQK(AM). October 1989: 93.9 mhz; 2 kw. 344 ft. TL: N35 42 06 W84 53 01. Web Site: www.wbacradio.com. Rep: D & R Radio. Format: Hot adult contemp. News: one hr wkly. Target aud: 25-54. ♦Duane Shannon, progmg dir; Ed Ramsey, pub affrs dir.

Springfield

WDBL(AM)— July 24, 1950: 1590 khz; 1 kw-D, 30 w-N. TL: N36 29 43 W86 54 26. (CP: 710 w-D. TL: N36 29 42 W86 54 22). 1640 Old Russellville Pike, Clarksburg 37043. Phone: (931) 648-7720. Fax: (931) 648-7769. Licensee: Lightning Broadcasting LLC (acq 7-28-2004; $150,000). Format: Contemp Christian. News staff: one; News: 16 hrs

Stations in the U.S. — Tennessee

Developers & Brokers of Radio Properties
contact American Media Services at our suite:
Philadelphia Marriott Downtown
215-625-2900
843-972-2200
americanmediaservices.com
Charleston, SC
Dallas, TX · Chicago, Il · Austin, TX
American Media Services, LLC

wkly. Target aud: 18 plus. Spec prog: Farm 10 hrs, gospel 10 hrs wkly. ♦ Susan Quesenberry, gen mgr; Lee Logan, opns mgr & progmg dir; J.C. Morrow, mus dir & chief of engrg.

WSGI(AM)— Dec 15, 1982: 1100 khz; 1 kw-D. TL: N36 31 00 W86 53 30. 722 S. Main St. 37172. Secondary address: PO Box 909 37172. Phone: (615) 384-9744. Fax: (615) 384-9746. E-mail: wsgi1100@yahoo.com. Licensee: Lightning Broadcasting LLC (acq 3-2001; $155,000). Format: Variety. Target aud: General. Spec prog: Relg, farm 5 hrs, gospel 16 hrs wkly. ♦ Jo Petersen, VP; Neil Petersen, pres & gen mgr; Billy Gray, gen sls mgr & news dir.

Static

WSBI(AM)— Apr 7, 1986: 1210 khz; 1 kw-D. TL: N36 37 22 W85 05 15. Box 160, Byrdstown 38549. Phone: (606) 387-6625. Fax: (606) 387-8126. E-mail: info@wsbiam.com. Web Site: www.wsbiam.com. Licensee: Donnie S. Cox. (acq 11-3-99; $60,000). Network: USA. Format: Country. News staff: one; News: 15 hrs wkly. Target aud: 25 plus. Spec prog: Gospel 10 hrs, bluegrass one hr wkly. ♦ Donnie Cox, gen mgr; Robert Huddleston, chief of engrg.

Surgoinsville

WEYE(FM)—Licensed to Surgoinsville. See Church Hill

Sweetwater

WDEH(AM)— 1955: 800 khz; 1 kw-D, 379 w-N. TL: N35 36 49 W84 27 33. Box 24250, Knoxville 37933. Phone: (423) 337-5025. Fax: (423) 337-5026. Licensee: Horne Radio L.L.C. Group owner: Horne Radio Group (acq 1999; $425,000. with co-located FM). Format: Gospel. ♦ Jim Christainsen, gen mgr; Todd Ethridge, progmg dir.

WLOD-FM—Co-owned with WDEH(AM). September 1967: 98.3 mhz; 6 kw. 135 ft. TL: N35 36 49 W84 27 33. Phone: (865) 675-4105. Fax: (865) 675-4859. Format: Bluegrass.

Tazewell

WCTU(FM)— October 1989: 105.9 mhz; 2.75 kw. Ant 492 ft. TL: N36 27 32 W83 35 07. Stereo. Box 215, 728 Essary Rd. 37879. Phone: (423) 626-7145. Fax: (423) 626-7145. E-mail: stair1@communication.com. Licensee: Stair Company Inc. Format: Country. News staff: one; News: 5 hrs wkly. Target aud: 25-90; people who buy the most in marketplace. ♦ Jim Stair, pres; Jim Gilbert, sls dir; Rhonda Stair, prom dir & progmg dir; Walter Stair, gen mgr, gen sls mgr, mus dir & news dir; Bob Wallace, chief of engrg.

WNTT(AM)— July 1, 1960: 1250 khz; 500 w-D. TL: N36 27 09 W83 34 23. Box 95, 115 Bluetop Rd. 37879-0095. Phone: (423) 626-4203. Fax: (423) 626-3040. E-mail: aileen@wntt1250am.co. Licensee: WNTT Inc. (acq 9-1-94; $90,000). Network: ABC. Format: Country, oldies, news. News: 12 hrs wkly. Target aud: 18-65; general. Spec prog: Gospel, bluegrass. ♦ Aileen S. Craft, CEO, gen sls mgr, progmg dir, progmg mgr & news dir; Darrell Turner, opns mgr & chief of opns; Mark England, sls VP & mus dir; Frank Folsom, chief of engrg.

Trenton

WTNE-FM— August 1980: 97.7 mhz; 50 kw. Ant 328 ft. TL: N36 05 10 W88 54 39. Stereo. Box 500 38382. Secondary address: 302 W. Eaton 38382. Phone: (731) 855-0098. Fax: (731) 855-1600. E-mail: wtkbwtne@bellsouth.net. Licensee: Grace Broadcasting Services Inc. Group owner: Thunderbolt Broadcasting Co./Gibson County Broadcasting (acq 1-7-2005; grpsl). Format: Country, sports. News staff: one. Target aud: 25-60. Spec prog: High school sports 10 hrs, college football 10 hrs wkly. ♦ Sherry Vaughn, gen mgr; Randy Gardner, sls dir; Steve Hilton, progmg dir; Robin Cude, news dir; Dave Hacker, chief of engrg.

WTNE(AM)— Dec 9, 1966: 1500 khz; 250 w-D, 6 w-N. TL: N35 58 52 W88 55 32. Phone: (731) 855-1500. Midsouth. Format: Adult contemp. Target aud: General; Gibson county, news oriented people. Spec prog: Sports. ♦ Dave Hacker, chief of engrg.

Tullahoma

*WAUT-FM— 1998: 88.5 mhz; 1.9 kw. 177 ft. TL: N35 20 30 W86 11 05. Box 3206, American Family Radio, Tupelo, MS 38803. Phone: (662) 844-8888. Phone: (662) 844-8893. Fax: (662) 842-6791. E-mail: comments@afr.net. Web Site: www.afr.net. Licensee: American Family Association. Group owner: American Family Radio Format: Relg. ♦ Marvin Sanders, gen mgr.

WHRP(FM)— July 1, 1962: 93.3 mhz; 100 kw. 981 ft. TL: N35 02 04 W86 22 52. Stereo. 1717 Hwy. 72 E., Athens, AL 35611. Phone: (256) 830-8300. Fax: (256) 232-6842. Web Site: www.power393.net. Licensee: Cumulus Licensing LLC. Group owner: Cumulus Media Inc. (acq 7-21-2003; grpsl). Gardner, Carton & Douglas. Format: Urban mainstream. News staff: 3. Target aud: 25-49; baby boomers graduating high school 1965-80. ♦ Bill West, gen mgr; John Holland, gen sls mgr; Wendy Black, gen sls mgr & prom dir; Phillip David, progmg dir; Marty Broman, news dir; Bill Schrode, chief of engrg.

WJIG(AM)— Aug 1, 1947: 740 khz; 250 w-D, 67 w-N. TL: N35 20 36 W86 12 00. WJIG AM 740, 607 E. Carroll St. 37388-3951. Phone: (931) 455-7426. Fax: (931) 455-7438. E-mail: wjig@cafes.net. Licensee: NRS Enterprises Inc. (acq 2-21-97; $163,000). Network: Salem Radio Network. Format: Southern gospel. ♦ Floyd "Bud" Miles, pres; Medford Donnell, gen mgr; Tom Wiseman, chief of engrg.

*WTML(FM)— 2001: 91.5 mhz; 1.55 kw. Ant 269 ft. TL: N35 23 53 W86 08 40. Nashville Public Radio, 630 Mainstream Dr., Nashville 37228-1204. Phone: (615) 760-2903. Fax: (615) 760-2904. Web Site: www.wpln.org. Licensee: Nashville Public Radio. Format: Classical, news, bluegrass. ♦ Robert Gordon, gen mgr; Scott Smith, opns mgr; Laura Landress, gen sls mgr; Henry Fennell, progmg dir; Will Griffin, mus dir; Anita Bugg, news dir; Tom Knox, chief of engrg.

Tusculum

WIKQ(FM)—Licensed to Tusculum. See Greeneville

Union City

WENK(AM)— Oct 26, 1946: 1240 khz; 1 kw-U. TL: N36 25 28 W89 02 17. Stereo. 1729 Nailling Dr. 38261. Phone: (731) 885-1240. Fax: (731) 885-3405. E-mail: wenk@charter.net. Licensee: WENK of Union City Inc. Group owner: WENK Broadcast Group Inc. (acq 1-74). Network: ABC Information & Entertainment. Rep: Rgnl Reps. Format: Oldies. News staff: 2; News: 15 hrs wkly. Target aud: 35-54. ♦ Terry Hailey, pres & gen mgr; Theresa James, sls dir; Robin Francis, news dir; Brad Hosford, chief of engrg.

WQAK(FM)— March 1994: 105.7 mhz; 6 kw. 328 ft. TL: N36 31 08 W89 05 25. 709 S. First St., Ste. A 38261. Phone: (731) 885-1057. Fax: (731) 885-0250. E-mail: programming@thequakerocks.com. Web Site: www.thequakerocks.com. Licensee: Twin States Broadcasting Inc. (acq 9-16-94; 10-24-94). Format: Rock alternative. ♦ Kathy Jo Roberts, gen mgr; Don Wilson, gen sls mgr & progmg dir; Rodney Holland, mus dir; Rodney Taylor, pres & news dir; Charles Holland, chief of engrg.

*WTNN(FM)—Not on air, target date: unknown: 88.9 mhz; 6 kw vert. Ant 115 ft. TL: N36 27 34 W89 00 02. Broadcasting for the Challenged Inc., 188 S. Bellevue, Suite 222, Memphis 38104. Phone: (901) 375-9324. Fax: (901) 375-0041. Licensee: Broadcasting for the Challenged Inc. ♦ Shea Flinn, gen mgr.

WYVY(FM)— Sept 20, 1974: 104.9 mhz; 3 kw. 298 ft. TL: N36 28 27 W88 56 42. (CP: 6 kw, ant 292 ft.). Stereo. Secondary address: 709 S. First St., Ste. A 38281. Phone: (731) 885-0051. Fax: (731) 885-0250. Web Site: www.todaysyoungcountry.com. Licensee: Twin States Broadcasting (acq 9-16-94; 10-24-94). Network: ABC Information & Entertainment. Format: Country. News staff: 2; News: 25 hrs wkly. Target aud: 18 plus. Spec prog: Farm 2 hrs, Black 5 hrs, gospel 7 hrs wkly. ♦ Rodney Taylor, pres; Kathy Jo Roberts, gen mgr & sls mgr; Don Wilson, opns mgr, gen mgr, progmg dir & news dir; Charles Holland, chief of engrg.

Wartburg

WECO(AM)— Aug 31, 1970: 940 khz; 5 kw-D. TL: N36 05 48 W84 35 31. Box 100 37887. Secondary address: 305 N. Church St. 37887. Phone: (423) 346-3900. Fax: (423) 346-7686. E-mail: wecoradio@highland.net. Licensee: Morgan County Broadcasting Co. Inc. Format: Gospel. ♦ Sandy Lavender, gen mgr; Gary Stone, progmg dir; Carl Stump, chief of engrg.

WECO-FM— August 1988: 101.3 mhz; 500 w. 770 ft. TL: N36 05 25 W78 38 05. (Acq 1-30-89). Format: Country. Target aud: 25-49.

Waverly

WQMV(AM)— Sept 25, 1963: 1060 khz; 1 kw-D. TL: N36 04 57 W87 50 05. Box 619, Ashland City 37015-0619. Phone: (615) 792-6789. Fax: (615) 792-7795. Licensee: C & L Broadcasting Corp. (acq 10-16-2003; $60,000). Format: News, sports, talk. ♦ Richard Albright, pres.

WVRY(FM)— Sept 26, 1972: 105.1 mhz; 50 kw. Ant 492 ft. TL: N36 05 16 W87 51 19. Stereo. 402 BNA Drive, Ste. 400, Nashville 37217. Phone: (615) 740-9879. Fax: (615) 740-7799. E-mail: info@salemmusicnetwork.com. Web Site: www.solidgospel105.com. Licensee: Reach Satellite Network Inc. Group owner: Salem Communications Corp. (acq 3-31-2000; $3.1 million. for stock with WBOZ(FM) Woodbury). Network: Salem Radio Network. Rep: Salem. Fletcher, Heald & Hildreth. Format: Christian country, Southern gospel. Target aud: 25-54. ♦ Jim Cumbee, CEO; Michael S. Miller, gen mgr; Carl Campbell, stn mgr; Wade Schoenemann, opns mgr; Kevin R. Anderson, rgnl sls mgr; Dick Marsh, prom dir; Les Butler, progmg dir.

Waynesboro

WWON(AM)— Jan 31, 1970: 930 khz; 500 w-D. TL: N35 18 30 W87 44 44. Box 1000, 100 Public Sq. S. 38485. Phone: (931) 722-3631. Fax: (931) 722-3632. E-mail: wwon@netease.net. Web Site: am930.net. Licensee: New Mind Broadcasting LLC (acq 1-27-2005; $92,000). Network: ABC Daytime Direction. Mullin, Rhyne, Emmons & Topel. Format: Oldies. News: 13 hrs wkly. Target aud: 18-54; listeners interested in rgnl & natl issues. ♦ Rob Edgar, sls VP & prom mgr; Shayne Riley, gen mgr, stn mgr, progmg dir & news dir; Kevin Kidd, chief of engrg.

White Bluff

WQSE(AM)— July 18, 1982: 1030 khz; 1 kw-D, DA-N. TL: N36 08 03 W87 12 58. 201 Hall Ln. 37187. Phone: (615) 797-9785. Fax: (615) 797-9788. E-mail: dvanedjwqse@aol.com. Licensee: Canaan Communications Inc. (acq 3-19-03; $85,000). Format: Southern gospel. ♦ Duane Jeffrey, pres & gen mgr; Kerry Lampley, sls dir; Mary Jeffrey, mus dir.

Winchester

WCDT(AM)— Mar 8, 1948: 1340 khz; 1 kw-U. TL: N35 10 51 W86 05 34. 1201 S. College St. 37398. Phone: (931) 967-2201. Phone: (931) 967-2202. Fax: (931) 967-2201. E-mail: wcdt@bellsouth.net. Web Site: www.wcdt1340.com. Licensee: Franklin County Radio & Broadcasting Co. Inc. (acq 8-1-56). Network: ABC. Format: Country. News staff: one; News: 15 hrs wkly. Target aud: General. Spec prog: Farm 15 hrs, Relg 6 hrs wkly. ♦ John T. Yarbrough, pres & VP; Tommy Yarbrough, gen mgr; Jeanetta Shields, gen sls mgr, progmg mgr & progmg; Sharon Holder, mktg dir & sls; Karen Shetters, prom mgr; Jan Tavalin, news dir; Karen Shetters, sls.

Woodbury

WBOZ(FM)— Oct 5, 1994: 104.9 mhz; 6 kw. Ant 328 ft. TL: N35 49 33 W86 09 28. Stereo. 312 S. Church St., Murfreesboro 37130. Secondary address: 402 BNA Dr., Suite 400, Nashville 37217. Phone: (615) 890-3233. Fax: (615) 890-2990. E-mail: webmaster@solidgospel.com. Web Site: www.solidgospel105.com. Licensee: Reach Satellite Network Inc. Group owner: Salem Communications Corp. (acq 4-1-00; $3.1

Tennessee

million. for stock with WVRY(FM) Waverly). Network: Salem Radio Network. Rep: Salem. Format: Christian country, southern gospel. News: 14 hrs wkly. Target aud: 25-54; adults. Spec prog: Sports 5 hrs wkly. ◆Greg R. Anderson, pres; Michael S. Miller, gen mgr; Kevin R. Anderson, stn mgr.

WBRY(AM)— Oct 24, 1963: 1540 khz; 500 w-D. TL: N35 49 53 W86 06 42. Box 7 37190. Secondary address: 153 Mile Valley Rd. 37190. Phone: (615) 563-2313. Fax: (615) 563-6229. E-mail: akus@wbry.com. Web Site: www.wbry.com. Licensee: Volunteer Broadcasting LLC (acq 3-2-2005; $130,000). Format: Traditional country. News staff: one; News: 7 hrs wkly. Target aud: 25 plus; adults. ◆Doug Combs, pres & gen mgr.

Texas

Abilene

*KACU(FM)— June 2, 1986: 89.7 mhz; 33 kw. 215 ft. TL: N32 28 34 W99 42 22. Stereo. ACU Box 29106 79699. Phone: (915) 674-2441. Fax: (915) 674-2417. E-mail: info@kacu.org. Web Site: www.kacu.org. Licensee: Abilene Christian University. Network: NPR. Format: Adult contemp, class, news. News: 42 hrs wkly. Target aud: 35 plus; middle-to-upper income professionals. Spec prog: Jazz 3 hrs wkly. ◆John Best, gen mgr & opns dir; Kim Seidman, dev dir.

*KAGT-FM— Nov 5, 2002: 90.5 mhz; 23 kw. Ant 341 ft. TL: N32 30 37 W99 44 28. Stereo. 500 Chestnut St. #1717 79602-6145. Phone: (325) 672-8484. Fax: (325) 672-8486. E-mail: mailbox@kagtfm.com. Web Site: kagtfm.com. Licensee: Gospel Radio Network (acq 10-28-02; $23,000. for CP). Network: USA. Format: Southern gospel/Christian talk. News: 10 hrs wkly. Target aud: 35+. ◆Tim Walker, pres & gen mgr; Tommy Fain, CFO; Russell Veckert, exec VP; Jo Ann Adams, stn mgr.

*KAQD(FM)— 1998: 91.3 mhz; 1 kw. Ant 177 ft. TL: N32 28 36 W99 44 56. Box 3206, American Family Radio, Tupelo, MS 38803. Phone: (662) 844-8888. Fax: (662) 844-9176. E-mail: comments@afr.net. Web Site: www.afr.net. Licensee: American Family Association. Group owner: American Family Radio Format: Inspirational Christian. ◆Marvin Sanders, gen mgr.

KBCY(FM)—See Tye

KEAN-FM—Listing follows KYYW(AM).

KEYJ-FM— Apr 30, 1961: 107.9 mhz; 100 kw. 670 ft. TL: N32 17 06 W99 38 38. Stereo. 3911 S. First St. 79605. Phone: (325) 677-7225. Phone: (325) 676-7711. Fax: (325) 676-3851. Web Site: www.keyj.com. Licensee: CCB Texas Licenses L.P. Group owner: Clear Channel Communications Inc. (acq 2000; grpsl). Format: Alternative rock. Target aud: 18-49; men. ◆Dale Harris, gen mgr; James Cameron, opns mgr; Frank Payne, progmg dir.

KFGL(FM)— September 1974: 100.7 mhz; 100 kw. 1,260 ft. TL: N32 24 48 W100 06 25. Stereo. 3911 S. First St. 79605. Phone: (325) 676-7711. Fax: (325) 676-3851. E-mail: reneegonzalez@clearchannel.com. Web Site: www.kissabilene.com. Licensee: CCB Texas Licenses L.P. Group owner: Clear Channel Communications Inc. (acq 2000; grpsl). Format: Classic rock. Target aud: 18-34; women. Spec prog: Oldies 2 hrs wkly. ◆Ted Warren, gen mgr; James Cameron, opns mgr; Renee Gonzalez, gen sls mgr.

*KGNZ(FM)— Mar 7, 1981: 88.1 mhz; 75 kw. 710 ft. TL: N32 17 46 W99 43 01. Stereo. 542 Butternut St. 79602. Secondary address: 1001 Cedar Crest St. 79601. Phone: (325) 673-3045. Fax: (325) 672-7938. E-mail: studio@kgnz.com. Web Site: www.kgnz.com. Licensee: Christian Broadcasting Co. Network: USA. Format: Adult contemp, Christian. Spec prog: Black 2 hrs, gospel 2 hrs wkly. ◆Larry Jack Hill, pres & gen mgr; Doug Harris, opns mgr; Randy Martinez, dev dir.

KKHR(FM)— June 1988: 106.3 mhz; 50 kw. Ant 184 ft. TL: N32 28 34 W99 42 22. Stereo. 402 Cypress St., Suite 709 79601. Phone: (915) 695-9898. Fax: (915) 691-9968. E-mail: star106@camalott.com. Web Site: www.star106.com. Licensee: Canfin Enterprises Inc. (acq 1-19-2005; $684,000). Rep: Lotus Entravision Reps LLC. Format: Sp. News: 3 hrs wkly. Target aud: 18-49. ◆Scott Powell, gen mgr; Amy Meridith, gen sls mgr; Ben Gonzalez, progmg dir & mus dir; James Thompson, chief of engrg.

KNCE(FM)—See Winters

KORQ(FM)—See Baird

KSLI(AM)— June 15, 1957: 1280 khz; 500 w-D, 226 w-N. TL: N32 26 30 W99 43 08. Box 3098 79604. Secondary address: 3911 S. First St. 79605. Phone: (325) 676-7711. Fax: (325) 676-3851. Licensee: CCB Texas Licenses L.P. Group owner: Clear Channel Communications Inc. (acq 2000; grpsl). Network: Network: ABC Information & Entertainment, Jones Radio Networks. Format: Music of your life. News: 4 hrs wkly. Target aud: 18-49; Hispanic. ◆Dale Harris, gen mgr.

KULL(FM)— Apr 1, 1998: 92.5 mhz; 50 kw. 492 ft. TL: N32 18 55 W99 59 24. (CP: 44 kw, ant 525 ft.). 3911 S. 1st St. 79605. Phone: (325) 677-7225. Fax: (325) 677-3851. Licensee: CCB Texas Licenses L.P. Group owner: Clear Channel Communications Inc. (acq 2000; grpsl). Network: ABC. Format: Oldies. ◆Ted Wrenn, VP; James Cameron, opns mgr.

KWKC(AM)— June 19, 1948: 1340 khz; 1 kw-U. TL: N32 25 14 W99 43 54. 1749 N. 2nd St. 79603. Phone: (325) 673-1455. Fax: (325) 673-3485. E-mail: jim@kwkc1340.com. Web Site: www.kwkc.com. Licensee: Abilene Radio Corp. (acq 12-8-2004; $550,000. with KZQQ(AM) Abilene). Format: News/talk. ◆Dave Boyll, opns VP & opns mgr; Jim Christopherson, sls VP.

KYYW(AM)— Oct 1, 1936: 1470 khz; 5 kw-D, 1 kw-N, DA-N. TL: N32 29 26 W99 45 02. 3911 S. First St. 79605. Phone: (915) 676-7711. Fax: (915) 676-3851. Web Site: www.keanradio.com. Licensee: CCB Texas Licenses L.P. Group owner: Clear Channel Communications Inc. (acq 2000; grpsl). Network: CBS. Kenkel & Associates. Format: Authentic country. Target aud: 30 plus; upscale, affluent. Spec prog: Farm 3 hrs, relg 5 hrs wkly. ◆Dale Harris, gen mgr; Justin Riggan, gen sls mgr; Renee Gonzalez, gen sls mgr; James Cameron, progmg dir; Gary Smith, engrg dir & chief of engrg.

KEAN-FM—Co-owned with KYYW(AM). July 1, 1969: 105.1 mhz; 100 kw. Ant 810 ft. TL: N32 16 35 W99 35 39. Stereo. E-mail: kean@keanradio.com. Web Site: www.keanradio.com. Network: ABC. Format: Country. ◆Rudy Fernandez, progmg dir.

KZQQ(AM)— Aug 29, 1962: 1560 khz; 500 w-D. TL: N32 27 21 W99 47 59. 1749 N. 2nd 79603. Phone: (325) 673-1455. Fax: (325) 673-3485. Web Site: www.kwkc.com. Licensee: Canfin Enterprises, Inc. (acq 12-8-2004; $550,000. with KWKC(AM) Abilene). Format: Sports/Talk. Target aud: 25 plus. Spec prog: Black 4 hrs wkly. ◆Jim Christoferson, gen mgr.

Alamo

KJAV(FM)— Aug 17, 1980: 104.9 mhz; 6 kw. Ant 328 ft. TL: N26 12 49 W98 05 21. BMP Radio LP, 1 Paseo del Prado, Bldg. 102, Edinburg 78539. Phone: (956) 686-8170. Fax: (956) 686-8415. E-mail: info@bmpradio.com. Web Site: www.bmpradio.com. Licensee: BMP RGV License Company L.P. (acq 12-14-2004; $7 million). Format: Sp. ◆Thomas Castro, pres.

Alamo Heights

KDRY(AM)—Licensed to Alamo Heights. See San Antonio

KLUP(AM)—See Terrell Hills

Alice

KNDA(FM)— Jan 1, 1974: 102.9 mhz; 50 kw. 492 ft. TL: N27 42 26 W97 46 54. Stereo. 2001 Saratoga, Suite 100, Corpus Christi 78417. Phone: (361) 814-1030. Phone: (361) 814-1029. Fax: (361) 814-1036. E-mail: lilricharddabomb@aol.com. Licensee: Encarnacion A. Guerra (acq 5-95). Format: Hip-hop, R&B. ◆Pat Rodriguez, gen mgr.

KOPY(AM)— 1947: 1070 khz; 1 kw-U, DA-N. TL: N27 46 39 W98 04 53. Box 731 78333. Secondary address: 2722 N. Business Hwy. 281 78332. Phone: (361) 664-1884. Fax: (361) 664-1886. Licensee: Alice Broadcast Co. (acq 1-1-96). Format: Country. News staff: 12; News: 2 hrs wkly. Target aud: 18-59. ◆Bobby Pena, gen mgr & stn mgr; Jackie Hinojosa, gen sls mgr, prom mgr, progmg dir & news dir.

KOPY-FM— Jan 20, 1976: 92.1 mhz; 3 kw. 300 ft. TL: N27 46 39 W98 04 53. Stereo. Format: Tejano. News: 8 hrs wkly. Target aud: General. ◆Bobby Pena, progmg dir.

Directory of Radio

KUKA(FM)—See San Diego

Allen

KESN(FM)— Dec 1, 1981: 103.3 mhz; 100 kw. Ant 1,968 ft. TL: N33 32 08 W96 49 54. Stereo. 2221 E. Lamar Blvd., Suite 300, Arlington 76006. Phone: (817) 695-3523. Fax: (817) 695-3516. Web Site: espn1033.com. Licensee: WBAP-KSCS Operating Ltd. Group owner: ABC Inc. (acq 8-9-00; $18 million). Format: Sports. Target aud: 25-54; males and females. Spec prog: Children 2 hrs wkly. ◆Marce Graves, CEO; Keri Korzeniewski, gen mgr.

Alpine

KALP(FM)— September 1986: 92.7 mhz; 2.37 kw. 328 ft. TL: N30 19 09 W103 37 04. Box 9650 79831. Secondary address: 500 Hendryx Ave. 79830. Phone: (432) 837-2144. Fax: (915) 837-3984. E-mail: alpineradio@brooksdata.net. Licensee: Rio Grande Broadcasting Co. Format: C&W. ◆Gene Ray Hendryx, gen mgr, progmg dir, chief of engrg & pres.

KVLF(AM)— Feb 27, 1947: 1240 khz; 1 kw-U. TL: N30 22 30 W103 39 36. Drawer 779 79831. Secondary address: 500 Hendryx Ave. 79831. Phone: (432) 837-2144. Fax: (432) 837-3984. E-mail: alpineradio @brooksdata.net. Licensee: Big Bend Broadcasters. Network: ABC. Format: Div. News: 21 hrs wkly. Spec prog: Sp 10 hrs wkly. ◆Gene Ray Hendryx Jr., pres; Ray Hendryx, gen mgr; Jerry Sotello, gen sls mgr.

Alvin

*KACC(FM)— Nov 1, 1993: 89.7 mhz; 5.6 kw. 338 ft. TL: N29 24 01 W95 12 13. Stereo. 3110 Mustang Rd. 77511. Phone: (281) 756-3765. Fax: (281) 756-3885. E-mail: cforsythe@alvincollege.edu. Web Site: www.kaccradio.com. Licensee: Alvin Community College. Garvey, Schubert & Barer. Format: AOR. News staff: one; News: 3 hrs wkly. Target aud: General. ◆A. Rodney Allbright, pres; Cathy Forsythe, gen mgr & prom dir; Mark Moss, chief of opns & progmg dir.

KTEK(AM)— November 1981: 1110 khz; 2.5 kw, DA. TL: N29 22 51 W95 14 15. 6161 Savoy, Suite 1200, Houston 77036. Phone: (713) 260-3600. Fax: (713) 260-3628. Web Site: www.kkht.com. Licensee: South Texas Broadcasting Inc. Group owner: Salem Communications Corp. (acq 7-2-98; $2.7 million. with KYCR(AM) Golden Valley, MN). Network: USA. Format: Christian talk. News: 6 hrs wkly. Target aud: 25-54; upscale families, 60% women, 40% male. Spec prog: Urdu-Hindi 3 hrs wkly. ◆Chuck Jewell, gen mgr; Paul Baker, opns mgr & mktg mgr; Dan Doster, gen sls mgr; Kendall Cockrell, progmg dir; Marsha Lambeth, progmg dir; Scott VanPelt, pub affrs dir; Sydney Jones, chief of engrg.

Amarillo

*KACV-FM— Mar 15, 1976: 89.9 mhz; 100 kw. 1,041 ft. TL: N35 20 33 W101 49 21. Stereo. Box 447 79178. Secondary address: 2408 S. Jackson 79109. Phone: (806) 371-5222. Fax: (806) 345-5576. E-mail: kacvfm90@actv.edu. Web Site: www.kacvfm.org. Licensee: Amarillo Junior College District. Format: Alternative / Block. Spec prog: Class 16 hrs, jazz 12 hrs, Black 8 hrs wkly. ◆Joyce Herring, gen mgr. Co-owned TV: *KACV-TV affil.

KAEZ(FM)— Dec 6, 1991: 105.7 mhz; 6 kw. 236 ft. TL: N35 12 28 W101 51 18. 1616 S. Kentucky St., Suite C-400 79102. Phone: (806) 353-4037. Fax: (806) 353-4665. E-mail: studio@thebreeze1057.com. Licensee: Kanza Society Inc. (acq 8-17-2004; $1.25 million). Network: ABC. Format: Christian. Target aud: General. ◆Tim Marx, gen mgr.

KARX(FM)—(Claude). Apr 12, 1992: 95.7 mhz; 100 kw. 391 ft. TL: N35 06 16 W101 39 28. Stereo. 301 S. Polk, Suite 100 79101. Phone: (806) 342-5200. Fax: (806) 342-5202. E-mail: chris.matchett@cumulus.com. Web Site: www.cumulus.com. Licensee: Cumulus Licensing Corp. Group owner: Cumulus Media Inc. (acq 2-2-98; $675,000). Format: Classic rock. News staff: one; News: 10 hrs wkly. Target aud: 25-54; male. ◆Rick Matchett, gen mgr; Stan Ross, sls dir; D'Lisa Pohnert, prom dir; Craig Vaughn, progmg dir; Dale Miller, mus dir; Matt Darby, news dir; J.P. Wolf, chief of engrg.

KATP(FM)— Mar 11, 1976: 101.9 mhz; 100 kw. 935 ft. TL: N35 20 33 W101 49 21. Stereo. 6214 W. 34th 79109. Phone: (806) 355-9777. Fax: (806) 359-0136. E-mail: katp@clearchannel.com. Web Site: www.catcountry1019.com. Licensee: AMFM Radio Licenses LLC. Group owner: Clear Channel Communications Inc. (acq 4-12-01; $1.5

Broadcasting & Cable Yearbook 2006

Developers & Brokers of Radio Properties
contact American Media Services at our suite: Philadelphia Marriott Downtown 215-625-2900
843-972-2200
americanmediaservices.com
Charleston, SC
Dallas, TX - Chicago, Il - Austin, TX
American Media Services, LLC

million). Format: Classic country. News: 2 hrs wkly. Target aud: 18-49. ♦Mike Ryan, gen mgr; Les Montgomery, dev mgr; Debbie Davis, gen sls mgr.

***KAVW(FM)**— July 1998: 90.7 mhz; 1 kw. 213 ft. TL: N35 11 50 W101 49 59. Box 3206, Tupelo, MS 38803. Phone: (662) 844-8888. Fax: (662) 842-6791. E-mail: comments@afr.net. Web Site: www.afr.net. Licensee: American Family Association. Group owner: American Family Radio Format: Inspirational Christian. ♦Marvin Sanders, gen mgr.

KBZD(FM)— March 1994: 99.7 mhz; 21.5 kw. 351 ft. TL: N35 06 50 W101 49 16. 3639 Wolflin Ave. 79103. Phone: (806) 355-1044. Fax: (806) 457-0642. Licensee: Tejas Broadcasting Ltd. LLP. Group owner: Amigo Broadcasting L.P. (acq 11-15-2004; grpsl). Format: Tejano/Regional Mexican. ♦Mac Douglas, gen mgr; Brad Gonzalez, gen sls mgr; Israel Salazar, progmg dir; Charlie Singleton, chief of engrg.

KTNZ(AM)—Co-owned with KBZD(FM). 1946: 1010 khz; 5 kw-D, 500 w-N, DA-2. TL: N35 11 03 W101 41 28. Format: Christian. ♦Israel Salazar, progmg VP & news dir.

KDJW(AM)— Sept 15, 1955: 1360 khz; 500 w-D, 137 w-N. TL: N35 14 49 W101 49 13. 1721 Avondale Ctr. 79106. Phone: (806) 331-2826. Fax: (806) 358-9285. E-mail: ffeedlot@aol.com. Web Site: www.kdjw.com. Licensee: Avondale Operating Inc. (acq 12-8-03). Format: Classic country. Target aud: 45 plus; adults with money. ♦Ron Slover, pres & gen mgr; Bill Howe, progmg dir & chief of engrg.

KGNC(AM)— May 19, 1922: 710 khz; 10 kw-U, DA-2. TL: N35 25 12 W101 33 20. Box 710 79189-0710. Secondary address: 3505 Olsen Blvd., Suite 117 79109. Phone: (806) 355-9801. Fax: (806) 354-8779. Fax: (806) 354-9450. Licensee: Morris Communications Corp. Group owner: Morris Communications Inc. (acq 12-22-97; grpsl). Network: ABC. Rep: Katz Radio. Wiley, Rein & Fielding. Format: News/talk, sports. News staff: 3; News: 35 hrs wkly. Target aud: General; upscale adults & agricultural business listeners. Spec prog: Farm 11 hrs, relg 4 hrs wkly. ♦Dan Gorman, gen mgr; Tim Butler, opns mgr; Doug Surlens, gen sls mgr; Chris Albracht, progmg dir; Barry King, news dir; Greg Wheeler, pub affrs dir; John Wolfe, chief of engrg.

KGNC-FM— Dec 24, 1958: 97.9 mhz; 100 kw. 1,285 ft. TL: N35 18 52 W101 50 47. Stereo. Format: Country. News: one hr wkly. Target aud: 25-54; upscale adults. ♦Dan Gorman, stn mgr; Jay Johnson, rgnl sls mgr & mktg mgr; Tim Butler, progmg mgr.

KIXZ(AM)— June 1947: 940 khz; 5 kw-D, 1 kw-N, DA-2. TL: N35 09 17 W101 45 28. 6214 W. 34th. 79109. Phone: (806) 355-9777. Fax: (806) 355-5832. E-mail: kixz@clearchannel.com. Web Site: www.newsradio940.com. Licensee: Capstar TX L.P. Group owner: Clear Channel Communications Inc. (acq 8-30-00; grpsl). Network: ABC Information & Entertainment. Akin, Gump, Strauss, Hauer & Feld. Format: News/talk. News staff: one; News: 8 hrs wkly. Target aud: General. Spec prog: Talk 2 hrs, gospel 6 hrs wkly. ♦Matt Martin, gen mgr; Dusty Cagle, sls dir & gen sls mgr; Lori Crofford, prom dir; David Emmons, progmg dir; Charles Fuller, news dir & chief of engrg.

KPRF(FM)—Co-owned with KIXZ(AM). October 1979: 98.7 mhz; 100 kw. 480 ft. TL: N35 11 02 W101 58 11. Stereo. E-mail: kprf@clearchannel.com. Web Site: www.power987.com. Network: ABC. Format: Contemp hit/top 40. News staff: one; News: 2 hrs wkly. Target aud: General. ♦Marshal Blevins, progmg dir.

***KJRT(FM)**— Apr 1, 1994: 88.3 mhz; 20 kw. 265 ft. TL: N35 11 57 W101 48 43. Box 8088, 5754 Canyon Dr. 79114. Phone: (806) 359-8855. Fax: (806) 354-2039. E-mail: kjrt@kingdomkeys.org. Web Site: www.kingdomkeys.org. Licensee: Top o'Texas Educational Broadcasting Foundation. Format: Relg, educ. ♦Ricky Pfeil, gen mgr.

KMML-FM— March 1985: 96.9 mhz; 100 kw. 613 ft. TL: N35 17 33 W101 50 48. Stereo. 6214 W. 34th St. 79109. Phone: (806) 355-9777. Fax: (806) 355-5832. E-mail: kmml@kmml.com. Web Site: www.969kmml.com. Licensee: Capstar TX L.P. Group owner: Clear Channel Communications Inc. (acq 8-30-00; grpsl). Network: ABC. Format: Real country. News staff: one; News: 2 hrs wkly. Target aud: General. ♦Mike Ryan, gen mgr; Les Montgomery, dev mgr & progmg dir; Debbie Davis, gen sls mgr; Lori Crofford, prom dir; Charlie Fuller, chief of engrg.

KMXJ-FM— March 1946: 94.1 mhz; 100 kw. 1,082 ft. TL: N35 20 33 W101 49 21. Stereo. 6214 W. 34th 79109. Phone: (806) 355-9777. Fax: (806) 355-5832. E-mail: kmxj@clearchannel.com. Web Site: www.mix941kmxj.com. Licensee: Capstar TX L.P. Group owner: Clear Channel Communications Inc. (acq 8-30-00; grpsl). Network: ABC. Format: Adult contemp. News staff: one; News: 2 hrs wkly. Target aud: General. ♦Mike Ryan, gen mgr; Les Montgomery, dev mgr; Debbie Davies, gen sls mgr; Lori Crofford, prom dir; Johnny McQueen, progmg dir & progmg mgr; Charlie Fuller, chief of engrg.

KPUR(AM)— Aug 1, 1949: 1440 khz; 5 kw-D, 1 kw-N, DA-N. TL: N35 07 20 W101 48 09. Stereo. 301 S. Polk, Suite 100 79101. Phone: (806) 342-5200. Fax: (806) 342-5202. E-mail: rickmatchett@cumulus.com. Web Site: www.cumulus.com. Licensee: Cumulus Licensing Corp. Group owner: Cumulus Media Inc. (acq 3-12-98; $820,000 with KPUR-FM Canyon). Format: Talk, sports. Target aud: 25-54. ♦Rick Matchett, gen mgr; Carolyn Reinert, sls dir; O'Lisa Pohnert, prom dir; Matt Darby, progmg dir; J.P. Wolf, chief of engrg.

KQFX(FM)—(Borger). March 1975: 104.3 mhz; 100 kw. 590 ft. TL: N35 25 54 W101 36 47. Stereo. 3639B Wolfin Ave. 79103. Phone: (806) 355-1044. Fax: (806) 457-0642. Licensee: Tejas Broadcasting Ltd. LLP. Group owner: Amigo Broadcasting L.P. (acq 11-15-2004; grpsl). Format: Regional. ♦Matt Douglas, gen mgr; Willie Palacios, sls dir & gen sls mgr; Israel Salavar, progmg dir; Charlie Singleton, chief of engrg.

KQIZ-FM— November 1976: 93.1 mhz; 100 kw. 700 ft. TL: N35 17 33 W101 50 48. Stereo. 301 S. Polk, Suite 100 79101. Phone: (806) 342-5200. Fax: (806) 342-5202. E-mail: rick.matchett@cumulus.com. Web Site: www.cumulus.com. Licensee: Cumulus Licensing Corp. Group owner: Cumulus Media L.L.C (acq 3-5-98; $3.057 million). Format: CHR. Target aud: 18-44; young families. Spec prog: Relg 2 hrs wkly. ♦Rick Matchett, gen mgr; Carolyn Reinert, sls dir; D'Lisa Pohnert, prom dir; Deanna McGuire, progmg dir; J.P. Wolf, chief of engrg.

KRGN(FM)— Oct 6, 1986: 103.1 mhz; 25 kw. 300 ft. TL: N35 16 04 W101 53 06. Box 10050 79116. Secondary address: 910 S. Lamar 79106. Phone: (806) 376-5746. Fax: (806) 376-4212. E-mail: krgn@flc.org. Web Site: www.krgn.org. Licensee: Family Life Broadcasting Inc. Group owner: Family Life Broadcasting System (acq 6-24-98; grpsl). Network: USA. Format: MOR Christian inspirational, news/talk, educ. News: 4 hrs wkly. Target aud: 28 plus; mature Christian, mainstream evangelical. ♦Steve Wright, stn mgr; Steve Johnson, news dir.

KXGL(FM)— November 1997: 100.9 mhz; 100 kw. Ant 1,305 ft. TL: N35 18 53 W101 50 47. Stereo. 1616 S. Kentucky, Suite C-215 79102. Phone: (806) 351-2345. Fax: (806) 331-3170. E-mail: bobrussell@1009theeagle.com. Licensee: JMJ Broadcasting Co. Inc. (acq 1-15-2004). Rep: Katz Radio. Larry Bernstein. Format: Classic hits. News staff: one; News: 5 hrs wkly. Target aud: 25-54. ♦Herbert W. McCord, pres; Bob Russell, gen mgr; Jamey Karr, opns mgr.

***KXLV(FM)**— August 1989: 89.1 mhz; 3 kw. 328 ft. TL: N35 15 39 W101 52 53. Stereo. 5700 W. Oaks Blvd., Rocklin, CA 95765. Phone: (916) 251-1600. Fax: (916) 251-1650. E-mail: klove@klove.com. Web Site: www.klove.com. Licensee: Educational Media Foundation. Group owner: EMF Broadcasting (acq 11-4-99; $450,000). Network: K-Love. Shaw Pittman. Format: Contemp Christian music. News staff: 3. Target aud: 25-44; Judeo Christian, female. ♦Richard Jenkins, pres; Mike Novak, VP & progmg dir; Lloyd Parker, gen mgr; Ed Lenane, opns dir & news dir; Keith Whipple, dev dir; Eric Allen, natl sls mgr; Russ Lloyd, rgnl sls mgr; Chris Joyce, prom dir; David Pierce, progmg mgr; Jon Rivers, mus dir; Sam Wallington, engrg dir.

***KXRI(FM)**— November 1993: 91.9 mhz; 2.25 kw. 292 ft. TL: N35 14 31 W101 48 43. 5700 W. Oakes Blvd., Rocklin, CA 95765. Phone: (916) 251-1600. Fax: (916) 251-1650. E-mail: info@air1.com. Web Site: www.air1.com. Licensee: Educational Media Foundation. Group owner: EMF Broadcasting (acq 5-1-2000; $750,000. with KKLU(FM) Lubbock). Network: Air 1. Shaw Pittman. Format: Contemp Christian. News staff: 3. Target aud: 18-35; Judeo Christian female. ♦Richard Jenkins, pres; Mike Novak, VP; Lloyd Parker, gen mgr; Keith Whipple, dev dir; Eric Allen, natl sls mgr; Russ Lloyd, rgnl sls mgr; Chris Joyce, prom dir.

KZIP(AM)— Sept 15, 1955: 1310 khz; 1 kw-D. TL: N35 11 02 W101 58 11. 3639 B. Wolflin 79102. Phone: (806) 355-1044. Fax: (806) 352-6525. Licensee: Del Norte Communications Inc. (acq 5-22-01). Rep: Caballero. Format: Talk radio. News staff: one; News: one hr wkly. Target aud: General. ♦Mac Douglas, gen mgr.

KZRK-FM—(Canyon). Sept 30, 1985: 107.9 mhz; 100 kw. 476 ft. TL: N35 13 36 W102 00 24. Stereo. 301 S. Polk, Suite 100 79101. Phone: (806) 342-5200. Fax: (806) 342-5202. E-mail: chris.knight@cumulus.com. Web Site: www.kzrk.com. Licensee: Cumulus Licensing Corp. Group owner: Cumulus Media Inc. (acq 3-3-98; $1 million. with co-located AM). Network: Westwood One. Rep: Roslin. Format: AOR. News staff: one; News: 3 hrs wkly. Target aud: 18-34; general. ♦Rick Matchett, gen mgr; Eric Slayter, opns mgr, prom mgr & progmg dir; Stan Ross, sls dir; D'Lisa Pohnert, mktg dir; Chris Collins, mus dir; J. Curry, asst music dir; J.P. Wolf, chief of engrg.

KZRK(AM)— May 8, 1962: 1550 khz; 1 kw-D, 219 w-N. TL: N34 58 54 W101 57 18. Web Site: www.kzrkam.com. Format: Sports talk.

Andrews

KACT(AM)— Jan 12, 1955: 1360 khz; 1 kw-D. TL: N32 20 50 W102 33 23. Box 524 79714. Phone: (915) 523-2845. Licensee: Zia Broadcasting Co. (acq 5-26-76). Format: Country. ♦Lonnie Allsup, pres; Gerald Reid, gen mgr & news dir; Roy Norman, gen sls mgr.

KACT-FM— 1980: 105.5 mhz; 3 kw. 210 ft. TL: N32 20 50 W102 33 23. Stereo.

Anson

KTLT(FM)— June 1988: 98.1 mhz; 50 kw. Ant 305 ft. TL: N32 39 49 W99 51 18. Stereo. 2525 S. Danville Dr., Abilene 79605. Phone: (325) 793-9700. Fax: (325) 692-1576. Web Site: www.98thelight.com. Licensee: Cumulus Licensing Corp. Group owner: Cumulus Media Inc. (acq 1999). Kaye, Scholer, Fierman, Hays & Handler. Format: Christian music. Target aud: 35 plus. ♦Trace Michaels, gen mgr; John Scott, progmg dir; Chris Andrews, chief of engrg.

Arlington

KLTY(FM)—Licensed to Arlington. See Dallas

Athens

KCKL(FM)—See Malakoff

KLVQ(AM)— May 17, 1948: 1410 khz; 1 kw-U. TL: N32 10 20 W95 50 36. Box 489, Hwy. 31 E., Malakoff 75148. Phone: (903) 489-1238. Fax: (903) 489-2671. E-mail: kcklklvq@tvec.com. Web Site: www.kcklklvq.com. Licensee: Love Radio Co. Group owner: Routt Radio Companies Inc. (acq 8-88). Network: Salem Radio Network. Format: Southern gospel. News staff: one; News: 7 hrs wkly. Target aud: 35 plus. Spec prog: Black one hr, relg 8 hrs wkly. ♦Adabeth Routt, pres & gen mgr; Pat Isaacson, opns mgr, sls dir & pub affrs dir; Rich Flowers, progmg dir & news dir; Wayne Blackwelder, chief of engrg.

Atlanta

KALT(AM)— 2001: . Stn currently dark 1610 khz; 10 kw-D, 1 kw-N. TL: N33 04 58 W94 10 58. Box 262550, Baton Rouge, LA 70826. Phone: (225) 768-3224. Fax: (225) 768-3729. Licensee: Family Worship Center Church Inc. (group owner; acq 2-26-02; grpsl). ♦David Whitelaw, gen mgr.

Broadcasting & Cable Yearbook 2006
D-473

KNRB(FM)— Dec 22, 1978: 100.1 mhz; 50 kw. Ant 492 ft. TL: N33 15 18 W94 05 16. Stereo. Box 262550, Baton Rouge, LA 70826. Phone: (225) 768-3224. Fax: (225) 768-3268. E-mail: wjme@sonliferadio.org. Web Site: www.jsm.org. Licensee: Family Worship Center Church Inc. (acq 3-7-2002; grpsl). Riley. Format: Southern gospel. News: 15 hrs wkly. Target aud: General. Spec prog: Trading Post show 18 hrs wkly. ♦David Whitelaw, chief of opns; John Santiago, progmg dir.

KPYN(AM)— Oct 18, 1950: 900 khz; 1 kw-D, 33 w-N. TL: N33 04 58 W94 10 58. Box 641405, Kenner, LA 70064. Phone: (504) 559-7047. Licensee: Freed AM Corp. (group owner; (acq 8-3-2005; $100,000). Format: Southern gospel. Target aud: . ♦Robert A. Delgiorno Jr., pres & gen mgr.

Austin

KAMX(FM)—See Luling

KASE-FM— Mar 30, 1969: 100.7 mhz; 100 kw. 1,100 ft. TL: N30 19 10 W97 48 06. Stereo. Clear Channel Radio KVET-KASE, 3601 South Congress, Bldg. F 78704. Phone: (512) 684-7300. Fax: (512) 684-7441. Web Site: www.kase101.com. Licensee: Capstar TX L.P. Group owner: Clear Channel Communications Inc. (acq 8-30-00; grpsl). Format: Country. Target aud: 18-44. ♦Dusty Black, gen mgr; Mac Daniels, opns mgr, gen sls mgr & progmg VP; Lise Hudson, sls dir & mktg dir; Tracy Walker, prom dir; Rachel Marisay, news dir; Jim Reese, chief of engrg.

KVET(AM)—Co-owned with KASE-FM. 1946: 1300 khz; 5 kw-D, 1 kw-N, DA-2. TL: N30 22 31 W97 42 59. Stereo. Web Site: www.sportsradio1300.com. Format: Talk, sports. News staff: 6; News: 25 hrs wkly. Target aud: 25-64. ♦Dusty Black, gen mgr; Trey Poston, progmg dir.

***KAZI-FM**— Aug 29, 1982: 88.7 mhz; 1.6 kw. 351 ft. TL: N30 16 37 W97 49 34. 8906 Wall St., Suite 203 78754. Phone: (512) 836-9544. Phone: (512) 836-9545. Fax: (512) 836-9563. E-mail: kazifm@msn.com. Web Site: www.kazifm.com. Licensee: Austin Community Radio. Haley, Bader & Potts. Format: Gospel, rap, rhythm and blues. News staff: one; News: 12 hrs wkly. Target aud: General; all ages, all ethnic groups. Spec prog: Reggae 6 hrs, blues 6 hrs, gospel 18 hrs, talk 10 hrs wkly. ♦David Bursell, chmn; Clayton Matthews, sls VP & gen sls mgr; Sharon Jones, mktg VP & prom mgr; Steven Savage, gen mgr & progmg dir; Pepper Thomas, mus dir; Richard Smith, news dir; Bob Moore, engrg VP & chief of engrg.

KBPA(FM)—(San Marcos). 1971: 103.5 mhz; 95.5 kw. 1,256 ft. TL: N30 02 42 W97 52 50. Stereo. 8309 N. Hwy 35, Suite 967 78753. Phone: (512) 832-4000. Fax: (512) 832-4071. Web Site: www.oldies103austin.com. Licensee: Emmis Austin Radio Broadcasting Co. L.P. Group owner: Emmis Communications Corp. (acq 4-25-2003; grpsl). Rep: Clear Channel. Wiley, Rein & Fielding. Format: Oldies. News staff: one; News: 4 hrs wkly. Target aud: 25-64. ♦Bruce Walden, gen mgr; Jeff Carrol, opns mgr; Brad Copland, gen sls mgr & natl sls mgr; Mike Paterson, prom dir; Bo Chase, progmg dir & progmg mgr; Lisa Melton, news dir; Jim Henkle, chief of engrg.

KFIT(AM)—(Lockhart). Feb 1, 1967: 1060 khz; 2 kw-D, DA. TL: N30 19 13 W97 38 59. Box 160158 78716. Secondary address: 110 Wild Basin Rd., Suite 375 78746. Phone: (512) 328-8400. Fax: (512) 328-8437. E-mail: kfit1060@texas.net. Licensee: KFIT Inc. (acq 6-25-91; $400,000; 7-15-91). Network: Westwood One. Dow, Lohnes & Albertson. Format: Gospel. News staff: 2. Target aud: 18-65. ♦Darrell Marshi, CEO; Terre Lewis, gen mgr, stn mgr & opns mgr.

KFON(AM)— 1922: 1490 khz; 1 kw-U. TL: N30 15 13 W97 42 25. Stereo. 2211 S. Hwy. 35, Suite 401 78741. Phone: (512) 416-1100. Web Site: www.bmpradio.com. Licensee: BMP Austin License Company L.P. (acq 2-10-2005; grpsl). Format: MOR, Tejano. Target aud: 18 plus; men. ♦Pedro Gasc, gen mgr.

KGSR(FM)—(Bastrop). 1966: 107.1 mhz; 46 kw. 518 ft. TL: N30 07 18 W97 34 45. Stereo. 8309 N. IH 35 78753. Phone: (512) 832-4000. Fax: (512) 832-4042. Web Site: www.kgsr.com. Licensee: LBJS Broadcasting Co. L.P. Group owner: Emmis Communications Corp. (acq 4-25-03; grpsl). Rep: McGavren Guild. Format: AAA. News staff: one. Target aud: 25-44; upscale, active, educated adults. Spec prog: Jazz 6 hrs wkly. ♦Beverley Wimer, VP; Scott Gillmore, VP; Bruce Walden, gen mgr; Bob Woche, gen sls mgr; Jyl Hershman-Ross, prom dir; Jody Denberg, progmg dir; Susan Castle, mus dir; Todd Feffries, news dir; Jim Henkel, chief of engrg.

KIXL(AM)—(Del Valle). Aug 8, 1959: 970 khz; 1 kw-U. TL: N30 19 13 W97 37 25. 11615 Angus Rd., Suite 120B 78759. Phone: (512) 372-9700. Fax: (512) 372-9088. E-mail: info@kixl.com. Web Site: www.kixl.com. Licensee: KIXL Broadcasting Corp. (acq 2-2-96). Network: Network: Moody, Salem Radio Network. Hardy, Carey & Chautin. Format: Christian, talk. News: 10 hrs wkly. Target aud: 25-54; conservative, family-oriented adults. Spec prog: Black 6 hrs wkly. ♦Gene Bender, gen mgr; Terry Haecker, gen sls mgr; Ed Sossen, progmg dir.

KJCE(AM)—Listing follows KKMJ-FM.

KKMJ-FM— Jan 5, 1968: 95.5 mhz; 100 kw horiz, 87 kw vert. Ant 1,000 ft. TL: N30 19 23 W97 47 58. Stereo. 4301 Westbank Dr., Escalade B, 3rd Fl. 78746. Phone: (512) 327-9595. Fax: (512) 329-6255. E-mail: jdhiatt@cbs.com. Web Site: www.majic.com. Licensee: Texas Infinity Radio L.P. (acq 10-13-98; grpsl). Rep: Katz Radio. Leventhal, Senter & Lerman. Format: Adult contemp. Target aud: 25-54. ♦Clint Culp, sr VP & sls dir; John Hiatt, sr VP & gen mgr.

KJCE(AM)—Co-owned with KKMJ-FM. Aug 12, 1958: 1370 khz; 5 kw-D, 500 w-N. TL: N30 18 16 W97 38 53. Web Site: www.talkradio137am.com. Group owner: Infinity Broadcasting Corp. . Network: Network: Network: Westwood One, ABC, Salem Radio Network. Format: Talk. News staff: one; News: 10 hrs wkly. Target aud: Males 18-54.

KLBJ(AM)— 1939: 590 khz; 5 kw-D, 1 kw-N, DA-N. TL: N30 14 14 W97 37 44. 8309 N. I-35 78753. Phone: (512) 832-4000. Fax: (512) 832-4081. Web Site: www.590klbj.com. Licensee: LBJS Broadcasting Co. L.P. Group owner: Emmis Communications Corp. (acq 4-25-03; grpsl). Network: Network: ABC, Wall Street. Rep: McGavren Guild. Format: News/talk. News staff: 6; News: 14 hrs wkly. ♦Brooke Gallagher, VP; Bruce Walden, gen mgr; Julie Springer, prom dir; Mark Caesar, progmg dir; Hal Kemp, news dir; Jim Henkel, engrg dir.

KLBJ-FM— 1960: 93.7 mhz; 100 kw. 1,050 ft. TL: N30 18 36 W97 47 33. Stereo. Web Site: www.klbjfm.com. Format: Rock. ♦Bob Sinclair, exec VP; Scott Gillmore, opns dir; Jeff Carroll, progmg dir; Loris Lowe, news dir.

***KMFA(FM)**— January 1967: 89.5 mhz; 40 kw. Ant 1,306 ft. TL: N30 19 23 W97 47 58. Stereo. 3001 N. Lamar, Suite 100 78705. Phone: (512) 476-5632. Fax: (512) 474-7463. E-mail: info@kmfa.org. Web Site: www.kmfa.org. Licensee: Capitol Broadcasting Association Inc. Garvey, Schubert, Barer. Format: Class. Target aud: General. Spec prog: Educ 2 hrs wkly. ♦Frank Bash, chmn; Jack Allen, gen mgr; Rich Upton, opns mgr.

KPEZ(FM)— Aug 13, 1976: 102.3 mhz; 20 kw. 685 ft. TL: N30 13 24 W97 49 39. Stereo. 3601 South Congress, #F 78704-7213. Phone: (512) 684-7300. Fax: (512) 684-7441. Web Site: www.z1023.com. Licensee: CCB Texas Licenses L.P. Group owner: Clear Channel Communications Inc. (acq 7-24-92). Rep: Clear Channel. Cohn & Marks. Format: Classic rock. News staff: one; News: 3 hrs wkly. Target aud: 25-54; young adults with families, above average income, education. ♦Kim Murray, VP & sls dir; Dusty Black, gen mgr; L. A. Lloyd, progmg dir; Jim Reese, chief of engrg; Andy Hancock, prom.

KQJZ(FM)—(Hutto). February 1980: . Stn currently dark 92.1 mhz; 1.65 kw. Ant 449 ft. TL: N30 32 04 W97 34 52. Stereo. 1707 N. Mays St., Round Rock 78664. Phone: (512) 218-0111. Licensee: Central Texas Radio Inc. (acq 3-23-2001). ♦Buddy McGregor, pres.

KTXZ(AM)—See West Lake Hills

***KUT(FM)**— Nov 10, 1958: 90.5 mhz; 100 kw. 680 ft. TL: N30 18 51 W97 51 58. Stereo. Univ.of Texas, KUT Radio, 1 University Station A0704 78712-1090. Phone: (512) 471-1631. Fax: (512) 471-3700. E-mail: kut@kut.org. Web Site: www.kut.org. Licensee: University of Texas at Austin. Network: Network: NPR, PRI. Cohn & Marks. Format: Div, jazz, news. News staff: 5; News: 25 hrs wkly. Target aud: 25-54; educated; influential decision makers & arts community. Spec prog: Folk 4 hrs, blues 6 hrs wkly. ♦Stewart Vanderwilt, gen mgr; Sylvia Carson, dev dir; Chris Collins, gen sls mgr & engrg mgr; Hawk Mendenhall, progmg dir; Emily Donahue, news dir.

KVET-FM— 1950: 98.1 mhz; 100 kw. 686 ft. TL: N30 13 24 W97 49 39. Stereo. 3601 South Congress, Bldg. F 78704. Phone: (512) 684-7300. Fax: (512) 684-7441. Web Site: www.kvet.com. Licensee: Capstar TX L.P. Group owner: Clear Channel Communications Inc. (acq 8-30-00; grpsl). Network: Westwood One. Format: Country. News staff: 4. Target aud: 35-64. ♦John Hogan, pres; Charlie Ranilly, sr VP; Dusty Black, gen mgr; Jason Kane, opns dir & progmg dir; Mel Jones, sls dir; Heather Lonsdale, natl sls mgr; Tracy Walker, prom dir; Janice Williams, mus dir; Chuck Meyer, news dir; Jim Reese, chief of engrg.

***KVRX(FM)**— November 1994: 91.7 mhz; 3 kw. 85 ft. TL: N30 16 00 W97 40 27. Box D, c/o UT Austin 78713. Phone: (512) 471-5106. Fax: (512) 471-8177. E-mail: kvrx@kvrx.com. Web Site: www.kvrx.org. Licensee: University of Texas at Austin. Format: Alternative. Target aud: 18-34; general. ♦William Blair, stn mgr; Alyx Vesey, progmg mgr; Michael Young, progmg mgr.

Azle

KTCY(FM)— June 29, 1967: 101.7 mhz; 92 kw. Ant 2,034 ft. TL: N33 26 13 W97 29 05. Stereo. 5307 E. Mockingbird Ln., Dallas 75206. Phone: (214) 887-9107. Fax: (214) 841-4215. Licensee: Entravision Holdings LLC. Group owner: Entravision Communications Corp. (acq 8-15-00; grpsl). Rep: Lotus Entravision Reps LLC. Format: Sp. Target aud: 18-34; Hispanics. ♦Scott Savage, gen mgr; Dean James, opns mgr, progmg dir & engrg dir; Ande Woods, gen sls mgr.

Baird

KORQ(FM)— Sept 9, 1999: 95.1 mhz; 100 kw. Ant 872 ft. TL: N32 17 06 W99 38 39. 1740 N. First, Abilene 79603. Phone: (325) 437-9596. Fax: (325) 673-1819. E-mail: doudmediagroup@aol.com. Web Site: www.95a.fm. Licensee: Doud Media Group LLC Acq 9-2-02 Dennis J. Kelly. Format: CHR. News staff: 2. Target aud: 18-49; women & teens. ♦Richard Doud, gen mgr; Brad Whitaker, gen sls mgr; Mark McGill, progmg dir; James Thompson, engrg dir.

Balch Springs

KSKY(AM)—Licensed to Balch Springs. See Dallas

Ballinger

KKCN(FM)— August 1977: 103.1 mhz; 100 kw. Ant 456 ft. TL: N31 39 37 W100 05 23. 1301 S. Abe St., San Angelo 76903. Phone: (325) 655-7161. Fax: (325) 658-7377. Web Site: www.kickin-country.com. Licensee: Encore Broadcasting of San Angelo LLC. Group owner: Encore Broadcasting LLC acq 1-26-2004; $875,000. with KNRX(FM) Sterling City). Format: Country. ♦John Kerr, gen mgr & gen sls mgr; Boomer Kingston, progmg dir; Tommy Jenkins, engr.

KRUN(AM)— August 1947: 1400 khz; 1 kw-U. TL: N31 43 31 W99 57 42. Box 230, 1920 Hutchings Ave. 76821. Phone: (325) 365-5500. Fax: (325) 365-3407. E-mail: krun1400@hotmail.com. Web Site: www.krunam.com. Licensee: Graham Brothers Communications L.L.C. (acq 12-11-98; $395,000. with co-located FM). Network: ABC. Format: Country, sports. News staff: one; News: 2 hrs wkly. Target aud: 25-54. Spec prog: Sp 4 hrs wkly. ♦Toby Virden, gen mgr.

Bandera

KEEP(FM)— July 11, 1981: 98.3 mhz; 1.65 kw. 430 ft. TL: N29 51 21 W99 05 26. Stereo. Box 311, 210 Woodcrest, Fredericksburg 78624. Phone: (830) 997-2197. Fax: (830) 997-2198. Web Site: www.texasrebelradio.com. Licensee: J. & J. Fritz Media Ltd. (group owner; acq 7-99; $108,000). Fletcher, Heald & Hildreth. Format: Americana AAA. News staff: one. ♦Jayson Fritz, pres, gen mgr & gen sls mgr; Jan Fritz, VP, mktg VP & adv mgr; Gloria Ottmers, opns mgr; Ariana Carruth Fritz, prom mgr; Mac McClennahan, progmg dir; Rick Star, mus dir; Duncan Black, chief of engrg.

Bastrop

KGSR(FM)—Licensed to Bastrop. See Austin

***KHIB(FM)**— 1998: 88.5 mhz; 4 kw. Ant 308 ft. TL: N30 12 57 W97 08 31. Houston Christian Broadcasters Inc., 2424 South Blvd., Houston 77098-5196. Phone: (713) 520-5200. Web Site: www.khcb.org. Licensee: Houston Christian Broadcasters Inc. (acq 1-19-2005; $112,000). Format: Christian. ♦Bruce Munsterman, pres & gen mgr.

Bay City

***KFRT(FM)**—Not on air, target date: unknown: 88.1 mhz; 45 kw. Ant 328 ft. TL: N28 42 08 W95 56 41. c/o WBFR(FM), 244 Goodwin Crest

Stations in the U.S. — Texas

Developers & Brokers of Radio Properties — contact American Media Services at our suite: Philadelphia Marriott Downtown 215-625-2900 · 843-972-2200 · americanmediaservices.com · Charleston, SC · Dallas, TX · Chicago, Il · Austin, TX — American Media Services, LLC

Dr., Suite 118, Birmingham, AL 35209. Phone: (205) 942-3530. Fax: (510) 568-6190. Licensee: Family Stations Inc. ♦Stanley Jackson, gen mgr.

KMKS(FM)— July 27, 1984: 102.5 mhz; 50 kw. 492 ft. TL: N28 47 47 W96 09 17. (CP: 100 kw). Stereo. Box 789 77404-0789. Secondary address: 2309 5th St. 77414. Phone: (979) 244-4242. Fax: (979) 245-0107. E-mail: kmks@kmks.com. Web Site: www.kmks.com. Licensee: Sandlin Broadcasting Co. Inc. Format: Hot C&W. News staff: 4; News: one hr wkly. Target aud: 24-54. ♦Margaret K. Sandlin, pres; Larry Sandlin, gen mgr, opns mgr & chief of engrg; Judith Gardiner, gen sls mgr & mktg mgr; Helen Linley, prom mgr & news dir; C.W. Simon, progmg dir; Teresa Kaufmann, pub affrs dir.

KXGJ(FM)— Sept 25, 1995: 101.7 mhz; 100 kw. 449 ft. TL: N28 43 53 W96 05 26. 3000 Bering Dr., Houston 77057. Phone: (713) 315-3400. Fax: (713) 314-3506. Licensee: Liberman Broadcasting of Houston License Corp. Group owner: Liberman Broadcasting Inc. (acq 8-22-02; $3.15 million. with KIOX-FM El Campo). Network: ABC. Format: Sp. ♦Leonard Liberman, CEO, pres & progmg mgr; Winter Horton, gen mgr; Daisy Ortiz, gen sls mgr; Mike Todd, engr.

***KZBJ(FM)**— 2005: 89.5 mhz; 35 kw. Ant 479 ft. TL: N29 08 58 W95 59 14. Box 187, Humble 77347. Phone: (281) 446-5725. Fax: (281) 540-2198. Web Site: www.ksbj.org. Licensee: KSBJ Educational Foundation (acq 5-31-2003). Format: Contemp Christian. ♦Tim McDermott, gen mgr.

Baytown

KWWJ(AM)— October 1947: 1360 khz; 5 kw-D, 1 kw-N, DA-2. TL: N29 46 28 W95 00 55. Stereo. Box 419 77522. Secondary address: 4638 Decker Dr. 77522. Phone: (281) 837-8777. Fax: (281) 424-7588. E-mail: d.martin@kwwj.org. Web Site: www.kwwj.org. Licensee: Salt of the Earth Broadcasting. (acq 8-88). Network: American Urban. Format: Relg. News staff: one. Target aud: General. ♦Darrell E. Martin, pres, gen mgr, gen sls mgr, prom mgr & pub affrs dir.

Beaumont

KFNC(FM)— 1948: 97.5 mhz; 100 kw. Ant 1,955 ft. TL: N29 41 52 W94 24 09. Stereo. 2700 Post Oak Blvd., Suite 2300, Houston 77056. Phone: (713) 300-3500. Fax: (713) 300-3585. Licensee: Cumulus Licensing Corp. Group owner: Cumulus Media Inc. Format: News/talk. Target aud: 18-49; active, responsive decision makers. ♦Pat Fant, mktg mgr.

KIKR(AM)— 1938: 1450 khz; 1 kw-U. TL: N30 03 52 W94 07 12. 755 S. 11th, Suite 102 77701. Phone: (409) 833-9421. Fax: (409) 833-9296. Web Site: www.cumulus.com. Licensee: Cumulus Licensing Corp. Group owner: Cumulus Media Inc. (acq 3-9-98; grpsl). Rep: McGavren Guild. Scott Johnson. Format: Sports. Target aud: 25-54. ♦Zanatta Kelley, gen mgr; Jim West, opns dir & mus dir; Mark Guzman, prom mgr; Greg Davis, chief of engrg.

***KLBT(FM)**—Not on air, target date: unknown: 88.1 mhz; 40 kw vert. Ant 216 ft. TL: N30 09 14 W94 28 23. American Educational Broadcasting Inc., 3185 S. Highland Dr., Suite 13, Las Vegas, NV 89109. Licensee: American Educational Broadcasting Inc.

KLVI(AM)— 1924: 560 khz; 5 kw-U, DA-N. TL: N30 02 42 W93 52 07. Stereo. 2885 Interstate 10 East 77702. Secondary address: 2885 I-10 E. 77726. Phone: (409) 896-5555. Fax: (409) 896-5599. Web Site: www.klvi.com. Licensee: Clear Channel Group owner: Clear Channel Communications Inc. (acq 8-30-00; grpsl). Network: ABC Information & Entertainment. Fisher, Wayland, Cooper, Leader & Zaragoza L.L.P. Format: News/talk. News staff: 4; News: 5 hrs wkly. Target aud: 25-54; informed professionals.John Hogan, CEO; Lowry Mays, CEO & chmn; Randall Mays, CFO; Charlie Rahilly, sr VP; Mark Kopelman, VP; Vesta Brandt, gen mgr; Trey Poston, opns dir; Jim Love, opns mgr & pub affrs dir; Elizabeth Blackstock, sls dir; Rob Windham, gen sls mgr & natl sls mgr; Shon Hodgkinson, prom dir; Al Caldwell, progmg dir; Neil Harrison, news dir; T. J. Bordelon, chief of engrg

KQBU-FM—See Houston

KQQK(FM)— July 10, 1967: 107.9 mhz; 100 kw. 1,000 ft. TL: N30 02 09 W94 08 31. Stereo. 3000 Bering Dr., Houston 77057. Phone: (731) 315-3400. Fax: (713) 314-3506. E-mail: julioesar@xoradio.com. Web Site: www.xoradio.com. Licensee: Liberman Broadcasting of Houston License Corp. Group owner: Liberman Broadcasting Inc. (acq 8-9-02; $24 million). Format: Sp, rock. Target aud: 18-49; bilingual Hispanics. ♦Leonard Liberman, pres; Winter Horton, gen mgr.

KQXY-FM— September 1966: 94.1 mhz; 100 kw. 1,099 ft. TL: N30 06 56 W94 00 00. Stereo. 755 S. 11th St., Suite 102 77701. Phone: (409) 833-9421. Fax: (409) 833-9296. E-mail: psanders@qt.rr.com. Web Site: www.kqxy.com. Licensee: Cumulus Licensing Corp. Group owner: Cumulus Media Inc. (acq 3-9-98; grpsl). Format: Contemp hit. News staff: one; News: 5 hrs wkly. Target aud: 18-49; skewed female. ♦Rick Prusator, gen mgr; Mike Simpson, gen sls mgr; Greg Davis, chief of engrg.

KRCM(AM)— July 1947: 1380 khz; 1 kw-D, 127 w-N. TL: N30 02 09 W94 08 31. Box 22257 77720-2257. Secondary address: 27 Sawyer St. 77702. Phone: (409) 835-2222. Fax: (409) 832-5686. E-mail: manager@newsradiofox.com. Web Site: www.newsradiofox.com. Licensee: Voice Broadcasting Inc. (acq 1-29-03). Format: News/talk. ♦Ralph McBride, pres & gen mgr; George Ferris, gen sls mgr; Debbie Wylde, prom mgr; Gail Ellison, progmg dir; Dominick Brascia, progmg mgr; Harold Mann, news dir; Jeff Roberts, pub affrs dir; Zach Wells, chief of engrg.

KTCX(FM)— 1996: 102.5 mhz; 50 kw. 492 ft. TL: N29 59 22 W94 14 44. 755 South 11th St., Suite 102, Box 870 77704. Phone: (409) 833-9421. Fax: (409) 833-9296. Web Site: www.ktcx.com. Licensee: Cumulus Licensing Corp. Group owner: Cumulus Media Inc. (acq 3-26-98; $3.6 million). Format: Adult urban. ♦Zanetta Kelley, gen mgr; Ed Turner, stn mgr; Jim West, opns mgr; Walter Brickhouse, sls VP; Wes Matejka, sls dir; Marco Camacho, rgnl sls mgr; Mark Guzman, prom dir; Douglas Harris, progmg dir; Adrian Scott, asst music dir; Greg Davis, chief of engrg.

***KTXB(FM)**— Jan 23, 1990: 89.7 mhz; 9 kw. 567 ft. TL: N30 09 27 W93 48 06. 550 Fannin St., Suite 1327 77701. Phone: (409) 745-1737. Web Site: www.familyradio.com. Licensee: Family Stations Inc. (group owner) Format: Christian relg. ♦Harold Camping, pres; Martha Tallent, stn mgr & opns mgr.

***KVLU(FM)**— 1974: 91.3 mhz; 40 kw. 450 ft. TL: N30 06 40 W94 03 10. Stereo. Box 10064 77710. Phone: (409) 880-8164. E-mail: kvlu@hal.lamar.edu. Web Site: www.kvlu.org. Licensee: Lamar University. Network: NPR. Format: Class, jazz, news. Target aud: 35 plus. Spec prog: Sp 5 hrs wkly. ♦Byron Balentine, gen mgr; Melanie Dishman, dev dir.

KYKR(FM)— Feb 1, 1966: 95.1 mhz; 100 kw. 500 ft. TL: N30 08 57 W94 07 59. Stereo. 2885 Interstate 10 E. 77702. Secondary address: 2885 Interstate 10 E. 77726. Phone: (409) 896-5555. Fax: (409) 896-5599. Web Site: www.kykr.com. Licensee: Capstar TX L.P. Group owner: Clear Channel Communications Inc. (acq 8-30-00; grpsl). Shaw Pittman. Format: Country. News staff: 3; News: 2 hrs wkly. Target aud: 18-54.John Hogan, CEO; Lowry Mays, chmn; Mark Mays, pres; Randall Mays, CFO; Charlie Rahilly, sr VP; Mark Kopelman, VP & opns mgr; Vesta Brandt, gen mgr; Trey Poston, opns dir; Elizabeth Blackstock, sls dir; Rod Windham, natl sls mgr; Shon Hodgkinson, prom dir; Mickey Ashworth, progmg dir; Neil Harrison, news dir; Jim Love, pub affrs dir; T. J. Bordelon, chief of engrg

KZZB(AM)— May 1, 1947: 990 khz; 1 kw-D, DA-1. TL: N30 08 57 W94 07 59. 2531 Calder Ave. 77702. Phone: (409) 833-0990. Fax: (409) 833-0995. Web Site: www.kzzbradio.com. Licensee: Martin Broadcasting Inc. (acq 7-28-92; 8-17-92). Rep: Christal. Haley, Bader & Potts. Format: Gospel. News staff: one. Target aud: 18-49. ♦Darrell Martin, pres & gen mgr; Willie Mae McIver, progmg dir.

Beeville

KIBL(AM)— Oct 20, 1949: 1490 khz; 1 kw-U. TL: N28 23 08 W97 43 42. Box 252, McAllen 78505. Phone: (956) 781-5528. Fax: (956) 686-2999. Licensee: Paulino Bernal. (acq 3-7-97; $50,600). Format: Christian, Sp Christian. ♦Eloy Bernal, gen mgr & progmg dir; John Ross, chief of engrg.

KVFM(FM)—Co-owned with KIBL(AM). 2000: 91.3 mhz; 1 kw vert. Ant 302 ft. TL: N28 26 42 W97 45 50. Licensee: Paulino Bernal Evangelism.

KRXB(FM)— Dec 2, 1988: 107.1 mhz; 1.25 kw. Ant 305 ft. TL: N28 25 40 W97 45 36. Stereo. Box 1664 78014. Phone: (361) 358-4941. Fax: (361) 358-0601. E-mail: krxbfm@nbnet.net. Licensee: Shaffer Communications Group Inc. (acq 10-95; $380,000). Network: Jones Radio Networks. Format: Classic rock. Target aud: 35 plus. ♦Joe Shaffer, pres; Gary Hoffman, gen mgr, opns mgr, progmg dir, news dir & chief of engrg; Cora Batch, gen sls mgr, natl sls mgr & mktg dir.

KTKO(FM)— Dec 12, 1976: 105.7 mhz; 25 kw. 328 ft. TL: N28 28 16 W97 48 39. Stereo. 2300 S. Washington 78102. Phone: (361) 358-1490. Fax: (361) 358-7814. E-mail: bebekicker106@lonestarinternet.net. Licensee: Texas Gulfwest Broadcasting Inc. (acq 6-01-02; $325,000). Gardner, Carton & Douglas. Format: Country. News staff: one; News: 13 hrs wkly. Target aud: 18-64. ♦Bebe Adamez, gen mgr, opns mgr & opns mgr.

Bellaire

KILE(AM)— June 7, 1961: 1560 khz; 500 w-D. TL: N29 37 15 W95 25 04. 3633 FM437 Farm to Market Rd., Rogers 76569. Secondary address: 10614 Rockley Rd., Houston 76569. Phone: (281) 564-7064. E-mail: Kile@sbcglobal.net. Licensee: The RAFTT Corp. (acq 12-31-2002; $75,000. with KWBC(AM) Navasota). Format: Multi ethnic. Target aud: 25-65; adult Hispanic 25 & older. Spec prog: Top-40. ♦Jerome Friemel, pres; Dan Cocozza, gen mgr.

Bells

KMKT(FM)— September 1997: 93.1 mhz; 6.8 kw. 626 ft. TL: N33 41 31 W96 26 36. 101 E. Main, Suite 255, Denison 75020. Phone: (903) 465-6200. Fax: (903) 463-9816. E-mail: jason@931kmkt.com. Web Site: www.931kmkt.com. Licensee: NM Licensing LLC. Group owner: NextMedia Group L.L.C. (acq 11-26-01; grpsl). Format: Country. ♦Steven Dinitz, CEO; Carl Hirsch, chmn; Bill Harrison, pres, VP & gen mgr; Skip Weller, pres; Sean Stover, CFO; David MacMullen, stn mgr; Jason Taylor, opns mgr & progmg dir; David Mac Mullen, sls dir; Jan Medders, gen sls mgr; Anne Oliver, prom dir; Tiffany Reynolds, news dir; Vince Richardson, chief of engrg.

Bellville

KNUZ(AM)— Aug 8, 1974: 1090 khz; 250 w-D. TL: N29 56 50 W96 15 54. 530 W. Main St., Brenham 77833. Phone: (979) 836-9411. Fax: (979) 836-9435. Licensee: Roy E. Henderson Group owner: Bayport Broadcast Group (acq 4-17-90; $150,000). Format: Adult contemp. ♦Roy Henderson, pres.

Belton

KOOC(FM)— Apr 25, 1970: 106.3 mhz; 11.5 kw. Ant 489 ft. TL: N31 03 46 W97 31 54. Stereo. 608 Moody Ln., Temple 76504. Phone: (254) 773-5252. Fax: (254) 773-0115. Web Site: www.b1063.com. Licensee: Cumulus Licensing LLC. Group owner: Cumulus Media Inc. (acq 2-2-2000; grpsl). Format: Rhythmic. Target aud: 25-54. ♦Bourdon Wooten, gen mgr; Brian Mack, stn mgr & progmg mgr; Mikie Cummings, gen sls mgr; Chris Cummings, news dir.

KTON(AM)— Dec 1, 1961: 940 khz; 1 kw-D, DA. TL: N31 02 37 W97 25 46. Box 1387 76513. Phone: (254) 939-9377. Fax: (254) 939-9458. Web Site: www.countrygold.com. Licensee: M&M Broadcasters Ltd. (group owner; acq 10-14-03; $400,000). Network: USA. Format: Country gold. Target aud: 25-54. ♦Gary Moss, pres; James Harrison, gen mgr, stn mgr & opns VP; Jim Cooper, engrg mgr.

Benbrook

KDXX(FM)— January 1990: 107.1 mhz; 74 kw. Ant 1,050 ft. TL: N32 35 10 W97 49 52. Stereo. 7700 Carpenter Fwy., Dallas 75247. Phone: (214) 525-0400. Fax: (214) 631-1196. Web Site: univision.com. Licensee: KCYT-FM License Corp. Group owner: Univision Radio (acq 9-22-2003; grpsl). Gammon & Grange. Format: Sp adult contemp. ♦ Frank Carter, gen mgr; Ivonne Flaherty, gen mgr; Andy Lockridge, opns dir; Cipriano Robles, sls dir; Betsy Galleguillos, natl sls mgr; Oscar Espinosa, prom dir; Herminio "Chayan" Ortuno, progmg dir; Patrick Parks, chief of engrg.

Big Lake

KPDB(FM)— 2001: 98.3 mhz; 50 kw. Ant 430 ft. TL: N31 11 45 W101 25 40. Radio Desafio, 4201 Ardmore Ave., Suite 3, Bakersfield, CA 93309. Phone: (661) 847-1065. E-mail: radiodesafio@radiodesafio.org. Web Site: www.radiodesafio.org. Licensee: Centro Cristiano de Fe Inc. (acq 5-13-02; $300,000). Format: Christian, Sp, relg.

KWTR(FM)— 2004: 104.1 mhz; 500 w. Ant 62 ft. TL: N31 11 54 W101 27 45. Box 1041 Phone: (325) 884-3451. Licensee: Woodrow Michael Warren. Group owner: Woodrow Michael Warren Stns. ♦ Woodrow Michael Warren, gen mgr.

Big Sandy

*KTAA(FM)— Nov 6, 1995: 90.7 mhz; 5.8 kw. Ant 515 ft. TL: N32 37 50 W94 53 44. One Academy Blvd. 75755. Phone: (903) 636-2000 ext 2701. E-mail: info@ktaa.org. Web Site: www.ktaa.org. Licensee: Institute in Basic Life Principles Inc. (acq 10-17-2000). Format: Christian. ♦ Timothy Baldridge, gen mgr.

Big Spring

*KBCX(FM)— 2001: 91.5 mhz; 250 w. Ant 331 ft. TL: N32 11 06 W101 27 56. Box 3206, Tupelo, MS 38803. Phone: (662) 844-8888. Fax: (662) 842-6791. E-mail: comments@afr.net. Web Site: www.afr.net. Licensee: American Family Association. Group owner: American Family Radio Format: Inspirational Christian. ♦ Marvin Sanders, gen mgr.

KBST(AM)— Dec 23, 1936: 1490 khz; 1 kw-U. TL: N32 15 44 W101 27 37. Stereo. Box 1632 79721. Secondary address: 608 Johnson St. 79720. Phone: (432) 267-1490. Fax: (432) 267-1579. E-mail: kbst@crcom.net. Licensee: Rhattigan Broadcasting (Texas) LP (group owner; acq 6-3-2004; grpsl). Network: ABC Information & Entertainment. Rep: Riley. Format: Talk, sports, nostalgic music. Target aud: 25 plus. ♦ Mike Rhattigan, CEO; John Weeks, gen mgr; Sam Stephens, gen sls mgr; Tim Knox, progmg dir; Mike Henry, news dir; Gary Graham, chief of engrg.

KBST-FM— 1961: 95.7 mhz; 33 kw. Ant 459 ft. TL: N32 13 13 W101 26 25. Stereo. Box 1632 79721. Secondary address: 608 Johnson St. 79720. Phone: (915) 267-6391. Fax: (915) 267-1579. E-mail: kbst@kbst.com. Web Site: www.kbst.com. Licensee: Rhattigan Broadcasting (Texas) LP. (group owner; acq 6-3-2004; grpsl). Format: News. ♦ John Weeks, gen mgr; Jim East, progmg dir; Steve Jess, news dir.

KBTS(FM)— Aug 14, 1995: 94.3 mhz; 8.3 kw. Ant 561 ft. TL: N32 13 13 W101 26 25. (CP: 15.4 kw, ant 420 ft.). Box 1632 79721. Secondary address: 608 Johnson St. 79720. Phone: (915) 267-6391. Fax: (915) 267-1579. E-mail: kbst@crcom.net. Licensee: Rhattigan Broadcasting (Texas) LP (group owner; acq 6-3-2004; grpsl). Format: Classic rock. ♦ John Weeks, gen mgr; Sam Stephens, opns mgr; Tim Knox, progmg dir; Mike Henry, news dir.

KBYG(AM)— 1948: 1400 khz; 1 kw-U. TL: N32 13 22 W101 28 35. 2801 Wasson Dr. 79720-7301. Phone: (432) 263-5294. Fax: (432) 263-6351. E-mail: kbyg@apex2000.net. Licensee: Ballard Drew. (acq 4-9-90). Format: Oldies, Sp, talk. News staff: one. Target aud: 25-54; Anglo-Hispanic. ♦ David M. Pappajohn, gen mgr; Raul Marquez, gen mgr; Jennifer Patton, stn mgr.

*KPBD(FM)— 2005: 89.3 mhz; 3 kw. Ant 328 ft. TL: N32 09 51 W101 25 27. Box 252, McAllen 78505. Phone: (956) 686-6382. Fax: (956) 686-2999. Licensee: Paulino Bernal Evangelism. ♦ Paulino Bernal Jr., pres.

Bishop

KMZZ(FM)— June 15, 1980: 106.9 mhz; 25 kw. Ant 298 ft. TL: N27 39 10 W97 54 59. (CP: Ant 246 ft. TL: N27 40 16 W97 44 17). Stereo. 701 Benys Rd., Corpus Christi 78408. Phone: (361) 289-0999. Fax: (361) 289-0810. Licensee: Gerald Benavides (acq 11-4-2004; $550,000). Baraff, Koerner & Olender. Format: Relg. News staff: one. Target aud: 18-49; people with buying power. ♦ Lionel Davila, gen mgr; Mike Aradillias, sls VP; Jeremy Lopez, progmg dir; George Sanders, chief of engrg.

Bloomington

*KHVT(FM)— Not on air, target date: unknown: 91.5 mhz; 25 kw. Ant 328 ft. TL: N28 50 39 W97 06 15. KHCB Radio Network, 2424 South Blvd., Houston 77098-5196. Phone: (713) 520-5200. Web Site: www.khvb.org. Licensee: Houston Christian Broadcasters Inc. (group owner). Format: Gospel. ♦ Bruce Munsterman, gen mgr.

KLUB(FM)— December 1992: 106.9 mhz; 25 w. 269 ft. TL: N28 42 16 W96 50 08. Stereo. 107 N. Star Dr., Victoria 77904. Secondary address: Box 3325, Victoria 77904. Phone: (361) 573-0777. Fax: (361) 578-0059. E-mail: klub@clearchannel.com. Web Site: www.1069therock.com. Licensee: Capstar TX L.P. Group owner: Clear Channel Communications Inc. (acq 8-30-00; grpsl). Format: Classic rock. News staff: one; News: 4 hrs wkly. Target aud: 25-59; listeners in a growth & acquisition mode. Spec prog: Blues. ♦ Jeff Lyon, gen mgr; Natalie Franz, gen sls mgr; Adam West, progmg mgr; James Love, news dir; Charles Smithey, engrg mgr & engr.

Boerne

KBRN(AM)— May 10, 1982: 1500 khz; 250 w-D. TL: N29 48 44 W98 43 41. 11737 Nelon Dr., Corpus Christi 78410. Phone: (361) 774-4354. Fax: (361) 241-7945. Licensee: Gerald Benavides (acq 6-25-2004; $200,000). Format: Sp. ♦ Gerry Benavides, gen mgr.

Bonham

KFYN(AM)— May 1948: 1420 khz; 250 w-D, 148 w-N. TL: N33 34 40 W96 09 55. Stereo. 811 E. Sam Rayburn Dr. 75418-4928. Secondary address: Box 248 75418-4928. Phone: (903) 583-3151. Fax: (903) 583-2728. E-mail: royv@netexas.net. Licensee: Vision Media Group Inc. (acq 12-4-02). Format: Country. Spec prog: Farm 6 hrs, relg 6 hrs, oldies rock 6 hrs wkly. ♦ C.L. Carter II, pres & gen mgr; Jeff Davis, opns mgr & progmg dir.

KFYZ-FM— Nov 1, 1979: 98.3 mhz; 12.5 kw. Ant 272 ft. TL: N33 33 16 W96 13 24. Stereo. Box 248 75418-4928. Secondary address: 811 E. Sam Rayburn Dr. 75418-4928. Phone: (903) 583-3151. Fax: (903) 583-2728. Licensee: North Texas Radio Group L.P. (acq 11-2-98; $1.15 million. with co-located AM). Format: Country. ♦ Roy Floyd, stn mgr.

Borger

*KASV(FM)— 1998: 88.7 mhz; 10 kw horiz, 3 kw vert. 203 ft. TL: N35 40 42 W101 23 18. Box 8088, Amarillo 79114. Phone: (806) 359-8855. Fax: (806) 354-2039. Web Site: www.kingdomkeys.org. Licensee: Top O' Texas Ed. Broadcasting. Format: Relg, educ. ♦ Ricky Pfeil, gen mgr.

*KAXH(FM)— 1998: 91.5 mhz; 290 w. 338 ft. TL: N35 38 17 W101 23 44. Box 3206, Tupelo, MS 38803. Phone: (662) 844-8888. Fax: (662) 842-6791. E-mail: comments@afr.net. Web Site: www.afr.net. Licensee: American Family Association. Group owner: American Family Radio Format: Christian. ♦ Marvin Sanders, gen mgr.

KQFX(FM)— Licensed to Borger. See Amarillo

KQTY(AM)— Jan 10, 1947: 1490 khz; 1 kw-U. TL: N35 41 05 W101 23 20. Stereo. Box 165, 113 Union 79007. Phone: (806) 273-7533. Phone: (806) 273-5889. Fax: (806) 273-3727. E-mail: kqtyradio@yahoo.com. Licensee: Zia Broadcasting. (acq 12-1-79). Network: ABC Information & Entertainment. Format: Country. News: 15 hrs wkly. Target aud: 25-54; blue collar workers with traditional values & beliefs. Spec prog: Relg one hrs, southern gospel 3 hrs, Christian country 5 hrs wkly. ♦ Lonnie Ausups, CEO; Roy Norman, gen mgr; George Grover, stn mgr.

KQTY-FM— 1999: 106.7 mhz; 6 kw. 259 ft. TL: N35 41 05 W101 23 12. Stereo. Box 165 79008-0165. Secondary address: 113 Union 79007. Phone: (806) 273-5889. Fax: (806) 273-3727. Licensee: Zia Broadcasting Co. Network: ABC Information & Entertainment. Format: Country. News: 15 hrs wkly. Target aud: 25-54. Spec prog: Christian gospel 5 hrs, southern gospe 3 hrs wkly. ♦ Derik Sullivan, gen mgr & stn mgr.

Bowie

KNTX(AM)— May 29, 1959: 1410 khz; 500 w-D, DA. TL: N33 35 10 W97 48 23. Stereo. Box 1080, State Hwy 59 & FM 1758 76230. Phone: (940) 872-2288. Fax: (940) 872-1228. E-mail: chenderson@kntxradio.com. Web Site: kntxradio.com. Licensee: Henderson Broadcasting Co. L.P. (acq 3-13-03). Network: CBS Radio. Rep: Riley, Reddy, Begley & McCormick. Format: Oldies. News staff: one; News: 15 hrs wkly. Target aud: 25-54. Spec prog: Farm 4 hrs, gospel 4 hrs wkly. ♦ Charley M. Henderson, pres, gen mgr, engrg dir & chief of engrg; Dee Blanton, opns dir & progmg dir; Pamela A. Henderson, VP, sls dir & prom VP; Ken Wood, mus dir; Doris McGuffey, news dir.

Brady

KNEL(AM)— December 1935: 1490 khz; 1 kw-U. TL: N31 07 48 W99 19 21. Box 630 76825. Secondary address: 117 S. Blackburn 76825. Phone: (915) 597-2119. Fax: (915) 597-1925. E-mail: knel@airmail.net. Web Site: www.knelradio.com. Licensee: Farris Broadcasting Inc. (acq 10-12-95; $475,000 with co-located FM). Network: ABC. Format: Oldies, rock & roll. Target aud: General. ♦ Lynn Farris, pres, gen mgr & gen sls mgr; Tracy Pitcox, progmg dir; Stan Cooper, chief of engrg.

KNEL-FM— Aug 21, 1979: 95.3 mhz; 3 kw. 299 ft. TL: N31 07 27 W99 21 34. Stereo. Web Site: www.knelradio.com. Network: ABC Daytime Direction. Format: Country. Target aud: General.

Breckenridge

KLXK(FM)— Listing follows KROO(AM).

KROO(AM)— September 1947: 1430 khz; 1 kw-D, 17 w-N. TL: N32 45 11 W98 55 57. Box 711 76424. Secondary address: 101 E. Walker St., Suite 201 76424. Phone: (254) 559-5766. Fax: (254) 559-6545. E-mail: klxk@brazosnet.com. Licensee: Graham Newspapers Inc. (group owner; acq 4-12-01; with co-located FM). Network: ABC Information & Entertainment. Format: Oldies. News staff: one; News: 2.5 hrs wkly. Target aud: 35+; adults. ♦ Roy Robinson, VP; Don Collett, gen mgr & progmg dir; Jim Jones, news dir & chief of engrg.

KLXK(FM)— Co-owned with KROO(AM). Aug 1, 1982: 93.5 mhz; 50 kw. 446 ft. TL: N32 45 31 W98 56 00. Stereo. Network: ABC. Format: Country. News staff: one; News: 4.5 hrs wkly. Target aud: 25-54; general. Spec prog: Relg 3 hrs wkly.

Brenham

KTTX(FM)— Listing follows KWHI(AM).

KULF(FM)— August 1988: 94.1 mhz; 6 kw. 328 ft. TL: N30 08 31 W96 25 00. Stereo. 530 W. Main 77833-9247. Phone: (979) 836-9411. Fax: (979) 836-9435. E-mail: fbbbrenham@sbcglobal.net. Licensee: Fort Bend Broadcasting Co. (group owner; acq 5-31-01; $1.5 million). Fletcher, Heald & Hildreth. Format: Adult contemp. News staff: one; News: 18 hrs wkly. Target aud: 18-49. Spec prog: Gospel 10 hrs wkly. ♦ Roy Henderson, pres & gen mgr; Ryan Henderson, gen sls mgr; Amber Kyle, progmg dir.

KWHI(AM)— Apr 15, 1947: 1280 khz; 1 kw-D, 89 w-N. TL: N30 10 05 W96 25 20. Box 1280 77834. Secondary address: 223 E. Main St. 77833. Phone: (979) 836-3655. Fax: (979) 830-8141. E-mail: mail@kwhi.com. Web Site: www.kwhi.com. Licensee: Tom S. Whitehead Inc. (acq 5-1-47). Network: ABC Information & Entertainment. Format: Country, news/talk. News staff: 2; News: 14 hrs wkly. Target aud: 25-54. Spec prog: Polka 2 hrs, relg 3 hrs, farm 3 hrs wkly. ♦ Tom S. Whitehead Jr., pres; Tom D. Whitehead, gen mgr, gen sls mgr & mktg dir; Shelly Granke, prom dir; Prentice Mearns, progmg dir; Frank Wagner, news dir; Mark Whitehead, chief of engrg.

KTTX(FM)— Co-owned with KWHI(AM). Sept 15, 1964: 106.1 mhz; 50 kw. 492 ft. TL: N30 21 49 W96 34 33. Stereo. Phone: (409) 776-1061. Fax: (409) 774-7545. E-mail: mail@ktex.com. Web Site: www.ktex.com. Format: Contemp country. News staff: one; News: 1.5 hrs wkly. Target

Stations in the U.S.   Texas

Developers & Brokers of Radio Properties — contact American Media Services at our suite: Philadelphia Marriott Downtown 215-625-2900; 843-972-2200; americanmediaservices.com; Charleston, SC; Dallas, TX · Chicago, Il · Austin, TX — American Media Services, LLC

aud: 18-49. ♦ Tom D. Whitehead, VP, gen sls mgr & natl sls mgr; Carolyn Warmke, rgnl sls mgr; Ken Murray, progmg dir; Shelly Granke, pub affrs dir.

Bridgeport

KBOC(FM)— Aug 2, 1982: 98.3 mhz; 6 kw. 226 ft. TL: N33 13 28 W97 47 51. Stereo. Box 156 76426. Secondary address: 708 FM 1658 76426. Phone: (940) 683-5486. Fax: (940) 683-3797. E-mail: info@kboc983.com. Web Site: www.kboc983.com. Licensee: North Texas Radio Group L.P. (acq 1999; $520,000). Format: Country. Target aud: 25-60; rural & business professionals. Spec prog: Farm 5 hrs, gospel 9 hrs wkly. ♦ Shari Johnson, gen mgr & pub affrs dir; Vicki Holder, sls dir & prom dir; Bob Bick, progmg VP & progmg dir; Doyle Hazle, chief of engrg.

Brookshire

KCHN(AM)— 2001: 1050 khz; 410 w-D, DA. TL: N29 52 45 W96 02 08. 1782 W. Sam Houston Pkwy. N., Houston 77043. Phone: (713) 490-2538. Fax: (713) 984-1721. Web Site: www.mrbi.net. Licensee: KCHN Licensee LLC. Format: Multi-ethnic. ♦ Barry Perrault, gen mgr, gen sls mgr & progmg dir; Terry Griffin, chief of engrg.

Brownfield

*KCWV(FM)—Not on air, target date: unknown: 90.7 mhz; 2 kw. Ant 220 ft. TL: N33 08 59 W102 16 46. Broadcasting for the Challenged Inc., 188 S. Bellevue, Suite 222, Memphis, TN 38104. Phone: (901) 726-8970. Licensee: Broadcasting for the Challenged Inc. ♦ George S. Flinn Jr., pres.

KKUB(AM)— August 1949: 1300 khz; 1 kw-D. TL: N33 10 49 W102 14 51. Box 411 79316-0411. Secondary address: 1722 Tahoka Rd. 79316. Phone: (806) 637-4531. Fax: (806) 637-4610. Licensee: Dios Llega Al Hombre Ministries (acq 5-10-2001). Format: Sp. ♦ Adolph Hernandez, gen mgr.

KLZK(FM)— Nov 12, 1984: 104.3 mhz; 50 kw. 466 ft. TL: N33 25 08 W102 08 58. Stereo. 9800 University Ave., Lubbock 79423. Phone: (806) 745-3434. Fax: (806) 748-2470. E-mail: idee@ramar.com. Web Site: www.stars1043.com. Licensee: Ramar Communications II Ltd. (group owner; acq 3-26-99; $1.025 million). Network: ABC Music Radio. Format: Soft AC. ♦ Diana Dee, gen sls mgr; Lew Dee, gen mgr & progmg dir.

*KPBB(FM)— 1999: 88.5 mhz; 4.5 kw. Ant 377 ft. TL: N33 09 18 W102 16 51. Box 252, McAllen 78505. Secondary address: 4501 N. McCall Rd., McAllen 78504. Phone: (956) 686-6382. Fax: (956) 686-2999. Licensee: Paulino Bernal Evangelism. Format: Spanish, Christian. ♦ Paulino Bernal, gen mgr.

Brownsville

*KBNR(FM)— Apr 10, 1984: 88.3 mhz; 5.5 kw. 289 ft. TL: N25 55 10 W97 31 44. Stereo. Box 5480 78523-5480. Secondary address: 216 W. Elizabeth 78520. Phone: (956) 542-6933. Fax: (956) 542-0523. E-mail: kbnr@hcjb.org. Web Site: www.radiokbnr.org. Licensee: World Radio Network Inc. Format: Relg, educ, Sp. News: 3 hrs wkly. Target aud: 20-45; Hispanic, middle & upper income. ♦ Ted Haney, pres; Abelardo Limon, VP; Moises Flores, stn mgr.

KKPS(FM)— Jan 17, 1978: 99.5 mhz; 100 kw. 1,034 ft. TL: N26 04 53 W97 49 44. Stereo. 2425 Olympic Blvd., Suite 6000 W., Santa Monica, CA 90404. Phone: (323) 900-6100. Licensee: Entravision Holdings L.L.C. Group owner: Entravision Communications Corp. (acq 7-20-00; grpsl). Rep: Caballero. Rosenman & Colin. Format: Sp mus, Tejano. News staff: one. Target aud: 18-49; Hispanic females, young adults. ♦ Scott Savage, gen mgr.

KRIO(AM)—See McAllen

KTEX(FM)— January 1975: 100.3 mhz; 100 kw. 1,125 ft. TL: N26 03 13 W97 44 39. Stereo. 901 E. Pike Blvd., Weslaco 78596. Phone: (956) 973-9202. Fax: (956) 973-9335. E-mail: ktexx@aol.com. Web Site: www.ktex.net. Licensee: Capstar TX L.P. Group owner: Clear Channel Communications Inc. (acq 8-15-00; grpsl). Rep: Allied Radio Partners. Format: Country. News staff: one. Target aud: 25-54; male & female. ♦ Billy Santiago, VP & opns mgr; Danny Fletcher, gen mgr.

KVNS(AM)— 1999: 1700 khz; 8.8 kw-D, 880 w-N. TL: N25 56 57 W97 33 15. Stereo. 901 E. Pike Blvd., Weslaco 78596. Phone: (956) 973-9202. Fax: (956) 973-9355. Licensee: Clear Channel Broadcasting Licenses Inc. Group owner: Clear Channel Communications Inc. (acq 12-9-2003; grpsl). Rep: Caballero. Shaw Pittman. Format: News/talk. ♦ Hilda Trevino, gen mgr; Gilda Gomez, opns mgr; Edgar C. Trevino, sls dir; John Ross, chief of engrg.

Brownwood

*KBUB(FM)— Mar 12, 1987: 90.3 mhz; 550 w. 308 ft. TL: N31 43 10 W99 00 57. Box 1549 76804. Phone: (325) 646-3420. Fax: (325) 643-9772. Licensee: Living Word Church of Brownwood Inc. (acq 12-18-96). Format: Christian praise music, teaching. ♦ Angelia Schum, gen mgr.

KBWD(AM)— Aug 17, 1941: 1380 khz; 1 kw-D, 500 w-N. TL: N31 42 36 W98 57 36. Box 280 76804. Secondary address: 300 Carnegie Blvd. 76801. Phone: (915) 646-3505. Fax: (915) 646-2220. E-mail: upfront@koxe.com. Web Site: www.koxe.com. Licensee: Brown County Broadcasting Co. Network: ABC Information & Entertainment. Format: Adult contemp. News staff: 2; News: 8 hrs wkly. Target aud: 25-54. ♦ Don Dillard, VP; Barbara McAnally, gen mgr; Bob James, progmg dir, chief of engrg & chief of engrg.

KOXE(FM)—Co-owned with KBWD(AM). May 17, 1975: 101.3 mhz; 100 kw. Ant 577 ft. TL: N31 43 45 W99 01 12. Stereo. Web Site: www.koxe.com. Format: C&W.

*KHPU(FM)— September 1998: 91.7 mhz; 290 w. 571 ft. TL: N31 43 32 W99 00 48. Stereo. HPU Station, 1000 Fisk St. 76801. Phone: (325) 649-8119. Fax: (325) 649-8901. E-mail: khpu@hputx.edu. Web Site: www.hputx.edu. Licensee: Howard Payne University. Cohen & Marks. Format: Christian, alternative. Target aud: 18-22; high school through college students. Spec prog: Gospel 4 hrs wkly. ♦ Jim Jones, gen mgr & opns dir; Jim Looby, dev dir.

*KPBE(FM)— 2000: 89.3 mhz; 6 kw. Ant 328 ft. TL: N31 46 37 W98 50 30. Box 252, McAllen 78505. Secondary address: 4501 N. McCall Rd., McAllen 78504. Phone: (956) 686-6382. Fax: (956) 686-2999. Licensee: Paulino Bernal Evangelism. Format: Sp, Christian. ♦ Paulino Bernal, pres & gen mgr.

KPSM(FM)— Apr 11, 1981: 99.3 mhz; 100 kw. Ant 446 ft. TL: N31 43 10 W99 00 57. Stereo. Box 1549 76804. Secondary address: 901 C.C. Woodson Rd. 76801. Phone: (915) 646-5993. Fax: (915) 643-9772. E-mail: rock@web-access.net. Web Site: www.kpsm.net. Licensee: Living Word Church of Brownwood Inc. (acq 1996). Network: Salem Radio Network. Format: Contemp Christian music. Spec prog: Children 3 hrs, Christian hip hop 5 hrs, Southern Gospel 2 hrs wkly. ♦ Jack Ruth, CEO; Angelia Schum, gen mgr; Brigitte Rittenour, stn mgr, opns dir, sls dir & mktg dir; Kevin Koontz, prom VP; Erich Schnitz, progmg dir; Tom Zintgraff, chief of engrg.

KXYL-FM— September 1965: 96.9 mhz; 74 kw. Ant 321 ft. TL: N31 42 16 W99 00 05. Stereo. Box 100, 600 Fisk Ave. 76804. Phone: (325) 646-3535. Fax: (325) 646-5347. Web Site: wattsradio.net. Licensee: Watts Communications Inc. (group owner; acq 7-7-94; $325,000 with co-located AM; 7-18-94). Network: Network: Network: ABC, Premiere Morning Drive AM, Premiere Morning Drive FM. Cohn & Marks. Format: News/talk. News staff: 3. Target aud: 18+. ♦ Cathy Hail, gen mgr & progmg dir; Helen Lehman, opns mgr & prom dir; Ted Wrenn, sls dir; Kyle Dennis, news dir; Stan Cooper, chief of engrg.

KXYL(AM)— 1953: 1240 khz; 1 kw-U. TL: N31 42 21 W98 59 45. Web Site: wattsradio.net. Rep: Roslin. Format: Btfl mus, Sp. News staff: 2; News: 8 hrs wkly. Target aud: 18+; Spanish. Spec prog: Christian Sp 36 hrs wkly. ♦ Chema Martinez, progmg dir.

Bryan

KAGC(AM)— Dec 27, 1977: 1510 khz; 500 w-D. TL: N30 41 21 W96 21 35. Box 4066 77805. Secondary address: 202 E. Carson St. 77801. Phone: (979) 779-1510. Fax: (979) 779-1587. E-mail: kagcradio@cox-internet.com. Licensee: Divcon Associates Inc. (acq 3-87). Network: Salem Radio Network. Verner, Liipfert, Bernhard, McPherson & Hand. Format: Contemp Christian. News: 6 hrs wkly. Target aud: 25-54; upscale, higher income & conservative. Spec prog: Black 2 hrs, Czech music 2 hrs, western swing 4 hrs wkly. ♦ Bob Bell, pres; Keith Kane, gen mgr, opns mgr, dev VP, gen sls mgr, prom mgr & progmg dir; Michele McNew, adv dir; Chester Leedecker, chief of engrg; Ed Loftis, chief of engrg.

KKYS(FM)— July 28, 1984: 104.7 mhz; 50 kw. 350 ft. TL: N30 42 59 W96 22 20. Stereo. 1716 Briarcrest Dr., Ste. 150 77802. Phone: (979) 846-5597. Fax: (979) 268-9090. Web Site: www.mix1047.com. Licensee: CCB Texas Licenses L.P. Group owner: Clear Channel Communications Inc. (acq 10-10-00; grpsl). Rep: McGavren Guild. Format: Hot adult contemp. News: 15 hrs wkly. Target aud: 18-49; heavy office lstng. ♦ Jan Stott, gen mgr; Kathy Vaughn, natl sls mgr & rgnl sls mgr; Nathan Peacock, rgnl sls mgr; Ed Loftis, chief of engrg.

KNDE(FM)—See College Station

KNFX-FM— Oct 7, 1991: 99.5 mhz; 3 kw. 328 ft. TL: N30 39 02 W96 20 57. 1716 Briarcrest Dr., Suite 150 77802. Phone: (979) 846-5597. Fax: (979) 268-9090. Web Site: www.995thefox.com. Licensee: CCB Texas Licenses L.P. Group owner: Clear Channel Communications Inc. (acq 7-20-01; $2.5 million). Rep: Caballero. Leventhal, Senter & Lerman. Format: Class rock. Target aud: General. ♦ Jan Stott, stn mgr; Kathy Vaughn, rgnl sls mgr; Nathan Peacock, rgnl sls mgr; Will Welch, progmg dir; Ed Loftis, engrg mgr & chief of engrg.

KORA-FM—Listing follows KTAM(AM).

KTAM(AM)— Sept 10, 1947: 1240 khz; 1 kw-U. TL: N30 39 02 W96 20 59. Box 3069 77805. Secondary address: 1240 Villa Maria 77802. Phone: (979) 776-1240. Fax: (979) 776-0123. Licensee: Equicom Inc. (group owner; acq 10-3-97; grpsl). Format: Sp. Target aud: 25 plus. ♦ Jim Ray, CEO & gen mgr; Glenn Hicks, sls dir; Carolyn Benavides, progmg dir; Gary Graham, engrg dir.

KORA-FM—Co-owned with KTAM(AM). Apr 1, 1966: 98.3 mhz; 900 w. 528 ft. TL: N30 39 02 W96 20 57. (CP: 2.3 kw). Stereo. Format: C&W. Target aud: 25-54. ♦ Amy Mattingly, progmg dir.

KZNE(AM)—See College Station

Buda

KROX-FM— Sept 1, 1984: 101.5 mhz; 12.5 kw. Ant 843 ft. TL: N30 19 23 W97 47 58. Stereo. 8309 N. IH 35, Austin 78753. Phone: (512) 832-4000. Fax: (512) 832-4071. Web Site: www.krox.com. Licensee: LBJS Broadcasting Co. L.P. Group owner: Emmis Communications Corp. (acq 4-25-03; grpsl). Rep: McGavren Guild. Format: Alternative, new rock. Target aud: 18-34; young adults. ♦ Bruce Walden, gen mgr; James White, sls dir; Melody Lee, progmg dir; Todd Jeffries, news dir; Jim Henkle, chief of engrg.

Burkburnett

KYYI(FM)— June 1, 1989: 104.7 mhz; 100 kw. 1,017 ft. TL: N34 05 35 W98 52 44. Stereo. 4302 Callfield Rd., Wichita Falls 76308. Phone: (940) 691-2311. Fax: (940) 696-2255. E-mail: bear104@bear104.com. Web Site: www.bear104.com. Licensee: Cumulus Licensing Corp. Group owner: Cumulus Media Inc. (acq 10-3-97; grpsl). Cohn & Marks. Format: Classic Rock. ♦ Lindy Parr, gen mgr; Brent Warner, opns mgr; Johnny Tidwell, gen sls mgr; Keith Vaughn, progmg dir; Jeff Chancey, chief of engrg.

Broadcasting & Cable Yearbook 2006

Texas

Burleson

KTFW(AM)— July 22, 1922: 1460 khz; 5 kw-D, 700 w-N, DA-2. TL: N32 34 43 W97 16 50. PO Box 1629, Cleburne 76033. Secondary address: 919 No. Main, Cleburne 76033. Phone: (817) 645-6643. Fax: (817) 645-6644. E-mail: info@countrygoldradio.com. Web Site: www.countrygoldradio.com. Licensee: M&M Broadcasters Ltd. (group owner; acq 4-26-99; $450,000). Format: Classic country. ◆ Gary Moss, gen mgr; Mike Crow, chief of opns.

Burnet

KBEY(FM)— April 1993: 92.5 mhz; 1.8 kw. Ant 604 ft. TL: N30 44 29 W98 19 05. 5226 Hwt. 281 N., Marblefalls 78654. Secondary address: Hwy. 2147, Ste. 112, Horseshoe Bay Phone: (830) 693-5551. Fax: (830) 693-5107. E-mail: realcountry@kbay.net. Web Site: www.radiohillcountry.com. Licensee: Munbilla Broadcasting Properties Ltd. (group owner). Format: Real country. ◆ Alan Barrows, gen mgr; Bill Woleben, opns dir.

KHLB(FM)—Listing follows KRHC(AM).

KRHC(AM)— Aug 19, 1963: 1340 khz; 1 kw-U. TL: N30 46 04 W98 13 49. Box 639, Marble Falls 78654. Phone: (830) 693-5551. Fax: (830) 693-5107. E-mail: comments@khlb.com. Web Site: www.khlb.com. Licensee: Munbilla Broadcasting Properties Ltd. (group owner; acq 12-4-2003); $1 million. with co-located FM). Network: ABC Information & Entertainment. Format: News, info, nostalgia. News staff: 2; News: 3 hrs wkly. Target aud: 35 plus. ◆ Margaret Ronquille, gen mgr & gen sls mgr; Paula Reed, progmg dir; Harold Mann, news dir; Gary Graham, chief of engrg.

KHLB(FM)—Co-owned with KRHC(AM). Dec 15, 1978: 106.9 mhz; 4.7 kw horiz, 4.6 kw vert. Ant 358 ft. TL: N30 44 12 W98 17 36. Stereo. Web Site: www.khlb.com. Network: ABC. Format: Country. News staff: 2; News: 3 hrs wkly. Target aud: 25-54.

Bushland

*KTXP(FM)— 2004: 91.5 mhz; 1 kw. Ant 262 ft. TL: N35 08 51 W102 05 56. High Plains Public Radio, 207 N. 7th St., Garden City, KS 67846. Phone: (806) 659-3730. Fax: (620) 275-7496. Web Site: www.hppr.org. Licensee: Kanza Society Inc. Network: NPR. Format: News, diversified. ◆ Deb Stout, progmg dir & progmg dir; Mary Palmer, mus dir; Chuck Springer, chief of engrg.

Byrne

*KLRW(FM)— 2004: 88.5 mhz; 500 w vert. Ant 522 ft. TL: N31 25 16 W100 32 36. 5700 West Oaks Blvd., Rocklin, CA 95765. Phone: (916) 251-1600. Fax: (916) 251-1650. Web Site: www.klove.com. Licensee: Educational Media Foundation. Group owner: EMF Broadcasting (acq 5-8-2003; $75,000. for CP). Network: K-Love. Format: Christian. ◆ Lloyd Parker, gen mgr.

Caldwell

KLTR(FM)— 2002: 107.3 mhz; 6 kw. Ant 328 ft. TL: N30 33 31 W96 34 50. 530 W. Main St., Brenham 77833. Phone: (979) 836-9411. Fax: (979) 836-9435. Licensee: Roy E. Henderson. Group owner: Bayport Broadcast Group Format: Adult contemp. ◆ Roy E. Henderson, pres; Lori Henderson, stn mgr; Ryan Henderson, rgnl sls mgr; Amber Kyle, progmg dir & news dir; Ray Nelson, chief of engrg.

Callisburg

*KPFC(FM)— April 1998: 91.9 mhz; 300 w. 62 ft. TL: N33 40 11 W97 00 50. Box 918, Camp Sweeney, Gainesville 76241. Phone: (940) 665-2011. Fax: (940) 665-9467. E-mail: kpfc@kpfc.org. Web Site: www.kpfc.org. Licensee: Camp Sweeney. Format: Contemporary hits. ◆ Dr. Ernie Fernandez, gen mgr; Skip Rigsby, progmg mgr.

Cameron

KMIL(AM)— September 1955: 1330 khz; 500 w-D, 97 w-N. TL: N30 50 48 W96 57 55. Drawer 832 76520. Secondary address: 901 E. First 76520. Phone: (254) 697-6633. Fax: (254) 697-6330. E-mail: kmil@tlab.net. Web Site: www.kmil.com. Licensee: Milam Broadcasting Co. (acq 12-31-97). Rep: Keystone (unwired net). Format: C&W, Sp. Target aud: General. Spec prog: Gospel 6 hrs, Czech 8 hrs wkly. ◆ Joe Smitherman, gen mgr, sls dir & news dir.

KNVR(FM)— 2002: . Stn currently dark 94.3 mhz; 1.25 kw. Ant 328 ft. TL: N30 51 30 W97 01 47. Cameron Broadcasting Co., 1110 W. William Cannon Dr., Suite 402, Austin 78745. Phone: (512) 383-1112. Licensee: Cameron Broadcasting Co. ◆ Clay Gish, gen mgr.

KXCS(FM)— Apr 8, 1985: 103.9 mhz; 25 kw. 695 ft. TL: N30 45 16 W96 54 30. (CP: 40 kw, ant 548 ft.). Stereo. Box 3069, Bryan 77805. Secondary address: 1240 E. Villa Maria, Bryan 77802. Phone: (979) 776-1240. Fax: (979) 776-6074. Web Site: www.1039thex.com. Licensee: Equicom Inc. Group owner: Equicom Inc. (acq 12-10-97; $4.5 million). Network: ABC. Fletcher, Heald & Hildreth. Format: Alternative rock. Target aud: 12-34; generation x. ◆ Dan Ginzel, gen mgr; Amy Mattingly, opns dir; Chuck Knugh, gen sls mgr; Bill Kaufmann, progmg dir; Gary Graham, chief of engrg.

Camp Wood

KAYG(FM)— 2001: 99.1 mhz; 965 w. Ant 226 ft. TL: N29 42 53 W100 00 56. Box 252, McAllen 78505. Secondary address: 4501 N. McCall Rd., McAllen 78504. Phone: (956) 686-6382. Fax: (956) 686-2999. Licensee: La Radio Cristiana Network Inc. Format: Sp, Christian. ◆ Paulino Bernal, pres & gen mgr.

Campbell

KRVA-FM— Aug 1, 1969: 107.1 mhz; 3.6 kw. Ant 423 ft. TL: N33 07 31 W95 44 35. Stereo. LKCM Radio Group L.P., 301 Commerce St., Fort Worth 76102. Phone: (817) 332-3235. Licensee: LKCM Radio Group L.P. (group owner; acq 3-15-2004; $1 million. with KRVF(FM) Kerens). Format: Oldies. News staff: 2. ◆ Kevin D. Prigel, gen mgr.

Canton

KVCI(AM)— Sept 12, 1963: 1510 khz; 500 w-D. TL: N32 41 02 W95 29 44. 1350 S. Hwy. 19, Suite C 75103. Phone: (903) 567-5566. Fax: (903) 567-5567. Web Site: www.kvciradio.com. Licensee: Canton Broadcasters Inc. (acq 7-9-98; $290,309). Format: Contemp Christian. News: 6 hrs wkly. Target aud: General. ◆ Eric Jontra, gen mgr & stn mgr; Dee Cox, opns mgr, sls dir & progmg dir.

Canyon

KPUR-FM— Jan 12, 1981: 107.1 mhz; 6 kw. 315 ft. TL: N35 05 09 W101 54 48. Stereo. 301 S. Polk, Suite 100, Amarillo 79101. Phone: (806) 342-5200. Fax: (806) 342-5202. E-mail: rickmatchett@cumulus.com. Web Site: www.kpur.com. Licensee: Cumulus Licensing Corp. Group owner: Cumulus Media L.L.C (acq 5-98; $820,000 with KPUR(AM) Amarillo). Format: Oldies. News staff: one; News: 5 hrs wkly. Target aud: 35-55; boomers. ◆ Rick Matchett, gen mgr; Eric Stevens, opns mgr & progmg dir; Carolyn Reinert, sls dir; D'Lisa Pohnert, prom dir; J.P. Wolf, chief of engrg.

*KWTS(FM)— 1971: 91.1 mhz; 6 kw. 141 ft. TL: N34 58 59 W101 55 10. Stereo. Box 1514, Wt. Stn 79016. Phone: (806) 651-2797. Phone: (806) 651-2911. Fax: (806) 651-2818. E-mail: kwts@mail.wtamu.edu. Web Site: www.wtamu.edu/kwts. Licensee: West Texas A & M University. Format: Rock. News staff: 2; News: 3 hrs wkly. Target aud: 16-25. Spec prog: Class 4 hrs, jazz 3 hrs, Black 3 hrs, techo 5 hrs, acoustic 3 hrs, Britsh rock 3 hrs, Sp 3 hrs wkly. ◆ Dr. Leigh Browning, pres; Evan Kolius, gen mgr; Elizabeth Wiseman, sls dir; Andi Law, prom dir; Anthony Smith, progmg dir; Randy Ray, chief of engrg.

KZRK(AM)—Licensed to Canyon. See Amarillo

KZRK-FM—Licensed to Canyon. See Amarillo

Carrizo Springs

KBEN(AM)— Aug 9, 1955: 1450 khz; 1 kw-U. TL: N28 31 15 W99 51 30. Box 707 78834. Secondary address: 203 S. 4th St. Phone: (210) 876-2210. Licensee: Sylvia Mijares (acq 9-30-97; $41,250). Borsari & Paxson. Format: Relg, Sp. Target aud: English & Sp listeners. ◆ Gordon Baehre, gen mgr.

KCZO(FM)— 1991: 92.1 mhz; 3 kw. 296 ft. TL: N28 33 24 W99 53 49. Box 252, McAllen 78505. Secondary address: 4501 N. Mc Call Rd., McAllen 78504. Phone: (956) 686-6382. Fax: (956) 686-2999. Licensee: Paulino Bernal Evangelism. Format: Sp, Christian. ◆ Eloy Bernal, gen mgr.

Carrollton

KJON(AM)— Dec 17, 1970: 850 khz; 5 kw-D, DA. TL: N33 16 42 W96 49 16. 521 E. Bolt St., Fort Worth 76110. Phone: (817) 923-3424. Fax: (817) 923-3451. Licensee: BMP DFW License Co. L.P. (acq 1-21-2005; $3.25 million). Network: ABC Daytime Direction. Format: Sp. ◆ Bob Prouse, gen mgr.

Carthage

KGAS(AM)— October 1955: 1590 khz; 2.5 kw-D, 130 w-N. TL: N32 09 12 W94 18 52. 215 S. Market St. 75633-2623. Phone: (903) 693-6668. Fax: (903) 693-7188. E-mail: info@kgasradio.com. Web Site: www.kgasradio.com. Licensee: Jerry T. Hanszen. (acq 9-1-88). Network: ABC Information & Entertainment. Format: Gospel. News staff: one; News: 20 hrs wkly. Target aud: General. Spec prog: Relg 10 hrs wkly. ◆ Jerry T. Hanszen, CEO, gen mgr & stn mgr; Judy McNatt, sls dir; Wanda Hanszen, progmg VP; Alan Mayton, mus dir & news dir.

KGAS-FM— Aug 1, 1992: 104.3 mhz; 6 kw. 328 ft. TL: N32 08 11 W94 23 07. Stereo. Web Site: www.kgasradio.com. Network: Network: ABC, Westwood One.

KTUX(FM)—Licensed to Carthage. See Shreveport LA

Cedar Park

KDHT(FM)— Aug 1, 1961: 93.3 mhz; 100 kw. Ant 1,948 ft. TL: N30 43 34 W97 59 23. Stereo. 8309 N. I-35, Austin 78753. Phone: (512) 832-4000. Fax: (512) 832-4081. Web Site: www.kxmg.com. Licensee: Emmis Austin Radio Broadcasting Co. L.P. Group owner: Emmis Communications Corp. (acq 4-25-03; grpsl). Format: CHR, dance. Target aud: 18-34; women & men who like current music. Spec prog: Pub service 2 hrs, Sp one hr, Latino one hr wkly. ◆ Bruce Walden, gen mgr; Jeff Carrol, opns mgr; Brad Copland, gen sls mgr; Bob Lewis, progmg dir; Bradley Grein, mus dir; Todd Jeffries, news dir; Jim Henkel, chief of engrg.

Center

KDET(AM)— Feb 22, 1949: 930 khz; 1 kw-D, 36 w-N. TL: N31 50 03 W94 12 53. Box 930, 307 San Augustine St. 75935. Phone: (936) 598-3304. Fax: (936) 598-9537. Licensee: Center Broadcasting Co. Inc. (group owner; acq 3-26-98; grpsl). Rep: Riley. Format: Southern gospel, country, Sp. ◆ Jack Russell, CEO & gen mgr; Chase Roberts, opns dir; Tracy Broadway, stn mgr & sls dir; Stuart Burson, adv dir, news dir & pub affrs dir.

KQBB(FM)—Co-owned with KDET(AM). July 5, 1978: 100.5 mhz; 2.05 kw. Ant 567 ft. TL: N31 43 34 W94 15 27. Stereo. Format: Country. News staff: one; News: 30 hrs wkly. Shelby County.

Centerville

KUZN(FM)— 2001: . Stn currently dark 105.9 mhz; 25 kw. Ant 328 ft. TL: N31 16 56 W95 53 42. 9 Inwood Manor, San Antonio 78248. Phone: (210) 408-0558. Licensee: William G. Hill, receiver (acq 4-11-2005). ◆ William G. Hill, gen mgr.

Childress

KCTX(AM)— May 8, 1947: 1510 khz; 250 w-D. TL: N34 25 41 W100 13 47. 1511 Ave. F N.W. 79201. Phone: (940) 937-6316. Fax: (940) 937-6551. E-mail: kctx@102online.com. Web Site: www.kctx.com. Licensee: Kenneth Paul Harris Sr. (acq 2-9-01; $28,800. assumption and forgiveness of debt). Format: Oldies. ◆ Paul Harris, gen mgr, opns mgr & gen sls mgr; Lisa Harris, progmg dir.

KCTX-FM— July 1, 1984: 96.1 mhz; 50 kw. 520 ft. TL: N34 26 20 W100 13 10. Stereo. 1511 Ave. F N.W. 79201. Phone: (940) 937-6316. Fax: (940) 937-6551. E-mail: kctx@io2online.com. Licensee: Kenneth Paul Harris Sr. (acq 8-00). Network: ABC Information & Entertainment. Rep: Riley. Format: Country. Target aud: General. Spec prog: Relg 5 hrs wkly. ◆ Paul Harris, gen mgr, progmg dir & news dir; Jim Turvaville, chief of engrg.

Clarendon

KEFH(FM)— September 2000: 99.3 mhz; 44 kw. Ant 522 ft. TL: N35 04 36 W100 53 33. Box 370 79226-0370. Phone: (806) 874-2296. Fax: (806) 874-4411. E-mail: kefh@anaonline.com. Licensee: RoHo

Stations in the U.S. — Texas

Developers & Brokers of Radio Properties
contact American Media Services at our suite:
Philadelphia Marriott Downtown
215-625-2900
843-972-2200
americanmediaservices.com
Charleston, SC
Dallas, TX • Chicago, Il • Austin, TX
American Media Services, LLC

Broadcasting Co. Format: Oldies. ♦ Ken Meinhart, gen mgr & progmg dir; Patrick Robertson, rgnl sls mgr; John Wolfe, chief of engrg.

Clarksville

KCAR(AM)— Apr 27, 1956: 1350 khz; 500 w-D, 50 w-N. TL: N33 36 41 W95 01 01. 228 W. Main St. 75426. Phone: (903) 427-3861. Fax: (903) 427-5524. E-mail: kool985@neato.net. Licensee: FFD Holdings I Inc. Group owner: Petracom Media LLC (acq 12-20-2004; grpsl). Network: Jones Radio Networks. Marjorie Esman. Format: Classic country. News: 10 hrs wkly. Target aud: General; rural, agricultural, middle-aged. Spec prog: Gospel 6 hrs, sports 10 hrs, farm 2 hrs wkly. ♦ Tex Phillips, gen mgr & sls dir; Mike Monday, progmg dir; Dale Gorsuch, chief of engrg.

KGAP(FM)—Co-owned with KCAR(AM). Dec 11, 1990: 98.5 mhz; 50 kw. 328 ft. TL: N33 35 47 W95 01 03. Stereo. Network: ABC. Format: Oldies. News: one hr wkly. Target aud: 25-64. ♦ Tex Phillips, CEO & sls dir.

Claude

KARX(FM)—Licensed to Claude. See Amarillo

Cleburne

KCLE(AM)— April 1947: 1140 khz; 850 w-D, 710 w-N, DA-2. TL: N32 16 54 W97 24 44. Box 1629 76033. Secondary address: 305 Milsap Hwy., Mineral Wells 76067. Phone: (817) 645-1140. Fax: (817) 645-3944. Licensee: First Broadcasting Capital Partners LLC Group owner: First Broadcasting Investment Partners LLC (acq 5-29-2003; $1.4 million). Format: Country. ♦ Chuck McKay, pres.

Cleveland

KTHT(FM)— Jan 17, 1993: 97.1 mhz; 100 kw. Ant 1,847 ft. TL: N30 32 06 W95 01 04. Stereo. 1990 Post Oak Blvd., Suite 2300, Houston 77056. Phone: (713) 622-5533. Fax: (713) 993-9300. Web Site: www.countrylegends971.com. Licensee: CXR Holdings L.L.C. Group owner: Cox Broadcasting (acq 8-15-2000; grpsl). Format: Country classics. ♦ Caroline Devine, gen mgr; Judy Lakin, gen sls mgr; John Chaing, progmg dir; Ed Wilson, engr.

Clifton

KWOW(FM)— 1989: 104.1 mhz; 16 kw. Ant 459 ft. TL: N31 44 05 W97 19 17. 6401 Cobbs Dr. Fl. A, Waco 76710-2536. Phone: (254) 776-1033. Fax: (254) 776-0642. E-mail: bbehnke@amigobroadcasting.com. Licensee: BMP Waco License Company L.P. Group owner: Amigo Broadcasting L.P. (acq 11-9-2004; grpsl). Rep: Lotus Entravision Reps LLC. Blooston, Mordkofsky, Jackson & Dickens. Format: Sp, Mexican rgnl. Target aud: 18-54; adults. ♦ Brad Behnke, VP, gen mgr, sls dir & prom dir; George Lopez, progmg dir; Ed Pryer, chief of engrg.

Cockrell Hill

KRVA(AM)—Licensed to Cockrell Hill. See Dallas

Coleman

KSTA(AM)— Nov 1, 1947: 1000 khz; 250 w-D. TL: N31 51 16 W99 25 36. Box 432 76834. Secondary address: 2500 N. Neches 76834. Phone: (325) 625-4188. Fax: (325) 625-3917. Fax: (325) 646-5347. E-mail: ksta@webaccess.com. Licensee: Watts Communications Inc. (group owner; acq 9-11-97; $300,000. with co-located FM). Format: Country. Target aud: General. Spec prog: Farm 14 hrs, Sp 5 hrs, gospel 7 hrs wkly. ♦ Mikey Wayne, gen mgr & progmg dir; Stan Cooper, chief of engrg.

KXCT(FM)—Co-owned with KSTA(AM). 1974: 102.3 mhz; 12 kw. Ant 689 ft. TL: N31 44 54 W99 19 57. Stereo. Format: Lite rock. ♦ Kyle Dennis, gen mgr & progmg dir.

College Station

*KAMU-FM— Mar 30, 1977: 90.9 mhz; 32 kw. 340 ft. TL: N30 37 48 W96 20 33. (CP: 2.4 kw horiz, 32 kw vert). Stereo. Moore Communications Ctr., 4244 TAMU 77843-4244. Phone: (979) 845-5613. Fax: (979) 845-1643. E-mail: kamu@tamu.edu. Web Site: kamutamu.edu. Licensee: Texas A&M University. Network: NPR, PRI. Format: Bluegrass, news, class, jazz. News: 35 hrs wkly. Target aud: General. Spec prog: Folk 3 hrs, new age 5 hrs, international 5 hrs wkly. ♦ Rodney L. Zent, gen mgr; Penny Zent, stn mgr; Elaine Hoyak, dev dir; Richard Howard, progmg dir; Ken Nelson, engrg dir; Ed Hadden, chief of engrg.

*KEOS(FM)— Mar 25, 1995: 89.1 mhz; 100 w vert. 254 ft. TL: N30 38 54 W96 23 23. (CP: 1 kw). Stereo. Box 78 77841. Secondary address: 207 E. Carson St., Bryan 77801-1404. Phone: (979) 779-5367. Fax: (979) 779-7259. E-mail: keos@keos.org. Web Site: www.keos.org. Licensee: Brazos Educational Radio. Network: PRI. Format: News/talk, educ. News staff: News progmg 25 hrs wkly Target aud: General. Spec prog: Folk 10 hrs, gospel 3 hrs, jazz 3 hrs, Jewish & Israeli 2 hrs wkly. ♦ Mark McCann, pres; Linda Gunderson, CFO; Jeff White, gen mgr & progmg dir; Tom Schwerdt, opns dir; Chad Brinkley, dev dir; John Roths, mus dir; George Weber, pub affrs dir; Lance Parr, chief of engrg.

KKYS(FM)—See Bryan

KNDE(FM)—Listing follows KZNE(AM).

KTAM(AM)—See Bryan

KZNE(AM)— Oct 2, 1922: 1150 khz; 1 kw-D, 500 w-N, DA-N. TL: N30 38 05 W96 21 20. Stereo. 2700 Earl Rudder Fwy. S., Suite 5000 77845. Phone: (979) 846-1150. Fax: (979) 846-1933. Web Site: www.kzne.com. Licensee: Bryan Broadcasting Corp. (group owner; acq 8-7-97; with co-located FM). Format: Sports. News staff: 3; News: 58 hrs wkly. Target aud: 25-54. Spec prog: Farm 10 hrs wkly. ♦ William R. Hicks, pres; Benjamin D. Downs, gen mgr; Sam Jones, sls dir & gen sls mgr; Louie Belina, progmg dir; Chace Murphy, news dir.

KNDE(FM)—Co-owned with KZNE(AM). Aug 8, 1964: 95.1 mhz; 36 kw. Ant 571 ft. TL: N30 41 18 W96 25 35. Stereo. Format: Top 40 hits. ♦ Bobby Mason, progmg dir.

WTAW(AM)— May 2000: 1620 khz; 10 kw-D, 1 kw-N. TL: N30 37 54 W96 21 28. Box 3248, Bryan 77805. Secondary address: 2700 Rudder Fwy., Suite 5000 77845. Phone: (979) 846-1150. Fax: (979) 846-1933. E-mail: radio@wtaw.com. Web Site: www.wtaw.com. Licensee: Bryan Broadcasting Corp. (group owner). Format: News/talk. ♦ Benjamin D. Downs, gen mgr; Sam Jones, gen sls mgr; Scott Delucia, progmg dir; Chris Dusterhoff, chief of engrg.

Colorado City

KAUM(FM)—Listing follows KVMC(AM).

KVMC(AM)— June 16, 1950: 1320 khz; 1 kw-D. TL: N32 23 15 W100 53 33. Box 990 79512. Phone: (915) 728-5224. Fax: (915) 728-5224. Web Site: www.realcountryonline.com. Licensee: James G. Baum (acq 2-13-81; $395,000;. FTR: 3-9-81). Format: Country. Spec prog: Farm 8 hrs wkly. ♦ James G. Baum, pres; Linda Baum, progmg dir; Gary Graham, chief of engrg.

KAUM(FM)—Co-owned with KVMC(AM). Mar 29, 1983: 107.1 mhz; 3 kw. Ant 157 ft. TL: N32 23 15 W100 53 33. Stereo. Web Site: www.realcountryonline.com.

Columbus

KULM(FM)— Sept 3, 1973: 98.3 mhz; 6 kw. Ant 253 ft. TL: N29 42 03 W96 34 24. Stereo. Box 111 78934. Secondary address: 325 Radio Ln. 78934. Phone: (979) 732-5766. Fax: (979) 732-6377. E-mail: cgeisradio@aol.com. Licensee: Roy E. Henderson. Group owner: Fort Bend Broadcasting Co. (acq 2-15-00; grpsl). Network: ABC. Format: C&W. News: 12 hrs wkly. Target aud: General. Spec prog: Polka 12 hrs wkly. ♦ Roy Henderson, pres; Steve Smith, CFO; Carl Geisler, stn mgr, sls dir & progmg dir; Ray Nelson, chief of engrg.

Comanche

KCOM(AM)— Apr 1, 1962: 1550 khz; 250 w-D. TL: N31 53 54 W98 35 14. Box 9, 105 N. Sand St. 76442. Phone: (325) 356-2558. Fax: (325) 356-5757. E-mail: kcom@comanchetx.com. Licensee: CCR-Stephenville III LLC. (acq 8-2-2005; $164,000). Format: C&W. Spec prog: Gospel 5 hrs wkly. ♦ Joseph Schwartz, pres; Marcus Nettleton, gen mgr & opns mgr; John Barnes, gen sls mgr; Peggy Vineyard, progmg dir & pub affrs dir; Stan Cooper, chief of engrg.

KYOX(FM)— March 1999: 94.3 mhz; 32 kw. 620 ft. TL: N31 54 51 W98 41 48. Stereo. 218 N. Austin St. 76442. Phone: (915) 356-3090. Fax: (915) 356-3120. E-mail: kyox@comanchetx.com. Licensee: CCR-Stephenville III LLC. Group owner: Cherry Creek Radio LLC (acq 6-10-2004; grpsl). Format: Traditional country. Target aud: 35-64; men & women. ♦ Richard Niblett, gen mgr; Jenni Lynn Robinson, gen sls mgr & mus dir; Pam Niblett, progmg dir & news dir; Justin McClure, chief of engrg.

Comfort

KCOR-FM— Feb 26, 1994: 95.1 mhz; 100 kw. Ant 925 ft. TL: N29 50 26 W98 49 32. Stereo. 1717 N. E. Loop 410, Suite 400, San Antonio 78217. Phone: (210) 829-1075. Licensee: Univision Radio License Corp. Group owner: Univision Radio (acq 9-22-2003; grpsl). Thompson, Hine & Flory. Format: Sp. News staff: one; News: 4 hrs wkly. Target aud: 25-54; average, middle income with small town & rural lifestyle. ♦ Mac Tichenor, pres; Dan Wilson, gen mgr; Rick Thomas, opns dir & opns mgr.

Commerce

*KETR(FM)— Apr 7, 1975: 88.9 mhz; 100 kw. 400 ft. TL: N33 14 17 W95 55 27. Stereo. Box 4504, Performing Arts Ctr., 2600 S. Neal 75429. Phone: (903) 886-5848. Fax: (903) 886-5850. Licensee: Board of Regents Texas A&M University-Commerce. Network: AP Radio. Format: Jazz, adult contemp, news. News staff: one; News: 7 hrs wkly. Target aud: 21-66; general. Spec prog: Bluegrass 3 hrs wkly. ♦ Beverly Nanos, gen sls mgr; Vicki Holloway, stn mgr & progmg dir; Mark Chapman, mus dir; Kevin Jeffries, news dir; Robert Goodwin, chief of engrg.

*KYJC(FM)— 2005: 91.3 mhz; 350 w horiz. Ant 174 ft. TL: N33 15 37 W95 52 59. CSN International Inc., 4022 N. 3300 E., Twin Falls, ID 83301. Licensee: CSN International Inc. Group owner: CSN International (acq 3-6-2003).

Conroe

*KAFR(FM)— October 1998: 88.3 mhz; 100 kw vert. Ant 443 ft. TL: N30 27 52 W95 30 20. American Family Radio, Box3206, Tupelo, MS 38803. Phone: (662) 844-8888. Fax: (662) 842-6791. E-mail: comments@afr.net. Web Site: www.afr.net. Licensee: American Family Association. Group owner: American Family Radio. Format: Inspirational Christian. ♦ Marvin Sanders, gen mgr.

KHPT(FM)— Feb 14, 1965: 106.9 mhz; 95 kw. Ant 1,128 ft. TL: N30 20 02 W95 12 51. Stereo. 1990 Post Oak Blvd., Suite 2300, Houston 77056. Phone: (713) 622-5533. Fax: (713) 993-9300. Web Site: www.1069thepoint.com. Licensee: CXR Holdings L.L.C. Group owner: Cox Broadcasting (acq 8-24-2000; grpsl). Format: '80s music. ♦ Caroline Devine, gen mgr; Doug Abernethy, sls dir; Bob MacKay, gen sls mgr; Bill Tatar, mktg dir; Bo Corona, prom dir; Johnny Chiang, progmg dir; Mike Murray, mus dir; Mike Mollett, pub affrs dir; Jed Wilkinson, chief of engrg.

KIOL(FM)—(Willis). 1992: 103.7 mhz; 15 kw. Ant 426 ft. TL: N30 26 55 W95 31 48. (CP: COL La Porte. 100 kw, ant 1,924 ft. TL: N30 02 45 W94 33 03). 1212 S. Frazier 77301. Phone: (936) 788-1035. Fax:

Texas Directory of Radio

(936) 788-2525. Fax: (936) 788-1089. Web Site: www.kstarcountry.com. Licensee: Cumulus Licensing LLC. Group owner: Cumulus Media Inc. (acq 5-13-2004; $32.2 million). Format: Rock. Target aud: 25-54; adults. ♦Ben Amato, CEO; Dave Ziebell, gen sls mgr; Laura Christian, prom dir & news dir; Matt Matthews, opns dir & mus dir.

KJOJ(AM)— Apr 16, 1951: 880 khz; 10 kw-D, 1 kw-N, DA-2. TL: N30 17 38 W95 25 55. Stereo. Little Saigon Radio, 6250 Westpark Dr. #112, Houston 77057. Phone: (832) 252-1234. Fax: (832) 252-1233. E-mail: radio@littlesaigonradio.com. Licensee: Liberman Broadcasting of Houston License Corp. Group owner: Liberman Broadcasting Inc. (acq 3-9-01; grpsl). Format: Vietnamese. ♦Anh Dang, gen mgr.

KYOK(AM)— Apr 13, 1981: 1140 khz; 5 kw-D, DA. TL: N30 20 40 W95 27 32. 300 E. Bryant Rd. 77301. Phone: (936) 441-1140. Fax: (936) 788-1140. Web Site: www.kyokradio.com. Licensee: Martin Broadcasting Inc. (acq 2-10-92; $175,000; 3-2-92). Format: Gospel. Target aud: 24-55. ♦Darrell Martin, pres & stn mgr; Nicholas Martin, stn mgr; Roland Booker, sls dir, prom dir & progmg dir; Dave Biondi, chief of engrg.

Copperas Cove

KNCT-FM—See Killeen

KSSM(FM)— Nov 21, 1977: 103.1 mhz; 8.6 kw. 276 ft. TL: N31 05 05 W97 57 07. Stereo. 608 Moody Ln., Temple 76504. Phone: (254) 773-5252. Fax: (254) 773-0115. E-mail: bourdon.wooter@cumulus.com. Web Site: www.1031kissfm.com. Licensee: Cumulus Licensing Corp. Group owner: Cumulus Media Inc. (acq 2-2-00). Network: ABC Information & Entertainment. Rep: Interep. Cohn & Marks. Format: Urban adult contemp. News: 3 hrs wkly. Target aud: 25-54. Spec prog: Gospel. ♦Bourdon Wooten, gen mgr; Mikie Cummings, gen sls mgr; Jamie Garrett, prom dir & news dir; Lisa Tanne, prom dir & adv mgr; Mark Raymond, progmg dir; Doug Bernhardt, chief of engrg & engr.

Corpus Christi

***KBNJ(FM)**— January 1985: 91.7 mhz; 5 kw. 500 ft. TL: N27 46 43 W97 37 57. Stereo. Box 270068 78427. Secondary address: 3766 Saturn Rd. 78413. Phone: (361) 855-0975/76. Fax: (361) 855-0977. E-mail: kbnj@hcjb.org. Web Site: www.kbnj.org. Licensee: World Radio Network Inc. (group owner; acq 6-5-84; $36,000; 5-21-84). Network: Network: Moody, USA. Format: Relg, educ, English. News: 7 hrs wkly. Target aud: General. ♦Joe Fahl, gen mgr, stn mgr & progmg mgr; Michael Barnes, mus dir & chief of engrg.

KBSO(FM)— 1992: 94.7 mhz; 3 kw. 285 ft. TL: N27 49 50 W97 32 34. 701 Benys Rd. 78408. Phone: (361) 289-0999. Fax: (361) 299-0810. E-mail: davilabroadcasti@bizstx.rr.com. Web Site: www.texasradio947.com. Licensee: Reina Broadcasting Inc. Format: Texas radio. ♦Manuel Davila Jr., gen mgr.

KCCT(AM)— June 1954: 1150 khz; 1 kw-D, 500 w-N, DA-2. TL: N27 48 01 W97 28 44. Stereo. 701 Benys Rd. 78408. Phone: (361) 289-0999. Fax: (361) 289-0810. E-mail: davilabroadcasti@bizstx.rr.com. Licensee: Radio KCCT Inc. (acq 8-15-74). Rep: Caballero. Format: Oldies. News staff: one; News: 14 hrs wkly. Target aud: 25-54; Hispanics. ♦Manuel Davila Jr., pres, VP, gen sls mgr & progmg dir; George Sanders, chief of engrg.

KCTA(AM)— Oct 24, 1959: 1030 khz; 50 kw-D. TL: N27 56 01 W97 15 34. 1602 S. Brownlee Blvd. 78404. Phone: (361) 882-7711. Fax: (361) 882-8038. Web Site: www.kcta.net. Licensee: Broadcasting Corp. of the Southwest. (acq 1959). Network: USA. Format: Relg. Target aud: 35 plus. Spec prog: Sp 6 hrs wkly. ♦Bill York, pres & gen mgr; David Freymiller, opns mgr.

KDAE(AM)—(Sinton). 1954: 1590 khz; 1 kw-D, 500 w-N, DA-2. TL: N28 01 16 W97 28 14. Stereo. Box 260715 78426. Secondary address: 929 N. Padre Island Dr. 78406. Phone: (361) 299-1982. Fax: (361) 299-1049. Web Site: www.radiolibertad.net. Licensee: The Worship Center of Kingsville. (acq 1-11-99). Network: ABC. Rep: McGavren Guild. Fisher, Wayland, Cooper, Leader & Zaragoza L.L.P. Format: MOR, Spanish, Christian. News staff: one; News: 2 hrs wkly. Target aud: 35-64. Spec prog: Farm 6 hrs wkly. ♦Rufino Sendejo, gen mgr; A.J. Solis, progmg dir; George Sanders, chief of engrg.

***KEDT-FM**— Mar 2, 1982: 90.3 mhz; 100 kw. 802 ft. TL: N27 39 12 W97 33 55. Stereo. 4455 S. Padre Island Dr., Suite 38 78411-4481. Phone: (361) 855-2213. Fax: (361) 855-3877. E-mail: info@kedt.pbs.org. Web Site: www.kedt.org. Licensee: South Texas Public Broadcasting System Inc. Network: NPR. Schwartz, Woods & Miller. Format: Class, news, jazz. Latin. News staff: one; News: 37 hrs wkly. Target aud: General. Spec prog: Sp 4 hrs wkly. ♦Don Dunlap, pres & gen mgr.

KEYS(AM)—Listing follows KZFM(FM).

KFTX(FM)—See Kingsville

KKBA(FM)—See Kingsville

***KKLM(FM)**— Mar 11, 1991: 88.7 mhz; 5 kw. 856 ft. TL: N27 44 28 W97 36 08. Stereo. 410 S. Padre Island Dr., Suite 207 78405. Phone: (361) 289-0887. Fax: (361) 289-0649. E-mail: bcrown@emfbroadcasting.com. Web Site: www.klove.com. Licensee: Educational Media Foundation. Group owner: EMF Broadcasting (acq 6-5-02; $500,000). Network: K-Love. Format: Comtemp Christian. News: 10 hrs wkly. Target aud: 35 plus. ♦Richard Jenkins, pres; Lloyd Parker, gen mgr; Brian Crown, stn mgr & chief of engrg; Mike Novak, progmg dir & news dir; David Pierce, pub affrs dir.

KKTX(AM)—Listing follows KRYS-FM.

KLTG(FM)— Sept 1, 1967: 96.5 mhz; 97 kw. 955 ft. TL: N27 44 28 W97 36 08. Stereo. Box 898 78403. Phone: (361) 883-1600. Fax: (361) 888-5685. Web Site: www.thebeach965online.com. Licensee: Tejas Broadcasting Ltd. LLP. Group owner: Amigo Broadcasting L.P. (acq 11-15-2004; grpsl). Format: Hot AC. Target aud: 25-54. ♦Gloria Apolinario, gen mgr.

KMIQ(FM)—(Robstown). July 23, 1989: 104.9 mhz; 3 kw. Ant 298 ft. TL: N27 40 39 W97 38 20. (CP: 104.9 mhz; 50 kw, ant 492 ft. TL: N27 56 08 W97 56 19). Stereo. Box 270547 78427. Phone: (361) 289-8877. Fax: (361) 289-7722. Licensee: Cotton Broadcasting. Rep: Caballero. Format: Tejano. Target aud: 18 plus. Spec prog: Relg 6 hrs wkly.

KMJR(FM)—See Portland

KMXR(FM)— January 1970: 93.9 mhz; 100 kw. 840 ft. TL: N27 46 50 W97 38 03. Stereo. 501 Tupper Ln. 78417. Phone: (361) 289-0111. Fax: (361) 289-5035. E-mail: oldies939@aol.com. Web Site: www.939online.com. Licensee: Capstar TX L.P. Group owner: Clear Channel Communications Inc. (acq 8-30-00; grpsl). Network: AP Radio. Format: Oldies. News staff: one; News: 5 hrs wkly. Target aud: 25-54. ♦Matt Martin, gen mgr.

KNCN(FM)—(Sinton). July 1, 1972: 101.3 mhz; 100 kw. 401 ft. TL: N27 55 24 W97 25 26. Stereo. Radio Plaza, 501 Tupper Ln. 78417. Phone: (361) 289-0111. Fax: (361) 289-5035. E-mail: c101@clearchannel.com. Web Site: www.c101.com. Licensee: Capstar TX L.P. Group owner: Clear Channel Communications Inc. (acq 8-30-00; grpsl). Format: Active rock. News: one hr wkly. Target aud: 18-49; active. Spec prog: Coastal Bend Forum one hr, In Concert 2 hrs, In the Studio one hr, Flashback 2 hrs wkly. ♦Matt Martin, gen mgr.

KOUL(FM)—(Sinton). May 20, 1968: 103.7 mhz; 100 kw. 941 ft. TL: N28 02 05 W97 26 10. Stereo. Box 898 78403. Secondary address: 1300 Antelope 78401. Phone: (361) 883-1600. Fax: (361) 883-9303. Licensee: Tejas Broadcasting Ltd. LLP. Group owner: Amigo Broadcasting L.P. (acq 11-15-2004; grpsl). Format: C&W. Target aud: 25-49; general. ♦Chuck Brooks, pres; Bert Clark, opns mgr; KC Sheperd, prom dir; Paul Danitz, stn mgr, gen sls mgr & adv mgr; Glenn Michaels, progmg dir; Lon Gonzalez, news dir; Lisa Del Rey, pub affrs dir; Henry Turner, chief of engrg.

KRYS-FM— Dec 5, 1982: 99.1 mhz; 100 kw. 1,049 ft. TL: N27 45 07 W97 38 18. (CP: 97 kw). Stereo. Radio Plaza, 501 Tupper Ln. 78417. Phone: (361) 289-0111. Fax: (361) 289-5024. Web Site: www.krysfm.com. Licensee: Capstar TX L.P. Group owner: Clear Channel Communications Inc. (acq 8-30-00; grpsl). Network: ABC. Format: Country. News staff: one. Target aud: 25-54. ♦Matt Martin, gen mgr; Zee Zepola, sls dir & gen sls mgr; Frank Edwards, prom dir & progmg dir; Lou Ramirez, mus dir; Russell Vaughn, chief of engrg.

KKTX(AM)—Co-owned with KRYS-FM. 2002: 1360 khz; 1 kw-U. TL: N27 48 01 W97 27 41. E-mail: scottjohnson@clearchannel.com. Web Site: www.1360online.com. Network: ABC. Format: News/talk. Target aud: 2-18; children. ♦Matt Martrin, gen mgr; Zee Zepola, sls dir; Scott Johnson, progmg dir; Russell Vaughan, chief of engrg.

KSIX(AM)— September 1947: 1230 khz; 1 kw-U. TL: N27 48 09 W97 27 14. Stereo. 710 Buffalo St., Suite 608 78416. Phone: (361) 882-5749. Fax: (361) 884-1240. E-mail: info@espn1230ksix.com. Web Site: www.espn1230ksix.com. Licensee: Withers Family Texas Holding LP (acq 10-28-02). Network: ESPN Radio. Format: Sports. ♦Jim Withers, gen mgr; Scott Howe, gen sls mgr; Bill Doerner, progmg dir.

KUNO(AM)— May 1950: 1400 khz; 1 kw-U. TL: N27 45 36 W97 26 14. Stereo. Radio Plaza, 501 Tupper Ln. 78417-9736. Phone: (361) 289-0111. Fax: (361) 289-5035. Licensee: Capstar TX L.P. Group owner: Clear Channel Communications Inc. (acq 8-30-00; grpsl). Format: Sp. News: 17 hrs wkly. Target aud: 25-64. ♦Matt Martin, gen mgr.

KZFM(FM)— Dec 7, 1964: 95.5 mhz; 100 kw. 994 ft. TL: N27 39 32 W97 34 10. Stereo. Box 9757 78469. Secondary address: 2117 Leopard St. 78408. Phone: (361) 883-3516. Fax: (361) 882-9767. E-mail: thechief@star94.net. Web Site: www.hotz95.com. Licensee: Malkan FM Associates L.P. Group owner: Malkan Broadcast Assoc. (acq 1976). Rep: Katz Radio. Thompson Hine. Format: CHR. Target aud: 18-34; female. ♦Glen Powers, pres & stn mgr; Janice Raleigh, gen sls mgr & prom dir; Gino Flores, prom dir; Ed Ocanas, progmg dir; Arlene Cordell, mus dir; John Gifford, chief of engrg.

KEYS(AM)—Co-owned with KZFM(FM). March 1941: 1440 khz; 1 kw-U, DA-N. TL: N27 47 02 W97 27 29. Phone: (361) 882-7411. Fax: (361) 882-9767. E-mail: johngifford1440@yahoo.com. Web Site: www.1440keys.com. Licensee: Malkan AM Associates L.P. (acq 1965). Network: ABC. Rep: Katz Radio. Thompson Hine. Format: News/talk, sports. Target aud: 25 plus; men. ♦Will Diaz, progmg dir.

Corsicana

KAND(AM)— May 17, 1937: 1340 khz; 1 kw-U. TL: N32 06 53 W96 27 47. 1504 N. Beaton St. 75110. Secondary address: Box 2998 75151. Phone: (903) 874-7421. Phone: (903) 874-1340. Fax: (903) 874-0789. Web Site: www.kand1340am.com. Licensee: Corsicana Media Inc. (acq 1-16-95; $500,000). Network: ABC Information & Entertainment. Format: Country, news. News staff: one; News: 25 hrs wkly. Target aud: General. ♦John Whetzell, pres; Mike Taylor, gen mgr; Mary Sikes, gen sls mgr; Bob Belcher, progmg dir; Dick Aldama, news dir; Jim Wiggins, chief of engrg.

Crane

KMMZ(FM)— 1995: 101.3 mhz; 100 kw. 485 ft. TL: N31 41 02 W102 19 13. Stereo. Box 60375, Midland 79711. Secondary address: 12200 W. I-20 E. 79711. Phone: (432) 563-2266. Fax: (432) 563-2288. E-mail: Sonny@kmmz.net. Licensee: Don L. Cook. Thompson, Hine & Flory. Format: Sp Top 40. Target aud: 25-54. ♦Don L. Cook, gen mgr.

KXOI(AM)— December 1959: 810 khz; 1 kw-D, 500 w-N, DA-1. TL: N31 28 39 W102 20 24. Box 2344, Odessa 79760. Phone: (432) 333-5061. Fax: (432) 333-6067. Licensee: Hispanic Outreach Ministries Inc. Format: Sp. Target aud: General. ♦Rev. Pedro Emiliano, pres; Eli Emiliano, gen mgr & progmg dir; Don Cook, chief of engrg.

Creedmoor

KZNX(AM)— Dec 8, 1962: 1530 khz; 10 kw-D, 990 w-CH. TL: N30 38 47 W97 40 08. Stereo. 4314 W. Baker Ln., Suite 1260, Austin 78759. Phone: (512) 346-8255. Fax: (512) 346-8262. E-mail: controlroom @espnaustin.com. Web Site: www.espnaustin.com. Licensee: Simmons-Austin, LS LLC. Group owner: Simmons Media Group (acq 6-2-2004; $2 million). Format: Talk, sports. News: 63 hrs wkly. Target aud: 25-54; 51% male, 49% female. ♦Daryl O'Neal, gen mgr; Jon Madani, chief of opns & progmg dir; Lori Hatter, sls dir; Courtney Cleland, prom mgr; J. Cole McClellan, chief of engrg.

Crockett

KBHT(FM)— Nov 15, 1982: 93.5 mhz; 50 kw. 479 ft. TL: N31 20 03 W95 47 13. Stereo. Box 130, Grapeland, 206 S. Main, Grapeland 75844. Secondary address: 212 West Oak, Palestine 75801. Phone: (936) 544-9350. Fax: (936) 544-9695. E-mail: nicolag@texcom.net. Web Site: www.kbht.com. Licensee: Nicol Broadcasting Ltd. (acq 9-7-93; $179,000; 9-27-93). Format: Classic country. Target aud: 25-54. Spec prog: Gospel 6 hrs wkly. ♦Tom Nicol, chmn; Ansel Bradshaw, pres, gen mgr & gen sls mgr; Tim O'Brien, progmg dir; Will Hatch, news dir; Chester Leeidtker, chief of engrg.

***KCKT(FM)**— February 2003: 88.5 mhz; 250 w. Ant 161 ft. TL: N31 19 37 W95 28 26. Box 3206, Tupelo, MS 38803. Phone: (662)

Stations in the U.S. Texas

Developers & Brokers of Radio Properties
contact American Media Services at our suite:
Philadelphia Marriott Downtown
215-625-2900
843-972-2200
americanmediaservices.com
Charleston, SC
Dallas, TX • Chicago, Il • Austin, TX
American Media Services, LLC

844-8888. Fax: (662) 842-6791. E-mail: comments@afr.net. Web Site: www.afr.net. Licensee: American Family Association. Group owner: American Family Radio (acq 1-17-01). Format: Christian. ♦Marvin Sanders, gen mgr.

KIVY(AM)— Nov 11, 1949: 1290 khz; 2.5 kw-D, 175 w-N. TL: N31 18 20 W95 27 06. 102 S. Fifth St. 75835. Phone: (936) 544-2171. Phone: (936) 544-KIVY. Fax: (936) 544-4891. Web Site: www.kivy.com. Licensee: Leon Hunt (acq 9-19-02; $1.1 million. with co-located FM). Network: ABC. Format: Classic oldies. Target aud: General. ♦Leon Hunt, pres, gen mgr, gen sls mgr & progmg dir; Chester Leediker, chief of engrg.

KIVY-FM— June 1, 1970: 92.7 mhz; 50 kw. 497 ft. TL: N31 18 18 W95 27 06. Stereo. Web Site: www.kivy.com. Network: ABC. Format: Country.

Crystal Beach

KPTI(FM)— November 1989: 105.3 mhz; 6 kw. Ant 180 ft. TL: N29 30 07 W94 31 15. Stereo. 1415 N. Loop West, Suite 550, Houston 77008. Phone: (713) 407-1415. Fax: (713) 407-1400. Licensee: Tichenor License Corp. Group owner: Univision Radio (acq 9-22-2003; grpsl). Format: Hip-hop. ♦Mark Masepohl, VP & gen mgr.

KSTB(FM)— 1996: 101.5 mhz; 14 kw. 449 ft. TL: N29 33 52 W94 23 59. Stereo. 755 S. 11th St., Ste.102, Beaumont 77701. Phone: (409) 833-9421. Fax: (409) 833-9296. Licensee: Cumulus Licensing Corp. Group owner: Cumulus Media Inc. (acq 5-20-02; $2.5 million). Rep: Roslin. Fisher, Wayland, Cooper, Leader & Zaragoza. Format: Country. News staff: 2; News: 12 hrs wkly. Target aud: 18-49. ♦Rick Prusater, gen mgr & stn mgr; Jim West, opns VP & progmg dir; Greg Davis, chief of engrg.

Crystal City

KHER(FM)— Sept 5, 1985: 94.3 mhz; 3 kw. 135 ft. TL: N28 39 57 W99 48 58. Old Big Wells Hwy., Farm Rd. 65, Box 707, Carri 20 S. 78839. Phone: (830) 374-2203. Phone: (830) 374-5730 (office). Fax: (830) 374-9658. E-mail: kherfm@yahoo.com. Licensee: Sylvia Mijares. (acq 9-4-97). Borsari & Paxson. Format: Sp, news/talk. Target aud: 18-54; 90% Hispanic, 10% non-minority. Spec prog: Relg 2 hrs wkly. ♦Sylvia Mijares, pres & gen mgr; Rudy Gomez, sls VP; Marie Thelma Martinez, news dir & pub affrs dir; Charlie Schmele, chief of engrg.

Cuero

***KTLZ(FM)**— 2003: . Stn currently dark 89.9 mhz; 5 kw. Ant 243 ft. TL: N29 02 23 W97 19 24. Box 5459, Twin Falls, ID 83303-5459. Phone: (208) 733-3551. Fax: (208) 733-3548. Web Site: www.radioassistministry.com. Licensee: Radio Assist Ministry Inc. (acq 9-21-2004; $50,000). ♦Clark Parrish, pres.

Cypress

KYND(AM)— December 1991: 1520 khz; 3 kw-D, DA. TL: N30 00 37 W95 41 40. Little Saigon Radio, 6250 Westpark Dr., #112, Houston 77057. Phone: (832) 252-1234. Fax: (832) 252-1233. E-mail: radio@littlesaigonradio.com. Web Site: www.littlesaigonradio.com. Licensee: Matthew Provenzano. Format: Vietnamese. Target aud: General. ♦Matt Provenzano, CEO; Anh Dang, gen mgr & stn mgr.

Daingerfield

KNGR(AM)— August 1966: 1560 khz; 1.5 kw-D, 60 w-N. TL: N33 01 35 W94 42 22. Stereo. Box 474 75638. Phone: (903) 645-4325. Web Site: www.kingcountry.org. Licensee: Network Communications Co. (acq 2-21-91; $50,000;. FTR: 3-11-91). Format: Gospel. ♦Bill R. Wright, chmn & gen mgr.

Dalhart

KXIT(AM)— 1948: 1240 khz; 1 kw-U. TL: N36 05 45 W102 30 38. Stereo. Box 1359, Hwy. 385 N. 79022. Phone: (806) 249-4747. Licensee: Dalhart Radio Inc. (acq 12-3-01; $325,000. with co-located FM). Format: Country. Spec prog: Farm 7 hrs wkly. ♦George Chambers, pres & gen mgr; Cheryl Riichard, rgnl sls mgr; Adam Taylor, progmg mgr; Auto Maxin, chief of engrg.

KXIT-FM— 1962: 96.3 mhz; 100 kw. Ant 472 ft. TL: N35 53 46 W102 23 03. Stereo. Format: Classic rock, oldies.

Dallas

KAAM(AM)—(Garland). 1973: 770 khz; 10 kw-D, 1 kw-N, DA-2. TL: N33 01 58 W96 34 31. Stereo. 3201 Royalty Row, Irving 75062. Phone: (972) 445-1700. Fax: (972) 438-6574. E-mail: cbcstand@aol.com. Web Site: www.kaamradio.com. Licensee: Dontron Inc. Group owner: Crawford Broadcasting Co. (acq 1979). Format: Adult standards. Target aud: 35 plus; Christian. ♦Don Crawford, pres; Don Crawford Jr., gen mgr.

KBFB(FM)— 1965: 97.9 mhz; 99 kw. 1,611 ft. TL: N32 35 15 W96 57 59. Stereo. 13331 Preston Rd., Suite 1180 75240. Phone: (972) 331-5400. Fax: (972) 331-5560. Web Site: www.979tlpbeat.com. Licensee: Radio One Licenses LLC. Group owner: Radio One Inc. (acq 2000; grpsl). Rep: CBS Radio. Format: Urban contemp. Target aud: 25-50. ♦Alfred Liggine, pres; George Laughlin, gen mgr; John Candelaria, opns mgr & progmg dir; Shawn Nunn, sls dir; Joe Libios, mktg dir & prom mgr; Tony Fields, progmg dir; Don Stevenson, chief of engrg.

***KCBI(FM)**— May 19, 1976: 90.9 mhz; 100 kw. 1,509 ft. TL: N32 35 22 W96 58 10. Stereo. Box 619000 75261-9000. Phone: (817) 792-3800. Fax: (817) 277-9929. E-mail: kcbi@kcbi.org. Web Site: www.kcbi.org. Licensee: Criswell College. (group owner) Network: AP Radio. Format: Inspirational, Christian. News staff: 4; News: 4 hrs wkly. Target aud: 35-54; Christian families. ♦Ronald L. Harris, CEO; Royce Laycock, chmn; Heidi Graham, pres & sls dir; Todd Chatman, stn mgr; Doug Price, opns VP; James Nance, dev VP; Troy Kriechbaum, prom dir & prom mgr; Marc Anderson, progmg VP & mus dir; L.B. Lyon, news dir; Doug Watson, engrg dir.

KDGE(FM)—See Fort Worth

KDMX(FM)— 1965: 102.9 mhz; 99 kw. 1,348 ft. TL: N32 34 54 W96 58 32. 14001 N. Dallas Pkwy., Suite 300 75240. Phone: (214) 866-8000. Fax: (214) 866-8201. E-mail: contactus@mix1029.listenernetwork.com. Web Site: www.mix1029.com. Licensee: Citicasters Licenses L.P. Group owner: Clear Channel Communications Inc. (acq 5-4-99; grpsl). Format: Adult contemp. News: 3 hrs wkly. Target aud: 25-49; upper income females. ♦Brenda Adrianee, gen mgr; Bill Alfano, gen sls mgr; Louis Sutton, chief of engrg.

KEGL(FM)—See Fort Worth

***KERA(FM)**— July 11, 1974: 90.1 mhz; 95 kw. 1,260 ft. TL: N32 34 43 W96 57 12. Stereo. 3000 Harry Hines Blvd. 75201. Phone: (214) 871-1390. Fax: (214) 740-9369. E-mail: kerafm@kera.org. Web Site: www.kera.org. Licensee: North Texas Public Broadcasting. Network: NPR, PRI. Arnold & Porter. Format: News/talk, progsv. News staff: 5; News: 80 hrs wkly. Target aud: 35-54; general. ♦Kevin Martin, COO, pres, pres, CFO & exec VP; Barger Tygart, chmn; Jeff Luchsinger, stn mgr; Patricia Lyons, dev VP & engrg dir.

KFJZ(AM)—See Fort Worth

KFLC(AM)—See Fort Worth

KFXR(AM)— 1947: 1190 khz; 50 kw-D, 5 kw-N, DA-2. TL: N32 47 10 W96 57 00. 720 N. Saint Paul St. 75201. Phone: (214) 855-0002. Licensee: Capstar TX L.P. Group owner: Clear Channel Communications Inc. (acq 3-27-01; $16 million). Network: Network: Westwood One,

CBS. Rep: CBS Radio. Leventhal, Senter & Lerman. News: 2 hrs wkly. Target aud: 25-54; general. Spec prog: Sports 6 hrs wkly.

KGGR(AM)— June 8, 1947: 1040 khz; 3.3 kw-D, 2.8 kw-CH. TL: N32 46 43 W96 43 51. 5787 S. Hampton Rd., Suite 285 75232. Phone: (972) 572-5447. Phone: (972) 988-1040. Fax: (214) 330-6133. Web Site: www.kggram.com. Licensee: Mortenson Broadcasting Co. of Texas Inc. Group owner: Mortenson Broadcasting Co. (acq 5-1-96; $1.15 million). Network: American Urban. Format: Relg, talk, Black. Target aud: 18 plus. ♦Ann Arnold, gen mgr; Christie Wafer, gen sls mgr.

KHKS(FM)—See Denton

KHVN(AM)—See Fort Worth

KJKK(FM)— Dec 25, 1965: 100.3 mhz; 97 kw. Ant 1,883 ft. TL: N32 35 05 W96 57 46. Stereo. 7901 Carpenter Fwy. 75247. Phone: (214) 630-3011. Fax: (214) 905-5052. Web Site: www.wild100.com. Licensee: Texas Infinity Broadcasting L.P. Group owner: Infinity Broadcasting Corp. (acq 11-13-98; grpsl). Network: ABC. Rep: CBS Radio. Format: CHR. Target aud: 18-49. ♦Mel Karmazin, CEO; Dave Siebert, gen mgr; David Henry, sls dir; Joel Gough, gen sls mgr; Amy Gomoll, prom dir; Alex Valentine, progmg dir; Bethany Parks, mus dir; Lori Dodd, pub affrs dir; Bob Henke, chief of engrg.

KKDA(AM)—See Grand Prairie

KKDA-FM— June 8, 1947: 104.5 mhz; 100 kw. 1,585 ft. TL: N32 35 22 W96 58 10. Stereo. Box 530860, Grand Prairie 75053. Secondary address: 1230 River Bend Dr., Ste. 111 75247. Phone: (972) 263-9911. Fax: (972) 558-0010. E-mail: staff@k104fm.com. Web Site: www.k104fm.com. Licensee: Service Broadcast Group. (acq 5-76). Rep: Christal. Format: Urban contemp. ♦Hymen Childs, pres; Chuck Smith, gen mgr; Vick Romanick, gen sls mgr; Liz Leos, prom mgr; Skip Cheatham, progmg dir; Sam Putney, news dir; Gary Wachter, chief of engrg.

KLIF(AM)— June 26, 1922: 570 khz; 5 kw-U, DA-2. TL: N32 56 40 W96 59 25. 3500 Maple Ave., Suite 1600 75219. Phone: (214) 526-2400. Phone: (214) 263-4141. Fax: (214) 520-4343. Web Site: www.klif.com. Licensee: KLIF Lico Inc. Group owner: Susquehanna Radio Corp. (acq 12-15-89). Network: ABC. Format: News/talk. News staff: 1; News: 15 hrs wkly. Target aud: 25-54; men.Peter P. Brubaker, chmn; David E. Kennedy, pres; Dan Halyburton, sr VP; Dan Bennett, VP; Lon Bason, gen mgr; Jim Quirk, sls dir & gen sls mgr; Jami Williams, natl sls mgr; Sharon Brown, mktg dir; Callie Hech, mktg mgr; Natalie Day, prom dir; Richard Fish, adv mgr; Jeff Hillery, progmg dir; Terese Arena, news dir; Annmarie Petitto, pub affrs dir; Rob Chickering, engrg dir; Hue Beavers, chief of engrg

KLLI(FM)— Apr 5, 1968: 105.3 mhz; 97 kw. Ant 1,883 ft. TL: N32 35 05 W96 57 46. Stereo. 7901 Carpenter Fwy 75247. Phone: (214) 630-3011. Fax: (214) 905-5052. Web Site: www.live1053.com. Licensee: Texas Infinity Broadcasting L.P. Group owner: Infinity Broadcasting Corp. (acq 11-13-98; grpsl). Network: Westwood One. Rep: CBS Radio. Leventhal, Senter & Lerman. Format: Talk. News staff: one; News: 3 hrs wkly. Target aud: 18-49; general. ♦Mel Karmazin, CEO; Brian Purdy, gen mgr; Steve Sullivan, gen sls mgr; Lynn Sornsen, natl sls mgr; Jeff Burkett, prom dir; Gavin Spittle, progmg dir; Bob Henke, chief of engrg.

KLNO(FM)—See Fort Worth

KLTY(FM)—(Arlington). April 1949: 94.9 mhz; 99 kw. Ant 1,666 ft. TL: N32 35 19 W96 58 05. Stereo. 6400 Belt Line Rd., Suite 120, Irving 75063. Phone: (972) 870-9949. Fax: (214) 561-2156. Web Site: www.klty.com. Licensee: Inspiration Media of Texas LLC. Group owner: Salem Communications Corp. Rep: Katz Radio. Format: Adult contemp Christian. News: 2 hrs wkly. Target aud: 25-54; female dominant, family oriented, upscale, conservative. ♦John L. Peroyea, VP & gen mgr.

KLUV-FM— 1961: 98.7 mhz; 98 kw. 1,584 ft. TL: N32 35 22 W96 58 10. Stereo. 4131 N. Central Expwy., Suite 700 75204. Phone: (214)

Broadcasting & Cable Yearbook 2006
D-481

Texas
Directory of Radio

526-9870. Fax: (214) 443-1570. Fax: (214) 522-5588. Web Site: www.kluv.com. Licensee: Texas Infinity Broadcasting L.P. Group owner: CBS Radio (acq 9-17-94; $51 million). Format: Oldies. News staff: 2. Target aud: 35-54. ◆ Mel Karmazin, pres; David Henry, gen mgr; John Phillips, gen sls mgr; Liz Balon, prom mgr; Jay Cresswell, mus dir; Kathy Jones, news dir & pub affrs dir; Bill Taylor, chief of engrg.

KMGS(AM)—See Highland Park

KMNY(AM)—See Hurst

KNIT(AM)— 1952: 1480 khz; 5 kw-D, 1.9 kw-N, DA-2. TL: N32 39 42 W96 39 20. 6400 N. Beltline Rd., Suite 110, Irving 75063. Phone: (214) 561-9673. Fax: (214) 561-9662. Licensee: Salem Media of Illinois LLC. Group owner: Univision Radio (acq 1-7-2005; with WIND(AM) Chicago, IL and KKHT-FM Winnie, TX in exchange for WPPN(FM) Des Plaines, IL). Format: Solid gospel. ◆ Pete Thomson, gen mgr.

*KNON(FM)— Aug 3, 1983: 89.3 mhz; 55 kw. Ant 850 ft. TL: N32 35 24 W96 58 21. Stereo. Box 710909 75371. Secondary address: 5353 Maples Ave. 75235. Phone: (214) 828-9500. Fax: (214) 823-3051. Web Site: www.knon.org. Licensee: Agape Broadcasting Foundation Inc. (acq 8-83). Format: Var. Target aud: General. ◆ Dave Chaos, stn mgr; Christian Lee, mus dir; Pamela Parker, sls dir & news dir.

KOAI(FM)—See Fort Worth

KPLX(FM)—See Fort Worth

KRLD(AM)— October 1926: 1080 khz; 50 kw-U, DA-N. TL: N32 53 25 W96 38 44. 1080 Ballpark Way, Arlington 76011. Phone: (817) 543-5400. Fax: (817) 543-5570. Web Site: www.krld.com. Licensee: Texas Infinity Broadcasting L.P. Group owner: Infinity Broadcasting Rep: CBS Radio. Format: News/talk, news, sports. News staff: 35; News: 119 hrs wkly. Target aud: 25-54. Spec prog: Texas Rangers baseball. ◆ Jerry Bobo, VP & gen mgr; Tom Bigby, opns dir.

KRVA(AM)—(Cockrell Hill). Sept 29, 1947: 1600 khz; 5 kw-D, 1 kw-N, DA-2. TL: N32 44 25 W96 42 38. 4965 Preston Park Blvd., Suite 120, Plano 75093. Phone: (972) 985-2902. Fax: (972) 985-2905. Licensee: Mortenson Broadcasting Co. of Texas Inc. (group owner; (acq 8-30-2004; $3.5 million). Format: Ethnic, Indian, Pakistani. ◆ Rehan Siddiqi, gen mgr; Norita Mittra, progmg dir.

KRVA-FM—See Campbell

KSKY(AM)—(Balch Springs). Sept 30, 1941: 660 khz; 10 kw-D, 660 w-N, DA-N. TL: N29 22 51 W95 14 15. 6400 N. Beltline, Suite 110, Irving 75063. Phone: (214) 561-9660. Fax: (214) 561-9662. E-mail: ksky@ksky.com. Web Site: www.ksky.com. Licensee: Bison Media Inc. Group owner: Salem Communications Corp. (acq 4-24-2000; $7.5 million, plus seller gets KMOM(FM) Fountain, CO). Latham & Watkins. Format: News, talk. Target aud: 35-59; middle income white female. Spec prog: High school, college sports. ◆ Pete Thomson, CFO, VP & gen mgr; David Darling, opns VP, opns mgr & progmg dir; Bots Johnson, gen sls mgr; Carol White, prom dir; Brian Heise, chief of engrg.

KSOC(FM)—(Gainesville). 1958: 94.5 mhz; 100 kw. 1,896 ft. TL: N33 33 36 W96 57 35. Stereo. 13331 Preston Rd., Suite 1180 75234. Phone: (972) 331-5400. Fax: (972) 726-0940. Licensee: Radio One Licenses LLC. Group owner: Radio One Inc. (acq 11-8-01; grpsl). Latham & Watkins. Format: Urban / adult contemp. News staff: one; News: one hr wkly. Target aud: 18-44; affluent generation X'ers. ◆ George Laughlin, gen mgr; John Candelaria, progmg dir.

KTCK(AM)— 1920: 1310 khz; 5 kw-D, 5 kw-N, DA-2. TL: N32 56 41 W96 56 25. Stereo. 3500 Maple Ave., Suite 1310 75219. Phone: (214) 526-7400. Fax: (214) 525-2525. Web Site: www.theticket.com. Licensee: KRBE Lico Inc. Group owner: Susquehanna Radio Corp. (acq 1996; $14 million). Network: CBS. Verner, Liipfert, Bernhard, McPherson & Hand. Format: Sports, talk. Target aud: 25-54; men & sport enthusiasts. ◆ Dave Kennedy, COO & pres; Pete Brubaker, CFO; Dan Bennett, VP, gen mgr & gen mgr; Jim Quirk, sls dir & mktg mgr; Ken Roberts, gen sls mgr; Jami Williams, natl sls mgr; Sharon Brown, stn mgr & mktg mgr; Jamey Garner, prom dir; Jeff Catlin, progmg dir & pub affrs dir; Mark Friedman, news dir; Rob Chickering, engrg dir.

KVIL-FM—See Highland Park

*KVTT(FM)— Jan 26, 1950: 91.7 mhz; 100 kw. 1,099 ft. TL: N32 35 24 W96 58 21. Stereo. 11061 Shady Tr. 75229. Phone: (214) 351-6655. Fax: (469) 522-0992. E-mail: kvtt@kvtt.org. Web Site: www.kvtt.org. Licensee: Covenant Educational Media Inc. (acq 9-21-2004; $16.5 million). Format: Talk, educ, music. ◆ Ron Evans, gen mgr & stn mgr; Bonnie Houston, opns mgr; Bryan Reeder, progmg dir & mus dir.

KZPS(FM)— Apr 1, 1948: 92.5 mhz; 100 kw. 1,590 ft. TL: N32 35 22 W96 58 10. Stereo. 14001 N. Dallas Pkwy., Suite 300 75240. Phone: (214) 866-8000. Fax: (972) 770-7747. Web Site: www.kzps.com. Licensee: AMFM Texas Licenses L.P. Group owner: Clear Channel Communications Inc. (acq 8-30-00; grpsl). Latham & Watkins. Format: Classic rock. News staff: one. Target aud: 25-44; upscale young adults. ◆ Brenda Adriance, gen mgr; Christie Banks, stn mgr; Sarah Frazier, gen sls mgr & rgnl sls mgr; Eric Landrum, prom dir; Anna DeHaro, progmg VP & news dir; Lewis Sutton, chief of engrg.

WBAP(AM)—See Fort Worth

WRR(FM)— 1948: 101.1 mhz; 100 kw. 1,510 ft. TL: N32 35 22 W96 58 10. Stereo. Box 159001 75315-9001. Secondary address: 1516 First Ave. 75210. Phone: (214) 670-8888. Fax: (214) 670-8394. Web Site: www.wrr101.com. Licensee: City of Dallas. Rep: McGavren Guild. Kaye, Scholer, Fierman, Hays & Handler. Format: Class. Target aud: 25-54; all ages. Spec prog: Children 2 hrs wkly. ◆ Gregory T. Davis, VP & gen mgr.

Decatur

*KDKR(FM)— 1998: 91.3 mhz; 21 kw vert. Ant 564 ft. TL: N33 23 12 W97 33 57. 5617 Diamond Oaks Dr. S., Fort Worth 76117. Phone: (817) 831-9130. E-mail: kdkr@csnradio.com. Web Site: www.kdkr.org. Licensee: CSN International (group owner; acq 7-12-2000). Format: Positive easy gospel, relg. ◆ Chris Rohloff, gen mgr; Stephanie Rohloff, progmg dir.

KRNB(FM)— Aug 15, 1968: 105.7 mhz; 100 kw. 492 ft. TL: N32 11 11 W98 17 26. (CP: Ant 1,673 ft.). Stereo. c/o KKDA(AM), Grand Prairie 75053. Phone: (972) 263-9911. Fax: (972) 558-0010. Web Site: www.krnb.com. Licensee: Service Broadcasting Corp. (acq 2-28-95; 5-22-95). Network: ABC. Format: Adult contemp. ◆ Hymen Childs, pres; Chuck Smith, gen mgr; Vick Romanick, gen sls mgr; Liz Leos, prom dir; Sam Weaver, progmg dir; Sam Putney, news dir; Gary Wachter, chief of engrg.

Del Mar Hills

KVOZ(AM)— Apr 15, 1952: 890 khz; 10 kw-D, 1 kw-N, DA-N. TL: N27 32 57 W99 22 21. Box 252, McAllen 78505. Phone: (956) 781-5528. Phone: (956) 686-6382. Fax: (956) 686-2999. Web Site: www.laradiochristiana.com. Licensee: Consolidated Radio Inc. (acq 3-27-97). Format: Sp gospel. Target aud: 18 plus. ◆ Paulino Bernal, gen mgr; Eloy Bernal, stn mgr; Pete Guzman, opns mgr.

Del Rio

KDLK-FM—Listing follows KTJK(AM).

KTDR(FM)— Mar 31, 1986: 96.3 mhz; 100 kw. 490 ft. TL: N29 32 25 W101 07 21. Stereo. 307 E. 8th St. 78840. Phone: (830) 775-6291. Phone: (830) 775-6291. Fax: (830) 775-6545. E-mail: production@themix96.com. Web Site: www.themix96.com. Licensee: Grande Broadcasting of Del Rio Inc. Network: ABC FM Connection. Borsari & Paxson. Format: Adult contemp. News: 1 hr wkly. Target aud: 25-54; male. Spec prog: Relg 3 hrs wkly. ◆ Frank Mendoza, pres & gen mgr; Chris Russell, gen sls mgr; Charlene Duncan, chief of engrg; Rodney Lyman, progmg mgr, news dir & chief of engrg.

KTJK(AM)— 1947: 1230 khz; 860 w-U. TL: N29 25 45 W100 54 17. Box 1489 78841-1489. Phone: (830) 775-9583. Fax: (830) 774-4009. Web Site: www.ktjk.com. Licensee: Forum Broadcasting Inc. (acq 12-10-02; with co-located FM). Format: Tejano music format. Target aud: 25-54. ◆ Larry Mariner, pres, pres & gen mgr; Rudy Briones, opns mgr; Jay Gonzalez, progmg mgr.

KDLK-FM—Co-owned with KTJK(AM). Aug 15, 1966: 94.1 mhz; 18 kw. Ant 276 ft. TL: N29 25 45 W100 54 17. Stereo. Web Site: www.kdlk.com. Network: Westwood One. Format: Country. Target aud: 18 plus.

KWMC(AM)— Aug 20, 1967: 1490 khz; 1 kw-U. TL: N29 22 17 W100 51 55. 903 E. Cortinas St. 78840. Phone: (830) 775-3544. Fax: (830) 775-3546. E-mail: kwmc1490@wcsonline.com. Licensee: Minerva Garza Valdez. Format: Rock oldies. News staff: 2. Spec prog: Relg 5 hrs wkly. ◆ Alfredo Garza, pres, gen mgr & chief of engrg; Minerva Garza-Valdez, VP; Guillermo Garza, stn mgr, prom dir & progmg dir; Javier Martinez, gen sls mgr.

Del Valle

KIXL(AM)—Licensed to Del Valle. See Austin

Denison

KJIM(AM)—See Sherman

Denison-Sherman

KYNG(AM)— Sept 26, 1948: 950 khz; 500 w-U, DA-2. TL: N33 41 08 W96 32 28. c/o Susquehanna Radio Corp., Box 1432, York, PA 17405-1069. Secondary address: Susquehanna Commerce Center, W, 221 West Philadelphia St. 17404. Phone: (717) 852-2132. Fax: (717) 771-1436. E-mail: rehan1999@aol.com. Licensee: KRBE Lico Inc. Group owner: Susquehanna Radio Corp. (acq 4-30-98; $2.672 million). Format: Brokered ethnic. Target aud: General; ethnic; Indian-Pakistani origin. ◆ Lon A. Bason, gen mgr; Rehan Siddigi, opns mgr.

Denton

KFZO(FM)— September 1988: 99.1 mhz; 100 kw. Ant 1,168 ft. TL: N33 23 22 W97 33 53. Stereo. 7700 Carpenter Fwy., Dallas 75247. Phone: (214) 525-0400. Phone: (214) 630-8531. Fax: (214) 689-3818. Fax: (214) 631-1196 (sales). Web Site: www.kick991.com. Licensee: KHCK-FM License Corp. Group owner: Univision Radio (acq 9-22-2003; grpsl). Rep: Katz Hispanic. Format: Sp, Tejano. News staff: one; News: one hr wkly. Target aud: 25-54; affluent/educated adults. ◆ Frank Carter, gen mgr; Andy Lockridge, opns dir; Howard Toole, sls dir; Cipriano Robles, gen sls mgr; Betsy Galleguillos, natl sls mgr; Oscar Espinosa, prom dir; Frank "Pancho" Gonzales, progmg dir; Myrna Vera, mus dir; Patrick Parks, chief of engrg.

KHKS(FM)— 1947: 106.1 mhz; 100 kw. 1,584 ft. TL: N32 35 22 W96 58 10. Stereo. 14001 N. Dallas Parkway, Suite 300, Dallas 75240. Phone: (214) 866-8000. Fax: (214) 866-8588. Web Site: www.1061kissfm.com. Licensee: AMFM Texas Licenses L.P. Group owner: Clear Channel Communications Inc. (acq 8-30-00; grpsl). Reed, Smith, Shaw & McClay. Format: CHR. News staff: one. Target aud: 18-49. ◆ Brenda Adriance, gen mgr; Chris Long, sls dir; Kelly Gunnersen, natl sls mgr; Grant Gold, rgnl sls mgr; Jon Volmar, mktg dir; Greg Sherrell, prom dir; Patrick Davis, progmg dir; Fernando ventura, mus dir; Louis Sutton, engrg dir & chief of engrg.

Devine

KRPT(FM)— Nov 17, 1982: 92.5 mhz; 50 kw. Ant 492 ft. TL: N28 55 32 W99 02 53. Stereo. 6222 N.W. IH 10, San Antonio 78201. Phone: (210) 736-9700. Fax: (210) 735-8811. Web Site: www.925krpt.com. Licensee: CCB Texas Licenses L.P. Group owner: Clear Channel Communications Inc. (acq 10-2-98; $1.5 million). Format: Progressive talk. ◆ Tom Glade, gen mgr.

Diboll

KAFX-FM—Licensed to Diboll. See Lufkin

KSML(AM)—Licensed to Diboll. See Lufkin

Dilley

KLMO-FM—Not on air, target date: unknown: 98.9 mhz; 50 kw. 492 ft. TL: N28 41 29 W99 10 34. Dilley Broadcasters, 115 West Ave. D, Robstown 78320. Phone: (210) 532-9858. Fax: (361) 289-7722. Licensee: Dilley Broadcasters. Format: Sp var.

Dimmitt

KDHN(AM)— Dec 22, 1963: 1470 khz; 500 w-D, 149 w-N. TL: N34 35 11 W102 18 35. 704 W. Cleveland St. 79027. Phone: (806) 647-4161. Fax: (806) 647-4715. E-mail: kdhn@highplains.net. Licensee: Collins Communications Co. (acq 12-12-84). Format: C&W, relg, Sp. News: 8 hrs wkly. Target aud: General. Spec prog: Sp 17 hrs wkly. ◆ Wayne Collins, pres & gen mgr.

| Stations in the U.S. | | Texas |

KNNK(FM)—Licensed to Dimmitt. See Hereford

Doss

*KGLF(FM)—Not on air, target date: unknown:. Stn currently dark 88.1 mhz; 6 kw. Ant 328 ft. TL: N30 22 22 W99 05 02. 103 Rare Eagle Ct., Austin 78734. Phone: (512) 608-0486. Licensee: Legacy Austin Broadcasting Foundation Inc. (acq 10-15-2003; $100,000 for CP). ♦ Rob Hand, gen mgr.

Dripping Springs

*KLOW(FM)—Not on air, target date: unknown: 91.9 mhz; 6 kw. Ant 276 ft. TL: N30 21 45 W98 18 08. 5700 West Oaks Blvd., Rocklin, CA 95765. Phone: (916) 251-1600. Fax: (916) 251-1650. Licensee: Educational Media Foundation. ♦ Lloyd Parker, gen mgr.

KXXS(FM)— 1984: 104.9 mhz; 2.35 kw. Ant 531 ft. TL: N30 11 54 W98 00 46. Stereo. 2211 IH 35, Suite 401, Austin 78741. Secondary address: 7524 N. Lamar Blvd., Austin 78752. Phone: (512) 416-1100. Fax: (512) 416-8205. Licensee: BMP Austin License Company L.P. Group owner: Amigo Broadcasting L.P. (acq 11-9-2004; grpsl). Kenkel & Associates. Format: Sp contemp. Target aud: 25-54; upscale, retired, affluent. ♦ Pedro Gasc, gen mgr; Javier Salgudo, progmg dir.

Dublin

KSTV-FM— Aug 15, 1968: 93.1 mhz; 7.9 kw. 580 ft. TL: N32 11 12 W98 17 44. Box 289, 3209 W. Washington (Dublin Hwy.), Stephenville 76401. Phone: (254) 968-2141. Fax: (254) 968-6221. E-mail: kstv@htcomp.net. Web Site: www.377net.com. Licensee: CCR-Stephenville III LLC. Group owner: Cherry Creek Radio LLC (acq 6-24-2004; grpsl). Format: Country. ♦ Robert Elliot, gen mgr; Robert Haschke, gen sls mgr; Tony Hart, progmg dir; Nyki Wyatt, news dir; Justin McClure, chief of engrg.

Dumas

KDDD-FM— June 29, 1960: 95.3 mhz; 3 kw. 260 ft. TL: N35 51 51 W101 55 45. Stereo. Box 555 79029. Secondary address: 408 N. Dumas Ave. 79029. Phone: (806) 935-4141. Fax: (806) 935-3836. Licensee: North River Investments Inc. (acq 3-18-2005; with co-located AM). Network: ABC. Format: Oldies. News staff: one; News: 13 hrs wkly. Target aud: 25-65; farmers, community, factory. Spec prog: Farm 5 hrs, gospel 5 hrs wkly. ♦ Kandi Bray, gen mgr & gen sls mgr; Steve Bayless, opns mgr & progmg dir; Ali Allison, news dir; Stephen White, chief of engrg.

KDDD(AM)— May 1, 1948: 800 khz; 250 w-D. TL: N35 51 42 W101 55 50. E-mail: kddd@amaonline.com. Format: Country. Target aud: General.

Eagle Pass

*KEPI(FM)— May 13, 1995: 88.7 mhz; 1 kw. 180 ft. TL: N28 39 26 W100 25 00. Box 873, 2477 El Indio Hwy. 78853. Phone: (830) 757-0887. Fax: (830) 757-8950. E-mail: kepi@hcjb.org. Licensee: World Radio Network Inc. Format: Contemp Christian. ♦ Amado Rodriguez, stn mgr; Saulo Alonzo Rodriguez, progmg mgr; Gary Lawson, chief of engrg.

KEPS(AM)— August 1957: 1270 khz; 1 kw-D. TL: N28 43 45 W100 29 30. Box 1123 78852. Secondary address: 127 Kilowatt Dr. 78852. Phone: (830) 773-9247. Fax: (830) 773-9500. Licensee: Rhattigan Broadcasting (Texas) LP (group owner; acq 6-3-2004; grpsl). Format: Tejano,. Target aud: 18-49; middle income, Texas-born Hispanics. ♦ Rosa T. De La Garza, gen mgr; Rosa T. De La Garza, gen sls mgr; Jose Perez, progmg dir; Mario Martinez, news dir; Gary Graham, chief of engrg.

KINL(FM)—Co-owned with KEPS(AM). Nov 2, 1971: 92.7 mhz; 20 kw. 184 ft. TL: N28 43 57 W100 29 34. Stereo. Format: Oldies 60, 70, 80. ♦ Cesar Galindo, progmg dir.

*KEPX(FM)— Sept 9, 1994: 89.5 mhz; 52 kw. 256 ft. TL: N28 39 26 W100 25 00. Stereo. Box 873, 2477 El Indio Hwy. 78853. Secondary address: Box 3333, McAllen 78853. Phone: (830) 757-0895. Phone: (830) 758-0895. Fax: (830) 757-8950. E-mail: kepx@hcjb.org. Web Site: kepx.net. Licensee: World Radio Network Inc. Bryan Cave. Format: Sp, Christian. News: 3 hrs wkly. Target aud: Hispanic; Mexican. ♦ Amado Rodriguez, VP & stn mgr.

Eastland

KATX(FM)— Sept 1, 1986: 97.7 mhz; 3 kw. Ant 203 ft. TL: N32 23 47 W98 46 26. Stereo. 611 W. Commerce 76448. Phone: (254) 629-2621. Fax: (254) 629-8520. E-mail: radio@txol.net. Licensee: Partnership Broadcasting Inc. (acq 2-1-2000; with co-located AM). Format: Country, talk. News staff: one; News: 8 hrs wkly. Target aud: 25-54; adults. ♦ David Bacon, pres; Chuck Statler, exec VP.

KEAS(AM)—Co-owned with KATX(FM). August 1953: 1590 khz; 500 w-D. TL: N32 23 47 W98 46 26. Network: Westwood One. News staff: one; News: 8 hrs wkly. Target aud: 25-54. Spec prog: Gospel 5 hrs wkly.

Edinburg

KBFM(FM)— February 1972: 104.1 mhz; 100 kw. 990 ft. TL: N26 05 59 W97 50 16. Stereo. 901 E. Pike St., Weslaco 78596. Phone: (956) 973-9202. Fax: (956) 973-9355. E-mail: kbfmm@aol.com. Web Site: www.b104.net. Licensee: Capstar TX L.P. Group owner: Clear Channel Communications Inc. (acq 8-15-00; grpsl). Network: ABC FM Connection. Rep: Christal. Format: CHR. News staff: one. Target aud: 18-34; females. Spec prog: Community affrs. ♦ Danny Fletcher, VP & gen mgr; Billy Santiago, opns mgr; Cyndi Torres, rgnl sls mgr; Bobby Macias, mus dir; Ken Meek, chief of engrg.

*KOIR(FM)— Feb 5, 1983: 88.5 mhz; 3 kw. 285 ft. TL: N26 07 49 W98 10 51. Stereo. 4300 S. Business Hwy. 281 78539-9699. Phone: (956) 380-8100. Phone: (956) 380-3435. Fax: (956) 380-8156. E-mail: correo@radioesparanza.com. Licensee: Rio Grande Bible Institute Inc. Bryan Cave. Format: Relg, educ, Sp. Target aud: General. ♦ Gerardo Lorenzo, gen mgr & progmg dir; Jerry Jeske, chief of engrg.

KURV(AM)— October 1947: 710 khz; 1 kw-U, DA-2. TL: N26 19 43 W98 09 35. 2921 N. Closner 78539. Phone: (956) 383-2777. Fax: (956) 383-2570. E-mail: talk@kurv.com. Web Site: www.kurv.com. Licensee: BMP RGV License Co. L.P. Group owner: Border Media Partners LLC (acq 1-9-2004; $7.5 million. with KSOX(AM) Raymondville). Network: Network: CBS, ABC News/Talk. Gammon & Grange. Format: News/talk, sports. News staff: 2; News: 30 hrs wkly. Target aud: 35-64. Spec prog: Farm 10 hrs wkly. ♦ Lance Hawkins, VP & gen mgr; Jim Hearn, opns mgr; Jane Smith, sls dir; Fred Alfaro, mktg dir & prom dir; Jeff Koch, progmg dir; Tim Sullivan, news dir; Joe Espinosa, chief of engrg.

KVLY(FM)— 1974: 107.9 mhz; 100 kw. 765 ft. TL: N26 15 01 W97 55 21. Stereo. 801 Jackson Rd., McAllen 78501. Phone: (956) 661-6000. Fax: (956) 661-6082. Licensee: Entravision Holdings L.L.C. Group owner: Entravision Communications Corp. (acq 7-20-00; grpsl). Rep: Allied Radio Partners. Format: Adult contemp Spanish. Target aud: 25-54. ♦ Willie Rosales, gen mgr, gen sls mgr, stn mgr, opns mgr & gen sls mgr; Alex Duran, progmg dir; Lilly Lopez, mus dir; Shirley Kennedy, news dir; Sonny Cavazos, chief of engrg.

Edna

KGUL(FM)— Sept. 20, 1998: 96.1 mhz; 13 kw. Ant 456 ft. TL: N29 06 05 W96 27 19. 102 Jason Plaza #2, Victoria 77901. Phone: (361) 572-0105. Fax: (361) 579-4105. Web Site: www.texasthunderradio.net. Licensee: Fort Bend Broadcasting Co. Inc. Group owner: Fort Bend Broadcasting Co. (acq 1-21-00; grpsl). Format: Country. ♦ Ryan Henderson, gen mgr.

KTMR(AM)— July 28, 1980: 1130 khz; 10 kw-D, DA. TL: N29 01 40 W96 40 05. 1302 N. Shepherd Dr., Houston 77008. Phone: (713) 868-9137. Fax: (713) 868-9631. E-mail: docarango@houston.rr.com. Licensee: SIGA Broadcasting Corp. (group owner); acq 5-4-99;

$333,750). Rep: Caballero. Format: Tejano. Spec prog: Black 3 hrs, Sp 12 hrs wkly. ♦ Gabriel Arango, gen mgr.

El Campo

KIOX-FM— September 1968: 96.9 mhz; 100 kw. 981 ft. TL: N29 05 44 W96 27 25. (CP: TL: N28 53 35 W96 21 40). 3000 Bering Dr., Houston 77057. Web Site: www.laraza.fm. Licensee: Liberman Broadcasting of Houston License Corp. Group owner: Liberman Broadcasting Inc. (acq 8-22-02; $3.15 million. with KXGJ(FM) Bay City). Pepper & Corazzini. Format: Hot country. Target aud: 18-49; college, plant workers, business & agriculture. ♦ Cheryl Kirk, gen mgr; Tim Michaels, opns mgr.

KULP(AM)— 1948: 1390 khz; 500 w-D, 180 w-N. TL: N29 12 34 W96 15 50. Box 390 77437. Secondary address: 515 E. Jackson St. 77437. Phone: (979) 543-3303. Fax: (979) 543-1546. E-mail: kulp@kulpradio.com. Web Site: www.kulpradio.com. Licensee: Wharton County Radio Inc. (acq 5-2-00; $240,000). Format: Classic country, news/talk, sports. News staff: 2; News: 5 hrs wkly. Target aud: 25 plus. Spec prog: Sp 14 hrs, Czech 5 hrs wkly. ♦ Bob Buckalew, pres & VP; Mike Wenglar, CFO & engrg dir; Jerry Aulds, gen mgr & sls VP; Stephen Zetsche, opns VP; Clint Robinson, opns mgr, mus dir & chief of engrg; Kate Manrriquez, prom mgr & pub affrs dir; Bob Nason, news dir.

El Paso

KAMA(AM)— July 13, 1972: . Stn currently dark 750 khz; 10 kw-D, 1 kw-N, DA-1. TL: N31 46 21 W106 16 56. South Bldg. 300, 2211 E. Missouri 79903. Phone: (915) 544-9797. Fax: (915) 544-1247. Web Site: www.netmio.com. Licensee: Tichenor Media System Inc. Group owner: Univision Radio (acq 9-22-2003; grpsl). Format: Sp, oldies. News staff: one; News: 8 hrs wkly. Target aud: 25-54; women. ♦ MacHenry Tichenor Jr., pres; Domingo Lopez, gen mgr; Margie LaFluer, rgnl sls mgr; Pedro Skaggs, progmg dir; Karla Hernandez, news dir; Andrew Kiska, chief of engrg.

KBNA(AM)— June 1947: 920 khz; 1 kw-D, 360 w-N, DA-N. TL: N31 45 41 W106 26 14. 2211 E. Missouri, Suite 5300 79903. Phone: (915) 544-9797. Fax: (915) 544-1247. Web Site: www.netmio.com. Licensee: Tichenor License Corp. Group owner: Univision Radio (acq 9-22-2003; grpsl). Rep: Katz Hispanic. Format: Sp. ♦ MacHenry Tichenor Jr., pres; Domingo Lopez, gen mgr; Margie LaFluer, gen sls mgr; Leo Lugo, prom mgr; Mario Castillo, progmg dir; Karla Hernandez, news dir; Andrew Kiska, chief of engrg.

KBNA-FM— Aug 15, 1969: 97.5 mhz; 100 kw horiz, 48 kw vert. 1,088 ft. TL: N31 47 34 W106 28 47. Stereo. Web Site: www.netmio.com. Rep: Katz Hispanic. ♦ Mario Castillo, progmg mgr.

KELP(AM)— Apr 10, 1959: 1590 khz; 5 kw-D, 800 w-N. TL: N31 46 12 W106 25 37. (CP: TL: N31 44 38 W106 23 45). Stereo. 6900 Commerce 79915. Phone: (915) 779-0016. Fax: (915) 779-6641. E-mail: info@kelppradio.com. Web Site: www.kelpradio.com. Licensee: McClatchey Broadcasting. (acq 2-14-84; $590,000; 1-30-84). Network: Salem Radio Network. Format: Christian talk, information. Target aud: 25-54; Christian community of El Paso, Las Cruces, Northern Mexico. Spec prog: Spanish 12 hrs wkkly. ♦ Arnold McClatchey, pres; Craig Rice, gen mgr & progmg; Joe Olivas, gen sls mgr & sls.

KHEY(AM)— Aug 22, 1929: 1380 khz; 5 kw-D, 500 w-N. TL: N31 45 42 W106 24 36. 4045 N. Mesa 79902. Phone: (915) 351-5400. Fax: (915) 351-3102. Web Site: www.khey1380.com. Licensee: CCB Texas Licenses L.P. Group owner: Clear Channel Communications Inc. (acq 5-29-98; $10.5 million. with co-located AM). Rep: Clear Channel. Format: Sports. Target aud: General. ♦ Bill Struck, gen mgr; Karen Daniels-Pearson, gen sls mgr; Chris Lucy, mktg dir; Frank Rodriquez, prom dir; Paul Whittler, progmg dir & pub affrs dir; Enrique Lopez, chief of engrg.

KTSM-FM—Co-owned with KHEY(AM). June 11, 1962: 99.9 mhz; 87 kw. 1,820 ft. TL: N31 48 19 W106 28 57. Stereo. Network: Network: CBS, ABC News/Talk. Format: Adult contemp. ♦ Bill Clifton Tole, progmg dir; Sam Cassiano, mus dir; Melissa Kerr, pub affrs dir; Enrique Lopez, engrg dir.

KHEY-FM—Listing follows KTSM(AM).

KHRO(AM)— Feb 11, 2004: 1650 khz; 8.5 kw-D, 850 w-N. TL: N31 45 13 W106 24 58. 5426 N. Mesa St. 79912-5421. Phone: (915) 581-1126. Fax: (915) 532-4970. Licensee: Entravision Holdings LLC. Group owner: Entravision Communications Corp. Format: Classic country. ♦David Candelaria, gen mgr; Phil Gabbard, sls dir; Jake Fritz, prom dir; Sergeant Preston, opns mgr & progmg dir; Jim Lotspeich, chief of engrg.

KINT-FM— July 4, 1975: 93.9 mhz; 96.2 kw. 1,420 ft. TL: N31 47 36 W106 28 50. 5426 N. Mesa St. 79912-5421. Phone: (915) 581-1126. Fax: (915) 585-4611. Licensee: Entravision Communications Co. L.L.C. Group owner: Entravision Communications Co. L.L.C. (acq 6-4-97; grpsl). Rep: Lotus Entravision Reps LLC. Format: Sp, adult contemp. News: 4 hrs wkly. Target aud: 25-54. ♦David Candelaria, gen mgr; Phil Gabbaard, gen sls mgr; Yvonne Orona, natl sls mgr; Abel Rodriguez, mktg VP & pub affrs dir; Maria Galnares, prom mgr; Norma Munoz, progmg dir; Javier Vargas, mus dir; Alfredo Durand, chief of engrg.

KSVE(AM)—Co-owned with KINT-FM. June 1958: 1150 khz; 5 kw-D, 380 w-N. TL: N31 45 15 W106 25 11. Stereo. Format: Oldies, Sp. Target aud: 18-54.

KLAQ(FM)—Listing follows KROD(AM).

KOFX(FM)— June 6, 1978: 92.3 mhz; 100 kw. 1,860 ft. TL: N31 48 55 W106 29 20. Stereo. 5426 N. Mesa 79912. Phone: (915) 581-1126. Fax: (915) 532-4970. Web Site: www.foxoldies.com. Licensee: Entravision Holdings L.L.C. Group owner: Entravision Communications Co. L.L.C. (acq 10-19-99). Format: Oldies. News staff: 2. Target aud: 25-54; upscale. ♦David Candelaria, gen mgr; Phil Gabbard, opns dir & gen sls mgr; Mike Preston, prom dir; Jim Lotspeich, chief of engrg.

KPAS(FM)—See Fabens

KPRR(FM)— Dec 5, 1969: 102.1 mhz; 100 kw horiz, 66 kw vert. 1,289 ft. TL: N31 47 34 W106 28 47. Stereo. 4045 N. Mesa 79902. Phone: (915) 351-5400. Fax: (915) 351-3102. Web Site: www.kprr.com. Licensee: CCB Texas Licenses L.P. Group owner: Clear Channel Communications Inc. (acq 5-16-96; grpsl). Rep: Clear Channel. Format: CHR. Target aud: 18-34. ♦L. Lowry Mays, CEO, chmn & pres; Randall T. Mays, CFO; Bill Struck, VP & gen mgr; Michelle Haston, gen sls mgr; Christopher Lucy, mktg dir; Frank Rodriguez, prom dir; Bobby Ramos, progmg dir; Patti Diaz, news dir; Andrea Thomas, pub affrs dir; Enriquez Lopez, chief of engrg.

KROD(AM)— June 1, 1940: 600 khz; 5 kw-U, DA-N. TL: N31 54 56 W106 23 33. 4150 Pinnacle 79902. Phone: (915) 544-9550. Fax: (915) 532-6342. Web Site: www.krod.com. Licensee: Regent Broadcasting of El Paso Inc. Group owner: Regent Communications Inc. (acq 12-1-99; grpsl). Rep: D & R Radio. Format: News/talk, sports. News staff: one; News: 3 hrs wkly. Target aud: 25-54; adult listeners who grew up on the roots of rock and roll. Spec prog: Dallas Cowboys football, UTEP sports. ♦Brad Dubow, gen mgr; Steve Kaplowitz, progmg dir; Ron Haney, chief of engrg.

KLAQ(FM)—Co-owned with KROD(AM). Oct 1, 1978: 95.5 mhz; 88 kw. 1,390 ft. TL: N31 47 47 W106 28 55. Stereo. Web Site: www.klaq.com. Format: Rock/AOR. Target aud: 18-49; adults who grew up on FM rock and roll. ♦Brad Dubow, gen mgr; Mike Ramey, progmg dir; Ron Haney, chief of engrg.

KSII(FM)— Dec 30, 1975: 93.1 mhz; 100 kw. 1,422 ft. TL: N31 47 34 W106 28 47. Stereo. 4150 Pinnacle, Suite 120 79902. Phone: (915) 544-9300. Fax: (915) 544-9536. Web Site: www.ksiiinfo.com. Licensee: Regent Broadcasting of El Paso Inc. Group owner: Regent Communications Inc. (acq 12-1-99; grpsl). Wilmer, Cutler & Pickering. Format: Hot adult contemp. News staff: one; News: 2 hrs wkly. Target aud: 25-54; 60% male, 40% female. ♦Brad Dubow, gen mgr; Kelly Calvillo, gen sls mgr; Chris Elliot, progmg dir; Diana Rivas, pub affrs dir; Robert King, chief of engrg.

***KTEP(FM)**— Sept 14, 1950: 88.5 mhz; 94 kw. 731 ft. TL: N31 47 17 W106 28 46. Stereo. 500 W. University Ave. 79968-0556. Phone: (915) 747-5152. Phone: (915) 880-5837. Fax: (915) 747-5641. E-mail: ktep@utep.edu. Web Site: www.ktep.org. Licensee: University of Texas at El Paso. Network: Network: PRI, NPR. Format: Class, jazz, news. News staff: one; News: 32 hrs wkly. Target aud: 35 plus; college educated, upper-income. Spec prog: Sp 2 hrs, gospel 4 hrs, folk 3 hrs wkly. ♦Dennis Woo, opns dir & mus dir; Joe Torres, dev dir & prom dir; Patrick J. Piotrowaski, gen mgr & progmg VP; Louie Saenz, news dir; Norbert Miles, chief of engrg.

KTSM(AM)— 1947: 690 khz; 10 kw-U, DA-2. TL: N31 58 11 W106 21 15. Stereo. 4045 N. Mesa 79902. Phone: (915) 351-5400. Fax: (915) 351-3102. Web Site: www.ktsmradio.com. Licensee: CCB Texas Licenses L.P. Group owner: Clear Channel Communications Inc. (acq 5-16-96; grpsl). Network: ABC Information & Entertainment. Rep: Clear Channel. Format: News/talk. Target aud: 25-54; men. Spec prog: Relg 3 hrs, radio health journal one hr, El Paso public forum one hr wkly. ♦L. Lowry Mays, CEO, chmn & pres; Randall T. May, CFO; Bill Struck, VP & gen mgr; Karen Daniels-Pearson, gen sls mgr; Christopher Lucy, mktg dir; Frank Rodriquez, prom dir; Tom Connelly, progmg mgr; Melissa Kerr, news dir; Michael Calderon, pub affrs dir; Enrique Lopez, chief of engrg.

KHEY-FM—Co-owned with KTSM(AM). Aug 1, 1974: 96.3 mhz; 100 kw. 1,390 ft. TL: N31 47 47 W106 28 55. Stereo. Web Site: www.khey.com. Network: ABC. Format: Country. Target aud: 25-54. ♦Michelle Haston, sls dir; Steve Gramzay, progmg dir; Bobby Gutierrez, news dir & pub affrs dir; Enrique Lopez, engrg dir.

***KVER(FM)**— Jan 1, 1993: 91.1 mhz; 510 w. 1,118 ft. TL: N31 47 34 W106 28 47. Stereo. Box 12008 79913-0008. Phone: (915) 544-9190. E-mail: kver91fm@aol.com. Licensee: World Network Radio Inc. (group owner) Format: Sp, relg, educ. Hispanic. ♦Alci Rengifo, stn mgr.

KVIV(AM)— Dec 3, 1949: 1340 khz; 1 kw-U. TL: N31 46 24 W106 24 52. 4900 Montana Ave. 79903. Phone: (915) 565-2999. Fax: (915) 562-3156. E-mail: radiovictoria@mail.com. Web Site: www.kviv.com. Licensee: Spanish Christian Broadcast of El Paso Inc. (acq 6-95; $550,000). Dow, Lohnes & Albertson. Format: Sp, relg. Target aud: Mexican-American. ♦Alfonso Cabrera, pres & gen mgr; Jesus Cruz, progmg dir.

***KXCR(FM)**— May 1, 1985: 89.5 mhz; 175 w. Ant 1,092 ft. TL: N31 47 34 W106 28 47. 5700 West Oaks Blvd., Rocklin, CA 95765. Phone: (916) 251-1600. Fax: (916) 251-1650. E-mail: klove@klove.com. Licensee: Educational Media Foundation. Group owner: EMF Broadcasting (acq 11-18-02; $1 million). Network: K-Love. Shaw Pittman. Format: Contemp Christian music. News staff: 3. Target aud: 25-44. ♦Richard Jenkins, pres; Mike Novak, VP & progmg dir; Lloyd Parker, gen mgr; Ed Lenane, opns dir & news dir; Keith Whipple, dev dir; Eric Allen, natl sls mgr; Felipe Agvillar, rgnl sls mgr; Chris Joyce, prom dir; David Pierce, progmg mgr; Jon Rivers, mus dir; Sam Wallington, engrg dir.

KXPL(AM)— Sept 16, 1985: 1060 khz; 10 kw-D. TL: N31 48 41 W106 31 53. 2211 E. Missouri Ave., E-237 79903-3837. Phone: (915) 587-8822. Fax: (915) 587-8602. E-mail: kxpl1060am@yahoo.com. Licensee: New Radio System Inc. (acq 7-21-2004). Format: Sp info/news. ♦Maria Elena Lazo, gen mgr; Jose Camacho, progmg dir; Paul Gregg, chief of engrg.

KYSE(FM)— Nov 29, 1958: 94.7 mhz; 97 kw horiz, 65 kw vert. Ant 1,191 ft. TL: N31 47 34 W106 28 47. Stereo. 5426 N. Mesa 79902. Phone: (915) 581-1126. Fax: (915) 532-4970. Web Site: www.superestrella947.com. Licensee: Entravision Holdings L.L.C. Group owner: Entravision Communications Co. L.L.C. (acq 10-19-99). Rep: Lotus Entravision Reps LLC. Format: Sp. Target aud: 18-34. ♦David Candelaria, gen mgr; Phil Gabbard, opns dir.

Electra

***KOLI(FM)**— January 1998: 94.9 mhz; 50 kw. 492 ft. TL: N34 05 01 W98 59 29. 4302 Callfield Rd., Wichita Falls 76308. Phone: (940) 691-2311. Fax: (940) 696-2255. Web Site: www.culumus.com. Licensee: Cumulus Licensing Corp. Group owner: Cumulus Media Inc. (acq 8-10-99; $238,400). Format: Classic Country. ♦Lindy Parr, gen mgr; Brent Warner, opns mgr & progmg dir; Andrea Lewis, gen sls mgr; Jim Russell, news dir; Jeff Chan, chief of engrg.

Elgin

KKLB(FM)— Aug 14, 1992: 92.5 mhz; 1.6 kw. 449 ft. TL: N30 19 00 W97 20 22. 7524 N. Lamar Blvd., Suite 200, Austin 78752. Phone: (512) 416-1100. Fax: (512) 416-8205. Licensee: BMP Austin License Company L.P. (acq 2-10-2005; grpsl). Network: CNN Radio. Rep: Caballero. Bechtel & Cole. Format: Sp, Tejano. ♦Pedro Gasc, gen mgr; Andrew Pulido, progmg mgr.

Fabens

KPAS(FM)— Mar 24, 1979: 103.1 mhz; 3 kw. 300 ft. TL: N31 35 42 W106 11 58. Stereo. Box 371010, El Paso 79937. Phone: (915) 851-3382. Licensee: Algie A. Felder. (acq 6-27-86; 5-12-86). Network: USA. Format: Christian. News: 6 hrs wkly. ♦Algie A. Felder, pres & gen mgr.

Fairfield

KNES(FM)— Dec 1, 1983: 99.1 mhz; 940 w. 500 ft. TL: N31 41 52 W96 09 44. Stereo. Box 347, 627 W. Commerce 75840. Phone: (903) 389-5637. Fax: (903) 389-7172. Web Site: www.knesfm.com. Licensee: J & J Communications Inc. (acq 11-19-90; $209,000; 12-10-90). Network: Jones Radio Networks. Rep: Riley. Format: Country. News staff: one; News: 6 hrs wkly. Target aud: General. Spec prog: Farm 3 hrs, talk 15 hrs, Black 3 hrs, gospel 3 hrs wkly. ♦Joe Reid, gen mgr & rgnl sls mgr; Buzz Russell, progmg dir; Lester Leediker, chief of engrg.

Falfurrias

KDFM(FM)—Not on air, target date: unknown: 103.3 mhz; 3 kw. 328 ft. TL: N27 15 28 W98 07 07. Box 252, McAllen 78505. Phone: (956) 686-6382. Phone: (956) 686-2992. Fax: (956) 686-2999. Licensee: La Radio Cristiana Network Inc. Format: Sp.

KLDS(AM)— Jan 1, 1953: 1260 khz; 500 w-D, 330 w-N. TL: N27 14 11 W98 10 22. Box 401 78355. Secondary address: 215 W. Adam St. 78355. Phone: (361) 325-1212. Fax: (361) 325-1212. Licensee: The Evangelistic Worship Center (acq 10-27-97; $75,000). Baraff, Koerner & Olender. Format: Christian. Target aud: General. ♦Timothy Trevino, gen mgr & progmg dir; Steve Cantu, chief of engrg.

KPSO-FM— Nov 1, 1983: 106.3 mhz; 6 kw. Ant 184 ft. TL: N27 14 11 W98 10 22. Stereo. 304 E. Rice St. 78355-3624. Phone: (361) 325-2112. Fax: (361) 325-2112. E-mail: kpso@awesomenet.net. Licensee: Brooks Broadcasting Corp. Koerner & Olender. Format: Tejano (Sp), country. News: 15 hrs wkly. Target aud: All groups. ♦Raymond O. Creely, gen mgr & chief of engrg; Steve Cantu, exec VP & gen sls mgr.

Fannett

***KZFT(FM)**— Oct 31, 2003: 90.5 mhz; 35 kw vert. Ant 361 ft. TL: N29 53 33 W94 08 06. Drawer 3206, Tupelo, MS 38803. Phone: (662) 844-8888. Fax: (662) 842-6791. Licensee: American Family Association. Group owner: American Family Radio. Format: Christian. ♦Marvin Sanders, gen mgr.

Farmersville

KFCD(AM)— November 1947: 990 khz; 7 kw-D, 920 w-N, DA-2. TL: N33 07 01 W96 16 47. Stereo. Box 12345, Dallas 75225. Phone: (972) 354-1990. Fax: (972) 354-0820. Licensee: DFW Radio License LLC (acq 2-5-2004; with KHSE(AM) Wylie). Network: CNN Radio. Format: Talk. Target aud: 35 plus; men. ♦Dave Schum, pres & chief of engrg; Jerry Overton, gen mgr; Dave Marcum, opns mgr, progmg mgr & pub affrs dir; Ed Wodka, rgnl sls mgr & adv mgr.

KXEZ(FM)— Sept 1, 1998: 92.1 mhz; 2.7 kw. 492 ft. TL: N33 16 31 W96 22 02. Stereo. Box 940670, Plano 75094. Phone: (903) 482-6750. Phone: (972) 396-1640. Fax: (972) 396-1643. E-mail: josh@khiy.com. Web Site: www.kxezfm.com. Licensee: Metro Broadcasters-Texas Inc. (acq 12-3-98). Network: Jones Radio Networks. Format: Music of your life. Target aud: 35-64; affluent, white collar, middle to upper income listeners. ♦Ken Jones, CEO, pres, gen mgr & chief of engrg; Glenda Jones, CFO; Jack Bishop, opns dir & pub affrs dir; Joshua Jones, sls dir, gen sls mgr, mktg VP, mktg dir & prom dir; Hal Mayfield, news dir; Ron Eudaly, engrg dir.

Farwell

KICA-FM— Sept 15, 1984: 98.3 mhz; 50 kw. Ant 223 ft. TL: N34 23 22 W103 10 27. (CP: 100 kw, ant 384 ft. TL: N34 29 36 W103 23 46). Stereo. 1000 Sycamore St., Clovis, NM 88101. Phone: (505) 762-6200. Fax: (505) 762-8800. Licensee: Broadcast Entertainment Corporation. (group owner; acq 10-27-99; grpsl). Format: World class rock. News staff: one; News: 3 hrs wkly. Target aud: 18-49. ♦Rick Keefer, CEO; Rick Kiefer, opns dir, engrg dir & chief of engrg; Ron Pierson, pres, gen mgr & gen sls mgr; Joe Daniels, progmg dir; Gena Wilkerson, mus dir & news dir.

Broadcasting & Cable Yearbook 2006

D-484

Stations in the U.S. — Texas

Developers & Brokers of Radio Properties
contact American Media Services at our suite:
Philadelphia Marriott Downtown
215-625-2900
843-972-2200
americanmediaservices.com
Charleston, SC
Dallas, TX · Chicago, Il · Austin, TX
American Media Services, LLC

KIJN(AM)— Apr 17, 1958: 1060 khz; 10 kw-D, DA. TL: N34 23 14 W103 01 51. Box 458 79325. Phone: (806) 481-3318. Fax: (806) 481-3835. E-mail: therock@kijn.net. Web Site: www.kijn.com. Licensee: Metropolitan Radio Group Inc. (group owner; acq 9-97; with co-located FM). Format: Christian music, relg. Target aud: General. Spec prog: Farm 3 hrs wkly. ♦ Rick Sanchez, gen mgr & progmg dir; Mike Richards, chief of engrg.

KIJN-FM— Aug 1, 1985: 92.3 mhz; 100 kw. Ant 354 ft. TL: N34 32 26 W102 47 56. Stereo. Format: Christian music, relg.

KMUL(AM)— July 6, 1956: 830 khz; 1.1 kw-D, 10 w-N. TL: N34 29 42 W103 23 39. Box 486, Muleshoe 79347. Secondary address: 600 W. 8th St., Muleshoe 79347. Phone: (806) 272-4273. Phone: (806) 272-4087. Fax: (806) 272-5067. Licensee: Broadcast Entertainment Corp. (group owner; acq 10-27-99; grpsl). Format: Sp. Spec prog: Farm 3 hrs wkly. ♦ Noe Anzaldua, gen mgr & progmg dir; Martha Alvarado, progmg dir; Rick Keefer, chief of engrg.

Ferris

KDFT(AM)— July 13, 1988: 540 khz; 1 kw-D, 249 w-N, DA-2. TL: N32 30 47 W96 34 28 (D), N32 30 52 W96 34 26 (N). 3304 W. Camp Wisdom, Suite 100, Dallas 75237. Phone: (972) 572-1540. Licensee: Way Broadcasting Licensee LLC (acq 4-19-2000; grpsl). Format: Sp Christian. Target aud: 25-59; Sp. ♦ Arthur Liu, pres; Francisco Martinez, CFO; James Glogowski, VP; Ted Sauceman, gen mgr.

Floresville

KTFM(FM)— June 15, 1977: 94.1 mhz; 40 kw. 548 ft. TL: N29 11 03 W98 30 49. Stereo. 7800 N.W. I-10, Suite 330, San Antonio 78230. Phone: (210) 340-1234. Fax: (210) 340-1775. Licensee: BMP San Antonio License Co. L.P. Group owner: Border Media Partners LLC (acq 12-23-2003; $24.4 million. with KSAH(AM) Universal City). Rep: Caballero. Bechtel &. Cole. Format: Mexican rgnl. News staff: one; News: 15 hrs wkly. Target aud: 18-49. ♦ Raul Rodriguez, gen mgr; Peggy McCormack, gen sls mgr; Lupe Contreras, prom dir; Manny Herrera, progmg dir; Minnie Ochoa, pub affrs dir; Brett Hudkins, chief of engrg.

*****KWCB(FM)**— 1993: 89.7 mhz; 9 kw. 138 ft. TL: N29 13 55 W98 03 05. 1905 10th St. 78114. Phone: (830) 393-6116. Fax: (830) 393-3817. E-mail: kwcb89fm@yahoo.com. Licensee: Wilson County Education Foundation Inc. Format: Christian/gospel, newtalk. Target aud: 35-55. ♦ Alfonso B. Gonzalez, pres; Cissy Gonzalez, gen mgr.

Flower Mound

KTYS(FM)— Apr 1, 1969: 96.7 mhz; 92 kw. 2,034 ft. TL: N33 26 13 W97 29 05. Stereo. 2221 E. Lomar Blvd., Suite 400, Arlington 76006. Secondary address: 3405 Loy Lake Rd. 76006. Phone: (817) 695-3500. Fax: (817) 695-3516. Web Site: www.967thetwister.com. Licensee: WBAP-KSCS Operating Ltd. Group owner: ABC Inc. (acq 9-30-98; $23 million). Network: ABC. Rep: McGavren Guild. Format: Country. News staff: one; News: 6 hrs wkly. Target aud: 18-34; adults. ♦ Keri Littlefield, gen mgr; David Klement, gen sls mgr; Greg Heitzman, natl sls mgr; Robert Shiflet, mktg mgr; Cari Swartzell, prom dir; Gayle Potect, progmg dir; Chris Huff, mus dir; Neal Peden, chief of engrg.

Floydada

KFLP(AM)— 1951: 900 khz; 250 w-D. TL: N33 58 20 W101 21 00. Box 658 79235. Phone: (806) 983-5704. Fax: (806) 983-5705. E-mail: kflp@kflp.net. Web Site: www.kflp.net. Licensee: Anthony L. Ricketts. (acq 8-4-99; with co-located FM). Target aud: General; contemp country mus lovers. Spec prog: Farm news, market reports, college football, Sunday worship. ♦ Tony St. James, gen mgr & progmg dir.

KFLP-FM— Apr 1, 1985: 95.3 mhz; 3 kw. 240 ft. TL: N33 58 07 W101 21 13. Stereo. Web Site: www.kflp.net.

Fort Stockton

KFST(AM)— May 8, 1954: 860 khz; 250 w-U. TL: N30 52 37 W102 53 30. 954 S US Hwy. 385 79735. Phone: (432) 336-2228. Phone: (432) 336-5834. Fax: (432) 336-5834. E-mail: kfst@ftstockton.net. Licensee: Fort Stockton Radio Co Inc. (acq 1-1-86). Network: ABC Information & Entertainment. Format: Adult contemp, relg. News staff: 2; News: 6 hrs wkly. Target aud: General. ♦ Ken Ripley, gen mgr, dev dir, progmg dir & chief of engrg.

KFST-FM— November 1974: 94.3 mhz; 3 kw. 236 ft. TL: N30 52 37 W102 53 30. Stereo. Format: Country, Sp.

Fort Worth

KBFB(FM)—See Dallas

KDGE(FM)— Apr 10, 1962: 102.1 mhz; 100 kw. Ant 1,447 ft. TL: N32 34 54 W96 58 32. Stereo. 14001 N. Dallas Pkwy., Suite 300, Addison 75001. Phone: (214) 866-8000. Licensee: Capstar TX L.P. Group owner: Clear Channel Communications Inc. (acq 8-30-00; grpsl). Rep: CBS Radio. Format: Alternative rock. News staff: one; News: 5 hrs wkly. Target aud: 20-44. ♦ Brenda Adriance, gen mgr; John Roberts, opns mgr.

KDMX(FM)—See Dallas

KDXX(FM)—See Benbrook

KEGL(FM)— April 1959: 97.1 mhz; 99 kw. Ant 1,666 ft. TL: N32 35 19 W96 58 05. Stereo. 14001 N. Dallas Pkwy., Suite 300, Dallas 75240. Phone: (214) 866-8000. Licensee: Citicasters Licenses L.P. Group owner: Clear Channel Communications Inc. (acq 5-4-99; grpsl). Format: Sp. ♦ Brenda Adriance, gen mgr; John Roberts, opns mgr.

KFJZ(AM)— Feb 15, 1947: 870 khz; 500 w-D. TL: N32 45 42 W97 18 49. 521 E. Bolt St. 76110. Phone: (817) 923-3424. Fax: (817) 923-3451. E-mail: sarita@radioluz.com. Licensee: BMP DFW License Co. L.P. (acq 3-11-2005; $2.5 million). Format: Sp. ♦ Bob Prouse, gen mgr.

KFLC(AM)— 1922: 1270 khz; 5 kw-U. TL: N32 43 36 W97 11 30. Stereo. 7700 Carpenter Fwy., Dallas 75247. Phone: (214) 525-0400. Fax: (214) 631-1196. Web Site: www.univision.com. Licensee: KESS-AM License Corp. Group owner: Univision Radio (acq 9-22-2003; grpsl). Rep: Katz Hispanic. Format: Sp, news/talk, sports. News staff: 2; News: 11 hrs wkly. Target aud: 25-54. ♦ Frank Carter, gen mgr; Andy Lockridge, opns dir; Cipriano Robles, sls dir; Ivonne Flaherty, gen sls mgr; Karen Hocking, natl sls mgr; Oscar Espinosa, prom dir; Herminio (Chayan) Ortuno, progmg dir; Myrna Vera, news dir; Patrick Parks, engrg mgr & chief of engrg.

KFXR(AM)—See Dallas

KHVN(AM)— Dec 6, 1946: 970 khz; 1 kw-D, 270 w-N. TL: N32 47 56 W97 17 43. 5787 S. Hampton Rd., Dallas 75232. Phone: (214) 331-5486. Fax: (214) 331-1908. E-mail: traffic@khvnam.com. Web Site: www.khvnam.com. Licensee: Mortenson Broadcasting Co. of Texas Inc. (group owner; acq 5-31-2002; $4.5 million. with KNAX(AM) Fort Worth). Network: ABC Daytime Direction. Rep: Interep. Format: Gospel. News staff: one; News: 10 hrs wkly. Target aud: 25-54. ♦ Jack Mortenson, CEO & VP; Dion Mortenson, gen mgr.

KJKK(FM)—See Dallas

KKDA-FM—See Dallas

KKGM(AM)— 2002: 1630 khz; 10 kw-D, 1 kw-N. TL: N32 47 56 W97 17 43. (CP: TL: N32 48 35 W97 07 24). 5787 S. Hampton Rd., Suite 108, Dallas 75232. Phone: (214) 337-5700. Fax: (214) 337-5707. E-mail: traffic@kkgmam.com. Web Site: www.kkgmam.com. Licensee: Mortenson Broadcasting Co. of Texas Inc. (group owner; acq 5-31-2002; with KHVN(AM) Fort Worth). Format: Southern gospel,

ministry, sports. Target aud: 30-64. ♦ Lon Sosh, gen mgr; Jack Davis, progmg dir; Mike Price, chief of engrg.

KLIF(AM)—See Dallas

KLLI(FM)—See Dallas

KLNO(FM)— Dec 24, 1964: 94.1 mhz; 100 kw. Ant 1,585 ft. TL: N32 35 22 W96 58 10. Stereo. 7700 Carpenter Hwy., Dallas 75247. Phone: (214) 525-0400. Fax: (214) 525-0473. Fax: (214) 631-1196 (sales). Licensee: HBC License Corp. Group owner: Univision Radio (acq 9-22-2003; grpsl). Network: ABC. Rep: Katz Hispanic. Format: Mexican regional. ♦ Frank Carter, gen mgr; Andy Lockridge, opns dir; Cipriane Robles, sls dir; Ivonne Flaherty, gen sls mgr; Karen Hecking, natl sls mgr; Oscar Espinosa, prom dir; Herminio (Chayan) Ortuno, progmg dir; Patrick Parks, chief of engrg.

KLTY(FM)—See Dallas

KLUV-FM—See Dallas

KOAI(FM)— Feb 8, 1965: 107.5 mhz; 25 kw. 1,647 ft. TL: N32 35 07 W96 58 06. (CP: 23 kw, ant 1,670 ft. TL: N32 35 05 W96 57 46). Stereo. 7901 Carpenter Fwy., Dallas 75247. Phone: (214) 526-9870. Fax: (214) 905-5052. Licensee: Texas Infinity Broadcasting L.P. Group owner: CBS Radio (acq 6-26-96; grpsl). Format: Smooth Jazz. Target aud: 25-54. ♦ Julie Davis, CEO; Mel Karmazin, pres; David Henry, gen mgr; Rick Frisch, gen sls mgr; Dave Dillon, natl sls mgr; Liz Balon, prom dir; Kurt Johnson, progmg dir; Mark Sanford, mus dir; Bill Taylor, news dir & chief of engrg; Vance Henley, engrg mgr.

KPLX(FM)— Dec 15, 1962: 99.5 mhz; 100 kw. 1,680 ft. TL: N32 34 54 W96 58 32. Stereo. 3500 Maple at Turtle Creek, Suite 1600, Dallas 75219. Phone: (214) 526-2400. Fax: (214) 520-4343. Web Site: www.995thewolf.com. Licensee: KPLX Lico Inc. Group owner: Susquehanna Radio Corp. (acq 1974). Format: Country. News staff: one; News: 4 hrs wkly. Target aud: 25-54; loyal listeners throughout the day.David E. Kennedy, COO & pres; Dan Halyburton, sr VP; Dan Bennett, VP; Lon A. Bason, gen mgr; Jim Quirk, sls dir; Jami Williams, natl sls mgr; Sharon Brown, mktg dir; Callie Hoch, mktg mgr; Marci Parrish, prom dir; Hank McMonigle, adv dir; Cindy Jones, adv mgr; Paul Williams, progmg dir; Cody Alan, mus dir; Chris Sommer, pub affrs dir; Rob Chickering, engrg mgr; Hue Beavers, chief of engrg

KRLD(AM)—See Dallas

KRVA(AM)—See Dallas

KSCS(FM)—Listing follows WBAP(AM).

KSKY(AM)—See Dallas

*****KTCU-FM**— Oct 6, 1964: 88.7 mhz; 3 kw. 320 ft. TL: N32 42 40 W97 22 00. Stereo. Box 298020, Moudy Bldg., Texas Christian Univ. 76129. Phone: (817) 257-7631. Phone: (817) 257-7634. Fax: (817) 257-7637. E-mail: ktcu@tcu.edu. Web Site: www.ktcu.tcu.edu. Licensee: Board of Trustees Texas Christian University. Format: Rock, class, jazz. ♦ JoAnna Woodell, gen mgr.

KZPS(FM)—See Dallas

WBAP(AM)— May 2, 1922: 820 khz; 50 kw-U. TL: N32 36 38 W97 10 00. Stereo. 2221 E. Lamar, Suite 300, Arlington 76006. Phone: (817) 695-1820. Fax: (817) 695-0014. Web Site: www.wbap.com. Licensee: WBAP-KSCS Operating Ltd. Group owner: ABC Inc. (acq 1974). Network: ABC Information & Entertainment. Rep: ABC Radio Sales. Format: News/talk. News staff: 7; News: 37 hrs wkly. Target aud: 25-54. Spec prog: Dallas Stars, farm 6 hrs wkly. ♦ Pete Dits, gen mgr & gen sls mgr; Stephanie Calahan, gen sls mgr; Bob Shomper, progmg dir; Neal Reden, chief of engrg.

KSCS(FM)—Co-owned with WBAP(AM). Mar 8, 1949: 96.3 mhz; 99 kw. 1,610 ft. TL: N32 35 15 W96 57 59. Stereo. Phone: (817) 640-1963. Fax: (817) 640-7065. Web Site: www.kscs.com. Rep: ABC

Broadcasting & Cable Yearbook 2006

Texas   **Directory of Radio**

Radio Sales. Format: Country. ♦ Greg Heitzman, natl sls mgr; Robert Shiflet, mktg dir; Ted Stecker, progmg dir; Rick Hadley, news dir.

Franklin

KZTR(FM)— Nov 7, 1994: 101.9 mhz; 25 kw. Ant 328 ft. TL: N30 56 04 W96 26 15. Box 3069, Bryan 77802. Phone: (979) 776-1240. Fax: (979) 776-0123. Licensee: Equicom Inc. (group owner; acq 1-22-99). Format: Adult contemp. ♦ Chuck Knuth, gen mgr & gen sls mgr; Dan Ginzel, opns mgr; Ron Elliott, progmg dir; Gary Graham, engrg dir.

Frankston

KOYE(FM)— June 15, 1970: 96.7 mhz; 50 kw. Ant 492 ft. TL: N32 02 22 W95 24 39. Stereo. Box 7820, Tyler 75711. Secondary address: 621 Chase, Tyler 75701. Phone: (903) 581-9966. Fax: (903) 534-5300. E-mail: request@koye.com. Web Site: www.koye967.com. Licensee: Access.1 Texas License Company LLC. Group owner: Waller Broadcasting (acq 1-7-2005; grpsl). Rep: McGavren Guild. Format: Rgnl Sp. News: 6 hrs wkly. Target aud: 18-49. ♦ Mary Ramos, gen mgr; Jim Hendrick, natl sls mgr; Richard Guest, gen mgr & mktg mgr; Jessie Duron, progmg dir.

KTXV(AM)— 2004: 890 khz; 250 w-D, 2 w-N. TL: N32 01 52 W95 40 07. Box 60991, Palo Alto, CA 94306. Phone: (650) 856-6823. Licensee: JNE Investments Inc. ♦ Jeffrey N. Eustis, pres.

Fredericksburg

KNAF(AM)— November 1947: 910 khz; 1 kw-D, 174 w-N. TL: N30 17 12 W98 52 58. Box 311 78624. Secondary address: 210 Woodcrest 78624. Phone: (830) 997-2197. Fax: (830) 997-2198. E-mail: texasrebelradio@fbgn. Licensee: J. & J. Fritz Media Ltd. (group owner; acq 1-23-91; FTR: 2-11-91). Format: Country, full service, talk. Spec prog: Farm 5 hrs, Polka 4.5 hrs wkly. ♦ Jayson Fritz, pres & gen mgr; Jan Fritz, sr VP; Arziana Carruth, prom dir; Rick Star, progmg dir; Holley Day, mus dir.

KNAF-FM— 2005: 105.7 mhz; 9.1 kw. Ant 538 ft. TL: N30 21 49 W98 54 47. Stereo. E-mail: txradio@ktc.com. (group owner). Format: Country. Target aud: 18-54. ♦ Jayson Fritz, engrg VP.

Freeport

KBRZ(AM)— October 1952: 1460 khz; 500 w-D, 214 w-N. TL: N28 58 59 W95 20 00. 912 Curtis Ave., Pasadena 77502. Phone: (713) 589-1336. Fax: (713) 589-1335. Licensee: Aleluya Christian Broadcasting Inc. (acq 3-1-01; $700,000). Network: ABC Information & Entertainment. Format: Sp Christian. ♦ Ruben Villarreal, gen mgr.

KJOJ-FM— 1987: 103.3 mhz; 100 kw. Ant 994 ft. TL: N28 48 57 W95 36 03. 3000 Bering Dr., Houston 77057. Fax: (713) 315-3565. Web Site: www.laraza.fm. Licensee: Liberman Broadcasting of Houston License Corp. Group owner: Liberman Broadcasting Inc. (acq 3-9-01; grpsl). Format: Rgnl Mexican. ♦ Winter Horton, gen mgr; Cheque Gonzalez, opns dir.

Freer

KBRA(FM)— Jan 18, 1985: 95.9 mhz; 190 w. 466 ft. TL: N27 51 17 W98 35 49. (CP: 2.1 kw, ant 397 ft.). Box 148, 208 E. Riley 78357. Phone: (361) 394-6959. Phone: (601) 932-1240. Fax: (601) 420-4114. Licensee: Cobra Broadcasting Co. L.L.C. Format: News/talk, sports. Target aud: 18 plus. ♦ William W. Fulgham, gen mgr; Dwight Martin, opns mgr & gen sls mgr.

*KPBN(FM)— 2004: 90.7 mhz; 700 w. Ant 312 ft. TL: N27 48 55 W98 41 45. Box 252, McAllen 78505. Phone: (956) 686-6382. Fax: (956) 686-2999. Licensee: Paulino Bernal Evangelism. Format: Sp, Christian. ♦ Paulino Bernal Jr., pres.

Friona

KGRW(FM)— Nov 1, 1994: 94.7 mhz; 50 kw. Ant 331 ft. TL: N34 41 17 W102 56 53. 3639 Wolfin Ave., Amarillo 79102. Phone: (806) 355-1044. Fax: (806) 457-0642. Licensee: Tejas Broadcasting Ltd. LLP. Group owner: Amigo Broadcasting L.P. (acq 11-15-2004; grpsl). Format: Sp, Tejano. Target aud: 25-54; working class Texas born Hispanic audience. ♦ Matt Douglas, gen mgr; Brad Gonzalez, gen sls mgr; Israel Salazar, progmg dir; Charles Singleton, chief of engrg.

Frisco

KXEB(AM)— October 1936: 910 khz; 1 kw-D, 500 w-N, DA-2. TL: N33 12 55 W96 53 56. 8828 N. Stemmons Fwy., Suite 106, Dallas 75247. Phone: (214) 634-7780. Fax: (214) 634-7523. Licensee: BMP DFW License Company L.P. Group owner: Amigo Broadcasting L.P. (acq 11-9-2004; grpsl). Format: Sp, sports. Target aud: Ages 18-44; Hispanic sports & music fans. ♦ Gus Perez, gen mgr; Fernando Gonzalez, sls dir; Arturo Canizalez, progmg dir.

Gainesville

KGAF(AM)— 1947: 1580 khz; 250 w-U, DA-N. TL: N33 37 42 W97 06 25. Box 368, Radio Hill Rd. 76241. Phone: (940) 665-5546. Fax: (940) 665-1580. E-mail: kgafadvertising@ntin.net. Licensee: First IV Media Inc. (acq 11-15-74). Format: C&W, news/talk. Spec prog: Farm 2 hrs, sports 3 hrs wkly. ♦ Linda Roller, dev dir; Shelley Carson, gen sls mgr; Jody Shotwell, progmg dir; Tom Carson, pres, gen mgr & news dir; Frank Bonner, chief of engrg.

KSOC(FM)—Licensed to Gainesville. See Dallas

Galveston

KGBC(AM)— May 1947: 1540 khz; 1 kw-D, 250 w-N, DA-N. TL: N29 18 51 W94 48 16. 1302 N. Shepherd Dr., Houston 77008. Phone: (409) 744-1540. Licensee: SIGA Broadcasting Corp. (group owner; acq 5-9-2002; $900,000). Network: ABC Information & Entertainment. Rep: Savalli. Format: Catholic talk. News staff: 2; News: 15 hrs wkly. Target aud: 30 plus; general. ♦ Gabriel Arango, pres; Dave Lane, gen mgr, opns dir, progmg dir & news dir; Sylvia Arango, VP & stn mgr.

KHCB(AM)—Licensed to Galveston. See Houston

KOVE-FM— July 2001: 106.5 mhz; 100 kw. Ant 1,322 ft. TL: N29 24 40 W94 57 04. Stereo. 1415 N. Loop W., 5th Fl., Houston 77008. Phone: (713) 407-1415. Fax: (713) 407-1400. Web Site: www.univision.com. Licensee: HBC License Corp. Group owner: Univision Radio (acq 9-22-2003; grpsl). Rep: Katz Hispanic. Format: Sp. News staff: one; News: 3 hrs wkly. Target aud: 18-49; assimilated Hispanics. ♦ Mark Masepohl, sr VP & VP; Dave Burdette, stn mgr; Arnulfo Ramirez, opns dir; Lisa Stout, gen sls mgr; Kim McBride, natl sls mgr; Frances Jones, prom dir; Nestor Enriquez, prom dir & prom mgr; Carlos Machado, progmg dir; Renzo Heredia, pub affrs dir; Marty Scruggs, engrg dir.

Ganado

KZAM(FM)— Nov 26, 1997: 104.7 mhz; 50 kw. 459 ft. TL: N28 55 37 W96 46 54. 102 Jason Plaza, Suite 2, Victoria 77901. Phone: (361) 572-0105. Fax: (361) 579-4105. Web Site: www.texasthunderradio.com. Licensee: Fort Bend Broadcasting Co. (group owner; acq 5-10-01; $1.5 million). Format: Country. ♦ Ryan Henderson, gen mgr.

Garland

KAAM(AM)—Licensed to Garland. See Dallas

Gatesville

*KVLZ(FM)— Apr 6, 1976: 98.3 mhz; 175 w. Ant 279 ft. TL: N31 27 07 W97 42 14. Stereo. Educational Media Foundation, 5700 West Oaks Blvd., Rocklin, CA 95765. Phone: (916) 251-1600. Fax: (916) 251-1650. Licensee: Educational Media Foundation. Group owner: EMF Broadcasting (acq 3-21-03; $100,000). Network: K-Love. Shaw Pittman. Format: Contemp Christian. News staff: 3. Target aud: 25-44; Judeo Christian, female. ♦ Richard Jenkins, pres; Mike Novak, VP & progmg dir; Lloyd Parker, gen mgr; Ed Lenane, opns dir & news dir; Keith Whipple, dev dir; Eric Allen, natl sls mgr; Chris Joyce, prom dir; David Pierce, progmg mgr; Jon Rivers, mus dir; Sam Wallington, engrg dir.

Georgetown

KHFI-FM— Mar 1, 1972: 96.7 mhz; 100 kw. 951 ft. TL: N30 19 20 W97 48 03. Stereo. 3601 S. Congress Ave., #F, Austin 78704-7213. Phone: (512) 684-7300. Fax: (512) 684-7441. Web Site: www.967kissfm.com. Licensee: CCB Texas Licenses L.P. Group owner: Clear Channel Communications Inc. (acq 3-9-93; $3.5 million;. FTR: 3-29-93). Rep: Clear Channel. Format: Hit rock. News staff: one; News: one hr wkly. Target aud: 18-49; adult women. ♦ Dusty Black, gen mgr; Laura Cullen, sls dir; Angie Hancock, prom dir; Jay Shannon, progmg dir.

KINV(FM)— Oct 31, 1991: 107.7 mhz; 25 kw. Ant 508 ft. TL: N30 42 17 W97 38 32. 911 W. Anderson Ln., Suite 107, Austin 78757. Phone: (512) 419-1077. Fax: (512) 419-9328. Web Site: www.netmio.com. Licensee: Univision Radio License Corp. Group owner: Univision Radio (acq 9-22-2003); grpsl). Rep: Allied Radio Partners. Jones, Waldo, Holbrook & McDonough. Format: Sp, alternative hits of the 80s & 90s. Target aud: 18-34; male. ♦ Mac Tichenor, CEO; Jeff Hinson, CFO; Tim McCoy, gen mgr; Chris Munoz, gen sls mgr; Chris Chappell, mktg dir & prom dir; Oscar Rios, progmg dir & progmg mgr; Cole McClellan, chief of engrg.

Giddings

*KANJ(FM)— Oct 28, 1999: 91.5 mhz; 8 kw. 335 ft. TL: N30 09 56 W96 52 16. 2424 South Blvd., Houston 77098. Phone: (713) 520-5200. Web Site: www.khcb.org. Licensee: Houston Christian Broadcasters Inc. (group owner) Network: Moody. Format: Christian. ♦ Bruce Munsterman, gen mgr.

Gilmer

KFRO-FM— July 24, 1980: 95.3 mhz; 5.9 kw. Ant 666 ft. TL: N32 37 50 W94 53 44. Stereo. Box 5818, Longview 75608. Secondary address: 481 Loop 281 E., Longview 75608. Phone: (903) 663-3700. Fax: (903) 663-9458. Web Site: www.wallerbroadcasting.com. Licensee: Walller Media LLC. Group owner: Waller Broadcasting (acq 6-15-98; $1.425 million. with KFRO(AM) Longview). Rep: Roslin, Kaye, Scholer, Fierman, Hays & Handler. Format: Oldies. Target aud: 25-49. Spec prog: Jazz 5 hrs wkly. ♦ Dudley Waller, CEO, pres & gen mgr; Richard Guest, COO; Debbie Tilley, CFO; Robert Taylor, gen sls mgr; Dru Laborde, progmg dir; Sans Hawkins, engrg dir.

KOFY(AM)— June 17, 1973: 1060 khz; 10 kw-D. TL: N32 43 51 W95 02 35. Box 4248, Tyler 75712. Phone: (903) 593-1744. Fax: (903) 535-8203. Licensee: Jerry Russell dba The Russell Co. (acq 5-7-01; with KWRD(AM) Henderson). Format: Sp mus. ♦ Jerry Russell, gen mgr; Henry Dunn, progmg dir; Porter Milton, chief of engrg.

Gladewater

KEES(AM)— 1947: 1430 khz; 5 kw-D, 1 kw-N, DA-N. TL: N32 31 46 W94 52 50. 1001 E. Southeast Loop 323, Suite 455, Tyler 75701-9600. Phone: (903) 593-2519. Fax: (903) 597-8378. Licensee: Gleiser Communications LLC (group owner; acq 11-21-03; grpsl). Network: Westwood One, ABC News/Talk. Rep: Riley. Format: Talk. ♦ Paul Gleiser, gen mgr & gen sls mgr; Mike LaRoux, chief of engrg.

Glen Rose

KTFW-FM— 1989: 92.1 mhz; 25 kw. 1,417 ft. TL: N32 16 31 W98 01 22. Stereo. Box 1629, 919 N. Main, Cleburne 76033. Phone: (817) 645-6643. Fax: (817) 645-6644. E-mail: info@countrygoldradio.com. Web Site: www.countrygoldradio.com. Licensee: M&M Broadcasters Ltd. (group owner; acq 12-19-97). Fletcher, Heald & Hildreth. Format: C&W. Target aud: 40 plus. ♦ Gary Moss, pres, gen mgr & chief of engrg; George Marti, VP; Mike Crow, stn mgr, progmg dir & progmg mgr; Norma Savage, gen sls mgr; Mary Montanez, mus dir.

Goliad

KHMC(FM)— 1995: 95.9 mhz; 6 kw. 328 ft. TL: N28 40 25 W97 20 24. Box 407, Victoria 77902. Phone: (361) 575-9533. Fax: (361) 575-9502. Licensee: Cinco de Mayo Broadcasting. Rep: Caballero. Format: Tejano. ♦ Homer Lopez, gen mgr; Ralph Salezar, gen sls mgr; Maggie Porres, progmg dir.

Gonzales

KCTI(AM)— Dec 17, 1947: 1450 khz; 1 kw-U. TL: N29 30 35 W97 24 51. 615 St. Paul St. 78629. Phone: (830) 672-3631. Fax: (830) 672-9603. E-mail: kcti@gvec.net. Web Site: www.kcti1450.com. Licensee: Gonzales Communications, a Texas L.P. (acq 3-1-95; with co-located FM; FTR: 5-22-95). Network: ABC Daytime Direction. Format: Country. Target aud: General. Spec prog: Polka 5 hrs, farm 5 hrs, Sp 6 hrs wkly. ♦ Marina Mann, CEO & pres; Joe Haynes, gen mgr, opns VP, gen sls mgr, mktg dir, adv dir & progmg dir; L.D. Decker, news dir; Bill Wolebon, chief of engrg.

*KITG(FM)—Not on air, target date: unknown: 88.1 mhz; 5 kw. Ant 328 ft. TL: N29 33 48 W97 25 44. 2702 Pine St., Laredo 78046. Phone: (956) 726-4738. Fax: (928) 569-0456. Licensee: Maranatha Church of Laredo Inc. ♦ Israel Tellez, gen mgr.

Broadcasting & Cable Yearbook 2006

Stations in the U.S.

Texas

Developers & Brokers of Radio Properties

contact American Media Services at our suite:
Philadelphia Marriott Downtown
215-625-2900
843-972-2200
americanmediaservices.com
Charleston, SC
Dallas, TX · Chicago, Il · Austin, TX
American Media Services, LLC

KQQT(FM)— March 1986: . Stn currently dark 106.3 mhz; 15 kw. Ant 423 ft. TL: N29 41 17 W97 40 39. 1707 North Mays St., Round Rock 78664. Phone: (512) 218-0111. Fax: (512) 218-0129. Licensee: Central Texas Radio Inc. (acq 4-2-2001). ♦ Mike McGregor, gen mgr.

Graham

KSWA(AM)— 1948: 1330 khz; 500 w-D. TL: N33 07 37 W98 35 35. Box 1507 76450. Phone: (940) 549-1330. Fax: (940) 549-8628. E-mail: sales@kwkq-kswa.com. Licensee: Graham Newspapers Inc. (group owner; acq 1996). Network: ABC. Rep: Riley. Baraff, Koerner & Olender. Format: Country. News staff: one; News: 10 hrs wkly. Target aud: 35 plus; adults. Spec prog: Bluegrass 2 hrs, gospel 2 hrs, Texas mus 2 hrs wkly. ♦ Roy Robinson, VP; Lee Parkinson, gen mgr & gen sls mgr; William Proffitt, progmg dir; James M. Jones, news dir & chief of engrg.

KWKQ(FM)— Co-owned with KSWA(AM). August 1975: 94.7 mhz; 10.5 kw. Ant 485 ft. TL: N33 02 30 W98 46 44. Stereo. Network: ABC. Format: CHR. News staff: one; News: 5 hrs wkly. Target aud: 12-49. Spec prog: Alternative 10 hrs wkly. ♦ Greg Tiller, progmg dir.

Granbury

KPIR(AM)— Mar 13, 1980: 1420 khz; 500 w-U, DA-2. TL: N32 27 43 W97 47 19. Box 1558 76049. Phone: (817) 579-7850. Fax: (817) 579-0192. Web Site: www.kpir.com. Licensee: Pirate Broadcasters Inc. (acq 8-13-02). Format: Real country. News staff: one; News: 21 hrs wkly. Target aud: 25-55; general. Spec prog: Farm one hr wkly. ♦ Bob Haschke, gen mgr & sls dir; Shayne Hollinger, progmg mgr; Justin McClure, chief of engrg.

Grand Prairie

KKDA(AM)— Aug 1, 1957: 730 khz; 500 w-U. TL: N32 45 52 W96 59 36. Box 530860 75053. Phone: (972) 263-9911. Fax: (972) 558-0010. Web Site: www.k104fm.com. Licensee: Service Broadcasting Corp. (acq 12-22-76). Format: Oldies. ♦ Hymen Childs, pres; Chuck Smith, gen mgr; Ken Johnson, gen sls mgr; Willis Johnson, progmg dir; Mike Crittender, engrg mgr; Gary Wachter, chief of engrg.

Greenville

KESN(FM)—See Allen

KGVL(AM)— Mar 26, 1946: 1400 khz; 1 kw-U. TL: N33 10 02 W96 05 55. Stereo. Box 1015 75403. Secondary address: 1517 Wolfe City Dr. 75401. Phone: (903) 455-1400. Phone: (903) 450-1400. Fax: (903) 455-5485. Licensee: Dynamic Broadcasting LLC (acq 1-11-2005; $500,000). Dow, Lohnes & Albertson. Format: 70, 80, 90 Country. Target aud: 25 plus. Spec prog: Black one hr, farm 5 hrs, relg 6 hrs wkly. ♦ Frank Janda, gen mgr; Jim Patrick, progmg dir; Jason Russell, chief of engrg.

KIKT(FM)— Sept 15, 1978: 93.5 mhz; 9.1 kw. Ant 328 ft. TL: N33 11 00 W96 03 19. Stereo. Box 1015 75403. Secondary address: 1517 Wolfe City Dr. 75401. Phone: (903) 450-0935. Phone: (903) 455-1460. Fax: (903) 455-5485. Web Site: www.kiktradio.com. Licensee: KRBE Lico Inc. (acq 9-2-99; with co-located AM). Network: ABC. Format: Country. News: 15 hrs wkly. Target aud: General. ♦ Frank Janda, gen mgr.

*KTXG(FM)—Not on air, target date: unknown: 90.5 mhz; 83 kw. Ant 276 ft. TL: N33 11 00 W96 03 19. Drawer 2440, Tupelo, MS 38801. Phone: (662) 844-8888. Fax: (662) 842-6791. Web Site: www.afr.net. Licensee: American Family Association. ♦ Marvin Sanders, gen mgr.

Gregory

KPUS(FM)— 1999: 104.5 mhz; 14 kw. 446 ft. TL: N27 52 00 W97 13 09. 826 S. Padre Island Dr., Corpus Christi 78416. Phone: (361) 814-3800. Fax: (361) 855-3770. Web Site: www.1045theoctopus.com. Licensee: Convergent Broadcasting Corpus Christi LP. Group owner: Convergent Broadcasting LLC (acq 1-12-2004; grpsl). Format: Modern adult contemp. ♦ Mark White, gen mgr; Dallas Garcia, gen sls mgr; Scott Holt, opns mgr & progmg dir; Molly Cox, mus dir.

Groves

KCOL-FM— Sept 17, 1983: 92.5 mhz; 50 kw. 440 ft. TL: N30 01 45 W93 52 59. Stereo. Box 5488, Beaumont 77726. Phone: (409) 896-5555. Fax: (409) 896-5566. Web Site: www.cool925.com. Licensee: Clear Channel Broadcasting Licenses Inc. Group owner: Clear Channel Communications Inc. (acq 1-29-2004; $4.5 million). Format: Oldies. Target aud: 35 plus. ♦ John Hogan, CEO; Randall Mays, CFO; Charlie Rahilly, sr VP; Mark Kopelman, VP; Vesta Brandt, gen mgr; Trey Poston, opns dir.

Hallettsville

KHLT(AM)— Sept 5, 1979: 1520 khz; 250 w-D. TL: N29 26 38 W96 57 22. 111 N. Main St. 77964. Phone: (361) 798-4333. Fax: (361) 798-3798. E-mail: texasthunderradio@yahoo.com. Licensee: Fort Bend Broadcasting Co. Inc. Group owner: Fort Bend Broadcasting Co. (acq 1-21-00; grpsl). Format: Rock, country. News staff: one; News: 13 hrs wkly. Target aud: General. Spec prog: Farm 6 hrs, Czech 3 hrs, Ger 3 hrs wkly. ♦ Laura Kremling, gen mgr, stn mgr, stn mgr & progmg dir; Ray Nelson, chief of engrg.

KTXM(FM)— Co-owned with KHLT(AM). Oct 29, 1997: 99.9 mhz; 6 kw. 131 ft. TL: N29 26 38 W96 57 22. Format: Rock, country.

Haltom City

KDBN(FM)— 1995: 93.3 mhz; 50 kw. 276 ft. TL: N32 54 44 W97 11 18. 3500 Maple Ave., 13th Fl., Dallas 75219. Phone: (214) 526-2400. Fax: (214) 525-2525. Web Site: www.thebonekdbn.com. Licensee: Texas Star Radio Inc. Group owner: Susquehanna Radio Corp. (acq 1-28-97). Format: Classic rock. ♦ Lon Bason, gen mgr; Todd Storch, gen sls mgr; Scott Strong, progmg dir; Bob Smith, news dir; Hugh Beavers, chief of engrg.

Hamilton

KCLW(AM)— May 22, 1948: 900 khz; 250 w-D. TL: N31 43 08 W98 08 39. Box 631 76531. Secondary address: 115 A N. Rice 76531. Phone: (254) 386-8804 phone/fax. E-mail: info@kclw.com. Web Site: www.kclw.com. Licensee: Lasting Value Broadcasting Group Inc. (acq 8-22-00; $380,000). Network: Network: CBS, Jones Radio Networks. Format: Classic country. News staff: one; News: 6 hrs wkly. Target aud: 18-65. Spec prog: Relg 6 hrs, Spanish 12 hrs wkly. ♦ Meredith Beal, pres; Sammie Casey, gen mgr; Ronald Beal, opns VP.

Hamlin

KCDD(FM)— Jan 30, 1987: 103.7 mhz; 100 kw. 985 ft. TL: N32 43 31 W100 04 19. Stereo. 2525 S. Danville Dr., Abilene 79605. Phone: (325) 793-9700. Fax: (915) 692-1576. Web Site: www.power103.com. Licensee: Cumulus Licensing Corp. Group owner: Cumulus Media Inc. (acq 2-13-98; grpsl). Format: CHR. ♦ Trace Michaels, gen mgr; Brad Elliott, progmg dir; Chris Andrews, chief of engrg.

Harker Heights

KRMY(AM)—See Killeen

KUSJ(FM)—Licensed to Harker Heights. See Temple

Harlingen

KBTQ(FM)—Listing follows KGBT(AM).

KFRQ(FM)— January 1960: 94.5 mhz; 100 kw. 1,158 ft. TL: N26 08 55 W97 49 17. Stereo. 801 N. Jackson Rd., McAllen 78501. Phone: (956) 661-6000. Fax: (956) 661-6082. Web Site: www.kfrq.com. Licensee: Entravision Holdings LLC. (group owner; acq 1996; $6.1 million with KKPS(FM) Brownsville). Rep: Allied Radio Partners. Format: Adult rock. News staff: one. Target aud: 25-54. ♦ Alex Duran, VP, gen mgr & progmg dir.

KGBT(AM)— 1941: 1530 khz; 50 kw-D, 10 kw-N, DA-N. TL: N26 22 29 W97 53 40. Stereo. 200 S. 10th, Suite 600, McAllen 78501. Phone: (956) 631-5499. Fax: (956) 631-0090. Web Site: www.netmio.com. Licensee: Tichenor License Corp. ("TLC"). Group owner: Univision Radio (acq 9-22-2003; grpsl). Rep: Katz Hispanic. Format: Sp. News staff: 2. Target aud: 18 plus. ♦ Joe Morales, gen mgr; Hugo Delacruz, progmg dir; Jorge Garza, chief of engrg.

KBTQ(FM)—Co-owned with KGBT(AM). July 1975: 96.1 mhz; 100 kw. 449 ft. TL: N26 10 34 W97 46 59. Stereo. Web Site: www.netmio.com. Format: Tejano. ♦ Alex Quintero, progmg dir.

*KMBH-FM— Apr 30, 1991: 88.9 mhz; 3 kw. 298 ft. TL: N26 10 46 W97 30 06. Stereo. Box 2147 78551. Secondary address: 1701 Tennessee 78551. Phone: (956) 421-4111. Fax: (956) 421-4150. E-mail: kmbhkhid@aol.com. Web Site: www.kmbh.org. Licensee: RGV Educational Broadcasting Inc. Network: NPR. Format: News, class, jazz. News: 34 hrs wkly. Target aud: General. Spec prog: Sp 3 hrs wkly. ♦ Fr. Pedro Briseno, CEO, pres & gen mgr; Chris Maley, progmg dir. Co-owned TV: *KMBH(TV) affil

Haskell

KVRP-FM— Apr 8, 1981: 97.1 mhz; 100 kw. 531 ft. TL: N33 09 40 W99 48 57. Stereo. Box 1118, 1406 N. First 79521. Phone: (940) 864-8505. Fax: (940) 864-8001. E-mail: gary@kvrp.com. Web Site: www.kvrp.com. Licensee: 1 Chronicles 14 L.P. (acq 8-4-2004; $700,000. with KVRP(AM) Stamford). Rep: Katz Radio. Format: Country, sports. News staff: one; News: 5 hrs wkly. Target aud: 25 plus. Spec prog: Farm 8 hrs, relg 6 hrs wkly. ♦ Greg Weston, pres & VP; Gary Barrett, stn mgr, gen sls mgr & prom mgr; Dave Harrison, progmg dir; Josh Roysdon, rgnl sls mgr & news dir.

Hearne

KVJM(FM)— May 15, 1985: 103.1 mhz; 5 kw horiz, 4.9 kw vert. 361 ft. TL: N30 45 35 W96 28 00. Box 3989, 219 N. Main, Bryan 77803. Phone: (979) 779-3337. Fax: (979) 779-3444. E-mail: kvjmv103@aol.com. Licensee: Equal Access Media Inc. Format: Urban contemp. Target aud: 18-54. Spec prog: Blues 4 hrs, gospel 6 hrs wkly. ♦ Pluria Marshall Jr., gen mgr & sls VP; Edward Sanchez, stn mgr, mus dir, asst music dir, news dir & pub affrs dir; Plyria Marshall Jr., natl sls mgr; Lester Pace, progmg dir; Ed Loftis, chief of engrg.

Hebronville

*KAZF(FM)— November 2000: 91.9 mhz; 3 kw. 266 ft. TL: N27 21 44 W98 40 09. Box 252, McAllen 78505. Phone: (956) 686-6382. Fax: (956) 686-2999. E-mail: paulinobernal@laradiocristina.com. Web Site: www.laradiocristina.com. Licensee: Paulino Bernal Evangelism. Format: Christian contemp. ♦ Gilbert Martinez, stn mgr.

KEKO(FM)— 2003: 101.7 mhz; 6 kw. Ant 328 ft. TL: N27 18 46 W98 39 51. Box 1614, Laredo 78044. Phone: (956) 726-4738. Fax: (928) 569-0456. Web Site: www.lacadenaradioluz.com/keko.htm. Licensee: La Nueva Cadena Radio Luz Inc. Format: Sp Christian. ♦ Israel Tellez, pres & gen mgr; Hiram Tellez, progmg mgr.

Helotes

KONO-FM— Feb 18, 1971: 101.1 mhz; 98 kw. 1,368 ft. TL: N29 50 26 W98 49 32. Stereo. 8122 Datapoint Dr., Suite 500, San Antonio 78229. Phone: (210) 615-5400. Fax: (210) 615-5300. Web Site: www.kono101.com. Licensee: CXR Holdings L.L.C. Group owner: Cox Broadcasting (acq 2-12-98; $23 million. with KONO(AM) San Antonio). Format: Oldies. News staff: one; News: one hr wkly. Target aud: 25-64; total audience appeal. ♦ Bob Neil, CEO; Marty Choate, VP & gen mgr; Roger Allen, opns VP & progmg dir; Connie Tyra Kremer, gen sls mgr; Jim Bratt, natl sls mgr; Julie Busse, mktg dir; Vera Flores, prom dir; Chrissie Murnin, news dir; Paul Reynolds, chief of engrg.

Texas

Hemphill

KPBL(AM)— Feb 16, 1978: . Stn currently dark 1240 khz; 1 kw-U. TL: N31 22 03 W93 50 10. R.R. 5 Box 2095 75948. Licensee: Phillip Burr Broadcasting Co. ♦ Phillip Burr, pres & gen mgr.

KTHP(FM)— November 2000: 103.9 mhz;; 6 kw. Ant 243 ft. TL: N31 20 28 W93 50 44. (CP: 4.5 kw, ant 377 ft. TL: N31 25 24 W93 50 30). 605 San Antonio Ave., Many, LA 71449. Phone: (409) 787-1039. Licensee: Baldridge-Dumas Communications Inc. (group owner). Format: Classic country. ♦ Rhonda Benson, gen mgr.

Hempstead

KEZB(FM)— 1999: 105.3 mhz; 9.2 kw. Ant 544 ft. TL: N30 18 19 W96 01 40. 530 W. Main St., Brenham 77833. Phone: (979) 836-9411. Fax: (979) 836-9435. Licensee: Farmers Communications. Group owner: Bayport Broadcast Group Robert J. Buenzle. Format: Adult comtemp. ♦ Roy E. Henderson, CEO & pres; Steve Britewell, engrg VP.

Henderson

KWRD(AM)— March 1956: 1470 khz; 5 kw-D. TL: N32 10 55 W94 47 49. 1101 Kilgore Dr. 75652. Phone: (903) 657-2324. Fax: (903) 657-6221. E-mail: kwrd@tyler.net. Licensee: Jerry Russell dba The Russell Co. (acq 5-7-2001; with KOFY(AM) Gilmer). Format: C&W, Southern gospel. Target aud: General. Spec prog: Farm 5 hrs wkly. ♦ Esther Milton, gen mgr; Henry Dunn, stn mgr & opns mgr.

Hereford

KJNZ(FM)— Dec 12, 2000: 103.5 mhz; 50 kw. Ant 249 ft. TL: N34 52 10 W102 34 47. 1220 Broadway, Suite 1035, Lubbock 79401. Phone: (806) 741-0701. Licensee: Tahoka Radio LLC Group owner: The Formby Stations Shaw Pittman. Format: Rgnl Mexican. ♦ Chip Formby, gen mgr.

KNNK(FM)— (Dimmitt). June 13, 1998: 100.5 mhz; 43 kw. Ant 489 ft. TL: N34 44 49 W102 29 37. Stereo. Box 1635, 207 S. 25-Mile Ave. 79045-9998. Phone: (806) 363-1005. Fax: (806) 364-0226. E-mail: knnk@wtrt.net. Web Site: www.knnk.net. Licensee: James D. Peeler. Network: Moody. Format: Southern gospel, beautiful music. Target aud: General; mature adults. Spec prog: Soft instrumentals 20 hrs wkly. ♦ James "Buddy" D. Peeler, gen mgr.

KPAN(AM)— August 1948: 860 khz; 250 w-D, 231 w-N. TL: N34 47 33 W102 25 45. Box 1757, 218 E. 5th St. 79045. Phone: (806) 364-1860. Fax: (806) 364-5814. E-mail: kpan@kpanradio.com. Web Site: www.kpanradio.com. Licensee: KPAN Broadcasters. Group owner: Formby Stations Network: CBS. Shaw Pittman. Format: Contemp country. News staff: one; News: 20 hrs wkly. Target aud: General. Spec prog: Tejano 15 hrs, farm 12 hrs wkly. ♦ Chip Formby, gen mgr.

KPAN-FM— Sept 1, 1965: 106.3 mhz; 30 kw. 259 ft. TL: N34 47 33 W102 25 45. Stereo. Web Site: www.kpanradio.com. Network: CBS Radio. Shaw Pittman. Target aud: General.

Highland Park

KMGS(AM)— Mar 1, 1960: 1160 khz; 35 kw-D, 1 kw-N, DA-2. TL: N33 10 37 W97 40 36. 750 N. St. Paul, 10th Fl., Dallas 75201. Phone: (214) 855-0002. Fax: (214) 855-5145. Licensee: First Broadcasting Capital Partners LLC. Group owner: First Broadcasting Investment Partners LLC (acq 4-10-2003; $3.25 million).

KVIL-FM—(Highland Park-Dallas). Aug 14, 1961: 103.7 mhz; 100 kw. Ant 1,571 ft. TL: N32 34 54 W96 58 32. Stereo. 4131 N. Central Expwy., Suite 1200, Dallas 75204. Phone: (214) 526-9870. E-mail: feedback@kvil.com. Web Site: www.kvil.com. Licensee: Texas Infinity Broadcasting L.P. Group owner: CBS Radio (acq 7-2-87). Network: CBS. Format: Light rock. ♦ David Henry, gen mgr.

Highland Park-Dallas

KVIL-FM—Licensed to Highland Park-Dallas. See Highland Park

Highland Village

KWRD-FM— Nov 15, 1988: 100.7 mhz; 100 kw. Ant 1,840 ft. TL: N33 33 37 W96 57 34. Stereo. 6400 N. Belt Line Rd., Suite 110, Irving 75063-6037. Phone: (214) 561-9673. Fax: (214) 561-9662. E-mail: theword@thewordfm.com. Web Site: www.thewordfm.com. Licensee: Inspiration Media of Texas LLC. Group owner: Salem Communications Corp. (acq 1-17-2001; grpsl). Format: Christian talk. ♦ Pete Thomson, gen mgr; David Darling, opns mgr & progmg; Easy Ezell, gen sls mgr; Carol White, prom dir; Brian Heise, chief of engrg.

Hillsboro

KBRQ(FM)— Oct 20, 1959: 102.5 mhz; 100 kw. Ant 449 ft. TL: N31 49 23 W97 09 35. Stereo. 314 W. State Hwy. 6, Waco 76712. Phone: (254) 776-3900. Fax: (254) 761-6371. E-mail: brenthenslee@clearchannel.com. Web Site: www.1025thebear.com. Licensee: Clear Channel Broadcasting Licenses Inc. Group owner: Clear Channel Communications Inc. (acq 11-12-2003; $300,000). Fisher, Wayland, Cooper, Leader & Zaragoza. Format: Classic rock. Target aud: 25-49; men. ♦ Evan Armstrong, gen mgr; Zack Owen, opns dir; Vernon Riggs, sls dir & gen sls mgr; Brent Henslee, progmg dir.

KHBR(AM)— May 21, 1948: 1560 khz; 250 w-D. TL: N32 01 00 W97 06 32. Box 569 76645. Secondary address: 335 Country Club Rd. 76645. Phone: (254) 582-3431. Fax: (254) 582-3800. E-mail: khbr@hillsboro.net. Web Site: www.khbrhillsboro.com. Licensee: KHBR Radio Inc. (acq 1955). Format: C&W. News: 18 hrs wkly. Target aud: General. Spec prog: Czech 2 hrs, gospel 6 hrs wkly. ♦ Roger Galle, pres; Rick Bailey, gen mgr.

Hondo

KCWM(AM)— Feb 13, 1970: 1460 khz; 500 w-D, 226 w-N. TL: N29 21 42 W99 07 42. Box 447 78861. Secondary address: 1605 Ave. K 78861. Phone: (830) 741-5296. Fax: (830) 426-3368. Licensee: Hondo Communications Inc. (acq 10-11-96). Rep: Keystone (unwired net). Format: C&W. News staff: one; News: 20 hrs wkly. Target aud: General. ♦ Mike Carr, pres, gen mgr & progmg dir; Tim Copeland, gen sls mgr, mktg dir & prom mgr; Paul McKay, chief of engrg.

KMFR(FM)— 1993:: 105.9 mhz; 6 kw. 328 ft. TL: N29 18 48 W99 16 03. Stereo. 8023 Vantage Dr., Suite 840, San Antonio 78230. Phone: (888) 522-7437. Fax: (210) 341-1777. Licensee: Hondo RadioWorks Ltd. (acq 12-12-2000; $74,925). Format: Classic rock. ♦ John W. Barger, CEO; J.R. Gulley, gen mgr; Robert Ruff, stn mgr.

Hooks

KPWW(FM)— Dec 22, 1985: 95.9 mhz; 11.5 kw. 449 ft. TL: N33 27 25 W94 10 59. (CP: 11.3 kw, ant 485 ft.). Stereo. 2324 Arkansas Blvd., Texarkana 71854. Phone: (870) 772-3771. Fax: (870) 772-0364. Web Site: www.power959.com. Licensee: Capstar TX L.P. Group owner: Clear Channel Communications Inc. (acq 8-30-00; grpsl). Rep: McGavren Guild. Format: Modern Top 40. News staff: one. Target aud: 18-49; contemp adults, upscale middle America. ♦ Ron Bird, gen mgr; Phil Robken, natl sls mgr; John Williams, news dir; Wes Spicher, progmg dir & chief of engrg.

Hornsby

*KOOP(FM)— November 1994: 91.7 mhz; 3.13 kw. 85 ft. TL: N30 16 00 W97 40 27. (CP: Ant 197 ft.). Stereo. Box 2116, Austin 78768. Secondary address: 304 E. 5th St., Austin 78701. Phone: (512) 472-1369. Phone: (512) 472-5667. Fax: (512) 472-6149. E-mail: info@koop.org. Web Site: www.koop.org. Licensee: Texas Educational Broadcasting Inc. Format: Var of mus & info. News: 14 hrs wkly. Spec prog: American Indian 1 hr, Black 2 hrs, folk 7 hrs, Ger .5 hrs, jazz 3 hrs, Pol .5 hrs, Spanish 10 hrs wkly. ♦ Amy Wright, stn mgr; Lonny Stern, prom dir; Joanna Garfinkel, mus dir.

Houston

KBME(AM)— Oct 16, 1944: 790 khz; 5 kw-U, DA-2. TL: N29 54 54 W95 27 42. Stereo. 200 West Loop S., Suite 300 77027. Phone: (713) 212-8000. Fax: (713) 212-8790. Web Site: www.790kbme.com. Licensee: AMFM Texas Licenses L.P. Group owner: Clear Channel Communications Inc. (acq 8-30-2000; grpsl). Network: ESPN Radio. Rep: Christal. Format: Sports. ♦ Mark Copelman, gen mgr; Pam McKay, gen sls mgr; Ken Charles, natl sls mgr & progmg VP; Dan Endom, rgnl sls mgr; Melissa Brezner, mktg dir & prom dir; Tim Collins, progmg dir; Bryan Erickson, news dir; Peggy Tuck, pub affrs dir; David Armstrong, chief of engrg.

KBXX(FM)— January 1958: 97.9 mhz; 100 kw. 1,920 ft. TL: N29 34 34 W95 30 36. Stereo. 24 Greenway Plaza, Suite 1508 77046. Phone: (713) 623-2108. Fax: (713) 623-0344. E-mail: scorpio@kbxx.com. Web Site: www.kbtt.com. Licensee: Radio One Licenses LLC. Group owner: Radio One Inc. (acq 2000). Rep: Clear Channel. Dickstein Shapiro Morin & Oshinsky L.L.P. Format: Hip hop. Target aud: 18-29; females. ♦ Ernest Jackson, pres; Carl Hamilton, VP; Mark McMillen, gen mgr; Tom Callococci, opns mgr.

KCOH(AM)— 1952: 1430 khz; 5 kw-D. TL: N29 45 22 W95 16 37. Stereo. 5011 Almeda Rd. 77004. Phone: (713) 522-1001. Fax: (713) 521-0769. E-mail: dsamuel@kcohradio.com. Web Site: www.kcohradio.com. Licensee: KCOH Inc. (acq 9-27-76). Network: American Urban. Rep: Roslin. Cavelli, Mertz & Davis. Format: Black, urban contemp, talk. News staff: 2; News: 15 hrs wkly. Target aud: 25-54; upbeat, knowledgeable, civic & politically minded adults. Spec prog: Sports. ♦ Mike Petrizzo, exec VP, gen mgr, gen sls mgr & adv dir; Michael Harris, progmg dir & news dir; Travis O. Gardner, VP, opns VP, prom mgr & mus dir; Don Samuel, asst music dir; J.D. Rigmaideu, engrg dir & chief of engrg.

KEYH(AM)— November 1974: 850 khz; 10 kw-D, 185 w-N, DA-1. TL: N29 39 19 W95 40 19. 3000 Bering Dr. 77057. Phone: (713) 315-3400. Fax: (713) 315-3506. Licensee: Liberman Broadcasting of Houston License Corp. Group owner: Liberman Broadcasting Inc. (acq 4-22-03; $5.70 million). Format: Sp. Target aud: 24-65; Hispanic, recent immigrants & primarily Sp speakers. ♦ Jeff Scott, pres & opns mgr; Winter Horton, gen mgr; Eddie Martiny, sls VP; Daisy Ortiz, gen sls mgr; Ezequiel Gonzalez, progmg dir; Meliza Posada, news dir; Errol Coker, chief of engrg.

*KHCB(AM)— (Galveston). 1922: 1400 khz; 1 kw-U. TL: N29 17 24 W94 50 12. 2424 South Blvd. 77098-5196. Phone: (713) 520-7900. Licensee: Houston Christian Broadcasters Inc. (group owner; acq 12-4-90; $150,000). Format: Sp, relg. News staff: one. Target aud: General. Spec prog: Chinese 13 hrs, Vietnamese 4 hrs wkly. ♦ Bruce Munsterman, pres, stn mgr & progmg dir; Dolly Martin, progmg mgr; Miguel Jacinto, mus dir & news dir; Dan Wales, chief of engrg.

KHCB-FM— Mar 10, 1962: 105.7 mhz; 100 kw. Ant 1,614 ft. TL: N29 34 06 W95 29 57. Stereo. Phone: (713) 520-5200. E-mail: khcb@nol.net. Web Site: www.khcb.org. Format: Christian. Spec prog: Sp 10 hrs, Chinese one hr wkly. ♦ Bruce Munsterman, gen mgr; Bonnie C. BeMent, mus dir & news dir; Dan Wales, engrg dir.

KHJZ-FM— Oct 4, 1959: 95.7 mhz; 100 kw. 1,971 ft. TL: N29 34 34 W95 30 36. Stereo. 24 Greenway Plaza, Suite 1900 77046. Phone: (713) 881-5100. Fax: (713) 881-5250. Web Site: www.khjz.com. Licensee: Texas Infinity Broadcasting L.P. Group owner: Infinity Broadcasting Corp. (acq 11-13-98; grpsl). Network: CBS. Rep: Infinity Radio Sales. Leventhal, Senter & Lerman. Format: Smooth Jazz / NAC. Target aud: 25-54. ♦ Laura Morris, VP; Diane Holt, sls dir; Maxine Todd, progmg dir; Dan Woodard, chief of engrg.

KHMX(FM)— 1961: 96.5 mhz; 100 kw. 1,952 ft. TL: N29 34 34 W95 30 36. Stereo. 3050 Post Oak Blvd., 12th Fl. 77056. Phone: (713) 212-8000. Fax: (713) 968-1044. Web Site: www.khmx.com. Licensee: Citicasters Licenses L.P. Group owner: Clear Channel Communications Inc. (acq 5-4-99; grpsl). Format: Adult contemp. Target aud: 25-40. ♦ Muriel Funches, VP; Rick Miles, gen sls mgr; Alan Ecklund, natl sls mgr; Marc Sherman, progmg dir; Lori Bradley, mus dir; Emma Villanueva, pub affrs dir.

KHPT(FM)—See Conroe

KIKK(AM)—See Pasadena

KILT(AM)— 1948: 610 khz; 5 kw-U, DA-2. TL: N29 55 04 W95 25 33. 24 Greenway Plaza, Suite 1900 77046. Phone: (713) 881-5100. Phone: (713) 881-5957. Fax: (713) 881-5150. Web Site: www.sportsradio610.com. Licensee: Texas Infinity Broadcasting L.P. Group owner: Infinity Broadcasting Corp. (acq 12-89). Rep: CBS Radio. Format: Sports, talk. ♦ Laura Morris, VP; Moose Rosenfeld, gen mgr; Bill Van Rysdam, progmg dir; Dan Woodard, chief of engrg.

KILT-FM— 1961: 100.3 mhz; 100 kw. 1,920 ft. TL: N29 34 34 W95 30 36. Stereo. Web Site: www.kilt.com. Format: Country. ♦ Nick Peterson, gen sls mgr; Jeff Garrison, progmg dir; Jim Carola, news dir.

KKBQ-FM—See Pasadena

KKRW(FM)— Jan 1, 1964: 93.7 mhz; 100 kw. 1,779 ft. TL: N29 34 27 W95 29 37. Stereo. 12th Fl., 3050 Post Oak Blvd. 77056. Phone:

Developers & Brokers of Radio Properties
contact American Media Services at our suite: Philadelphia Marriott Downtown 215-625-2900
843-972-2200
americanmediaservices.com
Charleston, SC
Dallas, TX - Chicago, Il - Austin, TX
American Media Services, LLC

(713) 212-8000. Fax: (713) 830-8099. Web Site: www.kkrw.com. Licensee: Capstar TX L.P. Group owner: Clear Channel Communications Inc. (acq 8-30-00; grpsl). Format: Classic rock. Target aud: 25-54. ♦Brian Purdy, gen mgr.

KLAT(AM)— July 31, 1961: 1010 khz; 5 kw-U, DA-2. TL: N29 53 47 W95 17 25. (CP: 3.6 kw-N). Stereo. 1415 N. Loop W., Suite 550 77008. Phone: (713) 407-1415. Fax: (713) 407-1400. Web Site: www.univision.com. Licensee: Tichenor License Corp. Group owner: Univision Radio (acq 9-22-2003; grpsl). Rep: Katz Hispanic. Format: Sp, news/talk. Target aud: 25-54; Hispanic. ♦Dave Burdette, VP & stn mgr; Mark Masepohl, VP, gen mgr & sls dir; Arnulfo Ramirez, opns mgr; Kim McBride, natl sls mgr & pub affrs dir; Manuel Cardona, rgnl sls mgr; Frances Jones, prom dir; Pilar Torres, prom mgr; Rolando Becerra, progmg dir; Renzo Heredia, news dir; Marty Scruggs, chief of engrg.

KQBU-FM—Co-owned with KLAT(AM). July 4, 1969: 93.3 mhz; 100 kw. Ant 594 ft. TL: N30 03 05 W94 31 37. Stereo. Web Site: www.univision.com. Rep: Katz Hispanic. Target aud: 25-54; Hispanics. ♦Mark Masepohl, sr VP; Jose Lopez, opns mgr; Arnulfo Ramirez, progmg VP; Renzo Heredia, prom dir & pub affrs dir.

KLDE(FM)—See Lake Jackson

KLOL(FM)—Listing follows KTRH(AM).

KLTN(FM)— Oct 4, 1960: 102.9 mhz; 100 kw. Ant 1,049 ft. TL: N29 45 26 W95 20 18. Stereo. 1415 N. Loop W., Suite 550 77008. Phone: (713) 407-1415. Fax: (713) 407-1400. Web Site: www.univision.com. Licensee: HBC Houston License Corp. Group owner: Univision Radio (acq 9-22-2003; grpsl). Rep: Katz Hispanic. Format: Sp. Target aud: 18-49; women. ♦Mark Masepoho, sr VP & gen mgr; Dave Burdette, stn mgr; Arnulfo Ramirez, opns mgr; Mark McMillen, gen sls mgr; Kim McBride, natl sls mgr; Frances Jones, prom dir; Raul Brindis, progmg dir; Renzo Heredia, news dir & pub affrs dir; Marty Scruggs, chief of engrg.

KLVL(AM)—See Pasadena

KMIC(AM)— 1955: 1590 khz; 5 kw-U, DA-N. TL: N29 50 38 W95 26 51. 3050 Post Oak Blvd., Suite 220 77056. Phone: (713 552-1590. Fax: (713) 552-1588. Web Site: www.disney.com. Licensee: Radio Disney Group LLC. Group owner: ABC Inc. (acq. 1999). Format: Top 40, CHR. Target aud: 6-14; 25-49; kids, parents. Spec prog: Children 10 hr wkly. ♦Fran Epstein, gen mgr, gen sls mgr & adv dir; Laura El-Messaoudi, prom mgr; Robin Jones, progmg dir; Laura JonesEl-Messaoudi, pub affrs dir; A. D. Ringmaiden, chief of engrg.

KMJQ(FM)— Feb 1, 1964: 102.1 mhz; 100 kw. 1,719 ft. TL: N29 34 27 W95 29 37. Stereo. 24 Greenway Plaza, Suite 1508 77046-2467. Secondary address: Box 22900 77227-2900. Phone: (713) 623-2108. Fax: (713) 623-0106. Web Site: www.kmjq.com. Licensee: Radio One Licenses LLC. Group owner: Radio One Inc. (acq 11-8-01; grpsl). Network: ABC. Rep: Clear Channel. Wiley, Rein & Fielding. Format: Adult urban contemp. News staff: 2. Target aud: 25-54; African-Americans. Spec prog: Talk 3 hrs wkly. ♦Carl Hamilton, VP; Mark McMillen, gen mgr; Tom Callococci, pres & opns mgr; Jerome Hutchinson, gen sls mgr; Brenda Ford-Jones, natl sls mgr; Cindy Webster, rgnl sls mgr; Bobrie Jefferson, prom mgr; Sam Choice, progmg dir & progmg mgr; Carmen Watkins, news dir; David Ainslie, engrg mgr & chief of engrg.

KNTH(AM)— Jan 17, 1968: 1070 khz; 10 kw-D, 5 kw-N, DA-2. TL: N29 59 33 W95 29 33. 6161 Savoy, Suite 1200 77036. Phone: (713) 260-3600. Fax: (713) 260-3628. Licensee: South Texas Broadcasting Inc. Group owner: Salem Communications Corp. (acq 1-6-95; $2.5 million;. FTR: 3-6-95). Rep: Salem. Format: News/talk. ♦Chuck Jewell, gen mgr; Paul Baker, opns mgr, mktg mgr & progmg dir; Dan Doster, gen sls mgr; Ken Garza, pub affrs dir; Sidney Jones, chief of engrg.

KODA(FM)— Nov 9, 1958: 99.1 mhz; 95 kw. 1,920 ft. TL: N29 34 34 W95 30 36. Stereo. 12th Fl., 3050 Post Oak Blvd. 77056. Phone: (713) 212-8000. Fax: (713) 830-8099. Web Site: www.sunny99.com. Licensee: AMFM Texas License L.P. Group owner: Clear Channel Communications Inc. (acq 8-30-00; grpsl). Latham & Watkins. Format: Adult contemp. News staff: one; News: 22 hrs wkly. Target aud: 25-54. Spec prog: Jazz 4 hrs wkly. ♦Mark Kopelman, gen mgr; Sandy Capell, gen sls mgr; Marc Sherman, progmg dir; Donna McCoy, mus dir.

***KPFT(FM)**— March 1970: 90.1 mhz; 100 kw. 433 ft. TL: N29 55 26 W95 32 17. (CP: 28 kw, ant 672 ft.). Stereo. 419 Lovett Blvd. 77006. Phone: (713) 526-4000. Fax: (713) 526-5750. Web Site: www.kpft.org. Licensee: Pacifica Foundation Inc. Group owner: Pacifica Foundation Inc. dba Pacifica Radio Network: PRI. Haley, Bader & Potts. Format: Div, news. Target aud: General. Spec prog: Black 15 hrs. ♦Dwande Bradlley, gen mgr; Donna Platt, dev dir; Otis Maclay, progmg dir; Phil Edwards, mus dir; Ernesto Aguilar, news dir; Renee Feltz, news dir; Steve Brightwell, engrg dir.

KPRC(AM)— May 9, 1925: 950 khz; 5 kw-U, DA-N. TL: N29 48 14 W95 16 42. 510 Lovett Blvd. 77006. Phone: (713) 526-5874. Fax: (713) 630-3666. Web Site: www.950kprc.com. Licensee: CCB Texas Licenses L.P. Group owner: Clear Channel Communications Inc. (acq 3-14-95; FTR: 6-5-95). Network: CBS. Rep: Clear Channel. Dow, Lohnes & Albertson. Format: News/talk. News staff: 15; News: 32 hrs wkly. Target aud: 25-54. Spec prog: Gardening 7 hrs, home handyman 6 hrs, automotive 3 hrs wkly. ♦Mark Kopelman, gen mgr; Pamela McKay, gen sls mgr; Ken Charles, progmg dir; Brian Erickson, news dir; David Armstrong, chief of engrg.

KPTY(FM)—(Missouri City). Aug 8, 1968: 104.9 mhz; 2.7 kw. Ant 981 ft. TL: N29 45 30 W95 22 03. Stereo. 1415 N. Loop West, Suite 550 77008. Phone: (713) 407-1415. Fax: (713) 407-1400. Web Site: www.party1049.com. Licensee: Tichenor License Corp. Group owner: Univision Radio (acq 9-22-2003; grpsl). Rep: Katz Hispanic. Format: Urban, hip hop, rhythm and blues. Target aud: 18-34; Urban/Latin audience. ♦Mark Masepohl, sr VP & gen mgr; Dave Burdette, stn mgr; J.D. Gonzales, opns VP; Kim McBride, natl sls mgr; Jeanette Perales, rgnl sls mgr; Frances Jones, prom dir; Estee Marquez, prom mgr; Marco Arias, progmg dir; Renzo Heredia, pub affrs dir; Marty Scruggs, chief of engrg; Claudetta Wallace, system mgr.

KQUE(AM)— Feb 18, 1948: 1230 khz; 1 kw-U. TL: N29 45 26 W95 20 18. 3000 Bering Dr., Suite 1170 77057. Phone: (713) 315-3400. Fax: (713) 315-3506. Licensee: Liberman Broadcasting of Houston License Corp. Group owner: Liberman Broadcasting Inc. (acq 3-9-01; grpsl). Rep: Allied Radio Partners. Fisher, Wayland, Cooper, Leader & Zaragoza L.L.P. Format: Mexican rgnl. News: 14 hrs wkly. Target aud: 35 plus; mature, upscale, high-income. ♦Leonard Liberman, VP; Winter Horton, gen mgr; Cheque Gonzalez, stn mgr; Jeff Scott, opns mgr; Eddie Martiny, sls VP; Daisy Ortiz, natl sls mgr; Gustavo Mentez, prom dir; Ezequiel Gonzalez, progmg dir; Errol Coker, chief of engrg.

KRBE(FM)— Nov 8, 1959: 104.1 mhz; 100 kw. 1,920 ft. TL: N29 34 34 W95 30 36. Stereo. 9801 Westheimer, Suite 700 77042. Phone: (713) 266-1000. Fax: (713) 954-2344. Web Site: www.104krbe.com. Licensee: KRBE Lico Inc. Group owner: Susquehanna Radio Corp. (acq 11-86; $25 million. with co-located AM; FTR: 10-6-86). Format: CHR. Target aud: 18-34; general.Peter Brubaker, chmn; David Kennedy, pres; Nancy Vaeth, sr VP; Mark Shecterle, gen mgr; Amy Dewbre, gen sls mgr; Beth Lavine, natl sls mgr; Mike Paterson, mktg dir; Lesley Brotamante, prom mgr & adv mgr; Tracy Austin, progmg dir & progmg mgr; Leslie Whittle, mus dir; Maria Todd, news dir; Benny Boone, pub affrs dir; Andy Hudack, engrg mgr; Chuck Underwood, chief of engrg

KROI(FM)—See Seabrook

KRTX(AM)—(Rosenberg-Richmond). Nov 15, 1948: 980 khz; 1 kw-D, 212 w-N. TL: N29 33 10 W95 47 00. (CP: 5 kw-U, DA-2). Stereo. 1415 N. Loop W., Suite 550 77008. Phone: (713) 407-1415. Fax: (713) 407-1400. Web Site: www.univision.com. Licensee: Tichenor Media System Inc. Group owner: Univision Radio (acq 9-22-2003; grpsl). Rep: Katz Hispanic. Cohn & Marks. Format: Tejano, Sp, var. Target aud: General; Hispanics. ♦Mark Maple, pres; Arnulfo Ramirez, opns VP & opns mgr; Lisa Stout, gen sls mgr; Kim McBride, natl sls mgr; Frances Jones, prom dir; Delores Frtiz, prom mgr & progmg dir; Ferando Hernandez, progmg dir; Renzo Heredia, mktg dir & pub affrs dir; Marty Scruggs, chief of engrg.

KTBZ-FM— Nov 1, 1964: 94.5 mhz; 100 kw. 2,000 ft. TL: N29 34 34 W95 30 36. Stereo. 3050 Post Oak Blvd., Suite 1200 77056. Phone: (713) 212-8000. Fax: (713) 968-1055. Web Site: www.thebuzz.com. Licensee: AMFM Texas Licenses L.P. Group owner: Clear Channel Communications Inc. (acq 8-30-00; grpsl). Rep: D & R Radio. Format: Oldies. Target aud: 25-54; baby boomers. Spec prog: Talk 2 hrs, relg one hr, pub affrs one hr wkly. ♦Ellen Cavanaugh, gen mgr; Jim Trapp, progmg dir.

KTEK(AM)—See Alvin

KTRH(AM)— Mar 29, 1930: 740 khz; 50 kw-U, DA-2. TL: N29 57 57 W94 56 32. 2000 West Loop South, Suite 300 77027. Phone: (713) 526-5874. Fax: (713) 360-3666. Web Site: www.ktrh.com. Licensee: AMFM Texas Licenses L.P. Group owner: Clear Channel Communications Inc. (acq 8-30-2000; grpsl). Network: ABC. Rep: Christal. Dow, Lohnes & Albertson. Format: News, sports. Target aud: 25-54. ♦Mark Kopelman, gen mgr; Betty Scott, progmg dir.

KLOL(FM)—Co-owned with KTRH(AM). 1947: 101.1 mhz; 100 kw. Ant 1,920 ft. TL: N29 34 34 W95 30 36. Stereo. 2000 West Loop S., Suite 300 77027. Phone: (713) 212-8000. Fax: (713) 212-8970. Web Site: www.klol.com. Rep: Christal. Format: Sp. Target aud: 18-54. ♦Paul Lambert, gen sls mgr; Alan Ecklund, natl sls mgr; Melissa Brezner, mktg VP; Rob Skinner, prom dir; Ken Charles, progmg VP; Vince Richards, progmg dir; Steve Fixx, mus dir; Laurent Fouilloud-Buyat, news dir & pub affrs dir; Bob Stroup, chief of engrg.

***KTRU(FM)**— May 20, 1971: 91.7 mhz; 50 kw. 492 ft. TL: N30 03 54 W95 16 10. Stereo. 6100 S. Main 77005. Phone: (713) 348-4098. Fax: (713) 348-4093. E-mail: ktru@ktru.org. Web Site: www.noise.ktru.org. Licensee: Rice University. Format: Div. Target aud: General. Spec prog: Class 8 hrs, jazz 14 hrs, reggae 6 hrs, folk 3 hrs, 60s mus 3 hrs, new age one hr wkly. ♦Will Robedee, gen mgr; Ben Horne, stn mgr; Allan McHale, news dir.

***KTSU(FM)**— October 1973: 90.9 mhz; 18.5 kw. 285 ft. TL: N29 43 25 W95 21 52. Stereo. 3100 Cleburne st. 77004. Phone: (713) 313-7591. Fax: (713) 313-7479. Licensee: Board of Regents Texas Southern University. Format: Educ, div, jazz. News staff: one; News: 10 hrs wkly. Target aud: 25-54. Spec prog: Reggae 8 hrs wkly. ♦Dr. Priscilla Slade, pres; George Thomas, gen mgr; Lindsey Williams, dev mgr, mktg dir, mktg mgr, adv dir & progmg dir; Cheryl Brooks, prom dir; Maurice Hopethompson, news dir; Dave Biondi, chief of engrg.

***KUHF(FM)**— Nov 6, 1950: 88.7 mhz; 100 kw. 1,800 ft. TL: N29 34 28 W95 29 37. Stereo. 4343 Elgin, 3rd Fl. 77204-0887. Phone: (713) 743-0887. Fax: (713) 743-0868. E-mail: kuhf@kuhf.org. Web Site: www.kuhf.org. Licensee: University of Houston. Network: Network: NPR, PRI. Dow, Lohnes & Albertson. Format: Class, news. News staff: 7; News: 25 hrs wkly. Target aud: 25 plus. ♦John Gladney Proffitt, CEO & gen mgr; Debra Fraser, stn mgr, prom dir & progmg mgr; Victor C. Kendell, dev dir; Robert Cahill, prom dir; Kathy Rogers, adv mgr; Dean Dalton, mus dir; Paul Pendergraft, news dir; Chris Hathaway, pub affrs dir; Alex Schneider, chief of engrg.

KXYZ(AM)— Aug 8, 1930: 1320 khz; 5 kw-U, DA-N. TL: N29 42 37 W95 10 29. 2700 Pasadena Fwy., Pasadena 77506. Phone: (713) 473-2500. Fax: (713) 984-1721. Web Site: www.radiounica.com. Licensee: Multicultural Radio Broadcasting Licensee LLC. Group owner: Multicultural Radio Broadcasting Inc. (acq 12-1-2003; grpsl). Rep: Caballero. Format: Contemp Sp, talk. ♦Barry Perrault, gen mgr & gen sls mgr.

Howe

KHYI(FM)— April 1949: 95.3 mhz; 16 kw. 413 ft. TL: N33 23 43 W96 35 50. Stereo. Box 940670, Plano 75094. Secondary address: 660 N. Central Expwy., Suite 120, Dlano 75074. Phone: (972) 633.0953. Fax: (972) 633-0957. E-mail: ken.jones@kxez.com. Web Site: www.khyi.com. Licensee: Metro Broadcasters-Texas Inc. Network: ABC. Fletcher, Heald & Hildreth. Format: Classic country. News staff: one; News: 3 hrs wkly. Target aud: 25-54; affluent, white collar, middle to upper income listeners. ♦Ken Jones, CEO, pres, gen mgr, news dir & chief of engrg; Glenda Jones, CFO; Lou Rogers, opns dir, opns mgr & pub

Texas   Directory of Radio

affrs dir; Joshua Jones, sls dir, gen sls mgr, mktg VP, mktg dir & prom dir; Bruce Kidder, progmg dir; Mike Doyal, engrg dir; Ron Eudaly, engrg dir.

Hudson

KLSN(FM)—Not on air, target date: unknown: 96.3 mhz; 1.35 kw. Ant 695 ft. TL: N31 21 55 W94 45 59. Box 111, Livingston 77351. Phone: (800) 600-5389. Fax: (936) 327-8477. Licensee: Lone Star Netwok (acq 5-11-01). Format: Country.

Humble

KGOL(AM)— July 18, 1984: 1180 khz; 50 kw-D, 1 kw-N, DA-3. TL: N30 08 21 W95 17 24. Stereo. 5821 Southwest Fwy., Suite 600, Houston 77057. Phone: (713) 349-9880. Fax: (713) 349-0647. E-mail: caguilar@entravision.com. Licensee: Entravision Holdings LLC. Group owner: Entravision Communications Corp. (acq 7-28-00; grpsl). Luther & Watkins. Format: Foreign/Ethnic. News staff: one. Target aud: General; ethnic & Asian. Spec prog: Hindi 15 hrs wkly. ♦ Walter Ulloa, CEO; Jeff Liberman, pres; Carmen Aguilar, gen mgr; David Padgett, opns mgr & progmg mgr; Rick Hunt, engrg VP.

*KSBJ(FM)— July 6, 1982: 89.3 mhz; 100 kw. Ant 840 ft. TL: N30 12 26 W95 05 28. Stereo. Box 187 77338. Secondary address: 327 Wilson Rd. 77347. Phone: (281) 446-5725. Fax: (281) 540-2198. Web Site: www.ksbj.org. Licensee: KSBJ Educational Foundation. Format: Contemp Christian. News staff: 31; News: 4 hrs wkly. Target aud: 25-49; Christian adults. ♦ Tim McDermott, gen mgr; Jason Ray, prom dir; Tom Carter, prom mgr; John Hull, progmg dir; Jim Beeler, mus dir; Amanda Carroll, news dir; George Schank, chief of engrg.

Huntington

KSML-FM— March 1, 1994: 101.9 mhz; 24.5 kw. Ant 666 ft. TL: N31 22 08 W94 38 45. Stereo. Yates Broadcasting, 121 Cotton Sq., Lufkin 75902. Phone: (936) 637-1019. Fax: (409) 632-5722. Web Site: www.kybi.com. Licensee: Yates Broadcasting Corp. Format: Adult contemp. ♦ Steven Yates, gen mgr.

Huntsville

*KHCH(AM)— Oct 4, 1982: 1400 khz; 600 w-D, 1 kw-N. TL: N30 43 07 W95 31 40. 2424 South Blvd., Houston 77098. Phone: (713) 520-5200. E-mail: khcb@nol.net. Web Site: www.khcb.org. Licensee: KHCB Inc. Group owner: Houston Christian Broadcasters Inc. (acq 10-97; $145,000). Network: Moody. Format: Christian, inspirational, easy lstng. Spec prog: Sp 8 hrs, Chinese 1 hr wkly. ♦ Bruce Munsterman, gen mgr.

KHVL(AM)— Nov 3, 1938: 1490 khz; 1 kw-U. TL: N30 41 48 W95 33 08. Box 330 77342. Secondary address: 622 Interstate 45 S. 77340. Phone: (936) 295-2651. Fax: (936) 295-8201. E-mail: ksam-fm@swbell.net. Web Site: www.khvl.com. Licensee: HEH Communications LLC (acq 12-11-00; $1.9 million. with co-located FM). Network: ABC. Format: Oldies. News staff: one. Target aud: 35 plus; general. Spec prog: Black 5 hrs wkly. ♦ Steve Everett, gen mgr; Brooke Addams, opns mgr; LeeAn Kelly, news dir.

KSAM-FM—Co-owned with KHVL(AM). Aug 1, 1965: 101.7 mhz; 6 kw. 420 ft. TL: N30 41 48 W95 33 08. Stereo. E-mail: ksammail@yahoo.com. Web Site: www.ksam1017.com. Format: Country. News staff: one; News: 2 hrs wkly. Target aud: 25-54; general.

*KSHU(FM)— October 1973: 90.5 mhz; 3 kw. 255 ft. TL: N30 42 50 W95 32 58. Stereo. Box 2207, 1804 Avenue J 77341. Phone: (936) 294-3939. Phone: (936) 294-1342. Fax: (936) 294-1888. E-mail: rtf_kshu@shsu.edu. Web Site: www.shsu.edu/~rtf_kshu. Licensee: Sam Houston State University. Format: Class, CHR, jazz. News. 25 hrs wkly. Target aud: General; rural. Spec prog: Sp 4 hrs wkly. ♦ Terry L. Rosati, gen mgr; Matt Orlando, opns dir; Adam Spry, progmg dir; Lowery Woodall, mus dir; Rachel Connner, news dir; Jenna Zibton, pub affrs dir; Steve Sandlin, chief of engrg.

Hurst

KMNY(AM)— April 1947: 1360 khz; 50 kw-D, 890 w-N, DA-2. TL: N32 46 28 W96 57 53. 3304 W. Camp Wisdom Rd., Suite 100, Dallas 75237. Phone: (972) 572-1540. Web Site: www.kdft.com. Licensee: Multicultural Radio Broadcasting Licensee LLC. Group owner: Multicultural Radio Broadcasting Inc. (acq 2-4-2004; grpsl). Network: USA. Format: Sp. ♦ Ted Sauceman, gen mgr.

Hutto

KQJZ(FM)—Licensed to Hutto. See Austin

Idalou

KRBL(FM)— Sept 18, 1995: 105.7 mhz; 6 kw. 328 ft. TL: N33 40 06 W101 37 52. 916 Main St., Suite 617, Lubbock 79401. Phone: (806) 749-1057. Fax: (806) 749-1177. Licensee: Triumph Communications Inc. Format: Classic country. Target aud: 24-64. ♦ Paul Beane, gen mgr, opns mgr & news dir; Steve Ritchie, gen sls mgr & adv dir; Anthony Garza, progmg dir & chief of engrg.

Ingleside

KJKE(FM)— 1996: 107.3 mhz; 14 kw. Ant 446 ft. TL: N27 52 00 W97 13 08. 826 S. Padre Island Dr., Corpus Christi 78416. Phone: (361)855-3974. Fax: (361) 855-3770. E-mail: 1073x@1073.com. Web Site: 1073thex.com. Licensee: Convergent Broadcasting Corpus Christi LP. Group owner: Convergent Broadcasting LLC (acq 1-12-2004; grpsl). Format: Alternative rock. ♦ Mark White, gen mgr; Dallas Garcia, adv mgr; Scott Holt, progmg dir; William Hooper, engr.

Ingram

*KTXI(FM)— November 1998: 90.1 mhz; 50 kw. 453 ft. TL: N30 06 14 W99 04 36. Stereo. Texas Public Radio, 8401 Datapoint Dr., Suite 800, San Antonio 78229. Phone: (210) 614-8977. Fax: (210) 614-8983. Web Site: www.ktxi.fm. Licensee: Texas Public Radio. Network: Network: NPR, PRI. Garvey, Schubert & Barer. Format: Class, news. Target aud: 25 plus. ♦ Joe Gwathmey, pres & gen mgr; Nathan Cone, opns mgr; Penny Dennis, progmg dir; Wayne Coble, engrg dir.

Jacksboro

KJKB(FM)— Oct 6, 1996: . Stn currently dark 95.5 mhz; 6 kw. Ant 328 ft. TL: N33 19 43 W98 16 46. 1032 S. Union Blvd., Lakewood, CO 80228. Phone: (303) 989-3920. Fax: (303) 989-3987. E-mail: huntmedia@aol.com. Licensee: Hunt Broadcasting Inc. Group owner: On-Air Family LLC (acq 1995; $6,000). ♦ Janice Hunt, CEO & gen mgr; Jim Hunt, exec VP.

Jacksonville

*KBJS(FM)— May 16, 1987: 90.3 mhz; 3 kw. 266 ft. TL: N31 58 16 W95 15 51. (CP: 19 kw, ant 1,286 ft. TL: N32 03 40 W95 18 50). Stereo. Box 193 75766. Phone: (903) 586-5257. Fax: (903) 586-4986. E-mail: info@kbjs.org. Web Site: www.kbjs.org. Licensee: East Texas Media Association Inc. Network: Moody. Format: Relg, Christian. Spec prog: Black one hr, Sp one hr wkly. ♦ Bob Shivery, pres & gen mgr; Randy Featherston, stn mgr; Eddie Baiseri, progmg dir & progmg mgr.

KEBE(AM)— Jan 12, 1947: 1400 khz; 1 kw-U. TL: N31 58 11 W95 15 52. Box 1648 75766. Secondary address: Radio Ctr., 402 S. Ragsdale 75766. Phone: (903) 586-2527. Fax: (903) 586-1394. Web Site: www.kooi.com. Licensee: Waller Broadcasting Inc. Group owner: Waller Broadcasting (acq 11-58; $75,000). Network: ABC Information & Entertainment. Rep: McGavren Guild. Format: Classic country. News staff: 2; News: 6 hrs wkly. Target aud: 25-54. Spec prog: Farm 9 hrs wkly. ♦ Dudley Waller, CEO, pres & gen mgr; Tina Harper, CFO; Jim Lord, opns dir & opns mgr.

KLJT(FM)— 1993: 102.3 mhz; 50 kw. Ant 492 ft. TL: N31 52 18 W95 10 00. Stereo. Box 1648 75766. Secondary address: 402 S. Ragsdale 75766. Phone: (903) 586-2527. Fax: (903) 589-0677. Web Site: www.wallerbroadcast.com. Licensee: Waller Media LLC. Group owner: Waller Broadcasting (acq 12-9-02). Network: ABC. Rep: McGavren Guild. David Tillotson. Format: Adult favorites. News: 6 hrs wkly. ♦ Dudley Waller, CEO & gen mgr.

KOOI-FM— Sept 9, 1967: 106.5 mhz; 100 kw. Ant 1,468 ft. TL: N32 03 40 W95 18 50. Stereo. Box 7820, Tyler 75711. Secondary address: 621 Chase, Tyler 75701. Phone: (903) 581-9966. Fax: (903) 534-5300. E-mail: codouglas@etradiogroup.com. Web Site: www.kooi.com. Licensee: Access.1 Texas License Company LLC. (acq 1-7-2005; grpsl). Network: ABC. Rep: McGavren Guild. Format: Adult contemp. News staff: 3. Target aud: 25-54; upscale adults. ♦ Mary Ramos, gen mgr & opns mgr; Jim Hendrick, gen sls mgr & natl sls mgr; Charlie O'Douglas, progmg dir, Rick Guest, mktg mgr & mus dir.

Jasper

KCOX(AM)— Aug 6, 1948: 1350 khz; 5 kw-D, 37 w-N. TL: N30 55 11 W93 68 13. Box 2008 75951. Phone: (409) 384-6801. Fax: (409) 384-3866. E-mail: kwyx@sabinenet.com. Web Site: www.jasperradio.com. Licensee: Lasting Value Radio Inc. (acq 5-11-00; $902,000. with co-located FM). Network: Network: Westwood One, ABC Daytime Direction. Format: News/talk. Spec prog: Farm 5 hrs, gospel 6 hrs wkly. ♦ Meredith Beal, pres; Shelly Williams, gen mgr, gen sls mgr & natl sls mgr; Clay Collins, progmg dir; Dade Moore, chief of engrg.

KTXJ-FM—Co-owned with KCOX(AM). November 1964: 102.7 mhz; 26 kw. 440 ft. TL: N31 03 36 W93 57 42. Stereo. Format: Country.

KJAS(FM)— 1996: 107.3 mhz; 8 kw. Ant 328 ft. TL: N30 58 31 W93 59 24. Stereo. 765 Hemphill St. 75951. Phone: (409) 384-2626. Fax: (409) 383-1979. E-mail: wb5rfk@jas.net. Web Site: www.kjas.com. Licensee: DBA Rayburn Broadcasting Co. Booth, Freret, Imlay & Tepper. Format: Adult contemp. News staff: one; News: 4 hrs wkly. Target aud: 24-54; females/buying group. Spec prog: Oldies 4 hrs wkly. ♦ Mike Lout, gen mgr; Melaney Dickerson, opns mgr; Debra Foster, sls VP & gen sls mgr; Crystal Mouton, pub affrs dir.

Jefferson

*KHCJ(FM)— 2003: 91.9 mhz; 3.1 kw. Ant 462 ft. TL: N32 49 23 W94 28 32. Houston Christian Broadcasters Inc., 2424 South Blvd., Houston 77098. Phone: (713) 520-5200. Web Site: www.khcb.org. Licensee: Houston Christian Broadcasters Inc. (group owner). Format: Christian. ♦ Bruce E. Munsterman, gen mgr.

KJTX(FM)— October 1990: 104.5 mhz; 3 kw. 423 ft. TL: N32 48 13 W94 22 26. (CP 2.3 kw, ant 531 ft.). Stereo. 625 kellyville Cutoff 75657. Phone: (903) 665-1150. Fax: (903) 665-1170. Web Site: www.kjtxgospel.com. Licensee: Wisdom Ministries Inc. (acq 4-16-93; $140,000; 5-3-93). Format: Gospel, Christian. News: 2 hrs wkly. Target aud: 25 plus. ♦ Leroy Richardson, pres, pres, gen mgr, progmg dir & chief of engrg.

Johnson City

KFAN-FM— 1991: 107.9 mhz; 37.2 kw. 492 ft. TL: N30 11 49 W98 38 19. Stereo. Box 311, 210 Woodcrest, Fredericksburg 78624. Phone: (830) 997-2197. Fax: (830) 997-2198. E-mail: texasrebelradio@fbg.net. Web Site: www.texasrebelradio.com. Licensee: J. & J. Fritz Media Ltd. (group owner). Format: Americana AAA. News staff: one. Target aud: 25-49. Spec prog: Jazz 5 hrs wkly. ♦ Jayson Fritz, pres, gen mgr & gen sls mgr; Jan Fritz, sr VP, mktg VP & adv VP; Jay Fritz, stn mgr; Ariana Perrum, prom VP; Mac McClennahan, progmg dir; Rick Star, mus dir; Kyle Province, news dir & pub affrs dir; Duncan Black, chief of engrg.

Jourdanton

KLEY-FM— 2001: 95.7 mhz; 12.5 kw. Ant 462 ft. TL: N28 56 59 W98 37 05. 9426 Old Katy Rd., Bldg. 10, Houston 77055. Phone: (817) 335-5999. Fax: (817) 335-1197. Licensee: BMP San Antonio License Co. L.P. (group owner; (acq 12-23-2004; $7.5 million). Format: Sp. ♦ Thomas Castro, gen mgr.

Junction

KMBL(AM)— 1953: 1450 khz; 1 kw-U. TL: N30 29 34 W99 45 41. 2125 Sidney Baker, Kerrville 78028. Secondary address: 214 Pecan St. 76899. Phone: (830) 896-1230. Fax: (830) 792-4142. E-mail: generalmanager@krvl.com. Licensee: Kimble County Communications Inc. Group owner: Hill Country Broadcasting Corp. (acq 7 7 08; $165,000. with co-located FM). Network: Westwood One. Format: Country. News staff: one; News: 6 hrs wkly. Target aud: General. Spec prog: Farm 6 hrs wkly. ♦ Kent Foster, CEO & pres; Monte Spearman, gen mgr, dev dir & mktg dir; Harley Belew, opns dir; Glen Taylor, prom dir; Monte Speaman, adv dir; A.J. Hernandez, progmg dir; Charles Rodiaquez, news dir; Carolyn Anderson, pub affrs dir; Steve Alex, stn mgr, sls dir & engrg VP.

KOOK(FM)— 1997: 93.5 mhz; 50 kw. 492 ft. TL: N30 29 31 W100 02 03. 2125 Sidney Baker St, Kerrville 78028. Phone: (830) 896-1230. Fax: (830) 792-4142. Licensee: Kimble County Communications Inc. Group owner: Hill Country Broadcasting Corp. (acq 8-16-00; grpsl). Network: ABC. Format: Country. Spec prog: Gospel 2 hrs wkly. ♦ Monte Spearman, gen mgr; Donna Keese, opns mgr.

Stations in the U.S. — Texas

Karnes City

KTXX(FM)— March 2005: 103.1 mhz; 34 kw. Ant 587 ft. TL: N29 00 52 W97 40 02. 2801 Via Fortuna Dr., Suite 675, Austin 78746. Phone: (512) 329-5843. Fax: (512) 329-5847. Licensee: Palm Broadcasting Co. Format: Talk. ♦Robert Walker, gen mgr.

Keene

*KJCR(FM)— June 13, 1974: 88.3 mhz; 23 kw. 180 ft. TL: N32 24 19 W97 19 55. Stereo. 304 N. College Dr. 76059. Phone: (817) 556-4788. Fax: (817) 556-4790. Web Site: www.kjcr.org. Licensee: Southwestern Adventist University. Donald E. Martin. Format: Relg. News: 8 hrs wkly. Target aud: 18 plus; general. ♦Don Sahly, pres; Randy Yates, gen mgr; Jon Armstrong, opns mgr & progmg dir; Jessica Protasio, sls dir & mus dir; Kristina Pascual, prom dir & news dir; Ron Macomber, chief of engrg.

Kenedy

KTNR(FM)—Licensed to Kenedy. See Kenedy-Karnes City

Kenedy-Karnes City

KAML(AM)— November 1954: 990 khz; 250 w-D, 70 w-N. TL: N28 51 02 W97 52 48. Rt. 1 Box 990, Kenedy 78119-9719. Secondary address: Box 990, Karnes City 78118. Phone: (830) 583-2990. Fax: (830) 583-0700. Licensee: SIGA Broadcasting Corp. (group owner; acq 1-17-2002). Rep: Dome. Format: Country, news, sports. News staff: 2; News: 8 hrs wkly. Target aud: 24-54; m-f. ♦Gabriel Arango, pres; Clyde Eckols, gen mgr; Clyde S. Eckols, mktg dir & sls; Steve Eckols, progmg dir.

KTNR(FM)—(Kenedy). Sept 1, 1982: 92.1 mhz; 3 kw. Ant 220 ft. TL: N28 45 35 W97 51 45. (CP: 6 kw, ant 262 ft). Stereo. Box 1614, Laredo 78044. Phone: (956) 726-4738. Fax: (956) 722-2184. Web Site: www.lacadenaradioluz.com/ktnr.htm. Licensee: Blue Texas Broadcasting LLC (acq 12-23-2003; $200,000). ♦Israel Tellez Sr., pres & gen mgr; Hiram G. Tellez, opns mgr.

Kerens

KRVF(FM)— May 23, 1979: 106.9 mhz; 21.5 kw. Ant 365 ft. TL: N32 06 12 W96 22 33. Stereo. 1373 S.E. Country Rd. 0070, Coriscana 75109. Phone: (903) 872-4757. Fax: (903) 885-9107. Licensee: LKCM Radio Group L.P. (group owner; (acq 3-15-2004; $1 million. with KRVA-FM Campbell). Format: Oldies. ♦Bert Goldman, exec VP; Chris McMurray, gen mgr.

Kermit

KERB(AM)— June 1950: 600 khz; 1 kw-D, DA. TL: N31 50 05 W103 08 10. Box 252, McAllen 78505. Phone: (956) 781-5528. Fax: (956) 686-2999. Licensee: La Radio Cristiana Network Inc. (acq 5-20-97; $80,000 with co-located FM). Rep: Keystone (unwired net). Format: Christian, Sp Christian. ♦Eloy Bernal, gen mgr; Gilbert Martinez, progmg dir.

KERB-FM— 1983: 106.3 mhz; 3 kw. 276 ft. TL: N31 50 05 W103 08 10. Web Site: www.laradiocristiana.com.

Kerrville

KCOR-FM—See Comfort

KERV(AM)— Nov 5, 1948: 1230 khz; 990 w-U. TL: N30 04 14 W99 11 07. Stereo. 2125 Sidney Baker N. 78028. Phone: (830) 896-1230. Phone: (800) 763-5785. Fax: (830) 792-4142. Web Site: www.kerv.com. Licensee: Barbwire Communications Inc. Group owner: Hill Country Broadcasting Corp. (acq 8-16-00; with co-located FM). Network: Network: Westwood One, ABC Information & Entertainment. Format: Nostalgia. News staff: one; News: 3 hrs wkly. Target aud: 45 plus; educated professionals. Spec prog: Relg 2 hrs, gospel one hr. ♦Kent Foster, pres; Harley Belew, progmg dir.

KRVL(FM)—Co-owned with KERV(AM). Sept 12, 1975: 94.3 mhz; 50 kw. 492 ft. TL: N30 15 45 W99 07 59. Stereo. Web Site: www.krvl.com. Network: ABC. Format: Country. Target aud: 25-49. Spec prog: Gospel 2 hrs, local church service 1 hr wkly.

*KHKV(FM)— 1998: 91.1 mhz; 300 w. 207 ft. TL: N30 02 37 W99 07 17. 2424 South Blvd., Houston 77098. Phone: (713) 520-5200. Web Site: www.khcb.org. Licensee: Houston Christian Broadcasters Inc. (group owner). Format: Christian, Sp. ♦Bruce Munsterman, gen mgr.

*KKER(FM)— Dec 8, 2000: 88.7 mhz; 5 kw. Ant 384 ft. TL: N30 06 07 W99 04 38. (CP: 100 kw, ant 380 ft). Houston Christian Broadcasters Inc., 2424 South Blvd, Houston 77098. Phone: (713) 520-5200. Web Site: www.khcb.org. Licensee: Houston Christian Broadcasters Inc. (group owner; acq 11-24-00; $3,500. for CP with CP of KHCP(FM) Paris). Format: Christian. ♦Bruce Munsterman, gen mgr.

KRNH(FM)— June 1994: 92.3 mhz; 44 kw. 403 ft. TL: N30 07 04 W99 11 40. 1216 B Sidney Baker S. 78028. Phone: (830) 896-4990. Fax: (830) 896-4991. E-mail: phylis@theranchfm92.com. Web Site: www.theranchfm92.com. Licensee: Radio Ranch Ltd. (acq 9-6-00; $245,000). Baraff, Koerner & Olender. Format: Country. Target aud: 18-64. Spec prog: Sp 4 hrs, gospel 3 hrs wkly. ♦Mark Grubbs, gen mgr; Leslie Klein, stn mgr.

Kilgore

KBGE(AM)—Listing follows KKTX-FM.

KKTX-FM— Dec 23, 1976: 96.1 mhz; 50 kw. Ant 492 ft. TL: N32 22 14 W94 56 20. Stereo. 3810 Brookside Dr., Tyler 75701. Phone: (903) 581-0606. Fax: (903) 581-2011. Web Site: www.kktx.com. Licensee: Capstar TX L.P. (acq 8-30-2000; grpsl). Format: Classic rock. Target aud: 25-54. ♦Craig Reininger, sls dir; Chris Jones, rgnl sls mgr; Lisa Nix, progmg dir.

KBGE(AM)—Co-owned with KKTX-FM. Dec 26, 1936: 1240 khz; 1 kw-U. TL: N32 25 02 W94 51 15. Web Site: www.kktx.com. Group owner: Clear Channel Communications Inc. Rep: Katz Radio, Target Broadcast Sales. Target aud: 25-54.

*KTPB(FM)— Feb 4, 1991: 88.7 mhz; 63 kw horiz, 79 kw vert. 551 ft. TL: N32 20 14 W95 02 41. Stereo. 904 Houston 75662. Phone: (903) 983-8625. Fax: (903) 984-8957. E-mail: ktpb@ballistic.com. Web Site: www.ktpb.com. Licensee: Kilgore College. Network: PRI. Arter & Hadden. Format: Class. News staff: one; News: 6 hrs wkly. Target aud: 35-50; higher socio-economic, educated. Spec prog: Jazz 4 hrs, new age 6 hrs, loc concerts 2 hrs, children one hr, show tunes 2 hrs, big band 4 wkly. ♦Kathy A. Housby, gen mgr; Manuel Almanza, opns dir.

Killeen

KIIZ-FM— Dec 10, 1990: 92.3 mhz; 3 kw. 259 ft. TL: N31 06 33 W97 39 00. Stereo. Box 2469, Harker Heights 76548. Phone: (254) 699-5000. Fax: (254) 680-4211. Web Site: www.kiiz.com. Licensee: Capstar TX L.P. Group owner: Clear Channel Communications Inc. (acq 8-30-00; grpsl). Format: Urban. News: 2 hrs wkly. Target aud: 18-49. ♦Tim Thomas, gen mgr & stn mgr; Jim Martin, gen sls mgr; Terry Steele, prom mgr; Julia Conner, news dir; Brett Gilbert, chief of engrg.

*KNCT-FM— Nov 23, 1970: 91.3 mhz; 50 kw. 1,170 ft. TL: N30 59 12 W97 37 47. Stereo. Box 1800, Central Texas College, 6200 W. Central Texas Expwy. 76542. Phone: (254) 526-1176. Fax: (254) 526-1850. Web Site: www.knct.org. Licensee: Central Texas College. Network: PRI. Format: Btfl mus, class. Target aud: 45 plus. Spec prog: Jazz 15 hrs wkly, big band 6 hrs wkly. ♦Max Rudolph, gen mgr; Dan Hull, progmg dir; Steve Sulzer, chief of engrg. Co-owned TV: *KNCT(TV) affil

KRMY(AM)— July 4, 1955: 1050 khz; 250 w-D. TL: N31 06 53 W97 42 00. Box 488 76540-0488. Secondary address: 314 N. 2nd St. 76514. Phone: (254) 628-7070. Fax: (254) 634-5263. Licensee: Martin Broadcasting Inc. (group owner; acq 11-89; grpsl; FTR: 11-27-89). Format: Gospel/Religious. Target aud: 18-44. ♦Darrell Martin, gen mgr; Horatio Martinez, progmg dir.

KUSJ(FM)—See Temple

Kingsville

KFTX(FM)— May 2, 1970: 97.5 mhz; 100 kw. 1,000 ft. TL: N27 30 54 W97 51 58. Stereo. 1520 S. Port Ave., Corpus Christi 78405. Phone: (361) 883-5987. Fax: (361) 883-3648. Web Site: www.kftx.com. Licensee: Quality Broadcasting Corp. (acq 12-23-88; $800,000; 1-23-89). Rep: Allied Radio Partners. Wood, Maines & Brown. Format: Country. News staff: one; News: 2 hrs wkly. Target aud: 25-49; educated, affluent young adults. ♦Bruce Nelson Stratton, gen mgr & stn mgr; Deborah DeSola, sls dir; Kenda West, gen sls mgr & natl sls mgr; Joshua Sandoval, prom VP; Chuck Abel, progmg dir; Austin Daniels, mus dir; Henry Turner, chief of engrg.

KINE(AM)— November 1948: 1330 khz; 1 kw-D, 250 w-N. TL: N27 36 36 W97 47 42. 115 W. Avenue D, Rob Towns 78380. Phone: (361) 855-1330. Fax: (361) 289-7722. Licensee: Cotton Broadcasting. (acq 9-28-90; $50,000; 10-22-90). Format: Rgnl Sp, relg. Target aud: 25-54. ♦Humberto L. Lopez, CEO; Humberto Lopez, pres; Carlos Lopez, gen mgr; Minerva R. Lopez, dev VP; Ernest Lopez, sls VP; Manuel Lopez, prom VP; Homer Lopez, mus dir; Tommy Greg, chief of engrg.

KKBA(FM)— November 1981: 92.7 mhz; 12.5 kw. 869 ft. TL: N27 32 07 W97 53 06. Stereo. Box 9757, Corpus Christi 78469. Secondary address: 2117 Leopard St., CorpusChristi 78408. Phone: (361) 883-3516. Fax: (361) 882-9767. E-mail: thechief@star94.net. Web Site: www.927kkba.com. Licensee: Malkan Broadcasting L.P. Group owner: Malkan Broadcast Assoc. (acq 9-13-95; FTR: 10-2-95). Rep: Katz Radio. Fletcher, Heald & Hildreth. Format: Adult contemp. News staff: one; News: 20 hrs wkly. Target aud: 25-54. ♦Glen Powers, pres & gen mgr; Janice Raleigh, sls dir; Norma Morales, prom dir; John Gifford, engrg dir & chief of engrg; Bart Allison, progmg.

*KTAI(FM)— Feb 23, 1970: 91.1 mhz; 100 w. 98 ft. TL: N27 31 24 W97 52 42. Stereo. 700 University Blvd., MSC 178, Texas A & M Univ.-Kingsville 78363. Phone: (361) 593-3489. E-mail: ktaifm@hotmail.com. Web Site: www.tamuk.edu/ktai. Licensee: Texas A&M University-Kingsville. Format: Rock. Target aud: 16-25; high school & college ages. Spec prog: Black 8 hrs, gospel 6 hrs, mus from India 3 hrs, mus from Mexico 3 hrs wkly. ♦Rumaldo Juarez, pres & gen mgr.

Krum

KNOR(FM)— Nov 11, 1984: 93.7 mhz; 12 kw. Ant 1,952 ft. TL: N33 26 13 W97 29 05. Stereo. Box 1487, Ardmore 73402. Secondary address: 115 W. Broadway St., Suite 501, Ardmore 73401. Phone: (580) 226-5105. Fax: (580) 226-5113. Web Site: www.kicm.com. Licensee: Liberman Broadcasting of Dallas License Corp. Group owner: Liberman Broadcasting Inc. (acq 5-13-2004; $15.5 million). Network: CBS. Rep: Roslin. Fletcher, Heald & Hildreth. Format: Progsv country. News staff: one; News: 8 hrs wkly. Target aud: 21-49; middle, upper-middle class listeners. ♦Curt Spain, gen mgr, gen sls mgr & progmg dir; Rob Carter, opns dir & opns mgr; Jodie Westerfelt, prom mgr; Steve Spain, mus dir; Pat Ownbey, news dir.

La Grange

KBUK(FM)—Listing follows KVLG(AM).

KVLG(AM)— June 27, 1959: 1570 khz; 250 w-D, DA-1. TL: N29 52 58 W96 51 57. Box 609 78945. Secondary address: FM 155 S. 78945. Phone: (979) 968-3173. Phone: (979) 743-4050. Fax: (979) 968-6196. Web Site: www.kvlgkbuk.com. Licensee: Fayette Broadcasting Corp. Format: Country. Target aud: General. Spec prog: Ger one hr, Black one hr, farm 4 hrs, Pol/Czech 12 hrs, relg 5 hrs wkly. ♦Roy Cerney, gen mgr & progmg dir.

Texas

Lake Jackson

KBRZ(AM)—See Freeport

KLDE(FM)— April 1963: 107.5 mhz; 100 kw. 2,000 ft. TL: N29 17 16 W95 13 53. Stereo. 1990 Post Oak Blvd., Suite 2300, Houston 77056. Phone: (713) 961-0093. Fax: (713) 993-9300. Web Site: www.klde.com. Licensee: CXR Holdings L.L.C. Group owner: Cox Television (acq 8-30-2000; grpsl). Format: Oldies. News staff: 2; News: 5 hrs wkly. Target aud: 25-54; college grads from the 60s, 70s & 80s. ◆ Caroline Devine, gen mgr; Doug Abernethy, sls dir; Bill Legrand, gen sls mgr; Mike Murray, natl sls mgr; Bill Tator, mktg dir; Cindy Bell, progmg dir; Ron Parker, progmg dir; Mike Mollett, pub affrs dir; Jed Wilkenson, engrg dir & chief of engrg.

*** KYBJ(FM)**— 1995: 91.1 mhz; 5 kw. 459 ft. TL: N29 02 37 W95 20 11. Box 187, c/o KSBJ(FM), Humble 77347. Phone: (979) 265-9191. Fax: (800) 966-5925. E-mail: kybj@massnet.net. Licensee: Educational Media Foundation of Brazosport. Format: Contemp Christian. Target aud: 25-49. ◆ Tim McDermott, gen mgr; Jon Hull, progmg dir; Amanda Carroll, news dir.

Lamesa

***KBKN(FM)**—Not on air, target date: unknown: 91.3 mhz; 250 w. Ant 157 ft. TL: N32 45 34 W101 57 09. 1406 E. Garden Ln., Midland 79702. Phone: (432) 638-1150. Fax: (432) 682-5230. Web Site: www.lapromesa.org. Licensee: La Promesa Foundation. (acq 5-4-2004; $108,000. including six translator stns). Format: Christian. ◆ Leonard Oswald, pres & gen mgr.

KPET(AM)— May 21, 1947: 690 khz; 250 w-U. TL: N32 42 27 W101 56 11. Box 1188, One Radio Rd. 79331. Phone: (806) 872-6511. Phone: (806) 872-6537. Fax: (806) 872-6514. E-mail: kpet@pics.net. Licensee: KPET Inc. (acq 8-7-91; $150,000). Network: ABC. Format: C&W. News staff: one; News: 2 hrs wkly. Target aud: 18-65. ◆ Don Sitton, chmn, gen mgr, opns dir & progmg dir; Elaine Githens, gen sls mgr & adv mgr; Grover Clifft, news dir; Anthony Garza, chief of engrg.

KTXC(FM)— May 1, 1988: 104.7 mhz; 100 kw. 800 ft. TL: N32 23 47 W101 57 24. Stereo. P.O. Box 60403, Midland 79711. Secondary address: 6 Destra Dr., Suite 6600, Midland 79705. Phone: (915) 570-6670. Fax: (915) 567-9992. Licensee: Graham Brothers Comm. L.L.C. (acq 1999; $270,000). Format: C&W. Target aud: 25-54; college-educated, upper-income families. ◆ Terry Graham, pres; Donn Holcomb, gen mgr & gen sls mgr; Tom Rivers, progmg dir.

Lampasas

KCYL(AM)— 1948: 1450 khz; 1 kw-U. TL: N31 04 31 W98 11 02. 505 N. Key Ave. 76550. Phone: (512) 556-6193. Phone: (512) 556-3671. Fax: (512) 556-2197. E-mail: kcylq102@igg-tx.net. Licensee: Ronald K. Witcher. (acq 2-12-85). Format: C&W. News staff: 3; News: 15 hrs wkly. Target aud: 30 plus; agriculture, farm & ranch. Spec prog: Farm 5 hrs, loc news & community service 14 hrs, sports 8 hrs, relg 10 hrs wkly. ◆ Joe Lombardi, prom mgr & progmg dir; Ronnie Witcher, pres, gen mgr, opns mgr, gen sls mgr & chief of engrg.

Laredo

***KBNL(FM)**— July 27, 1985: 89.9 mhz; 100 kw. Ant 604 ft. TL: N27 39 27 W99 35 10. Stereo. Box 440029 78044. Secondary address: 1620 E. Plum St. 78043. Phone: (956) 724-9090/724-9211. Fax: (956) 724-9919. E-mail: kbnlfm@hcjbeat.org. Licensee: World Radio Network Inc. (group owner; acq 10-24-85). Format: Relg, Sp. News: 2 hrs wkly. Target aud: General. ◆ Arturo Losano, gen mgr.

***KHOY(FM)**— November 1985: 88.1 mhz; 1.8 kw. 348 ft. TL: N27 31 14 W99 31 19. 1901 Corpus Christi 78043. Phone: (956) 722-4167. Fax: (956) 722-4464. Web Site: www.khoy.org. Licensee: Laredo Catholic Communications Inc. Format: Adult contemp, Sp. Target aud: General. ◆ Bennett McBride, gen mgr & news dir; Jose Angel Jimenez, progmg dir.

KJBZ(FM)— Dec 29, 1982: 92.7 mhz; 3 kw. 289 ft. TL: N27 31 04 W99 31 20. Stereo. 902 E. Calton Rd. 78041. Phone: (956) 726-9393. Fax: (956) 724-9915. Licensee: Encarnacion A. Guerra. (acq 12-14-89; $750,000; 1-8-90). Network: ABC Daytime Direction. Format: Tejano. News staff: one; News: 18 hrs wkly. Target aud: General; all ages. ◆ Belinda Guerra, VP, mktg dir & prom mgr; Elaine Matthews, opns dir & progmg dir; Roberto Estrada, gen mgr & gen sls mgr; Eric Navarro, mus dir; Joe Martinez, chief of engrg.

KLAR(AM)— 1956: 1300 khz; 1 kw-D, 80 w-N. TL: N27 31 45 W99 31 15. Stereo. Box 2517 78044. Secondary address: 3320 Anna Ave. 78040-1070. Phone: (956) 723-1300. Fax: (956) 723-9539. Licensee: Faith and Power Communications Inc. (acq 1996). Format: Sp Christian. News staff: 2; News: 18 hrs wkly. Target aud: 18-54; Hispanic & Anglo middle to upper-middle class. ◆ Hector Patino, pres, gen mgr & gen sls mgr.

KLNT(AM)— Apr 20, 1990: 1490 khz; 1 kw-U. Box 814 78042. Secondary address: 505 Houston St. 78042. Phone: (956) 725-1491. Phone: (956) 725-1492. Fax: (956) 725-3424. E-mail: talk@1490.com. Licensee: BMP 100.5 FM L.P. Group owner: Amigo Broadcasting L.P. (acq 11-9-2004; grpsl). Rep: Caballero. Fisher, Wayland, Cooper, Leader & Zaragoza L.L.P. Format: News/talk. News staff: 2; News: 6 hrs wkly. Target aud: 18-54. ◆ Thomas H. Castro, pres; Raul Rodriguez, gen mgr; Ruben Villarreal, opns dir; Joe Flores, sls.

KNEX(FM)— 1992: 106.1 mhz; 3 kw. 213 ft. TL: N27 33 12 W99 24 17. 505 Houston St. 78040. Phone: (956) 725-1491. Phone: (956) 725-1492. Fax: (956) 725-3424. Licensee: BMP 100.5 FM L.P. Group owner: Amigo Broadcasting L.P. (acq 11-9-2004; grpsl). Format: CHR, Sp. ◆ Miguel A. Villarreal Jr., gen mgr; Jorge Arredondo, gen sls mgr; Ruben Villarreal, opns mgr & progmg dir; Artura Serna, mus dir; Deyla Villarreal, news dir; Arturo Trevino, chief of engrg.

KQUR(FM)— Feb 2, 1972: 94.9 mhz; 100 kw. Ant 1,000 ft. TL: N27 31 14 W99 31 19. Stereo. 505 Houston St. 78040. Phone: (956) 725-1491. Fax: (956) 725-3424. Licensee: Border Broadcasters Inc. Rep: Roslin. Fisher, Wayland, Cooper, Leader & Zaragoza. Format: Classic hits. Target aud: 25-54; general. ◆ Miguel Villarreal, gen mgr; Ruben Villarreal, opns dir & opns mgr; Jorge Redando, gen sls mgr; Deyla Villarreal, progmg dir; Arturo Trevino, chief of engrg; Al Guevara, progmg.

KRRG(FM)— October 1982: 98.1 mhz; 100 kw. 737 ft. TL: N27 31 14 W99 31 19. Stereo. 902 E. Calton Rd. 78041. Phone: (956) 724-9800. Fax: (956) 724-9915. Licensee: Guerra Enterprises. (acq 11-20-92; $1.2 million; 12-21-92). Rep: D & R Radio. Format: Adult contemp, CHR. ◆ Belinda Guerra, pres & VP; Elaine Matthews, opns dir & progmg dir; Roberto Estrada, gen mgr, stn mgr & gen sls mgr; Joe Martinez, chief of engrg.

Leakey

KBLT(FM)— June 10, 1997: 104.3 mhz; 1 kw. 594 ft. TL: N29 41 34 W99 48 56. Box 56 78873. Secondary address: 935 East Main, Uvalde 78801. Phone: (830) 278-3693. Fax: (830) 278-2329. Licensee: Radio Cactus Ltd. (acq 10-23-00; $60,916. for 51% of stock with KBNU(FM) Uvalde). Format: Contemp Christian. Target aud: General. ◆ John Furr, pres & chief of engrg; Regenia Tumbarello, gen mgr.

Leander

KHHL(FM)— May 16, 1976: 98.9 mhz; 25 kw. Ant 538 ft. TL: N30 23 26 W97 50 13. Stereo. 7524 N. Lamar Blvd., Suite 200, Austin 78752. Phone: (512) 416-1100. Fax: (512) 416-8205. Licensee: BMP Austin License Company L.P. Group owner: Amigo Broadcasting L.P. (acq 11-9-2004; grpsl). Network: Network: ABC, Westwood One. Rep: D & R Radio. Wilkinson Barker Knauer. Format: Rgnl Mexican. Target aud: 25-54; adults. ◆ Pedro Gasc, gen mgr.

Levelland

KLVT(AM)— August 1949: 1230 khz; 1 kw-U. TL: N33 35 49 W102 23 09. Box 967 799336. Secondary address: 611 N. West Ave. 79336. Phone: (806) 894-3134. Fax: (806) 894-3135. E-mail: klvtlvl@aol.com. Licensee: Paul R. Beane (acq 6-1-00; $350,250. with co-located FM). Format: Gospel. ◆ Jody Rose, gen mgr, progmg dir & progmg dir; Anthony Garza, chief of engrg.

KLVT-FM— Nov 8, 1983: 105.3 mhz; 25 kw. Ant 298 ft. TL: N33 34 54 W102 23 48. Stereo. Format: Classic country. ◆ Steve Ritchie, opns mgr; Steve Richie, progmg dir.

Lewisville

KESS-FM— Apr 10, 1999: 107.9 mhz; 100 kw. Ant 981 ft. TL: N33 19 42 W97 03 56. 7700 John Carpenter Fwy., Dallas 75247. Phone: (214) 525-0400. Fax: (214) 631-1154. Web Site: www.univisionradio.com. Licensee: KECS-FM License Corp. Group owner: Univision Radio (acq 9-22-2003; grpsl). Rep: Katz Hispanic. Format: Mexican rgnl. ◆ Frank Carter, gen mgr; Andy Lockridge, opns dir; Cipriano Robles,

sls dir; Karen Hocking, natl sls mgr; Oscar Espinosa, prom dir; Herminio (Chayan) Ortuno, progmg dir.

Liberty

KSHN-FM— November 1977: 99.9 mhz; 26 kw. 679 ft. TL: N30 03 05 W94 31 37. Stereo. 2099 Sam Houston St. 77575-4817. Phone: (936) 336-5793. Fax: (936) 336-5250. E-mail: kshn@kshn.com. Web Site: www.kshn.com. Licensee: Trinity River Valley Broadcasting Co. (acq 11-77). Pepper & Corazzini. Format: Adult contemp, oldies, country. News staff: one; News: 36 hrs wkly. Target aud: 34 plus; Adults. Spec prog: Black 3 hrs, bluegrass 2 hrs, relg 5 hrs wkly. ◆ Bill Buchanan, CEO, pres, gen mgr, gen sls mgr & adv mgr; Tiffany York, dev dir & prom dir; Eric Latz, progmg dir; Pat Green, news dir; Barbara Moss, pub affrs dir; James Stephenson, chief of engrg.

Littlefield

KZZN(AM)— 1947: 1490 khz; 1 kw-U. TL: N33 56 17 W102 20 38. Box 510 79339. Secondary address: 338 Phelps Ave. 79339. Phone: (806) 385-4474. Phone: (806) 385-1490. Fax: (806) 385-6229. Licensee: Paul R. Beane (acq 11-02; $100,000). Network: USA. Format: Country, gospel. Target aud: General; try to reach all ages. Spec prog: Farm 7 hrs, relg 5 hrs wkly. ◆ Paul Beane, CEO & gen mgr; Mike Rader, opns mgr & progmg dir; Emil Macha, sls dir; Anthony Garza, chief of engrg.

Livingston

KETX(AM)— June 28, 1957: 1440 khz; 5 kw-D. TL: N30 44 23 W94 55 30. 3274 Radio Rd. 77351. Phone: (936) 327-8916. Fax: (936) 327-8477. Licensee: Harold J. Haley dba Polk County Broadcasting Co. Network: ABC. Eugene T. Smith. Format: Easy listening. News staff: 2. Target aud: General. ◆ Hal Haley, pres, gen mgr, progmg dir & chief of engrg.

KETX-FM— Sept 1, 1970: 92.3 mhz; 50 kw. 699 ft. TL: N30 44 23 W94 55 30. (CP: TL: N30 44 18 W94 55 23). Stereo. Format: Country.

Llano

KITY(FM)— 2004: 102.9 mhz; 2 kw. Ant 495 ft. TL: N30 40 37 W98 33 59. 1809 Lightsey Rd., Austin 78704. Phone: (512) 444-9268. Licensee: Bryan A. King (acq 3-9-2004; grpsl). Network: Network: CNN Radio, Westwood One. Format: Oldies. ◆ Bryan King, gen mgr.

KQBT(FM)— 2000: . Stn currently dark 96.3 mhz; 2.9 kw. 459 ft. TL: N30 41 12 W98 34 16. 3102 Oak Lawn Ave., Dallas 75219. Phone: (512) 383-1112. Licensee: Rawhide Radio LLC. Group owner: Univision Radio (acq 9-22-2003; grpsl). ◆ B. Shane Fox, gen mgr.

Lockhart

KFIT(AM)—Licensed to Lockhart. See Austin

Lometa

KACQ(FM)— 1996: 101.9 mhz; 6 kw. 328 ft. TL: N31 14 33 W98 19 19. 505 N. Key Ave., Lampasas 76550. Phone: (512) 556-6193. Fax: (512) 556-2197. Licensee: Debra L. Witcher. Format: Country. ◆ Norma Spinner, sls dir; Joe Lombardi, progmg dir; Lela Cooper, news dir; Ronnie Witcher, gen mgr & chief of engrg.

Longview

KFRO(AM)— Feb 6, 1935: 1370 khz; 1 kw-U, DA-N. TL: N32 30 07 W94 42 12. Stereo. 481 E. Loop 281 E. 75605. Phone: (903) 663-9800. Fax: (903) 663-9458. Web Site: www.kykx.com. Licensee: Access.1 Texas License Company LLC. Group owner: Waller Broadcasting (acq 1-7-2005; grpsl). Network: Network: ABC, Westwood One. Kaye, Scholer, Fierman, Hays & Handler L.L.P. Format: News/talk, sports. News staff: one; News: 30 hrs wkly. Target aud: 25-54; general. Spec prog: Black 3 hrs wkly. ◆ Sydney L. Small, CEO; Chesley Maddox-Dorsey, pres; Debbie Tilley, CFO; Richard Guest, gen mgr; Robert Taylor, sls dir; Dru Laborde, progmg dir; Sans Hawkins, engrg dir.

KYKX(FM)— July 1, 1974: 105.7 mhz; 100 kw. 1,156 ft. TL: N32 36 04 W94 52 15. Stereo. Box 5818, 481 E. Loop 281 75608-5818. Phone: (903) 663-9800. Fax: (903) 663-3700. Fax: (903) 663-9458. Web Site: www.kykx.com. Licensee: Access.1 Texas License Company LLC. Group owner: Waller Broadcasting (acq 1-7-2005; grpsl).

Stations in the U.S. — Texas

Developers & Brokers of Radio Properties — contact American Media Services at our suite: Philadelphia Marriott Downtown 215-625-2900. 843-972-2200. americanmediaservices.com. Charleston, SC. Dallas, TX · Chicago, Il · Austin, TX. American Media Services, LLC

Network: ABC Information & Entertainment. Rep: McGavren Guild. Format: Modern country. News staff: one; News: 6 hrs wkly. Target aud: General. ◆ Richard Guest, gen mgr; Ginger Nimmons, gen sls mgr; Dru LaBorde, progmg dir; Tom Metzger, gen mgr & news dir; Sans Hawkins, chief of engrg.

Lorenzo

KKCL(FM)— 1989: 98.1 mhz; 50 kw. 431 ft. TL: N33 36 32 W101 43 45. Stereo. 4413 82nd St., Suite 300, Lubbock 79424. Phone: (806) 798-9880. Web Site: 98kool.com. Licensee: Capstar TX L.P. Group owner: Clear Channel Communications Inc. (acq 8-30-00; grpsl). Network: ABC. Format: Oldies. News staff: 8; News: 14 hrs wkly. Target aud: 25-54; upscale 55% male, 45% female. Spec prog: Talk 17 hrs wkly. ◆ Scott Parsons, gen mgr.

Los Ybanez

KYMI(FM)— December 1990: 98.5 mhz; 50 kw. 459 ft. TL: N32 43 22 W102 01 50. Stereo. Box 15, 1919 County Rd. M. 79331-7939. Phone: (806) 872-6554. Fax: (806) 872-6244. Licensee: Israel Ybanez. (acq 3-8-90; 4-2-90). Network: Westwood One. Format: Sp, relg, Christian. News staff: one; News: 10 hrs wkly. Target aud: 25-49. Spec prog: Gospel 16 hrs, news/talk 10 hrs wkly. ◆ Israel Ybanez, pres & opns VP; Mary Ybanez, opns mgr; Genaro Guerrera, progmg dir; Patrick Park, chief of engrg.

Lubbock

*KAMY(FM)— Oct 1, 1990: 90.1 mhz; 200 w. 492 ft. TL: N33 30 08 W101 52 20. Stereo. 5124-C 69th St. 79424. Phone: (806) 794-1766. Fax: (806) 798-3251. E-mail: kamy@flc.org. Web Site: kamyfm.org. Licensee: Family Life Broadcasting Inc. Group owner: Family Life Broadcasting System (acq 6-24-98; grpsl). Format: Christian. Target aud: 28 plus; 35-54 female; Christian community of Lubbock. ◆ Dave Borowsky, prom dir; Don Webster, gen mgr, gen sls mgr & prom mgr.

KBZO(AM)— April 1953: 1460 khz; 1 kw-D, 250 w-N. TL: N33 32 53 W101 49 24. 1220 Broadway, Ste. 600 79401. Phone: (806) 763-6051. Fax: (806) 744-8363. E-mail: jsauceda@cntravision.com. Web Site: www.kboz.entravision.com. Licensee: Entravision Holdings LLC. Group owner: Entravision Communications Corp. (acq 10-7-99). Format: Mexican rgnl. Target aud: General. ◆ Jose Sauceda, gen mgr; Eben Fowler, stn mgr.

KDAV(AM)— May 14, 1947: 1590 khz; 1 kw-U, DA-2. TL: N33 31 16 W101 46 28. 1714 Buddy Holly Ave. 79401. Phone: (806) 770-5328. Fax: (806) 744-5888. E-mail: radio@door.net. Web Site: www.kdav.com. Licensee: Renaissance Broadcasting Inc. (acq 7-29-98; $150,000). Format: Oldies. ◆ Bill Clement, pres & gen mgr.

KEJS(FM)— 1993: 106.5 mhz; 34 kw. 587 ft. TL: N33 30 08 W101 52 20. 1607 13th St. 79401. Phone: (806) 747-5951. Fax: (806) 747-3524. E-mail: ebarton@kejsfm.com. Licensee: Barton Broadcasting Co. Format: Tejano. ◆ Ernest Barton, gen mgr; Debra Alcorte, mktg dir; Gilbert Esparza, progmg dir.

KFMX-FM—Listing follows KKAM(AM).

KFYO(AM)— Sept 6, 1927: 790 khz; 5 kw-D, 1 kw-N, DA-3. TL: N33 27 50 W101 55 30. Stereo. Box 53120 79464-4670. Secondary address: 4413 82nd St., Suite 300 79424. Phone: (806) 794-7979. Fax: (806) 744-1660. Licensee: Capstar TX L.P. Group owner: Clear Channel Communications Inc. (acq 8-30-00; grpsl). Network: CBS. Format: News/talk. News staff: 2; News: 12 hrs wkly. Target aud: General. Spec prog: Farm 15 hrs, relg 6 hrs wkly. ◆ Scott Parsons, gen mgr; Wes Nessman, opns dir; Matt Martin, sls dir; Robert Snyder, progmg dir; Roger Taylor, chief of engrg.

KZII-FM—Co-owned with KFYO(AM). Mar 10, 1982: 102.5 mhz; 100 kw. 850 ft. TL: N33 31 05 W101 51 25. Stereo. Format: CHR. News staff: one; News: 5 hrs wkly. Target aud: 18-49. ◆ Kidd Carson, progmg dir.

KJAK(FM)—(Slaton). Feb 12, 1978: 92.7 mhz; 100 kw. 584 ft. TL: N33 32 32 W101 50 14. Stereo. Box 6490 79493. Phone: (806) 745-6677. Fax: (806) 745-8140. E-mail: kjak@door.net. Web Site: www.kjak.com. Licensee: Williams Broadcasting Group. (acq 6-19-81; 7-13-81). Format: Christian. Target aud: General; Christians & those looking for answers to everyday problems. Spec prog: Sports 5 hrs wkly. ◆ Woody Van Dyke, gen mgr, gen sls mgr, prom mgr & mus dir; Bob Howell, news dir; Roger Taylor, chief of engrg.

KJTV(AM)—Listing follows KXTQ-FM.

KKAM(AM)— Jan 1, 1955: 1340 khz; 1 kw-U. TL: N33 33 24 W101 51 46. 4413 82nd St., Suite 300 79424-3366. Phone: (806) 798-7078. Fax: (806) 798-7052. Web Site: www.kfmx.com. Licensee: Capstar TX L.P. Group owner: Clear Channel Communications Inc. (acq 8-30-00; grpsl). Network: Network: ABC, CBS. Format: Sports. ◆ Scott Parsons, gen mgr; Wes Nessman, opns dir; Matt Martin, sls dir; Mark Finkner, progmg dir.

KFMX-FM—Co-owned with KKAM(AM). Aug 1, 1966: 94.5 mhz; 100 kw. 817 ft. TL: N33 31 05 W101 51 25. Stereo. Format: AOR. ◆ Wes Nessman, progmg dir.

*KKLU(FM)— Oct 24, 1993: 90.9 mhz; 13.5 kw. Ant 236 ft. TL: N33 32 30 W101 49 16. Stereo. 5700 W. Oaks Blvd., Rocklin 95765. Phone: (916) 251-1600. Fax: (916) 251-1650. Web Site: www.klove.com. Licensee: Educational Media Foundation. Group owner: EMF Broadcasting (acq 5-1-2000; $750,000. with KXRI(FM) Amarillo). Network: K-Love. Format: Contemp Christian mus. Target aud: All ages. ◆ Richard Jenkins, pres & gen mgr.

KLFB(AM)— Nov 15, 1966: 1420 khz; 500 w-U, DA-N. TL: N33 36 49 W101 52 30. 2700 Marshall St. 79415. Phone: (806) 765-8114. Fax: (806) 763-0428. Licensee: Drew Ballard. (acq 3-28-91; $40,000; 4-15-91). Rep: Caballero. Format: Sp. ◆ Shirley Ballard, gen mgr; Helen Castro, prom mgr & progmg dir; Bill Enloe, chief of engrg.

KLLL-FM— Mar 1, 1958: 96.3 mhz; 100 kw. 817 ft. TL: N33 31 05 W101 51 25. Stereo. 33 Briercroft Office Park. 70412. Phone: (806) 762-3000. Fax: (806) 770-5363. Web Site: www.klll.com. Licensee: Wilks License Co. -Lubbock LLC. Group owner: NextMedia Group L.L.C. (acq 8-19-2005; grpsl). Network: ABC. Format: Country. Target aud: 25-54. ◆ Scott Harris, gen mgr; Jeff Scott, opns mgr & progmg dir; Jay Richards, gen sls mgr; Rick Gilbert, prom dir & prom mgr; Kelly Greene, mus dir; Stacey James, news dir; Randy Hayes, chief of engrg.

*KOHM(FM)— January 1973: 89.1 mhz; 70 kw. Ant 567 ft. TL: N33 34 55 W101 53 25. Stereo. 1901 University Ave., Suite 603-B, Texas Tech Univ. 79410. Secondary address: Box 45891 79409. Phone: (806) 742-3100. Fax: (806) 742-3716. E-mail: kohm@ttv.edu. Web Site: www.kohm.org. Licensee: Texas Tech University. (acq 11-87). Network: NPR, PRI. Format: Classical. ◆ Derrick Ginter, gen mgr; Sherril Skibell, dev dir; Clinton Barrick, progmg dir; Cody Rogers, mus dir & news dir. Co-owned TV: *KTXT-TV affil.

KONE(FM)— 1975: 101.1 mhz; 100 kw. 882 ft. TL: N33 30 08 W101 52 20. Stereo. 33 Briercroft Office Park 79412. Phone: (806) 762-3000. Fax: (806) 762-8419. Web Site: www.cr101.com. Licensee: Wilks License Co.-Lubbock LLC. Group owner: NextMedia Group L.L.C. (acq 8-19-2005; grpsl). Network: ABC. Format: Soft adult contemp, classic rock. Target aud: 25-54. ◆ Scott Harris, gen mgr; Jeff Scott, opns mgr, progmg VP & progmg dir; Jay Richards, gen sls mgr; Rick Gilbert, prom dir; Kelly Greene, mus dir; Stacey James, news dir; Randy Hayes, chief of engrg.

KQBR(FM)— July 15, 1964: 99.5 mhz; 100 kw. 817 ft. TL: N33 31 05 W101 51 25. Stereo. Box 53120, 4413 82nd St., Suite 300 79424. Phone: (806) 798-7078. Fax: (806) 798-7052. E-mail: jacquineal@clearchannel.com. Web Site: www.kqbr.com. Licensee: Capstar TX L.P. Group owner: Clear Channel Communications Inc. (acq 8-30-00; grpsl). Format: Country. ◆ Scott Parsons, gen mgr; Wes Nessmann, opns mgr; Leslie Tucker, gen sls mgr; Tina Hill, gen sls mgr; Jackie Neal, progmg dir; Landon King, news dir; Roger Taylor, chief of engrg.

KRFE(AM)— Sept 19, 1953: 580 khz; 500 w-D, 290 w-N, DA-2. TL: N33 32 00 W101 49 14. 6602 Martin Luther King Blvd. 79404. Phone: (806) 745-1197. Fax: (806) 745-1088. Web Site: www.krfeam580.com. Licensee: KRFE Radio Inc. (acq 2-94). Network: ABC. Format: Easy lstng, news/talk. News staff: one; News: 5 hrs wkly. Target aud: 40 plus. Spec prog: News/talk 15 hrs wkly. ◆ Wade Wilkes, gen mgr & prom VP.

*KTXT-FM— Apr 1, 1961: 88.1 mhz; 35 kw. 423 ft. TL: N33 34 55 W101 53 25. Stereo. Box 43082, Texas Tech Univ. 79409. Phone: (806) 742-3916. Phone: (806) 742-3914. Fax: (806) 742-3906. Licensee: Texas Tech University. Format: Div. Spec prog: Black 6 hrs wkly. ◆ Clive Kinghorn, gen mgr; Marcus Parks, stn mgr & chief of engrg. Co-owned TV: *KTXT-TV affil.

KXTQ-FM— November 1963: 93.7 mhz; 100 kw. 740 ft. TL: N33 30 57 W101 50 54. Stereo. Box 3757 79452. Secondary address: 9800 University Ave. 79423. Phone: (806) 745-3434. Fax: (806) 748-2470. E-mail: cheinz@ramarcom.com. Web Site: www.magic937fm.com. Licensee: Ramar Communications II Ltd. (group owner; (acq 9-93; $362,500). Leventhal, Senter & Lerman. Format: Tejano, Sp. Target aud: 18-49. ◆ Brad Moran, pres; Chuck Heinz, gen mgr; Connie Hayes, sls VP & sls dir; Tony Samarripa, progmg dir & progmg VP; Tee Thomas, chief of engrg. Co-owned TV: KJTV-TV affil.

KJTV(AM)—Co-owned with KXTQ-FM. Nov 1, 1946: 950 khz; 5 kw-D, 500 w-N, DA-2. TL: N33 34 53 W101 49 38. Web Site: www.magic937fm.com. Format: News/talk. News staff: one; News: 147 hrs wkly. Target aud: 25-54. Spec prog: Sports. ◆ Chuck Heinz, sls dir; Tee Thomas, chief of engrg.

Lufkin

KAFX-FM—(Diboll). June 29, 1960: 95.5 mhz; 100 kw. Ant 567 ft. TL: N31 24 28 W94 45 53. Stereo. Box 2209, 1216 S. 1st St. 75901. Phone: (936) 634-4455. Fax: (936) 639-5503. E-mail: johnnylathrop@clearchannel.com. Web Site: kfox95.com. Licensee: Capstar TX L.P. Group owner: Clear Channel Communications Inc. (acq 8-30-00; grpsl). Format: Hot adult contemp. News staff: one; News: 2 hrs wkly. Target aud: 25-44; female. ◆ Johnny Lathrop, gen mgr; Tami Koonce, sls dir & natl sls mgr.

*KAVX(FM)— Dec 25, 1998: 91.9 mhz; 20 kw. 787 ft. TL: N31 22 08 W94 38 43. Stereo. Box 151340 75915-1340. Secondary address: 151 Holmes Rd., Lurkin 75904. Phone: (936) 639-5673. Fax: (936) 639-5677. E-mail: alross@kavx.org. Web Site: www.kavx.org. Licensee: Lufkin Educational Broadcasting Foundation. Network: USA. Gammon & Grange. Format: Teaching & talk. Target aud: 35 plus. ◆ Dwyan Calvert, chmn & gen mgr; Al Ross, stn mgr, opns mgr & prom mgr.

*KLDN(FM)— May 2, 1991: 88.9 mhz; 50 kw. Ant 649 ft. TL: N31 24 28 W94 45 53. Stereo. Box 5250, Shreveport, LA 71135. Phone: (318) 797-5150. Phone: (800) 552-8502. Fax: (318) 797-5153. E-mail: listenermail@redriverradio.org. Web Site: www.redriverradio.org. Licensee: Board of Supervisors of Louisiana State University. Network: Network: NPR, PRI. Format: Class, news, jazz. Target aud: 25+. ◆ Roy Gerritsen, gen mgr; Greg Hill, opns mgr.

KRBA(AM)— May 3, 1938: 1340 khz; 1 kw-U. TL: N31 21 51 W94 43 09. Box 1345 75901. Secondary address: 121 Cotton Sq. 75901. Phone: (936) 634-6661. Fax: (936) 632-5722. E-mail: kybi@lcc.net. Web Site: www.krba.net. Licensee: Stephen W. Yates. Format: Var/div. News staff: one; News: 7 hrs wkly. Target aud: General. ◆ Stephen Yates, gen mgr; Kevin Sims, progmg dir.

KYBI(FM)—Co-owned with KRBA(AM). May 1, 1978: 100.1 mhz; 25 kw. Ant 699 ft. TL: N31 24 28 W94 45 53. Stereo. Phone: (936) 634-5100. Web Site: www.kybi.com. Format: Adult contemp. Target aud: 25-54.

KSML(AM)—(Diboll). June 2, 1957: 1260 khz; 4.5 kw-D, 72 w-N. TL: N31 21 53 W94 43 08. 121 Cotton Sq. 75901. Phone: (936) 632-8444. Fax: (936) 632-8451. Licensee: Stephen W. & Karla Yates. (acq 5-95;

Broadcasting & Cable Yearbook 2006
D-493

Texas

5-22-95). Format: Sp. News staff: one; News: 14 hrs wkly. ◆Stephen W. Yates, pres & gen mgr; Oscar Chavez, progmg dir; Steve Comer, chief of engrg.

*KSWP(FM)— Aug 31, 1985: 90.9 mhz; 380 w. 174 ft. TL: N31 23 17 W94 46 43. (CP: 90.9 mhz, 30 kw, ant 787 ft.). Stereo. Rt. 17, Box 151340 75915. Secondary address: 151 Holmes Rd. 75904. Phone: (936) 639-5673. Fax: (936) 639-5677. Licensee: Lufkin Educational Broadcasting Foundation. Network: USA. Format: Christian mus. Spec prog: Pub affrs talk show 2 hrs wkly. ◆Dwyan Calvert, pres & gen mgr; Al Ross, opns mgr.

KYKS(FM)— July 9, 1976: 105.1 mhz; 100 kw. 1,066 ft. TL: N31 22 08 W94 38 45. Stereo. Box 2209 75901. Secondary address: 1216 S. First St. 75901. Phone: (936) 639-4455. Fax: (936) 632-5957. Fax: (936) 639-5540. E-mail: dannymerrell@kicks105.com. Web Site: www.kicks105.com. Licensee: Capstar TX L.P. Group owner: Clear Channel Communications Inc. (acq 8-30-00; grpsl). Fletcher, Heald & Hildreth. Format: Country. News staff: one. Target aud: 25-54. ◆Larry Gunter, gen mgr; Johnny Lathrop, sls dir; Danny Merrell, prom dir, progmg dir & pub affrs dir; Sean Ericson, mus dir; Morgan Mason, news dir.

Luling

KAMX(FM)— Mar 22, 1987: 94.7 mhz; 99 kw. 1,305 ft. TL: N30 19 23 W97 47 58. Stereo. 4301 Westbank Dr., Escalade B—3rd Fl., Bldg. B. Suite 350, Austin 78746. Phone: (512) 327-9595. Fax: (512) 329-6255. E-mail: jdhiatt@cbs.com. Web Site: mix947.com. Licensee: Texas Infinity Radio L.P. Group owner: Infinity Broadcasting Corp. (acq 11-13-98; grpsl). Rep: Katz Radio. Levanthal, Senter & Lerman. Format: Modern adult contemp. Target aud: 18-49; upscale adults. Spec prog: Pub affrs 2 hrs wkly. ◆Clint Culp, sr VP & sls dir; John Hiatt, sr VP, mktg dir & mktg mgr.

Lytle

*KZLV(FM)— Jan 20, 1990: 91.3 mhz; 2.95 kw. 302 ft. TL: N29 14 39 W98 44 27. Stereo. 1566 N.E. Loop 410, San Antonio 78209. Phone: (210) 824-9100. Fax: (210) 824-8870. Web Site: www.klove.com. Licensee: Educational Media Foundation. Group owner: EMF Broadcasting (acq 4-28-99). Network: K-Love. Format: Adult contemp, Christian. Target aud: 25-49; professional adult & parents. ◆Dick Jenkins, pres; Lloyd Parker, gen mgr; Ed Lenane, opns dir.

Madisonville

KAGG(FM)— Dec 5, 1989: 96.1 mhz; 50 kw. 500 ft. TL: N30 48 02 W96 07 00. Stereo. Box 4132, Bryan 77805. Secondary address: 1730 Briarcrest, Bryan 77802. Phone: (979) 268-9696. Fax: (979) 268-9090. E-mail: info@aggie96.com. Web Site: www.aggie96.com. Licensee: CCB Texas Licenses L.P. Group owner: Clear Channel Communications Inc. (acq 10-10-00; grpsl). Fletcher, Heald & Hildreth. Format: Country. ◆Jan Stott, gen mgr; Kathy Vaughan, gen sls mgr; Nathan Peacock, gen sls mgr; Jennifer Allen, progmg dir; Ed Loftus, chief of engrg.

*KHML(FM)—Not on air, target date: unknown: 91.5 mhz; 18 kw. Ant 321 ft. TL: N31 06 40 W95 57 09. 2424 South Blvd., Houston 77098-5110. Phone: (713) 520-5200. Web Site: www.khcb.org. Licensee: Houston Christian Broadcasters Inc. ◆Bruce Munsterman, pres & gen mgr.

KMVL(AM)— October 1989: 1220 khz; 500 w-D, 12 w-N. TL: N30 57 56 W95 53 52. 102 W. Main 77864. Phone: (409) 348-9200. Fax: (409) 348-9201. E-mail: kmvlradio@ev1.net. Web Site: www.kmvl.net. Licensee: Hunt Broadcasting. (acq 7-17-91; 8-5-91). Network: ABC Information & Entertainment. Format: Adult standards. News staff: one; News: 15 hrs wkly. Target aud: General. ◆Leon Hunt, gen mgr; Chester Leediker, chief of engrg.

KMVL-FM— April 1997: 100.5 mhz; 13 kw. 449 ft. TL: N31 00 42 W96 02 27. Web Site: www.kmvl.net. Network: ABC. Format: Country. Target aud: 25-49.

Malakoff

KCKL(FM)— Aug 8, 1983: 95.9 mhz; 6 kw. Ant 295 ft. TL: N32 08 48 W95 58 25. Stereo. Box 489, Hwy. 31 E. 75148. Phone: (903) 489-1238. Fax: (903) 489-2671. E-mail: kcklklvq@tvec.net. Web Site: www.kcklklvq.com. Licensee: Cedar Creek Radio Co. Group owner: Routt Radio Companies Inc. Network: ABC. Format: Real

country. News staff: one; News: 10 hrs wkly. Target aud: 25-54; country/city folk, weekenders & visitors to Cedar Creek Lake. Spec prog: Relg 7 hrs wkly. ◆Adabeth Routt, pres & gen mgr; Pat Isaacson, opns mgr & gen sls mgr; Mike Lallande, progmg dir; Rich Flowers, news dir; Wayne Blackwelder, chief of engrg.

Manor

KELG(AM)— Apr 22, 1981: 1440 khz; 800 w-D, 500 w-N, DA-2. TL: N30 19 36 W97 32 35. 7524 N. Lamar, Austin 78752. Phone: (512) 416-1100. Fax: (512) 416-8205. E-mail: kelg@austintejas.com. Web Site: www.bmpradio.com. Licensee: BMP Austin License Company L.P. (acq 2-10-2005; grpsl). Rep: Caballero. Bechtel & Cole. Format: Rgnl Mexican. ◆Thomas Castro, pres; Pedro Gasc, gen mgr; Mike Lozano, progmg dir; Steve Freeman, chief of engrg.

Marble Falls

*KBMD(FM)— 2002: 88.5 mhz; 6 kw. Ant 89 ft. TL: N30 33 12 W98 15 30. 1648 E. 6th St., Austin 78702. Phone: (512) 732-2777. Fax: (512) 347-7755. Licensee: La Promesa Foundation. (acq 2-24-2005; $130,000). Format: Catholic relg. ◆Leonard Oswald, pres; Dick Bigelow, gen mgr.

Marion

KBIB(AM)—Licensed to Marion. See San Antonio

Markham

KZRC(FM)— August 2000: 92.5 mhz; 6 kw. Ant 328 ft. TL: N28 52 26 W96 08 22. Stereo. PO Box 547, Bay City 77404. Phone: (979) 323-7771. Fax: (775) 719-2182. E-mail: kzrc@kzrc.com. Web Site: www.kzrc.com. Licensee: LBR Enterprises Inc. (acq 7-12-99; $250,000 for CP). Format: AOR, class rock, adult contemp. Target aud: 18-49; White equally mixed gender. Spec prog: Black 4 hrs, Gospel 4 hrs wkly. ◆Ms. Terry I. Marker, pres; Ernest Cunnar, gen mgr.

Marlin

KBBW(AM)—See Waco

KLRK(FM)— Apr 2, 1977: 92.9 mhz; 3 kw. 300 ft. TL: N31 19 31 W96 54 36. (CP: 50 kw, ant 492 ft. TL: 31 24 45 W97 12 40). Stereo. Box 8093, Waco 76714. Secondary address: 1018 N. Valley Mills Dr., Waco 76714. Phone: (254) 772-0930. Fax: (254) 772-1580. Web Site: www.klrk.com. Licensee: Simmons-Austin, LS LLC. Group owner: Simmons Media Group (acq 6-4-2004; grpsl). Rep: Roslin. Leventhal, Senter & Lerman. Format: Bright adult contemp. News staff: one; News: one hr wkly. Target aud: 25-49. Spec prog: Black 4 hrs, relg 2 hrs wkly. ◆Daryl O'Neal, gen mgr; Bill LeGrande, sls dir; Rob Reed, opns mgr & progmg dir; Cole McClellan, chief of engrg.

Marshall

*KBWC(FM)— March 1977: 91.1 mhz; 100 w. 110 ft. TL: N32 32 12 W94 22 29. Stereo. 711 Wiley Ave. 75670. Phone: (903) 927-3266. Phone: (903) 927-3307. Fax: (903) 935-0153. Licensee: Wiley College. Network: American Urban. Format: Urban/mix. Target aud: 18-34. ◆Shanon Levingston, gen mgr.

KCUL(AM)— Oct 7, 1957: 1410 khz; 500 w-D, 90 w-N, DA-2. TL: N32 29 30 W94 21 52. Box AA 75671. Phone: (903) 935-2500. Fax: (903) 938-9730. Licensee: Access. 1 Texas License Co. LLC. Group owner: Access.1 Communications Corp. (acq 5-9-00; grpsl). Format: Oldies, news, sports. News staff: one; News: 15 hrs wkly. Target aud: General. Spec prog: Farm 3 hrs wkly. ◆Phyllis Bailey, gen mgr; Mike Duncan, progmg dir; Eddie Thurmond, chief of engrg.

KCUL-FM— Jan 1, 1992: 92.3 mhz; 5.8 kw. Ant 328 ft. TL: N32 32 26 W94 24 03. Stereo. Target aud: 25 plus.

KMHT(AM)— 1947: 1450 khz; 1 kw-U. TL: N32 33 50 W94 21 04. 2323 Jefferson Ave. 75670. Phone: (903) 923-8000. Phone: (903) 935-6018. Fax: (903) 935-2481. E-mail: kmht@marshalltx.com. Licensee: Hanszen Broadcast Group Inc. (acq 9-10-02; $400,000. with co-located FM). Format: Country. ◆Jerry Hanszen, pres & sr VP; Chris Paddie, gen mgr; Alaina Pool, progmg dir; Rodney Andrews, chief of engrg.

KMHT-FM— Sept 4, 1977: 103.9 mhz; 3 kw. 300 ft. TL: N32 33 50 W94 21 04.

Mart

*KSUR(FM)—Not on air, target date: unknown: 88.9 mhz; 50 kw vert. Ant 489 ft. TL: N31 20 44 W97 01 16. Box 2440, Tupelo, MS 38803-2440. Phone: (662) 844-8888. Fax: (662) 842-6791. Web Site: www.afr.net. Licensee: American Family Association. ◆Marvin Sanders, gen mgr.

Mason

KHLE(FM)—Not on air, target date: unknown: 102.5 mhz; 50 kw. Ant 456 ft. TL: N30 42 03 W99 13 59. Box 8715, Horseshoe Bay 78657. Phone: (830) 693-5551. Fax: (830) 598-6534. Licensee: Munbilla Broadcasting Properties Ltd. (group owner). ◆Allan Barrows, gen mgr; Ben Shields, progmg dir; Bill Woleban, chief of engrg.

KOTY(FM)— 2004: 95.7 mhz; 50 kw. Ant 436 ft. TL: N30 33 53 W99 27 13. 1809 Lightsey Rd., Austin 78704. Phone: (512) 444-9268. Licensee: Bryan A. King (acq 2-13-2004; grpsl). ◆Bryan King, gen mgr.

McAllen

KGBT-FM— 1964: 98.5 mhz; 100 kw. 997 ft. TL: N26 07 14 W97 49 18. (CP: Ant 997 ft.). Stereo. 200 S. 10th, Suite 600 78501. Phone: (956) 631-5499. Fax: (956) 631-0090. Web Site: www.netmio /com/radio/kgbt-fm. Licensee: Tichenor License Corp. Group owner: Univision Radio (acq 9-22-2003; grpsl). Format: Mexican rgnl. ◆Mac Tichenor Jr., pres; Joe Morales, gen mgr; Angela Navarrete, gen sls mgr; Hugo de la Cruze, progmg dir; Odie Francisco Chavez, news dir; Jorge Garza, chief of engrg.

*KHID(FM)— July 16, 1992: 88.1 mhz; 2.1 kw. 253 ft. TL: N26 21 44 W98 19 26. Stereo. Box 2147, Harlingen 78551. Secondary address: 1701 E. Tennessee Ave., Harlingen 78550. Phone: (956) 421-4111. Fax: (956) 421-4150. E-mail: kmbhkhid@aol.com. Web Site: www.kmbh.org. Licensee: RGV Educational Broadcasting Inc. Format: News, class, jazz. News: 34 hrs wkly. Target aud: General. ◆Pedro Briseno, gen mgr.

KIRT(AM)—See Mission

KJAV(FM)—See Alamo

KRIO(AM)— 1947: 910 khz; 5 kw-U, DA-2. TL: N26 18 02 W98 12 38. 4300 S. Business 281, Edinburg 78539. Phone: (956) 380-3435. Fax: (956) 380-8156. E-mail: correo@radioesperanza.com. Web Site: www.radioesperanza.com. Licensee: Rio Grande Bible Institute Inc. (acq 5-30-86). Bryan Cave. Format: Relg, educ, Sp. News: 5 hrs wkly. Target aud: General. ◆Larry Windle, pres; Gerardo Lorenzo, gen mgr & progmg dir; Jerry Joske, chief of engrg.

KVLY(FM)—See Edinburg

KVMV(FM)— March 1972: 96.9 mhz; 100 kw. 1,160 ft. TL: N26 04 53 W97 49 44. Stereo. Box 3333 78502. Secondary address: 715 E. Thomas Dr., Pharr 78502. Phone: (956) 787-9700. Fax: (956) 787-9783. Web Site: www.kvmv.org. Licensee: World Radio Network Inc. (group owner; acq 8-27-84). Network: Moody. Format: Contemp Christian. News: 4 hrs wkly. Target aud: 30-65; general. ◆James Gamblin, gen mgr & progmg dir; Bob Malone, mus dir.

McCamey

KPBM(FM)—Not on air, target date: unknown: 95.3 mhz; 3 kw. 758 ft. TL: N31 12 42 W102 16 29. Box 252, McAllen 78502. Licensee: Paulino Bernal. ◆Paulino Bernal, gen mgr.

McCook

*KCAS(FM)— Jan 1, 2001: 91.5 mhz; 2.5 kw. Ant 358 ft. TL: N26 28 51 W98 23 45. Stereo. Faith Baptist Church Inc., 4301 N. Shary Rd., Mission 78574. Secondary address: P. O. Box 8106, Mission 78572. Phone: (956) 424-9098. Fax: (956) 581-7786. E-mail: kcasradio@juno.com. Web Site: www.greatradio.org. Licensee: Faith Baptist Church Inc. Network: USA. Format: Relg. News: 12 hrs wkly. Target aud: 30-85; male & female. ◆Joel Mangin, gen mgr, opns mgr & progmg dir; Jerry Jeske, chief of engrg.

Stations in the U.S. Texas

Developers & Brokers of Radio Properties

contact American Media Services at our suite:
Philadelphia Marriott Downtown
215-625-2900
843-972-2200
americanmediaservices.com
Charleston, SC
Dallas, TX · Chicago, Il · Austin, TX
American Media Services, LLC

McKinney

*KNTU(FM)— November 1969: 88.1 mhz; 100 kw. 443 ft. TL: N33 17 24 W97 08 10. Stereo. Box 310881, Denton 76203. Secondary address: 1216 Chestnut St., Suite 262, Denton 76201. Phone: (940) 565-3688. Phone: (940) 565-3459. Fax: (940) 565-2518. E-mail: kntu@unt.edu. Web Site: kntu.fm. Licensee: University of North Texas. Network: AP Radio. Format: Jazz. News: 8 hrs wkly. Target aud: 18 plus. Spec prog: Class 6 hrs, Sp 6 hrs, new mus 3 hrs, pub affrs 2 hrs wkly. ♦ Russ Campbell, gen mgr; Mark Lambert, opns dir; Aaron Brodie, news dir & chief of engrg.

McQueeney

KLTO-FM— July 1989: . Stn currently dark 97.7 mhz; 100 kw. Ant 981 ft. TL: N29 20 45 W97 38 44. 1777 N.E. Loop 410, San Antonio 78217. Phone: (210) 829-1075. Fax: (210) 824-9971. Licensee: Rawhide Radio LLC. Group owner: Univision Radio (acq 9-22-2003; grpsl). Format: Tejano. ♦ Dan Wilson, pres & gen mgr.

Memphis

KLSR-FM— 1982: 105.3 mhz; 100 kw. 485 ft. TL: N34 41 13 W100 30 23. Stereo. Box 400, 114 N. 7th 79245. Phone: (806) 259-3511. Web Site: www.klsrfm.com. Licensee: Davis Broadcast Company Inc. (acq 7-15-86; $78,348 with co-located AM; 7-28-86). Format: C&W, div. contemp. Spec prog: Sp 6 hrs, good time oldies 60s & 70s 10 hrs, relg 5 hrs wkly. ♦ Donna Davis, pres; Joe Davis, gen mgr.

Mercedes

KHKZ(FM)— Sept 10, 1982: 106.3 mhz; 1.65 kw. 649 ft. TL: N26 13 50 W98 20 18. Stereo. 901 E. Pike Blvd., Weslaco 78596. Phone: (866) 973-1041. Fax: (956) 544-0311. Licensee: Clear Channel Broadcasting Licenses Inc. Group owner: Clear Channel Communications Inc. (acq 12-9-2003; grpsl). Network: USA. Rep: Caballero. Fisher, Wayland, Cooper, Leader & Zaragoza. Format: Hot adult contemp. News staff: 3. Target aud: General. Spec prog: Black 3 hrs, southern gospel 2 hrs, Christian rock 3 hrs wkly. ♦ Danny Fletcher, gen mgr; Billy Santiago, opns mgr; Cyndia Torres, gen sls mgr; J. Contu, progmg dir; Ken Meek, chief of engrg.

Merkel

KHXS(FM)— Nov 4, 1983: 102.7 mhz; 100 kw. 1,486 ft. TL: N32 22 00 W99 58 42. Stereo. 2525 S. Danville, Abilene 79608. Phone: (325) 793-9700. Fax: (325) 692-1576. Web Site: www.102thebear.com. Licensee: Cumulus Licensing Corp. Group owner: Cumulus Media Inc. (acq 6-15-98; $1.6 million). Format: Classic rock. ♦ Trace Michaels, gen mgr; Kelly Jay, opns mgr; Kim Creshaw, gen sls mgr; Justin Case, prom dir; John Miller, progmg dir; Cindy Stephens, news dir; Chris Andrews, chief of engrg.

KMXO(AM)— June 1, 1963: 1500 khz; 250 w-D. TL: N32 28 17 W100 00 19. 604 N. 2nd St. 79536. Phone: (325) 928-3060. Fax: (325) 928-4683. Licensee: Ray R. Silva. Format: Chirstian. ♦ Zacarias Serrato, gen mgr.

Mertzon

*KMEO(FM)—Not on air, target date: unknown: 91.9 mhz; 6.5 kw vert. Ant 522 ft. TL: N31 25 16 W100 32 36. Box 2440, Tupelo, MS 38803. Phone: (662) 844-8888. Fax: (662) 842-6791. Licensee: American Family Association. (acq 7-25-2005). ♦ Marvin Sanders, gen mgr.

Mesquite

*KEOM(FM)— Sept 4, 1984: 88.5 mhz; 61 kw. 514 ft. TL: N32 45 46 W96 38 04. Stereo. 2600 Motley Dr., Suite 300 75150. Phone: (972) 288-6411. E-mail: jgriffin@mosquiteisd.org. Web Site: www.keom.fm. Licensee: Mesquite Independent School District. Format: Div. Target aud: General; citizens of Mesquite & surrounding area. ♦ James Griffin, stn mgr.

Mexia

KRQX(AM)— May 21, 1956: 1590 khz; 500 w-D, 128 w-N. TL: N31 41 10 W96 27 18. Box 1590 76667. Secondary address: 1006-B Milam St. 76667. Phone: (254) 562-5328. Fax: (254) 562-6729. E-mail: radio@kycxfm.com. Licensee: Simmons-Austin, LS LLC. (acq 7-28-2005; $390,000. with co-located FM). Network: ABC. Format: Country, Christian, relg. Target aud: General; 20-59. Spec prog: Farm 12 hrs, Gospel 3 hrs wkly. ♦ Susan Cholopisa, gen mgr; Bill Ferris, opns dir & gen sls mgr; Jan Phillips, news dir.

KYCX-FM—Co-owned with KRQX(AM). Aug 29, 1983: 104.9 mhz; 2.1 kw. Ant 351 ft. TL: N31 42 25 W96 31 23. Stereo. E-mail: susan@kycxfm.com. Web Site: www.kycxfm.com. Network: CBS. Roy F. Perkins. Format: Oldies. ♦ Bill Ferris, chief of opns; Susan Cholopisa, stn mgr & progmg dir.

Midland

KBAT(FM)— 1974: 93.3 mhz; 100 kw. 500 ft. TL: N31 57 30 W102 03 59. Stereo. 11300 Hwy 191, Bldg. 2 79707. Phone: (432) 563-5499. Fax: (915) 563-5530. Web Site: www.b93.net. Licensee: Cumulus Licensing Corp. Group owner: Cumulus Media Inc. (acq 12-17-98; grpsl). Format: Contemporary Hit/Top-40. News staff: one; News: 2 hrs wkly. Target aud: 18-44. ♦ John Moesch, opns mgr; Kevin Meyer, gen sls mgr; Kent Cooper, mktg mgr; Kris Moore, prom dir; Spencer Bennett, progmg dir; Gary Vaughn, chief of engrg.

KCHX(FM)— Aug 15, 1988: 106.7 mhz; 100 kw. 613 ft. TL: N31 54 53 W101 57 49. Stereo. 1330 E. 8th St., Suite 207, Odessa 79761. Phone: (432) 563-9102. Fax: (432) 580-9102. Web Site: www.mymix1067.com. Licensee: Capstar TX L.P. Group owner: Clear Channel Communications Inc. (acq 8-30-00; grpsl). Format: Adult contemp. News: 2 hrs wkly. Target aud: 25-54; general. ♦ Gloria Apolinario, gen mgr; Laura Florez, gen sls mgr; Rob Norris, chief of engrg & engr.

KCRS(AM)— Dec 20, 1935: 550 khz; 5 kw-D, 1 kw-N, DA-2. TL: N32 04 10 W102 01 46. 1330 E. 8th St., Suite 207, Odessa 79761. Phone: (432) 563-9102. Fax: (432) 580-9102. Web Site: www.newstalkkcrs.com. Licensee: CCB Texas Licenses L.P. Group owner: Clear Channel Communications Inc. (acq 6-15-00; with co-located FM). Dow, Lohnes & Albertson. Format: News/talk. News staff: 2; News: 30 hrs wkly. Target aud: 25-54. ♦ Gloria Apolinario, gen mgr; Robert Hallmark, opns mgr, prom dir, progmg dir & pub affrs dir; Steve Driscoll, opns mgr; Jesse Grimes, news dir; Rod Norris, engrg mgr.

KCRS-FM— May 25, 1976: 103.3 mhz; 100 kw. 920 ft. TL: N32 05 11 W102 17 11. Web Site: www.1033kissfm.net. Format: Adult contemp. ♦ Ric Elliott, progmg dir; Jesse Grimes, pub affrs dir.

KJBC(AM)— Aug 6, 1950: 1150 khz; 1 kw-D. TL: N31 58 55 W102 03 30. 1903 S. Lamesa Rd. 79701. Phone: (432) 638-1150. Fax: (432) 682-5230. E-mail: matt@guadaluperadionetwork.org. Web Site: www.lapromesa.org. Licensee: La Promesa Foundation. (acq 2-11-2002; $85,000). Format: Catholic progmg. ♦ Matt Jolley, gen mgr; Toya Hall, progmg dir.

KMCM(FM)—See Odessa

KMND(AM)— Nov 27, 1963: 1510 khz; 500 w-D. TL: N31 37 48 W102 04 53. (CP: 2.4 kw-D). Bldg. #2, 11300 Hwy. 191 79707. Phone: (432) 563-5636. Fax: (432) 563-3823. E-mail: jmesher@aol.com. Web Site: www.kmnd.com. Licensee: Cumulus Licensing Corp. Group owner: Cumulus Media Inc. (acq 12-17-98; grpsl). Network: ESPN Radio. Format: Sports. Spec prog: Jazz one hr wkly. ♦ Kent Cooper, gen mgr; Mike Baer, sls dir & gen sls mgr; Robi Burns, progmg dir; Garry Vaughn, chief of engrg.

KNFM(FM)—Co-owned with KMND(AM). Nov 2, 1959: 92.3 mhz; 100 kw. Ant 985 ft. TL: N32 05 51 W102 17 21. Stereo. Web Site: www.lonestar92.com. Network: ABC Information & Entertainment. Format: Country. ♦ John Moesch, progmg dir.

*KPBJ(FM)— 2005: 90.1 mhz; 1.85 kw. Ant 417 ft. TL: N31 57 39 W101 54 25. Box 252, McAllen 78505. Phone: (956) 686-6382. Fax: (956) 686-2999. Licensee: Paulino Bernal Evangelism. Format: Sp. ♦ Paulino Bernal Jr., pres.

KPOE(AM)—Not on air, target date: unknown: 880 khz; 2 kw-D, 500 w-N, DA-2. TL: N31 48 00 W102 10 30 (day), N32 00 03 W102 05 55 (night). 906 W. Ave. I, Lovington, NM 88260. Phone: (505) 397-3906. Licensee: SIBR Inc. ♦ Winford Carlile, pres.

KQRX(FM)—Licensed to Midland. See Odessa

KWEL(AM)— April 1957: 1070 khz; 2.5 kw-D. TL: N31 57 44 W102 04 07. 1110 E. Scharbauer Dr. 79705. Phone: (432) 620-9393. Fax: (432) 620-9394. E-mail: craiganderson@kwel.com. Web Site: www.kwel.com. Licensee: Faustino Quiroz. (acq 5-1-93; $140,000; 4-5-93). Network: ABC. Format: Talk, news. News: 60 hrs wkly. Target aud: General; Adults 35+. ♦ Faustino Quiroz, CEO; Craig Anderson, gen mgr; Doris Anderson, opns.

Mineola

KMOO-FM— Sept 1, 1977: 99.9 mhz; 6 kw. 295 ft. TL: N32 45 04 W95 33 18. Stereo. Box 628 75773. Secondary address: Hwy. 69 N. 75773. Phone: (903) 569-3823. Fax: (903) 569-6641. E-mail: jason@kmoo.com. Web Site: www.kmoo.com. Licensee: KMOO Inc. (acq 5-26-98; $600,000 for stock). Format: Country. News staff: one; News: 3 hrs wkly. Target aud: 25-64. ♦ Jason Hightower, pres, gen mgr, gen sls mgr & progmg dir; Amy Castleberry, opns dir; Kenny Smith, prom dir; Pat Thurman, pub affrs dir.

Mineral Wells

KFWR(FM)— Mar 1, 1970: 95.9 mhz; 80 kw. Ant 1,079 ft. TL: N32 39 50 W98 09 47. Stereo. 115 W. 3rd St., Fort Worth 76102. Phone: (817) 332-0959. Fax: (817) 348-8373. Web Site: 959theranch.com. Licensee: LKCM Radio Group L.P. (group owner; acq 9-30-02; $6 million). Format: Tex country. Target aud: 25-54; local, Texas country. ♦ Gerry Schlegel, pres; Joel Gough, sls dir; Rick Lovett, progmg dir.

KJSA(AM)— Dec 1, 1946: 1120 khz; 250 w-D. TL: N32 47 12 W98 05 53. 305 Millsap Hwy. 76067. Phone: (940) 325-1140. Fax: (940) 325-1164. Licensee: First Broadcasting Investment Partners LLC. (group owner; acq 6-13-2005; grpsl). Format: Classic country. ♦ Chuck McKay, gen mgr.

Mirando City

KBDR(FM)— Apr 1, 1993: 100.5 mhz; 42 kw. Ant 551 ft. TL: N27 21 17 W99 13 52. Stereo. 107 Calle Del Norte, Suite 102, Laredo 78041. Phone: (956) 725-1000. Fax: (956) 718-1000. E-mail: ss@bmpradio.com. Licensee: BMP 100.5 FM LP. Group owner: Border Media Partners LLC (acq 5-30-2003; $8 million. with KBUC(FM) Raymondville). Format: Regional Sp. Target aud: 18-45; upper-income bracket. ♦ Tom Castro, CEO; Hugo Del Pozzo, CFO; Steve Stephenson, VP & gen mgr; Nestor Cobos, stn mgr; Issac Carrillo, opns mgr & sls dir; Robert Garcia, prom dir; Joe Flores, adv dir; Rogelio Botello Rios, progmg dir; Joe Espinoza, chief of engrg.

Mission

KGBT-FM—See McAllen

KIRT(AM)— Feb 23, 1958: 1580 khz; 1 kw-D, 302 w-N. TL: N26 17 36 W89 19 50. 608 S. 10th St., McAllen 78501. Phone: (956) 686-2111. Fax: (956) 668-0370. E-mail: kirtradio@aol.com. Licensee: Bravo Broadcasting Co. Inc. (acq 10-25-01). Rep: Caballero. Format: Sp. ♦ Humberto Pedraza, gen mgr; Rosie Pedraza, gen sls mgr; Armando Pedraza, progmg dir; John Pankratz, chief of engrg.

KQXX-FM— 1989: 105.5 mhz; 3 kw. 300 ft. TL: N26 13 50 W98 20 18. Stereo. 1050 McIntosh St., Brownsville 78521. Phone: (956) 544-1600. Fax: (956) 544-0311. Licensee: Clear Channel Broadcasting Licenses Inc. Group owner: Clear Channel Communications Inc. (acq

Broadcasting & Cable Yearbook 2006

Texas

12-9-2003; grpsl). Rep: Caballero. Format: Oldies. News staff: 3. ♦ Danny Fletcher, gen mgr; Billy Santiago, opns mgr; Cyndia Torres, gen sls mgr; Ken Meek, chief of engrg.

Missouri City

KPTY(FM)—Licensed to Missouri City. See Houston

Monahans

KFZX(FM)— Jan 9, 1984: 102.1 mhz; 100 kw. 977 ft. TL: N31 57 55 W102 46 10. Stereo. Box 4716, Odessa 79760. Secondary address: 1330 E. 8th St., Suite 207, Odessa 79760. Phone: (915) 563-9102. Fax: (915) 580-9102. Fax: (915) 580-4800. Licensee: Capstar TX L.P. Group owner: Clear Channel Communications (acq 8-30-00; grpsl). Format: Classic rock. Target aud: 25-54. ♦ Gloria Apolinario, gen mgr & gen sls mgr; Steve Driscoll, progmg dir; Jesse Grimes, news dir; Amy Parker, pub affrs dir; Rodney Norris, chief of engrg.

KGEE(FM)—Licensed to Monahans. See Odessa

KLBO(AM)— Mar 12, 1947: 1330 khz; 5 kw-D, 1 kw-N, DA-N. TL: N31 38 45 W103 00 04. Box 270, 1706 E. Sealy St. 79756. Phone: (432) 943-2588. Fax: (432) 943-7314. E-mail: klboradio@apex2000.net. Web Site: www.klboradio.com. Licensee: Sandhills Communication Inc. (acq 2001; $175,000). Network: Network: UPI, CBS. Rep: Riley. Roberts & Eckard. Format: Oldies. News staff: one. Target aud: 25-54; general. Spec prog: Gospel 3 hrs wkly. ♦ Rick Anderson, gen mgr; David McCaffity, progmg dir; Allen Martin, news dir.

Mount Enterprise

KTEZ(FM)—Not on air, target date: unknown: 99.9 mhz; 4.6 kw. 371 ft. TL: N31 59 26 W94 43 39. 605 San Antonio Ave., Many, LA 71449. Phone: (318) 256-5924. Licensee: Baldridge-Dumas Communications Inc. (group owner; acq 2-14-02). ♦ Rusty Reynolds, pres.

Mount Pleasant

KIMP(AM)— Oct 8, 1948: 960 khz; 1 kw-D, 75 w-N. TL: N33 09 54 W95 00 27. Box 990 75456. Secondary address: 1798 U.S. Hw. 67 West 75455. Phone: (903) 572-8726. Fax: (903) 572-7232. Web Site: easttexasradio.com. Licensee: East Texas Broadcasting Inc. (group owner; acq 11-21-91; $850,000. with co-located FM; FTR: 12-16-91). Network: ABC. Format: Classic country, Sp. News staff: 10; News: 10 hrs wkly. Target aud: General. Spec prog: Sp 25 hrs. ♦ John Mitchell, chmn; Bud Kitchens, pres, VP & gen mgr; Darrin Tripp, opns dir & progmg dir; Bryan Frimesth, gen sls mgr; Clint Cooper, news dir & pub affrs dir; Bill Hughes, chief of engrg.

Muenster

KZZA(FM)— Dec 23, 1991: 106.5 mhz; 6 kw. 328 ft. TL: N33 38 34 W97 19 15. Stereo. 5307 E. Mockingbird Ln., Suite 500, Dallas 75206. Phone: (214) 887-9107. Fax: (214) 841-4215. Web Site: casa1067.com. Licensee: Entravision Holdings LLC. Group owner: Entravision Communications Corp. (acq 11-7-2000; swap for KRVA-FM McKinney and KRVF(FM) Terrell). Thompson Hine. Format: Rythmic CHR. Target aud: 18-34. ♦ Scott Savage, gen mgr; Pamela A. Henderson, opns mgr & prom VP; Ande Woods, sls dir & gen sls mgr; Dean James, progmg dir & engrg mgr.

Muleshoe

KMUL-FM— Feb 6, 1966: 103.1 mhz; 3.6 kw. Ant 403 ft. TL: N34 12 58 W102 43 42. Stereo. Box 7000, Clovis, NM 88101. Secondary address: 1000 Sycamore 88101. Phone: (505) 762-6200. Fax: (505) 762-8800. Licensee: Broadcast Entertainment Corp. (acq 10-27-99; grpsl). Format: Country. ♦ Rick Keefer, opns mgr; Ron Pierson, gen mgr & progmg dir.

Nacogdoches

KJCS(FM)— May 1967: 103.3 mhz; 100 kw. 476 ft. TL: N31 34 51 W94 40 16. Stereo. 910 North St. 75961. Phone: (936) 559-8800. Fax: (936) 559-8801. Licensee: Radio Licensing Inc. Network: ABC. Format: Country. Spec prog: Gospel 3 hrs wkly. ♦ Bill Vance Jr., gen mgr; Carolyn Gage, stn mgr & natl sls mgr; Della Huse, gen sls mgr; Lou Bennett, progmg dir & pub affrs dir.

***KSAU(FM)**— July 5, 1975: 90.1 mhz; 3.5 kw. 450 ft. TL: N31 37 45 W94 40 44. Stereo. Box 13048 75962. Phone: (936) 468-4000. Fax: (936) 468-1331. E-mail: ksau@sfasu.edu. Web Site: www.sfasu.edu/ksau. Licensee: Stephen F. Austin State University. Network: ABC. Format: Jazz, progsv, new age. News: 3 hrs wkly. Target aud: 18-54. Spec prog: Blues 2 hrs, reggae 2 hrs, urban contemp 4 hrs, classic rock 14 hrs, contemp Christian 2 hrs wkly. ♦ Sherry Williford, gen mgr.

KSFA(AM)— June 2, 1947: 860 khz; 1 kw-D, 500 w-N. TL: N31 36 40 W94 37 50. Stereo. 1216 South First, Lufkin 75901. Phone: (936) 639-4455. Fax: (936) 639-4440. Web Site: www.ksfa860.com. Licensee: Capstar TX L.P. Group owner: Clear Channel Communications Inc. (acq 8-30-00; grpsl). Format: News/talk. Target aud: 25 plus; upscale, upper income level men. Spec prog: Houston Astros baseball, farm 7 hrs wkly. ♦ Larry Gunter, gen mgr; Danny Merrell, progmg dir.

KTBQ(FM)—Co-owned with KSFA(AM). July 15, 1967: 107.7 mhz; 50 kw. 492 ft. TL: N31 42 30 W94 41 18. Stereo. Web Site: www.q1077.com. Format: Classic rock. News staff: one. Target aud: 18-49; upscale women.

KYKS(FM)—See Lufkin

Navasota

KHTZ(FM)— Mar 1, 1989: 92.5 mhz; 6 kw. 263 ft. TL: N30 24 58 W96 04 43. Stereo. Box 306, E. Main St., Brenham 77833. Phone: (979) 836-9411. Fax: (979) 836-9435. E-mail: ftb@sbcglobal.net. Web Site: www.sunykltr.com. Licensee: Fort Bend Broadcasting Co. (group owner; acq 5-31-2001; $900,000). Network: Jones Radio Networks. Format: Adult contemp. News: one hr wkly. Target aud: 25-54. Spec prog: Gospel 4 hrs wkly. ♦ Rebecca Hanson, gen mgr.

KWBC(AM)— Sept 21, 1960: . Stn currently dark 1550 khz; 250 w-D, 26 w-N. TL: N30 22 48 W96 06 01. 303 E. Washington, Suite A 77868. Phone: (936) 825-9007. Fax: (936) 825-1019. E-mail: news@navasotanews.com. Web Site: navasotanews.com. Licensee: The RAFTT Corp. (acq 12-31-2002;. $75,000. with KILE(AM) Bellaire). Format: Local news/talk. ♦ Ben Downs, gen mgr; Dave Hill, stn mgr; Tom Turner, news dir; Chris Dusterhoff, chief of engrg.

Nederland

KBED(AM)— Jan 11, 1969: 1510 khz; 5 kw-D, DA-D. TL: N30 03 35 W93 58 49. 755 S. 11th St., Suite 102, Beaumont 77704. Phone: (409) 833-9421. Fax: (409) 833-9296. Web Site: www.cumulus.com. Licensee: Cumulus Licensing Corp. Group owner: Cumulus Media Inc. (acq 3-9-98; grpsl). Network: ESPN Radio. Format: Sports. News staff: one; News: 5 hrs wkly. Target aud: 18-49; males. Spec prog: Relg 4 hrs wkly. ♦ Zanetta Kelley, gen mgr; Wes Matejka, sls dir; Mark Guzman, prom dir; Jim West, progmg dir; Richard Core, news dir; Greg Davis, chief of engrg.

New Boston

KEWL-FM— July 1995: 95.1 mhz; 25 kw. Ant 325 ft. TL: N33 26 15 W94 25 11. 1323 College Dr., Texarkana 75503. Phone: (903) 793-1109. Fax: (903) 794-4717. Web Site: www.oldiesoldies.com. Licensee: FFD Holdings I Inc. Group owner: Petracom Media LLC (acq 12-20-2004; grpsl). Format: Oldies. Target aud: 25-54. ♦ Norm Mason, CEO & chief of engrg; Terrill Metheny, gen mgr; Don Waloshin, gen sls mgr.

KNBO(AM)— Nov 16, 1969: 1530 khz; 2.5 kw-D. TL: N33 28 56 W94 25 25. Box 848, F.M. Rd. 992 75570. Phone: (903) 628-2561. Phone: (903) 628-2562. Licensee: Bowie County Broadcasting Co. Inc. Format: MOR, Christian. Target aud: General. ♦ Richard E. Knox, pres & gen mgr.

KZRB(FM)— Nov 16, 1997: 103.5 mhz; 50 kw. 492 ft. TL: N33 24 54 W94 38 10. Stereo. Box 1055, Hooks 75561. Secondary address: 710 W. Ave. A, Hooks 75561. Phone: (903) 547-3223. Fax: (903) 547-3095. Web Site: kzrb.com. Licensee: B & H Broadcasting System Inc. (acq 4-16-93; $1.5 million;. FTR: 5-3-93). Network: Network: ABC, CNN Radio. Format: Adult contemp, oldies, urban contemp. News staff: one; News: 9 hrs wkly. Target aud: 25-54; all age buyers. ♦ Ray C. Bursey Jr., CEO, pres, gen mgr, opns mgr & sls VP; Ray C. Bursey, prom VP; Larry Stuart, progmg VP & mus dir; Wayne Duncan, engrg VP.

New Braunfels

KGNB(AM)— Apr 1, 1950: 1420 khz; 1 kw-D, 196 w-N. TL: N29 39 45 W98 10 29. 1540 Loop 337 N. 78130. Phone: (830) 625-7311. Fax: (830) 625-7336. Web Site: www.kgnb.com. Licensee: New Braunfels Communications Inc. Network: Network: CNN Radio, Sporting News Radio Network. Southmayd & Miller, P.C. Format: Loc news, sports talk. News staff: 3; News: 26 hrs wkly. Target aud: 25-54; men. ♦ Bill Rainer, CEO; Fred Stockwell, gen mgr.

KNBT(FM)—Co-owned with KGNB(AM). Nov 22, 1968: 92.1 mhz; 6 kw. 300 ft. TL: N29 43 50 W98 07 15. Stereo. Web Site: www.knbtfm.com. Format: Americana. Target aud: 25-54. Spec prog: Relg 3 hrs wkly.

New Ulm

KNRG(FM)— 1999: 92.3 mhz; 6 kw. Ant 328 ft. TL: N29 53 50 W96 32 35. Box 111, Columbus 78934. Phone: (979) 732-5766. Fax: (979) 732-6377. Licensee: New Ulm Broadcasting Co. Group owner: Bayport Broadcast Group Format: Classic hits. ♦ Carl Geisler, gen mgr.

Nolanville

KLFX(FM)— 1994: 107.3 mhz; 980 w. Ant 581 ft. TL: N31 05 23 W97 35 55. 100 W. Central Texas Expwy., Suite 306, Harker Heights 76548. Phone: (254) 699-5000. Fax: (254) 680-4212. E-mail: klfx@klfx.com. Web Site: 1073rocks.com. Licensee: Clear Channel Broadcasting Licenses Inc. Group owner: Clear Channel Communications Inc. (acq 1-15-2004; $2.6 million). Format: Rock. ♦ Evan Armstrong, gen mgr.

Odem

KLHB(FM)— Feb 18, 1985: 98.3 mhz; 50 kw. Ant 433 ft. TL: N27 47 26 W97 27 02. Stereo. 1300 Antelope, Corpus Christi 78401. Phone: (361) 883-1600. Fax: (361) 883-9303. E-mail: johnnyo@johnnyoradio.com. Web Site: club983.com. Licensee: Tejas Broadcasting Ltd. LLP. Group owner: Amigo Broadcasting L.P. (acq 11-15-2004; grpsl). Format: Sp. Target aud: 18-49; progsv, affluent, middle class Hispanics. ♦ Paul Danitz, gen mgr; Bert Clark, opns mgr.

Odessa

***KBMM(FM)**— 2004: 89.5 mhz; 25 kw. Ant 535 ft. TL: N31 40 35 W102 21 32. Drawer 3206, Tupelo, MS 38803. Phone: (662) 844-8888. Web Site: afr.net. Licensee: American Family Association. Group owner: American Family Radio Format: Christian. ♦ Marvin Sanders, gen mgr.

***KFLB(AM)**— Jan 29, 1947: 920 khz; 1 kw-D, 500 w-N, DA-1. TL: N31 49 14 W102 25 42. Box 3509 79760. Secondary address: 808 Tower Dr., Suite 6 79761. Phone: (432) 580-5352. Fax: (432) 332-1044. E-mail: kfb@flc.org. Web Site: www.flr.org. Licensee: Family Life Broadcasting System. (group owner; acq 6-24-98; grpsl). Format: Christian, relg. Target aud: 34-59; females. ♦ Dave Borowsky, gen mgr; Merri Jo Leonard, opns dir & opns mgr.

KFLB-FM— Sept 1, 1989: 90.5 mhz; 28 kw. 453 ft. TL: N31 53 50 W102 33 57. Web Site: www.flc.org. Licensee: Family Life Broadcasting Inc.

KFZX(FM)—See Monahans

KGEE(FM)—(Monahans). Nov 1, 1983: 99.9 mhz; 100 kw. Ant 574 ft. TL: N31 45 40 W102 31 28. Stereo. 11300 Hwy. 191, Bldg. 2, Midland 79707. Phone: (432) 563-5499. Fax: (432) 563-5530. Web Site: www.kgee.com. Licensee: Cumulus Licensing Corp. Group owner: Cumulus Media Inc. (acq 12-17-98; grpsl). Jones, Waldo, Holbrook & McDonough. Format: Contemp Christian. Target aud: 25-54; general. ♦ Kent Cooper, gen mgr & mktg mgr; John Moesch, opns mgr; Kevin Meyer, gen sls mgr; Kris Moore, prom dir & mus dir; Spencer Bennett, progmg dir; Gary Vaughn, chief of engrg.

KHKX(FM)— July 1, 1977: 99.1 mhz; 100 kw. Ant 407 ft. TL: N32 03 10 W102 17 38. Stereo. Box 9400, Midland 79708. Phone: (432) 520-9912. Fax: (432) 520-0112. Licensee: Encore Broadcasting L.L.C. (group owner; acq 3-14-01; $1.475 million). Network: USA. Format: Country. News: one hr wkly. Target aud: 25-54; general. ♦ Tommy Vascocu, CEO & gen mgr.

Stations in the U.S. Texas

Developers & Brokers of Radio Properties — contact American Media Services at our suite: Philadelphia Marriott Downtown 215-625-2900 · 843-972-2200 · americanmediaservices.com · Charleston, SC · Dallas, TX · Chicago, Il · Austin, TX — American Media Services, LLC

KMCM(FM)— January 1961: 96.9 mhz; 100 kw. 500 ft. TL: N32 05 13 W102 17 12. Stereo. 3303 N. Midkiff Rd., Suite 115, Midland 79705. Phone: (432) 520-9912. Fax: (432) 520-0112. Web Site: www.97gold.com. Licensee: Encore Broadcasting L.L.C. (group owner; acq 9-1-02; $2.5 million). Rep: Katz Radio. Wiley, Rein & Fielding. Format: Golden oldies. News: 2 hrs wkly. Target aud: 25-54; men. ◆ Tommy R. Vascocu, pres & gen mgr; Cathy Fowler, opns mgr.

KMRK-FM— Aug 23, 1991: 96.1 mhz; 27.5 kw. Ant 948 ft. TL: N32 05 11 W102 17 10. Stereo. 1330 E. 8th St., Suite 207 79761. Phone: (432) 563-9102. Fax: (432) 580-9102. Fax: (915) 580-4800. E-mail: gloriaapolinario@clearchannel.com. Web Site: www.wild961.com. Licensee: Capstar TX L.P. Group owner: Clear Channel Communications Inc. (acq 8-30-00; grpsl). Network: American Urban. Format: CHR, urban hip hop. News staff: one; News: 2 hrs wkly. Target aud: 18-34. ◆ Gloria Apolinario, gen mgr; Steve Driscoll, opns mgr.

KNFM(FM)—See Midland

*KOCV(FM)— Jan 6, 1964: 91.3 mhz; 5 kw. 300 ft. TL: N31 51 30 W102 23 00. (CP: Ant 289 ft.). Stereo. Odessa College, 201 W. University Blvd. 79764. Phone: (432) 580-9130. Fax: (915) 337-0529. E-mail: kocv@oc.odessa.edu. Web Site: www.odessa.edu. Licensee: Odessa College. Network: NPR. Format: News, eclectic, class. News staff: one; News: 33 hrs wkly. Target aud: 35 plus; educated, affluent adults. Spec prog: Jazz 4 hrs, opera 4 hrs, folk 4 hrs, blues 4 hrs, bluegrass 2 hrs, Celtic 4 hrs wkly. ◆ Chad Hauris, gen mgr, opns mgr & mus dir; Doug Cole, gen mgr.

KODM(FM)— 1965: 97.9 mhz; 100 kw. 361 ft. TL: N31 47 40 W102 10 44. Stereo. 11300 Hwy. 191, Bldg. 2, Midland 79707. Phone: (432) 563-5499. Fax: (432) 563-5330. Web Site: www.kodm.com. Licensee: Cumulus Licensing Corp. Group owner: Cumulus Media Inc. (acq 12-17-98; grpsl). Network: ABC. Format: Lite rock, adult contemp. Target aud: 25-54; women. ◆ Kent Cooper, gen mgr & mktg mgr; John Moesch, opns mgr; Kevin Meyer, gen sls mgr; Kris Moore, prom dir; Spencer Bennett, progmg dir; Gary Vaughn, chief of engrg.

KOZA(AM)— Jan 20, 1947: . Stn currently dark 1230 khz; 1 kw-U. TL: N31 49 52 W102 22 09. Box 553 79760. Secondary address: 1100 S. Grant Ave. 79761. Phone: (432) 335-0064. Fax: (432) 333-3044. Licensee: Stellar Media Inc. (acq 4-20-89). Format: Sp. Target aud: 18-54. ◆ Benjamin Velasquez, gen mgr; Daniel Melendez, progmg dir.

KQLM(FM)— Mar 11, 1996: 107.9 mhz; 100 kw. 846 ft. TL: N32 05 51 W102 17 21. 1319 S. Crane 79763. Phone: (432) 333-1227. Fax: 432) 335-0064. Licensee: Stellar Media Inc. (acq 12-30-02). Haley, Bader & Potts. Format: Sp, contemp. News: 10 hrs wkly. Target aud: General; Hispanics/Latinos. ◆ Benjamin Velasquez, CEO & gen mgr.

KQRX(FM)—(Midland). Oct 20, 1995: 95.1 mhz; 10.35 kw. Ant 505 ft. TL: N32 03 10 W102 17 38. 3303 N. Midkiff, Suite 115, Midland 79705. Phone: (432) 520-9510. Fax: (432) 520-9505. Web Site: www.95x.net. Licensee: Encore Broadcasting L.L.C. (group owner; (acq 3-14-2001). Fletcher, Heald & Hildreth. Format: Alternative rock. Target aud: 18-24. ◆ Tommy Vascocu, pres & gen mgr; Michael Todd, progmg dir.

KRIL(AM)— June 1946: 1410 khz; 1 kw-U, DA-N. TL: N31 49 00 W102 21 00. 11300 Hwy 191, Bldg. 2, Midland 79707. Phone: (432) 563-5636. Fax: (432) 563-3823. Web Site: www.kmnd.com. Licensee: Cumulus Licensing Corp. Group owner: Cumulus Media Inc. (acq 8-10-99; $110,000). Network: ESPN Radio. Format: Sports. Target aud: 25 plus; higher educ level, higher income level. ◆ Kent Cooper, gen mgr; Robie Burns, progmg dir; Gary Vaugn, chief of engrg.

KXOI(AM)—See Crane

Orange

KIOC(FM)— Feb 28, 1977: 106.1 mhz; 100 kw. 1,225 ft. TL: N30 09 31 W93 59 11. Stereo. 2885 Interstate 10 E., Beaumont 77702. Phone: (409) 896-5555. Fax: (409) 896-5599. E-mail: bigdog106@bigdog106.com. Web Site: www.bigdog106.com. Licensee: Capstar TX L.P. Group owner: Clear Channel Communications Inc.

(acq 8-30-00; grpsl). Format: Classic rock. Target aud: 18-49; adults who have discretionary income. John Hogan, CEO; Lowry Mays, chmn; Mark Mays, pres; Randall Mays, CFO; Charlie Rahilly, sr VP; Mark Kopelman, VP; Vesta Brandt, gen mgr; Gaile Darbone, opns dir; Trey Poston, opns dir; Elizabeth Blackstock, sls dir; Rod Windham, natl sls mgr & rgnl sls mgr; Shon Hodgkinson, prom dir & chief of engrg; Mike Davis, progmg dir; Jim Love, pub affrs dir; T.J. Bordelon, chief of engrg

KKMY(FM)— 1972: 104.5 mhz; 100 kw. 440 ft. TL: N30 08 07 W93 50 39. (CP: 98 kw, ant 984 ft. TL: N30 08 04 W93 56 59). Stereo. 2885 Interstate 10 E., Beaumont 77702. Phone: (409) 896-5555. Fax: (409) 896-5500. Web Site: www.mix1045.com. Licensee: Capstar TX L.P. Group owner: Clear Channel Communications Inc. (acq 8-30-00; grpsl). Fisher, Wayland, Cooper, Leader & Zaragoza. Format: Adult contemp. Target aud: 25-54; at-work lstng audience.John Hogan, CEO; Lowry Mays, chmn; Mark Mays, pres; Randall Mays, CFO; Charlie Rahilly, sr VP; Mark Kopelman, VP; Vesta Brandt, gen mgr; Trey Poston, opns dir & progmg dir; Gaile Darbone, opns mgr; Elizabeth Blackstock, sls dir; Rod Windham, natl sls mgr; Shon Hodgkinson, prom dir & progmg dir; Neil Harrison, news dir; Jim Love, pub affrs dir; T. J. Bordelon, chief of engrg

KOGT(AM)— January 1948: 1600 khz; 1 kw-U, DA-N. TL: N30 08 25 W93 45 11. Box 1667 77631-1667. Secondary address: 5304 Meeks Dr. 77632. Phone: (409) 883-4381. Fax: (409) 883-7996. E-mail: news@kogt.com. Web Site: www.kogt.com. Licensee: G-CAP Communications Inc. (acq 8-7-92; 8-24-92). Format: C&W, news, sports. Target aud: 25 plus. ◆ Gary Stelly, pres, gen mgr & progmg dir; Richard Corder, gen sls mgr; Glenn Earle, news dir; Russ Ingram, engrg dir.

Ore City

KAZE(FM)— May 1991: 106.9 mhz; 8.2 kw. 502 ft. TL: N32 41 54 W94 37 04. 2020 Bill Owens Pkwy, Ste 200, Long View 75604. Phone: (903) 845-2259. Fax: (903) 759-5189. Web Site: www.theblaze.tv. Licensee: Reynolds Radio Inc. (group owner; acq 1-9-97). Format: Rhythmic Contemporary Hit Radio. ◆ Rusty Reynolds, pres; Rick Reynolds, gen mgr; Bob Woodman, gen sls mgr; Lance Thomas, progmg dir; Marcus Love, mus dir; James McWain, engrg dir.

Overton

KPXI(FM)— Oct 8, 1961: 100.7 mhz; 8.1 kw. Ant 571 ft. TL: N32 09 07 W95 03 27. Stereo. 6400 N. Belt Line Rd., Suite 110, Irving 75063-6037. Phone: (214) 561-9673. Fax: (214) 561-9662. Web Site: www.thewordfm.com. Licensee: Inspiration Media of Texas LLC. Group owner: Sunburst Media L.P. (acq 11-6-2000; with KWRD-FM Highland Village). Format: Christian talk. ◆ Pete Thomson, gen mgr; Easy Ezell, gen sls mgr.

Ozona

KYXX(FM)— Nov 25, 1976: 94.3 mhz; 13 kw. 456 ft. TL: N30 42 43 W101 07 30. Stereo. HC 65 Box 50, Sonora 76950. Phone: (325) 387-3553. Fax: (325) 387-3554. E-mail: khoskyxx@sonoratx.net. Licensee: Ozona Broadcasting Inc. Group owner: Hill Country Broadcasting Corp. (acq 8-16-00; grpsl). Format: Real country. News: 5 hrs wkly. Target aud: 12-50 plus; ranchers, oil field, general, travelers. ◆ Kent Foster, pres; Monte Spearman, gen mgr; Donna Keese, stn mgr; Eddy Smith, engr.

Palacios

KROY(FM)— November 1996: 99.7 mhz; 50 kw. 331 ft. TL: N28 43 53 W96 05 26. 102 Jason Plaza, Suite 2, Victoria 77901. Phone: (361) 572-0105. Fax: (361) 798-3798. Licensee: Fort Bend Broadcasting Co. (group owner; acq 1-22-99). Format: Texas country. ◆ Egon Barthels, gen mgr; Ryan Henderson, opns mgr; Lori Beusin, gen sls mgr; Robi Austynn, progmg dir; Ray Nelson, chief of engrg.

Palestine

KNET(AM)— Jan 2, 1936: 1450 khz; 1 kw-U. TL: N31 46 26 W95 37 00. Box 3649 75802. Secondary address: 800 W. Palestine Ave. 75801. Phone: (903) 729-6077. Fax: (903) 729-4742. E-mail: traffic@kyyk.com. Web Site: www.kyyk.com. Licensee: Tomlinson-Leis Communications L.P. (acq 8-9-2005); $1.2 million. with co-located FM). Woble, Carlyle, Sandridge & Rice. Format: Classic country. News staff: one; News: 6 hrs wkly. Target aud: 35 plus. Spec prog: Relg 7 hrs, farm 6 hrs wkly. ◆ Edward B. Tomlinson II, pres; Jason Hightower, gen mgr; Tamie Armstrong, opns dir & sls dir; Dave Peterson, progmg dir.

KYYK(FM)—Co-owned with KNET(AM). Aug 20, 1976: 98.3 mhz; 50 kw. 492 ft. TL: N31 46 26 W95 37 00. Stereo. Web Site: www.kyyk.com. Format: Country. News staff: one; News: 2 hrs wkly. Target aud: 18-54.

*KYFP(FM)— May 15, 2000: 89.1 mhz; 25 kw. 420 ft. TL: N32 00 13 W95 43 06. Stereo. Bible Broadcasting Network, 8030 Arrowridge Blvd., Charlotte, NC 28241. Phone: (704) 523-5555. Fax: (704) 522-1967. Web Site: www.bbnradio.org. Licensee: Bible Broadcasting Network Inc. Group owner: Bible Broadcasting Network Smithwick & Belendiuk PC. Format: Relg. ◆ Lowell Davey, pres; Richard Johnson, opns mgr; Hank Iarrior, progmg dir; Ron Muffley, chief of engrg.

Pampa

*KAVO(FM)— July 1998: 90.9 mhz; 250 w. 207 ft. TL: N35 30 47 W100 57 18. Box 3206, Tupelo, MS 38803. Phone: (662) 844-8888. Fax: (662) 842-6791. E-mail: comments@afr.net. Web Site: www.afr.net. Licensee: American Family Association. Group owner: American Family Radio Format: Inspirational Christian. ◆ Marvin Sanders, gen mgr.

KGRO(AM)— 1947: 1230 khz; 1 kw-U. TL: N35 34 39 W100 57 08. Box 1779 79066-1779. Phone: (806) 669-6809. Fax: (806) 669-0662. E-mail: kgrokomx@pampa.com. Licensee: Pampa Broadcasters Inc. (acq 8-1-67). Network: Network: ABC Information & Entertainment, Jones Radio Networks. Format: Adult contemp. Target aud: 18-45. ◆ James Hughes, pres; Darrell Sehorn, gen mgr, gen sls mgr & progmg dir; Donny Hooper, news dir; Greg Campbell, chief of engrg.

KOMX(FM)—Co-owned with KGRO(AM). May 18, 1981: 100.3 mhz; 32 kw. 300 ft. TL: N35 34 39 W100 57 08. Stereo. Network: ABC. Format: Country. Target aud: 20 plus.

Paris

KBUS(FM)— June 3, 1985: 101.9 mhz; 50 kw. 500 ft. TL: N33 37 15 W95 32 50. Stereo. Box 1038 75461. Phone: (903) 785-1068. Fax: (903) 785-7176. E-mail: jyoung@easttexasradio.com. Web Site: www.easttexasradio.com. Licensee: East Texas Broadcasting Inc. (group owner; acq 5-11-01; grpsl). Network: ABC Information & Entertainment. Pepper & Corazzini. Format: Classic rock, news. News staff: one; News: 20 hrs wkly. Target aud: 25-54. Spec prog: Farm 6 hrs wkly. ◆ Bud Kitchens, pres; Jimmy Young, gen mgr; Trey Elliott, opns mgr; Jay James, progmg dir & pub affrs dir; Dave Johnson, news dir.

*KHCP(FM)— Jan 10, 2001: 89.3 mhz; 21 kw. Ant 354 ft. TL: N33 49 36 W95 27 49. Houston Christian Broadcasters Inc, 2424 South Blvd, Houston 77098. Phone: (713) 520-5200. Web Site: www.khcb.org. Licensee: Houston Christian Broadcasters Inc. (group owner; acq 11-24-00; $3,500. for CP with CP of KKER(FM) Kerrville). Format: Christian. ◆ Bruce Munsterman, gen mgr.

KOYN(FM)— Oct 6, 1988: 93.9 mhz; 50 kw. 492 ft. TL: N33 49 36 W95 27 49. Stereo. Box 1038 75461. Secondary address: 2810 Pine Mill Rd. 75461. Phone: (903) 785-1068. Fax: (903) 785-7176. E-mail: jyoung@easttexasradio.com. Web Site: www.easttexasradio.com. Licensee: East Texas Broadcasting Inc. (group owner; acq 5-11-01; grpsl). Network: USA. Pepper & Corazzini. Format: Country. News staff: 2; News: 3 hrs wkly. Target aud: 12 plus. ◆ Bud Kitchens, exec VP;

Broadcasting & Cable Yearbook 2006

Texas

Jimmy Young, gen mgr & stn mgr; Trey Elliott, opns mgr; Jay James, progmg dir; Dave Johnson, news dir.

KPJC(AM)— September 1950: 1250 khz; 500 w-D, 95 w-N. TL: N33 43 21 W95 32 50. Stereo. Paris Junior College, 2400 Clarksville St. 75460. Phone: (903) 782-0792. Fax: (903) 782-0259. E-mail: mprice@parisjc.edu. Web Site: www.parisjc.edu. Licensee: Paris Junior College. (acq 11-16-98). Format: Smooth jazz. ♦ Mel Price, gen mgr & stn mgr; Jesse Gilbert, opns dir.

KPLT(AM)— Nov 19, 1936: 1490 khz; 1 kw-U. TL: N33 38 07 W95 33 14. Box 9 75461. Secondary address: 2305 S.E. 3rd St. 75461. Phone: (903) 785-1068. Fax: (903) 785-7176. Web Site: www.kpltfm.com. Licensee: East Texas Broadcasting Inc. (group owner; acq 5-11-01; grpsl). Network: ABC. Pepper & Corazzini. Format: Classic country. Target aud: General. Spec prog: Gospel 15 hrs wkly. ♦ John Mitchell, pres; Bob Gipson, exec VP, gen mgr, sls dir & gen sls mgr; Kim Good, prom dir & prom mgr; Trey Elliott, opns dir, opns mgr, progmg VP & progmg dir; Dave Johnson, news dir; Christy Storey, pub affrs dir; Bill Hughes, engrg dir & chief of engrg.

KPLT-FM— Aug 14, 1966: 107.7 mhz; 50 kw. Ant 492 ft. TL: N33 44 55 W95 24 53. Web Site: www.kpltfm.com. Network: ABC. Format: Hot adult contemp. Target aud: 18-35; heavy female/listen at work.

Pasadena

*****KFTG(FM)**— February 1981: 88.1 mhz; 440 w. Ant 110 ft. TL: N29 40 02 W95 09 17. 912 Curtis Ave. 77502. Phone: (713) 589-1336. Fax: (713) 589-1335. Licensee: Aleluya Christian Broadcasting Inc. (acq 3-21-03; $482,500). Format: Southern gospel. ♦ Roberto R. Villarreal, gen mgr.

KHJZ-FM—See Houston

KIKK(AM)— October 1957: 650 khz; 250 w-D. TL: N29 41 18 W95 10 29. Suite 1900, 24 Greenway Plaza, Houston 77046. Phone: (713) 881-5100. Fax: (713) 881-5250. Web Site: www.businessradio650.com. Licensee: Texas Infinity Broadcasting L.P. Group owner: Infinity Broadcasting Corp. (acq 10-20-93; 11-8-93). Network: CBS. Rep: CBS Radio. Format: Business radio. Target aud: 25-44. ♦ Laura Morris, VP & gen mgr; Josh Mednick, sls dir; Dan Blanchard, gen sls mgr & natl sls mgr; Richard Topper, natl sls mgr; Pam Kehoe, mktg dir & prom mgr; Brent Clanton, progmg dir; Dan Woodard, chief of engrg.

KKBQ-FM— August 1962: 92.9 mhz; 100 kw. 1,919 ft. TL: N29 34 34 W95 30 36. Stereo. 1990 Post Oak Blvd. #2300, Houston 77056. Phone: (713) 961-0093. Fax: (713) 993-9300. Web Site: www.KKBQ.com. Licensee: CXR Holdings L.L.C. Group owner: Cox Broadcasting (acq 8-7-2000; grpsl). Reed, Smith, Shaw & McClay. Format: Country. Target aud: 25-54. ♦ Caroline Devine, gen mgr; Doug Abernethy, sls dir; Judy Lakin, gen sls mgr; Mike Murray, natl sls mgr; Bill Tatar, mktg dir; Remo Mazzini, prom dir; Christi Brooks, mus dir; Mike Mollett, pub affrs dir; Jed Wilkinson, chief of engrg.

KLVL(AM)— May 5, 1950: 1480 khz; 1 kw-D, 500 w-N, DA-N. TL: N29 41 49 W95 11 09. 1302 N. Shepherd Dr., Houston 77008. Phone: (713) 665-8994. Phone: (713) 868-6166. Fax: (713) 868-9631. E-mail: diddierugalde@hotmail.com. Web Site: www.klvl.com. Licensee: SIGA Broadcasting Corp. (group owner; acq 5-16-97; $1.25 million). Format: Sp var. Spec prog: Black 4 hrs wkly. ♦ Dr. Gabriel Arango, pres; Hector Guevara, gen mgr.

Pearsall

KRIO-FM— Aug 4, 2002: 104.1 mhz; 100 kw. Ant 981 ft. TL: N28 44 53 W98 50 14. 7800 IH 10 W., San Antonio 78213. Phone: (210) 340-1234. Fax: (210) 340-1234. Licensee: BMP San Antonio License Co. L.P. (acq 7-23-2004; $10.25 million). Fletcher, Heald & Hildreth. Format: Sp contemp. ♦ Paula Furr, CFO; John Barger, gen mgr.

KVWG(AM)— Nov 3, 1962: 1280 khz; 500 w-D. TL: N28 53 13 W99 06 40. Box K 78061. Secondary address: 205 S. Walnut St. 78061. Phone: (830) 334-8900. Fax: (830) 334-3448. Licensee: Pearsall Radio Works Ltd. (acq 10-20-98; $200,000. with co-located FM). Format: Classic country, farm. ♦ J.R. Gully, gen mgr, gen sls mgr, prom mgr, progmg dir, news dir & chief of engrg.

KVWG-FM— March 1984: 95.3 mhz; 3 kw. 203 ft. TL: N28 53 13 W99 06 40. Stereo. Box K 78061.

Pecan Grove

KREH(AM)— 1952: 900 khz; 2.5 kw-D, 10 w-N. TL: N29 38 38 W96 05 46. 5821 Southwest Fwy., Suite 600, Houston 77057. Phone: (713) 917-0050. Fax: (713) 917-0213. E-mail: info@radio.viet.com. Web Site: www.radiosaigonhouston.com. Licensee: Bustos Media Holdings LLC. Group owner: Bustos Media Holdings (acq 6-11-02). Format: Oldies, var, country. ♦ Thuy Vu, gen mgr.

Pecos

KIUN(AM)— Oct 23, 1935: 1400 khz; 1 kw-U. TL: N31 26 09 W103 30 14. Box 469 79772. Phone: (915) 445-2497. Fax: (915) 445-4092. E-mail: kivn@classicnet.net. Web Site: www.98xfm.com. Licensee: Pecos Radio Co. (acq 6-15-78). Rep: Riley. Format: Country. Target aud: General. Spec prog: Farm 3 hrs wkly. ♦ Bill Cole, gen mgr, progmg dir & chief of engrg.

KPTX(FM)— Co-owned with KIUN(AM). Aug 3, 1981: 98.3 mhz; 3 kw. 160 ft. TL: N31 26 09 W103 30 14. Stereo. E-mail: kptx@classicnet.net. Web Site: www.98xfm.com. Network: ABC Information & Entertainment. Format: Adult contemp.

KKLY(FM)— 1999: 97.3 mhz; 100 kw. Ant 413 ft. TL: N31 30 54 W103 11 25. 11300 Hwy. 191, Bldg. 2, Midland 79707. Phone: (432) 563-5636. Fax: (432) 563-3823. Web Site: www.lonestar92.com. Licensee: Cumulus Licensing LLC. (acq 6-11-2002; $1 million). Format: Country. ♦ Kent Cooper, gen mgr.

Perryton

KEYE(AM)— Nov 19, 1948: 1400 khz; 1 kw-U. TL: N36 23 20 W100 49 37. Box 630 79070. Phone: (806) 435-5458. Fax: (806) 435-5393. E-mail: keye@arn.net. Web Site: www.keye.net. Licensee: Perryton Radio Inc. (acq 8-69). Format: Country. Spec prog: Farm 2 hrs, relg 3 hrs wkly. ♦ Chris Samples, gen mgr, gen sls mgr & progmg dir.

KEYE-FM— January 1978: 96.1 mhz; 8.5 kw. 400 ft. TL: N36 21 54 W100 46 48. Stereo. Web Site: www.keye.net. Format: Oldies.

Pflugerville

KOKE(AM)— 2001: 1600 khz; 5 kw-D, 700 w-N, DA-2. TL: N30 20 44 W97 32 46. 2211 S. IH 35, Suite 401, Austin 78741. Phone: (512) 416-1100. Fax: (512) 416-8205. Licensee: BMP Austin License Company L.P. Group owner: Amigo Broadcasting L.P. (acq 11-9-2004; . grpsl). Format: Sp, news, talk. ♦ Paul Danitz, gen mgr; Tim Harper, rgnl sls mgr; Javier Salgado, progmg dir.

Pharr

KVJY(AM)— February 1985: 840 khz; 5 kw-D, 1 kw-N, DA-2. TL: N26 19 00 W98 06 16. Stereo. 730 W. Nolana Loop, 2nd Fl., McAllen 78509. Phone: (212) 966-1059. Phone: (956) 992-8895. Fax: (956) 992-8897. Web Site: www.radiounica.com. Licensee: Multicultural Radio Broadcasting Licensee LLC. Group owner: Multicultural Radio Broadcasting Inc. (acq 2-4-2004; grpsl). Network: ABC Information & Entertainment. Format: Country. ♦ Andrew Goldman, exec VP; Blaine Decker, sr VP; Virginia Lennon, VP; Pilar Gonzalez, gen mgr; Juan Manuel Diaz, opns dir.

Pilot Point

KZMP-FM— Oct 17, 1983: 104.9 mhz; 15.7 kw. Ant 1,755 ft. TL: N33 33 37 W96 57 34. Stereo. 5307 E. Mockingbird Ln., Suite 500, Dallas 75206. Phone: (214) 887-9107. Fax: (214) 841-4215. Licensee: Entravision Holdings LLC. Group owner: Entravision Communications Corp. (acq 8-9-02; $35 million). Format: Sp. ♦ Scott Savage, gen mgr; Dean James, opns mgr & progmg dir; Ande Woods, gen sls mgr.

Pittsburg

KDVE(FM)— Dec 15, 1986: 103.1 mhz; 10 kw. Ant 672 ft. TL: N32 52 50 W94 58 13. Stereo. Box 1648, Jacksonville 75766. Secondary address: 402 S. Ragsdale, Jacksonville 75766. Phone: (903) 586-2527. Fax: (903) 589-0677. Licensee: Waller Media LLC. (group owner; acq 8-9-2005; $975,000 with KXAL-FM Tatum). Format: Talk. ♦ Dudley Waller, gen mgr.

*****KKXI(FM)**— 2003: 91.1 mhz; 800 w vert. Ant 128 ft. TL: N33 01 41 W95 02 57. Stereo. 403 S. Madison Ave., Ste 6, Mount Pleasant 75455. Phone: (903) 575-9191. Fax: (903) 575-1984. E-mail: leo@kkxi.com. Web Site: www.kkxi.com. Licensee: Millennium Broadcasting Corp. Format: 80s/90s rock. News staff: one; News: 10 hrs wkly. Target aud: 30-55+. ♦ Stacy Ashcraft, pres & gen mgr; Leo Ashcraft, engrg VP.

KSCN(FM)— Mar 1, 1999: 96.9 mhz; 14 kw. 390 ft. TL: N33 00 31 W95 04 14. Stereo. Box 990, Mount Pleasant 75456. Secondary address: 1798 US Hwy. 67 W., Mount Pleasant 75455. Phone: (903) 572-8726. Fax: (903) 572-7232. E-mail: bud@easttexasradio.com. Web Site: www.easttexasradio.com. Licensee: East Texas Broadcasting Inc. (group owner). Format: Country. News staff: 2; News: 3 hrs wkly. Target aud: 25-54; general. ♦ John Mitchell, chmn; Bud Kitchens, pres & gen mgr; Darrin Tripp, opns dir & progmg dir; Bryan Friesth, gen sls mgr; Clint Cooper, news dir & pub affrs dir; Bill Hughes, chief of engrg.

Plains

*****KPHS(FM)**— Nov 14, 1977: 90.3 mhz; 220 w. 135 ft. TL: N33 11 16 W102 49 20. Box 479 79355. Phone: (806) 456-7401. Fax: (806) 456-4325. Licensee: Plains Independent School District. Format: Educ. ♦ Rennetta O'Quinn, gen mgr.

Plainview

*****KBAH(FM)**— Mar 18, 2004: 90.5 mhz; 75 kw. Ant 426 ft. TL: N34 03 58 W101 42 16. Box 3206, Tupelo, MS 38803. Phone: (662) 844-8888 ext. 204. Web Site: afr.net. Licensee: American Family Association. Group owner: American Family Radio Format: Christian. ♦ Marvin Sanders, gen mgr.

KKYN-FM—Listing follows KVOP(AM).

*****KPMB(FM)**— Not on air, target date: unknown: 88.5 mhz; 3 kw. Ant 282 ft. TL: N34 13 14 W101 42 52. Box 252, McAllen 78505. Phone: (956) 686-6382. Fax: (956) 686-2999. Licensee: Paulino Bernal Evangelism. Format: Sp relg.

KREW(AM)— Aug 14, 1944: 1400 khz; 1 kw-U. TL: N34 12 20 W101 42 59. 3218 N. Quincy 79072. Secondary address: Box 1420 79072. Phone: (806) 293-2661. Fax: (806) 293-5732. Web Site: kkyn.net. Licensee: Rhattigan Broadcasting (Texas) LP (group owner; acq 6-3-2004; grpsl). Network: ABC News/Talk. Format: Sp, oldies. News: 7 hrs wkly. Target aud: Adults 35+; baby boomers. ♦ John Weeks, gen mgr; Cherie Griffith, sls dir; Jerry Larsen, gen sls mgr; Brandy Haines, progmg dir; Tom Hall, stn mgr & news dir; Gary Graham, chief of engrg.

KRIA(FM)—Co-owned with KREW(AM). 1999: 106.9 mhz; 50 kw. 469 ft. TL: N34 15 47 W101 40 30. Web site: kkyn.net. Network: CSN. Fisher, Wayland, Cooper, Leader & Zaragoza. Format: Adult contemp. News: 10 hrs wkly. Target aud: Hispanic; 18-49. ♦ Jim Ray, CEO; Dimas Garcia, progmg dir.

KSTQ-FM— September 1961: . Stn currently dark 97.3 mhz; 100 kw. Ant 440 ft. TL: N34 15 45 W101 40 05. Box 3757, Lubbock 79452. Phone: (806) 745-3434. Licensee: Ramar Communications II Ltd. (group owner; acq 7-12-2002; $750,000). ♦ Chuck Heinz, gen mgr.

KVOP(AM)— Oct 1, 1974: 1090 khz; 5 kw-D, 500 w-N, DA-2. TL: N34 05 32 W101 38 26. 3218 N. Quincy 79072. Secondary address: Box 147 79072. Phone: (806) 296-2771. Fax: (806) 293-5732. Licensee: Rhattigan Broadcasting (Texas) LP (group owner; acq 6-3-2004; grpsl). Network: ABC Information & Entertainment. Rep: Katz Radio. Format: Talk. News: 10 hrs wkly. Target aud: Adults; 25-54. Spec prog: Farm 12 hrs wkly. ♦ John Weeks, gen mgr; Chekie Griffith, sls dir; Brandy Haines, progmg dir; Tom Hall, stn mgr & news dir; Gary Graham, chief of engrg.

KKYN-FM—Co-owned with KVOP(AM). 1987: 106.9 mhz; 50 kw. Ant 469 ft. TL: N34 15 47 W101 40 30. Stereo. Web Site: www.kkyn.net. Network: ABC News/Talk. Format: Country. News staff: one; News: 5 hrs wkly. Target aud: 35 plus. ♦ Jerry Larsen, stn mgr; Tom Hall, mktg dir, prom dir & pub affrs dir.

*****KWLD(FM)**— 1952: 91.5 mhz; 370 w. 105 ft. TL: N34 11 14 W101 43 32. Stereo. 1900 W. 7th St., #230, , PLainview 79072. Phone: (806) 291-1091. Fax: (806) 291-1963. E-mail: kwld@wbu.edu. Web Site: www.wbu.edu. Licensee: Wayland Baptist University. Network: USA. Format: CHR, Christian music, jazz. News: 14 hrs wkly. Target aud: 15-30; high school through college, young adult, afternoon & evening. ♦ Paul Armes, pres; Jim Smith, CFO; Bill Hardage, exec VP; Betty

Stations in the U.S.

Texas

Developers & Brokers of Radio Properties

contact American Media Services at our suite:
Philadelphia Marriott Downtown
215-625-2900
843-972-2200
americanmediaservices.com
Charleston, SC
Dallas, TX · Chicago, Il · Austin, TX

American Media Services, LLC

Donaldson, VP; Claude Lusk, VP; Steve Long, gen mgr; Paul Sutton, stn mgr & progmg dir; David Carr, chief of engrg.

Plano

KMKI(AM)— July 15, 1939: 620 khz; 5 kw-D, 4.5 kw-N, DA-2. TL: N33 14 34 W96 32 29. Stereo. 2221 E. Lamar Blvd., Suite 300, Arlington 76006. Phone: (817) 695-1333. Fax: (817) 695-3556. Web Site: www.radiodisney.com. Licensee: Radio Disney Dallas LLC. Group owner: ABC Inc. (acq 9-4-98; $12.1 million). Network: Radio Disney. Rep: Interep. Format: Children. Target aud: Women 18-34; adults 25-49. ◆ Keri Littlefield, pres & gen mgr; Robin Jones, opns VP; Jamie Ramsey, gen sls mgr; Greg Heitzman, natl sls mgr; Molly Borsh, prom dir.

Pleasanton

KFNI(AM)— Feb 8, 1951: 1380 khz; 4 kw-D, 160 w-N, DA-D. TL: N29 00 00 W98 31 50. 7800 IH 10 W., Suite 330, San Antonio 78230. Phone: (210) 340-1234. Fax: (210) 340-1775. Licensee: BMP Radio LP. Group owner: Border Media Partners LLC (acq 4-4-2004). Format: Christian, Sp. News: 2 hrs wkly. Target aud: 25-55; middle & working class. Spec prog: Farm 3 hrs wkly. ◆ Tom Castro, pres; Raul Rodrguez, gen mgr; Jennifer Rodriguez, stn mgr & progmg dir; Jesse Muniz, mus dir; Bret Huggins, news dir, engrg VP & chief of engrg; Lisa Moreno, pub affrs dir.

Point Comfort

KAJI(FM)— Dec 10, 1998: 94.1 mhz; 25 kw. 194 ft. TL: N28 46 08 W96 42 39. Stereo. 102 Jason Plaza, Suite 2, Victoria 77901. Phone: (361) 572-0105. Fax: (361) 798-3798. Licensee: Fort Bend Broadcasting Co. Inc. Group owner: Fort Bend Broadcasting Co. (acq 4-13-01; $400,000). Format: Classic rock. Target aud: Baby Boomers; Active, Affluent Adults. ◆ Ryan Henderson, gen mgr & progmg dir.

Port Arthur

***KDEI(AM)**— August 1934: 1250 khz; 5 kw-D, 1 kw-N, DA-N. TL: N29 57 04 W93 52 46. 601 Washington St., Alexandria, LA 71301. Phone: (318) 561-6145. Fax: (318) 449-9954. E-mail: info.usa@radiomaria.org. Web Site: www.radiomaria.us. Licensee: Radio Maria Inc. (group owner; acq 9-20-99). Network: American Urban. Format: Relg. News: 10.5 hrs wkly. Target aud: General; isolated and under-represented groups in society, sick, elderly etc. Spec prog: Cajun 1/2 hr wkly; Sp 2 hrs wkly. ◆ Dale dePerrodil, gen sls mgr; Duane Stenzel, gen mgr & progmg dir; Danny Brou, chief of engrg.

KOLE(AM)— 1947: 1340 khz; 1 kw-U. TL: N29 54 15 W93 56 10. Box 22257, Beaumont 77720-2257. Secondary address: 27 Sawyer St., Beaumont 77702. Phone: (409) 835-2222. Phone: (866) 835-1340. Fax: (409) 832-5686. E-mail: mamager@newsradiofox.com. Web Site: www.newsradiofox.com. Licensee: CityGate Media Inc. (acq 10-95; $80,000). Network: USA. Format: News/talk. News staff: 2. Target aud: 25 plus. ◆ Ralph McBride, pres & gen mgr; George Ferris, gen sls mgr; Debbie Wylde, prom mgr; Dominick Brascia, progmg dir & progmg mgr; Harold Mann, news dir; Jeff Roberts, pub affrs dir; Zach Wells, chief of engrg.

KQBU-FM—Licensed to Port Arthur. See Houston

KTJM(FM)— Apr 15, 1963: 98.5 mhz; 100 kw. Ant 1,952 ft. TL: N30 03 05 W94 31 37. Stereo. 3000 Bering Dr., Houston 77057. Phone: (281) 493-2900. Fax: (281) 596-9608. Web Site: www.laraza.fm. Licensee: Liberman Broadcasting of Houston License Corp. Group owner: Liberman Broadcasting Inc. (acq 3-9-01; grpsl). Format: Rgnl Mexican. ◆ Cheque Gonzalez, gen mgr.

Port Isabel

KNVO-FM— 1992: 101.1 mhz; 3 kw. 360 ft. TL: N25 57 52 W97 14 38. Stereo. 801 Jackson Rd., McAllen 78501. Phone: (956) 661-6000. Fax: (956) 661-6081. Licensee: Entravision Holdings L.L.C. Group owner: Entravision Communications Co. L.L.C. (acq 7-20-00; grpsl).

Network: Westwood One. Fletcher, Heald & Hildreth. Format: Sp contemp. News staff: one; News: one hr wkly. Target aud: 25-55. ◆ Willie Rosales, gen mgr & gen sls mgr; Mando Sanroman, progmg dir; Sonny Cabazos, chief of engrg.

Port Lavaca

KITE(FM)—Licensed to Port Lavaca. See Victoria

Port Neches

KUHD(AM)— June 13, 1959: 1150 khz; 500 w-D, 63 w-N, DA-2. TL: N30 04 45 W93 57 05. 419 Stadium Rd., Port Arthur 77642. Phone: (409) 983-4256. Fax: (409) 983-5858. Licensee: Vision Latina Broadcasting Inc. (acq 9-8-93; $75,000; 9-27-93). Format: Sp. ◆ Eloy Castro, pres & gen mgr; Marco Mata, gen sls mgr; Patricia Montenegro, progmg dir; Richard Ryele, chief of engrg.

Portland

KMJR(FM)— Dec 15, 1979: 105.5 mhz; 1.9 kw. 354 ft. TL: N27 47 48 W97 23 51. Stereo. 1300 Antelope, Corpus Christi 78401. Phone: (361) 883-1600. Fax: (361) 888-5685. Licensee: Tejas Broadcasting Ltd. LLP. Group owner: Amigo Broadcasting L.P. (acq 11-15-2004; grpsl). Format: Rgnl Mexican. Target aud: 18-49; general. ◆ Eddie Alonzo, gen mgr; Julie Garza, progmg dir; Lon Gonzalez, news dir; Henry Turner, chief of engrg.

KOUL(FM)—See Corpus Christi

***KSGR(FM)**— October 2000: 91.1 mhz; 3 kw. Ant 298 ft. TL: N28 00 06 W97 15 01. 3001 Rodd Field Rd., Corpus Christi 78414. Phone: (361) 814-7775. Fax: (361) 814-7779. E-mail: ksgr@csnradio.com. Licensee: CSN International (group owner; acq 6-8-99). Format: Contemp Christian. ◆ Jim Sheperd, gen mgr.

Post

KPOS(FM)— May 1, 1991: 107.3 mhz; 22 kw. Ant 748 ft. TL: N33 13 23 W101 26 26. 5700 W. Oaks Blvd., Rocklin, CA 95765. Phone: (916) 251-1600. Fax: (916) 251-1650. Licensee: Educational Media Foundation. Group owner: EMF Broadcasting (acq 5-21-2004; $550,000). Network: Air 1. Format: Christian contemp. ◆ Lloyd Parker, gen mgr.

Prairie View

***KPVU(FM)**— Nov 26, 1981: 91.3 mhz; 98.3 kw. 410 ft. TL: N30 05 21 W95 59 46. Stereo. Box 156, Hilliard Hall 77446. Phone: (936) 857-4511. Phone: (936) 857-4515. Fax: (936) 857-2729. Web Site: www.pvamu.edu. Licensee: Prairie View A&M University. Format: Smooth jazz, adult contemp, gospel. News staff: News progmg 14 hrs wkly Target aud: 18-55. Spec prog: Black 6 hrs wkly. ◆ Larry Coleman, gen mgr; Charles Porter, opns mgr, progmg dir & news dir; Gwen Johnson, dev dir, sls dir, mktg mgr, prom dir & adv mgr; Dave Cassels, chief of engrg.

Premont

KMFM(FM)— 1989: 104.9 mhz; 3 kw. 299 ft. TL: N27 22 19 W98 11 21. (CP: 100.7 mhz, 25 kw, ant 285 ft. TL: N27 28 30 W98 03 23). Box 252, McAllen 78502. Phone: (956) 686-6382. Fax: (956) 686-2999. Licensee: Radio Cristiana Network. Format: Sp, relg. ◆ Eloy Bernal, gen mgr; Paulino Bernal Jr., stn mgr & progmg dir; John Ross, chief of engrg.

Quanah

KIXC(AM)— Sept 1, 1982: 100.9 mhz; 3 kw; 192 ft. TL: N34 18 58 W99 44 49. (CP: 50 kw, ant 420 ft.). Stereo. Box 29, 221 N. Main St. 79252. Phone: (940) 663-6363. Fax: (940) 663-6364. E-mail: kixc@broadcast.net. Web Site: www.kixc.com. Licensee: Michael Augustus. (acq 8-26-99). Format: Country. News: 10 hrs wkly. Target aud: General. Spec prog:

Farm 3 hrs, relg 2 hrs wkly. ◆ Glen Ingram, pres & gen sls mgr; Michael Reeves, gen mgr; John White, opns dir & progmg dir.

KREL(AM)— May 11, 1951: 1150 khz; 500 w-D, DA. TL: N34 18 58 W99 44 49. 404 Hughes St. 79252. Phone: (940) 663-5711. Fax: (214) 855-5963. Licensee: First Broadcasting Investment Partners LLC. (group owner; (acq 6-13-2005); grpsl). Format: Classic country. Target aud: General.

Ralls

KCLR(AM)— May 31, 1963: 1530 khz; 5 kw-D, 1 kw-CH. TL: N33 40 00 W101 22 44. Box 252, McAllen 78505. Phone: (956) 686-6382. Fax: (956) 686-2999. E-mail: paulinobernal@hotmail.com. Web Site: www.laradiocristiana.com. Licensee: Paulino Bernal (acq 10-19-01). Format: Sp, Christian. ◆ Paulino Bernal, gen mgr; Eloy Bernal, stn mgr; Pete Guzman, opns mgr.

Raymondville

KBIC(FM)— October 1996: 105.7 mhz; 1.35 kw. 420 ft. TL: N26 26 49 W97 42 02. c/o KRGE, Weslaco 78599. Phone: (956) 968-7777. Fax: (956) 968-5143. Licensee: Christian Ministries of the Valley Inc. (acq 2-4-93; 3-1-93). Format: Christian, gospel. ◆ Enrique Garza, gen mgr & progmg dir; Elias Garza, chief of engrg.

KBUC(FM)— 1979: 102.1 mhz; 17.9 kw. Ant 758 ft. TL: N26 38 09 W97 50 10. Stereo. Bldg. 102, One Paseo Del Prado, Edinburg 78539. Phone: (956) 686-8170. Fax: (956) 686-8415. Licensee: BMP RGV License Company L.P. Group owner: Border Media Partners LLC (acq 5-30-2003; $8 million. with KBDR(FM) Mirando City). Format: Regional Mexican. ◆ Jose Luis Munoz, gen mgr; Rogelio Botelleo Rios, opns mgr; Maria Alvarez, gen sls mgr; Joe Espinoza, chief of engrg.

KSOX(AM)— June 1, 1957: 1240 khz; 1 kw-U. TL: N26 27 28 W97 46 55. 2921 North Closner, Edinburg 78541. Phone: (956) 383-2777. Fax: (956) 383-2570. Licensee: BMP RGV License Co. L.P. Group owner: Border Media Partners LLC (acq 1-9-2004; $7.5 million. with KURV(AM) Edinburg). Format: Sports. Target aud: 25-55. ◆ Lance Hawkins, gen mgr; Jim Hearn, opns mgr; Mary Robigurz, gen sls mgr; John Duncan, prom dir; Jeff Koch, progmg dir; Joe Espinosa, chief of engrg.

Refugio

KTKY(FM)— Oct 5, 1979: . Stn currently dark 106.1 mhz; 25 kw. Ant 328 ft. TL: N28 08 15 W97 12 45. (CP: COL Taft. 50 kw, ant 446 ft. TL: N27 52 00 W97 13 08). Stereo. Pacific Broadcasting of Missouri L.L.C., 7755 Carondelet Ave., Clayton, MO 63105. Phone: (314) 345-1030. Licensee: Pacific Broadcasting of Missouri L.L.C. (acq 4-24-98; $725,000). ◆ James G. Withers, gen mgr.

Richmond

KPTY(FM)—See Houston

KRTX(AM)—See Houston

Rio Grande City

KQBO(FM)— April 1985: 107.5 mhz; 1.41 kw. 420 ft. TL: N26 25 47 W98 49 25. Stereo. 102 KCTM-FM 103 Rd. 78582-9805. Phone: (956) 487-8224. Fax: (815) 361-6185. Licensee: Gustavo Valadez Jr. (acq 6-13-03). Rep: Caballero. Format: Latin pop. News: 5 hrs wkly. Target aud: 18-45. ◆ Gustavo "Gus" Valadez Jr., pres.

Robinson

KHCK-FM— Nov 1, 1972: 107.9 mhz; 6 kw. Ant 328 ft. TL: N31 30 33 W97 10 03. Stereo. 10801 N. Mopac Expwy. 2-250, Austin 78759-5457. Phone: (214) 525-0400. Phone: (512) 419-1077. Web Site: www.netmio.com. Licensee: KICI-FM License Corp. Group owner: Univision Radio (acq

Broadcasting & Cable Yearbook 2006

D-499

Texas

Directory of Radio

9-22-2003; grpsl). Rep: Caballero. Format: Mexican, rgnl. Target aud: 18-54. ♦ Mac Tichenor, pres; Tim McCoy, gen mgr; Chris Munoz, gen sls mgr; Oscar Rios, progmg dir.

Robstown

*KLUX(FM)— Mar 17, 1985: 89.5 mhz; 60 kw. Ant 954 ft. TL: N27 46 50 W97 38 03. Stereo. 1200 Lantana, Corpus Christi 78407. Phone: (361) 289-6437/289-2487. Fax: (361) 289-1420. E-mail: klux@goccn.org. Web Site: www.klux.org. Licensee: Diocesan Telecommunications Corp. Network: USA. Ross & Hardies. Format: Easy lstng. News staff: one; News: 13 hrs wkly. Target aud: 35 plus; total persons. Spec prog: Sp 3 hrs wkly. ♦ Rev. Msgr. Michael Howell, chmn; Marty Wind, exec VP & gen mgr; Russ Martin, opns dir, opns mgr & dev dir.

KMIQ(FM)—Licensed to Robstown. See Corpus Christi

KROB(AM)— Feb 22, 1963: 1510 khz; 500 w-D. TL: N27 46 39 W97 37 55. 400 SPID, Suite 107, Corpus Christi 78405. Phone: (361) 774-4354. Fax: (361) 299-6002. E-mail: krobam1510@sbcglobal.net. Licensee: B Communications Joint Venture (acq 1-4-02). Format: Oldies. ♦ Jerry Benavides, pres; Jerry Benavides, gen mgr; Ben Benavides, sls dir; Bob Pena, progmg dir; Gary Graham, chief of engrg.

KSAB(FM)— Oct 13, 1966: 99.9 mhz; 96 kw. 955 ft. TL: N27 44 28 W97 36 08. Stereo. 501 Tupper Ln., Radio Plaza, Corpus Christi 78417. Phone: (361) 289-0111. Fax: (361) 289-5035. E-mail: ksabfm@aol.com. Web Site: www.ksabfm.com. Licensee: Capstar TX L.P. Group owner: Clear Channel Communications Inc. (acq 8-30-00; grpsl). Format: Tejano, Sp. ♦ Matt Martin, gen mgr; Dan Pena, prom dir & progmg dir.

Rockdale

KRXT(FM)— Feb 27, 1989: 98.5 mhz; 6 kw. 328 ft. TL: N30 38 32 W97 02 13. Stereo. 1095 W. Highway 79 76567. Phone: (512) 446-6985. Fax: (512) 446-6987. E-mail: krxtl@tlab.net. Web Site: www.krxt.com. Licensee: KRXT Inc. Network: ABC Information & Entertainment. Format: Country. News staff: one; News: 20 hrs newa progmg wkly. Target aud: General. Spec prog: Spanish, Czech. ♦ Charles W. McGregor, pres, gen mgr & stn mgr.

Rockport

KKPN(FM)— October 1986: 102.3 mhz; 50 kw. 371 ft. TL: N28 00 03 W97 04 34. 826 S. Padre Island Dr., Corpus Christi 78416. Phone: (361) 855-3974. Fax: (361) 855-3770. E-mail: planet103@planet1023.com. Licensee: Convergent Broadcasting Corpus Christi LP. Group owner: Convergent Broadcasting LLC (acq 1-12-2004; grpsl). Format: CHR. ♦ Mark White, gen mgr; Dallas Garcia, gen sls mgr & adv mgr; Scott Holt, progmg dir; William Hooper, chief of engrg.

KTKY(FM)—See Refugio

Rollingwood

KJCE(AM)—Licensed to Rollingwood. See Austin

Roma

KBMI(FM)— Apr 30, 1983: 97.7 mhz; 3 kw. 298 ft. TL: N26 24 22 W99 00 37. Box 627 78584. Secondary address: 100 S. Bethel St. 78584. Phone: (956) 849-3022. Fax: (956) 849-3022. Licensee: Horizon Broadcasting Inc. (acq 10-26-98; $119,742). Format: Sp, relg. Target aud: General; Sp speaking audience. ♦ Arturo Gonzalez, gen mgr; progmg dir & chief of engrg.

Rosenberg-Richmond

KRTX(AM)—Licensed to Rosenberg-Richmond. See Houston

Round Rock

KFMK(FM)— October 1998: 105.9 mhz; 4.5 kw. 1,302 ft. TL: N30 19 23 W97 47 58. 3601 South Congress, Bldg. F, Austin 78704. Phone: (512) 684-7300. Fax: (512) 684-7441. Web Site: www.jammin1059.com. Licensee: Capstar TX L.P. Group owner: Clear Channel Communications Inc. (acq 8-30-00; grpsl). Format: Rhythmic adult contemp. ♦ Mack Daniels, chief of opns; Debbie Harris, gen sls mgr; George Bradshaw, engr.

*KNLE-FM— Aug 17, 1981: 88.1 mhz; 3 kw. 233 ft. TL: N30 26 58 W98 48 48. Stereo. Box 907 78680. Secondary address: 12703 Research Dr., Suite 222, Austin 78680. Phone: (512) 257-8881. Fax: (512) 257-8880. E-mail: webmaster@candle88.com. Web Site: www.candle88.com. Licensee: Ixoye Productions Inc. (acq 6-23-03). Format: Adult contemp, CHR. News: 6 hrs wkly. Target aud: 18-49; primarily female. Spec prog: Children 4 hrs wkly. ♦ Sherland Priest, gen mgr, progmg dir, news dir & chief of engrg.

KZNX(AM)—See Creedmoor

Rudolph

*KTER(FM)—Not on air, target date: unknown: 90.7 mhz; 2.4 kw. 282 ft. TL: N26 41 13 W97 45 52. Faith Pleases God Church Corp., 4501 West Expwy. 83, Harlingen 78552. Phone: (956) 412-5600. Fax: (956) 428-7556. Licensee: Faith Pleases God Church Corp. Format: Educ, Christian, Sp. Target aud: General. Spec prog: Children 4 hrs wkly. ♦ Aracelis Ortiz, CEO; Clark Ortiz, pres; Ricardo Mejia, gen mgr; Tonya Porter, opns VP.

Rusk

KTLU(AM)— 1955: 1580 khz; 840 w-D, 165 w-N. TL: N31 49 12 W95 10 19. Box 475 75785. Secondary address: 618 N. Main St. 75785. Phone: (903) 586-7771. Phone: (903) 683-2257. Fax: (903) 683-5104. E-mail: kwrw@mediactr.com. Licensee: E.H. Whitehead. Network: ABC. Format: Oldies. News staff: one; News: 3 hrs wkly. Target aud: 35-65. Spec prog: Sp 10 hrs wkly. ♦ Marie Whitehead, pres; Robert Gonzalez, gen mgr.

KWRW(FM)—Co-owned with KTLU(AM). July 1, 1981: 97.7 mhz; 14.5 kw. 407 ft. TL: N31 49 12 W95 10 19. Stereo. Target aud: 25-54. Spec prog: Sp 10 hrs wkly.

San Angelo

KCLL(FM)— Aug 17, 1995: 100.1 mhz; 50 kw. Ant 385 ft. TL: N31 31 49 W100 29 05. 422 N. Van Buren St., #424 76901-3147. Phone: (325) 658-2995. Fax: (325) 659-2239. E-mail: kyzzfm@cs.com. Licensee: Foster Communications Co. Inc. (group owner; (acq 5-19-2004; $450,000). Format: Tejano. Target aud: 18-49; Hispanics, demographics. ♦ Fred M. Key, pres; Audrey Carver Luna, gen mgr, gen sls mgr, natl sls mgr, prom mgr & pub affrs dir; Wilburn Luna, CFO & opns mgr; Freddy Maskill, prom mgr; Juan Vela, progmg dir, progmg mgr & news mgr; Richard Whitworth, chief of engrg.

KCRN(AM)— 1947: 1340 khz; 1 kw-U. TL: N31 28 43 W100 27 50. Box 32 76902-0032. Secondary address: 17 S. Chadbourne, Suite 500 76903. Phone: (325) 655-6917. Fax: (325) 655-7806. E-mail: mm.kcrn@kcrn.org. Web Site: www.kcrn.org. Licensee: Criswell College. (group owner; (acq 6-18-91; $350,000 with co-located FM; 7-8-91). Format: Inspirational Christian, relg. News: 2 hrs wkly. Target aud: 35-54; adults with children in the home. ♦ Ron Harris, CEO; Mark Mohr, stn mgr; Steve Hayes, progmg dir; Doug Watson, chief of engrg.

KCRN-FM— Feb 1, 1965: 93.9 mhz; 100 kw. Ant 710 ft. TL: N31 42 11 W100 19 20. Stereo. Web Site: www.kcrn.org. News: 2 hrs wkly. Target aud: 25 plus.

KDCD(FM)— June 1, 1980: 92.9 mhz; 100 kw. 729 ft. TL: N31 26 08 W100 34 08. Stereo. 3434 Sherwood Way 76901. Phone: (915) 947-0899. Phone: (325) 947-0899. Fax: (915) 947-0996. E-mail: kdcd@wcc.net. Web Site: www.cdcountry.fm. Licensee: Regency Broadcasting Inc. (acq 8-10-92; $186,000, 9-21-92). Format: Young country. Target aud: 18-49. Spec prog: Relg 2 hrs wkly. ♦ Beth Auldridge, CEO, sr VP & gen mgr; Jack Auldridge, chmn & pres; Jack Auldridge Jr., CFO & VP; J. Pat McKaye, opns mgr; JoAnna Alexander, sls VP, gen sls mgr & mktg dir; Lynn Ashley, prom dir, progmg dir & pub affrs dir; Len Martinez, chief of engrg.

KELI(FM)— November 1986: 98.7 mhz; 100 kw. 1,290 ft. TL: N31 22 01 W100 02 48. Stereo. 1301 S. Abe St. 76903. Phone: (915) 655-7161. Fax: (915) 658-7377. Web Site: www.kickin-country.com. Licensee: Encore Broadcasting of San Angelo LLC. Group owner: Encore Broadcasting LLC (acq 1-26-2004; grpsl). Format: Oldies. News staff: one; News: 6 hrs wkly. Target aud: 25-54. Spec prog: Relg 6 hrs wkly. ♦ John Kerr, exec VP, gen mgr, gen sls mgr & adv dir; Boomer Kingston, progmg dir; Tommy Jenkins, prom mgr & engr.

KGKL(AM)— Dec 4, 1928: 960 khz; 5 kw-D, 1 kw-N, DA-N. TL: N31 29 39 W100 24 55. Box 1878 76902. Secondary address: 1301 S. Abe

76903. Phone: (325) 655-7161. Fax: (325) 658-7377. Web Site: kgkl960.com. Licensee: Encore Broadcasting of San Angelo LLC. Group owner: Encore Broadcasting LLC (acq 1-26-2004; grpsl). Network: ABC Information & Entertainment. Rep: Katz Radio. Format: News, talk, ESPN sports. Target aud: 35 plus. Spec prog: Farm 6 hrs wkly. ♦ John Kerr, gen mgr.

KGKL-FM— Dec 24, 1965: 97.5 mhz; 100 kw. 500 ft. TL: N31 29 46 W100 24 50. Stereo. Web Site: www.kgkl975.com. Network: ABC Information & Entertainment. Kenkel & Associates. News: 3 hrs wkly. Target aud: 25-54.

KIXY-FM—Listing follows KKSA(AM).

*KJJN(FM)—Not on air, target date: unknown: 89.3 mhz; 1 kw. Ant 800 ft. TL: N31 41 59 W100 26 30. Broadcasting for the Challenged Inc., 188 S. Bellevue, Suite 222, Memphis, TN 38104. Phone: (901) 375-9324. Fax: (901) 375-0041. Licensee: Broadcasting for the Challenged Inc. ♦ George S. Flinn Jr., pres & gen mgr.

KKSA(AM)— Nov 28, 1954: 1260 khz; 540 w-D, 71 w-N. TL: N31 29 14 W100 26 57. Stereo. Box 2191 76902. Secondary address: KIXY Complex, 2824 Sherwood Way 76901. Phone: (325) 949-2112. Fax: (325) 944-0851. Web Site: www.kksa-am.com. Licensee: Foster Communications Company Inc. Group owner: Foster Communications Co. (acq 4-9-84). Network: Network: Network: Westwood One, CBS, ABC News/Talk. Rep: McGavren Guild. Leventhal, Senter & Lerman. Format: News/talk, sports. News staff: one; News: 20 hrs wkly. Target aud: 25-54. ♦ Fred M. Key, CEO & pres; Jay Michaels, opns mgr; Randy Phair, gen sls mgr.

KIXY-FM— Co-owned with KKSA(AM). October 1966: 94.7 mhz; 100 kw. 446 ft. TL: N31 29 14 W100 26 57. Stereo. 2824 Sherwood Way 76901. Phone: (325) 949-3333. E-mail: kixy@kixyfm.com. Web Site: www.kixyfm.com. Network: CNN Radio. Rep: McGavren Guild. Format: Top-40, adult contemp. News staff: one. Target aud: 18-49. ♦ Shannon J. Roach, CFO.

KMDX(FM)— Dec 5, 1998: 106.1 mhz; 50 kw. Ant 456 ft. TL: N31 26 08 W100 34 08. 3434 Sherwood Way 76901. Phone: (325) 947-0899. Fax: (325) 947-0996. E-mail: mixguy@wcc.net. Web Site: www.mix106.fm. Licensee: Regency Broadcasting Inc. Format: CHR, rock/AOR. ♦ Jack Auldridge, CEO & pres; Beth Auldridge, chmn, sr VP & gen mgr; Jack Auldridge Jr., CFO & VP; J. Pat McKaye, opns mgr, prom dir & mus dir; JoAnna Alexander, gen sls mgr & adv VP; J.Pat McKaye, progmg VP; Lynn Ashley, news dir; Len Martinez, engrg VP.

*KPEB(FM)—Not on air, target date: unknown: 90.9 mhz; 15 kw vert. Ant 144 ft. TL: N31 24 45 W100 25 54. 6080 Mt. Moriah Ext., Memphis, TN 38115. Phone: (901) 375-9324. Licensee: Broadcasting for the Challenged Inc. ♦ George S. Flinn Jr., pres & gen mgr.

KSJT-FM— Oct 7, 1985: 107.5 mhz; 100 kw. 656 ft. TL: N31 26 19 W100 34 18. Stereo. 209 W. Beauregard Ave. 76903. Phone: (325) 655-1717. Fax: (325) 6557-0601. Licensee: La Unica Broadcasting Co. Format: Sp. Target aud: 18-55. ♦ Louis Perez, pres; Armando Martinez, stn mgr; Cody Austin, gen sls mgr; Jesus Zapata, progmg dir; Arturo Madrid, news dir.

*KUTX(FM)— Apr 1, 1996: 90.1 mhz; 5 kw. 909 ft. TL: N31 35 21 W100 31 00. 1 University Station A 0704, Univ. of Texas, Austin 78712-1090. Phone: (512) 471-1631. Fax: (512) 471-3700. Licensee: University of Texas at Austin. Network: Network: NPR, PRI. Cohn & Marks. Format: Div, news, jazz. Target aud: 25-54; educated opinions, leaders and arts community. Spec prog: Folk 4 hrs, blues 6 hrs wkly. ♦ Stewart Vanderwilt, gen mgr.

KWFR(FM)— November 1995: 101.9 mhz; 100 kw. 807 ft. TL: N31 29 29 W100 26 03. Box 2191 76902. Secondary address: KIXY Complex, 2824 Sherwood Way 76901. Phone: (325) 949-2112. Fax: (325) 944-0851. Web Site: www.kwfrfm.com. Licensee: Foster Communications Co. Inc. (group owner; acq 12-1-94; $219,000. with KFXJ(FM) Abilene; FTR: 2-13-95). Format: Classic rock. ♦ Fred M. Key, pres; John M. Kerr, gen mgr; Jay Michaels, opns mgr & progmg dir; J. Randall Phair, gen sls mgr; Jeff Rottman, news dir; Adolph Ganza, chief of engrg.

San Antonio

KAHL(AM)— 1948: 1310 khz; 5 kw-D, 280 w-N, DA-2. TL: N29 24 53 W98 20 36. 1777 N.E. Loop 410, Suite 400 78217. Phone: (210) 829-1075. Fax: (210) 822-2372. Web Site: www.kxtn.com. Licensee:

Developers & Brokers of Radio Properties
contact American Media Services
at our suite:
Philadelphia Marriott Downtown
215-625-2900
843-972-2200
americanmediaservices.com
Charleston, SC
Dallas, TX · Chicago, Il · Austin, TX
American Media Services, LLC

Tichenor License Corp. Group owner: Univision Radio (acq 9-22-2003; grpsl). Rep: Katz Hispanic. Cohn & Marks. Format: Tejano, Sp. Target aud: 25-44; upscale Hispanic appeal. ♦Mac Tichenor, CEO & pres; Gary Stone, COO; Jeff Hinson, CFO; Dan Wilson, gen mgr; J.D. Gonzalez, opns mgr; Abbe Cherkaoul, sls dir; Fran Yacovone, gen sls mgr; Robert De La Garza, prom dir; Jon Ramirez, progmg dir; Mike Pesina, news dir; Bret Huggins, chief of engrg.

KXTN-FM—Co-owned with KAHL(AM). Dec 31, 1967: 107.5 mhz; 100 kw. 1,514 ft. TL: N29 16 29 W98 15 52. Stereo. 1777 N.E. Loop 410, Suite 400 78217. Phone: (210) 829-1075. Fax: (210) 822-2372. Web Site: www.kxtn.com. Format: Tejano, Sp. Target aud: 25-49; contemp Sp, affluent, upscale. ♦Rosemary Scott, progmg dir.

KAJA(FM)—Listing follows WOAI(AM).

***KBIB(AM)**—(Marion). Sept 21, 1989: 1000 khz; 250 w-D, DA. TL: N29 34 09 W98 09 47. 290 N. Santa Clara Rd., Marion 78124. Phone: (830) 914-2083. E-mail: kbibam@juno.com. Web Site: www.kbib.org. Licensee: Hispanic Community College. Wiley, Rein & Fielding. Format: Relg, Sp. Target aud: General. ♦Pastor Ken Hutchinson, gen mgr.

KCHL(AM)— June 1960: 1480 khz; 2.5 kw-D, 90 w-N, DA-2. TL: N29 24 45 W98 24 52. 1211 W. Hein Rd. 78220. Phone: (210) 337-1480. Fax: (210) 333-0081. E-mail: 1480@netscape.net. Licensee: Martin Broadcasting Inc. (group owner; acq 6-4-92; 6-22-92). Rep: McGavren Guild. Latham & Watkins. Format: Gospel. News staff: one. Target aud: 25-54. ♦Darrel Martin, gen mgr; "Skud R. Jones, gen sls mgr; "Skud R." Jones, progmg dir; Brett Huggins, chief of engrg.

KCOR(AM)— Feb 1, 1946: 1350 khz; 5 kw-U, DA-N. TL: N29 31 27 W98 37 05. 1777 N.E. Loop 410, Suite 400 78217. Phone: (210) 821-6548. Fax: (210) 804-7820. Web Site: www.netmio.com. Licensee: Tichenor License Corp. Group owner: Univision Radio (acq 9-22-2003; grpsl). Rep: Katz Hispanic. Cohn & Marks. Format: Sp, news/talk. Target aud: 25-54; adults. ♦McHenry Tichenor, CEO & pres; Gary Stone, COO; Jeff Hinson, CFO; Mark Masepohz, sr VP; Dan Wilson, gen mgr; JD Gonzalez, opns mgr; Ernie Quinones, gen sls mgr; Robert De La Garza, prom dir; Rogelio Leal, progmg dir; Frank Cortez, pub affrs dir; Bret Huggins, chief of engrg.

KROM(FM)—Co-owned with KCOR(AM). June 1947: 92.9 mhz; 100 kw. 1,016 ft. TL: N29 11 03 W98 30 49. Stereo. Fax: (210) 804-7825. Web Site: www.netmio.com. Rep: Katz Hispanic. Cohn & Marks. Format: Regional Mexican, Sp. Target aud: 19-49; male. ♦Jd Gonzalez, opns dir.

KCYY(FM)—Listing follows KKYX(AM).

KDRY(AM)—(Alamo Heights). Nov 8, 1963: 1100 khz; 11 kw-D, 1 kw-N, DA-N. TL: N29 33 26 W98 22 35. 16414 San Pedro Ave., Suite 575 78232-2246. Phone: (210) 545-1100. Fax: (210) 545-1139. Web Site: www.am1100.com. Licensee: KDRY Radio Inc. Target aud: General. Spec prog: Southern Gospel.

KEDA(AM)— Mar 17, 1966: 1540 khz; 5 kw-D, 1 kw-N, DA-N. TL: N29 21 30 W98 21 05. Stereo. 510 S. Flores St. 78204. Phone: (210) 226-5254. Phone: (210) 226-5810. Fax: (210) 227-7937. E-mail: kedakid@aol.com. Licensee: D & E Broadcasting Co. (acq 3-7-66). Rep: Caballero. Format: Tex Mex, Cajun. Target aud: 25-54. Spec prog: Salsa 4 hrs wkly. ♦Madeline Davila, pres; Alberto P. Davila, VP, gen mgr, natl sls mgr & mktg VP; Ricardo P. Davila, progmg dir; Bret Huggins, chief of engrg.

KELZ-FM—See Terrell Hills

KFIT EXP STN— 1989: 1060 khz; 1 kw-D, DA. TL: N29 17 32 W98 31 57. Box 160158, Austin 78716. Secondary address: 110 Wild Basin Rd., Suite 375, Austin 78716. Phone: (512) 328-8400. Fax: (512) 328-8437. Licensee: KFIT Inc. Format: Gospel. ♦Rev. Darrell Martin, gen mgr; Terri Lewis, progmg dir.

KISS-FM— December 1946: 99.5 mhz; 100 kw. 1,112 ft. TL: N29 16 29 W98 15 52. Stereo. 8930 Four Winds Dr., Suite 500 78239. Phone: (210) 646-0105. Fax: (210) 646-9711. E-mail: virgil.thompson@cox.com. Web Site: www.kissrocks.com. Licensee: CXR Holdings L.L.C. Group owner: Cox Broadcasting (acq 8-4-97; grpsl). Rep: Christal. Format: AOR. Target aud: 18-44; men. ♦Virgil Thompson, gen mgr; Janis Maxymof, gen sls mgr; Jennifer Schultz, prom dir; Kevin Vargas, progmg dir; C.J. Cruz, mus dir & asst music dir; Steve Hahn, news dir & pub affrs dir; Richard Schuh, chief of engrg.

KKYX(AM)— 1926: 680 khz; 50 kw-D, 10 kw-N, DA-N. TL: N29 30 03 W98 49 54. Stereo. 8122 Datapoint, # 500 78229. Phone: (210) 615-5400. Fax: (210) 615-5300. Web Site: www.kkyx.com. Licensee: CXR Holdings L.L.C. Group owner: Cox Broadcasting (acq 3-28-97; grpsl). Network: UPI. Format: Country. News staff: one; News: 3 hrs wkly. Target aud: 35-64. Spec prog: Pub affrs 2 hrs wkly. ♦Bob Neil, CEO; Ben Reed, VP & gen mgr; Marty Choate, gen sls mgr; Jim Bratt, natl sls mgr; Julie Busse, mktg dir; Jim Kinney, prom dir; George King, progmg dir & progmg mgr; Chrissie Murnin, news dir & pub affrs dir; Paul Reynolds, chief of engrg.

KCYY(FM)—Co-owned with KKYX(AM). June 25, 1966: 100.3 mhz; 100 kw. 984 ft. TL: N29 31 25 W98 43 25. Stereo. Web Site: www.y100fm.com. Network: UPI. News staff: one. Target aud: 25-54. ♦Alyce Ian, pub affrs dir.

KONO(AM)— January 1927: 860 khz; 5 kw-D, 1 kw-N, DA-N. TL: N29 26 14 W98 25 19. Stereo. 8122 Datapoint Dr., Suite 500 78229. Phone: (210) 615-5400. Fax: (210) 615-5339. Web Site: www.kono101.com. Licensee: CXR Holdings L.L.C. Group owner: Cox Broadcasting (acq 2-12-98; $23 million. with KONO-FM Helotes). Bechtel & Cole. Format: Oldies. News staff: one; News: one hr wkly. Target aud: 25-64; total audience appeal. ♦Ben Reed, VP; Marty Choate, gen mgr; Connie Tyra-Kremer, gen sls mgr; Roger Allen, progmg dir; Paul Reynolds, chief of engrg.

KONO-FM—See Helotes

***KPAC(FM)**— Nov 7, 1982: 88.3 mhz; 100 kw. 656 ft. TL: N29 31 25 W98 43 25. Stereo. 8401 Datapoint Dr., Suite 800 78229. Phone: (210) 614-8977. Fax: (210) 614-8983. Web Site: www.tpr.org. Licensee: Texas Public Radio. Network: PRI. Garvey, Schubert & Barer. Format: Class. News: 3 hrs wkly. Target aud: 25 plus; educated, upscale financially, mature, influential opinion leaders. ♦Joe Gwathmey, pres & gen mgr; Nathan Cone, opns mgr; Penny Dennis, progmg dir; Wayne Coble, engrg dir.

KQXT(FM)— Nov 19, 1967: 101.9 mhz; 100 kw. 700 ft. TL: N29 25 08 W98 29 00. Stereo. 6222 N.W. IH-10 78201. Phone: (210) 736-9700. Fax: (210) 736-9776. Fax: (210) 735-8811. Licensee: CCB Texas Licenses L.P. Group owner: Clear Channel Communications Inc. (acq 1-27-93; $8 million;. FTR: 3-8-93). Clear Channel. Format: Soft adult contemp. News staff: one; News: 2 hrs wkly. Target aud: 25-54; core target is women 30-44. Spec prog: Contemp jazz 4 hrs, relg 2 hrs, pub affrs one hr wkly. ♦L. Lowry Mays, CEO; Mark Mays, COO & pres; Randall Mays, CFO; Linda Hardy, gen mgr & gen sls mgr; Tom Glade, gen mgr; Mike McDonald, sls dir; Marian Holdsworth, natl sls mgr; Sue Nicholas, natl sls mgr; Tim Kiesling, mktg dir; Bill Rohde, prom dir; Ed Scarborough, progmg dir; Stan Kelly, news dir; Dan Walthers, chief of engrg.

KRDY(AM)— Nov 13, 1961: 1160 khz; 10 kw-D, 1 kw-N, DA-2. TL: N29 32 11 W98 41 08. Stereo. Radio Disney, 2221 E. Lamar Blvd., Suite 300, Arlington 76006. Phone: (817) 695-1333. Fax: (817) 695-0805. Web Site: psc.disney.go.com/radiodisney/mystation/sanantonio. Licensee: Radio Disney Group LLC. Group owner: ABC Inc. (acq 5-30-03; $3.2 million). Network: Radio Disney. Format: Children. ♦Keri Korzeniewski, gen mgr.

***KRTU(FM)**— Jan 22, 1976: 91.7 mhz; 8.9 kw. 120 ft. TL: N29 27 51 W98 28 56. Stereo. Trinity University, One Trinity Place 78212-7200. Phone: (210) 999-8313. Fax: (210) 999-8355. E-mail: krtu@trinity.edu. Web Site: www.krtu.org. Licensee: Trinity University. Cohn & Marks. Format: Jazz. News: 5 hrs wkly. Target aud: 35-64; people from all walks of life who love jazz music. Spec prog: Christian rock 2 hrs. ♦Dr. William G. Christ, gen mgr; Dr. Rob Huesea, stn mgr; Ryan Weber, opns mgr; Chris Helfrich, dev dir; Aaron Prado, progmg dir; Brett Huggins, chief of engrg.

KSAH(AM)—See Universal City

KSLR(AM)— Dec 26, 1926: 630 khz; 5 kw-U, DA-2. TL: N29 23 24 W98 21 00. 9601 McAllister Fwy., Suite 1200 78216-4686. Phone: (210) 344-8481. Fax: (210) 340-1213. E-mail: kslr@kslr.com. Web Site: www.kslr.com. Licensee: Salem Media of Texas Inc. Group owner: Salem Communications Corp. (acq 8-6-94). Network: Salem Radio Network. Format: Christian, educ teaching, talk. News staff: one. Target aud: 18-54; women & families. Spec prog: Sp 18 hrs wkly. ♦David Ziebell, gen mgr; Baron Wiley, opns mgr; James Herring, gen mgr & gen sls mgr.

KSRX(FM)—Listing follows KTSA(AM).

***KSTX(FM)**— October 1988: 89.1 mhz; 100 kw. 656 ft. TL: N29 31 33 W98 43 21. Stereo. 8401 Datapoint Dr., Suite 800 78229. Phone: (210) 614-8977. Fax: (210) 614-8983. Web Site: www.tpr.org. Licensee: Texas Public Radio. Network: Network: NPR, PRI. Format: News & info. News staff: 3; News: 67 hrs wkly. Target aud: 25 plus; educated, upscale financially, influential opinion leaders. Spec prog: Jazz 6 hrs, var talk 6 hrs, folk 5 hrs, blues 6 hrs wkly. ♦Joe N. Gwathmey, pres & gen mgr; Nathan Cone, opns mgr; Penny Dennis, progmg dir; Wayne Coble, news dir & engrg dir.

***KSYM-FM**— Sept 15, 1966: 90.1 mhz; 5.7 kw. 128 ft. TL: N29 26 50 W98 29 55. Stereo. 1300 San Pedro Ave. 78212-4299. Phone: (210) 733-2787. Fax: (210) 733-2801. E-mail: ksym@accd.edu. Web Site: www.ksym.org. Licensee: San Antonio College. Format: AAA, Texas mus., new alternative. Target aud: 12-54; depending on block format. ♦John Onderdonk, gen mgr; Marlene Romo, sls dir; Michael Botsford, progmg dir; Shalom Topps, mus dir; Victor Pfau, chief of engrg.

KTKR(AM)— May 10, 1984: 760 khz; 50 kw-D, 1 kw-N, DA-2. TL: N29 26 58 W98 18 33. Stereo. 6222 N.W. IH-10 78201. Phone: (210) 736-9700. Fax: (210) 735-8811. Web Site: www.ticketssports.com. Licensee: CCB Texas Licenses L.P. Group owner: Clear Channel Communications Inc. (acq 6-16-93; $800,000;. FTR: 7-5-93). Network: Westwood One. Rep: Clear Channel. Format: Sports. Target aud: 25-49; male. ♦L.L. Mays, CEO, chmn & opns dir; Randall Mays, CFO; Tom Glade, gen mgr; Tom Gebhart, gen sls mgr; Nate Lundy, progmg dir.

KTSA(AM)— May 9, 1922: 550 khz; 5 kw-U, DA-N. TL: N29 29 41 W98 24 52 (D), N29 29 46 W98 24 54 (N). 4050 Eisenhauer Rd. 78218. Phone: (210) 528-5500. Fax: (210) 599-5588. Web Site: www.ktsa.com. Licensee: Texas Infinity Broadcasting L.P. Group owner: Infinity Broadcasting Corp. (acq 7-1-2000; $90 million;. in stock; tax-free merger with co-located FM). Network: ABC Daytime Direction. Cohn & Marks. Format: News/talk. News staff: 11; News: 35 hrs wkly. Target aud: 25-54. ♦Reid Reker, gen mgr; Ann Edwards, opns mgr; Tim Germadnik, pres & progmg dir.

KSRX(FM)—Co-owned with KTSA(AM). 1969: 102.7 mhz; 100 kw horiz, 70 kw vert. 670 ft. TL: N29 25 09 W98 29 06. Stereo. Web Site: www.ktfm.com. Format: CHR, top-40. Target aud: 12 plus. ♦John Cook, progmg dir.

KXXM(FM)— May 5, 1964: 96.1 mhz; 100 kw. 479 ft. TL: N29 38 00 W98 37 50. (CP: 99 kw, ant 328 ft.). Stereo. 6222 N.W. I-10 78201. Phone: (210) 736-9700. Fax: (210) 736-8811. E-mail: mix961@mic961.com. Web Site: www.mix961.com. Licensee: CCB Texas Licenses L.P. Group owner: Clear Channel Communications Inc. (acq 6-19-98; $15 million). Format: CHR. News staff: one; News: 3 hrs wkly. Target aud: 18-34; females. ♦Tom Glade, VP & gen mgr; Mike Hall, gen sls mgr; Tim Kiesling, mktg dir; Cesar Campa, prom dir.

***KYFS(FM)**— Nov 7, 1982: 90.9 mhz; 100 kw. 476 ft. TL: N29 40 20 W98 14 43. Stereo. 9330 Corporate Dr., Suite 808, Selma 78154. Phone: (210) 651-9093. Fax: (210) 651-9093. E-mail: kyfs@bbnradio.org. Web Site: www.bbnradio.org. Licensee: Bible Broadcasting Network

Texas

Inc. (group owner; acq 11-20-91; $75,000; 12-9-91). Smithwick & Belendiuk. Format: Christian. Target aud: 2 plus. ♦John D. Woolery, gen mgr & opns mgr.

KZDC(AM)— Jan 1, 1953: 1250 khz; 1 kw-U, DA-N. TL: N29 24 29 W98 26 39. Stereo. 7800 W. IH 10, Suite 330 10017. Phone: (210) 280-4000. Fax: (210) 822-9668. Web Site: www.radiounica.com. Licensee: Multicultural Radio Broadcasting Licensee LLC. Group owner: Multicultural Radio Broadcasting Inc. (acq 2-4-2004; grpsl). Format: Mexican rgnl. ♦Scott Keebler, gen mgr; Theo Alvarado, progmg dir; Roy Pressman, chief of engrg.

KZEP-FM— Oct 1, 1966: 104.5 mhz; 100 kw. 735 ft. TL: N29 25 09 W98 29 06. Stereo. 427 E. 9th St. 78215. Phone: (210) 226-6444. Fax: (210) 225-5736. E-mail: kzepp@kzep.com. Web Site: www.kzep.com. Licensee: Texas Lotus Corp. Group owner: Lotus Communications Corp. Rep: D & R Radio. Format: Classic rock. News staff: one; News: 3 hrs wkly. Target aud: 25-54; males. ♦Jay A. Levine, pres, VP & gen mgr; Trish Levine, prom dir; Craig Chambers, progmg dir; Tom Scheppke, mus dir; Dave Delgado, news dir; Eddie Miles, chief of engrg.

WOAI(AM)— Sept 29, 1922: 1200 khz; 50 kw-U. TL: N29 30 05 W98 07 09. 6222 N.W. IH-10 78201. Phone: (210) 736-9700. Fax: (210) 735-8811. Web Site: www.woai.com. Licensee: CCB Texas Licenses L.P. Group owner: Clear Channel Communications Inc. (acq 1975). Network: ABC. Rep: Clear Channel. Format: News/talk. News staff: 13; News: 20 hrs wkly. Target aud: 35-64; general. ♦L. Lowry Mays, pres & CEO; Tom Glade, gen mgr; Nate Lundy, opns dir & progmg dir; Mike McDonald, sls dir; Tom Gebhart, gen sls mgr; Marian Holdsworth, natl sls mgr; Sue Nicholas, natl sls mgr; Tim Kiesling, mktg dir; Bill Rohde, prom mgr; Jim Forsyth, news dir; Dan Walthers, chief of engrg.

KAJA(FM)— Co-owned with WOAI(AM). 1951: 97.3 mhz; 100 kw. 984 ft. TL: N29 25 20 W98 29 22. Stereo. 6222 N.W. IH-10 78201. Web Site: www.kj97.com. Rep: Clear Channel. Format: Country. News: 2 hrs wkly. Target aud: 18-54. ♦Alan Furst, opns mgr; Dean Phillips, gen sls mgr; Clayton Allen, prom mgr & progmg dir.

San Augustine

KQSI(FM)— Dec 29, 1993: 92.5 mhz; 1.4 kw. Ant 220 ft. TL: N31 31 44 W94 05 59. Box 930, Center 75935. Phone: (936) 275-3242. Fax: (936) 598-9537. Licensee: Center Broadcasting Co. Inc. (group owner; acq 3-26-98; grpsl). Network: ABC. Format: C & W, Sp. News staff: one. Target aud: 35-65. ♦Tracy Broadway, gen mgr & gen sls mgr; Rob Rockett, progmg dir; Daniel Christie, news dir; Harlan Riley, chief of engrg.

San Diego

KUKA(FM)— July 14, 1993: 105.9 mhz; 25 kw. 450 ft. TL: N27 45 04 W98 07 28. Stereo. 810 Alviar St., Alice 78045. Phone: (361) 668-6666. Fax: (361) 668-6661. Licensee: Ideal Media Inc. dba KUKA Tejano FM 106. (acq 12-5-96). Akin, Gump, Strauss, Hauer & Feld. Format: Sp. News staff: one; News: one hr wkly. Target aud: 18-34; middle to upper class. ♦Armando Marroquin Jr., pres, mktg mgr, prom mgr & adv mgr; Teo Pena, gen mgr; Estela Nava, opns mgr & chief of engrg; Zulema Z. Marroquin, dev VP; Javier Villanueva, rgnl sls mgr; Tio Pena, mktg dir; Pedro Vasquez, progmg dir; Peter Vasquez, news dir; Henry Turner, chief of engrg.

San Juan

KUBR(AM)— 1991: 1210 khz; 10 kw-D, 1 kw-N, DA-2. TL: N26 14 41 W98 05 25. Box 252, McAllen 78505. Phone: (956) 686-6382. Fax: (956) 686-2999. E-mail: paylinobernal@hotmail.com. Web Site: www.laradiocristiana.com. Licensee: Radio Christiana Network. Format: Sp, Christian. ♦Paulino Bernal, gen mgr; Eloy Bernal, stn mgr; Pete Guzman, opns mgr.

San Marcos

KBPA(FM)— Licensed to San Marcos. See Austin

*****KTSW(FM)**— Apr 15, 1992: 89.9 mhz; 10.5 kw. Ant 213 ft. TL: N29 39 20 W98 07 59. Stereo. Old Main 106, 601 University Dr. 78666-4616. Phone: (512) 245-3485. Fax: (512) 245-3732. E-mail: ktsw@txstate.edu. Web Site: www.ktsw.txstate.edu. Licensee: Texas State University-San Marcos (acq 4-16-92; $150,000;. FTR: 5-11-92). Booth, Freret, Imlay & Tepper. Format: College alternative, news/talk, sports. Target aud: 18-25; college students. ♦Dan Schumachev, gen mgr; Liz Castro, stn mgr & sls dir; Bryant Martin, sls dir & prom dir; Angela Maldonado, progmg mgr; Whitney Barclay, mus dir; Tom Bruce, engrg dir.

KUOL(AM)— 1948: 1470 khz; 250 w-U, DA-N. TL: N29 53 53 W97 54 44. Box 252, McAllen 78505. Phone: (956) 686-6382. Fax: (956) 686-2999. E-mail: paulinobernal@hotmail.com. Web Site: www.laradiocristiana.com. Licensee: Radio Christiana Network. (acq 3-26-97). Format: Sp, Christian. ♦Paulino Bernal, gen mgr; Eloy Bernal, stn mgr; Pete Guzman, opns mgr.

San Saba

KBAL(AM)— 1954: 1410 khz; 800 w-D, 203 w-N. TL: N31 11 26 W98 42 55. Box 126 76877. Secondary address: Building D-2, 2402 Broadmoor, Bryon 77802. Phone: (915) 372-5225. Fax: (915) 372-3817. E-mail: kabal@centex.net. Web Site: www.kbalradio.com. Licensee: Roy E. Henderson. (acq 2-15-00; grpsl). Fletcher, Heald & Hildreth. Format: Adult contemp. News staff: 2; News: 6 hrs wkly. Rural all ages. Spec prog: Farm 2 hrs,gospel 7 hrs wkly. ♦Steve Smith, CFO; Shay Hardy, gen mgr, opns dir, progmg dir & news dir; Sherry Spinks, gen mgr & sls dir.

KBAL-FM— 1996: 106.1 mhz; 3 kw. Ant 20 ft. TL: N31 11 26 W98 42 55. 705 Live Oak 76877. Web Site: www.kbalradio.com. Format: Country. News staff: one; News: 5 hrs wkly. Target aud: General.

Sanger

KTDK(FM)— December 1989: 104.1 mhz; 6.2 kw. Ant 630 ft. TL: N33 28 47 W97 09 32. Stereo. 3500 Maple Ave., Suite 1310, Dallas 75219. Phone: (214) 526-7400. Fax: (214) 525-2525. Web Site: www.merge933.net. Licensee: KRBE Lico Inc. Group owner: Susquehanna Radio Corp. (acq 4-30-98; $3.683 million). Format: Sports. Target aud: 24-55. ♦Dan Bennett, gen mgr; Joan Leonard, opns mgr; Jim Quirk, sls dir; Kim Roberts, gen sls mgr; Jeff Catlin, progmg dir; Jimmy Christopher, news dir; Rob Chickering, chief of engrg.

*****KVRK(FM)**— July 8, 1999: 89.7 mhz; 14 kw. 1,699 ft. TL: N33 33 36 W96 57 35. Research Educational Foundation Inc., 11061 Shady Tr., Dallas 75229. Phone: (214) 351-6655. Fax: (214) 351-6809. E-mail: chris@897powerfm.com. Web Site: www.897powerfm.com. Licensee: Research Educational Foundation Inc. Format: Christian, rock. ♦Stanley Thomas, gen mgr; Ron Evans, stn mgr; Devin Wickham, opns dir; Krystal Coleman, prom dir; Chris Goodwin, progmg dir; Kent Loney, chief of engrg.

Schertz

KBBT(FM)— Feb 1, 1976: 98.5 mhz; 97 kw. Ant 991 ft. TL: N29 31 25 W98 43 25. Stereo. 1777 N.E. Loop 410, Suite 400, San Antonio 78217. Phone: (210) 829-1075. Fax: (210) 804-7825. Web Site: www.netmio.com. Licensee: Univision Radio License Corp. Group owner: Univision Radio (acq 9-22-2003; grpsl). Format: Hip Hop. ♦Mac Tichenor, CEO & pres; Jeff Hinson, CFO; Dan Wilson, gen mgr; J. D. Gonzalez, opns mgr.

Seabrook

KROI(FM)— Apr 23, 1984: 92.1 mhz; 50 kw. Ant 981 ft. TL: N29 16 33 W95 22 45. Stereo. 24 Greenway Plaza, Suite 900, Houston 77046. Phone: (713) 623-2108. Fax: (713) 623-8166. Licensee: Radio One Licenses LLC. Group owner: Radio One Inc. (acq 7-20-2004; $72.5 million). Target aud: General. ♦Alfred C. Liggins III, pres; Scott R. Royster, exec VP; Dough Abernethy, gen mgr.

Seadrift

KMAT(FM)— May 1999: 105.1 mhz; 40 kw. Ant 407 ft. TL: N28 25 44 W96 26 54. Stereo. 866 N. Wilcrest, Houston 77079. Phone: (713) 722-0169. Fax: (713) 468-5773. E-mail: bcordell@houston.rr.com. Web Site: www.kmat.cc. Licensee: William E. Cordell. Leventhal, Senter & Lerman. Format: Christian. News: 2 hrs wkly. Target aud: 30-50. ♦Bill Cordell, pres & gen mgr.

Seguin

KSMG(FM)— Sept 9, 1970: 105.3 mhz; 100 kw. 1,240 ft. TL: N29 16 29 W98 15 52. Stereo. 8930 Four Winds Dr., Suite 500, San Antonio 78239. Phone: (210) 646-0105. Fax: (210) 646-9711. E-mail: virgil.thompson@cox.com. Web Site: www.magic1053.com. Licensee: CXR Holdings L.L.C. Group owner: Cox Broadcasting (acq 8-4-97; grpsl). Rep: Christal. Leventhal, Senter & Lerman. Format: Hot adult contemp. News staff: one; News: 5 hrs wkly. Target aud: 25-49; females. ♦Virgil Thompson, gen mgr; Rory Charitan, gen sls mgr; Robert John, progmg dir; Katrina Curtiss, mus dir; Karen Clauss, news dir & pub affrs dir; Richard Schuh, chief of engrg.

KWED(AM)— Sept 9, 1948: 1580 khz; 1 kw-D, 253 w-N. TL: N29 34 48 W97 59 05. 609 E. Court St. 78155. Phone: (830) 379-2234. Fax: (830) 379-2238. Web Site: www.kwed1580.com. Licensee: Seguin Media Group Ltd. (acq 6-10-02; $940,000). Network: Network: Westwood One, CNN Radio. Womble,Caryle,Sandridge & Rice. Format: Country, news/talk. News staff: 5; News: 30 hrs wkly. Target aud: General. Spec prog: Farm 6 hrs wkly. ♦Hal Widsten, pres, gen mgr & gen sls mgr; Darren Dunn, opns mgr & news mgr; Sarah Masterson, pub affrs dir; Richard Schuh, chief of engrg.

Seminole

KIKZ(AM)— Apr 15, 1954: 1250 khz; 1 kw-D, 250 w-N. TL: N32 41 58 W102 38 12. 105 N.W. 11th St. 79360. Phone: (915) 758-5878. Fax: (915) 758-5474. E-mail: kikz-kssem@midtech.net. Licensee: Gaines County Broadcasting Ltd. (acq 6-9-93; $193,276 with co-located FM; 7-5-93). Network: ABC. Format: Country, Sp. News staff: one; News: 7 hrs wkly. Target aud: General. Spec prog: Farm 5 hrs, Ger one hr, relg 6 hrs wkly. ♦Danny Curtis, gen mgr, prom mgr, progmg dir & engrg mgr; Mike Elder, gen sls mgr; Audie Cox, news dir.

KSEM-FM— Co-owned with KIKZ(AM). Mar 15, 1985: 106.3 mhz; 3 kw. 174 ft. TL: N32 41 58 W102 38 12. Stereo. Format: Country.

Seymour

KSEY(AM)— Oct 26, 1950: 1230 khz; 1 kw-U. TL: N33 35 49 W99 16 42. 700 eighth St., Suite 210, Wichita Falls 76301. Phone: (940) 767-0011. Fax: (940) 767-0164. E-mail: kseytejano1230am@aol.com. Licensee: Mark Aulabaugh. (acq 11-95). Format: Sp. ♦Tommy Cobos, gen mgr; Orlando Jariez, progmg dir.

KSEY-FM— June 26, 1981: 94.3 mhz; 3 kw. 112 ft. TL: N33 35 49 W99 16 42. (CP: 93.9 mhz, 50 kw, ant 492 ft. TL: N33 42 00 W99 08 12). Stereo. Box 471 76380. Phone: (940) 889-2637. Fax: (940) 889-2637. E-mail: fmksey@aol.com. Web Site: www.radioksey.com. Format: Full service. ♦Mark Aulabaugh, gen mgr; Joe Gaither, progmg dir.

Shamrock

KBKH(FM)— Sept 15, 1997: 92.9 mhz; 50 kw. Ant 253 ft. TL: N35 20 29 W100 14 33. Stereo. Box 688 79079-0688. Phone: (806) 256-1221. Fax: (806) 256-1223. E-mail: kbkh@kbkh.com. Web Site: www.kbkh.com. Licensee: Terry Keith Hammond (acq 8-26-2002). Format: Adult contemp, oldies, news/talk. News staff: one; News: 32 hrs wkly. Target aud: 25-75; adults. Spec prog: Farm 25 hrs, gospel 6 wkly. ♦Keith Hammond, pres, gen mgr, mktg dir & engrg dir.

Sherman

KJIM(AM)— Dec 19, 1947: 1500 khz; 1 kw-D, DA. TL: N33 41 30 W96 33 29. 4367 Woodlawn Rd., Denison 75021-8037. Phone: (903) 893-1197. Fax: (908) 893-1197. Licensee: Bob Mark Allen Productions Inc. Network: Network: Westwood One, CBS. Format: Original hits of the 50s, 60s, 70s & 80s, news, sports. Target aud: 40-65. ♦Bob Mark Allen, pres.

KKLF(AM)— 1999: 1700 khz; 10 kw-D, 700 w-N. TL: N33 25 23 W96 39 45. 3500 Maple Ave., Suite 1310, Dallas 75219. Phone: (214) 526-7400. Fax: (214) 525-2525. Web Site: www.theticket.com. Licensee: KRBE Lico Inc. Group owner: Susquehanna Radio Corp. (acq 4-30-98). Format: Sports. ♦Peter P. Brubaker, CEO & chmn; David E. Kennedy, pres; Joe Barlek, CFO; Dan Bennett, VP; Jim Quirk, sls dir; Ken Roberts, gen sls mgr; Jami Williams, natl sls mgr; Callie Hoch, mktg dir; Sharon Brown, mktg mgr; Jamey Garner, prom dir; Jeff Catlin, progmg dir; Mark Friedman, pub affrs dir; Rob Chickering, engrg dir.

KYNG(AM)— See Denison-Sherman

Silsbee

KAYD-FM— June 21, 1980: 101.7 mhz; 10.5 kw. Ant 502 ft. TL: N30 06 54 W93 59 56. Stereo. 755 S. 11th St., Suite 102, Beaumont 77704. Phone: (409) 833-9421. Fax: (409) 833-9296. Web Site:

Stations in the U.S. — Texas

Developers & Brokers of Radio Properties

contact American Media Services at our suite:
Philadelphia Marriott Downtown
215-625-2900
843-972-2200
americanmediaservices.com
Charleston, SC
Dallas, TX · Chicago, Il · Austin, TX

American Media Services, LLC

www.kayd.com. Licensee: Cumulus Licensing LLC. (acq 11-8-2004); $2.1 million). Format: Country. News: 20 hrs wkly. Target aud: 25-54; persons. ♦Zanetta Kelley, gen mgr; Jim West, opns mgr & progmg dir; Wes Matejka, sls dir; Mark Guzman, prom mgr.

KSET(AM)— Oct 13, 1959: 1300 khz; 500 w-D. TL: N30 21 02 W94 13 39. Box 455 77656. Phone: (409) 385-2883. Fax: (409) 386-1001. E-mail: kset@kset1300.com. Web Site: www.kset1300.com. Licensee: Proctor-Williams Inc. (acq 2-14-01; with co-located FM). Format: All sports. Target aud: General. ♦Dave Collier Sr., CEO & gen mgr.

Sinton

KDAE(AM)—Licensed to Sinton. See Corpus Christi

KNCN(FM)—Licensed to Sinton. See Corpus Christi

KOUL(FM)—Licensed to Sinton. See Corpus Christi

Slaton

KJAK(FM)—Licensed to Slaton. See Lubbock

Snyder

KLYD(FM)— 2003: 98.9 mhz; 5.6 kw. Ant 341 ft. TL: N32 45 23 W100 54 09. Box 1008 79550. Phone: (325) 573-9322. Fax: (325) 573-7445. Licensee: Delbert Foree. Format: Modern rock. ♦Dink Foree, gen mgr.

KSNY(AM)— Dec 22, 1949: 1450 khz; 1 kw-U. TL: N32 43 33 W100 56 30. Box 1008 79550. Secondary address: 2301 Ave. R 79549. Phone: (325) 573-9322. Fax: (325) 573-7445. E-mail: ksnyfm@snydertex.com. Licensee: Snyder Broadcasting Co. (acq 1952). Network: ABC. Format: Christian. Target aud: General. ♦Bill Jamar, pres; Lydia Foree, VP; Dink Foree, gen mgr, prom mgr, progmg dir & progmg dir.

KSNY-FM— Sept 2, 1980: 101.5 mhz; 35 kw. 500 ft. TL: N32 53 29 W101 06 29. Stereo. Format: Country. News staff: one; News: 5 hrs wkly. Target aud: 25-54.

Somerset

KSJL(AM)— Mar 1, 1988: 810 khz; 250 w-U, DA-2. TL: N29 18 48 W98 30 29. 6222 NW I-10, San Antonio 78201. Phone: (210) 736-9700. Fax: (210) 735-8811. Web Site: www.ksjl.com. Licensee: Maranatha Broadcasting Inc. (Group owner: Clear Channel (acq 3-11-98; $750,000). Format: Urban contemp. News: 10 hrs wkly. ♦Tom Glade, VP & gen mgr; Ken North, opns mgr & rgnl sls mgr; Tim Kiesling, mktg dir; Ed Scarborough, progmg dir.

Sonora

KHOS(AM)— Apr 9, 1976: 980 khz; 1 kw-D, 260 w-N. TL: N30 33 08 W100 39 24. c/o KMXO(AM), 604 N. Second St., Merkel 79536. Phone: (325) 928-3060. Fax: (325) 928-4683. Licensee: Zacarias Serrato. (acq 7-7-99; $5,000). Format: Christian, Sp, educ. ♦Zacarias Serrato, gen mgr.

KHOS-FM— May 1979: 92.1 mhz; 3 kw. 298 ft. TL: N30 33 33 W100 37 54. Stereo. HC65, Box 50, Hwy. 277 S. 76950. Phone: (325) 387-3553. Fax: (325) 387-3554. E-mail: khoskyxx@sonoratx.net. Licensee: Sonora Broadcasting Co. Group owner: Hill Country Broadcasting Corp. (acq 8-16-00; grpsl). Network: ABC. Format: Real country. News: 3 hrs wkly. Target aud: 12-50 plus. ♦Kent Foster, pres; Monte Spearman, gen mgr; Donna Keese, stn mgr; Eddy Smith, engr.

South Padre Island

KESO(FM)— Aug 27, 1996: 92.7 mhz; 3 kw. 298 ft. TL: N26 04 04 W97 13 16. Stereo. 1004 Padre Blvd., 4th Fl. 78597. Phone: (956) 761-2270. Fax: (956) 761-1656. Web Site: www.alternative927.com. Licensee: BMP RGV License Company L.P. (acq 12-6-2004; $6.6 million. with KZSP(FM) South Padre Island). Format: Alternative rock. Target aud: 25-44. ♦Terry Kimball, gen mgr & stn mgr; Jim Wilson, progmg dir.

KZSP(FM)— July 27, 1990: 95.3 mhz; 2.5 kw. 353 ft. TL: N26 04 04 W97 13 16. Stereo. 1004 Padre Blvd., 4th Fl. 78597. Phone: (956) 761-2270. Fax: (956) 761-1656. Web Site: www.love953.com. Licensee: BMP RGV License Company L.P. (acq 12-6-2004; $6.6 million. with KESO(FM) South Padre Island). Format: Light jazz. News: 2 hrs wkly. Target aud: 25-54; success-oriented adults. ♦Terry Kimball, gen mgr & stn mgr; Jim Wilson, progmg dir & chief of engrg.

Spearman

*KTOT(FM)— 2003: 89.5 mhz; 100 kw. Ant 1,066 ft. TL: N36 03 44 W101 01 56. High Plains Public Radio, 207 N. 7th St., Garden City, KS 67846. Phone: (620) 275-7444. Web Site: www.hppr.org. Licensee: Kanza Society Inc. Format: Class music, news. ♦Richard Hicks, gen mgr; Debra Stout, progmg mgr.

KXDJ(FM)— Dec 16, 1963: . Stn currently dark 98.3 mhz; 17.6 kw. Ant 836 ft. TL: N36 03 44 W101 01 56. Stereo. Box 307, 605 E. Kenneth Ave. 79081. Phone: (806) 659-2529. Licensee: George Chambers (acq 12-15-2003; $280,000). ♦George Chambers, pres & VP.

Springtown

*KSQX(FM)— August 1985: 89.1 mhz; 3 kw. Ant 184 ft. TL: N32 58 53 W97 42 18. 905 Palopinto St., Weatherford 76086. Phone: (817) 341-8950. Fax: (817) 598-1661. Web Site: www.kyqx.com. Licensee: CSSI Non-Profit Educational Broadcasting Corp. (acq 5-21-02). Format: Adult contemp. ♦Melinda Beard, gen mgr; Dave Cowley, progmg dir; Brent Baker, news dir.

Stamford

KLGD(FM)— Feb 22, 1999: 106.9 mhz; 40 kw. Ant 548 ft. TL: N32 56 16 W99 57 20. 209 S. Danville, Suite B-105, Abilene 79605. Phone: (915) 691-5400. Fax: (915) 691-5653. E-mail: bruce@texas96.com. Web Site: countrylegends.com. Licensee: Texas Gulfwest Communications Corp. (acq 6-26-01). Format: Country. Target aud: 35 plus; adults. ♦Bill Hooten, CEO & gen mgr; Pete Garcia, progmg mgr & mus dir.

KVRP(AM)— July 1947: 1400 khz; 1 kw-U. TL: N32 55 52 W99 47 00. Box 1118, 1406 N. First St., Haskell 79521. Phone: (940) 864-8505. Fax: (940) 864-8001. E-mail: gary@kvrp.com. Web Site: www.kvrp.com. Licensee: 1 Chronicles 14 L.P. (acq 8-4-2004; $700,000. with KVRP-FM Haskell). Rep: Katz Radio. Format: Country. News staff: one. Target aud: 25 plus. ♦Gregg Weston, pres & gen mgr; Gary Barrett, stn mgr & gen sls mgr; Josh Roysdon, natl sls mgr & news dir; Dave Harrison, progmg mgr; Megan Cox, chief of engrg.

Stanton

*KFRI(FM)—Not on air, target date: unknown: 88.1 mhz; 100 kw. Ant 377 ft. TL: N32 05 48 W101 46 26. Stereo. 5700 W. Oaks Blvd., Rocklin, CA 95765. Phone: (916) 251-1600. Fax: (916) 251-1650. E-mail: info@air1.com. Web Site: www.air1.com. Licensee: Educational Media Foundation. Group owner: EMF Broadcasting. Network: Air 1. Shaw Pittman. Format: Contemp Christian. News staff: 3. Target aud: 18-35. ♦Richard Jenkins, pres; Mike Novak, VP & progmg dir; Lloyd Parker, gen mgr; Keith Whipple, dev dir; Eric Allen, natl sls mgr; Russ Lloyd, rgnl sls mgr; Chris Joyce, prom dir; Bryan O'Neal, progmg mgr; Liz Morton, mus dir; Ed Lenane, news dir; Sam Wallington, engrg dir.

KKJW(FM)— 1998: 105.9 mhz; 37 kw. 400 ft. TL: N31 51 19 W101 47 32. 24 Smith Rd., Midland 79705. Phone: (915) 620-8282. Fax: (915) 620 0498. Licensee: Unique Broadcasting L.L.C. (acq 7-23-97). Format: Classic country. ♦Dick Baze, gen mgr.

Stephenville

KCUB-FM— July 1, 1990: 98.3 mhz; 3 kw. 328 ft. TL: N32 12 46 W98 15 19. Stereo. Box 1137 76401. Secondary address: 471 Harbin Dr., Suite 102 76401. Phone: (254) 968-7459. Fax: (254) 968-6258. E-mail: kcub@kcubonline.com. Web Site: www.kcubonline.com. Licensee: Reese Broadcasting L.L.C. (acq 11-13-98; $665,000). Network: Jones Radio Networks. Format: Texas country. News staff: 2; News: 7 hrs wkly. Target aud: 20-65; all-important age group of today's buying public. ♦John Hollinger, gen mgr; Jonathon Boev, gen sls mgr & progmg dir; Jim Rhodes, chief of engrg.

*KEQX(FM)—Not on air, target date: unknown: 89.7 mhz; 3.5 kw vert. Ant 328 ft. TL: N32 06 50 W98 07 01. 905 Palo Pinto St., Weatherford 76086. Phone: (817) 341-8950. Fax: (817) 596-9842. Web Site: kyqx.com. Licensee: CSSI Non-Profit Educational Broadcasting Corp. ♦Melinda Beard, gen mgr.

*KQXS(FM)— 2004: 89.1 mhz; 1.2 kw vert. Ant 424 ft. TL: N32 16 09 W98 18 51. 905 Palo Pinto St., Weatherford 76086. Phone: (817) 341-8950. Fax: (817) 596-9842. Web Site: kyqx.com. Licensee: CSSI Non-Profit Educational Broadcasting Corp. (acq 11-25-2002). ♦Melinda Beard, gen mgr.

KSTV(AM)— 1947: 1510 khz; 500 w-D. TL: N32 12 08 W98 14 54. Box 289, 3209 W. Washington 76401. Phone: (254) 968-2141. Fax: (254) 968-6221. Web Site: www.kstvfm.com. Licensee: CCR-Stephenville III LLC. Group owner: Cherry Creek Radio LLC (acq 6-24-2004; grpsl). Network: ABC Daytime Direction. Format: Mexician hits. Target aud: 54 plus; general. Spec prog: Farm 5 hrs, relg 6 hrs wkly. ♦Robert Elliott, gen mgr; Bob Haschke, gen sls mgr; Jose Perez, prom mgr & progmg dir; Loena Rodriquez, news dir; Justin McClure, chief of engrg.

Sterling City

KNRX(FM)— Dec 1, 1998: 96.5 mhz; 40 kw. Ant 544 ft. TL: N31 35 56 W100 50 42. 1301 S. Abe St., San Angelo 76903. Phone: (325) 655-7161. Fax: (325) 658-7377. Web Site: www.kickin-country.com. Licensee: Encore Broadcasting of San Angelo LLC. Group owner: Encore Broadcasting LLC (acq 1-26-2004; $875,000. with KKCN(FM) Ballinger). Format: Alternative rock. Target aud: 18-34. ♦John Kerr, gen mgr & adv dir; Boomer Kingston, progmg dir; Tommy Jenkins, engrg dir.

Sulphur Springs

KSCH(FM)— Aug 30, 1982: 95.9 mhz; 6 kw. 285 ft. TL: N33 09 07 W95 36 12. Stereo. Box 564 75483. Secondary address: 930 S. Gilmer 75483. Phone: (903) 885-1546. Fax: (903) 885-1101. E-mail: hitmusic@klake.net. Web Site: www.easttexasradio.com. Licensee: East Texas Broadcasting Inc. (group owner; acq 9-30-99). Fletcher, Heald & Hildreth. Format: Sp, CHR. News staff: 3; News: 13 hrs wkly. Target aud: 18-60. ♦J.R. "Bud" Kitchens Jr., pres; Daniel Osuna, gen mgr & gen sls mgr.

KSST(AM)— March 1947: 1230 khz; 1 kw-U. TL: N33 07 00 W95 35 05. Box 284 75483. Secondary address: 717 Shannon Rd. 75483. Phone: (903) 885-3111. Fax: (903) 885-4160. E-mail: ksst@neto.com. Web Site: www.ksstradio.com. Licensee: Hopkins County Broadcasting Co. (acq 1948). Network: ABC Information & Entertainment. Format: Full service, adult standards. News staff: 2; News: 30 hrs wkly. Target aud: 25-54. ♦Dwayne Grimes, opns dir, gen sls mgr & progmg dir; Enola Gay, prom dir & mus dir; Patsy Bradford, adv dir; Jimmy Rogers, news dir & pub affrs dir; William Bradford, CEO, pres, gen mgr & chief of engrg.

Sweetwater

KXOX(AM)— November 1939: 1240 khz; 1 kw-U. TL: N32 29 16 W100 23 31. Stereo. Box 570 79556. Secondary address: 1801 Hoyt Ln. 79556. Phone: (325) 236-6655. Fax: (325) 235-4391. E-mail: kxox@bigcountry.net. Licensee: Stein Broadcasting Inc. (acq 1956). Format: Country. News: 2 plus hrs wkly. Target aud: 25-54. Spec prog:

Broadcasting & Cable Yearbook 2006

Texas
Directory of Radio

Farm 5 hrs, Sp 8 hrs, gospel 4 hrs wkly. ♦ Jack Stein, pres; Jeff Stein, gen mgr, prom mgr & news dir; Richard Ferguson, progmg dir; Gary Graham, chief of engrg.

KXOX-FM— Apr 7, 1976; 96.7 mhz; 2.9 kw. 154 ft. TL: N32 29 16 W100 23 31. Stereo. News staff: one.

Tahoka

KAMZ(FM)— 2001: 103.5 mhz; 20 kw. Ant 328 ft. TL: N33 19 26 W101 48 15. 1220 Broadway, Suite 1035, Lubbock 79401. Phone: (806) 741-0701. Fax: (806) 741-0705. Licensee: Albert Benavides. Format: Mexican regional. ♦ Albert Benavides, gen mgr; Rick Benavides, natl sls mgr; Bob Benavides, mus dir; Bill Enloe, chief of engrg.

KMMX(FM)— Aug 13, 1987: 100.3 mhz; 100 kw. 800 ft. TL: N33 26 30 W101 52 42. Stereo. 33 Briercroft Park, Lubbock 79412. Phone: (806) 762-3000. Fax: (806) 762-8419. Web Site: www.kmmx.com. Licensee: Wilks License Co.-Lubbock LLC. Group owner: NextMedia Group L.L.C. (acq 8-19-2005; grpsl). Network: ABC. Format: Adult contemp. News staff: one; News: 5 hrs wkly. Target aud: 25-54; females. ♦ Scott Harris, gen mgr; Jeff Scott, opns mgr; Jay Richards, gen sls mgr; Damon Scott, progmg dir; Stacey James, news dir; Randy Hayes, chief of engrg.

Tatum

KXAL-FM— Aug 1, 1965: 100.3 mhz; 2.45 kw. Ant 518 ft. TL: N32 22 37 W94 34 18. Stereo. Box 1648, Jacksonville 75766. Secondary address: 402 Ragsdale, Jacksonville 75766. Phone: (903) 586-2527. Fax: (903) 589-0677. Licensee: Waller Media LLC. Group owner: On-Air Family LLC (acq 8-9-2005; $975,000 with KDVE(FM) Pittsburg). Format: Sp. ♦ Dudley Waller, gen mgr; Chris Ousley, gen sls mgr; Victor Covarrubias, progmg dir.

Taylor

KWNX(AM)— Apr 1, 1948: 1260 khz; 1 kw-D. TL: N30 36 19 W97 24 51. 4314 W. Baker Ln., Suite 1260, Austin 78759. Phone: (512) 346-8255. Fax: (512) 346-8262. E-mail: controlroom@espnaustin.com. Web Site: www.espnaustin.com. Licensee: Simmons-Austin, LS LLC. Group owner: Simmons Media Group (acq 5-17-2004; $950,000). Format: News/talk, sports. ♦ Daryl O'Neal, gen mgr; Jon Madani, opns dir & progmg dir; Lori Hatter, sls dir; Courtney Cleland, prom mgr; J. Cole McClellan, chief of engrg.

KXBT(FM)— Apr 4, 1975: 104.3 mhz; 48 kw. Ant 492 ft. TL: N30 26 04 W97 21 53. Stereo. Escalade B-Third Fl., 4301 Westbank Dr., Austin 78746. Phone: (512) 327-9595. Fax: (512) 329-6255. Web Site: www.beat1043.com. Licensee: Infinity Radio Inc. Group owner: Infinity Broadcasting Corp. (acq 11-13-98; grpsl). Format: Contemporary hit radio. News staff: one. Target aud: 12-34. ♦ John Sykes, CEO; John Full, pres; Ted Siry, CFO; Brian Ongaro, sr VP & sls VP; John Hiatt, VP & gen mgr; Tatjana Deegan, gen sls mgr; Geneva Duncan, natl sls mgr; Joe McCormack, mktg dir; Carla Spears, prom dir; Dusty Hayes, progmg VP; Jason Kidd, progmg dir; Preston Lowe, mus dir; Dave Matyis, engrg dir & chief of engrg.

Temple

***KBDE(FM)**—Not on air, target date: unknown: 89.9 mhz; 11.5 kw vert. Ant 489 ft. TL: N31 16 05 W97 21 34. Box 3206, Tupelo, MS 38803. Phone: (662) 844-8888 ext. 204. Web Site: afr.net. Licensee: American Family Association. Group owner: American Family Radio Format: Christian. ♦ Marvin Sanders, gen mgr.

KLTD(FM)— 1995: 101.7 mhz; 16.5 kw. 410 ft. TL: N31 16 24 W97 23 31. 108 E. Ave. E., Copperas Cove 76522. Phone: (254) 773-5252. Fax: (254) 547-2394. Web Site: www.cumulus.com. Licensee: Cumulus Licensing Corp. Group owner: Cumulus Media Inc. (acq 4-20-01; $1.5 million. including $50,000 noncompete clause). Format: Classic Rock. ♦ Bourdon Wooten, gen mgr; Mikie Cummings, gen sls mgr; Jamie Garrett, prom dir; Tom Rivers, progmg dir; Chris Cummings, news dir; Doug Bernhardt, chief of engrg.

KTEM(AM)— Nov 25, 1936: 1400 khz; 950 w-U. TL: N31 04 01 W97 23 57. 608 Moody Ln. 76504. Phone: (254) 773-5252. Fax: (254) 773-0115. E-mail: mailbox@ktem.com. Web Site: www.ktem.com. Licensee: Cumulus Licensing Corp. Group owner: Cumulus Media Inc. (acq 3-12-01; $425,000). Network: CBS. Format: News/talk, sports. News staff: one; News: 30 hrs wkly. Target aud: 35-64; affluent, educated, politically active. Spec prog: Czech 3 hrs wkly. ♦ Bourdon Wooten, gen mgr & natl sls mgr; Mike Cummings, gen sls mgr; Lisa Tanner, prom mgr; Dave Hodges, progmg dir & news dir; Troy Carrell, chief of engrg.

KUSJ(FM)—(Harker Heights). June 1987: 105.5 mhz; 930 w. 587 ft. TL: N31 05 23 W97 35 55. (CP: 33 kw, ant 600 ft. TL: N30 59 09 W97 37 51). Stereo. 608 Moody Ln. 76504. Phone: (254) 773-5252. Fax: (254) 773-0015. E-mail: bourdon.wooten@cumulus.com. Web Site: us105.com. Licensee: Cumulus Licensing Corp. Group owner: Cumulus Media Inc. (acq 2-2-00; grpsl). Format: Country. Target aud: 25-54. ♦ Bourdon Wooten, gen mgr; Mikie Cummings, gen sls mgr; Jamie Garrett, prom dir; Lisa Tanner, prom dir; Doug Bernhardt, chief of engrg & engr.

***KVLT(FM)**— May 1, 2003: 88.5 mhz; 5 kw vert. Ant 617 ft. TL: N30 59 08 W97 37 56. Stereo. American Educational Broadcasting Inc., 3185 S. Highland Dr. #13, Las Vegas, NV 89109. Secondary address: 3411 Market Loop, Studio,Suite 108 76504. Phone: (254) 791-5251. Fax: (254) 791-0200. E-mail: james@kvltfm.com. Licensee: American Educational Broadcasting Inc. Network: K-Love. Fletcher, Heald & Hildreth. Format: Contemp Christian music. ♦ Carl J. Auel, pres; James E. Auel, gen mgr.

Terrell

KPYK(AM)— October 1947: 1570 khz; 250 w-D, 6 w-N. TL: N32 44 35 W96 18 18 (day), N32 45 18 W96 18 58 (night). Box 157 75160. Phone: (972) 524-5795. Fax: (972) 524-5795. E-mail: KRYK@broadcast.net. Web Site: www.kpyk .com. Licensee: Mohnkern Electronics Inc. (acq 4-1-92; $25,000 plus assumption of debt; 3-16-92). Format: Btfl mus, big band, old radio programs. News staff: one; News: 8 hrs wkly. Target aud: 40 plus; mature adults. Spec prog: Sp one hr, Black 5 hrs, relg 11 hrs, drama 7 hrs, children one hr weekly. ♦ Len Mohnkern, pres, gen mgr, gen sls mgr & news mgr; Chuck Mohnkern, chief of opns, progmg dir & chief of engrg; Liz Mohnkern, asst music dir; Susan Pinson, prom dir & pub affrs dir.

Terrell Hills

KELZ-FM— July 18, 1979: 106.7 mhz; 100 kw. Ant 1,017 ft. TL: N29 11 03 W98 30 49. Stereo. 8122 Datapoint Dr., # 500, San Antonio 78229. Phone: (210) 615-5400. Fax: (210) 615-5300. Web Site: www.jamz.com. Licensee: CXR Holdings L.L.C. Group owner: Cox Communications Inc. (acq 3-28-97; grpsl). Latham & Watkins. Format: Contemp hit. News staff: one. Target aud: 18-34. ♦ Bob Neil, CEO; Ben Reed, VP; Marty Choate, gen mgr; Roger Allen, opns mgr; Mark Bowka, gen sls mgr; Jim Bratt, natl sls mgr; Julie Busse, mktg mgr; Joey Farris, prom dir; Doug Bennett, progmg dir; Lee Mick, chief of engrg.

KLUP(AM)— Oct 17, 1947: 930 khz; 5 kw-D, 1 kw-N, DA-N. TL: N29 31 06 W98 24 25. 9601 McAllister Fwy., Suite 1200, San Antonio 78216. Phone: (210) 344-8481. Fax: (210) 340-1213. E-mail: myopinion@klup.com. Web Site: www.klup.com. Licensee: South Texas Broadcasting Inc. Group owner: Salem Communications Corp. (acq 7-27-00; grpsl). Network: Salem Radio Network. Format: News/talk. Target aud: 35-64; upper & middle income, empty nesters. ♦ Baron Wiley, gen mgr, opns mgr, progmg dir & progmg dir; David Ziebell, gen mgr & gen sls mgr; James Herring, gen sls mgr.

Texarkana

KCMC(AM)— Feb 26, 1932: 740 khz; 1 kw-U, DA-1. TL: N33 26 17 W94 08 33. 615 Olive St. 75501. Phone: (903) 793-4671. Fax: (903) 792-4261. Licensee: ArkLaTex LLC. (group owner; (acq 1-4-2002; grpsl). Network: ESPN Radio. Rep: McGavren Guild. Format: Sports. Target aud: 18-59; sports fans. ♦ Mike Simpson, gen mgr; Alex Rain, opns mgr & progmg dir.

KEWL(AM)— 1946: 1400 khz; 1 kw-U. TL: N33 26 28 W94 03 16. 1323 College Dr. 75503. Phone: (903) 793-1100. Fax: (903) 794-4717. Licensee: FFD Holdings I Inc. Group owner: Petracom Media LLC (acq 12-20-2004; grpsl). Format: Oldies. ♦ Mike Basso, gen mgr.

KEWL-FM—See New Boston

KHTA(FM)—See Wake Village

KKYR-FM— July 15, 1965: 102.5 mhz; 100 kw. 445 ft. TL: N33 22 24 W94 01 00. Stereo. 2324 Arkansas Blvd., AR 71854. Phone: (870) 772-3771. Fax: (870) 772-0364. Web Site: www.kkyr.com. Licensee: Capstar TX L.P. Group owner: Clear Channel Communications Inc. (acq 8-30-00; grpsl). Format: Country. Target aud: General. ♦ Ron Bird, gen mgr; Phil Robken, gen sls mgr; Mario Garcia, progmg dir; John Williams, news dir; Wes Spicher, chief of engrg.

KOSY(AM)—See Texarkana, AR

KRMD(AM)—See Shreveport, LA

KRMD-FM—See Shreveport, LA

KTAL-FM— 1945: 98.1 mhz; 100 kw horiz, 61 kw vert. 1,360 ft. TL: N32 54 11 W94 00 22. 208 N. Thomas Dr., Shreveport, LA 71107. Phone: (318) 222-3122. Fax: (318) 459-1493. Fax: (318) 222-2957. Licensee: Access. 1 Louisiana Holding Co. LLC. Group owner: Access.1 Communications Corp. (acq 12-20-02; grpsl). Format: Classic rock. ♦ Cary Camp, gen mgr; Howard Clark, opns mgr; Don Zimmerman, gen sls mgr; Tom Michaels, progmg dir & news dir; Eddie Thurmond, chief of engrg.

KTFS(AM)— Oct 23, 1961: 940 khz; 2.5 kw-D, 11 w-N. TL: N33 24 28 W94 02 45. 615 Olive St. 75501. Phone: (903) 793-4671. Fax: (903) 792-4261. Licensee: ArkLaTex LLC (group owner; acq 1-4-02; grpsl). Network: Network: CBS Radio, CNN Radio. Rep: McGavren Guild. Format: News/talk. News staff: one; News: 2 hrs wkly. Target aud: 35 plus. Spec prog: Rush Limbaugh, Black gospel 2 hrs wkly. ♦ Mike Simpson, gen mgr; Jay Calhoun, opns dir & news dir.

***KTXK(FM)**— Feb 1, 1984: 91.5 mhz; 5.2 kw. 335 ft. TL: N33 23 33 W94 14 44. Stereo. 2500 N. Robinson 75599. Phone: (903) 838-4541. Fax: (903) 832-5030. E-mail: ktxktc@texarkanacollege.edu. Licensee: Texarkana College. Network: PRI, NPR. Format: Btfl mus, class. News staff: one; News: 35 hrs wkly. Target aud: 35 plus. Spec prog: Jazz 15 hrs wkly. ♦ Steve Mitchell, pres, gen mgr & chief of opns.

Texas City

KYST(AM)— November 1947: 920 khz; 5 kw-D, 1 kw-N, DA-2. TL: N29 25 03 W94 56 12. 7322 S.W. Fwy., Suite 500, Houston 77074. Phone: (713) 779-9292. Fax: (713) 779-1651. Web Site: www.radiodeporte.com. Licensee: Hispanic Broadcasting Inc. (acq 10-1-93; $548,000; 10-18-93). Format: Sp. ♦ Cruz Velasquez, gen mgr.

Thorndale

KJAZ(FM)—Not on air, target date: unknown: 99.3 mhz; 6 kw. Ant 328 ft. TL: N30 29 21 W97 17 58. 1110 W. William Cannon Dr., Suite 402, Austin 78745. Phone: (512) 383-1112. Licensee: Jackson Lake Broadcasting Co.

Three Rivers

KEMA(FM)— 2003: 94.5 mhz; 48 kw. Ant 492 ft. TL: N28 43 10 W98 02 34. 1110 W. William Cannon Dr., Suite 401, Austin 78745. Phone: (512) 383-1112. Licensee: Roy E. Henderson (acq 3-24-2000; $25,000. for CP). ♦ Roy E. Henderson, gen mgr.

Tomball

KSEV(AM)— Dec 1, 1986: 700 khz; 25 kw-D, 1 kw-N, DA-2. TL: N30 11 34 W95 35 40. 11451 Katy Fwy., Suite 215, Houston 77079. Phone: (281) 588-4800. Fax: (832) 358-9556. E-mail: thevoice@ksevradio.com. Web Site: www.ksevradio.com. Licensee: Liberman Broadcasting of Houston License Corp. Group owner: Liberman Broadcasting Inc. (acq 3-9-01; grpsl). Format: News/talk. ♦ Dan Patrick, VP & gen mgr; Louis Wright, opns mgr; Bonnie English, sls dir; Pam McKay, gen sls mgr; Doug Roach, progmg dir; Chuck McLeod, chief of engrg.

Tulia

KBTE(FM)— Apr 1, 1991: 104.9 mhz; 96.6 kw. Ant 977 ft. TL: N33 57 35 W101 35 22. 33 Briercroft Office Park, Lubbock 79412. Phone: (806) 762-3000. Fax: (806) 770-5363. Licensee: Dove Media L.L.P. Format: Rhythm and blues, hip hop. Target aud: General. Spec prog: Loc sports. ♦ Jay Richard, gen mgr; Jeff Scott, opns mgr; Robbie Cruise, gen mgr & progmg dir; Randy Hayes, chief of engrg.

KTUE(AM)— November 1954: 1260 khz; 1 kw-D, 53 w-N. TL: N34 31 34 W101 46 56. Dove Media Inc., 598 Westwood Dr., Suite 208, Abilene 79603. Phone: (325) 677-3900. Fax: (325) 677-3910. E-mail:

Stations in the U.S.   Texas

Developers & Brokers of Radio Properties

contact American Media Services
at our suite:
Philadelphia Marriott Downtown
215-625-2900
843-972-2200
americanmediaservices.com
Charleston, SC
Dallas, TX • Chicago, Il • Austin, TX

American Media Services, LLC

bhc1000@aol.com. Licensee: Paulino Bernal (acq 7-13-2004). Format: Sp relg. Target aud: General. ◆ Bruce Campbell, gen mgr.

Tye

KBCY(FM)— October 1983: 99.7 mhz; 100 kw. 744 ft. TL: N32 24 39 W100 06 26. Stereo. Box 3157, 2525 S. Danvile, Abilene 79608. Phone: (325) 793-9700. Fax: (325) 692-1576. Web Site: www.kbcy.com. Licensee: Cumulus Licensing Corp. Group owner: Cumulus Media Inc. (acq 2-13-98; grpsl). Format: Country. News: 21 hrs wkly. Target aud: 25-49; upscale adults. Spec prog: Relg 5 hrs wkly. ◆ Kelly Jay, opns mgr; Kim Crenshaw, gen sls mgr; Trace Michaels, gen mgr & mktg mgr; Justin Case, prom dir; Doc Alexander, progmg dir; Chris Andrews, chief of engrg.

KWFA(AM)—Not on air, target date: unknown: 1030 khz; 5 kw-D, 370 w-N, DA-2. TL: N32 27 37 W99 50 03. 6720 Lakeview Dr., Carmichael, CA 95608. Licensee: Marlene V. Borman. ◆ Marlene V. Borman, gen mgr.

Tyler

KDOK(FM)— November 1975: 92.1 mhz; 9.6 kw. Ant 443 ft. TL: N32 22 28 W95 16 24. Stereo. Box 92 75710-0092. Phone: (903) 593-2519. Phone: (903) 592-5200. Fax: (903) 597-4141. Web Site: www.kdok.com. Licensee: Gleiser Communications LLC acq 11-21-2003; grpsl). Format: Oldies. News staff: one; News: 2 hrs wkly. Target aud: 35 plus. Spec prog: Tyler Junior Collete football, Saturday Night Big Band Dance Party. ◆ Paul Gleiser, gen mgr, opns mgr & gen sls mgr; Paul Berry, progmg dir & news dir; Mark Lavoux, chief of engrg.

KGLD(AM)— May 11, 1956: 1330 khz; 1 kw-D, 77 w-N. TL: N32 22 35 W95 15 55. Stereo. Box 1330 75710-1330. Secondary address: 1001 E. S.E. Loop 323 75701. Phone: (903) 593-2519. Fax: (903) 597-8378. Web Site: www.kdok.com. Licensee: Salt of the Earth Broadcasting Inc. (acq 4-13-2004; $160,000). Network: ABC. Gardner, Carton & Douglas. Format: Oldies. Spec prog: S. ◆ Paul Gleiser, gen mgr; Roger Gray, progmg dir; Mike LaRoux, chief of engrg.

*****KGLY(FM)**— June 1988: 91.3 mhz; 12 kw. 462 ft. TL: N32 21 06 W95 16 00. Stereo. Box 8525 75711. Secondary address: 2721 E. Erwin St. 75708. Phone: (903) 593-5863. Fax: (903) 593-2663. E-mail: kkgly@kgly.com. Web Site: www.encouraagementfm.com. Licensee: Educational Radio Foundation of East Texas Inc. Network: Network: Moody, USA. Format: Relg. News: 3 hrs wkly. Target aud: 35 plus. ◆ Dan Bolin, gen mgr; John Paul Little, stn mgr; Leah Coombs, mus dir; Sans Hawkins, chief of engrg.

KISX(FM)—See Whitehouse

KKUS(FM)— 1990: 104.1 mhz; 50 kw. 492 ft. TL: N32 29 40 W95 28 55. Box 7820 75711. Secondary address: 621 Chase Dr. 75701. Phone: (903) 581-9966. Fax: (903) 534-5300. E-mail: kkus@etradiogroup.com. Web Site: www.theranch1041.com. Licensee: Access.1 Texas License Company LLC. Group owner: Waller Broadcasting. (acq 1-7-2005; grpsl). Network: CNN Radio. Rep: McGavren Guild. Format: Classic Country. Target aud: 35+. ◆ Mary Ramos, gen mgr; Jim Hendrick, natl sls mgr; Rick Guest, mktg mgr; Bob Mauldin, progmg dir.

KNUE(FM)— Dec 31, 1964: 101.5 mhz; 100 kw. 1,074 ft. TL: N32 15 35 W94 57 02. Stereo. 3810 Brookside 75701. Phone: (903) 581-0606. Fax: (903) 581-2011. Web Site: www.knue.com. Licensee: Capstar TX L.P. Group owner: Clear Channel Communications Inc. (acq 8-30-00; grpsl). Format: Country. Target aud: General. ◆ Steve Joos, gen mgr; Craig Reininger, sls dir; Chris Jones, prom dir & adv dir; Michael Gibson, progmg dir & mus dir; Dave Goldman, news dir.

KTBB(AM)— Aug 28, 1947: 600 khz; 5 kw-D, 2.5 kw-N, DA-2. TL: N32 16 18 W95 12 23. Stereo. Box 6 75710-0006. Phone: (903) 593-2519. Fax: (903) 593-4918. Web Site: www.ktbb.com. Licensee: Gleiser Communications LLC (group owner; acq 11-21-2003; grpsl). Network: Network: ABC Information & Entertainment, ABC News/Talk. Gardner, Carton & Douglas. Format: Full service, news/talk, sports & info. News staff: 7; News: 70 hrs wkly. Target aud: 35 plus. Spec prog: Gospel 5 hrs wkly. ◆ Paul L. Gleiser, CEO, pres, gen mgr & sls dir; Roger Gray, progmg dir; Mike LaRoux, chief of engrg.

KTYL-FM— February 1966: 93.1 mhz; 82 kw. Ant 938 ft. TL: N32 15 35 W94 57 02. Stereo. 3810 Brookside Dr. 75701-9420. Phone: (903) 581-0606. Fax: (903) 581-2011. Web Site: www.mix931.com. Licensee: Capstar TX L.P. Group owner: Clear Channel Communications Inc. (acq 8-30-00; grpsl). Format: Hot adult contemp. Target aud: 18-54. ◆ Steve Joos, gen mgr; Craig Reininger, sls dir; Chris Jones, gen sls mgr; Jeff Evans, progmg dir.

*****KVNE(FM)**— Oct 15, 1983: 89.5 mhz; 100 kw. 899 ft. TL: N32 32 21 W95 13 16. (CP: 96 kw). Stereo. Box 8525 75711. Phone: (903) 593-5863. Web Site: www.kvne.com. Licensee: Educational Radio Foundation of East Texas Inc. Format: Relg. News: 6 hrs wkly. Target aud: 20-45; families. Spec prog: Gospel 4 hrs, children 4 hrs, Sp 2 hrs wkly. ◆ Mike Harper, stn mgr.

KYZS(AM)— 1930: 1490 khz; 1 kw-U. TL: N32 22 30 W95 16 05. Stereo. Box 6 75710. Phone: (903) 593-2519. Fax: (903) 597-4141. Web Site: www.kdok.com. Licensee: Gleiser Communications LLC (group owner; acq 11-21-2003; grpsl). Format: ESPN radio-sports. ◆ Paul Gleiser, gen mgr & opns mgr; Robert Gray, progmg dir; Robert LaRoux, chief of engrg.

KZEY(AM)— 1958: 690 khz; 1 kw-D, 92 w-N, DA-2. TL: N32 22 52 W95 20 52. Box 4248, Lake Park Dr. 75712. Phone: (903) 593-1744. Fax: (903) 593-2666. Licensee: Community Broadcast Group Inc. Format: Urban contemp. News staff: one. Target aud: General. Spec prog: Gospel 16 hrs wkly. ◆ Esther Milton, gen mgr, gen sls mgr & mus dir; Darrell Bowdre, news dir.

Universal City

KSAH(AM)— Nov 1, 1986: 720 khz; 10 kw-D, 1 kw-N, DA-2. TL: N29 31 51 W98 10 39. Stereo. 7800 1-10 West, Suite 330, San Antonio 78230. Phone: (210) 340-1234. Fax: (210) 340-1775. Licensee: BMP San Antonio License Co. L.P. Group owner: Border Media Partners LLC (acq 12-23-2003; $24.4 million. with KTFM(FM) Floresville). Format: Sp. News staff: one; News: 2 hrs wkly. Target aud: 18-49. ◆ Peggy McCormick, gen mgr & natl sls mgr; Raoul Rodriquez, gen mgr; Lupe Contreras, prom dir; Manny Herrera, progmg dir; Brett Huggins, chief of engrg.

University Park

KTNO(AM)— 1938: 1440 khz; 15 kw-D, 350 w-N, DA-2. TL: N32 45 02 W96 43 22. 5787 S. Hampton Rd., Suite 340, Dallas 75232. Phone: (214) 330-5866. Fax: (214) 330-9885. Web Site: www.ktnoam.com. Licensee: Mortensen Broadcasting Co. of Texas Inc. (group owner; acq 8-8-97; $650,000). Network: ABC. Rep: Caballero. Format: Sp, talk info, Christian. News staff: 2; News: 40 hrs wkly. Target aud: 25 plus. ◆ Jose Alfredo Castillo, gen mgr, gen sls mgr & progmg dir; Mike Benhauser, chief of engrg.

KZMP(AM)— 1999: 1540 khz; 33 kw-D, 1 kw-N, DA. TL: N32 48 45 W97 00 31. 5307 E. Mockingbird Ln., Suite 500, Dallas 75206. Phone: (214) 887-9107. Fax: (214) 841-4215. Licensee: Entravision Holdings L.L.C. Group owner: Entravision Communications Corp. (acq 8-15-00; grpsl). Fisher, Wayland, Cooper, Leader & Zaragoza. Format: Sp. Target aud: 18-49; Hispanics. ◆ Scott Savage, gen mgr; Dean James, opns mgr, prom dir & progmg dir; Ande Woods, gen sls mgr.

Uvalde

KBNU(FM)— 1996: 93.9 mhz; 25 kw horiz, 14.3 kw vert. Ant 292 ft. TL: N29 16 34 W99 41 44. Stereo. 935 East Main St. 78801. Phone: (830) 278-3693. Fax: (830) 278-2329. E-mail: themessage@sbcglobal.net. Web Site: www.message.fm. Licensee: Radio Cactus Inc (acq 10-23-00; $60,916. for 51% of stock with KBLT(FM) Leakey). Format: Christian hit radio, adult contemp. News staff: one. Target aud: General; 18-49. ◆ John Furr, CEO & chief of engrg; Paula Furr, CFO; Regenia Tumbarello, gen mgr, gen sls mgr, prom dir & progmg dir.

KUVA(FM)— Aug 20, 1984: 102.3 mhz; 3 kw. 280 ft. TL: N29 11 46 W99 46 48. Stereo. Box 758, 1400 Batesville Rd. 78801. Phone: (830) 278-2555. Fax: (830) 278-9461. E-mail: production@uvalderadio.com. Web Site: www.uvalderadio.com. Licensee: Rhattigan Broadcasting (Texas) LP (group owner; acq 6-3-2004; grpsl). Baraff, Koerner & Olender. Format: Sp, Tejano. News staff: one; News: 6 hrs wkly. Target aud: 16-60; Hispanic. ◆ Justin Rue, gen mgr.

KVOU(AM)— Apr 4, 1947: 1400 khz; 1 kw-U. TL: N29 11 16 W99 46 36. Box 758 78802-0758. Secondary address: 1400 Batesville Rd. 78801. Phone: (830) 278-2555/2557. Fax: (830) 278-9461. E-mail: production@uvalde.com. Web Site: www.uvalderadio.com. Licensee: Rhattigan Broadcasting (Texas) LP (group owner; acq 6-3-2004; grpsl). Network: ABC Information & Entertainment. Baraff, Koerner & Olender. Format: Oldies. News staff: one; News: 15 hrs wkly. Target aud: 25-54; general. Spec prog: Farm 12 hrs wkly. ◆ Kevin L. Bonner, gen mgr.

KVOU-FM— Sept 9, 1976: 104.9 mhz; 25 kw. 263 ft. TL: N29 11 16 W99 46 36. Stereo. Box 758 78802-0758. Secondary address: 1400 Batesville Rd. 78801. Phone: (830) 278-2555. Fax: (830) 278-2557. Fax: (830) 278-9461. E-mail: production@uvalderadio.com. Web Site: www.uvalderadio.com. Licensee: Rhattigan Broadcasting (Texas) LP (group owner; acq 6-3-2004; grpsl). Network: ABC. Baraff, Koerner & Olender. Format: Country. News: 15 hrs wkly. Target aud: 18-49. Spec prog: High school play-by-play sports, Texas A&M football. ◆ Justin Rue, gen mgr.

Vernon

KVWC(AM)— July 1939: 1490 khz; 1 kw-U. TL: N34 09 12 W99 16 09. Box 1419 76385. Secondary address: 304 E. Wilbarger 76384. Phone: (940) 552-6221. Fax: (940) 553-4222. E-mail: kvwc@kvwc.com. Web Site: www.kvwc.com. Licensee: KVWC Inc. (acq 6-1-61). Rep: Riley. Format: Oldies, farm, country. News staff: one; News: 10 hrs wkly. Target aud: General; Wilbarger & surrounding counties. Spec prog: Gospel 16 hrs wkly. ◆ Mike Klappenbach, pres, gen mgr, progmg dir & chief of engrg.

KVWC-FM— Apr 10, 1972: 103.1 mhz; 6 kw. Ant 141 ft. TL: N34 09 12 W99 16 09. Stereo. Web Site: www.kvwc.com.

Victoria

*****KAYK(FM)**— October 2003: 88.5 mhz; 50 kw vert. Ant 282 ft. TL: N28 46 43 W97 02 51. Drawer 2440, Tupelo, MS 38803. Phone: (662) 844-8888. Web Site: www.afr.net. Licensee: American Family Association. Group owner: American Family Radio Format: Christian. ◆ Marvin Sanders, gen mgr.

KEPG(FM)— Feb 2, 1989: 100.9 mhz; 6 kw. Ant 272 ft. TL: N28 47 20 W97 03 00. Box 3487 77903. Secondary address: 3613 N. Main St. 77901. Phone: (361) 576-6111. Fax: (361) 572-0014. Licensee: Victoria RadioWorks Ltd. (group owner; (acq 1999; $27,500). Format: CHR. ◆ Cindy Cox, gen mgr.

KITE(FM)—(Port Lavaca). Aug 1, 1976: 93.3 mhz; 100 kw. Ant 318 ft. TL: N28 42 22 W96 48 03. Stereo. Box 3487 77903. Secondary address: 3613 N. Main St. 77903. Phone: (361) 576-6111. Fax: (361) 572-0014. Licensee: Victoria RadioWorks Ltd. (group owner; (acq 10-29-98; $500,000). Rep: McGavren Guild. Format: Oldies. Spec prog: Farm one hr wkly. ◆ Cindy Cox, gen mgr.

KIXS(FM)— Dec 4, 1980: 107.9 mhz; 100 kw. 362 ft. TL: N28 46 03 W96 59 11. Stereo. Box 3325 77903. Secondary address: 107 North Star Dr. 77904. Phone: (361) 573-0777. Fax: (361) 578-0059. E-mail: kixs@clearchannel.com. Web Site: www.kixs.com. Licensee: Capstar TX L.P. Group owner: Clear Channel Communications Inc. (acq 8-30-00; grpsl). Format: C&W. Target aud: 25-49; listeners in a growth & acquisition mode. ◆ Jeff Lyon, gen mgr; Natalie Franz, gen sls mgr & natl sls mgr; James Love, prom dir, news dir & pub affrs dir; Eric Sharp, progmg dir; Joe Bob Burris, mus dir; Charles Smithey, chief of engrg.

KNAL(AM)— Apr 16, 1948: 1410 khz; 500 w-U, DA-N. TL: N28 46 48 W97 00 08. Box 3487 77903. Secondary address: 3613 N. Main St. 77901. Phone: (361) 576-6111. Fax: (361) 572-0014. Licensee: Victoria RadioWorks Ltd. (group owner; (acq 2-1-2002; $100,000). Fletcher, Heald & Hildreth. Format: Adult standards. ♦Cindy Cox, gen mgr.

KQVT(FM)— Dec 1, 1990: 92.3 mhz; 6 kw. Ant 298 ft. TL: N28 46 04 W96 59 12. Stereo. 107 North Star Dr. 77904. Phone: (361) 573-0777. Fax: (361) 578-0059. E-mail: kqvt@clearchannel.com. Web Site: www.kqvt.com. Licensee: Capstar TX L.P. Group owner: Clear Channel Communications Inc. (acq 8-2-01; $650,000). Format: Adult contemp. ♦Jeff Lyon, gen mgr; Natalie Franz, gen sls mgr & natl sls mgr; James Love, prom dir, prom dir, news dir & pub affrs dir; J.P. Stone, progmg mgr; Charles Smithey, chief of engrg.

KTXN-FM— Dec 1, 1994: 98.7 mhz; 100 kw. 253 ft. TL: N28 48 46 W97 03 45. Stereo. 302 Sam Houston Dr. 77901. Phone: (361) 573-2121. Fax: (361) 573-5872. Web Site: www.texasmix.com. Licensee: Cosmopolitan Enterprises of Victoria Inc. Network: Westwood One. Dennis J. Kelly. Format: Texas blues, classic rock, zydeco. News staff: 2; News: 2 hrs wkly. Target aud: 18-54; general. ♦Steve Coffman, gen mgr, opns mgr, sls dir & progmg dir; Steve Pingel, stn mgr; Bob Nancy, news dir; Jim Koenig, engrg dir.

KVIC(FM)—Listing follows KVNN(AM).

KVNN(AM)— January 1940: 1340 khz; 1 kw-U. TL: N28 49 49 W97 00 33. Box 3487 77903. Secondary address: 3613 N. Main St. 77901. Phone: (361) 576-6111. Fax: (361) 572-0014. Licensee: Victoria RadioWorks Ltd. (group owner; (acq 10-26-98; $2.1 million. with co-located FM). Rep: McGavren Guild. Format: Traditional country. Target aud: 25-54; adults. ♦Cindy Cox, gen mgr.

KVIC(FM)—Co-owned with KVNN(AM). Apr 8, 1976: 95.1 mhz; 13 kw. Ant 459 ft. TL: N28 46 55 W96 56 29. Stereo. Format: Adult contemp, CHR. Target aud: 18-49.

***KVRT(FM)**— 1995: 90.7 mhz; 30 kw. 328 ft. TL: N28 46 55 W96 56 30. 4455 S. Padre Island Dr., Suite 38, Corpus Christi 78411-1690. Phone: (361) 855-2213. Fax: (361) 855-3877. Licensee: South Texas Public Broadcasting System Inc. Format: Class, news, jazz. ♦Don Dunlap, chmn, pres & gen mgr; Myra Lombardo, exec VP; Anita Herbert, sls dir; Davita Underbrink, prom dir; Jeff Felts, progmg dir; Bill Clough, news dir; Cody Blount, chief of engrg.

***KXBJ(FM)**— Sept 1, 1994: 89.3 mhz; 18.5 kw. 336 ft. TL: N28 49 20 W96 58 20. Stereo. Box 187, Humble 77347. Secondary address: 2207 Wildwood St. 77901. Phone: (361) 574-8936. Fax: (361) 575-0175. E-mail: kxbj@vipx.org. Web Site: www.kxbj.org. Licensee: Educational Media Foundation of Victoria. Network: USA. Hardy & Carey. Format: Contemp Christian mus, relg. Target aud: 25-54. ♦Dr. Billy Powell, pres; Tim McDermott, gen mgr; Bard Letsinger, stn mgr; Jon Hull, progmg dir.

Waco

KBBW(AM)— April 1953: 1010 khz; 10 kw-D, 2.5 kw-N, DA-2. TL: N31 34 09 W97 00 00. 1019 Washington St. 76701. Phone: (254) 757-1010. Fax: (254) 752-5339. E-mail: info@1010kbw.com. Licensee: Steve Williams dba American Broadcasting of Texas. (acq 6-16-86; 5-12-86). Format: Christian. Target aud: 25-54. ♦Elizabeth Layne, stn mgr & opns dir; Ryan Williams, opns dir; Allen Newton, gen sls mgr; Jeremy Beutel, prom dir & news dir; Steve Williams, pres, gen mgr & progmg dir; Dave Fricker, chief of engrg.

KBCT-FM— Aug 1, 1996: 94.5 mhz; 3.2 kw. 453 ft. TL: N31 30 31 W97 10 03. 4701 W. Waco Dr. 76710. Phone: (254) 388-5945. E-mail: mail@lonestar.com. Web Site: www.lonestar94.com. Licensee: Kennelwood Broadcasting Co. Inc. Format: Country. Target aud: 25-54; upper income professionals. ♦Jerry Lenamon, pres & gen mgr.

KBGO(FM)— Sept 6, 1959: 95.7 mhz; 24 kw. 505 ft. TL: N31 30 51 W97 11 43. Stereo. 314 W. State Hwy. 6 76712. Phone: (254) 776-3900. Fax: (254) 761-6371. E-mail: brenthenslee@clearchannel.com. Web Site: www.oldies95online.com. Licensee: Capstar TX L.P. Group owner: Clear Channel Communications Inc. (acq 8-30-00; grpsl). Format: Oldies. Target aud: 35-64. ♦Evan Armstrong, gen mgr; Zack Owen, opns dir & opns mgr; Vernon Riggs, sls dir; Brett Henslee, progmg dir & chief of engrg.

KBRQ(FM)—See Hillsboro

KQRL(AM)— Oct 8, 1962: 1580 khz; 1 kw-D, 500 w-N, DA-2. TL: N31 31 04 W97 05 16. Box 8093 76714-8093. Secondary address: 1018 N. Valley Mills Dr. 76710. Phone: (254) 772-0930. Fax: (254) 772-1580. E-mail: productioni@hot.rr.net. Licensee: Simmons-Austin, LS LLC. Group owner: Simmons Media Group (acq 6-4-2004; grpsl). Rep: Roslin. Leventhal, Senter & Lerman. Format: Sports. News staff: one; News: 2 hrs wkly. Target aud: 25-54. Spec prog: Black 4 hrs, Sp 14 hrs wkly. ♦Daryl O'Neal, gen mgr; Bill Le Grand, sls dir; Tom Barfield, opns mgr & progmg dir.

KRZI(AM)— 2001: 1660 khz; 10 kw-D, 1 kw-N. TL: N31 24 46 W97 12 18. Box 8093 76714-8093. Secondary address: 1018 N. Valley Mills Dr. 76710. Phone: (254) 772-0930. Fax: (254) 772-1580. E-mail: production@hot.rr.com. Web Site: www.1660espn.com. Licensee: Simmons-Austin, LS LLC. Group owner: Simmons Media Group (acq 6-4-2004; grpsl). Network: ESPN Radio. Format: Sports. ♦Daryl O'Neal, gen mgr; Bill Le Grand, sls dir; Tom Barfield, opns mgr & progmg dir.

***KVLW(FM)**— 2005: 88.1 mhz; 16.5 kw vert. Ant 1,096 ft. TL: N31 18 53 W97 19 36. American Educational Broadcasting Inc., 3185 S. Highland Dr., Suite 13, Las Vegas, NV 89109. Secondary address: 3411 Market Loop, Studio, Suite 108, Temple 76502. Phone: (254) 791-5251. Fax: (254) 791-0200. Licensee: American Educational Broadcasting Inc. Network: K-Love. Fletcher, Heald & Hildreth. Format: Contemp Christian music. ♦Carl Auel, pres; James E. Auel, gen mgr.

***KWBU-FM**— Mar 15, 1966: 107.1 mhz; 3 kw. 190 ft. TL: N31 31 51 W97 09 10. Box 97368, KWBU, Baylor Univ. 76798. Phone: (254) 710-4470. Phone: (254) 710-6909. Fax: (254) 710-1563. E-mail: kwbu@baylor.edu. Web Site: www.baylor.edu/kwbu. Licensee: Baylor University. Format: Class, div. News staff: one; News: 10 hrs wkly. Target aud: under 45; college age. Spec prog: Jazz 10 hrs wkly. ♦Frank Fallon, pres & gen mgr; Brian Potter, sls dir & adv dir; Aubrey Abbott, prom dir; Kateigh Axness, mus dir; Aron Watman, asst music dir; Lauren Lewis, news dir; Ron Stephens, engrg dir.

KWTX(AM)— May 1, 1946: 1230 khz; 5 kw-D, 250 w-N, DA-2. TL: N31 31 42 W97 07 14. 314 W. State Hwy. 6 76712. Phone: (254) 776-3900. Fax: (254) 761-6371. Web Site: newstalk1230.com. Licensee: Capstar TX L.P. Group owner: Clear Channel Communications Inc. (acq 8-30-2000; grpsl). Network: ABC. Rep: Clear Channel. Format: News/talk. Target aud: 35-64; adults. ♦Michael Oppenheimer, gen mgr; Zack Owen, opns mgr; Evan Armstrong, gen sls mgr; Gloria Norris, natl sls mgr; Max Watson, progmg dir; Steve Keating, chief of engrg.

KWTX-FM— Dec 1, 1970: 97.5 mhz; 97 kw. 1,568 ft. TL: N31 19 19 W97 18 58. Stereo. Web Site: www.975online.com. Format: CHR. Target aud: 25-49; women. ♦Jay Charles, progmg dir.

WACO-FM— June 1960: 99.9 mhz; 90 kw. 1,660 ft. TL: N31 20 15 W97 18 37. Stereo. 314 W. State Hwy. 6 76712. Phone: (254) 776-3900. Fax: (254) 761-6371. E-mail: info@waco100.com. Web Site: www.waco100.com. Licensee: Capstar TX L.P. Group owner: Clear Channel Communications Inc. (acq 8-30-00; grpsl). Format: Country. ♦Evan Armstrong, gen mgr & gen sls mgr; Zack Owen, opns dir & progmg dir; Brett Gilbert, chief of engrg.

Wake Village

***KHTA(FM)**— Sept 22, 2000: 92.5 mhz; 25 kw. Ant 328 ft. TL: N33 24 53 W93 58 12. Houston Christian Broadcasters Inc., 2424 South Blvd., Houston 77098. Phone: (713) 520-5200. E-mail: khcb@nol.net. Web Site: www.khcb.org. Licensee: Houston Christian Broadcasters Inc. (group owner) Format: Bible teaching, inspirational mus. Target aud: General; all ages, families. ♦Bruce Munsterman, pres & stn mgr.

Waxahachie

KBEC(AM)— June 1955: 1390 khz; 480 w-D, 260 w-N, DA-2. TL: N32 26 45 W96 48 15. 711 Ferris Ave. 75165. Phone: (972) 923-1390. Phone: (972) 938-1390. Fax: (972) 935-0871. E-mail: info@kbec.com. Web Site: www.kbec.com. Licensee: Faye and Richard Tuck Inc. Format: Classic country. News: 15 hrs wkly. Target aud: 25-54. Spec prog: Farm 3 hrs, Pol 2 hrs wkly. ♦Barry Wolverton, sls dir & gen sls mgr; Ken Roberts, gen mgr, stn mgr & progmg dir.

Weatherford

***KMQX(FM)**—Not on air, target date: unknown: 88.5 mhz; 5.5 kw. Ant 492 ft. TL: N32 49 17 W98 09 36. 905 Palo Pinto St., Weatherton 76086. Phone: (817) 341-2337. Fax: (817) 598-1661. Licensee: CSSI Non-Profit Educational Broadcast Inc. ♦Charles H. Beard, pres; Melinda Beard, gen mgr.

***KYQX(FM)**— Jan 5, 1986: 89.5 mhz; 4.5 kw. Ant 518 ft. TL: N32 51 05 W98 06 31. 905 Palo Pinto St. 76086. Secondary address: 203 Eden St. 76086. Phone: (817) 594-1220. Phone: (817) 341-2337. Fax: (817) 598-1661. Web Site: www.kyqx.com. Licensee: CSSI Non Profit Educational Broadcasting Corp. (acq 8-14-98; $55,000). Format: Lite rock. ♦Charles Beard, pres; Melinda Beard, gen mgr, opns mgr & progmg dir.

KZEE(AM)— Aug 12, 1956: 1220 khz; 500 w-D, 8 w-N. TL: N32 47 09 W97 47 55. Box 54803, Hurst 76054. Phone: (817) 594-1220. Phone: (817) 849-1971. Fax: (817) 427-3931. Web Site: www.radio1220am.com. Licensee: Tarrant Radio Broadcasting Inc. (acq 9-5-01; $800,000). Format: Christian Gospel. ♦Parvez Malik, pres; Cima Hernandez, gen mgr.

Weslaco

KHKZ(FM)—See Mercedes

KRGE(AM)— 1926: 1290 khz; 5 kw-U, DA-N. TL: N26 12 36 W97 54 33. Box 1290, Mile 6 3/4 W. Business 83 78599. Phone: (956) 968-7777. Fax: (956) 968-5143. E-mail: egarza@radiovida.com. Web Site: www.radiovida.com. Licensee: Christian Ministries of the Valley. (acq 1-31-91; 2-18-91). Format: Christian, Sp. News: 3 hrs wkly. Target aud: 18-34. ♦Enrique Garza, gen mgr.

West Lake Hills

KTXZ(AM)— June 9, 1982: 1560 khz; 2.5 kw-U, DA-2. TL: N30 21 38 W97 39 11. 7524 N. Lamar, Austin 78752. Phone: (512) 416-1100. Fax: (512) 458-0700. Licensee: BMP Austin License Company L.P. (acq 2-10-2005; grpsl). Format: Sp contemp. News: 14 hrs wkly. Target aud: 18-54; bilingual, Hispanic, male & female. Spec prog: Christian mus 6 hrs wkly. ♦Barbara Crawford, gen mgr & adv mgr; Joe Garcia, gen mgr; Alicia Vertuche, progmg dir; Steve Freeman, chief of engrg.

West Odessa

***KLVW(FM)**— 2001: 88.7 mhz; 100 kw. Ant 426 ft. TL: N31 50 53 W102 27 04. 5700 West Oaks Blvd., Rocklin, CA 95765. Phone: (916) 251-1600. Fax: (916) 251-1650. E-mail: klove@klove.com. Web Site: www.klove.com. Licensee: Educational Media Foundation. Group owner: EMF Broadcasting. Network: K-Love. Shaw Pittman. Format: Contemp Christian. News staff: 3. Target aud: 25-44; Judeo Christian, female. ♦Richard Jenkins, pres; Mike Novak, VP & progmg dir; Lloyd Parker, gen mgr; Ed Lenane, opns dir & news dir; Keith Whipple, dev dir; Eric Allen, natl sls mgr; Russ Lloyd, rgnl sls mgr; Chris Joyce, prom dir; David Pierce, progmg mgr; Jon Rivers, mus dir; Sam Wallington, engrg dir.

Wharton

KANI(AM)— June 17, 1962: 1500 khz; 500 w-U, DA-N. TL: N29 19 22 W96 03 32. Box 350 77488. Secondary address: 215 E. Milam St. 77488. Phone: (979) 532-3800. Fax: (979) 532-8510. Licensee: Ammerman Enterprises Inc. (acq 6-1-82; $250,000; 6-14-82). Format: Religious. Spec prog: Sp 3 hrs, Pol 6 hrs wkly. ♦Sandra Stuart, gen mgr, gen sls mgr, progmg dir & news dir.

Wheeler

***KPDR(FM)**— Aug 31, 1986: 90.5 mhz; 10 kw. 482 ft. TL: N35 25 57 W100 16 31. Stereo. Box 8088, 5754 Canyon Dr., Amarillo 79114. Phone: (806) 359-8855. Fax: (806) 354-2039. E-mail: kjrt@kingdomkeys.org. Web Site: www.kingdomkeys.org. Licensee: Top O' Texas Educational Broadcasting Foundation. Network: USA. Dow, Lohnes & Albertson. Format: Relg, educ. Target aud: General. Spec prog: Sp 5 hrs wkly. ♦Ricky Pfeil, pres & gen mgr.

White Oak

KLBL(FM)— May 17, 2002: 99.3 mhz; 34 kw. Ant 541 ft. TL: N32 35 17 W94 58 53. 2020 Bill Owens Pkwy., Suite 200, Longview 75604. Phone: (903) 844-0993. Fax: (903) 759-5189. Web Site: www.thebull993.com. Licensee: Reynolds Radio Inc. (group owner)

Stations in the U.S.   Texas

Format: Country. ♦Bob Gambill, gen mgr; Kathleen Adams, gen sls mgr; Sherri Stallsworth, prom mgr; Don John, progmg dir; Ryan Fox, mus dir.

Whitehouse

KISX(FM)— Aug 15, 1982: 107.3 mhz; 50 kw. 500 ft. TL: N32 17 19 W95 11 56. Stereo. 3810 Brookside Dr., Tyler 75701. Phone: (903) 581-0606. Fax: (903) 581-2011. E-mail: stevejoos@clearchannel.com. Web Site: kiss107i.com. Licensee: Capstar TX L.P. Group owner: Clear Channel Communications Inc. (acq 8-30-00; grpsl). Format: CHR. Target aud: 18-44. ♦Steve Joos, gen mgr; Craig Reininger, sls dir; Larry Thompson, progmg dir.

Whitesboro

KMAD-FM— June 1, 1985: 102.5 mhz; 18 kw. Ant 672 ft. TL: N33 41 31 W96 26 36. Stereo. 101 E. Main St., Suite 255, Denison 75021. Phone: (903) 463-6800. Fax: (903) 463-9816. Web Site: www.theclassicrockexperience.com. Licensee: NM Licensing LLC. Group owner: NextMedia Group L.L.C. (acq 11-26-2001; grpsl). Format: Classic rock. ♦David Smith, gen mgr.

Wichita Falls

KBZS(FM)— Nov 15, 1984: 106.3 mhz; 2.4 kw. 423 ft. TL: N33 53 18 W98 34 08. (CP: 15.5 kw, ant 899 ft. TL: N33 53 23 W98 33 31). Stereo. 2525 Kell Blvd., Suite 200 76308. Phone: (940) 763-1111. Fax: (940) 322-3166. Web Site: www.1063thebuzz.com. Licensee: CCB Texas Licenses L.P. Group owner: Clear Channel Communications Inc. (acq 10-23-00; grpsl). Network: Westwood One. Rep: McGavren Guild. Format: AOR, adult contemp. Target aud: 18-49. ♦Bruce Holberg, pres; Kim Dodds, gen mgr; Chris Walters, opns mgr & news dir; Melissa Detrick, sls dir; Kara Tucker, prom dir; Liz Ryan, progmg dir; Scott Maingi, chief of engrg.

KLUR(FM)— Apr 14, 1963: 99.9 mhz; 100 kw. Ant 808 ft. TL: N33 54 04 W98 32 21. Stereo. 4302 Callfield Rd. 76308. Phone: (940) 691-2311. Fax: (940) 696-2255. Web Site: www.klur.com. Licensee: Cumulus Licensing Corp. Group owner: Cumulus Media Inc. (acq 10-3-97; grpsl). Network: ABC Information & Entertainment. Format: New country. ♦Jim Marks, gen mgr & natl sls mgr; Lindy Parr, sls dir; Andrea Lewis, rgnl sls mgr; Zach Morton, progmg dir; Jeff Chancey, chief of engrg.

*KMCU(FM)—Not on air, target date: unknown: 88.7 mhz; 5 w horiz, 3 kw vert. Ant 253 ft. TL: N33 56 30 W98 34 06. Stereo. Lawton,Clinton,Ardmore,Altus, Oaklahoma, 90% c/o KCCU(FM), Cameron University, 2800 W. Gore Blvd., Lawton, OK 73505. Phone: (580) 581-2425. Fax: (580) 581-5571. E-mail: kccu@cameron.edu. Web Site: www.cameron.edu/kccu/. Licensee: Cameron University. Network: Network: NPR, PRI. Format: NPR news-classical & jazz music. News staff: 2; News: 36 hrs wkly. Target aud: 35 plus. ♦Mark Norman, gen mgr; Michael Leal, stn mgr & progmg dir; Kristin Gordon, opns dir & pub affrs dir; Nadia Sikes, adv mgr; Terry Anderson, adv mgr; Debbie Taylor, news dir; Charlie Thurston, chief of engrg.

*KMOC(FM)— July 9, 1987: 89.5 mhz; 3 kw. 672 ft. TL: N33 54 04 W98 32 21. (CP: 10 kw). Box 41 76307. Secondary address: 4010 W. Wenonah St. 76307. Phone: (940) 767-3303. Fax: (940) 723-5807. E-mail: kmocfm@wf.net. Web Site: www.kmocfm.com. Licensee: Christian Service Foundation Inc. Network: Moody. Format: Christian. ♦Doug Salvi, progmg dir.

KNIN-FM— May 12, 1975: 92.9 mhz; 100 kw. 930 ft. TL: N33 54 04 W98 32 21. Stereo. 2525 Kell Blvd., Suite 200 76308. Phone: (940) 763-1111. Fax: (940) 322-3166. E-mail: info@929nin.com. Web Site: www.929nin.com. Licensee: CCB Texas Licenses L.P. Group owner: Clear Channel Communications Inc. (acq 10-23-00; grpsl). Rep: McGavren Guild. Format: CHR. Target aud: 18-49. ♦Kim Dodds, gen mgr; Chris Walters, opns mgr; Melissa Detrick, sls dir & Kara Tucker, prom dir; Liz Ryan, progmg dir; Vicki Vox, asst music dir; Scott Maingi, chief of engrg.

KQXC-FM— Jan 7, 1994: 103.9 mhz; 4.5 kw. Ant 315 ft. TL: N33 56 30 W98 34 07. Stereo. 4302 Callfield Rd. 76308. Phone: (940) 691-2311. Fax: (940) 696-2255. Web Site: www.cumulus.com. Licensee: Cumulus Licensing Corp. Group owner: Cumulus Media Inc. (acq 10-3-97; grpsl). Network: ABC. Format: Rhythmic CHR. Target aud: 18-45; males. ♦Jim Marks, gen mgr, opns mgr & natl sls mgr; Belda Holt, rgnl sls mgr; Susan Adkins, mktg dir & prom dir; Zach Morton, progmg dir; Jeff Chancey, chief of engrg.

*KTEO(FM)— Sept 1, 1993: 90.5 mhz; 7 kw. 782 ft. TL: N33 53 50 W98 32 33. Box 905 76307. Secondary address: 2906 Avenue H 76309. Phone: (940) 767-4905. Web Site: www.kteo.hiskidsradio.net. Licensee: Cornerstone Baptist Educational Ministries (acq 1-22-92; $1 for CP; 2-10-92). Format: Children. Target aud: 3-12; children. ♦Dr. Rex Rogers, pres; Lee Geysbeek, VP; David Malin, gen mgr & dev dir; Janet Briggs, opns mgr.

KWFS(AM)— 1948: 1290 khz; 5 kw-D, 250 w-N. TL: N33 57 38 W98 33 42. 2525 Kell Blvd., Suite 200 76308. Phone: (940) 763-1111. Fax: (940) 322-3166. Web Site: www.newstalk1290.com. Licensee: CCB Texas Licenses L.P. Group owner: Clear Channel Communications Inc. (acq 10-23-00; grpsl). Rep: Clear Channel. Format: News/talk. News staff: one:; News: 12 hrs wkly. Target aud: 25 plus. Spec prog: Sp 4 hrs wkly. ♦Chris Walters, pres, opns mgr & progmg dir; Kim Dodds, gen mgr; Melissa Detrick, gen sls mgr; Kara Tucker, prom dir; Scott Maingi, chief of engrg.

KWFS-FM— 1961: 102.3 mhz; 100 kw. Ant 449 ft. TL: N33 53 51 W98 32 32. Stereo. E-mail: info@lonestar1023.com. Web Site: www.lonestar1023.com. Format: Country. News: one hr wkly. Target aud: 18-49.

Willis

KIOL(FM)—Licensed to Willis. See Conroe

KVST(FM)— 1998: 99.7 mhz; 2.55 kw. Ant 504 ft. TL: N30 26 55 W95 31 48. 1212 S. Frazier, Conroe 77301. Phone: (936) 788-1035. Fax: (936) 788-2525. Web Site: www.kvst.com. Licensee: New Wavo Communication Group Inc. (acq 7-16-98; $158,218). Format: Country. ♦Ben Amato, pres & gen mgr; William Boggs, gen sls mgr; Larry Galla, progmg mgr; Mike Shilo, news dir; Dade Moore, engrg dir.

Winfield

KALK(FM)— Sept 27, 1987: 97.7 mhz; 22.5 kw. 328 ft. TL: N33 11 01 W95 12 32. Stereo. Box 990, Mount Pleasant 75456. Secondary address: 1798 US Hwy. 67 W., Mount Pleasant 75455. Phone: (903) 577-9770. Phone: (903) 572-8726. Fax: (903) 572-7232. E-mail: hitmusic@klake.net. Web Site: www.easttexasradio.com. Licensee: East Texas Broadcasting Inc. (group owner; acq 1999; $600,000). Format: Hot adult contemp. News staff: one; News: one hr wkly. Target aud: 18-54; younger, upwardly mobile, white collar. Spec prog: Gospel one hr wkly. ♦Bud Kitchens, pres, VP & gen mgr; John Mitchell, chmn & pres; Darrin Tripp, opns dir.

Winnie

KKHT-FM— Dec 1, 1987: 100.7 mhz; 100 kw. Ant 1,952 ft. TL: N30 03 05 W94 31 37. Stereo. 6161 Savoy, Suite 1200, Houston 77036. Phone: (713) 260-3600. Fax: (713) 260-3628. E-mail: comments@kkht.com. Web Site: www.kkht.com. Licensee: Salem Media of Illinois LLC. Group owner: Univision Radio (acq 1-7-2005; with WIND(AM) Chicago, IL and KNIT(AM) Dallas in exchange for WPPN(FM) Des Plaines, IL). Rep: Salem. Format: Christian talk. ♦Chuck Jewell, gen mgr; Paul Baker, opns mgr, mktg mgr & progmg dir; Dan Doster, gen sls mgr; Marsha Lambeth, mus dir; Ken Garza, pub affrs dir; Sidney Jones, chief of engrg.

Winnsboro

KWNS(AM)— Sept 1, 1983: 104.7 mhz; 3 kw. 282 ft. TL: N32 56 32 W95 18 53. Stereo. Box 54, 215 Market St. 75494. Phone: (903) 342-3501. E-mail: kwnsfm@peoplescom.net. Licensee: Richard E.

Foster. (acq 11-1-89; $10,000; 11-20-89). Network: USA. Format: Southern gospel. News staff: one. Target aud: 35-70. ♦Lottie Foster, pres & gen mgr.

Winona

KBLZ(FM)—Not on air, target date: unknown: 102.7 mhz; 9.3 kw. 531 ft. TL: N32 23 09 W95 06 43. Box 11196, College Station 77842. Phone: (903) 581-5259. Phone: (903) 939-3473. Web Site: www.theblaze.cc. Licensee: S.O. 2,000 LLC. Group owner: Reynolds Radio Inc. (acq 8-26-99). Format: Urban Contemporary. ♦Rick Reynolds, gen mgr.

Winters

KNCE(FM)— Nov 1, 1981: 96.1 mhz; 50 kw. Ant 492 ft. TL: N32 12 52 W99 53 22. Stereo. 1740 N. 1st St., Abilene 79603. Phone: (325) 437-9596. Fax: (325) 673-1819. Licensee: Doud Media Group LLC Dennis Kelly. Format: Country. Target aud: 25-54; women. ♦Richard Doud, gen mgr; Mark McGill, opns dir; Brad Whitaker, gen sls mgr; James Thompson, engrg dir.

Wolfforth

KAIQ(FM)— 2000: 95.5 mhz; 100 kw. Ant 676 ft. TL: N33 31 03 W101 51 24. 1220 Broadway, Suite 500, Lubbock 79401. Phone: (806) 763-6051. Fax: (806) 744-8363. Licensee: Entravision Holdings LLC. (acq 2-10-2005; $1.5 million). ♦Jose Sauceda, gen mgr.

Woodville

KVLL-FM— 1993: 94.7 mhz; 50 kw. 492 ft. TL: N31 00 32 W94 24 14. Box 1345, Lufkin 75901. Secondary address: 121 Cotton Sq., Lufkin 75901. Phone: (936) 634-4584. Phone: (888) 644-8170. Fax: (936) 632-5722. Web Site: www.yatesbroadcasting.com. Licensee: Stephen W. Yates dba Yates Broadcasting Co. (acq 5-3-99; $550,000). Format: Hot country, news/talk. ♦Stephen W. Yates, pres & gen mgr; Generose Lopez, progmg dir.

KWUD(AM)— Jan 4, 1968: 1490 khz; 1 kw-U. TL: N30 44 52 W94 25 56. Box 129 75979. Secondary address: 105 E Wheat 75979. Phone: (409) 283-2777. Fax: (409) 283-2283. E-mail: wkud1490@samlink.com. Licensee: Carroll Texas Broadcasting Ltd. Group owner: Jimmy Ray Carroll Stns (acq 10-5-01). Network: ABC, Jones Radio Networks. Format: Oldies, Country, other. News staff: one; News: 12 hrs wkly. Target aud: 18-55. Spec prog: Farm 2 hrs, gospel 6 hrs, relg 3 hrs wkly. ♦Jim Carroll, pres; Elmer Luck, gen mgr, sls VP, gen sls mgr & gen sls mgr; Jeanette Luck, opns dir; Chester Leediker, chief of engrg.

Wylie

KHSE(AM)— 2004: 700 khz; 250 w-U, DA-2. TL: N33 01 58 W96 17 56. Box 12345, Dallas 75225. Phone: (214) 369-2900. Licensee: DFW Radio License LLC (acq 2-5-2004; with KFCD(AM) Farmersville). ♦Dave Schum, pres.

Yoakum

KYKM(FM)— January 1982: 92.5 mhz; 3 kw. 300 ft. TL: N29 21 03 W97 11 32. Stereo. 111 N. Main St., Hallettsville 77964. Phone: (361) 798-4333. Fax: (361) 798-3798. E-mail: texasthunderradio@yahoo.com. Licensee: Fort Bend Broadcasting Co. Inc. Group owner: Fort Bend Broadcasting Co. (acq 1-21-00; grpsl). Format: Country. News staff: one; News: 12 hrs wkly. Target aud: General. Spec prog: Polka 9 hrs wkly. ♦Laura Kremling, gen mgr, opns mgr, dev mgr & progmg dir; Ray Nelson, chief of engrg.

Zapata

KBAW(FM)—Not on air, target date: unknown: 93.5 mhz; 25 kw. 328 ft. TL: N26 54 43 W99 17 09. 2702 Pine St., Laredo 78043. Phone: (956) 726-4738. E-mail: radioluz@border.net. Web Site:

Utah | Directory of Radio

www.lacadenaradioluz.com/kbaw-93.htm. Licensee: La Nueva Cadena Radio Luz Inc. Format: Sp, Christian. ♦ Isreal Tellez, stn mgr.

Utah

Blanding

KBDX(FM)—Not on air, target date: unknown: 92.7 mhz; 594 w horiz. 255 w vert. Ant 3,405 ft. TL: N37 50 24 W109 27 41. 200 E. Broadway, Farmington, NM 87401. Phone: (505) 325-1716. Fax: (505) 325-6797. Web Site: www.bigdog969.com. Licensee: KBDX Blanding L.L.C. (acq 12-10-03; $300,000). Format: Classic rock. ♦ William Schmidt, gen mgr; Dan Kelley, opns dir & progmg dir; Barry Shainman, gen sls mgr; Bill Kruger, mktg VP; Randy Burton, prom dir; Jim Burt, chief of engrg.

Bountiful

KJMY(FM)— Mar 15, 1988: 99.5 mhz; 39 kw. Ant 2,952 ft. TL: N40 36 29 W112 09 33. 2801 S. Decker Lake Dr., Salt Lake City 84119. Phone: (801) 908-1300. Fax: (801) 908-1449. Web Site: www.my995fm.com. Licensee: Citicasters Licenses L.P. Group owner: Clear Channel Communications Inc. (acq 1999; grpsl). Rep: Clear Channel, Katz Radio. Hogan & Hartson. Format: Modern alternative, retro classics. Target aud: 18-49; adults. ♦ Stu Stanek, gen mgr; Bill Betts, opns mgr; Bill Matthews, sls dir & prom dir; Emily Hunt, gen sls mgr; Mark Christiansen, progmg dir.

Brian Head

KREC(FM)— Nov 14, 1988: 98.1 mhz; 56 kw. 2,526 ft. TL: N37 32 32 W113 04 05. Stereo. 750 W. Ridgeview Dr., Suite 204, Saint George 84770. Phone: (435) 673-3579. Fax: (435) 673-8900. E-mail: star98fm@bonnevillesg.com. Licensee: Bonneville Holding Co. Group owner: Bonneville International Corp. (acq 11-24-2003; grpsl). Format: Soft adult contemp. Target aud: 25-54. ♦ Don Shelline, gen mgr; Kevin Fry, gen sls mgr; Gary Smith, chief of engrg.

Brigham City

KEGH(FM)— June, 2002: 100.7 mhz; 81 kw. Ant 2,165 ft. TL: N41 47 08 W112 13 55. Simmons Media Group, 515 S. 700 E., Suite 1C, Salt Lake City 84102. Phone: (801) 524-2600. Fax: (801) 521-9234. Web Site: www.kjq.com. Licensee: Simmons-SLC, LS LLC. Group owner: Simmons Media Group (acq 4-4-2001; grpsl). Format: Modern rock.

KRAR(FM)— Oct 20, 1972: 106.9 mhz; 81 kw. Ant 2,165 ft. TL: N41 47 03 W112 13 55. Stereo. 2801 S. Decker Lake Dr., Salt Lake City 84119. Phone: (801) 908-4100. Fax: (801) 908-4122. Web Site: www.kosy.com. Licensee: Simmons-SLC, LS LLC. Group owner: Simmons Media Group (acq 4-19-2004; $3.95 million). Format: Hip hop, rhythm and blues.

KXOL(AM)— July 1, 1998: 1660 khz; 10 kw-D, 1 kw-N. TL: N41 18 54 W112 04 43. 515 S. 700 E., Salt Lake City 84102. Phone: (801) 325-3126. Fax: (801) 731-9666. Licensee: Simmons-SLC, LS, LLC. Group owner: Simmons Media Group (acq 4-1-2003; $925,000). with KSOS(AM) Brigham City). Format: Oldies. ♦ Bev Snyder, opns mgr.

Cedar City

KNNZ(AM)— 1971: 940 khz; 10 kw-D. TL: N37 45 51 W113 06 15. 251 W. Hilton Dr., Saint George 84770. Phone: (435) 586-5900. Fax: (435) 673-8228. Web Site: www.mbmediagroup.com. Licensee: MB Media Group Inc. (group owner; acq 7-6-01; with co-located FM). Network: ABC Information & Entertainment. Allied Radio Partners. Format: News. ♦ Brent Miner, pres, gen mgr & gen sls mgr; Dale Nelson, progmg dir; Dan Hobson, chief of engrg.

KXBN(FM)—Co-owned with KNNZ(AM). May 10, 1974: 94.9 mhz; 25.5 kw. 1,681 ft. TL: N37 38 41 W113 22 28. Stereo. Web Site: www.949967.com. Network: ABC FM Connection. Format: CHR. ♦ Tim Nesmith, sls dir & progmg dir.

KSUB(AM)— July 4, 1937: 590 khz; 5 kw-D, 1 kw-N, DA-N. TL: N37 41 55 W113 10 44. 251 W. Hilton Dr., Saint George 84770. Phone: (435) 586-5900. Fax: (435) 673-8228. Web Site: www.590ksub.com. Licensee: MB Media Group Inc. (group owner; acq 7-6-01; with co-located FM). Network: CBS. Target Radio. Format: News/talk, info. News staff: one; News: 15 hrs wkly. Target aud: 35-65; adults. Spec prog: Relg, loc talk, farm 6 hrs wkly. ♦ Brent Miner, pres & gen mgr; Steve Miner, progmg dir; Dan Hobson, chief of engrg.

KXFF(FM)—Co-owned with KSUB(AM). Oct 15, 1976: 92.5 mhz; 41.6 kw. 1,690 ft. TL: N37 38 41 W113 22 28. Stereo. Web Site: www.fox1023.com. Network: Jones Radio Networks. Format: Oldies. News: 5 hrs wkly.

***KSUU(FM)**— October 1966: 91.1 mhz; 10 kw. -462 ft. TL: N37 38 55 W113 05 32. Stereo. 351 W. Ctr. 84720. Phone: (435) 865-8224. Fax: (435) 865-8352. E-mail: ksuu@suu.edu. Web Site: www.suu.edu/ksuu. Licensee: Southern Utah University. Format: CHR. News: 2 hrs wkly. Target aud: 12-34; children, university students. Spec prog: News, class 3 hrs, rhythm and blues 4 hrs, rock 4 hrs wkly. ♦ Cal Rollins, stn mgr; Alex May, progmg dir; Alisia Brooks, mus dir; Camie Stables, news dir; Lance Jackson, chief of engrg.

Centerville

KRRD(AM)— Dec 1, 1957: 1600 khz; 5 kw-D, 1 kw-N, DA-N. TL: N40 54 08 W111 55 40. Stereo. 2722 S. Redwood Rd., Suite 1, Salt Lake City 84119. Phone: (801) 908-8777. Fax: (801) 908-8782. Licensee: Bustos Media of Utah License LLC. Group owner: Bustos Media Holdings (acq 9-1-2004; $1.5 million). Format: Sp. ♦ Jose Tovar, gen mgr.

KXRV(FM)— Dec 24, 1979: 105.7 mhz; 25 kw. Ant 3,739 ft. TL: N40 39 34 W112 12 05. Stereo. 2801 S. Decker Lake Dr., Salt Lake City 84119. Phone: (801) 908-1300. Fax: (801) 908-1569. Web Site: www.river1057.com. Licensee: Citicasters Licenses L.P. Group owner: Clear Channel Communications Inc. (acq 2-27-2004; $22 million. with KOSY-FM Spanish Fork). Rep: Clear Channel, Katz Radio. Format: Adult rock. Target aud: 25-54; adults. ♦ Stu Stanek, gen mgr; Bill Betts, opns mgr; Bill Matthews, sls dir & chief of engrg; Deborah Wallace, gen sls mgr; Frank Bell, progmg dir.

Coalville

KJQN(FM)— 2004: 103.1 mhz; 89 kw horiz. Ant 2,122 ft. TL: N40 52 16 W110 59 43. Simmons Media Group, 515 South 700 East, Salt Lake City 84102. Phone: (801) 524-2600. Fax: (801) 524-6002. Web Site: www.simmonsmedia.com. Licensee: Simmons-SLC, LS LLC. Group owner: Simmons Media Group (acq 5-20-2004; $4.4 million. for CP). Format: Alternative. ♦ G. Craig Hanson, gen mgr.

Delta

KMGR(FM)— Sept 5, 1989: 95.9 mhz; 100 kw horiz. Ant 961 ft. TL: N39 43 58 W111 56 34. Stereo. 3 Point Media - Delta LLC, 980 N. Michigan Ave., Suite 1880, Chicago, IL 60611. Phone: (312) 204-9900. Licensee: 3 Point Media - Delta LLC. (acq 8-1-2003; $1.25 million). ♦ Bruce Buzil, gen mgr.

KNAK(AM)— Feb 25, 1974: 540 khz; 1 kw-U. TL: N39 20 12 W112 33 21. Box 636 84624-0626. Secondary address: 1259 N. 100 W., American Fork 84003. Phone: (435) 864-5111. Fax: (801) 406-0067. Web Site: www.radioforthefamily.com. Licensee: Sam Bushman (acq 8-12-96; $120,000). Format: Relg. News: 15 hrs wkly. Target aud: 20-50. Spec prog: Farm 5 hrs wkly. ♦ Curt Crosby, gen sls mgr & news dir; Sam Bushman, pres, gen mgr, stn mgr & progmg dir.

Ephraim

***KAGJ(FM)**—Not on air, target date: unknown: 89.5 mhz; 100 w. -321 ft. TL: N39 21 37 W111 34 54. Snow College, 150 E. College Ave. 84627. Phone: (435) 283-7425/7000. E-mail: kagj_fm@hotmail.com. Web Site: www.snow.edu/~kage. Licensee: Snow College. Format: Classic rock with a kick. ♦ Gary Chidester, gen mgr.

Garland

KYLZ(FM)—See Tremonton

Kanab

KPLD(FM)— 1986: 101.1 mhz; 99 kw. 786 ft. TL: N36 43 18 W112 12 57. Stereo. 204 Playa Della Rosita, Washington 84780. Phone: (435) 628-3643. Fax: (435) 673-1210. E-mail: kony@infowest.com. Licensee: Marathon Media Group L.L.C. (acq 1999; $1.75 million. with KUNF(AM) Washington). Format: Alternative. ♦ Carl Lamar, VP & gen mgr.

Levan

KCFM(FM)—Not on air, target date: fall 2003: 96.7 mhz; 67 kw horiz. Ant 1,919 ft. TL: N39 20 12 W111 27 06. 930 S. State St., Suite 20, Orem 84097. Phone: (801) 226-2655. Fax: (801) 226-2655. Licensee: Zeta Holdings LLC. Format: Sp var. ♦ Robert H. Morey, gen mgr.

Logan

KBLQ-FM—Listing follows KLGN(AM).

KGNT(FM)—See Smithfield

KLGN(AM)— March 1968: 1390 khz; 5 kw-D, 500 w-N, DA-N. TL: N41 44 04 W111 51 13. Box 3369 84323. Secondary address: 810 W. 200 N. 84321. Phone: (435) 752-1390. Fax: (435) 752-1392. Web Site: www.1390.com. Licensee: Sun Valley Radio Inc. (group owner; acq 12-27-91; $572,279. with co-located FM). Network: Network: Westwood One, CBS. Rep: Allied Radio Partners. Format: Adult standards, memories MOR. Target aud: 45 plus. Spec prog: Talk. ♦ Kent Frandsen, pres; Jay Eubanks, gen mgr, gen sls mgr, mktg mgr & prom mgr; Michael Carver, opns mgr & progmg dir; Dan Baker, chief of engrg.

KBLQ-FM—Co-owned with KLGN(AM). August 1977: 92.9 mhz; 50 kw. 154 ft. TL: N41 52 18 W111 48 31. Stereo. Web Site: www.q92.fm. Format: Adult contemp. Target aud: 25-54; general. Spec prog: Gospel 8 hrs, jazz 4 hrs wkly.

***KUSR(FM)**— March 1999: 89.5 mhz; 800 w. -617 ft. TL: N41 44 44 W111 48 16. Utah Public Radio, 8505 Old Main Hill 84322-8505. Phone: (435) 797-3138. Fax: (435)797-3150. E-mail: upr@upr.usu.edu. Web Site: www.upr.org. Licensee: Utah State University of Agricultural and Applied Science. Network: NPR. Format: Classical, News/Talk. ♦ Richard Meng, gen mgr.

***KUSU-FM**— April 1953: 91.5 mhz; 90 kw. 1,140 ft. TL: N41 53 11 W112 04 17. Stereo. Utah Public Radio, 8505 Old Main Hill 84322-8505. Phone: (435) 797-3138. Phone: (800) 826-1495. Fax: (435) 797-3150. E-mail: upr@upr.usu.edu. Web Site: www.upr.org. Licensee: Utah State University. Network: Network: NPR, PRI. Dow, Lohnes & Albertson. Format: Class, news/talk. News staff: 2. Target aud: General. ♦ Richard Meng, gen mgr; Lee Austin, progmg dir; Nora Zambreno, pub affrs dir; Clifford J. Smith, chief of engrg.

KVFX(FM)—Listing follows KVNU(AM).

KVNU(AM)— Nov 20, 1938: 610 khz; 5 kw-D, 1 kw-N, DA-N. TL: N41 40 30 W111 56 06. Box 267, 1350 N. 200 W. 84323-0267. Phone: (801) 752-5141. Licensee: Sun Valley Radio Inc. (group owner; acq 1996; $900,000. with co-located FM). Network: ABC Information & Entertainment. Rep: Allied Radio Partners. Format: News/talk. News staff: one; News: 15 hrs wkly. Target aud: General. Spec prog: Farm 2 hrs, relg 3 hrs wkly. ♦ Al Lewis, gen mgr & progmg dir; James Murdock, gen sls mgr; Jennie Christensen, news dir; Dan Baker, chief of engrg.

KVFX(FM)—Co-owned with KVNU(AM). Nov 11, 1974: 94.5 mhz; 70 kw. 1,148 ft. TL: N41 53 50 W111 57 39. Stereo. Format: CHR. News: 2 hrs wkly. Target aud: 18-35. ♦ Blair Carter, progmg dir & progmg mgr.

***KZCL(FM)**—Not on air, target date: unknown: 90.5 mhz; 300 w. Ant 1,246 ft. TL: N41 53 43 W112 04 43. 1971 West North Temple, Salt Lake City 84116. Phone: (801) 363-1818. Fax: (801) 533-9136. Licensee: Listeners Community Radio of Utah Inc. ♦ Donna Land Maldonado, gen mgr.

Manti

KMTI(AM)— June 7, 1976: 650 khz; 10 kw-D, 1 kw-N, DA-2. TL: N39 17 39 W111 38 13. Box 40, 1600 W. 500 N. 84642. Phone: (435) 835-7301. Fax: (435) 835-2250. Web Site: www.kmtiradio.com. Licensee: Sanpete County Broadcasting Co. Network: ABC Information & Entertainment. Rosenman & Colin. Format: Country, news. News staff: one; News: 20 hrs wkly. Target aud: 25-50. Spec prog: Farm 5 hrs wkly. ♦ Douglas Barton, pres & gen mgr; Dave Gunderson, gen sls mgr; Larry Masco, progmg dir; Mike Traina, news dir; Kirk Williams, chief of engrg.

Broadcasting & Cable Yearbook 2006

Stations in the U.S. — Utah

KNJQ(FM)— December 1978: 105.1 mhz; 74 kw horiz. Ant 2,244 ft. TL: N39 45 37 W111 34 38. Stereo. 515 S. 700 E., Suite 1C, Salt Lake City 84102. Phone: (801) 524-2600. Fax: (801) 521-9234. Web Site: www.kjq.com. Licensee: Millcreek Broadcasting L.L.C. (group owner; acq 4-17-01). Format: Alternative. ♦Douglas Barton, gen mgr; Sam Penrod, mus dir.

Midvale

KQMB(FM)— 1995: 102.7 mhz; 25 kw. Ant 3,739 ft. TL: N40 39 34 W112 12 05. Stereo. 55 North 300 West, Salt Lake City 84180. Phone: (801) 575-5555. Fax: (801) 526-1070. Web Site: www.ksl.com. Licensee: Bonneville Holding Co. Group owner: Bonneville International Corp. (acq 12-5-2003; grpsl). Format: News/talk, sports. ♦Chris Redgrave, gen mgr.

Moab

KCYN(FM)— Sept 20, 1998: 97.1 mhz; 29 kw. Ant 1,292 ft. TL: N38 31 37 W109 18 21. Box 1119 84532. Secondary address: 1030 S. Bowling Alley Ln. #3 84532. Phone: (435) 259-1035. Fax: (435) 259-1037. E-mail: kcyn@citilink.net. Web Site: www.kcyn97fm.com. Licensee: Moab Communications LLC. (acq 8-15-97). Format: Country. News: 12 hrs wkly. Target aud: 18-54. ♦Phillip Mueller, gen mgr & gen sls mgr; Kenneth Meyer, chief of engrg.

*KZMU(FM)— April 1992: 89.7 mhz; 100 w. -581 ft. TL: N38 32 47 W109 31 03. Stereo. Box 1076 84532. Secondary address: 1734 Rocky Rd. 84532. Phone: (435) 259-4897. Fax: (435) 259-8824. Fax: (435) 259-8763. E-mail: kzmu@citylink.net. Web Site: www.kzmu.org. Licensee: Moab Public Radio. Format: Var/div, public radio. News staff: one; News: 8 hrs wkly. Target aud: General. Spec prog: Asian one hr, American Indian 5 hrs, Black 3 hrs, Sp one hr, folk 6 hrs, blues 19 hrs wkly. ♦Jeff Flanders, gen mgr; Christy Williams, progmg dir; Glen Peart, mus dir & asst music dir; Lewis Downey Jr., engrg dir.

Murray

KJQS(AM)— Nov 8, 1948: 1230 khz; 1 kw-U. TL: N40 39 57 W111 54 26. Stereo. 434 Bearcat Dr., Salt Lake City 84115. Phone: (801) 485-6700. Fax: (801) 487-5369. Licensee: Citadel Broadcasting Co. Group owner: Citadel Broadcasting Corp. (acq 2-29-00; $104,202). Format: Sports. ♦Eric Hauenstein, gen mgr; Jeff Austin, opns mgr & progmg dir; Terry Mathis, gen sls mgr; Richard Bauer, chief of engrg.

Naples

KCUA(FM)— 1993: 92.5 mhz; 840 w. Ant 1,660 ft. TL: N40 32 16 W109 41 57. 800 South and 2000 East, Roosevelt 84066. Phone: (801) 412-6080. Licensee: 3 Point Media - Coalville LLC. (acq 5-28-2004; $1.7 million). Format: Classic Rock. ♦Joe Evans, stn mgr.

Nephi

KUDE(FM)— May 9, 1990: 103.9 mhz; 74 kw horiz. Ant 2,244 ft. TL: N39 45 37 W111 34 38. Stereo. 2835 East 3300 South, Salt Lake City 84109. Phone: (801) 412-6040. Fax: (801) 412-6041. Licensee: Millcreek Broadcasting L.L.C. (group owner; acq 4-17-01). Format: CHR/POP. Target aud: 18-45. ♦Randy Rodgers, gen mgr; Brian Michel, opns mgr; Lutisha Merrill, gen sls mgr; Scott St. John, mktg mgr; Kevin Terry, engrg VP.

North Ogden

*KNKL(FM)— Jan 29, 2004: 88.7 mhz; 7.3 kw vert. Ant 984 ft. TL: N41 35 30 W112 14 57. 5700 W. Oaks Blvd., Rocklin, CA 95765. Phone: (916) 251-1600. Fax: (916) 251-1650. E-mail: klove@klove.com. Web Site: www.klove.com. Licensee: Educational Media Foundation. Group owner: EMF Broadcasting. Network: K-Love. Shaw Pittman. Format: Contemp Christian. News staff: 3. Target aud: 25-44; female-Judeo Christian. ♦Richard Jenkins, pres; Mike Novak, VP & progmg dir; Lloyd Parker, gen mgr; Ed Lenane, opns dir & news dir; Keith Whipple,

dev dir; Eric Allen, natl sls mgr; Dan Beck, rgnl sls mgr; Chris Joyce, prom dir; David Pierce, progmg mgr; Jon Rivers, mus dir; Sam Wallington, engrg dir.

North Salt Lake City

KALL(AM)— Sept 22, 1981: 700 khz; 50 kw-D, 1 kw-N, DA-2. TL: N40 53 29 W111 56 28 (D), N40 53 32 W111 56 28 (N). Stereo. 2801 S. Decker Lake Dr., Salt Lake City 84119-2330. Phone: (801) 908-1300. Fax: (801) 908-1459. Web Site: www.hotticket700.com. Licensee: Citicasters Licenses L.P. Group owner: Clear Channel Communications Inc. (acq 1999; grpsl). Rep: Clear Channel. Format: Sports/talk. News staff: 1; News: 20 hrs wkly. Target aud: 18-49; men. ♦Stu Stanek, gen mgr; Bill Betts, opns mgr; Bill Mathews, sls dir; Steve Pearson, natl sls mgr; Jason Wilmot, progmg dir.

Oakley

KEGA(FM)— 2003: 101.5 mhz; 89 kw horiz, 38 kw vert. Ant 2,122 ft. TL: N40 52 16 W110 59 43. Simmons Media Group, 515 South 700 E. #1C, Salt Lake City 84102. Phone: (801) 524-2600. Fax: (801) 521-8100. Web Site: www.1015theeagle.com. Licensee: Simmons-SLC, LS LLC. Group owner: Simmons Media Group (acq 4-4-2001; grpsl). Format: Country. ♦Craig Hanson, pres; Stephen Johnson, gen mgr.

Ogden

KBER(FM)— July 13, 1976: 101.1 mhz; 25 kw. 3,740 ft. TL: N40 39 35 W112 12 05. Stereo. 434 Bearcat Dr., Salt Lake City 84115. Phone: (801) 485-6700. Fax: (801) 487-5369. Web Site: www.kber.com. Licensee: Citadel Broadcasting Co. Group owner: Citadel Broadcasting Corp. (acq 1996; $7.7 million). Network: ABC. Rep: Allied Radio Partners. Format: AOR. News staff: one. Target aud: 18-49; men. ♦Eric Hauenstein, gen mgr; Bruce James, opns mgr; Terry Mathis, gen sls mgr; Lindsay Randall, natl sls mgr; Joel Smith, prom dir & mus dir; Kelly Hamer, progmg dir; Richie Bauer, engrg dir.

KBZN(FM)— 1978: 97.9 mhz; 26 kw. 3,770 ft. TL: N40 39 35 W112 12 05. 257 E. 200 S., Suite 400, Salt Lake City 84111. Phone: (801) 364-9836. Fax: (801) 364-8068. E-mail: breeze@kbzn.com. Web Site: www.kbzn.com. Licensee: Capitol Broadcasting Inc. (acq 4-5-91; 4-29-91). Format: Smooth jazz, new age. ♦John Webb, gen mgr; Rob Riesen, opns dir; Cris Winn, gen sls mgr.

KLO(AM)— 1924: 1430 khz; 5 kw-U, DA-N. TL: N41 10 44 W112 04 09. (CP: TL: N41 02 48 W112 01 38). 4155 Harrison Blvd., Suite 206 84003-2463. Phone: (801) 627-1430. Fax: (801) 627-0317. Web Site: www.kloradio.com. Licensee: KLO Broadcasting Co. Network: ABC Information & Entertainment. Format: Talk. ♦John Webb, pres & gen mgr; Dan Jessop, opns mgr & progmg dir; Jan Bagley, gen sls mgr; Patrick Gleason, chief of engrg.

KPQP(FM)— Aug 1, 1964: 101.9 mhz; 25 kw. Ant 3,739 ft. TL: N40 39 34 W112 12 05. Stereo. 2835 E. 3300 S., Suite 800, Salt Lake City 84107. Phone: (801) 412-6040. Fax: (801) 412-6041. Web Site: www.kkat.com. Licensee: Citadel Broadcasting Co. Group owner: Citadel Broadcasting Corp. (acq 7-20-2004; $16 million). Network: ABC. Format: Modern country. News staff: one; News: 6 hrs wkly. Target aud: 25-54. ♦Randy Rodgers, gen mgr.

KSVN(AM)— Jan 1, 1946: 730 khz; 1 kw-D, 66 w-N. TL: N41 11 17 W112 04 52. 4215 W. 4000 S., West Haven 84401. Phone: (801) 292-1799. Fax: (801) 731-4445. Licensee: Azteca Broadcasting Corp. (group owner; acq 2-1-86). Format: Rgnl Mexican. ♦Alex Collantes, pres, gen mgr & progmg dir; Maria Coria, gen sls mgr.

*KWCR-FM— May 21, 1966: 88.1 mhz; 3 kw. -470 ft. TL: N41 11 30 W111 56 37. (CP: Ant 315 ft.). Stereo. 2188 University Cir. 84408-2188. Phone: (801) 626-8800. Fax: (801) 626-6935. E-mail: kwcrradio@mail.weber.edu. Web Site: www.weber.edu/kwcr. Licensee: Weber State University Board of Trustees. Format: Contemp hits, rock. News: 4 hrs wkly. Target aud: 18-26; college students, male & female. Spec prog: Relg 3 hrs, gospel 3 hrs, Sp 16 hrs wkly. ♦Mark Howard, gen mgr & sls mgr.

*KYFO(AM)— April 1948: 1490 khz; 1 kw-U. TL: N41 14 23 W111 59 08. 1506 Gibson Ave. 84404. Phone: (801) 254-9000. Fax: (435) 628-6636. Licensee: AM Radio 1490 Inc. (acq 12-6-2004; $520,000). Network: Network: CNN Radio, Westwood One. Dan J. Alpert. Format: Adult standard. ♦E. Morgan Skinner Jr., CEO & pres.

*KYFO-FM— June 1983: 95.5 mhz; 100 kw. Ant 718 ft. TL: N41 14 59 W112 14 11. Stereo. 1506 Gibson Ave. 84404. Phone: (801) 394-8833. Web Site: www.bbnradio.org. Licensee: Bible Broadcasting Network. (acq 1994). Format: Christian. ♦Lowell Davey, pres; Tom Gearhart, gen mgr.

Orem

KENZ(FM)— Nov 15, 1978: 107.5 mhz; 45 kw. 2,850 ft. TL: N40 16 48 W111 56 05. Stereo. 434 Bearcat Dr., Salt Lake City 84115-2520. Phone: (801) 485-6700. Fax: (801) 487-5369. Web Site: www.1075.com. Licensee: Citadel Broadcasting Co. Group owner: Citadel Broadcasting Corp. (acq 12-18-96). Format: Alternative. Target aud: 25-54. ♦Eric Hauenstein, gen mgr; Diane Curtis, adv mgr; Bruce Jones, progmg dir; Kurt Johnson, prom.

*KOHS(FM)— October 1994: 91.7 mhz; 1.75 kw. -831 ft. TL: N40 17 48 W111 41 04. (CP: Ant -869 ft. TL: N40 17 32 W111 40 56). Stereo. 175 S. 400 E. 84058. Phone: (801) 224-9236. Fax: (801) 538-5690. Licensee: Orem HI. Sch. Format: Alternative.

KSRR(AM)—See Provo

Park City

*KPCW(FM)— July 2, 1980: 91.9 mhz; 105 w. Ant -23 ft. TL: N40 40 59 W111 31 22. Stereo. Box 1372 84060. Secondary address: KPCW City Hall Bldg., 445 Marsac 84060. Phone: (435) 649-9004. Fax: (435) 645-9063. E-mail: letters@kpcw.org. Web Site: www.kpcw.org. Licensee: Community Wireless of Park City. Format: AAA, news. Spec prog: Class 17 hrs, C&W 18 hrs, jazz 12 hrs wkly. ♦Blair Feulner, gen mgr; Karen Thomas, progmg dir; Leslie Thatcher, news dir; Dennis Silver, chief of engrg.

Parowan

KENT(AM)— September 2003: 1400 khz; 800 w-U. TL: N37 48 22 W112 56 40. Box 1450, St. George 84771-1450. Secondary address: 210 North 1000 East, St. George 84770. Phone: (435) 477-1400. Fax: (435) 628-6636. Licensee: AM Radio 1400 Inc. Group owner: Diamond Broadcasting Corp. Dan J. Alpert. Format: News/sports. ♦E. Morgan Skinner Jr., CEO & pres; Lavon Randall, chmn; R. Michael Bull, CFO.

Payson

KTCE(FM)— November 1993: 92.1 mhz; 125 w. Ant 2,155 ft. TL: N40 05 21 W111 49 15. 2835 E. 3300 S., Salt Lake City 84603. Phone: (801) 412-6040. Fax: (801) 412-6041. Licensee: Moenkopi Communications Inc. Format: Hip hop, rhythm and blues.

Pleasant Grove

*KPGR(FM)— May 1976: 88.1 mhz; 115 w. -1,128 ft. TL: N40 21 48 W111 43 30. Stereo. 700 E. 200 S. 84062. Phone: (801) 785-5747. Phone: (801) 785-8700. Fax: (801) 785-8744. Web Site: www.kpgr.tripod.com. Licensee: Alpine School District. Format: Var. Target aud: 12-18; students. Spec prog: All Pleasant Grove High football, basketball, baseball games 4 hrs wkly.

Price

KARB(FM)— July 1977: 98.3 mhz; 3 kw. -145 ft. TL: N39 36 36 W110 48 52. (CP: 7 kw). Stereo. Box 875 84501. Secondary address: 1899 North Carbonville Rd. 84501. Phone: (435) 637-1167. Fax: (435) 637-1177. E-mail: koal@emerytelcom.net. Web Site: www.koal.net.

Utah Directory of Radio

Licensee: Eastern Utah Broadcasting Co. Network: ABC FM Connection. Format: Country. ♦Tom Anderson, gen mgr.

KOAL(AM)— October 1936: 750 khz; 10 kw-U, 6.8 kw-N, DA-N. TL: N39 34 02 W110 47 53. Box 875 84501. Phone: (435) 637-1167. Fax: (435) 637-1177. E-mail: koal@castlenet.com. Web Site: www.koal.net. Licensee: Eastern Utah Broadcasting Co. Network: ABC Information & Entertainment. Format: News/talk, sports. Spec prog: Farm 5 hrs wkly. ♦Keith Mason, progmg dir; Thomas Anderson, pres, gen mgr & chief of engrg.

KSLL(AM)— Sept 6, 1980: 1080 khz; 10 kw-D. TL: N39 33 43 W110 46 36. Stereo. Box 1080 84501. Secondary address: 163 E. 100 N. 84501. Phone: (435) 637-1080. Fax: (435) 637-8191. E-mail: kusa@emerytelcom.net. Web Site: www.kusaonline.com. Licensee: Against the Wind Broadcasting Inc. (acq 6-21-02; $250,000. with co-located FM). Format: Country. Target aud: General. ♦Randy J. Timothy, pres; David B. Smith, gen mgr & progmg dir; Dennis Silver, chief of engrg.

KWSA(FM)—Co-owned with KSLL(AM). December 1985: 100.9 mhz; 3 kw. 111 ft. TL: N39 32 42 W110 48 56. Stereo. Web Site: www.kusaonline.com. Format: Adult contemp.

Provo

***KBYU-FM**— November 1960: 89.1 mhz; 32 kw. 2,913 ft. TL: N40 36 28 W112 09 33. Stereo. C302 Harris Fine Arts Ctr. 84602. Phone: (801) 422-3552. Fax: (801) 422-0922. E-mail: kbyu@byu.edu. Web Site: www.kbyu.org. Licensee: Brigham Young University. Network: PRI. Format: Class, news/talk. Target aud: 35 plus. ♦John Reim, CEO; Walter B. Rudolph, gen mgr; Derek Marquis, dev dir & sls dir; James Bell, mktg dir & prom dir; Bruce Seely, progmg dir; Christine Nokleby, progmg mgr; Eric Glissmeyer, mus dir; Rebecca Cressman, news dir; Lynn Edwards, engrg dir. Co-owned TV: *KBYU-TV affil.

***KEYY(AM)**— December 1949: 1450 khz; 1 kw-U. TL: N40 13 49 W111 41 12. 307 S. 1600 W. 84601-3932. Phone: (801) 374-5210. Fax: (801) 374-2910. E-mail: mail@keyy.com. Web Site: www.keyy.com. Licensee: Biblical Ministries Worldwide. (acq 5-10-88). Network: Network: Moody, Salem Radio Network. Garvey, Schubert & Barer. Format: Christian. News: 13 hrs wkly. Target aud: General. Spec prog: Sp 5 hrs wkly. ♦Steven A. Barsuhn, gen mgr.

KHTB(FM)— November 1979: 94.9 mhz; 47 kw. Ant 2,798 ft. TL: N40 16 58 W111 56 11. Stereo. 2835 E. 3300 S., Suite 800, Salt Lake City 84107. Phone: (801) 412-6040. Fax: (801) 412-6041. Web Site: www.949zht.com. Licensee: 3 Point Media-Salt Lake City LLC. (acq 2-23-2004; $26 million. with KPQP(FM) Ogden). Format: CHR. Target aud: 18-34; females. ♦Randy Rodgers, gen mgr.

KOVO(AM)— Sept 12, 1939: 960 khz; 5 kw-D, 1080 w-N, DA-N. TL: N40 12 44 W111 40 13. 26 W. Center 84601. Phone: (801) 818-1074. Phone: (801) 818-9600. Fax: (801) 818-3308. Web Site: www.1280thezone.com. Licensee: Simmons-SLC, LS LLC. Group owner: Simmons Media Group (acq 4-19-2004; $1 million). Network: ABC Information & Entertainment. Rep: D & R Radio. Format: All sports. Target aud: 35 plus; upper income affluent males & females 35-65. ♦Craig Hanson, pres; Randy Rogers, gen mgr; Ryan Hatch, progmg dir.

KSRR(AM)— Nov 24, 1947: 1400 khz; 1 kw-U. TL: N40 15 29 W111 42 24. Box 828, Orem 84058. Secondary address: 1454 W. Business Park Dr., Orem 84058. Phone: (801) 224-1400. Licensee: Zeta Holdings LLC (acq 8-27-97). Format: Adult contemp. News: one hr wkly. Target aud: 18-54. ♦Robert H. Morey, gen mgr.

KXRK(FM)— Feb 14, 1968: 96.3 mhz; 38 kw. Ant 2,952 ft. TL: N40 36 28 W112 09 26. Stereo. 515 South 700 East, Suite 1C, Salt Lake City 84102. Phone: (801) 524-2600. Fax: (801) 521-9234. E-mail: xmail@x96.com. Web Site: www.x96.com. Licensee: Simmons-SLC, LS LLC. Group owner: Simmons Media Group (acq 4-4-2001; grpsl). Fletcher, Heald & Hildreth. Format: Alternative. Target aud: 18-34; young, affluent executives. ♦Craig Hanson, pres; Bruce Thomas, CFO; Stephen C. Johnson, gen mgr; Alan Hague, opns dir; Mike Lund, gen sls mgr; Kris Burton, natl sls mgr; Natalie Divino, mktg dir & prom dir; Todd Nukem, progmg dir; Scott Matthews, chief of engrg.

Randolph

KDUT(FM)— 2001: 102.3 mhz; 89 kw horiz. Ant 2,122 ft. TL: N40 52 16 W110 59 43. 2722 S. Redwood Rd., Suite 1, Salt Lake City 84119. Phone: (801) 908-8777. Fax: (801) 908-8782. Web Site: www.bustosmedia.com. Licensee: Bustos Media of Utah License LLC. Group owner: Bustos Media Holdings (acq 7-1-2004; $9 million). Format: Sp CHR. ♦Edward Distel, gen mgr.

Richfield

KCYQ(FM)— 2000: 97.5 mhz; 56 kw. Ant 2,353 ft. TL: N39 19 17 W111 46 11. (CP: COL Elsinore. 97.7 mhz; 41 kw, ant 2,883 ft. TL: N38 32 30 W112 03 31). Stereo. Box 40, Manti 84642. Phone: (435) 835-7301. Fax: (435) 835-2250. Web Site: www.kcyq.com. Licensee: Sanpete County Broadcasting Co. (acq 5-3-2001; $250,000). Format: Super hits. ♦Douglas Barton, CEO, pres & gen mgr; Dave Gunderson, sls VP; J.D. Fox, progmg VP & mus dir; Kirk Williams, engrg VP.

KLGL(FM)—Listing follows KSVC(AM).

KSVC(AM)— September 1947: 980 khz; 5 kw-D, 1 kw-N, DA-N. TL: N38 45 40 W112 04 35. 390 E. Annabella Rd. 84701. Phone: (435) 896-4456. Fax: (435) 896-9333. E-mail: ksvcnews@ksvcradio.com. Web Site: www.ksvcradio.com. Licensee: Mid-Utah Radio Inc. (acq 9-15-94; $275,000 with co-located FM; 10-24-94). Network: ABC Information & Entertainment. Borsari & Paxson. Format: News/talk, sports. News: 18 hrs wkly. Target aud: 18-54. Spec prog: Farm one hr wkly. ♦Kevin Kitchen, gen mgr, sls dir, mus dir & news dir; Kirk Williams, chief of engrg.

KLGL(FM)—Co-owned with KSVC(AM). 1978: 93.7 mhz; 41 kw. Ant 2,883 ft. TL: N38 32 30 W112 03 31. (CP: 56.1 kw, ant 2,355 ft. TL: N39 19 17 W111 46 11). Stereo. Web Site: www.klgl.com. Network: Network: Westwood One, ABC Information & Entertainment. Format: Country. News staff: one; News: 11 hrs wkly. Target aud: General. ♦Michael Ray, mus dir.

Roosevelt

KIFX(FM)— Dec 14, 1987: 98.5 mhz; 2.65 kw. 1,853 ft. TL: N40 31 15 W109 42 17. (CP: 3.19 kw, ant 1,689 ft. TL: N40 32 16 W109 41 57). Stereo. The Fox 98.5, Rt. 2, Box 2384 84066. Secondary address: 2242 E. 1000 S. 84066. Phone: (435) 722-5011. Phone: (435) 789-5101. Fax: (435) 722-5012. Web Site: www.hitsandfavorites.com. Licensee: Evans Broadcasting Inc. (acq 5-31-91; $283,750; 6-24-91). Art Moore. Format: Adult contemp. News staff: one; News: 5 hrs wkly. Target aud: 21-45. ♦Joseph L. Evans, pres & gen mgr; Teddie Evans, VP; Vickie Reary, opns dir; Teena Christopherson, gen sls mgr; Earl Hawkins, progmg dir; Jean Liddell, news dir; Steve Sprouce, chief of engrg.

KNEU(AM)— Jan 6, 1978: 1250 khz; 5 kw-D, 129 w-N. TL: N40 17 13 W109 57 32. Rt. 2, Box 2384, Ballard 84066. Secondary address: 1800 E. 800S, Ballard 84066. Phone: (435) 722-5011. Phone: (435) 789-5101. Fax: (435) 722-5012. E-mail: radio@ubtanet.com. Licensee: Country Gold Broadcasting. (acq 2-84; $419,419; 2-20-84). Format: C&W. News staff: one; News: 10 hrs wkly. Target aud: 25-54. ♦Joseph L. Evans, pres & gen mgr; Teddie Evans, VP & gen sls mgr; Bob Fox, gen mgr; Tenna Christopherson, gen sls mgr; Earl Hawkins, progmg dir & news dir; Jim Leonard, chief of engrg.

KXRQ(FM)— Dec 18, 1998: 94.3 mhz; 17.5 kw. Ant 1,863 ft. TL: N40 31 15 W109 42 25. 1420 E. 2850 S., Suite 200, Vernal 84078. Phone: (435) 722-0940. Phone: (435) 781-1100. Fax: (435) 781-1500. E-mail: cruise@iwworeko.com. Web Site: www.kxrq.com. Licensee: Uinta Broadcasting L.C. (acq 2-15-01; $450,000). Format: CHR. hot adult contemp. Target aud: 25-54. Spec prog: Religion 6 hrs wkly. ♦Charles D. Hahl, gen mgr; Charles Hall, opns dir, engrg dir & chief of engrg; Ray Wanty, gen sls mgr & prom dir; Mark Christiansen, progmg dir.

Roy

***KANN(AM)**— September 1961: 1120 khz; 10 kw-D, 1 kw-N, DA-2. TL: N41 03 31 W112 04 10. Box 3880, Ogden 84409. Secondary address: 2500 W. 3700 S., Syracuse 84075. Phone: (801) 776-0249. E-mail: bobalzu6arat@aol.com. Web Site: www.sosradio.net. Licensee: Faith Communications. Format: Christian. News: 6 hrs wkly. Target aud: 25-44; young families. ♦Jack French, pres; Bob Alzugarat, gen mgr; Brad Staley, opns mgr.

KUDD(FM)— September 1986: 107.9 mhz; 67 kw. 2,383 ft. TL: N41 15 27 W112 26 24. 2835 E. 3300 S., Suite 800, Salt Lake City 84107. Phone: (801) 412-6040. Fax: (801) 412-6041. Licensee: Millcreek Broadcasting L.L.C. (group owner; (acq 4-17-2001; grpsl). Robert Olender. Format: CHR. Target aud: General. ♦Randy Rodgers, gen mgr; Lutisha Merrill, gen sls mgr; Scott St. John, prom VP; Brian Michel, progmg dir; Kevin Terry, chief of engrg.

Saint George

***KAER(FM)**—Not on air, target date: unknown: 89.3 mhz; 900 w. Ant -112 ft. TL: N37 06 54 W113 34 23. 5700 W. Oaks Blvd., Rocklin, CA 95765. Phone: (916) 251-1600. Fax: (916) 251-1650. E-mail: info@air1.com. Web Site: www.air1.com. Licensee: Educational Media Foundation. Group owner: EMF Broadcasting. Network: Air 1. Shaw Pittman. Format: Contemp Christian. News staff: 3. Target aud: 19-35; Judeo Christian female. ♦Richard Jenkins, pres; Mike Novak, VP & progmg dir; Lloyd Parker, gen mgr; Keith Whipple, dev dir; Eric Allen, natl sls mgr; Dan Beck, rgnl sls mgr; Chris Joyce, prom dir; Bryan O'Neal, progmg mgr; Liz Morton, mus dir; Ed Lenane, news dir; Sam Wallington, engrg dir.

KDXU(AM)— July 3, 1957: 890 khz; 10 kw-U, DA-N. TL: N37 04 04 W113 31 04. 750 W. Ridgeview Dr., Suite 204 84770. Phone: (435) 673-3579. Fax: (435) 673-8900. Licensee: Bonneville Holding Co. Group owner: Bonneville International Corp. (acq 11-24-03; grpsl). Network: ABC Information & Entertainment. Format: News/talk. Target aud: 25-54. Spec prog: Relg 4 hrs wkly. ♦C. Craig Hanson, pres; Don Shelline, gen mgr; Kevin Fry, gen sls mgr; Bryan Hyde, progmg dir; Gary Smith, chief of engrg.

KSNN(FM)—Co-owned with KDXU(AM). June 15, 1973: 93.5 mhz; 3 kw. -125 ft. TL: N37 06 54 W113 34 23. Stereo. Format: Adult contemp. Target aud: 12-49. ♦Bryan Benware, progmg dir.

KONY(FM)— Nov 12, 1994: 99.9 mhz; 89 kw. Ant 2,053 ft. TL: N36 50 49 W113 29 28. Stereo. Box 910850 84791. Phone: (435) 628-3643. Fax: (435) 673-1210. Web Site: kony.us. Licensee: Canyon Media Corp. Group owner: Legacy Communications Corp. Format: Country. ♦M. Kent Frandsen, pres; Carl Lamar, gen mgr.

***KRDC-FM**— 1975: 91.7 mhz; 105 w. -312 ft. TL: N37 06 16 W113 33 55. Stereo. 225 S. 700 E. 84770. Phone: (435) 652-7891. Phone: (435) 652-7500. Web Site: www.dixie.edu. Licensee: Dixie College. Format: Alternative, urban contemp, specialty shows. Target aud: 14-25; college & high school students. Spec prog: Class 15 hrs, jazz 10 hrs wkly. ♦Lex De Azevedo, gen mgr; Paul Graves, stn mgr.

***KSGU(FM)**—Not on air, target date: unknown: 90.7 mhz; 2 kw. Ant 1,820 ft. TL: N36 50 49 W113 29 28. 1289 S. Torrey Pines Dr., Las Vegas, NV 89146. Phone: (702) 258-9895. Fax: (702) 258-5646. Web Site: www.knpr.org. Licensee: Nevada Public Radio (acq 3-10-2005; $250,000. for CP). ♦Lamar Marchese, gen mgr.

KUNF(AM)—(Washington). June 6, 1982: 1210 khz; 10 kw-D, 250 w-N. TL: N37 08 38 W113 30 03. 750 W. Ridge View Dr., Suite 204, St. George 84770. Phone: (435) 673-3579. Phone: (435) 673-9398. Fax: (435) 673-8900. Licensee: Bonneville Holding Co. Group owner: Bonneville International Corp. (acq 11-24-03; grpsl). Format: Nostalgia, adult standards. News: 5 hrs wkly. Target aud: 18-64. ♦Don Shelline, gen mgr; Bob Paterson, stn mgr & progmg dir; Kevin Fry, gen sls mgr; Jessica Paterson, pub affrs dir; Gary Smith, chief of engrg.

KZHK(FM)— January 1997: 95.9 mhz; 96.6 kw. 1,965 ft. TL: N36 50 50 W113 29 28. 204 Playa Della Rosita, Washington 84780. Phone: (435) 628-3643. Fax: (435) 673-1210. E-mail: kony@infowest.com. Licensee: Marvin Kent Frandsen. Group owner: Sun Valley Radio Inc. Format: Classic rock. ♦M.K. Frandsen, pres; Carl Lamar, gen mgr & news dir; John Van Wagoner, gen sls mgr; Aaronee Allen, mktg dir, prom dir & pub affrs dir; Marty Lane, stn mgr & progmg dir; Kelton Llyod, chief of engrg.

KZNU(AM)— Oct 9, 1957: 1450 khz; 1 kw-U. TL: N37 05 02 W113 33 26. Stereo. Box 910850 84791. Phone: (435) 628-3643. Phone: (435) 673-1210. Fax: (435) 628-6636. Licensee: Canyon Media Corp. Group owner: Legacy Communications Corp. (acq 7-31-2004). Format: News/talk.

Salt Lake City

KALL(AM)—See North Salt Lake City

KBEE(FM)— 1947: 98.7 mhz; 40 kw. 2,932 ft. TL: N40 36 30 W112 09 34. Stereo. 434 Bearcat Dr. 84115. Phone: (801) 485-6700. Fax: (801) 487-5369. Web Site: www.b987.com. Licensee: Citadel Broadcasting Co. Group owner: Citadel Broadcasting Corp. (acq 7-18-97; $2,873,027. with co-located AM). Format: Adult contemp. Target aud: General.

Stations in the U.S. Utah

Developers & Brokers of Radio Properties

contact American Media Services at our suite:
Philadelphia Marriott Downtown
215-625-2900
843-972-2200
americanmediaservices.com
Charleston, SC
Dallas, TX · Chicago, Il · Austin, TX
American Media Services, LLC

♦ Eric Hauenstein, gen mgr; Ed Hill, opns mgr; Jim Bratt, gen sls mgr; Jaelyn Carillo, prom dir; Rusty Keys, progmg dir; Richie Bauer, chief of engrg.

KFNZ(AM)—Co-owned with KBEE(FM). 1923: 1320 khz; 50 kw-D, 200 w-N. TL: N40 38 36 W111 55 24. Stereo. Format: Sports. ♦ Zandi Wilcox, gen sls mgr; Joel Smith, prom dir; Jeff Austin, progmg dir.

KBJA(AM)—(Sandy). June 2001: 1640 khz; 10 kw-D, 1 kw-N. TL: N40 42 47 W111 55 53. 2250 S. Redwood Rd. 84119. Phone: (801) 765-1480. Phone: (801) 746-0946. Fax: (801) 746-0326. E-mail: radiounica@hotmail.com. Web Site: www.radiounicautah.com. Licensee: United Broadcasting Co. Inc. Network: CNN en Espanol. Format: Sp. News staff: 5; News: 41 1/2 hrs wkly. Target aud: Hispanic adults; Adult hispanic market. ♦ David C. Kifuri, gen mgr, opns dir, adv dir & progmg dir; Jose L. Rivera, stn mgr, sls dir & news dir; Magdalena Garcia, dev dir; Patricia Rivera, mktg dir; Enrique Corona, prom dir & mus dir; Jessica M. Kifuri, asst music dir; Elizabeth Amores, news dir & pub affrs dir; Jose A. Sanchez, pub affrs dir; Dennis Silver, chief of engrg.

*KCPW-FM— 1992: 88.3 mhz; 750 w. Ant -587 ft. TL: N40 45 33 W111 49 48. Box 510730 84151-0730. Phone: (801) 359-5279. Fax: (801) 746-2708. E-mail: news@kcpw.org. Web Site: www.kcpw.org. Licensee: Community Wireless of Park City Inc. Network: Network: NPR, PRI. Format: News/talk. Target aud: 25 plus. ♦ Vicki Mann, gen mgr; Bryan Schott, stn mgr & mus dir.

KDYL(AM)—(South Salt Lake). Sept 2, 1967: 1060 khz; 10 kw-D, 149 w-N. TL: N40 32 18 W112 04 38. Box 57760 84157. Secondary address: 3606 South 500 West 84115. Phone: (801) 262-5624. Fax: (801) 266-1510. E-mail: kdylam@aros.net. Web Site: www.kdylam.com. Licensee: Holiday Broadcasting Co. Group owner: Carlson Communications International (acq 5-8-84). Network: Network One. Format: Adult standards. News: 13 hrs wkly. Target aud: 35-64; general. ♦ R. Steve Carlson, sr VP; Brent J. Carlson, VP; Ralph J. Carlson, CEO, pres & gen mgr; Ralph J Carlson, stn mgr; R. Steve Carlson, opns VP.

KJQS(AM)—See Murray

KKAT(AM)— Nov 15, 1955: 860 khz; 10 kw-D, 195.8 w-N, 3 kw-CH. TL: N40 42 47 W111 55 53. Stereo. 434 Bearcat Dr. 84115. Phone: (801) 485-6700. Fax: (801) 487-5369. Licensee: Citadel Broadcasting Co. Group owner: Citadel Broadcasting Co. Rep: Christal. Format: Disney. Target aud: 25-54. ♦ Larry Wilson, CEO & chmn; Bob Proffitt, sr VP; Eric Hauenstein, gen mgr; Susie Harris Carlson, gen sls mgr; Rusty Keys, prom mgr & progmg dir; Richie Bauer, chief of engrg.

KUBL-FM—Co-owned with KKAT(AM). July 31, 1965: 93.3 mhz; 25 kw. Ant 3,739 ft. TL: N40 39 34 W112 12 05. Stereo. Web Site: www.kbull93.com. Format: Country 90s. ♦ Ed Hill, opns mgr & progmg dir; Terry Mathis, sls dir & gen sls mgr; Randi P' Poll, prom VP & prom dir; Richie Bauer, chief of engrg.

KMRI(AM)—(West Valley City). Nov 16, 1956: 1550 khz; 10 kw-D, 500 w-N. TL: N40 43 29 W112 00 43. 314 S. Redwood Rd. 84104. Secondary address: Box 352 84110. Phone: (801) 886-1550. Fax: (801) 973-7145. E-mail: kmri1550@aol.com. Licensee: KMRI Radio L.L.C. (acq 12-11-97; $500,000). Wood, Maines & Borwn. Format: Christian, rgnl Mexican music. News staff: 2; News: 40 hrs wkly. Target aud: 16-50. ♦ Pat Openshaw, pres; Dennis Ermel, gen mgr; Micah Coleman, opns mgr; Jessica Lockwood, sls dir & chief of engrg; Isaac Velasquez, progmg dir.

KNRS(AM)— Aug 1, 1938: 570 khz; 5 kw-U, DA-2. TL: N40 49 09 W111 55 56. 2801 S. Decker Lake Dr. 84119. Phone: (801) 908-1300. Fax: (801) 908-1459. Web Site: www.knrs.com. Licensee: Citicasters Licenses L.P. Group owner: Clear Channel Communications Inc. (acq 1999; grpsl). Rep: Clear Channel. Format: News/Talk. News staff: one; News: 2 hrs wkly. Target aud: 25-54; adults. ♦ Stu Stanek, gen mgr; Bill Betts, opns mgr; Bill Mathews, sls dir & mgr; Jason Wilmot, progmg dir; Jim Vandiver, sls. Co-owned TV: KTVX(TV)

KODJ(FM)— Dec 1, 1968: 94.1 mhz; 40 kw. Ant 3,060 ft. TL: N40 36 22 W112 09 49. Stereo. 2801 S. Decker Lake Dr. 84119. Phone: (801) 908-1300. Fax: (801) 908-1429. Web Site: www.kodj.com. Licensee: Citicasters Licenses L.P. Group owner: Clear Channel Communications Inc. (acq 5-4-99; grpsl). Rep: Clear Channel, Katz Radio. Format: Hits of the 60s & 70s. News: 2 hrs wkly. Target aud: 25-54; adults. ♦ Stu Stanek, gen mgr; Bill Betts, opns mgr; Deborah Wallace, gen sls mgr; Rob Boshard, progmg dir. Co-owned TV: KUTV(TV) affil

KPQP(FM)—See Ogden

*KRCL(FM)— Dec 3, 1979: 90.9 mhz; 16.5 kw. 3,770 ft. TL: N40 39 35 W112 12 05. Stereo. 1971 W. North Temple 84116-3046. Phone: (801) 363-1818. Fax: (801) 533-9136. E-mail: mailman@krcl.org. Web Site: www.krcl.org. Licensee: Listeners Community Radio of Utah Inc. Format: Div, educ, folk. News staff: one; News: 3 hrs wkly. Target aud: General. Spec prog: Black 20 hrs, Sp 9 hrs, American Indian 4 hrs, Asian 4 hrs, Polynesian one hr, wkly. ♦ Donna Land Maldonado, pres & gen mgr; Kami St. John, dev VP, dev dir & mktg dir; Troy Mumm, opns dir & progmg dir; Doug Young, mus dir; Gena Edualson, pub affrs dir; Felix Gonzalez, engrg mgr; Lewis Downey, chief of engrg.

KRRD(AM)—See Centerville

KRSP-FM— Aug 21, 1968: 103.5 mhz; 25 kw. Ant 3,739 ft. TL: N40 39 34 W112 12 05. Stereo. 55 North 300 West 84180. Phone: (801) 575-5555. Fax: (801) 526-1070. Web Site: www.arrow1035.com. Licensee: Bonneville Holding Co. Group owner: Bonneville International Corp. (acq 12-5-2003; grpsl). Format: Classic rock. Target aud: 18-34. ♦ Chris Redgrave, gen mgr.

KSFI(FM)— Dec 26, 1946: 100.3 mhz; 25 kw. Ant 3,740 ft. TL: N40 39 34 W112 12 05. Stereo. 55 North 300 West 84180. Phone: (801) 575-5555. Fax: (801) 526-1070. Web Site: www.fm100.com. Licensee: Bonneville Holding Co. Group owner: Bonneville International Corp. (acq 12-5-2003; grpsl). Format: Adult contemp. Target aud: 25-54; general. ♦ Chris Redgrave, gen mgr; Paulette Cary, sls dir; Dain Craig, progmg dir; Christa Lee Durrant, mus dir; Peggy Ijams, news dir.

KSL(AM)— May 6, 1922: 1160 khz; 50 kw-U. TL: N40 46 46 W112 05 56. Stereo. Box 1160 84110-1160. Secondary address: Broadcast House, 55 N. 300 W., Salt lake City 84180. Phone: (801) 575-7600. Fax: (801) 575-7625. Web Site: www.ksl.com. Licensee: Bonneville International Corp. (group owner) Network: CBS. Format: News/talk, sports. News staff: 12. Target aud: 25-54. ♦ Bruce Reese, CEO; Richard Mecham, pres & gen mgr; Robert Johnson, CFO; Chris Redgrave, gen mgr & gen sls mgr; Lora Woodbury, natl sls mgr; Paulette Cary, rgnl sls mgr; Rochelle Beatty, prom mgr; Rod Arquette, progmg dir; Janine Baker, pub affrs dir; John Dehnel, chief of engrg. Co-owned TV: KSL-TV affil.

KSOP(AM)—(South Salt Lake). Feb 1, 1955: 1370 khz; 5 kw-D, 500 w-N, DA-N. TL: N40 43 12 W111 55 42. Box 25548 84119. Secondary address: 1285 W. 2320 S. 84119. Phone: (801) 972-1043. Fax: (801) 974-0868. Licensee: KSOP Inc. Format: Classic country. News staff: one. Target aud: 25-54. ♦ Greg Hilton, pres, gen mgr & gen sls mgr; Don Hilton, progmg dir; Debbie Turpin, mus dir; Dick Jacobson, news dir; Bill Traue, chief of engrg.

KSOP-FM— Dec 10, 1964: 104.3 mhz; 25 kw. 3,650 ft. TL: N40 39 35 W112 12 05. Stereo. Web Site: www.ksopcountry.com.

KTKK(AM)—(Sandy). May 13, 1960: 630 khz; 1 kw-D, 500 w-N, DA-2. TL: N40 41 30 W111 55 30. 10348 S. Redwood Rd., South Jordan 84095. Phone: (801) 253-4883. Fax: (801) 253-9085. E-mail: webmaster@k-talk.com. Web Site: www.k-talk.com. Licensee: United Broadcasting Co. (acq 12-1-63). Format: Talk. Target aud: 35 plus. ♦ Richard Perry, pres & gen mgr; Janet Kelly, sls dir, prom dir & sls; Tom Draschil, progmg dir & news dir; Dennis Silver, engrg dir.

*KUER(FM)— June 4, 1960: 90.1 mhz; 38 kw. Ant 2,900 ft. TL: N40 36 30 W112 09 34. Stereo. Univ. of Utah, 101 Wasatch Dr. 84112. Phone: (801) 581-6625. Fax: (801) 581-5426. E-mail: radiowest@kuer.org. Web Site: www.kuer.org. Licensee: University of Utah. Network: Network: NPR, PRI. Format: News, class, jazz. Spec prog: Gospel 3 hrs wkly. ♦ John Greene, gen mgr; Jenny Brundin, news dir.

*KUFR(FM)— Dec 14, 1989: 91.7 mhz; 250 w. -354 ft. TL: N40 48 59 W111 55 19. 136 E. S. Temple, Suite 1630 84111. Phone: (801) 359-3147. Fax: (801) 359-8112. Web Site: www.familyradio.com. Licensee: Family Stations Inc. (group owner) Format: Christian relg. ♦ Harold Camping, pres & gen mgr; Roger Crawford, stn mgr & chief of engrg; James Abrahamson, opns mgr; Thad McKinney, rgnl sls mgr.

KWDZ(AM)— 1945: 910 khz; 5 kw-D, 1 kw-N, DA-2. TL: N40 30 48 W112 00 23. Stereo. 2801 S. Decker Lake Dr., Suite 100 84119. Phone: (801) 908-5152. Fax: (801) 908-7844. Web Site: www.radiodisney.com. Licensee: Radio Disney Group LLC. Group owner: ABC Inc. (acq 4-30-03; $3.7 million). Network: Radio Disney. Format: Children. ♦ Celia Willette, gen mgr; Meradyth Moore, mktg dir & prom dir; Barry McClellen, chief of engrg.

KXRV(FM)—See Centerville

KZHT(FM)— Feb 1, 1961: 97.1 mhz; 25 kw. Ant 3,739 ft. TL: N40 39 34 W112 12 05. Stereo. 2801 S. Decker Lake Dr. 84119. Phone: (801) 908-1300. Fax: (801) 908-1389. Web Site: www.971zht.com. Licensee: Clear Channel Broadcasting Licenses Inc. Group owner: Clear Channel Communications Inc. (acq 7-10-00). Rep: Katz Radio. Format: CHR. Target aud: 18-49. ♦ Bill Betts, gen mgr & opns mgr; Bill Mathews, sls dir; Emily Hunt, gen sls mgr; Stacy Sappenfield, prom dir; Jeff McCartney, progmg dir.

KZNS(AM)— February 1945: 1280 khz; 5 kw-D, 500 w-N, DA-N. TL: N40 44 47 W111 54 42. 515 S. 700 East, Suite 1C 84102. Phone: (801) 524-2600. Fax: (801) 521-9234. Web Site: www.1280kzn.com. Licensee: Simmons-SLC, LS LLC. Group owner: Simmons Media Group (acq 4-4-2001; grpsl). Network: Network: Westwood One, CNN Radio. Rep: CBS Radio. Format: Sports talk. Target aud: 35 plus; retired, affluent, responsible & loyal. ♦ David Simmons, chmn; G. Craig Hanson, pres; Stephen C. Johnson, gen mgr; Amanda Traeger, sls dir & gen sls mgr; Eric Ray, news dir; Scott Matthews, chief of engrg.

Sandy

KBJA(AM)—Licensed to Sandy. See Salt Lake City

KTKK(AM)—Licensed to Sandy. See Salt Lake City

Smithfield

KGNT(FM)— February 1983: 103.9 mhz; 3 kw. Ant -131 ft. TL: N41 48 44 W111 47 31. 810 W. 200 N., Logan 84321. Phone: (435) 752-1390. Fax: (435) 752-1392. Web Site: www.thegiant.com. Licensee: Frandsen Media Co. LLC. Group owner: Sun Valley Radio Inc. (acq 2-4-02; $775,000). Network: Network: CBS, Westwood One. Dan J. Alpert. Format: Oldies. Target aud: 18-49; 55% female, 45% male middle class. ♦ Jay Eubanks, stn mgr; Lori Gill, gen sls mgr; David Denton, progmg dir & news dir; Paul Anderson, chief of engrg.

South Jordan

KUUU(FM)— Sept 1, 1979: 92.5 mhz; 500 w. Ant 3,929 ft. TL: N40 39 35.2 W112 12 04.7. Stereo. 2835 E. 3300 S., Salt Lake City 84109. Phone: (801) 412-6040. Fax: (801) 412-6041. Licensee: Millcreek Broadcasting L.L.C. (group owner; (acq 4-17-2001; grpsl). Rep: Allied Radio Partners. Format: Hip hop, rhythm and blues. News staff: one; News: 15 hrs wkly. Target aud: General. ♦ Randy Rodgers, gen mgr; Brian Michel, opns mgr; Lutisha Merrill, gen sls mgr; Scott St. John, prom mgr; Kevin Cruise, mus dir; Kevin Terry, engrg VP.

South Salt Lake

KDYL(AM)—Licensed to South Salt Lake. See Salt Lake City

KSOP(AM)—Licensed to South Salt Lake. See Salt Lake City

Utah

Spanish Fork

KHQN(AM)— July 24, 1960: 1480 khz; 1 kw-D. TL: N40 04 30 W111 39 42. 8628 S. State St. 84660. Phone: (801) 798-3559. Licensee: Sace Broadcasting Corp. Network: UPI. Format: New age, progsv, relg. Spec prog: Farm 4 hrs wkly. ◆Chris Warden, pres; Christine Warden, gen mgr.

KOSY-FM— Nov 1, 1967: 106.5 mhz; 25 kw. Ant 3,739 ft. TL: N40 39 34 W112 12 05. 2801 S. Decker Lake Dr., Salt Lake City 84119. Phone: (801) 908-1300. Fax: (801) 908-1459. Web Site: www.kosy.com. Licensee: Citicasters Licenses L.P. Group owner: Clear Channel Communications Inc. (acq 2-27-2004); $22 million. with KXRV(FM) Centerville). Rep: Clear Channel, Katz Radio. Format: Soft adult contemp. Target aud: 25-44; women. ◆Stu Stanek, gen mgr; Bill Betts, opns mgr; Bill Matthews, sls dir; Jim Vandiver, gen sls mgr; Steve Clem, progmg dir.

Taylorsville

KUTR(AM)—Not on air, target date: unknown: 820 khz; 50 kw-D, 2.5 kw-N, 10 kw-CH, DA-3. TL: N40 19 46 W112 04 11. 55 North 300 West, Salt Lake City 84180. Phone: (801) 575-5555. Fax: (801) 526-1070. Licensee: Bonneville Holding Co. Group owner: Bonneville International Corp. (acq 12-5-2003; grpsl). ◆Chris Redgrave, gen mgr.

Tooele

KCPW(AM)— July 3, 1956: 1010 khz; 50 kw-D, 13 w-N. TL: N40 32 36 W112 18 33. Box 510730, Salt Lake City 84151-0730. Phone: (801) 359-5279. Fax: (801) 746-2708. Web Site: www.kiqn1010.com. Licensee: Community Wireless of Park City Inc. (acq 10-1-2003). Network: Network: NPR, PRI. Rep: Katz Radio. Format: News/talk info. ◆Blair Feulner, gen mgr.

Tremonton

KNFL(AM)— 2002: . Stn currently dark 1470 khz; 10 kw-D, 1 kw-N, DA-2. TL: N41 34 28 W112 05 57. AM Radio 1470, Inc., St. George 84771. Phone: (435) 628-1000. Licensee: AM Radio 1470 Inc. Group owner: Diamond Broadcasting Corp. (acq 12-6-2004; grpsl). Dan J. Alpert. ◆E. Morgan Skinner Jr., CEO.

KYLZ(FM)— July 1, 1983: 104.9 mhz; 99 kw. 1,059 ft. TL: N41 43 34 W112 12 33. Stereo. Box 3369, Logan 84321. Phone: (435) 752-1390. Fax: (435) 752-1392. Licensee: 3 Point Media - Utah LLC. (acq 11-28-2001; $1.73 million). Network: Network: CBS, Jones Radio Networks. Dan J. Alpert. Format: Classic country. News staff: 3. Target aud: 25-54; 60% female, 40% male middle to upper class. ◆Kent Frandsen, pres; Jay Eubanks, gen mgr & stn mgr; Lori Gill, gen sls mgr; David Denton, progmg dir & news dir; Paul Anderson, chief of engrg.

Vernal

KLCY-FM—Listing follows KVEL(AM).

KVEL(AM)— Jan 19, 1947: 920 khz; 4.5 kw-D, 1 kw-N, DA-N. TL: N40 29 30 W109 31 45. Box 307, 2425 N. Vernal Ave. 84078. Phone: (435) 789-0920. Phone: (435) 789-1059. Fax: (435) 789-6977. E-mail: kvel@ubtanet.com. Licensee: Ashley Communications Inc. (acq 8-11-98; $10,000 for stock with co-located FM). Network: ABC Information & Entertainment. Reddy, Begley & McCormick. Format: Sports, news/talk. News staff: one; News: 20 hrs wkly. Target aud: 35-64; affluent, upscale. Spec prog: Farm 2 hrs, relg, Sp, pub affrs one hr wkly. ◆Steve Evans, gen mgr & gen sls mgr; Clay Johnson, progmg dir; Steve Sprouse, chief of engrg.

KLCY-FM—Co-owned with KVEL(AM). May 1, 1975: 105.9 mhz; 2.9 kw. Ant 413 ft. TL: N40 24 50 W109 35 34. (CP: 105.5 mhz; 3.3 kw, ant 1,699 ft. TL: N40 32 16 W109 41 57). Network: Network: ABC, Jones Radio Networks. Format: Eagle country. News: 2 hrs wkly. Target aud: 18-54; active.

Washington

KUNF(AM)—Licensed to Washington. See Saint George

West Jordan

KLLB(AM)— 1982: 1510 khz; 10 kw-D. TL: N40 33 06 W111 58 17. 868 E. 5900 South, Salt Lake City 84107. Phone: (801) 487-0247. Fax: (801) 262-6200. Licensee: United Security Financial Inc. (acq 6-18-91; $180,001; 7-8-91). Format: Gospel. ◆Lois Johnson, gen mgr; Joel Cosby, sls dir; D.J. Stone, progmg dir; Darrell Cosby, chief of engrg.

West Valley City

KMRI(AM)—Licensed to West Valley City. See Salt Lake City

Vermont

Addison

WUSX(FM)— 1999: 93.7 mhz; 21 kw. Ant 354 ft. TL: N44 13 15 W73 24 37. 372 Dorset St., South Burlington 05403. Phone: (802) 863-1010. Fax: (802) 860-4721. Licensee: Addison Broadcasting Co. Inc. Group owner: Northeast Broadcasting Company Inc. (acq 12-19-2000; $434,000). Format: Classic country. ◆Rich Delancy, gen mgr.

Barre

***WCMD-FM**— Aug 1, 1998: 89.9 mhz; 940 w. 590 ft. TL: N44 07 32 W72 28 36. Stereo. 134 Main St., Essex Junction 05452. Secondary address: Box 8310, Essex 05451-8310. Phone: (802) 878-8885. Fax: (802) 879-6835. E-mail: cmi.radio@verizon.net. Web Site: cmiradio.com. Licensee: Christian Ministries Inc. Network: Moody. Joseph E. Dunne III. Format: Inspirational. News: 15 hrs wkly. Target aud: General; Christian, middle income. ◆Mark Kinsley, pres; Richard McClary, gen mgr; Karlo Salminen, opns dir; Peter Morton, chief of engrg.

WORK(FM)—Listing follows WSNO(AM).

WSKI(AM)—See Montpelier

WSNO(AM)— Oct 13, 1959: 1450 khz; 1 kw-U. TL: N44 11 40 W72 30 52. 41 Jacques St. 05641. Phone: (802) 476-4168. Fax: (802) 479-5893. Web Site: www.wsno1450.net. Licensee: Nassau Broadcasting III L.L.C. Group owner: Nassau Broadcasting Partners L.P. (acq 8-2-2004; grpsl). Network: CBS. Format: News/talk, sports. ◆Ken Barlow, gen mgr; Jim Severance, progmg dir.

WORK(FM)—Co-owned with WSNO(AM). Aug 5, 1974: 107.1 mhz; 1.5 kw. 410 ft. TL: N44 09 30 W72 28 46. Web Site: www.1071workfm.com. Format: Hot adult contemp. ◆T.J. Michaels, progmg dir.

Bellows Falls

WZLF(FM)— November 1981: 107.1 mhz; 1 kw. 530 ft. TL: N43 12 33 W72 19 58. Stereo. Box 1230, Claremont, NH 03743. Phone: (603) 542-7735. Fax: (603) 542-8721. Web Site: www.bobcountrysm.com. Licensee: Nassau Broadcasting III L.L.C. Group owner: Nassau Broadcasting Partners L.P. (acq 8-2-2004; grpsl). Rep: Roslin. Format: Country. News staff: one; News: 5 hrs wkly. Target aud: 25-54; general. Spec prog: Farm one hr wkly. ◆Courtney Galluzzo, gen mgr, gen sls mgr & rgnl sls mgr; Doug Daniels, opns mgr; Heath Cole, progmg dir & news dir; Neil Langer, chief of engrg.

Bennington

WBTN(AM)— Sept 23, 1953: 1370 khz; 1 kw-D. TL: N42 54 19 W73 12 32. WBTN Svc., 982 Mansion Dr. 05201. Secondary address: 407 Harwood Hill 05201. Phone: (802) 442-6321. Fax: (802) 442-3112. E-mail: wbtn@svc.edu. Licensee: Southern Vermont College (acq 8-20-03). Network: Westwood One. Format: News/talk, music; student progmg. Target aud: 24-54. ◆Barbara Sirvis, pres; Barbara Snyder, gen mgr.

WBTN-FM— Nov 4, 1978: 94.3 mhz; 3 kw. 110 ft. TL: N42 56 52 W73 10 36. Stereo. 20 Troy Ave., Colchester 05446. Phone: (802) 655-9451. Fax: (802) 655-2799. E-mail: contact@vpr.net. Web Site: www.vpr.net. Licensee: Vermont Public Radio. (acq 11-24-99; $901,000 with co-located AM). Format: Classical. News staff: one; News: 4 hrs wkly. Target aud: 18-45. ◆Mark Vogelzang, gen mgr & stn mgr; Kevin O'Malley, opns dir, mktg dir & mus dir; Robert Harrington, sls dir; Bob Harrington, adv dir.

Directory of Radio

Berlin

WWFY(FM)— Apr 2, 1975: 100.9 mhz; 5.2 kw. Ant 718 ft. TL: N44 07 38 W72 28 48. Stereo. 41 Jacques St., Barre 05641. Phone: (802) 476-4168. Fax: (802) 479-5893. Web Site: www.froggy1009.com. Licensee: Nassau Broadcasting III L.L.C. Group owner: Nassau Broadcasting Partners L.P. (acq 8-2-2004); grpsl). Gardner, Carton & Douglas. Format: Country. Target aud: 18-49; young professionals. ◆Jim Severance, gen mgr; Ken Barlow, sls VP.

Bolton

***WGLY-FM**— 1996: 91.5 mhz; 1 kw. Ant 935 ft. TL: N44 21 53 W72 55 52. Stereo. 134 B Main St., Essex Junction 05452. Secondary address: Box 8310, Essex 05451-8310. Phone: (802) 878-8885. Fax: (802) 879-6835. E-mail: cmi@radio@verizon.net. Web Site: cmiradio.com. Licensee: Christian Ministries Inc. Network: Moody. Joseph E. Dunne III. Format: Inspirational. ◆Mark Kinsley, pres; Richard McClary, gen mgr; Karlo Salminen, opns dir & dev mgr; Peter Morton, chief of engrg.

Brandon

WEXP(FM)— May 2000: 101.5 mhz; 350 w. Ant 1,305 ft. TL: N43 39 31 W73 06 26. Stereo. 1 Scale Ave., Suite 84, Rutland 05761-4459. Phone: (802) 773-9264. Fax: (802) 747-0553. Web Site: www.101thefox.com. Licensee: Nassau Broadcasting III L.L.C. Group owner: Vox Radio Group L.P. (acq 1-21-2005; $2.5 million. with WVAY(FM) Wilmington). Network: Westwood One. Format: Rock/AOR, classic rock. Target aud: 25-54; male. ◆John Gales, gen mgr; Glenn Novak, gen sls mgr; Kemy Chambers, prom dir; Kelly Kowalski, progmg dir.

Brattleboro

WINQ(FM)—See Winchester, NH

WKVT(AM)— Nov 29, 1959: 1490 khz; 1 kw-U. TL: N42 50 51 W72 34 56. 458 Williams St. 05301. Phone: (802) 254-2343. Fax: (802) 254-6683. Web Site: www.wkvt.com. Licensee: Saga Communications of New England LLC. Group owner: Saga Communications Inc. (acq 5-1-02; grpsl). Network: CBS. Format: News/talk. News staff: one; News: 30 hrs wkly. Target aud: 35-64; news & info oriented adults. ◆Mike Trombly, gen mgr; Peter Case, progmg dir & news dir.

WKVT-FM— 1980: 92.7 mhz; 6 kw. 610 ft. TL: N42 53 45 W72 39 49. Stereo. Network: AP Radio. Format: Classic rock. News staff: one; News: 8 hrs wkly. Target aud: 18-44.

WTSA(AM)— Apr 19, 1950: 1450 khz; 1 kw-U. TL: N42 52 13 W72 33 35. Box 819 05302. Secondary address: 827 Western Ave. 05301. Phone: (802) 254-4577. Fax: (802) 257-4644. E-mail: info@wtsa.net. Web Site: www.wtsa.net. Licensee: Tri-State Broadcasters Inc. (acq 7-1-86; grpsl; 5-26-86). Rep: D & R Radio. Cohn & Marks. Format: Sports. News staff: one. Target aud: General. ◆John Kilduff, pres & opns dir; Tim Johnson, news dir & chief of engrg.

WTSA-FM— Dec 15, 1975: 96.7 mhz; 5.2 kw. Ant 167 ft. TL: N42 53 21 W72 36 47. Stereo. Web Site: www.wtsa.net. Licensee: Tri-State Broadcasters Inc. Format: Adult contemp. Target aud: 12 plus. Spec prog: Oldies 16 hrs wkly.

WYRY(FM)—See Keene, NH

Burlington

WEZF(FM)— July 19, 1968: 92.9 mhz; 46 kw. 2,703 ft. TL: N44 31 40 W72 48 58. Stereo. 265 Hegeman Ave., Colchester 05446. Secondary address: Box 1093 05402-1093. Phone: (802) 655-0093. Fax: (802) 655-0478. Web Site: www.star929.com. Licensee: Capstar TX L.P. Group owner: Clear Channel Communications Inc. (acq 8-30-00; grpsl). Rep: Clear Channel, Wiley, Rein & Fielding. Format: Adult contemp. News staff: one; News: 7 hrs wkly. Target aud: 25-54. ◆Karen Marshall, gen mgr; Gale Parmalee, opns mgr.

WIZN(FM)—(Vergennes). Nov 15, 1983: 106.7 mhz; 50 kw. 373 ft. TL: N44 18 40 W73 14 34. Stereo. Box 1067 05402. Phone: (802) 860-2440. Fax: (802) 860-1818. E-mail: wizn@wizn.com. Web Site: www.wizn.com. Licensee: Burlington Broadcasters Inc. Group owner: Deer River Broadcasting Group (acq 8-85; $64,000; 8-26-85). Format: Rock/AOR, live. Target aud: 18-49. Spec prog: Oldies 3 hrs, reggae one hr, progsv one hr, blues 3 hrs wkly. ◆Arthur J. La Vigne, pres; Jennifer McCann, gen mgr; Mike Luoma, progmg dir & mus dir.

Stations in the U.S. — Vermont

Developers & Brokers of Radio Properties

contact American Media Services at our suite: Philadelphia Marriott Downtown 215-625-2900
843-972-2200
americanmediaservices.com
Charleston, SC
Dallas, TX · Chicago, Il · Austin, TX

American Media Services, LLC

WJOY(AM)— Sept 14, 1946: 1230 khz; 1 kw-U. TL: N44 27 03 W73 11 51. Box 4489 05406-4489. Secondary address: 70 Joy Dr. 05403. Phone: (802) 658-1230. Fax: (802) 862-0786. E-mail: wjoy@hallradio.com. Web Site: www.wjoy.com. Licensee: Hall Communications Inc. (group owner; acq 12-1-83; 12-5-83). Network: Westwood One. Rep: D & R Radio. Fletcher, Heald & Hildreth. Format: News, MOR. News staff: one; News: 4 hrs wkly. Target aud: General; affluent, empty nesters, well educated. ◆ Bonnie Rowbotham, chmn; Arthur J. Rowbotham, pres; Richard P. Reed, exec VP; Bill Baldwin, sr VP; Dan Dubonnet, gen mgr; Steve Pelkey, opns dir & progmg dir; Lee Bodette, gen sls mgr; Wendy Naylor, prom dir; Ginny McGehee, news dir & pub affrs dir; Dennis Snyder, chief of engrg.

WOKO(FM)—Co-owned with WJOY(AM). June 26, 1962: 98.9 mhz; 100 kw. 307 ft. TL: N44 27 03 W73 11 51. Stereo. Web Site: www.woko.com. Format: Country. ◆ Dan Dubonnet, VP; Margot St. John, mus dir.

*WRUV(FM)— Oct 3, 1965: 90.1 mhz; 460 w. 145 ft. TL: N44 28 37 W73 11 59. (CP: Ant 131 ft.). Stereo. Univ. of Vermont, Billings Student Ctr. 05405. Phone: (802) 656-4399. Phone: (802) 656-0796. Fax: (802) 656-2281. E-mail: wruv@zoo.uvm.edu. Web Site: www.wruv.org. Licensee: University of Vermont & State Agricultural College. Format: Div, educ, jazz. Spec prog: Non-commercial free format, progmg varies. ◆ Jake Davignon, stn mgr.

WTWK(AM)—See Plattsburgh, NY

WVAA(AM)— Apr 19, 1954: 1390 khz; 5 kw-U, DA-N. TL: N44 29 47 W73 12 49. Stereo. 372 Dorset Str., South Burlington 05403. Phone: (802) 655-6753. Phone: (802) 655-6754. Fax: (802) 860-4721. E-mail: wvaa@radiovermont.com. Licensee: Radio Vermont, KDR L.L.C. Group owner: Radio Vermont Group Inc. (acq 5-17-99; $428,000). Network: AP Radio. Rep: McGavren Guild. Format: Talk. Target aud: 25-54; affluent, upscale baby boomer generation. Spec prog: Sports 10 hrs wkly. ◆ Bob Rowe, pres & stn mgr.

WVMT(AM)— May 20, 1922: 620 khz; 5 kw-U, DA-N. TL: N44 29 47 W73 12 49. Box 620, 118 Malletts Bay Ave, Colchester 05446. Phone: (802) 655-1620. Fax: (802) 655-1329. E-mail: paulg@95triplex.com. Web Site: www.am620wvmt.com. Licensee: Sison Broadcasting Inc. (acq 3-3-97; $2,939,014 with WXXX(FM) South Burlington). Network: CBS, ABC Daytime Direction. Rep: McGavren Guild. Format: News/talk & sports. News staff: 2; News: 14 hrs wkly. Target aud: 35-65. ◆ Paul S. Goldman, pres & gen mgr; Mark Esbjerg, opns mgr; Charlie Papillo, prom mgr; Mark Ebjerg, progmg dir; Ernie Farrar, news dir.

*WVPS(FM)— Oct 15, 1980: 107.9 mhz; 50 kw. 2,640 ft. TL: N44 31 32 W72 48 54. Stereo. 365 Troy Ave., Colchester 05446. Phone: (802) 655-9451. Fax: (802) 655-2799. Fax: (802) 655-9117. E-mail: contract@vpr.net. Web Site: www.vpr.net. Licensee: Vermont Public Radio. Network: Network: NPR, PRI. Haley, Bader & Potts. Format: Class, jazz, news. News staff: 9; News: 43 hrs wkly. Target aud: General. Spec prog: Switchboard call-in progmg 3 hrs, opera 5 hrs, folk 4 hrs, children .5 hrs wkly. ◆ Mark Vogelzang, CEO, pres & gen mgr; Cindy Shuman, CFO & VP; Victoria St. John, opns dir; Robin Turnau, dev dir; Tammy West, gen sls mgr; Jody Evans, progmg dir; Walter Parker, mus dir; John Van Hoesen, news dir; Richard Parker, chief of engrg.

Castleton

*WIUV(FM)— Oct 1, 1976: 91.3 mhz; 227 w. -235 ft. TL: N43 36 29 W73 10 54. Castleton State College, 86 Seminary St. 05735. Phone: (802) 468-5611. Phone: (802) 468-1264. Fax: (802) 468-5237. Web Site: www.castleton.edu. Licensee: Board of Trustees. Format: Progsv, variety. Target aud: General; smart people. Spec prog: Jazz 10 hrs, reggae 6 hrs, rap-urban 5 hrs, folk 4 hrs, Sp one hr wkly. ◆ Robert Gershon, gen mgr.

Colchester

*WWPV-FM— Aug 10, 1973: 88.7 mhz; 100 w. 82 ft. TL: N44 29 38 W73 09 51. St. Michaels College, Box 274, Winooski Park 05439.

Phone: (802) 654-2334. Fax: (802) 654-2336. E-mail: wwpv@smcvt.edu. Web Site: personalweb.smcvt.edu/wwpv. Licensee: Board of Trustees, St. Michaels College. Format: Free-form. Target aud: 14-65; varies by time of day & progmg. ◆ Mike McCarthy, stn mgr; Jon Van Luling, progmg dir.

Danville

WDOT(FM)— 1996: 95.7 mhz; 3.8 kw. Ant 246 ft. TL: N44 24 58 W72 03 32. Box 374, St. Johnsbury 05819. Phone: (802) 748-4055. Phone: (877) 367-6468. Fax: (802) 223-1520. Web Site: www.pointfm.com. Licensee: Montpelier Broadcasting Inc. Group owner: Northeast Broadcasting Company Inc. (acq 1996; $152,500 for CP). Format: AAA. ◆ Kim Buckminster, gen mgr.

Derby Center

WMOO(FM)— Apr 1, 1991: 92.1 mhz; 2.25 kw. 619 ft. TL: N44 58 23 W72 04 30. Stereo. Box 92, Derby/Newport Rd. 05829. Phone: (802) 766-9236. Fax: (802) 766-8067. Web Site: www.northstarhits.com. Licensee: Nassau Broadcasting III L.L.C. (acq 12-22-2004; $2.35 million. with WIKE(AM) Newport). Network: ABC Information & Entertainment. Shaw Pittman. Format: Hot adult contemp. News staff: one; News: 16 hrs wkly. Target aud: General. Spec prog: Community events 8 hrs wkly. ◆ Dawn Prudhomme, opns mgr & adv dir; Ken Wells, gen sls mgr; Dan Macek, mktg dir & mus dir; Bill Maxwell, prom dir; Steve Savage, progmg dir; Nic Macek, asst music dir; Tod Pronto, news dir & pub affrs dir; William J. Macek, gen mgr & chief of engrg.

Hartford

WWOD(FM)— Mar 15, 1992: 104.3 mhz; 5.6 kw. Ant 495 ft. TL: N43 39 15 W72 21 32. Stereo. 106 N. Main St., West Lebanon, NH 03784. Phone: (603) 298-2953. Phone: (603) 542-7735. Fax: (603) 298-7554. E-mail: info@bestoldies104.com. Web Site: www.bestoldies104.com. Licensee: Family Broadcasting Inc. Group owner: Nassau Broadcasting Partners L.P. (acq 8-2-2004; grpsl). Network: USA. May & Dunne. Format: Oldies. News staff: one. Target aud: 25 plus. Spec prog: Children 3 hrs, country gospel 2 hrs wkly. ◆ Courtney Galluzzo, pres; Neil Langer, natl sls mgr; Heath Cole, progmg dir.

Johnson

*WJSC-FM— July 16, 1972: 90.7 mhz; 200 w. Ant -489 ft. TL: N44 38 29 W72 40 20. Stereo. Box 75, c/o Johnson State College. 05656. Phone: (802) 635-1355. Phone: (802) 635-1434. Fax: (802) 635-1202. E-mail: wjsc907@hotmail.com. Web Site: www.wjsc.findhere.org. Licensee: Board of Trustees, Vermont State College. Format: Alternative, div. Spec prog: Class 3 hrs, C&W 3 hrs wkly. ◆ Andrew Frappier, gen mgr.

Killington

WEBK(FM)— Aug 4, 1993: 105.3 mhz; 50 kw. 2,240 ft. TL: N43 38 22 W72 50 12. Stereo. Box 30, Rutland 05702. Phone: (802) 775-7500. Fax: (802) 775-7555. E-mail: webk@catamountradio.com. Licensee: 6 Johnson Road Licenses Inc. Group owner: Pamal Broadcasting Ltd. (acq 10-19-2001; grpsl). Verner, Liipfert, Bernhard, McPherson & Hand. Format: AAA. News: one hr wkly. Target aud: 24-48; baby boomers. ◆ Harry Weinhagen, gen mgr; Paul Hatin, sls dir & gen sls mgr; Sheila Bigelow, mktg dir & mktg mgr; Spider Glen, progmg VP & progmg dir; Peter Morton, chief of engrg.

Lyndon

WGMT(FM)— May 19, 1990: 97.7 mhz; 600 w. 1,883 ft. TL: N44 34 15 W71 53 40. Stereo. Box 97, 10 Church St., Lyndonville 05851. Phone: (802) 626-9800. Phone: (802) 626-0977. Fax: (802) 626-8500. E-mail: wgmt@kingcon.com. Web Site: www.kingcon.com. Licensee: Vermont Broadcast Associates Inc. Rep: Roslin. Bryan Cave. Format: Adult contemp. News staff: 2; News: 5 hrs wkly. Target aud: 22-54; families, more female, disposable income, mobile. ◆ Bruce James, pres & gen mgr; Steve Nichols, gen sls mgr; Lynn Beaudoin, natl sls mgr & rgnl sls mgr; Jan Clausing, prom mgr; Mike Barrett, progmg dir; Todd Wellington, news dir; Judy Masure, pub affrs dir; Don Smith, chief of engrg.

Lyndonville

*WWLR(FM)— Feb 4, 1977: 91.5 mhz; 3 kw. -75 ft. TL: N44 32 04 W72 01 36. Stereo. Box F, Lyndon State College 05851. Phone: (802) 626-6214. Fax: (802) 626-4806. E-mail: impulse915@hotmail.com. Web Site: www.lsc.vsc.edu. Licensee: Board of Trustees, Vermont State Colleges. Format: Rock/AOR. Target aud: Everyone. Spec prog: Class 2 hrs, jazz 3 hrs wkly. ◆ P.J. Cioffi, gen mgr; Jim Champine, opns dir.

Manchester

WEQX(FM)— November 1984: 102.7 mhz; 1.25 kw. 2,490 ft. TL: N43 09 58 W73 06 59. Stereo. Box 1027 05254. Secondary address: 161 Elm St., Manchester Center 05255. Phone: (802) 362-4800. Phone: (802) 362-4875. Fax: (802) 362-5555. Fax: (802) 362-4885. E-mail: eqx@weqx.com. Web Site: www.weqx.com. Licensee: Northshire Communications Inc. Format: Alternative. News: 5 hrs wkly. Target aud: 25-44. Spec prog: Jazz 4 hrs, AAA 4 hrs, locl 2 hrs, new music 3 hrs wkly. ◆ A. Brooks Brown, pres, gen mgr, adv mgr & chief of engrg; Melinda Brown, VP & opns mgr; Tim Bronson, progmg dir; Pete O'Callaghan, mus dir & news dir; Nikki Alexander, news dir.

Marlboro

WRSY(FM)— July 1996: 101.5 mhz; 120 w. Ant 745 ft. TL: N42 50 46 W72 41 16. Box 1230, Claremont, NH 03743. Secondary address: 100 Main St., Northampton, MA 01060. Phone: (603) 542-7735. Phone: (413) 585-9555. Fax: (603) 542-8721. Fax: (413) 585-8501. E-mail: dj@wrsi.com. Web Site: www.wrsi.com. Licensee: Saga Communications of New England LLC. Group owner: Saga Communications Inc. (acq 2-13-2004; grpsl). Format: AAA. Target aud: 35 plus; women. ◆ Ted Bilodeau, gen mgr & opns dir; Sean O'Mealy, news dir; Bob Shotwell, chief of engrg.

Middlebury

WFAD(AM)— Dec 24, 1965: 1490 khz; 1 kw-U. TL: N43 59 57 W73 09 35. Box 500, 74 Exchange St. 05753. Phone: (802) 388-9000. Fax: (802) 388-3000. Web Site: www.wfad.com. Licensee: Addison Broadcasting Co. Inc. Group owner: Northeast Broadcasting Company Inc. (acq 6-22-01). Network: ABC. Mullin, Rhyne, Emmons & Topel. Format: Full svc, oldies. News: 15 hrs wkly. Target aud: 35 plus; people looking for loc information. Spec prog: Farm one hr, sports 10 hrs, big band 21 hrs, talk of Vermont 10 hrs wkly. ◆ Bob Rowe, gen mgr; David John, sls dir; Gerry Germain, news dir; Jon Hosford, chief of engrg.

*WRMC-FM— May 1949: 91.1 mhz; 2.9 kw. Ant -30 ft. TL: N44 00 25 W73 10 40. Stereo. Middlebury College 05753. Phone: (802) 443-2471. Phone: (802) 443-6324. Fax: (802) 443-5108. E-mail: wrmc@wrmc.middlebury.edu. Web Site: www.wrmc.middlebury.edu. Licensee: President and Fellows of Middlebury College. Format: Div, progsv. News: 8 hrs wkly. Target aud: General. Spec prog: Urban contemp 12 hrs, class 15 hrs, folk 15 hrs, relg one hr, blues 10 hrs, jazz 10 hrs, Sp one hr wkly. ◆ Ryan Abernnathey, gen mgr.

Montpelier

WNCS(FM)— June 13, 1977: 104.7 mhz; 1.9 kw. 2,093 ft. TL: N44 18 14 W72 37 18. Stereo. 169 River St. 05602-3724. Phone: (802) 223-2396. Fax: (802) 223-1520. Web Site: www.pointfm.com. Licensee: Montpelier Broadcasting Co. Inc. Group owner: Northeast Broadcasting Company Inc. (acq 2-12-87). Format: AAA. Target aud: 25-40; above-average income & educated, baby boomers. Spec prog: Folk 4 hrs, jazz 5 hrs wkly. ◆ Steven Silberberg, pres; Ed Flanagan, gen mgr; Tanya Stepasiuk, prom dir; Mark Miller, progmg dir; Jon Hosford, chief of engrg.

WORK(FM)—See Barre

WSKI(AM)— Dec 7, 1947: 1240 khz; 1 kw-U. TL: N44 14 40 W72 32 47. Stereo. 169 River St. 05602. Phone: (802) 223-5275. Fax: (802) 223-1520. Licensee: Galloway Communications Inc. Group owner: Northeast Broadcasting Company Inc. (acq 5-2-00; grpsl). Format:

Vermont   **Directory of Radio**

Oldies. Target aud: 35-64; 60% female, 40% male. ♦ Ed Flanagan, gen mgr & sls dir; Tom McCloud, progmg mgr; Jon Hosford, chief of engrg.

WSNO(AM)—See Barre

Morrisville

WLVB(FM)— August 1993: 93.9 mhz; 5.4 kw. 121 ft. TL: N44 34 24 W72 38 11. Box 94 05661. Phone: (802) 888-4294. Fax: (802) 888-8523. E-mail: wlvb@radiovermont.com. Web Site: www.wlvbradio.com. Licensee: Radio Vermont Inc. Group owner: Radio Vermont Group Inc. Format: Country. ♦ Ken Squier, pres; Eric Michaels, gen mgr; Craig Ladd, opns mgr; Mark Struhsacker, rgnl sls mgr; Roland Lajoie, progmg dir & pub affrs dir; Rich Haskell, news dir; Tom Laffan, chief of engrg.

Newport

WIKE(AM)— Oct 12, 1952: 1490 khz; 1 kw-U. TL: N44 56 28 W72 13 35. Stereo. Box 1490 05855. Secondary address: Derby Newport Rd., Derby 05829. Phone: (802) 766-9236. Fax: (802) 766-8067. Web Site: www.northstarhits.com. Licensee: Nassau Broadcasting III L.L.C. (acq 12-22-2004; $2.35 million. with WMOO(FM) Derby Center). Covington & Burling. Format: Country. News staff: one; News: 4 hrs wkly. Target aud: 18 plus. Spec prog: Loc info/entertainment 5 hrs wkly. ♦ William J. Macek, gen mgr; Dawn Prudhomme, opns mgr.

Northfield

*WNUB-FM— Dec 8, 1967: 88.3 mhz; 285 w. -387 ft. TL: N44 08 32 W72 39 31. Stereo. 158 Harmon Dr., Comm. Ctr., Norwich Univ. 05663. Phone: (802) 485-2483. Fax: (802) 485-2565. E-mail: wnub@norwich.edu. Web Site: www.norwich.edu. Licensee: The Trustees of Norwich University. Format: Rock/AOR, Triple A, Modern. Target aud: 15-40. ♦ Doug Smith, gen mgr.

Norwich

*WNCH(FM)— 2004: 88.1 mhz; 110 w horiz, 1.7 kw vert. Ant 2,211 ft. TL: N43 26 15 W72 27 08. Vermont Public Radio, 365 Troy Ave., Colchester 05446. Phone: (802) 655-9451. Fax: (802) 655-2799. Web Site: www.vpr.net. Licensee: Vermont Public Radio. Format: Cultural music svc. ♦ Mark Vogelzang, pres & gen mgr.

Plainfield

*WGDR(FM)— May 11, 1973: 91.1 mhz; 800 w. -350 ft. TL: N44 17 04 W72 26 28. Stereo. Box 336, Goddard College 05667. Phone: (802) 454-7762. Phone: (802) 454-9962. E-mail: wgdr@goddard.edu. Web Site: www.wgdr.org. Licensee: Goddard College Corp. Format: Div. Target aud: Multiple. Spec prog: Folk 10 hrs, Black 8 hrs, jazz 6 hrs, class 3 hrs, farm one hr, American Indian one hr wkly. ♦ Amanda Gustafson, gen mgr.

Poultney

WVNR(AM)— Aug 1, 1981: 1340 khz; 1 kw-U. TL: N43 30 16 W73 12 11. Box 568, East Poultney 05741. Secondary address: 1214 Rt. 30 S. 05764. Phone: (802) 287-9030. E-mail: wvnrwnyv@yahoo.com. Licensee: Pine Tree Broadcasting Co. (acq 4-86). Format: Adult contemp, country, oldies. News staff: one; News: 3 hrs wkly. Target aud: 25-54; active, community oriented, working and professional, and families. Spec prog: Big band 3 hrs, loc sports 6 hrs, swap shop one hr, Polish one hr, gospel one hr wkly. ♦ Michael J. Leech, pres; Judith E. Leech, exec VP & gen mgr.

Putney

*WCMK(FM)— 2003: 91.9 mhz; 80 w. Ant 758 ft. TL: N42 58 28 W72 36 12. Box 8310, Essex 05451-8310. Phone: (802) 878-8885. Fax: (802) 879-6835. E-mail: cmi.radio@verizon.net. Web Site: www.cmiradio.com. Licensee: Christian Ministries Inc. Format: Christian. ♦ Ríc McClary, gen mgr.

Randolph

WCVR-FM—Listing follows WWWT(AM).

WWWT(AM)— Nov 26, 1968: 1320 khz; 1 kw-D, 66 w-N. TL: N43 56 21 W72 38 13. Box 249, Randolph Center 05061. Secondary address: 62 Radio Dr. 05060. Phone: (802) 728-4411. Fax: (802) 728-4013. E-mail: randolphradio@clearchannel.com. Licensee: Capstar TX L.P. Group owner: Clear Channel Communications Inc. (acq 12-22-00; grpsl). Rep: Savalli. Fisher, Wayland, Cooper, Leader & Zaragoza L.L.P. Format: News/talk. Target aud: 18-49. ♦ Tim Plante, gen mgr; Karen Warner, stn mgr.

WCVR-FM—Co-owned with WWWT(AM). Oct 25, 1982: 102.1 mhz; 11 kw. 436 ft. TL: N43 57 20 W72 36 10. Stereo. Web Site: www.champrocks.com. Format: Classic rock. News: 6 hrs wkly. Target aud: 25-54; 50/50 men and women.

Randolph Center

*WVTC(FM)— Aug 29, 1983: 90.7 mhz; 300 w horiz. 203 ft. TL: N43 56 07 W72 36 10. Stereo. Vermont Technical College, Box 500 05061. Phone: (802) 728-1550. Fax: (802) 728-1550. Web Site: www.wvtc.net. Licensee: Vermont State Colleges Vermont Technical College. Format: Punk, rap, rock, alternative. Target aud: General. ♦ Shaun Tulley, gen mgr; Matt DeJackome, stn mgr.

Royalton

WRJT(FM)— 1996: 103.1 mhz; 1.35 kw. 682 ft. TL: N43 46 28 W72 23 55. c/o WNCS(FM), 169 River St., Montpelier 05602. Phone: (802) 223-2396. Fax: (802) 223-1520. Web Site: www.pointfm.com. Licensee: Lisbon Communications Inc. Group owner: Northeast Broadcasting Company Inc. (acq 11-30-01). Format: AAA. ♦ Ed Flanagan, gen mgr; Tanya Stepasiuk, prom dir; Mark Miller, progmg dir; Jon Hosford, chief of engrg.

Rupert

WMNV(FM)— Apr 10, 1990: 104.1 mhz; 4.3 kw horiz. Ant 200 ft. TL: N43 16 01 W73 15 21. Stereo. 30 Park Ave., Cohoes, NY 12047-3330. Phone: (518) 237-1330. Fax: (518) 235-4468. E-mail: info@whaz.com. Web Site: www.whaz.com. Licensee: Capital Media Corp. (group owner; acq 4-15-97). Format: Adult Christian. Target aud: 25-75. Spec prog: Gospel, relg. ♦ Paul F. Lotters, pres, gen mgr & progmg mgr; Steven L. Klob, opns dir, dev dir, sls dir, mktg dir & adv dir; Rex P. Gregory, progmg dir, mus dir, news dir & pub affrs dir; Charles S.W. Fitch, chief of engrg.

Rutland

*WFTF(FM)— Jan 10, 1987: 90.5 mhz; 720 w. -560 ft. TL: N43 37 09 W72 59 04. 2 Meadow Ln. 05701. Phone: (802) 775-0358. Phone: (802) 773-2863. Web Site: www.cbcvt.org. Licensee: Calvary Bible Church. Network: Moody. Format: Christian. ♦ Ronald Systo, pres & gen mgr.

WJEN(FM)— October 1988: 94.5 mhz; 6 kw. 389 ft. TL: N43 36 49 W73 01 33. Stereo. Box 30 05702. Phone: (802) 775-7500. Fax: (802) 775-7555. E-mail: catcountrymornings@hotmail.com. Web Site: www.catcountry.net. Licensee: 6 Johnson Road Licenses Inc. Group owner: Pamal Broadcasting Ltd. (acq 10-19-2001; grpsl). Network: Network: ABC, Westwood One, Motor Racing Net. Format: New country. News: one hr wkly. Target aud: 18-49; adult, income $35,000 plus, homeowners. Spec prog: Sports/NASCAR 4 hrs wkly. ♦ Harry Weinhagen, gen mgr; Paul Hatin, stn mgr & gen sls mgr; Sheila Bigelow, prom mgr; D. B. James, progmg dir; Peter Morton, chief of engrg.

WJJR(FM)— Mar 25, 1971: 98.1 mhz; 1.15 kw. 2,591 ft. TL: N43 36 17 W72 49 14. Stereo. Box 30 05702. Secondary address: 67 Merchants Row, Rutland 05702. Phone: (802) 775-7500. Fax: (802) 775-7555. E-mail: wjjr@catamountradio.com. Web Site: www.wjjr.net. Licensee: 6 Johnson Road Licenses Inc. Group owner: Pamal Broadcasting Ltd. (acq 10-19-2001; grpsl). Hogan & Hartson. Format: Adult contemp. News staff: one; News: one hr wkly. Target aud: 25-54; in-office managerial, professional. Spec prog: News, pub affrs one hr wkly. ♦ Harry Weinhagen, gen mgr; Paul Hatin, gen sls mgr; Terry Jarrosak, progmg dir; Nanci Gordon, news dir; Peter Morton, chief of engrg.

*WRVT(FM)— Jan 10, 1989: 88.7 mhz; 2.77 kw. 1,328 ft. TL: N43 39 32 W73 06 25. 20 Troy Ave., Colchester 05446. Phone: (802) 655-9451. Fax: (802) 655-2799. Fax: (802) 655-1801. E-mail: contact@vpr.net. Web Site: www.vpr.net. Licensee: Vermont Public Radio. Network: Network: NPR, PRI. Haley, Bader & Potts. Format: Class, jazz, news. Target aud: General. Spec prog: Switchboard call-in 3 hrs, folk 4 hrs wkly. ♦ Mark Vogelzang, pres & gen mgr; Cindy Shuman, CFO; Victoria St. John, opns dir; Robin Turnau, dev dir; Gail

England, gen sls mgr; Jody Evans, progmg dir; Walter Parker, mus dir; John Van Hoesen, news dir; Richard Parker, chief of engrg.

WSYB(AM)— Dec 10, 1930: 1380 khz; 5 kw-D, 1 kw-N, DA-D. TL: N43 35 35 W72 59 25. Box 940 05702-0940. Secondary address: 250 Dorr Dr. 05701. Phone: (802) 775-5597. Fax: (802) 775-6637. Licensee: Capstar TX L.P. Group owner: Clear Channel Communications Inc. (acq 12-22-00; grpsl). Rep: McGavren Guild. Format: News/talk. Target aud: 35-64. ♦ Dave Ryeron, progmg dir; Glen Dudley, chief of engrg.

WZRT(FM)—Co-owned with WSYB(AM). 1974: 97.1 mhz; 1.15 kw. 2,591 ft. TL: N43 36 17 W72 49 14. Stereo. Format: Adult contemp. News staff: 2; News: 5 hrs wkly. Target aud: 18-49.

Saint Albans

WLFE-FM—Listing follows WRSA(AM).

WRSA(AM)— 1930: 1420 khz; 1 kw-D, 110 w-N. TL: N44 50 12 W73 04 57. Box 712, 2 Main St. 05478. Phone: (802) 524-2133. Fax: (802) 527-1450. E-mail: wlfe.fm@tverizonr.net. Licensee: Champlain Communications Corp. Group owner: Northeast Broadcasting Company Inc. (acq 9-18-98; $500,000. with co-located FM). Format: Talk radio. News staff: one; News: 20 hrs wkly. Target aud: General. ♦ Mike Kmack, gen mgr, opns mgr & progmg dir.

WLFE-FM—Co-owned with WRSA(AM). April 1970: 102.3 mhz; 440 w. 800 ft. TL: N44 46 56 W73 03 54. Stereo. Format: Country. News staff: one; News: 5 hrs wkly. Target aud: 18-54.

Saint Johnsbury

*WCKJ(FM)— Aug 1, 1998: 90.5 mhz; 1 kw. 738 ft. TL: N44 24 40 W71 58 13. Stereo. Box 8310, Essex 05451-8310. Secondary address: 134-B Main St., Essec Junction 05452. Phone: (802) 878-8885. Fax: (802) 879-6835. E-mail: cmi.radio@verizon.net. Web Site: www.cmiradio.com. Licensee: Christian Ministries Inc. Network: Moody. Joseph E. Dunne III. Format: Inspirational. ♦ Ric McClary, gen mgr.

WKXH(FM)—Listing follows WSTJ(AM).

WSTJ(AM)— July 10, 1949: 1340 khz; 1 kw-U. TL: N44 25 06 W71 59 45. Box 249, 1303 Concord Ave. 05819. Phone: (802) 748-1340. Fax: (802) 748-2361. E-mail: kix105@kix1055.com. Licensee: Vermont Broadcast Associates Inc. (acq 4-3-98; $630,000 with co-located FM). Network: Network: ABC, Jones Radio Networks. Bryan Cave. Format: Adult standards. News staff: one; News: 20 hrs wkly. Target aud: 35-75; adults and work places. ♦ Bruce James, pres & gen mgr; Candis Leopold, opns mgr; Dave Labounty, progmg dir; Don Smith, chief of engrg.

WKXH(FM)—Co-owned with WSTJ(AM). Aug 1, 1985: 105.5 mhz; 400 w. 712 ft. TL: N44 24 38 W71 58 13. Stereo. Phone: (802) 748-2345. Network: Network: ABC, Westwood One. Format: Hot country. News staff: 2. Target aud: 24-55; families.

*WVPA(FM)— 1999: 88.5 mhz; 290 w vert. Ant 1,863 ft. TL: N44 34 15 W71 53 38. Vermont Public Radio, 20 Troy Ave., Colchester 05446. Phone: (802) 655-9451. Fax: (802) 655-2799. Web Site: www.vpr.net. Licensee: Vermont Public Radio. Format: Class, jazz, news. ♦ Mark Vogelzang, gen mgr.

South Burlington

WXXX(FM)— Nov 16, 1984: 95.5 mhz; 25 kw. 236 ft. TL: N44 30 35 W73 11 05. Stereo. Box 620, Colchester 05446. Secondary address: Malletts Bay Ave., Colchester 05446. Phone: (802) 655-9550. Fax: (802) 655-1329. Web Site: www.95triplex.com. Licensee: Sison Broadcasting Inc. (acq 3-3-97; $2,939,014 with WVMT(AM) Burlington). Rep: McGavren Guild. Format: CHR. News staff: one; News: one hr wkly. Target aud: 18-49. ♦ Mark Esbjerg, opns mgr; Paul Goldman, gen mgr & gen sls mgr; Ben Hamilton, progmg dir; Chantal Paulino, news dir.

Springfield

WNBX(AM)— May 26, 1954: 1480 khz; 5 kw-D. TL: N43 16 54 W72 29 21. 19 Main St. 05156-2914. Phone: (603) 885-1480. Phone: (603) 448-0500. Fax: (603) 448-6601. Fax: (603) 526-9372. E-mail: realoldies1480@vermontel.net. Web Site: www.WNBX.com. Licensee:

Stations in the U.S. — Virginia

Developers & Brokers of Radio Properties
contact American Media Services at our suite:
Philadelphia Marriott Downtown
215-625-2900
843-972-2200
americanmediaservices.com
Charleston, SC
Dallas, TX · Chicago, Il · Austin, TX
American Media Services, LLC

KOOR Communications Inc. (group owner; acq 12-19-01; $75,000). Format: Talk. News staff: one; News: 7 hrs wkly. Target aud: 45 plus; 35-54. ♦ Bob Vinikoor, pres; Ray Lemire, gen mgr, opns dir & progmg dir.

WTSM(FM)— Jan 1, 1972: 93.5 mhz; 3 kw. 300 ft. TL: N43 16 54 W72 29 21. Stereo. 31 Hanover St., Suite 4, Lebanon, NH 03766. Phone: (603) 448-1400. Fax: (603) 448-1755. E-mail: pd@rock1017.com. Web Site: www.xl92.com. Licensee: Clear Channel Broadcasting Licenses Inc. Group owner: Clear Channel Communications Inc. (acq 2-16-2001; $2 million. with WMXR(FM) Woodstock). Format: Lite rock. Target aud: 25-50. ♦ Tim Plante, gen mgr.

Stowe

WCVT(FM)— Feb 28, 1977: 101.7 mhz; 130 w. 2,066 ft. TL: N44 25 14 W72 49 42. Stereo. Box 3536, Mountain Rd. 05672. Secondary address: 9 Stowe St., Waterbury 05676. Phone: (802) 244-1764. Fax: (802) 244-1771. E-mail: wcvt@classicvermont.com. Web Site: www.wcvtradio.com. Licensee: Radio Vermont Classics L.L.C. Group owner: Radio Vermont Group Inc. (acq 6-19-97; $450,000). Rep: McGavren Guild. Format: Classical. Target aud: 25-54; educated, upscale adults & families with active lifestyles. Spec prog: Children one hr wkly. ♦ Eric Michaels, gen mgr; Thomas B. Beardsley, stn mgr; Frankie Allen, opns dir.

Sunderland

WJAN(FM)— May 1, 1991: 95.1 mhz; 96 w. 2,398 ft. TL: N43 09 58 W73 07 02. Stereo. Box 30, Rutland 05702. Phone: (802) 775-7500. Fax: (802) 775-7555. E-mail: catcountrymornings@hotmail.com. Web Site: www.catcountry.net. Licensee: 6 Johnson Road Licenses Inc. Group owner: Pamal Broadcasting Ltd. (acq 10-19-2001; grpsl). Format: Country. News staff: one; News: one hr wkly. Target aud: 18-49. ♦ Harry Weinhagen, gen mgr; Paul Hatin, gen sls mgr; Sheila Bigelow, prom mgr; D. B. James, progmg dir; Peter Morton, chief of engrg.

Vergennes

WIZN(FM)—Licensed to Vergennes. See Burlington

Warren

WDEV-FM— Aug 11, 1989: 96.1 mhz; 3 kw. 4,000 ft. TL: N44 07 37 W72 55 43. Stereo. Box 550, Waterbury 05676. Secondary address: 9 Stowe St., Waterbury 05676. Phone: (802) 244-7321. Fax: (802) 244-1771. E-mail: wdev@radiovermont.com. Web Site: www.wdevradio.com. Licensee: Radio Vermont Inc. Group owner: Radio Vermont Group Inc. (acq 10-15-92; $643,000 with WKDR(AM) Burlington; 11-23-92). Wiley, Rein & Fielding. Format: News/talk, sports, music. News staff: one; News: 2 hrs wkly. Target aud: 25-54; affluent, upscale baby boomer generation. ♦ Ken D. Squier, pres; Eric Michaels, gen mgr; Jack Donovan, progmg dir.

Waterbury

WDEV(AM)— July 16, 1931: 550 khz; 5 kw-D, 1 kw-N, DA-2. TL: N44 21 09 W72 45 06. Box 550, 9 Stowe St. 05676. Phone: (802) 244-7321. Fax: (802) 244-1771. E-mail: wdev@radiovermont.com. Web Site: www.wdevradio.com. Licensee: Radio Vermont Inc. Group owner: Radio Vermont Group Inc. (acq 1969). Format: News, sports, div. Spec prog: Class one hr wkly. ♦ Eric Michaels, gen mgr & gen sls mgr; Jack Donovan, progmg dir; Rich Haskell, news dir; Tom Laffin, chief of engrg.

WWMP(FM)— Feb 14, 1985: 103.3 mhz; 3 kw. 912 ft. TL: N44 21 52 W72 55 53. Stereo. Box 590, Middlebury 05753. Phone: (802) 388-9000. Fax: (802) 388-3000. Licensee: Radio Broadcasting Services Inc. Group owner: Northeast Broadcasting Company Inc. (acq 5-4-2000). Network: USA. Joseph E. Dunne III. Format: Adult contemp. News staff: one; News: 16 hrs wkly. Target aud: 25-54. Spec prog: Children 3 hrs wkly. ♦ Bob Rowe, gen mgr & stn mgr; T. J. Michaels, prom mgr; Jon Hosford, chief of engrg.

Wells River

WTWN(AM)— Oct 3, 1976: 1100 khz; 5 kw-D. TL: N44 08 55 W72 04 02. Box 675, 1047 Rt. 302 05081. Phone: (802) 757-3311. Fax: (802) 757-2774. E-mail: wtwngch@kingcon.com. Web Site: www.wtwnradio.com. Licensee: Puffer Broadcasting Inc. (acq 10-3-73). Network: USA. Rep: Roslin. Shaw Pittman. Format: Relg. News: 9 hrs wkly. Target aud: 25 plus. Spec prog: Children, gospel. ♦ Stephen J. Puffer, pres, gen mgr, sls dir, gen sls mgr, prom mgr & progmg VP; Glenn Hatch, stn mgr & mktg dir; Teresa Puffer, opns mgr & progmg dir; Don Smith, chief of engrg.

White River Junction

WNHV(AM)— Feb 28, 1963: 910 khz; 1 kw-D, 84 w-N. TL: N43 37 19 W72 21 04. Box 5229, West Lebanon, NH 03784. Secondary address: 106 N. Main St., West Lebanon, NH 03784. Phone: (603) 298-2953. Fax: (603) 298-7554. E-mail: espnthescore@aol.com. Web Site: www.scoreradio.com. Licensee: Nassau Broadcasting III L.L.C. Group owner: Nassau Broadcasting Partners L.P. (acq 8-2-2004; grpsl). Rep: Roslin. Format: Sports. Target aud: 18-55. ♦ Jim Whedon, gen mgr; Doug Daniels, progmg dir; Neil Langer, chief of engrg.

WXLF(FM)—Co-owned with WNHV(AM). Feb 1, 1969: 95.3 mhz; 3 kw. 225 ft. TL: N43 39 14 W72 17 43. Stereo. Web Site: www.bobcountryfm.com. Format: Hot country. News: one hr wkly. Target aud: 35-54. Spec prog: Jazz. ♦ Heath Cole, progmg dir; Ram Reed, news dir.

WTSL(AM)—See Hanover, NH

WXXK(FM)—See Lebanon NH

Wilmington

WVAY(FM)— June 1, 1989: 100.7 mhz; 135 w. Ant 1,460 ft. TL: N42 57 33 W72 55 22. Stereo. 1 Scale Ave., Skuite 84, Rutland 05761-4459. Secondary address: Box 850, West Dover 05356. Phone: (802) 464-1350. Fax: (802) 464-1112. Web Site: www.101thefox.com. Licensee: Nassau Broadcasting III L.L.C. (group owner; (acq 1-21-2005); $2.5 million. with WEXP(FM) Brandon). Rep: McGavren Guild. Dan Alpert. Format: Classic rock. Target aud: 25-54; residents, tourists, upscale Mt. ♦ John Gales, gen mgr & stn mgr; Kelly Kowalski, progmg dir.

Windsor

*WVPR(FM)— Aug 13, 1977: 89.5 mhz; 1.78 kw. 2,160 ft. TL: N43 26 17 W72 27 08. Stereo. 20 Troy Ave., Colchester 05446. Phone: (802) 655-9451. Fax: (802) 655-2799. Fax: (802) 655-9117. Web Site: www.vpr.net. Licensee: Vermont Public Radio. Network: Network: NPR, PRI. Haley, Bader & Potts. Format: Jazz, class, news. Target aud: General. Spec prog: Switchboard call-in 3 hrs, folk 6 hrs wkly. ♦ Mark Vogelzang, CEO, pres & gen mgr; Cindy Shuman, CFO & VP; Michael Crane, opns dir & progmg dir; Sam Sanders, opns mgr; Robin Turnau, dev dir; Tammy West, gen sls mgr; Walter Parker, mus dir; Steve Young, news dir; Richard Parker, chief of engrg.

Woodstock

*WGLV(FM)— 2003: 91.7 mhz; 100 w. Ant 2,276 ft. TL: N43 38 22 W72 50 12. Box 8310, Essex 05451-8310. Secondary address: 134-B Main St., Essex Junction 05452. Phone: (802) 878-8885. Fax: (802) 879-6835. E-mail: cmi.radio@verizon.net. Web Site: www.cmiradio.com. Licensee: Christian Ministries Inc. Format: Inspirational. ♦ Ric McClary, gen mgr.

WMXR(FM)— Apr 18, 1989: 93.9 mhz; 670 w. Ant 682 ft. TL: N43 36 17 W72 28 03. Stereo. 31 Hanover St., Suite 4, Lebanon, NH 03766. Phone: (603) 448-1400. Fax: (603) 448-1755. E-mail: pd@rock1017.com. Web Site: www.wvrrfm.com. Licensee: Clear Channel Broadcasting Licenses Inc. Group owner: Clear Channel Communications Inc. (acq 2-16-2001; $2 million. with WTSM(FM) Springfield). Format: Rock. ♦ Tim Plante, gen mgr.

Virginia

Abingdon

WABN(AM)— Dec 10, 1956: 1230 khz; 1 kw-U. TL: N36 43 07 W81 56 55. Box 151, Vansant 24656. Phone: (276) 676-3806. Fax: (276) 676-3572. Licensee: Appalachian Educational Communication Corp. (acq 5-5-2004; $50,000). Format: Relg. ♦ Rev. Michael Smith, pres & gen mgr; Lisa Smith, progmg dir; Billy Ray Dotson, chief of engrg.

WFHG-FM— Dec 10, 1966: 92.7 mhz; 1.8 kw. 371 ft. TL: N36 43 07 W81 56 55. Stereo. Bristol Broadcasting Co. Inc., 901 E. Valley Dr., Bristol 24201. Phone: (276) 669-8112. Fax: (276) 669-0541. Web Site: www.supertalkwfhg.com. Licensee: Bristol Broadcasting Co. Inc. (group owner; acq 11-30-99; with co-located AM). Format: News talk. News: 2 hrs wkly. Target aud: 12 plus; progsv, contemp & urban. ♦ Ryland Sutherland, mus dir.

Accomac

WVES(FM)— Aug 13, 1990: 99.3 mhz; 22 kw. 344 ft. TL: N37 47 05 W75 36 16. Stereo. 27214 Muttonhunk Rd., Parksley 23421. Phone: (757) 665-6500. Fax: (757) 665-6178. E-mail: hotcountry@tassnet.net. Web Site: www.wevs.com. Licensee: Chincoteague Broadcasting Corp. (acq 5-18-98; $350,000). Network: Network: USA, Westwood One. Format: Hot country. News: 3 hrs wkly. Target aud: 25 plus. ♦ Stephen Marks, pres; Mark Dodds, gen mgr, stn mgr, opns mgr, gen sls mgr, prom mgr, prom mgr & mus dir; Dave Bralley, news dir; Kelli Spragg, pub affrs dir; Tom Reynolds, chief of engrg.

Alberta

WWDW(FM)— 2001: 103.1 mhz; 2.2 kw. Ant 535 ft. TL: N36 52 02 W77 53 31. Box 910, Roanoke Rapids, NC 27870. Phone: (252) 536-0209. Fax: (252) 538-0378. E-mail: info@wsmy1400.com. Web Site: www.wsmy1400.com. Licensee: First Media Radio LLC. (group owner; (acq 12-3-2003); grpsl). Format: Gospel. ♦ Alan Garrick, gen mgr.

Alexandria

WKDL(AM)—Licensed to Alexandria. See Washington DC

Altavista

WKDE(AM)— Apr 29, 1962: 1000 khz; 1 kw-D. TL: N37 07 20 W79 17 20. Box 390, 200 Frazier Rd. 24517. Phone: (434) 369-5588. Fax: (434) 369-1632. Licensee: DJ Broadcasting Corp. (acq 1-13-92; $300,000 with co-located FM; 2-10-92). Network: CNN Radio. Format: News. News: one hr wkly. Target aud: General. Spec prog: Southern gospel 5 hrs wkly. ♦ David Hoehne, pres & gen mgr; Edith Edward, chief of engrg.

WKDE-FM— June 30, 1969: 105.5 mhz; 6 kw. 328 ft. TL: N37 09 37 W79 13 28. Stereo. E-mail: info@kdcountry.com. Web Site: www.kdcountry.com. Format: C&W. News: one hr wkly. Target aud: 25-54. Spec prog: Black gospel 5 hrs, bluegrass 10 hrs wkly.

Amherst

WAMV(AM)— Oct 1, 1976: 1420 khz; 2.2 kw-D, 17 w-N. TL: N37 34 29 W79 01 14. Box 1420, 132 School Rd. 24521. Phone: (434) 946-9000. Fax: (434) 946-2201. E-mail: wamvradio@aol.com. Licensee: Community First Broadcasters Inc. (acq 4-1-88; $40,000). Network: USA. Format: Adult standards. Target aud: 50+. ♦ Robert Langstaff, pres, gen mgr, sls dir & progmg dir; Lee Parr, chief of engrg.

WYYD(FM)— Jan 27, 1981: 107.9 mhz; 20.5 kw. 1,768 ft. TL: N37 28 13 W79 22 30. Stereo. 3305 Old Forest Rd., Lynchburg 24501. Phone: (434) 385-8298. Fax: (434) 385-7279. Web Site: www.wyyd.cc. Licensee: Capstar TX L.P. Group owner: Clear Channel Communications Inc. (acq 8-30-00; grpsl). Network: ABC. Rep: McGavren Guild.

Virginia

Format: Country. News staff: one. Target aud: 25-54; those with moderate high expendable income. ◆ Chris Clendenen, gen mgr; Ron Gaylor, sls dir; Dave Carwile, gen sls mgr; Tom Sweat, natl sls mgr & rgnl sls mgr; Bobbi Crowder, prom dir; Joel Dearing, progmg dir; Jason Osborne, pub affrs dir; Jeff Parker, chief of engrg.

Appalachia

WAXM(FM)—See Big Stone Gap

Appomattox

WOWZ(AM)— June 1, 1974: 1280 khz; 1 kw-U. TL: N37 22 19 W78 50 06. Box 552, Forest 24551. Phone: (434) 534-0400. Fax: (434) 534-0401. E-mail: news1280@msn.com. Web Site: news1280.com. Licensee: Perception Media Inc. (acq 1-28-2004; $150,000). Format: News. ◆ Ben Peyton, pres.

WSNZ(FM)— May 17, 1989: 102.7 mhz; 22 kw. Ant 745 ft. TL: N37 28 07 W79 00 27. Stereo. 3305 Old Forest Rd., Lynchburg 24501. Phone: (434) 385-8298. Fax: (434) 385-8991. E-mail: stevencross @clearchannel.com. Web Site: www.magicfm.cc. Licensee: Capstar TX L.P. Group owner: Clear Channel Communications Inc. (acq 8-30-2000; grpsl). Format: Classic hits. Target aud: 35-54. Spec prog: New age 8 hrs wkly. ◆ Chris Clendenen, gen mgr; Dave Carwile, gen sls mgr & adv mgr; Tom Sweat, natl sls mgr; Bobbi Crowder, prom dir; Ron Gaylor, adv VP; Sarah Macomber, adv dir; Bill Cahill, progmg VP; Steve Cross, progmg dir; Jeff Parker, chief of engrg.

WTTX-FM— September 1976: 107.1 mhz; 3 kw. 300 ft. TL: N37 22 19 W78 50 06. Box 637 24522. Phone: (434) 352-7607. Fax: (434) 352-2451. E-mail: wttx@lynchburg.net. Web Site: users.lynchberg.net/jsaves/wttxfm. Licensee: CLL Inc. Format: Southern gospel. ◆ Terry Cook, pres, gen mgr & gen sls mgr; Laura Coflin, mus dir; Glen Reinheimer, chief of engrg.

Arlington

WABS(AM)— Nov 7, 1946: 780 khz; 5 kw-D. TL: N38 53 44 W77 08 04. 1901 N. Moore St., Suite 200 22209. Phone: (703) 807-2266. Fax: (703) 807-2248. E-mail: comment@wabs.com. Web Site: www.wabs.com. Licensee: Salem Media of Virginia Inc. Group owner: Salem Communications Corp. (acq 1-10-00). Network: Salem Radio Network. Rep: Salem. Fletcher Heald & Hildreth. Format: Contemp praise, worship, talk. News: 4 hrs wkly. Target aud: 25-54. ◆ Edward Atsinger, CEO & pres; Stu Epperson, chmn; David Evans, CFO; Joe Davis, sr VP; David Ruleman, VP, gen mgr & opns VP; Rich ee, opns mgr.

WAVA(FM)—Licensed to Arlington. See Washington DC

WZHF(AM)— Apr 7, 1947: 1390 khz; 5 kw-U, DA-2. TL: N38 54 15 W77 09 54. Stereo. Way Broadcasting Inc., 12216 Parklawn Dr., Suite 203, Rockville, MD 20852. Phone: (301) 424-9292. Fax: (301) 424-8266. Licensee: Way Broadcasting Licensee LLC. Group owner: Multicultural Radio Broadcasting Inc. (acq 5-30-00; grpsl). Format: Sp. ◆ Bill Parris, gen mgr & progmg dir; Raoul Lopez Bastidas, sls mgr; David Song, chief of engrg.

Ashland

WHAN(AM)— May 1, 1962: 1430 khz; 1 kw-U. TL: N37 44 46 W77 29 44. (CP: 5 kw-D. TL: N37 44 45 W77 29 44). Box 148, 11337 W. Ashcake Rd. 23005. Phone: (804) 798-1010. Phone: (804) 345-1430. Fax: (804) 798-7933. E-mail: clear@msn.com. Web Site: www.whan1430.com. Licensee: Fifth Estate Broadcasting. (acq 2-23-98). Network: Network: USA, Moody. Format: Talk. News: 7 hrs wkly. Target aud: 18-35; general. ◆ William Roberts, pres & stn mgr; Roger Reynolds, gen sls mgr & prom dir; Skip Andrews, progmg dir; Brian Edwards, chief of engrg.

WYFJ(FM)— Dec 7, 1967: 100.1 mhz; 6 kw. 321 ft. TL: N37 19 14 W79 37 59. Stereo. 407 S. Washington Hwy. 23005. Phone: (804) 798-3248. Phone: (704) 523-5555. E-mail: wyfj@bbnradio.org. Web Site: www.bbnradio.org. Licensee: Bible Broadcasting Network Inc. (group owner; acq 2-1-80). Network: USA. Format: Relg, Christian. News: 9 hrs wkly. ◆ Lowell Davey, pres; Randy Adams, gen mgr & stn mgr.

Bassett

WCBX(AM)— Oct 1, 1960: 900 khz; 1.1 kw-D, 180 w-N, DA-2. TL: N36 46 47 W80 00 35. Box 192, Martinsville 24114. Secondary address: 1675 Grandview Dr., Martinsville 24112. Phone: (276) 638-5235. Fax: (276) 638-6089. Web Site: thesportsaddictnetwork.com. Licensee: Base Communications Inc. (acq 4-17-98). Format: Fox sports radio affiliate. News staff: one; News: 12 hrs wkly. Target aud: 35-55. ◆ Edward A. Baker, pres & gen mgr; Brian Sanders, stn mgr; Michael Carter, opns mgr & progmg dir.

Bayside

WBVA(AM)—Licensed to Bayside. See Virginia Beach

Bedford

WLEQ(FM)— Oct 20, 1992: 106.9 mhz; 290 w. Ant 1,276 ft. TL: N37 19 14 W79 37 59. 19-C Wadsworth St., Lynchburg 24501. Phone: (434) 845-3698. Fax: (434) 845-2063. Licensee: Centennial Broadcasting LLC. Group owner: Cumulus Media Inc. (acq 8-11-2005; $1.9 million). Format: Oldies. ◆ J. Davis, gen mgr.

Berryville

WWRE(FM)— May 19, 1980: 105.5 mhz; 3 kw. 300 ft. TL: N39 07 03 W77 58 22. Stereo. Box 3300, Winchester 22604. Secondary address: 520 N. Pleasant Valley Rd., Winchester 22601. Phone: (540) 667-2224. Fax: (540) 722-3295. Web Site: www.realclassicrock.com. Licensee: Mid Atlantic Network Inc. Group owner: Mid Atlantic Network (acq 5-28-97; $850,000). with WWRT(FM) Strasburg). Cole, Raywid & Braverman. Format: Classic Rock. Target aud: 18 plus. ◆ John P. Lewis, pres; Chris Lewis, gen mgr & gen sls mgr; Jeff Adams, opns mgr; Don Wilson, progmg dir; Steve Edwards, news dir; Archie McKay, chief of engrg.

Big Stone Gap

WAXM(FM)—Listing follows WLSD(AM).

WLSD(AM)— Aug 20, 1953: 1220 khz; 1 kw-D, 45 w-N. TL: N36 50 26 W82 44 14. Stereo. Drawer W, 1600 Intermont Heights 24219. Phone: (276) 523-1700. Phone: (276) 679-1901. Fax: (276) 679-1198. E-mail: 93.5@waxm.com. Licensee: Valley Broadcasting Inc. (acq 5-1-80; $359,000; 5-12-80). Network: CBS. Jerry Miller. Format: Relg. Target aud: 19-60. ◆ Greg Kress, pres; William Stanley, gen mgr, sls VP, gen sls mgr & rgnl sls mgr; Paul Miller, adv dir; Rick Phillips, progmg dir; Jack Starnes, chief of engrg.

WAXM(FM)—Co-owned with WLSD(AM). Apr 8, 1975: 93.5 mhz; 2.45 kw, 1,883 ft. TL: N36 54 50 W82 53 40. Stereo. 724 Park Ave., Norton 24273. Phone: (276) 679-1901. Fax: (276) 679-1198. Network: CBS. Format: Country. ◆ Kim Swecker, prom dir.

Blacksburg

WBRW(FM)— December 1964: 105.3 mhz; 3.8 kw. 472 ft. TL: N37 11 12 W80 28 54. (CP: 12 kw). Stereo. Box 3788, Radford 24143. Secondary address: 7080 Lee Hwy., Rayford 24141. Phone: (540) 633-5330. Fax: (540) 633-2998. Licensee: Cumulus Licensing LLC. Group owner: Cumulus Media Inc. (acq 3-31-2004; grpsl). Format: Classic rock. News staff: 2; News: 10 hrs wkly. Target aud: 18-49. ◆ Scott Claytons, opns dir & gen sls mgr; Scott Stevens, opns mgr & sls dir; Courtney Quinn, progmg dir; Marty Gordon, news dir; Dave Dalesky, chief of engrg.

WFNR(AM)— 1973: 710 khz; 10 kw-D, DA. TL: N37 08 01 W80 21 17. 7080 Lee Hwy., Radford 24141. Phone: (540) 633-5330. Fax: (540) 633-2998. E-mail: wwatson@valleybroadcasting.com. Web Site: www.nrvtoday.com. Licensee: Cumulus Licensing LLC. Group owner: Cumulus Media Inc. (acq 3-31-2004; grpsl). Network: UPI. Format: News/talk. Target aud: 25 plus; general. ◆ Joe Mule, gen mgr; Scott Stevens, opns mgr.

WKEX(AM)— July 10, 1969: 1430 khz; 1 kw-D, 62 w-N. TL: N37 13 57 W80 26 40. (CP: 5 kw-U, DA-2). Box 889 24063. Secondary address: 1501 Lark Ln. 24060. Phone: (540) 951-9791. Fax: (540) 961-2021. E-mail: wkexam@yahoo.com. Web Site: www.thesportsadditictnetwork.com. Licensee: Base Communications Inc. Group owner: Baker Family Stations (acq 6-30-98; $60,000). Network: USA. Format: Sports talk. Target aud: 35 plus; mature adults, all income levels. Spec prog: Gospel 5 hrs, relg 3 hrs wkly, 3 hrs syndicated, sports 4 hrs. ◆ Edward Baker, pres; Brian Sanders, gen mgr, dev dir, sls dir & progmg dir; Drake Anderson, opns dir & progmg dir; Andrew Matney, prom dir; Tammy Chase, pub affrs dir; Tim Pauley, engrg dir.

Directory of Radio

*WUVT-FM— Oct 23, 1969: 90.7 mhz; 3 kw. 156 ft. TL: N37 13 28 W80 24 30. Stereo. 350 Squires Student Ctr. 24061-0546. Phone: (540) 231-9880. Fax: (208) 692-5239. E-mail: wuvtamfm@vt.edu. Web Site: www.wuvt.vt.edu. Licensee: Educational Media Corporation at Virginia Tech. Format: Div. Target aud: general; college students. Spec prog: American Indian 2 hrs, Greek 2 hrs, Chinese 2 hrs, Turkish 2 hrs, African 2 hrs, Latin 2 hrs wkly. ◆ Jake Faber, gen mgr & opns mgr.

WWVT(AM)—See Christiansburg

Blackstone

WBBC-FM—Listing follows WKLV(AM).

WKLV(AM)— 1947: 1440 khz; 5 kw-D. TL: N37 03 14 W78 01 15. Stereo. Box 300, 950 Kenbridge Rd. 23824. Phone: (434) 292-4146. Fax: (434) 292-7669. E-mail: wbbc@meckcom.net. Web Site: www.bobcatcountryradio.com. Licensee: Denbar Communications Inc. (acq 7-26-91; $175,000 with co-located FM; 6-10-91). Format: Sports. Target aud: 25-54. ◆ Dennis Royer, pres, progmg dir & chief of engrg; Dennis Royer Jr., gen sls mgr.

WBBC-FM—Co-owned with WKLV(AM). Nov 17, 1975: 93.5 mhz; 17.5 kw. 394 ft. TL: N37 03 14 W78 01 15. (CP: 17.5 kw). Stereo. Network: Westwood One. Format: Hot country. Target aud: 25-54; middle class, with two cars, homeowners.

Bluefield

WBDY(AM)— Nov 17, 1980: 1190 khz; 10 kw-D, DA. TL: N37 16 19 W81 19 05. 900 Bluefield Ave., WV 24701. Phone: (304) 327-7114. Fax: (304) 325-7850. Licensee: Monterey Licenses LLC. Group owner: Triad Broadcasting Co. LLC (acq 7-18-00; grpsl). Rep: Rgnl Reps. Format: ESPN radio. Target aud: 25 plus; working & retired adults with disposable income. ◆ John Halford, gen mgr; Dave Crosier, opns dir; Danny Clemons, gen sls mgr; Joseph Echoles, progmg dir; Keith Brown, chief of engrg.

WHKX(FM)—Co-owned with WBDY(AM). December 1970: 106.3 mhz; 3 kw. 1,122 ft. TL: N37 15 30 W81 10 36. Stereo. Network: Westwood One. Format: Contemp country. News: 17 hrs wkly. ◆ Dave Crosier, progmg dir.

Bowling Green

WWUZ(FM)— 1998: 96.9 mhz; 2.8 kw. 472 ft. TL: N37 57 56 W77 22 19. 616 Armelia St., Fredericksburg 22401. Phone: (540) 374-5500. Fax: (540) 374-5525. Web Site: www.classicrock969.com. Licensee: The Free Lance-Star Publishing Co. of Fredericksburg, Virginia. Group owner: The Free Lance-Star Publishing Co. (acq 8-23-01; $2.15 million). Format: Classic rock. ◆ Josiah Rowe III, pres; John Moen, gen mgr; Jon Reed, gen mgr & progmg dir; Jim Butler, sls dir; Bridgette Dean, prom dir; Rich Creeger, mus dir; Frank Hammon, news dir & pub affrs dir; Chris Wilk, chief of engrg.

Bridgewater

WBHB-FM— Mar 3, 1989: 105.1 mhz; 6 kw. Ant 328 ft. TL: N38 24 30 W78 54 04. Stereo. 130 Media Lane, Harrisonburg 22801. Phone: (540) 434-0331. Fax: (540) 434-7087. Web Site: www.valleyradio.com. Licensee: M. Belmont VerStandig Inc. Group owner: VerStandig Broadcasting (acq 1993; $10,000. with WHBG(AM) Harrisonburg; FTR: 9-13-93). Format: Oldies. News staff: 2. Target aud: 24-54. ◆ Susanne Fitzpatrick, gen mgr.

Bristol

WFHG(AM)— January 1947: 980 khz; 5 kw-D, 1 kw-N, DA-N. TL: N36 36 30 W82 09 36. Box 1389 24203. Secondary address: 901 E. Valley Dr. 24201. Phone: (276) 669-8112. Fax: (276) 669-0541. E-mail: bhagy@wxbq.com. Web Site: www.supertalkwfhg.com. Licensee: Bristol Broadcasting Inc. Group owner: Nininger Stations (acq 1972). Network: ABC Information & Entertainment. Rep: McGavren Guild. Shaw Pittman. Format: News/talk, sports. ◆ W.L. Nininger, pres; Bill Hagy, gen mgr; Jennifer Worley, opns dir; Winnie Quaintance, sls dir; Roger Bouldin, prom dir; Chuck Lawson, chief of engrg.

WIGN(AM)—See Bristol, TN

WQUT(FM)—See Johnson City, TN

Stations in the U.S. | Virginia

Developers & Brokers of Radio Properties
contact American Media Services at our suite: Philadelphia Marriott Downtown 215-625-2900
843-972-2200
americanmediaservices.com
Charleston, SC
Dallas, TX · Chicago, Il · Austin, TX
American Media Services, LLC

WXBQ-FM—See Bristol, TN

WZAP(AM)— 1946: 690 khz; 10 kw-D, 14 w-N. TL: N36 37 51 W82 09 53. Box 369 24203. Secondary address: 11373 Wallace Pike 24202. Phone: (276) 669-6950. Phone: (276) 669-6900. Fax: (276) 669-0794. E-mail: wzapradio@aol.com. Licensee: RAM Communications Inc. (acq 1-10-77; $375,000). Network: USA. Format: Relg. News: 8 hrs wkly. Target aud: General. ♦R.A. Morris, pres, gen mgr & gen sls mgr; Tommy Tester, stn mgr, prom mgr & progmg dir; Glen Harlow, mus dir; Al Morris, news dir; Joyce Boyd, pub affrs dir; John Faniola, chief of engrg.

Broadway

WJDV(FM)—Licensed to Broadway. See Broadway-Timberville

Broadway-Timberville

WBTX(AM)— May 18, 1972: 1470 khz; 5 kw-D, DA. TL: N38 37 24 W78 48 52. Box 337, 166 Main St., Broadway 22815. Phone: (540) 896-8933. Fax: (540) 896-1448. E-mail: info@positive-radio.com. Web Site: www.positive-radio.com. Licensee: Massanutten Broadcasting Co. Inc. Network: USA. Rep: Salem. Format: Southern gospel. News: 8 hrs wkly. Target aud: 25-54. Spec prog: Farm one hr wkly. ♦David Eshleman, pres; Thomas Watson, gen mgr; Denise David, gen sls mgr; Jim Snavely, progmg dir & news dir; Bill Fawcett, chief of engrg.

WLTK(FM)—Co-owned with WBTX(AM). 1997: 103.3 mhz; 2.1 kw. 544 ft. TL: N38 36 31 W78 54 07. Stereo. Phone: (540) 896-9585. Web Site: www.positive-radio.com. (Acq 8-8-2001; exchange for WJDV(FM) Broadway plus $1.25 million). Network: USA. Rep: Salem. Format: Contemp Christian. News: 9 hrs wkly. Target aud: 25-44. ♦Greg Crabtree, progmg dir.

WJDV(FM)—(Broadway). Dec 18, 1989: 96.1 mhz; 2.6 kw. Ant 1,010 ft. TL: N38 33 50 W78 57 00. Stereo. 130 Media Lane, Harrisonburg 22801. Phone: (540) 434-0331. Fax: (540) 434-7084. Web Site: www.valleyradio.com. Licensee: HJV L.P. Group owner: VerStandig Broadcasting (acq 3-12-2001; swap with WLTK(FM) New Market). Format: Lite rock. Target aud: 25-44. ♦Susanne Fitzpatrick, gen mgr.

Brookneal

WODI(AM)— Feb. 1, 1997: 1230 khz; 1 kw-U. TL: N37 02 17 W78 56 30. 1230 Radio Rd. 24528-3141. Phone: (434) 376-1230. Fax: (434) 376-9634. E-mail: wodi@wodiradio.com. Web Site: www.wodiradio.com. Licensee: D & M Communications Inc. (acq 9-5-96; $47,000). Network: UPI. Format: Oldies, talk. Target aud: 25-54; general. ♦David L. Marthouse, pres, gen mgr & progmg dir; Anthony R. DeNicola, VP, opns mgr & asst music dir; Anthony W. DeNicola, gen sls mgr & mktg mgr; Dianne D. DeNicola, prom mgr; Brian R. DeNicola, mus dir; Bob O'Brien, pub affrs dir; John Gers, engrg dir; Harry Kane, chief of engrg.

Buena Vista

WWZW(FM)— 1981: 96.7 mhz; 2 kw. Ant 1,135 ft. TL: N37 43 37 W79 18 24. Stereo. Box 902, Lexington 24450. Secondary address: 312 S. Main St., Lexington 24450. Phone: (540) 463-2161. Fax: (540) 463-9524. E-mail: info@wrel.com. Licensee: First Media Radio LLC (group owner; (acq 6-21-2004; $1.33 million. with WREL(AM) Lexington). Network: ABC. Format: Hot country. Target aud: 25-54. Spec prog: Farm 3 hrs, bluegrass 4 hrs wkly. ♦Alex Kolobielski, pres; Dave Peach, gen mgr; Scott M. Lancey, sls dir; Mark Smith, engrg dir.

Buffalo Gap

WZXI(FM)—Licensed to Buffalo Gap. See Staunton

Cape Charles

***WAZP(FM)**— 2000: 90.7 mhz; 13 kw. Ant 512 ft. TL: N37 10 53 W75 57 47. EMF Broadcasting, 5700 W. Oaks Blvd., Rocklin, CA 95765. Phone: (916) 251-1600. Fax: (916) 251-1650. E-mail: klove@klove.com.

Web Site: www.klove.com. Licensee: Delmarva Educational Association. Network: K-Love. Shaw Pittman. Format: Contemp Christian. News staff: 3. Target aud: 25-44; Judeo Christian, female. ♦Lloyd Parker, gen mgr; Keith Whipple, dev dir; Eric Allen, natl sls mgr; Chris Joyce, prom dir; Mike Novak, progmg dir; David Pierce, progmg mgr; Jon Rivers, mus dir; Ed Lenane, news dir.

Cedar Bluff

WHQX(FM)— 1989: 107.7 mhz; 550 w. 751 ft. TL: N37 09 49 W81 46 06. 900 Bluefield Ave., Bluefield, WV 24701. Phone: (304) 327-7114. Fax: (304) 325-7850. Web Site: www.kickscountry.com. Licensee: Monterey Licenses LLC. Group owner: Triad Broadcasting Co. LLC (acq 7-18-00; grpsl). Format: Country. News staff: one. ♦John Halford, gen mgr & gen sls mgr; Dave Crouiser, progmg dir; Keith Bowman, chief of engrg.

WYRV(AM)— March 1985: 770 khz; 5 kw-D. TL: N37 05 05 W81 46 07. Box 70 24609. Secondary address: 504 Middlecreek Rd. 24609. Phone: (276) 964-9619. Phone: (276) 964-5167. Fax: (276) 964-9610. E-mail: brad@youradio.net. Web Site: www.youradio.net. Licensee: Faith Christian Music Broadcasting Ministries Inc. (acq 4-12-01). Positive Radio (contemp Christian/mainstream). News staff: one; News: 3 hrs wkly. Target aud: 30 plus. ♦Brad Ratliff, gen mgr, adv mgr & progmg dir; Greg Webb, mus dir; Acie T. Rasnake, chief of engrg.

Charles City

***WAUQ(FM)**— 2000: 89.7 mhz; 10 kw. Ant 351 ft. TL: N37 25 58 W77 11 38. Box 3206, Tupelo, MS 38803. Phone: (662) 844-8888. Fax: (662) 842-6791. Web Site: www.afr.net. Licensee: American Family Association. Group owner: American Family Radio Format: Christian, inspirational. ♦Marvin Sanders, gen mgr.

Charlottesville

WCHV(AM)— 1930: 1260 khz; 5 kw-D, 2.5 kw-N, DA-2. TL: N38 06 52 W78 27 18. Stereo. 1150 Pepsi Pl., Suite 300 22901. Phone: (434) 978-4408. Fax: (434) 978-1109. Web Site: www.wchv.com. Licensee: Clear Channel Broadcasting Licenses Inc. (group owner; (acq 9-13-2000; $450,000). Format: News/talk. ♦Phil Robken, gen mgr; Regan Keith, opns mgr; Mike Chiumento, gen sls mgr.

WCJZ(FM)— 1995: 107.5 mhz; 300 w. 983 ft. TL: N37 59 00 W78 28 53. 1150 Pepsi Pl., Suite 300 22901. Phone: (434) 978-4408. Phone: (434) 964-1075. Fax: (978) 978-1190. Licensee: Clear Channel Broadcasting Licenses Inc. (acq 11-19-2004; $5.9 million). Format: Rock, adult contemp, smooth jazz. ♦David Mitchel, gen mgr; Kevin McCabe, gen sls mgr; Kishore Persaud, engrg dir & chief of engrg.

WHTE-FM—(Ruckersville). Mar 29, 1990: 101.9 mhz; 6 kw. 223 ft. TL: N38 13 06 W78 22 03. 1150 Pepsi Pl., Suite 300 22901. Phone: (434) 978-4408. Fax: (434) 978-1109. Web Site: www.1019hot.com. Licensee: Clear Channel Broadcasting Licenses Inc. Group owner: Clear Channel Communications Inc. (acq 8-6-99; grpsl). Network: AP Network News. Format: Top-40. News: 5 hrs wkly. Target aud: 30 plus; middle to upper middle class. ♦Phil Robken, gen mgr; Regan Keith, opns mgr; Mike Chiumento, gen sls mgr.

WINA(AM)— September 1949: 1070 khz; 5 kw-U, DA-N. TL: N38 05 22 W78 30 14. 1140 Rose Hill Dr. 22903. Phone: (434) 220-2300. Fax: (434) 220-2304. Web Site: www.wina.com. Licensee: Charlottesville Communications LLC. (group owner; (acq 12-13-2004; grpsl). Network: Network: CBS, ABC Information & Entertainment. Rep: Christal. Smithwick & Belendiuk. Format: News/talk, sports. News staff: 4; News: 20 hrs wkly. Target aud: General. ♦Brad Eure, pres, gen mgr & progmg dir.

WQMZ(FM)—Co-owned with WINA(AM). Oct 1954: 95.1 mhz; 6 kw. 144 ft. TL: N38 02 54 W78 28 12. Stereo. Web Site: www.z95.net. Format: Adult contemp.

WKAV(AM)— October 1957: 1400 khz; 1 kw-U. TL: N38 01 49 W78 29 22. 1150 Pepsi Pl., Suite 300 22901. Phone: (434) 978-4408. Fax:

(434) 978-1109. Web Site: www.wkav.com. Licensee: Clear Channel Broadcasting Licenses Inc. Group owner: Clear Channel Communications Inc. (acq 6-13-00; $450,000). Format: Sports. Target aud: 35 plus. ♦Phil Robken, gen mgr; Regan Keith, opns mgr; Mike Chiumento, gen sls mgr.

***WNRN(FM)**— September 1996: 91.9 mhz; 320 w. 1,066 ft. TL: N37 58 55 W78 29 03. 2250 Old Ivy Rd., Suite 2 22903. Phone: (434) 971-4096. Fax: (434) 971-6562. E-mail: wnrn@wnrn.org. Web Site: www.wnrn.org. Licensee: Stu-Comm Inc. Davis Wright Tremaine. Format: Alternative, AAA, urban contemp. Target aud: 18-49; educated, upscale young professionals and students. Spec prog: Folk 19 hrs, techno 6 hrs, industrial 2 hrs, punk 2 hrs wkly. ♦Mike Friend, gen mgr, dev dir, progmg dir & chief of engrg; Anne Williams, mktg dir; Mike Momson, mus dir; Steve Mendenhall, news dir.

WSUH(FM)—See Crozet

***WTJU(FM)**— May 10, 1957: 91.1 mhz; 600 w. 1,066 ft. TL: N37 58 55 W78 29 03. Stereo. Box 400811 22904-4811. Secondary address: 2nd Floor 22904. Phone: (434) 924-0885. Fax: (434) 924-8996. E-mail: wtju@virginia.edu. Web Site: wtju.radio.virginia.edu. Licensee: University of Virginia. Network: PRI. Format: Var/div. News: 5 hrs wkly. Target aud: General; from rural population to college educated. Spec prog: Black 8 hrs, children 2 hrs, folk 20 hrs, Gospel 1 hr Sp 2 hrs wkly. ♦Chuck Taylor, gen mgr & stn mgr.

WUVA(FM)— June 22, 1979: 92.7 mhz; 6 kw. 3,000 ft. TL: N37 59 06 W78 28 51. Stereo. 1928 Arlington Blvd., Suite 312 22903. Phone: (434) 817-6880. Fax: (434) 817-6884. E-mail: info@92.7kissfm.com. Web Site: www.92.7kissfm.com. Licensee: WUVA Inc. Rep: Katz Radio. Format: Adult urban contemp. News staff: 20; News: 20 hrs wkly. Target aud: 18-54. ♦Sharon Sant, gen mgr, sls, mktg & adv; Tanisha Thompson, opns mgr, progmg dir & progmg.

***WVTU(FM)**— Jan 8, 1991: 89.3 mhz; 195 w horiz, 160 w vert. 1,696 ft. TL: N38 03 58 W78 47 54. (CP: 3.2 kw). Stereo. 3520 Kingsburg Ln., Roanoke 24014. Phone: (540) 989-8900. Fax: (540) 776-2727. Web Site: www.wvtf.org. Licensee: Virginia Tech. Foundation Inc. Network: NPR, PRI. Dow, Lohnes & Albertson. Format: Class, jazz, npr (simulcast @ wvtf). ♦Glenn Gleixner, gen mgr & dev dir; Seth Williamson, mus dir; Rick Mattoni, news dir; Paxton Durham, chief of engrg.

***WVTW(FM)**— 1997: 88.5 mhz; 120 w. 1,089 ft. TL: N37 58 49 W78 29 21. 3520 Kingsburg Ln., Roanoke 24014. Phone: (540) 989-8900. Fax: (540) 776-2727. Web Site: www.wvtf.org. Licensee: Virginia Tech Foundation Inc. Network: NPR. Format: Class, jazz, NPR. ♦Glenn Gleixner, gen mgr & dev dir; Seth Williamson, mus dir; Rick Mattoni, news dir; Paxton Durham, chief of engrg.

WWWV(FM)— 1959: 97.5 mhz; 8.9 kw. Ant 1,132 ft. TL: N37 59 05 W78 28 49. Stereo. 1140 Rose Hill Dr. 22903. Phone: (434) 220-2300. Fax: (434) 220-2304. Web Site: www.3wv.com. Licensee: Charlottesville Communications LLC. (group owner; (acq 12-13-2004; grpsl). Rep: Christal. Smithwick & Belendiuk. Format: Classic rock. Target aud: 18-49. ♦Brad Eure, pres & gen mgr; Rick Daniels, opns mgr.

Chase City

WFXQ(FM)— Feb 1, 1993: 99.9 mhz; 12 kw. Ant 469 ft. TL: N36 48 17 W78 20 59. (CP: COL Creedmoor, NC. 22 kw, ant 292 ft. TL: N36 04 52 W78 28 27). Stereo. Hwy. 47 W., South Hill 23970. Phone: (434) 447-4007. Fax: (434) 447-4789. Licensee: Capitol Broadcasting Co. Inc. Group owner: Joyner Radio Inc. (acq 4-13-2005; $7.25 million). Network: ABC. Format: Adult standards. ♦Jerry E. Brown, exec VP & opns dir; Greg Thrift, VP, gen mgr, prom VP, prom VP, progmg dir & mus dir; John Hart, chief of engrg.

***WMVE(FM)**— April 2007: 90.1 mhz; 8 kw. Ant 371 ft. TL: N36 46 29 W78 20 41. 23 Sesame St., Richmond 23235. Phone: (804) 320-1301. Fax: (804) 320-8729. Web Site: www.ideastations.org. Licensee: Commonwealth Public Broadcasting Corp. Network: Network: NPR, PRI. ♦Bill Miller, gen mgr.

Broadcasting & Cable Yearbook 2006

Virginia

Chatham

WKBY(AM)— June 8, 1966: 1080 khz; 1 kw-D. TL: N36 46 54 W79 23 29. 12932 U.S. Hwy. 29 24531. Phone: (434) 432-8108. Fax: (434) 432-1523. E-mail: wkby1080@gamewood.net. Licensee: William L. Bonner. (acq 11-15-90; $250,000; 12-3-90). Format: Black, gospel. ♦William L. Bonner, pres; Van Jay, gen mgr; Lois Stephens, gen sls mgr; Vickie Pritchett, progmg dir; Tim Walker, chief of engrg.

Cheriton

*WWIP(FM)— 2005: 89.1 mhz; 20 kw. Ant 449 ft. TL: N37 10 53 W75 57 47. Delmarva Educational Association, 3780 Will Scarlet Rd., Winston-Salem, NC 27104. Phone: (336) 768-1041. Licensee: Delmarva Educational Association. ♦Nancy A. Epperson, pres.

Chesapeake

WCDG(FM)—See Moyock, NC

WCPK(AM)— 1967: 1600 khz; 5 kw-D, 27 kw-N. TL: N36 48 10 W76 16 58. 645 Church St., Suite 400, Norfolk 23501. Phone: (757) 622-4600. Fax: (757) 624-6515. E-mail: martinpepian@aol.com. Licensee: Christian Broadcasting of Chesapeake Inc. (acq 10-17-97; $200,000). Winston & Strawn. Format: Gospel. News staff: one. Target aud: 25-54; white collar, upscale professionals. ♦L.E. Willis, pres; Katrina Chase, gen mgr; Jonathan Willis, opns dir, opns mgr & progmg dir; Alvin Rooks, sls dir & gen sls mgr; Martin Culpeper, mktg dir & prom dir; James Phillips, news dir; Terry Love, chief of engrg.

*WFOS(FM)— Sept 14, 1973: 88.7 mhz; 15 kw. 172 ft. TL: N76 18 03 W36 43 18. Stereo. 1617 Cedar Rd. 23320-7111. Phone: (757) 547-1036. Phone: (757) 547-0134. Fax: (757) 547-0160. Licensee: Chesapeake School Board. Format: Big band, blues, oldies, class, educ. Target aud: High school. ♦W. Randolph Nichols, pres; Richie Babb, gen mgr.

WPYA(FM)— Nov 30, 1973: 93.7 mhz; 100 kw. 997 ft. TL: N36 32 57 W76 11 21. Stereo. 500 Dominion Tower, 999 Waterside Dr., Norfolk 23510. Phone: (757) 640-8500. Fax: (757) 640-8552. Web Site: bob-fm.com. Licensee: Commonwealth Radio L.L.C. Group owner: Sinclair Communications Inc. (acq 1996; $8.1 million. with WTAR(AM) Norfolk). Rep: McGavren Guild. Format: Adult hits. News staff: one; News: 2 hrs wkly. Target aud: 25-54. ♦Bob Sinclair, pres; Lisa Sinclair, gen mgr; Dave Morgan, stn mgr & opns mgr.

Chester

WDYL(FM)— December 1968: 101.1 mhz; 4 kw. Ant 367 ft. TL: N37 26 21 W77 25 57. Stereo. 812 Moorefield Park Dr., Richmond 23236. Phone: (804) 330-5700. Fax: (804) 330-4079. Web Site: y101rocks.com. Licensee: CXR Holdings L.L.C. Group owner: Cox Communications Inc. (acq 2-1-2001; grpsl). Format: New rock/alternative rock. ♦Mike Murphy, progmg dir; Jon Bennett, chief of engrg.

WGGM(AM)— September 1964: 820 khz; 10 kw-D, 1 kw-N, DA-2. TL: N37 22 58 W77 25 21. 4301 W. 100 Rd. 23831. Phone: (804) 717-2000. Fax: (804) 717-2009. E-mail: pscott4u@yahoo.com. Web Site: www.am820.net. Licensee: Hoffman Communications Inc. (acq 10-76). Network: USA. Steve Yelverton. Format: Relg. Target aud: 25-49. ♦Hubert Hoffman, pres; Paul Scott Bulifant, VP & gen mgr.

Chincoteague

WCTG(FM)— 2004: 96.5 mhz; 5.3 kw. Ant 344 ft. TL: N37 55 14 W75 23 07. Sebago Broadcasting L.L.C., 6819 Franklin Park Rd., McLean 22101. Phone: (703) 761-5013. Fax: (703) 761-5023. Licensee: Sebago Broadcasting Co. L.L.C. Gammon & Grange. Format: Classic rock, oldies. ♦A. Wray Fitch III, pres.

Christiansburg

WBRW(FM)—See Blacksburg

WFNR-FM— 1990: 100.7 mhz; 3 kw. 328 ft. TL: N37 08 01 W80 21 17. (CP: Ant 453 ft.). Box 3788, Radford 24143. Secondary address: 7080 Lee Hwy., Radford 24141. Phone: (540) 633-5330. Fax: (540) 633-2998. Web Site: www.nrvtoday.com. Licensee: Cumulus Licensing LLC. Group owner: Cumulus Media Inc. (acq 3-31-2004; grpsl). Network: UPI. Format: News talk. News: 7 hrs wkly. Target aud: 25 plus. ♦Ronald Walton, gen mgr; Scott Stevens, opns mgr; Wes Watson, progmg dir; Dave Dalesky, chief of engrg.

WWVT(AM)— October 1954: 1260 khz; 2.8 kw-D, 28 w-N. TL: N37 09 11 W80 24 57. 3520 Kingsbury Ln., Roanoke 24014. Phone: (540) 989-8900. Fax: (540) 776-2727. E-mail: mail@wvtf.org. Web Site: www.wvtf.org. Licensee: Virginia Tech Foundation Inc. (acq 5-22-98). Network: Network: NPR, PRI. Format: Talk. News: 60 hrs wkly. Target aud: 30-54; business professionals. ♦Glenn Gleixner, gen mgr; Rick Mattioni, progmg dir; Paxton Durham, chief of engrg.

Churchville

WBOP(FM)—Licensed to Churchville. See Harrisonburg

WNLR(AM)— Mar 9, 1962: 1150 khz; 2.5 kw-D, 30 w-N. TL: N38 12 39 W79 07 53. Box 400 24421. Secondary address: Rt. 250 W. Phone: (540) 885-8600. Phone: (540) 885-1150. Fax: (540) 886-8624. E-mail: wnlr@nlministries.org. Web Site: www.nlministries.org. Licensee: New Life Ministries Inc. (acq 12-8-93; $200,000; 1-3-94). Network: Moody, USA. Format: Relg, adult contemp. Target aud: 22-55; females with family size above average. ♦Bill Garvey, pres; Tom Watson, gen mgr; Russ Whitesell, opns mgr.

Claremont

WPMH(AM)— Aug 19, 1997: 670 khz; 20 kw-D, 3 w-N, DA-2. TL: N37 10 29 W76 53 49. 2202 Jolliss Rd., Chesapeake 23321. Phone: (757) 465-6700. Fax: (757) 488-7761. Web Site: wpmhradio.com. Licensee: Chesapeake-Portsmouth Broadcasting Corp. (acq 3-2-2001; $950,000). Format: Christian talk. ♦Henry Hoot, gen mgr & opns mgr.

Clarksville

WLUS-FM— Jan 1, 1984: 98.3 mhz; 17.5 kw. Ant 394 ft. TL: N36 44 24 W78 44 49. Stereo. Box 1603, Oxford, NC 27565. Secondary address: 615 B Lewis St., Oxford, NC 27565. Phone: (919) 693-7900. Fax: (919) 693-9585. Web Site: www.bestcountryaround.com. Licensee: Lakes Media Holding Company LLC. (group owner; acq 2-1-2005; grpsl). Network: ABC. Format: Country. News staff: 3; News: 2 hrs wkly. Target aud: 25-54; male & female. ♦Thomas C. Birch, pres; Jerry E. Brown, VP & gen mgr; Mike Elliott, opns mgr & gen sls mgr; Melissa P. Wilkerson, gen sls mgr & news dir; John Hart, chief of engrg.

Clifton Forge

WXCF(AM)— Oct 19, 1950: 1230 khz; 1 kw-U, DA-1. TL: N37 49 18 W79 48 46. Box 710, 1047 Ingalls St. 24422. Phone: (540) 862-5751. Phone: (540) 962-1133. Fax: (540) 862-2120. Web Site: www.bigcountry101.com. Licensee: Quorum Radio Partners of Virginia Inc. (acq 5-03; with co-located FM). Format: Adult contemp. News: one hr wkly. Target aud: 40 & up. ♦Marcia Smith, gen sls mgr & prom dir; Michael Stone, pres, gen mgr, sls dir & progmg dir; Lawrence Mason, chief of engrg.

WXCF-FM— Nov 20, 1982: 103.9 mhz; 150 w. Ant 1,909 ft. TL: N37 54 12 W79 52 15. Stereo. Format: Hits of the 70s, 80s & 90s. News staff: one. Target aud: 18-54; Targeting mostly women 25-54.

Clinchco

WDIC(AM)— May 1961: 1430 khz; 5 kw-D. TL: N37 08 42 W82 23 22. Stereo. Box 412, Rt. 1, Clintwood 24228. Phone: (276) 835-8626. Fax: (276) 835-8627. E-mail: wdic@wdicradio.com. Licensee: Dickenson County Broadcasting Corp. Group owner: Richard W. Edwards (acq 1-84; $366,850). FTR: 1-30-84). Network: ABC. Rgnl Reps. Smithwick & Belendiuk. Format: Country. News: 8 hrs wkly. Target aud: General. Spec prog: Farm one hr, relg 12 hrs wkly. ♦Richard W. Edwards, pres; Rufus E. Nickles, gen mgr, adv mgr & adv; Betty N. Fleming, opns mgr; Tammy Hill, progmg mgr & progmg.

WDIC-FM— July 2, 1989: 92.1 mhz; 2.5 kw. Ant 505 ft. TL: N37 08 42 W82 23 22. Stereo. Web Site: www.wdicradio.com. Network: ABC. Rep: Rgnl Reps. Smithwick & Belendiuk. Format: Oldies, news, loc sports. News: 3 hrs wkly. Target aud: 25-55; baby boomers.

Coeburn

WVSG(FM)— Apr 15, 1991: 99.7 mhz; 3 kw. 2,850 ft. TL: N36 56 44 W82 29 50. Stereo. Box 729, Whitesburg, KY 41858. Phone: (276) 395-3997. Fax: (606) 633-3314. E-mail: wvsg@msn.com. Licensee: Preston Communications Group Inc. (acq 11-6-01). Network: USA. Format: Southern gospel. Target aud: 18-54. ♦Preston L. Salyer, pres & gen mgr; Stephen Mullins, opns mgr; C.J. Kincer, progmg dir; Matthew Caudill, chief of engrg.

Collinsville

WFIC(AM)— Mar 1, 1970: 1530 khz; 1 kw-D, 250 w-CH. TL: N36 42 56 W79 55 15. Box 192, Martinsville 24114. Secondary address: 1675 Grandview Rd., Martinsville 24112. Phone: (276) 638-5235. Fax: (276) 638-6089. E-mail: eddie@spiritfm.com. Licensee: BASE Communications Inc. Group owner: Baker Family Stations (acq 9-3-97; $60,000). Network: USA. Format: Southern Gospel. Target aud: 35 plus; general. ♦Brian Sanders, gen mgr; Michael Carter, opns mgr & gen sls mgr; Wendall Minter, progmg dir.

Colonial Beach

WGRQ(FM)— May 3, 1986: 95.9 mhz; 2.4 kw. Ant 525 ft. TL: N38 13 45 W77 07 10. Stereo. 4414 Lafayette Blvd. #100, Fredericksburg 22408. Phone: (540) 891-9696. Fax: (540) 891-1656. E-mail: tcooper@oldies959.com. Web Site: www.oldies959.com. Licensee: Telemedia Broadcasting Inc. (acq 1-20-88). Network: ABC. Rep: Roslin. Format: Oldies. News staff: one; News: 3 hrs wkly. Target aud: 25 plus; baby boomers. ♦Carl W. Hurlebaus, pres; Thomas P. Cooper, gen mgr; Bill Keeler, sls dir; Branch Harper, prom dir; Jim Herring, progmg dir; Cathy Sato, pub affrs dir.

Colonial Heights

WDZY(AM)—Licensed to Colonial Heights. See Richmond

WKHK(FM)—Licensed to Colonial Heights. See Richmond

Covington

WIQO-FM—Listing follows WKEY(AM).

WKEY(AM)— May 23, 1941: 1340 khz; 1 kw-U. TL: N37 46 09 W79 58 59. Box 710, 508 W. Oak St. 24426. Phone: (540) 962-1133. Web Site: www.big country101.com. Licensee: Quorum Radio Partners of Virginia Inc., debtor-in-possession Group owner: Quorum Radio Partners of Virginia Inc. (acq 4-20-2005; with co-located FM). Fletcher, Heald & Hildreth. Format: Oldies. News staff: one; News: 12 hrs wkly. Target aud: 25 plus; younger country listeners. Spec prog: Black one hr, gospel 2 hrs wkly. ♦Marcia Smith, gen sls mgr; Michael Stone, pres, gen mgr & progmg dir; Dwight Rohr, news dir; Lawrence Mason, chief of engrg.

WIQO-FM—Co-owned with WKEY(AM). October 1964: 100.9 mhz; 560 w. 1,059 ft. TL: N37 47 36 W79 55 57. Web Site: www.bigcountry101.com. Network: ABC Information & Entertainment. Format: Country. News staff: one; News: 10 hrs wkly. Target aud: 25-54; general.

Crewe

WPZZ(FM)— June 9, 1949: 104.7 mhz; 100 kw horiz, 84 kw vert. Ant 981 ft. TL: N37 10 15 W77 57 16. Stereo. 2809 Emerywood Pkwy., Suite 300, Richmond 23294. Phone: (804) 672-9299. Fax: (804) 672-9314. Licensee: Radio One Licenses LLC. Group owner: Radio One Inc. (acq 11-8-2001; grpsl). Hogan & Hartson. Format: Gospel. Target aud: 18-34; adults. Spec prog: Farm 10 hrs wkly. ♦Alfred Liggins, CFO; Sheri Sawyer, gen mgr; Kevin Gardner, opns mgr & progmg dir; Yvonne Hagen, gen sls mgr; Bobby Walden, natl sls mgr; Dottie Brooks, mktg dir; June Grant, prom dir; Clovia Lawrence, pub affrs dir; Chris Lawless, chief of engrg.

WSVS(AM)— Apr 7, 1947: 800 khz; 5 kw-D, 275 w-N. TL: N37 11 43 W78 10 01. Box 47, 800 Melody Ln. 23930. Phone: (434) 645-7734. Phone: (434) 645-7735. Fax: (434) 645-1701. E-mail: wsvs@meckcom.net. Licensee: Colonial Broadcasting of Crewe Inc. Network: Family Radio. Format: C&W. News staff: one; News: 7 hrs wkly. Target aud: 35 plus. ♦John Wilson, CEO & pres; Francis Wood, gen mgr; Elliott Irving, stn mgr; Eddie Higgins, opns dir; Steve Winn, progmg dir.

Crozet

*WMRY(FM)— May 1995: 103.5 mhz; 270 w. 1,515 ft. TL: N37 57 00 W78 43 38. Stereo. Box 1292, c/o WMRA(FM), Harrisonburg 22803. Secondary address: 821 S. Main St., Harrisonburg 22807. Phone:

Stations in the U.S. — Virginia

(540) 568-6221. Fax: (540) 568-3814. Web Site: www.wmra.org. Licensee: James Madison University Board of Visitors. Network: Network: NPR, PRI. Format: Class, news. News staff: one; News: 32 hrs wkly. Target aud: 35-64; well educated adults. Spec prog: Folk 8 hrs, blues 4 hrs wkly. ♦Tom DuVal, gen mgr; Diane Halke, dev dir.

WSUH(FM)— September 1980: 102.3 mhz; 4.9 kw. 360 ft. TL: N38 04 47 W78 44 22. Stereo. Box 7703, Suite 300, Charlottesville 22906. Secondary address: 1150 Pepsi Pl., Charlottesville 22901. Phone: (434) 978-4408. Fax: (804) 434-1109. Web Site: www.1023thefox.com. Licensee: Clear Channel Broadcasting Licenses Inc. Group owner: Clear Channel Communications Inc. (acq 8-6-99). Format: Classic hits of the 60s & 70s. Target aud: 35-54; general. ♦Phil Robken, gen mgr & progmg dir; Regan Keith, opns mgr; Mike Chiumento, gen sls mgr.

Culpeper

*WARN(FM)— 1997: 91.5 mhz; 930 w. 121 ft. TL: N38 27 15 W77 59 10. Box 3206, American Family Radio, Tupelo, MS 38803. Phone: (662) 844-8888. Fax: (662) 842-6791. Web Site: www.afr.net. Licensee: American Family Association. Group owner: American Family Radio Format: Christian, inspirational. ♦Marvin Sanders, gen mgr.

WCVA(AM)— February 1949: 1490 khz; 1 kw-U. TL: N38 29 04 W77 59 22. Box 699, One Radio Ln. 22701. Phone: (540) 825-3900. Fax: (540) 825-4237. Web Site: www.cruisincountry.com. Licensee: Piedmont Communications Inc. (group owner; acq 11-21-2003; grpsl). Network: ABC Information & Entertainment. Format: Nostalgia. News staff: one; News: 10 hrs wkly. Target aud: General. ♦John Schick, pres & gen mgr; Ann Velez, gen sls mgr; Yon O'Connor, progmg dir; Chris Wilk, chief of engrg.

WJMA-FM— Co-owned with WCVA(AM). Dec 4, 1971: 103.1 mhz; 3 kw. 300 ft. TL: N38 29 04 W77 59 22. (CP: 3.3 kw). Stereo. Web Site: www.cruisincountry.com. Format: Modern country.

*WPER(FM)— 1999: 89.9 mhz; 50 kw. Ant 331 ft. TL: N38 40 42 W77 47 18. Box 889, Blacksburg 24063. Phone: (540) 961-2377. Fax: (540) 951-5282. E-mail: mail@spiritfm.com. Web Site: www.spiritfm.com. Licensee: Positive Alternative Radio Inc. Group owner: Baker Family Stations (Positive Radio Group) Booth, Freret, Imlay & Tepper. Format: Relg, teaching, contemp Christian. ♦Barry Armstrong, gen mgr.

Danville

WAKG(FM)—Listing follows WBTM(AM).

WBTM(AM)— May 24, 1930: 1330 khz; 5 kw-D, 1 kw-N, DA-N. TL: N36 36 36 W79 25 47. Stereo. Box 1629 24543. Secondary address: 710 Grove St. 24541. Phone: (434) 793-4411. Fax: (434) 797-3918. Web Site: www.wbtm1330.com. Licensee: Piedmont Broadcasting Corp. Network: ABC Information & Entertainment. Format: Oldies. News staff: 2; News: 5 hrs wkly. Target aud: 24 plus; young working adults. ♦Bob Ashby, CEO, chmn, pres & gen mgr; Dave Hutcheson, opns mgr; Mike Wimmer, gen sls mgr & natl sls mgr; Carol Metz, prom mgr; Alex Vardavas, progmg dir; Chuck Vipperman, news dir; Allen Boaz, chief of engrg.

WAKG(FM)—Co-owned with WBTM(AM). June 3, 1968: 103.3 mhz; 100 kw. 630 ft. TL: N36 44 28 W79 23 05. Stereo. Phone: (434) 797-4290. Web Site: www.wakg.com. Format: Modern country. Target aud: 18-54. ♦Dave Hutcheson, opns VP; Mike Wimmer, sls VP; Sherri Crowder, progmg mgr; Allan Rowe, mus dir.

WDVA(AM)— June 29, 1947: 1250 khz; 5 kw-U, DA-N. TL: N36 34 53 W79 26 33. Stereo. One Radio Ln. 24541. Phone: (434) 797-1250. Phone: (434) 797-1266. Fax: (434) 797-1255. Licensee: Mitchell Communications Inc. (acq 6-28-93; 7-19-93). Network: CBS. Latham & Watkins. Format: Gospel. News: 12 hrs wkly. Target aud: 18 plus. ♦C.G. Hairston, pres & gen mgr.

WILA(AM)— Aug 25, 1957: 1580 khz; 1 kw-D. TL: N36 34 03 W79 22 50. Box 3444 24543. Secondary address: 865 Industrial Ave. 24541. Phone: (434) 792-2133. Fax: (434) 792-2134. E-mail: wilaradio@gamewood.net. Licensee: Tol-Tol Communications Inc. (acq 12-29-92; $250,000; 1-25-93). Network: American Urban. Rep: Savalli. Format: Black, gospel, oldies. Target aud: General; ethnic (Black) and citizens who enjoy div progmg. ♦Lawrence A. Toller, pres, gen mgr, sls dir, progmg dir & pub affrs dir.

*WOKD-FM— 1998: 91.1 mhz; 18 kw. 466 ft. TL: N56 44 30 W79 23 07. Box 889, Blacksburg 24063. Phone: (540) 961-2377. Fax: (540) 951-5282. E-mail: mail@spiritfm.com. Web Site: www.spiritfm.com. Licensee: Positive Alternative Radio Inc. Group owner: Baker Family Stations Format: Christian adult contemp. ♦Barry Armstrong, gen mgr.

Deltaville

WSRV(FM)— Jan 5, 1999: 92.3 mhz; 2.4 kw. Ant 525 ft. TL: N37 29 37 W76 26 30. 6558 Main St., Suite 2, Gloucester 23061. Phone: (804) 695-0100. Fax: (804) 695-1650. Web Site: www.tideradio.com. Licensee: Bullseye Broadcasting LLC (acq 3-3-2005). Format: Triple A. News staff: one. ♦Sherry Campana, pres; Tom Davis, gen mgr.

Dillwyn

WBNN-FM— July 2000: 105.3 mhz; 6 kw. Ant 328 ft. TL: N37 34 50 W78 37 18. Stereo. Hwy. 15 23936. Secondary address: 18498 N. Madison Hwy. 23936. Phone: (434) 983-6621. Fax: (434) 983-6772. E-mail: mail@bigcountry1053.com. Web Site: www.bigcountry1053.com. Licensee: WKGM Inc. Group owner: Baker Family Stations Booth, Freret, Imlay & Tepper P. Format: Classical country. Target aud: 35-55. Spec prog: Relg. ♦Vernon H. Bayer, CEO; Greg Breeden, progmg dir.

Dublin

WPIN(AM)— 1995: 810 khz; 4.2 kw-D. TL: N37 07 55 W80 37 07. Box 889, Blacksburg 24063. Phone: (540) 961-2377. Fax: (540) 961-2021. Licensee: Dublin Radio. Booth, Freret, Imlay & Tepper. Format: Fox sports. ♦Edward A. Baker, pres & gen mgr; Brian Sanders, stn mgr.

*WPIN-FM— 1994: 91.5 mhz; 100 w horiz, 90 w vert. 1,204 ft. TL: N37 01 27 W80 44 47. Box 889, Blacksburg 24060. Phone: (540) 552-8073. Fax: (540) 951-5282. Web Site: www.spiritfm.com. Licensee: Positive Alternative Radio Inc. Group owner: Baker Family Stations (Positive Radio Group) Booth, Freret, Imlay & Tepper. Format: Christian adult contemp. ♦Barry Armstrong, CEO & gen mgr; Vernon H. Baker, chmn; Edward A. Baker, pres.

Duffield

WDUF(AM)— Aug 12, 1986: 1120 khz; 1 kw-D. TL: N36 42 30 W82 47 30. Box 391 24244. Phone: (276) 431-4357. Licensee: Duffield Broadcasting Co. Format: Var/div, bluegrass, gospel, country. Target aud: General; miners, industrial & agricultural workers, seniors. Spec prog: Lunchtime farm 5 hrs wkly. ♦Jay Marion Smith, stn mgr.

Dumfries-Triangle

WPWC(AM)— Dec 22, 1961: 1480 khz; 1 kw-D, 500 w-N, DA-2. TL: N38 34 06 W77 20 20. 14416 Jefferson Davis Hwy., Suite 20, Woodbridge 22191. Phone: (703) 494-0100. Phone: (703) 490-1579. Fax: (703) 490-1579. E-mail: radiofiesta1480@yahoo.com. Licensee: JMK Communications Inc. (acq 1-19-00; $900,000). Format: Sp. ♦Grant Chang, pres; Carlos Aragon, gen mgr; Clasa Marshall, gen sls mgr; Jose Luis Liriano, progmg dir.

Earlysville

WKTR(AM)— Feb 17, 1991: 840 khz; 8.2 kw-D, DA. TL: N38 15 57 W78 24 53. Box 309, Spotswood Business Park Cir., Quinque 22965. Secondary address: Spotswood Business Park Circle, Quinque 22965. Phone: (434) 985-8585. Fax: (757) 365-0412. E-mail: larrycobb@cox.net. Licensee: Rural Radio Service. Group owner: Baker Family Stations Booth, Freret, Imlay & Tepper. Format: Relg. ♦Edward A. Baker, pres; Larry W. Cobb, VP & gen mgr.

Edinburg

*WOTC(FM)— Apr 1, 1994: 88.3 mhz; 1 kw. 403 ft. TL: N38 48 12 W78 41 23. 408 Stony Creek Rd. 22824. Phone: (540) 984-8665 ext 206. Fax: (540) 984-9877. Web Site: www.valleybaptistchurch.net. Licensee: Valley Baptist Church-Christian School. Network: USA. Format: Educ, relg, news. Target aud: General; relg, children. ♦Ed Dorrin, gen mgr.

Elkton

WACL(FM)— Mar 6, 1989: 98.5 mhz; 900 w. Ant 1,607 ft. TL: N38 23 36 W78 46 14. Stereo. 207 University Blvd., Harrisonburg 22801. Phone: (540) 434-1777. Fax: (540) 432-9968. E-mail: radio@goodradio.com. Web Site: www.goodradio.com. Licensee: Capstar TX L.P. Group owner: Clear Channel Communications Inc. (acq 3-12-01; grpsl). Format: Mainstream rock. News staff: one; News: one hr wkly. Target aud: 35-49. ♦Steve Davis, gen mgr; Jeff Caudell, chief of engrg.

Emory

*WEHC(FM)— Nov 15, 1994: 90.7 mhz; 100 w. 95 ft. TL: N36 46 20 W81 49 56. Box 947, Keller, Garnand Dr. 24327-0947. Phone: (276) 944-4161. Phone: (276) 944-6822. Fax: (276) 944-6934. E-mail: tdkeller@ehc.edu. Web Site: www.ehcweb.ehc.edu/masscomm/wehc. Licensee: Emory and Henry College. Format: Div, CHR, progsv. News: 3 hrs wkly. Target aud: College community. ♦Dr. Teresa Keller, gen mgr; Jay Webb, stn mgr; Ron Taylor, chief of engrg.

Emporia

WEVA(AM)— Nov 4, 1952: 860 khz; 1 kw-D. TL: N36 41 56 W77 32 55. Box 1056, 705 Washington St. 23847. Secondary address: 705 Washington Street 23847. Phone: (434) 634-2133. Fax: (434) 634-5050. E-mail: info@wevaradio.com. Web Site: www.wevaradio.com. Licensee: Colonial Media Corp. Dec. 2001 Network: Network: CBS, Westwood One. Wilkinson, Barker, Knauer & Quinn. Format: Adult contemp, news/talk. News: 14 hrs wkly. Target aud: 25 plus; Adults 25-64. Spec prog: Gospel 6 hrs, garden 3 hrs, news 14 hrs. ♦James Vavtrout, CEO; George A. Sperry, gen mgr, sls VP & prom mgr; Andy Lucy, progmg mgr & mus dir; Joseph Wetherbee, chief of engrg.

*WJYA(FM)— January 1999: 89.3 mhz; 2 kw vert. Ant 443 ft. TL: N36 46 04 W77 43 39. Stereo. 1320 Central Park Blvd., Suite 253, Fredericksburg 22401. Phone: (540) 786-5960. Fax: (540) 786-0001. E-mail: wjya@csnradio.org. Web Site: www.csnvirginia.org. Licensee: CSN International (group owner; acq 3-8-02; $3.32 million. with WJYJ(FM) Fredericksburg). Format: Contemp Christian. ♦Chuck Smith, gen mgr.

WYTT(FM)— 2003: 99.5 mhz; 1.27 kw. Ant 501 ft. TL: N36 39 20 W77 34 22. Box 910, Roanoke Rapids, NC 27890. Phone: (252) 536-0597. Fax: (252)538-0378. Web Site: www.firstmediarr.com. Licensee: First Media Radio LLC. Group owner: The MainQuad Group. (acq 12-3-2003; grpsl). Format: Hits & Oldies. ♦Alan Garrick, gen mgr & progmg dir; Frank White, chief of engrg.

Ettrick

WJZV(FM)— 2001: 93.1 mhz; 5.2 kw. Ant 348 ft. TL: N37 16 21 W77 33 59. 300 Arboretum Pl., Suite 590, Richmond 23236. Phone: (804) 327-9902. Fax: (804) 327-9911. Licensee: Richmond Broadcasting Inc. Format: Country. ♦Kevin Lein, gen mgr.

Exmore

WROX-FM—Licensed to Exmore. See Virginia Beach

Fairfax

WDCT(AM)— Sept 25, 1955: 1310 khz; 5 kw-D, 500 w-N, DA-2. TL: N38 51 08 W77 18 57. 3251 Old Lee Hwy., Suite 506 22030. Phone: (703) 273-4000. Fax: (703) 273-1015. E-mail:

Virginia

1310@radiowashingtonnews.com. Web Site: www.radiowashingtonnews.com. Licensee: Family Radio Ltd. (acq 1995). Network: Moody. Format: Korean. Target aud: 25-54; 60% female, 40% male. ♦Kenneth Shin, gen mgr & chief of engrg; Young Jang, sls dir; Ronnie Shin, progmg dir.

Fairlawn

WKNV(AM)— 1998: 890 khz; 10 kw-D, DA. TL: N37 08 26 W80 36 49. Box 889, Blacksburg 24063. Phone: (540) 961-2377. Fax: (540) 951-5282. Licensee: Base Communications Inc. Group owner: Baker Family Stations Format: Relg. ♦Edward A. Baker, pres & gen mgr; Brian Sanders, stn mgr & progmg dir; Winston Hawkins, chief of engrg.

Falls Church

WFAX(AM)—Licensed to Falls Church. See Washington DC

Falmouth

WGRX(FM)— May 17, 2001: 104.5 mhz; 2.7 kw. Ant 492 ft. TL: N38 16 31 W77 32 34. Stereo. 4414 Lafayette Blvd. #100, Fredericksburg 22408. Phone: (540) 891-9696. Fax: (540) 891-1656. E-mail: wgrx@thunder1045.com. Web Site: ww.thunder1045.com. Licensee: Telemedia Broadcasting Inc. (acq 4-17-01; $1.8 million. for two-thirds). Rep: Roslin. Format: Country. News: 3 hrs wkly. Target aud: 18-49; male audience, working class. ♦Carl W. Hurlebaus, pres; Thomas P. Cooper, gen mgr; Bill Keeler, sls dir; Tim Stone, progmg dir; Cathy Sato, pub affrs dir.

Farmville

WFLO(AM)— August 1947: 870 khz; 1 kw-D. TL: N37 19 35 W78 23 09. Box 367, 1582 Cumberland Rd. 23901. Phone: (434) 392-4195. Fax: (434) 392-5724. E-mail: wflo@moonstar.com. Web Site: www.wflo.net. Licensee: Colonial Broadcasting Co. Inc. (acq 4-71). Rep: Salem. Format: C&W, news/talk. News staff: one; News: 4 hrs wkly. Target aud: 25 plus. Spec prog: Relg 10 hrs wkly. ♦John D. Wilson, pres; Henry Fulcher, sr VP; Francis E. Wood Jr., gen mgr; Chris Wood, opns dir & progmg dir; Chris Brochon, prom dir; Elliott Irving, news dir; Polly Davis, sls.

WFLO-FM— May 1961: 95.7 mhz; 50 kw. 492 ft. TL: N37 19 35 W78 23 09. Stereo. Network: Network: Jones Radio Networks, AP Radio. Format: Adult contemp. News staff: one; News: 4 hrs wkly. Target aud: 25 plus. ♦John Wilson, chmn.

*WMLU(FM)— 1988: 91.3 mhz; 1 w horiz, 150 w vert. Ant 72 ft. TL: N37 17 50 W78 23 42. Longwood University, 201 High St., Virginia 23909. Phone: (434) 395-2475. Phone: (434) 395-2792. Fax: (434) 395-2378. E-mail: wlcx@longwood.edu. Web Site: http://lancer.longwood.edu/org/wlcx. Licensee: Longwood University. Format: Div, progsv. Target aud: 18-23; div college students. ♦Matt Taylor, gen mgr; Bryan Lee, progmg VP & progmg dir; John Gross, chief of engrg.

WPAK(AM)— June 15, 1978: 1490 khz; 1 kw-U. TL: N38 18 47 W78 23 41. 446 Plank Rd. 23901. Phone: (434) 392-8114. Fax: (434) 392-8115. Licensee: Great Virginia Venture Inc. (acq 5-11-98; $201,000). Format: Relg. Spec prog: Farm one hr, gospel 12 hrs wkly. ♦George H. Granger, pres; Mark Neimand, gen mgr.

WVHL(FM)— Sept 1, 1997: 92.9 mhz; 6 kw. 328 ft. TL: N37 17 06 W78 29 39. Drawer T, 116 North St. 23901. Secondary address: 116 North St. 23901. Phone: (434) 392-9393. Fax: (434) 392-6091. E-mail: v93@wvhl.net. Web Site: www.wvhl.net. Licensee: The Farmville Herald Inc. Network: ABC. Format: Country. Target aud: General. ♦Steve Wall, gen mgr; Sherry Massaro, opns mgr.

Ferrum

*WFFC(FM)— January 1989: 89.9 mhz; 100 w. Ant -40 ft. TL: N36 55 46 W80 01 27. Stereo. WFFC Radio, Ferrum College 24088. Phone: (540) 365-4482. Fax: (540) 365-5589. E-mail: wffc@ferrum.edu. Web Site: www.radioif.org. Licensee: Virginia Tech Foundation Inc. (acq 1-23-2004; $10). Format: Class, progsv. ♦John wojtowicz, stn mgr.

Fieldale

WODY(AM)— July 1, 1993: 1160 khz; 5 kw-D, 250 w-N, DA-2. TL: N36 42 36 W79 57 58. Box 192, Martinsville 24114. Secondary address: 1675 Grandview R., Martinsville 24112. Phone: (276) 638-5235. Fax: (276) 638-6089. E-mail: mcarter@thesportsaddictnetwork.com. Web Site: thesportsaddictnetwork.com. Licensee: Base Communications Inc. Group owner: Baker Family Stations (acq 4-17-98). Network: USA. Format: ESPN. Target aud: 25-54. ♦Vernon H. Baker, pres & CFO; Edward A. Baker, exec VP & gen mgr; Brian Sanders, stn mgr & sls dir; Michael Carter, opns mgr; Winston Hawkins, chief of engrg.

Floyd

WGFC(AM)— Apr 20, 1985: 1030 khz; 1 kw-D. TL: N36 55 53 W80 16 34. Box 495 24091. Secondary address: 401 Shooting Creek Rd. S.E. 24091. Phone: (540) 745-9811. Fax: (540) 745-9812. E-mail: wgfc@wgfcradio.com. Web Site: www.nlcm.net/radio.htm. Licensee: New Life Christian Communications Inc. (acq 7-1-02). Format: Bluegrass, southern gospel. News staff: 2; News: 10 hrs wkly. Target aud: Loc community interest & general audience. ♦R. Leon Goad, CEO, pres & gen mgr; Sandra Haga, exec VP; Jackie Goad, VP.

Fort Lee

WKLR(FM)—Licensed to Fort Lee. See Richmond

Franklin

WLQM(AM)— Oct 13, 1956: 1250 khz; 1 kw-D. TL: N36 40 57 W76 55 43. Box 735 23851. Secondary address: 320 Franklin St. 23851. Phone: (757) 562-3135. Fax: (757) 562-2345. E-mail: wlqm@wlqmradio.com. Web Site: www.wlqmradio.com. Licensee: Franklin Broadcasting Corp. (acq 8-10-59). Format: Urban Gospel. Target aud: 25-49. Spec prog: Gospel 12 hrs wkly. ♦Peter E. Clark, pres; Michael E. Clark, gen mgr; Tim Parsons, opns VP; Johnny Hart, gen sls mgr & prom mgr; Michael Clark, natl sls mgr; Walter Hale, rgnl sls mgr & progmg dir; Peter Clark, news dir; Mickel Pruden, chief of engrg.

WLQM-FM— January 1988: 101.7 mhz; 6 kw. 469 ft. TL: N36 41 17 W77 00 58. Web Site: www.wlqmradio.com. Network: ABC. Pepper & Corazzini. Format: Contemp country. ♦Tim Parsons, progmg dir.

Fredericksburg

WBQB(FM)—Listing follows WFVA.

WFLS-FM—Listing follows WYSK(AM).

WFVA(AM)— Sept 8, 1939: 1230 khz; 1 kw-U. TL: N38 16 50 W77 26 11. Box 269, 1914 Mimosa St. 22405. Phone: (540) 373-7721. Fax: (540) 899-3879. E-mail: wfva@am1230wfva.com. Web Site: www.am1230wfva.com. Licensee: Mid-Atlantic Network Inc. (group owner) Network: ABC Information & Entertainment. Cole, Raywid & Braverman. Format: MOR, talk. News staff: 3; News: 15 hrs wkly. Target aud: 35 plus. Spec prog: Washington Redskins football. ♦John P. Lewis, pres; Shawn Sloan, gen mgr; Brian Demay, opns dir; Kat Kammer, gen sls mgr; Jessica Beadel, prom dir; Rod Spencer, progmg mgr; Veronica Robinson, news dir; John Diamantis, chief of engrg.

WGRQ(FM)—See Colonial Beach

*WJYJ(FM)— May 6, 1983: 90.5 mhz; 38 kw. Ant 500 ft. TL: N38 11 48 W77 33 45. Stereo. 1320 Central Park Blvd. 22404. Phone: (540) 786-5960. Fax: (540) 786-0001. E-mail: wjyj@csnradio.com. Web Site: www.csnvirginia.org. Licensee: CSN International (group owner; acq 3-8-02; $3.32 million. with WJYA from Emporia). Format: Contemp Christian. News staff: one; News: 14 hrs wkly. Target aud: 25-49. ♦Chuck Smith, pres; Steve Wang, gen mgr & stn mgr; Chris Wilk, chief of engrg.

WYSK(AM)— July 15, 1960: 1350 khz; 1 kw-D, 37 w-N. TL: N38 18 46 W77 26 20. 616 Amelia St. 22401. Phone: (540) 373-1500. Fax: (540) 374-5525. Web Site: www.wysk.com. Licensee: The Free Lance-Star Publishing Co. (group owner). Format: Latino. News staff: 3; News: 12 hrs wkly. Target aud: General. ♦John Moen, gen mgr & progmg dir; Chris Wilk, chief of engrg.

WFLS-FM—Co-owned with WYSK(AM). June 12, 1962: 93.3 mhz; 50 kw. 492 ft. TL: N38 18 46 W77 26 20. Stereo. Web Site: www.wfls.com. Format: Country. News staff: 3. ♦Jon Reed, progmg mgr; Dick Ritchie, pub affrs dir.

Front Royal

WFQX(FM)— Jan 17, 1973: 99.3 mhz; 3 kw. 295 ft. TL: N39 00 11 W78 20 28. Stereo. 510 Pegasus Ct., Winchester 22602. Phone: (540) 662-5101. Fax: (540) 662-8610. Web Site: ww.993thefox.com. Licensee: Capstar TX L.P. Group owner: Clear Channel Communications Inc. (acq 8-30-00; grpsl). Format: Rock/AOR. News staff: 3; News: one hr wkly. Target aud: 25-49; men. ♦Jim Shea, CEO; Chuck Peterson, gen mgr; David Miller, opns mgr & progmg mgr; Marcella Vance, sls dir; Justin Maglione, prom dir, prom dir & mus dir; Ben Gates, pub affrs dir; Mark Kesner, chief of engrg.

WFTR(AM)— Sept 19, 1948: 1450 khz; 1 kw-U. TL: N38 54 31 W78 10 37. Box 192 22630. Secondary address: 1106 Elm St. 22630. Phone: (540) 635-4121. Fax: (540) 635-9387. E-mail: wftr@shentel.net. Web Site: www.realcountryonline.com. Licensee: Royal Broadcasting Inc. (acq 8-15-00; $950,000 with co-located FM). Network: ABC. Commercial Media Sales. Format: Country. News staff: one; News: 20 hrs wkly. Target aud: 25-54. Spec prog: Bluegrass 2 hrs wkly. ♦Andrew Shearer, CEO; Mike O'Dell, COO, gen mgr, gen sls mgr & progmg dir; Shae Parker, opns mgr.

WZRV(FM)—Co-owned with WFTR(AM). 1981: 95.3 mhz; 6 kw. 300 ft. TL: N38 58 29 W78 12 09. Stereo. Phone: (540) 665-9595. E-mail: wzrv953@shentel.net. Web Site: www.oldiesradioonline.com. Network: ABC. Format: Oldies. News staff: one. Target aud: 25-54. ♦Mike O'Dell, sls dir; Randy Woodward, progmg mgr; Mario Retrosi, news dir.

Galax

WBRF(FM)— Dec 15, 1961: 98.1 mhz; 100 kw. 1,756 ft. TL: N36 34 50 W80 58 23. Stereo. Box 838 24333. Secondary address: 325 Poplar Knob Rd. 24333. Phone: (276) 236-9273. Fax: (276) 236-7198. E-mail: brc98@adelphia.net. Licensee: Blue Ridge Radio Inc. (acq 4-19-85; 12-31-84). Network: CBS. Format: Country. Target aud: General. Spec prog: Pub affrs one hr wkly. ♦Debby Sizer Stringer, gen mgr, stn mgr, gen sls mgr & adv mgr; Ray Bass, prom mgr; Betty Liddle, prom mgr & progmg dir; Jason Blevins, mus dir; John Mullins, chief of engrg.

*WOKG(FM)— 2005: 90.3 mhz; 2.7 kw. Ant 538 ft. TL: N36 39 27 W80 54 22. Box 889, Blacksburg 24063. Licensee: Positive Alternative Radio Inc. Group owner: Baker Family Stations.

WWWJ(AM)— Feb 1, 1947: 1360 khz; 5 kw-D. TL: N36 39 48 W80 54 52. Box 270, 325 Poplar Knob Rd. 24333. Phone: (276) 236-2921. Fax: (276) 236-2922. Licensee: Twin County Broadcasting Corp. (acq 4-19-85; $200,000; 4-8-85). Network: CBS. Format: Gospel. News: 1 hr wkly. Target aud: 18 plus. Spec prog: Sp 20 hrs, farm one hr wkly. ♦Deborah E. Stringer, pres & gen mgr; J. Brice Parks, gen sls mgr; Carole Bonn, progmg dir; Samantha Farmer, mus dir; John Mullins, chief of engrg.

Gate City

WGAT(AM)— July 24, 1959: 1050 khz; 1 kw-D, 266 w-N. TL: N36 37 59 W82 34 56. 117 E. Jackson, Suite 2 24251. Phone: (276) 386-7025. Fax: (276) 386-3600. E-mail: wgatradio@earthlink.net. Licensee: Tri-Cities Broadcasting Corp. (acq 11-28-90; $70,000;. FTR: 12-17-90). Network: Network: CNN Radio, Jones Radio Networks. Dow, Lohnes & Albertson. Format: Sports, talk. News staff: one; News: 10 hrs wkly. Target aud: 25 plus. ♦Alan Giles, pres; Mike Long, gen mgr.

Glen Allen

WTOX(AM)—Not on air, target date: unknown: 1480 khz; 6.3 kw-D, 1.5 kw-N, DA-2. TL: N37 40 56 W77 33 49. 308 W. Broad St., Richmond 23220. Phone: (804) 643-0990. Fax: (804) 474-3770. Licensee: Radio Richmond 1480 Inc. Group owner: 4M Communications Inc. ♦Gloria Kurtlin, stn mgr.

Gloucester

WXGM(AM)— Jan 20, 1957: 1420 khz; 740 w-D. TL: N37 24 36 W76 32 52. Stereo. Box 634, 6267 Professional Dr. 23061. Phone: (804)

Stations in the U.S. — Virginia

Developers & Brokers of Radio Properties — contact American Media Services at our suite: Philadelphia Marriott Downtown 215-625-2900. 843-972-2200. americanmediaservices.com. Charleston, SC. Dallas, TX · Chicago, IL · Austin, TX. American Media Services, LLC

693-2105. Phone: (804) 693-9946. Fax: (804) 693-2182. E-mail: office@xtra99.com. Web Site: www.xtra99.com. Licensee: WXGM Inc. (acq 7-91; 6-22-81). Network: ABC. Verner, Liipfert, Bernhard, McPherson & Hand. Format: Adult contemp. News staff: one; News: 7 hrs wkly. Target aud: 25-54. Spec prog: Farm 2 hrs, relg 2 hrs wkly. ♦ Thomas W. Robinson, pres & gen mgr; Harvey King, opns mgr & progmg dir; Iris Lassister, gen sls mgr; Herman King, news dir; Bill Swartz, chief of engrg.

WXGM-FM— July 29, 1991: 99.1 mhz; 6 kw. 328 ft. TL: N37 24 36 W76 32 52. Stereo. Web Site: www.xtra99.com. Format: Adult contemp.

Goochland

WZEZ(FM)— 2001: 100.5 mhz; 4.8 kw. Ant 262 ft. TL: N37 38 16 W77 54 21. 4301 W. 100 Rd., Chester 23831. Phone: (804) 717-2000. Fax: (804) 717-2009. E-mail: wzez@cavtel.net. Web Site: www.wzezradio.com. Licensee: Hubert N. Hoffman III, executor (acq 9-12-02). Network: USA. Format: Nostalgia. ♦ Paul Scott, gen mgr.

Gretna

WMNA(AM)— Aug 11, 1956: 730 khz; 1 kw-D, 28 w-N, DA. TL: N36 55 31 W79 19 50. Box 730, 677 Zion Rd. 24557. Phone: (434) 656-1234. Fax: (434) 847-5709. Web Site: www.wlni.com. Licensee: 3 Daughters Media Inc. Group owner: Burns Media Strategies Inc. (acq 11-14-2002; $300,000. with co-located FM). Womble, Carlyle, Sandridge & Rice. Format: Country. News staff: one; News: 19 hrs wkly. Target aud: 18-55; family groups. Spec prog: Farm 8 hrs, Black 2 hrs, bluegrass 20 hrs, sports 10 hrs, gospel 15 hrs wkly. ♦ Gary E. Burns, CEO, pres & gen mgr; Mike Slenski, gen mgr; Charlotte Wells, progmg dir; Dale Cook, chief of engrg.

WMNA-FM— Feb 28, 1959: 106.3 mhz; 6 kw. 260 ft. TL: N36 55 31 W79 19 50. Stereo. Network: ABC Information & Entertainment. Format: Talk. News: 10 hrs wkly. Target aud: 24-54; active & mature. ♦ Rich Roth, progmg dir.

Grundy

WMJD(FM)—Listing follows WNRG(AM).

WNRG(AM)— Nov 16, 1955: 940 khz; 5 kw-D, 14 w-N. TL: N37 18 08 W82 07 04. Box 2045 24614. Secondary address: Rt. 460 W. 24614. Phone: (276) 935-7227. Fax: (276) 935-2587. E-mail: wnrg940@hotmail.com. Web Site: www.wnrg-wmjd-tv7.com. Licensee: Peggy Sue Broadcasting Corp. (group owner; acq 3-29-2004; $200,000. with co-located FM). Network: UPI. Format: Country. Spec prog: Farm 5 hrs wkly. ♦ Ron Cole, gen mgr, opns mgr, gen sls mgr & progmg dir; Arthur Stiltner, mus dir & chief of engrg.

WMJD(FM)—Co-owned with WNRG(AM). June 21, 1965: 97.7 mhz; 1.4 kw. 490 ft. TL: N37 18 08 W82 07 04. Stereo. Phone: (276) 935-7227. E-mail: wmjd97@hotmail.com. Web Site: www.wnrg-wmjd-tv7.com. Format: Adult contemp, oldies. ♦ Ron Cole, stn mgr; Elliott Stewart, mus dir & news dir.

Hampden-Sydney

*****WWHS-FM**— Oct 11, 1972: 92.1 mhz; 10 w. 140 ft. TL: N37 14 19 W78 27 48. (CP: Ant 216 ft.). Stereo. Box 606, Hampden-Sydney College 23943. Phone: (434) 223-6009. E-mail: wwhs@hsc.edu. Web Site: people.hsc.edu. Licensee: President & Board of Trustees of Hampden-Sydney College. Format: CHR, div, progsv. News: 5 hrs wkly. Target aud: 18-25; college community. Spec prog: Blues 2 hrs, class 2 hrs, jazz 6 hrs, reggae 4 hrs, funk 4 hrs wkly. ♦ Elijah Wallace, gen mgr.

Hampton

*****WHOV(FM)**— Mar 5, 1964: 88.1 mhz; 2 kw horiz, 8 kw vert. 200 ft. TL: N37 01 03 W76 20 13. Stereo. Dept. of Mass Media Arts, Hampton Univ. 23668. Phone: (757) 727-5407. Phone: (757) 727-5711.

Fax: (757) 727-5084. E-mail: info@whovfm.com. Web Site: www.whovfm.com. Licensee: Hampton University. Format: Var/div. News: 2 hrs wkly. Target aud: 18-54. Spec prog: Sp 12 hrs, blues 3 hrs, reggae 4 hrs wkly. ♦ Leon Scott, pres; Jay Wright, gen mgr, gen sls mgr, adv mgr & progmg dir; Rebecca Milbourne, opns mgr; Robert Grau, chief of engrg.

WLRT(AM)— July 1, 1948: 1490 khz; 1 kw-U. TL: N37 01 46 W76 22 35. 2845 N. Armistead Ave., Suite C 23666. Phone: (757) 766-9262. Fax: (757) 766-7439. Web Site: www.racetalklive.com.racetalklive.com. Licensee: Hampton Radio II Inc. (acq 12-9-86; $485,000;. FTR: 10-20-86). Network: Network: ABC, Motor Racing Net. Hazes Associates. Format: News, sports. ♦ Joseph Russo, pres; George Greenlaw, gen sls mgr; Keith Bennett, progmg dir; Ralph Stevens, chief of engrg.

WWDE-FM— June 1, 1962: 101.3 mhz; 50 kw. 499 ft. TL: N36 49 41 W76 15 05. Stereo. 236 Clearfield Ave., Suite 206, Virginia Beach 23462. Phone: (757) 497-2000. Fax: (757) 456-5458. Web Site: www.2wd.com. Licensee: Entercom Norfolk License LLC. Group owner: Entercom Communications Corp. (acq 12-13-99; grpsl). Rep: D & R Radio. Bryan Cave. Format: Adult contemp. News: one hr wkly. ♦ David J. Field, CEO, pres & opns dir; Steve Fisher, CFO & exec VP; John C. Donlevie, exec VP; Steve Godofsky, VP; Skip Schmidt, gen mgr; Don London, opns mgr.

Harrisonburg

WBOP(FM)—(Churchville). Mar 2, 1991: 106.3 mhz; 10 kw. Ant 574 ft. TL: N38 09 52 W79 08 24. Stereo. 1866 E. Market St. , Suite 325 22801-5111. Secondary address: 639 N. Main St., Mount Crawford 22841. Phone: (540) 432-1063. Fax: (540) 433-9267. E-mail: wbop@rica.net. Web Site: www.wbopfm.com. Licensee: Force 5 Communications LLC (group owner; acq 2-28-2005; $3.1 million. with WSIG(FM) Mount Jackson). Southmayd & Miller. Format: Classic, new rock. Target aud: 18-49. ♦ Tom Manley, gen mgr.

*****WEMC(FM)**— 1955: 91.7 mhz; 1.85 kw. 190 ft. TL: N38 28 20 W78 52 57. Stereo. Eastern Mennonite Univ., 1200 Park Rd. 22802. Phone: (540) 432-4288. Phone: (540) 432-4287. Fax: (540) 432-4444. E-mail: wemc@emu.edu. Web Site: www.emu.edu/wemc. Licensee: Eastern Mennonite University. Booth, Freret, Imlay & Tepper. Format: Classical, Jazz, World. News: 34 hrs wkly. Target aud: General. Spec prog: Folk/bluegrass 12 hrs, 50s 1 hr wkly. ♦ Jon Kauffmann-Kennel, gen mgr & progmg dir.

WHBG(AM)— August 1956: 1360 khz; 4.7 kw-D, 20 w-N. TL: N38 24 30 W78 54 04. Stereo. 130 Media Ln. 22801. Phone: (540) 434-0331. Fax: (540) 434-7087. Web Site: www.valleyradio.com. Licensee: M. Belmont VerStandig Inc. Group owner: VerStandig Broadcasting Format: Sports. Target aud: 24-50. ♦ Susanne FitzPatrick, gen mgr.

WKCY(AM)— May 11, 1967: 1300 khz; 5 kw-D. TL: N38 27 52 W78 50 53. Box 1107 22801. Secondary address: 207 University Blvd. 22801. Phone: (540) 434-1777. Fax: (540) 432-9968. Web Site: www.goodradio.com. Licensee: Capstar TX L.P. Group owner: Clear Channel Communications Inc. (acq 3-12-01; grpsl). Network: USA. Format: Talk. Target aud: 55 plus. Spec prog: Relg 2 hrs wkly. ♦ Steve Davis, gen mgr; Susie Smith, gen sls mgr; Steve Knupp, progmg dir; David Burman, news dir; Jeff Caudell, chief of engrg.

WKCY-FM— November 1980: 104.3 mhz; 50 kw. 409 ft. TL: N38 23 40 W79 08 26. Stereo. Web Site: www.goodradio.com. Format: Country. Target aud: 25-54. ♦ Dennis Hughes, progmg dir.

*****WMRA(FM)**— June 18, 1975: 90.7 mhz; 10.5 kw, 1,046 ft. TL: N38 33 40 W78 56 56. Stereo. Box 1292, 821 S. Main St. 22807. Phone: (540) 568-6221. Fax: (540 568-3814. Web Site: www.wmra.org. Licensee: James Madison University Board of Visitors. Network: Network: PRI, NPR. Format: Class, news. News staff: one; News: 32 hrs wkly. Target aud: 35-64; well-educated. Spec prog: Folk 8 hrs, blues 4 hrs wkly. ♦ Tom DuVal, gen mgr; Diane Halke, dev dir.

WQPO(FM)—Listing follows WSVA(AM).

WSVA(AM)— June 9, 1935: 550 khz; 5 kw-D, 1 kw-N, DA-N. TL: N38 27 04 W78 54 29. Box 752 22803. Secondary address: 130 Media Ln. 22801. Phone: (540) 434-0331. Web Site: www.valleyradio.com. Licensee: M. Belmont VerStandig Inc. Group owner: VerStandig Broadcasting (acq 4-17-87). Network: ABC Information & Entertainment. Format: News/talk. News staff: 5. Target aud: 35 plus. Spec prog: Farm 8 hrs wkly. ♦ John D. VerStandig, pres; Susanne Mowbray, gen mgr; Dennis Burchill, sls dir; Frank Wilt, progmg dir; Ellsworth Neff, chief of engrg.

WQPO(FM)—Co-owned with WSVA(AM). Dec 3, 1946: 100.7 mhz; 50 kw. 492 ft. TL: N38 27 08 W78 54 32. (CP: 3.8 kw, ant 1,617 ft. TL: N38 23 37 W78 46 14). Stereo. Web Site: www.valleyradio.com. Format: CHR. News staff: 3. ♦ Dennis Burchill, sls dir; Jeremy Lee, progmg dir.

*****WXJM(FM)**— September 1990: 88.7 mhz; 390 w. 62 ft. TL: N38 26 22 W78 52 21. Stereo. Anthony Seeger Hall, James Madison Univ. 22807. Phone: (540) 568-6878. Phone: (540) 568-3425. Fax: (540) 568-7907. E-mail: wxjm@jmv.edu. Web Site: www.jmu.edu/wxjm. Licensee: Board of Trustees of James Madison University. (acq 9-1-89). Format: Progsv. News: 7 hrs wkly. Target aud: General. Spec prog: Jazz 14 hrs, relg 2 hrs, Sp 3 hrs wkly. ♦ Carissa Page, gen mgr; Nathan Marsh, opns mgr; Jess Wodward, progmg dir.

Heathsville

*****WCNV(FM)**— April 2006: 89.1 mhz; 5 kw vert. Ant 305 ft. TL: N37 54 22 W76 29 09. Community Idea Stations, 23 Sesame St., Richmond 23235. Phone: (804) 320-1301. Fax: (804) 320-8729. Web Site: www.ideastations.org. Licensee: Commonwealth Public Broadcasting Corp. Network: Network: NPR, PRI. ♦ Bill Miller, gen mgr.

Highland Springs

WCLM(AM)— May 18, 1959: 1450 khz; 960 w-U. TL: N37 32 39 W77 20 47. Box 24888, 3165 Hull St., Richmond 23224. Phone: (804) 231-2186. Fax: (804) 231-2186. Web Site: www.wclmradio.com. Licensee: World Media Broadcast Co. (acq 10-25-94; 11-14-94). Network: ABC. Format: Var/div. Target aud: 25-65. Spec prog: Gospel, blues 5 hrs wkly. ♦ George Lacey, dev dir; Jean Trimble, sls dir & mktg mgr; Kimberly Osacio, gen sls mgr; Preston T. Brown, CEO, pres, VP, gen mgr, opns VP & progmg dir; John Trimble, mus dir; Jim Grainger, chief of engrg.

*****WHCE(FM)**— Sept 29, 1980: 91.1 mhz; 3 kw horiz. Ant 105 ft. TL: N37 32 18 W77 19 27. Henrico County Schools, 100 Tech Dr. 23075. Phone: (804) 328-4075. Phone: (804) 328-4078. Fax: (804) 328-4074. Licensee: Henrico County Schools. Format: CHR. Target aud: 12-20; teenagers, young adults. ♦ Bob Kaufman, gen mgr.

Hillsville

WHHV(AM)— Sept 16, 1961: 1400 khz; 1 kw-U. TL: N36 45 00 W80 43 20. Box 648 24333. Secondary address: 343 Virginia St. 24343. Phone: (276) 728-9114. Fax: (276) 728-9968. E-mail: whhv@whhvradio.com. Web Site: www.nlcm.net. Licensee: New Life Christian Communications Inc. (acq 4-2-01). Format: Gospel. News: 20 hrs wkly. Target aud: General. Spec prog: Farm one hr wkly. ♦ Leon Goad, pres & chief of engrg; Jackie Goad, VP, progmg dir & news dir; R. Leon Goad, gen mgr & adv dir; Sandra Haga, opns dir.

Hopewell

WHAP(AM)— Jan 16, 1949: 1340 khz; 1 kw-U. TL: N37 17 46 W77 18 50. 306 W. Broad St., Richmond 23220. Phone: (804) 643-0990. Fax: (804) 643-4990. E-mail: whap@radiorichmond.com. Web Site: www.radiorichmond.com. Licensee: MainQuad Communications Inc. (acq 1-14-2005; $200,000). Network: CBS. Cohn & Marks. Format: Talk. ♦ Mike Mazursky, gen mgr; Steve Miller, opns mgr.

Virginia   Directory of Radio

Hot Springs

*WCHG(FM)— September 1995: 107.1 mhz; 160 w. 1,407 ft. TL: N38 01 53 W79 46 52. Stereo. Drawer G 24445. Phone: (540) 839-5400. Fax: (540) 839-5403. E-mail: wchg@tds.net. Licensee: Pocahontas Communications Cooperative Corp. (acq 11-23-93; $2,000; 12-13-93). Format: Country plus. News: 15 hrs wkly. Target aud: General. ♦Cheryl Kinderman, gen mgr; Heather Dooley, news dir; Chuck Niday, chief of engrg.

Jonesville

WJNV(FM)— 2000: 99.1 mhz; 4 kw. Ant 403 ft. TL: N36 42 05 W83 10 14. Box 996 24263. Phone: (276) 346-2000. Fax: (276) 346-2049. E-mail: wjnvfm@naxs.net. Licensee: Regina Kay Moore. Format: Country.

Kilmarnock

WKWI(FM)— Sept 1, 1975: 101.7 mhz; 3 kw. 328 ft. TL: N37 43 26 W76 23 27. Stereo. Box 819, 101 Radio Rd. 22482. Phone: (804) 435-1414. Phone: (804) 435-1313. Fax: (804) 435-0484. E-mail: wkwi@rivnet.net. Licensee: Two Rivers Communications Inc. (acq 4-7-2004; $900,000). Network: AP Network News. Format: Adult contemp. Target aud: 25-64. Spec prog: Farm 2 hrs, Black 6 hrs, Gospel 5 hrs wkly. ♦William C. Sherard, pres; Charlie Lassitor, gen mgr; Carl Christiansen, sls dir; Joanne Chewning, mus dir; Joe Patton, chief of engrg.

Lawrenceville

WHFD(FM)— Sept 1, 1991: 105.5 mhz; 6 kw. 154 ft. TL: N36 45 10 W77 51 49. Box 4 23868. Secondary address: 2162 Plank Rd. 23868. Phone: (434) 848-9433. Fax: (434) 848-9434. E-mail: whfd1055@aol.com. Web Site: www.whfdradio.com. Licensee: Willis Broadcasting Corp. (group owner; acq 4-27-99; $350,000 with co-located AM). Format: Gospel. ♦Katrina Chase, gen mgr.

WLES(AM)— September 1959: 580 khz; 500 w-D. TL: N36 45 10 W77 51 49. 233 Main St. 23868. Secondary address: 2202 Jolliff Road, Chesapeake 23321. Phone: (434) 848-8870. Fax: (434) 848-4020. E-mail: info@1010wpmh.com. Licensee: Chesapeake-Portsmouth Broadcasting Corp. (acq 7-19-00). Network: UPI. Format: Oldies. ♦Nancy Epperson, pres; Henry Hoot, VP; Doug Stewart, gen mgr.

Lebanon

WLRV(AM)— Oct 28, 1974: 1380 khz; 1 kw-D, 63 w-N. TL: N36 55 18 W82 06 16. Box 939, 303 W. Main St. 24266-0939. Phone: (276) 889-1380. Fax: (276) 889-1388. E-mail: wrlv@youmax.com. Web Site: www.wlrv.com. Licensee: Gary W. Ward Broadcasting Corp. (acq 12-13-99; $161,250). Network: USA. Format: Bluegrass, gospel, soft 60's rock & roll. Target aud: 25 plus. ♦Gary W. Ward, pres & gen mgr; Mike Lowe, opns dir, prom dir, progmg dir & news dir; Barbara Jessee, gen sls mgr, adv dir & adv mgr; Rick Lang, chief of engrg.

WXLZ-FM— Feb 1, 1993: 107.3 mhz; 530 w. 774 ft. TL: N36 50 38 W82 11 04. Stereo. Box 1299 24266. Secondary address: Russell County Industrial Park, WXLZ Dr. 24266. Phone: (276) 889-1073. Fax: (276) 889-3677. E-mail: wxlz1073@mounet.com. Web Site: www.wxlz.net. Licensee: Yeary Broadcasting Inc. Network: CBS. Format: Modern country. News staff: 2; News: 3 hrs wkly. Target aud: 18 plus; students, farmers, miners, executives & rural residents. ♦Lannis Yeary, pres & gen mgr; Gary Scott, progmg dir; Richard Quillen, mus dir; Ron Keane, chief of engrg.

Leesburg

WAGE(AM)— Mar 6, 1958: 1200 khz; 5 kw-D, 1 kw-N, DA-N. TL: N39 06 36 W77 35 03. 711 Wage Dr. S.W. 20175. Phone: (703) 777-1200. Fax: (703) 777-7431. E-mail: wage@wage.com. Web Site: www.wage.com. Licensee: Radio WAGE Inc. (acq 3-80). Leventhal, Senter & Lerman. Format: News, full service, talk. News staff: one; News: 114 hrs wkly. Target aud: 25 plus; above average income, families, homeowners. ♦Grenville Emmet III, pres; Dene Hill, stn mgr; Karen E. Snoots, natl sls mgr & mktg dir; Chris King, progmg VP; Tim Jon, news dir; Fran Little, chief of engrg.

Lexington

*WLUR(FM)— Feb 27, 1967: 91.5 mhz; 175 w. Ant -75 ft. TL: N37 47 17 W79 26 36. Stereo. WLUR, Washington and Lee Univ. 24450-0303. Phone: (540) 458-4017. Fax: (540) 458-4079. E-mail: wlur@wlu.edu. Web Site: wlur.wlu.edu. Licensee: Washington & Lee University. Format: Div. News: 2 hrs wkly. Target aud: General; college students, city and county residents. ♦Tom Burish, pres; Jeremy Franklin, gen mgr; Angela Ernst, opns dir & prom dir; Benjamin Losi, opns dir; Amy McCamphill, mus dir; Derrick Barksdale, mus dir.

*WMRL(FM)— June 1992: 89.9 mhz; 100 w. 196 ft. TL: N37 42 22 W79 26 11. Stereo. Box 1292, Harrisonburg 22803. Phone: (540) 568-6221. Fax: (540) 568-3814. Web Site: www.wmra.org. Licensee: James Madison University Board of Visitors. Network: Network: NPR, PRI. Format: Class, news. News staff: one; News: 32 hrs wkly. Target aud: 35-64; well-educated. Spec prog: Folk 8 hrs, blues 4 hrs wkly. ♦Tom DuVal, gen mgr; Diane Halke, dev dir.

WREL(AM)— Nov 14, 1948: 1450 khz; 1 kw-U. TL: N37 46 00 W79 25 56. 312 Main St. 24450. Phone: (540) 463-2161. Fax: (540) 463-9524. E-mail: info@wrel.com. Web Site: www.wrel.com. Licensee: First Media Radio LLC (group owner; acq 6-21-2004; $1.33 million. with WWZW-FM Buena Vista). Rep: Keystone (unwired net). Format: News/talk, sports. News staff: one; News: 6 hrs wkly. Target aud: 35 plus. ♦James Putgrese, gen mgr; Scott Lancey, sls dir & gen sls mgr; Russ Brown, progmg dir & chief of engrg; Jim Bresnahan, news dir.

Louisa

WOJL(FM)— July 10, 1980: 105.5 mhz; 3.3 kw. 325 ft. TL: N38 01 37 W78 01 05. Stereo. Box 277 23093. Secondary address: 21128 Louisa Rd. 23093. Phone: (540) 967-1142. Fax: (540) 967-1150. Web Site: www.louisa.net. Licensee: Piedmont Communications Inc. (group owner; acq 12-1-2003; $550,000). Format: Country. News: 2 hrs wkly. Target aud: 25-54. Spec prog: Farm 2 hrs, bluegrass 14 hrs, relg 3 hrs, gospel 3 hrs wkly. ♦John Schick, pres; J. David Watt, gen mgr & progmg dir; James Granger, chief of engrg.

Luray

WMXH-FM— Listing follows WRAA(AM).

WRAA(AM)— October 1962: 1330 khz; 1 kw-D, 40 w-N. TL: N38 39 34 W78 29 28. 130 University Blvd., Suite B, Harrisonburg 22801. Phone: (540) 801-1057. Fax: (540) 564-2873. E-mail: production @easyradioinc.com. Licensee: EZ Radio Inc. (acq 6-2-88; $585,000 with co-located FM). Rep: Keystone (unwired net). Format: Country, Smith & Hargrove. Format: Country. Target aud: 18-49; middle to upper income, mobile. Spec prog: Relg 7 hrs wkly. ♦Jason Cave, pres, gen sls mgr, progmg dir & chief of engrg; Joshua Cave, VP.

WMXH-FM— Co-owned with WRAA(AM). Oct 16, 1979: 105.7 mhz; 440 w. 1,079 ft. TL: N38 30 41 W78 29 15. Stereo. Web Site: www.stardust1057.com. Format: MOR, music of your life. Target aud: 18-54; working people with disposable income interested in mus, news & sports. Spec prog: Relg 5 hrs wkly.

WYFT(FM)— October 1986: 103.9 mhz; 6 kw. Ant 302 ft. TL: N38 38 17 W78 24 06. Stereo. 598 5th St. 22835. Phone: (540) 743-7602. Phone: (704) 523-5555. Fax: (540) 743-7602. E-mail: wyft@bbnradio.org. Web Site: www.bbnradio.org. Licensee: Bible Broadcasting Network Inc. (group owner; acq 12-22-86). Format: Relg. News: 13 hrs wkly. Target aud: General. ♦Lowell Davey, pres; Ron Muffley, chief of engrg.

Lynchburg

WBRG(AM)— Sept 6, 1956: 1050 khz; 1 kw-D, 100 w-N. TL: N37 25 15 W79 06 55. Box 1079 24505. Secondary address: 239 Ragland Rd., Madison Heights 24572. Phone: (434) 845-5916. E-mail: wbrg@rev.net. Licensee: Tri-County Broadcasting Inc. (acq 7-1-67). Network: Network: ABC, Westwood One, Motor Racing Net. Format: News/talk, sports. News staff: 2; News: 12 hrs. wkly. Target aud: 25-54; College educated, professional/management, high household income, married with children. ♦Brent Epperson, gen mgr.

WJJX(FM)— Listing follows WVGM(AM).

WKPA(AM)— July 7, 1988: 1390 khz; 4.7 kw-D, 34 w-N. TL: N37 27 52 W79 07 21. 942 Kyle Ave., Roanoke 24012. Secondary address: 2043 10th St., Roanoke 24012. Phone: (540) 343-5597. Fax: (540) 345-4064. Web Site: www.radiowkpa.com. Licensee: Seven Hills Media Inc. Booth, Freret, Imlay & Tepper P. Format: Relg. Target aud: General. ♦Dorothy Durrett, gen mgr, opns dir, progmg dir & chief of engrg; Zeke Leonard, sls dir; Sharon M. Moran, prom mgr; Buddy Durrett, mus dir.

WLLL(AM)— Nov 1, 1963: 930 khz; 9 kw-D, 42 w-N. TL: N37 24 25 W79 13 57. Box 11375 24506. Secondary address: 105 Whitehall Rd. 24501. Phone: (434) 385-9555. Fax: (434) 385-6073. E-mail: wlllam930@aol.com. Web Site: www.llllradio.com. Licensee: Hubbards Advertising Agency Inc. (acq 1-28-02). Format: Gospel. ♦Fletcher Hubbard, pres, gen mgr, sls dir & progmg dir.

WLNI(FM)— Feb 2, 1994: 105.9 mhz; 6 kw. Ant 266 ft. TL: N37 25 37 W79 07 26. Box 11798 24506. Secondary address: 19-C Wadsworth St. 24501. Phone: (434) 845-5463. Fax: (434) 847-5709. E-mail: wlni@aol.com. Web Site: www.wlni.com. Licensee: Centennial Broadcasting LLC. Group owner: Burns Media Strategies Inc. (acq 1-7-2005; grpsl). Network: Network: ABC, Westwood One. Format: Talk, sports. ♦Allen B. Shaw, CEO; J. Davis, gen mgr; Mike Slenski, sls VP & prom dir; Rich Roth, progmg dir.

WLVA(AM)— Apr 21, 1930: 590 khz; 5 kw-D, 1 kw-N, DA-2. TL: N37 25 39 W79 13 23. Stereo. Box 552, Forest 24551. Phone: (434) 534-0400. Fax: (434) 534-0401. E-mail: news1280@msn.com. Licensee: Kovas Communications of Inidana Inc. (group owner; acq 6-7-2002). Format: All news. Target aud: 25-54; upscale, decision makers & professionals. ♦Vic Bosiger, gen mgr & progmg dir.

*WRVL(FM)— June 19, 1981: 88.3 mhz; 50 kw. 1,082 ft. TL: N37 11 50 W79 21 07. Stereo. 1971 University Blvd. 24502-2269. Phone: (434) 582-3688. Fax: (434) 582-2994. E-mail: wrvl@liberty.edu. Web Site: www.wrvlfm.com. Licensee: Liberty University. Fletcher, Heald & Hildreth. Format: Relg. News staff: one; News: 8 hrs wkly. Target aud: 25 plus. Spec prog: Liberty Univ. football & basketball. ♦David Young, sr VP; Jerry Edwards, gen mgr, stn mgr & mus dir; Mark Edwards, mus dir; Erick Petersen, pub affrs dir; Vangie Alban, pub affrs dir; Rob Branch, engrg dir; Chris Wygal, chief of engrg.

WVBE-FM— 1948: 100.1 mhz; 20 kw. 646 ft. TL: N37 20 56 W79 10 06. (CP: Ant 328 ft. TL: N37 28 06 W79 05 50). Stereo. Box 92, Roanoke 24022. Secondary address: 3934 Electric Rd. S.W., Roanoke 24018. Phone: (540) 774-9200. Fax: (540) 774-5667. E-mail: info@vibe100.com. Web Site: www.vibe100.com. Licensee: Mel Wheeler Inc. (group owner; acq 3-12-97; $7.5 million. with WXLK(FM) Roanoke). Format: Urban contemp. News: one hr wkly. Target aud: 25-54; skew women, skew black. ♦Leonard Wheeler, CEO, pres & gen mgr.

WVGM(AM)— Feb 22, 1962: 1320 khz; 1 kw-U. TL: N37 25 37 W79 07 26. 3807 Brandon Ave. S.W., Suite 2350, Roanoke 24018. Phone: (540) 725-1220. Fax: (540) 725-1245. Web Site: www.gameradio.go.com. Licensee: Capstar TX L.P. Group owner: Clear Channel Communications Inc. (acq 8-30-00; grpsl). Rep: Katz Radio. Format: Sports talk, ESPN. Spec prog: Gospel 19 hrs wkly. ♦Chris Clendenen, gen mgr; Steve Curtis, progmg dir; Jeff Parker, chief of engrg.

WJJX(FM)— Co-owned with WVGM(AM). Aug 1, 1964: 101.7 mhz; 3.4 kw. 300 ft. TL: N37 25 37 W79 07 26. Stereo. Web Site: www.wjjs.com. Format: Top-40. Target aud: 18-54; general. ♦David Lee Michaels, progmg dir.

*WWMC(FM)— February 1993: 90.9 mhz; 100 w. 604 ft. TL: N37 20 56 W79 10 05. Stereo. 1971 Univ. Blvd. 24502. Phone: (434) 582-3691. Fax: (434) 582-7461. E-mail: wwmcfm@liberty.edu. Web Site: www.thelightonline.com. Licensee: Liberty University Inc. Format: Christian, sports, var/div. News: 5 hrs wkly. Target aud: 16-30; high school, college and young adult; general: 12-45. ♦Jamie Hall, stn mgr.

WYYD(FM)— See Amherst

WZZU(FM)— Sept 1, 1970: 97.9 mhz; 570 w. Ant 1,925 ft. TL: N37 33 46 W79 11 38. Stereo. 19-C Wadsworth St. 24501. Phone: (434) 845-3698. Fax: (434) 845-2063. E-mail: z101mgt@aol.com. Web Site: www.oldies979.com. Licensee: Centennial Broadcasting LLC. (group owner; (acq 11-23-2004; $4.15 million. with WZZI(FM) Vinton). Format: Oldies. Target aud: 25-54. Spec prog: Relg one hr wkly. ♦J. Davis, gen mgr & stn mgr.

Manassas

WJFK-FM— Licensed to Manassas. See Washington DC

Stations in the U.S.   Virginia

Developers & Brokers of Radio Properties
contact American Media Services at our suite: Philadelphia Marriott Downtown
215-625-2900
843-972-2200
americanmediaservices.com
Charleston, SC
Dallas, TX · Chicago, Il · Austin, TX

American Media Services, LLC

WKDV(AM)— Oct 1, 1957: 1460 khz; 5 kw-U, DA-2. TL: N38 45 00 W77 30 49. 9540 Godwin Dr. 20110. Phone: (703) 330-8022. Web Site: www.metroradioinc.com. Licensee: Metro Radio Inc. Group owner: Multicultural Radio Broadcasting Inc. (acq 8-1-2005; exchange for WFBR(AM) Glen Burnie, MD). Format: Mexican rgnl. ◆Kelly Koonce, gen mgr.

WTOP-FM—See Warrenton

Marion

WMEV(AM)— Dec 12, 1948: 1010 khz; 1 kw-D, 30 w-N. TL: N36 51 23 W81 30 21. 1041 Radio Hill Rd. 24354. Phone: (276) 783-3151. Phone: (276) 783-9400 (STUDIO). Fax: (276) 783-3152. E-mail: supercountry@fm94.com. Web Site: www.fm94.com. Licensee: Holston Valley Broadcasting Corp. Group owner: Glenwood Communications Corp. (acq 7-1-98; $1.65 million with co-located FM). Network: Network: Motor Racing Net, Salem Radio Network. Format: Southern Gospel. News: 3 hrs wkly. Target aud: 18-54. Spec prog: Gospel 2 hrs, relg 8 hrs wkly. ◆George E. DeVault Jr., pres; Jim Mabe, opns dir; Anita Dixon, sls dir; N. David Widener, gen mgr & natl sls mgr; Lynn Rutledge, progmg dir; Duane Nelson, news dir.

WMEV-FM— June 21, 1961: 93.9 mhz; 100 kw. 1,480 ft. TL: N36 54 08 W81 32 33. Stereo. Format: Hot country. ◆N. David Widener, gen mgr; Anita Dixon, sls VP; Lynn Rutledge, progmg dir; Lyle Musser, chief of engrg.

WOLD(AM)— Apr 25, 1962: . Stn currently dark 1330 khz; 5 kw-D, 31 w-N. TL: N36 49 11 W81 28 12. Box 2061, Bristol, TN 37621-2061. Phone: (423) 878-6391. Fax: (423) 878-6520. Licensee: Appalachian Educational Communication Corp. (acq 11-3-2003; $35,000). ◆Kenneth C. Hill, pres & gen mgr.

WOLD-FM— Mar 14, 1968: 102.5 mhz; 440 w. Ant 1,204 ft. TL: N36 54 10 W81 32 27. Stereo. Box 1047 24354-1047. Phone: (276) 783-7100. Licensee: Emerald Sound Inc. Network: CNN Radio. Format: Adult contemp. ◆Robert S. Dix, pres & gen mgr; Patricia Ann Dix, stn mgr & opns mgr.

*****WVTR(FM)**— Nov 22, 1991: 91.9 mhz; 4.5 kw. 1,489 ft. TL: N36 44 52 W81 18 15. c/o WVTF, 3520 Kingsbury Ln., Roanoke 24014. Phone: (540) 989-8900. Fax: (540) 776-2727. Web Site: www.wvtf.org. Licensee: Virginia Tech Foundation Inc. Network: NPR. Format: Class, jazz, NPR. ◆Glenn Gleixner, stn mgr & dev dir.

WZVA(FM)— Sept 2, 1996: 103.5 mhz; 1.35 kw. -36 ft. TL: N36 52 07 W81 26 07. Box 85 24354. Phone: (276) 783-4042. Fax: (276) 783-2120. E-mail: staff@z-103.com. Web Site: www.z-103.com. Licensee: T.E.C.O. Broadcasting Inc. (acq 11-7-97; $125,000). Format: CHR, adult contemp. Target aud: 18-49; women & men. ◆Tom Copenhaver, CEO; Darla Gross, stn mgr.

Martinsville

WHEE(AM)— Aug 4, 1954: 1370 khz; 5 kw-D, 500 w-N. TL: N36 41 09 W79 54 14. Drawer 3551 24115. Secondary address: 40 Franklin St. 24112. Phone: (276) 632-9811. Phone: (276) 632-5433. Fax: (276) 632-9813. E-mail: news@whee.net. Web Site: www.wheeradio.com. Licensee: Patrick Henry Broadcasting Corp. (acq 1-5-98; $200,000 for stock). Network: CBS. Wilkinson, Barker, Knauer & Quinn. Format: Talk. Target aud: 17-60; agriculture & mfg area audience. ◆Bill Wyatt, pres, gen mgr, gen sls mgr & progmg dir; Teddy Thomas, prom mgr; T.L. Walker, chief of engrg.

*****WPIM(FM)**— 1997: 90.5 mhz; 4 kw. 326 ft. TL: N36 42 16 W79 50 06. Box 929, Blacksburg 24063. Phone: (540) 552-8073. Fax: (540) 951-5282. E-mail: mail@spiritfm.com. Web Site: www.spiritfm.com. Licensee: Positive Alternative Radio Inc. Group owner: Baker Family Stations (Positive Radio Group) Booth, Freret, Imlay & Tepper. Format: Christian adult contemp. ◆Vernon H. Baker, CEO & chmn; Edward A. Baker, pres & VP; Barry Armstrong, gen mgr & stn mgr.

WROV-FM— January 1950: 96.3 mhz; 13.8 kw. 2,076 ft. TL: N36 43 00 W79 51 07. Stereo. 3807 Brandon Ave., Suite 2350, Roanoke 24018. Phone: (540) 725-1220. Fax: (540) 725-1245. Web Site: www.96-3rov.com. Licensee: Capstar TX L.P. Group owner: Clear Channel Communications Inc. (acq 8-30-00; grpsl). Rep: D & R Radio. Format: AOR. Target aud: 18-49; general. ◆Chris Clendenen, gen mgr; Ron Gaylor, gen sls mgr; Aaron Roberts, progmg dir; Ed Kilbane, news dir; Jeff Parker, chief of engrg.

Mechanicsville

WCDX(FM)— Oct 7, 1985: 92.1 mhz; 4.5 kw. Ant 770 ft. TL: N37 42 50 W77 30 23. Stereo. 2809 Emerywood Pkwy., Suite 300, Richmond 23294. Phone: (804) 672-9299. Fax: (804) 672-9314. Fax: (804) 672-9316. Licensee: Radio One Licenses LLC. Group owner: Radio One Inc. (acq 11-8-2001; grpsl). Rep: Allied Radio Partners. Fletcher, Heald & Hildreth. Format: Urban contemp. Target aud: 18-44. ◆Larry Jones, gen sls mgr; June Grant, prom mgr; Reggie Baker, progmg dir & mus dir; Ladonna Monet, news dir.

Midlothian

WCUL(FM)— Nov 22, 1971: 98.9 mhz; 4.8 kw. Ant 746 ft. TL: N37 36 52 W77 30 56. Stereo. Box 271, Orange 22960-0157. Phone: (540) 672-1000. Fax: (540) 672-0282. Licensee: MainQuad Communications Inc. Group owner: The MainQuad Group (acq 1-2-2004; $6.25 million). Format: Var. ◆John Schick, gen mgr.

Moneta

WCQV(AM)— November 1991: 880 khz; 900 w-D. TL: N37 10 00 W70 37 50. 1848 Clay St. S.E., Roanoke 24013. Phone: (540) 343-7109. Fax: (540) 343-2306. Web Site: www.wcqv.com. Licensee: Perception Media Group Inc. (group owner; acq 1999; $75,000). Format: Adult standards. Target aud: 35 plus; mostly middle aged, affluent, cosmopolitan. Spec prog: Relg 5 hrs wkly. ◆Ben Peyton, pres, stn mgr & sls dir; Barbara Evans, progmg dir; Dale Cook, chief of engrg.

Monterey

*****WVLS(FM)**— September 1995: 89.7 mhz; 200 w. 1,460 ft. TL: N38 20 39 W79 35 47. Stereo. Box 185 24465. Phone: (540) 468-1897. Phone: (540) 468-1234. Fax: (540) 468-1233. E-mail: wvls@htcnet.net. Web Site: wvls.cfw.com. Licensee: Pocahontas Communications Cooperative Corp. Format: Country plus. Target aud: General. ◆Cheryl Kinderman, gen mgr; Carson Raleton, stn mgr; Shaun Harvey, progmg dir & mus dir; Heather Dooley, news dir; Chuck Niday, chief of engrg.

Mount Jackson

WSIG(FM)— October 1988: 96.9 mhz; 7 kw. Ant 558 ft. TL: N38 36 31 W78 54 07. 1866 E. Market St., Suite 325, Harrisonburg 22801. Phone: (540) 432-1063. Fax: (540) 433-9267. E-mail: wsig@shentel.net. Licensee: Vox Communications Group LLC. (group owner; acq 7-13-2005; $2 million). Network: AP Radio. Southmayd & Miller. Format: Classic country. Spec prog: Bluegrass 6 hrs, gospel 4 hrs wkly. ◆Tom Manley, gen mgr.

WSVG(AM)— Apr 23, 1954: 790 khz; 1 kw-D, 40 w-N. TL: N38 46 15 W78 37 17. Box 425 22842. Phone: (540) 477-4443. Fax: (540) 477-4407. Licensee: Hometown Broadcasting of Mt. Jackson LLC (acq 2-25-2005). Format: Big band. ◆Alan Arehart, gen mgr; Patty Shaffer, gen mgr.

Narrows-Pearisburg

WNRV(AM)— August 1953: 990 khz; 5 kw-D, 10 w-N. TL: N37 20 39 W80 46 36. 1848 Clay St. S.E., Roanoke 24013. Phone: (540) 343-7109. Fax: (540) 343-2306. Web Site: www.radio3wr.com. Licensee: Perception Media Group Inc. (group owner; acq 6-2-99). Format: Gospel. ◆Ben Peyton, pres; Barbara Evans, stn mgr, sls dir & progmg dir; Blair Peyton, mus dir; Dale Cook, chief of engrg.

Nassawadox

*****WJCN(FM)**— 2005: 90.1 mhz; 450 w vert. Ant 199 ft. TL: N37 33 27 W75 49 44. CSN International, 3232 W. MacArthur Blvd., Santa Ana, CA 92704. Phone: (208) 734-6633. Fax: (208) 736-1958. E-mail: feedback@csnradio.com. Web Site: csnradio.com. Licensee: CSN International (group owner). ◆Mike Keslter, pres; Mike Stocklin, opns dir.

New Market

WLTK(FM)—Licensed to New Market. See Broadway-Timberville

Newport News

WCMS(AM)—Listing follows WGH-FM.

WGH-FM— November 1948: 97.3 mhz; 74 kw. 415 ft. TL: N36 57 47 W76 24 42. Stereo. 5589 Greenwich Rd., Virginia Beach 23462. Phone: (757) 671-1000. Fax: (757) 671-1010. Web Site: www.eagle97.com. Licensee: MHR License LLC. Group owner: Barnstable Broadcasting Inc. (acq 3-18-2005; grpsl). Format: Contemp country. Target aud: 25-34. ◆Andy Graham, gen mgr; Frankie Roman, mktg dir & prom mgr; John Shomby, progmg dir; Keith O'Malley, chief of engrg.

WNVZ(FM)—See Norfolk

WTJZ(AM)— November 1947: 1270 khz; 1.5 kw-D, 900 w-N, DA-N. TL: N37 01 52 W76 22 00. Box 610, Hampton 23669-0610. Secondary address: 553 Michigan, Hampton 23669. Phone: (757) 723-1270. Fax: (757) 723-0820. Licensee: Chesapeake-Portsmouth Broadcasting Corp. (acq 1999; $380,000). Format: Gospel, inspirational. ◆Jerome Barber, gen mgr & opns mgr; Greg Roberts, progmg dir.

Norfolk

WCMS(AM)—See Newport News

WFOG(FM)—See Suffolk

WGH-FM—See Newport News

WGPL(AM)—See Portsmouth

*****WHRO-FM**— 1990: 90.3 mhz; 23 kw. 630 ft. TL: N36 48 32 W76 30 13. Stereo. 5200 Hampton Blvd. 23508. Phone: (757) 889-9400. Fax: (757) 489-0007. E-mail: info@whro.org. Web Site: www.whro.org. Licensee: Hampton Roads Educational Telecommunications Association Inc. Network: Network: NPR, PRI. Format: Class, fine arts. Target aud: 35 plus; well-educated, executives, leaders. ◆Joseph Widoff, CEO & pres; Regina Brayboy, COO; Carol Vollbrecht, CFO; John Heimerl, VP & stn mgr; Heather Fleming Mazzoni, opns mgr & chief of opns; Virginia Thumm, dev dir. Co-owned TV: *WHRO-TV affil.

*****WHRV(FM)**— 1974: 89.5 mhz; 23 kw. 730 ft. TL: N36 48 32 W76 30 13. Stereo. 5200 Hampton Blvd. 23508. Phone: (757) 889-9400. Fax: (757) 489-0007. Web Site: www.whro.org. Licensee: Hampton Roads Educational Telecommunications Association, Inc. (acq 2-86). Network: Network: NPR, PRI. Format: News/talk, pub affrs, jazz. News staff: one; News: 105 hrs wkly. Target aud: 35 plus. Spec prog: Progsv 14 hrs, folk 7 hrs wkly. ◆Joseph Widoff, CEO; Regina Brayboy, COO; Carol Vollbrecht, CFO; John Heimerl, gen mgr; Heather Fleming, opns mgr & chief of opns; Virginia Thumm, dev VP & dev dir. Co-owned TV: *WHRO-TV affil.

WJOI(AM)— 1949: 1230 khz; 1 kw-U. TL: N36 50 03 W76 16 12. 870 Greenbriar Cir., Suite 399, Chesapeake 23320. Phone: (757) 366-9900. Fax: (757) 366-0022. Licensee: Tidewater Communications LLC. Group owner: Saga Communications Inc. (acq 9-15-86). Rep: McGavren Guild. Format: Adult Standards. ◆Dave Paulus, pres, VP & gen mgr; Don Crowder, chief of engrg.

Broadcasting & Cable Yearbook 2006

Virginia

WNOR(FM)—Co-owned with WJOI(AM). 1961: 98.7 mhz; 46 kw. Ant 518 ft. TL: N36 50 04 W76 16 11. Stereo. Web Site: www.fm99.com. Smithwick & Belendiuk. Format: Rock/AOR. ♦Harvey Najen, progmg dir.

WKUS(FM)—Licensed to Norfolk. See Portsmouth

WLRT(AM)—See Hampton

WNIS(AM)— Sept 21, 1923: 790 khz; 5 kw-U, DA-1. TL: N37 04 23 W76 17 28. Stereo. 500 Dominion Tower, 999 Waterside Dr. 23510. Phone: (757) 640-8500. Fax: (757) 640-8552. Fax: (757) 622-6397. E-mail: wnis@wnis.com. Web Site: www.WNIS.com. Licensee: Sinclair Communications Inc. (group owner). Network: Network: ABC, Westwood One. Rep: McGavren Guild. Format: News/talk. Target aud: 25-54. Spec prog: Sports, relg 2 hrs wkly. ♦Bob Sinclair, CEO & gen mgr; Lisa Sinclair, stn mgr; Dave Morgan, opns mgr.

*WNSB(FM)— Mar 22, 1980: 91.1 mhz; 8.1 kw. 422 ft. TL: N36 46 32 W76 23 11. (CP: 18 kw, ant 299 ft. TL: N36 45 23 W76 23 06). Stereo. 700 Park Ave., Suite 129 23504-8015. Phone: (757) 823-9672. Fax: (757) 823-2385. E-mail: wnsb@nsu.edu. Web Site: www.hot91.com. Licensee: Norfolk State University Board of Visitors. Network: NPR. Format: Urban. Target aud: 18-24. ♦Dr. Emmanuel Onyedike, gen mgr; Edward Turner, stn mgr.

WNVZ(FM)— July 1967: 104.5 mhz; 50 kw. 480 ft. TL: N37 02 20 W76 18 30. Stereo. 236 Clearfield Ave., Suite 206, Virginia Beach 23462. Phone: (757) 497-2000. Fax: (757) 497-7158. Web Site: www.z104.com. Licensee: Entercom Norfolk License LLC. Group owner: Entercom Communications Corp. (acq 12-13-99; grpsl). Rep: D & R Radio. Format: CHR. News staff: News progmg one hr wkly Target aud: 18-34; females.David J. Field, CEO & pres; Steve Fisher, CFO & exec VP; Steve Godofsky, VP; Skip Schmidt, gen mgr; Don London, opns mgr & progmg dir; Mark Warlaumont, sls dir; Bernardo Nogueira, natl sls mgr; Nathan James, prom dir; Suzanne McGovern, adv dir; Ernie Warinner, mus dir & chief of engrg; Jay West, mus dir; Tricia Harris, pub affrs dir; John C. Donlevie, engrg VP

WOWI(FM)— June 1948: 102.9 mhz; 50 kw. 500 ft. TL: N36 45 23 W76 23 06. Stereo. 1003 Norfolk Sq. 23502. Phone: (757) 466-0009. Fax: (757) 466-7043. Web Site: www.103jamz.com. Licensee: Clear Channel Radio Licenses Inc. Group owner: Clear Channel Communications Inc. (acq 1996; grpsl). Rep: McGavren Guild. Format: Urban contemp. Target aud: 18-34. ♦Lowry Mays, CEO, chmn & pres; Reggie Jordan, VP & stn mgr; Eric Mychaels, opns mgr, progmg dir & progmg dir; Terry Ratliff, sls dir; Bob Rischitelli, gen sls mgr; Toni Bailey Jones, prom mgr; D.J. Law, mus dir; Cheryl Wilkerson, news dir; Doc Christian, pub affrs dir; Greg Gabriel, chief of engrg.

WPCE(AM)—See Portsmouth

WRJR(AM)—See Portsmouth

WTAR(AM)— September 1952: 850 khz; 50 kw-D, 25 kw-N, DA-2. TL: N36 51 39 W76 21 13. 500 Dominion Tower, 999 Waterside Dr. 23510. Phone: (757) 640-8500. Fax: (757) 640-8552. Web Site: www.wtar.com. Licensee: Sinclair Communications Inc. (group owner) (acq 9-87; $725,000;. FTR: 9-21-87). Network: Network: CNN Radio, Westwood One. Rep: McGavren Guild. Format: News/talk. Target aud: 25-54; 35 plus. ♦Bob Sinclair, CEO & gen mgr; Lisa Sinclair, stn mgr.

WTJZ(AM)—See Newport News

WVAB(AM)—(Virginia Beach). Dec 10, 1954: 1550 khz; 5 kw-D, 249 w-N. TL: N36 49 20 W76 05 30. Box 55285, Virginia Beach 23471. Phone: (757) 412-4321. Phone: (757) 481-6982. Fax: (757) 490-8704. E-mail: wvab@email.com. Web Site: www.wvab.com. Licensee: Ronald W. Cowan Jr. Network: CNN Radio. Format: News. ♦Ronald W. Cowan Jr., gen mgr, CEO & pres; Richard Harris, sls dir.

WVKL(FM)— Sept 21, 1961: 95.7 mhz; 40 kw. Ant 881 ft. TL: N36 48 56 W76 28 00. Stereo. 236 Clearfield Ave., Suite 206, Virginia Beach 23462. Phone: (757) 497-2000. Fax: (757) 456-5458. Web Site: www.957rnb.com. Licensee: Entercom Norfolk License LLC. Group owner: Entercom Communications Corp. (acq 12-13-99; grpsl). Format: Rhythm and blues. ♦David J. Field, CEO & pres; Steve Fisher, CFO & exec VP; John C. Donleive, exec VP; Steve Godofsky, VP; Skip Schmidt, gen mgr; Don London, opns mgr; Karen Parker-Chesson, news dir.

WVXX(AM)— July 1, 1954: 1050 khz; 5 kw-D, 358 w-N, DA-2. TL: N36 49 44 W76 12 26. Radisson Hotel, 700 Monticello Ave., Suite 301 23510. Phone: (704) 873-4802. Fax: (704) 873-4803. Licensee: Davidson Media Virginia Stations LLC. Group owner: Barnstable Broadcasting Inc. (acq 12-23-2004; $975,000). Format: Sp. ♦Peter W. Davidson, gen mgr.

WWDE-FM—See Hampton

WXMM(FM)— Oct 1, 1962: 100.5 mhz; 50 kw. Ant 500 ft. TL: N36 49 44 W76 12 26. Stereo. 5589 Greenwich Rd., Suite 200, Virginia Beach 23462. Phone: (757) 671-1000. Fax: (757) 671-1010. Web Site: www.maxfm.fm. Licensee: MHR License LLC. (acq 3-18-2005; grpsl). Format: Country. ♦Andy Graham, gen mgr.

WYFI(FM)— Oct 2, 1971: 99.7 mhz; 50 kw. 456 ft. TL: N36 49 41 W76 15 05. Stereo. 4310 Indian River Rd., Suite 5, Chesapeake 23325. Phone: (757) 420-9505. Fax: (757) 420-9505. E-mail: wyfi@bbnradio.org. Web Site: www.bbnradio.org. Licensee: Bible Broadcasting Network Inc. (group owner; acq 12-24-70). Format: Relg. ♦Lowell Davey, pres; Dennis Gast, gen mgr.

WYRM(AM)— Apr 6, 1976: . Stn currently dark 1110 khz; 50 kw-D, DA. TL: N36 56 34 W76 31 56. Word Broadcasting Network Inc., Box 19229, Louisville, KY 40259. Phone: (502) 968-1220, ext 16. Phone: (757) 622-9256. Fax: (502) 962-3143. Licensee: Word Broadcasting Network Inc. (group owner; acq 7-29-2003; $1.25 million. with WYMM(AM) Jacksonville, FL). Format: Religious. ♦Larry Cobb, gen mgr.

Norton

WNVA(AM)— March 1946: 1350 khz; 5 kw-D. TL: N36 57 58 W82 35 17. Box 500 24273. Phone: (276) 328-2244. Fax: (276) 328-0024. E-mail: wnva@mounet.com. Licensee: Radio-Wise Inc. Regnl Reps Format: Adult contemp. News: 2 hrs wkly. Target aud: 25-65; adults & young adults. Spec prog: Gospel 15 hrs, relg 2 hrs wkly. ♦Willliam G. Stallard, VP; William G. Stallard, gen mgr; Deborah Baker, opns dir & sls dir; Gerald Hibbitts, chief of engrg.

WNVA-FM— July 25, 1969: 106.3 mhz; 1.65 kw. 613 ft. TL: N36 57 58 W82 35 17. Stereo. Network: Jones Radio Networks. Regnl Reps Format: CHR country. News: 10 hrs wkly. Target aud: 18-45; young adults. ♦Debbie Baker, sls dir.

Onley-Onancock

WESR(AM)— Jan 23, 1958: 1330 khz; 5 kw-D, 51 w-N. TL: N37 43 02 W75 41 01. Box 100, Tasley 23441. Secondary address: 22479 Front St., Accomac 23301. Phone: (757) 787-3852. Fax: (757) 787-3819. Web Site: www.west.net. Licensee: Eastern Shore Radio Inc. (acq 1-23-97; $148,300 for stock with co-located FM). Network: ABC. Rep: Dome. Format: Country classics, talk. ♦Charles Russell, gen mgr; Bill LeCato, progmg dir.

WESR-FM— 1968: 103.3 mhz; 50 kw. 320 ft. TL: N37 43 02 W75 41 01. Stereo. Web Site: www.wesr.net. Network: ABC. Format: Adult contemp.

Orange

WVCV(AM)— Sept 10, 1949: 1340 khz; 1 kw-U. TL: N38 15 14 W78 07 15. Box 271 22960-0157. Secondary address: 207 Spicers Mill Rd. 22960. Phone: (540) 672-1000. Fax: (540) 672-0282. E-mail: advertising@wjmafm.com. Licensee: Piedmont Communications Inc. (group owner; acq 2-18-93; $30,000. with co-located FM; FTR: 3-8-93). Network: CBS. Format: Oldies, talk. Target aud: 18-54. Spec prog: Gospel 2 hrs, relg one hr, news 18 hrs wkly. ♦John Schick, gen mgr; Gary Harrison, opns mgr, prom dir, progmg dir, pub affrs dir & chief of engrg; Ann Velez, gen sls mgr; Phil Goodwin, news dir.

Pearisburg

WNRV(AM)—See Narrows-Pearisburg

Pennington Gap

WSWV(AM)— June 1, 1959: 1570 khz; 2.3 kw, 191 w-N. TL: N36 44 02 W83 02 34. Box 630, 203 W. Morgan Ave. 24277. Phone: (276) 546-2520. Fax: (276) 546-1356. E-mail: wswv@optidynamic.com. Web Site: www.wswv.net. Licensee: B C Broadcasting Co. Inc. (acq 6-6-2005; $105,000 with co-located FM). Network: AP Network News. Rep: Rgnl Reps. Format: Adult contemp, relg. Target aud: 24-54; young, working adults. ♦Kathy Laufer, gen mgr & adv VP; Nicole Clontz, stn mgr, opns dir, gen sls mgr, progmg VP & mus dir; Mary Lou Clontz, asst music dir & mktg dir; Mike Cook, chief of engrg.

WSWV-FM— 1973: 105.5 mhz; 3.5 kw. 276 ft. TL: N36 44 02 W83 02 34. Stereo. Phone: (276) 546-2521. Web Site: www.wswv.net. Format: Adult contemp. ♦Nicole Clontz, opns mgr, prom mgr & progmg dir; Kathy Laufer, adv mgr; Rob McLaughlin, mktg dir & mus dir; Johnny Woliver, asst music dir.

Petersburg

WARV-FM— December 1992: 100.3 mhz; 4.7 kw. 328 ft. TL: N37 08 57 W77 24 54. 300 Arboretum Pl., Suite 590, Richmond 23236. Phone: (804) 327-9902. Fax: (804) 327-9911. Licensee: MainQuad Communications Inc. (acq 2-24-2003). Format: Oldies. ♦Dan Berman, pres; William McCutchen, exec VP; Kevin Lein, gen mgr & gen sls mgr; Joey Butler, opns dir & progmg dir; Mike McClain, prom mgr; Kelly Fever, pub affrs dir; Frank White, chief of engrg.

WKJM(FM)—Listing follows WROU(AM).

WROU(AM)— May 7, 1945: 1240 khz; 1 kw-U. TL: N37 14 01 W77 22 36. 4301 W. Hundred Rd., Chester 23831. Phone: (804) 717-2000. Fax: (804) 717-2009. E-mail: wgcv@cavte.net. Web Site: www.am1240.net. Licensee: Radio One Licenses LLC. Group owner: Radio One Inc. (acq 7-26-99; grpsl). Rep: McGavren Guild. Format: Gospel. Target aud: 25-54. ♦Paul Scott, gen mgr.

WKJM(FM)—Co-owned with WROU(AM). Oct 1, 1966: 99.3 mhz; 3 kw. Ant 328 ft. TL: N37 14 01 W77 22 36. Stereo. 2809 Emory Wood Pkwy., Suite 300, Richmond 23294. Phone: (804) 672-9299. Fax: (804) 672-9314. Format: Urban adult contemp. Target aud: 25-54; Black adults.

*WVST-FM— July 12, 1987: 91.3 mhz; 2.2 kw vert. Ant 167 ft. TL: N37 14 15 W77 24 55. Stereo. Box 9067, 130 Harris Hall, Virginia State Univ. 23806. Phone: (804) 524-5000. Fax: (804) 524-5826. Web Site: www.vsu.edu/wvst. Licensee: Virginia State University. Format: Diversified, jazz. Target aud: 25 plus; general. Spec prog: Gospel 13 hrs wkly. ♦Dr. Moadab, gen mgr; Yolie Thomas, stn mgr & opns mgr; Hugh Mannah, chief of opns.

Poquoson

WZNR(FM)— April 2001: 106.1 mhz; 2.6 kw. Ant 502 ft. TL: N37 04 24 W76 17 33. Stereo. 500 Dominion Tower, 999 Waterside Dr., Norfolk 23510. Phone: (757) 640-8500. Fax: (757) 640-8552. Web Site: www.zone1061.com. Licensee: Commonwealth Broadcasting L.L.C. (acq 8-24-2001; $1.883 million. for CP). Rep: McGavren Guild. Format: CHR, top-40. Target aud: 18-44. ♦Lisa Sinclair, gen mgr; Jay Michaels, progmg dir.

Portsmouth

WGPL(AM)— January 1942: 1350 khz; 5 kw-U, DA-2. TL: N36 53 00 W76 22 22. 645 Church St., Suite 400, Norfolk 23501. Phone: (757) 622-4600. Fax: (757) 624-6515. E-mail: martinpepion@aol.com. Licensee: Christian Broadcasting of Norfolk Inc. Group owner: Willis Broadcasting Corp. Network: ABC FM Connection. Format: Gospel. News staff: 2; News: 6 hrs wkly. Target aud: 25-54. ♦L. E. Willis, pres; Katrina Chase, gen mgr & opns mgr; Alvin Rooks, sls dir; Martha Culpeper, mktg dir & prom dir; Jonathan Willis, progmg dir; Terry Love, chief of engrg.

WHKT(AM)— 1999: 1650 khz; 10 kw-D, 1 kw-N. TL: N36 48 10 W76 16 58. 5041 Corporate Woods Dr., Ste 165, Virginia Beach 23462. Phone: (757) 519-9171. Fax: (757) 519-9147. Web Site: www.radiodisney.com. Licensee: Radio Disney Group LLC. Group owner: ABC Inc. (acq 6-5-2002; $1.08 million. with WRJR(AM) Portsmouth). Format: Radio Disney. ♦Monica Rae Clanin, mktg mgr, prom mgr & pub affrs dir; Richard Bowen, stn mgr, opns dir, gen sls mgr & chief of engrg.

WKUS(FM)—(Norfolk). Aug 3, 1962: 105.3 mhz; 50 kw. 499 ft. TL: N36 48 43 W76 27 49. Stereo. Clear Channel Communications Inc., 1003 Norfolk Sq., Norfolk 23502. Phone: (757) 466-0009. Fax: (757) 466-4043. E-mail: vibe@clearchannel.com. Web Site: www.vibezone.com. Licensee: Clear Channel Broadcasting Licenses Inc. Group owner: Clear Channel Communications Inc. (acq 1996; grpsl). Network: ABC Daytime Direction. Rep: Roslin. Format: Adult urban. Target aud: 25-54. ♦Janet Armstead, gen mgr; Michelle Smith, prom mgr.

Stations in the U.S. — Virginia

Developers & Brokers of Radio Properties
contact American Media Services at our suite:
Philadelphia Marriott Downtown
215-625-2900
843-972-2200
americanmediaservices.com
Charleston, SC
Dallas, TX · Chicago, Il · Austin, TX
American Media Services, LLC

WPCE(AM)— Jan 11, 1964: 1400 khz; 1 kw-U. TL: N36 49 45 W76 19 23. 645 Church St., Suite 400, Norfolk 23501. Phone: (757) 622-4600. Fax: (757) 624-6515. E-mail: martinpepion@aol.com. Licensee: Christian Broadcasting of Portsmouth Inc. (group owner; acq 3-4-92; grpsl; 3-23-92). Format: Inspirational. ♦ L.E. Willis, pres; Katrina Chase, gen mgr; Jonathan Willis, opns mgr & progmg dir; Alvin Rooks, sls dir; Cindy Perkins, gen sls mgr; Martin Culpeper, mktg dir & prom dir; James Phillips, mus dir & news dir; Terry Love, chief of engrg.

WRJR(AM)— Jan 9, 1972: 1010 khz; 5 kw-D, 449 w-N, DA-2. TL: N36 49 20 W76 26 38. 2202 Jolliff Rd., Chesapeake 23321. Phone: (757) 488-1010. Web Site: www.wpmhradio.com. Licensee: Radio Disney Group LLC. Group owner: ABC Inc. (acq 6-5-2002; $1.08 million. with WHKT(AM) Portsmouth). Format: Relg, news/talk. ♦ Henry W. Hoot, gen mgr.

Pound

WDXC(FM)— 1990: 102.3 mhz; 280 w. 992 ft. TL: N37 09 07 W82 37 57. (CP: 35 kw, ant 1,315 ft.). Stereo. 12552 Orby Cantrell Hwy. 24279. Phone: (276) 796-5411. Fax: (276) 796-5412. E-mail: chase@wdxcfm.com. Web Site: www.wdxcfm.com. Licensee: WDXC Radio Inc. (acq 6-90; 6-4-90). Format: Country. Target aud: General. ♦ Howard Cornett, pres, gen mgr & sls VP; Jackie Cornett, exec VP; Jeff Mullins, progmg dir; Celvin Eldridge, chief of engrg.

Powhatan

WBBT-FM— 1999: 107.3 mhz; 1.4 kw. Ant 679 ft. TL: N37 30 15 W77 42 14. 300 Arboretum Pl., Suite 590, Ricmond 23236. Phone: (804) 327-9902. Fax: (804) 327-9911. Web Site: www.oldies1073.net. Licensee: MainQuad Inc. Group owner: The MainQuad Group (acq 11-29-96; grpsl). Format: Oldies. ♦ Dan Berman, pres & gen mgr; Kevin Lein, gen mgr & gen sls mgr; Joey Butler, opns dir & progmg dir; William McCutchen, exec VP & mktg VP; Mike McClain, prom mgr; Kelly Fever, pub affrs dir; Frank White, chief of engrg.

Pulaski

WPSK-FM— Dec 1, 1967: 107.1 mhz; 25 kw. 1,207 ft. TL: N37 01 28 W80 44 47. Stereo. Box 3788, Radford 24143-3788. Secondary address: 7080 Lee Hwy., Radford 24141. Phone: (540) 633-5330. Phone: (540) 633-1071. Fax: (540) 633-2998. Web Site: nrvtoday.com. Licensee: Cumulus Licensing LLC. Group owner: Cumulus Media Inc. (acq 3-31-2004; grpsl). Format: Country. News staff: one; News: 10 hrs wkly. Target aud: 25-54. ♦ Ronald Walton, gen mgr; Scott Stevens, opns mgr; Sean Summer, progmg dir; Dave Dalesky, chief of engrg.

Quantico

WPWC(AM)—See Dumfries-Triangle

Radford

WRAD(AM)— 1950: 1460 khz; 5 kw-D, 500 w-N, DA-N. TL: N37 08 35 W80 34 38. Stereo. Box 3788 24143. Secondary address: 7080 Lee Hwy. 24141. Phone: (540) 633-5330. Fax: (540) 633-6300. Licensee: Cumulus Licensing LLC. Group owner: Cumulus Media Inc. (acq 3-31-2004; grpsl). Format: Classic hits of the 60s, 70s & 80s, sports. Target aud: 25 plus. ♦ Ron Walton, gen mgr; Scott Stevens, gen sls mgr; David Dalesky, chief of engrg.

WWBU(FM)—Co-owned with WRAD(AM). 1965: 101.7 mhz; 3 kw. 66 ft. TL: N37 08 33 W80 34 39. Stereo. Format: Classic country. ♦ Randy Thompson, gen sls mgr.

*WVRU(FM)— Oct 9, 1978: 89.9 mhz; 500 w. 15 ft. TL: N37 08 26 W80 33 11. Stereo. Box 6973 24142. Secondary address: 236 Porterfield 24142. Phone: (540) 831-5171. Phone: (540) 831-6059. Fax: (540) 831-5893. E-mail: wvru@radford.edu. Web Site: www.wvru.org. Licensee: Radford University. Format: Jazz, triple A, BBC. News: 6 hrs wkly. Target aud: General. Spec prog: Jazz 19 hrs, class 15 hrs, Black 6 hrs, folk one hr, blues 7 hrs, oldies 5 hrs, public affrs 6 hrs, new age 3 hrs wkly. ♦ Ashlee B. Claud, gen mgr, dev VP & progmg VP; Jonathan Benfield, opns dir; Randy McCallister, engrg VP.

Richlands

WGTH-FM— Jan 3, 1977: 105.5 mhz; 450 w. 800 ft. TL: N37 09 20 W81 46 11. Box 370 24641. Phone: (276) 964-2502. Fax: (276) 964-4500. E-mail: wgth@wgth.net. Web Site: www.wgth.net. Licensee: High Knob Broadcasters Inc. Network: Salem Radio Network. Format: Relg, southern gospel. News: 8 hrs wkly. Target aud: General. ♦ Ron Brown, pres & gen mgr.

WGTH(AM)— Oct 5, 1951: 540 khz; 1 kw-D, 97 w-N. TL: N37 05 01 W81 46 58. (Acq 2-28-95; 5-22-95). News: 10 hrs wkly. Target aud: General.

WRIC-FM— November 1989: 100.7 mhz; 1.3 kw. 705 ft. TL: N37 09 04 W81 53 56. Stereo. Box 838, 1600 Front St., Suite 202 24641. Phone: (276) 964-4066. Phone: (276) 963-4400. Fax: (276) 963-4927. E-mail: wric@netscope.net. Licensee: Peggy Sue Broadcasting Corp. (group owner; acq 12-1-98; $190,000). Network: USA. Wilkinson, Barker, Knauer & Quinn. Format: Hot adult contemp. News staff: 3; News: 2 hrs wkly. Target aud: 24-54; young adult professionals. ♦ Henry Beam, pres; Dirk Hall, sr VP, gen mgr, gen sls mgr, mktg VP & prom VP; Jennie Casey, opns mgr; Dave Mann, chief of opns, progmg mgr & news dir; Wayne Boone, chief of engrg.

Richmond

WBTJ(FM)— May 1957: 106.5 mhz; 7.6 kw. Ant 1,233 ft. TL: N37 30 14 W77 41 53. Stereo. 3245 Basic Rd 23228. Phone: (804) 474-0000. Fax: (804) 474-0090. E-mail: sheilahbelle@clearchannel.com. Web Site: www.1065thebeat.com. Licensee: Capstar TX L.P. Group owner: Clear Channel Communications Inc. (acq 8-30-00; grpsl). Rep: Christal. Pepper & Corazzini. Format: Oldies, urban contemp. News staff: one; News: 5 hrs wkly. Target aud: 18-44. ♦ Mark Mays, pres; Tracy Onskell, sls dir; Ruth Jones, gen sls mgr; Ronda Steers, natl sls mgr; I.L. Scout, prom dir; Aaron Maxwell, progmg dir; Mike Street, mus dir; Sheilah Belle, news dir & pub affrs dir; Mike Fleming, engrg VP; Jon Bennett, chief of engrg.

WBTK(AM)— September 1926: 1380 khz; 5 kw-U, DA-2. TL: N37 37 13 W77 26 57. 9401 Courthouse Rd., Suite 307, Chesterfield 23832. Phone: (804) 717-5600. Fax: (804) 717-5602. E-mail: info@wbtk.com. Web site: www.wbtk.com. Licensee: SCA License Corp. Group owner: Salem Communications Corp. (acq 2001; $735,000). Format: Christian talk. Target aud: 35 plus; older, upscale. ♦ David Ruleman, VP; David Jackson, gen mgr & gen sls mgr; Dave Terry, opns mgr & prom dir; Glen Motto, progmg dir & pub affrs dir.

WCDX(FM)—See Mechanicsville

WCLM(AM)—See Highland Springs

*WCVE(FM)— May 6, 1988: 88.9 mhz; 17.5 kw. Ant 840 ft. TL: N37 34 00 W77 28 36. Stereo. 23 Sesame St. 23235. Phone: (804) 320-1301. Fax: (804) 320-8729. Web Site: www.ideastations.org. Licensee: Commonwealth Public Broadcasting Corp. Network: Network: NPR, PRI. Format: Class, news. News staff: one; News: 35 hrs wkly. Target aud: 35 plus. Spec prog: Folk 6 hrs, blues 5 hrs, jazz 13 hrs wkly. ♦ Bill Miller, VP & stn mgr; Peter Solomon, opns mgr; Lisa Tait, dev VP & dev dir. Co-owned TV: *WCVE-TV affil.

*WDCE(FM)— Sept 7, 1977: 90.1 mhz; 100 w. 118 ft. TL: N37 34 48 W77 32 35. Stereo. Box 85, Univ. of Richmond, 28 W. Hampton Way 23173. Phone: (804) 289-8698. Fax: (804) 289-8996. Web Site: www.student.richmond.edu. Licensee: University of Richmond. Format: Progsv, div, new mus. News: 3 hrs wkly. Target aud: 15-30. Spec prog: Class 3 hrs, jazz 9 hrs, relg 3 hrs wkly. ♦ Dan Inglis, gen mgr.

WDZY(AM)—(Colonial Heights). 1955: 1290 khz; 5 kw-D, 41 w-N. TL: N37 15 30 W77 23 40. (CP: 25 kw-D). 413 Stuart Cir., Suite 110 23220. Phone: (804) 353-7200. Fax: (804) 353-2633. Web Site: www.radiodisney.com/wdzy/290. Licensee: Radio Disney Group LLC. Group owner: ABC Inc. (acq 8-22-00; grpsl). Format: Family progmg. News: 7 hrs wkly. Target aud: 2-12, 25-54; children & women. ♦ Laura Haemker, stn mgr & gen sls mgr; Amy Garelick, prom mgr.

WFTH(AM)— June 16, 1964: 1590 khz; 5 kw-D, 19 w-N. TL: N37 30 02 W77 27 28. 227 E. Belt Blvd. 23224. Phone: (804) 233-0765. Fax: (804) 233-3725. Web Site: www.faith1590.com. Licensee: Tri-City Christian Radio Inc. (acq 3-22-90; $450,000; 4-16-90). Format: Gospel. ♦ Jack Johnson, pres; Mary Johnson, VP; Bryant Johnson, gen mgr, stn mgr & opns mgr.

WGGM(AM)—See Chester

WKHK(FM)—(Colonial Heights). Nov 17, 1972: 95.3 mhz; 17.5 kw. 393 ft. TL: N37 26 21 W77 25 57. Stereo. Gateway Crossing, 351 Tilghmen Rd., Salisbury 21804. Phone: (410) 742-1923. Fax: (410) 742-2329. Web Site: k9sscountry.com. Licensee: Cox Radio Inc. Group owner: Cox Broadcasting (acq 8-31-00; grpsl). Hogan & Hartson. Format: Country. News staff: one; News: 8 hrs wkly. Target aud: 25-54. ♦ Doug Hillard, gen mgr; Frank Hamilton, sls dir; Dixie Penner, prom dir; Kenny Love, progmg dir; Walt Barcus, mus dir, mus dir & pub affrs dir; Jon Bennett, chief of engrg.

WKJM(FM)—See Petersburg

WKJS(FM)— 1996: 105.7 mhz; 2.3 kw. Ant 531 ft. TL: N37 30 52 W77 30 28. 2809 Emerywood Pkwy., Suite 300 23294. Phone: (804) 672-9299. Fax: (804) 672-9314. Licensee: Radio One Licenses LLC. Group owner: Radio One Inc. (acq 11-8-2001; grpsl). Network: CBS. Rep: Allied Radio Partners. Fletcher, Heald & Hildreth. Format: Urban adult contemp. Target aud: 25-54; general. ♦ Bob Rich, gen mgr; Larry Jones, gen sls mgr; Bob Walden, natl sls mgr; Eric Cunningham, prom dir; Phil Daniels, progmg dir; Mikki Spencer, pub affrs dir.

WKLR(FM)—(Fort Lee). July 29, 1963: 96.5 mhz; 50 kw. 453 ft. TL: N37 20 22 W77 24 31. Stereo. 812 Moorefield Park Dr., Suite 300 23236. Phone: (804) 330-5700. Fax: (320) 330-4079. Web Site: www.965theplanet.com. Licensee: Cox Radio Inc. Group owner: Cox Broadcasting (acq 8-31-00; grpsl). Format: Classic rock. News staff: one; News: 5 hrs wkly. Target aud: 25-49. ♦ James Kennedy, chmn; Bob Willoughby, sls dir; Kevin Meek, gen sls mgr; Ronda Steers, natl sls mgr; Micki Long, mktg VP; Scott Weimer, progmg dir; Leslie Taylor, pub affrs dir; Scott Swingle, engrg dir; Jon Bennett, engrg mgr & chief of engrg.

WLEE(AM)— May 4, 1951: 990 khz; 1 kw-D, 13 w-N. TL: N37 31 40 W77 22 48. 306 W. Broad St. 23220. Phone: (804) 643-0990. Fax: (804) 474-5070. E-mail: wlee@radiorichmond.com. Web Site: www.radiorichmond.com. Licensee: 4M of Richmond Inc. Group owner: 4M Communications Inc. (acq 6-28-96; $75,000). Format: Talk. News staff: 2; News: 144 hrs wkly. Target aud: 25-64; white collar, upscale professionals. ♦ Peter Davidson, pres; Gloria Kirkland, exec VP & gen sls mgr; Mike Mazursky, gen mgr; Steve Miller, opns VP & progmg mgr.

WMXB(FM)— Dec 23, 1961: 103.7 mhz; 18.5 kw. 750 ft. TL: N37 30 31 W77 34 37. Stereo. 812 Moorefield Park Dr., Suite 300 23236. Phone: (804) 330-5700. Fax: (804) 330-4079. Fax: (804) 323-1524 sls. Web Site: www.mix1037.com. Licensee: Cox Radio Inc. Group owner: Cox Broadcasting (acq 8-00; grpsl). Network: ABC. Rep: McGavren Guild. Format: Adult contemp. News staff: one; News: 8 hrs wkly. Target aud: 25-54; predominately female. ♦ James Kennedy, CEO & COO; Steve McCall, gen mgr; Bob Willoughby, sls dir; Russ DeVries, gen sls mgr; Ronda Steers, natl sls mgr; Mark Nelson, prom dir; Tim Baldwin, progmg dir; Jackie Cunningham, news dir; Jon Bennett, chief of engrg.

WREJ(AM)— May 8, 1964: 1540 khz; 10 kw-D, DA-D. TL: N37 37 08 W77 25 27. 306 W. Broad St. 23220. Phone: (804) 643-0990. Fax: (804) 474-5070. E-mail: wrej@radiorichmond.com. Web Site: www.radiorichmond.com. Licensee: Radio Richmond 1540 Inc. (acq 10-26-99; $600,000). Network: Network: ABC, USA. Format: Urban inspirational. News staff: 3; News: 90 hrs wkly. Target aud: 35-64; individuals concerned about financial, civic & economic issues. Spec prog: Indian one hr, gospel one hr, lt one hr wkly. ♦Peter Davidson, pres; Mike Mazursky, gen mgr; Steve Miller, opns VP; Gloria Kirkland, gen sls mgr.

WRNL(AM)— Nov 15, 1937: 910 khz; 5 kw-U, DA-N. TL: N37 36 52 W77 30 49. 3245 Basie Rd. 23228. Phone: (804) 345-1140. Fax: (804) 474-0168. Web Site: www.sportsradio910.com. Licensee: Clear Channel Radio Licenses Inc. Group owner: Clear Channel Communications Inc. (acq 8-10-93; $9.75 million with co-located FM; 8-30-93). Format: Sports. Target aud: 25-54; men. ♦Ruth Jones, VP & gen mgr; Rebecca Gilreath, gen sls mgr; Dawna Ellis, mktg dir & adv dir; June Snead, prom dir.

WROU(AM)—See Petersburg

WRVA(AM)— Nov 2, 1925: 1140 khz; 50 kw-U, DA-1. TL: N37 24 13 W77 18 59. 3245 Basie Rd. 23228. Phone: (804) 345-1140. Phone: (804) 474-0000. Fax: (804) 474-0168. Web Site: www.wrva.com. Licensee: Clear Channel Broadcasting Inc. (group owner: Clear Channel Communications Inc. acq 6-26-92; grpsl; 7-20-92). Network: ABC. Rep: Clear Channel. Format: News/talk. News staff: 10; News: 24 hrs wkly. Target aud: 35-54. Spec prog: Relg 10 hrs, computers 2 hrs, gardening 3 hrs, home care 2 hrs, legal one hr wkly. ♦Ruth Jones, sr VP & gen mgr; Bill Cahill, gen sls mgr; Nina James, natl sls mgr; Dawna Ellis, mktg dir & adv dir; June Snead, prom dir; Deanna Malone, news dir; Mike Fleming, chief of engrg.

WRVQ(FM)— Aug 4, 1948: 94.5 mhz; 200 kw. Ant 455 ft. TL: N37 24 13 W77 18 59. Stereo. 3245 Basie Rd. 23228. Phone: (804) 474-0000. Fax: (804) 474-0090. Web Site: www.q94radio.com. Licensee: Clear Channel Broadcasting Licenses Inc. Group owner: Clear Channel Communications Inc. Format: Mainstream. Target aud: 18-44; women. ♦Ruth Jones, gen mgr; Tracy Driskol, gen sls mgr; Skip Sher, prom dir; Billy Surf, progmg dir; Mike Fleming, chief of engrg.

WRXL(FM)— Mar 4, 1949: 102.1 mhz; 140 kw. 320 ft. TL: N37 36 52 W77 30 49. (CP: 20 kw, ant 786 ft.). Stereo. 3245 Basie Rd. 23228. Phone: (804) 474-0000. Fax: (804) 474-0092. Web Site: www.1021thex.com. Licensee: Clear Channel Radio Licenses Inc. Format: AOR, new rock. Target aud: 25-44. ♦Ruth Jones, gen mgr.

WTVR-FM— February 1946: 98.1 mhz; 50 kw. 1,004 ft. TL: N37 34 00 W77 28 36. Stereo. 3245 Basie Rd. 23228. Phone: (804) 474-0000. Fax: (804) 474-0090. Web Site: www.lite98.com. Licensee: Clear Channel Broadcasting Licenses Inc. Group owner: Clear Channel Communications Inc. (acq 1996; $18 million. with co-located AM). Rep: Clear Channel. Format: Adult contemp. ♦Ruth Jones, gen mgr; Bill Cahill, progmg dir; Mike Fleming, chief of engrg.

WVNZ(AM)— September 1955: 1320 khz; 5 kw-D, DA. TL: N37 28 00 W77 27 08. 306 W. Broad St. 23220. Phone: (804) 643-0990. Fax: (804) 474-5070. E-mail: wvnz@radiorichmond.com. Web Site: www.radiorichmond.com. Licensee: RadioRichmond 1320 Inc. Group owner: 4M Communications Inc. (acq 12-2-99; $400,000). Network: ABC. Format: Spanish. News staff: 3; News: 15 hrs wkly. Target aud: 35 plus; Hispanic population. ♦Peter Davidson, pres; Michael Mazursky, gen mgr; Steve Miller, opns mgr; Gloria Kirkland, gen sls mgr & progmg dir.

WXGI(AM)— Oct 1, 1947: 950 khz; 5 kw-D, 64 w-N. TL: N37 30 52 W77 30 28. 701 German School Rd. 23225. Phone: (804) 233-7666. Fax: (804) 233-7681. E-mail: info@espn950am.com. Web Site: espn950am.com. Licensee: Gee Communications Inc. Network: ESPN Radio. Format: All sports/ESPN Radio. Target aud: 30 plus. ♦David Gee, CEO & pres; Sharon Eichenlaub, CFO; Howard H. Keller, opns dir; Peter Cowley, gen sls mgr; Peter Crowley, progmg dir; Clellan Jarrell, pub affrs dir; John McCune, chief of engrg.

WYFJ(FM)—See Ashland

Roanoke

WFIR(AM)— June 20, 1924: 960 khz; 5 kw-U, DA-N. TL: N37 15 20 W79 57 20. 3934 Electric Rd. 24018. Secondary address: 3509 Hounds Chase Ln. 24014. Phone: (540) 345-1511. Fax: (504) 342-2270. E-mail: wfir@bellatlantic.net. Licensee: Mel Wheeler Inc. (group owner; acq 3-31-00; with co-located FM). Network: CBS. Rep: Christal. Format: News/talk. Target aud: 35-54. ♦Leonard Wheeler, pres; Anne Booze, gen sls mgr; Kathy Rilee, mktg dir; Kevin LaRue, progmg dir; Mike Ward, news dir; J. J. Largen, chief of engrg.

WSLC-FM—Co-owned with WFIR(AM). November 1948: 94.9 mhz; 100 kw. Ant 1,979 ft. TL: N37 11 41 W80 09 22. Stereo. 1002 Newman Dr., Salem 24153. Secondary address: Box 6002, Salem 24153. Phone: (540) 774-0201. Fax: (540) 774-5667. Web Site: www.949starcountry.com. Format: Country. Target aud: 25-54. ♦Leonard Wheeler, gen mgr; Stan Reynolds, gen sls mgr; Kim Adams, prom mgr; Brett Sharp, progmg dir; Robynn James, mus dir.

WGMN(AM)— 1946: 1240 khz; 1 kw-U. TL: N37 16 12 W79 58 14. 3807 Brandon Ave., Suite 2350 24018. Phone: (540) 725-1220. Fax: (540) 725-1245. Web Site: www.espnradio.com. Licensee: Capstar TX L.P. Group owner: Clear Channel Communications Inc. (acq 8-30-00; grpsl). Network: ABC Daytime Direction. Rep: D & R Radio. Format: Sports. Target aud: 25-54. ♦Chris Clendenen, gen mgr; Ron Gaylor, sls dir & gen sls mgr; Aaron Roberts, progmg dir; Steve Curtiss, news dir; Jeff Parker, chief of engrg.

WKBA(AM)—(Vinton). Oct 9, 1961: 1550 khz; 10 kw-D, DA. TL: N37 17 24 W79 55 22. 2043 10th St. N.E. 24012. Phone: (540) 343-5597. Fax: (540) 345-4064. Licensee: Tinker Creek Broadcasters Inc. (acq 2-1-83). Booth, Freret, Imlay & Tepper P. Format: Relg. Target aud: General. Spec prog: Black 10 hrs wkly. ♦David H. Moran, pres & gen mgr; Sharon M. Moran, stn mgr & sls dir; Dorothy Durrett, progmg dir; Dale Cook, chief of engrg.

WPAR(FM)—See Salem

WRIS(AM)— Feb 28, 1953: 1410 khz; 5 kw-D, 72 w-N. TL: N37 16 47 W79 59 29. Box 6099, 219 Luckett St. N.W. 24017. Phone: (540) 342-1410. Phone: (540) 342-7811. Fax: (540) 342-5952. E-mail: wrisam@aol.com. Licensee: WRIS L.L.C. (acq 1-15-98). Rep: Allied Radio Partners. Blair, Joyce & Silva. Format: Relg, inspirational. News staff: one. Target aud: 35-75. ♦Lloyd Gochenour, pres, gen mgr & gen sls mgr; Russ Brown, opns mgr, progmg dir & news dir.

WROV-FM—See Martinsville

***WRXT(FM)**— July 31, 1994: 90.3 mhz; 5.5 kw. 1,112 ft. TL: N37 23 09 W79 40 10. 20276A Timberlake Road, Lynchburg 24502. Phone: (434) 237-9798. Fax: (434) 237-1025. Web Site: www.spiritfm.com. Licensee: Positive Alternative Radio Inc. Group owner: Baker Family Stations (acq 1-23-02). Format: Contemp Christian. ♦Barry Armstrong, gen mgr; Brian Sumner, mus dir.

WSLQ(FM)— Nov 1, 1947: 99.1 mhz; 200 kw. 1,985 ft. TL: N37 11 42 W80 09 22. Stereo. 3934 Electric Rd. 24018. Secondary address: Box 92 24018. Phone: (540) 387-0234. E-mail: q99@bellatlantic.net. Web Site: www.q99fm.com. Licensee: Mel Wheeler Inc. Rep: Katz Radio. Format: Adult contemp. News: 1 hr wkly. Target aud: 25-54; skew female.

WSNV(FM)—See Salem

WVBE(AM)— Oct 1, 1940: 610 khz; 5 kw-D, 1 kw-N, DA-2. TL: N37 18 11 W80 02 33. 3934 Electric Rd. 24018. Secondary address: Box 92 24022. Phone: (540) 774-9200. Fax: (540) 774-5667. E-mail: info@vibe100.com. Web Site: www.vibe100.com. Licensee: Mel Wheeler Inc. (group owner; (acq 10-1-76). Network: Motor Racing Net. Rep: Katz Radio. Pepper & Corazzini. Format: Urban adult contemp. Target aud: Adult 25-54; skew female, skew black. Spec prog: VA Tech football & basketball, coaches live call-in. ♦Leonard Wheeler, pres & gen mgr.

***WVTF(FM)**— Aug 1, 1973: 89.1 mhz; 100 kw. 1,970 ft. TL: N37 11 56 W80 09 02. Stereo. 3520 Kingsbury Ln. 24014-1348. Phone: (540) 989-8900. Fax: (540) 776-2727. E-mail: wvtf@vt.edu. Web Site: www.wvtf.org. Licensee: Virginia Tech Foundation Inc. (acq 1-1-82). Network: Network: PRI, NPR. Dow, Lohnes & Albertson. Format: Class, jazz, news. News staff: 3; News: 39 hrs wkly. Target aud: General. ♦Glenn Gleixner, gen mgr & dev dir.

WWWR(AM)— April 1957: 910 khz; 1 kw-D, 84 w-N. TL: N37 16 06 W79 54 46. 1848 Clay St. S.E. 24013. Phone: (540) 343-7109. Fax: (540) 343-2306. Web Site: www.3wradio.com. Licensee: Perception Media Group Inc. (group owner; acq 4-25-91; $150,000;. FTR: 5-13-91). Network: USA. Format: Gospel. Target aud: 35-64. ♦Ben Peyton, pres; Barbara Evans, stn mgr, sls dir & progmg dir; Dale Cook, chief of engrg.

WXLK(FM)— Dec 17, 1960: 92.3 mhz; 93 kw. 2,050 ft. TL: N37 11 56 W80 09 03. Stereo. Box 92 24022. Secondary address: 3934 Electric Rd. S.W. 24018. Phone: (540) 774-9200. Fax: (540) 774-5667. Web Site: www.k92radio.com. Licensee: Mel Wheeler Inc. (group owner; acq 3-12-97; $7.5 million. with WVBE-FM Lynchburg). Format: CHR. Target aud: 18-44; women. ♦Leonard Wheeler, CEO, pres & gen mgr.

WZBL(FM)— November 1993: 104.9 mhz; 14.5 kw. Ant 925 ft. TL: N37 22 23 W79 55 40. 3305 Old Forest Rd., Lynchburg 24501. Phone: (434) 385-8298. Fax: (434) 385-8991. Web Site: www.magicfm.cc. Licensee: Capstar TX L.P. Group owner: Clear Channel Communications Inc. (acq 8-30-2000; grpsl). Format: Adult contemp. News staff: 2. ♦Chris Clendenen, pres & gen mgr; Tom Sweat, natl sls mgr & rgnl sls mgr; Steve Cross, progmg dir; Jason Osborne, pub affrs dir; Jeff Parker, chief of engrg.

Rocky Mount

WYTI(AM)— Mar 31, 1957: 1570 khz; 2.5 kw-D, 220 w-N. TL: N36 58 37 W79 53 45. Drawer 430, 275 Glenwood Dr. 24151. Phone: (540) 483-9955. Phone: (540) 483-2166. Fax: (540) 483-7802. E-mail: wyti@cablenet-va.com. Licensee: WYTI Inc. (acq 1-71). Network: ABC. Format: Traditional country, bluegrass, gospel. Target aud: 30 plus; general. Spec prog: NASCAR races, relg 10 hrs wkly. ♦Susan Mullins, exec VP, gen mgr & opns mgr; William E. Jefferson, pres & stn mgr.

Ruckersville

WHTE-FM—Licensed to Ruckersville. See Charlottesville

Rural Retreat

WCRR(AM)— May 15, 1985: 660 khz; 550 w-D. TL: N36 55 17 W81 14 34. Box 660 24368. Phone: (276) 686-4111. Fax: (276) 686-4112. Licensee: Ora Robert Smallwood III (acq 5-20-2003). Network: UPI. Pepper & Corazzini. Format: Country, relg. Target aud: General. ♦Bob Smallwood, pres, gen sls mgr & chief of engrg; Rodney Allen, gen mgr & progmg dir.

WXBX(FM)— June 11, 1992: 95.3 mhz; 6 kw. Ant 400 ft. TL: N36 55 17 W81 14 34. Stereo. Box 1247, Three Rivers Media Corp., 110 W. Spiller St., Wytheville 24382. Phone: (276) 228-3185. Fax: (276) 228-9261. E-mail: wyve/wxbx@netva.com. Web Site: www.wyve.com. Licensee: Three Rivers Media Corp. (acq 10-01-98; $200,000). Network: Network: AP Network News, Jones Radio Networks. Rgnl Reps Brooks, Pierce, McLendon, Humphrey & Leonard. Format: Oldies. News staff: one; News: 12 hrs wkly. Target aud: 25+. ♦Gary W. Hagerich, CEO, pres & gen mgr; Danny Gordon, news dir; Sam Parks, chief of engrg.

Saint Paul

WXLZ(AM)— Nov 3, 1981: 1140 khz; 2.5 kw-D. TL: N36 52 15 W82 18 21. Box 250, Mew Rd., Castlewood 24224. Phone: (276) 762-5595. Fax: (276) 889-3677. E-mail: wxlz1073@mounet.com. Web Site: www.wxlz.net. Licensee: Yeary Broadcasting Inc. Network: CBS. Format: Relg. News staff: 3; News: 3 hrs wkly. Target aud: 25 plus; students, farmers, miners & rural area residents. Spec prog: Gospel 15 hrs wkly. ♦Lannis Yeary, CEO, gen sls mgr & prom mgr; Donna Yeary, exec VP; Gary Scott, stn mgr & progmg dir; Wilma Kiser, mktg dir; Pat Jenkins, news dir & pub affrs dir; Ron Keene, chief of engrg.

Salem

***WPAR(FM)**— April 1994: 91.3 mhz; 3.3 kw horiz, 3 kw vert. 902 ft. TL: N37 22 23 W79 55 40. Stereo. Box 889, Blacksburg 24063. Phone: (540) 961-2377. Fax: (540) 951-5282. E-mail: mail@spiritfm.com. Web Site: www.spiritfm.com. Licensee: Positive Alternative Radio Inc. Group owner: Baker Family Stations (acq 5-90; FTR: 5-21-90). Network: USA. Booth, Freret, Imlay & Tepper. Format: Christian adult contemp. Target aud: 25-54; adults with families. ♦Barry Armstrong, gen mgr.

WSNV(FM)— Mar 7, 1969: 93.5 mhz; 5.8 kw. 98 ft. TL: N37 16 47 W79 59 29. Stereo. 3807 Brandon Ave. S.W., Suite 2350, Roanoke 24018. Phone: (540) 725-1220. Fax: (540) 725-1245. Web Site: www.j93.com. Licensee: Capstar TX L.P. Group owner: Clear Channel Communications Inc. (acq 8-30-00; grpsl). Network: Westwood One. Rep: Allied Radio Partners. Format: Soft adult contemp. News: one hr wkly. Target aud: 24 plus. ♦Chris Clendenen, gen mgr & gen sls mgr; Steve Cross, progmg dir; Ed Kilbane, mus dir & news dir.

WTOY(AM)— Sept 7, 1956: 1480 khz; 5 kw-D. TL: N37 16 21 W80 04 52. 504 23rd St., Roanoke 24017. Phone: (540) 344-9869. Fax: (540) 344-0976. Licensee: Ward Broadcasting Corp. (acq 3-2-92). Format: Adult urban contemp. ♦Irving L. Ward Sr., gen mgr, chief of engrg, pres & sls dir; Carter G., progmg VP & progmg dir.

Stations in the U.S. — Virginia

Saltville

WXMY(AM)— Nov 5, 1981: 1600 khz; 5 kw-D. TL: N36 51 43 W81 43 29. (CP: 10 kw-D, 10 w-N, DA-2). Box 5555, Chilhowie 24319. Phone: (276) 496-0016. Fax: (276) 496-0005. E-mail: wxmy@aol.com. Web Site: www.1600wxmy.com. Licensee: Continental Media Group LLC (acq 4-11-01; $62,000). Format: Classic country, bluegrass, gospel. Target aud: 25-54. ♦ Jeff Raynor, gen mgr, stn mgr & gen sls mgr; J.C. Heath, mus dir.

Smithfield

WKGM(AM)— Dec 18, 1974: 940 khz; 10 kw-D, 3 kw-N, DA-N. TL: N36 57 16 W76 37 48. Box 339 23431. Secondary address: 13379 Great Spring Rd. 23430. Phone: (757) 357-9546. Phone: (757) 622-9546. Fax: (757) 365-0412. E-mail: wkgm@hotmail.com. Licensee: WKGM Inc. Group owner: Baker Family Stations Format: Relg. News: one hr wkly. Target aud: 25 plus. Spec prog: Farm 2 hrs, Ger one hr, Sp one hr, gospel 5 hrs wkly. ♦ Vernon H. Baker, pres; Larry W. Cobb, VP, gen mgr, gen sls mgr & chief of engrg; Robert Stallings, pub affrs dir.

South Boston

WHLF(FM)— Sept 1, 1992: 95.3 mhz; 6 kw. 246 ft. TL: N36 43 59 W78 56 03. Stereo. Box 526, 1210 Porter Ln. 24592. Phone: (434) 572-2988. Fax: (434) 572-1662. E-mail: whlf@whlf.com. Web Site: www.whlf.com. Licensee: JLC Properties Inc. (acq 4-1-93; FTR: 4-19-93). Network: ABC. Format: Adult hit contemp. News staff: one; News: 8 hrs wkly. Target aud: 25-54; those that have spendable income. Spec prog: Gospel. ♦ John L. Cole III, pres; Catherine M. Cole, dev dir & gen sls mgr; Nick Long, sls dir; Kelly Redd, mus dir; Sonny Riddle, news dir.

WQOK(FM)—Licensed to South Boston. See Raleigh NC

WSBV(AM)— 1980: 1560 khz; 2.5 kw-D, DA-1. TL: N36 42 24 W78 52 28. Box 778, 1180 Plywood Tr. 24592. Phone: (434) 572-4418. Fax: (434) 572-9245. Licensee: Linda Waller-Barton Format: Contemp Christian, Multi-Cultural. Target aud: 40 plus. Spec prog: Farm one hr wkly. ♦ Linda Waller-Barton, gen mgr; April Warf, stn mgr & progmg dir; James W. Barton, opns dir; Karen Newman, sls VP; Wendy Coleman, mktg mgr; Kevin Pearson, prom VP; Rodney Logan, progmg mgr; Willie Yancey, mus dir; Maria Spooner, asst music dir; Barbara Claiborne, pub affrs dir; Tim Walker, chief of engrg.

South Hill

WKSK-FM—Listing follows WSHV(AM).

WSHV(AM)— Nov 1, 1953: 1370 khz; 5 kw-D. TL: N36 44 39 W78 09 42. Box 216 23970. Phone: (434) 447-8997. Phone: (434) 447-4007. Fax: (434) 447-4789. E-mail: wshv@hotmail.com. Licensee: Lakes Media Holding Company LLC. Group owner: Joyner Radio Inc. (acq 2-1-2005; grpsl). Network: ABC. Format: Black. News staff: one. Target aud: General. ♦ Jerry E. Brown, sr VP; Greg Thirft, gen mgr; Robert Wilson, progmg mgr; Robby McMulian, news dir; John Hart, chief of engrg.

WKSK-FM—Co-owned with WSHV(AM). Dec 23, 1966: 101.9 mhz; 6 kw. Ant 315 ft. TL: N36 44 39 W78 09 42. Stereo. E-mail: wjws@yahoo.com. Network: ABC. Format: Country. News staff: one; News: 2 hrs wkly. Target aud: General; adults 25-54. ♦ Steve Howell, progmg dir.

Spotsylvania

*WWED(FM)—Not on air, target date: unknown: 89.5 mhz; 380 w vert. Ant 433 ft. TL: N38 11 48 W77 33 45. Box 905 22553. Licensee: Educational Media Corp.

WYSK-FM— Mar 31, 1988: 99.3 mhz; 3 kw. 295 ft. TL: N38 08 31 W77 41 38. 616 Amelia St., Fredericksburg 22401. Phone: (540) 582-2405. Phone: (540) 374-5500. Fax: (540) 374-5525. Web Site: www.wysk.com. Licensee: The Free Lance-Star Publishing Co. (group owner; acq 4-19-93; $200,000;. FTR: 5-3-93). Format: Rock alternative. News staff: 3. Target aud: 25-49. ♦ Josiah P Rowe, III, pres; John Moen, gen mgr; James T. Butler, sls dir & gen sls mgr; Bridgette Dean, prom dir; Jon Reed, progmg dir; Frank Wells, mus dir; Frank Hammon, news dir; Chris Wilk, chief of engrg.

Stanleytown

WZBB(FM)— March 1989: 99.9 mhz; 3.6 kw. 722 ft. TL: N36 54 50 W79 57 07. Stereo. 10899 Virginia Ave., Bassett 24055. Phone: (540) 489-9999. Fax: (276) 629-8399. E-mail: kristib@wzbbfm.com. Web Site: www.wzbbfm.com. Licensee: WNLB Radio Inc. Format: Country. Target aud: 21 plus. ♦ Donny Brook, pres; Glenn Lynch, VP; Kristi Banks, gen mgr, mktg dir & adv dir; Kristie Banks, gen sls mgr & rgnl sls mgr; Tiffany Purcell, prom dir; Craig Richards, progmg dir; Dan Taylor, mus dir; Lisa Layne, asst music dir & news dir; Paxton Durham, chief of engrg.

Staunton

WCYK-FM— September 1984: 99.7 mhz; 3.3 kw. 1,692 ft. TL: N38 03 52 W78 48 18. Stereo. Box 7703, Charlottesville 22906. Secondary address: 1150 Pepsi Pl., Suite 300, Charlottesville 22901. Phone: (434) 978-4408. Fax: (434) 978-1109. Web Site: www.country997.com. Licensee: Clear Channel Broadcasting Licenses Inc. Group owner: Clear Channel Communications Inc. (acq 8-6-99; grpsl). Rep: Clear Channel, Katz Radio. Format: Country. Target aud: 25-54. ♦ Phil Robken, gen mgr & natl sls mgr; Mike Chiumento, gen sls mgr & chief of engrg; Regan Keith, opns mgr & progmg dir.

WKCI(AM)—See Waynesboro

WKDW(AM)— April 1954: 900 khz; 2.5 kw-D, 128 w-N. TL: N38 10 27 W79 04 12. Stereo. Box 2189 24401. Phone: (540) 886-2376. Fax: (540) 885-8662. E-mail: wkdw@ntelos.net. Web Site: www.goodradio.com. Licensee: Clear Channel Broadcasting Licenses Inc. Group owner: Clear Channel Communications Inc. (acq 11-15-00; grpsl). Holland & Knight. Format: Country. News staff: one; News: 15 hrs wkly. Target aud: 25-54. Spec prog: Farm one hr, blue grass one hr wkly. ♦ Steve Davis, gen mgr; Kris Losh, progmg dir; Jeff Caudell, chief of engrg.

WSVO(FM)—Co-owned with WKDW(AM). May 29, 1959: 93.1 mhz; 2.8 kw. 338 ft. TL: N38 10 27 W79 04 12. (CP: TL: N38 10 32 W79 04 12). Stereo. Web Site: www.goodradio.com. Format: Oldies. News staff: one; News: 15 hrs wkly. Target aud: 35-54.

WNLR(AM)—See Churchville

WTON(AM)— Mar 9, 1946: 1240 khz; 1 kw-U. TL: N38 08 30 W79 02 33. Box 1085 24402-1085. Secondary address: 304 W. Beverly St. 24401. Phone: (540) 885-5188. Fax: (540) 885-1240. E-mail: star94@cfw.com. Web Site: www.pioneermediaalliance.com. Licensee: High Impact Communications Inc. (acq 3-1-96; $1 million). Network: Network: CBS, ESPN Radio. Reddy & Begley. Target aud: 18-49. ♦ Brenda Ratcliff, gen mgr; J. Gary Ratcliff, pres & gen mgr; Barry Bland, sls VP; Cass Johnson, progmg dir.

WTON-FM— November 1990: 94.3 mhz; 330 w. 2,263 ft. TL: N38 09 55 W79 18 51. Stereo. Phone: (800) 978-2794. Web Site: www.star943fm.com. Network: CBS. Rgnl Reps Reddy & Begley. Format: Classic hits. News: 3 hrs wkly. Target aud: 18-49; 60% women, 40% men.

WZXI(FM)—(Buffalo Gap). 1988: 95.5 mhz; 6 kw. Ant 308 ft. TL: N38 10 55 W79 13 34. Stereo. 130 University Blvd., Harrisonburg 22801. Secondary address: Broadcast House, 420 N. New St. 24402. Phone: (540) 801-1057. Fax: (540) 564-2873. E-mail: wzxi@easyradioinc.com. Web Site: www.wzxi.com. Licensee: Vox Communications Group LLC. (acq 7-13-2005; $900,000). Format: Talk radio. News staff: one. Target aud: 18-49. ♦ Jeff Wilson, gen sls mgr.

Stephens City

WKSI-FM—Listing follows WMRE(AM).

Strasburg

WWRT(FM)— Jan 1, 1987: 104.9 mhz; 3 kw. 219 ft. TL: N39 01 22 W78 25 35. Stereo. Box 3300, Winchester 22604. Secondary address: 520 N. Pleasant Valley Rd., Winchester 22601. Phone: (540) 667-2224. Fax: (540) 722-3295. Web Site: www.realclassicrock.fm. Licensee: Mid Atlantic Network Inc. Group owner: Mid Atlantic Network (acq 7-8-97; $850,000. with WWRE(FM) Berryville). Cole, Raywid & Braverman. Format: Classic Rock. Target aud: 18 plus. ♦ John P. Lewis, pres; Chris Lewis, gen mgr & gen sls mgr; Jeff Adams, opns mgr; Don Wilson, progmg dir; Steve Edwards, news dir; Archie McKay, chief of engrg.

Stuart

WHEO(AM)— Oct 12, 1959: 1270 khz; 5 kw-D. TL: N36 37 25 W80 15 50. 3824 Wayside Rd. 24171. Phone: (276) 694-3114. Fax: (276) 694-2241. E-mail: wheo@sitesstar.net. Web Site: www.wheo.net. Licensee: Mountain View Communications Inc. (acq 6-86). Network: CNN Radio. Format: Country. News staff: one; News: 25 hrs wkly. Target aud: General. Spec prog: Farm 4 hrs, relg 10 hrs, loc news 10 hrs wkly. ♦ Dean Goad, pres; Jamie Clark, VP, opns mgr & gen sls mgr; La Vergne Collins, sls dir; Richard Rogers, progmg dir; Bruce Dollarhite, chief of engrg & engr.

Suffolk

WAFX(FM)— Dec 12, 1983: 106.9 mhz; 100 kw. 984 ft. TL: N36 48 16 W76 45 17. Stereo. 870 Greenbriar Cir., Suite 399, Chesapeake 23320. Phone: (757) 366-9900. Fax: (757) 366-0022. Web Site: www.1069thefox.com. Licensee: Tidewater Communications LLC. Group owner: Saga Communications Inc. (acq 3-15-94; $4 million;. FTR: 5-9-94). Rep: McGavren Guild. Format: Classic rock. Target aud: 18-49. ♦ Dave Paulus, gen mgr; Barry Haugh, gen sls mgr; Mike Beck, progmg dir.

WFOG(FM)— December 1965: 92.9 mhz; 50 kw. 480 ft. TL: N36 52 35 W76 23 28. Stereo. 5589 Greenwich Rd., Suite 200, Virginia Beach 23462. Phone: (757) 671-1000. Fax: (757) 671-1010. Web Site: www.929oldies.com. Licensee: MHR License LLC. Group owner: Barnstable Broadcasting Inc. (acq 3-18-2005; grpsl). Format: Oldies. Target aud: 25-54; women. Spec prog: Relg 2 hrs, Sunday Morning Magazine one hr wkly. ♦ Andy Graham, gen mgr; Cynthia Johnson, sls dir; Frankie Roman, prom dir; John Shomby, progmg dir; Keith McMalley, chief of engrg.

Sweet Briar

*WNRS-FM— 1980: 89.9 mhz; 30 w. Ant 1,942 ft. TL: N37 33 50 W79 11 34. Stereo. Box 143 24595. Phone: (434) 381-6187. Fax: (434) 381-6173. E-mail: wnrs@sbc.edu. Web Site: www.wnrs-fm.sbc.edu. Licensee: Sweet Briar College. Format: Modern rock. Target aud: General. ♦ Erin Coleman, gen mgr; Virginia Wood, stn mgr; Joelle Andrews, opns mgr; Collean Lawey, adv VP; John Jaffe, progmg dir; Suzie Sweetbrier, mus dir.

Tappahannock

WRAR(AM)— Nov 1, 1970: 1000 khz; 500 w-D. TL: N37 57 08 W76 48 57. Box 1023 22560. Secondary address: 156 Prince St. 22560. Phone: (804) 443-4321. Fax: (804) 443-1055. E-mail: danny@wrarfm.com. Web Site: www.wrarfm.com. Licensee: Rappahanock Communications Inc. (acq 1-85). Network: ABC Information & Entertainment. Format: Black gospel. ♦ Danny C. Wadsworth, pres & gen mgr; Rich Morgan, gen sls mgr; Jay Atkins, progmg dir; Frank S. Miner, chief of engrg.

WRAR-FM— July 26, 1971: 105.5 mhz; 6 kw. 328 ft. TL: N37 52 27 W76 43 37. Stereo. Web Site: www.wrarfm.com. Format: Adult contemp. ♦ Jay Davis, progmg dir; Tom Davis, news dir.

Broadcasting & Cable Yearbook 2006

Virginia

Tasley

WESR-FM—See Onley-Onancock

Tazewell

WKQY(FM)—Listing follows WTZE(AM).

WTZE(AM)— Apr 22, 1966: 1470 khz; 5 kw-D. TL: N37 07 57 W81 33 21. 900 Bluefield Ave., Bluefield, WV 24701. Phone: (304) 327-7114. Fax: (304) 325-7850. Licensee: Monterey Licenses LLC. Group owner: Triad Broadcasting Co. LLC (acq 7-18-00; grpsl). Network: Motor Racing Net. Format: News/talk. News: 5 hrs wkly. Target aud: 21-54. Spec prog: Gospel 5 hrs wkly. ♦ John Halford, gen mgr; Dave Crosier, opns dir; Joseph Echoles, progmg dir; Keith Bowman, chief of engrg.

WKQY(FM)—Co-owned with WTZE(AM). Sept 1, 1968: 100.1 mhz; 4.2 kw. 395 ft. TL: N37 08 00 W81 35 43. Stereo. Format: Oldies. News staff: one. Target aud: 25 plus.

Vinton

WJJS-FM— 1994: 106.1 mhz; 6 kw. Ant 95 ft. TL: N37 17 03 W79 59 14. 3807 Brandon Ave. S.W., Suite 2350, Roanoke 24018. Phone: (540) 725-1220. Fax: (540) 725-1245. Web Site: www.wjjs.cc. Licensee: Capstar TX L.P. Group owner: Clear Channel Communications Inc. (acq 8-30-2000; grpsl). Format: Top-40. ♦ Chris Clendenen, gen mgr; Ron Gaylor, gen sls mgr & rgnl sls mgr; David Lee Michaels, progmg dir; Ed Kilbane, news dir; Jeff Parker, chief of engrg.

WKBA(AM)—Licensed to Vinton. See Roanoke

WZZI(FM)— Dec 12, 1995: 101.5 mhz; 630 w. 705 ft. TL: N37 21 57 W79 52 01. 210 1st St., Suite 240, Roanoke 24011. Phone: (540) 344-2800. Fax: (540) 344-4001. E-mail: oldies1015t@aol.com. Licensee: Centennial Broadcasting LLC. (group owner; (acq 11-23-2004; $4.15 million. with WZZU(FM) Lynchburg). Format: Oldies. ♦ Allen B. Shaw, pres; Henry Guess, gen sls mgr; Dale Cook, chief of engrg.

Virginia Beach

WBVA(AM)—(Bayside). May 1999: 1450 khz; 1 kw-U. TL: N36 51 29 W76 09 28. Box 55285 23471. Phone: (757) 481-9282. Phone: (757) 412-4321. Fax: (757) 490-8704. E-mail: wbva@email.com. Web Site: www.expage.com/wbva. Licensee: Ronald W. Cowan Jr. (acq 5-21-2001). Network: Sporting News Radio Network. Format: Talk, weekend sports. ♦ Ronald W. Cowan Jr., CEO, pres & gen mgr; Richard Harris, sls dir.

***WJLZ(FM)**— Feb 12, 1989: 88.5 mhz; 1.2 kw. Ant 118 ft. TL: N36 50 30.7 W76 05 37. 3500 Virginia Beach Blvd., Suite 201 23452. Phone: (757) 498-9632. Fax: (757) 498-8609. E-mail: info@wjlz.com. Web Site: www.wjlz.com. Licensee: Virginia Beach Educational Broadcasting Foundation Inc. Format: Christian. Target aud: General. ♦ Anne Verebely, VP, gen mgr & mus dir; Lisa Herrera, prom dir; William M. Verebely Jr., pres & engrg dir; Bill Verebely, chief of engrg.

WPTE(FM)— May 5, 1984: 94.9 mhz; 50 kw. 499 ft. TL: N36 48 38 W76 16 57. Stereo. 236 Clearfield Ave., Suite 206 23462. Phone: (757) 497-2000. Fax: (757) 456-5458. Web Site: www.pointradio.com. Licensee: Entercom Norfolk License LLC. Group owner: Entercom Communications Corp. (acq 12-13-99; grpsl). Rep: D & R Radio. Format: Modern adult comtemp. News: one hr wkly. Target aud: 18-49. ♦ David J. Field, CEO; David J. Field, pres; Skip Schmidt, gen mgr.

WPYA(FM)—See Chesapeake

WROX-FM—(Exmore). 1986: 96.1 mhz; 23 kw. Ant 722 ft. TL: N37 15 45 W76 00 45. Stereo. 500 Dominion Tower, 999 Waterside Dr., Norfolk 23510. Phone: (757) 640-8500. Fax: (757) 640-8552. Web Site: www.96x.fm. Licensee: Sinclair Telecable Inc. Group owner: Sinclair Communications Inc. (acq 9-28-93; $1.3 million;. FTR: 10-25-93). Rep: McGavren Guild. Format: Modern rock. News staff: one. Target aud: 18-34; men. ♦ Bob Sinclair, pres; Lisa Sinclair, gen mgr; Dave Morgan, opns mgr.

WVAB(AM)—Licensed to Virginia Beach. See Norfolk

WWHV(FM)— 2002: 102.1 mhz; 6 kw. Ant 167 ft. TL: N36 49 58 W75 58 16. 545 South Birdneck Rd., Suite 100 23450. Phone: (757) 422-6421. Fax: (757) 422-6437. E-mail: hot102va@aol.com. Web Site: www.hot102fm.com. Licensee: On Top Communications of Virginia Inc. Group owner: On Top Communications Inc. (acq 1-8-02; grpsl). Format: Hip hop, rhythm and blues. ♦ Parish Brown, progmg djr.

WXMM(FM)—See Norfolk

Warrenton

WBPS-FM— Nov 2, 1978: 94.3 mhz; 3 kw. 397 ft. TL: N38 40 42 W77 47 18. Stereo. 8121 Georgia Ave., 10th Fl., Silver Springs 20910. Phone: (301) 588-6200. Fax: (301) 589-4376. Licensee: Mega Communications of Warrenton Licensee L.L.C. Group owner: Mega Communications Inc. (acq 6-30-2000; $5.25 million). Network: ABC Daytime Direction. Format: Sp tropical. ♦ Elio Aguilar, gen mgr; Mark Kreider, progmg dir.

WKCW(AM)— Dec 7, 1957: 1420 khz; 10 kw-D, 17 w-N. TL: N38 45 05 W77 44 38. 320 B. Maple Ave. E., Vienna 22180. Phone: (540) 347-1421. Phone: (703) 319-3400. Fax: (703) 319-3390. Web Site: www.wkcw1420am.com. Licensee: Metro Radio Inc. (group owner; (acq 1-2-2004; $400,000). Format: Sp tropical. News staff: one; News: 2 hrs wkly. Target aud: 25-54; mature adults with discretionary income of $30,000 plus. Spec prog: Bluegrass, farm one hr, rel 6 hrs wkly. ♦ Bruce A. Houston, pres; Bill Parris, gen mgr, gen sls mgr & mktg mgr; Tom Casey, opns mgr, progmg dir & news dir; Jim Richardson, chief of engrg.

WPRZ(AM)— Nov 21, 1957: 1250 khz; 5 kw-D, 32 w-N, DA-2. TL: N38 43 52 W77 46 42. 7351 Hunton St. 20187-2222. Phone: (540) 349-1250. Fax: (540) 349-2726. E-mail: info@wprz.org. Web Site: www.wprz.org. Licensee: Praise Communications Inc. (acq 12-83; $400,000). Network: Network: USA, Moody. Bentley Law Office. Format: Christian mus & programs. News: 5 hrs wkly. Target aud: 25-54; Christian. Spec prog: Children 7 hrs wkly. ♦ Sally L. Buchanan, gen mgr & gen sls mgr; Steve W. Buchanan, pres, opns mgr & sls mgr.

WTOP-FM— Mar 28, 1966: 107.7 mhz; 33 kw. 1,199 ft. TL: N38 44 31 W77 50 07. Stereo. 3400 Idaho Ave. N.W., Washington, DC 20016. Phone: (202) 895-5000. Fax: (202) 895-5140. Web Site: www.wtopnews.com. Licensee: Bonneville Holding Co. Group owner: Bonneville International Corp. (acq 4-27-98). Network: CBS. Format: News. News staff: 60; News: 168 hrs wkly. Target aud: 25-54. ♦ Bruce Reese, CEO; Bob Johnson, CFO; Joel Oxley, VP & gen mgr; Matt Mills, gen sls mgr; Leo Donohoe, natl sls mgr; Janie Floyd, rgnl sls mgr; Mary Kay Le May, mktg mgr; Jim Farley, progmg VP; Lisa Wolfe, progmg mgr; Mike McMearty, news dir; Melvin Chase, pub affrs dir; Dave Garner, chief of engrg.

Warsaw

WNNT-FM— Mar 1, 1967: 100.9 mhz; 3 kw. 305 ft. TL: N37 56 39 W76 45 05. Stereo. Box 877 22572. Secondary address: 194 Islington Rd. 22572. Phone: (804) 333-4900. Phone: (804) 333-3711. Fax: (804) 333-4531. E-mail: rivercountry@rivercountry1009.com. Web Site: www.rivercountry1009.com. Licensee: Northern Neck & Tidewater Communications (acq 9-16-93; $400,000;. FTR: 10-11-93). Format: Country.

Waynesboro

WKCI(AM)— Mar 10, 1965: 970 khz; 5 kw-D, 1 kw-N, DA-2. TL: N38 05 12 W78 54 42. 207 University Blvd., Harrisonburg 22801. Phone: (540) 434-1777. Fax: (540) 432-9968. Web Site: www.shenandoahradio.com. Licensee: Clear Channel Broadcasting Licenses Inc. Group owner: Clear Channel Communications Inc. (acq 11-16-00; grpsl). Format: News/talk. News staff: one; News: 2 hrs wkly. Target aud: 25-54. Spec prog: Black 3 hrs, farm 2 hrs wkly. ♦ Steve Davis, gen mgr; Steve Knupp, opns mgr & progmg VP; Susie Smith, gen sls mgr; Mark Ness, chief of engrg.

***WPVA(FM)**— 1999: 90.1 mhz; 2.5 kw. Ant 961 ft. TL: N38 01 16 W78 52 38. 1320 Central Park Blvd., Suite 253, Fredericksburg 22401. Phone: (540) 786-5960. Fax: (540) 786-0001. E-mail: wpva@csnradio.com. Web Site: www.csnvirginia.org. Licensee: CSN International. (group owner; acq 10-5-99; $70,000). Booth, Freret, Imlay & Tepper. Format: Contemp Christian. ♦ Steve Wang, gen mgr.

West Point

WTYD(FM)— July 1991: 107.9 mhz; 6 kw. Ant 328 ft. TL: N37 27 02 W76 48 48. (CP: 4 kw. TL: N37 27 00 W76 48 46). Stereo. 5000 New Point Rd., Suite 2102, Williamsburg 23188. Phone: (757) 565-1079. Fax: (757) 565-7094. Web Site: www.tideradio.com. Licensee: Davis Media LLC (acq 6-17-2005; $1.13 million). Format: Triple A. ♦ Thomas G. Davis, pres & gen mgr; Derek Mason, gen sls mgr; Betsy Balkcom, prom mgr; Amy Miller, mus dir.

White Stone

WNDJ(FM)— Sept 1, 1995: 104.9 mhz; 6 kw. 282 ft. TL: N37 43 26 W76 23 27. Box 896, Urbanna 22578. Phone: (804) 758-9635. Fax: (804) 758-5835. E-mail: windyradio@windy105fm.com. Web Site: windy105fm.com. Licensee: Windmill Communications Inc. Network: Westwood One. Format: Adult standards, talk. Target aud: 25-54. ♦ Millard S. Younts, pres; Richard Swift, exec VP; Mitt Younts, gen mgr; Carter Mills, stn mgr & prom dir; Sharon Lambertti, opns dir; Jack Davis, sls VP & sls dir; Scott Simpson, engrg dir & chief of engrg.

Williamsburg

***WCWM(FM)**— Sept 28, 1959: 90.9 mhz; 13.5 kw. Ant 269 ft. TL: N37 21 16 W76 59 58. Stereo. Campus Ctr., College of Wiliam & Mary, Box 8793 23186. Phone: (757) 221-3287. Fax: (757) 221-2118. E-mail: wcwm@wm.edu. Web Site: www.wm.edu/so/wcwm. Licensee: College of William & Mary. Network: Moody. Format: Div, alternative new mus, progsv. News: 3 hrs wkly. Target aud: General. Spec prog: Jazz 13 hrs, class 11 hrs, reggae 6 hrs, blues 3 hrs wkly. ♦ Mariana Cruz, gen mgr & stn mgr.

WMBG(AM)— Jan 1, 1958: 740 khz; 500 w-D, 8 w-N. TL: N37 16 37 W76 45 07. 1005 Richmond Rd. 23185. Phone: (757) 229-7400. E-mail: info@wmbgradio.com. Licensee: Williamsburg's Radio Station Inc. Network: CNN Radio. Format: Adult standards. News staff: one; News: one hr wkly. Target aud: 45 plus; wealthy & mature in Williamsburg. Spec prog: Gospel 5 hrs wkly. ♦ Bob Sheeran, opns dir; Greg Granger, pres, gen mgr, stn mgr & opns mgr.

Winchester

WINC(AM)— June 15, 1941: 1400 khz; 1 kw-U. TL: N39 11 12 W78 09 06. Box 3300 22604. Secondary address: 520 N. Pleasant Valley Rd. 22601. Phone: (540) 667-2224. Fax: (540) 722-3295. Web Site: www.winc.fm. Licensee: Mid-Atlantic Network Inc. (group owner) Network: Network: Westwood One, CBS. Cole, Raywid & Braverman. Format: News/talk, sports. News staff: 3; News: 128 hrs wkly. Target aud: 25 plus; mid-to-upscale active adults. ♦ John Lewis, pres; Chris Lewis, gen mgr & gen sls mgr; Jeff Adams, opns mgr & progmg dir; Steve Edwards, news dir; Archie McKay, chief of engrg.

WINC-FM— October 1946: 92.5 mhz; 22 kw. 1,424 ft. TL: N38 57 21 W78 01 28. Stereo. Web Site: www.winc.fm. Network: Westwood One. Format: Hot adult contemp. News staff: 4; News: 6 hrs wkly. Target aud: 18-49; active, upscale listeners. ♦ Pam Christian, mktg dir.

WTFX(AM)— Jan 27, 1961: 610 khz; 500 w-U, DA-2. TL: N39 11 53 W78 13 13. 510 Pegasus Ct. 22602. Phone: (540) 662-5101. Fax: (540) 662-8610. Web Site: sportstalk610.com. Licensee: Capstar TX L.P. Group owner: Clear Channel Communications Inc. (acq 8-30-00; grpsl). Network: Network: ABC, USA. Format: Christian. News staff: one; News: 20 hrs wkly. Target aud: General; educated, affluent. Spec prog: Sports. ♦ Jim Shea, pres; Chuck Peterson, gen mgr; David Miller, opns mgr & progmg dir; Marcellla T. Vance, sls dir; Justin Maglione, prom dir; Harve Allen, progmg VP; Ben Gates, pub affrs dir; Mark Kesner, chief of engrg.

WUSQ-FM—Co-owned with WTFX(AM). Dec 10, 1965: 102.5 mhz; 31 kw. 630 ft. TL: N39 10 38 W78 15 53. Stereo. Web Site: www.wusq.com. Format: Modern country. News: one hr wkly. Target aud: 25-54; males.

***WTRM(FM)**— July 1986: 91.3 mhz; 6.1 kw. Ant 1,348 ft. TL: N39 10 59 W78 23 23. Stereo. Box 3438 22604. Phone: (540) 869-4997. Fax: (540) 869-7173. E-mail: wtrm@wtrm.org. Web Site: www.wtrm.org. Licensee: Timber Ridge Ministries Inc. Network: USA. Lauren A. Colby. Format: Southern gospel. Target aud: General. ♦ Richard Choy, CEO, VP, gen mgr, stn mgr & chief of engrg; Leona Choy, pres; Tim Bates, mus dir.

Windsor

WJCD(FM)— May 1990: 107.7 mhz; 3 kw. 328 ft. TL: N36 48 58 W76 41 35. (CP: 2.4 kw, ant 522 ft.). Stereo. 1003 Norfolk Sq., Norfolk 23502. Phone: (757) 466-0009. Fax: (757) 466-9523. E-mail: contact@litefmnorfolk.com. Web Site: wjcd.com. Licensee: Clear

Stations in the U.S. — Washington

Developers & Brokers of Radio Properties
contact American Media Services at our suite: Philadelphia Marriott Downtown
215-625-2900
843-972-2200
americanmediaservices.com
Charleston, SC
Dallas, TX • Chicago, Il • Austin, TX
American Media Services, LLC

Channel Broadcasting Licenses Inc. Group owner: Clear Channel Communications Inc. (acq 9-10-96; grpsl). Format: Smooth jazz. Target aud: 25-34; women. Spec prog: Talk 5 hrs wkly. ◆ Janet Armstead, gen mgr; Greg Gabriel, chief of engrg.

Wise

*WISE-FM— Aug 1, 1999: 90.5 mhz; 220 w. 669 ft. TL: N36 57 39 W82 30 56. Stereo. Office of College Relations, One College Ave. 24293. Phone: (540) 328-0300. Fax: (540) 328-0255. E-mail: wisefm@virginia.edu. Web Site: www.wisefm.org. Licensee: Clinch Valley College of the University of Virginia. Network: Network: NPR, PRI. Format: Class, educ, news. News: 45 hrs wkly. Target aud: General. Spec prog: Jazz 9 hrs, Celtic 2 hrs wkly. ◆ Jay Lemons (chancellor), CEO; Scott Pippin, stn mgr, dev dir, mktg dir, progmg dir & pub affrs dir; Don Mussell, engrg mgr.

WNVA-FM—See Norton

Woodbridge

WJZW(FM)—Licensed to Woodbridge. See Washington DC

Woodstock

WAMM(AM)— Oct 9, 1981: 1230 khz; 1 kw-U. TL: N38 51 11 W78 31 30. Box 542 22664. Secondary address: 118 N. Main St. 22664. Phone: (540) 459-5700. Fax: (540) 459-7241. E-mail: retro@shentel.net. Web Site: www.radioshenandoah.com. Licensee: Hometown Broadcasting LLC (acq 9-13-02; $140,000). Format: Adult standards. News staff: one; News: 9 hrs wkly. Target aud: 45+. ◆ Margaret Boston, pres; Bernard Boston, gen mgr; Alan Arehart, stn mgr; Craig Orndorff, progmg dir; Michael Reed, sls dir & chief of engrg.

WAZR(FM)— Oct 18, 1985: 93.7 mhz; 8.5 kw. Ant 420 ft. TL: N38 37 04 W78 42 39. Stereo. 207 University Blvd., Harrisonburg 22801. Phone: (540) 434-1777. Fax: (540) 432-9968. Web Site: www.937kissfm.com. Licensee: Clear Channel Broadcasting Licenses Inc. Group owner: Clear Channel Communications Inc. (acq 6-3-02; $1.35 million. including five-year noncompete agreement). Format: CHR. ◆ Steve Davis, gen mgr.

Wytheville

WYVE(AM)— Sept 21, 1949: 1280 khz; 2.5 kw-D, 164 w-N. TL: N36 57 54 W81 04 55. Stereo. Box 1247, 110 West Spiller St., Suite. 1 24382. Phone: (276) 228-3185. Phone: (276) 228-6308. Fax: (276) 228-9261. E-mail: trmedia@msn.com. Web Site: www.wyve. Licensee: Three Rivers Media Corp. (acq 10-1-98; $250,000). Format: C&W, loc news, sports, info. News staff: one; News: 10 hrs wkly. Target aud: 25 plus; general. Spec prog: Gospel 4 hrs wkly. ◆ Gary W. Hagerich, CEO, pres & stn mgr; Danny Gordon, opns dir; Sam Parks, chief of engrg.

Yorktown

WXEZ(FM)— July 4, 1975: 94.1 mhz; 50 kw. 500 ft. TL: N37 29 37 W76 26 30. (CP: 40 kw, ant 531 ft.). Stereo. 5589 Greenwich Rd., Suite 200, Virginia Beach 23462. Phone: (757) 671-1000. Fax: (757) 518-9364. Web Site: www.wxez941.com. Licensee: MHR License LLC. Group owner: Barnstable Broadcasting Inc. (acq 3-18-2005; grpsl). Format: Gospel. News staff: 8. Target aud: 35-64. ◆ Wes Eure, gen sls mgr; Dale Murray, progmg dir.

*WYCS(FM)— February 1966: 91.5 mhz; 1.3 kw horiz, 20 kw vert. Ant 371 ft. TL: N37 12 17 W76 30 07. Stereo. Box 1924, Tulsa, OK 74101. Phone: (918) 455-5693. Phone: (757) 886-7490. E-mail: mail@oasisnetwork.org. Web Site: www.oasisnetwork.org. Licensee: Creative Educational Media Corp. Inc. (acq 9-30-97; $449,000). Fletcher, Heald & Hildreth. Format: Christian/southern gospel. Target aud: 25-40; educated, employed, sentimental. ◆ David Ingles, pres & gen mgr.

Washington

Aberdeen

KBKW(AM)— Aug 1, 1949: 1450 khz; 1 kw-U. TL: N46 56 59 W123 49 13. Box 1198 98520. Secondary address: 1520 Simpson Ave. 98520. Phone: (360) 533-3000. Fax: (360) 532-1456. E-mail: bossbill@jodesha.com. Web Site: www.jodesha.com. Licensee: Jodesha Broadcasting Inc. (group owner; acq 2-28-03; $750,000. with KSWW(FM) Montesano). Network: Network: ABC Information & Entertainment, AP Network News. Rep: Tacher. Format: news/talk, Spanish. Target aud: 25-54. ◆ Wm J. Wolfenbarger, pres; Bill Wolfenbarger, gen mgr; Gabrielle Jordan, opns dir.

KDDS-FM—(Elma). 1981: 99.3 mhz; 41 kw. Ant 2,034 ft. TL: N47 19 12 W123 20 41. Stereo. Box 11232, Tacoma 98411. Fax: (360) 704-3146. Web Site: www.kayofm.com. Licensee: Bustos Media of Seattle License LLC. (acq 7-28-2005; $20 million). Format: Rgnl Mexican. ◆ Bill Bradley, gen mgr; Ed Bruno, sls VP; Heidi Persson, rgnl sls mgr; Craig Sullivan, progmg dir; Jeff Turnbow, news dir & pub affrs dir.

KDUX-FM—Listing follows KXRO(AM).

KWOK(AM)—See Hoquiam

KXRO(AM)— May 28, 1928: 1320 khz; 5 kw-D, 1 kw-N, DA-N. TL: N46 57 28 W123 48 26. 1308 Coolidge Rd. 98520. Phone: (360) 533-1320. Fax: (360) 532-0935. Web Site: www.kxro.com. Licensee: Morris Communications Corp. Group owner: Morris Communications Inc. (acq 10-15-98; grpsl). Network: CBS. Rep: McGavren Guild. Covington & Burling. Format: News/talk. News staff: 2; News: 6 hrs wkly. Target aud: 35-64. ◆ Donna Rosi, gen mgr & gen sls mgr; Pat Anderson, opns dir & progmg dir; Liz Miller, news dir & pub affrs dir; Jay White, chief of engrg.

KDUX-FM—Co-owned with KXRO(AM). Oct 4, 1964: 104.7 mhz; 48 kw. 360 ft. TL: N46 56 00 W123 43 49. Stereo. Web Site: www.kdux.com. Rep: Interep, McGavren Guild. Format: Classic rock. News staff: one. Target aud: 25-54. ◆ Pat Anderson, opns mgr & progmg dir.

KXXK(FM)—See Olympia

Airway Heights

KXLX(AM)— October 1986: 700 khz; 10 kw-D, 600 w-N, DA-N. TL: N47 36 31 W117 22 25. 500 W. Boone Ave., Spokane 99201. Phone: (509) 324-4000. Fax: (509) 324-8992. Licensee: QueenB Radio Inc. (acq 9-1-2005; $236,000). Network: ESPN Radio. Format: Sports. ◆ Stephen Herling, exec VP; Chris Garras, VP & gen mgr; Teddi Gibbon, stn mgr; Roger Nelson, sls dir; Bud Nameck, progmg dir.

Anacortes

KLKI(AM)— Dec 18, 1957: 1340 khz; 1 kw-U. TL: N48 29 44 W122 36 15. Box 96, 25th & Commercial Ave. 98221. Phone: (360) 293-3141. Phone: (360) 336-3500. Fax: (360) 293-9463. E-mail: klki@klki.com. Web Site: www.klki.com. Licensee: Berry Entertainment Inc. (acq 6-11-98). Network: Network: Network: Westwood One, CBS, ABC. Format: Sports, news/talk, adult contemp, big band. News staff: 3; News: 30 hrs wkly. Target aud: 25-60. Spec prog: Sp hrs, relg one hr wkly. ◆ Lynn Mc Mullen, opns VP & prom dir; Dedrick Allen, opns mgr & news dir; William T. Berry, CEO, chmn, gen mgr & gen sls mgr; Glen Harris, progmg dir.

Asotin

KCLK(AM)—Licensed to Asotin. See Clarkston

KCLK-FM—See Clarkston

Auburn

*KGRG(FM)— December 1974: 89.9 mhz; 250 w. 367 ft. TL: N47 15 23 W122 13 07. Stereo. 12401 S.E. 320th St. 98092-3699. Phone: (253) 833-9111. Fax: (253) 288-3439. E-mail: tkrause@greenriver.edu. Web Site: www.kgrg.com. Licensee: Green River Community College. Format: Modern rock. News: 2 hrs wkly. Target aud: 16-34. Spec prog: Loc mus 3 hrs, rap 3 hrs, metal 2 hrs, reggae/ska 4 hrs, industrial 2 hrs, electronic 2 hrs wkly. ◆ Tom Evans Krause, gen mgr; Mary Lue, sls dir & gen sls mgr; Nadine Bedford, prom dir; Jennifer Biesold, progmg dir; Derne Hoffman, mus dir; Aaron Richards, news dir; Jon Kasprick, chief of engrg.

Auburn-Federal Way

KWMG(AM)— Aug 6, 1958: 1210 khz; 27 kw-D, 10 kw-N. TL: N47 18 20 W122 14 51. Stereo. 1820 Eastlake Ave. E., Seattle 98102. Phone: (206) 343-9700. Fax: (206) 726-6888. Licensee: Bustos Media of Washington License LLC. Group owner: Entercom Communications Corp. (acq 1-21-2005; $6 million). Rep: D & R Radio. Format: Talk. ◆ David Pridemore, VP & gen mgr; Ethan Kelly, natl sls mgr; Cathy Cangiano, mktg dir & prom dir; Ken Berry, progmg dir; Ursula Reutin, news dir & pub affrs dir; Tom Pierson, chief of engrg.

Bellevue

*KASB(FM)— Mar 22, 1971: 89.3 mhz; 10 w. 289 ft. TL: N47 36 17 W122 11 47. 10416 E. Wolverine Way 98004-6698. Phone: (425) 456-7119. Fax: (425) 456-7110. E-mail: kasb89@hotmail.com. Web Site: www.bsd405.org. Licensee: Bellevue School District No. 405. Format: Alternative, news. Spec prog: News magazine 3 hrs, sports 6 hrs wkly. ◆ Wes Zujko, gen mgr.

*KBCS(FM)— Feb 3, 1973: 91.3 mhz; 7.9 kw. 216 ft. TL: N47 35 07 W122 08 39. Stereo. 3000 Landerholm Cir. S.E. 98007. Phone: (425) 564-2427. Fax: (425) 564-5697. E-mail: kbcs@ctc.edu. Web Site: kbcs.fm. Licensee: Bellevue Community College. Format: Jazz, folk, world mus. News: 4 hrs wkly. Target aud: General. ◆ Steve Ramsey, gen mgr; Kristen Walsh, progmg dir; Bruce Wirth, mus dir & pub affrs dir; Sam Roffe, chief of engrg.

KLSY-FM— November 1964: 92.5 mhz; 58 kw. 2,342 ft. TL: N47 30 14 W121 58 29. Stereo. 3650 131st Ave. S.E., Suite 550 98006. Phone: (425) 653-9462. Fax: (425) 653-9464. Web Site: www.klsyradio.com. Licensee: Bellevue Radio Inc. Group owner: Sandusky Radio Rep: Christal. Format: Adult contemp. News: one hr wkly. Target aud: 25-49; working women & families. ◆ Norman Rau, pres; Marc S. Kaye, VP & gen mgr; Susan Hoffman, sls dir; Julie Judge, natl sls mgr; Tarah Smigun, rgnl sls mgr & prom mgr; Bill West, progmg dir; Darla Thomas, mus dir; Jim Kampmann, news dir; Kate Daniels, pub affrs dir; George Bisso, chief of engrg.

KXPA(AM)— March 1958: 1540 mhz; 5 kw-U, DA-N. TL: N47 35 29 W122 10 56. 114 Lakeside Ave., Seattle 98122-6542. Phone: (206) 292-7800. Fax: (206) 292-2140. Licensee: Multicultural Radio Broadcasting Licensee LLC. Group owner: Multicultural Radio Broadcasting Inc. (acq 2-13-98; grpsl). Format: Sp, ethnic, div. Spec prog: Ethiopian 2 hrs, German 1 1/2 hrs, Vietnamese 5 1/2 hrs, Hawaiian 1 1/2 hrs wkly. ◆ Arthur Liu, pres; Lisa Shepherd, gen mgr; Dennis Hartley, opns mgr, progmg dir & pub affrs dir; Lisa A. Shepherd, gen sls mgr.

Bellingham

KAFE(FM)—Listing follows KPUG(AM).

KARI(AM)—See Blaine

KBAI(AM)— Apr 4, 1958: 930 khz; 1 kw-D, 500 w-N, DA-N. TL: N48 47 52 W122 28 01. (CP: COL: Bellingham). 2219 Yew Street Rd. 98229. Phone: (360) 734-9790. Fax: (360) 733-4551. Licensee: Saga Broadcasting LLC. Group owner: Saga Communications Inc. (acq 3-8-99; $1 million). Rep: Tacher. Garvey, Schubert & Barer. Format: Adult contemp. News staff: one; News: 5 hrs wkly. Target aud: 25-35. ◆ Ed Christian, pres; Rick Staeb, gen mgr.

Washington

KGMI(AM)— 1927: 790 khz; 5 kw-D, 1 kw-N, DA-N. TL: N48 41 09 W122 26 43. 2219 Yew Street Rd. 98229. Phone: (360) 734-9790. Web Site: www.kgmi.com. Licensee: Saga Broadcasting LLC. Group owner: Saga Communications Inc. (acq 9-24-98; $8 million. with co-located FM). Network: ABC Information & Entertainment. Rep: McGavren Guild. Format: News/talk. Target aud: 35-64. ◆ Ed Christian, pres; Rick Staeb, gen mgr & natl sls mgr; Krista Kay, prom dir & news dir; Brett Bonner, progmg dir; Will Vos, chief of engrg.

KISM(FM)—Co-owned with KGMI(AM). March 1960: 92.9 mhz; 50 kw. 2,440 ft. TL: N48 40 48 W122 50 24. Stereo. Web Site: www.kism.com. Format: Classic rock. Target aud: 25-44. ◆ Carol Dooley, progmg dir & mus dir.

KPUG(AM)— Feb 29, 1948: 1170 khz; 10 kw-D, 5 kw-N, DA-N. TL: N40 46 34 W122 26 21. 2219 Yew Street Rd. 98226-8855. Phone: (360) 734-9790. Fax: (360) 734-5233. Web Site: www.1170kpug.com. Licensee: Saga Broadcasting LLC. Group owner: Saga Communications Inc. (acq 10-30-98; $5,825,000. with co-located FM). Rep: McGavren Guild. Format: Sports/talk. News staff: 3; News: 24 hrs wkly. Target aud: 25-54. ◆ Ed Chrtistian, pres & opns dir; Rick Staeb, gen mgr; Doug Lange, progmg dir; Will Vos, engrg dir & chief of engrg.

KAFE(FM)—Co-owned with KPUG(AM). July 2, 1965: 104.3 mhz; 60 kw. 2,310 ft. TL: N48 40 48 W122 50 24. Stereo. Web Site: www.kafe.com. Format: Adult contemp. ◆ Scotty Kvipers, prom dir; Don Hurley, progmg dir & chief of engrg.

*KUGS(FM)— Jan 29, 1974: 89.3 mhz; 100 w. Ant 384 ft. TL: N48 44 11 W122 28 47. (CP: 700 w, ant 482 ft). Licensee: Western Wash. Univ., 700 Viking Union Bldg. 98225. Phone: (360) 650-4771. Phone: (360) 650-5847. Fax: (360) 650-6507. Web Site: www.kugs.org. Licensee: Western Washington University. Format: Progsv, news/talk. News: 17 hrs wkly. Target aud: 18-34; college students & adults. Spec prog: Black 10 hrs, Hawaiian 2 hrs wkly. ◆ Jamie Hoover, gen mgr; Aaron Chamberlain, chief of engrg.

*KZAZ(FM)— Sept 1, 1991: 91.7 mhz; 120 w. 334 ft. TL: N48 48 04 W122 27 40. Stereo. 1609 Broadway, Suite E 98225. Phone: (360) 738-9170. Fax: (360) 738-4605. E-mail: nwpr@wsu.edu. Web Site: www.nwpr.org. Licensee: Washington State University. (acq 7-29-97). Network: Network: NPR, PRI. Dow, Lohnes & Albertson. Format: Class, jazz, NPR news. News: 40 hrs wkly. Target aud: 25-54; general. Spec prog: Folk 8 hrs, world music 7 hrs wkly. ◆ Karen Olstad, gen mgr; Roger Johnson, stn mgr, sls dir & rgnl sls mgr; Scott Weatherly, opns mgr; Sarah McDaniel, dev mgr; Mary Hawkins, progmg dir; Robin Rilette, mus dir; Ralph Hogan, chief of engrg.

Benton City

KZTB(FM)— Aug 1, 1974: 96.7 mhz; 1.4 kw. Ant 692 ft. TL: N46 15 33 W119 21 55. Stereo. 2730 West Lewis #B, Pasco 99301. Phone: (509) 543-3334. Fax: (509) 543-3337. Web Site: www.radiozorro.com. Licensee: Bustos Media of Eastern Washington License LLC. (acq 11-18-2004; grpsl). Format: Sp. News staff: one; News: 22 hrs wkly. Target aud: 25 plus. ◆ Bob Berry, gen mgr.

Blaine

KAFE(FM)—See Bellingham

KARI(AM)— Feb 12, 1960: 550 khz; 5 kw-D, 2.5 kw-N, DA-2. TL: N48 57 15 W122 44 36. 4840 Lincoln Rd. 98230. Phone: (360) 371-5500. Phone: (604) 536-7733. Fax: (360) 371-7617. E-mail: kari@kari55.com. Web Site: www.kari55.com. Licensee: Way Broadcasting Licensee LLC (acq 7-20-00; $3 million. with KVRI(AM) Blaine). Format: Relg, news/talk. Target aud: 35 plus. Spec prog: Ger 2 hrs, Ukrainian one hr, Arabic one hr wkly. ◆ Arthur Liu, pres; Yvonne Liu, VP; Gary Nawman, gen mgr, opns mgr, gen sls mgr & progmg dir; Michael Gilbert, chief of engrg.

KVRI(AM)— Jan 1, 2001: 1600 khz; 50 kw-D, 10 kw-N. TL: N48 57 15 W122 44 36. 4840 Lincoln Rd. 98230. Phone: (360) 371-5500. Fax: (360) 371-7617. E-mail: kuri@kari55.com. Web Site: www.kari55.com. Licensee: Way Broadcasting Licensee LLC (acq 5-23-00; with KARI(AM) Blaine). Format: Punjabi. ◆ Arthur Liu, pres; Yvonne Liu, VP; Gary Nawman, gen mgr, opns mgr & progmg dir; Michael Gilbert, chief of engrg.

Bremerton

KBRO(AM)— May 1947: 1490 khz; 1 kw-U. TL: N47 33 52 W122 39 26. Box 4024, Seattle 98104. Phone: (206) 583-0811. Fax: (206) 467-9425. E-mail: kbro@worldnet.att.net. Licensee: Seattle Streaming Radio LLC. (acq 7-22-2005; $900,000 with KNTB(AM) Lakewood). Format: Hits of the 80s. News staff: one; News: 20 hrs wkly. Target aud: 25-54; Kitsap county residents. Spec prog: Samoan 4 hrs, Filipino 4 hrs wkly. ◆ Chris Hanley, gen mgr.

KRWM(FM)— Aug 22, 1964: 106.9 mhz; 100 kw. 820 ft. TL: N47 36 57 W122 18 26. (CP: 55 kw, ant 1,243 ft.). Stereo. 3650 131 Ave. S.E., Suite 550, Bellevue 98006. Phone: (425) 373-5545. Fax: (425) 653-1188. Web Site: www.warm1069.com. Licensee: Seascape Radio Inc. Group owner: Sandusky Radio (acq 9-12-96; $29.25 million). Rep: CBS Radio. Reed, Smith, Shaw & McClay. Format: Soft adult contemp. Target aud: 35-54; educated, upscale professionals, family oriented, white/blue collar. ◆ Marc Kaye, gen mgr; Erik Kreman, gen sls mgr & rgnl sls mgr; Heather Gardner, prom dir; Gary Nolan, progmg dir; George Bisso, chief of engrg.

Burien-Seattle

KGNW(AM)— Oct 10, 1970: 820 khz; 50 kw-D, 5 kw-N, DA-2. TL: N47 26 00 W121 28 02. 2815 2nd Ave., Suite 550, Seattle 98121. Phone: (206) 443-8200. Fax: (206) 777-1133. Web Site: www.kgnw.com. Licensee: Inspiration Media Inc. Group owner: Salem Communications Corp. (acq 1984). Rep: Salem. Format: Relg, Christian talk. News: 3 hrs wkly. Target aud: 35 plus. Spec prog: Talk, women, loc affrs, health. ◆ Stuart Epperson, chmn; Edward G. Atsinger III, pres; Eric H. Halvorson, VP; David Fitts, gen mgr; Chuck Olmstead, opns mgr; Bill Montgomery, gen sls mgr; Lyn-Felice Calvin, prom dir & prom mgr; Charles A. Olmstead, progmg dir; Monte Passmore, chief of engrg.

Camas

KNRK(FM)—Licensed to Camas. See Portland OR

Cashmere

KYSN(FM)—See Wenatchee

KZPH(FM)— 1993: 106.7 mhz; 6 kw. 513 ft. TL: N47 30 35 W120 31 24. Stereo. 231 N. Wenatchee Ave., Wenatchee 98801. Phone: (509) 665-6565. Fax: (509) 663-1150. Web Site: www.therock1067.com. Licensee: Fisher Radio Regional Group Inc. Group owner: Fisher Broadcasting Company (acq 11-15-97). Rep: McGavren Guild. Fisher, Wayland, Cooper, Leader & Zaragoza. Format: Classic rock. Target aud: 25-54. ◆ Jim Senst, gen mgr.

Castle Rock

KRQT(FM)— January 1994: 107.1 mhz; 740 w. 1,732 ft. TL: N46 20 35 W123 05 54. 1130 14th Ave., Longview 98632. Phone: (360) 425-1500. Fax: (360) 425-1500. Web Site: www.theclassicrockexperience.com. Licensee: Bicoastal Longview LLC. Group owner: Entercom Communications Corp. (acq 1-27-2005; grpsl). Format: Classic rock & roll. ◆ Gayle Kessinger, stn mgr.

Centralia

KCED(FM)—Licensed to Centralia. See Centralia-Chehalis

KNBQ(FM)—Licensed to Centralia. See Centralia-Chehalis

Centralia-Chehalis

*KCED(FM)—(Centralia). Feb 17, 1975: 91.3 mhz; 1 kw. -72 ft. TL: N46 42 54 W122 57 39. (CP: 1.2 kw, ant 131 ft.). Stereo. 600 W. Locust St., Centralia 98531-4099. Phone: (360) 736-9391 x343. Fax: (360) 330-7509. Fax: www.centralia.ctc.edu. Licensee: Board of Trustees, Centralia College. Format: Variety/diversified, Sp. Spec prog: Sports 3 hrs wkly. ◆ Wade Fisher, gen mgr, progmg dir & pub affrs dir; Bill Schoelkopf, chief of engrg.

KELA(AM)— Nov 1, 1937: 1470 khz; 5 kw-D, 1 kw-N. TL: N46 41 47 W122 57 23. 1635 S. Gold St., Centralia 98531. Phone: (360) 736-3321. Phone: (360) 748-3321. Fax: (360) 736-0150. E-mail: johndimeoe@clearchannel.com. Web site: www.kelaam.com. Licensee: Citicasters Licenses L.P. Group owner: Clear Channel Communications Inc. (acq 5-4-99; grpsl). Network: ABC Information & Entertainment. Rep: Clear Channel. Format: News/talk, sports. News staff: 2; News: 28 hrs wkly. Target aud: 35 plus. Spec prog: Big band 3 hrs, class 2 hrs wkly. ◆ John DiMeo Jr., gen mgr; Larry Miner, gen sls mgr; Steve Richert, progmg dir; Doug Adamson, news dir; Dan Smith, chief of engrg.

KNBQ(FM)—Co-owned with KELA(AM). Aug 24, 1965: 102.9 mhz; 70 kw. Ant 2,191 ft. TL: N46 58 31 W123 08 16. Stereo. Web Site: www.kmnt.com. Format: Country. News staff: 2; News: 7 hrs wkly. Target aud: 18 plus. ◆ Deborah Lemmons, progmg dir.

KITI(AM)—(Chehalis-Centralia). October 1954: 1420 khz; 5 kw-U, DA-2. TL: N46 42 08 W122 55 58. 1133 Kresky, Centralia 98531. Phone: (360) 736-1355. Fax: (360) 736-4761. E-mail: mshannon@live95.com. Licensee: Premier Broadcasters Inc. (acq 10-77). Network: ABC Information & Entertainment. Rep: Allied Radio Partners. Leventhal, Senter & Lerman. Format: Oldies. News staff: one; News: 15 hrs wkly. Target aud: 25-54. ◆ Rod Etherton, pres & gen mgr.

Chehalis

*KACS(FM)— Aug 18, 1993: 90.5 mhz; 3 kw. Ant 187 ft. TL: N46 43 52 W123 01 28. (CP: 6 kw). Stereo. 2401 N.E. Kresky, Suite B 98532. Phone: (360) 740-9436. Fax: (360) 740-9415. E-mail: manager@kacs.org. Web Site: www.kacs.org. Licensee: Chehalis Valley Educational Foundation. Donald E. Martin. Format: Relg. Target aud: 35-49. ◆ Kerry O'Connor, chmn; Camerson Beirle, gen mgr, stn mgr & progmg dir; Marilyn Remer, chief of engrg.

KITI(AM)—See Centralia-Chehalis

KMNT(FM)— 2005: 104.3 mhz; 2.35 kw. Ant 1,056 ft. TL: N46 33 18 W123 03 27. 1635 S. Gold St., Centralia 98531. Phone: (360) 330-0777. Fax: (360) 736-0150. Web Site: www.kmnt.com. Licensee: Citicasters Licenses L.P. Format: Country. ◆ John DiMeo Jr., gen mgr.

Chehalis-Centralia

KITI(AM)—Licensed to Chehalis-Centralia. See Centralia-Chehalis

Chelan

KOZI(AM)— Mar 1, 1957: 1230 khz; 1 kw-U. TL: N47 50 50 W120 00 29. Box 819 98816. Secondary address: 123 E. Johnson 98816. Phone: (509) 682-4033. Fax: (509) 682-4035. Web Site: www.kozi.com. Licensee: Icicle Broadcasting Co. Group owner: (acq 8-26-99; grpsl). Rep: Target Broadcast Sales. Haley, Bader & Potts. Format: Adult contemp, news/talk. News staff: 3; News: 32 hrs wkly. Target aud: General. Spec prog: Farm 3 hrs, Sp 5 hrs wkly. ◆ Harriet Bullitt, pres; Gary Mathews, gen mgr; Joe Fiala, stn mgr; Steve Byquist, opns mgr & progmg dir; Vicky Chandler, gen sls mgr; Michael Dickes, mus dir; Clint Strand, news dir.

KOZI-FM— Aug 26, 1981: 93.5 mhz; 590 w. 1,040 ft. TL: N47 51 07 W119 52 18. Stereo. Web Site: www.kozi.com. Format: Adult contemp news/talk.

Cheney

*KEWU-FM— Apr 3, 1964: 89.5 mhz; 10 kw. 1,407 ft. TL: N47 34 43 W117 17 50. Stereo. Electronic Media & Film, 104 RTV Bldg. 99004-2495. Phone: (509) 359-2440. Fax: (509) 359-4841. Licensee: Eastern Washington University Board of Trustees. Format: Jazz. ◆ Marvin Smith, gen mgr.

KEYF-FM— May 4, 1986: 101.1 mhz; 100 kw. 1,607 ft. TL: N47 35 35 W117 17 46. Stereo. 1601 E. 57th, Spokane 99223. Phone: (509) 448-1000. Phone: (509) 232-1011. Fax: (509) 448-7015. Web Site: www.oldies1011.com. Licensee: Citadel Broadcasting Co. Group owner: Citadel Broadcasting Corp. (acq 4-22-99; grpsl). Format: Music of the 70s & 80s. News staff: one; News: 15 hrs wkly. Target aud: 25-54. ◆ Jim Votaw, gen mgr; Christa McDonald, gen sls mgr; Tim Cotter, opns mgr & progmg dir; Dave Ratener, chief of engrg.

Clarkston

KCLK-FM— 1974: 94.1 mhz; 100 kw. 1,233 ft. TL: N46 27 27 W117 06 03. Stereo. 403 C St., Lewiston, ID 83501. Phone: (509) 758-3361. Phone: (208) 743-6564. Fax: (509) 758-4986. E-mail: kclkfm@aol.com. Licensee: Pacific Empire Radio Corp. Group owner: Pacific Empire

Stations in the U.S. — Washington

Developers & Brokers of Radio Properties
contact American Media Services at our suite:
Philadelphia Marriott Downtown
215-625-2900
843-972-2200
americanmediaservices.com
Charleston, SC
Dallas, TX • Chicago, Il • Austin, TX
American Media Services, LLC

Communications Corp. (acq 9-26-2000; grpsl). Network: Westwood One. Format: Mainstream country. News staff: one. Target aud: 25 plus. ♦Glenn Heffley, progmg dir; Mark Bolland, pres, pres, gen mgr, sls dir & chief of engrg.

KCLK(AM)— Mar 2, 1971: 1430 khz; 5 kw-D, 1 kw-N, DA-2. TL: N46 18 59 W117 02 24. 1859 Fifth Ave., Asotin 99403. Phone: (509) 758-3362. E-mail: kclkam@aol.com. Format: Sports, talk. News staff: one. Target aud: 15 plus; sports interested. ♦Patti Vassar, chief of engrg.

KNWV(FM)— July 11, 1995: 90.5 mhz; 250 w. 1,063 ft. TL: N46 27 26 W117 06 00. Box 642530, 382 Murrow Ctr., Pullman 99164-2530. Phone: (509) 335-6500. Fax: (509) 335-3772. E-mail: nwpr@wsu.edu. Web Site: www.nwpr.org. Licensee: Washington State University. Dow, Lohnes & Albertson. Format: Class, news. News staff: 37 hrs wkly. ♦Karen Olstad, COO & gen mgr; Dennis Haarsager, gen mgr; Roger Johnson, stn mgr & sls dir; Scott Weatherly, opns mgr; Sarah McDaniel, dev dir; Mary Hawkins, progmg dir; Robin Rilette, mus dir; Ralph Hogan, engrg dir.

KQQQ(AM)—See Pullman

KRLC(AM)—See Lewiston, ID

KVAB(FM)— July 15, 1997: 102.9 mhz; 440 w. 1,171 ft. TL: N46 27 27 W117 06 03. 403 C St., Lewiston, ID 83501. Secondary address: 1859 5th Ave. 99403. Phone: (509) 758-3362. Fax: (509) 758-4986. E-mail: kvabfm@aol.com. Web Site: kvabfm.com. Licensee: Pacific Empire Radio Corp. Group owner: Pacific Empire Communications Corp. (acq 9-26-2000; grpsl). Network: Westwood One. Rep: Tacher. Format: Classic rock. Target aud: 25-55. ♦Mark Bolland, CEO & pres; Jay Mlazgor, gen mgr; Scott Matthews, opns mgr & gen sls mgr; Mark Bone, progmg dir; Patti Vassar, chief of engrg.

Cle Elum

KXAA(FM)— Nov., 2002: 93.7 mhz; 6 kw. Ant 95 ft. TL: N47 09 06 W120 47 23. Stereo. 717 N.E. 12th St., East Wenatchee 98802. Secondary address: 115 N Harris Ave. 98922. Phone: (509) 674-0937. Fax: (509) 674-4042. Licensee: Wheeler Broadcasting Inc. (group owner; acq 5-28-2004; exercise of option). Network: Jones Radio Networks. Format: Classic Hits. ♦Mike Andler, gen mgr; Kelly Hart, stn mgr; Jeri Trantham, opns dir; Mark Wheeler, sls dir; Kelly Alford, engrg dir.

Colfax

KCLX(AM)—Listing follows KRAO-FM.

KMAX(AM)— 1998: 840 khz; 10 kw-D, 280 w-N. TL: N46 54 50 W117 19 28. Box 710 99111. Secondary address: 840 W. Fairview Rd. 99111. Phone: (509) 397-3441. Fax: (509) 397-4752. E-mail: kzzlkrow@stjohncable.com. Web Site: www.palousecountry.com. Licensee: Inland Northwest Broadcasting LLC. (group owner). (acq 6-28-2005; grpsl). Network: Westwood One. Format: Talk radio. News staff: 2; News: 15 hrs wkly. Target aud: 25; established professional aged people - young marrieds couples. ♦Robert G. Hauser, gen mgr, sls dir & prom dir; Glen Vaagen, progmg dir & news dir.

KRAO-FM— Oct 10, 1994: 102.5 mhz; 2.2 kw. 1,073 ft. TL: N46 51 44 W117 10 20. Stereo. Box 710, 840 Fairview Rd. W. 99111. Phone: (509) 397-6371. Fax: (509) 397-4752. E-mail: kzzlkrow@stjohncable.com. Web Site: www.palousecountry.com. Licensee: Inland Northwest Broadcasting LLC. (group owner; (acq 6-28-2005; grpsl). Format: Classic rock. Target aud: 18-45; college, young budding professionals to professional business people. ♦Robert G. Hauser, gen mgr & gen sls mgr; Robert Hauser, opns mgr; Randy Byers, progmg dir; Glenn Vaagen, news dir; Steve Franco, chief of engrg.

KCLX(AM)—Co-owned with KRAO-FM. 1950: 1450 khz; 1 kw-U. TL: N46 52 17 W117 22 37. Phone: (509) 397-3441. Web Site: www.palousecountry.com. Rep: Farmakis. Format: Classic country.

Target aud: 25 plus; agricultural-urban. Spec prog: Farm 5 hrs, sports 7 hrs wkly. ♦Robert Hauser, stn mgr & opns mgr.

College Place

KGTS(FM)— Oct 5, 1963: 91.3 mhz; 4.6 kw. 1,297 ft. TL: N45 59 20 W118 10 29. Stereo. 204 S. College Ave. 99324. Phone: (509) 527-2991. Fax: (509) 527-2611. Web Site: www.plr.org. Licensee: Walla Walla College. Network: USA. Format: Christian contemp. Target aud: 35-54. ♦Jon Dybdahl, pres; Kevin Krueger, gen mgr; Don Godman, opns dir.

Colville

KCRK-FM—Listing follows KCVL(AM).

KCVL(AM)— Nov 15, 1955: 1240 khz; 1 kw-U. TL: N48 31 15 W117 54 28. Box 111, 187 Mantz & Ricky Rd. 99114. Phone: (509) 684-5031. Fax: (509) 684-5034. Web Site: www.kcvl.com. Licensee: North Country Broadcasting. (acq 1996). Network: ABC Information & Entertainment. Rep: Tacher. Format: Country. ♦Eric Carpenter, pres, pres & gen mgr; Mike Eakins, sls dir.

KCRK-FM— Co-owned with KCVL(AM). Oct 13, 1981: 92.1 mhz; 3 kw. Ant -790 ft. TL: N48 31 15 W117 54 28. Stereo. Phone: (509) 684-5032. Network: Westwood One. Format: Adult contemp.

Davenport

KKRS(FM)— 1998: 97.3 mhz; 5.1 kw. Ant 722 ft. TL: N47 35 14 W117 53 26. 12720 W. Sunset Hwy., Suite C, Airway Heights 99001. Phone: (509) 244-5577. Fax: (509) 244-2232. E-mail: kkrs@csnradio.com. Licensee: CSN International. (group owner; acq 1999; $111,425). Format: Christian talk, educ, music. ♦Barney Dasovich, gen mgr & progmg dir.

Dayton

KZHR(FM)— December 1992: 92.5 mhz; 54 kw. Ant 1,243 ft. TL: N46 19 14 W117 58 46. Box 2623, Tri Cities 99302. Secondary address: 2823 W. Lewis St., Pasco 99301. Phone: (509) 546-0313. Fax: (509) 546-2678. Licensee: CCR-Tri Cities IV LLC. Group owner: Cherry Creek Radio LLC (acq 12-19-2003; grpsl). Format: Mexican rgnl. ♦Dennis W. Goodman, COO, exec VP & gen mgr; Willy Contreras, progmg dir.

Deer Park

KAZZ(FM)— September 1983: . Stn currently dark 107.1 mhz; 25 kw. Ant 328 ft. TL: N48 01 45 W117 35 57. Stereo. Box 1640 99006. Secondary address: 518 S. Fir 99006. Phone: (509) 276-8816. Phone: (509) 276-8817. Fax: (509) 276-2790. E-mail: kazzfm@sisna.com. Licensee: First Broadcasting Investment Partners LLC (group owner; acq 10-20-03; $1 million). Format: Adult standards. ♦Jason Johnson, gen mgr.

Dishman

KEYF(AM)— Oct 3, 1984: 1050 khz; 5 kw-D, 260 w-N. TL: N47 36 27 W117 21 40. 1601 E. 57th Ave, Spokane 99223. Phone: (509) 448-1000. Fax: (509) 448-7015. E-mail: barrywatkins@sitcomm.com. Licensee: Citadel Broadcasting Co. Group owner: Citadel Broadcasting Corp. (acq 4-22-99; grpsl). Network: ABC Information & Entertainment. Format: Adult standards. News staff: one; News: 15 hrs wkly. Target aud: 25-54. ♦Jim Botaw, gen mgr; Christa McDonald, sls dir; Joe Chabala, gen mgr & prom dir; Barry Watkins, progmg dir; Dave Ratener, chief of engrg.

KSPO(FM)— 1996: 106.5 mhz; 6 kw. 328 ft. TL: N47 36 10 W117 16 13. (CP: 2.55 kw, ant 508 ft.). Box 31000, Spokane 99223. Phone: (509) 443-1000. Fax: (509) 448-3811. E-mail: acn@acn-network.com. Web Site: www.acn-network.com. Licensee: Thomas W. Read dba Classical Broadcasting. (acq 1996; $100,000). Network: USA. Pepper

& Corazzini. Format: Relg, talk. Target aud: 35 plus. ♦Melinda Read, sr VP; Thomas W. Read, pres & gen mgr.

East Wenatchee

KTRW-FM—Not on air, target date: unknown: 88.1 mhz; 600 w. Ant -131 ft. TL: N47 22 52 W120 17 16. Box 31000, Spokane 99223. Phone: (509) 443-1000. Fax: (509) 448-3811. Licensee: Douglas County Educational Radio Association. ♦Thomas W. Read, pres.

KYSN(FM)—Licensed to East Wenatchee. See Wenatchee

Eatonville

KFNK(FM)— 1995: 104.9 mhz; 17 kw. Ant 407 ft. TL: N46 50 24 W122 15 27. 351 Elliott Ave. W., 3rd Fl., Seattle 98119. Phone: (206) 494-2000. Fax: (206) 286-2376. E-mail: bobcase@clearchannel.com. Web Site: www.funkymonkey1049.fm. Licensee: Ackerley Media Group Inc. Group owner: Clear Channel Communications Inc. (acq 2-12-03; $4.5 million). Format: Alternative rock. ♦Michele Grosenick, gen mgr; Bob Case, opns mgr & progmg dir; Corrie Westmorland, prom mgr; Sean Shannon, gen sls mgr & adv mgr; Doug Irwin, chief of engrg.

Edmonds

KCIS(AM)—Listing follows KCMS(FM).

KCMS(FM)— Mar 11, 1960: 105.3 mhz; 54 kw. Ant 1,263 ft. TL: N47 32 40 W122 06 26. Stereo. 19303 Fremont Ave. N., Seattle 98133. Phone: (206) 546-7350. Fax: (206) 546-7372. E-mail: comments@spirit1053.com. Web Site: www.spirit1053.com. Licensee: Crista Ministries. Format: Adult contemp, Christian mus. News: one hr wkly. Target aud: 25-44. ♦Tim Beltz, exec VP; Tony Bollen, VP & gen mgr; Melene Thompson, sls dir; Scott Valentine, progmg dir.

KCIS(AM)— Co-owned with KCMS(FM). 1954: 630 khz; 5 kw-D, 2.5 kw-N, DA-N. TL: N47 46 06 W122 21 07. Box 330300, Seattle 98133-9700. Secondary address: 19303 Fremont Ave. N., Seattle 98133. E-mail: comments@kcisradio.com. Web Site: www.kcisradio.com. Group owner: Crista Broadcasting Network: Network: Network: USA, Moody, AP Radio. Format: Christian, inspirational. News staff: one; News: 40 hrs wkly. Target aud: 35-55. ♦Mark Holland, progmg dir.

Ellensburg

KCSH(FM)— 1998: 88.9 mhz; 380 w. 548 ft. TL: N47 10 02 W120 45 50. 111 W. 6th Ave., Studio B 98926. Phone: (509) 964-2061. Fax: (509) 964-2825. Web Site: www.lifetalk.net. Licensee: Lifetalk Broadcasting Association. Format: Relg, inspirational. ♦Kermit Netteburg, pres; Philip Follet, CEO & pres; Don Zacharias, gen mgr; Jeremy Woodruff, progmg dir; Jerry Mathis, chief of engrg.

KCWU(FM)— Apr 30, 1999: 88.1 mhz; 500 w. Ant -194 ft. TL: N47 00 21 W120 30 55. Stereo. Central Washington Univ., 400 E. University Way 98926-7594. Phone: (509) 963-2283, 2282. Fax: (509) 963-1688. E-mail: kcwu@cwu.edu. Web Site: www.881theburg.com. Licensee: Trustees of Central Washington University. Morrison & Foerster. Format: Modern rock, alternative, div. News: 5 hrs wkly. Target aud: 15-49; 18-34 core. ♦Chris Hull, gen mgr & dev dir.

KNWR(FM)— June 1992: 90.7 mhz; 5 kw. 2,552 ft. TL: N47 15 48 W120 23 31. Box 642530, 382 Murrow Ctr., Pullman 99164-2530. Phone: (509) 335-6500. Fax: (509) 335-3772. E-mail: nwpr@wsu.edu. Web Site: www.nwpr.org. Licensee: Washington State University. Network: Network: NPR, PRI. Format: Class, news. News staff: one; News: 37 hrs wkly. Target aud: General. Spec prog: Jazz, folk. ♦Karen Olstad, COO & gen mgr; Dennis Haarsager, gen mgr; Roger Johnson, stn mgr & sls dir; Scott Weatherly, opns mgr; Sarah McDaniel, dev dir; Mary Hawkins, progmg dir; Robin Rilette, mus dir; Ralph Hogan, engrg dir.

KQBE(FM)— Nov 24, 1983: 103.1 mhz; 2 kw. 1,273 ft. TL: N47 00 21 W120 30 55. Stereo. Box 1032 98926. Secondary address: 5th & Pine St. 98926. Phone: (509) 962-2823. Fax: (509) 962-5105. E-mail:

Washington

kqbe@elltel.net. Licensee: Peak Communications Inc. (acq 5-1-89; $265,000; 5-1-89). Format: Adult contemp. Target aud: 18-49. ♦ Jack Kelleher, pres, gen mgr & opns mgr; Keith Marshall, gen sls mgr; Keith Danson, progmg dir & news dir; Steve Douglas, chief of engrg.

KXLE(AM)— 1946: 1240 khz; 1 kw-U. TL: N47 00 00 W120 31 40. 1311 Vantage Hwy. 98926. Phone: (509) 925-1488. Fax: (509) 962-7882. E-mail: kxle@elltel.net. Licensee: KXLE Inc. (acq 6-82). Network: CBS. Rep: Tacher. Bosari & Paxson. Format: News/talk, sports. News staff: 4; News: 40 hrs wkly. Target aud: 25-54; adults. ♦ Sol M. Tacher, pres; Brad Tacher, VP & gen mgr; Jim Ridgway, sls dir; Patti Burke, prom mgr; Richard James, progmg dir & news dir; Kevin Whitaker, engrg dir.

KXLE-FM— 1972: 95.3 mhz; 51 kw. 423 ft. TL: N47 09 49 W120 47 34. Stereo. Rep: Tacher. Format: Country. News: 6 hrs wkly. Target aud: 18-59; male & female. ♦ Sol Tacher, CEO; Brad Tacher, gen mgr; Patti Burke, prom dir; Steve Scellick, progmg dir; Robert Lowery, news dir.

Elma

KDDS-FM—Licensed to Elma. See Aberdeen

Enumclaw

KENU(AM)— Mar 1, 1992: 1330 khz; 500 w-D, 26 w-N. TL: N47 12 53 W121 58 19. 12401 S.E. 320 St., Auburn 98092-3699. Phone: (360) 802-1330. Phone: (253) 288-3388. Fax: (253) 288-3460. E-mail: kenuradio@hotmail.com. Web Site: www.kenuradio.com. Licensee: Green River Foundation. (acq 9-17-96; $40,000). Format: Dance/techno. Target aud: 12-34. ♦ Tom Evans Krause, gen mgr.

Ephrata

KTAC(FM)—Listing follows KTBI(AM).

KTBI(AM)— Aug 17, 1950: 810 khz; 50 kw-D. TL: N47 21 22 W119 28 56. Box 31000, Spokane 99223. Phone: (509) 754-2000. Fax: (509) 448-3811. E-mail: ktbi@ktbi.com. Web Site: www.ktbi.com. Licensee: Tacoma Broadcasters Inc. Pepper & Corazzini. Format: Relg, talk. Target aud: 35 plus. Spec prog: Farm 15 hrs wkly. ♦ Melinda Read, VP; John Tillman, opns mgr; Thomas W. Read, pres, gen mgr & progmg dir; George Frese, engrg dir.

KTAC(FM)—Co-owned with KTBI(AM). 1998: 93.9 mhz; 18 kw. 384 ft. TL: N47 19 13 W119 34 22. Box 31000, Spokane 99223. E-mail: ktac@ktac.com. Web Site: www.ktac.com. Licensee: TRMR Inc.

KULE(AM)— 1952: 730 khz; 1 kw-D, 29 w-N. TL: N47 19 01 W119 33 46. Box 2888, Yakima 98907. Secondary address: 910 Basin S.W. 98823. Phone: (509) 457-1000. Fax: (509) 452-0541. E-mail: zorro@radiozorro.com. Web Site: www.radiozorro.com. Licensee: Bustos Media of Eastern Washington License LLC. (group owner; (acq 11-18-2004); grpsl). Network: Network: Westwood One, CBS. Rep: Tacher. Timothy K. Brady. Format: News/talk, sports. News staff: one; News: 20 hrs wkly. Target aud: 25-54. Spec prog: Farm 1 hr wkly. ♦ Amador S. Bustos, pres; Bob Berry, gen mgr; Keith Teske, opns mgr; Judith McInnis, prom dir; Martin Ortiz, progmg dir.

KULE-FM— Dec 25, 1982: 92.3 mhz; 26 kw. 460 ft. TL: N47 19 14 W119 34 21. Stereo. Fax: (509) 754-4110. E-mail: kule@kule.com. Web Site: www.radiozorro.com. Network: CBS. Format: Country. ♦ Bob Berry, gen mgr; Keith Teske, opns VP; Tom Vinup, news dir.

Everett

KRKO(AM)— Aug 1, 1920: 1380 khz; 5 kw-U, DA-N. TL: N47 55 32 W122 11 19. Stereo. 2707 Colby Ave. #1380 98201. Phone: (425) 304-1381. Fax: (425) 304-1382. E-mail: andrew.skotdal@krko.com. Web Site: www.krko.com. Licensee: S & R Broadcasting. (acq 1987). Network: Network: Westwood One, ESPN Radio. Cohn & Marks. Format: Talk, sports. News staff: one; News: 24 hrs wkly. Target aud: men 25-54; residents of Northern Puget Sound. ♦ Andrew P. Skotdal, pres, gen mgr, dev mgr & adv dir; Ed Ramirez, gen sls mgr; Tony Stevens, opns mgr, mktg dir, prom dir, progmg dir & news dir; George Bisso, chief of engrg.

*KSER(FM)— Feb 9, 1991: 90.7 mhz; 5.8 kw. 302 ft. TL: N48 01 28 W122 06 41. Stereo. 2623 Wetmore Ave 98201. Phone: (425) 303-9070. Fax: (425) 303-9075. E-mail: kser@aol.com. Web Site: www.kser.org. Licensee: KSER Foundation. (acq 1996). Network: PRI. Bechtel & Cole. Format: Div. News staff: one; News: 17 hrs wkly. Target aud: General. Spec prog: American Indian 2 hrs, folk 2 hrs, jazz 2 hrs, Reggae 2 hrs, soca 2 hrs, Blues 6 hrs wkly. ♦ Ed Bremer, gen mgr.

KWYZ(AM)— July 21, 1957: 1230 khz; 1 kw-U. TL: N47 58 06 W122 10 24. 807 S. 336 St., Federal Way 98003. Phone: (253) 815-1212. Fax: (253) 815-1913. Web Site: www.radiohankook.com. Licensee: Jean J. Suh dba Radio Hankook. (acq 1999; $480,000). Rep: Roslin. Format: Korean. ♦ Doris Haan, gen mgr; Kenneth Son, gen sls mgr & prom dir; Herman Han, adv dir; Larry Gruber, chief of engrg.

Ferndale

KRPI(AM)— May 1963: 1550 khz; 50 kw-D, 10 kw-N, DA-2. TL: N48 50 35 W122 36 05. Box 3213 98248. Secondary address: 5538 Imhoff Rd. 98248. Phone: (360) 384-5117. Fax: (360) 380-4202. E-mail: krpi@krpiradio.com. Web Site: www.krpiradio.net. Licensee: BBC Broadcasting Inc. (acq 4-19-02; $600,000). Format: East Indian. News: 13.75 hrs wkly. Target aud: 35+; East Indian adults. ♦ Suki Badh, gen mgr; Andy Struiksma, stn mgr.

Forks

KBDB-FM—Listing follows KBIS(AM).

KBIS(AM)— October 1967: 1490 khz; 1 kw-U. TL: N47 57 16 W124 23 20. Box 450 98331. Secondary address: 260 Cedar 9833331. Phone: (360) 374-6233. Fax: (360) 374-6852. E-mail: kllm@centurytel.net. Licensee: First Broadcasting Investment Partners LLC. (group owner; (acq 12-18-2003; $300,000. with co-located FM). Tacher. Format: Rock, CHR. News staff: 2; News: 2 hrs wkly. Target aud: 25-54; general. Spec prog: NFL, Sonics, college & high school football, Mariners 20 hrs, gospel 6.5 hrs wkly. ♦ Gary Lawrence, pres; Al Monroe, gen mgr, progmg dir & chief of engrg; Marcia Nearhoff, gen sls mgr.

KBDB-FM—Co-owned with KBIS(AM). 1985: 103.9 mhz; 3 kw. -75 ft. TL: N47 57 16 W124 23 20. Format: CHR.

Gig Harbor

*KGHP(FM)— Aug 30, 1988: 89.9 mhz; 1.5 kw. 190 ft. TL: N47 14 29 W122 46 14. Stereo. 14105 62nd Ave. N.W. 98329. Phone: (253) 857-3513. Phone: (253) 857-3589. Fax: (253) 853-5841. E-mail: kghp@wednet.edu. Web Site: www.kghp.wednet.edu. Licensee: Peninsula School District No. 401. Format: AAA, eclectic, community info. News: 10 hrs wkly. Target aud: General; diverse community audience. ♦ Leland Smith, gen mgr; Kate Hamilton, dev dir, progmg dir, asst music dir & pub affrs dir; Keith Stiles, chief of engrg.

Goldendale

KLCK(AM)— Sept 4, 1984: 1400 khz; 1 kw-U. TL: N45 49 14 W120 50 15. Box 305, 514 S. Columbus 98620. Phone: (509) 773-3300. Fax: (509) 773-3301. E-mail: klck@gorge.net. Web Site: www.klck1400.com. Licensee: Klickitat Valley Broadcasting Services Inc. (acq 12-18-01; $400,000. with KYYT(FM) Goldendale). Rep: Tacher. Format: Oldies. ♦ Danny V. Manciu, pres & gen mgr; Betsy Hadden, sls dir; Kevin Malcolm, progmg dir; Julian Notestine, news dir; Colin Malcolm, chief of engrg.

KYYT(FM)— Jan 6, 1992: 102.3 mhz; 1.8 kw. 574 ft. TL: N45 48 02 W120 47 35. Box 1023, The Dalles 97058. Secondary address: 620 E. 3rd St., The Dalles 97058. Phone: (541) 296-9102. Fax: (541) 298-7775. E-mail: kyyt@gorge.net. Web Site: www.y102country.com. Licensee: Haystack Broadcasting Inc. (acq 12-18-01; $400,000. with KLCK(AM) Goldendale). Format: Country. ♦ Danny V. Manciu, pres & gen mgr; Colin B. Malcolm, stn mgr & chief of engrg; Betsy Hadden, gen sls mgr; Kevin B. Malcolm, prom dir & progmg dir; Hannah Settje, news dir.

Grand Coulee

KEYG(AM)— 1979: 1490 khz; 1 kw-U. TL: N47 52 58 W118 58 20. Drawer K 99133. Phone: (509) 633-2020. Phone: (509) 633-1490. Fax: (509) 633-1014. E-mail: keygfm@bigdam.net. Web Site: www.keygfm.com. Licensee: Wheeler Broadcasting Inc. (group owner; acq 12-6-85). Format: Country. News staff: one; News: 4 hrs wkly. Target aud: 25 plus. Spec prog: Class 4 hrs, mus to remember 4 hrs, big band 4 hrs wkly. ♦ Verl D. Wheeler, CEO; Mark Wheeler, gen mgr, gen sls mgr & progmg dir; Mike Helgerson, chief of engrg.

KEYG-FM— Feb 10, 1984: 98.5 mhz; 100 kw horiz, 85 kw vert. 994 ft. TL: N47 49 18 W118 55 59. Stereo. Format: Classic hits.

Grandview

KARY-FM— Aug 21, 1989: 100.9 mhz; 6.9 kw. 1,269 ft. TL: N46 29 12 W120 00 12. Stereo. 1200 Chesterly Dr., Suite 160, Yakima 98902-7345. Phone: (509) 248-2900. Fax: (509) 452-9661. Web Site: cherryfm.com. Licensee: New Northwest Broadcasters LLC (group owner; acq 10-20-98; grpsl). Rep: Allied Radio Partners. Format: Oldies. Target aud: 25-54. Spec prog: Relg 8 hrs wkly. ♦ Pete Benedetti, CEO; Joe Benedetti, pres & gen mgr; Dewey Boynton, opns mgr & sls dir; Ron King, natl sls mgr & rgnl sls mgr; Charlie Brooks, prom dir; Lou Bartelli, progmg dir & news dir; David Wooten, chief of engrg.

Hoquiam

KWOK(AM)— Nov 16, 1961: 1490 khz; 1 kw-U. TL: N46 58 22 W123 51 10. Stereo. 1308 Coolidge Rd., Aberdeen 98520. Phone: (360) 533-1320. Fax: (360) 532-0935. Licensee: Morris Communications Corp. Group owner: Morris Communications Inc. (acq 2-18-00; $650,000 with KXXK(FM) Hoquiam-Aberdeen). Format: Sports/talk-ESPN. Target aud: 26-65. ♦ Donna Rosi, gen mgr & gen sls mgr; Pat Anderson, opns mgr & progmg dir; Liz Miller, news dir; Jay White, chief of engrg.

Hoquiam-Aberdeen

KXXK(FM)—Licensed to Hoquiam-Aberdeen. See Olympia

Ilwaco

KVAS(FM)— 2000: 103.9 mhz; 10 kw. Ant 171 ft. TL: N46 18 51 W124 03 07. 1006 W. Marine Dr., Astoria, OR 97103. Phone: (503) 325-2911. Fax: (503) 325-5570. E-mail: kastnews@newnw.com. Licensee: New Northwest Broadcasters LLC (group owner; acq 8-25-99; $250,000. for CP). Format: Country. ♦ Paul Mitchell, gen mgr; Brian Riffe, gen sls mgr; Jeff Nelson, news dir; Tom Freel, opns mgr, progmg dir & chief of engrg.

Kelso

KLOG(AM)— Oct 8, 1949: 1490 khz; 1 kw-U. TL: N46 07 00 W122 53 07. Stereo. Box 90 98626. Secondary address: 506 Cowlitz Way W. 98626. Phone: (360) 636-0110. Fax: (360) 577-6949. Web Site: www.klog.com. Licensee: Washington Interstate Broadcasting Co. Inc. (acq 6-5-02; with co-located FM). Rep: Tacher. Richard Hayes. Format: Adult contemp. News staff: 2. Target aud: 25-54. ♦ Joel Hanson, gen mgr; Bill Dodd, progmg dir.

KUKN(FM)—Co-owned with KLOG(AM). July 7, 1962: 105.5 mhz; 700 w. Ant 859 ft. TL: N46 09 52 W122 51 13. Stereo. Web Site: www.kukn.com. Acq 4-12-02; in exchange for KLYK(FM) Kelso). Format: Country. News staff: 2; News: 2 hrs wkly. ♦ Joel Hanson, natl sls mgr & rgnl sls mgr; Jadd Curtis, prom dir; Beth Jensen, pub affrs dir.

KLYK(FM)—Licensed to Kelso. See Longview

*KTJC(FM)— 2004: 91.1 mhz; 17 w horiz, 8 kw vert. Ant 620 ft. TL: N46 19 46 W122 57 50. 803 Vandercook Way, Longview 98632-4039. Phone: (360) 501-5852. Fax: (208) 736-1958. E-mail: ktjc@csnradio.com. Web Site: csnradio.com. Licensee: CSN International (group owner). Format: Christian. ♦ Lee Flory, stn mgr.

Kennewick

*KBLD(FM)— 1998: 91.7 mhz; 800 w. 836 ft. TL: N46 14 10 W119 19 15. Box 6389, Calvary Chapel of Tri-Cities 99336. Secondary address: 301 S. Washington 99336. Phone: (509) 585-2653. Fax: (509) 586-0521. E-mail: kbld@csnradio.com. Web Site: www.kbld.com. Licensee: CSN International (group owner; acq 6-12-97; $14,120). Format: Christian, var/div. ♦ Marty Atkins, gen mgr.

KONA(AM)—Licensed to Kennewick. See Richland-Pasco-Kennewick

KONA-FM—Licensed to Kennewick. See Richland-Pasco-Kennewick

Stations in the U.S. Washington

Developers & Brokers of Radio Properties

contact American Media Services at our suite: Philadelphia Marriott Downtown 215-625-2900
843-972-2200
americanmediaservices.com
Charleston, SC
Dallas, TX · Chicago, Il · Austin, TX

American Media Services, LLC

KTCR(AM)—Licensed to Kennewick. See Richland-Pasco-Kennewick

KTCV(FM)—Licensed to Kennewick. See Richland-Pasco-Kennewick

Kirkland

*KARR(AM)— 1964: 1460 khz; 5 kw-D, 2.5 kw-N, DA-2. TL: N47 40 24 W122 10 07. Box 883 98083-0883. Phone: (510) 568-6200. E-mail: farrradio@familyradio.com. Web Site: www.familyradio.com. Licensee: Family Stations Inc. (group owner; acq 10-22-86; $50,000; 8-11-86). Format: Relg. News: 5 hrs wkly. Target aud: General; conservative Christians & evangelicals. ♦ Harold Camping, pres; Bob Walther, gen mgr & opns mgr; William Thornton, VP & dev VP.

KJAQ(FM)—See Seattle

Lacey

KBRD(AM)— June 1, 1986: 680 khz; 250 w-D. TL: N47 00 41 W122 49 53. Box 434, Olympia 98507. Secondary address: 125 N. Turner, Olympia 98506. Phone: (360) 491-6800. Licensee: BJ & Skip's for the Music (acq 11-3-2004; with KLDY(AM) Lacey). Network: AP Radio. Format: Big band, country, hits of the 20s, 30s, 40s & 50s, var/div. Target aud: General. Spec prog: Jazz one hr wkly. ♦ Adrian DeBee, gen mgr.

KLDY(AM)— Sept 22, 1983: 1280 khz; 1 kw-D, 500 w-N. TL: N47 03 44 W122 49 49. Stereo. Box 434, Olympia 98507. Secondary address: 125 N. Turner, Olympia 98507. Phone: (360) 491-6800. Licensee: BJ & Skip's for the Music (acq 11-3-2004; with KBRD(AM) Lacey). Format: The musical arts & classical. Target aud: General. ♦ Adrian DeBee, gen mgr.

Lakewood

KLAY(AM)—Licensed to Lakewood. See Tacoma

KNTB(AM)—Licensed to Lakewood. See Tacoma

Leavenworth

KOHO-FM— 1998: 101.1 mhz; 6 kw. -872 ft. TL: N47 35 32 W120 38 35. 7475 KOHO Pl. 98826. Phone: (509) 548-1011. Fax: (509) 548-3222. E-mail: gmathews@kohoradio.com. Web Site: www.kohoradio.com. Licensee: Icicle Broadcasting Inc. (group owner; acq 8-26-99; grpsl). Format: Bluegrass, jazz, classical. ♦ Gary Mathews, gen mgr; Vicky Chandler, gen sls mgr; Michael Dickes, progmg dir; Ian Dunne, news dir; Jim Hobson, chief of engrg.

Long Beach

KAQX(FM)— May 1987: 94.3 mhz; 3 kw. 233 ft. TL: N46 18 51 W124 03 07. Stereo. 1006 W. Marine Dr., Astoria, OR 97103. Phone: (503) 325-2911. Fax: (503) 325-5570. E-mail: kaqx@newnw.com. Web Site: kastnewsradio.com. Licensee: New Northwest Broadcasters LLC (group owner; acq 8-24-99; grpsl). Rep: Tacher. Format: CHR. News staff: one; News: 6 hrs wkly. Target aud: 25-54; 35 plus female, some college students. ♦ Paul Mitchell, gen mgr; Brian Riffe, sls dir; Jeff Nelson, news dir; Tom Freel, opns mgr, progmg dir & chief of engrg.

Longview

KBAM(AM)— Aug 15, 1955: 1270 khz; 5 kw-D, 83 w-N. TL: N46 10 58 W122 57 28. 1130 14th Ave. 98632. Phone: (360) 423-1210. Fax: (360) 423-1554. E-mail: dcrowe@entercom.com. Web Site: www.realcountryonline.com. Licensee: Bicoastal Longview LLC. Group owner: Entercom Communications Corp. (acq 1-27-2005; grpsl). Network: CBS. Rep: McGavren Guild. Format: Real country. ♦ Julie Laird, gen mgr, sls dir & progmg dir; Doug Fisher, chief of engrg.

KEDO(AM)— May 1938: 1400 khz; 1 kw-U. TL: N46 08 57 W122 58 29. Broadcast Ctr., 1130 14th Ave. 98632. Phone: (360) 425-1500. Fax: (360) 423-1554. Web Site: www.oldiesradioonline.com. Licensee: Bicoastal Longview LLC. Group owner: Entercom Communications Corp. (acq 1-27-2005; grpsl). Network: ABC Information & Entertainment. Art Moore. Leventhal, Senter & Lerman. Format: News, oldies. News staff: one; News: 15 hrs wkly. Target aud: 25-54. Spec prog: Pub affrs 2 hrs wkly. ♦ Gayle Kessinger, gen mgr, stn mgr, progmg mgr & news dir; Doug Fisher, chief of engrg.

KLYK(FM)—Co-owned with KEDO(AM). Aug 7, 1991: 94.5 mhz; 3 kw. Ant 476 ft. TL: N46 16 49 W122 52 34. Stereo. Web Site: www.todaysbesthits.com. Network: Westwood One. Format: Hot adult contemp. News: 2 hrs wkly. Target aud: 18-49. ♦ Gayle Kessinger, progmg dir.

*KJVH(FM)— 1988: 89.5 mhz; 100 w. 780 ft. TL: N46 09 52 W122 51 13. 136 E. S. Temple, Suite 1630, Salt Lake City, UT 84111. Phone: (801) 359-3147. Fax: (801) 359-8112. Web Site: www.familyradio.com. Licensee: Family Stations Inc. (group owner) Format: Christian relg. ♦ Harold Camping, pres; Roger Crawford, gen mgr & stn mgr.

KLOG(AM)—See Kelso

KUKN(FM)—Licensed to Longview. See Kelso

*KWYQ(FM)— Oct 22, 1987: 90.3 mhz; 500 kw. 735 ft. TL: N46 10 12 W122 56 43. Stereo. Box 1000, Kelso 98626. Phone: (360) 578-1929. Fax: (360) 636-1357. Web Site: wayfm.com. Licensee: WAY-FM Media Group Inc. (group owner; (acq 8-1-2003 with KWYA(FM) Astoria, OR). Format: Contemp Christian. Target aud: 19-34. ♦ Robert D. Augsburg, pres; Danny Houle, gen mgr.

Lynden

KWPZ(FM)— Nov 8, 1960: 106.5 mhz; 68 kw. Ant 2,332 ft. TL: N48 40 45 W122 50 31. Stereo. 1843 Front St., Suite A 98264. Phone: (360) 354-5596. Fax: (360) 354-7517. E-mail: praise@crista.org. Web Site: www.praise1065.com. Licensee: CRISTA Ministries Inc. Group owner: CRISTA Broadcasting (acq 12-80). Format: Relg, Christian. Target aud: 25-54; female. ♦ James Gwinn, pres; Tony Bollen, VP & gen mgr; Marvin Mickley, stn mgr & opns mgr; Jim Bouma, opns mgr; Roger Burke, sls dir & gen sls mgr; Lynette Schulz, prom mgr.

Mabton

KLES(FM)— 1997: . Stn currently dark 98.7 mhz; 11.5 kw. Ant 874 ft. TL: N46 28 33 W120 08 37. 152101 W. Country Rd. 12, Prosser 99350. Phone: (509) 789-1209. Fax: (509) 786-1181. Licensee: MBProsser Licensee LLC. Group owner: Moon Broadcasting (acq 2-6-2004; $1.9 million). Format: Sp contemp. ♦ Frank Allec, gen mgr.

McCleary

KGY-FM— October 1992: 96.9 mhz; 2.33 kw. 1,056 ft. TL: N47 05 08 W123 11 19. Box 1249, Olympia 98507. Phone: (360) 943-1240. Fax: (360) 352-1222. E-mail: kgysales@kgyradio.com. Web Site: www.realcountryonline.com. Licensee: KGY Inc. Haley, Bader & Potts. Format: Country. News staff: 2. Target aud: 25-49. ♦ Barbara O. Kerry, pres; Dick Pust, gen mgr; Darrell Wray, gen sls mgr, mktg dir, prom dir & adv dir; Larry Bailey, progmg dir; Jeanna Spain, mus dir; Ian Fox, news dir; Loni Leitgeb, pub affrs dir; Tom Trotzer, chief of engrg.

Medical Lake

KTSL(FM)— Mar 7, 1989: 101.9 mhz; 12 kw. 495 ft. TL: N47 41 30 W117 46 00. Stereo. 1212 N. Washington, Suite 124, Spokane 99201. Phone: (509) 326-9500. Fax: (509) 326-1560. E-mail: spirit101.9 @spirit1019.com. Web Site: www.spirit1019.com. Licensee: Pamplin Broadcasting-Washington Inc. Group owner: Pamplin Broadcasting (acq 7-24-98; $1.3 million). Fisher, Wayland, Cooper, Leader & Zaragoza. Format: Contemp Christian. News staff: one. Target aud: 18-49; young families. ♦ Karen Dineen, gen mgr & sls dir; Conrad Agte, chief of engrg.

Mercer Island

*KMIH(FM)— February 1970: 104.5 mhz; 30 w. Ant 226 ft. TL: N47 34 21 W122 13 01. Stereo. 9100 S.E. 42nd 98040-4107. Phone: (206) 236-3296. Fax: (206) 236-3342. Web Site: www.x104.fm. Licensee: Mercer Island School District No. 400. Pepper & Corazzini. Format: CHR. Target aud: 15-35; young, progsv students. ♦ Nick De Vogel, gen mgr; Mike Payne, chief of engrg.

Mercer Island-Seattle

KIXI(AM)—Licensed to Mercer Island-Seattle. See Seattle

Montesano

KSWW(FM)— 1998: 102.1 mhz; 50 kw. Ant 440 ft. TL: N46 56 30 W123 47 07. Box 1198, Aberdeen 98520. Secondary address: 1520 Simpson Ave., Aberdeen 98520. Phone: (360) 533-3000. Fax: (360) 532-1456. Web Site: www.jodesha.com. Licensee: Jodesha Broadcasting Inc. (group owner; acq 2-28-03; $750,000. with KBKW(AM) Aberdeen). Network: ABC. Tacher David Tillotson. Format: Adult contemp. Target aud: 25-54. ♦ Gabrielle Jordan, opns mgr; Jerry Anderson, gen sls mgr; Rhys Davis, progmg dir; William J. Wolfenbarger, pres, gen mgr & engrg dir.

Moses Lake

KBSN(AM)— November 1947: 1470 khz; 5 kw-D, 1 kw-N, DA-2. TL: N47 06 16 W119 17 32. Drawer B 98837. Secondary address: 2241 W. Main 98837. Phone: (509) 765-3441. Fax: (509) 766-0273. E-mail: kddrmsales@atnet.net. Licensee: KSEM Inc. Network: ABC Information & Entertainment. Format: News/talk, sports, farm. Target aud: General. Spec prog: Sp 9 hrs wkly. ♦ Jim Davis, gen mgr, opns mgr & prom mgr; Stacey Lehman, gen sls mgr; Gary Roberts, progmg dir; Andy Patrick, news dir; Will Vos, chief of engrg.

KDRM(FM)—Co-owned with KBSN(AM). Oct 1, 1980: 99.3 mhz; 3 kw. 275 ft. TL: N47 05 54 W119 17 47. Stereo. Format: Hot adult contemp. Target aud: 18-34. ♦ Emilio Vela, gen mgr; Dennis Clay, prom mgr; Dave Heaverlo, progmg dir.

*KLWS(FM)— Apr 10, 1997: 91.5 mhz; 7.2 kw. Ant 686 ft. TL: N47 18 50 W119 34 55. Box 642530, Murrow Communications Ctr., Washington State Univ., Rm. 382, Pullman 99164-2530. Phone: (509) 335-6500. Fax: (509) 335-6577. E-mail: nwpr@wsu.edu. Web Site: www.nwpr.org. Licensee: Washington State University. Dow, Lohnes & Albertson. Format: News & views. ♦ Karen Olstad, COO & gen mgr; Dennis Haarsager, gen mgr; Roger Johnson, stn mgr & sls dir; Scott Weatherly, opns mgr; Sarah McDaniel, dev mgr; Mary Hawkins, progmg dir; Robin Rilette, mus dir; Ralph Hogan, engrg dir.

*KMLW(FM)— May 4, 1997: 88.3 mhz; 4 kw. 817 ft. TL: N46 56 31 W119 25 41. 5408 S. Freya, Spokane 99223. Secondary address: 820 N. LaSalle Blvd., Chicago, IL 60610. Phone: (509) 448-2555. Phone: (312) 329-4301. Fax: (509 448-6855. Fax: (312) 329-4468. E-mail: kmbi@moody.edu. Web Site: www.moody.edu. Licensee: Moody Bible Institute of Chicago. (group owner) Format: Relg. Target aud: 35-54; Christians. Spec prog: Class one hr wkly. ♦ Rich Monteith, stn mgr; Gary Leonard, progmg dir.

KWIQ(AM)—(Moses Lake North). Feb 20, 1956: 1020 khz; 2 kw-D, 440 w-N, DA-D. TL: N47 09 48 W119 21 39. Box 999 98837. Secondary address: 11768 Kittleson Rd., Moses Lake North 98837. Phone: (509) 765-1761. Phone: (509) 765-1762. Fax: (509) 765-8901. Licensee: Morris Communications Corp. Group owner: Morris Communications Inc. (acq 10-15-98; grpsl). Network: ESPN Radio. Rep: Katz Radio. Format: Sports. News staff: one; News: 6 hrs wkly. Target aud: 18-49; men. ♦ Gary Patrick, gen mgr; Jeff Dahlstrom, sls dir & gen sls mgr; John Windus, progmg dir; Jay White, chief of engrg.

KWIQ-FM— May 22, 1968: 100.3 mhz; 100 kw. 194 ft. TL: N47 06 09 W119 14 26. Stereo. Web Site: www.kwiq.com. Rep: Katz Radio. Allied Radio Partners. Format: Country. News staff: one. ♦ Jeff Dahlstrom, natl sls mgr.

Broadcasting & Cable Yearbook 2006

D-533

Washington

Moses Lake North

KWIQ(AM)—Licensed to Moses Lake North. See Moses Lake

Mount Vernon

KAPS(AM)— Mar 17, 1963: 660 khz; 10 kw-D, 1 kw-N. TL: N48 26 22 W122 20 45. 2029 Freeway Dr. 98273. Phone: (360) 424-0660. Fax: (360) 424-1660. E-mail: country@kapsradio.com. Web Site: www.kapsradio.com. Licensee: Valley Broadcasters Inc. (acq 8-13-93; 8-30-93). Network: ABC Information & Entertainment. McGaven Guild Format: Country. News staff: one; News: hourly. Target aud: General. ♦ Jim Keane, pres; Jerry Keane, gen sls mgr; Mike Yeoman, progmg dir.

KBRC(AM)— Dec 11, 1946: 1430 khz; 5 kw-D, 1 kw-N, DA-N. TL: N48 25 22 W122 21 10. Stereo. Box 250 98273. Secondary address: 2029 Freeway Dr. 98273. Phone: (360) 424-4278. Phone: (360) 424-1430. Fax: (360) 424-1660. E-mail: oldies@kbrcradio.com. Web Site: kbrcradio.com. Licensee: Valley Broadcasting. (acq 1996; Network: ABC. Tacher. Covington & Burling. Format: Oldies. News staff: 2. Target aud: 25-54. Spec prog: Sp 3 hrs, farm 5 hrs wkly. ♦ James Keane, pres & gen mgr; Jerry Keane, gen sls mgr & mktg dir; Guy Ovenell, progmg dir; Kirk Tollifson, news dir; Paul Thompson, chief of engrg.

*****KMWS(FM)**— May 4, 1973: 90.1 mhz; 100 w hoirz. Ant -161 ft. TL: N48 26 13 W122 18 36. Northwest Public Radio, Box 642530, Pullman 99164-2530. Phone: (509) 335-6536. E-mail: dahmen@wsu.edu. Web Site: www.nwpr.org. Licensee: Washington State University (acq 3-31-2003). Format: News/talk. ♦ Dennis Haahnsager, gen mgr.

*****KSVR(FM)**— 2002: 91.7 mhz; 170 w. Ant 669 ft. TL: N48 23 49 W122 18 26. Skagit Valley College, 2405 E. College Way 98273. Phone: (360) 416-7711. Fax: (360) 416-7822. E-mail: mail@ksvr.org. Web Site: www.ksvr.org. Licensee: Board of Trustees of Skagit Valley College (acq 4-19-00). Format: Progsv, Sp, news/talk. ♦ Rip Robbins, gen mgr, opns dir & progmg dir; Bill McCuskey, chief of engrg.

Naches

KQSN(FM)— November 2000: 99.3 mhz; 790 w. Ant 899 ft. TL: N46 36 02 W120 52 06. 4010 Summitview Ave., Yakima 98908. Phone: (509) 972-3461. Fax: (509) 972-3540. Web Site: 993thehawk.com. Licensee: Capstar TX L.P. Group owner: Clear Channel Communications Inc. (acq 3-12-01; $1.3 million). Format: Classic rock. ♦ Cheryl Salomone, gen mgr; Ron Harris, progmg dir.

KZTA(FM)—Licensed to Naches. See Yakima

Newport

KMJY-FM— December 1989: 104.5 mhz; 930 w. Ant 2,867 ft. TL: N48 19 54 W116 41 35. Stereo. Box 17400, Oldtown, ID 83822. Secondary address: 282 Memory Ln., Oldtown, ID 83822. Phone: (208) 437-5700. Fax: (208) 437-5887. E-mail: kmjy@kmjy.com. Web Site: www.kmjy.com. Licensee: Radio Station KMJY LLC (acq 1-28-2004; $1.3 million). Format: Hits of the 60s & 70s. ♦ Chris Gilbreth, gen mgr.

*****KUBS(FM)**— Sept 10, 1973: 91.5 mhz; 150 w. -538 ft. TL: N48 10 23 W117 03 15. Box 70, Newport High School 99156-0070. Phone: (509) 447-4931. Fax: (509) 447-4354. Licensee: Newport Consolidated School District #56415. Format: CHR.

Nile

*****KSBC(FM)**— 2003: . Stn currently dark 88.1 mhz; 200 w. Ant -1,145 ft. TL: N46 50 02 W120 56 13. Stereo. 5700 W. Oaks Blvd., Rocklin, CA 95765. Phone: (916) 251-1600. Fax: (916) 251-1650. E-mail: klove@klove.com. Web Site: www.klove.com. Licensee: Educational Media Foundation. Group owner: EMF Broadcasting (acq 10-2-2003; grpsl). Network: K-Love. Shaw Pittman. Format: Contemp Christian. News staff: 3. Target aud: 25-44; Judeo Christian female. ♦ Richard Jenkins, pres; Mike Novak, VP & progmg dir; Lloyd Parker, gen mgr; Ed Lenane, opns dir & news dir; Keith Whipple, dev dir; Eric Allen, natl sls mgr; Chris Joyce, prom dir; David Pierce, progmg mgr; Jon Rivers, mus dir; Sam Wallington, engrg dir.

Oak Harbor

KWDB(AM)— Dec 14, 1984: 1110 khz; 500 w-D. TL: N48 17 27 W122 42 28. (CP: 1520 khz, 1 kw-D. TL: N48 16 55 W122 42 26). Box 1455, 3170 D N. Heller Rd. 98277. Phone: (360) 675-7320. Phone: (360) 240-1520. Fax: (360) 675-0166. E-mail: kwdb@kwdb.com. Web Site: www.kwdb.com. Licensee: West Beach Broadcasting Corp. (acq 3-20-00; $55,000). Format: Adult standards, big band, oldies. News staff: 2; News: 12 hrs wkly. Target aud: 20-60. Spec prog: Gospel 6 hrs wkly. ♦ Richard Bell, gen mgr.

Ocean Park

*****KLOP(FM)**—Not on air, target date: unknown: 88.1 mhz; 550 w. Ant 1,044 ft. TL: 46 41 46 W123 46 17. EMF Broadcasting, 5700 W. Oaks Blvd., Rocklin, CA 95765. Phone: (916) 251-1600. Fax: (916) 251-1650. E-mail: klove@klove.com. Web Site: www.klove.com. Licensee: Educational Media Foundation. Group owner: EMF Broadcasting. Network: K-Love. Shaw Pittman. Format: Contemp Christian. News staff: 3. Target aud: 25-44; Judeo Christian, female. ♦ Richard Jenkins, pres; Mike Novak, VP & progmg dir; Lloyd Parker, gen mgr; Ed Lenane, opns dir & news dir; Keith Whipple, dev dir; Eric Allen, natl sls mgr; Ted Gillette, rgnl sls mgr; Chris Joyce, prom dir; David Pierce, progmg mgr; Jon Rivers, mus dir; Sam Wallington, engrg dir.

Olympia

*****KAOS(FM)**— Jan 1, 1973: 89.3 mhz; 1.5 kw. -19 ft. TL: N47 04 22 W122 58 51. Stereo. CAB 301 98505. Phone: (360) 867-6000. Phone: (360) 867-6895. Fax: (360) 866-6797. E-mail: kaos@evergreen.edu. Web Site: www.kaosradio.org. Licensee: Evergreen State College. Network: PRI. Format: Div. News: 5 hrs wkly. Target aud: 18-35. Spec prog: Folks 16 hrs, Asian 3 hrs, American Indian 3 hrs, Sp 6 hrs wkly. ♦ Donna DiBianco, opns mgr & pub affrs dir; Jerry Drummond, gen mgr, dev dir & dev dir.

KGTK(AM)—Licensed to Olympia. See Tacoma

KGY(AM)— Apr 15, 1922: 1240 khz; 1 kw-U. TL: N47 03 31 W122 54 09. Box 1249 98507. Secondary address: 1240 N. Washington St. 98501. Phone: (360) 943-1240. Fax: (360) 352-1222. E-mail: kgysales@kgyradio.com. Web Site: www.kgyradio.com. Licensee: KGY Inc. (acq 1-15-39). Format: Full service, adult contemp. News staff: 2. Target aud: General. ♦ Barbara Kerry, pres; Dick Pust, gen mgr & progmg mgr; Darrell Wray, gen sls mgr; Jeanna Spain, mus dir; Ian Fox, news dir; Loni Leitgeb, pub affrs dir; Tom Trotzer, chief of engrg.

KLDY(AM)—See Lacey

*****KWGV(FM)**— 2005: . Stn currently dark 90.1 mhz; 100 w. Ant -59 ft. TL: N47 02 20 W122 54 00. 121st and Park Ave. S., Tacoma 98447-0003. Phone: (253) 536-5009. Fax: (253) 535-8332. Licensee: Pacific Lutheran University Inc. (acq 8-19-2005; $400,000). ♦ Martin J. Neeb, gen mgr.

KXXK(FM)—(Hoquiam-Aberdeen). Sept 3, 1965: 95.3 mhz; 3 kw. 449 ft. TL: N46 55 53 W123 44 02. (CP: 5 kw, ant 436 ft. TL: N46 56 30 W123 47 07). Stereo. 1308 Coolidge Rd., Aberdeen 98520. Phone: (360) 533-1320. Fax: (360) 532-0935. Licensee: Morris Communications Corp. Group owner: Morris Communications Inc. (acq 2-18-00; $650,000 with KWOK(AM) Hoquiam). Format: Hot country. Target aud: 26-54. ♦ Donna Rosi, gen mgr & gen sls mgr; Patrick Anderson, opns mgr; Ryan Dokke, progmg dir; Liz Miller, news dir; Jay White, chief of engrg.

KXXO(FM)— Jan 16, 1990: 96.1 mhz; 72 kw. Ant 2,099 ft. TL: N46 38 07 W122 28 01. Stereo. Box 7937 98507. Secondary address: Rockway/Leland Bldg., 119 N. Washington Ave. 98507. Phone: (360) 943-9937. Phone: (360) 624-3712. Fax: (360) 352-3643. E-mail: admin@mixx96.com. Web Site: www.mixx96.com. Licensee: 3 Cities Inc. Format: Adult contemp. News staff: one; News: one hr wkly. Target aud: 25-54; general. ♦ David Rauh, pres & gen mgr; Toni Holm, sr VP & stn mgr; Brian Butler, gen sls mgr; Sanrica Marquez, prom dir; John Foster, progmg dir; Ann D'Angelo, news dir; Tim Vik, chief of engrg.

Omak

KNCW(FM)—Listing follows KOMW(AM).

Directory of Radio

KOMW(AM)—Sept 30, 1947: 680 khz; 5 kw-D. TL: N48 23 40 W119 32 00. Box 151 98841. Secondary address: 320 Emery St. 98841. Phone: (509) 826-0100. Fax: (509) 826-3929. Web Site: www.komw.net. Licensee: North Cascades Broadcasting Inc. (group owner; acq 7-90). Network: ABC. Rep: Tacher. Format: Adult standards, talk. Target aud: 18-45. Spec prog: Farm 2 hrs, Sp 2 hrs wkly. ♦ John P. Andrist, CEO, pres, gen mgr, prom dir & prom mgr; Rebecca L. Andrist, CFO & sr VP; Rick Duck, gen sls mgr; Chris Schmidt, progmg dir; Steve Hardy, news dir; Randy Gates, pub affrs dir; Jerry Robinson, chief of engrg.

KNCW(FM)—Co-owned with KOMW(AM). Apr 10, 1978: 92.7 mhz; 4.1 kw. 941 ft. TL: N48 19 12 W119 32 18. Stereo. Web Site: www.komw.net. Format: Country. Target aud: General.

*****KQWS(FM)**— Jan 6, 1999: 90.1 mhz; 3 kw. Ant 2,457 ft. TL: N48 44 37 W119 37 16. Box 642530, Murrow Communications Ctr., Washington State Univ., Pullman 99164-2530. Phone: (509) 335-6500. Fax: (509)335-3772. E-mail: nwpr@wsu.edu. Web Site: www.nwpr.org. Licensee: Washington State University. Dow, Lohnes & Albertson. Format: News, class. News staff: one; News: 60 hrs wkly. ♦ Karen Olstad, COO & gen mgr; Dennis Haarsager, gen mgr; Roger Johnson, stn mgr; Scott Weatherly, opns mgr; Sarah McDaniel, dev dir; Mary Hawkins, progmg dir; Robin Bilette, mus dir; Ralph Hogan, engrg dir.

KZBE(FM)— June 22, 1998: 104.3 mhz; 3.5 kw. 981 ft. TL: N48 19 12 W119 32 18. Box 151 98841. Phone: (509) 826-0100. Fax: (509) 826-3929. E-mail: news@komw.net. Web Site: www.komw.net. Licensee: North Cascades Broadcasting Inc. (group owner; acq 10-14-97; $47,606). Network: ABC. Format: Contemp hit/Top-40. News staff: 2; News: 3 hrs wkly. Target aud: 18 plus. ♦ John P. Andrist, CEO, pres & gen mgr; Rebecca L. Andrist, CFO, sr VP & opns mgr; Rick Duck, gen sls mgr; Chris Schmidt, progmg dir; Jerry Robinson, chief of engrg.

Opportunity

KIXZ-FM— Apr 1, 1961: 96.1 mhz; 56 kw. 2,378 ft. TL: N47 34 11 W117 05 00. Stereo. 808 East Sprague, Spokane 99202. Phone: (509) 242-2100. Fax: (509) 242-1160. Web Site: www.kix961.com. Licensee: Capstar TX L.P. Group owner: Clear Channel Communications Inc. (acq 8-30-00; grpsl). Rep: Allied Radio Partners. Shaw Pittman. Format: Country. Target aud: 25-54. ♦ Kosta Panidis, gen mgr & gen sls mgr; Jerry Jensen, natl sls mgr; Joe Chabala, prom dir; Paul Neumann, progmg dir; Kent Abendroth, chief of engrg.

KXLI(AM)— November 1955: 630 khz; 530 w-D, 53 w-N. TL: N47 36 31 W117 22 25. Box 31000, Spokane 99223. Phone: (509) 443-1000. Fax: (509) 448-3811. E-mail: acn@quest.net. Web Site: www.acn-network.com. Licensee: Mutual Broadcasting System LLC Group owner: Morgan Murphy Stations (acq 9-1-2005; $375,000). Format: Relg. ♦ Thomas W. Read, gen mgr.

Othello

KOLW(FM)— February 1992: 97.5 mhz; 4.6 kw. Ant 656 ft. TL: N46 45 55 W119 16 49. (CP: COL Basin City. 50 kw, ant 620 ft. TL: N46 17 23 W119 25 28). Stereo. 45 Campbell Rd., Walla Walla 99362. Phone: (509) 527-1000. Fax: (509) 529-5534. E-mail: kzln@teleu98.com. Licensee: Capstar TX L.P. (acq 11-9-2004; exchange for KHTO(FM) Milton-Freewater, OR). Network: Jones Radio Networks. Wheeler Broadcasting. Format: CHR. Target aud: 25-49; 60% male, 40% female. ♦ Mark Wheeler, gen mgr.

KRSC(AM)— Sept 1, 1957: 1400 khz; 1 kw-U. TL: N46 49 29 W119 11 26. 128 S. 1st Ave. 99344. Phone: (509) 488-0606. Fax: (509) 488-0909. Licensee: Rafael C. Guerrero (acq 8-22-01). Format: Sp, Mexican, sports, talk. ♦ Gaudencio Felipe, gen mgr; Maria Maya, sls dir; Jose Luis Cruz, progmg dir.

Pasco

KEYW(FM)— June 30, 1986: 98.3 mhz; 3 kw. 197 ft. TL: N46 08 48 W119 05 59. Stereo. 2621 W. A St. 99301. Phone: (509) 547-9791. Fax: (509) 547-8509. E-mail: thekey@keyw.com. Web Site: www.keyw.com. Licensee: Capstar TX L.P. Group owner: Clear Channel Communications Inc. (acq 2-15-02; grpsl). Format: Adult contemp. Target aud: 18-49. ♦ Eric Van Winkle, gen mgr; Grant Linnen, gen sls mgr; Crystal Struthers, prom dir; Paul Drake, progmg dir; Chuck Ince, chief of engrg.

KFLD(AM)—Licensed to Pasco. See Richland-Pasco-Kennewick

KGDN(FM)—Licensed to Pasco. See Richland-Pasco-Kennewick

Stations in the U.S.

Washington

Developers & Brokers of Radio Properties
contact American Media Services at our suite: Philadelphia Marriott Downtown 215-625-2900
843-972-2200
americanmediaservices.com
Charleston, SC
Dallas, TX · Chicago, Il · Austin, TX
American Media Services, LLC

KGSG(FM)— Apr 1, 1997: 93.7 mhz; 600 w. 958 ft. TL: N46 04 59 W119 09 38. Box 2852 99302. Phone: (509) 547-5196. Fax: (509) 547-5203. Web Site: www.kgsg.org. Licensee: Gospel Music Broadcasting Corp. (acq 3-26-98). Format: Southern gospel. ♦ Martin L. Gibbs, pres, gen mgr & chief of engrg; Marlin Schultz, gen sls mgr; Sharon Harmon, progmg dir.

*KOLU(FM)— Sept 1, 1971: 90.1 mhz; 3.99 kw. 93 ft. TL: N46 14 59 W119 09 10. (CP: 7.5 kw, ant 1,000 ft.). Stereo. 4921 W. Wernett 99301. Phone: (509) 547-2062. Fax: (509) 544-0340. Web Site: www.riverviewbaptist.org. Licensee: Riverview Baptist Christian Schools. Format: Relg. ♦ Pastor J. Towne, gen mgr & progmg dir; Martin Gibbs, chief of engrg.

Port Angeles

KIKN(AM)— June 16, 1961: 1290 khz; 1 kw-D, 149 w-N, DA-1. TL: N48 05 55 W123 24 21. 2815 2nd Ave., Suite 550, Seattle 98121. Phone: (206) 443-8200. Fax: (206) 771-1133. Web Site: www.1300kol.com. Licensee: Common Ground Broadcasting Inc. Group owner: Salem Communications Corp. (acq 10-17-01; $525,000). Network: Salem Radio Network. Format: Talk. News staff: one; News: 10 hrs wkly. Target aud: 25-49; heavy buyers, strong family base. Spec prog: Relg one hr wkly. ♦ David Fitts, gen mgr; Chuck Olmstead, opns mgr & gen sls mgr.

*KNWP(FM)— Mar 23, 1998: 90.1 mhz; 1.6 kw. Ant 197 ft. TL: N48 09 03 W123 40 09. Box 642530, 382 Murrow Ctr., Pullman 99164-2530. Phone: (509) 335-6500. Fax: (509) 335-3772. E-mail: nwpr@wsu.edu. Web Site: www.nwpr.org. Licensee: Washington State University. Dow, Lohnes & Albertson. Format: Classical, news. News staff: one; News: 37 hrs wkly. ♦ Karen Olstad, COO & gen mgr; Dennis Haarsager, gen mgr; Roger Johnson, stn mgr & sls dir; Scott Weatherly, opns mgr; Sarah McDaniel, dev dir; Mary Hawkins, progmg dir; Robin Rilette, mus dir; Ralph Hogan, engrg dir.

KONP(AM)— 1945: 1450 khz; 1 kw-U. TL: N48 07 19 W123 26 13. Box 1450, 313 W. First 98362. Phone: (360) 457-1450. Fax: (360) 457-9114. E-mail: office@konp.com. Web Site: www.konp.com. Licensee: Radio Pacific Inc. (acq 2-12-02; $850,000). Network: ABC Information & Entertainment. Rep: Tacher. Format: News/talk. Target aud: 28-54. ♦ Brown Maloney, chmn; Stan Comeau, gen sls mgr; Todd Ortloff, opns mgr, sls dir, progmg dir, news dir & chief of engrg.

*KVIX(FM)— Mar 22, 2005: 89.3 mhz; 600 w. Ant 489 ft. TL: N48 09 03 W123 40 09. c/o KPLU-FM, 121st and Park Ave., Tacoma 98447. Phone: (253) 535-7758. Fax: (253) 535-8332. Web Site: www.kplu.org. Licensee: Pacific Lutheran University Inc. Network: NPR. Format: News, jazz. ♦ Martin J. Neeb, gen mgr; Kerry Swansey, dev VP; Kay Steik, sls VP; Joey Cohn, progmg VP; Nick Morrison, mus dir; Erin Hennessey, news dir; Lowell Kiesow, engrg VP.

Prosser

KMNA(FM)— Sept 6, 1962: 101.7 mhz; 3.5 kw. 865 ft. TL: N46 11 12 W119 45 13. Stereo. 152101 W. County Rt. 12 99350. Phone: (509) 786-4532. Fax: (509) 786-1181. Licensee: MBProsser Licensee LLC. Group owner: Moon Broadcasting (acq 2-15-2000; $750,000). Rep: Target Broadcast Sales. Format: Hispanic. Target aud: 18-49. ♦ Frank Allec, gen mgr, opns mgr & gen sls mgr; Rubin Muniz, gen sls mgr; Juan Tejeda, prom mgr; Piomar Marin, progmg dir & news dir.

KZXR(AM)—Co-owned with KMNA(FM). Dec 14, 1956: 1310 khz; 5 kw-D, 66 w-N. TL: N46 14 03 W119 48 49. Phone: (509) 786-1310. (Acq 2-24-2000; $500,000). Rep: Tacher. Format: News/talk, sports. Target aud: 25-54. ♦ Frank Allec, gen mgr, opns mgr, gen sls mgr & news dir; Todd Summers, progmg dir & chief of engrg.

Pullman

KFFR(FM)— 2005: 97.7 mhz; 650 w. Ant 987 ft. TL: N46 40 52 W116 58 16. 840 S.E. Bishop Blvd. 99163. Phone: (866) 977-3473. Fax: (888) 550-6847. Web Site: www.977thefire.com. Licensee: Royal Communications of Washington (acq 6-16-2004; $225,000. for CP). Format: Contemp Christian and positive pop. ♦ Christopher Gilbreth, gen mgr.

KHTR(FM)—Listing follows KQQQ(AM).

KQQQ(AM)— 1938: 1150 khz; 11 kw-D, 27 w-N. TL: N46 43 36 W117 12 23. 801 Old Wawawai Rd. 99163. Secondary address: Box 1 99163. Phone: (509) 332-6551. Fax: (509) 332-5151. E-mail: khtr@aol.com. Web Site: www.hot104.net. Licensee: Radio Palouse Inc. (group owner; acq 12-74). Network: Network: ABC Information & Entertainment, ABC News/Talk. Allied Radio Partners. David Tillotson. Format: News/talk. News staff: one; News: 28 hrs wkly. Target aud: General. Spec prog: Farm 3 hrs, loc news 10 hrs wkly. ♦ Bill Weed, gen mgr; Larry Weir, opns mgr; Rod Schwartz, gen sls mgr; Evan Ellis, news dir; Steve Franko, chief of engrg.

KHTR(FM)—Co-owned with KQQQ(AM). 1967: 104.3 mhz; 24 kw. 1,669 ft. TL: N46 48 40 W116 54 55. Stereo. Box 1 99163. Secondary address: 801 Old Wawawai Rd. 99163. Web Site: www.hot104.net. Format: CHR. News staff: one; News: 24 hrs wkly. Target aud: General. ♦ Jeremy West, mus dir.

KRFA-FM—See Moscow, ID

*KRLF(FM)— July 1, 1991: 88.5 mhz; 420 w vert. 794 ft. TL: N46 38 01 W117 05 13. Stereo. S.W. 345 Kimball 99163. Phone: (509) 332-3545. Fax: (509) 332-5433. E-mail: krlf@lffmtc.org. Licensee: Living Faith Fellowship Educational Ministries. Gammon & Grange. Format: Christian adult contemp, inspirational, praise & worship. News: 18 hrs wkly. Target aud: 18-54. Spec prog: Black one hr, children 5 hrs wkly. ♦ Phillip J. Vance, pres; Alan King, stn mgr; Aaron Atkinson, opns mgr & progmg dir; Frank Younce, engrg mgr.

KUUX(AM)—Not on air, target date: unknown: 650 khz; 3 kw-D, 250 w-N, DA-N. TL: N46 46 03 W117 11 03. Box 1 99163. Phone: (509) 332-6551. Fax: (509) 332-5151. Licensee: Radio Palouse Inc. (group owner). ♦ Bill Weed, gen mgr; Rod Schwartz, sls dir; Larry Weir, progmg mgr; Evan Ellis, news dir; Steve Frenko, engrg mgr.

*KWSU(AM)— June 1922: 1250 khz; 5 kw-U. TL: N46 41 47 W117 14 44. Box 642530, Murrow Communications Ctr., Washington State Univ., Rm. 382 99164-2530. Phone: (509) 335-6500. Fax: (509) 335-6577. E-mail: nwpr@wsu.edu. Web Site: www.nwpr.org. Licensee: Washington State Univ. Network: NPR. Dow, Lohnes & Albertson. Format: News, class. News staff: one; News: 60 hrs wkly. Target aud: General. Spec prog: Jazz 14 hrs wkly. ♦ Karen Olstad, COO; Dennis Haarsager, gen mgr; Roger Johnson, stn mgr & sls dir; Scott Weatherly, opns mgr; Sarah McDaniel, dev dir; Mary Hawkins, progmg dir & engrg mgr; Robin Rilette, mus dir; Ralph Hogan, engrg dir & engrg mgr. Co-owned TV: *KWSU-TV affil.

*KZUU(FM)— Sept 21, 1979: 90.7 mhz; 800 w. 105 ft. TL: N46 43 51 W117 09 08. Stereo. CUB Rm 311, Washington State Univ. 99164-7204. Phone: (509) 335-2208. Fax: (509) 335-3772. Licensee: Washington State University Board of Regents. Format: Rock, jazz, diversified. News staff: one; News: 5 hrs wkly. Target aud: 18-49; college students. Spec prog: Jazz 12 hrs, Black 12 hrs, folk 4 hrs, Sp 3 hrs, new mus 10 hrs, environmental protection 2 hrs wkly. ♦ Dan Maher, pres; Andy Hurst, gen mgr & mus dir; Lori Stewart, prom dir; Jackie Kaiser, progmg dir; Mike Guay, gen mgr & progmg mgr.

KZZL-FM— Nov 1991: 99.5 mhz; 81.4 kw. 1,059 ft. TL: N46 40 52 W116 58 19. Stereo. Box 710, Colfax 99111. Secondary address: 840 Fairview Rd., Colfax 99111. Phone: (509) 397-3441. Fax: (509) 397-4752. E-mail: kzzlkrow@stjohncable.com. Web Site: www.palousecountry.com. Licensee: Inland Northwest Broadcasting LLC. (group owner). (acq 6-28-2005; grpsl). Dow, Lohnes & Albertson. Format: Country. News staff: one; News: 2 hrs wkly. Target aud: 25 plus. ♦ Robert G. Hauser, gen mgr & gen sls mgr; Robert Hauser, sls dir; Randy Byers, progmg dir; Glenn Vaagen, news dir; Terri Linderman, chief of engrg.

Puyallup

KSUH(AM)— Dec 1, 1951: 1450 khz; 1 kw-U. TL: N47 10 41 W122 16 24. (CP: 1440 khz; 5 kw-D, 2 kw-N, DA-2). 807 S. 336 St., Federal Way 98003. Phone: (253) 815-1212. Fax: (253) 815-1913. Web Site: www.radiohankook.com. Licensee: Jean J. Suh. (acq 4-4-97; $350,000). Format: Korean, var/div. News staff: 2. Target aud: 25-65; working folks. ♦ Doris Haan, gen mgr; Kenneth Son, gen sls mgr & prom dir; Herman Han, progmg dir; Larry Gruber, chief of engrg.

Quincy

KWNC(AM)— Sept 10, 1957: 1370 khz; 1 kw-D, 40 w-N. TL: N47 16 15 W119 51 13. Box159, Wenatchee 98807. Phone: (509) 787-4461. Fax: (509) 664-6799. E-mail: news@kwnc.com. Licensee: Wescoast Broadcasting Co. Inc. (acq 3-8-99). Rep: Tacher. Format: News, farm. News staff: 3; News: 168 hrs wkly. Target aud: 35 plus; farm-oriented. Spec prog: Farm 5 hrs wkly. ♦ Jim Wallace Jr., pres & gen mgr; Debbie Capestrini, opns dir & progmg dir; Greg McEwen, gen sls mgr; Steve Hair, news dir; Pete Peterson, chief of engrg.

KWWW-FM— Aug 29, 1985: 96.7 mhz; 440 w. 1,079 ft. TL: N47 19 13 W199 48 00. Stereo. 231 N. Wenatchee Ave., Wenatchee 98801. Phone: (509) 665-6565. Fax: (509) 663-1150. Web Site: www.kw3.com. Licensee: Fisher Radio Regional Group Inc. Group owner: Fisher Broadcasting Company. Rep: McGavren Guild. Shaw Pittman. Format: CHR, 80s & 90s. Target aud: 18-49. ♦ Bill Krippaehne, CEO; Ben Tucker, chmn; Larry Roberts, pres; Jim Senst, gen mgr & adv mgr; Leona Frank, sls dir; Dave Herald, gen sls mgr & natl sls mgr; Dale Roth, prom mgr & progmg dir; Dave Bernstein, news dir; Lisa Rodriguez, pub affrs dir; Manuel Garcia, chief of engrg.

KZML(FM)— October 1998: 95.9 mhz; 2.51 kw. 1,046 ft. TL: N47 19 13 W119 47 59. Box 2888, Yakima 98907. Secondary address: 706 Butterfield Rd., Yakima 98901. Phone: (509) 457-1000. Fax: (509) 452-0541. E-mail: zorro@radiozorro.com. Web Site: www.radiozorro.com. Licensee: Bustos Media of Eastern Washington License LLC. (group owner; (acq 11-18-2004; grpsl). Rep: Tacher. Tacher Format: Mexican regional. News staff: one; News: 3 hrs wkly. Target aud: 18-35; Hispanic. ♦ Bob Berry, gen mgr; Keith Teske, opns mgr; Martin Ortiz, progmg dir.

Raymond

KFMY(FM)— Oct 26, 1984: 97.7 mhz; 44 kw. Ant 1,322 ft. TL: N46 54 05 W123 25 07. Stereo. Box 7489, Olympia 98507. Secondary address: 1803 State Ave. N.E., Olympica 98506. Phone: (360) 918-9000. Fax: (360) 704-3146. Web Site: www.977theeagle.com. Licensee: Sound South Broadcasting LLC (acq 3-1-2003; $2.28 million). Network: ABC. Rep: Tacher. Format: Classic hits. News: 10 hrs wkly. Target aud: 25-54; adults. ♦ Bill Bradley, gen mgr & gen sls mgr; Craig Sullivan, opns mgr, progmg dir & mus dir; Ed Bruno, sls VP; Heidi Persson, natl sls mgr; Jeff Turnbow, news dir & pub affrs dir.

Renton

KRIZ(AM)— Feb 2, 1982: 1420 khz; 1 kw-D, 500 w-N, DA-2. TL: N47 26 25 W122 12 09. 2600 S. Jackson St., Seattle 98144. Secondary address: Box 22462, Seattle 98122-0462. Phone: (206) 323-3070. Fax: (206) 322-6518. E-mail: ztwins@aol.com. Web Site: www.ztwins.com. Licensee: KRIZ Broadcasting Inc. (acq 2-84; $400,000; 3-5-84). Network: American Urban. Format: Black oldies, blues. Target aud: 18 plus. Spec prog: Relg 18 hrs wkly. ♦ Christopher H. Bennett, pres, stn mgr & sls mgr; Gloria V. Bennett, VP; Frank P. Barrow, chief of opns; Jawann Bennett, progmg dir; Terry Denbrook, chief of engrg.

KYIZ(AM)— 1998: 1620 khz; 10 kw-D, 1 kw-N. TL: N47 26 25 W122 12 09. 2600 S. Jackson St., Seattle 98144. Secondary address: Box 22462, Seattle 98144. Phone: (206) 323-3070. Fax: (206) 322-6518. E-mail: ztwins@aol.com. Web Site: www.ztwins.com. Licensee: KRIZ Broadcasting Inc. Format: Urban contemp, rhythm & blues. ♦ Christopher H. Bennett, pres, gen mgr & sls mgr; Gloria V. Bennett, VP, gen mgr & stn mgr; Frank P. Barrow, chief of opns; Jawann Bennett, progmg dir; Terry Denbrook, chief of engrg.

Washington Directory of Radio

Richland

KALE(AM)—Licensed to Richland. See Richland-Pasco-Kennewick

KEGX(FM)—Licensed to Richland. See Richland-Pasco-Kennewick

KFAE-FM—Licensed to Richland. See Richland-Pasco-Kennewick

KIOK(FM)—Licensed to Richland. See Richland-Pasco-Kennewick

KORD-FM—Licensed to Richland. See Richland-Pasco-Kennewick

Richland-Pasco-Kennewick

KALE(AM)—(Richland). Apr 1, 1950: 960 khz; 5 kw-D, 1 kw-N, DA-N. TL: N46 14 34 W119 10 48. 830 N. Columbia Center Blvd., Suite B-2, Kennewick 99336. Phone: (509) 783-0783. Fax: (509) 735-8627. Web Site: www.am960.com. Licensee: New Northwest Broadcasters LLC (group owner; acq 12-10-99; grpsl). Rep: Tacher, D & R Radio. Haley, Bader & Potts. Format: ESPN sports. News staff: one. Target aud: 25 plus; general. ♦Don Morin, gen mgr.

KIOK(FM)—Co-owned with KALE(AM). Oct 3, 1978: 94.9 mhz; 100 kw. 1,250 ft. TL: N46 05 47 W119 11 36. Stereo. Web Site: www.thundercountry949.com. Format: Country.

KEGX(FM)—Listing follows KTCR(AM).

***KFAE-FM**—(Richland). July 1982: 89.1 mhz; 100 kw. 1,148 ft. TL: N46 05 43 W119 11 41. Stereo. Box 642530, Murrow Communications Ctr., Washington State Univ., Rm 382, Pullman 99164-2530. Secondary address: Washington State Univ. at Tri-Cities, 100 Sprout Rd., Richland 99164-2530. Phone: (509) 335-6500. Fax: (509) 335-3772. E-mail: nwpr@wsu.edu. Web Site: www.nwpr.org. Licensee: Washington State University. Network: Network: PRI, NPR. Dow, Lohnes & Albertson. Format: Class, news. News staff: one; News: 37 hrs wkly. Target aud: General. Spec prog: Folk, jazz 15 hrs wkly. ♦Karen Olstad, COO & gen mgr; Dennis Haarsager, gen mgr; Roger Johnson, stn mgr & sls dir; Scott Weatherly, opns dir; Sarah McDaniel, dev mgr; Mary Hawkins, progmg dir; Robin Rilette, mus dir; Ralph Hogan, engrg dir. Co-owned TV: *KTNW(TV) affil.

KFLD(AM)—(Pasco). July 28, 1956: 870 khz; 10 kw-U. TL: N46 13 41 W119 07 32. Box 2485, Pasco 99301. Secondary address: 2621 W.A. St., Pasco 99301. Phone: (509) 547-9791. Fax: (509) 547-8509. Web Site: www.sportsradio870.com. Licensee: Capstar TX L.P. Group owner: Clear Channel Communications Inc. (acq 2-15-01; grpsl). Art Moore. Format: Sports. News staff: one; News: 3 hrs wkly. Target aud: 18-64. ♦Eric Van Winkle, gen mgr; Grant Linnen, gen sls mgr; Curt Cartier, progmg dir; Chuck Ince, chief of engrg.

KORD-FM—Co-owned with KFLD(AM). Oct 15, 1965: 102.7 mhz; 100 kw. 1,100 ft. TL: N46 05 47 W119 11 36. Stereo. Web Site: www.1027kord.com. Format: Country. Target aud: 25-54. ♦Paul Drake, progmg dir.

KGDN(FM)—(Pasco). February 1992: 101.3 mhz; 2.75 kw. 1,000 ft. TL: N46 05 47 W119 11 36. Box 3258, Tri Cities 99302. Secondary address: 830 N. Columbia Center Blvd., Suite B3, Pasco 99336. Phone: (509) 783-8600. Fax: (509) 448-3811. E-mail: kgdn@kgdn.com. Web Site: www.kgdn.com. Licensee: West Pasco Fine Arts Radio. Pepper & Corazzini. Format: Christian. Target aud: 35 plus. ♦Thomas W. Read, gen mgr; Bill Glenn, stn mgr, opns dir & engrg dir; Melinda Read, sls dir; Joseph Spinelli, progmg dir.

KONA(AM)—(Kennewick). January 1948: 610 khz; 5 kw-U, DA-2. TL: N46 13 41 W119 04 07. Stereo. 2823 W. Lewis, Pasco 99301. Secondary address: Box 2623, Tri Cities 99302. Phone: (509) 547-1618. Fax: (509) 546-2678. E-mail: kona@konaradio.com. Web Site: www.konaradio.com. Licensee: CCR-Tri Cities IV LLC. (group owner; (acq 12-19-2003; grpsl). Network: ABC Information & Entertainment. Rep: Allied Radio Partners. Pepper & Corazzini. Format: News/talk. News staff: 2; News: 25 hrs wkly. Target aud: 25-54. Spec prog: Farm 3 hrs, sports 8 hrs wkly. ♦Dennis W. Goodman, gen mgr; Scott Smith, gen sls mgr; Todd Nevard, prom dir, prom dir & progmg dir; Dennis Shannon, news dir; Art Blum, chief of engrg.

KONA-FM— Aug 1, 1969: 105.3 mhz; 100 kw. 1,180 ft. TL: N46 05 48 W119 11 36. Stereo. Web Site: www.konaradio.com. Allied Radio Partners. Format: Light adult contemp. News staff: 2; News: 3 hrs wkly. ♦Dennis W. Goodman, COO, exec VP & stn mgr; Scott Smith, sls VP & sls dir; Todd Nevard, progmg VP.

KTCR(AM)—(Kennewick). August 1945: 1340 khz; 1 kw-U. TL: N46 13 16 W119 11 20. 830 N. Columbia Ctr. Blvd., Suite B-2, Kennewick 99336. Phone: (509) 783-0783. Fax: (509) 735-8627. Web Site: www.ktcr.com. Licensee: New Northwest Broadcasters LLC (group owner; acq 12-10-99; grpsl). Rep: Christal. Format: News/talk. Target aud: 25-64. Spec prog: Sports. ♦Don Morin, gen mgr.

KEGX(FM)—Co-owned with KTCR(AM). June 10, 1992: 106.5 mhz; 100 kw. 1,082 ft. TL: N46 05 51 W119 11 30. Stereo. Web Site: www.kegx.com. Format: Classic rock. Target aud: 25-54.

***KTCV(FM)**—(Kennewick). Dec 10, 1984: 88.1 mhz; 320 w. 92 ft. TL: N46 13 05 W119 12 17. Stereo. 5929 W. Metaline, Kennewick 99336. Phone: (509) 734-3621. Phone: (509) 734-3622. Fax: (509) 734-3609. E-mail: dailed@ksd.org. Web Site: www.ktcv.net. Licensee: Kennewick School District No. 17. Format: Alternative rock. ♦Ed Dailey, gen mgr; Bill Glenn, chief of engrg.

Rock Island

KAAP(FM)— Sept 19, 1990: 99.5 mhz; 5 kw. 167 ft. TL: N47 22 52 W120 17 15. (CP: 5.3 kw, ant -82 ft.). Stereo. 231 N. Wenatchee Ave., Wenatchee 98801. Phone: (509) 665-6565. Fax: (509) 663-1150. Web Site: www.applefm.com. Licensee: Fisher Radio Regional Group Inc. Group owner: Fisher Broadcasting Company (acq 3-1-95). Rep: McGavren Guild. Shaw Pittman. Format: Adult contemp,. News staff: one. Target aud: 25-54. ♦Bill Krippaehne, CEO; Ben Tucker, chmn; Larry Roberts, pres; Jim Senst, gen mgr & mktg dir; Leona Frank, gen sls mgr; Todd Johnson, prom mgr; Joe Bowers, engrg dir; Manuel Garcia, chief of engrg.

Roy

***KWFJ(FM)**— September 1995: 89.7 mhz; 1 kw. 98 ft. TL: N46 57 59 W122 32 56. Box 401 98580. Secondary address: 9006 320 St. S. 98580. Phone: (206) 843-1692. E-mail: cbcroy@cbcroy.org. Licensee: Calvary Baptist Church. Network: Bible Bcstg Net. Format: Christian. ♦Bernie Brill, gen mgr.

Royal City

KRCW(FM)— 1995: 96.3 mhz; 19.5 kw. 790 ft. TL: N46 45 55 W119 16 51. Stereo. 508 W. Lewis St., Pasco, CA 99301. Phone: (509) 545-0700. Fax: (509) 543-4100. E-mail: lourdesbautista@campesina.com. Web Site: www.campesina.com. Licensee: Farmworker Educational Radio Network. Borsari & Paxson. Format: Sp. Target aud: 25-54; Hispanic market. ♦Anthony Chavez, pres, gen mgr & sls VP; Paul Chavez, VP; Lourdes Bautista, stn mgr; Jesse Portillo, opns dir, dev VP & progmg dir; Mario Hildalgo, mktg VP; Cenovio Nunez, prom VP; Armando Ameta, adv VP & mus dir; Carlos Ortiz, news dir; David Whitehead, engrg VP.

Seattle

***KBLE(AM)**— 1948: 1050 khz; 5 kw-D, 440 w-N. TL: N47 33 41 W122 21 34. Box 2482, Kirkland 98083. Phone: (425) 867-2340. E-mail: info@sacredheartradio.org. Web Site: www.kble.com. Licensee: Sacred Heart Radio Inc. (acq 1-11-01). Pepper & Corazzini. Format: Relg. ♦Ron Belter, gen mgr & opns mgr.

KBSG-FM—See Tacoma

KCMS(FM)—See Edmonds

***KEXP-FM**— 1972: 90.3 mhz; 3.3 kw. Ant 692 ft. TL: N47 36 58 W122 18 28. Stereo. 113 Dexter Ave. 98109. Phone: (206) 520-KEXP. Fax: (206) 520-5899. Web Site: www.kexp.org. Licensee: Regents of University of Washington. Network: NPR. Dow,Lohnes & Albertson. Format: Progsv, div, alternative. Target aud: 18-44; educated, culturally interested, active outdoors, prof/mngr/tech positions. ♦Tom Mara, gen mgr; Jack Walters, opns mgr; Monica Ramsey, dev dir; Courtney Miller, mktg dir; Kevin Cole, progmg dir; Don Yates, mus dir; Mike McCormick, news dir; Jamie Alls, chief of engrg.

KGNW(AM)—See Burien-Seattle

KHHO(AM)—(Tacoma). August 1942: 850 khz; 10 kw-D, 1 kw-N, DA-2. TL: N47 13 56 W122 23 22. Stereo. 351 Elliott Ave. W., Suite 300 98119. Phone: (206) 494-2000. Fax: (206) 286-2376. Web Site: khho-am.clearchannel.com. Licensee: AK Media Group Inc. Group owner: Clear Channel Communications Inc. (acq 6-14-02; grpsl). Format: Sports. Target aud: 25-55. ♦Michele Grosenick, pres & gen mgr; Sean Shannon, sls dir & adv dir; Gus Swanson, mktg dir; Gina Gray, prom dir; Rich Moore, progmg dir; Stephen Kilbreath, news dir; Doug Irwin, chief of engrg.

KING-FM— 1947: 98.1 mhz; 58 kw. 2,342 ft. TL: N47 30 55 W122 58 29. Stereo. 10 Harrison St., Suite 100 98109. Phone: (206) 691-2981. Fax: (206) 691-2982. E-mail: web@king.org. Web Site: www.king.org. Licensee: Classic Radio Inc. (acq 2-92; $9.75 million. with co-located AM). Format: Class. News: 2 hrs wkly. ♦Jennifer Ridewood, gen mgr; Kirsten Cummings, sls dir; Jen Pirak, mktg dir; Shawna Keen, prom mgr; Bob Goldfarb, progmg dir; Tom Olsen, mus dir; Aaron Stoess, asst music dir; Buzz Anderson, chief of engrg.

KIRO(AM)— 1927: 710 khz; 50 kw-U, DA-N. TL: N47 23 55 W122 26 01. 1820 Eastlake Ave. E. 98102-3711. Phone: (206) 726-7000. Fax: (206) 726-5446. Web Site: www.710kiro.com. Licensee: Entercom Seattle License LLC. Group owner: Entercom Communications Corp. (acq 3-6-97; grpsl). Network: CBS. Format: News/talk, sports. News staff: 20. Target aud: 25-54. ♦David Pridemore, gen mgr; Dennis McCormick, gen sls mgr; Tom Lendening, progmg dir.

KISW(FM)— 1950: 99.9 mhz; 100 kw. 1,150 ft. TL: N47 32 41 W122 06 28. Stereo. 1100 Olive Way, Suite 1650 98101. Phone: (206) 285-7625. Fax: (206) 215-9355. Web Site: www.kisw.com. Licensee: Entercom Seattle License LLC. Group owner: Entercom Communications Corp. (acq 1996). Rep: D & R Radio. Format: Rock/AOR. Target aud: 18-49. ♦David Field, pres; Melissa Forrest, VP & gen mgr; Bob Nordberg, gen sls mgr; Dan O'Shea, natl sls mgr; Erron Sorensen, mktg dir; Kerri Lewis, prom dir; Ryan Castle, progmg dir; Ashley Wilson, mus dir; Gary Engard, engrg dir.

KIXI(AM)—(Mercer Island-Seattle). 1947: 880 khz; 50 kw-D, 10 kw-N, DA-2. TL: N47 34 59 W122 10 52. 3650 131st Ave. S.E., Suite 550, Bellevue 98006. Phone: (425) 653-9462. Fax: (425) 653-1088. E-mail: bobb@kixi.com. Web Site: www.kixi.com. Licensee: Bellevue Radio Inc. Group owner: Sandusky Radio (acq 11-15-91; $3.5 million; 12-3-91). Rep: Christal. Format: Adult standards. Target aud: 35 plus; mature active adults. ♦Marc S. Kaye, VP & gen mgr; Susan Hoffman, sls dir; Julie Judge, natl sls mgr; Lois Mares, rgnl sls mgr; Tarah Smigun, prom mgr; Bob Brooks, progmg dir; Jim Kampmann, news dir & pub affrs dir; George Bisso, chief of engrg.

KJAQ(FM)— 1959: 96.5 mhz; 100 kw. 1,223 ft. TL: N47 32 39 W122 06 32. Stereo. 1000 Dexter Ave. N., Suite 100 98109. Phone: (206) 805-1100. Fax: (206) 805-0920. Web Site: www.965thepoint.com. Licensee: Infinity Radio Holdings Inc. Group owner: Infinity Broadcasting Corp. (acq 11-13-98; grpsl). Format: 80s pop/rock. Target aud: 25-54. ♦Dave McDonald, pres; Lisa Decker, gen mgr & sls VP; Lisa McDonald, gen mgr; Nils Olsen, gen sls mgr; Lisa Adams, prom dir; Jim Trapp, progmg dir; Anita Moffett, news dir; Tom McGinley, chief of engrg.

KJR(AM)— 1921: 950 khz; 5 kw-U, DA-N. TL: N47 34 57 W122 21 46. 351 Elliot Ave. W., Suite 300 98119. Phone: (206) 285-2295. Fax: (206) 286-2376. Web Site: www.kjram.com. Licensee: AK Media Group Inc. Group owner: Clear Channel Communications Inc. (acq 6-14-02; grpsl). Rep: D & R Radio. Format: Sports. Target aud: 25-54. ♦Michelle Grosnick, VP & gen mgr; Sean Shannon, sls dir & adv mgr; Gus Swanson, mktg dir; Gina Gray, prom dir; Rich Moore, progmg dir; Tom Benton, pub affrs dir; Doug Irwin, chief of engrg.

KJR-FM— May 25, 1960: 95.7 mhz; 100 kw. 1,150 ft. TL: N47 32 41 W122 06 28. Stereo. Phone: (206) 494-2000. Web Site: www.957kjrfm.com. Format: Classic hits. Target aud: 30-44. ♦Rick Carter, gen sls mgr; Valerie Koch, prom dir; Bob Case, progmg dir; Stephen Kilbreath, mus dir & news dir.

KKDZ(AM)— May 15 1993: 1250 khz; 5 kw-U, DA-N. TL: N47 33 41 W122 21 34. 200 First Ave. W., Suite 104 98119. Phone: (206) 281-5300. Fax: (206) 281-8881. Web Site: www.radiodisney.com. Licensee: WMAL Inc. Group owner: ABC Inc. (acq 1-21-98; $1.2 million). Format: Children's. News staff: 5. Target aud: Kids 6-14; Moms 25-49. ♦Bob Nordberg, gen mgr; Laura Dunham, prom mgr.

KKNW(AM)—Listing follows KWJZ(FM).

KKOL(AM)— 1922: 1300 khz; 5 kw-U, DA-N. TL: N47 35 09 W122 20 56. 2815 2nd Ave., Suite 550 98121. Phone: (206) 443-8200. Fax: (206) 777-1133. Licensee: Inspiration Media Inc. Group owner: Salem Communications Corp. (acq 4-17-97; $2 million). Rep: Salem. Format: News/talk. Target aud: 35 plus; men & women. ♦David Fitts, gen mgr;

Developers & Brokers of Radio Properties
contact American Media Services
at our suite:
Philadelphia Marriott Downtown
215-625-2900
843-972-2200
americanmediaservices.com
Charleston, SC
Dallas, TX - Chicago, Il - Austin, TX
American Media Services, LLC

Charles Olmstead, opns dir; Bill Montgomery, gen sls mgr; Lyn-Felice Calvin, prom mgr; Chuck Olmstead, progmg dir & progmg mgr; Monte Passmore, chief of engrg.

KLFE(AM)— Sept 10, 1956: 1590 khz; 5 kw-U, DA-N. TL: N47 39 19 W122 31 06. 2815 2nd Ave., Suite 550 98121. Phone: (206) 443-8200. Fax: (206) 777-1133. Licensee: Inspiration Media Inc. Group owner: Salem Communications Corp. (acq 1994; $500,000). Rep: Salem. Format: Christian talk. Target aud: 25-54. Spec prog: Ethiopian 2 hrs, Russian 12 hrs, Saimoan 4 hrs wkly. ♦David Fitts, gen mgr; Charles A. Olmstead, opns mgr & progmg mgr; Bill Montgomery, natl sls mgr & prom dir; Lyn-Felice Calvin, prom mgr; Monte Passmore, chief of engrg.

KLSY-FM—See Bellevue

KMPS-FM— July 8, 1961: 94.1 mhz; 57 kw. 2,342 ft. TL: N47 30 14 W121 58 29. Stereo. Box 24888 98124. Secondary address: 1000 Dexter Ave., N., Suite 100 98109. Phone: (206) 805-1100. Fax: (206) 805-0911. E-mail: email@kmps.com. Web Site: www.kmps.com. Licensee: Infinity Radio Holdings Inc. Group owner: Infinity Broadcasting Corp. (acq 11-13-98; grpsl). Format: Country. Target aud: General. ♦Dave McDonald, gen mgr; Becky Brenner, opns mgr & progmg dir; Rod Krebs, gen sls mgr; Judi Yazzolino, natl sls mgr; Apryl Battin, prom dir; Tony Thomas, mus dir; Don Riggs, news dir; Tom McGinley, chief of engrg.

KMTT(FM)—(Tacoma). June 2, 1958: 103.7 mhz; 58 kw. 2,343 ft. TL: N47 30 14 W121 58 29. Stereo. 1100 Olive Way, Suite 1650 98101-1827. Phone: (206) 233-1037. Fax: (206) 233-8979. E-mail: studio@kmtt.com. Web Site: www.kmtt.com. Licensee: Entercom Seattle License L.L.C. Group owner: Entercom Communications Corp. (acq 6-73; with co-located AM). Rep: D & R Radio. Format: AAA. News staff: one; News: 3 hrs wkly. Target aud: 25-49. ♦Joseph M. Field, pres; Kevin McCarthy, VP & gen mgr; Chris Mays, stn mgr & progmg dir; Blaine Shepherd, gen sls mgr; Erron Sorenson, mktg mgr; Jennifer Orr, prom dir; Shawn Stewart, mus dir; Lauren Daniels, news dir; Marty Hadfield, engrg dir; Stephen Dimitroff, chief of engrg.

KNDD(FM)— Mar 9, 1985: 107.7 mhz; 100 kw. 1,194 ft. TL: N47 32 35 W122 06 25. (CP: 57.3 kw, ant 2,342 ft.). Stereo. 1100 Olive Way, Suite 1650 98101. Phone: (206) 622-3251. Fax: (206) 682-8349. Web Site: www.1077theend.com. Licensee: Entercom Seattle License L.L.C. Group owner: Entercom Communications Corp. (acq 1996). Rep: D & R Radio. Format: Alternative. News staff: one. Target aud: 18-34; well educated active adults. ♦Steve Oshin, CEO; Joseph M. Field, pres; Steve Fisher, CFO; Kevin McCarthy, VP & gen mgr; Jim Keller, sls dir & news dir; Ron Steinman, sls dir; Dan O'Shea, natl sls mgr; Erron Sorensen, mktg dir; Katie Moreland, prom dir; Phil Manning, progmg dir; Andrew Harms, mus dir; Stephen Dimitroff, chief of engrg.

***KNHC(FM)**— Jan 25, 1971: 89.5 mhz; 8.5 kw. Ant 1,220 ft. TL: N47 32 35 W122 06 25. Stereo. 10750 30th Ave. N.E., Suite 219 98125. Phone: (206) 252-3800. Phone: (206) 421-8989. Fax: (206) 252-3805. E-mail: info@c895fm.com. Web Site: www.c895fm.com. Licensee: Seattle Public Schools. Wilmer, Cutler & Pickering. Format: CHR, educ. News: 9 hrs wkly. Target aud: 18-34; male & female. Spec prog: Black, gospel 6 hrs, gothic/industrial 6 hrs wkly. ♦Gregg Neilson, gen mgr; Judy Rudow, opns mgr & gen sls mgr; Jon McDaniel, progmg dir.

KOMO(AM)— 1926: 1000 khz; 50 kw-U, DA-N. TL: N47 27 54 W122 26 27. 140 4th Ave. N. 98109. Phone: (206) 404-4000. Fax: (206) 404-3646. E-mail: comments@KOMO1000news.com. Web Site: www.KOMO1000news.com. Licensee: Fisher Broadcasting - Seattle Radio L.L.C. Group owner: Fisher Broadcasting Company (acq 12-5-01; grpsl). Network: ABC. Format: News. News staff: 9; News: 11 hrs wkly. Target aud: 25-54. Spec prog: Seattle Mariners. ♦Rob Dunlop, gen mgr; Joe Heslet, gen sls mgr; Gary Greenberg, natl sls mgr; Kari Jean Korsgren, prom dir; Dennis Kelly, progmg dir & news dir; Kelly Alford, engrg mgr. Co-owned TV: KOMO-TV affil.

KPLZ(FM)— Sept 1, 1959: 101.5 mhz; 100 kw. 1,150 ft. TL: N47 32 42 W122 06 29. Stereo. Fisher Plaza, 140 Fourth Ave. N., Suite 340 98109. Phone: (206) 404-4000. Fax: (206) 404-3644. Web Site: www.star1015.com. Licensee: Fisher Broadcasting - Seattle Radio L.L.C. Group owner: Fisher Broadcasting Company (acq 12-5-01; grpsl). Format: Adult contemp. Target aud: 18-44; women. ♦Rob Dunlop, gen mgr; Kerie Swetson, opns mgr & gen sls mgr; Bryce Phillippy, gen sls mgr & natl sls mgr; Jennifer Pirak, prom dir; Kent Phillips, progmg dir; Leonard Barokas, news dir; Kelly Alfred, chief of engrg.

KVI(AM)—Co-owned with KPLZ(FM). 1929: 570 khz; 5 kw-U. TL: N47 25 19 W122 25 44. Phone: (206) 404-3648. Web Site: www.570kvi.com. Network: ABC. Format: Talk. Target aud: 25-54. ♦John Sandzig, gen sls mgr; Alyson Soma, prom mgr; Paul Duckworth, progmg dir.

KPTK(AM)— 1927: 1090 khz; 50 kw-U, DA-2. TL: N47 23 38 W122 25 25. 1000 Dexter Ave. N., Suite 100 98109. Phone: (206) 805-1090. Fax: (206) 805-0911. Web Site: www.am1090seattle.com. Licensee: Infinity Radio Holdings Inc. Group owner: Infinity Broadcasting Corp. (acq 11-13-98; grpsl). Format: Progressive talk. ♦Dave McDonald, gen mgr; Rod Krebs, sls dir; Jim Trapp, progmg dir; Tom McGinley, chief of engrg.

KQBZ(FM)— 1946: 100.7 mhz; 57 kw horiz, 52 kw vert. 2,342 ft. TL: N47 30 14 W121 58 29. Stereo. 1100 Olive Way, Suite 1650 98101. Phone: (206) 285-7625. Fax: (206) 381-0997. Web Site: www.1007thebuzz.com. Licensee: Entercom Seattle License LLC. Group owner: Entercom Communications Corp. Format: News/talk. News: 15 hrs wkly. Target aud: 18-34; men who like entertaining talk. ♦Joseph M. Field, pres; Kevin McCarthy, VP & gen mgr; Chris Mays, stn mgr; Melissa Forrest, opns mgr; Ann Marie Mulholland, gen sls mgr; Kerri Lewis, prom dir; Dave Richards, progmg dir; Liz Sommers, news dir; Stephen Dimitroff, chief of engrg.

KTFH(AM)— Mar 31, 2003: 1680 khz; 10 kw-D, 1 kw-N. TL: N47 39 20 W122 31 05. 2815 2nd Ave., Suite 550 98121. Phone: (206) 443-8200. Fax: (206) 777-1133. Licensee: Inspiration Media Inc. Group owner: Salem Communications Corp. Format: Multi-cultural. ♦David Fitts, gen mgr; Charles Olmstead, opns dir & progmg dir.

KTTH(AM)— 1925: 770 khz; 50 kw-D, 5 kw-N, DA-2. TL: N47 23 38 W122 25 25. 1820 Eastlake Ave. E. 98102-3711. Phone: (206) 726-7000. Fax: (206) 726-5446. Licensee: Entercom Seattle License LLC. Group owner: Entercom Communications Corp. (acq 3-6-97; grpsl). Network: ABC Daytime Direction. Fletcher, Heald & Hildreth. Format: News. News staff: 6. Target aud: 25-54; adults. ♦David Pridemore, gen mgr; Ken Berry, stn mgr.

KUBE(FM)— May 6, 1964: 93.3 mhz; 100 kw. 1,291 ft. TL: N47 32 39 W122 06 29. Stereo. 351 Elliott Ave. W. #300 98119. Phone: (206) 285-2295. Fax: (206) 286-2376. Web Site: www.kube93.com. Licensee: Clear Channel Radio Licenses Inc. Group owner: Clear Channel Communications Inc. (acq 6-14-02; grpsl). Format: Rythmic dance, CHR. ♦Michele Grosenick, pres & gen mgr; Shellie Hart, opns mgr; Alison Hesse, sls dir & progmg dir; Gus Swanson, mktg dir; Jen Dalton, prom dir; Eric Powers, progmg dir; Karen Wild, mus dir; Stephen Kilbreath, news dir; Doug Irwin, chief of engrg; John Miller, chief of engrg.

***KUOW(FM)**— Jan 16, 1952: 94.9 mhz; 100 kw. 730 ft. TL: N47 36 58 W122 18 28. Stereo. 4518 University Way N.E., Suite 310 98105. Phone: (206) 543-2710. Fax: (206) 616-9125. E-mail: letters@kuow.org. Web Site: www.kuow.org. Licensee: University of Washington. Network: Network: NPR, PRI. Ernest Sanchez. Format: News, info. News staff: 15; News: 60 hrs wkly. Target aud: 25-54; highly educated, influential,decision makers. Spec prog: Sp 2 hrs, jazz 5 hrs wkly. ♦Wayne Roth, gen mgr; Dane Johnson, opns dir; Marcia Scholl, dev dir; John Hill, rgnl sls mgr; Jeff Hansen, progmg dir; Guy Nelson, news dir; Terry Denbrook, chief of engrg.

KWJZ(FM)— Nov 1, 1954: 98.9 mhz; 100 kw. 1,110 ft. TL: N47 32 41 W122 06 28. (CP: 58 kw, ant 2,342 ft. TL: N47 30 14 W121 58 29). Stereo. 3650 131st Ave. S.E., Suite 550, Bellevue 98006. Phone: (425) 373-5536. Fax: (425) 653-1133. Web Site: www.kwjz.com. Licensee: Orca Radio Inc. Group owner: Sandusky Radio (acq 1996; $26 million with co-located AM). Network: Network: Westwood One, ABC Information & Entertainment. Rep: Christal. Wiley, Rein & Fielding. Format: Smooth jazz, new adult contemp. News staff: 2; News: 9 hrs wkly. Target aud: 25-54; younger active, mid to upper income adults. ♦Marc Kaye, gen mgr; Susan Hoffman, sls dir; Ann Marie Mulholland, gen sls mgr; Cindy Gilsdorf, mktg dir & prom dir; Carol Handley, progmg mgr; Dianna Rose, mus dir; George Bisso, chief of engrg.

KKNW(AM)—Co-owned with KWJZ(FM). 1926: 1150 khz; 10 kw-U, DA-N. TL: N47 35 11 W122 11 11. Fax: (425) 373-5507. Web Site: www.newschannel1150.com. Format: News/talk. News staff: one; News: 10 hrs wkly. Target aud: 35-64; active, well educated adults with middle to upper income. Spec prog: Loc sports 15 hrs, Russian 5 hrs wkly. ♦Eric Burris, opns mgr & progmg dir; Erik Krema, stn mgr & gen sls mgr.

KZOK-FM— December 1964: 102.5 mhz; 100 kw. 1,170 ft. TL: N47 32 35 W122 06 25. (CP: 58 kw, ant 2,342 ft.). Stereo. 1000 Dexter Ave. N., Suite 100 98109. Phone: (206) 805-1100. Fax: (206) 441-1411. Web Site: www.kzok.com. Licensee: Infinity Radio Holdings Inc. Group owner: Infinity Broadcasting Corp. (acq 11-13-98; grpsl). Format: Classic rock. Target aud: 25-49; adults with a primary, men. ♦Carey Curelop, gen mgr & opns mgr; Dave McDonald, pres & gen mgr.

Selah

KBBO(AM)—Licensed to Selah. See Yakima

Shelton

KMAS(AM)— Sept 21, 1962: 1030 khz; 10 kw-D, 1 kw-N. TL: N47 13 17 W123 04 46. Box 760, 210 W. Cota St. 98584. Phone: (360) 426-1030. Fax: (360) 427-5268. E-mail: kmas@kmas.com. Web Site: www.kmas.com. Licensee: Sound Broadcasting Inc. (acq 4-1-87). Network: ABC Information & Entertainment. Tacher. Format: Adult contemp. News staff: 2; News: 20 hrs wkly. Target aud: 25-64. Spec prog: Sp 2.5 hrs, Christian 4 hrs wkly. ♦Harold S. Greenberg, pres, gen mgr & gen sls mgr; Marian Greenberg, VP & pub affrs dir; Steve George, progmg dir; Mike Hanna, mus dir; Dedrick Allan, news dir; Tom Trotzer, chief of engrg.

KRXY(FM)— October 1998: 94.5 mhz; 710 w. 954 ft. TL: N47 08 18 W123 08 28. 2124 Pacific Ave. S.E., Olympia 98506-4753. Phone: (360) 236-1010. Fax: (360) 236-1133. E-mail: krxy@krxy.com. Web Site: www.krxy.com. Licensee: Premier Broadcasters Inc. Group owner: Premier Group Rep: Allied Radio Partners. Leventhal, Senter, Lerman. Format: Top-40, Hits of the 80s & 90s. ♦Derek Shannon, gen mgr; Bob Hart, gen sls mgr & progmg dir; Matt Shannon, mus dir; Paul Walker, news dir; Rod Etherton, chief of engrg.

Silverdale

KITZ(AM)— Oct 26, 1948: 1400 khz; 1 kw-D, 890 w-N. TL: N47 37 45 W122 39 52. 1700 Mile Hill Dr., Suite 201A, Port Orchard 98366. Phone: (360) 876-1400. Fax: (360) 876-7920. E-mail: info@kittz1400.com. Web Site: kitz1400.com. Licensee: KITZ Radio Inc. (acq 12-8-2000; $500,000. for 60%). Network: Westwood One. Pepper & Corazzini. Format: Megatalk. Target aud: 35-64; adults 25+. ♦Alan Gottlieb, chmn & pres; Paul Lyle, gen mgr; Kevin Corcoran, opns VP; Chris Van Dyk, sls VP; Nicole Englestad, prom dir; Jerry Hill, engrg dir.

South Bend

KJET(FM)— July 1999: 105.7 mhz; 14 kw. 950 ft. TL: N46 41 44 W123 46 17. Stereo. Box 1198, Aberdeen 98520. Secondary address: 1520 Simpson Ave., Aberdeen 98520. Phone: (360) 538-3000. Fax: (360) 532-1456. E-mail: info@jodesha.com. Web Site: www.jodesha.com. Licensee: Jodesha Broadcasting Inc. (group owner) Network: ABC. Rep: Tacher. David Tillotson. Format: Adult top-40. News: 7 hrs wkly. Target aud: 18-49. ♦William J. Wolfenbarger, pres & gen mgr; Gabrielle Jordan, opns mgr.

Spokane

***KAGU(FM)**— Mar 16, 1988: 88.7 mhz; 100 w. -141 ft. TL: N47 40 06 W117 24 05. Stereo. 502 E. Boone Ave. 99258. Phone: (509)

Broadcasting & Cable Yearbook 2006

D-537

328-4220. Fax: (509) 324-5718. Web Site: www.gonzaga.edu/kagu/. Licensee: Gonzaga University Telecommunications Association. (acq 12-4-91). Format: Adult contemp. Spec prog: Class 2 hrs, jazz 2 hrs, folk 2 hrs, drama 2 hrs wkly. ♦Fr. Robert Lyons, gen mgr; Matt Caputo, prom dir.

KBBD(FM)— 1988: 103.9 mhz; 5.5 kw. Ant 1,417 ft. TL: N47 36 04 W117 17 53. Stereo. 1601 E. 57th 99223. Phone: (509) 448-1000. Fax: (509) 448-7015. Web Site: www.wild1039.com. Licensee: Citadel Broadcasting Co. Group owner: Citadel Broadcasting Corp. (acq 1999; $4.15 million). Network: ABC. Pepper & Corazzini. Format: Hip Hop. Target aud: 18-34. ♦Jim Votaw, gen mgr; Steve Kicklighter, gen mgr & progmg dir; Tim Cotter, opns mgr; Christa McDonald, gen sls mgr; Joe Chabala, prom dir; Chuck Wright, mus dir; Dave Ratener, chief of engrg.

KCDA(FM)—(Post Falls).ID June 29, 1979: 103.1 mhz; 9.4 kw. 2,450 ft. TL: N47 34 14 W117 04 55. Stereo. 808 E. Sprague 99202. Phone: (509) 242-2400. Fax: (509) 448-4043. Web Site: www.mix1031.com. Licensee: Capstar TX L.P. Group owner: Clear Channel Communications Inc. (acq 10-18-00; $4.7 million). Rep: Roslin. Pepper & Corazzini. Format: Alternative music. News staff: 2; News: one hr wkly. Target aud: 25-54; active & affluent. ♦Kosta Panidis, gen mgr.

KDRK-FM—Listing follows KGA(AM).

***KEEH(FM)**— July 1, 1991: 104.9 mhz; 10.5 kw. Ant 1,548 ft. TL: N47 34 45 W117 17 51. Stereo. Box 19039 99219. Secondary address: 3715 S. Grove Rd. 99219. Phone: (509) 456-4870. Fax: (509) 838-4882. E-mail: keeh@plr.org. Web Site: www.plr.org. Licensee: Upper Columbia Media Association (acq 9-8-93; $148,000;. FTR: 10-4-93). Network: USA. Format: Christian. Target aud: General. ♦John Dolrymple, gen mgr.

KEYF-FM—See Cheney

KEZE(FM)— Dec 25, 1992: 96.9 mhz; 6 kw. 535 ft. TL: N47 41 39 W117 20 03. 500 W. Boone Ave. 99201. Phone: (509) 324-4000. Fax: (509) 324-8992. Web Site: www.star969.com. Licensee: QueenB Radio Inc. Group owner: Morgan Murphy Stations. Network: USA. Rep: Katz Radio. Format: Hits of the 80s & 90s. Target aud: 25 plus; general. ♦Elizabeth M. Burns, pres; Steve Herling, exec VP; Chris Garros, VP; Chris Garras, gen mgr; Teddie Gibbon, stn mgr; Ken Hopkins, opns mgr; Tery Garras, sls dir; Ken Richards, progmg dir.

KGA(AM)— 1926: 1510 khz; 50 kw-U, DA-N. TL: N47 35 44 W117 22 15. Box 30013 99223-3000. Secondary address: E. 1601 57th St. 99223. Phone: (509) 448-1000. Fax: (509) 448-7015. Web Site: www.1510kga.com. Licensee: Citadel Broadcasting Co. Group owner: Citadel Broadcasting Corp. (acq 5-18-92; grpsl, including co-located FM; FTR: 6-8-92). Format: News/talk. News staff: 3; News: 183 hrs wkly. Target aud: 25-54; general. Spec prog: Farm one hr wkly. ♦Christa McDonald, gen mgr & gen sls mgr; Ray Edwards, gen mgr; Chuck DeBruin, progmg dir; Ken Broeffle, chief of engrg.

KDRK-FM—Co-owned with KGA(AM). 1965: 93.7 mhz; 60 kw. Ant 2,424 ft. TL: N47 34 14 W117 04 55. Stereo. Web Site: www.catcountry94.com. Format: Country. ♦Toby Howell, prom dir; Tony Trovato, progmg dir. Co-owned TV: KHQ-TV affil

KISC(FM)—Listing follows KQNT(AM).

KJRB(AM)— 1947: 790 khz; 5 kw-U, DA-N. TL: N47 36 16 W117 23 11. Box 30013 99223. Secondary address: E. 1601 57th 99223. Phone: (509) 448-1000. Fax: (509) 448-7015. Web Site: www.790kfan.com. Licensee: Citadel Broadcasting Co. Group owner: Citadel Broadcasting Corp. (acq 9-20-93; $125,000;. FTR: 10-11-93). Format: Sports, talk. News staff: one; News: 168 hrs wkly. Target aud: 25-54. Spec prog: GSL football & basketball, North Idaho Vandals football & basketball, Bloomsday. ♦Christa McDonald, gen mgr, opns mgr & gen sls mgr; Ray Edwards, gen mgr; Toby Howell, prom dir & progmg dir; Chuck DeBruin, news dir; Ken Broeffle, engrg mgr & chief of engrg.

KZBD(FM)—Co-owned with KJRB(AM). Nov 8, 1965: 105.7 mhz; 100 kw. 1,910 ft. TL: N47 34 44 W117 17 46. Stereo. Web Site: www.1057thebuzzard.com. (Acq 3-22-93; $2.75 million. with co-located AM; FTR: 4-12-93). Network: ABC. Format: Classic rock. ♦Victoria Frederick, progmg dir.

KKZX(FM)—Listing follows KPTQ(AM).

***KMBI-FM**— July 1, 1974: 107.9 mhz; 64 kw. 2,380 ft. TL: N47 34 15 W117 05 00. Stereo. 5408 S. Freya St. 99223. Phone: (509) 448-2555. Fax: (509) 448-6855. E-mail: kmbi@moody.edu. Web Site: www.kmbi.org. Licensee: Moody Bible Institute. Group owner: The Moody Bible Institute of Chicago Southmayd & Miller. Format: Relg. News: 9 hrs wkly. Target aud: 35-54; Christian men & women. ♦Rich Monteith, gen mgr, stn mgr & opns mgr; Gordon Canaday, chief of engrg.

KMBI(AM)— July 12, 1959: 1330 khz; 5 kw-D. TL: N47 36 17 W117 21 27. (Acq 6-74). News: 6 hrs wkly. Target aud: 35-54; Christian men & women. ♦D. Gary Leonard, stn mgr; Steve Stewart, pub affrs dir.

***KPBX-FM**— 1970: 91.1 mhz; 56 kw. 2,380 ft. TL: N47 34 13 W117 05 00. Stereo. 2319 N. Monroe St. 99205. Phone: (509) 328-5729. Fax: (509) 328-5764. E-mail: rkunkel@kpbx.org. Web Site: www.kpbx.org. Licensee: Spokane Public Radio Inc. Network: Network: NPR, PRI. Format: Class, news, jazz. News staff: 3; News: 50 hrs wkly. Target aud: General; educated. Spec prog: Jazz, folk, world mus, new age/space, new mus. ♦Richard Kunkel, CEO, pres & gen mgr; Brian Flick, opns dir; Kathy Sackett, sls dir; Jancan Jorgenson, mktg dir; Janean Jorgenson, prom dir; Verne Windham, progmg dir & mus dir; Doug Nadvornick, news dir & pub affrs dir; Jerry Olson, chief of engrg.

KPTQ(AM)— 1965: 1280 khz; 5 kw-D, DA. TL: N47 36 27 W117 21 40. 808 E. Sprague Ave. 99202. Phone: (509) 242-2400. Fax: (509) 242-2581. Web Site: www.kaqq1280.com. Licensee: Capstar TX L.P. Group owner: Clear Channel Communications Inc. (acq 8-30-2000; grpsl). Network: USA. Rep: D & R Radio. Tacher. Arent, Fox, Kintner, Plotkin & Kahn. Format: Progressive talk. News: one hr wkly. Target aud: General. ♦Garth Trimble, gen sls mgr; Kosta Panidis, gen mgr & gen sls mgr; Barry Watkins, progmg dir.

KKZX(FM)—Co-owned with KPTQ(AM). Oct 10, 1975: 98.9 mhz; 100 kw. 1,614 ft. TL: N47 35 35 W117 17 46. Stereo. Web Site: www.kkzx.com. Format: Classic rock. News: one hr wkly. Target aud: 25-54. Spec prog: Blues 2 hrs wkly. ♦Jon McGann, progmg dir.

KQNT(AM)— 1922: 590 khz; 5 kw-U. TL: N47 36 59 W117 22 12. 808 E. Spague Ave. 99202. Phone: (509) 242-2400. Fax: (509) 242-2581. Web Site: www.newstalk590.com. Licensee: Capstar TX L.P. Group owner: Clear Channel Communications Inc. (acq 8-30-00; grpsl). Rep: Allied Radio Partners. Fisher, Wayland, Cooper, Leader & Zaragoza L.L.P. Format: News/talk. Target aud: 35-64. Spec prog: Farm 6 hrs wkly. ♦Garth Trimble, gen sls mgr; Kosta Panidis, gen mgr & gen sls mgr; Jerry Jensen, natl sls mgr; Joe Chabala, prom dir; Dean Allen, progmg dir; Harv Clark, news dir; Kent Abendroth, chief of engrg.

KISC(FM)—Co-owned with KQNT(AM). May 1, 1966: 98.1 mhz; 94 kw. 2,030 ft. TL: N47 34 53 W117 17 47. Stereo. Web Site: www.literockkiss.com. Format: Adult contemp. ♦Rob Harder, progmg dir.

KSBN(AM)— September 1921: 1230 khz; 1 kw-U. TL: N47 39 30 W117 25 08. 506 W. 1st Ave. 99201. Phone: (509) 838-4000. Fax: (509) 838-4800. E-mail: ksbn@ksbn.net. Web Site: www.ksbn.net. Licensee: KSBN Radio Inc. (acq 6-95). Format: Business, financial, talk, news. News staff: one; News: 24 hrs wkly. Target aud: 30-65; upscale; business owners. ♦Alan Gottlieb, chmn; Angela Watkins, gen mgr; Patrick Carey, gen sls mgr; Bradley Kemmer, progmg mgr & news dir; Conrad Agte, chief of engrg.

***KSFC(FM)**— March 1973: 91.9 mhz; 100 w. 92 ft. TL: N47 40 37 W117 27 31. 2319 N. Monroe St. 99205. Phone: (509) 328-5729. Fax: (509) 328-5764. E-mail: rkunkel@kpbx.org. Web Site: www.ksfc.org. Licensee: Spokane Public Radio Inc. Format: News. Target aud: Curious. Spec prog: American Indian 5 hrs, black 2 hrs wkly. ♦Richard Kunkel, pres & gen mgr; Doug Nadvornick, progmg dir & news dir; Jerry Olson, engrg dir & chief of engrg.

KTRW(AM)— 1947: 970 khz; 5 kw-D, 1 kw-N, DA-N. TL: N47 36 59 W117 21 55. Box 31000 99223. Phone: (509) 443-1000. Fax: (509) 448-3811. E-mail: acn@qwest.net. Licensee: Sacred Heart Radio Inc. (acq 9-7-2005;. $850,000). Format: Relg. Target aud: 25-54. ♦Joe Spinelli, gen mgr; George Kessler, gen sls mgr; Mike Ellis, prom mgr; Dave Spencer, progmg mgr; Tim Anderson, chief of engrg.

***KWRS(FM)**— Sept 16, 1991: 90.3 mhz; 10 w. -89 ft. TL: N47 45 30 W117 25 00. Stereo. Stn 40, Whitworth College 99251. Phone: (509) 777-4575. Fax: (509) 777-3710. E-mail: kwrsuc@mail.witworth.edu. Web Site: www.whitworth.edu/kwrs. Licensee: Whitworth College. Format: CHR, progsv, rock/AOR. News staff: one; News: 2 hrs wkly. Target aud: 15-35; mostly college & high school students. Spec prog: Black 12 hrs, folk 8 hrs, relg 4 hrs, Sp 2 hrs wkly. ♦Katie Thompson, gen mgr; Sara Edlin-Marlowe, stn mgr.

KXLY(AM)— October 1922: 920 khz; 5 kw-U. TL: N47 36 30 W117 22 25. W. 500 Boone Ave. 99201. Phone: (509) 324-4000. Fax: (509) 324-8992. E-mail: kxly@kyly920.com. Web Site: www.kxly.com. Licensee: Spokane Radio Inc. Group owner: Morgan Murphy Stations (acq 3-21-62). Network: Network: Network: CBS, Wall Street, ABC News/Talk. Rep: Katz Radio. Format: News/talk. News staff: 25; News: 30 hrs wkly. Target aud: Adults 35 plus; upper end education & income levels. Spec prog: Sports talk 5 hrs, sports play-by-play 20 hrs, local talk 15 hrs wkly. ♦Stephen R. Herling, VP; Chris Garras, gen mgr; Teddie Gibbon, stn mgr; Roger Nelson, opns mgr & sls dir; Dick Brantley, rgnl sls mgr & mktg dir; Gina Mauro, prom dir.

KXLY-FM— September 1959: 99.9 mhz; 37 kw. 2,998 ft. TL: N47 55 18 W117 06 48. Stereo. Fax: (509) 324-8992. E-mail: classy@classy99.cox. Web Site: www.classy99.com. Network: Network: Westwood One, Jones Radio Networks. Rep: Katz Radio. Format: Adult contemp. Target aud: 25-64; adults, upper end income & education levels. ♦Tery Garras, sls dir; Joe Via, rgnl sls mgr. Co-owned TV: KXLY-TV affil.

KZZU-FM— September 1955: 92.9 mhz; 81 kw. 2,080 ft. TL: N47 35 42 W117 17 53. Stereo. 500 W. Boone Ave. 99201. Phone: (509) 324-4000. Fax: (509) 324-8992. Web Site: www.kzzu.com. Licensee: QueenB Radio Inc. Group owner: Morgan Murphy Stations (acq 4-1-96; $1.75 million. with co-located AM). Format: CHR. Target aud: 18-49. ♦Steve Herling, VP; Chris Garras, gen mgr & gen sls mgr; Teddie Gibbon, stn mgr; Brew Michaels, opns dir & progmg dir; George Kessler, natl sls mgr & natl sls mgr; Joe via, rgnl sls mgr; Brian Paul, mktg dir, prom dir & adv dir; Casey Christopher, mus dir; Tim Anderson, chief of engrg. Co-owned TV: KXLY-TV.

Sumner

KZIZ(AM)— 1990: 1560 khz; 5 kw-D. TL: N47 12 48 W122 13 25. Box 22462, Seattle 98122-0462. Secondary address: 2600 S. Jackson St., Seattle 98144. Phone: (206) 323-3070. Fax: (206) 322-6518. E-mail: ztwins@aol.com. Web Site: www.ztwins.com. Licensee: KRIS Bennett Broadcasting Inc. Network: American Urban. Format: Gospel. Target aud: 12 plus; African-American. Spec prog: Relg 18 hrs wkly. ♦Christopher H. Bennett, gen mgr & sls dir; Gloria Bennett, stn mgr; Frank P. Barrow, chief of opns; Jawann Bennett, progmg dir; Terry Denbrook, chief of engrg.

Sunnyside

***KAYB(FM)**— 1998: 88.1 mhz; 250 w. -190 ft. TL: N46 19 53 W120 00 51. Box 3206, Tupelo, MS 38803. Phone: (662) 844-8888. Fax: (662) 842-6791. E-mail: comments@afr.net. Web Site: www.afr.net. Licensee: American Family Association. Group owner: American Family Radio Format: Christian, inspirational. ♦Marvin Sanders, gen mgr.

KZTS(AM)— September 1950: 1210 khz; 10 kw-D, 1 kw-N. TL: N46 19 49 W120 02 10. Box 2888, Yakima 98907. Secondary address: 706 Butterfield Rd., Yakima 98901. Phone: (509) 457-1000. Fax: (509) 452-0541. E-mail: zorro@radiozorro.com. Web Site: www.radiozorro.com. Licensee: Bustos Media of Eastern Washington License LLC. (group owner; (acq 11-18-2004; grpsl). Rep: Tacher. Format: Sp. News staff: one. Target aud: 25-55; Hispanic. ♦Amador S. Bustos, pres; Bob Berry, gen mgr; Keith Teske, opns dir; Martin Ortiz, progmg dir; Earld Clark, news dir.

Tacoma

KBKS-FM— May 1959: 106.1 mhz; 55 kw. 699 ft. TL: N47 18 15 W122 23 44. Stereo. 1000 Dexter Ave. N., Suite 100, Seattle 98109. Phone: (206) 805-1061. Fax: (206) 805-0920. Web Site: www.kiss1061radio.com. Licensee: Infinity Radio Holdings Inc. Group owner: Infinity Broadcasting Corp. (acq 11-13-98; grpsl). Leventhal, Senter & Lerman. Format: CHR. Target aud: 25-54. ♦Dave McDonald, sr VP, gen mgr & opns mgr; Bill Sigmar, gen sls mgr; Judi Yazzolino, natl sls mgr; Gina Thompson, prom dir; Mike Preston, progmg dir; Paul Anthony, mus dir; Allan Hines, news dir; Arne Skoog, chief of engrg.

KBSG-FM— Oct 26, 1948: 97.3 mhz; 52 kw. 2,391 ft. TL: N47 30 14 W121 58 29. Stereo. 1820 Eastlake Ave. E., Seattle 98102-3711. Phone: (206) 343-9700. Fax: (206) 623-7677. E-mail: kbsg@kbsg.com. Web Site: www.kbsg.com. Licensee: Entercom Seattle License L.L.C. Group owner: Entercom Communications Corp. Rep: D & R Radio. Format: Oldies. News staff: one. Target aud: 25-54. ♦Joseph M. Field,

Stations in the U.S. Washington

Developers & Brokers of Radio Properties

contact American Media Services at our suite:
Philadelphia Marriott Downtown
215-625-2900
843-972-2200
americanmediaservices.com
Charleston, SC
Dallas, TX · Chicago, Il · Austin, TX

American Media Services, LLC

CEO; Steve Fisher, CFO; Kevin McCarthy, VP; Mark Pitts, gen mgr; David Pridemore, sls dir; Andre Riley, gen sls mgr; Kathy Cangiano, mktg dir; Cheryl Rodriguez, prom dir; Jay Kelly, progmg dir; Tom Pierson, chief of engrg.

KGTK(AM)—(Olympia). October 1956: 920 khz; 3 kw-D, 7 w-N. TL: N47 03 44 W122 49 49. Stereo. 12500 N.E. Tenth Pl., Bellevue 98005. Secondary address: 1700 Mile High Dr., Suite 201A, Port Orchard 98366. Phone: (360) 876-1400. Fax: (360) 876-7920. Licensee: KITZ Radio Inc. (acq 4-30-2004; $300,000). Network: USA. Format: Talk. News: 7 hrs wkly. Target aud: 18-65; diversified adults. ♦ Alan Gottlieb, pres; Julie Versnel, VP; Kevin Corcoran, gen mgr & progmg dir.

KHHO(AM)—Licensed to Tacoma. See Seattle

KKMO(AM)— 1922: 1360 khz; 5 kw-U. TL: N47 18 19 W122 26 33. 2815 2nd Ave., Suite 550, Seattle 98121. Phone: (206) 443-8200. Fax: (206) 443-1561. E-mail: reception@inspirationradio.com. Web Site: www.kgnw.com. Licensee: Inspiration Media Inc. Group owner: Salem Communications Corp. (acq 8-12-98; $500,000). Format: Sp talk and music. Target aud: 35 plus. ♦ David Fitts, gen mgr; Chuck Olmstead, opns dir, opns mgr, progmg dir & progmg mgr; Violetta Strash, gen sls mgr; Luciana Bosio, prom mgr; Jaime Mendez, progmg mgr; Monte Passmore, chief of engrg.

KLAY(AM)—(Lakewood). 1991: 1180 khz; 5 kw-D, 1 kw-N, DA-N. TL: N47 09 00 W122 24 38. 10025 Lakewood Dr. S.W., Suite B 98499. Phone: (253) 581-0324. Fax: (253) 581-0326. E-mail: klay11800@qwest.net. Web Site: www.klay1180.com. Licensee: Clay Frank Huntington. Format: Talk. News staff: 4; News: 11 hrs wkly. Target aud: 30-65. ♦Clay Frank Huntington, pres; Evan Brown, opns dir & pub affrs dir; Bob McCluskey, sls VP; Walker Mattson, progmg VP; Lynn Benson, news dir; Nick Winter, engrg dir.

KMTT(FM)—Licensed to Tacoma. See Seattle

KNTB(AM)—(Lakewood). September 1978: 1480 khz; 1 kw-D, 111 w-N, DA-2. TL: N47 09 56 W122 34 32. 4301 S. Pine St. #30 98409. Phone: (253) 476-5944. Licensee: Seattle Streaming Radio LLC. (acq 7-22-2005; $900,000 with KBRO(AM) Bremerton). Format: Hits of the 60s, 70s & 80s. ♦ Chris Hanley, gen mgr.

*KPLU-FM— November 1966: 88.5 mhz; 58 kw. 2,356 ft. TL: N47 28 50 W122 31 58. Stereo. 12180 Park Ave. S. 98447-0885. Secondary address: 2601 4th Ave., Suite 150, Seattle 98121. Phone: (253) 535-7758. Fax: (253) 535-8332. E-mail: kplu@plu.edu. Web Site: www.kplu.org. Licensee: Pacific Lutheran University. Network: Network: NPR, PRI. Dow, Lohnes & Albertson. Format: Jazz, news. News staff: 9; News: 54 hrs wkly. Target aud: 25-54; upscale, highly educated professionals. Spec prog: Blues 12 hrs, car talk 2 hrs wkly. ♦ Martin J. Neeb, gen mgr; Kerry A. Swanson, opns dir & dev dir; Kay Steik, sls dir; Kirk Nelson, rgnl sls mgr; Joe Cohn, progmg dir; Nick Morrison, mus dir; Erin Hennessey, news dir; Lowell Kiesow, chief of engrg.

*KUPS(FM)— Feb 28, 1978: 90.1 mhz; 100 w. 65 ft. TL: N47 15 48 W122 28 37. Stereo. 1500 N. Warner 98416. Phone: (253) 879-3288. Fax: (253) 879-3147. E-mail: thesound@ups.edu. Web Site: kups.ups.edu. Licensee: University of Puget Sound. Format: Progsv. News staff: one; News: 7 hrs wkly. Target aud: 18-45. Spec prog: Black 18 hrs, jazz 12 hrs, reggae 6 hrs, world mus 4 hrs, blues 6 hrs, metal 8 hrs wkly. ♦ Ryan Cunningham, gen mgr; Adam Gehrke, chief of opns.

*KVTI(FM)— Nov 15, 1955: 90.9 mhz; 51 kw. 364 ft. TL: N47 09 39 W122 34 35. Stereo. 4500 Steilacoom Blvd. S.W., Lakewood 98499-4098. Phone: (253) 589-5884. Fax: (253) 589-5797. E-mail: i-91fm@mail.cptc.edu. Web Site: www.i91.ctc.edu. Licensee: Clover Park Technical College. Garvey, Shubert & Barer. Format: CHR, Top-40. News: 2 hrs wkly. Target aud: 12-34; young adults & teens. Spec prog: Live mus 3 hrs, talk 4 hrs wkly. ♦ John L. Mangan, gen mgr & progmg dir; Beth Valiant, mus dir; Al Bednarczyk, chief of engrg.

*KXOT(FM)— June 1, 1949: 91.7 mhz; 7.9 kw. Ant 553 ft. TL: N47 18 15 W122 23 44. Stereo. 113 Dexter Ave. N., Seattle 98109. Phone: (206) 520-5800. Fax: (206) 520-5899. Web Site: www.kexp.org.

Licensee: PRC Tacoma — I LLC (acq 1-31-2005; $5 million). Format: Eclectic alternative. Target aud: . ♦ Tom Mara, gen mgr; Gary Rubin, gen sls mgr; Kevin Cole, progmg dir. Co-owned TV: .

Toppenish

KDBL(FM)— Oct 31, 1977: 92.9 mhz; 17 kw. 843 ft. TL: N46 30 15 W120 23 33. Stereo. 4010 Summitview, Yakima 98908. Phone: (509) 972-3461. Fax: (509) 972-3542. Web Site: www.929thebull.com. Licensee: Citicasters Licenses L.P. Group owner: Clear Channel Communications Inc. (acq 10-26-99; grpsl). Rep: McGavren Guild. Shaw Pittman. Format: Country. News staff: 2. Target aud: 18-49. ♦Gary Donovan, pres & exec VP; Lzrry Miner, gen mgr; Ron Harris, opns mgr; Rick Michaels, progmg dir.

KYNR(AM)— May 16, 1954: 1490 khz; 1 kw-U. TL: N46 22 33 W120 19 18. Box 151 98948-0151. Secondary address: 711 King Ln. 98948. Phone: (509) 865-5363. Fax: (509) 865-2129. E-mail: kyn@yakama.com. Web Site: www.kynr.com. Licensee: Confederated Tribes and Bands of the Yakama Nation (acq 2-9-01; $300,000). Format: Classic rock, Country, Diversified, Jazz, Oldies, News, Sports, Urban contemp. News: one hr wkly. Target aud: 18-58. Spec prog: American Indian 20 hrs wkly. ♦ Ron Washines, gen mgr; Reggie George, progmg dir; John Sodini, engrg mgr.

Tumwater

KVSN(AM)— August 1987: 1340 khz; 1 kw-U. TL: N47 00 25 W122 55 07. 5333 Lambskin St. 98512-8017. Secondary address: Box 14778 98511-4778. Phone: (360) 943-9834. Fax: (360) 943-8209. E-mail: info@kvsn.net. Web Site: www.kvsn.net. Licensee: Evergreen Broadcasting Inc. Network: Network: USA, Moody. Gary Preble. Format: Relg, christian. Target aud: General. ♦ Donald Trosper, opns mgr & progmg dir; Lawrence Adams, gen mgr, stn mgr, sls dir, adv dir & engrg mgr.

Twisp

KVLR(FM)— June 1993: 106.3 mhz; 220 w. Ant 1,633 ft. TL: N48 19 06 W120 06 46. PO Box 637 98856. Phone: (509) 997-5857. Fax: (509) 997-5859. E-mail: kvlr@kvlr.com. Web Site: www.kvlr.com. Licensee: Valley Air LLC (acq 3-24-2003). Format: Mainstream Country. ♦ Debbie Griggs, gen mgr, gen sls mgr & mus dir; Lonnie England, chief of engrg.

Union Gap

KYXE(AM)— Sept 13, 1983: 1020 khz; 4 kw-D, 400 w-N, DA-D. TL: N46 34 17 W120 27 15 (D), N46 34 14 W120 27 15 (N). Box 2888, Yakima 98907. Secondary address: 706 Butterfield Rd. 98907. Phone: (509) 457-1000. Fax: (509) 452-0541. E-mail: zorro@radiozorro.com. Web Site: www.radiozorro.com. Licensee: Bustos Media of Eastern Washington License LLC. (group owner; (acq 11-18-2004); grpsl). Tacher. Format: Sp. Target aud: 25-49; Hispanic adults. ♦ Bob Berry, gen mgr; Keith Teske, opns mgr; Martin Ortiz, progmg & news dir.

Vancouver

KBMS(AM)— 1955: 1480 khz; 1 kw-D, 2.5 kw-N, DA-N. TL: N45 36 06 W122 43 06. Box 251 98666. Phone: (360) 699-1881. Licensee: Chris Bennett Broadcasting Inc. Network: ABC. Format: Urban contemp. ♦Chris Bennett, gen mgr; Angela Jenkins, stn mgr.

KKAD(AM)— Aug 10, 1963: 1550 khz; 50 kw-D, 12 kw-N, DA-N. TL: N45 38 47 W122 30 51. 888 S.W. 5th Ave., Suite 790, Portland, OR 97204. Phone: (503) 223-4321. Fax: (503) 294-0074. E-mail: markail@kpam.com. Web Site: www.sunny1550kkad.com. Licensee: Pamplin Broadcasting-Washington Inc. Group owner: Pamplin Broadcasting (acq 11-20-98; $1.65 million). Network: AP Network News. Rep: Tacher. The Tacher Co., INc. Format: Adult standards/music of your life. News staff: 2; News: 5.6 hrs wkly. Target aud: 35-64. Spec prog: Portland Beaver baseball 18 hrs wkly. ♦ Paul Clithero, gen mgr; Mark L. Ail, stn mgr & opns mgr; Margaret Evans, gen sls mgr; Jeanne Winters, natl sls dir; Misty Osko, prom mgr; Paul Duckworth, progmg dir; Bill Gallagher, news dir; Dave Bischoff, chief of engrg.

KKSN(AM)— Sept 1, 1946: 910 khz; 5 kw-U, DA-2. TL: N45 33 28 W120 30 09. 0700 S.W. Bancroft, Portland, OR 97239. Phone: (503) 223-1441. Web Site: www.kisnam.com. Licensee: Entercom Portland License LLC. Group owner: Entercom (acq 4-23-98; grpsl). Rep: D & R Radio. Format: Oldies. Target aud: 25-54; men. ♦ David Field, pres; Jack Hutchinson, stn mgr; Allan Davis, opns dir.

KRVO(FM)— 2001: 105.9 mhz; 5.9 kw, 1,141 ft. TL: N45 40 46 W122 22 06. 4949 S.W. Macadam Ave., Portland, OR 97201. Phone: (503) 226-0100. Phone: (503) 323-6400. Fax: (503) 802-1640. Web Site: www.1059theriver.com. Licensee: Citicasters Licenses L.P. Group owner: Clear Channel Communications Inc. (acq 1999; grpsl). Format: First Class Rock, Hits of the 60s, 70s & 80s. ♦ Mary Lou Gunn, gen mgr; Tony Coles, opns mgr.

KXMG(AM)—See Portland, OR

KYCH-FM—See Portland, OR

Walla Walla

KGDC(AM)— Dec 6, 1956: 1320 khz; 1 kw-D, 660 w-N. TL: N46 02 13 W118 21 07. 38 E. Main St., Suite 11 99362. Phone: (509) 525-7878. E-mail: comments@kgdcradio.com. Licensee: Two Hearts Communications LLC (acq 8-20-01). Format: News/talk. News: 5 hrs wkly. Target aud: General. ♦ Rod Fazzari, pres, stn mgr, progmg dir & chief of engrg.

KGTS(FM)—See College Place

KHSS(FM)— Nov 5, 1986: 100.7 mhz; 1.3 kw. 1,374 ft. TL: N46 04 04 W118 20 21. (CP: Ant 1,414 ft. TL: N45 59 04 W118 10 08). Stereo. 38 E. Main St. 99362. Phone: (509) 525-7878. Fax: (509) 522-2046. E-mail: comments@khssradio.com. Web Site: www.khssradui.com. Licensee: Two Hearts Communications L.L.C. (acq 3-26-98; $160,000). Rep: Katz Radio. Pepper & Corazzini. Format: Catholic talk. Target aud: 18-34. Spec prog: Relg 3 hrs wkly. ♦ Rodney Fazzari, gen mgr & progmg dir; Todd Brandenburg, chief of engrg.

KNLT(FM)— Jan 1, 1980: 95.7 mhz; 100 kw. 1,401 ft. TL: N45 59 04 W118 10 08. Stereo. 830 N. Columbia Center Blvd., Suite B-2, Kennewick 99336. Phone: (509) 783-0783. Fax: (509) 735-8627. Web Site: www.oldies957fm.com. Licensee: New Northwest Broadcasters LLC (group owner; acq 1999). Rep: Christal. Format: Oldies. Target aud: 25-54. ♦ Jim Richmond, VP & gen mgr; Don Morin, gen mgr & natl sls mgr; Lon Martin, progmg dir; Allison Crawford, news dir & pub affrs dir; Rob Meadows, chief of engrg.

*KRKL(FM)— May 10, 1977: 93.3 mhz; 42 kw. Ant 1,378 ft. TL: N45 59 19 W118 10 28. Stereo. 5700 W. Oaks Blvd., Rocklin, CA 95765. Phone: (916) 251-1600. Fax: (916) 251-1650. Web Site: www.klove.com. Licensee: Educational Media Foundation. Group owner: EMF Broadcasting (acq 4-1-02; $1 million). Network: K-Love. Shaw Pittman. Format: Contemp Christian. News staff: 3. Target aud: 25-44; Judeo Christian, female. ♦ Richard Jenkins, pres; Mike Novak, VP & progmg dir; Lloyd Parker, gen mgr; Ed Lenane, opns dir & news dir; Keith Whipple, dev dir; Eric Allen, natl sls mgr; Ted Gillette, rgnl sls mgr; Chris Joyce, prom dir; David Pierce, progmg mgr; Jon Rivers, mus dir; Sam Wallington, engrg dir.

KTEL(AM)— October 1946: 1490 khz; 1 kw-U. TL: N46 20 33 W118 20 20. 13 1/2 E. Main St., Suite 202 99362. Phone: (541) 522-1383. Fax: (509) 522-0211. E-mail: rmckone@uci.net. Licensee: WW2 L.L.C. Group owner: Capps Broadcast Group (acq 6-2-03). Network: Network: Jones Radio Networks, ABC. Rep: Tacher. Tacher Format: Oldies. Target aud: 25 plus; general. Spec prog: Farm 5 hrs wkly. ♦ Dave Capps, pres; Colleen Doyle, opns mgr; Liz Halley, sls VP & sls dir; Randy McKone, VP, gen mgr & progmg dir; Andrew Holt, news dir.

KUJ(AM)— 1928: 1420 khz; 5 kw-U, DA-N. TL: N46 04 03 W118 24 08. 45 Campbell Rd. 99362. Phone: (509) 527-1000. Fax: (509) 529-5534. E-mail: kujam@bmi.net. Licensee: Alexandra Communications Inc. (acq 4-13-2001). Network: Westwood One. Tacher. Taylor,

Washington Directory of Radio

Theimann & Aitken. Format: News/talk, sports. News staff: one; News: 15 hrs wkly. Target aud: 25 plus. ♦Cheryl Hodgins, exec VP; Tom Hodgins, CEO & gen mgr.

KUJ-FM— 1997: 99.1 mhz; 2.1 kw. 1,125 ft. TL: N45 59 38 W118 10 47. 45 Campbell Rd. 99362. Phone: (509) 248-2900. Fax: (509) 529-5534. E-mail: kujam@bmi.net. Licensee: New Northwest Broadcasters LLC (group owner; acq 6-22-2004; $1.68 million). Format: Top-40. ♦Joe Benedetti, gen mgr.

***KWCW(FM)**— 1971: 90.5 mhz; 160 w. Ant -52 ft. TL: N46 04 11 W118 19 51. Stereo. Whitman College 99362. Phone: (509) 527-5285. Web Site: www.kwcw.net. Licensee: The Associated Students of Whitman College Radio Committee. Format: Free form. News staff: one; News: 2.5 hrs wkly. ♦Travis Kiefer, gen mgr.

***KWWS(FM)**— Mar 6, 1997: 89.7 mhz; 3.2 kw. 1,345 ft. TL: N45 59 04 W118 10 08. Box 642530, Murrow Communications Ctr., Washington State Univ., Pullman 99164-2530. Phone: (509) 335-6500. Fax: (509) 335-6577. E-mail: nwpr@wsu.edu. Web Site: www.nwpr.org. Licensee: Washington State University. Dow, Lohnes & Albertson. Format: News/talk. ♦Karen Olstad, COO & gen mgr; Dennis Haarsager, gen mgr; Roger Johnson, stn mgr; Scott Weatherly, opns dir; Sarah McDaniel, dev dir; Mary Hawkins, progmg dir; Robin Rilette, mus dir; Ralph Hogan, engrg dir.

KXRX(FM)— August 1977: 97.1 mhz; 50 kw. Ant 1,338 ft. TL: N45 59 04 W118 10 08. (CP: 100 kw, ant 1,328 ft. TL: N45 59 04 W118 10 09). Stereo. 2621 W. A St., Pasco 99301. Phone: (509) 547-9791. Fax: (509) 547-8509. Web Site: www.97rock.fm. Licensee: Capstar TX L.P. Group owner: Clear Channel Communications Inc. (acq 2-15-01; grpsl). Format: Rock. News staff: one; News: one hr wkly. Target aud: 25 plus; middle to upper income level listeners. ♦Eric Van Winkle, gen mgr.

Wapato

***KSOH(FM)**— Mar 6, 1992: 89.5 mhz; 9.5 kw. 974 ft. TL: N46 31 42 W120 31 16. 1006 S. Fair Ave, Yakima 98901. Phone: (509) 248-4673. Fax: (509) 248-1579. E-mail: lifetalk@compuserve.com. Web Site: www.lifetalk.net/ksoh. Licensee: Life Talk Broadcasting Association. Format: Btfl mus, relg, talk. Target aud: 25-50; families, singles needing courage, hope & answers to societal ills. ♦Lynette Wilson, stn mgr; Ed Sorrels, opns mgr, gen sls mgr, mktg dir, progmg mgr & pub affrs dir; Jeremy Woodruff, progmg dir.

Wenatchee

KKRT(AM)— Nov 17, 1956: 900 khz; 1 kw-D, 78 w-N. TL: N47 27 45 W120 19 24. Box 79, 2nd Fl., 32 N. Mission St. 98801. Phone: (509) 663-5186. Fax: (509) 663-8779. Web Site: www.kkrt.com. Licensee: Morris Communications Corp. Group owner: Morris Communications Inc. (acq 10-15-98; grpsl). Network: ESPN Radio. Rep: Katz Radio. Format: Sports. Target aud: 18-54; men. ♦William Morris III, CEO; Michael Osterhont, exec VP; Gary Patrick, gen mgr; Jeff Dahlstrom, sls dir; John Windus, progmg dir; Jay White, chief of engrg.

KKRV(FM)—Co-owned with KKRT(AM). May 1, 1976: 104.7 mhz; 6.5 kw. Ant 1,322 ft. TL: N47 28 44 W120 12 49. Stereo. Web Site: www.kkrv.com. Format: New country. Target aud: 25-54; women.

***KPLW(FM)**— 1996: 89.9 mhz; 6 kw. 1,222 ft. TL: N47 19 10 W120 14 17. 606 N. Western Ave. 98801. Phone: (509) 665-6641. Fax: (509) 665-3126. E-mail: kplw@plr.org. Web Site: www.plr.org. Licensee: Growing Christian Foundation. Format: Relg, Christian. News: 2 hrs wkly. Target aud: 35-54; female. ♦Kevin Krueger, chmn & pres; Sean Ruud, gen mgr.

KPQ(AM)— December 1929: 560 khz; 5 kw-U, DA-N. TL: N47 27 12 W120 19 43. Box 159 98807-0159. Secondary address: 32 N. Mission 98801. Phone: (509) 663-5121. Fax: (509) 664-6799. E-mail: kpq@crcwnet.com. Web Site: www.kpq.com. Licensee: Wescoast Broadcasting Co. Network: ABC Information & Entertainment. Rep: Tacher. Davis Wright Tremaine. Format: News/talk. News: 165 hrs wkly. Target aud: 35 plus. Spec prog: Farm 3 hrs wkly. ♦Jim Wallace Jr., pres & gen mgr; Debi Campestrini, opns dir & opns mgr; Greg McEwen, gen sls mgr & mktg dir; Steve Hair, news dir; Pete Peterson, chief of engrg.

KPQ-FM— December 1967: 102.1 mhz; 35 kw. 2,655 ft. TL: N47 16 28 W120 25 30. Stereo. E-mail: info@thequake1021.com. Web Site: www.thequake1021.com. Format: Classic rock, CHR. News: one hr wkly. Target aud: 25 plus. ♦Kelly Hart, mus dir.

KWWX(AM)— 1948: 1340 khz; 1 kw-U. TL: N47 23 50 W120 16 25. 231 N. Wenatchee Ave. 98801. Phone: (509) 665-6565. Fax: (509) 663-1150. Web Site: www.lasuperz.com. Licensee: Fisher Radio Regional Group Inc. Group owner: Fisher Broadcasting Company (acq 1996). Rep: McGavren Guild. Shaw Pittman. Format: Sp. News staff: one; News: 10 hrs wkly. Target aud: General; Hispanic. ♦Bill Krippaenne, CEO; Ben Tucker, chmn & prom mgr; Larry Roberts, pres; Jim Senst, gen mgr; Leona Frank, sls dir, adv VP & adv dir; Dave Herald, natl sls mgr; Elsa Esparza, prom dir & progmg dir; Manuel Garcia, chief of engrg.

KYSN(FM)—(East Wenatchee). Dec 25, 1980: 97.7 mhz; 7 kw. -150 ft. TL: N47 22 52 W120 17 16. Stereo. 231 N. Wenatchee Ave. 98801. Phone: (509) 665-6565. Fax: (509) 663-1150. E-mail: production@nw-tel.net. Web Site: www.kysn.com. Licensee: Fisher Radio Regional Group Inc. Group owner: Fisher Broadcasting Company (acq 12-28-94; grpsl; FTR: 2-20-95). Format: Country. News staff: one; News: 20 hrs wkly. Target aud: 25-54. Spec prog: Farm one hr, relg one hr wkly. ♦Bill Krippaehne, CEO; Ben Tucker, chmn; Larry Roberts, pres; Jim Senst, gen mgr; John Ross, opns mgr & progmg dir; Leona Frank, sls dir; Dave Herald, natl sls mgr; Dave Bernstein, news dir; Lisa Rodriguez, pub affrs dir; Manuel Garcia, chief of engrg.

White Salmon

***KBNO-FM**— 2001: 89.3 mhz; 20 w vert. Ant 1,102 ft. TL: N45 43 23 W121 26 42. 2650 Montello Ave., Hood River, OR 97031. Phone: (541) 386-8810. Web Site: www.hcjb.org/wrn. Licensee: World Radio Network Inc. Format: Relg, Sp. ♦John Estey, gen mgr.

Wilson Creek

KWLN(FM)— November 1994: 103.3 mhz; 25 kw. 243 ft. TL: N47 16 40 W119 00 00. Box 79, Wenatchee 98807. Phone: (509) 663-5186. Fax: (509) 663-8779. Web Site: www.lanuevaradio.com. Licensee: Morris Communications Corp. Group owner: Morris Communications Inc. (acq 10-15-98; grpsl). Rep: Katz Radio. Wiley, Rein & Fielding. Format: Sp. Target aud: 15 plus. ♦Gary Patrick, gen mgr; Jeff Dahlstrom, sls dir; Jose Luis High, progmg dir; Jay White, chief of engrg.

Winlock

KITI-FM— Aug 15, 1995: 95.1 mhz; 380 w. Ant 879 ft. TL: N46 32 35 W123 01 14. Stereo. 1133 Kresky Rd., Centralia 98531. Phone: (360) 736-1355. Fax: (360) 736-9108. Fax: (360) 736-4761. E-mail: live95@live95.com. Web Site: www.live95.com. Licensee: Premier Broadcasters Inc. Allide Leventhal, Senter & Lerman. Format: Hot adult contemp. News staff: one. Target aud: 25-49. ♦Rod Etherton, pres; Rob Etherton, gen mgr; Andy West, opns mgr; Rick Petty, gen sls mgr & natl sls mgr; Matt Shannon, progmg dir; Harvey Brooks, engrg dir & chief of engrg.

Winthrop

KTRT(FM)—Not on air, target date: unknown: 97.5 mhz; 330 w. Ant 1,650 ft. TL: N48 19 06 W120 06 47. 30 Grizzly Mtn Rd. 98862. Phone: (509) 996-3125. Licensee: Tin Can Communications LLC. ♦Richard T. Mills, gen mgr.

Yakima

KATS(FM)—Listing follows KIT(AM).

KBBO(AM)—(Selah). 1955: 980 khz; 5 kw-D, 500 w-N, DA-N. TL: N46 36 46 W120 28 24. 1200 Chesterley Dr., #160 98902. Phone: (509) 248-2900. Fax: (509) 452-9661. Licensee: New Northwest Broadcasters LLC (group owner; acq 12-1-98; grpsl). Network: Network: ABC, USA. Allied Radio Partners. Dow, Lohnes & Albertson. Format: Talk, news, sports. News staff: one. Target aud: 35-64. ♦Pete Benedetti, CEO; Trila Bumstead, COO; Brent Phillipy, VP; Lou Barfelli, opns dir, progmg dir & pub affrs dir; Kit Osborne, sls dir; Ron King, natl sls mgr & rgnl sls mgr; Jenifer Wilde, prom dir; Tim Mauch, chief of engrg.

KXDD(FM)—Co-owned with KBBO(AM). July 1, 1971: 104.1 mhz; 61 kw. 781 ft. TL: N46 30 48 W120 24 05. (CP: 100 kw, ant 1,128 ft. TL: N46 38 27 W120 23 42). Stereo. Format: Country. Target aud: 18-54. ♦Dewey Boynton, opns mgr & mus dir; Stace Whitmire, prom mgr.

***KDNA(FM)**— Dec 19, 1979: 91.9 mhz; 18.5 kw. 920 ft. TL: N46 31 42 W120 31 03. Stereo. Box 800, 121 Sunnyside Ave., Granger 98932. Phone: (509) 854-1900. Fax: (509) 854-2223. E-mail: info@kdna.org. Web Site: www.radiokdna.org. Licensee: Northwest Communities Educational Center. Format: Sp, informational. News staff: one; News: 8 hrs wkly. Target aud: General; Sp speaking farm workers. Spec prog: Relg 4 hrs, children 5 hrs, Sp 106 hrs wkly. ♦Ricardo Garcia, gen mgr; Gabriel Martinez, stn mgr & chief of engrg; Amelia Ramon, dev dir; Elizabeth Torres, sls dir & adv mgr; Jesus Sosa, prom dir; Antonio Baldras, progmg mgr & mus dir; Jose Rios, news dir.

KFFM(FM)—Listing follows KUTI(AM).

KHHK(FM)— Dec 1, 1984: 99.7 mhz; 7.6 kw. 584 ft. TL: N46 31 53 W120 26 58. Stereo. 1200 Chesterley Dr., Suite 160 98902. Phone: (509) 248-2900. Fax: (509) 452-9661. Web Site: newhot997.com. Licensee: New Northwest Broadcasters LLC (group owner; acq 12-1-98; grpsl). Format: Urban contemp. Target aud: 18-34. ♦Pete Benedetti, CEO & pres; Kit Osborne, gen mgr; Matt Boynton, progmg dir.

KIT(AM)— Apr 8, 1929: 1280 khz; 5 kw-D, 1 kw-N. TL: N46 34 19 W120 29 41. Stereo. 4010 Summitview Ave. 98908-2966. Phone: (509) 972-3461. Fax: (509) 972-3540. Fax: (509) 972-3542. E-mail: daveetel@clearchannel.com. Web Site: www.1280kit.com. Licensee: Citicasters Licenses L.P. Group owner: Clear Channel Communications Inc. (acq 10-26-99; grpsl). Network: Network: CBS, ABC Information & Entertainment. Rep: McGavren Guild. Fisher, Wayland, Cooper, Leader & Zaragoza. Format: News/talk. News staff: 2. Target aud: 25-64; professional, mature. Spec prog: Farm 6 hrs wkly. ♦Gary Donovan, exec VP; Cheryl Salomone, gen mgr; Ron Harris, opns mgr; Connie Johnston, sls dir; Dave Ettl, progmg dir; Lance Tormey, news dir; John Wilbanks, chief of engrg.

KATS(FM)—Co-owned with KIT(AM). Dec 15, 1968: 94.5 mhz; 100 kw. 850 ft. TL: N46 31 59 W120 30 14. Stereo. E-mail: katsfm@hotmail.com. Web Site: www.katsfm.com. Format: Rock/AOR. News staff: one. Target aud: 20-45. ♦Ron Harris, mus dir.

KJOX(AM)— 1947: 1390 khz; 5 kw-D, 500 w-N, DA-2. TL: N46 34 17 W120 27 15. (CP: 400 w-N). 1200 Chesterly Dr., Suite 160 98902-7345. Phone: (509) 248-2990. Fax: (509) 452-9661. Licensee: New Northwest Broadcasters LLC (group owner; acq 10-20-98; grpsl). Network: USA. Rep: Allied Radio Partners. Format: Relg, Christian adult contemp. News staff: 2; News: 12 hrs wkly. Target aud: 35-64; family oriented. Spec prog: Black 2 hrs, gospel 2 hrs wkly. ♦Pete Benedetti, CEO; Trila Bumstead, COO & pres; Trila Houston, CFO; Brent Phillipy, VP; Kit Osborne, sls dir; Ron King, natl sls mgr & rgnl sls mgr; Jenifer Wilde, prom dir; Lou Bartelli, progmg dir & pub affrs dir; Tim Mauch, chief of engrg.

KRSE(FM)—Co-owned with KJOX(AM). Aug 18, 1977: 105.7 mhz; 100 kw. 584 ft. TL: N46 42 45 W120 37 46. Stereo. Web Site: k105.com. Format: Adult contemp. Target aud: 25-64; upscale listener, primarily women. ♦Gail Dahl, prom dir; Kendall Weaver, opns mgr & progmg dir.

***KNWY(FM)**— Feb 20, 1993: 90.3 mhz; 5 kw. Ant 895 ft. TL: N46 31 57 W120 30 37. Box 642530, 382 Murrow Ctr., Pullman 99164-2530. Phone: (509) 335-6500. Fax: (509) 335-3772. E-mail: nwpr@wsu.edu. Web Site: www.nwpr.org. Licensee: Washington State University. Dow, Lohnes & Albertson. Format: News, class. News staff: one; News: 37 hrs wkly. ♦Karen Olstad, COO & gen mgr; Dennis Haarsager, gen mgr; Roger Johnson, stn mgr & sls dir; Scott Weatherly, opns mgr; Sarah McDaniel, dev mgr; Mary Hawkins, progmg dir; Robin Rilette, mus dir; Ralph Hogan, engrg mgr.

KUTI(AM)— Oct 19, 1944: 1460 khz; 5 kw-U, 3.7 kw-N, DA-N. TL: N46 33 29 W121 27 02. 4010 Summitview Ave. 98908-2966. Phone: (509) 972-3461. Fax: (509) 972-3540. E-mail: jackbalzer@clearchannel.com. Web Site: www.1460kuti.com. Licensee: Citicasters Licenses L.P. Group owner: Clear Channel Communications Inc. (acq 10-26-99; grpsl). Rep: McGavren Guild. Fisher, Wayland, Cooper, Leader & Zaragoza. Format: Classic Country. News staff: one; News: 2 hrs wkly. Target aud: 35 plus. ♦Gary Donavan, exec VP; Cheryl Salomone, gen mgr; Ron Harris, opns mgr; Jack Balzer, progmg dir; Lance Tormey, news dir; John Wilbanks, chief of engrg.

KFFM(FM)—Co-owned with KUTI(AM). Aug 31, 1970: 107.3 mhz; 100 kw. 1,500 ft. TL: N46 38 27 W120 23 42. Stereo. E-mail: steverocha @clearchannel.com. Web Site: www.kffm.com. Rep: McGavren Guild. Shaw Pittman. Format: CHR. News staff: one; News: one hr wkly. Target aud: 18-34. ♦Steve Rocha, progmg dir.

Stations in the U.S. — West Virginia

Developers & Brokers of Radio Properties

contact American Media Services at our suite:
Philadelphia Marriott Downtown
215-625-2900
843-972-2200
americanmediaservices.com
Charleston, SC
Dallas, TX • Chicago, Il • Austin, TX

American Media Services, LLC

KYAK(AM)— Oct 17, 1962: 930 khz; 10 kw-D, 127 w-N. TL: N46 36 48 W120 28 51. Box 31000, Spokane 99223. Phone: (509) 452-5925. Fax: (509) 448-3811. E-mail: kyak@kyak.com. Licensee: Thomas W. Read dba Yakima Christian Broadcasting. (acq 6-1-98; $150,000). Pepper & Corazzini. Format: Christian. ♦Melinda Read, gen mgr; Mike Bastonelli, stn mgr.

*KYPL(FM)— Oct 15, 1997: 91.1 mhz; 26 kw. Ant 797 ft. TL: N46 30 48 W120 24 05. Stereo. 204 South College Ave., College Place 99324. Secondary address: 3205 River Rd. 98902. Phone: (509) 527-2991. Fax: (509) 527-2611. E-mail: plr@plr.org. Web Site: www.plr.org. Licensee: Growing Christian Foundation. Format: Inspirational Christian. News: 8 hrs wkly. Target aud: 35-54; family-oriented, Christian. ♦Kevin Krueger, chmn; Kevin Kreuger, gen mgr; Harry Watts, sls VP & prom mgr; Breanna Mayne, progmg dir; Walter Cox, engrg dir.

*KYVT(FM)— September 1980: 88.5 mhz; 3 kw. -254 ft. TL: N46 35 06 W120 31 41. Stereo. Yakima Valley Technical Ctr., 1116 S. 15th Ave. 98902. Phone: (509) 573-5013. Phone: (509) 573-5000. Fax: (509) 573-5023. Web Site: yvtech.us. Licensee: Yakima School District No. 7. Format: Alternative. News staff: one; News: 2 hrs wkly. Target aud: 18-25; student & working people. Spec prog: Urban alternative 3 hrs wkly. ♦John Schieche, pres; Randy Beckstead, gen mgr, chief of opns, dev dir & chief of engrg; Andy Ward, prom dir; Ryan Ricigliano, mus dir; Aaron Tamburro, news dir.

KYXE(AM)—See Union Gap

KZTA(FM)—(Naches). Oct 25, 1988: 96.9 mhz; 14 kw. Ant 935 ft. TL: N46 35 59 W120 52 08. Stereo. Box 2888 98901. Secondary address: 706 Butterfield Rd. 98901. Phone: (509) 457-1000. Fax: (509) 452-0541. E-mail: zorro@radiozorro.com. Web Site: www.radiozorro.com. Licensee: Bustos Media of Eastern Washington License LLC. (group owner; (acq 11-18-2004; grpsl). Rep: Tacher. Format: Sp. News: 3 hrs wkly. Target aud: 18-35; Hispanic. ♦Amador S. Bustos, pres; Bob Berry, gen mgr; Keith Teske, opns mgr; Judy Ernesti, sls dir; Judith McInnes, progmg dir.

West Virginia

Barrackville

WBVQ(FM)— July 1993: 93.1 mhz; 2.6 kw. 495 ft. TL: N39 31 23 W80 12 00. Box 2377, Buckhannon 26201. Secondary address: WBUC Rd., Buckhannon 26201. Phone: (304) 472-1460. Fax: (304) 472-1528. E-mail: B93@verizon.net. Licensee: Cat Radio Inc. Group owner: McGraw/Elliott Group Stations (acq 3-1-95). Network: ABC. Dome. Fisher, Wayland, Cooper, Leader & Zaragoza. Format: Oldies. News staff: one. Target aud: 25-54; active adults. ♦Dick McGraw, CEO & chief of engrg; Karen McGraw, pres & VP; Harry Elliott, CFO; Todd Elliott, gen mgr & opns VP; Brian Elliott, dev VP, sls VP, gen sls mgr, mktg VP, prom VP & progmg VP; Jack Logar, mus dir; Jennifer Huffman, asst music dir; Nancy Boyce, news dir & pub affrs dir.

Beckley

WCIR-FM—Listing follows WIWS(AM).

WIWS(AM)— Nov 14, 1966: 1070 khz; 10 kw-D. TL: N37 45 18 W81 14 12. 306 S. Karawha St. 25801-5619. Phone: (304) 253-7000. Fax: (304) 255-1044. Licensee: Southern Communications Corp. (acq 1976). Format: Oldies. Target aud: 18-54; traveling motorists. ♦Jay Quesenberry, gen mgr; Rennolt Madrazo, sls dir; Rick Pizer, prom dir & progmg dir; Randy Kerbawy, chief of engrg.

WCIR-FM—Co-owned with WIWS(AM). June 1971: 103.7 mhz; 5 kw. 1,485 ft. TL: N37 56 51 W81 18 32. Stereo. E-mail: 103cir@103cir.com. Web Site: www.103cir.com. Rep: Katz Radio. Borsari & Paxson. Format: CHR. News staff: 2; News: 2 hrs wkly. Target aud: 25-54.

WJLS-FM— Nov 6, 1946: 99.5 mhz; 34 kw. 1,050 ft. TL: N37 35 23 W81 06 51. Stereo. Box 5499 25801. Secondary address: WJLS Bldg., 102 N. Kanawha St. 25801. Phone: (304) 253-7311. Fax: (304) 253-3466. E-mail: dawg@wjls.com. Web Site: www.wjls.com. Licensee: First Media Radio LLC (group owner; acq 2-1-02; $3.6 million. with co-located AM). Network: CNN Radio. Dome, Rgnl Reps. Format: Country. News staff: 15; News: 10 hrs wkly. Target aud: 25-54. ♦Mark Reid, gen mgr, sls dir & gen sls mgr; Darrell Ramsay, progmg dir; Bob Cannon, news dir; Charles Marlow, chief of engrg.

WJLS(AM)— Mar 5, 1939: 560 khz; 4.5 kw-D, 470 w-N, DA-N. TL: N37 45 32 W81 11 12. Web Site: www.wjls.com. Network: CNN Radio. Rep: Dome, Rgnl Reps. Format: Relg, southern gospel. News staff: 5; News: 4 hrs wkly. Target aud: 25-54. Spec prog: Sports 3 hrs wkly. ♦Sandi Smith-Milam, progmg dir; Gary Hosey, mus dir.

WOAY(AM)—See Oak Hill

*WVPB(FM)— May 1, 1974: 91.7 mhz; 10.5 kw. 917 ft. TL: N37 53 46 W80 59 21. Stereo. 600 Capitol St., Charleston 25301. Phone: (304) 556-4900. Fax: (304) 556-4960. E-mail: feedback@wvpubcast.org. Web Site: www.wvpubcast.org. Licensee: West Virginia Educational Broadcasting Authority. Network: Network: NPR, PRI. Format: News, class, jazz. ♦Marilyn DiVita, gen mgr & dev dir; Rita Ray, gen mgr; James Muhammad, progmg dir; Greg Collard, news dir; Chuck Wells, chief of engrg.

WWNR(AM)— Aug 9, 1946: 620 khz; 5 kw-D, 25 w-N. TL: N37 45 18 W81 14 12. 306 S. Kanawha St. 25801. Phone: (304) 253-7000. Fax: (304) 255-1044. E-mail: wwnr@netphase.net. Web Site: www.newstalk620.com. Licensee: Southern Communications Corp. (group owner; acq 1-26-2004). Network: CBS Radio. Pepper & Corazzini. Format: News/talk. News staff: 2; News: 35 hrs wkly. Target aud: 25-54. ♦R. Shane Southern, pres; Jay Quesenberry, gen mgr, stn mgr & opns mgr; Rennold Madrazo, sls dir; Shane Sothern, gen sls mgr; Rick Rizer, prom dir & progmg dir; Warren Ellison, news dir; Randy Kerbawy, chief of engrg.

Berkeley Springs

WCST(AM)— Sept 7, 1958: 1010 khz; 250 w-D, 17 w-N. TL: N39 37 00 W78 13 03. 440 Radio Station Ln. 25411. Phone: (304) 258-1010. Fax: (304) 258-1976. E-mail: wdhc@stargate.net. Licensee: Capper Broadcasting Co. Network: ABC Information & Entertainment. Format: Country. ♦Michael Fagan, gen mgr, sls dir & progmg dir; Fran Little, chief of engrg.

WDHC(FM)—Co-owned with WCST(AM). December 1965: 92.9 mhz; 3.2 kw. Ant 456 ft. TL: N39 37 00 W78 13 03. Stereo. ♦Mike Fagan, gen mgr.

Bethany

*WVBC(FM)— Jan 1, 1967: 88.1 mhz; 1.1 kw. 410 ft. TL: N40 12 58 W80 33 31. Stereo. Bethany House, Bethany College 26032. Phone: (304) 829-7853. Licensee: Bethany College. Network: AP Radio. Format: Div, educ, progsv. News staff: News progmg 1 hr wkly Target aud: 18-34; high school & college students. Spec prog: Christian rock 4 hrs, folk 2 hrs, classic rock 8 hrs, class 2 hrs wkly. ♦Patrick Sutherland, gen mgr.

Bethlehem

WUKL(FM)— Feb 27, 2004: 105.5 mhz; 13.5 kw. Ant 312 ft. TL: N40 03 17 W80 42 26. Stereo. Box 448, Bellaire, OH 43906. Phone: (740) 676-5661. Fax: (740) 676-2742. Web Site: oldiesradioonline.com. Licensee: Keymarket Licenses LLC Group owner: Keymarket Communications LLC (acq 2-4-2004; $1.35 million). Network: ABC. Format: Oldies. News staff: one. Target aud: 35-54. ♦Gerald A. Getz, pres; John Crawford, gen mgr.

Bluefield

WHAJ(FM)—Listing follows WHIS(AM).

WHIS(AM)— June 27, 1929: 1440 khz; 5 kw-D, 500 w-N. TL: N37 16 33 W81 15 06. Stereo. 900 Bluefield Ave. 24701. Phone: (304) 327-7114. Fax: (304) 325-7850. Licensee: Monterey Licenses LLC. Group owner: Triad Broadcasting Co. LLC (acq 7-18-00; grpsl). Format: News/talk. Target aud: 35 plus; upper income, leaders of the community. ♦John Halford, gen mgr; Danny Clemons, sls dir; Joseph Echles, progmg dir; Keith Bowman, chief of engrg.

WHAJ(FM)—Co-owned with WHIS(AM). Apr 23, 1963: 104.5 mhz; 100 kw. 1,200 ft. TL: N37 15 21 W81 10 55. Stereo. Web Site: www.1045.com. Format: Adult contemp. Target aud: 25-54. ♦Dave Harris, progmg dir.

WKEZ(AM)— May 18, 1948: 1240 khz; 1 kw-U. TL: N37 15 57 W81 11 20. 900 Bluefield Ave. 24701. Phone: (304) 327-7114. Fax: (304) 325-7850. Licensee: Monterey Licenses LLC. Group owner: Triad Broadcasting Co. LLC (acq 7-18-00; grpsl). Format: Oldies. Target aud: 40 plus. Spec prog: Relg 5 hrs wkly. ♦David Benjamin, CEO & pres; John Halford, gen mgr, natl sls mgr & rgnl sls mgr; Danny Clemons, gen sls mgr; Ed Weiland, progmg dir; Keith Bowman, engrg mgr.

*WPIB(FM)— September 1995: 90.9 mhz; 740 w horiz, 700 w vert. 1,102 ft. TL: N37 15 26 W81 10 43. Box 929, Blacksburg, VA 24063. Fax: (540) 200-3215. E-mail: office@spiritfm.com. Web Site: www.spiritfm.com. Licensee: Positive Alternative Radio Inc. Group owner: Baker Family Stations (Positive Radio Group) (acq 4-22-92). Network: USA. Format: Adult contemp, contemp Christian. ♦Vernon H. Baker, pres; Edward A. Baker, opns VP.

Bridgeport

WDCI(FM)— June 29, 1991: 104.1 mhz; 3 kw. 328 ft. TL: N39 17 59 W80 17 30. (CP: 2.45 kw, ant 518 ft.). Stereo. Box 360 26330. Phone: (304) 842-8644. Fax: (304) 842-8653. E-mail: rtgresak@aol.com. Licensee: WDCI Radio Inc. (acq 8-18-98; $405,000). Network: Jones Radio Networks. Dome. William D. Silva. Format: Soft adult contemp. Target aud: 25-54. ♦Bruce Wallace, pres & gen mgr; Tom Thompson, dev mgr, gen sls mgr, mktg mgr, prom mgr & adv mgr; Tina Grefak, progmg mgr; Hank Vest, chief of engrg.

Buckhannon

WBRB(FM)—Listing follows WBUC(AM).

WBTQ(FM)— 1984: 93.5 mhz; 16 kw. 417 ft. TL: N38 58 11 W80 01 58. Stereo. 228 Randolph Ave., Elkins 26241. Phone: (304) 472-1400. Fax: (304) 472-1740. Licensee: Elkins Radio Corp. Group owner: McGraw/Elliott Group Stations (acq 1996; $205,000). Network: Jones Radio Networks. Rep: Rgnl Reps. Dome. Format: Good time oldies. News staff: one; News: 3 hrs wkly. Target aud: 25-49. ♦Richard H. McGraw, CEO; Karen McGraw, pres; Harry Elliott, CFO; Todd Elliott, gen mgr & opns mgr; Brian Elliott, gen sls mgr; Jane Birdsong, mus dir, news dir & pub affrs dir; Bill Davisson, chief of engrg.

WBUC(AM)— Dec 13, 1959: 1460 khz; 5 kw-D, 87 w-N. TL: N39 00 07 W80 15 50. Stereo. Box 2377, WBUC Rd., Rt. 33 26201. Phone: (304) 472-1460. Fax: (304) 472-1528. Licensee: Cat Radio Inc. Group owner: McGraw/Elliott Group Stations (acq 9-4-86; $395,000;. FTR: 8-4-86). Format: Talk. News staff: one. Target aud: General. Spec prog: Relg 7 hrs wkly. ♦Dick McGraw, CEO & chief of engrg; Karen McGraw, pres; Harry Elliott, CFO; Todd Elliott, gen mgr & opns VP; Brian Elliott, sls VP, gen sls mgr & adv VP; Ron Roth, prom VP & progmg VP; Tamara Cicogna, adv mgr; Nancy Boyce, news dir & pub affrs dir.

WBRB(FM)—Co-owned with WBUC(AM). June 16, 1990: 101.3 mhz; 50 kw. 497 ft. TL: N38 56 40 W80 10 46. Stereo. Format: Country. News staff: one; News: 4 hrs wkly. Target aud: 25-54; upper middle class, white collar, craftsman.

*WVPW(FM)— September 1968: 88.9 mhz; 14 kw. 840 ft. TL: N39 02 04 W80 33 47. Stereo. 600 Capitol St., Charleston 25301. Phone: (304) 556-4900. Fax: (304) 556-4960. E-mail: feedback@wvpubcast.org.

West Virginia

Web Site: www.wvpubcast.org. Licensee: West Virginia Education Broadcasting Authority. Network: Network: NPR, PRI. Format: News, class, jazz. ◆ Marilyn DiVita, gen mgr & dev dir; Rita Ray, gen mgr; James Muhammad, progmg dir; Greg Collard, news dir; Chuck Wells, engrg dir.

*WVWC(FM)— Sept 15, 1997: 92.1 mhz; 10 w. 85 ft. TL: N38 59 24 W80 13 10. Box 167, 59 College Ave. 26201-2999. Phone: (304) 473-8292. Fax: (304) 472-2571. E-mail: c92@wvwc.edu. Web Site: www.wvwc.edu/c92. Licensee: West Virginia Wesleyan College. Format: Classic rock, progsv, div. Target aud: 12-25; high school & college audience. Spec prog: Black 4 hrs, class 2 hrs, jazz 8 hrs, relg 4 hrs, blues 2 hrs wkly. ◆ Phillips B. Kolsun, gen mgr.

Charles Town

WMRE(AM)— May 28, 1962: 1550 khz; 5 kw-D, DA. TL: N39 16 23 W77 51 56. 510 Pegasus Ct., Winchester, VA 22602-4596. Phone: (540) 662-5101. Fax: (540) 662-8610. Licensee: AMFM Radio Licenses LLC. Group owner: Clear Channel Communications Inc. (acq 2-16-2001; $1.525 million. with co-located FM). Rep: Roslin. Format: Adult standards. News staff: 2. Target aud: 25-54; adults. Spec prog: Relg. ◆ Chuck Peterson, gen mgr; David Miller, opns mgr; Marcella Vance, sls dir; Justin Maglione, prom dir; Maark Kesner, chief of engrg.

WKSI-FM—Co-owned with WMRE(AM). Aug 28, 1966: 98.3 mhz; 1.75 kw. Ant 617 ft. TL: N39 10 38 W78 15 53. Stereo. Web Site: wxva.com. Format: Country. Target aud: 25-54. ◆ Jay Flanagan, mus dir.

Charleston

WBES(AM)—(Dunbar). Nov 4, 1946: 1240 khz; 1 kw-U. TL: N38 23 08 W81 42 51. Box 871 25323. Secondary address: 4250 Washington St. 25313. Phone: (304) 744-7020. Fax: (304) 744-8562. Licensee: Bristol Broadcasting Co. Inc. (group owner; acq 8-90; grpsl). Format: Talk, sports. Target aud: 18-49. ◆ Mike Robinson, gen mgr; John Gush, natl sls mgr & rgnl sls mgr; Dan King, rgnl sls mgr.

WVSR-FM—Co-owned with WBES. September 1964: 102.7 mhz; 50 kw. Ant 403 ft. TL: N38 21 26 W81 40 05. Stereo. Web Site: www.electric102.com. Format: CHR.

WCAW(AM)— 1946: 680 khz; 50 kw-D, 250 w-N, DA-2. TL: N38 19 15 W81 36 31. 1111 Virginia St. E. 25301. Phone: (304) 342-8131. Fax: (304) 344-4745. Licensee: West Virginia Radio Corp. of Charleston. (acq 7-14-93; $1.1 million with co-located FM; 8-9-93). Network: ABC. Format: Classic country. News staff: one. Target aud: 25-54. ◆ John Anthony, progmg dir.

WVAF(FM)—Co-owned with WCAW(AM). Feb 1, 1965: 99.9 mhz; 50 kw. 490 ft. TL: N38 19 15 W81 36 31. Stereo. Web Site: www.v100radio.com. Format: Adult contemp. Target aud: Female skew. ◆ Dale Miller, gen sls mgr; Rich Johnson, progmg dir; Greg Johnson, asst music dir; Nikki Walters, pub affrs dir.

WCHS(AM)— Sept 15, 1927: 580 khz; 5 kw-U, DA-N. TL: N38 21 49 W81 46 05. 1111 Virginia St. E. 25301. Phone: (304) 342-8131. Fax: (304) 344-4745. E-mail: 58live@wvradio.com. Licensee: West Virginia Radio Corp. of Charleston. (acq 6-1-92; $1.74 million with co-located FM; 6-22-92). Network: CBS. Rep: McGavren Guild. Format: News/talk, sports. News staff: 2. Target aud: 25-54. ◆ Dale Miller, pres & opns dir; Sean Banks, pres & gen mgr; Noel Richardson, opns VP & chief of engrg; Rick Johnson, opns dir & progmg dir.

WKWS(FM)—Co-owned with WCHS-TV. Sept 16, 1969: 96.1 mhz; 50 kw. 360 ft. TL: N38 21 24 W81 36 19. (CP: Ant 550 ft. TL: N38 21 51 W81 46 05). Stereo. Web Site: www.kick96.com. Format: Hot country hits. ◆ Christian Miller, gen sls mgr; John Anthony, progmg VP; Rick Johnson, opns mgr & pub affrs dir.

WKAZ(FM)—See Miami

WQBE-FM—Listing follows WVTS(AM).

WSWW(AM)— 1939: 1490 khz; 1 kw-U. TL: N38 21 28 W81 37 00. 1111 Virginia St. E. 25301. Phone: (304) 342-8131. Fax: (304) 344-4745. Licensee: West Virginia Radio Corp. (group owner; acq 6-5-97; $2.15 million with WKAZ(FM) Miami). Rep: D & R Radio. Format: ESPN-All sports/talk. ◆ John Raese, chmn; Dale Miller, pres; Sean Banks, gen mgr; Dave Harmon, opns dir & progmg dir; Vince Wardell, gen sls mgr; Noel Richardson, chief of engrg.

*WVPN(FM)— May 8, 1979: 88.5 mhz; 50 kw. Ant 299 ft. TL: N38 22 32 W81 29 25. Stereo. 600 Capitol St. 25301. Phone: (304) 556-4900. Fax: (304) 556-4960. E-mail: feedback@wvpubcast.org. Web Site: www.wvpubcast.org. Licensee: West Virginia Educational Broadcasting Authority. Network: Network: NPR, PRI. Format: News, class, jazz. ◆ Rita Ray, gen mgr; Marilyn DiVita, dev mgr; James Muhammad, progmg dir; Laura Harbert-Allen, mus dir; Greg Collard, news dir; Chuck Wells, engrg dir.

WVTS(AM)— Feb 16, 1957: 950 khz; 5 kw-D, 1 kw-N, DA-N. TL: N38 23 00 W81 42 52. Box 871, 4250 Washington St. W. 25323. Phone: (304) 744-7020. Fax: (304) 744-8562. Licensee: Bristol Broadcasting Co. Inc. (group owner; acq 5-1-64). Network: ABC Information & Entertainment. Rep: McGavren Guild. Format: Talk. ◆ Mike Robinson, gen mgr; John Gush, natl sls mgr & rgnl sls mgr; Dan King, rgnl sls mgr.

WQBE-FM—Co-owned with WVTS(AM). Feb 16, 1957: 97.5 mhz; 50 kw. 500 ft. TL: N38 24 22 W81 43 26. Web Site: www.wqbe.com. Format: Educ.

Clarksburg

WGIE(FM)—Listing follows WXKX(AM).

*WKJL(FM)— October 1992: 88.1 mhz; 32.5 kw. 712 ft. TL: N39 18 02 W80 20 37. Stereo. Box 540, He's Alive Inc. Corp. Offices, 34 Springs Rd., Grantsville, MD 21536-0540. Phone: (301) 895-3292. Fax: (301) 895-3293. E-mail: hesalive@hesalive.net. Web Site: www.hesalive.net. Licensee: He's Alive Inc. Network: USA. Format: Gospel, adult contemp, Christian, relg. Target aud: 18-35. ◆ Dewayne Johnson, pres; Monte Palmer, gen mgr & stn mgr.

WOBG(AM)— Apr 12, 1936: 1400 khz; 1 kw-U. TL: N39 17 46 W80 18 16. 1489 Locust Ave., #C, Fairmont 26554-1337. Secondary address: Old Weatherservice Bldg., Unit St. 50 E. 26301. Phone: (304) 624-1400. Fax: (304) 624-1402. Licensee: Clarksburg Radio Co. Group owner: Burbach Broadcasting Group (acq 1-11-99; $330,000 with WOBG-FM Salem). Commercial Media Sales. Format: Adult standards. Target aud: 35 plus. Spec prog: Italian one hr wkly. ◆ Nicholas A. Galli, pres; David Branham, gen mgr; David Branham, gen sls mgr; Greg Bolgard, progmg dir; Debbie Southern, pub affrs dir; Larry Smith, chief of engrg.

WPDX(AM)— Aug 19, 1947: 750 khz; 1 kw-D. TL: N39 14 40 W80 23 05. 105 Oak Mound Rd. 26301. Phone: (304) 624-6425. Fax: (304) 622-3560. E-mail: wpdx@iolinc.net. Licensee: Tschudy Broadcasting Corp. Group owner: Tschudy Broadcast Group (acq 11-5-91; $405,000 with co-located FM; 12-2-91). Network: AP Radio. Commercial Media Sales Format: Music of your life. Target aud: 35-54; male & female. ◆ Earl Judy Jr., pres; Mike King, gen mgr & sls VP; John Conrad, mus dir.

WPDX-FM— Aug 19, 1974: 104.9 mhz; 7.4 kw. Ant 597 ft. TL: N39 15 22 W80 06 46. Stereo. Phone: (304) 624-6426. (Acq 1992). Network: AP Radio. Commercial Media Sales Format: Classic country. News: 5 hrs wkly. Target aud: 35-54; blue collar. ◆ John Conrad, prom dir.

WWLW(FM)— 1973: 106.5 mhz; 50 kw. 500 ft. TL: N39 11 14 W80 32 45. Stereo. 1065 Radio Park Dr., Mt. Clare 26408. Phone: (304) 623-6546. Fax: (304) 623-6547. Licensee: West Virginia Radio Corp. of Clarksburg. (acq 3-2-93; $1.2 million;. FTR: 3-22-93). Format: Adult contemp. News staff: one; News: 2 hrs wkly. ◆ Dale B. Miller, pres & gen mgr; Christian Miller, stn mgr; Harvey Kercheval, opns VP; Larry Cottrill, gen sls mgr; Chad Perry, progmg dir; Noel Richardson, engrg VP; Ralph Messer, chief of engrg.

WXKX(AM)— Nov 28, 1946: 1340 khz; 1 kw-U. TL: N39 17 27 W80 18 56. 1489 Locust Ave., #C, Fairmont 26554-1337. Phone: (304) 624-1400. Fax: (304) 624-1402. Licensee: Burbach of DE LLC. Group owner: Burbach Broadcasting Group (acq 11-2-00; $435,000 cash. with co-located FM). Network: ESPN Radio. Rep: Roslin, Rgnl Reps. Baraff, Koerner & Olender. Format: Sports. News: 14 hrs wkly. Target aud: 35 plus; office workers, retirees, upper income. Spec prog: Pittsburgh Pirates, Alderson-Broadus College basketball, high school football. ◆ Nick Galli, pres; Dan Barham, gen mgr; David Branham, gen sls mgr; Greg Bolgard, prom dir; Larry Smith, chief of engrg.

WGIE(FM)—Co-owned with WXKX(AM). 1975: 92.7 mhz; 620 w. 600 ft. TL: N39 17 27 W80 18 56. Stereo. Format: Country. News: 3 hrs wkly. Target aud: 25-45; young professionals.

Directory of Radio

Danville

WZAC-FM— Oct 9, 1989: 92.5 mhz; 610 w. 697 ft. TL: N38 05 01 W81 48 17. Stereo. Box 87 25053. Secondary address: 457 Main St., Madison 25130. Phone: (304) 369-5200. Phone: (304) 369-5201. Fax: (304) 369-5200. Licensee: Price Broadcasting Co. Format: Classic country. Target aud: General. ◆ Wayne Price, gen mgr.

Dunbar

WBES(AM)—Licensed to Dunbar. See Charleston

WZJO(FM)— Oct 13, 1988: 94.5 mhz; 9.6 kw. Ant 525 ft. TL: N38 25 11 W81 43 24. Stereo. Box 871, Charleston 25323. Secondary address: 4250 Washington St., Charleston 25313. Phone: (304) 744-7020. Fax: (304) 744-8562. Web Site: www.mix945online.com. Licensee: Bristol Broadcasting Co. Inc. (group owner; acq 1996; grpsl). Network: Network: Moody, Westwood One, ABC Information & Entertainment. Rep: Dome, Rgnl Reps, Katz Radio. Format: Adult contemp, 80s format. Spec prog: Class 2 hrs wkly. ◆ Mike Robinson, gen mgr; Barrie Hamm, prom mgr; Dave Evans, progmg dir; Randy Justice, chief of engrg.

Elizabeth

WRZZ(FM)— 1986: 106.1 mhz; 3 kw. 469 ft. TL: N39 09 48 W81 26 12. Stereo. P.O. Box 5559, Vienna 26105. Secondary address: 6006 Grand Ave., Vienna 26105. Phone: (304) 295-6070. Phone: (304) 580-0106. Fax: (304) 295-4389. Web Site: www.classicrockz106.com. Licensee: Burbach of DE LLC. Group owner: Clear Channel Communications Inc. (acq 7-29-2005; $750,000). Network: Westwood One. Rep: Clear Channel. Koerner & Olender. Format: Classic rock. Target aud: 25-54; baby boomer rock listeners. ◆ Chuck Poet, gen mgr.

Elkins

*WBHZ(FM)— 1999: 91.9 mhz; 280 w. 1,118 ft. TL: N38 52 18 W79 55 39. Box 2440, Tupelo, MS 38803. Phone: (662) 844-8888. Fax: (662) 842-6791. Web Site: www.afr.net. Licensee: American Family Association. Group owner: American Family Radio Format: Christian. ◆ Marvin Sanders, gen mgr.

WDNE(AM)— February 1948: 1240 khz; 1 kw-U. TL: N38 55 25 W79 51 33. Box 1337 26241. Phone: (304) 636-1300. Fax: (304) 636-2200. E-mail: wdne@wvradio.com. Licensee: West Virginia Radio Corp. of Elkins. Group owner: West Virginia Radio Corp. (acq 6-17-97; $750,000 with co-located FM). Format: Adult Standards. News staff: one. Target aud: 18 plus. ◆ Rick Cooper, gen mgr & gen sls mgr; Howard Swick, prom dir; Roger Taylor, progmg dir; Joe Gaynor, mus dir; Noel Richardson, chief of engrg.

WDNE-FM— June 15, 1985: 98.9 mhz; 3 kw. 328 ft. TL: N38 51 53 W79 48 26. (CP: 5.1 kw, ant 725 ft. TL: N38 54 36 W79 47 18). Stereo. Format: Country.

WELK(FM)— Oct 17, 1982: 94.7 mhz; 5 kw. 728 ft. TL: N38 54 43 W79 47 19. Stereo. 228 Randolph Ave. 26241. Phone: (304) 636-8800. Fax: (304) 636-8801. E-mail: radiosales@3wlogic.net. Licensee: Elkins Radio Corp. Group owner: McGraw/Elliott Group Stations. Fisher, Wayland, Cooper, Leader & Zaragoza. Format: Adult contemp, Top-40. News staff: one; News: 3 hrs wkly. Target aud: 18-49; female. ◆ Richard H. McGraw, CEO; Karen McGraw, pres; Harry Elliot, CFO; Todd Elliott, VP, gen mgr & opns dir; Brian Elliott, gen sls mgr; Brad Elliott, progmg dir; Jane Birdsong, news dir & pub affrs dir; Bill Davisson, chief of engrg.

Fairmont

WKKW(FM)— October 1975: 97.9 mhz; 32 kw. 600 ft. TL: N39 25 04 W80 03 44. Stereo. 1251 Earl L. Core Rd., Morgantown 26505. Phone: (304) 296-0029. Fax: (304) 296-3876. E-mail: jshaffer@wvradio.com. Licensee: Descendants Trust, Lauren M. Kelley, trustee. (acq 9-13-00; $1.5 million). Network: ABC Daytime Direction. Putbrese, Hunsaker & Trent. Format: Country. Target aud: 25-54; young professionals. ◆ Dave Jecklin, gen mgr; Christian Miller, sls dir; John Thomas, progmg dir.

WMMN(AM)— Dec 22, 1928: 920 khz; 5 kw-D, DA-N. TL: N39 28 03 W80 12 20. (CP: 5 kw-D, 200 w-N, DA-N). Box 1549 26555. Phone: (304) 366-3700. Fax: (304) 366-3706. Web Site: www.920wmmn.com. Licensee: Fantasia Broadcasting Inc. Commercial Media Sales.

Stations in the U.S. — West Virginia

Developers & Brokers of Radio Properties
contact American Media Services at our suite: Philadelphia Marriott Downtown 215-625-2900
843-972-2200
americanmediaservices.com
Charleston, SC
Dallas, TX · Chicago, Il · Austin, TX
American Media Services, LLC

Format: Sports. Target aud: 45 plus. ◆Nick L. Fantasia, pres, gen mgr & opns mgr; Bill Dunn, sls dir & progmg dir; Bob Ice, chief of engrg.

WRLF(FM)—Listing follows WTCS(AM).

WTCS(AM)— January 1948: 1490 khz; 1 kw-U. TL: N39 28 19 W80 08 27. Box 1549 26555. Secondary address: 450 Leonard Ave. 26554. Phone: (304) 366-3700. Fax: (304) 366-3706. Licensee: Fairmont Broadcasting Co. (acq 5-1-56). Commercial Media Sales. Putbrese, Hunsaker & Trent. Format: Christian. Target aud: 25-55. Spec prog: It 3 hrs wkly. ◆Nick Fantasia, pres, gen mgr & opns mgr; Bill Dunn, gen sls mgr; Bob Ice, chief of engrg.

WRLF(FM)—Co-owned with WTCS(AM). Aug 26, 1989: 94.3 mhz; 3.6 kw. 249 ft. TL: N39 28 03 W80 12 20. Stereo. Web Site: www.wrlf.com. Format: Rock/AOR. Target aud: 25-55; 60% male, 40% female.

Fisher

WELD(AM)— Aug 1, 1956: 690 khz; 2 kw-D. TL: N39 03 08 W79 00 21. 126 Kessel Rd. 26818. Phone: (304) 538-6062. Fax: (304) 538-7032. E-mail: WELD@hardynet.com. Web Site: weldamfm.com. Licensee: Thunder Associates LLC (acq 02-01-04 $600,000. with WELD-FM Petersburg). Network: ABC. Rep: Dome. Reddy, Begley & McCormick. Format: Oldies. News: 3 hrs wkly. Target aud: 25+; 25+. Spec prog: Farm 3 hrs, relg 10 hrs wkly. ◆Curtis Durst, pres; Sandra Durst, exec VP; Alan Yokum, gen mgr.

WQWV(FM)— July 1998: 103.7 mhz; 310 w. 1,384 ft. TL: N39 02 16 W79 05 23. Box 55, Petersburg 26847. Secondary address: 2 Alt Ave., Petersburg 26847. Phone: (304) 257-4432. Fax: (304) 257-9733. E-mail: wqwv@wqwv.com. Web Site: www.wqwv.com. Licensee: McGuire Broadcasting L.L.C. (acq 5-20-99). Network: CNN Radio. Format: Contemp hit/Top-40, Variety/diverse. ◆Eric McGuire, gen mgr; Kevin Spencer, opns mgr; Angel Blizzard, gen sls mgr.

Fort Gay

*****WFGH(FM)**— June 4, 1973: 90.7 mhz; 7.8 kw. 205 ft. TL: N38 07 58 W82 35 37. Box 410 25514. Phone: (304) 648-5752. Fax: (304) 648-5447. E-mail: wfgh907@radio.com. Web Site: www.tolisarebels.org /tech/broadcasting.htm. Licensee: Wayne County Board of Education. Format: Oldies, country, gospel. News staff: 2; News: 15 hrs wkly. Target aud: General. Spec prog: Oldies. ◆Hazel B. Damron, progmg dir; Vernon R. Stanfill, gen mgr, opns dir & chief of engrg.

Frost

*****WVMR(AM)**— Aug 17, 1981: 1370 khz; 5 kw-D. TL: N38 17 25 W79 55 52. Box 139, Rte. 1, Dunmore 24934. Phone: (304) 799-6004. Fax: (304) 799-7444. E-mail: amrinet@starband.net. Licensee: Pocahontas Communications Cooperative Corp. Format: Country. Target aud: General. Spec prog: Farm 5 hrs, relg 10 hrs, big band 3 hrs, bluegrass 5 hrs wkly. ◆Bill Ellenburg, pres.

Grafton

*****WDKL(FM)**— Sept 10, 1979: 95.9 mhz; 3 kw. 150 ft. TL: N39 21 16 W80 01 27. Stereo. 5700 W. Oaks Blvd., Rocklin, CA 95765. Phone: (916) 251-1600. Fax: (916) 251-1650. E-mail: klove@klove.com. Web Site: www.klove.com. Licensee: Educational Media Foundation Group owner: EMF Broadcasting. (acq 5-28-02). Network: K-Love. Shaw Pittman. Format: Contemp Christian. News staff: 3. Target aud: 25-44; female-Judeo Christian. ◆Richard Jenkins, pres; Mike Novak, VP & progmg dir; Lloyd Parker, gen mgr; Richard Hunt, gen mgr; Ed Lenane, opns dir & news dir; Keith Whipple, dev dir; Eric Allen, natl sls mgr; Tom Cody, rgnl sls mgr; Chris Joyce, prom dir; David Pierce, progmg mgr; Jon Rivers, mus dir; Sam Wallington, engrg dir.

WTBZ(AM)— January 1948: 1260 khz; 500 w-D. TL: N39 21 01 W80 02 40. Box 2 26354. Phone: (304) 265-2200. Fax: (304) 265-0972. E-mail: wtbz@go.com. Licensee: Appalachian Radio LLC (acq 8-12-2002). Reddy, Begley & McCormick LLP. Format: Adult contemp, news/talk.

News: 15 hrs wkly. Target aud: 18-65. Spec prog: Farm 1 hrs, relg 8 hrs wkly. ◆Melanie Tocco, gen mgr.

Green Valley

WAMN(AM)— January 1987: 1050 khz; 1.5 kw-D. TL: N37 18 20 W81 07 30. (CP: 1050 khz; 1.43 kw-D, 250 w-N). Box 6350, Bluefield 24701. Secondary address: 4415 Blue Prince Rd. 24701. Phone: (304) 327-9266. Phone: (304) 325-8058. Fax: (7040 325-8058. Licensee: WAMN Inc. Group owner: Baker Family Stations (acq 2-8-89). Format: Southern gospel. ◆Vernon H. Baker, pres; Dwayne Addison, gen mgr.

Hinton

WMTD(AM)— Jan 11, 1963: 1380 khz; 1 kw-D. TL: N37 40 49 W80 54 24. 306 S. Kanawha St., Beckley 25801. Phone: (304) 253-7000. Fax: (304) 255-1044. Licensee: Southern Communications Corp. (group owner; (acq 4-19-2000); $107,000. with co-located FM). Network: CBS. Format: News/talk, oldies. News staff: 3; News: 9 hrs wkly. Target aud: General. ◆R. Shane Southern, pres; Jay Quesenberry, gen mgr; Rennold Madrazo, sls dir; Steve Coleman, rgnl sls mgr; Rick Rizer, progmg VP & chief of engrg; Randy Kerbawy, engrg VP.

WMTD-FM— Oct 1, 1985: 102.3 mhz; 160 w. 1,008 ft. TL: N37 42 56 W80 56 55. (CP: 368 w, ant 1,273 ft.). Stereo. News staff: one; News: 1 hr wkly. Target aud: Adults 18-49.

Huntington

WAMX(FM)—(Milton). Oct 1, 1980: 106.3 mhz; 560 w. 1,092 ft. TL: N38 30 21 W82 12 33. Stereo. 134 4th Ave. 25701. Phone: (304) 525-7788. Fax: (304) 525-3299. E-mail: x1063@x1063.com. Web Site: www.x1063.com. Licensee: Capstar TX L.P. Group owner: Clear Channel Communications Inc. (acq 8-30-00; grpsl). Format: Active rock. News staff: one; News: 4 hrs wkly. Target aud: 25-49; males in their late teens to late '40s. ◆Judi Jennings, gen mgr; Kevin Beller, gen sls mgr; Paul Oslund, progmg dir & progmg mgr; Bill Cornwell, news dir; Scott Hensley, chief of engrg.

WCMI(AM)—See Ashland, KY

WDGG(FM)—See Ashland, KY

WEMM(AM)— 1946: 1470 khz; 5 kw-D, 72 w-N. TL: N38 24 22 W82 29 04. 703 3rd Ave. 25701. Phone: (304) 525-5141. Fax: (304) 525-0748. Web Site: www.wemmam.com. Licensee: Mortenson Broadcasting Co. of West Virginia LLC. Group owner: Mortenson Broadcasting Co. (acq 11-12-03). Format: Southern gospel. Target aud: 25-50; general. ◆Jack Mortenson, pres; Anita Jones, gen mgr.

WEMM-FM— Sept 6, 1971: 107.9 mhz; 50 kw. 500 ft. TL: N38 28 33 W82 15 00. Stereo. 703 3rd Ave. 25701. Phone: (304) 525-5141. Phone: (304) 525-9366. Fax: (304) 525-0748. Web Site: www.wemmfm.com. Licensee: Mortenson Broadcasting Co. (group owner). Network: USA. Format: Christian, gospel. News: 4 hrs wkly. Target aud: 35 plus; responsive, loyal, family oriented. ◆Jack M. Mortenson, pres; Anita G. Jones, gen mgr.

WKEE-FM—Listing follows WVHU(AM).

WMEJ(FM)—See Proctorville, OH

*****WMUL(FM)**— Nov 1, 1961: 88.1 mhz; 1.15 kw. -56 ft. TL: N38 25 26 W82 25 39. Stereo. Comm. Bldg., One John Marshall Dr. 25755-2635. Phone: (304) 696-6640. Phone: (304) 696-6651. Fax: (304) 696-3232. E-mail: wmul@marshall.edu. Web Site: www.marshall.edu/wmul. Licensee: Marshall University Board of Governors (acq 8-7-01). Network: ABC FM Connection. William D. Silva. Format: Div. News: 7 hrs wkly. Target aud: General. ◆Michael J. Farrell, pres; Dr. Chuck G. Bailey, gen mgr; Vince Payne, stn mgr; Chuck Cook, chief of opns.

WRVC(AM)— Oct 23, 1923: 930 khz; 5 kw-D, 1 kw-N, DA-N. TL: N38 24 03 W82 29 42. Box 1150 25713. Secondary address: 401 11th St., Suite 200 25701. Phone: (304) 523-8401. Fax: (304) 523-4848. Web Site: www.wrvc.am. Licensee: Fifth Avenue Broadcasting Co. Inc. Group owner: Kindred Communications Inc. (acq 6-1-70). Network: Westwood One. Arent, Fox, Kintner, Plotkin & Kahn. Format: News/talk, sports. News: 40 hrs wkly. Target aud: 35 plus; affluent. Spec prog: Relg 3 hrs wkly. ◆Tom Wolf, pres; Mike Kirtner, gen mgr & gen sls mgr; Cameron Smith, opns dir, progmg dir & chief of engrg; Nwman Adkins, sls VP; Newman Adkins, natl sls mgr, mktg dir & adv dir; Rich Mhyrwold, rgnl sls mgr; Jeff Crawford, prom dir; Jay Nunley, prom mgr.

WTCR(AM)—See Kenova

WTCR-FM— May 1, 1966: 103.3 mhz; 50 kw. 490 ft. TL: N38 25 11 W82 24 06. 9801 Radio Park Rd., Catlettsburg, KY 41129. Phone: (606) 739-8427. Fax: (606) 739-6009. E-mail: wtcr@wtcr.com. Web Site: wtcr.com. Licensee: Capstar TX L.P. Group owner: Clear Channel Communications Inc. (acq 8-30-00; grpsl). Network: ABC Information & Entertainment. Rep: Rgnl Reps, Katz Radio. Format: Country. ◆Judy Jennings, gen mgr; Randy Dunn, sls dir; Gloria Ward, gen sls mgr; Judy Eaton, progmg dir; Dave Poole, mus dir; Bill Cornwell, news dir; Scott Hensley, chief of engrg.

WVHU(AM)— July 1947: 800 khz; 5 kw-D, 185 w-N. TL: N38 23 35 W82 28 24. Stereo. Box 2288 25724. Secondary address: 134 4th Ave. 25701. Phone: (304) 525-7788. Fax: (304) 525-6281. E-mail: paulswann@clearchanneler. Web Site: www.800wvhu.com. Licensee: Capstar TX L.P. Group owner: Clear Channel Communications Inc. (acq 8-30-00; grpsl). Alan Campbell. Format: News/talk. Target aud: 25-54; older, professional, higher income. ◆Judy Jennings, gen mgr; Matt Tweel, sls dir; Kym Blake, natl sls mgr; Truezy Robinette, prom dir; Paul Swann, progmg dir; Bill Cornwell, news dir; Scott Hensley, chief of engrg.

WKEE-FM—Co-owned with WVHU(AM). November 1947: 100.5 mhz; 53 kw. 561 ft. TL: N38 23 35 W82 28 24. Stereo. Web Site: www.wkee.com. Format: Chr, pop. Target aud: 18-42. ◆Jim Davis, progmg dir; Gary Miller, mus dir.

*****WVWV(FM)**— Nov 28, 1977: 89.9 mhz; 8.1 kw. 1,200 ft. TL: N38 29 42 W82 12 03. Stereo. 600 Capitol St., Charleston 25301. Phone: (304) 556-4900. Fax: (304) 556-4981. E-mail: feedback@wvpubcast.org. Web Site: www.wvpubcast.org. Licensee: West Virginia Educational Broadcasting Authority. Network: Network: NPR, PRI. Format: News, class, jazz. ◆Marilyn DiVita, gen mgr & dev dir; Rita Ray, gen mgr; James Muhammad, progmg dir; Greg Collard, news dir; Chuck Wells, engrg dir.

Hurricane

WOKU(AM)— July 2, 1971: 1080 khz; 1 kw-D. TL: N38 26 41 W82 00 54. 3006 Mt. Vernon Rd., Suite 1080 25526. Phone: (304) 757-9661. Fax: (304) 757-9620. E-mail: woku@wv-cis.net. Web Site: www.woku.com. Licensee: Big River Radio Inc. Group owner: Baker Family Stations (acq 1996; $20,000). Format: Adult contemporary Christian. ◆Vernon H. Baker, pres; Randy Parsons, gen mgr; Matt Curry, opns mgr & progmg dir; Winston Hawkins, chief of engrg.

Kenova

WDNQ(FM)—Not on air, target date: unknown: 97.9 mhz; 3.5 kw. Ant 436 ft. TL: N38 25 26 W82 32 08. 136 Main St., Suite 202, Westport, CT 06880-3304. Phone: (203) 227-1978. Licensee: Connoisseur Media LLC. ◆Michael O. Driscoll, gen mgr.

WTCR(AM)— August 1954: 1420 khz; 5 kw-D, 500 w-N, DA-N. TL: N38 24 42 W82 36 13. 9801 Radio Park Rd., Catlettsburg, KY 41129. Secondary address: Box 2186, Huntington 25722. Phone: (606) 739-8427/739-8420. Fax: (606) 739-6009. E-mail: wtcr@clearchannel.com. Licensee: Capstar TX L.P. Group owner: Clear Channel Communications Inc. (acq 8-30-00; grpsl). Network: ABC Information & Entertainment. Rep: Rgnl Reps, Katz Radio. Format: Christian. Target aud: 35 plus. ◆Judy Jennings, gen mgr; Judy Eaton, stn mgr; Kim York-Blake, sls dir; Clint McElroy, progmg dir; Scott Hensley, chief of engrg.

Broadcasting & Cable Yearbook 2006

West Virginia

Keyser

WCBC-FM— January 1990: 107.1 mhz; 530 w. 783 ft. TL: N39 31 26 W78 51 44. Stereo. Box 1290,, 35 Baltimore St., Cumberland, MD 21502. Phone: (301) 786-4335. Fax: (301) 722-8336. E-mail: wcbc@1270am.com. Licensee: Prosperitas Broadcasting System. (acq 9-7-89; $300,000; 9-25-89). Format: Oldies. ♦David Aydelotte, gen mgr; Jim Robey, stn mgr & progmg dir; Mary Clites, gen sls mgr; Bryan Gowans, news dir; Martin White, chief of engrg.

WKLP(AM)— Aug 31, 1965: 1390 khz; 1 kw-D, 74 w-N. TL: N39 26 12 W78 57 21. Box F, Rt. 46 E. 26726. Phone: (304) 788-1662. Fax: (304) 788-1662. E-mail: wqzk@wqzk.com. Web Site: www.wqzk.com. Licensee: Starcast Systems Inc. (group owner; acq 1-1-82; $300,000; 1-11-82). Network: ABC Information & Entertainment. Format: MOR. Target aud: 35 plus. Spec prog: Big band. ♦Jack Mullen II, gen mgr, pres & chief of engrg; Jack Mullen III, progmg dir; Mark Allen, mus dir; Pat Sullivan, news dir.

WQZK-FM—Co-owned with WKLP(AM). Sept 15, 1973: 94.1 mhz; 15 kw. 801 ft. TL: N39 25 08 W78 57 13. Stereo. Web Site: www.wqzk.com. Format: Classic rock. Target aud: 18-49.

Kingwood

WFSP(AM)— Aug 25, 1967: 1560 khz; 1 kw-D, 250 w-CH. TL: N39 20 01 W79 43 10. Box 567 26537. Phone: (304) 329-1780. Fax: (304) 329-1781. E-mail: wfspradio@labyrinth.net. Web Site: www.prestoncounty.com/wfsp. Licensee: WFSP Inc. (acq 8-24-79). Network: CBS. Rep: Dome. Format: Christion, relg. News staff: one; News: 6 hrs wkly. Target aud: 20 plus. ♦Arthur W. George, pres; Donna Nestor, opns mgr; Dave Wills, mus dir; Kathy Casseday, news dir & pub affrs dir; Chuck Clemence, chief of engrg.

WFSP-FM— June 10, 1991: 107.7 mhz; 1.6 kw. 449 ft. TL: N39 28 50 W79 43 11. Stereo. Web Site: www.prestoncounty.com/wfsp. Network: Westwood One. Format: Adult contemp. News staff: one; News: 25 hrs wkly. Target aud: 18-45.

WKMM(FM)— Dec 1, 1986: 96.7 mhz; 300 w. 797 ft. TL: N39 27 29 W79 35 18. Stereo. 106 E. Main St. 26537. Phone: (304) 329-0967. Fax: (304) 329-2131. E-mail: jcrogan@wkmmfm.com. Web Site: www.wkmmfm.com. Licensee: MarPat Corp. (acq 8-1-93; $190,000; 8-23-93). Network: Westwood One. Format: Country. Target aud: 25-55. ♦P.J. Crogan, pres & opns mgr; Marty White, chief of engrg.

Lewisburg

WKCJ(FM)— October 1981: 103.1 mhz; 25 kw. 781 ft. TL: N37 42 43 W80 30 20. Stereo. Box 610, Rt. 60 W. Harts Run, White Sulphur Springs 24986. Phone: (304) 536-1310. Phone: (304) 645-1191. Fax: (304) 536-1311. Licensee: Quorum Radio Partners of Virginia Inc., debtor-in-possession. (group owner; acq 4-20-2005; grpsl). Network: ABC Information & Entertainment. Rep: Rgnl Reps. Format: Modern & traditional country. News: 12 hrs wkly. Target aud: 25-55. Spec prog: Gospel 6 hrs, relg 4 hrs, farm 3 hrs wkly. ♦Rita McClung, sls VP & sls dir; James Perrow, mus dir; Dwight Rohr, news dir; Wayne Beone, chief of engrg.

WRON-FM—See Ronceverte

Lindside

***WHFI(FM)**— September 1990: 106.7 mhz; 3 kw. 303 ft. TL: N37 28 56 W80 39 40. Box 97, Rt. 1 24951. Phone: (304) 753-9971. Fax: (304) 753-9792. Web Site: www.whfi-fm.com. Licensee: Monroe County Board of Education (acq 5-1-89). Format: MOR. ♦James W. Higginbotham, gen mgr.

Logan

WVOW(AM)— May 1954: 1290 khz; 5 kw-D, 1 kw-N, DA-N. TL: N37 51 28 W81 58 16. Box 1776 25601. Secondary address: 204 Main St., Suite 201 25601. Phone: (304) 752-5080. Fax: (304) 752-5711. E-mail: amfmwvow@mountain.net. Licensee: Logan Broadcasting Corp. Network: ABC Information & Entertainment. Format: Adult contemp. News staff: 2. Target aud: General. ♦Martha Jane Becker, pres, gen sls mgr & prom mgr; Larry Bevins, gen mgr; Rhonda Bryant, progmg dir; Bill France, mus dir; Bob Weisner, news dir; Terry Bucklew, chief of engrg.

WVOW-FM— August 1969: 101.9 mhz; 15 kw. 830 ft. TL: N37 51 28 W81 58 16. Format: Adult contemp.

Lost Creek

WOTR(FM)— Dec 9, 1991: 96.3 mhz; 6 kw horiz. 302 ft. TL: N39 08 43 W80 19 40. Stereo. Box 505 26385. Phone: (304) 745-4243. Web Site: www.wotr.tsx.org. Licensee: James W. Allman. William D. Silva. Format: Gospel, relg. Target aud: 25-99. ♦Bill Allman, gen mgr; James W. Allman, CEO & chief of opns.

Mannington

WGYE(FM)— December 1992: 102.7 mhz; 3.2 kw. 453 ft. TL: N39 32 18 W80 20 16. 1489 Locust Ave., Suite C, Fairmont 26554. Phone: (304) 363-8888. Fax: (304) 367-1885. E-mail: 1027production@results.netassoc.net. Licensee: Burbach of DE LLC. Group owner: Burbach Broadcasting Group (acq 6-20-2000; grpsl). Format: Country. News staff: one; News: 4 hrs wkly. Target aud: 25-54. ♦Nicholas A. Galli, pres; David Bronham, gen mgr; Greg Bolyard, mus dir; Larry Smith, engrg mgr.

Marmet

***WKVW(FM)**— June 30, 1995: 93.3 mhz; 4.1 kw. Ant 397 ft. TL: N38 13 09 W81 25 05. 5700 W. Oaks Blvd., Rocklin, CA 95765-3719. Phone: (916) 251-1600. Fax: (916) 251-1650. Web Site: www.klove.com. Licensee: Educational Media Foundation Group owner: EMF Broadcasting (acq 7-1-2002; $500,000). Network: K-Love. Shaw Pittman. Format: Contemp Christian. News staff: 3. Target aud: 25-44; Judeo Christian, female. ♦Richard Jenkins, pres; Mlke Novak, VP; Lloyd Parker, gen mgr; Ed Lenane, opns dir & mktg dir; Keith Whipple, dev dir; Eric Allen, natl sls mgr; Tom Cody, rgnl sls mgr; Chris Joyce, prom dir; David Pierce, progmg dir; Mike Novak, progmg dir; Jon Rivers, mus dir; Sam Wallington, engrg dir.

Martinsburg

WEPM(AM)— Oct 13, 1946: 1340 khz; 1 kw-U. TL: N39 27 48 W77 59 11. 1606 W. King St. 25401. Phone: (304) 263-8868. Fax: (304) 263-8906. Licensee: Prettyman Broadcasting Co. (group owner; acq 1-1-87; $2 million;. FTR: 11-10-86). Network: CBS. Rep: Katz Radio. Format: News/talk, sports. Target aud: 35 plus. Spec prog: Relg 6 hrs wkly. ♦Yogi Yoder, gen mgr; Chuck Thornton, sls dir; Jay Young, progmg dir; Rodney Rockwell, chief of engrg.

WLTF(FM)—Co-owned with WEPM(AM). 1949: 97.5 mhz; 11.4 kw. Ant 1,036 ft. TL: N39 27 33 W78 03 48. Stereo. Web Site: www.lite975.com. Format: Adult contemp. Target aud: 30-49. ♦Stacey Drake, progmg dir.

WRNR(AM)— Apr 16, 1976: 740 khz; 500 w-D, 21 w-N, DA-2. TL: N39 28 25 W77 55 57. Box 709, 1762 Eagle School Rd. 25402. Phone: (304) 263-6586. Fax: (304) 263-3082. Licensee: Shenandoah Communications Inc. Network: Network: Westwood One, CBS. Rep: Rgnl Reps. Format: News/talk, sports. News staff: 3; News: 28 hrs wkly. Target aud: 35 & above; middle to upper age & income. ♦Richard S. Wachtel, pres, gen mgr & gen sls mgr; Gregg M. Wachtel, exec VP; Matt Miller, opns dir; Tom Tucker, progmg dir; Richard Strader, news dir; Fran Little, chief of engrg.

***WVEP(FM)**— Feb 11, 1987: 88.9 mhz; 3.6 kw. 1,623 ft. TL: N39 08 38 W78 26 09. Stereo. 600 Capitol St., Charleston 25301. Phone: (304) 556-4900. Fax: (304) 556-4981. E-mail: feedback@wvpubcast.org. Web Site: www.wvpubcast.org. Licensee: West Virginia Educational Broadcasting Authority. Network: NPR, PRI. Format: News, jazz, class. ♦Marilyn DiVita, gen mgr & dev dir; Rita Ray, gen mgr; James Muhammad, progmg dir; Greg Collard, news dir; Chuck Wells, engrg dir.

Matewan

WHJC(AM)— Dec 2, 1951: 1360 khz; 1 kw-D. TL: N37 37 02 W82 10 04. Box 68 25678. Secondary address: 156 Radio Hill, McCarr, KY 41544. Phone: (606) 427-7261. Fax: (606) 427-7260. E-mail: pwr1067@bellsouth.net. Licensee: Three States Broadcasting Co. Inc. Format: Hot adult contemp. Target aud: 45 plus. ♦George D. Warren, pres, gen mgr & news dir; Evelyn Warren, sls dir; Melissa White, gen sls mgr & progmg dir; Russell Laferty, chief of engrg.

WVKM(FM)—Co-owned with WHJC(AM). Aug 30, 1989: 106.7 mhz; 4.3 kw. Ant 751 ft. TL: N37 36 49 W82 11 22. Stereo. Format: Hot adult contemp, CHR. Target aud: 18-49; women & men.

Miami

WKAZ(FM)— November 1985: 107.3 mhz; 50 kw. 600 ft. TL: N38 25 W81 31 27. Stereo. 1111 Virginia St. E., Charleston 25301. Phone: (304) 342-8131. Fax: (304) 344-4745. Licensee: West Virginia Radio Corp of Charleston. (group owner; (acq 6-5-97; $2.15 million. with WCZR(AM) Charleston). Rep: D & R Radio. Format: Oldies. Target aud: 25-54. ♦Sean Banks, gen mgr; Max Wulf, progmg dir; Noel Richardson, chief of engrg.

Middlebourne

***WRSG(FM)**— 2001: 91.5 mhz; 900 w. Ant 157 ft. TL: N39 30 59 W80 54 00. 1993 Silver Knight Dr., Sistersville 26175. Phone: (304) 758-9007. Fax: (304) 758-9006. E-mail: wrsgfm@yahoo.com. Web Site: tchs.tyle.k12.wv.us/ths/wrsg/wrsg.htm. Licensee: Tyler County Board of Education. Format: Var. ♦Becki Ferrebee, progmg dir; Bob Eddy, chief of engrg; Tom Taggert, chief of engrg; Greg Goodfellow, system mgr.

Milton

WAMX(FM)—Licensed to Milton. See Huntington

WZZW(AM)— June 26, 1973: 1600 khz; 6 kw-D, 26 w-N. TL: N38 25 46 W82 06 21. 134 4th Ave., Huntington 25701. Phone: (304) 525-7788. Fax: (304) 525-6281. Web Site: www.havejoy.com. Licensee: Capstar TX L.P. Group owner: Clear Channel Communications Inc. (acq 8-30-00; grpsl). Network: ABC News/Talk. Format: Contemp Christian. Target aud: 25-44; adult, upscale baby boomers. ♦Judy Jennings, gen mgr; Kym York Blake, gen mgr & sls dir; Clint McElroy, progmg dir; Scott Hensley, chief of engrg.

Montgomery

WMON(AM)— July 14, 1946: 1340 khz; 1 kw-U. TL: N38 10 48 W81 20 06. 100 Kanawha Terr., St. Albans 25177. Phone: (304) 722-3808. Fax: (304) 727-1300. E-mail: info@wjyp.com. Web Site: www.wjyp.com. Licensee: L.M. Communications of Kentucky LLC. Group owner: L.M. Communications Inc. (acq 4-1-03; grpsl). Network: CBS. Rep: Keystone (unwired net). Format: Chirstian. Target aud: 25 plus. ♦Lynn Martin, pres & VP; Richard Findley, gen mgr; Chris Akers, sls dir; Chris Colagrosso, progmg dir; Lisa Parr, pub affrs dir; Fred Francis, chief of engrg.

Morgantown

WAJR(AM)— Dec 7, 1940: 1440 khz; 5 kw-D, 500 w-N, DA-2. TL: N39 40 34 W80 00 12. 1251 Earl Core Rd. 26505. Phone: (304) 296-0029. Fax: (304) 296-3876. Web Site: www.wajr.com. Licensee: West Virginia Radio Corp. Network: ABC Information & Entertainment. Putbrese, Hunsaker & Trent, P. Format: News/talk. News staff: 7; News: 15 hrs wkly. Spec prog: Rush Limbaugh, sports. ♦Dale B. Miller, pres & gen mgr; Harvey Kercheval, opns VP; Gary Mertins, sls dir; Tim Loughry, prom dir; Jim Stallings, progmg dir; Shawm Falkenstein, news dir; Kay Murray, pub affrs dir; Noel Richardson, engrg VP; Ralph Messer, chief of engrg.

WVAQ(FM)—Co-owned with WAJR(AM). 1948: 101.9 mhz; 50 kw. 500 ft. TL: N39 36 30 W79 59 07. Stereo. Web Site: www.wvaq.com. Format: CHR. News staff: 2; News: one hr wkly. Target aud: 18-49. ♦Hoppy Kercheval, opns dir; Lacy Neff, progmg dir.

WCLG(AM)— December 1954: 1300 khz; 2.5 kw-D, 44 w-N. TL: N39 37 40 W79 58 11. Stereo. Box 885 26507. Secondary address: 343 High St. 26505. Phone: (304) 292-2222. Fax: (304) 292-2224. Web Site: www.wclg.com. Licensee: Bowers Broadcasting Corp. (acq 12-19-59). Rep: Dome. Format: Oldies. ♦Garry Bowers, pres & gen mgr; Rebecca Hunn, sls dir; Jeffrey Miller, progmg dir; Ken Tennant, chief of engrg.

WCLG-FM— Sept 28, 1974: 100.1 mhz; 6 kw. 300 ft. TL: N39 37 40 W79 58 11. Stereo. Web Site: www.wclg.com. Format: Classic rock.

***WVPM(FM)**— May 27, 1981: 90.9 mhz; 5 kw. 1,440 ft. TL: N39 41 45 W79 45 45. Stereo. 600 Capitol St., Charleston 25301. Phone: (304) 556-4900. Fax: (304) 556-4960. E-mail: feedback@wvpubcast.org. Web Site: www.wvpubcast.org. Licensee: West Virginia Educational

Stations in the U.S. West Virginia

Developers & Brokers of Radio Properties

contact American Media Services at our suite:
Philadelphia Marriott Downtown
215-625-2900
843-972-2200
americanmediaservices.com
Charleston, SC
Dallas, TX · Chicago, Il · Austin, TX

American Media Services, LLC

Broadcasting Authority. Network: Network: NPR, PRI. Format: News, class, jazz. ♦ Marilyn DiVita, gen mgr; James Muhammad, progmg dir.

*WWVU-FM— Aug 20, 1982: 91.7 mhz; 2.6 kw. 180 ft. TL: N39 38 09 W79 56 38. Stereo. Box 6446, Mountainlair, West Virginia Univ. 26506-6446. Phone: (304) 293-3329. Fax: (304) 293-7363. E-mail: u92@mail.wvu.edu. Web Site: u92.wvu.edu. Licensee: West Virginia University Board of Governors (acq 8-10-01). Network: ABC FM Connection. William D. Silva. Format: Educ, div, progsv. News: 2 hrs wkly. Target aud: 18-35; mostly college & high school students. Spec prog: New age 6 hrs, reggae 5 hrs, metal 3 hrs, bluegrass one hr, oldies 8 hrs, big band 2 hrs wkly. ♦ Kim Harrison, gen mgr.

WZST(FM)—See Westover

Moundsville

WRKP(FM)— Jan 15, 1990: 96.5 mhz; 1.9 kw. Ant 594 ft. TL: N39 50 51 W80 45 23. Stereo. 2002 First St. 26041. Phone: (304) 845-1052. Fax: (304) 845-1054. E-mail: ronking@wrkp.com. Web Site: www.wrkp.com. Licensee: RKP International Corp. Network: Network: USA, Salem Radio Network. Rep: Salem. CMS Format: Contemp Christian mus, talk. News staff: one; News: 5 hrs wkly. Target aud: 12-45; 60% female, 40% male. ♦ LuAnn Jerin, opns mgr, progmg dir & mus dir; Roger Rolson, rgnl sls mgr; Ronald W. King, CEO, pres, gen mgr, sls dir & adv dir; Marg King, engrg VP; Allen Fox, chief of engrg.

WVLY(AM)— Oct 1, 1950: 1370 khz; 5 kw-D, 20 w-N. TL: N39 54 20 W80 46 42. 98 16th St., Wheeling 26003. Phone: (304) 233-9859. Fax: (304) 214-9859. E-mail: wvlyradio@aol.com. Licensee: Monroe Communications LLC (acq 1-9-2004; $75,000). Network: CNN Radio. Format: News/talk. News: 14 hrs wkly. Target aud: 25-54; adults. ♦ Howard Monroe, pres; Mark Bohack, chief of engrg.

Mount Hope

WTNJ(FM)— June 1, 1980: 105.9 mhz; 50 kw. 500 ft. TL: N37 53 12 W81 11 40. 306 S. Karawha St., Beckley 25801-5619. Phone: (304) 253-7000. Fax: (304) 255-1044. Licensee: Southern Communications Group owner: Southern Communications Corp. (acq 3-12-01; $2.375 million). Network: ABC Information & Entertainment. Format: Country. News staff: one; News: 12 hrs wkly. Target aud: 25-54. Spec prog: NASCAR races, West Virginia Univ. sports. ♦ Jay Quesenberry, gen mgr & gen sls mgr; Rick Reiser, opns mgr; Rick Peiser, progmg dir; Warren Ellison, news dir; Randy Kerbawy, chief of engrg.

Mullens

WPMW(FM)— Sept 30, 1981: 92.7 mhz; 1.65 kw. 443 ft. TL: N37 35 39 W81 23 49. Stereo. 213 Howard Ave. 25882. Phone: (304) 294-4405. Fax: (304) 294-5616. E-mail: ranny@c92.com. Web Site: www.c92.com. Licensee: Castle Rock Investments L.L.C (acq 12-31-97; $175,000). Format: Classic rock. ♦ Debra Toler, gen sls mgr; Jeff Halsey, progmg dir & news dir; Mike Muscari, mus dir; Ranny Parks, gen mgr & chief of engrg.

New Martinsville

WETZ(AM)— May 25, 1953: 1330 khz; 1 kw-D, 60 w-N. TL: N39 39 27 W80 51 34. Box 10 26155. Secondary address: 325 N.Main St. 26155. Phone: (304) 455-1111. Fax: (304) 455-1170. Licensee: Dailey Corp. (group owner; acq 2-1-2001; grpsl). Network: ABC. Reddy, Begley & McCormick. Format: Stardust Timeless Classic. News: 10 hrs wkly. Target aud: 25-64. ♦ Calvin Dailey Jr., pres; Dennis Gage, gen mgr.

WETZ-FM— December 1977: 103.9 mhz; 2.5 kw. Ant 502 ft. TL: N39 39 10 W80 54 47. Stereo. Web Site: www.powercountry104.com. Network: ABC. News: 10 hrs wkly. Target aud: 25-54; country.

WXCR(FM)— 2002: 92.3 mhz; 3.2 kw. Ant 453 ft. TL: N39 40 16 W80 53 04. Stereo. Box 564 26155. Secondary address: Box 374, Saints Marys 26170. Phone: (304) 684-3400. Fax: (304) 684-9241. Licensee: Seven Ranges Radio Co. Inc. Reddy, Begley & McCormick. Format: Classic rock. Target aud: 25-54; 70% men, 30% women. ♦ Sam Yoho, pres & gen mgr; Lou Petronio, opns mgr.

WYMJ(FM)— Dec 1, 2002: 99.5 mhz; 2.7 kw. Ant 482 ft. TL: N39 39 10 W80 54 47. Stereo. Box 10 26155. Phone: (304) 455-1111. Fax: (304) 455-1170. Web Site: www.oldiesradioonline.com. Licensee: Dailey Corp. (group owner; acq 2-6-2001; grpsl). Network: ABC. Reddy, Begley, McCormick. Format: Adult contemp. News staff: 3. ♦ Dex Gage, gen mgr, opns mgr, gen sls mgr & progmg dir; Ed Wilhelm, chief of engrg.

Oak Hill

WAXS(FM)— 1948: 94.1 mhz; 26 kw. 650 ft. TL: N37 57 30 W81 09 03. Stereo. 306 S. Karawha St., Beckley 25801. Phone: (304) 253-7000. Fax: (304) 255-1044. Licensee: Plateau Broadcasting Inc. Group owner: Southern Communications Corp. (acq 3-12-01; $875,000). Network: ABC. Format: Oldies. News staff: one; News: 2 hrs wkly. Target aud: General; baby boomers. ♦ Jay Quesenberry, gen mgr & gen sls mgr; Rick Reiser, opns mgr & progmg dir; Warren Ellison, adv dir & news dir; Randy Kerbawy, chief of engrg.

WOAY(AM)— Feb 22, 1947: 860 khz; 10 kw-D, 11 w-N, 5 kw-CH. TL: N37 57 30 W81 09 03. Box 140, 240 Central Ave. 25901. Phone: (304) 465-0534. Fax: (304) 465-1486. E-mail: woayradio@aol.com. Licensee: Commissioned Communications Corp. (acq 8-90; FTR: 8-6-90). Network: Network: Moody, USA. Format: Relg. News: 10 hrs wkly. Target aud: General. ♦ Eugene Ellison, CEO, pres & gen mgr; Judy Ellison, VP; Stephanie Gibson, chief of engrg.

WTNJ(FM)—See Mount Hope

Parkersburg

WADC(AM)— Apr 9, 1954: 1050 khz; 5 kw-D, 144 w-N. TL: N39 15 29 W81 33 49. Box 4739 26104-4739. Phone: (304) 485-4565. Fax: (304) 424-6955. Licensee: Burbach of Delaware, LLC. Group owner: Burbach Broadcasting Group (acq 3-19-98; $1.775 million. with co-located FM). Network: CNN Radio. Koerner & Olender. Format: Adult standards. News: 12 hrs wkly. Target aud: 35-64. Spec prog: Relg 3 hrs wkly. ♦ Don Staats, gen mgr; Larry Smith, chief of engrg.

WGGE(FM)—Co-owned with WADC(AM). Sept 1, 1965: 99.1 mhz; 11.5 kw. 485 ft. TL: N39 15 29 W81 33 49. Stereo. Web Site: www.froggy99.net. Format: Mainstream country. Target aud: 25-54; loyal modern country listeners. Spec prog: Farm 2 hrs, NASCAR 5 hrs wkly.

WHBR-FM—Listing follows WVNT(AM).

WHNK(AM)— July 12, 1935: 1450 khz; 1 kw-U. TL: N39 17 23 W81 31 36. Box 5559, 6006 Grand Central Ave., Vienna 26105. Phone: (304) 295-6070. Fax: (304) 295-4389. E-mail: johnchalfant@clearchannel.com. Web Site: www.whnk.com. Licensee: Clear Channel Broadcasting Licenses Inc. Group owner: Clear Channel Communications Inc. (acq 4-17-01). Format: Class country. News staff: one; News: 3 hrs wkly. Target aud: 25-54; middle-aged, with higher income. ♦ Chuck Poet, gen mgr; John Chalfant, opns mgr & progmg dir; Kirk McCall, gen sls mgr; Rachel Greenwalt, prom mgr; Doug Hess, news dir & pub affrs dir; Jerry Kuhn, chief of engrg.

WVNT(AM)— September 1947: 1230 khz; 1 kw-U. TL: N39 16 56 W81 33 17. Box 4739 26104-4739. Phone: (304) 485-4565. Fax: (304) 424-6955. Licensee: Burbach of Delaware, LLC. Group owner: Burbach Broadcasting Group (acq 1-1-97; grpsl). Network: CNN Radio. Rep: McGavren Guild. Format: News/talk. News staff: one. Target aud: 30-50. Spec prog: Gospel 4 hrs wkly. ♦ Don Staats, gen mgr.

WHBR-FM—Co-owned with WVNT(AM). March 1967: 103.1 mhz; 2.1 kw. Ant 561 ft. TL: N39 21 00 W81 33 56. Stereo. Network: ABC Information & Entertainment. Format: Active rock. News staff: one; News: 6 hrs wkly. Target aud: 18-49; active/modern rock listeners.

*WVPG(FM)— April 4, 1985: 90.3 mhz; 9 kw. 321 ft. TL: N39 12 44 W81 35 30. Stereo. 600 Capitol St., Charleston 25301. Phone: (304) 556-4900. Fax: (304) 556-4960. E-mail: feedback@wvpubcast.org. Web Site: www.wvpubcast.org. Licensee: West Virginia Educational Broadcasting Authority. Network: Network: NPR, PRI. Format: News, class, jazz. News staff: 2. Spec prog: Mountain Stage 2 hrs, children one hr wkly. ♦ Rita Ray, CEO; Marilyn DiVita, gen mgr; Peggy Dorsey, dev mgr; Beth Carenbauer, adv mgr; James Muhammad, progmg dir; Laura H. Allen, mus dir; Giles Snyder, news dir & pub affrs dir; David McClanahan, chief of engrg.

WXIL(FM)— Sept 1, 1975: 95.1 mhz; 50 kw. 500 ft. TL: N39 14 47 W81 28 19. Stereo. 5 Rosemar Circle 26104. Secondary address: 1715 St. Mary's Ave. 26101. Phone: (304) 485-7425. Phone: (304) 485-4565. Fax: (304) 424-6955. Web Site: www.95xil.net. Licensee: PBBC Inc. Group owner: Burbach Broadcasting Group (acq 9-1-80; $1 million;. FTR: 7-7-80). Format: Hot Adult Contemp. News staff: one; News: 6 hrs wkly. Target aud: 25-54; women. ♦ Nicholas A. Galli, chmn & pres; Don Staats, VP & gen mgr; Brian Steel, opns dir & progmg dir; Mebi Haddox, sls dir; Eddie Gaydosh, prom dir; Larry Hughes, mus dir; Julie Williams, news dir.

Petersburg

*WAUA(FM)— Dec 1, 1997: 89.5 mhz; 10 kw. Ant 1,056 ft. TL: N39 12 07 W79 16 31. 600 Capitol St., Charleston 25301. Phone: (304) 556-4900. Fax: (304) 556-4981. Licensee: West Virginia Educational Broadcasting Authority. Network: Network: NPR, PRI. Format: Classical, news, public affairs. ♦ James Muhammad, gen mgr; Peggy Dorsey, dev mgr; David McClanahan, chief of engrg.

WELD-FM— Feb 6, 1987: 101.7 mhz; 1.9 kw horiz, 1.85 kw vert. Ant 515 ft. TL: N38 58 34 W79 01 13. Stereo. 126 Kessel Rd., Fisher 26818. Phone: (304) 538-6062. Fax: (304) 538-7032. E-mail: weld@chardynet.com. Web Site: www.weldamfm.com. Licensee: Thunder Associates LLC (acq 12-1-03; $600,000. with WELD(AM) Fisher). Network: ABC. Rep: Dome, Keystone (unwired net). Reddy, Begley & McCormick. Format: Country, relg, farm. News staff: one; News: 3 hrs wkly. Target aud: 25 plus. Spec prog: Gospel 3 hrs wkly. ♦ Curtis Durst, pres; Sandra Durst, exec VP; Alan Yokum, gen mgr.

Philippi

*WQAB(FM)— October 1975: 91.3 mhz; 7.2 kw. 180 ft. TL: N39 09 52 W80 02 57. Stereo. Box 2097, Withers-Brandon Hall, Alderson-Broaddus College 26416. Phone: (304) 457-6281. Phone: (304) 457-2916. Fax: (304) 457-6239. Licensee: Alderson-Broaddus College. Format: Div, CHR, adult contemp. News: 8 hrs wkly. Target aud: 15-40; college students. Spec prog: Jazz 4 hrs, Black 2 hrs, radio drama 2 hrs, children's 2 hrs wkly. ♦ Harry Hancock, stn mgr; George Sommer, engrg VP.

Pineville

WWYO(AM)— 1949: 970 khz; 1 kw-D, 26 w-N. TL: N37 35 20 W81 32 25. Stereo. Box 647, Bluefield 24701. Secondary address: Rt. 10, One Radio Rd. 24701. Phone: (304) 327-5651. Phone: (304) 732-8552. Fax: (304) 327-5651. E-mail: am970wwyo@citlink.net. Web Site: www.am970wwyo.bizland.com. Licensee: MRJ Inc. (acq 4-20-90; $125,000). Format: Southern gospel, country, MOR. Target aud: 25-65; housewives. Spec prog: Folk one hr, sports 18 hrs, educ 2 hrs, community 8 hrs wkly. ♦ Rudolph D. Jennings, pres & gen mgr.

Pocatalico

WRVZ(FM)— 1995: 98.7 mhz; 63 w. 617 ft. TL: N38 23 53 W81 41 06. 1111 Virginia St. E., Charleston 25301. Phone: (304) 342-8131. Fax: (304) 344-4745. Licensee: West Virginia Radio Corp. of Charleston. Group owner: West Virginia Radio Corp. (acq 3-12-01; $800,000). Format: CHR. ♦ Robert Benns, pres; Sean Banks, gen mgr; Woody Woods, progmg dir; Noel Richardson, chief of engrg.

West Virginia

Point Pleasant

WBGS(AM)— 1994: 1030 khz; 10 kw-D, DA. TL: N38 48 42 W82 05 59. 303 8th St., VA 25550. Phone: (304) 675-2763. Fax: (304) 675-2771. Licensee: Big River Radio Inc. Group owner: Baker Family Stations (Positive Radio Group) Booth, Freret, Imlay & Tepper. Format: Relg, teaching, gospel music. ♦ Vernon H. Baker, CEO, chmn & pres; Edward A. Baker, VP; Kevin Nott, gen mgr & progmg dir; Shari Cochron, sls dir; Tom Payne, mus dir; Winston Hawkins, chief of engrg.

WBYG(FM)— Co-owned with WBGS(AM). 1994: 99.5 mhz; 4.7 kw. 328 ft. TL: N38 47 52 W82 10 07. 303 8th St. 25550. Phone: (304) 675-2763. Fax: (304) 675-2771. Web Site: www.wbyg.com. (Acq 1-28-92). Format: Country. ♦ Kathy Wise, gen mgr.

*WPCN(FM)— Dec 21, 2000: 88.1 mhz; 3 kw. Ant 289 ft. TL: N38 50 49 W82 07 50. 303 8th Street 25550. Phone: (304) 675-2727. Fax: (304) 675-2771. E-mail: joyfm881@yahoo.com. Web Site: www.joyfm881.com. Licensee: Positive Alternative Radio Inc. Group owner: Baker Family Stations (Positive Radio Group) Booth, Freret, Imley & Tepper. Format: Southern gospel. ♦ Randy Parson, gen mgr, opns mgr & progmg dir.

Princeton

WAEY(AM)— December 1947: 1490 khz; 1 kw-U. TL: N37 23 23 W81 05 58. Box 5588 24740. Secondary address: Lilly Grove Addition, 1 Radio Ln. 24740. Phone: (304) 425-2151. Fax: (304) 487-2016. Licensee: Princeton Broadcasting Inc. Format: Gospel. News staff: one; News: 14 hrs wkly. Target aud: 25 plus; blue collar. ♦ Linda Witt, pres; Pat Tolley, VP; Bob Spencer, gen mgr & gen sls mgr; Jason Reed, opns mgr & prom dir; Ron Witt, progmg dir; Wayne Boone, chief of engrg.

WSTG(FM)— Co-owned with WAEY(AM). Apr 1, 1973: 95.9 mhz; 6 kw. 285 ft. TL: N37 23 23 W81 05 58. (CP: 480 w, ant 1,141 ft. TL: N37 15 30 W81 10 37). Stereo. Web Site: www.star95.com. Licensee: L & P Broadcasting Inc. Network: ABC Information & Entertainment. Format: Adult Top-40s. News staff: one.

WKOY-FM— April 1983: 100.9 mhz; 630 w. 641 ft. TL: N37 18 20 W81 07 30. Stereo. 900 Bluefield Ave., Bluefield 24701. Phone: (304) 327-7114. Fax: (304) 325-7850. Web Site: www.theeaglefm.com. Licensee: Monterey Licenses LLC. Group owner: Triad Broadcasting Co. LLC (acq 7-18-00; grpsl). Format: Classic Rock. News staff: one. Target aud: 25 plus. ♦ John Halford, gen mgr; Ken Deitz, opns dir; Danny Clemmon, gen sls mgr; Ed Weiland, progmg dir; Keith Bowman, chief of engrg.

*WPWV(FM)— September 2003: 90.1 mhz; 2.5 kw vert. Ant 1,040 ft. TL: N37 30 35 W81 12 55. Box 3206, Tupelo, MS 38801. Phone: (662) 844-8888. Fax: (662) 842-6791. Web Site: www.afr.net. Licensee: American Family Association. Group owner: American Family Radio. Format: Christian. ♦ Marvin Sanders, gen mgr.

Rainelle

WRLB(FM)— February 1977: 95.3 mhz; 3.1 kw. 460 ft. TL: N37 57 28 W80 45 45. (CP: 12.9 kw). Stereo. Box 1727, Lewisburg 24901. Phone: (304) 647-3606. Web Site: www.wrlb.com. Licensee: Faith Communications Network Inc. (acq 10-25-01). Format: Inspirational, Christian. Target aud: 25-54.

WRRL(AM)— 1973: 1130 khz; 1 kw-D. TL: N37 57 28 W80 45 45. H.C. 61, Box 383, Danese 25831. Phone: (304) 438-8537 phone/fax. E-mail: wrrlam@mountain.net. Licensee: Faith Mountain Communications Inc. (acq 2-8-01; $60,000). Format: Gospel, Christian, News/talk. Target aud: 35+. ♦ Nancy Whitt, CEO; Allen R. Whitt, pres & gen mgr.

Ravenswood

WLWF(FM)— July 15, 1996: 93.1 mhz; 3.3 kw. 446 ft. TL: N38 53 36 W81 46 52. Box 669, Gibbs & Gallatin St. 26164-0669. Phone: (304) 273-2544. Fax: (304) 273-3020. E-mail: thewolf@wirefire.com. Licensee: Legend Communications of West Virginia LLC. Group owner: Legend Communications L.L.C. (acq 11-14-01). Format: Country. Target aud: 18-50; general. Spec prog: American Indian one hr, Black one hr, farm one hr, folk 2 hrs, gospel 7 hrs, relg 7 hrs wkly. ♦ Rex Osborne, CEO.

WMOV(AM)— 1953: 1360 khz; 1 kw-U. TL: N38 57 52 W81 46 09. 527 Gibbs St. 26164. Phone: (304) 273-2544. Fax: (304) 273-3020.

E-mail: wmovam@aol.com. Licensee: Shay Hill, executor (acq 2-9-2004). Network: USA. Format: Full service. News staff: one; News: 14 hrs wkly. Target aud: 16 plus; emphasis on 25 plus. Spec prog: Talk 2 hrs, Pol one hr, folk 2 hrs, jazz 2 hrs, bluegrass 10 hrs wkly. ♦ Burke Allen, pres; Greg Carter, gen mgr, opns VP & opns dir.

Richwood

WKQV(FM)— Not on air, target date: unknown: 105.5 mhz; 3.96 kw. Ant 824 ft. TL: N38 21 34 W80 38 51. 1717 Dixie Hwy., Suite 650, Ft. Wright, KY 41011. Phone: (859) 331-9100. Licensee: Radioactive LLC. ♦ Benjamin L. Homel, pres & gen mgr.

WVAR(AM)— 1956: 600 khz; 1 kw-D. TL: N38 13 50 W80 32 49. 202 Back Fork St., Webster Springs 26288. Phone: (304) 847-5141. Fax: (304) 847-5149. Licensee: J & K Broadcasting Inc. (group owner; (acq 5-16-2005); with WAFD(FM) Webster Springs for 50% of stock). Rep: Dome. Format: Real country. News staff: one; News: 13 hrs wkly. Target aud: 25 plus; general. ♦ James A. Hardman, pres, gen mgr, sls dir, progmg dir & chief of engrg; Kimberly Stewart, stn mgr & news dir.

Ridgeley

WDYK(FM)— Not on air, target date: unknown: 100.5 mhz; 6 kw. Ant 163 ft. TL: N39 41 13 W78 40 54. 1717 Dixie Hwy., Suite 650, Fort Wright, KY 41011. Phone: (859) 331-9100. Licensee: Radioactive LLC. ♦ Benjamin L. Homel, pres.

Ripley

WCEF(FM)— Feb 24, 1981: 98.3 mhz; 3 kw. 300 ft. TL: N38 46 04 W81 41 09. Stereo. Box 798, 98 Cedar Lakes Rd. 25271. Phone: (304) 372-9800. Fax: (304) 372-9811. E-mail: shadow@c98.com. Web Site: www.c98.com. Licensee: Big River Radio Inc. Group owner: Baker Family Stations (acq 1-31-2003; $762,500). Format: Country. Target aud: 25-54. ♦ Ric Shannon, gen mgr & gen sls mgr; Rich Lacey, gen mgr, prom dir & progmg dir; Larry Koenig, chief of engrg.

*WLKV(FM)— Mar 26, 1994: 90.7 mhz; 3 kw. Ant 328 ft. TL: N38 51 44 W81 41 27. 5700 West Oaks Blvd., Rocklin, CA 95765. Phone: (916) 251-1600. Fax: (916) 251-1650. Web Site: www.klove.com. Licensee: Educational Media Foundation. (acq 3-31-2005; $700,000. with WLKP(FM) Belpre, OH). Network: K-Love. Format: Christian. ♦ Lloyd Parker, gen mgr.

Romney

WDZN(FM)— Aug 29, 1988: 100.1 mhz; 480 w. 823 ft. TL: N39 25 20 W78 47 25. Stereo. Box 477, Cumberland, MD 21501-0477. Phone: (301) 724-6000. Fax: (301) 724-0617. Web Site: www.radiodisney.com. Licensee: Charter Equities Inc. Network: Jones Radio Networks. Baraff, Koerner & Olender. Format: Disney. News staff: one; News: 15 hrs wkly. Target aud: 25-54; adult decision makers. ♦ Warren Gregory, pres & gen mgr; Travis Medcalf, sls dir & news dir; Rick Williams, chief of engrg.

*WVSB(FM)— Mar 30, 1973: 104.1 mhz; 100 w. Ant 781 ft. TL: N39 18 56 W78 43 04. Stereo. 301 E. Main St. 26757. Phone: (304) 822-4838. Fax: (304) 822-4896. E-mail: gpark@access.k12.wv.us. Licensee: West Virginia Schools for the Deaf & Blind. Format: Classic country. Target aud: General. Spec prog: West Virginia tourism information. ♦ Jane McBride, pres; Connie Newhouse, VP; George S. Park, gen mgr, chief of opns & progmg mgr.

Ronceverte

WRON(AM)— 1947: 1400 khz; 1 kw-U. TL: N37 45 36 W80 27 18. 276 Seneca Trail N. 24970. Phone: (304) 645-1400. Phone: (304) 645-1327. Fax: (304) 647-4802. E-mail: wron@wron.net. Web Site: www.wron.com. Licensee: Michael J. Kidd dba Greenbrier Radio. (acq 10-1-97; $450,000 with co-located FM). Network: Jones Radio Networks. Rep: Dome, Rgnl Reps. Format: Adult contemp, talk. News: 14 hrs wkly. Target aud: 35 & under. Spec prog: Relg 5 hrs wkly. ♦ Michael J. Kidd, stn mgr, opns mgr, progmg dir & news dir; T.C. Johnston, gen sls mgr & prom mgr; Grace Boxwell, pub affrs dir; Larry Carver, chief of engrg.

WRON-FM— Dec 6, 1983: 97.7 mhz; 1 kw. 800 ft. TL: N37 47 54 W80 30 55. Stereo. Web Site: www.wron.com. Rep: Rgnl Reps. Format: Oldies. Target aud: 25-60. ♦ Michael J. Kidd, dev mgr & progmg mgr; T.C. Johnston, mktg mgr; Larry Carver, engrg mgr.

Rupert

WYKM(AM)— Dec 9, 1981: 1250 khz; 5 kw-D, 32 w-N. TL: N37 59 35 W80 41 03. Box 627 25984. Secondary address: 714 Nicholas St. 25984. Phone: (304) 392-6003. Fax: (304) 392-5352. E-mail: bettydcrookshan@citynet.net. Licensee: Mountain State Broadcasting Co. Network: CBS. Format: Country, gospel. News: 7 hrs wkly. ♦ Betty D. Crookshanks, pres, gen mgr, gen sls mgr & progmg dir; Donald Crookshanks, exec VP; Wayne Boone, chief of engrg.

Saint Albans

WJYP(AM)— Jan 14, 1956: 1300 khz; 1 kw-D, 49 w-N. TL: N38 23 43 W81 51 00. 100 Kanawha Terr. 25177. Phone: (304) 722-3308. Fax: (304) 727-1300. E-mail: buywklc@wklc.com. Web Site: www.wklc.com. Licensee: WKLC Inc. Group owner: L.M. Communications Inc. (acq 2-23-80). Leventhal, Senter & Lerman. Format: Christian, news/talk, sports. News staff: one. Target aud: 18-49. ♦ Dick Findley, gen mgr; Bill Knight, opns mgr; Terri Outlaw, sls dir; Jesse Corliss, prom dir & progmg dir; Mark Atkinson, news dir & pub affrs dir; Fred Francis, chief of engrg.

WKLC-FM— Co-owned with WJYP(AM). Jan 1, 1966: 105.1 mhz; 50 kw. 1,663 ft. TL: N38 25 15 W81 55 27. Stereo. E-mail: rock105@intelos.com. Web Site: www.wklc.com. Network: ABC. Format: Rock/AOR. ♦ Bill Knight, progmg dir.

Saint Marys

WJAW(AM)— October 1984: 630 khz; 1 kw-D. TL: N39 23 42 W81 13 49. 925 Lancaster St., Marietta, OH 45750. Phone: (740) 373-1490. Fax: (740) 373-1717. E-mail: swiles@wmoa1490.com. Web Site: www.mariettaonline.com. Licensee: JAWCO Inc. (acq 2-26-2001; $25,000). Format: Sports. ♦ John Wharff III, gen mgr, sls dir & mktg dir; Dan Castelli, progmg dir; Ralph Metheny, chief of engrg.

WRRR-FM— Nov 16, 1983: 93.9 mhz; 17 kw. Ant 390 ft. TL: N39 22 49 W81 11 36. Stereo. Box 374 26170. Phone: (304) 684-3400. Fax: (304) 684-9241. Licensee: Seven Ranges Radio Co. Inc. Network: ABC News/Talk. Reddy, Begley & McCormick, LLP. Format: Adult contemp. News staff: one; News: 9 hrs wkly. Target aud: 25-49. ♦ Sam Yoho, pres & gen mgr; Lou Petronio, opns mgr.

Salem

WOBG-FM— Nov 1, 1990: 105.7 mhz; 6 kw. 581 ft. TL: N39 19 06 W80 26 18. Stereo. Box 2208, Old Weatherservice Bldg., Old Rt. 50 E., Clarksburg 26301. Phone: (304) 624-1400. Fax: (304) 624-1402. Licensee: Burbach of DE LLC. Group owner: Burbach Broadcasting Group (acq 5-17-00; grpsl). Network: ABC Information & Entertainment. Commercial Media Sales. Format: Classic rock. Target aud: 25-54. ♦ Nicholas A. Galli, pres; David Branhom, gen mgr & gen sls mgr; Larry Nelson, prom dir; Greg Bolyard, progmg dir; Larry Smith, chief of engrg.

Shepherdstown

*WSHC(FM)— 1974: 89.7 mhz; 950 w. -10 ft. TL: N39 25 53 W77 48 18. Stereo. WSHC-FM, Shepherd College, King St. 25443. Phone: (304) 876-5134. E-mail: wshc@shepherd.edu. Web Site: www.897wshc.org. Licensee: Shepherd College Board of Governors (acq 8-28-01). Network: ABC. Format: Alternative. News: 7 hrs wkly. Target aud: 18-24; college/young adult. ♦ Buck Lam, gen mgr; Ben Townsend, stn mgr.

South Charleston

WMXE(FM)—Listing follows WSCW(AM).

WSCW(AM)— Dec 13, 1963: 1410 khz; 5 kw-D. TL: N38 22 34 W81 42 13. 100 Kanawha Terr., St. Albans 25177. Phone: (304) 744-5388. E-mail: info@praise101.com. Web Site: www.praise101.com. Licensee: L.M. Communications of Kentucky LLC. Group owner: L.M. Communications Inc. (acq 4-1-03; grpsl). Format: Southern Gospel. Target aud: 25-64. ♦ Dick Findley, gen mgr; Terri Outlaw, sls dir; Chris Colagrasso, progmg dir.

WMXE(FM)— Co-owned with WSCW(AM). July 29, 1985: 100.9 mhz; 3 kw. 285 ft. TL: N38 22 34 W81 42 13. Stereo. Format: Adult contemp, relg. Target aud: 25-54. ♦ Bill Knight, opns mgr; Terri Outlaw, sls VP; Bob Campbell, progmg dir.

Stations in the U.S. — West Virginia

Developers & Brokers of Radio Properties

contact American Media Services at our suite:
Philadelphia Marriott Downtown
215-625-2900
843-972-2200
americanmediaservices.com
Charleston, SC
Dallas, TX · Chicago, Il · Austin, TX

American Media Services, LLC

---

*WWLA(FM)—Not on air, target date: unknown: 89.3 mhz; 300 w. Ant 528 ft. TL: N38 26 37 W81 36 08. 188 S. Bellevue, Suite 222, Memphis, TN 38104. Phone: (901) 726-8970. Fax: (901) 375-0041. Licensee: Broadcasting for the Challenged Inc. ♦ George S. Flinn Jr., pres.

Spencer

WVRC(AM)— Sept 12, 1961: 1400 khz; 1 kw-U. TL: N38 48 23 W81 21 40. 106 Radio St. 25276. Phone: (304) 927-3760. Fax: (304) 927-2877. E-mail: mail@wvrcradio.com. Web Site: www.wvrcradio.com. Licensee: Star Communications Inc. (acq 9-22-82; $40,000; 10-11-82). Rep: Rgnl Reps. Format: Gospel. ♦ Larry Koenig, pres & chief of engrg; Bob Edwards, VP, gen mgr, gen sls mgr & progmg dir; Zachary Zdanek, news dir.

WVRC-FM— October 1992: 104.7 mhz; 3 kw. 328 ft. TL: N38 47 40 W81 17 36. Web Site: www.wvrcradio.com. (Acq 3-1-91; 3-25-91). Format: Country.

Summersville

WCWV(FM)— Mar 13, 1983: 92.9 mhz; 11 kw. 900 ft. TL: N38 21 37 W80 38 49. Stereo. 713 Main St. 26651. Phone: (304) 872-5202. Fax: (304) 872-6904. E-mail: wcwv@c93net.com. Web Site: www.c93net.com. Licensee: R-S Broadcasting Co. Inc. Network: AP Radio, Jones Radio Networks. Rep: Dome. Format: Adult contemp. News: 23 hrs wkly. Target aud: 18-54. Spec prog: Gospel 15 hrs, relg 18 hrs wkly. ♦ Vivian Jean Brown, pres; Michael D. Brown, VP, gen mgr, chief of opns, news dir & engrg dir; Wes Brown, gen sls mgr, mktg dir & prom dir; Tanya Pitsenbarger, mus dir & pub affrs dir.

WDBS(FM)—See Sutton

*WMLJ(FM)— 1993: 90.5 mhz; 11 kw. Ant 1,033 ft. TL: N38 06 42 W80 35 52. Box 1014 26651. Phone: (304) 872-4612. Licensee: Grace Missionary Baptist Church. (acq 5-3-93; 5-24-93). Format: Gospel, children. Target aud: General. Spec prog: Sp one hr wkly. ♦ Clyde I. Ebron, pres; Chris Brown, gen mgr; Mike Tyler, chief of engrg.

Sutton

WDBS(FM)—Listing follows WSGB(AM).

WSGB(AM)— Jan 22, 1964: 1490 khz; 1 kw-U. TL: N38 39 11 W80 43 10. 180 Main St. 26601. Phone: (304) 765-7373. Fax: (304) 765-7836. E-mail: thebuzz@theboss97fm.com. Web Site: www.theboss97fm.com. Licensee: Summit Media Broadcasting L.L.C. (acq 12-30-99; $250,000. with co-located FM). Network: ABC. Rep: Dome. Dome, Regnl Reps Format: Adult contemp. Target aud: 18-34; young adults. ♦ Al Sergi, pres & gen mgr; Daniel Finch, CFO.

WDBS(FM)—Co-owned with WSGB(AM). Apr 25, 1987: 97.1 mhz; 22 kw. Ant 751 ft. TL: N38 27 05 W80 27 14. Stereo. Web Site: theboss97fm.com. Network: Network: Jones Radio Networks, AP Radio. Rep: Rgnl Reps. Format: Country classic, bluegrass. News: 9 hrs wkly. Target aud: 25-54; young adults females/males.

Vienna

WDMX(FM)— May 22, 1989: 100.1 mhz; 1.65 kw. 440 ft. TL: N39 20 18 W81 30 01. Stereo. Box 5559, 6006 Grand Central Ave. 26105. Phone: (304) 295-6070. Phone: (304) 375-6558. Fax: (304) 295-4389. E-mail: oldies@radio1.netassoc.net. Web Site: www.wdmx.com. Licensee: Clear Channel Broadcasting Licenses Inc. Group owner: Clear Channel Communications Inc. (acq 4-17-01; grpsl). Network: ABC. Rep: Clear Channel. Format: Oldies. News staff: 2; News: 2 hrs wkly. Target aud: 25-54. ♦ Chuck Poet, gen mgr; Jim Grywalsky, opns mgr.

Webster Springs

WAFD(FM)— Feb 1, 1996: 100.3 mhz; 33 kw. Ant 594 ft. TL: N38 27 38 W80 25 18. 202 Backfork St. 26288. Phone: (304) 847-5141. Fax: (304) 847-5149. Licensee: J&K Broadcasting Inc. (group owner). (acq 5-16-2005; with WVAR(AM) Richwood for 50% of stock). Format: Southern gospel. ♦ James A. Hardman, gen mgr, opns mgr, progmg dir & chief of engrg.

Weirton

WEIR(AM)— Sept 15, 1950: 1430 khz; 1 kw-U, DA-2. TL: N40 26 45 W80 37 36. Stereo. 2307 Pennsylvania Ave. 26062. Phone: (304) 723-1444. Fax: (304) 723-1688. E-mail: weir1430@weir.net. Web Site: www.unforgettablefavorites.com. Licensee: Priority Communications Ohio L.L.C. Group owner: Priority Communications (acq 12-4-98; $475,000 with WCDK(FM) Cadiz, OH). Network: Westwood One. Dome Pepper & Corazzini. Format: Talk morning, adult standards. News staff: one; News: 25 hrs wkly. Target aud: General. Spec prog: It 3 hrs, Gr 1 hr wkly. ♦ Jay Philippone, pres & gen mgr; Judy Vavrek, stn mgr, gen sls mgr & mktg dir; Tammie Beagle, opns mgr, progmg dir & news dir; Hank Segle, chief of engrg.

Welch

WELA(AM)—Not on air, target date: unknown: 1340 khz; 1 kw-U. TL: N37 25 50 W81 35 33. 115 Farwood Dr., Moreland, OH 44022. Phone: (216) 381-6037. Licensee: C. Douglas Thomas. ♦ C. Douglas Thomas, gen mgr.

WELC(AM)— Aug 19, 1950: 1150 khz; 5 kw-D. TL: N37 25 01 W81 36 58. Box 949 24801. Secondary address: U.S. Rt. 52 24801. Phone: (304) 436-2131. Fax: (304) 436-2132. E-mail: mail@welcamfm.com. Web Site: www.welcamfm.com. Licensee: Pocahontas Broadcasting Co. Rgnl Reps. Format: Adult contemp. Target aud: 21-54. Spec prog: Relg 15 hrs wkly. ♦ Sam Sidote, pres, gen mgr, gen sls mgr & prom mgr; Mary Sidote, progmg dir; John Sidote, mus dir, news dir & chief of engrg.

WELC-FM— Feb 1, 1990: 102.9 mhz; 1.8 kw. 423 ft. TL: N37 25 01 W81 36 58. Stereo. Web Site: www.welcamfm.com. Format: Adult contemp. Target aud: 18-49.

West Liberty

*WGLZ(FM)— Sept 4, 1990: 91.5 mhz; 150 w. 213 ft. TL: N40 09 49 W80 36 06. Box 13, West Liberty State College 26074. Phone: (304) 336-8045. Phone: (304) 336-8037. Fax: (304) 336-8286. Licensee: West Liberty State College. Format: Alternative/mix. ♦ Christian H. Lee, stn mgr & chief of engrg.

Weston

WFBY(FM)— Aug 29, 1972: 102.3 mhz; 940 w. 489 ft. TL: N39 04 15 W80 31 13. (CP: 10 kw, ant 509 ft.) 1065 Radio Park Dr., Mount Clare 26408. Phone: (304) 296-0029. Fax: (304) 296-3876. Licensee: West Virginia Radio Corp. (group owner; acq 1994; $250,000). Putbrese, Hunsaker & Trent. Format: Classic Rock. Target aud: 25-44. ♦ Dale Miller, pres & gen mgr; Christian Miller, CFO & stn mgr; Harvey Kercheval, opns VP; Larry Cottrill, natl sls mgr & rgnl sls mgr; Tina Clark, prom mgr; Chad Perry, progmg dir; Noel Richardson, engrg VP & engrg dir; Ralph Messor, chief of engrg.

WHAW(AM)— Feb 14, 1948: 980 khz; 1 kw-D, 50 w-N. TL: N39 02 25 W80 27 16. 300 Harrison Rd. 26452. Phone: (304) 269-5555. Fax: (304) 269-4800. E-mail: whaw@aol.com. Web Site: www.whawradio.com. Licensee: Stephen R. Peters. (acq 4-16-98). Network: ABC. Format: Real country, talk, oldies. News staff: one; News: 2 hrs wkly. Target aud: General. Spec prog: Folk 4 hrs, gospel 18 hrs wkly. ♦ Della Jane Woofter, sls dir & adv dir; Stephen R. Peters, gen mgr, progmg dir & engrg mgr.

Westover

WZST(FM)— Jan 5, 1983: 100.9 mhz; 3 kw. 198 ft. TL: N39 32 44 W79 55 58. Stereo. 401 Grand Central Station Dr., Suite 7000, Morgantown 26505. Secondary address: 15 Campbell St., Luray, VA 26505. Phone: (304) 292-1101. Fax: (304) 363-3852. E-mail: star100radio@aol.com. Licensee: Tschudy Communications Corp. Group owner: Tschudy Broadcast Group (acq 5-88). Format: Hot country. Spec prog: Relg mus 2 hrs wkly. ♦ Earl Judy, pres; Dick Yoder, gen mgr; Brian Dulaney, opns mgr & news dir; Judy King, gen sls mgr; Mike Donota, progmg dir; Rick Williams, chief of engrg.

Wheeling

WBBD(AM)— May 2, 1941: 1400 khz; 1 kw-U. TL: N40 05 49 W80 42 06. 1015 Main St. 26003. Phone: (304) 232-1170. Fax: (304) 234-0041. Licensee: Capstar TX L.P. Group owner: Clear Channel Communications Inc. (acq 8-30-00; grpsl). Format: Big band, adult standards. Target aud: 35 plus. Spec prog: Pol 2 hrs wkly. ♦ Scott Miller, gen mgr; Mark Carter, gen sls mgr; Jimmy Elliott, progmg dir; Jack Reese, chief of engrg.

WKWK-FM—Co-owned with WBBD(AM). Mar 17, 1948: 97.3 mhz; 50 kw. 470 ft. TL: N40 05 49 W80 42 06. Stereo. Web Site: www.wk973.com. Network: ABC Information & Entertainment. Format: Var/div. Target aud: 25-54. ♦ Scott Miller, VP & gen mgr; Mark Carter, sls VP; Missy Tschappat, prom dir; Jim Connor, progmg dir; Tammie Beagle, news dir; Jack Rees, engrg dir.

WEGW(FM)— October 1966: 107.5 mhz; 10.5 kw. 882 ft. TL: N40 03 41 W80 45 08. Stereo. 1015 Main St. 26003. Phone: (304) 232-1170. Fax: (304) 234-0041. Web Site: www.wegw.com. Licensee: Capstar TX L.P. Group owner: Clear Channel Communications Inc. (acq 8-30-00; grpsl). Format: Rock/AOR. Target aud: 25-54. ♦ James T. Shea, pres; Scott Miller, VP & gen mgr; Karen Hardy, sls dir & gen sls mgr; Missy Tschappat, prom dir; Dana Kelly, progmg dir; Jeff Jagger, mus dir; Tammie Beagle, asst music dir; Jack Rees, chief of engrg.

WKKX(AM)— Apr 7, 1963: 1600 khz; 5 kw-D, 33 w-N. TL: N40 05 26 W80 42 11. Box 231 26003. Phone: (304) 214-1610. Fax: (304) 232-8488. E-mail: tsanthony@stratuswave.net. Web Site: www.espn1600.com. Licensee: RCK 1 Group LLC (acq 7-19-2004; $400,000). Network: ESPN Radio. Rep: Christal. Format: Sports talk. Target aud: 25-54; men. ♦ Tom Anthony, gen mgr.

WOVK(FM)—Listing follows WWVA.

*WPHP(FM)— Apr 4, 1977: 91.9 mhz; 1 kw. 259 ft. TL: N40 04 07 W80 39 04. 1976 Parkview Rd. 26003. Phone: (304) 243-0400. Fax: (304) 243-0449. Licensee: Ohio County Board of Education. Format: Top-40. Spec prog: Black 4 hrs, jazz one hr wkly. ♦ Carolyn Ihlenfeld, gen mgr; Caroline Ihlenfeld, progmg dir.

*WVNP(FM)— Oct 7, 1981: 89.9 mhz; 25 kw. Ant 499 ft. TL: N40 12 58 W80 33 31. Stereo. 600 Capitol St., Charleston 25301. Phone: (304) 556-4900. Fax: (304) 556-4960. E-mail: feedback@wvpubcast.org. Web Site: www.wvpubcast.org. Licensee: West Virginia Educational Broadcasting Authority. Network: Network: NPR, PRI. Format: News, class, jazz. ♦ Marilyn DiVita, gen mgr & dev dir; Rita Ray, gen mgr; James Muhammad, progmg dir; Greg Callard, news dir; Chuck Wells, engrg dir.

WWVA(AM)— December 1926: 1170 khz; 50 kw-U, DA-2. TL: N40 06 07 W80 52 02. 1015 Main St. 26003. Phone: (304) 232-1170. Fax: (304) 234-0041. Fax: (304) 234-0036. Web Site: www.wwva.com. Licensee: Capstar TX L.P. Group owner: Clear Channel Communications Inc. (acq 8-30-00; grpsl). Rep: McGavren Guild. Format: News/talk. Target aud: 25-54. Spec prog: Farm 2 hrs wkly. ♦ Scott Miller, gen mgr; Scott Peel, natl sls mgr; Jim Harrington, progmg dir; Tammie Beagle, news dir.

West Virginia

WOVK(FM)— Co-owned with WWVA. September 1947: 98.7 mhz; 50 kw. 390 ft. TL: N40 04 58 W80 46 18. (CP: 15 kw, ant 906 ft., TL: N40 04 48 W80 46 06). Web Site: www.wovk.com. Format: Country. ♦ Jim Elliott, progmg dir.

White Sulphur Springs

WSLW(AM)— 1971: 1310 khz; 5 kw-D. TL: N37 48 17 W80 21 03. Box 610, Rt. 60 W. Harts Run 24986. Phone: (304) 536-1310. Fax: (304) 536-1311. E-mail: radio@wkejwslw.com. Licensee: Quorum Radio Partners of Virginia Inc., debtor-in-possession. (group owner; acq 4-20-2005; grpsl). Network: ABC Information & Entertainment. Rep: Rgnl Reps. Format: Adult standards. News: 8 hrs wkly. Target aud: 25-60; secondary 16-25 & 60 plus. ♦ Michael Stone, gen mgr & progmg dir; Rita McClung, gen sls mgr & prom mgr; Chuck Harper, news dir; Wayne Boone, chief of engrg.

Williamson

WBTH(AM)— Apr 19, 1939: 1400 khz; 1 kw-U. TL: N37 40 09 W82 16 09. Box 1409, 5 1/2 E. Second Ave. 25661. Phone: (304) 235-3600. Fax: (304) 235-8118. Licensee: East Kentucky Radio Network Inc. (group owner; acq 4-4-00; $630,000. with co-located FM). Format: Adult contemp, oldies. Target aud: 25-54. ♦ Dwayne Amburgey, gen mgr & sls dir; Vernon Roberts, gen mgr, opns mgr & progmg dir; Joe Kinzer, opns mgr & news dir; Paul Manuel, mus dir & chief of engrg; Walter Clyde Dingus, chief of engrg.

WXCC(FM)— Co-owned with WBTH(AM). Oct 27, 1978: 96.5 mhz; 50 kw. 500 ft. TL: N37 40 09 W82 16 09. E-mail: wxcc@mikrotec.com. Web Site: www.wxccfm.com. Format: Contemp country.

Williamstown

WVVV(FM)— 2000: 96.9 mhz; 3.51 kw. 423 ft. TL: N39 20 18 W81 30 01. Box 5559, Vienna 26105. Phone: (304) 295-6070. Fax: (304) 295-4389. Web Site: www.z969radio.net. Licensee: Bennco Inc. (acq 11-2-01; $1.625 million). Format: Var/div. ♦ Jack Horton, gen mgr.

Wisconsin

Adams

WDKM(FM)— Oct 8, 1993: 106.1 mhz; 6 kw. 328 ft. TL: N43 57 29 W89 49 43. Stereo. 408 Hillwood Ln., Friendship 53934. Secondary address: 1040 W. Center St. 53910. Phone: (608) 339-3221. Fax: (608) 339-2403. E-mail: heidi@wdkmfm.com. Web Site: www.wdkmfm.com. Licensee: Roche-A-Cri Broadcasting. Format: Oldies. Spec prog: Polka 14 hrs wkly. ♦ Drew Smith, stn mgr, mus dir & engrg VP; Audrey Babcock, sls dir; Heidi Roekle, gen mgr & progmg VP; Harry Davis, news dir.

Algoma

WBDK(FM)— Nov 12, 1986: 96.7 mhz; 8 kw. 538 ft. TL: N44 42 26 W87 24 26. Stereo. 3030 Park Dr., Suite 3, Sturgeon Bay 54235. Phone: (920) 746-9430. Fax: (920) 746-9433. Web Site: www.doorradio.com. Licensee: Nicolet Broadcasting Inc. (group owner; acq 9-3-93; 9-27-93). Pepper & Corazzini. Format: Oldies of 50's & 60's. News staff: 3. Target aud: 34 plus. ♦ Paul Schmitt, sr VP; Roger Utnehmer, pres & gen mgr; Karen Leitzinger, opns mgr & mus dir; Kathy Robinson, progmg dir & progmg mgr; James Wyngaard, news dir; John Zecherle, chief of engrg.

WRLU(FM)— Aug 1, 1999: 104.1 mhz; 6 kw. 328 ft. TL: N44 40 02 W87 23 55. 3030 Park Dr., Suite 3, Sturgeon Bay 54235. Phone: (920) 746-9430. Fax: (920) 746-9433. Web Site: www.doorradio.com. Licensee: Nicolet Broadcasting Inc. (group owner) Format: Country. News: 3 hrs wkly. ♦ Roger Utnehmer, pres & gen mgr; Kathy Robinson, progmg dir.

Allouez

WJLW(FM)— 1996: 106.7 mhz; 25 kw. 328 ft. TL: N44 29 03 W87 56 12. Stereo. 810 Victoria St., Green Bay 54302. Phone: (920) 468-4100. Fax: (920) 468-0250. Licensee: Cumulus Licensing Corp. Group owner: Cumulus Media Inc. (acq 8-7-98; $2.5 million). Format: Class rock. News staff: one; News: 5 hrs wkly. Target aud: 25-54; educated/affluent adults. ♦ Greg Jessen, CEO, CEO & gen mgr;

Jimmy Clark, CFO & opns mgr; Buck Hein, gen sls mgr; Kurt Petersen, mktg mgr & news dir; Scott Klohn, progmg dir; Chris Gielow, chief of engrg.

Altoona

WDVM(AM)— See Eau Claire

WISM-FM— Nov 15, 1991: 98.1 mhz; 10 kw. Ant 174 ft. TL: N44 46 36 W91 28 30. 619 Cameron St., Eau Claire 54703. Phone: (715) 830-4000. Fax: (715) 835-9680. Web Site: www.mix981.com. Licensee: Clear Channel Broadcasting Licenses Inc. Group owner: Clear Channel Communications Inc. (acq 11-1-2002; $2.4 million). Format: Adult contemp. Target aud: 25-54. ♦ Rick Hencley, gen mgr; Mike Cushman, opns mgr; Steve Potter, sls dir; Jim Finn, progmg dir; Paul Orth, chief of engrg.

Amery

WXCE(AM)— Jan 23, 1978: 1260 khz; 5 kw-U, DA-2. TL: N45 15 25 W92 22 00. Box 1260 54001. Secondary address: 328 S. 100th St. 54001. Phone: (715) 268-7185. Fax: (715) 268-7187. E-mail: wxce@spacestar.net. Web Site: www.wxce.com. Licensee: Lake Country Broadcasting Corp. (acq 1-14-99). Network: ABC. Format: News/talk. News staff: one; News: 20 hrs wkly. Target aud: 35 plus. ♦ Darren Van Blaricom, gen mgr & progmg mgr; Ray Ose, rgnl sls mgr; Greg Marston, news dir; Reynold Lark, chief of engrg.

Antigo

WACD(FM)— 1998: 106.1 mhz; 10 kw. 276 ft. TL: N45 06 23 W89 09 09. Box 509 54409. Phone: (715) 623-4124. Licensee: Results Broadcasting Inc. (group owner; acq 4-29-2005; $500,000. with WATK(AM) Antigo). Format: Adult standards. ♦ Shaughn Novy, gen mgr; K.B. Butler, opns mgr.

WATK(AM)— Mar 15, 1948: 900 khz; 250 w-D, 196 w-N. TL: N45 06 50 W89 08 20. Box 509, N. 2237 Hwy. 45 S. 54409. Phone: (715) 623-4124. Fax: (715) 627-4497. E-mail: wrlo@marathonmedianorth.net. Web Site: www.wrlo1053.com. Licensee: Results Broadcasting Inc. (group owner; acq 4-29-2005; $500,000. with WACD(FM) Antigo). Network: Jones Radio Networks. Format: Adult standards. News staff: 2; News: 12 hrs wkly. Target aud: 25-59; two-income families. Spec prog: Gospel 2 hrs wkly. ♦ Tom Hopfensperger, gen mgr; Duff Damos, progmg dir & opns mgr; Shaughn Novy, gen sls mgr; Dave St. Peter, progmg dir & news dir; Cliff Groth, chief of engrg.

WRLO-FM— Nov 11, 1973: 105.3 mhz; 100 kw. Ant 541 ft. TL: N45 22 04 W89 08 20. Stereo. 3616 Hwy. 47 N., Rhinelander 54501. Phone: (715) 362-1975. Fax: (715) 362-1973. Web Site: www.wrlo1053.com. Licensee: NewRadio Group LLC (acq 12-20-2002; grpsl). Format: Classic rock. Target aud: 21-54. ♦ Michele Krueger, sls dir; Shaughn Novy, rgnl sls mgr; Duff Damos, progmg dir; John Burton, news dir; Jim Zastrow, chief of engrg.

Appleton

WAPL-FM— Dec 24, 1965: 105.7 mhz; 100 kw. 1,175 ft. TL: N44 21 32 W87 59 07. Stereo. Box 1519 54912. Secondary address: 2727 E. Radio Rd. 54915. Phone: (920) 734-9226. Fax: (920) 733-3291. E-mail: wapl@wcinet.com. Web Site: www.wapl.com. Licensee: Woodward Communications Inc. (group owner; acq 3-75). Rep: McGavren Guild. Hogan & Hartson. Format: Mainstream rock. News: 2 hrs wkly. Target aud: 20-plus; professional and semi-professional adults. ♦ Greg Bell, gen mgr, stn mgr & opns mgr; Joe Calgaro, sls dir & progmg dir; Ed Walters, natl sls mgr & news dir; Elle Wood, prom dir; Steve Brown, chief of engrg.

*WEMI(FM)— 1994: 91.9 mhz; 3.1 kw. Ant 328 ft. TL: N44 15 17 W88 26 13. 1909 W. 2nd St. 54914. Phone: (920) 749-9456. Fax: (920) 749-0474. Web Site: christianfamilyradio.net. Licensee: Evangel Ministries Inc. Network: Network: Network: Moody, USA, Salem Radio Network. Leventhal, Senter & Lerman. Format: Relg. News: 10 hrs wkly. Target aud: 35-49; women. Spec prog: Sp one hr wkly. ♦ Mary B. Lieb, chmn; Paul Cameron, gen mgr; Phil Pannier, opns dir; Heidi Prahl, dev dir.

*WLFM(FM)— Mar 10, 1956: 91.1 mhz; 10.5 kw. 120 ft. TL: N44 15 42 W88 23 47. Stereo. 420 E. College Ave. 54911. Phone: (920) 832-6566. Phone: (920) 832-6567. Fax: (920) 832-6904. E-mail: wlfm@lawrence.edu. Web Site: www.lawrenceu.edu/sorg/wlfm. Licensee: Lawrence University. Network: Network: NPR, PRI. Format: Talk, div.

Directory of Radio

News: 15 hrs wkly. Target aud: 45 plus; socially active, educated. Spec prog: Class 10 hrs wkly. ♦ Lauren Semivan, stn mgr; Nolan Riegler, stn mgr.

WSCO(AM)— 1952: 1570 khz; 1 kw-D, 331 w-N. TL: N44 13 04 W88 24 33. PO Box 1519, 2800 E. College Ave. 54912. Phone: (920) 733-6639. Fax: (920) 739-0494. Licensee: Woodward Communications Inc. (group owner; acq 12-3-01; $450,000). Format: Sports. Target aud: 35 plus. ♦ Bill Skemp, CEO & sls dir; Tom Yumt, pres; Greg Bell, VP & gen mgr; John Wanie, sls dir; Jay Van Stiphoup, progmg dir; Steve Brown, chief of engrg.

Ashland

WATW(AM)— May 1, 1940: 1400 khz; 1 kw-U. TL: N46 34 23 W90 51 56. (CP: 480 w-U. TL: N46 34 25 W90 51 56). Stereo. 2320 Ellis Ave. 54806. Phone: (715) 682-2727. Phone: (715) 682-2728. Fax: (715) 682-9338. E-mail: production@baybroadcasting.net. Web Site: www.baybroadcasting.net. Licensee: Heartland Communications License LLC. (group owner; acq 4-23-2004; grpsl). Network: ABC Information & Entertainment. Lauren A. Colby. Format: Hits of the 40s, 50s & 60s, news. News staff: one; News: 17 hrs wkly. Target aud: 40 plus; middle to upper income adults. Spec prog: Big band, polka one hr, relg 5 hrs wkly. ♦ Jerry Hackman, gen mgr; Skip Hunter, progmg dir & chief of engrg.

WJJH(FM)— Co-owned with WATW(AM). Aug 1, 1970: 96.7 mhz; 50 kw. 246 ft. TL: N46 34 25 W90 51 56. Stereo. Network: ABC FM Connection. Format: Classic rock. Target aud: 25-45.

WBSZ(FM)— July 25, 1994: 93.3 mhz; 100 kw. 246 ft. Stereo. 2320 Ellis Ave. 54806. Phone: (715) 682-2727. Fax: (715) 682-9338. E-mail: production@baybroadcasting.net. Web Site: www.baybroadcasting.net. Licensee: Heartland Communications License LLC. (group owner; acq 4-23-2004; grpsl). Network: Network: ABC, Westwood One. Lauren A. Colby. Format: Hot country. Target aud: 18-49. ♦ John "Jay" Nix, gen mgr, sls VP & mktg VP; Dave Morris, dev VP; Skip Hunter, opns VP & mus dir.

WEGZ(FM)— See Washburn

Auburndale

*WLBL(AM)— 1922: 930 khz; 5 kw-D. TL: N44 36 52 W90 02 08. 518 S. 7th Ave., Wausau 54401-5362. Phone: (715) 261-6298. Fax: (715) 848-28. E-mail: listener@wpr.org. Web Site: www.wpr.org. Licensee: State of Wisconsin, Education Communications Board. Network: Network: NPR, PRI. Format: News/talk, MOR. News staff: 4. ♦ Phil Corriveau, gen mgr; Rick Reyer, stn mgr & dev dir.

Balsam Lake

WLMX-FM— Feb 14, 1997: 104.9 mhz; 22 kw. 348 ft. TL: N45 25 07 W92 14 34. Stereo. Box 476, Milltown 54858. Secondary address: 97 W. Main St., Milltown 54858. Phone: (715) 825-4240. Fax: (715) 825-4244. E-mail: studio@mix105.ws. Web Site: mix105.ws. Licensee: Quarnstrom Media Group LLC (group owner; acq 3-28-2003; $1.2 million. with WXCX(FM) Siren). Network: ABC. Format: Adult contemp. News: 5 hrs wkly. Target aud: 18-49; adults. ♦ Alan Quarnstrom, pres; Don Welch, VP; Dale Brooks, gen mgr; Neil Novotny, opns mgr.

Baraboo

WOLX-FM— Licensed to Baraboo. See Madison

WRPQ(AM)— June 1967: 740 khz; 250 w-D, 6.4 w-N. TL: N43 27 19 W89 45 13. Stereo. Box 456 53913. Secondary address: 407 Oak St. 53913. Phone: (608) 356-3974. Fax: (608) 355-9952. E-mail: jeffsmith@wrpq.com. Web Site: www.wrpq.com. Licensee: Baraboo Broadcasting Co. (acq 7-1-91; $125,000; 7-13-81). Network: CNN Radio. Koerner & Olender. Format: Adult contemp. News staff: one; News: 8 hrs wkly. Target aud: 25-54. Spec prog: Relg 4 hrs wkly. ♦ Gregory Buchwald, VP & engrg VP; Jeff Smith, pres, gen mgr, sls dir, prom dir, adv mgr, progmg dir & news dir.

Barron

WAQE-FM— 1999: 97.7 mhz. 15.5 kw. Ant 289 ft. TL: N45 32 16 W91 45 50. Box 703, 1859 21st Ave., Rice Lake 54868. Phone: (715) 234-9059. Fax: (715) 234-6942. E-mail: info@waqe.com. Web Site: www.waqe.com. Licensee: TKC Inc. Shaw Pittman. Format: Hits of the 80s, 90s & today. News staff: one; News: 5 hrs wkly. Target aud:

Broadcasting & Cable Yearbook 2006

Stations in the U.S.   Wisconsin

Developers & Brokers of Radio Properties

contact American Media Services
at our suite:
Philadelphia Marriott Downtown
215-625-2900
843-972-2200
americanmediaservices.com
Charleston, SC
Dallas, TX • Chicago, Il • Austin, TX

American Media Services, LLC

25-54; general. ♦Brian Schultz, gen mgr & stn mgr; Tom Koser, gen mgr; Mike Bigner, progmg dir; Mike Murrey, chief of engrg.

Beaver Dam

WBEV(AM)— Mar 21, 1951: 1430 khz; 1 kw-U, DA-N. TL: N43 25 43 W88 53 33. Box 902 533916. Secondary address: 100 Stoddart St. 533916. Phone: (920) 885-4442. Fax: (920) 885-2152. Licensee: Good Karma Broadcasting L.L.C. (group owner; acq 12-2-97; grpsl). Network: ABC Information & Entertainment. Format: Adult contemp, news/talk. News staff: 3; News: 20 hrs wkly. Target aud: 30 plus; general. Spec prog: Farm 8 hrs, sports 18 hrs wkly. ♦Craig Karmazin, pres & gen mgr; Rick Armon, chief of opns & progmg dir; John Moser, gen sls mgr & news dir; Warren Jorgenson, chief of engrg.

WXRO(FM)—Co-owned with WBEV(AM). July 15, 1968: 95.3 mhz; 6 kw. 328 ft. TL: N43 28 09 W88 49 32. Stereo. Format: Modern country. News staff: 3; News: 10 hrs wkly. Target aud: 25-54; general. Spec prog: Farm 6 hrs wkly. ♦Craig Karmazin, chmn; John A. Moser, sls dir; Rick Armon, prom dir.

Beloit

***WBCR-FM**— Nov 30, 1965: 90.3 mhz; 100 w. 44 ft. TL: N42 30 13 W89 01 55. (CP: 130 w). Beloit College, 700 College St. 53511. Phone: (608) 363-2402. Fax: (608) 363-2718. E-mail: wbcr@stubeloit.edu. Web Site: www.beloit.edu/~wbcr/. Licensee: Beloit College. Format: Educ, div. ♦Kyle McKenzie, gen mgr; Andrew Falk, progmg dir; Emily Eagle, progmg dir; Seth Porter, mus dir.

WGEZ(AM)— Sept 26, 1948: 1490 khz; 1 kw-U. TL: N42 29 45 W89 01 03. Box 416 53512. Secondary address: 622 Public Ave. 53511. Phone: (608) 365-8865. Fax: (608) 365-8867. E-mail: wgezam@hotmail.com. Licensee: Alliance Communications Inc. (acq 2-18-2005; $325,000). Network: CBS. Format: Oldies. Target aud: 25-54; baby boomers. ♦Edward J. Moskal, pres; Paul Roden, gen mgr & progmg dir; Jeff Haas, sls dir; Alex Ruano, news dir; Todd Housser, chief of engrg.

WTJK(AM)—(South Beloit).IL May 18, 1948: 1380 khz; 5 kw-U, DA-N. TL: N42 27 34 W89 01 43. Stereo. 1 Parker Place, Suite 485, Janesville 53545. Phone: (608) 758-9025. Fax: (608) 758-9550. E-mail: espn1380@hotmail.com. Web Site: www.espn1380.com. Licensee: Good Karma Broadcasting L.L.C. (group owner; acq 9-13-00; $235,000). Network: ESPN Radio. Rep: McGavren Guild. Format: Sports, info. News: 40 hrs wkly. Target aud: Males 25-54. ♦Keith Williams, gen mgr; Laurie Clark, gen sls mgr; Sean Thompson, progmg dir; Warren Jorgensen, chief of engrg.

Berlin

WBJZ(FM)— July 31, 1972: 104.7 mhz; 3.4 kw. Ant 351 ft. TL: N43 53 57 W88 53 37. 112 Watson St., Ripon 54971. Phone: (920) 748-9205. Fax: (920) 748-5530. Licensee: Caxambas Corp. Format: Smooth jazz. Target aud: 35-54; upscale, adults. ♦Jason Mansmith, gen mgr, stn mgr, gen sls mgr & progmg dir; Mike Enfelt, chief of engrg.

WISS(AM)— June 28, 1971: 1090 khz; 500 w-D. TL: N43 56 55 W88 59 09. Box 71 54923. Secondary address: 112 N. Pearl St. 54923. Phone: (920) 361-3551. Fax: (920) 361-3737. E-mail: production @hometownbroadcasting.com. Web Site: www.hometownbroadcasting.com. Licensee: Hometown Broadcasting LLC (acq 12-1-99; $165,000). Format: Classic country, sports, local news/talk. News staff: one; News: 10 hrs wkly. Target aud: 25-54; local community. ♦Margaret Corrente, gen mgr, sls dir & prom dir; Tom Boyson, gen mgr; Bernie Phillips, progmg dir & news dir; Andy Disterhaft, chief of engrg.

Birnamwood

WYNW(FM)— 2003: 92.9 mhz; 250 w. Ant 46 ft. TL: N44 55 49 W89 12 33. Starboard Network, 2300 Riverside Drive, Green Bay 54301. Phone: (920) 469-3021. Fax: (920) 469-3023. Web Site: www.relevantradio.com. Licensee: Starboard Media Foundation Inc. Group owner: Relevant Radio (acq 7-9-2002). Format: Catholic radio. ♦Mike Strub, gen mgr.

Black River Falls

WWIS(AM)— Aug 23, 1958: 1260 khz; 580 w-D. TL: N44 19 11 W90 53 31. W11573 Town Creek Rd. 54615. Phone: (715) 284-4391. Fax: (715) 284-9740. E-mail: wwis@wwisradio.com. Web Site: www.wwisradio.com. Licensee: WWIS Radio Inc. (acq 5-1-68). Miller & Miller, P.C. Format: Oldies. News: 6 hrs wkly. Target aud: General. ♦Robert E. Smith, chmn; Nelson Lent, pres; Robert A. Gabrielson, gen mgr.

WWIS-FM— Jan 21, 1991: 99.7 mhz; 25 kw. 328 ft. TL: N44 19 11 W90 53 31. Stereo. W. 11573 Town Creek Rd. 54615. Phone: (715) 284-4391. Fax: (715) 284-9740. E-mail: wwis@cuttingedge.net. Web Site: www.wisradio.com. Licensee: WWIS Radio Inc. Network: CBS. Format: Adult contemp. News: 12 hrs wkly. ♦Robert Smith, chmn; Nelson Lent, pres & gen mgr; Robert Gabrielson, gen mgr & opns mgr.

Bloomer

WQRB(FM)— 1993: 95.1 mhz; 8.9 kw. 430 ft. TL: N45 01 59 W91 21 09. Stereo. Box 45, Eau Claire 54703. Phone: (715) 830-4000. Fax: (715) 835-9680. Web Site: www.b95radio.com. Licensee: Capstar TX L.P. Group owner: Clear Channel Communications Inc. (acq 2000; grpsl). Format: Hot country. Target aud: 25-54. ♦Rick Hencley, gen mgr; Mike Cushman, opns mgr; Steve Potter, gen sls mgr; Mike McKay, progmg dir; Keith Edwards, news dir; Paul Orth, chief of engrg.

Brillion

WDUZ-FM— March 1993: 107.5 mhz; 6 kw. 328 ft. TL: N44 15 28 W88 11 43. (CP: 5 kw). 810 Victoria St., Green Bay 54302. Phone: (920) 468-4100. Fax: (920) 468-0250. Licensee: Cumulus Licensing Corp. Group owner: Cumulus Media Inc. (acq 8-7-98; $2.065 million). Fisher, Wayland, Cooper, Leader & Zaragoza. Format: Sports/talk. Target aud: 18-49; educated, affluent, upper-income. Spec prog: Sp 2 hrs wkly. ♦Greg Jessen, gen mgr; Buck Hein, gen sls mgr; Brian Stenzel, prom dir; Jimmy Clark, opns mgr, sls dir & progmg dir; Chris Gielow, engrg mgr.

Brookfield

WFMR(FM)— Aug 18, 1995: 106.9 mhz; 3 kw. 154 ft. TL: N43 07 41 W88 05 36. 5407 W. McKinley Ave., Milwaukee 53208. Phone: (414) 978-9000. Fax: (414) 978-9001. Web Site: www.wfmr.com. Licensee: Saga Communications of Milwaukee LLC. Group owner: Saga Communications Inc. (acq 5-9-97; $5 million. with WFMR(FM) Menomonee Falls). Format: Classical. Target aud: 25-54. ♦Thomas Joerres, pres & gen mgr; Annmarie King, gen sls mgr; Cindy Gaudion, natl sls mgr; Steve Murphy, progmg dir; Andrea Williams, pub affrs dir; Dave Popovich, chief of engrg.

Brule

***WHSA(FM)**— Sept 14, 1952: 89.9 mhz; 38 kw. 550 ft. TL: N46 27 59 W91 33 56. Stereo. P.O. Box 2000, Superior 54880. Secondary address: 1800 Grand Ave., Superior 54880. Phone: (715) 394-8530. Fax: (715) 394-8404. E-mail: jmunson@uwsuper.edu. Web Site: www.wpr.org. Licensee: State of Wisconsin Educational Communications Board. Network: NPR. Format: Class, news/talk. News staff: one; News: 39 hrs wkly. Target aud: 34 plus. Spec prog: Folk 3 hrs, jazz 6 hrs wkly. ♦John A. Munson, gen mgr.

Burlington

***WBSD(FM)**— Apr 7, 1975: 89.1 mhz; 300 w. 107 ft. TL: N42 40 14 W88 16 18. Stereo. 400 McCanna prkwy 53105. Phone: (262) 763-0195. Fax: (262) 763-0207. Web Site: www.wbsdfm.com. Licensee: Burlington Area School District. Format: Alternative, progsv rock.

Target aud: 25-54. Spec prog: Jazz 4 hrs, reggae 3 hrs, ska/punk 2 hrs, metal 3 hrs, blues 3 hrs, folk 5 hrs wkly. ♦Terry Havel, gen mgr; Ryan Rutz, opns VP.

Chetek

WATQ(FM)— May 17, 1997: 106.7 mhz; 50 kw. 492 ft. TL: N45 14 31 W91 44 43. Stereo. Box 45, Eau Claire 54702. Secondary address: 619 Cameron St. 54702. Phone: (715) 830-4000. Fax: (715) 835-9680. Web Site: www.moose106.com. Licensee: Capstar TX L.P. Group owner: Clear Channel Communications Inc. (acq 2000; grpsl). Network: CBS. Format: Country. News staff: 2. Target aud: 35-64. ♦Rick Hencley, gen mgr; Steve Potter, gen sls mgr; Mike Cushman, progmg dir; Keith Edwards, news dir; Paul Orth, chief of engrg.

Chilton

WMBE(AM)— May 25, 1984: 1530 khz; 250 w-D. TL: N44 01 10 W88 09 32. Box 1450, Fond du Lac 54936. Secondary address: 354 Winnebago Dr., Fond du Lac 54935. Phone: (920) 921-1071. Fax: (920) 921-0757. E-mail: info@espnradio1530.com. Web Site: www.espnradio1530.com. Licensee: Maszka-Pacer Radio Inc. (acq 12-28-90; $4,469; 1-14-91). Network: USA. Format: Sports. News staff: 2. Target aud: Males 18-54; Sports fans. ♦R.B. Hopper, gen mgr; Mark Kastein, gen sls mgr & prom mgr; Shawn A. Kiser, progmg dir; Stu Muck, engrg dir.

Chippewa Falls

WAXX(FM)—See Eau Claire

WCFW(FM)— Oct 20, 1968: 105.7 mhz; 25 kw. 305 ft. TL: N44 52 18 W91 17 11. Stereo. 318 Well St. 54729. Phone: (715) 723-2257. Fax: (715) 723-8276. Licensee: Roland L. Bushland dba Bushland Radio/WCFW. Format: Adult contemp. News: 8 hrs wkly. Target aud: 35 plus; upscale. Spec prog: Relg 2 hrs wkly. ♦Roland L. Bushland, gen mgr; Patricia Bushland, gen sls mgr & progmg dir.

WEAQ(AM)— Sept 7, 1958: 1150 khz; 5 kw-D. TL: N45 53 05 W91 23 25. Box 1, Eau Claire 54702. Secondary address: 944 Harlem St., Altoona 54720. Phone: (715) 832-1530. Fax: (715) 832-5329. Web Site: www.espn1150.com. Licensee: Maverick Media of Eau Claire License LLC. Group owner: Maverick Media LLC (acq 6-13-2003; grpsl). Network: ABC Information & Entertainment. Rep: Katz Radio. Format: Sports/talk. Target aud: 40 plus; general. ♦Gary Rozynek, pres; George Roberts, VP; Bruce Butler, gen mgr; Dave Craig, stn mgr & opns dir; Jim Casey, chief of opns.

Cleveland

WLKN(FM)— Apr 25, 1985: 98.1 mhz; 5.8 kw. Ant 292 ft. TL: N43 59 03 W87 45 55. Stereo. Box 26, 1050 Linden St. 53015. Phone: (920) 693-3103. Fax: (920) 693-3104. Web Site: www.wlkn.com. Licensee: Radio K-T Inc. (acq 10-15-99; $980,000). Network: AP Network News. Shook, Hardy & Bacon. Format: Adult contemp. News staff: one; News: 7 hrs wkly. Target aud: 25-54; active, upscale. ♦Jack Taddeo, CEO & pres; David Jetzer, stn mgr & gen sls mgr; Terry Matthews, progmg dir; Jackie Goetsch, news dir & pub affrs dir; Ken Ebneter, chief of engrg.

Clintonville

WFCL(AM)— Feb 28, 1983: 1380 khz; 5 kw-D, 2.5 kw-N, DA-2. TL: N44 34 00 W88 44 36. 33 E. 3rd St. 54929. Phone: (715) 823-5128. Phone: (800) 236-1380. Fax: (715) 823-1367. E-mail: wjmqnews@yahoo.com. Web Site: resultsbroadcasting.com. Licensee: Results Broadcasting Inc. Group owner: Results Broadcasting (acq 1996). Network: Jones Radio Networks. Miller & Miller, P.C. Format: MOR. News staff: one; News: 12 hrs wkly. Target aud: 25-54. Spec prog: Farm 8 hrs wkly. ♦Bruce Grassman, pres & gen mgr; Andy Richards, opns mgr; Shaughn Novy, gen sls mgr; Doug Rogers, prom mgr & progmg dir; Kay Weinig, prom dir; Doug Erdmann, news dir; Rick Eby, chief of engrg.

Broadcasting & Cable Yearbook 2006
D-549

Wisconsin

WJMQ(FM)— Co-owned with WFCL(AM). Oct 27, 1986: 92.3 mhz; 6 kw. 328 ft. TL: N44 34 00 W88 44 36. Stereo. Web Site: resultsbroadcasting.com. Format: Country. News staff: one; News: 12 hrs wkly. Target aud: 12-plus. ◆Doug Rogers, opns dir, prom dir & mus dir.

Columbus

WTLX(FM)— July 16, 1990: 100.5 mhz; 6 kw. 328 ft. TL: N43 24 19 W89 06 24. Stereo. Box 902, Beaver Dam 53916. Phone: (920) 885-4442. Fax: (920) 885-2152. Web Site: www.100xmadison.com. Licensee: Good Karma Broadcasting L.L.C. (group owner; acq 12-2-97; grpsl). Format: Talk, sports. News staff: one; News: 8 hrs wkly. Target aud: 25-50. ◆Craig Karmazin, pres & gen mgr; Scott Trentadue, stn mgr & sls dir; Rick Armon, opns dir; Jim Stowell, pub affrs dir; Warren Jorgensen, chief of engrg.

Cornell

WDRK(FM)— 2001: 99.9 mhz; 25 kw. Ant 328 ft. TL: N45 07 22 W91 24 23. Box 1, Eau Claire 54702. Secondary address: 944 Harlem St., Altoona 54720. Phone: (715) 832-1530. Fax: (715) 832-5329. Web Site: www.999thecarponline.com. Licensee: Maverick Media of Eau Claire License LLC. Group owner: Maverick Media LLC (acq 6-13-2003; grpsl). Format: Rock. News staff: 3; News: one hr wkly. ◆George Roberts, gen mgr, mktg VP & mktg mgr; Rick Roberts, stn mgr & progmg mgr; Al Shannon, opns mgr & mus dir; Lynn Bieritz, sls dir; Dan Gainey, natl sls mgr & rgnl sls mgr; Sue Savage, prom dir; Mike Simon, news dir; Jim Casey, chief of engrg.

De Forest

WHIT-FM— 2003: 93.1 mhz; 6 kw horiz, 5.4 kw vert. Ant 321 ft. TL: N43 09 34 W89 12 55. Box 2058, Madison 53701. Phone: (608) 273-1000. Fax: (608) 271-8182. Licensee: Mid-West Management Inc. Group owner: The Mid-West Family Broadcast Group (acq 8-13-02). Format: Variety. ◆John Hunt, gen sls mgr; Mark Van Allen, gen mgr & progmg dir.

De Pere

WKSZ(FM)—Licensed to De Pere. See Green Bay

Delafield

*****WHAD(FM)**— May 30, 1948: 90.7 mhz; 72 kw. Ant 682 ft. TL: N43 01 42 W88 23 32. 111 E. Kilbourn Ave., Suite 2375, Milwaukee 53202. Phone: (414) 227-2040. Fax: (414) 227-2043. E-mail: whad@wpr.org. Web Site: www.wpr.org. Licensee: State of Wisconsin Educational Communications Board. Network: NPR. Format: Pub radio, news/talk. News staff: one; News: 11 hrs wkly. Target aud: 35-55; general. ◆Bill Estes, stn mgr; Shavonn Montgomery-Brown, gen sls mgr; Lisa Nalbandian, prom mgr; Chuck Quirmbach, news dir; David Schank, chief of engrg.

Denmark

WPCK(FM)— Sept 1, 1969: 104.9 mhz; 10 kw. Ant 515 ft. TL: N44 24 38 W87 34 20. Stereo. 810 Victoria St., Green Bay 54302. Phone: (920) 468-4100. Fax: (920) 468-0250. E-mail: country@wpkr.com. Web Site: www.kicks104.com. Licensee: Cumulus Licensing LLC. Group owner: Cumulus Media Inc. (acq 11-10-2003; $8.1 million. with WPKR(FM) Omro). Rep: Christal. Cohn & Marks. Format: Country. News staff: 2; News: 4 hrs wkly. Target aud: 25-54; adults. Spec prog: Relg 3 hrs wkly. ◆Greg Jessen, gen mgr; Jimmy Clark, VP & opns mgr.

Dickeyville

WVRE(FM)— 2/1/03; 101.1 mhz; 3.7 kw. Ant 423 ft. TL: N42 31 43 W90 36 56. Stereo. Box 659, Dubuque, IA 52004. Phone: (563) 690-0800. Fax: (563) 588-5688. Licensee: Radio Dubuque Inc. (group owner; acq 8-1-01). Rep: McGavren Guild. Format: Country. News staff: one. Target aud: Adults; 25-54. ◆Thomas Parsley, gen mgr.

Dodgeville

WDMP(AM)— Nov 1, 1968: 810 khz; 250 w-D, 10 w-N. TL: N42 55 10 W90 08 06. Box 9 53533. Secondary address: 2163 Hwy. 151 S. 53523. Phone: (608) 935-2302. Fax: (608) 935-3464. Web Site: www.d99point3.com. Licensee: Dodge-Point Broadcasting Co. Format: Country. News staff: one; News: 5 hrs wkly. Target aud: General.

◆Louise E. Hamlin, pres; Kurt Reinicke, gen mgr & gen sls mgr; Kenny Jay, progmg dir; Robert Brainerd, news dir.

WDMP-FM— Nov 1, 1968: 99.3 mhz; 1.55 kw. 459 ft. TL: N42 55 10 W90 08 06. Stereo. E-mail: mail@d99point3.com. Web Site: www.d99point3.com.

Durand

WDMO(FM)— Oct 24, 1973: 95.9 mhz; 1.3 kw. Ant 498 ft. TL: N44 34 53 W91 54 44. Stereo. 313 Main St., Menomonie 54751. Phone: (715) 231-9500. Fax: (715) 231-9505. Web Site: www.thunder959.com. Licensee: Zoe Communications Inc. (group owner; (acq 7-31-2001; with co-located AM). Format: Country. ◆Bo Landry, opns mgr, progmg dir & news dir; Wendy Oberg, gen mgr & gen sls mgr; Mike Oberg, chief of engrg.

WQOQ(AM)— Co-owned with WDMO(FM). Nov 21, 1968: 1430 khz; 2 kw-D, 152 w-N. TL: N44 38 28 W91 55 22.

Eagle River

WERL(AM)— May 23, 1961: 950 khz; 1 kw-D, 51 w-N. TL: N45 58 38 W89 14 52. Stereo. Box 309, 909 Railroad St. 54521. Phone: (715) 479-4451. Fax: (715) 479-6511. E-mail: wrjo@wrjo.com. Web Site: www.wrjo.com. Licensee: Heartland Communications License LLC. (acq 12-7-2004; $2.2 million. with co-located FM). Format: Adult standards. News staff: one; News: 7 hrs wkly. Target aud: General. ◆Mary Jo Berner, pres; Jeff Wagner, gen mgr & gen sls mgr; Jeff Litscher, prom dir & progmg dir; Chris Oatman, news dir; Del Dayton, chief of engrg.

WRJO(FM)— Co-owned with WERL(AM). July 31, 1971: 94.5 mhz; 50 kw. 492 ft. TL: N45 58 38 W89 14 52. Stereo. Web Site: www.wrjo.com. Format: Oldies, rock and roll.

Eau Claire

WAXX(FM)— February 1965: 104.5 mhz; 100 kw. 1,830 ft. TL: N44 39 51 W90 57 41. Stereo. Box 1 54702. Secondary address: 944 Harlem St., Altoona 54720. Phone: (715) 832-1530. Fax: (715) 832-5329. Web Site: www.waxx104online.com. Licensee: Maverick Media of Eau Claire License LLC. Group owner: Maverick Media LLC (acq 6-13-2003; grpsl). Format: Country. News staff: 4. Target aud: 25-54; metro & rgnl adults. Spec prog: Farm 15 hrs wkly. ◆Gary Rozynek, pres; George Roberts, gen mgr & mktg mgr; George House, stn mgr, opns mgr, progmg dir & mus dir; Lynn Bieritz, sls dir; Dan Gainlebbb, gen sls mgr; Marty Green, natl sls mgr; Dan Gainey, rgnl sls mgr; John Murphy, prom dir; Mike Simon, news dir; Terry West, pub affrs dir; Jim Casey, chief of engrg.

WAYY(AM)— May 1937: 790 khz; 5 kw-U, DA-N. TL: N44 49 51 W91 26 58. Box One 54702-0001. Phone: (715) 832-1530. Fax: (715) 832-5329. E-mail: crgmarty@charter.net. Licensee: Maverick Media of Eau Claire License LLC. Group owner: Maverick Media LLC (acq 6-13-2003; grpsl). Network: ABC Information & Entertainment. Pepper & Corazzini. Format: News/talk. News staff: 4. Target aud: 35 plus; general. Spec prog: Farm 5 hrs wkly. ◆George Roberts, gen mgr; Dave Craig, opns mgr & progmg dir; Lynn Bieritz, gen sls mgr; John Murphy, prom dir; Mike Simon, news dir; Del Dayton, chief of engrg.

WIAL(FM)— Co-owned with WAYY(AM). 1948: 94.1 mhz; 85 kw. 350 ft. TL: N44 49 48 W91 26 48. Stereo. 944 Harlem Ave., Altoona 54720. E-mail: i94@charter.net. Format: Adult contemp. Target aud: 18-54. ◆George Roberts, gen mgr; Rick Roberts, stn mgr, opns mgr & mus dir; Curt Pufahl, prom dir & progmg dir; Sue Kelly, prom mgr.

WBIZ(AM)— Nov 11, 1947: 1400 khz; 1 kw-U. TL: N44 48 48 W91 31 15. Box 45 54702. Secondary address: 619 Cameron St. 54702. Phone: (715) 830-4000. Fax: (715) 835-9680. Web Site: www.wbiz.com. Licensee: Capstar TX L.P. Group owner: Clear Channel Communications Inc. (acq 2000; grpsl). Network: CBS. Format: All sports. Target aud: 25-54. ◆Rick Hencley, gen mgr; Mike Cushman, opns mgr; Steve Potter, gen sls mgr; Mike Cush, progmg mgr; Keith Edwards, news dir; Paul Orth, chief of engrg.

WBIZ-FM— December 1967: 100.7 mhz; 100 kw. 740 ft. TL: N44 47 58 W91 27 59. Stereo. Web Site: www.z100radio.com. Format: CHR. ◆Rick Hencley, VP & gen sls mgr; Audrey Phillips, progmg dir; Jare E. Jordan, mus dir; Keith Edwards, news dir.

Directory of Radio

*****WDVM(AM)**— April 1948: 1050 khz; 1 kw-D, 500 w-N. TL: N44 46 36 W91 28 30. Stereo. Relevant Radio 1050 AM, WDVM, 1752 Bracket Ave. 54701. Phone: (715) 855-1439. Phone: (715) 577-0943. Fax: (715) 855-1471. Web Site: www.relevantradio.com. Licensee: Starboard Media Foundation Inc. Group owner: Relevant Radio (acq 7-6-2001). Rep: Allied Radio Partners. Format: Talk, religious. News staff: one. Target aud: 35 plus; mature adults. ◆Mark Follett, CEO; Sherry Brownrigg, pres; Raymond P. Jay, stn mgr; Martin Jury, opns dir.

*****WHEM(FM)**— Aug 22, 1995: 91.3 mhz; 350 w. Ant 216 ft. TL: N44 45 50 W91 31 06. (CP: 300 w, ant 285 ft). 228 E. Lowes Creek Rd. 54701. Phone: (715) 838-9595. E-mail: whem@discover-net.net. Web Site: www.whem.com. Licensee: Fourth Dimension Inc. (acq 7-2-93; $2,810; 8-2-93). Format: Christian. ◆Harlan Reinders, gen mgr & chief of engrg; Phyllis Reinders, progmg dir.

*****WUEC(FM)**— Oct 27, 1975: 89.7 mhz; 5.2 kw. 630 ft. TL: N44 47 58 W91 27 59. Stereo. Wisconsin Public Radio, 1221 W. Clairemont Ave. 54701. Phone: (715) 839-3868. Fax: (715) 839-2939. E-mail: kallenbach@wpr.org. Web Site: www.wpr.org. Licensee: Board of Regents, University of Wisconsin. Network: NPR. Dow, Lohnes & Albertson. Format: Class, news, jazz. News: 24 hrs wkly. Target aud: General. Spec prog: Folk 3 hrs, blues 3 hrs wkly. ◆Dean Kallenbach, stn mgr; Marvin Spielman, dev dir & mktg dir; Reid Sollberger, prom dir; Jennifer Haukohl, mus dir; Mary Jo Wagner, news dir; Mike Mueller, chief of engrg.

*****WVCF(FM)**— 1997: 90.5 mhz; 980 w. 279 ft. TL: N44 57 29 W91 28 58. VCY/America Inc., 3434 W. Kilbourn Ave., Milwaukee 53208. Phone: (414) 935-3000. Fax: (414) 935-3015. E-mail: wvcf@vcyamerica.org. Web Site: www.vcyamerica.org. Licensee: VCY America Inc. (group owner) Network: Network: USA, Moody. Format: Relg, Christian. ◆Dr. Randall Melchert, pres; Victor Eliason, VP & gen mgr; Jim Schneider, progmg dir; Tom Schlueter, mus dir; Gordon Morris, news dir; Andy Eliason, chief of engrg.

Elk Mound

WECL(FM)— March 1, 2004: 92.9 mhz; 3.3 kw. 446 ft. TL: N44 53 40 W91 35 40. Stereo. 944 Harlem St., Altoona 54720. Secondary address: Box 1(one), Eau Claire 54702. Phone: (715) 832-1530. Fax: (715) 832-5329. Web site: www.929classicrock.com. Licensee: Maverick Media of Eau Claire License LLC. Group owner: Maverick Media LLC (acq 6-13-2003; grpsl). Pepper & Corazzini. Target aud: 35-54; Adults. Spec prog: Flashback, 4hrs. ◆George Roberts, gen mgr; Dan Lea, opns dir; Rick Roberts, stn mgr & opns mgr; Lynn Bieritz, sls dir; Dan Gainey, natl sls mgr.

Elm Grove

WGLB(AM)— Dec 6, 1963: 1560 khz; 185 w-D, 250 w-N, DA-2. TL: N43 00 32 W88 02 06. 5181 N. 35th St., Milwaukee 53209. Phone: (414) 527-4365. Fax: (414) 527-4367. E-mail: wglb@wglbam1560.com. Web Site: wglbam1560.com. Licensee: Joel J. Kinlow (acq 7-25-95; with co-located FM; FTR: 8-21-95). Format: Gospel. ◆Joel Kinlow, CEO; Joel Kinlow, pres & gen mgr; Willis H. Payne Jr., stn mgr & sls dir.

Evansville

WKPO(FM)— Aug 17, 1989: 105.9 mhz; 1.7 kw. 493 ft. TL: N42 43 38 W89 15 02. Stereo. One Parker Pl., Suite 485, Janesville 53545. Phone: (608) 758-9025. Fax: (608) 758-9550. E-mail: hot1059@hotmail.com. Web Site: hot1059.net. Licensee: Good Karma Broadcasting L.L.C. (acq 10-2-97; $1.5 million). Format: CHR rhythm. News staff: one; News: 3 hrs wkly. Target aud: 25-54. ◆Craig Kanmazin, CEO & pres; Keith Williams, gen mgr & stn mgr; Rick Armon, prom dir & opns mgr; Caroline Riegel, prom dir; Dan Hunt, progmg dir; Matt Gritzmacher, pub affrs dir; Warren Jorgensen, engrg dir & chief of engrg.

Fond du Lac

KFIZ(AM)— July 6, 1922: 1450 khz; 1 kw-U. TL: N43 47 28 W88 28 16. Stereo. Box 1450 54936-1450. Secondary address: 254 Winnebago Dr. 54935. Phone: (920) 921-1071. Fax: (920) 921-0757. E-mail: info@kfiz.com. Web Site: www.kfiz.com. Licensee: RBH Enterprises Inc. Group owner: Mountain Dog Media (acq 1-23-97; $1. plus assumption of liabilities with co-located FM). Format: News/talk, sports. Target aud: 35-64; Men & Women. Spec prog: Farm 10 hrs wkly. ◆R.B. Hopper, pres & gen mgr.

WFDL-FM—(Lomira). April 1993: 97.7 mhz; 4 kw. Ant 400 ft. TL: N43 39 14 W88 26 25. (CP: 17.5 kw). 210 S. Main St. 54935. Phone: (920)

Stations in the U.S. Wisconsin

Developers & Brokers of Radio Properties
contact American Media Services at our suite:
Philadelphia Marriott Downtown
215-625-2900
843-972-2200
americanmediaservices.com
Charleston, SC
Dallas, TX · Chicago, Il · Austin, TX
American Media Services, LLC

924-9697. Fax: (920) 929-8865. E-mail: info@sunny97-7.com. Web Site: www.wfdl.com. Licensee: Radio Plus of Fond du Lac Inc. (acq 4-96). Haley, Bader & Potts. Format: Adult contemp. News staff: one. Target aud: 25-54. ♦ Chris Bernier, pres; Terry Davis, VP, gen mgr & gen sls mgr; Mike Enfelt, opns mgr & chief of engrg; Todd Dehring, progmg dir; Greg Stensland, news dir.

WFON(FM)— Oct 5, 1967: 107.1 mhz; 3 kw. Ant 312 ft. TL: N43 50 22 W88 22 06. Stereo. 254 Winnebago Dr. 54935. Phone: (920) 921-1071. Fax: (920) 921-0757. Web Site: www.k107.com. Licensee: RBH Enterprises Inc. Group owner: Mountain Dog Media (acq 1-23-97). Format: Hot adult contemp. News staff: one; News: 1 hr wkly. Target aud: Women 25-54. ♦ Randy Hopper, gen mgr.

***WLWR(FM)**— 2005: 91.7 mhz; 20 kw vert. Ant 357 ft. TL: N43 39 35 W88 26 26. 194 Godfrey Rd., Edgewater, FL 32141. Phone: (386) 423-2013. Fax: (386) 423-9058. E-mail: cornerstoneradio@aol.com. Licensee: Cornerstone Community Radio Inc. Network: USA. Format: Christian. News: 8 hrs wkly. Spec prog: Children 8 hrs wkly. ♦ Richard Van Zandt, pres; Ken Hettinea, gen mgr.

WRPN(AM)—(Ripon). Sept 15, 1957: 1600 khz; 5 kw-U, DA-2. TL: N43 49 01 W88 50 49. 112 Watson St., Ripon 54971. Phone: (920) 748-5111. Fax: (920) 748-5530. E-mail: wrpn@wrpnam.com. Web Site: www.wrpnam.com. Licensee: Radio Broadcasting L.P. Network: Network: CBS, ABC. Rep: Farmakis. Haley, Bader & Potts. Format: News/talk. News staff: 4; News: 25 hrs wkly. Target aud: 25 plus; Fond du Lac, Green Lake counties. Spec prog: Pol 2 hrs, sports 15 hrs wkly. ♦ Tom Biolo, gen mgr; Jason Mansmith, sls dir; Jason Marsmith, progmg dir; Justin Cleveland, news dir; Mike Enfelt, chief of engrg.

WTCX(FM)—Co-owned with WRPN(AM). Feb 1, 1965: 96.1 mhz; 2 kw. 403 ft. TL: N43 49 10 W88 43 20. (CP: 3.94 kw). Stereo. 210 South Main St., Fon du Lac 54935. Phone: (920) 929-8865. Fax: (920) 929-8865. Web Site: www.961themix.com. Format: Classic hits, new rock. News staff: one; News: 3 hrs wkly. Target aud: 25-54; women. ♦ Mike Enfelt, opns mgr; Terry Davis, VP, gen mgr & gen sls mgr; Gregg Owens, progmg dir; Jean Hoffmann, chief of engrg.

***WVFL(FM)**—Not on air, target date: unknown: 89.9 mhz; 1.4 kw vert. Ant 341 ft. TL: N43 48 09 W88 20 18. 3434 W. Kilbourn Ave., Milwaukee 53208-3313. Phone: (414) 935-3000. Fax: (414) 935-3015. E-mail: vcy@vcyamerica.org. Licensee: VCY America Inc. ♦ Vic Eliason, VP & gen mgr.

Forestville

WRKU(FM)— Aug 1, 1999: 102.1 mhz; 6 kw. 328 ft. TL: N44 46 58 W87 22 24. 3030 Park Dr., Suite 3, Sturgeon Bay 54235. Phone: (920) 746-9430. Fax: (920) 746-9433. Web Site: www.doorradio.com. Licensee: Nicolet Broadcasting Inc. (group owner) Format: Oldies. News: 3 hrs wkly. ♦ Roger Utnehmer, pres & gen mgr; Kathy Robinson, prom dir.

Fort Atkinson

WFAW(AM)— Jan 24, 1963: 940 khz; 500 w-D, 550 w-N, DA-2. TL: N42 54 24 W88 45 06. Box 94 53538. Phone: (920) 563-9329. Fax: (920) 563-0315. Licensee: NewRadio Group LLC (group owner; acq 7-16-2003; grpsl). Network: ABC Information & Entertainment. Rep: McGavren Guild. Format: Sports, news/talk. News staff: one. ♦ Mary Quass, CEO & VP; Lindsay Wood-Davis, COO & stn mgr; Tami Gillmore, CFO; Benjamin D. Rosenthal, gen mgr; Gary Douglas, opns dir; Jim Vriezen, sls VP, sls dir & rgnl sls mgr; Gary Moen, progmg dir; Michael Clish, news dir; Clif Groth, engrg VP & chief of engrg.

WSJY(FM)—Co-owned with WFAW(AM). Sept 4, 1959: 107.3 mhz; 26 kw. 676 ft. TL: N42 50 48 W88 51 16. Stereo. Box 2107, Janesville 54547. Phone: (608) 756-0747. Fax: (608) 755-1252. Rep: McGavren Guild. Format: Lite adult contemp. News staff: one. Target aud: 25-54. ♦ Gary Doublas, opns mgr; Clif Groth, engrg dir.

Goodman

***WMVM(FM)**— May 3, 1993: . Stn currently dark 91.3 mhz; 422 w. Ant 118 ft. TL: N45 37 36 W88 21 28. (CP: 90.7 mhz; 9 kw, ant 156 ft. TL: N45 46 27 W88 24 28). Box 212, Suring 54174. Phone: (920) 842-2900. Fax: (920) 842-2704. Licensee: WRVM Inc. (acq 9-11-02; $20,000). ♦ Michael A. Cornell, gen mgr; Brian Hay, sls dir & mus dir; Rich Frischkorn, asst music dir; Alan Kilgore, engrg dir.

Green Bay

WAPL-FM—See Appleton

WDUZ(AM)— June 19, 1947: 1400 khz; 1 kw-U. TL: N44 29 36 W87 59 13. Stereo. 810 Victoria St. 54302. Phone: (920) 468-4100. Fax: (920) 468-0250. Web Site: www.supertalk1400.cumulus.com. Licensee: Cumulus Licensing Corp. Group owner: Cumulus Media Inc. (acq 6-27-2002; $6 million. with WQLH(FM) Green Bay). Network: Network: ABC Information & Entertainment, ESPN Radio. Rep: Allied Radio Partners. Format: News/talk. News staff: one. Target aud: 18-64; high income, male skew. ♦ Greg Jessen, gen mgr & natl sls mgr; Buck Hein, gen sls mgr & natl sls mgr; Brian Stenzel, prom dir; Curt Petersen, adv dir, news dir & pub affrs dir; Jimmy Clark, opns mgr & progmg dir; Chris Gielow, chief of engrg.

***WEMY(FM)**— Aug 26, 1974: 91.5 mhz; 710 w. TL: N44 21 32 W87 59 07. Stereo. 1909 W. 2nd St., Appleton 54914. Phone: (920) 749-9456. Fax: (920) 749-0474. Web Site: www.christianfamilyradio.net. Licensee: Evangel Ministries Inc. (group owner; acq 3-10-98). Network: Network: Salem Radio Network, USA. Leventhal, Senter & Lerman. Format: Relg. News: 10 hr wkly. Target aud: 35-49; women. Spec prog: Sp one hr wkly. ♦ Mary B. Lieb, chmn; Paul Cameron, gen mgr; Phil Pannier, opns dir; Heidi Prahl, dev dir.

***WHID(FM)**— April 1997: 88.1 mhz; 17 kw. 1,023 ft. TL: N44 21 32 W87 59 07. Stereo. 2420 Nicolet Dr. 54311-7001. Phone: (920) 465-2444. Fax: (920) 465-2576. E-mail: slaatsg@uwgb.edu. Web Site: www.wpr.org. Licensee: Board of Regents of University of Wisconsin Systems. Network: Network: NPR, PRI. Dow, Lohnes & Albertson. Format: Talk. News staff: one; News: 18 hrs wkly. Target aud: 35 plus; socially active, life-long learners. Spec prog: Sp 3 hrs, Asian 2 hrs wkly. ♦ Glen Slaats, gen mgr & adv mgr; Ellen Clark, dev mgr; Rick Peyer, adv mgr; Patty Murray, news dir; Mark Friedman, chief of engrg.

WIXX(FM)—Listing follows WTAQ(AM).

WJLW(FM)—See Allouez

WKSZ(FM)—(De Pere). Oct 1, 1984: 95.9 mhz; 4.5 kw. 774 ft. TL: N44 21 32 W87 59 07. Stereo. Box 1519, Appleton 54912. Secondary address: 1263 main St., Suite #225 54301. Phone: (920) 431-0959. Fax: (920) 431-8490. Web Site: www.mixvariety.com. Licensee: Woodward Communications Inc. (group owner; acq 1995). Rep: McGavren Guild. Hogan & Hartson. Format: Adult contemp. Target aud: 18-34; females. ♦ Bill Skemp, CEO; Tom Yunt, pres; Greg Bell, VP & gen mgr; Kelly Radandt, natl sls dir; Nicole Ehlers, rgnl sls mgr; Dayton Kane, progmg dir; Ed Walters, news dir; Steve Brown, chief of engrg.

WNFL(AM)— Dec 12, 1947: 1440 khz; 5 kw-D, 1 kw-N, DA-2. TL: N44 28 40 W88 00 00. 115 S. Jefferson St. 54301. Secondary address: Box 23333 54305. Phone: (920) 435-3771. Fax: (920) 444-1155. Licensee: Midwest Communications Inc. (group owner; acq 12-10-96; grpsl). Network: Network: ABC, CBS. Rep: Christal. Miller & Neely. Format: Talk. News staff: 3; News: 100 hrs wkly. Target aud: 35-64; people in upper-income level with above average education. Spec prog: Sports 15 hrs wkly. ♦ Duke Wright, pres & gen mgr; Gary Tesch, exec VP; Shelley Lukasik, gen sls mgr; Dan Stone, progmg dir & progmg mgr; Mark Daniels, news dir; Tim Laes, chief of engrg.

***WORQ(FM)**— Feb 1, 1994: 90.1 mhz; 11 kw. Ant 646 ft. TL: N44 21 32 W87 59 07. 1075 Brookwood Dr., Suite 2C 54304. Phone: (920) 494-9010. Fax: (920) 494-7602. E-mail: email@q90fm.com. Web Site: www.q90fm.com. Licensee: Lakeshore Communications Inc. Network:

USA. Wiley, Rein & Fielding. Format: Christian. News: 7 hrs wkly. Target aud: Under 30; rock and roll generation. ♦ Mike LeMay, gen mgr; Jim Kidraider, progmg dir; Scott Grathen, chief of engrg.

***WPNE-FM**— Jan 15, 1973: 89.3 mhz; 100 kw. 940 ft. TL: N44 24 35 W88 00 05. 2420 Nicolet Dr. 54311-7001. Phone: (920) 465-2444. Fax: (920) 465-2576. Web Site: www.wpr.org. Licensee: State of Wisconsin Educational Communications Board. Network: Network: NPR, PRI. Dow, Lohnes & Albertson. Format: Class music, news. News staff: 2; News: 29 hrs wkly. Target aud: 35 plus; socially aware, artistically stimulated. Spec prog: Jazz 10 hrs, folk 8 hrs, American Indian 2 hrs wkly. ♦ Glen Slaats, gen mgr & adv mgr; Ellen Clark, dev mgr; Rick Reyer, adv mgr; Patty Murray, news dir; Steve Konopka, chief of engrg.

WQLH(FM)— July 1, 1967: 98.5 mhz; 100 kw. 1,254 ft. TL: N44 38 41 W88 08 13. Stereo. 810 Victoria St. 54302. Phone: (920) 468-4100. Fax: (920) 468-0250. Web Site: star98.cumulus.com. Licensee: Cumulus Licensing Corp. Group owner: Cumulus Media Inc. (acq 6-27-2002; $6 million. with WDUZ(AM) Green Bay). Format: Hot AC. Target aud: Adults 25-54. ♦ Jimmy Clark, pres & opns mgr; Greg Jessen, gen mgr; Buck Hein, gen sls mgr; Brian Stenzel, prom dir; Jim Clark, progmg dir; Steve Davis, mus dir; Chris Gielow, chief of engrg.

WTAQ(AM)— Apr 6, 1925: 1360 khz; 5 kw-U, DA-N. TL: N44 25 51 W88 04 51. (CP: 10 kw-D, 5 kw-N, DA-2). Stereo. Box 23333 54301. Secondary address: 115 South Jefferson St. 54301. Phone: (414) 435-3771. Fax: (414) 455-1155. Licensee: Midwest Communications Inc. (group owner; acq 1975). Network: CBS. Rep: Christal. Miller & Miller. Format: News/talk. News staff: 4. Target aud: 30 plus. Spec prog: Farm 5 hrs wkly. ♦ D.E. Wright, pres & gen mgr; Gary Tesch, CFO & exec VP; Shelley LuKasik, gen sls mgr; Aaron Vorass, prom dir & prom mgr; Dan Stone, progmg dir; Mark Daniels, news dir; Tim Laes, chief of engrg.

WIXX(FM)—Co-owned with WTAQ(AM). Nov 1, 1960: 101.1 mhz; 100 kw. 1,080 ft. TL: N44 24 35 W88 00 05. Stereo. Format: CHR. ♦ Don Snyder, sls VP; Mary Kay Wright, gen sls mgr; Jeff McCarthy, progmg VP; David Burns, progmg dir.

Greenfield

WMCS(AM)—Licensed to Greenfield. See Milwaukee

Hallie

WOGO(AM)—Listing follows WWIB(FM).

WWIB(FM)— Dec 30, 1972: 103.7 mhz; 100 kw. 706 ft. TL: N45 06 35 W91 09 43. Stereo. 2396 State Hwy. 53, Suite One, Chippewa Falls 54729. Phone: (715) 723-1037. Phone: (715) 723-4626. Fax: (715) 723-1348. Web Site: www.wwib.com. Licensee: Stewards of Sound Inc. (acq 10-29-93; with WOGO(AM) Hallie; 11-15-93). Network: USA. Format: Adult Christian contemp. News staff: one; News: 16 hrs wkly. Target aud: 25-54. ♦ Terri Steward, gen mgr & stn mgr; Steven Slater, gen sls mgr; Greg Steward, progmg mgr; Mark Halversen, news dir; Patrick Wahl, chief of engrg.

WOGO(AM)—Co-owned with WWIB(FM). June 1985: 680 khz; 2.5 kw-D, 500 w-N, DA-2. TL: N44 53 22 W91 23 03. Stereo. Web Site: www.wwib.com. (Acq 10-29-93; with WWIB(FM) Ladysmith; 11-15-93). Network: USA. Format: News/talk. News staff: one; News: 16 hrs wkly. Target aud: 25-54.

Hartford

WTKM(AM)— 1951: 1540 khz; 500 w-D. TL: N43 16 48 W88 23 02. Box 270216, 27 N. Main St. 53027. Phone: (262) 673-3550. Phone: (262) 252-4567. Fax: (262) 673-5472. E-mail: wtkm@nconnect.net. Web Site: www.wtkm.com. Licensee: Kettle Moraine Broadcasting Co. Inc. (acq 3-12-90; grpsl; 4-2-90). Rep: Farmakis. Format: Polka, country. News staff: 2; News: 20 hrs wkly. Target aud: 35 plus. ♦ Scott Lopas, pres & gen mgr; Tom Shanahan, stn mgr.

Broadcasting & Cable Yearbook 2006

Wisconsin

WTKM-FM— Oct 1, 1973: 104.9 mhz; 5.8 kw. 300 ft. TL: N43 16 48 W88 23 02. Stereo. News staff: 2.

Hayward

WHSM(AM)— Dec 21, 1957: 910 khz; 5 kw-D, 75 w-N. TL: N45 59 07 W91 32 21. Stereo. 16880 W. US Hwy. 63 54843. Phone: (715) 634-4836. Phone: (800) 845-8984. Fax: (715) 634-8256. E-mail: radio@whsm.com. Web Site: www.whsm.com. Licensee: QB Broadcasting Ltd. (acq 5-30-94; $200,000). Format: Music of your life. News staff: one; News: 2 hrs wkly. Target aud: 25-54. ◆ Al Quarnstrom, pres; Don Welch, exec VP, gen mgr & gen sls mgr; Bobi Hopp, opns mgr & progmg dir; Joe Lancello, news dir; Bill Meys, chief of engrg.

WHSM-FM— June 21, 1980: 101.1 mhz; 1.45 kw. 410 ft. TL: N45 59 07 W91 32 23. Stereo. Web Site: www.whsm.com. Format: Bright adult contemp, adult hit radio.

WRLS-FM— Apr 16, 1968: 92.3 mhz; 6 kw. 321 ft. TL: N46 01 17 W91 30 41. Stereo. Box 1008, Radio Hill Rd. 54843. Phone: (715) 634-4871. Fax: (715) 634-3025. E-mail: wrls@cheqnet.net. Web Site: www.wrlsfm.com. Licensee: Vacationland Broadcasting Inc. (acq 12-9-92; 1-4-93). Network: Network: CNN Radio, AP Radio. Format: Adult contemp. News: News progmg 10 hrs wkly. Target aud: 25 plus; general. ◆ Tom Koser, pres; Robert Koser, VP; Steve Kaner, gen mgr; Shad Harper, opns mgr.

Highland

*WHHI(FM)— Sept 14, 1952: 91.3 mhz; 100 kw. 560 ft. TL: N43 02 58 W90 22 00. Wisconsin Public Radio, 821 University Ave., Madison 53706-1496. Phone: (608) 263-3970. Fax: (608) 263-9763. E-mail: schnirring@wpr.org. Web Site: www.wpr.org. Licensee: State of Wisconsin Educational Communications Board. Network: Network: NPR, PRI. Dow, Lohnes & Albertson. Format: Educ, news/talk. News staff: 9. Target aud: 35-54; Skews female: issue oriented talk-variety of perspectives. ◆ Phil Corriveau, gen mgr; Mary Kay Sherer, dev dir, mktg dir, prom dir & pub affrs dir; Connie Walker, news dir; Allen Rieland, engrg dir.

Holmen

WKBH(AM)— July 28, 1984: 1570 khz; 1 kw-D, 500 w-N. TL: N43 55 32 W91 16 02. 1407 2nd Ave. N., Onalaska 54650. Phone: (608) 779-4415. Fax: (608) 779-4419. Web Site: www.relevantradio.com. Licensee: Starboard Media Foundation Inc. Group owner: Relevant Radio (acq 1-17-2003; $210,000). Smithwick & Belendiuk. Format: Catholic talk. News staff: one; News: 35 hrs wkly. Target aud: 40 plus; those interested in Catholic news, talk & opinion. ◆ Jack Socha, stn mgr.

Hudson

WDGY(AM)—Licensed to Hudson. See Minneapolis-St. Paul MN

WMIN(AM)— Dec 14, 1983: 740 khz; 1.1 kw-DA. TL: N44 58 05 W92 40 01. Box 25130, St. Paul, MN 55125. Phone: (651) 436-4000. Fax: (651) 436-6770. Licensee: Borgen Broadcasting Corp. (acq 12-11-89; $300,000; 1-1-90). Format: Talk. Target aud: 25-54. ◆ Gregory Borgen, pres & gen mgr; Dave Akey, gen sls mgr; Tom Witschen, prom dir & progmg dir; Paul Orth, chief of engrg.

Hurley

WHRY(AM)— Mar 1, 1985: 1450 khz; 1 kw-U. TL: N46 24 56 W90 09 34. Box 1450 54534. Secondary address: 209 Harrison St., Ironwood, MI 49938. Phone: (906) 932-5234. Fax: (906) 932-1548. E-mail: wupm@wupm-whry.com. Licensee: Big G Little O Inc. Format: Oldies, Hits of the 50s, 60s & 70s. ◆ Charles H. Gervasio, pres, gen mgr, sls VP & news dir; Norma Rigoni, VP; Laura Keller, progmg dir; Al Harrison, chief of engrg.

Iron River

WNXR(FM)— November 1994: 107.3 mhz; 50 kw. 380 ft. TL: N46 31 27 W91 16 18. Stereo. 2320 Ellis Ave., Ashland 54806. Phone: (715) 372-5400. Fax: (715) 682-9338. E-mail: production@baybroadcasting.net. Web Site: www.baybroadcasting.net. Licensee: Heartland Communications License LLC. (group owner; (acq 4-23-2004; grpsl). Network: Westwood One. Format: Hits of the 50s, 60s & 70s. ◆ Rich Collins, gen mgr & progmg dir; Darla Isham, gen sls mgr; Skip Hunter, chief of engrg.

Jackson

WRRD(AM)— May 1, 1964: 540 khz; 400 w-U, DA-2. TL: N43 20 00 W88 09 11. Stereo. 135 S. 84th St., #310, Milwaukee 53214-1477. Phone: (414) 258-1700. Web Site: www.540theword.com. Licensee: SCA License Corp. Group owner: Salem Communications Corp. (acq 12-18-00; $7 million. with WWTC(AM) Minneapolis, MN). Lance Riley. Format: Christian talk/ministries. News: 6 hrs wkly. Target aud: 25-54; Christians. Spec prog: Croation 2 hrs, Latino 2 hrs wkly. ◆ Bob Emory, gen mgr; Lil Roohara, sls dir.

Janesville

WCLO(AM)— July 1930: 1230 khz; 1 kw-U. TL: N42 39 35 W89 02 32. Box 5001 53545. Secondary address: One S. Parker Dr. 53545. Phone: (608) 752-7895. Fax: (608) 752-4438. E-mail: programming@wclo.com. Licensee: Southern Wisconsin Broadcasting L.L.C. Group owner: Bliss Communications Inc. Dow, Lohnes & Albertson. Format: News/talk. Target aud: General. ◆ Robert Dailey, gen mgr; Ken Scott, progmg dir.

WJVL(FM)—Co-owned with WCLO(AM). October 1947: 99.9 mhz; 11 kw. 502 ft. TL: N42 43 47 W89 10 10. Stereo. Web Site: www.wvl.com. Format: C&W. Target aud: 25-34. ◆ Robert S. Dailey, exec VP; Mike O'Brien, gen sls mgr; Tim Bremel, progmg dir; Stan Stricker, news dir; Ja Mielkey, chief of engrg.

WSJY(FM)—See Fort Atkinson

Kaukauna

WJOK(AM)— Sept 25, 1965: 1050 khz; 1 kw-D, 500 w-N, DA-2. TL: N44 14 51 W88 18 00. 2300 Riverside Dr., Green Bay 54301. Phone: (920) 469-3021. Fax: (920) 469-3023. Web Site: www.1050am.org. Licensee: Starboard Media Foundation Inc. Group owner: Relevant Radio (acq 8-28-2001; $500,000). Network: Network: USA, Moody. Leventhal, Senter & Lerman. Format: Catholic. Target aud: 35-54. Spec prog: Relg 2 hrs wkly. ◆ Dave Nier, gen mgr.

WOGB(FM)— 1996: 103.1 mhz; 3.6 kw. 879 ft. TL: N44 21 32 W87 59 07. 810 Victoria St., Green Bay 54302. Phone: (920) 468-4100. Fax: (920) 468-0250. Web Site: www.cumulus.com. Licensee: Cumulus Licensing Corp. Group owner: Cumulus Media L.L.C. (acq 6-30-97; grpsl). Format: Oldies. Target aud: 35-54; affluent baby-boomers, mild 40's. ◆ Greg Jessen, gen mgr; Jimmy Clark, opns mgr; Buck Hein, sls dir; Brian Stemzel, prom dir; Dan Markus, progmg dir; Chris Gielow, news dir & engrg mgr; Charlene Bielinski, chief of engrg.

Kenosha

*WGTD(FM)— Dec 23, 1975: 91.1 mhz; 5 kw. 134 ft. TL: N42 36 28 W87 50 55. Stereo. 3520 30th Ave. 53144. Phone: (262) 564-3800. Fax: (262) 564-3801. E-mail: coled@gtc.edu. Web Site: wgtd.org. Licensee: Gateway Technical College. Network: NPR. Format: News, classical music. News staff: 2. Target aud: General. Spec prog: Ger one hr. ◆ David Cole, gen mgr.

WIIL(FM)—Listing follows WLIP(AM).

WLIP(AM)— May 11, 1947: 1050 khz; 250 w-U. TL: N42 33 10 W87 53 38. 8500 Green Bay Rd., Pleasant Prairie 53158. Phone: (262) 694-7800. Fax: (262) 694-7767. Web Site: www.wlip.com. Licensee: NM Licensing LLC. Group owner: NextMedia Group L.L.C. (acq 11-26-00; grpsl). Format: Talk. News staff: 2. Target aud: 35 plus. ◆ Kara Lafond, gen mgr; John Perry, opns mgr & progmg dir; Rory Fraley, sls dir; Stewart Wattles, news dir.

WIIL(FM)—Co-owned with WLIP(AM). 1961: 95.1 mhz; 50 kw. 384 ft. TL: N42 33 10 W87 53 38. Stereo. Web Site: www.95wiil.com. Format: Rock. Target aud: 18-54.

WWDV(FM)—See Zion, IL

Kewaunee

WAUN(FM)— 1973: 92.7 mhz; 6 kw. Ant 328 ft. TL: N44 29 50 W87 35 12. Box 12003, Green Bay 54307. Phone: (920) 388-9286. Fax: (920) 743-9183. Licensee: Magnum Broadcasting Inc. (acq 12-2-98). Format: Talk. News staff: one; News: 15 hrs wkly. Target aud: 25-54. Spec prog: Czech one hr, farm 10 hrs, relg 3 hrs wkly. ◆ Dave Magnum, pres; Jim Coursolle, gen mgr; Rick Jensen, opns mgr & news dir; Russ Nelson, gen sls mgr; Steve Peterson, progmg dir.

Kiel

*WSTM(FM)—Not on air, target date: unknown: 91.3 mhz; 100 w hoirz, 1.25 kw vert. Ant 459 ft. TL: N43 43 32 W88 03 07. Box 259, Plymouth 53073. Phone: (920) 893-2661. Fax: (920) 892-2706. E-mail: wjub@excel.net. Web Site: wjub.org. Licensee: Jubilation Ministries Inc. Format: Christian. ◆ Susan Noordyk, progmg dir.

Kimberly

WHBY(AM)— Dec 1, 1925: 1150 khz; 5 kw-U, DA-2. TL: N44 08 48 W88 28 54. Stereo. Box 1519, Appleton 54912. Secondary address: 2800 E. College Ave., Appleton 54915. Phone: (920) 733-6639. Fax: (920) 739-0494. E-mail: whby@wcinet.com. Web Site: www.whby.com. Licensee: Woodward Communications Inc. (group owner; (acq 3-75). Rep: McGavren Guild. Format: News/talk. News staff: 3; News: 25 hrs wkly. Target aud: 35 plus; upper middle class, educated. ◆ Bill Skemp, CEO; Tom Yumt, CEO & pres; Greg Bell, VP & gen mgr; Kelly Radandt, natl sls mgr; John Wanie, rgnl sls mgr; Jay Van Stiphout, progmg dir; Ed Walters, news dir; Steve Brown, chief of engrg.

La Crosse

KQEG(FM)—(La Crescent).MN Apr 5, 1989: 102.7 mhz; 4.3 kw. 863 ft. TL: N43 44 53 W91 17 51. Stereo. 1407 Second Ave. N., Onalaska 54650. Phone: (608) 782-8335. Fax: (608) 782-8340. Web Site: oldiesradioonline.net. Licensee: White Eagle Broadcasting Inc. Group owner: La Crosse Radio Group (acq 2-4-2000; $2 million). Rep: Allied Radio Partners. O'Malley. Format: Oldies. News: 4 hrs wkly. Target aud: 25-54. ◆ Pat Smith, gen mgr.

*WHLA(FM)— Nov 21, 1950: 90.3 mhz; 100 kw. 1,010 ft. TL: N43 48 17 W91 22 06. Wisconsin Public Radio, Whitney Centa, LaCrosse 54601. Phone: (608) 785-8380. Fax: (608) 785-5005. E-mail: purcell@wpr.org. Web Site: www.wpr.org. Licensee: State of Wis. Educational Communications Board. Network: Network: NPR, PRI. Dow, Lohnes & Albertson. Format: Educ, talk. News staff: 9. Target aud: 35-54; Skews Female: issue oriented talk-variety of perspectives. ◆ Wendy Wink, CEO; Rolf Wegenke, chmn; Ted Tobie, CFO; Gene Purcell, gen mgr; Monika Petkus, mktg dir; Joy Cardin, progmg dir & pub affrs dir; Connie Walker, news dir; Dennis Behr, engrg VP; Pete Kingslien, engrg dir.

WIZM(AM)— Jan 2, 1923: 1410 khz; 5 kw-U, DA-N. TL: N43 50 48 W91 13 03. Box 99, 201 State St. 54602. Phone: (608) 782-1230. Phone: (608) 796-2505. Fax: (608) 782-1170. E-mail: dickr@familyradioinc.com. Web Site: www.familyradio.com. Licensee: Family Radio Inc. Group owner: Mid-West Family Broadcast Group (acq 7-12-71; $500,000). Network: Network: Westwood One, CBS. Rep: Christal. Shaw Pittman. Format: News/talk. News staff: 5; News: 18 hrs wkly. Target aud: 35 plus. Spec prog: Asian 2 hrs wkly. ◆ Dick Record, pres & gen mgr; Howard Gloede, sls dir & gen sls mgr; Kevan Kavanaugh, rgnl sls mgr; Theresa Timm, rgnl sls mgr; Mike Hayes, prom mgr; Scott Robert Shaw, progmg dir & news dir; Keith Carr, pub affrs dir; Chris O'Hearn, chief of engrg.

WIZM-FM— 1966: 93.3 mhz; 100 kw. 1,000 ft. TL: N43 44 23 W91 22 04. Stereo. Web Site: www.familyradio.com. (Acq 6-15-76). Format: Top-40. News staff: 5; News: 2 hrs wkly. Target aud: 18-49. ◆ Jeff Nix, progmg dir.

WKBH-FM— (West Salem). Mar 15, 1982: 100.1 mhz; 3.6 kw. 426 ft. TL: N43 51 02 W91 12 08. Stereo. Box 1624 54602-1624. Secondary address: 1407 2nd Ave. N., Onalaska 54650. Phone: (608) 779-9524. Phone: (608) 783-3100. Fax: (608) 782-8340. Licensee: Mississippi Valley Broadcasters LLC. Group owner: La Crosse Radio Group (acq 12-16-2000). Format: Classic rock. News staff: one. Target aud: 25-54. ◆ Lee Norman, pres; Todd Wohlert, stn mgr; Mike Schmidt, gen sls mgr; Brucie Bumchuckles, prom dir; Shellia Fillner, progmg dir; Patrick Delaney, chief of engrg.

WKTY(AM)— May 1948: 580 khz; 5 kw-D, 1 kw-N, DA-2. TL: N43 44 25 W91 12 21. Box 99, 201 State St. 54602. Phone: (608) 782-1230. Fax: (608) 782-1170. Licensee: Family Radio Inc. Group owner: The Mid-West Family Broadcast Group (acq 1996; $1.3 million). Network: ABC Information & Entertainment. Rep: Christal. Shaw Pittman. Format: Sports, talk. News staff: 5; News: 18 hrs wkly. Target aud: 25-54. Spec prog: Farm 10 hrs wkly. ◆ Dick Record, pres & gen mgr; Howard Gloede, gen sls mgr; Kevan Kavanaugh, rgnl sls mgr; Mike

Stations in the U.S.   **Wisconsin**

Kearns, prom dir; Scott Robert Shaw, progmg dir & news dir; Keith Carr, pub affrs dir; Chris O'Hearn, chief of engrg.

WRQT(FM)—Co-owned with WKTY(AM). January 1972: 95.7 mhz; 50 kw. 410 ft. TL: N43 44 30 W91 18 14. Stereo. Format: Active rock. News: 5 hrs wkly. Target aud: General. ◆ Brian Michaels, progmg dir.

WLFN(AM)— May 1947: 1490 khz; 1 kw-U. TL: N43 49 42 W91 14 27. Stereo. Box 2017 54602-2017. Secondary address: 1407 Second Ave. N., Onalaska 54650. Phone: (608) 782-8335. Fax: (608) 782-8340. Licensee: Mississippi Valley Broadcasters L.L.C. Group owner: La Crosse Radio Group. Rep: Allied Radio Partners. Format: Original Hits. News staff: one; News: 5 hrs wkly. Target aud: 35 plus. ◆ Pat Smith, gen mgr; Mike Schmitz, sls dir; Pete Schreier, progmg dir; Lucy Lemar, news dir; Patrick Delaney, chief of engrg.

WLXR-FM—Co-owned with WLFN(AM). March 1975: 104.9 mhz; 1.35 kw. 430 ft. TL: N43 45 28 W91 17 26. (CP: 3.4 kw). Stereo. Web Site: www.wlxr.com. Format: Adult contemp. Target aud: 18-49. ◆ Debbie Brague, progmg dir.

*****WLSU(FM)**— Jan 4, 1971: 88.9 mhz; 8.2 kw. Ant 928 ft. TL: N43 48 17 W91 22 06. Stereo. Univ. of Wisconsin-La Crosse, 1725 State St. 54601. Phone: (608) 785-8380. Fax: (608) 785-5005. Web Site: www.wpr.org. Licensee: University of Wisconsin System. Network: Network: NPR, PRI. Dow, Lohnes & Albertson. Format: Class, jazz, news. News staff: 3; News: 40 hrs wkly. Target aud: General. ◆ Gene Purcell, gen mgr, opns dir & progmg dir; Marvin Spielman, dev dir; Sandra Harris, news dir; Steve Roisum, pub affrs dir.

WQCC(FM)— Mar 31, 1994: 106.3 mhz; 12 kw. 476 ft. Box 2017 54602-2017. Phone: (608) 782-1063. Phone: (608) 782-8335. Fax: (608) 779-5945. E-mail: wlxr/wqcc@aol.com. Licensee: Mississippi Valley Broadcasters L.L.C. Group owner: La Crosse Radio Group (acq 12-31-96). Format: Country. ◆ Pat Smith, gen mgr; Mike Schmitz, gen sls mgr; John Stevenson, progmg dir; Lucy Lemar, news dir; Patrick Delaney, chief of engrg.

Ladysmith

WJBL(FM)—Listing follows WLDY(AM).

WLDY(AM)— September 1948: 1340 khz; 1 kw-U. TL: N45 27 52 W91 07 26. Box 351 54848-0351. Secondary address: W8746 Hwy. 8 54848. Phone: (715) 532-5588. Fax: (715) 532-7357. E-mail: wldy@centurytel.net. Licensee: Roth Broadcasting Inc. (acq 1-9-2004; $924,722. with co-located FM). Network: ABC. Format: Country, news/talk. News staff: one; News: 15 hrs wkly. Target aud: 35 plus; mature audience. Spec prog: Polka 3 hrs wkly. ◆ Sandra Roth, pres & gen mgr; David Roth, gen sls mgr & progmg dir; Jocelyn Kilmer, progmg dir; Tom Costello, news dir; Del Dayton, chief of engrg.

WJBL(FM)—Co-owned with WLDY(AM). October 1984: 93.1 mhz; 4.9 kw. 358 ft. TL: N45 27 59 W91 07 23. Stereo. Network: ABC. Format: Oldies. News staff: one; News: 10 hrs wkly. Target aud: 25-54.

Lake Geneva

WLKG(FM)— June 6, 1994: 96.1 mhz; 6 kw. 328 ft. TL: N42 36 34 W88 26 36. Box 996, 500 Interchange N. 53147. Phone: (262) 249-9600. Fax: (262) 249-9630. E-mail: lake96@wlkg.com. Web Site: www.wlkg.com. Licensee: CTJ Communications Ltd. Shaw Pittman. Format: Hot AC. News: 15 hrs wkly. Target aud: 25-54; mainly female. Spec prog: Hits of the 70's 10 hrs, sports 2 hrs wkly. ◆ Tom Kwiatkowski, pres; Barb Kwiatkowski, VP; Nancy Douglass, gen mgr.

WZRK(AM)— May 15, 1964: 1550 khz; 1 kw-D, DA. TL: N42 35 40 W88 23 19. Box 695 53147. Secondary address: 6715 Hwy. 50 53147. Phone: (262) 248-1005. Fax: (262) 248-2002. E-mail: wzrk@relevantradio.com. Web Site: www.relevantradio.com. Licensee: Starboard Media Foundation Inc. Group owner: Relevant Radio (acq 5-31-2001). Donald E. Martin. Format: Catholic talk. Target aud: 25 plus. Spec prog: Farm. ◆ Ted Ehlen, gen mgr & stn mgr.

Lancaster

WGLR(AM)— Sept 9, 1977: 1280 khz; 500 w-D. TL: N42 50 22 W90 40 19. Box 587, 206 S. Sheridan St. 53813. Phone: (608) 723-7671. Fax: (608) 723-7674. Licensee: QueenB Radio Wisconsin Inc. Group owner: Morgan Murphy Stations (acq 3-18-98; $1.66 million with co-located FM). Format: C&W. Spec prog: Farm 10 hrs wkly. ◆ Danny Sullivan, gen mgr; Doug Wagen, opns dir & news dir; Rick Sanson, sls dir & gen sls mgr; Rob Spangler, progmg dir.

WGLR-FM— Sept 9, 1982: 97.7 mhz; 3 kw. 235 ft. TL: N42 50 18 W90 40 14. (CP: 25 kw, ant 328 ft.). Stereo. Format: Country.

*****WJTY(FM)**— Mar 12, 1983: 88.1 mhz; 7 kw horiz, 50 kw vert. Ant 476 ft. TL: N42 57 08 W90 25 47. Stereo. 341 S. Washington 53813. Phone: (608) 723-7888. Fax: (608) 723-4557. E-mail: info@wjty.org. Web Site: www.wjty.org. Licensee: Joy Public Broadcasting Corp. Network: Network: Moody, USA. Format: Relg, contemp, MOR. News staff: one; News: 11 hrs wkly. Target aud: 30-90; families. ◆ Lowell M. Bush, CEO, pres, gen mgr & dev dir; Joyce Bush, progmg dir & news dir; Dennis Baldridge, chief of engrg.

Lomira

WFDL-FM—Licensed to Lomira. See Fond du Lac

Madison

*****WERN(FM)**— Mar 30, 1947: 88.7 mhz; 20.5 kw. 990 ft. TL: N43 03 18 W89 28 42. Stereo. 821 University Ave. 53706-1496. Phone: (608) 263-3970. Phone: (608) 263-4120. Fax: (608) 263-9763. E-mail: schnirring@wpr.org. Web Site: www.wpr.org. Licensee: State of Wisconsin Educational Communications Board. Network: Network: NPR, PRI. Format: News, class. News staff: 9; News: 29 hrs wkly. Target aud: 25-64; persons seeking quality music & intellectual stimulation. ◆ Phil Corriveau, gen mgr; Ben Spindler, dev dir; Monik Petkus, prom dir; Connie Walker, news dir; Allen Rieland, chief of engrg.

*****WHA(AM)**— 1922: 970 khz; 5 kw-D, 51 w-N. TL: N43 02 30 W89 24 31. 821 University Ave. 53706. Phone: (608) 263-3970. Fax: (608) 263-9763. E-mail: listener@wpr.org. Web Site: www.wpr.org. Licensee: Regents of University of Wisconsin System. Network: Network: NPR, PRI. Format: Educ, talk, news. News staff: 9. Target aud: 35-54; male/female, educated, skews female: issue oriented talk-variety of perspectives. ◆ Phil Corriveau, gen mgr; Tom Martin-Erickson, opns dir & opns mgr; Ben Spindler, dev dir, dev mgr & mktg dir; Connie Walker, news dir; Allen Rieland, chief of engrg. Co-owned TV: *WHA-TV affil

WIBA(AM)— Apr 2, 1925: 1310 khz; 5 kw-U, DA-N. TL: N42 59 53 W89 25 42. Stereo. 2651 S. Fish Hatchery Rd. 53711. Phone: (608) 274-5450. Fax: (608) 274-5521. Web Site: www.wiba.com. Licensee: Capstar TX L.P. Group owner: Clear Channel Communications Inc. (acq 8-30-00; grpsl). Network: Network: CBS, Wall Street. Dow, Lohnes & Albertson. Format: News/talk. Target aud: 25-64. ◆ Jeff Tyler, gen mgr & opns mgr; Kurt Peterson, sls dir; Tim Scott, progmg dir; Josh Wescott, news dir; Tim Wagner, chief of engrg.

WIBA-FM— Mar 1947: 101.5 mhz; 50 kw. 450 ft. TL: N43 03 22 W89 32 07. (CP: Ant 1,013 ft.). Stereo. Web Site: www.wibafm.com. Format: Classic rock. ◆ Mike Ferris, progmg dir.

WLMV(AM)— September 1948: 1480 khz; 5 kw-U, DA-N. TL: N43 01 30 W89 23 48. Stereo. Box 2058 53701. Secondary address: 2740 Ski Ln. 53713. Phone: (608) 271-1484. Phone: (608) 273-1000. Fax: (608) 271-0400. Licensee: Mid-West Management Inc. Group owner: The Mid-West Family Broadcast Group. Rep: McGavren Guild. Shaw Pittman. Format: Sp. Target aud: General; Latino community. ◆ Thomas A. Walker, pres & gen mgr; Ted Waldbillig, sls VP & gen sls mgr; Bill Mann, natl sls mgr; Luis Montoto, progmg dir; Robin Colbert, news dir; John Bauer, chief of engrg.

WMGN(FM)—Co-owned with WLMV(AM). September 1948: 98.1 mhz; 38 kw. 581 ft. TL: N42 57 46 W89 22 46. Stereo. 2740 Ski Ln. 53713. Phone: (608) 271-1000. Fax: (608) 271-8182. E-mail: info@magic98.com. Web Site: www.magic98.com. Rep: McGavren Guild. Shaw Pittman. Format: Adult contemp. Target aud: 25-54. ◆ Bill Mann, sls VP; Pat O'Neill, opns dir & progmg dir; Mark Van Allen, mus dir.

WMAD(FM)—(Sauk City). Sept 18, 1964: 96.3 mhz; 5.1 kw. 672 ft. TL: N43 12 37 W89 35 57. Stereo. 2651 S. Fish Hatchery Rd. 53711. Phone: (608) 274-5450. Fax: (608) 274-5521. Web Site: www.wmad.com. Licensee: Capstar TX L.P. Group owner: Clear Channel Communications Inc. (acq 8-30-00; grpsl). Rep: Christal. Leventhal, Senter & Lerman. Format: Alternative. News staff: one; News: one hr wkly. Target aud: 25-49. ◆ Jeff Tyler, gen mgr; Kurt Peterson, gen sls mgr; Curtis Gross, progmg dir; Joe McCall, chief of engrg.

WNWC(AM)—See Sun Prairie

*****WNWC-FM**— Apr 30, 1959: 102.5 mhz; 50 kw. 460 ft. TL: N43 02 07 W89 30 25. Stereo. 5606 Medical Cir. 53719. Phone: (608) 271-1025. Fax: (608) 271-1150. E-mail: wnwc@nwc.edu. Web Site: www.wnwc.org. Licensee: Northwestern College. Group owner: Northwestern College & Radio (acq 1-19-73). Network: AP Radio. Format: Contemp Christian Music. News staff: one; News: 20 hrs wkly. Target aud: 35-45. ◆ Greg Walters, gen mgr.

WOLX-FM—(Baraboo). Mar 3, 1946: 94.9 mhz; 37 kw. 1,299 ft. TL: N43 25 40 W89 39 14. Stereo. 7601 Ganser Way 53719. Phone: (608) 826-0077. Fax: (608) 826-1244. Web Site: www.wolx.com. Licensee: Entercom Madison Licensee LLP. Group owner: Entercom Communications Corp. (acq 7-10-00; grpsl). Rep: Christal. Rosenman & Colin. Format: Oldies. News staff: 2; News: 2 hrs wkly. Target aud: 25-54. ◆ David Field, pres; Ed Schulz, VP; Michael Weber, CFO & opns mgr; Lindsay Wood Davis, mktg mgr.

*****WORT(FM)**— Dec 1, 1975: 89.9 mhz; 2 kw. 900 ft. TL: N43 03 01 W89 29 15. Stereo. 118 S. Bedford St. 53703. Phone: (608) 256-2695/256-2001. Fax: (608) 256-3704. E-mail: wort@terracom.net. Web Site: www.wort-fm.org. Licensee: Back Porch Radio Broadcasting Inc. Format: Div, class. News staff: one; News: 3 hrs wkly. Target aud: 25-34. Spec prog: Black 3 hrs, jazz 15 hrs wkly. ◆ Norman Stockwell, opns dir; Sybil Augustine, mus dir; Nathan Moore, news dir.

*****WSUM(FM)**— 2003: 91.7 mhz; 5.5 kw. Ant 338 ft. TL: N42 54 16 W89 33 20. Box 260020 53726-0020. Phone: (608) 262-1864. Web Site: www.wsum.org. Licensee: Board of Regents of the University of Wisconsin. Format: Educ. ◆ Dave Black, gen mgr.

WTDY(AM)— 1998: 1670 khz; 10 kw-D, 1 kw-N. TL: N43 01 30 W89 23 48. Box 2058 53701. Secondary address: 2740 Ski Lane 53713. Phone: (608) 273-1000. Fax: (608) 271-0400. Fax: (608) 271-8182. Web Site: www.wtdy.com. Licensee: Mid-West Management Inc. Group owner: The Mid-West Family Broadcast Group Network: CNN Max. Rep: McGavren Guild. Shaw Pittman. Format: News/talk. News staff: 5; News: 15 hrs wkly. Target aud: Male 25-54; Young to middle aged males. ◆ Tom Walker, pres & gen mgr; Ted Waldbillig, sls dir; John Sylvester, progmg dir; Robin Colbert, news dir; John Bauer, chief of engrg.

WTSO(AM)— January 1948: 1070 khz; 10 kw-D, 5 kw-N, DA-2. TL: N42 59 45 W89 18 50. 2651 S. Fishhatchery Rd. 53711. Phone: (608) 274-5450. Fax: (608) 274-5521. Web Site: www.espn1070.com. Licensee: Capstar TX L.P. Group owner: Clear Channel Communications Inc. (acq 8-30-00; grpsl). Network: ABC Information & Entertainment. Dow, Lohnes & Albertson. Format: Sports. News staff: 6. Target aud: 25-54. Spec prog: Farm 20 hrs wkly. ◆ Jeff Tyler, gen mgr & opns mgr; Kurt Peterson, sls dir; Tim Scott, progmg dir; Tim Wagner, chief of engrg.

WZEE(FM)—Co-owned with WTSO(AM). 1948: 104.1 mhz; 9.4 kw. 1,119 ft. TL: N43 03 09 W89 28 42. Stereo. Web Site: www.z104fm.com. Format: Adult contemp, CHR. News staff: 2; News: one hr wkly. ◆ Tommy Bodean, progmg dir.

Wisconsin

WTUX(AM)— Aug 14, 1964: 1550 khz; 5 kw-D, DA. TL: N43 00 08 W89 23 08. Box 2058 53071. Secondary address: 2740 Ski Ln. 53713. Phone: (608) 273-1000. Fax: (608) 271-0400. Web Site: www.wtux.com. Licensee: Mid-West Management Inc. Group owner: The Mid-West Family Broadcast Group (acq 8-12-97; $6.4 million. with WWQM-FM Middleton). Network: ABC Information & Entertainment. Rep: Christal. Format: Music of your life. Target aud: 25-54. ♦Tom Walker, pres & gen mgr; Mark Van Allen, progmg dir; John Hunt, chief of engrg.

WWQM-FM—See Middleton

WXXM(FM)—See Sun Prairie

Manitowoc

WCUB(AM)—(Two Rivers). November 1952: 980 khz; 5 kw-U, DA-2. TL: N44 03 50 W87 41 49. Box 1990 54221-1990. Secondary address: 1915 Mirro Dr. 54220. Phone: (920) 683-6800. Fax: (920)683-6807. Web Site: www.cubradio.com. Licensee: Cub Radio Inc. (acq 1-1-61). Rep: Katz Radio. Format: C&W, farm. News staff: 2; News: 16 hrs wkly. Target aud: 35 plus. ♦Lee Davis, pres, gen mgr & gen sls mgr; Kyle Kristofer, progmg dir; Dan Deicher, news dir.

WLTU(FM)—Co-owned with WCUB(AM). Sept 1, 1966: 92.1 mhz; 3.7 kw. 420 ft. TL: N44 07 31 W87 37 41. Stereo. Web Site: www.cubradio.com. Format: Oldies. News staff: one. Target aud: 25-64.

WOMT(AM)— Nov 8, 1926: 1240 khz; 1 kw-U. TL: N44 07 31 W87 37 41. Box 1385, 3730 Mangin St. 54221-1385. Phone: (920) 682-0351. Fax: (920) 682-1008. E-mail: womt@lakefield.net. Web Site: www.womtradio.com. Licensee: Seehafer Broadcasting Corp. (acq 1-1-70). Network: CBS. Miller & Neely. Format: Full service, adult contemp, MOR. News staff: 2; News: 45 hrs wkly. Target aud: 25-64; business executives, males/females. Spec prog: News 18 hrs wkly. ♦Don Seehafer, pres & gen mgr; Ben Jaket, stn mgr; Russ Matar, gen sls mgr; Lindy Lukes, mktg dir; Mark Seehafer, adv VP; Tim Strews, progmg dir; Fred Barry, news dir; Harley Engel, chief of engrg.

WQTC-FM—Co-owned with WOMT(AM). Nov 19, 1965: 102.3 mhz; 3 kw. 328 ft. TL: N44 07 31 W87 37 41. Stereo. Format: Classic rock. Target aud: 18-49.

WTRW(AM)—See Two Rivers

Marathon

WKQH(FM)— 1988: 104.9 mhz; 21 kw. 358 ft. TL: N44 50 13 W89 45 57. 500 Division St., Stevens Point 54481. Phone: (715) 341-9800. Fax: (715) 341-0000. E-mail: rmuzzy@1010WSQT.com. Web Site: www.rock1049.com. Licensee: RLM Communications Inc. Group owner: Muzzy Broadcasting L.L.C. (acq 1994; $150,000). Format: Active rock. ♦Richard L. Muzzy, gen mgr & gen mgr.

Marinette

WAGN(AM)—See Menominee, MI

WHYB(FM)—See Menominee, MI

WLST(FM)—Listing follows WMAM(AM).

WMAM(AM)— Oct 8, 1939: 570 khz; 250 w-D, 100 w-N. TL: N45 06 02 W87 37 30. N. 2880 Roosevelt Rd. 54143. Phone: (715) 735-6631. Fax: (715) 732-0125. Licensee: Badger Communications L.L.C. (group owner; acq 4-4-97) $1 million. with co-located FM including telephone answering service) Network: CBS. Rep: Michigan. Format: Talk, sports. News staff: one; News: 4 hrs wkly. Target aud: 25 plus; upscale. Spec prog: Milwaukee Brewers, Green Bay Packers, farm 3 hrs wkly. ♦Shawn Katzbeck, gen mgr & gen sls mgr; Jim Medley, progmg dir; Chuck Gennaro, chief of engrg.

WLST(FM)—Co-owned with WMAM(AM). Sept 1, 1976: 95.1 mhz; 100 kw. 500 ft. TL: N45 03 48 W87 39 26. (CP: 133 kw). Stereo. Web Site: www.live95.net. Format: Adult contemp. News: 2 hrs wkly. Target aud: 25-49; females. Spec prog: Dick Clark's American Mus Survey.

Marshall

*****WJWD(FM)**— 2003: 90.3 mhz; 51 w horiz, 9.9 kw vert. Ant 312 ft. TL: N43 20 40 W89 06 10. 152 McCrae Rd., Fall River 53932. Phone: (920) 484-6220. Fax: (920) 484-3753. E-mail: wjwd@csnradio.com. Licensee: CSN International (group owner). Format: Relg. ♦Patrick Lannoye, gen mgr & opns mgr.

Marshfield

WDLB(AM)— Feb 2, 1947: 1450 khz; 1 kw-U. TL: N44 41 49 W90 09 20. Box 630, 1710 N. Central Ave. 54449. Phone: (715) 384-2191. Fax: (715) 387-3588. Web Site: wdlb@mmwi.net. Licensee: NewRadio Group LLC (group owner; acq 12-20-2002; grpsl). Network: ABC Information & Entertainment. Miller & Fields, P.C. Format: News/talk, sports. News staff: 3; News: 13 hrs wkly. Target aud: 25-49; general. Spec prog: Farm 14 hrs wkly. ♦Wayne Ripp, gen mgr & opns mgr, progmg dir & news dir; Arnie Peck, gen sls mgr & adv VP; George Nicholas, engrg dir.

WLJY(FM)—Co-owned with WDLB(AM). Dec 1, 1965: 106.5 mhz; 100 kw. 800 ft. TL: N44 38 41 W89 51 11. Stereo. Format: Soft adult contemp. Target aud: 25-54. Spec prog: Relg 2 hrs wkly. ♦Arnie Peck, rgnl sls mgr.

Mauston

WRJC(AM)— Jan 4, 1962: 1270 khz; 500 w-D. TL: N43 49 52 W90 04 51. Box 200, Fairway Ln. 53948. Phone: (608) 847-6565. Fax: (608) 847-6249. Licensee: WRJC Broadcasting Co. (acq 2-15-86; 12-23-85). Network: CBS. Womble, Carlyle, Sandridge & Rice. Format: MOR. News staff: one; News: 8 hrs wkly. Target aud: 25 plus; general. ♦Rick Charles, pres, gen mgr & gen sls mgr; Greg Lawrence, prom VP & mus dir; June Gill, news dir; Ken Ebneter, chief of engrg.

WRJC-FM— 1976: 92.1 mhz; 2.0 kw. 600 ft. TL: N43 47 16 W90 11 52. (CP: Ant 571 ft.). Stereo. E-mail: wrjc@mwj.net. Web Site: www.wrjc.com. Licensee: WRJC Inc. Network: CBS. Format: Adult contemp. News staff: one; News: 10 hrs wkly. Target aud: 21 plus; adults. ♦Rick Charles, CEO.

Mayville

WMDC(FM)— Oct 31, 1998:: 98.7 mhz; 6 kw. 246 ft. TL: N43 28 53 W88 28 45. 132 N. Main St. 53050. Phone: (920) 387-0000. Fax: (920) 387-2222. E-mail: bigsky@dotnet.com. Web Site: www.great98.com. Licensee: Radio Plus Inc. Format: 60s & 70s hits. News staff: one. Target aud: 25-54. ♦Tom Biolo, gen mgr; Norm Grey, gen sls mgr; Michael Casper, progmg dir; Scot Neu, news dir; Mike Enfeldt, engrg dir.

Medford

WIGM(AM)— Oct 26, 1941: 1490 khz; 1 kw-U, DA-1. TL: N45 07 55 W90 19 54. Box 59 54451. Secondary address: 630 S. 8th 54451. Phone: (715) 748-2566. Web Site: www.k99wigm.com. Licensee: WIGM Inc. (acq 6-55). Network: Network: ABC Information & Entertainment, ESPN Radio. Format: Country, sports. News staff: one; News: 14 hrs wkly. Target aud: 21 plus. Spec prog: Farm 10 hrs wkly. ♦Brad Dahlvig, pres & gen mgr; Karen Dahlvig, sls dir; Paula Liske, news dir; Del Dayton, chief of engrg.

WKEB(FM)—Co-owned with WIGM(AM). September 1991: 99.3 mhz; 23 kw. 342 ft. TL: N45 07 55 W90 19 54. Stereo. Network: CBS. Format: Adult contemp. ♦Brad Dahlvig, CEO; Del Dayton, sls VP & engrg VP; Karen Dahlvig, sr VP, dev dir, sls VP & mktg dir.

Menomonee Falls

WJMR-FM— June 26, 1956: 98.3 mhz; 6 kw. 328 ft. TL: N43 09 00 W88 07 25. (CP: Ant 292 ft.). Stereo. 5407 W. McKinley Ave., Milwaukee 53208-2540. Phone: (414) 978-9000. Fax: (414) 978-9001. Web Site: www.wjmr.com. Licensee: Lakefront Communications LLC. Group owner: Saga Communications Inc. (acq 4-24-97; $5 million. with WFMR(FM) Brookfield). Rep: McGavren Guild. Smithwick & Belendiuk. Format: Urban adult comtemp. News: 4 hrs wkly. Target aud: 25 plus. ♦Tom Joerres, pres & gen mgr; Roger Williams, gen sls mgr; Lauri Jones, progmg dir; Andrea Williams, news dir & pub affrs dir; David Popovich, chief of engrg.

Menomonie

*****WHWC(FM)**— June 28, 1950: 88.3 mhz; 70 kw. Ant 1,050 ft. TL: N45 02 47 W91 51 42. 1221 W. Clairemont Ave., Eau-Claire 54701. Secondary address: 821 University Ave., Madison 53706-1496. Phone: (715) 839-3868. Fax: (715) 839-2939. Web Site: www.wpr.org. Licensee: State of Wisconsin Educational Communications Board. Network: Network: NPR, PRI. Dow, Lohnes & Albertson. Format: Educ, talk. Target aud: 35-54. Spec prog: Folk 7 hrs wkly. ♦Dean Kallenbach, gen mgr.

WMEQ(AM)— May 1951: 880 khz; 10 kw-D, 210 w-N. TL: N44 48 48 W91 55 34. Stereo. Box 45, Eau Claire 54702. Secondary address: 619 Cameron ST., Eau Claire 54703. Phone: (715) 830-4000. Fax: (715) 835-9680. Web Site: www.wmeq.com. Licensee: Capstar TX L.P. Group owner: Clear Channel Communications Inc. (acq 2000; grpsl). Format: News/talk, sports. Target aud: 35 plus. Spec prog: Farm 15 hrs wkly. ♦Mike Cushman, opns mgr; Rick Hencley, gen mgr & gen sls mgr; Jay Moore, progmg dir; Paul Orth, chief of engrg.

WMEQ-FM— July 19, 1967: 92.1 mhz; 17.5 kw. Ant 718 ft. TL: N44 54 59 W91 41 55. Stereo. Web Site: www.rock921.com. Format: Classic rock. Target aud: 25-54. ♦Mike Cushman, opns mgr; Rick Hencley, VP & sls dir.

*****WVSS(FM)**— Apr 22, 1969: 90.7 mhz; 590 w. Ant 426 ft. TL: N44 54 56 W92 04 34. Stereo. 1221 W. Clairemont Ave., Eau-Claire 54701. Phone: (715) 839-3868. Fax: (715) 839-2939. Licensee: Board of Regents, University of Wisconsin Systems. Format: Class, news/talk. Target aud: 45-64. Spec prog: Folk 6 hrs, jazz 5 hrs wkly. ♦Dean Kallenbach, gen mgr; Marvin Spielman, dev mgr; Mary Jo Wagner, news dir.

Merrill

WJMT(AM)— May 10, 1960: 730 khz; 1 kw-D, 127 w-N. TL: N45 10 45 W89 38 20. 120 S. Mill St. 54452-2508. Phone: (715) 536-6262. Fax: (715) 536-6208. Licensee: Roberts Broadcasting Inc. Group owner: Badger Communications L.L.C. (acq 6-4-01; grpsl). Rep: D & R Radio. Format: Adult contemp, MOR, talk. News staff: one. Target aud: 35-59. Spec prog: Relg 3 hrs, farm 7 hrs, Pol 3 hrs wkly. ♦David Winters, pres; Steven Resnick, gen mgr; Christine Vorpagel, gen sls mgr; Nick Summers, progmg dir; Joe Weniger, news dir; Chuck Genarro, chief of engrg.

WMZK(FM)—Co-owned with WJMT(AM). Aug 25, 1968: 104.1 mhz; 24 kw. 617 ft. TL: N45 06 14 W89 43 05. Stereo. E-mail: advertising@z104rocks.com. Web Site: www.z104rocks.com. Format: Rock/AOR. News staff: one. Target aud: 18-49.

Middleton

WTUX(AM)—See Madison

WWQM-FM— Oct 20, 1970: 106.3 mhz; 4.5 kw. 374 ft. TL: N43 03 03 W89 29 13. Stereo. 2740 Ski Ln., Madison 53713. Secondary address: Box 2058, Madison 53744-4408. Phone: (608) 273-1000. Phone: (608) 273-1000. Fax: (608) 271-8182. Web Site: www.q106.com. Licensee: Mid-West Management Inc. Group owner: The Mid-West Family Broadcast Group (acq 8-15-97; $6.4 million. with WTUX(AM) Madison). Rep: McGavren Guild. Shaw Pittman. Format: Country. Target aud: 25-54; general. ♦Thomas A. Walker, pres & gen mgr; Ted Waldbillig, sls VP & gen sls mgr; Brent Allen, prom mgr; Mark Grantin, progmg dir & progmg mgr; Mel McKenzie, mus dir; Robin Colbert, news dir; John Bauer, chief of engrg.

Milladore

*****WGNV(FM)**— Feb 13, 1986: 88.5 mhz; 50 kw. 584 ft. TL: N44 38 37 W89 50 48. Stereo. Box 88, 10945 Hwy. N. 54454. Phone: (715) 457-2988. Fax: (715) 457-2987. Web Site: christianfamilyradio.net. Licensee: Evangel Ministries Inc. Network: Network: Moody, Salem Radio Network. Leventhal, Senter & Leman. Format: Christian adult contemp. News: 10 hrs wkly. Target aud: Women; 35-49. Spec prog: Children 4 hrs wkly. ♦Paul Cameron, gen mgr; Andrew Kilgas, mktg dir & progmg dir; Andy Kilgas, adv dir & adv mgr; Todd Christopher, mus dir; Jim Jensen, engrg dir.

Milwaukee

WHQG(FM)—Listing follows WJYI(AM).

WISN(AM)— 1922: 1130 khz; 50 kw-D, 10 kw-N, DA-2. TL: N42 45 18 W88 04 53. 12100 W. Howard Ave., Greenfield 53228. Phone: (414) 545-8900. Fax: (414) 327-3200. Web Site: www.newstalk1130.com. Licensee: Capstar TX L.P. Group owner: Clear Channel Communications Inc. (acq 8-30-2000; grpsl). Network: Network: Westwood One, ABC Information & Entertainment. Format: Talk, news. News staff: 4. Target

Stations in the U.S. — Wisconsin

aud: 25-54. ♦Cindy McDowell, gen mgr; Keith Bratel, sls dir; Phil Kurth, gen sls mgr; Jerry Bott, progmg dir; Harold Mester, news dir; Al Hajny, chief of engrg.

WQBW(FM)—Co-owned with WISN(AM). January 1961: 97.3 mhz; 15.5 kw. 980 ft. TL: N43 06 41 W87 55 38. Stereo. Web Site: www.light97.com. Network: ABC. Format: Adult contemp. ♦Tom Buettner, sls dir; Dan Atkinson, progmg dir.

WJYI(AM)— 1955: 1340 khz; 1 kw-U. TL: N43 02 49 W87 58 52. 5407 W. McKinley Ave. 53208. Phone: (414) 978-9000. Fax: (414) 978-9001. Web Site: www.joy1340.com. Licensee: Lakefront Communications LLC. Group owner: Saga Communications Inc. (acq 2-23-94; $7 million. with co-located FM; FTR: 3-14-94). Network: Network: CBS, ABC FM Connection. Format: Contemporary Christian. Target aud: 18-54. ♦Tom Joerres, pres & gen mgr; Ryan Salzer, opns mgr; Cindy Gaudion, natl sls mgr; Terry Qualls, rgnl sls mgr; Brad Wallace, prom dir; Dave Popovich, chief of engrg.

WHQG(FM)—Co-owned with WJYI(AM). October 1960: 102.9 mhz; 50 kw. ant 440 ft. TL: N43 02 49 W87 58 52. Stereo. Web Site: www.1029thehog.com. Format: Active rock. ♦Ann Marie King, sls dir; Scott Schubert, prom dir; Sean Elliott, progmg dir.

WJZI(FM)— June 1958: 93.3 mhz; 12.6 kw. Ant 992 ft. TL: N43 05 15 W87 54 12. Stereo. 2979 N. Mayfair Rd. 53222. Phone: (414) 778-1933. Fax: (414) 771-3036. Web Site: www.wjzi.com. Licensee: Milwaukee Radio Alliance L.L.C. (group owner; acq 9-23-97; grpsl). Rep: Allied Radio Partners. Format: Smooth jazz. Target aud: 25-54; general. ♦Willie D. Davis, chmn; William R. Lynett, pres; Bill Hurwitz, gen mgr; Traci Northrup, opns dir & sls dir; Jerry Arndt, natl sls dir; Kate Svehlek, prom mgr; Stan Atkinson, progmg dir; John Church, chief of engrg.

WKKV-FM—See Racine

WKLH(FM)— 1958: 96.5 mhz; 20 kw. 810 ft. TL: N43 05 48 W87 54 19. Stereo. 5407 W. McKinley Ave. 53208. Phone: (414) 978-9000. Fax: (414) 978-9001. Web Site: www.wklh.com. Licensee: Lakefront Communications LLC. Group owner: Saga Communications Inc. (acq 7-18-90). Format: Classic rock. News staff: one. Target aud: 25-44; baby boomers. ♦Tom Joerres, pres & gen mgr; Annmarie King, gen sls mgr; Cindy Gaudion, natl sls mgr; Brad Wallace, prom dir; Bob Bellini, progmg dir; Carole Caine, news dir; Dave Popovich, chief of engrg.

WKTI(FM)—Listing follows WTMJ(AM).

WLUM-FM—Listing follows WMCS(AM).

WMCS(AM)—(Greenfield). Apr 27, 1947: 1290 khz; 5 kw-U, DA-2. TL: N42 55 11 W87 59 17. Stereo. 4222 W. Capitol Dr. 53216. Phone: (414) 444-1290. Fax: (414) 444-1409. Web Site: www.1290wmcs.com. Licensee: Milwaukee Radio Alliance L.L.C. (group owner; acq 9-23-97; grpsl). Network: ESPN Radio. Rep: Allied Radio Partners. Format: Talk. News staff: one; News: 7 hrs wkly. Target aud: 25-54; upwardly mobile Blacks. Spec prog: Blues 6 hrs, gospel 5 hrs, Sp 5 hrs, church 3.25 hrs wkly. ♦Don Rosette, gen mgr & gen sls mgr; Eric Von, opns mgr; Tyrene Jackson, progmg dir; Keith Murphy, news dir; John Church, chief of engrg.

WLUM-FM—Co-owned with WMCS(AM). September 1960: 102.1 mhz; 20 kw. Ant 761 ft. TL: N43 05 48 W87 54 19. Stereo. 2979 N. Mayfair Rd. 53222-4301. Phone: (414) 771-1021. Fax: (414) 771-3036. Web Site: www.rock102.com. Format: Rock. Target aud: 18-49; teens & adults. ♦Bill Hurwitz, gen mgr; Jerry Arndt, sls dir & natl sls dir; Traci Northrup, gen sls mgr; Tommy Wilde, progmg dir; Stan Atkinson, news dir; John Church, chief of engrg.

WMIL(FM)—See Waukesha

*WMSE(FM)— Mar 14, 1981: 91.7 mhz; 1 kw. 125 ft. TL: N43 02 43 W87 54 57. (CP: 3.2 kw, ant 128 ft.). Stereo. 1025 N. Broadway 53202. Phone: (414) 277-7247. Fax: (414) 277-7149. Web Site: www.wmse.org. Licensee: Milwaukee School of Engineering. Format: Mix. Target aud: 18-35; young adults. Spec prog: Black 13 hrs, jazz 15 hrs, It 3 hrs, Sp 3 hrs, class 3 hrs wkly. ♦Tom Crawford, gen mgr; Mike Bereiter, mus dir; Julie Cudahy, chief of engrg.

*WMWK(FM)— Dec 7, 1990: 88.1 mhz; 170 w. 955 ft. TL: N43 05 24 W87 53 47. Stereo. 290 Hegenberger Rd., Oakland, CA 94621. Secondary address: Box 11552, 1100 E. Capitol Dr., Shorewood 53211. Phone: (414) 964-9794. Phone: (800) 543-1495. Web Site: www.familyradio.com. Licensee: Family Stations Inc. (group owner) Network: UPI. Format: Christian. ♦Harold Camping, pres; John Rorvik, gen mgr.

WMYX(FM)—Listing follows WSSP(AM).

WNOV(AM)— Aug 15, 1946: 860 khz; 250 w-D, 5 w-N. TL: N43 02 20 W87 54 17. (CP: TL: N43 04 20 W87 57 07). Box 06438, 3815 N. Teutonia Ave. 53206. Phone: (414) 449-9668. Fax: (414) 449-9945. E-mail: wnov860@yahoo.com. Web Site: www.wnov.com. Licensee: Courier Communications Corp. (acq 1-2-73). Format: Urban contemp. ♦Jerrel W. Jones, CEO & pres; Sandra Robinson, gen mgr, opns mgr & gen sls mgr; Laura Taylor, prom dir; Homer Blow, progmg dir & chief of engrg.

WOKY(AM)— 1947: 920 khz; 5 kw-D, 1 kw-N, DA-2. TL: N42 58 32 W88 03 56. Stereo. 12100 W. Howard Ave., Greenfield 53228. Phone: (414) 545-5920. Fax: (414) 546-9654. Web Site: www.am920woky.com. Licensee: Clear Channel Radio Licenses Inc. Group owner: Clear Channel Communications Inc. (acq 3-17-97; $40 million with WMIL(FM) Waukesha). Network: ABC. Rep: Clear Channel. Format: Adult standards. News staff: 3; News: 15 hrs wkly. Target aud: 35-64. ♦Cindy McDowell, VP & stn mgr; Keith Bratel, sls dir; Joe Stribl, gen sls mgr & prom dir; Phil Kurth, sls dir & gen sls mgr; Harold Mester, progmg dir & news dir; Jerry Bott, progmg dir; Gregory Jon, mus dir; Al Hajny, chief of engrg.

WRIT-FM— May 10, 1961: 95.7 mhz; 34 kw. 610 ft. TL: N43 05 25 W87 54 54. Stereo. Box 20920 53220-0920. Secondary address: 12100 W. Howard Ave., Greenfield 53228. Phone: (414) 545-8900. Fax: (414) 327-3200. Licensee: Clear Channel Radio Licenses Inc. Group owner: Clear Channel Communications Inc. (acq 10-97; $14.5 million). Rep: Clear Channel. Format: Hits of the 60s & 70s. Target aud: 25-54; baby boomers. ♦Cindy McDowell, gen mgr; Jeff Lynn, stn mgr & progmg dir; Kerry Wolfe, opns mgr; Keith Bratel, gen sls mgr; Ken Kohl, prom dir; Harold Mester, news dir; Al Hajny, chief of engrg.

WRRD(AM)—See Jackson

WSSP(AM)— Oct 14, 1935: 1250 khz; 5 kw-U, DA-2. TL: N42 56 44 W88 03 39. 11800 W. Grange Ave., Hales Corners 53130. Phone: (414) 529-1250. Fax: (414) 529-2122. Licensee: Entercom Milwaukee License LLC. Group owner: Entercom Communications Corp. (acq 12-13-99; grpsl). Akin, Gump, Strauss, Hauer & Feld. Format: Christian radio. Target aud: 25-49. Spec prog: Relg 3 hrs, Ger 8 hrs, Sp 3 hrs wkly. ♦Craig Hodgson, gen mgr; Alan Kirshbom, sls dir; Andrea Biebel, natl sls mgr; Jim Morales, prom dir; Glenn Redd, progmg dir & progmg mgr; Michael Clemens, news dir; Chris Tarr, chief of engrg.

WMYX(FM)—Co-owned with WSSP(AM). Nov 1, 1962: 99.1 mhz; 50 kw. 450 ft. TL: N42 56 44 W88 03 39. Stereo. Web Site: www.99wmyx.com. Network: Westwood One. Rep: D & R Radio. Format: Hot adult contemp. Target aud: 25-49; women. Spec prog: Relg one hr wkly. ♦Tom Gjerdrum, progmg mgr; Jane Matenaer, pub affrs dir.

WTMJ(AM)— July 25, 1927: 620 khz; 50 kw-D, 10 kw-N. TL: N43 01 56 W88 07 54. Stereo. 720 E. Capitol Dr. 53212. Secondary address: Box 693 53201. Phone: (414) 332-9611. Fax: (414) 967-5378. Web Site: www.620wtmj.com. Licensee: Journal Broadcast Corp. Group owner: Journal Broadcast Group Inc. Network: ABC. Rep: Christal. Hogan & Hartson. Format: News/talk, sports. Target aud: General. Spec prog: Relg 2 hrs wkly. ♦Doug Kiel, CEO; Jon Schweitzer, gen mgr & chief of engrg; Jeff Kuether, sls VP; Diana Paul, mktg VP; Rick Belcher, opns VP & progmg dir; Dan Shelley, news dir; Randy Price, engrg VP.

WKTI(FM)—Co-owned with WTMJ(AM). June 1959: 94.5 mhz; 15.5 kw. 911 ft. TL: N43 05 29 W87 54 07. Stereo. Web Site: www.wkti.com. Format: Adult contemp. News staff: one. Target aud: 25-54. ♦Jon Schweitzer, stn mgr; Lisa Letterman, mktg VP; Bob Walker, progmg dir. Co-owned TV: WTMJ-TV affil

*WUWM(FM)— Sept 24, 1964: 89.7 mhz; 15 kw. 871 ft. TL: N43 05 24 W87 53 47. Stereo. Box 413 53201. Secondary address: 161 W. Wisconsin Ave. 53202. Phone: (414) 227-3355. Fax: (414) 270-1297. E-mail: wuwm@uwn.edu. Web Site: www.wuwm.com. Licensee: Board of Regents of University of Wisconsin. Network: Network: PRI, NPR. Format: News, AAA. News staff: 5. Target aud: General. ♦Dave Edwards, CEO & gen mgr; Susan Baran, dev mgr; Betsy Neldner, mktg mgr; Bruce Winter, progmg dir; Marge Pitrof, news dir; Tom May, chief of engrg.

WVCY-FM— 1961: 107.7 mhz; 43 kw. Ant 528 ft. TL: N42 57 46 W88 04 23. 3434 W. Kilbourn Ave. 53208. Phone: (414) 935-3000. Fax: (414) 935-3015. E-mail: wvcyfm@vcyamerica.org. Web Site: www.vcyamerica.org. Licensee: VCY/America Inc. (group owner; acq 1-70). Network: Network: USA, Moody. Format: Relg, Christian. ♦Dr. Randall Melchert, pres; Victor Eliason, VP & gen mgr; Gordon Morris, opns mgr & news dir; Jim Schneider, progmg dir; Tom Schlueter, mus dir; Andy Eliason, chief of engrg.

WXSS(FM)—See Wauwatosa

*WYMS(FM)— Mar 5, 1973: 88.9 mhz; 1.5 kw. 870 ft. TL: N43 05 21 W87 53 47. Stereo. 5225 W. Vliet St. 53208. Phone: (414) 475-8989/8890. Fax: (414) 475-8413. E-mail: wyms@milwaukee12.wi.us. Web Site: www.wyms.org. Licensee: Milwaukee Board of School Directors. Hogan & Hartson. Format: Jazz, educ. News: 10 hrs wkly. Target aud: General.

Minocqua

WLKD(AM)— Aug 1, 1978: 1570 khz; 5 kw-D, 500 w-N. TL: N45 49 13 W89 43 27. Stereo. Box 96 54548. Secondary address: 7380 Hwy. 51 S. 54548. Phone: (715) 356-9696. Fax: (715) 356-1977. Web Site: www.wmqa.com. Licensee: Raven Broadcasting Corp. Group owner: NewRadio Group LLC (acq 12-20-2002; grpsl). Network: ABC Information & Entertainment. Leventhal, Senter & Lerman. Format: ESPN Sports. News staff: one; News: 18 hrs wkly. Target aud: 45 plus. Spec prog: Relg 3 hrs wkly. ♦Casey Kelly, stn mgr; Duff Damos, opns mgr; Michelle Hartzheim, rgnl sls mgr; Mike Ell, prom dir; Mike Wolf, progmg mgr & mus dir; John Burton, news dir; Al Johnson, chief of engrg.

WMQA-FM—Co-owned with WLKD(AM). Apr 3, 1975: 95.9 mhz; 25 kw. 289 ft. TL: N45 52 14 W89 42 35. Stereo. E-mail: wmqa@n5gnorthwoods.net. Web Site: www.wmqa.com. Network: ABC Information & Entertainment. Leventhal, Senter & Lerman. Format: Soft rock. News staff: one; News: 18 hrs wkly. Target aud: 25-54. ♦Mike Wolf, prom mgr.

Mishicot

WZOR(FM)— Dec 17, 1994: 94.7 mhz; 21.5 kw. Ant 354 ft. TL: N44 20 30 W87 47 10. Box 1519, Appleton 54912. Secondary address: 2727 E. Radio Rd., Appleton 54915. Phone: (920) 734-9226. Fax: (920) 733-2391. E-mail: razor@wcinet.com. Web Site: www.razor947.com. Licensee: Woodward Communications Inc. (group owner; acq 1-27-00). Rep: McGavren Guild. Hogan & Hartson. Format: Active rock. ♦Roxanne Steele, gen mgr; Jeff Sharkey, progmg dir; Ed Walters, news dir; Steve Brown, chief of engrg.

Monroe

WEKZ(AM)— July 27, 1951: 1260 khz; 1 kw-D, 19 w-N. TL: N42 35 41 W89 35 35. W4765 Radio Ln. 53566. Phone: (608) 325-2161. Phone: (608) 325-4869. Fax: (608) 325-2164. E-mail: wekz@wekz.com. Web Site: www.wekz.com. Licensee: Green County Broadcasting Corp. (acq 4-96; $1,445,000). Network: Network: ABC, ABC Information & Entertainment. Format: Country classic. News staff: 4; News: 16 hrs wkly. Target aud: 50 plus. Spec prog: Ger 3 hrs, Swiss 3 hrs wkly.

Wisconsin — Directory of Radio

♦ Scott Thompson, gen mgr & gen sls mgr; Wyatt Herrmann, progmg dir; Don Jacobson, news dir; Gary Gulalski, pub affrs dir; Todd Hauser, chief of engrg.

WEKZ-FM— June 1959: 93.7 mhz; 36 kw. 581 ft. TL: N42 34 36 W89 41 34. Stereo. Web Site: www.wekz.com. Licensee: Ronald M. Spielman, Scott A. Thompson dba Green County Broadcasting. (Acq 2-28-96). Network: ABC. Format: Adult contemp. News staff: 4; News: 10 hrs wkly. Target aud: 35-55. ♦ Scott Thompson, stn mgr.

Mosinee

WOFM(FM)— Oct 7, 1991: 94.7 mhz; 50 kw. 492 ft. TL: N44 59 18 W89 59 42. Stereo. 557 Scott St., Wausau 54403-1206. Phone: (715) 842-1672. Fax: (715) 848-3158. E-mail: theoldiesstation @theoldiesstation.com. Web Site: www.wofm.com. Licensee: WRIG Inc. Group owner: Midwest Communications Inc. (acq 9-24-97; $35,000 for 70%). Format: Oldies. News staff: one; News: 3 hrs wkly. Target aud: 25-54; upscale baby boomers. Spec prog: Polka 3 hrs wkly. ♦ Duke Wright, pres; Gary Tesch, exec VP; Brett Lucht, gen mgr; Ken Clark, opns mgr; Greg Stump, gen sls mgr; Bob Jung, progmg dir; Chris Conley, news dir; Frank Zastrow, engrg VP.

Mukwonago

WFZH(FM)— 2002: 105.3 mhz; 1.65 kw. Ant 633 ft. TL: N42 58 05 W88 11 20. 135 S. 84th St., Suite 310, Milwaukee 53214. Phone: (414) 258-1700. Fax: (414) 266-5353. E-mail: studio@1053thefish.com. Web Site: wfzh.salemwebnetwork.com. Licensee: Caron Broadcasting Inc. Group owner: Salem Communications Corp. (acq 10-22-01). Format: Christian. ♦ Danny Clayton, progmg dir.

Neenah-Menasha

WNAM(AM)— May 23, 1947: 1280 khz; 5 kw-U. TL: N44 09 36 W88 27 57. Stereo. 491 S. Washburn, Suite 400, Oshkosh 54904. Phone: (920) 426-3239. Fax: (920) 231-0145. Licensee: Cumulus Broadcasting L.L.C. Group owner: Cumulus Media L.L.C. (acq 6-30-97; grpsl). Network: ABC Information & Entertainment. Rep: Allied Radio Partners. Format: Easy lstng. News staff: 3; News: 13 hrs wkly. Target aud: 35 plus. ♦ Jeffrey A. Schmidt, gen mgr; Larry Phillip, sls dir.

WNCY-FM— Sept 9, 1977: 100.3 mhz; 45 kw. 489 ft. TL: N44 15 27 W88 11 41. Stereo. Box 23333, Green Bay 54305. Secondary address: 115 S. Jefferson St., Green Bay 54301. Phone: (920) 435-3771. Fax: (920) 444-1155. Web Site: www.wncy.com. Licensee: Midwest Communications Inc. (group owner; acq 12-10-96; grpsl). Format: Country. ♦ D.E. Wright, pres; Gary Tesch, exec VP; Jeff McCarthy, VP; Craig Von Able, gen sls mgr; Randy Shannon, progmg dir; Mark Daniels, news dir; Tim Laes, engrg dir.

WROE(FM)— November 1971: 94.3 mhz; 13 kw. 459 ft. TL: N44 09 30 W88 17 03. Stereo. Box 23333, Green Bay 54301. Phone: (920) 435-3771. Fax: (920) 444-1155. Licensee: Midwest Communications Inc. (group owner; acq 12-10-96; grpsl). Format: Soft adult contemp. Target aud: 25-54. ♦ Duke Wright, CEO; D.E. Wright, gen mgr; David Fries, gen sls mgr; Aaron Vorass, prom mgr; Denny Luell, progmg dir; Tim Laes, chief of engrg.

WWWX(FM)—See Oshkosh

Neillsville

WCCN(AM)— Sept 22, 1957: 1370 khz; 5 kw-D, 42 w-N. TL: N44 34 18 W90 35 15. Box 387, 1201 E. Division St. 54456. Phone: (715) 743-2222. Phone: (715) 743-3333. Fax: (715) 743-2288. Licensee: Central Wisconsin Broadcasting Inc. (group owner; acq 12-87; FTR: 3-25-91). Network: ABC. Miller & Fields, P.C. Format: Big Band, nostalgia. News staff: one; News: 20 hrs wkly. Target aud: 45 plus. Spec prog: Farm 19 hrs, Polka 2 hrs wkly. ♦ J. Kevin Grap, pres; Margaret L. Grap, VP.

WCCN-FM— July 1964: 107.5 mhz; 100 kw. Ant 577 ft. TL: N44 35 30 W90 37 09. Stereo. E-mail: 1075therock@tds.net. Web Site: www.1075therock.com. Network: ABC. Miller & Fields, P.C. Format: Rock. News staff: one. Target aud: 25-40.

WPKG(FM)— February 2004: 92.7 mhz; 3.4 kw. Ant 440 ft. TL: N44 35 30 W90 37 09. 1201 E. Division St. 54456. Phone: (715) 743-3333. Fax: (715) 743-2288. Licensee: Central Wisconsin Broadcasting Inc. (group owner). Format: Adult contemp. Females. ♦ J. Kevin Grap, gen mgr.

Nekoosa

WMMA(FM)— 2002: 93.9 mhz; 25 kw. Ant 318 ft. TL: N44 13 23 W89 49 46. Box 1103, Wisconsin Rapids 54495. Secondary address: 321 Market St., Wisconsin Rapids 54494. Phone: (715) 424-5050. Fax: (715) 424-5656. Web Site: www.relevantradio.com. Licensee: Starboard Media Foundation Inc. Group owner: Relevant Radio (acq 12-20-2001; $2.3 million. with WIBU(AM) Wisconsin Dells). Format: Relg. ♦ Jack O'Keefe, gen mgr.

WUSP(FM)—Not on air, target date: unknown:. Stn currently dark 105.5 mhz; 6 kw. Ant 279 ft. TL: N44 21 45 W90 03 58. 2307 Princess Ann St., Greensboro, NC 27408. Phone: (336) 286-2087. Licensee: Todd P. Robinson Inc. ♦ Todd P. Robinson, pres.

New London

WOZZ(FM)— Oct 6, 1967: 93.5 mhz; 50 kw. 528 ft. TL: N44 21 35 W88 42 46. (CP: Ant 492 ft.). Stereo. 1500 N. Casaloma Dr., Suite 307, Appleton 54913-8220. Phone: (920) 733-4990. Fax: (920) 733-5507. Web Site: www.wozz.com. Licensee: Midwest Communications of Iowa Inc. Group owner: Midwest Communications Inc. (acq 6-30-93; $1.85 million. with WLYD(FM) Sturgeon Bay; FTR: 7-26-93). Format: Classic rock. News staff: 2; News: 8 hrs wkly. Target aud: 25-44. ♦ David Fries, gen mgr, gen sls mgr & gen sls mgr; David Louis, progmg dir; Tim Laef, chief of engrg.

New Richmond

WIXK(AM)—Licensed to New Richmond. See Minneapolis-St. Paul MN

Oconto

WOCO(AM)— Mar 11, 1966: 1260 khz; 1 kw-D. TL: N45 53 31 W87 57 18. 3829 Hwy.22 54153. Phone: (920) 834-3540. Fax: (920) 834-3532. E-mail: wocoamfm@bayland.net. Licensee: Lamardo Inc. (acq 3-25-99; with co-located FM). Format: C&W, var. Target aud: 29 plus. ♦ Larry Kaszynski, gen sls mgr, adv mgr & mus dir; Terri Kaszynski, rgnl sls mgr, prom mgr & news dir; Dorothy Kaszynski, progmg dir; Walter P. Kaszynski, pres, gen mgr & chief of engrg.

WOCO-FM— Aug 1, 1968: 107.1 mhz; 3 kw. 210 ft. TL: N44 53 31 W87 57 18. Format: Easy lstng.

Omro

WPKR(FM)—Licensed to Omro. See Oshkosh

Oshkosh

WOSH(AM)— Dec 31, 1941: 1490 khz; 1 kw-U. TL: N44 02 46 W88 31 44. 491 S. Washburn, Suite 400 54904. Phone: (920) 426-3239. Fax: (920) 231-0145. Web Site: www.cumulus.com. Licensee: Cumulus Broadcasting Inc. Group owner: Cumulus Media LLC. (acq 9-1-97; grpsl). Rep: D & R Radio. Format: News/talk, sports. Target aud: 25 plus. ♦ Jeffrey Schmidt, gen mgr; Larry Phillip, gen sls mgr; John Stiloski, prom dir; Bob Burnell, progmg dir; Jonathan Krause, news dir; Steve Griesbach, chief of engrg.

WVBO(FM)— Co-owned with WOSH(AM). Sept 1, 1966: 103.9 mhz; 25 kw. 318 ft. TL: N44 02 47 W88 31 44. Stereo. Web Site: www.1039vbo.com. Network: Westwood One. Format: Oldies. Target aud: 35-54. ♦ Brian Roberts, progmg dir.

WPKR(FM)— (Omro). July 12, 1990: 99.5 mhz; 50 kw. 420 ft. TL: N43 50 51 W88 51 31. Stereo. 491 S. Washburn St., Suite 400 54904. Phone: (920) 426-3239. Fax: (920) 231-0145. Web Site: wpkr.com. Licensee: Cumulus Licensing LLC. Group owner: Cumulus Media Inc. (acq 11-10-2003; $8.1 million. with WPCK(FM) Denmark). Rep: Allied Radio Partners. Format: Country. News staff: one; News: 2 hrs wkly. Target aud: 25-54. Spec prog: Farm one hr wkly. ♦ Jeff Schmidt, gen mgr.

*****WRST-FM**— Apr 20, 1966: 90.3 mhz; 960 w. 125 ft. TL: N44 01 45 W88 33 08. Stereo. 800 Algoma Blvd. 54901. Phone: (920) 424-3113. Phone: (920) 424-1234. Fax: (920) 424-1279. Licensee: Board of Regents, University of Wisconsin System. Network: NPR. Format: Div. Target aud: General. ♦ Ben Jarman, gen mgr; Kelly Bougneit, stn mgr; Nick Rusch, progmg dir; Bob Knudsen, news dir; Dwight Poppy, chief of engrg.

*****WVCY(AM)**— July 1, 1969: 690 khz; 250 w-D, 77 w-N, DA-2. TL: N44 04 51 W88 33 53. 3434 W. Kilbourn Ave., Milwaukee 53208. Phone: (414) 935-3000. Fax: (414) 935-3015. E-mail: wvcyam@vcyamerica.org. Web Site: www.vcyamerica.org. Licensee: VCY/America Inc. (group owner; acq 1-19-95). Network: USA. Format: Relg. ♦ Dr. Randall Melchert, pres; Vic Eliason, VP & gen mgr; Jim Schneider, progmg dir & pub affrs dir; Tom Schlueter, mus dir; Gordon Morris, news dir; Andy Eliason, chief of engrg.

WWWX(FM)— Jan 30, 1967: 96.9 mhz; 6 kw. 328 ft. TL: N44 03 51 W88 31 44. 491 S. Washburn St., Suite 400 54904. Phone: (920) 426-3239. Fax: (920) 231-0145. Web Site: www.fox969.com. Licensee: Cumulus Broadcasting Inc. Group owner: Cumulus Media Inc. (acq 6-30-97; grpsl). Network: ABC. Rep: Allied Radio Partners. Format: Rock. Target aud: 25-54. ♦ Jeff Schmidt, gen mgr.

Park Falls

WCQM(FM)—Listing follows WNBI(AM).

*****WHBM-FM**— Nov 11, 1988: 90.3 mhz; 17.5 kw. 727 ft. TL: N45 56 43 W90 16 28. 518 S. 7th Ave., Wausau 54401. Phone: (715) 261-6298. Fax: (715) 848-2890. E-mail: reyer@wpr.org. Web Site: www.wpr.org. Licensee: State of Wisconsin Educational Communications Board. Dow, Lohnes & Albertson. Format: News/talk. News staff: 9. Target aud: 35-54; Skews Female: Issue oriented talk-variety of perspectives. ♦ Wendy Wink, CEO; Ted Tobie, CFO; Greg Schnirring, gen mgr; Rick Reyer, gen mgr & stn mgr; Tom Martin-Erickson, opns dir & opns mgr; Ben Spindler, gen sls mgr; Connie Walker, news dir; Dennis Behr, engrg VP; Pete Kingslien, engrg dir & chief of engrg.

WNBI(AM)— 1953: 980 khz; 1 kw-D, 105 w-N. TL: N45 55 04 W90 26 58. Box 309 54552. Secondary address: Hwy. 13 St. 54552. Phone: (715) 762-3221. Fax: (715) 762-2358. E-mail: wnbi@pctcnet.net. Licensee: Heartland Communications License LLC. (group owner; acq 7-30-2002; $850,000. with co-located FM). Network: ABC. Format: Sports. News staff: 2; News: 12 hrs wkly. Target aud: 25-54; adults with disposable income. Spec prog: Relg one hr, loc community talk 5 hrs wkly. ♦ James Gregori, gen mgr; Darla Isham, gen sls mgr; Joel Karnick, opns dir, progmg dir & news dir; Arthur Dunham, chief of engrg.

WCQM(FM)— Co-owned with WNBI(AM). Apr 13, 1968: 98.3 mhz; 57 kw. 233 ft. TL: N45 55 04 W90 26 58. Web Site: www.wcqm.com. Network: ABC. Format: Country. News staff: one; News: 6 hrs wkly. Target aud: 20-70.

Peshtigo

WSFQ(FM)— Aug 5, 1996: 96.3 mhz; 49 kw. 482 ft. TL: N45 07 19 W87 51 07. Stereo. N. 2880 Roosevelt Rd., Marinette 54143. Phone: (715) 735-6631. Fax: (715) 732-0125. Web Site: www.badgerb-bayarearadio.com. Licensee: Badger Communications L.L.C. (group owner; acq 8-6-98; grpsl). Network: ABC. Format: Oldies. News staff: one. Target aud: 49; male. ♦ David Winters, pres; Jim Medley, opns dir & progmg VP; Shawn Katzbeck, sls dir; Mike Wolfe, progmg dir; Glenn King, news dir.

Platteville

WPVL(AM)— Feb 22, 1955: 1590 khz; 1 kw-D, 500 w-N, DA-N. TL: N42 44 46 W90 28 28. Box One, 1245 N. 4th St. 53818. Phone: (608) 348-2775. Fax: (608) 348-2780. E-mail: wpvl@n2.com. Licensee: QueenB Radio Wisconsin Inc. Group owner: Morgan Murphy Stations (acq 3-18-98; $825,000 with co-located FM). Network: ABC. Robert Olender. Format: ESPN/Sports. News staff: 2; News: 10 hrs wkly. Target aud: 35 plus. Spec prog: Farm 12 hrs, sports 15 hrs wkly. ♦ Dan Sullivan, gen mgr.

WPVL-FM— Sept 1, 1966: 107.1 mhz; 4.1 kw. 235 ft. TL: N42 44 45 W90 38 27. Stereo. Format: Oldies. News staff: one; News: 10 hrs wkly. Target aud: 30 plus; general adults.

*****WSUP(FM)**— Feb 25, 1964: 90.5 mhz; 1 kw. 146 ft. TL: N42 43 57 W90 29 09. Stereo. One Univ. Plaza, 42 Pioneer Tower 53818. Phone: (608) 342-1165. Phone: (608) 342-1291. Fax: (608) 342-1290. E-mail: wsup@uwplatt.edu. Web Site: ums.uwplatt.edu/~wsup/. Licensee: Board of Regents, University of Wisconsin System. Dow, Lohnes & Albertson. Format: AOR. News: 10 hrs wkly. Target aud: 18-24; college-age. Spec prog: Class 4 hrs, jazz 3 hrs, alternative 6 hrs, metal 6 hrs, dance 4 hrs wkly. ♦ George E. Smith, gen mgr; Laura Lohfink, stn mgr.

Stations in the U.S.   Wisconsin

Developers & Brokers of Radio Properties
contact American Media Services at our suite: Philadelphia Marriott Downtown
215-625-2000
843-972-2200
americanmediaservices.com
Charleston, SC
Dallas, TX · Chicago, Il · Austin, TX
American Media Services, LLC

Plymouth

WJUB(AM)— April 1954: 1420 khz; 500 w-D, 62 w-N. TL: N43 44 33 W87 56 21. Box 259, N. 5569 State Hwy. 57 53073-0259. Phone: (920) 893-2661. Phone: (920) 467-4891. Fax: (920) 892-2706. E-mail: 1420amthebreeze@jmiradio.org. Web Site: www.1420thebreeze.com. Licensee: Jubilation Ministries Inc. (acq 12-17-90; $185,000; 1-7-91). Network: USA. Format: Adult Standards. News: 11 hrs wkly. Target aud: 25-54. Spec prog: Farm 5 hrs wkly. ♦ Gerry Krebsbach, pres; William Horsch, gen mgr; David Hendrickson, progmg dir.

WXER(FM)— Oct. 3, 2000: 104.5 mhz; 6 kw. 328 ft. TL: N43 43 32 W88 03 07. Stereo. 1102 Fond Du Lac Ave., Sheboygan Falls 53085. Phone: (920) 467-0200. Fax: (920) 467-4300. E-mail: wxer@excel.net. Web Site: www.1045thepoint.com. Licensee: RBH Enterprises Inc. dba Yellow Dog Broadcasting. Group owner: Mountain Dog Media (acq 6-23-00; $700,000. with WCLB(AM) Sheboygan). Format: Adult contemp. Target aud: 29-54. Spec prog: Ger 3 hrs wkly. ♦ Randall B. Hopper, pres & stn mgr; Steve Schouten, opns mgr; Dave Riley, progmg dir; Stuart Muck, chief of engrg.

Port Washington

WPJP(FM)— October 1969: . Stn currently dark 100.1 mhz; 6 kw. Ant 318 ft. TL: N43 25 14 W87 59 40. Stereo. Box 10707, Green Bay 54307. Phone: (920) 469-3021. Fax: (262) 784-2149. Licensee: Starboard Media Foundation Inc. Group owner: Relevant Radio (acq 5-15-2003; $900,000.) ♦ Mark Follett, CEO & pres; Neil Robbins, stn mgr.

Portage

WBKY(FM)— 1998: 95.9 mhz; 5.4 kw. Ant 321 ft. TL: N43 38 17 W89 34 16. Box 360 53901. Secondary address: 1420 E. Wisconsin St. 53901. Phone: (608) 635-7341. Fax: (608) 635-7343. Licensee: Magnum Communications Inc. Network: AP Radio. Fisher, Wayland, Cooper, Leader & Zaragoza. Format: Country. News staff: 2; News: 7 hrs wkly. ♦ Dave Magnum, gen mgr; Rick Jensen, opns mgr.

WDDC(FM)—Listing follows WPDR(AM).

WPDR(AM)— July 31, 1952: 1350 khz; 1 kw-D, 41 w-N. TL: N43 31 40 W89 25 52. Box 448 53901. Secondary address: N6912 Hwy. 51 53901. Phone: (608) 742-1001. Fax: (608) 742-1688. E-mail: wpdr@jvlnet.com. Licensee: Zoe Communications Inc. (group owner; acq 2003; $1.1 million. with co-located FM). Network: ABC Information & Entertainment. Format: News/talk, adult contemp. News staff: 2; News: 14 hrs wkly. Target aud: 35 plus. Spec prog: Farm 6 hrs wkly. ♦ Mike Oberg, pres, gen mgr & chief of engrg; Lyric Klaske, gen mgr; Wendy Oberg, pres, exec VP & gen mgr; Robert Hoffer, sls dir; Susann Gamble, progmg dir & news dir.

WDDC(FM)—Co-owned with WPDR(AM). Nov 8, 1966: 100.1 mhz; 3.3 kw. 300 ft. TL: N43 31 40 W89 25 52. (CP: 1.84 kw. TL: N43 31 42 W89 26 01). Stereo. Network: ABC Information & Entertainment. Format: Country. News staff: 2. Target aud: 25-45; office workers, young adults. ♦ Kevin Todryk, progmg dir.

Poynette

WHFA(AM)— July 1925: 1240 khz; 1 kw-U. TL: N43 21 38 W89 24 08. 2300 Riverside Dr., Green Bay 54301. Phone: (920) 469-3021. Fax: (608) 833-7117. E-mail: whfa@relevantradio.com. Web Site: www.relevantradio.com. Licensee: Starboard Media Foundation Inc. Group owner: Relevant Radio (acq 6-28-2001; $1 million). Network: ABC. Format: Catholic. News: 3 hrs wkly. Target aud: 35-64. ♦ Martin Jury, opns mgr & dev dir.

Prairie du Chien

WPRE(AM)— Dec 11, 1952: 980 khz; 1 kw-D. TL: N43 03 39 W91 09 26. Box 90 53821. Secondary address: 640 North Villa Louis Rd. 53821. Phone: (608) 326-2411. Fax: (608) 326-2412. E-mail: wqpcwpre@mwt.net. Web Site: www.wpre.cjb.com. Licensee: Robinson Corp. Group owner: Robinson Corporation (acq 1-7-98; with co-located FM). Network: Westwood One. Format: Oldies. News staff: one. ♦ David Robinson, pres & gen mgr; Jeff Robinson, opns mgr.

WQPC(FM)—Co-owned with WPRE(AM). 1968: 94.3 mhz; 36 kw. 525 ft. TL: N43 03 35 W91 06 02. Stereo. Web Site: www.q94.us. Format: Country.

Racine

WBJX(AM)— June 4, 1950: 1460 khz; 500 w-D, 65 w-N. TL: N42 45 06 W87 49 55. 2310 C S. Greenbay Rd., #305 53406. Phone: (262) 635-7463. Fax: (262) 637-9994. Phone: (847) 336-0179. E-mail: rcjeffers@aol.com. Web Site: www.wbjx.com. Licensee: WBJX Inc. (acq 1996; $275,000). Rep: Allied Radio Partners. Format: Sp. Target aud: 25-54; upscale adults, professionals, upper income executives, college grads. Spec prog: Gospel 8 hrs wkly. ♦ Bob Jeffers, gen mgr; Patricia Marinez, opns mgr; Robert Jeffers, engrg mgr.

WEZY(FM)—Listing follows WRJN(AM).

WKKV-FM— August 1948: 100.7 mhz; 50 kw. 500 ft. TL: N42 48 18 W88 02 54. Stereo. 12100 W. Howard Ave., Greenfield 53228. Phone: (414) 321-1007. Fax: (414) 327-3200. Web Site: www.v100.com. Licensee: Clear Channel Radio Licenses Inc. Group owner: Clear Channel Communications Inc. (acq 1996; grpsl). Network: American Urban. Rep: Clear Channel. Format: Urban rhythm and blues. Target aud: 18-44; general. Spec prog: Gospel 4 hrs wkly. ♦ L. Lowry Mays, CEO; Mark Mays, pres; Cindy McDowell, gen mgr; Randy Wanek, sls dir; Byron Miller, prom dir; Doc Love, progmg dir & progmg mgr; Harold Mester, news dir; Al Hajny, chief of engrg.

WRJN(AM)— December 1926: 1400 khz; 1 kw-U. TL: N42 42 39 W87 49 48. 4201 Victory Ave. 53405. Phone: (262) 634-3311. Fax: (262) 634-6515. E-mail: wrjn@wi.net. Licensee: Racine Broadcasting L.L.C. Group owner: Bliss Communications Inc. (acq 7-11-97; $5 million with co-located FM). Network: ABC Information & Entertainment. Rep: Christal. Format: News/talk. News staff: 2; News: 40 hrs wkly. Target aud: 35 plus. Spec prog: Class 2 hrs, It 2.5, Serbian 2 hrs wkly. ♦ Skip Bliss, pres; Rob Lisser, CFO; Bob Dailey, exec VP; Tim Etes, VP & gen mgr; Ron Richards, opns dir; Leo Edelstein, gen sls mgr & adv mgr; Lew Turner, prom dir; Don Rosen, progmg dir; Tom Karkow, news dir; Bill Lawrence, pub affrs dir; Bob Gorjance, chief of engrg.

WEZY(FM)—Co-owned with WRJN(AM). Aug 6, 1962: 92.1 mhz; 6 kw. 275 ft. TL: N42 40 55 W87 50 59. (CP: 2.7 kw, ant 495 ft.). Stereo. Format: Easy Listening. News staff: 2; News: 4 hrs wkly. Target aud: 25-54. ♦ Don Rosen, mus dir.

Reedsburg

WBDL(FM)— 1997: 102.9 mhz; 3.6 kw. 423 ft. TL: N43 35 32 W90 00 42. 410 Oak St., Baraboo 53913. Phone: (608) 356-3661. Fax: (608) 356-3561. E-mail: wbdl@baraboo.com. Licensee: NewRadio Group LLC (group owner; acq 12-20-2002; grpsl). Format: Soft Rock. ♦ Tommy Lee Bychinski, gen mgr; Kent Penshorn, gen sls mgr; Kevin Kellogg, progmg dir; Steve Miller, news dir; Cliff Groth, chief of engrg.

WNFM(FM)—Listing follows WRDB(AM).

WRDB(AM)— Feb 6, 1953: 1400 khz; 1 kw-U. TL: N43 32 30 W90 02 05. Box 349 E. 53959. Phone: (608) 524-1400. Phone: (608) 524-1049. Fax: (608) 524-2474. E-mail: saukbroad@mwt.net. Licensee: NewRadio Group LLC (group owner; acq 12-20-2002; grpsl). Network: ABC Information & Entertainment. Miller & Fields, P.C. Format: Oldies, farm, news. News staff: one; News: 14 hrs wkly. Target aud: 25-54. ♦ Tommy Lee Bychinski, gen mgr.

WNFM(FM)—Co-owned with WRDB(AM). July 16, 1967: 104.9 mhz; 1.6 kw. 449 ft. TL: N43 32 30 W90 02 05. (CP: 3.2 kw). Stereo. Format: C&W. News staff: one; News: 10 hrs wkly. Target aud: 25 plus.

Reserve

*WOJB(FM)— Apr 1, 1982: 88.9 mhz; 100 kw. 604 ft. TL: N45 52 16 W91 20 56. Stereo. 13386 W. Trepania Rd., Hayward 54843. Phone: (715) 634-2100. Fax: (715) 634-4070. E-mail: generalmanager@wojb.org. Web Site: www.wojb.org. Licensee: Lac Courte Oreilles Ojibwe Public Broadcasting Corp. Network: Network: NPR, PRI. Format: Div. Spec prog: Indian 15 hrs, country 15 hrs, jazz 10 hrs, bluegrass 2 hrs wkly. ♦ Carolyn Nayquonabe, gen mgr.

Rhinelander

WHDG(FM)— Sept 1, 1994: 97.5 mhz; 100 kw. 551 ft. TL: N45 22 50 W89 11 22. 3616 Hwy. 47 N. 54501. Phone: (715) 362-1975. Fax: (715) 362-1973. E-mail: whdg@whdg.net. Web Site: www.whdg.com. Licensee: Raven Broadcasting Corp. Group owner: NewRadio Group LLC (acq 12-20-2002; grpsl). Leventhal, Senter & Lerman. Format: Country. News staff: one; News: 10 hrs wkly. Target aud: 25-54. ♦ Duff Damos, gen mgr & opns dir; Bill Mitchell, progmg dir; John Burton, news dir; Al Johnson, chief of engrg.

WOBT(AM)— Mar 9, 1947: 1240 khz; 1 kw-U. TL: N45 38 07 W89 22 21. 3616 Hwy. 47 N. 54501. Phone: (715) 362-6140. Fax: (715) 362-1973. Licensee: NewRadio Group LLC (group owner; acq 12-20-2002; grpsl). Network: ABC Information & Entertainment. Fisher, Wayland, Cooper, Leader & Zaragoza L.L.P. Format: ESPN sports. News staff: one; News: 10 hrs wkly. Target aud: 25-55. ♦ Maxy Quass, pres; Lindshy Wood Dhuis, gen mgr; Michele Krueger, gen sls mgr & adv mgr; Duff Damos, progmg dir; John Burton, news dir; Al Johnson, chief of engrg.

WRHN(FM)—Co-owned with WOBT(AM). Jan 26, 1966: 100.1 mhz; 25 kw. 385 ft. TL: N45 38 08 W89 22 42. (CP: 100 kw, ant 981 ft. TL: N45 24 03 W89 28 54). Stereo. Web Site: www.wrhnfm.com. Format: Contemp hits. Target aud: 30-55.

*WXPR(FM)— Apr 24, 1983: 91.7 mhz; 100 kw. 403 ft. TL: N45 46 28 W89 14 54. Stereo. 303 W. Prospect St. 54501. Phone: (715) 362-6000. Fax: (715) 362-6007. E-mail: wxpr@wxpr.org. Web Site: www.wxpr.org. Licensee: White Pine Community Broadcasting Inc. Network: NPR. Format: Div, class, folk. Spec prog: Jazz 8 hrs wkly. ♦ Mick Fiocchi, pres & gen mgr; Walt Gander, opns mgr; Chris Moran, dev dir; Jessie Dick, mktg dir; Jeff Dabel, mus dir; Ken Krall, news dir & pub affrs dir; Elmer Goetsch, chief of engrg.

Rice Lake

WAQE(AM)— Aug 6, 1979: 1090 khz; 5 kw-D. TL: N45 32 16 W91 45 50. Stereo. Box 703, 1859 21st Ave. 54868. Phone: (715) 234-9059. Fax: (715) 234-6942. E-mail: info@wage.com. Web Site: www.waqe.com. Licensee: TKC Inc. Group owner: Koser Radio Group (acq 1999). Shaw Pittman. Format: Classic country. News staff: one; News: 5 hrs wkly. Target aud: 24-59; traditional country mus listeners. ♦ Brian Schultz, gen mgr, stn mgr & sls dir; Tom Koser, gen mgr; Dane Jensen, sls VP; Mike Bigner, progmg dir; Mike Murrey, chief of engrg.

WKFX(FM)—Co-owned with WAQE(AM). Nov 20, 1980: 99.1 mhz; 44 kw. 522 ft. TL: N45 22 23 W91 55 22. (CP: 44 kw, ant 522 ft. TL: N45 22 23 W91 55 22). Box 352 54868. E-mail: info@fox99.com. Web Site: www.fox99.com. Format: Classic hits. News staff: one; News: 3 hrs wkly. Target aud: 18-49; young, upscale adults. ♦ Peter Neuser, stn mgr.

WJMC(AM)— 1938: 1240 khz; 1 kw-U. TL: N45 30 27 W91 46 28. Box 703, 1859 21st Ave. 54868. Phone: (715) 234-2131. Fax: (715) 234-6942. E-mail: info@wjmc.com. Web Site: www.wjmcradio.com. Licensee: TKC Inc. Group owner: Koser Radio Group (acq 1-1-89). Fisher, Wayland, Cooper, Leader & Zaragoza L.L.P. Format: Farm, news/talk, adult contemp. Target aud: 25-54. ♦ Thomas A. Koser, pres & gen mgr; Dane Jensen, stn mgr & gen sls mgr; Mike Bigner, progmg dir; Ken DeNucci, news dir; Mike Murrey, chief of engrg.

Broadcasting & Cable Yearbook 2006

Wisconsin

WJMC-FM— 1947: 96.1 mhz; 50 kw. Ant 482 ft. TL: N45 37 14 W91 44 44. Stereo. Web Site: www.wjmcradio.com. Format: Hot country. Target aud: 25-54. ♦Dane Jensen, stn mgr.

Richland Center

WRCO(AM)— Oct 18, 1949: 1450 khz; 1 kw-U. TL: N43 18 58 W90 22 31. Box 529, 2111 Bohmann Dr. 53581-0529. Phone: (608) 647-2111. Fax: (608) 647-8025. E-mail: wrco@wrco.net. Web Site: www.wrco.net. Licensee: Fruit Broadcasting LLC. (acq 1994). Network: CBS. Format: Adult Standards. News staff: one; News: 20 hrs wkly. Target aud: 25-54; general. Spec prog: Farm 2.hrs wkly. ♦Ron Fruit, pres, gen mgr & opns mgr; Alice Schulte, gen sls mgr; Phil Nee, progmg dir; Aaron Joyce, news dir; Dennis Baldridge, chief of engrg.

WRCO-FM— August 1965: 100.9 mhz; 6 kw. 240 ft. TL: N43 20 14 W90 22 44. Stereo. Web Site: www.wrco.com. Network: CBS Radio. Format: Country, news. News staff: one; News: 45 hrs wkly. Target aud: General; adult. Spec prog: Farm 18 hrs, Gospel 6 hrs wkly. ♦Alice Schulte, sls dir; Phil Nee, progmg dir; Ron Fruit, pub affrs dir; Dennis Baldridge, chief of engrg.

Ripon

WRPN(AM)—Licensed to Ripon. See Fond du Lac

*WRPN-FM— Sept 15, 1957: 90.1 mhz; 231 w. 110 ft. TL: N43 50 37 W88 50 31. Stereo. Box 248, Harwood Memorial Union, 300 Seward St. 54971-0248. Phone: (920) 748-8147. Phone: (920) 748-8115 (college). Fax: (920) 748-7243. E-mail: wrpnfm@yahoo.com. Web Site: www.homestead.com. Licensee: Board of Trustees of Ripon College. Network: CBS, ABC. Rep: Farmakis. Haley, Bader & Potts. Format: Classic rock, div, progsv. News staff: 4; News: 25 hrs wkly. Spec prog: Pol 2 hrs, sports 15 hrs wkly. ♦Guy McHendry, gen mgr; Joe Laedtke, opns dir; Stephanie Hasz, progmg mgr; Brandon Mumm, mus dir.

WTCX(FM)—Licensed to Ripon. See Fond du Lac

River Falls

WEVR(AM)— Sept 14, 1969: 1550 khz; 1 kw-D. TL: N44 53 19 W92 39 04. 178 Radio Rd. 54022. Phone: (715) 425-1111. Phone: (612) 381-1111. Licensee: Hanten Broadcasting Co. Inc. (acq 6-1-74). Network: USA. Format: Lite adult contemp, sports. News: 18 hrs wkly. Target aud: General. Spec prog: Farm 18 hrs wkly. ♦Carol Hanten, pres & gen mgr.

WEVR-FM— Sept 30, 1970: 106.3 mhz; 6 kw. 300 ft. TL: N44 53 19 W92 39 04. Stereo. Phone: (715) 381-1111. Format: News. News: 18 hrs wkly.

*WRFW(FM)— Nov 2, 1968: 88.7 mhz; 3 kw. 82 ft. TL: N44 53 08 W92 39 20. Stereo. Univ. of Wisconsin River Falls, 306 North Hall, 410 S. 3rd St., MN 54022. Phone: (715) 425-3886/3887. Fax: (715) 425-3532. E-mail: urfw@uwrf.edu. Web Site: www.uwrf.edu/wrfw. Licensee: University of Wisconsin System. Format: Div, AOR, news/talk. Spec prog: CHR, educ, jazz, new age, oldies, AOR, talk, country, farm 10 hrs wkly. ♦Rick Burgsteiner, gen mgr; Andy Kagol, stn mgr.

Rudolph

WIZD(FM)— Sept 30, 1990: 99.9 mhz; 13 kw. Ant 453 ft. TL: N44 20 19 W89 38 55. Stereo. Box 850, 2460 Plover Rd., Plover 54467. Phone: (715) 344-6050. Phone: (715) 421-4040. Fax: (715) 341-8070. Web Site: www.wizd.com. Licensee: WRIG Inc. Group owner: Midwest Communications Inc. (acq 1999; $1.4 million). Network: ABC. Format: Oldies. News staff: 3; News: 3 hrs wkly. Target aud: 35 plus; upper income. Spec prog: Polka 3 hrs wkly. ♦Duke Wright, pres; Brett Luechit, gen mgr; Jeff McCarthy, progmg VP; Don Clark, progmg dir.

Sauk City

WMAD(FM)—Licensed to Sauk City. See Madison

Schofield

WRIG(AM)— Aug 1, 1958: 1390 khz; 5 kw-U, DA-2. TL: N44 52 42 W89 38 29. Stereo. Box 2048, Wausau 54402-2048. Secondary address: 920 Grand Ave. 54476. Phone: (715) 842-1672. Fax: (715) 848-3158. E-mail: ken@bigwrig.com. Web Site: www.bigwrig.com.

Licensee: WRIG Inc. Group owner: Midwest Communications Inc. Network: Westwood One. Format: MOR. News staff: one; News: 4 hrs wkly. Target aud: 50 plus. ♦D.E. Wright, pres; Gary Tesch, exec VP; Brett Lucht, gen mgr; Samantha Milanowski, gen sls mgr; Ken Clark, progmg dir; Frank Zastrow, chief of engrg.

Seymour

WECB(FM)— May 1998: 104.3 mhz; 5.6 kw. Ant 341 ft. TL: N44 31 26 W88 19 56. Box 1519, Appleton 54912. Phone: (920) 734-9226. Fax: (920) 739-0494. Web Site: www.1043thebreeze.com. Licensee: Woodward Communications Inc. (group owner; acq 6-23-2003; $1.75 million). Hogan & Hartson. Format: Soft adult contemp 70s & 80s. ♦Greg Bell, gen mgr; Nicole Ehlers, gen sls mgr.

Shawano

WOWN(FM)—Listing follows WTCH(AM).

WTCH(AM)— Sept 3, 1948: 960 khz; 1 kw-U, DA-N. TL: N49 46 47 W88 37 53. 1456 E. Green Bay St. 54166. Phone: (715) 524-2194. Fax: (715) 524-9980. Web Site: www.wtcham960.com. Licensee: Results Broadcasting Inc. Group owner: Results Broadcasting (acq 12-23-96; $2,704,670. for 50% of stock with co-located FM). Network: CBS. Format: Classic country. News staff: one; News: 25 hrs wkly. Target aud: 25-54; northeast Wisconsin adults. Spec prog: Farm 21 hrs wkly. ♦Bruce Grassman, chmn, pres & gen mgr; Trisha Peterson, VP.

WOWN(FM)— Co-owned with WTCH(AM). December 1966: 99.3 mhz; 14 kw. 440 ft. TL: N44 45 14 W88 20 01. Stereo. Network: ABC. Format: Oldies. News staff: one; News: 13 hrs wkly. Target aud: 20-45. ♦Bruce Grassman, CEO.

Sheboygan

WBFM(FM)—Listing follows WHBL(AM).

WCLB(AM)— January 1956: 950 khz; 500 w-D, DA. TL: N43 44 33 W87 49 00. 1102 Fond Du Lac Ave., Sheboygan Falls 53085. Phone: (920) 467-0200. Fax: (920) 467-4300. E-mail: wbates@mdogmedia.com. Web Site: www.sheboygansespn950.com. Licensee: RBH Enterprises Inc. dba Yellow Dog Broadcasting. Group owner: Mountain Dog Media (acq 6-23-00; $700,000. with WXER(FM) Plymouth). Network: Westwood One. Holland & Knight. Format: Sports. News staff: 2; News: 8 hrs wkly. Target aud: 35-64. ♦Randal B. Mupper, pres; Wade Bates, progmg dir; Stu Muck, chief of engrg.

WHBL(AM)— Jan 1, 1926: 1330 khz; 5 kw-D, 1 kw-N, DA-2. TL: N43 43 14 W87 44 04. Box 27 53082. Secondary address: 2100 Washington Ave. 53081. Phone: (920) 458-2107. Fax: (920) 458-9775. E-mail: studio@whbl.com. Licensee: Midwest Communications Inc. (group owner; acq 8-8-00; grpsl). Network: ABC Information & Entertainment. Format: News/talk. News staff: 2; News: 24 hrs wkly. Target aud: 25-55. Spec prog: Farm 10 hrs wkly. ♦Roxanne Charles, gen mgr & gen sls mgr; Nick Reed, progmg dir; Mike Kinzel, news dir; Bob Gorjance, chief of engrg.

WBFM(FM)— Co-owned with WHBL(AM). Mar 1, 1977: 93.7 mhz; 6 kw. 253 ft. TL: N43 43 12 W87 44 04. Stereo. 920 Washinton Ave. 53081. Web Site: wbfm93radio.com. Format: Country. News staff: news progmg 24 hrs wkly News: 2; . Target aud: 25-54; adults in Sheboygan county/Northern Milwaukee metro area. ♦Ron Simonet, progmg dir.

*WSHS(FM)— Nov 19, 1971: 91.7 mhz; 180 w. 82 ft. TL: N43 46 37 W87 43 08. Stereo. 1042 School Ave. 53083. Phone: (920) 459-3610. Fax: (920) 803-7612. E-mail: wshs@sheboygan.kiz.wi.us. Licensee: Sheboygan Area School District. Network: NPR. Glenn Slatts Format: Adult contemp, AOR. Target aud: 18-45; young adults & teens. Spec prog: Hmong 3 hrs, Sp 3 hrs wkly. ♦Ron Rindfleish, pres; Jon Etter, gen mgr; Jackson Sohn, prom mgr; Erik Shircel, news dir; Tom Lang, chief of engrg.

Sheboygan Falls

WHBZ(FM)— April 1997: 106.5 mhz; 6 kw. 239 ft. TL: N43 43 16 W87 44 03. 2100 Washington Ave., Sheboygan 53081. Phone: (920) 458-2107. Fax: (920) 458-9775. E-mail: thebuzz@whbzfm.com. Web Site: www.WHBZ.fm. Licensee: Midwest Communications Inc. (group owner; acq 8-8-00; grpsl). Format: Rock. ♦Roxanne Charles, gen mgr; Jay Morris, progmg dir; Ron Simonet, mus dir.

Directory of Radio

Shell Lake

WCSW(AM)— Dec 30, 1967: 940 khz; 1 kw-D. TL: N45 41 36 W91 57 57. Box 190 54871. Secondary address: 345 Hwy. 63 S. 54871. Phone: (715) 468-9500. Fax: (715) 468-9505. Licensee: Zoe Communications Inc. (group owner; acq 1-1-00; with co-located FM). Network: Network: ABC, ABC Information & Entertainment. Format: Talk. Target aud: General. Spec prog: Farm 3 hrs wkly. ♦Wendy Oberg, gen mgr; Loren Miller, gen sls mgr; Mike Oberg, progmg dir, news dir & chief of engrg.

WGMO(FM)— Co-owned with WCSW(AM). December 1974: 95.3 mhz; 7.1 kw. 512 ft. TL: N45 40 28 W91 58 52. Stereo. Web Site: www.95wgmo.com. Network: Westwood One. Format: Classic rock. News staff: one.

Siren

WXCX(FM)— 2000: 105.7 mhz; 6 kw. Ant 328 ft. TL: N45 52 21 W92 27 39. Stereo. 97 W. Main St., Suite C, Milltown 54858. Phone: (715) 825-4240. Fax: (715) 825-4244. E-mail: millpine@lakeland.wsx. Web Site: oldies1057.ws. Licensee: Quarnstrom Media Group LLC (group owner; acq 3-15-2003; $1.2 million. with WLMX-FM Balsam Lake). Network: Jones Radio Networks. Rep: Midwest Radio. MidwestRadio Format: Classic hits. News staff: one. Target aud: 35-64. ♦Alan Quarnstrom, pres; Don Welch, VP; Dale Brooks, gen mgr; Neil Novotny, progmg dir.

Sister Bay

*WHDI(FM)— 2000: 91.9 mhz; 3.4 kw. Ant 476 ft. TL: N45 14 19 W87 05 27. 3319 W. Beltline Hwy., Network HQ, Madison 53713. Phone: (608) 264-9600. Fax: (608) 264-9664. Web Site: www.ecb.org. Licensee: State of Wisconsin-Educational Communications Board. Dow, Lohnes & Albertson. Format: Talk. ♦Wendy Wink, gen mgr; Phil Corrivean, stn mgr.

*WHND(FM)— Sept. 16, 1999: 89.7 mhz; 3.4 kw. 538 ft. TL: N45 14 19 W87 05 27. 2420 Nicolet Dr., Green Bay 54311. Secondary address: 821 University Ave., Madison 53706. Phone: (920) 465-2444. Fax: (920) 465-2576. E-mail: slaats@wpr.org. Web Site: www.wpr.org. Licensee: State of Wisconsin Educational Communications Board. Network: Network: NPR, PRI. Dow, Lohnes & Albertson. Format: News, class music. News staff: one; News: 29 hrs wkly. Target aud: 35 plus; socially aware, educated & financially secure. Spec prog: American Indian 2 hrs, blues 2 hrs, folk 2 hrs, jazz 10 hrs wkly. ♦Glen Slaats, gen mgr & adv mgr; Ellen Clark, adv mgr; Patty Murray, news dir; Steve Konopka, chief of engrg.

Sparta

WCOW-FM— Mar 1, 1960: 97.1 mhz; 100 kw. 587 ft. TL: N43 58 06 W90 51 35. Stereo. 113W. Oak St. 54656-1712. Phone: (608) 269-3307. Phone: (608) 269-3100. Fax: (608) 269-5170. Web Site: www.cow97.com. Licensee: Sparta-Tomah Broadcasting Co. Inc. Network: ABC Information & Entertainment. Miller & Miller. Format: Contemp country. News staff: 3; News: 15 hrs wkly. Target aud: 25 plus; rural & city residents. Spec prog: Green Bay Packers. ♦Gary Michaelson, gen sls mgr; Jeff Harvey, gen mgr, gen sls mgr, prom dir & progmg dir; Jason Jennings, news dir.

WKLJ(AM)— Co-owned with WCOW-FM. June 1951: 1290 khz; 5 kw-D, 59 w-N. TL: N43 58 06 W90 51 35. (Acq 1-19-89). Format: News/talk, relg. News staff: 3. Target aud: 35 plus; rural & city residents.

Spencer

WOSQ(FM)— Sept 20, 1984: 92.3 mhz; 6 kw. 300 ft. TL: N44 48 35 W90 21 51. Stereo. Box 630, Marshfield 54449. Secondary address: 1710 N. Central Ave. 54449. Phone: (715) 384-3921. Fax: (715) 387-3588. E-mail: wosq@mmwi.net. Licensee: NewRadio Group LLC (group owner; acq 12-20-2002; grpsl). Miller & Miller. Format: Country. News staff: one; News: 7 hrs wkly. Target aud: 25-54. Spec prog: Loc sports play-by-play, farm. ♦Wayne Ripp, gen mgr; Jay Latsch, opns mgr; Arnie Peck, gen sls mgr; George Nicholas, engrg dir.

Spooner

WPLT(FM)—Not on air, target date: unknown: 106.3 mhz; 6 kw. Ant 279 ft. TL: N45 47 40 W91 55 03. Box 190, Shell Lake 54871. Phone: (715) 468-9500. Fax: (715) 468-9505. Web Site: www.zoestations.com.

Stations in the U.S. — Wisconsin

Licensee: Zoe Communications Inc. (group owner; acq 12-6-00; $439,000. for CP). Format: Country. ◆Wendy Oberg, gen mgr; Tasha Hagberg, gen sls mgr; Mike Oberg, progmg dir & chief of engrg.

Stevens Point

WSPT(AM)— 1949: 1010 khz; 1 kw-D. TL: N44 32 17 W89 35 43. 500 Division St. 54481. Phone: (715) 341-9800. Fax: (715) 341-0000. E-mail: rmuzzy@1010wspt.com. Web Site: 1010wspt.com. Licensee: Americus Communications L.L.C. Group owner: Muzzy Broadcasting L.L.C. (acq 1996; $1.2 million with co-located FM). Format: News/talk. Target aud: 25-54; upscale, male-orientated. Spec prog: Pol one hr wkly. ◆Richard L. Muzzy, pres & gen mgr.

WSPT-FM— May 1, 1961: 97.9 mhz; 100 kw. Ant 338 ft. TL: N44 32 17 W89 35 43. Stereo. Web Site: 979wspt.com. Format: Adult contemp.

***WWSP(FM)**— Sept 28, 1968: 89.9 mhz; 11.5 kw. 325 ft. TL: N44 28 55 W89 40 34. Stereo. 105 CAL, UWSP, Reserve St. 54481. Phone: (715) 346-3755. Fax: (715) 346-4012. E-mail: wwsp@uwsp.edu. Web Site: www.uwsp.edu/stuorg/wwsp. Licensee: Board of Regents, University of Wisconsin System. Dow, Lohnes & Albertson. Format: Jazz, progsv. Target aud: College students. Spec prog: Hmong one hr, pub affrs 5 hrs, sports 3 hrs, blues 4 hrs wkly. ◆Mark Tolstedt, gen mgr; Courtney Sikorski, stn mgr; Cynthia Atchison, dev dir; Jackie Klish, sls dir; Melissa Basler, prom dir; Rebecca Pollesch, prom dir; Jon Henseler, progmg dir; Tom Behake, mus dir; Stephen Raschke, news dir; Rick Westenberger, chief of engrg.

Sturgeon Bay

WDOR(AM)— Sept 8, 1951: 910 khz; 1 kw-D. TL: N44 49 38 W87 21 27. Box 549, 800 S. 15th Ave. 54235. Phone: (920) 487-2822. Fax: (920) 743-2334. E-mail: email@wdor.com. Licensee: Door County Broadcasting Inc. Network: ABC Information & Entertainment. Shaw Pittman. Format: Adult contemp. News staff: one; News: 23 hrs wkly. Target aud: 21-50; general. ◆Edward Allen III, sls dir, pres, gen mgr, gen sls mgr & progmg dir; Dan Allen, mus dir; Roger Levendusky, news dir; Steve Konopka, engrg dir.

WDOR-FM— Dec 12, 1966: 93.9 mhz; 77 kw. 640 ft. TL: N44 54 23 W87 22 15. Stereo. Phone: (920) 743-4411. Format: Sports. News: 25 hrs wkly. Target aud: 20-40; general. Spec prog: Sports, farm 5 hrs wkly.

WLYD(FM)— Mar 4, 1982: 99.7 mhz; 46 kw. 512 ft. TL: N44 38 08 W87 37 37. Stereo. Box 23333, 115 S. Jefferson St., Green Bay 54305. Secondary address: 115 S. Jefferson St., Green Bay 54301. Phone: (920) 435-3771. Fax: (920) 444-1155. E-mail: studio@wlyd997.com. Web Site: www.wild997.com. Licensee: Midwest Communications Inc. (group owner; acq 6-18-93; $3.5 million. with WOZZ(FM) New London; FTR: 7-5-93). Rep: Christal. Miller & Miller. Format: Hip Hop, Rhythmic CHR. News staff: one; News: 3 hrs wkly. Target aud: 13-34; young, active, hip. ◆Duke Wright, pres & gen mgr; Jeff Wright, gen sls mgr; Jason Hillary, progmg dir; Jerry Bader, news dir; Tim Laes, chief of engrg.

*WPFF(FM)— August 1991: 90.5 mhz; 100 kw. 653 ft. TL: N44 54 23 W87 22 15. Stereo. Box 28, 1715 Michigan St. 54235. Phone: (920) 743-7443. E-mail: wpff@wpff.com. Web Site: www.wpff.com. Licensee: Family Educational Broadcasting Corp. Network: USA. Shaw Pittman. Format: Christian, CHR. News: 12 hrs wkly. Target aud: 25-49; baby boomers. ◆Mark Schwarzbauer, gen mgr; Andy King, stn mgr.

*WRGX(FM)— July 1998: 88.5 mhz; 50 kw. 518 ft. TL: N44 54 14 W87 22 13. Box 28 54235. Secondary address: 1723 Michigan St. 54235. Phone: (920) 743-7443. Fax: (920) 743-7543. E-mail: wrgx@wrgx.com. Web Site: www.wrgx.com. Licensee: Family Educational Broadcasting Corp. of Door County Wisconsin. Format: Christian; Rock/AOR. Target aud: 13-35; teens & generation x listeners. ◆Dr. Mark Schwarzbaur, CEO & gen mgr.

WSRG(FM)— Apr 18, 1988: 97.7 mhz; 6 kw. 400 ft. TL: N44 54 21 W87 22 15. (CP: Ant 554 ft.). Stereo. 1009 Egg Harbor Rd., Suite 113 54235. Phone: (920) 743-6677. Fax: (920) 743-9183. Web Site: www.wsrgstar97.com. Licensee: Magnum Broadcasting Inc. (acq 11-30-98; $200,000). Network: Jones Radio Networks. Leventhal, Senter & Lerman. Format: Adult contemp. News staff: 2. Target aud: 25-54. ◆Rick Jensen, opns mgr; Frank DeVillers, adv mgr; Steve Peterson, progmg mgr; Pete Holiday, news dir.

Sturtevant

WEXT(FM)— June 18, 1993: 104.7 mhz; 4.2 kw. Ant 338 ft. TL: N42 51 20 W87 50 41. 8500 Green Bay Rd., Pleasant Prairie 53158. Phone: (262) 694-7800. Fax: (262) 694-7767. Web Site: www.extremecountry.com. Licensee: NM Licensing LLC. Group owner: NextMedia Group L.L.C. acq 11-26-01; grpsl). Network: Westwood One. Reddy, Begley & McCormick. Format: Country. News staff: 2. Target aud: 25-54; adult families with school-age children. ◆Jim Hooker, pres; Kira LaFond, gen mgr; Roy Fraley, gen sls mgr; Tammy Myers, prom dir; Tim Allen, opns mgr & progmg dir; Stuart James, news dir; Eugene McEffe, pub affrs dir & chief of engrg.

Sun Prairie

*WNWC(AM)— Jan 12, 1982: 1190 khz; 1 kw-D, DA. TL: N43 09 36 W89 12 41. 5606 Medical Cir., Madison 53719. Phone: (608) 271-1025. Fax: (608) 271-1150. E-mail: wnwc@nwc.edu. Web Site: www.wnwc.org. Licensee: Northwestern College. Group owner: Northwestern College & Radio (acq 12-19-96; $250,000). Format: Relg, talk. ◆Greg Walters, gen mgr.

WXXM(FM)— Apr 12, 1972: 92.1 mhz; 3.7 kw. Ant 410 ft. TL: N43 10 10 W89 15 38. Stereo. 2651 S. Fish Hatchery Rd., Madison 53711. Phone: (608) 274-5450. Fax: (608) 274-5521. Web Site: www.wmad.com. Licensee: Capstar TX L.P. Group owner: Clear Channel Communications Inc. (acq 8-30-00; grpsl). Format: Adult contemp. ◆Jeff Tyler, gen mgr; Brian Sines, gen sls mgr; Tim Scott, opns mgr & gen sls mgr; Jon Reilly, progmg dir; Josh Westscott, news dir; Joe McCall, chief of engrg.

Superior

KKCB(FM)—See Duluth, MN

KRBR(FM)—Listing follows WDSM(AM).

KTCO(FM)—See Duluth, MN

*KUWS(FM)— Jan 31, 1966: 91.3 mhz; 83 kw. 646 ft. TL: N46 47 21 W92 06 51. Stereo. Box 2000 54880. Phone: (715) 394-8530. Fax: (715) 394-8404. E-mail: jmunson@facstaffuwsuper.edu. Web Site: www.kuws.fm. Licensee: Board of Regents, University of Wisconsin System. Network: NPR. Format: Div, news/talk, educ. News staff: one; News: 20 hrs wkly. Target aud: 12 plus; above average income & education. Spec prog: Alternative 16 hrs, Black 4 hrs, jazz 15 hrs, sports 6 hrs wkly. ◆John Munson, stn mgr; Patrick Olsen, opns mgr.

WDSM(AM)— October 1939: 710 khz; 10 kw-D, 5 kw-N, DA-N. TL: N46 39 14 W92 08 51. 715 E. Central Entrance, Duluth, MN 55811. Phone: (218) 722-4321. Fax: (218) 722-5423. Web Site: www.allsports710.com. Licensee: Midwest Communications Inc. (group owner; acq 8-1-01; grpsl). Network: Westwood One, CBS. Rosenman & Colin. Format: Talk. Target aud: 25-54. ◆Alicia Ridley, gen mgr & opns mgr; Dale Johnson, gen sls mgr & mktg mgr; Mark Fleischer, progmg dir; John Talcott, chief of engrg.

KRBR(FM)—Co-owned with WDSM(AM). Sept 9, 1979: 102.5 mhz; 100 kw. 600 ft. TL: N46 47 21 W92 07 09. Stereo. Web Site: www.krbr.com. Format: Modern rock. News: 3 hrs wkly. Target aud: 18-49. ◆Susan Smith, gen sls mgr & mktg mgr; Ray Styles, prom mgr & progmg dir; Dave Strandberg, news dir.

WGEE(AM)— June 18, 1959: 970 khz; 1 kw-D, 27 w-N. TL: N46 43 28 W92 07 11. Midwest Communications, 715 E. Central Entrance, Duluth, MN 55811. Phone: (218) 722-4321. Fax: (218) 722-5423. Licensee: Midwest Communications Inc. (group owner; acq 8-1-01; grpsl). Network: ABC Daytime Direction. Hyett/Ramsland. Rosenman & Colin. Format: Radio Disney. News staff: 6. Target aud: 2-12. ◆Duke Wright, CEO & pres; Gay Tesch, exec VP; David Drew, opns dir; Don Snyder, sls VP; Dale Johnson, mktg dir & mktg mgr; David Kuharski, prom dir & prom mgr; Jeff McCarthy, progmg VP; Mark Fleischer, progmg dir & progmg mgr; Dave Strandberg, news dir; John Talcott, chief of engrg.

Suring

*WRVM(FM)— Sept 17, 1967: 102.7 mhz; 100 kw. 980 ft. TL: N44 59 50 W88 23 49. Stereo. Box 212, Hwy. 32 N. 54174. Phone: (920) 842-2839. Fax: (920) 842-2704. E-mail: wrvmfm@wrvm.org. Web Site: www.wrvm.org. Licensee: WRVM Inc. (acq 5-15-68). Network: Moody. Kenkel & Associates. Format: Relg. Target aud: General; family stn with children's programs. ◆Michael A. Cornell, gen mgr; Dennis Jones, progmg dir; Alan Kilgore, chief of engrg.

Sussex

WKSH(AM)— July 1998: 1640 khz; 10 kw-D, 1 kw-N. TL: N43 04 38 W88 11 32. W.223 N.3251 Shady Ln., Pewaukee 53072. Phone: (262) 695-9500. Fax: (262) 691-2378. E-mail: debra.1bratel@abc.com. Web Site: www.radiodisney.com. Licensee: Radio Disney Group LLC. Group owner: ABC Inc. (acq 9-26—02; $2.6 million). Network: Network: ABC, Radio Disney. Rep: Interep. Format: Top 40. Target aud: Under 14; children & the grown ups that love them. ◆Debra Bratel, gen mgr & stn mgr; Melissa Macco, gen sls mgr; Rich Padgen, prom dir.

Three Lakes

WLSL(FM)— August 1994: 93.7 mhz; 100 kw. Ant 407 ft. TL: N45 46 30 W89 14 55. 38 W. Davenport St., Rhinelander 54501. Phone: (715) 369-9575. Fax: (715) 369-9475. E-mail: b93perry@newnorth.net. Licensee: Results Broadcasting of Rhinelander Inc. Group owner: Results Broadcasting (acq 3-10-2000; $500,000). Format: Classic hits. ◆Bruce Grassman, CEO; Perry Pokrandt, gen mgr & gen sls mgr; Brian Roberts, progmg dir.

Tomah

WBOG(AM)— Apr 19, 1959: 1460 khz; 1 kw-D, 42 w-N. TL: N43 58 07 W90 30 50. 1021 N. Superior Ave., Suite 5 54660. Phone: (608) 372-9600. Fax: (608) 372-7566. E-mail: magnumradio@charter.net. Web Site: www.magnumradiogroup.com. Licensee: Magnum Radio Inc. (group owner; acq 1994; $275,000. with co-located FM). Network: Network: ABC Information & Entertainment, Jones Radio Networks. Format: Oldies. News staff: one; News: 10 hrs wkly. Target aud: 35 plus. Spec prog: Big band 3 hrs, polka 2 hrs wkly. ◆Dave Magnum, pres; Brian Winnekins, opns dir; Diane Pergande, sls dir; Steve Peterson, gen mgr, prom dir & progmg mgr; Clary Harris, news dir; Darrell Sanders, chief of engrg.

WTMB(FM)—Co-owned with WBOG(AM). July 11, 1990: 94.5 mhz; 8.3 kw. 564 ft. TL: N43 53 56 W90 29 23. Stereo. 1021 N. Superior Ave., Suite 5 Web Site: www.magnumradiogroup.com. Network: ABC Information & Entertainment. News staff: one; News: 6 hrs wkly. Target aud: 25-54.

*WVCX(FM)— Jan 29, 1965: 98.9 mhz; 100 kw. 991 ft. TL: N43 51 13 W90 27 28. Stereo. 3434 W. Kilbourn Ave., Milwaukee 53208. Phone: (414) 935-3000. Fax: (414) 935-3015. E-mail: wvcx@vcyamerica.org. Web Site: www.vcyamerica.org. Licensee: VCY/America Inc. (group owner; acq 1984). Network: Network: USA, Moody. Format: Relg, talk, Christian. ◆Dr. Randall Melchert, pres; Vic Eliason, VP & gen mgr; Jim Schneider, progmg dir; Tom Schlueter, mus dir; Gordon Morris, news dir; Andy Eliason, chief of engrg.

WXYM(FM)— Mar 11, 1992: 96.1 mhz; 44 kw. 525 ft. TL: N44 01 32 W90 48 58. Stereo. 1021 N. Superior Ave., Suite 5 54660. Phone: (608) 372-9600. Fax: (608) 372-7566. E-mail: magnumradio@charter.net. Web Site: www.magnumradiogroup.net. Licensee: Magnum Radio Inc.

(acq 9-27-91; 10-14-91). Format: Hot AC. News staff: 2; News: 6 hrs wkly. Target aud: 25-54. ♦Dave Magnum, pres; Steve Peterson, gen mgr; Debbie Doyle, opns mgr.

Tomahawk

WJJQ(AM)— August 1968: 810 khz; 980 w-D. TL: N45 29 27 W89 43 36. Box 10, 81 E. Mohawk Dr. 54487. Phone: (715) 453-4482. Phone: (715) 457-4481. Fax: (715) 453-7169. E-mail: wjjq@wjjq.com. Web Site: www.wjjq.com. Licensee: Albert Broadcasting II LLC (acq 6-11-84). Network: Network: Network: CBS, ESPN Radio, Westwood One. Shaw Pittman. Format: Sports, talk. News staff: one; News: 15 hrs wkly. Target aud: 25 plus. ♦Gregg Albert, pres & gen mgr; Margaruite Albert, VP; Tim Albert, prom mgr & progmg dir.

WJJQ-FM— Oct 15, 1984: 92.5 mhz; 25 kw. 259 ft. TL: N45 29 27 W89 43 36. Stereo. Secondary address: 81 E. Mohawk Drive 54487. Phone: (715) 453-4482. Fax: (715) 453-7169. E-mail: galbert@wjjq.com. Web Site: www.wjjq.com. Network: CBS Radio. Regional Reps Shaw Pittman. Format: Lite hits, news, sports,oldies. News staff: one; News: 25 hrs wkly. Target aud: 25 plus. ♦Mary Lu Voermans, adv mgr; Tim Albert, mus dir.

Trempealeau

WFBZ(FM)— Nov 24, 1984: 105.5 mhz; 3 kw. 531 ft. TL: N43 56 33 W91 26 03. Stereo. 1407 2nd Ave. N., Onalaska 54650. Phone: (608) 782-8335. Fax: (608) 782-8340. Web Site: www.espnradio.105.com. Licensee: S & S Broadcasting. Group owner: La Crosse Radio Group (acq 3-28-2003; $520,000). Format: Sports. News staff: one; News: 24 hrs wkly. Target aud: 25-54. ♦Joe Roskos, pres; Pat Smith, gen mgr; Chuck Wolfe, stn mgr; Mike Schmitz, gen sls mgr; Audrey Philips, prom dir; Jon Resaris, progmg dir; Patrick Delaney, chief of engrg.

Two Rivers

WCUB(AM)—Licensed to Two Rivers. See Manitowoc

WLTU(FM)—See Manitowoc

WTRW(AM)— Oct 29, 1951: 1590 khz; 1 kw-D, 33 w-N. TL: N44 10 23 W87 35 37. 1414 16th St. 54241-3031. Phone: (920) 794-1800. Fax: (920) 794-8791. E-mail: wtrw@hotmail.net. Web Site: www.wtrw.net. Licensee: WTRW Inc. Network: Network: Network: CNN Radio, NBC, Westwood One. Format: Oldies. News staff: one; News: 10 hrs wkly. Target aud: 25-54; baby boomers & professionals. ♦Mark Heller, pres.

Verona

WMMM-FM— July 4, 1991: 105.5 mhz; 4.4 kw. 384 ft. TL: N42 57 42 W89 29 32. 7601 Ganser Way, Madison 53719. Phone: (608) 826-0077. Fax: (608) 826-1244. Web Site: www.1055triplem.com. Licensee: Entercom Madison Licensee LLP. Group owner: Entercom Communications Corp. (acq 7-10-00; grpsl). Format: AAA. Target aud: 25-44; upscale, college educated adults. ♦David Field, pres; Steve Fisher, CFO; Lindsay Wood Davis, mktg mgr.

Viroqua

WVRQ(AM)— Feb 25, 1958: 1360 khz; 1 kw-D, 23 w-N. TL: N43 32 04 W90 52 23. E7601A County Rd. SS 54665. Phone: (608) 637-7200. Fax: (608) 637-7299. E-mail: wvrq@mwt.net. Web Site: www.wvrq.com. Licensee: Robinson Corp. Group owner: Robinson Corporation. Network: Network: CBS, ABC. Format: Oldies. News staff: one; News: 14 hrs wkly. Target aud: 25 plus. Spec prog: Farm 2 hrs, relg 6 hrs, polka 6 hrs wkly. ♦David Robinson, pres & gen mgr.

WVRQ-FM— Oct 6, 1967: 102.3 mhz; 3.3 kw. 298 ft. TL: N43 31 27 W90 51 51. Stereo. Web Site: www.wvrq.com. Network: ABC Daytime Direction. Format: Country. News: 20 hrs wkly. Target aud: 25-54. Spec prog: Bluegrass 2 hrs, farm 5 hrs wkly. ♦Jeff Robinson, opns mgr & progmg dir.

Washburn

***WEGZ(FM)**— Oct 5, 1981: 105.9 mhz; 98 kw. Ant 741 ft. TL: N46 41 31 W90 59 27. Stereo. 3434 W. Kilbourn Ave., Milwaukee 53208. Phone: (414) 935-3000. Fax: (414) 935-3015. E-mail: wegz@vcyamerica.org. Web Site: www.vcyamerica.org. Licensee: Keweenaw Bay Broadcasting Inc. Group owner: VCY/America Inc. (acq 4-19-02; $465,000). Format: Religious, Christian music, talk. ♦Dr. Randall Melchert, pres; Vic Eliason, VP & gen mgr; Gordon Morris, opns dir & news dir; Jim Schneider, progmg dir & pub affrs dir; Andy Eliason, chief of engrg.

Watertown

WJJO(FM)— Aug 1, 1961: 94.1 mhz; 50 kw. 492 ft. TL: N43 11 43 W88 45 17. Stereo. Box 2058, Madison 53701. Secondary address: 2740 Ski Ln., Madison 53713. Phone: (608) 273-1000. Fax: (608) 271-8182. Web Site: www.wjjo.com. Licensee: Mid-West Management Inc. Group owner: Mid-West Family Stations (acq 6-18-93; $1.6 million; 7-5-93). Rep: McGavren Guild. Shaw Pittman. Format: Rock. Target aud: 21-49; male. ♦Ted Waldbillig, sls dir & prom mgr; Tom Walker, pres, gen mgr & gen sls mgr; Randy Hawke, progmg dir; Blake Patton, mus dir & pub affrs dir; John Bauer, chief of engrg.

WTTN(AM)— Apr 2, 1950: 1580 khz; 1 kw-D, 7.8 w-N. TL: N43 11 43 W88 45 17. Box 509, 615 E. Main St. 53094. Phone: (920) 261-1580. Fax: (920) 261-0624. Licensee: Good Karma Broadcasting L.L.C. (group owner; acq 8-26-99; $525,000). Network: CNN Radio. Format: Country legends, local news/talk, oldies, farm. News staff: 3; News: 15 hrs wkly. Target aud: 25-64. Spec prog: Relg 4 hrs wkly. ♦Craig . Karmazin, CEO & pres; Scott M. Trentadue, gen mgr & prom VP; Rick Armon, opns mgr; John Moser, sls VP, gen sls mgr, adv VP & adv mgr; Jim Stowell, progmg dir & pub affrs dir; Mike Kissling, news dir; Warren Jorgensen, engrg dir & chief of engrg.

Waukesha

WAUK(AM)— Mar 27, 1947: 1510 khz; 10 kw-D, DA. TL: N43 01 00 W88 11 42. Stereo. 1801 Coral Dr. 53186. Phone: (262) 544-6800. Fax: (262) 544-1705. E-mail: www.wauksportsradio@msn.com. Web Site: www.espn1510.com. Licensee: Good Karma Broadcasting L.L.C. (group owner; acq 4-9-2004; $2 million). Network: ABC. Hough & Cook. Format: Sports/Talk. News staff: 2; News: 6 hrs wkly. Target aud: 25 plus; male. Spec prog: NASCAR racing. ♦Craig Karmazin, pres; Craig Karmazn, stn mgr; C. J. Knee, opns dir; Bill Johnson, progmg dir; C.J. Knee, news dir; Warren Jorgenson, chief of engrg.

***WCCX(FM)**— Sept 1, 1978: 104.5 mhz; 10 w. 50 ft. TL: N43 00 16 W88 13 39. 100 N. E. Ave. 53186. Phone: (262) 524-7355. Fax: (262) 524-7139. E-mail: wccx_dj@cc.edu. Web Site: wccx.cc.edu. Licensee: Trustees Carroll College. Format: Div. Target aud: General; high school & college students. Spec prog: Sp 8 hrs, metal 3 hrs, rap 3 hrs wkly. ♦Rey Monis, gen mgr & stn mgr; Jennifer Ball-Sharp, prom dir; Phil Mineff, progmg dir; Bill Aper, mus dir; Ray Newpert, news dir; LeRoy Wolinkowski, chief of engrg.

WMIL(FM)— Jan 1, 1982: 106.1 mhz; 50 kw. 976 ft. TL: N43 05 18 W87 54 12. Stereo. 12100 W. Howard Ave., Greenfield 53228. Phone: (414) 545-8900. Phone: (414) 545-5920. Fax: (414) 546-8058. Web Site: www.fm106.com. Licensee: Clear Channel Broadcasting Inc. Group owner: Clear Channel Communications Inc. (acq 3-17-97; $40 million with WOKY(AM) Milwaukee). Rep: Clear Channel. Format: Country. News staff: 4; News: 1.5 hrs wkly. Target aud: 25-54; middle America. ♦L. Lowry Mays, CEO & chmn; Mark Mays, pres; Cindy McDowell, gen mgr; Keith Bratel, sls dir; Colleen Kurth, natl sls mgr & pub affrs dir; Jean Kemp, natl sls mgr & rgnl sls mgr; Enid Parkinson, prom dir; Kerry Wolfe, progmg dir; Mitch Morgan, mus dir.

Waunakee

WCHY(FM)— Apr 20, 1992: 105.1 mhz; 6 kw. 328 ft. TL: N43 13 20 W89 18 01. Stereo. 7601 Ganser Way, Madison 53719. Phone: (608) 826-0077. Fax: (608) 826-1244. Web Site: www.y105.com. Licensee: Entercom Madison Licensee LLP. Group owner: Entercom Communications Corp. (acq 7-10-2000; grpsl). Format: 70's & 80's. Target aud: 18-49. ♦David Field, pres; Steve Fisher, CFO; Ed Schulz, gen mgr.

Waupaca

WDUX(AM)— Apr 29, 1956: 800 khz; 5 kw-D, 500 w-N, DA-1. TL: N44 21 15 W89 03 29. Box 247 54981. Secondary address: 200 Tower Rd. 54981. Phone: (715) 258-5528. Fax: (715) 258-7711. E-mail: wdux@waupacaonline.net. Web Site: www.wdux.net. Licensee: Laird Broadcasting Co. (acq 12-30-99; grpsl). Network: Network: ABC, Jones Radio Networks. Rep: Katz Radio. Format: Classic country. News staff: one; News: 20 hrs wkly. Target aud: 35 plus. Spec prog: Farm 6 hrs wkly. ♦William L. Laird, pres; Tina Grenlie, stn mgr, gen sls mgr & prom mgr; Jack Barry, opns mgr, progmg dir & news dir.

WDUX-FM— Jan 29, 1967: 92.7 mhz; 6 kw. 243 ft. TL: N44 21 14 W89 03 44. Stereo. Web Site: www.wdux.net. Network: Network: Network: ABC, CBS Radio, Westwood One. Format: Adult contemp. Target aud: 25-54. Spec prog: Sports 15 hrs wkly. ♦Rick Winters, progmg mgr.

Waupun

WFDL(AM)— May 26, 1966: 1170 khz; 1 kw-D. TL: N43 38 30 W88 43 22. 609 Home Ave. 53963. Phone: (920) 324-4441. Fax: (920) 324-3139. E-mail: wmrh1170@yahoo.com. Web Site: www.am1170.com. Licensee: Radio Plus Inc. (acq 7-90; $170,000;. FTR: 7-2-90). Network: CBS Radio. Format: News/talk. Target aud: 35 plus; mature adults. Spec prog: Farm 5 hrs wkly. ♦Chris Bernier, pres; Terry Davis, gen mgr; Todd Dehring, progmg dir; Greg Stensland, news dir; Mike Enfelt, news dir & engrg mgr.

Wausau

***WCLQ(FM)**— May 23, 1988: 89.5 mhz; 8.5 kw. 328 ft. TL: N44 58 58 W89 36 06. Stereo. 4111 Schofield Ave., Suite 10, Schofield 54476. Phone: (715) 355-5151. Fax: (715) 359-3128. E-mail: 89q@89q,org. Web Site: www.89q.org. Licensee: Christian Life Communications Inc. Network: USA. Format: Contemp hit/Top-40. News: 9 hrs wkly. Target aud: 18-35; Christian/young family. ♦Coy Sawyer, CFO, gen mgr, chief of opns, dev mgr & sls dir; Scott Michaels, mus dir; Frank Zastrow, chief of engrg.

WDEZ(FM)— Mar 27, 1964: 101.9 mhz; 100 kw. 489 ft. TL: N44 58 58 W89 36 06. (CP: 98 kw, ant 1,076 ft. TL: N44 55 14 W89 41 31). Stereo. Box 2048 54402-2048. Phone: (715) 842-1672. Fax: (715) 848-3158. E-mail: wdez@wdez.com. Web Site: www.wdez.com. Licensee: WRIG Inc. Group owner: Midwest Communications Inc. Rep: Christal. Format: Country. News staff: one; News: 4 hrs wkly. Target aud: 25-54. Spec prog: Farm 4 hrs wkly. ♦D.E. Wright, pres; Gary Tesch, VP; Brett Lucht, gen mgr; Dave Weir, sls dir; Carrie VanDeraa, prom dir; Vanessa Ryan, progmg dir & mus dir; Pat Snyder, news dir; Frank Zastrow, chief of engrg; Eddie Hill, sls.

***WHRM(FM)**— June 10, 1949: 90.9 mhz; 77kw. TL: N44 55 14 W89 41 31. Stereo. 518 S. 7th Ave. 54401. Phone: (715) 848-1978. Fax: (715) 848-2890. E-mail: reyer@wpr.org. Web Site: www.wpr.org. Licensee: State of Wisconsin Educational Communications Board. Network: Network: NPR, PRI. Dow, Lohnes & Albertson. Format: Class, educ. News: 29 hrs wkly. Target aud: 25-64; male/female. ♦Wendy Wink, CEO; Ted Tobie, CFO; Greg Schnirring, gen mgr; Rick Reyer, stn mgr & rgnl sls mgr; Maru Nonn, opns dir; Tom Martin-Erickson, opns dir & chief of opns; Ben Spindler, gen sls mgr; Vivki Noon, mus dir; Connie Walker, news dir; Dennis Behr, engrg VP; Allen Rieland, engrg dir; Pete Kingslien, chief of engrg.

WIFC(FM)—Listing follows WSAU(AM).

***WLBL-FM**— November 1995: 91.9 mhz; 560 w. 823 ft. TL: N44 55 14 W89 41 31. 518 S. 7th Ave. 54401. Phone: (715) 848-1978. Fax: (715) 848-2890. E-mail: reyer@wpr.org. Web Site: www.wpr.org. Licensee: State of Wisconsin-Educational Communications Board. Network: NPR. Format: Call-in talk. Spec prog: Folk 3 hrs wkly. ♦Wendy Wink, CEO; Greg Schnirring, gen mgr; Rick Reyer, gen mgr, stn mgr & dev mgr; Connie Walker, news dir.

WLRK(FM)—Listing follows WXCO(AM).

WRIG(AM)—See Schofield

WSAU(AM)— Jan 30, 1937: 550 khz; 5 kw-U, DA-2. TL: N44 51 26 W89 35 13. Box 2048 54402-2048. Secondary address: 557 Scott St. 54403. Phone: (715) 842-1672. Fax: (715) 848-3158. E-mail: wsau@wsau.com. Web Site: www.wsau.com. Licensee: WRIG Inc. Group owner: Midwest Communications Inc. (acq 1996; $3.5 million with co-located FM). Network: ABC Information & Entertainment. Rep: Christal. Format: News/talk. News staff: 2. Target aud: 35-64. Spec prog: Farm 5 hrs, Polish 3 hrs, religious 3 hrs wkly. ♦Brett Lucht, gen mgr; Patrick Snyder, opns mgr & progmg dir; Samantha Milanwwski, stn mgr & sls dir; Carrie Van Deraa, prom dir; Frank Zastrow, chief of engrg.

WIFC(FM)—Co-owned with WSAU(AM). 1947: 95.5 mhz; 98 kw. 1,150 ft. TL: N44 55 14 W89 41 31. Stereo. E-mail: wifc@wifc.com. Web Site: www.wifc.com. Format: CHR. News staff: 2. Target aud: 18-49. ♦Brett Lucht, sls dir; Chris Pickett, progmg dir.

WXCO(AM)— Aug 1, 1953: 1230 khz; 1 kw-U. TL: N44 58 10 W89 36 25. Box 778 54402. Secondary address: 1110 E. Wausau Ave. 54403.

Stations in the U.S.

Phone: (715) 845-8218. Fax: (715) 845-6582. E-mail: wxco@wxco.com. Web Site: www.wxco.com. Licensee: Badger Communications. Group owner: Badger Communications L.L.C. (acq 9-17-03; $3.4 million. with co-located FM). Network: Network: Network: CBS, Westwood One, ABC News/Talk. Format: News. News staff: one; News: 10 hrs wkly. Target aud: 25 plus; professionals/business. ♦ Jeff Cecil, opns dir & progmg dir; Ken Rajek, gen mgr & gen sls mgr; Bob Starr, chief of engrg.

WLRK(FM)—Co-owned with WXCO(AM). Feb 1, 1985: 107.9 mhz; 100 kw. 1,019 ft. TL: N45 03 33 W89 26 10. Stereo. E-mail: wyco@wycofm.com. Web Site: www.wycofm.com. Format: CHR. Target aud: 25-49; upscale adults, female.

*WXPW(FM)— February 1996: 91.9 mhz; 560 w. 823 ft (ST WLBL-FM). TL: N44 55 14 W89 41 31. 303 W. Prospect St., Rhinelander 54501. Phone: (715) 362-6000. Fax: (715) 362-6007. E-mail: wxpr@wxpr.org. Web Site: www.wxpr.org. Licensee: White Pine Community Broadcasting Inc. Format: NPR news, great music. ♦ Mick Fiocchi, pres & gen mgr; Walt Gander, opns mgr; Chris Moran, dev dir; Jessie Dick, mktg dir; Jeff Dabel, mus dir; Ken Krall, news dir & pub affrs dir; Elmer Goetsch, chief of engrg.

Wautoma

WAUH(FM)— 2001: 102.3 mhz; 5.3 kw. Ant 3,490 ft. TL: N44 01 54 W89 09 07. Box 492, 103 W. Main St. 54982. Phone: (902) 787-7220. Fax: (902) 787-0128. E-mail: classichits@wauhradio.com. Web Site: www.wauhradio.com. Licensee: Hometown Broadcasting LLC (acq 8-9-02). Format: Classic hits. ♦ Tom Boyson, gen mgr; Margaret Corrente, gen sls mgr; Greg Mantiss, progmg dir; Andy Disterhaft, chief of engrg.

Wauwatosa

WXSS(FM)— Jan 1, 1961: 103.7 mhz; 19.5 kw. 840 ft. TL: N43 05 48 W87 54 19. Stereo. 11800 W. Grange Ave., Hales Corners 53130. Phone: (414) 529-1250. Fax: (414) 529-2122. Licensee: Entercom Milwaukee License LLC. Group owner: Entercom Communications Corp. (acq 12-13-99; grpsl). Network: ABC. Format: CHR. News staff: one. Target aud: 18-44; women. ♦ Craig Hodgson, gen mgr; Alan Kirshbon, sls dir; Andrea Biebel, natl sls mgr; Brian Kelly, progmg dir; Perry Faulknar, mus dir; Glenn Redd, pub affrs dir; Chris Tarr, chief of engrg.

West Bend

WBKV(AM)— November 1950: 1470 khz; 2.5 kw-U, DA-2. TL: N43 22 14 W88 09 58. Box 933 53095. Secondary address: 2410 S. Main St., Suite A 53095. Phone: (262) 334-2344. Fax: (262) 334-1512. E-mail: jhodges@westbendradio.com. Web Site: wbkvam.com. Licensee: West Bend Broadcasting Inc. Group owner: Bliss Communications Inc. (acq 10-18-70). Network: CNN Radio. Dow, Lohnes & Albertson. Format: Classic country. News staff: one; News: 20 hrs wkly. Target aud: 35-64; info-hungry adults interested in loc events & classic country music. ♦ Skip Bliss, pres; Rob Lisser, CFO; James N. Hodges, VP, gen mgr & natl sls mgr; Mike Elliott, opns dir; James Hodges, gen sls mgr; Bob Bonenfant, progmg dir; Judy Steffes, news dir; Jason Mielke, chief of engrg.

WBWI-FM—Co-owned with WBKV(AM). September 1958: 92.5 mhz; 17.5 kw. 565 ft. TL: N43 25 45 W88 17 53. Stereo. News staff: one; News: 2 hrs wkly. Target aud: 25-54; country mus listeners with disposable income.

West Salem

WKBH-FM—Licensed to West Salem. See La Crosse

Whitehall

WHTL-FM— Sept 10, 1981: 102.3 mhz; 3 kw. 450 ft. TL: N44 24 47 W91 17 03. Stereo. Box 66, N35609 Hwy. 53 54773. Phone: (715) 538-4341. Phone: (715) 538-4341. Fax: (715) 538-4360. E-mail: whtl@triwest.net. Licensee: The WHTL Group L.L.C. (acq 7-21-98; $60,000). Bosari & Paxson. Format: Oldies. News staff: one; News: 24 hrs wkly. Target aud: 25 plus; adult fans who make household buying decisions. Spec prog: Farm 5 hrs wkly. ♦ Tim Harrington, CFO, opns mgr, sls dir & pub affrs dir; Mary Little, progmg mgr & mus dir; Todd A. Harrington, gen mgr & chief of engrg.

Whitewater

WKCH(FM)— Jan 2, 1998: 106.5 mhz; 6 kw. 200 ft. TL: N42 54 24 W88 45 06. Box 94, Fort Atkinson 53538. Phone: (262) 473-9524. Fax: (920) 563-0315. Licensee: NewRadio Group LLC (group owner; acq 7-16-2003; grpsl). Format: Oldies. ♦ Mary Quass, CEO; Lindsay Wood Davis, COO; Tami Billmore, CFO; Benjamin D. Rosenthal, gen mgr; Gary Douglas, opns dir; Jim Vriezen, sls dir; Michael Clish, news dir.

WSLD(FM)— Nov 16, 1992: 104.5 mhz; 6 kw. 328 ft. TL: N42 35 47 W88 43 16. Stereo. Box 709, N. 6534 Hwy. 89 53190. Phone: (608) 883-6677. Fax: (608) 883-2054. Licensee: WPW Broadcasting Inc. (group owner; acq 8-4-99; $700,000). Format: Country. News staff: one; News: 10 hrs wkly. Target aud: General. ♦ David Madison, CEO; Nora Karbash, gen mgr; Penny Helms, natl sls mgr; Sarah Lofgren, news dir.

*WSUW(FM)— Jan 10, 1965: 91.7 mhz; 1.3 kw. 185 ft. TL: N42 50 10 W88 44 36. Stereo. UW Whitewater, 1201 Anderson Library 53190. Phone: (262) 472-1323. Phone: (262) 472-1314. Fax: (262) 472-5029. E-mail: wsuw@uww.edu. Web Site: www.wsuw.org. Licensee: Board of Regents University of Wisconsin System. Format: Hip Hop, Alternative, jazz. Target aud: 18-44. Spec prog: Heavy metal 14 hrs, jazz/world beat 6 hrs, urban contemp 14 hrs wkly. ♦ Wilfred Tremblay, gen mgr; Ashley Nixon, mktg mgr; Brian O'Shea, progmg dir; Andy King, mus dir.

Whiting

WYTE(FM)— Oct 21, 1985: 96.7 mhz; 50 kw. 492 ft. TL: N44 29 24 W89 32 54. Stereo. Box 1030, Stevens Point 54481. Phone: (715) 341-8858. Fax: (715) 387-9744. Web Site: www.wyte.com. Licensee: NewRadio Group LLC (group owner; acq 12-20-2002; grpsl). Rep: Interep. Miller & Miller. Format: Country. News staff: one; News: 7 hrs wkly. Target aud: 25-54. ♦ Mary Quegg, CFO; Tami Gillmore, CFO; Wayne A. Ridd, gen mgr; Mark Skibba, opns mgr & progmg dir; Ed Paulson, mus dir; Kelli Martin, asst music dir.

Winneconne

WVBO(FM)—Licensed to Winneconne. See Oshkosh

Wisconsin Dells

WDLS(AM)— May 1969: 900 khz; 1 kw-D, 229 w-N. TL: N43 38 23 W89 43 14. Box 204 53965. Secondary address: 121 Broadway 53965. Phone: (608) 254-2546. Fax: (608) 745-5771. Web Site: wdlsam.com. Licensee: Magnum Communications Inc. Group owner: Magnum Radio Inc. (acq 2-10-99; $775,000. with co-located FM). Network: Network: Jones Radio Networks, AP Radio. Format: Var. News staff: one; News: 6 hrs wlky. Target aud: 18-45; men. Spec prog: Medical 5 hrs wkly. ♦ Dave Magnum, chmn; JIm Coursole, gen mgr.

WNNO-FM—Co-owned with WDLS(AM). May 1974: 106.9 mhz; 6 kw. Ant 321 ft. TL: N43 38 23 W89 43 14. Stereo. Box 360, Portage 53901. Web Site: mix106wnno.com. Format: Adult contemp. News staff: one; News: 7 hrs wkly. Target aud: 18-40.

Wisconsin Rapids

WFHR(AM)— Nov 5, 1940: 1320 khz; 5 kw-D, 500 w-N, DA-N. TL: N44 24 56 W89 50 06. Box 8022, 645 25th Ave. N. 54495-8022. Phone: (715) 424-1300. Fax: (715) 424-1347. Web Site: www.wfhrradio.com. Licensee: NewRadio Group LLC (group owner; acq 7-30-2004; $4.01 million. with co-located FM). Network: CBS. Format: News/talk, info, full service. ♦ Mary Quass, pres; Wayne Ripp, gen mgr; Joe Steckbauer, gen sls mgr; Greg Gack, progmg dir; Carl Hilke, news dir.

WGLX-FM—Co-owned with WFHR(AM). Aug 1, 1946: 103.3 mhz; 100 kw. 331 ft. TL: N44 24 56 W89 50 10. Stereo. 2301 PLover Road, Plover 54467. Phone: (715) 341-8838. Fax: (715) 341-9744. E-mail: onradio@wglx.com. Web Site: www.wglx.com. Format: Classic rock. Target aud: 25-49. ♦ Panama Jack, progmg dir.

Wittenberg

*WVRN(FM)—Not on air, target date: unknown: 89.9 mhz; 25 kw. Ant 482 ft. TL: N44 57 54 W89 00 18. 3434 W. Kilbourn Ave., Milwaukee 53208-3313. Phone: (414) 935-3000. Fax: (414) 935-3015. Licensee: VCY America Inc. ♦ Vic Eliason, VP & gen mgr.

Wyoming

Afton

KRSV(AM)— Aug 13, 1985: 1210 khz; 5 kw-D, 250 w-N. TL: N42 43 22 W110 57 39. Box 1210, Wyoming Hwy. 238 83110. Phone: (307) 885-5778. E-mail: hansenjw@silverstar.com. Licensee: Western Wyoming Radio Inc. Network: ABC. Format: Modern country, loc news, sports. ♦ Jerry Hansen, pres & gen mgr; Jennie Hansen, sls dir & progmg dir; Dan Dockstader, news dir.

KRSV-FM— Nov 13, 1985: 98.7 mhz; 3 kw. Ant -289 ft. TL: N42 51 02 W110 58 46.

*KUWA(FM)— July 1, 1998: 91.3 mhz; 400 w. -312 ft. TL: N42 51 02 W110 58 46. Box 3984, Laramie 82071. Phone: (307) 766-4240. Fax: (307) 766-6184. E-mail: wpr@uwyo.edu. Web Site: wyomingpublicradio.net. Licensee: University of Wyoming. Network: Network: NPR, PRI. Format: Progsv, news/talk, class. News: 4 hrs wkly. Target aud: 25-54 plus; demographic, high income, education. Spec prog: Folk 5 hrs, jazz 5 hrs wkly. ♦ Jon Schwartz, gen mgr; Peg Arnold, dev dir; Roger Adams, opns mgr & progmg dir; Don Woods, mus dir; Bob Beck, news dir.

Albin

KKAW(FM)— 2001: 107.3 mhz; 9.3 kw. Ant 531 ft. TL: N41 29 31 W104 05 07. 2109 E. 10th St., Cheyenne 82001. Phone: (307) 638-8921. Fax: (307) 638-8922. Licensee: Chisholm Trail Broadcasting LLC Group owner: Northeast Broadcasting Company Inc. (acq 2-25-2005; $850,000. with KREO(FM) Pine Bluffs). Format: Country. ♦ Larry Proietti, gen mgr.

Basin

KZMQ(AM)—See Greybull

Buffalo

KBBS(AM)— Apr 17, 1956: 1450 khz; 1 kw-U. TL: N44 20 33 W106 40 54. 1221 Fort St. 82834. Phone: (307) 684-7070. Fax: (307) 684-7676. E-mail: kbbs@vcn.com. Web Site: www.kix93.com. Licensee: Legend Communications of Wyoming L.L.C. Group owner: Legend Communications LLC (acq 9-1-00; $1.05 million with KLGT(FM) Buffalo). Network: ABC Information & Entertainment. Rep: McGavren Guild. Format: Oldies, News/talk, Sports. News: 10 hrs wkly. Target aud: 35-64; age group with the most money to spend. ♦ Larry Patrick, CEO; Roger Gelder, COO; Larry Patrick, pres; Travis Reeves, VP; Albert L. Wildeman, gen mgr; Steve Lawrence, stn mgr, opns dir, progmg dir & chief of engrg; Robin Harnden, sls dir; Penny Lauahan, news dir; Charles Dozier, engrg dir & engrg dir.

*KBUW(FM)— 2000: 90.5 mhz; 430 w. Ant -197 ft. TL: N44 20 50 W106 43 25. Box 3984, Laramie 82071. Phone: (307) 766-4240. Fax: (307) 766-6184. E-mail: rgriscom@uwyo.edu. Web Site:

uwadmnweb.uwyo.edu/WPR. Licensee: University of Wyoming. Format: News, AAA. ♦Jon Schwartz, gen mgr; Peg Arnold, dev dir; Roger Adams, adv dir; Bob Beck, news dir; Larry Dean, chief of engrg.

KLGT(FM)— Mar 7, 1983: 92.9 mhz; 100 kw. Ant 358 ft. TL: N44 34 32 W106 52 23. Stereo. 1221 Fort St. 82834. Phone: (307) 684-5126. Phone: (307) 684-2584. Fax: (307) 684-7676. E-mail: klgt@vcn.com. Web Site: www.kix93.com. Licensee: Legend Communications of Wyoming L.L.C. Group owner: Legend Communications L.L.C. (acq 9-1-00). Network: Jones Radio Networks. Rep: McGavren Guild. Format: Country. News staff: one; News: 9 hrs wkly. Target aud: 24-54; those with spendable income. Spec prog: Relg one hr wkly. ♦Larry Patrick, CEO & pres; Roger Gelder, COO; Nicki Williams, CFO; Travis Reeves, VP, gen mgr & stn mgr; Ed Cwik, opns mgr, progmg dir & chief of engrg; Robin Harnden, sls dir; Arron Lee, news dir; Charles Dozier, engrg dir.

Burns

KIGN(FM)— Sept 26, 1990: 101.9 mhz; 50 kw. 492 ft. TL: N41 07 01 W104 40 07. Stereo. 101.9 KING FM, 1912 Capitol Ave., Suite 300, Cheyenne 82001. Phone: (307) 632-4400. Fax: (307) 632-1818. E-mail: kingfm@hotmail.com. Web Site: www.kingfm.com. Licensee: Citicasters Licenses L.P. Group owner: Clear Channel Communications Inc. (acq 9-7-99; $1.2 million). Format: Country. News staff: one; News: 3 hrs wkly. Target aud: 25-54. ♦Craig Cochran, gen mgr; Tim Davidson, progmg dir; Quin Morrison, chief of engrg.

Casper

KASS(FM)— Oct 15, 1990: 106.9 mhz; 94 kw. Ant 1,765 ft. TL: N42 44 37 W106 18 31. Stereo. 218 N. Wolcott St. 82602. Phone: (307) 265-1984. Fax: (307) 473-7461. E-mail: kass@wyomingradio.com. Web Site: www.wyomingradio.com. Licensee: Mount Rushmore Broadcasting Inc. (group owner; (acq 1995; $150,000). Format: Classic rock. ♦Roger Ashley, gen mgr; Roger Arnt, gen sls mgr; Donny Rood, prom mgr & news dir; Steve Fritz, chief of engrg.

***KCSP-FM**— 1992: 90.3 mhz; 100 kw. 1,922 ft. TL: N42 44 24 W106 18 23. Stereo. 6363 Hwy. 50 E., Carson City 89701. Phone: (775) 883-5647. Fax: (775) 883-5704. Licensee: Western Inspirational Broadcasters Inc. (acq 10-3-90). Network: USA. Format: Contemp Christian. News: 16 hrs wkly. Target aud: General. ♦Tom Hesse, gen mgr.

KHOC(FM)— 1998: 102.5 mhz; 100 kw. Ant 1,696 ft. TL: N42 44 37 W106 18 31. Stereo. 218 N. Wolcott St. 82601. Phone: (307) 265-1984. Fax: (307) 266-3295. E-mail: info@wyomingradio.com. Web Site: www.wyomingradio.com. Licensee: Mount Rushmore Broadcasting Inc. (group owner; (acq 10-29-98; $300,000). Format: Hot adult contemp. ♦Roger Ashley, gen mgr; Roger Arndt, sls dir; Donnie Rood, prom dir & progmg dir; Steve Fritz, engrg dir.

KKTL(AM)— 1999: 1400 khz; 1 kw-U. TL: N42 51 22 W106 21 41. 150 N. Nichols Ave. 82601. Phone: (307) 266-5252. Fax: (307) 235-9143. E-mail: kktl@clearchannel.com. Licensee: Citicasters Licenses L.P. Group owner: Clear Channel Communications Inc. (acq 5-4-99; grpsl). Format: Sports. ♦Bob Price, gen mgr & sls dir; Staci Owens, mktg dir; Bob Davis, progmg dir; Dave Nutter, chief of engrg.

***KLWC(FM)**— 2005: 89.1 mhz; 1.5 kw vert. Ant 1,848 ft. TL: N42 44 03 W106 20 00. 5700 West Oaks Blvd., Rocklin, CA 95765. Phone: (916) 251-1600. Fax: (916) 251-1650. Web Site: www.klove.com. Licensee: Educational Media Foundation. (acq 1-11-2005; $100,000. for CP with CP for KLRV(FM) Billings, MT). Network: K-Love. Format: Christian. ♦Lloyd Parker, gen mgr.

KMGW(FM)—Listing follows KTWO(AM).

KMLD(FM)— Oct 1, 1967: 94.5 mhz; 63 kw. Ant 1,909 ft. TL: N42 44 03 W106 20 00. Stereo. 218 N. Wolcott St. 82601. Phone: (307) 265-1984. Fax: (307) 473-7461. E-mail: kmld@wyomingradio.com. Web Site: www.wyomingradio.com. Licensee: Mt. Rushmore Broadcasting Inc. Group owner: Mount Rushmore Broadcasting Inc. (acq 3-12-2001; grpsl). Format: Oldies. Target aud: 35-64. ♦Roger Ashley, gen mgr; Roger Arnt, gen sls mgr; Donny Rood, prom mgr; Donny Rood, progmg dir; Steve Fritz, chief of engrg.

KQLT(FM)— Oct 7, 1983: 103.7 mhz; 97 kw. Ant 1,860 ft. TL: N42 44 37 W106 18 31. Stereo. 218 N. Wolcott St. 82601. Phone: (307) 265-1984. Fax: (307) 473-7461. E-mail: kqlt@wyomingradio.com. Web Site: www.wyomingradio.com. Licensee: Mount Rushmore Broadcasting Inc. (group owner; (acq 8-17-94; $230,000;. FTR: 9-12-94). Rep: McGavren Guild. Dow, Lohnes & Albertson. Format: Country. Target aud: General. ♦Jan Charles Gray, pres; Roger Ashley, gen mgr; Don Rood, opns mgr; Roger Arnt, gen sls mgr; Donny Rood, prom mgr, progmg dir & news dir; Steve Fritz, chief of engrg.

KTRS-FM— January 1997: 104.7 mhz; 18 w. 1,774 ft. TL: N42 44 37 W106 18 26. 150 N. Nichols Ave. 82601. Phone: (307) 266-5252. Fax: (307) 235-9143. E-mail: ktrs@clearchannel.com. Licensee: Clear Channel Broadcasting Licenses Inc. Group owner: Clear Channel Communications Inc. (acq 3-29-01; grpsl). Format: CHR. Target aud: 12-24. ♦Bob Price, gen mgr, gen sls mgr & news dir; Donovan Short, opns mgr, gen sls mgr & progmg dir; Dave Nutter, chief of engrg.

KTWO(AM)— Jan 2, 1930: 1030 khz; 50 kw-U, DA-N. TL: N42 50 34 W106 13 07. 150 N. Nichols Ave. 82601. Phone: (307) 266-5252. Fax: (307) 235-9143. E-mail: ktwo@clearchanel.com. Web Site: www.k2radio.com. Licensee: Citicasters Licenses L.P. Group owner: Clear Channel Communications Inc. (acq 5-4-99; grpsl). Network: CBS. Cohn & Marks. Format: Talk. Target aud: 25-54. ♦Bob Price, gen mgr, opns mgr & gen sls mgr; Bob Davis, progmg dir; Vicki Daniels, news dir; David Nutter, chief of engrg.

KMGW(FM)—Co-owned with KTWO(AM). 1998: 96.7 mhz; 2.85 kw. Ant 1,771 ft. TL: N42 44 37 W106 18 26. E-mail: kmgw@clearchannel.com. Web Site: www.hitsandfavorites.com. Licensee: Clear Channel Broadcasting Licenses Inc. (acq 3-12-01; grpsl). Format: Adult contemp. ♦Donovan Short, progmg dir.

***KUWC(FM)**— 2000: 91.3 mhz; 530 w. Ant 1,784 ft. TL: N42 44 26 W106 21 34. Box 3984, Laramie 82071. Phone: (307) 766-4240. Fax: (307) 766-6184. E-mail: jbs@uwyo.edu. Web Site: uwadmnweb.uwyo.edu. Licensee: University of Wyoming. Format: News, AAA. ♦Jon Schwartz, gen mgr; Peg Arnold, prom dir; Roger Adams, progmg dir; Larry Dean, mus dir; Bob Beck, news dir.

KVOC(AM)— Sept 29, 1946: 1230 khz; 1 kw-U. TL: N42 50 05 W106 17 44. 218 N. Wolcott St. 82601. Phone: (307) 265-1984. Fax: (307) 473-7461. E-mail: mtrushmore@mrbradio.com. Web Site: www.wyomingradio.com. Licensee: Mount Rushmore Broadcasting Inc. (group owner; (acq 6-12-97; $105,000). Network: Network: ABC Information & Entertainment, ESPN Radio. Format: Sports. ♦Jan Charles Gray, pres; Roger Ashley, gen mgr; Roger Arndt, sls dir; Donny Rood, prom dir & progmg dir; Steve Fritz, chief of engrg.

KWYY(FM)— Nov 30, 1981: 95.5 mhz; 100 kw. 1,920 ft. TL: N42 44 37 W106 18 26. Stereo. 251 W. First St. 82601. Secondary address: 105 North Nichols Phone: (307) 266-5252. Fax: (307) 235-9143. E-mail: kwyy@clearchannel.com. Licensee: Clear Channel Broadcasting Licenses Inc. Group owner: Clear Channel Communications Inc. (acq 3-29-01; grpsl). Rep: Allied Radio Partners. Format: Country. Target aud: 25-54. ♦Bob Price, gen mgr & gen sls mgr; Donovan Short, opns mgr & progmg dir; Dave Nutter, chief of engrg.

Cheyenne

KFBC(AM)— 1940: 1240 khz; 1 kw-U. TL: N41 07 17 W104 50 22. 1806 Capitol Ave. 82001. Phone: (307) 634-4461. Fax: (307) 632-8586. Licensee: Montgomery Broadcasting L.L.C. (acq 7-1-93; $250,000). Network: ABC. Format: Full service, news, sports. News staff: 5; News: 25 hrs wkly. Target aud: 35-54. ♦Dave Montgomery, pres, gen mgr & sls dir; J.D. Harris, stn mgr; Dagan Miller, news dir.

KGAB(AM)—(Orchard Valley). 1952: 650 khz; 8.5 kw-D, 500 w-N, DA-N. TL: N41 03 09 W104 49 53. 1912 Capitol Ave., Suite 300 82001. Phone: (307) 632-4400. Fax: (307) 632-1818. Web Site: www.kgab.com. Licensee: Citicasters Licenses L.P. Group owner: Clear Channel Communications Inc. (acq 1999; grpsl). Format: News/talk. News staff: 3. Target aud: 25-64. ♦Craig Cochran, gen mgr; Dave Chaffin, opns mgr & progmg dir; Amy Richards, news dir; Quin Morrison, chief of engrg.

KOLZ(FM)—Co-owned with KGAB(AM). August 1961: 100.7 mhz; 100 kw. 490 ft. TL: N41 06 01 W105 00 23. Stereo. Web Site: www.kolz.com. Format: Country. ♦Jeff Brown, progmg dir.

KIGN(FM)—See Burns

KJUA(AM)— 1952: 1380 khz; 1 kw-D, 8 w-N. TL: N41 07 22 W104 48 07. Stereo. 110 East 17th St., Suite 205 82001. Phone: (307) 635-8787. Fax: (307) 635-8788. E-mail: kjjl@kjjl.com. Web Site: www.kjjl.com. Licensee: Christus Broadcasting Inc. Network: CNN Radio. Booth, Freret, Imlay. Format: Adult contemp. News staff: 2; News: 22 hrs wkly. Target aud: 35 plus; mature adults. Spec prog: Gospel one hr wkly. ♦Paul Montoya, pres.

KKPL(FM)— 1997: 99.9 mhz; 50 kw. Ant 492 ft. TL: N40 59 22 W105 03 47. 3201 E. Mulberry St., Unit H, Fort Collins, CO 80524. Phone: (970) 407-9099. Fax: (970) 407-0584. Web Site: www.999thepoint.com. Licensee: Regent Broadcasting of Ft. Collins Inc. Group owner: Regent Communications Inc. (acq 1-8-2004; $7.75 million. with KARS-FM Laramie). Format: Alternative. ♦Cal Hall, gen mgr; Mark Callaghan, opns mgr; Lisa Schneider, sls dir; Mark Callagham, progmg dir; Kama McDonald, news dir; Quin Morrison, chief of engrg.

KLEN(FM)— Sept 26, 1983: 106.3 mhz; 3 kw. -3 ft. TL: N41 08 08 W104 48 12. Stereo. 1912 Capitol Ave., Suite 300 82001. Phone: (307) 632-4400. Fax: (307) 632-1818. E-mail: cheyenneaudio@clearchannel.com. Web Site: www.1063klen.com. Licensee: Citicasters Licenses L.P. Group owner: Clear Channel Communications Inc. (acq 5-4-99; grpsl). Format: News/talk. News staff: 3. Target aud: 25-54. ♦Craig Cochran, gen mgr; Dave Chaffin, opns mgr & gen sls mgr; Amy Richards, prom dir & news dir; Curt Jackson, progmg dir; Quin Morrison, chief of engrg.

KQLF(FM)— Sept 1, 1968: 97.9 mhz; 100 kw. 541 ft. TL: N41 06 01 W105 00 23. Stereo. 1612 La Porte, Suite 300, Fort Collons, CO 80521. Phone: (970) 482-5991. Fax: (970) 482-5994. Licensee: Citicasters Licenses L.P. Group owner: Clear Channel Communications Inc. (acq 1999; grpsl). Format: Adult contemp. News staff: 3; News: 2 hrs wkly. Target aud: 25-54. ♦Stu Haskell, gen mgr; Chris Kelly, opns mgr & progmg dir; Kathy Arias, gen sls mgr; Scott James, mus dir; Rich Bircumshaw, news dir; Cliff Mikkelson, chief of engrg.

KRAE(AM)— Apr 29, 1961: 1480 khz; 1 kw-D, 67 w-N. TL: N41 07 26 W104 49 10. Stereo. 2109 E. 10th St. 82001. Phone: (307) 638-8921. Fax: (307) 638-8922. E-mail: news@1049krrr.com. Licensee: Brahmin Broadcasting Corp. Group owner: Northeast Broadcasting Company Inc. (acq 5-10-2004; grpsl). Network: CBS. Rep: Mountain Media. Format: News/ talk, sports. Spec prog: Sp 2 hrs wkly. ♦Larry Proietti, gen mgr; Jessica Cooper, sls dir; Larry Proeitti, progmg dir; R.J. Fox, news dir; Rob Thomas, chief of engrg.

KRRR(FM)—Co-owned with KRAE(AM). 1997: 104.9 mhz; 25.5 kw. Ant 115 ft. TL: N41 08 04 W104 41 32. Stereo. Format: Oldies. Target aud: 25-54.

KSHF(FM)—Not on air, target date: unknown: 93.7 mhz; 25 kw. Ant 115 ft. TL: N41 08 04 W104 41 32. White Park Broadcasting Inc., 288 S. River Rd., Bedford, NH 03110. Phone: (603) 668-6470. Licensee: White Park Broadcasting Inc. ♦Steven A. Silberberg, pres.

***KWYH(FM)**—Not on air, target date: unknown: 88.1 mhz; 900 w. Ant 236 ft. TL: N41 03 09 W104 49 53. Drawer 3206, Tupelo, MS 38803. Phone: (662) 844-8888. Fax: (662) 842-6791. Web Site: www.afr.net. Licensee: American Family Association. ♦Marvin Sanders, gen mgr.

Chugwater

KCUG(FM)—Not on air, target date: unknown: 99.5 mhz; 6 kw. Ant 272 ft. TL: N41 46 09 W104 48 57. White Park Broadcasting Inc., 288 S. River Rd., Bedford, NH 03110. Phone: (603) 668-9999. Fax: (603) 668-6470. Licensee: White Park Broadcasting Inc. ♦Steven A. Silberberg, pres & gen mgr.

***KLWV(FM)**— 2004: 90.9 mhz; 100 kw. Ant 1,183 ft. TL: N41 18 39 W105 27 12. EMF Broadcasting, 5700 W. Oaks Blvd., Rocklin, CA 95765. Phone: (916) 251-1600. Fax: (916) 251-1650. E-mail: klove@klove.com. Web Site: www.klove.com. Licensee: Educational Media Foundation. Group owner: EMF Broadcasting (acq 10-2-03; grpsl). Network: K-Love. Shaw Pittman. Format: Contemp Christian. News staff: 3. Target aud: 25-44; Judeo Christian, female. ♦Richard Jenkins, pres; Mike Novak, VP & progmg dir; Lloyd Parker, gen mgr; Ed Lenane, opns dir & news dir; Keith Whipple, dev dir; Eric Allen, natl sls mgr; Roger Chapman, rgnl sls mgr; Chris Joyce, prom dir; David Pierce, progmg mgr; Jon Rivers, mus dir; Sam Wallington, engrg dir.

Cody

KODI(AM)— March 1947: 1400 khz; 1 kw-U. TL: N44 30 30 W109 04 05. Box 1210, 1949 Mountain View Dr. 82414. Phone: (307) 578-5000. Fax: (307) 527-5045. E-mail: rgelder@bhrnwy.com. Web Site: www.bighornradio.com. Licensee: Legend Communications of Wyoming LLC. Group owner: Legend Communications LLC (acq 6-29-99;

Stations in the U.S. — Wyoming

Developers & Brokers of Radio Properties
contact American Media Services at our suite: Philadelphia Marriott Downtown 215-625-2900
843-972-2200
americanmediaservices.com
Charleston, SC
Dallas, TX · Chicago, Il · Austin, TX
American Media Services, LLC

$890,000 with co-located FM). Format: News/talk, sports. News: 20 hrs wkly. Target aud: 35 plus. ♦ Larry Patrick, pres; Roger Gelder, exec VP; Carol Kary, VP, gen mgr & gen sls mgr; Rita Conners, opns mgr; Mack Frost, news dir; Tom Morrison, progmg dir & pub affrs dir; Charles Dozier, chief of engrg.

KTAG(FM)—Co-owned with KODI(AM). Nov 30, 1981: 97.9 mhz; 100 kw. 1,901 ft. TL: N44 29 44 W109 09 13. Stereo. Rep: Allied Radio Partners. Format: Adult contemp. News: 6 hrs wkly. Target aud: 25-39; upper middle class, young families, suburban w/some college, 60% female. ♦ Larry Patrick, CEO; Roger Gelder, COO.

Diamondville

KDWY(FM)— 2000: 105.3 mhz; 16 kw. Ant 886 ft. TL: N41 50 18 W110 30 12. c/o Radio Station KMER(AM), Box 432, Kemmerer 83101. Phone: (307) 877-4422. Fax: (307) 877-5537. E-mail: kmer@onewest.net. Licensee: Simmons-SLC, LS LLC. Group owner: Simmons Media Group (acq 4-19-2004; grpsl). Network: ABC. Format: Country. News staff: one; News: one hr wkly. Target aud: 25-55. ♦ Jim Carroll, gen mgr; Jim Thoeny, opns dir.

Douglas

KBOG(FM)—Not on air, target date: unknown: 92.5 mhz; 5.4 kw. Ant 3,188 ft. TL: N42 16 05 W105 26 33. 288 S. River Rd., Bedford, NH 03110. Phone: (603) 668-6470. Licensee: White Park Broadcasting Inc. ♦ Steven A. Silberberg, pres & gen mgr.

*KDUW(FM)— 2000: 91.7 mhz; 450 w. Ant -52 ft. TL: N42 44 41 W105 20 09. Box 3984, Laramie 82071. Phone: (307) 766-4240. Fax: (307) 766-6184. E-mail: hgriscom@uwyo.edu. Web Site: www.wyomingpublicradio.org. Licensee: University of Wyoming. Format: News, progsv. class. ♦ Jon Schwartz, gen mgr; Peg Arnold, progmg dir; Roger Adams, progmg dir; Larry Dean, chief of engrg.

KKTY(AM)— June 22, 1957: 1470 khz; 1 kw-D, 500 w-N. TL: N42 45 48 W105 23 32. Box 135, 247 Russell Ave. 82633. Phone: (307) 358-3636. Fax: (307) 358-4010. E-mail: kkty@netcommander.com. Web Site: www.kktyonline.com. Licensee: Douglas Broadcasting Inc. (acq 2-11-93; $120,000 with co-located FM; 3-8-93). Network: Network: Westwood One, CNN Radio. Regnl Reps Format: Oldies. News: 28 hrs wkly. Target aud: General. ♦ Dennis Switzer, pres & gen mgr.

KKTY-FM— Dec 6, 1982: 99.3 mhz; 813 w. 530 ft. TL: N42 43 42 W105 31 46. Stereo. Web Site: www.kktyonline.com. Network: Network: Jones Radio Networks, CNN Radio. Format: Country. News staff: one; News: 28 hrs wkly. Target aud: General.

KTED(FM)—Not on air, target date: unknown: 100.9 mhz; 31 kw. Ant 626 ft. TL: N42 45 30 W105 47 49. 288 S. River Rd., Bedford, NH 03110. Phone: (603) 668-6470. Licensee: White Park Broadcasting Inc. ♦ Steven A. Silberberg, pres.

Ethete

*KWRR(FM)— 2000: 89.5 mhz; 85 kw. Ant 1,820 ft. TL: N43 27 30 W108 11 39. Box 327, Kinnear 82516. Phone: (307) 335-8659. Phone: (307) 335-8658. Fax: (307) 335-8740. Licensee: Business Council of the Northern Arapaho Tribe. (acq 8-11-98). Format: Variety. ♦ Steven White, gen mgr.

Evanston

KBMG(FM)— June 1982: 106.1 mhz; 89 kw horiz. Ant 2,122 ft. TL: N40 52 16 W110 59 43. Stereo. 2722 S. Redwood Rd., Suite 1, Salt Lake City, UT 84119. Phone: (801) 908-8777. Fax: (801) 908-8782. Licensee: Bustos Media of Utah License LLC. Group owner: Bustos Media Holdings (acq 7-1-2004; $3 million). Format: Sp. ♦ Edward Distel, gen mgr.

*KCWW(FM)—Not on air, target date: unknown: 88.1 mhz; 92 w. Ant 1,348 ft. TL: N41 21 10 W110 54 29. Box 1372, Park City, UT 84060-1372. Phone: (435) 649-9004. Fax: (435) 645-9063. Licensee: Community Wireless of Park City Inc. ♦ Blair Feulner, gen mgr.

KEVA(AM)— June 27, 1953: 1240 khz; 1 kw-U. TL: N41 15 29 W111 00 51. Box 190, 568 Airport Rd. 82931. Phone: (307) 789-9101. Phone: (307) 789-9102. Fax: (307) 789-8521. E-mail: keva@vcn.com. Web Site: 1240keva.com. Licensee: Sagebrush Broadcasting Co. Inc. Group owner: Jimmy Ray Carroll Stns (acq 1-23-2001). Format: Country. Target aud: 25-54. ♦ Linda Burris, gen mgr, gen sls mgr, prom dir & prom mgr; Mike Richard, progmg mgr; Dennis Silver, chief of engrg.

Evansville

KUYO(AM)— Aug 23, 1985: 830 khz; 25 kw-D. TL: N42 52 13 W106 12 12. Box 50607, Casper 82605-0607. Secondary address: 1423 S. Beverly, Casper 82609. Phone: (307) 577-5896. Web Site: www.kuyo.com. Licensee: Wyoming Christian Broadcasting Co. (acq 6-1-99; $75,000). Format: Classic Christian, talk. Target aud: 35-65; general. ♦ Aaron Remington, VP; Steve Stumbo, pres & gen mgr.

Fort Bridger

KNYN(FM)— 2001: 99.1 mhz; 27.5 kw. Ant 1,604 ft. TL: N41 21 10 W110 54 26. Box 271, Kemmerer 83101. Phone: (307) 789-9101. Fax: (307) 789-8521. Licensee: M. Kent Frandsen. (acq 6-22-99; $125,000). Format: Adult contemp.

Fox Farm

KRND(AM)— 1998: 1630 khz; 10 kw-D, 1 kw-N. TL: N41 07 22 W104 48 07. 110 E. 17th St., Suite 205, Cheyenne 82001. Phone: (307) 635-8787. Fax: (307) 635-8788. E-mail: kwy@kwyradio.com. Web Site: www.kwyradio.com. Licensee: Christus Broadcasting Inc. Network: AP Network News. Booth, Freret & Imlay. Format: Classic country. News staff: 1; News: 22 hrs wkly. Target aud: 35 plus; mature adults. ♦ Paul Montoya, pres, gen mgr & chief of opns.

Gillette

KAML-FM—Listing follows KIML(AM).

*KAXG(FM)— Mar 27, 2003: 89.7 mhz; 250 w. Ant 89 ft. TL: N44 13 50 W105 27 45. Box 2426, Havre, MT 59501-2426. Phone: (406) 265-5845. Fax: (406) 265-8860. E-mail: ynop@ynopradio.org. Web Site: www.ynopradio.org. Licensee: Hi-Line Radio Fellowship Inc. (acq 3-13-03; $65,000). Format: Christian Inspirational. Target aud: General; those looking for inprirational Christian music & progmg. ♦ Ed Matter, gen mgr; Brenda Boyum, opns mgr; Roger Lonnquist, dev dir; Brian Jackson, progmg dir.

KGWY(FM)— Jan 5, 1983: 100.7 mhz; 100 kw. 635 ft. TL: N44 14 35 W105 32 19. Stereo. Box 1179 82717. Secondary address: 2810 Southern Dr. 82718. Phone: (307) 686-2242. Fax: (307) 686-7736. E-mail: thefox@basinsradio.com. Web Site: www.basinsradio.com. Licensee: Legend Communications of Wyoming LLC. Group owner: Legend Communications L.L.C. (acq 5-29-01; $1.9 million). Network: ABC. Format: Country. News staff: one. Target aud: 20-45. ♦ Larry Patrick, pres; Don Clonch, gen mgr; John English, opns mgr.

KIML(AM)— Sept 13, 1957: 1270 khz; 5 kw-D, 1 kw-N, DA-N. TL: N44 18 12 W015 59 52. Stereo. Box 1179 82717. Phone: (307) 686-2242. Fax: (307) 686-7736. Web Site: www.basinsradio.com. Licensee: Gillette Broadcasting Co. (acq 5-29-01; $1.2 million. for stock, including $100,000 consulting agreement, with co-located FM). Format: News, talk, sports. News staff: one; News: 40 hrs wkly. Target aud: 25 plus. ♦ Don Clonch, gen mgr; John English, opns mgr & gen sls mgr.

KAML-FM—Co-owned with KIML(AM). May 1976: 96.9 mhz; 100 kw. 456 ft. TL: N44 18 10 W105 27 00. Stereo. Web Site: www.basinsradio.com. Format: CHR, rock. News staff: one. Target aud: 25-54.

*KLWD(FM)— 2001: 91.9 mhz; 1 kw. Ant 226 ft. TL: N44 17 00 W105 31 00. Stereo. Box 1492 82717. Phone: (307) 682-9553. Fax: (307) 682-8509. E-mail: klwd@csnradio.com. Web Site: klwd.vcn.com. Licensee: CSN International (group owner; acq 5-8-00; $10,000. for CP). Format: Inspirational, relg. ♦ Don Wight, pres, gen mgr & progmg dir.

*KUWG(FM)— 1997: 90.9 mhz; 450 w. 459 ft. TL: N44 12 33 W105 28 05. Box 3984, Univ. Station, Laramie 82071. Phone: (307) 766-4240. Fax: (307) 766-6184. E-mail: wpr@uwyo.edu. Web Site: uwadmnweb.uwyo.edu. Licensee: University of Wyoming. Format: News, progsv, class. ♦ Jon Schwartz, gen mgr; Hank Arnold, dev dir; Roger Adams, progmg dir; Bob Beck, news dir; Larry Dean, chief of engrg.

KXXL(FM)— 2004: 103.9 mhz; 50 kw. Ant 392 ft. TL: N44 13 50 W105 27 45. Box 2230 82717. Phone: (307) 687-1003. Fax: (307) 687-1006. Licensee: Keyhole Broadcasting LLC. Format: Classic rock. ♦ Don Howe, gen mgr.

Glendo

KYOD(FM)— July 10, 1999: 100.1 mhz; 55 kw. Ant 456 ft. TL: N42 46 13 W105 13 21. Stereo. 1837 Madora Ave., Suite B, Douglas 82633. Phone: (307) 358-6177. Fax: (307) 358-0978. E-mail: kyod@netcommander.com. Web Site: www.kyod.com. Licensee: Canned Ham Communications LLC (acq 5-23-00; $150,000. for CP). Rep: Interep. Shaw Pittman. Format: Morden adult contemp. News: one hr wkly. Target aud: 25-54. Spec prog: Hard rock 2 hrs wkly. ♦ Darrell Woolsey, gen mgr; Mary Woolsey, stn mgr.

Glenrock

KGRK(FM)—Not on air, target date: unknown: 98.3 mhz; 200 w. Ant -249 ft. TL: N42 51 49 W105 52 15. 6807 Foxglove Dr., Cheyenne 82009. Phone: (307) 778-9318. Licensee: Michael Radio Group LLC. ♦ Victor A. Michael Jr., gen mgr.

Green River

KFRZ(FM)—Listing follows KUGR(AM).

KSIT(FM)—See Rock Springs

KUGR(AM)— June 18, 1976: 1490 khz; 1 kw-U. TL: N41 30 56 W109 26 11. Box 970 82935. Secondary address: 40 Shoshone Ave. 82935. Phone: (307) 875-6666. Fax: (307) 875-5847. E-mail: kugr@sweetwater.net. Web Site: www.kugr.net. Licensee: Wagon Wheel Communications Corp. (acq 1-1-79). Network: Network: CBS, Westwood One. Format: Soft adult contemp. News staff: one; News: 4 hrs wkly. Target aud: 30 plus. Spec prog: Sp 5 hrs wkly. ♦ Al Harris, CEO & pres; Steve Core, gen mgr & opns dir; Jeff Driggs, gen sls mgr; Sean Maxwell, progmg dir, chief of engrg & chief of engrg; Adam Dormoth, news dir.

KFRZ(FM)—Co-owned with KUGR(AM). Sept 23, 1999: 92.1 mhz; 90 kw. 1,138 ft. TL: N41 29 47 W109 20 44. E-mail: kugr@sweetwater.net. Web Site: www.kfrz.net. Network: Westwood One. Format: Country. News staff: one; News: 3 hrs wkly. Target aud: General.

KZWB(FM)— 2005: 97.9 mhz; 10.5 kw. Ant 1,073 ft. TL: N41 29 47 W109 20 44. 40 Shoshone Ave. 82935. Phone: (307) 875-6666. Fax: (307) 875-5847. Licensee: Wagonwheel Communications Corp. ♦ Alan W. Harris, pres.

Greybull

KZMQ(AM)— May 20, 1979: 1140 khz; 10 kw-D. TL: N44 27 01 W108 02 56. Box 1210, 1949 Mountain View Dr., Cody 82414. Phone: (307) 578-5000. Fax: (307) 527-5045. E-mail: rgelder@bhrnway.com. Web Site: www.bighornradio.com. Licensee: Legend Communications of Wyoming L.L.C. Group owner: Legend Communications LLC (acq 1-27-98; $1.5 million with co-located FM). Format: Real country. Target aud: 25-49. ♦ Larry Patrick, pres; Roger Gelder, exec VP & gen mgr; Carol Kary, stn mgr & gen sls mgr; Rita Conners, opns dir & opns mgr;

Wyoming

Barbara Greene, sls VP & sls dir; Jerry Dunning, progmg dir; Mack Frost, news dir; Charlie Dozier, chief of engrg.

KZMQ-FM— Feb 21, 1986: 100.3 mhz; 56 kw. 2,443 ft. TL: N44 48 41 W107 55 06. Stereo. Format: Country. ◆ Carol Kary, gen mgr.

Guernsey

KANT(FM)— Not on air, target date: unknown: 104.1 mhz; 50 kw. Ant 417 ft. TL: N42 20 51 W105 01 54. White Park Broadcasting Inc., 288 S. River Rd., Bedford, NH 03110. Phone: (603) 668-6470. Licensee: White Park Broadcasting Inc. ◆ Steven A. Silberberg, pres & gen mgr.

Jackson

KJAX(FM)— 2000: 93.3 mhz; 100 kw. Ant 1,069 ft. TL: N43 27 40 W110 45 09. c/o KSGT(AM) and KMTN(FM), Box 100 83001. Phone: (307) 733-2120. Fax: (307) 733-4760. Licensee: Chaparral Broadcasting Inc. Group owner: Chaparral Communications (acq 3-29-2000; $393,787. for stock). Format: Country. ◆ Scott Anderson, gen mgr.

KMTN(FM)— Listing follows KSGT(AM).

*KNIL(FM)— Not on air, target date: unknown: 88.3 mhz; 2.35 kw. Ant 1,073 ft. TL: N43 27 40 W110 45 09. 6080 Mt. Moriah Ext., Memphis, TN 38115. Phone: (901) 375-9324. Licensee: Broadcasting for the Challenged Inc. ◆ George S. Flinn Jr., pres & gen mgr.

KSGT(AM)— July 20, 1962: 1340 khz; 1 kw-U. TL: N43 30 22 W110 45 16. Box 100 83001. Secondary address: 645 S. Cache St. 83001. Phone: (307) 733-2120. Fax: (307) 733-4760. Web Site: www.jacksonholeradio.com. Licensee: Chaparral Broadcasting Inc. (group owner; acq 11-30-92; $215,000 with KMER(AM) Kemmerer; 12-21-92). Network: ABC Information & Entertainment. Keck, Mahin & Cate. Format: Country. Target aud: 25 plus. ◆ Del Ray, progmg dir; Scott Anderson, gen mgr, opns VP, gen sls mgr, prom VP & chief of engrg.

KMTN(FM)— Co-owned with KSGT(AM). Dec 16, 1974: 96.9 mhz; 48 kw. 940 ft. TL: N43 27 42 W110 45 10. Stereo. Web Site: www.jacksonholeradio.com. Network: ABC. Format: AOR. Target aud: 18-54. ◆ Mark Fishman, progmg dir.

*KURT(FM)— Not on air, target date: unknown: 89.1 mhz; 2.2 kw. Ant 1,102 ft. TL: N43 27 40 W110 45 09. 6080 Mt. Moriah Ext., Memphis, TN 38115. Phone: (901) 375-9324. Licensee: Broadcasting for the Challenged Inc. ◆ George S. Flinn Jr., pres & gen mgr.

*KUWJ(FM)— November 1992: 90.3 mhz; 3 kw. 1,105 ft. TL: N43 27 40 W110 45 09. Stereo. Department 3984, 1000 E. University Ave., Laramie 82071. Phone: (307) 766-4240. Fax: (307) 766-6184. E-mail: wpr@uwyo.edu. Web Site: www.wyomingpublicradio.net. Licensee: University of Wyoming. Network: Network: NPR, PRI. Format: News, class, progsv. News staff: 3; News: 42 hrs wkly. Target aud: 25-54; educated, upper-income professionals. Spec prog: Folk 10 hrs, jazz 6 hrs, state news 3 hrs wkly. ◆ Jon B. Schwartz, gen mgr; Peg Arnold, dev dir & adv dir; Don Woods, mus dir; Bob Beck, news dir; Larry Dean, engrg dir.

KZJH(FM)— July 13, 1989: 95.3 mhz; 100 kw. 1,056 ft. TL: N43 27 40 W110 45 09. Box 2620 83001. Phone: (307) 733-1770. Fax: (307) 733-4760. E-mail: kz95@blissnet.com. Licensee: Chaparral Broadcasting Co. Group owner: Chaparral Communications (acq 8-25-00; $1.1 million). Network: ABC. Format: Classic rock. News staff: one. Target aud: 18-55. ◆ Scott Anderson, gen mgr & chief of engrg; Silver Jacobson, gen sls mgr; Jay Martin, progmg dir; Brian Karre, mus dir; Dee Dee Dudley, news dir.

Kemmerer

KAOX(FM)— Oct. 1, 1999: 107.3 mhz; 16 kw. Ant 886 ft. TL: N41 50 18 W110 30 12. Stereo. Box 432, c/o KMER (AM) 83101. Secondary address: 436 Fossil Butte 83101. Phone: (307) 877-4422. Fax: (307) 877-5537. E-mail: kmer@onewest.net. Licensee: Simmons-SLC, LS LLC. Group owner: Simmons Media Group (acq 4-19-2004; grpsl). Network: CBS. Format: Adult standards. News staff: one; News: 2 hrs wkly. Target aud: 35 plus; male / female. ◆ Jim Carroll, gen mgr; Jim Thoeny, chief of opns.

KMER(AM)— Dec 7, 1962: 950 khz; 5 kw-D, 500 w-N. TL: N41 47 57 W110 32 44. Box 432 83101. Secondary address: 436 Fossil Butte Dr.

83101. Phone: (307) 877-4422. Fax: (307) 877-5537. E-mail: kmer@onewest.net. Licensee: Simmons-SLC, LS LLC. Group owner: Simmons Media Group (acq 5-20-2004; grpsl). Network: ABC Information & Entertainment. Format: Oldies. News staff: one; News: one hr wkly. Target aud: 25-54. Spec prog: News/talk 7 hrs, farm 3 hrs wkly. ◆ Jim Carroll, gen mgr; Jim Thoeny, opns dir.

Lander

KDLY(FM)— Listing follows KOVE(AM).

KOVE(AM)— 1947: 1330 khz; 5 kw-D, 1 kw-N, DA-N. TL: N42 50 35 W108 44 38. 1530 Main St. 82520. Phone: (307) 332-5683. Fax: (307) 332-5548. E-mail: radio1@wyoming.com. Web Site: www.kovekdly.com. Licensee: Fremont Broadcasting Inc. Network: CBS. Format: C&W. Target aud: 25 plus. Spec prog: Talk 15 hrs wkly. ◆ Joe Kenney, pres, gen mgr, gen sls mgr & progmg dir; Leslie Myers, news dir; Lincoln Scott, chief of engrg.

Laramie

*KAIW(FM)— Not on air, target date: unknown: 88.9 mhz; 400 w. Ant 645 ft. TL: N41 17 46 W105 53 30. 5700 West Oaks Blvd., Rocklin, CA 95765. Phone: (916) 251-1600. Fax: (916) 251-1650. Licensee: Educational Media Foundation. ◆ Lloyd Parker, gen mgr.

KARS-FM— Sept 23, 1974: 102.9 mhz; 100 kw. Ant 1,220 ft. TL: N41 18 39 W105 27 12. Stereo. 600 Main St., Windsor, CO 80550. Phone: (970) 686-2791. Fax: (970) 686-7491. Licensee: Regent Broadcasting of Ft. Collins Inc. Group owner: Regent Communications Inc. (acq 1-8-2004; $7.75 million. with KKPL(FM) Cheyenne). Format: Classic rock. Target aud: 18-44. ◆ K.W. Graybow, progmg dir.

KCGY(FM)— Nov 7, 1983: 95.1 mhz; 100 kw. 1,070 ft. TL: N41 18 34 W105 27 11. Stereo. Box 1290 82073. Secondary address: 3525 Soldier Springs Rd. 82070. Phone: (307) 745-4888. Fax: (307) 742-4576. Licensee: Clear Channel Broadcasting Licenses Inc. Group owner: Clear Channel Communications Inc. (acq 4-15-2002). Format: Mainstream country. ◆ Andrew W. Hoefer, gen mgr; Larry Lindstrom, gen sls mgr; John Campbell, progmg dir; Cliff Nikkolson, chief of engrg; Jim Mross, chief of engrg.

KHAT(AM)— Feb 27, 1962: 1210 khz; 10 kw-D, 1 kw-N, DA-N. TL: N41 15 19 W105 33 01. Stereo. 302 S. 2nd St., Suite 204 82070. Phone: (307) 745-5208. Fax: (307) 745-8570. E-mail: mix105@fiberpipe.net. Licensee: Appaloosa Broadcasting Co. Group owner: Northeast Broadcasting Company Inc. (acq 3-2-2004; $160,000). Network: CBS. Format: Classic country, news. Target aud: 25-54. Spec prog: Farm one hr wkly. ◆ Dan Conway, gen mgr, opns mgr & gen sls mgr; Tammy Foster, mktg dir; Reed Fletcher, chief of engrg.

KHIH(FM)— Not on air, target date: unknown: 98.7 mhz; 110 w. Ant 1,073 ft. TL: N41 18 39 W105 27 12. 6807 Foxglove Dr., Cheyenne 82009. Phone: (307) 778-9318. Fax: (307) 745-8570. Licensee: Laramie Mountain Broadcasting LLC. (acq 4-18-2005; $750,000 for CP with KVUW(FM) Wendover, NV).

KIMX(FM)— 2002: 96.7 mhz; 6.5 kw. Ant 932 ft. TL: N41 17 07 W105 26 41. 302 S. 2nd St., Suite 204 82070. Phone: (307) 745-5208. Fax: (307) 745-8570. Licensee: Appaloosa Broadcasting Co. Inc. Group owner: Northeast Broadcasting Company Inc. (acq 11-12-03; $775,000). Format: Adult contemp. ◆ Dan Conway, gen mgr, opns mgr & gen sls mgr; Tammy Foster, mktg dir; Eric Monocle, progmg dir; Reed Fletcher, chief of engrg.

KOWB(AM)— Feb 20, 1948: 1290 khz; 5 kw-D, 1 kw-N, DA-2. TL: N41 17 02 W105 34 51. Box 1290 82073. Secondary address: 3525 Soldier Springs Rd. 82070. Phone: (307) 745-4888. Fax: (307) 742-4576. Licensee: Clear Channel Broadcasting Licenses Inc. Group owner: Clear Channel Communications Inc. (acq 4-15-2002; $850,000). Network: ABC Information & Entertainment. Rep: Keystone (unwired net). Format: News/talk, sports. News staff: one; News: 7 hrs wkly. Target aud: 25-54. ◆ Andrew W. Hoefer, gen mgr; Larry Lindstrom, gen sls mgr; Dwight Gulley, progmg dir & progmg mgr; Will Maxwell, pub affrs dir; Matt Schilz, engrg mgr; Chris Nikkelson, chief of engrg; Jim Mross, chief of engrg.

KRQU(FM)— 2000: 104.5 mhz; 3 kw. Ant 951 ft. TL: N41 17 08 W105 26 41. 302 S. 2nd St., Suite 204 82070. Phone: (307) 745-5208. Fax: (307) 745-8570. E-mail: mix105@fiberpipe.net. Licensee: Laramie Mountain Broadcasting LLC. Group owner: Kona Coast Radio LLC (acq 6-20-2002). Format: Classic rock and roll. ◆ Dan Conway, gen

mgr, opns mgr & gen sls mgr; Tammy Foster, mktg dir; Eric Monocle, progmg dir; Reed Fletcher, chief of engrg.

*KUWR(FM)— Sept 10, 1966: 91.9 mhz; 100 kw. 1,128 ft. TL: N41 18 39 W105 27 12. Stereo. Department 3984, 1000 E. University Ave. 82071. Phone: (307) 766-4240. Fax: (307) 766-6184. E-mail: wpr@uwyo.edu. Web Site: www.wyomingpublicradio.net. Licensee: University of Wyoming. Network: Network: NPR, PRI. Format: News, progsv, class. News staff: 3; News: 42 hrs wkly. Target aud: 25-54; educated, college graduates, professionals, upper income. Spec prog: Folk 10 hrs, jazz 6 hrs, state news 3 hrs wkly. ◆ Jon Schwartz, gen mgr; Don Woods, dev VP & mus dir; Peg Arnold, dev dir, sls dir & adv dir; Roger Adams, prom mgr & progmg dir; Bob Beck, news dir; Larry Dean, chief of engrg.

Lost Cabin

KWYW(FM)— 2001: 99.1 mhz; 50 kw. Ant 1,896 ft. TL: N43 26 18 W107 59 37. 320 Senior Ave., Thermopolis 82443. Phone: (307) 864-2119. Fax: (307) 864-3937. E-mail: kthe@directairnet.com. Licensee: Jimmy Ray Carroll. Group owner: Jimmy Ray Carroll Stns (acq 6-25-01; $30,000. for CP). Format: Adult contemp. ◆ Jimmy Ray Carroll, pres; Dick Howe, gen mgr & progmg dir; Amber Phipps, news dir.

Lovell

KROW(FM)— Not on air, target date: unknown: 107.1 mhz; 64 kw. Ant 2,375 ft. TL: N44 48 38 W107 55 18. 288 S. River Rd., Bedford, NH 03110. Phone: (603) 668-6470. Licensee: White Park Broadcasting Inc. ◆ Steven A. Silberberg, pres & gen mgr.

Marbleton

KFMR(FM)— Not on air, target date: unknown: 95.7 mhz; 7 kw. Ant 1,394 ft. TL: N42 19 28 W110 19 12. Box 36148, Tucson, AZ 85740. Phone: (520) 797-4434. Licensee: Skywest Media L.L.C. ◆ Ted Tucker, gen mgr.

Midwest

KRVK(FM)— 2001: 107.9 mhz; 100 kw. Ant 1,948 ft. TL: N42 44 37 W106 18 26. 150 N. Nichols, Casper 82601. Phone: (307) 266-5252. Fax: (307) 235-9143. E-mail: krvk@clearchannel.com. Web Site: theriver1079.com. Licensee: Clear Channel Broadcasting Licenses Inc. Group owner: Clear Channel Communications Inc. (acq 3-28-01). Format: Classic rock. ◆ Robert Price, gen mgr; Donovan Short, progmg dir; Dave Nutter, chief of engrg.

Mills

KHAD(FM)— Not on air, target date: unknown: 105.5 mhz; 3.4 kw. Ant 1,683 ft. TL: N42 44 30 W106 18 29. 288 S. River Rd., Bedford, NH 03110. Phone: (603) 668-6470. Licensee: White Park Broadcasting Inc. ◆ Steven A. Silberberg, pres & gen mgr.

Newcastle

KASL(AM)— July 10, 1953: 1240 khz; 1 kw-U. TL: N43 50 47 W104 12 45. 933 W. Main St. 82701. Phone: (307) 746-4433. Fax: (307) 746-4435. E-mail: kasl@vcn.com. Licensee: KASL L.L.C. (acq 7-28-99; $125,000). Network: ABC Information & Entertainment. Smithwick & Belendiuk. Format: C&W. News staff: one; News: 35 hrs wkly. Target aud: General; town & county residents, children through adults. Spec prog: Farm 5 hrs, relg 2 hrs wkly. ◆ Val Cook, CEO, gen mgr, opns mgr, gen sls mgr & adv mgr; Ed Schlup, progmg dir; Jay Ingalls, chief of engrg.

KRKI(FM)— 2003: 99.5 mhz; 400 w. Ant 146 ft. TL: N43 49 57 W104 13 08. Box 969 82701. Secondary address: 1807 W. Main St. 82701. Phone: (307) 746-9614. Licensee: Michael Radio Group. ◆ Dick Hinker, gen mgr.

*KUWN(FM)— 1998: 90.5 mhz; 400 w. 203 ft. TL: N43 49 57 W104 13 08. Department 3984, 1000 E. University Ave., Laramie 82071. Phone: (307) 766-4240. Fax: (307) 766-6184. E-mail: wpr@uwyo.edu. Web Site: www.wyomingpublicradio.net. Licensee: University of Wyoming. Format: News, progsv, class. ◆ Jon Schwartz, gen mgr; Peg Arnold, dev dir, sls dir & adv dir; Roger Adams, progmg dir; Don Woods, mus dir; Bob Beck, news dir; Larry Dean, chief of engrg.

Wyoming

Developers & Brokers of Radio Properties
contact American Media Services at our suite:
Philadelphia Marriott Downtown
215-625-2900
843-972-2200
americanmediaservices.com
Charleston, SC
Dallas, TX · Chicago, Il · Austin, TX
American Media Services, LLC

Orchard Valley

KGAB(AM)—Licensed to Orchard Valley. See Cheyenne

*KWYC(FM)—Not on air, target date: unknown: 90.3 mhz; 20 kw. Ant 425 ft. TL: N41 13 01 W104 26 53. Stereo. CSN International, 4002 N. 3300 E., Twin Falls, ID 83301. Phone: (208) 734-6633. Fax: (208) 736-1958. Licensee: CSN International. (group owner; (acq 1-9-2004; $1. for CP). Format: Contemp Chrisitan talk.

Pine Bluffs

KJJL(AM)—Not on air, target date: unknown: 540 khz; 900 w-D, 700 w-N, DA-2. TL: N41 11 13 W104 11 05. 965 S. Irving St., Denver 80219. Phone: (303) 935-1156. Licensee: Timothy C. Cutforth. ♦ Timothy C. Cutforth, gen mgr.

KREO(FM)— December 2000: 105.3 mhz; 400 w. Ant 157 ft. TL: N41 09 55 W104 04 31. (CP: 6 kw, ant 249 ft. TL: N41 17 17 W104 00 21). Stereo. 2109 E. 10th St., Cheyenne 82001. Phone: (307) 638-8921. Fax: (307) 638-8922. E-mail: news@1049krrr.com. Licensee: Chisholm Trail Broadcasting LLC Group owner: Northeast Broadcasting Company Inc. (acq 2-25-2005; $850,000. with KKAW(FM) Albin). Format: Oldies. Target aud: 25-54. ♦ Larry Proietti, gen mgr.

Pinedale

KPIN(FM)— December 1997: 101.1 mhz; 211 w. -180 ft. TL: N42 51 59 W109 52 08. Box 2000 82941. Phone: (307) 367-2000. Fax: (307) 367-3300. E-mail: kpin@wyoming.com. Licensee: Robert R. Rule dba Rule Communications. Format: Country, oldies. ♦ Robert R. Rule, gen mgr.

*KUWX(FM)— 2000: 90.9 mhz; 450 w. Ant 440 ft. TL: N42 50 40 W109 55 24. Department 3984, 1000 E. Wyoming Ave., Laramie 82071. Phone: (307) 766-4240. Fax: (307) 766-6184. E-mail: wpr@uwyo.edu. Web Site: www.wyomingpublicradio.net. Licensee: University of Wyoming. Format: News, progsv, class. ♦ Jon Schwartz, gen mgr; Peg Arnold, dev dir, sls dir & adv dir; Roger Adams, progmg dir; Don Woods, mus dir; Bob Beck, news dir; Larry Dean, chief of engrg.

Powell

KCGL(FM)— Nov 26, 2001: 104.1 mhz; 100 kw. Ant 1,942. TL: N44 29 46 W109 09 16. Box 1210, Cody 82414. Secondary address: 1949 Mountain View Dr., Cody 82414. Phone: (307) 578-5000. Fax: (307) 527-5045. E-mail: rgelder@bhmwy.com. Licensee: Legend Communications of Wyoming LLC. Group owner: Legend Communications L.L.C. (acq 4-3-02; $450,000). Format: Classic rock. ♦ Larry Patrick, pres; Roger Gelder, exec VP; Carol Kary, VP, gen mgr & sls dir; Donny Anderson, progmg dir; Charles Dozler, chief of engrg.

KLZY(FM)—Listing follows KPOW(AM).

KPOW(AM)— Mar 30, 1941: 1260 khz; 5 kw-D, 1 kw-N, DA-N. TL: N44 42 00 W108 46 00. Box 968 82435. Secondary address: 912 Ln. 11 1/2 82435. Phone: (307) 754-5183. Phone: (307) 527-5949. Fax: (307) 754-9667. E-mail: kpow-z92@wir.net. Licensee: Chaparral Broadcasting Inc. Group owner: Chaparral Communications (acq 11-30-92; $215,000 with co-located FM; 12-21-92). Network: ABC Information & Entertainment. Keck, Mahin & Cate. Format: News, Talk. News: 38 hrs wkly. Target aud: 29-64. Spec prog: Farm 19 hrs wkly. ♦ Scott Anderson, gen mgr, progmg mgr & chief of engrg; Scott Mangold, sls dir & news dir.

KLZY(FM)—Co-owned with KPOW(AM). May 15, 1982: . Stn currently dark 92.5 mhz; 100 kw. 1,857 ft. TL: N44 29 49 W109 09 19. Stereo. NOT IN OPERATION, Powell-Cody Phone: (307) 754-5186. Network: ABC Daytime Direction. Format: Hot country. News: 4 hrs wkly. Target aud: 17-49. ♦ Russ Graham, progmg dir; Jim Estabrook, mus dir.

*KUWP(FM)— 2000: 90.1 mhz; 430 w. Ant 1,624 ft. TL: N44 35 14 W108 51 08. Department 3984, 1000 E. Wyoming Ave., Laramie 82071. Phone: (307) 766-4240. Fax: (307) 766-6184(. E-mail: wpr@uwyo.edu. Web Site: www.wyomingpublicradio.net. Licensee: University of Wyoming. Format: News, progsv, class. ♦ Jon Schwartz, gen mgr; Peg Arnold, dev dir, sls dir & adv dir; Roger Adams, progmg dir; Don Woods, mus dir; Bob Beck, news dir; Larry Dean, chief of engrg.

Powell-Cody

KLZY(FM)—Licensed to Powell-Cody. See Powell

Rawlins

KIQZ(FM)—Listing follows KRAL(AM).

KRAL(AM)— February 1947: 1240 khz; 1 kw-U. TL: N41 46 55 W107 15 40. 2346 W. Spruce 82301. Phone: (307) 324-3315. Fax: (307) 324-3509. E-mail: jackmorgan@vcn.com. Web Site: www.kiqz-kral.com. Licensee: Mount Rushmore Broadcasting Inc. (group owner; (acq 8-6-93; $80,000. with co-located FM; FTR: 8-23-93). Network: ABC. Format: Adult contemp. Target aud: 14 plus. ♦ Jack Morgan, progmg dir & news dir.

KIQZ(FM)—Co-owned with KRAL(AM). Nov 12, 1981: 92.7 mhz; 3 kw. Ant 298 ft. TL: N41 46 16 W107 14 15. Stereo. Web Site: www.kiqz-kral.com.

Riverton

*KCWC-FM— March 1974: 88.1 mhz; 3 kw. 1,449 ft. TL: N42 34 59 W108 42 36. Stereo. 2660 Peck Ave. 82501. Phone: (307) 855-2121. Phone: (307) 855-2268. Fax: (307) 856-3893. E-mail: dsmith@cwc.com. Licensee: Central Wyoming College. Format: Jazz, new age, progsv. ♦ JoAnne McFarland, pres; Dale Smith, stn mgr.

KTAK(FM)—Listing follows KVOW(AM).

KTRZ(FM)— Dec 4, 1984: 93.1 mhz; 100 kw. 884 ft. TL: N42 43 10 W108 08 41. Stereo. Box 808 82501. Secondary address: 1002 N. 8th West 82501. Phone: (307) 856-2922. Fax: (307) 856-7552. E-mail: ktrz@tcinc.net. Web Site: www.ktrzfm.com. Licensee: Jimmy Ray Carroll. Group owner: Jimmy Ray Carroll Stns (acq 4-1-02). Network: CNN Radio. Pepper & Corazzini. Format: Classic & modern rock. News staff: one; News: 2 hrs wkly. Target aud: 25 plus; rgnl/loc tourists, agribusiness, core population. ♦ Jim Carroll, CEO; Smokey Wildeman, gen mgr & stn mgr; Dan Preston, opns mgr.

KVOW(AM)— July 2, 1948: 1450 khz; 1 kw-U. TL: N43 01 35 W108 20 45. 603 E. Pershing Ave. 82501. Phone: (307) 856-2251. Fax: (307) 856-0252. E-mail: kvow@wyoming.com. Web Site: www.kvowradio.com. Licensee: Edwards Communications L.C. (group owner; (acq 6-22-99; $875,000. with co-located FM). Network: ABC Information & Entertainment. Format: Info, oldies. Spec prog: Farm 5 hrs wkly. ♦ Larry Cross, gen mgr & gen sls mgr; Jeff Kehl, progmg dir & news dir; Lonnie Fairfield, chief of engrg.

KTAK(FM)—Co-owned with KVOW(AM). Dec 15, 1976: 93.9 mhz; 50 kw. 951 ft. TL: N42 43 10 W108 08 45. Stereo. E-mail: ktak@wyoming.com. Web Site: www.ktakradio.com. Network: ABC Information & Entertainment. Format: Country.

Rock River

KVAN(FM)—Not on air, target date: unknown: 95.9 mhz; 3.4 kw. Ant 440 ft. TL: N41 42 24 W105 54 48. 6807 Foxglove Dr., Cheyenne 82009. Phone: (307) 778-9318. Fax: (307) 632-9349. Licensee: Kona Coast Radio LLC. ♦ Victor A. Michael Jr., gen mgr.

Rock Springs

KQSW(FM)—Listing follows KRKK(AM).

KRKK(AM)— 1938: 1360 khz; 5 kw-D, 1 kw-N, DA-N. TL: N41 37 12 W109 14 20. Box 2128 82902. Secondary address: 2717 Yellowstone Rd. 82901. Phone: (307) 362-3793. Fax: (307) 362-8727. E-mail: wyoradio@wyoradio.com. Web Site: www.wyoradio.com. Licensee: Big Thicket Broadcasting Co. of Wyoming Inc. (acq 1996). Format: Oldies. ♦ Bill Luzmoore, pres, pres & progmg dir; Jon Collins, gen mgr & chief of engrg; Tom Ellis, gen sls mgr; Doug Randall, news dir.

KQSW(FM)—Co-owned with KRKK(AM). January 1977: 96.5 mhz; 100 kw. 1,680 ft. TL: N41 25 54 W109 07 01. Format: Country.

KSIT(FM)— October 1981: 104.5 mhz; 100 kw. 1,630 ft. TL: N41 26 00 W109 07 02. Stereo. Box 2128 82902. Secondary address: 2717 Yellowstone Rd. 82902. Phone: (307) 362-7034. Phone: (307) 362-3793. Fax: (307) 362-8727. Web Site: www.wyoradio.com. Licensee: Big Thicket Broadcasting Company of W. (acq 12-1-84). Arent, Fox, Kintner, Plotkin & Kahn. Format: Classic rock. News staff: one; News: 10 hrs wkly. Target aud: 18-45; general. ♦ Bill Luzmoor, pres; John Collins, gen mgr, opns mgr & chief of engrg; Tom Ellis, gen sls mgr & prom mgr; Bill Luzmoore, progmg dir.

*KUWZ(FM)— November 1994: 90.5 mhz; 100 kw. 1,135 ft. TL: N41 29 47 W109 20 47. Stereo. Department 3984, 1000E. Wyoming Ave., Laramie 82071. Phone: (307) 766-4240. Fax: (307) 766-6184. E-mail: wpr@uwyo.edu. Web Site: www.wyomingpublicradio.net. Licensee: University of Wyoming. (group owner) Network: Network: NPR, PRI. Format: Class, progsv, news. News staff: 3; News: 52 hrs wkly. Target aud: 25-54; college graduates, professionals, mgrs, upper income. Spec prog: Folk 10 hrs, jazz 6 hrs, state news 3 hrs wkly. ♦ Jon Schwartz, gen mgr; Peg Arnold, dev dir, sls dir & adv dir; Roger Adams, progmg dir; Don Woods, mus dir; Bob Beck, news dir; Larry Dean, engrg dir & chief of engrg.

KYCS(FM)— Oct 1, 1986: 95.1 mhz; 100 kw. 1,635 ft. TL: N41 29 50 W109 20 36. Stereo. 40 Shoshone Ave., Green River 82902. Phone: (307) 362-6746. Fax: (307) 875-5847. E-mail: kugr@sweetwater.net. Web Site: www.theradionetwork.net. Licensee: Faith Broadcasting Corporation. Format: Top-40. ♦ Faith Harris, pres; Steve Core, gen mgr; Jeff Driggs, gen sls mgr; Al Harris, mus dir & chief of engrg.

Saratoga

KTGA(FM)—Not on air, target date: unknown: 99.3 mhz; 30 kw. Ant -7 ft. TL: N41 28 24 W106 44 56. 3611 Cherry Hill Dr., Greensboro, NC 27410. Phone: (336) 286-2087. Licensee: United States CP LLC. ♦ W. Philip Robinson, gen mgr.

Sheridan

*KOHR(FM)— 2004: 88.7 mhz; 500 w. Ant 7 ft. TL: N44 47 54 W106 55 51. Box 2426, Hevre, MT 59501. Phone: (406) 265-5845. Fax: (406) 265-8860. Licensee: Hi-Line Radio Fellowship Inc. (acq 7-31-2003; $10,000. for CP). Format: Christian Inspirational. ♦ Ed Matter, gen mgr; Brenda Boyum, opns mgr; Roger Lonnquist, dev dir; Brian Jackson, progmg dir.

*KPRQ(FM)—Not on air, target date: unknown: 88.1 mhz; 450 w. Ant 1,118 ft. TL: N44 37 26 W107 07 02. Montana State University-Billings, 1500 N. 30th St., Billings, MT 59101. Phone: (406) 657-2941. Fax: (406) 657-2977. Web Site: www.yellowstonepublicradio.org. Licensee: Montana State University-Billings. ♦ Marvin Granger, gen mgr.

KROE(AM)— Mar 18, 1961: 930 khz; 5 kw-D, 117 w-N. TL: N44 47 54 W106 55 51. Box 5086 82801. Secondary address: 1716 KROE Ln. 82801. Phone: (307) 672-7421. Fax: (307) 672-2933. E-mail: kimlove@sheridanmedia.com. Web Site: www.sheridanmedia.com. Licensee: Lovcom Inc. (group owner). Network: CBS. Rep: Target Broadcast Sales. Pepper & Corazzini. Format: Oldies, div, news/talk. News staff: one; News: 20 hrs wkly. Target aud: 25-54; general. ♦ Kim Love, pres & gen mgr; Steve Sisson, opns dir; Jim Schellinger, gen sls mgr; Nick Tyler, progmg dir; Clark Jessop, news dir; Tony Cuesta, engrg mgr & chief of engrg.

Broadcasting & Cable Yearbook 2006

Wyoming

KZWY(FM)—Co-owned with KROE(AM). December 1977: 94.9 mhz; 75 kw. 1,207 ft. TL: N44 37 20 W107 06 57. Stereo. E-mail: info@sheridanmedia.com. Web Site: www.sheridanmedia.com. Format: Classic rock. Target aud: 18-49; general. ♦Steve Sisson, chief of opns; Tony Cuesta, chief of engrg.

*KSUW(FM)— 1998: 91.3 mhz; 450 w. 1,161 ft. TL: N44 56 09 W106 55 51. Department 3984, 1000 E. Wyoming Ave., Laramie 82071. Phone: (307) 766-4240. Fax: (307) 766-6184. E-mail: wpr@uwyo.edu. Web Site: www.wyomingpublicradio.net. Licensee: University of Wyoming. Format: News, progsv, class. ♦Jon Schwartz, gen mgr; Peg Arnold, dev dir & adv dir; Roger Adams, progmg dir; Don Woods, mus dir; Bob Beck, news dir; Larry Dean, chief of engrg.

*KWCF(FM)—Not on air, target date: unknown: 88.9 mhz; 1 kw. Ant 961 ft. TL: N44 36 10 W106 55 42. CSN International, 3232 W. MacArthur Blvd., Santa Ana, CA 92704. Phone: (714) 825-9663. Fax: (714) 825-9660. Web Site: www.calvarychapel.org. Licensee: CSN International (group owner). ♦Mike Kestler, pres; Jeff Smith, VP; Mike Stocklin, opns dir; Don Mills, progmg dir; Kelly Carlson, engrg dir.

KWYO(AM)— July 9, 1934: 1410 khz; 5 kw-D, 500 w-N. TL: N44 46 15 W106 55 37. Box 5087 82801. Secondary address: 1716 Kroe Ln 82801. Phone: (307) 672-0701. Fax: (307) 672-2933. Web Site: www.sheridanmedia.com. Licensee: Lovcom Inc. (group owner; acq 9-11-03). Network: ABC Information & Entertainment. Pepper & Corazzini. Format: adult standards. News staff: one; News: 20 hrs wkly. Target aud: 25-54. ♦W.K. Love, pres; Kim Love, gen mgr; Bob Grammens, opns VP; Steve Sisson, opns mgr; Jim Schellinger, gen sls mgr; Michael Gallagher, progmg dir; Tony Cuesta, chief of engrg.

KYTI(FM)— September 1978: 93.7 mhz; 75 kw. 1,207 ft. TL: N44 37 20 W107 06 57. Stereo. Box 5086, 1716 KROE Ln 82801. Phone: (307) 672-7421. Fax: (307) 672-2933. Web Site: www.sheridanmedia.com. Licensee: Lovcom Inc. (group owner; acq 5-15-97). Network: ABC. Format: Country. News: 4 hrs wkly. Target aud: 25-50. ♦Kim Love, gen mgr & opns mgr; Jim Schellinger, gen sls mgr; Nick Tyler, progmg dir; Clark Jessop, news dir; Tony Cuesta, chief of engrg.

Story

KZZS(FM)— Nov 13, 2003: 98.3 mhz; 100 kw. Ant 272 ft. TL: N44 34 32 W106 52 23. Stereo. 1221 Fort St., Buffalo 82834. Secondary address: 610 Illinois St., Buffalo 82834. Phone: (307) 684-7070. Fax: (307) 684-7676. Web Site: www.kzzsradio.com. Licensee: Legend Communications of Wyoming L.L.C. Group owner: Legend Communications LLC. (acq 5-31-00; $200,000. for CP). Format: Hot adult hits. News staff: one; News: 6 hrs wkly. Target aud: 18-35. ♦Larry Patrick, CEO & pres; Roger Gelder, COO; Travis Reeves, VP, gen mgr & stn mgr; Ed Cwik, opns mgr & progmg dir; Robin Harnden, sls dir; Aaron Lee, news dir; Charles Dozier, engrg VP & engrg dir.

Sundance

*KUWD(FM)— 2000: 91.5 mhz; 430 w. Ant 1,591 ft. TL: N44 28 35 W104 26 54. Department 3984, 1000 E. Wyoming Ave., Laramie 82071. Phone: (307) 766-4240. Fax: (307) 766-6184. E-mail: wpr@uwyo.edu. Web Site: www.wyomingpublicradio.net. Licensee: University of Wyoming. Format: News, progsv, class. ♦Jon Schwartz, gen mgr; Peg Arnold, dev dir, sls dir & adv dir; Roger Adams, progmg dir; Don Woods, mus dir; Bob Beck, news dir; Larry Dean, chief of engrg.

KYDT(FM)— November 1997: 103.1 mhz; 25.2 kw. 1,650 ft. TL: N44 28 35 W104 26 54. Stereo. Box 787, Belle Fourche, SD 57717. Phone: (605) 892-2571. Fax: (605) 892-2573. E-mail: wyodak@hotmail.com. Web Site: www.kydt.com. Licensee: Ultimate Caps Inc. Network: Network: ESPN Radio, Westwood One, AP Network News. Format: Country, sports, news, talk. News: 25 hrs wkly. Target aud: General; rural, suburban, country mus, sports fans. ♦Cynthia Grimmelmann, pres; Karl Grimmelmann, exec VP, gen mgr & opns VP.

Thayne

KTYN(FM)—Not on air, target date: unknown: 105.9 mhz; 370 w. Ant 2,332 ft. TL: N43 06 18 W111 07 17. College Creek Broadcasting Inc., 980 N. Michigan Ave., Suite 1875, Chicago, IL 60611. Phone: (312) 204-9900. Licensee: College Creek Broadcasting Inc. ♦Neal J. Robinson, pres & gen mgr.

Thermopolis

KDNO(FM)— Aug 30, 2001: 101.7 mhz; 16.25 kw. Ant 1,901 ft. TL: N43 26 18 W107 59 37. Box 591 82443-0501. Secondary address: 320 Senior Ave. 82443. Phone: (307) 864-2119. Fax: (307) 864-3937. E-mail: kthe@directairnet.com. Licensee: Carjim LLC. Group owner: Jimmy Ray Carroll Stns (acq 9-13-2001; $20,000. for CP). Format: Classic country. ♦Jim Carroll, pres; Dick Howe, gen mgr, gen sls mgr & progmg dir; Amber Phipps, news dir.

KTHE(AM)— April 1957: 1240 khz; 1 kw-U. TL: N43 38 42 W108 12 15. Box 591 82443-0591. Secondary address: 320 Senior Ave. 82443. Phone: (307) 864-2119. Fax: (307) 864-3937. E-mail: kthe@directairnet.com. Licensee: Carjim LLC. Group owner: Jimmy Ray Carroll Stns (acq 5-7-2002). Format: Adult contemp, oldies. Target aud: 25-54; varied. ♦Jim Carroll, pres; Dick Howe, gen mgr, gen sls mgr & progmg dir; Amber Phipps, news dir; Joyce Howe, chief of engrg.

KUWT(FM)— 2001: 91.3 mhz; 450 w. Ant 253 ft. TL: N43 39 07 W108 15 07. Department 3984, 1000 E. Wyoming Ave., Laramie 82071. Phone: (307) 766-4240. Fax: 307 766-6184. E-mail: wpr@uwyo.edu. Web Site: www.wyomingpublicradio.net. Licensee: University of Wyoming. Format: News, progsv, class. ♦Jon Schwartz, gen mgr; Peg Arnold, dev dir, sls dir & adv dir; Roger Adams, progmg dir; Don Woods, mus dir; Bob Beck, news dir; Larry Dean, chief of engrg.

Torrington

KERM(FM)—Listing follows KGOS(AM).

KGOS(AM)— May 15, 1950: 1490 khz; 1 kw-U. TL: N42 04 20 W104 13 40. Box 40 82240. Secondary address: Rt. 2 & Radio Rd. 82240. Phone: (307) 532-2158. Fax: (307) 532-2641. Licensee: Mount Rushmore Broadcasting Inc. (group owner). Network: ABC Information & Entertainment. Art Moore. Format: Country. News staff: one; News: 20 hrs wkly. Target aud: 20 plus; general. Spec prog: Sp one hr, farm 20 hrs wkly. ♦Grant Kath, gen mgr & gen sls mgr; Greg Kath, gen mgr, opns mgr & progmg dir.

KERM(FM)—Co-owned with KGOS(AM). Dec 15, 1976: 98.3 mhz; 3 kw. Ant 300 ft. TL: N41 59 41 W104 12 05. Stereo.

West Laramie

*KRWT(FM)—Not on air, target date: unknown: 89.9 mhz; 100 kw vert. Ant 571 ft. TL: N41 54 19 W106 32 37. CSN International, 4002 N. 3300 E., Twin Falls, ID 83301. Phone: (208) 734-6633. Fax: (208) 736-1958. Web Site: www.csnradio.com. Licensee: CSN International (group owner). Format: Contemp Christian talk.

Wheatland

KYCN(AM)— Nov 16, 1960: 1340 khz; 250 w-U. TL: N42 02 44 W104 56 47. Box 248 82201. Secondary address: 450 E. Cole 32201. Phone: (307) 322-5926. Phone: (307) 322-5927. Fax: (307) 322-9300. E-mail: info@kycn-kzew.com. Web Site: www.kycn-kzew.com. Licensee: Smith Broadcasting Inc. (acq 12-6-91; with co-located FM). Network: ABC. Rep: Target Broadcast Sales. Bryan Cave. Format: Country. News staff: one; News: 14 hrs wkly. Target aud: General. Spec prog: Farm 7 hrs wkly. ♦Catherine Smith, gen sls mgr, mktg mgr, prom mgr & adv mgr; Derek Barton, news dir; Kent G. Smith, pres, gen mgr, mus dir & chief of engrg.

KZEW(FM)—Co-owned with KYCN(AM). February 1985: 101.7 mhz; 3 kw. 156 ft. TL: N42 02 44 W104 56 47. Stereo. Web Site: www.kycn-kzew.com. Network: Jones Radio Networks. Format: Adult contemp. ♦Kent G. Smith, chief of opns, progmg dir & pub affrs dir.

Worland

KKLX(FM)—Listing follows KWOR(AM).

KWOR(AM)— Mar 7, 1946: 1340 khz; 1 kw-U. TL: N44 01 01 W107 58 14. 1340 Radio Dr. 82401. Phone: (307) 347-3231. Fax: (307) 347-4880. E-mail: kwor@rtconnect.net. Web Site: www.kworkklx.com. Licensee: KWOR Inc. (acq 3-21-97; $265,000 with co-located FM). Network: ABC Information & Entertainment. Eugene T. Smith. Format: Oldies. Target aud: General. ♦Bill Harrington, gen mgr, progmg dir & progmg dir; Tony Cuesta, chief of engrg.

Directory of Radio

KKLX(FM)—Co-owned with KWOR(AM). Dec 1, 1980: 96.1 mhz; 50 kw. 400 ft. TL: N44 04 06 W107 51 57. Stereo. Network: ABC Information & Entertainment. Format: Mus of the 80s & 90s & today.

American Samoa

Leone

KNWJ(FM)— 2001: 104.7 mhz; 280 w. Ant 1,499 ft. TL: N14 19 21 W170 45 47. Stereo. Box 997777, Pago Pago 96799. Phone: (684) 699-8123. E-mail: info@fm104.org. Web Site: www.fm104.org. Licensee: Showers of Blessings Radio (acq 5-26-00; $70,000. for CP). Format: Today's Christian hits. ♦Dan Dalle, gen mgr.

Pago Pago

KKHJ(FM)— May 1, 2000: 93.1 mhz; 420 w. Ant 1,489 ft. TL: N14 16 12 W170 41 10. Stereo. Box 6758 96799. Phone: (684) 633-7793. Phone: (702) 898-4669. Fax: (684) 633-4493. Fax: (208) 567-6865. Web Site: www.983khj.fm. Licensee: South Seas Broadcasting. Group owner: Contemporary Communications. Wood, Maines & Brown, Chartered. Format: CHR. News staff: one. Target aud: General. ♦Larry G. Fuss, pres; Joey Cummings, gen mgr.

KSBS-FM— Apr 14, 1988: 92.1 mhz; 3 kw. -135 ft. TL: S14 17 41 W170 39 44. (CP: 15 kw, ant -92 ft.). Stereo. Box 793 96799-0793. Phone: (684) 633-7000. Fax: (684) 633-5727. E-mail: prescott.esther@ksbsfm.com. Web Site: www.ksbsfm.com. Licensee: Samoa Technologies Inc. Format: Adult contemp. Target aud: Working adults. ♦Barney Sene ., pres; Esther Prescott, gen mgr.

Tafuna

KJAL(AM)— 2005: 585 khz; 5 kw-U. TL: S14 21 28 W170 46 36. Box 218, Pago Pago 96799. Phone: (684) 699-2253. Licensee: District Council of the Assemblies of God in AS. ♦Vickie Haleck, stn mgr.

Guam

Agat

*KSDA-FM— Nov 22, 1990: 91.9 mhz; 3.8 kw. 1,000 ft. TL: N13 25 53 W144 42 36. Stereo. 290 Chalan Palasyo, Agana Heights 96910. Phone: (671) 472-5732. Fax: (671) 477-4678. E-mail: mail@joy92.net. Web Site: www.joy92.net. Licensee: Good News Broadcasting Corp. (acq 8-9-01; charitable contribution). Format: Inspirational, Christian. News: 7 hrs wkly. Target aud: 25-54. Spec prog: Chuukese one hr, Tagalog one hr, Cebuano one hr, Korean one hr, Japanese one hr, Chinese one hr wkly. ♦Robert Gibbons, chmn & pres; Matt Dodd, gen mgr & stn mgr.

Barrigada

*KHMG(FM)— Mar 26, 1996: 88.1 mhz; 8 kw. 472 ft. TL: N13 29 17 W144 49 53. Stereo. Box 23189, 170C Machaute St. 96921. Phone: (671) 477-6341. Fax: (671) 477-7136. E-mail: khmg@harvestministries.net. Web Site: www.harvestministries.net. Licensee: Harvest Christian Academy. Garvey, Schubert & Barer. Format: Relg, Christian. News: 5 hrs wkly. Target aud: General; Christian, church and school families. Spec prog: Children 2 hrs wkly. ♦Dr. Marty Herron, pres; John Collier, stn mgr & progmg dir.

Dededo

KGUM-FM— Feb 28, 1999: 105.1 mhz; 12 kw. Ant 502 ft. TL: N13 29 17 W144 49 30. 111 W. Santo Papa, Suite 800, Hagatna 96910. Phone: (671) 477-5700. Fax: (671) 477-3982. Web Site: www.105therock.com. Licensee: Sorensen Pacific Broadcasting Inc. (group owner; acq 6-23-03; grpsl). Format: Rock. ♦Jon Anderson, pres; Rex W. Sorensen, CEO, chmn & gen mgr; Albert Juan, stn mgr.

Hagatna

KGUM(AM)— February 1975: 567 khz; 10 kw-U, DA-1. TL: N13 23 21 E144 45 34. 111 W. Chalan Santo Papa, Suite 800 96910. Phone: (671) 477-5700. Fax: (671) 477-3982. Web Site: www.radiopacific.com. Licensee: Sorensen Pacific Broadcasting Inc. (group owner; acq

Stations in the U.S.   Puerto Rico

Developers & Brokers of Radio Properties
contact American Media Services at our suite: Philadelphia Marriott Downtown 215-625-2900
843-972-2200
americanmediaservices.com
Charleston, SC
Dallas, TX · Chicago, Il · Austin, TX
American Media Services, LLC

6-23-03; grpsl). Network: Network: CBS, Westwood One. Format: News/talk. News staff: 5; News: 20 hrs wkly. Target aud: 35 plus; adults with high income & education. Spec prog: Educ one hr, computer 3 hrs, police one hr, health & fitness one hr, environmental one hr, drug recovery one hr wkly. ♦Kathy Sorensen, VP & gen mgr.

KZGZ(FM)— Co-owned with KGUM(AM). December 1986: 97.5 mhz; 40 kw. 538 ft. TL: N13 29 17 W144 49 30. Stereo. Format: Hip hop. News: 15 hrs wkly. Target aud: 18-34; young affluent adults.

KISH(FM)— 2003: 102.9 mhz; 25 kw. Ant 535 ft. TL: N13 29 17 W144 49 53. Inter-Island Communications Inc., 1868 Halsey Dr., Piti 96915. Phone: (671) 477-9448. Fax: (671) 477-5786. Licensee: Inter-Island Communications Inc. (group owner). Format: Chamorro music-language of Guam and Marianas Islands. News staff: one; News: 15 hrs wkly. Target aud: General; indegnious residents of Marianas Islands. ♦Frances W. Poppe, CEO; Edward H. Poppe Jr., pres & gen mgr; Edward H. Poppe III, exec VP; Rosalin Kosss, progmg dir.

KOKU(FM)— Apr 28, 1984: 100.3 mhz; 5 kw. 190 ft. TL: N13 26 28 W144 42 40. Stereo. 424 W. O'Brien Dr., 107 Julace Ctr. 96910. Fax: (671) 477-5658. E-mail: marketing@hitradio.com. Web Site: www.hitradio100.com. Licensee: Moy Communications Inc. (acq 4-29-2004; $350,000). Dow, Lohnes & Albertson. Format: Top-40. Target aud: 18-34; females. ♦Kurt S. Moylan, pres; Rick Nauta, progmg dir & chief of engrg; Vince R. Limuaco, gen mgr, sls & mktg.

*KPRG(FM)— Jan 27, 1994: 89.3 mhz; 2.8 kw. 485 ft. TL: N13 29 17 W144 49 30. Stereo. KPRG, UoG Stn., Mangilao 96923. Phone: (671) 734-8930. Fax: (671) 734-2958. E-mail: kprg@kprg.org. Web Site: www.kprg.org. Licensee: Guam Educational Radio Foundation. Network: NPR. Format: News, div, class. ♦Olympia Terral, gen mgr; Gene Ficker, progmg dir.

KSTO(FM)— September 1973: 95.5 mhz; 25 kw. 530 ft. TL: N13 29 17 E144 49 53. Stereo. 1868 Halsey Dr., Piti 96915. Phone: (671) 477-7108. Phone: (671) 477-9448. Fax: (671) 477-6411. E-mail: ksto@ite.net. Licensee: Inter-Island Communications Inc. (group owner; acq 11-77). Format: Adult contemp. News staff: one; News: 14 hrs wkly. Target aud: 25-54. Spec prog: Country 12 hrs, gospel 6 hrs wkly. ♦Edward H. Poppe Jr., pres & gen mgr; Frances Poppe, CFO; Edward H. Poppe III, exec VP; Michelle Poppe-Aguon, opns dir; Rosalin Koss, progmg dir.

KTKB(FM)— 2003: 101.9 mhz; 50 kw. Ant 492 ft. TL: N13 29 16 W144 49 36. KM Broadcasting of Guam L.L.C., 3654 W. Jarvis Ave., Skokie, IL 60076. Phone: (847) 674-0864. Phone: (671) 647-1019. Fax: (847) 674-9188. Fax: (671) 648-1019. Web Site: www.ktkb.com. Licensee: KM Broadcasting of Guam L.L.C. Group owner: KM Communications Inc. Format: Filipino. ♦Myoung Bae, pres; Kevin Bae, gen mgr; Rolando Manuntag, stn mgr.

KTWG(AM)— August 1975: 801 khz; 10 kw-U. TL: N13 27 07 W144 42 32. 1868 Halsey Dr., Asan, NC 96910. Phone: (671) 477-5894. Fax: (671) 477-6411. E-mail: ktwg@ktwg.com. Web Site: www.ktwg.com. Licensee: Edward H. Poppe Jr. and Frances W. Poppe. Group owner: Inter-Island Communications Inc. (acq 2-20-2002). Format: Relg. News staff: one; News: 5 hrs wkly. Target aud: 25-49; Christian. ♦K. Leilani S. Dahilig, stn mgr & opns mgr.

KUAM(AM)— Mar 14, 1954: 612 khz; 10 kw-U. TL: N13 26 53 E144 45 22. 600 Harmon Loop Rd. #102, Dededo 96912. Phone: (671) 637-5826. Fax: (671) 637-9865. Web Site: www.kuam.com/i94. Licensee: Pacific Telestations Inc. (acq 9-27-77). Network: CBS. Format: MOR, adult contemp. Spec prog: Chamorro 5 hrs, Tagalog 5 hrs, Japanese 3 hrs wkly. ♦Joey Calvo, gen mgr.

KUAM-FM— Sept 1, 1966: 93.9 mhz; 2 kw. 950 ft. TL: N13 25 53 E144 42 36. (CP: 5.2 kw, ant 948 ft). Phone: (671) 637-0094. Web Site: www.kuam.com/i94. Format: Urban contemp, rhythm & blues.. Co-owned TV: KUAM-TV affil.

Tumon

KIJI(FM)— Not on air, target date: unknown: 104.3 mhz; 850 w. Ant 72 ft. TL: N13 30 37.3 E144 48 17.6. La Casa de Colina, 3rd Fl., 200 Chichirica St., Tamuning 96913-4217. Phone: (671) 647-4703. Licensee: Guam Broadcast Services Inc. ♦Gary W.F. Gumataotao, pres & gen mgr.

Puerto Rico

Adjuntas

WOQI(AM)— 1997: 1020 khz; 1 kw-D, 280 w-N. TL: N18 09 04 W66 42 48. Box 982 00601. Phone: (787) 829-1453. Fax: (787) 829-1453. E-mail: Coki@coqui.net. Licensee: WPAB Inc. (acq. 6-23-01; $450,000). Format: Sp, var/div. News: 15 hrs wkly. Target aud: General; General Public. ♦Alphoso Jimenez-Luchete, gen mgr.

Aguada

WFDT(FM)— 1975: 105.5 mhz; 3 kw. 1,036 ft. TL: N18 18 57 W67 10 54. Stereo. Box 363222, San Juan 00936. Phone: (787) 758-1300. Fax: (787) 767-9343. Web Site: www.fidelitypr.com. Licensee: Arso Radio Corp. Group owner: Uno Radio Group (acq 4-19-01; $3.2 million). Format: Adult contemp, easy lstng. News staff: 4. Target aud: 25-49; middle class. ♦Luis Soto, pres & VP.

Aguadilla

WABA(AM)— Nov 15, 1951: 850 khz; 5 kw-D, 1 kw-N. TL: N18 24 02 W67 09 27. Box 188, No. 6, Calle Munoz Rivera 00605. Phone: (787) 891-1230. Fax: (787) 882-2282. E-mail: wabaradio@hotmail.com. Web Site: www.waba850.com. Licensee: Aquadilla Radio & TV Corp. Inc. (acq 1973). Format: Adult contemp, Sp. ♦Hector Richard Carbona, pres; Rosipa Pellot, gen mgr; Mereida Nieves, gen sls mgr & news dir; Tito R. Areicaga, adv dir & progmg dir; Juan Rivera, chief of engrg.

WIVA-FM— Apr 16, 1964: 100.3 mhz; 22 kw. 2,014 ft. TL: N18 09 07 W66 59 15. Stereo. Box 1331 00605. Phone: (787) 834-2320. Fax: (787) 831-7969. E-mail: ventas@unoradio.com. Web Site: www.salsoul.com. Licensee: Arso Radio Corp. Group owner: Uno Radio Group (acq 3-85). Network: UPI. Format: Salsa. News staff: one; News: 5 hrs wkly. Target aud: 12 plus. ♦Jesus M. Soto, CEO & pres; Luis A. Soto, pres & chief of engrg; Maida Bedaya, gen mgr; Raymond Totti, gen sls mgr; Anthony Soto, progmg dir.

WTPM(FM)— May 27, 1971: 92.9 mhz; 50 kw. 1,223 ft. TL: N18 18 52 W67 10 58. Stereo. Box 1629, Mayaguez 00681. Phone: (787) 831-9200. Phone: (787) 834-6340. Fax: (787) 831-9292. Web Site: www.wtpm.com. Licensee: Corp. of the 7th Day Adventists of West Puerto Rico (acq 2-80; $125,000). Format: Sp adult contemp. News: 11 hrs wkly. Target aud: General; traditional Christian groups. Spec prog: English one hr, class 7 hrs wkly. ♦Daniel Ponce, gen mgr & opns dir.

WWNA(AM)— 1956: 1340 khz; 950 w-U. TL: N18 24 00 W67 09 48. Box 7, Moca 00676. Secondary address: Rd. 111, Aquadilla 00605. Phone: (787) 252-1730. Fax: (787) 868-1340. Licensee: Dominga Barreto Santiago (acq 1-25-2005; $500,000). Format: Sp var. Target aud: 20-55. Spec prog: Jazz 3 hrs wkly. ♦Aureo Matos, gen mgr, gen sls mgr & progmg dir; Ron Cushing, chief of engrg.

Arecibo

WCMN(AM)— June 24, 1947: 1280 khz; 5 kw-D, 1 kw-N. TL: N18 28 52 W66 41 16. Box 436 00613. Secondary address: 55 Gonzalo Marin St. 00612. Phone: (787) 878-0070. Phone: (787) 781-6303. Fax: (787) 880-1112. E-mail: wcmn@xsn.net. Licensee: Caribbean Broadcasting Corp. Group owner: Uno Radio Group (acq 4-7-2004; $5.75 million. for stock with co-located FM). Fisher, Wayland, Cooper, Leader & Zaragoza L.L.P. Format: Sp, news/talk. News staff: 3; News: 50 hrs wkly. Target aud: 30 plus. ♦Byron Mitchell, VP & gen mgr; Maria M. Mitchell, sls dir, prom dir & progmg dir; Juan Rivera, chief of engrg.

WCMN-FM— Jan 1, 1967: 107.3 mhz; 50 kw. 3,000 ft. TL: N18 14 52 W66 48 43. Stereo. Web Site: www.delta107.com. Format: Sp, Top-40. Target aud: 18-42; young adults.

WMIA(AM)— Feb 21, 1957: 1070 khz; 500 w-D, 2.5 kw-N. TL: N18 27 33 W66 45 20. Box 1055 00613-1055. Secondary address: 1168 Miramar Ave. 00612. Phone: (787) 878-1275. Phone: (787) 878-2727. Web Site: www.am-radio.us. Licensee: Abacoa Radio Corp. Booth, Freret, Imlay & Tepper. Format: Adult contemp, Sp, news/talk. News staff: 7; News: 80 hrs wkly. Target aud: 25 plus; the buying power in the area. Spec prog: Oldies, Sp 16 hrs, relg 3 hrs wkly. ♦Epifanio Rodriguez-Velez, gen mgr & chief of opns.

WNIK(AM)— 1957: 1230 khz; 1 kw-U. TL: N18 27 20 W66 44 24. Box 142041 00614. Phone: (787) 880-2461. Fax: (787) 879-1011. Licensee: Unik Broadcasting System Corp. (acq 12-10-2004; $335,000). Format: Div, Sp. Target aud: General. ♦Manuel Santiago, gen mgr.

WNIK-FM— July 17, 1965: 106.5 mhz; 25 kw. Ant 20 ft. TL: N18 27 20 W66 44 24. Stereo. Box 556 00613. Phone: (787) 880-2613. Fax: (787) 879-1011. Licensee: Kelly Broadcasting System Inc. (acq 4-87). Format: Ballads. ♦Raul Santiago, gen mgr.

Barceloneta-Manati

WBQN(AM)— Mar 1, 1975: 1160 khz; 5 kw-D, 2.5 kw-N, DA-D. TL: N18 26 23 W66 33 07. Box 1625, Manati 00674. Phone: (787) 854-2450. Phone: (787) 854-3738. Fax: (787) 854-3738. E-mail: riveraolmo@hotmail.com. Licensee: Radio Borinquen Inc. Format: Top-40 CHR, Sp. Target aud: General. ♦Angel M. Rivera, pres; Luis R. Rivera Jr., gen mgr.

Barranquitas

WOLA(AM)— March 1986: 1380 khz; 1 kw-U. TL: N18 11 01 W66 18 24. Box 669-A, Carr 719 KMo1 Bo Halachal 00794. Phone: (787) 857-1380. Fax: (787) 857-1381. E-mail: wola@prtc.com. Licensee: R and R Broadcasting Format: Sp/tropical. Target aud: General. Spec prog: Jazz 5 hrs wkly. ♦Edgardo Rivera, pres, gen mgr & progmg dir; Edgardo Riviera, gen sls mgr; Jesus R. Gomez, chief of engrg.

Bayamon

WLUZ(AM)— 1966: 1600 khz; 5 kw-U. TL: N18 21 38 W66 09 30. Box 9394, San Juan 00908-0394. Secondary address: 403 Del Parque, 15 th Fl., Santurce 00912-3709. Phone: (787) 785-1600. Phone: (787) 729-1600. Fax: (787) 785-2094. Fax: (787) 723-8685. E-mail: tony-trelles@yahoo.com. Licensee: Marketing Promotion Network Inc. (acq 11-1-98; $1.6 million. plus $800,000 penthouse). Fletcher, Heald & Hildreth, P. L. C. Format: Romantic ballads, nostalgia, Sp, talk. Target aud: 35 plus. Spec prog: Comedy. ♦Tony Trelles, pres; Martha Villanueva, opns dir.

WODA(FM)— Dec 3, 1959: 94.7 mhz; 31 kw. Ant 1,837 ft. TL: N18 16 44 W65 51 12. Stereo. Box 949, Guayanbo 00970-0949. Secondary address: Amelia Industrial Park, Calle Frances 42, Guaynabo 00968. Phone: (787) 622-9700. Fax: (787) 622-9478. Web Site: www.onda94.com. Licensee: WLDI Inc. Group owner: Spanish Broadcasting System Inc. (acq 11-29-99; grpsl). Booth, Freret, Imlay & Tepper. Format: Sp, Top-40. Target aud: 12-24; males & females, middle/upper socio-economic. ♦Raul Alarcon, pres; Ismael Nieves, gen mgr; Marie Elena Martinez, gen sls mgr; Luis Enrique Rivera, prom VP; Jose Nelson Diaz, progmg dir; Alejandro Luciano, chief of engrg.

WRSJ(AM)— 1947: 1560 khz; 5 kw-D, 750 w-N. TL: N18 24 05 W66 07 14. 1554 Bori St., San Juan 00927-6113. Phone: (787) 274-1800. Fax: (787) 281-9758. Licensee: International Broadcasting Corp. (group owner; (acq 7-6-2004; $1.45 million. with WCHQ(AM) Quebradillas). Format: Sp. ♦Pedro Roman Collazo, pres; Margarita Nazario, gen mgr.

Broadcasting & Cable Yearbook 2006

D-567

Puerto Rico

WXYX(FM)— Feb 1, 1979: 100.7 mhz; 50 kw. 1,092 ft. TL: N18 16 58 W66 10 47. Stereo. HC67 Box 15390 00956-9535. Secondary address: Rd 174, KM 5.0 Bo. Guaraguao 00956-9535. Phone: (787) 785-9390. Phone: (787) 785-9100. Fax: (787) 785-9377. E-mail: info@lax.fm. Web Site: www.lax.fm. Licensee: RAAD Broadcasting Corp. Format: Top 40 pop. Target aud: 12-34; young teens, adults. ♦Roberto Davila, pres, gen mgr & opns mgr; Eduardo Cora, gen sls mgr; Michelle Torres, prom dir; Herman Davila, progmg dir; Juan Rivera, chief of engrg.

Cabo Rojo

WMIO(FM)—Listing follows WYAC(AM).

WYAC(AM)— Jan 9, 1970: 930 khz; 2.5 kw-U. TL: N18 06 05 W67 09 17. Box 489, Mayaguez 00681. Secondary address: Radio Centre, Post & Bosgue Sts., Mayaguez 00684. Phone: (787) 620-9898. Web Site: www.radiopr740.com. Licensee: Bestov Broadcasting Inc. of Puerto Rico (acq 4-14-99; $3.65 million. with co-located FM). Reddy, Begley & McCormick. Format: News/talk, Sp. News staff: . Target aud: General; Mayaguez county residents. ♦Luis Majia, pres; Francisco Acosta, gen mgr.

WMIO(FM)—Co-owned with WYAC(AM). Jan 10, 1988: 102.3 mhz; 3 kw. 680 ft. TL: N17 59 37 W67 10 27. Stereo. Box 9023916, San Juan 00922. Phone: (787) 798-7878. Fax: (787) 620-0720. Reddy, Begley & McCormick. Format: Adult contemp. Target aud: 18-45; general. ♦Alan Mejia, gen mgr.

Caguas

WBRQ(FM)—See Cidra

WNEL(AM)— July 21, 1947: 1430 khz; 5 kw-U. TL: N18 14 53 W66 01 25. Box 487 00726-0487. Phone: (787) 744-3131. Fax: (787) 743-0252. E-mail: leon@unoradio.com. Licensee: Turabo Radio Corp. Group owner: Uno Radio Group (acq 4-1-73). Network: UPI. John P. Bankson Jr. Format: Latin Oldies. Target aud: 24 plus. ♦Jesus M. Soto, CEO & chmn; Luis M. Soto, pres; Luis Gonzales, CFO; Luis Leon, gen mgr, gen sls mgr & progmg dir; Raymond Totti, sls VP; Tanya Ramos, mktg dir; Aracelis Cruz, prom VP; Anthony Soto, progmg VP; Alberto Pereira, chief of engrg.

WPRM-FM—See San Juan

WVJP(AM)— Nov 24, 1947: 1110 khz; 2.5 kw-D, 500 w-N. TL: N18 13 25 W66 01 11. Box 207 00726. Secondary address: Tomas de Castro #2 00626. Phone: (787) 743-5790. Fax: (787) 746-6996. Licensee: Borinquen Broadcasting Co. (acq 7-7-99; $700,000 for 12). Format: Adult contemp, btfl mus, Sp. ♦Jancel Pereira, CEO; Bienvenido Rodriguez, gen mgr; Norma Rodriguez-Trinidad, progmg dir; Jesus R. Gomez, chief of engrg.

WVJP-FM— October 1968: 103.3 mhz; 28 kw. 1,906 ft. TL: N18 16 41 W65 51 09. Stereo. Format: Sp, romantic.

Camuy

WDIN(FM)— Aug 15, 1968: 102.9 mhz; 50 kw. 303 ft. TL: N18 28 49 W66 51 14. Box 780 00627. Phone: (787) 743-5790. Fax: (787) 746-6996. Web Site: www.dimension.fm. Licensee: HQ 103 Inc. (acq 5-28-86). Format: Sp variety. ♦Bienvenido Rodriguez, gen mgr & progmg dir; Maggie Lopez, progmg dir.

Canovanas

WGIT(AM)— 2001: 1660 khz; 10 kw-D, 1 kw-N. TL: N18 23 09 W65 55 16. 1554 Calle Bori, San Juan 00927. Phone: (787) 274-1800. Fax: (787) 281-9758. Licensee: International Broadcasting Corp. (group owner; acq 5-29-03; $1.3 million). Format: Sp, sports, music. ♦Pedro Roman-Collazo, gen mgr; Margarita Nazario, stn mgr.

Carolina

WIDA(AM)— Mar 16, 1964: 1400 khz; 1 kw-U. TL: N18 23 49 W65 56 06. Box 188 00986. Secondary address: Ignacio Arzuaga 203-7 00987. Phone: (787) 757-1414. Phone: (787) 757-1717. Fax: (787) 769-4103. E-mail: radiovida@cadenaradiovida.com. Web Site: www.cadenaradiovida.com. Licensee: Christian Broadcasting Corp. (acq 7-80; $750,000; 7-28-80). Network: UPI. Format: Sp. ♦Dr. Federico Iglesias, gen mgr; Edwin Carrasquillo, progmg dir; Alberto Periera, chief of engrg.

WIDA-FM— August 1983: 90.5 mhz; 25 kw. 1,900 ft. TL: N18 06 48 W66 03 07. Web Site: www.cadenaradiovida.com. Format: Educ.

WVOZ-FM— Mar 3, 1967: 107.7 mhz; 50 kw. 1,636 ft. TL: N18 24 10 W66 03 21. (CP: 12 kw, ant 2,758 ft.). Stereo. 1554 Calle Bori, Rio Piedras 00927. Phone: (787) 274-1800. Fax: (787) 281-9758. Licensee: International Broadcasting Corp. (group owner). Format: Adult contemp. ♦Pedro Roman-Collazo, pres; Margarita Nazario, gen mgr & progmg dir.

Cayey

WLEY(AM)— Dec 3, 1965: 1080 khz; 250 w-U. TL: N18 06 55 W66 08 28. 100 Gran Bulevar Paseo, Suite 403A, San Juan 00926. Phone: (787) 292-1700. Fax: (787) 292-1717. Licensee: Media Power Group Inc. (group owner; (acq 9-30-2003; grpsl). ♦Joe Pagan, gen mgr.

Ceiba

WFAB(AM)— 1993: 890 khz; 250 w-U. TL: N18 12 16 W65 42 40. Box 318, Rio Blanco 00744. Phone: (787) 874-0890. Fax: (787) 874-0190. Web Site: www.lanaveprdc.net. Licensee: Daniel Rosario Diaz. (acq 12-18-98). Format: Relg. ♦Daniel Rosario Diaz, pres & gen mgr; Jose N. Garcia, stn mgr.

Cidra

WBRQ(FM)— Mar 1, 1972: 97.7 mhz; 5 kw. Ant 876 ft. TL: N18 13 30 W66 05 53. Stereo. Box 6715, Caguas 00726-9297. Phone: (787) 745-9700. Phone: (787) 745-9770. Fax: (787) 745-9777. E-mail: nuevavida@nuevavidafm.com. Web Site: www.nuevavidafm.com. Licensee: New Life Broadcasting Inc. (acq 3-20-01; $3.6 million). Roy F. Perkins. Format: Sp, Contemp Christian. Target aud: 25-49; women. ♦Dominga Bareto Santiago, pres; Orlando Mercado, gen mgr & progmg dir.

Coamo

WCPR(AM)— 1967: 1450 khz; 1 kw-U. TL: N18 05 29 W66 22 15. Box 1863 00769. Phone: (787) 825-7061. Fax: (787) 825-1905. Licensee: Coamo Broadcasting Corp. Format: Adult contemp. News: 9 hrs wkly. Target aud: General. ♦Jose David Soler, pres & gen mgr.

Corozal

WORO(FM)— July 1968: 92.5 mhz; 50 kw. 1,197 ft. TL: N18 15 09 W66 19 58. 415 Carbonell St., San Juan 00918. Secondary address: Box 9021967, San Juan 00902. Phone: (787) 751-1380. Fax: (787) 758-9967. Licensee: Catholic Apostolic & Roman Church San Juan Archdiocese. (acq 1981; $1 million; 3-2-81). Format: Btfl mus. ♦Roberto Octavio Gonzalez, pres; Allan Corales, gen mgr; Elsa Feernandez, sls dir; Carlos Rodriguez, progmg dir; Jesus Gomez, chief of engrg; Jose Gomez, chief of engrg.

Culebra

*****WJVP(FM)**— 1998: 89.3 mhz; 30 kw vert. 577 ft. TL: N18 19 37 W65 18 21. Box 40000, Bayamon 00958. Secondary address: An 167 Calle Granada AM Alahambra, Bayamon 00956. Phone: (787) 288-4336. Phone: (787) 288-4332. Fax: (787) 740-7104. Web Site: www.clamorpr.org. Licensee: Clamor Broadcasting Network Inc. Format: Relg, civic, cultural. ♦Jorde Raschke, gen mgr.

WXZX(FM)— December 1996: 98.7 mhz; 6 kw. Ant 584 ft. TL: N18 19 19 W65 17 59. Stereo. Box 1047, Fajardo 00738. Phone: (787) 860-1065. Fax: (787) 860-1055. Licensee: La Gigante Radio Corp. (acq 2-25-2002). Format: Sp, Christian, tropical music. News staff: 4. Target aud: 25-54. ♦Aureo Matos, gen mgr.

Fajardo

WCMA-FM— Feb 15, 1969: 96.5 mhz; 11.5 kw. 2,795 ft. TL: N18 18 36 W65 47 41. Box 949, Guaynabo 00970-0949. Secondary address: Amelia Industrial Park, Calle Frances #42, Guaynabo 00968. Phone: (787) 622-9700. Fax: (787) 622-9478. Web Site: www.spanishbroadcastingsystem.com. Licensee: WCMA Licensing Inc. Group owner: Spanish Broadcasting System Inc. (acq 8-4-98; $8.25 million). Format: Music of the 80s & 90s. ♦Falex Bonnet, gen mgr.

WIOA(FM)—See San Juan

WMDD(AM)— May 31, 1947: 1480 khz; 5 kw-U. TL: N18 21 46 W65 38 24. Box 948 00738. Phone: (787) 863-0202. Phone: (787) 793-0669. Fax: (787) 863-0166. Licensee: Pan Caribbean Broadcasting de P.R. Inc. (acq 3-19-03; with WZIN(FM) Charlotte Amalie, VI). Format: Tropical. Target aud: 25-49. ♦Rita Friedman, pres & opns mgr.

WTTP(FM)—See Las Piedras

Guayama

*****WCRP(FM)**— 1991: 88.1 mhz; 27 kw. 1,889 ft. TL: N18 06 47 W66 03 08. Box 344 00785-0344. Phone: (787) 864-3658. Fax: (787) 864-6780. Licensee: Ministerio Radial Cristo Viene Pronto Inc. Format: Educ, Christian. ♦Carmita Rodriguez, pres & gen mgr.

WIBS(AM)— Mar 1, 1981: 1540 khz; 1 kw-D. TL: N17 59 44 W66 04 39. Calle Bori 1554, San Juan 00927. Phone: (787) 274-1800. Fax: (787) 281-9758. Licensee: International Broadcasting Corp. (group owner; acq 12-3-01; $300,000). Format: Sp, tropical. ♦Pedro Roman-Collazo, CEO; Margarita Nazario, gen mgr & progmg dir.

WMEG(FM)— November 1966: 106.9 mhz; 25 kw. 1,994 ft. TL: N18 06 48 W66 03 07. Stereo. Box 949, Guaynabo 00970-0949. Secondary address: Amelia Industrial Park, Calle Frances 42, Guaynabo 00968. Phone: (787) 622-9700. Fax: (787) 622-9478. Web Site: www.broadcastingsystem.com. Licensee: WMEG Licensing Inc. Group owner: Spanish Broadcasting System Inc. (acq 3-15-99; $16 million. with WZET(FM) Hormigueros). Format: Rock, English. ♦Falex Bonnet, gen mgr & gen sls mgr.

WXRF(AM)— July 1948: 1590 khz; 1 kw-U. TL: N17 57 40 W66 08 20. Calle Bori 1554, San Juan 00927. Phone: (787) 274-1800. Fax: (787) 281-9758. Licensee: International Broadcasting Corp. (acq 10-7-2001; $1,382,961. with WVEO(TV) Aguadilla). Format: Sports, Music. ♦Pedro Roman-Collazo, pres; Margarita Nazario, gen mgr, gen sls mgr & progmg dir.

Guayanilla

WOIZ(AM)— Oct 1, 1986: 1130 khz; 200 w-D, 700 w-N. TL: N18 01 03 W66 46 22. Stereo. Box 561130 00656. Phone: (787) 835-1130. Phone: (787) 835-3130. Fax: (787) 835-3130. Licensee: Radio Antillas of Harriet Broadcasters. Format: Adult contemp, oldies, news/talk. News: 10 hrs wkly. Target aud: 35+. ♦Luis A. Rodriguez III, pres, gen mgr, opns mgr & gen sls mgr; Maria de los Angeles Rivera, VP.

Hatillo

WMSW(AM)— 1980: 1120 khz; 5 kw-U. TL: N18 28 15 W66 50 24. Box 140961, Arecibo 00614. Phone: (787) 879-4094. Fax: (787) 880-0441. Licensee: Aurora Broadcasting Corp. (acq 11-23-2004). Format: News/talk, music. ♦Manuel Santiago Santos, pres & progmg dir; Hector Santiago Santos, VP; Lloyd Santiago Santos, gen sls mgr; Ronald Cushing, chief of engrg.

Hormigueros

WRRH(FM)— 1998: 106.1 mhz; 800 w. Ant 1,932 ft. TL: N18 08 33 W66 58 56. Box 1061 00660. Phone: (787) 849-1061. Fax: (787) 849-6106. E-mail: renacer1061@yahoo.com. Web Site: www.renacer1061.com. Licensee: Renacer Broadcasters Corp. Format: Contemp Christian music. ♦Larry W. Ramos, gen mgr & gen sls mgr; Kehmuel Ramos, progmg dir.

WZET(FM)— Oct 12, 1980: 92.1 mhz; 3 kw. 581 ft. TL: N18 11 15 W67 07 04. (CP: 2 kw, ant 1,105 ft.). Stereo. Box 949, Gauynabo 00970-0949. Secondary address: Amelia Industrial Park, Calle Frances 42, Guaynabo 00968. Phone: (787) 622-9700. Fax: (787) 622-9478. Web Site: www.spanishbroadcastingsystem.com. Licensee: WSMA Licensing Inc. Group owner: Spanish Broadcasting System Inc. (acq 3-15-99; $16 million. with WMEG(FM) Guayama). Format: Sp, tropical. ♦Falex Bonnet, gen mgr.

Stations in the U.S. Puerto Rico

Developers & Brokers of Radio Properties
contact American Media Services at our suite:
Philadelphia Marriott Downtown
215-625-2900
843-972-2200
americanmediaservices.com
Charleston, SC
Dallas, TX · Chicago, Il · Austin, TX

American Media Services, LLC

Humacao

WALO(AM)— Feb 11, 1958: 1240 khz; 1 kw-U. TL: N18 08 49 W65 48 49. Box 9230 00792. Phone: (787) 852-1240. Fax: (787) 852-1280. E-mail: wlo@prtc.net. Licensee: Ochoa Broadcasting Corp. (acq 4-70; $400,000). Fletcher, Heald & Hildreth. Format: Sp, news/talk, music, sports, MOR. News staff: 2; News: 60 hrs wkly. Target aud: Adult 18-54, male 25-54; general. Spec prog: Relg 2 hrs wkly. ♦ Efrain Archilla-Roig, CEO, chmn & pres; Beatriz Archilla, gen mgr; Maribel Ortiz-Del Valle, opns dir; Ken Allen, dev dir.

Isabela

WISA(AM)— Oct 19, 1961: 1390 khz; 1 kw-U. TL: N18 30 08 W67 01 38. Box 750 00662. Phone: (787) 872-0100. Phone: (787) 872-2030. Fax: (787) 872-0802. Licensee: Isabela Broadcasting Inc. (acq 4-87). Format: MOR. ♦ David Marda, gen mgr; Edwin Nieves, progmg dir.

WKSA-FM—Co-owned with WISA(AM).Not on air, target date: unknown: 101.5 mhz; 42 kw. Ant -26 ft. TL: N18 26 36 W67 08 50. Phone: (787) 798-7878. Format: Ballads.

Juana Diaz

WCGB(AM)— Nov 23, 1967: 1060 khz; 5 kw-D, 500 w-N. TL: N17 59 35 W66 28 33. Box 1414 00795. Secondary address: Carretera Hwy. 1, KM 112.0 00795. Phone: (787) 837-1060. Fax: (787) 260-1060. E-mail: wcgbam@prtc.net. Licensee: Calvary Evangelistic Mission Inc. (acq 11-5-2004; $500,000). Format: Relg, var/div, Sp. News: 10 hrs wkly. Target aud: Adult. ♦ Lawrence Trumbower, gen mgr & opns dir.

Juncos

WRRE(AM)— 1971: 1460 khz; 500 w-U, DA-2. TL: N18 12 54 W65 54 33. Box 1460, Las Piedras 00771. Phone: (787) 874-5244. Fax: (787) 716-0808. Web Site: www.sonidosantidad.welcome.to. Licensee: Hacienda San Eladio Inc. (acq 4-16-03; $625,000). Format: Sp relg. ♦ Areel Rivera Garcia, pres & gen mgr.

Lajas

WSQD(AM)— 1986: 1510 khz; 1 kw-U, DA-1. TL: N18 02 11 W67 04 58. Box 1689 00667. Phone: (787) 899-5724. Fax: (787) 899-5475. Licensee: Perry Broadcasting Systems (acq 4-1-2002; $535,500). Format: Sp news/talk. ♦ Oscar Vega, gen mgr.

WXLX(FM)— Jan 5, 1994: 103.7 mhz; 50 kw. 456 ft. TL: N17 59 37 W67 11 09. Stereo. HC 67, Bayamon 00956-9535. Phone: (787) 255-2325. Phone: (787) 785-9390. Fax: (787) 785-9377. Licensee: Radio X Broadcasting Corp. (acq 1-20-98; $3 million). Format: CHR. ♦ Roberto Davila, pres & gen mgr; Roberto Davila Rios, opns mgr.

Lares

WGDL(AM)— February 1983: 1200 khz; 250 w-D. TL: N18 17 40 W66 53 50. Box 872 00669. Phone: (787) 897-1200. Phone: (787) 897-3889. Fax: (787) 897-7821. E-mail: wgdl1200@yahoo.com. Licensee: Lares Broadcasting Corp. Network: UPI. John P. Bankson Jr. Format: Tropical, Sp. News staff: one; News: 20 hrs wkly. Target aud: General. ♦ Pedro Hernandez, pres; Julia Bello, gen mgr & gen sls mgr; Angel Perez, progmg dir.

Las Piedras

WTTP(FM)— Nov 4, 1978: 98.3 mhz; 760 w. Ant 1,958 ft. TL: N18 16 44 W65 51 12. Stereo. 1058 Ponce De Leon, San Juan 00907. Phone: (787) 691-3636. Fax: (787) 721-6767. Licensee: La Mas Z Radio Inc. (acq 7-6-2004; $1.99 million). Format: Romantic, Latin. ♦ Raisaac Colon, pres, gen sls mgr & mus dir; Mr. Raisaac Colon-Rios, gen mgr; Rafaol Acosta, chief of engrg.

Levittown

*WPLI(FM)— Oct 1, 1986: 88.5 mhz; 35 w. Ant 121 ft. TL: N18 26 55 W66 10 26. 2288.5 PMB 286, Box 607071, Bayamon 00959. Phone: (787) 798-8850. Fax: (787) 798-8851. Web Site: www.plenitudfm.com. Licensee: Family Educational Association (acq 4-7-2004; $800,000). Format: Relg. ♦ Shay Garcya, stn mgr.

Luquillo

WZOL(FM)— 1976: 92.1 mhz; 4.6 kw. Ant 915 ft. TL: N18 19 54 W65 41 11. Box 29027, Rio Piedras 00929. Phone: (787) 767-1005. Fax: (787) 758-1055. Web Site: www.radiosol.org. Licensee: Radio Sol 92, WZOL Inc. Format: Relg. ♦ Pedro M. Canales, pres; William H. Irizarry, gen mgr; Willie Lopez, progmg dir; Raymond Hernandez, chief of engrg.

Manati

WBQN(AM)—See Barceloneta-Manati

WMNT(AM)— May 1961: 1500 khz; 1 kw-D, 250 w-N. TL: N18 26 06 W66 29 54. Box 6 00674. Secondary address: Delta St. #1305 Caparra Terr., San Juan 00920. Phone: (787) 854-2223. Fax: (787) 781-7647. Fax: (787) 854-2713. E-mail: radio@atenas.com. Web Site: www.radioatenas.com. Licensee: Manati Radio Corp. (acq 9-4-97; $200,000. for 100%). Shaw Pittman. Format: News/talk, sports, Sp. News staff: 2; News: 25 hrs wkly. Target aud: 25 plus; men & women. Spec prog: NBA, World Series in Sp. ♦ Jose Ariras Dominicci, CEO; Jose A. Ribas-Dominicci, pres; Freddy Ribas, VP, gen mgr & sls dir; Maria Elena Rodriguez, stn mgr.

WNRT(FM)— 1973: 96.9 mhz; 50 kw. Ant 882 ft. TL: N18 15 41 W66 32 19. Box 13324, San Juan 00908. Phone: (787) 758-8562. Fax: (787) 758-8833. Web Site: www.radiotriunfo.com. Licensee: La Voz Evangelica de Puerto Rico Inc. Format: Christian. ♦ Luis Barajas, pres; Mosses Flores, gen mgr; Moises Flores, opns mgr & dev mgr; Virgen Perez, sls VP; Carlos Vazquez Flecha, progmg dir; Jorge Figueroa, engrg dir.

Maricao

WAEL(AM)—See Mayaguez

WAEL-FM— July 1970: 96.1 mhz; 24.2 kw. 2,011 ft. TL: N18 09 07 W66 49 15. Stereo. Box 1370, Mayaguez 00681-1370. Secondary address: Ramirez Peben Final, Guanajibo Homes, Mayaguez 00681. Phone: (787) 832-4560/ 832-0600. Fax: (787) 792-3140. E-mail: ssales@waelfm96.com. Web Site: www.waelfm96.com. Licensee: WAEL Inc. Booth, Freret, Imlay & Tepper. Format: CHR, tropical mus. Target aud: 12-24. ♦ Luis Pirallo, gen mgr & progmg dir; Angel Peerez, opns mgr & prom dir; Maria del Pilar-Pirallo, pres & gen sls mgr; Ivan Selin, chief of engrg.

Mayaguez

WAEL(AM)— 1949: 600 khz; 5 kw, DA-1. TL: N18 10 46 W67 10 14. (CP: 5 kw). Box 1370 00681-1370. Secondary address: 600 Ramirez Pabon , Guanajibo Homes 00680. Phone: (787) 832-0600. Phone: (787) 832-4560. Fax: (787) 792-3140. E-mail: mgmt@waelfm96.com. Web Site: www.waelfm96.com. Licensee: WAEL Inc. (acq 1957). Booth, Freret, Imlay & Tepper P. Format: Oldies, sports. Target aud: 25 plus. ♦ Maria del Pilar Pirallo, pres; Luis Pirallo, opns mgr, progmg dir & engrg dir; Maria Pirallo, gen sls mgr; Ivan Seliu, engrg dir.

WAEL-FM—See Maricao

WEGM(FM)—See San German

WIOB(FM)— Oct 12, 1947: 97.5 mhz; 25 kw. 990 ft. TL: N18 19 33 W67 10 13. (CP: 50 kw). Box 949, Guaynabo 00970-0949. Secondary address: Amelia Industrial Park, Calle Frances 42, Guaynabo 00968. Phone: (787) 622-9700. Fax: (787) 622-9478. Web Site: www.spanishbroadcastingsystem.com. Licensee: Cadena Estereotempo

Inc. Group owner: Spanish Broadcasting System Inc. (acq 11-29-99; grpsl). Hogan & Hartson. Format: Sp, ballads. Target aud: 30-50; women. ♦ Falex Bonnet, gen mgr.

WIVA-FM—See Aguadilla

WKJB(AM)— Dec 6, 1946: 710 khz; 10 kw-D, 750 w-N. TL: N18 10 08 W67 09 03. Box 1293 00681. Phone: (787) 834-6666. Fax: (787) 831-6925. Licensee: WKJB-AM Inc. Format: News/talk. Spec prog: Sp 1 hr wkly. ♦ Dennis Bechara, pres; Jose A. Bechara Jr., exec VP & gen mgr; Ada Ramos, gen sls mgr; Eric Graniela, progmg dir; Rafy Aviles, news dir; Pedro Velez Jr., chief of engrg.

WNOD(FM)— 1960: 94.1 mhz; 25 kw. 2,967 ft. TL: N18 09 05 W66 59 20. Stereo. Box 949, Guaynabo 00970-0949. Phone: (787) 265-9494. Fax: (787) 622-9700. Web Site: www.lamega.fm. Licensee: WOYE Inc. Group owner: Spanish Broadcasting System Inc. (acq 11-29-99; grpsl). Hogan & Hartson. Format: Top-40. News staff: one; News: 10 hrs wkly. Target aud: 18-49; young adults. ♦ Raul Alarcon, chmn; Ismael Nieves, gen mgr; Marie Elena Martinez, gen sls mgr & rgnl sls mgr; Luis Enriquez Rivera, mktg dir; Pedro Arroyo, progmg dir; Alejandro Luciano, chief of engrg; Demare Ramirez, chief of engrg.

WORA(AM)— May 12, 1947: 760 khz; 5 kw-D, DA-1. TL: N18 11 30 W67 09 28. Box 363222, San Juan 00936-3222. Phone: (787) 758-1300. Fax: (787) 751-2319. E-mail: noticias@notiuno.com. Web Site: www.notiuno.com. Licensee: Arso Radio Corp. Group owner: Uno Radio Group (acq 5-10-01; grpsl). Format: News. ♦ Luis Soto, pres & gen mgr; Raymond Totti, gen sls mgr; Tanya Ramos, mktg dir; Ray Cruz, progmg dir; Betsey Rivera, news dir; Alberto Pereira, chief of engrg.

WPRA(AM)— Oct 16, 1937: 990 khz; 1 kw-U. TL: N18 10 52 W67 10 07. Stereo. Box 1293, 637 S. Post St. 00681. Phone: (787) 834-6666. Phone: (787) 265-9910. Fax: (787) 831-6925. Licensee: WPRA Inc. (acq 1996). Kenkel & Associates. Format: Top-40, Sp. Target aud: General. ♦ Dennis Bechara, pres; Jose A. Bechara, VP & gen mgr; Ada Ramos, sls dir & gen sls mgr; Eric Graniela, progmg dir; Pedro Velez Jr., chief of engrg.

*WRUO(FM)— December 1998: 88.3 mhz; 2 kw. 1,004 ft. TL: N18 19 31 W67 10 13. Box 21305 STNC, San Juan 00931. Phone: (787) 763-4699. Fax: (787) 763-5205. E-mail: lcandelas@wrtu.org. Web Site: www.wrtu.org. Licensee: University of Puerto Rico. Format: News, jazz, classical. ♦ Laura Candelas, gen mgr.

WTIL(AM)— November 1950: 1300 khz; 1 kw-U. TL: N18 11 00 W67 10 04. 261 Castilla St., Sultana Park, Naywest 00680. Secondary address: Post & Bosque Sts. 00680. Phone: (787) 652-0633. Fax: (787) 652-1292. Licensee: International Broadcasting Corp. (group owner; acq 5-12-2004; $700,000). Format: Talk, oldies, Sp, adult contemp. Target aud: 35 plus. ♦ Jose Ramiez, gen mgr.

WTPM(FM)—See Aguadilla

WUKQ-FM— Jan 15, 1963: 99.1 mhz; 50 kw. 1,963 ft. TL: N18 09 05 W66 59 19. Stereo. Box 364668, San Juan 00936. Phone: (787) 833-9910. Fax: (787) 833-9911. Licensee: El Mundo Broadcasting Corp. Group owner: Univision Radio (acq 8-1-2003; grpsl). Format: Top 40. Spec prog: Jazz 6 hrs wkly. ♦ Huberto E. Biagi, VP & gen mgr; Raul Muxo, gen mgr; Miguel Rodrigio, rgnl sls mgr; Carlos Gonzalez, progmg dir & chief of engrg; Antonio Gonzalez Caballero, news dir; Grafton Olivera, engrg dir.

Moca

WZNA(AM)— December 1983: 1040 khz; 5 kw-D, 245 w-N, DA-1. TL: N18 16 38 W67 10 01. Stereo. Box 6715, Caguas 00725. Phone: (787) 745-9770. Fax: (787) 745-9777. E-mail: nuevavuda@nuevavidafm.com. Web Site: www.nuevavidafm.com. Licensee: Western New Life Inc. (acq 8-9-2004; $950,000). Format: Contemp Christian. ♦ Juan Carlos Matos Barreto, pres; Orlando Mercede, gen mgr & opns mgr.

Broadcasting & Cable Yearbook 2006

Puerto Rico

Morovis

WEKO(AM)— December 1981: 1580 khz; 5 kw-D, 2.5 kw-N, DA-D. TL: N18 20 32 W66 25 08. Calle Bori 1554, San Juan 00927. Phone: (787) 274-1800. Fax: (787) 281-9758. Licensee: International Broadcasting Corp. (group owner; acq 9-29-98; $315,000). Fletcher, Heald & Hildreth. Format: Pop Latin & American mus, news. Target aud: 30 plus. ♦Pedro Roman-Collazo, pres; Margarita Nazario, gen mgr & progmg dir.

Naguabo

WYQE(FM)— December 1994: 92.9 mhz; 3.9 kw. 853 ft. TL: N18 16 49 W65 40 12. Stereo. Box 9300 00718. Secondary address: Apt. 2-A 00718. Phone: (809) 847-9300. Phone: (809) 874-9300. Fax: (809) 874-9290. E-mail: wyqe@yunque93.com. Web Site: www.yunque93.com. Licensee: Fajardo Broadcasting Co. Inc. (acq 12-29-99). Format: Sp tropical. News staff: 2; News: 20 hrs wkly. Target aud: 18 plus; general. ♦Efrain Archilla-Diez, pres, gen mgr & chief of engrg; Raul Rivera, VP, opns mgr, prom dir, progmg mgr & mus dir; Edwin Glass, sls dir; Vanessa Jimenez, natl sls mgr.

Pastillo

*****WWQS(FM)**—Not on air, target date: unknown: 90.1 mhz; 200 w. Ant -121 ft. TL: N17 59 40 W66 27 33. Box 8072, Ponce 00732. Licensee: Gamma Community Services Corp.

Patillas

WEXS(AM)— 1991: 610 khz; 250 w-D, 1 kw-N, DA-D. TL: N18 00 36 W66 01 28. Box 640 00723. Phone: (787) 839-0610. Fax: (787) 839-0960. Licensee: Community Broadcasting Inc. Format: Adult contemp, CHR, news. Target aud: 18-55. Spec prog: Relg 2 hrs, sports 6 hrs wkly. ♦Enrique Garcia, gen mgr.

Penuelas

WENA(AM)—See Yauco

WPPC(AM)— May 25, 1976: 1570 khz; 1 kw-D, 126 w-N. TL: N18 03 47 W66 43 04. Box 9064, Pompanos Stn., Ponce 00732-9064. Phone: (809) 836-1570. Phone: (809) 848-4670. Fax: (787) 848-4670. E-mail: radiofelicidad@yahoo.com. Licensee: Radio Felicidad Inc. (acq 6-18-81; $125,000; 7-13-81). Format: MOR, relg, Sp. Target aud: General. ♦Carlos Morales, pres; Ezequiel Pacheco, adv mgr; Jose L. Torres, chief of engrg.

Ponce

WDEP(AM)— Feb 1, 1973: 1490 khz; 5 kw-D, 1 kw-N. TL: N17 58 52 W66 36 51. Stereo. 100 Gran Bulevar Paseo, Suite 403A, San Juan 00926. Phone: (787) 292-1700. Fax: (787) 292-1717. Licensee: Media Power Group Inc. (group owner; (acq 9-30-2003; grpsl). Format: Sp, news/talk, variety. ♦Joe Pagan, gen mgr.

WIOC(FM)— January 1970: 105.1 mhz; 47 kw. Ant -200 ft. TL: N17 59 27 W66 37 45. Box 949, Guaynabo 00970-0949. Secondary address: Amelia Industrial Park, Calle Frances 42, Guaynabo 00978. Phone: (787) 622-9700. Fax: (787) 622-9478. Web Site: www.lamega.fm. Licensee: Cadena Estereotempo Inc. Group owner: Spanish Broadcasting System Inc. (acq 11-29-99; grpsl). Hogan & Hartson. Format: Adult contemp. News staff: one; News: one hr wkly. Target aud: 30-50; women. ♦Raul Alarcon, pres; Ismael Nieves, gen mgr; Marie Elena Martinez, gen sls mgr; Luis Enrique Rivera, prom dir; Pedro Arroyo, progmg dir; Alejandro Luciano, chief of engrg.

WISO(AM)— Sept 15, 1953: 1260 khz; 1 kw-U. TL: N17 59 22 W66 37 11. 134 Domenech Ave., Hato Rey 00918-3502. Phone: (787) 763-1066. Fax: (787) 763-4195. E-mail: jblanco25@hotmail.com. Web Site: www.waparadio.net. Licensee: Wilfredo G. Blanco Pi. (acq 1996; $500,000). Format: News/talk. News: 26 hrs wkly. Target aud: Adults. ♦Wilfredo G. Blanco, pres & gen mgr; Jorge Blanco, opns mgr, prom mgr, progmg dir, news dir & chief of engrg; Carmen Blanco, gen sls mgr.

WLEO(AM)— Nov 3, 1956: 1170 khz; 250 w-U. TL: N17 58 52 W66 36 51. Box 7213 00732. Secondary address: WLEO/WZAR, 46 Sector Purto Viejo, Playa De Ponce 00732. Phone: (787) 842-0048. Fax: (787) 841-1011. Fax: (787) 840-0049. Licensee: Uno Radio of Ponce Inc. Group owner: Uno Radio Group (acq 2-18-00; grpsl). Borsari & Paxson. Format: Oldies. News staff: 2; News: 50 hrs wkly. Target aud: 25 plus; mature, blue-collar & professionals. Spec prog: Sports. ♦Jose Juan Santiago, stn mgr; Carlos Conesa, rgnl sls mgr; Ray Cruz, progmg mgr & news dir; Oscar Vega, chief of engrg.

WZAR(FM)—Co-owned with WLEO(AM). Mar 17, 1966: 101.9 mhz; 14 kw. 2,580 ft. TL: N18 01 40 W66 39 14. Stereo. Phone: (787) 842-0048. Fax: (787) 840-0049. Format: Adult contemp, Sp. News: 12 hrs wkly. Target aud: 18-49; blue & white collar, adults, professionals. Spec prog: Talk show 15 hrs wkly. ♦Jose Juan Santiago, opns mgr; Pedro Gonzales, progmg mgr; Rafael Acosta, engrg mgr.

WPAB(AM)— Aug 14, 1940: 550 khz; 5 kw-U. TL: N17 59 27 W66 37 46. Box 7243 00732-7243. Secondary address: 1831 Ave. Eduardo Ruberte 00716. Phone: (787) 840-5550. Fax: (787) 840-7077. Licensee: WPAB Inc. (acq 8-21-97; $3 million for stock with co-located FM). Network: CNN en Espanol. Sayda Ortiz Booth, Freret, Imlay & Tepper PC. Format: Sp news/talk. News staff: 7. Target aud: 25 plus; concerned adults. ♦Alfonso Gimenez Porrata, CEO & pres; Alfonso Gimenez Lucchetti, VP & gen mgr; Maria Luisa Gimenez-Lucchztti, opns VP; Sayda Ortiz, sls VP & gen sls mgr; Jose Elias Torres, progmg dir; William Batista, chief of engrg.

WPRP(AM)— 1936: 910 khz; 5 kw-U. TL: N17 59 49 W66 37 31. Box 7213 00732. Secondary address: WLEO/WZAR Bldg., Sector Puerto Viejo, Paseo Sauri, Playa de Ponce 00732. Phone: (787) 842-0048. Fax: (787) 840-0049. E-mail: jsantiago@unoradio.com. Web Site: www.unoradio.com. Licensee: Arso Radio Corp. Group owner: Uno Radio Group (acq 5-8-01; grpsl). Format: News/talk, Sp. Target aud: 35 plus. ♦Jose Juan Santiago, pres, gen mgr & opns VP; Carlos Conesa, sls dir & gen sls mgr; Glerys Rivera, prom dir; Ray Cruz, progmg dir & pub affrs dir; Oscar Vega, engrg dir.

*****WPUC-FM**— May 17, 1984: 88.9 mhz; 10.8 kw. 2,912 ft. TL: N18 10 27 W66 35 32. Stereo. 2250 Ave. Las Americas, Suite 529 00717-0777. Phone: (787) 651-2000. Fax: (787) 651-2022. Web Site: www.catolicaradio.com. Licensee: Catholic University of Puerto Rico Service Association. Format: Adult contemp. News staff: 3; News: 30 hrs wkly. Target aud: General; professionals, young adults, retirees, mid & upper middle class. Spec prog: Educ. ♦Julio Ramirez, gen mgr; Axel Cruz Sanchez, stn mgr, opns mgr & progmg dir; Rey Morira, chief of engrg.

WRIO(FM)— 1986: 101.1 mhz; 34 kw. 1,768 ft. TL: N18 09 15 W66 33 15. Box 7213 00732. Phone: (787) 842-0048. Fax: (787) 840-0049. Web Site: www.salsoul.com. Licensee: Arso Radio Corp. Group owner: Uno Radio Group. Format: Sp Salsa. ♦Jose Santiago, gen mgr; Vicente Veldodere, sls dir; Vicente Bergodere, gen sls mgr; Donny Cruz, progmg dir; Alberto Pereira, chief of engrg.

WUKQ(AM)— May 1, 1957: 1420 khz; 1 kw-U. TL: N17 59 23 W66 37 21. Box 364668, San Juan 00936. Phone: (787) 758-5800. Fax: (787) 763-1854. Web Site: www.wkaqradio.com. Licensee: El Mundo Broadcasting Corp. Group owner: Univision Radio (acq 8-1-2003; grpsl). Format: News/talk info. Target aud: 25-55; young professionals, retirees, middle & upper income. Spec prog: Pub affrs interviews. ♦Hubert E. Blagui, gen mgr.

WZMT(FM)— May 1969: 93.3 mhz; 14.5 kw. -225 ft. TL: N17 59 26 W66 37 43. Stereo. Box 949, Guaynabo 00970-0949. Secondary address: Amelia Industrial Park, Calle Frances 42, Guaynabo 00968. Phone: (787) 622-9700. Fax: (787) 622-9478. Web Site: www.lamega.fm. Licensee: Potorican American Broadcasting Inc. Group owner: Spanish Broadcasting System Inc. (acq 2000; grpsl). Latham & Watkins. Format: Modern, tropical, Sp. News staff: one; News: 6 hrs wkly. Target aud: 18-49; affluent young adults. ♦Raul Alarcon, pres; Ismael Nieves, gen mgr; Maria Elena Martinez, gen sls mgr & rgnl sls mgr; Luis Enrique Rivera, prom dir; Pedro Arroyo, progmg dir; Alejandro Luciano, chief of engrg.

Quebradillas

WCHQ(AM)— February 1998: 960 khz; 1 kw-D, 1.7 kw-N, DA-2. TL: N18 26 38 W66 57 43. Box 4039, Carolina 00984. Phone: (787) 750-4090. Fax: (787) 750-6440. Licensee: International Broadcasting Corp. (group owner; (acq 7-6-2004); $1.45 million. with WRSJ(AM) Bayamon). Format: Sp, relg. ♦Luis Rosado, pres; Josue Salgado, progmg dir.

WIDI(FM)— Nov 17, 1974: 98.3 mhz; 3 kw. Ant 1,000 ft. TL: N18 23 33 W66 59 46. Stereo. Box 1553 00678. Phone: (787) 895-2725. Phone: (787) 895-0000. Fax: (787) 895-4198. E-mail: magic973@prtc.net. Licensee: Jose J. Arzuaga. (acq 7-10-79). Format: Tropical, oldies, Sp. News: 2 hrs wkly. Target aud: General. ♦Jose J. Arzuaga, pres, exec VP & gen mgr; Idalia Arzuaga, sr VP; Idalia Arrieta, opns VP; Joshua Arzuaga, dev VP; Rosidalia Villafane, dev dir.

Rio Grande

WDGT(FM)— 2003: 97.3 mhz; 800 w. Ant 1,906 ft. TL: N18 16 46 W65 51 12. Box 1553, Quebradillas 00678. Phone: (787) 895-0000. Fax: (787) 895-4198. E-mail: magic973@prtc.net. Web Site: www.magic973.com. Licensee: Josantonio Mellado Romero, et al (acq 11-18-2002). Irwin, Campbell & Tannenwald. Format: Oldies. ♦Idalia Arzuagi, gen mgr; Nitza Mercado, opns dir; Eva Cordero, dev dir; Marimel Almodovar, sls dir & adv dir; Joshua Arluaga, progmg dir; Rafael Brito, news dir; Victor Gonsalez, pub affrs dir; Jose Arluaga, engrg dir.

Rio Piedras

WFID(FM)— Nov 17, 1958: 95.7 mhz; 50 kw. 941 ft. TL: N18 16 00 W66 05 05. Stereo. Box 363222, San Juan 00936-3222. Secondary address: 1581 Ponce DeLeon St. 00926. Phone: (787) 758-1300. Fax: (787) 757-8545. Web Site: www.unoradiogroup.com. Licensee: Madifide Inc. Group owner: Uno Radio Group (acq 3-26-98; $11,537,500). Wiley, Rein & Fielding. Format: Easy lstng, adult contemp. Target aud: 25-49; middle & upper income. ♦Luis Soto, pres & gen mgr; Ana Velez, sls VP & mktg VP; Raymond Totti, sls dir; Alberto Pereira, chief of engrg.

WSKN(AM)—See San Juan

WVOZ(AM)—See San Juan

Sabana

WJIT(AM)— Mar. 31, 2000: 1250 khz; 1 kw-N, 250 w-D. TL: N18 25 28 W66 20 17. Box 878, Vega Alta 00692. Secondary address: Road #2 km 30.5, Vega Alta 00769. Phone: (787) 449-9304. Fax: (787) 825-1905. Licensee: WJIT Broadcasting Corp. Format: Var. ♦Olga Fernandez, pres; Jose David Soler, progmg dir & chief of engrg.

Sabana Grande

WYKO(AM)— 1990: . Stn currently dark 880 khz; 1 kw-D, 500 w-N. TL: N18 04 21 W66 57 06. 34 Doctor Felix Tio St. 00637. Fax: (787) 873-5795. Licensee: Juan Galiano Rivera (acq 8-3-90; $450,000;. FTR: 8-6-90). ♦Juan Galiano Rivera, pres & gen mgr.

Salinas

WHOY(AM)— Apr 6, 1967: 1210 khz; 5 kw-U, DA-2. TL: N17 58 38 W66 18 14. Box 1148 00751. Phone: (787) 824-2755. Fax: (787) 824-8054. E-mail: whoyam@coquinet.com. Licensee: Colon Radio Corp. (acq 1-31-97; $700,000). Fletcher, Heald & Hildreth. Format: Sp. ♦Martin Colon, gen mgr, gen sls mgr, prom mgr, progmg dir & news dir; Rafael Pagan, chief of engrg.

San German

WEGM(FM)— Feb 1, 1969: 95.1 mhz; 25 kw. 1,970 ft. TL: N18 08 55 W66 58 54. Box 949, Guaynabo 00970-0949. Secondary address: Amelia Industrial Park, Calle Frances 42, Guaynabo 00968. Phone: (787) 622-9700. Fax: (787) 622-9478. Web Site: www.lamega.fm. Licensee: WRPC Inc. Group owner: Spanish Broadcasting System Inc. (acq 11-29-99; grpsl). Format: CHR-English. Target aud: 18-49; men. ♦Raul Alarcon, pres; Ismael Nieves, gen mgr; Marie Elena Martinez, gen sls mgr & progmg VP; Luis Enriquez Rivera, prom dir; Pedro Arroyo, progmg dir; Roque Gallart, progmg dir; Alejandro Luciano, chief of engrg.

*****WNNV(FM)**— Nov 14, 1996: 91.7 mhz; 5 kw. 436 ft. TL: N18 04 08 W67 02 54. Box 847, Mayaguez 00681. Phone: (787) 883-7100. Fax: (787) 833-7940. Licensee: Centro Cristiano de Restauracion de Cabo Rojo Inc. (acq 1-4-2005; $1 million). Format: Contemp Christian. Target aud: 25-49. ♦Miguel Marquez, progmg dir.

WPRA(AM)—See Mayaguez

WSOL(AM)— 1955: 1090 khz; 250 w-D, 730 w-N. TL: N18 04 44 W67 01 18. (CP: TL: N18 08 18 W67 07 43). Stereo. Box 5000-442 00683. Phone: (787) 892-2216/892-2975. Fax: (787) 264-1090. E-mail: wsol@isla.net. Web Site: www.wsol.com. Licensee: San German Broadcasters Group. Roy F. Perkins. Format: Tropical, Sp, news.

Stations in the U.S.   Puerto Rico

Developers & Brokers of Radio Properties
contact American Media Services at our suite:
Philadelphia Marriott Downtown
215-625-2900
843-972-2200
americanmediaservices.com
Charleston, SC
Dallas, TX · Chicago, Il · Austin, TX
American Media Services, LLC

Target aud: Adults. Spec prog: Farm 2 hrs wkly. ♦ Alfredo Cardona, pres; Luz Maria Rivera, gen mgr & progmg dir; Gloria Silva, stn mgr, opns mgr, gen sls mgr & prom mgr; Lucy Rivera, opns dir, mktg dir & prom dir; Yolanda Ramos, asst music dir.

San Juan

WAPA(AM)— Jan 15, 1947: 680 khz; 10 kw-U, DA-N. TL: N18 24 17 W65 56 55. 134 Domenech Ave., Hato Rey 00918-3502. Phone: (787) 763-1066. Fax: (787) 763-4195. E-mail: jblanco25@hotmail.com. Web Site: www.waparadio.net. Licensee: Wifredo G. Blanco Pi (acq 2-25-91). Format: Sp, news/talk. ♦ Wilfredo G. Blanco, gen mgr; Jorge Blanco, opns mgr.

WBMJ(AM)— July 19, 1968: 1190 khz; 10 kw-D, 5 kw-N, DA-2. TL: N18 21 00 W66 06 50. Box 367000 00936-7000. Phone: (787) 724-1190. Phone: (787) 724-2727. Fax: (787) 722-5395. Fax: (787) 723-9633. E-mail: radio@vrockradio.org. Licensee: Calvary Evangelistic Mission Inc. (acq 11-85). Network: Network: Moody, USA, Salem Radio Network. Format: Relg, talk, MOR (English). News: 7 hrs wkly. Target aud: General; religious community of central Puerto Rico. ♦ Janet Luttrell, CEO & VP.

WCAD(FM)— Mar 5, 1968: 105.7 mhz; 50 kw. 1,100 ft. TL: N18 16 54 W66 06 46. Stereo. Box 9024188 00902-4188. Secondary address: 1667 Fernandez Juncos Ave., San Turce 00910. Phone: (787) 726-6144. Fax: (787) 268-3313. E-mail: alfa@alfarock.com. Web Site: www.alfarock.com. Licensee: Broadcasting & Programming Systems of Puerto Rico Inc. Format: Rock (AOR). ♦ Ralph Perez, gen mgr, stn mgr & gen sls mgr; Pedro Davila, progmg dir; Ada Cox, pub affrs dir; T. Morales, engrg dir.

WCMA-FM—See Fajardo

WFID(FM)—See Rio Piedras

WIAC(AM)— 1947: 740 khz; 10 kw-U, DA-1. TL: N18 25 25 W66 08 20. Box 9023916 00902-3916. Phone: (787) 620-9898. Fax: (787) 620-0730. E-mail: tcarrasquillo@radiopr740.com. Web Site: www.radiopr740.com. Licensee: Bestov Broadcasting Inc. of Puerto Rico (acq 1954). John P. Bankson Jr. Format: News,politics. Target aud: General. ♦ Luis A. Mejia, pres; Valerie Majia, VP & gen mgr; Luis Penchi, news dir; Rey Moraira, chief of engrg.

WIAC-FM— Mar 1, 1961: 102.5 mhz; 50 kw. 1,139 ft. TL: N18 25 25 W66 08 20. Stereo. Web Site: www.systema102.com. Format: Pop, soft music. ♦ Danny Gonzalez, chief of opns; Glenn Valares, sls dir; Valerie Mejia, progmg dir.

WIOA(FM)— Mar 1, 1961: 99.9 mhz; 31 kw. Ant 1,837 ft. TL: N18 16 44 W65 51 12. Stereo. Box 949, Guaynabo 00970-0949. Secondary address: Amelia Industrial Park, Calle Frances 42, Guaynabo 00968. Phone: (787) 622-9700. Fax: (787) 622-9478. Web Site: www.lamega.fm. Licensee: Cadena Estereotempo Inc. Group owner: Spanish Broadcasting System Inc. (acq 11-29-99; grpsl). Format: Adult contemp, ballads, Sp. Target aud: 18-49; predominantly women. ♦ Raul Alarcon, pres; Ismael Nieves, gen mgr; Maria Elena Martinez, sls mgr; Luis Enrique Rivera, prom dir; Fernando de Hostas, progmg mgr; Alejandro Luciano, chief of engrg.

***WIPR(AM)**— Jan 26, 1948: 940 khz; 10 kw-U, DA-1. TL: N18 25 36 W66 08 29. Box 190909 00919. Phone: (787) 766-0505. Fax: (787) 250-7694. Web Site: tutv.puertorico.pr. Licensee: Puerto Rico Corp. for Public Broadcasting. Network: NPR. Format: Newstalk. News staff: 7; News: 7 hrs wkly. ♦ Luis Agrait, chmn; Linda Hernandez, pres; Yolanda Zavala, exec VP; Raul Carbonell, gen mgr, progmg dir & progmg mgr; Vilma Reyes, stn mgr; Susan Marte, opns VP; Ileana Rivera, dev dir; Luis Santiago, sls dir & mktg VP; Jorge Gonzalez, engrg dir & chief of engrg; Osvaldo Torres, chief of engrg.

WIPR-FM— June 3, 1960: 91.3 mhz; 125 kw. 2,719 ft. TL: N18 06 42 W66 03 05. (CP: 105 kw, ant 2,706 ft.). Web Site: tutv.puertorico.pr. (Acq 8-87). Format: Class.

WKAQ(AM)— Dec 3, 1922: 580 khz; 10 kw-U, DA-1. TL: N18 25 55 W66 08 07. Box 364668 00936-4668. Secondary address: 383 F.D. Roosevelt Ave., Hato Rey 00918. Phone: (787) 758-5800. Fax: (787) 763-1854. Licensee: El Mundo Broadcasting Corp. Group owner: Univision Radio (acq 8-1-2003; grpsl). Format: News/talk. News staff: 22. Target aud: General. ♦ Huberto Biaggi, gen mgr; Marisol Seda, news dir; Grafton Olivera, chief of engrg.

WKAQ-FM— Oct 8, 1958: 104.7 mhz; 50 kw. 1,220 ft. TL: N18 16 51 W66 06 38. Stereo. Fax: (787) 756-5220. Web Site: www.kq105fm.com. Format: Top-40. ♦ Huberto E. Biaggi, exec VP; Raul Muxo, gen sls mgr; Carlos Gonzalez, progmg dir.

WKVM(AM)— 1951: 810 khz; 50 kw-U, DA-1. TL: N18 21 47 W66 08 13. 415 Carbonell St., Hato Rey 00918. Secondary address: c/o Arquidiocesis de San Juan, Apartado 1967 00901-1967. Phone: (787) 751-1018. Fax: (787) 758-9967. Licensee: Catholic, Apostolic & Roman Church, San Juan Archdiocese. (acq 3-4-82; $1.01 million; 1-18-82). Format: Oldies (daytime), relg Catholic (evenings). ♦ Roberto Gonzalez, pres; Allan Corales, stn mgr; Mrs. Elsa Fernandez, sls VP; Jose Antonio Cruz, progmg dir; Jose Gomez, chief of engrg.

WNEL(AM)—See Caguas

WODA(FM)—See Bayamon

WORO(FM)—See Corozal

WOSO(AM)— Nov 21, 1977: 1030 khz; 10 kw-U, DA-1. TL: N18 22 07 W66 15 17. Box 9023940 00902-3940. Phone: (787) 724-4242. Fax: (787) 723-9676. Web Site: www.woso.com. Licensee: Sherman Broadcasting Corp. Network: Network: Wall Street, CBS. Format: News/talk. News staff: 2; News: 6 hrs wkly. Target aud: 25-49. ♦ Sherman Wildman, pres; Sergio Fernandez, gen mgr; Mariano Calderon, opns dir & progmg dir; Gary Tuominen, news dir; Rodolfo Rivas, chief of engrg.

WPRM-FM— April 1959: 98.5 mhz; 25 kw. 1,910 ft. TL: N18 06 45 W66 03 07. Stereo. Box 487, Caguas 00726-0487. Phone: (787) 744-3131. Fax: (787) 743-0252. Web Site: www.salsoul.com. Licensee: Arso Radio Corp. Group owner: Uno Radio Group (acq 4-1-73). Drinker Biddle & Reath. Format: Salsoul. News staff: one; News: 3 hrs wkly. Target aud: 18-49. ♦ Jesus M. Soto, CEO & chmn; Luis A. Soto, pres; Luis A. Gonzalez, CFO; Maida Bedaya, gen mgr; Raymond Totti, gen sls mgr; Anthony Soto, progmg dir.

WQBS(AM)— Nov 1, 1954: 870 khz; 10 kw-U, DA-1. TL: N18 22 17 W66 12 17. 1508 Calle Bori 00927-6116. Phone: (787) 756-8700. Fax: (787) 765-2965. E-mail: angel@aercobroadcasting.com. Licensee: Aerco Broadcasting Corp. (acq 1-11-2005). Format: Div, Sp. ♦ Luz Alvarez, gen mgr; Nec Hernandez, progmg dir; Rudy Rivas, chief of engrg. Co-owned TV: WSJU-TV

WQII(AM)— 1947: 1140 khz; 10 kw-U, DA-1. TL: N18 21 30 W66 08 05. Cobians Plaza GM01, 1607 Ponce de Leon Ave., Stop 24, Santurce 00909. Secondary address: Box 906 6590 00906-6590. Phone: (787) 723-4848. Fax: (787) 723-4035. E-mail: postmaster@1140qpr.com. Licensee: Communications Council Group Inc. Format: Talk shows (women's). ♦ Nieves Gonzalez Avreu, pres; Jorge Rudolfo Marquina, gen mgr; William Padilla, sls dir; Danny Gonzalez, progmg dir; Raymond Hernandez, chief of engrg.

WRSJ(AM)—See Bayamon

***WRTU(FM)**— Feb 8, 1980: 89.7 mhz; 50 kw. 796 ft. TL: N18 16 00 W66 05 05. Stereo. Box 21305, Stn. C 00931-1305. Secondary address: Mariana Bracetti St., Ponce de Leon Ave., Rio Piedras 00931. Phone: (787) 763-4699. Phone: (787) 464-0000 ext 5728. Fax: (787) 763-5205. E-mail: lcandelas@wrtu.org. Web Site: www.wrtu.org. Licensee: University of Puerto Rico. Dow, Lohnes & Albertson. Format: Class, jazz, Sp. News staff: 5; News: 8 hrs wkly. Target aud: General; young, professional & highly educated. Spec prog: News 7 hrs, talk 2 hrs wkly. ♦ Laura Candelas, gen mgr.

WSKN(AM)— Oct 15, 1949: 1320 khz; 5 kw-D, 2.3 kw-N. TL: N18 23 00 W66 04 01. 100 Gran Bulevar Paseo, Suite 403A 00926. Phone: (787) 292-1700. Fax: (787) 292-1717. Licensee: Media Power Group Inc. (group owner; acq 9-30-2003; grpsl). Format: Sp. ♦ Joe Pagan, gen mgr.

WUNO(AM)— Jan 11, 1960: 630 khz; 5 kw-U, DA-2. TL: N18 26 00 W66 07 29. Box 363222 00936-3222. Secondary address: 1581 Ponce de Leon St., Rio Peidras 00926. Phone: (787) 758-1300. Fax: (787) 756-8545. E-mail: info@notiuno.com. Web Site: www.notiuno.com. Licensee: Madifide Inc. Group owner: Uno Radio Group (acq 5-8-01; grpsl). Format: News/talk. News staff: 22; News: 168 hrs wkly. Target aud: 25 plus. ♦ Jesus M. Soto, CEO; Luis Soto, pres & gen mgr; Ray Cruz, progmg dir.

WVOZ(AM)— July 4, 1949: 1520 khz; 10 kw-U, DA-1. TL: N18 21 00 W66 09 25. 1554 Calle Bori 00927. Phone: (787) 764-1077. Phone: (787) 274-1800. Fax: (787) 281-9758. Licensee: Pedro Roman Collazo. Freret & Imlay. Format: Tropical, sports. Target aud: 35 plus; medium and low income individuals. Spec prog: Puerto Rican & Latin hits. ♦ Pedro Roman-Collazo, pres; Margarita Nazario, gen mgr.

WZNT(FM)— 1959: 93.7 mhz; 50 kw. 280 ft. TL: N18 22 42 W66 07 04. Stereo. Box 949, Guaynabo 00970-0949. Secondary address: Amelia Industrial Park, Calle Frances 42, Guaynabo 00968. Phone: (787) 622-9700. Fax: (787) 622-9478. Web Site: www.lamega.fm. Licensee: WZNT Inc. Group owner: Spanish Broadcasting System Inc. (acq 2000; grpsl). Fletcher, Heald & Hildreth. Format: Tropical, salsa & merengue. Target aud: 18-49; male. ♦ Raul Alarcon, pres; Ismael Nieves, gen mgr & stn mgr; Marie Elena Martinez, sls VP & gen sls mgr; Luis Enrique Rivera, prom dir; Billie Fourquet, progmg VP; Pedro Arroyo, progmg mgr; Nestor Rodriguez, progmg mgr; Alejandro Luciano, chief of engrg.

San Sebastian

WLRP(AM)— Feb 15, 1965: 1460 khz; 500 w-U. TL: N18 20 50 W66 59 56. (CP: 2.5 kw). Box 1670 00685. Phone: (787) 896-1460. Fax: (787) 896-8100. E-mail: radioraices@prtc.net. Licensee: Las Raices Pepinianas Inc. Format: Adult contemp. ♦ Ramon Colon Pratts, pres; Alfredo Perez, gen mgr & gen sls mgr; Ramon E. Pratts, prom mgr; Jose M. Chaparro, mus dir; Juan Felin, chief of engrg.

WNOD(FM)—See Mayaguez

WRSS(AM)— April 1984: 1410 khz; 1 kw-D, DA-1. TL: N18 19 14 W66 58 45. Box 1410 00685. Secondary address: Segundo Ruez # 52 St. 00685. Phone: (787) 896-2121. Fax: (787) 896-5753. E-mail: tunuevafamilia@hotmail.com. Licensee: Angel Vera-Maury (acq 2-9-03; $250,000). Format: Talk, oldies, Sp. News staff: 6; News: over 30 hrs wkly. Target aud: 30 plus. Spec prog: Div. ♦ Angel Vera Maury, pres; Cesar Vera, gen mgr; Arturo Soto, gen sls mgr; Nestor Gonzalez, progmg VP & progmg dir.

Utuado

WERR(FM)— Feb 1, 1970: 104.1 mhz; 50 kw. 255 ft. TL: N18 17 31 W66 39 28. Stereo. P.O. Box 29404, San Juan 00929. Secondary address: San Felipe # 205, Arecibo 00612. Phone: (787) 751-6318. Phone: (787) 751-1310. Fax: (787) 751-6854. E-mail: jrivera@redentor104fm.com. Web Site: www.redentor104fm.com. Licensee: Radio Redentor Inc. (acq 6-75). Fletcher, Heald & Hildreth. Format: Adult contemp, Sp, Christian. Target aud: General. ♦ Rev. Ricardo Apunte, pres; Jesus M. Rivera, gen mgr; Rev. Abimael Reyes, mktg dir & mktg mgr; Rev. Ramon Rivera, engrg dir.

WUPR(AM)— Apr 18, 1964: 1530 khz; 1 kw-D, 250 w-N. TL: N18 16 02 W66 42 38. Box 868 00641. Phone: (787) 894-2460. Fax: (787) 894-4955. Web Site: www.coqui.net. Licensee: Central Broadcasting Corp. Format: Sp, news/talk. News staff: 2; News: 11 hrs wkly. Target aud: 18-49; middle income adults. ♦ Jose A. Martinez, pres, gen mgr, gen sls mgr & progmg dir; Manuel E. Andujar, mus dir; Manuel B. Martinez, news dir; Epifanio Rodriguez Velez, chief of engrg.

Vega Baja

WEGA(AM)— October 1971: 1350 khz; 2.5 kw-U, DA-2. TL: N18 28 38 W66 23 43. Box 1488 00694-1488. Phone: (787) 858-0386. Fax: (787) 855-0916. Licensee: A Radio Company Inc. (acq 9-1-2004; $850,000). Format: Var/div. ♦Gerardo Angulo, pres; Carmelo Santiago, gen mgr; Hector Santiago, sls VP & progmg dir; Lloyd Santiago, mktg VP; Ronald Cushing, chief of engrg.

Vieques

WIVV(AM)— Dec 8, 1956: 1370 khz; 5 kw-D, 1 kw-N. TL: N18 06 19 W65 28 03. Box 367000, San Juan 00936-7000. Phone: (787) 724-1190. Phone: (787) 741-8717. Fax: (787) 722-5395. Fax: (787) 741-8717. E-mail: radio@vrockradio.org. Licensee: Calvary Evangelistic Mission Inc. Network: Salem Radio Network. Format: Relg, talk, MOR, Sp. News: 7 hrs wkly. Target aud: General; eastern Puerto Rico & the Leeward Islands. Spec prog: News 7 hrs wkly. ♦Janet L. Luttrell, CEO & VP.

Yabucoa

WXEW(AM)— Jan 1, 1978: 840 khz; 5 kw-D, 1 kw-N, DA-N. TL: N18 02 58 W65 52 07. (CP: 5 kw-U). 203 Font Martelo Ave., Humacao 00971. Secondary address: Box 100 00767. Phone: (787) 893-3065. Phone: (787) 850-0840. Fax: (787) 850-4055. E-mail: victor@victoria840.com. Web Site: www.victoria840.com. Licensee: Radio Victoria Inc. (acq 9-19-83). Format: MOR, Sp, talk. ♦Victoria Vargas, pres; Victor M. Calderon, VP & gen mgr; Caly Burmudez, gen sls mgr; Brenda Calderon, mktg dir; Jose Calderon, prom mgr & mus dir; Luis Calderon, progmg dir; Angel Bena, news dir; Alberto Pereira, chief of engrg.

Yauco

WENA(AM)— Nov 11, 1978: 1330 khz; 2 kw-D, 1.4 kw-N, DA-1. TL: N18 02 04 W66 51 48. Stereo. Box 1338, 25 DeJullo St., Condominio Torres Navel Bldg. 00698. Phone: (787) 267-1330. Phone: (787) 856-1330. Fax: (787) 267-1340. E-mail: wena@cogui.net. Web Site: www.yaucoweb.com/wena/. Licensee: Southern Broadcasting Corp. Roy F. Perkins. Format: Adult contemp, CHR, news/talk. News staff: 5; News: 28 hrs wkly. Target aud: 25 plus; young adults & women. ♦Nephtali Rodriguez, pres & gen mgr; Israel Rodriguez, VP & opns VP; Ramon Ramos, dev mgr; Pedro Gregory, sls dir; Juan Diaz, adv mgr; Guillermo Valls, progmg dir; Isaac Pagan, engrg dir; Ronald Cushing, engrg mgr.

WKFE(AM)— Nov 3, 1961: 1550 khz; 250 w-U. TL: N18 01 24 W66 52 02. 100 Gran Bulevar Paseo, Suite 403A, San Juan 00926. Phone: (787) 292-1700. Fax: (787) 292-1717. Licensee: Media Power Group Inc. (group owner; (acq 9-30-2003; grpsl). Fletcher, Heald & Hildreth. Format: Sp news/talk. News staff: 2; News: 40 hrs wkly. Target aud: 25 plus; 50% men, 50% women. ♦Eduardo Rivero, pres; Jose Pagan, gen mgr; Orlando Morales, progmg dir.

Virgin Islands

Charlotte Amalie

WGOD(AM)— 1992: 1090 khz; 250 w-D. TL: N18 18 57 W64 53 02. Box 305012, St. Thomas 00803. Phone: (340) 774-4498. Fax: (340) 777-9978. Licensee: Three Angels Broadcasting Corp. Inc. (acq 7-5-89). Format: Gospel. ♦Charles Saunders, pres & gen mgr.

WGOD-FM— Sept 1, 1980: 97.9 mhz; 50 kw. 295 ft. TL: N18 21 25 W64 58 00. Stereo. (Acq 8-15-85). Format: Relg, educ.

***WIUJ(FM)**— Oct 5, 1979: 102.9 mhz; 1.5 kw. 1,427 ft. TL: N18 21 26 W64 56 50. Stereo. Box 2477, St. Thomas 00803. Phone: (340) 776-1029. Phone: (340) 777-9485. Fax: (340) 774-0004. Licensee: Virgin Islands Youth Development Radio. (acq 8-6-90). Format: Adult contemp, jazz, Sp, btfl music, big band. News staff: one. Target aud: General. Spec prog: Class 5 hrs, jazz 6 hrs, Fr 4 hrs, Sp 4 hrs wkly. ♦Leo Morone, gen mgr; F. Ottley, opns mgr; Greg Cyntje, progmg dir; Mike Morone, asst music dir; Ron Hall, chief of engrg.

WIVI(FM)— Apr 26, 1992: 96.1 mhz; 2.4 kw. 1,500 ft. TL: N18 21 33 W64 58 18. Stereo. Box 304383, St. Thomas 00803-4383. Phone: (340) 774-1972. Phone: (340) 776-9696. Fax: (340) 776-7060. Web Site: www.pirateradiovi.com. Licensee: Rox Radio Enterprises Inc. (acq 11-20-98; $30,000 for 60% of stock). Format: AAA. News: one hr wkly. Target aud: 25-54; general. Spec prog: Rock. ♦Lou Lambert, gen mgr; Doreen Carl, sls dir; Kevin Simmons, progmg dir.

WSTA(AM)— Aug 1, 1950: 1340 khz; 1 kw-U. TL: N18 20 10 W64 57 17. Box 1340, # 121 Subbase, St. Thomas 00804. Secondary address: 121 Sub Base, St. Thomas 00802. Phone: (340) 774-1340. Phone: (340) 777-4500. Fax: (340) 776-1316. E-mail: addie@wsta.com. Web Site: www.WSTA.com. Licensee: Ottley Communications Corp. (acq 12-1-84). Network: Network: ABC, CNN Radio. Miller & Neely, P.C. Format: Div, oldies, adult urban contemp. News staff: 2; News: 20 hrs wkly. Target aud: General. ♦Athneil Ottley, pres; Athniel Ottley, gen mgr; Athneil C. Ottley, stn mgr; Irvin Brown, chief of opns; Jean Forde, sls dir, mktg dir & mus dir; Peter E. Ottley, progmg mgr; Lee Carle, news dir; Manny Centeno, chief of engrg.

WVGN(FM)— 2002: 107.3 mhz; 1.4 kw. Ant 1,565 ft. TL: N18 21 31 W64 58 20. 714 Nisky Mail Box, PMB PP-105, Saint Thomas 00802. Phone: (340) 774-2012. Fax: (340) 776-5362. E-mail: NPR@wvgn.org. Web Site: www.wvgn.org. Licensee: LKK Group Corp. (acq 6-27-02; $290,000). Network: NPR. Format: News/talk. ♦Patricia Bourne, VP, gen mgr, stn mgr & progmg dir.

WVJZ(FM)— Mar 15, 1986: 105.3 mhz; 7.7 kw. 1,490 ft. TL: N18 21 33 W64 58 18. Stereo. Box 305678, 13 Crown Bay Fill, St. Thomas 00803-5678. Secondary address: Box 8209, Bluebeards's Castle, Suite 255, St. Thomas 00801. Phone: (340) 776-5260. Phone: (340) 776-5260. Fax: (340) 776-5357. Fax: (340) 776-5357. E-mail: contact@kasvi.net. Web Site: www.wvjz.net. Licensee: Gark LLC. Group owner: Knight Quality Stations (acq 6-4-98). Pepper & Corazzini. Format: Urban. News staff: 2. Target aud: 18-34; young adults, business professionals & college students. ♦Randolph H. Knight, pres; Mark P. Bastin, gen mgr, sls dir, mktg dir & progmg dir; Jean Greaux Jr., opns dir & chief of engrg; Anthony Peets, mus dir.

WVWI(AM)— Nov 19, 1962: 1000 khz; 5 kw-D, 1 kw-N. TL: N18 20 11 W64 41 38. Box 305678, 13 Crown Bay Fill, St. Thomas 00803-5678. Phone: (340) 776-1000. Fax: (340) 776-5357. E-mail: contact@kqsvi.net. Web Site: www.wvwi.net. Licensee: Knight Communications of the Virgin Islands Inc. Group owner: Knight Quality Stations (acq 1996; $250,000). Network: Network: CBS, Westwood One. Pepper & Corazzini. Format: Sports, news/talk. News staff: 2; News: 25 hrs wkly. Target aud: 25-54; middle/upper income professionals. Spec prog: Relg 6 hrs, West Indian one hr, East Indian one hr wkly. ♦Randolph H. Knight, pres; Mark P. Bastin, gen mgr, sls dir, mktg dir & progmg dir; Jean Greaux Jr., opns dir, news dir & chief of engrg.

WZIN(FM)— Nov 2, 1976: 104.3 mhz; 19.5 kw. Ant 1,545 ft. TL: N18 21 31 W64 58 20. Stereo. Nisky Mall Center, PMB 357, St. Thomas, PR 00802. Phone: (340) 776-1043. Fax: (340) 775-3446. E-mail: info@buzzrocks.com. Web Site: www.buzzrocks.com. Licensee: Pan Caribbean Broadcasting de P.R. Inc. (acq 7-11-02; $1 million). Arter & Hadden. Format: Alternative rock. Target aud: 18-34. ♦Alan Friedman, VP & gen mgr.

Christiansted

***WIVH(FM)**— July 1993: 90.1 mhz; 1 kw. 731 ft. TL: N17 44 10 W64 42 04. 2457 Rt. 118, Hunlock Creek, PA 18621. Secondary address: 5007 Estate Mt. Washington 00820-4565. Phone: (570) 477-3688. Phone: (340) 778-2852. Fax: (340) 719-3076. E-mail: wrgn@epix.net. Web Site: www.wrgn.org/wivh.htm. Licensee: Gospel Media Institute Inc. Format: Relg. Target aud: General. ♦Burl F. Updyke, pres & gen mgr.

WJKC(FM)— Oct 29, 1983: 95.1 mhz; 50 kw. 886 ft. TL: N17 44 07 W64 40 46. (CP: Ant 791 ft.). Stereo. Box 25680, St.Croix 00824-1680. Phone: (340) 773-0995. Fax: (340) 773-9093. Web Site: www.viradio.com. Licensee: Radio 95 Inc. Rosenman & Colin. Format: Urban, Reggae, hip-hop. Target aud: General. ♦Jonathan K. Cohen, pres & gen mgr; Troy Brown, progmg dir; Herb Schoenbohm, chief of engrg.

WMNG(FM)— 1997: 104.9 mhz; 6 kw. 699 ft. TL: N17 44 08 W64 40 47. Box 25680, St. Croix 00824-1680. Phone: (340) 773-0995. Fax: (340) 773-9093. E-mail: jkc95@aol.com. Web Site: www.viradio.com. Licensee: Clara Communications Corp. Format: Classic hits. ♦Jonathan K. Cohen, gen mgr; Amanda Cohen, gen sls mgr; Tom Yarbaugh, progmg dir; Herb Schoenbahm, chief of engrg.

WVIQ(FM)— May 17, 1965: 99.5 mhz; 10.5 kw. 1,080 ft. TL: N17 45 20 W64 47 55. Stereo. Box 25680, St. Croix 00824-1680. Phone: (340) 773-1180. Fax: (340) 773-9093. E-mail: www.jkc95@aol.com. Web Site: www.viradio.com. Licensee: JKC Communications of the Virgin Islands Inc. (acq 1999; $590,000). Format: Adult contemp. ♦Jonathan Cohen, gen mgr & gen sls mgr; Tom Yarborough, progmg dir; Herb Schoenbohm, chief of engrg.

WYAC-FM— Feb 26, 1989: 93.5 mhz; 11.5 kw. Ant 735 ft. TL: N17 44 08 W64 40 47. Stereo. Box 25868 00824. Secondary address: 118 Estate Mt. Welcome 00824. Phone: (340) 773-3693. Fax: (340) 719-1800. E-mail: rogerwmorgan@juno.com. Licensee: Philip E. Kuhlman and Ellen N. Kuhlman, joint tenants (acq 7-8-2004; $300,000). Format: Adult contemp. News: one hr wkly. Target aud: General; affluent young adult permanent residents. Spec prog: Relg 3 hrs wkly. ♦Francisce "Francky" Velasquez, stn mgr; Roger Morgan, pres, gen mgr, prom mgr & progmg dir; Herb Schoerbaum, chief of engrg.

Cruz Bay

WWKS(FM)— Feb 3, 1997: 101.3 mhz; 48 kw. 1,302 ft. TL: N18 20 17 W64 43 40. Stereo. Box 305678, St. Thomas 00803-5678. Secondary address: Box 8209, Bluebeard's Castle, St. Thomas 00801. Phone: (340) 776-4585. Phone: (340) 776-1013. Fax: (340) 776-5357. Fax: (340) 774-4455. Web Site: www.wwks.net. Licensee: Knight V.I. Radio Corp. Group owner: Knight Quality Stations (acq 1996; $225,000). Network: ABC. Pepper & Corazzini. Format: Urban contemp. News staff: 2; News: 2 hrs wkly. Target aud: 25-54; middle/upper income professionals. Spec prog: West Indian/calypso 25 hrs wkly. ♦Randolph H. Knight, pres; Mark P. Bastin, gen mgr, sls dir, mktg dir & progmg dir; Jean Greaux Jr., opns dir, news dir & chief of engrg.

Frederiksted

WAXJ(FM)— 1999: 103.5 mhz; 6 kw. Ant -33 ft. TL: N17 43 28 W64 53 03. 79-A Castle Coakley, Christiansted 00820. Phone: (340) 719-1620. Phone: (340) 778-2753. Fax: (340) 778-1686. E-mail: wrra@islands.vi. Web Site: www.wrra.vi. Licensee: Reef Broadcasting Inc. (acq 6-27-98). Format: Div music. ♦Hugh Pemberton, gen mgr & chief of engrg; Beverley Meyers, gen sls mgr; Hugh Pembeton, progmg dir.

WDHP(AM)— May 1999: 1620 khz; 10 kw-D, 1 kw-N. TL: N17 43 28 W64 53 03. 79A Estate Castle Coakley 00820. Phone: (340) 719-1620. Fax: (340) 778-1686. E-mail: wrra@islands.vi. Web Site: www.wrra.vi. Licensee: Reef Broadcasting Inc. Format: Diversified, talk, beautiful music. ♦Beverley Meyers, sls dir; Hugh Pemberton, gen mgr, progmg dir & chief of engrg.

WEVI(FM)— 2003: 101.7 mhz; 900 w. Ant 790 ft. TL: N17 43 15 W64 51 26. Box 892, Christiansted 00821. Phone: (340) 719-1400. Fax: (340) 719-1733. E-mail: info@frontlinemissions.org. Web Site: www.frontlinemissions.org. Licensee: Frontline Missions International Inc. (acq 3-12-02). Format: Christian Carribbean music, Bible teachings. ♦Anthony Whitehead, gen mgr & progmg dir.

WMYP(FM)— 2002: 98.3 mhz; 1.9 kw. Ant 915 ft. TL: N17 44 51 W64 50 11. Box 8294, Christiansted 00823. Phone: (340) 772-0098. Fax: (340) 772-9852. E-mail: latino98@viaccess.net. Licensee: Juan G. Padin & Jose J. Martiniez (acq 10-15-99). Format: Sp, tropical/pop. Target aud: 18-49. ♦Jose Martinez, gen mgr; Johnny Daly, gen sls mgr; Junior Martinez, opns mgr & progmg dir.

WRRA(AM)— 1976: 1290 khz; 500 w-D, 250 w-N. TL: N17 43 28 W64 53 03. 79A Estate Castle Coakley, Christiansted 00820. Phone: (340) 778-1620. Fax: (340) 778-1686. E-mail: wrra@islands.vi. Web Site: www.wrra.vi. Licensee: Reef Broadcasting Inc. Roy F. Perkins. Format: Gospel. News staff: 2; News: 25 hrs wkly. Target aud: 18-56. Spec prog: Black, jazz 6 hrs, gospel 12 hrs, relg 10 hrs wkly. ♦Beverley Meyers, sls dir; Hugh Pemberton, gen mgr & progmg dir.

St. Thomas

WTTP(FM)—See Las Piedras, PR

Mexico

Tijuana

XETRA(AM)—Licensed to Tijuana. See San Diego CA

XETRA-FM—Licensed to Tijuana. See San Diego CA

XHRM-FM—Licensed to Tijuana. See San Diego CA

Federated States of Micronesia

Pohnpei

V6AH(AM)— 1964: 1449 khz; 10 kw-U. Box 1086, Kolonia Pohnpei 96941. Phone: (691) 320-2296. Fax: (691) 320-5212. E-mail: v6ah_radio@mail.fm. Web Site: www.fm/ppbc. Licensee: Oltrick D. Santos. Format: CHR. News: 20 hrs wkly. Target aud: General. Spec prog: Farm 20 hrs, folk 20 hrs, gospel 2 hrs, relg 2 hrs wkly. ♦ Oltrick D. Santos, gen mgr.

Truk

V6AK(AM)— 1962: 1593 khz; 5 kw-U, DA-1. Box 2222, Weno, Chuuk 96942. Phone: (691) 330-2596. Licensee: Dept. of Public Affairs/Government. Format: News. Target aud: General. ♦ Johnny Esa, gen mgr.

Yap

*V6AI(AM)— June 9, 1965: 1494 khz; 10 kw-U. Box 117, Colonia YAP State Western Caroline Islands 96943. Phone: (691) 350-2174. Fax: (691) 350-4426. E-mail: petergar@mail.fm. Licensee: Yap State Government. Format: CHR, country, news. News staff: 2; News: 20 hrs wkly. Target aud: General. Spec prog: Yapese 10 hrs, Micronesian 10 hrs, Japanese 5 hrs, Filipino 5 hrs wkly. ♦ Peter Garamfel, gen mgr; Bernie Tiningmow, progmg dir; John Gilmatam, mus dir; Jovencio David, chief of engrg. Co-owned TV: *WAAB-TV affil

Northern Mariana Islands

Chalan Kanoa-Saipan

*KRNM(FM)— Feb 28, 1998: 88.1 mhz; 1.8 kw. Ant 125 ft. TL: N15 09 05 E145 43 11. Stereo. Box 501250, Northern Marianas College, Saipan 96950. Phone: (670) 234-3690 ext 1520. Fax: (670) 235-0915. E-mail: carlp@nmcnet.edu. Web Site: www.nmcnet.edu. Licensee: Northern Marianas College. Network: Network: NPR, PRI. Format: Classical, jazz, news/talk. Spec prog: Chamorro 2 hrs, Korean 1 hrs, Chinese 1 hr wkly. ♦ Carl Pogue, gen mgr.

Garapan-Saipan

KCNM(AM)— October 1984: 1080 khz; 5 kw-U. TL: N15 09 00 W145 42 52. Box 500914, Saipan 96950. Secondary address: Box 20249, Guam Main Facility 96921. Phone: (670) 234-7239. Phone: (670) 234-8644. Fax: (670) 234-0447. E-mail: kzmi-fm@vzpavifica.net. Licensee: Inter-Island Communications Inc. (group owner; (acq 8-6-84). Network: AP Network News. Format: News/talk. News staff: one; News: 168 hrs wkly. Target aud: General. Spec prog: Chamorro. ♦ Harry B. Blalock, gen mgr; Bob Webb, gen sls mgr; Louie Tenorio, progmg dir.

KCNM-FM— 1999: 101.1 mhz; 3.2 kw. Ant 827 ft. TL: N15 11 00 W145 44 06. 1868 Halsey Dr., Piti, GU 96915. Phone: (671) 477-7108. Fax: (671) 477-6411. E-mail: kcnm@ite.net. Web Site: www.kcnmkzmi.com. Licensee: Inter-Island Communications Inc. (group owner). Format: Ethnic. ♦ Edward H. Poppe Jr., pres; Frances Poppe, CFO; Edward Poppe, gen mgr; Harry Blalock, stn mgr; Michelle Poppe-Aguon, opns dir; Lewis Tenorio, progmg dir.

KPXP(FM)— Nov 5, 1992: 99.5 mhz; 6.5 kw. 1,492 ft. TL: N15 11 10 W145 44 25. Stereo. 111 W. Chalan Santo Papa St., Hagatna, GU 96910. Phone: (670) 235-7996. Phone: (670) 235-7997. Fax: (670) 235-7998. E-mail: rex@spbguam.com. Web Site: www.power99.com. Licensee: Sorensen Pacific Broadcasting Inc. (group owner; acq 6-23-03; grpsl). Kaye, Scholer, Fierman, Hays & Handler. Format: CHR. News staff: one; News: 14 hrs wkly. Target aud: 14-39; affluent adults. ♦ Jon A. Anderson, pres; Rex W. Sorensen, CEO, chmn & CFO; Curtis Dancoe, stn mgr, sls dir & gen sls mgr; Laurence Bejerana, prom mgr; Raymond Gibson, progmg dir; Marvin Palmer, chief of engrg.

KRSI(FM)— July 1992: 97.9 mhz; 4.5 kw. Ant 1,519 ft. TL: N15 11 09 E145 44 29. Stereo. 111 W. Chalan Santo Papa St., Hagatna, GU 96910. Phone: (670) 235-7996. Fax: (670) 235-7998. E-mail: rex@spbguam.com. Web Site: www.radiopacific.com. Licensee: Sorensen Pacific Broadcasting Inc. (group owner; acq 6-23-03; grpsl). Cohn & Marks. Format: Classic rock, div, rock. News: one hr wkly. Target aud: 25-49. Spec prog: Blues 6 hrs, reggae 19 hrs, Hawaiian 2 hrs, Chamdru 4 hrs, jazz one hr wkly. ♦ Rex Sorensen, CEO & pres; Curtis Dancoe, gen mgr & gen sls mgr; Laurence Bejerana, prom mgr; Raymond Gibson, progmg dir; Marvin Palmer, chief of engrg.

KWAW(FM)— 1999: 100.3 mhz; 2.5 kw. Ant 3 ft. TL: N15 12 28 W145 42 52. (CP: 1.1 kw, ant 1,512 ft. TL: N15 11 05 W145 44 26). Boon Bldg., 1270 N. Marine Dr., Tamuning, GU 96911. Phone: (670) 234-5929 (request line). Fax: (670) 234-2262. Web Site: www.magic100radio.com. Licensee: Leon Padilla Ganacias. (acq 8-13-98; $25,615). ♦ Leon Padilla Ganacias, gen mgr.

KZMI(FM)— 1997: 103.9 mhz; 3.2 kw. 300 ft. Stereo. 1868 Halsey Drive, Piti, GU 96915. Phone: (670) 235-5064. Fax: (670) 234-0447. Web Site: www.itecrmi.com. Licensee: Inter-Island Communications Inc. (group owner). Format: Adult contemp. ♦ Edward H. Poppe Jr., pres; Frances Poppe, CFO; Edward H. Poppe III, exec VP; Harvey Blalock, stn mgr; Michelle Poppe-Aguon, opns mgr; Lewis Tenovio, progmg dir.

Directory of Radio Stations in Canada

Alberta

Athabasca

CKBA(AM)— Aug 1, 1989: 850 khz; 1 kw-D. Unit 2, 4907 51st St., Venture Pl. P9S 1E7. Phone: (780) 675-5301. Fax: (780) 675-4938. E-mail: JPeckham@ab.ncc.ca. Licensee: 3937844 Canada Inc. Group owner: NewCap Inc. (acq 4-19-02; grpsl). Format: Today's country. News staff: one. Target aud: 25-54. ♦ Al Anderson, VP; Joanne Peckham, gen mgr.

Blairmore

CJPR-FM— 2004: 94.9 mhz; 760 w. Box 840 T0K 0E0. Phone: (403) 562-2806. Fax: (403) 562-8114. Licensee: 3937844 Canada Inc. Format: Full country. ♦ L. Anderson, VP; Darryl Ferguson, stn mgr.

Brooks

CIBQ(AM)— Apr 15, 1973: 1340 khz; 1 kw-D, DA-1. Unit 8-403 2nd Ave., West Brooks T1R 1S3. Phone: (403) 362-3418. Phone: (403) 362-6000 (NEWS). Fax: (403) 362-8168. Web Site: www.eidnet.org/local/Q13. Licensee: 3937844 Canada Inc. Group owner: NewCap Broadcasting Ltd. acq 4-19-02; grpsl). Format: Contemp country. News staff: one; News: 12 hrs wkly. Target aud: 25-54. ♦ Al Anderson, gen mgr; John Petrie, stn mgr.

Calgary

CBCX-FM— 2003: 89.7 mhz; 10 kw. 1724 Westmount Blvd. N.W. T2N 3G7. Phone: (403) 521-6000. Web Site: radio-canada.ca/regions/alberta. Licensee: CBC. Network: Chaine Culturelle. Format: Fr. ♦ Rene Fontaine, gen mgr.

*CBR(AM)— Oct 1, 1964: 1010 khz; 50 kw-U, DA-2. Box 2640 T2P 2M7. Secondary address: 1724 Westmount Blvd. N.W. T2N 3G7. Phone: (403) 521-6000. Fax: (403) 521-6271. Web Site: www.cbc.ca. Licensee: CBC. Format: Info, div, news/talk. News: 24 hrs wkly. ♦ David Gray, gen mgr; Ashley Demulder, opns mgr; Harry Wagter, mktg mgr; Helen Henderson, progmg mgr; Donna McElligott, news dir.

CBR-FM— Sept 29, 1975: 102.1 mhz; 100 kw. 788 ft. Stereo. Network: CBC Radio Two. Format: Class, blues.

CBRF-FM— 2002: 103.7 mhz; 22 kw. Box 2640 T2P 2M7. Secondary address: 1724 Westmount Blvd. N.W. T2N 3G7. Phone: (403) 521-6000. Fax: (403) 521-6262. Web Site: radio-canada.ca/regions/alberta. Licensee: Canadian Broadcasting Corp. Network: Premiere Chaine. Format: Fr. ♦ Francois Pageau, gen mgr; Mike Spear, progmg dir; Chris Franklin, news dir.

CFAC(AM)— May 1922:: 960 khz; 50 kw-U. Stereo. 2723 37th Ave. N.E. T1Y 5R8. Phone: (403) 291-0000. Fax: (403) 291-4368. Licensee: Rogers Broadcasting Ltd. (acq 12-89). Format: All sports. News staff: 3; News: 15 hrs wkly. Target aud: 55 plus. Spec prog: Agriculture, rural 10 hrs wkly. ♦ Tony Viner, pres; Gary Miles, exec VP; Kevin McKenna, VP, gen mgr & opns VP; Jim Dunlop, gen sls mgr; Dawn Buffam, mktg dir & progmg dir; Paul Williams, adv dir; Bob MacDonald, engrg dir.

CHFM-FM—Co-owned with CFAC(AM). Aug 29, 1962: 95.9 mhz; 48 kw. Ant 480 ft. TL: N51 03 37 W114 10 13. Stereo. Web Site: www.chfm.com. Rep: Canadian Broadcast Sales. Format: Adult contemp. News staff: one. Target aud: 35-54; females. ♦ Tony Viner, CEO; Kevin McKenna, stn mgr; Brian Depoe, mktg dir & progmg dir; Jennifer Reynolds, prom dir; Darren Robson, mus dir; David Spence, news dir; Tanya Berner, pub affrs dir.

CFFR(AM)— Jan 10, 1984: 660 khz; 50 kw, DA-2. Stereo. 2723 37 Ave. N.E. T1Y 5R8. Phone: (403) 291-0000. Fax: (403) 291-5342. Licensee: Rogers (Alberta) Ltd. Group owner: Rogers Broadcasting Ltd. (acq 9-10-99; grpsl). Format: Oldies. News staff: 5; News: 10 hrs wkly. Target aud: 25-49. Spec prog: Sports 15 hrs wkly. ♦ Kevin McKenna, gen mgr; Brian Depoe, prom dir & progmg dir; Jennifer Reynolds, prom dir & progmg dir; Darren Robson, mus dir; David Spence, news dir.

CKIS-FM—Co-owned with CFFR(AM). June 3, 1996: 96.9 mhz; 48 kw. 686 ft. TL: N51 02 18 W114 13 28. Format: Classic rock. ♦ Vince Cownden, VP & progmg dir; K. Kirch, mus dir; K. Crook, engrg VP.

CFGQ-FM— Apr 15, 1982: 107.3 mhz; 100 kw. Ant 638 ft. TL: N51 03 54 W114 12 47. Stereo. 630 3rd Ave. S.W., Suite 105 T2P 4L4. Phone: (403) 716-6500. Fax: (403) 716-2111. Web Site: www.q107fm.ca. Licensee: CKIK-FM Ltd. Group owner: Corus Entertainment Inc. (acq 7-6-2000; grpsl). Format: Classic rock. Target aud: 25-44. ♦ Garry McKenzie, gen mgr; Doug Young, gen sls mgr; Christian Hall, progmg dir; Natasha Rapchuk, news dir; Wade Wensink, chief of engrg.

CHQR(AM)—Co-owned with CFGQ-FM. November 1964: 770 khz; 50 kw-U, DA-2. Stereo. Web Site: www.qr77.com. (Acq 4-15-70). Rep: Canadian Broadcast Sales, Dora-Clayton. Format: News/talk, sports. News staff: 11; News: 17 hrs wkly. Target aud: 35 plus. ♦ Conan Daly, prom dir & engrg VP; Jay Donald, progmg dir. Co-owned TV: CICT-TV affil

CHKF-FM— Nov 14, 1998: 94.7 mhz; 53 kw. 2723-37 Ave. N.E. #109 T1Y 5R8. Phone: (403) 717-1940. Fax: (403) 717-1945. E-mail: general@fm947.com. Web Site: www.fm947.com. Licensee: Fairchild Radio (Calgary FM) Ltd. Format: Ethnic. News staff: 2; News: 21 hrs wkly. Target aud: General. ♦ Thomas Fung, chmn; George Lee, sr VP, VP & gen mgr; Christine Leung, stn mgr & mktg mgr.

CIBK-FM— Sept 6, 2002: 98.5 mhz; 100 kw. Box 2750, Stn M T2P 4P8. Phone: (403) 240-5800. Fax: (403) 240-5801. Web Site: www.vibe985.com. Licensee: Standard Radio Inc. Group owner: Standard Broadcasting Corp. (acq 4-19-02; grpsl). Format: Urban rhythm. ♦ Tom Peacock, gen mgr.

CIQX-FM— Aug 30, 2002: 103.1 mhz; 100 kw. Stereo. The Breeze 103.1 FM, Suite 100, 1110 Centre St. N.E., Suite 100 T2E 2R2. Phone: (403) 271-6366. Fax: (403) 278-6772. E-mail: info@thebreeze103.com. Web Site: www.thebreeze103.com. Licensee: 3937844 Canada Inc. Group owner: NewCap Broadcasting Ltd. (acq 4-19-02; grpsl). Rep: Integrated Media Sales. Format: Adult contemp, smooth jazz. News staff: one; News: 35 hrs wkly. Target aud: 35-54. ♦ Stephen Peck, gen mgr.

CJAY-FM—Listing follows CKMX(AM).

CJSI-FM— December 1997: 88.9 mhz; 47 kw. Ant 979 ft. TL: N51 03 54 W114 12 47. Suite 100, 4510 Macleod Trail S. T2G 0A4. Phone: (403) 276-1111. Fax: (403) 276-1114. E-mail: shine@homefm.com. Web Site: www.shinefm.com. Licensee: Touch Canada Broadcasting Inc. Format: Contemp Christian. ♦ Allan Hunsperger, CEO, pres & gen mgr.

*CJSW-FM— Jan 15, 1985: 90.9 mhz; 4 kw. Stereo. Rm. 127-MacEwan Hall, 2500 University Dr. N.W. T2N 1N4. Phone: (403) 220-3902. Phone: (403) 220-3904. Fax: (403) 289-8212. Web Site: www.cjsw.com. Licensee: The University of Calgary Student Radio Society. Format: Alternative, jazz, community. News: 5 hrs wkly. Target aud: General; young, trendy & well-heeled. Spec prog: Fr one hr, Ger 2 hrs, It one, Sp one hr wkly. ♦ Chad Saunders, gen mgr.

CKMX(AM)— May 18, 1922: 1060 khz; 50 kw-U, DA-N. TL: N50 54 02 W26 113 52. Stereo. Box 2750, Broadcast House T2P 4P8. Phone: (403) 240-5800. Fax: (403) 240-5801. Web Site: www.cjay92.com. Licensee: Standard Radio Inc. Group owner: Standard Broadcasting Corp. (acq 6-19-92). Format: Adult contemp. News staff: one. Target aud: 45 plus. Spec prog: Jazz 5 hrs wkly. ♦ Tom Peacock, gen mgr & gen sls mgr.

CJAY-FM—Co-owned with CKMX(AM). June 1, 1977: 92.1 mhz; 100 kw. Ant 979 ft. TL: N51 03 37 W114 10 13. Stereo. Fax: (403) 242-6956. Web Site: www.cjay92.com. Format: Rock. ♦ Ryan Dryden, mktg dir; Bob Harris, progmg dir; Ben Jeffery, mus dir; Ken Pasolli, engrg dir.

CKRY-FM— July 9, 1982: 105.1 mhz; 100 kw. Ant 400 ft. Stereo. 630 3rd Ave. S.W., Suite 105 T2P 4L4. Phone: (403) 716-2105. Fax: (403) 716-2111. Web Site: www.country105.com. Licensee: Corus Entertainment Inc. (group owner) Rep: Canadian Broadcast Sales. Format: Country. News staff: 6; News: 7 hrs wkly. Target aud: 25-54. ♦ Garry McKenzie, gen mgr & stn mgr.

Camrose

CFCW(AM)— Nov 2, 1954: 790 khz; 50 kw-U, DA-2. Stereo. 5241 Calvary Trail, NW, Suite 600, Edmonton T5T 4M2. Phone: (780) 468-3939. Fax: (780) 435-0844. Licensee: CFCW Broadcasting. Group owner: NewCap Inc. Rep: Canadian Broadcast Sales. Format: Country. News: 11 hrs wkly. Target aud: 25-54; country mus, sports & hockey listeners in Edmonton region. Spec prog: Sports open line, farm 5 hrs wkly. ♦ Al Anderson, gen mgr.

Canmore

CHMN-FM— February 1998: 106.5 mhz; 510 w. Peschl's Corner, 749 Railway Ave. T1W 1P2. Phone: (403) 678-2222. Phone: (403) 678-2223. Fax: (403) 678-6844. Licensee: Rogers Broadcasting Ltd. (group owner). Rep: Canadian Broadcast Sales. Format: Hot adult contemp. ♦ Kevin McKenna, gen mgr.

Drayton Valley

CIBW-FM— 1994: 92.9 mhz; 7.4 kw. Postal Bag 929 T7A 1V3. Phone: (780) 542-9290. Fax: (780) 542-9319. E-mail: bwcprod@telusplanet.net. Licensee: Jim Pattison Broadcast Group Ltd. (the general partner) and Jim Pattison Industries Ltd. (the limited partner) carrying on business as Jim Pattison Broadcast Group L.P. Group owner: The Jim Pattison Broadcast Group (acq 9-7-95). Rep: Canadian Broadcast Sales. Format: Country. News staff: one; News: 16 hrs wkly. Target aud: General; people with money to spend. ♦ Rick Arnish, pres; Paul Mason, gen mgr.

Drumheller

CKDQ(AM)— 1958: 910 khz; 50 kw-U, DA-2. Stereo. Box 1480 T0J 0Y0. Secondary address: 515 Hwy. 10 E. T0J 0Y0. Phone: (403) 823-3384. Fax: (403) 823-7241. E-mail: bbrown@ab.ncc.ca. Licensee: 3937844 Canada Inc. Group owner: NewCap Broadcasting Ltd. (acq 4-19-02; grpsl). Rep: CBS Radio. Format: Country. News staff: 2; News: 11 hrs wkly. Target aud: 25-54. Spec prog: Farm 8 hrs, relg 2 hrs wkly. ♦ Hugh MacDonald, gen mgr.

Edmonton

CBX(AM)— 1948: 740 khz; 50 kw-U, DA-2. Box 555 T5J 2P4. Secondary address: Edmonton City Ctr., 10062-102 Ave., Suite 123, Alberta T5J 24G. Phone: (780) 468-7500. Fax: (780) 468-7419. E-mail: cbx_edmonton@cbc.ca. Web Site: www.edmonton.cbc.ca. Licensee: CBC. Network: CBC Radio One. Format: Info, news/talk. Target aud: 35 plus; college educated. ♦ Judy Piercey, VP; Don Orchard, progmg dir.

CBX-FM—Not on air, target date: unknown: 90.9 mhz; 100 kw. Ant 633 ft. Stereo. Web Site: www.edmonton.cdc.ca. Network: CBC Radio Two. Format: Btfl mus, class, news.

CFBR-FM—Listing follows CFRN(AM).

CFCW(AM)—See Camrose

CFRN(AM)— 1934: 1260 khz; 50 kw-U, DA-N. 18520 Stony Plain Rd., Suite 100 T5S 2E2. Phone: (780) 486-2800. Fax: (780) 489-6927. Web Site: www.cfrn.com. Licensee: Standard Radio Inc. Group owner: Standard Broadcasting Corp. (acq 6-19-92). Format: Sports. Target aud: 45 plus. Spec prog: Adult standards, nostalgia. ♦ Marty Forbes, gen mgr.

CFBR-FM—Co-owned with CFRN(AM). Apr 25, 1951: 100.3 mhz; 100 kw. 482 ft. Stereo. Format: Rock, classic rock.

CHBN-FM— Feb 17, 2005: 91.7 mhz; 100 kw. 10212 Jasper Ave. N.W. T5J 5A3. Phone: (780) 424-2222. Fax: (780) 401-1600. Web Site: www.thebounce.ca. Licensee: CHUM Ltd./Milestone Media Broadcasting

Broadcasting & Cable Yearbook 2006

Directory of Radio
Alberta

Ltd., partners in a partnership to be established. Format: Urban contemp. Target aud: 15-39. ♦ James Stuart, gen mgr.

CHDI-FM— May 9, 2005: 102.9 mhz; 100 kw. 5915 Gateway Blvd. T6H 2H3. Phone: (780) 423-2005. Fax: (780) 437-5129. Web Site: www.radiosonic.fm. Licensee: O.K. Radio Group Ltd. Format: Modern rock. ♦ Diana Parker, gen mgr.

CHED(AM)— Mar 3, 1954: 630 khz; 50 kw-U, DA-N. Stereo. 5204-84 St. T6E 5N8. Phone: (780) 440-6300. Fax: (780) 468-6739. Fax: (780) 469-5937. E-mail: info@630ched.com. Web Site: www.630ched.com. Licensee: Corus Premium Television Ltd. Group owner: Corus Entertainment Inc. (acq 7-6-00; grpsl). Format: Sports, talk. ♦ Doug Rutherford, gen mgr; Daryl Hooks, progmg dir; Tom Davies, chief of engrg.

CKNG-FM— Co-owned with CHED(AM). Aug 11, 1982: 92.5 mhz; 100 kw. 900 ft. Stereo. E-mail: info@power92.com. Format: Top-40. ♦ James Stuart, progmg dir.

*CHFA(AM)— Nov 20, 1949: 680 khz; 10 kw-U, DA-1. Box 555 T5J 2P4. Secondary address: 7909 51st. Ave. T6E 5L9. Phone: (780) 468-7800. Fax: (780) 468-7812. Licensee: CBC. (acq 4-1-74). Format: Div, MOR, news/talk. News staff: 8; News: 8 hrs wkly. Target aud: 20-60; Fr speaking. ♦ Robert Rabinovitch, pres; Sylvain LaFrance, exec VP; Rene Fontaine, gen mgr.

CHQT(AM)— Listing follows CISN-FM.

CIRK-FM— 1949: 97.3 mhz; 100 kw. Stereo. 2394 W. Edmonton Mall, 8882 170 St. TST 2MQ. Phone: (780) 437-4996. Fax: (780) 436-9803. Web Site: www.k-rock973.com. Licensee: NewCap Inc. Group owner: NewCap Broadcasting Ltd. (acq 2-17-99; C$10 million). Format: Classic rock. Target aud: 18-54; mobile adults. ♦ Al Anderson, gen mgr.

CISN-FM— June 5, 1982: 103.9 mhz; 100 kw. 757 ft. Stereo. 5204 84th St. T6E 5N8. Phone: (780) 428-1104. Fax: (780) 469-5937. E-mail: info@cisnfm.com. Web Site: www.cisnfm.com. Licensee: Corus Radio Co. Group owner: Corus Entertainment Inc. (acq 7-6-00; grpsl). Format: Contemp country. ♦ Doug Rutherford, gen mgr & stn mgr; Neil Cunningham, gen sls mgr; Khazma Tichon, prom dir; James Stuart, progmg dir; Bob Layton, news dir; Tom Davies, chief of engrg.

CHQT(AM)— Co-owned with CISN-FM. Aug 19, 1965: 880 khz; 50 kw-U, DA-N. E-mail: info@cool880.com. Format: Hits of the 60s & 70s.

CJCA(AM)— May 22, 1922: 930 khz; 50 kw-U, DA-N. 4207 98th St. N.W., Suite 204 T6E 5R7. Phone: (780) 466-4930. Fax: (780) 469-5335. Web Site: www.cjca.ca. Licensee: The Partners of the CJCA L.P. (Rosedale Meadows Development Inc., Touch Canada Broadcasting Ltd. and C.R.A. Investments Ltd). (acq 4-12-94). Format: Contemp Christian. News: 6 hrs wkly. Target aud: 25-54. ♦ Allan Hunsperger, CEO, pres & gen mgr; Rebecca Greet, prom dir; Corri Allan, progmg dir; Gord Craig, news dir.

CJRY-FM— Co-owned with CJCA(AM).Not on air, target date: unknown: 105.9 mhz; 100 kw. Ant 633 ft. Web Site: www.cjry.ca/cms. Licensee: Touch Canada Broadcasting Inc. Format: Contemp Christian music.

CJSR-FM— 1984: 88.5 mhz; 900 w. Stereo. Room 0-09, Students' Union Bldg., Univ. of Alberta T6G 2J7. Phone: (780) 492-5244. Fax: (780) 492-3121. Web Site: www.cjsr.com. Licensee: The First Alberta Campus Radio Association. Format: Alternative progmg. Target aud: General; everyone who looks for something new in the mus industry. Spec prog: American Indian 2 hrs, Black 7 hrs, class 2 hrs, folk 16 hrs, Fr one hr, gospel 2 hrs, Pol 2 hrs, Sp 2 hrs wkly. ♦ Charlotte Bourne, gen mgr.

CKER-FM— 1996: 101.9 mhz; 100 kw. Stereo. 6005 Gateway Blvd. T6H 2H3. Phone: (780) 438-1019. Fax: (780) 437-5129. E-mail: cker@cker.ca. Web Site: www.cker.ca. Licensee: OK Radio Group Ltd. Format: Ethnic, Christian, Chinese. News staff: 2; News: 14 hrs wkly. Target aud: General; ethnic audience (24 languages), and Christian. Spec prog: It 3 hrs, Sp 8 hrs, Por 2 hrs, Ukrainian 10 hrs, Dutch 3 hrs, Pol 6 hrs, E.Indian 7 hrs wkly. ♦ Roger Charest Sr., pres; Diana Parker, gen mgr; Roger Charest Jr., opns mgr.

CKRA-FM— Nov 15, 1979: 96.3 mhz; 100 kw. 757 ft. Stereo. 2394 W. Edmonton Mall, 8882 170th St. TST 2HQ. Phone: (780) 437-4996. Fax: (780) 436-9803. Web Site: www.96x.ca. Licensee: NewCap Inc.

Group owner: NewCap Broadcasting Ltd. Rep: Canadian Broadcast Sales. Format: Hot AC. News staff: 6; News: 5 hrs wkly. Target aud: 25-54; urban young adults. ♦ Al Anderson, gen mgr.

*CKUA-FM— June 28, 1948: 94.9 mhz; 100 kw. 400 ft. Stereo. 4th Fl., 10526 Jasper Ave. T5J 1Z7. Phone: (780) 428-7595. Fax: (780) 428-7624. E-mail: radio@ckua.org. Web Site: www.ckua.com. Licensee: CKUA Radio Foundation. (acq 5-29-95). Format: Div, class, jazz. News staff: 4; News: 6 hrs wkly. Target aud: General; Alberta population. ♦ Ken Regan, gen mgr & opns mgr; Judy Ham, gen sls mgr; Sonia Kochansky, prom dir; Brian Dunsmore, progmg dir; Peter North, mus dir; Neil Lutes, chief of engrg.

CKUA(AM)— Nov 21, 1927: 580 khz; 10 kw-U, DA-2. TL: N53 20 34 W113 27 27. Format: Diversified.

Edson

CJYR(AM)— Apr 4, 1968: 970 khz; 10 kw-U, DA-1. Box 7800 T7E 1V8. Secondary address: 422 50th St. T7E 1T1. Phone: (780) 723-4461. Fax: (780) 723-3765. Licensee: 3937844 Canada Inc. Group owner: NewCap Broadcasting Ltd. (acq 4-19-02; grpsl). Format: Adult contemp, CHR. News staff: 3. Target aud: 18-55. Spec prog: Farm 2 hrs wkly. ♦ Al Anderson, VP; Dave Schuck, gen mgr & stn mgr.

Falher

*CKRP-FM— Nov 2, 1996: 95.7 mhz; 671 w. TL: N55 44 07 W117 11 34. Stereo. Rebroadcasts CITE-FM Montreal 65% Box 718, Association Canadienne-Francaise de l'Alberta, Regionale de Riviere-la-Paix T0H 1M0. Phone: (780) 837-2346. Fax: (780) 837-2092. Web Site: www.ckrp.info.ca. Licensee: Association canadienne-francaise de l'Alberta-Regionale de Riviere-la-Paix. Format: French, adult contemp, community service. Target aud: French population. ♦ Chantal Gelinas, pres.

Fort McMurray

CJOK-FM— 2003: 93.3 mhz; 10.7 kw. TL: N56 41 16 W111 19 55. 9912 Franklin Ave. T9H 2K5. Phone: (780) 743-2246. Fax: (780) 791-7250. Fax: (780) 743-8662. Web Site: my.mymcmurray.com. Licensee: OK Radio Group Ltd. Format: Contemp country. News staff: 3; News: 4 hrs wkly. Target aud: 25-44. ♦ Roger Charest, CEO; Stu Morton, CEO & pres; Kelly Boyd, gen mgr.

CKYX-FM— March 1985: 97.9 mhz; 3 kw. Stereo. 9912 Franklin Ave. T9H 2K5. Phone: (780) 743-2246. Fax: (780) 791-7250. Fax: (780) 743-8662. Web Site: my.mymcmurray.com. Licensee: OK Radio Group Ltd. Format: Classic rock. News staff: 3; News: 5 hrs wkly. Target aud: 18-44. ♦ Roger Charest, CEO; Stu Morton, pres; Kelly Boyd, gen mgr.

Fort Vermilion

CIAM-FM— Jan 27, 2003: 92.7 mhz; 30 w. Box 609 T0H 1N0. Secondary address: 4709 River Road T0H 1N0. Phone: (780)-927-2426. Fax: (780) 927-2427. E-mail: ciam@telus.net. Licensee: Care Radio Broadcasting Association. Format: Var/div/multingual. ♦ Michael Sandstrom, gen mgr; James Neufeld, news dir; Phil Peters, progmg dir & chief of engrg.

Grand Centre (Cold Lake)

CJXK-FM— Sept 3, 2004: 95.3 mhz; 100 kw. B5412 55th St., Cold Lake T9M 1R5. Phone: (780) 594-2459. Fax: (780) 594-3001. Licensee: 3937844 Canada Inc. Format: Classic rock. ♦ Carla Loffer, stn mgr.

Grande Prairie

CFGP-FM— June 20, 1996: 97.7 mhz; 70 kw. TL: N55 27 57 W118 45 32. Stereo. 9835 101 Ave., Suite 200 T8V 5V4. Phone: (780) 539-9700. Fax: (780) 532-1600. Fax: (780) 539-0367. Web Site: www.sunfm.com. Licensee: O.K. Radio Group Ltd. Format: Hot adult contemp. News staff: 4; News: 4 hrs wkly. Target aud: 25-55. ♦ Roger Charest, CEO, chmn & pres; Stu Morton, exec VP; Tom Bedore, gen mgr & opns mgr.

CJXX-FM— Nov 1, 2000: 93.1 mhz; 100 kw. TL: N55 03 08 W118 51 59. 9817 101st Ave., Suite 202, Grand Prairie T8V 0X6. Phone: (780) 532-0840. Fax: (780) 538-1266. Fax: (780) 539-6397. E-mail:

general@bigcountryxx.com. Web Site: www.bigcountryxx.com. Licensee: Jim Pattison Broadcast Group Ltd. (the general partner) and Jim Pattison Industries Ltd. (the limited partner) carrying on business as Jim Pattison Broadcast Group L.P. Group owner: The Jim Pattison Broadcast Group (acq 12-21-2000; grpsl). Format: C&W. News staff: 5; News: 14 hrs wkly. Target aud: 25-49; adults who love country music. ♦ Rick Arnish, pres; Ken Truhn, gen mgr.

High Level

CKHL-FM— July 1999: 102.1 mhz; 8.765 kw. Box 3759 T0H 1Z0. Phone: (780) 926-4531. Fax: (780) 926-4564. Web Site: www.ylcountry.com. Licensee: 912038 Alberta Ltd. Format: Country. ♦ Cynthia Babiy, VP; Terry Babiy, gen mgr & sls dir; Doug Longard, rgnl sls mgr; Kevin Becker, progmg dir; Mike Matthews, chief of engrg.

High Prairie

CKVH(AM)— 1990: 1020 khz; 1 kw-D, 400 w-N. Box 2219 T0G 1E0. Phone: (780) 523-5111. Fax: (780) 523-3360. E-mail: rturner@ab.ncc.ca. Licensee: 3937844 Canada Inc. Group owner: NewCap Broadcasting Ltd. (acq 4-19-02; grpsl). Format: Country. ♦ Randy Turner, gen mgr & opns mgr.

High River

CFXL-FM— Listing follows CHRB(AM).

CHRB(AM)— Dec 5, 1977: 1140 khz; 50 kw-D, 46 kw-N, DA-2. TL: N50 55 25 W113 49 58. 11 5th Ave. S.E. TIV 1G2. Phone: (403) 652-2472. Fax: (403) 652-7861. E-mail: am1140@am1140radio.com. Web Site: www.am1140radio.com. Licensee: Golden West Broadcasting Ltd. (group owner). Rep: Canadian Broadcast Sales. Format: C&W, relg. News staff: 2; News: 10 hrs wkly. Target aud: General. Spec prog: Farm 5 hrs wkly. ♦ Elmer Hildebrand, CEO; Lyndon Friesen, sr VP; Keith Leask, stn mgr, gen sls mgr, prom dir & progmg dir; Menno Friesen, sls VP; Don McCracken, news dir; Vern Moores, chief of engrg.

CFXL-FM— Co-owned with CHRB(AM). 2003: 100.9 mhz; 100 kw.

High River-Okotoks

CFXL-FM— Licensed to High River-Okotoks. See High River

Hinton

CIYR-FM— July 2004: 97.5 mhz; 1.2 kw. 506 Carmichael Ln., #102 T7V 1S4. Phone: (780) 865-8804. Fax: (780) 865-7792. Licensee: 3937844 Canada Inc. Format: Hot adult contemp. Target aud: 18-54. ♦ Dave Schuck, gen mgr.

Lac La Biche

CFWE-FM— 1990: 89.9 mhz; 13245 146th St., Edmonton T5L 4S8. Phone: (780) 447-2393. Fax: (780) 454-2820. E-mail: cfwe@ammsa.com. Web Site: www.ammsa.com/cfwe. Licensee: Aboriginal Multi-Media Society of Alberta. Format: Aboriginal, country. Target aud: General; Cree, Blackfoot, Stoney, Dene & English language listeners. ♦ Bert Crowfoot, CEO & gen mgr; Al Standerwick, stn mgr.

Lethbridge

CFRV-FM— 1979: 107.7 mhz; 100 kw. 600 ft. TL: N49 42 23 W112 43 11. Stereo. 1015 3rd Ave S. T1K 0J3. Phone: (403) 328-1077. Fax: (403) 380-1539. Web Site: www.1077theriver.ca. Licensee: Rogers Broadcasting Ltd. (group owner) Format: Adult contemp, classic rock, CHR. News staff: 1; News: 2 hrs wkly. Target aud: 18-49; Males. ♦ Terry Voth, gen mgr.

CHLB-FM— 1997: 95.5 mhz; 100 kw. Stereo. 401 Mayor Magrath Dr. S. T1J 3L8. Phone: (403) 329-0955. Fax: (403) 329-0195. Web Site: www.country95.fm. Licensee: Jim Pattison Broadcast Group Ltd. (the general partner) and Jim Pattison Industries Ltd. (the limited partner) carrying on business as Jim Pattison Broadcast Group L.P. Group owner: The Jim Pattison Broadcast Group (acq 12-21-2000; grpsl). Format: Country. News staff: 5. Target aud: 25-54. ♦ Rob Bye, gen mgr.

CJRX-FM— Nov 3, 2000: 106.7 mhz; 100 kw. 600 ft. TL: N49 42 23 W112 43 11. Stereo. Box 820, 1015 3rd Ave S. T1K 0J3. Phone: (403)

Alberta

320-1220. Fax: (403) 380-1539. Web Site: www.rock106.ca. Licensee: Rogers Broadcasting Ltd. (group owner) Format: Rock. News staff: 1; News: 2 hrs wkly. Target aud: 25-44; Female. ♦ Terry Voth, gen mgr.

CJTS-FM— 2001: 97.1 mhz; 50 w. Spirit FM, 508B 5th Ave. S. T1J 0T9. Phone: (403) 394-0971. Fax: (403) 394-0938. E-mail: 97@spiritfm.ca. Web Site: www.spiritfm.ca. Licensee: Spirit Broadcasting. Format: Contemp Christian. ♦ Terry R. Fleming, CEO, pres & gen mgr.

Lloydminster

CKLM-FM— May 18, 2001: 106.1 mhz; 100 kw. Stereo. Box 21 T9V 0K2. Secondary address: 5012 49th St. T9V 0K2. Phone: (780) 875-5400. Fax: (780) 875-4628. Web Site: www.borderrock.com. Licensee: 912038 Alberta Ltd. (acq 8-17-01). Format: Rock/AOR. News staff: 3. Target aud: 12-54; male. ♦ Anita B. Dent, VP; J. Stewart Dent, pres & gen mgr.

CKSA-FM— Aug 29, 2003: 95.9 mhz; 100 kw. 5026 50th St. T9V 1P3. Phone: (780) 875-3321. Fax: (780) 875-4704. E-mail: mwb@cksa.com. Licensee: NewCap Inc. Group owner: Midwest Broadcasting. (acq 12-22-2004; C$6,246,000. with CILR-FM Lloydminster). Format: Country's best mix. ♦ Mike Keller, gen mgr.

Medicine Hat

CFMY-FM— Feb 1, 1999: 96.1 mhz; 100 kw. 10 Boundary Rd. S.E., Redcliff T0J 2P0. Phone: (403) 548-8282. Fax: (403) 548-8270. E-mail: myfm@jpbg.com. Web Site: www.my96fm.com. Licensee: Jim Pattison Broadcast Group Ltd. (the general partner) and Jim Pattison Industries Ltd. (the limited partner) carrying on business as Jim Pattison Broadcast Group L.P. Group owner: The Jim Pattison Broadcast Group (acq 12-21-2000; grpsl). Format: Adult contemp. ♦ Rick Arnish, pres; Dwaine Dietrich, gen mgr.

CHAT(AM)— Nov 1, 1946: 1270 khz; 10 kw-U, DA-2. Box 1270 T1A 7H5. Phone: (403) 529-1270. Fax: (403) 529-1292. Licensee: Jim Pattison Broadcast Group Ltd. (the general partner) and Jim Pattison Industries Ltd. (the limited partner) carrying on business as Jim Pattison Broadcast Group L.P. Group owner: The Jim Pattison Broadcast Group (acq 12-21-2000; grpsl). Rep: Canadian Broadcast Sales. Format: Country. News staff: 4; News: 14 hrs wkly. Target aud: General. ♦ Rick Arnish, pres; Dwaine Dietrich, gen mgr. Co-owned TV: CHAT-TV affil.

CJLT-FM— April 2003: 99.5 mhz; 48 w. 901 3rd Ave. S.W. T1A 4Z2. Phone: (403) 529-9599. Fax: (403) 529-2824. E-mail: alive995@telus.net. Web Site: www.alivefm.com. Licensee: Lighthouse Broadcasting Ltd. Format: Christian. ♦ Scott Raible, pres & opns mgr.

Okotoks

CFXL-FM—See High River

Olds

CKLJ-FM— Feb 2, 2004: 97.7 mhz; 13 kw. #6, 4526 49 Ave. T4H 1A4. Phone: (403) 556-2628. Fax: (403) 556-2637. E-mail: cklj@telus.net. Licensee: CAB-K Broadcasting Ltd. Format: Country. ♦ Brian Hepp, gen mgr.

Peace River

CKKX-FM— July 1997: 106.1 mhz; 990 w. Bag Service No. 300 T8S 1T5. Phone: (780) 624-2535. Fax: (780) 624-5424. E-mail: reception@ylcountry.com. Web Site: www.kix106.net. Licensee: 912038 Alberta Ltd. Format: Hot adult contemp. ♦ Cynthia Babiy, VP; Terry Babiy, pres & gen mgr.

CKYL(AM)— Nov 1, 1954: 610 khz; 10 kw-U, DA-2. Bag Service No. 300 T8S 1T5. Phone: (780) 624-2535. Fax: (780) 624-5424. Web Site: www.ylcountry.com. Licensee: Peace River Broadcasting Ltd. (acq 12-15-95). Rep: Target Broadcast Sales. Format: Country. ♦ Terry Babiy, gen mgr.

Red Deer

CFDV-FM— Nov 8, 2004: 106.7 mhz; 100 kw. 2840 Bremner Ave. T4R 1M9. Phone: (403) 343-7105. Fax: (403) 343-2573. E-mail: onair@1067thedrive.fm. Web Site: www.1067thedrive.fm. Licensee: Jim Pattison Broadcast Group Ltd. (the general partner) and Jim Pattison Industries Ltd. (the limited partner) carrying on business as Jim Pattison Broadcast Group L.P. Rep: Target Broadcast Sales. Format: Classic rock. News staff: 3. Target aud: 25-54; adults, primary demo-males. ♦ Jim Pattison, CEO; Rick Arnish, pres; Paul Mason, gen mgr; Bryn James, gen sls mgr.

CHUB-FM— 1949: 105.5 mhz; 100 kw. 2840 Bremner Ave. T4R 1M9. Phone: (403) 343-7105. Fax: (403) 343-2573. Licensee: Jim Pattison Broadcast Group Ltd. (the general partner) and Jim Pattison Industries Ltd. (the limited partner) carrying on business as Jim Pattison Broadcast Group L.P. Group owner: The Jim Pattison Broadcast Group (acq 12-21-2000; grpsl). Rep: Target Broadcast Sales. WTR Media Sales Format: Hot adult contemp. News staff: 3. Target aud: Adults 25-49; primary demo-females. ♦ Jim Pattison, CEO; Rick Arnish, pres; Paul Mason, gen mgr; Bryn James, gen sls mgr.

CIZZ-FM— Nov 1, 1987: 98.9 mhz; 100 kw. 800 ft. Stereo. Box 5339 T4N 6W1. Secondary address: 4920 59th Ave. T4N 2N1. Phone: (403) 343-1303. Fax: (403) 346-1230. E-mail: zedfm@corusent.com. Web Site: www.zedfm.com. Licensee: Newcap Inc. Group owner: Corus Entertainment Inc. (acq 8-10-2005; C$8,392,714 with CKGY-FM Red Deer). Format: Adult contemp, CHR. News staff: 6. Target aud: 18-49; male 55%, female 45%. ♦ Doug Rutherford, VP; Ron Thompson, gen mgr & stn mgr.

CKGY-FM— April 2001: 95.5 mhz; 100 kw. 800 ft. Stereo. Bag 5339 T4N 6W1. Secondary address: 4920 59th St. T4N 2N1. Phone: (403) 348-0955. Fax: (403) 346-1230. E-mail: kgcountry@corusent.com. Web Site: www.ckgy.com. Licensee: Newcap Inc. Group owner: Corus Entertainment Inc. (acq 8-10-2005; C$8,392,714 with CIZZ-FM Red Deer). Rep: Canadian Broadcast Sales. Format: Today's hottest country. News staff: 6. Target aud: 25-54; 50% male, 50% female. ♦ Doug Rutherford, VP; Ron Thompson, gen mgr.

Rocky Mountain House

CHBW-FM— 1997: 94.5 mhz; 720 w. 4814B 49th St. T4T 1S8. Phone: (403) 844-9450. Fax: (403) 844-4770. E-mail: bigshow@telus.net. Licensee: Jim Pattison Broadcast Group Ltd. (the general partner) and Jim Pattison Industries Ltd. (the limited partner) carrying on business as Jim Pattison Broadcast Group L.P. Group owner: The Jim Pattison Broadcast Group. Format: Country. ♦ Paul Mason, gen mgr; Barry Simon, stn mgr.

Saint Albert

CFMG-FM— Aug 29, 1994: 104.9 mhz; 100 kw. 18520 Stony Plain Rd., Suite 100, Edmonton T5S 2E2. Phone: (780) 435-1049. Fax: (780) 489-6927. E-mail: cfmg@sri.ca. Web Site: www.ezrock1049.com. Licensee: Standard Radio Inc. Group owner: Standard Broadcasting Corp. (acq 4-19-2002; grpsl). Format: Adult contemp. News staff: 2; News: 4 hrs wkly. Target aud: 25-54; middle to upper income families. ♦ Marty Forbes, pres & gen mgr; Karl Stark, gen sls mgr; Steve Moore, progmg dir; Bruce Bedford, engrg dir & chief of engrg.

Saint Paul

CHLW(AM)— 1975: 1310 khz; 10 kw-U, DA-2. 201-4341 50th Ave., St. Paul T0A 3A3. Phone: (780) 645-4425. Fax: (780) 645-2383. E-mail: dwhite@ab.ncc.ca. Web Site: www.angelfire.com/ca/chlw. Licensee: 3937844 Canada Inc. Group owner: NewCap Broadcasting Ltd. (acq 4-19-02; grpsl). Format: New country. News staff: one; News: 4 hrs wkly. Target aud: 25-49. Spec prog: Farm 5 hrs, relg 5 hrs wkly. ♦ Mark Maheu, pres; Roger Thorpe, stn mgr; Al Anderson, opns dir.

Siksika

CHDH-FM— 2002: 97.7 mhz; 50 w. Box 1490 T0J 3W0. Phone: (403) 734-5339. Fax: (403) 734-5497. E-mail: siksikamedia@siksikanation.com. Licensee: Dale Hinves, on behalf of a society to be incorporated. Format: News/talk, education, native music. ♦ Paul Melting Tallow, gen mgr.

Slave Lake

CKWA(AM)— Nov 1, 1985: 1210 khz; 1 kw-U, DA-1. Box 2470,#207 Slave Lake Plaza, 201 Main St. T0G 2A0. Phone: (780) 849-2577. Fax: (780) 849-4833. E-mail: ckwa@ab.nec.cs. Licensee: 3937844 Canada Inc. Group owner: NewCap Broadcasting Ltd. (acq 4-19-02; grpsl). Format: Country. Target aud: 25-54. Spec prog: Rock 5 hrs wkly. ♦ Ida May Mulligan, stn mgr.

Stations in Canada

Stettler

CKSQ(AM)— Dec 15, 1976: 1400 khz; 1 kw-U, DA-2. 4703 58th St. T0C 2L1. Phone: (403) 742-2930. Fax: (403) 742-0660. E-mail: cksq@ab.ncc.ca. Licensee: 3937844 Canada Inc. Group owner: NewCap Broadcasting Ltd. (acq 4-19-02; grpsl). Format: Country. News staff: one; News: 7 hrs wkly. Target aud: 25-54; 55% female, 45% male. ♦ Rick Garrison, gen mgr & stn mgr.

Taber

CJBZ-FM— 2000: 93.3 mhz; 50 kw. 401 Mayor Magrath Dr., Lethbridge T1J 3L8. Phone: (403) 394-9300. Fax: (403) 329-0195. E-mail: bye@country95.fm. Web Site: www.b93.fm. Licensee: Jim Pattison Broadcast Group Ltd. (the general partner) and Jim Pattison Industries Ltd. (the limited partner) carrying on business as Jim Pattison Broadcast Group L.P. Group owner: The Jim Pattison Broadcast Group (acq 12-21-2000; grpsl). Format: Classic hits. News staff: 4. Target aud: 40 plus. ♦ Rick Arnish, pres; Rob Bye, gen mgr.

Wainwright

CKKY(AM)— February 1984: 830 khz; 10 kw-D, 3.5 kw-N. 1037 2nd Ave., 2nd fl T9W 1K7. Phone: (780) 842-4311. Fax: (780) 842-4636. E-mail: ckky@ab.ncc.ca. Licensee: 3937844 Canada Inc. Group owner: NewCap Broadcasting Ltd. (acq 5-20-2002; grpsl). Format: C&W. News staff: 2; News: 14 hrs wkly. Target aud: 20-45; agriculture-related working class. Spec prog: Farm 10 hrs wkly. ♦ Ron Prochner, gen mgr.

CKWY-FM—Co-owned with CKKY(AM).Not on air, target date: unknown: 93.7 mhz; 100 kw. Format: Adult contemp.

Westlock

CFOK(AM)— Aug 19, 1975: 1370 khz; 10 kw-U, DA-2. 10030-106 St., Suite 17 T7P 2K4. Phone: (780) 349-4421. Fax: (780) 349-6259. E-mail: wbetts@ab.ncc.ca. Licensee: 3937844 Canada Inc. Group owner: NewCap Broadcasting Ltd. (acq 4-19-02; grpsl). Rep: Canadian Broadcast Sales. Format: Today's country. News staff: one; News: 15 hrs wkly. Target aud: 25-54. Spec prog: Farm 5 hrs, relg 6 hrs wkly. ♦ Al Anderson, gen mgr & opns VP; Wray Betts, stn mgr.

Wetaskiwin

CIHS-FM— December 2000: 93.5 mhz; 1.7 kw. Ant 230 ft. 5206 50th Ave. T9A 0S8. Phone: (780) 352-2508. Fax: (780) 352-2502. E-mail: cihs@incentre.net. Web Site: www.wtc.ab.calcihs.ca. Licensee: Tag Broadcasting. Format: Old country, country gospel. ♦ Christie-Anne Tessier, exec VP; Tony Greengrass, CEO, chmn, pres & gen mgr; Paula Osha, stn mgr.

CKJR(AM)— 1971: 1440 khz; 10 kw-U, DA-2. 5241 Calgary Trail N.W., Suite 600, Edmonton T6H 5G8. Phone: (780) 468-3939. Fax: (780) 435-0844. Licensee: 3937844 Canada Inc. Group owner: NewCap Broadcasting Ltd. (acq 4-19-02; grpsl). Format: Hot new country. Spec prog: Greek 2 hrs wkly. ♦ Al Anderson, gen mgr.

British Columbia

100 Mile House

CKBX(AM)— July 30, 1971: 840 khz; 1 kw-D, 250 w-N, DA-1. Box 939 V0K 2E0. Phone: (250) 395-3848. Fax: (250) 395-4147. E-mail: radioman@bcinternet.net. Web Site: wildcountryradio.com. Licensee: Cariboo Broadcasters Ltd. Group owner: Cariboo Central Interior Radio Inc. (acq 1981). Format: Country. Spec prog: Class one hr wkly. ♦ Terry Shepherd, CEO & gen mgr; Brad McGuire, stn mgr.

Abbotsford

CKQC-FM— September 2001: 107.1 mhz; 215 w. Stereo. 45715 Hocking Ave., Suite 520, Chilliwack V2P 6Z6. Phone: (604) 859-5277. Fax: (604) 702-3212. Licensee: Rogers Radio (British Columbia) Ltd. Group owner: Rogers Broadcasting Ltd. Format: Country. ♦ Ken Geiger, gen mgr; Mary Kemmis, gen sls mgr; Murray Olfert, prom dir.

Directory of Radio

British Columbia

Boston Bar

CKGO-FM-1— July 4, 1980: 106.1 mhz; 91 w. -2,871 ft. 520 45715 Hocking Ave., Chilliwack 2p676. Phone: (604) 795-5711. Fax: (604) 702-3212. Web Site: www.starfm.com. Licensee: Rogers Broadcasting Ltd. (group owner; acq 9-10-99; grpsl). Format: Hot adult contemp. News staff: 3. ◆Ken Geiger, gen mgr, stn mgr & progmg dir; Mary Kemmis, gen sls mgr; Murray Olfert, prom mgr; Terry Chan, mus dir.

Burnaby

*****CJSF-FM**— Feb 6, 2003: 90.1 mhz; 450 w. CJSF Radio, TC 216, Simon Fraser University V5A 1S6. Phone: (604) 291-3727. Fax: (604) 291-3695. Web Site: www.cjsf.ca. Licensee: Simon Fraser Campus Radio Society. Format: Var. Spec prog: Persian 2 hrs, Portugese 2 hrs, Sp 4 hrs wkly. ◆Magnus Thyvold, stn mgr; Elvira Balakshin, progmg dir; Ed Blake, mus dir; Frieda Werden, pub affrs dir.

Burns Lake

CFLD(AM)— November 1965: 760 khz; 1 kw-U. Box 600, Evergreen Mall V0J 1E0. Secondary address: 355 Smithers V0J 2NO. Phone: (250) 692-3414. Fax: (250) 847-9411. Licensee: Cariboo Central Interior Radio Inc. (group owner) Format: Adult contemp. ◆Allan Collison, gen mgr; Bill Waugh, stn mgr & progmg dir.

Campbell River

CFWB(AM)— September 1968: 1490 khz; 1 kw-U. 909 Ironwood Rd. V9W 3E5. Phone: (250) 287-7106. Fax: (250) 287-7170. E-mail: coastradio@coastradio.com. Licensee: CFCP Radio Ltd. Rep: Target Broadcast Sales. Format: Country. News staff: 3. Target aud: 20-45. ◆Norma Browne, CEO; Greg Phelps, gen mgr; Alan Buxton, opns mgr.

Castlegar

CKQR-FM— 1998: 99.3 mhz; 333 w. TL: N 49 18 54 W117 37 27. 525 11th Ave. V1N 1J6. Phone: (250) 365-7600. Fax: (250) 365-8480. E-mail: dg@bkradio.com. Web Site: www.bkradio.com. Licensee: BKR-Boundary Kootenay Radio. Rep: Canadian Broadcast Sales. Format: Soft rock. News staff: one; News: 6 hrs wkly. Target aud: 18-49; median target demo, 36 yr old female. ◆J.W. Gillespie, CEO, chmn & pres; Dennis Gerein, gen mgr & gen sls mgr; Jamie Swetlikoe, progmg dir.

Chetwynd

CHET-FM— 1997: 94.5 mhz; 25 w. 4612 N. Access Rd. V0C 1J0. Phone: (250) 788-9452. Fax: (250) 788-9402. E-mail: info@peacefm.ca. Web Site: www.chetchad.com. Licensee: Chetwynd Communications Society. Format: Hits of the 60s thru today, MOR, div. ◆Charlie Lasser, chmn; Leo Sabulsky, gen mgr; Dave Allen, progmg mgr; Karen Patterson, mus dir; Mike Sabulsky, chief of engrg; Sadie Hasketh, sls.

Chilliwack

CKCL-FM— Sept 29, 1986: 107.5 mhz; 303 w. Stereo. 2440 Ash St., Vancouver V5Z 4J6. Phone: (604) 877-6357. Fax: (604) 877-4443. Web Site: www.1049clearfm.com. Licensee: Rogers Radio (British Columbia) Ltd. Group owner: Rogers Broadcasting Ltd. (acq 9-10-99; grpsl). Format: MOR. News: 6 hrs wkly. Target aud: 35 plus. ◆Tony Viner, CEO; Rael Merson, pres; Laura Nixon, CFO; Gary Miles, exec VP; Paul Fisher, VP; David Larsen, progmg dir.

CKSR-FM— Aug 31, 2001: 98.3 mhz; 2.34 kw. Stereo. # 520, 45715 Hocking Ave. V2P 6Z6. Phone: (604) 795-5711. Fax: (604) 702-3212. Web Site: www.starfm.com. Licensee: Rogers Radio (British Columbia) Ltd. Group owner: Rogers Broadcasting Ltd. Rep: Canadian Broadcast Sales. Format: Adult contemp. News staff: 3. Target aud: 25-54; general. Spec prog: Farm 2 hrs wkly. ◆Tony Viner, CEO; Rael Merson, pres; Ken Geiger, gen mgr.

Clearwater

CHNL-1(AM)— May 1, 1970: 1400 khz; 1 kw-D, 250 w-N. c/o CHNL(AM), 611 Lansdowne St., Kamloops V2C 1Y6. Phone: (250) 372-2292. Fax: (250) 372-2293. E-mail: info@radionl.com. Licensee: NL Broadcasting Ltd. Format: Adult contemp, oldies. Target aud: 25-54; family oriented adults, middle-upper income. ◆Robbie Dunn, CEO, pres, gen mgr & adv mgr; Ravinder Dhaliwal, CFO & chief of engrg.

opns; Jim Reynolds, dev mgr & progmg dir; Peter Angle, rgnl sls mgr & mktg dir; T. Tyler, mus dir; Jim Harrison, news dir; Dave Coulter, chief of engrg.

Courtenay

CFCP-FM— 1959: 98.9 mhz; 2.685 kw. Stereo. 1625-A McPhee Ave. V9N 3A6. Phone: (250) 334-2421. Fax: (250) 334-1977. E-mail: coastradio@coastradio.com. Web Site: www.coastradio.com. Licensee: CFCP Radio Ltd. Format: Adult contemp. News staff: 4; News: 16 hrs wkly. Target aud: 25-54; women. ◆Norma Browne, pres; Greg Phelps, gen mgr.

CKLR-FM— 1998: 97.3 mhz; 4.7 kw. 801B 29th St. V9N 7Z5. Phone: (250) 703-2200. Fax: (250) 703-9611. Web Site: www.973theeagle.com. Licensee: Central Island Broadcasting Ltd. Format: Adult comtemp. ◆Paul Larsen, gen mgr; Richard Skinner, rgnl sls mgr; Glennis Lane, prom mgr.

Cranbrook

CHBZ-FM— Oct 1, 1995: 104.7 mhz; 1.26 kw. 19 9th Ave. S. V1C 2L9. Phone: (250) 426-2224. Fax: (250) 426-5520. E-mail: info@b104.ca. Web Site: www.b104.ca. Licensee: Jim Pattison Broadcast Group Ltd. (the general partner) and Jim Pattison Industries Ltd. (the limited partner) carrying on business as Jim Pattison Broadcast Group L.P. Group owner: The Jim Pattison Broadcast Group (acq 2-1-2001; grpsl). Rep: Target Broadcast Sales. Format: Country. News staff: 3. Target aud: 18-54. ◆Rick Arnish, pres; Rod Schween, gen mgr; Bruce Davis, sls VP; Dave Walker, gen sls mgr; Derek Kortschaga, progmg dir.

CHDR-FM— 2002: 102.9 mhz; 1.6 kw. 19 9th Ave. S. V1C 2L9. Phone: (250) 426-2224. Fax: (250) 426-5520. E-mail: info@thedrivefm.ca. Web Site: www.thedrivefm.ca. Licensee: Jim Pattison Broadcast Group Ltd. (the general partner) and Jim Pattison Industries Ltd. (the limited partner) carrying on business as Jim Pattison Broadcast Group L.P. Group owner: The Jim Pattison Broadcast Group. Rep: Target Broadcast Sales. Format: Adult rock. News staff: 3. Target aud: 25-54. ◆Rick Arnish, pres; Rod Schween, gen mgr; Bruce Davis, sls VP; Dave Walker, gen sls mgr; Rene Ross, progmg dir.

Crawford Bay

CBTE-FM— 1988: 89.9 mhz; 135 w. TL: N49 38 54 W116 50 53. c/o CBTK-FM, 243 Lawrence Ave., Kelowna V1Y 6L2. Phone: (250) 861-3781. Fax: (250) 861-6644. E-mail: kelowna@cbc.ca. Web Site: www.vancouver.cbc.ca/daybreaksouth. Licensee: Canadian Broadcasting Corp. Format: News, pub affrs, entertainment. ◆Charlie Chessius, opns mgr.

CKKC-FM—Licensed to Crawford Bay. See Nelson

Creston

CFKC(AM)— Sept 21, 1968: 1340 khz; 250 w-U, DA-1. 1560 2nd Ave., Trail V1R 1M4. Secondary address: 138-10 Ave. N. V0B 1G0. Phone: (250) 368-5510. Fax: (250) 368-8471. E-mail: kbs@bc.tri.ca. Licensee: Standard Radio Inc. Group owner: Standard Broadcasting Corp. (acq 4-19-02; grpsl). Rep: Target Broadcast Sales. Format: MOR. Spec prog: Ethnic mus 2 hrs wkly. ◆Gary Dorosz, gen mgr; Darren Robertson, progmg dir; Drew Wilson, news dir.

Dawson Creek

CHAD-FM— 2003: 104.1 mhz; 50 w. c/o CHET-FM, Box 214, Chetwynd V0C 1J0. Phone: (250) 784-1880. Fax: (250) 782-7566. E-mail: info@chetchad.com. Web Site: www.chetchad.com. Licensee: Chetwynd Communications Society. Format: MOR, div, oldies. ◆Leo Sabulsky, gen mgr; Mike Sabulsky, chief of engrg.

CJDC-FM— Dec 15, 1947: 890 khz; 10 kw-U. 901-102 Ave. V1G 2B6. Phone: (250) 782-3341. Fax: (250) 782-3154. Licensee: Standard Radio Inc. Group owner: Standard Broadcasting Corp. (acq 4-19-02; grpsl). Format: Country. News staff: 7. Target aud: General. Spec prog: Rock 4 hrs wkly. ◆Tracey Card, gen mgr; Angie Clowry, opns mgr & chief of engrg.

Duncan

CJSU-FM— August 2000: 89.7 mhz; 1.862 kw. #205 2700 Beverly St. V9L 5C7. Phone: (250) 746-0897. Fax: (250) 748-1517. E-mail: cam@897sunfm.com. Web Site: www.897sunfm.com. Licensee: Drew Media Inc. Rep: Target Broadcast Sales, Canadian Broadcast Sales. Format: Adult contemp. News staff: 2; News: 12 hrs wkly. Target aud: 35-54. Spec prog: Oldies 12 hrs wkly. ◆Jason Mann, gen mgr; Ron Larson, progmg dir.

Egmont

CIEG-FM— July 1985: 107.5 mhz; 50 w. 300 ft. Box 1068, Squamish V0N 3G0. Phone: (604) 892-1021. Phone: (604) 683-8060. Fax: (604) 892-6383. E-mail: mountainfm@mountainfm.com. Web Site: www.mountainfm.com. Licensee: Rogers Broadcasting. Rep: Canadian Broadcast Sales. Format: Adult contemp. News staff: 3; News: 16 hrs wkly. Target aud: 25-44. ◆Gary Miles, pres; Paul Fisher, VP; Ken Geiger, gen mgr; Janis Eorreia, gen sls mgr & prom mgr.

Fernie

CJDR-FM— Aug 30, 2002: 99.1 mhz; 470 w. 19 9th Ave. S., Cranbrook V1C 2L9. Phone: (250) 426-2224. Fax: (250) 426-5520. E-mail: info@thedrivefm.ca. Web Site: www.thedrivefm.ca. Licensee: Jim Pattison Broadcast Group Ltd. (the general partner) and Jim Pattison Industries Ltd. (the limited partner) carrying on business as Jim Pattison Broadcast Group L.P. Group owner: The Jim Pattison Broadcast Group. Rep: Target Broadcast Sales. Format: Adult rock. News staff: one. ◆Rick Arnish, pres; Rod Schween, gen mgr; Bruce Davis, sls VP; Dave Walker, gen sls mgr; Rene Ross, progmg dir.

Fort Nelson

CKRX-FM— 1998: 102.3 mhz; 1.8 kw. Box 880 V0C 1R0. Secondary address: 5152 Liard St. V0C 1R0. Phone: (250) 774-2525. Fax: (250) 774-2577. E-mail: kjohnson@sri.ca. Licensee: Standard Radio Inc. Group owner: Standard Broadcasting Corp. (acq 4-19-02; grpsl). Format: CHR. ◆Gary Slaight, CEO & pres; David Coriat, CFO & exec VP; Tracey Gard, gen mgr; Ken Johnson, stn mgr; Angie Clowry, progmg dir & progmg mgr.

Fort St. John

CHRX-FM—Not on air, target date: unknown: 98.5 mhz; 50 kw. 10532 Alaska Rd. V1J 1B3. Phone: (250) 785-6634. Fax: (250) 785-4544. Licensee: Standard Radio Inc. Group owner: Standard Broadcasting Corp. (acq 4-19-2002; grpsl). Format: Rock. ◆Angie Clowry, opns mgr.

CKFU-FM— Sept 1, 2003: 100.1 mhz; 50 w. 10423 101st Ave. V1J 2B7. Phone: (250) 787-7100. Fax: (250) 263-9749. E-mail: reception@moosefm.ca. Web Site: www.moosefm.ca. Licensee: Russ Wagg, on behalf of a corporation to be incorporated. Format: Lite rock 80s & 90s. ◆Kerry Mann, pres; Russ Beerlling, gen mgr; Erin Epp, prom mgr; Rob MacNamara, progmg VP.

CKNL-FM— 2003: 101.5 mhz; 40 kw. 10532 Alaska Rd. V1J 1B3. Phone: (250) 785-6634. Fax: (250) 785-4544. Licensee: Standard Radio Inc. Group owner: Standard Broadcasting Corp. Format: Classic rock. ◆Angie Cloury, opns mgr.

Gibsons

CISC-FM— October 1984: 107.5 mhz; 820 w. Ant 1,000 ft. Box 1068, Squamish V0N 3G0. Phone: (604) 892-1021. Phone: (604) 683-8060. Fax: (604) 892-6383. E-mail: mountainfm@mountainfm.com. Web Site: www.mountainfm.com. Licensee: Rogers Broadcasting. Format: Hot adult contemp. News staff: 3; News: 16 hrs wkly. Target aud: 25-44. Spec prog: Magazine show 3 hrs wkly. ◆Gary Miles; Paul Fisher, VP; Ken Geiger, gen mgr & opns mgr; Mary Kemmis, opns mgr.

Golden

CKGR(AM)— 1973: 1400 khz; 1 kw-D, DA-1. Box 1403 V0A 1H0. Phone: (250) 832-2161. Fax: (250) 344-7233. Web Site: www.myezrock.com. Licensee: Standard Radio Inc. Group owner: Standard Broadcasting Corp. (acq 4-19-02; grpsl). Rep: Target Broadcast Sales. Format: Easy rock. ◆Ron Langridge, gen mgr.

British Columbia

Greenville

CILZ-FM— 1990: . Stn currently dark 96.1 mhz; 7.9 w. Greenville Television Association, 289 Church St. V0J 1X0. Phone: (250) 621-3212. Fax: (250) 621-3320. E-mail: tiffanym@nisgaa.net. Licensee: Greenville Television Association. Format: Contemp country.

Greenwood

CKGF-FM-2— 2003: 96.7 mhz; 40 w horiz. Ant 1,886 ft. TL: N49 05 29 W118 36 36. 525 11th Ave., Castlegar V1N 1J6. Phone: (250) 365-7600. Fax: (250) 365-8480. Licensee: Boundary Broadcasting Ltd. Format: Soft rock. Target aud: 25-54. ◆ Bill Gillespie, pres; Dennis Gerein, gen mgr & gen sls mgr; Doug Johnston, news dir.

Hope

CFSR-FM— 2001: 100.5 mhz; 157 w. 45715 Hocking Ave., Suite 520, Chilliwack V2P 6Z6. Phone: (604) 869-9313. Fax: (604) 702-3212. Web Site: www.starfm.com. Licensee: Rogers Radio (British Columbia) Ltd. Group owner: Rogers Broadcasting Ltd. Format: Adult contemp. ◆ Ken Geiger, gen mgr; Mary Kemmis, gen sls mgr; Murray Olfert, prom mgr.

Invermere

CKIR(AM)— December 1989: 870 khz; 1 kw-U. Box 1403, Golden V0A 1H0. Phone: (250) 832-2161. Fax: (250) 344-7233. E-mail: ckir@rockies.net. Web Site: www.myezrock.com. Licensee: Standard Radio Inc. Group owner: Standard Broadcasting Corp. (acq 4-19-02); grpsl). Format: Easy rock. ◆ Ron Langridge, gen mgr.

Kamloops

CFBX-FM— Apr 2, 2001: 92.5 mhz; 4.9 w. 900 McGill Rd., House 8 V2C 5N3. Phone: (250) 377-3988. Fax: (250) 372-5055. E-mail: radio@cariboo.bc.ca. Web Site: www.thex.ca. Licensee: The Kamloops Campus/Community Radio Society. Format: Div. ◆ Brant Zwicker, stn mgr; Brant Zwieker, prom dir; Steve Marlow, prom dir & progmg dir.

CHNL(AM)— May 1, 1970: 610 khz; 25 kw-D, 5 kw-N, DA-N. 611 Lansdowne St. V2C 1Y6. Phone: (250) 372-2292. Phone: (250) 372-2197. Fax: (250) 372-2293. E-mail: info@radionl.com. Licensee: NL Broadcasting Ltd. Format: Adult contemp, oldies. News staff: 5; News: 15.5 hrs wkly. Target aud: 25-54; family oriented, middle-upper class income. ◆ Robbie Dunn, pres, gen mgr & adv mgr; Ravinder Dhaliwal, CFO; Peter Angle, gen sls mgr; Jim Reynolds, progmg dir; T. Tyler, mus dir; Jim Harrison, news dir; Dave Coulter, chief of engrg.

CKRV-FM—Co-owned with CHNL(AM). Jan 28, 1984: 97.5 mhz; 5 kw. Stereo. Phone: (250) 372-2197. (Acq 6-10-93; $925,000.). Format: Top 40. News staff: one; News: 5 hrs wkly. Target aud: 25-54; professionals, office personnel. ◆ Tim Thompson, mus dir.

CIFM-FM— 1961: 98.3 mhz; 4.3 kw. Stereo. 460 Pemberton Terr. V2C 1T5. Phone: (250) 372-3322. Fax: (250) 374-0445. E-mail: info@98.3cifm.com. Web Site: www.98.3cifm.com. Licensee: Jim Pattison Broadcast Group Ltd. (the general partner) and Jim Pattison Industries Ltd. (the limited partner) carrying on business as Jim Pattison Broadcast Group L.P. Group owner: The Jim Pattison Broadcast Group (acq 1987). Format: Adult rock. News staff: 6; News: 9 hrs wkly. Target aud: 30-40; baby boomers with disposable income. ◆ Rick Arnish, pres, gen mgr & stn mgr; Doug Collins, chief of opns. Co-owned TV: CFJC-TV affil.

CKBZ-FM— 2001: 100.1 mhz; 3.5 kw. Stereo. 460 Pemberton Terr. V2C 1T5. Phone: (250) 372-3322. Fax: (250) 374-0445. E-mail: info@b100.ca. Web Site: www.b100.ca. Licensee: Jim Pattison Broadcast Group Ltd. (the general partner) and Jim Pattison Industries Ltd. (the limited partner) carrying on business as Jim Pattison Broadcast Group L.P. Group owner: The Jim Pattison Broadcast Group. Format: Adult contemp. News staff: 6; News: 10 hrs wkly. Target aud: 25-44; large, loyal audience with disposable income. ◆ Rick Arnish, pres & gen mgr; Doug Collins, opns mgr. Co-owned TV: CFJC-TV affil.

Kelowna

***CBTK-FM—** November 1987: 88.9 mhz; 4.7 kw. 1,676 ft. 243 Lawrence Ave. V1Y 6L2. Phone: (250) 861-3781. Fax: (250) 861-6644. E-mail: kelowna@cbc.ca. Web Site: www.vancouver.cbc.ca/daybreaksouth.

Licensee: Canadian Broadcasting Corp. Network: CBC Radio One. Format: News, pub affrs, entertainment. ◆ Charlie Chessius, opns mgr & progmg dir.

CHSU-FM—Listing follows CKFR(AM).

CILK-FM— June 21, 1985: 101.5 mhz; 11 kw. 1,246 ft. (CP: 10.3 kw.). Stereo. 1598 Pandosy St. V1Y 1P4. Phone: (250) 860-1010. Fax: (250) 860-0505. E-mail: info@silk.fm. Web Site: www.silk.fm. Licensee: Silk FM Broadcasting Ltd. Format: Adult contemp 80s & 90s. News staff: 2; News: 2 hrs wkly. Target aud: 25-54; women. Spec prog: Gospel 3 hrs wkly. ◆ Nick Frost, pres; Rick Dyer, gen mgr & gen sls mgr.

CKFR(AM)— Nov 8, 1971: 1150 khz; 10 kw-U, DA-N. 300-435 Bernard Ave. V1Y 6N8. Phone: (250) 860-8600. Fax: (250) 860-8856. Licensee: Standard Radio Inc. Group owner: Standard Broadcasting Corp. (acq 4-19-02; grpsl). Format: Oldies. Target aud: 25-54. Spec prog: Home improvements 2 hrs, Top-20 countdown 2 hrs, NHL hockey play-by-play 10 hrs, country 4 hrs wkly. ◆ Don Shafer, gen mgr; Dallas Gray, gen sls mgr & mktg mgr; Jason Mann, progmg dir; Betty Selin, news dir.

CHSU-FM—Co-owned with CKFR(AM). Sept 21, 1995: 99.9 mhz; 13 kw. Web Site: www.thesun.net. Format: Adult comtemp.

CKLZ-FM—Listing follows CKOV(AM).

CKOV(AM)— Nov 4, 1931: 630 khz; 5 kw-D, 1 kw-N. TL: N49 50 42 W119 29 07. Stereo. 3805 Lakeshore Rd. V1W 3K6. Phone: (250) 762-3331. Fax: (250) 762-2141. E-mail: ckov@cnx.net. Licensee: Jim Pattison Broadcast Group Ltd. (the general partner) and Jim Pattison Industries Ltd. (the limited partner) carrying on business as Jim Pattison Broadcast Group L.P. Group owner: The Jim Pattison Broadcast Group (acq 6-30-98). Format: News, info, talk. News staff: 5; News: 13 hrs wkly. Target aud: 29-59. ◆ Rick Arnish, pres & VP; Bruce Davis, gen mgr & gen sls mgr; Hugh Dixon, prom mgr; Rob Bye, progmg mgr; Matt Cherrille, news dir; Victor Deveall, chief of engrg.

CKLZ-FM—Co-owned with CKOV(AM). 1964: 104.7 mhz; 3.8 kw. 1,611 ft. TL: N49 46 06 W119 29 59. Stereo. Phone: (250) 763-1047. E-mail: rob@power104.fm. Web Site: www.power104.fam. Format: AOR. News staff: 2; News: 4 hrs wkly. Target aud: 25-49. ◆ Rob Bye, mus dir.

Kitimat

CKTK-FM— 2004: 97.7 mhz; 170 w. 4625 Lazelle Ave., Terrace V8G 1S4. Phone: (250) 635-6316. Fax: (250) 638-6320. Licensee: Standard Radio Inc. Group owner: Standard Broadcasting Corp. Format: CHR. ◆ Doug Anderson, stn mgr.

Lillooet

CHLS-FM— 2001: 100.5 mhz; 5 w. Box 2124 V0K 1V0. Secondary address: Box 760 V0K 1V0. Phone: (250) 256-2457. Fax: (250) 256-7405. E-mail: twilley@gw.sd74.bc.ca. Web Site: www.lillooetradiotv.ca. Licensee: Radio Lillooet Society. Format: Var/div. News: 5 hrs wkly. Target aud: All ages; coomunity of Lillooet. Spec prog: First nations 16 hrs wkly. ◆ Tom Willey, pres & stn mgr; Louis McIvor, prom VP; Vivian Birch-Jones, progmg dir; Sasha LeBaron, engrg dir.

MacKenzie

CHMM-FM— Oct 27, 2003: 103.5 mhz; 900 w. 86 Centennial Ave., Box 547 V0J 2C0. Phone: (250) 997-6277. Fax: (250) 997-6222. E-mail: jd@chmm.ca. Web Site: www.mackbc.com/mackenzieradio. Licensee: MacKenzie and Area Community Radio Society. Format: Var. ◆ J.D. McKenzie, stn mgr.

Merritt

CJNL(AM)— 1970: 1230 khz; 1 kw-D, 250 w-N. TL: N50 06 29 W120 46 06. Box 1630 V1K 1B8. Secondary address: 2196 Quilchena Ave., Unit 201 V1K 1B8. Phone: (250) 378-4288. Fax: (250) 378-6979. Licensee: Merritt Broadcasting Ltd. (acq 1-30-95; C$214,800). Rep: Target Broadcast Sales. Format: Adult contemp, oldies, news. News staff: one; News: 2 hrs wkly. Target aud: General; working family all ages. ◆ Robbie Dunn, CEO & pres; Elizabeth Laird, gen mgr; Brian Wiebe, opns dir.

Nanaimo

CHLY-FM— Sept 21, 2001: 101.7 mhz; 1.3 kw. Ant 312 ft. TL: N49 13 20 W124 00 07. #2-34 Victoria Crescent V9R 5B8. Phone: (250) 716-3400. Phone: (740) 250-1017 (main). Fax: (250) 716-1082. E-mail: admin@chly.fm. Web Site: www.chly.fm. Licensee: Radio Malaspina Society. Format: Div. ◆ Elan Goldenblatt, opns dir; James Booker, progmg mgr; George Miller, mus dir.

CHWF-FM— Oct 1, 2001: 106.9 mhz; 1.6 kw. 4550 Wellington Rd. V9T 2H3. Phone: (250) 758-1131. Fax: (250) 758-4644. E-mail: info@islandradio.bc.ca. Web Site: www.1069thewolf.com. Licensee: Central Island Broadcasting Ltd. Rep: Canadian Broadcast Sales. Format: Rock. News staff: 2. Target aud: 25-54; general. ◆ Hugh McKinnon, pres; Bob Adshead, VP; Paul Larsen, gen mgr; Bob McCheyne, sls dir; Kimberly Strain, prom dir; Kent Wilson, mus dir.

CKWV-FM— Jan 2, 1995: 102.3 mhz; 1.3 kw. Stereo. 4550 Wellington Rd. V9T 2H3. Phone: (250) 758-1131. Fax: (250) 758-4644. E-mail: info@islandradio.bc.ca. Web Site: www.islandradio.bc.ca. Licensee: Central Island Broadcasting Ltd. Rep: Canadian Broadcast Sales. Format: Adult contemp. News staff: 2. Target aud: 25-54; general. ◆ Hugh McKinnon, pres; Bob Adshead, VP; Bob McCheyne, sls dir; Kimberly Strain, prom dir; Paul Larsen, gen mgr & progmg mgr; Ken Schumaker, mus dir; D'Arcy Rinald, news dir; Barry Mandziak, chief of engrg.

Nelson

CJLY-FM— 2002: 93.5 mhz; 70 w. Kootenay Cooperative Radio, Box 767 V1L 5R4. Phone: (250) 352-9600. Fax: (250) 352-9653. E-mail: kcr@kootenaycoopradio.com. Web Site: www.kootenaycoopradio.com. Licensee: Kootenay Co-operative Radio. Format: Div. ◆ Bill Metcalfe, opns mgr; Terry Brennan, progmg dir.

CKKC(AM)— July 15, 1939: 880 khz; 1 kw-D, 700 w-N, DA-1. 1560 2nd Ave., Trail V1R 1M4. Phone: (250) 352-5510. Phone: (250) 368-5510. Fax: (250) 352-9189. Fax: (250) 368-8471. Web Site: www.kbs.fm. Licensee: Standard Radio Inc. Group owner: Standard Broadcasting Corp. (acq 4-19-02; grpsl). Rep: Target Broadcast Sales. Format: MOR. ◆ Ross Haus, gen mgr & sls dir.

CKKC-FM— Sept 1, 1989: 101.9 mhz; 140 w. TL: N49 38 54 W116 50 53.

New Denver

CKZX-FM— October 1981: 93.5 mhz; 100 w. c/o Radio Station CKKC(AM), 1560 2nd Ave., Trail V1R 1M4. Phone: (250) 368-5510. Fax: (250) 368-8471. Web Site: www.kbsradio.ca. Licensee: Standard Radio Inc. Group owner: Standard Broadcasting Corp. (acq 4-19-2002; grpsl). Format: Adult Contemp. ◆ Ross Hawse, gen mgr; Kevin Einarson, gen sls mgr; Darren Robertson, progmg dir; Larry King, chief of engrg.

New Westminster

CFMI-FM—Licensed to New Westminster. See Vancouver

CKNW(AM)—Licensed to New Westminster. See Vancouver

Osoyoos

CJOR(AM)— December 1966: 1240 khz; 1 kw-U, DA-1. 33 Carmi Ave., Penticton V2A 364. Phone: (250) 492-2800. Fax: (250) 493-0370. Licensee: Standard Radio Inc. Group owner: Standard Broadcasting Corp. (acq 4-19-02; grpsl). Rep: Canadian Broadcast Sales. Format: Adult contemp,. Target aud: 25-49. Spec prog: Por 3 hrs wkly. ◆ Lee Sterry, gen mgr.

Parksville

CIBH-FM— Jan 14, 2002: 88.5 mhz; 960 w. Box 1370 V9P 2H3. Phone: (250) 248-4211. Fax: (250) 248-4210. E-mail: info@islandradio.bc.ca. Web Site: www.885thebeach.com. Licensee: Central Island Broadcasting Ltd. Format: Adult contemp, oldies soft rock. News staff: 2. ◆ Hugh McKinnon, pres; Bob Adshead, VP; Bob McCheyne, sls dir; Paul Larson, gen mgr & progmg dir.

Directory of Radio

British Columbia

Pemberton

CISP-FM— Oct 5, 1982: 104.5 mhz; 400 w. 1,000 ft. Box 1068, Squamish V0N 3G0. Phone: (604) 892-1021. Phone: (604) 683-8060. Fax: (604) 892-6383. E-mail: mountainfm@mountainfm.com. Web Site: www.mountainfm.com. Licensee: Rogers Broadcasting Ltd. (group owner) Format: Hot adult contemp. News staff: 3; News: 16 hrs wkly. Target aud: 25-45. ♦ Gary Miles, pres; Paul Fisher, VP; Ken Geiger, gen mgr; Mary Kemmis, opns mgr; Rebecca Hall, prom dir.

Pender Harbour

CIPN-FM— October 1984: 104.7 mhz; 750 w. 1,500 ft. Box 1068, Squamish V0N 3G0. Phone: (604) 892-1021. Phone: (604) 683-8060. Fax: (604) 892-6383. E-mail: mountainfm@mountainfm.com. Web Site: www.mountainfm.com. Licensee: Rogers Broadcasting. Format: Hot adult contemp. News staff: 3; News: 16 hrs wkly. ♦ Gary Miles, pres; Paul Fisher, VP; Ken Geiger, gen mgr.

Penticton

CIGV-FM— Oct 18, 1981: 100.7 mhz; 6.3 kw. Ant 2,486 ft. TL: N49 42 46 W119 36 26. Stereo. 125 Nanaimo Ave. W. V2A 1N2. Phone: (250) 493-6767. Fax: (250) 493-0098. E-mail: info@giantfm.com. Web Site: www.giantfm.ca. Licensee: Great Valleys Radio Ltd. Rep: Target Broadcast Sales. Format: Country, adult contemp. News staff: 3; News: 16 hrs wkly. Target aud: 18 plus. Spec prog: Class 2 hrs, farm one hr wkly. ♦ James Robinson, CEO, pres & gen mgr; Rae Slavens, gen sls mgr; Carl Harris, mus dir; Harry Shaw, chief of engrg.

CJMG-FM—Listing follows CKOR(AM).

CKOR(AM)— September 1948: 800 khz; 10 kw-D, 500 w-N. 33 Carmi Ave. V2A 3G4. Phone: (250) 492-2800. Fax: (250) 493-0370. Licensee: Standard Radio Inc. Group owner: Standard Broadcasting Corp. (acq 4-19-02; grpsl). Format: Gold. ♦ Ross Hawse, gen mgr.

CJMG-FM—Co-owned with CKOR(AM). June 1, 1965: 97.1 mhz; 1.8 kw. 755 ft. Stereo. Format: AOR.

Port Alberni

CJAV(AM)— Apr 1, 1946: 1240 khz; 1 kw-U. TL: N49 16 41 W124 46 51. 2970 3rd Ave. V9Y 2A7. Phone: (250) 723-2455. Fax: (250) 723-0797. Web Site: www.av1240.com. Licensee: CJAV Ltd. (acq 4-1-72). Rep: Canadian Broadcast Sales. Format: Adult contemp, country. News: 14 hrs wkly. Target aud: General. Spec prog: European one hr wkly. ♦ Christine Gibson, pres; Chris Talbot, gen mgr & opns mgr; Paul Larson, gen mgr & gen sls mgr.

Port Hardy

CFNI(AM)— Sept 1, 1979: 1240 khz; 1 kw-U, DA-1. Box 1240, 5050 Beaver Harbour Rd. V0N 2P0. Phone: (250) 949-6500. Phone: (250) 334-2421. Fax: (250) 949-6580. Licensee: CFCP Ltd. Format: Adult contemp. News staff: one. Target aud: General. ♦ Norma Browne, CEO & pres; Gregory T. Phelps, gen mgr; Carole Ford, stn mgr.

Powell River

CHQB(AM)— Mar 21, 1967: 1280 khz; 1 kw-U, DA-1. TL: N49 48 10 W124 36 10. 6816 Courtenay St. V8A 1X1. Phone: (604) 485-4207. Fax: (604) 485-4210. E-mail: chqb@onelink.ca. Web Site: www.coastradio.com. Licensee: CFCP Radio Ltd. (acq 11-18-97). Network: Bible Bcstg Net. Target. Format: Country. News staff: one; News: 14 hrs wkly. Target aud: General. ♦ Norma Browne, pres; Gregory T. Phelps, gen mgr.

CJMP-FM— 3.6 w: 90.1 mhz; 4476 A Marine Ave. V8A 2K2. Phone: (604) 485-2688. Fax: (604) 485-2683. E-mail: modelcommunity@prcn.org. Licensee: Powell River Model Community Project for Persons with Disabilities. Format: Var. ♦ Geraldine Braak, gen mgr.

Prince George

CBYG-FM—Not on air, target date: unknown: 91.5 mhz; 100 kw. 890 Victoria St., Unit 1 V2L 5P1. Phone: (250) 562-6701. Fax: (250) 562-4777. E-mail: daybreaknorth@cbc.ca. Web Site: www.vancouver.cbc.ca/daybreaknorth. Licensee: CBC. Network: CBC Radio One. Format: Current affrs. ♦ Deborah Irvine, stn mgr.

CFUR-FM— 2002: 88.7 mhz; 4.3 w. 3333 University Way V2N 4Z9. Phone: (250) 960-7664. Fax: (250) 960-5995. E-mail: info@cfur.ca. Web Site: www.cfur.ca. Licensee: Education Alternative Radio Society. Format: Div. Target aud: Community of Prince George. ♦ Christopher Earl, stn mgr; Bryndis Ogmundson, progmg dir; Glen Yakemchuk, engrg dir.

CIRX-FM— Oct 1, 1983: 94.3 mhz; 3.5 kw. Ant 1,145 ft. Stereo. 1940 3rd Ave. V2M 1G7. Phone: (250) 564-2524. Fax: (250) 562-6611. Web Site: www.94xfm.com. Licensee: Cariboo Central Interior Radio Inc. (group owner). Format: Rock. Target aud: 18-34. ♦ Terry Shepherd, gen mgr; Gary Russell, progmg mgr; Richard Davis, chief of engrg.

CJCI-FM— Aug 5, 2003: 97.3 mhz; 12 kw. The Wolf, 1940 3rd Ave. V2M 1G7. Phone: (250) 564-2524. Fax: (250) 562-6611. E-mail: thewolf@97fm.ca. Web Site: www.97fm.ca. Licensee: Cariboo Central Interior Radio Inc. (group owner). Format: Modern country, southern rock. News staff: 3. Target aud: 25-54. ♦ Terry Shepherd, gen mgr; Alice George, gen sls mgr; Darren Coogan, progmg mgr; Richard Davis, chief of engrg.

CKDV-FM— 2003: 99.3 mhz; 9.3 kw. 1810 3rd Ave. V2M 1G4. Phone: (250) 564-8861. Fax: (250) 562-8768. E-mail: ckpgmail@ckpg.bc.ca. Web Site: www.993thedrive.com. Licensee: Jim Pattison Broadcast Group Ltd. (the general partner) and Jim Pattison Industries Ltd. (the limited partner) carrying on business as Jim Pattison Broadcast Group L.P. Group owner: The Jim Pattison Broadcast Group. Format: Classic rock. ♦ Ken Kilcullen, gen mgr; Gord Wilkinson, gen sls mgr; Ron Pollillo, progmg dir; Mike Woodworth, news dir.

CKKN-FM— Mar 1, 1981: 101.3 mhz; 10 kw. Ant 1,000 ft. Stereo. 2nd Fl. 1810 3rd Ave. V2M 1G4. Phone: (250) 564-8861. Fax: (250) 562-8768. Fax: (250) 562-7681. E-mail: ckpgmail@ckpg.bc.cn. Web Site: www.993thedrive.com. Licensee: Jim Pattison Broadcast Group Ltd. (the general partner) and Jim Pattison Industries Ltd. (the limited partner) carrying on business as Jim Pattison Broadcast Group L.P. Group owner: The Jim Pattison Broadcast Group (acq 12-21-2000; grpsl). Format: CHR. ♦ Rick Arnish, pres; Gord Wilkinson, gen mgr; Ken Kilcullen, gen mgr; Ron Polillo, progmg mgr; Rick Kelly, mus dir; Mike Woodworth, news dir. Co-owned TV: CKPG-TV affil.

Prince Rupert

*CFPR(AM)— 1936: 860 khz; 10 kw-U, DA-1. 222 Third Ave. W., Suite 1 V8J 1L1. Phone: (250) 624-2161. Fax: (250) 627-8594. E-mail: daybreaknorth@vancouver.cbc.ca. Web Site: www.cbc.ca. Licensee: CBC. (acq 1953). Network: CBC Radio One. Format: CBC info, news/talk. Target aud: General. Spec prog: Current affrs. ♦ Ian Giesbrecht, gen mgr.

CHTK(AM)— 1965: 560 khz; 1 kw-D, 250 w-N. 215 Cowbay Rd., Unit 212 V8J 1A2. Phone: (250) 627-8255. Fax: (250) 624-3100. E-mail: gsimpson@sri.ca. Licensee: Standard Radio Inc. Group owner: Standard Broadcasting Corp. (acq 4-19-02; grpsl). Format: CHR. ♦ Mike Lunn, gen mgr.

CIAJ-FM— 2000: 100.7 mhz; 26.5 w. 531 6th Ave. W. V8J 1Z7. E-mail: cfirm@citytel.net. Licensee: Canadian Christians In Action Ministries. Format: Christian. ♦ Prescott Sandhu, gen mgr.

Princeton

CIOR(AM)— June 1972: 1400 khz; 1 kw-U, DA-1. TL: N49 26 50 W120 30 42. Box 539, 203 8309 Main St., Osoyoos V0H 1V0. Phone: (250) 492-2800. Fax: (250) 495-7228. Licensee: Okanagan Skeena Group Ltd. Rep: Canadian Broadcast Sales. Format: Adult contemp. ♦ Ross Hawse, stn mgr.

Qualicum

CIBH-FM—See Parksville

Quesnel

CKCQ-FM— 2004: 100.3 mhz; 1.8 kw. 160 Front St. V2J 2K1. Phone: (250) 992-7046. Fax: (250) 992-2354. Web Site: www.thewolfpack.ca. Licensee: Cariboo Central Interior Radio Inc. Format: Modern country, southern rock. News staff: 4. ♦ Al Manderson, gen mgr.

Revelstoke

CKCR(AM)— Nov 21, 1965: 1340 khz; 1 kw-D, 250 w-N. Box 1420 V0E 2S0. Secondary address: 208 E. 1st. St. V0E 2S0. Phone: (250) 837-2149. Fax: (250) 837-5577. E-mail: ckcr@rctvonline.net. Web Site: www.myezrock.com. Licensee: Standard Radio Inc. Group owner: Standard Broadcasting Corp. (acq 4-19-02; grpsl). Format: Easy rock. ♦ Ron Langridge, pres & gen mgr.

Richmond

CISL(AM)— May 1, 1980: 650 khz; 10 kw-U, DA-2. No. 20, 11151 Horseshoe Way V7A 4S5. Phone: (604) 272-6500. Fax: (604) 272-0917. Web Site: www.650cisl.com. Licensee: Standard Radio Inc. Group owner: Standard Broadcasting Corp. (acq 5-8-96; C$18 million with CKZZ-FM Vancouver). Format: Oldies. ♦ Gary Slaight, pres; Gary Russell, VP & gen mgr.

Salmon Arm

CKXR(AM)— Nov 18, 1965: 580 khz; 10 kw-D, 1 kw-N, DA-2. Box 69 V1E 4N2. Phone: (250) 832-2161. Fax: (250) 832-2240. Web Site: myezrock.com. Licensee: Standard Radio Inc. Group owner: Standard Broadcasting Corp. (acq 4-19-02; grpsl). Format: Adult contemp. News staff: 2. Target aud: 25-54. ♦ Ron Langridge, gen mgr & stn mgr.

Sechelt

CKKS-FM— July 1985: 104.7 mhz; 750 w. 2,000 ft. Box 1068, Squamish V0N 3G0. Phone: (604) 892-1021. Phone: (604) 683-8060. Fax: (604) 892-6383. E-mail: mountainfm@mountainfm.com. Web Site: www.mountainfm.com. Licensee: Rogers Broadcasting Ltd. (group owner). Rep: Canadian Broadcast Sales. Format: Hits of the 80s & 90s. News staff: 3; News: 16 hrs wkly. Target aud: 25-45. Spec prog: Magazine show 3 hrs wkly. ♦ Gary Miles, pres; Ken Geiger, gen mgr, opns mgr & progmg dir; Mary Kemmis, opns mgr; Paul Fisher, gen sls mgr; Rebecca Hall, prom dir.

Smithers

CFBV(AM)— Oct 25, 1963: 870 khz; 1 kw-D, 250 w-N. Box 335 V0J 2N0. Secondary address: 1139 Queen St. V0J 2N0. Phone: (250) 847-2521. Fax: (250) 847-9411. Licensee: Cariboo Central Interior Radio Inc. (group owner) Format: Adult contemp. ♦ Al Collison, gen mgr.

Squamish

CISQ-FM— Nov 30, 1981: 107.1 mhz; 12.48 kw. Ant 800 ft. Box 1068 V0N 3G0. Phone: (604) 892-1021. Fax: (604) 892-6383. Web Site: www.mountainfm.com. Licensee: Rogers Broadcasting. Rep: Canadian Broadcast Sales. Format: Hot adult contemp. News staff: 3; News: 5 hrs wkly. Target aud: 18-54. Spec prog: Talk 5 hrs wkly. ♦ Ken Geiger, gen mgr.

Summerland

CHOR(AM)— 1972: 1450 khz; 1 kw-U, DA-1. Box 1170, 13415 Rosedale V0H 1Z0. Phone: (250) 494-0333. Fax: (250) 493-0370. Web Site: www.thesun.net. Licensee: Okanagan Radio Ltd. Rep: Canadian Broadcast Sales. Format: Oldies. Spec prog: Class 3 hrs, jazz 3 hrs wkly. ♦ Lee Sterry, gen mgr; Lee Sterry, stn mgr; Dustin Collins, progmg dir.

Terrace

CFNR-FM— 1995: 92.1 mhz; 43 w. 4562B Queensway Dr. V8G 3X6. Phone: (250) 638-8137. Fax: (250) 638-8027. E-mail: cfnrmailbag@monarch.net. Web Site: www.cfnr.net. Starchoice Ch. 851 Licensee: Northern Native Broadcasting (Terrace, B.C.). Format: Classic rock, sportstalk. News: 10 hrs wkly. Target aud: General; 35+. Spec prog: First nations 9 hrs, gospel 1 hr wkly. ♦ Clarence Martin, CEO; Barry Wall, gen sls mgr & mktg mgr; Ron Taylor, progmg dir.

CFTK(AM)— 1960: 590 khz; 1 kw-U, DA-1. 4625 Lazelle Ave. V8G 1S4. Phone: (250) 635-6316. Fax: (250) 638-6320. Licensee: Standard Radio Inc. Group owner: Standard Broadcasting Corp. (acq 4-19-02; grpsl). Format: MOR. ♦ Brian Langston, gen mgr.

CJFW-FM—Co-owned with CFTK(AM). December 1983: 103.1 mhz; Format: Contemp country.. Co-owned TV: CFTK-TV affil.

Trail

CJAT-FM— 1996: 95.7 mhz; 13.5 kw. 1560 2nd Ave. V1R 1M4. Phone: (250) 368-5510. Fax: (250) 368-8471. E-mail: kbs@sri.ca. Web Site: www.kbsradio.ca. Licensee: Standard Radio Inc. Group owner: Standard Broadcasting Corp. (acq 4-19-02; grpsl). Rep: Target Broadcast Sales. Format: Adult contemp. Spec prog: Ethnic mus 2 hrs wkly. ♦Ross Hawse, gen mgr & gen sls mgr; Darren Robertson, progmg dir; Larry King, chief of engrg.

Vancouver

***CBU(AM)**— 1925: 690 khz; 50 kw-U, DA-1. (Digital radio: 1459.792 mhz). Box 4600, 700 Hamilton St. V6B 4A2. Phone: (604) 662-6000. Fax: (604) 662-6088. Web Site: www.vancouver.cbc.ca. Licensee: Canadian Broadcasting Corp. Format: Class, jazz, news/talk. ♦Joan Anderson, gen mgr; Joan Athey, prom dir; Brett Ballah, news dir; Dave Newbury, engrg dir.

CBU-FM— 1947: 105.7 mhz; 100 kw. 1,823 ft. (Digital radio: 1459.792 mhz). Stereo. Web Site: vanconver.cbc.ca. ♦Tod Elvidge, mus dir.

CBUF-FM— Dec 1, 1967: 97.7 mhz; 50 kw. Ant 1,823 ft. (Digital radio: 1459.792 mhz). Stereo. 700 Hamilton St. V6B 4A2. Secondary address: Box 4600 V6B 4A2. Phone: (604) 662-6169. Fax: (604) 662-6161. Web Site: www.radio-canada.ca/c-b. Licensee: CBC. Network: Premiere Chaine. Format: Div. ♦Stephane Boisjoly, gen mgr; Mario Deschamps, progmg dir.

CBUX-FM— Sept 22, 2002: 90.9 mhz; 1.28 kw. 700 Hamilton St. V6B 4A2. Phone: (604) 662-6000. Fax: (604) 662-6335. Web Site: www.radio-canada.ca/c-b. Licensee: Canadian Broadcasting Corp. Network: Chaine Culturelle. Format: Var, Fr. ♦Stephanie Boisjoly, gen mgr; Mario Deschamps, progmg dir.

CFBT-FM— February 2002: 94.5 mhz; 46 kw. #A301 - 770 Pacific Blvd., Plaza of Nations V6B 5E7. Phone: (604) 699-2328. Fax: (604) 484-4912. E-mail: info@thebeat.com. Web Site: www.thebeat.com. Licensee: Focus Entertainment Group Inc. (acq 8-3-01). Format: Rythmic CHR, Top 40. News staff: one; News: 2 hrs wkly. ♦Barry Duggan, exec VP; Jennifer Smith, VP & gen sls mgr; Scot Turner, progmg dir.

CFMI-FM—Listing follows CKNW(AM).

CFOX-FM—Listing follows CHMJ(AM).

***CFRO-FM**— Apr 22, 1975: 102.7 mhz; 5.5 kw. 1,005 ft. 110 - 360 Columbia St. V6A 4J1. Phone: (604) 684-8494. Fax: (604) 681-5310. E-mail: vcrstaff@vcn.bc.ca. Web Site: www.vcn.bc.ca/cfro. Licensee: Vancouver Co-Op Radio. Format: Community, news/talk, alternative pub affrs. Target aud: General; alternative community. Spec prog: Black 14 hrs, Chinese 2 hrs, Greek one hr, hip hop 17 hrs, jazz 16 hrs, Latin American 7 hrs, Pol 5 hrs wkly. ♦Allen Jensen, progmg mgr; Leela Chinniah, progmg mgr; Rob Gauvin, mus dir; Danjel van Tijn, engrg dir; Voja Furtula, engrg dir.

CFUN(AM)—Listing follows CHQM-FM.

CHKG-FM— Sept 6, 1997: 96.1 mhz; 46 kw. 525 W. Broadway, Suite A-1 V5Z 4K5. Phone: (604) 708-1234. Fax: (604) 708-1201. E-mail: general@fm961.com. Web Site: www.fm961.com. Licensee: Fairchild Radio (Vancouver FM) Ltd. Rep: Target Broadcast Sales. Format: Ethnic. News staff: 10; News: 10 hrs wky. ♦Brenda Lo, sr VP & dev VP; George Lee, sr VP & gen mgr; Thomas Fung, chmn & VP; Alan Kwok, opns mgr.

CHMB(AM)— Dec 10, 1959: 1320 khz; 50 kw-U, DA-2. TL: N49 09 55 W123 02 28. 1200 W. 73rd Ave., Suite 100 V6P 6G5. Phone: (604) 263-1320. Fax: (604) 261-0310. E-mail: info@am1320.com. Web Site: www.am1320.com. Licensee: Mainstream Broadcasting Corp. (acq 12-14-93; C$1.8 million). Format: Chinese, multicultural. News staff: 6; News: 30 hrs wkly. Target aud: 18-65; multilingual, multicultural, mainly Chinese. Spec prog: American Indian one hr, It one hr, Japanese 7 hrs, Sp one hr, Vietnamese 2 hrs wkly. ♦James Ho, CEO, chmn & pres; George Feng, dev VP, sls VP & mktg VP; Susanna Low, sls dir; Kay Lai, gen sls mgr; Raymond Chow, progmg mgr; Stella Ho, news dir; Calvin Kwok, pub affrs dir; K.K. Wong, chief of engrg.

CHMJ(AM)— June 1954: 730 khz; 50 kw-U, DA-2. Stereo. 700 W. Georgia St., Suite 2000 V7Y 1K9. Phone: (604) 681-7511. Fax: (604) 331-2722. Web Site: www.mojoradio.ca. Licensee: Corus Radio Co. Group owner: Corus Entertainment Inc. (acq 7-6-00; grpsl). Format: All news. ♦Lou Del Gobbo, gen mgr; Shari Wong, gen sls mgr; April Cruz, prom dir; Tom Plasteras, progmg dir.

CFOX-FM—Co-owned with CHMJ(AM). October 1964: 99.3 mhz; 100 kw. 2,243 ft. Stereo. Phone: (604) 684-7221. Format: AOR. ♦Bob Mills, progmg dir.

CHQM-FM— Aug 10, 1960: 103.5 mhz; 53 kw. Ant 2,026 ft. (Digital radio: 1463.280 mhz). Stereo. 380 W. 2nd Ave., Suite 300 V5Y 1C8. Phone: (604) 871-9000. Fax: (604) 871-2901. E-mail: qmfmmail@qmfm.com. Web Site: www.qmfm.com. Licensee: CHUM (Western) Ltd. Group owner: CHUM Ltd. (acq 8-23-69). Format: Adult contemp. News staff: 5; News: 2 hrs wkly. Target aud: 25-54. ♦Barry O'Donnell, gen sls mgr; Carl LeGrice, prom dir; Neil Gallagher, progmg mgr; Clara Carotenuto, mus dir; Dave Youell, chief of engrg.

CFUN(AM)—Co-owned with CHQM-FM. Apr 20, 1922: 1410 khz; 50 kw-U, DA-2. (Digital radio: 1463.280 mhz). E-mail: cfunmail@cfun.cim. Web Site: www.cfun.com. (Acq 1-1-73). Format: Talk. Target aud: 25-49; upscale, well-educated females.

***CITR-FM**— Apr 1, 1982: 101.9 mhz; 1.8 kw. 170 ft. Stereo. Univ. of British Columbia, 233-6138 Sub Blvd. V6T 1Z1. Phone: (604) 822-3017. Fax: (604) 822-9364. E-mail: citrmgr@ams.ubc.ca. Web Site: www.citr.ca. Licensee: Student Radio Society of University of British Columbia. Format: Div. News: 10 hrs wkly. Target aud: General; campus/community. Spec prog: Black 18 hrs, Fr 2 hrs, Sp 2 hrs, East Indian 2 hrs, Greek one hr wkly. ♦Harry Hertscheg, chmn; Dave Gwilliam, pres; Paul Lambert, VP; Lydia Masemola, stn mgr & chief of opns; Luke Meat, mus dir; Lucas Teddoro Da Silva, news dir.

CJJR-FM—Listing follows CKBD(AM).

CJVB(AM)— June 18, 1972: 1470 khz; 50 kw-U, DA-2. TL: N49 11 36 W123 01 17. Stereo. A1-525 West Broadway V5Z 4K5. Phone: (604) 708-1234. Fax: (604) 708-1201. E-mail: general@am1470.com. Web Site: www.am1470.com. Licensee: Fairchild Radio Group Ltd. Rep: Major Market Broadcasters Ltd, Target Broadcast Sales. In House Format: Ethnic, Chinese. News staff: 10; News: 23 hrs wkly. Target aud: 30 plus; new Canadians. ♦Thomas Fung, chmn & pres; Brenda Lo, sr VP & dev VP; George Lee, sr VP, VP & gen mgr; Alan Kwok, opns mgr.

CKBD(AM)— July 13, 1926: 600 khz; 10 kw-U, DA-N. Stereo. 300-1401 W. 8th Ave. V6H 1C9. Phone: (604) 731-6111. Fax: (604) 731-0493. E-mail: 600am@600am.com. Web Site: www.600am.com. Licensee: Jim Pattison Broadcast Group Ltd. (the general partner) and Jim Pattison Industries Ltd. (the limited partner) carrying on business as Jim Pattison Broadcast Group L.P. Group owner: The Jim Pattison Broadcast Group (acq 1965). Rep: Canadian Broadcast Sales. Format: MOR. News staff: 3; News: 6 hrs wkly. Target aud: 45; mature adults. ♦Jim Pattison, CEO & chmn; Gerry Siemens, VP & gen mgr; Mark Rogers, gen sls mgr; Brian Pritchard, rgnl sls mgr; Sheila Dunn, prom dir; Gord Eno, progmg dir; Mark Patric, mus dir; Campbell McCubbin, news dir; Dave Linder, engrg mgr.

CJJR-FM—Co-owned with CKBD(AM). July 1, 1986: 93.7 mhz; 75 kw. 2,250 ft. Stereo. 1501 W. 8th Ave. V6H 1C9. Phone: (604) 731-7772. Fax: (604) 731-1329. Format: Contemp country. News staff: 2. Target aud: 25-54. ♦Mark Rogers, gen sls mgr; Brian Pritchaad, natl sls mgr; Karen Seaboyer, prom dir; Gordon End, progmg dir; Mark Patric, mus dir; Campbell McCubbin, news dir; Shiral Tobin, pub affrs dir; David Linder, engrg mgr.

CKLG-FM—Listing follows CKWX(AM).

CKNW(AM)—(New Westminster). Sept 1, 1944: 980 khz; 50 kw-U, DA-2. Stereo. 700 W. Georgia St., Suite 2000 V7Y 1K9. Phone: (604) 331-2711. Fax: (604) 331-2722. E-mail: info@cknw.com. Web Site: www.cknw.com. Licensee: Corus Premium Television Ltd. Group owner: Corus Entertainment Inc. (acq 7-6-2000; grpsl). Rep: Canadian Broadcast Sales. Format: MOR, news/talk, sports. News staff: 20; News: 14 hrs wkly. Target aud: General. ♦Lou Delgobbo, gen mgr; Al Anaka, sls VP; Steve Scarrow, prom dir; Tom Plasteras, progmg dir; Steve Parsons, mus dir; Gord Macdonald, news dir; Ian Koenigsfest, pub affrs dir; Dave Glasstetter, engrg VP.

CFMI-FM—Co-owned with CKNW(AM). Mar 22, 1970: 101.1 mhz; 100 kw. 3,500 ft. Stereo. Phone: (604) 331-2808. Fax: (604) 331-2727. E-mail: rock101@rock101.com. Web Site: www.rock101.com. Format: Classic rock. Target aud: 25-49. ♦Ross Winters, progmg dir; Graham Hatch, news dir.

CKST(AM)— Jan 19, 1963: 1040 khz; 50 kw-U, DA-2. Stereo. 300-380 W. 2nd Ave., Suite 300 V5Y 1C8. Phone: (604) 871-9000. Fax: (604) 871-2901. E-mail: live@team1040.ca. Web Site: www.team1040.ca. Licensee: CHUM Ltd. (group owner; acq 2-10-03). Rep: Canadian Broadcast Sales. Format: All sports. News staff: 4; News: 8 hrs wkly. Target aud: 40 plus; intelligent, socially conscious, older demographic. ♦Paul Ski, gen mgr & opns VP.

CKWX(AM)— Apr 1, 1923: 1130 khz; 50 kw-U, DA-N. TL: N49 09 22 W123 04 00. 2440 Ash St. V5Z 4J6. Phone: (604) 877-4488. Phone: (604) 872-2557. Fax: (604) 877-4494. Web Site: www.news1130.com. Licensee: Rogers Broadcasting Ltd. (group owner; acq 1989). Rep: CBS Radio. Format: All news. News staff: 45; News: 168 hrs wkly. Target aud: 35-54; men. ♦Ted Rogers, CEO & chmn; Tony Viner, pres; Laura Nixon, CFO; Gary Miles, exec VP; Paul Fisher, gen mgr & opns mgr; May Lam, prom mgr; Jacquie Donaldson, progmg dir & news dir; Rick Dal Farra, chief of engrg.

CKLG-FM—Co-owned with CKWX(AM). Mar 1, 1980: 96.9 mhz; 100 kw. 2,500 ft. TL: N49 21 29 W122 57 09. Stereo. Web Site: www.969jackfm.com. Format: Adult contemp. ♦May Lam, prom dir; Doreen Copeland, mus dir; Rick dal Farva, engrg mgr.

CKZZ-FM— May 1991: 95.3 mhz; 75 kw. #20, 11151 Horseshoe Way, Richmond V7A 4S5. Phone: (604) 241-0953. Fax: (604) 272-0917. E-mail: info@z95.com. Web Site: www.z95.com. Licensee: Standard Radio Inc. Group owner: Standard Broadcasting Corp. (acq 5-8-96; C$18 million with CISL(AM) Richmond). Format: Hot adult contemp. ♦Gary Slaight, pres; Gary Russell, VP & gen mgr.

Vanderhoof

CIVH(AM)— November 1973: 1340 khz; 1 kw-D, 500 w-N, DA-1. TL: N54 01 00 W123 59 00. Box 1370, 150 W. Columbia St. V0J 3A0. Phone: (250) 567-4914. Fax: (250) 567-4982. E-mail: ciradio@hwy16.com. Licensee: Cariboo Central Interior Radio. (group owner) Rep: Target Broadcast Sales. Format: Modern country & best southern rock. Target aud: General. Spec prog: Relg 5 hrs wkly. ♦Ron A. East, CEO; Terry Shepard, gen mgr; Alice George, gen sls mgr; Jacqui Ryks, prom mgr & mus dir; Bill Russell, progmg VP; Tom Bulmer, stn mgr, rgnl sls mgr & progmg mgr; Eryn Collins, news dir.

Vernon

CICF-FM— 2001: 105.7 mhz; 46 kw. 2800 31st St. V1T 5H4. Phone: (250) 545-9222. Fax: (250) 542-2083. E-mail: vernonmail@sri.ca. Web Site: www.thesun.net/vernon. Licensee: Standard Radio Inc. Group owner: Standard Broadcasting Corp. Format: Hot adult contemp. ♦Gord Leighton, gen mgr; Jason Mann, progmg dir; Larry King, chief of engrg.

CKIZ-FM— Nov 8, 2001: 107.5 mhz; 46 kw. 3313 32nd Ave. V1T 2E1. Phone: (250) 545-2141. Fax: (250) 545-9008. E-mail: kissfm@1075kiss.com. Web Site: www.1075kiss.com. Licensee: Rogers Broadcasting Ltd. (group owner). Rep: Canadian Broadcast Sales. Format: Hot adult contemp, news. ♦Patrick Nicol, gen mgr; Gord Wiens, gen sls mgr; Don Weglo, progmg dir; Duane Schindel, chief of engrg.

Victoria

***CBCV-FM**— Sept 28, 1998: 90.5 mhz; 3 kw. 1025 Pandora Ave. V8V 3P6. Phone: (250) 360-2227. Fax: (250) 360-2600. E-mail: victoria@cbc.ca. Web Site: www.vancouver.cbc.ca/ontheisland. Licensee: CBC. Network: CBC Radio One. Format: Var, news/talk. News staff: 8; News: 13 hrs wkly. ♦Peter Hutchinson, stn mgr & progmg mgr.

CFAX(AM)— Sept 4, 1959: 1070 khz; 10 kw-U, DA-1. TL: N48 23 50 W123 18 20. Stereo. Mellor Bldg., 825 Broughton St. V8W 1E5. Phone: (250) 386-1070. Fax: (250) 381-2329. E-mail: cfax@cfax1070.com. Web Site: www.cfax1070.com. Licensee: CHUM Ltd. (acq 10-1-2004;. C$7.5 million. with co-located FM). Rep: Target Broadcast Sales. Target Broadcast Sales Format: News/talk. News staff: 7; News: 21 hrs wkly. Target aud: 45 plus; 50% males, 50% females. ♦Mel Cooper, gen mgr; Kevin Bell, sls dir; Jack Simmons, gen sls mgr & natl sls mgr; Shannon Kowalko, adv dir; Terry Spence, exec VP, opns VP & progmg dir; Al Ferraby, mus dir; Beth Myers, news dir; Bud Goes, chief of engrg.

Directory of Radio

CHBE-FM—Co-owned with CFAX(AM). Aug 23, 2002: 107.3 mhz; 20 kw. TL: N48 25 06 W123 30 35. 825 Broughton St. V8W 1E5. Phone: (250) 382-1073. Fax: (250) 386-5775. Web Site: www.b1073.ca. Format: Classic hits. News: 1.5 hrs. Target aud: 35-49. ♦ Terry Spence, opns dir; Brad Edwards, opns mgr & progmg dir; Jack Simmons, rgnl sls mgr; Jim Scanlon, mktg VP; Mandy Butler, prom dir & adv dir; Rick Ball, news dir.

*CFUV-FM— Dec 17, 1984: 101.9 mhz; 2.29 kw. 265 ft. Stereo. Box 3035 V8W 3P3. Phone: (250) 721-8607. Phone: (250) 721-8702. Fax: (250) 721-7111. Web Site: www.cfuv.uvic.ca. Licensee: University of Victoria Student Radio Society. Format: Div. News: 8.5 hrs wkly. Target aud: General; people tired of commercial radio, on campus & in the community. Spec prog: It 2 hrs, American Indian 1 hrs; Fr 2 hrs, Pol one hr, Sp 3 hrs wkly. ♦ Randy Gelling, stn mgr; Zeta Lay, progmg dir.

CHTT-FM— September 2000: 103.1 mhz; 50 w. TL: N48 26 52 W123 19 19. Stereo. 817 Fort St. V8W 1H6. Phone: (250) 382-0900. Fax: (250) 382-4358. Web Site: www.1031jackfm.ca. Licensee: Rogers Broadcasting Ltd. (group owner) Rep: Canadian Broadcast Sales. News: 5 hrs wkly. ♦ Kim Hesketh, gen mgr; Tony Marsh, gen sls mgr; Gorde Edlund, progmg dir.

CIOC-FM— Mar 18, 1965: 98.5 mhz; 100 kw. 567 ft. Stereo. 817 Fort St. V8W 1H6. Phone: (250) 382-0900. Fax: (250) 382-4358. Web Site: www.ocean985.com. Licensee: Rogers Broadcasting Ltd. (group owner) Format: Lite rock, adult contemp. News staff: one; News: 2 hrs wkly. Target aud: 35-54; female. ♦ Kim Hesketh, VP & stn mgr; Dawn Kaysoe, opns dir; Dean Fox, chief of engrg.

CJZN-FM— May 2000: 91.3 mhz; 1.766 kw. (Digital radio: 1,472.000 mhz; 2 kw). Stereo. Top Floor, 2750 Quadra St. V8T 4E8. Phone: (250) 475-6611. Fax: (250) 475-3299. E-mail: modernrock@TheZone.fm. Web Site: www.thezone.fm. Licensee: O.K. Radio Group Ltd. Format: Modern rock. Target aud: 25-64. ♦ Stu Morton, pres; Dan McAllister, gen mgr; John Shields, opns mgr; Brian Blackburn, sls VP; Sarah Morton, prom dir; Al Ford, progmg dir.

CKKQ-FM— Dec 12, 1987: 100.3 mhz; 100 kw. Ant 1,620 ft. TL: N48 35 41 W123 32 37. (Digital radio: 1,472.000 mhz; 2 kw). Stereo. Top Floor, 2750 Quadra St. V8T 4E8. Phone: (250) 475-0100. Fax: (250) 475-3299. E-mail: theCrew@theQ.fm. Web Site: www.theq.fm. Licensee: OK Radio Group Ltd. Rep: Canadian Broadcast Sales. Format: Rock. News staff: 2; News: 4 hrs wkly. Target aud: 25-49. ♦ Stu Morton, pres; Dan McAllister, gen mgr & natl sls mgr; John Shields, opns mgr.

*CKMO(AM)— Sept 4, 2000: 900 khz; 10 kw-U, DA-1. Stereo. 3100 Four Bay Rd. V8P 5J2. Phone: (250) 370-3658. Fax: (250) 370-3679. E-mail: info@village900.ca. Web Site: www.village900.ca. Licensee: CKMO Radio Society. Format: Educ, Roots, Folk, World. News: 5 hrs wkly. Spec prog: Class, folk, country, blues, news/talk, Portuegese 3 hrs, world beat 3 hrs wkly. ♦ Doug Ozeroff, gen mgr.

Whistler

CISW-FM— Feb 25, 1982: 102.1 mhz; 586 w. 2,250 ft. Box 1068, Squamish VON 1B4. Phone: (604) 892-1021. Phone: (604) 683-8060. Fax: (604) 892-6383. E-mail: mountainfm@mountainfm.ca. Web Site: www.mountainfm.ca. Licensee: Rogers Broadcasting Ltd. (group owner). Format: Hot adult contemp. ♦ Gary MilesMatches, pres; Paul Fisher, VP; Ken Geiger, gen mgr; Mary Kemmis, opns mgr.

Williams Lake

CFFM-FM—Listing follows CKWL(AM).

CKWL(AM)— Feb 25, 1960: 570 khz; 1 kw-U, DA-2. 83 S. First Ave. V2G 1H4. Phone: (250) 392-6551. Fax: (250) 392-4142. E-mail: brad@cffmthemax.com. Web Site: www.thewolfpack.ca. Licensee: Cariboo Broadcasters Ltd. Group owner: Cariboo Central Interior Radio Inc. Rep: Canadian Broadcast Sales, Target Broadcast Sales. Format: Modern country, southern rock. Target aud: 25-54 plus. ♦ Brad McGuire, stn mgr; Terry Shepherd, CEO & gen sls mgr.

CFFM-FM—Co-owned with CKWL(AM). Aug 31, 1987: 97.5 mhz; Stereo. Phone: (250) 398-2336. Web Site: www.cffmthemax.com. (Acq 12-23-92). Rep: Target Broadcast Sales, Canadian Broadcast Sales. Format: Rock and pop. News staff: 2. Target aud: 18-44.

Manitoba

Altona

CFAM(AM)— Mar 13, 1957: 950 khz; 10 kw-U, DA-2. Box 950, 201-125 Centre Avenue R0G 0B0. Phone: (204) 324-6464. Fax: (204) 324-8918. E-mail: cfam@gordenwestradio.com. Web Site: www.cfamradio.com. Licensee: Golden West Broadcasting Ltd. (group owner) Rep: Canadian Broadcast Sales. Format: Agriculture, MOR. News staff: 8; News: 12 hrs wkly. Target aud: General. Spec prog: Class 15 hrs wkly. ♦ Elmer Hildebrand, CEO & pres; Ang Enns, stn mgr.

Boissevain

CJRB(AM)— 1973: 1220 khz; 10 kw-U. Box 1220 R0K 0E0. Phone: (204) 324-6464. Fax: (204) 324-8918. Licensee: Golden West Broadcasting Ltd. (group owner) Format: Easy lstng, inspirational, agriculture. News staff: one. Target aud: General. ♦ E. Hildebrand, pres; Lyndon Friesen, exec VP; Menno Friesen, gen sls mgr; Al Friesen, progmg mgr; Laverne Siemens, engrg dir.

Brandon

CJJJ-FM— May 2003: 106.5 mhz; 930 w. Assiniboine Community College, 1430 Victoria Ave. E., Rm 223 R7A 2A9. Phone: (204) 571-3900. Fax: (204) 726-7014. Licensee: Assiniboine Campus-Community Radio Society Inc. Format: Var. ♦ Bob Crighton, stn mgr.

CKLF-FM— June 1, 2000: 94.7 mhz; 100 kw. 624 14th St. E. R7A 7E1. Phone: (204) 726-8888. Fax: (204) 726-1270. E-mail: tyler@starfmradio.com. Web Site: www.starfmradio.com. Licensee: Riding Mountain Broadcasting Ltd. Format: Adult contemp. News staff: 7. Target aud: 25-54; adults. ♦ Don Kille, CEO & gen mgr.

CKLQ(AM)— October 1977: 880 khz; 10 kw-U, DA-2. 624 14th St. R7A 7E1. Phone: (204) 726-8888. Fax: (204) 726-1270. E-mail: qcountry@cklq.mb.ca. Web Site: www.ckcq.mb.ca. Licensee: Riding Mountain Broadcasting Ltd. Format: Country. News staff: 7. Target aud: 35 plus. Spec prog: Farm 18 hrs wkly. ♦ Don Kille, pres & gen mgr.

CKXA-FM— February 2000: 101.1 mhz; 100 kw. 2940 Victoria Ave. R7B 3Y3. Phone: (204) 728-1150. Fax: (204) 725-3794. E-mail: hot101@hot101.ca. Web Site: www.hot101.ca. Licensee: Standard Radio Inc. Group owner: Standard Broadcasting Corp. (acq 2-1-02; grpsl). Format: Country. ♦ Sharon Taylor, VP & gen mgr; Kevin Grexton, opns mgr.

CKX-FM— Dec 16, 1963: 96.1 mhz; 100 kw. 1,042 ft. Stereo. 2940 Victoria Ave. R7B 3Y3. Phone: (204) 728-1150. Fax: (204) 727-1150. Fax: (204) 727-2505. Licensee: Standard Radio Inc. Group owner: Standard Broadcasting Corp. (acq 2-1-02; grpsl). Format: Classic rock. ♦ Lee Sterry, gen mgr; Kevin Grexton, opns mgr & progmg dir; Gyl Tosheck, gen sls mgr; Norine Mitchell, rgnl sls mgr; Donna Smith, prom dir; Angela Greis, asst music dir; Bob Bruce, news dir.

Churchill

CHFC(AM)— Sept 13, 1959: 1230 khz; 250 w-U, DA-1. c/o CBC, Winnipeg R3C 2H1. Phone: (204) 788-3222. Fax: (204) 788-3225. E-mail: communications@winnipeg.cbc.ca. Licensee: Canadian Broadcasting Corp. Network: CBC Radio One. Format: Var/div. ♦ John Bertrand, gen mgr.

Cross Lake

CFNC-FM— 1990: 1490 khz; 50 w. Box 129 R0B 0J0. Phone: (204) 676-2331. Phone: (204) 676-2248. Fax: (204) 676-2911. Licensee: Native Communications Inc. Format: Community. ♦ Dina Monias, pres.

Dauphin

CKDM(AM)— Jan 6, 1951: 730 khz; 10 kw-D, 5 kw-N, DA-N. 27 3rd Ave. N.E. R7N 0Y5. Phone: (204) 638-3230. Fax: (204) 638-8257/8891. E-mail: 730ckdm@mb-sympatico.ca. Web Site: www.730ckdm.com. Licensee: Dauphin Broadcasting Co. Ltd. (acq 11-23-93). News staff: 3. ♦ Alan Truman, VP & gen mgr.

Manitoba

Flin Flon

CFAR(AM)— Nov 14, 1937: 590 khz; 10 kw-D, 1 kw-N, DA-2. 316 Green St. R8A 0H2. Phone: (204) 687-3469. Phone: (204) 687-8300. Fax: (204) 687-6786. E-mail: cfar@arcticradio.ca. Web Site: www.arcticradio.ca. Licensee: Arctic Radio (1982) Ltd. (acq 9-1-82). Format: Oldies. News staff: 2; News: 15 hrs wkly. Target aud: General. Spec prog: Cree mus. ♦ Tom O'Brien, pres & gen mgr; Maureen Kozar, stn mgr.

Portage la Prairie

CFRY(AM)— Oct 18, 1956: 920 khz; 25 kw-D, 15 kw-N, DA-2. 350 River Rd. R1N 0N6. Phone: (204) 239-5111. Fax: (204) 857-3456. Licensee: Golden West Broadcasting Ltd. Group owner: Golden West Broadcasting Ltd. (acq 7-26-2000; with co-located FM). Format: C&W. Spec prog: Farm 4 hrs wkly. ♦ Warren Neufeld, stn mgr.

CFRY-FM— 1996: 93.1 mhz; 27 kw.

CJPG-FM— May 4, 2004: 96.5 mhz; 24 kw. Box 920 R1N 0N6. Secondary address: 350 River Rd. R1N 0N6. Phone: (204) 239-5111. Fax: (204) 857-3456. Web Site: www.mix965fm.com. Licensee: Golden West Broadcasting Ltd. Format: CHR. ♦ Warren Neufeld, stn mgr.

Pukatawagan

CFPX-FM— Sept 19, 1971: 98.3 mhz; 34.8 w. Missinnippi River Native, Communications Inc. R0B 1G0. Phone: (204) 553-2155. Fax: (204) 553-2158. Licensee: Missinnippi River Native Communications Inc. Format: Country, rock. ♦ John Colomb, gen mgr.

Saint Boniface

*CKSB(AM)— May 27, 1946: 1050 khz; 10 kw-U. 607 Langevin St. R2H 2W2. Phone: (204) 788-3236. Fax: (204) 788-3245. Web Site: www.radiocanada.ca/radio/manitoba. Licensee: Societe Radio Canada. (acq 4-1-73). Format: Div, Fr. Target aud: General. ♦ Robert Rabinovitch, CEO; Huguette Le Gall, mktg mgr; Rene Fontaine, progmg dir; Gilles Frechette, progmg mgr; Michel Boucher, news dir.

CKXL-FM— October 1991: 91.1 mhz; 61 kw. 340 Provencher Blvd., Winnipeg R2H 0G7. Phone: (204) 233-4243. Phone: (204) 231-3691. Fax: (204) 233-3646. E-mail: info@envol91.mb.ca. Web Site: www.envol91.mb.ca. Licensee: La Radio Communautaire du Manitoba Inc. Format: Soft rock, div, Fr. Target aud: General; Francophone 20-50. Spec prog: Folk 2 hrs, jazz 4 hrs, Sp 2 hrs, blues 2 hrs, reggae 2 hrs, dance 5 hrs, techno 4 hrs wkly, disco 2 hrs. ♦ Annie Bedard, gen mgr; Martin Gauteron, progmg dir.

Selkirk

CFQX-FM— Nov 9, 1981: 104.1 mhz; 100 kw. 500 ft. (CP: 95.3 mhz.). Stereo. 177 Lombard Ave., 3rd Fl., Manitoba R3B 0W5. Phone: (204) 944-1031. Fax: (204) 943-7687. E-mail: jtrecarten@qx104fm.com. Web Site: www.qx104fm.com. Licensee: Standard Radio Inc. Group owner: Standard Broadcasting Corp. (acq 2-1-02; grpsl). Format: Country. News staff: 2. Target aud: 25-54. ♦ Sharon Taylor, VP, gen mgr & gen mgr; Gyl Toshack, gen sls mgr & natl sls mgr; Janet Trecarten, progmg dir.

CICY-FM— 2000: 105.5 mhz; 100 kw. Stereo. 1507 Inkster Blvd., Winnipeg R2X 1R2. Phone: (204) 772-8255. Fax: (204) 779-5628. E-mail: info@ncifm.com. Web Site: www.ncifm.com. Licensee: Native Communication Inc. Format: Div in English, Cree, Saulteaux, Ojibiway languages; CHR, country. News staff: 2. Target aud: 25 and up; aboriginal. ♦ Ron Nadeau, CEO; Rita Ducharme, pres; Dave McLeod, gen mgr.

Steinbach

CHSM(AM)— Mar 19, 1964: 1250 khz; 10 kw-U, DA-2. 250 Main St. R5G 148. Phone: (204) 326-3737. Fax: (204) 326-2299. Web Site: www.steinbachonline.com. Licensee: Golden West Broadcasting Ltd. (group owner) Rep: Canadian Broadcast Sales. Format: MOR. News staff: 3; News: 12 hrs wkly. Target aud: General. Spec prog: Farm. ♦ Elmer Hildebrand, pres; Laverne Tappel, gen mgr; Al Friesen, progmg dir; Laverne Siemens, engrg dir & chief of engrg.

Broadcasting & Cable Yearbook 2006

Manitoba

CILT-FM— Co-owned with CHSM(AM). Sept 29, 1998: 96.7 mhz; 50 kw. Phone: (204) 346-5483. Web Site: www.steinbachonline.com. Format: Light adult contemp.

The Pas

CJAR(AM)— 1974: 1240 khz; 1 kw-U, DA-1. Box 2980 R9A 1R7. Phone: (204) 623-5307. Fax: (204) 623-5337. E-mail: cjar@articradio.ca. Web Site: www.articradio.ca. Licensee: Arctic Radio Corp. Ltd. Format: Adult contemp, AOR, C&W. Spec prog: Aboriginal 5 hrs wkly. ♦ Tom O'Brien, chmn & pres; Jeremy Walchal, gen mgr.

Thompson

*CBWK-FM— 1980: 100.9 mhz; 9.4 kw. 7 Selkirk Ave. R8N 0M4. Phone: (204) 677-1680. Fax: (204) 677-9517. E-mail: north@winnpeg.cbc.ca. Web Site: www.winnipeg.cbc.ca. Licensee: CBC. Network: CBC Radio One. Format: Div, talk. ♦ Mark Sislo, gen mgr & progmg dir; Charles Altiman, news dir; Doug MacPherson, chief of engrg.

CHTM(AM)— Mar 29, 1964: 610 khz; 1 kw-U. 103 Cree R8N 0B9. Phone: (204) 778-7361. Fax: (204) 778-5252. E-mail: chtm@articradio.ca. Web Site: www.articradio.com. Licensee: Arctic Radio (1982) Ltd. Format: Adult contemp, classic rock, country. News staff: 2; News: 15 hrs wkly. Target aud: General. Spec prog: Relg 12 hrs, Cree (American Indian) 10 hrs wkly. ♦ Tom O'Brien, pres; Dave Moore, gen mgr, opns mgr & gen sls mgr; Don Barkman, mus dir.

CINC-FM— 1994: 96.3 mhz; 86 w. 76 Severn Crescent R8N 1M6. Phone: (204) 778-8343. Fax: (204) 778-6559. E-mail: info@ncifm.com. Web Site: www.ncifm.com. Licensee: Native Communications Inc. Format: Div in English, Cree, Saulteaux, Ojibway languages. ♦ Dave McLeod, gen mgr; Rey St. Jermain, progmg dir.

Winkler

CJEL-FM— Oct 4, 2000: 93.5 mhz; 100 kw. Box 399 R6W 4A6. Secondary address: 201-295 Main St. R6W 4A6. Phone: (204) 331-9300. Fax: (204) 325-2206. E-mail: info@eagle935fm.com. Web Site: www.eagle935fm.com. Licensee: Golden West Broadcasting Ltd. (group owner) Format: Adult contemp. ♦ Elmer Hildebrand, CEO, chmn & pres; Bill Hildebrand, stn mgr.

Winkler-Morden

CKMW(AM)— Aug 1, 1980: 1570 khz; 10 kw-U, DA-2. 300-561 Main St., Winkler R6W 1G3. Phone: (204) 325-9506. Fax: (204) 325-2206. E-mail: country1570@goldenwestradio.com. Web Site: www.ckmwradio.com. Licensee: Golden West Broadcasting Ltd. (group owner) Rep: Canadian Broadcast Sales. Format: Country. News staff: 2. Target aud: General. ♦ Bill Hildebrand, gen mgr & stn mgr; Elmer Hildebrand, CEO, pres & engrg dir.

Winnipeg

CBW(AM)— Sept 3, 1948: 990 khz; 50 kw-D, 46 kw-N. Box 160 R3C 2H1. Phone: (204) 788-3222. Fax: (204) 788-3227. Web Site: www.cbc.ca. Licensee: Canadian Broadcasting Corp. Network: CBC Radio One. Format: Div. Spec prog: Farm 6 hrs, class 8 hrs, C&W one hr wkly. ♦ John Berfrand, gen mgr.

CBW-FM— Oct 11, 1965: 98.3 mhz; 354 kw. Stereo. Network: CBC Radio Two. Format: Class, div.. Co-owned TV: CBWT(TV) affil

CFEQ-FM— 2003: 107.1 mhz; 920 w. 738 Osborne St. R3L 2C2. Phone: (204) 944-8961. Fax: (204) 772-5854. E-mail: tom@freq107.com. Web Site: www.freq107.com. Licensee: Kesitah Inc. Format: Alternative. ♦ Tom Hiebert, gen mgr; Jarret Hannah, mktg dir & progmg dir.

CFRW(AM)— Nov 1, 1963: 1290 khz; 10 kw-U, DA-2. Stereo. 1445 Pembina Hwy. R3T 5C2. Phone: (204) 477-5120. Fax: (204) 453-0815. Licensee: CHUM Ltd. (group owner; acq 7-74). Format: Oldies. ♦ Brian Stone, gen mgr; Scott Bodnarchuk, gen sls mgr; Howard Kroeger, progmg dir.

CHIQ-FM— Co-owned with CFRW(AM). Nov 1, 1963: 94.3 mhz; 100 kw. 450 ft. Stereo. Format: CHR.

CFWM-FM— June 13, 1996: 99.9 mhz; 100 kw. 1445 Pembina Hwy. R3T 5C2. Phone: (204) 477-5120. Fax: (204) 453-8777. E-mail: bryan@chumwinnipeg.com. Web Site: www.999bobfm.com. Licensee: CHUM Ltd. (group owner; acq 12-20-2001; C$7 million. swap with CHOM-FM Montreal, PQ). Format: Adult contemp. News staff: one; News: 5 hrs wkly. Target aud: 25-54. ♦ Alan Waters, CEO; Jay Switzer, pres; Bryan Stone, VP & gen mgr.

CHNR-FM— Dec 7, 2002: 100.7 mhz; 1.3 kw. 3586 Portce Ave. R3K 0Z8. Phone: (204) 889-2586. Fax: (204) 831-1512. E-mail: chnr@shawbiz.ca. Web Site: www.thebreezefm.com. Licensee: CKVN Radiolink System Inc. Format: Soft adult contemp, adult standards. News staff: one. ♦ Russ Tyson, progmg dir; Lynette Lyndon, news dir.

CHVN-FM— Sept 14, 2000: 95.1 mhz; 100 kw. TL: N49 46 15 W97 30 35. Stereo. Box 1812 R3C 3R1. Secondary address: 1111 Chevrier Blvd. R3T 1Y2. Phone: (204) 949-3395. Fax: (204) 949-3349. E-mail: chvn@chvnradio.com. Web Site: www.chvnradio.com. Licensee: Golden West Broadcasting Ltd. (acq 2004). Network: Salem Radio Network. Format: Christian music. Target aud: 18-49; families. Spec prog: Children 1 hr, Gospel 4 hrs, teens 6 hrs wkly. ♦ Elmer Hildebrand, CEO; Wade Kehler, gen mgr; Terry Van Veen, progmg dir.

CITI-FM— 1962: 92.1 mhz; 100 kw. Ant 700 ft. Stereo. 166 Osborne St., Unit 4 R3L 1Y8. Phone: (204) 788-3400. Fax: (204) 788-3401. E-mail: geoff.poulton@winnipegradio.rogers.com. Web Site: www.92citi.ca. Licensee: Rogers Broadcasting Ltd. (group owner; acq 8-20-92). Format: Classic rock. ♦ Geoff Poulton, gen mgr; Gayle Zarbatany, progmg dir; Frank Andrews, mus dir.

CJKR-FM— Listing follows CJOB(AM).

CJOB(AM)— 1946: 680 khz; 50 kw-U, DA-N. 930 Portage Ave. R3G 0P8. Phone: (204) 786-2471. Fax: (204) 783-4512. Fax: (204) 780-9750. Licensee: Corus Premium Television Ltd. Group owner: Corus Entertainment Inc. (acq 7-6-2000; grpsl). Rep: Canadian Broadcast Sales. Format: News/talk. News staff: 25; News: 56 hrs wkly. Target aud: 25-54. ♦ Garth Buchko, pres, gen mgr, stn mgr & mktg mgr; Sherrie Johnston, opns mgr; Steve Dubois, gen sls mgr; Robin Bonne, prom dir; Paul Graham, mus dir; Vic Grant, progmg dir & news dir; Jack Hoeppner, chief of engrg.

CJKR-FM— Co-owned with CJOB(AM). March 1948: 97.5 mhz; 310 kw. 228 ft. Stereo. Fax: (204) 780-9750. Web Site: www.power97.com. Format: Winning best rock. Target aud: 25-44; males. ♦ Steve Parsons, progmg dir; Lochlin Cross, mus dir.

CJUM-FM— Sept 4, 1998: 101.5 mhz; 1.2 kw. Stereo. UMFM, 308 University Center, University of Manitoba R3T 2N2. Phone: (204) 474-6518. Fax: (204) 269-1299. E-mail: station.manager@umfm.com. Web Site: www.umfm.com. Licensee: The University of Manitoba Students' Union. Format: Diversified. News: 12 hrs wkly. Target aud: 18-58; All genders, all ages who prefer non-commercial music and culture. ♦ Liz Clayton, gen mgr & stn mgr; Jared McKetiak, progmg dir.

CJWV-FM— Not on air, target date: unknown: 107.9 mhz; 200 w. 262 Niagara St. R3N 0V2. Licensee: N.I.B. 95.5 Cable FM Inc. ♦ Paul McCrea, gen mgr.

CJZZ-FM— March 2003: 99.1 mhz; 63.7 kw. Stereo. 30th Fl. CanWest Global Pl., 201 Portage Ave. R3B 3K6. Phone: (204) 253-2665. Fax: (204) 926-1674. Licensee: Global Communications Ltd. Group owner: CanWest Global Communications Corp. Format: Smooth jazz. News staff: one. Target aud: 35-45. ♦ Brian Wortley, opns mgr & gen sls mgr; Jay Thomas, prom dir; Barry Horne, progmg dir. Co-owned TV: CKND-TV

CKIC-FM— March 2004: 92.9 mhz; 201 w. W302-160 Princess St. R3B 1K9. Phone: (204) 949-8480. Fax: (204) 949-0057. Licensee: Red River College Radio. Format: Var. ♦ Rick Everett, stn mgr.

CKJS(AM)— Mar 25, 1975: 810 khz; 10 kw-U, DA-1. 520 Corydon Ave. R3L 0P1. Phone: (204) 477-1221. Fax: (204) 453-8244. E-mail: info@ckjs.com. Web Site: www.ckjs.com. Licensee: CKJS Ltd. Direct. Format: Ethnic, Christian. Target aud: General. Spec prog: Ger 6 hrs, It 5 hrs, Pol 7 hrs, Sp 3 hrs, Por 8 hrs, Greek one hr, Filipino 20 hrs wkly. ♦ Tony Carta, gen mgr.

CKMM-FM— Feb 14, 1980: 103.1 mhz; 70 kw. Ant 676 ft. Stereo. 177 Lombard Ave., 3rd. Fl. R3B 0N5. Phone: (204) 943-1687. E-mail: staylor@hotqx.com. Web Site: www.hot103live.com. Licensee: Standard Radio Inc. Group owner: Standard Broadcasting Corp. (acq 2002; grpsl). Format: CHR. ♦ Sharon Taylor, gen mgr; Curtis Strange, progmg dir; Jaxon Hawks, mus dir.

*CKUW-FM— Mar 1, 1999: 95.9 mhz; 450 w. TL: N49 52 51 W97 08 56. Stereo. 515 Portage Ave., Rm. 4C M11 R3B 2E9. Phone: (204) 786-9782. Fax: (204) 783-7080. E-mail: ckuw@uwinnipeg.ca. Web Site: www.ckuw.ca. Licensee: The Winnipeg Campus/Community Radio Society. Format: Urban contemp, rock/AOR, news/talk. News: 5 hrs wkly. Target aud: General; Our community. Spec prog: Children 2 hrs, class 4 hrs, folk 10 hrs, jazz 10 hrs wkly. ♦ Rob Schmidt, stn mgr; Art Ladd, progmg dir; Don Baily, mus dir.

CKY-FM— Jan 21, 2004: 102.3 mhz; 70 kw. 166 Osborne St., Unit 4 R3L 1Y8. Phone: (204) 788-3400. Fax: (204) 788-3401. E-mail: geoff.poulton@winnipegradio.rogers.com. Web Site: www.102clearfm.com. Licensee: Rogers Broadcasting Ltd. (group owner). Format: Adult contemp. ♦ Geoff Poulton, VP & gen mgr; Gayle Zarbatany, progmg dir; Craig Pfeifer, mus dir.

New Brunswick

Balmoral

CIMS-FM— 1994: 103.9 mhz; 7.295 kw. 1991 Ave. CP2561, des Pionniers E8E 2W7. Phone: (506) 826-1040. Fax: (506) 826-2400. E-mail: cimsfm@nbnet.nb.ca. Web Site: www.cimsfm.ca. Licensee: Cooperative Radio Restigouche Ltee. Format: Var. ♦ Allain Jolicoeur, rgnl sls mgr; Camille Deschenes, rgnl sls mgr; Pierre Morais, gen mgr & progmg dir; Camille Levesque, chief of engrg.

Bathurst

CKBC-FM— Jan 22, 2004: 104.9 mhz; 20 kw. Stereo. 176 Main St. E2A 1A4. Phone: (506) 547-1360. Fax: (506) 547-1367. Licensee: Astral Media Radio Atlantic Inc. Group owner: Astral Media Inc. Rep: Canadian Broadcast Sales. Format: Adult contemp. News staff: 3; News: 9 hrs wkly. Target aud: 25-49. Spec prog: Fr 9 hrs wkly. ♦ Jacques Parisien, pres; John Eddy, exec VP; Jamie Robichaud, gen mgr & gen sls mgr; Pat Brenan, sls VP; Eva George, prom mgr; Bob Fowlie, progmg dir; Peter Assaff, news dir.

CKLE-FM— Mar 29, 1990: 92.9 mhz; 100 kw. Stereo. 195 Main St. E2A 1A7. Phone: (506) 546-4600. Phone: (506) 546-1122. Fax: (506) 546-6611. E-mail: ckleadmin@mb.aibn.com. Licensee: Radio De LaBaie Ltd. Format: Light rock. Spec prog: Jazz 2 hrs wkly. ♦ Armand Roussy, gen mgr, gen sls mgr, adv dir & progmg dir; Rene Lanpeigne, mus dir.

Blackville

CJFY-FM— 2004: 107.5 mhz; 45 w. 401 Main St. E9B 1T3. Phone: (506) 843-2208. Fax: (506) 843-2603. E-mail: news@life1075.com. Web Site: www.life1075.com. Licensee: Miramichi Fellowship Center Inc. Format: Christian music. ♦ John D. Stewart, CEO; Shaun Mackenzie, gen mgr.

Campbellton

CKNB(AM)— 1939: 950 khz; 10 kw-D, 1 kw-N, DA-2. Box 340, 74 Water Street E3N 3G7. Phone: (506) 753-4415. Fax: (506) 789-9505. E-mail: cknb@nb.sympatico.ca. Licensee: Maritime Broadcasting System Ltd. Format: Adult contemp, country, CHR. News: 10 hrs wkly. Target aud: General. Spec prog: Fr 18 hrs wkly. ♦ Merv Russell, pres; David Montgomery, gen mgr; Mark Firth, progmg dir & news dir.

Caraquet

CJVA(AM)— Sept 15, 1977: 810 khz; 10 kw-U, DA-2. 195 Main St., Bathurst E2A 1A7. Phone: (506) 727-4605. Fax: (506) 727-6611. Licensee: Radio Acadie Ltd. Rep: Canadian Broadcast Sales. Format: Div, adult contemp, MOR. Target aud: 25 plus. Spec prog: C&W 15 hrs wkly. ♦ Rufino Landry, pres; Armand Roussy, gen mgr.

Edmundston

CFAI-FM— Jan 15, 1991: 101.1 mhz; 4 kw. TL: N47 23 25 W68 18 59. Stereo. 165 Blvd. Hebert E3V 2S8. Phone: (506) 737-5060. Fax: (506) 737-5084. E-mail: cfai@101rock105.com. Web Site: www.101rock105.com. Licensee: La Cooperative des Montagnes

Directory of Radio   New Brunswick

Ltee. Format: Top-40, soft rock. News: 6 hrs wkly. Target aud: 12-50. Spec prog: Jazz. ♦ Ron Cromier, pres; Jacques Bard, gen sls mgr & adv dir; Guy Soucy, progmg dir; Serge Parent, gen mgr, dev dir, rgnl sls mgr, mktg mgr, prom VP, prom dir & progmg dir; Jonathan Gaston Guay, mus dir; Ron Cormier, chief of engrg.

CJEM-FM— July 1998: 92.7 mhz; 40.75 kw. TL: N47 21 47 W68 17 21. Stereo. 174 Church St. E3V 1K2. Phone: (506) 735-3351. Fax: (506) 739-5803. E-mail: cjem@nbnet.nb.ca. Licensee: Radio Edmundston Inc. Rep: Canadian Broadcast Sales. Format: Hot adult contemp, CHR. News staff: 2; News: 6 hrs wkly. Target aud: 25-54. ♦ Jean Marc Michaud, pres; Murillo Soucy, gen mgr.

Fredericton

CBZF-FM— 2004: 99.5 mhz; 3.2 kw. Box 2200 E3B 5G4. Secondary address: 1160 Regent St. E3B 5G4. Phone: (506) 451-4000. Fax: (506) 451-4170. Web Site: www.cbc.ca. Licensee: Canadian Broadcasting Corp. Network: CBC Radio One. Format: Div. ♦ Gary Arsenault, opns mgr.

*CBZ-FM— January 1978: 101.5 mhz; 100 kw. Stereo. Box 2200 E3B 5G4. Secondary address: 1160 Regent St. E3B 5G4. Phone: (506) 451-4000. Fax: (506) 451-4170. Web Site: www.cbc.ca. Licensee: Canadian Broadcasting Corp. Network: CBC Radio Two. Format: Classics & beyond, news/talk. ♦ Gary Arsenault, gen mgr.

CFRK-FM— 2005: 92.3 mhz; 93 kw. NewCap Inc., 745 Windmill Rd., Dartmouth, NS B3B 1C2. Phone: (902) 468-7557. Fax: (902) 468-7558. Web Site: www.ncc.ca. Licensee: Newcap Inc. Format: Classic rock.

CFXY-FM—Listing follows CKHJ(AM).

CHSR-FM— Jan 24, 1961: 97.9 mhz; 250 w. Ant 157 ft. Stereo. Box 4400, Student Union Bldg., Univ. of New Brunswick E3B 5A3. Phone: (506) 453-4985. Fax: (506) 453-4999. E-mail: chsr@unb.ca. Web Site: www.unb.ca/chsr. Licensee: CHSR Broadcasting Inc. Format: Alternative, diverse. News: 6 hrs wkly. Target aud: General. Spec prog: Fr 2 hrs, ethnic 5 hrs, American Indian one hr, class 6 hrs, jazz 6 hrs, Chinese 3 hrs wkly. ♦ Tristis Ward, stn mgr; Linda Pelletier, dev mgr & prom mgr; Pierre Loiselle, adv mgr & progmg mgr.

CIBX-FM— June 11, 1996: 106.9 mhz; 100 kw. (CP: 78 kw.). 206 Rookwood Ave. E3B 2M2. Phone: (506) 455-1069. Fax: (506) 452-2345. Licensee: Astral Media Radio Atlantic Inc. Group owner: Astral Media Inc. (acq 4-19-2002; grpsl). Rep: Canadian Broadcast Sales. Format: Lite rock. News staff: 4; News: 8 hrs wkly. Target aud: 25-54. ♦ John Eddy, pres; Pat Brennan, gen mgr & gen sls mgr; Tom Blizzard, progmg dir; Dick Cleveland, chief of engrg.

CIXN-FM— Apr 8, 2001: 96.5 mhz; 27 w. Joy FM, 60 Bishop Dr. E3C 1B2. Phone: (506) 454-9600. Fax: (506) 443-0091. E-mail: welcome@joyfm.ca. Web Site: www.joyfm.ca. Licensee: The Joy FM Network Inc. Format: Christian. ♦ Garth McCrea, gen mgr; Tim Hatfield, gen sls mgr; Allen Price, progmg dir.

CJPN-FM— August 1997: 90.5 mhz; 840 w. 715 Priestman St. E3B 5W7. Phone: (506) 454-2576. Fax: (506) 453-3958. E-mail: cjpn@nbnet.nb.ca. Web Site: www.cjpn.ca. Licensee: Radio Fredericton Inc. Format: Adult contemp. ♦ Carole Theriault, gen mgr; Caarole Theriault, gen sls mgr; Francois Albert, progmg dir & chief of engrg.

CKHJ(AM)— Aug 19, 1977: 1260 khz; 10 kw-U, DA-N. 206 Rookwood Ave. E3B 2M2. Phone: (506) 451-9111. Fax: (506) 452-2345. Licensee: Astral Media Radio Atlantic Inc. Group owner: Astral Media Inc. Format: Country. Spec prog: Fr one hr wkly. ♦John Eddy, gen mgr; Pat Brennan, gen sls mgr.

CFXY-FM— Co-owned with CKHJ(AM). July 15, 1983: 105.3 mhz; 78 kw. 800 ft. Stereo. Format: C&W, rock.

Fredericton Centre

CKTP-FM— 2002: 95.7 mhz; 50 w. 120 Paul St., Fredericton E3A 2V8. Phone: (506) 474-1636. Fax: (506) 454-7187. Web Site: cap.ic.gc.ca/nb/stmarys. Licensee: Maliseet Nation Radio Inc. Format: Talk. ♦ Timothy Paul, gen mgr.

Grand Falls

CIKX-FM— 2001: 93.5 mhz; 5.3 kw. 399 Broadway Blvd. E3Z 2K5. Phone: (506) 473-9393. Fax: (506) 473-3893. E-mail: grdprod@radioatl.ca. Licensee: Astral Media Radio Atlantic Inc. Group owner: Astral Media Inc. (acq 2003; grpsl). Format: Hot adult contemp. ♦ Pat Brennan, gen mgr; Jacques Lafrance, gen sls mgr; Rick McGuire, progmg dir; Ian Scott, news dir; Dick Cleveland, chief of engrg.

CKMV-FM— August 2000: 95.1 mhz; 975 w. Stereo. 174 Church St., Edmundston E3V 1K2. Phone: (506) 735-3351. Fax: (506) 739-5803. E-mail: cjem@nbnet.nb.ca. Licensee: Radio Edmundston Inc. Rep: Canadian Broadcast Sales. Format: Hot adult contemp, CHR. Target aud: 25-54. ♦ Jean-Marc Michaud, pres; Murillo Soucy, gen mgr, gen sls mgr & chief of engrg; Paul Clavette, progmg dir; Jean Rousselle, news dir.

Kedgwick

*CFJU-FM— 1991: 90.1 mhz; 3 kw. TL: N47 35 05 W67 21 47. Stereo. C.P. 1043 E8B 1Z9. Phone: (506) 235-9000. Fax: (506) 235-9001. E-mail: cfjufm@nbnet.nb.ca. Licensee: La Radio Communautaire des Hauts-Plateaux Inc. Rep: Radio Unie Target, Major Market Broadcasters Ltd. Format: Div, Fr. News: 8 hrs wkly. Target aud: 25-55. Spec prog: Country 12 hrs wkly. ♦ M. Victor St- Pierre, pres; Lucille Theriault, gen mgr.

Miramichi City

CFAN-FM— Jan 10, 2003: 99.3 mhz; 17.8 kw. Box 338 E1V 3M4. Secondary address: 396 Pleasant St. E1V 1X3. Phone: (506) 622-3311. Fax: (506) 627-0335. E-mail: cfan@nb.sympatico.ca. Web Site: www.993theriver.com. Licensee: Maritime Broadcasting System Ltd. Group owner: Maritime Broadcasting. Format: Adult contemp. News staff: one; News: 8 hrs wkly. Target aud: General. Spec prog: Relg 4 hrs, folk 2 hrs wkly. ♦ Brent Preston, gen mgr & gen sls mgr; Paddy Quinn, progmg mgr; Rodney McQuade, chief of engrg.

Moncton

CBA(AM)— 1939: 1070 khz; 50 kw-U. Box 950, 250 University Ave. E1C 8N8. Phone: (506) 853-6666. Fax: (506) 853-6400. Web Site: www.cbc.ca. Licensee: CBC. Network: CBC Radio One. Format: News, current affrs.

CBA-FM— March 1982: 95.5 mhz; 100 kw. Web Site: www.cbc.ca. Network: CBC Radio Two. Format: Class.

*CBAF-FM— 1982: 88.5 mhz; 95 kw. 250 University Ave. E1C 5K3. Phone: (506) 853-6666. Fax: (506) 867-8000. Web Site: www.cbc.radio-canada.ca. Licensee: Radio Canada. Network: Radio Canada. Format: Var, news/talk. ♦ Benoit Quenneville, gen mgr; Claire Hendy, opns mgr & chief of engrg; Cynthia Boudreau, mktg mgr; Louis Mills, news dir; Michel LeBlanc, engrg mgr.

CBAL-FM— 1983: 98.3 mhz; 77 kw. Ant 577 ft. TL: N46 08 41 W64 54 14. Stereo. Box 950 E1C 8N8. Phone: (506) 853-6666. Fax: (506) 853-6739. Web Site: www.cbc.radio-canada.ca. Licensee: Societe Radio Canada. Network: Chaine Culturelle. Format: Var. ♦ Benoit Quenneville, gen mgr; Claire Hendy, opns mgr & chief of opns; Cynthia Boudreau, prom mgr & news mgr; Michel LeBlanc, engrg mgr.

CFQM-FM— 1976: 103.9 mhz; 25 kw. 1000 St. George Blvd. E1E 4M7. Phone: (506) 858-1220. Fax: (506) 858-1209. E-mail: magic104@radiomoncton.com. Web Site: www.radiomoncton.com. Licensee: Maritime Broadcasting System Ltd. Format: Adult contemp. ♦ Dan Barton, gen mgr & mus dir; Wayne Keeping, gen sls mgr; Rodney McQuade, progmg dir; Dave Lockhart, news dir; Oakes, chief of engrg.

CHOY-FM— Feb 19, 2001: 99.9 mhz; 9.5 kw. 1000 St. George Blvd. E1E 4M7. Phone: (506) 858-1220. Fax: (506) 858-1209. E-mail: choix@radiomoncton.com. Web Site: www.radiomoncton.com. Licensee: CHOIX-FM Ltee. Group owner: Maritime Broadcasting. Format: Fr. ♦ Dan Barton, gen mgr; Wayne Keeping, gen sls mgr; Rodney Mcquade, progmg dir; Mathieu Friolet, mus dir; Bob Oakes, chief of engrg.

CITA-FM— January 2001: 105.9 mhz; 50 w. 3170 Mountain Rd. E1G 2W8. Phone: (506) 384-5825. Phone: (506) 384-1059. Fax: (506) 854-8609. E-mail: harvest@nbnet.nb.ca. Web Site: www.citafm.com. Licensee: International Harvesters for Christ Evangelistic Association

Inc. Format: Christian music. ♦ Jeff Lutes, pres, stn mgr & engrg dir; Marcel Cormier, opns dir, progmg dir & engrg mgr.

CJMO-FM— June 19, 1987: 103.1 mhz; 46.8 kw. Stereo. 27 Arsenault Ct. E1E 4J8. Phone: (506) 858-5525. Fax: (506) 858-5539. E-mail: c103@c103.com. Web Site: www.c103.com. Licensee: Atlantic Stereo Ltd. Rep: Canadian Broadcast Sales. Format: Classic rock. News staff: 4; News: 5 hrs wkly. Target aud: 25-54; adults. Spec prog: Jazz 2 hrs wkly. ♦ Mark Maheu, pres; David Murray, CFO & opns VP; Hilary Montbourquette, gen mgr.

CJXL-FM— November 2000: 96.9 mhz; 100 kw. 27 Arsenault Ct. E1E 4J8. Phone: (506) 858-5525. Fax: (506) 858-5539. E-mail: xl96@xl96.com. Web Site: www.xl96.com. Licensee: Atlantic Stereo Ltd. Format: Today's best country. Target aud: 25-54; adults. ♦ Mark Maheu, pres; Hilary Montbourquette, gen mgr; Dave Murray, opns VP; Dave Ostler, gen sls mgr; Tom Manton, natl sls mgr; Paul Thomas, prom mgr; Andrew Stewart, progmg dir; Brian Affleck, chief of engrg.

CKCW-FM— January 2001: 94.5 mhz; 19 kw. 1000 St. George Blvd. E1E 4M7. Phone: (506) 858-1220. Fax: (506) 858-1209. E-mail: k94@radiomoncton.com. Web Site: www.radiomoncton.com. Licensee: Maritime Broadcasting System Ltd. Format: Today's newest music. Target aud: 18-44; adults. ♦ Dan Barton, gen mgr & mus dir; Wayne Keeping, gen sls mgr; Rodney McQuade, progmg dir; Bob Oakes, chief of engrg.

CKNI-FM—Not on air, target date: unknown: 91.9 mhz; 70 kw. 70 Assomption Blvd. E1C 1A1. Phone: (902) 493-7133. Licensee: Rogers Broadcasting Ltd. Format: News/talk. ♦ Rael Merson, pres; Jim Hamm, gen mgr.

CKOE-FM— November 2000: 107.3 mhz; 50 w. Ant 82 ft. 3030 Mountain Rd. E1G 2W8. Phone: (506) 388-6212. Fax: (506) 383-9699. E-mail: x101fm@radiochristian.com. Web Site: www.radiochristian.com. Licensee: Houssen Broadcasting Ltd. Format: Christian hit radio. ♦ James Houssen, gen mgr & engrg mgr; Kurt Parks, progmg dir.

CKUM-FM— 1982: 93.5 mhz; 250 w. 98 ft. TL: N46 06 16 W64 46 57. Stereo. Universite de Moncton, Centre etudiant, 2e etage E1A 3E9. Phone: (506) 858-3750. Fax: (506) 858-4524. Web Site: www.radioj935.com. Licensee: Les Medias Acadiens Universitaires Inc. Format: Var/div, Fr. Target aud: 15-40. Spec prog: Jazz 4 hrs wkly. ♦ Christian Boudreau, pres; Boris Salou, VP; Eric Gauvin, VP & gen sls mgr; Sheila Layace, VP; Michele Routier, gen mgr; Jason Deiren, progmg dir; Martin Gautreau, mus dir.

Pokemouche

CKRO-FM— 1988: 97.1 mhz; 50 kw. Radio Peninsule Inc., 142 Rt. 113 E8P 1K7. Phone: (506) 336-9706. Fax: (506) 336-9058. E-mail: info@ckro.ca. Licensee: Radio Peninsule Inc. Format: Fr., MOR. Target aud: General. ♦ Lester Young, pres; Rachel Savoie, VP; Donald Noel, gen mgr, stn mgr, gen sls mgr & adv mgr; Marilyne McLaughlin, natl sls mgr, mktg mgr & prom mgr; Janique Doiron, mus dir; Rejean Hebert, progmg dir & news dir; Alphe Theriault, engrg dir & engrg mgr.

Sackville

*CHMA-FM— 1985: 106.9 mhz; Suite 303, 152A Main St. E4L 1B4. Phone: (506) 364-2221. Fax: (506) 536-4230. E-mail: chma@mta.ca. Web Site: www.mta.ca/chma. Licensee: Attic Broadcasting Ltd. (acq 8-24-00). Format: Div. ♦ Pierre Malloi, gen mgr; Tori Weldon, progmg dir.

Saint John

CBD-FM— April 1981: 91.3 mhz; 80 kw. Box 2358 E2L 3V6. Phone: (506) 632-7744. Fax: (506) 632-7761. Web Site: www.nb.cbc.ca. Licensee: Canadian Broadcasting Corp. Network: CBC Radio One. Format: Talk, info. ♦ Susan Lambert, stn mgr; Bill Preeper, chief of engrg.

CFBC(AM)— Nov 21, 1946: 930 khz; 50 kw-U, DA-2. TL: N45 13 55 W66 06 15. Stereo. 226 Union St. E2L 1B1. Phone: (506) 658-5100. Fax: (506) 658-5116. Licensee: Maritime Broadcasting System Ltd. Group owner: Maritime Broadcasting (acq 9-29-98; C$2 million. with co-located FM). Format: Oldies. ♦ Mark Lee, gen mgr; Dave Clarkson, gen sls mgr; Dan Roman, progmg dir; Brian McLain, news dir; Roger Vautour, chief of engrg.

New Brunswick

CJYC-FM—Co-owned with CFBC(AM). Mar 12, 1965: 98.9 mhz; 12 kw. 350 ft. TL: N45 18 49 W66 04 43. Format: Classic rock. Target aud: 25-34; young, upwardly, mobile, family oriented. ♦Paul Jensen, progmg dir.

CFHA-FM— Oct 20, 2003: 103.5 mhz; 49.6 w. Ant 200 ft. TL: N45 16 31 W65 04 25. (CP: Ant 102 ft). 28 King St., Suite 3E E2L 1G3. Phone: (506) 657-4242. Fax: (506) 642-7408. E-mail: cfha@nb.aibn.com. Web Site: www.cfharadio.com. Licensee: TFG Communications Inc. Format: Comedy. News staff: one; News: 20 hrs wkly. Target aud: 25-54. ♦Tom Gamblin, CEO & gen mgr; Geoff Banks, stn mgr & progmg dir; Dave Dean, sls dir; Jim MacIntosh, news dir.

CFMH-FM— January 2001: 92.5 mhz; 49.6 w. c/o Student Services, UNB Saint John, Box 5050 E2L 4L5. Phone: (506) 648-5667. Fax: (506) 648-5541. E-mail: cfmh@unbsj.ca. Web Site: www.cfmhradio.com. Licensee: Campus Radio Saint John Inc. Format: Var. ♦Linda Pellties, stn mgr; Chuck Teed, adv mgr; Dave Arthurss, progmg dir; Derek Wurts, progmg dir; Dan Jones, mus dir; Jana Randall, asst music dir; Troy Chenier, news dir; Matt McQuade, chief of engrg.

CHNI-FM—Not on air, target date: unknown: 88.9 mhz; 79 kw. 55 Waterloo St. E2L 4V9. Phone: (902) 493-7133. Licensee: Rogers Broadcasting Ltd. Format: News/talk. ♦Rael Merson, pres; Jim Hamm, gen mgr.

CHSJ-FM— Jan 7, 1998: 94.1 mhz; 50.4 kw. Box 2000, 58 King St. E2L 3T4. Phone: (506) 633-3323. Fax: (506) 644-3485. E-mail: chsj@radioabl.com. Licensee: Acadia Broadcasting Ltd. (group owner). Network: CBS Radio. Format: C&W. Target aud: 25-54. ♦Jim MacMullin, gen mgr; Troy Wallace, gen sls mgr; Lori Carle, prom dir & mus dir; Bruce Weaver, progmg dir; Gary MacDonald, news dir; Hugh Morrison, engrg mgr.

CHWV-FM— 2001: 97.3 mhz; 55 kw. Box 2000 E2L 3T4. Phone: (506) 633-3323. Fax: (506) 644-3485. E-mail: thewave@radioabl.com. Licensee: Acadia Broadcasting Ltd. (group owner). Format: Adult contemp. ♦Jim MacMullin, gen mgr; Troy Wallace, gen sls mgr; Lori Carle, prom dir; Bruce Weaver, progmg dir; Gary MacDonald, news dir; Hugh Morrison, chief of engrg.

CINB-FM— Nov 16, 2000: 96.1 mhz; 50 w. NewSong FM, Box 96 E2L 3X1. Phone: (506) 657-9600. Fax: (506) 657-7664. E-mail: programming@newsongfm.com. Web Site: www.newsongfm.com. Licensee: Newsong Communications Ltd. Format: Contemp Christian. ♦Don Mabee, stn mgr; Mike Stackhouse, gen sls mgr; Gary Stackhouse, progmg dir.

CIOK-FM— Aug 10, 1987: 100.5 mhz; 100 kw. 1,650 ft. 226 Union St. E2L 1B1. Phone: (506) 658-5100. Fax: (506) 658-5116. E-mail: mlee@nb.aibn.com. Licensee: Maritime Broadcasting Systems. Group owner: Maritime Broadcasting Format: Adult contemp. News staff: 5; News: 7 hrs wkly. Target aud: 25-49; housewives, families, professionals. Spec prog: Real radio 4 hrs wkly. ♦Merv Russell, pres; Mark Lee, gen mgr; Dave Clarkson, gen sls mgr; Dan Roman, mktg mgr; Tina Campbell, prom mgr; Allen Gidyk, progmg dir; Roger Vautour, chief of engrg.

Saint Stephen

CHTD-FM— May 31, 2001: 98.1 mhz; 40 kw. Stereo. 73 Milltown Blvd., Suite 108, Ganong Pl., St. Stephen E3L 1G5. Phone: (506) 466-1000. Fax: (506) 466-4500. E-mail: mail@thetide.ca. Web Site: www.thetide.ca. Licensee: Acadia Broadcasting Ltd. (group owner). Format: Country. News staff: 2. Target aud: 25-54. ♦Jim MacMullin, gen mgr; Mark Downey, stn mgr.

Shediac

CJSE-FM— July 26, 1994: 89.5 mhz; 20.445 kw. 96 Rue Providence E4P2M9. Phone: (506) 532-0080. Fax: (506) 532-0120. E-mail: gilles@cjse.ca. Web Site: www.cjse.ca. Licensee: Radio Beausejour Inc. Format: Var. ♦Gilles Arseneault, gen mgr; John Richard, sls VP; Yvon Michaud, progmg dir; Normand Cormier, mus dir; Roger LeBlanc, chief of engrg.

Sussex

CJCW(AM)— June 1975: 590 khz; 1 kw-D, 250 w-N, DA-2. Box 5900 E4E 4N3. Phone: (506) 432-2529. Fax: (506) 433-4900. E-mail: cjcw@nbnet.nb.ca. Licensee: Maritime Broadcasting System Ltd. Group owner: Maritime Broadcasting Format: Adult contemp. Target aud: General. Spec prog: Relg 4 hrs wkly. ♦Robert Pace, CEO; Merv Russell, pres; Louis McNamara, gen mgr.

Woodstock

CJCJ-FM— June 1, 2001: 104.1 mhz; 10 kw. Unit One, 131 Queen St. E7M 2M8. Phone: (506) 325-3030. Fax: (506) 325-3031. E-mail: wskprod@radioatl.ca. Licensee: Astral Media Radio Atlantic Inc. Group owner: Astral Media Inc. (acq 4-19-2002; grpsl). Format: Adult contemp. ♦Pat Brennan, gen mgr; Jacques Lafrance, gen sls mgr; Rick McGuire, progmg dir; Dick Cleveland, chief of engrg.

Newfoundland

Argentia

CFOZ-FM— 1980: 100.3 mhz; 5 kw. c/o CHOZ-FM, Box 2020, 446 Logy Bay Rd., St. John's A1C 5S2. Phone: (709) 726-2922. Fax: (709) 726-3300. Web Site: www.ozfm.com. Licensee: Newfoundland Broadcasting Co. Ltd. Rep: Canadian Broadcast Sales. Format: CHR, adult contemp, classic rock. News staff: 2. Target aud: 18-49. ♦Geoff Stirling, chmn; Frank Collins, CFO; Doug Neal, gen mgr, chief of opns & chief of engrg; Lorraine Pope, sls dir, gen sls mgr & progmg dir; Jesse Stirling, mktg VP & mktg dir; Scott G. Stirling, CEO, pres & progmg dir; Maurice Fitzgerald, mus dir; Larry Davis, news dir.

Baie Verte

CKIM(AM)— 1979: 1240 khz; 1 kw-D, 500 w-N. Box 620, Grenfell Heights A2A 2K2. Phone: (709) 489-2192. Fax: (709) 489-8626. Web Site: www.vocm.com. Licensee: NewCap Inc. Group owner: NewCap Broadcasting Ltd. (acq 6-00; grpsl). Format: Rock. ♦Dave Hillier, gen mgr; Denn Dillion, gen sls mgr; Richard King, progmg dir; Roger Barnett, news dir; Harold Steele, chief of engrg.

Bonavista Bay

CBGY(AM)— Aug 25, 1977: 750 khz; 10 kw-U, DA-2. c/o Radio Stn CBG, Box 369, Gander A1V 1W7. Phone: (709) 256-4311. Fax: (709) 651-2021. Licensee: CBC. Format: News, current affrs. ♦Robert Rabinowitz, CEO; Chris Norman, gen mgr; Larry O'Brian, stn mgr.

CJOZ-FM— 1979: 92.1 mhz; 50 kw. c/o CHOZ-FM, 446 Logy Bay Rd., Box 2020, St. John's A1C 5S2. Phone: (709) 726-2922. Fax: (709) 726-3300. Web Site: www.ozfm.com. Licensee: Newfoundland Broadcasting Co. (group owner) Rep: Canadian Broadcast Sales. Format: CHR, adult contemp, classic rock. News staff: 2. Target aud: 18-49. ♦Geoff Stirling, chmn; Scott Stirling, CEO & pres; Frank Collins, CFO; Doug Neal, gen mgr, chief of opns & chief of engrg; Jesse Stirling, gen sls mgr & mktg dir; Lorraine Pope, gen sls mgr & progmg dir; Maurice Fitzgerald, mus dir; Larry Davis, news dir.

Carbonear

CHVO(AM)— Oct 7, 1980: 560 khz; 5 kw-U, DA-1. One CHVO Dr. A1Y 1A2. Phone: (709) 596-1560. Fax: (709) 596-8626. E-mail: chvo@vocm.com. Licensee: NewCap Inc. Group owner: NewCap Broadcasting Ltd. (acq 6-00; grpsl). Format: Country. Spec prog: Irish/Newfoundland 8 hrs wkly. ♦John Steele, pres; John Murphy, gen mgr; Aiden Hibbs, stn mgr; Ron Ryan, gen sls mgr & prom mgr; Ken Ash, progmg dir; Gerry Phalen, news dir; Harold Steele, chief of engrg.

Churchill Falls

CFLC-FM— 1974: 97.9 mhz; 8 w. 50 ft. c/o CFCB(AM), Box 570, Corner Brook A2H 6H5. Phone: (709) 634-3111. Fax: (709) 634-4081. Licensee: NewCap Inc. Group owner: NewCap Broadcasting Ltd. (acq 4-2-01; grpsl). Format: Country. ♦Michael Murphy, gen mgr & stn mgr; Ken Ash, progmg dir & progmg mgr.

Clarenville

CJKK-FM— 1988: 105.3 mhz; 2.07 kw. c/o CHOZ-FM, 446 Logy Bay Rd., St. John's A1C 5R6. Phone: (709) 726-2922. Fax: (709) 726-3300. Web Site: www.ozfm.com. Licensee: Newfoundland Broadcasting Co. (group owner) Rep: Canadian Broadcast Sales. Format: CHR, adult contemp, classic rock. News staff: 2. Target aud: 18-49. ♦Geoff Stirling, chmn; Scott Stirling, CEO & pres; Frank Collins, CFO; Doug Neal, gen mgr, opns mgr & chief of opns.

CKVO(AM)— Nov 15, 1974: 710 khz; 10 kw-U. c/o VOCM(AM), Box 8590, Stn. A, 391 Kenmount Rd., St. John's A1B 3P5. Phone: (709) 466-2710. Fax: (709) 726-8626/726-4633. E-mail: feedback@vocm.com. Web Site: www.vocm.com. Licensee: NewCap Inc. Group owner: NewCap Broadcasting Ltd. (acq 6-00; grpsl). Format: Contemp country. ♦John Murphy, gen mgr; Ken Ash, opns mgr; Dennis Dillon, gen sls mgr; Paul Raynes, progmg dir; Gerry Phelan, news dir; Harold Steele, chief of engrg.

Corner Brook

***CBY(AM)**— Apr 1, 1949: 990 khz; 10 kw-U, DA-1. Box 610 A2H 6G1. Phone: (709) 637-1150. Fax: (709) 634-8506. Licensee: CBC. Network: CBC Radio One. Format: News/talk, var. Target aud: 30 plus; mature. ♦Robert Rabinowitz, CEO; Gordon Lannon, gen mgr.

CFCB(AM)— Oct 3, 1960: 570 khz; 1 kw-D. Box 570 A2H 6H5. Phone: (709) 634-4570. Fax: (709) 634-4081. Licensee: Newcap Inc. Group owner: NewCap Broadcasting Ltd. (acq 4-2-01; grpsl). Rep: Canadian Broadcast Sales. Format: Country. ♦Harry Steele, pres; J. Steele, VP; Michael Murphy, gen mgr; Darryl Stevens, opns mgr & progmg dir.

CKOZ-FM— 1979: 92.3 mhz; 50 kw. c/o CHOZ-FM, 446 Logy Bay Rd., Box 2020, St. John's A1C 5S2. Phone: (709) 726-2922. Fax: (709) 726-3300. Web Site: www.ozfm.com. Licensee: Newfoundland Broadcasting Co. (group owner) Rep: Canadian Broadcast Sales. Format: CHR, adult contemp, classic rock. News staff: 2. Target aud: 18-49. ♦Geoff Stirling, chmn; Scott Stirling, CEO & pres; Frank Collins, CFO; Doug Neal, gen mgr, chief of opns & chief of engrg; Lorraine Pope, gen sls mgr & progmg dir; Jesse Stirling, mktg dir; Maurice Fitzgerald, mus dir; Larry Davis, news dir.

CKXX-FM— June 20, 1997: 103.9 mhz; 40 kw. Stereo. P.O. Box570, 345 O'Connell Dr., Corner Brook, NL A2H6H5. Phone: (709) 634-4570. Fax: (709) 634-4081. Web Site: k-rock1039.com. Licensee: NewCap Inc. Group owner: NewCap Broadcasting Ltd. (acq 8-29-90). Rep: Canadian Broadcast Sales. Format: Rock. News staff: 2. Target aud: 25-54. Spec prog: Oldies 3 hrs wkly. ♦Michael Murphy, gen mgr; Daryl Stevens, opns mgr.

Gander

***CBG(AM)**— 1949: 1400 khz; 4 kw-U. Box 369 A1V 1W7. Phone: (709) 256-4311. Fax: (709) 651-2021. Licensee: CBC. Format: Info. ♦Robert Rabinowitz, CEO; Larry O'Brien, gen mgr.

CKGA(AM)— 1969: 650 khz; 5 kw-U, DA-2. Box 650 A1V 1X2. Phone: (709) 651-3650. Fax: (709) 651-2542. Licensee: NewCap Inc. Group owner: NewCap Broadcasting Ltd. (acq 6-00; grpsl). ♦Dave Hillier, gen mgr; Dennis Dillon, gen sls mgr; Dean Clarke, progmg dir; Robet Tuck, news dir; Harold Steele, chief of engrg.

CKXD-FM— November 2000: 98.7 mhz; 6 kw. Box 650 A1V 1X2. Phone: (709) 651-3650. Fax: (709) 651-2542. E-mail: ckxd.ckga.psa@vocm.com. Web Site: www.vocm.com. Licensee: Newcap Inc. Group owner: NewCap Broadcasting Ltd. Format: Classic rock. Spec prog: Newfoundland & Irish 12 hrs wkly. ♦John Murphy, gen mgr; Dennis Dillon, gen sls mgr; Ken Ash, progmg dir; Harold Steele, chief of engrg.

Goose Bay

CFGB-FM—See Happy Valley

CFLN(AM)— Aug 1, 1974: 1230 khz; 1 kw-D, 250 w-N, DA-1. Box 160, Station C, Happy Valley Goose Bay A0P-1C0. Phone: (709) 896-2968. Fax: (709) 896-8708. Licensee: NewCap Inc. Group owner: NewCap Broadcasting Ltd. (acq 4-2-01; grpsl). Format: Adult contemp. ♦Harry Steele, chmn; Robert G. Steele, pres.

Grand Falls

CKCM(AM)— October 1962: 620 khz; 10 kw-D, DA-1. Box 620, Grand Falls-Windsor A22 2K2. Secondary address: 35 A Grenfell Heights, Grand Falls-Windsor A2A 2K2. Phone: (709) 489-2192. Fax: (709) 489-8626. Web Site: www.vocm.com. Licensee: NewCap Inc. Group owner: NewCap Broadcasting Ltd. (acq 6-00; grpsl). Format: Contemp

Directory of Radio

country. ♦ Dave Hillier, gen mgr; Dennis Dillon, gen sls mgr; Richard King, progmg dir; Roger Barnett, news dir; Harold Steele, chief of engrg.

Grand Falls-Windsor

CBT(AM)— July 1, 1949: 540 khz; 10 kw-U. 2 Harris Ave. A2A 2Y4. Phone: (709) 489-2102. Fax: (709) 489-1055. Licensee: CBC. Format: Info. ♦ Robert Rabinowitz, CEO; Diane Humber, gen mgr; Chris Norman, stn mgr.

CKXG-FM— 2001: 102.3 mhz; 20 kw. Box 620 A2A 2K2. Phone: (709) 489-2192. Fax: (709) 489-8626. E-mail: vocm.krock.psa@vocm.com. Web Site: www.vocm.com. Licensee: NewCap Broadcasting Ltd. Group owner: NewCap Broadcasting Ltd. Format: Classic rock. ♦ Dave Hillier, gen mgr; Dennis Dillon, gen sls mgr; Richard King, progmg dir; Harold Steele, chief of engrg.

Happy Valley

*CFGB-FM— Feb 23, 1959: 89.5 mhz; 1 kw-w. Box 1029, Stn C, 12 Loring Dr., Happy Valley-Goose Bay A0P 1CO. Phone: (709) 896-2911. Fax: (709) 896-8900. E-mail: labmorning@stjohns.cbc.ca. Web Site: www.stjohns.cbc.ca. Licensee: CBC. Network: CBC Radio One. Format: Info. ♦ Diane Humber, gen mgr; Cynthia Wall, progmg mgr; Lorne Burry, engrg mgr.

Labrador City

CBDQ-FM— 1997: 96.3 mhz; 255 w. Box 576 A2V 2L3. Phone: (709) 944-3616. Fax: (709) 944-5472. Web Site: www.stjohns.cbc.ca. Licensee: CBC. Format: Talk, info. ♦ Diane Humber, gen mgr.

CJRM-FM— Sept 23, 1992: 97.3 mhz; 500 w. 1,998 ft. TL: N52 57 01 W66 55 01. Stereo. C.P. 453, 308 Hudson Dr. A2V 2K7. Phone: (709) 944-7600. Phone: (709) 944-2973. Fax: (709) 944-5125. E-mail: cjrm@crrstv.net. Licensee: Radio Communautaire du Labrador Inc. (acq 9-4-92). Format: Fr, English, div. Target aud: General; English & Fr speaking audience in Labrador West. ♦ Norman Gillespie, pres; Dean Baker, exec VP & mus dir; linda McLean, stn mgr.

Lewisporte

CIFX-FM— 2002: 93.7 mhz; 50 w. Stereo. Box 601 A0G 3A0. Secondary address: 37 George Street AOG 3AO. Phone: (709) 535-6000. Phone: (708) 535-2546. Fax: (709) 535-6600. E-mail: mixfm@cablerocket.com. Licensee: Mix FM Inc. Format: Div, hot adult contemp/CHR. Target aud: 18-49. ♦ Todd Foss, stn mgr, mus dir & progmg; Vicki Fudge, pub affrs dir; Koren Hurley, sls; Angela Brenton, prom; Peter Ginn, engr.

Marystown

CHCM(AM)— 1961: 740 khz; 10 kw-U, DA-N. Box 560 A0E 2M0. Phone: (709) 279-2560. Phone: (709) 279-2426. Fax: (709) 279-3538. Fax: (709) 279-2800. E-mail: chem.frontdesk@vocm.com. Licensee: NewCap Inc. Group owner: NewCap Broadcasting Ltd. (acq 5-4-00; grpsl). Format: Country. ♦ Russell Murphy, gen mgr, opns mgr & gen sls mgr; Harry Myles, progmg dir; Bob Tower, news dir; Harold Steele, chief of engrg.

CIOZ-FM— 1979: 96.3 mhz; 25 kw. c/o CHOZ-FM, 446 Logy Bay Rd., Box 2020, St. John's A1C 5S2. Phone: (709) 726-2922. Fax: (709) 726-3300. Web Site: www.ozfm.com. Licensee: Newfoundland Broadcasting Co. (group owner) Rep: Canadian Broadcast Sales. Format: CHR, adult contemp, classic rock. News staff: 2. Target aud: 18-49. ♦ Geoff Stirling, chmn; Scott Stirling, CEO & pres; Frank Collins, CFO; Doug Neal, gen mgr, chief of engrg; Lorraine Pope, gen sls mgr & progmg; Jesse Stirling, mktg VP, mktg dir & prom VP; Maurice Fitzgerald, mus dir & asst music dir; Larry Davis, news dir.

Mount Pearl

*VOAR(AM)— 1930: 1210 khz; 10 kw, DA-1. TL: N47 32 01 W52 49 01. 1041 Topsail Rd. A1N 5E9. Phone: (709) 745-VOAR. Fax: (709)745-1600. E-mail: voar@voar.org. Web Site: www.voar.org. Licensee: Seventh-Day Adventist Church in Newfoundland. Format: Relg, gospel. News: 12 hrs wkly. Target aud: 25-44; individuals interested in family life & traditional values. ♦ Gary Hodder, pres; Sherry Griffin, stn mgr & opns mgr.

Port au Choix

CFNW(AM)— 1960: 790 khz; 1 kw-U, DA-1. c/o CFCB(AM), 345 O'Connell Dr., Corner Brook A2H 6H5. Phone: (709) 634-4570. Fax: (709) 634-4081. Licensee: Newcap Inc. Group owner: NewCap Broadcasting Ltd. (acq 4-2-01; grpsl). Rep: Integrated Media Sales. Format: Country. ♦ Harry Steele, pres; Michael Murphy, gen mgr; Darryl Stevens, opns mgr.

Rattling Brook

CHOS-FM— 1979: 95.9 mhz; 50 kw. c/o CHOZ-FM, 446 Logy Bay Rd., Box 2020, St. John's A1C 5S2. Phone: (709) 726-2922. Fax: (709) 726-3300. Web Site: www.ozfm.com. Licensee: Newfoundland Broadcasting Co. (group owner) Rep: Canadian Broadcast Sales. Format: CHR, adult contemp, classic rock. News staff: 2. Target aud: 18-49. ♦ Geoff Stirling, chmn; Scott G. Sterling, CEO & pres; Frank Collins, CFO; Doug Neal, gen mgr & chief of opns.

Red Rocks

CKSS-FM— 1994: 96.9 mhz; 520 w. c/o CHOZ-FM, 466 Logy Bay Rd., Box 2020, St. John's A1C 5S2. Phone: (709) 726-2922. Fax: (709) 726-3300. Web Site: www.ozfm.com. Licensee: Newfoundland Broadcasting Co. (group owner) Rep: Canadian Broadcast Sales. Format: CHR, adult contemp, classic rock. News staff: 2. Target aud: 18-49. ♦ Geoff Stirling, chmn; Scott Stirling, CEO & pres; Frank Collins, CFO; Doug Neal, gen mgr, chief of opns & chief of engrg; Lorraine Pope, gen sls mgr & progmg dir; Jesse Stirling, mktg dir; Larry Davis, news dir.

Saint Andrews

CFCV-FM— 1974: 97.7 mhz; 60 West St., Stephenville A2N 1C6. Secondary address: C/o CFGN(AM), Port-aux-Basques A0M 1C0. Phone: (709) 695-2183. Phone: (709) 643-2191. Fax: (709) 695-9614. E-mail: cfsx@vocm.com. Web Site: www.vocm.com. Licensee: NewCap Inc. Group owner: NewCap Broadcasting Ltd. Format: Country, oldies. ♦ Michael Murphy, gen mgr; Gerry Murphy, gen sls mgr; Larry Bennett, progmg dir; Harold Steele, chief of engrg.

Saint John's

*CBN(AM)— Apr 1, 1949: 640 khz; 10 kw-U. Box 12010, Stn A, 342-44 Duckworth St. A1B 3T8. Phone: (709) 576-5000. Fax: (709) 576-5205. Web Site: www.cbc.ca. Licensee: CBC. Network: CBC Radio One. Format: Div. News staff: 6; News: 10 hrs wkly. Target aud: General. Spec prog: Fisheries 3 hrs wkly. ♦ Diane Humber, gen mgr & news dir; Larry O'Brien, opns dir; Lori Wheeler, prom mgr; Liz Lacey, mus dir.

CBN-FM— July 1, 1975: 106.9 mhz; 100 kw. 300 ft. Stereo. Network: CBC Radio Two. Format: Class, news/talk.. Co-owned TV: *CBNT-TV affil

*CHMR-FM— January 1986: 93.5 mhz; 50 w. -10 ft. Stereo. Memorial University, MUNSU, South Annex, Rm 2009 A1C 5S7. Phone: (709) 737-4777. Phone: (709) 737-4778. Fax: (709) 737-7688. E-mail: chmr@mun.ca. Web Site: www.mun.ca/chmr. Licensee: Memorial University of Newfoundland Radio Society Inc. Format: Div, alternative. News: 7 hrs wkly. Target aud: General. Spec prog: Fr 2 hrs, jazz 6 hrs, relg 4 hrs, blues 6 hrs, rap 2 hrs, reggae 2 hrs, Indian one hr wkly. ♦ Kathy Rowe, gen mgr, opns mgr, dev mgr, rgnl sls mgr, adv mgr & mus dir; Ernst Rollmann, progmg dir & asst music dir; Nancy Earle, mktg mgr, prom mgr, progmg dir, asst music dir & news dir; Craig Peterman, chief of engrg.

CHOZ-FM— June 15, 1977: 94.7 mhz; 100 kw. 821 ft. TL: NN47 31 36 W52 42 50. Stereo. Box 2050, 446 Logy Bay Rd. A1C 5R6. Phone: (709) 722-5015. Fax: (709) 726-3300. E-mail: ntvsales@ntv.ca. Web Site: www.ozfm.com. Licensee: Newfoundland Broadcasting Co. Ltd. Group owner: Newfoundland Broadcasting Co. Rep: Canadian Broadcast Sales. Format: CHR, adult contemp, classic rock. News staff: 2. Target aud: 18-49. ♦ Geoff Stirling, chmn; Scott G. Stirling, CEO & pres; Frank Collins, CFO; Jesse Stirling, VP, sls dir, mktg VP, mktg dir & prom mgr; Doug Neal, gen mgr, opns mgr, chief of opns, engrg dir & chief of engrg; Dave Lawrence, stn mgr; Lorraine Pope, natl sls mgr & mus dir; Paul Kinsman, progmg dir; Larry Davis, news dir. Co-owned TV: CJON-TV affil.

CJYQ(AM)—Listing follows CKIX-FM.

Broadcasting & Cable Yearbook 2006

D-585

Northwest Territories

CKIX-FM— Oct 15, 1983: 99.1 mhz; 100 kw. Ant 930 ft. Stereo. Box 8590, Station A, St. John's A1B 3P5. Phone: (709) 726-5590. Fax: (709) 726-4633. Web Site: www.991hitsfm.com. Licensee: Newcap Inc. Group owner: NewCap Broadcasting Ltd. (acq 1-17-83). Format: CHR. ♦ John Murphey, gen mgr; Randy Snow, progmg dir; Brad Michaels, mus dir.

CJYQ(AM)— Co-owned with CKIX-FM. 1951: 930 khz; 50 kw-U. Format: Country.

CKSJ-FM— 2004: 101.1 mhz; 20 kw. Box 28106 A1B 4J8. Phone: (709) 754-6748. Fax: (709) 754-6749. E-mail: onair@coast1011.com. Web Site: www.coast1011.com. Licensee: Andrew Newman and Andrew Bell, on behalf of a corporation to be incorporated. Format: Adult contemp. ♦ Andrew Newman, gen mgr.

VOCM(AM)— Oct 19, 1936: 590 khz; 20 kw-U, DA-2. Stereo. Box 8590, Stn A, 391 Kenmount Rd. A1B 3P5. Phone: (709) 726-5590. Fax: (709) 726-4633. Fax: (709) 726-8626. E-mail: feedback@vocm.com. Web Site: www.vocm.com. Licensee: NewCap Inc. Group owner: NewCap Broadcasting Ltd. (acq 6-00; grpsl). Rep: Canadian Broadcast Sales. Format: Adult contemp, country, news/talk. News staff: 16. Target aud: 25 plus. ♦ John Steele, pres; John Murphy, gen mgr; Ken Ash, opns mgr; Ron Ryan, sls VP; Paul Magee, progmg dir; Gerry Phelan, news dir; Harold Steele, engrg dir.

VOCM-FM— September 1982: 97.5 mhz; 100 kw. Stereo. Web Site: www.k-rock975.com. Format: Classic rock. News: 7 hrs wkly. Target aud: Adults 25-54. ♦ Dave Newberry, rgnl sls mgr; Mike Campbell, progmg dir & mus dir.

*VOWR(AM)— June 20, 1924: 800 khz; 10 kw-D, 2.5 kw-N, DA-1. TL: N47 34 16 W52 45 13. Box 7430, Patrick St., St. John's A1E 3Y5. Phone: (709) 579-9233. Fax: (709) 579-9232. Web Site: www.vowr.org. Licensee: Wesley United Church Radio Board. Format: Div, oldies, folk. Target aud: 40 plus. Spec prog: Relg 10 hrs, folk 15 hrs wkly. ♦ Cecil Strickland, chmn; John Tessier, gen mgr & opns mgr.

Stephenville

CFSX(AM)— Nov 14, 1964: 870 khz; 500 w-U. 60 West St. A2N 1C6. Phone: (709) 643-2191. Fax: (709) 643-5025. Web Site: www.vocm.com. Licensee: NewCap Inc. Group owner: NewCap Broadcasting Ltd. (acq 2001; grpsl). Format: Country. News staff: 2. Target aud: General. Spec prog: Relg one hr wkly. ♦ Harry Steele, chmn; Robert G. Steele, pres; John Murphy, gen mgr; Gerry Murphy, stn mgr.

CIOS-FM— 1979: 98.5 mhz; 10 kw. c/o CHOZ-FM, 446 Logy Bay Rd., Box 2020, St. John's A1C 5S2. Phone: (709) 726-2922. Fax: (709) 726-3300. Web Site: www.ozfm.com. Licensee: Newfoundland Broadcasting Co. (group owner) Format: CHR, adult contemp, classic rock. News staff: 2. Target aud: 18-49. ♦ Geoff Stirling, chmn; Scott Stirling, CEO & pres; Frank Collins, CFO; Doug Neal, gen mgr, opns mgr & chief of opns.

Wabush

CFLW(AM)— 1971: 1340 khz; 250 w-U, DA-1. Box 6000, 4 Grenfell Dr. A0R 1B0. Phone: (709) 282-3602. Phone: (709) 282-3601. Fax: (709) 282-5543. Licensee: Newcap Inc. Group owner: NewCap Broadcasting Ltd. (acq 4-2-01; grpsl). Format: Country. Target aud: General. ♦ Harry Steele, chmn; Robert G. Steele, pres; Mike Murphy, gen mgr.

Northwest Territories

Hay River

CJCD-FM-1— Sept 15, 1986: 100.1 mhz; 300 w. 175 ft. Stereo. Box 218, Yellowknife X1A 2N2. Phone: (867) 920-4636. Fax: (867) 920-4033. E-mail: info@cjcd.ca. Web Site: www.cjcd.ca. Licensee: CJCD Radio Ltd. (acq 3-8-00). Rep: Canadian Broadcast Sales. Format: Hot adult contemp. Target aud: 25-49. ♦ Eileen Dent, pres & gen mgr; Bryan Edwards, VP; Tim Jaworski, gen sls mgr; Joanne Cochrane, progmg dir; Norm Bryatt, news dir; Jim Pook, chief of engrg.

Northwest Territories

CKHR-FM— January 1979: 107.3 mhz; 32 w. 185 ft. Box 4394 X0E 1G3. Phone: (867) 874-2547. Web Site: www.tvradioworld.com. Licensee: Hay River Broadcasting Society. Format: MOR, var. ♦ Al Erickson, pres; Ray Lawson, stn mgr.

Inuvik

*CHAK(AM)— Nov 26, 1960: 860 khz; 1 kw-D, DA-1. Bag 8 X0E 0T0. Phone: (867) 777-7600. Fax: (867) 777-7640. Licensee: CBC. Format: News/talk. Target aud: General. Spec prog: Inuvialuktun 9 hrs, Gwich'in 9 hrs wkly. ♦ Peter Skinner, gen mgr.

Tuktoyaktuk

CFCT(AM)— 1971: 600 khz; 1 kw-U. c/o Radio Station CHAK, Bag 8, Inuvik X0E 0T0. Phone: (867) 777-7600. Fax: (867) 777-7640. Licensee: CBC. (acq 1982). Network: CBC Radio One. Format: Div. Spec prog: Eskimo 5 hrs wkly. ♦ Peter Skinner, gen mgr.

Yellowknife

*CFYK(AM)— Dec 13, 1958: 1340 khz; 2.5 kw-U. Box 160 X1A 2N2. Phone: (867) 920-5400. Fax: (867) 920-5410 (ADMIN). Fax: (867) 920-5440 PROG. Licensee: CBC. Format: Div, news/talk. Target aud: General. Spec prog: Slavey 8 hrs, Dogrib 4 hrs, Chipewayan 4 hrs wkly. ♦ Peter Skinner, gen mgr; David McNaughton, opns mgr.

CIVR-FM— 2001: 103.5 mhz; 164 w. Box 1586 X1A 2P2. Phone: (867) 873-3292. E-mail: civr@franco-nord.com. Web Site: www.radiotaiga.ca. Licensee: L'Association franco-culturelle de Yellowknife. Format: Fr. News: 2 hrs wkly. Spec prog: Worldbeat 3 hrs, jazz 4 hrs wkly. ♦ Jeff Hipfner, pres; Sylvie Boisclair, gen mgr.

CJCD-FM— 1998: 100.1 mhz; 400 w. TL: N62 27 00 W114 19 00. Box 218 X1A 2N2. Phone: (867) 920-4636. Fax: (867) 920-4033. E-mail: info@cjcd.ca. Web Site: www.cjcd.ca. Licensee: CJCD Radio Ltd. (acq 3-8-00). Rep: Canadian Broadcast Sales. Format: Hot Adult contemp. Target aud: 25-54. ♦ Eileen Dent, CEO, pres & gen mgr.

CKLB-FM— Dec 11, 1985: 101.9 mhz; 130 w. 162 ft. Stereo. Box 1919 X1A 2P4. Phone: (867) 920-2277. Fax: (867) 920-4205. E-mail: ncs@internorth.com. Licensee: Native Communications Society of the Western N.W.T. Format: C&W. News staff: 3. Spec prog: Black one hr wkly. ♦ Elizabeth Biscaye, gen mgr.

Nova Scotia

Amherst

CKDH(AM)— Oct 25, 1957: 900 khz; 1 kw-U, DA-N. Box 670 B4H 4B8. Phone: (902) 667-3875. Fax: (902) 667-4490. E-mail: ckdh@ckdh.net. Web Site: www.ckdh.net. Licensee: Maritime Broadcasting System Ltd., Maclean Hunter Broadcast Division. (acq 1989). Rep: Canadian Broadcast Sales. Format: Light rock. Target aud: 25-49 & 18-34; general. Spec prog: C&W 11 hrs, farm 2 hrs wkly. ♦ Dave March, gen mgr & progmg dir; Jeff DeGanz, news dir.

Antigonish

CJFX-FM— 2003: 98.9 mhz; 75.39 kw. Stereo. Box 5800 B2G 2R9. Secondary address: 85 Kirk St. Phone: (902) 863-4580. Fax: (902) 863-6300. E-mail: cjfx@cjfx.ca. Web Site: www.cjfx.ca. Licensee: Atlantic Broadcasters Ltd. Rep: Canadian Broadcast Sales. Canadian Broadcast Sales Format: CHR, maritime. News staff: 3; News: 24 hrs wkly. Target aud: 18+. ♦ David MacLean, gen mgr.

Barrington

CJLS-FM-1— 1982: 96.3 mhz; 5.5 kw. c/o CJLS(AM), 328 Main St., Suite 201, Yarmouth B5A 1E4. Phone: (902) 742-7175. Fax: (902) 742-3143. E-mail: cjls@cjls.com. Web Site: www.cjls.com. Licensee: Radio CJLS Ltd. (acq 7-1-98). Format: Adult contemp. ♦ Chris Perry, VP & progmg mgr; Ray Zinck, pres & gen mgr; Dave Hall, gen sls mgr; Gary Nickerson, news dir; Jim Harris, engrg dir.

Bridgewater

CKBW-FM— February 2002: 98.1 mhz; 32 kw. 215 Dominion St. B4V 2G8. Phone: (902) 543-2401. Fax: (902) 543-1208. E-mail: ckbw@ckbw.com. Web Site: www.ckbw.com. Licensee: Acadia Broadcasting Ltd. (group owner). Format: Classic rock, CHR, hot rock. News staff: 2; News: 11 hrs wkly. Target aud: General; rural & small town urban. ♦ John Wiles, gen mgr, opns mgr & progmg dir; Barry Smith, gen sls mgr & natl sls mgr; Brian Tepper, prom dir; Sheldon MacLeod, news dir & pub affrs dir; Frank Grayney, chief of engrg.

Cheticamp

*CKJM-FM— 1995: 106.1 mhz; 3 kw. TL: N46 36 55 W61 02 52. Stereo. Box 699, Les Trois Pignons, Main Rd. B0E 1H0. Phone: (902) 224-1242. Fax: (902) 224-1770. E-mail: ckjm@auracom.com. Web Site: www.ckjm.info.ca. Licensee: La Cooperative Radio Cheticamp Ltee. Format: Var, country, Fr. Target aud: General. Spec prog: Gaelic one hr wkly, jazz 3 hrs wkly. ♦ Claudie Deveau, pres; Angus Lefort, gen mgr, opns mgr, mktg dir & engrg dir; Nicolle Desveaux, natl sls mgr & adv dir; Ginette Chiasson, progmg dir.

Dartmouth

CFDR(AM)— Dec 5, 1962: 780 khz; 50 kw-D, 15 kw-N. 2900 Agricola St., Halifax B3K 6B2. Phone: (902) 453-2524. Fax: (902) 453-3132. Licensee: New Cap Broadcasting Ltd. (group owner) Rep: Canadian Broadcast Sales. Format: Hot country. ♦ Tom Manton, sls VP; Ted Hyland, gen sls mgr; J. C. Douglas, progmg dir; Rich Horner, news dir; Walter Labucki, chief of engrg.

CFRQ-FM— Co-owned with CFDR(AM). Nov 28, 1983: 104.3 mhz; 100 kw. 400 ft. Stereo. Web Site: www.q104.ca. Format: Classic rock.

Digby

CKDY(AM)— Feb 2, 1970: 1420 khz; 1 kw-U, DA-1. Box 1420 B0V 1A0. Secondary address: 53 Sydney St. B0V 1A0. Phone: (902) 245-2111. Fax: (902) 678-9720. E-mail: programming@avrnetwork.com. Web Site: www.avrnetwork.com. Licensee: Maritime Broadcasting. (group owner; acq 8-79). Format: Contemp country. Spec prog: Farm 7 hrs wkly. ♦ Diane Best, gen mgr; Scott Baines, stn mgr; Karen Corey, gen sls mgr; Amanda Misner, progmg dir; Dave Chaulk, news dir; Garth Faulkner, chief of engrg.

Eastern Passage

CFEP-FM— 2002: 94.7 mhz; 50 w. Seaside-FM, Box 196 B3G 1M5. Phone: (902) 465-9900. Fax: (902) 469-0966. E-mail: seasidefm@ns.sympatico.ca. Web Site: www.seasidefm.com. Licensee: Seaside Broadcasting Organization. Format: Easy lstng, big band, adult standards. ♦ Wayne Harrett, gen mgr & progmg dir.

Eskasoni Indian Reserve

CICU-FM— 1994: 94.1 mhz; 1 w. Box 7100, Eskasoni B1W 1A1. Secondary address: 130 Anslum Rd., Eskasoni Indian Reserve, Eskasoni B0A 1J0. Phone: (902) 379-2955. Fax: (902) 379-2966. E-mail: greguj@ns.sympaatico.ca. Licensee: Greg Johnson. Format: Micmac-language (32and English-language (75%) progmg. ♦ Greg Johnson, gen mgr & chief of engrg; Linda Johnson, progmg dir.

Halifax

CBAX-FM— September 2003: 91.5 mhz; 77.5 kw. TL: N44 39 03 W63 39 28. c/o CBAL-FM, 250 University Ave., Moncton, NB E1C 5K3. Phone: (506) 853-6666. Fax: (506) 867-8000. Licensee: Societe Radio-Canada. Network: Chaine Culturelle. Format: Fr classical. ♦ Benoit Quennecille, gen mgr; Andree Girard, progmg dir.

CBHA-FM— 1989: 90.5 mhz; 91 kw. 711 ft. Box 3000 B3J 3E9. Phone: (902) 420-8311. Fax: (902) 420-4357. Fax: (902) 420-4429. E-mail: mainstreet@halifax.cbc.ca. Web Site: www.cbc.ca. Licensee: CBC. Network: CBC Radio One. Format: News, jazz, div. ♦ Robert Rabinovitch, CEO, pres & gen mgr; Carole Taylor, chmn; Susan Mitton, opns dir; Nicole Vautour, progmg dir.

*CBH-FM— June 1, 1976: 102.7 mhz; 81 kw. 711 ft. Stereo. Box 3000 B3J 3E9. Phone: (902) 420-8311. Fax: (902) 420-4429. Fax: (902) 420-4089. E-mail: weekender@halifax.cbc.ca. Web Site: www.cbc.ca. Licensee: CBC. Network: CBC Radio One. Format: Div, class. Target aud: General. ♦ Robert Rabinovitch, CEO & chmn; Carole Taylor, chmn; Robert Rabinoitch, pres; Susan Mitton, opns dir; Nicole Vautour, progmg dir.

CHAL-FM—Not on air, target date: unknown: 105.1 mhz; 32 kw. Global Halifax, 14 Akerley Blvd., Dartmouth B3B 1J3. Phone: (902) 481-7400. Fax: (902) 468-2154. Licensee: Global Communications Ltd. Format: Easy lstng. ♦ Barry Saunders, gen mgr.

CHFX-FM—Listing follows CHNS(AM).

CHNS(AM)— May 12, 1926: 960 khz; 10 kw-U, DA-2. Box 400 B3J 2R2. Secondary address: 5121 Sackville St., 3rd Fl. B3J1K1. Phone: (902) 422-1651. Fax: (902) 422-5330. E-mail: christa.webber@chfradio.com. Licensee: Maritime Broadcasting System. (acq 6-94). Format: Oldies. News staff: 5; News: 7 hrs wkly. Target aud: 25-54. ♦ Merv Russell, pres; Nancy Hilchie, gen mgr; Michael Halverson, opns mgr; Shauna Williams, prom dir; Mike Cranston, news dir.

CHFX-FM—Co-owned with CHNS(AM). Feb 9, 1970: 101.9 mhz; 100 kw. 546 ft. Stereo. E-mail: chfx@ns.sympatico.ca. Format: Country. News staff: 5; News: 6 hrs wkly. Target aud: 25-44. ♦ John Gold, mus dir.

CIOO-FM—Listing follows CJCH(AM).

CJCH(AM)— Nov 4, 1944: 920 khz; 25 kw-U, DA-D. TL: N44 38 10 W63 40 22. Stereo. 2900 Agricola St. B3K 6B2. Phone: (902) 453-2524. Fax: (902) 453-3120. Fax: (902) 453-3132. Web Site: www.cjch.net. Licensee: CJCH 920/C100 FM Division of CHUM Ltd. Group owner: CHUM Ltd. Format: Yesterday. News staff: 5. ♦ Scott Bodnarchuk, gen mgr; Bill Bodnarchuk, gen sls mgr; Terry Williams, progmg mgr; Earle Mader, mus dir; Rick Howe, news dir & pub affrs dir; Walter Labrucci, engrg dir.

CIOO-FM—Co-owned with CJCH(AM). November 1977: 100.1 mhz; 100 kw. 770 ft. TL: N44 39 05 W63 39 51. Stereo. Web Site: www.c100.net. Format: Adult contemp. ♦ Trent McGrath, prom dir.

CJNI-FM—Not on air, target date: unknown: 95.7 mhz; 65 kw. 6080 Young St. B3K 5L2. Phone: (902) 493-7133. Licensee: Rogers Broadcasting Ltd. Format: News/talk. ♦ Rael Merson, pres; Jim Hamm, gen mgr.

*CKDU-FM— February 1985: 97.5 mhz; 3.2 kw. Ant 300 ft. Dalhousie SUB, 6136 University Ave. B3H 4J2. Phone: (902) 494-6479. E-mail: ckdu@ckdu.ca. Web Site: www.ckdu.ca. Licensee: CKDU-FM Society Ltd. Format: Div. News staff: one; News: 4 hrs wkly. Target aud: General. ♦ Michael Catano, stn mgr.

CKHZ-FM—Not on air, target date: unknown: 103.5 mhz; 78 kw. Evanov Radio Group, 5302 Dundas St. W., Toronto, ON M9B 1B2. Phone: (416) 213-1035. Fax: (416) 233-8617. Licensee: CKMW Radio Ltd., on behalf of a corporation to be incorporated. Format: Youth contemp. ♦ Bill Evanov, gen mgr.

CKUL-FM— August 1990: 96.5 mhz; 100 kw. 2900 Agricola St. B3K 4P5. Phone: (902) 453-4004. Fax: (902) 453-3132. E-mail: fm965@mrg.ca. Web Site: www.planetkool.ca. Licensee: Sun Radio Ltd. Group owner: NewCap Broadcasting Ltd. (acq 12-17-2001). Rep: Canadian Broadcast Sales. Format: Classic hits 60s & 70s & 80s. News staff: 3; News: 3 hrs wkly. Target aud: 35-54. ♦ Mark Maheu, pres; Scott Bodnarchuk, gen mgr; Tom Manton, sls VP; Trent McGrath, prom mgr; Gary Greer, progmg mgr; Rich Horner, news dir & pub affrs dir; Walter Labucki, chief of engrg.

Kentville

CKEN-FM— Mar 14, 1965: 97.7 mhz; 18 kw. Ant 680 ft. Stereo. Box 310 B4N 1H5. Secondary address: 29 Oakdene Ave. B4N 1H5. Phone: (902) 678-2111. Fax: (902) 678-9894. E-mail: avr@avrnetwork.com. Web Site: www.avrnetwork.com. Licensee: Maritime Broadcasting System Ltd. Group owner: Maritime Broadcasting (acq 1998; grpsl). Rep: Canadian Broadcast Sales. Format: Country. News staff: 5. Target aud: 18-49. Spec prog: Farm 5 hrs wkly. ♦ Dianne Best, gen mgr; Karen Corey, gen sls mgr; Amanda Misner, progmg dir; James Cormier, mus dir; Garth Faulkner, chief of engrg.

CKWM-FM— 2003: 94.9 mhz; 100 kw. Box 310 B4N 1H5. Secondary address: 29 Oakdene Ave. B4N 1H5. Phone: (902) 678-2111. Fax: (902) 678-9894. E-mail: magic949@magic949.ca. Web Site:

Directory of Radio   Ontario

www.magic949.ca. Licensee: Maritime Broadcasting System Ltd. Group owner: Maritime Broadcasting. Format: Adult contemp. ♦Dianne Best, gen mgr; Karen Corey, gen sls mgr; Angela Rose, progmg dir; Garth Faulkner, chief of engrg.

Liverpool

CKBW-FM-1— Sept 15, 1980: 94.5 mhz; 8.7 kw. Ant 250 ft. Stereo. c/o CKBW(AM), 215 Dominion St., Bridgewater B4V 2G8. Phone: (902) 543-2401. Fax: (902) 543-1208. E-mail: ckbw@ckbw.com. Web Site: www.ckbw.com. Licensee: Acadia Broadcasting Ltd. (group owner; acq 8-31-89). Canadian Broadcast Sales. Format: Classic rock, CHR, hot rock. News staff: 2; News: 11 hrs wkly. Target aud: General; rural & small town urban. ♦John Wiles, gen mgr, opns mgr, progmg dir & mus dir; Barry Smith, gen sls mgr & natl sls mgr; Brian Tepper, prom dir; Sheldon MacLeod, news dir & pub affrs dir; Frank Grayney, chief of engrg.

Middleton

CKAD(AM)— 1962: 1350 khz; 1 kw-U, DA-1. Box 550 B0S 1P0. Phone: (902) 825-3429. Fax: (902) 678-9894. E-mail: programming @avrnetwork.com. Licensee: Maritime Broadcasting. (group owner; acq 6-26-79). Format: Country. Spec prog: Farm 3 hrs wkly. ♦Diane Best, gen mgr; Scott Baines, stn mgr; Karen Corey, gen sls mgr; Amanda Misner, progmg dir & progmg mgr; Dave Chaulk, news dir; Garth Faulkner, chief of engrg.

New Glasgow

CKEC(AM)— Dec 23, 1953: 1320 khz; 25 kw-U, DA-N. Box 519, CKEC Radio Bldg., 84 Provost St. B2H 5E7. Phone: (902) 752-4200. Phone: (902) 755-1320. Fax: (902) 755-2468. Fax: (902) 928-1320. E-mail: ckec@ckec.com. Licensee: D. Freeman. (acq 1964). Rep: Canadian Broadcast Sales. Format: Adult contemp, classic rock, MOR, country. News staff: 3; News: 15 hrs wkly. Target aud: General. Spec prog: Scottish. ♦D.B. Freeman, CEO; M.D. Freeman, exec VP & gen mgr.

New Tusket

CJLS-FM-2— 1982: 93.5 mhz; 3 kw. c/o Radio Station CJLS(AM), 328 Main St., Suite 201, Yarmouth B5A 1E4. Phone: (902) 742-7175. Fax: (902) 742-3143. E-mail: cjls@cjls.com. Web Site: www.cjls.com. Licensee: Radio CJLS Ltd. Format: Adult contemp. ♦Chris Perry, VP & progmg mgr; Ray Zinck, pres & gen mgr; Dave Hall, gen sls mgr; Gary Nickerson, news dir; Jim Harris, engrg dir.

Port Hawkesbury

CIGO-FM— 2000: 101.5 mhz; 19 kw. TL: N45 39 00 W61 28 00. 11 MacIntosh Ave. B9A 3K4. Secondary address: Port Hawkesbury Business Park, MacIntosh Ave. B9A 3K4. Phone: (902) 625-1220. Phone: (902) 625-1015. Fax: (902) 625-2664. Fax: (902) 625-6397. E-mail: 1015thehawk@1015thehawk.com. Web Site: www.1015thehawk.com. Licensee: MacEachern Broadcasting Ltd. Format: Adult contemp. News staff: 2; News: 4 hrs wkly. Target aud: 18-49; blue collar, high school education, married. Spec prog: Scottish 2 hrs, Irish one hr wkly. ♦Bob MacEachern, pres & stn mgr.

Shelburne

CKBW-FM-2— Sept 15, 1980: 93.1 mhz; 8.6 kw. Stereo. c/o CKBW(AM), 215 Dominion St., Bridgewater B4V 2G8. Phone: (902) 543-2401. Fax: (902) 543-1208. E-mail: ckbw@ckbw.com. Web Site: www.ckbw.com. Licensee: Acadia Broadcasting Ltd. (group owner; acq 8-31-89). Canadian Broadcast Sales. Format: Classic rock, CHR, hot rock. Target aud: General; rural & small town urban. ♦John Wiles, gen mgr, opns mgr, progmg dir & mus dir; Barry Smith, gen sls mgr & natl sls mgr; Brian Tepper, prom dir; Sheldon MacLeod, news dir & pub affrs dir; Frank Grayney, chief of engrg.

Sydney

CBI(AM)— Nov 1, 1948: 1140 khz; 10 kw-U, DA-2. Box 700 B1P 6H7. Phone: (902) 539-5050. Fax: (902) 563-4170. Web Site: www.cbc.ca. Licensee: CBC. Network: CBC Radio One. Format: Info. ♦Hank Vanleeuween, gen mgr.

CBI-FM— July 1977: 105.1 mhz; 20 kw. 400 ft. Stereo. Web Site: www.cbc.ca. Network: CBC Radio Two. Format: Classics, lite classics.

CHER(AM)— Dec 21, 1985: 950 khz; 10 kw-U, DA-1. 318 Charlotte St. B1P 1C5. Phone: (902) 564-5596. Fax: (902) 564-1873. Licensee: Bras d'Or Broadcasting Ltd. Group owner: Maritime Broadcasting (acq 8-10-01; C$300,000. for 55% of the shares). Rep: Canadian Broadcast Sales. Format: Oldies. ♦Alan Peddle, gen mgr & gen sls mgr; Rod DeViller, opns mgr; Phil Thompson, progmg dir; Gary Andrea, news dir; Roy MacIntosh, chief of engrg.

CJCB(AM)— Feb 14, 1929: 1270 khz; 10 kw-U, DA-N. Stereo. Radio Bldg., 318 Charlotte St. B1P 1C8. Phone: (902) 564-5596. Fax: (902) 564-1057. Licensee: Maritime Broadcasting System Ltd. Format: Today's country. News staff: 9. Target aud: General. ♦Rod Deviller, opns mgr; Alan Peddle, gen mgr & gen sls mgr; Phil Thompson, prom mgr; Roy MacIntosh, engrg mgr & chief of engrg.

CKPE-FM—Co-owned with CJCB(AM). September 1962: 94.9 mhz; 61 kw. 210 ft. Stereo. Format: Best mix of the 80s & 90s. ♦Phil Thompson, prom dir & prom mgr; Joe Purdy, mus dir; Roy MacIntosh, chief of engrg.

CJIJ-FM— June 2, 2003: 99.9 mhz; 50 w. C99 FM Radio, 49 Tupsi Dr., Membertou B1S 3K6. Phone: (902) 562-0009. Fax: (902) 539-6645. E-mail: c99fm@hotmail.com. Web Site: c99fm.homestead.com. Licensee: Membertou Radio Association Inc. Format: Classic hits, classic rock. ♦Peter Christmas Jr., gen mgr; Jay Bedford, gen sls mgr; progmg dir & chief of engrg; Alex Morrison, prom mgr & chief of engrg.

Truro

CINU-FM— 2004: 98.5 mhz; 50 w. Box 25012 B2N 7B8. Secondary address: 883 Prince St. B2N 1H2. Phone: (902) 843-4673. Fax: (902) 662-2879. E-mail: hopefmministries@eastlink.ca. Licensee: Hope FM Ministries Ltd. Format: Christian music. ♦Barry Reid, pres & gen mgr.

CKTO-FM— 1965: 100.9 mhz; 50 kw. Ant 189 ft. Stereo. 187 Industrial Ave. B2N 6V3. Phone: (902) 893-6060. Fax: (902) 893-7771. Licensee: Astral Media Radio Atlantic Inc. Group owner: Astral Media Inc. (acq 4-19-2002; grpsl). Rep: Canadian Broadcast Sales. Format: Adult contemp, rock. News staff: 3; News: 6 hrs wkly. Target aud: 25-49. ♦John Eddy, exec VP; Mike Worsley, stn mgr; Chris Van Tassel, progmg dir; James Cormier, mus dir; Dave Guy, news dir.

CKTY-FM— 2001: 99.5 mhz; 16.75 kw. 187 Industrial Ave. B2N 6V3. Phone: (902) 893-6060. Fax: (902) 893-7771. Licensee: Astral Media Radio Atlantic Inc. Group owner: Astral Media Inc. (acq 4-19-2002; grpsl). Rep: Canadian Broadcast Sales. Format: Country. ♦John Eddy, exec VP; Mike Worsley, gen sls mgr; Chris Van Tassel, progmg dir; James Cormier, mus dir; Dave Guy, news dir.

Windsor

CFAB(AM)— 1945: 1450 khz; 1 kw-U. Box 278 B0N 2T0. Phone: (902) 798-2111. Fax: (902) 798-8140. E-mail: avr@avrnetwork.com. Web Site: www.avrnetwork.com. Licensee: Maritime Broadcasting System Ltd. Group owner: Maritime Broadcasting. Format: Country. News staff: 5; News: 9 hrs wkly. Target aud: 25-54. ♦Dianne Best, gen mgr; Scott Baines, stn mgr; Karen Corey, gen sls mgr; Amanda Misner, progmg dir; Dave Chaulk, news dir; Garth Faulkner, engrg dir & chief of engrg.

Yarmouth

CIFA-FM— Sept 28, 1990: 104.1 mhz; 39.3 w. 475 ft. Stereo. Box 8, Saulnierville B0W 2Z0. Phone: (902) 769-2432. Fax: (902) 769-3101. E-mail: cifa@ns.sympatico.com. Web Site: www.cifa.fm. Licensee: Radio Clare. Format: Div, community news. Target aud: General. ♦Alphonsind Saulnier, pres; Darlene Comeau, gen mgr; Jean Louis Belliveau, gen sls mgr; Emile Blinn, progmg dir & engrg mgr.

CJLS-FM— 2003: 95.5 mhz; 18 kw. Stereo. 328 Main St., Suite 201 B5A 1E4. Phone: (902) 742-7175. Fax: (902) 742-3143. E-mail: CJLS@cjls.com. Web Site: www.cjls.com. Licensee: Radio CJLS Ltd. Format: Adult contemp. ♦Ray Zinck, gen mgr; Dave Hall, gen sls mgr; Chris Perry, progmg dir; Jim Harris, chief of engrg.

Nunavut

Baker Lake

CKQN-FM— 1973: 99.3 mhz; 60 w. -50 ft. Box 13 X0C 0A0. Phone: (867) 793-2962. Fax: (867-793-2726). Web Site: www.tvradioworld.com. Licensee: Qamani'tuap Naalautaa Society. Network: CBC Radio One. Format: Eskimo, Inuit.

Iqaluit

CFFB(AM)— Feb 6, 1961: 1230 khz; 1 kw-U, DA-1. Box 490 X0A 0H0. Phone: (867) 979-6100. Fax: (867) 979-6147. E-mail: cbcnorth@cbc/ca. Web Site: cbc.ca/north. Licensee: CBC. Format: News/talk, Inuktitut language. ♦Pat Nagle, gen mgr.

CFRT-FM— 1994: 107.3 mhz; 27 w. C.P. 880 X0A 0H0. Phone: (867) 979-4606. Fax: (867) 979-0800. E-mail: cfrt@nunafranc.ca. Web Site: www.franconunavut.ca. Licensee: Association des francophones de Nunavut. Format: Fr. ♦Daniel Cuerrier, gen mgr.

CKIQ-FM— May 26, 2003: 99.9 mhz; 537 w. Box 417 X0A 0H0. Secondary address: 1036 Airport Rd. X0A 0H0. Phone: (867) 975-2547. Fax: (867) 975-2598. E-mail: 99.9@ckiq.com. Web Site: www.ckiq.ca. Licensee: Nunavut Natautinga Ltd. Rep: Target Broadcast Sales. Format: Classic rock. ♦Terri Chegwyn, gen mgr.

Rankin Inlet

CBQR-FM— 1988: 105.1 mhz; 87 w. Box 130 X0C 0G0. Phone: (867) 645-2244. Fax: (867) 645-2820. Web Site: www.north.cbc.ca. Licensee: CBC Radio. Network: CBC Radio One. Format: Adult contemp, talk, div. Spec prog: Inuktitut 10 hrs wkly. ♦Elizabeth Kusugak, gen mgr.

Ontario

Ajax

CJKX-FM— 1994: 95.9 mhz; 19.94 kw. Ant 330 ft. Stereo. 1200 Airport Blvd., Suite 207, Oshawa L1J 8P5. Phone: (905) 428-9600. Fax: (905) 571-1150. E-mail: kx96@kx96.fm. Web Site: www.kx96.fm. Licensee: Durham Radio Inc. (group owner). Format: New country. News staff: 3; News: 1.5 hrs wkly. Target aud: 25-54; . ♦Douglas E. Kirk, pres & gen mgr; Steve Kassay, opns VP & opns mgr; Steve Macaulay, sls VP & gen sls mgr.

Akwesasne

CKON-FM— Oct 1, 1984: 97.3 mhz; 150 w. 150 ft. Box 140, Rooseveltown, NY 13683. Secondary address: Box 1496 K6H 5V5. Phone: (613) 575-2100. Phone: (518) 358-3426 (US). Fax: (613) 575-2566. E-mail: ckon@ckonfm.com. Web Site: www.ckonfm.com. Licensee: Mohawk Nation Council. Group owner: Akwesasne Communication Society Format: Div. Target aud: General. Spec prog: Mohawk. ♦Judy Laffin, gen mgr; Larry Edwards, gen mgr & progmg dir.

Alexandria

CHOD-FM—See Cornwall

Atikokan

CKDR-6(AM)— May 1977: 1240 khz; 50 w. c/o CKDR, Box 580, Dryden P8N 2Z3. Phone: (807) 223-2355. Fax: (807) 223-5090. E-mail: mail@ckdr.net. Web Site: www.ckdr.net. Licensee: Fawcett Broadcasting. Group owner: Fawcett Broadcasting Ltd. Format: Contemp hits of the 60s, 70s, 80s & 90s. News staff: one. Target aud: 25-54. ♦Bruce Walchuk, gen mgr & gen sls mgr; Randy Pike, news dir.

Aylmer

CHPD-FM— September 2003: 105.9 mhz; 250 w. TL: N42 45 40 W80 56 03. 16 Talbot St. N5H 1H4. Phone: (519) 773-8555. Fax: (519) 773-8606. E-mail: radio@mccayl.org. Licensee: Aylmer and Area Inter-Mennonite Community Council. Format: Low German, Christian.

Broadcasting & Cable Yearbook 2006

Ontario

News staff: one; News: one hr wkly. ♦ Abe Harms, CEO; Philip Wiebe, chmn & pres; Peter Bergen, VP; Henry Rempel, stn mgr.

Bancroft

CHMS-FM— May 2001: 97.7 mhz; 50 kw. Box 1240 K0L 1C0. Phone: (613) 332-1423. Fax: (613) 332-0841. E-mail: moose977@hbgradio.com. Web Site: www.moosefm.com. Licensee: The Haliburton Broadcasting Group Inc. Group owner: Haliburton Broadcasting Group Inc. Format: Hot adult contemp. Target aud: General. Spec prog: Relg one hr, loc talk 5 hrs, sports 2 hrs wkly. ♦ Steve Skelly, opns mgr.

Barrie

CFJB-FM— Oct 7, 1988: 95.7 mhz; 46 kw. Ant 500 ft. Box 95, 400 Bayfield St., Suite 205 L4M 5A1. Phone: (705) 725-7304. Fax: (705) 721-7842. E-mail: dbingley@rock95.com. Web Site: www.rock95.com. Licensee: Rock 95 Broadcasting (Barrie-Orillia) Ltd. (acq 2-7-94). Format: Classic rock, new rock, 80s rock. News staff: 3; News: 4 hrs wkly. Target aud: 18-49; broad-based, well-educated, above-average income. ♦ Doug Bingley, CEO, pres & gen mgr; Jim Cowden, VP & gen sls mgr; Tom Harrison, gen sls mgr; Dave Carr, progmg dir.

CHAY-FM— May 21, 1977: 93.1 mhz; 100 kw. Ant 1,000 ft. Stereo. Box 937,, 1125 Bayfield St. N. L4M 4Y6. Phone: (705) 737-3511. Fax: (705) 737-0603. E-mail: knoel@corusent.com. Web Site: www.thenewchay.com. Licensee: Corus Radio Co. Group owner: Corus Entertainment Inc. Format: Adult contemp. News staff: 3; News: 13 hrs wkly. Target aud: 25-64; general. ♦ John Hayes, pres; Kim Noel, gen mgr; Frank Allinson, gen sls mgr; Keith Talbert, prom mgr; Darren Stevens, progmg dir.

CIQB-FM— November 1994: 101.1 mhz; 4.3 kw. Box 937 L4M 4S9. Secondary address: 1125 Bayfield St. N. L4M 4S9. Phone: (705) 726-1011. Fax: (705) 726-0022. E-mail: knoel@corusent.com. Web Site: www.b101fm.com. Licensee: 591989 B.C. Ltd. Group owner: Corus Entertainment Inc. (acq 3-24-2000; grpsl). Format: Adult contemp. News staff: 3; News: 11 hrs wkly. Target aud: 25-54; women 35-49 & 25-54 & at work people. ♦ John Hayes, pres & VP; Kim Noel, gen mgr; Dave Pinder, mktg dir & prom; Darren Stevens, progmg dir.

CJLF-FM— Aug 15, 1999: 100.3 mhz; 18.7 kw. 115 Bell Farm Rd, Unit 111 L4M 5G1. Phone: (705) 735-3370. Fax: (705) 735-3301. Web Site: www.lifeonline.fm. Licensee: Trust Communications Ministries. Format: Christian music. ♦ Scott Jackson, stn mgr; Jen Taylor, prom dir; Ben Davy, progmg dir; Christy Burton, news dir.

CKMB-FM— 2001: 107.7 mhz; 20 kw. 400 Bayfield St., Suite 205 L4M 5A1. Phone: (705) 725-7304. Fax: (705) 721-7842. Web Site: www.star1075.com. Licensee: Rock 95 Broadcasting (Barrie-Orillia) Ltd. Format: Top 40/contemp hits. ♦ Doug Bingley, CEO, pres, gen mgr & chief of engrg; Jim Cowden, sls VP & mktg VP; Helen Mathers, prom dir; Dale Smith, progmg mgr & chief of engrg.

Belleville

CHCQ-FM— 2001: 100.1 mhz; 21 kw. Stereo. 354 Pinnacle St. K8N 3B4. Phone: (613) 966-0955. Fax: (613) 967-2565. Web Site: www.cool100.fm. Licensee: Starboard Communications Ltd. (acq 7-26-02; C$541,351). Rep: CHUM Group Radio Sales. Format: Country. Target aud: 25-54; adults. ♦ John Sherratt, pres & gen mgr.

CIGL-FM—Listing follows CJBQ(AM).

CJBQ(AM)— Aug 12, 1946: 800 khz; 10 kw-U, DA-2. Box 488 K8N 5B2. Secondary address: 10 S. Front St. K8N2Y3. Phone: (613) 969-5555. Fax: (613) 969-8122. Web Site: www.cjbq.com. Licensee: Quinte Broadcasting Ltd. (group owner). Rep: Hooper Jones. Format: Country. Spec prog: Farm 3 hrs wkly. ♦ Bill Morton, gen mgr & gen sls mgr; Peter Thompson, progmg dir.

CIGL-FM—Co-owned with CJBQ(AM). August 1962: 97.1 mhz; 50 kw. Web Site: www.mix97.com. Format: Hot adult contemp.

CJLX-FM— October 1992: 91.3 mhz; 3.4 kw. TL: N44 09 50 W77 23 24. Stereo. Box 4200, Loyalist College, Wallbridge-Loyalist Rd. K8N 5B9. Phone: (613) 966-0923. Fax: (613) 966-1993. E-mail: cjlx@loyalistc.on.ca. Web Site: www.cjlx.fm. Licensee: Loyalist College Radio Inc. (acq 11-13-90). Rep: Target Broadcast Sales. Format: Rock, community service. News: 6 hrs wkly. Target aud: 18-34; primary, ages 50 plus secondary. Spec prog: Fr one hr, folk one hr, jazz 4 hrs, Greek one hr, Dutch one hr wkly. ♦ Greg Schatzmann,

CEO & gen mgr; Sandi Ramsan, sls dir & gen sls mgr; Len Arminio, news dir; Tim Rorabeck, chief of engrg.

CJOJ-FM— Dec 1, 1993: 95.5 mhz; 42 kw. Stereo. 354 Pinnacle St. K8N 3B4. Phone: (613) 966-0955. Fax: (613) 967-2565. Web Site: www.classichits955.fm. Licensee: Starboard Communications Ltd. (acq 7-26-02; C$1,456,610). Rep: CHUM Group Radio Sales. Format: CHR, adult contemp. Target aud: 25-54; adults - skewed females 60%, males 40%. ♦ John Sherratt, pres & stn mgr.

CKJJ-FM— Oct 18, 2003: 102.3 mhz; 45 kw. Box 23095 K8P 5J3. Secondary address: 214 Pinnacle St. K8P 3A6. Phone: (613) 966-4822. Fax: (613) 966-3211. E-mail: info@ucbcanada.com. Web Site: www.ucbcanada.com. Licensee: United Christian Broadcasters Canada. Format: Christian music. ♦ Garry Quinn, gen mgr; Alan Baker, progmg dir.

Bracebridge

CFBG-FM— May 1988: 99.5 mhz; 12 kw. Box 960,, 25 Highland St., Haliburton K0M 1S0. Phone: (705) 645-2218. Fax: (705) 645-6957. E-mail: moose995@hbgradio.com. Web Site: www.hbgradio.com. Licensee: The Haliburton Broadcasting Group Inc. Group owner: Haliburton Broadcasting Group Inc. (acq 12-10-97; C$295,000). Format: Hot adult contemp. Target aud: 34-45; older adult contemporary. Spec prog: Jazz 2 hrs, big band one hr, loc magazine one hr wkly. ♦ Christopher Grossman, pres & gen mgr; Kimberley Ward, VP & opns mgr; Sean Connon, gen sls mgr.

Brampton

CFNY-FM— Aug 8, 1960: 102.1 mhz; 35 kw. Ant 1,378 ft. TL: N43 38 33 W79 23 15. (Digital radio: Dec 3, 1998: 1465.024 mhz; 5.084 kw). Stereo. One Dundas St. W., Suite 1600, Toronto M5G 1Z3. Phone: (416) 408-3343. Fax: (416) 847-3300. Web Site: www.edge.ca. Licensee: Corus Radio Co. Group owner: Corus Entertainment Inc. (acq 1995; C$16.75 million). Rep: Canadian Broadcast Sales. Format: Modern rock, progsv. News staff: 2; News: 3 hrs wkly. Target aud: 18-34; self motivated, mus loving, active, young at heart people. ♦ John Cassaday, CEO & pres; Heather Shaw, chmn; Tom Peddie, CFO; Jim Johnston, gen mgr.

CIAO(AM)— Dec 23, 1953: 530 khz; 1 kw-D, 250 w-N, DA-2. (Digital radio: 1466.768 mhz; 5.084 kw). 5302 Dundas S. W., Toronto M9B-1B2. Phone: (416) 213-1035. Fax: (416) 233-8617. Web Site: www.am530.ca. Licensee: CKMW Radio Ltd. Group owner: Evanov Radio Group (acq 9-26-83). Rep: Target Broadcast Sales. Format: Ethnic, multilingual. ♦ Bill Evanov, pres; Paul Evanov, exec VP.

Brantford

CFWC-FM— 2002: 93.9 mhz; 250 w. 271 Greenwich St. N3S 2X9. Phone: (519) 759-2339. Fax: (519) 753-1157. E-mail: info@power93.ca. Web Site: www.power93.ca. Licensee: 1486781 Ontario Ltd. Format: Christian music. ♦ Dean Johnston, gen mgr.

CKPC(AM)— December 1923: 1380 khz; 10 kw-U, DA-2. (CP: 25 kw). 571 West St. N3T 5P8. Phone: (519) 759-1000. Fax: (519) 753-1470. Web Site: www.ckpc.on.ca. Licensee: Telephone City Broadcast Ltd. Rep: Target Broadcast Sales. Format: Classic hits. News staff: 7; News: 9 hrs wkly. Target aud: 35-64. ♦ Richard D. Buchanan, pres & gen mgr; Peter Jackman, sls VP & gen sls mgr.

CKPC-FM— May 1949: 92.1 mhz; 50 kw. 750 ft. Stereo. Web Site: www.ckpc.on.ca. Format: Adult contemp. News: 7 hrs wkly. Target aud: 25-49.

Brockville

CFJR-FM— 2003: 104.9 mhz; 5.6 kw. 601 Stewart Blvd. K6V 5V9. Phone: (613) 345-1666. Fax: (613) 342-2438. E-mail: comments@hometownradio.ca. Web Site: www.hometownradio.ca. Licensee: CHUM Ltd. (group owner). Format: Adult contemp. News staff: 3; News: 5 hrs wkly. Target aud: 35-54; female slant. ♦ Jay Smitzer, pres; Greg Hinton, gen mgr & progmg dir; Rick Moran, gen sls mgr; Warren Davies, chief of engrg.

CJPT-FM— July 28, 1988: 103.7 mhz; 100 kw. Ant 495 ft. TL: N44 23 58 W75 58 21. 601 Stewart Blvd. K6V 5V9. Phone: (613) 345-1666. Fax: (613) 342-2438. E-mail: info@bob.fm. Web Site: www.bob.fm. Licensee: CHUM Ltd. (group owner). Format: Hits of the 80s. News

Stations in Canada

staff: 3. Target aud: 18-44; male. ♦ Jay Switzer, pres; Paul Ski, exec VP; Greg Hinton, gen mgr & progmg dir; Rick Moran, rgnl sls mgr; Alison MacLean, prom dir.

Burlington

CIWV-FM—See Hamilton

CJXY-FM— Sept 23, 1976: 107.9 mhz; 26.4 kw. Ant 672 ft. TL: N43 23 12 W79 52 34. Stereo. 875 Main St. West, Hamilton L85 4R1. Phone: (905) 521-9900. Fax: (905) 521-2306. Web Site: www.y108.ca. Licensee: Corus Radio Co. Group owner: Corus Entertainment Inc. Format: Mainstream rock, adult contemp. News staff: 3; News: 2 hrs wkly. Target aud: 25-54. ♦ Suzanne Carpenter, gen mgr.

Cambridge

CJDV-FM— 1998: 107.5 mhz; 2.5 kw. Stereo. 1315 Bishop St. N., Unit 100 N1R 6Z2. Phone: (519) 621-7510. Fax: (519) 621-0165. E-mail: cross@davefm.com. Web Site: www.davefm.com. Licensee: 591989 B.C. Ltd. Group owner: Corus Entertainment Inc. (acq 4-2000; grpsl). Format: Hot adult contemp. News staff: 2. Target aud: 18-49. Spec prog: Por 2 hrs wkly. ♦ Clyde Ross, gen mgr, gen sls mgr & news dir; Lucia Zdeb, prom dir; Kneale Mann, progmg dir; Brian Clemens, engrg VP & chief of engrg.

Campbellford

CKOL-FM— 1993: 93.7 mhz; 500 w. Box 551 K0L 1L0. Secondary address: 15 Ragland St. S. K0L 1L0. Phone: (705) 653-1089. Fax: (705) 653-1089. E-mail: ckl-radio@excite.com. Licensee: Campbellford Area Radio Association. Format: Div. Spec prog: Gospel 3 hrs, bluegrass 3 hrs wkly. ♦ Dave Lockwood, gen mgr; David Lockwood, gen sls mgr, progmg dir & chief of engrg.

Cape Croker (Neyaashiinigmiing)

CHFN-FM— 2003: 100.1 mhz; 72 w. RR 5, Wiarton N0H 2T0. Phone: (519) 534-1003. Fax: (519) 534-0063. E-mail: chfn@bellnet.ca. Web Site: www.nawash.ca/chfn. Licensee: Jessica Nadjiwon, on behalf of a non-profit corporation to be incorporated. Format: Aboriginal news & programs relevant to the Ojibway people. News: 12 hrs wkly. Target aud: 18-65; progmg is div. ♦ Jake Linklater, pres; Peter Akiwenzie, VP; Jessica Nadjiwon, gen mgr; Beedahsega Elliott, mktg mgr; Johnathan Pedoniquotte, progmg mgr.

Chatham

CFCO(AM)— 1926: 630 khz; 10 kw-D, 6 kw-N, DA-2. TL: N42 20 03 W82 16 53. Stereo. Box 100 N7M 5K1. Secondary address: 117 Keil Dr. S. N7M 5K1. Phone: (519) 352-3000. Phone: (519) 354-2200. Fax: (519) 354-2880. Fax: (519) 352-9690. E-mail: info@630cfco.com. Web Site: www.630cfco.com. Licensee: Bea-Ver Communications Inc. (acq 3-20-97). Rep: Target Broadcast Sales. Format: MOR. News staff: 6; News: 6 hrs wkly. Target aud: 35 plus. Spec prog: Farm 3 hrs, gospel 2 hrs wkly. ♦ Carl Veroba, CEO, pres & gen mgr; Doug Kirk, VP; Walter Ploegman, opns mgr; Phil Ceccacci, gen sls mgr; Mike Regnier, prom dir; Rob Henderson, progmg dir; Simon Crouch, news dir; Ron Wilken, chief of engrg.

CKSY-FM— Nov 17, 1999: 94.3 mhz; 50 kw. Ant 495 ft. TL: N42 26 14 W82 06 23. Box 100 N7M 5K1. Secondary address: 117 Keil Dr. S. N7M 5K1. Phone: (519) 354-2200. Phone: (519) 354-0311. Fax: (519) 354-2880. E-mail: info@cksyfm.com. Web Site: www.cksyfm.com. Licensee: Bea-Ver Communications Inc. Format: Adult contemp. News staff: 5; News: 5 hrs wkly. Target aud: 18-54. Spec prog: Gospel 2 hrs wkly. ♦ Carl Veroba, CEO, pres & gen mgr; Doug Kirk, VP; Phil Ceccacci, gen sls mgr; Shannon Snoes, prom dir; Jay Poole, progmg mgr.

CKUE-FM— July 1, 1986: 95.1 mhz; 42 kw. Ant 495 ft. TL: N42 26 14 W82 06 23. Stereo. Box 100 N7M 5K1. Secondary address: 117 Keil Dr. S. N7M 5K1. Phone: (519) 354-2853. Fax: (519) 354-2880. E-mail: info@therock951.com. Web Site: www.therock951.com. Licensee: Bea-Ver Communications Inc. Format: AOR. News staff: 2. Target aud: 18-49. ♦ Carl Veroba, CEO, pres & gen mgr; Doug Kirk, VP; Justin Oliphant, prom dir; Walter Ploegman, progmg dir; Ron Wilken, chief of engrg.

Directory of Radio   Ontario

Christian Island

CKUN-FM—Not on air, target date: unknown: 101.3 mhz; 900 w. Ant 156 ft. Beausoleil First Nation Band Council no. 30 & 30A, Administration Office, 1 O'Gema St. L0K 1C0. Phone: (705) 247-2456. Phone: (705) 247-2051. Fax: (705) 247-2239. Web Site: www.chimnissing.ca /xtras/radio.html. Licensee: Chimnissing Communications. Format: Div music. ♦Edna King, gen mgr; Kim Anderson, progmg dir; Richard Sutherland, progmg dir & engrg mgr.

Cobourg

CFMX-FM— 1978: 103.1 mhz; 86.7 kw. 825 ft. TL: N01 44 04 W01 78 09. (Digital radio: 1466.768 mhz; 5.084 kw). Stereo. 550 Queen St. E., Suite 205, Toronto M5A 1VZ. Secondary address: Box 1031, One Queen St. K9A 1M8. Phone: (905) 367-5353. Fax: (905) 367-1742. E-mail: info@cfmx.com. Web Site: www.classical96fm.com. Licensee: Trumar Communications Inc. (acq 11-30-83; C$50,000). Robson Broadcast Consultants. Format: Class. News staff: 3; News: 4 hrs wkly. Target aud: 35 plus; well-educated, upscale, owners/managers/professionals. ♦Peter Webb, CEO, pres & gen mgr; Truus Rosenthal, VP; Roberta Hunt, opns mgr; Al Kingdon, rgnl sls mgr; Marissa Colalillo, prom dir; John van Driel, progmg dir & mus dir; David Franco, news dir; Wassim Saikali, chief of engrg.

CHUC(AM)— Aug 27, 1957: 1450 khz; 8 kw-D, 1 kw-N, DA-2. TL: N43 57 20 W78 13 09. (CP: 1580 khz; 10 kw-U). Box 520 K9A 4L3. Secondary address: 7805 Telephone Rd. K9A 4J7. Phone: (905) 372-5401. Fax: (905) 372-6280. E-mail: chuc@chuc1450.com. Licensee: Pineridge Broadcasting Inc. (acq 7-31-92). Format: Soft pop, oldies, country. News staff: 3; News: 7 hrs wkly. Target aud: 25-54; predominantely female. ♦Don Conway, pres & gen mgr.

CKSG-FM—Co-owned with CHUC(AM). July 18, 2002: 93.3 mhz; 2.1 kw. E-mail: info@star933.com. Web Site: www.star933.com. Format: Adult contemp. News staff: one; News: one hr wkly. Target aud: 25-54; predoninately female.

Cochrane

CHPB-FM— 2004: 98.1 mhz; 50 w. 32 Mountjoy St. N., Suite 103, Timmins P4N 4V6. Phone: (705) 267-6070. Fax: (705) 267-6095. E-mail: moose981@hbgradio.com. Licensee: The Haliburton Broadcasting Group Inc. Group owner: Haliburton Broadcasting Group Inc. (acq 11-19-2003; with CJWL-FM Iroquois Falls). Format: Adult contemp. News staff: one. Target aud: 18-65. ♦Christopher Grossman, gen mgr; Kent Matheson, progmg dir; Mike Fry, mus dir; Todd Hamblin, news dir; Diane Bradley, sls.

Collingwood

CKCB-FM— Mar 29, 1996: 95.1 mhz; 350 w. 1400 Hwy. 26 E. L9Y 4W2. Phone: (705) 446-9510. Fax: (705) 444-6776. E-mail: jeaton@thepeakfm.com. Web Site: www.thepeakfm.com. Licensee: 591989 B.C. Ltd. Group owner: Corus Entertainment Inc. (acq 3-24-00; grpsl). Rep: Major Market Broadcasters Ltd. Format: Adult contemp. News staff: one; News: 11 hrs wkly. Target aud: 25-54. ♦John Eaton, gen mgr; John Nichols, opns mgr, gen sls mgr & progmg dir; Kim Di Girolamo, prom dir; Dale West, news dir.

Cornwall

CFLG-FM— 1973: 104.5 mhz; 15 kw. 300 ft. TL: N45 03 30 W74 44 45. Stereo. 237 Water St. E. K6H 1A2. Phone: (613) 932-5180. Fax: (613) 938-0355. E-mail: derrickscott@variety104.com. Web Site: www.seawayvalley.com. Licensee: Corus Radio Co. Group owner: Corus Entertainment Inc. (acq 11-19-01; grpsl). Rep: Canadian Broadcast Sales. Format: Adult contemp. News staff: 4; News: 5 hrs wkly. Target aud: 25-54; predominantly female professionals & housewives. ♦Tim Wieczorek, gen mgr; Rob Sequin, prom dir; Derrick Scott, progmg dir.

CHOD-FM— May 1, 1994: 92.1 mhz; 19.2 kw. Stereo. 1111 Montreal Rd., Suite 202 K6H 1E1. Phone: (613) 936-2463. Fax: (613) 936-2568. Web Site: www.chod.fm.ca. Licensee: Radio Communautaire Cornwall-Alexandria Inc. Format: Adult pop, French. News staff: one; News: 10 hrs wkly. Target aud: 25-54. Spec prog: Class 4 hrs, jazz 4 hrs wkly. ♦Norman Couture, pres; Marc Charbonneau, gen mgr.

CJSS-FM— 1999: 101.9 mhz; 1.42 kw. TL: N45 03 30 W74 44 45. Box 969, 237 Water St. E. K6H 5V1. Phone: (613) 932-5180. Fax: (613) 938-0355. E-mail: onaircjss@rock1019.com. Web Site: www.seawayvalley.com. Licensee: Corus Radio Co. Group owner: Corus Entertainment Inc. (acq 11-19-01; grpsl). Rep: Canadian Broadcast Sales. Format: Rock. News staff: 4; News: 2 hrs wkly. Target aud: 35 plus; well informed—interested in loc news & info including talk radio. Spec prog: Relg one hr wkly. ♦Tim Wieczorek, gen mgr.

CJUL(AM)—Co-owned with CJSS-FM. Nov 24, 2000: 1220 khz; 1 kw-U. E-mail: onaircjul@seawayvalley.com. Format: Oldies. News staff: 4; News: 4 hrs wkly. Target aud: 45 plus.

Dryden

*CJIV-FM— March 2003: 97.3 mhz; 50 w. Box 112 P8N 2Y7. Phone: (807) 937-9731. Fax: (807) 937-6490. E-mail: cjiv@canada.com. Web Site: www.cjiv973.net. Licensee: Way of Life Broadcasting. Format: Christian. News: 2 hrs wkly. Target aud: All ages; interested in Christian radio bcsts. ♦Gordon Robinson, gen mgr; Jake Letkeman, progmg mgr.

CKDR(AM)— August 1963: 800 khz; 1 kw-D, 700 w-N. Box 580 P8N 2Z3. Phone: (807) 223-2355. Fax: (807) 223-5090. E-mail: mail@ckdr.net. Web Site: www.ckdr.net. Licensee: Fawcett Broadcasting Ltd. (group owner) Format: Oldies, CHR. Target aud: 25 plus. ♦Bruce Walchuk, gen mgr & gen sls mgr.

Elliot Lake

CKNR-FM— Mar 3, 1997: 94.1 mhz; 90 kw. 15 Charles Walk P5A 2A2. Phone: (705) 848-3608. Fax: (705) 848-1378. E-mail: moose941@hbgradio.com. Web Site: www.hbgradio.com. Licensee: The Haliburton Broadcasting Group Inc. Group owner: Haliburton Broadcasting Group Inc. (acq 3-12-2004; C$625,000). Rep: Canadian Broadcast Sales. Format: Adult contemp. Target aud: 35-54. ♦Christopher Grossman, pres & gen mgr; Kimberly Ward, VP; Ericka MacLellan, opns mgr; Chris Waschuk, sls; Patricia Orser, news dir & mktg; Bob Alexander, prom.

Englehart

CJBB-FM— January 2000: 103.1 mhz; 1.6 kw. Stereo. Box 665, 50 Third St. P0J 1H0. Phone: (705) 544-1121. Fax: (705) 544-2286. E-mail: cjbb@ntl.sympatico.ca. Licensee: 1353151 Ontario Inc. Format: Adult contemp, rock. News staff: 5; News: 5 hrs wkly. ♦Boyd Woods, CEO; Rick Stow, progmg dir.

Fort Erie

CKEY-FM— May 19, 1991: 101.1 mhz; 19.7 kw. TL: N42 53 52 W78 57 27. Stereo. 4668 St. Clair Ave., Niagara Falls L2E 6X7. Phone: (905) 356-6710. Fax: (905) 356-0696. E-mail: cjrniz@niagara.com. Web Site: www.wild101.com. Licensee: CJRN 710 Inc. Format: Top-40, CHR. Target aud: 18-44; upper income adults. ♦David J. Dancy, pres & gen sls mgr; Elizabeth Lewis, gen mgr; Heather Vigna, prom dir; Robert White, progmg dir; Mike Ridley, chief of engrg.

Fort Frances

CFOB-FM— June 4, 2002: 93.1 mhz; 21 kw. 242 Scott St. P9A 1G7. Phone: (807) 274-5341. Phone: (218) 283-4420. Fax: (807) 274-2033. E-mail: alad@b93.ca. Licensee: Fawcett Broadcasting Ltd. (group owner). Rep: TeleRep. Format: Adult contemp. News staff: 2. Target aud: 25-54; International Falls/N. Central MN. ♦Ala Dulas, gen mgr; Doug Cain, rgnl sls mgr; Laurie Beadle, rgnl sls mgr; Mike Connors, mus dir.

Georgina Island

CFGI-FM— 2004: 102.7 mhz; 250 w. 102.7 Nish Radio, Box N-13, Sutton West L0E 1R0. Phone: (705) 437-3748. Fax: (705) 437-3748. Licensee: Georgina Island First Nations Communications. Format: Var. ♦Sally Charles, gen mgr.

Guelph

CFRU-FM— Jan 28, 1980: 93.3 mhz; 250 w. 1,085 ft. TL: N43 32 07 W80 13 25. Stereo. Level 2 Univ. Ctr., Univ. of Guelph N1G 2W1. Phone: (519) 824-4120, Ext. 5302. Fax: (519) 763-9603. E-mail: info@cfru.ca. Web Site: www.cfru.ca. Licensee: University of Guelph Radio-Radio Gryphon. Format: Multicultural, Div. News staff: one; News: 12 hrs wkly. Target aud: General. Spec prog: It one hr, relg one hr, Sp. ♦MacKenzie Jenkins, opns mgr; Lori Guest, progmg dir; Helen Spitzer, mus dir; Jennifer Moore, news dir.

CIMJ-FM—Listing follows CJOY(AM).

CJOY(AM)— June 14, 1948: 1460 khz; 10 kw-U. Stereo. 75 Speedvale Ave. E. N1E 6M3. Phone: (519) 824-7000. Fax: (519) 824-4118. E-mail: cjoy@cjoy.com. Licensee: 591989 B.C. Ltd. Group owner: Corus Entertainment Inc. (acq 3-24-00; grpsl). Format: Oldies. News staff: 4; News: 8 hrs wkly. Target aud: 25-54. ♦Guus Hazelaar, gen mgr; Larry Mellott, progmg mgr; Mike Stevens, engrg VP.

CIMJ-FM—Co-owned with CJOY(AM). 1969: 106.1 mhz; 50 kw. 249 ft. Stereo. E-mail: kkelly@magic106.com. Web Site: www.magic106.com. Format: Adult contemp. News: 6 hrs wkly. Target aud: 18-49. ♦Kevin Kelly, progmg mgr; Curtis Dunat, mus dir.

Haliburton

CKHA-FM— July 2003: 100.9 mhz; 3.4 kw. Box 1125 K0M 1S0. Phone: (705) 457-9603. Fax: (705) 457-9522. E-mail: ccanoefm@bellnet.ca. Web Site: www.canoefm.com. Licensee: Haliburton County Community Radio Association. Format: Var. ♦Dave Sovereign, stn mgr.

Hamilton

*CFMU-FM— Jan 13, 1978: 93.3 mhz; 166 w. 300 ft. TL: N47 14 41 W79 54 58. Stereo. McMaster Univ. Student Center, Rm. B119 L8S 4S4. Phone: (905) 525-9140, EXT. 22053. Fax: (905) 529-3208. E-mail: cfmunews@msu.mcmaster.ca. Web Site: cfmu.mcmaster.ca. Licensee: CFMU Radio Inc. (acq 1978). Format: Div, pub affrs, multicultural. News: 15 hrs wkly. Target aud: General; univ students, people with an adventurous outlook towards life. Spec prog: Class 5 hrs, Sp one hr, blues 5 hrs, Canadian Indian one hr, Fr one hr, It one hr wkly. ♦Sandeep Bhandari, stn mgr; James Hayashi-Tennant, progmg dir; Craig Nordemann, mus dir; Stefan Lozinski, prom.

CHAM(AM)— November 1959: 820 khz; 50 kw-U, DA-2. Stereo. 883 Upper WentWorth, Suite 401 L9A 4Y6. Phone: (905) 574-1150. Fax: (905) 575-6429. E-mail: info@820cham.com. Web Site: www.820cham.com. Licensee: Standard Radio Inc. Group owner: Standard Broadcasting Corp. (acq 4-29-02; grpsl). Format: Country. News staff: 4; News: 26 hrs wkly. Target aud: 25-54. ♦Gary Slaight, CEO & pres; Tom Cooke, VP & gen mgr; Rancy Redden, sls dir; Wendy Haennel, mktg dir & prom dir; Tom Tompkins, prom mgr & progmg dir; Robyn Foley, news dir; Carrie Arnold, pub affrs dir; Charlie Tryon, chief of engrg.

CHML(AM)— May 27, 1927: 900 khz; 50 kw-U, DA-1. Stereo. 875 Main St. W. L8S 4R1. Phone: (905) 521-9900. Fax: (905) 521-2306. Licensee: Corus Premium Television Ltd. Group owner: Corus Entertainment Inc. (acq 7-6-2000; grpsl). Network: Telemedia. Rep: Canadian Broadcast Sales. Format: News/talk, sports. Target aud: 35 plus. ♦Suzanne Carpenter, gen mgr; Greg Hinton, progmg dir; Mike Rose, mus dir.

CING-FM—Co-owned with CHML(AM). Sept 14, 1964: 95.3 mhz; 100 kw. Ant 1,000 ft. Stereo. 64 Jefferson Ave., Unit 18, Toronto M6K 3H4. Secondary address: 875 Main St. W., Suite 900 L8S 4R1. Phone: (416) 534-1191. Phone: (905) 521-9900. Fax: (416) 583-4133. Fax: (905) 540-2453. Web Site: www.country953.com. Rep: Canadian Broadcast Sales. Format: Country. Target aud: 25-54; female. ♦Ginny Townson Sedik, gen sls mgr; Nadia Cerelli-Fiore, prom dir; Steve Parsons, progmg dir; Rick Walters, mus dir; Ted Townsend, engrg dir.

*CIOI-FM— 1998: 101.5 mhz; 240 w. TL: N43 14 12 W79 53 13. Stereo. Mohawk College, 135 Fennell Ave. W. L8N 3T2. Phone: (905) 575-2175. Fax: (905) 575-2385. Licensee: The Mohawk College Radio Corp. Format: College alternative. News: 6 hrs wkly. Target aud: 17-24; college students & the div communities they represent. Spec prog: Sp 3 hrs, Indian one hr, Assyrian one hr wkly. ♦Les Palango, gen mgr.

CIWV-FM— Sept 1, 2000: 94.7 mhz; 11.39 kw. Ant 446 ft. TL: N43 12 21 W79 43 50. Stereo. 589 Upper Wellington St. L9A 3P8. Phone: (905) 388-8911. Fax: (905) 388-7947. E-mail: smoothjazz@wave947.fm. Web Site: www.wave947.fm. Licensee: Burlingham Communications Inc. Rep: Target Broadcast Sales. Format: Smooth jazz. News staff: 2. Target aud: 35-64. ♦Douglas E. Kirk, chmn, pres & gen mgr; Thomas A. Pippy, CFO; Steve Kassay, opns VP; Simon Constam, gen sls mgr.

CKLH-FM—Listing follows CKOC(AM).

Broadcasting & Cable Yearbook 2006

Ontario

CKOC(AM)— May 20, 1922: 1150 khz; 50 kw-U, DA-2. TL: N43 03 04 W79 48 42. Stereo. 883 Upper Wentworth St., Suite 401 L9A 4Y6. Phone: (905) 574-1150. Fax: (905) 575-6429. Web Site: www.oldies1150.com. Licensee: Standard Radio Inc. Group owner: Standard Broadcasting Corp. (acq 4-29-02; grpsl). Rep: Canadian Broadcast Sales. Format: Oldies. News staff: 4; News: 3 hrs wkly. Target aud: 25-54. ◆ Tom Cooke, gen mgr & gen sls mgr; Christopher Randall, prom dir & prom mgr; Sunni Genesco, asst music dir.

CKLH-FM—Co-owned with CKOC(AM). Oct 7, 1986: 102.9 mhz; 40.5 kw. TL: N43 20 12 W79 52 07. Stereo. E-mail: info@k-litefm.com. Web Site: www.l-litefm.com. Format: Adult contemp. Target aud: 25-54; working women, owners, mgrs, professionals.

Hanover

CFBW-FM— 2001: 91.3 mhz; 5 w. Stereo. 275 10 St., Suite 4 N4N 1P1. Phone: (519) 364-0200. Fax: (519) 364-5175. E-mail: bluewaterradio@on.aibn.com. Web Site: www.bluewaterradio.ca. Licensee: Bluewater Community Radio. Format: Div. Target aud: 12-75; Ontario audience rural agricultural/urban. Spec prog: Gospel 7 hrs, Scottish 2 hrs wkly. ◆ Andrew McBride, stn mgr.

Hawkesbury

CHPR-FM— February 1986: 102.1 mhz; 789 w. 70 ft. TL: N45 35 01 N45 35 01. 115 Principale E., Suite 101, Oxbury K6A 1A1. Secondary address: 11 Argentevel, Lachute, PQ J8H 1X8. Phone: (613) 632-1000. Phone: (450) 562-8862. Fax: (450) 562-1902. Fax: (613) 632-1110. E-mail: infocouleurfmm@radionord.vom. Web Site: www.radionord.com. Licensee: Radio Fusion Inc. Group owner: Radio Nord Inc. (acq 8-22-89). Format: Adult contemp. News staff: one. Target aud: 25 plus. ◆ Jean-Pierre Major, gen mgr; Yves Trottier, gen sls mgr; Marc Dupuis, progmg dir; Marie Josee Clermont, mus dir; Daniel Racicot, chief of engrg.

Hearst

CHOH-FM— 1996: 92.9 mhz; 140 w. 32 Mountjoy St., N., Suite 103, Timmins P4N 4V6. Phone: (705) 267-6070. Fax: (705) 267-6095. E-mail: chycfm@hbgradio.com. Web Site: www.hbgradio.com. Licensee: Haliburton Broadcasting Group Inc. (group owner; acq 8-31-99; grpsl). Format: Hot AC, French, English. Spec prog: Sp one hr wkly. ◆ Christopher Grossman, pres & gen mgr.

*CINN-FM— 1988: 91.1 mhz; 5.5 w. 298 ft. TL: N49 38 50 W83 30 50. Box 2648, 1004, rue Prince P0L 1N0. Phone: (705) 372-1011. Fax: (705) 362-7411. E-mail: cinnfm@cinn.com. Web Site: www.cinnfm.com. Licensee: Radio de l'Epinette Noire Inc. Format: Adult contemp. News staff: 2. Target aud: 18-35. ◆ Jrelle Abin Larose, pres; Gabtane Morrissette, gen mgr.

Huntsville

CFBK-FM— September 1957: 105.5 mhz; 5 kw. Unit 2, 15 Main St. E. P1H 2C6. Phone: (705) 789-4461. Fax: (705) 789-1269. Web Site: www.zevler.com. Licensee: Muskoka-Parry Sound Broadcasting Ltd. (acq 9-13-94). Format: Adult contemp. ◆ Ian Byers, CEO, chmn, pres, gen mgr & gen sls mgr; Margaret Byers, opns dir & progmg mgr.

Iroquois Falls

CJWL-FM— Dec 8, 1998: 101.1 mhz; 50 w. 32 Mountjoy St. N., Suite 103, Timmins P4N 4V6. Phone: (705) 267-6070. Fax: (705) 267-6095. E-mail: moose1011@hbgradio.com. Web Site: www.hbgradio.com.no Licensee: The Haliburton Broadcasting Group Inc. Group owner: Haliburton Broadcasting Group Inc. (acq 11-19-03; with CHPB-FM Cochrane). Format: Adult contemp. News staff: one; News: 15 hrs wkly. Target aud: 25+. ◆ Christopher Grossman, pres & gen mgr; Kent Matheson, progmg dir; Todd Hamblin, news dir; Diane Bradley, sls.

Kaministiquia

CFQK-FM— 2002: 104.5 mhz; 50 w. 584 Red River Rd., Suite 200, Thunder Bay P7B 1H3. Phone: (807) 768-5048. Fax: (807) 767-7634. E-mail: max104@tbaytel.net. Licensee: Northwest Broadcasting Inc. Format: Country. ◆ Ari Lahdekorpi, gen mgr; Rich Fleming, progmg dir.

Kapuskasing

CKAP-FM— September 2001: 100.9 mhz; 12 kw. Box 960, Haliburton K0M 1S0. Phone: (705) 335-2379. Fax: (705) 337-6391. Web Site: www.hbgradio.com. Licensee: The Haliburton Broadcasting Group Inc. Group owner: Haliburton Broadcasting Group Inc. Format: CHR. News staff: 2. Target aud: General. ◆ Christopher Grossman, pres; Valerie Isaac, opns mgr.

CKGN-FM— October 1993: 89.7 mhz; 3 kw. 77 chemin Brunelle Nd. P5N 2M1. Phone: (705) 335-5915. Fax: (705) 335-3508. E-mail: ckgnfm@nt.net. Licensee: Radio communautaire KapNord Inc. Format: Fr, var/div, adult contemp. News staff: 2. Target aud: General. Spec prog: Children 2 hrs, gospel one hrs wkly. ◆ Claude Chabot, gen mgr.

Kenora

CBQX-FM— Mar 28, 1978: 98.7 mhz; 38 kw. 213 Miles St. E., Thunder Bay P7C 1J5. Phone: (807) 625-5000/(416) 205-3700. Fax: (416) 205-3111. Web Site: www.nwo.cbc.ca. Licensee: CBC. Network: CBC Radio One. Format: Info. ◆ Kelly McInnes, gen mgr & stn mgr.

CJRL-FM— 2004: 89.5 mhz; 40 kw. TL: N49 46 45 W94 27 25. 128 Main St. S. P9N 1S9. Phone: (807) 468-3181. Fax: (807) 468-4188. E-mail: newsroom@895mix.fm. Licensee: Fawcett Broadcasting Ltd. Format: Hot adult contemp. Target aud: 25-54. Spec prog: Ukrainian one hr wkly. ◆ H.G. Fawcett, pres; Hugh Syrja, gen mgr.

Kettle Point

CKTI-FM— Apr 26, 2004: 107.7 mhz; 420 w. Points' Eagle Radio, R.R. 2, Forest N0N 1J0. Secondary address: 9111 W. Ipperwash Rd., Unit 6 N0N 1J0. Phone: (519) 786-3883. Fax: (519) 786-2834. E-mail: points_eagle_radio@hotmail.com. Web Site: www.angelfire.com/rock3/points_eagle_radio. Licensee: Point Eagle Radio Inc. Format: Country, classic rock. ◆ Connie George, opns dir.

Killaloe

CHCR-FM— 1998: 102.9 mhz; 33 w. Box 195 K0J 2A0. Secondary address: 7A Lake St., 2nd Fl. K0J 2A0. Phone: (613) 757-0657. Fax: (613) 757-0818. E-mail: stationmanager@chcr.org. Web Site: www.chcr.org. Licensee: Homegrown Community Radio. Format: Div. Spec prog: Canadian fiddle 8 hrs, Fr 8 hrs, Pol 1 hr, traditional bluegrass 6 hrs wkly. ◆ Daryl Andermann, gen mgr.

Kingston

CBBK-FM— May 21, 1979: 92.9 mhz; 1.6 kw. 395 ft. TL: N44 17 32 W76 28 50. Stereo. Box 500, Station A, Toronto M5W 1E6. Phone: (416) 205-3700. Fax: (416) 205-6063. Web Site: www.cbc.ca. Licensee: Canadian Broadcasting Corp. Network: CBC Radio Two. Format: Public radio. ◆ Robert Raeinobitch, CFO & progmg dir.

CFFX(AM)— Aug 31, 1942: 960 khz; 10 kw-D, 5 kw-N, DA-2. Stereo. 170 Queen St. K7K 1B2. Phone: (613) 549-1911. Fax: (613) 544-5508. Web Site: www.oldies960.com. Licensee: 591989 B.C. Ltd. Group owner: Corus Entertainment Inc. (acq 3-24-00; grpsl). Rep: CBS Radio. Format: Oldies. News staff: one; News: 3 hrs wkly. Target aud: 35-64; female. Spec prog: Toronto Blue Jays, Toronto Maple Leafs, Kingston Hockey. ◆ Mike Ferguson, VP & gen mgr; Jim Elyot, opns mgr & prom mgr.

CFMK-FM—Co-owned with CFFX(AM). Aug 31, 1942: 96.3 mhz; 14 kw. Ant 500 ft. Stereo. Phone: (613) 544-2340. Web Site: www.963joefm.com. Format: 80s based Gold. News staff: one; News: new progmg 2 hrs wkly. Target aud: 25-54. Co-owned TV: CKWS-TV affil.

CFLY-FM—Listing follows CKLC(AM).

*CFRC-FM— January 1953: 101.9 mhz; 3 kw. 295 ft. TL: N44 17 24 W77 25 55. Stereo. Queens Univ., Carruthers Hall K7L 3N6. Phone: (613) 533-2121. Fax: (613) 533-6049. E-mail: cfrc@ams.queensu.ca. Licensee: Radio Queen's University. Format: Div. News: 5 hrs wkly. Target aud: General. ◆ Stuart Mills, stn mgr.

CIKR-FM— Feb 19, 2001: 105.7 mhz; 24 kw. Stereo. 863 Princess, Suite 301 K7L 5N4. Phone: (613) 549-1057. Fax: (613) 549-5302. Web Site: www.krock1057.ca. Licensee: K-Rock 1057 Inc. Format: Rock. News staff: 2. Target aud: 18-44; adults. ◆ John P. Wright, pres & gen mgr.

CKLC(AM)— Nov 18, 1953: 1380 khz; 10 kw-U, DA-1. Stereo. Box 1380, 168 Wellington St. K7L 4Y5. Phone: (613) 544-1380. Fax: (613) 546-9751. E-mail: jrobb@kos.net. Licensee: Chum Radio Group. (acq 5-14-76). Format: All time favorites. News staff: 4; News: 3 hrs wkly. Target aud: 35-55. ◆ James Waters, pres; Gary Perrin, gen mgr & gen sls mgr; Greg Hinton, opns mgr & opns mgr; Kelly Spanton, sls dir & adv mgr; Renee Demers, prom dir, prom dir & prom mgr; Darcy Magee, progmg dir & progmg dir; Jacquie Beckett, mus dir & mus dir; Shauna Cunningham, news dir & news dir; Tony Orr, news dir; Terry Kelly, chief of engrg.

CFLY-FM—Co-owned with CKLC(AM). 1963: 98.3 mhz; 100 kw. 400 ft. Stereo. E-mail: flyfm@flyfmkingston.com. Web Site: www.flyfmkingston.com. Format: Adult contemp. News staff: 2; News: 5 hrs wkly. Target aud: 25-44.

CKVI-FM— 1997: 91.9 mhz; 6.5 w. 235 Frontenac St. K7L 3S7. Phone: (613) 544-7864. Fax: (613) 544-8795. E-mail: ckvi@limestone.on.ca. Web Site: www.thecave.ca. Licensee: KCVI Educational Radio Station Inc. Format: Div. ◆ Anthony Harty, stn mgr, progmg dir & chief of engrg.

Kirkland Lake

CJKL-FM— 1997: 101.5 mhz; 23 kw. Stereo. Box 430 P2N 3J4. Phone: (705) 567-3366. Fax: (705) 567-6101. E-mail: cjkl@cjklfm.com. Web Site: www.cjklfm.com. Licensee: Connelly Communications Corp. Rep: Canadian Broadcast Sales. Format: Adult contemp. News staff: 2. ◆ Ann Connelly, gen sls mgr; Rob Connelly, pres, stn mgr & progmg dir; Elesha Teskey, news dir; Don Eluidge, engrg dir.

Kitchener

CFCA-FM—Licensed to Kitchener. See Waterloo

CHYM-FM—Listing follows CKGL(AM).

CKGL(AM)— 1929: 570 khz; 10 kw-U, DA-1. 305 King St. W. N2G 4E4. Phone: (519) 743-2611. Fax: (519) 743-7510. Licensee: Rogers Broadcasting Ltd. Network: CBS. Format: News/talk. Target aud: 25-54. ◆ Gavin Tucker, gen mgr.

CHYM-FM— Co-owned with CKGL(AM). 1949: 96.7 mhz; 25 kw. 658 ft. (CP: 100 kw). Stereo. Format: Lite rock. ◆ Gavin Tucker, progmg dir; Neil Beaumont, mus dir; Mike McCabe, engrg mgr.

CKKW(AM)—Licensed to Kitchener. See Waterloo

CKWR-FM—Licensed to Kitchener. See Waterloo

Kitchener/Paris

CJIQ-FM— Jan 8, 2001: 88.3 mhz; 4 kw. Rm 3B15, Conestoga College, 299 Doon Valley Dr., Kitchener N2G 4M4. Phone: (519) 748-5220. E-mail: cjiqinfo@cjiq.fm. Web Site: www.cjiq.fm. Licensee: Conestoga College Communications Corp. Format: Div. ◆ Mark Burley, stn mgr.

Kitchener-Waterloo

CIKZ-FM— Feb 6, 2004: 106.7 mhz; 1.7 kw. Ant 657 ft. 490 Dutton Dr., Unit C2, Waterloo N2L 6H7. Phone: (519) 746-3331. Fax: (519) 746-3364. E-mail: plarche@kicxfm.com. Web Site: www.kicx995fm.com. Licensee: Larche Communications Inc. Format: New country. ◆ Paul Larche, pres & gen mgr; Jordan Cooledge, gen sls mgr; Ron Funnell, gen sls mgr; Derm Carnduff, progmg dir.

CJTW-FM— February 2004: 94.3 mhz; 50 w. Stereo. Faith FM, Box 1433, Stn C, Unit 202, Kitchener N2G 4H6. Secondary address: 659 King St. E., Kitchener N2G 2M4. Phone: (519) 575-9090. Fax: (519) 575-9119. E-mail: info@faithfm.org. Web Site: www.faithfm.org. Licensee: Sound of Faith Broadcasting. Format: Christian. ◆ Robert Reid, pres; Dave MacDonald, gen mgr; Brad Loveday, progmg dir.

CKBT-FM— January 2004: 91.5 mhz; 3.6 kw. Stereo. 235 King St. E., Kitchener N2G 4N5. Phone: (519) 741-9915. Fax: (519) 568-6390.

Directory of Radio   Ontario

Web Site: www.915thebeat.com. Licensee: Global Communications Ltd. Group owner: CanWest Global Communications Corp. Format: Rhythmic CHR. Target aud: 18-34. ♦ David Jones, gen mgr; Sandra Henein, prom mgr; Ed Ringward, sls; Mike Blake, sls.

Leamington

CHYR-FM— Aug 23, 1993: 96.7 mhz; 19.32 kw. 100 Talbot St. E. N8H 1L3. Phone: (519) 326-6171. Fax: (519) 322-1110. E-mail: 96.7@chyr.com. Web Site: www.chyr.com. Licensee: Blackburn Radio Inc. Group owner: Blackburn Group Inc. (acq 12-19-94; grpsl). Rep: Integrated Media Sales. Format: Hot adult contemp. Target aud: 25-54. Spec prog: lt 3 hrs, relg 3 hrs wkly. ♦ Terry Regier, gen mgr; Cordell Green, progmg dir; Kevin Black, news dir; Tim O'Neil, gen sls mgr, sls & adv.

Lindsay (city of Kawartha Lakes)

CKLY-FM— May 16, 1998: 91.9 mhz; 5.27 kw. 249 Kent St. W., Lindsay K9V 2Z3. Phone: (705) 324-9103. Fax: (705) 324-4149. E-mail: y92@y92.net. Web Site: www.chumlimited.com. Licensee: CHUM Ltd. (group owner; acq 12-21-00; C$800,000). Rep: Canadian Broadcast Sales. Format: Adult contemp. News staff: 2; News: 14 hrs wkly. Target aud: 30-65. ♦ Rick Ringer, opns mgr; Dave Illman, progmg dir; Steve Fawcett, gen mgr, gen sls mgr & engrg mgr.

Little Current

CFRM-FM— 2002: 101.1 mhz; 5 w. Stereo. 10 Campbell St. E. P0P 1K0. Phone: (705) 368-1419. Fax: (705) 368-1080. E-mail: radio@manitoulin.net. Web Site: www.101rocks.com. Licensee: Manitoulin Radio Communication Inc. Format: Classic rock. News staff: 2. Target aud: General; baby boomer. Spec prog: Blues 2 hrs, country 5 hrs, gospel 2 hrs wkly. ♦ Craig Timmermans, CEO & pres; Rick Nelson, stn mgr; Sam Nardi, opns VP; Bob Clark, news dir.

London

CBBL-FM— Oct 1, 1978: 100.5 mhz; 22.5 kw. TL: N42 57 20 W81 21 20. Stereo. Box 500, Station A, Toronto M5W 1E6. Phone: (416) 205-3700. Fax: (416) 205-6063. Web Site: www.cbc.ca. Licensee: Canadian Broadcasting Corp. Network: CBC Radio Two. Format: Public radio. ♦ Robert Raeinobitch, CFO & chief of engrg.

CBCL-FM— June 1998: 93.5 mhz; 69.3 kw. 208 Piccadilly St., Unit 4 N6A 1S1. Phone: (519) 667-1990. Fax: (519) 667-1557. Web Site: www.cbc.ca. Licensee: Canadian Broadcasting Corp. Network: CBC Radio One. Format: Public radio. Spec prog: News 10 hrs wkly. ♦ Robert Raeinobitch, CFO & gen mgr.

CFHK-FM—See St. Thomas

CFPL(AM)— September 1922: 980 khz; 10 kw-D, 5 kw-N, DA-2. TL: N42 53 29 W81 12 02. Stereo. 380 Wellington St., Rm. 222 N6A 5B5. Phone: (519) 931-6000. Fax: (519) 667-4623. Fax: (519) 438-2415. Web Site: www.am980.net. Licensee: Corus Radio Co. Group owner: Corus Entertainment Inc. Format: Sports, adult contemp, news/talk. News staff: 8; News: 10 hrs wkly. Target aud: 35-54. ♦ Dean Sinclair, gen mgr; Bob Fisher, sls dir, gen sls mgr & prom dir; Rick Jackiw, rgnl sls mgr; Gord Harris, progmg dir & news dir; Andy Bingle, engrg dir.

CFPL-FM— 1948: 95.9 mhz; 179 kw. 885 ft. TL: N42 57 15 W81 15 58. Stereo. Phone: (519) 433-3696. Web Site: www.fm96.com. Format: New rock. Target aud: 25-49.

CHJX-FM— 2003: 105.9 mhz; 10 w. 100 Fullarton St. N6A 1K1. Phone: (519) 679-9882. Fax: (519) 679-2459. E-mail: gracefm_administration@skynet.ca. Web Site: www.gracefm.ca. Licensee: Sound of Faith Broadcasting. Format: Contemp Christian music. ♦ Doug Chaplin, gen mgr.

*CHRW-FM— Oct 31, 1981: 94.9 mhz; 3.5 kw. Ant 128 ft. TL: N43 00 30 W81 16 36. 250 Univ. Community Ctr., Univ. of Western Ontario, Room 250 N6A 3K7. Phone: (519) 661-3601. Fax: (519) 661-3372. E-mail: chrwgm@uwo.ca. Web Site: www.chrwradiio.com. Licensee: Radio Western Inc. Format: Alternative, multicultural, jazz,blues,metal. News staff: one; News: 5 hrs wkly. ♦ Grant Stein, stn mgr & progmg VP; Alicks Girowski, prom dir & mus dir; Zoltan Harasztyn, adv mgr & progmg.

CHST-FM— Sept 1, 2000: 102.3 mhz; 4.77 kw. Stereo. 102.3 Bob FM, 1 Communication Rd. N6A 6E9. Phone: (519) 690-0102. Fax: (519) 686-5942. Web Site: www.1023bob.com. Licensee: CHUM Ltd. (group owner) Format: Classic hits. News staff: one; News: one hr wkly. ♦ Jay Switzer, CEO; Jim Blundell, gen mgr; Ann LaRocque, gen sls mgr; Al Smith, progmg dir. Co-owned TV: CFPL-TV.

CIQM-FM— June 1, 1986: 97.5 mhz; 50 kw. 300 ft. Stereo. 743 Wellington Rd. S. N6C 4R5. Phone: (519) 686-2525. Fax: (519) 686-3658. Web Site: www.q975.com. Licensee: Standard Radio Inc. Group owner: Standard Broadcasting Corp. (acq 4-19-02; grpsl). Format: Adult contemp. Target aud: 25-54; female. ♦ Gary Slaight, CEO; Braden Doerr, exec VP, VP & gen mgr; Barry Smith, opns mgr & progmg dir.

*CIXX-FM— Oct 31, 1978: 106.9 mhz; 3 kw. Ant 150 ft. Stereo. 1460 Oxford St. E. N5V 1W2. Phone: (519) 453-2810. Fax: (519) 453-2250. E-mail: mstoparczyk@1069fm.ca. Web Site: www.1069fm.ca. Licensee: Radio Fanshawe Inc. Format: Urban contemp. News staff: 2. Target aud: 12-34; primarily college, univ, high school. Spec prog: Christian 3 hrs, educ 4 hrs hrs wkly. ♦ Steve Andruiak, gen mgr; Barry Sutherland, opns mgr, gen sls mgr & prom mgr.

CJBC-FM-4— Sept 3, 1978: 99.3 mhz; 22.5 kw. 91 ft. TL: N42 57 20 W81 21 20. Box 500, Stn A, Toronto M5W 1E6. Phone: (416) 205-3311. Fax: (416) 205-7795. Web Site: www.torontocbc.ca. Licensee: Canadian Broadcasting Corp. Network: Premiere Chaine. Format: Div, Fr. ♦ Claire Margetti, gen mgr & progmg dir.

CJBK(AM)— Jan 25, 1967: 1290 khz; 10 kw-U, DA-2. TL: N42 52 08 W81 13 58. Stereo. 743 Wellington Rd. S. N6C 4R5. Phone: (519) 686-2525. Fax: (519) 686-3658. Fax: (519) 686-1156. Web Site: www.cjbk.com. Licensee: Standard Radio Inc. Group owner: Standard Broadcasting Corp. (acq 4-19-00; grpsl). Format: News/talk. News staff: 4. Target aud: 35-54. ♦ Gary Slaight, CEO; Braden Doerr, pres & gen mgr.

CJBX-FM—Co-owned with CJBK(AM). Mar 3, 1980: 92.7 mhz; 50 kw. 400 ft. Stereo. Web Site: www.bx93.com. Format: Country.

CKSL(AM)— June 1956: 1410 khz; 10 kw-U, DA-2. Stereo. 743 Wellington Rd. S. N6C4R5. Phone: (519) 686-2525. Fax: (519) 686-3658. E-mail: comments@oldies1410.com. Web Site: www.oldies1410.com. Licensee: Standard Radio Inc. Group owner: Standard Broadcasting Corp. (acq 4-19-02; grpsl). Rep: Integrated Media Sales. Format: Oldies. News staff: one; News: 1 hr wkly. Target aud: 35-54; Adults 35-54. ♦ Gary Slaight, CEO; Braden Doerr, gen mgr; Barry Smith, opns mgr; Dan MacGillivray, gen sls mgr.

Marathon

CFNO-FM— July 17, 1982: 93.1 mhz; 50 kw. 879 ft. Stereo. Box 1000 P0T 2E0. Secondary address: 93 Evergreen Dr. P0T 2E0. Phone: (807) 229-1010. Fax: (807) 229-1686. E-mail: sales@cfno.fm. Licensee: North Superior Broadcasting Ltd. (acq 1982). Format: Adult contemp. Spec prog: C&W 12 hrs wkly.

Midland

CICZ-FM— September 1993: 104.1 mhz; 9.354 kw. Box 609, 355 Cranston Crescent L4R 4L3. Phone: (705) 526-2268. Fax: (705) 526-3060. E-mail: plarche@kicxfm.com. Web Site: www.kicx104fm.com. Licensee: Larche Communications Inc. Format: New country. ♦ Mora Austin, gen mgr & gen sls mgr; Paul Larche, pres & gen mgr; Drem Carnduff, progmg dir; Glen Prinz, chief of engrg.

Mississauga

CJMR(AM)— June 17, 1974: 1320 khz; 20 kw-U. (Digital radio: 1466.768 mhz; 5.084 kw). Broadcasting Ctr., 284 Church St., Oakville L6J 7N2. Phone: (905) 845-2821. Fax: (905) 271-1320. Fax: (905) 842-1250. E-mail: hmcdonald@whiteoaksgroup.ca. Licensee: Trafalgar Broadcasting Ltd. Rep: Target Broadcast Sales. Format: Ethnic. ♦ Harry McDonald, sls VP & sls dir; Michael Caine, pres, gen mgr & progmg dir.

Moosonee

*CHMO(AM)— Feb 29, 1976: 1450 khz; 50 w. TL: N51 16 39 W80 38 40. Box 400 P0L 1Y0. Secondary address: 38 First St. P0L 1Y0. Phone: (705) 336-2466. Fax: (705) 336-2186. Licensee: James Bay Broadcasting Corp. Format: Div, country. News staff: one; News: 10 hrs progm wkly. Target aud: General. Spec prog: Cree Indian. ♦ John Kirk, pres; Ernest Hunter, stn mgr; Ron Spencer, prom mgr & progmg dir; Jack Williams, mus dir; George Witham, chief of engrg.

New Liskeard

CJTT-FM— June 26, 1998: 104.5 mhz; 10 kw. PO Box 1058 P0J 1P0. Secondary address: 55 Whitewood Ave. P0J 1P0. Phone: (705) 647-7334. Fax: (705) 647-8660. E-mail: cjtt@nt.net. Licensee: Connelly Communications Corp. (acq 9-79). Format: Mix. News staff: one. ♦ Gail Moore, gen mgr.

Newmarket

CKDX-FM— September 1994: 88.5 mhz; 11.3 kw. 5302 Dundas St. W., Etobicoke M9B 1B2. Phone: (416) 213-1035. Fax: (416) 233-8617. E-mail: rebecca@foxy885.com. Web Site: www.foxy885.com. Licensee: CKDX Radio Ltd. Group owner: Evanov Radio Group (acq 12-21-2000). Format: Adult favorites. ♦ Bill Evanov, pres; Don Currie, gen mgr; Rebecca Shay, prom mgr, progmg dir & sls.

Niagara Falls

CFLZ-FM— 1996: 105.1 mhz; 7.2 kw. Box 710 L2E 6X7. Secondary address: 4668 St. Clair Ave. L2E 6X7. Phone: (905) 356-6710. Fax: (905) 356-0696. E-mail: robwhite@niagara.com. Web Site: www.river.fm. Licensee: 788813 Ontario Inc. Rep: Canadian Broadcast Sales. Format: Modern adult contemp. News staff: 3; News: 5 hrs wkly. ♦ David J. Dancy, pres & gen sls mgr; Elizabeth Lewis, gen mgr; Robert White, progmg dir.

North Bay

CHUR-FM— 1996: 100.5 mhz; 100 kw. Stereo. Box 3000 P1B 8K8. Phone: (705) 474-2000. Fax: (705) 474-7761. Web Site: www.ezrocknorthbay.com. Licensee: Rogers Broadcasting Ltd. (group owner; acq 4-19-2002; grpsl). Rep: Integrated Media Sales. Format: Adult contemp, soft rock. Target aud: 25-54. ♦ Ted Rogers, CEO & pres; Peter Mckeown, gen mgr & stn mgr.

CKAT(AM)— Mar 3, 1931: 600 khz; 10 kw-D, 5 kw-N, DA-1. Box 3000 P1B 8K8. Phone: (705) 474-2000. Fax: (705) 474-7761. Licensee: Rogers Broadcasting Ltd. (group owner; acq 4-19-02; grpsl). Format: Country. News staff: 5; News: 6 hrs wkly. Target aud: 25-54. ♦ Rick Doughty, gen mgr; James Dahlke, gen sls mgr; Peter McKeown, prom dir; Dean Belanger, asst music dir; Clint Thomas, news dir; Csaba Senyi, engrg dir.

CKFX-FM—Co-owned with CKAT(AM). Jan 19, 1967: 101.9 mhz; 100 kw. Ant 350 ft. Stereo. Format: Rock. ♦ Kevin Ochefski, prom dir; Mike Belanger, progmg dir.

North York

CILQ-FM—Licensed to North York. See Toronto

Oakville

CJYE(AM)— Nov 17, 1956: 1250 khz; 10 kw-D, 5 kw-N, DA-2. Broadcasting Ctr., 284 Church St. L6J 7N2. Phone: (905) 845-2821. Phone: (905) 271-1320. Fax: (905) 842-1250. E-mail: dmillar@joy1250.ca. Web Site: www.christianradio.ca/station/cjye. Licensee: Trafalgar Broadcasting Ltd. Format: Contemp Christian music. ♦ Harry H. McDonald, sr VP; Michael Caine, pres & gen mgr.

Ohsweken

*CKRZ-FM— 1991: 100.3 mhz; 250 w. Stereo. Box 189 N0A 1M0. Phone: (519) 445-4140. Fax: (519) 445-0177. E-mail: sonics@bellnet.ca. Licensee: Southern Onkwehon: We Nishinabec Indigenous Communications Society. Format: Div, country, classic contemp rock. News staff: one; News: 4.5 hrs wkly. Target aud: General.

Orangeville

CIDC-FM— May 1, 1987: 103.5 mhz; 30.7 kw. Stereo. 5302 Dundas St., W., Etobicoke M9B 1B2. Phone: (416) 213-1035. Fax: (416) 233-8617. E-mail: info@z1035.com. Web Site: www.z1035.com. Licensee: Dufferin Communications Inc. Group owner: Evanov Radio Group (acq 9-28-94). Rep: Canadian Broadcast Sales. Format: Dance, Top-40. News staff: one. Target aud: 18-44. ♦ Bill Evanov, pres; Don Currie, gen mgr; Paul Evanov, progmg dir.

Ontario

Orillia

CICX-FM— Sept 7, 1943: 105.9 mhz; 43 kw. Stereo. 7 Progress Dr., Box 550 L3V 6K2. Phone: (705) 326-3511. Fax: (705) 326-1816. E-mail: jack@1059jackfm.com. Web Site: www.1059jackfm.com. Licensee: Rogers Broadcasting Ltd. (group owner; acq 4-19-02; grpsl). Format: Hot adult contemp. News staff: 2; News: 2 hrs wkly. Target aud: 25-54; upscale, educated, white collar, female skewed. ♦ Gary Miles, CEO; Rael Merson, pres; Rick Doughty, gen mgr; Jack Latimer, progmg dir.

Oshawa

CKDO(AM)— 1946: 1350 khz; 10 kw-D, 5 kw-N, DA-2. Stereo. 1200 Airport Blvd., Suite 207 L1J 8P5. Phone: (905) 571-0949. Fax: (905) 571-1150. Licensee: Durham Radio Inc. (group owner; (acq 4-23-03; C$3.9 million. with co-located FM). Format: Golden oldies. News staff: 4; News: 9 hrs wkly. Target aud: 35-54. Spec prog: Relg one hr wkly. ♦ Doug Freeman, gen mgr.

CKGE-FM— Co-owned with CKDO(AM). Sept 12, 1957: 94.9 mhz; 50 kw. 474 ft. TL: N43 57 15 W78 48 24. Stereo. Format: Classic rock, news. News staff: 4; News: 5 hrs wkly. Target aud: 45 plus.

Ottawa

*CBOF-FM— Sept 12, 1974: 90.7 mhz; (Digital radio: 1482.464 mhz). Stereo. Box 3220, Station C K1Y 1E4. Phone: (613) 724-1200. Phone: (613) 562-8521. Fax: (613) 562-8520. Web Site: www.cbc.radio-canada.ca/regions/ottawa. Licensee: Societe Radio-Canada. Network: Radio Canada. Format: Var/div. ♦ Jean-Francois Rioux, gen mgr.

*CBO-FM— Jan 7, 1991: 91.5 mhz; 20 kw. (Digital radio: 1482.464 mhz). Box 3220, Station C K1Y 1E4. Secondary address: Ottawa Broadcast Centre, 181 Queen St. K1P 1K9. Phone: (613) 724-1200. Phone: (613) 562-8422. Fax: (613) 562-8430. Fax: (613) 562-8408. Web Site: www.ottawa.cbc.ca. Licensee: CBC. Network: CBC Radio One. Format: Var/div. ♦ Guylaine Saucier, chmn; Robert Rabinovitch, CEO & pres; Miriam Fry, gen mgr; Gilles R. Tessier, opns dir.

*CBOQ-FM— Feb 18, 1947: 103.3 mhz; 70 kw. (Digital radio: 1482.464 mhz). Stereo. Box 3220, Station C K1Y 1E4. Phone: (613) 724-1200. Phone: (613) 562-8422. Fax: (613) 562-8430. Fax: (613) 562-8408. Web Site: www.ottawa.cbc.ca. Licensee: CBC. Network: CBC Radio Two. Format: Div. class. ♦ Robert Rabinovitch, CEO & pres; Miriam Fry, gen mgr; Gilles R. Tessier, opns dir.

*CBOX-FM— 1990: 102.5 mhz; 70 kw. Ant 1,077 ft. (Digital radio: 1482.464 mhz). Stereo. Box 3220, Station C K1Y 1E4. Phone: (613) 724-1200. Phone: (613) 562-8521. Fax: (613) 562-8520. Web Site: www.radio-canada.ca/regions/ottawa. Licensee: Societe Radio-Canada. Network: Radio Canada. Format: Div, class. ♦ Jean-Francois Rioux, gen mgr.

CFGO(AM)— June 7, 1964: 1200 khz; 50 kw-U, DA-2. (Digital radio: 1487.696 mhz). Stereo. Team 1200, 87 George St. K1N 9H7. Phone: (613) 789-2486. Fax: (613) 738-2881. Web Site: www.team1200.com. Licensee: CHUM (Ottawa) Ltd. Group owner: CHUM Ltd. (acq 9-10-99; for 87.5%). Format: Sports, talk. News staff: 5. Target aud: 18-34; men. ♦ Allan Waters, CEO; Jim Waters, VP; Chris Gordon, opns mgr & progmg dir; Don Holtby, sls VP; Mark Maheu, gen mgr & gen sls mgr; Brad Boechler, natl sls dir; Al Macartney, mktg dir; J. R. Ello, prom dir & prom mgr; John Brenner, news dir; Harrie Jones, engrg dir & chief of engrg.

CJMJ-FM— Co-owned with CFGO(AM). Aug 13, 1991: 100.3 mhz; 100 kw. (Digital radio: 1487.696 mhz). Stereo. Fax: (613) 750-0100. Web Site: www.majic100.fm. Format: Adult contemp, oldies. Target aud: 25-44; female. ♦ Brad Boechler, rgnl sls mgr; Jack Derouin, rgnl sls mgr; Craig Heward, prom mgr; Kent Newson, progmg mgr; Codi Jeffreys, mus dir.

CFRA(AM)— May 3, 1947: 580 khz; 50 kw-D, 10 kw-N, DA-2. (Digital radio: 1487.696 mhz). 87 George St. K1N 9H7. Phone: (613) 789-2486. Fax: (613) 523-6423. Fax: (613) 738-5024. Web Site: www.cfra.com. Licensee: CHUM Ltd. (group owner). Network: ABC. Format: News/talk. News: 24 hrs wkly. Target aud: 35-54. ♦ Jim Waters, pres; Don Holtby, VP & sls dir; Chris Gordon, opns mgr; Brad Boechler, rgnl sls mgr; Jack Derouin, rgnl sls mgr; Al Macartney, mktg dir; Craig Heward, prom mgr; Dave Mitchell, progmg dir; John Brenner, news dir; Linda Ulmer, pub affrs dir; Harrie Jones, engrg mgr & chief of engrg.

CKKL-FM— Co-owned with CFRA(AM). 1959: 93.9 mhz; 95 kw. Ant 1,077 ft. (Digital radio: 1487.696 mhz). Stereo. Phone: (613) 526-9393. Fax: (613) 739-4040. Web Site: www.939bobfm.com. Network: ABC. Format: Hits of the 80s & 90s. News staff: 2; News: one hr wkly. Target aud: 18-34. ♦ Don Holtby, sls VP; JR Ello, prom dir; Chris Gordon, progmg dir; Jay Lawrence, mus dir & asst music dir; Harrie Jones, engrg mgr.

CHEZ-FM— Mar 25, 1977: 106.1 mhz; 100 kw. Ant 998 ft. (Digital radio: 1484.208 mhz). Stereo. 2001 Thurston Dr. K1G 6C9. Phone: (613) 736-2001. Fax: (613) 736-2002. Web Site: www.chez106.com. Licensee: Rogers Broadcasting Ltd. (acq 7-2-99; grpsl). Format: Classic rock. News staff: 3; News: 2 hrs wkly. Target aud: 25-54; Males. ♦ Scott Parsons, chmn, pres, VP & gen mgr.

CHLX-FM— See Gatineau, PQ

CHRI-FM— Mar 6, 1997: 99.1 mhz; 25.3 kw. 551 ft. TL: N45 13 01 W75 37 51. Stereo. 1010 Thomas Spratt Pl., Suite 3 K1G 5L5. Phone: (613) 247-1440. Phone: (613) 247-7128. Fax: (613) 247-7128. E-mail: chri@chri.ca. Web Site: www.chri.ca. Licensee: Christian Hit Radio Inc. Format: Contemp Christian mus. News staff: one; News: 2 hrs wkly. Target aud: 18-44; Christians. Spec prog: Children 2 hrs wkly. ♦ Gerry Turcotte, pres; Robert Du Broy, gen mgr; Charles Shefler, gen sls mgr.

*CHUO-FM— May 31, 1991: 89.1 mhz; 18.2 kw. TL: N45 30 11 W75 51 02. Stereo. 372 Rideau St., Suite 201 K1N 1G7. Phone: (613) 562-5965. Fax: (613) 562-5969. E-mail: info@chuo.fm. Web Site: www.chuo.fm. Licensee: Radio Ottawa Inc. Format: English/French. Target aud: General. Spec prog: Ger 2 hrs, jazz 5 hrs, relg 2 hrs, Sp 3 hrs, Chinese 2 hrs, Haitian 2 hrs, African 4 hrs wkly.

CIHT-FM— February 2003: 89.9 mhz; 27 kw. 1504 Merivale Rd. K2E 6Z5. Phone: (613) 723-8990. Fax: (613) 723-7016. Web Site: www.hot899.com. Licensee: NewCap Inc. Group owner: NewCap Broadcasting Ltd. Format: CHR, Top-40. ♦ Eric Stafford, VP; Eric Stafford, gen mgr; Rob Mise, stn mgr.

CIMF-FM— See Gatineau, PQ

CISS-FM— Listing follows CIWW(AM).

CIWW(AM)— June 1, 1949: 1310 khz; 50 kw-U, DA-2. (Digital radio: 1484.208 mhz). 2001 Thurston Dr. K1G 6C9. Phone: (613) 736-2001. Fax: (613) 736-2002. Web Site: www.oldies1310.com. Licensee: Rogers Media. Format: Oldies. ♦ Scott Anderson, gen mgr.

CISS-FM— Co-owned with CIWW(AM). Oct 29, 1969: 105.3 mhz; 100 kw. Ant 1,077 ft. (Digital radio: 1484.208 mhz). Stereo. Web Site: www.1053kissfm.com. Format: Adult contemp, top-40. ♦ Al Campagnola, progmg dir.

CJLL-FM— 2003: 97.9 mhz; 6.77 kw. CHIN Radio Ottawa, 30 Murray St., Suite 100 K1N 5M4. Phone: (613) 244-0979. Fax: (613) 244-3858. E-mail: chinottawa@chinradio.com. Web Site: www.chinradio.com/ottawa.asp. Licensee: Radio 1540 Ltd. Format: Ethnic. ♦ Edward Ylanen, gen mgr; Ed Ylanen, gen sls mgr; Gary Michaels, progmg dir.

CJRC(AM)— (Gatineau).PQ June 3, 1968: 1150 khz; 50 kw-D, 5 kw-N, DA-2. (Digital radio: 1463.280 mhz). 150, rue d'Edmonton, Gatineau, PQ J8y 3s6. Phone: (819) 561-8801. Fax: (819) 561-9439. E-mail: nouvelles@cjrc1150.com. Web Site: www.cjrc1150.com. Licensee: 591991 B.C. Ltd. Group owner: Astral Media. Inc. (acq 1-21-2005; grpsl). Network: Radiomedia. Format: News/talk. News staff: 3; News: 49 hrs wkly. Target aud: 35-64; Adults-Babyboomers 50% males %0% females. ♦ Kathleen Michaud, sls dir; Sylvie Charette, gen mgr & progmg dir; Louis-Philippe Brule, news dir.

CKCU-FM— Nov 15, 1975: 93.1 mhz; 12 kw. 853 ft. TL: N45 30 11 W75 51 02. Stereo. 517 Unicentre, 1125 Colonel By Dr. K1S 5B6. Phone: (613) 520-2898. Fax: (613) 520-4060. E-mail: info@ckcufm.com. Web Site: www.ckcufm.com. Licensee: Radio Carleton Inc. Format: Progsv, div, community, campus. News staff: 2; News: 25 hrs wkly. Target aud: General; alternative music, spoken word, ethnic audience. Spec prog: Jazz 15 hrs, Black 12 hrs, Fr 2 hrs, Pol one hr, Vietnamese one hr, Canadian Indian 2 hrs, folk 12 hrs, It 1 hr, relg 3 hrs wkly. ♦ Matthew Crosier, stn mgr.

*CKDJ-FM— Oct 3, 1994: 107.9 mhz; 100 w. 1385 Woodroffe Ave., Algonquin College, Rm. N 101 K2G 1V8. Phone: (613) 727-4723, ext. 7740. Fax: (613) 727-7689. Web Site: www.ckdj.net. Licensee: CKDJ-FM Algonquin Radio. Format: Hip Hop / Alternative. Target aud: 17-24; collegel students. ♦ Don Crockford, gen mgr; Ryan Lindsay, stn mgr.

CKQB-FM— Sept 1, 1994: 106.9 mhz; 84 kw. (Digital radio: 1487.696 mhz). Stereo. 1504 Merivale Rd. K2E 6Z5. Phone: (613) 225-1069. Fax: (613) 226-3381. E-mail: bearinfo@thebear.net. Web Site: www.thebear.fm. Licensee: Standard Radio Inc. Network: Telemedia. Format: Mainstream Rock. News staff: 3; News: one hr wkly. Target aud: 18-34; professionals. ♦ Gary Slaight, pres; Eric Stafford, VP & gen mgr; Scott Broderick, gen sls mgr; Gord Taylor, progmg dir.

Owen Sound

CFOS(AM)— Mar 1, 1940: 560 khz; 7.5 kw-D, 1 kw-N. TL: N44 32 40 W80 54 08. Box 280 N4K 5P5. Phone: (519) 376-2030. Fax: (519) 371-4242. E-mail: bayshore@radioowensound.com. Web Site: www.radioowensound.com. Licensee: Bayshore Broadcasting Corp. Format: News/talk, oldies. News staff: 7; News: 12 hrs wkly. ♦ Jamie Petit, gen mgr, prom dir & progmg dir; Rob Brignell, dev dir & mktg dir; Deb Shaw, gen sls mgr; Robin Woods, mus dir; Manny Paiva, news dir.

CIXK-FM— Co-owned with CFOS(AM). Jan 3, 1989: 106.5 mhz; 100 kw. 555 ft. TL: N44 44 37 W80 54 16. Stereo. Web Site: www.radioowensound.com. Format: Today's hits, yesterday's classics. News staff: 7. Target aud: 18-40. ♦ J.D. Moffat, prom dir & progmg dir; Don Vail, mus dir.

CKYC-FM— Sept 4, 2001: 93.7 mhz; 31.6 kw. 270 9th St. E. N4K 5P5. Phone: (519) 376-2030. Fax: (519) 371-4242. E-mail: timblack@bmts.com. Web Site: www.radioowensound.com. Licensee: Bayshore Broadcasting Corp. Format: New country. Target aud: 25-54; adult. ♦ Ross Kentner, gen mgr.

Parry Sound

CKLP-FM— July 1986: 103.3 mhz; 50 kw. 400 ft. (CP: 46.6 kw.). Stereo. 60 James St., Suite 301 P2A 1T5. Phone: (705) 746-2163. Fax: (705) 746-4292. E-mail: moose1033@hbgradio.com. Web Site: www.moosefm.com/cklp. Licensee: The Haliburton Broadcasting Group Inc. Group owner: Haliburton Broadcasting Group Inc. (acq 11-9-01; C$2,025,000). Rep: Target Broadcast Sales. Format: Adult contemp. News staff: 2; News: 12 hrs wkly. Target aud: General. Spec prog: Canadian Indian 1 hr, Gospel 1 hr wkly. ♦ Christopher Grossman, pres; Dave Keeble, stn mgr; Kimberly Ward-Grossman, opns VP.

Pembroke

CHVR-FM— May 6, 1996: 96.7 mhz; 100 kw. Stereo. 595 Pembroke St. E. K8A 3L7. Phone: (613) 735-9670. Fax: (613) 735-7748. E-mail: music@star96.ca. Web Site: www.star96.ca. Licensee: Standard Radio Inc. Group owner: Standard Broadcasting Corp. (acq 4-19-02; grpsl). Format: Country. Target aud: 25-54. ♦ Al Kennedy, gen mgr & gen sls mgr; Rick Johnston, progmg dir.

Penetanguishene

*CFRH-FM— Sept 24, 1999: 88.1 mhz; 8.6 kw. TL: N44 46 10 W79 59 25. C.P. 5099 L9M 2G3. Secondary address: 63 rue Main L9M 2G3. Phone: (705) 549-3116. Fax: (705) 549-6463. E-mail: cfrh@lacle.ca. Web Site: www.lacle.ca. Licensee: La Cle d'la Baie en Huronie - Association culturelle francophone. (acq 2-17-99). Format: Fr. Target aud: Francophone; francophone minority in mid-southern Ontario. ♦ Michelle Laurin, opns VP & mktg VP; Peter Hominuk, CEO, gen mgr & sls dir.

Peterborough

*CFFF-FM— 1969: 92.7 mhz; 700 w. 715 George St., N. K9H 3T2. Phone: (705) 741-4011. E-mail: info@trentradio.ca. Web Site: www.trentu.ca/trentradio. Licensee: Trent Radio. Format: Div. Target aud: General. ♦ John Muir, gen mgr.

CKKK-FM— 2004: 99.5 mhz; 50 w. 80 Hunter St. K9H 1G5. Phone: (705) 876-0404. Fax: (705) 755-0688. E-mail: info@kaosradio.com. Web Site: www.kaosradio.com. Licensee: King's Kids Promotions Outreach Ministries Inc. Format: Christian music.

Directory of Radio   Ontario

CKPT(AM)— December 1959: 1420 khz; 10 kw-D, 5 kw-N, DA-2. TL: N44 16 13 W78 17 23. Box 177 K9J 6Y8. Phone: (705) 742-8844. Fax: (705) 742-1417. E-mail: radio@ckpt.com. Web Site: www.ckpt.com. Licensee: CKPT/CKQM Division of CHUM Ltd. Format: Memories. News staff: 2. Target aud: 25-54; 60% women. ♦Allan Waters, chmn; Jim Waters, pres; Taylor Baiden, CFO; Steve Fawcett, gen mgr; Ray Hebert, prom dir; Angela Rose, progmg dir; George Gall, news dir; Ed Crompton, engrg dir.

CKQM-FM—Co-owned with CKPT(AM). Sept 16, 1977: 105.1 mhz; 50 kw. 301 ft. TL: N44 17 36 W78 21 20. Stereo. E-mail: radio@ckgm.com. Web Site: www.country105.fm. Format: Country. Target aud: 25-64. ♦Brian Young, mus dir.

CKRU(AM)— Mar 21, 1942: 980 khz; 10 kw-D, 7.5 kw-D, DA-2. 159 King St. K9J 2R8. Phone: (705) 748-6101. Fax: (705) 742-7708. Web Site: www.980kruz.net. Licensee: 591989 B.C. Ltd. Group owner: Corus Entertainment Inc. (acq 3-24-00; grpsl). Format: Oldies. ♦Kathleen McNair, gen mgr; Brian Ellis, progmg dir.

CKWF-FM—Co-owned with CKRU(AM). July 24, 1968: 101.5 mhz; 15.2 kw. Ant 896 ft. Stereo. E-mail: info@thewolf.com. Web Site: www.thewolf.ca. Format: Classic rock.

Port Elgin

CFPS-FM— 2005: 97.9 mhz; 3.8 kw. Box 280, Owen Sound N4K 5P5. Phone: (519) 376-2030. Fax: (519) 371-4242. Web Site: www.98thebeach.ca. Licensee: Bayshore Broadcasting Corp. Format: Oldies. Target aud: 18-54. ♦Ross Kentner, gen mgr.

Port Hope

CKSG-FM—See Cobourg

Quinte West

CJTN-FM— 2004: 107.1 mhz; 3.64 kw. 31 Quinte St. K8V 3S7. Phone: (613) 392-1237. Fax: (613) 394-6430. E-mail: billmorton@mix97.com. Web Site: www.cjtn.com. Licensee: Quinte Broadcasting Co. Ltd. Format: Lite rock. Spec prog: Scottish one hr wkly. ♦Bill Morton, pres; Bob Rowbotham, gen mgr & gen sls mgr; Lorne Brooker, prom.

Red Lake

CKDR-5(AM)— Aug 1, 1981: 1340 khz; 250 w-U, DA-1. c/o CKDR, Box 580, Dryden P8N 2Z3. Phone: (807) 223-2355. Fax: (807) 223-5090. E-mail: mail@ckdr.net. Web Site: www.ckdr.net. Licensee: Fawcett Broadcasting Ltd. (group owner) Format: Contemp hits/top 40. ♦Bruce Walchuk, gen mgr.

Renfrew

CHMY-FM— August 2004: 96.1 mhz; 1.66 kw. Box 961 K7V 1R6. Secondary address: 321-B Raglan St. S. K7V 4H4. Phone: (613) 432-6936. Fax: (613) 432-1086. Web Site: www.myfmradio.ca. Licensee: Jon Pole & Andrew Dickson, on behalf of a corporation to be incorporated. Format: Adult contemp. ♦Andrew Dickson, gen mgr.

Saint Catharines

CFBU-FM— 1997: 103.7 mhz; 250 w. Stereo. % Brock University, 500 Glenridge Ave., St. Catharines L2S 3A1. Phone: (905) 688-5550, ext. 1-4909. Fax: (905) 641-7581. E-mail: pd@cfbu.ca. Web Site: www.cfbu.ca. Licensee: Brock University Student Radio. Format: Var. Spec prog: American Indian one hr, jazz 4 hrs, Sp 4 hrs, Por 2 hrs wkly. ♦Russell Gragg, stn mgr & opns mgr.

CHRE-FM— Mar 1, 1967: 105.7 mhz; 50 kw. 438 ft. Stereo. Box 610, 12 Yates St. L2R 6Z4. Phone: (905) 688-1057. Fax: (905) 684-4800. Web Site: www.1057ezrock.com. Licensee: Standard Radio Inc. Group owner: Standard Broadcasting Corp. (acq 4-19-02; grpsl). Format: Soft rock. News staff: 4. Target aud: 25-54. ♦Tom Cooke, gen mgr.

CHSC(AM)— Mar 20, 1967: 1220 khz; 10 kw-U, DA-2. 36 Queenston St. L2R 2Y9. Phone: (905) 682-6692. Fax: (905) 682-9434. E-mail: pssa@1220chsc.ca. Website: www.1220chsc.ca. Licensee: Pellpropco Inc. (acq 6-19-02; C$725,000). Rep: Canadian Broadcast Sales. Format: Adult contemp, news. Target aud: 25-54; female. ♦Domick Pellgrino, gen mgr.

CHTZ-FM—Listing follows CKTB(AM).

CKTB(AM)— 1930: 610 khz; 10 kw-D, 5 kw-N, DA-1. Box 977 L2R6Z4. Secondary address: 12 Yates St. L2R6X7. Phone: (905) 984-6610. Fax: (905) 684-4800. E-mail: newsroom@610cktb.com. Web Site: www.610cktb.com. Licensee: Standard Radio Inc. Group owner: Standard Broadcasting Corp. (acq 4-19-02; grpsl). Format: News/talk. Target aud: 35-65. ♦Tom Cook, gen mgr, opns VP & gen sls mgr; Joe Gurney, chief of engrg.

CHTZ-FM—Co-owned with CKTB(AM). February 1949: 97.7 mhz; 50 kw. 414 ft. Stereo. Box 977 L2R 6Z4. Phone: (905) 688-0977. Web Site: www.htzfm.com. Format: Rock/AOR.

Sarnia

CBEG-FM— Nov 27, 1977: 90.3 mhz; 50 kw. 375 ft. Box 500 Stn A, Toronto M5W 1E6. Phone: (519) 255-3411. Fax: (519) 255-3443. Web Site: www.windsor.cbc.ca. Licensee: CBC. Network: CBC Radio One. Format: Info. ♦Janice Stein, stn mgr.

CFGX-FM— Sept 14, 1981: 99.9 mhz; 27 kw. TL: N42 52 12 W82 23 50. Stereo. 1415 London Rd. N7S 1P6. Phone: (519) 542-5500. Fax: (519) 542-1520. Web Site: www.foxfm.com. Licensee: Blackburn Radio Inc. Group owner: Blackburn Group Inc. (acq 12-19-94; grpsl). Format: Adult contemp. Target aud: 25-54; females in the workplace. Spec prog: New age 7 hrs wkly. ♦Terry Regier, gen mgr; Ron Dann, opns mgr & mktg mgr; George Hayes, progmg dir; Larry Gordon, news dir.

CHKS-FM— 1999: 106.3 mhz; 35 kw. 1415 London Rd. N7S 1P6. Phone: (519) 542-5500. Fax: (519) 542-1520. E-mail: rock@k106fm.com. Web Site: www.k106fm.com. Licensee: Blackburn Radio Inc. Group owner: Blackburn Group Inc. Format: Rock. ♦Terry Regier, gen mgr; Ron Dann, opns mgr & mktg mgr; George Hayes, progmg dir; Larry Gordon, news dir.

CHOK(AM)— July 26, 1946: 1070 khz; 10 kw-U, DA-2. TL: N42 53 30 W82 19 20. Stereo. 1415 London Rd. N7S 1P6. Phone: (519) 542-5500. Fax: (519) 542-1520. E-mail: radio@chok.com. Web Site: www.chok.com. Licensee: Sarnia Broadcasters (1993) Ltd. Group owner: Blackburn Group Inc. (acq 12-18-98; C$902,600). Rep: Canadian Broadcast Sales. Format: Baby boomers classics. News staff: 3; News: 11 hrs wkly. Target aud: 25-54. Spec prog: Toronto Blue Jays baseball, Toronto Maple Leaf hockey, Jr. "A" Sting hockey. ♦Terry Regier, gen mgr; Ron Dann, opns mgr, sls dir & mktg mgr; Larry Gordon, prom dir & news dir; George Hays, progmg dir.

Sault Ste. Marie

CHAS-FM— May 15, 1964: 100.5 mhz; 13.9 kw. 103 ft. TL: N46 35 40 W84 21 00. Stereo. 642 Great Northern Rd. P6B 4Z9. Phone: (705) 759-9200. Fax: (705) 946-3575. Web Site: www.ezrocksoo.com. Licensee: Rogers Broadcasting Ltd. (group owner; acq 4-19-2002; grpsl). Format: Adult contemp. News staff: 3. Target aud: 25-54; adults. Spec prog: Class 5 hrs, jazz 2 hrs, lt 2 hrs wkly. ♦Derek Patterson, gen sls mgr; Lydia McNeice, prom dir; Scott Sexsmith, gen mgr & progmg dir; Craig Perdue, news dir; Harvey Parent, chief of engrg.

CJQM-FM— May 13, 1964: 104.3 mhz; 100 kw. Ant 1,000 ft. Stereo. 642 Great Northern Rd. P6B 4Z9. Phone: (705) 759-9200. Fax: (705) 946-3575. Web Site: www.qcountry.ca. Licensee: Rogers Broadcasting Ltd. (group owner; acq 4-19-2002; grpsl). Format: Country. News: 3 hrs wkly. Target aud: 25-54; adults. Spec prog: It 4 hrs wkly. ♦Derek Patterson, gen sls mgr; Lydia McNeice, prom dir; Scott Sexsmith, gen mgr & progmg dir; Craig Perdue, news dir; Harvey Parent, chief of engrg.

Savant Lake

CBQL-FM— January 1977: 104.9 mhz; 78 w. 287 ft. 213 Miles St. E., Thunder Bay P7C 1J5. Phone: (807) 625-5000. Phone: (416) 205-3700. Fax: (807) 625-5035. Fax: (416) 205-3311. Licensee: CBC. Network: CBC Radio One. Format: Info. ♦Tom Grand, stn mgr.

Simcoe

CHCD-FM— 1997: 98.9 mhz; 14.37 kw. Ant 500 Ft. Stereo. Box 98 N3Y 4K8. Secondary address: 55 Park Rd. N3Y 4K8. Phone: (519) 426-7700. Fax: (519) 426-8574. Web Site: www.cd989.com. Licensee: CHCD Inc. (acq 2-26-01; C$1.05 million). Rep: Canadian Broadcast

Sales. Format: Adult contemp. News staff: 3. Target aud: Women; 25-54. ♦Jim MacLeod, pres; Blair Daggett, gen mgr; Gerry Hamill, prom mgr; Kate Buick, news dir.

Sioux Narrows

CBQS-FM— May 1977: 95.7 mhz; 1.3 kw. 134 ft. c/o CBC Radio, 213 Miles St. E., Thunder Bay P7C 1J5. Phone: (807) 625-5000, EXT. 5021. Fax: (807) 625-5035. Web Site: www.cbc.ca/ottowa. Licensee: CBC. Format: Public radio. Spec prog: Canadian Indian one hr wkly. ♦Tom Grand, gen mgr & stn mgr.

Smiths Falls

CJET-FM— November 2000: 92.3 mhz; 9.3 kw. Box 630 K7A 2B1. Phone: (613) 283-4630. Fax: (613) 283-7243. E-mail: webmaster@923jackfm.com. Web Site: www.923jackfm.com. Licensee: Rogers Broadcasting Ltd., on behalf of CHEZ-FM Inc. Format: Hits from 80s to present. ♦Scott Parsons, gen mgr.

CKBY-FM— Jan 29, 1969: 101.1 mhz; 100 kw. Ant 500 ft. Stereo. 2001 Thurston Dr, Ottawa K1G 6C9. Phone: (613) 736-2001. Fax: (613) 736-2002. Web site: www.y101.fm. Licensee: CHEZ-FM Inc. Group owner: Rogers Broadcasting Ltd. (acq 7-2-99; grpsl). Format: Country. News staff: 2; News: 6 hrs wkly. Target aud: 35-54; female. ♦Scott Parsons, chmn, pres & gen mgr.

St. Thomas

CFHK-FM— July 8, 1994: 103.1 mhz; 50 kw. 492 ft. TL: N42 50 57 W81 08 52. Stereo. 380 Wellington St., Rm. 222, London N6A 5B5. Phone: (519) 931-6000. Fax: (519) 679-1967. E-mail: jeff@energy103.ca. Web Site: www.energy103.ca. Licensee: Corus Radio Co. Group owner: Corus Entertainment Inc. (acq 8-23-99; grpsl). Format: Top 40. Target aud: 18-39. ♦Dave Farough, gen mgr; Bob Fisher, gen sls mgr & natl sls mgr; Jim McCourtie, progmg dir & progmg mgr.

Stratford

CHGK-FM—Listing follows CJCS(AM).

CJCS(AM)— 1924: 1240 khz; 1 kw-U, DA-1. 376 Romeo St. S. N5A 4T9. Phone: (519) 271-2450. Fax: (519) 271-3102. Web site: www.cjcsradio.com. Licensee: Raedio Inc. Network: Telemedia. Format: Oldies. Target aud: 25-54. ♦Steve Rae, pres, gen mgr & sls dir; Jim Fewer, prom dir; Eddie Matthews, progmg mgr; Michael Stoparczyck, mus dir; Tanya McIntyre, news dir; Bill Tofflemire, chief of engrg.

CHGK-FM—Co-owned with CJCS(AM). Sept 2, 2003: 107.7 mhz; 2.805 kw. Format: Adult contemp.

Sturgeon Falls

CFSF-FM— Apr 4, 2003: 99.3 mhz; 1.35 kw. 12006 Hwy. 17, Unit 7 P2B 3K8. Phone: (705) 753-6776. Fax: (705) 753-6776. E-mail: jocorequest@yahoo.com. Web Site: www.joco.ca. Licensee: JOCO Communications Inc. Format: Top-40, adult contemp, Fr (20%). ♦Joseph Cormier, gen mgr.

Sudbury

CBBS-FM— Mar 29, 2001: 90.1 mhz; 50 kw. CBC Radio, 15 MacKenzie St. P3C 4Y1. Phone: (705) 688-3200. Fax: (705) 688-3220. Web Site: www.sudbury.cbc.ca. Licensee: Canadian Broadcasting Corp. Network: CBC Radio Two. Format: Classical jazz. ♦Kelly McInnes, gen mgr.

CBBX-FM— Mar 29, 2001: 90.9 mhz; 50 kw. c/o CBFX-FM, Box 6000, Montreal, PQ H3C 3A8. Phone: (514) 597-6000. E-mail: auditoire@radio-canada.ca. Web site: www.cbc.radio-canada.ca. Licensee: Canadian Broadcasting Corp. Network: Chaine Culturelle. Format: Var. ♦Sylvain LaFrance, VP.

*****CBCS-FM**— June 17, 1978: 99.9 mhz; 50 kw. 250 ft. 15 Mackenzie St. P3C 4Y1. Phone: (705) 688-3200. Fax: (705) 688-3220. Web Site: www.sudbury.cbc.ca. Licensee: Radio-Canada/CBC. Network: CBC Radio One. Format: Info, news/talk. News staff: 4; News: 3 hrs wkly. Target aud: 30 plus; College/university educated/professional. ♦Kelly McInnes, progmg mgr.

***CBON-FM**— June 19, 1978: 98.1 mhz; 50 kw. 800 ft. Stereo. 15 Mackenzie St. P3C 4Y1. Phone: (705) 688-3200. Fax: (705) 688-3220. Web Site: www.radio-canada.ca. Licensee: Radio-Canada/CBC. Network: CBC Radio One. Format: Var. ♦Guy Babineau, gen mgr.

CHNO-FM— February 2000: 103.9 mhz; 11 kw. 493-B Barrydowne Rd. P3A 3T4. Phone: (705) 560-8323. Fax: (705) 560-7765. E-mail: z103@z103fm.com. Web Site: www.z103fm.com. Licensee: NewCap Inc. Group owner: NewCap Broadcasting Ltd. (acq 11-9-01; C$2,843,000). Format: Top-40. News staff: one; News: 7 hrs wkly. Target aud: 35-64; middle-income. Spec prog: American Indian 1 hr wkly. ♦Mark Maheu, pres; Dave Murray, opns VP; Rick Tompkins, progmg dir.

CHYC-FM— 2000: 98.9 mhz; 1 kw. 493-B Barrydowne Rd. P3A 3T4. Phone: (705) 560-8323. Fax: (705) 560-2492. E-mail: sbncher@nbgradio.com. Web Site: www.chycfm.com. Licensee: The Haliburton Broadcasting Group Inc. Group owner: Haliburton Broadcasting Group Inc. Format: CHR, adult contemp. Target aud: General. ♦Christopher Grossman, pres & gen mgr.

CIGM(AM)— Aug 23, 1935: 790 khz; 50 kw-U, DA-2. 880 LaSalle Blvd. P3A 1X5. Phone: (705) 566-4480. Fax: (705) 560-7232. E-mail: cjohnson@rci.rogers.com. Web Site: www.wowsudbury.com/music/cigm.asp. Licensee: Rogers Broadcasting Ltd. (group owner; (acq 4-19-2002; grpsl). Format: New country. ♦Ted Rogers, pres; Rick Doughty, gen mgr; Gerry Currie, gen sls mgr; Gary Duguay, prom dir & prom mgr; Chris Johnson, progmg dir; Henri Belanger, chief of engrg.

CJRQ-FM—Co-owned with CIGM(AM). September 1965: 92.7 mhz; 100 kw. 889 ft. Stereo. Web Site: www.q92rocks.com. Format: Rock. ♦Bryan Bailey, mus dir.

CJMX-FM— 1980: 105.3 mhz; 100 kw. Ant 780 ft. TL: N46 30 02 W81 01 16. Stereo. 880 Lasalle Blvd. P3A 1X5. Phone: (705) 566-4480. Fax: (705) 560-7232. Web Site: www.ezrocksudbury.com. Licensee: Rogers Broadcasting Ltd. (group owner; (acq 4-19-2002; grpsl). Rep: Canadian Broadcast Sales. Format: Adult contemp, soft rock. News staff: 4; News: 1 hr wkly. Target aud: 25-49; working women. ♦Ted Rogers, pres; Rick Doughty, gen mgr.

CJTK-FM— 1998: 95.5 mhz; 1.4 kw. Stereo. 417 Notre Dame Ave. P3C 5K6. Phone: (705) 674-2585. Fax: (705) 688-1081. E-mail: mail@cjtk.com. Web Site: cjtk.com. Licensee: Eternacom Inc. Format: Relg, Christian. News staff: one; News: 2 hrs wkly. Target aud: General. ♦Curtis Belcher, CEO, chmn & pres; Louis Depatie, chief of opns.

***CKLU-FM**— Apr 30, 1997: 96.7 mhz; 1.3 kw. TL: N46 25 29 W81 00 54. Stereo. 935 Ramsey Lake Rd. P3E 2C6. Phone: (705) 673-6538. Phone: (705) 675-1151. Fax: (705) 675-4878. E-mail: chef@ckfu.ujyf.ca. Licensee: Laurentian Student and Community Radio Corp. Format: News/talk, div, jazz. News: 3 hrs wkly. Target aud: General. Spec prog: It one hr, Polish one hr, Fr 19 hrs, Sp 1 hr, Ger 1 hr wkly. ♦Dan Welch, pres; Lindsey Chrysler, VP; Carl Jorgensen, opns mgr.

Thunder Bay

***CBQ-FM**— July 5, 1984: 101.7 mhz; 23.5 kw. 900 ft. Stereo. 213 Miles St. E. P7C 1J5. Phone: (807) 625-5000. Fax: (807) 625-5035. Web Site: www.cbc.ca. Licensee: CBC. Network: CBC Radio One. Format: Talk/news, public radio. ♦Robert Rabinovitch, pres & stn mgr; Tom Grand, gen mgr.

***CBQT-FM**— August 1990: 88.3 mhz; 23.5 kw. 213 Miles St. E. P7C 1J5. Phone: (807) 625-5000. Fax: (807) 625-5035. Web Site: www.cbc.ca. Licensee: CBC. Network: CBC Radio One. Format: News, current affairs. Target aud: General; northwestern Ontario residents. Spec prog: Canadian Indian one hr wkly. ♦Robert Rabinovitch, CEO & progmg mgr; Tom Grand, gen mgr.

***CJOA-FM**— Dec 20, 1998: 95.1 mhz; 50 w. 63 Carrie St., Rm 42 P7A 4J2. Phone: (807) 344-9525. Fax: (807) 344-9525. E-mail: info@cjoa.org. Web Site: www.cjoa.org. Licensee: Thunder Bay Christian Radio. Format: Christian music. All ages. ♦Ray Gauthier, pres; Bonnie Gauthier, gen mgr.

CJSD-FM—Listing follows CKPR(AM).

CJUK-FM— August 2001: 99.9 mhz; 37 w. Magic 99.9 FM, 995 Memorial Ave. P7B 4A1. Phone: (807) 345-9999. Fax: (807) 345-9939. E-mail: magicmail@magic999.fm. Web Site: www.magic999.fm. Licensee: Newcap Inc. (acq 5-10-2005; C$2.3 million). Format: Soft rock, adult contemp. ♦Dennis Landriault, pres & gen mgr.

CKPR(AM)— Feb 3, 1931: 580 khz; 5 kw-D, 1 kw-N. Stereo. 87 N. Hill St. P7A 5V6. Phone: (807) 346-2600. Fax: (807) 345-9923. Web Site: ckpr.com. Licensee: C.J.S.D. Inc. (acq 5-25-92). Rep: Canadian Broadcast Sales. Format: Adult contemp. News staff: 6. Target aud: 25-54; families & office workers. Spec prog: News/talk 10 hrs wkly. ♦H.F. Dougall, pres.

CJSD-FM—Co-owned with CKPR(AM). October 1948: 94.3 mhz; 93 kw. 1,009 ft. Stereo. E-mail: rock@rock94.fm. Web Site: rock94.com. Format: Adult rock. Target aud: 18-44. Co-owned TV: CKPR-TV, CHFD-TV affils.

CKTG-FM— March 1996: 105.3 mhz; 100 kw. 180 Park Ave., Suite 200 7V5 6J4. Phone: (807) 346-2006. Fax: (807) 345-9923. E-mail: hits@hot105.fm. Web Site: www.thenewhot105.com. Licensee: NewCap Broadcasting Ltd. (group owner) Rep: Canadian Broadcast Sales. Format: Classic rock. News staff: 5; News: 4 hrs wkly. Target aud: 25 plus. Spec prog: It, relg, Finnish one hr wkly. ♦Bob Templeton, pres; K. Klein, VP, gen mgr & gen mgr.

Tillsonburg

CKOT(AM)— Apr 30, 1955: 1510 khz; 10 kw-D, DA-D. Box 10, 77 Broadway N4G 4H3. Phone: (519) 842-4281. Fax: (519) 842-4284. Licensee: Tillsonburg Broadcasting Co. Ltd. Rep: Target Broadcast Sales. Format: Country. News staff: 5; News: 7 hrs wkly. Target aud: 18-50; general. Spec prog: Ger one hr, Hungarian one hr, Belgian one hr, Dutch one hr wkly. ♦John Lamers, pres & gen mgr; Robin Henry, sls VP.

CKOT-FM— Dec 1, 1965: 101.3 mhz; 50 kw. 454 ft. Stereo. Format: Easy lstng. Target aud: 30 plus; general. Spec prog: Gospel one hr wkly.

Timmins

***CHIM-FM**— 1996: 102.3 mhz; 84 w. 226 Delnite Rd. P4N 7C2. Phone: (705) 264-2150. E-mail: chimfm@vianet.ca. Web Site: www.chimfm.com. Licensee: 1158556 Ontario Ltd. Format: Christian music. ♦Roger de Brabant, chmn; Karen Turner, stn mgr.

CHMT-FM— July 12, 2001: 93.1 mhz; 3.6 kw. 32 Mountjoy St. N. P4N 4V6. Phone: (705) 267-6070. Fax: (705) 267-6095. E-mail: moose931@hbgradio.com. Web Site: www.hbgradio.com. Licensee: The Haliburton Broadcasting Group Inc. Group owner: Haliburton Broadcasting Group Inc. Format: Country. News staff: 2; News: 5 hrs wkly. Target aud: 25-49; female. ♦Christopher Grossman, pres & gen mgr; Kimberly Ward, VP & opns VP; Penny Proulx, opns mgr.

CHYK-FM— 2000: 104.1 mhz; 3.5 kw. 32 Mountjoy St. N., Suite 103 P4N 4V6. Phone: (705) 267-6070. Fax: (705) 267-6095. E-mail: chykfm@hbgradio.com. Web Site: www.hbgradio.com. Licensee: Haliburton Broadcasting Group Inc. (group owner). Rep: Canadian Broadcast Sales. Format: Adulte contemp, Fr. News staff: one; News: 4 hrs wkly. Target aud: 18-65. ♦Christopher Grossman, gen mgr & sls dir; Kimberly Ward, opns VP; Sean Connon, gen sls mgr; Sylvain Boucher, progmg dir; Gilles Lafortune, news dir; Sylvie Bealieu, sls.

CJQQ-FM— Sept 6, 1976: 92.1 mhz; 40 kw. Ant 400 ft. Stereo. Box 1046 P4N 7H8. Secondary address: 260 2nd Ave. P4N 7H8. Phone: (705) 264-2351. Fax: (705) 264-2984. Web Site: www.rogers.ca. Licensee: Rogers Broadcasting Ltd. (group owner; acq 4-19-02;. grpsl). Format: AOR. Target aud: 18-44. ♦Mick Weaver, gen mgr; Angelo Leader, gen sls mgr.

CKGB-FM— August 2001: 99.3 mhz; 40 kw. Box 1046 P4N 7H8. Secondary address: 260 2nd Ave. P4N 7H8. Phone: (705) 264-2351. Fax: (705) 264-2984. Web Site: www.rogers.ca. Licensee: Rogers Broadcasting Ltd. (group owner; (acq 4-19-2002; grpsl). Format: Easy rock. News staff: 2; News: 4 hrs wkly. Target aud: 35-55. ♦Mick Weaver, gen mgr; Angelo Leader, gen sls mgr.

Toronto

CBLA-FM— Apr 19, 1998: 99.1 mhz; 55.1 kw. (Digital radio: Dec 3, 1998: 1461.536 mhz; 5.084 kw). Box 500, Station A M5W 1E6. Phone: (416) 205-7400. Fax: (416) 205-6336. Web Site: www.cbc.ca. Licensee: CBC. Network: CBC Radio One. Format: Talk, public radio. ♦Robert Rabinovitch, CEO & pres; Tom Grand, gen mgr.

CBL-FM— 1946: 94.1 mhz; 55.7 kw. 389 ft. (Digital radio: Dec 3, 1998: 1461.536 mhz; 5.084 kw). Box 500, Station A. M5W 1E6. Secondary address: Box 3220, Station C., Ottawa K1Y 1E4. Phone: (416) 205-7400. Fax: (416) 205-6336. Web Site: www.cbc.ca. Licensee: CBC. Network: CBC Radio Two. Format: Class, public radio. ♦Robert Rabinovitch, CEO & pres; Tom Grand, gen mgr.

CFIE-FM— Dec 13, 2002: 106.5 mhz; 1.1 kw. 366 Adelaide St., Suite 323 M5A 3X9. Phone: (416) 703-1287. Fax: (416) 703-4328. E-mail: info@aboriginalradio.com. Web Site: www.aboriginalradio.com. Licensee: Aboriginal Voices Radio Inc. Format: Canadian aboriginal and world aboriginal. ♦Mark MacLeod, opns mgr; Roy Hennessy, opns mgr; Patrice Mousseau, progmg dir.

CFMJ(AM)— July 1, 1957: 640 khz; 50 kw-U, DA-2. (Digital radio: Dec 3, 1998: 1465.024 mhz; 5.084 kw). Stereo. One Dundas St. W., Suite 1600 5G123. Phone: (416) 221-6400. Fax: (416) 847-3300. E-mail: onair@mojoradio.com. Web Site: www.mojoradio.com. Licensee: Corus Premium Corp. Group owner: Corus Entertainment Inc. (acq 7-6-00; grpsl). Rep: Canadian Broadcast Sales. Format: News/talk. News staff: 6. Target aud: 35-64; upscale, mature, female. Spec prog: Sports/NHL hockey. ♦J.J. Johnston, gen mgr; Scott Armstrong, progmg dir; Ross MacLeod, news dir.

CFMX-FM-1— 1988: 96.3 mhz; 24.5 kw. Ant 930 ft. TL: N56 43 38 W55 79 22. Stereo. 550 Queen St. E., Suite 205 M5A 1V2. Phone: (416) 367-5353. Fax: (416) 367-1742. E-mail: info@classical1963.com. Web Site: www.classical963fm.com. Licensee: Trumar Communications Inc. (acq 7-7-98). Network: BN Audio. Rep: CHUM Group Radio Sales. Format: Class. News staff: 3; News: 4 hrs wkly. Target aud: 35 plus; well educated, upscale, owners/managers/professionals. ♦Peter Webb, CEO, pres & gen mgr; Truus Rosenthal, VP; Roberta Hunt, opns mgr.

CFNY-FM—See Brampton

CFRB(AM)— Feb 19, 1927: 1010 khz; 50 kw-U, DA-2. (Digital radio: Dec 3, 1998: 1458.048 mhz; 5.084 kw). Stereo. 2nd Fl., 2 St. Clair Ave. W. M4V 1L6. Phone: (416) 924-5711. Fax: (416) 872-8683. Web Site: www.cfrb.com. Licensee: Standard Broadcasting Corp. Ltd. Group owner: Standard Broadcasting Corp. (acq 1985). Rep: Integrated Media Sales. Format: News/talk. News staff: 2; News: 40 hrs wkly. Target aud: 25-64; general. Spec prog: Class 7 hrs, farm 2 hrs wkly. ♦Gary Slaight, CEO; Alan Slaight, chmn; Ian Laurie, CFO; Pat Holiday, gen mgr; Bill Herz, sls dir; G. Scott Johns, rgnl sls mgr; Robb Collis, mktg dir, prom dir & pub affrs dir; Steve Kowch, opns mgr & progmg dir; Dave Trafford, news dir; Dave Simon, engrg VP.

CKFM-FM—Co-owned with CFRB(AM). July 1, 1961: 99.9 mhz; 40 kw. 1,550 ft. TL: N43 38 33 W79 23 15. (Digital radio: Dec 3, 1998: 1458.048 mhz; 5.084 kw). Stereo. Phone: (416) 922-9999. Fax: (416) 323-6800. Web Site: www.mix999.fm.com. Format: Hit radio. Target aud: 25-49. ♦Blair Bartrem, pres, opns mgr & progmg dir; Karen Steele, mktg mgr & prom dir; Wayne Webster, mus dir; Anastasia Moshona, asst music dir; Dave Simon, engrg dir.

CFTR(AM)— Aug 8, 1962: 680 khz; 50 kw-U. (Digital radio: Dec 3, 1998: 1456.304 mhz; 5.084 kw). Stereo. 777 Jarvis St. M4Y 3B7. Phone: (416) 935-8468. Fax: (416) 935-8480. Web Site: www.680news.com. Licensee: Rogers Broadcasting Ltd. Network: ABC. Rep: Canadian Broadcast Sales. Format: News. News staff: 50; News: 168 hrs wkly. Target aud: 25-54; owners, managers, professionals. ♦Anthony P. Viner, CEO & pres; Sandy Sanderson, exec VP; Derek Berghuis, gen mgr, sls VP & gen sls mgr; Vicky Belfiore, mktg dir & prom mgr; John Hinnen, progmg VP; Connie Ricciuti, news dir; Kirk Nesbitt, chief of engrg.

CHFI-FM—Co-owned with CFTR(AM). Feb 8, 1957: 98.1 mhz; 44 kw. 1,815 ft. (Digital radio: Dec 3, 1998: 1456.304 mhz; 5.084 kw). Stereo. Phone: (416) 935-8298. Format: Soft adult contemp. Target aud: 25-54. ♦Julie Adam, VP, gen mgr, progmg VP & progmg dir; Victor Dann, gen sls mgr; Vicky Belfiore, prom dir & adv dir; Drew Keith, mus dir.

CFXJ-FM— Feb 9, 2001: 93.5 mhz; 1.058 kw. Ant 980 ft. (Digital radio: 1454.56 mhz; 5.084 kw). 211 Yonge St., Suite 400 M5B 1M4. Phone: (416) 214-5000. Fax: (416) 214-0660. Web Site: www.flow935.com. Licensee: Milestone Radio Inc. Format: Urban. News staff: one. Target aud: 18-35. ♦Denham Jolly, CEO & pres; Nicole Jolly, opns VP; Vanessa Santos, prom mgr; Wayne Williams, progmg dir; Scott Palmateer, chief of engrg.

CHEV— 2005: 1610 khz; 99 w. 254 Main St., Markham L3P 1Y7. Phone: (905) 294-0033. E-mail: info@chevradioam.com. Web Site:

Directory of Radio Ontario

www.chevradioam.com. Licensee: BAF Audio Visual Inc. Format: Sports. ♦Tom Neo, pres; Bruce Ferrergson, stn mgr.

CHHA(AM)— Nov 21, 2004: 1610 khz; 1 kw-U. 22 Wenderly Dr. M6B 2N9. Phone: (416) 782-2953. E-mail: sanlorenzo@rogers.com. Licensee: San Lorenzo Latin American Community Centre. Format: Sp, ethnic. ♦Herman Astudillo, gen mgr.

CHIN(AM)— 1966: 1540 khz; 50 kw-D, 30 kw-N, DA-2. TL: N43 35 32 W79 39 22. Stereo. 622 College St. M6G 1B6. Phone: (416) 531-9991. Fax: (416) 531-5274. E-mail: sales@chinradio.com. Web Site: www.chinradio.com.ANIK e-z, KUBAND (digital) Licensee: Radio 1540 Ltd. Format: Ethnic, multilingual (21 languages). News staff: 4; News: 9 hrs wkly. Target aud: 30 plus; immigrants in the Toronto census metropolitan area. ♦Johnny Lombardi, CEO; Lenny Lombardi, pres & exec VP; Theresa Lombardi, sr VP; Joe Mulvihill, gen mgr; Donina Lombardi, pub affrs dir; Michael Evans, engrg dir.

CHIN-FM— 1967: 100.7 mhz; 8.5 kw. 1,700 ft. TL: N48 38 33 W79 23 15. (Digital radio: Dec 3, 1998: 1465.024 mhz; 5.084 kw). Stereo. News: 10 hrs wkly. Target aud: 30 plus; multi-ethnic, first & second generation immigrants.

CHKT(AM)— Feb 21, 1951: 1430 khz; 50 kw-U, DA-2. Unit 7, 135 East Beaver Creek Rd. L4B 1E2. Phone: (905) 763-3350. Fax: (905) 889-9828. Licensee: Fairchild Radio Group Ltd. (acq 10-3-96; C$1.8 million). Format: Multicultural. News staff: 3; News: 18 hrs wkly. Chinese and other ethnic groups. Spec prog: News 18 hrs wkly. ♦Joe Chan, CEO; Thomas Fung, chmn; Louis Cheng, VP; Cyril Lai, gen mgr; Gary Nobody, stn mgr; Castro Liu, progmg dir; Mary Yang, news dir & pub affrs dir; Fred Cheung, engrg mgr.

CHRY-FM— 1987: 105.5 mhz; 50 w. 413 Student Ctr., York University, 4700 Keele St. M3J 1P3. Phone: (416) 736-5293. Fax: (416) 650-8052. E-mail: chry@yorku.ca. Web Site: www.yorku.ca/chry. Licensee: CHRY Community Radio Inc. Format: Black, alternative, div. News staff: 4; News: 10 hrs wkly. Target aud: General; campus community. Spec prog: Afghan, African, Black, Chinese, environment, Fr, gospel, jazz, Sp, Hebrew. ♦Susy Glass, gen mgr & stn mgr; Anderson Rouse, opns mgr; Neil Armstrong, progmg dir.

CHUM(AM)— October 1944: 1050 khz; 50 kw-U, DA-2. (Digital radio: Dec 3, 1998: 1456.304 mhz; 5.084 kw). Stereo. 1331 Yonge St. M4T 1Y1. Phone: (416) 925-6666. Fax: (416) 926-4026. Web Site: www.1050chum.com. Licensee: CHUM Ltd. (group owner) Format: Oldies. News staff: 6. ♦Jim Waters, pres; Bill Bodnarchuk, gen mgr; Marc Charlebois, gen sls mgr; Brad Jones, progmg dir; Jeff Howatt, news dir; Larry Keats, chief of engrg.

CHUM-FM— Sept 15, 1963: 104.5 mhz; 40 kw. 1,380 ft. (Digital radio: Dec 3, 1998: 1456.304 mhz; 5.084 kw). Stereo. Web Site: www.chumfm.com. Format: Adult contemp. News: 6 hrs wkly. ♦Loretta Tate, prom dir; Rob Farina, progmg dir.

CHWO(AM)— Jan 8, 2001: 740 khz; 50 kw-U. TL: N43 34 30 W79 49 03. (Digital radio: 1454.56 mhz; 5.084 kw). Box 740, Station A M5W 4K6. Secondary address: Broadcasting Ctr., 284 Church St., Oakville L6J 7N2. Phone: (905) 845-2821. Phone: (416) 544-0740. Fax: (905) 842-1250. Web Site: www.am740.ca. Licensee: AM 740 Prime Time Radio L.P. Format: Adult standard. News: 9 hrs wkly. Target aud: 50 plus. Spec prog: Por 11 hrs, It 4 hrs, Pol 2 hrs, Sp 3 hrs, East Indian 8 hrs wkly. ♦J. E. Caine, CEO; Michael Caine, pres & gen mgr; Jacqui Gerrard, opns mgr.

CIAO(AM)—See Brampton

CILQ-FM—(North York). May 22, 1977: 107.1 mhz; 40 kw. 1,380 ft. (Digital radio: Dec 3, 1998: 1465.024 mhz; 5.084 kw). Stereo. 1 Dundas St., Suite 1600 M5G 1Z3. Phone: (416) 221-0107. Fax: (416) 847-3300. Web Site: www.q107.com. Licensee: Corus Premium Television Ltd. Group owner: Corus Entertainment Inc. (acq 7-2000; grpsl). Format: Classic rock. News staff: 5; News: 15 hrs wkly. Target aud: 18-44. ♦John Cassaday, CEO; John P Hayes Jr., pres; J. J. Johnston, gen mgr; Dave Farough, progmg dir; Ross Macleod, news dir; Michelle Dyer, prom.

CIRV-FM— 1986: 88.9 mhz; 1.88 kw. (Digital radio: 1466.768 mhz; 5.084 kw). 1087 Dundas St. W. M6J 1W9. Phone: (416) 537-1088. Phone: (416) 588-2472. Fax: (416) 537-2463. E-mail: info@cirvfm.com. Web Site: www.cirvfm.com. Licensee: CIRC Radio Inc. Format: Multicultural/ethnic. News staff: 5. ♦Alberto Elmir, VP; Frank Alvarez, CEO, pres & gen mgr.

***CIUT-FM**— 1986: 89.5 mhz; 15 kw. Stereo. 91 St. George St. M5S 2E8. Phone: (416) 595-0909. Fax: (416) 946-7004. E-mail: b.burchell@ciut.fm. Web Site: www.ciut.fm. Licensee: University of Toronto Community Radio Inc. Format: Var/div. News: 3 hrs wkly. Target aud: General. Spec prog: American Indian 2 hrs, Fr 2 hrs, Sp 4 hrs hrs wkly. ♦Brian Burchell, stn mgr; Ken Stowar, progmg dir.

CJAQ-FM— Jan 26, 1993: 92.5 mhz; 9.1 kw. (Digital radio: Dec 3, 1998: 1456.304 mhz; 5.084 kw). 777 Jarvis St. M4Y 3B7. Phone: (416) 935-8392. Fax: (416) 935-8410. Web Site: www.925jackfm.com. Licensee: Rogers (Toronto) Ltd. Group owner: Rogers Broadcasting Ltd. (acq 9-10-99; grpsl). Format: All hits. News staff: 4; News: 6 hrs wkly. Target aud: 25-54. ♦Gary L. Miles, CEO; Rael Merson, pres; Laura Nixon, CFO; Pat Cardinal, gen mgr.

CJBC(AM)— 1947: 860 khz; 50 kw-U. (Digital radio: Dec 3, 1998: 1461.536 mhz; 5.084 kw). Box 500, Station A M5W 1E6. Phone: (416) 205-3311. Fax: (416) 205-5622. Web Site: www.cbc.ca. Licensee: CBC. Format: Educ, cultural, var. ♦Alain Dorion, gen mgr.

CJBC-FM— 1993: 90.3 mhz; 5.73 kw. 1,414 ft. TL: N43 38 33 W79 23 15. (Digital radio: Dec 3, 1998: 1461.536 mhz; 5.084 kw). Stereo. Phone: (416) 205-2522. Fax: (416) 205-7660. Network: Radio Canada. Format: Class. ♦Manon Cote, gen mgr.

CJCL(AM)— 1944: 590 khz; 50 kw-U, DA-1. (Digital radio: Dec 3, 1998: 1458.048 mhz; 5.084 kw). Stereo. 777 Jarvis St. M4Y 3B7. Phone: (416) 935-0590. Fax: (416) 413-4116. E-mail: contact@fan590.com. Web Site: www.fan590.com. Licensee: Rogers Broadcasting Ltd. (group owner; acq 4-19-02; grpsl). Network: Telemedia. Format: Sports, talk. Target aud: 25-54; men. ♦Nelson Millmen, stn mgr.

CJEZ-FM— May 24, 1987: 97.3 mhz; 28.9 kw. Ant 1,500 ft. (Digital radio: Dec 3, 1998: 1458.048 mhz; 5.084 kw). 40 Eglington Ave. E., Suite 600 M4P 3B6. Phone: (416) 482-0973. Fax: (416) 486-5696. E-mail: info@ezrock.com. Web Site: www.ezrock.com. Licensee: Standard Radio Inc. Group owner: Standard Broadcasting Corp. (acq 4-19-02; grpsl). Format: EZ listening/soft rock. Target aud: 35-54. ♦Gary Slaight, CEO; Pat Holiday, gen mgr.

CJMR(AM)—See Mississauga

***CJRT-FM**— 1949: 91.1 mhz; 100 kw. 1,300 ft. (Digital radio: Dec 3, 1998: 1458.048 mhz; 5.084 kw). Stereo. 150 Mutual M5B 2M1. Phone: (416) 595-0404. Fax: (416) 595-9413. E-mail: info@jazz.fm. Web Site: www.jazz.fm. Licensee: CJRT-FM Inc. (acq 1974). Format: Jazz. Target aud: 35 plus. ♦B. Webber, chmn; Brad Barker, opns dir; Joy Gooding, dev dir; Heather Bambrick, progmg; Donnie Tong, engr.

CJSA-FM— 2004: 101.3 mhz; 373 w. Canadian Multicultural Radio, 306 Rexdale Rd., Unit 7 M9W 1R6. Phone: (416) 292-4059. Fax: (416) 292-4574. E-mail: info@cmr24.com. Web Site: www.cmr24.com. Licensee: 3885275 Canada Inc. Format: Ethnic. ♦Sivakumaran Sivapaphafundaram, gen mgr.

CKIE-FM— 2005: 105.1 mhz; 425 W. Adelaide St., 3rd Fl. M5V 3C1. Phone: (416) 599-2666. Fax: (416) 599-2666. E-mail: info@radiotoronto.coop. Web Site: www.radiotoronto.coop. Licensee: La Cooperative radiophonique de Toronto inc. Format: Fr variety. ♦Nathalie Le Roc'h, pres; Christian Martel, gen mgr.

***CKLN-FM**— July 1983: 88.1 mhz; 250 w. c/o CKLN Radio Inc., 380 Victoria St. M5B 1W7. Phone: (416) 595-1477. Fax: (416) 595-0226. E-mail: stationmanager@ckln.fm. Web Site: www.ckln.fm. Licensee: CKLN Radio Inc. Format: Alternative. ♦Tim May, progmg dir.

Wahta Mohawk Territory near Bala

CFWP-FM— 2003: 98.3 mhz; 1.06 kw. Box 711, 2350 Muskoka Rd. 38, Bala P0C 1A0. Phone: (705) 762-1274. Web Site: www.wahta.com/hawkradio. Licensee: Wahta Communications Society. Format: Var. ♦Cal White, gen mgr.

Waterloo

CFCA-FM—Listing follows CKKW(AM).

CIKZ-FM—See Kitchener-Waterloo

CKKW(AM)—(Kitchener). Aug 1, 1959: 1090 khz; 10 kw-U, DA-2. TL: N43 17 20 W80 24 16. Stereo. 255 King St. N., Suite 207 N2J 4V2. Phone: (519) 884-4470. Fax: (519) 884-6482. Web Site: www.oldies1090.com. Licensee: CHUM Ltd. (group owner; acq 7-30-93; C$5 million). Format: Oldies. ♦Jay Switzer, pres; Paul Cugliari, gen mgr; John Yost, gen sls mgr; Jay Nijhuis, prom mgr; Pete Travers, progmg dir.

CFCA-FM—Co-owned with CKKW(AM). Apr 3, 1967: 105.3 mhz; 100 kw. 820 ft. TL: N43 24 15 W80 38 05. Stereo. Web Site: www.koolfm.com. Format: Classic rock.

***CKMS-FM**— Oct 16, 1977: 100.3 mhz; 250 w. 110 ft. Stereo. 200 University Ave. W. N2L 3G1. Phone: (519) 886-2567. Fax: (519) 884-3530. E-mail: ckmsfm@web.ca. Web Site: www.ckmsfm.uwaterloo.ca. Licensee: Radio Waterloo Inc. Format: Div, campus. News staff: one. ♦Heather Majaury, stn mgr; Bob Trevison, mus dir; Paul Heap, news dir; Bill Wharrie, engrg VP.

CKWR-FM—(Kitchener). Mar 23, 1974: 98.5 mhz; 15.2 kw. Ant 576 ft. Stereo. 375 University Ave. E. N2k 3M7. Phone: (519) 886-9870. Fax: (519) 886-0090. E-mail: general@ckwr.com. Web Site: www.yourfm.ca. Licensee: Wired World Inc. Rep: CHUM Group Radio Sales. Format: Adult contemp; speciality & multicultural. News staff: 2; News: 8 hrs wkly. Target aud: 35-64; mature audience. Spec prog: Romanian 2 hrs, Ger 3 hrs, Greek 2 hrs, Serbian 2 hrs, Pol 4 hrs, Por 5 hrs, Sp 4 hrs wkly. ♦Scott Jensen, pres; John Champion, VP; Vic Folliott, stn mgr; Anne-Marie Scarlett, gen sls mgr; Stacey Englehart, prom dir & news dir.

Wawa

CJWA-FM— 1996: 107.1 mhz; 210 w. 55 Broadway Ave. P0S 1K0. Phone: (705) 856-4555. Phone: (888) 465-2592. Fax: (705) 856-1520. Licensee: North Superior Broadcasting Ltd. Rep: Canadian Broadcast Sales. Format: Adult contemp. Target aud: 25-54. ♦Rick Labbe, pres, gen mgr, sls dir & progmg dir; Mark Capeless, progmg dir & news dir; Vern Valois, chief of engrg.

Welland

CIXL-FM— May 20, 1999: 91.7 mhz; 27.42 kw. TL: N52 42 56 W19 79 16. 860 Forks Road West L3B 5R6. Phone: (905) 732-4433. Fax: (905) 732-4780. E-mail: info@giantfm.org. Web Site: www.giantfm.com. Licensee: R.B. Communications, LTD. Rep: Canadian Broadcast Sales. Format: CHR. News staff: 4; News: 23 hrs wkly. Target aud: 25 plus; professional, blue collar adults. ♦Pat St. John, pres; Peter Morena, opns mgr & chief of opns.

Windsor

***CBE(AM)**— July 1, 1950: 1550 khz; 10 kw-U, DA-1. (Digital radio: 1484.208 mhz; 4.369 kw). 825 Riverside Dr. W. N9A 5K9. Phone: (519) 255-3411. Fax: (519) 255-3443. Web Site: www.cbc.ca. Licensee: CBC. Network: CBC Radio One. Format: Div, news/talk. Spec prog: Class 4 hrs, jazz 2 hrs wkly. ♦Janice Stein, gen mgr.

CBE-FM— Oct 15, 1978: 89.9 mhz; 100 kw. 538 ft. (Digital radio: 1484.208 mhz; 4.369 kw). Stereo. Web Site: www.cbc.ca. Network: CBC Radio Two. Format: Class, div. ♦Bill Conway, stn mgr & stn mgr.

CBEF(AM)— May 1970: 540 khz; 2.5 kw-D, 5 kw-N, DA-1. 825 Riverside Dr. W. N9A 5K9. Phone: (519) 255-3411. Phone: (519) 255-3588. Fax: (519) 255-3565. Licensee: CBC. Network: CBC Radio One. Format: Div. ♦Alain Dorion, stn mgr; Jackie Kervoelen, mus dir; Maryse Durette, news dir; Manny Pacheko, engrg mgr.

CIDR-FM—Listing follows CKLW(AM).

CIMX-FM—Listing follows CKWW(AM).

***CJAM-FM**— November 1983: 91.5 mhz; 456 w. 401 Sunset Ave. N9B 3P4. Phone: (519) 971-3606. Fax: (519) 971-3605. E-mail: news@cjam.ca. Web Site: www.cjam.com. Licensee: Student Media, University of Windsor. Format: Progsv, info, ethnic. Target aud: General; listeners in Windsor/Detroit area. Spec prog: Black 10 hrs, class 4 hrs, folk 4 hrs, jazz 6 hrs, Pol one hr, Sp one hr wkly. ♦Armondo Correia, pres; Christien Gagnier, stn mgr & progmg dir.

CKLW(AM)— June 1, 1932: 800 khz; 50 kw-U, DA-2. (Digital radio: 1484.208 mhz; 4.369 kw). 1640 Ouellette Ave. N8X 1L1. Phone: (519) 258-8888. Fax: (519) 258-0182. Web Site: www.am800cklw.com. Licensee: CHUM Ltd. (group owner; acq 1-29-93). Rep: McGavren

Ontario

Guild. Format: News/talk. Target aud: 25-54. ♦ Jay Switzer, pres; Eric Proksch, gen mgr; Sandra Neposlan, gen sls mgr; Heidi Baiden, prom dir; Keith Chinnery, progmg dir; Jason Moore, news dir; Jim Valvasori, engrg dir & chief of engrg.

CIDR-FM— Co-owned with CKLW(AM). 1949: 93.9 mhz; 100 kw. 700 ft. (Digital radio: 1484.208 mhz; 4.369 kw). Stereo. Phone: (313) 961-9811. Fax: (313) 961-1603. E-mail: feedback@l93.9fmradio.com. Web Site: www.literock939fm.com. Format: Adult contemp. ♦ Curtis Paul, prom dir; Wendy Duff, progmg dir.

CKWW(AM)— Mar 29, 1964: 580 khz; 500 w-U, DA-1. (Digital radio: 1484.208 mhz; 4.369 kw). 1640 Ouellette Ave. N8X 1L1. Secondary address: 30100 Telegraph Rd., Suite 460, Bingham Farms, MI 48025. Phone: (519) 258-8888. Phone: (313) 961-9811. Fax: (519) 258-0182. Fax: (313) 961-1603. E-mail: eprokch@am800cklw.com. Licensee: Division of CHUM Ltd. Group owner: CHUM Ltd. (acq 9-5-85). Rep: McGavren Guild. Format: Nostalgia, MOR. Target aud: 45 plus. ♦ Eric Proksch, gen mgr; Marie Madison, progmg dir.

CIMX-FM—Co-owned with CKWW(AM). July 10, 1967: 88.7 mhz; 100 kw. 577 ft. (Digital radio: 1484.208 mhz; 4.369 kw). Stereo. Format: Modern rock. Target aud: 18-34. ♦ Craig Posegay, prom mgr; Murray Brookshaw, progmg dir; Matt Franklin, mus dir.

Wingham

CKNX(AM)— Feb 20, 1926: 920 khz; 10 kw-D, 1 kw-N, DA-2. 215 Carling Terr. N0G 2W0. Phone: (519) 357-1310. Fax: (519) 357-1897. E-mail: news@cknxradio.com. Licensee: Blackburn Radio Inc. Group owner: Blackburn Group Inc. Format: Country. News staff: 7; News: 10 hrs wkly. Target aud: 35-54. Spec prog: Relg 6 hrs wkly. ♦ Jack Gillespie, gen mgr.

CKNX-FM— Apr 17, 1977: 101.7 mhz; 65.766 kw. Ant 741 ft. Stereo. Format: Adult contemp. Target aud: 25-49. Co-owned TV: CKNX-TV affil.

Woodstock

CJFH-FM— 2004: 94.3 mhz; 50 w. 419C Dundas St. N4S 1B8. Phone: (519) 539-2304. E-mail: faithfmwoodstock@execulink.com. Licensee: Sound of Faith Broadcasting. Format: Christian. ♦ Gary Hill, gen mgr.

CKDK-FM— July 1, 1987: 103.9 mhz; 52 kw. 400 ft. Stereo. Box 100, 290 Dundas St. N4S 7W7. Phone: (519) 539-1040. Fax: (519) 539-7479. E-mail: dave.farough@corusent.com. Web Site: www.thehawk.ca. Licensee: Corus Radio Group owner: Corus Entertainment Inc. (acq 1991). Rep: Canadian Broadcast Sales. Format: Classic Rock. News staff: 3; News: 9 hrs wkly. Target aud: 25-54. ♦ John Cassaday, CEO; John Hayes, pres; Dave Farough, gen mgr; Gord Harris, progmg dir.

Prince Edward Island

Charlottetown

*CBCT-FM— 1972: 96.1 mhz; 93.5 kw. 540 ft. Box 2230, 430 University Ave. C1A 8B9. Phone: (902) 629-6400. Fax: (902) 629-6518. Fax: (902) 629-6520. Web Site: pei.cbc.ca. Licensee: CBC. Network: CBC Radio One. Format: Talk. News: 11 hrs wkly. ♦ Barbara Nymark, gen mgr; John Channing, sls dir; Susan Mitton, progmg dir & news dir.

CFCY(AM)— Aug 15, 1924: 630 khz; 10 kw-U, DA-2. Box 1060 C1A 7M7. Secondary address: 5 Prince St. C1A 7M7. Phone: (902) 892-1066. Fax: (902) 566-1338. E-mail: requests@cfcy.pe.ca. Web Site: www.cfcy.pe.ca. Licensee: Maritime Broadcasting Ltd. Format: Country. News staff: 3; News: 6 hrs wkly. ♦ Robert Pace, chmn; Merv Russell, pres; Frank Lewis, gen mgr; Nicole Pugh, prom dir; Lee Drake, mus dir; Scott Chapman, news dir; Walter Corney, chief of engrg.

CHLQ-FM—Co-owned with CFCY(AM). March 1982: 93.1 mhz; 25 kw. Stereo. E-mail: requests@magic93.pe.ca. Web Site: www.magic93.pe.ca. Format: Lite rock. News: 4 hrs wkly. Target aud: 25-54. ♦ Frank Lewis, stn mgr; Jim Ferguson, opns mgr & progmg mgr; Heather Tedford, gen sls mgr; Paul Alan, mus dir; Walter Corney, engrg mgr.

CHTN(AM)— Dec 25, 1974: 720 khz; 10 kw-D, 7.5 kw-N, DA-D. TL: N46 11 22 W63 09 54. 5 Prince St. C1A 7M7. Phone: (902) 892-1066. Fax: (902) 566-1338. Licensee: NewCap Broadcasting Ltd. (group owner; acq 10-7-81). Rep: Canadian Broadcast Sales. Format: Oldies. News staff: 2; News: 17 hrs wkly. Target aud: 25-54. ♦ Mark Maheu, exec VP; Frank Lewis, gen mgr; Jim Ferguson, opns mgr; Heather Tedford, gen sls mgr; Nicole Pugh, prom mgr; Gerard Murphy, progmg mgr; Anne MacRae, news dir; Walter Corney, chief of engrg.

Summerside

CJRW-FM— 2000: 102.1 mhz; 11 kw. 763 Water St. E. C1N 4J3. Phone: (902) 436-2201. Fax: (902) 436-8573. Licensee: Maritime Broadcasting System Ltd. Group owner: Maritime Broadcasting (acq 8-10-00; C$650,000. for approximately 92.9% of the common shares). Format: Hit country. News staff: one. Target aud: General. ♦ Lois E. Schurman, chmn; Paul M. Schurman, pres; Brent Schurman, VP; Dave Chamberlain, gen mgr; Harry McLellan, gen sls mgr; Gina Cole, prom dir; Trisha Smith, progmg dir; Kevin Warren, mus dir; Ken Kingston, news dir & pub affrs dir; Steve Harvey, engrg dir.

Quebec

Acton Vale

CFID-FM— 2004: 103.7 mhz; 1.65 kw. C.P. 130 J0H 1A0. Phone: (450) 546-1037. Fax: (450) 546-7521. E-mail: info@radio-acton.com. Web Site: www.radio-acton.com. Licensee: Radio-Acton inc. Format: Fr, var. ♦ Gaetan Chevanelle, gen mgr.

Alma

CFGT(AM)— October 1953: 1270 khz; 10 kw-D, 5 kw-N, DA-2. 460 Sacre Coure W., Suite 200 G8B 1L9. Phone: (418) 662-6673. Fax: (418) 662-6070. E-mail: klykfm@commercial.dejecom.qu.ca. Licensee: Radio CKYK-FM Inc. Group owner: Group Radio Antenne 6 Inc. (acq 8-18-94). Network: Radiomutuel. Format: Talk AC some Country. ♦ Rosaire Leclere, gen mgr; Jean-Philippe Tremblay, progmg dir & mus dir.

CKYK-FM—Co-owned with CFGT(AM). 1995: 95.7 mhz; 100 kw. TL: N48 24 05 W72 05 23. Phone: (418) 662-6888. Licensee: Radio CKYK FM Inc. Format: Rock of the 80's.

Amqui

CFVM-FM— 2003: 99.9 mhz; 23.8 kw. 111 rue de l'Hopital G5J 2K1. Phone: (418) 629-2025. Fax: (418) 629-2599. E-mail: cfvm@globetrotter.net. Web Site: www.lamatapedia.com/cfvm. Licensee: Astral Media Radio inc. Group owner: Corus Entertainment Inc. (acq 1-21-2005; grpsl). Format: Adult contemp, classic rock, CHR. News staff: 2; News: 6 hrs wkly. Target aud: 18 plus. ♦ Adalbert Levesque, gen mgr & sls dir; Jean Lemay, progmg dir; Jean Fournier, engrg mgr.

Asbestos

CJAN-FM— AM 1972;FM 2001: 99.3 mhz; 11.1 kw. 185 du Roi, PE J1T 1S4. Phone: (819) 879-5439. Phone: (819) 879-5430. Fax: (819) 879-7922. E-mail: info@fm993.ca. Licensee: Radio Plus B.M.D. inc. Rep: Target Broadcast Sales. Format: Adult contemp, MOR. News staff: one. Target aud: 35-75; general. ♦ Marie-Paule Drouin, pres.

Baie Comeau

CBMI-FM— May 28, 1974: 93.7 mhz; 3 kw. c/o CBVE-FM, 888 Saint-Jean St., Quebec G1R 5H6. Phone: (418) 691-3613. Fax: (418) 691-3610. Licensee: Canadian Broadcasting Corp. Network: CBC Radio One. Format: Pub affrs, info. ♦ David Kyle, gen mgr.

CHLC-FM— 1996: 97.1 mhz; 4.21 kw. Stereo. 907 Rue de Puyjalon G5C 1N3. Phone: (418) 589-3771. Fax: (418) 589-9086. E-mail: info@chlc.com. Web Site: www.chlc.com. Licensee: 9022-6242 Quebec Inc. (acq 4-29-96). Format: Adult contemp, MOR. Target aud: General. ♦ Yvon Savoes, pres; Francois Morache, VP; George Daviault, gen mgr, sls dir & news dir; Mike Mainville, progmg dir; Mark Andre Halle, news dir.

Stations in Canada

Carleton

CIEU-FM— 1983: 94.9 mhz; 25 kw. 1,466 ft. TL: N48 08 27 W66 06 32. 1645 Perron Est. G0C 1J0. Phone: (418) 364-7094. Fax: (418) 364-3150. E-mail: cieufm@cieufm.com. Web Site: www.cieufm.com. Licensee: Diffusion Communautaire Baie des Chaleurs Inc. Format: CHR, adult contemp. News staff: 2; News: 7 hrs wkly. Target aud: General. Spec prog: Blues 5 hrs, class 3 hrs, folk 3 hrs, jazz 3 hrs wkly. ♦ Jacques Veillette, pres; Louis St-Laurent, gen mgr; Carol Boudreau, mus dir.

Chapais

CFED(AM)— 1969: 1340 khz; 250 w-U. c/o CHRL, 568 Boul. St. Joseph, Roberval G8H 2K6. Secondary address: 539 Zieme Rue, Chibougamau G8P 1N8. Phone: (418) 275-1831. Phone: (418) 748-3931. Fax: (418) 275-2475. Fax: (418) 748-3931. Web Site: contacteantenne6.com. Licensee: Radio Chibougamau Inc. Group owner: Group Radio Antenne 6 Inc. (acq 1-6-93). Format: Pop music. News staff: one; News: 20 hrs wkly. Target aud: General; mainly adults. ♦ Marc-Andre Levesque, pres; Louis Arcand, mus dir.

Charlesbourg

CIMI-FM— Aug 10, 2001: 103.7 mhz; 20 w. Radio Charlesbourg - Haute St-Charles, 385 rue Jean XXIII G2N 1V4. Phone: (418) 841-4445. Phone: (418) 624-0700. Fax: (418) 841-3330. Web Site: www.cimifm.com. Format: Alternative. ♦ Stephane Tremblay, pres; Francois Beaule, opns mgr; Stephane Bertrand, sls dir; Dominic Tessier, progmg dir & engrg dir; Annie Bouchard, news dir.

Chateauguay

CHAI-FM— 1980: 101.9 mhz; 100 w. Stereo. 25 boul. St. Francis J6J 1Y6. Phone: (450) 698-3131. Phone: (450) 698-3138. Fax: (450) 698-3330. Licensee: Radio Communautaires de Chateauguay Inc. Format: Adult contemp, CHR. News staff: 2; News: 4 hrs wkly. Target aud: General; all ages. ♦ Christian Laberge, pres; Sylvain Poirier, opns dir & progmg dir.

Chibougamau

CJMD(AM)— Nov 21, 1969: 1240 khz; 1 kw-U. TL: N49 54 35 W74 22 08. c/o CHRL, 568 Boul. St. Joseph, Roberval G8H 2K6. Secondary address: 539 Zieme Rue, Chibougamau G8P 1N8. Phone: (418) 275-1831. Phone: (418) 748-3931. Fax: (418) 275-2475. Fax: (418) 748-3931. E-mail: contact@antenne6.com. Licensee: Radio Chibougamau Inc. Group owner: Group Radio Antenne 6 Inc. (acq 1-6-93). Network: Radiomedia. Format: Pop music. News staff: one; News: 20 hrs wkly. Target aud: General; mainly adults.

Chicoutimi

CBJE-FM— 1976: 102.7 mhz; 30 kw. Ant 294 ft. TL: N48 25 29 W71 06 32. CP 6000, c/o CBM(AM), Montreal H3C 3A8. Phone: (514) 597-4444. Fax: (514) 597-4416. Licensee: CBC. Format: Talk radio. ♦ Patricia Pleszczynska, gen mgr; Judith Bleier, opns mgr; Kate Arthur, prom mgr; Sally Caudwell, news dir.

CBJ-FM— 2001: 93.7 mhz; 50 kw. Ant 1,719 ft. TL: N48 36 04 W70 49 46. 500 rue Des Sagueneens G7H 6N4. Phone: (418) 696-6600. Fax: (418) 696-6689. Licensee: Canadian Broadcasting Corp. Network: Premiere Chaine. Format: Var, talk, adlult contemp. News staff: 7. Target aud: 35 and up; adlut, news-oriented. ♦ Armano Dubois, gen mgr; Armand Dubois, prom dir & news dir.

*CBJX-FM— Sept 20, 1933: 100.9 mhz; 98 kw. Ant 294 ft. TL: N48 25 29 W71 06 32. 500 rue Des Sagueneens G7H 6N4. Phone: (418) 696-6600. Fax: (418) 696-6689. Licensee: Canadian Broadcasting Corp. Network: Chaine Culturelle. Format: Classical. ♦ Armand Dubois, opns mgr.

CFIX-FM— July 31, 1987: 96.9 mhz; 43.8 kw. 267 est, rue Racine G7H 5K3. Phone: (418) 543-9797. Fax: (418) 543-7968. E-mail: cfix@rock-detente.com. Web Site: www.rock-detente.com. Licensee: Astral Media Inc. Group owner: Radio Nord (acq 5/04 grpsl). Format: Adult contemp, MOR. ♦ Pierre Brosseau, pres; Marc Andre Levesque, opns mgr; Marc Andre LeVesque, mktg dir; Louis Arcand, progmg dir & news dir.

Degelis

CFVD-FM— 1995: 95.5 mhz; 12.47 kw. 300 ft. TL: N47 33 02 W68 43 48. Stereo. 654 6ieme rue est, Ville Degelis G5T 1Y1. Phone: (418) 853-2370. Phone: (418) 853-3370. Fax: (418) 853-3321. E-mail: cfvd@fm95.ca. Web Site: www.infotennis.com. Licensee: Radio Degelis Inc. Rep: MPV Radio. Format: CHR, country, adult contemp. News staff: 10. Target aud: General. ♦Gilles Caron, pres & gen mgr; Real Provencher, VP.

Dolbeau-Mistassini

CHVD-FM— 2003: 100.3 mhz; 21.4 kw. 1975 Boul Wallberg, Dolbeau G8L 1J5. Phone: (418) 276-3333. Fax: (418) 276-6755. Licensee: Radio CHVD Inc. Group owner: Radio Nord 5/04 Format: MOR. ♦Pierre Broseau, pres; Marc Andre Levesque, opns mgr & sls dir; Louis Arcand, progmg dir & news dir.

CKII-FM— 2004: 101.3 mhz; 250 w. 1709 boul. Wallberg G8L 1H6. Phone: (418) 239-2544. Fax: (418) 239-0842. Licensee: L'Alliance Laurentienne des metis et indiens sans statut, Local 30 Mistassini inc. Format: Fr. ♦Michel Bouchard, gen mgr.

Donnacona

CKNU-FM— 1997: 100.9 mhz; 3.1 kw. 274 rue Notre-Dame G0A 1T0. Phone: (418) 285-2568. Fax: (418) 285-5483. Licensee: 6087329 Canada Inc. (acq 11-24-98). Format: News/talk. ♦Patrice Denerse, pres & opns mgr.

Drummondville

CHRD-FM— 1997: 105.3 mhz; 2.9 kw. Stereo. 2070 rue St. Georges J2C 5G6. Phone: (819) 475-1480. Phone: (819) 478-0099. Fax: (819) 475-5180. E-mail: chrd@hy.cgocable.ca. Licensee: Astral Media Radio Inc. Group owner: Astral Media Inc. (acq 8-13-2001). Format: Adult contemp, MOR, news. News staff: 3; News: 15 hrs wkly. Target aud: 18 plus; general. Spec prog: Relg one hr wkly. ♦Joel Rioux, pres, gen mgr, opns dir, sls dir & prom dir; Martin Tremblay, progmg dir; David Rivet, news dir; Michel Cournoyer, chief of engrg.

CJDM-FM— Aug 15, 1987: 92.1 mhz; 3 kw. 300 ft. Stereo. 412 Heriot, Suite 203 J2B 1B5. Phone: (819) 474-1892. Fax: (819) 474-6610. E-mail: cjdm@cgocable.ca. Web Site: www.cjdm.ca. Licensee: Astral Media Radio inc. Group owner: Corus Entertainment Inc. (acq 1-21-2005; grpsl). Rep: Canadian Broadcast Sales. Format: Adult contemp, Fr. News staff: 2; News: 5 hrs wkly. Target aud: 18-44. ♦Pierre Gaudreau, gen mgr & sls dir; Martine Pichette, prom dir; Claude Rene Piette, progmg dir; Alain Rivard, mus dir; Claude Boucher, news dir; Daniel Pelletier, engrg dir.

Fermont

CBMR-FM— 1982: 105.1 mhz; 16 w. 1400 Rene Levesque E., c/o CBM(AM) - A 4, Montreal H2L 8M2. Phone: (514) 597-4444. Fax: (514) 597-4416. Licensee: Canadian Broadcasting Corp. ♦Patricia Pleszczynska, opns mgr; Judith Bleier, opns mgr.

CFMF-FM— 1980: 103.1 mhz; 50 w. 100 ft. Stereo. Box 280 G0G 1J0. Phone: (418) 287-5147. Fax: (418) 287-5776. E-mail: diffusion1.ferment@sympatico.ca. Web Site: www.diffusionfermont.ca. Licensee: Radio Communautaire de Fermont Inc. Format: Div, Fr, adult contemp. Target aud: 7-55. Spec prog: Jazz one hr, C&W 4 hrs wkly. ♦D. Brouard, pres; Pierre McKinnon, sr VP; Diane Levesque, gen mgr; Johanne Chasse, gen sls mgr; Marjonne Lavoie, progmg mgr; Frederic Harrisson, mus dir; Genevieve Vincent, news dir.

Forestville

CFRP(AM)— 1977: 620 khz; 1 kw-U. 907 Rue de Puyjalon, Baie Cameau G5C 1N3. Phone: (418) 589-3771. Fax: (418) 589-9086. Licensee: 9022-6242 Quebec Inc. (acq 3-29-96). Format: Adult contemp, MOR. ♦Yvon Savoie, pres; George Baviauet, gen mgr.

Fort Coulonge

CHIP-FM— May 2, 1981: 101.7 mhz; 10 kw. 299 ft. TL: N45 45 41 W76 35 01. Stereo. Box 820, La Radio du Pontiac, 33 Romain St., Fort Colonge J0X 1V0. Phone: (819) 683-3155. Fax: (819) 683-3211. E-mail: chip-fm@qc.aira.com. Web Site: www.chipfm.com. Licensee: La Radio du Pontiac Inc. Format: Country in Fr & English. News: 5 hrs wkly. Target aud: 35 yrs & up; rural people. farming communities, small towns. Spec prog: Oldies, rock, gospel 7 hrs, class 2 hrs wkly. ♦Fern Laliberte, pres; Frank Doyle, gen mgr.

Gaspe

CJRG-FM— December 1978: 94.5 mhz; 4.15 kw. 1,150 ft. Stereo. 162 Jacques Cartier G4X 1M9. Phone: (418) 368-3511. Fax: (418) 368-1663. Licensee: Radio Gaspesie Inc. Format: MOR. Spec prog: Class 2 hrs, jazz 2 hrs wkly. ♦Jacques Chartier, gen mgr, progmg dir, mus dir, asst music dir & news dir; Paul Minville, gen sls mgr; Yvan DuPuis, engrg dir.

Gatineau

CHLX-FM— Sept 23, 2002: 97.1 mhz; 12.6 kw. 125 rue Jean-Proulx J8Z 1T4. Phone: (819) 770-9710. Fax: (819) 770-9740. E-mail: classique@radionord.com. Web Site: www.radionord.com/radio-classic/index.html. Licensee: Radio Nord Communications Inc. Group owner: Radio Nord Communications Inc. (acq 8-25-2004). Format: Fr, classical, jazz. ♦Jean-Pierre Major, gen mgr; Diane Pelletier, sls dir; Yurs Trottier, progmg dir.

CIMF-FM— Jan 1, 1970: 94.9 mhz; 84 kw horiz. Ant 1,059 ft. TL: N45 30 11 W75 51 02. (Digital radio: 1463.280 mhz). Stereo. 15 Taschereau J8Y 2V6. Phone: (819) 770-2463. Fax: (819) 770-9338. E-mail: cimf@rockdetente.com. Web Site: www.rockdetente.com. Licensee: Astral Media Radio Inc. Group owner: Astral Media Inc. (acq 10-28-2002; grpsl). Format: Soft rock. News staff: 2; News: 3 hrs wkly. ♦Ian Greenberg, pres; Carmen Rodrigue, gen mgr; Claude Raymond, sls dir & gen sls mgr; Eric St-Louis, prom mgr; Patrice Croteau, progmg mgr; Jean-Guy Faucher, mus dir; Mano Aube, news dir; Pierre Sylvestre, chief of engrg.

CJLL-FM—See Ottawa, ON

CJRC(AM)—Licensed to Gatineau. See Ottawa ON

CKTF-FM— Mar 11, 1988: 104.1 mhz; 19 kw. Ant 1,077 ft. TL: N45 30 11 W75 51 02. (Digital radio: 1463.280 mhz). Stereo. 15 rue Taschereau J8Y 2V6. Phone: (819) 243-5555. Fax: (819) 243-6816. Web Site: www.radioenergie.com. Licensee: Astral Media Radio Inc. Group owner: Astral Media Inc. Format: Dance, top-40, AOR. ♦Carmen Rodrigue, gen mgr; Vincent Pons, sls dir; Melany Gauvin, prom mgr; Astral Musique, mus dir; Pierre Sylvestre, engrg dir.

Harrington Harbour

*CFTH-FM-1— Oct 30, 1991: 97.7 mhz; 180 w. Stereo. Box 88, Harrington Harbour, Duplessis G0G 1N0. Phone: (418) 795-3349. Fax: (418) 795-3200. E-mail: cfth@globetrotter.qc.ca. Licensee: Radio Communautaire de Harrington Harbour. Format: Adult contemp, Country, Oldies. Target aud: General; five fishing villages. Spec prog: News/talk. ♦Lana Shattler, gen mgr; Quenton Lessard, progmg dir; Rowena Osborne, progmg dir; Betty Strickland, news dir.

Havre-Saint-Pierre

CILE-FM— 1987: 95.1 mhz; 1.496 kw. Ant 201 ft. 992 Rue du Bouleau G0G 1P0. Phone: (418) 538-2453. Phone: (418) 538-2451. Fax: (418) 538-3870. E-mail: cilemf@globetrotter.net. Web Site: www.cilemf.com. Licensee: Radio & Television Communautaire Havre-St. Pierre. Format: MOR. ♦Berchmens Boudreau, gen mgr & progmg dir; Catherine Ramoisy, news dir; Gerald Gallant, engrg mgr.

Iles-de-la-Madeleine

CFIM-FM— Nov 15, 1981: 92.7 mhz; 6.3 kw. Stereo. C.P. 490, 1172 Chemin Laverniere, Cap-aux-Meules G0B 1B0. Phone: (418) 986-5233. Fax: (418) 986-5319. E-mail: cfimmf@sympatico.ca. Licensee: Diffusion Communautaire des Iles Inc. Diffusion Communautaire des Iles Format: Div, news/talk. Target aud: General. ♦Charles Eugene Cyr, gen mgr; Linda Noel, mktg VP; Suzanne Richard, gen mgr & progmg dir; Helen Fauteux, news dir; Paul Turbide, engrg dir.

Joliette

CJLM-FM— 1996: 103.5 mhz; 3 kw. TL: N45 59 0 W73 25 52. Stereo. 540 St. Thomas J6E 3R4. Phone: (450) 756-1035. Fax: (450) 756-8097. Licensee: Cooperative de Radiodiffusion MF 103.5 de Lanaudiere. Cooperative de Radiodiffusion MF 103.5 de Lanaudiere Format: MOR. Target aud: 25-49. Spec prog: Oldies 6 hrs wkly. ♦Marie Josee, prom VP; Jacques Plante, progmg mgr & news dir; Normand Masse, gen mgr, sls dir & engrg dir.

Jonquiere

CKAJ-FM— Apr 11, 1977: 92.5 mhz; 2.693 kw. Stereo. C.P. 872 G7X 7M8. Secondary address: Pavillon Manicougan, 3791, De La Fabrique G7X 7W8. Phone: (418) 546-2525. Phone: (418) 546-2526. Fax: (418) 546-2528. E-mail: informations@ckaj.org. Web Site: www.ckaj.org. Licensee: Radio Communautaire du Saguenay Inc. Format: Div, classic rock, country. News staff: one; News: 6 hrs wkly. Target aud: 25-54. Spec prog: Fr. ♦Anick Bilodau, pres; Alec Tremblay, opns dir; Pierre Boivin, progmg dir; Henri Girard, chief of engrg.

Kahnawake

*CKRK-FM— Mar 30, 1981: 103.7 mhz; 250 w. 75 ft. Stereo. Box 1050 J0L 1B0. Phone: (450) 638-1313. Phone: (450) 638-1407. Fax: (450) 638-4009. E-mail: programming@k103radio.com. Web Site: www.k103radio.com. Licensee: Mohawk Radio Kahnawake Association. (acq 8-4-94). Format: Adult contemp, C&W, contemp hit. News staff: 2; News: 3 hrs wkly. Target aud: General; young adults in Montreal suburban area. Spec prog: Mohawk 10 wkly. ♦Lois Williams, gen sls mgr; Christin Jerome, progmg dir, mus dir & news dir.

Kuujjuaq

CKUJ-FM— 1992: 97.3 mhz; 394 w. Box 1082 J0M 1C0. Phone: (819) 964-2921. Fax: (819) 964-2229. Licensee: Minister Council of Kuujjuaq. Format: Inuit. ♦Michael Gordon, pres; Mary Gordon, opns dir & news dir.

La Malbaie

*CBV-FM-6— Sept 20, 1979: 99.3 mhz; 820 w. Ant 108 ft. TL: N47 41 02 W70 08 06. 888 Saint-Jean St., Quebec G1R 5H6. Phone: (418) 654-1341. Fax: (418) 656-8842. Licensee: CBC. Network: Premiere Chaine. Format: Current Affairs/News. ♦Susan Campbell, gen mgr; Claude- Saindon, opns mgr; Sally Caldwell, news dir; Gaston LeBlanc, engrg mgr.

La Pocatiere

CHOX-FM— Apr 23, 1992: 97.5 mhz; 25 kw. Stereo. 601 lere rue, Suite 50 G0R1Z0. Phone: (418) 856-1310. Fax: (418) 856-3747. E-mail: choxfm@globetrotter.net. Web Site: cibm107.com. Licensee: CHOX-FM Inc. Format: CHR. ♦Guy Simard, pres; Gilles Gosselin, opns mgr & progmg VP; Diane Bouchard, dev VP; Georgette Charent, sls VP; Renee Giard, mktg VP; Michel Cloutier, prom VP; Michel Farvey, mus dir; Jacques Dufour, news dir; Clement Lavoie, engrg VP.

La Tabatiere

CFTH-FM-2— 1991: 98.5 mhz; 70 w. Box 88, Harrington Harbour G0G 1N0. Phone: (418) 795-3349. Fax: (418) 795-3200. Licensee: Radio communautaire de Harrington Harbour. Format: Var.

La Tuque

CFLM(AM)— Oct 3, 1959: 1240 khz; 1 kw-U, DA-2. C.P. 850, 529 St. Louis G9X 3P6. Phone: (819) 523-4575. Fax: (819) 676-8000. E-mail: radio.h-m@sympatico.ca. Licensee: Radio Haute Mauricle Inc. (acq 1982). Format: Var; adult contemp; CHR. News staff: one. Target aud: General. ♦Rejean LeClerc, pres, gen mgr & opns dir.

Lac Megantic

CJIT-FM— 2002: 106.7 mhz; 4.25 kw. 4766 rue Laval G6B 1C7. Phone: (819) 583-0663. Fax: (819) 583-0665. Licensee: 9063-0104 Quebec inc., doing business under the name of Radio Gae-Rit Lac Megantic Rep: Target Broadcast Sales. Format: Top-40, MOR. ♦Ritha Bregon, pres; Michel Brochu, opns mgr & progmg dir; Rachel Frigon, gen sls mgr; Mathieu Beaumont, news dir; Michel Mathieu, engrg dir.

Lac-Brome

CIDI-FM—Not on air, target date: unknown: 99.1 mhz; 496 w. 305B Knowlton Rd., Box 473, Knowlton J0E 1V0. Phone: (450) 242-2272. E-mail: rcm99.1fm@bellnet.ca. Web Site: www.sunnymead.org/cidi. Licensee: Radio Communautaire Missisquoi.

Quebec

Lac-Etchemin

*CFIN-FM— Mar 27, 1992: 100.5 mhz; 6.7 kw. 676 ft. TL: N46 24 41 W70 35 44. Stereo. 201 Claude-Bilodeau St. G0R 1S0. Phone: (418) 625-3737. Fax: (418) 625-3730. E-mail: cfinfm@sogetel.net. Web Site: www.cfinfm.com. Licensee: Radio Bellechasse. Target. Format: MOR, Country, Flashback. News staff: one; News: 30 hrs wkly. Target aud: 35-60. Spec prog: Fr, Sp, class 4 hrs, jazz 6 hrs, relg one hr, country 6 hrs wkly. ◆ Raymond Boutin, pres; Martin Roy, VP; Jean-Pierre Pampalon, stn mgr, sls dir & prom dir; Isabelle Giasson, progmg dir & mus dir; Cassio Pee Du Bois, news dir & pub affrs dir.

Lachute

CJLA-FM— Dec 1, 1974: 104.9 mhz; 3 kw. Stereo. 385 Rue Principale J8H 1Y1. Phone: (450) 562-8862. Fax: (450) 562-1902. E-mail: fusionfm@citenet.net. Licensee: Radio Nord Communications Inc. (group owner; acq 8-22-89). Format: Adult contemp. News staff: one; News: 8 hrs wkly. Target aud: 25-59. ◆ Pierre Brosseau, pres; Jean-Pierre Major, gen mgr; Marc Dubois, opns mgr & progmg dir; Yves Trottier, gen sls mgr; Olivier Proulx, news dir; Gaston Tousignant, chief of engrg.

Lac-Simon (Louvicourt)

CHUT-FM— 2000: 95.3 mhz; 97.9 w. 1016 rue Wabanonik, Lac-Simon J0Y 3M0. Phone: (819) 736-4501. Fax: (819) 736-2333. Licensee: Radio communautaire MF Lac Simon inc. Format: Community/aboriginal. ◆ Alain Flamand, gen mgr.

Laval

CFAV(AM)— January 2004: 1570 khz; 10 kw-U. Radio Nostalgie, 2040 Autoroute Laval H7S 2M9. Phone: (450) 680-1570. E-mail: avidtoire@nostalgie1570.com. Web Site: www.nostalgie1570.com. Licensee: Gilles Lajoie and Colette Chabot, on behalf of a corporation to be incorporated. Format: Nostalgia. ◆ Colette Chabot, gen mgr.

CFGL-FM— September 1968: 105.7 mhz; 41 kw. TL: N45 30 20 W73 35 32. (Digital radio: 1454.56 mhz; 1.594 kw at Laval, 1.4 kw at Montreal). Stereo. 2830 Boul. St. Martin E. H7E 5A1. Phone: (450) 664-1500. Phone: (514) 381-5903. Fax: (450) 664-4138. Fax: (450) 664-1651. Web Site: www.rythmefm.com. Licensee: Newco, a wholly owned subsidiary of Cogeco Radio Television Inc. Group owner: Cogeco Inc. Format: Adult contemp. News staff: 2; News: 2 hrs wkly. Target aud: 25-54; those preferring soft & easy lstng hits. ◆ Richard LaChance, gen mgr; Sylvain Venne, chief of opns; Daniel Brouilette, prom dir; Andre St-Amand, progmg dir; Lilianne Randall, mus dir; Jean Arcand, engrg dir.

Lennoxville

*CJMQ-FM— 2004: 88.9 mhz; 500 w. Stereo. Box 2135, Student Union Bldg., Bishop's University J1M 1Z7. Phone: (819) 822-9600, EXT. 2689. Phone: (819) 822-9600. Fax: (819) 822-9747. E-mail: cjmq@ubishops.ca. Web Site: www.ubishops.ca/cjmq. Licensee: Radio Bishop's Inc. Format: Campus/community. News: 5 hrs wkly. Target aud: General; campus & community. ◆ David Teasdale, stn mgr; Joel Heath, prom dir; Maureen Teasdale, progmg dir; Zaheed Bardai, mus dir; David Humble, engrg dir; Wayne Stacey, chief of engrg.

Les Escoumins

CHME-FM— 1994: 94.9 mhz; 5kw. C.P. 730 G0T 1K0. Secondary address: 34 rue de la Reserve G0T 1K0. Phone: (418) 233-2700. Fax: (418) 233-3326. E-mail: chme@b2b2c.ca. Licensee: Radio Essipit Haute Cote-Nord inc. Format: Fr. ◆ Gilles LaBelle, gen mgr.

Levis

CFOM-FM— 1992: 102.9 mhz; 16.8 kw. Stereo. 2136.ch.Ste-foy, Quebec G1V 1R8. Phone: (418) 694-1029. Fax: (418) 682-8430. E-mail: radioflashback@cfom1029.com. Web Site: www.cfom1029.com. Licensee: 591991 B.C. Ltd. Group owner: Astral Media Inc. (acq 1-21-2005; grpsl). Format: Hits of the 60s, 70s, 80s & 90s. Target aud: 25 plus. ◆ Pierre DeMondehare, gen mgr; Jean-Paul Lemire, sls dir; Annie Anglehart, prom dir; Mario Paquin, progmg dir.

Listuguj

CFIC-FM— 2000: 105.1 mhz; 50 w. Box 304 G0C 2R0. Secondary address: 44A Riverside E. G0C 2R0. Phone: (418) 788-5166. Fax: (418) 788-3524. Web Site: www.105hotcountry.com. Licensee: Societe d'Art, de Culture et d'Histoire Micmacs. Format: Country. ◆ Gerald Dedam, pres; Chris Dedam, gen mgr & engrg dir; Linda Gilbert, sls dir & news dir.

Longueuil

CHAA-FM— 1987: 103.3 mhz; 64 w. Stereo. 91 St. Jean J4H 2W8. Phone: (450) 646-6800. Fax: (450) 646-7378. E-mail: admin@chaamf.qc.ca. Web Site: www.chaafm.qc.ca. Licensee: Radio Communautaire de la Rive-Sud Inc. Rep: Target Broadcast Sales. Format: Adult contemp. News staff: 2; News: 5 hrs wkly. Target aud: 18-54; general. Spec prog: Fr 18 hrs, retro oldies 9 hrs, Greek 5 hrs, Vietnamese 4 hrs, Sp 3 hrs wkly. ◆ Eric Tetreault, chmn & gen mgr; Richard Boileau, sls dir & mktg dir; France Dube, progmg dir.

CHMP-FM— Apr 9, 1977: 98.5 mhz; 40.8 kw. Ant 623 ft. Stereo. 211 avenue Gordon, Verdun H4G 2R2. Phone: (514) 767-2435. Fax: (514) 761-0985. Web Site: www.fm985.ca. Licensee: Diffusion Metromedia CMR Inc. Group owner: Corus Entertainment Inc. (acq 1-26-2001; grpsl). Rep: Canadian Broadcast Sales. Format: Talk. News: 5 hrs wkly. Target aud: 18-44. ◆ Pierre Beland, pres; Pierre Accand, VP; Jacques Papin, gen mgr; David Therrien, sls dir; Michel Lacroix, gen sls mgr; Maurice Tietolman, natl sls mgr; Pierre Tremblay, prom mgr; Denis Fortin, progmg dir; Michel Belleau, mus dir; Real Terrault, chief of engrg.

Lourdes-de-Blanc-Sablon

CFBS-FM— 1989: 89.9 mhz; 178 w. C.P. 8 G0G 1W0. Phone: (418) 461-2445. Fax: (418) 461-2425. E-mail: cfbs@globetrotter.qc.ca. Licensee: Radio Blanc-Sablon inc. Format: Current affrs. ◆ Vicky Driscol, pres; Patrick Bereburbe, progmg dir; Dominique Jones, news dir & engrg mgr.

Magog

CIMO-FM— 1979: 106.1 mhz; 50 kw. 1845 King W., #200, Sherbrooke J1J 2E4. Phone: (819) 347-1414. Fax: (819) 347-1061. Web Site: www.radioenergie.com. Licensee: Astral Media Radio Inc. Group owner: Astral Media Inc. Format: Top 40. Target aud: 18-34. ◆ Nathalie Johnson, gen mgr; Isabelle Gagnon, sls dir; Anne-Marie Bercier, prom dir & progmg dir; Marc Toussaint, news dir; J.P. Maheu, chief of engrg.

Maliotenam

CKAU-FM— 1993: 104.5 mhz; 50 w. C.P. 338, Sept-Iles G4R 4K6. Phone: (418) 927-2440. Fax: (418) 927-2800. E-mail: dels@globetrotter.net. Web Site: www.ckau.com. Licensee: Corporation de Radio Kushapetsheken Apetuamiss Uashat. Format: Var. ◆ Yves Rock, gen mgr; Reginald Thomas, adv dir; Mathieu McKenzie, engrg mgr.

Maniwaki

CBOF-1(AM)— Oct 22, 1973: 990 khz; 40 w, DA-1. Box 3220, Stn C, Ottawa, ON K1Y 1E4. Phone: (613) 288-6000. Fax: (613) 288-6560. Web Site: cbc.ca. Licensee: Canadian Broadcasting Corp. Format: Div. ◆ Robert Rabinowitz, CEO; Denis Simard, gen mgr.

CFOR-FM— August 1994: 99.3 mhz; 2.4 kw. 184 Notre Dame St. J9E 2J5. Phone: (819) 441-0993. Fax: (819) 441-3488. E-mail: cfor993@b2b2c.ca. Licensee: 9116-1299 Quebec Inc. (acq 4-22-02). Format: Rock music. News staff: 3. Target aud: 15-45. ◆ Laure Voilquin, gen sls mgr; Rock Lepine, pres, gen mgr & progmg dir.

CHGA-FM— Nov 1980: 97.3 mhz; 2.8 kw. 163 Laurier Maniwaki J9E 2K6. Phone: (819) 449-3959. Phone: (819) 449-5590. Fax: (819) 449-7331. E-mail: chga@bellnet.ca. Web Site: www.chga.qc.ca. Licensee: Radio Communautaire Type B. Format: Div, adult contemp. News staff: one; News: 15 hrs wkly. Spec prog: Class one hr, jazz 3 hrs, country 8 hrs, folk 5 hrs wkly. ◆ Hubert Tremblay, pres; Lise Morissette, gen mgr; Lise Morisette, opns dir; Gaitam Bussiere, dev dir, gen sls mgr, mktg dir & progmg dir; Linda Lemieux, rgnl sls mgr; Kim Lacaille, mus dir; Georges Vasiloff, engrg dir.

Maniwaki (Kitigan Zibi Anishinabeg Reserve)

CKWE-FM— 1987: 103.9 mhz; 50 w. River Desert Indian Band, Box 309, Maniwaki J9E 3C9. Phone: (819) 449-5170. Phone: (819) 449-5097. Fax: (819) 449-5673. E-mail: anita.tenasco@kza.qc.ca. Licensee: Jean-Guy Whiteduck. Format: Talk, var, community news. ◆ Anita Penasco, gen mgr, sls dir & progmg dir; Eleanor Whiteduck, opns mgr.

Maria (Reserve)

CHRG-FM— 1991: 101.7 mhz; 10 w. Box 118 G0C 1Y0. Secondary address: 120 School St. G0C 1Y0. Phone: (418) 759-5424. Fax: (418) 759-5424. E-mail: radio@globetrotter.net. Licensee: Douglas Martin. Format: Country, oldies, var/div. ◆ Douglas Martin, gen mgr & progmg dir; Veronica Jerome, gen sls mgr & news dir.

Mashteuiatsh (Pointe-Bleue)

CHUK-FM— 1996: 107.3 mhz; 50 w. 1491 rue Ouiatchouan, Mashteuiatsh G0W 2H0. Phone: (418) 275-4684. Fax: (418) 275-7964. Web Site: www.chukfm.ca. Licensee: Corporation Mediatique Teuehikan. Format: Montagnais, Fr. ◆ Marc Gill, gen mgr; Jean Denis Gill, progmg dir & progmg dir.

Matagami

CHEF-FM— 2001: 99.9 mhz; 36 w. 110 boulevard Matagami, C.P. 39 J0Y 2A0. Phone: (819) 739-9990. Fax: (819) 739-6003. Licensee: Radio Matagami. Format: Fr, MOR. ◆ M. Jean-Claude Constantineau, pres; Marie-Eve C. Gallant, gen mgr; Daniel Cliche, dev dir; David Chabot, news dir.

Matane

CBGA-FM— 2004: 102.1 mhz; 42.93 kw. 155 rue Saint-Sacrement G4W 1Y9. Phone: (418) 562-0290. Phone: (418) 566-2322. Fax: (418) 562-3555. E-mail: communications_matane@radiocanada.ca. Web Site: radio-canada.ca/gaspesie. Licensee: CBC. Network: Premiere Chaine. Format: CHR, div, news/talk. News staff: 5; News: 3 hrs wkly. Target aud: General. ◆ Louis Pelletier, gen mgr; Johanne LaBrie, prom mgr; Richard Morisset, mus dir.

CHOE-FM— May 1991: 95.3 mhz; 30 kw. Stereo. 800 Ouest du Phare G4W 1V7. Phone: (418) 562-8181. Fax: (418) 562-0778. E-mail: choe.routage@globetrotter.net. Licensee: Les Communications Matane Inc. Format: Light rock. Target aud: 18-34; young workers. ◆ Kenneth Gagne, pres; Kenneth Gagne Jr., gen mgr, chief of opns & progmg dir; Michel Desrosiers, sls dir; Carol St-Pierre, news dir; Jacques Tremblay, chief of engrg.

CHRM-FM— April 2001: 105.3 mhz; 30 kw. 800 avenue du Phare Ouest G4W 1V7. Phone: (418) 562-4141. Fax: (418) 562-0778. Licensee: Les Communications Matane inc. Format: MOR. ◆ Kenneth Gagne, pres; Kenneth Gagne Jr., gen mgr, chief of opns & progmg dir; Michel Desrosiers, sls dir; Carol St-Pierre, news dir.

Mont-Laurier

CFLO-FM— 1995: 104.7 mhz; 10.98 kw. Stereo. 332 de la Madone J9L 1R9. Phone: (819) 623-5610. Phone: (819) 623-6610. Fax: (819) 623-7406. E-mail: cflofm@sympatico.ca. Web Site: www.cflofm@sypatico.ca. Licensee: Soneme Inc. Soneme Inc. (acq 1988). Rep: MPV Radio. Format: Adult contemp, French. News: 3 hrs wkly. Target aud: 24-54. ◆ Alain Desjardins, pres & stn mgr.

Montmagny

CFEL-FM— 1987: 102.1 mhz; 8.7 kw. 443 ft. TL: N46 56 21 W70 30 29. Stereo. 191 Chemen des Poirier G5V 4L2. Secondary address: 5245 Boulevard De La Rive-Sud Levis, Levis G6V4ZA. Phone: (418) 248-1122. Fax: (418) 248-1951. E-mail: cfel@globetrotter.net. Licensee: 5191991 B.C. Ltd. Group owner: Corus Entertainment Inc. (acq 3-24-2000; grpsl). Format: Adult contemp. News staff: one. Target aud: 25-49. ◆ Michel Montminy, gen mgr & opns VP; Rene' Nadeau, sls VP & progmg dir.

Directory of Radio Quebec

Montreal

CBF-FM— 1947: 95.1 mhz; 100 kw. 823 ft. (Digital radio: 1458.048 mhz; 11.724 kw). Stereo. Box 6000 H3C 3A8. Phone: (514) 597-6000. Fax: auditoire@radio-canada.ca. Web Site: www.cbc.radio-canada.ca. Licensee: CBC. Format: Class. ♦Sylvain LaFrance, VP; Bertrand Emond, gen mgr. Co-owned TV: CBFT(TV) affil.

CBFX-FM— 1998: 100.7 mhz; 100 kw. (Digital radio: 1458.048 mhz; 11.724 kw). Box 6000 H3C 3A8. Phone: (514) 597-6000. Fax: (416) 205-3714. Web Site: www.cbc.radio-canada.ca. Licensee: CBC. Network: Chaine Culturelle. Format: Var. ♦Sylvain LaFrance, VP; Bertrand Emond, stn mgr & progmg dir; Alain Saulnier, news dir.

CBME-FM— 1998: 88.5 mhz; 16.9 kw. (Digital radio: 1458.048 mhz; 11.724 kw). Box 6000 H3C 3A8. Phone: (514) 597-4444. Fax: (514) 597-4142. Web Site: www.radio-canada.ca. Licensee: Canadian Broadcasting Corp. Network: CBC Radio One. Format: News, current affrs. ♦Patricia Pleszczynska, stn mgr; Judith Bleier, opns mgr; Sally Caldwell, progmg dir & news dir.

CBM-FM— 1947: 93.5 mhz; 24.6 kw. 823 ft. (Digital radio: 1458.048 mhz; 11.724 kw). Stereo. Box 6000 H3C 3A8. Phone: (514) 597-6000. Fax: (514) 597-4416. Licensee: Canadian Broadcasting Corp. Format: Class. ♦Patricia Pleszczynska, stn mgr; Judith Bleier, opns mgr; Patricia Plesczynska, progmg dir. Co-owned TV: CBMT(TV) affil.

CFMB(AM)— Dec 21, 1962: 1280 khz; 50 kw-U, DA-2. TL: N45 19 31 W73 32 55. 35 York St., Westmount H3Z 2Z5. Phone: (514) 483-2362. Fax: (514) 483-1362. E-mail: admin@cfmb.ca. Web Site: www.cfmb.ca. Licensee: CFMB Ltee. Format: Ethnic. ♦Andrew Mielewczyk, pres & gen sls mgr; A.M. St. Germain-Stanczykowski, exec VP; Luigi Valente, stn mgr & chief of engrg; Marcello Silveri, rgnl sls mgr; Ivana Bombardieri, prom mgr; Walter Centa, natl sls mgr & progmg dir; Tony Ferrara, mus dir; Nino Di Stefano, news dir; Teddy Colantonio, pub affrs dir.

CFQR-FM—Listing follows CINW(AM).

CFZZ-FM—(Saint Jean-Iberville). 1992: 104.1 mhz; 1.35 kw. 104 rue Richelieu, St. Jean-Sur-Richelieu J3B 6X3. Phone: (450) 346-0104. Fax: (450) 348-2274. E-mail: z104@z104.fm. Web Site: www.z104.fm. Licensee: Astral Media Radio inc. Group owner: Corus Entertainment Inc. (acq 1-21-2005; grpsl). Format: Adult contemp. ♦Luc Lalonde, gen mgr & mktg dir; Ghislaine Plourde, progmg dir & news dir.

CHOM-FM— July 16, 1963: 97.7 mhz; 47.1 kw. Ant 979 ft. TL: N45 30 20 W73 35 32. (Digital radio: 1452.816 mhz; 11.724 kw). Stereo. 1411 Du Fort, 3rd Fl. H3H 2R1. Phone: (514) 931-2466. Fax: (514) 846-4747. Web Site: www.chom.com. Licensee: Standard Radio Inc. Group owner: Standard Broadcasting Corp. (acq 12-20-01; C$15 million. in swap for CFWM-FM Winnipeg, MB). Format: Rock. ♦Bob Harris, opns mgr; Jacques Bolduc, sls dir; Matt Cundill, progmg dir; Rob Braide, gen mgr & mus dir; Derek Conton, news dir; Mark Kavanagh, engrg mgr.

***CIBL-FM**— Apr 26, 1980: 101.5 mhz; 315 w. Stereo. 2nd Fl., 1691 Boul. Pie IX H1V 2C3. Phone: (514) 526-2581. Fax: (514) 526-3583. E-mail: info@cibl.cam.org. Web Site: www.cibl.cam.org. Licensee: Radio Communautaire Francophone de Montreal Inc. Format: Music/talk. News staff: 4; News: 14 hrs wkly. Target aud: General. Spec prog: Black 13 hrs, class 4 hrs, jazz 14 hrs, reggae 4 hrs, world beat 8 hrs wkly. ♦Andre Cyr, sls dir; Elizabeth Dery, gen mgr & mktg dir.

CINF(AM)—(Verdun). Nov 3, 1946: 690 khz; 50 kw-U, DA-2. 215 Jacques, Bureau 333 H2Y 1M6. Phone: (514) 849-1690. Fax: (514) 849-0733. Web Site: www.info690.com. Licensee: Metromedia CMR Montreal Inc. Group owner: Corus Entertainment Inc. (acq 1-26-01; grpsl). Format: News. ♦Pierre Arcand, pres; Maurice Tietolman, gen mgr; Christian Chalifour, sls dir; Marie Claude Baribault, prom dir; Yvon Vadnais, progmg dir; Kim Bickerdike, chief of engrg.

CKOI-FM—Co-owned with CINF(AM). 1953: 96.9 mhz; 307 kw. 712 ft. Stereo. Web Site: www.info690.com. Format: CHR. ♦Andre St. Amard, progmg dir.

CINQ-FM— Jan 27, 1975: 102.3 mhz; 1.29 kw. Ant 180 ft. Stereo. 5212 Boul. St. Laurent H2T 1S1. Phone: (514) 495-2597. Fax: (514) 495-2429. Web Site: www.radiocentreville.com. Licensee: Radio Centre-Ville Saint Louis Inc. Format: Multilingual, Fr, world music. News staff: one. Target aud: 25-54; Fr & multilingual. Spec prog: Sp 16, Portugese 13 hrs, Greek 13 hrs, Chinese 5 hrs, Haitian 6 hrs, Creole 12, English 16 hrs wkly. ♦Evan Kapelanakis, pres; Magalie Pare, stn mgr; Frantz Joachim, gen sls mgr & adv mgr; Ricardo Costa (English), progmg mgr; Suzanne Charland (Fr), progmg mgr; Robert Laplante, news dir; Marc Provencher, chief of engrg.

CINW(AM)— November 1999: 940 khz; 50 kw-U. 215 St. Jacques, Suite 333 H2Y 1M6. Phone: (514) 849-0940. Fax: (514) 849-0733. E-mail: news@940news.com. Web Site: www.940news.com. Licensee: Metromedia CMR Broadcasting Inc. Group owner: Corus Entertainment Inc. (acq 1-26-2001; grpsl). Rep: Canadian Broadcast Sales. Format: News. News staff: 4; News: 168 hrs wkly. Target aud: 35-54. ♦Pierre Beland, pres; Pierre Arcand, exec VP; Maurice Tietolman, gen mgr; George Weiss, sls VP & sls dir; Marie Claude Baribault, prom dir & prom mgr; Yven G. Vadnais, progmg dir & progmg mgr; Kim Bickerdike, chief of engrg.

CFQR-FM—Co-owned with CINW(AM). November 1966: 92.5 mhz; 41.4 kw. 979 ft. Stereo. Box 925 H4G 3M1. Secondary address: 211 Gordon Ave, Verdum Quebec H4F-2R2. Phone: (514) 767-9250. Web Site: www.940news.com. Format: Light rock. Target aud: 25-54. ♦Kathie Murphy, prom mgr; Ted Silver, progmg dir.

CIRA-FM— 1994: 91.3 mhz; 36.2 kw. 505 du Mont-Cassin Ave. H3L 1W7. Phone: (514) 382-3913. Fax: (514) 858-0965. E-mail: cira@radiovm.com. Web Site: www.radiovm.com. Licensee: Radio Ville-Marie. Format: Relg, div music. ♦Jean-Guy Roy, gen mgr; Andre Rocheleau, sls dir & progmg dir; Therese Miron, progmg dir; Mario Bard, news dir; Joe Pachecho, engrg mgr; Michael Forest, chief of engrg.

***CISM-FM**— March 1991: 89.3 mhz; 10 kw. Box 6128, C-1509, 2332 Edouard Montpetit H3C 3J7. Phone: (514) 343-7511. Fax: (514) 343-2418. E-mail: cism@cam.org. Web Site: www.cismfm.qc.ca. Licensee: Communications du Versant Nord. Format: Alternative. ♦Dave Ouellet, gen mgr; Guillaume St-Onge, prom dir; Candide Proulx, progmg dir; Martin Roussy, mus dir; Cecile Boumati, news dir; Luc Guillox, engrg dir.

CITE-FM— May 20, 1977: 107.3 mhz; 42.9 kw. 700 ft. (Digital radio: 1452.816 mhz; 11.724 kw). Stereo. 1717 Rene Levesque Est H2L 4T9. Phone: (514) 845-2483. Fax: (514) 288-1073. E-mail: cite@rock-detente.com. Web Site: www.rock-detente.com. Licensee: Astral Media Radio Inc. Group owner: Astral Media Inc. (acq 4-19-2002; grpsl). Rep: Integrated Media Sales. Format: Adult contemp. Target aud: 25-49. ♦Jacques Parisien, pres; Sylvain Langlois, VP; Luc Tremblay, gen mgr.

CJAD(AM)— Dec 8, 1945: 800 khz; 50 kw-D, 10 kw-N, DA-2. (Digital radio: 1454.56 mhz; 1.4 kw in Montreal, 1.594 kw in Laval). Stereo. 1411 Rue du Fort H3H 2R1. Phone: (514) 989-2523. Fax: (514) 989-3868. Web Site: www.cjad.com. Licensee: Standard Radio Inc. Group owner: Standard Broadcasting Corp. Format: News/talk, info. News staff: 15; News: 14 hrs wkly. ♦Rob Braide, VP & gen mgr; Blair Bartrem, opns mgr; Jacques Bolduc, gen sls mgr; Marie-Claude Baribeau, prom mgr; Rick Moffat, progmg mgr; Derek Conlon, news dir; Mark Kavanagh, engrg dir.

CJFM-FM—Co-owned with CJAD(AM). Oct 1, 1962: 95.9 mhz; 41.2 kw. 979 ft. (Digital radio: 1454.56 mhz; 1.4 kw in Montreal, 1.594 kw in Laval). Stereo. Phone: (514) 989-2536. Fax: (514) 989-2525. Web Site: www.themix.com. Format: Adult contemp. ♦Matthew Wood, prom mgr; Blair Bartrem, progmg mgr; Ray Scott, mus dir; Mark Kavanagh, chief of engrg.

CJPX-FM— June 25, 1998: 99.5 mhz; Radio Classique Montreal Inc., Iles Notre Dame, Parc Jean-Drapeau H3C 1A9. Phone: (514) 871-0995. Fax: (514) 871-0990. Licensee: Radio Classique Montreal Inc. Format: Class. ♦Jean-Pierre Coallier, CEO; Pierre Barbeau, VP; Francois Pare, gen mgr; Rejean Beaulieu, sls dir.

CJWI(AM)— 2002: 1610 khz; 1 kw-U. 3733 Jarry St. E. H1Z 2G1. Phone: (514) 287-1288. Fax: (514) 287-3299. Licensee: CPAM Radio Union.com inc. Format: Ethnic. ♦Jean Ernest Pierre, gen mgr.

CKAC(AM)— Sept 22, 1922: 730 khz; 50 kw-U, DA-1. (Digital radio: 1452.816 mhz; 11.724 kw). 1411 Peel St., BUR. 400 H3A 1S5. Phone: (514) 845-5151. Fax: (514) 845-2229. Web Site: www.ckac.com. Licensee: 591991 B.C. Ltd. Group owner: Astral Media Inc. (acq 1-21-2005; grpsl). Network: UPI. Format: MOR, news/talk. News: 20 hrs wkly. Target aud: 35-54. ♦Sylvain Chamberland, gen mgr; Julie Gagnon, opns dir.

CKDG-FM— January 2004: 105.1 mhz; 141 w. 5899 Park Ave. H2V 4H4. Phone: (514) 273-2481. Fax: (514) 273-3707. Web Site: www.chcr.ca. Licensee: Canadian Hellenic Cable Radio Ltd. Format: Ethnic. ♦John DeParis, pres; Francis Bergeron, gen mgr; Marie Griffths, gen mgr; Marie Grif, progmg dir; Tony Choundalas, news dir; Jean Frechette, engrg mgr.

CKGM(AM)— Dec 7, 1959: 990 khz; 50 kw-U. TL: N45 17 43 W73 43 20. (Digital radio: 1452.816 mhz; 11.724 kw). 1310 Greene Ave. H3Z 2B5. Phone: (514) 931-4487. Fax: (514) 931-4079. Web Site: www.team990.com. Licensee: CHUM Ltd. (group owner; acq 9-5-85). Rep: Hooper Jones. Format: Sports. ♦Lee Hambleton, gen mgr; Wayne Bews, sls dir & natl sls mgr.

CKLX-FM— 2004: 91.9 mhz; 1.9 kw. Ant 633 ft. 1 Place Ville Marie, Bureau 1523 H3B 2B5. Phone: (514) 866-8686. Fax: (514) 866-8056. Licensee: 9115-0318 Quebec inc. Group owner: Radio Nord Communications Inc. Format: Jazz and blues. Target aud: 35-64. ♦Jean-Pierre Major, gen mgr.

CKMF-FM— May 11, 1964: 94.3 mhz; 41.4 kw. 979 ft. (Digital radio: 1452.816 mhz; 11.724 kw). Stereo. 1717 Rene Levesque E. H2L 4T9. Phone: (514) 529-3229. Fax: (514) 529-9308. E-mail: Lsabbatini @radio.astral.com. Web Site: www.radioenergie.com. Licensee: Astral Media Radio Inc. Group owner: Astral Media Inc. (acq 1-12-2000; grpsl). Network: Radiomutuel. Format: CHR. News: one hr wkly. Target aud: 18-34. Spec prog: Disco. ♦Ian Greenburg, CEO; Jacques Parisien, chmn & pres; Luc Sabbatini, exec VP & opns mgr; Charles Benoit, VP; Luc Tremblay, gen mgr; Robert Latreille, stn mgr & engrg dir; Marie Josee Lefelbvre, natl sls mgr; Michel Tartif, rgnl sls mgr; Andre Allara, mktg dir; Johanne Cloutier, mktg mgr; Sylvain Legare, prom dir; Sylvain Simard, progmg dir.

***CKUT-FM**— November 1987: 90.3 mhz; 3647 University H3A 2B3. Phone: (514) 398-6787. Phone: (514) 398-6788. Fax: (514) 398-8261. Web Site: www.ckut.ca. Licensee: Radio McGill Inc. Format: Div. News staff: one; News: 6 hrs wkly. Spec prog: Black, Fr, Sp, folk, Gospel. ♦Louise Burns, sls VP & mktg dir; Suhrid Manchanda, prom dir; Steve Guimond, progmg dir, mus dir & pub affrs dir; Alex Moskos, asst music dir; Gretchen King, news dir; Valentine Latty, chief of engrg.

Natashquan

CKNA-FM— Jan 30, 1983: 104.1 mhz; 6.56 kw. C.P. 9 G0G 2E0. Secondary address: 29 chemin d'en Haut G0G 2E0. Phone: (418) 726-3284. Phone: (418) 726-3240. Fax: (418) 726-3367. E-mail: ckna@globetrotter.net. Web Site: pages.globetrotter.net/ckna/. Licensee: La Radio Communautaire CKNA Inc. Format: MOR. ♦Carmen Rodrigue, gen mgr; Vincent Pons, sls dir; Melanie Gauvin, prom mgr; Charles Benoit, progmg VP; Genevieve Moreau, mus dir.

New Carlisle

CHNC(AM)— Dec 23, 1933: 610 khz; 10 kw-D, 5 kw-N, DA-1. TL: N48 01 19 W65 14 52. Box 610 G0C 1Z0. Secondary address: 153 Rt. 132 G0C 1Z0. Phone: (418) 752-2215. Fax: (418) 752-6939. E-mail: radiochnc@globtrotter.net. Licensee: Radio CHNC Ltee. Network: Radiomedia. Format: Adult contemp, CHR. Target aud: General; Adult. ♦Art Houde, pres & gen mgr; Francois LePage, adv mgr; Gaetan Pelletier, progmg dir; Linda Gagnon, mus dir; Francis Remillard, asst music dir; Michel Merin, news dir.

Pikogan

CKAG-FM— 1993: 100.1 mhz; 50 w. 45 rue Migwan J9T 3A3. Phone: (819) 727-3237. Fax: (819) 732-1569. E-mail: ckagfm@cableamos.com. Licensee: Societe de Communication Ikito Pikogan Ltee.

Plessisville

CKYQ-FM— 1996: 95.7 mhz; 1 kw. Box 142 G6L 2Y6. Phone: (819) 362-3737. Fax: (819) 362-3414. E-mail: ckyq-fm@ivic.qc.ca. Web Site: www.kyqfm.com. Licensee: Societe CKYQ Radio Media Enr. Network: Telemedia. Format: MOR. ♦Hugh Laroche, news dir; Stephane Dion, pres, stn mgr, mktg dir, progmg dir & chief of engrg.

Pohenegamook

CFVD-FM-2— Sept 10, 1983: 92.1 mhz; 294 w. 654 6th St. E., Degelis G5T 1Y1. Phone: (418) 853-3370. Phone: (418) 853-2370. Fax: (418) 853-3321. E-mail: cfvd@fm95.ca. Web Site: infotennis.com. Licensee:

Radio Degelis Inc. Rep: MPV Radio. Format: Div, CHR. News staff: 10. Target aud: General. ♦Gilles Caron, pres, gen mgr & dev dir; Real Provencher, VP.

Port-Cartier

CIPC-FM— 1995: 99.1 mhz; 13 kw. Stereo. 52 Elie Roche Fort G5B 1N2. Phone: (418) 766-6868. Fax: (418) 766-6870. Licensee: Radio Port-Cartier Inc. Format: Top-40. ♦Patrick Guerard, pres, gen mgr & gen sls mgr; Danny Gravel, progmg dir; Sophie Paradis, news dir; Rosaire Lessard, chief of engrg.

Port-Menier

CJBE-FM— 1989: 90.1 mhz; 10 w. C.P. 15, Port-Menier (Ile d'Anticosti) G0G 2Y0. Phone: (418) 535-0292. Fax: (418) 535-0292. E-mail: radioanticosti@hotmail.com. Licensee: Radio Anticosti Inc. Format: Var. ♦Sandra Dussault, pres; Denis Tremblay, gen mgr & progmg dir.

Quebec

CBVE-FM— March 1979: 104.7 mhz; 100 kw. 411 ft. 888 Saint-Jean St. G1R 5H6. Phone: (418) 691-3613. Fax: (418) 691-3610. E-mail: quebecam@cbc.ca. Web Site: www.cbc.ca. Licensee: Canadian Broadcasting Corp. Network: CBC Radio One. Format: News/talk, div. ♦Claude Saindon, gen mgr & progmg dir; Judith Bleier, opns dir.

***CBV-FM**— 1974: 106.3 mhz; 100 kw. Ant 541 ft. TL: N46 51 40 W71 04 46. 888 Saint-Jean St. G1R 5H6. Phone: (418) 654-1341. Fax: (418) 656-8842. Web Site: www.cbc.ca. Licensee: Societe Radio Canada. Network: Premiere Chaine. Format: Div, news/talk. News: 15 hrs wkly. Target aud: General. ♦Marleine Simard, gen mgr; Robert Rabinovitch, pres & gen mgr; Marlene Simard, progmg dir; Norman LaCombe, news dir; Robert Jacques, engrg mgr. Co-owned TV: *CBVT-TV affil.

***CBVX-FM**— 1998: 95.3 mhz; 100 kw. 541 ft. TL: N46 51 40 W71 04 46. Stereo. 888 Saint-Jean St. G1R 5H6. Phone: (418) 654-1341. Fax: (418) 656-8212. Web Site: www.cbc.ca. Licensee: Societe Radio Canada. Network: Radio Canada. Format: Class. Target aud: General. Spec prog: Jazz 16 hrs, news 7 hrs wkly. ♦Marleine Simard, gen mgr & progmg dir; Real Jean, opns mgr.

CHIK-FM— Aug 1, 1982: 98.9 mhz; 41 kw. 1,355 ft. TL: N46 49 22 W71 29 43. 900 d'Youville St., 1st Floor G1R 3P7. Phone: (418) 687-9900. Fax: (418) 687-3106. Web Site: www.radioenergie.com. Licensee: Astral Media Radio Inc. Group owner: Astral Media Inc. Format: Adult contemp. ♦Daniel Tremblay, gen mgr; Real Marcotte, sls dir; Julie Durand, prom dir; Jean Alexandre, progmg dir; Rejean Bergeron, news dir; Michel Duval, engrg dir.

CHRC(AM)— Apr 1, 1926: 800 khz; 50 kw-U, DA-1. 2136 Chemin Sainte-Foy, Sainte.-Foy G1V 1R8. Phone: (418) 688-8080. Fax: (418) 670-1234. Web Site: www.chrc.com. Licensee: 591991 B.C. Ltd. Group owner: Astral Media Inc. (acq 1-21-2005; grpsl). Network: Telemedia. Format: Sports. Target aud: 35 plus. Spec prog: French.

***CION-FM**— Sept 19, 1995: 90.9 mhz; 5.69 kw. 1,364 ft. TL: N46 49 17 W71 29 48. Stereo. 2511 Chemin Ste-Foy, Suite 200 G1V 1T7. Phone: (418) 659-9090. Phone: (418) 650-1572. Fax: (418) 650-3306. E-mail: cionfm@radiogalilee.qc.ca. Licensee: Radio Galilee. Format: Relg, adult contemp, btfl mus. Target aud: General. ♦Alexandre St. Hilaire, pres; Denis Veilleux, gen mgr & progmg dir; Mario Blouin, mus dir; Jacques Fortin, news dir; Daniel Coulombe, engrg mgr.

CITF-FM— July 22, 1982: 107.5 mhz; 37.8 kw. 500 ft. Stereo. 900 Dyouville St., 1st Fl. G1R 3P7. Phone: (418) 527-3232. Fax: (418) 687-3106. Web Site: www.rockdetente.com. Licensee: Astral Media Radio Inc. Group owner: Astral Media Inc. (acq 4-19-2002; grpsl). Rep: Integrated Media Sales. Radio Plus. Format: Adult contemp. News staff: 2. Target aud: 25-54. ♦Michel Duval, CEO & chief of engrg; Daniel Tremblay, gen mgr; Suzie Baronet, sls dir; Julie Durand, prom dir; Marc Tanguay, progmg dir.

CJEC-FM— August 2003: 91.9 mhz; 14.45 kw. 1305 Chemin Ste-Foy, 4e etage G1S 4Y5. Phone: (418) 688-0919. Fax: (418) 527-0919. Web Site: www.rythmefm.com/qbc_rythme01.html. Licensee: Cogeco Diffusion Inc. Group owner: Cogeco Radio-Television Inc. Format: Adult contemp. ♦Louis Audet, pres; Geoffrey O. Brown, gen mgr; Carole Vezina, sls dir; Daniel Plante, mktg dir, prom dir & progmg dir; Lilianne Randall, mus dir; Martin Perkins, engrg dir.

CJMF-FM— Sept 15, 1979: 93.3 mhz; 32.96 kw. Ant 1,275 ft. Stereo. 1305 Chemin Ste-Foy, 4e etage G1S 4Y5. Phone: (418) 687-9330. Fax: (418) 687-0211. E-mail: commentaire@cjmf.com. Web Site: www.le933.com. Licensee: Cogeco Diffusion Inc. Group owner: Cogeco Radio-Television Inc. (acq 11-87; $8 million). Format: Talk, classic rock. News staff: 27; News: 5 hrs wkly. Target aud: 25-54; mostly female with upscale income. ♦Louis Audet, pres; Jean-Paul Lemue, gen mgr.

CKIA-FM— Oct 31, 1984: 88.3 mhz; 350 w. 700 ft. TL: N46 48 28 W71 12 57. 600 Cote d'Abraham G1R 1A1. Phone: (418) 529-9026. Fax: (418) 529-4156. E-mail: ckiafm@moso.com. Web Site: www.meduse.org/ckiafm. Licensee: Radio Basse-Ville Inc. Format: Classic rock, country, div. News staff: one; News: 2 hrs wkly. Target aud: 18-35; general. Spec prog: Class 3 hrs, jazz 4 hrs, Sp 4 hrs, Haitian 2 hrs, African one hr wkly. ♦Jacynthe Huard, gen mgr; Reynald Poirier, gen sls mgr; Sophie Anne Mailloux, progmg dir & news dir; Denis Roberge, chief of engrg.

***CKRL-FM**— Feb 15, 1973: 89.1 mhz; 1.4 kw. 700 ft. TL: N46 48 27 W71 13 02. Stereo. 405 3rd Ave. G1L 2W2. Phone: (418) 640-2575. Fax: (418) 640-1588. E-mail: ckrl@ckrl.qc.ca. Web Site: www.ckrl.qc.ca. Licensee: CKRL MF 89.1 Inc. Format: Adult contemp, jazz, class, rock. News staff: one. Spec prog: Sp 2 hrs, It 2 hrs, Black 6 hrs, Arab 3 hrs wkly. ♦Dany Fortin, gen mgr & sls dir; Daniel Deslauriers, mktg dir; Bastien Gagnon La France, progmg dir; Daniel Marcoux, mus dir.

Radisson

CIAU-FM— 1996: 103.1 mhz; 17 w. Box 285 J0Y 2X0. Secondary address: 143 rue Jolliet J0Y 2X0. Phone: (819) 638-7033. Phone: (819) 638-1031. Fax: (819) 638-7033. E-mail: ciaufm@lino.com. Web Site: www.ciaufm.com. Licensee: Radio communautaire de Radisson (acq 4-23-2004). Format: Var. News staff: one; News: 3 hrs wkly. Spec prog: Fr 8 hrs, Jazz 3 hrs wkly. ♦Eric Hamel, pres, dev dir & sls dir; Martin Beaucage, stn mgr, opns dir, prom dir & adv dir; Martin Beaucaage, progmg dir.

Restigouche

CHRQ-FM— 1991: 106.9 mhz; 31 w. Box 180 G0C 2R0. Phone: (418) 788-2449. Fax: (418) 788-2653. E-mail: chrq1069@globetrotter.net. Licensee: Gespegewag Communications Society. Format: English-language & Micmac-laguage community radio. News staff: 5; News: one hr wkly. Community members all ages. ♦Sandra Bulmer, stn mgr; Chad Gedeon, rgnl sls mgr; Karen Duguay, prom mgr; Steve Clement, progmg mgr.

Rimouski

***CBRX-FM**— Feb 28, 1959: 101.5 mhz; 50 kw. 931 ft. Stereo. 273 rue St-Jean Baptiste Ouest G5L 4J8. Phone: (418) 723-2217. Fax: (418) 723-6126. Licensee: Canadian Broadcasting Corp. Network: Chaine Culturelle. Format: Class, jazz, talk. ♦Bernard Labarge, pres & news dir; Bernard Lebarge, gen mgr; Bernard Labarbe, progmg dir.

CIKI-FM— Feb 14, 1988: 98.7 mhz; 76 kw. Stereo. 875 Boul. St. Germain Ouest G5L 3T9. Phone: (418) 723-2323. Fax: (418) 722-7508. E-mail: ciki@pqm.net. Web Site: www.ciki.fm. Licensee: Astral Media Radio inc. Group owner: Corus Entertainment Inc. (acq 1-21-2005; grpsl). Format: AOR. ♦Bertrand Bellavance, gen mgr; Jean Fournier, opns mgr & chief of engrg; Ghislain Desgardins, sls dir; Francois La Fond, progmg dir; Alain Rivard, mus dir; Martin Bressard, news dir.

CJBR-FM— 2000: 89.1 mhz; 19.4 kw. 273 rue St-Jean Baptiste Ouest G5L 4J8. Phone: (418) 723-2217. Fax: (418) 723-6126. Licensee: Canadian Broadcasting Corp. Format: MOR, adult contemp, news/talk. Spec prog: Fr. ♦Bernard Labarge, gen mgr & news dir.

CJOI-FM— Oct 22, 2000: 102.9 mhz;; 33.6 kw. 875 Boul. St. Germain Ouest G5L 3T9. Phone: (418) 723-2323. Fax: (418) 722-7508. E-mail: cjoi@pqm.net. Web Site: www.cjoi.fm. Licensee: Astral Media Radio inc. Group owner: Corus Entertainment Inc. (acq 1-21-2005; grpsl). Format: MOR. ♦Bertrand Bellavance, gen mgr; Jean Fournier, opns mgr & chief of engrg; Francois La Fond, progmg dir; Martin Bressard, news dir.

Rimouski-Mont Joli

CKMN-FM— June 4, 1990: 96.5 mhz; 6.4 kw. TL: N48 22 32 W68 35 43. Stereo. 323 Montee Industrielle, Rimouski G5M 1A7. Phone: (418) 722-2566. Fax: (418) 724-7815. E-mail: ckmn-fm@cgocable.ca. Licensee: La Radio Communautaire du Comte. Format: Adult contemp, CHR, country. News staff: 5. Target aud: 25-55; general. Spec prog: Oldies 3 hrs, classical 3 hrs wkly. ♦Antonini Michaud, exec VP; Jean-Claude Pinel, exec VP; Claude Marmen, mktg dir; Renie Langlois, prom dir & progmg dir; Michel Vallee, chief of engrg.

Riviere au Renard

CJRE-FM— 1979: 97.9 mhz; 56 w. 594 ft. 162 Jacques Cartier, Gaspe G4X 1M9. Phone: (418) 368-3511. Fax: (418) 368-1663. Licensee: Radio Gaspesie Inc. Format: MOR. ♦Jacques Chartier, gen mgr; Paul Mainville, sls dir; Jacques Henri, progmg dir; Genevieve Gelinas, news dir; Yvan Dupuis, engrg dir.

Riviere du Loup

CIBM-FM— 1966: 107.1 mhz; 100 kw. Ant 244 ft. 64 Hotel de Ville G5R 1L5. Phone: (418) 867-1071. Fax: (418) 862-7704. Web Site: www.cibm107.com. Licensee: CIBM Mont-Bleu. Network: Radiomedia. Format: Pop rock. ♦Guy Simard, gen mgr; Renee Giard, gen sls mgr & prom dir; Daniel St. Pierre, progmg dir; Martin Pelletier, news dir; Clement Lavore, engrg dir.

CIEL-FM— Dec 15, 1994: 103.7 mhz; 60 kw. Ant 1,050 ft. TL: N47 34 53 W69 22 20. 64 Hotel-de-Ville G5R 1L5. Phone: (418) 862-8241. Fax: (418) 862-7704. Web Site: www.103rockdouceur.com/ciel. Licensee: Radio CJFP (1986) Ltee. Format: Adult contemp. ♦Guy Simard, pres & gen mgr; Renee Giard, sls dir, natl sls mgr, rgnl sls mgr, mktg dir & prom dir; Daniel St. Pierre, progmg dir, mus dir, asst music dir & news dir; Clement LaVoie, engrg dir.

Roberval

CHRL-FM— March 1, 2002: 99.5 mhz; 16.6 kw. TL: N48 26 25 W72 06 47. 568 Blvd. St. Joseph G8H 2K6. Phone: (418) 275-1831. Fax: (418) 275-2475. E-mail: chrl@antenne6.com. Licensee: Radio Roberval inc. Group owner: Group Radio Antenne 6 Inc. Network: Radiomedia. Format: Div, info, music. News staff: one; News: 20 hrs wkly. Target aud: General; mainly adults. ♦Marc-Henri Levesque, gen mgr; Lewis Gagnon, sls dir; Louis Arcand, progmg dir & news dir.

Rouyn-Noranda

CHIC-FM— 2003: 88.7 mhz; 50 w. C.P. 2185 J9X 5A6. Phone: (819) 797-4242. Fax: (819) 797-3803. Licensee: Communications CHIC (C.H.I.C.). Format: Fr, Christian music. ♦Andre Curadeau, gen mgr; Vic Cimon, stn mgr & opns dir; Jocelyn Cote, sls dir & progmg dir.

CHOA-FM— Sept 21, 1990: 96.5 mhz; 55 kw. 600 ft. Stereo. 380 Ave. Murdoch J9X 1G5. Phone: (819) 762-0741. Fax: (819) 762-2280. Licensee: Radio Nord Communications Inc. (group owner). Format: Adult contemp. Target aud: 25-54. ♦Pierre R. Brosseau, CEO & pres; Jean-Pierre Major, gen mgr; Frantz Boivin, sls dir; Jean Gagnon, news dir; Gerald Landry, chief of engrg. Co-owned TV: CFEM-TV, CKRN-TV affils.

CJMM-FM— June 17, 1988: 99.1 mhz; 3.5 kw. Ant 200 ft. Stereo. 33B Gamble Ouest J9X 2R3. Phone: (819) 797-2566. Fax: (819) 797-1664. E-mail: mtrottier@radioenergie.astral.com. Web Site: www.radioenergie.com. Licensee: Astral Media Radio Inc. Group owner: Astral Media Inc. (acq 1-12-2000; grpsl). Format: Adult contemp. News staff: one; News: 5 hrs wkly. Target aud: 18-44. ♦Marlene Trottier, gen mgr & sls dir; Stefan Baillargeon, natl sls mgr, rgnl sls mgr, prom dir, prom mgr, progmg dir & mus dir; Guy Champoux, news dir; Mathieu Barrette, engrg mgr.

Saguenay

CJAB-FM— May 25, 1979: 94.5 mhz; 44.2 kw. Stereo. 121 Racine Est., Chicoutimi G7H 5G4. Phone: (418) 545-9450. Fax: (418) 545-9186. Licensee: Astral Media Radio Inc. Group owner: Astral Media Inc. (acq 8-21-92). Network: Radiomutuel. Format: Pop. ♦Richard Turcotte, gen mgr; Carol Tremblay, sls dir; Katia Boivin, progmg dir; Jean-Francois Cote, news dir; Stephane Villeneuve, engrg mgr.

CKRS(AM)— June 23, 1947: 590 khz; 25 kw-D, 7.5 kw-N. 121 Racine St., Chicoutimi G7H 5G4. Phone: (418) 545-2577. Fax: (418) 545-9186. Web Site: www.ckrs.com. Licensee: 591991 B.C. Ltd. Group owner: Astral Media Inc. (acq 1-21-2005; grpsl). Network: Radiomutuel. Format: Oldies, news/talk. Target aud: 25-54. ♦Richard

Turcotte, gen mgr; Michel Gaguou, sls dir; Brigette Simard, prom VP; Daniel Coto, prom VP; Eric Arsene;aut, chief of engrg.

Saint Augustin

CJAS-FM— 1992: 93.5 mhz; 100 w. C.P. 100, Comte Duplessis, Riviere Saint-Augustin G0G 2R0. Phone: (418) 947-2239. Fax: (418) 947-2664. E-mail: sajcr@globetrotter.com. Licensee: La Radio Communautaire de Riviere St-Augustin Inc. Format: Adult contemp. ♦ Laurette Gallibois, gen mgr, sls dir & mktg dir; Maria Shattler, progmg dir; Lindsey Durepos, mus dir; Rachel Bilodeau, news dir.

Saint Constant

CJMS(AM)— May 1999: 1040 khz; 10 kw-D, 5 kw-N. Rm. 102, 200B St. Pierre J5A 2G9. Phone: (514) 990-2567. Fax: (450) 632-0528. Web Site: www.cjms.ca. Licensee: 3553230 Canada Inc. (acq 3-29-01). Network: Radio Unica. Format: Country. News staff: 2. ♦ Alex Azoulay, pres; Jean-Francois DuBois, gen mgr.

Saint Gabriel-de-Brandon

CFNJ-FM— Aug 10, 1985: 99.1 mhz; 9.75 kw. Ant 1,300 ft. C.P. 120, 30 rue des Ecoles J0K 2N0. Phone: (450) 835-3437. Phone: (450) 835-3438. Fax: (450) 835-3581. E-mail: cfng99@pandora.qc.ca. Licensee: Radio Nord-Joli Inc. Format: MOR. Spec prog: Black one hr, class 2 hrs, C&W 4 hrs, jazz 2 hrs. ♦ Denis Roch, pres, pres & gen mgr; Audrey Turenne, sls dir; Nicolas Bellemare, progmg dir.

Saint Georges

CHJM-FM— June 22, 1987: 99.7 mhz; 100 kw. 350 ft. Stereo. C.P. 100, Saint Georges-de-Beauce G5Y 5C4. Secondary address: 170 120ieme rue, Saint Georges-de-Beauce G5Y 5C4. Phone: (418) 227-0997. Phone: (418) 228-5535. Fax: (418) 228-0096. E-mail: adminrb@cgocable.ca. Web Site: www.mix997.som. Licensee: Radio Beauce Inc. (acq 10-24-02; C$432,000. with CKRB-FM Saint Georges-de-Beauce). Format: Rock. News staff: one; News: 4 hrs wkly. Target aud: 18-35. ♦ Guy Simard, pres; Marie Jalbert, gen mgr; Renee Giard, sls dir; Jacques Goulet, natl sls mgr; Louis Poulin, prom mgr; Marcel Rancourt, mus dir; Susanne Bougie, news dir; Gaston Guay, chief of engrg.

Saint Georges-de-Beauce

CKRB-FM— October 1953: 103.5 mhz; 17 kw. Stereo. C.P. 100 G5Y 5C4. Secondary address: 170, 120th Rue G5Y 5C4. Phone: (418) 228-1460. Phone: (418) 228-5535. Fax: (418) 228-0096. E-mail: adminrb@ckrb1033.com. Web Site: www.ckrb1033.com. Licensee: Radio Beauce Inc. (acq 10-24-02; C$432,000. with CHJM-FM Saint Georges). Format: Adult contemp. News staff: 2; News: 11 hrs wkly. Target aud: 35 plus. ♦ Guy Simard, pres; Maurice Marcotte, gen mgr; Renee Giard, sls dir; Jacques Goulet, natl sls mgr; Louis Poulin, prom mgr; Marcel Rancourt, mus dir; Suzanne Bougie, news dir; Gaston Guay, chief of engrg.

Saint Hilarion

CIHO-FM— Oct 10, 1986: 96.3 mhz; 315 Cartier Nord G0A 3V0. Phone: (418) 457-3333. Fax: (418) 457-3518. E-mail: ciho@charlevoix.net. Licensee: Radio MF Charlevoix Inc. Format: MOR. Spec prog: Class 2 hrs, jazz 2 hrs wkly. ♦ Gervais Desbiens, gen mgr; Rene Belanger, adv mgr; Pierre Beauchesne, progmg dir & engrg mgr; Dave Kid, news dir.

Saint Hyacinthe

CFEI-FM— 1988: 106.5 mhz; 3 kw. 855 rue Ste. Marie J2S 4R9. Phone: (450) 774-6486. Fax: (450) 774-7785. E-mail: cfei@cgocable.ca. Web Site: www.boomfm.astral.com. Licensee: Astral Media Radio Inc. Group owner: Astral Media Inc. (acq 8-13-2001). Format: 60s, 70s. ♦ Jacques Parisien, pres; Martin Tremblay, gen mgr, opns mgr & sls dir; Jean-Frrancois Herbert, progmg dir; Anddre Lalier, mus dir.

Saint Jean-Iberville

CFZZ-FM—Licensed to Saint Jean-Iberville. See Montreal

Saint Jerome

CIME-FM— Mar 25, 1977: 103.9 mhz; 11.7 kw. Stereo. 120 Delagare St. J7Z 2C2. Phone: (450) 431-2463. Fax: (450) 565-9755. E-mail: ventes@cime.fm. Licensee: Diffusion Metromedia CMR Inc. Group owner: Corus Entertainment Inc. (acq 1-26-01; grpsl). Format: Adult contemp. ♦ John Cassidy, pres; Norman Martel, gen mgr.

Saint Pamphile

CJDS-FM— Dec 7, 2001: 94.7 mhz; 24 w. C.P. 550 G0R 3X0. Phone: (418) 356-1303. Fax: (418) 356-2586. E-mail: cjdsradio@globetrotter.net. Licensee: 3819914 Canada inc. Format: MOR. ♦ Jean-Claude Dignard, pres & gen mgr; Claire Soulieres, opns mgr & sls dir; Ann Dignard, dev dir & progmg dir; J. C. Dignard, pub affrs dir.

Saint Remi

*****CHOC-FM**— 1999: 104.9 mhz; 250 w. 107 Chevrefils J0L 2L0. Phone: (450) 454-5500. Fax: (450) 454-9435. E-mail: chocfm@cam.org. Web Site: webchoc.fr.fm. Licensee: Radio Communautaire Intergeneration Jardin du Quebec. Format: Community radio. News staff: one; News: 10 hrs wkly. ♦ Yvon Potvin, pres.

Sainte Anne des Monts

CBGN(AM)— 1972: 1340 khz; 1 kw-D, 250 w-N. 155 St. Sacrament St., Matane G4W 1Y9. Phone: (418) 562-0290. Fax: (418) 566-6068. Licensee: CBC. (acq 9-1-72). Format: Talk, news. ♦ Louis Pelletier, gen mgr.

CJMC-FM— March 1996: 100.3 mhz; 2.51 kw. 170 Boul. Ste. Anne G4V 1N1. Phone: (418) 763-5522. Phone: (418) 763-5523. Fax: (418) 763-7211. Web Site: cjmc@quebectel.com. Licensee: Radio du Golfe Inc. Format: MOR. Spec prog: Class 2 hrs, western 2 hrs wkly. ♦ Jacques Vallee, pres, opns dir, sls dir & mktg dir; Olivier Vallee, prom dir; Stephane Cyr, progmg dir, mus dir, news dir & chief of engrg.

Sainte Foy

*****CHYZ-FM**— Jan 29, 1997: 94.3 mhz; 6 kw. Stereo. Pavillon Pollack, Cite Universitaire, Suite 023 G1K 7P4. Phone: (418) 656-2131 ext. 4595. Fax: (418) 656-3660. E-mail: chyz@public.ulaval.ca. Web Site: www.chyz.qc.ca. Licensee: Radio Campus Laval. Format: Fr, div, techno/electronica. News staff: 4; News: 10 hrs wkly. Target aud: 18-30; univ students. Spec prog: Hip-hop/rap 15 hrs wkly. ♦ Jean-Philippe Lessard, gen mgr.

Sainte-Marie-de-Beauce

CHEQ-FM— Nov 29, 1998: 101.3 mhz; 4.677 kw. 1068 boul. Vachon N., Suite 101 G6E 1M6. Phone: (418) 387-1013. Fax: (418) 387-3757. E-mail: cheqfm@globetrotter.net. Web Site: www.cheqfm.qc.ca. Licensee: 9079-3670 Quebec Inc. (acq 8-16-00). Format: MOR, adult contemp. ♦ Jacques Poulin, pres; Sylvie Paulin, gen mgr & opns mgr.

Senneterre

CIBO-FM— 1982: 100.5 mhz; C.P. 1150 J0Y 2M0. Phone: (819) 737-2222. Fax: (819) 737-8599. E-mail: cibofm@yahoo.ca. Licensee: Radio communautaire M.F. de Senneterre Inc. Format: Community. ♦ Guy Bilodeau, pres & gen mgr.

Sept-Iles

*****CBSI-FM**— Nov 1, 1982: 98.1 mhz; 96.7 kw. 350 ft. 350 rue Smith, bur. 30 G4R 3X2. Phone: (418) 968-0720. Phone: (800) 463-1731. Fax: (418) 968-9219. Fax: (418) 962-1344. E-mail: cbsi@radio-canada.ca. Web Site: www.radio-canada.ca/cote-nord. Licensee: CBC. Format: Div, educ, talk. Target aud: General. ♦ Pierre Lafreniere, stn mgr.

CKCN-FM— December 1998: 94.1 mhz; 4.88 kw. 437 Arnaud St. G4R 3B3. Phone: (418) 962-3838. Fax: (418) 968-6662. E-mail: ckcn@globetrotter.net. Licensee: Radio Sept-Iles Inc. Network: Radiomedia. Rep: Radio Unie Target. Format: Adult contemp, news/talk. News: 16 hrs wkly. Target aud: 25-54. Spec prog: Country 8 hrs wkly. ♦ Pierre Bergeron, pres & gen mgr; Dominique Marquis, stn mgr.

Shawinigan

CFUT-FM— Feb 7, 2005: 91.1 mhz; 5 w. 5655 boulevard des Hetres G9N 4V9. Phone: (819) 539-5493, ext 232. Fax: (819) 539-1749. Licensee: La radio campus communautaire francophone de Shawinigan inc. ♦ Denis Benoit, gen mgr.

CKSM(AM)— Apr 30, 1951: 1220 khz; 10 kw-D, 2.5 kw-N, DA-2. 1350 rue Royale, Bureau 1200, Trois Rivieres G9A 4J4. Phone: (819) 374-3556. Fax: (819) 374-3222. Licensee: Astral Media Radio Inc. Group owner: Astral Media Inc. Format: Adult contemp, news/talk, sports. ♦ Jean Martin, gen mgr; Diane Marchand, sls dir; Claude Bolduc, prom dir, adv dir & progmg dir.

Sherbrooke

CFAK-FM— 2003: 88.3 mhz; 490 w. Radio CFAK, 2500 boul. de Universite, local 116 J1K 2R1. Phone: (819) 821-8000 ext 2693. Fax: (819) 821-7930. E-mail: dq@cfak.qc.ca. Web Site: www.cfak.qc.ca. Licensee: Comite de la radio etudiante universitaire de Sherbrooke (CREUS). Format: Fr. ♦ Steve Bazinet, gen mgr.

CFGE-FM— July 2004: 93.7 mhz; 1.78 kw. 3720 boulevard Industriel J1L 1Z9. Phone: (819) 822-0937. Fax: (819) 822-2112. Web Site: www.rythmefm.com/estrie. Licensee: Cogeco Diffusion inc. Format: Adult contemp. News staff: one. ♦ Michel Cloutier, gen mgr; Andre' David, gen sls mgr; Dominc D'Anjou, progmg dir.

CFLX-FM— 1984: 95.5 mhz; 1.35 kw. TL: N45 22 50 W71 54 51. Stereo. 67 N Wellington St. J1H 5A9. Phone: (819) 566-2787. Fax: (819) 566-7331. E-mail: cflx@cflx.qc.ca. Web Site: www.cflx.qc.ca. Licensee: Radio communautaire de l'Estrie. Format: News/talk, div, Fr. News staff: 2; News: 10 hrs wkly. Target aud: 18-35; college degree. Spec prog: Class 7 hrs, jazz 8 hrs, Sp 3 hrs wkly. ♦ Daniel Bergeron, pres; Jose Deschenes, gen mgr & opns mgr.

CHLT(AM)— June 1937: 630 khz; 10 kw-D, 5 kw-N. TL: N45 18 16 W71 51 59. 4020 boul. de Portland J1L 2V6. Phone: (819) 563-6363. Fax: (819) 566-4222. Licensee: 591991 B.C. Ltd. Group owner: Astral Media Inc. (acq 1-21-2005; grpsl). Network: Radiomedia. Format: News/talk. News staff: 4; News: 20 hrs wkly. Target aud: 18 plus. ♦ Marc Fabi, gen mgr & sls dir; Gilles Morin, prom dir; Jocelyn Proulx, progmg dir; Michel Laroche, chief of engrg.

CIGR-FM— 2004: 104.5 mhz; 1.3 kw. 4020 Boul. Portland J1L 2V6. Phone: (819) 829-1045. Fax: (819) 829-1315. E-mail: info@grock.fm. Web Site: www.generationrock.fm. Licensee: Groupe Generation Rock. Format: Fr, rock. ♦ Jean-Pierre Beaudoin, gen mgr.

CIMO-FM—See Magog

CITE-FM-1— September 1962: 102.7 mhz; 92.8 kw. Ant 1,851 ft. Stereo. 1845 King West, Suite 200 J1J 2E4. Phone: (819) 566-6655. Fax: (819) 566-1011. Licensee: Astral Media Radio Inc. (acq 4-19-2002; grpsl). Format: Adult contemp. ♦ Natalie Johnson, gen mgr.

CKTS(AM)— July 1, 1946: 900 khz; 10 kw-U, DA-2. TL: N45 26 00 W72 01 00. 4020 boul. de Portland J1L 2V6. Phone: (819) 347-1414. Fax: (819) 566-4222. Licensee: 591991 B.C. Ltd. Group owner: Astral Media Inc. (acq 1-21-2005; grpsl). Format: Talk. ♦ Jocelyn Proulx, gen mgr.

Sorel

CJSO-FM— Sept 27, 1989: 101.7 mhz; 3.5 kw. 327 ft. 100 boul. Couillard Despres, Sorel-Tracy J3P 5C1. Phone: (450) 743-2772. Fax: (450) 743-0293. E-mail: cjso@cjso.qc.ca. Web Site: www.cjso.qc.ca. Licensee: Radio Diffusion Sorel-Tracy Inc. (acq 4-21-95). Rep: MPV Radio. Format: Soft rock. News staff: 2; News: 5 hrs wkly. Spec prog: Class 2 hrs wkly. ♦ Claude St. Germain, gen mgr; Jean Lemay, progmg dir; Valerie Ferland, mus dir; Jean-Marc Lebeau, news dir.

Thetford Mines

CFJO-FM— July 15, 1989: 97.3 mhz; 100 kw. Ant 270 ft. 55 St. Jean Baptiste, Victoriaville G6P 6T3. Secondary address: 327 Rue Labbe G6G 5S3. Phone: (418) 338-1009. Phone: (819) 752-2785. Fax: (819) 338-0386. Fax: (819) 752-3182. Web Site: www.o973.com. Licensee: Reseau des Appalaches (FM) Ltee. Group owner: Gestion Appalaches inc. Rep: Broadcast Sales, Target Broadcast Sales. Format: Classic rock, AOR. News staff: 15. Target aud: 18-40. ♦ Annie Labbe, pres.

Quebec

CKLD-FM— 1950: 105.5 mhz; 6 kw. Stereo. Box 69, 327 Rue Labbe G6G 5S3. Phone: (418) 335-7533. Fax: (418) 335-9009. Web Site: www.passionrock.com. Licensee: Radio Megantic Ltee. Group owner: Gestion Appalaches inc. Rep: Broadcast Sales, Target Broadcast Sales. Format: Hot adult contemp. News staff: 5. Target aud: 35-64. ♦ Annie Labbe, gen mgr & opns dir.

Trois Rivieres

CBF-FM-1— July 21, 1977: 104.3 mhz; 100 kw. 1,000 ft. TL: N46 29 27 W72 39 00. Stereo. Box 6000, Montreal H3C 3A8. Phone: (514) 597-6000. Fax: (514) 597-4510. Web Site: www.cbc.radio-canada.ca. Licensee: CBC French. Network: Radio Canada. Format: Class, cultural, drama. ♦ Sylvain La France, gen mgr; Louise Carriere, progmg dir.

CFOU-FM— Sept 7, 1997: 89.1 mhz; 250 w. Stereo. Universite du Quebec a Trois-Rivieres, 1002 Pavillon Neree-Beauchemin, 3351 boulevard des Forges G9A 5H7. Phone: (819) 697-2368. Fax: (819) 697-3888. E-mail: cfou@uqtr.uquebec.ca. Web Site: www.cfoufm.com. Licensee: Radio campus des etudiants de l"Universite du Quebec a Trois-Rivieres. Format: Div. ♦ Eric Leclair, gen mgr; Louis Rousseau, prom dir; Alain Lefebvre, progmg dir.

CHEY-FM— Aug 22, 1990: 94.7 mhz; 100 kw. 1500 rue Royale, Bur 1200 G9A 4J4. Phone: (819) 376-0947. Fax: (819) 373-5555. E-mail: chey@rockdetente.com. Web Site: www.rockdetente.com. Licensee: Astral Media Radio Inc. (acq 4-19-2002; grpsl). Format: Soft rock. ♦ Jean Martin, gen mgr; Rene Rivard, sls dir; Stephanie Fournier, prom dir; Sylvie Roberge, progmg dir.

CHLN(AM)— Oct 17, 1937: 550 khz; 10 kw-D, 5 kw-N, DA-2. 1500 Rue Royale, Bur 1200 G9A 4J4. Phone: (819) 374-3556. Fax: (819) 374-3222. Web Site: www.chln550.com. Licensee: 591991 B.C. Ltd. Group owner: Astral Media Inc. (acq 1-21-2005; grpsl). Format: News/talk, sports, MOR, top-40. Spec prog: Pub affrs 8 hrs wkly. ♦ Jean Martin, gen mgr; Diane Marchand, sls dir; Claude Bolduc, prom dir & progmg dir; Cluade Bolduc, adv dir.

CIGB-FM— Aug 27, 1979: 102.3 mhz; 11 kw. Stereo. 1500 Royale, Bureau 260 G9A 6J4. Phone: (819) 378-1023. Fax: (819) 378-1360. Web Site: www.radioenergie.com. Licensee: Astral Media Radio Inc. Group owner: Astral Media Inc. (acq 8-24-90). Format: CHR. News staff: 5; News: 3 hrs wkly. Target aud: 18-49. ♦ Jean Martin, gen mgr.

CJEB-FM— June 8, 2004: 100.1 mhz; 30.61 kw. Ant 1,177 ft. 4141 boul. St. Jean G9B 2M8. Phone: (819) 691-1001. Fax: (819) 691-1002. E-mail: g.garceau@rythmefm.com. Web Site: www.rythmefm.com/maur. Licensee: Cogeco Radio-Television inc. Format: Fr adult contemp. ♦ Michel Cloutier, gen mgr.

Val d'Or

CHGO-FM— 2000: 104.3 mhz; 100 kw. 1729 3e Ave. J9X 1G5. Phone: (819) 825-0010. Fax: (819) 825-7313. Web Site: www.gofm.net. Licensee: Radio-Nord Communications Inc. (group owner). Network: Radiomedia. Format: Classic rock. ♦ Pierre R. Brosseau, CEO & pres; Jean-Pierre Major, gen mgr; Ghislain Beaulieu, opns mgr.

CJMV-FM— June 17, 1989: 102.7 mhz; 65 kw. 200 ft. 173 Perreault St. J9P 2H3. Phone: (819) 825-2568. Fax: (819) 825-2840. Web Site: www.radioenergie.com. Licensee: Astral Media Radio Inc. Group owner: Astral Media Inc. (acq 1-12-2000; grpsl). Format: Top-40. Target aud: 18-49. ♦ Ian Greenberg, pres; Marlene Trottier, gen mgr & opns dir.

Valleyfield

CKOD-FM— June 6, 1994: 103.1 mhz; 3 kw. 167 ft. TL: N45 16 08 W74 05 50. (CP: 103.1 mhz). Stereo. 249 Victoria St. J6T 1A9. Phone: (450) 373-0103. Phone: (450) 452-0103. Fax: (450) 373-4297. E-mail: fm103@ckod.qc.ca. Web Site: www.ckod.qc.ca. Licensee: Radio Express Inc. Rep: Target Broadcast Sales. Format: Adult contemp. News staff: one; News: 7 hrs wkly. Target aud: 18-54; general. ♦ Robert Brunet, pres & gen mgr; Martin Leblanc, opns dir & progmg dir; Dean Nevins, sls dir.

Verdun

CINF(AM)—Licensed to Verdun. See Montreal

CKOI-FM—Licensed to Verdun. See Montreal

Victoriaville

CFDA-FM— 1999: 101.9 mhz; 1.35 kw. Box 490 G6P 6T3. Secondary address: 55 St. Jean Baptiste St. G6P 6T3. Phone: (819) 752-5545. Fax: (819) 752-7552. Web Site: www.passionrock.com. Licensee: Radio Victoriaville Ltee. Group owner: Gestion Appalaches inc. Rep: Broadcast Sales, Target Broadcast Sales. Format: Adult contemp. News staff: 7. Target aud: 35-65. Spec prog: Country 3 hrs, retro/oldies 3 hrs wkly. ♦ Annie Labbe, gen mgr.

Ville-Marie

CKVM-FM— 2004: 93.1 mhz; 18.4 kw. TL: N47 19 57 W79 25 38. Stereo. 62 Suite Anne J9V 2B7. Secondary address: 62 Ste. Anne J9V 2B7. Phone: (819) 629-2710. Fax: (819) 622-0716. E-mail: ckvm@ckvm.qc.ca. Licensee: Radio Temiscamingue Inc. Network: Radiomedia. Format: Adult contemp. News staff: one; News: 11 hrs wkly. Target aud: General. ♦ Claude Gagnon, pres; Jacquelin Bastien, VP; Serge Lalonde, stn mgr.

Westmount

CKGM(AM)—See Montreal

Windsor

CIAX-FM— 2000: 98.3 mhz; 426 w. 49 Sixth Ave. J1S 1T2. Phone: (819) 845-5900. Phone: (819) 845-2692. Fax: (819) 845-2692. E-mail: unite@qc.aira.ca. Licensee: Carrefour Jeunesse Emploi - Comte Johnson. Format: Div. ♦ Patrick Levesque, pres & gen mgr; Julie Lupien, progmg dir.

Saskatchewan

Caronport

CJOS-FM— July 1995: 92.7 mhz; 5 w. Stereo. 510 College Dr. S0H 0S0. Phone: (306) 756-3292. Phone: (306) 756-3238. Fax: (306) 756-5533. E-mail: cjos@briercrest.com. Licensee: Briercrest Community Radio Inc. Format: Contemp Christian, news. News: one hr wkly. Target aud: 14 plus; student along with the community. ♦ Peter Miko, gen mgr; Joel Armstrong, stn mgr.

Cumberland House

CJCF-FM— 1990: 89.9 mhz; 30.5 w. Box 100 S0E 0S0. Phone: (306) 888-2176. Phone: (306) 888-4444. Fax: (306) 888-2103. Licensee: Cumberland House Radio & Television Committee Inc. Format: Ethnic. ♦ Rachel Fiddler, gen mgr.

Estevan

CHSN-FM—Listing follows CJSL(AM).

CJSL(AM)— August 1959: 1280 khz; 10 kw-U, DA-N. 200-1236 Fifth St. S4A 0Z6. Phone: (306) 634-1280. Fax: (306) 634-6364. Licensee: Golden West Broadcasting Ltd. (group owner; acq 3-95). Rep: Canadian Broadcast Sales. Format: Contemp country. Target aud: General. Spec prog: Farm 4 hrs, relg 10 hrs wkly. ♦ Elmer Hildebrand, CEO & pres; Laverne Pappel, stn mgr & gen sls mgr.

CHSN-FM— Co-owned with CJSL(AM). 2001: 102.3 mhz; 100 kw. Format: Light rock.

Gravelbourg

*CBKF-1(AM)— 1952: 540 khz; 5 kw-U, DA-2. 2440 Broad St., Regina S4P 4A1. Phone: (306) 347-9540. Fax: (306) 347-9635. Web Site: www.cbc.ca. Licensee: CBC French. Format: Div. ♦ Rikki Bote, gen mgr; Robert Rabinowitz, CEO & progmg dir.

CFRG-FM— 2003: 93.1 mhz; 48 w. C.P. 176 S0H 1X0. Phone: (506) 737-5060. Fax: (506) 737-5084. E-mail: cfaidirection@hotmail.com. Licensee: Association communautaire fransaskoise de Gravelbourg Inc. Format: Fr.

Hudson Bay

CFMQ-FM— Sept 15, 1994: 98.1 mhz; 38.2 w. TL: N52 54 03 W102 23 31. Stereo. Box 1272 S0E 0Y0. Phone: (306) 865-3065. Fax: (306) 865-2227. E-mail: cfmq@sk.sympatico.ca. Licensee: HB Communications Inc. Format: Easy lstng, div, country. News: one hr wkly. Target aud: General. Spec prog: AOR, talk. ♦ Mark Brann, pres; Dan Brann, gen mgr, sls VP, progmg mgr, news dir & engrg mgr.

Kindersley

CFYM(AM)— July 29, 1987: 1210 khz; 1 kw-U. Box 490, Rosetown S0L 2VO. Phone: (306) 463-4411. Fax: (306) 882-3037. Web Site: www.cjym.com. Licensee: Golden West Broadcasting Ltd. Group owner: Golden West Broadcasting Ltd. (acq 10-21-99). Rep: Target Broadcast Sales. Format: Hit Gold, adult contemp. Spec prog: Farm news. ♦ Elmer Hildebrand, pres.

CKVX-FM—Co-owned with CFYM(AM).Not on air, target date: unknown: 104.9 mhz; 50 w. Format: Contemp country.

La Ronge

*CBKA-FM— September 1979: 105.9 mhz; 80 w. Box 959 S0J 1L0. Phone: (306) 347-9540. Fax: (306) 425-2270. Web Site: www.sask.cbc.ca. Licensee: CBC. Network: CBC Radio One. Format: Rgnl current affrs. Spec prog: Cree & Dene 20 hrs wkly. ♦ David Kyle, gen mgr.

CJLR-FM— 1990: 89.9 mhz; 216 w. Ant 151 ft. Box 1529 S0J 1L0. Phone: (306) 425-4003. Fax: (306) 425-3123. E-mail: mbcradio@mbcradio.com. Web Site: www.mbcradio.com. Licensee: Natotawin Broadcasting Inc. (acq 9-2-93). Format: Ethnic, country, div. Target aud: General. Spec prog: Cree & Dene languages. ♦ Deborah Charles, CEO & gen mgr; William Dumais, pres; Keith Kratchmer, CFO; Teddy Clark, VP; Dallas Hicks, stn mgr & progmg dir.

Meadow Lake

CFDM-FM— 2001: 105.7 mhz; 46.5 w. Box 8168, Flying Dust First Nation S9X 1T8. Phone: (306) 236-1445. Fax: (306) 236-2861. Licensee: FDB Broadcasting Inc. Format: Country, top-40. ♦ Duwayne Derocher, stn mgr.

CJNS(AM)— Nov 1, 1977: 1240 khz; 1 kw-U, DA-1. Box 1660 S0M 1V0. Phone: (306) 236-6494. Fax: (306) 236-6141. Licensee: Northwestern Radio Partnership Group owner: Rawlco Radio Ltd. (acq 1-7-2003; grpsl). Format: Contemp country. ♦ David Dekker, gen mgr, gen sls mgr & adv mgr; Ken Schiller, opns mgr.

CJNS-FM—Not on air, target date: unknown: 102.3 mhz; 45 kw.

Melfort

CJVR-FM—Listing follows CKJH(AM).

CKJH(AM)— Oct 8, 1966: 750 khz; 25 kw-U, DA-N. TL: N52 47 57 W104 35 25. Stereo. Box 750, 611 Main St. S0E 1A0. Phone: (306) 752-2587. Fax: (306) 752-5932. Fax: (306) 752-6339. E-mail: cjvr@cjvr.com. Web Site: www.cjvr.com. Licensee: Radio CJVR Ltd. (acq 9-27-90). Rep: Target Broadcast Sales. Format: Just the hits. News staff: 4; News: 15 hrs wkly. Target aud: General. Spec prog: Relg 9 hrs wkly. ♦ Eugene Fabro Sr., chmn; Eugene W. Fabro, pres; Gary Fitz, VP, gen mgr & natl sls mgr; Karen Anderson, prom dir; Bill Wood, progmg dir; Cal Gratton, mus dir; Neil Shewchuk, news dir; Bayne Opseth, chief of engrg.

CJVR-FM—Co-owned with CKJH(AM). March 1, 2002: 105.1 mhz; 100 kw. Format: Country.

Moose Jaw

CHAB(AM)— Apr 22, 1922: 800 khz; 10 kw-U, DA-N. TL: N50 22 38 W105 23 35. Stereo. 1704 Main St. N. S6J 1L4. Phone: (306) 694-0800. Fax: (306) 692-8880. E-mail: country800@sk.simpatico.ca. Licensee: Golden West Broadcasting Ltd. (group owner; acq 8-20-92). Rep: Canadian Broadcast Sales. Format: Greatest hits. News staff: 3. Target aud: 25-54. ♦ Elmer Hildebrand, CEO & pres; Barry Vice, stn mgr & progmg dir; Abbey White, prom mgr; Rob Carnie, news dir.

Directory of Radio

Saskatchewan

CILG-FM—Co-owned with CHAB(AM). 2002: 100.7 mhz; 100 kw. Phone: (306) 692-1007. Format: Country.

Nipawin

CIOT-FM— January 2005: 104.1 mhz; 200 w. Box 1240 S0E 1E0. Phone: (306) 862-2468. Fax: (306) 862-2660. Web Site: www.lighthousefm.ca. Licensee: Wilderness Ministries Inc. Format: Christian.

CJNE-FM— June 2002: 94.7 mhz; 14.8 kw. Box 220 S0E 1E0. Phone: (306) 862-9478. Fax: 862-2334. E-mail: sales@cjnefm.com. Web Site: www.cjnefm.com. Licensee: CJNE FM Radio Inc. Format: Classic rock, golden oldies. ♦ Norm Rudock, gen mgr & gen sls mgr; Treana Rudock, stn mgr; Les Blair, prom mgr.

North Battleford

CJCQ-FM—Listing follows CJNB(AM).

CJNB(AM)— Jan 28, 1947: 1050 khz; 10 kw-U, DA-1. Box 1460 S9A 2Z5. Phone: (306) 445-2477. Fax: (306) 445-4599. Licensee: Northwestern Radio Partnership. Group owner: Rawlco Radio Ltd. (acq 1-7-2003;. grpsl). Rep: Canadian Broadcast Sales. Format: Country. Spec prog: Farm 7 hrs, relg 10 hrs wkly. ♦ Gord Rawlinson, pres; David Dekker, gen mgr & gen sls mgr; Harry M. Dekker, prom mgr; Doug Harrison, progmg dir; Dave Senft, chief of engrg.

CJCQ-FM—Co-owned with CJNB(AM). September 2001: 97.9 mhz; 100 kw. Format: Pop rock.

Pinehouse Lake

CFNK-FM— 1996: 89.9 mhz; 7 w. General Delivery, Box 370 S0J 2B0. Phone: (306) 884-2011. Phone: (306) 884-2016. Fax: (306) 884-2365. Web Site: www.cfnk.radiok.sympatico.ca. Licensee: Pinehouse Communications Society Inc. Format: Cree language, adult contemp, oldies. ♦ Peter Smith, gen mgr; Vince Natomagan, progmg dir.

Prince Albert

CFMM-FM—Listing follows CKBI(AM).

CHQX-FM— June 18, 2001: 101.5 mhz; 100 kw. Ant 606 ft. Stereo. Box 900 S6V 7R4. Phone: (306) 763-7421. Fax: (306) 764-1850. E-mail: mix101@rawlco.com. Licensee: Rawlco Radio Ltd. (group owner). Format: Adult rock. ♦ Jim Scarrow, gen mgr & opns mgr; Karl Johnson, gen sls mgr.

CKBI(AM)— 1934: 900 khz; 10 kw-U, DA-N. Box 900 S6V 7R4. Phone: (306) 763-7421. Fax: (306) 764-1850. Licensee: Rawlco Radio Ltd. (group owner; acq 1946). Rep: Canadian Broadcast Sales. Format: Adult contemp, MOR, oldies. Target aud: 34 plus; working women. Spec prog: Farm 2 hrs wkly. ♦ Jim Scarrow, gen mgr; Dave Hryhor, rgnl sls mgr; Neil Headrick, progmg dir; Jeff White, news dir; Dale Zimmerman, engrg mgr.

CFMM-FM—Co-owned with CKBI(AM). Jan 30, 1982: 99.1 mhz; 100 kw. 606 ft. Stereo. Format: Classic rock mix 101, contemp hit, news. ♦ Garth Kalin, progmg mgr.

Regina

*CBK(AM)— July 29, 1939: 540 khz; 50 kw-D, DA. Box 540, 2440 Broad St. S4P 4A1. Phone: (306) 347-9540. Fax: (306) 347-9524. E-mail: bill-gerald@cbc.ca. Licensee: CBC. Network: CBC Radio One. Format: Div, news, talk. Spec prog: Farm 5 hrs wkly. ♦ Bill Gerald, stn mgr; Debbie Carpentier, gen mgr & opns dir; David Kyle, news dir.

CBK-FM— May 1, 1977: 96.9 mhz; 100 kw. 501 ft. Stereo. Phone: (360) 956-7400. Fax: (306) 956-7417. Web Site: www.sask.cbc.ca. Network: CBC Radio Two. Format: Var/div, jazz, classical.. Co-owned TV: *CBKT(TV) affil

CBKF-FM— Sept 1, 1973: 97.7 mhz; 13.7 kw. 501 ft. Box 540 S4P 4A1. Secondary address: 2440 Broad St. S4P-3Z4. Phone: (306) 347-9540. Fax: (306) 347-9493. Web Site: www.cbc.ca. Licensee: Radio Canada. Network: CBC Radio Two. Format: Div. ♦ Rene Fontaine, gen mgr; Anne Brochu, progmg dir & news mgr; Steve Tomchuk, engrg mgr. Co-owned TV: CBKF(TV) affil.

CFWF-FM—Listing follows CKRM(AM).

CHMX-FM— Feb 4, 1966: 92.1 mhz; 100 kw. 499 ft. Stereo. 2060 Halifax St. S4P 1T7. Phone: (306) 546-6200. Web Site: lite92fm.com. Licensee: Harvard Broadcasting Inc. (acq 3-1-81). Format: Adult Contemp. ♦ Les Schuster, opns dir & gen sls mgr.

CIZL-FM—Listing follows CJME(AM).

CJME(AM)— July 27, 1926: 980 khz; 10 kw-D, 5 kw-N, DA-2. 2401 Saskatchewan Dr., Suite 210 S4P 4H8. Phone: (306) 525-0000. Fax: (306) 347-8557. Licensee: Rawlco Radio Ltd. (group owner); acq 11-30-2001). Format: News/talk. ♦ Tom Newton, gen mgr; Keith Black, rgnl sls mgr; Marcie Watson, prom dir; Don Kollins, progmg dir; Murray Wood, news dir.

CIZL-FM—Co-owned with CJME(AM). June 1982: 98.9 mhz; 100 kw. 435 ft. Stereo. (Acq 4-67). Format: AOR, classic hits, adult contemp. Target aud: 18-49. ♦ Craig Romanyk, rgnl sls mgr; Marci Watsen, prom mgr; Tom Newton, progmg dir.

*CJTR-FM— Nov 1, 2001: 91.3 mhz; 480 w. TL: N50 27 18 W104 36 30. Stereo. Box 334, Station Main S4P 3A1. Phone: (306) 525-7274. Fax: (306) 525-9741. E-mail: radius@cjtr.ca. Web Site: www.cjtr.ca. Licensee: Radius Communications Inc. Div. News: 10 hrs wkly. Spec prog: American Indian 4 hrs, Black 2 hrs, Chinese one hr, It one hr, Portugese one hr wkly. ♦ Rick August, pres; Dave Kuzenko, VP; Keith Colhoun, gen mgr.

CKCK-FM— Aug 9, 2002: 94.5 mhz; 100 kw. 2401 Saskatchewan Dr., Suite 210 S4P 4H8. Phone: (306) 525-0000. Fax: (306) 347-8557. Licensee: Rawlco Radio Ltd. (group owner). Format: Classic rock. ♦ Gord Rawlinson, pres; Ralph Bird, gen sls mgr; Tom Newton, gen mgr & progmg dir; Michael Zaplitny, news dir; Gord Stankey, engrg mgr.

CKRM(AM)— July 29, 1922: 620 khz; 10 kw-U, DA-2. 2060 Halifax St. S4P 1T7. Phone: (306) 546-6200. Fax: (306) 781-7338. Web Site: www.620ckrm.com. Licensee: HDL Investments Inc. (acq 11-30-01; C$4.2 million. with co-located FM). Format: C&W, farm. ♦ Mike Olstrom, stn mgr.

CFWF-FM—Co-owned with CKRM(AM). Apr 15, 1982: 104.9 mhz; 100 kw. 400 ft. Stereo. Web Site: www.620ckrm.com. (Acq 8-25-95). Rep: Canadian Broadcast Sales. Format: Classic rock.

Rosetown

CJYM(AM)— Aug 8, 1966: 1330 khz; 10 kw-U, DA-1. Box 490 S0L 2V0. Secondary address: 208 Hwy.4 S0L 2V0. Phone: (306) 882-2686. Fax: (306) 882-3037. Web Site: www.cjym.com. Licensee: Dace Broadcasting Corp. Group owner: Golden West Broadcasting Ltd. (acq 10-21-99). Rep: Target Broadcast Sales. Format: Classic hits. News staff: 2. Target aud: General. ♦ Barb Bell, gen mgr.

Saskatoon

CBKF-2(AM)— Nov 6, 1952: 860 khz; 10 kw-U, DA-2. 144 2nd Ave. S7K 1K5. Phone: (306) 956-7400. Fax: (306) 956-7476. Web Site: www.sask.cbc.ca. Licensee: CBC French. Format: Div. Target aud: General. ♦ David Kyle, gen mgr; Robert Rabinowitz, progmg dir.

*CBKS-FM— July 1, 1978: 105.5 mhz; 98 kw. 586 ft. Stereo. 144 2nd Ave. S. S7K 1K5. Phone: (306) 956-7400. Fax: (306) 956-7417. Web Site: www.sask.cbc.ca. Licensee: CBC. Network: CBC Radio One. Format: Div, jazz, class. ♦ David Kyle, stn mgr & progmg dir; Carley Caverly, gen sls mgr; John Calver, news dir; Steve Tomchuk, chief of engrg.

CFCR-FM— 1991: 90.5 mhz; 1.48 kw. Stereo. Box 7544, 103 3rd Ave. N. S7K 4L4. Phone: (306) 664-6678. Fax: (306) 933-0038. E-mail: cfcr@quadrant.net. Web Site: www.cfcr.ca. Licensee: Community Radio Society of Saskatoon Inc. Format: Var. News: one hr wkly. Target aud: General. Spec prog: Fr one hr, Ger 2 hrs, It one hr, Pol one hr, Sp 2 hrs wkly. ♦ Dian Deminchuk, pres; Ron Sprizziri, gen mgr; Bob Greenhough, sls dir; Theo Kivol, progmg VP.

CFMC-FM—Listing follows CKOM(AM).

CFQC-FM—Listing follows CJWW(AM).

CJDJ-FM— June 1990: 102.1 mhz; 100 kw. 715 Saskatchewan Crescent West S7M 5V7. Phone: (306) 934-2222. Fax: (306) 477-0002. Licensee: Rawlco Radio Ltd. (group owner, (acq 12-21-2000); C$870,000. for all the issued and outstanding shares). Format: Rock. News staff: 3; News: 4 hrs wkly. Target aud: 25-49; well educated, well paid professionals. Spec prog: Relg 6 hrs wkly. ♦ Jamie Wall, pres & gen mgr; Pam Leyland, pres & gen mgr.

CJMK-FM— May 2001: 98.3 mhz; 100 kw. 345 Fourth Ave. S. S7K 5S5. Phone: (306) 244-1975. Fax: (306) 665-5501. Web Site: www.magic983.fm. Licensee: 629112 Saskatchewan Ltd. (group owner). Format: Adult gold contemp. ♦ Elmer Hildebrand, pres; Vic Dubois, gen mgr; Ken McFarlane, gen sls mgr; Steve Chisholm, progmg dir; Matt Bradley, mus dir; Eldon Duchscher, news dir; Al Pippen, chief of engrg.

CJWW(AM)— January 1976: 600 khz; 25 kw-D, 8 kw-N, DA-N. Stereo. 345 Fourth Ave. S. S7K 5S5. Phone: (306) 244-1975. Fax: (306) 665-5730. Fax: (306) 665-5501. Web Site: www.cjwwradio.com. Licensee: 629112 Saskatchewan Ltd. (group owner; acq 12-21-00; C$7,450,000). Rep: Canadian Broadcast Sales. Format: Country, info. News staff: 7. Target aud: General; 35-64 central; 18+ full coverage. Spec prog: Gospel 3 hrs wkly. ♦ Elmer Hildebrand, chmn & pres; Irene Osborn, CFO; V. Dubois, gen mgr; Ken McFarlane, gen sls mgr; Rod Kitter, progmg dir; D. Woroniuk, mus dir; Jay Richards, asst music dir; E. Duchscher, news dir; Steve Shannon, pub affrs dir; J. Hayes, chief of engrg.

CFQC-FM—Co-owned with CJWW(AM). Feb 6, 1995: 92.9 mhz; 100 kw. Format: New country. News staff: 2. Target aud: General. ♦ Warren Cargill, progmg dir; Jeff Hayes, engrg dir.

CKOM(AM)— June 8, 1951: 650 khz; 10 kw-U, DA-2. 715 Saskatchewan Crescent W. S7M 5V7. Phone: (306) 934-2222. Fax: (306) 373-7587. Licensee: Rawlco Radio Ltd. (group owner). Format: News/talk. ♦ Jamie Wall, gen mgr.

CFMC-FM—Co-owned with CKOM(AM). Dec 12, 1965: 95.1 mhz; 100 kw. Ant 110 ft. Stereo. Format: Today's best music.

Shaunavon

CJSN(AM)— Dec 6, 1966: 1490 khz; 1 kw-U. 407 Centre St. S0N 2M0. Phone: (306) 297-2671. Fax: (306) 297-3051. Web Site: www.swiftcurrentonline.com. Licensee: Frontier City Broadcasting. Group owner: Golden West Broadcasting Ltd. (acq 1973). Format: C&W, MOR. ♦ Deborah Gauger, gen mgr & opns mgr; Darwin Gooding, progmg dir.

Swift Current

CIMG-FM— Oct 20, 1979: 94.1 mhz; 100 kw. 400 ft. Stereo. 134 Central Ave. N. S9H 0L1. Phone: (306) 773-4605. Fax: (306) 773-6390. E-mail: eaglecontrol@goldenwestradio.com. Web Site: www.eagle94.com. Licensee: Golden West Broadcasting Ltd. (group owner; (acq 11-8-95; C$97,500). Rep: Canadian Broadcast Sales. Format: Classic hits. News staff: 3; News: 4 hrs wkly. Target aud: 18-35. ♦ Elmer Hildebrand, CEO; Menno Friesen, VP; Deborah Gauger, stn mgr, gen sls mgr & adv mgr; Lisa Ray, prom dir; Kim Johnston, progmg dir; Ryan Suitzer, mus dir; Anita Irwin, news dir; David Funk, chief of engrg.

CKFI-FM—Not on air, target date: unknown: 97.1 mhz; 100 kw. 134 Central Ave. N. S9H 0L1. Phone: (306) 773-4605. Fax: (306) 773-6390. Licensee: Golden West Broadcasting Ltd. Format: Contemp rock. ♦ Deborah Gauger, stn mgr.

CKSW(AM)— June 1, 1956: 570 khz; 10 kw-U, DA-2. 134 Central Ave. S9H 0L1. Phone: (306) 773-4605. Fax: (306) 773-6390. Web Site: www.swiftcurrentonline.com. Licensee: Golden West Broadcasting Ltd. Group owner: Golden West Broadcasting Ltd. Rep: Canadian Broadcast Sales. Format: Country, regl. News staff: 5; News: 9 hrs wkly. Target aud: 25-54. Spec prog: Farm 5 hrs, Ger one hr wkly. ♦ Jill Ahrens, gen sls mgr & rgnl sls mgr; Darwin Gooding, progmg dir; Kim Johnston, adv mgr & progmg dir; Dave Funk, chief of engrg.

Weyburn

CFSL(AM)— Aug 16, 1957: 1190 khz; 10 kw-D, 5 kw-N, DA-N. 305 Souris Ave. S4H 2K2. Phone: (306) 848-1190. Fax: (306) 842-2720. Licensee: Soo Line Broadcasting Ltd. Group owner: Golden West Broadcasting Ltd. (acq 2-16-95). Rep: Canadian Broadcast Sales.

Saskatchewan

Format: C&W. News staff: 3. Target aud: 25 plus. Spec prog: Farm 3 hrs, relg 9 hrs wkly. ◆Elmer Hildenbrand, CEO; Cameron Birnie, stn mgr & news dir.

White Bear Lake Resort

CIDD-FM— 2002: 97.7 mhz; 46.5 w. The Moose, Box 121, Kenosee Lake S0C 2S0. Phone: (306) 577-2450. Licensee: White Bear Children's Charity Inc. Format: Div. ◆Lana Littlechief, gen mgr.

Yorkton

CFGW-FM—Listing follows CJGX(AM).

CJGX(AM)— Aug 19, 1927: 940 khz; 50 kw-D, 10 kw-N. 120 Smith St. E. S3N 3V3. Phone: (306) 782-2256. Fax: (306) 783-4994. Licensee: Yorkton Broadcasting Ltd. and Walsh Investments Inc., partners of GX Radio, a gen partnership. (acq 2-15-89). Format: Country. ◆George G. Gallagher, pres; Lyle J. Walsh, gen mgr; Bryan Mireau, engrg dir.

CFGW-FM—Co-owned with CJGX(AM). July 1, 2001: 94.1 mhz; 100 kw. Format: Hot adult contemp.

Zenon Park

CKZP-FM— January 2002: 102.7 mhz; 5.4 w. Box 100 S0E 1W0. Phone: (306) 767-2451. Fax: (306) 767-2548. E-mail: legeru@tsd53.ca. Web Site: www.thinkfast.ca/tsd/tsdpromo2/zpradio.htm. Licensee: Radio Zenon Park Inc. Format: Var (English and French progmg). ◆J. Ulysse Leger, gen mgr.

Yukon Territory

Tagish

CFET-FM— June 1, 2003: 106.7 mhz; 50 w. Mile 234 Y0B 1T0. Phone: (867) 667-6397. Fax: (867) 668-2633. E-mail: cfet@tagishtel.ca. Web Site: www.tagishtel.ca/radio. Licensee: Robert G. Hopkins. Format: Variety/classic rock. ◆Robert G. Hopkins, gen mgr.

Whitehorse

***CFWH(AM)—** 1958: 570 khz; 5 kw-U, DA-1. 3103 Third Ave. Y1A 1E5. Phone: (867) 668-8400. Fax: (867) 668-8408. Licensee: CBC. Network: CBC Radio One. Format: Talk, info. Spec prog: Fr one hr wkly. ◆Mike Liudee, opns dir; Frank Fry, opns mgr.

CHON-FM— Feb 1, 1985: 98.1 mhz; 4.261 kw. 250 ft. Stereo. 4230 A 4th Ave. Y1A 1K1. Phone: (867) 668-6629. Fax: (867) 668-6612. E-mail: nnby@nnby.net. Licensee: Northern Native Broadcasting. Format: C&W, classic rock. Spec prog: Yukon native language 15 hrs wkly. ◆Elsie Hume, chmn; Shirley Adamson, gen mgr; Denis Gerard, opns mgr & engrg mgr; Les Carpenter, progmg dir.

CIAY-FM— 2003: 100.7 mhz; 50 w. 91806 Alaska Hwy. Y1A 5B7. Phone: (867) 393-2429. Fax: (867) 393-2439. E-mail: stnmgr@newlifefmyukon.ca. Web Site: www.newlifefmyukon.ca. Licensee: Bethany Pentecostal Tabernacle. Format: Christian. ◆Rod Carby, stn mgr; Wade Meszaros, sls dir; Ean McDonald, progmg dir.

CKRW(AM)— November 1969: 610 khz; 1 kw-U, DA-1. 203-4103 4th Ave., Suite 203 Y1A 1H6. Phone: (867) 688-6100. Fax: (867) 668-4209. E-mail: marketing@ckrw.com. Web Site: www.ckrw.com. Licensee: Klondike Broadcasting Co. Ltd. Rep: Canadian Broadcast Sales. Format: CHR. ◆Rolf Hougen, CEO; Wendy Tayler, gen mgr; Jennifer Johnstone, opns mgr; Eva Bidrman, gen sls mgr.

Michigan

Detroit

CIDR-FM—See Windsor, ON

CKLW(AM)—See Windsor, ON

Miscellaneous Radio Services

American Forces Radio & Television Service (AFRTS), Department of Defense, American Forces Info Service, 601 N. Fairfax St., Alexandria, VA 22314. Phone: (703) 428-0616. Melvin Russell, dir; Kathi Blevins, deputy dir.

March Air Reserve Base, CA 92518-2017. AFRTS Broadcast Center, 1363 Z St, Bldg. 2730. Phone: (909) 413-2201. Lt. Col. Roberto Garza, commander; Bob Matheson, dir progmg; Tom Weber, industry liaison.

AFRTS has radio & TV outlets located in 177 countries & on board U.S. Navy ships. AFRTS stns operate in 18 countries providing rgnl & loc info to large concentrations of U.S. forces. All of the entertainment progmg, U.S sporting events, & natl. & international news is provided to the outlets either directly via international satellites from the AFRTS Broadcast Center at March Air Reserve Base, Calif., or through the AFRTS operated stns which insert their rgnl & loc radio drive-time programs & radio & TV news & spot announcements. A rgnl AFRTS service in Europe delivers the AFRTS fed progmg & rgnl news & info via EUTELSAT to affils located in seven nations as well as directly to cable head-ends, remote transmitters, and homes throughout Europe & the Middle East. The worldwide AFRTS-TV progmg consists of: an entertainment service time shifted for the various parts of the globe & providing the best of U.S. network TV progmg; a news service providing natl & international news from CNN & the major U.S. networks; a sports channel providing sports news & sporting events from ESPN, ESPN2 & the major U.S. networks; & a fourth service devoted to alternative entertainment progmg primarily oriented on family-type programs from PBS & from U.S.cable TV channels. AFRTS-Radio satellite progmg consists of two continuous news info & sporting events svcs, a NPR service & entertainment svcs with mus for practically all tastes & likes of AFRTS' authorized audience which is all active duty military & Department of Defense civilian personnel & their families stationed overseas. Access to the AFRTS worldwide satellite svcs is restricted through the use of the Scientific Atlanta Power-Vu MPEG-2 digital compression encoding system.

Radio Free Asia

Radio Free Asia, 2025 M St. N.W., Suite 300, Washington, DC 20036. Phone: (202) 530-4900. Web Site: www.rfa.org. Richard Richter, pres; Patrick Taylor, CFO; Daniel Southerland, VP progmg/exrec editor; Sarah Jackson-Han, dir of communications.

Provides information, news. & commentary about events in the respective countries of Asia & elsewhere. The service is intended to be a forum for a variety of opinions & voices from within Asian nations whose people do not fully enjoy freedom of expression.

Radio Free Europe/Radio Liberty

Radio Free Europe/Radio Liberty, (RFE/RL Inc.). 1201 Connecticut Ave. NW, Washington, DC 20036. Phone: (202) 457-6947. Fax: (202) 457-6992. Web Site: www.rferl.org. Thomas A. Dine, pres/CEO; Don Jensen, dir of communications.

110 00 Prague 1, NO Czech Republic, Vinohradska 1. Phone: (420-2) 2112-1111. Anna Rausova, media relations coord.

Bcsts to East Europe in Bulgarian, Czech, Slovak, Romanian, Lithuanian, Estonian, & Latvian; bcsts to the Commonwealth of Independent States in Russian, Ukrainian, Belorussian, Armenian, Azeri, Bosnian, Georgian, Tatar-Bashkir, Kazak, Kirghiz, Tajik, Turkmen, Uzbek. Also bcsts to the former Yugoslavia in Serbian & Croatian, bcsts in Persian to Iran & in Arabic to Iraq.

Broadcasting Board of Governors, 330 Independence Ave. S.W., Rm. 3360, Washington, DC 20237. Phone: (202) 203-4545. Fax: (202) 203-4585. Web Site: www.bbg.gov/. Brian T. Conniff, exec dir; Janet Stormes, CFO.

The board makes & supervises grants to Radio Free Europe, Radio Liberty, & Radio Free Asia; & assures that funds are applied consistently with the broad foreign policy objectives of the U.S. govt.

U.S. International Radio

Adventist World Radio, 12501 Old Columbia Pike, Silver Spring, MD 20904-6600. Phone: (301) 680-6304. Fax: (301) 680-6303. E-mail: info@awr.org. Greg Scott, sr VP; Benjamin D. Schoun, pres.

The international radio service of the General Conference of Seventh-day Adventists, AWR is made up of four regions: the Americas, Africa, Asia-Pacific, & Europe. AWR programs are produced in more than 50 studios around the world & is currently broadcasting, in more than 50 languages, more than 1,200 programs each week worldwide.

Blue Ridge Communications Inc., Shortwave Radio Station WWRB, c/o Airline Transport Communications, Box 7, Manchester, TN 37349-0007. Phone: (931) 841-0492. Fax: (931) 728-6087. Web Site: www.wwrb.org.

WWRB Manchester, TN. Worldwide broadcasting utilizing 5 shortwave transmitters and 6 major antenna systems (azimuths); more than 10 years of well established global audience.

Family Stations Inc., 10400 N.W. 240th St., Okeechobee, FL 34972. Phone: (863) 763-0281. Fax: (863) 763-8867. E-mail: fsiyfr@okeechobee.com. Web Site: www.familyradio.com. Harold Camping, pres/gen mgr; David Hoff, mgr international department; Dan Elyea, engrg mgr.

WYFR Okeechobee, Fla. Twelve 100 kw transmitters & two 50 kw transmitters in Florida. Bcstg on various frequencies, in English to Europe, Africa & the Americas (including Caribbean area), in German to Europe, in Russian to East Europe, in Arabic to West Africa, in French to Europe, North Africa & the Americas & in Sp to Southern Europe, Central & South America, in Portuguese to Europe, South America & West Africa, in It to Europe. Format: Relg.

Far East Broadcasting Co. Inc., Box 1, La Mirada, CA 90637. Phone: (562) 947-4651. Fax: (310) 943-0160. E-mail: febc@febc.org. Web Site: www.febc.org. Gregg Harris, pres.

Broadcasts 560 hrs of progmg in 150 languages, to a potential audience of more than 2.5 billion people. FEBC's broadcasts are heard in many countries with limited access to Christian ministry, or where there is tremendous political and cultural opposition to the gospel.

Fundamental Broadcasting Network, c/o Grace Missionary Baptist Church, 520 Roberts Rd., Newport, NC 28570. Phone: (252) 223-4600. Fax: (252) 223-2201. E-mail: fbn@clis.com. Web Site: www.fbnradio.com. David Robinson, engr.

WBOH Newport, N.C. Broadcasts on 5.920 mhz 24 hrs a day. **WTJC Newport, N.C.** Broadcasts on 9.370 mhz 24 hrs a day.

Good News World Outreach, WRNO Worldwide, Box 895, Fort Worth, TX 76101-0895. Phone: (817) 850-9990. Fax: (817) 850-9994. E-mail: wrnoradio@mailup.net. Web Site: www.wrnoworldwide.org. Robert E. Mawire, chmn/CEO.

WRNO New Orleans. 50 kw shortwave transmitter reaching North America, Central America, Europe, & Far East. Format: news, talk (educational, Christian), sports, music.

International Fellowship of Churches Inc., dba IMF World Missions. Radio Station KIMF, 9746 6th St., Rancho Cucamonga, CA 91730. E-mail: james@plancktech.com.

Broadcasts on 5.835 mhz and 11.885 mhz with two 50 kw transmitters.

La Voz de Restauracion Broadcasting Inc., Box 56320, Los Angeles, CA 90056. Phone: (323) 766-2454. Fax: (323) 766-2458. E-mail: info@restauracion.com. Web Site: www.restauracion.com. Rene F. Molina, dir.

KVOH Rancho Simi, CA Format: Sp.

Our Lady's Youth Center, 230 High Valley Rd., Vado, NM 88072. Phone: (505) 233-2090. Fax: (505) 233-3019.

Operates **KJES Vado, N.M.**

Radio Miami International, 175 Fontainebleau Blvd., Suite 1N4, Miami, FL 33172. Phone: (305) 559-9764. Fax: (305) 559-8186. E-mail: info@wrmi.net. Web Site: www.wrmi.net. Jeff White, gen mgr.

WRMI Miami. Stn sells block airtime for $1/minute to organizations wanting to reach any part of the Americas in any language. 7,385 & 9,955 & 15,725 khz shortwave, 50 kw power.

Trans World Radio, Box 8700, Cary, NC 27512-8700. Phone: (919) 460-3700. Fax: (919) 460-3702. E-mail: info@twr.org. Web Site: www.gospelcom.net. Joe Fort; Glenn W. Sink, dir ministry dev.

KTWR Agana, Guam. Guam E-mail: twrguamk@twr.hafa.net.gu Four 100-kw shortwave transmitters to bcst to Australia, Bali, China, the eastern & central part of the Commonwealth of Independent States, Far East, India, Indonesia, Japan, Korea, Myanmar, Southeast Asia. Format: Relg (23 languages). Edmund Spieker, rgnl dir; Edward Stortro, stn dir; Chuck White, chief engr.

Trinity Broadcasting Network, KTBN/Shortwave, Box 18147, Salt Lake City, UT 84118. Phone: (801) 250-4111 (office). "Skinny" Johnny Mitchell.

KTBN, 6475 W. 5400 South, West Valley City, Utah 84118.

United Nations, Audio-Visual Promotion & Distribution. Room S-805, United Nations, New York, NY 10017. Phone: (212) 963-6982. Fax: (212) 963-6869. E-mail: audio-visual@un.org. Web Site: www.un.org/av. Kofi Annan; Kensaku Hogen, under sec-gen for public info; Barbara Sue-Ting-Len, chief & audio-visual promotion & distribution.

TV coverage of UN meetings & events & the production, promotion & distribution of documentary programs. All major UN events are also recorded on audio for radio distribution. Offices in 124 countries.

The Voice of the OAS, 17th & Constitution N.W., Washington, DC 20006. Phone: (202) 458-3986. Fax: (202) 458-3930. E-mail: informacion-publica@oas.org. Web Site: www.oas.org. Von Martin, producer; Claudio Lessa, producer.

Radio programs with news, interviews, info & music from Latin America. Concentrating on the acitivities of the Organization of American States.

WBCQ Radio, 274 Britton Rd., Monticello, ME 04760-3110. Phone: (207) 538-9180. Fax: (207) 985-7547 (same as phone; call first for switch). E-mail: wbcq@wbcq.com. Web Site: www.wbcq.com.

WBCQ Monticello, Me. International bcst shortwave stn. Lease & program time available. 5.105 mhz, 7.415 mhz, 9.330 mhz & 17.495 mhz.

WEWN Global Catholic Radio, 5817 Old Leeds Rd., Birmingham, AL 35210-2164. Phone: (205) 271-2900. Fax: (205) 271-2926. E-mail: wewn@ewtn.com. Web Site: www.ewtn.com. R.W. Steltemeier, CEO; Michael Warsaw, pres; Frank Leurck, stn mgr; Thom Price, progmg dir; Jim Duffy, dir mktg; Dennis Dempsey, chief engr.

WEWN Vandiver, Ala. Catholic progmg in English & Sp, 24 hours a day, worldwide via shortwave & satellite delivered international AM-FM service.

WJIE International Shortwave, Box 197309, Louisville, KY 40259. Phone: (502) 968-1220. Fax: (502) 964-4228. E-mail: wjiesw@hotmail.com. Web Site: www.wjiesw.com. Robert W. Rodgers, pres; Greg Holt, VP; Doug Rumsey, dir.

WJIE Millerstown, Ky. On two sw frequencies operating 24 hours daily. Target areas: Europe & Asia. Also operates WJIE-FM on 88.5 mhz with 24.5 kw horiz, 18.5 kw vert in Okolona, Ky.

WMLK Radio, Assemblies of Yahweh, Box C, Bethel, PA 19507. Phone: (717) 933-4518. Web Site: www.assembliesofyahweh.com. Elder Jacob O. Meyer, pres.

Branch offices in Metro-Manila, Phillippines; San Juan, Port of Spain, Trinidad & Tobago; Leeds, England. **WMLK Bethel, Pa.** Bcstg to Europe & the Middle East 10 hours, six days each week, Sunday-Friday, with religious instruction content.

WNQM Inc., Group owner: F.W. Robbert Broadcasting Co.. 1300 WWCR Ave., Nashville, TN 37218. Phone: (615) 255-1300. Phone: (800) 238-5576. Fax: (615) 255-1311. E-mail: wwcr@aol.com. Web Site: www.wwcr.com. Fred P. Westenberger, pres; George McClintock, gen mgr; Adam Lock, program dir; William Hair, chief engr.

WWCR Nashville. Frequencies: 3.210 mhz, 5.070 mhz, 5.935 mhz, 7.465 mhz, 9.475 mhz, 12.160 mhz, 15.825 mhz.

World Christian Broadcasting Corp., Operations Center, 605 Bradley Court, Franklin, TN 37067-8200. Phone: (615) 371-8707. Fax: (615) 371-8791. E-mail: dward@worldchristian.org. Web Site: www.knls.org. Charles H. Caudill, pres/CEO; Dale R. Ward, exec producer; Kevin Chambers, chief engr; Andy Baker, dev VP.

Anchor Point, AK 99556. KNLS, Box 473. Phone: (907) 235-8262. (907) 235-8462. Kevin Chambers, chief eng.

KNLS Anchor Point, Alaska (transmission facilities): Relg & secular progmg beamed to Asia, eastern Europe & the Pacific Rim on the international shortwave bands.

World Harvest Radio International, Box 12, South Bend, IN 46624. Phone: (574) 291-8200. Fax: (574) 291-9043. E-mail: whr@lesea.com. Web Site: www.whr.org. Steve Sumrall, pres; Peter Sumrall, VP/gen mgr; Joe Hill, sls & opns mgr; Douglas Garlinger, chief engr.

WHRI Indianapolis. Two 100 kw transmitters serving

Miscellaneous Radio Services

Europe, North, Central & South America. **KWHR Naalehu, Hawaii.** Two 100 kw transmitters serving primarily Asia, & also Oceania & Australia/New Zealand. **WHRA Greenbush, Me.** One 250 kw transmitter serving Africa & The Middle East. Shortwave transmitters are available for lease (time sls).

World International Broadcasters Inc., Box 88, Red Lion, PA 17356. Phone: (717) 246-1681, EXT. 140. Fax: (717) 244-9316. John H. Norris, pres; Patricia Norris-Slaughter, sec; John C. Norris, dir; Mary Norris-Michel, dir; Fred Wise, dir.

WINB Red Lion, Pa. Shortwave progmg of programs to Western Europe, the Mediterranean, North Africa, Mexico, Philippines, Guam, Formosa, Australia. Format: Relg.

Voice of America, 330 Independence Ave. S.W., Washington, DC 20237. Phone: (202) 619-2538. Fax: (202) 619-1241. E-mail: VOANews@VOANews.com. Myrna R. Whitworth, dir; Joe O'Connell, dir pub affrs; Beth Knisley, dir media rel.

Facilities: VOA transmitters are located at 13 relay stns in the U.S. & abroad in Belize, Botswana, Germany, Greece (Kavalla & Rhodes), Kuwait, Morocco, the Philippines, Sao Tome, Sri Lanka, & Thailand. Two other sites located in the U.S. are Delano, Calif., & Greenville, N.C. Programs originate in the Washington, D.C., studios at VOA headquarters. A 150-channel master control panel is used to route them onto appropriate satellite circuits for delivery to the relay stns, & two centers to record reports from VOA correspondents around the world.

Satellite Services

SIRIUS Satellite Radio
1221 Avenue of the Americas, New York, NY 10020. Phone: (212) 584-5100; Customer service: (888) 539-SIRIUS (7474). Website: www.sirius.com.

Management: Mel Karmazin, CEO; Joseph P. Clayton, chairman of the board of directors; Scott Greenstein, president, entertainment and sports; James E. Meyer, president, operations and sales; Patrick L. Donnelly, EVP and general counsel; David J. Frear, EVP and CFO; Mary Pat Ryan, EVP, subscriber sales and operation; Jay Clark, EVP, programming; Tola Murphy-Baran, SVP, marketing; Terry Smith, SVP of engineering; Larry Pesce, SVP, services; Douglas Wilsterman, SVP, general manager OEM division; Robert F. Law, SVP, general manager consumer electronics division; Stan Kozlowski, SVP, retail distribution; Doug Kaplan, SVP, business affairs and business development, entertainment and sports; Patrick Reilly, SVP, communications; John H. Schultz, SVP, human resources; William C. Pratt, chief information officer; Jeremy Coleman, VP of talk, information and entertainment programming; Steve Blatter, SVP, music programming; Ross Zapin, VP, promotions; Jim Collins, VP, corporate communications.

For $12.95 a month, SIRIUS offers over 120 channels of satellite radio: 65 devoted to commercial-free music, and over 55 channels dedicated to sports, news and entertainment. SIRIUS also broadcasts live play-by-play games of the NHL and NFL, and is the official satellite radio partner of the NFL.

The service can be used in cars, trucks, RVs, homes, offices, stores, and even outdoors. Boaters around the country, and up to 200 miles offshore, can also tune into SIRIUS.

The receiver product line starts with transportable Plug & Play radios and continues to high-end receivers with motorized touch-control display screens, as well as radios that are found in new cars and trucks. These units are manufactured by leading consumer electronics brands, including Alpine, Blaupunkt, Clarion, Eclipse, Jensen, JVC, Kenwood, Panasonic, Sanyo and U.S. Electronics.

DaimlerChrysler, Ford and BMW are SIRIUS' exclusive automotive partners, and their production represents over 40% of the new cars and light trucks sold annually in the United States. SIRIUS radios are currently offered in vehicles from Audi, BMW, Chrysler, Dodge, Ford, Infiniti, Jeep, Lincoln-Mercury, Lexus, Mazda, Mercedes-Benz, MINI, Nissan, Porsche, Scion, Toyota, Volkswagen and Volvo.

XM Satellite Radio
1500 Eckington Place, NE, Washington, DC 20002. Phone: (866) 962-2557; Fax: (202) 380-4500.

Technology and Innovation Center 7777 Glades Rd., Suite 400, Boca Raton, FL 33434. Phone: (561) 226-1200 or (561) 967-2346; Fax: (561) 883-5642. Website: www.xmradio.com.

OEM Liason Office 39810 Grand River, Suite 180, Novi, MI 48375-2138. Phone: (248) 478-6500; Fax: 248-427-9958.

Japan Office XM Satellite Radio, c/o Eugene Moosa-Mikami, Bellhouse B, 27-18 Honmoku Wada, Nakaku, Yokohama, Japan 231-0827. Phone/Fax: 81-45-621-4519.

XM Studios-New York Economist Building, 111 W. 57th St., New York, NY 10019. Phone: (212) 956-5656.

XM Studios-Nashville Country Music Hall of Fame & Museum, 222 5th Ave. S., Nashville, TN 37203.

Management: Hugh Panero, president and CEO; Gary Parsons, chairman; Lee Abrams, chief programming officer; Greg Cole, VP, treasurer; Steve Cook, EVP, sales and marketing; Eric Logan, EVP, production; Derek de Bastos, VP, engineering; Joseph J. Euteneuer, EVP and CFO; Gary Hahn, SVP, advertising and brand management; Steve Harris, VP, external programming; Patricia Kesling, SVP, marketing and operations; Ann Kontner, SVP, human resources; Mary Malone, VP, corporate controller; Lon Levin, SVP, regulatory; Paul Marko, SVP, subscriber technology; Anthony J. Masiello, SVP, operations; Michael J. Morrison, VP, terrestrial network and business operations; Dan Murphy, SVP, production marketing and dstribution; Frank Patry, VP, enterprise information technology; Stell Patsiokas, EVP, technology and engineering; Chance Patterson, VP, corporate affairs; Jeff Snyder, SVP, systems engineering; Melanie Stensrud, VP, Listener Care; Joseph Titlebaum, EVP, general counsel and secretary; Dan Turner, VP, programming operations.

For $12.95 a month, XM offers 68 commercial-free music channels; 33 channels of news, sports and talk; and 21 channels of XM traffic and weather. XM's equity partners include General Motors, the largest U.S. auto and truck manufacturer; Honda Motors; Clear Channel, the largest U.S. radio station operator. It has receiver and retailing partnerships with such leading audio manufacturers as Delphi, Pioneer, Alpine and Sony, and with such electronics retailers as Walmart, Best Buy, Circuit City, Sears and participating Radio Shack franchise dealers.

XM Satellite Radio Inc. is a wholly owned subsidiary of the publicly traded XM Satellite Radio Holdings Inc. (NASDAQ: XMSR).

U.S. AM Stations by Call Letters

KAAA Kingman AZ
KAAB Batesville AR
KAAM(AM) Garland TX
KAAN Bethany MO
KAAY Little Rock AR
KABC Los Angeles CA
KABI Abilene KS
KABL(AM) Salinas CA
KABN(AM) Concord CA
KABQ Albuquerque NM
*KABR Alamo Community NM
KACE(AM) Birch Tree MO
KACH Preston ID
KACI The Dalles OR
KACT Andrews TX
KADA Ada OK
KADI(AM) Springfield MO
KADR Elkader IA
KADS Elk City OK
KAFF Flagstaff AZ
KAFY(AM) Bakersfield CA
KAGC Bryan TX
KAGE Winona MN
KAGH Crossett AR
*KAGI Grants Pass OR
KAGO Klamath Falls OR
KAGV(AM) Big Lake AK
KAGY Port Sulphur LA
KAHI Auburn CA
KAHL(AM) San Antonio TX
KAHS(AM) El Dorado KS
KAHZ(AM) Pomona CA
KAIR Atchison KS
KAJO Grants Pass OR
KAKC(AM) Tulsa OK
KAKK(AM) Walker MN
KALE Richland WA
KALI West Covina CA
KALL(AM) North Salt Lake City UT
KALM Thayer MO
KALN Iola KS
KALT(AM) Atlanta TX
KALV Alva OK
KALY Los Ranchos de Albuquerque NM
KAMA El Paso TX
KAMI Cozad NE
KAML Kenedy-Karnes City TX
KAMQ Carlsbad NM
KANA(AM) Anaconda MT
KAND Corsicana TX
KANE New Iberia LA
KANI Wharton TX
*KANN Roy UT
KAOI(AM) Kihei HI
KAOK Lake Charles LA
KAOL Carrollton MO
KAPE Cape Girardeau MO
*KAPL(AM) Phoenix OR
KAPR Douglas AZ
KAPS Mount Vernon WA
KAPZ Bald Knob AR
KARI Blaine WA
KARN Little Rock AR
*KARR Kirkland WA
KARS Belen NM
KART Jerome ID
KARV Russellville AR
KASA Phoenix AZ
KASI Ames IA
KASL Newcastle WY
KASM Albany MN
KASO Minden LA
KAST Astoria OR
KATA Arcata CA
KATD Pittsburg CA
KATE Albert Lea MN
KATK Carlsbad NM
KATL Miles City MT
KATO Safford AZ
KATQ Plentywood MT
KATZ Saint Louis MO

KAUS Austin MN
KAVA Pueblo CO
KAVL Lancaster CA
KAVP(AM) Colona CO
KAVT Fresno CA
*KAWC Yuma AZ
KAWL York NE
KAWW(AM) Heber Springs AR
KAXX Eagle River AK
KAYL Storm Lake IA
KAYR Van Buren AR
KAYS Hays KS
KAZA(AM) Gilroy CA
KAZG(AM) Scottsdale AZ
KAZM(AM) Sedona AZ
KAZN Pasadena CA
KBAD Las Vegas NV
KBAI(AM) Bellingham WA
KBAL(AM) San Saba TX
KBAM Longview WA
KBAR Burley ID
*KBBI Homer AK
KBBO(AM) Selah WA
KBBR(AM) North Bend OR
KBBS Buffalo WY
KBBW Waco TX
KBCH Lincoln City OR
KBCK(AM) Deer Lodge MT
KBCL(AM) Bossier City LA
KBCR Steamboat Springs CO
KBCV(AM) Hollister MO
KBDB(AM) Sparks NV
KBEC Waxahachie TX
KBED(AM) Nederland TX
KBEL Idabel OK
KBEN Carrizo Springs TX
KBET(AM) Winchester NV
KBEW Blue Earth MN
KBFI(AM) Bonners Ferry ID
KBFS Belle Fourche SD
KBGE(AM) Kilgore TX
KBGG(AM) Des Moines IA
KBGN Caldwell ID
KBHB Sturgis SD
KBHC Nashville AR
KBHS(AM) Hot Springs AR
*KBIB Marion TX
KBID Bakersfield CA
KBIF Fresno CA
KBIM Roswell NM
KBIS(AM) Forks WA
KBIX Muskogee OK
KBIZ Ottumwa IA
KBJA Sandy UT
KBJD Denver CO
KBJM Lemmon SD
KBJT Fordyce AR
KBKB Fort Madison IA
KBKO Santa Barbara CA
KBKR Baker City OR
KBKW Aberdeen WA
KBLA Santa Monica CA
*KBLE(AM) Seattle WA
KBLF Red Bluff CA
KBLG Billings MT
KBLI Blackfoot ID
KBLJ(AM) La Junta CO
KBLL Helena MT
KBLU Yuma AZ
KBME Houston TX
KBMO(AM) Benson MN
KBMR Bismarck ND
KBMS Vancouver WA
KBMW Breckenridge MN
KBNA(AM) El Paso TX
KBND Bend OR
KBNN Lebanon MO
KBNO(AM) Denver CO
KBNP Portland OR
KBOA Kennett MO
KBOE Oskaloosa IA

KBOI Boise ID
KBOK(AM) Malvern AR
KBOV(AM) Bishop CA
KBOW Butte MT
KBOZ Bozeman MT
*KBPS Portland OR
KBRB Ainsworth NE
KBRC(AM) Mount Vernon WA
KBRD Lacey WA
KBRF Fergus Falls MN
KBRH Baton Rouge LA
KBRI Brinkley AR
KBRK Brookings SD
KBRL McCook NE
KBRN Boerne TX
KBRO Bremerton WA
KBRT Avalon CA
KBRV Soda Springs ID
*KBRW(AM) Barrow AK
KBRX O'Neill NE
KBRZ Freeport TX
KBSF Springhill LA
KBSN Moses Lake WA
KBSR Laurel MT
KBST Big Spring TX
*KBSU Boise ID
KBSZ Wickenburg AZ
KBTA Batesville AR
KBTB(AM) Las Vegas NV
KBTC Houston MO
KBTM(AM) Jonesboro AR
KBTN Neosho MO
KBUF(AM) Holcomb KS
KBUL Billings MT
KBUN Bemidji MN
KBUR Burlington IA
KBUY Ruidoso NM
KBWD Brownwood TX
KBYG Big Spring TX
KBYO Tallulah LA
KBYR(AM) Anchorage AK
KBZO Lubbock TX
KBZY Salem OR
KBZZ(AM) Sparks NV
KCAA(AM) Loma Linda CA
KCAB Dardanelle AR
KCAL Redlands CA
KCAM Glennallen AK
KCAP Helena MT
KCAR Clarksville TX
*KCAT Pine Bluff AR
KCBC Riverbank CA
KCBF Fairbanks AK
KCBL Fresno CA
KCBQ San Diego CA
KCBR Monument CO
KCBS San Francisco CA
KCCB Corning AR
KCCC Carlsbad NM
KCCR Pierre SD
KCCS Salem OR
KCCT Corpus Christi TX
KCCV Overland Park KS
KCEO Vista CA
KCFC(AM) Boulder CO
KCFJ(AM) Alturas CA
KCFO Tulsa OK
*KCFR(AM) Denver CO
KCGS Marshall AR
KCHA Charles City IA
KCHE(AM) Cherokee IA
KCHI Chillicothe MO
KCHJ Delano CA
KCHK New Prague MN
KCHL San Antonio TX
KCHN Brookshire TX
KCHR Charleston MO
KCHS Truth or Consequences NM
*KCHU(AM) Valdez AK
KCID Caldwell ID
KCII(AM) Washington IA

KCIK(AM) Blue Lake CA
KCIM Carroll IA
KCIS(AM) Edmonds WA
KCJB Minot ND
KCJJ(AM) Iowa City IA
KCKK Lakewood CO
KCKN(AM) Kansas City KS
KCKX Stayton OR
KCKY Coolidge AZ
KCLA Pine Bluff AR
KCLE(AM) Cleburne TX
KCLI Clinton OK
KCLK Asotin WA
KCLN Clinton IA
KCLR Ralls TX
KCLV Clovis NM
KCLW Hamilton TX
KCLX Colfax WA
KCMC Texarkana TX
KCMD(AM) Portland OR
KCMN Colorado Springs CO
KCMO Kansas City MO
KCMX Phoenix OR
KCNI Broken Bow NE
KCNM(AM) Garapan-Saipan NP
KCNN East Grand Forks MN
KCNR(AM) Shasta CA
KCNW(AM) Fairway KS
KCNZ(AM) Cedar Falls IA
KCOB Newton IA
KCOG Centerville IA
KCOH Houston TX
KCOL(AM) Wellington CO
KCOM Comanche TX
KCON(AM) Conway AR
KCOR(AM) San Antonio TX
KCOW Alliance NE
KCOX(AM) Jasper TX
KCPS Burlington IA
KCPW(AM) Tooele UT
KCQL Aztec NM
KCRC Enid OK
KCRG Cedar Rapids IA
KCRN San Angelo TX
KCRO Omaha NE
KCRS(AM) Midland TX
KCRT Trinidad CO
KCRV Caruthersville MO
KCRX Roswell NM
KCSJ Pueblo CO
KCSP(AM) Kansas City MO
KCSR Chadron NE
KCST Florence OR
KCTA Corpus Christi TX
KCTC Sacramento CA
KCTE Independence MO
KCTI(AM) Gonzales TX
KCTO(AM) Cleveland MO
KCTX Childress TX
KCUB Tucson AZ
KCUE Red Wing MN
KCUL Marshall TX
KCUP(AM) Toledo OR
KCUV(AM) Littleton CO
KCUZ Clifton AZ
KCVL Colville WA
KCVR Lodi CA
KCWJ(AM) Blue Springs MO
KCWM Hondo TX
KCXL Liberty MO
KCYL Lampasas TX
KCZZ(AM) Mission KS
KDAC Fort Bragg CA
KDAE Sinton TX
KDAK Carrington ND
KDAL Duluth MN
KDAO Marshalltown IA
KDAP Douglas AZ
KDAV Lubbock TX
KDAZ Albuquerque NM
KDBM Dillon MT

KDBS Alexandria LA
KDBV(AM) Salinas CA
KDCC Dodge City KS
KDCE Espanola NM
KDDD Dumas TX
KDDR Oakes ND
KDDZ Arvada CO
KDEC Decorah IA
KDEF Albuquerque NM
*KDEI(AM) Port Arthur TX
KDET Center TX
KDEX Dexter MO
KDFN Doniphan MO
KDFO(AM) Bakersfield CA
KDFT Ferris TX
KDGO Durango CO
KDHL Faribault MN
KDHN Dimmitt TX
KDIA Vallejo CA
KDIF Riverside CA
KDIO Ortonville MN
KDIS(AM) Pasadena CA
KDIX Dickinson ND
KDIZ Golden Valley MN
KDJI Holbrook AZ
KDJQ(AM) Meridian ID
KDJS Willmar MN
KDJW(AM) Amarillo TX
KDKA Pittsburgh PA
KDKD Clinton MO
KDLA De Ridder LA
*KDLG Dillingham AK
KDLM Detroit Lakes MN
KDLR Devils Lake ND
KDLS Perry IA
KDMA Montevideo MN
KDMO Carthage MO
KDMS El Dorado AR
KDNZ(AM) Cedar Falls IA
KDOM Windom MN
KDOX Henderson NV
KDQN De Queen AR
KDRO Sedalia MO
KDRS Paragould AR
KDRY Alamo Heights TX
KDSJ Deadwood SD
KDSN Denison IA
KDTA Delta CO
KDTH Dubuque IA
KDUN(AM) Reedsport OR
KDUS Tempe AZ
KDUZ Hutchinson MN
KDWA(AM) Hastings MN
KDWN Las Vegas NV
KDXE(AM) North Little Rock AR
KDXU Saint George UT
KDYA Vallejo CA
KDYL(AM) South Salt Lake UT
KDYN Ozark AR
KDZR(AM) Lake Oswego OR
KEAS Eastland TX
KEBC(AM) Midwest City OK
KEBE Jacksonville TX
*KEBR Rocklin CA
*KECR El Cajon CA
KEDA San Antonio TX
KEDO Longview WA
KEEL(AM) Shreveport LA
KEES Gladewater TX
KEIN Great Falls MT
KEJO Corvallis OR
KELA Centralia-Chehalis WA
KELD El Dorado AR
KELE Mountain Grove MO
KELG(AM) Manor TX
KELK Elko NV
KELO(AM) Sioux Falls SD
KELP El Paso TX
KELY Ely NV
KENA(AM) Mena AR
KENI Anchorage AK

U.S. AM Stations by Call Letters

KENN Farmington NM	*KFNW(AM) West Fargo ND	KGOS Torrington WY	KIHN Hugo OK	KJOK(AM) Yuma AZ
KENO Las Vegas NV	KFNX Cave Creek AZ	KGRE Greeley CO	KIHR Hood River OR	KJOL(AM) Grand Junction CO
KENT(AM) Parowan UT	KFNZ Salt Lake City UT	KGRN Grinnell IA	KIID(AM) Sacramento CA	KJON(AM) Carrollton TX
KENU Enumclaw WA	KFON Austin TX	KGRO Pampa TX	KIIS(AM) Thousand Oaks CA	KJOP(AM) Lemoore CA
KEOR Atoka OK	KFOR Lincoln NE	KGRV Winston OR	KIIX(AM) Fort Collins CO	KJOX(AM) Yakima WA
KEPS Eagle Pass TX	KFOX(AM) Torrance CA	KGRZ Missoula MT	KIJN Farwell TX	KJPG(AM) Frazier Park CA
KERB Kermit TX	KFPT(AM) Clovis CA	KGSO(AM) Wichita KS	KIJV Huron SD	KJPR(AM) Shasta Lake City CA
KERI(AM) Wasco-Greenacres CA	KFPW Fort Smith AR	KGST Fresno CA	KIKC Forsyth MT	KJPW Waynesville MO
KERN Bakersfield CA	KFQD Anchorage AK	KGTK(AM) Olympia WA	KIKK Pasadena TX	KJQS(AM) Murray UT
KERR Polson MT	KFRA Franklin LA	KGTL Homer AK	KIKN Port Angeles WA	KJR Seattle WA
KERV Kerrville TX	KFRC San Francisco CA	KGTO Tulsa OK	KIKO Miami AZ	KJRB Spokane WA
KESM El Dorado Springs MO	KFRM(AM) Salina KS	KGU Honolulu HI	KIKR Beaumont TX	KJRG Newton KS
KESP(AM) Modesto CA	*KFRN Long Beach CA	KGUM(AM) Hagatna GU	KIKZ Seminole TX	KJSA Mineral Wells TX
KESQ Indio CA	KFRO Longview TX	KGVL Greenville TX	KILE Bellaire TX	KJSK Columbus NE
KEST San Francisco CA	KFRU Columbia MO	KGVO Missoula MT	KILJ Mount Pleasant IA	KJSL Saint Louis MO
KETX Livingston TX	KFSA Fort Smith AR	KGVW Belgrade MT	KILR Estherville IA	KJTV(AM) Lubbock TX
KEUN Eunice LA	KFSD(AM) Escondido CA	KGVY Green Valley AZ	KILT Houston TX	KJUA(AM) Cheyenne WY
KEVA Evanston WY	KFSG(AM) Roseville CA	KGWA Enid OK	KIMB Kimball NE	KJUG Tulare CA
KEVT Cortaro AZ	KFST Fort Stockton TX	KGY Olympia WA	KIML Gillette WY	KKAA Aberdeen SD
KEWE(AM) Oroville CA	KFTA(AM) Rupert ID	KGYN Guymon OK	KIMM Rapid City SD	KKAD(AM) Vancouver WA
KEWI(AM) Benton AR	KFTI(AM) Wichita KS	KHAC Tse Bonito NM	KIMP(AM) Mount Pleasant TX	KKAM Lubbock TX
KEWL(AM) Texarkana TX	KFTM Fort Morgan CO	KHAR Anchorage AK	KINA Salina KS	KKAN Phillipsburg KS
KEX Portland OR	KFUN Las Vegas NM	KHAS Hastings NE	KIND Independence KS	KKAQ Thief River Falls MN
KEXO Grand Junction CO	*KFUO(AM) Clayton MO	KHAT(AM) Laramie WY	KINE Kingsville TX	KKAR Omaha NE
KEXS Excelsior Springs MO	KFVR Crescent City CA	KHBC(AM) Hilo HI	KINF(AM) Roswell NM	KKAT(AM) Salt Lake City UT
KEYE Perryton TX	KFWB Los Angeles CA	KHBM Monticello AR	KINN Alamogordo NM	KKAY White Castle LA
KEYF(AM) Dishman WA	KFXD(AM) Boise ID	KHBR Hillsboro TX	KINO Winslow AZ	KKBJ(AM) Bemidji MN
KEYG Grand Coulee WA	KFXN Minneapolis MN	KHBZ(AM) Honolulu HI	KINS Eureka CA	KKCQ Fosston MN
KEYH Houston TX	KFXR(AM) Dallas TX	*KHCB Galveston TX	KINY Juneau AK	KKDA Grand Prairie TX
KEYL Long Prairie MN	KFXX(AM) Portland OR	*KHCH(AM) Huntsville TX	KIOU Shreveport LA	KKDD San Bernardino CA
*KEYQ Fresno CA	KFXZ(AM) Lafayette LA	KHCM(AM) Honolulu HI	KIOV Payette ID	KKDZ Seattle WA
KEYS Corpus Christi TX	KFYI(AM) Phoenix AZ	KHDN Hardin MT	KIPA(AM) Hilo HI	KKEA(AM) Honolulu HI
*KEYY(AM) Provo UT	KFYN Bonham TX	KHEY(AM) El Paso TX	KIQI San Francisco CA	KKEE(AM) Astoria OR
KEYZ Williston ND	KFYO Lubbock TX	KHGG(AM) Van Buren AR	KIQQ Barstow CA	KKFN Denver CO
*KEZJ Twin Falls ID	KFYR Bismarck ND	KHHO Tacoma WA	KIQS Willows CA	KKGM(AM) Fort Worth TX
KEZM Sulphur LA	KGA Spokane WA	KHIL Willcox AZ	KIRN(AM) Simi Valley CA	KKGO(AM) Beverly Hills CA
KEZW Aurora CO	KGAB Orchard Valley WY	KHIT Reno NV	KIRO Seattle WA	KKGR East Helena MT
*KEZX(AM) Medford OR	KGAF Gainesville TX	KHJ(AM) Los Angeles CA	KIRT Mission TX	KKHK(AM) Kansas City KS
KEZY(AM) San Bernardino CA	KGAK Gallup NM	KHLO Hilo HI	KIRV Fresno CA	KKIM Albuquerque NM
KEZZ Estes Park CO	KGAL Lebanon OR	KHLP(AM) Omaha NE	KIRX Kirksville MO	KKIN Aitkin MN
KFAB Omaha NE	KGAM Palm Springs CA	KHLT Hallettsville TX	KIST(AM) Santa Barbara CA	KKJL San Luis Obispo CA
KFAL Fulton MO	KGAS Carthage TX	KHMO Hannibal MO	KIT Yakima WA	KKJX(AM) Klamath Falls OR
KFAN Minneapolis MN	KGBC Galveston TX	KHNC Johnstown CO	KITA Little Rock AR	KKJY(AM) Albuquerque NM
KFAQ(AM) Tulsa OK	KGBT Harlingen TX	KHND Harvey ND	KITI Chehalis-Centralia WA	KKLE(AM) Winfield KS
KFAR Fairbanks AK	KGDC Walla Walla WA	KHNR(AM) Honolulu HI	KITO Vinita OK	KKLF(AM) Sherman TX
KFAX San Francisco CA	KGDD(AM) Oregon City OR	KHOB Hobbs NM	KITZ Silverdale WA	KKLL Webb City MO
KFAY Farmington AR	KGDP(AM) Orcutt CA	KHOJ(AM) Saint Charles MO	KIUL Garden City KS	KKLO Leavenworth KS
KFBC Cheyenne WY	KGEM Boise ID	KHOL Beulah ND	KIUN Pecos TX	KKLS Rapid City SD
KFBK Sacramento CA	KGEN Tulare CA	KHOS Sonora TX	KIUP Durango CO	KKMC Gonzales CA
KFBX(AM) Fairbanks AK	KGEO Bakersfield CA	KHOT Madera CA	KIVY Crockett TX	KKML(AM) Colorado Springs CO
KFCD(AM) Farmersville TX	KGET(AM) Bakersfield CA	KHOW Denver CO	KIWA Sheldon IA	KKMO Tacoma WA
KFCR Custer SD	KGEZ Kalispell MT	KHOZ Harrison AR	KIXI Mercer Island-Seattle WA	KKMS Richfield MN
KFEL Pueblo CO	KGFF Shawnee OK	KHPI(AM) Moreno Valley CA	KIXL(AM) Del Valle TX	KKNE(AM) Waipahu HI
KFEQ(AM) Saint Joseph MO	KGFL Clinton AR	KHPP(AM) Waukon IA	KIXW Apple Valley CA	KKNO Gretna LA
KFFA Helena AR	KGFW Kearney NE	KHPY(AM) Moreno Valley CA	KIXZ Amarillo TX	KKNS(AM) Corrales NM
*KFFF(AM) Boone IA	KGFX Pierre SD	KHQN Spanish Fork UT	*KIYU Galena AK	KKNT(AM) Phoenix AZ
KFFK(AM) Rogers AR	KGGF Coffeyville KS	KHRA(AM) Honolulu HI	KJAA Globe AZ	KKNW(AM) Seattle WA
KFFN Tucson AZ	KGGN Gladstone MO	KHRO(AM) El Paso TX	KJAL(AM) Tafuna AS	KKNX Eugene OR
KFGO Fargo ND	KGGR Dallas TX	KHRT Minot ND	KJAM(AM) Madison SD	KKOB-EX Santa Fe NM
KFH(AM) Wichita KS	KGHF Pueblo CO	KHSE(AM) Wylie TX	KJAN Atlantic IA	KKOB Albuquerque NM
KFI Los Angeles CA	KGHL Billings MT	KHSN(AM) Coos Bay OR	KJAY Sacramento CA	KKOH Reno NV
KFIA Carmichael CA	KGHS International Falls MN	KHTK Sacramento CA	KJBC(AM) Midland TX	KKOJ Jackson MN
KFIG Fresno CA	KGHT Sheridan AR	KHTS(AM) Canyon Country CA	KJBN Little Rock AR	KKOL Seattle WA
KFIL Preston MN	KGIM Aberdeen SD	KHUB Fremont NE	KJCB Lafayette LA	KKON(AM) Kealakekua HI
KFIR Sweet Home OR	KGIR Cape Girardeau MO	KHVH Honolulu HI	KJCE Rollingwood TX	KKOW Pittsburg KS
KFIT-EX San Antonio TX	KGIW Alamosa CO	KHVL(AM) Huntsville TX	KJCK Junction City KS	KKOY Chanute KS
KFIT Lockhart TX	KGKL San Angelo TX	KHVN Fort Worth TX	KJDJ San Luis Obispo CA	KKOZ Ava MO
KFIV Modesto CA	KGLA Gretna LA	KHWG John Day OR	KJDY John Day OR	KKPC Pueblo CO
KFIZ Fond du Lac WI	KGLD Tyler TX	KIAL(AM) Unalaska AK	KJEF(AM) Jennings LA	KKPZ(AM) Portland OR
KFJB Marshalltown IA	KGLE Glendive MT	KIAM Nenana AK	KJFF(AM) Festus MO	KKRT Wenatchee WA
KFJZ Fort Worth TX	KGLN Glenwood Springs CO	KIBL Beeville TX	KJFK(AM) Reno NV	KKRX Lawton OK
KFKA(AM) Greeley CO	KGLO Clovis NM	KICA Clovis NM	KJIM Sherman TX	KKSA San Angelo TX
KFLA Scott City KS	KGLO(AM) Mason City IA	KICD Spencer IA	KJIN(AM) Houma LA	KKSL(AM) Lake Oswego OR
*KFLB(AM) Odessa TX	KGME(AM) Phoenix AZ	KICE(AM) Bend OR	KJJD(AM) Windsor CO	*KKSM Oceanside CA
KFLC(AM) Fort Worth TX	KGMI Bellingham WA	KICO Calexico CA	KJJK Fergus Falls MN	KKSN(AM) Vancouver WA
KFLD Pasco WA	KGMS(AM) Tucson AZ	KICS Hastings NE	KJJL(AM) Pine Bluffs WY	KKTL Casper WY
KFLG(AM) Bullhead City AZ	KGMT Fairbury NE	KICY Nome AK	KJJQ Volga SD	KKTX(AM) Corpus Christi TX
KFLN Baker MT	KGMY Springfield MO	KID Idaho Falls ID	KJJR Whitefish MT	KKTY Douglas WY
KFLP Floydada TX	KGNB New Braunfels TX	KIDD Monterey CA	KJLL South Tucson AZ	KKUB Brownfield TX
KFLS Klamath Falls OR	KGNC Amarillo TX	KIDO(AM) Nampa ID	*KJLT North Platte NE	KKUZ Sallisaw OK
*KFLT Tucson AZ	KGNM Saint Joseph MO	KIDR Phoenix AZ	KJME(AM) Fountain CO	KKVV(AM) Las Vegas NV
KFMB San Diego CA	KGNO Dodge City KS	KIEV(AM) Culver City CA	KJMJ(AM) Alexandria LA	KKXL Grand Forks ND
KFMO Park Hills MO	*KGNU(AM) Denver CO	KIFG Iowa Falls IA	KJMP(AM) Pierce CO	KKXX Paradise CA
KFMZ(AM) Brookfield MO	KGNW Burien-Seattle WA	KIFW Sitka AK	KJNO Juneau AK	KKYX San Antonio TX
KFNI Pleasanton TX	KGO San Francisco CA	KIGO(AM) Saint Anthony ID	*KJNP North Pole AK	KKZN(AM) Thornton CO
KFNN Mesa AZ	KGOE Eureka CA	KIGS Hanford CA	KJOC Davenport IA	KKZZ(AM) Ventura CA
KFNS(AM) Wood River IL	KGOL Humble TX	*KIHM(AM) Reno NV	KJOJ Conroe TX	KLAC Los Angeles CA

Broadcasting & Cable Yearbook 2006

D-609

U.S. AM Stations by Call Letters

KLAM Cordova AK	KLYC(AM) McMinnville OR	KNBO New Boston TX	KODI Cody WY	*KPMO(AM) Mendocino CA
KLAR Laredo TX	KLYQ Hamilton MT	KNBR San Francisco CA	KODL The Dalles OR	KPMP(AM) Modesto CA
KLAT Houston TX	KLYR Clarksville AR	KNBY Newport AR	KODY North Platte NE	KPNS(AM) Duncan OK
KLAV(AM) Las Vegas NV	KLZ Denver CO	KNCB Vivian LA	KOEL(AM) Oelwein IA	KPNW Eugene OR
KLAY(AM) Lakewood WA	KLZS(AM) Eugene OR	KNCK Concordia KS	KOFC Fayetteville AR	KPOC(AM) Pocahontas AR
KLBB Saint Paul MN	KMA Shenandoah IA	KNCO Grass Valley CA	KOFE Saint Maries ID	KPOD Crescent City CA
KLBJ Austin TX	KMAD Madill OK	KNCR Fortuna CA	KOFI Kalispell MT	KPOE(AM) Midland TX
KLBM La Grande OR	KMAJ Topeka KS	KNCY Nebraska City NE	KOFO Ottawa KS	*KPOF Denver CO
KLBO Monahans TX	KMAL(AM) Malden MO	KNDC Hettinger ND	KOFY(AM) Gilmer TX	KPOJ(AM) Portland OR
KLBP(AM) Brooklyn Park MN	KMAM Butler MO	KNDI Honolulu HI	KOGA Ogallala NE	KPOK Bowman ND
KLBS Los Banos CA	KMAN Manhattan KS	KNDK Langdon ND	KOGO(AM) San Diego CA	KPOW Powell WY
KLCB Libby MT	KMAQ Maquoketa IA	KNDN Farmington NM	KOGT Orange TX	KPQ(AM) Wenatchee WA
KLCK Goldendale WA	KMAS Shelton WA	KNDY Marysville KS	KOHI Saint Helens OR	KPRC Houston TX
KLCL Lake Charles LA	KMAV Mayville ND	KNEA(AM) Jonesboro AR	KOHU Hermiston OR	KPRK Livingston MT
KLCN Blytheville AR	KMAX Colfax WA	KNEB Scottsbluff NE	KOIL(AM) Plattsmouth NE	KPRL Paso Robles CA
KLCY East Missoula MT	KMBD Tillamook OR	KNED McAlester OK	KOIT San Francisco CA	KPRM Park Rapids MN
KLDC Brighton CO	*KMBI Spokane WA	KNEK Washington LA	KOJM Havre MT	KPRO Riverside CA
KLDS Falfurrias TX	KMBL Junction TX	KNEL Brady TX	KOKA Shreveport LA	KPRT Kansas City MO
KLDY Lacey WA	KMBS West Monroe LA	KNEM Nevada MO	KOKB Blackwell OK	KPRV Poteau OK
KLEA Lovington NM	KMBX(AM) Soledad CA	KNET Palestine TX	KOKC(AM) Oklahoma City OK	KPRZ San Marcos-Poway CA
KLEB Golden Meadow LA	KMBZ Kansas City MO	KNEU Roosevelt UT	KOKE Pflugerville TX	KPSA(AM) Roswell NM
KLEE Ottumwa IA	KMCD Fairfield IA	KNEW Oakland CA	KOKK Huron SD	KPSI Palm Springs CA
KLEM(AM) Le Mars IA	KMCL(AM) Donnelly ID	KNFL(AM) Tremonton UT	KOKL Okmulgee OK	KPSZ(AM) Des Moines IA
KLER Orofino ID	KMDO Fort Scott KS	KNFT Bayard NM	KOKO Warrensburg MO	KPTK(AM) Seattle WA
KLEX Lexington MO	KMED Medford OR	KNFX Austin MN	KOKP Perry OK	KPTL Carson City NV
KLEY(AM) Wellington KS	KMER Kemmerer WY	KNGL McPherson KS	KOKX Keokuk IA	KPTO(AM) Pocatello ID
KLFB Lubbock TX	KMET Banning CA	*KNGN McCook NE	KOLE Port Arthur TX	KPTQ(AM) Spokane WA
KLFD Litchfield MN	KMFS(AM) Guthrie OK	KNGR(AM) Daingerfield TX	KOLM(AM) Rochester MN	KPUA Hilo HI
KLFE Seattle WA	KMFX Wabasha MN	KNHD Camden AR	KOLT Scottsbluff NE	KPUG Bellingham WA
KLFF(AM) Arroyo Grande CA	KMGS(AM) Highland Park TX	KNIA Knoxville IA	KOLY Mobridge SD	KPUR Amarillo TX
KLFJ Springfield MO	KMHI Mountain Home ID	KNIM(AM) Maryville MO	KOMC Branson MO	KPWB Piedmont MO
KLGA Algona IA	KMHL Marshall MN	KNIR New Iberia LA	KOMJ(AM) Omaha NE	KPXQ(AM) Glendale AZ
KLGN Logan UT	KMHS Coos Bay OR	KNIT(AM) Dallas TX	KOMO Seattle WA	KPYK Terrell TX
KLGR Redwood Falls MN	KMHT Marshall TX	KNJY(AM) Boise ID	KOMW Omak WA	KPYN(AM) Atlanta TX
KLHT Honolulu HI	KMIA(AM) Black Canyon City AZ	KNLV Ord NE	KOMY(AM) La Selva Beach CA	KPZA(AM) Hot Springs AR
KLIB(AM) Roseville CA	KMIC(AM) Houston TX	KNML(AM) Albuquerque NM	KONA Kennewick WA	KPZK(AM) Little Rock AR
KLIC(AM) Monroe LA	KMIK Tempe AZ	KNMX Las Vegas NM	KONO San Antonio TX	KQAB Lake Isabella CA
KLID Poplar Bluff MO	KMIL Cameron TX	KNND Cottage Grove OR	KONP Port Angeles WA	KQAD(AM) Luverne MN
KLIF(AM) Dallas TX	KMIN Grants NM	KNNS Larned KS	KOOQ North Platte NE	KQAM Wichita KS
KLIK(AM) Jefferson City MO	KMIS Portageville MO	KNNZ(AM) Cedar City UT	KOPT(AM) Eugene OR	KQCV Oklahoma City OK
KLIM Limon CO	KMJ Fresno CA	KNOC Natchitoches LA	KOPY Alice TX	KQDI Great Falls MT
KLIN Lincoln NE	KMJC Mount Shasta CA	KNOE Monroe LA	KORC Waldport OR	KQDJ Jamestown ND
KLIV San Jose CA	KMJM(AM) Cedar Rapids IA	*KNOM Nome AK	KORE Springfield-Eugene OR	KQDS Duluth MN
KLIX Twin Falls ID	KMKI Plano TX	KNOT(AM) Prescott AZ	KORL(AM) Honolulu HI	KQEN(AM) Roseburg OR
KLIZ Brainerd MN	KMKY Oakland CA	KNOX Grand Forks ND	KORN Mitchell SD	KQEQ Fowler CA
KLKC(AM) Parsons KS	KMLB Monroe LA	KNPT Newport OR	KORT Grangeville ID	KQIK Lakeview OR
KLKI Anacortes WA	KMMJ Grand Island NE	KNRC(AM) Englewood CO	KOSE Wilson AR	KQKD Redfield SD
KLLA Leesville LA	KMMO Marshall MO	KNRO(AM) Redding CA	KOSY(AM) Texarkana AR	KQKE(AM) Oakland CA
KLLB West Jordan UT	KMMS Bozeman MT	KNRS Salt Lake City UT	KOTA Rapid City SD	KQLO(AM) Sun Valley NV
KLLK Willits CA	KMND Midland TX	KNRY Monterey CA	KOTC Kennett MO	KQLX Lisbon ND
KLMR Lamar CO	KMNS Sioux City IA	KNSA Unalakleet AK	KOTN Pine Bluff AR	KQMG Independence IA
KLMS(AM) Lincoln NE	KMNY(AM) Hurst TX	KNSI Saint Cloud MN	KOTS Deming NM	KQMS Redding CA
KLMX Clayton NM	KMOG Payson AZ	KNSP Staples MN	*KOTZ Kotzebue AK	KQNA(AM) Prescott Valley AZ
KLNG(AM) Council Bluffs IA	KMON Great Falls MT	KNSS(AM) Wichita KS	KOUU Pocatello ID	KQNG Lihue HI
KLNT Laredo TX	KMOX Saint Louis MO	KNST Tucson AZ	KOVC Valley City ND	KQNK Norton KS
KLO Ogden UT	KMOZ Rolla MO	KNTB Lakewood WA	KOVE Lander WY	KQNM(AM) Milan NM
KLOA Ridgecrest CA	KMPC(AM) Los Angeles CA	KNTH(AM) Houston TX	KOVO Provo UT	KQNT(AM) Spokane WA
KLOC(AM) Turlock CA	KMPG Hollister CA	KNTR(AM) Lake Havasu City AZ	KOWB Laramie WY	KQQQ Pullman WA
KLOE Goodland KS	KMRB San Gabriel CA	KNTS(AM) Palo Alto CA	KOWL(AM) South Lake Tahoe CA	KQRL(AM) Waco TX
KLOG Kelso WA	KMRC Morgan City LA	KNTX(AM) Bowie TX	KOWZ(AM) Waseca MN	KQTL Sahuarita AZ
KLOH Pipestone MN	KMRF Marshfield MO	KNUI Kahului HI	KOXR Oxnard CA	KQTY Borger TX
KLOK San Jose CA	KMRI West Valley City UT	KNUJ(AM) New Ulm MN	KOY Phoenix AZ	KQUE Houston TX
KLOO Corvallis OR	KMRN Cameron MO	KNUS Denver CO	KOZA Odessa TX	KQV Pittsburgh PA
KLPL Lake Providence LA	KMRS Morris MN	KNUU(AM) Paradise NV	KOZE Lewiston ID	KQWB(AM) West Fargo ND
KLPW(AM) Union MO	KMRY Cedar Rapids IA	KNUV(AM) Tolleson AZ	KOZI Chelan WA	KQWC Webster City IA
KLPZ Parker AZ	KMSD Milbank SD	KNUZ Bellville TX	KOZN(AM) Bellevue NE	KQYX(AM) Joplin MO
KLSD(AM) San Diego CA	KMTA Miles City MT	KNWA Bellefonte AR	KOZQ Waynesville MO	KRAE Cheyenne WY
KLSQ(AM) Whitney NV	KMTI Manti UT	*KNWC(AM) Sioux Falls SD	KOZY Grand Rapids MN	KRAI Craig CO
KLTC Dickinson ND	KMTL Sherwood AR	KNWH(AM) Twentynine Palms CA	KPAM Troutdale OR	KRAK(AM) Hesperia CA
KLTF Little Falls MN	KMTX Helena MT	KNWQ(AM) Palm Springs CA	KPAN(AM) Hereford TX	KRAL Rawlins WY
KLTI Macon MO	KMUL(AM) Farwell TX	*KNWS Waterloo IA	KPAY Chico CA	KRAM West Klamath OR
KLTK South West City MO	KMUR(AM) Pryor OK	KNWT(AM) Thousand Palms CA	KPBL Hemphill TX	KRBA Lufkin TX
KLTT Commerce City CO	KMUS(AM) Sperry OK	KNWZ(AM) Coachella CA	KPCO Quincy CA	KRBI(AM) Saint Peter MN
KLTX Long Beach CA	KMUZ Gresham OR	KNX Los Angeles CA	KPCR(AM) Quincy IL	KRBT Eveleth MN
KLTZ Glasgow MT	KMVI Wailuku HI	KNXN Sierra Vista AZ	KPDQ Portland OR	KRCM Beaumont TX
KLUP(AM) Terrell Hills TX	KMVL Madisonville TX	KNZR Bakersfield CA	KPEL Lafayette LA	KRCN(AM) Longmont CO
KLVI Beaumont TX	KMVP Phoenix AZ	KNZZ(AM) Grand Junction CO	KPET Lamesa TX	KRCO Prineville OR
KLVL Pasadena TX	KMXA Aurora CO	KOA Denver CO	KPGE Page AZ	KRDD Roswell NM
*KLVP(AM) Tigard OR	KMXE(AM) Orange CA	*KOAC Corvallis OR	KPGM(AM) Pawhuska OK	KRDM(AM) Redmond OR
KLVQ(AM) Athens TX	KMXO Merkel TX	KOAK Red Oak IA	KPHN Kansas City MO	KRDO Colorado Springs CO
KLVT Levelland TX	KMYC(AM) Marysville CA	KOAL Price UT	KPHX Phoenix AZ	KRDU Dinuba CA
KLVZ(AM) Denver CO	KMZK Billings MT	KOAQ Terrytown NE	KPIG(AM) Piedmont CA	KRDY(AM) San Antonio TX
KLWJ Umatilla OR	KNAB Burlington CO	KOBB Bozeman MT	KPIR(AM) Granbury TX	KRDZ Wray CO
KLWN(AM) Lawrence KS	KNAF Fredericksburg TX	KOBE Las Cruces NM	KPJC(AM) Paris TX	KREA(AM) Honolulu HI
KLWT Lebanon MO	KNAK Delta UT	KOBO Yuba City CA	KPKE(AM) Gunnison CO	KREB(AM) Bentonville-Bella Vista AR
KLXR(AM) Redding CA	KNAL Victoria TX	KOCR Joplin MO	KPLT Paris TX	KREF(AM) Norman OK
KLXX Bismarck-Mandan ND	KNAX(AM) McCook NE	KOCY Del City OK	KPLY(AM) Reno NV	KREH Pecan Grove TX

Broadcasting & Cable Yearbook 2006

D-610

U.S. AM Stations by Call Letters

KREI Farmington MO
KREL(AM) Quanah TX
KREW(AM) Plainview TX
KRFE Lubbock TX
KRFO Owatonna MN
KRFS Superior NE
KRFT(AM) De Soto MO
KRGE Weslaco TX
KRGI Grand Island NE
KRGS(AM) Rifle CO
KRHC(AM) Burnet TX
KRHW Sikeston MO
KRIB(AM) Mason City IA
KRIL Odessa TX
KRIO(AM) McAllen TX
KRIZ Renton WA
KRJO(AM) Monroe LA
KRKC(AM) King City CA
KRKE(AM) Albuquerque NM
KRKK Rock Springs WY
KRKO Everett WA
KRKS(AM) Denver CO
KRKY(AM) Granby CO
KRLA(AM) Glendale CA
KRLC Lewiston ID
KRLD Dallas TX
KRLL(AM) California MO
KRLN(AM) Canon City CO
KRLV Las Vegas NV
KRLW Walnut Ridge AR
KRMD Shreveport LA
KRMG Tulsa OK
KRML Carmel CA
KRMO(AM) Cassville MO
KRMP(AM) Oklahoma City OK
KRMS Osage Beach MO
KRMX Pueblo CO
KRMY Killeen TX
KRND(AM) Fox Farm WY
*KRNI(AM) Mason City IA
KRNR Roseburg OR
KRNT Des Moines IA
KROB(AM) Robstown TX
KROC(AM) Rochester MN
KROD El Paso TX
KROE(AM) Sheridan WY
KROF Abbeville LA
KROO Breckenridge TX
KROP(AM) Brawley CA
KROS Clinton IA
KROX Crookston MN
KRPI(AM) Ferndale WA
KRPL Moscow ID
KRQX Mexia TX
KRRD(AM) Centerville UT
KRRP(AM) Coushatta LA
KRRS Santa Rosa CA
KRRZ Minot ND
KRSA Petersburg AK
KRSC Othello WA
KRSL Russell KS
KRSN(AM) Los Alamos NM
KRSV Afton WY
KRSX(AM) Victorville CA
KRSY(AM) Alamogordo NM
KRTA Medford OR
KRTK Chubbuck ID
KRTN Raton NM
KRTR(AM) Honolulu HI
KRTX Rosenberg-Richmond TX
KRUD(AM) Honolulu HI
KRUI Ruidoso Downs NM
KRUN Ballinger TX
KRUS Ruston LA
KRVA Cockrell Hill TX
KRVM Eugene OR
KRVN Lexington NE
KRVT(AM) Claremore OK
KRVZ Springerville-Eagar AZ
KRWB Roseau MN
KRWC Buffalo MN
KRXA(AM) Carmel Valley CA
KRXK(AM) Rexburg ID
KRXR Gooding ID
KRZE Farmington NM
KRZI(AM) Waco TX
KRZY Albuquerque NM

KSAC(AM) Sacramento CA
KSAH(AM) Universal City TX
KSAL Salina KS
KSAZ(AM) Marana AZ
KSBN Spokane WA
KSBQ Santa Maria CA
KSCB Liberal KS
KSCJ Sioux City IA
KSCO Santa Cruz CA
KSCR(AM) Eugene OR
KSDG Julian CA
KSDN Aberdeen SD
KSDO San Diego CA
*KSDP Sand Point AK
KSDR Watertown SD
KSDT Hemet CA
KSEI Pocatello ID
KSEK Pittsburg KS
KSEL Portales NM
KSEN Shelby MT
KSEO Durant OK
KSET(AM) Silsbee TX
KSEV Tomball TX
KSEY Seymour TX
KSFA Nacogdoches TX
KSFN North Las Vegas NV
KSFO San Francisco CA
KSFT Saint Joseph MO
KSGF(AM) Springfield MO
KSGL Wichita KS
KSGM(AM) Chester IL
KSGT Jackson WY
KSHO Lebanon OR
KSHP North Las Vegas NV
KSIB Creston IA
KSID Sidney NE
KSIG Crowley LA
KSIM Sikeston MO
KSIR Brush CO
KSIS(AM) Sedalia MO
KSIV(AM) Clayton MO
KSIW Woodward OK
KSIX Corpus Christi TX
KSJB Jamestown ND
*KSJK Talent OR
KSJL Somerset TX
KSJX(AM) San Jose CA
KSKE(AM) Buena Vista CO
KSKY(AM) Balch Springs TX
KSL Salt Lake City UT
KSLD(AM) Soldotna AK
KSLG(AM) Saint Louis MO
KSLI(AM) Abilene TX
KSLJ(AM) Blackfoot ID
KSLL(AM) Price UT
KSLM Salem OR
KSLO Opelousas LA
KSLR San Antonio TX
KSLV Monte Vista CO
KSMA Santa Maria CA
KSMH(AM) West Sacramento CA
KSML Diboll TX
KSMM Shakopee MN
KSMO Salem MO
KSNM(AM) Las Cruces NM
KSNY Snyder TX
KSOK Arkansas City KS
KSON San Diego CA
KSOO(AM) Sioux Falls SD
KSOP South Salt Lake UT
KSOU Sioux Center IA
KSOX Raymondville TX
KSPA(AM) Ontario CA
KSPD Boise ID
KSPI Stillwater OK
KSPN(AM) Los Angeles CA
KSPT(AM) Sandpoint ID
KSQB(AM) Sioux Falls SD
KSQP(AM) Pierre SD
KSRA Salmon ID
KSRM Soldotna AK
KSRO Santa Rosa CA
KSRR Provo UT
KSRV Ontario OR
KSSK(AM) Honolulu HI
KSSL(AM) Idaho Falls ID
KSSR Santa Rosa NM

KSST Sulphur Springs TX
KSTA Coleman TX
KSTC Sterling CO
KSTE Rancho Cordova CA
KSTL Saint Louis MO
KSTN Stockton CA
KSTP Saint Paul MN
KSTV Stephenville TX
KSUB Cedar City UT
KSUD West Memphis AR
KSUE Susanville CA
KSUH Puyallup WA
KSUM Fairmont MN
KSUN Phoenix AZ
KSVA(AM) Albuquerque NM
KSVC Richfield UT
KSVE El Paso TX
KSVN Ogden UT
KSVP Artesia NM
KSWA Graham TX
KSWB Seaside OR
KSWD Seward AK
KSWM Aurora MO
KSWV Santa Fe NM
KSXT(AM) Loveland CO
KSYB(AM) Shreveport LA
*KSYC(AM) Yreka CA
KSYL Alexandria LA
KSZL Barstow CA
KTAM Bryan TX
KTAN(AM) Sierra Vista AZ
KTAP Santa Maria CA
KTAR(AM) Phoenix AZ
KTAT Frederick OK
KTBA Tuba City AZ
KTBB Tyler TX
KTBI Ephrata WA
KTBL(AM) Los Ranchos de Albuquerque NM
*KTBR(AM) Roseburg OR
KTBZ(AM) Tulsa OK
KTCH Wayne NE
KTCK Dallas TX
KTCR Kennewick WA
KTCS Fort Smith AR
KTCT San Mateo CA
KTDD(AM) San Bernardino CA
KTEK Alvin TX
KTEL Walla Walla WA
KTEM Temple TX
KTFH(AM) Seattle WA
KTFI Twin Falls ID
KTFJ Dakota City NE
KTFS(AM) Texarkana TX
KTFW(AM) Burleson TX
KTFX Sand Springs OK
KTGE Salinas CA
*KTGG Spring Arbor MI
KTGO Tioga ND
KTGR Columbia MO
KTHE Thermopolis WY
KTHH(AM) Albany OR
KTHO South Lake Tahoe CA
KTHS Berryville AR
KTIB Thibodaux LA
KTIC West Point NE
KTIE(AM) San Bernardino CA
KTIK Nampa ID
KTIP Porterville CA
KTIQ(AM) Merced CA
*KTIS Minneapolis MN
KTIX Pendleton OR
KTJK Del Rio TX
KTJS Hobart OK
KTKK Sandy UT
KTKN Ketchikan AK
KTKR San Antonio TX
KTKT Tucson AZ
KTKZ Sacramento CA
KTLK(AM) Los Angeles CA
KTLO Mountain Home AR
KTLQ Tahlequah OK
KTLR(AM) Oklahoma City OK
KTLU Rusk TX
KTLV Midwest City OK
KTMC McAlester OK
KTME Lompoc CA

KTMM(AM) Grand Junction CO
KTMR Edna TX
KTMS Santa Barbara CA
KTMT Ashland OR
KTNC Falls City NE
KTNF(AM) Saint Louis Park MN
KTNM Tucumcari NM
KTNN Window Rock AZ
KTNO(AM) University Park TX
KTNQ Los Angeles CA
KTNS Oakhurst CA
KTNZ Amarillo TX
KTOB(AM) Petaluma CA
KTOE(AM) Mankato MN
KTOK(AM) Oklahoma City OK
KTON Belton TX
KTOP Topeka KS
KTOQ Rapid City SD
KTOX Needles CA
KTOZ Springfield MO
KTPA Prescott AR
KTPI(AM) Mojave CA
KTRB Modesto CA
KTRC(AM) Santa Fe NM
KTRF Thief River Falls MN
KTRH Houston TX
KTRS Saint Louis MO
KTRW Spokane WA
KTSA San Antonio TX
KTSM(AM) El Paso TX
KTTH(AM) Seattle WA
KTTN(AM) Trenton MO
KTTP(AM) Pineville LA
KTTR Rolla MO
KTTT Columbus NE
KTUC Tucson AZ
KTUE Tulia TX
KTUI Sullivan MO
KTWG(AM) Hagatna GU
KTWO Casper WY
KTXV(AM) Frankston TX
KTXZ West Lake Hills TX
KTYM Inglewood CA
KTZN Anchorage AK
KUAI Eleele HI
KUAM(AM) Hagatna GU
KUAU Haiku HI
*KUAZ(AM) Tucson AZ
KUBA Yuba City CA
KUBC(AM) Montrose CO
KUBR San Juan TX
KUDO(AM) Anchorage AK
KUGN Eugene OR
KUGR Green River WY
KUGT Jackson MO
KUHD Port Neches TX
KUHL Santa Maria CA
KUIK(AM) Hillsboro OR
KUJ Walla Walla WA
KUKI Ukiah CA
KUKU(AM) Willow Springs MO
KULE Ephrata WA
KULP El Campo TX
KULY Ulysses KS
KUMA Pendleton OR
KUMU Honolulu HI
KUNF(AM) Washington UT
KUNO Corpus Christi TX
KUNX(AM) Santa Paula CA
KUOA(AM) Siloam Springs AR
KUOL San Marcos TX
*KUOM Minneapolis MN
KUPA(AM) Pearl City HI
KUPI(AM) Ammon ID
KURL Billings MT
KURM Rogers AR
KURS San Diego CA
KURV Edinburg TX
KURY Brookings OR
KUTI(AM) Yakima WA
KUTR(AM) Taylorsville UT
KUTY Palmdale CA
KUUX(AM) Pullman WA
KUVR Holdrege NE
KUYL(AM) Stockton CA
KUYO Evansville WY

KUZZ Bakersfield CA
KVAK(AM) Valdez AK
KVBL Visalia CA
KVBR Brainerd MN
KVCI Canton TX
KVCK(AM) Wolf Point MT
KVCL Winnfield LA
KVCU Boulder CO
KVDW(AM) England AR
KVEC San Luis Obispo CA
KVEL Vernal UT
KVEN Ventura CA
KVET Austin TX
KVFC Cortez CO
KVFD(AM) Fort Dodge IA
KVGB Great Bend KS
KVI Seattle WA
KVIN(AM) Ceres CA
*KVIP Redding CA
KVIS Miami OK
KVIV El Paso TX
KVJY Pharr TX
KVKK(AM) Verndale MN
KVLE(AM) Vail CO
KVLF Alpine TX
KVLG La Grange TX
KVLH Pauls Valley OK
KVLV(AM) Fallon NV
KVMA Magnolia AR
KVMC Colorado City TX
KVML(AM) Sonora CA
KVNA(AM) Flagstaff AZ
KVNI Coeur d'Alene ID
KVNN Victoria TX
KVNR Santa Ana CA
KVNS(AM) Brownsville TX
KVNU Logan UT
KVOC Casper WY
KVOE Emporia KS
KVOI Tucson AZ
KVOK Kodiak AK
KVOL Lafayette LA
KVOM Morrilton AR
KVON Napa CA
KVOP(AM) Plainview TX
KVOR Colorado Springs CO
KVOT(AM) Taos NM
KVOU Uvalde TX
KVOW Riverton WY
KVOX Moorhead MN
KVOZ Del Mar Hills TX
KVPI Ville Platte LA
KVRC Arkadelphia AR
KVRH Salida CO
KVRI(AM) Blaine WA
KVRP Stamford TX
KVSA McGehee AR
KVSF(AM) Santa Fe NM
KVSH Valentine NE
KVSI Montpelier ID
KVSL Show Low AZ
KVSN Tumwater WA
KVSO(AM) Ardmore OK
KVSV Beloit KS
KVTA Port Hueneme CA
KVTK(AM) Vermillion SD
KVTO Berkeley CA
KVVN Santa Clara CA
KVWC Vernon TX
KVWG(AM) Pearsall TX
KVWM(AM) Show Low AZ
KWAC Bakersfield CA
KWAD Wadena MN
KWAI Honolulu HI
KWAK Stuttgart AR
KWAL Wallace ID
KWAM Memphis TN
KWAS Joplin MO
KWAT Watertown SD
KWAY Waverly IA
KWBC Navasota TX
KWBE Beatrice NE
KWBG Boone IA
KWBW Hutchinson KS
KWBY Woodburn OR
KWCK Searcy AR
KWDB(AM) Oak Harbor WA

Broadcasting & Cable Yearbook 2006

D-611

U.S. AM Stations by Call Letters

KWDF Ball LA
KWDJ(AM) Ridgecrest CA
KWDZ(AM) Salt Lake City UT
KWEB(AM) Rochester MN
KWED Seguin TX
KWEI Weiser ID
KWEL Midland TX
KWEY Weatherford OK
KWFA(AM) Tye TX
KWFM(AM) Tucson AZ
KWFS Wichita Falls TX
*KWG(AM) Stockton CA
KWHI Brenham TX
KWHN(AM) Fort Smith AR
KWHW Altus OK
KWIK Pocatello ID
KWIL Albany OR
KWIP Dallas OR
KWIQ(AM) Moses Lake North WA
KWIX Moberly MO
KWJL(AM) Lancaster CA
KWKA Clovis NM
KWKC Abilene TX
KWKH(AM) Shreveport LA
KWKU(AM) Pomona CA
KWKW Los Angeles CA
KWKY Des Moines IA
KWLA Many LA
*KWLC Decorah IA
KWLM Willmar MN
KWLO Waterloo IA
KWLS Pratt KS
KWMC Del Rio TX
KWMG(AM) Auburn-Federal Way WA
KWMO Washington MO
KWMT Fort Dodge IA
KWNA Winnemucca NV
KWNC Quincy WA
KWNO Winona MN
KWNX(AM) Taylor TX
KWOA Worthington MN
KWOC Poplar Bluff MO
KWOF Waterloo IA
KWOK(AM) Hoquiam WA
KWON Bartlesville OK
KWOR Worland WY
KWOS(AM) Jefferson City MO
KWPC Muscatine IA
KWPM West Plains MO
KWRD Henderson TX
KWRE Warrenton MO
KWRF Warren AR
KWRM Corona CA
KWRN Apple Valley CA
KWRO Coquille OR
KWRT(AM) Boonville MO
KWRU(AM) Fresno CA
KWSH Wewoka OK
KWSL Sioux City IA
KWSN(AM) Sioux Falls SD
KWST(AM) El Centro CA
*KWSU Pullman WA
KWSW Eureka CA
*KWTL(AM) Grand Forks ND
KWTO Springfield MO
KWTX Waco TX
KWUD(AM) Woodville TX
KWUF(AM) Pagosa Springs CO
KWVR Enterprise OR
KWWJ Baytown TX
KWWN(AM) Las Vegas NV
KWWX Wenatchee WA
KWXI Glenwood AR
KWXT Dardanelle AR
KWXY Cathedral City CA
KWYD Colorado Springs CO
KWYN Wynne AR
KWYO Sheridan WY
KWYR(AM) Winner SD
KWYS West Yellowstone MT
KWYZ Everett WA
KXAM Mesa AZ
KXAR Hope AR
KXBX Lakeport CA
KXCA(AM) Lawton OK
KXEB(AM) Frisco TX
KXEG(AM) Phoenix AZ

KXEL Waterloo IA
KXEN(AM) Saint Louis MO
KXEO Mexico MO
KXEQ Reno NV
KXEW South Tucson AZ
KXEX Fresno CA
KXGF Great Falls MT
KXGN Glendive MT
KXIC Iowa City IA
KXIT Dalhart TX
KXJK Forrest City AR
KXKS Albuquerque NM
KXL Portland OR
KXLE Ellensburg WA
KXLI(AM) Opportunity WA
KXLO Lewistown MT
KXLQ Indianola IA
KXLX(AM) Airway Heights WA
KXLY Spokane WA
KXMG(AM) Portland OR
KXMR Bismarck ND
KXMX(AM) Anaheim CA
KXNO(AM) Des Moines IA
KXNT North Las Vegas NV
KXO(AM) El Centro CA
KXOI Crane TX
KXOL Brigham City UT
KXOR(AM) Junction City OR
KXOX Sweetwater TX
KXPA Bellevue WA
KXPL(AM) El Paso TX
KXPN(AM) Kearney NE
KXPO Grafton ND
KXPS(AM) Thousand Palms CA
KXRA Alexandria MN
KXRB(AM) Sioux Falls SD
KXRE Manitou Springs CO
KXRO Aberdeen WA
KXSP(AM) Omaha NE
KXSS(AM) Waite Park MN
KXTD Wagoner OK
KXTK(AM) Arroyo Grande CA
KXTL Butte MT
KXTO Reno NV
KXTR(AM) Kansas City KS
KXXA(AM) Conway AR
KXXT(AM) Tolleson AZ
KXXX Colby KS
KXYL(AM) Brownwood TX
KXYZ Houston TX
KXZZ Lake Charles LA
KYAA(AM) Soquel CA
KYAK Yakima WA
KYAL(AM) Sapulpa OK
KYBC(AM) Cottonwood AZ
KYCA(AM) Prescott AZ
KYCN Wheatland WY
KYCR Golden Valley MN
KYCY San Francisco CA
KYDZ(AM) Bellevue NE
KYET Williams AZ
*KYFO(AM) Ogden UT
*KYFR Shenandoah IA
KYHN(AM) Fort Smith AR
KYIZ Renton WA
KYKK(AM) Hobbs NM
KYKN Keizer OR
KYLS Fredericktown MO
KYLT Missoula MT
KYLW(AM) Lockwood MT
KYMN Northfield MN
KYMO East Prairie MO
KYND Cypress TX
KYNG(AM) Denison-Sherman TX
KYNO Fresno CA
KYNR(AM) Toppenish WA
KYNS(AM) San Luis Obispo CA
KYNT Yankton SD
KYOK(AM) Conroe TX
KYOO Bolivar MO
KYOS Merced CA
KYPA Los Angeles CA
KYRO Potosi MO
KYSM Mankato MN
KYST Texas City TX
*KYUK Bethel AK
KYUU Liberal KS

KYVA(AM) Gallup NM
KYW Philadelphia PA
KYXE(AM) Union Gap WA
KYYW(AM) Abilene TX
KYZS Tyler TX
KZDC San Antonio TX
KZEE Weatherford TX
KZER(AM) Santa Barbara CA
KZEY Tyler TX
KZFX(AM) Salinas CA
KZGX(AM) Watertown MN
KZIM Cape Girardeau MO
KZIP Amarillo TX
KZIZ Sumner WA
KZMP(AM) University Park TX
KZMQ Greybull WY
KZMX Hot Springs SD
KZNE(AM) College Station TX
KZNG Hot Springs AR
KZNS(AM) Salt Lake City UT
KZNT(AM) Colorado Springs CO
KZNU(AM) Saint George UT
KZNX(AM) Creedmoor TX
KZNY(AM) Milwaukie OR
KZOO Honolulu HI
KZPA Fort Yukon AK
KZQQ(AM) Abilene TX
KZRA Springdale AR
KZRK(AM) Canyon TX
KZSB(AM) Santa Barbara CA
KZSF San Jose CA
KZSJ(AM) San Martin CA
KZTD(AM) Cabot AR
KZTS(AM) Sunnyside WA
KZUE El Reno OK
KZXR Prosser WA
KZZB Beaumont TX
KZZJ Rugby ND
KZZN Littlefield TX
KZZR(AM) Burns OR
KZZZ(AM) Bullhead City AZ
V6AH Pohnpei FM
*V6AI Yap FM
V6AK Truk FM
WAAA Winston-Salem NC
WAAM Ann Arbor MI
WAAV Leland NC
WAAX Gadsden AL
WABA Aguadilla PR
WABB Mobile AL
WABC(AM) New York NY
WABF(AM) Fairhope AL
WABG(AM) Greenwood MS
WABH Bath NY
WABI Bangor ME
WABJ Adrian MI
WABL Amite LA
WABN Abingdon VA
WABO Waynesboro MS
WABQ Cleveland OH
WABS Arlington VA
WABV(AM) Abbeville SC
WABY(AM) Mechanicville NY
WACA Wheaton MD
WACB Taylorsville NC
WACC Hialeah FL
WACE Chicopee MA
WACK(AM) Newark NY
WACM West Springfield MA
WACQ(AM) Carrville AL
WACT Tuscaloosa AL
WACV Montgomery AL
WADA Shelby NC
WADB Asbury Park NJ
WADC Parkersburg WV
WADE Wadesboro NC
WADK Newport RI
WADM Decatur IN
WADO New York NY
WADR Remsen NY
WADS Ansonia CT
WADV Lebanon PA
WAEB Allentown PA
WAEC Atlanta GA
WAEL Mayaguez PR
WAEW Crossville TN
WAEY Princeton WV

WAFC Clewiston FL
WAFS(AM) Atlanta GA
WAFZ Immokalee FL
WAGE Leesburg VA
WAGF Dothan AL
WAGG(AM) Birmingham AL
WAGL Lancaster SC
WAGN Menominee MI
WAGR Lumberton NC
WAGS Bishopville SC
WAHT Clemson SC
WAIA(AM) Beaver Dam KY
WAIK Galesburg IL
WAIM Anderson SC
WAIN Columbia KY
WAIS Buchtel OH
WAIT(AM) Chicago IL
WAIZ(AM) Hickory NC
WAJD Gainesville FL
WAJF Decatur AL
WAJQ Alma GA
WAJR Morgantown WV
WAKE Valparaiso IN
WAKI McMinnville TN
WAKK(AM) McComb MS
WAKM Franklin TN
WAKO Lawrenceville IL
WAKR Akron OH
WAKV Otsego MI
WAKY Greensburg KY
WALD Walterboro SC
WALE Greenville RI
WALG Albany GA
WALH Mountain City GA
WALK(AM) East Patchogue NY
WALL Middletown NY
WALO(AM) Humacao PR
WALR Atlanta GA
WALT Meridian MS
WAMA Tampa FL
WAMB(AM) Nashville TN
WAMC(AM) Albany NY
WAMD Aberdeen MD
WAME(AM) Statesville NC
WAMF(AM) Fulton NY
WAMG(AM) Dedham MA
WAMI Opp AL
WAML Laurel MS
WAMM Woodstock VA
WAMN Green Valley WV
WAMO(AM) Millvale PA
WAMS(AM) Newark DE
WAMT(AM) Pine Castle-Sky Lake FL
WAMV Amherst VA
WAMW(AM) Washington IN
WAMY Amory MS
WANA(AM) Anniston AL
WANG Havelock NC
WANI Opelika AL
WANO Pineville KY
WANR Warren OH
WANS Anderson SC
WANY Albany KY
WAOC(AM) Saint Augustine FL
WAOK Atlanta GA
WAOS(AM) Austell GA
WAOV Vincennes IN
WAPA San Juan PR
WAPF(AM) McComb MS
WAPI Birmingham AL
WAPZ Wetumpka AL
WAQE Rice Lake WI
WAQI Miami FL
WARE Ware MA
WARF(AM) Akron OH
WARK Hagerstown MD
WARL(AM) Attleboro MA
WARM Scranton PA
WARR Warrenton NC
WARU Peru IN
WARV Warwick RI
WASB Brockport NY
WASC Spartanburg SC
WASG Atmore AL
WASK Lafayette IN
WASN(AM) Youngstown OH
WASO Covington LA

WASP Brownsville PA
WASR Wolfeboro NH
WATA Boone NC
WATB Decatur GA
WATH Athens OH
WATK Antigo WI
WATN Watertown NY
WATO Oak Ridge TN
WATR(AM) Waterbury CT
WATS Sayre PA
WATT Cadillac MI
WATV Birmingham AL
WATW Ashland WI
WATX Algood TN
WATZ Alpena MI
WAUB Auburn NY
WAUC Wauchula FL
WAUD Auburn AL
WAUG New Hope NC
WAUK Waukesha WI
WAUR Sandwich IL
WAVG(AM) Jeffersonville IN
WAVL Apollo PA
WAVN Southaven MS
WAVO Rock Hill SC
WAVP(AM) Avon Park FL
WAVS Davie FL
WAVU(AM) Albertville AL
WAVZ New Haven CT
WAWK Kendallville IN
WAXO Lewisburg TN
WAXY South Miami FL
WAYE Birmingham AL
WAYN Rockingham NC
*WAYR Orange Park FL
WAYS(AM) Macon GA
WAYY(AM) Eau Claire WI
WAZL Hazleton PA
WAZN(AM) Watertown MA
WAZS(AM) Summerville SC
WAZX Smyrna GA
WAZZ Fayetteville NC
*WBAA West Lafayette IN
WBAC(AM) Cleveland TN
WBAE Portland ME
WBAF Barnesville GA
WBAG Burlington-Graham NC
WBAJ Blythwood SC
WBAL Baltimore MD
WBAP Fort Worth TX
WBAT Marion IN
WBAU(AM) Fort Walton Beach FL
WBAX Wilkes-Barre PA
WBBA Pittsfield IL
WBBD Wheeling WV
WBBF(AM) Buffalo NY
WBBK Blakely GA
WBBL Grand Rapids MI
WBBM Chicago IL
WBBP Memphis TN
WBBR New York NY
WBBT Lyons GA
WBBW Youngstown OH
WBBX Kingston TN
WBBZ Ponca City OK
WBCA Bay Minette AL
WBCB Levittown-Fairless Hills PA
WBCE Wickliffe KY
WBCF(AM) Florence AL
WBCH Hastings MI
WBCK Battle Creek MI
WBCO Bucyrus OH
WBCP Urbana IL
WBCR Alcoa TN
WBCU Union SC
WBDY Bluefield VA
WBEC Pittsfield MA
WBEJ Elizabethton TN
WBEN Buffalo NY
WBES(AM) Dunbar WV
WBET Brockton MA
WBEV Beaver Dam WI
WBEX Chillicothe OH
WBFC Stanton KY
WBFD(AM) Bedford PA
WBFJ Winston-Salem NC
WBGC Chipley FL

Broadcasting & Cable Yearbook 2006

D-612

U.S. AM Stations by Call Letters

WBGG(AM) Pittsburgh PA
WBGN(AM) Bowling Green KY
WBGR Baltimore MD
WBGS Point Pleasant WV
WBGX(AM) Harvey IL
WBGZ Alton IL
WBHB Fitzgerald GA
WBHF(AM) Cartersville GA
WBHN Bryson City NC
WBHP Huntsville AL
WBHR Sauk Rapids MN
WBHV(AM) Somerset PA
WBHY Mobile AL
WBIB Centreville AL
WBIC Royston GA
WBIG Aurora IL
WBIL Tuskegee AL
WBIN Benton TN
WBIP Booneville MS
WBIS(AM) Annapolis MD
WBIW Bedford IN
WBIX(AM) Natick MA
WBIZ Eau Claire WI
WBJX Racine WI
WBKC Painesville OH
WBKV West Bend WI
WBKZ Jefferson GA
WBLA Elizabethtown NC
WBLC Lenoir City TN
WBLF Bellefonte PA
WBLJ(AM) Dalton GA
WBLL Bellefontaine OH
WBLO(AM) Thomasville NC
WBLR Batesburg SC
WBMC McMinnville TN
WBMD Baltimore MD
WBMJ San Juan PR
WBML Macon GA
WBMQ Savannah GA
WBNC Conway NH
WBNL(AM) Boonville IN
WBNR Beacon NY
WBNS Columbus OH
WBNW Concord MA
WBOB Florence KY
WBOG(AM) Tomah WI
WBOK New Orleans LA
WBOL Bolivar TN
WBOW(AM) Terre Haute IN
WBOX Bogalusa LA
WBPZ Lock Haven PA
WBQN(AM) Barceloneta-Manati PR
WBRD Palmetto FL
WBRG Lynchburg VA
WBRI Indianapolis IN
WBRK Pittsfield MA
WBRM Marion NC
WBRN Big Rapids MI
WBRT Bardstown KY
WBRV Boonville NY
WBRY Woodbury TN
WBSA Boaz AL
WBSC Bennettsville SC
WBSL Bay St. Louis MS
WBSM New Bedford MA
WBSR Pensacola FL
WBT Charlotte NC
WBTA Batavia NY
WBTC Uhrichsville OH
WBTE Windsor NC
WBTG Sheffield AL
WBTH Williamson WV
WBTK(AM) Richmond VA
WBTM Danville VA
WBTN Bennington VT
WBTO Linton IN
WBTX Broadway-Timberville VA
WBUC Buckhannon WV
WBUD Trenton NJ
*WBUR(AM) West Yarmouth MA
WBUT Butler PA
WBVA(AM) Bayside VA
WBVP Beaver Falls PA
WBWL Jacksonville FL
WBXR Hazel Green AL
WBYE Calera AL
WBYS Canton IL

WBYU New Orleans LA
WBZ Boston MA
WBZI Xenia OH
WBZK York SC
WBZQ Huntington IN
WBZT(AM) West Palm Beach FL
WBZU(AM) Scranton PA
WBZZ(AM) Seffner FL
WCAB(AM) Rutherfordton NC
WCAM Camden SC
WCAO Baltimore MD
WCAP Lowell MA
WCAR Livonia MI
WCAW Charleston WV
WCAZ Carthage IL
WCBA Corning NY
WCBC Cumberland MD
WCBG(AM) Waynesboro PA
WCBL Benton KY
WCBM Baltimore MD
WCBQ Oxford NC
WCBR Richmond KY
WCBS New York NY
WCBT Roanoke Rapids NC
WCBW(AM) Highland IL
WCBX(AM) Bassett VA
WCBY Cheboygan MI
WCCD(AM) Parma OH
WCCF(AM) Punta Gorda FL
WCCM(AM) Haverhill MA
WCCN Neillsville WI
WCCO Minneapolis MN
WCCS Homer City PA
WCCW(AM) Traverse City MI
WCCY Houghton MI
WCDL(AM) Carbondale PA
WCDO Sidney NY
WCDS(AM) Glasgow KY
WCDT Winchester TN
WCEC(AM) Salem NH
WCED DuBois PA
WCEH Hawkinsville GA
WCEM Cambridge MD
WCEO(AM) Columbia SC
WCER Canton OH
WCEV Cicero IL
WCFI(AM) Ocala FL
WCFJ Chicago Heights IL
WCGA Woodbine GA
WCGB Juana Diaz PR
WCGC Belmont NC
WCGL Jacksonville FL
WCGO Chicago Heights IL
WCGR Canandaigua NY
WCGW Nicholasville KY
WCHA Chambersburg PA
WCHB Taylor MI
WCHE West Chester PA
WCHI Chillicothe OH
WCHJ Brookhaven MS
WCHK Canton GA
WCHL Chapel Hill NC
WCHM Clarkesville GA
WCHN Norwich NY
WCHO(AM) Washington Court House OH
WCHP Champlain NY
WCHQ(AM) Quebradillas PR
WCHR(AM) Flemington NJ
WCHS Charleston WV
WCHT Escanaba MI
WCHV Charlottesville VA
WCIE Spring Lake NC
WCIL Carbondale IL
WCIN Cincinnati OH
WCIS Morganton NC
WCJU Columbia MS
WCJW(AM) Warsaw NY
WCKB Dunn NC
WCKD(AM) Lebanon TN
WCKI Greer SC
WCKL Catskill NY
WCKS(AM) Jacksonville AL
WCKW(AM) Garyville LA
WCKY(AM) Cincinnati OH
WCLA Claxton GA
WCLB(AM) Sheboygan WI

WCLC Jamestown TN
WCLD Cleveland MS
WCLE Cleveland TN
WCLG Morgantown WV
WCLM Highland Springs VA
WCLN Clinton NC
WCLO Janesville WI
WCLT(AM) Newark OH
WCLU(AM) Glasgow KY
WCLW Eden NC
WCLY Raleigh NC
WCMA(AM) Daleville AL
WCMC(AM) Wildwood NJ
WCMD(AM) Cumberland MD
WCMI Ashland KY
WCMN Arecibo PR
WCMP Pine City MN
WCMS(AM) Newport News VA
WCMT(AM) Martin TN
WCMX Leominster MA
WCMY(AM) Ottawa IL
WCNB(AM) Connersville IN
WCNC(AM) Elizabeth City NC
WCND Shelbyville KY
WCNM(AM) Lewiston ME
WCNN North Atlanta GA
WCNS Latrobe PA
WCNW Fairfield OH
WCNX(AM) Hope Valley RI
WCNZ(AM) Marco Island FL
WCOA Pensacola FL
WCOC(AM) Dora AL
WCOG Greensboro NC
WCOH Newnan GA
WCOJ(AM) Coatesville PA
WCOK Sparta NC
WCON Cornelia GA
WCOR Lebanon TN
WCOS Columbia SC
WCPA Clearfield PA
WCPC Houston MS
WCPH Etowah TN
WCPK Chesapeake VA
WCPM Cumberland KY
WCPR Coamo PR
WCPS Tarboro NC
WCPT(AM) Crystal Lake IL
WCQV(AM) Moneta VA
WCRA Effingham IL
WCRE Cheraw SC
WCRK(AM) Morristown TN
WCRL Oneonta AL
WCRM Fort Myers FL
WCRN Worcester MA
WCRO Johnstown PA
WCRR Rural Retreat VA
WCRS Greenwood SC
WCRV Collierville TN
WCSA Ripley MS
WCSI(AM) Columbus IN
WCSJ(AM) Morris IL
WCSL Cherryville NC
WCSM Celina OH
WCSR Hillsdale MI
WCSS Amsterdam NY
WCST Berkeley Springs WV
WCSV Crossville TN
WCSW Shell Lake WI
WCSZ(AM) Sans Souci SC
WCTA Alamo TN
WCTC(AM) New Brunswick NJ
*WCTF Vernon CT
WCTN Potomac-Cabin John MD
WCTR(AM) Chestertown MD
WCTS Maplewood MN
WCTT Corbin KY
WCTZ Clarksville TN
WCUB(AM) Two Rivers WI
*WCUE Cuyahoga Falls OH
WCUG Cuthbert GA
WCUM Bridgeport CT
WCVA Culpeper VA
WCVC Tallahassee FL
WCVG Covington KY
WCVL Crawfordville IN
WCVP Murphy NC
WCWA Toledo OH

WCXI(AM) Fenton MI
WCXN Claremont NC
WCYN Cynthiana KY
WCZZ(AM) Greenwood SC
WDAD Indiana PA
WDAE(AM) Saint Petersburg FL
WDAK Columbus GA
WDAL Dalton GA
WDAN(AM) Danville IL
WDAO Dayton OH
WDAP Huntingdon TN
WDAS Philadelphia PA
WDAY Fargo ND
WDBC Escanaba MI
WDBL(AM) Springfield TN
WDBO Orlando FL
WDBQ Dubuque IA
WDBZ(AM) Cincinnati OH
WDCD(AM) Albany NY
WDCF Dade City FL
WDCR Hanover NH
WDCT Fairfax VA
WDCY Douglasville GA
WDDD Johnston City IL
WDDO Macon GA
WDDV(AM) Venice FL
WDDY(AM) Albany NY
WDDZ(AM) Pawtucket RI
WDEA Ellsworth ME
WDEB Jamestown TN
WDEE Reed City MI
WDEF Chattanooga TN
WDEH Sweetwater TN
WDEL Wilmington DE
WDEO(AM) Ypsilanti MI
WDEP(AM) Ponce PR
WDER Derry NH
WDEV Waterbury VT
WDEX Monroe NC
WDFB Junction City KY
WDFN Detroit MI
WDGR Dahlonega GA
WDGY(AM) Hudson WI
WDHP Frederiksted VI
WDIA Memphis TN
WDIC(AM) Clinchco VA
WDID(AM) Highland IL
WDIG Steubenville OH
WDIS Norfolk MA
WDIZ Panama City FL
WDJA(AM) Delray Beach FL
WDJL Huntsville AL
WDJS Mount Olive NC
WDJZ Bridgeport CT
WDKD Kingstree SC
WDKN Dickson TN
WDLA Walton NY
WDLB Marshfield WI
WDLC Port Jervis NY
WDLK Dadeville AL
*WDLM East Moline IL
WDLS(AM) Wisconsin Dells WI
WDLT Fairhope AL
WDLW Lorain OH
WDLX Washington NC
WDMG Douglas GA
WDMJ Marquette MI
WDMN(AM) Rossford OH
WDMP(AM) Dodgeville WI
WDMV(AM) Poolesville MD
WDNC(AM) Durham NC
WDND(AM) South Bend IN
WDNE Elkins WV
WDNG Anniston AL
WDNT(AM) Dayton TN
WDNY(AM) Dansville NY
WDNZ(AM) Raleigh NC
WDOC Prestonsburg KY
WDOD Chattanooga TN
WDOE Dunkirk NY
WDOG Allendale SC
WDOR Sturgeon Bay WI
WDOS Oneonta NY
WDOV Dover DE
WDOW Dowagiac MI
WDPC Dallas GA
WDPN Alliance OH

WDQN Du Quoin IL
WDRC(AM) Hartford CT
WDRD(AM) Newburg KY
WDRF(AM) Woodruff SC
WDRU(AM) Wake Forest NC
WDSC Dillon SC
WDSK Cleveland MS
WDSL Mocksville NC
WDSM Superior WI
WDSR Lake City FL
WDSS(AM) Ada MI
WDTK(AM) Detroit MI
WDTM Selmer TN
WDTW(AM) Dearborn MI
WDUF Duffield VA
WDUN Gainesville GA
WDUR Durham NC
WDUX Waupaca WI
WDUZ(AM) Green Bay WI
WDVA Danville VA
WDVH(AM) Gainesville FL
*WDVM(AM) Eau Claire WI
WDWD Atlanta GA
WDWS(AM) Champaign IL
WDXE Lawrenceburg TN
WDXI Jackson TN
WDXL Lexington TN
WDXQ(AM) Cochran GA
WDXR Paducah KY
WDXY Sumter SC
WDYZ(AM) Orlando FL
WDZ(AM) Decatur IL
WDZK Bloomfield CT
WDZY Colonial Heights VA
WEAC Gaffney SC
WEAE Pittsburgh PA
WEAL Greensboro NC
WEAM Columbus GA
WEAQ Chippewa Falls WI
WEAV Plattsburgh NY
WEBC Duluth MN
WEBJ Brewton AL
WEBO Owego NY
WEBQ Harrisburg IL
WEBS(AM) Calhoun GA
WEBY(AM) Milton FL
WECK Cheektowaga NY
WECM Milton FL
WECO Wartburg TN
WECR Newland NC
WECU(AM) Winterville NC
WECZ Punxsutawney PA
WEDI(AM) Eaton OH
WEDO McKeesport PA
WEEB Southern Pines NC
WEED(AM) Rocky Mount NC
WEEF Highland Park IL
WEEI Boston MA
WEEN(AM) Lafayette TN
WEEO(AM) Shippensburg PA
WEEP(AM) Virginia MN
WEEU Reading PA
WEEX Easton PA
WEEZ Laurel MS
WEFL(AM) Tequesta FL
WEGA Vega Baja PR
WEGG Rose Hill NC
WEGO Concord NC
WEGP Presque Isle ME
WEHH Elmira Heights-Horseheads NY
WEIC Charleston IL
WEIM Fitchburg MA
WEIR Weirton WV
WEIS Centre AL
WEJL Scranton PA
WEKB(AM) Elkhorn City KY
WEKC Williamsburg KY
WEKG Jackson KY
WEKO(AM) Morovis PR
WEKR Fayetteville TN
WEKT Elkton KY
WEKY Richmond KY
WEKZ Monroe WI
WELA(AM) Welch WV
WELB Elba AL
WELC Welch WV
WELD(AM) Fisher WV

Broadcasting & Cable Yearbook 2006

D-613

U.S. AM Stations by Call Letters

WELE Ormond Beach FL
WELI New Haven CT
WELM Elmira NY
WELO Tupelo MS
WELP(AM) Easley SC
WELR Roanoke AL
WELS Kinston NC
WELW Willoughby-Eastlake OH
WELY Ely MN
WELZ Belzoni MS
WEMB Erwin TN
WEMD(AM) Easton MD
WEMG(AM) Camden NJ
WEMJ Laconia NH
WEMM(AM) Huntington WV
WEMR Tunkhannock PA
WENA Yauco PR
WENC Whiteville NC
WENE(AM) Endicott NY
WENG Englewood FL
WENI(AM) Corning NY
WENK Union City TN
WENO Nashville TN
WENR Engelwood TN
WENT Gloversville NY
WENU(AM) South Glens Falls NY
WENY Elmira NY
WEOA Evansville IN
WEOK Poughkeepsie NY
WEOL Elyria OH
WEPG South Pittsburg TN
WEPM Martinsburg WV
WEPN(AM) New York NY
WERC Birmingham AL
WERE Cleveland OH
WERH Hamilton AL
WERL Eagle River WI
WERT Van Wert OH
WESB Bradford PA
WESL East St. Louis IL
WESO Southbridge MA
WESR Onley-Onancock VA
WEST Easton PA
WESX Salem MA
WESY Leland MS
WETB Johnson City TN
WETC Wendell-Zebulon NC
WETR(AM) Knoxville TN
WETZ New Martinsville WV
WEUP Huntsville AL
WEUS(AM) Orlovista FL
WEUV(AM) Huntsville AL
WEVA(AM) Emporia VA
WEVR River Falls WI
WEW Saint Louis MO
WEWC(AM) Callahan FL
WEWO Laurinburg NC
WEXL Royal Oak MI
WEXS Patillas PR
WEXY Wilton Manors FL
WEZC Neon KY
WEZE Boston MA
WEZJ Williamsburg KY
WEZS Laconia NH
WFAB Ceiba PR
WFAD Middlebury VT
WFAI(AM) Salem NJ
WFAM(AM) Augusta GA
WFAN New York NY
WFAS(AM) White Plains NY
WFAU Gardiner ME
WFAW Fort Atkinson WI
WFAX Falls Church VA
WFAY(AM) Fayetteville NC
WFBG Altoona PA
WFBL(AM) Syracuse NY
WFBR(AM) Glen Burnie MD
WFBS(AM) Berwick PA
WFCL Clintonville WI
*WFCM Smyrna TN
WFCV Fort Wayne IN
WFDF Flint MI
WFDL(AM) Waupun WI
WFDR Manchester GA
WFEA Manchester NH
WFEB Sylacauga AL
WFED(AM) Silver Spring MD

WFFF Columbia MS
WFFG Marathon FL
WFFX Meridian MS
WFGI(AM) Charleroi PA
WFGL Fitchburg MA
WFGM(AM) Sandy Springs GA
WFGN Gaffney SC
WFGW Black Mountain NC
WFHG(AM) Bristol VA
WFHK Pell City AL
WFHR Wisconsin Rapids WI
WFIA Louisville KY
WFIC(AM) Collinsville VA
WFIF Milford CT
WFIL(AM) Philadelphia PA
WFIN Findlay OH
WFIR(AM) Roanoke VA
WFIS Fountain Inn SC
WFIW(AM) Fairfield IL
*WFKJ Cashtown PA
WFKN Franklin KY
WFKY Frankfort KY
WFLA(AM) Tampa FL
WFLE Flemingsburg KY
WFLF(AM) Pine Hills FL
WFLI Lookout Mountain TN
WFLL(AM) Fort Lauderdale FL
WFLN(AM) Arcadia FL
WFLO Farmville VA
WFLR Dundee NY
WFLT Flint MI
WFLW Monticello KY
WFMB(AM) Springfield IL
WFMC Goldsboro NC
WFMD(AM) Frederick MD
WFMH(AM) Cullman AL
WFMO Fairmont NC
WFMW Madisonville KY
WFNA(AM) Charlotte NC
WFNC Fayetteville NC
WFNN(AM) Erie PA
WFNO Norco LA
WFNR Blacksburg VA
WFNS(AM) Blackshear GA
WFNT Flint MI
WFNW(AM) Naugatuck CT
WFNY(AM) Gloversville NY
WFNZ Charlotte NC
WFOB Fostoria OH
WFOM Marietta GA
WFOR Hattiesburg MS
WFOY(AM) Saint Augustine FL
WFPA(AM) Fort Payne AL
WFPB Orleans MA
WFPR Hammond LA
WFRA Franklin PA
WFRB Frostburg MD
*WFRF(AM) Tallahassee FL
WFRL Freeport IL
WFRM Coudersport PA
WFRN Elkhart IN
WFRX West Frankfort IL
WFSC Franklin NC
WFSH Valparaiso-Niceville FL
WFSP Kingwood WV
WFSR Harlan KY
*WFST(AM) Caribou ME
WFTD Marietta GA
WFTG London KY
WFTH Richmond VA
WFTL(AM) West Palm Beach FL
WFTM Maysville KY
WFTN Franklin NH
WFTR Front Royal VA
WFTU(AM) Riverhead NY
WFTW Fort Walton Beach FL
WFUL(AM) Fulton KY
WFUN Ashtabula OH
WFUR Grand Rapids MI
WFVA(AM) Fredericksburg VA
WFVR Valdosta GA
WFWL(AM) Camden TN
WFXH Hilton Head Island SC
WFXJ(AM) Jacksonville FL
WFXN(AM) Moline IL
WFXY Middlesboro KY
WFYC(AM) Alma MI

WFYL(AM) McConnellsburg PA
WGAA Cedartown GA
WGAB Newburgh IN
WGAC Augusta GA
WGAD Gadsden AL
WGAI Elizabeth City NC
WGAN(AM) Portland ME
WGAP Maryville TN
*WGAS South Gastonia NC
WGAT Gate City VA
WGAU Athens GA
WGAW Gardner MA
WGBB Freeport NY
WGBF Evansville IN
WGBN New Kensington PA
WGBR Goldsboro NC
WGCD Chester SC
WGCH(AM) Greenwich CT
WGCL Bloomington IN
WGCM Gulfport MS
WGCR Brevard NC
WGCV(AM) Cayce SC
WGDL Lares PR
WGDN Gladwin MI
WGEA Geneva AL
WGEE(AM) Superior WI
WGEM Quincy IL
WGEN Geneseo IL
WGET Gettysburg PA
WGEZ Beloit WI
WGFA(AM) Watseka IL
WGFC Floyd VA
WGFP Webster MA
WGFS Covington GA
WGFT(AM) Campbell OH
WGFY Charlotte NC
WGGA Gainesville GA
WGGG Gainesville FL
WGGH Marion IL
WGGM Chester VA
WGGO Salamanca NY
WGGT(AM) North Palm Beach FL
WGHB Farmville NC
WGHC(AM) Clayton GA
WGHN Grand Haven MI
WGHQ Kingston NY
WGHT Pompton Lakes NJ
WGIG(AM) Brunswick GA
WGIL Galesburg IL
WGIN Rochester NH
WGIP Exeter NH
WGIR Manchester NH
WGIT(AM) Canovanas PR
WGJK(AM) Rome GA
WGKA(AM) Atlanta GA
WGL Fort Wayne IN
WGLB(AM) Elm Grove WI
WGLD(AM) Red Lion PA
WGLH La Follette TN
WGLL Auburn IN
WGLR Lancaster WI
WGMA Spindale NC
WGMI Bremen GA
WGML Hinesville GA
WGMN Roanoke VA
WGN(AM) Chicago IL
WGNC Gastonia NC
*WGNR Anderson IN
WGNS Murfreesboro TN
WGNU(AM) Granite City IL
WGNY Newburgh NY
WGNZ Fairborn OH
WGOC Blountville TN
WGOD Charlotte Amalie VI
WGOH Grayson KY
WGOK Mobile AL
WGOL Russellville AL
WGOM Marion IN
WGOP(AM) Pocomoke City MD
WGOS High Point NC
WGOV Valdosta GA
WGOW Chattanooga TN
WGPA(AM) Bethlehem PA
WGPC Albany GA
WGPL Portsmouth VA
WGR Buffalo NY
WGRA Cairo GA

WGRB(AM) Chicago IL
WGRM Greenwood MS
WGRO Lake City FL
WGRP Greenville PA
WGRV Greeneville TN
WGRY Grayling MI
WGSB Mebane NC
WGSF(AM) Memphis TN
WGSM Huntington NY
WGSO New Orleans LA
WGSP Charlotte NC
WGST Atlanta GA
WGSV Guntersville AL
WGTA Summerville GA
WGTH Richlands VA
WGTJ(AM) Murrayville GA
WGTK(AM) Louisville KY
WGTM Wilson NC
WGTN Georgetown SC
WGTO Cassopolis MI
WGTX De Funiak Springs FL
WGUN Atlanta GA
WGUS(AM) Augusta GA
WGVA Geneva NY
WGVL Greenville SC
WGVM Greenville MS
WGVS(AM) Muskegon MI
*WGVU Kentwood MI
WGWM London KY
WGY Schenectady NY
WGYM(AM) Hammonton NJ
WGYV Greenville AL
WGZS Dothan AL
*WHA Madison WI
WHAG Halfway MD
WHAK Rogers City MI
WHAL(AM) Phenix City AL
WHAM Rochester NY
WHAN Ashland VA
WHAP Hopewell VA
WHAS Louisville KY
WHAT Philadelphia PA
WHAW Weston WV
WHAZ Troy NY
WHB Kansas City MO
WHBB Selma AL
WHBC Canton OH
WHBG Harrisonburg VA
WHBK Marshall NC
WHBL(AM) Sheboygan WI
WHBN(AM) Harrodsburg KY
WHBQ Memphis TN
WHBS(AM) Moultrie GA
WHBT(AM) Tallahassee FL
WHBU Anderson IN
WHBY(AM) Kimberly WI
WHCG Metter GA
WHCO(AM) Sparta IL
WHCU Ithaca NY
WHDL Olean NY
WHDM McKenzie TN
WHEE Martinsville VA
WHEN Syracuse NY
WHEO Stuart VA
WHEP Foley AL
WHEW Franklin TN
WHFA(AM) Poynette WI
WHFB(AM) Benton Harbor-St. Joseph MI
WHGG(AM) Kingsport TN
WHGH Thomasville GA
WHGM(AM) Savannah GA
WHGS(AM) Hampton SC
WHGT(AM) Chambersburg PA
WHHO Hornell NY
WHHQ Elizabethton TN
WHHV Hillsville VA
WHIC(AM) Rochester NY
WHIE Griffin GA
WHIM Apopka FL
WHIN Gallatin TN
WHIO Dayton OH
WHIP Mooresville NC
WHIR Danville KY
WHIS Bluefield WV
WHIY Moulton AL
WHIZ Zanesville OH

WHJB(AM) Bedford PA
WHJC Matewan WV
WHJJ Providence RI
WHK(AM) Cleveland OH
WHKP Hendersonville NC
WHKT Portsmouth VA
WHKW(AM) Cleveland OH
WHKY(AM) Hickory NC
WHKZ(AM) Warren OH
WHLD Niagara Falls NY
WHLI Hempstead NY
WHLM(AM) Bloomsburg PA
WHLN Harlan KY
WHLO Akron OH
WHLS Port Huron MI
WHLX(AM) Marine City MI
WHLY(AM) South Bend IN
WHMA Anniston AL
WHMP Northampton MA
WHMQ(AM) Greenfield MA
WHMT Humboldt TN
WHNC Henderson NC
WHNK(AM) Parkersburg WV
WHNP(AM) East Longmeadow MA
WHNR Cypress Gardens FL
WHNY McComb MS
WHNZ(AM) Tampa FL
WHO(AM) Des Moines IA
WHOC Philadelphia MS
WHOG Hobson City AL
WHOL Allentown PA
WHON Centerville IN
WHOO(AM) Kissimmee FL
WHOP(AM) Hopkinsville KY
WHOS Decatur AL
WHOW Clinton IL
WHOY Salinas PR
WHP Harrisburg PA
WHPY Clayton NC
WHRY Hurley WI
WHSC Hartsville SC
WHSM Hayward WI
WHSR Pompano Beach FL
WHSY(AM) Hattiesburg MS
WHTB Fall River MA
WHTC(AM) Holland MI
WHTG Eatontown NJ
WHTH Heath OH
WHTK Rochester NY
WHUB Cookeville TN
WHUC Hudson NY
WHUN Huntingdon PA
WHVN Charlotte NC
WHVO(AM) Hopkinsville KY
WHVR Hanover PA
WHVW Hyde Park NY
WHWH Princeton NJ
WHYL Carlisle PA
WHYM(AM) Lake City SC
WHYN Springfield MA
WIAC San Juan PR
WIAM Williamston NC
WIAN Ishpeming MI
WIBA Madison WI
WIBC(AM) Indianapolis IN
WIBG Ocean City NJ
WIBH Anna IL
WIBM Jackson MI
WIBQ(AM) Sarasota FL
WIBR Baton Rouge LA
WIBS Guayama PR
WIBW Topeka KS
WIBX Utica NY
WICC Bridgeport CT
WICH Norwich CT
WICK Scranton PA
WICO(AM) Salisbury MD
WICY Malone NY
WIDA Carolina PR
WIDG Saint Ignace MI
WIDS Russell Springs KY
WIDU(AM) Fayetteville NC
WIEL Elizabethtown KY
WIEZ Lewistown PA
WIFA(AM) Knoxville TN
WIFI Florence NJ
WIGG Wiggins MS

Broadcasting & Cable Yearbook 2006

D-614

U.S. AM Stations by Call Letters

WIGM Medford WI
WIGN(AM) Bristol TN
*WIHM Taylorville IL
WIIN Ridgeland MS
WIJD(AM) Prichard AL
WIJK Evergreen AL
WIKB Iron River MI
WIKC Bogalusa LA
WIKE Newport VT
WIL(AM) Saint Louis MO
WILA Danville VA
WILB(AM) Canton OH
WILC Laurel MD
WILD Boston MA
WILE Cambridge OH
WILI(AM) Willimantic CT
WILK Wilkes-Barre PA
*WILL(AM) Urbana IL
WILM Wilmington DE
WILO Frankfort IN
WILS Lansing MI
WILY Centralia IL
WIMA Lima OH
WIMG Ewing NJ
WIMO Winder GA
WIMS Michigan City IN
WINA Charlottesville VA
WINC Winchester VA
WIND Chicago IL
WINE Brookfield CT
WING Dayton OH
WINI(AM) Murphysboro IL
WINK(AM) Fort Myers FL
WINR Binghamton NY
WINS New York NY
WINT(AM) Melbourne FL
WINU(AM) Shelbyville IL
WINV(AM) Beverly Hills FL
WINW Canton OH
WINY Putnam CT
WINZ(AM) Miami FL
WIOD Miami FL
WIOI New Boston OH
WIOJ(AM) Jacksonville Beach FL
WION Ionia MI
WIOO Carlisle PA
WIOS Tawas City MI
WIOU Kokomo IN
WIOV Reading PA
WIOZ Pinehurst NC
WIP Philadelphia PA
WIPC(AM) Lake Wales FL
*WIPR(AM) San Juan PR
WIPS Ticonderoga NY
WIQB(AM) Conway SC
WIQR Prattville AL
WIRA Fort Pierce FL
WIRB(AM) Level Plains AL
WIRD Lake Placid NY
WIRJ Humboldt TN
WIRL(AM) Peoria IL
WIRO Ironton OH
WIRV Irvine KY
WIRY Plattsburgh NY
WISA Isabela PR
WISE Asheville NC
WISK Americus GA
WISL Shamokin PA
WISN Milwaukee WI
WISO Ponce PR
WISP Doylestown PA
WISR Butler PA
WISS Berlin WI
WISW Columbia SC
WITA Knoxville TN
WITH(AM) Baltimore MD
WITK(AM) Pittston PA
WITS(AM) Sebring FL
WITY Danville IL
WITZ Jasper IN
WIVV Vieques PR
WIWS Beckley WV
WIXC(AM) Titusville FL
WIXE(AM) Monroe NC
WIXI(AM) Jasper AL
WIXK(AM) New Richmond WI
WIXN Dixon IL

WIXT(AM) Little Falls NY
WIYD Palatka FL
WIZE Springfield OH
WIZK(AM) Bay Springs MS
WIZM La Crosse WI
WIZR Johnstown NY
WIZS Henderson NC
WIZZ(AM) Greenfield MA
WJAE Westbrook ME
WJAG Norfolk NE
WJAK Jackson TN
WJAS Pittsburgh PA
WJAT Swainsboro GA
WJAW(AM) Saint Marys WV
WJAX Jacksonville FL
WJAY Mullins SC
WJBB Haleyville AL
WJBC Bloomington IL
WJBD Salem IL
WJBI Batesville MS
WJBM Jerseyville IL
WJBO Baton Rouge LA
WJBS Holly Hill SC
WJBW(AM) Jupiter FL
WJBY(AM) Rainbow City AL
WJCC(AM) Miami Springs FL
WJCI Rantoul IL
WJCM(AM) Sebring FL
WJCV Jacksonville NC
WJCW Johnson City TN
WJDA Quincy MA
WJDB Thomasville GA
WJDJ(AM) Hartsville SC
WJDM Elizabeth NJ
WJDX Jackson MS
WJDY(AM) Salisbury MD
WJEH Gallipolis OH
WJEJ Hagerstown MD
WJEP Ochlocknee GA
WJER Dover-New Philadelphia OH
WJES Johnston SC
WJET(AM) Erie PA
WJFC Jefferson City TN
WJFJ Tryon NC
WJFK Baltimore MD
WJGK(AM) Kingston NY
WJGR Jacksonville FL
WJHX(AM) Lexington AL
WJIB Cambridge MA
WJIG Tullahoma TN
WJIL Jacksonville IL
WJIM(AM) Lansing MI
WJIT Sabana PR
WJJB(AM) Brunswick ME
WJJC Commerce GA
WJJG Elmhurst IL
WJJL Niagara Falls NY
WJJM Lewisburg TN
WJJQ Tomahawk WI
WJJT Jellico TN
*WJKN(AM) Jackson MI
WJKY Jamestown KY
WJLD Fairfield AL
WJLE Smithville TN
WJLG Savannah GA
WJLS Beckley WV
WJMC Rice Lake WI
WJML(AM) Petoskey MI
WJMO Cleveland Heights OH
WJMP Kent OH
WJMS Ironwood MI
WJMT Merrill WI
WJMX Florence SC
WJNA(AM) Royal Palm Beach FL
WJNC Jacksonville NC
WJNO(AM) West Palm Beach FL
WJNT Pearl MS
WJNX(AM) Fort Pierce FL
WJNZ(AM) Kentwood MI
WJOB Hammond IN
WJOC Chattanooga TN
WJOE(AM) Orange-Athol MA
WJOI Norfolk VA
WJOK Kaukauna WI
WJOL Joliet IL
WJON Saint Cloud MN
WJOT Wabash IN

WJOX Birmingham AL
WJOY Burlington VT
WJPA Washington PA
WJPF Herrin IL
WJQI(AM) Fort Campbell KY
WJR Detroit MI
WJRD(AM) Tuscaloosa AL
WJRI Lenoir NC
WJRM Troy NC
WJSA Jersey Shore PA
WJSB Crestview FL
WJSM Martinsburg PA
WJSS(AM) Havre de Grace MD
WJST(AM) New Castle PA
WJTB North Ridgeville OH
WJTH Calhoun GA
WJTN Jamestown NY
WJTO Bath ME
WJUB(AM) Plymouth WI
WJUN Mexico PA
WJUS Marion AL
WJWF(AM) Columbus MS
WJWK Seaford DE
WJWL Georgetown DE
WJYI Milwaukee WI
WJYM Bowling Green OH
WJYP(AM) Saint Albans WV
WJYZ Albany GA
WJZM Clarksville TN
WJZN(AM) Augusta ME
WKAC Athens AL
WKAM Goshen IN
WKAN Kankakee IL
WKAP Allentown PA
WKAQ San Juan PR
*WKAR East Lansing MI
WKAT North Miami FL
WKAV Charlottesville VA
WKAX Russellville AL
WKBA Vinton VA
WKBC North Wilkesboro NC
WKBF Rock Island IL
WKBH Holmen WI
WKBI Saint Marys PA
WKBK(AM) Keene NH
WKBL(AM) Covington TN
WKBN Youngstown OH
WKBO Harrisburg PA
WKBR Manchester NH
WKBV(AM) Richmond IN
WKBY Chatham VA
WKBZ(AM) Muskegon MI
WKCB Hindman KY
WKCE Maryville TN
WKCI(AM) Waynesboro VA
WKCM Hawesville KY
WKCT(AM) Bowling Green KY
WKCU Corinth MS
WKCW Warrenton VA
WKCY Harrisonburg VA
WKDA(AM) Nashville TN
WKDE Altavista VA
WKDI Denton MD
WKDK Newberry SC
WKDL(AM) Alexandria VA
WKDM(AM) New York NY
WKDO Liberty KY
WKDP Corbin KY
WKDV Manassas VA
WKDW Staunton VA
WKDX Hamlet NC
WKDZ Cadiz KY
WKEI(AM) Kewanee IL
WKEN(AM) Dover DE
WKEU Griffin GA
WKEW Greensboro NC
WKEX Blacksburg VA
WKEY Covington VA
WKEZ Bluefield WV
WKFB(AM) Jeannette PA
WKFE Yauco PR
WKFI Wilmington OH
WKFL Bushnell FL
WKFN(AM) Clarksville TN
*WKGC Panama City Beach FL
WKGM Smithfield VA
WKGN Knoxville TN

WKGQ Milledgeville GA
WKGX Lenoir NC
WKHB(AM) Irwin PA
WKHM(AM) Jackson MI
WKHZ(AM) Ocean City MD
WKIC Hazard KY
WKII(AM) Solana FL
WKIK La Plata MD
WKIN Kingsport TN
WKIP Poughkeepsie NY
WKIQ Eustis FL
WKIZ Key West FL
WKJB Mayaguez PR
WKJG(AM) Fort Wayne IN
WKJK Louisville KY
WKJQ Parsons TN
WKKD Aurora IL
WKKP McDonough GA
WKKS Vanceburg KY
WKKX(AM) Wheeling WV
WKLA Ludington MI
WKLB Manchester KY
WKLJ Sparta WI
WKLK Cloquet MN
WKLP Keyser WV
WKLV Blackstone VA
WKLY Hartwell GA
WKLZ Kalamazoo MI
WKMB Stirling NJ
WKMC Roaring Spring PA
WKMG Newberry SC
WKMI Kalamazoo MI
WKMQ(AM) Tupelo MS
WKMT Kings Mountain NC
WKND(AM) Manchester CT
WKNG Tallapoosa GA
WKNR(AM) Cleveland OH
WKNV Fairlawn VA
WKNW Sault Ste. Marie MI
WKNY Kingston NY
WKOK Sunbury PA
WKOR(AM) Starkville MS
WKOX Framingham MA
WKOZ Kosciusko MS
WKPA Lynchburg VA
WKPR Kalamazoo MI
WKPT Kingsport TN
WKQW Oil City PA
WKRA Holly Springs MS
WKRC Cincinnati OH
WKRD(AM) Louisville KY
WKRK Murphy NC
WKRM Columbia TN
WKRO Cairo IL
WKRS Waukegan IL
WKRT Cortland NY
WKSC Kershaw SC
WKSH(AM) Sussex WI
WKSK(AM) West Jefferson NC
WKSN Jamestown NY
WKSR Pulaski TN
WKST(AM) New Castle PA
WKTA Evanston IL
WKTE Ring NC
WKTF(AM) Vienna GA
WKTP Jonesborough TN
WKTQ South Paris ME
WKTR Earlysville VA
WKTT(AM) Saraland AL
WKTX Cortland OH
WKTY La Crosse WI
WKUN Monroe GA
WKVA Lewistown PA
WKVG Jenkins KY
WKVI Knox IN
WKVL(AM) Knoxville TN
WKVM San Juan PR
WKVQ Eatonton GA
WKVT Brattleboro VT
WKVX Wooster OH
WKWF Key West FL
WKWH(AM) Shelbyville IN
WKWL Florala AL
WKWN Trenton GA
WKXG Greenwood MS
WKXI Jackson MS
WKXL(AM) Concord NH

WKXM Winfield AL
WKXO Berea KY
WKXR Asheboro NC
WKXV Knoxville TN
WKXW(AM) Atlantic City NJ
WKY Oklahoma City OK
WKYH(AM) Paintsville KY
WKYK Burnsville NC
WKYO Caro MI
WKYX Paducah KY
WKZE Sharon CT
WKZI Casey IL
WKZK North Augusta SC
WKZN(AM) West Hazleton PA
WKZO Kalamazoo MI
WKZV Washington PA
WLAA(AM) Winter Garden FL
WLAC Nashville TN
WLAD Danbury CT
WLAF La Follette TN
WLAG La Grange GA
WLAM(AM) Lewiston ME
WLAN Lancaster PA
WLAP Lexington KY
WLAQ Rome GA
WLAR Athens TN
WLAS(AM) Lafayette IN
WLAT(AM) New Britain CT
WLAY Muscle Shoals AL
WLBA Gainesville GA
WLBB(AM) Carrollton GA
WLBE Leesburg FL
WLBG Laurens SC
WLBH Mattoon IL
WLBK De Kalb IL
*WLBL Auburndale WI
WLBN Lebanon KY
WLBQ Morgantown KY
WLBR Lebanon PA
WLBY(AM) Saline MI
WLCC Brandon FL
WLCG Macon GA
WLCK(AM) Scottsville KY
WLCM Charlotte MI
WLCR(AM) Mt. Washington KY
WLDR(AM) Kingsley MI
WLDS Jacksonville IL
WLDX Fayette AL
WLDY Ladysmith WI
WLEA Hornell NY
WLEC Sandusky OH
WLEE(AM) Richmond VA
WLEM Emporium PA
WLEO(AM) Ponce PR
WLES(AM) Lawrenceville VA
WLET Toccoa GA
WLEW Bad Axe MI
WLEY Cayey PR
WLFJ(AM) Greenville SC
WLFN La Crosse WI
WLGC Greenup KY
WLGN Logan OH
WLGZ(AM) Rochester NY
WLHN Muncie IN
WLIB New York NY
WLIE(AM) Islip NY
WLIJ Shelbyville TN
WLIK Newport TN
WLIL(AM) Lenoir City TN
WLIM Patchogue NY
WLIP Kenosha WI
WLIS Old Saybrook CT
WLIV Livingston TN
WLJM Lima OH
*WLJN Elmwood Township MI
WLJW(AM) Cadillac MI
WLKD Minocqua WI
WLKF Lakeland FL
WLKM Three Rivers MI
WLKR(AM) Norwalk OH
WLKS West Liberty KY
WLKW(AM) West Warwick RI
WLLH Lowell MA
WLLL Lynchburg VA
WLLM Lincoln IL
*WLLN Lillington NC
WLLQ(AM) Chapel Hill NC

U.S. AM Stations by Call Letters

WLLV Louisville KY	WMBD Peoria IL	WMOR Morehead KY	WNEM(AM) Bridgeport MI	WOAI San Antonio TX
WLLY Wilson NC	WMBE Chilton WI	WMOU Berlin NH	WNER(AM) Watertown NY	WOAM(AM) Peoria IL
WLMC Georgetown SC	WMBG Williamsburg VA	WMOV Ravenswood WV	WNES Central City KY	WOAP Owosso MI
WLMR(AM) Chattanooga TN	WMBH(AM) Joplin MO	WMOX Meridian MS	WNEX Macon GA	WOAY Oak Hill WV
WLMV(AM) Madison WI	*WMBI(AM) Chicago IL	*WMPC(AM) Lapeer MI	WNEZ(AM) Windsor CT	WOBG Clarksburg WV
WLNA(AM) Peekskill NY	WMBM Miami Beach FL	WMPL Hancock MI	WNFL Green Bay WI	WOBL Oberlin OH
WLNC Laurinburg NC	WMBN(AM) Petoskey MI	WMPM Smithfield NC	WNFO Ridgeland SC	WOBM Lakewood NJ
WLNL Horseheads NY	WMBS Uniontown PA	WMPO Middleport-Pomeroy OH	WNGO(AM) Mayfield KY	WOBT Rhinelander WI
WLNO New Orleans LA	WMC(AM) Memphis TN	WMPS(AM) Bartlett TN	WNHV White River Junction VT	WOBX(AM) Wanchese NC
WLNR Kinston NC	WMCA New York NY	WMPX Midland MI	WNIK Arecibo PR	WOC Davenport IA
WLOA(AM) Farrell PA	WMCB Martinsville IN	WMQM(AM) Lakeland TN	WNIL Niles MI	WOCA Ocala FL
WLOB Portland ME	WMCH Church Hill TN	WMRB Columbia TN	WNIO(AM) Youngstown OH	WOCC Corydon IN
WLOC(AM) Munfordville KY	WMCJ(AM) Cullman AL	WMRC Milford MA	WNIS Norfolk VA	WOCN Miami FL
WLOD Loudon TN	WMCL McLeansboro IL	WMRD Middletown CT	WNIV Atlanta GA	WOCO Oconto WI
WLOE Eden NC	WMCP Columbia TN	WMRE Charles Town WV	WNIX(AM) Greenville MS	WOCV Oneida TN
WLOH Lancaster OH	WMCR Oneida NY	WMRK Selma AL	WNJC Washington Township NJ	WODI Brookneal VA
WLOI La Porte IN	WMCS Greenfield WI	WMRN Marion OH	WNKX Centerville TN	WODJ(AM) Whitehall MI
WLOK Memphis TN	WMCT Mountain City TN	WMRO(AM) Gallatin TN	WNLA Indianola MS	WODT New Orleans LA
WLOL(AM) Minneapolis MN	WMCW(AM) Harvard IL	WMSA Massena NY	WNLK(AM) Norwalk CT	WODY Fieldale VA
WLON Lincolnton NC	WMDB Nashville TN	WMSG Oakland MD	WNLR Churchville VA	WOEG Hazlehurst MS
WLOP Jesup GA	WMDD Fajardo PR	WMSH Sturgis MI	WNLS Tallahassee FL	WOEN(AM) Olean NY
WLOR Huntsville AL	WMDH New Castle IN	WMSK(AM) Morganfield KY	WNMA Miami Springs FL	WOF(AM) Andover NJ
WLOU Louisville KY	*WMDR Augusta ME	WMSP Montgomery AL	WNMB(AM) North Myrtle Beach SC	WOFE(AM) Rockwood TN
WLOV Washington GA	WMEL Melbourne FL	WMSR Manchester TN	WNML(AM) Knoxville TN	WOFX(AM) Troy NY
WLPA Lancaster PA	WMEQ(AM) Menomonie WI	WMST(AM) Mt. Sterling KY	WNMT Nashwauk MN	WOGO Hallie WI
WLPH Irondale AL	WMER Meridian MS	WMSW Hatillo PR	WNNC Newton NC	WOGR Charlotte NC
WLPO La Salle IL	WMET Gaithersburg MD	WMSX Brockton MA	WNNG(AM) Warner Robins GA	WOHI East Liverpool OH
WLPR Prichard AL	WMEV Marion VA	WMT Cedar Rapids IA	WNNJ Newton NJ	WOHS Shelby NC
WLQH Chiefland FL	WMFA(AM) Raeford NC	WMTA(AM) Central City KY	WNNR(AM) Jacksonville FL	*WOI Ames IA
WLQM Franklin VA	WMFC Monroeville AL	WMTC Vancleve KY	WNNW(AM) Lawrence MA	WOIC(AM) Columbia SC
WLQR Toledo OH	WMFD Wilmington NC	WMTD Hinton WV	WNNZ Westfield MA	WOIR Homestead FL
WLQV Detroit MI	WMFG Hibbing MN	WMTE Manistee MI	WNOG Naples FL	WOIZ Guayanilla PR
WLQY Hollywood FL	WMFJ Daytona Beach FL	WMTL Leitchfield KY	WNOO Chattanooga TN	WOKA(AM) Douglas GA
WLRB Macomb IL	WMFN Zeeland MI	WMTM Moultrie GA	WNOP Newport KY	WOKB Winter Garden FL
WLRC Walnut MS	WMFR High Point NC	WMTN Morristown TN	WNOS New Bern NC	WOKC Okeechobee FL
WLRM(AM) Millington TN	WMGC Murfreesboro TN	WMTR Morristown NJ	WNOV Milwaukee WI	WOKS Columbus GA
WLRP San Sebastian PR	WMGG(AM) Largo FL	WMTY(AM) Farragut TN	WNOW Mint Hill NC	WOKT Cannonsburg KY
WLRT(AM) Hampton VA	WMGJ Gadsden AL	WMUF Paris TN	WNPC Newport TN	WOKU Hurricane WV
WLRV Lebanon VA	WMGO Canton MS	WMUU Greenville SC	WNPV Lansdale PA	WOKV Jacksonville FL
WLS Chicago IL	WMGR Bainbridge GA	WMVB Millville NJ	WNPZ(AM) Knoxville TN	WOKY Milwaukee WI
WLSB Copperhill TN	WMGT(AM) Stillwater MN	WMVG Milledgeville GA	WNQM Nashville TN	WOL Washington DC
WLSC Loris SC	WMGW Meadville PA	WMVO(AM) Mount Vernon OH	WNRG Grundy VA	WOLA Barranquitas PR
WLSD Big Stone Gap VA	WMGY Montgomery AL	WMVP Chicago IL	WNRI Woonsocket RI	WOLB(AM) Baltimore MD
WLSG(AM) Wilmington NC	WMHG(AM) Muskegon MI	WMWR(AM) Dry Branch GA	WNRP(AM) Gulf Breeze FL	WOLD Marion VA
WLSH Lansford PA	WMIA Arecibo PR	WMXF(AM) Waynesville NC	WNRR(AM) Augusta GA	WOLF Syracuse NY
WLSI Pikeville KY	WMIC(AM) Sandusky MI	WMYF Portsmouth NH	WNRS Herkimer NY	WOLS Florence SC
WLSP Lapeer MI	WMID(AM) Atlantic City NJ	WMYM(AM) Miami FL	WNRV(AM) Narrows-Pearisburg VA	WOLY Battle Creek MI
WLSS(AM) Sarasota FL	WMII(AM) Manistique MI	WMYN Mayodan NC	WNSG Nashville TN	WOMI(AM) Owensboro KY
WLSV Wellsville NY	WMIK Middlesboro KY	WMYQ Newton MS	WNSH Beverly MA	WOMN(AM) Franklinton LA
WLTA Alpharetta GA	WMIN Hudson WI	WMYR Fort Myers FL	WNSI(AM) Robertsdale AL	WOMP Bellaire OH
WLTC Gastonia NC	WMIQ Iron Mountain MI	WMYT Carolina Beach NC	WNSR Brentwood TN	WOMT Manitowoc WI
WLTG Panama City FL	WMIR Atlantic Beach SC	WNAE Warren PA	WNSS(AM) Syracuse NY	WONA Winona MS
WLTH Gary IN	WMIS Natchez MS	WNAH Nashville TN	WNST Towson MD	WOND Pleasantville NJ
WLTN Littleton NH	WMIX Mount Vernon IL	WNAK Nanticoke PA	WNSW Newark NJ	WONE Dayton OH
WLTP(AM) Marietta OH	WMIZ Vineland NJ	WNAM Neenah-Menasha WI	WNTA Rockford IL	WONG Canton MS
WLTQ(AM) Charleston SC	WMJH Rockford MI	WNAP Norristown PA	WNTD Chicago IL	WONN Lakeland FL
WLUA(AM) Belton SC	WMJL Marion KY	WNAT Natchez MS	WNTF Bithlo FL	WONQ Oviedo FL
WLUV Loves Park IL	WMJR Winchester KY	WNAU New Albany MS	WNTJ(AM) Johnstown PA	WONW Defiance OH
WLUZ(AM) Bayamon PR	WMKI(AM) Boston MA	WNAV(AM) Annapolis MD	WNTK Newport NH	WONX Evanston IL
WLVA Lynchburg VA	WMKM Inkster MI	WNAW North Adams MA	WNTN Newton MA	WOOD Grand Rapids MI
WLVF Haines City FL	WMKT(AM) Charlevoix MI	WNAX(AM) Yankton SD	WNTP(AM) Philadelphia PA	WOOF Dothan AL
WLVJ(AM) Boynton Beach FL	WMLB(AM) East Point GA	WNBF Binghamton NY	WNTR(AM) Dunedin FL	WOON(AM) Woonsocket RI
WLVL Lockport NY	WMLC(AM) Monticello MS	WNBH New Bedford MA	WNTS Beech Grove IN	WOPI Bristol TN
WLVP(AM) Gorham ME	WMLM Saint Louis MI	WNBI Park Falls WI	WNTT Tazewell TN	WOPP Opp AL
WLVU(AM) Dunedin FL	WMLP Milton PA	WNBN(AM) Meridian MS	WNTW(AM) Somerset PA	WOQI(AM) Adjuntas PR
WLVV Mobile AL	WMLR Hohenwald TN	WNBP(AM) Newburyport MA	WNTX(AM) Brookport IL	WOR New York NY
WLW Cincinnati OH	WMLT Dublin GA	WNBS Murray KY	WNUZ Talladega AL	WORA Mayaguez PR
WLWI(AM) Montgomery AL	WMMB Melbourne FL	WNBT Wellsboro PA	WNVA Norton VA	WORC Worcester MA
WLWL Rockingham NC	WMMG Brandenburg KY	WNBX Springfield VT	WNVI North Vernon IN	WORD(AM) Spartanburg SC
WLXE(AM) Rockville MD	WMMI Shepherd MI	WNBY Newberry MI	WNVR Vernon Hills IL	WORL Altamonte Springs FL
WLXG Lexington KY	WMML Glens Falls NY	WNBZ Saranac Lake NY	WNVY Cantonment FL	WORM Savannah TN
WLXN Lexington NC	WMMN Fairmont WV	WNCA Siler City NC	*WNWC(AM) Sun Prairie WI	WORV Hattiesburg MS
WLYC Williamsport PA	WMMV Cocoa FL	WNCC(AM) Northern Cambria PA	WNWF(AM) Destin FL	WOSH Oshkosh WI
WLYJ(AM) Jasper AL	WMMW Meriden CT	WNCO Ashland OH	WNWI Oak Lawn IL	WOSO San Juan PR
WLYN Lynn MA	WMNA Gretna VA	WNCT Greenville NC	WNWN Portage MI	*WOSU Columbus OH
WLYV Fort Wayne IN	WMNC Morganton NC	WNDA(AM) De Land FL	WNWR Philadelphia PA	WOTS Kissimmee FL
WLZR(AM) Canton NC	WMNE(AM) Riviera Beach FL	WNDB Daytona Beach FL	WNWS Brownsville TN	*WOUB Athens OH
WMAC Macon GA	WMNI Columbus OH	WNDC Baton Rouge LA	WNWZ Grand Rapids MI	WOWO Fort Wayne IN
WMAF Madison FL	WMNT(AM) Manati PR	WNDE Indianapolis IN	WNXT Portsmouth OH	WOWW Germantown TN
WMAJ State College PA	WMNZ Montezuma GA	WNDI Sullivan IN	*WNYC New York NY	WOWZ(AM) Appomattox VA
WMAL Washington DC	WMOA Marietta OH	WNDV South Bend IN	WNYG Babylon NY	WOYE(AM) Saint Cloud FL
WMAM Marinette WI	WMOB Mobile AL	WNDZ Portage IN	WNYY(AM) Ithaca NY	WOYK York PA
WMAN Mansfield OH	WMOG Brunswick GA	WNEA Newnan GA	WNZK Dearborn Heights MI	WOYL Oil City PA
WMAS Springfield MA	WMOH Hamilton OH	WNEB Worcester MA	WNZS(AM) Veazie ME	WOZK Ozark AL
WMAX Bay City MI	WMOK Metropolis IL	*WNED Buffalo NY	WNZT(AM) Hermon ME	WPAB Ponce PR
WMAY(AM) Springfield IL	WMON Montgomery WV	WNEG Toccoa GA	WNZZ Montgomery AL	WPAD Paducah KY
WMBA Ambridge PA	WMOP Ocala FL	WNEL Caguas PR	WOAD Jackson MS	WPAK Farmville VA

Broadcasting & Cable Yearbook 2006

D-616

U.S. AM Stations by Call Letters

WPAM Pottsville PA
WPAQ Mount Airy NC
WPAT Paterson NJ
WPAX Thomasville GA
WPAY Portsmouth OH
WPAZ Pottstown PA
WPBC Decatur GA
WPBQ(AM) Flowood MS
WPBR Lantana FL
WPBS(AM) Conyers GA
WPCC Clinton SC
WPCE Portsmouth VA
WPCF(AM) Panama City Beach FL
WPCH(AM) North Augusta SC
WPCI Greenville SC
WPCM Burlington NC
WPDC Elizabethtown PA
WPDM Potsdam NY
WPDR Portage WI
WPDX(AM) Clarksburg WV
WPEH Louisville GA
WPEK(AM) Fairview NC
*WPEL Montrose PA
WPEN Philadelphia PA
WPEO Peoria IL
WPEP Taunton MA
WPET Greensboro NC
WPFB Middletown OH
WPFC Port Allen LA
WPFD Fairview TN
WPFJ Franklin NC
WPFM Darlington SC
WPFR(AM) Terre Haute IN
WPGA Perry GA
WPGC Morningside MD
*WPGM Danville PA
WPGR(AM) Monroeville PA
WPGS Mims FL
WPGW Portland IN
WPGY(AM) Ellijay GA
WPHB Philipsburg PA
WPHE Phoenixville PA
WPHM Port Huron MI
WPHT Philadelphia PA
WPHX(AM) Sanford ME
WPHY(AM) Trenton NJ
WPIC Sharon PA
WPID Piedmont AL
WPIE Trumansburg NY
WPIN Dublin VA
WPIP Winston-Salem NC
WPIT Pittsburgh PA
WPJK Orangeburg SC
WPJL Raleigh NC
WPJM Greer SC
WPJS Conway SC
WPJX(AM) Zion IL
WPKE Pikeville KY
WPKY Princeton KY
WPLK Palatka FL
WPLM Plymouth MA
WPLN(AM) Madison TN
WPLO Grayson GA
WPLV West Point GA
*WPLX(AM) Germantown TN
WPLY(AM) Mount Pocono PA
WPMB Vandalia IL
WPMH(AM) Claremont VA
WPMI(AM) Mobile AL
WPMP(AM) Pascagoula-Moss Point MS
WPMZ Providence RI
WPNA Oak Park IL
WPNH Plymouth NH
WPNI(AM) Amherst MA
WPNN(AM) Pensacola FL
WPNT(AM) Connellsville PA
WPNW(AM) Zeeland MI
WPOL Winston-Salem NC
WPON Walled Lake MI
WPOP Hartford CT
WPPA Pottsville PA
WPPC Penuelas PR
WPRA Mayaguez PR
WPRD Winter Park FL
WPRE Prairie du Chien WI
WPRN Butler AL

WPRO Providence RI
WPRP Ponce PR
WPRR(AM) Johnstown PA
WPRS Paris IL
WPRT Prestonsburg KY
WPRX Bristol CT
WPRY Perry FL
WPRZ Warrenton VA
WPSE Erie PA
WPSL(AM) Port St. Lucie FL
WPSN(AM) Honesdale PA
WPSO New Port Richey FL
WPSP Royal Palm Beach FL
WPTB(AM) Statesboro GA
WPTF Raleigh NC
WPTK(AM) Pine Island Center FL
WPTL(AM) Canton NC
WPTN Cookeville TN
WPTT McKeesport PA
WPTW Piqua OH
WPTX(AM) Lexington Park MD
WPUL South Daytona FL
WPUT(AM) Brewster NY
WPVL Platteville WI
WPWA Chester PA
WPWC Dumfries-Triangle VA
WPWT(AM) Colonial Heights TN
WPYB Benson NC
WPYR(AM) Baton Rouge LA
WPYT(AM) Wilkinsburg PA
WQAH(AM) Priceville AL
WQAM Miami FL
WQBA Miami FL
WQBB Powell TN
WQBC Vicksburg MS
WQBN Temple Terrace FL
WQBQ Leesburg FL
WQBS San Juan PR
WQCH La Fayette GA
WQCR(AM) Alabaster AL
WQCT Bryan OH
WQEW New York NY
WQFX Gulfport MS
WQHL(AM) Live Oak FL
WQII San Juan PR
WQIS(AM) Camden SC
WQIZ Saint George SC
WQJM(AM) Myrtle Beach SC
WQKI(AM) Saint Matthews SC
WQKR Portland TN
WQLS Ozark AL
WQMA Marks MS
WQMC Sumter SC
WQMS(AM) Quitman MS
WQMV(AM) Waverly TN
WQNT(AM) Charleston SC
WQNX Aberdeen NC
WQOP Atlantic Beach FL
WQOQ Durand WI
WQOR(AM) Olyphant PA
WQPM Princeton MN
WQRX Valley Head AL
WQSC Charleston SC
WQSE White Bluff TN
WQSN Kalamazoo MI
WQST Forest MS
WQSV Ashland City TN
WQSY(AM) Cordele GA
WQTH Hanover NH
WQTK(AM) Moncks Corner SC
WQTM(AM) Orlando FL
WQTW Latrobe PA
WQUN(AM) Hamden CT
WQVA(AM) Lexington SC
WQXA York PA
WQXI Atlanta GA
WQXL Columbia SC
WQXM(AM) Bartow FL
WQXO Munising MI
WQXY Hazard KY
WRAA Luray VA
WRAB Arab AL
WRAD Radford VA
WRAG Carrollton AL
WRAK Williamsport PA
WRAM Monmouth IL
WRAR Tappahannock VA

WRAW Reading PA
WRAY Princeton IN
WRBE Lucedale MS
WRBZ Raleigh NC
WRCA Waltham MA
WRCC Battle Creek MI
WRCG Columbus GA
WRCO Richland Center WI
WRCR(AM) Spring Valley NY
WRCS Ahoskie NC
WRCY(AM) Mount Vernon IN
WRDB Reedsburg WI
WRDD Ebensburg PA
WRDT(AM) Monroe MI
WRDW(AM) Augusta GA
WRDZ La Grange IL
WREC(AM) Memphis TN
WREF Ridgefield CT
WREJ Richmond VA
WREL Lexington VA
WREM Monticello ME
WREV Reidsville NC
WRFC Athens GA
WRFD(AM) Columbus-Worthington OH
WRFS(AM) Alexander City AL
WRGA Rome GA
WRGC Sylva NC
WRGM Ontario OH
WRGS Rogersville TN
WRHB(AM) Kendall FL
WRHC Coral Gables FL
WRHI Rock Hill SC
WRHL Rochelle IL
WRIB Providence RI
WRIE Erie PA
WRIG Schofield WI
WRIN Rensselaer IN
WRIS Roanoke VA
WRIV Riverhead NY
WRIX Homeland Park SC
WRJC Mauston WI
WRJN Racine WI
WRJR(AM) Portsmouth VA
WRJW Picayune MS
WRJX(AM) Jackson AL
WRJZ Knoxville TN
WRKB Kannapolis NC
WRKD Rockland ME
WRKK Hughesville PA
WRKL New City NY
WRKM Carthage TN
WRKO Boston MA
WRKQ Madisonville TN
WRKY(AM) Murray KY
WRLA(AM) West Point GA
WRLL(AM) Johnston City IL
WRLV Salyersville KY
WRLZ Eatonville FL
WRMD Saint Petersburg FL
WRMG Red Bay AL
WRMN Elgin IL
WRMQ Orlando FL
WRMS Beardstown IL
WRMT(AM) Rocky Mount NC
WRNA China Grove NC
WRNE Pensacola FL
WRNI(AM) Providence RI
WRNJ Hackettstown NJ
WRNL Richmond VA
WRNR Martinsburg WV
WRNS Kinston NC
WRNY Rome NY
WROA Gulfport MS
WROB(AM) West Point MS
WROC(AM) Rochester NY
WROD Daytona Beach FL
WROK Rockford IL
WROL Boston MA
WROM Rome GA
WRON Ronceverte WV
WROS Jacksonville FL
WROU(AM) Petersburg VA
WROW Albany NY
WROX Clarksdale MS
WROY Carmi IL
WRPM Poplarville MS
WRPN Ripon WI

WRPQ Baraboo WI
WRRA Frederiksted VI
WRRD(AM) Jackson WI
WRRE Juncos PR
WRRL Rainelle WV
WRRZ Clinton NC
WRSA(AM) Saint Albans VT
WRSB Canandaigua NY
WRSC State College PA
WRSJ(AM) Bayamon PR
WRSL Stanford KY
WRSM Sumiton AL
WRSS San Sebastian PR
WRSW Warsaw IN
WRTA Altoona PA
WRTG Garner NC
WRTK(AM) Niles OH
WRTM Vicksburg MS
WRTO(AM) Chicago IL
WRUF Gainesville FL
WRUN Utica NY
WRUS Russellville KY
WRVA Richmond VA
WRVC Huntington WV
WRVK Mt. Vernon KY
WRWB(AM) Harrogate TN
WRWD(AM) Ellenville NY
WRWH Cleveland GA
WRXB Saint Petersburg Beach FL
WRXO(AM) Roxboro NC
WRYM New Britain CT
*WRYT(AM) Edwardsville IL
WRZN Hernando FL
WSAI(AM) Cincinnati OH
*WSAJ Grove City PA
WSAL Logansport IN
WSAM Saginaw MI
WSAO Senatobia MS
WSAR Fall River MA
WSAT Salisbury NC
WSAU Wausau WI
WSB Atlanta GA
WSBA York PA
WSBB New Smyrna Beach FL
WSBC(AM) Chicago IL
WSBI Static TN
WSBM(AM) Florence AL
WSBR Boca Raton FL
WSBS Great Barrington MA
WSBT South Bend IN
WSBV South Boston VA
WSCG(AM) Greenville MI
WSCO(AM) Appleton WI
WSCP Sandy Creek-Pulaski NY
WSCR(AM) Chicago IL
WSCW South Charleston WV
WSDE(AM) Cobleskill NY
WSDO(AM) Sanford FL
WSDQ Dunlap TN
WSDR Sterling IL
WSDS(AM) Salem Township MI
WSDT Soddy-Daisy TN
WSDX(AM) Brazil IN
WSDZ Belleville IL
WSEL Pontotoc MS
WSEM Donalsonville GA
WSEN(AM) Baldwinsville NY
WSEV Sevierville TN
WSEZ Paoli IN
WSFB Quitman GA
WSFC Somerset KY
WSFE(AM) Burnside KY
WSFN Brunswick GA
WSFW Seneca Falls NY
WSFZ(AM) Jackson MS
WSGB(AM) Sutton WV
WSGC(AM) Elberton GA
WSGF(AM) Augusta GA
WSGH Lewisville NC
WSGI Springfield TN
WSGO Oswego NY
WSGW Saginaw MI
WSHE(AM) Columbus GA
WSHN Fremont MI
WSHO New Orleans LA
*WSHU(AM) Westport CT
WSHV(AM) South Hill VA

WSIC Statesville NC
WSIP Paintsville KY
WSIR Winter Haven FL
WSIV East Syracuse NY
WSJC Magee MS
WSJM Saint Joseph MI
WSJS Winston-Salem NC
WSKI Montpelier VT
WSKN(AM) San Juan PR
WSKO Providence RI
WSKR Denham Springs LA
WSKW Skowhegan ME
WSKY(AM) Asheville NC
WSLA Slidell LA
WSLB Ogdensburg NY
WSLM Salem IN
WSLV(AM) Ardmore TN
WSLW White Sulphur Springs WV
WSM Nashville TN
WSMB New Orleans LA
WSME(AM) Camp Lejeune NC
WSMG Greeneville TN
WSMI Litchfield IL
WSML Graham NC
WSMN Nashua NH
WSMT Sparta TN
WSMX Winston-Salem NC
WSMY Weldon NC
WSNG Torrington CT
WSNH(AM) Nashua NH
WSNJ Bridgeton NJ
WSNL(AM) Flint MI
WSNO Barre VT
WSNR(AM) Jersey City NJ
WSNT Sandersville GA
WSNW(AM) Seneca SC
WSOK Savannah GA
WSOL San German PR
WSOM Salem OH
WSON Henderson KY
WSOO Sault Ste. Marie MI
WSOS(AM) Saint Augustine Beach FL
WSOY(AM) Decatur IL
WSPA(AM) Spartanburg SC
WSPC Albemarle NC
WSPD Toledo OH
WSPG(AM) Spartanburg SC
WSPL(AM) Streator IL
WSPQ(AM) Springville NY
WSPR Springfield MA
WSPT Stevens Point WI
WSPY(AM) Geneva IL
WSPZ(AM) South Haven MI
WSQD Lajas PR
WSQL Brevard NC
WSQR Sycamore IL
WSRA(AM) Albany GA
WSRC Durham NC
WSRF Fort Lauderdale FL
WSRO(AM) Ashland MA
WSRP(AM) Jacksonville NC
WSRQ(AM) Sarasota FL
WSRW Hillsboro OH
WSRY(AM) Elkton MD
WSSA Morrow GA
WSSC Sumter SC
WSSO(AM) Starkville MS
WSSP(AM) Milwaukee WI
WSTA(AM) Charlotte Amalie VI
WSTC(AM) Stamford CT
WSTJ Saint Johnsbury VT
WSTN Somerville TN
WSTP Salisbury NC
WSTT Thomasville GA
WSTU(AM) Stuart FL
WSTV Steubenville OH
WSUA Miami FL
WSUB Groton CT
*WSUI Iowa City IA
WSVA Harrisonburg VA
WSVG(AM) Mount Jackson VA
WSVM(AM) Valdese NC
WSVS Crewe VA
*WSWI Evansville IN
WSWN Belle Glade FL
WSWV Pennington Gap VA
WSWW Charleston WV

U.S. AM Stations by Call Letters

WSYB Rutland VT
WSYD Mount Airy NC
WSYL Sylvania GA
WSYR Syracuse NY
WSYW Indianapolis IN
WSYY(AM) Millinocket ME
WTAB Tabor City NC
WTAD Quincy IL
WTAG Worcester MA
WTAL Tallahassee FL
WTAM Cleveland OH
WTAN Clearwater FL
WTAQ(AM) Green Bay WI
WTAR(AM) Norfolk VA
WTAW(AM) College Station TX
WTAX(AM) Springfield IL
WTAY Robinson IL
WTBC Tuscaloosa AL
WTBF Troy AL
WTBI Pickens SC
WTBN(AM) Pinellas Park FL
WTBO Cumberland MD
WTBQ Warwick NY
WTBZ Grafton WV
WTCA Plymouth IN
WTCH Shawano WI
WTCJ Tell City IN
WTCL Chattahoochee FL
WTCM(AM) Traverse City MI
WTCO Campbellsville KY
WTCR Kenova WV
WTCS Fairmont WV
WTCW Whitesburg KY
WTCY Harrisburg PA
WTDY Madison WI
WTEL(AM) Red Springs NC
WTEM Washington DC
WTFX(AM) Winchester VA
WTGA Thomaston GA
WTGM Salisbury MD
WTHB Augusta GA
WTHE Mineola NY
WTHV Hahira GA
WTIC Hartford CT
WTIF Tifton GA
WTIG Massillon OH
WTIK Durham NC
WTIL Mayaguez PR
WTIQ Manistique MI
WTIR(AM) Cocoa Beach FL
WTIS Tampa FL
WTIV Titusville PA
WTIX New Orleans LA
WTJH East Point GA
WTJK South Beloit IL
WTJS Jackson TN
WTJZ Newport News VA
WTKA Ann Arbor MI
WTKG Grand Rapids MI
WTKI(AM) Huntsville AL
WTKM(AM) Hartford WI
WTKN(AM) Corinth MS
WTKS(AM) Savannah GA
WTKT(AM) Harrisburg PA
WTKY Tompkinsville KY
WTKZ Allentown PA
WTLA North Syracuse NY
WTLB Utica NY
WTLC Indianapolis IN
WTLK Taylorsville NC
WTLM Opelika AL
WTLN Orlando FL
WTLO Somerset KY
WTLS Tallassee AL
WTMA Charleston SC
WTMC(AM) Wilmington DE
WTME(AM) Rumford ME
WTMI(AM) West Hartford CT
WTMJ Milwaukee WI
WTMM Rensselaer NY
WTMN(AM) Gainesville FL
WTMP Egypt Lake FL
WTMR Camden NJ
WTMT Louisville KY
WTMY Sarasota FL
WTMZ Dorchester Terrace-Brentwood SC

WTNE Trenton TN
WTNI(AM) Biloxi MS
WTNK(AM) Hartsville TN
WTNL Reidsville GA
WTNS Coshocton OH
WTNT(AM) Bethesda MD
WTNY Watertown NY
WTOB Winston-Salem NC
WTOD Toledo OH
WTOE Spruce Pine NC
WTON Staunton VA
WTOP Washington DC
WTOR Youngstown NY
WTOT Marianna FL
WTOX(AM) Glen Allen VA
WTOY Salem VA
WTPG(AM) Columbus OH
WTPR Paris TN
WTRB Ripley TN
WTRC Elkhart IN
WTRE Greensburg IN
WTRI Brunswick MD
WTRN Tyrone PA
WTRO Dyersburg TN
WTRP La Grange GA
WTRU(AM) Kernersville NC
WTRW Two Rivers WI
WTRX Flint MI
WTSA Brattleboro VT
WTSB(AM) Selma NC
WTSJ Cincinnati OH
WTSK Tuscaloosa AL
WTSL Hanover NH
WTSN Dover NH
WTSO Madison WI
WTSV Claremont NH
WTSZ(AM) Eminence KY
WTTB Vero Beach FL
WTTC Towanda PA
WTTF Tiffin OH
WTTI Dalton GA
WTTL Madisonville KY
WTTM Princeton NJ
WTTN Watertown WI
WTTR(AM) Westminster MD
WTTT(AM) Boston MA
WTUP Tupelo MS
WTUX(AM) Madison WI
WTVB(AM) Coldwater MI
WTVL(AM) Waterville ME
WTVN(AM) Columbus OH
WTWA Thomson GA
WTWB Auburndale FL
WTWD(AM) Plant City FL
WTWG(AM) Columbus MS
WTWK(AM) Plattsburgh NY
WTWN Wells River VT
WTWZ Clinton MS
WTXY Whiteville NC
WTYL Tylertown MS
WTYM Kittanning PA
WTYS Marianna FL
WTYX(AM) Watkins Glen NY
WTZE Tazewell VA
WTZN(AM) Troy PA
WTZQ(AM) Hendersonville NC
WTZX Sparta TN
WUAM(AM) Saratoga Springs NY
WUAT Pikeville TN
WUCO(AM) Marysville OH
WUFE Baxley GA
WUFF Eastman GA
*WUFL Sterling Heights MI
WUFO Amherst NY
WUHN Pittsfield MA
WUKQ(AM) Ponce PR
WULA Eufaula AL
WULM(AM) Springfield OH
WUMP Madison AL
WUNA Ocoee FL
*WUNN(AM) Mason MI
WUNO(AM) San Juan PR
WUNR Brookline MA
WUPR Utuado PR
WURD(AM) Philadelphia PA
WURL Moody AL
WURP(AM) Braddock PA

WUSS(AM) Pleasantville NJ
WUST Washington DC
WUTQ Utica NY
WUUS(AM) Rossville GA
WUVR(AM) Lebanon NH
WVAA(AM) Burlington VT
WVAB Virginia Beach VA
WVAE(AM) Biddeford ME
WVAL Sauk Rapids MN
WVAM Altoona PA
WVAR Richwood WV
WVBE(AM) Roanoke VA
WVBF(AM) Middleborough Center MA
WVBS Burgaw NC
WVCB(AM) Shallotte NC
WVCC(AM) Hogansville GA
WVCD(AM) Bamberg-Denmark SC
WVCG Coral Gables FL
WVCH Chester PA
WVCV Orange VA
*WVCY Oshkosh WI
WVEI(AM) Worcester MA
WVEL Pekin IL
WVFN(AM) East Lansing MI
WVGB Beaufort SC
WVGM Lynchburg VA
WVHI Evansville IN
WVHU(AM) Huntington WV
WVIP Mount Kisco NY
WVJP Caguas PR
WVJS(AM) Owensboro KY
WVKO Columbus OH
WVKZ Schenectady NY
WVLD Valdosta GA
WVLG(AM) Wildwood FL
WVLK Lexington KY
WVLN Olney IL
WVLY(AM) Moundsville WV
WVLZ(AM) Knoxville TN
WVMC Mount Carmel IL
*WVMR Frost WV
WVMT Burlington VT
WVNA Tuscumbia AL
WVNE(AM) Leicester MA
WVNJ Oakland NJ
WVNN Athens AL
WVNR Poultney VT
WVNT(AM) Parkersburg WV
WVNZ(AM) Richmond VA
WVOA(AM) Dewitt NY
WVOC Columbia SC
WVOE Chadbourn NC
WVOG New Orleans LA
WVOH Hazlehurst GA
WVOI(AM) Marco Island FL
WVOJ(AM) Fernandina Beach FL
WVOK(AM) Oxford AL
WVOL Berry Hill TN
WVON Cicero IL
WVOP Vidalia GA
WVOS Liberty NY
WVOT(AM) Wilson NC
WVOW Logan WV
WVOX New Rochelle NY
WVOZ San Juan PR
WVPO Stroudsburg PA
WVRC Spencer WV
WVRQ(AM) Viroqua WI
WVSA Vernon AL
WVSM Rainsville AL
WVTJ Pensacola FL
WVTL(AM) Amsterdam NY
WVTS(AM) Charleston WV
WVVI Charlotte Amalie VI
WVXX(AM) Norfolk VA
WVZN Columbia PA
WWAA(AM) Avondale Estates GA
WWAB Lakeland FL
WWAM Jasper TN
WWBA Pinellas Park FL
WWBC Cocoa FL
WWBF Bartow FL
WWBG Greensboro NC
WWCA Gary IN
WWCB Corry PA
WWCH Clarion PA
WWCK Flint MI

WWCL Lehigh Acres FL
WWCN North Fort Myers FL
WWCO(AM) Waterbury CT
WWCS Canonsburg PA
WWDB(AM) Philadelphia PA
WWDJ Hackensack NJ
WWDR(AM) Murfreesboro NC
WWFE Miami FL
WWFL Clermont FL
WWFT(AM) Nicholasville KY
WWGA(AM) Waycross GA
WWGB Indian Head MD
WWGC(AM) Albertville AL
WWGE(AM) Loretto PA
WWGP(AM) Sanford NC
WWGS(AM) Georgetown SC
WWHN Joliet IL
WWIC Scottsboro AL
WWII Shiremanstown PA
WWIL Wilmington NC
WWIN Baltimore MD
WWIO(AM) Saint Mary's GA
WWIS Black River Falls WI
WWJ Detroit MI
WWJB(AM) Brooksville FL
WWJC Duluth MN
WWJZ Mount Holly NJ
WWKB Buffalo NY
WWKK(AM) Petoskey MI
WWL(AM) New Orleans LA
WWLE Cornwall NY
WWLF(AM) Auburn NY
WWLG(AM) Pikesville MD
WWLK Eddyville KY
WWLS Moore OK
WWLX Lawrenceburg TN
WWLZ Horseheads NY
WWMI Saint Petersburg FL
WWMK Cleveland OH
WWNA(AM) Aguadilla PR
WWNB New Bern NC
WWNC Asheville NC
WWNH Madbury NH
WWNL(AM) Pittsburgh PA
WWNN Pompano Beach FL
WWNR Beckley WV
WWNS Statesboro GA
WWNT Dothan AL
WWNZ(AM) Veazie ME
WWOF(AM) Walhalla SC
WWOL Forest City NC
WWON(AM) Waynesboro TN
WWOW Conneaut OH
WWPA Williamsport PA
WWPG Tuscaloosa AL
WWPR Bradenton FL
WWRC(AM) Washington DC
WWRF(AM) Lake Worth FL
WWRL New York NY
WWRU(AM) Jersey City NJ
*WWRV New York NY
WWSC Glens Falls NY
WWSD Quincy FL
WWSJ Saint Johns MI
WWSM Annville-Cleona PA
WWSZ(AM) New Albany IN
WWTC Minneapolis MN
WWTK(AM) Lake Placid FL
WWTM(AM) Decatur AL
WWTQ(AM) Memphis TN
WWTR(AM) Bridgewater NJ
WWTX(AM) Wilmington DE
WWVA(AM) Wheeling WV
WWVT Christiansburg VA
WWWC(AM) Wilkesboro NC
WWWE(AM) Hapeville GA
WWWI(AM) Baxter MN
WWWJ Galax VA
WWWR Roanoke VA
WWWS Buffalo NY
WWWT Randolph VT
WWXL Manchester KY
WWYO Pineville WV
WWZN(AM) Boston MA
WWZQ Aberdeen MS
WXAG Athens GA
WXAL Demopolis AL

WXAM(AM) Buffalo KY
WXBD Biloxi MS
WXCE Amery WI
WXCF Clifton Forge VA
WXCO Wausau WI
WXCT(AM) Southington CT
WXEM Buford GA
WXEW Yabucoa PR
WXFN Muncie IN
WXGI Richmond VA
WXGM Gloucester VA
WXGO Madison IN
WXIC Waverly OH
WXIT Blowing Rock NC
WXJC(AM) Birmingham AL
WXJO(AM) Gordon GA
WXKL Sanford NC
WXKO Fort Valley GA
WXKS Everett MA
WXKX(AM) Clarksburg WV
WXLA Dimondale MI
WXLI Dublin GA
WXLW Indianapolis IN
WXLZ Saint Paul VA
WXMC Parsippany-Troy Hills NJ
WXMY Saltville VA
WXNC(AM) Monroe NC
WXNH(AM) Jaffrey NH
WXNI(AM) Westerly RI
WXNT(AM) Indianapolis IN
WXOK Baton Rouge LA
WXOL(AM) Delaware OH
WXQK(AM) Spring City TN
WXRA(AM) Georgetown KY
WXRF Guayama PR
WXRL Lancaster NY
WXRP Hanceville AL
WXRQ(AM) Mount Pleasant TN
WXRS Swainsboro GA
WXTC Charleston SC
WXTN Lexington MS
WXTR Frederick MD
WXVI Montgomery AL
*WXXI Rochester NY
WXXP(AM) Waynesburg PA
WXYB Indian Rocks Beach FL
WXYT Detroit MI
WYAC(AM) Cabo Rojo PR
WYAL Scotland Neck NC
WYAM(AM) Hartselle AL
WYBC New Haven CT
WYBG Massena NY
WYBT Blountstown FL
WYCB Washington DC
WYCK Plains PA
WYCV Granite Falls NC
WYDE(AM) Birmingham AL
WYEA Sylacauga AL
WYFN Nashville TN
*WYFQ(AM) Charlotte NC
WYFY Rome NY
WYGH Paris KY
WYGL Selinsgrove PA
WYGR Wyoming MI
WYHG(AM) Young Harris GA
WYIS McRae GA
WYKC Grenada MS
WYKM Rupert WV
WYKO Sabana Grande PR
WYLD New Orleans LA
WYLF(AM) Penn Yan NY
WYLL(AM) Chicago IL
WYLS York AL
WYMB Manning SC
WYMC Mayfield KY
WYMM(AM) Jacksonville FL
WYMR(AM) Bridgeport AL
WYNC Yanceyville NC
WYND De Land FL
WYNE(AM) North East PA
WYNI Monroeville AL
WYNN Florence SC
WYNS Lehighton PA
WYNY(AM) Cross City FL
WYOS(AM) Binghamton NY
WYPC Wellston OH
WYRD Greenville SC

U.S. AM Stations by Call Letters

WYRE Annapolis MD
WYRM(AM) Norfolk VA
WYRN(AM) Louisburg NC
WYRV Cedar Bluff VA
WYSH Clinton TN
WYSK Fredericksburg VA
WYSL Avon NY
WYSR(AM) High Point NC
WYTH Madison GA
WYTI Rocky Mount VA
WYUS Milford DE
WYVE Wytheville VA

WYWY Barbourville KY
WYXC(AM) Cartersville GA
WYXE Gallatin TN
WYXI Athens TN
WYYZ Jasper GA
WYZD Dobson NC
WYZE Atlanta GA
WZAM Ishpeming MI
WZAN Portland ME
WZAP(AM) Bristol VA
WZAZ Jacksonville FL
WZBK(AM) Keene NH

WZBO(AM) Edenton NC
WZCT Scottsboro AL
WZEP(AM) De Funiak Springs FL
WZFB(AM) Fair Bluff NC
WZGX(AM) Bessemer AL
WZHF Arlington VA
WZHR(AM) Zephyrhills FL
WZJY Mt. Pleasant SC
WZKY Albemarle NC
WZMG Pepperell AL
WZNA(AM) Moca PR
WZNG Shelbyville TN

WZNN(AM) Black Mountain NC
WZNO Pensacola FL
WZNZ Jacksonville FL
WZOB Fort Payne AL
WZOE Princeton IL
WZON Bangor ME
WZOT Rockmart GA
WZQK(AM) Brandon MS
WZQZ(AM) Trion GA
WZRC New York NY
WZRH(AM) Dallas NC
WZRK(AM) Lake Geneva WI

WZRX Jackson MS
WZSK(AM) Everett PA
WZTA(AM) Vero Beach FL
WZTQ(AM) Centre AL
WZUM Carnegie PA
WZYX(AM) Cowan TN
WZZA(AM) Tuscumbia AL
WZZB Seymour IN
WZZK(AM) Birmingham AL
WZZW Milton WV
WZZX Lineville AL
XETRA Tijuana MEX

U.S. FM Stations by Call Letters

KAAK(FM) Great Falls MT
KAAN-FM Bethany MO
KAAP(FM) Rock Island WA
KAAQ(FM) Alliance NE
KAAR(FM) Butte MT
KAAT(FM) Oakhurst CA
*KAAX(FM) Avenal CA
*KABF(FM) Little Rock AR
KABG(FM) Los Alamos NM
KABK-FM Augusta AR
KABQ-FM Santa Fe NM
*KABU(FM) Fort Totten ND
KABX-FM Merced CA
KABZ(FM) Little Rock AR
*KACC(FM) Alvin TX
KACI-FM The Dalles OR
KACL(FM) Bismarck ND
KACO(FM) Ardmore OK
KACQ(FM) Lometa TX
*KACS(FM) Chehalis WA
KACT-FM Andrews TX
*KACU(FM) Abilene TX
*KACV-FM Amarillo TX
KACW(FM) North Bend OR
KACY(FM) Arkansas City KS
KACZ(FM) Riley KS
KADA-FM Ada OK
KADD(FM) Logandale NV
KADI-FM Republic MO
KADL(FM) Imperial NE
KADQ-FM Rexburg ID
*KADU(FM) Hibbing MN
*KADV(FM) Modesto CA
KADX(FM) Houston AK
KAEH(FM) Beaumont CA
*KAEN(FM) Melbourne AR
*KAER(FM) Saint George UT
KAEZ(FM) Amarillo TX
KAFC(FM) Anchorage AK
KAFE(FM) Bellingham WA
KAFF-FM Flagstaff AZ
*KAFH(FM) Great Falls MT
*KAFM(FM) Grand Junction CO
KAFN(FM) Gould AR
*KAFR(FM) Conroe TX
KAFX-FM Diboll TX
KAGB(FM) Waimea HI
KAGE-FM Winona MN
KAGG(FM) Madisonville TX
KAGH-FM Crossett AR
*KAGJ(FM) Ephraim UT
KAGL(FM) El Dorado AR
KAGM(FM) Los Lunas NM
KAGO-FM Klamath Falls OR
*KAGT-FM Abilene TX
*KAGU(FM) Spokane WA
*KAHJ(FM) Bunkie LA
KAHM(FM) Prescott AZ
*KAHR(FM) Poplar Bluff MO
*KAIB(FM) Whitehall MT
*KAIC(FM) Tucson AZ
*KAIG(FM) Dodge City KS
*KAIH(FM) Lake Havasu City AZ
*KAIK(FM) Tillamook OR
KAIM-FM Honolulu HI
*KAIO(FM) Idaho Falls ID
KAIQ(FM) Wolfforth TX
KAIR-FM Horton KS
*KAIS(FM) Redwood Valley CA
*KAIW(FM) Laramie WY
*KAIZ(FM) Mesquite NV
KAJA(FM) San Antonio TX
*KAJC(FM) Salem OR
KAJI(FM) Point Comfort TX
KAJK-FM Ferndale CA
KAJM(FM) Payson AZ
KAJN-FM Crowley LA
*KAJP(FM) Firebaugh CA
*KAJX(FM) Aspen CO
KAJZ(FM) Rio Rancho NM
*KAKA(FM) Salina KS

KAKJ(FM) Marianna AR
*KAKL(FM) Anchorage AK
KAKN(FM) Naknek AK
*KAKO(FM) Ada OK
KAKQ-FM Fairbanks AK
KAKS(FM) Huntsville AR
KAKT(FM) Phoenix OR
*KAKX(FM) Mendocino CA
*KALA(FM) Davenport IA
KALC(FM) Denver CO
KALF(FM) Red Bluff CA
KALI-FM Santa Ana CA
KALK(FM) Winfield TX
KALP(FM) Alpine TX
KALQ-FM Alamosa CO
*KALR(FM) Hot Springs AR
KALS(FM) Kalispell MT
KALT-FM Alturas CA
*KALU(FM) Langston OK
*KALW(FM) San Francisco CA
*KALX(FM) Berkeley CA
KALZ(FM) Fresno CA
*KAMB(FM) Merced CA
KAMD-FM Camden AR
KAMJ-FM Gosnell AR
KAML-FM Gillette WY
KAMO-FM Rogers AR
KAMS(FM) Mammoth Spring AR
*KAMU-FM College Station TX
KAMX(FM) Luling TX
*KAMY(FM) Lubbock TX
KAMZ(FM) Tahoka TX
*KANH(FM) Emporia KS
*KANJ(FM) Giddings TX
*KANL(FM) Baker City OR
*KANO(FM) Hilo HI
KANR(FM) Belle Plaine KS
KANS(FM) Emporia KS
KANT(FM) Guernsey WY
*KANU(FM) Lawrence KS
*KANV(FM) Olsburg KS
*KANW(FM) Albuquerque NM
*KANX(FM) Sheridan AR
*KANZ(FM) Garden City KS
KAOC(FM) Cavalier ND
KAOD(FM) Babbitt MN
*KAOG(FM) Jonesboro AR
KAOI-FM Wailuku HI
*KAOR(FM) Vermillion SD
*KAOS(FM) Olympia WA
*KAOW(FM) Fort Smith AR
KAOX(FM) Kemmerer WY
KAOY(FM) Kealakekua HI
KAPA(FM) Hilo HI
KAPB-FM Marksville LA
*KAPC(FM) Butte MT
*KAPG(FM) Bentonville AR
*KAPI(FM) Ruston LA
*KAPK(FM) Grants Pass OR
*KAPM(FM) Alexandria LA
KAPW(FM) Cotton Plant AR
*KAQA(FM) Kilauea HI
*KAQD(FM) Abilene TX
KAQF(FM) Clovis NM
KAQX(FM) Long Beach WA
*KARA(FM) Williams CA
KARB(FM) Price UT
*KARF(FM) Independence KS
*KARG(FM) Poteau OK
*KARH(FM) Forrest City AR
*KARJ(FM) Kuna ID
KARL-FM Tracy MN
*KARM(FM) Visalia CA
KARN-FM Sheridan AR
KARO(FM) Nyssa OR
KARP-FM Dassel MN
*KARQ(FM) East Sonora CA
KARS-FM Laramie WY
*KARU(FM) Cache OK
KARV-FM Ola AR
KARX(FM) Claude TX

KARY-FM Grandview WA
KARZ(FM) Marshall MN
*KASB(FM) Bellevue WA
*KASD(FM) Rapid City SD
KASE-FM Austin TX
*KASF(FM) Alamosa CO
KASH-FM Anchorage AK
*KASK(FM) Fairfield CA
KASR(FM) Conway AR
KASS(FM) Casper WY
KAST-FM Astoria OR
*KASU(FM) Jonesboro AR
*KASV(FM) Borger TX
*KATB(FM) Anchorage AK
KATF(FM) Dubuque IA
KATI(FM) California MO
KATJ-FM George CA
KATK-FM Carlsbad NM
KATM(FM) Modesto CA
KATP(FM) Amarillo TX
KATQ-FM Plentywood MT
KATR-FM Otis CO
KATS(FM) Yakima WA
KATT-FM Oklahoma City OK
KATW(FM) Lewiston ID
KATX(FM) Eastland TX
KATY-FM Idyllwild CA
KATZ-FM Alton IL
*KAUF(FM) Kennett MO
KAUJ(FM) Grafton ND
KAUL(FM) Ellington MO
KAUM(FM) Colorado City TX
*KAUR(FM) Sioux Falls SD
KAUS-FM Austin MN
KAVD(FM) Limon CO
*KAVE(FM) Oakridge OR
KAVH(FM) Eudora AR
KAVJ(FM) Sutherlin OR
*KAVK(FM) Many LA
*KAVO(FM) Pampa TX
KAVV(FM) Benson AZ
KAVW(FM) Amarillo TX
*KAVX(FM) Lufkin TX
*KAWC-FM Yuma AZ
KAWK(FM) Custer SD
*KAWS(FM) Boise ID
KAWW(FM) Lihue HI
KAWW-FM Heber Springs AR
*KAWZ(FM) Twin Falls ID
*KAXE(FM) Grand Rapids MN
*KAXG(FM) Gillette WY
*KAXH(FM) Borger TX
*KAXL(FM) Green Acres CA
*KAXR(FM) Arkansas City KS
*KAXV(FM) Bastrop LA
*KAYA(FM) Hubbard NE
*KAYB(FM) Sunnyside WA
*KAYC(FM) Durant OK
KAYD-FM Silsbee TX
*KAYE-FM Tonkawa OK
KAYG(FM) Tulsa OK
*KAYH(FM) Fayetteville AR
*KAYK(FM) Victoria TX
KAYL-FM Storm Lake IA
*KAYM(FM) Weatherford OK
*KAYP(FM) Burlington IA
KAYQ(FM) Warsaw MO
*KAYT(FM) Jena LA
KAYW(FM) Meeker CO
KAYX(FM) Richmond MO
*KAZC(FM) Tishomingo OK
KAZE(FM) Ore City TX
*KAZF(FM) Hebronville TX
*KAZI-FM Austin TX
KAZR(FM) Pella IA
*KAZU(FM) Pacific Grove CA
KAZX(FM) Kirtland NM
KAZY(FM) Woodward OK
KAZZ(FM) Deer Park WA
KBAC(FM) Las Vegas NM
*KBAH(FM) Plainview TX

KBAJ(FM) Deer River MN
KBAL-FM San Saba TX
*KBAN(FM) De Ridder LA
*KBAQ-FM Phoenix AZ
KBAT(FM) Midland TX
KBAW(FM) Zapata TX
KBAY(FM) Gilroy CA
KBAZ(FM) Hamilton MT
KBBB(FM) Billings MT
KBBD(FM) Spokane WA
KBBE(FM) McPherson KS
*KBBF(FM) Santa Rosa CA
*KBBG(FM) Waterloo IA
*KBBK(FM) Lincoln NE
KBBM(FM) Jefferson City MO
KBBN-FM Broken Bow NE
KBBQ-FM Fort Smith AR
KBBT(FM) Schertz TX
KBBU(FM) Modesto CA
KBBX-FM Nebraska City NE
KBBY-FM Ventura CA
KBBZ(FM) Kalispell MT
KBCE(FM) Boyce LA
*KBCM(FM) Blytheville AR
KBCN-FM Marshall AR
KBCO-FM Boulder CO
KBCQ(FM) Roswell NM
KBCR-FM Steamboat Springs CO
*KBCS(FM) Bellevue WA
KBCT-FM Waco TX
*KBCU(FM) North Newton KS
*KBCW(FM) McAlester OK
*KBCX(FM) Big Spring TX
KBCY(FM) Tye TX
*KBDA(FM) Great Bend KS
KBDB-FM Forks WA
*KBDC(FM) Mason City IA
*KBDD(FM) Winfield KS
*KBDE(FM) Temple TX
*KBDG(FM) Turlock CA
*KBDH(FM) San Ardo CA
KBDN(FM) Bandon OR
*KBDO(FM) Des Arc AR
KBDR(FM) Mirando City TX
KBDS(FM) Taft CA
KBDX(FM) Blanding UT
KBDZ(FM) Perryville MO
KBEA-FM Muscatine IA
KBEB-FM Rayne LA
KBEE(FM) Salt Lake City UT
KBEF(FM) Gibsland LA
KBEK(FM) Mora MN
KBEL-FM Idabel OK
*KBEM-FM Minneapolis MN
KBEQ-FM Kansas City MO
KBER(FM) Ogden UT
*KBES(FM) Ceres CA
KBEV-FM Dillon MT
KBEW-FM Blue Earth MN
KBEY(FM) Burnet TX
KBEZ(FM) Tulsa OK
KBFB(FM) Dallas TX
KBFC(FM) Forrest City AR
KBFL(FM) Buffalo MO
KBFM(FM) Edinburg TX
KBFO(FM) Aberdeen SD
*KBFR(FM) Bismarck ND
KBFX(FM) Anchorage AK
KBFZ(FM) Kimball NE
*KBGA(FM) Missoula MT
KBGL(FM) Larned KS
*KBGM(FM) Park Hills MO
KBGO(FM) Waco TX
KBGR(FM) Beebe AR
KBGX(FM) Keaau HI
KBGY(FM) Faribault MN
*KBHE-FM Rapid City SD
*KBHG(FM) Alexandria MN
KBHH(FM) Kerman CA
KBHI(FM) Miner MO
KBHL(FM) Osakis MN

*KBHN(FM) Booneville AR
KBHP(FM) Bemidji MN
KBHR(FM) Big Bear City CA
KBHT(FM) Crockett TX
*KBHU-FM Spearfish SD
*KBHW(FM) International Falls MN
*KBHZ(FM) Willmar MN
*KBIA(FM) Columbia MO
KBIC(FM) Raymondville TX
KBIG-FM Los Angeles CA
*KBIL(FM) Park City MT
KBIM-FM Roswell NM
*KBIO(FM) Natchitoches LA
*KBIQ(FM) Manitou Springs CO
KBIU(FM) Lake Charles LA
*KBIY(FM) Van Buren MO
*KBJQ(FM) Bronson KS
*KBJS(FM) Jacksonville TX
KBJX(FM) Shelley ID
KBKB-FM Fort Madison IA
*KBKC(FM) Moberly MO
KBKG(FM) Corning AR
KBKH(FM) Shamrock TX
KBKK(FM) Ball LA
*KBKL(FM) Grand Junction CO
*KBKN(FM) Lamesa TX
KBKO-FM Bakersfield CA
KBKS-FM Tacoma WA
*KBKY(FM) Merced CA
KBKZ(FM) Raton NM
KBLB(FM) Nisswa MN
*KBLD(FM) Kennewick WA
KBLL-FM Helena MT
KBLO(FM) Corcoran CA
KBLP(FM) Lindsay OK
KBLQ-FM Logan UT
KBLR-FM Blair NE
KBLS(FM) North Fort Riley KS
KBLT(FM) Leakey TX
*KBLW(FM) Billings MT
KBLX-FM Berkeley CA
KBLZ(FM) Winona TX
KBMB(FM) Sacramento CA
*KBMC(FM) Bozeman MT
*KBMD(FM) Marble Falls TX
KBMG(FM) Evanston WY
*KBMH(FM) Holbrook AZ
KBMI(FM) Roma TX
*KBMJ(FM) Heber Springs AR
*KBMK(FM) Bismarck ND
*KBMM(FM) Odessa TX
*KBMP(FM) Enterprise KS
*KBMQ(FM) Monroe LA
KBMV-FM Birch Tree MO
KBMX(FM) Proctor MN
KBNA-FM El Paso TX
KBNF(FM) Chester CA
KBNG(FM) Ridgway CO
*KBNJ(FM) Corpus Christi TX
*KBNL(FM) Laredo TX
*KBNO-FM White Salmon WA
KBNR(FM) Brownsville TX
KBNU(FM) Uvalde TX
*KBNV(FM) Fayetteville AR
KBOA-FM Piggott AR
KBOB-FM Geneseo IL
KBOC(FM) Bridgeport TX
KBOE-FM Oskaloosa IA
KBOG(FM) Douglas WY
*KBOJ(FM) Worthington MN
KBOM(FM) Santa Fe NM
KBON(FM) Mamou LA
*KBOO(FM) Portland OR
KBOQ(FM) Carmel CA
KBOS-FM Tulare CA
KBOT(FM) Pelican Rapids MN
KBOX(FM) Lompoc CA
KBOY-FM Medford OR
KBOZ-FM Bozeman MT
KBPA(FM) San Marcos TX
*KBPB(FM) Harrison AR

U.S. FM Stations by Call Letters

*KBPG(FM) Montevideo MN
KBPI(FM) Denver CO
*KBPK(FM) Buena Park CA
*KBPN(FM) Brainerd MN
*KBPR(FM) Brainerd MN
*KBPS-FM Portland OR
*KBPU(FM) De Queen AR
*KBPW(FM) Hampton AR
*KBQC(FM) Independence KS
KBQI(FM) Albuquerque NM
KBQQ(FM) Pinesdale MT
KBRA(FM) Freer TX
KBRB-FM Ainsworth NE
KBRE(FM) Atwater CA
KBRG(FM) San Jose CA
KBRJ(FM) Anchorage AK
KBRK-FM Brookings SD
KBRQ(FM) Hillsboro TX
KBRU-FM Fort Morgan CO
*KBRW-FM Barrow AK
*KBRX-FM O'Neill NE
*KBSA(FM) El Dorado AR
*KBSB(FM) Bemidji MN
KBSG-FM Tacoma WA
*KBSJ(FM) Jackpot NV
*KBSK(FM) McCall ID
*KBSM(FM) McCall ID
KBSO(FM) Corpus Christi TX
*KBSQ(FM) McCall ID
*KBSS(FM) Sun Valley ID
KBST-FM Big Spring TX
*KBSU-FM Boise ID
*KBSW(FM) Twin Falls ID
*KBSX(FM) Boise ID
*KBSY(FM) Burley ID
KBTA-FM Batesville AR
KBTE(FM) Tulia TX
*KBTL(FM) El Dorado KS
KBTN-FM Neosho MO
KBTO(FM) Bottineau ND
KBTQ(FM) Harlingen TX
KBTS(FM) Big Spring TX
KBTT(FM) Haughton LA
KBTW(FM) Lenwood CA
KBUA(FM) San Fernando CA
*KBUB(FM) Brownwood TX
KBUC(FM) Raymondville TX
KBUD(FM) Sardis MS
KBUE(FM) Long Beach CA
KBUG(FM) Malin OR
KBUK(FM) La Grange TX
KBUL-FM Carson City NV
KBUS(FM) Paris TX
*KBUT(FM) Crested Butte CO
*KBUW(FM) Buffalo WY
KBUX(FM) Quartzsite AZ
*KBUZ(FM) Topeka KS
KBVA(FM) Bella Vista AR
KBVC(FM) Buena Vista CO
KBVL(FM) Pawhuska OK
*KBVM(FM) Portland OR
*KBVR(FM) Corvallis OR
KBVU-FM Alta IA
*KBWA(FM) Brush CO
*KBWC(FM) Marshall TX
KBWS-FM Sisseton SD
KBXB(FM) Sikeston MO
KBXG-FM Lake Charles LA
KBXL(FM) Caldwell ID
*KBXO(FM) Coachella CA
KBXR(FM) Columbia MO
KBXX(FM) Houston TX
KBYB(FM) Hope AR
*KBYI(FM) Rexburg ID
KBYN(FM) Arnold CA
KBYO-FM Tallulah LA
*KBYR-FM Rexburg ID
*KBYU-FM Provo UT
KBYZ(FM) Bismarck ND
KBZB(FM) Pioche NV
KBZD(FM) Amarillo TX
KBZE(FM) Berwick LA
KBZI(FM) Deerfield MO
KBZM(FM) Big Sky MT
KBZN(FM) Ogden UT
KBZQ(FM) Lawton OK
KBZS(FM) Wichita Falls TX

KBZT(FM) San Diego CA
KBZU(FM) Albuquerque NM
KBZZ-FM Morgan City LA
*KCAC(FM) Camden AR
KCAD(FM) Dickinson ND
KCAJ-FM Roseau MN
KCAL-FM Redlands CA
KCAQ(FM) Oxnard CA
KCAR-FM Galena KS
*KCAS(FM) McCook TX
*KCAW(FM) Sitka AK
KCAY(FM) Russell KS
*KCBI(FM) Dallas TX
KCBS-FM Los Angeles CA
*KCBX(FM) San Luis Obispo CA
KCBZ(FM) Cannon Beach OR
*KCCD(FM) Moorhead MN
*KCCK-FM Cedar Rapids IA
KCCL(FM) Shingle Springs CA
*KCCM-FM Moorhead MN
KCCN-FM Honolulu HI
KCCQ(FM) Ames IA
*KCCU(FM) Lawton OK
KCCV-FM Olathe KS
KCCY(FM) Pueblo CO
KCDA(FM) Post Falls ID
KCDD(FM) Hamlin TX
KCDL(FM) Cordell OK
KCDQ(FM) Douglas AZ
*KCDS(FM) Deadhorse AK
KCDU(FM) Carmel CA
KCDV(FM) Cordova AK
KCDX(FM) Florence AZ
KCDY(FM) Carlsbad NM
*KCDZ(FM) Twentynine Palms CA
*KCEA(FM) Atherton CA
KCEC-FM Wellton AZ
*KCED(FM) Centralia WA
KCEE(FM) Grass Valley CA
KCEL(FM) California City CA
*KCEP(FM) Las Vegas NV
KCEZ(FM) Los Molinos CA
KCFA(FM) Arnold CA
*KCFB(FM) Saint Cloud MN
KCFM(FM) Levan UT
*KCFN(FM) Wichita KS
*KCFP(FM) Pueblo CO
*KCFS(FM) Sioux Falls SD
*KCFV(FM) Ferguson MO
KCFX(FM) Harrisonville MO
*KCFY(FM) Yuma AZ
KCGB(FM) Hood River OR
KCGL(FM) Powell WY
KCGM(FM) Scobey MT
KCGN-FM Ortonville MN
KCGQ-FM Gordonville MO
KCGR(FM) Cottage Grove OR
KCGY(FM) Laramie WY
KCHA-FM Charles City IA
KCHC(FM) Willows CA
KCHE-FM Cherokee IA
KCHI-FM Chillicothe MO
*KCHO(FM) Chico CA
KCHQ(FM) Driggs ID
KCHX(FM) Midland TX
KCHZ(FM) Ottawa KS
*KCIC(FM) Grand Junction CO
KCIE(FM) Dulce NM
*KCIF(FM) Hilo HI
KCII-FM Washington IA
KCIJ(FM) Atlanta LA
KCIL(FM) Houma LA
*KCIR(FM) Twin Falls ID
KCIV(FM) Mount Bullion CA
*KCIX(FM) Garden City ID
KCJC(FM) Dardanelle AR
KCJF(FM) Earle AR
*KCJH(FM) Livingston CA
KCJK(FM) Garden City MO
*KCJL(FM) Lincoln ND
*KCJX(FM) Carbondale CO
KCKL(FM) Malakoff TX
KCKS(FM) Concordia KS
*KCKT(FM) Crockett TX
KCLB-FM Coachella CA
*KCLC(FM) Saint Charles MO
KCLD-FM Saint Cloud MN

KCLH(FM) Caledonia MN
KCLK-FM Clarkston WA
KCLL(FM) San Angelo TX
KCLQ(FM) Lebanon MO
KCLR-FM Boonville MO
KCLS(FM) Ely NV
KCLT(FM) West Helena AR
*KCLU(FM) Thousand Oaks CA
KCLV-FM Clovis NM
KCLY(FM) Clay Center KS
KCMB(FM) Baker City OR
*KCME(FM) Manitou Springs CO
*KCMF(FM) Fergus Falls MN
*KCMH(FM) Mountain Home AR
KCMI(FM) Terrytown NE
*KCML(FM) Saint Joseph MN
KCMM(FM) Belgrade MT
KCMO-FM Kansas City MO
*KCMP(FM) Northfield MN
KCMQ(FM) Columbia MO
*KCMR(FM) Mason City IA
KCMS(FM) Edmonds WA
*KCMT(FM) Oro Valley AZ
KCMX-FM Ashland OR
KCMY(FM) Gardnerville-Minden NV
KCNA(FM) Cave Junction OR
*KCND(FM) Bismarck ND
KCNE-FM Chadron NE
KCNL(FM) Sunnyvale CA
KCNM-FM Garapan-Saipan NP
KCNO(FM) Alturas CA
KCNQ(FM) Kernville CA
*KCNT(FM) Hastings NE
KCNV(FM) Las Vegas NV
KCNY(FM) Bald Knob AR
KCOB-FM Newton IA
KCOL-FM Groves TX
KCOO(FM) Coolidge AZ
KCOR-FM Comfort TX
*KCOU(FM) Columbia MO
*KCOZ(FM) Point Lookout MO
KCPI(FM) Albert Lea MN
*KCPR(FM) San Luis Obispo CA
*KCPW-FM Salt Lake City UT
KCQQ(FM) Davenport IA
*KCRB-FM Bemidji MN
KCRE-FM Crescent City CA
KCRF-FM Lincoln City OR
*KCRH(FM) Hayward CA
*KCRI(FM) Indio CA
KCRK-FM Colville WA
*KCRL(FM) Sunrise Beach MO
KCRN-FM San Angelo TX
KCRR(FM) Grundy Center IA
KCRS-FM Midland TX
KCRT-FM Trinidad CO
*KCRU(FM) Oxnard CA
KCRV-FM Caruthersville MO
*KCRW(FM) Santa Monica CA
KCRX-FM Seaside OR
*KCRY(FM) Mojave CA
KCRZ(FM) Tipton CA
*KCSB-FM Santa Barbara CA
*KCSC(FM) Edmond OK
*KCSD(FM) Sioux Falls SD
*KCSH(FM) Ellensburg WA
KCSI(FM) Red Oak IA
*KCSM(FM) San Mateo CA
*KCSN(FM) Northridge CA
KCSP-FM Casper WY
*KCSS(FM) Turlock CA
KCST-FM Florence OR
*KCSU-FM Fort Collins CO
KCTN(FM) Garnavillo IA
KCTR-FM Billings MT
KCTT-FM Yellville AR
KCTX-FM Childress TX
KCTY-FM Plattsmouth NE
KCUA(FM) Naples UT
KCUB-FM Stephenville TX
KCUF(FM) El Jebel CO
KCUG(FM) Chugwater WY
*KCUK(FM) Chevak AK
KCUL-FM Marshall TX
*KCUR-FM Kansas City MO
KCUV(FM) New Castle CO
KCVI(FM) Blackfoot ID

*KCVJ(FM) Osceola MO
*KCVK(FM) Otterville MO
KCVM(FM) Hudson IA
*KCVN(FM) Cozad NE
*KCVO-FM Camdenton MO
KCVR-FM Columbia CA
*KCVS(FM) Salina KS
*KCVT(FM) Silver Lake KS
KCVW(FM) Kingman KS
*KCVX(FM) Salem MO
*KCVZ(FM) Dixon MO
KCWC-FM Riverton WY
KCWD(FM) Harrison AR
KCWN(FM) New Sharon IA
KCWR(FM) Bakersfield CA
*KCWU(FM) Ellensburg WA
*KCWV(FM) Brownfield TX
*KCWW(FM) Evanston WY
*KCXR(FM) Taft OK
KCXX(FM) Lake Arrowhead CA
*KCXY(FM) East Camden AR
KCYN(FM) Moab UT
KCYQ(FM) Richfield UT
KCYS(FM) Seaside OR
*KCYY(FM) San Antonio TX
KCZE(FM) New Hampton IA
*KCZO(FM) Carrizo Springs TX
*KCZQ(FM) Cresco IA
KDAA(FM) Rolla MO
KDAG(FM) Farmington NM
KDAI(FM) Ontario CA
KDAL-FM Duluth MN
KDAM(FM) Hope ND
KDAO-FM Eldora IA
*KDAP-FM Douglas AZ
*KDAQ(FM) Shreveport LA
KDAR(FM) Oxnard CA
KDAT(FM) Cedar Rapids IA
KDAY(FM) Redondo Beach CA
KDB(FM) Santa Barbara CA
KDBB(FM) Bonne Terre MO
KDBH(FM) Natchitoches LA
KDBI(FM) Emmett ID
KDBL(FM) Toppenish WA
KDBN(FM) Haltom City TX
KDBR(FM) Kalispell MT
KDBX(FM) Clear Lake SD
KDBZ(FM) Anchorage AK
KDCD(FM) San Angelo TX
KDCQ(FM) Coos Bay OR
*KDCR(FM) Sioux Center IA
*KDCV-FM Blair NE
KDDB(FM) Waipahu HI
KDDD-FM Dumas TX
KDDG(FM) Albany MN
KDDK(FM) Franklin LA
KDDQ(FM) Comanche OK
KDDS-FM Elma WA
KDDX(FM) Spearfish SD
KDEC-FM Decorah IA
KDEL-FM Arkadelphia AR
KDEM(FM) Deming NM
KDEP(FM) Garibaldi OR
KDES-FM Palm Springs CA
KDEW-FM De Witt AR
KDEX-FM Dexter MO
KDEZ(FM) Jonesboro AR
KDFC-FM San Francisco CA
KDFM(FM) Falfurrias TX
KDFO-FM Delano CA
*KDFR(FM) Des Moines IA
KDGE(FM) Fort Worth TX
KDGL(FM) Yucca Valley CA
KDGS(FM) Andover KS
*KDHT(FM) Cedar Park TX
*KDHX(FM) Saint Louis MO
*KDIM(FM) Coweta OK
KDIS-FM Little Rock AR
*KDJC(FM) Baker City OR
*KDJE(FM) Jacksonville AR
KDJK(FM) Mariposa CA
KDJM(FM) Broomfield CO
KDJR(FM) De Soto MO
*KDJS(FM) Willmar MN
KDJT(FM) Harwood ND
KDKB(FM) Mesa AZ

KDKD-FM Clinton MO
KDKK-FM Park Rapids MN
*KDKL(FM) Coalinga CA
*KDKR(FM) Decatur TX
KDKS-FM Blanchard LA
KDLD(FM) Santa Monica CA
KDLE(FM) Newport Beach CA
KDLK-FM Del Rio TX
*KDLL(FM) Kenai AK
KDLO-FM Watertown SD
KDLS-FM Perry IA
KDLX(FM) Makawao HI
KDLY(FM) Lander WY
KDMG(FM) Burlington IA
*KDMR(FM) Mitchellville IA
KDMX(FM) Dallas TX
*KDNA(FM) Yakima WA
*KDND(FM) Sacramento CA
*KDNE(FM) Crete NE
*KDNI(FM) Duluth MN
*KDNK(FM) Glenwood Springs CO
KDNN(FM) Honolulu HI
KDNO(FM) Thermopolis WY
KDNS(FM) Downs KS
*KDNW(FM) Duluth MN
KDOG(FM) North Mankato MN
KDOK(FM) Tyler OK
KDOM-FM Windom MN
KDON-FM Salinas CA
KDOT(FM) Reno NV
*KDOV(FM) Medford OR
KDPR(FM) Dickinson ND
KDQN-FM De Queen AR
KDRB(FM) Ankeny IA
*KDRE(FM) Sterling CO
KDRF(FM) Albuquerque NM
*KDRH(FM) King City CA
KDRK-FM Spokane WA
KDRM(FM) Moses Lake WA
KDRS-FM Paragould AR
*KDSC(FM) Thousand Oaks CA
*KDSD-FM Pierpont SD
KDSK(FM) Grants NM
KDSN-FM Denison IA
KDSR(FM) Williston ND
KDSS(FM) Ely NV
KDST(FM) Dyersville IA
*KDSU(FM) Fargo ND
KDTR(FM) Florence MT
*KDUB(FM) Dubuque IA
KDUC(FM) Barstow CA
*KDUK-FM Florence OR
KDUQ(FM) Ludlow CA
*KDUR(FM) Durango CO
KDUT(FM) Randolph UT
*KDUV(FM) Visalia CA
*KDUW(FM) Douglas WY
KDUX-FM Aberdeen WA
KDVA(FM) Buckeye AZ
KDVE(FM) Pittsburg TX
*KDVL(FM) Devils Lake ND
*KDVS(FM) Davis CA
*KDVV(FM) Topeka KS
KDWB-FM Richfield MN
KDWD(FM) Emmetsburg IA
*KDWG(FM) Dillon MT
KDWY(FM) Diamondville WY
*KDXL(FM) Saint Louis Park MN
KDXX(FM) Benbrook TX
KDXY(FM) Lake City AR
KDYN-FM Ozark AR
KDZA-FM Pueblo CO
KDZN(FM) Glendive MT
KDZY(FM) McCall ID
KEAG(FM) Anchorage AK
KEAN-FM Abilene TX
*KEAR(FM) San Francisco CA
KEBN(FM) Garden Grove CA
*KECC(FM) Miles City MT
*KECG(FM) El Cerrito CA
KECH-FM Sun Valley ID
KECO(FM) Elk City OK
KEDD(FM) Johannesburg CA
KEDG(FM) Alexandria LA
KEDJ(FM) Gilbert AZ
*KEDM(FM) Monroe LA
*KEDP(FM) Las Vegas NM

U.S. FM Stations by Call Letters

*KEDR(FM) Sacramento CA
*KEDT-FM Corpus Christi TX
*KEEH(FM) Spokane WA
KEEI(FM) Hanapepe HI
KEEP(FM) Bandera TX
KEEY-FM Saint Paul MN
KEEZ-FM Mankato MN
KEFH(FM) Clarendon TX
KEFM(FM) Omaha NE
*KEFR(FM) Le Grand CA
*KEFS(FM) North Powder OR
*KEFX(FM) Twin Falls ID
KEGA(FM) Oakley UT
KEGH(FM) Brigham City UT
KEGK(FM) Wahpeton ND
*KEGL(FM) Fort Worth TX
*KEGR(FM) Fort Dodge IA
KEGX(FM) Richland WA
KEHK(FM) Brownsville OR
KEJJ(FM) Gunnison CO
KEJL(FM) Eunice NM
KEJS(FM) Lubbock TX
KEKA-FM Eureka CA
KEKB(FM) Fruita CO
*KEKL(FM) Mesquite NV
KEKO(FM) Hebronville TX
KELD-FM Hampton AR
KELE-FM Mountain Grove MO
KELI(FM) San Angelo TX
KELN(FM) North Platte NE
KELO-FM Sioux Falls SD
*KELP(FM) Mesquite NM
KELR-FM Chariton IA
KELT(FM) Riverside CA
KELZ-FM Terrell Hills TX
KEMA(FM) Three Rivers TX
*KEMC(FM) Billings MT
KEMX(FM) Locust Grove OK
KENA-FM Mena AR
KEND(FM) Roswell NM
*KENW-FM Portales NM
KENZ(FM) Orem UT
KEOJ(FM) Caney KS
KEOK(FM) Tahlequah OK
*KEOL(FM) La Grande OR
*KEOM(FM) Mesquite TX
*KEOS(FM) College Station TX
*KEPC(FM) Colorado Springs CO
KEPG(FM) Victoria TX
*KEPI(FM) Eagle Pass TX
*KEPX(FM) Eagle Pass TX
*KEQX(FM) Stephenville TX
*KERA(FM) Dallas TX
KERB-FM Kermit TX
KERM(FM) Torrington WY
KERX(FM) Paris AR
KESC(FM) Wilburton OK
*KESD(FM) Brookings SD
KESM-FM El Dorado Springs MO
KESN(FM) Allen TX
KESO(FM) South Padre Island TX
KESR(FM) Shasta Lake City CA
KESS-FM Lewisville TX
KESY(FM) Cuba MO
KESZ(FM) Phoenix AZ
*KETR(FM) Commerce TX
KETX-FM Livingston TX
KEUG(FM) Veneta OR
*KEUL(FM) Girdwood AK
KEUN(FM) Eunice LA
KEWB(FM) Anderson CA
KEWL-FM New Boston TX
*KEWU-FM Cheney WA
KEXA(FM) Salinas CA
KEXL(FM) Norfolk NE
*KEXP-FM Seattle WA
*KEYA(FM) Belcourt ND
KEYB(FM) Altus OK
KEYE-FM Perryton TX
KEYF-FM Cheney WA
KEYG-FM Grand Coulee WA
KEYJ-FM Abilene TX
KEYN-FM Wichita KS
KEYW(FM) Pasco WA
KEZA(FM) Fayetteville AR
KEZB(FM) Hempstead TX
KEZE(FM) Spokane WA

KEZG(FM) Calico Rock AR
KEZJ-FM Twin Falls ID
KEZK-FM Saint Louis MO
KEZL(FM) Fowler CA
KEZN(FM) Palm Desert CA
KEZO-FM Omaha NE
KEZP(FM) Bunkie LA
KEZQ(FM) West Yellowstone MT
KEZR(FM) San Jose CA
KEZS-FM Cape Girardeau MO
KFAB-FM Kindred ND
*KFAE-FM Richland WA
*KFAI(FM) Minneapolis MN
KFAN-FM Johnson City TX
KFAT(FM) Anchorage AK
KFAV(FM) Warrenton MO
KFBD-FM Waynesville MO
*KFBN(FM) Fargo ND
KFBZ(FM) Haysville KS
*KFCF(FM) Fresno CA
KFCM(FM) Cherokee Village AR
KFDI-FM Wichita KS
*KFDN(FM) Lakewood CO
KFEB(FM) Campbell MO
KFEG(FM) Klamath Falls OR
*KFER(FM) Santa Cruz CA
KFFA-FM Helena AR
KFFB-FM Fairfield Bay AR
*KFFF-FM Boone IA
KFFG(FM) Los Altos CA
KFFM(FM) Yakima WA
KFFR(FM) Pullman WA
*KFFW(FM) Cabool MO
KFFX(FM) Emporia KS
KFGE(FM) Milford NE
KFGI(FM) Crosby ND
KFGL(FM) Abilene TX
KFGY(FM) Healdsburg CA
KFH-FM Clearwater KS
*KFHL(FM) Wasco CA
KFIL-FM Preston MN
KFIN(FM) Jonesboro AR
KFIS(FM) Scappoose OR
KFIX(FM) Plainville KS
*KFJC(FM) Los Altos CA
*KFJM(FM) Grand Forks ND
KFKF-FM Kansas City KS
*KFKX(FM) Hastings NE
*KFLB-FM Odessa TX
KFLG-FM Kingman AZ
KFLI(FM) Des Arc AR
*KFLL(FM) Susanville CA
KFLP-FM Floydada TX
*KFLQ(FM) Albuquerque NM
*KFLR-FM Phoenix AZ
KFLS-FM Tulelake CA
*KFLT-FM Tucson AZ
*KFLV(FM) Wilber NE
KFLW(FM) Saint Robert MO
KFLX(FM) Kachina Village AZ
KFLY(FM) Corvallis OR
KFMA(FM) Green Valley AZ
KFMB-FM San Diego CA
KFMC(FM) Fairmont MN
KFMF(FM) Chico CA
KFMG(FM) Juneau AK
KFMH(FM) Belle Fourche SD
KFMI(FM) Eureka CA
KFMJ(FM) Ketchikan AK
KFMK(FM) Round Rock TX
KFML(FM) Little Falls MN
KFMM(FM) Thatcher AZ
KFMN(FM) Lihue HI
KFMQ(FM) Gallup NM
KFMR(FM) Marbleton WY
KFMS(FM) Franklin ID
KFMT(FM) Fremont NE
KFMU-FM Oak Creek CO
KFMW(FM) Waterloo IA
KFMX-FM Lubbock TX
KFMY(FM) Raymond WA
KFNC(FM) Beaumont TX
KFNF(FM) Oberlin KS
KFNK(FM) Eatonville WA
*KFNO(FM) Fresno CA
KFNS-FM Troy MO
KFNV-FM Ferriday LA

KFNW-FM Fargo ND
KFOG(FM) San Francisco CA
KFPB(FM) Chino Valley AZ
*KFPR(FM) Redding CA
*KFRB(FM) Bakersfield CA
KFRC-FM San Francisco CA
*KFRD(FM) Butte MT
KFRG(FM) San Bernardino CA
*KFRI(FM) Stanton TX
*KFRJ(FM) China Lake CA
KFRO-FM Gilmer TX
*KFRP(FM) Coalinga CA
KFRQ(FM) Harlingen TX
KFRR(FM) Woodlake CA
*KFRS(FM) Soledad CA
*KFRT(FM) Bay City TX
*KFRW(FM) Great Falls MT
KFRX(FM) Lincoln NE
*KFRY(FM) Pueblo CO
*KFRZ(FM) Green River WY
KFSH-FM Anaheim CA
*KFSI(FM) Rochester MN
*KFSK(FM) Petersburg AK
KFSO-FM Visalia CA
*KFSR(FM) Fresno CA
KFST-FM Fort Stockton TX
KFTE(FM) Breaux Bridge LA
*KFTG(FM) Pasadena TX
KFTK(FM) Florissant MO
KFTT(FM) Bagdad AZ
KFTX(FM) Kingsville TX
KFTZ(FM) Idaho Falls ID
KFUO-FM Clayton MO
KFVR-FM La Junta CO
KFWR(FM) Mineral Wells TX
KFXI(FM) Marlow OK
KFXJ(FM) Augusta KS
KFXR-FM Chinle AZ
KFXS(FM) Rapid City SD
*KFXT(FM) Sulphur OK
KFXX-FM Hugoton KS
*KFYE(FM) Kingsburg CA
KFYV(FM) Ojai CA
KFYX(FM) Texarkana AR
KFYZ-FM Bonham TX
KFZO(FM) Denton TX
KFZX(FM) Monahans TX
*KGAC(FM) Saint Peter MN
KGAP(FM) Clarksville TX
KGAS-FM Carthage TX
KGBA-FM Holtville CA
*KGB-FM San Diego CA
*KGBI-FM Omaha NE
*KGBM(FM) Randsburg CA
KGBR(FM) Gold Beach OR
KGBT-FM McAllen TX
KGBX-FM Nixa MO
*KGBY(FM) Sacramento CA
*KGCB(FM) Prescott AZ
*KGCR-FM Goodland KS
KGCX(FM) Sidney MT
KGDN(FM) Pasco WA
*KGDP-FM Santa Maria CA
KGEE(FM) Monahans TX
KGEN-FM Hanford CA
*KGFA(FM) Great Falls MT
*KGFC(FM) Great Falls MT
KGFM(FM) Bakersfield CA
KGFT(FM) Pueblo CO
KGFX-FM Pierre SD
KGFY(FM) Stillwater OK
KGGF-FM Fredonia KS
KGGG(FM) Sterling KS
KGGI(FM) Riverside CA
KGGL(FM) Missoula MT
KGGM(FM) Delhi LA
KGGO(FM) Des Moines IA
KGHL-FM Billings MT
*KGHP(FM) Gig Harbor WA
*KGHR(FM) Tuba City AZ
KGIM-FM Redfield SD
KGKL-FM San Angelo TX
KGKS(FM) Scott City MO
KGLC(FM) Miami OK
*KGLF(FM) Doss TX
KGLI(FM) Sioux City IA
KGLM-FM Anaconda MT

*KGLP(FM) Gallup NM
*KGLT(FM) Bozeman MT
*KGLV(FM) Shafter CA
KGLX(FM) Gallup NM
*KGLY(FM) Tyler TX
KGMG(FM) Oracle AZ
KGMN(FM) Kingman AZ
KGMO(FM) Cape Girardeau MO
KGMX(FM) Lancaster CA
KGMZ-FM Aiea HI
*KGNA-FM Arnold MO
KGNC-FM Amarillo TX
KGNN-FM Cuba MO
KGNT(FM) Smithfield UT
*KGNU-FM Boulder CO
*KGNV(FM) Washington MO
KGNZ(FM) Abilene TX
KGON(FM) Portland OR
KGOR(FM) Omaha NE
*KGOT(FM) Anchorage AK
*KGOU(FM) Norman OK
KGOZ(FM) Gallatin MO
KGPQ(FM) Monticello AR
*KGPR(FM) Great Falls MT
KGPZ(FM) Coleraine MN
KGRA(FM) Jefferson IA
KGRC(FM) Hannibal MO
*KGRD(FM) Orchard NE
KGRG(FM) Auburn WA
*KGRI(FM) Lebanon OR
KGRK(FM) Glenrock WY
*KGRM(FM) Grambling LA
KGRR(FM) Epworth IA
KGRS(FM) Burlington IA
KGRT-FM Las Cruces NM
KGRW(FM) Friona TX
*KGSF(FM) Anderson MO
KGSG(FM) Pasco WA
*KGSP(FM) Parkville MO
KGSR(FM) Bastrop TX
KGTM(FM) Rexburg ID
KGTR(FM) Larned KS
*KGTS(FM) College Place WA
KGTW(FM) Ketchikan AK
*KGUD(FM) Longmont CO
KGUL(FM) Edna TX
KGUM-FM Dededo GU
*KGVA(FM) Fort Belknap Agency MT
KGVE(FM) Grove OK
KGWY(FM) Gillette WY
KGY-FM McCleary WA
*KGZO(FM) Shafter CA
KHAD(FM) Mills WY
KHAK(FM) Cedar Rapids IA
KHAL(FM) Condon OR
KHAM(FM) Britt IA
*KHAP(FM) Chico CA
KHAY(FM) Ventura CA
KHAZ(FM) Hays KS
KHBM-FM Monticello AR
KHBQ(FM) Sulphur LA
KHBT(FM) Humboldt IA
KHBZ-FM Oklahoma City OK
KHCA(FM) Wamego KS
*KHCB-FM Houston TX
*KHCC-FM Hutchinson KS
*KHCD(FM) Salina KS
*KHCJ(FM) Jefferson TX
KHCK-FM Robinson TX
KHCL(FM) Arcadia LA
*KHCO(FM) Hayden CO
*KHCP(FM) Paris TX
KHCR(FM) Bismarck MO
*KHCS(FM) Palm Desert CA
*KHCT(FM) Great Bend KS
*KHDC(FM) Chualar CA
KHDR(FM) Lenwood CA
KHDV(FM) King City CA
*KHDX(FM) Conway AR
KHER(FM) Crystal City TX
KHEV(FM) Houma LA
KHEY-FM El Paso TX
*KHFD(FM) Hereford TX
KHFI-FM Georgetown TX
KHFM(FM) Santa Fe NM
*KHFR(FM) Santa Maria CA
KHGN(FM) Kirksville MO

KHGQ(FM) Quincy CA
KHHK(FM) Yakima WA
KHHL(FM) Leander TX
KHHT(FM) Los Angeles CA
KHHZ(FM) Oroville CA
*KHIB(FM) Bastrop TX
*KHID(FM) McAllen TX
KHIH(FM) Laramie WY
*KHII(FM) Cloudcroft NM
*KHIM(FM) Mangum OK
KHIP(FM) Gonzales CA
KHIX(FM) Carlin NV
*KHJC(FM) Lihue HI
KHJQ(FM) Susanville CA
KHJZ-FM Houston TX
KHKC-FM Atoka OK
KHKE(FM) Cedar Falls IA
KHKI(FM) Des Moines IA
KHKK(FM) Modesto CA
*KHKL(FM) Laytonville CA
KHKN(FM) Benton AR
KHKR-FM East Helena MT
KHKS(FM) Denton TX
*KHKV(FM) Kerrville TX
KHKX(FM) Odessa TX
KHKZ(FM) Mercedes TX
KHLA(FM) Jennings LA
KHLB(FM) Burnet TX
KHLE(FM) Mason TX
KHLL(FM) Richwood LA
KHLS(FM) Blytheville AR
*KHLV(FM) Helena MT
KHMB(FM) Hamburg AR
KHMC(FM) Goliad TX
KHME(FM) Winona MN
*KHMG(FM) Barrigada GU
*KHML(FM) Madisonville TX
*KHMS(FM) Victorville CA
KHMX(FM) Houston TX
KHMY(FM) Pratt KS
*KHNE-FM Hastings NE
KHNR-FM Honolulu HI
*KHNS(FM) Haines AK
KHOC(FM) Casper WY
KHOE(FM) Fairfield IA
KHOK(FM) Hoisington KS
KHOM(FM) Salem OR
KHOP(FM) Oakdale CA
KHOS-FM Sonora TX
KHOT-FM Paradise Valley AZ
KHOV-FM Wickenburg AZ
*KHOY(FM) Laredo TX
KHOZ-FM Harrison AR
KHPA(FM) Hope AR
KHPE(FM) Albany OR
KHPO(FM) Merced CA
KHPQ(FM) Clinton AR
*KHPR(FM) Honolulu HI
KHPT(FM) Conroe TX
*KHPU(FM) Brownwood TX
KHQT(FM) Las Cruces NM
KHRD(FM) Weaverville CA
*KHRI(FM) Hollister CA
KHRN(FM) Huron CA
KHRQ(FM) Baker CA
KHRT-FM Minot ND
KHSL-FM Paradise CA
*KHSR(FM) Crescent City CA
KHSS(FM) Walla Walla WA
KHST(FM) Lamar MO
*KHSU-FM Arcata CA
*KHTA(FM) Wake Village TX
KHTB(FM) Provo UT
KHTE-FM England AR
KHTN(FM) Planada CA
KHTO(FM) Milton-Freewater OR
KHTQ(FM) Hayden ID
KHTR(FM) Pullman WA
KHTS-FM El Cajon CA
KHTT(FM) Muskogee OK
KHTZ(FM) Navasota TX
KHUI(FM) Honolulu HI
KHUM(FM) Garberville CA
KHUS(FM) Bennington NE
KHUT(FM) Hutchinson KS
*KHVT(FM) Bloomington TX
KHWD(FM) Roseville CA

U.S. FM Stations by Call Letters

KHWI(FM) Hilo HI	KIOD(FM) McCook NE	*KJCH(FM) Coos Bay OR	KJWL(FM) Fresno CA	KKJK(FM) Ravenna NE
KHWK(FM) Tonopah NV	KIOI(FM) San Francisco CA	KJCK-FM Junction City KS	KJYE(FM) Grand Junction CO	KKJM(FM) Saint Joseph MN
KHWY(FM) Essex CA	KIOK(FM) Richland WA	*KJCM(FM) Snyder OK	*KJYL(FM) Eagle Grove IA	KKJO(FM) Saint Joseph MO
KHWZ(FM) Ludlow CA	KIOL(FM) Willis TX	*KJCQ(FM) Quincy CA	KJYO(FM) Oklahoma City OK	KKJQ(FM) Garden City KS
KHXS(FM) Merkel TX	KIOO(FM) Porterville CA	*KJCR(FM) Keene TX	*KJZA(FM) Drake AZ	KKJW(FM) Stanton TX
KHYI(FM) Howe TX	*KIOS-FM Omaha NE	KJCS(FM) Nacogdoches TX	KJZI(FM) Minneapolis MN	*KKJZ(FM) Long Beach CA
KHYL(FM) Auburn CA	KIOT(FM) Los Lunas NM	*KJCU(FM) Laytonville CA	KJZS(FM) Sparks NV	KKLA-FM Los Angeles CA
*KHYM(FM) Copeland KS	KIOW(FM) Forest City IA	*KJCV(FM) Country Club MO	KJZY(FM) Sebastopol CA	KKLB(FM) Elgin TX
KHYT(FM) Tucson AZ	KIOX-FM El Campo TX	KJCY(FM) Saint Ansgar IA	*KJZZ(FM) Phoenix AZ	KKLD(FM) Prescott Valley AZ
KHYZ(FM) Mountain Pass CA	KIOZ(FM) San Diego CA	KJDX(FM) Susanville CA	KKAC(FM) Vandalia MO	KKLH(FM) Marshfield MO
KHZR(FM) Potosi MO	*KIPO(FM) Honolulu HI	KJDY-FM Canyon City OR	KKAJ-FM Ardmore OK	KKLI(FM) Widefield CO
*KIAD(FM) Dubuque IA	KIPR(FM) Pine Bluff AR	KJEB(FM) Strasburg CO	KKAL(FM) Paso Robles CA	*KKLJ(FM) Klamath Falls OR
KIAI(FM) Mason City IA	KIQK(FM) Rapid City SD	KJEE(FM) Montecito CA	KKAW(FM) Albin WY	*KKLM(FM) Corpus Christi TX
KIAK-FM Fairbanks AK	KIQO(FM) Atascadero CA	KJEL(FM) Lebanon MO	KKBA(FM) Kingsville TX	KKLN(FM) Atwater MN
KIAQ(FM) Clarion IA	KIQQ-FM Newberry Springs CA	KJET(FM) South Bend WA	KKBB(FM) Bakersfield CA	*KKLP(FM) La Pine OR
*KIBC(FM) Burney CA	KIQX(FM) Durango CO	KJEZ(FM) Poplar Bluff MO	KKBC-FM Baker City OR	KKLR(FM) Poplar Bluff MO
KIBG(FM) Wallace ID	KIQZ(FM) Rawlins WY	KJFA(FM) Albuquerque NM	KKBD(FM) Sallisaw OK	KKLS-FM Sioux Falls SD
KIBR(FM) Sandpoint ID	KIRC(FM) Seminole OK	KJFM(FM) Louisiana MO	KKBG(FM) Hilo HI	*KKLT(FM) Texarkana AR
KIBS(FM) Bishop CA	KIRK(FM) Macon MO	*KJFT(FM) Arlee MT	KKBI(FM) Broken Bow OK	*KKLU(FM) Lubbock TX
KIBT(FM) Fountain CO	KISC(FM) Spokane WA	KJFX(FM) Fresno CA	KKBJ-FM Bemidji MN	KKLV(FM) Turrell AR
*KIBX(FM) Bonners Ferry ID	KISD(FM) Pipestone MN	*KJHA(FM) Houston AK	KKBL(FM) Monett MO	*KKLW(FM) Willmar MN
KIBZ(FM) Crete NE	KISF(FM) Las Vegas NV	*KJHK(FM) Lawrence KS	KKBN(FM) Twain Harte CA	KKLX(FM) Worland WY
KICA-FM Farwell TX	KISH(FM) Hagatna GU	KJIA(FM) Spirit Lake IA	KKBO(FM) Alamogordo NM	KKLY(FM) Pecos TX
*KICB(FM) Fort Dodge IA	*KISL(FM) Avalon CA	KJIK(FM) Duncan AZ	KKBQ(FM) Pasadena TX	KKLZ(FM) Las Vegas NV
KICD-FM Spencer IA	KISM(FM) Bellingham WA	*KJIL(FM) Copeland KS	KKBR(FM) Billings MT	KKMA(FM) Le Mars IA
KICK-FM Palmyra MO	KISN(FM) Belgrade MT	*KJIR(FM) Hannibal MO	KKBS(FM) Guymon OK	KKMG(FM) Pueblo CO
KICM(FM) Healdton OK	KISQ(FM) San Francisco CA	KJIW-FM Helena AR	KKBT(FM) Los Angeles CA	KKMI(FM) Burlington IA
KICR(FM) Coeur d'Alene ID	KISR(FM) Fort Smith AR	KJJJ(FM) Lake Havasu City AZ	KKBX(FM) Fargo ND	KKMJ-FM Austin TX
KICT-FM Wichita KS	KISS-FM San Antonio TX	KJJK-FM Fergus Falls MN	KKBZ(FM) Clarinda IA	KKMK(FM) Rapid City SD
KICX-FM McCook NE	KIST-FM Santa Barbara CA	KJJM(FM) Baker MT	KKCA(FM) Fulton MO	KKMR(FM) Arizona City AZ
KICY-FM Nome AK	*KISU-FM Pocatello ID	*KJJN(FM) San Angelo TX	KKCB(FM) Duluth MN	KKMT(FM) Columbia Falls MT
*KIDE(FM) Hoopa CA	KISV(FM) Bakersfield CA	KJJY(FM) West Des Moines IA	*KKCC(FM) Clovis NM	KKMV(FM) Rupert ID
KID-FM Idaho Falls ID	KISW(FM) Seattle WA	KJJZ(FM) Indio CA	KKCD(FM) Omaha NE	KKMX(FM) Tri City OR
*KIDH(FM) Jordan Valley OR	KISX(FM) Whitehouse TX	KJKB(FM) Jacksboro TX	KKCH(FM) Glenwood Springs CO	KKMY(FM) Orange TX
KIDI(FM) Guadalupe CA	KISY(FM) Gooding ID	KJKE(FM) Ingleside TX	KKCI(FM) Goodland KS	KKND(FM) Port Sulphur LA
KIDN-FM Hayden CO	KISZ-FM Cortez CO	KJKJ(FM) Grand Forks ND	*KKCJ(FM) Cannon AFB NM	KKNG-FM Newcastle OK
KIDX(FM) Ruidoso NM	KITE(FM) Port Lavaca TX	KJKK(FM) Dallas TX	KKCK(FM) Marshall MN	KKNL(FM) New London IA
KIFG-FM Iowa Falls IA	*KITG(FM) Gonzales TX	*KJKL(FM) Selma OR	KKCL(FM) Lorenzo TX	KKNM(FM) Gallup NM
KIFM(FM) San Diego CA	KITH(FM) Kapaa HI	KJKS(FM) Kahului HI	KKCN(FM) Ballinger TX	KKNN(FM) Delta CO
KIFS(FM) Ashland OR	KITI-FM Winlock WA	KJLH-FM Compton CA	KKCQ-FM Bagley MN	KKNS-FM Missoula MT
KIFX(FM) Roosevelt UT	KITN(FM) Worthington MN	KJLO-FM Monroe LA	*KKCR(FM) Hanalei HI	KKNU(FM) Springfield-Eugene OR
*KIGC(FM) Oskaloosa IA	KITO-FM Vinita OK	*KJLP(FM) Palmer AK	KKCS-FM Colorado Springs CO	KKOA(FM) Volcano HI
KIGL(FM) Seligman MO	KITS(FM) San Francisco CA	KJLS(FM) Hays KS	KKCT(FM) Bismarck ND	KKOB-FM Albuquerque NM
KIGN(FM) Burns WY	KITT(FM) Soda Springs ID	*KJLT-FM North Platte NE	KKCV(FM) Rozel KS	KKOK(FM) Morris MN
KIHK(FM) Rock Valley IA	KITX(FM) Hugo OK	*KJLU(FM) Jefferson City MO	KKCW(FM) Beaverton OR	KKOR(FM) Gallup NM
*KIHS(FM) Adel IA	KITY(FM) Llano TX	KJLV(FM) Hoxie AR	KKCY(FM) Colusa CA	KKOT(FM) Columbus NE
KIHT(FM) Saint Louis MO	KIVA(FM) Santa Rosa NM	KJLY(FM) Blue Earth MN	KKDA-FM Dallas TX	KKOW-FM Pittsburg KS
KIIK-FM Fairfield IA	KIVY-FM Crockett TX	KJMB(FM) Blythe CA	KKDC(FM) Dolores CO	KKOY(FM) Chanute KS
KIIM-FM Tucson AZ	KIWA-FM Sheldon IA	*KJMC(FM) Des Moines IA	KKDG(FM) Fresno CA	KKOZ-FM Ava MO
KIIS-FM Los Angeles CA	KIWI(FM) McFarland CA	KJMD(FM) Pukalani HI	KKDJ(FM) Delano CA	KKPL(FM) Cheyenne WY
KIIZ-FM Killeen TX	*KIWR(FM) Council Bluffs IA	KJMG(FM) Bastrop LA	KKDM(FM) Des Moines IA	KKPN(FM) Rockport TX
KIJI(FM) Tumon GU	KIXA(FM) Lucerne Valley CA	KJMH(FM) Lake Arthur LA	KKDQ(FM) Thief River Falls MN	KKPR-FM Kearney NE
KIJN-FM Farwell TX	KIXB(FM) El Dorado AR	KJMK(FM) Webb City MO	*KKDU(FM) El Dorado AR	KKPS(FM) Brownsville TX
KIKC-FM Forsyth MT	KIXC-FM Quanah TX	KJML(FM) Columbus KS	KKDV(FM) Walnut Creek CA	KKPT(FM) Little Rock AR
KIKD(FM) Lake City IA	KIXF(FM) Baker CA	KJMM(FM) Bixby OK	KKDY(FM) West Plains MO	KKQQ(FM) Volga SD
KIKF(FM) Cascade MT	KIXN(FM) Hobbs NM	KJMN(FM) Castle Rock CO	KKED(FM) Fairbanks AK	KKQY(FM) Hill City KS
KIKI-FM Honolulu HI	KIXO(FM) Sulphur OK	KJMO(FM) Jefferson City MO	KKEG(FM) Fayetteville AR	KKQZ(FM) Wellington CO
*KIKL(FM) Lafayette LA	KIXQ(FM) Joplin MO	KJMS(FM) Memphis TN	KKEN(FM) Duncan OK	KKRB(FM) Klamath Falls OR
KIKN-FM Salem SD	KIXR(FM) Ponca City OK	KJMX(FM) Reedsport OR	KKEQ(FM) Fosston MN	KKRC(FM) Granite Falls MN
KIKO-FM Claypool AZ	KIXS(FM) Victoria TX	KJMY(FM) Bountiful UT	*KKER(FM) Kerrville TX	*KKRD(FM) Enid OK
KIKS-FM Iola KS	KIXT(FM) Bay City OR	KJMZ(FM) Lawton OK	KKEX(FM) Preston ID	KKRE(FM) Hollis OK
KIKT(FM) Greenville TX	KIXW-FM Lenwood CA	KJNA-FM Jena LA	KKEZ(FM) Fort Dodge IA	KKRF(FM) Stuart IA
KIKV-FM Sauk Centre MN	KIXX(FM) Watertown SD	KJNI(FM) Rainier OR	KKFC(FM) Coalgate OK	KKRG(FM) Santa Fe NM
KIKX(FM) Ketchum ID	KIXY-FM San Angelo TX	*KJNP-FM North Pole AK	KKFG(FM) Bloomfield NM	*KKRI(FM) Pocola OK
KILJ-FM Mount Pleasant IA	KIXZ-FM Opportunity WA	KJNZ(FM) Hereford TX	*KKFI(FM) Kansas City MO	KKRK(FM) Coffeyville KS
KILO(FM) Colorado Springs CO	KIYS(FM) Jonesboro AR	KJOE(FM) Slayton MN	KKFM(FM) Colorado Springs CO	KKRL(FM) Carroll IA
KILR-FM Estherville IA	KIYX(FM) Sageville IA	KJOJ-FM Freeport TX	KKFR(FM) Glendale AZ	*KKRO(FM) Redding CA
KILS(FM) Minneapolis KS	KIZN(FM) Boise ID	KJOT(FM) Boise ID	KKFS(FM) Lincoln CA	KKRQ(FM) Iowa City IA
KILT-FM Houston TX	KIZS(FM) Broken Arrow OK	*KJOV(FM) Woodward OK	KKGB(FM) Sulphur LA	*KKRS(FM) Davenport WA
*KILV(FM) Castana IA	KIZZ(FM) Minot ND	KJOY(FM) Stockton CA	KKGL(FM) Nampa ID	KKRV(FM) Wenatchee WA
KILX(FM) Hatfield AR	*KJAB-FM Mexico MO	KJPW-FM Waynesville MO	KKHB(FM) Eureka CA	KKRW(FM) Houston TX
KIMN(FM) Denver CO	KJAC(FM) Timnath CO	KJQN(FM) Coalville UT	KKHI(FM) Kremmling CO	KKRY(FM) Miles City MT
KIMX(FM) Laramie WY	KJAE(FM) Leesville LA	*KJRF(FM) Lawton OK	KKHJ(FM) Pago Pago AS	KKRZ(FM) Portland OR
KIMY(FM) Watonga OK	KJAK(FM) Slaton TX	KJR-FM Seattle WA	KKHQ-FM Oelwein IA	*KKSB(FM) Scottsbluff NE
KINB(FM) Kingfisher OK	KJAM-FM Madison SD	KJRL(FM) Herington KS	KKHR(FM) Abilene TX	KKSD(FM) Milbank SD
KIND-FM Independence KS	KJAQ(FM) Seattle WA	*KJRT(FM) Amarillo TX	KKHT-FM Winnie TX	KKSF(FM) San Francisco CA
KINE-FM Honolulu HI	KJAS(FM) Jasper TX	KJRV(FM) Wessington Springs SD	KKIA(FM) Ida Grove IA	KKSI(FM) Eddyville IA
KING-FM Seattle WA	KJAV(FM) Alamo TX	KJSN(FM) Modesto CA	KKID(FM) Salem MO	KKSJ(FM) Maurice LA
*KINI(FM) Crookston NE	KJAX(FM) Jackson WY	KJSR(FM) Tulsa OK	KKIK(FM) Horseshoe Bend AR	KKSR(FM) Sartell MN
KINK(FM) Portland OR	KJAZ(FM) Thorndale TX	*KJTA(FM) Flagstaff AZ	KKIN-FM Aitkin MN	KKSS(FM) Santa Fe NM
KINL(FM) Eagle Pass TX	*KJBB(FM) Watertown SD	*KJTH(FM) Ponca City OK	KKIQ(FM) Livermore CA	KKST(FM) Oakdale LA
KINT-FM El Paso TX	KJBL(FM) Julesburg CO	KJTX(FM) Jefferson TX	KKIS-FM Soldotna AK	KKTC(FM) Taos NM
KINV(FM) Georgetown TX	KJBR(FM) Marked Tree AR	*KJTY(FM) Topeka KS	KKIT(FM) Angel Fire NM	KKTN(FM) Victor ID
KINX(FM) Great Falls MT	KJBX(FM) Trumann AR	KJUG-FM Tulare CA	KKIX(FM) Fayetteville AR	*KKTO(FM) Tahoe City CA
KINZ(FM) Humboldt KS	KJBZ(FM) Laredo TX	KJUL(FM) North Las Vegas NV	*KKJA(FM) Redmond OR	*KKTR(FM) Kirksville MO
KIOA(FM) Des Moines IA	*KJCC(FM) Carnegie OK	KJVC(FM) Mansfield LA	KKJG(FM) San Luis Obispo CA	KKTX-FM Kilgore TX
KIOC(FM) Orange TX	KJCD(FM) Longmont CO	*KJVH(FM) Longview WA	KKJJ(FM) Henderson NV	KKTY-FM Douglas WY

Broadcasting & Cable Yearbook 2006

D-623

U.S. FM Stations by Call Letters

KKTZ(FM) Lakeview AR	*KLFS(FM) Van Buren AR	KLQP(FM) Madison MN	KLXS-FM Pierre SD	KMJE(FM) Gridley CA
*KKUA(FM) Wailuku HI	*KLFV(FM) Grand Junction CO	KLQV(FM) San Diego CA	*KLXV(FM) Glenwood Springs CO	*KMJG(FM) Homer AK
KKUL(FM) Lincoln NE	KLFX(FM) Nolanville TX	*KLRB(FM) Stuart OK	KLYD(FM) Snyder TX	KMJI(FM) Ashdown AR
*KKUP(FM) Cupertino CA	KLGA-FM Algona IA	*KLRC(FM) Siloam Springs AR	KLYK(FM) Kelso WA	KMJJ-FM Shreveport LA
KKUS(FM) Tyler TX	KLGD(FM) Stamford TX	*KLRD(FM) Yucaipa CA	KLYR-FM Clarksville AR	KMJK(FM) Lexington MO
KKUU(FM) Indio CA	KLGL(FM) Richfield UT	*KLRE-FM Little Rock AR	*KLYT(FM) Albuquerque NM	KMJM-FM Columbia IL
*KKVO(FM) Altus OK	*KLGQ(FM) Grants NM	*KLRF(FM) Milton-Freewater OR	KLYV(FM) Dubuque IA	KMJQ(FM) Houston TX
KKVS(FM) Truth or Consequences NM	KLGR-FM Redwood Falls MN	*KLRH(FM) Sparks NV	KLYY(FM) Riverside CA	KMJR(FM) Portland TX
KKVU(FM) Stevensville MT	KLGT(FM) Buffalo WY	*KLRI(FM) Rigby ID	KLZA(FM) Falls City NE	KMJV(FM) Soledad CA
KKWD(FM) Edmond OK	KLHB(FM) Odem TX	KLRJ(FM) Aberdeen SD	KLZK(FM) Brownfield TX	KMJX(FM) Conway AR
KKWK(FM) Cameron MO	KLHI-FM Lahaina HI	KLRK(FM) Marlin TX	KLZN(FM) Susanville CA	KMJY-FM Newport WA
KKWQ(FM) Warroad MN	*KLHS-FM Lewiston ID	KLRM(FM) San Luis Obispo CA	KLZR(FM) Lawrence KS	KMKF(FM) Manhattan KS
KKWS(FM) Wadena MN	*KLHV(FM) Fort Collins CO	*KLRO(FM) Hot Springs AR	*KLZV(FM) Sterling CO	*KMKL(FM) North Branch MN
*KKXI(FM) Pittsburg TX	KLIL(FM) Moreauville LA	*KLRQ(FM) Clinton MO	KLZX(FM) Weston ID	KMKR(FM) Oakridge OR
KKXK(FM) Montrose CO	KLIP(FM) Monroe LA	KLRR(FM) Redmond OR	KLZY(FM) Powell-Cody WY	KMKS(FM) Bay City TX
KKXL-FM Grand Forks ND	KLIQ(FM) Hastings NE	KLRS(FM) Chico CA	KLZZ(FM) Waite Park MN	KMKT(FM) Bells TX
KKXS(FM) Shingletown CA	KLIR(FM) Columbus NE	*KLRV(FM) Billings MT	KMAC(FM) Gainesville MO	KMKX(FM) Willits CA
KKXX-FM Shafter CA	KLIT(FM) Fountain Valley CA	*KLRW(FM) Byrne TX	KMAD-FM Whitesboro TX	KMLA(FM) El Rio CA
KKYA(FM) Yankton SD	KLIX-FM Twin Falls ID	*KLRX(FM) Wapello IA	KMAG(FM) Fort Smith AR	KMLD(FM) Casper WY
KKYC(FM) Clovis NM	KLIZ-FM Brainerd MN	*KLRY(FM) Gypsum CO	KMAJ-FM Topeka KS	KMLE(FM) Chandler AZ
KKYN(FM) Plainview TX	KLJA(FM) Jamestown ND	KLRZ(FM) Larose LA	KMAK(FM) Orange Cove CA	KMLK(FM) El Dorado AR
KKYR-FM Texarkana TX	*KLJC(FM) Kansas City MO	*KLSA(FM) Alexandria LA	KMAQ-FM Maquoketa IA	KMLO(FM) Lowry SD
KKYS(FM) Bryan TX	KLJH(FM) Bayfield CO	KLSC(FM) Malden MO	KMAR-FM Winnsboro LA	KMLT(FM) Thousand Oaks CA
KKYY(FM) Whiting IA	KLJR-FM Santa Paula CA	*KLSE-FM Rochester MN	KMAT(FM) Seadrift TX	*KMLV(FM) Ralston NE
KKYZ(FM) Sierra Vista AZ	KLJT(FM) Jacksonville TX	*KLSI(FM) Moss Beach CA	KMAV-FM Mayville ND	*KMLW(FM) Moses Lake WA
KKZQ(FM) Tehachapi CA	*KLJV(FM) Scottsbluff NE	KLSK(FM) Great Falls MT	*KMBH-FM Harlingen TX	KMMG(FM) Weston OR
KKZR(FM) Bryant AR	KLJZ(FM) Yuma AZ	KLSN(FM) Hudson TX	*KMBI-FM Spokane WA	KMML-FM Amarillo TX
KKZX(FM) Spokane WA	*KLKA(FM) Globe AZ	*KLSP(FM) Angola LA	*KMBN(FM) Las Cruces NM	KMMM(FM) Madera CA
KKZY(FM) Bemidji MN	KLKC-FM Parsons KS	KLSR-FM Memphis TX	KMBQ(FM) Wasilla AK	KMMO-FM Marshall MO
KLAA(FM) Tioga LA	KLKK(FM) Clear Lake IA	KLSS-FM Mason City IA	KMBR(FM) Butte MT	KMMR(FM) Malta MT
KLAD-FM Klamath Falls OR	KLKL(FM) Minden LA	*KLSU(FM) Baton Rouge LA	KMBY-FM Seaside CA	KMMS-FM Bozeman MT
*KLAI(FM) Laytonville CA	*KLKM(FM) Kalispell MT	KLSX(FM) Los Angeles CA	KMCH(FM) Manchester IA	KMMT(FM) Mammoth Lakes CA
KLAK(FM) Durant OK	KLKO(FM) Elko NV	KLSY-FM Bellevue WA	KMCJ(FM) Colstrip MT	KMMX(FM) Tahoka TX
KLAL(FM) Wrightsville AR	KLKS(FM) Breezy Point MN	KLSZ-FM Van Buren AR	KMCK(FM) Siloam Springs AR	KMMY(FM) Muskogee OK
KLAN(FM) Glasgow MT	KLKX(FM) Rosamond CA	KLTA(FM) Breckenridge MN	KMCL-FM McCall ID	KMMZ(FM) Crane TX
KLAQ(FM) El Paso TX	KLKY(FM) Stanfield OR	KLTB(FM) Boise ID	KMCM(FM) Odessa TX	KMNA(FM) Prosser WA
KLAW(FM) Lawton OK	KLLC(FM) San Francisco CA	KLTC-FM Superior MT	KMCO(FM) McAlester OK	*KMNE-FM Bassett NE
KLAX-FM East Los Angeles CA	KLLE(FM) North Fork CA	KLTD(FM) Temple TX	KMCQ(FM) The Dalles OR	*KMNR(FM) Rolla MO
KLAZ(FM) Hot Springs AR	KLLI(FM) Dallas TX	KLTE(FM) Kirksville MO	KMCR(FM) Montgomery City MO	KMNT(FM) Chehalis WA
KLBA-FM Albia IA	KLLL-FM Lubbock TX	KLTG(FM) Corpus Christi TX	*KMCU(FM) Wichita Falls TX	*KMOC(FM) Wichita Falls TX
KLBC(FM) Durant OK	KLLN(FM) Newark AR	KLTH(FM) Lake Oswego OR	*KMCV(FM) High Point MO	KMOD-FM Tulsa OK
KLBJ-FM Austin TX	KLLP(FM) Chubbuck ID	KLTI-FM Ames IA	KMCX(FM) Ogallala NE	KMOE(FM) Butler MO
KLBL(FM) White Oak TX	KLLT(FM) Spencer IA	KLTN(FM) Houston TX	KMDL(FM) Kaplan LA	*KMOJ(FM) Minneapolis MN
KLBN(FM) Auberry CA	*KLLU(FM) Gallup NM	KLTO-FM McQueeney TX	KMDX(FM) San Angelo TX	KMOK(FM) Lewiston ID
KLBQ(FM) El Dorado AR	KLLY(FM) Oildale CA	KLTQ(FM) Lincoln NE	*KMDY(FM) Keokuk IA	KMON-FM Great Falls MT
*KLBR(FM) Bend OR	KLLZ-FM Walker MN	KLTR(FM) Caldwell TX	KMDZ(FM) Las Vegas NM	KMOO-FM Mineola TX
*KLBT(FM) Beaumont TX	KLMA(FM) Hobbs NM	*KLTU(FM) Mammoth AZ	KMEL(FM) San Francisco CA	KMOQ(FM) Baxter Springs KS
KLBU(FM) Pecos NM	*KLMF(FM) Klamath Falls OR	KLTW-FM Prineville OR	KMEM-FM Memphis MO	KMOR(FM) Scottsbluff NE
*KLBV(FM) Steamboat Springs CO	KLMG(FM) Jackson CA	KLTY(FM) Arlington TX	KMEN(FM) Mendota CA	*KMOU(FM) Roswell NM
KLBZ(FM) Reserve NM	KLMJ(FM) Hampton IA	KLUA(FM) Kailua-Kona HI	KMEO(FM) Mertzon TX	KMOZ-FM Grand Junction CO
KLCA(FM) Tahoe City CA	KLMM(FM) Morro Bay CA	KLUB(FM) Bloomington TX	KMEZ(FM) Belle Chasse LA	*KMPO(FM) Modesto CA
*KLCC(FM) Eugene OR	KLMO-FM Dilley TX	KLUC-FM Las Vegas NV	*KMFA(FM) Austin TX	*KMPQ(FM) Roseburg OR
*KLCD(FM) Decorah IA	KLMP(FM) Rapid City SD	KLUE(FM) Poplar Bluff MO	KMFB(FM) Mendocino CA	*KMPR(FM) Minot ND
KLCE(FM) Blackfoot ID	KLMR-FM Lamar CO	*KLUH(FM) Poplar Bluff MO	KMFC(FM) Centralia MO	KMPS-FM Seattle WA
KLCH(FM) Lake City MN	*KLMT(FM) Billings MT	KLUK(FM) Needles CA	KMFG(FM) Nashwauk MN	KMQA(FM) East Porterville CA
KLCI(FM) Princeton MN	KLMY(FM) Lincoln NE	KLUN(FM) Paso Robles CA	KMFM(FM) Premont TX	KMQS(FM) Victor ID
KLCM(FM) Lewistown MT	*KLMZ(FM) Fouke AR	KLUR(FM) Wichita Falls TX	KMFR(FM) Hondo TX	*KMQX(FM) Weatherford TX
*KLCO(FM) Newport OR	*KLNB(FM) Grand Island NE	KLUV-FM Dallas TX	KMFX-FM Lake City MN	KMRJ(FM) Rancho Mirage CA
*KLCQ(FM) Eaton CO	*KLND(FM) Little Eagle SD	*KLUX(FM) Robstown TX	KMFY(FM) Grand Rapids MN	KMRK-FM Odessa TX
KLCR(FM) Lakeview OR	*KLNE-FM Lexington NE	*KLVA(FM) Casa Grande AZ	KMGA(FM) Albuquerque NM	*KMRL(FM) Buras LA
*KLCU(FM) Ardmore OK	*KLNI(FM) Decorah IA	*KLVB(FM) Red Bluff CA	KMGC(FM) Camden AR	*KMRO(FM) Camarillo CA
*KLCV(FM) Lincoln NE	KLNO(FM) Fort Worth TX	*KLVC(FM) Magalia CA	KMGE(FM) Eugene OR	KMRQ(FM) Manteca CA
KLCX(FM) Saint Charles MN	*KLNR(FM) Panaca NV	KLVE(FM) Los Angeles CA	KMGG(FM) Denver CO	KMRR(FM) Globe AZ
KLCY-FM Vernal UT	KLNV(FM) San Diego CA	KLVF(FM) Las Vegas NM	KMGI(FM) Pocatello ID	KMRX(FM) El Dorado AR
KLDE(FM) Lake Jackson TX	KLNZ(FM) Glendale AZ	*KLVG(FM) Garberville CA	KMGJ(FM) Grand Junction CO	*KMSA(FM) Grand Junction CO
KLDG(FM) Liberal KS	KLOA-FM Ridgecrest CA	*KLVH(FM) San Luis Obispo CA	KMGK(FM) Glenwood MN	*KMSC(FM) Sioux City IA
KLDJ(FM) Duluth MN	*KLOB(FM) Thousand Palms CA	*KLVJ(FM) Julian CA	KMGL(FM) Oklahoma City OK	*KMSE(FM) Rochester MN
*KLDN(FM) Lufkin TX	KLOK-FM Greenfield CA	*KLVK(FM) Fountain Hills AZ	KMGM(FM) Montevideo MN	*KMSI(FM) Moore OK
KLDR(FM) Harbeck-Fruitdale OR	KLOL(FM) Houston TX	KLVM(FM) Prunedale CA	KMGN(FM) Flagstaff AZ	*KMSK(FM) Austin MN
*KLDV(FM) Morrison CO	*KLON(FM) Rockaway Beach OR	*KLVN(FM) Livingston CA	KMGO(FM) Centerville IA	*KMSL(FM) Mansfield LA
*KLDZ(FM) Medford OR	KLOO-FM Corvallis OR	KLVO(FM) Belen NM	KMGQ(FM) Goleta CA	*KMSM-FM Butte MT
KLEA-FM Lovington NM	*KLOP(FM) Ocean Park WA	*KLVP-FM Cherryville OR	KMGR(FM) Delta UT	KMSO(FM) Missoula MT
*KLEF(FM) Anchorage AK	KLOQ(FM) Winton CA	*KLVR(FM) Santa Rosa CA	KMGV(FM) Fresno CA	*KMSU(FM) Mankato MN
KLEN(FM) Cheyenne WY	KLOR-FM Ponca City OK	*KLVS(FM) Grass Valley CA	KMGW(FM) Casper WY	KMSW(FM) The Dalles OR
KLEO(FM) Kahaluu HI	KLOS(FM) Los Angeles CA	KLVT-FM Levelland TX	KMGX(FM) Bend OR	*KMSX(FM) Maumelle AR
KLER-FM Orofino ID	KLOU(FM) Saint Louis MO	*KLVU(FM) Sweet Home OR	KMGZ(FM) Lawton OK	KMTB(FM) Murfreesboro AR
KLES(FM) Mabton WA	*KLOV(FM) Winchester OR	*KLVV(FM) Ponca City OK	*KMHA(FM) Four Bears ND	*KMTC(FM) Russellville AR
*KLEU(FM) Lewistown MT	*KLOW(FM) Dripping Springs TX	*KLVW(FM) West Odessa TX	*KMHD(FM) Gresham OR	*KMTG(FM) San Jose CA
KLEY-FM Jourdanton TX	*KLOX(FM) Creston IA	*KLVY(FM) Fairmead CA	KMHK(FM) Hardin MT	*KMTH(FM) Maljamar NM
KLEZ(FM) Malvern AR	*KLOY(FM) Astoria OR	*KLWC(FM) Casper WY	KMHM(FM) Lutesville MO	KMTK(FM) Bend OR
*KLFC(FM) Branson MO	KLOZ(FM) Eldon MO	*KLWD(FM) Gillette WY	KMHT-FM Marshall TX	KMTN(FM) Jackson WY
*KLFF-FM San Luis Obispo CA	*KLPI-FM Ruston LA	*KLWG(FM) Lompoc CA	KMHX(FM) Windsor CA	*KMTS(FM) Glenwood Springs CO
*KLFH(FM) Ojai CA	KLPL-FM Lake Providence LA	*KLWS(FM) Moses Lake WA	*KMIH(FM) Mercer Island WA	KMTT(FM) Tacoma WA
*KLFM(FM) Great Falls MT	*KLPR(FM) Kearney NE	*KLWV(FM) Chugwater WY	KMIQ(FM) Robstown TX	KMTX-FM Helena MT
KLFN(FM) Sunburg MN	KLPW-FM Union MO	*KLXA-FM Alexandria LA	KMIT(FM) Mitchell SD	KMTY(FM) Holdrege NE
*KLFO(FM) Florence OR	KLPX(FM) Tucson AZ	KLXK(FM) Breckenridge TX	KMIX(FM) Tracy CA	*KMUD(FM) Garberville CA
*KLFR(FM) Reedsport OR	KLQL(FM) Luverne MN	KLXQ(FM) Mountain Pine AR	*KMJC-FM Mount Shasta CA	*KMUE(FM) Eureka CA

U.S. FM Stations by Call Letters

KMUL-FM Muleshoe TX	KNEN(FM) Norfolk NE	KNUJ-FM Sleepy Eye MN	KOMT(FM) Mountain Home AR	KPDQ-FM Portland OR
*KMUN(FM) Astoria OR	*KNEO(FM) Neosho MO	KNUQ(FM) Paauilo HI	KOMX(FM) Pampa TX	*KPDR(FM) Wheeler TX
*KMUW(FM) Wichita KS	KNES(FM) Fairfield TX	KNUW(FM) Santa Clara NM	KONA-FM Kennewick WA	*KPEB(FM) San Angelo TX
*KMVC(FM) Marshall MO	KNEV(FM) Reno NV	KNVO-FM Port Isabel TX	KOND(FM) Clovis CA	KPEK(FM) Albuquerque NM
KMVL-FM Madisonville TX	KNEX(FM) Laredo TX	KNVR(FM) Cameron TX	KONE(FM) Lubbock TX	KPEL-FM Abbeville LA
KMVR(FM) Mesilla Park NM	*KNFA(FM) Grand Island NE	KNWB(FM) Hilo HI	KONI(FM) Lanai City HI	KPEN-FM Soldotna AK
KMVX(FM) Jerome ID	KNFM(FM) Midland TX	*KNWC-FM Sioux Falls SD	KONO-FM Helotes TX	KPER(FM) Hobbs NM
*KMWR(FM) Brookings OR	KNFO(FM) Basalt CO	*KNWD(FM) Natchitoches LA	*KONQ(FM) Dodge City KS	KPEZ(FM) Austin TX
*KMWS(FM) Mount Vernon WA	*KNFR(FM) Butte MT	*KNWF(FM) Fergus Falls MN	KONY(FM) Saint George UT	*KPFA(FM) Berkeley CA
KMXA-FM Minot ND	KNFT-FM Bayard NM	KNWI(FM) Osceola IA	KOOC(FM) Belton TX	*KPFB(FM) Berkeley CA
KMXB(FM) Henderson NV	KNFX-FM Bryan TX	KNWJ(FM) Leone AS	KOOI-FM Jacksonville TX	*KPFC(FM) Callisburg TX
KMXC(FM) Sioux Falls SD	*KNGA(FM) Saint Peter MN	KNWM(FM) Madrid IA	KOOK(FM) Junction TX	*KPFK(FM) Los Angeles CA
KMXD(FM) Des Moines IA	*KNGM(FM) Emporia KS	*KNWO(FM) Cottonwood ID	KOOL-FM Phoenix AZ	KPFM(FM) Mountain Home AR
KMXE-FM Red Lodge MT	KNGS(FM) Coalinga CA	*KNWP(FM) Port Angeles WA	*KOOP(FM) Hornsby TX	KPFN(FM) Seward AK
KMXF(FM) Lowell AR	KNGY(FM) Alameda CA	*KNWR(FM) Ellensburg WA	KOOS(FM) North Bend OR	*KPFR(FM) Pine Grove OR
KMXG(FM) Clinton IA	*KNHA(FM) Hastings NE	*KNWS-FM Waterloo IA	KOOU(FM) Hardy AR	*KPFT(FM) Houston TX
KMXH(FM) Alexandria LA	*KNHC(FM) Seattle WA	*KNWV(FM) Clarkston WA	KOOZ(FM) Myrtle Point OR	*KPFX(FM) Fargo ND
KMXI(FM) Chico CA	*KNHM(FM) Bayside CA	*KNWY(FM) Yakima WA	*KOPB-FM Portland OR	*KPGB(FM) Pryor MT
KMXJ-FM Amarillo TX	*KNHT(FM) Rio Dell CA	KNXR(FM) Rochester MN	*KOPJ(FM) Sebeka MN	KPGG(FM) Ashdown AR
*KMXK(FM) Cold Spring MN	KNID(FM) Alva OK	KNXX(FM) Donaldsonville LA	*KOPN(FM) Columbia MO	*KPGR(FM) Pleasant Grove UT
KMXL(FM) Carthage MO	KNIK-FM Anchorage AK	*KNYD(FM) Broken Arrow OK	KOPR(FM) Butte MT	*KPGS(FM) Pagosa Springs CO
KMXM(FM) Colorado City AZ	*KNIL(FM) Jackson WY	KNYE(FM) Pahrump NV	KOPY-FM Alice TX	*KPHF(FM) Phoenix AZ
KMXN(FM) Osage City KS	KNIM-FM Maryville MO	KNYN(FM) Fort Bridger WY	KOQL(FM) Ashland MO	*KPHL(FM) Pahala HI
KMXP(FM) Phoenix AZ	KNIN-FM Wichita Falls TX	*KNYR(FM) Yreka CA	KOQO-FM Fresno CA	KPHR(FM) Ortonville MN
KMXQ(FM) Socorro NM	*KNIS(FM) Carson City NV	KNZA(FM) Hiawatha KS	KORA-FM Bryan TX	*KPHS(FM) Plains TX
KMXR(FM) Corpus Christi TX	KNIX-FM Phoenix AZ	*KOAB-FM Bend OR	KORD-FM Richland WA	KPHT(FM) Rocky Ford CO
KMXS(FM) Anchorage AK	KNJQ(FM) Manti UT	KOAI(FM) Fort Worth TX	KORI(FM) Mansfield LA	KPHW(FM) Kaneohe HI
*KMXT(FM) Kodiak AK	KNKK(FM) Needles CA	*KOAP(FM) Lakeview OR	*KORM(FM) Astoria OR	KPIG-FM Freedom CA
KMXV(FM) Kansas City MO	*KNKL(FM) North Ogden UT	KOAS(FM) Dolan Springs AZ	KORQ(FM) Baird TX	*KPIJ(FM) Junction City OR
KMXW(FM) Newton KS	KNKN(FM) Pueblo CO	KOBB-FM Bozeman MT	KORR(FM) American Falls ID	KPIN(FM) Pinedale WY
KMXX(FM) Imperial CA	KNKT(FM) Armijo NM	*KOBC(FM) Joplin MO	KORT-FM Grangeville ID	*KPJP(FM) Greenville CA
KMXY(FM) Grand Junction CO	*KNLB(FM) Lake Havasu City AZ	*KOBK(FM) Baker City OR	KOSB(FM) Perry OK	*KPKJ(FM) Mentmore NM
KMXZ-FM Tucson AZ	*KNLE-FM Round Rock TX	KOCN(FM) Pacific Grove CA	KOSI(FM) Denver CO	*KPKK(FM) Amargosa Valley NV
KMYI(FM) San Diego CA	KNLF(FM) Quincy CA	KOCP(FM) Camarillo CA	*KOSJ(FM) Mitchell NE	KPKX(FM) Phoenix AZ
KMYT(FM) Temecula CA	*KNLG(FM) New Bloomfield MO	*KOCU(FM) Altus OK	*KOSN(FM) Ketchum OK	KPKY(FM) Pocatello ID
KMYX-FM Arvin CA	*KNLH(FM) Cedar Hill MO	*KOCV(FM) Odessa TX	KOSO(FM) Patterson CA	KPLA(FM) Columbia MO
KMYY(FM) Rayville LA	*KNLK(FM) Santa Rosa NM	KODA(FM) Houston TX	KOSP(FM) Willard MO	KPLD(FM) Kanab UT
KMYZ-FM Pryor OK	*KNLM(FM) Marshfield MO	KODJ(FM) Salt Lake City UT	KOSS(FM) Rosamond CA	*KPLG(FM) Plains MT
KMZA(FM) Seneca KS	*KNLN(FM) Vienna MO	KODM(FM) Odessa TX	KOST(FM) Los Angeles CA	KPLM(FM) Palm Springs CA
KMZE(FM) Woodward OK	*KNLP(FM) Potosi MO	KODS(FM) Carnelian Bay CA	*KOSU(FM) Stillwater OK	KPLN(FM) San Diego CA
*KMZL(FM) Missoula MT	*KNLQ(FM) Cuba MO	KODZ(FM) Eugene OR	KOSY-FM Spanish Fork UT	KPLO-FM Reliance SD
*KMZO(FM) Hamilton MT	KNLR(FM) Bend OR	KOEA(FM) Doniphan MO	KOTE(FM) Eureka KS	KPLT-FM Paris TX
KMZT-FM Los Angeles CA	KNLT(FM) Walla Walla WA	KOEL-FM Cedar Falls IA	KOTM-FM Ottumwa IA	*KPLU-FM Tacoma WA
KMZU(FM) Carrollton MO	KNLV-FM Ord NE	KOFH(FM) Nogales AZ	*KOTO(FM) Telluride CO	*KPLW(FM) Wenatchee WA
KMZZ(FM) Bishop TX	*KNMA(FM) Socorro NM	KOFM(FM) Enid OK	KOTY(FM) Mason TX	KPLX(FM) Fort Worth TX
*KNAA(FM) Show Low AZ	KNMB(FM) Cloudcroft NM	KOFX(FM) El Paso TX	KOUL(FM) Sinton TX	KPLZ(FM) Seattle WA
KNAB-FM Burlington CO	*KNMC(FM) Havre MT	KOGA-FM Ogallala NE	KOUT(FM) Rapid City SD	*KPMB(FM) Plainview TX
*KNAC(FM) Earlimart CA	*KNMI(FM) Farmington NM	KOGM(FM) Opelousas LA	*KOUX(FM) Blytheville AR	KPMW(FM) Haliimaile HI
*KNAD(FM) Page AZ	KNMO(FM) Nevada MO	*KOGR(FM) Rosedale CA	KOUZ(FM) Blanchard LA	KPMX(FM) Sterling CO
KNAF-FM Fredericksburg TX	KNMZ(FM) Alamogordo NM	*KOHL(FM) Fremont CA	KOVE-FM Galveston TX	KPNC-FM Ponca City OK
*KNAG(FM) Grand Canyon AZ	*KNNB(FM) Whiteriver AZ	KOHM(FM) Lubbock TX	*KOWI(FM) Lamoni IA	KPND(FM) Sandpoint ID
*KNAI(FM) Phoenix AZ	KNNG(FM) Sterling CO	*KOHN(FM) Sells AZ	KOWZ-FM Blooming Prairie MN	*KPNE-FM North Platte NE
*KNAQ(FM) Prescott AZ	KNNK(FM) Dimmitt TX	KOHO-FM Leavenworth WA	KOXE(FM) Brownwood TX	*KPNO(FM) Norfolk NE
KNAS(FM) Nashville AR	KNNN(FM) Shasta Lake City CA	*KOHR(FM) Sheridan WY	KOYE(FM) Frankston TX	KPNT(FM) Sainte Genevieve MO
*KNAU(FM) Flagstaff AZ	*KNNU(FM) Newton IA	*KOHS(FM) Orem UT	KOYN(FM) Paris TX	KPNY(FM) Alliance NE
*KNBA(FM) Anchorage AK	KNOB(FM) Healdsburg CA	*KOHT(FM) Marana AZ	KOYT(FM) Elko NV	KPOA(FM) Lahaina HI
KNBB(FM) Ruston LA	KNOD(FM) Harlan IA	*KOIR(FM) Edinburg TX	KOZB(FM) Livingston MT	KPOC-FM Pocahontas AR
*KNBJ(FM) Bemidji MN	KNOE-FM Monroe LA	KOIT-FM San Francisco CA	KOZE(FM) Lewiston ID	KPOD-FM Crescent City CA
KNBQ(FM) Centralia WA	KNOF(FM) Saint Paul MN	*KOJI(FM) Okoboji IA	KOZI(FM) Chelan WA	KPOI-FM Honolulu HI
KNBT-FM New Braunfels TX	*KNOG(FM) Nogales AZ	*KOJO(FM) Lake Charles LA	*KOZO(FM) Branson MO	*KPOO(FM) San Francisco CA
*KNBU(FM) Baldwin City KS	*KNOM-FM Nome AK	KOJY(FM) Bloomfield IA	KOZT(FM) Fort Bragg CA	KPOR(FM) Emporia KS
KNBZ(FM) Redfield SD	*KNON(FM) Dallas TX	KOKF(FM) Edmond OK	KOZX(FM) Cabool MO	KPOS(FM) Post TX
*KNCA(FM) Burney CA	KNOR(FM) Krum TX	KOKO-FM Kerman CA	KOZY-FM Gering NE	KPOW-FM La Monte MO
KNCB-FM Vivian LA	KNOU(FM) Empire LA	KOKR(FM) Newport AR	KOZZ-FM Reno NV	KPPC(FM) Pocatello ID
*KNCC(FM) Elko NV	*KNOW-FM Minneapolis-St. Paul MN	*KOKS(FM) Poplar Bluff MO	*KPAC(FM) San Antonio TX	KPPL(FM) Poplar Bluff MO
KNCE(FM) Winters TX	KNOX-FM Grand Forks ND	KOKU(FM) Hagatna GU	*KPAE(FM) Erwinville LA	*KPPN(FM) Pollock Pines CA
KNCI(FM) Sacramento CA	*KNPR(FM) Las Vegas NV	KOKX-FM Keokuk IA	KPAK(FM) Alva OK	*KPPR(FM) Williston ND
*KNCM(FM) Appleton MN	KNRB(FM) Atlanta TX	KOKY(FM) Sherwood AR	KPAN-FM Hereford TX	KPPT-FM Toledo OR
KNCN(FM) Sinton TX	KNRG(FM) New Ulm TX	KOKZ(FM) Waterloo IA	*KPAQ(FM) Plaquemine LA	KPPV(FM) Prescott Valley AZ
KNCO-FM Grass Valley CA	*KNRI(FM) Bismarck ND	KOLA(FM) San Bernardino CA	KPAS(FM) Fabens TX	KPQ-FM Wenatchee WA
KNCQ(FM) Redding CA	KNRJ(FM) Payson AZ	*KOLI(FM) Electra TX	KPAT(FM) Orcutt CA	KPQP(FM) Ogden UT
*KNCT-FM Killeen TX	KNRK(FM) Camas WA	KOLL-FM Lonoke AR	KPAW(FM) Fort Collins CO	KPQX(FM) Havre MT
KNCU(FM) Newport OR	KNRQ(FM) Eugene OR	KOLS(FM) Dodge City KS	*KPBB(FM) Brownfield TX	*KPRA(FM) Ukiah CA
KNCW(FM) Omak WA	KNRX(FM) Sterling City TX	KOLT-FM Bridgeport NE	*KPBD(FM) Big Spring TX	KPRB(FM) Brush CO
KNCY-FM Auburn NE	*KNSE(FM) Austin MN	*KOLU(FM) Pasco WA	*KPBE(FM) Brownwood TX	KPRC-FM Salinas CA
KNDA(FM) Alice TX	KNSG(FM) Springfield MN	KOLV(FM) Olivia MN	*KPBJ(FM) Midland TX	*KPRD(FM) Hays KS
KNDD(FM) Seattle WA	*KNSQ(FM) Mount Shasta CA	KOLW(FM) Othello WA	KPBM(FM) McCamey TX	*KPRE(FM) Vail CO
KNDE(FM) College Station TX	*KNSR(FM) Collegeville MN	KOLX(FM) Barling AR	*KPBN(FM) Freer TX	*KPRF(FM) Amarillo TX
KNDK-FM Langdon ND	*KNSU(FM) Thibodaux LA	KOLY-FM Mobridge SD	KPBQ-FM Pine Bluff AR	*KPRG(FM) Hagatna GU
*KNDL(FM) Angwin CA	*KNSW(FM) Worthington-Marshall MN	KOLZ(FM) Cheyenne WY	*KPBS-FM San Diego CA	*KPRH(FM) Montrose CO
KNDR(FM) Mandan ND	KNSX(FM) Steelville MO	KOMA(FM) Oklahoma City OK	*KPBX-FM Spokane WA	KPRI(FM) Encinitas CA
KNDY-FM Marysville KS	KNTI(FM) Lakeport CA	KOMB(FM) Fort Scott KS	*KPCC(FM) Pasadena CA	*KPRJ(FM) Jamestown ND
KNEB-FM Scottsbluff NE	*KNTK(FM) Weed CA	KOMC-FM Kimberling City MO	KPCH(FM) Dubach LA	*KPRN(FM) Grand Junction CO
KNEC(FM) Yuma CO	*KNTN(FM) Thief River Falls MN	KOMG(FM) Ozark MO	KPCL(FM) Farmington NM	*KPRQ(FM) Sheridan WY
KNEI-FM Waukon IA	*KNTO(FM) Chowchilla CA	KOMP(FM) Las Vegas NV	KPCW(FM) Park City UT	KPRR(FM) El Paso TX
KNEK-FM Washington LA	*KNTU(FM) McKinney TX	KOMR(FM) Sun City AZ	KPDB(FM) Big Lake TX	KPRS(FM) Kansas City MO
KNEL-FM Brady TX	KNUE(FM) Tyler TX	KOMS(FM) Poteau OK	*KPDO(FM) Pescadero CA	*KPRU(FM) Delta CO

Broadcasting & Cable Yearbook 2006

D-625

U.S. FM Stations by Call Letters

KPRV-FM Heavener OK	KQLB(FM) Los Banos CA	KRAT(FM) Altamont OR	*KRLX(FM) Northfield MN	*KRUC(FM) Las Cruces NM
KPRW(FM) Perham MN	KQLF(FM) Cheyenne WY	KRAV(FM) Tulsa OK	*KRMB(FM) Bisbee AZ	KRUE(FM) Waseca MN
*KPRX(FM) Bakersfield CA	KQLK(FM) De Ridder LA	*KRAW(FM) Sterling AK	*KRMC(FM) Douglas AZ	KRUF(FM) Shreveport LA
KPSA-FM Lordsburg NM	KQLL-FM Owasso OK	KRAY-FM Salinas CA	KRMD-FM Shreveport LA	*KRUI-FM Iowa City IA
*KPSC(FM) Palm Springs CA	KQLM(FM) Odessa TX	KRAZ(FM) Santa Ynez CA	KRMH-FM Red Mesa AZ	KRUP(FM) Dillingham AK
KPSD(FM) Faith SD	KQLQ(FM) Columbia LA	KRBB(FM) Wichita KS	KRMQ-FM Clovis NM	*KRUX(FM) Las Cruces NM
*KPSH(FM) Coachella CA	KQLS(FM) Colby KS	*KRBD(FM) Ketchikan AK	KRMR(FM) Hayden CO	KRUZ(FM) Santa Barbara CA
KPSI-FM Palm Springs CA	KQLT(FM) Casper WY	KRBE(FM) Houston TX	KRMS-FM Osage Beach MO	KRVA-FM Campbell TX
KPSL-FM Bakersfield CA	*KQLU(FM) Belgrade MT	KRBI-FM Saint Peter MN	KRNA(FM) Iowa City IA	KRVB(FM) Nampa ID
KPSM(FM) Brownwood TX	*KQLV(FM) Bosque Farms NM	KRBK(FM) Booneville AR	KRNB(FM) Decatur TX	KRVE(FM) Brusly LA
KPSO-FM Falfurrias TX	KQLX-FM Lisbon ND	KRBL(FM) Idalou TX	*KRNE-FM Merriman NE	KRVF(FM) Kerens TX
*KPSU(FM) Goodwell OK	KQMA-FM Phillipsburg KS	*KRBM(FM) Pendleton OR	KRNG(FM) Fallon NV	KRVG(FM) Glenwood Springs CO
KPTE(FM) Durango CO	KQMB(FM) Midvale UT	KRBR(FM) Superior WI	KRNH(FM) Kerrville TX	KRVH(FM) Rio Vista CA
KPTI(FM) Crystal Beach TX	*KQMC(FM) Hawthorne NV	*KRBW(FM) Ottawa KS	*KRNL-FM Mount Vernon IA	KRVI(FM) Detroit Lakes MN
KPTX(FM) Pecos TX	KQMG-FM Independence IA	KRBZ(FM) Kansas City MO	*KRNM(FM) Chalan Kanoa-Saipan NP	KRVK(FM) Midwest WY
KPTY(FM) Missouri City TX	*KQMN(FM) Thief River Falls MN	*KRCB-FM Santa Rosa CA	KRNO(FM) Incline Village NV	KRVL(FM) Kerrville TX
*KPUB(FM) Flagstaff AZ	KQMO(FM) Shell Knob MO	*KRCC(FM) Colorado Springs CO	KRNQ(FM) Keokuk IA	KRVM-FM Eugene OR
KPUR-FM Canyon TX	KQMQ-FM Honolulu HI	KRCD(FM) Inglewood CA	*KRNU(FM) Lincoln NE	KRVN-FM Lexington NE
KPUS(FM) Gregory TX	KQMT(FM) Denver CO	KRCH(FM) Rochester MN	KRNV-FM Reno NV	KRVO(FM) Vancouver WA
*KPVL(FM) Postville IA	KQMX(FM) Clinton OK	KRCK(FM) Mecca CA	*KRNW(FM) Chillicothe MO	KRVR(FM) Copperopolis CA
KPVR(FM) Bowling Green MO	*KQNC(FM) Quincy CA	*KRCL(FM) Salt Lake City UT	KRNY(FM) Kearney NE	*KRVS(FM) Lafayette LA
KPVS(FM) Hilo HI	KQNG-FM Lihue HI	KRCQ(FM) Detroit Lakes MN	*KROA(FM) Grand Island NE	KRVV(FM) Bastrop LA
*KPVU(FM) Prairie View TX	KQNK-FM Norton KS	KRCS(FM) Sturgis SD	KROC-FM Rochester MN	KRVX(FM) Wimbledon ND
KPVW(FM) Aspen CO	KQNS-FM Lindsborg KS	*KRCU(FM) Cape Girardeau MO	KROG(FM) Grants Pass OR	KRVY-FM Starbuck MN
KPWB-FM Piedmont MO	KQOB(FM) Enid OK	KRCV(FM) West Covina CA	KROI(FM) Seabrook TX	KRWA-FM Waldron AR
KPWR(FM) Los Angeles CA	KQOD(FM) Stockton CA	KRCW(FM) Royal City WA	KROJ(FM) Vinton IA	*KRWG(FM) Las Cruces NM
KPWW(FM) Hooks TX	KQOL-FM Las Vegas NV	KRCX-FM Marysville CA	KROK(FM) South Fort Polk LA	KRWM(FM) Bremerton WA
KPXI(FM) Overton TX	KQOR(FM) Mena AR	KRCY-FM Lake Havasu City AZ	KROL(FM) Las Cruces NM	KRWN(FM) Farmington NM
KPXP(FM) Garapan-Saipan NP	*KQPD(FM) Ardmore OK	*KRDC-FM Saint George UT	KROM(FM) San Antonio TX	KRWP(FM) Stockton MO
KPYG(FM) Cambria CA	KQPM(FM) Ukiah CA	KRDE(FM) Globe AZ	KROQ(FM) Pasadena CA	KRWQ(FM) Gold Hill OR
*KPYR(FM) Craig CO	KQPR(FM) Albert Lea MN	KRDG(FM) Shingletown CA	KROR(FM) Hastings NE	*KRWT(FM) West Laramie WY
KPZA-FM Jal NM	KQPT(FM) Colusa CA	KRDJ(FM) New Iberia LA	*KROU(FM) Spencer OK	KRXB(FM) Beeville TX
KPZE-FM Carlsbad NM	KQQK(FM) Beaumont TX	KRDO-FM Colorado Springs CO	KROW(FM) Lovell WY	KRXL(FM) Kirksville MO
KPZK-FM Cabot AR	KQQL(FM) Anoka MN	*KRDR(FM) Red River NM	KROX-FM Buda TX	KRXO(FM) Oklahoma City OK
KQAK(FM) Bend OR	KQQT(FM) Gonzales TX	KRDS-FM New Prague MN	KROY(FM) Palacios TX	KRXQ(FM) Sacramento CA
*KQAL(FM) Winona MN	KQRA(FM) Brookline MO	KRDX(FM) Nogales AZ	KRPM(FM) Houston AK	KRXT(FM) Rockdale TX
KQAY-FM Tucumcari NM	KQRB(FM) Windom MN	KREC(FM) Brian Head UT	KRPQ(FM) Rohnert Park CA	KRXV(FM) Yermo CA
KQAZ(FM) Springerville-Eagar AZ	KQRC-FM Leavenworth KS	KRED-FM Eureka CA	*KRPR(FM) Rochester MN	KRXX(FM) Kodiak AK
KQBA(FM) Los Alamos NM	*KQRI(FM) Socorro NM	KREJ(FM) Medicine Lodge KS	*KRPS(FM) Pittsburg KS	KRXY(FM) Shelton WA
KQBB(FM) Center TX	KQRK(FM) Ronan MT	KREK(FM) Bristow OK	KRPT(FM) Devine TX	KRYD(FM) Norwood CO
KQBE(FM) Ellensburg WA	KQRN(FM) Mitchell SD	KREO(FM) Pine Bluffs WY	KRQK(FM) Lompoc CA	KRYE(FM) Rye CO
KQBL(FM) Billings MT	KQRQ(FM) Rapid City SD	KREP(FM) Belleville KS	KRQQ(FM) Tucson AZ	*KRYI(FM) Rye CO
KQBO(FM) Rio Grande City TX	KQRS-FM Golden Valley MN	KRER(FM) Hamilton City CA	KRQR(FM) Orland CA	KRYK(FM) Chinook MT
KQBR(FM) Lubbock TX	KQRT(FM) Las Vegas NV	KRES(FM) Moberly MO	KRQS(FM) Alberton MT	KRYS-FM Corpus Christi TX
KQBT(FM) Llano TX	KQRV(FM) Deer Lodge MT	KREU(FM) Roland OK	KRQT(FM) Castle Rock WA	*KRZA(FM) Alamosa CO
KQBU-FM Port Arthur TX	KQRX(FM) Midland TX	KREZ(FM) Chaffee MO	KRQU(FM) Laramie WY	KRZK(FM) Branson MO
KQBZ(FM) Seattle WA	*KQSC(FM) Santa Barbara CA	*KRFA-FM Moscow ID	*KRQZ(FM) Lompoc CA	KRZN(FM) Billings MT
KQCH(FM) Omaha NE	*KQSD-FM Lowry SD	*KRFC(FM) Fort Collins CO	*KRRC(FM) Portland OR	KRZQ-FM Sparks NV
KQCL(FM) Faribault MN	KQSI(FM) San Augustine TX	KRFM(FM) Show Low AZ	KRRG(FM) Laredo TX	KRZR(FM) Hanford CA
KQCM(FM) Joshua Tree CA	KQSK(FM) Chadron NE	KRFO-FM Owatonna MN	KRRK(FM) Lake Havasu City AZ	KRZS(FM) Flagstaff AZ
KQCR-FM Parkersburg IA	KQSM-FM Bentonville AR	*KRFR(FM) Bozeman MT	KRRM(FM) Rogue River OR	KRZY-FM Santa Fe NM
KQCS(FM) Bettendorf IA	KQSN(FM) Naches WA	KRFS-FM Superior NE	KRRN(FM) Kingman AZ	KRZZ(FM) San Francisco CA
KQCV-FM Shawnee OK	KQSR(FM) Yuma AZ	KRFX(FM) Denver CO	KRRO(FM) Sioux Falls SD	*KSAB(FM) Robstown TX
KQDD(FM) Osceola AR	KQSS(FM) Miami AZ	KRGI-FM Grand Island NE	KRRQ(FM) Lafayette LA	KSAJ-FM Abilene KS
KQDI-FM Great Falls MT	KQST(FM) Sedona AZ	KRGN(FM) Amarillo TX	KRRR(FM) Cheyenne WY	*KSAK(FM) Walnut CA
KQDJ-FM Valley City ND	KQSW(FM) Rock Springs WY	KRGT(FM) Indian Springs NV	KRRV-FM Alexandria LA	KSAL-FM Salina KS
KQDS-FM Duluth MN	KQTA(FM) Homedale ID	KRGY-FM Aurora NE	KRRW(FM) Saint James MN	KSAM-FM Huntsville TX
KQDY(FM) Bismarck ND	KQTP(FM) Saint Marys KS	*KRHS(FM) Overland MO	KRRX(FM) Burney CA	KSAN(FM) San Mateo CA
*KQED-FM San Francisco CA	KQTY-FM Borger TX	KRHV(FM) Big Pine CA	KRRY(FM) Canton MO	KSAR(FM) Thayer MO
KQEG(FM) La Crescent MN	KQTZ(FM) Hobart OK	KRIA(FM) Plainview TX	KRSB-FM Roseburg OR	KSAS-FM Caldwell ID
*KQEI-FM North Highlands CA	*KQUJ(FM) Ada OK	KRIG-FM Nowata OK	*KRSC-FM Claremore OK	*KSAU(FM) Nacogdoches TX
KQEO(FM) Idaho Falls ID	KQUL(FM) Lake Ozark MO	KRIO-FM Pearsall TX	*KRSD(FM) Sioux Falls SD	KSAY(FM) Fort Bragg CA
KQEW(FM) Fordyce AR	KQUR(FM) Laredo TX	KRIT(FM) Parker AZ	KRSE(FM) Yakima WA	*KSBA(FM) Coos Bay OR
KQEZ(FM) Houston AK	KQUS-FM Hot Springs AR	KRJB(FM) Ada MN	KRSH(FM) Healdsburg CA	*KSBC(FM) Nile WA
KQFC(FM) Boise ID	KQVO(FM) Calexico CA	KRJC(FM) Elko NV	KRSI(FM) Garapan-Saipan NP	KSBH(FM) Coushatta LA
*KQFE(FM) Springfield OR	KQVT(FM) Victoria TX	KRJM(FM) Mahnomen MN	KRSJ(FM) Durango CO	*KSBJ(FM) Humble TX
KQFM(FM) Hermiston OR	KQWB-FM Moorhead MN	KRJT(FM) Elgin OR	KRSK(FM) Molalla OR	KSBL(FM) Carpinteria CA
*KQFR(FM) Rapid City SD	KQWC-FM Webster City IA	KRKA(FM) Erath LA	KRSP-FM Salt Lake City UT	*KSBR(FM) Mission Viejo CA
KQFX(FM) Borger TX	*KQWS(FM) Omak WA	KRKC-FM King City CA	KRSQ(FM) Laurel MT	KSBS-FM Pago Pago AS
KQHC(FM) Burns OR	KQXC-FM Wichita Falls TX	KRKD(FM) Dermott AR	*KRSR(FM) Roswell NM	KSBV(FM) Salida CO
KQHN(FM) Oil City LA	KQXL-FM New Roads LA	KRKI(FM) Newcastle WY	*KRSS(FM) Tarkio MO	*KSBX(FM) Santa Barbara CA
*KQHR(FM) Hood River OR	KQXR(FM) Payette ID	*KRKL(FM) Walla Walla WA	KRST(FM) Albuquerque NM	KSBZ(FM) Sitka AK
KQHT(FM) Crookston MN	*KQXS(FM) Stephenville TX	KRKN(FM) Eldon IA	*KRSU(FM) Appleton MN	KSCA(FM) Glendale CA
KQIB(FM) Idabel OK	KQXT(FM) San Antonio TX	KRKR(FM) Lincoln NE	KRSV-FM Afton WY	KSCB-FM Liberal KS
KQIC(FM) Willmar MN	KQXX(FM) Mission TX	KRKS-FM Boulder CO	*KRSW(FM) Worthington MN	KSCH(FM) Sulphur Springs TX
KQID(FM) Alexandria LA	KQXY-FM Beaumont TX	KRKT-FM Albany OR	KRSX-FM Yermo CA	*KSCL(FM) Shreveport LA
KQIK-FM Lakeview OR	KQYB(FM) Spring Grove MN	KRKU(FM) McCook NE	KRSY-FM La Luz NM	KSCN(FM) Pittsburg TX
KQIS(FM) Basile LA	KQYK(FM) Lake Crystal MN	KRKV(FM) Las Animas CO	KRTH(FM) Los Angeles CA	KSCQ(FM) Silver City NM
KQIZ-FM Amarillo TX	KQZB(FM) Troy ID	KRKX(FM) Billings MT	KRTI(FM) Grinnell IA	KSCR-FM Benson MN
KQJZ(FM) Hutto TX	KQZR(FM) Craig CO	KRKZ(FM) Altus OK	*KRTM(FM) Temecula CA	*KSCS(FM) Fort Worth TX
KQKI(FM) Bayou Vista LA	KQZZ(FM) Devils Lake ND	*KRLF(FM) Pullman WA	KRTN-FM Raton NM	*KSCU(FM) Santa Clara CA
KQKK(FM) Walker MN	KRAB(FM) Green Acres CA	KRLI(FM) Malta Bend MO	KRTQ(FM) Sand Springs OK	*KSCV(FM) Springfield MO
*KQKL(FM) Selma CA	KRAI-FM Craig CO	*KRLJ(FM) La Junta CO	KRTR-FM Kailua HI	KSCY(FM) Big Sky MT
KQKQ-FM Council Bluffs IA	KRAJ(FM) Johannesburg CA	KRLS(FM) Knoxville IA	*KRTU(FM) San Antonio TX	KSD(FM) Saint Louis MO
KQKS(FM) Lakewood CO	KRAO-FM Colfax WA	KRLT(FM) South Lake Tahoe CA	KRTY(FM) Los Gatos CA	*KSDA-FM Agat GU
KQKY(FM) Kearney NE	KRAQ(FM) Jackson MN	KRLU(FM) Roswell NM	KRTZ(FM) Cortez CO	KSDB-FM Manhattan KS
KQLA(FM) Ogden KS	KRAR(FM) Brigham City UT	KRLW-FM Walnut Ridge AR	*KRUA(FM) Anchorage AK	*KSDJ(FM) Brookings SD

U.S. FM Stations by Call Letters

KSDL(FM) Sedalia MO
KSDM(FM) International Falls MN
KSDN-FM Aberdeen SD
KSDR-FM Watertown SD
*KSDS(FM) San Diego CA
KSDZ(FM) Gordon NE
KSEA(FM) Greenfield CA
KSEC(FM) Bentonville AR
KSED(FM) Sedona AZ
*KSEF(FM) Farmington MO
KSEG(FM) Sacramento CA
KSEH(FM) Brawley CA
KSEK-FM Girard KS
KSEL-FM Portales NM
KSEM-FM Seminole TX
KSEQ(FM) Visalia CA
*KSER(FM) Everett WA
KSES-FM Seaside CA
KSEY-FM Seymour TX
KSEZ(FM) Sioux City IA
*KSFC(FM) Spokane WA
*KSFH(FM) Mountain View CA
*KSFI(FM) Salt Lake City UT
KSFM(FM) Woodland CA
KSFQ(FM) White Rock NM
*KSFR(FM) Santa Fe NM
*KSFS(FM) Sioux Falls SD
KSFT-FM South Sioux City NE
KSFX(FM) Roswell NM
KSGC(FM) Tusayan AZ
KSGF-FM Ash Grove MO
*KSGN(FM) Riverside CA
*KSGR(FM) Portland TX
*KSGU(FM) Saint George UT
KSHA(FM) Redding CA
KSHE(FM) Crestwood MO
KSHF(FM) Cheyenne WY
*KSHI(FM) Zuni NM
KSHK(FM) Kekaha HI
KSHL(FM) Gleneden Beach OR
KSHN-FM Liberty TX
KSHR-FM Coquille OR
*KSHU(FM) Huntsville TX
KSIB-FM Creston IA
KSID-FM Sidney NE
KSII(FM) El Paso TX
KSIQ(FM) Brawley CA
KSIR-FM Bennett CO
*KSIT(FM) Rock Springs WY
*KSIV-FM Saint Louis MO
*KSJD(FM) Cortez CO
*KSJE(FM) Farmington NM
KSJJ(FM) Redmond OR
*KSJM(FM) Winfield KS
*KSJN(FM) Minneapolis MN
KSJO(FM) San Jose CA
KSJQ(FM) Savannah MO
*KSJR-FM Collegeville MN
*KSJS(FM) San Jose CA
KSJT-FM San Angelo TX
*KSJV(FM) Fresno CA
*KSJY(FM) Saint Martinville LA
KSJZ(FM) Jamestown ND
*KSKA(FM) Anchorage AK
KSKB(FM) Brooklyn IA
KSKD(FM) Livingston CA
KSKE-FM Vail CO
*KSKF(FM) Klamath Falls OR
KSKG(FM) Salina KS
KSKI-FM Sun Valley ID
KSKK(FM) Staples MN
KSKL(FM) Scott City KS
KSKS(FM) Fresno CA
KSKU(FM) Hutchinson KS
KSKX(FM) Security CO
KSKZ(FM) Copeland KS
*KSLC(FM) McMinnville OR
KSLE(FM) Wewoka OK
KSLG-FM Hydesville CA
KSLK(FM) Visalia CA
KSLQ(FM) Washington MO
KSLS(FM) Liberal KS
KSLT(FM) Spearfish SD
*KSLU(FM) Hammond LA
KSLV-FM Monte Vista CO
KSLX-FM Scottsdale AZ
KSLY-FM San Luis Obispo CA

KSLZ(FM) Saint Louis MO
KSMA-FM Osage IA
KSMB(FM) Lafayette LA
*KSMC(FM) Moraga CA
KSMD(FM) Pangburn AR
KSME(FM) Greeley CO
*KSMF(FM) Ashland OR
KSMG(FM) Seguin TX
KSMJ(FM) Shafter CA
KSML-FM Huntington TX
*KSMR(FM) Winona MN
*KSMS-FM Point Lookout MO
KSMT(FM) Breckenridge CO
KSMU(FM) Springfield MO
*KSMW(FM) West Plains MO
KSMX(FM) Clovis NM
KSMY(FM) Lompoc CA
KSND(FM) Monmouth OR
KSNE-FM Las Vegas NV
KSNI-FM Santa Maria CA
KSNN(FM) Saint George UT
KSNO-FM Snowmass Village CO
KSNP(FM) Burlington KS
KSNQ(FM) Twin Falls ID
KSNR(FM) Thief River Falls MN
*KSNS(FM) Medicine Lodge KS
KSNX(FM) Show Low AZ
KSNY-FM Snyder TX
KSOC(FM) Gainesville TX
KSOF(FM) Dinuba CA
*KSOH(FM) Wapato WA
KSOK-FM Winfield KS
KSOL(FM) San Francisco CA
KSOM(FM) Audubon IA
KSON-FM San Diego CA
KSOP-FM Salt Lake City UT
KSOQ-FM Escondido CA
*KSOR(FM) Ashland OR
*KSOS(FM) Las Vegas NV
KSOU-FM Sioux Center IA
*KSPB(FM) Pebble Beach CA
*KSPC(FM) Claremont CA
KSPE-FM Ellwood CA
KSPI-FM Stillwater OK
KSPK(FM) Walsenburg CO
*KSPL(FM) Kalispell MT
KSPN-FM Aspen CO
KSPO(FM) Dishman WA
KSPQ(FM) West Plains MO
KSPW(FM) Sparta MO
KSPZ(FM) Colorado Springs CO
KSQB-FM Dell Rapids SD
KSQL(FM) Santa Cruz CA
KSQQ(FM) Morgan Hill CA
*KSQX(FM) Springtown TX
KSQY(FM) Deadwood SD
KSRA-FM Salmon ID
*KSRC(FM) Kansas City MO
*KSRD(FM) Saint Joseph MO
KSRF(FM) Poipu HI
*KSRG(FM) Ashland OR
*KSRH(FM) San Rafael CA
KSRI(FM) Santa Cruz CA
KSRJ(FM) Juneau AK
KSRN(FM) Kings Beach CA
*KSRQ(FM) Thief River Falls MN
*KSRS(FM) Roseburg OR
KSRT(FM) Cloverdale CA
KSRV-FM Ontario OR
KSRW(FM) Independence CA
KSRX(FM) San Antonio TX
KSRZ(FM) Omaha NE
KSSA(FM) Ingalls KS
KSSB(FM) Calipatria CA
KSSC(FM) Ventura CA
KSSD(FM) Fallbrook CA
KSSE(FM) Arcadia CA
KSSH(FM) Ingalls KS
KSSI(FM) China Lake CA
KSSJ(FM) Fair Oaks CA
KSSK-FM Waipahu HI
KSSM(FM) Copperas Cove TX
KSSN(FM) Little Rock AR
KSSO(FM) Norman OK
KSSS(FM) Bismarck ND
*KSSU(FM) Durant OK
KSSW(FM) Nashville AR

*KSSX(FM) Chickasha OK
KSSZ(FM) Fayette MO
KSTB(FM) Crystal Beach TX
KSTH(FM) Holyoke CO
KSTJ(FM) Boulder City NV
*KSTK(FM) Wrangell AK
*KSTM(FM) Indianola IA
KSTN-FM Stockton CA
KSTO(FM) Hagatna GU
KSTP-FM Saint Paul MN
KSTQ-FM Plainview TX
KSTR-FM Montrose CO
KSTT-FM Los Osos-Baywood Park CA
KSTV-FM Dublin TX
*KSTX(FM) San Antonio TX
KSTY(FM) Canon City CO
KSTZ(FM) Des Moines IA
*KSUA(FM) Fairbanks AK
*KSUI(FM) Iowa City IA
*KSUL(FM) Port Sulphur LA
KSUP(FM) Juneau AK
*KSUR(FM) Mart TX
*KSUT(FM) Ignacio CO
*KSUU(FM) Cedar City UT
*KSUW(FM) Sheridan WY
KSUX(FM) Winnebago NE
KSVL(FM) Smith NV
*KSVR(FM) Mount Vernon WA
*KSVY(FM) Sonoma CA
*KSWC(FM) Winfield KS
KSWF(FM) Aurora MO
KSWG(FM) Wickenburg AZ
*KSWH(FM) Arkadelphia AR
KSWI(FM) Atlantic IA
KSWN(FM) McCook NE
*KSWP(FM) Lufkin TX
KSWW(FM) Montesano WA
KSXX(FM) Payson AZ
KSXY(FM) Middletown CA
KSYC-FM Yreka CA
KSYD(FM) Reedsport OR
*KSYE(FM) Frederick OK
*KSYM-FM San Antonio TX
KSYN(FM) Joplin MO
KSYR(FM) Benton LA
KSYU(FM) Corrales NM
KSYV(FM) Solvang CA
KSYZ-FM Grand Island NE
KSZR(FM) Oro Valley AZ
KTAA(FM) Big Sandy TX
KTAC(FM) Ephrata WA
KTAD(FM) Sterling CO
KTAG(FM) Cody WY
*KTAH(FM) Steamboat Springs CO
*KTAI(FM) Kingsville TX
KTAK(FM) Riverton WY
KTAL-FM Texarkana TX
KTAO(FM) Taos NM
*KTBG(FM) Warrensburg MO
KTBH-FM Kurtistown HI
*KTBJ(FM) Festus MO
KTBQ(FM) Nacogdoches TX
KTBT(FM) Collinsville OK
KTBZ-FM Houston TX
*KTCB(FM) Tillamook OR
*KTCC(FM) Colby KS
KTCE(FM) Payson UT
*KTCF(FM) Dolores CO
KTCH-FM Wayne NE
KTCL(FM) Fort Collins CO
KTCM(FM) Kingman KS
KTCN(FM) Eureka Springs AR
KTCO(FM) Duluth MN
KTCS-FM Fort Smith AR
*KTCU-FM Fort Worth TX
*KTCV(FM) Kennewick WA
KTCX(FM) Beaumont TX
KTCY(FM) Azle TX
KTCZ-FM Minneapolis MN
*KTDB(FM) Ramah NM
KTDE-FM Gualala CA
KTDK(FM) Sanger TX
KTDR(FM) Del Rio TX
*KTDU(FM) Trimble CO
KTDY(FM) Lafayette LA
KTEA(FM) Cambria CA
*KTEC(FM) Klamath Falls OR

KTED(FM) Douglas WY
KTEG(FM) Bosque Farms NM
*KTEI(FM) Placerville CO
*KTEO(FM) Wichita Falls TX
KTEP(FM) El Paso TX
*KTER(FM) Rudolph TX
KTEX(FM) Brownsville TX
KTEZ(FM) Mount Enterprise TX
KTFC(FM) Sioux City IA
KTFG(FM) Sioux Rapids IA
KTFM(FM) Floresville TX
KTFR(FM) Chelsea OK
KTFW-FM Glen Rose TX
KTFX-FM Warner OK
*KTFY(FM) Buhl ID
KTGA(FM) Saratoga WY
KTGL(FM) Beatrice NE
*KTGS(FM) Ada OK
KTGV(FM) Jonesville LA
*KTGW(FM) Fruitland NM
KTHC(FM) Sidney MT
*KTHI(FM) Caldwell ID
KTHK(FM) Idaho Falls ID
*KTHN(FM) La Junta CO
KTHP(FM) Hemphill TX
KTHQ(FM) Eagar AZ
KTHR(FM) Wichita KS
KTHS-FM Berryville AR
*KTHT(FM) Cleveland TX
KTHU(FM) Corning CA
KTHX-FM Dayton NV
KTIG(FM) Pequot Lakes MN
KTIJ(FM) Elk City OK
KTIL-FM Tillamook OR
*KTIS-FM Minneapolis MN
*KTJC(FM) Kelso WA
KTJJ(FM) Farmington MO
KTJM(FM) Port Arthur TX
*KTJO-FM Ottawa KS
KTJZ(FM) Tallulah LA
KTKB(FM) Hagatna GU
KTKC(FM) Springhill LA
KTKE(FM) Truckee CA
*KTKL(FM) Stigler OK
KTKO(FM) Beeville TX
KTKS(FM) Versailles MO
KTKU(FM) Juneau AK
KTKY(FM) Refugio TX
KTLB(FM) Twin Lakes IA
*KTLC(FM) Canon City CO
*KTLF(FM) Colorado Springs CO
KTLI(FM) El Dorado KS
*KTLN(FM) Thibodaux LA
KTLO-FM Mountain Home AR
KTLS-FM Holdenville OK
KTLT(FM) Anson TX
*KTLW(FM) Lancaster CA
*KTLX(FM) Columbus NE
KTLZ(FM) Cuero TX
KTMC-FM McAlester OK
KTMG(FM) Prescott AZ
*KTMH(FM) Colona MO
*KTMK(FM) Tillamook OR
*KTMO(FM) New Madrid MO
KTMQ(FM) Temecula CA
KTMT-FM Medford OR
KTMX(FM) York NE
*KTNA(FM) Talkeetna AK
*KTNE-FM Alliance NE
KTNR(FM) Kenedy TX
KTNT(FM) Eufaula OK
KTNX(FM) Arcadia MO
KTNY(FM) Libby MT
*KTOC(FM) Jonesboro AR
KTOH(FM) Kalaheo HI
KTOM-FM Marina CA
*KTOO(FM) Juneau AK
KTOR(FM) Westwood CA
*KTOT(FM) Spearman TX
KTOY(FM) Texarkana AR
KTOZ-FM Pleasant Hope MO
*KTPB(FM) Kilgore TX
*KTPH(FM) Tonopah NV
KTPI-FM Tehachapi CA
KTPK(FM) Topeka KS
*KTPL(FM) Pueblo CO
KTPO(FM) Kootenai ID

*KTPR(FM) Fort Dodge IA
*KTPS(FM) Pagosa Springs CO
*KTPT(FM) Rapid City SD
KTPZ(FM) Mountain Home ID
KTQM-FM Clovis NM
KTQX(FM) Bakersfield CA
KTRA-FM Farmington NM
KTRI-FM Mansfield MO
*KTRM(FM) Kirksville MO
KTRN(FM) White Hall AR
KTRQ(FM) Colt AR
KTRR(FM) Loveland CO
KTRS-FM Casper WY
*KTRU(FM) Houston TX
*KTRW-FM East Wenatchee WA
KTRX(FM) Dickson OK
KTRY-FM Bastrop LA
KTRZ(FM) Riverton WY
KTSC-FM Pueblo CO
*KTSD-FM Reliance SD
KTSE-FM Patterson CA
KTSJ(FM) Opelousas LA
KTSL(FM) Medical Lake WA
KTSM-FM El Paso TX
KTSO(FM) Glenpool OK
KTSR(FM) De Quincy LA
*KTST(FM) Oklahoma City OK
*KTSU(FM) Houston TX
*KTSW(FM) San Marcos TX
*KTSY(FM) Caldwell ID
KTTA(FM) Esparto CA
*KTTB(FM) Glencoe MN
KTTG(FM) Mena AR
KTTI(FM) Yuma AZ
*KTTK(FM) Lebanon MO
KTTL(FM) Alva OK
KTTN-FM Trenton MO
KTTR-FM Saint James MO
KTTS-FM Springfield MO
KTTX(FM) Brenham TX
KTUF-FM Kirksville MO
*KTUH(FM) Honolulu HI
KTUI-FM Sullivan MO
KTUM(FM) Tatum NM
KTUN(FM) Eagle CO
KTUX(FM) Carthage TX
KTUZ-FM Okarche OK
*KTVR-FM La Grande OR
KTWA(FM) Ottumwa IA
*KTWB(FM) Sioux Falls SD
*KTWD(FM) Wallace ID
KTWS(FM) Bend OR
*KTWV(FM) Los Angeles CA
*KTXB(FM) Beaumont TX
KTXC(FM) Lamesa TX
*KTXG(FM) Greenville TX
*KTXI(FM) Ingram TX
KTXJ-FM Jasper TX
*KTXK(FM) Texarkana TX
KTXM(FM) Hallettsville TX
*KTXN-FM Victoria TX
*KTXP(FM) Bushland TX
KTXR(FM) Springfield MO
*KTXT-FM Lubbock TX
KTXX(FM) Karnes City TX
KTXY(FM) Jefferson City MO
KTYD(FM) Santa Barbara CA
KTYL-FM Tyler TX
KTYN(FM) Thayne WY
KTYS(FM) Flower Mound TX
KTZA(FM) Artesia NM
KTZR-FM Green Valley AZ
KTZU(FM) Velva ND
KTZZ(FM) Conrad MT
*KUAC(FM) Fairbanks AK
KUAD-FM Windsor CO
*KUAF(FM) Fayetteville AR
KUAL-FM Brainerd MN
KUAM-FM Hagatna GU
*KUAP(FM) Pine Bluff AR
*KUAR(FM) Little Rock AR
*KUAT-FM Tucson AZ
*KUAZ-FM Tucson AZ
KUBB(FM) Mariposa CA
KUBE(FM) Seattle WA
KUBL-FM Salt Lake City UT
*KUBO(FM) Calexico CA

Broadcasting & Cable Yearbook 2006

D-627

U.S. FM Stations by Call Letters

KUBQ(FM) La Grande OR	*KUTX(FM) San Angelo TX	KVMX(FM) Banks OR	KWHF(FM) Harrisburg AR	*KWTM(FM) June Lake CA
*KUBS(FM) Newport WA	KUUB(FM) Sun Valley NV	KVNA-FM Flagstaff AZ	KWHL(FM) Anchorage AK	KWTO-FM Springfield MO
*KUCA(FM) Conway AR	KUUL(FM) East Moline IL	*KVNE(FM) Tyler TX	KWHQ-FM Kenai AK	KWTR(FM) Big Lake TX
KUCD(FM) Pearl City HI	KUUR(FM) Carbondale CO	*KVNF(FM) Paonia CO	KWHT(FM) Pendleton OR	*KWTS(FM) Canyon TX
*KUCI(FM) Irvine CA	KUUS(FM) San Joaquin CA	*KVNO(FM) Omaha NE	KWIC(FM) Topeka KS	*KWTU(FM) Tulsa OK
*KUCR(FM) Riverside CA	KUUU(FM) South Jordan UT	*KVOD(FM) Denver CO	KWID(FM) Las Vegas NV	*KWTW(FM) Bishop CA
*KUCV(FM) Lincoln NE	*KUUZ(FM) Lake Village AR	KVOE-FM Emporia KS	KWIE(FM) San Jacinto CA	KWTX-FM Waco TX
KUDD(FM) Roy UT	KUVA(FM) Uvalde TX	KVOM-FM Morrilton AR	KWIM(FM) Window Rock AZ	KWTY(FM) Cartago CA
KUDE(FM) Nephi UT	*KUVO(FM) Denver CO	KVOO-FM Tulsa OK	KWIN(FM) Lodi CA	KWUF-FM Pagosa Springs CO
*KUDL(FM) Kansas City KS	*KUWA(FM) Afton WY	KVOU-FM Uvalde TX	KWIQ-FM Moses Lake WA	*KWUR(FM) Clayton MO
*KUDU(FM) Tok AK	*KUWC(FM) Casper WY	*KVOV(FM) Carbondale CO	*KWIT(FM) Sioux City IA	*KWVA(FM) Eugene OR
KUEL-FM Fort Dodge IA	*KUWD(FM) Sundance WY	KVOX-FM Moorhead MN	KWIZ(FM) Santa Ana CA	KWVE-FM San Clemente CA
*KUER(FM) Salt Lake City UT	*KUWG(FM) Gillette WY	KVPI-FM Ville Platte LA	*KWJC(FM) Liberty MO	*KWVI(FM) Waverly IA
*KUFM(FM) Missoula MT	*KUWJ(FM) Jackson WY	KVPR(FM) Fresno CA	*KWJG(FM) Kasilof AK	*KWVK(FM) Kasilof AK
*KUFN(FM) Hamilton MT	*KUWL(FM) College AK	KVRD-FM Cottonwood AZ	KWJJ-FM Portland OR	KWVR-FM Enterprise OR
KUFO-FM Portland OR	*KUWN(FM) Newcastle WY	KVRE(FM) Hot Springs Village AR	KWJM(FM) Farmerville LA	KWVV-FM Homer AK
*KUFR(FM) Salt Lake City UT	*KUWP(FM) Powell WY	KVRH-FM Salida CO	*KWJT(FM) Rathdrum ID	*KWVZ(FM) Florence OR
KUFX(FM) San Jose CA	*KUWR(FM) Laramie WY	*KVRK(FM) Sanger TX	KWJZ(FM) Seattle WA	*KWWC-FM Columbia MO
*KUGS(FM) Bellingham WA	*KUWS(FM) Superior WI	*KVRN(FM) Marvell AR	KWKJ(FM) Windsor MO	KWWK(FM) Rochester MN
*KUHB-FM Saint Paul AK	KUWT(FM) Thermopolis WY	KVRO(FM) Stillwater OK	*KWKK(FM) Russellville AR	KWWR(FM) Mexico MO
*KUHF(FM) Houston TX	*KUWX(FM) Pinedale WY	KVRP-FM Haskell TX	*KWKL(FM) Grandfield OK	*KWWS(FM) Walla Walla WA
*KUHM(FM) Helena MT	*KUWZ(FM) Rock Springs WY	*KVRS(FM) Lawton OK	KWKM(FM) Saint Johns AZ	KWWV(FM) Santa Margarita CA
KUIC(FM) Vacaville CA	*KUYI(FM) Hotevilla AZ	KVRT(FM) Victoria TX	KWKQ(FM) Graham TX	KWWW-FM Quincy WA
KUJ-FM Walla Walla WA	KUZN(FM) Centerville TX	KVRV(FM) Monte Rio CA	*KWKR(FM) Leoti KS	*KWXC(FM) Grove OK
KUJZ(FM) Creswell OR	KUZZ-FM Bakersfield CA	KVRW(FM) Lawton OK	*KWKZ(FM) Charleston MO	KWXD(FM) Asbury MO
KUKA(FM) San Diego TX	*KVAB(FM) Clarkston WA	*KVRX(FM) Austin TX	*KWLD(FM) Plainview TX	KWXE(FM) Glenwood AR
KUKI-FM Ukiah CA	KVAK-FM Valdez AK	*KVSC(FM) Saint Cloud MN	KWLF(FM) Fairbanks AK	KWXX-FM Hilo HI
*KUKL(FM) Kalispell MT	KVAN(FM) Rock River WY	KVSP(FM) Anadarko OK	*KWLN(FM) Wilson Creek WA	*KWXY-FM Cathedral City CA
KUKN(FM) Longview WA	KVAR(FM) Pine Ridge SD	*KVSS(FM) Omaha NE	KWLR(FM) Maumelle AR	*KWYA(FM) Astoria OR
KUKU-FM Willow Springs MO	KVAS(FM) Ilwaco WA	*KVST(FM) Willis TX	*KWLT(FM) North Crossett AR	*KWYC(FM) Orchard Valley WY
KULE-FM Ephrata WA	KVAY(FM) Lamar CO	KVSV-FM Beloit KS	*KWLV(FM) Many LA	KWYE(FM) Fresno CA
KULF(FM) Brenham TX	*KVAZ(FM) Henryetta OK	*KVTI(FM) Tacoma WA	KWLY(FM) Moapa Valley NV	*KWYH(FM) Cheyenne WY
KULH(FM) Wheeling MO	KVBE(FM) Hanford CA	*KVTT(FM) Dallas TX	KWLZ-FM Warm Springs OR	*KWYI(FM) Kawaihae HI
KULL(FM) Abilene TX	*KVCF(FM) Freeman SD	KVTY(FM) Lewiston ID	*KWMD(FM) Kasilof AK	KWYK-FM Aztec NM
KULM(FM) Columbus TX	KVCK-FM Wolf Point MT	KVUU(FM) Pueblo CO	KWME(FM) Wellington KS	KWYL(FM) South Lake Tahoe CA
KULO(FM) Alexandria MN	*KVCL-FM Winnfield LA	KVUW(FM) Wendover NV	*KWMR(FM) Point Reyes Station CA	KWYN-FM Wynne AR
*KULV(FM) Ukiah CA	*KVCM(FM) Helena MT	KVVA-FM Apache Junction AZ	KWMT-FM Tucson AZ	*KWYQ(FM) Longview WA
KUMA-FM Pendleton OR	*KVCO(FM) Concordia KS	KVVF(FM) Santa Clara CA	*KWMU(FM) Saint Louis MO	KWYR-FM Winner SD
*KUMD-FM Duluth MN	*KVCR(FM) San Bernardino CA	KVVP(FM) Leesville LA	KWMW(FM) Maljamar NM	KWYS-FM Island Park ID
*KUMM(FM) Morris MN	*KVCX(FM) Gregory SD	KVVR(FM) Dutton MT	KWMX(FM) Williams AZ	KWYW(FM) Lost Cabin WY
*KUMR(FM) Rolla MO	*KVCY(FM) Fort Scott KS	KVVS(FM) Mojave CA	KWNA-FM Winnemucca NV	KWYY(FM) Casper WY
KUMU-FM Honolulu HI	*KVDP(FM) Dry Prong LA	KVVZ(FM) San Rafael CA	*KWND(FM) Springfield MO	KXAA(FM) Cle Elum WA
*KUMX(FM) North Fort Polk LA	KVEG(FM) Mesquite NV	KVWC-FM Vernon TX	KWNE(FM) Ukiah CA	KXAC(FM) Saint James MN
*KUNA(FM) La Quinta CA	*KVER(FM) El Paso TX	KVWG-FM Pearsall TX	KWNG(FM) Red Wing MN	KXAL-FM Tatum TX
*KUNC-FM Greeley CO	KVET-FM Austin TX	KVYB(FM) Santa Barbara CA	KWNM(FM) Hurley NM	KXAZ(FM) Page AZ
*KUND-FM Grand Forks ND	*KVFG(FM) Victorville CA	KVYN(FM) Saint Helena CA	KWNN(FM) Turlock CA	*KXBA(FM) Nikiski AK
*KUNI(FM) Cedar Falls IA	*KVFL(FM) Pierre SD	KWAK-FM Stuttgart AR	KWNO-FM Rushford MN	*KXBJ(FM) Victoria TX
*KUNM(FM) Albuquerque NM	*KVFM(FM) Beeville TX	*KWAR(FM) Waverly IA	KWNR(FM) Henderson NV	KXBL(FM) Henryetta OK
KUNQ(FM) Houston MO	*KVFR(FM) Laytonville CA	KWAV(FM) Monterey CA	KWNS(FM) Winnsboro TX	KXBN(FM) Cedar City UT
*KUNR(FM) Reno NV	KVFX(FM) Logan UT	KWAW(FM) Garapan-Saipan NP	KWNZ(FM) Sun Valley NV	*KXBR(FM) International Falls MN
*KUNV(FM) Las Vegas NV	KVGB-FM Great Bend KS	*KWAX(FM) Eugene OR	KWOA-FM Worthington MN	KXBT(FM) Taylor TX
*KUNY(FM) Mason City IA	KVGO(FM) Spring Valley MN	KWAY-FM Waverly IA	KWOD(FM) Sacramento CA	KXBX-FM Lakeport CA
*KUNZ(FM) Ottumwa IA	KVGS(FM) Laughlin NV	KWBF-FM North Little Rock AR	*KWOF-FM Hiawatha IA	*KXBZ(FM) Manhattan KS
*KUOI(FM) Moscow ID	*KVHS(FM) Concord CA	*KWBI(FM) Great Bend KS	*KWOI(FM) Carroll IA	*KXCI(FM) Tucson AZ
*KUOM-FM Saint Louis Park MN	KVHT(FM) Vermillion SD	KWBU-FM Waco TX	KWOL-FM Whitefish MT	KXCL(FM) Placerville CA
KUOO(FM) Spirit Lake IA	KVIB(FM) Sun City West AZ	*KWBX(FM) Salem OR	KWOW(FM) Clifton TX	*KXCM(FM) Twentynine Palms CA
*KUOP(FM) Stockton CA	KVIC(FM) Victoria TX	KWBZ(FM) Monroe City MO	KWOX(FM) Woodward OK	*KXCR(FM) El Paso TX
*KUOW(FM) Seattle WA	*KVID(FM) Barstow CA	KWCA(FM) Weaverville CA	KWOZ(FM) Mountain View AR	KXCS(FM) Cameron TX
KUPD-FM Tempe AZ	KVIL-FM Highland Park-Dallas TX	*KWCB(FM) Floresville TX	KWPK-FM Sisters OR	*KXCT(FM) Coleman TX
KUPH(FM) Mountain View MO	*KVIP-FM Redding CA	KWCC(FM) Muscatine IA	KWPN-FM West Point NE	*KXCV(FM) Maryville MO
KUPI-FM Idaho Falls ID	*KVIX(FM) Port Angeles WA	KWCD(FM) Bisbee AZ	*KWPR(FM) Lund NV	KXDC(FM) Estes Park CO
KUPL-FM Portland OR	*KVJC(FM) Globe AZ	KWCF(FM) Sheridan WY	KWPT(FM) Fortuna CA	KXDD(FM) Yakima WA
*KUPR(FM) Alamogordo NM	KVJM(FM) Hearne TX	KWCK-FM Searcy AR	KWPZ(FM) Lynden WA	KXDG(FM) Webb City MO
*KUPS(FM) Tacoma WA	*KVKI-FM Shreveport LA	KWCL-FM Oak Grove LA	KWQW(FM) Boone IA	*KXDJ(FM) Spearman TX
KUQL(FM) Wessington Springs SD	*KVKL(FM) Las Vegas NV	KWCO-FM Chickasha OK	*KWRB(FM) Bisbee AZ	KXDL(FM) Browerville MN
KUQQ(FM) Milford IA	KVLB(FM) Bend OR	*KWCR-FM Ogden UT	*KWRC(FM) Rapid City SD	KXDR(FM) Hamilton MT
KURB(FM) Little Rock AR	KVLC(FM) Hatch NM	KWCW(FM) Walla Walla WA	KWRD-FM Highland Village TX	KXDZ(FM) Templeton CA
*KURE(FM) Ames IA	KVLD(FM) Atkins AR	KWCX(FM) Willcox AZ	KWRF-FM Warren AR	*KXEI(FM) Havre MT
KURK(FM) Reno NV	KVLE-FM Gunnison CO	*KWDM(FM) West Des Moines IA	*KWRI(FM) Bartlesville OK	KXEZ(FM) Farmersville TX
KURM-FM South West City MO	KVLI-FM Lake Isabella CA	KWDO(FM) Waldo AR	*KWRK(FM) Window Rock AZ	KXFE(FM) Dumas AR
KURQ(FM) Grover Beach CA	*KVLK(FM) Belen NM	KWDQ(FM) Woodward OK	KWRL(FM) La Grande OR	*KXFF(FM) Cedar City UT
*KURT(FM) Jackson WY	KVLL-FM Woodville TX	KWEI-FM Fruitland ID	KWRP(FM) Pecos NM	KXFG(FM) Sun City CA
KURY-FM Brookings OR	KVLO(FM) Humnoke AR	KWEN(FM) Tulsa OK	KWRQ(FM) Clifton AZ	KXFM(FM) Santa Maria CA
*KUSC(FM) Los Angeles CA	*KVLQ(FM) Lincoln ND	KWES(FM) Ruidoso NM	*KWRR(FM) Ethete WY	KXFX(FM) Santa Rosa CA
*KUSD(FM) Vermillion SD	KVLR(FM) Twisp WA	KWEY-FM Weatherford OK	*KWRS(FM) Spokane WA	*KXGA(FM) Glennallen AK
*KUSF(FM) San Francisco CA	*KVLT(FM) Temple TX	*KWFC(FM) Springfield MO	KWRT-FM Boonville MO	KXGE(FM) Dubuque IA
KUSJ(FM) Harker Heights TX	*KVLU(FM) Beaumont TX	*KWFH(FM) Parker AZ	*KWRV(FM) Sun Valley ID	KXGJ(FM) Bay City TX
KUSN(FM) Dearing KS	KVLV-FM Fallon NV	*KWFJ(FM) Roy WA	KWRW(FM) Rusk TX	KXGL(FM) Amarillo TX
KUSO(FM) Albion NE	*KVLW(FM) Waco TX	*KWFL(FM) Roswell NM	*KWRX(FM) Redmond OR	KXGO(FM) Arcata CA
*KUSP(FM) Santa Cruz CA	KVLY(FM) Edinburg TX	KWFR(FM) San Angelo TX	KWSA(FM) Price UT	KXGT(FM) Jamestown ND
*KUSR(FM) Logan UT	*KVLZ(FM) Gatesville TX	KWFS-FM Wichita Falls TX	*KWSB-FM Gunnison CO	KXHT(FM) Marion AR
KUSS(FM) Carlsbad CA	KVMA-FM Shreveport LA	KWFX(FM) Woodward OK	*KWSC(FM) Wayne NE	*KXHV(FM) Sacramento CA
*KUSU-FM Logan UT	KVMG(FM) Dunnigan CA	KWGB(FM) Colby KS	KWSF(FM) Flandreau SD	KXIA(FM) Marshalltown IA
*KUSW(FM) Farmington NM	*KVMI(FM) Arthur ND	*KWGL(FM) Ouray CO	*KWSO(FM) Warm Springs OR	KXIO(FM) Clarksville AR
KUT(FM) Austin TX	*KVMR(FM) Nevada City CA	KWGO(FM) Burlington ND	KWSZ(FM) Lompoc CA	KXIT-FM Dalhart TX
*KUTE(FM) Ignacio CO	*KVMT(FM) Montrose CO	*KWGS(FM) Tulsa OK	*KWTD(FM) Ridgecrest CA	KXIX(FM) Bend OR
KUTT(FM) Fairbury NE	*KVMV(FM) McAllen TX	*KWGV(FM) Olympia WA	*KWTH(FM) Barstow CA	*KXJH(FM) Linton IN

Broadcasting & Cable Yearbook 2006

D-628

U.S. FM Stations by Call Letters

KXJM(FM) Portland OR
*KXJS(FM) Sutter CA
*KXJZ(FM) Sacramento CA
KXKC(FM) New Iberia LA
KXKK(FM) Park Rapids MN
KXKL-FM Denver CO
*KXKM(FM) McCarthy AK
KXKQ(FM) Safford AZ
KXKS-FM Shreveport LA
KXKT(FM) Glenwood IA
KXKU(FM) Lyons KS
KXKX(FM) Knob Noster MO
KXKZ(FM) Ruston LA
KXLB(FM) Livingston MT
*KXLC(FM) La Crescent MN
KXLE-FM Ellensburg WA
KXLM(FM) Oxnard CA
KXLP(FM) New Ulm MN
KXLR(FM) Fairbanks AK
KXLS(FM) Lahoma OK
KXLT-FM Eagle ID
*KXLU(FM) Los Angeles CA
*KXLV(FM) Amarillo TX
KXLY-FM Spokane WA
KXMO-FM Owensville MO
*KXMS(FM) Joplin MO
KXMT(FM) Taos NM
KXNA(FM) Springdale AR
*KXNE-FM Norfolk NE
KXNP(FM) North Platte NE
KXO-FM El Centro CA
KXOJ-FM Sapulpa OK
KXOL-FM Los Angeles CA
KXOO(FM) Elk City OK
KXOQ(FM) Kennett MO
KXOR-FM Thibodaux LA
*KXOT(FM) Tacoma WA
KXOX-FM Sweetwater TX
KXPC(FM) Lebanon OR
KXPK(FM) Evergreen CO
*KXPR(FM) Sacramento CA
KXPT(FM) Las Vegas NV
KXRA-FM Alexandria MN
*KXRD(FM) Victorville CA
*KXRI(FM) Amarillo TX
*KXRJ(FM) Russellville AR
KXRK(FM) Provo UT
KXRQ(FM) Roosevelt UT
KXRR(FM) Monroe LA
KXRS(FM) Hemet CA
*KXRT(FM) Idabel OK
KXRV(FM) Centerville UT
KXRX(FM) Walla Walla WA
KXRZ(FM) Alexandria MN
KXSA-FM Dermott AR
KXSB(FM) Big Bear Lake CA
KXSE(FM) Davis CA
KXSM(FM) Hollister CA
*KXSR(FM) Groveland CA
KXTC(FM) Thoreau NM
KXTE(FM) Pahrump NV
*KXTH(FM) Seminole OK
KXTN-FM San Antonio TX
KXTQ-FM Lubbock TX
KXTS(FM) Calistoga CA
KXTY(FM) Morro Bay CA
KXTZ(FM) Pismo Beach CA
*KXUA(FM) Fayetteville AR
*KXUL(FM) Monroe LA
KXUS(FM) Springfield MO
*KXWA(FM) Loveland CO
*KXWY(FM) Rye CO
KXXI(FM) Gallup NM
KXXK(FM) Hoquiam-Aberdeen WA
KXXL(FM) Gillette WY
KXXM(FM) San Antonio TX
KXXO(FM) Olympia WA
KXXQ(FM) Milan NM
KXXR(FM) Minneapolis MN
KXXS(FM) Dripping Springs TX
KXXY-FM Oklahoma City OK
KXXZ(FM) Barstow CA
KXYL-FM Brownwood TX
KXZM(FM) Felton CA
KYBA(FM) Stewartville MN
KYBB(FM) Canton SD
KYBE(FM) Frederick OK

KYBI(FM) Lufkin TX
*KYBJ(FM) Lake Jackson TX
KYBR(FM) Espanola NM
*KYCC(FM) Stockton CA
KYCH-FM Portland OR
KYCK(FM) Crookston MN
KYCS(FM) Rock Springs WY
*KYCU(FM) Clinton OK
KYCX-FM Mexia TX
KYDL(FM) Hot Springs AR
*KYDS(FM) Sacramento CA
KYDT(FM) Sundance WY
KYEE(FM) Alamogordo NM
KYEL(FM) Danville AR
KYEZ(FM) Salina KS
*KYFL(FM) Monroe LA
KYFM(FM) Bartlesville OK
*KYFO-FM Ogden UT
*KYFP(FM) Palestine TX
*KYFS(FM) San Antonio TX
*KYFW(FM) Wichita KS
KYGL(FM) Texarkana AR
KYGO-FM Denver CO
KYIS(FM) Oklahoma City OK
KYIX(FM) South Oroville CA
*KYJC(FM) Commerce TX
KYKC(FM) Byng OK
KYKD(FM) Bethel AK
*KYKL(FM) Tracy CA
KYKM(FM) Yoakum TX
KYKR(FM) Beaumont TX
KYKS(FM) Lufkin TX
KYKX(FM) Longview TX
KYKY(FM) Saint Louis MO
KYKZ(FM) Lake Charles LA
KYLA(FM) Homer LA
*KYLC(FM) Lake Charles LA
KYLD(FM) San Francisco CA
KYLS-FM Ironton MO
*KYLU(FM) Tehachapi CA
*KYLV(FM) Oklahoma City OK
KYLZ(FM) Tremonton UT
*KYMC(FM) Ballwin MO
KYMG(FM) Anchorage AK
*KYMI(FM) Los Ybanez TX
KYMO-FM East Prairie MO
KYMX(FM) Sacramento CA
KYNF(FM) Prairie Grove AR
KYNU(FM) Carrington ND
KYNZ(FM) Lone Grove OK
KYOD(FM) Glendo WY
KYOE(FM) Point Arena CA
KYOO-FM Halfway MO
*KYOR(FM) Newport OR
KYOT-FM Phoenix AZ
KYOX(FM) Comanche TX
*KYPL(FM) Yakima WA
KYQQ(FM) Arkansas City KS
*KYQX(FM) Weatherford TX
*KYRM(FM) Yuma AZ
*KYRV(FM) Concordia MO
KYRX(FM) Marble Hill MO
KYSC(FM) Fairbanks AK
KYSE(FM) El Paso TX
KYSF(FM) Bonanza OR
KYSJ(FM) Coos Bay OR
KYSL(FM) Frisco CO
KYSM-FM Mankato MN
KYSN(FM) East Wenatchee WA
KYSR(FM) Los Angeles CA
KYSS-FM Missoula MT
KYTC(FM) Northwood IA
KYTE(FM) Newport OR
KYTI(FM) Sheridan WY
KYTT-FM Coos Bay OR
KYTZ(FM) Walhalla ND
KYVA-FM Grants NM
*KYVT(FM) Yakima WA
*KYWA(FM) Wichita KS
*KYWH(FM) Lockwood MT
KYXK(FM) Gurdon AR
KYXX(FM) Ozona TX
KYXY(FM) San Diego CA
KYYA(FM) Billings MT
KYYI(FM) Burkburnett TX
KYYK(FM) Palestine TX
KYYS(FM) Kansas City MO

KYYT(FM) Goldendale WA
KYYX(FM) Minot ND
KYYY(FM) Bismarck ND
KYYZ(FM) Williston ND
KYZK(FM) Sun Valley ID
KYZX(FM) Pueblo West CO
KZAM(FM) Ganado TX
*KZAN(FM) Hays KS
KZAP(FM) Paradise CA
KZAT-FM Belle Plaine IA
*KZAZ(FM) Bellingham WA
KZBB(FM) Poteau OK
KZBD(FM) Spokane WA
KZBE(FM) Omak WA
*KZBJ(FM) Bay City TX
KZBK(FM) Brookfield MO
KZBL(FM) Natchitoches LA
KZBQ(FM) Pocatello ID
KZBR(FM) San Francisco CA
KZCD(FM) Lawton OK
KZCH(FM) Derby KS
*KZCL(FM) Logan UT
KZCR(FM) Fergus Falls MN
KZDX(FM) Burley ID
KZDY(FM) Cawker City KS
KZEG(FM) Clinton IA
KZEL-FM Eugene OR
KZEN(FM) Central City NE
KZEP-FM San Antonio TX
KZEW(FM) Wheatland WY
KZFM(FM) Corpus Christi TX
KZFN(FM) Moscow ID
*KZFR(FM) Chico CA
*KZFT(FM) Fannett TX
KZGL(FM) Cottonwood AZ
KZGZ(FM) Hagatna GU
KZHE(FM) Stamps AR
KZHK(FM) Saint George UT
KZHR(FM) Dayton WA
KZHT(FM) Salt Lake City UT
KZIA(FM) Cedar Rapids IA
KZID(FM) Orofino ID
*KZIG(FM) Cave City AR
KZII-FM Lubbock TX
KZIN-FM Shelby MT
KZIO(FM) Two Harbors MN
KZIQ-FM Ridgecrest CA
*KZJB(FM) Pocatello ID
KZJH(FM) Jackson WY
KZJK(FM) Saint Louis Park MN
KZKE(FM) Seligman AZ
KZKK(FM) Huron SD
KZKS(FM) Rifle CO
KZKX(FM) Seward NE
KZKZ-FM Greenwood AR
KZLA-FM Los Angeles CA
KZLE(FM) Batesville AR
KZLG(FM) Mansura LA
KZLK(FM) Rapid City SD
KZLS(FM) Great Bend KS
KZLT-FM East Grand Forks MN
*KZLU(FM) Inyokern CA
*KZLV(FM) Lytle TX
KZLZ(FM) Kearny AZ
KZMA(FM) Naylor MO
KZMG(FM) New Plymouth ID
KZMI(FM) Garapan-Saipan NP
KZMK(FM) Sierra Vista AZ
KZML(FM) Quincy WA
KZMN(FM) Kalispell MT
KZMP-FM Pilot Point TX
KZMQ-FM Greybull WY
KZMT(FM) Helena MT
*KZMU(FM) Moab UT
KZMX-FM Hot Springs SD
KZMY(FM) Bozeman MT
KZMZ(FM) Alexandria LA
*KZNA(FM) Hill City KS
KZNC(FM) Huron SD
KZNM(FM) Los Alamos NM
KZNN(FM) Rolla MO
KZOK-FM Seattle WA
KZON(FM) Phoenix AZ
KZOQ(FM) Missoula MT
KZOR(FM) Hobbs NM
KZOZ(FM) San Luis Obispo CA
KZPE(FM) Ford City CA

*KZPH(FM) Cashmere WA
*KZPI(FM) Deming NM
KZPK(FM) Paynesville MN
KZPL(FM) Lee's Summit MO
KZPO(FM) Lindsay CA
KZPR(FM) Minot ND
KZPS(FM) Dallas TX
KZPT(FM) Tucson AZ
KZQD(FM) Liberal KS
KZRB(FM) New Boston TX
KZRC(FM) Markham TX
KZRD(FM) Dodge City KS
*KZRI(FM) Welches OR
KZRK-FM Canyon TX
KZRM(FM) Chama NM
KZRO(FM) Dunsmuir CA
KZRQ-FM Mount Vernon MO
KZRR(FM) Albuquerque NM
KZRV(FM) Billings MT
KZRX(FM) Dickinson ND
KZRZ(FM) West Monroe LA
*KZSC(FM) Santa Cruz CA
*KZSD-FM Martin SD
*KZSE(FM) Rochester MN
KZSN(FM) Hutchinson KS
KZSP(FM) South Padre Island TX
KZSQ(FM) Sonora CA
KZSR(FM) Onawa IA
KZST(FM) Santa Rosa CA
*KZSU(FM) Stanford CA
KZTA(FM) Naches WA
KZTB(FM) Benton City WA
KZTQ(FM) Carson City NV
KZTR(FM) Franklin TX
KZUA(FM) Holbrook AZ
KZUL-FM Lake Havasu City AZ
*KZUM(FM) Lincoln NE
*KZUU(FM) Pullman WA
KZWA(FM) Moss Bluff LA
KZWB(FM) Green River WY
KZWY(FM) Sheridan WY
KZXY-FM Apple Valley CA
KZYP(FM) Pine Bluff AR
KZYQ(FM) Lake Village AR
KZYR(FM) Avon CO
*KZYX(FM) Philo CA
*KZYZ(FM) Willits CA
KZZA(FM) Muenster TX
KZZE(FM) Eagle Point OR
KZZI(FM) Belle Fourche SD
KZZK(FM) New London MO
KZZL-FM Pullman WA
KZZO(FM) Sacramento CA
KZZP(FM) Mesa AZ
KZZQ(FM) Winterset IA
KZZS(FM) Story WY
KZZT(FM) Moberly MO
KZZU(FM) Spokane WA
KZZX(FM) Alamogordo NM
KZZY(FM) Devils Lake ND
WAAC(FM) Valdosta GA
*WAAE(FM) New Bern NC
WAAF(FM) Worcester MA
WAAG(FM) Galesburg IL
WAAI(FM) Hurlock MD
*WAAJ(FM) Benton KY
WAAL(FM) Binghamton NY
WAAO-FM Andalusia AL
*WAAQ(FM) Onsted MI
WAAW(FM) Williston SC
WAAZ-FM Crestview FL
WABB-FM Mobile AL
*WABE(FM) Atlanta GA
WABK-FM Gardiner ME
WABO-FM Waynesboro MS
*WABR(FM) Tifton GA
WABT(FM) Mechanicville NY
WABX(FM) Evansville IN
WABZ(FM) Sherman IL
WACD(FM) Antigo WI
WACF(FM) Paris IL
*WACG-FM Augusta GA
WACL(FM) Elkton VA
WACO-FM Waco TX
WACR-FM Aberdeen MS
WADI(FM) Corinth MS
WADW(FM) Pickford MI

WAEB-FM Allentown PA
*WAEF(FM) Cordele GA
WAEG(FM) Evans GA
WAEL-FM Maricao PR
*WAER(FM) Syracuse NY
*WAES(FM) Lincolnshire IL
WAEV(FM) Savannah GA
WAEZ(FM) Greeneville TN
WAFC-FM Clewiston FL
WAFD(FM) Webster Springs WV
*WAFG(FM) Fort Lauderdale FL
*WAFJ(FM) Belvedere SC
WAFL(FM) Milford DE
WAFM(FM) Amory MS
WAFN-FM Arab AL
*WAFR(FM) Tupelo MS
WAFT(FM) Valdosta GA
WAFX(FM) Suffolk VA
WAFY(FM) Middletown MD
WAFZ-FM Immokalee FL
WAGF-FM Dothan AL
WAGH(FM) Fort Mitchell AL
WAGI-FM Gaffney SC
*WAGO(FM) Snow Hill NC
*WAGP(FM) Beaufort SC
WAGR-FM Lexington MS
WAGX(FM) Manchester OH
*WAHI-FM Augusta IL
WAHR(FM) Huntsville AL
*WAHS(FM) Auburn Hills MI
WAIB(FM) Tallahassee FL
*WAIC(FM) Springfield MA
WAID(FM) Clarksdale MS
*WAIH(FM) Potsdam NY
*WAII(FM) Hattiesburg MS
*WAIJ(FM) Grantsville MD
WAIL(FM) Key West FL
WAIN-FM Columbia KY
*WAIR(FM) Lake City MI
WAIV(FM) Cape May NJ
*WAJC(FM) Wilson NC
WAJI(FM) Fort Wayne IN
*WAJJ(FM) McKenzie TN
WAJK(FM) La Salle IL
WAJM(FM) Atlantic City NJ
WAJQ-FM Alma GA
*WAJS(FM) Tupelo MS
WAJV(FM) Brooksville MS
WAJZ(FM) Voorheesville NY
WAKB(FM) Wrens GA
*WAKD(FM) Sheffield AL
WAKG(FM) Danville VA
WAKH(FM) McComb MS
*WAKJ(FM) De Funiak Springs FL
*WAKL(FM) Flint MI
WAKO-FM Lawrenceville IL
WAKQ(FM) Paris TN
WAKS(FM) Akron OH
WAKT-FM Callaway FL
WAKU(FM) Crawfordville FL
WAKW(FM) Cincinnati OH
WAKX(FM) Narragansett Pier RI
WAKY-FM Springfield KY
WAKZ(FM) Sharpsville PA
WALC(FM) Charleston SC
*WALF(FM) Alfred NY
WALI(FM) Walterboro SC
WALK-FM Patchogue NY
*WALN(FM) Carrollton GA
WALR-FM La Grange GA
WALS(FM) Oglesby IL
WALV(FM) Cleveland TN
WALX(FM) Selma AL
WALY(FM) Bellwood PA
WALZ-FM Machias ME
WAMB-FM Nashville TN
*WAMC-FM Albany NY
*WAMH(FM) Amherst MA
WAMI-FM Opp AL
WAMJ(FM) Mableton GA
*WAMK(FM) Kingston NY
WAMO-FM Beaver Falls PA
*WAMP(FM) Jackson TN
*WAMQ(FM) Great Barrington MA
WAMR-FM Miami FL
*WAMU(FM) Washington DC
WAMW-FM Washington IN

U.S. FM Stations by Call Letters

WAMX(FM) Milton WV
WAMZ(FM) Louisville KY
WANB-FM Waynesburg PA
*WANC(FM) Ticonderoga NY
*WANM(FM) Tallahassee FL
WANT(FM) Lebanon TN
WANY-FM Albany KY
WAOA-FM Melbourne FL
WAOL(FM) Ripley OH
WAOQ(FM) Brantley AL
WAOR(FM) Niles MI
WAOX(FM) Staunton IL
*WAOY(FM) Gulfport MS
*WAPB(FM) Madison FL
*WAPD(FM) Campbellsville KY
WAPE-FM Jacksonville FL
*WAPJ(FM) Torrington CT
WAPL-FM Appleton WI
*WAPN(FM) Holly Hill FL
*WAPO(FM) Mount Vernon IL
*WAPR(FM) Selma AL
*WAPS(FM) Akron OH
*WAPX-FM Clarksville TN
*WAQB(FM) Tupelo MS
WAQE-FM Barron WI
*WAQG(FM) Ozark AL
*WAQL(FM) McComb MS
*WAQQ(FM) Rogers Heights MI
*WAQU(FM) Selma AL
*WAQV(FM) Crystal River FL
WAQX-FM Manlius NY
WAQY(FM) Springfield MA
WAQZ(FM) Fort Thomas KY
*WARC(FM) Meadville PA
*WARG(FM) Summit IL
WARH(FM) Granite City IL
WARM-FM York PA
*WARN(FM) Culpeper VA
WARO(FM) Naples FL
WARQ(FM) Columbia SC
WARU-FM Roann IN
WARV-FM Petersburg VA
WARW(FM) Bethesda MD
*WARY(FM) Valhalla NY
WASE-FM Radcliff KY
WASH(FM) Washington DC
WASJ(FM) Panama City Beach FL
WASK-FM Battle Ground IN
WASL(FM) Dyersburg TN
*WASM(FM) Natchez MS
*WASU-FM Boone NC
*WASW(FM) Waycross GA
WATD-FM Marshfield MA
WATG(FM) Trion GA
*WATI(FM) Vincennes IN
*WATP(FM) Laurel MS
WATQ(FM) Chetek WI
*WATU(FM) Port Gibson MS
*WATY(FM) Folkston GA
WATZ-FM Alpena MI
*WAUA(FM) Petersburg WV
WAUH(FM) Wautoma WI
*WAUI(FM) Shelby OH
*WAUM(FM) Duck Hill MS
WAUN(FM) Kewaunee WI
*WAUO(FM) Hohenwald TN
*WAUQ(FM) Charles City VA
*WAUS(FM) Berrien Springs MI
*WAUT-FM Tullahoma TN
*WAUV(FM) Ripley TN
*WAUZ(FM) Greensburg IN
WAVA(FM) Arlington VA
WAVC(FM) Mio MI
WAVF(FM) Hanahan SC
WAVH(FM) Daphne AL
*WAVI(FM) Oxford MS
WAVJ(FM) Princeton KY
WAVK(FM) Marathon FL
*WAVM(FM) Maynard MA
*WAVQ(FM) Key West FL
WAVR(FM) Waverly NY
WAVT-FM Pottsville PA
WAVV(FM) Marco FL
WAVW(FM) Stuart FL
*WAVX(FM) Schuyler Falls NY
WAWC(FM) Syracuse IN
*WAWF(FM) Kankakee IL

*WAWH(FM) Dublin GA
*WAWI(FM) Lawrenceburg TN
*WAWJ(FM) Marion IL
*WAWL-FM Red Bank TN
*WAWN-FM Franklin PA
WAWZ(FM) Zarephath NJ
*WAXG(FM) Mt. Sterling KY
WAXI(FM) Rockville IN
WAXJ(FM) Frederiksted VI
WAXL(FM) Santa Claus IN
WAXM(FM) Big Stone Gap VA
WAXQ(FM) New York NY
*WAXR(FM) Geneseo IL
WAXS(FM) Oak Hill WV
*WAXU(FM) Troy AL
WAXX(FM) Eau Claire WI
WAXZ(FM) Georgetown OH
WAYA(FM) Spring City TN
WAYB-FM Graysville TN
WAYC(FM) Bedford PA
*WAYD(FM) Auburn KY
*WAYF(FM) West Palm Beach FL
*WAYG(FM) Grand Rapids MI
*WAYH(FM) Harvest AL
*WAYJ(FM) Fort Myers FL
*WAYK(FM) Kalamazoo MI
*WAYL(FM) Saint Augustine FL
*WAYM(FM) Columbia TN
*WAYQ(FM) Clarksville TN
*WAYR-FM Brunswick GA
*WAYT(FM) Thomasville GA
WAYV(FM) Atlantic City NJ
*WAYW(FM) New Johnsonville TN
WAYZ(FM) Hagerstown MD
WAZA(FM) Liberty MS
*WAZD(FM) Savannah TN
WAZO(FM) Southport NC
*WAZP(FM) Cape Charles VA
WAZR(FM) Woodstock VA
WAZS-FM McClellanville SC
WAZU(FM) Circleville OH
WAZX-FM Cleveland GA
*WAZY-FM Lafayette IN
*WBAA-FM West Lafayette IN
WBAB(FM) Babylon NY
WBAD(FM) Leland MS
*WBAI(FM) New York NY
WBAM-FM Montgomery AL
WBAQ(FM) Greenville MS
WBAR-FM Lake Luzerne NY
WBAV-FM Gastonia NC
WBAW-FM Barnwell SC
*WBAZ(FM) Bridgehampton NY
WBBA-FM Pittsfield IL
WBBB(FM) Raleigh NC
*WBBC-FM Blackstone VA
WBBG(FM) Niles OH
WBBI(FM) Endwell NY
WBBK-FM Blakely GA
WBBM-FM Chicago IL
*WBBN(FM) Taylorsville MS
WBBO(FM) Ocean Acres NJ
WBBQ-FM Augusta GA
WBBS(FM) Fulton NY
WBBT-FM Powhatan VA
WBBV(FM) Vicksburg MS
WBCG(FM) Murdock FL
WBCH-FM Hastings MI
*WBCI(FM) Bath ME
*WBCJ(FM) Spencerville OH
*WBCL(FM) Fort Wayne IN
WBCM(FM) Boyne City MI
WBCN(FM) Boston MA
*WBCR-FM Beloit WI
WBCT(FM) Grand Rapids MI
*WBCX(FM) Gainesville GA
*WBCY(FM) Archbold OH
WBDB(FM) Ogdensburg NY
WBDC(FM) Huntingburg IN
*WBDG(FM) Indianapolis IN
WBDI(FM) Copenhagen NY
WBDL(FM) Algoma WI
WBDR(FM) Cape Vincent NY
WBDX(FM) Trenton GA
WBEA(FM) Southold NY
WBEB(FM) Philadelphia PA

WBEC-FM Pittsfield MA
WBEE-FM Rochester NY
WBEI(FM) Reform AL
*WBEL(FM) Cairo IL
WBEN-FM Philadelphia PA
*WBEQ(FM) Morris IL
*WBER(FM) Rochester NY
*WBEW(FM) Chesterton IN
WBEY-FM Crisfield MD
*WBEZ(FM) Chicago IL
WBFA(FM) Smiths AL
WBFB(FM) Belfast ME
WBFG(FM) Parker's Crossroads TN
*WBFH(FM) Bloomfield Hills MI
*WBFI(FM) McDaniels KY
*WBFJ-FM Winston-Salem NC
WBFM(FM) Sheboygan WI
*WBFO(FM) Buffalo NY
*WBFR(FM) Birmingham AL
WBFX(FM) Grand Rapids MI
*WBFY(FM) Pinehurst NC
WBFZ(FM) Selma AL
WBGA(FM) Saint Simons Island GA
WBGB(FM) Ponte Vedra Beach FL
*WBGD(FM) Brick Township NJ
WBGE(FM) Bainbridge GA
WBGF(FM) Belle Glade FL
WBGG-FM Fort Lauderdale FL
WBGJ(FM) Sylvan Beach NY
WBGK(FM) Newport Village NY
*WBGL(FM) Champaign IL
*WBGM(FM) New Berlin PA
*WBGO(FM) Newark NJ
WBGQ(FM) Bulls Gap TN
WBGU(FM) Bowling Green OH
WBGV(FM) Marlette MI
*WBGW(FM) Fort Branch IN
*WBGY(FM) Naples FL
WBHB-FM Bridgewater VA
WBHC-FM Hampton SC
*WBHD(FM) Olyphant PA
WBHJ(FM) Tuscaloosa AL
*WBHK(FM) Warrior AL
*WBHM(FM) Birmingham AL
*WBHT(FM) Mountain Top PA
*WBHW(FM) Loogootee IN
WBHX(FM) Tuckerton NJ
*WBHY-FM Mobile AL
*WBHZ(FM) Elkins WV
*WBIA(FM) Shelbyville TN
*WBIE(FM) Delphos OH
WBIG-FM Washington DC
*WBIK-FM Pleasant City OH
*WBIM-FM Bridgewater MA
WBIO(FM) Philpot KY
*WBIY(FM) La Belle FL
WBIZ-FM Eau Claire WI
*WBJB-FM Lincroft NJ
*WBJC(FM) Baltimore MD
*WBJD(FM) Atlantic Beach NC
WBJI(FM) Blackduck MN
*WBJV(FM) Steubenville OH
*WBJW(FM) Albion IL
*WBJY(FM) Americus GA
WBJZ(FM) Berlin WI
*WBKE-FM North Manchester IN
*WBKG(FM) Macon GA
WBKK(FM) Amsterdam NY
WBKN(FM) Brookhaven MS
WBKR(FM) Owensboro KY
WBKS(FM) Ironton OH
WBKT(FM) Norwich NY
*WBKU(FM) Ahoskie NC
WBKX(FM) Fredonia NY
*WBKY(FM) Portage WI
*WBLD(FM) Orchard Lake MI
WBLE(FM) Batesville MS
WBLI(FM) Patchogue NY
WBLJ-FM Shamokin PA
WBLK(FM) Depew NY
WBLM(FM) Portland ME
*WBLQ(FM) Westerly RI
WBLS(FM) New York NY
*WBLU-FM Grand Rapids MI
*WBLV(FM) Twin Lake MI
*WBLW(FM) Gaylord MI
WBLX-FM Mobile AL

*WBMF(FM) Crete IL
WBMH(FM) Grove Hill AL
WBMI(FM) West Branch MI
*WBMK(FM) Morehead KY
*WBMR(FM) Telford PA
*WBMT(FM) Boxford MA
*WBMV(FM) Mount Vernon IL
WBMW(FM) Ledyard CT
WBMX(FM) Boston MA
WBMZ(FM) Metter GA
WBNE(FM) Wrightsville Beach NC
*WBNH(FM) Pekin IL
*WBNI-FM Orland IN
WBNN-FM Dillwyn VA
WBNO-FM Bryan OH
*WBNQ(FM) Bloomington IL
WBNS-FM Columbus OH
WBNT-FM Oneida TN
WBNU(FM) Shallotte NC
WBNV(FM) Barnesville OH
*WBNY(FM) Buffalo NY
WBNZ(FM) Frankfort MI
*WBOI(FM) Fort Wayne IN
WBON-FM Westhampton NY
WBOP(FM) Churchville VA
WBOQ(FM) Gloucester MA
*WBOR(FM) Brunswick ME
WBOS(FM) Brookline MA
WBOT(FM) Brockton MA
WBOW-FM Terre Haute IN
WBOX-FM Varnado LA
WBOZ(FM) Woodbury TN
WBPC(FM) Ebro FL
WBPM(FM) Saugerties NY
*WBPR(FM) Worcester MA
WBPS-FM Warrenton VA
WBPT(FM) Birmingham AL
*WBPW(FM) Presque Isle ME
WBQB(FM) Fredericksburg VA
WBQI(FM) Bar Harbor ME
WBQQ(FM) Kennebunk ME
WBQW(FM) Scarborough ME
WBQX(FM) Thomaston ME
WBRB(FM) Buckhannon WV
WBRF(FM) Galax VA
*WBRH(FM) Baton Rouge LA
WBRK-FM Pittsfield MA
*WBRO(FM) Marengo IN
WBRQ(FM) Cidra PR
WBRR(FM) Bradford PA
*WBRS(FM) Waltham MA
WBRU(FM) Providence RI
WBRV-FM Boonville NY
WBRW(FM) Blacksburg VA
WBRX(FM) Patton PA
*WBSB(FM) Anderson IN
*WBSD(FM) Burlington WI
*WBSH(FM) Hagerstown IN
*WBSJ(FM) Portland IN
*WBSL-FM Sheffield MA
*WBSN-FM New Orleans LA
*WBST(FM) Muncie IN
*WBSU(FM) Brockport NY
*WBSW(FM) Marion IN
WBSX(FM) Hazleton PA
WBSZ(FM) Ashland WI
WBTF(FM) Midway KY
WBT-FM Chester SC
WBTG-FM Sheffield AL
WBTI(FM) Lexington MI
WBTJ(FM) Richmond VA
WBTN-FM Bennington VT
WBTO-FM Petersburg IN
WBTP(FM) Clearwater FL
WBTQ(FM) Buckhannon WV
WBTR-FM Carrollton GA
WBTS(FM) Doraville GA
WBTT(FM) Naples Park FL
WBTU(FM) Kendallville IN
WBTY(FM) Homerville GA
WBTZ(FM) Plattsburgh NY
WBUF(FM) Buffalo NY
WBUG-FM Fort Plain NY
*WBUK(FM) Ottawa OH
*WBUL(FM) Lexington KY
*WBUQ(FM) Bloomsburg PA
*WBUR-FM Boston MA

WBUS(FM) Boalsburg PA
WBUV(FM) Moss Point MS
*WBUX(FM) Buxton NC
WBUZ(FM) La Vergne TN
*WBVB(FM) Coal Grove OH
*WBVC(FM) Pomfret CT
WBVD(FM) Melbourne FL
WBVE(FM) Bedford PA
*WBVI(FM) Fostoria OH
*WBVM(FM) Tampa FL
*WBVN(FM) Carrier Mills IL
WBVQ(FM) Barrackville WV
WBVR-FM Auburn KY
WBVV(FM) Booneville MS
WBVX(FM) Carlisle KY
WBWB(FM) Bloomington IN
*WBWC(FM) Berea OH
WBWI-FM West Bend WI
WBWN(FM) Le Roy IL
WBWR(FM) Bedford VA
WBWT(FM) Midway FL
WBWZ(FM) New Paltz NY
WBXB(FM) Edenton NC
WBXE(FM) Baxter TN
*WBXL(FM) Baldwinsville NY
WBXQ(FM) Cresson PA
WBXX(FM) Battle Creek MI
WBXY(FM) La Crosse FL
WBYA(FM) Islesboro ME
WBYG(FM) Point Pleasant WV
*WBYH(FM) Hawley PA
WBYL(FM) Salladasburg PA
WBYN(FM) Boyertown PA
*WBYO(FM) Sellersville PA
WBYP(FM) Belzoni MS
WBYR(FM) Van Wert OH
WBYT(FM) Elkhart IN
*WBYX(FM) Stroudsburg PA
WBYY(FM) Somersworth NH
WBYZ(FM) Baxley GA
*WBZA(FM) Rochester NY
*WBZC(FM) Pemberton NJ
WBZD-FM Muncy PA
WBZE(FM) Tallahassee FL
WBZF(FM) Hartsville SC
WBZG(FM) Peru IL
WBZH(FM) Harriman TN
WBZN(FM) Old Town ME
WBZO(FM) Bay Shore NY
WBZR(FM) Tunkhannock PA
WBZS-FM Prince Frederick MD
WBZT-FM Mauldin SC
WBZV(FM) Hudson MI
WBZX(FM) Columbus OH
WBZY(FM) Bowdon GA
WCAA(FM) Newark NJ
WCAD(FM) San Juan PR
*WCAI(FM) Woods Hole MA
*WCAL(FM) California PA
*WCAN(FM) Canajoharie NY
*WCAT-FM Carlisle PA
WCBC-FM Keyser WV
*WCBE(FM) Columbus OH
*WCBH(FM) Casey IL
WCBJ(FM) Campton KY
WCBK-FM Martinsville IN
WCBL-FM Benton KY
*WCBN-FM Ann Arbor MI
WCBS-FM New York NY
*WCBU(FM) Peoria IL
*WCBW-FM East St. Louis IL
WCCC-FM Hartford CT
*WCCE(FM) Buie's Creek NC
WCCG(FM) Hope Mills NC
*WCCH(FM) Holyoke MA
WCCI(FM) Savanna IL
*WCCK(FM) Calvert City KY
*WCCL(FM) Central City PA
WCCN-FM Neillsville WI
WCCP-FM Clemson SC
*WCCQ(FM) Crest Hill IL
WCCR(FM) Clarion PA
*WCCT-FM Harwich MA
*WCCV(FM) Cartersville GA
WCCW-FM Traverse City MI
*WCCX(FM) Waukesha WI
WCDA(FM) Versailles KY

Broadcasting & Cable Yearbook 2006

D-630

U.S. FM Stations by Call Letters

*WCDB(FM) Albany NY
WCDD(FM) Canton IL
WCDG(FM) Moyock NC
WCDJ(FM) Truro MA
WCDK(FM) Cadiz OH
WCDO-FM Sidney NY
WCDQ(FM) Crawfordsville IN
*WCDR-FM Cedarville OH
WCDV(FM) Hammond LA
WCDW(FM) Susquehanna PA
WCDX(FM) Mechanicsville VA
WCDZ(FM) Dresden TN
*WCEB(FM) Corning NY
WCEF(FM) Ripley WV
WCEI-FM Easton MD
*WCEL(FM) Plattsburgh NY
WCEM-FM Cambridge MD
WCEN-FM Hemlock MI
WCEZ(FM) Carthage IL
WCFB(FM) Daytona Beach FL
WCFF(FM) Urbana IL
*WCFL(FM) Morris IL
*WCFM(FM) Williamstown MA
WCFR-FM Walpole NH
WCFW(FM) Chippewa Falls WI
WCFX(FM) Clare MI
WCGQ(FM) Columbus GA
*WCHC(FM) Worcester MA
*WCHG(FM) Hot Springs VA
WCHO-FM Washington Court House OH
WCHR-FM Manahawkin NJ
*WCHW-FM Bay City MI
WCHX(FM) Lewistown PA
WCHY(FM) Waunakee WI
WCHZ(FM) Harlem GA
WCIB(FM) Falmouth MA
*WCIC(FM) Pekin IL
*WCID(FM) Friendship NY
WCIF(FM) Melbourne FL
*WCIG(FM) Carbondale PA
*WCIH(FM) Elmira NY
*WCII(FM) Spencer NY
*WCIK(FM) Bath NY
WCIL-FM Carbondale IL
WCIR-FM Beckley WV
*WCIT(FM) Trout Run PA
*WCIY(FM) Canandaigua NY
WCIZ-FM Watertown NY
WCJC(FM) Van Buren IN
WCJK(FM) Murfreesboro TN
*WCJL(FM) Morgantown IN
WCJM-FM West Point GA
WCJO(FM) Jackson OH
WCJU-FM Prentiss MS
WCJX(FM) Five Points FL
WCJZ(FM) Charlottesville VA
WCKC(FM) Cadillac MI
WCKG(FM) Elmwood Park IL
*WCKJ(FM) Saint Johnsbury VT
WCKK(FM) Carthage MS
WCKM-FM Lake George NY
WCKQ(FM) Campbellsville KY
WCKR(FM) Hornell NY
WCKS-FM Fruithurst AL
WCKT(FM) Port Charlotte FL
WCKX(FM) Columbus OH
WCKY-FM Tiffin OH
WCKZ(FM) Roanoke IN
WCLC-FM Jamestown TN
WCLD-FM Cleveland MS
WCLE-FM Calhoun TN
WCLG-FM Morgantown WV
*WCLH(FM) Wilkes-Barre PA
*WCLK(FM) Atlanta GA
WCLN-FM Clinton NC
*WCLQ(FM) Wausau WI
*WCLR(FM) Arlington Heights IL
*WCLT-FM Newark OH
WCLU-FM Munfordville KY
WCLV(FM) Lorain OH
WCLX(FM) Westport NY
WCLZ(FM) Brunswick ME
WCMA-FM Fajardo PR
*WCMB-FM Oscoda MI
*WCMD-FM Barre VT
WCME(FM) Boothbay Harbor ME

WCMF-FM Rochester NY
WCMG(FM) Latta SC
WCMJ(FM) Cambridge OH
*WCMK(FM) Putney VT
*WCML-FM Alpena MI
WCMM(FM) Gulliver MI
*WCMN-FM Arecibo PR
*WCMO(FM) Marietta OH
*WCMP-FM Pine City MN
WCMQ-FM Hialeah FL
WCMT-FM South Fulton TN
*WCMU-FM Mount Pleasant MI
*WCMW-FM Harbor Springs MI
*WCMZ-FM Sault Ste. Marie MI
WCNA(FM) Potts Camp MS
WCNF(FM) Benton Harbor MI
WCNG(FM) Murphy NC
*WCNI(FM) New London CT
WCNK(FM) Key West FL
*WCNO(FM) Palm City FL
WCNV(FM) Heathsville VA
WCNY-FM Syracuse NY
WCOD-FM Hyannis MA
WCOE(FM) La Porte IN
*WCOF(FM) Arcade NY
*WCOG-FM Galeton PA
WCOL-FM Columbus OH
WCON-FM Cornelia GA
WCOO(FM) Kiawah Island SC
WCOS-FM Columbia SC
*WCOT(FM) Jamestown NY
*WCOU(FM) Warsaw NY
*WCOV-FM Clyde NY
WCOW-FM Sparta WI
WCOY(FM) Quincy IL
WCOZ(FM) Laporte PA
*WCPE(FM) Raleigh NC
*WCPI(FM) McMinnville TN
*WCPN(FM) Cleveland OH
WCPR-FM D'Iberville MS
WCPV(FM) Essex NY
WCPZ(FM) Sandusky OH
*WCQL(FM) Glens Falls NY
WCQM(FM) Park Falls WI
*WCQR-FM Kingsport TN
*WCQS(FM) Asheville NC
WCRB(FM) Waltham MA
WCRC(FM) Effingham IL
*WCRF(FM) Cleveland OH
WCRG(FM) Williamsport PA
*WCRH(FM) Williamsport MD
WCRI(FM) Block Island RI
*WCRJ(FM) Jacksonville FL
WCRP(FM) Guayama PR
*WCRQ(FM) Dennysville ME
*WCRT(FM) Terre Haute IN
*WCRX(FM) Chicago IL
WCRZ(FM) Flint MI
*WCSB(FM) Cleveland OH
WCSF(FM) Joliet IL
*WCSG(FM) Grand Rapids MI
WCSJ-FM Morris IL
*WCSK(FM) Kingsport TN
WCSM-FM Celina OH
WCSN-FM Orange Beach AL
*WCSO(FM) Columbus MS
*WCSP-FM Washington DC
WCSQ(FM) Manning SC
WCSR-FM Hillsdale MI
*WCSU-FM Wilberforce OH
WCSX(FM) Birmingham MI
WCSY-FM South Haven MI
WCTB(FM) Fairfield ME
WCTG(FM) Chincoteague VA
WCTH(FM) Plantation Key FL
WCTK(FM) New Bedford MA
WCTL(FM) Union City PA
WCTO(FM) Easton PA
WCTQ(FM) Sarasota FL
WCTT-FM Corbin KY
WCTU(FM) Tazewell TN
WCTW(FM) Catskill NY
WCTY(FM) Norwich CT
*WCUC-FM Clarion PA
WCUL(FM) Orange VA
WCUP(FM) L'Anse MI
*WCUR(FM) West Chester PA

*WCUW(FM) Worcester MA
WCUZ(FM) Bear Lake MI
*WCVE(FM) Richmond VA
*WCVF-FM Fredonia NY
*WCVH(FM) Flemington NJ
*WCVJ(FM) Jefferson OH
*WCVK(FM) Bowling Green KY
*WCVM(FM) Bronson MI
*WCVO(FM) Gahanna OH
WCVP-FM Robbinsville NC
WCVQ(FM) Fort Campbell KY
WCVR-FM Randolph VT
WCVS-FM Virden IL
WCVT(FM) Stowe VT
WCVU(FM) Solana FL
*WCVV(FM) Belpre OH
*WCVY(FM) Coventry RI
*WCVZ(FM) South Zanesville OH
*WCWM(FM) Williamsburg VA
*WCWP(FM) Brookville NY
*WCWS(FM) Wooster OH
*WCWT-FM Centerville OH
WCWV(FM) Summersville WV
*WCXL(FM) Kill Devil Hills NC
WCXR(FM) Lewisburg PA
WCXT(FM) Hart MI
WCXU(FM) Caribou ME
WCXX(FM) Madawaska ME
WCYI(FM) Lewiston ME
*WCYJ-FM Waynesburg PA
WCYK-FM Staunton VA
WCYN-FM Cynthiana KY
WCYO(FM) Irvine KY
*WCYT(FM) Lafayette Township IN
WCYY(FM) Biddeford ME
WCZE(FM) Harbor Beach MI
WCZQ(FM) Monticello IL
WCZR(FM) Vero Beach FL
WCZT(FM) Villas NJ
WCZW(FM) Charlevoix MI
WCZX(FM) Hyde Park NY
WCZY-FM Mount Pleasant MI
WDAC(FM) Lancaster PA
WDAF-FM Liberty MO
WDAI(FM) Pawley's Island SC
WDAQ(FM) Danbury CT
WDAR-FM Darlington SC
WDAS-FM Philadelphia PA
*WDAV(FM) Davidson NC
WDAY-FM Fargo ND
WDBA(FM) DuBois PA
*WDBK(FM) Blackwood NJ
*WDBM(FM) East Lansing MI
WDBN(FM) Wrightsville GA
WDBQ-FM Galena IL
WDBR(FM) Springfield IL
WDBS(FM) Sutton WV
WDBT(FM) Headland AL
*WDBX(FM) Carbondale IL
WDBY(FM) Patterson NY
*WDCB(FM) Glen Ellyn IL
*WDCC(FM) Sanford NC
*WDCE(FM) Richmond VA
WDCG(FM) Durham NC
*WDCI(FM) Bridgeport WV
*WDCL-FM Somerset KY
*WDCO-FM Cochran GA
*WDCV-FM Carlisle PA
WDCX(FM) Buffalo NY
WDDB(FM) Columbia City IN
WDDC(FM) Portage WI
WDDD-FM Marion IL
WDDH(FM) Saint Marys PA
WDDJ(FM) Paducah KY
WDDK(FM) Greensboro GA
WDDQ(FM) Adel GA
WDEB-FM Jamestown TN
WDEC-FM Americus GA
WDEE-FM Reed City MI
WDEF-FM Chattanooga TN
WDEK(FM) De Kalb IL
WDEN-FM Macon GA
*WDEQ-FM De Graff OH
*WDET-FM Detroit MI
WDEV-FM Warren VT
WDEZ(FM) Wausau WI
*WDFB(FM) Danville KY

*WDFH(FM) Ossining NY
WDFM(FM) Defiance OH
WDFX(FM) Cleveland MS
*WDGC-FM Downers Grove IL
WDGG(FM) Ashland KY
WDGL(FM) Baton Rouge LA
WDGM(FM) Greensboro AL
WDGT(FM) Rio Grande PR
WDHA-FM Dover NJ
WDHC(FM) Berkeley Springs WV
WDHI(FM) Delhi NY
WDHR(FM) Pikeville KY
WDHT(FM) Springfield OH
WDIC-FM Clinchco VA
WDIF(FM) Marion OH
*WDIH(FM) Salisbury MD
WDIN(FM) Camuy PR
*WDIY(FM) Allentown PA
WDJC-FM Birmingham AL
*WDJM-FM Framingham MA
WDJR(FM) Enterprise AL
*WDJW(FM) Somers CT
WDJX(FM) Louisville KY
WDKB(FM) De Kalb IL
WDKC(FM) Covington PA
WDKF(FM) Englewood OH
*WDKL(FM) Grafton WV
WDKM(FM) Adams WI
WDKR(FM) Maroa IL
WDKS(FM) Newburgh IN
WDKX(FM) Rochester NY
WDKZ(FM) Salisbury MD
WDLA-FM Walton NY
WDLD(FM) Halfway MD
WDLJ(FM) Breese IL
*WDLM-FM East Moline IL
WDLT-FM Chickasaw AL
WDLZ(FM) Murfreesboro NC
WDME-FM Dover Foxcroft ME
WDMG-FM Ocilla GA
*WDMK(FM) Detroit MI
WDML(FM) Woodlawn IL
WDMO(FM) Durand WI
WDMP-FM Dodgeville WI
WDMS(FM) Greenville MS
WDMT(FM) Pittston PA
WDMX(FM) Vienna WV
*WDNA(FM) Miami FL
WDNB(FM) Jeffersonville NY
WDNE-FM Elkins WV
WDNH-FM Honesdale PA
WDNL(FM) Danville IL
WDNQ(FM) Kenova WV
*WDNR(FM) Chester PA
WDNS(FM) Bowling Green KY
WDNT-FM Dayton TN
*WDNX(FM) Olive Hill TN
WDNY-FM Dansville NY
WDOD-FM Chattanooga TN
WDOG-FM Allendale SC
*WDOH(FM) Delphos OH
WDOK(FM) Cleveland OH
*WDOM(FM) Providence RI
WDOR-FM Sturgeon Bay WI
WDOT(FM) Danville VT
WDOW-FM Dowagiac MI
WDOX(FM) North Cape May NJ
*WDPG(FM) Greenville OH
*WDPR(FM) West Carrollton OH
*WDPS(FM) Dayton OH
WDPT(FM) Piqua OH
WDQN(FM) Du Quoin IL
WDQX(FM) Morton IL
WDQZ(FM) Lexington IL
WDRC-FM Hartford CT
WDRE(FM) Calverton-Roanoke NY
WDRK(FM) Cornell WI
WDRM(FM) Decatur AL
WDRQ(FM) Detroit MI
*WDRS(FM) Dorsey IL
WDRV(FM) Chicago IL
WDSD(FM) Smyrna DE
WDSJ(FM) Greenville OH
WDSN(FM) Reynoldsville PA
*WDSO(FM) Chesterton IN
WDST(FM) Woodstock NY
WDSY-FM Pittsburgh PA

WDTH(FM) Wildwood Crest NJ
WDTL-FM Cleveland MS
*WDTR(FM) Monroe MI
WDTW-FM Detroit MI
*WDUB(FM) Granville OH
WDUK(FM) Havana IL
WDUQ(FM) Pittsburgh PA
WDUV(FM) New Port Richey FL
WDUX-FM Waupaca WI
WDUZ-FM Brillion WI
WDVD(FM) Detroit MI
WDVE(FM) Pittsburgh PA
WDVH-FM Trenton KY
*WDVR(FM) Delaware Township NJ
WDVT(FM) Harwichport MA
*WDVV(FM) Wilmington NC
*WDVW(FM) La Place LA
*WDVX(FM) Clinton TN
WDWG(FM) Rocky Mount NC
*WDWN(FM) Auburn NY
WDXB(FM) Jasper AL
WDXC(FM) Pound VA
WDXE-FM Lawrenceburg TN
WDXO(FM) Hazlehurst MS
WDXQ-FM Cochran GA
WDXX(FM) Selma AL
*WDYF(FM) Dothan AL
WDYK(FM) Ridgeley WV
*WDYL(FM) Chester VA
*WDYN-FM Chattanooga TN
WDYW(FM) Romney WV
WDZQ(FM) Decatur IL
WDZZ-FM Flint MI
*WEAA(FM) Baltimore MD
WEAI(FM) Lynnville IL
WEAM-FM Buena Vista GA
WEAS-FM Savannah GA
WEAT-FM West Palm Beach FL
*WEAX(FM) Angola IN
*WEAZ(FM) Holly Hill FL
WEBB(FM) Waterville ME
WEBE(FM) Westport CT
WEBK(FM) Killington VT
WEBL(FM) Warner Robins GA
WEBN(FM) Cincinnati OH
WEBQ-FM Eldorado IL
*WEBT(FM) Valley AL
WEBX(FM) Tuscola IL
WEBZ(FM) Port St. Joe FL
WECB(FM) Seymour WI
*WECC-FM Folkston GA
*WECI(FM) Richmond IN
WECL(FM) Elk Mound WI
WECO-FM Wartburg TN
WECR-FM Beech Mountain NC
*WECS(FM) Willimantic CT
*WECW(FM) Elmira NY
WEDG(FM) Buffalo NY
WEDJ(FM) Danville IN
*WEDM(FM) Indianapolis IN
WEDR(FM) Miami FL
*WEDW-FM Stamford CT
*WEEC(FM) Springfield OH
WEEI-FM Westerly RI
*WEEM(FM) Pendleton IN
WEEO-FM McConnellsburg PA
WEFG-FM Whitehall MI
WEFM(FM) Michigan City IN
*WEFR(FM) Erie PA
*WEFT(FM) Champaign IL
WEFX(FM) Norwalk CT
WEGC(FM) Sasser GA
WEGH(FM) Northumberland PA
WEGI(FM) Oak Grove KY
WEGK(FM) Charlestown IN
*WEGL(FM) Auburn AL
WEGM(FM) San German PR
WEGQ(FM) Scotia NY
WEGR(FM) Memphis TN
*WEGS(FM) Milton FL
WEGT(FM) Lafayette TN
WEGW(FM) Wheeling WV
WEGX(FM) Dillon SC
*WEGZ(FM) Washburn WI
*WEHC(FM) Emory VA
WEHM(FM) Southampton NY
WEIB(FM) Northampton MA

U.S. FM Stations by Call Letters

*WEIU(FM) Charleston IL	WEZF(FM) Burlington VT	WFLE-FM Flemingsburg KY	*WFUV(FM) New York NY	WGLO(FM) Pekin IL
*WEJC(FM) White Star MI	WEZG(FM) Sturgis KY	WFLK(FM) Geneva NY	WFWI(FM) Fort Wayne IN	WGLQ(FM) Escanaba MI
*WEJF(FM) Palm Bay FL	WEZJ-FM Williamsburg KY	WFLM(FM) White City FL	*WFWM(FM) Frostburg MD	WGLR-FM Lancaster WI
WEJT(FM) Shelbyville IL	WEZL(FM) Charleston SC	WFLO-FM Farmville VA	*WFWR(FM) Attica IN	*WGLS-FM Glassboro NJ
WEJZ(FM) Jacksonville FL	WEZN-FM Bridgeport CT	WFLQ(FM) French Lick IN	WFXA-FM Augusta GA	*WGLT(FM) Normal IL
*WEKF(FM) Corbin KY	WEZQ(FM) Bangor ME	**WFLR-FM Dundee NY**	WFXC(FM) Durham NC	*WGLV(FM) Woodstock VT
*WEKH(FM) Hazard KY	WEZV(FM) North Myrtle Beach SC	**WFLS-FM Fredericksburg VA**	WFXD(FM) Marquette MI	*WGLX-FM Wisconsin Rapids WI
WEKL(FM) Augusta GA	WEZX(FM) Scranton PA	**WFLY(FM) Troy NY**	WFXE(FM) Columbus GA	*WGLY-FM Bolton VT
WEKS(FM) Zebulon GA	WEZY(FM) Racine WI	**WFLZ-FM Tampa FL**	WFXF(FM) Honeoye Falls NY	*WGLZ(FM) West Liberty WV
*WEKU(FM) Richmond KY	WEZZ(FM) Clanton AL	**WFMB-FM Springfield IL**	WFXH-FM Hilton Head Island SC	WGMC(FM) Greece NY
WEKX(FM) Jellico TN	*WFAE(FM) Charlotte NC	*WFME(FM) Newark NJ	WFXJ-FM North Kingsville OH	WGMD(FM) Rehoboth Beach DE
WEKZ-FM Monroe WI	WFAF(FM) Mount Kisco NY	**WFMF(FM) Baton Rouge LA**	WFXK(FM) Tarboro NC	WGMG(FM) Crawford GA
WELC-FM Welch WV	*WFAR(FM) Danbury CT	WFMG(FM) Richmond IN	WFXM(FM) Gordon GA	WGMK(FM) Donalsonville GA
WELD-FM Petersburg WV	WFAS-FM White Plains NY	WFMH-FM Holly Pond AL	WFXN-FM Galion OH	WGMM(FM) Corning NY
*WELH(FM) Providence RI	WFAT(FM) Portage MI	WFMI(FM) Southern Shores NC	WFXO(FM) Iuka MS	WGMO(FM) Shell Lake WI
*WELJ(FM) Brewton AL	WFBC-FM Greenville SC	WFMK(FM) East Lansing MI	WFXQ(FM) Chase City VA	WGMR(FM) Tyrone PA
WELK(FM) Elkins WV	WFBE(FM) Flint MI	WFML(FM) Vincennes IN	WFXX(FM) Georgiana AL	WGMS-FM Washington DC
*WELL-FM Dadeville AL	*WFBF(FM) Buffalo NY	WFMM(FM) Sumrall MS	*WFYI-FM Indianapolis IN	WGMT(FM) Lyndon VT
WELR-FM Roanoke AL	*WFBI(FM) Greenville MS	WFMN(FM) Flora MS	WFYN(FM) Waynesboro PA	WGMX(FM) Marathon FL
WELS-FM Kinston NC	WFBQ(FM) Indianapolis IN	WFMP(FM) Coon Rapids MN	WFYR(FM) Elmwood IL	WGMZ(FM) Glencoe AL
WELT(FM) East Dublin GA	WFBX(FM) Parker FL	*WFMQ(FM) Lebanon FL	*WFYV-FM Atlantic Beach FL	WGNA-FM Albany NY
WELY-FM Ely MN	WFBY(FM) Weston WV	WFMR(FM) Brookfield WI	WFYY(FM) Bloomsburg PA	WGNB(FM) Zeeland MI
*WEMC(FM) Harrisonburg VA	WFBZ(FM) Trempealeau WI	WFMS(FM) Indianapolis IN	WFZH(FM) Mukwonago WI	WGNE-FM Palatka FL
*WEMI(FM) Appleton WI	WFCA(FM) Ackerman MS	WFMT(FM) Chicago IL	WFZX(FM) Searsport ME	WGNG(FM) Tchula MS
WEMM-FM Huntington WV	WFCC-FM Chatham MA	*WFMU(FM) East Orange NJ	WGAC-FM Warrenton GA	*WGNI(FM) Wilmington NC
*WEMU(FM) Ypsilanti MI	*WFCF(FM) Saint Augustine FL	WFMV(FM) South Congaree SC	*WGAJ(FM) Deerfield MA	*WGNJ(FM) Saint Joseph IL
WEMX(FM) Kentwood LA	WFCG(FM) Tylertown MS	WFMX(FM) Statesville NC	WGAO(FM) Franklin MA	WGNL(FM) Greenwood MS
*WEMY(FM) Green Bay WI	*WFCH(FM) Charleston SC	WFMZ(FM) Hertford NC	WGAR-FM Cleveland OH	*WGNN(FM) Fisher IL
WEND(FM) Salisbury NC	*WFCI(FM) Franklin IN	WFNC-FM Lumberton NC	*WGBE(FM) Bryan OH	*WGNR-FM Anderson IN
WENI-FM Big Flats NY	WFCJ(FM) Miamisburg OH	WFNK(FM) Lewiston ME	WGBF-FM Henderson KY	*WGNV(FM) Milladore WI
WENN(FM) Hoover AL	*WFCM-FM Murfreesboro TN	*WFNM(FM) Lancaster PA	WGBG(FM) Seaford DE	WGNX(FM) Vero Beach FL
WENU-FM Hudson Falls NY	*WFCO(FM) Lancaster OH	*WFNP(FM) Rosendale NY	*WGBH(FM) Boston MA	WGNY-FM Newburgh NY
WENY-FM Elmira NY	*WFCR(FM) Amherst MA	WFNQ(FM) Nashua NH	*WGBK(FM) Glenview IL	*WGOD-FM Charlotte Amalie VI
WENZ(FM) Cleveland OH	*WFCS(FM) New Britain CT	WFNR-FM Christiansburg VA	WGBT(FM) Eden NC	WGOG(FM) Walhalla SC
*WEOS(FM) Geneva NY	WFCT(FM) Apalachicola FL	WFNU(FM) Repton AL	WGBZ(FM) Cape May Court House NJ	*WGOJ(FM) Conneaut OH
WEOW(FM) Key West FL	WFCX(FM) Leland MI	WFNX(FM) Lynn MA	*WGCA-FM Quincy IL	WGOR(FM) New Ellenton SC
*WEPC(FM) Belton SC	*WFDD-FM Winston-Salem NC	*WFOF(FM) Covington IN	*WGCC-FM Batavia NY	WGOW-FM Soddy-Daisy TN
*WEPR(FM) Greenville SC	WFDL-FM Lomira WI	WFOG(FM) Suffolk VA	*WGCF(FM) Paducah KY	*WGPH(FM) Vidalia GA
*WEPS(FM) Elgin IL	WFDT(FM) Aguada PR	WFON(FM) Fond du Lac WI	WGCI-FM Chicago IL	WGPR(FM) Detroit MI
WEQX(FM) Manchester VT	*WFDU(FM) Teaneck NJ	*WFOS(FM) Chesapeake VA	WGCM-FM Gulfport MS	*WGPS(FM) Elizabeth City NC
*WERB(FM) Berlin CT	WFDX(FM) Atlanta MI	WFOX(FM) Gainesville GA	WGCO(FM) Midway GA	WGQR(FM) Elizabethtown NC
*WERG(FM) Erie PA	WFEN(FM) Rockford IL	*WFPB-FM Falmouth MA	WGCS(FM) Goshen IN	WGRC(FM) Lewisburg PA
WERH-FM Hamilton AL	WFEX(FM) Peterborough NH	WFPG-FM Atlantic City NJ	*WGCU-FM Fort Myers FL	WGRD-FM Grand Rapids MI
WERK(FM) Muncie IN	WFEZ(FM) Avoca PA	*WFPK(FM) Louisville KY	WGCX(FM) Navarre FL	*WGRE(FM) Greencastle IN
*WERN(FM) Madison WI	*WFFC(FM) Ferrum VA	*WFPL(FM) Louisville KY	WGCY(FM) Gibson City IL	WGRF(FM) Buffalo NY
WERO(FM) Washington NC	WFFF-FM Columbia MS	WFPS(FM) Freeport IL	*WGDE(FM) Defiance OH	WGRK-FM Greensburg KY
WERQ-FM Baltimore MD	WFFG-FM Corinth NY	*WFQS(FM) Franklin NC	WGDN-FM Gladwin MI	WGRM-FM Greenwood MS
WERR(FM) Utuado PR	WFFH(FM) Smyrna TN	WFQX(FM) Front Royal VA	WGDQ(FM) Hattiesburg MS	*WGRN(FM) Greenville IL
*WERS(FM) Boston MA	WFFI(FM) Kingston Springs TN	WFRB-FM Frostburg MD	*WGDR(FM) Plainfield VT	WGRQ(FM) Colonial Beach VA
*WERU-FM Blue Hill ME	*WFFL(FM) Panama City FL	*WFRC(FM) Columbus GA	WGEL(FM) Greenville IL	WGRR(FM) Hamilton OH
WERV-FM Aurora IL	WFFM(FM) Ashburn GA	WFRD(FM) Hanover NH	WGEM-FM Quincy IL	*WGRS(FM) Guilford CT
WERX-FM Columbia NC	*WFFN(FM) Cordova AL	WFRE(FM) Frederick MD	WGER(FM) Saginaw MI	WGRT(FM) Port Huron MI
WERZ(FM) Exeter NH	WFFY(FM) Destin FL	*WFRF-FM Monticello FL	*WGES(FM) Key Largo FL	*WGRW(FM) Anniston AL
WESC-FM Greenville SC	WFGA(FM) Hicksville OH	WFRG-FM Utica NY	*WGEV(FM) Beaver Falls PA	WGRX(FM) Falmouth VA
WESE(FM) Baldwyn MS	*WFGB(FM) Kingston NY	*WFRH(FM) Kingston NY	WGFA-FM Watseka IL	WGRY-FM Grayling MI
*WESM(FM) Princess Anne MD	WFGE(FM) Murray KY	WFRI(FM) Winamac IN	WGFB(FM) Rockton IL	*WGSG(FM) Mayo FL
*WESN(FM) Bloomington IL	WFGF(FM) Lima OH	*WFRJ(FM) Johnstown PA	WGFG(FM) Branchville SC	*WGSK(FM) South Kent CT
WESP(FM) Dothan AL	*WFGH(FM) Fort Gay WV	WFRM-FM Coudersport PA	WGFM(FM) Cheboygan MI	*WGSL(FM) Loves Park IL
WESR-FM Onley-Onancock VA	WFGI-FM Johnstown PA	WFRN-FM Elkhart IN	WGFN(FM) Glen Arbor MI	WGSQ(FM) Cookeville TN
*WESS(FM) East Stroudsburg PA	WFGO(FM) Erie PA	WFRO-FM Fremont OH	*WGFR(FM) Glens Falls FL	WGSS(FM) Kingstree SC
*WESU(FM) Middletown CT	WFGR(FM) Grand Rapids MI	*WFRP(FM) Americus GA	WGFX(FM) Gallatin TN	*WGSU(FM) Geneseo NY
*WETA(FM) Washington DC	WFGY(FM) Altoona PA	WFRR(FM) Walton IN	WGGC(FM) Bowling Green KY	WGSY(FM) Phenix City AL
*WETD(FM) Alfred NY	WFGZ(FM) Lobelville TN	*WFRS(FM) Smithtown NY	WGGE(FM) Parkersburg WV	*WGTC(FM) Hickory MS
*WETH(FM) Hagerstown MD	*WFHB(FM) Bloomington IN	*WFRW(FM) Webster NY	WGGI(FM) Benton PA	*WGTD(FM) Kenosha WI
WETL(FM) South Bend IN	*WFHE(FM) Hickory NC	WFRY-FM Watertown NY	*WGGL-FM Houghton MI	WGTE-FM Toledo OH
*WETN(FM) Wheaton IL	WFHG-FM Abingdon VA	*WFSE(FM) Edinboro PA	WGGN(FM) Castalia OH	*WGTF(FM) Dothan AL
*WETS(FM) Johnson City TN	*WFHL(FM) New Bedford MA	WFSH-FM Athens GA	WGGY(FM) Scranton PA	WGTH-FM Richlands VA
WETZ-FM New Martinsville WV	WFHM-FM Cleveland OH	*WFSI(FM) Annapolis MD	WGH-FM Newport News VA	WGTN-FM Andrews SC
*WEUL(FM) Kingsford MI	*WFHN(FM) Nashville TN	*WFSK(FM) Nashville TN	WGHN-FM Grand Haven MI	WGTR(FM) Bucksport SC
WEUP-FM Moulton AL	*WFHU(FM) Henderson TN	WFSL(FM) Thomasville GA	*WGHW(FM) Lockwoods Folly Town NC	*WGTS(FM) Takoma Park MD
WEUZ(FM) Minor Hill TN	WFIA-FM New Albany IN	WFSO(FM) Olivebridge NY	*WGIB(FM) Birmingham AL	WGTY(FM) Gettysburg PA
*WEVC(FM) Gorham NH	WFID(FM) Rio Piedras PR	WFSP-FM Kingwood WV	WGIC(FM) Cookeville TN	WGTZ(FM) Eaton OH
WEVE-FM Eveleth MN	*WFIT(FM) Melbourne FL	*WFSQ(FM) Tallahassee FL	WGIE(FM) Clarksburg WV	*WGUC(FM) Cincinnati OH
*WEVH(FM) Hanover NH	*WFIU(FM) Bloomington IN	WFSS(FM) Fayetteville NC	*WGIR-FM Manchester NH	WGUF(FM) Marco FL
WEVI(FM) Frederiksted VI	WFIW-FM Fairfield IL	*WFSU-FM Tallahassee FL	WGIX-FM Gouverneur NY	*WGUR(FM) Milledgeville GA
*WEVJ(FM) Jackson NH	*WFIX(FM) Florence AL	WFSW(FM) Panama City FL	WGKC(FM) Mahomet IL	*WGUY(FM) Dexter ME
*WEVL(FM) Memphis TN	WFJA(FM) Sanford NC	WFSY(FM) Panama City FL	WGKL(FM) Gladstone MI	*WGVC(FM) Simpsonville SC
*WEVN(FM) Keene NH	WFJO(FM) Folkston GA	WFTA(FM) Fulton MS	*WGKR(FM) Grand Gorge NY	WGVE(FM) Gary IN
*WEVO(FM) Concord NH	*WFJS(FM) Hazlet NJ	*WFTF(FM) Rutland VT	WGKS(FM) Paris KY	WGVS-FM Whitehall MI
WEVR-FM River Falls WI	WFJX(FM) Hilliard OH	*WFTI-FM Saint Petersburg FL	WGKX(FM) Memphis TN	*WGVU-FM Allendale MI
*WEVS(FM) Nashua NH	WFKL(FM) Fairport NY	WFTM-FM Maysville KY	WGKY(FM) Wickliffe KY	WGVX(FM) Lakeville MN
WEVX(FM) Rantoul IL	WFKP(FM) Ellenville NY	WFTN-FM Franklin NH	WGLC-FM Mendota IL	WGVY(FM) Cambridge MN
WEXC(FM) Greenville PA	WFKS(FM) Neptune Beach FL	WFTZ(FM) Manchester TN	*WGLE(FM) Lima OH	WGVZ(FM) Eden Prairie MN
WEXP(FM) Brandon VT	WFKX(FM) Henderson TN	*WFUM-FM Flint MI	*WGLF(FM) Tallahassee FL	WGWD(FM) Gretna FL
WEXT(FM) Sturtevant WI	WFKZ(FM) Plantation Key FL	WFUN-FM Bethalto IL	WGLI(FM) Hancock MI	*WGWG(FM) Boiling Springs NC
WEYE(FM) Surgoinsville TN	WFLB(FM) Laurinburg NC	WFUR-FM Grand Rapids MI	*WGLE(FM) Lima OH	*WGWR(FM) Liberty NY
WEZB(FM) New Orleans LA	WFLC(FM) Miami FL	WFUS(FM) Bradenton FL	WGLM(FM) West Lafayette IN	WGXL(FM) Hanover NH

Broadcasting & Cable Yearbook 2006

D-632

U.S. FM Stations by Call Letters

WGYE(FM) Mannington WV	WHLJ(FM) Statenville GA	WHYB(FM) Menominee MI	WINX-FM Cambridge MD	*WJCH(FM) Joliet IL
WGYI(FM) Oil City PA	*WHLP(FM) Hanna IN	*WHYC(FM) Swanquarter NC	WIOA(FM) San Juan PR	*WJCJ(FM) Ladoga IN
WGYL(FM) Vero Beach FL	WHLW(FM) Luverne AL	WHYI-FM Fort Lauderdale FL	WIOB(FM) Mayaguez PR	*WJCK(FM) Piedmont AL
WGYY(FM) Meadville PA	WHLZ(FM) Marion SC	WHYN-FM Springfield MA	WIOC(FM) Ponce PR	WJCL-FM Savannah GA
WGZB-FM Lanesville IN	WHMA-FM Ashland AL	*WHYT(FM) Goodland Township MI	WIOG(FM) Bay City MI	*WJCN(FM) Nassawadox VA
WGZO(FM) Parris Island SC	*WHMC-FM Conway SC	*WHYY(FM) Philadelphia PA	WIOK(FM) Falmouth KY	*WJCO(FM) Montpelier IN
WGZR(FM) Bluffton SC	WHMD(FM) Hammond LA	WHZQ(FM) Cross Hill SC	WIOL(FM) Greenville GA	*WJCP(FM) Austin IN
*WHAB(FM) Acton MA	WHME(FM) South Bend IN	WHZR(FM) Royal Center IN	WIOQ(FM) Philadelphia PA	*WJCQ(FM) Jackson MI
*WHAD(FM) Delafield WI	WHMH-FM Sauk Rapids MN	WHZT(FM) Seneca SC	WIOT(FM) Toledo OH	*WJCR-FM Upton KY
WHAI(FM) Greenfield MA	WHMI-FM Howell MI	WHZZ(FM) Lansing MI	WIOV-FM Ephrata PA	*WJCS(FM) Allentown PA
WHAJ(FM) Bluefield WV	*WHMR(FM) Ledbetter KY	*WIAA(FM) Interlochen MI	WIOZ(FM) Southern Pines NC	*WJCT-FM Jacksonville FL
WHAK-FM Rogers City MI	WHMS(FM) Champaign IL	*WIAB(FM) Mackinaw City MI	*WIPA(FM) Pittsfield IL	*WJCU(FM) University Heights OH
WHAL-FM Horn Lake MS	*WHMX(FM) Lincoln ME	WIAC-FM San Juan PR	*WIPR-FM San Juan PR	WJCX(FM) Pittsfield ME
WHAY(FM) Whitley City KY	*WHND(FM) Sister Bay WI	WIAL(FM) Eau Claire WI	*WIQH(FM) Concord MA	*WJCY(FM) Cicero IN
WHBC-FM Canton OH	*WHNI(FM) Rochester IN	WIBA-FM Madison WI	WIQO-FM Covington VA	*WJCZ(FM) Milford IL
WHBE(FM) East Hampton NY	WHNN(FM) Bay City MI	WIBB(FM) Fort Valley GA	WIQQ(FM) Leland MS	WJDB(FM) Thomasville AL
*WHBM-FM Park Falls WI	WHOD(FM) Jackson AL	*WIBI(FM) Carlinville IL	WIRE(FM) Lebanon IN	WJDF(FM) Orange MA
WHBQ-FM Germantown TN	WHOG-FM Ormond-by-the-Sea FL	WIBL(FM) Augusta GA	WIRK-FM West Palm Beach FL	WJDK-FM Seneca IL
WHBR-FM Parkersburg WV	*WHOJ(FM) Terre Haute IN	WIBN(FM) Earl Park IN	*WIRN(FM) Buhl MN	*WJDQ(FM) Meridian MS
WHBX(FM) Tallahassee FL	WHOK(FM) Lancaster OH	WIBT(FM) Shelby NC	*WIRP(FM) Pennsuco FL	*WJDR(FM) Prentiss MS
WHBZ(FM) Sheboygan Falls WI	WHOM(FM) Mt. Washington NH	WIBV(FM) Mount Vernon IL	WIRQ(FM) Rochester NY	*WJDS(FM) Sparta GA
*WHCB(FM) Bristol TN	WHOP-FM Hopkinsville KY	WIBW-FM Topeka KS	*WIRR(FM) Virginia-Hibbing MN	*WJDT(FM) Rogersville TN
WHCC(FM) Ellettsville IN	WHOT-FM Youngstown OH	WIBZ(FM) Wedgefield SC	WIRX(FM) Saint Joseph MI	*WJDV(FM) Broadway VA
*WHCE(FM) Highland Springs VA	*WHOU-FM Houlton ME	*WICA(FM) Traverse City MI	*WISE-FM Wise VA	WJEC(FM) Vernon AL
*WHCF(FM) Bangor ME	*WHOV(FM) Hampton VA	WICB(FM) Ithaca NY	WISG(FM) Fishers IN	*WJED(FM) Dogwood Lakes Estate FL
*WHCI(FM) Hartford City IN	WHOW-FM Clinton IL	*WICE(FM) Ironwood MI	WISH-FM Galatia IL	*WJEF(FM) Lafayette IN
*WHCJ(FM) Savannah GA	WHPA(FM) Northern Cambria PA	WICI(FM) Sumter SC	WISK-FM Americus GA	*WJEL(FM) Indianapolis IN
*WHCL-FM Clinton NY	*WHPC(FM) Garden City NY	WICL(FM) Williamsport MD	WISM-FM Altoona WI	WJEN(FM) Rutland VT
*WHCM(FM) Palatine IL	WHPE-FM High Point NC	*WICN(FM) Worcester MA	WIST(FM) Thomasville NC	WJEQ(FM) Macomb IL
*WHCN(FM) Hartford CT	*WHPK-FM Chicago IL	WICO-FM Salisbury MD	*WISU(FM) Terre Haute IN	WJER-FM Dover OH
*WHCR-FM New York NY	*WHPL(FM) West Lafayette IN	*WICR(FM) Indianapolis IN	WISY(FM) Canandaigua NY	WJEZ(FM) Dwight IL
WHCY(FM) Blairstown NJ	WHPO(FM) Hoopeston IL	*WICV(FM) East Jordan MI	*WITC(FM) Cazenovia NY	WJFD-FM New Bedford MA
WHDG(FM) Rhinelander WI	*WHPR(FM) Highland Park MI	WIDA-FM Carolina PR	WITF-FM Harrisburg PA	*WJFF(FM) Jeffersonville NY
*WHDI(FM) Sister Bay WI	WHPT(FM) Sarasota FL	WIDI(FM) Quebradillas PR	WITL-FM Lansing MI	WJFK-FM Manassas VA
WHDQ(FM) Claremont NH	WHPZ(FM) Bremen IN	WIDL(FM) Caro MI	*WITR(FM) Henrietta NY	*WJFL(FM) Tennille GA
WHDR(FM) Miami FL	WHQG(FM) Milwaukee WI	*WIDR(FM) Kalamazoo MI	WITX(FM) Beaver Falls PA	*WJFM(FM) Baton Rouge LA
WHDX(FM) Buxton NC	WHQO(FM) Skowhegan ME	WIFC(FM) Wausau WI	WITZ-FM Jasper IN	*WJFP(FM) Fort Pierce FL
WHDZ(FM) Buxton NC	WHQQ(FM) Neoga IL	WIFE(FM) Connersville IN	*WIUJ(FM) Charlotte Amalie VI	*WJFR(FM) Jacksonville FL
WHEB(FM) Portsmouth NH	*WHQR(FM) Wilmington NC	*WIFF(FM) Binghamton NY	*WIUM(FM) Macomb IL	WJFX(FM) New Haven IN
*WHEI(FM) Tiffin OH	*WHQT(FM) Coral Gables FL	WIFL(FM) Inglis FL	*WIUP-FM Indiana PA	WJGA-FM Jackson GA
WHEL(FM) Helen GA	WHQX(FM) Cedar Bluff VA	WIFM-FM Elkin NC	*WIUS(FM) Macomb IL	*WJGL(FM) Jacksonville FL
*WHEM(FM) Eau Claire WI	WHRB(FM) Cambridge MA	WIFN(FM) Macon GA	*WIUV(FM) Castleton VT	WJGO(FM) Tice FL
WHER(FM) Heidelberg MS	*WHRK(FM) Memphis TN	WIFO-FM Jesup GA	*WIUW(FM) Warsaw IL	*WJHD(FM) Portsmouth RI
WHFB-FM Benton Harbor MI	WHRL(FM) Albany NY	WIFX-FM Jenkins KY	WIVA-FM Aguadilla PR	*WJHM(FM) Daytona Beach FL
*WHFC(FM) Bel Air MD	*WHRM(FM) Wausau WI	*WIGH(FM) Lexington TN	*WIVH(FM) Christiansted VI	*WJHS(FM) Columbia City IN
WHFD(FM) Lawrenceville VA	*WHRO-FM Norfolk VA	WIGL(FM) Saint Matthews SC	WIVI(FM) Charlotte Amalie VI	WJHT(FM) State College PA
*WHFH(FM) Flossmoor IL	WHRP(FM) Tullahoma TN	WIGY(FM) Madison ME	WIVK-FM Knoxville TN	*WJIA(FM) Guntersville AL
*WHFI(FM) Lindside WV	*WHRS(FM) Cookeville TN	WIHC(FM) Newberry MI	WIVQ(FM) Spring Valley IL	*WJIC(FM) Zanesville OH
WHFM(FM) Southampton NY	*WHRV(FM) Norfolk VA	WIHN(FM) Normal IL	WIVR(FM) Kentland IN	*WJIE-FM Okolona KY
*WHFR(FM) Dearborn MI	WHRW(FM) Binghamton NY	*WIHS(FM) Middletown CT	WIVY(FM) Morehead KY	*WJIF(FM) Opp AL
WHFS(FM) Catonsville MD	*WHSA(FM) Brule WI	WIHT(FM) Washington DC	WIXM(FM) Millville NJ	*WJIJ(FM) Norlina NC
WHFX(FM) Darien GA	WHSB(FM) Alpena MI	WIII(FM) Cortland NY	*WIXO(FM) Bartonville IL	WJIM-FM Lansing MI
WHGL-FM Canton PA	*WHSD(FM) Hinsdale IL	WIIL(FM) Kenosha WI	*WIXQ(FM) Millersville PA	*WJIR(FM) Key West FL
*WHGN(FM) Crystal River FL	WHSM-FM Hayward WI	WIIS(FM) Key West FL	WIXV(FM) Savannah GA	*WJIS(FM) Bradenton FL
*WHHB(FM) Holliston MA	*WHSN(FM) Bangor ME	*WIIT(FM) Chicago IL	WIXX(FM) Green Bay WI	WJIV(FM) Cherry Valley NY
WHHH(FM) Indianapolis IN	*WHSS(FM) Hamilton OH	WIIZ(FM) Blackville SC	WIXY(FM) Champaign IL	*WJIW(FM) Greenville MS
*WHHI(FM) Highland WI	WHST(FM) Tawas City MI	WIJY(FM) Franklin IN	WIYN(FM) Deposit NY	WJIZ-FM Albany GA
WHHM-FM Henderson TN	WHSX(FM) Edmonton KY	WIKB-FM Iron River MI	WIYY(FM) Baltimore MD	*WJJB-FM Topsham ME
*WHHS(FM) Havertown PA	WHTA(FM) Hampton GA	WIKI(FM) Carrollton KY	*WIZB(FM) Abbeville AL	*WJJE(FM) Delaware OH
WHHT(FM) Horse Cave KY	WHTD-FM Mount Clemens MI	WIKK(FM) Newton IL	WIZD(FM) Rudolph WI	*WJJH(FM) Ashland WI
WHHY-FM Montgomery AL	WHTE-FM Ruckersville VA	*WIKL(FM) Greencastle IN	WIZF(FM) Erlanger KY	WJJJ(FM) Greensburg PA
WHHZ(FM) Newberry FL	WHTF(FM) Havana FL	WIKQ(FM) Tusculum TN	WIZM-FM La Crosse WI	WJJK(FM) Noblesville IN
*WHID(FM) Green Bay WI	WHTG-FM Eatontown NJ	WIKS(FM) New Bern NC	*WIZN(FM) Vergennes VT	*WJJM-FM Lewisburg TN
*WHIF(FM) Palatka FL	WHTI(FM) Alexandria IN	WIKX(FM) Charlotte Harbor FL	WJAA(FM) Austin IN	*WJJN(FM) Columbia AL
*WHIJ(FM) Ocala FL	WHTL-FM Whitehall WI	WIKY-FM Evansville IN	*WJAB(FM) Huntsville AL	WJJO(FM) Watertown WI
*WHIL-FM Mobile AL	WHTO(FM) Iron Mountain MI	WIKZ(FM) Chambersburg PA	WJAD(FM) Leesburg GA	WJJQ-FM Tomahawk WI
WHIR-FM Danville KY	WHTQ(FM) Orlando FL	WILE-FM Byesville OH	WJAM-FM Orrville AL	WJJR(FM) Rutland VT
WHIT-FM De Forest WI	WHTS-FM Rock Island IL	WIL-FM Saint Louis MO	WJAN(FM) Sunderland VT	*WJJS-FM Vinton VA
WHIZ-FM Zanesville OH	WHTT-FM Buffalo NY	WILI-FM Willimantic CT	WJAQ(FM) Marianna FL	*WJJW(FM) North Adams MA
*WHJE(FM) Carmel IN	WHTY(FM) Hartford City IN	*WILL-FM Urbana IL	WJAW-FM McConnelsville OH	WJJX(FM) Lynchburg VA
WHJT(FM) Clinton MS	WHTZ(FM) Newark NJ	WILN(FM) Panama City FL	*WJAZ(FM) Summerdale PA	WJJY-FM Brainerd MN
WHJX(FM) Baldwin FL	WHUD(FM) Peekskill NY	WILQ(FM) Williamsport PA	WJBB-FM Haleyville AL	*WJJZ(FM) Philadelphia PA
WHJY(FM) Providence RI	WHUG(FM) Jamestown NY	WILT(FM) Jacksonville NC	WJBD-FM Salem IL	*WJKA(FM) Jacksonville NC
WHKB(FM) Houghton MI	WHUR-FM Washington DC	WILV(FM) Chicago IL	WJBL(FM) Ladysmith WI	WJKC(FM) Christiansted VI
*WHKC(FM) Columbus OH	*WHUS(FM) Storrs CT	WILW(FM) Avalon NJ	WJBQ(FM) Portland ME	WJKI(FM) Bethany Beach DE
WHKF(FM) Harrisburg PA	WHUZ(FM) Saegertown PA	WILZ(FM) Saginaw MI	WJBR-FM Wilmington DE	WJKK(FM) Vicksburg MS
*WHKL(FM) Crenshaw MS	WHVE(FM) Russell Springs KY	WIMC(FM) Crawfordsville IN	*WJBT(FM) Green Cove Springs FL	WJKL(FM) Elgin IL
*WHKN(FM) Millen GA	*WHVP(FM) Hudson NY	WIMI(FM) Ironwood MI	WJBW(FM) Jupiter FL	*WJKN-FM Spring Arbor MI
WHKO(FM) Dayton OH	*WHVT(FM) Clyde OH	WIMK(FM) Iron Mountain MI	WJBX(FM) Fort Myers Beach FL	*WJKQ(FM) Jackson MI
WHKR(FM) Rockledge FL	*WHWC(FM) Menomonie WI	WIMT(FM) Lima OH	WJBZ-FM Seymour TN	WJKS(FM) Canton NJ
WHKS(FM) Port Allegany PA	*WHWE(FM) Howe IN	WIMX(FM) Gibsonburg OH	*WJCA(FM) Albion NY	WJKW(FM) Athens OH
WHKX(FM) Bluefield VA	*WHWG(FM) Trout Lake MI	WIMZ-FM Knoxville TN	*WJCB(FM) Clewiston FL	*WJKX(FM) Ellisville MS
*WHLA(FM) La Crosse WI	WHWK(FM) Binghamton NY	WINC-FM Winchester VA	WJCD(FM) Windsor VA	WJLB(FM) Detroit MI
WHLC(FM) Highlands NC	WHWL(FM) Marquette MI	WINK-FM Fort Myers FL	*WJCE(FM) Elkton MI	WJLE-FM Smithville TN
WHLF(FM) South Boston VA	WHXQ(FM) Kennebunkport ME	WINL(FM) Linden NY	*WJCF(FM) Morristown IN	*WJLF(FM) Gainesville FL
WHLG(FM) Port St. Lucie FL	WHXR(FM) North Windham ME	WINN(FM) Columbus IN	*WJCG(FM) Monee IL	*WJLH(FM) Flagler Beach FL
WHLH(FM) Jackson MS	WHXT(FM) Orangeburg SC	WINQ(FM) Winchester NH		WJLK-FM Asbury Park NJ

Broadcasting & Cable Yearbook 2006

D-633

U.S. FM Stations by Call Letters

WJLQ(FM) Pensacola FL
*WJLR(FM) Seymour IN
WJLS-FM Beckley WV
WJLT(FM) Evansville IN
*WJLU(FM) New Smyrna Beach FL
WJLW(FM) Allouez WI
*WJLY(FM) Ramsey IL
*WJLZ(FM) Virginia Beach VA
WJMA-FM Culpeper VA
WJMC-FM Rice Lake WI
WJMD(FM) Hazard KY
*WJMF(FM) Smithfield RI
WJMG(FM) Hattiesburg MS
WJMH(FM) Reidsville NC
WJMI(FM) Jackson MS
*WJMJ(FM) Hartford CT
WJMK(FM) Chicago IL
WJMM-FM Keene KY
WJMN(FM) Boston MA
WJMQ(FM) Clintonville WI
WJMR-FM Menomonee Falls WI
*WJMU(FM) Decatur IL
WJMX-FM Cheraw SC
WJMZ-FM Anderson SC
*WJNF(FM) Marianna FL
WJNG(FM) Johnsonburg PA
*WJNI(FM) Ladson SC
WJNR-FM Iron Mountain MI
WJNS-FM Yazoo City MS
WJNV(FM) Jonesville VA
*WJNY(FM) Watertown NY
*WJOD(FM) Asbury IA
*WJOG(FM) Good Hart MI
*WJOH(FM) Raco MI
*WJOJ(FM) Harrisville MI
*WJOM(FM) Eagle MI
WJOR-FM Saint Joseph TN
WJOT-FM Wabash IN
WJPA-FM Washington PA
WJPD(FM) Ishpeming MI
*WJPG(FM) Cape May Court House NJ
*WJPH(FM) Woodbine NJ
WJPT-FM Fort Myers Villas FL
*WJPZ-FM Syracuse NY
WJQB(FM) Spring Hill FL
WJQK(FM) Zeeland MI
WJQZ(FM) Wellsville NY
*WJRC(FM) Lewistown PA
WJRE(FM) Galva IL
*WJRF(FM) Duluth MN
*WJRH(FM) Easton PA
WJRL-FM Ozark AL
WJRR(FM) Cocoa Beach FL
WJRS(FM) Jamestown KY
WJRZ-FM Manahawkin NJ
WJSA-FM Jersey Shore PA
*WJSC-FM Johnson VT
WJSE(FM) Petersburg NJ
WJSG(FM) Hamlet NC
WJSH(FM) Folsom LA
WJSJ(FM) Fernandina Beach FL
*WJSL(FM) Houghton NY
WJSM-FM Martinsburg PA
WJSN-FM Jackson KY
*WJSO(FM) Pikeville KY
*WJSP-FM Warm Springs GA
WJSQ(FM) Athens TN
*WJSR(FM) Birmingham AL
*WJSU(FM) Jackson MS
*WJSV(FM) Morristown NJ
WJSZ(FM) Ashley MI
*WJTA(FM) Kosciusko MS
*WJTF(FM) Panama City FL
*WJTG(FM) Fort Valley GA
*WJTL(FM) Lancaster PA
WJTT(FM) Red Bank TN
*WJTY(FM) Lancaster WI
WJUC(FM) Swanton OH
*WJUF(FM) Inverness FL
WJUN-FM Mexico PA
WJUX(FM) Monticello NY
*WJVK(FM) Owensboro KY
WJVL(FM) Janesville WI
WJVO(FM) South Jacksonville IL
*WJVP(FM) Culebra PR
WJVS(FM) Cincinnati OH

*WJWD(FM) Marshall WI
*WJWJ-FM Beaufort SC
*WJWT(FM) Gardner MA
*WJWV(FM) Fort Gaines GA
WJWZ(FM) Wetumpka AL
WJXA(FM) Nashville TN
WJXB-FM Knoxville TN
WJXM(FM) De Kalb MS
WJXN-FM Utica MS
WJXQ(FM) Jackson MI
WJXR(FM) Macclenny FL
WJXY(FM) Conway SC
*WJYA(FM) Emporia VA
*WJYC(FM) Delhi Hills OH
WJYD(FM) London OH
WJYE(FM) Buffalo NY
WJYF(FM) Nashville GA
*WJYJ(FM) Fredericksburg VA
WJYO(FM) Fort Myers FL
*WJYW(FM) Union City IN
WJYY(FM) Concord NH
WJZA(FM) Lancaster OH
*WJZB(FM) Starkville MS
WJZD(FM) Long Beach MS
WJZE(FM) Oak Harbor OH
WJZI(FM) Milwaukee WI
WJZJ(FM) Glen Arbor MI
WJZK(FM) Richwood OH
WJZO(FM) Shelbyville KY
WJZQ(FM) Cadillac MI
WJZR(FM) Rochester NY
WJZS(FM) Block Island RI
WJZT(FM) Woodville FL
WJZV(FM) Ettrick VA
WJZW(FM) Woodbridge VA
WJZZ-FM Roswell GA
WKAA(FM) Willacoochee GA
WKAB(FM) Berwick PA
WKAD(FM) Harrietta MI
WKAI(FM) Macomb IL
WKAK(FM) Albany GA
WKAQ-FM San Juan PR
*WKAR-FM East Lansing MI
WKAY(FM) Knoxville IL
WKAZ(FM) Miami WV
WKBB(FM) West Point MS
WKBC-FM North Wilkesboro NC
WKBE(FM) Warrensburg NY
WKBH-FM West Salem WI
WKBI-FM Saint Marys PA
WKBQ(FM) Covington TN
WKBU(FM) Kenner LA
WKBX(FM) Kingsland GA
WKCA(FM) Owingsville KY
WKCB-FM Hindman KY
*WKCC(FM) Kankakee IL
WKCG(FM) Augusta ME
WKCH(FM) Whitewater WI
WKCI-FM Hamden CT
WKCJ(FM) Lewisburg WV
*WKCL(FM) Ladson SC
WKCN(FM) Lumpkin GA
*WKCO(FM) Gambier OH
WKCQ(FM) Saginaw MI
*WKCR-FM New York NY
*WKCS(FM) Knoxville TN
WKCX(FM) Rome GA
WKCY-FM Harrisonburg VA
WKDB(FM) Laurel DE
WKDD(FM) Canton OH
WKDE-FM Altavista VA
WKDF(FM) Nashville TN
WKDG(FM) Martinez GA
WKDJ-FM Clarksdale MS
*WKDN-FM Camden NJ
WKDO(FM) Liberty KY
WKDP-FM Corbin KY
WKDQ(FM) Henderson KY
*WKDS(FM) Kalamazoo MI
*WKDU(FM) Philadelphia PA
WKDZ-FM Cadiz KY
WKEA-FM Scottsboro AL
WKEB(FM) Medford WI
WKED-FM Frankfort KY
WKEE-FM Huntington WV
WKEQ(FM) Somerset KY
WKES(FM) Lakeland FL

*WKET(FM) Kettering OH
*WKEU-FM The Rock GA
WKEY-FM Key West FL
WKEZ-FM Tavenier FL
*WKFA(FM) Saint Catherine FL
WKFM(FM) Huron OH
WKFR-FM Battle Creek MI
WKFS(FM) Milford OH
WKFX(FM) Rice Lake WI
WKGA(FM) Dadeville AL
WKGB-FM Susquehanna PA
*WKGC-FM Panama City FL
WKGL-FM Loves Park IL
WKGO(FM) Cumberland MD
WKGR(FM) Fort Pierce FL
WKGS(FM) Irondequoit NY
WKHC(FM) Dahlonega GA
WKHG(FM) Leitchfield KY
WKHI(FM) Fruitland MD
WKHJ(FM) Mountain Lake Park MD
WKHK(FM) Colonial Heights VA
WKHL(FM) Stamford CT
WKHM-FM Brooklyn MI
*WKHN(FM) Hubbard Lake MI
WKHQ-FM Charlevoix MI
*WKHR(FM) Bainbridge OH
*WKHS(FM) Worton MD
WKHT(FM) Knoxville TN
WKHW(FM) Pocomoke City MD
WKHX-FM Marietta GA
WKHY(FM) Lafayette IN
WKIB(FM) Anna IL
WKID(FM) Vevay IN
WKIE(FM) Arlington Heights IL
WKIF(FM) Kankakee IL
WKIK-FM California MD
WKIS(FM) Boca Raton FL
WKIT-FM Brewer ME
WKIX(FM) Goldsboro NC
WKJC(FM) Tawas City MI
*WKJL(FM) Clarksburg WV
WKJM(FM) Petersburg VA
WKJQ(FM) Parsons TN
*WKJR(FM) Jasper IN
WKJS(FM) Richmond VA
WKJT(FM) Teutopolis IL
WKJX(FM) Elizabeth City NC
WKJY(FM) Hempstead NY
WKJZ(FM) Hillman MI
WKKB(FM) Middletown RI
*WKKC(FM) Chicago IL
WKKF(FM) Ballston Spa NY
WKKG(FM) Columbus IN
WKKI(FM) Celina OH
WKKJ(FM) Chillicothe OH
*WKKL(FM) West Barnstable MA
WKKO(FM) Toledo OH
WKKQ(FM) Barbourville KY
WKKR(FM) Auburn AL
WKKS-FM Vanceburg KY
WKKT(FM) Statesville NC
WKKV-FM Racine WI
WKKW(FM) Fairmont WV
WKKY(FM) Geneva OH
WKKZ(FM) Dublin GA
WKLA-FM Ludington MI
WKLB(FM) Lowell MA
WKLC-FM Saint Albans WV
WKLD(FM) Oneonta AL
WKLG(FM) Rock Harbor FL
WKLH(FM) Milwaukee WI
WKLI-FM Albany NY
WKLK-FM Cloquet MN
WKLL(FM) Frankfort NY
WKLM(FM) Millersburg OH
WKLN(FM) Wilmington OH
WKLO(FM) Hardinsburg IN
WKLQ(FM) Greenville MI
WKLR(FM) Fort Lee VA
WKLS(FM) Atlanta GA
WKLT(FM) Kalkaska MI
WKLU(FM) Brownsburg IN
WKLW-FM Paintsville KY
WKLX(FM) Beaver Dam KY
WKLZ(FM) Petoskey MI
WKMJ(FM) Hancock MI
WKML(FM) Lumberton NC

WKMM(FM) Kingwood WV
WKMO(FM) Hodgenville KY
*WKMS-FM Murray KY
WKMX(FM) Enterprise AL
*WKMY(FM) Winchendon MA
WKNA(FM) Senatobia MS
WKNB(FM) Clarendon PA
*WKNC-FM Raleigh NC
WKNE(FM) Keene NH
WKNG-FM Heflin AL
*WKNH(FM) Keene NH
*WKNJ-FM Union Township NJ
WKNL(FM) New London CT
WKNN-FM Pascagoula MS
*WKNO-FM Memphis TN
*WKNP(FM) Jackson TN
*WKNQ(FM) Dyersburg TN
WKNS(FM) Kinston NC
WKNU(FM) Brewton AL
WKNZ(FM) Collins MS
WKOA(FM) Lafayette IN
WKOE(FM) Ocean City NJ
WKOL(FM) Plattsburgh NY
WKOM(FM) Columbia TN
WKOQ(FM) Newaygo MI
WKOR-FM Columbus MS
WKOS(FM) Kingsport TN
WKOT(FM) Marseilles IL
WKOV-FM Wellston OH
WKOY(FM) Princeton WV
*WKPB(FM) Henderson KY
WKPE-FM Orleans MA
WKPK(FM) Gaylord MI
WKPL(FM) Ellwood City PA
WKPO(FM) Evansville WI
WKPQ(FM) Hornell NY
*WKPS(FM) State College PA
*WKPW(FM) Knightstown IN
*WKPX(FM) Sunrise FL
WKQB(FM) Southern Pines NC
WKQC(FM) Charlotte NC
WKQH(FM) Marathon WI
WKQI(FM) Detroit MI
WKQL(FM) Brunswick GA
WKQQ(FM) Winchester KY
WKQS-FM Negaunee MI
WKQV(FM) Richwood WV
WKQW-FM Oil City PA
WKQX(FM) Chicago IL
WKQY(FM) Tazewell VA
WKQZ(FM) Midland MI
WKRA-FM Holly Springs MS
*WKRB(FM) Brooklyn NY
WKRF(FM) Tobyhanna PA
WKRH(FM) Minetto NY
*WKRJ(FM) New Philadelphia OH
WKRK-FM Detroit MI
WKRL-FM North Syracuse NY
WKRO-FM Edgewater FL
WKRQ(FM) Cincinnati OH
WKRR(FM) Asheboro NC
WKRV(FM) Vandalia IL
*WKRW(FM) Wooster OH
WKRX(FM) Roxboro NC
*WKRY(FM) Versailles IN
WKRZ-FM Wilkes-Barre PA
WKSA-FM Isabela PR
WKSB(FM) Williamsport PA
WKSC-FM Chicago IL
WKSD(FM) Paulding OH
WKSE(FM) Niagara Falls NY
WKSF(FM) Asheville NC
*WKSG(FM) Cedar Creek KY
WKSI-FM Stephens City VA
WKSJ-FM Mobile AL
WKSK-FM South Hill VA
WKSM(FM) Fort Walton Beach FL
WKSO(FM) Natchez MS
WKSP(FM) Aiken SC
WKSQ(FM) Ellsworth ME
WKSR-FM Pulaski TN
WKSS(FM) Hartford CT
WKST-FM Pittsburgh PA
*WKSU-FM Kent OH
*WKSV(FM) Thompson OH
WKSW(FM) Urbana OH
WKSX(FM) Johnston SC

WKSY(FM) Picayune MS
WKSZ(FM) De Pere WI
WKTG(FM) Madisonville KY
WKTI(FM) Milwaukee WI
WKTJ-FM Farmington ME
WKTK(FM) Crystal River FL
*WKTL(FM) Struthers OH
WKTM(FM) Soperton GA
WKTN(FM) Kenton OH
*WKTO(FM) Edgewater FL
*WKTS(FM) Kingston TN
WKTU(FM) Lake Success NY
*WKTZ-FM Jacksonville FL
WKUB(FM) Blackshear GA
*WKUE(FM) Elizabethtown KY
WKUL(FM) Cullman AL
WKUS(FM) Norfolk VA
WKUZ(FM) Wabash IN
WKVB(FM) Port Matilda PA
*WKVC(FM) North Myrtle Beach SC
WKVE(FM) Semora NC
*WKVF(FM) Byhalia MS
*WKVH(FM) Monticello FL
WKVI-FM Knox IN
*WKVJ(FM) Dannemora NY
WKVK(FM) Honor MI
WKVL-FM Loudon TN
*WKVR-FM Huntingdon PA
WKVS(FM) Lenoir NC
WKVT-FM Brattleboro VT
*WKVU(FM) Utica NY
*WKVW(FM) Marmet WV
*WKVY(FM) Somerset KY
WKVZ(FM) Ripley TN
*WKWC(FM) Owensboro KY
WKWH-FM Rushville IN
*WKWI(FM) Kilmarnock VA
WKWK-FM Wheeling WV
*WKWR(FM) Key West FL
WKWS(FM) Charleston WV
WKWX(FM) Savannah TN
WKWY(FM) Tompkinsville KY
*WKWZ(FM) Syosset NY
WKXA-FM Findlay OH
WKXB(FM) Burgaw NC
WKXC-FM Aiken SC
WKXD(FM) Monterey TN
*WKXH(FM) Saint Johnsbury VT
WKXI-FM Magee MS
WKXJ(FM) Signal Mountain TN
WKXK(FM) Pine Hill AL
WKXM-FM Winfield AL
WKXN(FM) Greenville AL
WKXP(FM) Kingston NY
WKXQ(FM) Rushville IL
WKXS-FM Leland NC
WKXU(FM) Louisburg NC
WKXW-FM Trenton NJ
WKXX(FM) Attalla AL
WKXY(FM) Clarksdale MS
WKXZ(FM) Norwich NY
WKYA(FM) Greenville KY
WKYE(FM) Johnstown PA
*WKYJ(FM) Rouses Point NY
WKYL(FM) Lawrenceburg KY
WKYM(FM) Monticello KY
WKYQ(FM) Paducah KY
WKYR-FM Burkesville KY
WKYS(FM) Washington DC
*WKYU-FM Bowling Green KY
WKYW(FM) Frankfort KY
WKYZ(FM) Key Colony Beach FL
WKZA(FM) Lakewood NY
WKZB(FM) Stonewall MS
WKZC(FM) Scottville MI
*WKZE-FM Salisbury CT
WKZJ(FM) Eufaula AL
WKZL(FM) Winston-Salem NC
*WKZM(FM) Sarasota FL
WKZP(FM) Spencer TN
WKZQ-FM Myrtle Beach SC
WKZR(FM) Milledgeville GA
WKZS(FM) Covington IN
WKZU(FM) Ripley MS
WKZW(FM) Bay Springs MS
WKZX-FM Lenoir City TN
WKZY(FM) Cross City FL

U.S. FM Stations by Call Letters

WKZZ(FM) Tifton GA
*WLAB(FM) Fort Wayne IN
WLAK-FM Huntingdon PA
WLAN-FM Lancaster PA
WLAV-FM Grand Rapids MI
WLAY-FM Tuscumbia AL
*WLAZ(FM) Kissimmee FL
WLBC-FM Muncie IN
*WLBF(FM) Montgomery AL
WLBH-FM Mattoon IL
*WLBL-FM Wausau WI
*WLBS(FM) Bristol PA
WLBW(FM) Fenwick Island DE
*WLCA(FM) Godfrey IL
*WLCH(FM) Lancaster PA
WLCN(FM) Atlanta IL
WLCS(FM) North Muskegon MI
WLCT(FM) Lafayette TN
WLCY(FM) Blairsville PA
WLDA(FM) Fort Rucker AL
WLDE(FM) Fort Wayne IN
WLDI(FM) Fort Pierce FL
WLDR-FM Traverse City MI
WLEG(FM) Ligonier IN
WLEN(FM) Adrian MI
WLER-FM Butler PA
WLEV(FM) Allentown PA
WLEW-FM Bad Axe MI
WLEY-FM Aurora IL
*WLFA(FM) Asheville NC
*WLFC(FM) Findlay OH
WLFE-FM Saint Albans VT
WLFF(FM) Brookston IN
*WLFJ-FM Greenville SC
*WLFM(FM) Appleton WI
*WLFR(FM) Pomona NJ
*WLFS(FM) Port Wentworth GA
WLFW(FM) Chandler IN
WLFX(FM) Berea KY
WLGC-FM Greenup KY
*WLGH(FM) Leroy Township MI
*WLGI(FM) Hemingway SC
WLGL(FM) Riverside PA
WLGN-FM Logan OH
WLGP(FM) Harkers Island NC
WLGT(FM) Washington NC
*WLGY(FM) Nanty Glo PA
WLHC(FM) Robbins NC
WLHK(FM) Shelbyville IN
WLHM(FM) Logansport IN
*WLHS(FM) West Chester OH
WLHT-FM Grand Rapids MI
*WLHW(FM) Casey IL
*WLIC(FM) Frostburg MD
WLIE-FM Golconda IL
WLIF(FM) Baltimore MD
WLIH(FM) Whitneyville PA
WLIN-FM Durant MS
WLIR-FM Hampton Bays NY
WLIT-FM Chicago IL
*WLIU(FM) Southampton NY
WLIV-FM Monterey TN
WLJA-FM Ellijay GA
WLJC(FM) Beattyville KY
WLJE(FM) Valparaiso IN
*WLJH(FM) Glens Falls NY
WLJI(FM) Summerton SC
*WLJK(FM) Aiken SC
*WLJN-FM Traverse City MI
*WLJP(FM) Monroe NY
*WLJR(FM) Birmingham AL
*WLJS-FM Jacksonville AL
WLJY(FM) Marshfield WI
WLJZ(FM) Mackinaw City MI
WLKC(FM) Campton NH
WLKE(FM) Bar Harbor ME
WLKG(FM) Lake Geneva WI
WLKH(FM) Somerset PA
WLKI(FM) Angola IN
WLKJ(FM) Portage PA
WLKK(FM) Wethersfield Township NY
*WLKL(FM) Mattoon IL
WLKM-FM Three Rivers MI
WLKN(FM) Cleveland WI
*WLKP(FM) Belpre OH
WLKQ-FM Buford GA
WLKR-FM Norwalk OH

WLKS-FM West Liberty KY
WLKT(FM) Lexington-Fayette KY
*WLKV(FM) Ripley WV
WLKX-FM Forest Lake MN
WLKZ(FM) Wolfeboro NH
WLLD(FM) Holmes Beach FL
WLLE(FM) Clinton KY
WLLF(FM) Mercer PA
WLLG(FM) Lowville NY
WLLJ(FM) Etowah TN
WLLK-FM Somerset KY
WLLR-FM Davenport IA
WLLT(FM) Polo IL
WLLW(FM) Seneca Falls NY
WLLX(FM) Lawrenceburg TN
WLMD(FM) Bushnell IL
WLME(FM) Cannelton IN
WLMG(FM) New Orleans LA
*WLMH(FM) Morrow OH
WLMI(FM) Kane PA
WLMS(FM) Lecanto FL
*WLMU(FM) Harrogate TN
*WLMW(FM) Manchester NH
WLMX-FM Balsam Lake WI
WLNG(FM) Sag Harbor NY
WLNH-FM Laconia NH
WLNI(FM) Lynchburg VA
WLNK(FM) Charlotte NC
WLNX(FM) Lincoln IL
*WLNZ(FM) Lansing MI
WLOB-FM Rumford ME
WLOD-FM Sweetwater TN
WLOF(FM) Attica NY
*WLOG(FM) Markleysburg PA
WLOQ(FM) Winter Park FL
WLOW(FM) Port Royal SC
*WLPE(FM) Augusta GA
*WLPF(FM) Ocilla GA
*WLPG(FM) Florence SC
*WLPJ(FM) New Port Richey FL
*WLPT(FM) Jesup GA
WLPW(FM) Lake Placid NY
WLQB(FM) Ocean Isle Beach NC
WLQI(FM) Rensselaer IN
WLQK(FM) Livingston TN
WLQM-FM Franklin VA
WLQT(FM) Kettering OH
*WLRA(FM) Lockport IL
WLRD(FM) Willard OH
*WLRH(FM) Huntsville AL
WLRK(FM) Wausau WI
*WLRN-FM Miami FL
WLRO(FM) Richmond KY
WLRQ-FM Cocoa FL
WLRR(FM) Milledgeville GA
WLRS(FM) Shepherdsville KY
WLRW(FM) Champaign IL
*WLRY(FM) Rushville OH
WLSK(FM) Lebanon KY
WLSL(FM) Three Lakes WI
WLSM-FM Louisville MS
*WLSN(FM) Grand Marais MN
*WLSO(FM) Sault Ste. Marie MI
WLSQ-FM Dyer TN
WLSR(FM) Galesburg IL
WLST(FM) Marinette WI
*WLSU(FM) La Crosse WI
WLSW(FM) Scottdale PA
WLSZ(FM) Humboldt TN
WLTB(FM) Johnson City NY
WLTE(FM) Minneapolis MN
WLTF(FM) Martinsburg WV
WLTI(FM) Syracuse NY
WLTJ(FM) Pittsburgh PA
WLTK(FM) New Market VA
*WLTL(FM) La Grange IL
WLTM(FM) Atlanta GA
WLTN-FM Lisbon NH
WLTO(FM) Nicholasville KY
WLTQ-FM Venice FL
*WLTR(FM) Columbia SC
*WLTS(FM) State College PA
WLTT(FM) Shallotte NC
WLTU(FM) Manitowoc WI
WLTW(FM) New York NY
WLTY(FM) Cayce SC
WLUE(FM) Louisville KY

*WLUJ(FM) Springfield IL
WLUM-FM Milwaukee WI
WLUP-FM Chicago IL
*WLUR(FM) Lexington VA
WLUS-FM Clarksville VA
*WLUW(FM) Chicago IL
WLVB(FM) Morrisville VT
WLVE(FM) Miami Beach FL
*WLVF-FM Haines City FL
WLVG(FM) Center Moriches NY
WLVH(FM) Hardeeville SC
WLVK(FM) Fort Knox KY
WLVQ(FM) Columbus OH
*WLVR(FM) Bethlehem PA
WLVS-FM Clifton TN
WLVX(FM) Elberton GA
WLVY(FM) Elmira NY
WLWD(FM) Columbus Grove OH
*WLWF(FM) Ravenswood WV
WLWI-FM Montgomery AL
*WLWJ(FM) Petersburg IL
*WLWR(FM) Fond du Lac WI
WLXC(FM) Lexington SC
*WLXO(FM) Stamping Ground KY
*WLXP(FM) Savannah GA
WLXR-FM La Crosse WI
WLXT(FM) Petoskey MI
WLXV(FM) Cadillac MI
WLXX(FM) Lexington KY
WLYD(FM) Sturgeon Bay WI
WLYE-FM Glasgow KY
WLYF(FM) Miami FL
WLYT(FM) Hickory NC
WLYU(FM) Lyons GA
WLZA(FM) Eupora MS
WLZK(FM) Paris TN
WLZL(FM) Annapolis MD
WLZN(FM) Macon GA
WLZQ(FM) South Whitley IN
WLZS(FM) Beaver Springs PA
WLZT(FM) Chillicothe OH
WLZW(FM) Utica NY
WLZX(FM) Northampton MA
WLZZ(FM) Montpelier OH
*WMAB-FM Mississippi State MS
WMAD(FM) Sauk City WI
*WMAE-FM Booneville MS
WMAG(FM) High Point NC
*WMAH-FM Biloxi MS
*WMAO-FM Greenwood MS
WMAS-FM Springfield MA
*WMAU-FM Bude MS
*WMAV-FM Oxford MS
*WMAW-FM Meridian MS
WMAX-FM South Pittsburg TN
WMBC-FM Columbus MS
*WMBI-FM Chicago IL
*WMBJ(FM) Murrell's Inlet SC
*WMBL(FM) Mitchell IN
*WMBR(FM) Cambridge MA
*WMBU(FM) Forest MS
*WMBV(FM) Dixons Mills AL
*WMBW(FM) Chattanooga TN
WMBX(FM) Jensen Beach FL
*WMBZ(FM) Germantown TN
WMCD(FM) Claxton GA
*WMCE(FM) Erie PA
WMC-FM Memphis TN
WMCG(FM) Milan GA
WMCI(FM) Mattoon IL
WMCM(FM) Rockland ME
*WMCN(FM) Saint Paul MN
*WMCO(FM) New Concord OH
*WMCQ(FM) Muskegon MI
WMCR-FM Oneida NY
*WMCU(FM) Miami FL
*WMCX(FM) West Long Branch NJ
WMDC(FM) Mayville WI
WMDH-FM New Castle IN
WMDJ-FM Allen KY
*WMDM-FM Lexington Park MD
*WMDR-FM Oakland ME
*WMEA(FM) Portland ME
*WMEB-FM Orono ME
*WMED(FM) Calais ME
WMEE(FM) Fort Wayne IN
WMEF(FM) Fort Kent ME

WMEG(FM) Guayama PR
*WMEH(FM) Bangor ME
*WMEJ(FM) Proctorville OH
*WMEM(FM) Presque Isle ME
*WMEP(FM) Camden ME
WMEQ-FM Menomonie WI
WMEV-FM Marion VA
*WMEW(FM) Waterville ME
WMEX(FM) Farmington NH
WMEZ(FM) Pensacola FL
WMFC-FM Monroeville AL
*WMFE-FM Orlando FL
WMFG-FM Hibbing MN
*WMFL(FM) Florida City FL
*WMFM(FM) Key West FL
*WMFO(FM) Medford MA
WMFQ(FM) Ocala FL
WMFS(FM) Bartlett TN
*WMFT(FM) Tuscaloosa AL
*WMFX(FM) Saint Andrews SC
WMGB(FM) Montezuma GA
WMGC-FM Detroit MI
WMGE(FM) Miami Beach FL
WMGF(FM) Mount Dora FL
WMGH-FM Tamaqua PA
WMGI(FM) Terre Haute IN
WMGK(FM) Philadelphia PA
WMGL(FM) Ravenel SC
WMGM(FM) Atlantic City NJ
WMGN(FM) Madison WI
WMGP(FM) Hogansville GA
WMGQ(FM) New Brunswick NJ
WMGS(FM) Wilkes-Barre PA
WMGV(FM) Newport NC
WMGX(FM) Portland ME
WMGZ(FM) Eatonton GA
*WMHB(FM) Waterville ME
*WMHC(FM) South Hadley MA
*WMHD-FM Terre Haute IN
*WMHI(FM) Cape Vincent NY
*WMHK(FM) Columbia SC
*WMHN(FM) Webster NY
*WMHQ(FM) Malone NY
*WMHR(FM) Syracuse NY
*WMHS(FM) Pike Creek DE
*WMHT-FM Schenectady NY
*WMHW-FM Mount Pleasant MI
WMHX(FM) Hershey PA
WMIB(FM) Fort Lauderdale FL
*WMIE(FM) Cocoa FL
WMIK-FM Middlesboro KY
*WMIL(FM) Waukesha WI
WMIO(FM) Cabo Rojo PR
WMIT(FM) Black Mountain NC
WMIX-FM Mount Vernon IL
WMJC(FM) Smithtown NY
WMJD(FM) Grundy VA
WMJE(FM) Clarkesville GA
WMJI(FM) Cleveland OH
WMJJ(FM) Birmingham AL
WMJK(FM) Clyde OH
WMJL-FM Marion KY
WMJM(FM) Jeffersontown KY
WMJO(FM) Essexville MI
WMJQ(FM) Brockport NY
WMJU(FM) Bude MS
WMJW(FM) Cleveland MS
WMJX(FM) Boston MA
WMJY(FM) Biloxi MS
WMJZ-FM Gaylord MI
WMKB(FM) Earlville IL
*WMKC(FM) Saint Ignace MI
*WMKJ(FM) Mt. Sterling KY
*WMKL(FM) Key Largo FL
*WMKO(FM) Marco FL
WMKR(FM) Pana IL
*WMKV(FM) Reading OH
*WMKW(FM) Crossville TN
WMKX(FM) Brookville PA
*WMKY(FM) Morehead KY
WMKZ(FM) Monticello KY
*WMLJ(FM) Summersville WV
*WMLL(FM) Bedford NH
*WMLN-FM Milton MA
*WMLS(FM) Grand Marais MN
*WMLU(FM) Farmville VA
*WMLV(FM) Butler AL

WMLX(FM) Saint Mary's OH
WMMA(FM) Nekoosa WI
WMMC(FM) Marshall IL
WMME-FM Augusta ME
WMMG-FM Brandenburg KY
WMMJ(FM) Bethesda MD
WMMM-FM Verona WI
WMMO(FM) Orlando FL
WMMQ(FM) East Lansing MI
WMMR(FM) Philadelphia PA
WMMS(FM) Cleveland OH
*WMMT(FM) Whitesburg KY
WMMX(FM) Dayton OH
WMMY(FM) Jefferson NC
WMMZ(FM) Meridian MS
WMNA-FM Gretna VA
WMNB(FM) North Adams MA
WMNC-FM Morganton NC
*WMNF(FM) Tampa FL
WMNG(FM) Christiansted VI
*WMNJ(FM) Madison NJ
*WMNR(FM) Monroe CT
WMNV(FM) Rupert VT
WMNX(FM) Wilmington NC
*WMOC(FM) Lumber City GA
WMOD(FM) Bolivar TN
WMOI(FM) Monmouth IL
WMOJ(FM) Fairfield OH
WMOM(FM) Pentwater MI
WMOO(FM) Derby Center VT
WMOQ(FM) Bostwick GA
WMOR-FM Morehead KY
WMOS(FM) Montauk NY
*WMOT(FM) Murfreesboro TN
WMOZ(FM) Moose Lake MN
*WMPG(FM) Gorham ME
*WMPH(FM) Wilmington DE
WMPI(FM) Scottsburg IN
*WMPN-FM Jackson MS
*WMPR(FM) Jackson MS
WMPW(FM) Munford TN
*WMPZ(FM) Ringgold GA
WMQA-FM Minocqua WI
*WMQT(FM) Ishpeming MI
WMQX-FM Winston-Salem NC
*WMQZ(FM) Colchester IL
*WMRA(FM) Harrisonburg VA
WMRF-FM Lewistown PA
*WMRI(FM) Marion IN
*WMRL(FM) Lexington VA
WMRN-FM Marion OH
WMRR(FM) Muskegon Heights MI
WMRS(FM) Monticello IN
*WMRT(FM) Marietta OH
WMRV-FM Endicott NY
WMRX-FM Beaverton MI
*WMRY(FM) Crozet VA
WMRZ(FM) Dawson GA
*WMSC(FM) Upper Montclair NJ
*WMSD(FM) Rose Township MI
*WMSE(FM) Milwaukee WI
WMSH-FM Sturgis MI
WMSI(FM) Jackson MS
*WMSJ(FM) Freeport ME
WMSK-FM Morganfield KY
*WMSL(FM) Athens GA
WMSO(FM) Newton MS
*WMSQ(FM) Marlette MI
WMSR-FM Collinwood TN
*WMSS(FM) Middletown PA
WMSU(FM) Starkville MS
*WMSV(FM) Starkville MS
*WMTB-FM Emmittsburg MD
WMTC-FM Vancleve KY
WMTD-FM Hinton WV
*WMTE-FM Manistee MI
WMT-FM Cedar Rapids IA
*WMTH(FM) Park Ridge IL
WMTK(FM) Littleton NH
WMTM-FM Moultrie GA
WMTR-FM Archbold OH
*WMTS-FM Murfreesboro TN
WMTT(FM) Tioga PA
*WMTU-FM Houghton MI
WMTX(FM) Tampa FL
*WMUA(FM) Amherst MA
*WMUB(FM) Oxford OH

U.S. FM Stations by Call Letters

*WMUC-FM College Park MD
WMUF-FM Henry TN
*WMUH(FM) Allentown PA
*WMUK(FM) Kalamazoo MI
*WMUL(FM) Huntington WV
WMUS(FM) Muskegon MI
WMUT(FM) Grenada MS
WMUU-FM Greenville SC
WMUZ(FM) Detroit MI
*WMVE(FM) Chase City VA
*WMVL(FM) Linesville PA
*WMVM(FM) Goodman WI
WMVR-FM Sidney OH
*WMVV(FM) Griffin GA
*WMVX(FM) Cleveland OH
WMVY(FM) Tisbury MA
*WMWK(FM) Milwaukee WI
*WMWM(FM) Salem MA
WMWV(FM) Conway NH
WMXA(FM) Opelika AL
WMXB(FM) Richmond VA
WMXC(FM) Mobile AL
WMXD(FM) Detroit MI
WMXE(FM) South Charleston WV
WMXG(FM) Stephenson MI
WMXH-FM Luray VA
WMXI(FM) Laurel MS
WMXJ(FM) Pompano Beach FL
WMXK(FM) Morristown TN
WMXL(FM) Lexington KY
*WMXM(FM) Lake Forest IL
WMXN-FM Stevenson AL
WMXO(FM) Olean NY
WMXQ(FM) Jacksonville FL
WMXR(FM) Woodstock VT
WMXS(FM) Montgomery AL
WMXT(FM) Pamplico SC
WMXU(FM) Starkville MS
WMXV(FM) Russellville AL
WMXW(FM) Vestal NY
WMXX-FM Jackson TN
WMXY(FM) Youngstown OH
WMXZ(FM) De Funiak Springs FL
WMYB(FM) Myrtle Beach SC
WMYI(FM) Hendersonville NC
*WMYJ(FM) Oolitic IN
WMYK(FM) Peru IN
WMYP(FM) Frederiksted VI
WMYU(FM) Karns TN
WMYX(FM) Milwaukee WI
WMYY(FM) Schoharie NY
WMZD(FM) Statesboro GA
WMZK(FM) Merrill WI
WMZQ-FM Washington DC
*WNAA(FM) Greensboro NC
WNAK-FM Carbondale PA
*WNAN(FM) Nantucket MA
*WNAS(FM) New Albany IN
WNAX-FM Yankton SD
*WNAZ-FM Nashville TN
WNBB(FM) Bayboro NC
WNBQ(FM) Mansfield PA
WNBR-FM Windsor NC
WNBT-FM Wellsboro PA
WNBY-FM Newberry MI
WNCB(FM) Homewood AL
WNCC-FM Franklin NC
WNCD(FM) Youngstown OH
*WNCH(FM) Norwich VT
WNCI(FM) Columbus OH
*WNCK(FM) Nantucket MA
WNCL(FM) Milford DE
WNCO-FM Ashland OH
WNCQ-FM Canton NY
WNCS(FM) Montpelier VT
WNCT-FM Greenville NC
*WNCU(FM) Durham NC
WNCV(FM) Niceville FL
*WNCW(FM) Spindale NC
WNCX(FM) Cleveland OH
WNCY-FM Neenah-Menasha WI
WNDD(FM) Silver Springs FL
WNDH(FM) Napoleon OH
WNDI-FM Sullivan IN
*WNDJ(FM) White Stone VA
WNDN(FM) Chiefland FL
WNDT(FM) Alachua FL

*WNDV-FM South Bend IN
*WNDY(FM) Crawfordsville IN
*WNEC-FM Henniker NH
*WNED-FM Buffalo NY
*WNEE(FM) Jasper GA
*WNEF(FM) Newburyport MA
*WNEK-FM Springfield MA
WNEW(FM) New York NY
*WNFA(FM) Port Huron MI
WNFB(FM) Lake City FL
WNFK(FM) Perry FL
WNFM(FM) Reedsburg WI
WNFN(FM) Belle Meade TN
*WNFR(FM) Sandusky MI
WNFZ(FM) Oak Ridge TN
WNGC(FM) Toccoa GA
*WNGE(FM) Negaunee MI
*WNGN(FM) Argyle NY
*WNGU(FM) Dahlonega GA
WNGZ(FM) Montour Falls NY
WNHT(FM) Churubusco IN
*WNHU(FM) West Haven CT
WNHW(FM) Belmont NH
WNIC(FM) Dearborn MI
*WNIE(FM) Freeport IL
*WNIJ(FM) De Kalb IL
WNIK-FM Arecibo PR
*WNIN-FM Evansville IN
*WNIQ(FM) Sterling IL
WNIR(FM) Kent OH
*WNIU(FM) Rockford IL
*WNIW(FM) La Salle IL
*WNJA(FM) Jamestown NY
*WNJB(FM) Bridgeton NJ
*WNJM(FM) Manahawkin NJ
*WNJN-FM Atlantic City NJ
*WNJP(FM) Sussex NJ
*WNJR(FM) Washington PA
*WNJS-FM Berlin NJ
*WNJT-FM Trenton NJ
*WNJZ(FM) Cape May Court House NJ
WNKI(FM) Corning NY
*WNKJ(FM) Hopkinsville KY
WNKL(FM) Wauseon OH
WNKO(FM) Newark OH
WNKR(FM) Williamstown KY
WNKS(FM) Charlotte NC
WNKT(FM) Saint George SC
*WNKU(FM) Highland Heights KY
WNKX-FM Centerville TN
WNLA-FM Indianola MS
WNLC(FM) East Lyme CT
*WNLE(FM) Fernandina Beach FL
WNLF(FM) Macomb IL
WNLT(FM) Harrison OH
*WNMC-FM Traverse City MI
*WNMH(FM) Northfield MA
WNML-FM Loudon TN
*WNMU-FM Marquette MI
WNMX-FM Waxhaw NC
WNNH(FM) Henniker NH
WNNJ-FM Newton NJ
WNNK-FM Harrisburg PA
WNNL(FM) Fuquay-Varina NC
WNNO-FM Wisconsin Dells WI
WNNS(FM) Springfield IL
WNNT-FM Warsaw VA
*WNNV(FM) San German PR
WNNX(FM) Atlanta GA
WNOD(FM) Mayaguez PR
WNOE-FM New Orleans LA
WNOI(FM) Flora IL
WNOK(FM) Columbia SC
WNOR(FM) Norfolk VA
WNOU(FM) Indianapolis IN
WNOX(FM) Oak Ridge TN
WNPC-FM Newport TN
WNPQ(FM) New Philadelphia OH
*WNPR(FM) Norwich CT
WNPT-FM Linden AL
*WNRK(FM) Norwalk OH
*WNRN(FM) Charlottesville VA
WNRQ(FM) Nashville TN
*WNRS-FM Sweet Briar VA
WNRT(FM) Manati PR
*WNRX(FM) Jefferson City TN

*WNRZ(FM) Dickson TN
*WNSB(FM) Norfolk VA
*WNSC-FM Rock Hill SC
WNSI-FM Atmore AL
WNSL(FM) Laurel MS
WNSN(FM) South Bend IN
WNSP(FM) Bay Minette AL
WNSV(FM) Nashville IL
WNSX(FM) Winter Harbor ME
WNSY(FM) Talking Rock GA
WNTC(FM) Drakesboro KY
*WNTE(FM) Mansfield PA
*WNTH(FM) Winnetka IL
*WNTI(FM) Hackettstown NJ
WNTK-FM New London NH
*WNTQ(FM) Syracuse NY
WNUA(FM) Chicago IL
*WNUB-FM Northfield VT
WNUE-FM Titusville FL
WNUQ(FM) Albany GA
*WNUR-FM Evanston IL
WNUS(FM) Belpre OH
WNUY(FM) Bluffton IN
WNVA-FM Norton VA
WNVE(FM) South Bristol Township NY
WNVZ(FM) Norfolk VA
*WNWC-FM Madison WI
WNWN-FM Coldwater MI
WNWS-FM Jackson TN
WNWV(FM) Elyria OH
WNXR(FM) Iron River WI
WNXT-FM Portsmouth OH
WNXX(FM) Jackson LA
*WNYC-FM New York NY
*WNYE(FM) New York NY
*WNYK(FM) Nyack NY
WNYN-FM Athol MA
*WNYO(FM) Oswego NY
WNYQ(FM) Queensbury NY
WNYR-FM Waterloo NY
*WNYU-FM New York NY
WNYV(FM) Whitehall NY
*WNZN(FM) Lorain OH
*WNZR(FM) Mount Vernon OH
WOAB(FM) Ozark AL
WOAD-FM Pickens MS
WOAH(FM) Glennville GA
*WOAK(FM) La Grange GA
*WOAS(FM) Ontonagon MI
WOBB(FM) Tifton GA
*WOBC-FM Oberlin OH
WOBE(FM) Crystal Falls MI
WOBG-FM Salem WV
WOBM-FM Toms River NJ
*WOBN(FM) Westerville OH
WOBO(FM) Batavia OH
WOBR-FM Wanchese NC
WOBX-FM Manteo NC
WOCE(FM) Benton TN
*WOCG(FM) Huntsville AL
WOCL(FM) De Land FL
WOCM(FM) Selbyville DE
WOCN-FM South Yarmouth MA
WOCO-FM Oconto WI
WOCQ(FM) Berlin MD
*WOCR(FM) Olivet MI
*WOCS(FM) Lerose KY
WOCY(FM) Carrabelle FL
WODA(FM) Bayamon PR
WODB(FM) Delaware OH
WODE-FM Easton PA
WODR(FM) Fair Bluff NC
WODS(FM) Boston MA
WODZ-FM Rome NY
*WOEL-FM Elkton MD
*WOES(FM) Ovid-Elsie MI
*WOEZ(FM) Maynardville TN
WOFE-FM Rockwood TN
WOFM(FM) Mosinee WI
*WOFN(FM) Beach City OH
*WOFR(FM) Schoolcraft MI
WOFX-FM Cincinnati OH
WOGB(FM) Kaukauna WI
WOGF(FM) East Liverpool OH
WOGG(FM) Oliver PA
WOGH(FM) Burgettstown PA
WOGI(FM) Charleroi PA

WOGK(FM) Ocala FL
WOGL(FM) Philadelphia PA
WOGR-FM Salisbury NC
WOGT(FM) East Ridge TN
*WOHC(FM) Chillicothe OH
WOHF(FM) Bellevue OH
*WOHP(FM) Portsmouth OH
WOHT(FM) Grenada MS
*WOI-FM Ames IA
*WOJB(FM) Reserve WI
*WOJC(FM) Crothersville IN
WOJG(FM) Bolivar TN
WOJL(FM) Louisa VA
WOJO(FM) Evanston IL
WOKA-FM Douglas GA
*WOKD-FM Danville VA
WOKE(FM) Garrison KY
*WOKG(FM) Galax VA
*WOKI(FM) Oliver Springs TN
WOKK(FM) Meridian MS
*WOKL(FM) Troy OH
WOKN(FM) Southport NY
WOKO(FM) Burlington VT
WOKQ(FM) Dover NH
WOKR(FM) Remsen NY
WOKW(FM) Curwensville PA
WOKZ(FM) Fairfield IL
WOLC(FM) Princess Anne MD
WOLD-FM Marion VA
WOLF-FM Oswego NY
*WOLG(FM) Carlinville IL
WOLI(FM) Easley SC
WOLL(FM) Hobe Sound FL
*WOLN(FM) Olean NY
*WOLR(FM) Lake City FL
WOLT(FM) Greer SC
WOLV(FM) Houghton MI
*WOLW(FM) Cadillac MI
WOLX-FM Baraboo WI
WOLZ(FM) Fort Myers FL
WOMC(FM) Detroit MI
WOMG(FM) Columbia SC
WOMP-FM Bellaire OH
*WOMR(FM) Provincetown MA
WOMX-FM Orlando FL
WONA-FM Winona MS
*WONB(FM) Ada OH
*WONC(FM) Naperville IL
WONE-FM Akron OH
*WONU(FM) Kankakee IL
*WONY(FM) Oneonta NY
WOOD-FM Grand Rapids MI
WOOF-FM Dothan AL
WOOZ-FM Harrisburg IL
WOPR(FM) Lacombe LA
WOQL(FM) Winchendon MA
WORC-FM Webster MA
WORD-FM Pittsburgh PA
WORG(FM) Elloree SC
WORK(FM) Barre VT
WORM-FM Savannah TN
WORO(FM) Corozal PR
*WORQ(FM) Green Bay WI
*WORT(FM) Madison WI
*WORW(FM) Port Huron MI
WORX-FM Madison IN
WOSB(FM) Marion OH
WOSC(FM) Bethany Beach DE
*WOSE(FM) Coshocton OH
WOSM(FM) Ocean Springs MS
WOSN(FM) Indian River Shores FL
*WOSP(FM) Portsmouth OH
WOSQ(FM) Spencer NY
*WOSR(FM) Middletown NY
*WOSS(FM) Ossining NY
WOSU-FM Columbus OH
*WOSV(FM) Mansfield OH
WOTC(FM) Edinburg VA
*WOTJ(FM) Morehead City NC
*WOTL(FM) Toledo OH
WOTR(FM) Lost Creek WV
WOTT(FM) Henderson NY
*WOUB-FM Athens OH
*WOUC-FM Cambridge OH
WOUF(FM) Beulah MI
*WOUH-FM Chillicothe OH
*WOUL-FM Ironton OH

WOUR(FM) Utica NY
*WOUZ(FM) Zanesville OH
*WOVI(FM) Novi MI
WOVK(FM) Wheeling WV
WOVO(FM) Glasgow KY
WOWE(FM) Vassar MI
WOWF(FM) Crossville TN
WOWI(FM) Norfolk VA
*WOWL(FM) Burnsville MS
WOWN(FM) Shawano WI
WOWQ(FM) DuBois PA
WOWY(FM) University Park PA
WOXD(FM) Oxford MS
WOXL-FM Biltmore Forest NC
WOXO-FM Norway ME
WOXX(FM) Franklin PA
WOXY(FM) Oxford OH
WOYS(FM) Apalachicola FL
WOZI(FM) Presque Isle ME
*WOZQ(FM) Northampton MA
WOZW(FM) New Carlisle IN
WOZZ(FM) New London WI
WPAC(FM) Ogdensburg NY
*WPAE(FM) Centreville MS
WPAL-FM Ridgeville SC
WPAP-FM Panama City FL
*WPAR(FM) Salem VA
*WPAS(FM) Pascagoula MS
WPAT-FM Paterson NJ
WPAY-FM Portsmouth OH
WPBG(FM) Peoria IL
WPBH(FM) Mexico Beach FL
WPBX(FM) Crossville TN
WPBZ(FM) Indiantown FL
*WPCD(FM) Champaign IL
*WPCJ(FM) Pittsford MI
WPCK(FM) Denmark WI
*WPCL(FM) Northern Cambria PA
*WPCN(FM) Point Pleasant WV
*WPCR-FM Plymouth NH
*WPCS(FM) Pensacola FL
WPCV(FM) Winter Haven FL
*WPDA(FM) Jeffersonville NY
*WPDD(FM) Norco LA
WPDH(FM) Poughkeepsie NY
WPDT(FM) Johnsonville SC
WPDX-FM Clarksburg WV
*WPEA(FM) Exeter NH
*WPEB(FM) Philadelphia PA
WPEG(FM) Concord NC
WPEH-FM Louisville GA
*WPEL-FM Montrose PA
*WPER(FM) Culpeper VA
WPEZ(FM) Jeffersonville GA
*WPFB-FM Middletown OH
*WPFF(FM) Sturgeon Bay WI
*WPFL(FM) Century FL
WPFM-FM Panama City FL
*WPFR-FM Clinton IN
*WPFW(FM) Washington DC
*WPFX-FM North Baltimore OH
WPGA-FM Perry GA
WPGB(FM) Pittsburgh PA
WPGC-FM Morningside MD
WPGG(FM) Evergreen AL
WPGI(FM) Horseheads NY
*WPGL(FM) Pattersonville NY
*WPGM-FM Danville PA
*WPGP(FM) Tafton PA
*WPGT(FM) Roanoke Rapids NC
WPGU(FM) Urbana IL
WPGW-FM Portland IN
*WPHD(FM) South Waverly PA
*WPHH(FM) Waterbury CT
WPHI-FM Media PA
*WPHK(FM) Blountstown FL
*WPHN(FM) Gaylord MI
*WPHP(FM) Wheeling WV
WPHR(FM) Auburn NY
*WPHS(FM) Warren MI
WPHX-FM Sanford ME
WPIA(FM) Eureka IL
*WPIB(FM) Bluefield WV
WPIG(FM) Olean NY
WPIK(FM) Summerland Key FL
*WPIL(FM) Heflin AL
*WPIM(FM) Martinsville VA

U.S. FM Stations by Call Letters

*WPIN-FM Dublin VA
*WPIO(FM) Titusville FL
WPIQ(FM) Manistique MI
*WPIR(FM) Hickory NC
*WPJC(FM) Pontiac IL
WPJP(FM) Port Washington WI
WPKE-FM Coal Run KY
*WPKF(FM) Poughkeepsie NY
WPKG(FM) Neillsville WI
WPKL(FM) Uniontown PA
*WPKM(FM) Montauk NY
*WPKN(FM) Bridgeport CT
WPKO-FM Bellefontaine OH
WPKQ(FM) North Conway NH
WPKR(FM) Omro WI
*WPKT(FM) Meriden CT
WPKX(FM) Enfield CT
WPLA(FM) Callahan FL
*WPLH(FM) Tifton GA
*WPLI(FM) Levittown PR
WPLJ(FM) New York NY
WPLM-FM Plymouth MA
*WPLN-FM Nashville TN
WPLR(FM) New Haven CT
WPLT(FM) Spooner WI
WPMA(FM) Buckhead GA
WPMJ(FM) Chillicothe IL
WPMW(FM) Mullens WV
WPMX(FM) Statesboro GA
WPNC-FM Plymouth NC
*WPNE-FM Green Bay WI
WPNG(FM) Pearson GA
WPNH-FM Plymouth NH
*WPNR-FM Utica NY
*WPOB-FM Plainview NY
WPOC(FM) Baltimore MD
WPOI(FM) Saint Petersburg FL
WPOR(FM) Portland ME
WPOS-FM Holland OH
WPOW(FM) Miami FL
*WPOZ(FM) Union Park FL
WPPL(FM) Blue Ridge GA
WPPN(FM) Des Plaines IL
*WPPR(FM) Demorest GA
WPPT(FM) Mercersburg PA
WPPZ-FM Jenkintown PA
*WPQZ(FM) Muskegon MI
WPRB(FM) Princeton NJ
*WPRC(FM) Princeton IL
WPRF(FM) Reserve LA
*WPRG(FM) Columbia MS
*WPRJ(FM) Coleman MI
*WPRK(FM) Winter Park FL
*WPRL(FM) Lorman MS
WPRM-FM San Juan PR
WPRN-FM Lisman AL
WPRO-FM Providence RI
WPRW-FM Martinez GA
*WPSA(FM) Paul Smiths NY
*WPSB(FM) Kane PA
*WPSC-FM Wayne NJ
WPSK-FM Pulaski VA
*WPSM(FM) Fort Walton Beach FL
*WPSR(FM) Evansville IN
WPST(FM) Trenton NJ
*WPSU(FM) State College PA
*WPTC(FM) Williamsport PA
WPTE(FM) Virginia Beach VA
*WPTH(FM) Olney IL
WPTI(FM) Louisville KY
*WPTJ(FM) Paris KY
WPTM(FM) Roanoke Rapids NC
WPTQ(FM) Cave City KY
WPTR(FM) Clifton Park NY
*WPTS-FM Pittsburgh PA
WPUB-FM Camden SC
*WPUC-FM Ponce PR
*WPUM(FM) Rensselaer IN
WPUP(FM) Royston GA
WPUR(FM) Atlantic City NJ
*WPVA(FM) Waynesboro VA
WPVL-FM Platteville WI
WPVQ(FM) Greenfield MA
*WPWB(FM) Byron GA
WPWQ(FM) Mount Sterling IL
*WPWV(FM) Princeton WV
WPWX(FM) Hammond IN

WPWZ(FM) Pinetops NC
WPXC(FM) Hyannis MA
WPXN(FM) Paxton IL
WPXY-FM Rochester NY
WPXZ-FM Punxsutawney PA
WPYA(FM) Chesapeake VA
WPYO(FM) Maitland FL
WPYX(FM) Albany NY
WPZE(FM) Fayetteville GA
WPZS(FM) Albemarle NC
WPZX(FM) Pocono Pines PA
WPZZ(FM) Crewe VA
*WQAB(FM) Philippi WV
*WQAC(FM) Alma MI
WQAH-FM Addison AL
WQAK(FM) Union City TN
WQAL(FM) Cleveland OH
*WQAQ(FM) Hamden CT
WQAR(FM) Stillwater NY
WQBE-FM Charleston WV
WQBJ(FM) Cobleskill NY
WQBK-FM Rensselaer NY
WQBR(FM) Avis PA
WQBT(FM) Savannah GA
WQBW(FM) Milwaukee WI
WQBX(FM) Alma MI
WQBZ(FM) Fort Valley GA
WQCB(FM) Brewer ME
WQCC(FM) La Crosse WI
WQCD(FM) New York NY
WQCK(FM) Clinton LA
WQCM(FM) Greencastle PA
*WQCS(FM) Fort Pierce FL
WQCY(FM) Quincy IL
WQDK(FM) Ahoskie NC
WQDR(FM) Raleigh NC
WQDY-FM Calais ME
*WQED-FM Pittsburgh PA
*WQEJ(FM) Johnstown PA
WQEL(FM) Bucyrus OH
WQEM(FM) Columbiana AL
WQEN(FM) Gadsden AL
WQFL(FM) Rockford IL
WQFM(FM) Nanticoke PA
WQFN(FM) Forest City PA
*WQFS(FM) Greensboro NC
WQFX-FM Russell PA
WQGN-FM Groton CT
WQHH(FM) Dewitt MI
WQHK-FM Decatur IN
WQHL-FM Live Oak FL
WQHQ(FM) Ocean City-Salisbury MD
WQHR(FM) Presque Isle ME
WQHT(FM) New York NY
WQHY(FM) Prestonsburg KY
WQHZ(FM) Erie PA
WQIC(FM) Lebanon PA
WQIK-FM Jacksonville FL
WQIL(FM) Chauncey GA
WQIO(FM) Mount Vernon OH
WQJB(FM) State College MS
WQJQ(FM) Kosciusko MS
*WQJU(FM) Mifflintown PA
WQJZ(FM) Ocean Pines MD
WQKC(FM) Seymour IN
*WQKE(FM) Plattsburgh NY
WQKI-FM Orangeburg SC
WQKL(FM) Ann Arbor MI
*WQKO(FM) Howe IN
WQKQ(FM) Carthage IL
WQKS-FM Montgomery AL
WQKT(FM) Wooster OH
WQKX(FM) Sunbury PA
WQKY(FM) Emporium PA
WQKZ(FM) Ferdinand IN
WQLA-FM La Follette TN
WQLB(FM) Tawas City MI
WQLC(FM) Watertown FL
WQLF(FM) Lena IL
WQLH(FM) Green Bay WI
WQLI(FM) Pelham GA
WQLJ(FM) Oxford MS
WQLK(FM) Richmond IN
*WQLN-FM Erie PA
WQLR(FM) Kalamazoo MI
WQLT(FM) Florence AL
WQLV(FM) Millersburg PA

WQLZ(FM) Taylorville IL
WQME(FM) Anderson IN
WQMF(FM) Jeffersonville IN
WQMG-FM Greensboro NC
WQMJ(FM) Forsyth GA
WQMR(FM) Snow Hill MD
WQMT(FM) Chatsworth GA
WQMU(FM) Indiana PA
WQMX(FM) Medina OH
WQMZ(FM) Charlottesville VA
*WQNA(FM) Springfield IL
WQNC(FM) Harrisburg NC
*WQNN(FM) Brownsville TN
WQNQ(FM) Fletcher NC
WQNR(FM) Tallassee AL
WQNS(FM) Waynesville NC
WQNY(FM) Ithaca NY
WQNZ(FM) Natchez MS
WQOK(FM) South Boston VA
WQOL(FM) Vero Beach FL
WQON(FM) Roscommon MI
*WQOX(FM) Memphis TN
WQPC(FM) Prairie du Chien WI
WQPO(FM) Harrisonburg VA
*WQPR(FM) Muscle Shoals AL
WQPW(FM) Valdosta GA
WQQB(FM) Rantoul IL
WQQK(FM) Hendersonville TN
WQQL(FM) Springfield IL
WQQQ(FM) Sharon CT
WQQR(FM) Mayfield KY
WQRB(FM) Bloomer WI
WQRC(FM) Barnstable MA
*WQRI(FM) Bristol RI
WQRJ(FM) Mitchell IN
WQRK(FM) Bedford IN
WQRL(FM) Benton IL
WQRM(FM) Smethport PA
*WQRP(FM) Dayton OH
WQRT(FM) Salamanca NY
WQSA(FM) Unadilla GA
WQSB(FM) Albertville AL
WQSD(FM) Briarcliff Acres SC
*WQSG(FM) Lafayette IN
WQSI(FM) Union Springs AL
WQSL(FM) Jacksonville NC
WQSM(FM) Fayetteville NC
WQSO(FM) Rochester NH
WQSR(FM) Baltimore MD
WQSS(FM) Camden ME
WQST-FM Forest MS
*WQSU(FM) Selinsgrove PA
WQSX(FM) Lawrence MA
WQTC-FM Manitowoc WI
WQTE(FM) Adrian MI
*WQTQ(FM) Hartford CT
WQTU(FM) Rome GA
WQTX(FM) Charlotte MI
WQTY(FM) Linton IN
WQUA(FM) Citronelle AL
*WQUB(FM) Quincy IL
WQUE-FM New Orleans LA
WQUL(FM) West Frankfort IL
WQUS(FM) Lapeer MI
WQUT(FM) Johnson City TN
WQVE(FM) Camilla GA
*WQVI(FM) Forest MS
WQWK(FM) Pleasant Gap PA
WQWV(FM) Fisher WV
WQXA-FM York PA
WQXB(FM) Grenada MS
WQXC-FM Otsego MI
*WQXE(FM) Elizabethtown KY
WQXK(FM) Salem OH
WQXQ(FM) Central City KY
WQXR-FM New York NY
WQXZ(FM) Cordele GA
WQYK-FM Saint Petersburg FL
WQYX(FM) Clearfield PA
WQYZ(FM) Ocean Springs MS
WQZK-FM Keyser WV
WQZL(FM) Belhaven NC
WQZQ(FM) Dickson TN
WQZS(FM) Meyersdale PA
WQZX(FM) Greenville AL
WQZY(FM) Dublin GA
WQZZ(FM) Eutaw AL

WRAC(FM) West Union OH
*WRAE(FM) Raeford NC
*WRAF-FM Toccoa Falls GA
WRAK-FM Bainbridge GA
WRAL(FM) Raleigh NC
WRAN(FM) Tower Hill IL
WRAR-FM Tappahannock VA
*WRAS(FM) Atlanta GA
WRAT(FM) Point Pleasant NJ
WRAX(FM) Helena AL
WRAY-FM Princeton IN
WRBA(FM) Springfield FL
*WRBB(FM) Boston MA
WRBC(FM) Lewiston ME
WRBE-FM Lucedale MS
*WRBH(FM) New Orleans LA
WRBI(FM) Batesville IN
*WRBK(FM) Richburg SC
WRBN(FM) Clayton GA
WRBO(FM) Como MS
WRBP(FM) Hubbard OH
WRBQ-FM Tampa FL
WRBR-FM South Bend IN
WRBS(FM) Baltimore MD
WRBT(FM) Harrisburg PA
WRBV(FM) Warner Robins GA
WRBX(FM) Reidsville GA
WRCD(FM) Canton NY
WRCH(FM) New Britain CT
WRCI(FM) Webster NY
*WRCJ-FM Detroit MI
WRCK(FM) Utica NY
WRCL(FM) Frankenmuth MI
*WRCM(FM) Wingate NC
WRCN-FM Riverhead NY
WRCO-FM Richland Center WI
WRCQ(FM) Dunn NC
WRCT(FM) Pittsburgh PA
*WRCU-FM Hamilton NY
WRCV(FM) Dixon IL
WRCZ(FM) Ravena NY
WRDA(FM) Jerseyville IL
*WRDL(FM) Ashland OH
WRDO(FM) Fitzgerald GA
*WRDR(FM) Freehold Township NJ
WRDU(FM) Wilson NC
*WRDV(FM) Warminster PA
WRDW-FM Philadelphia PA
WRDX(FM) Dover DE
WRDZ-FM Plainfield IN
WREB(FM) Greencastle IN
WRED(FM) Saco ME
*WREH(FM) Cypress Quarters FL
WREK(FM) Atlanta GA
WREO-FM Ashtabula OH
WREQ(FM) Ridgebury PA
WREZ(FM) Metropolis IL
*WRFE(FM) Chesterfield SC
*WRFG(FM) Atlanta GA
WRFL(FM) Lexington KY
*WRFM(FM) Wadesville IN
WRFQ(FM) Mt. Pleasant SC
*WRFT(FM) Indianapolis IN
*WRFW(FM) River Falls WI
WRFX-FM Kannapolis NC
WRFY-FM Reading PA
*WRGF(FM) Greenfield IN
*WRGN(FM) Sweet Valley PA
WRGO(FM) Cedar Key FL
*WRGP(FM) Homestead FL
WRGR(FM) Tupper Lake NY
*WRGX(FM) Sturgeon Bay WI
WRHD(FM) Williamston NC
WRHK(FM) Danville IL
WRHL-FM Rochelle IL
WRHM(FM) Lancaster SC
WRHN(FM) Rhinelander WI
*WRHO(FM) Oneonta NY
WRHQ(FM) Richmond Hill GA
WRHT(FM) Morehead City NC
*WRHU(FM) Hempstead NY
*WRHV(FM) Poughkeepsie NY
WRHY(FM) Centre AL
WRIC-FM Richlands VA
WRIF(FM) Detroit MI
*WRIH(FM) Richmond VA
*WRIJ(FM) Masontown PA

WRIK-FM Metropolis IL
WRIL(FM) Pineville KY
WRIO(FM) Ponce PR
WRIP(FM) Windham NY
WRIT-FM Milwaukee WI
*WRIU(FM) Kingston RI
WRIX-FM Honea Path SC
*WRJA-FM Sumter SC
WRJB(FM) Camden TN
WRJC(FM) Mauston WI
WRJH(FM) Brandon MS
WRJL-FM Eva AL
WRJM-FM Geneva AL
WRJO(FM) Eagle River WI
WRJT(FM) Royalton VT
WRJY(FM) Brunswick GA
*WRKA(FM) Saint Matthews KY
*WRKC(FM) Wilkes-Barre PA
*WRKF(FM) Baton Rouge LA
WRKG(FM) Drew MS
WRKH(FM) Mobile AL
WRKI(FM) Brookfield CT
WRKK-FM Sparta TN
WRKP(FM) Moundsville WV
WRKR(FM) Portage MI
WRKS(FM) New York NY
WRKT(FM) North East PA
WRKU(FM) Forestville WI
*WRKW(FM) Johnstown PA
WRKX(FM) Ottawa IL
WRKY-FM Hollidaysburg PA
WRKZ(FM) Pittsburgh PA
WRLB(FM) Rainelle WV
*WRLC(FM) Williamsport PA
WRLD-FM Valley AL
WRLF(FM) Fairmont WV
*WRLI-FM Southampton NY
WRLO-FM Antigo WI
WRLS-FM Hayward WI
WRLT(FM) Franklin TN
WRLU(FM) Algoma WI
WRLV-FM Salyersville KY
WRLX(FM) West Palm Beach FL
WRMA(FM) Fort Lauderdale FL
*WRMB(FM) Boynton Beach FL
*WRMC-FM Middlebury VT
WRMF(FM) Palm Beach FL
WRMJ(FM) Aledo IL
WRML(FM) Pageland SC
WRMM-FM Rochester NY
WRMO(FM) Milbridge ME
WRMS-FM Beardstown IL
*WRMU(FM) Alliance OH
WRMX-FM Norris TN
WRNB(FM) Pennsauken NJ
*WRNF(FM) Selma AL
WRNN(FM) Socastee SC
WRNO-FM New Orleans LA
WRNQ(FM) Poughkeepsie NY
WRNR-FM Grasonville MD
WRNS-FM Kinston NC
WRNX(FM) Amherst MA
WRNZ(FM) Lancaster KY
WROE(FM) Neenah-Menasha WI
WROG(FM) Cumberland MD
WROI(FM) Rochester IN
WRON-FM Ronceverte WV
WROO(FM) Jacksonville FL
WROQ(FM) Anderson SC
WROR-FM Framingham MA
WROU-FM West Carrollton OH
WROV-FM Martinsville VA
WROX-FM Exmore VA
WROZ(FM) Lancaster PA
WRPG(FM) Hawkinsville GA
*WRPI(FM) Troy NY
*WRPJ(FM) Port Jervis NY
*WRPN-FM Ripon WI
*WRPR(FM) Mahwah NJ
*WRPS(FM) Rockland MA
WRPW(FM) Colfax IL
WRQC(FM) Estero FL
WRQK(FM) Canton OH
*WRQM(FM) Rocky Mount NC
WRQN(FM) Bowling Green OH
WRQO(FM) Monticello MS
WRQQ(FM) Goodlettsville TN

U.S. FM Stations by Call Letters

WRQR(FM) Wilmington NC	WRXS(FM) Ocean City MD	WSIP-FM Paintsville KY	*WSQE(FM) Corning NY	*WTGN(FM) Lima OH
WRQT(FM) La Crosse WI	*WRXT(FM) Roanoke VA	*WSIU(FM) Carbondale IL	*WSQG-FM Ithaca NY	*WTGP(FM) Greenville PA
WRQX(FM) Washington DC	*WRXV(FM) State College PA	WSIX-FM Nashville TN	*WSQH(FM) Forest MS	WTGR(FM) Union City OH
WRR(FM) Dallas TX	WRXW(FM) Pearl MS	*WSJB-FM Standish ME	*WSQX-FM Binghamton NY	WTGV-FM Sandusky MI
WRRB(FM) Arlington NY	WRXX(FM) Centralia IL	WSJD(FM) Princeton IN	WSRB(FM) Lansing IL	WTGY(FM) Charleston MS
*WRRC(FM) Lawrenceville NJ	WRXZ(FM) Sylvester GA	WSJF(FM) Saint Augustine Beach FL	WSRG(FM) Sturgeon Bay WI	WTGZ(FM) Tuskegee AL
*WRRG(FM) River Grove IL	WRYV(FM) Gallipolis OH	*WSJI(FM) Cherry Hill NJ	WSRI(FM) Sugar Grove IL	WTHB-FM Waynesboro GA
WRRH(FM) Hormigueros PR	WRZA(FM) Park Forest IL	*WSJL(FM) Northport AL	WSRK(FM) Oneonta NY	*WTHD(FM) Lagrange IN
WRRK(FM) Braddock PA	WRZE(FM) Nantucket MA	WSJO(FM) Egg Harbor City NJ	WSRM(FM) Coosa GA	WTHI-FM Terre Haute IN
WRRM(FM) Cincinnati OH	WRZI(FM) Vine Grove KY	WSJR(FM) Dallas PA	WSRN-FM Swarthmore PA	WTHK(FM) Trenton NJ
WRRN(FM) Warren PA	WRZK(FM) Colonial Heights TN	WSJT(FM) Lakeland FL	WSRS(FM) Worcester MA	*WTHL(FM) Somerset KY
WRRR-FM Saint Marys WV	WRZQ-FM Greensburg IN	WSJW(FM) Starview PA	WSRV(FM) Deltaville VA	*WTHN(FM) Sault Ste. Marie MI
WRRV(FM) Middletown NY	WRZR(FM) Loogootee IN	WSJY(FM) Fort Atkinson WI	WSRW-FM Hillsboro OH	WTHO-FM Thomson GA
WRRX(FM) Gulf Breeze FL	WRZX(FM) Indianapolis IN	WSJZ-FM Sebastian FL	*WSRX(FM) Naples FL	*WTHS(FM) Holland MI
WRSA-FM Decatur AL	WRZZ(FM) Elizabeth WV	WSKB(FM) Westfield MA	WSRZ-FM Coral Cove FL	WTHT(FM) Auburn ME
*WRSD(FM) Folsom PA	WSAE(FM) Spring Arbor MI	WSKE(FM) Everett PA	WSSB-FM Orangeburg SC	WTHX(FM) Lebanon Junction KY
*WRSE(FM) Elmhurst IL	WSAG(FM) Pinconning MI	*WSKG-FM Binghamton NY	*WSSD(FM) Chicago IL	WTHZ(FM) Lexington NC
WRSF(FM) Columbia NC	WSAJ-FM Grove City PA	WSKL(FM) Veedersburg IN	WSSJ(FM) Hinesville GA	WTIC-FM Hartford CT
*WRSG(FM) Middlebourne WV	WSAK(FM) Hampton NH	WSKO-FM Wakefield-Peacedale RI	*WSSK(FM) Saratoga Springs NY	WTIF-FM Omega GA
*WRSH(FM) Rockingham NC	WSAQ(FM) Port Huron MI	WSKQ(FM) New York NY	WSSL-FM Gray Court SC	*WTIM-FM Taylorville IL
WRSI(FM) Turners Falls MA	*WSBF-FM Clemson SC	WSKS(FM) Whitesboro NY	WSSM(FM) Havelock NC	*WTIP(FM) Grand Marais MN
*WRSK(FM) Slippery Rock PA	WSB-FM Atlanta GA	WSKT(FM) Spencer IN	WSSQ(FM) Sterling IL	WTIX-FM Galliano LA
WRSN(FM) Burlington NC	WSBG(FM) Stroudsburg PA	WSKU(FM) Little Falls NY	WSSR(FM) Joliet IL	*WTJB(FM) Columbus GA
WRSR(FM) Owosso MI	*WSBU(FM) Saint Bonaventure NY	WSKV(FM) Stanton KY	WSSX-FM Charleston SC	*WTJT(FM) Baker FL
*WRST-FM Oshkosh WI	WSBY-FM Salisbury MD	WSKY-FM Micanopy FL	WSTB(FM) Streetsboro OH	*WTJU(FM) Charlottesville VA
*WRSU-FM New Brunswick NJ	*WSBZ(FM) Miramar Beach FL	WSKZ(FM) Chattanooga TN	WSTF(FM) Andalusia AL	*WTJY(FM) Asheboro NC
WRSV(FM) Rocky Mount NC	*WSCB(FM) Springfield MA	WSLC-FM Roanoke VA	WSTG(FM) Princeton WV	WTKB-FM Atwood TN
WRSW-FM Warsaw IN	WSCC-FM Goose Creek SC	WSLD(FM) Whitewater WI	WSTH-FM Alexander City AL	*WTKC(FM) Findlay OH
WRSY(FM) Marlboro VT	*WSCD-FM Duluth MN	*WSLE(FM) Salem IL	WSTI-FM Quitman GA	WTKE(FM) Holt FL
*WRTC-FM Hartford CT	*WSCF-FM Vero Beach FL	*WSLJ(FM) Watertown NY	WSTK(FM) Aurora NC	WTKF(FM) Atlantic NC
*WRTE(FM) Chicago IL	WSCG-FM Lakeview MI	WSLL(FM) Saranac Lake NY	*WSTM(FM) Kiel WI	WTKK(FM) Boston MA
*WRTI(FM) Philadelphia PA	*WSCH(FM) Aurora IN	WSLM-FM Salem IN	WSTO(FM) Owensboro KY	*WTKL(FM) New Orleans LA
*WRTL(FM) Ephrata PA	*WSCI(FM) Charleston SC	*WSLN(FM) Delaware OH	WSTQ(FM) Streator IL	WTKM-FM Hartford WI
WRTM-FM Port Gibson MS	*WSCL(FM) Salisbury MD	*WSLO(FM) Malone NY	WSTR(FM) Smyrna GA	WTKS-FM Cocoa Beach FL
WRTN(FM) New Rochelle NY	*WSCN(FM) Cloquet MN	WSLQ(FM) Roanoke VA	WSTS(FM) Fairmont NC	WTKU(FM) Ocean City NJ
WRTO-FM Goulds FL	WSCP-FM Pulaski NY	WSLT(FM) Clearwater SC	WSTW(FM) Wilmington DE	WTKV(FM) Oswego NY
*WRTP(FM) Roanoke Rapids NC	*WSCS(FM) New London NH	*WSLU(FM) Canton NY	WSTZ-FM Vicksburg MS	WTKW(FM) Bridgeport NY
*WRTQ(FM) Ocean City NJ	*WSCT(FM) Springfield IL	*WSLX(FM) New Canaan CT	*WSUC-FM Cortland NY	WTKX-FM Pensacola FL
WRTR(FM) Brookwood AL	WSCY(FM) Moultonborough NH	WSLY(FM) York AL	WSUE(FM) Sault Ste. Marie MI	WTKY-FM Tompkinsville KY
*WRTS(FM) Erie PA	*WSDH(FM) Sandwich MA	*WSMA(FM) Scituate MA	*WSUF(FM) Noyack NY	WTLC-FM Greenwood IN
WRTT-FM Huntsville AL	*WSDL(FM) Ocean City MD	WSMC-FM Collegedale TN	WSUH(FM) Crozet VA	*WTLD(FM) Jesup GA
*WRTU(FM) San Juan PR	WSDM-FM Brazil IN	WSMD-FM Mechanicsville MD	*WSUL(FM) Monticello NY	*WTLG(FM) Starke FL
*WRTX(FM) Dover DE	*WSDP(FM) Plymouth MI	WSM-FM Nashville TN	*WSUM(FM) Madison WI	*WTLI(FM) Bear Creek Township MI
*WRTY(FM) Jackson Township PA	WSEA(FM) Atlantic Beach SC	WSMI-FM Litchfield IL	WSUN-FM Holiday FL	WTLQ-FM Punta Rassa FL
*WRUC(FM) Schenectady NY	*WSEB(FM) Englewood FL	WSMJ(FM) Baltimore MD	*WSUP(FM) Platteville WI	*WTLR(FM) State College PA
WRUF-FM Gainesville FL	WSEI(FM) Olney IL	WSMK(FM) Buchanan MI	WSUS(FM) Franklin NJ	WTLT(FM) Naples FL
WRUL(FM) Carmi IL	WSEK(FM) Burnside KY	*WSMM(FM) Selmer TN	*WSUW(FM) Whitewater WI	WTLX(FM) Columbus WI
WRUM(FM) Orlando FL	WSEL-FM Pontotoc MS	WSMO(FM) Thomaston AL	WSUY(FM) Charleston SC	*WTLY(FM) Thomasville GA
*WRUO(FM) Mayaguez PR	WSEN-FM Baldwinsville NY	*WSMR(FM) Sarasota FL	*WSVH(FM) Savannah GA	WTLZ(FM) Saginaw MI
WRUP(FM) Munising MI	WSEO(FM) Nelsonville OH	WSMS(FM) Artesia MS	WSVO(FM) Staunton VA	*WTMB(FM) Tomah WI
*WRUR-FM Rochester NY	WSEV-FM Gatlinburg TN	*WSMU-FM North Dartmouth MA	WSWR(FM) Shelby OH	*WTMD(FM) Towson MD
*WRUV(FM) Burlington VT	*WSEW(FM) Sanford ME	WSMW(FM) Greensboro NC	WSWT(FM) Peoria IL	WTMG(FM) Williston FL
*WRUW-FM Cleveland OH	WSEY(FM) Oregon IL	WSNA(FM) South Webster OH	WSWV-FM Pennington Gap VA	*WTMK(FM) Lowell IN
WRVA-FM Rocky Mount NC	WSFL-FM New Bern NC	*WSNC(FM) Winston-Salem NC	*WSYC-FM Shippensburg PA	*WTML(FM) Tullahoma TN
WRVB(FM) Marietta OH	WSFM(FM) Oak Island NC	*WSND-FM Notre Dame IN	WSYE(FM) Houston MS	WTMP-FM Dade City FL
WRVC-FM Catlettsburg KY	WSFQ(FM) Peshtigo WI	WSNE-FM Taunton MA	WSYN(FM) Georgetown SC	*WTMQ(FM) Lumpkin GA
*WRVD(FM) Syracuse NY	*WSFR(FM) Corydon IN	WSNI(FM) Philadelphia PA	WSYR-FM Gifford FL	*WTMV(FM) Youngsville PA
WRVE(FM) Schenectady NY	*WSFX(FM) Nanticoke PA	WSNN(FM) Potsdam NY	WSYY-FM Millinocket ME	WTMX(FM) Skokie IL
WRVF(FM) Toledo OH	WSGA(FM) Hinesville GA	WSNT-FM Sandersville GA	WTAK-FM Hartselle AL	WTNE-FM Trenton TN
*WRVG(FM) Georgetown KY	WSGC-FM Elberton GA	WSNU(FM) Lock Haven PA	WTAO-FM Murphysboro IL	*WTNJ(FM) Mount Hope WV
WRVH(FM) Williamsport PA	*WSGE(FM) Dallas NC	WSNV(FM) Salem VA	*WTBB(FM) Gadsden AL	WTNM(FM) Water Valley MS
WRVI(FM) Valley Station KY	*WSGG(FM) Norfolk CT	WSNX-FM Muskegon MI	WTBF-FM Brundidge AL	*WTNN(FM) Union City TN
*WRVJ(FM) Watertown NY	WSGL(FM) Naples FL	WSNY(FM) Columbus OH	WTBG(FM) Brownsville TN	WTNR(FM) Holland MI
*WRVL(FM) Lynchburg VA	WSGM(FM) Coalmont TN	WSNZ(FM) Appomattox VA	*WTBI-FM Greenville SC	WTNS-FM Coshocton OH
*WRVM(FM) Suring WI	*WSGN(FM) Gadsden AL	WSOC-FM Charlotte NC	WTBJ(FM) Oxford AL	WTNT-FM Tallahassee FL
*WRVN(FM) Utica NY	WSGP(FM) Glasgow KY	*WSOE(FM) Elon NC	WTBK(FM) Manchester KY	WTNV(FM) Jackson TN
*WRVO(FM) Oswego NY	*WSGR-FM Port Huron MI	*WSOF-FM Madisonville KY	WTBM(FM) Mexico ME	*WTOH(FM) Mobile AL
WRVQ(FM) Richmond VA	WSGS(FM) Hazard KY	WSOG(FM) Spring Valley IL	WTBX(FM) Hibbing MN	WTOJ(FM) Carthage NY
WRVR-FM Memphis TN	*WSHA(FM) Raleigh NC	*WSOH(FM) New Washington IN	WTCB(FM) Orangeburg SC	WTON-FM Staunton VA
*WRVS-FM Elizabeth City NC	WSHC(FM) Shepherdstown WV	WSOL-FM Brunswick GA	*WTCC(FM) Springfield MA	WTOP-FM Warrenton VA
*WRVT(FM) Rutland VT	*WSHD(FM) Eastport ME	*WSOR(FM) Naples FL	WTCD(FM) Indianola MS	WTOS-FM Skowhegan ME
*WRVU(FM) Nashville TN	WSHH(FM) Pittsburgh PA	WSOS-FM Saint Augustine FL	WTCJ-FM Tell City IN	*WTOT-FM Graceville FL
WRVV(FM) Harrisburg PA	*WSHJ(FM) Southfield MI	*WSOU(FM) South Orange NJ	*WTCK(FM) Charlevoix MI	WTPA(FM) Mechanicsburg PA
WRVW(FM) Lebanon TN	WSHK(FM) Kittery ME	WSOX(FM) Red Lion PA	WTCM-FM Traverse City MI	*WTPC(FM) Elsah IL
WRVX(FM) Eufaula AL	*WSHL-FM Easton MA	WSOY-FM Decatur IL	WTCQ(FM) Vidalia GA	WTPI(FM) Indianapolis IN
WRVY-FM Henry IL	WSHP(FM) Attica IN	WSPA-FM Spartanburg SC	WTCR-FM Huntington WV	*WTPL(FM) Hillsboro NH
WRVZ(FM) Pocatalico WV	*WSHR(FM) Lake Ronkonkoma NY	WSPI(FM) Mount Carmel PA	WTCX(FM) Ripon WI	WTPM(FM) Aguadilla PR
*WRWA(FM) Dothan AL	*WSHS(FM) Sheboygan WI	WSPK(FM) Poughkeepsie NY	WTDA(FM) Westerville OH	WTPR-FM McKinnon TN
WRWD-FM Highland NY	*WSHU(FM) Fairfield CT	*WSPM(FM) Cloverdale IN	WTDK(FM) Federalsburg MD	WTPT(FM) Forest City NC
*WRWJ(FM) Murrysville PA	WSHW(FM) Frankfort IN	*WSPN(FM) Saratoga Springs NY	WTDR(FM) Talladega AL	*WTQR(FM) Winston-Salem NC
WRWK(FM) Delta OH	WSHZ(FM) Muskegon MI	*WSPS(FM) Concord NH	*WTEB(FM) New Bern NC	WTRB-FM Sylacauga AL
*WRXC(FM) Shelton CT	*WSIA(FM) Staten Island NY	WSPT-FM Stevens Point WI	*WTFH(FM) Helen GA	WTRG(FM) Gaston NC
*WRXH(FM) Plymouth IN	WSIB(FM) Selmer TN	WSPX(FM) Bowman SC	WTFM(FM) Kingsport TN	WTRH(FM) Ramsey IL
WRXK-FM Bonita Springs FL	*WSIE(FM) Edwardsville IL	WSPY-FM Plano IL	WTFX-FM Clarksville IN	*WTRK(FM) Bay City MI
WRXL(FM) Richmond VA	*WSIF(FM) Wilkesboro NC	WSPZ-FM Hartford MI	WTGA-FM Thomaston GA	*WTRM(FM) Winchester VA
WRXQ(FM) Coal City IL	WSIG(FM) Mount Jackson VA	*WSQA(FM) Hornell NY	WTGE(FM) Baker LA	WTRS-FM Dunnellon FL
WRXR-FM Rossville GA	WSIM(FM) Bishopville SC	*WSQC(FM) Oneonta NY	WTGG(FM) Amite LA	*WTRT(FM) Benton KY

Broadcasting & Cable Yearbook 2006

D-638

U.S. FM Stations by Call Letters

WTRV(FM) Walker MI
WTRX-FM Pontiac IL
WTRY-FM Rotterdam NY
WTRZ-FM McMinnville TN
WTSA-FM Brattleboro VT
*WTSC-FM Potsdam NY
*WTSE(FM) Benton TN
*WTSG(FM) Carlinville IL
WTSH-FM Rockmart GA
WTSM(FM) Springfield VT
*WTSR(FM) Trenton NJ
WTSS(FM) Buffalo NY
*WTSU(FM) Troy AL
WTSX(FM) Port Jervis NY
WTSZ-FM Eminence KY
WTTC-FM Towanda PA
WTTH(FM) Margate City NJ
WTTP(FM) Las Piedras PR
WTTS(FM) Bloomington IN
*WTTU(FM) Cookeville TN
WTTX-FM Appomattox VA
WTUA(FM) Saint Stephen SC
WTUE(FM) Dayton OH
WTUF(FM) Boston GA
WTUG(FM) Tuscaloosa AL
WTUK(FM) Harlan KY
*WTUL(FM) New Orleans LA
WTUN(FM) Ringgold GA
*WTUR(FM) Upland IN
WTUZ(FM) Uhrichsville OH
WTVR-FM Richmond VA
WTVY-FM Dothan AL
WTWR-FM Monroe MI
WTWV(FM) Mashpee MA
WTWX-FM Guntersville AL
WTXM(FM) Maryville TN
WTXQ(FM) Saint Johns MI
*WTXR(FM) Toccoa Falls GA
WTXT(FM) Fayette AL
WTYB(FM) Springfield GA
WTYD(FM) West Point VA
WTYE(FM) Robinson IL
WTYJ(FM) Fayette MS
WTYL-FM Tylertown MS
WTYS-FM Marianna FL
WTZB(FM) Englewood FL
WTZR(FM) Elizabethton TN
*WUAG(FM) Greensboro NC
*WUAL-FM Tuscaloosa AL
*WUAW(FM) Erwin NC
WUBB(FM) York Center ME
WUBE-FM Cincinnati OH
*WUBJ(FM) Jamestown NY
*WUBS(FM) South Bend IN
WUBT(FM) Russellville KY
WUBU(FM) South Bend IN
WUBZ-FM Philipsburg PA
*WUCF-FM Orlando FL
*WUCX-FM Bay City MI
WUCZ-FM Carthage TN
*WUDR(FM) Dayton OH
*WUEC(FM) Eau Claire WI
*WUEV(FM) Evansville IN
WUEZ(FM) Carterville IL
WUFF-FM Eastman GA
WUFK(FM) Fort Kent ME
*WUFM(FM) Columbus OH
*WUFN(FM) Albion MI
*WUFR(FM) Bedford PA
*WUFT-FM Gainesville FL
*WUGA(FM) Athens GA
*WUGN(FM) Midland MI
WUGO(FM) Grayson KY
WUHT(FM) Birmingham AL
WUHU(FM) Smiths Grove KY
*WUIN(FM) Carolina Beach NC
*WUIS(FM) Springfield IL
*WUJC(FM) Saint Marks FL
WUJM(FM) Gulfport MS
WUKL(FM) Bethlehem WV
WUKQ-FM Mayaguez PR
WUKS(FM) Saint Pauls NC
*WUKY(FM) Lexington KY
WULF(FM) Hardinsburg KY
WULS(FM) Broxton GA
*WUMB-FM Boston MA
*WUMC(FM) Elizabethton TN

WUME-FM Paoli IN
*WUMF-FM Farmington ME
*WUML(FM) Lowell MA
*WUMR(FM) Memphis TN
WUMS(FM) University MS
WUMX(FM) Rome NY
*WUNC(FM) Chapel Hill NC
*WUND-FM Manteo NC
*WUNH(FM) Durham NH
*WUNV(FM) Albany GA
*WUNY(FM) Utica NY
*WUOG(FM) Athens GA
*WUOL(FM) Louisville KY
*WUOM(FM) Ann Arbor MI
*WUOT(FM) Knoxville TN
WUPE(FM) Pittsfield MA
*WUPI(FM) Presque Isle ME
WUPK(FM) Marquette MI
WUPM(FM) Ironwood MI
WUPS(FM) Houghton Lake MI
*WUPX(FM) Marquette MI
WUPY(FM) Ontonagon MI
WURB(FM) Windsor NC
*WURC(FM) Holly Springs MS
*WURI(FM) Manteo NC
WURK(FM) Elwood IN
*WUSB(FM) Stony Brook NY
*WUSC-FM Columbia SC
WUSE(FM) Fairview PA
*WUSF(FM) Tampa FL
*WUSI(FM) Olney IL
WUSJ(FM) Jackson MS
WUSL(FM) Philadelphia PA
*WUSM-FM Hattiesburg MS
WUSN(FM) Chicago IL
*WUSO(FM) Springfield OH
WUSP(FM) Nekoosa WI
WUSQ-FM Winchester VA
*WUSR(FM) Scranton PA
WUSV(FM) San Carlos Park FL
WUSW(FM) Hattiesburg MS
WUSY(FM) Cleveland TN
WUSZ(FM) Virginia MN
*WUTC(FM) Chattanooga TN
*WUTK-FM Knoxville TN
*WUTL(FM) Tallahassee FL
*WUTM(FM) Martin TN
*WUTS(FM) Sewanee TN
WUUF(FM) Sodus NY
WUUU(FM) Franklinton LA
WUUZ(FM) Cooperstown PA
WUVA(FM) Charlottesville VA
*WUVT-FM Blacksburg VA
*WUWF(FM) Pensacola FL
*WUWG(FM) Carrollton GA
*WUWM(FM) Milwaukee WI
WUZR(FM) Bicknell IN
WUZZ-FM Lima OH
*WVAC-FM Adrian MI
WVAF(FM) Charleston WV
WVAQ(FM) Morgantown WV
*WVAS(FM) Montgomery AL
WVAY(FM) Wilmington VT
WVAZ(FM) Oak Park IL
*WVBC(FM) Bethany WV
WVBE-FM Lynchburg VA
WVBG(FM) Redwood MS
*WVBH(FM) Beach Haven West NJ
WVBO(FM) Winneconne WI
WVBR-FM Ithaca NY
*WVBU-FM Lewisburg PA
*WVBV(FM) Medford Lakes NJ
WVBZ(FM) High Point NC
*WVCF(FM) Eau Claire WI
*WVCM(FM) Iron Mountain MI
*WVCN(FM) Baraga MI
WVCO(FM) Loris SC
*WVCP(FM) Gallatin TN
*WVCR-FM Loudonville NY
*WVCT(FM) Keavy KY
*WVCX-FM Tomah WI
WVCY-FM Milwaukee WI
*WVDA(FM) Valdosta GA
WVEE(FM) Atlanta GA
WVEK-FM Cumberland KY
*WVEL-FM Glasford IL
*WVEP(FM) Martinsburg WV

WVES(FM) Accomac VA
WVEZ(FM) Louisville KY
*WVFA(FM) Lebanon NH
WVFB(FM) Celina TN
WVFJ-FM Manchester GA
*WVFL(FM) Fond du Lac WI
*WVFS(FM) Tallahassee FL
WVGA(FM) Lakeland GA
WVGN(FM) Charlotte Amalie VI
*WVGR(FM) Grand Rapids MI
*WVGS(FM) Statesboro GA
*WVHC(FM) Herkimer NY
WVHL(FM) Farmville VA
*WVHM(FM) Benton KY
*WVHR(FM) Huntingdon TN
*WVIA-FM Scranton PA
WVIB(FM) Holton MI
WVIC(FM) Jackson MI
*WVIJ(FM) Port Charlotte FL
*WVIK(FM) Rock Island IL
WVIL(FM) Virginia IL
WVIM-FM Coldwater MS
WVIN-FM Bath NY
WVIQ(FM) Christiansted VI
WVIV-FM Highland Park IL
WVIX(FM) Joliet IL
*WVJC(FM) Mount Carmel IL
WVJP-FM Caguas PR
WVJZ(FM) Charlotte Amalie VI
*WVKC(FM) Galesburg IL
*WVKF(FM) Shadyside OH
WVKL(FM) Norfolk VA
WVKM(FM) Matewan WV
WVKO-FM Johnstown OH
*WVKR-FM Poughkeepsie NY
WVKS(FM) Toledo OH
WVKX(FM) Irwinton GA
WVLC(FM) Mannsville KY
WVLE(FM) Scottsville KY
WVLF(FM) Norwood NY
*WVLI(FM) Kankakee IL
*WVLS(FM) Monterey VA
WVLT(FM) Vineland NJ
WVLY-FM Milton PA
*WVMC-FM Mansfield OH
*WVME(FM) Meadville PA
WVMG(FM) Normal IL
*WVMJ(FM) Conway NH
*WVML(FM) Millersburg OH
*WVMM(FM) Grantham PA
*WVMN(FM) New Castle PA
*WVMS(FM) Sandusky OH
WVMV(FM) Detroit MI
*WVMW-FM Scranton PA
WVMX(FM) Cincinnati OH
WVNA-FM Muscle Shoals AL
*WVNH(FM) Concord NH
WVNI(FM) Nashville IN
*WVNL(FM) Vandalia IL
WVNO-FM Mansfield OH
WVNP(FM) Wheeling WV
WVNU(FM) Greenfield OH
WVNV(FM) Malone NY
WVNW(FM) Burnham PA
WVOA-FM Mexico NY
*WVOB(FM) Dothan AL
WVOD(FM) Manteo NC
*WVOF(FM) Fairfield CT
WVOH-FM Hazlehurst GA
WVOK-FM Oxford AL
WVOM(FM) Howland ME
WVOR-FM Rochester NY
WVOS-FM Liberty NY
WVOW-FM Logan WV
WVOZ-FM Carolina PR
*WVPA(FM) Saint Johnsbury VT
WVPB(FM) Beckley WV
*WVPE(FM) Elkhart IN
WVPG(FM) Parkersburg WV
*WVPH(FM) Piscataway NJ
WVPM(FM) Morgantown WV
*WVPN(FM) Charleston WV
*WVPR(FM) Windsor VT
*WVPS(FM) Burlington VT
*WVPW(FM) Buckhannon WV
WVRB(FM) Wilmore KY
WVRC-FM Spencer WV

WVRE(FM) Dickeyville WI
*WVRI(FM) Pavo GA
WVRK(FM) Columbus GA
*WVRN(FM) Wittenberg WI
WVRQ-FM Viroqua WI
WVRR(FM) Newport NH
WVRT(FM) Mill Hall PA
*WVRU(FM) Radford VA
WVRV(FM) East St. Louis IL
WVRY(FM) Waverly TN
*WVSB(FM) Romney WV
*WVSD(FM) Itta Bena MS
WVSG(FM) Coeburn VA
*WVSH(FM) Huntington IN
*WVSI(FM) Mount Vernon IL
*WVSO(FM) South Vienna OH
WVSR-FM Charleston WV
*WVSS(FM) Menomonie WI
*WVST-FM Petersburg VA
*WVSU-FM Birmingham AL
WVSZ(FM) Chesterfield SC
*WVTC(FM) Randolph Center VT
*WVTF(FM) Roanoke VA
*WVTI(FM) Holland MI
*WVTK(FM) Port Henry NY
*WVTR(FM) Marion VA
*WVTU(FM) Charlottesville VA
*WVTW(FM) Charlottesville VA
*WVUA-FM Tuscaloosa AL
*WVUB(FM) Vincennes IN
*WVUD(FM) Newark DE
*WVUM(FM) Coral Gables FL
*WVUR-FM Valparaiso IN
WVVE(FM) Panama City Beach FL
WVVR(FM) Hopkinsville KY
*WVVS(FM) Valdosta GA
WVVV(FM) Williamstown WV
WVWA(FM) Peachtree City GA
*WVWC(FM) Buckhannon WV
WVWN(FM) Heyworth IL
*WVWV(FM) Huntington WV
*WVXA(FM) Rogers City MI
*WVXG(FM) Mount Gilead OH
*WVXH(FM) Harrison MI
*WVXM(FM) Manistee MI
*WVXR(FM) Richmond IN
*WVXU(FM) Cincinnati OH
*WVXW(FM) West Union OH
*WVYA(FM) Williamsport PA
WVYB(FM) Holly Hill FL
*WVYC(FM) York PA
WVZA(FM) Herrin IL
WWAG(FM) McKee KY
WWAV-FM Santa Rosa Beach FL
WWAX(FM) Hermantown MN
WWBB(FM) Providence RI
WWBD(FM) Bamberg SC
WWBE(FM) Mifflinburg PA
WWBL(FM) Washington IN
*WWBM(FM) Yates GA
WWBN(FM) Tuscola MI
WWBR(FM) Big Rapids MI
WWBU(FM) Radford VA
WWBX(FM) Bangor ME
WWCD(FM) Grove City OH
*WWCF(FM) McConnellsburg PA
*WWCJ(FM) Cape May NJ
WWCK-FM Flint MI
WWCM(FM) Standish MI
WWCT(FM) Farmington IL
*WWCU(FM) Cullowhee NC
WWDC-FM Washington DC
WWDE-FM Hampton VA
WWDG(FM) DeRuyter NY
WWDL-FM Scranton PA
WWDM(FM) Sumter SC
*WWDS(FM) Muncie IN
WWDV(FM) Zion IL
WWDW(FM) Alberta VA
*WWEB(FM) Wallingford CT
*WWEC(FM) Elizabethtown PA
*WWED(FM) Spotsylvania VA
WWEG(FM) Hagerstown MD
WWEL(FM) London KY
*WWET(FM) Valdosta GA
*WWEV(FM) Cumming GA

WWFG(FM) Ocean City MD
*WWFM(FM) Trenton NJ
WWFN-FM Lake City SC
*WWFP(FM) Brigantine NJ
*WWFR(FM) Stuart FL
WWFX(FM) Southbridge MA
WWFY(FM) Berlin VT
WWGF(FM) Donalsonville GA
WWGM(FM) Alamo TN
*WWGN(FM) Ottawa IL
*WWGO(FM) Charleston IL
WWGR(FM) Fort Myers FL
WWGY(FM) Grove City PA
WWHA(FM) Oriental NC
WWHC(FM) Oakland MD
*WWHI(FM) Muncie IN
WWHK(FM) Concord NH
WWHP(FM) Farmer City IL
WWHQ(FM) Meredith NH
*WWHR(FM) Bowling Green KY
*WWHS-FM Hampden-Sydney VA
WWHT(FM) Syracuse NY
WWHV(FM) Virginia Beach VA
*WWHW(FM) Dillon SC
*WWIA(FM) Palm Bay FL
WWIB(FM) Hallie WI
*WWIL-FM Wilmington NC
WWIN-FM Glen Burnie MD
WWIO-FM Brunswick GA
*WWIP(FM) Cheriton VA
WWIS-FM Black River Falls WI
WWIZ(FM) Mercer PA
*WWJD(FM) Pippa Passes KY
WWJK(FM) Jackson MS
WWJM(FM) New Lexington OH
WWJO(FM) Saint Cloud MN
*WWJS(FM) Watertown NY
WWKA(FM) Orlando FL
WWKC(FM) Caldwell OH
WWKF(FM) Fulton KY
*WWKG(FM) Clermont FL
WWKI(FM) Kokomo IN
WWKL(FM) Palmyra PA
*WWKM(FM) Imlay City MI
WWKN(FM) Marshall MI
WWKO(FM) Belleview FL
WWKR(FM) Pentwater MI
WWKS(FM) Cruz Bay VI
WWKT-FM Kingstree SC
WWKX(FM) Woonsocket RI
WWKY(FM) Providence KY
WWKZ(FM) Columbus MS
*WWLA(FM) South Charleston WV
*WWLC(FM) Cross City FL
WWLD(FM) Cairo GA
WWLI(FM) Providence RI
WWLL(FM) Sebring FL
*WWLR(FM) Lyndonville VT
WWLS-FM Bethany OK
WWLT(FM) Manchester KY
*WWLU(FM) Lincoln University PA
WWLW(FM) Clarksburg WV
WWLY(FM) Huntingdon PA
*WWMC(FM) Lynchburg VA
WWMG(FM) Millbrook AL
WWMJ(FM) Ellsworth ME
WWMP(FM) Waterbury VT
*WWMS(FM) Oxford MS
*WWMU(FM) Muncie IN
WWMX(FM) Baltimore MD
WWMY(FM) Raleigh NC
WWMY(FM) Kinston NC
*WWNJ(FM) Dover Township NJ
WWNK(FM) Farmville NC
*WWNO(FM) New Orleans LA
WWNQ(FM) Forest Acres SC
WWNU(FM) Irmo SC
*WWNW(FM) New Wilmington PA
WWOC(FM) Hatteras NC
WWOD(FM) Hartford VT
WWOG(FM) Cookeville TN
WWOJ(FM) Avon Park FL
WWOT(FM) Altoona PA
*WWOZ(FM) New Orleans LA
*WWPH(FM) Princeton Junction NJ
WWPJ(FM) Pen Argyl PA
WWPN(FM) Westernport MD

U.S. FM Stations by Call Letters

WWPR-FM New York NY
*WWPT(FM) Westport CT
*WWPV-FM Colchester VT
WWQM-FM Middleton WI
WWQQ-FM Wilmington NC
*WWQS(FM) Pastillo PR
WWRE(FM) Berryville VA
WWRK(FM) Scranton SC
WWRM(FM) Tampa FL
WWRQ-FM Valdosta GA
WWRT(FM) Strasburg VA
WWRX(FM) Pawcatuck CT
WWRZ(FM) Fort Meade FL
WWSE(FM) Jamestown NY
WWSL(FM) Philadelphia MS
WWSN(FM) Waycross GA
*WWSP(FM) Stevens Point WI
WWST(FM) Sevierville TN
*WWSU(FM) Dayton OH
WWSW-FM Pittsburgh PA
WWSY(FM) Seelyville IN
*WWTA(FM) Marion MA
WWTB(FM) Topsail Beach NC
*WWTE(FM) Wellfleet MA
WWTH(FM) Oscoda MI
WWTN(FM) Manchester TN
*WWTS(FM) Logansport IN
WWUF(FM) Waycross GA
*WWUH(FM) West Hartford CT
WWUN-FM Clarksdale MS
WWUS(FM) Big Pine Key FL
WWUZ(FM) Bowling Green VA
WWVA-FM Canton GA
WWVR(FM) West Terre Haute IN
*WWVU-FM Morgantown WV
WWVV(FM) Ridgeland SC
WWVZ(FM) Braddock Heights MD
WWWA(FM) Winslow ME
WWWD(FM) Bolingbroke GA
WWWI-FM Pillager MN
WWWK(FM) Marathon FL
WWWM-FM Sylvania OH
WWWQ(FM) College Park GA
WWWV(FM) Charlottesville VA
WWWW(FM) Ann Arbor MI
WWWX(FM) Oshkosh WI
WWWY(FM) North Vernon IN
WWWZ(FM) Summerville SC
*WWXC(FM) Albany GA
WWXM(FM) Garden City SC
WWXQ(FM) Trinity AL
WWYL(FM) Chenango Bridge NY
WWYN(FM) McKenzie TN
WWYW(FM) Dundee IL
WWYY(FM) Belvidere NJ
WWYZ(FM) Waterbury CT
WWZD-FM New Albany MS
*WWZP(FM) Freeland MI
WWZW(FM) Buena Vista VA
WWZY(FM) Long Branch NJ
WWZZ(FM) Waldorf MD
WXAB(FM) McLain MS
*WXAC(FM) Reading PA
WXAJ(FM) Hillsboro IL
WXAL-FM Addison VT
WXAN(FM) Ava IL
*WXBA(FM) Brentwood NY
WXBC(FM) Hardinsburg KY
*WXBE(FM) Beaufort NC
WXBM-FM Milton FL
WXBQ-FM Bristol TN
WXBT(FM) West Columbia SC
WXBX(FM) Rural Retreat VA
WXCC(FM) Williamson WV
WXCF-FM Clifton Forge VA
WXCH(FM) Versailles IN
*WXCI(FM) Danbury CT
WXCL(FM) Pekin IL
WXCM(FM) Whitesville KY
WXCR(FM) New Martinsville WV
WXCV(FM) Homosassa Springs FL
WXCX(FM) Siren WI
WXCY(FM) Havre de Grace MD
WXDJ(FM) North Miami Beach FL
*WXDU(FM) Durham NC
WXDX-FM Pittsburgh PA
WXEF(FM) Effingham IL
WXEG(FM) Beavercreek OH
*WXEL(FM) West Palm Beach FL
WXER(FM) Plymouth WI
WXET(FM) Arcola IL
WXEZ(FM) Yorktown VA
WXFL(FM) Florence AL
WXFM(FM) Mount Zion IL
WXFX(FM) Prattville AL
WXGL(FM) Saint Petersburg FL
WXGM-FM Gloucester VA
*WXGN(FM) Egg Harbor Township NJ
WXHB(FM) Richton MS
WXHC(FM) Homer NY
*WXHD(FM) Mount Hope NY
*WXHL-FM Christiana DE
WXHT(FM) Madison FL
WXIL(FM) Parkersburg WV
WXIS(FM) Erwin TN
WXIZ(FM) Waverly OH
WXJB(FM) Harrogate TN
WXJC-FM Cordova AL
*WXJM(FM) Harrisonburg VA
WXJN(FM) Lewes DE
WXJY(FM) Georgetown SC
WXJZ(FM) Gainesville FL
WXKB(FM) Cape Coral FL
WXKC(FM) Erie PA
WXKE(FM) Huntington IN
WXKQ(FM) Whitesburg KY
WXKR(FM) Port Clinton OH
WXKS-FM Medford MA
WXKT(FM) Washington GA
WXKY-FM Stanford KY
WXKZ-FM Prestonsburg KY
WXLC(FM) Waukegan IL
WXLF(FM) White River Junction VT
*WXLG(FM) North Creek NY
*WXLH(FM) Blue Mountain Lake NY
WXLK(FM) Roanoke VA
WXLM(FM) Stonington CT
WXLO(FM) Fitchburg MA
WXLP(FM) Moline IL
WXLR(FM) Harold KY
WXLT(FM) Christopher IL
*WXLU(FM) Peru NY
*WXLV(FM) Schnecksville PA
WXLX(FM) Lajas PR
WXLY(FM) North Charleston SC
WXLZ-FM Lebanon VA
WXMA(FM) Louisville KY
WXMD(FM) Pocomoke City MD
WXMG(FM) Upper Arlington OH
WXMK(FM) Dock Junction GA
*WXML(FM) Upper Sandusky OH
WXMM(FM) Norfolk VA
WXMP(FM) Peoria IL
WXMX(FM) Millington TN
WXMZ(FM) Hartford KY
WXNR(FM) Grifton NC
WXOF(FM) Yankeetown FL
WXOQ(FM) Selmer TN
WXOT(FM) Mount Union PA
*WXOU(FM) Auburn Hills MI
*WXPH(FM) Harrisburg PA
WXPK(FM) Briarcliff Manor NY
*WXPL(FM) Fitchburg MA
*WXPN(FM) Philadelphia PA
*WXPR(FM) Rhinelander WI
*WXPW(FM) Wausau WI
WXQL(FM) Carrollton MI
WXQR(FM) Jacksonville NC
WXQW(FM) Meridianville AL
*WXRB(FM) Dudley MA
WXRC(FM) Hickory NC
WXRD(FM) Crown Point IN
WXRG(FM) Pascagoula MS
*WXRI(FM) Winston-Salem NC
WXRK(FM) New York NY
WXRO(FM) Beaver Dam WI
WXRR(FM) Hattiesburg MS
WXRS-FM Swainsboro GA
WXRT-FM Chicago IL
WXRV(FM) Haverhill MA
WXRX(FM) Belvidere IL
WXRZ(FM) Corinth MS
WXSR(FM) Quincy FL
WXSS(FM) Wauwatosa WI
WXST(FM) Hollywood SC
WXTA(FM) Edinboro PA
WXTB(FM) Clearwater FL
WXTK(FM) West Yarmouth MA
WXTM(FM) Cleveland Heights OH
WXTQ(FM) Athens OH
*WXTS-FM Toledo OH
WXTT(FM) Danville IL
WXTU(FM) Philadelphia PA
WXTW(FM) Auburn IN
WXUR(FM) Herkimer NY
*WXUT(FM) Toledo OH
*WXVS(FM) Waycross GA
*WXVU(FM) Villanova PA
*WXVW(FM) Veedersburg IN
WXXB(FM) Delphi IN
*WXXE(FM) Fenner NY
WXXF(FM) Loudonville OH
*WXXI-FM Rochester NY
WXXK(FM) Lebanon NH
WXXL(FM) Tavares FL
WXXM(FM) Sun Prairie WI
WXXO(FM) Cambridge Springs PA
WXXQ(FM) Freeport IL
WXXR(FM) Fredericktown OH
WXXS(FM) Lancaster NH
WXXX(FM) South Burlington VT
*WXXY-FM Port Republic NJ
WXXZ(FM) Grand Marais MN
*WXYC(FM) Chapel Hill NC
WXYK(FM) Gulfport MS
WXYM(FM) Tomah WI
WXYX(FM) Bayamon PR
WXZO(FM) Willsboro NY
WXZQ(FM) Piketon OH
WXZX(FM) Culebra PR
WXZZ(FM) Georgetown KY
WYAB(FM) Yazoo City MS
WYAC-FM Christiansted VI
*WYAJ(FM) Sudbury MA
WYAK-FM Surfside Beach SC
*WYAR(FM) Yarmouth ME
WYAV(FM) Myrtle Beach SC
WYAY(FM) Gainesville GA
*WYAZ(FM) Yazoo City MS
WYBB(FM) Folly Beach SC
WYBC-FM New Haven CT
*WYBF(FM) Radnor Township PA
WYBL(FM) Ashtabula OH
WYBR(FM) Big Rapids MI
WYBZ(FM) Crooksville OH
WYCA(FM) Crete IL
WYCD(FM) Detroit MI
*WYCE(FM) Wyoming MI
WYCL(FM) Pensacola FL
*WYCM(FM) Charlton MA
WYCR(FM) York-Hanover PA
*WYCS(FM) Yorktown VA
WYCT(FM) Pensacola FL
WYCY(FM) Hawley PA
WYDE-FM Cullman AL
WYDL(FM) Middleton TN
*WYDM(FM) Monroe MI
WYDS(FM) Decatur IL
WYEC(FM) Kewanee IL
*WYEP-FM Pittsburgh PA
WYEZ(FM) Murrell's Inlet SC
WYFA(FM) Waynesboro GA
*WYFB(FM) Gainesville FL
*WYFC(FM) Clinton TN
*WYFD(FM) Decatur AL
*WYFE(FM) Tarpon Springs FL
*WYFG(FM) Gaffney SC
*WYFH(FM) North Charleston SC
WYFI(FM) Norfolk VA
WYFJ(FM) Ashland VA
*WYFK(FM) Columbus GA
WYFL(FM) Henderson NC
WYFM(FM) Sharon PA
*WYFO(FM) Lakeland FL
*WYFP(FM) Harpswell ME
*WYFQ-FM Wadesboro NC
*WYFS(FM) Savannah GA
WYFT(FM) Luray VA
*WYFU(FM) Masontown PA
*WYFV(FM) Cayce SC
*WYFW(FM) Winder GA
WYFX(FM) Mount Vernon IN
WYGB(FM) Edinburgh IN
WYGC(FM) High Springs FL
WYGE(FM) London KY
*WYGG(FM) Asbury Park NJ
WYGL-FM Elizabethville PA
WYGO(FM) Madisonville TN
WYGS(FM) Columbus IN
WYGY(FM) Lebanon OH
WYHT(FM) Mansfield OH
WYHY(FM) Winnebago IL
WYJB(FM) Albany NY
*WYJC(FM) Greenville FL
WYJZ(FM) Lebanon IN
WYKK(FM) Quitman MS
*WYKL(FM) Crestline OH
WYKR-FM Haverhill NH
WYKS(FM) Gainesville FL
WYKT(FM) Wilmington IL
WYKX(FM) Escanaba MI
WYKZ(FM) Beaufort SC
WYLD-FM New Orleans LA
WYLT(FM) Fort Wayne IN
*WYLV(FM) Alcoa TN
WYLZ(FM) Pinconning MI
WYMG(FM) Jacksonville IL
WYMJ(FM) New Martinsville WV
*WYMS(FM) Milwaukee WI
WYMV(FM) Madisonville KY
WYMX(FM) Greenwood MS
WYMY(FM) Goldsboro NC
WYNA(FM) Calabash NC
WYND-FM Hatteras NC
WYNF(FM) Gray GA
WYNG(FM) Mount Carmel IL
WYNK-FM Baton Rouge LA
WYNN-FM Florence SC
WYNR(FM) Waycross GA
WYNT(FM) Upper Sandusky OH
WYNU(FM) Milan TN
WYNW(FM) Birnamwood WI
WYNZ(FM) Westbrook ME
WYOK(FM) Atmore AL
WYOO(FM) Springfield FL
WYOT(FM) Ebensburg PA
WYOY(FM) Gluckstadt MS
*WYPF(FM) Frederick MD
*WYPL(FM) Memphis TN
*WYPR(FM) Baltimore MD
WYPW(FM) Nappanee IN
WYPY(FM) Baton Rouge LA
WYQE(FM) Naguabo PR
*WYQS(FM) Mars Hill NC
WYRB(FM) Genoa IL
WYRK(FM) Buffalo NY
WYRO(FM) McArthur OH
WYRQ(FM) Little Falls MN
*WYRS(FM) Manahawkin NJ
WYRY(FM) Hinsdale NH
*WYSA(FM) Wauseon OH
WYSC(FM) McRae GA
WYSF(FM) Birmingham AL
WYSK-FM Spotsylvania VA
*WYSM(FM) Lima OH
*WYSO(FM) Yellow Springs OH
WYSP(FM) Philadelphia PA
WYSS(FM) Sault Ste. Marie MI
WYST(FM) Fairbury IL
*WYSU(FM) Youngstown OH
WYSX(FM) Morristown NY
*WYSZ(FM) Maumee OH
WYTE(FM) Whiting WI
*WYTF(FM) Indianola MS
*WYTJ(FM) Linton IN
WYTK(FM) Rogersville AL
*WYTL(FM) Wyomissing PA
WYTM-FM Fayetteville TN
*WYTN(FM) Youngstown OH
WYTR(FM) Brookville PA
WYTT(FM) Emporia VA
WYTZ(FM) Bridgman MI
WYUL(FM) Chateaugay NY
WYUM(FM) Mount Vernon GA
WYUU(FM) Safety Harbor FL
WYVK(FM) Middleport OH
WYVN(FM) Saugatuck MI
WYVR(FM) Petersburg IL
WYVY(FM) Union City TN
WYXB(FM) Indianapolis IN
WYXL(FM) Ithaca NY
WYXY(FM) Boonville IN
WYYD(FM) Amherst VA
WYYL(FM) Tunica MS
WYYS(FM) Streator IL
WYYU(FM) Dalton GA
WYYW(FM) Marion MS
WYYX(FM) Bonifay FL
WYYY(FM) Syracuse NY
WYZB(FM) Mary Esther FL
WYZK(FM) Valdosta GA
WYZY(FM) Saranac Lake NY
WZAA(FM) Garden City NY
WZAC-FM Danville WV
WZAD(FM) Wurtsboro NY
WZAI(FM) Brewster MA
WZAK(FM) Cleveland OH
WZAQ(FM) Louisa KY
WZAR(FM) Ponce PR
WZAT(FM) Savannah GA
WZAX(FM) Nashville NC
WZBA(FM) Westminster MD
WZBB(FM) Stanleytown VA
*WZBC(FM) Newton MA
WZBD(FM) Berne IN
WZBG(FM) Litchfield CT
WZBH(FM) Georgetown DE
WZBL(FM) Roanoke VA
WZBN(FM) Sylvester GA
WZBQ(FM) Carrollton AL
*WZBT(FM) Gettysburg PA
WZBX(FM) Sylvania GA
WZBZ(FM) Pleasantville NJ
WZCR(FM) Hudson NY
WZDM(FM) Vincennes IN
WZDQ(FM) Humboldt TN
WZEB(FM) Ocean View DE
WZEC(FM) Hoosick Falls NY
WZEE(FM) Madison WI
WZET(FM) Hormigueros PR
WZEW(FM) Fairhope AL
WZEZ(FM) Goochland VA
WZFJ(FM) Pequot Lakes MN
WZFL-FM Centreville MS
WZFX(FM) Whiteville NC
WZGC(FM) Atlanta GA
WZHT(FM) Troy AL
WZID(FM) Manchester NH
WZIN(FM) Charlotte Amalie VI
*WZIP(FM) Akron OH
WZIQ(FM) Smithville GA
WZJO(FM) Dunbar WV
WZJS(FM) Banner Elk NC
WZJZ(FM) Lehigh Acres FL
WZKB(FM) Wallace NC
WZKF(FM) Salem IN
WZKL(FM) Alliance OH
*WZKM(FM) Waynesboro MS
WZKR(FM) Decatur MS
WZKS(FM) Union MS
WZKX(FM) Bay St. Louis MS
WZKZ(FM) Alfred NY
WZLA-FM Abbeville SC
WZLD(FM) Petal MS
WZLF(FM) Bellows Falls VT
WZLK(FM) Virgie KY
WZLM(FM) Talladega AL
WZLQ(FM) Tupelo MS
WZLR(FM) Xenia OH
WZLT(FM) Lexington TN
WZLX(FM) Boston MA
*WZLY(FM) Wellesley MA
*WZMB(FM) Greenville NC
WZMJ(FM) Batesburg SC
WZMQ(FM) Key Largo FL
WZMR(FM) Altamont NY
WZMT(FM) Ponce PR
WZMX(FM) Hartford CT
*WZNB(FM) New Bern NC
WZNE(FM) Brighton NY
WZNF(FM) Lumberton MS
WZNJ(FM) Demopolis AL
WZNL(FM) Norway MI
WZNR(FM) Poquoson VA
WZNS(FM) Fort Walton Beach FL

Broadcasting & Cable Yearbook 2006

D-640

U.S. FM Stations by Call Letters

WZNT(FM) San Juan PR	WZPR(FM) Nags Head NC	WZSP(FM) Nocatee FL	WZXL(FM) Wildwood NJ	WZZK-FM Birmingham AL
WZNX(FM) Sullivan IL	WZPT(FM) New Kensington PA	WZSR(FM) Woodstock IL	*WZXM(FM) Middletown PA	WZZL(FM) Reidland KY
WZOC(FM) Plymouth IN	WZPW(FM) Peoria IL	WZST(FM) Westover WV	*WZXQ(FM) Chambersburg PA	WZZN(FM) Chicago IL
WZOE-FM Princeton IL	WZQQ(FM) Hyden KY	WZTK(FM) Burlington NC	WZXR(FM) South Williamsport PA	WZZO(FM) Bethlehem PA
WZOK(FM) Rockford IL	*WZRD(FM) Chicago IL	WZTZ(FM) Elba AL	WZXV(FM) Palmyra NY	WZZP(FM) Hopkinsville KY
WZOL(FM) Luquillo PR	*WZRI(FM) Spring Lake NC	WZUN(FM) Phoenix NY	*WZXX(FM) Lawrenceburg TN	WZZR(FM) Riviera Beach FL
WZOM(FM) Defiance OH	*WZRN(FM) Norlina NC	WZUP(FM) Rose Hill NC	WZYP(FM) Athens AL	WZZS(FM) Zolfo Springs FL
WZOO-FM Edgewood OH	WZRR(FM) Birmingham AL	WZUS(FM) Macon IL	WZYQ(FM) Mound Bayou MS	WZZT(FM) Morrison IL
WZOQ(FM) Wapakoneta OH	*WZRS(FM) Pana IL	WZUU(FM) Allegan MI	WZYY(FM) Renovo PA	WZZU(FM) Lynchburg VA
WZOR(FM) Mishicot WI	WZRT(FM) Rutland VT	WZVA(FM) Marion VA	*WZYZ(FM) Spencer TN	WZZY(FM) Winchester IN
WZOW(FM) Goshen IN	*WZRU(FM) Roanoke Rapids NC	WZVN(FM) Lowell IN	*WZZD(FM) Warwick PA	WZZZ(FM) Portsmouth OH
WZOZ(FM) Oneonta NY	WZRV(FM) Front Royal VA	WZWW(FM) Bellefonte PA	*WZZE(FM) Glen Mills PA	XETRA-FM Tijuana MEX
*WZPE(FM) Bath NC	WZRX-FM Fort Shawnee OH	WZWZ(FM) Kokomo IN	*WZZH(FM) Honesdale PA	XHRM-FM Tijuana MEX
WZPL(FM) Greenfield IN	WZSN(FM) Greenwood SC	WZXI(FM) Buffalo Gap VA	WZZI(FM) Vinton VA	

Canadian AM Stations by Call Letters

CBA(AM) Moncton NB
*CBE(AM) Windsor ON
CBEF(AM) Windsor ON
*CBG(AM) Gander NF
CBGN(AM) Sainte Anne des Monts PQ
CBGY(AM) Bonavista Bay NF
CBI(AM) Sydney NS
*CBK(AM) Regina SK
*CBKF-1(AM) Gravelbourg SK
CBKF-2(AM) Saskatoon SK
*CBN(AM) Saint John's NF
CBOF-1(AM) Maniwaki PQ
*CBR(AM) Calgary AB
CBT(AM) Grand Falls-Windsor NF
*CBU(AM) Vancouver BC
CBW(AM) Winnipeg MB
CBX(AM) Edmonton AB
*CBY(AM) Corner Brook NF
CFAB(AM) Windsor NS
CFAC(AM) Calgary AB
CFAM(AM) Altona MB
CFAR(AM) Flin Flon MB
CFAV(AM) Laval PQ
CFAX(AM) Victoria BC
CFBC(AM) Saint John NB
CFBV(AM) Smithers BC
CFCB(AM) Corner Brook NF
CFCO(AM) Chatham ON
CFCT(AM) Tuktoyaktuk NT
CFCW(AM) Camrose AB
CFCY(AM) Charlottetown PE
CFDR(AM) Dartmouth NS
CFED(AM) Chapais PQ
CFFB(AM) Iqaluit NU
CFFR(AM) Calgary AB
CFFX(AM) Kingston ON
CFGO(AM) Ottawa ON
CFGT(AM) Alma PQ
CFKC(AM) Creston BC
CFLD(AM) Burns Lake BC
CFLM(AM) La Tuque PQ
CFLN(AM) Goose Bay NF
CFLW(AM) Wabush NF
CFMB(AM) Montreal PQ
CFMJ(AM) Toronto ON

CFNC(AM) Cross Lake MB
CFNI(AM) Port Hardy BC
CFNW(AM) Port au Choix NF
CFOK(AM) Westlock AB
CFOS(AM) Owen Sound ON
CFPL(AM) London ON
*CFPR(AM) Prince Rupert BC
CFRA(AM) Ottawa ON
CFRB(AM) Toronto ON
CFRN(AM) Edmonton AB
CFRP(AM) Forestville PQ
CFRW(AM) Winnipeg MB
CFRY(AM) Portage la Prairie MB
CFSL(AM) Weyburn SK
CFSX(AM) Stephenville NF
CFTK(AM) Terrace BC
CFTR(AM) Toronto ON
CFUN(AM) Vancouver BC
CFWB(AM) Campbell River BC
*CFWH(AM) Whitehorse YT
*CFYK(AM) Yellowknife NT
CFYM(AM) Kindersley SK
CHAB(AM) Moose Jaw SK
*CHAK(AM) Inuvik NT
CHAM(AM) Hamilton ON
CHAT(AM) Medicine Hat AB
CHCM(AM) Marystown NF
CHED(AM) Edmonton AB
CHER(AM) Sydney NS
CHEV Toronto ON
*CHFA(AM) Edmonton AB
CHFC(AM) Churchill MB
CHHA(AM) Toronto ON
CHIN(AM) Toronto ON
CHKT(AM) Toronto ON
CHLN(AM) Trois Rivieres PQ
CHLT(AM) Sherbrooke PQ
CHLW(AM) Saint Paul AB
CHMB(AM) Vancouver BC
CHMJ(AM) Vancouver BC
CHML(AM) Hamilton ON
*CHMO(AM) Moosonee ON
CHNC(AM) New Carlisle PQ
CHNL(AM) Kamloops BC
CHNL-1(AM) Clearwater BC

CHNS(AM) Halifax NS
CHOK(AM) Sarnia ON
CHOR(AM) Summerland BC
CHQB(AM) Powell River BC
CHQR(AM) Calgary AB
CHQT(AM) Edmonton AB
CHRB(AM) High River AB
CHRC(AM) Quebec PQ
CHSC(AM) Saint Catharines ON
CHSM(AM) Steinbach MB
CHTK(AM) Prince Rupert BC
CHTM(AM) Thompson MB
CHTN(AM) Charlottetown PE
CHUC(AM) Cobourg ON
CHUM(AM) Toronto ON
CHVO(AM) Carbonear NF
CHWO(AM) Toronto ON
CIAO(AM) Brampton ON
CIBQ(AM) Brooks AB
CIGM(AM) Sudbury ON
CINF(AM) Verdun PQ
CINW(AM) Montreal PQ
CIOR(AM) Princeton BC
CISL(AM) Richmond BC
CIVH(AM) Vanderhoof BC
CIWW(AM) Ottawa ON
CJAD(AM) Montreal PQ
CJAR(AM) The Pas MB
CJAV(AM) Port Alberni PQ
CJBC(AM) Toronto ON
CJBK(AM) London ON
CJBQ(AM) Belleville ON
CJCA(AM) Edmonton AB
CJCB(AM) Sydney NS
CJCH(AM) Halifax NS
CJCL(AM) Toronto ON
CJCS(AM) Stratford ON
CJCW(AM) Sussex NB
CJDC(AM) Dawson Creek BC
CJGX(AM) Yorkton SK
CJMD(AM) Chibougamau PQ
CJME(AM) Regina SK
CJMR(AM) Mississauga ON
CJMS(AM) Saint Constant PQ
CJNB(AM) North Battleford SK

CJNL(AM) Merritt BC
CJNS(AM) Meadow Lake SK
CJOB(AM) Winnipeg MB
CJOR(AM) Osoyoos BC
CJOY(AM) Guelph ON
CJRB(AM) Boissevain MB
CJRC(AM) Gatineau PQ
CJSL(AM) Estevan SK
CJSN(AM) Shaunavon SK
CJUL(AM) Cornwall ON
CJVA(AM) Caraquet NB
CJVB(AM) Vancouver BC
CJWI(AM) Montreal PQ
CJWW(AM) Saskatoon SK
CJYE(AM) Oakville ON
CJYM(AM) Rosetown SK
CJYQ(AM) Saint John's NF
CJYR(AM) Edson AB
CKAC(AM) Montreal PQ
CKAD(AM) Middleton NS
CKAT(AM) North Bay ON
CKBA(AM) Athabasca AB
CKBD(AM) Vancouver BC
CKBI(AM) Prince Albert SK
CKBX(AM) 100 Mile House BC
CKCM(AM) Grand Falls NF
CKCR(AM) Revelstoke BC
CKDH(AM) Amherst NS
CKDM(AM) Dauphin MB
CKDO(AM) Oshawa ON
CKDQ(AM) Drumheller AB
CKDR(AM) Dryden ON
CKDR-5(AM) Red Lake ON
CKDR-6(AM) Atikokan ON
CKDY(AM) Digby NS
CKEC(AM) New Glasgow NS
CKFR(AM) Kelowna BC
CKGA(AM) Gander NF
CKGL(AM) Kitchener ON
CKGM(AM) Montreal PQ
CKGR(AM) Golden BC
CKHJ(AM) Fredericton NB
CKIM(AM) Baie Verte NF
CKIR(AM) Invermere BC
CKJH(AM) Melfort SK

CKJR(AM) Wetaskiwin AB
CKJS(AM) Winnipeg MB
CKKC(AM) Nelson BC
CKKW(AM) Kitchener ON
CKKY(AM) Wainwright AB
CKLC(AM) Kingston ON
CKLQ(AM) Brandon MB
CKLW(AM) Windsor ON
*CKMO(AM) Victoria BC
CKMW(AM) Winkler-Morden MB
CKMX(AM) Calgary AB
CKNB(AM) Campbellton NB
CKNW(AM) New Westminster BC
CKNX(AM) Wingham ON
CKOC(AM) Hamilton ON
CKOM(AM) Saskatoon SK
CKOR(AM) Penticton BC
CKOT(AM) Tillsonburg ON
CKOV(AM) Kelowna BC
CKPC(AM) Brantford ON
CKPR(AM) Thunder Bay ON
CKPT(AM) Peterborough ON
CKRM(AM) Regina SK
CKRS(AM) Saguenay PQ
CKRU(AM) Peterborough ON
CKRW(AM) Whitehorse YT
*CKSB(AM) Saint Boniface MB
CKSL(AM) London ON
CKSM(AM) Shawinigan PQ
CKSQ(AM) Stettler AB
CKST(AM) Vancouver BC
CKSW(AM) Swift Current SK
CKTB(AM) Saint Catharines ON
CKTS(AM) Sherbrooke PQ
CKUA(AM) Edmonton AB
CKVH(AM) High Prairie AB
CKVO(AM) Clarenville NF
CKWA(AM) Slave Lake AB
CKWL(AM) Williams Lake BC
CKWW(AM) Windsor ON
CKWX(AM) Vancouver BC
CKXR(AM) Salmon Arm BC
CKYL(AM) Peace River AB
*VOAR(AM) Mount Pearl NF
VOCM(AM) Saint John's NF
*VOWR(AM) Saint John's NF

Canadian FM Stations by Call Letters

*CBAF-FM Moncton NB
CBA-FM Moncton NB
CBAL-FM Moncton NB
CBAX-FM Halifax NS
CBBK-FM Kingston ON
CBBL-FM London ON
CBBS-FM Sudbury ON
CBBX-FM Sudbury ON
CBCL-FM London ON
*CBCS-FM Sudbury ON
*CBCT-FM Charlottetown PE
*CBCV-FM Victoria BC
CBCX-FM Calgary AB
CBD-FM Saint John NB
CBDQ-FM Labrador City NF
*CBE-FM Windsor ON
CBEG-FM Sarnia ON
CBF-FM Montreal PQ
CBF-FM-1 Trois Rivieres PQ
CBFX-FM Montreal PQ
CBGA-FM Matane PQ
CBHA-FM Halifax NS
*CBH-FM Halifax NS
CBI-FM Sydney NS
CBJE-FM Chicoutimi PQ
CBJ-FM Chicoutimi PQ
*CBJX-FM Chicoutimi PQ
*CBKA-FM La Ronge SK
CBKF-FM Regina SK
*CBK-FM Regina SK
*CBKS-FM Saskatoon SK
CBLA-FM Toronto ON
CBL-FM Toronto ON
CBME-FM Montreal PQ
CBM-FM Montreal PQ
CBMI-FM Baie Comeau PQ
CBMR-FM Fermont PQ
*CBN-FM Saint John's NF
*CBOF-FM Ottawa ON
*CBO-FM Ottawa ON
*CBON-FM Sudbury ON
*CBOQ-FM Ottawa ON
*CBOX-FM Ottawa ON
*CBQ-FM Thunder Bay ON
CBQL-FM Savant Lake ON
CBQR-FM Rankin Inlet NU
CBQS-FM Sioux Narrows ON
*CBQT-FM Thunder Bay ON
CBQX-FM Kenora ON
CBRF-FM Calgary AB
*CBR-FM Calgary AB
*CBRX-FM Rimouski PQ
*CBSI-FM Sept-Iles PQ
CBTE-FM Crawford Bay BC
*CBTK-FM Kelowna BC
CBUF-FM Vancouver BC
CBU-FM Vancouver BC
CBUX-FM Vancouver BC
CBVE-FM Quebec PQ
*CBV-FM Quebec PQ
*CBV-FM-6 La Malbaie PQ
*CBVX-FM Quebec PQ
CBW-FM Winnipeg MB
*CBWK-FM Thompson MB
CBX-FM Edmonton AB
CBYG-FM Prince George BC
CBZF-FM Fredericton NB
*CBZ-FM Fredericton NB
CFAI-FM Edmundston NB
CFAK-FM Sherbrooke PQ
CFAN-FM Miramichi City NB
CFBG-FM Bracebridge ON
CFBK-FM Huntsville ON
CFBR-FM Edmonton AB
CFBS-FM Lourdes-de-Blanc-Sablon PQ
CFBT-FM Vancouver BC
CFBU-FM Saint Catharines ON
CFBW-FM Hanover ON
CFBX-FM Kamloops BC
CFCA-FM Kitchener ON
CFCP-FM Courtenay BC

CFCR-FM Saskatoon SK
CFCV-FM Saint Andrews NF
CFDA-FM Victoriaville PQ
CFDM-FM Meadow Lake SK
CFDV-FM Red Deer AB
CFEI-FM Saint Hyacinthe PQ
CFEL-FM Montmagny PQ
CFEP-FM Eastern Passage NS
CFEQ-FM Winnipeg MB
CFET-FM Tagish YT
*CFFF-FM Peterborough ON
CFFM-FM Williams Lake BC
*CFGB-FM Happy Valley NF
CFGE-FM Sherbrooke PQ
CFGI-FM Georgina Island ON
CFGL-FM Laval PQ
CFGP-FM Grande Prairie AB
CFGQ-FM Calgary AB
CFGW-FM Yorkton SK
CFGX-FM Sarnia ON
CFHA-FM Saint John NB
CFHK-FM St. Thomas ON
CFIC-FM Listuguj PQ
CFID-FM Acton Vale PQ
CFIE-FM Toronto ON
CFIM-FM Iles-de-la-Madeleine PQ
*CFIN-FM Lac-Etchemin PQ
CFIX-FM Chicoutimi PQ
CFJB-FM Barrie ON
CFJO-FM Thetford Mines PQ
CFJR-FM Brockville ON
*CFJU-FM Kedgwick NB
CFLC-FM Churchill Falls NF
CFLG-FM Cornwall ON
CFLO-FM Mont-Laurier PQ
CFLX-FM Sherbrooke PQ
CFLY-FM Kingston ON
CFLZ-FM Niagara Falls ON
CFMC-FM Saskatoon SK
CFMF-FM Fermont PQ
CFMG-FM Saint Albert AB
CFMH-FM Saint John NB
CFMI-FM New Westminster BC
CFMK-FM Kingston ON
CFMM-FM Prince Albert SK
CFMQ-FM Hudson Bay SK
*CFMU-FM Hamilton ON
CFMX-FM Cobourg ON
CFMX-FM-1 Toronto ON
CFMY-FM Medicine Hat AB
CFNJ-FM Saint Gabriel-de-Brandon PQ
CFNK-FM Pinehouse Lake SK
CFNO-FM Marathon ON
CFNR-FM Terrace BC
CFNY-FM Brampton ON
CFOB-FM Fort Frances ON
CFOM-FM Levis PQ
CFOR-FM Maniwaki PQ
CFOU-FM Trois Rivieres PQ
CFOX-FM Vancouver BC
CFOZ-FM Argentia NF
CFPL-FM London ON
CFPS-FM Port Elgin ON
CFPX-FM Pukatawagan MB
CFQC-FM Saskatoon SK
CFQK-FM Kaministiquia ON
CFQM-FM Moncton NB
CFQR-FM Montreal PQ
CFQX-FM Selkirk MB
*CFRC-FM Kingston ON
CFRG-FM Gravelbourg SK
*CFRH-FM Penetanguishene ON
CFRK-FM Fredericton NB
CFRM-FM Little Current ON
*CFRO-FM Vancouver BC
CFRQ-FM Dartmouth NS
CFRT-FM Iqaluit NU
CFRU-FM Guelph ON
CFRV-FM Lethbridge AB
CFRY-FM Portage la Prairie MB
CFSF-FM Sturgeon Falls ON

CFSR-FM Hope BC
*CFTH-FM-1 Harrington Harbour PQ
CFTH-FM-2 La Tabatiere PQ
CFUR-FM Prince George BC
CFUT-FM Shawinigan PQ
*CFUV-FM Victoria BC
CFVD-FM Degelis PQ
CFVD-FM-2 Pohenegamook PQ
CFVM-FM Amqui PQ
CFWC-FM Brantford ON
CFWE-FM Lac La Biche AB
CFWF-FM Regina SK
CFWM-FM Winnipeg MB
CFWP-FM Wahta Mohawk Territory near Bala ON
CFXJ-FM Toronto ON
CFXL-FM High River-Okotoks AB
CFXY-FM Fredericton NB
CFZZ-FM Saint Jean-Iberville PQ
CHAA-FM Longueuil PQ
CHAD-FM Dawson Creek BC
CHAI-FM Chateauguay PQ
CHAL-FM Halifax NS
CHAS-FM Sault Ste. Marie ON
CHAY-FM Barrie ON
CHBE-FM Victoria BC
CHBN-FM Edmonton AB
CHBW-FM Rocky Mountain House AB
CHBZ-FM Cranbrook BC
CHCD-FM Simcoe ON
CHCQ-FM Belleville ON
CHCR-FM Killaloe ON
CHDH-FM Siksika AB
CHDI-FM Edmonton AB
CHDR-FM Cranbrook BC
CHEF-FM Matagami PQ
CHEQ-FM Sainte-Marie-de-Beauce PQ
CHET-FM Chetwynd BC
CHEY-FM Trois Rivieres PQ
CHEZ-FM Ottawa ON
CHFI-FM Toronto ON
CHFM-FM Calgary AB
CHFN-FM Cape Croker (Neyaashiinigmiing) ON
CHFX-FM Halifax NS
CHGA-FM Maniwaki PQ
CHGK-FM Stratford ON
CHGO-FM Val d'Or PQ
CHIC-FM Rouyn-Noranda PQ
CHIK-FM Quebec PQ
*CHIM-FM Timmins ON
CHIN-FM Toronto ON
CHIP-FM Fort Coulonge PQ
CHIQ-FM Winnipeg MB
CHJM-FM Saint Georges PQ
CHJX-FM London ON
CHKF-FM Calgary AB
CHKG-FM Vancouver BC
CHKS-FM Sarnia ON
CHLB-FM Lethbridge AB
CHLC-FM Baie Comeau PQ
CHLQ-FM Charlottetown PE
CHLS-FM Lillooet BC
CHLX-FM Gatineau PQ
CHLY-FM Nanaimo BC
*CHMA-FM Sackville NB
CHME-FM Les Escoumins PQ
CHMM-FM MacKenzie BC
CHMN-FM Canmore AB
CHMP-FM Longueuil PQ
*CHMR-FM Saint John's NF
CHMS-FM Bancroft ON
CHMT-FM Timmins ON
CHMX-FM Regina SK
CHMY-FM Renfrew ON
CHNI-FM Saint John NB
CHNO-FM Sudbury ON
CHNR-FM Winnipeg MB
CHOA-FM Rouyn-Noranda PQ
*CHOC-FM Saint Remi PQ
CHOD-FM Cornwall ON
CHOE-FM Matane PQ

CHOH-FM Hearst ON
CHOI-FM Quebec PQ
CHOM-FM Montreal PQ
CHON-FM Whitehorse YT
CHOS-FM Rattling Brook NF
CHOX-FM La Pocatiere PQ
CHOY-FM Moncton NB
CHOZ-FM Saint John's NF
CHPB-FM Cochrane ON
CHPD-FM Aylmer ON
CHPR-FM Hawkesbury ON
CHQM-FM Vancouver BC
CHQX-FM Prince Albert SK
CHRD-FM Drummondville PQ
CHRE-FM Saint Catharines ON
CHRG-FM Maria (Reserve) PQ
CHRI-FM Ottawa ON
CHRL-FM Roberval PQ
CHRM-FM Matane PQ
CHRQ-FM Restigouche PQ
*CHRW-FM London ON
CHRX-FM Fort St. John BC
CHRY-FM Toronto ON
CHSJ-FM Saint John NB
CHSN-FM Estevan SK
CHSR-FM Fredericton NB
CHST-FM London ON
CHSU-FM Kelowna BC
CHTD-FM Saint Stephen NB
CHTT-FM Victoria BC
CHTZ-FM Saint Catharines ON
CHUB-FM Red Deer AB
CHUK-FM Mashteuiatsh (Pointe-Bleue) PQ
CHUM-FM Toronto ON
*CHUO-FM Ottawa ON
CHUR-FM North Bay ON
CHUT-FM Lac-Simon (Louvicourt) PQ
CHVD-FM Dolbeau-Mistassini PQ
CHVN-FM Winnipeg MB
CHVR-FM Pembroke ON
CHWF-FM Nanaimo BC
CHWV-FM Saint John NB
CHYC-FM Sudbury ON
CHYK-FM Timmins ON
CHYM-FM Kitchener ON
CHYR-FM Leamington ON
*CHYZ-FM Sainte Foy PQ
CIAJ-FM Prince Rupert BC
CIAM-FM Fort Vermilion AB
CIAU-FM Radisson PQ
CIAX-FM Windsor PQ
CIAY-FM Whitehorse YT
CIBH-FM Parksville BC
CIBK-FM Calgary AB
*CIBL-FM Montreal PQ
CIBM-FM Riviere du Loup PQ
CIBO-FM Senneterre PQ
CIBW-FM Drayton Valley AB
CIBX-FM Fredericton NB
CICF-FM Vernon BC
CICU-FM Eskasoni Indian Reserve NS
CICX-FM Orillia ON
CICY-FM Selkirk MB
CICZ-FM Midland ON
CIDC-FM Orangeville ON
CIDD-FM White Bear Lake Resort SK
CIDI-FM Lac-Brome PQ
CIDR-FM Windsor ON
CIEG-FM Egmont BC
CIEL-FM Riviere du Loup PQ
CIEU-FM Carleton PQ
CIFA-FM Yarmouth NS
CIFM-FM Kamloops BC
CIFX-FM Lewisporte NF
CIGB-FM Trois Rivieres PQ
CIGL-FM Belleville ON
CIGO-FM Port Hawkesbury NS
CIGR-FM Sherbrooke PQ
CIGV-FM Penticton BC
CIHO-FM Saint Hilarion PQ
CIHS-FM Wetaskiwin AB

CIHT-FM Ottawa ON
CIKI-FM Rimouski PQ
CIKR-FM Kingston ON
CIKX-FM Grand Falls NB
CIKZ-FM Kitchener-Waterloo ON
CILE-FM Havre-Saint-Pierre PQ
CILG-FM Moose Jaw SK
CILK-FM Kelowna BC
CILQ-FM North York ON
CILT-FM Steinbach MB
CILZ-FM Greenville BC
CIME-FM Saint Jerome PQ
CIMF-FM Gatineau PQ
CIMG-FM Swift Current SK
CIMI-FM Charlesbourg PQ
CIMJ-FM Guelph ON
CIMO-FM Magog PQ
CIMS-FM Balmoral NB
CIMX-FM Windsor ON
CINB-FM Saint John NB
CINC-FM Thompson MB
CING-FM Hamilton ON
*CINN-FM Hearst ON
CINQ-FM Montreal PQ
CINU-FM Truro NS
CIOC-FM Victoria BC
*CIOI-FM Hamilton ON
CIOK-FM Saint John NB
*CION-FM Quebec PQ
CIOO-FM Halifax NS
CIOS-FM Stephenville NF
CIOT-FM Nipawin SK
CIOZ-FM Marystown NF
CIPC-FM Port-Cartier PQ
CIPN-FM Pender Harbour BC
CIQB-FM Barrie ON
CIQM-FM London ON
CIQX-FM Calgary AB
CIRA-FM Montreal PQ
CIRK-FM Edmonton AB
CIRV-FM Toronto ON
CIRX-FM Prince George BC
CISC-FM Gibsons BC
*CISM-FM Montreal PQ
CISN-FM Edmonton AB
CISP-FM Pemberton BC
CISQ-FM Squamish BC
CISS-FM Ottawa ON
CISW-FM Whistler BC
CITA-FM Moncton NB
CITE-FM Montreal PQ
CITE-FM-1 Sherbrooke PQ
CITF-FM Quebec PQ
CITI-FM Winnipeg MB
*CITR-FM Vancouver BC
*CIUT-FM Toronto ON
CIVR-FM Yellowknife NT
CIWV-FM Hamilton ON
CIXK-FM Owen Sound ON
CIXL-FM Welland ON
CIXN-FM Fredericton NB
*CIXX-FM London ON
CIYR-FM Hinton AB
CIZL-FM Regina SK
CIZZ-FM Red Deer AB
CJAB-FM Saguenay PQ
*CJAM-FM Windsor ON
CJAN-FM Asbestos PQ
CJAQ-FM Toronto ON
CJAS-FM Saint Augustin PQ
CJAT-FM Trail BC
CJAY-FM Calgary AB
CJBB-FM Englehart ON
CJBC-FM Toronto ON
CJBC-FM-4 London ON
CJBE-FM Port-Menier PQ
CJBR-FM Rimouski PQ
CJBX-FM London ON
CJBZ-FM Taber AB
CJCD-FM Yellowknife NT
CJCD-FM-1 Hay River NT

Canadian FM Stations by Call Letters

CJCF-FM Cumberland House SK
CJCI-FM Prince George BC
CJCJ-FM Woodstock NB
CJCQ-FM North Battleford SK
CJDJ-FM Saskatoon SK
CJDM-FM Drummondville PQ
CJDR-FM Fernie BC
CJDS-FM Saint Pamphile PQ
CJDV-FM Cambridge ON
CJEB-FM Trois Rivieres PQ
CJEC-FM Quebec PQ
CJEL-FM Winkler MB
CJEM-FM Edmundston NB
CJET-FM Smiths Falls ON
CJEZ-FM Toronto ON
CJFH-FM Woodstock ON
CJFM-FM Montreal PQ
CJFW-FM Terrace BC
CJFX-FM Antigonish NS
CJFY-FM Blackville NB
CJIJ-FM Sydney NS
CJIQ-FM Kitchener/Paris ON
CJIT-FM Lac Megantic PQ
*CJIV-FM Dryden ON
CJJJ-FM Brandon MB
CJJR-FM Vancouver BC
CJKK-FM Clarenville NF
CJKL-FM Kirkland Lake ON
CJKR-FM Winnipeg MB
CJKX-FM Ajax ON
CJLA-FM Lachute PQ
CJLF-FM Barrie ON
CJLL-FM Ottawa ON
CJLM-FM Joliette PQ
CJLR-FM La Ronge SK
CJLS-FM Yarmouth NS
CJLS-FM-1 Barrington NS
CJLS-FM-2 New Tusket NS
CJLT-FM Medicine Hat AB
CJLX-FM Belleville ON
CJLY-FM Nelson BC
CJMC-FM Sainte Anne des Monts PQ
CJMF-FM Quebec PQ
CJMG-FM Penticton BC
CJMJ-FM Ottawa ON
CJMK-FM Saskatoon SK
CJMM-FM Rouyn-Noranda PQ
CJMO-FM Moncton NB
CJMP-FM Powell River BC
*CJMQ-FM Lennoxville PQ
CJMV-FM Val d'Or PQ
CJMX-FM Sudbury ON
CJNE-FM Nipawin SK

CJNI-FM Halifax NS
CJNS-FM Meadow Lake SK
*CJOA-FM Thunder Bay ON
CJOI-FM Rimouski PQ
CJOJ-FM Belleville ON
CJOK-FM Fort McMurray AB
CJOS-FM Caronport SK
CJOZ-FM Bonavista Bay NF
CJPG-FM Portage la Prairie MB
CJPN-FM Fredericton NB
CJPR-FM Blairmore AB
CJPT-FM Brockville ON
CJPX-FM Montreal PQ
CJQM-FM Sault Ste. Marie ON
CJQQ-FM Timmins ON
CJRE-FM Riviere au Renard PQ
CJRG-FM Gaspe PQ
CJRL-FM Kenora ON
CJRM-FM Labrador City NF
CJRQ-FM Sudbury ON
*CJRT-FM Toronto ON
CJRW-FM Summerside PE
CJRX-FM Lethbridge AB
CJRY-FM Edmonton AB
CJSA-FM Toronto ON
CJSD-FM Thunder Bay ON
CJSE-FM Shediac NB
*CJSF-FM Burnaby BC
CJSI-FM Calgary AB
CJSO-FM Sorel PQ
CJSR-FM Edmonton AB
CJSS-FM Cornwall ON
CJSU-FM Duncan BC
*CJSW-FM Calgary AB
CJTK-FM Sudbury ON
CJTN-FM Quinte West ON
*CJTR-FM Regina SK
CJTS-FM Lethbridge AB
CJTT-FM New Liskeard ON
CJTW-FM Kitchener-Waterloo ON
CJUM-FM Winnipeg MB
CJVR-FM Melfort SK
CJWA-FM Wawa ON
CJWL-FM Iroquois Falls ON
CJWV-FM Winnipeg MB
CJXK-FM Grand Centre (Cold Lake) AB
CJXL-FM Moncton NB
CJXX-FM Grande Prairie AB
CJXY-FM Burlington ON
CJYC-FM Saint John NB
CJZN-FM Victoria BC

CJZZ-FM Winnipeg MB
CKAG-FM Pikogan PQ
CKAJ-FM Jonquiere PQ
CKAP-FM Kapuskasing ON
CKAU-FM Maliotenam PQ
CKBC-FM Bathurst NB
CKBT-FM Kitchener-Waterloo ON
CKBW-FM Bridgewater NS
CKBW-FM-1 Liverpool NS
CKBW-FM-2 Shelburne NS
CKBY-FM Smiths Falls ON
CKBZ-FM Kamloops BC
CKCB-FM Collingwood ON
CKCK-FM Regina SK
CKCL-FM Chilliwack BC
CKCN-FM Sept-Iles PQ
CKCQ-FM Quesnel BC
CKCU-FM Ottawa ON
CKCW-FM Moncton NB
CKDG-FM Montreal PQ
*CKDJ-FM Ottawa ON
CKDK-FM Woodstock ON
*CKDU-FM Halifax NS
CKDV-FM Prince George BC
CKDX-FM Newmarket ON
CKEN-FM Kentville NS
CKER-FM Edmonton AB
CKEY-FM Fort Erie ON
CKFI-FM Swift Current SK
CKFM-FM Toronto ON
CKFU-FM Fort St. John BC
CKFX-FM North Bay ON
CKGB-FM Timmins ON
CKGE-FM Oshawa ON
CKGF-FM-2 Greenwood BC
CKGN-FM Kapuskasing ON
CKGO-FM-1 Boston Bar BC
CKGY-FM Red Deer AB
CKHA-FM Haliburton ON
CKHL-FM High Level AB
CKHR-FM Hay River NT
CKHZ-FM Halifax NS
CKIA-FM Quebec PQ
CKIC-FM Winnipeg MB
CKIE-FM Toronto ON
CKII-FM Dolbeau-Mistassini PQ
CKIQ-FM Iqaluit NU
CKIS-FM Calgary AB
CKIX-FM Saint John's NF
CKIZ-FM Vernon BC
CKJJ-FM Belleville ON
*CKJM-FM Cheticamp NS
CKKC-FM Crawford Bay BC

CKKK-FM Peterborough ON
CKKL-FM Ottawa ON
CKKN-FM Prince George BC
CKKQ-FM Victoria BC
CKKS-FM Sechelt BC
CKKX-FM Peace River AB
CKLB-FM Yellowknife NT
CKLD-FM Thetford Mines PQ
CKLE-FM Bathurst NB
CKLF-FM Brandon MB
CKLG-FM Vancouver BC
CKLH-FM Hamilton ON
CKLJ-FM Olds AB
CKLM-FM Lloydminster AB
*CKLN-FM Toronto ON
CKLP-FM Parry Sound ON
CKLR-FM Courtenay BC
*CKLU-FM Sudbury ON
CKLX-FM Montreal PQ
CKLY-FM Lindsay (city of Kawartha Lakes) ON
CKLZ-FM Kelowna BC
CKMB-FM Barrie ON
CKMF-FM Montreal PQ
CKMM-FM Winnipeg MB
CKMN-FM Rimouski-Mont Joli PQ
*CKMS-FM Waterloo ON
CKMV-FM Grand Falls NB
CKNA-FM Natashquan PQ
CKNG-FM Edmonton AB
CKNI-FM Moncton NB
CKNL-FM Fort St. John BC
CKNR-FM Elliot Lake ON
CKNU-FM Donnacona PQ
CKNX-FM Wingham ON
CKOD-FM Valleyfield PQ
CKOE-FM Moncton NB
CKOI-FM Verdun PQ
CKOL-FM Campbellford ON
CKON-FM Akwesasne ON
CKOT-FM Tillsonburg ON
CKOZ-FM Corner Brook NF
CKPC-FM Brantford ON
CKPE-FM Sydney NS
CKQB-FM Ottawa ON
CKQC-FM Abbotsford BC
CKQM-FM Peterborough ON
CKQN-FM Baker Lake NU
CKQR-FM Castlegar BC
CKRA-FM Edmonton AB
CKRB-FM Saint Georges-de-Beauce PQ
*CKRK-FM Kahnawake PQ

*CKRL-FM Quebec PQ
CKRO-FM Pokemouche NB
*CKRP-FM Falher AB
CKRV-FM Kamloops BC
CKRX-FM Fort Nelson BC
CKRY-FM Calgary AB
*CKRZ-FM Ohsweken ON
CKSA-FM Lloydminster AB
CKSG-FM Cobourg ON
CKSJ-FM Saint John's NF
CKSR-FM Chilliwack BC
CKSS-FM Red Rocks NF
CKSY-FM Chatham ON
CKTF-FM Gatineau PQ
CKTG-FM Thunder Bay ON
CKTI-FM Kettle Point ON
CKTK-FM Kitimat BC
CKTO-FM Truro NS
CKTP-FM Fredericton Centre NB
CKTY-FM Truro NS
*CKUA-FM Edmonton AB
CKUE-FM Chatham ON
CKUJ-FM Kuujjuaq PQ
CKUL-FM Halifax NS
CKUM-FM Moncton NB
CKUN-FM Christian Island ON
*CKUT-FM Montreal PQ
*CKUW-FM Winnipeg MB
CKVI-FM Kingston ON
CKVM-FM Ville-Marie PQ
CKVX-FM Kindersley SK
CKWE-FM Maniwaki (Kitigan Zibi Anishinabeg Reserve) PQ
CKWF-FM Peterborough ON
CKWM-FM Kentville NS
CKWR-FM Kitchener ON
CKWV-FM Nanaimo BC
CKWY-FM Wainwright AB
CKXA-FM Brandon MB
CKXD-FM Gander NF
CKX-FM Brandon MB
CKXG-FM Grand Falls-Windsor NF
CKXL-FM Saint Boniface MB
CKXX-FM Corner Brook NF
CKYC-FM Owen Sound ON
CKY-FM Winnipeg MB
CKYK-FM Alma PQ
CKYQ-FM Plessisville PQ
CKYX-FM Fort McMurray AB
CKZP-FM Zenon Park SK
CKZX-FM New Denver BC
CKZZ-FM Vancouver BC
VOCM-FM Saint John's NF

U.S. AM Stations by Frequency

540 khz
KRXA(AM) Carmel Valley CA
*KVIP(AM) Redding CA
WFLF(AM) Pine Hills FL
WDAK(AM) Columbus GA
KWMT(AM) Fort Dodge IA
KNOE(AM) Monroe LA
WGOP(AM) Pocomoke City MD
WETC(AM) Wendell-Zebulon NC
WXNH(AM) Jaffrey NH
KNMX(AM) Las Vegas NM
WLIE(AM) Islip NY
WWCS(AM) Canonsburg PA
WYNN(AM) Florence SC
WKFN(AM) Clarksville TN
KDFT(AM) Ferris TX
KNAK(AM) Delta UT
WGTH(AM) Richlands VA
WRRD(AM) Jackson WI
KJJL(AM) Pine Bluffs WY

550 khz
KTZN(AM) Anchorage AK
WASG(AM) Atmore AL
KFYI(AM) Phoenix AZ
KUZZ(AM) Bakersfield CA
KRAI(AM) Craig CO
*WAYR(AM) Orange Park FL
WDUN(AM) Gainesville GA
KMVI(AM) Wailuku HI
KFRM(AM) Salina KS
KTRS(AM) Saint Louis MO
KBOW(AM) Butte MT
WIOZ(AM) Pinehurst NC
WAME(AM) Statesville NC
KFYR(AM) Bismarck ND
WGR(AM) Buffalo NY
WKRC(AM) Cincinnati OH
*KOAC(AM) Corvallis OR
WPAB(AM) Ponce PR
WDDZ(AM) Pawtucket RI
KCRS(AM) Midland TX
KTSA(AM) San Antonio TX
WSVA(AM) Harrisonburg VA
WDEV(AM) Waterbury VT
KARI(AM) Blaine WA
WSAU(AM) Wausau WI

560 khz
KVOK(AM) Kodiak AK
WOOF(AM) Dothan AL
KBLU(AM) Yuma AZ
KSFO(AM) San Francisco CA
KLZ(AM) Denver CO
WQAM(AM) Miami FL
WIND(AM) Chicago IL
WMIK(AM) Middlesboro KY
WHYN(AM) Springfield MA
WFRB(AM) Frostburg MD
WGAN(AM) Portland ME
WRDT(AM) Monroe MI
WEBC(AM) Duluth MN
KWTO(AM) Springfield MO
KMON(AM) Great Falls MT
WGAI(AM) Elizabeth City NC
WCKL(AM) Catskill NY
WFIL(AM) Philadelphia PA
WVOC(AM) Columbia SC
WNSR(AM) Brentwood TN
WHBQ(AM) Memphis TN
KLVI(AM) Beaumont TX
KPQ(AM) Wenatchee WA
WJLS(AM) Beckley WV

567 khz
KGUM(AM) Hagatna GU

570 khz
WAAX(AM) Gadsden AL
KCFJ(AM) Alturas CA
KLAC(AM) Los Angeles CA
WTBN(AM) Pinellas Park FL
KQNG(AM) Lihue HI

WKYX(AM) Paducah KY
WIDS(AM) Russell Springs KY
WTNT(AM) Bethesda MD
WWNC(AM) Asheville NC
WDNZ(AM) Raleigh NC
KSNM(AM) Las Cruces NM
WMCA(AM) New York NY
WSYR(AM) Syracuse NY
WKBN(AM) Youngstown OH
WNAX(AM) Yankton SD
KLIF(AM) Dallas TX
KNRS(AM) Salt Lake City UT
KVI(AM) Seattle WA
WMAM(AM) Marinette WI

580 khz
KRSA(AM) Petersburg AK
WBIL(AM) Tuskegee AL
KSAZ(AM) Marana AZ
KMJ(AM) Fresno CA
KUBC(AM) Montrose CO
WDBO(AM) Orlando FL
WGAC(AM) Augusta GA
KIDO(AM) Nampa ID
*WILL(AM) Urbana IL
WIBW(AM) Topeka KS
KJMJ(AM) Alexandria LA
WTAG(AM) Worcester MA
WTCM(AM) Traverse City MI
WELO(AM) Tupelo MS
KANA(AM) Anaconda MT
WKSK(AM) West Jefferson NC
KTMT(AM) Ashland OR
WHP(AM) Harrisburg PA
WKAQ(AM) San Juan PR
KZMX(AM) Hot Springs SD
WOFE(AM) Rockwood TN
KRFE(AM) Lubbock TX
WLES(AM) Lawrenceville VA
WKTY(AM) La Crosse WI
WCHS(AM) Charleston WV

585 khz
KJAL(AM) Tafuna AS

590 khz
KHAR(AM) Anchorage AK
WRAG(AM) Carrollton AL
KPZA(AM) Hot Springs AR
KTIE(AM) San Bernardino CA
KTHO(AM) South Lake Tahoe CA
KCSJ(AM) Pueblo CO
WAFC(AM) Clewiston FL
WDIZ(AM) Panama City FL
WDWD(AM) Atlanta GA
KSSK(AM) Honolulu HI
KID(AM) Idaho Falls ID
KFNS(AM) Wood River IL
WVLK(AM) Lexington KY
WEZE(AM) Boston MA
WJMS(AM) Ironwood MI
WKZO(AM) Kalamazoo MI
KGLE(AM) Glendive MT
WCAB(AM) Rutherfordton NC
WGTM(AM) Wilson NC
KXSP(AM) Omaha NE
WROW(AM) Albany NY
KUGN(AM) Eugene OR
WARM(AM) Scranton PA
WMBS(AM) Uniontown PA
WWLX(AM) Lawrenceburg TN
KLBJ(AM) Austin TX
KSUB(AM) Cedar City UT
WLVA(AM) Lynchburg VA
KQNT(AM) Spokane WA

600 khz
KVNA(AM) Flagstaff AZ
KOGO(AM) San Diego CA
KCOL(AM) Wellington CO
WICC(AM) Bridgeport CT
WBWL(AM) Jacksonville FL
WMT(AM) Cedar Rapids IA

WKYH(AM) Paintsville KY
WVOG(AM) New Orleans LA
WCAO(AM) Baltimore MD
*WFST(AM) Caribou ME
WCHT(AM) Escanaba MI
WSNL(AM) Flint MI
KGEZ(AM) Kalispell MT
WCVP(AM) Murphy NC
WSJS(AM) Winston-Salem NC
KSJB(AM) Jamestown ND
WSOM(AM) Salem OH
WFRM(AM) Coudersport PA
WAEL(AM) Mayaguez PR
WREC(AM) Memphis TN
KROD(AM) El Paso TX
KERB(AM) Kermit TX
WTBB(AM) Tyler TX
WVAR(AM) Richwood WV

610 khz
WAGG(AM) Birmingham AL
KARV(AM) Russellville AR
KAVL(AM) Lancaster CA
KFRC(AM) San Francisco CA
KVLE(AM) Vail CO
WSNG(AM) Torrington CT
WIOD(AM) Miami FL
WVTJ(AM) Pensacola FL
WPLO(AM) Grayson GA
WCEH(AM) Hawkinsville GA
WRUS(AM) Russellville KY
KDAL(AM) Duluth MN
KCSP(AM) Kansas City MO
KOJM(AM) Havre MT
WFNZ(AM) Charlotte NC
KCSR(AM) Chadron NE
WGIR(AM) Manchester NH
KNML(AM) Albuquerque NM
WTVN(AM) Columbus OH
KRTA(AM) Medford OR
WIP(AM) Philadelphia PA
WEXS(AM) Patillas PR
KILT(AM) Houston TX
KVNU(AM) Logan UT
WVBE(AM) Roanoke VA
WTFX(AM) Winchester VA
KONA(AM) Kennewick WA

612 khz
KUAM(AM) Hagatna GU

620 khz
KGTL(AM) Homer AK
WJHX(AM) Lexington AL
KTAR(AM) Phoenix AZ
KIGS(AM) Hanford CA
KMJC(AM) Mount Shasta CA
KJOL(AM) Grand Junction CO
WDAE(AM) Saint Petersburg FL
WTRP(AM) La Grange GA
KIPA(AM) Hilo HI
KMNS(AM) Sioux City IA
KWAL(AM) Wallace ID
WTMT(AM) Louisville KY
WZON(AM) Bangor ME
WJDX(AM) Jackson MS
WDNC(AM) Durham NC
WSNR(AM) Jersey City NJ
WHEN(AM) Syracuse NY
KPOJ(AM) Portland OR
WKHB(AM) Irwin PA
WGCV(AM) Cayce SC
WRJZ(AM) Knoxville TN
KMKI(AM) Plano TX
WVMT(AM) Burlington VT
WTMJ(AM) Milwaukee WI
WWNR(AM) Beckley WV

630 khz
KJNO(AM) Juneau AK
KIAM(AM) Nenana AK
WAVU(AM) Albertville AL
WJDB(AM) Thomasville AL

KVMA(AM) Magnolia AR
KIDD(AM) Monterey CA
KHOW(AM) Denver CO
WMAL(AM) Washington DC
WBMQ(AM) Savannah GA
WNEG(AM) Toccoa GA
KFXD(AM) Boise ID
WLAP(AM) Lexington KY
KJSL(AM) Saint Louis MO
WAIZ(AM) Hickory NC
WMFD(AM) Wilmington NC
KLEA(AM) Lovington NM
KPLY(AM) Reno NV
KWRO(AM) Coquille OR
WEJL(AM) Scranton PA
WUNO(AM) San Juan PR
WPRO(AM) Providence RI
KSLR(AM) San Antonio TX
KTKK(AM) Sandy UT
KCIS(AM) Edmonds WA
KXLI(AM) Opportunity WA
WDGY(AM) Hudson WI
WJAW(AM) Saint Marys WV

640 khz
*KYUK(AM) Bethel AK
KFI(AM) Los Angeles CA
WJNA(AM) Royal Palm Beach FL
WVLG(AM) Wildwood FL
WGST(AM) Atlanta GA
*WOI(AM) Ames IA
KTIB(AM) Thibodaux LA
WNNZ(AM) Westfield MA
WMFN(AM) Zeeland MI
KGVW(AM) Belgrade MT
WFNC(AM) Fayetteville NC
WWJZ(AM) Mount Holly NJ
WHLO(AM) Akron OH
WWLS(AM) Moore OK
WGOC(AM) Blountville TN
WCRV(AM) Collierville TN

650 khz
KENI(AM) Anchorage AK
KSTE(AM) Rancho Cordova CA
KRTR(AM) Honolulu HI
WSRO(AM) Ashland MA
WMII(AM) Manistique MI
WNMT(AM) Nashwauk MN
WSM(AM) Nashville TN
KIKK(AM) Pasadena TX
KUUX(AM) Pullman WA
KGAB(AM) Orchard Valley WY

660 khz
KFAR(AM) Fairbanks AK
WDLT(AM) Fairhope AL
KTNN(AM) Window Rock AZ
KGDP(AM) Orcutt CA
WORL(AM) Altamonte Springs FL
WMIC(AM) Sandusky MI
WBHR(AM) Sauk Rapids MN
KEYZ(AM) Williston ND
KCRO(AM) Omaha NE
WFAN(AM) New York NY
WXIC(AM) Waverly OH
KXOR(AM) Junction City OR
WPYT(AM) Wilkinsburg PA
WLFJ(AM) Greenville SC
KSKY(AM) Balch Springs TX
WCRR(AM) Rural Retreat VA
KAPS(AM) Mount Vernon WA

670 khz
*KDLG(AM) Dillingham AK
WYLS(AM) York AL
KWXI(AM) Glenwood AR
KIRN(AM) Simi Valley CA
KLTT(AM) Commerce City CO
WWFE(AM) Miami FL
KPUA(AM) Hilo HI
KBOI(AM) Boise ID

WSCR(AM) Chicago IL
KBTB(AM) Las Vegas NV
WIEZ(AM) Lewistown PA
WMTY(AM) Farragut TN
WPMH(AM) Claremont VA

680 khz
*KBRW(AM) Barrow AK
KNBR(AM) San Francisco CA
WRMD(AM) Saint Petersburg FL
WCNN(AM) North Atlanta GA
WCTT(AM) Corbin KY
WDRD(AM) Newburg KY
WRKO(AM) Boston MA
WCBM(AM) Baltimore MD
WDBC(AM) Escanaba MI
KFEQ(AM) Saint Joseph MO
KKGR(AM) East Helena MT
WPTF(AM) Raleigh NC
WRGC(AM) Sylva NC
KWKA(AM) Clovis NM
WINR(AM) Binghamton NY
WISR(AM) Butler PA
WAPA(AM) San Juan PR
WWTQ(AM) Memphis TN
KKYX(AM) San Antonio TX
KBRD(AM) Lacey WA
KOMW(AM) Omak WA
WOGO(AM) Hallie WI
WCAW(AM) Charleston WV

690 khz
WJOX(AM) Birmingham AL
KEWI(AM) Benton AR
KVOI(AM) Tucson AZ
KRMX(AM) Pueblo CO
KRGS(AM) Rifle CO
WADS(AM) Ansonia CT
WOKV(AM) Jacksonville FL
KORL(AM) Honolulu HI
KSLJ(AM) Blackfoot ID
KGGF(AM) Coffeyville KS
WTIX(AM) New Orleans LA
XETRA(AM) Tijuana MEX
WNZK(AM) Dearborn Heights MI
KFXN(AM) Minneapolis MN
KSTL(AM) Saint Louis MO
KOAQ(AM) Terrytown NE
KRCO(AM) Prineville OR
WPHE(AM) Phoenixville PA
KTSM(AM) El Paso TX
KPET(AM) Lamesa TX
KZEY(AM) Tyler TX
WZAP(AM) Bristol VA
*WVCY(AM) Oshkosh WI
WELD(AM) Fisher WV

700 khz
KBYR(AM) Anchorage AK
WGZS(AM) Dothan AL
KMBX(AM) Soledad CA
WJOE(AM) Orange-Athol MA
WDMV(AM) Poolesville MD
KNAX(AM) McCook NE
WLW(AM) Cincinnati OH
KGRV(AM) Winston OR
KSEV(AM) Tomball TX
KHSE(AM) Wylie TX
KALL(AM) North Salt Lake City UT
KXLX(AM) Airway Heights WA

710 khz
WPMI(AM) Mobile AL
KAPZ(AM) Bald Knob AR
KMIA(AM) Black Canyon City AZ
KFIA(AM) Carmichael CA
KSPN(AM) Los Angeles CA
KNUS(AM) Denver CO
WAQI(AM) Miami FL
WUFF(AM) Eastman GA
WROM(AM) Rome GA
WEKC(AM) Williamsburg KY
KEEL(AM) Shreveport LA

U.S. AM Stations by Frequency

WREM(AM) Monticello ME
KCMO(AM) Kansas City MO
WEGG(AM) Rose Hill NC
KXMR(AM) Bismarck ND
WOR(AM) New York NY
WKJB(AM) Mayaguez PR
WQKI(AM) Saint Matthews SC
WTPR(AM) Paris TN
*WFCM(AM) Smyrna TN
KGNC(AM) Amarillo TX
KURV(AM) Edinburg TX
WFNR(AM) Blacksburg VA
KIRO(AM) Seattle WA
WDSM(AM) Superior WI

720 khz
*KOTZ(AM) Kotzebue AK
WRZN(AM) Hernando FL
WVCC(AM) Hogansville GA
KUAI(AM) Eleele HI
WGN(AM) Chicago IL
WGCR(AM) Brevard NC
WQTH(AM) Hanover NH
KDWN(AM) Las Vegas NV
WVOA(AM) Dewitt NY
KFIR(AM) Sweet Home OR
WWII(AM) Shiremanstown PA
KSAH(AM) Universal City TX

730 khz
WUMP(AM) Madison AL
KSUD(AM) West Memphis AR
WWTK(AM) Lake Placid FL
WSTT(AM) Thomasville GA
*KBSU(AM) Boise ID
KLOE(AM) Goodland KS
WFMW(AM) Madisonville KY
WMTC(AM) Vancleve KY
WASO(AM) Covington LA
WACE(AM) Chicopee MA
WJTO(AM) Bath ME
WVFN(AM) East Lansing MI
KWOA(AM) Worthington MN
KWRE(AM) Warrenton MO
KURL(AM) Billings MT
WFMC(AM) Goldsboro NC
WOHS(AM) Shelby NC
KDAZ(AM) Albuquerque NM
WDOS(AM) Oneonta NY
WJYM(AM) Bowling Green OH
*KEZX(AM) Medford OR
WNAK(AM) Nanticoke PA
WPIT(AM) Pittsburgh PA
WLTQ(AM) Charleston SC
WLIL(AM) Lenoir City TN
KKDA(AM) Grand Prairie TX
KSVN(AM) Ogden UT
WKDL(AM) Alexandria VA
WMNA(AM) Gretna VA
KULE(AM) Ephrata WA
WJMT(AM) Merrill WI

740 khz
WMSP(AM) Montgomery AL
KIDR(AM) Phoenix AZ
KBRT(AM) Avalon CA
KCBS(AM) San Francisco CA
KVOR(AM) Colorado Springs CO
KVFC(AM) Cortez CO
WSBR(AM) Boca Raton FL
WQTM(AM) Orlando FL
KBOE(AM) Oskaloosa IA
WVLN(AM) Olney IL
WNOP(AM) Newport KY
WJIB(AM) Cambridge MA
WPAQ(AM) Mount Airy NC
KATK(AM) Carlsbad NM
WGSM(AM) Huntington NY
KRMG(AM) Tulsa OK
WVCH(AM) Chester PA
WIAC(AM) San Juan PR
WRWB(AM) Harrogate TN
WIRJ(AM) Humboldt TN
WJIG(AM) Tullahoma TN
KTRH(AM) Houston TX
KCMC(AM) Texarkana TX
WMBG(AM) Williamsburg VA
WRPQ(AM) Baraboo WI

WMIN(AM) Hudson WI
WRNR(AM) Martinsburg WV

750 khz
KFQD(AM) Anchorage AK
WSB(AM) Atlanta GA
WNTX(AM) Brookport IL
WNDZ(AM) Portage IN
KKNO(AM) Gretna LA
WBMD(AM) Baltimore MD
WWKK(AM) Petoskey MI
KBNN(AM) Lebanon MO
KERR(AM) Polson MT
WAUG(AM) New Hope NC
KMMJ(AM) Grand Island NE
KHWG(AM) Fallon NV
KSEO(AM) Durant OK
KXL(AM) Portland OR
WQOR(AM) Olyphant PA
KAMA(AM) El Paso TX
KOAL(AM) Price UT
WPDX(AM) Clarksburg WV

760 khz
WURL(AM) Moody AL
KMTL(AM) Sherwood AR
KFMB(AM) San Diego CA
KKZN(AM) Thornton CO
WLCC(AM) Brandon FL
WEFL(AM) Tequesta FL
KGU(AM) Honolulu HI
KCCV(AM) Overland Park KS
WVNE(AM) Leicester MA
WJR(AM) Detroit MI
WCIS(AM) Morganton NC
WCPS(AM) Tarboro NC
WCHP(AM) Champlain NY
WORA(AM) Mayaguez PR
WETR(AM) Knoxville TN
WENO(AM) Nashville TN
KTKR(AM) San Antonio TX

770 khz
*KCHU(AM) Valdez AK
WVNN(AM) Athens AL
KCBC(AM) Riverbank CA
WWCN(AM) North Fort Myers FL
WYHG(AM) Young Harris GA
WCGW(AM) Nicholasville KY
KJCB(AM) Lafayette LA
*KUOM(AM) Minneapolis MN
WEW(AM) Saint Louis MO
KATL(AM) Miles City MT
WLWL(AM) Rockingham NC
KKOB(AM) Albuquerque NM
KKOB Exp Stn Santa Fe NM
WABC(AM) New York NY
WTOR(AM) Youngstown NY
WAIS(AM) Buchtel OH
WKFB(AM) Jeannette PA
KAAM(AM) Garland TX
WYRV(AM) Cedar Bluff VA
KTTH(AM) Seattle WA

780 khz
*KNOM(AM) Nome AK
WZZX(AM) Lineville AL
KAZM(AM) Sedona AZ
WBBM(AM) Chicago IL
WTME(AM) Rumford ME
WIIN(AM) Ridgeland MS
WCKB(AM) Dunn NC
WWOL(AM) Forest City NC
WJAG(AM) Norfolk NE
KKOH(AM) Reno NV
KSPI(AM) Stillwater OK
WPTN(AM) Cookeville TN
WABS(AM) Arlington VA

790 khz
KCAM(AM) Glennallen AK
WTSK(AM) Tuscaloosa AL
KURM(AM) Rogers AR
KOSY(AM) Texarkana AR
KNST(AM) Tucson AZ
KFPT(AM) Clovis CA
KWSW(AM) Eureka CA
KABC(AM) Los Angeles CA
WLBE(AM) Leesburg FL

WPNN(AM) Pensacola FL
WAXY(AM) South Miami FL
WQXI(AM) Atlanta GA
WSFN(AM) Brunswick GA
WGRA(AM) Cairo GA
WKON(AM) Kealakekua HI
KSPD(AM) Boise ID
KBRV(AM) Soda Springs ID
WRMS(AM) Beardstown IL
KXXX(AM) Colby KS
WKRD(AM) Louisville KY
WSGW(AM) Saginaw MI
WGHL(AM) Billings MT
WBLO(AM) Thomasville NC
KBET(AM) Winchester NV
WTNY(AM) Watertown NY
WLSV(AM) Wellsville NY
WHTH(AM) Heath OH
KWIL(AM) Albany OR
WAEB(AM) Allentown PA
WPIC(AM) Sharon PA
WSKO(AM) Providence RI
WVCD(AM) Bamberg-Denmark SC
WQSV(AM) Ashland City TN
WETB(AM) Johnson City TN
WMC(AM) Memphis TN
KBME(AM) Houston TX
KFYO(AM) Lubbock TX
WSVG(AM) Mount Jackson VA
WNIS(AM) Norfolk VA
KGMI(AM) Bellingham WA
KJRB(AM) Spokane WA
WAYY(AM) Eau Claire WI

800 khz
KINY(AM) Juneau AK
WHOS(AM) Decatur AL
WMGY(AM) Montgomery AL
KAGH(AM) Crossett AR
KVOM(AM) Morrilton AR
KDFO(AM) Bakersfield CA
KLDC(AM) Brighton CO
WLAD(AM) Danbury CT
WPLK(AM) Palatka FL
WJAT(AM) Swainsboro GA
KXIC(AM) Iowa City IA
WKZI(AM) Casey IL
WSHO(AM) New Orleans LA
WNNW(AM) Lawrence MA
KQAD(AM) Luverne MN
WVAL(AM) Sauk Rapids MN
KREI(AM) Farmington MO
WKBC(AM) North Wilkesboro NC
WTMR(AM) Camden NJ
KQCV(AM) Oklahoma City OK
KPDQ(AM) Portland OR
WCHA(AM) Chambersburg PA
WDSC(AM) Dillon SC
WPJM(AM) Greer SC
WDEH(AM) Sweetwater TN
KDDD(AM) Dumas TX
WSVS(AM) Crewe VA
WDUX(AM) Waupaca WI
WVHU(AM) Huntington WV

801 khz
KTWG(AM) Hagatna GU

810 khz
WCKS(AM) Jacksonville AL
KGO(AM) San Francisco CA
WEUS(AM) Orlovista FL
WTHV(AM) Hahira GA
WBIC(AM) Royston GA
WDDD(AM) Johnston City IL
WSYW(AM) Indianapolis IN
WEKG(AM) Jackson KY
WYRE(AM) Annapolis MD
WMJH(AM) Rockford MI
WHB(AM) Kansas City MO
WSJC(AM) Magee MS
KSWV(AM) Santa Fe NM
WGY(AM) Schenectady NY
WEDO(AM) McKeesport PA
WKVM(AM) San Juan PR
WQIZ(AM) Saint George SC
KBHB(AM) Sturgis SD

WCTA(AM) Alamo TN
WMGC(AM) Murfreesboro TN
KXOI(AM) Crane TX
KSJL(AM) Somerset TX
WPIN(AM) Dublin VA
KTBI(AM) Ephrata WA
WDMP(AM) Dodgeville WI
WJJQ(AM) Tomahawk WI

820 khz
KCBF(AM) Fairbanks AK
WMGG(AM) Largo FL
WAIT(AM) Chicago IL
*WSWI(AM) Evansville IN
WXTR(AM) Frederick MD
WWLZ(AM) Horseheads NY
*WNYC(AM) New York NY
*WOSU(AM) Columbus OH
KORC(AM) Waldport OR
WWAM(AM) Jasper TN
WBAP(AM) Fort Worth TX
KUTR(AM) Taylorsville UT
WGGM(AM) Chester VA
KGNW(AM) Burien-Seattle WA

830 khz
*KSDP(AM) Sand Point AK
*KFLT(AM) Tucson AZ
KNCO(AM) Grass Valley CA
KMXE(AM) Orange CA
WACC(AM) Hialeah FL
WFGM(AM) Sandy Springs GA
KHVH(AM) Honolulu HI
WFNO(AM) Norco LA
WCRN(AM) Worcester MA
WMMI(AM) Shepherd MI
WCCO(AM) Minneapolis MN
KOTC(AM) Kennett MO
WTRU(AM) Kernersville NC
WKTX(AM) Cortland OH
WEEU(AM) Reading PA
KMUL(AM) Farwell TX
KUYO(AM) Evansville WY

840 khz
WBHY(AM) Mobile AL
KPMP(AM) Modesto CA
WRYM(AM) New Britain CT
WPGS(AM) Mims FL
WHGH(AM) Thomasville GA
WHAS(AM) Louisville KY
WKDI(AM) Denton MD
KTIC(AM) West Point NE
KXNT(AM) North Las Vegas NV
KKNX(AM) Eugene OR
KSWB(AM) Seaside OR
WVPO(AM) Stroudsburg PA
WXEW(AM) Yabucoa PR
WCEO(AM) Columbia SC
KVJY(AM) Pharr TX
WKTR(AM) Earlysville VA
KMAX(AM) Colfax WA

850 khz
KICY(AM) Nome AK
WXJC(AM) Birmingham AL
KIIS(AM) Thousand Oaks CA
KOA(AM) Denver CO
WREF(AM) Ridgefield CT
WRUF(AM) Gainesville FL
WFTL(AM) West Palm Beach FL
WCUG(AM) Cuthbert GA
WPTB(AM) Statesboro GA
KHLO(AM) Hilo HI
KWOF(AM) Waterloo IA
WCPT(AM) Crystal Lake IL
WEEI(AM) Boston MA
WGVS(AM) Muskegon MI
WWJC(AM) Duluth MN
*KFUO(AM) Clayton MO
WQST(AM) Forest MS
WLRC(AM) Walnut MS
WRBZ(AM) Raleigh NC
WYLF(AM) Penn Yan NY
WKNR(AM) Cleveland OH
WNTJ(AM) Johnstown PA
WABA(AM) Aguadilla PR

WPFD(AM) Fairview TN
WKVL(AM) Knoxville TN
KJON(AM) Carrollton TX
KEYH(AM) Houston TX
WTAR(AM) Norfolk VA
KHHO(AM) Tacoma WA

860 khz
WAMI(AM) Opp AL
KWRF(AM) Warren AR
KOSE(AM) Wilson AR
KMVP(AM) Phoenix AZ
KTRB(AM) Modesto CA
WNTR(AM) Dunedin FL
WAEC(AM) Atlanta GA
WDMG(AM) Douglas GA
KWPC(AM) Muscatine IA
WGOM(AM) Marion IN
KKOW(AM) Pittsburg KS
WSON(AM) Henderson KY
WSBS(AM) Great Barrington MA
WBGR(AM) Baltimore MD
KNUJ(AM) New Ulm MN
WFMO(AM) Fairmont NC
WACB(AM) Taylorsville NC
KARS(AM) Belen NM
KPAM(AM) Troutdale OR
WAMO(AM) Millvale PA
WWDB(AM) Philadelphia PA
WLBG(AM) Laurens SC
WTZX(AM) Sparta TN
KFST(AM) Fort Stockton TX
KPAN(AM) Hereford TX
KSFA(AM) Nacogdoches TX
KONO(AM) San Antonio TX
KKAT(AM) Salt Lake City UT
WEVA(AM) Emporia VA
WNOV(AM) Milwaukee WI
WOAY(AM) Oak Hill WV

870 khz
WQRX(AM) Valley Head AL
KRLA(AM) Glendale CA
KJMP(AM) Pierce CO
KHNR(AM) Honolulu HI
WINU(AM) Shelbyville IL
WMTL(AM) Leitchfield KY
WWL(AM) New Orleans LA
WLVP(AM) Gorham ME
*WKAR(AM) East Lansing MI
KPRM(AM) Park Rapids MN
KAAN(AM) Bethany MO
KLSQ(AM) Whitney NV
WHCU(AM) Ithaca NY
WQBS(AM) San Juan PR
WPWT(AM) Colonial Heights TN
KFJZ(AM) Fort Worth TX
WFLO(AM) Farmville VA
KFLD(AM) Pasco WA

880 khz
KGHT(AM) Sheridan AR
KKMC(AM) Gonzales CA
WBKZ(AM) Jefferson GA
WCBW(AM) Highland IL
KJJR(AM) Whitefish MT
WRRZ(AM) Clinton NC
WPEK(AM) Fairview NC
WPIP(AM) Winston-Salem NC
KRVN(AM) Lexington NE
KHAC(AM) Tse Bonito NM
WCBS(AM) New York NY
WRFD(AM) Columbus-Worthington OH
KWIP(AM) Dallas OR
KCMX(AM) Phoenix OR
WYKO(AM) Sabana Grande PR
WMDB(AM) Nashville TN
KJOJ(AM) Conroe TX
KPOE(AM) Midland TX
WCQV(AM) Moneta VA
KIXI(AM) Mercer Island-Seattle WA
WMEQ(AM) Menomonie WI

890 khz
*KBBI(AM) Homer AK
WYAM(AM) Hartselle AL
KLFF(AM) Arroyo Grande CA
KSDG(AM) Julian CA

Broadcasting & Cable Yearbook 2006
D-646

U.S. AM Stations by Frequency

KJME(AM) Fountain CO
KDJQ(AM) Meridian ID
WLS(AM) Chicago IL
WAMG(AM) Dedham MA
KGGN(AM) Gladstone MO
WEEZ(AM) Laurel MS
WHNC(AM) Henderson NC
KQLX(AM) Lisbon ND
KTLR(AM) Oklahoma City OK
*WFKJ(AM) Cashtown PA
WFAB(AM) Ceiba PR
WBAJ(AM) Blythwood SC
KVOZ(AM) Del Mar Hills TX
KTXV(AM) Frankston TX
KDXU(AM) Saint George UT
WKNV(AM) Fairlawn VA

900 khz
KZPA(AM) Fort Yukon AK
WATV(AM) Birmingham AL
WGOK(AM) Mobile AL
WOZK(AM) Ozark AL
KHOZ(AM) Harrison AR
KBIF(AM) Fresno CA
KALI(AM) West Covina CA
WJWL(AM) Georgetown DE
WSWN(AM) Belle Glade FL
WMOP(AM) Ocala FL
WJTH(AM) Calhoun GA
WBML(AM) Macon GA
WJLG(AM) Savannah GA
KNUI(AM) Kahului HI
KSGL(AM) Wichita KS
WWLK(AM) Eddyville KY
WFIA(AM) Louisville KY
WLSI(AM) Pikeville KY
WILC(AM) Laurel MD
WJJB(AM) Brunswick ME
*KTIS(AM) Minneapolis MN
KFAL(AM) Fulton MO
WYCV(AM) Granite Falls NC
WAYN(AM) Rockingham NC
WIAM(AM) Williamston NC
KJSK(AM) Columbus NE
WSNH(AM) Nashua NH
WBRV(AM) Boonville NY
WUAM(AM) Saratoga Springs NY
WCER(AM) Canton OH
WCPA(AM) Clearfield PA
WURD(AM) Philadelphia PA
WNMB(AM) North Myrtle Beach SC
WKXV(AM) Knoxville TN
WCOR(AM) Lebanon TN
KPYN(AM) Atlanta TX
KFLP(AM) Floydada TX
KCLW(AM) Hamilton TX
KREH(AM) Pecan Grove TX
WCBX(AM) Bassett VA
WKDW(AM) Staunton VA
KKRT(AM) Wenatchee WA
WATK(AM) Antigo WI
WDLS(AM) Wisconsin Dells WI

910 khz
*KIYU(AM) Galena AK
WZMG(AM) Pepperell AL
KLCN(AM) Blytheville AR
KGME(AM) Phoenix AZ
*KECR(AM) El Cajon CA
KRAK(AM) Hesperia CA
KNEW(AM) Oakland CA
KOXR(AM) Oxnard CA
*KPOF(AM) Denver CO
WLAT(AM) New Britain CT
WTWD(AM) Plant City FL
WFVR(AM) Valdosta GA
*WSUI(AM) Iowa City IA
WAKO(AM) Lawrenceville IL
KINA(AM) Salina KS
WSFE(AM) Burnside KY
WNDC(AM) Baton Rouge LA
WABI(AM) Bangor ME
WGTO(AM) Cassopolis MI
WFDF(AM) Flint MI
WALT(AM) Meridian MS
KBLG(AM) Billings MT
WSRP(AM) Jacksonville NC
KCJB(AM) Minot ND

KBIM(AM) Roswell NM
WRKL(AM) New City NY
WLTP(AM) Marietta OH
WPFB(AM) Middletown OH
KVIS(AM) Miami OK
KURY(AM) Brookings OR
WAVL(AM) Apollo PA
WBZU(AM) Scranton PA
WSBA(AM) York PA
WPRP(AM) Ponce PR
WTMZ(AM) Dorchester Terrace-Brentwood SC
WSPA(AM) Spartanburg SC
KJJQ(AM) Volga SD
WMRB(AM) Columbia TN
WJCW(AM) Johnson City TN
WEPG(AM) South Pittsburg TN
KNAF(AM) Fredericksburg TX
KXEB(AM) Frisco TX
KRIO(AM) McAllen TX
KWDZ(AM) Salt Lake City UT
WRNL(AM) Richmond VA
WWWR(AM) Roanoke VA
WNHV(AM) White River Junction VT
KKSN(AM) Vancouver WA
WHSM(AM) Hayward WI
WDOR(AM) Sturgeon Bay WI

920 khz
KSRM(AM) Soldotna AK
WGOL(AM) Russellville AL
KARN(AM) Little Rock AR
KVIN(AM) Ceres CA
KPSI(AM) Palm Springs CA
KVEC(AM) San Luis Obispo CA
KLMR(AM) Lamar CO
WMEL(AM) Melbourne FL
WGKA(AM) Atlanta GA
WVOH(AM) Hazlehurst GA
*KYFR(AM) Shenandoah IA
WGNU(AM) Granite City IL
WMOK(AM) Metropolis IL
*WBAA(AM) West Lafayette IN
WTCW(AM) Whitesburg KY
WBOX(AM) Bogalusa LA
WMPL(AM) Hancock MI
KDHL(AM) Faribault MN
KWAD(AM) Wadena MN
KWYS(AM) West Yellowstone MT
WPCM(AM) Burlington NC
WPTL(AM) Canton NC
WPHY(AM) Trenton NJ
KSVA(AM) Albuquerque NM
KBAD(AM) Las Vegas NV
*KIHM(AM) Reno NV
WKRT(AM) Cortland NY
WGHQ(AM) Kingston NY
WIRD(AM) Lake Placid NY
WMNI(AM) Columbus OH
KSHO(AM) Lebanon OR
WKVA(AM) Lewistown PA
WHJJ(AM) Providence RI
WYMB(AM) Manning SC
KKLS(AM) Rapid City SD
WLIV(AM) Livingston TN
KBNA(AM) El Paso TX
*KFLB(AM) Odessa TX
KYST(AM) Texas City TX
KVEL(AM) Vernal UT
KGTK(AM) Olympia WA
KXLY(AM) Spokane WA
WOKY(AM) Milwaukee WI
WMMN(AM) Fairmont WV

930 khz
KTKN(AM) Ketchikan AK
KNSA(AM) Unalakleet AK
WYNI(AM) Monroeville AL
WJBY(AM) Rainbow City AL
KAPR(AM) Douglas AZ
KAFF(AM) Flagstaff AZ
KHJ(AM) Los Angeles CA
KKXX(AM) Paradise CA
KIUP(AM) Durango CO
KRKY(AM) Granby CO
WYUS(AM) Milford DE
WLVF(AM) Haines City FL
WFXJ(AM) Jacksonville FL

WLSS(AM) Sarasota FL
WMGR(AM) Bainbridge GA
KSEI(AM) Pocatello ID
WTAD(AM) Quincy IL
WAUR(AM) Sandwich IL
WHON(AM) Centerville IN
WKCT(AM) Bowling Green KY
WFMD(AM) Frederick MD
WBCK(AM) Battle Creek MI
KKIN(AM) Aitkin MN
KWOC(AM) Poplar Bluff MO
WSFZ(AM) Jackson MS
WLCY(AM) East Missoula MT
*WYFQ(AM) Charlotte NC
WDLX(AM) Washington NC
KOGA(AM) Ogallala NE
WGIN(AM) Rochester NH
WPAT(AM) Paterson NJ
KCCC(AM) Carlsbad NM
WBEN(AM) Buffalo NY
WIZR(AM) Johnstown NY
WEOL(AM) Elyria OH
WKY(AM) Oklahoma City OK
*KAGI(AM) Grants Pass OR
WHLM(AM) Bloomsburg PA
WYAC(AM) Cabo Rojo PR
KSDN(AM) Aberdeen SD
WSEV(AM) Sevierville TN
WWON(AM) Waynesboro TN
KDET(AM) Center TX
KLUP(AM) Terrell Hills TX
WLLL(AM) Lynchburg VA
KBAI(AM) Bellingham WA
KYAK(AM) Yakima WA
*WLBL(AM) Auburndale WI
WRVC(AM) Huntington WV
KROE(AM) Sheridan WY

940 khz
KGMS(AM) Tucson AZ
KWRU(AM) Fresno CA
WINE(AM) Brookfield CT
WLQH(AM) Chiefland FL
WINZ(AM) Miami FL
WMAC(AM) Macon GA
KKNE(AM) Waipahu HI
KPSZ(AM) Des Moines IA
WMIX(AM) Mount Vernon IL
WCND(AM) Shelbyville KY
WYLD(AM) New Orleans LA
WGFP(AM) Webster MA
WIDG(AM) Saint Ignace MI
WSPZ(AM) South Haven MI
KSWM(AM) Aurora MO
WCPC(AM) Houston MS
WKYK(AM) Burnsville NC
KVSH(AM) Valentine NE
WLJM(AM) Lima OH
KICE(AM) Bend OR
KWBY(AM) Woodburn OR
WFGI(AM) Charleroi PA
WGRP(AM) Greenville PA
WADV(AM) Lebanon PA
*WIPR(AM) San Juan PR
WECO(AM) Wartburg TN
KIXZ(AM) Amarillo TX
KTON(AM) Belton TX
KTFS(AM) Texarkana TX
KNNZ(AM) Cedar City UT
WNRG(AM) Grundy VA
WKGM(AM) Smithfield VA
WFAW(AM) Fort Atkinson WI
WCSW(AM) Shell Lake WI

950 khz
KSWD(AM) Seward AK
WNZZ(AM) Montgomery AL
KXJK(AM) Forrest City AR
KFSA(AM) Fort Smith AR
KAHI(AM) Auburn CA
KKFN(AM) Denver CO
WTLN(AM) Orlando FL
WGTA(AM) Summerville GA
WGOV(AM) Valdosta GA
KOEL(AM) Oelwein IA
KNJY(AM) Boise ID
KOZE(AM) Lewiston ID
WNTD(AM) Chicago IL

WXLW(AM) Indianapolis IN
KJRG(AM) Newton KS
WYWY(AM) Barbourville KY
KRRP(AM) Coushatta LA
WROL(AM) Boston MA
WCTN(AM) Potomac-Cabin John MD
WWJ(AM) Detroit MI
KTNF(AM) Saint Louis Park MN
KWOS(AM) Jefferson City MO
WHSY(AM) Hattiesburg MS
KMTX(AM) Helena MT
WPET(AM) Greensboro NC
KNFT(AM) Bayard NM
KDCE(AM) Espanola NM
WHVW(AM) Hyde Park NY
WROC(AM) Rochester NY
WIBX(AM) Utica NY
WDIG(AM) Steubenville OH
*KTBR(AM) Roseburg OR
WNCC(AM) Northern Cambria PA
WPEN(AM) Philadelphia PA
WQTK(AM) Moncks Corner SC
WORD(AM) Spartanburg SC
KWAT(AM) Watertown SD
WAKM(AM) Franklin TN
KYNG(AM) Denison-Sherman TX
KPRC(AM) Houston TX
KJTV(AM) Lubbock TX
WXGI(AM) Richmond VA
KJR(AM) Seattle WA
WERL(AM) Eagle River WI
WCLB(AM) Sheboygan WI
WVTS(AM) Charleston WV
KMER(AM) Kemmerer WY

960 khz
WERC(AM) Birmingham AL
WLPR(AM) Prichard AL
KCGS(AM) Marshall AR
KKNT(AM) Phoenix AZ
KIXW(AM) Apple Valley CA
KQKE(AM) Oakland CA
WELI(AM) New Haven CT
WGRO(AM) Lake City FL
WGGT(AM) North Palm Beach FL
WJYZ(AM) Albany GA
WRFC(AM) Athens GA
KMA(AM) Shenandoah IA
KSRA(AM) Salmon ID
*WDLM(AM) East Moline IL
WSBT(AM) South Bend IN
WPRT(AM) Prestonsburg KY
KROF(AM) Abbeville LA
WFGL(AM) Fitchburg MA
WTGM(AM) Salisbury MD
WHAK(AM) Rogers City MI
KLTF(AM) Little Falls MN
KZIM(AM) Cape Girardeau MO
WABG(AM) Greenwood MS
KFLN(AM) Baker MT
WZRH(AM) Dallas NC
WRNS(AM) Kinston NC
KNEB(AM) Scottsbluff NE
KNDN(AM) Farmington NM
WEAV(AM) Plattsburgh NY
WKVX(AM) Wooster OH
KGWA(AM) Enid OK
KKJX(AM) Klamath Falls OR
WHYL(AM) Carlisle PA
WPLY(AM) Mount Pocono PA
WATS(AM) Sayre PA
WCHQ(AM) Quebradillas PR
WGLH(AM) La Follette TN
WBMC(AM) McMinnville TN
KIMP(AM) Mount Pleasant TX
KGKL(AM) San Angelo TX
KOVO(AM) Provo UT
WFIR(AM) Roanoke VA
KALE(AM) Richland WA
WTCH(AM) Shawano WI

970 khz
KFBX(AM) Fairbanks AK
WERH(AM) Hamilton AL
WTBF(AM) Troy AL
KNEA(AM) Jonesboro AR
KVWM(AM) Show Low AZ
KGET(AM) Bakersfield CA

KNWZ(AM) Coachella CA
KESP(AM) Modesto CA
KFEL(AM) Pueblo CO
WNNR(AM) Jacksonville FL
WFLA(AM) Tampa FL
WNIV(AM) Atlanta GA
WVOP(AM) Vidalia GA
KFTA(AM) Rupert ID
WMAY(AM) Springfield IL
WFSR(AM) Harlan KY
WGTK(AM) Louisville KY
KSYL(AM) Alexandria LA
WESO(AM) Southbridge MA
WAMD(AM) Aberdeen MD
WZAN(AM) Portland ME
WZAM(AM) Ishpeming MI
WKHM(AM) Jackson MI
KNFX(AM) Austin MN
WZQK(AM) Brandon MS
KBUL(AM) Billings MT
WRCS(AM) Ahoskie NC
WLZR(AM) Canton NC
WDAY(AM) Fargo ND
*KJLT(AM) North Platte NE
WWDJ(AM) Hackensack NJ
KNUU(AM) Paradise NV
*WNED(AM) Buffalo NY
WCHN(AM) Norwich NY
WFUN(AM) Ashtabula OH
WATH(AM) Athens OH
KCFO(AM) Tulsa OK
KCMD(AM) Portland OR
WBLF(AM) Bellefonte PA
WBGG(AM) Pittsburgh PA
WJMX(AM) Florence SC
WXQK(AM) Spring City TN
KIXL(AM) Del Valle TX
KHVN(AM) Fort Worth TX
WKCI(AM) Waynesboro VA
KTRW(AM) Spokane WA
*WHA(AM) Madison WI
WGEE(AM) Superior WI
WWYO(AM) Pineville WV

980 khz
KCAB(AM) Dardanelle AR
KNTR(AM) Lake Havasu City AZ
KINS(AM) Eureka CA
*KEYQ(AM) Fresno CA
KFWB(AM) Los Angeles CA
KDBV(AM) Salinas CA
KGLN(AM) Glenwood Springs CO
WSUB(AM) Groton CT
WTEM(AM) Washington DC
WDVH(AM) Gainesville FL
WTOT(AM) Marianna FL
WRNE(AM) Pensacola FL
WHSR(AM) Pompano Beach FL
WKLY(AM) Hartwell GA
WPGA(AM) Perry GA
WUUS(AM) Rossville GA
KUPI(AM) Ammon ID
KSGM(AM) Chester IL
WITY(AM) Danville IL
WGWM(AM) London KY
KOKA(AM) Shreveport LA
WCAP(AM) Lowell MA
WAKV(AM) Otsego MI
KKMS(AM) Richfield MN
KMBZ(AM) Kansas City MO
WAKK(AM) McComb MS
WKOR(AM) Starkville MS
WAAV(AM) Leland NC
WAAA(AM) Winston-Salem NC
KICA(AM) Clovis NM
KMIN(AM) Grants NM
KVLV(AM) Fallon NV
WOFX(AM) Troy NY
WONE(AM) Dayton OH
WILK(AM) Wilkes-Barre PA
WAZS(AM) Summerville SC
WBZK(AM) York SC
KDSJ(AM) Deadwood SD
WYFN(AM) Nashville TN
KRTX(AM) Rosenberg-Richmond TX
KHOS(AM) Sonora TX
KSVC(AM) Richfield UT

U.S. AM Stations by Frequency

WFHG(AM) Bristol VA
KBBO(AM) Selah WA
WNBI(AM) Park Falls WI
WPRE(AM) Prairie du Chien WI
WCUB(AM) Two Rivers WI
WHAW(AM) Weston WV

990 khz
WEIS(AM) Centre AL
WLDX(AM) Fayette AL
KTKT(AM) Tucson AZ
KATD(AM) Pittsburg CA
KTMS(AM) Santa Barbara CA
KRKS(AM) Denver CO
WXCT(AM) Southington CT
WMYM(AM) Miami FL
WDYZ(AM) Orlando FL
WGML(AM) Hinesville GA
KHBZ(AM) Honolulu HI
KAYL(AM) Storm Lake IA
WCAZ(AM) Carthage IL
WITZ(AM) Jasper IN
WLHN(AM) Muncie IN
KRSL(AM) Russell KS
WGSO(AM) New Orleans LA
WDEO(AM) Ypsilanti MI
KRMO(AM) Cassville MO
WABO(AM) Waynesboro MS
WEEB(AM) Southern Pines NC
WBTE(AM) Windsor NC
KSVP(AM) Artesia NM
WLGZ(AM) Rochester NY
WJEH(AM) Gallipolis OH
WTIG(AM) Massillon OH
KTHH(AM) Albany OR
WNTP(AM) Philadelphia PA
WNTW(AM) Somerset PA
WPRA(AM) Mayaguez PR
WALE(AM) Greenville RI
WNML(AM) Knoxville TN
WKAM(AM) Memphis TN
KZZB(AM) Beaumont TX
KFCD(AM) Farmersville TX
KAML(AM) Kenedy-Karnes City TX
WNRV(AM) Narrows-Pearisburg VA
WLEE(AM) Richmond VA

1000 khz
WDJL(AM) Huntsville AL
WNSI(AM) Robertsdale AL
KFLG(AM) Bullhead City AZ
KCEO(AM) Vista CA
WYBT(AM) Blountstown FL
WJBW(AM) Jupiter FL
WMVP(AM) Chicago IL
WKVG(AM) Jenkins KY
WCMX(AM) Leominster MA
WXTN(AM) Lexington MS
WRTG(AM) Garner NC
WOF(AM) Andover NJ
KKIM(AM) Albuquerque NM
WLNL(AM) Horseheads NY
WCCD(AM) Parma OH
KTOK(AM) Oklahoma City OK
WIOO(AM) Carlisle PA
WWOF(AM) Walhalla SC
KXRB(AM) Sioux Falls SD
WMUF(AM) Paris TN
KSTA(AM) Coleman TX
*KBIB(AM) Marion TX
WKDE(AM) Altavista VA
WRAR(AM) Tappahannock VA
WVWI(AM) Charlotte Amalie VI
KOMO(AM) Seattle WA

1010 khz
WCOC(AM) Dora AL
KXXT(AM) Tolleson AZ
KCHJ(AM) Delano CA
KIQI(AM) San Francisco CA
KXPS(AM) Thousand Palms CA
KSIR(AM) Brush CO
WIOJ(AM) Jacksonville Beach FL
WBZZ(AM) Seffner FL
WGUN(AM) Atlanta GA
*KRNI(AM) Mason City IA
WCSI(AM) Columbus IN
KIND(AM) Independence KS

KDLA(AM) De Ridder LA
WCKW(AM) Garyville LA
WOLB(AM) Baltimore MD
KCHI(AM) Chillicothe MO
KXEN(AM) Saint Louis MO
WMOX(AM) Meridian MS
WSPC(AM) Albemarle NC
WFGW(AM) Black Mountain NC
WELS(AM) Kinston NC
WNTK(AM) Newport NH
WINS(AM) New York NY
WIOI(AM) New Boston OH
KZNY(AM) Milwaukie OR
WHIN(AM) Gallatin TN
WORM(AM) Savannah TN
KTNZ(AM) Amarillo TX
KLAT(AM) Houston TX
KBBW(AM) Waco TX
KCPW(AM) Tooele UT
WMEV(AM) Marion VA
WRJR(AM) Portsmouth VA
WSPT(AM) Stevens Point WI
WCST(AM) Berkeley Springs WV

1020 khz
KAXX(AM) Eagle River AK
KTNQ(AM) Los Angeles CA
WKZE(AM) Sharon CT
WRHB(AM) Kendall FL
WJEP(AM) Ochlocknee GA
WCIL(AM) Carbondale IL
WPEO(AM) Peoria IL
KJJK(AM) Fergus Falls MN
KOIL(AM) Plattsmouth NE
WIBG(AM) Ocean City NJ
KINF(AM) Roswell NM
KOKP(AM) Perry OK
KDKA(AM) Pittsburgh PA
WOQI(AM) Adjuntas PR
WRIX(AM) Homeland Park SC
KWIQ(AM) Moses Lake North WA
KYXE(AM) Union Gap WA

1030 khz
KFAY(AM) Farmington AR
KEVT(AM) Cortaro AZ
KJDJ(AM) San Luis Obispo CA
WONQ(AM) Oviedo FL
WEBS(AM) Calhoun GA
WNVR(AM) Vernon Hills IL
KBUF(AM) Holcomb KS
WBZ(AM) Boston MA
WWGB(AM) Indian Head MD
*WUFL(AM) Sterling Heights MI
WCTS(AM) Maplewood MN
KCWJ(AM) Blue Springs MO
WNOW(AM) Mint Hill NC
WDRU(AM) Wake Forest NC
KDUN(AM) Reedsport OR
WOSO(AM) San Juan PR
WGSF(AM) Memphis TN
WQSE(AM) White Bluff TN
KCTA(AM) Corpus Christi TX
KWFA(AM) Tye TX
WGFC(AM) Floyd VA
KMAS(AM) Shelton WA
WBGS(AM) Point Pleasant WV
KTWO(AM) Casper WY

1040 khz
KURS(AM) San Diego CA
KCBR(AM) Monument CO
WLVJ(AM) Boynton Beach FL
WWBA(AM) Pinellas Park FL
WPBS(AM) Conyers GA
KLHT(AM) Honolulu HI
WHO(AM) Des Moines IA
WOKT(AM) Cannonsburg KY
WLCR(AM) Mt. Washington KY
WSGH(AM) Lewisville NC
WCHR(AM) Flemington NJ
WYSL(AM) Avon NY
WJTB(AM) North Ridgeville OH
*KLVP(AM) Tigard OR
WZSK(AM) Everett PA
WZNA(AM) Moca PR
WQBB(AM) Powell TN
KGGR(AM) Dallas TX

1050 khz
WRFS(AM) Alexander City AL
WWIC(AM) Scottsboro AL
KJBN(AM) Little Rock AR
KTBA(AM) Tuba City AZ
KJPG(AM) Frazier Park CA
KCAA(AM) Loma Linda CA
KTCT(AM) San Mateo CA
WJSB(AM) Crestview FL
WROS(AM) Jacksonville FL
WJCM(AM) Sebring FL
WFAM(AM) Augusta GA
WMNZ(AM) Montezuma GA
WDZ(AM) Decatur IL
WTCA(AM) Plymouth IN
WNES(AM) Central City KY
KLPL(AM) Lake Providence LA
KVPI(AM) Ville Platte LA
WMSG(AM) Oakland MD
WFED(AM) Silver Spring MD
WTKA(AM) Ann Arbor MI
KLOH(AM) Pipestone MN
KMIS(AM) Portageville MO
KSIS(AM) Sedalia MO
WTWG(AM) Columbus MS
KMTA(AM) Miles City MT
WFSC(AM) Franklin NC
WLON(AM) Lincolnton NC
WWGP(AM) Sanford NC
WBNC(AM) Conway NH
KTBL(AM) Los Ranchos de Albuquerque NM
WSEN(AM) Baldwinsville NY
WYBG(AM) Massena NY
WEPN(AM) New York NY
WTSJ(AM) Cincinnati OH
KKRX(AM) Lawton OK
KGTO(AM) Tulsa OK
KORE(AM) Springfield-Eugene OR
WBUT(AM) Butler PA
WLYC(AM) Williamsport PA
WIQB(AM) Conway SC
WSMT(AM) Sparta TN
KCHN(AM) Brookshire TX
KRMY(AM) Killeen TX
WGAT(AM) Gate City VA
WBRG(AM) Lynchburg VA
WVXX(AM) Norfolk VA
KEYF(AM) Dishman WA
*KBLE(AM) Seattle WA
*WDVM(AM) Eau Claire WI
WJOK(AM) Kaukauna WI
WLIP(AM) Kenosha WI
WAMN(AM) Green Valley WV
WADC(AM) Parkersburg WV

1060 khz
KAYR(AM) Van Buren AR
KDUS(AM) Tempe AZ
KTNS(AM) Oakhurst CA
KRCN(AM) Longmont CO
WIXC(AM) Titusville FL
WKGQ(AM) Milledgeville GA
WKNG(AM) Tallapoosa GA
KHBC(AM) Hilo HI
KBGN(AM) Caldwell ID
WMCL(AM) McLeansboro IL
WRHL(AM) Rochelle IL
WFLE(AM) Flemingsburg KY
WJKY(AM) Jamestown KY
WLNO(AM) New Orleans LA
WBIX(AM) Natick MA
WHFB(AM) Benton Harbor-St. Joseph MI
KFIL(AM) Preston MN
KTOZ(AM) Springfield MO
WKMQ(AM) Tupelo MS
WGSB(AM) Mebane NC
WXNC(AM) Monroe NC
WCOK(AM) Sparta NC
KNLV(AM) Ord NE
KKVV(AM) Las Vegas NV
WILB(AM) Canton OH
KYW(AM) Philadelphia PA
WCGB(AM) Juana Diaz PR
KGFX(AM) Pierre SD
WNPC(AM) Newport TN
WQMV(AM) Waverly TN

KXPL(AM) El Paso TX
KIJN(AM) Farwell TX
KOFY(AM) Gilmer TX
KFIT(AM) Lockhart TX
KFIT EXP STN San Antonio TX
KDYL(AM) South Salt Lake UT

1070 khz
WAPI(AM) Birmingham AL
KNX(AM) Los Angeles CA
WKII(AM) Solana FL
*WFRF(AM) Tallahassee FL
KILR(AM) Estherville IA
WIBC(AM) Indianapolis IN
KFTI(AM) Wichita KS
WEKT(AM) Elkton KY
KBCL(AM) Bossier City LA
KVKK(AM) Verndale MN
KHMO(AM) Hannibal MO
KATQ(AM) Plentywood MT
WNCT(AM) Greenville NC
WGOS(AM) High Point NC
WKMB(AM) Stirling NJ
WTWK(AM) Plattsburgh NY
WSCP(AM) Sandy Creek-Pulaski NY
KRAM(AM) West Klamath OR
WKOK(AM) Sunbury PA
WMIA(AM) Arecibo PR
WCSZ(AM) Sans Souci SC
WFLI(AM) Lookout Mountain TN
WDIA(AM) Memphis TN
KOPY(AM) Alice TX
KNTH(AM) Houston TX
KWEL(AM) Midland TX
WINA(AM) Charlottesville VA
WTSO(AM) Madison WI
WIWS(AM) Beckley WV

1080 khz
KUDO(AM) Anchorage AK
WKAC(AM) Athens AL
KGVY(AM) Green Valley AZ
KSCO(AM) Santa Cruz CA
WTIC(AM) Hartford CT
WVCG(AM) Coral Gables FL
WHOO(AM) Kissimmee FL
WFTD(AM) Marietta GA
KWAI(AM) Honolulu HI
KOAK(AM) Red Oak IA
KVNI(AM) Coeur d'Alene ID
*WRYT(AM) Edwardsville IL
WNWI(AM) Oak Lawn IL
WKJK(AM) Louisville KY
WOAP(AM) Owosso MI
KYMN(AM) Northfield MN
KYMO(AM) East Prairie MO
WKGX(AM) Lenoir NC
WWDR(AM) Murfreesboro NC
KNDK(AM) Langdon ND
KCNM(AM) Garapan-Saipan NP
WUFO(AM) Amherst NY
KFXX(AM) Portland OR
WWNL(AM) Pittsburgh PA
WLEY(AM) Cayey PR
WALD(AM) Walterboro SC
KRLD(AM) Dallas TX
KSLL(AM) Price UT
WKBY(AM) Chatham VA
WOKU(AM) Hurricane WV

1090 khz
WWGC(AM) Albertville AL
KAAY(AM) Little Rock AR
KNCR(AM) Fortuna CA
KMXA(AM) Aurora CO
WNVY(AM) Cantonment FL
WBAF(AM) Barnesville GA
KSOU(AM) Sioux Center IA
*KNWS(AM) Waterloo IA
WCRA(AM) Effingham IL
WFCV(AM) Fort Wayne IN
WILD(AM) Boston MA
WBAL(AM) Baltimore MD
WCAR(AM) Livonia MI
WKBZ(AM) Muskegon MI
KEXS(AM) Excelsior Springs MO
KBOZ(AM) Bozeman MT
WKTE(AM) King NC

WTSB(AM) Selma NC
KTGO(AM) Tioga ND
WKFI(AM) Wilmington OH
KLWJ(AM) Umatilla OR
WSOL(AM) San German PR
WCZZ(AM) Greenwood SC
WENR(AM) Englewood TN
WTNK(AM) Hartsville TN
WHGG(AM) Kingsport TN
KNUZ(AM) Bellville TX
KVOP(AM) Plainview TX
WGOD(AM) Charlotte Amalie VI
KPTK(AM) Seattle WA
WISS(AM) Berlin WI
WAQE(AM) Rice Lake WI

1100 khz
KFNX(AM) Cave Creek AZ
KAFY(AM) Bakersfield CA
KFAX(AM) San Francisco CA
KNZZ(AM) Grand Junction CO
WWWE(AM) Hapeville GA
WCGA(AM) Woodbine GA
KKLL(AM) Webb City MO
WMYQ(AM) Newton MS
KQNM(AM) Milan NM
KWWN(AM) Las Vegas NV
WHLI(AM) Hempstead NY
WTAM(AM) Cleveland OH
WGPA(AM) Bethlehem PA
WSGI(AM) Springfield TN
KDRY(AM) Alamo Heights TX
WTWN(AM) Wells River VT

1110 khz
KAGV(AM) Big Lake AK
WBCA(AM) Bay Minette AL
WBIB(AM) Centreville AL
KGFL(AM) Clinton AR
KDIS(AM) Pasadena CA
KLIB(AM) Roseville CA
WTIS(AM) Tampa FL
KAOI(AM) Kihei HI
*WMBI(AM) Chicago IL
WKDZ(AM) Cadiz KY
WCBR(AM) Richmond KY
WOMN(AM) Franklinton LA
KTTP(AM) Pineville LA
WUHN(AM) Pittsfield MA
*WUNN(AM) Mason MI
WJML(AM) Petoskey MI
WKRA(AM) Holly Springs MS
WBT(AM) Charlotte NC
KFAB(AM) Omaha NE
WCEC(AM) Salem NH
KYKK(AM) Hobbs NM
WSFW(AM) Seneca Falls NY
WTBQ(AM) Warwick NY
WGNZ(AM) Fairborn OH
KEOR(AM) Atoka OK
KBND(AM) Bend OR
WJSM(AM) Martinsburg PA
WNAP(AM) Norristown PA
WKZV(AM) Washington PA
WVJP(AM) Caguas PR
WPMZ(AM) Providence RI
WSLV(AM) Ardmore TN
WUAT(AM) Pikeville TN
KTEK(AM) Alvin TX
WYRM(AM) Norfolk VA
KWDB(AM) Oak Harbor WA

1120 khz
WHOG(AM) Hobson City AL
KZSJ(AM) San Martin CA
KLIM(AM) Limon CO
WPRX(AM) Bristol CT
WUST(AM) Washington DC
WNWF(AM) Destin FL
WXJO(AM) Gordon GA
WBNW(AM) Concord MA
KMOX(AM) Saint Louis MO
WTWZ(AM) Clinton MS
WSME(AM) Camp Lejeune NC
WBBF(AM) Buffalo NY
KPNW(AM) Eugene OR
WKQW(AM) Oil City PA
WMSW(AM) Hatillo PR

U.S. AM Stations by Frequency

WKCE(AM) Maryville TN
KJSA(AM) Mineral Wells TX
*KANN(AM) Roy UT
WDUF(AM) Duffield VA

1130 khz
WACQ(AM) Carrville AL
KAAB(AM) Batesville AR
KQNA(AM) Prescott Valley AZ
KRDU(AM) Dinuba CA
KSDO(AM) San Diego CA
WWBF(AM) Bartow FL
WLBA(AM) Gainesville GA
KRUD(AM) Honolulu HI
KILJ(AM) Mount Pleasant IA
WSDX(AM) Brazil IN
KLEY(AM) Wellington KS
WRKY(AM) Murray KY
KWKH(AM) Shreveport LA
WDFN(AM) Detroit MI
KFAN(AM) Minneapolis MN
WQFX(AM) Gulfport MS
WPYB(AM) Benson NC
WCLW(AM) Eden NC
WECR(AM) Newland NC
KBMR(AM) Bismarck ND
WBBR(AM) New York NY
WEDI(AM) Eaton OH
WASP(AM) Brownsville PA
WOIZ(AM) Guayanilla PR
WQIS(AM) Camden SC
WFXH(AM) Hilton Head Island SC
WYXE(AM) Gallatin TN
KTMR(AM) Edna TX
WISN(AM) Milwaukee WI
WRRL(AM) Rainelle WV

1140 khz
KSLD(AM) Soldotna AK
WBXR(AM) Hazel Green AL
KQAB(AM) Lake Isabella CA
KNWQ(AM) Palm Springs CA
KHTK(AM) Sacramento CA
KNAB(AM) Burlington CO
WQBA(AM) Miami FL
WRMQ(AM) Orlando FL
KGEM(AM) Boise ID
WVEL(AM) Pekin IL
WAWK(AM) Kendallville IN
WMMG(AM) Brandenburg KY
WRLV(AM) Salyersville KY
WJNZ(AM) Kentwood MI
KCXL(AM) Liberty MO
KPWB(AM) Piedmont MO
KLTK(AM) South West City MO
WAPF(AM) McComb MS
WSAO(AM) Senatobia MS
WRNA(AM) China Grove NC
KSFN(AM) North Las Vegas NV
WCJW(AM) Warsaw NY
KRMP(AM) Oklahoma City OK
WQII(AM) San Juan PR
KSOO(AM) Sioux Falls SD
WLOD(AM) Loudon TN
KCLE(AM) Cleburne TX
KYOK(AM) Conroe TX
WRVA(AM) Richmond VA
WXLZ(AM) Saint Paul VA
KZMQ(AM) Greybull WY

1150 khz
WGEA(AM) Geneva AL
WJRD(AM) Tuscaloosa AL
KCKY(AM) Coolidge AZ
KTLK(AM) Los Angeles CA
KNRC(AM) Englewood CO
WMRD(AM) Middletown CT
WDEL(AM) Wilmington DE
WNDB(AM) Daytona Beach FL
WTMP(AM) Egypt Lake FL
WXKO(AM) Fort Valley GA
KCPS(AM) Burlington IA
KWKY(AM) Des Moines IA
WGGH(AM) Marion IL
KSAL(AM) Salina KS
WMST(AM) Mt. Sterling KY
WLOC(AM) Munfordville KY
WJBO(AM) Baton Rouge LA

WTTT(AM) Boston MA
KASM(AM) Albany MN
KRMS(AM) Osage Beach MO
WONG(AM) Canton MS
KSEN(AM) Shelby MT
WBAG(AM) Burlington-Graham NC
WGBR(AM) Goldsboro NC
KDEF(AM) Albuquerque NM
WRUN(AM) Utica NY
*WCUE(AM) Cuyahoga Falls OH
WIMA(AM) Lima OH
KNED(AM) McAlester OK
KAGO(AM) Klamath Falls OR
KXMG(AM) Portland OR
WHUN(AM) Huntingdon PA
WGBN(AM) New Kensington PA
WAVO(AM) Rock Hill SC
WSNW(AM) Seneca SC
KIMM(AM) Rapid City SD
WGOW(AM) Chattanooga TN
WCRK(AM) Morristown TN
WDTM(AM) Selmer TN
KZNE(AM) College Station TX
KCCT(AM) Corpus Christi TX
KSVE(AM) El Paso TX
KJBC(AM) Midland TX
KUHD(AM) Port Neches TX
KREL(AM) Quanah TX
WNLR(AM) Churchville VA
KQQQ(AM) Pullman WA
KKNW(AM) Seattle WA
WEAQ(AM) Chippewa Falls WI
WHBY(AM) Kimberly WI
WELC(AM) Welch WV

1160 khz
WKTT(AM) Saraland AL
WEWC(AM) Callahan FL
WOYE(AM) Saint Cloud FL
WMLB(AM) East Point GA
KHPP(AM) Waukon IA
WYLL(AM) Chicago IL
WBOB(AM) Florence KY
WKCM(AM) Hawesville KY
WMET(AM) Gaithersburg MD
WSKW(AM) Skowhegan ME
WCXI(AM) Fenton MI
KCTO(AM) Cleveland MO
WTEL(AM) Red Springs NC
WJFJ(AM) Tryon NC
WOBM(AM) Lakewood NJ
WVNJ(AM) Oakland NJ
WABY(AM) Mechanicville NY
WPIE(AM) Trumansburg NY
WCCS(AM) Homer City PA
WYNS(AM) Lehighton PA
WBQN(AM) Barceloneta-Manati PR
WAMB(AM) Nashville TN
KMGS(AM) Highland Park TX
KRDY(AM) San Antonio TX
KSL(AM) Salt Lake City UT
WODY(AM) Fieldale VA

1170 khz
*KJNP(AM) North Pole AK
WXRP(AM) Hanceville AL
WACV(AM) Montgomery AL
KCBQ(AM) San Diego CA
KLOK(AM) San Jose CA
KJJD(AM) Windsor CO
*WCTF(AM) Vernon CT
WKFL(AM) Bushnell FL
WAVS(AM) Davie FL
WSOS(AM) Saint Augustine Beach FL
KHCM(AM) Honolulu HI
KJOC(AM) Davenport IA
WLBH(AM) Mattoon IL
WDFB(AM) Junction City KY
WDIS(AM) Norfolk MA
WFPB(AM) Orleans MA
KOWZ(AM) Waseca MN
KUGT(AM) Jackson MO
WCXN(AM) Claremont NC
WCLN(AM) Clinton NC
WWTR(AM) Bridgewater NJ
WWLE(AM) Cornwall NY
KFAQ(AM) Tulsa OK
WLEO(AM) Ponce PR

WQVA(AM) Lexington SC
*WPLX(AM) Germantown TN
KPUG(AM) Bellingham WA
WFDL(AM) Waupun WI
WWVA(AM) Wheeling WV

1180 khz
KYET(AM) Williams AZ
KERI(AM) Wasco-Greenacres CA
WZQZ(AM) Trion GA
WLDS(AM) Jacksonville IL
WGAB(AM) Newburgh IN
WXLA(AM) Dimondale MI
WJNT(AM) Pearl MS
KOFI(AM) Kalispell MT
WMYT(AM) Carolina Beach NC
KYDZ(AM) Bellevue NE
WHAM(AM) Rochester NY
WCNX(AM) Hope Valley RI
WFGN(AM) Gaffney SC
WVLZ(AM) Knoxville TN
KGOL(AM) Humble TX
KLAY(AM) Lakewood WA

1190 khz
WHIY(AM) Moulton AL
KREB(AM) Bentonville-Bella Vista AR
KNUV(AM) Tolleson AZ
KXMX(AM) Anaheim CA
KDYA(AM) Vallejo CA
KVCU(AM) Boulder CO
WAMT(AM) Pine Castle-Sky Lake FL
WPSP(AM) Royal Palm Beach FL
WAFS(AM) Atlanta GA
WWIO(AM) Saint Mary's GA
KDAO(AM) Marshalltown IA
WOWO(AM) Fort Wayne IN
KVSV(AM) Beloit KS
KNEK(AM) Washington LA
WBIS(AM) Annapolis MD
KKOJ(AM) Jackson MN
KMFX(AM) Wabasha MN
KRFT(AM) De Soto MO
KPHN(AM) Kansas City MO
WBSL(AM) Bay St. Louis MS
WIXE(AM) Monroe NC
KXKS(AM) Albuquerque NM
WSDE(AM) Cobleskill NY
WLIB(AM) New York NY
KEX(AM) Portland OR
WBMJ(AM) San Juan PR
WJES(AM) Johnston SC
WSDQ(AM) Dunlap TN
WHMT(AM) Humboldt TN
KFXR(AM) Dallas TX
WBDY(AM) Bluefield VA
*WNWC(AM) Sun Prairie WI

1200 khz
WQLS(AM) Ozark AL
KYAA(AM) Soquel CA
WPTK(AM) Pine Island Center FL
WRTO(AM) Chicago IL
WBCE(AM) Wickliffe KY
WKOX(AM) Framingham MA
WCHB(AM) Taylor MI
KYOO(AM) Bolivar MO
WXIT(AM) Blowing Rock NC
WSML(AM) Graham NC
*KFNW(AM) West Fargo ND
WJGK(AM) Kingston NY
WTLA(AM) North Syracuse NY
WRKK(AM) Hughesville PA
WKST(AM) New Castle PA
WGDL(AM) Lares PR
WMIR(AM) Atlantic Beach SC
WKDA(AM) Nashville TN
WOAI(AM) San Antonio TX
WAGE(AM) Leesburg VA

1210 khz
KQTL(AM) Sahuarita AZ
KQEQ(AM) Fowler CA
*KEBR(AM) Rocklin CA
KPRZ(AM) San Marcos-Poway CA
WNMA(AM) Miami Springs FL
WDGR(AM) Dahlonega GA
KZOO(AM) Honolulu HI

WILY(AM) Centralia IL
WSKR(AM) Denham Springs LA
WLDR(AM) Kingsley MI
WDAO(AM) Dayton OH
KGYN(AM) Guymon OK
WPHT(AM) Philadelphia PA
WHOY(AM) Salinas PR
KOKK(AM) Huron SD
WMPS(AM) Bartlett TN
WSBI(AM) Static TN
KUBR(AM) San Juan TX
KUNF(AM) Washington UT
KWMG(AM) Auburn-Federal Way WA
KZTS(AM) Sunnyside WA
KRSV(AM) Afton WY
KHAT(AM) Laramie WY

1220 khz
WAYE(AM) Birmingham AL
WABF(AM) Fairhope AL
KVSA(AM) McGehee AR
KHTS(AM) Canyon Country CA
KNTS(AM) Palo Alto CA
KWKU(AM) Pomona CA
KLVZ(AM) Denver CO
WQUN(AM) Hamden CT
WJAX(AM) Jacksonville FL
WOTS(AM) Kissimmee FL
WIBQ(AM) Sarasota FL
WZOT(AM) Rockmart GA
KJAN(AM) Atlantic IA
KQMG(AM) Independence IA
WLPO(AM) La Salle IL
WKRS(AM) Waukegan IL
WSLM(AM) Salem IN
KOFO(AM) Ottawa KS
WFKN(AM) Franklin KY
WPHX(AM) Sanford ME
WBCH(AM) Hastings MI
WMGT(AM) Stillwater MN
KOMC(AM) Branson MO
KGIR(AM) Cape Girardeau MO
KLPW(AM) Union MO
WOEG(AM) Hazlehurst MS
WKMT(AM) Kings Mountain NC
WREV(AM) Reidsville NC
WENC(AM) Whiteville NC
KDDR(AM) Oakes ND
WZBK(AM) Keene NH
WGNY(AM) Newburgh NY
WHKW(AM) Cleveland OH
WERT(AM) Van Wert OH
KTLV(AM) Midwest City OK
KCCS(AM) Salem OR
WJUN(AM) Mexico PA
WRIB(AM) Providence RI
WFWL(AM) Camden TN
WCPH(AM) Etowah TN
WAXO(AM) Lewisburg TN
KMVL(AM) Madisonville TX
KZEE(AM) Weatherford TX
WLSD(AM) Big Stone Gap VA
WFAX(AM) Falls Church VA

1230 khz
KIFW(AM) Sitka AK
KVAK(AM) Valdez AK
WAUD(AM) Auburn AL
WKWL(AM) Florala AL
WJBB(AM) Haleyville AL
WBHP(AM) Huntsville AL
WRJX(AM) Jackson AL
WNUZ(AM) Talladega AL
WTBC(AM) Tuscaloosa AL
KCON(AM) Conway AR
KFPW(AM) Fort Smith AR
KBTM(AM) Jonesboro AR
KAAA(AM) Kingman AZ
KOY(AM) Phoenix AZ
KATO(AM) Safford AZ
KINO(AM) Winslow AZ
KGEO(AM) Bakersfield CA
KSZL(AM) Barstow CA
KBOV(AM) Bishop CA
KXO(AM) El Centro CA
KDAC(AM) Fort Bragg CA
KYPA(AM) Los Angeles CA
KPRL(AM) Paso Robles CA

KLXR(AM) Redding CA
*KWG(AM) Stockton CA
KEXO(AM) Grand Junction CO
KKPC(AM) Pueblo CO
KBCR(AM) Steamboat Springs CO
KSTC(AM) Sterling CO
WKND(AM) Manchester CT
WGGG(AM) Gainesville FL
WONN(AM) Lakeland FL
WMAF(AM) Madison FL
WSBB(AM) New Smyrna Beach FL
WZNO(AM) Pensacola FL
WWSD(AM) Quincy FL
WBZT(AM) West Palm Beach FL
WNRR(AM) Augusta GA
WBLJ(AM) Dalton GA
WXLI(AM) Dublin GA
WFOM(AM) Marietta GA
WSOK(AM) Savannah GA
WWGA(AM) Waycross GA
KFJB(AM) Marshalltown IA
KBAR(AM) Burley ID
KORT(AM) Grangeville ID
KRXK(AM) Rexburg ID
WJBC(AM) Bloomington IL
WFXN(AM) Moline IL
WHCO(AM) Sparta IL
WJOB(AM) Hammond IN
WSAL(AM) Logansport IN
WTCJ(AM) Tell City IN
WHIR(AM) Danville KY
WHOP(AM) Hopkinsville KY
WANO(AM) Pineville KY
KLIC(AM) Monroe LA
WBOK(AM) New Orleans LA
KSLO(AM) Opelousas LA
WNAW(AM) North Adams MA
WESX(AM) Salem MA
WNEB(AM) Worcester MA
WITH(AM) Baltimore MD
WCMD(AM) Cumberland MD
WNZT(AM) Hermon ME
WTKG(AM) Grand Rapids MI
WGRY(AM) Grayling MI
WIKB(AM) Iron River MI
*WMPC(AM) Lapeer MI
WSOO(AM) Sault Ste. Marie MI
WMSH(AM) Sturgis MI
WKLK(AM) Cloquet MN
KGHS(AM) International Falls MN
KYSM(AM) Mankato MN
KMRS(AM) Morris MN
KTRF(AM) Thief River Falls MN
KWNO(AM) Winona MN
KWAS(AM) Joplin MO
KLWT(AM) Lebanon MO
KWIX(AM) Moberly MO
WTKN(AM) Corinth MS
WSSO(AM) Starkville MS
KOBB(AM) Bozeman MT
KHDN(AM) Hardin MT
KXLO(AM) Lewistown MT
KLCB(AM) Libby MT
WSKY(AM) Asheville NC
WFAY(AM) Fayetteville NC
WMFR(AM) High Point NC
WLNR(AM) Kinston NC
WNNC(AM) Newton NC
WCBT(AM) Roanoke Rapids NC
KDIX(AM) Dickinson ND
KTNC(AM) Falls City NE
KHAS(AM) Hastings NE
WMOU(AM) Berlin NH
WTSV(AM) Claremont NH
WCMC(AM) Wildwood NJ
KRSY(AM) Alamogordo NM
KOTS(AM) Deming NM
KYVA(AM) Gallup NM
KFUN(AM) Las Vegas NM
KPSA(AM) Roswell NM
KELY(AM) Ely NV
KLAV(AM) Las Vegas NV
KJFK(AM) Reno NV
WECK(AM) Cheektowaga NY
WENY(AM) Elmira NY
WMML(AM) Glens Falls NY
WHUC(AM) Hudson NY

U.S. AM Stations by Frequency

WIXT(AM) Little Falls NY
WFAS(AM) White Plains NY
WDBZ(AM) Cincinnati OH
WTPG(AM) Columbus OH
WIRO(AM) Ironton OH
WCWA(AM) Toledo OH
KADA(AM) Ada OK
WBBZ(AM) Ponca City OK
KKEE(AM) Astoria OR
KZZR(AM) Burns OR
KHSN(AM) Coos Bay OR
KMUZ(AM) Gresham OR
KQIK(AM) Lakeview OR
*KSJK(AM) Talent OR
KCUP(AM) Toledo OR
WBVP(AM) Beaver Falls PA
WEEX(AM) Easton PA
WKBO(AM) Harrisburg PA
WCRO(AM) Johnstown PA
WBPZ(AM) Lock Haven PA
WTIV(AM) Titusville PA
WNIK(AM) Arecibo PR
WXNI(AM) Westerly RI
WAIM(AM) Anderson SC
WOIC(AM) Columbia SC
WOLS(AM) Florence SC
KWSN(AM) Sioux Falls SD
WMLR(AM) Hohenwald TN
WAKI(AM) McMinnville TN
KSIX(AM) Corpus Christi TX
KTJK(AM) Del Rio TX
KQUE(AM) Houston TX
KERV(AM) Kerrville TX
KLVT(AM) Levelland TX
KOZA(AM) Odessa TX
KGRO(AM) Pampa TX
KSEY(AM) Seymour TX
KSST(AM) Sulphur Springs TX
KWTX(AM) Waco TX
KJQS(AM) Murray UT
WABN(AM) Abingdon VA
WODI(AM) Brookneal VA
WXCF(AM) Clifton Forge VA
WFVA(AM) Fredericksburg VA
WJOI(AM) Norfolk VA
WAMM(AM) Woodstock VA
WJOY(AM) Burlington VT
KOZI(AM) Chelan WA
KWYZ(AM) Everett WA
KSBN(AM) Spokane WA
WCLO(AM) Janesville WI
WXCO(AM) Wausau WI
WVNT(AM) Parkersburg WV
KVOC(AM) Casper WY

1240 khz
WEBJ(AM) Brewton AL
WULA(AM) Eufaula AL
WBCF(AM) Florence AL
WMGJ(AM) Gadsden AL
WLYJ(AM) Jasper AL
KVRC(AM) Arkadelphia AR
KTLO(AM) Mountain Home AR
KWAK(AM) Stuttgart AR
KJAA(AM) Globe AZ
KPOD(AM) Crescent City CA
KJOP(AM) Lemoore CA
KNRY(AM) Monterey CA
KLOA(AM) Ridgecrest CA
KSAC(AM) Sacramento CA
KEZY(AM) San Bernardino CA
KSON(AM) San Diego CA
KSMA(AM) Santa Maria CA
KSUE(AM) Susanville CA
KRDO(AM) Colorado Springs CO
KDGO(AM) Durango CO
KSLV(AM) Monte Vista CO
KCRT(AM) Trinidad CO
WWCO(AM) Waterbury CT
WBGC(AM) Chipley FL
WYNY(AM) Cross City FL
WKIQ(AM) Eustis FL
WINK(AM) Fort Myers FL
WMMB(AM) Melbourne FL
WFOY(AM) Saint Augustine FL
WBHB(AM) Fitzgerald GA
WGGA(AM) Gainesville GA

WLAG(AM) La Grange GA
WDDO(AM) Macon GA
WWNS(AM) Statesboro GA
WPAX(AM) Thomasville GA
WTWA(AM) Thomson GA
KDEC(AM) Decorah IA
*KWLC(AM) Decorah IA
KBIZ(AM) Ottumwa IA
KICD(AM) Spencer IA
KMCL(AM) Donnelly ID
KMHI(AM) Mountain Home ID
KWIK(AM) Pocatello ID
KOFE(AM) Saint Maries ID
WSBC(AM) Chicago IL
WEBQ(AM) Harrisburg IL
WTAX(AM) Springfield IL
WSDR(AM) Sterling IL
WHBU(AM) Anderson IN
KIUL(AM) Garden City KS
KFH(AM) Wichita KS
WLLV(AM) Louisville KY
WFTM(AM) Maysville KY
WPKE(AM) Pikeville KY
WSFC(AM) Somerset KY
KASO(AM) Minden LA
KANE(AM) New Iberia LA
WHMQ(AM) Greenfield MA
*WBUR(AM) West Yarmouth MA
WCEM(AM) Cambridge MD
WJEJ(AM) Hagerstown MD
WCNM(AM) Lewiston ME
WSYY(AM) Millinocket ME
WATT(AM) Cadillac MI
WCBY(AM) Cheboygan MI
WIAN(AM) Ishpeming MI
WJIM(AM) Lansing MI
WMFG(AM) Hibbing MN
WJON(AM) Saint Cloud MN
KLIK(AM) Jefferson City MO
KNEM(AM) Nevada MO
KFMO(AM) Park Hills MO
WWZQ(AM) Aberdeen MS
WPBQ(AM) Flowood MS
WGRM(AM) Greenwood MS
WGCM(AM) Gulfport MS
WMIS(AM) Natchez MS
WAVN(AM) Southaven MS
KMZK(AM) Billings MT
KLTZ(AM) Glasgow MT
KLYQ(AM) Hamilton MT
KBLL(AM) Helena MT
WSQL(AM) Brevard NC
WHVN(AM) Charlotte NC
WCNC(AM) Elizabeth City NC
WJNC(AM) Jacksonville NC
WPJL(AM) Raleigh NC
WWWC(AM) Wilkesboro NC
KDLR(AM) Devils Lake ND
KFOR(AM) Lincoln NE
KODY(AM) North Platte NE
WFTN(AM) Franklin NH
WSNJ(AM) Bridgeton NJ
KAMQ(AM) Carlsbad NM
KCLV(AM) Clovis NM
KALY(AM) Los Ranchos de Albuquerque NM
KELK(AM) Elko NV
WGBB(AM) Freeport NY
WGVA(AM) Geneva NY
WJTN(AM) Jamestown NY
WVOS(AM) Liberty NY
WNBZ(AM) Saranac Lake NY
WVKZ(AM) Schenectady NY
WATN(AM) Watertown NY
WBBW(AM) Youngstown OH
WHIZ(AM) Zanesville OH
KVSO(AM) Ardmore OK
KADS(AM) Elk City OK
KBEL(AM) Idabel OK
KOKL(AM) Okmulgee OK
KEJO(AM) Corvallis OR
KTIX(AM) Pendleton OR
KRDM(AM) Redmond OR
KQEN(AM) Roseburg OR
WRTA(AM) Altoona PA
WIOV(AM) Reading PA
WYGL(AM) Selinsgrove PA

WBAX(AM) Wilkes-Barre PA
WALO(AM) Humacao PR
WOON(AM) Woonsocket RI
WLSC(AM) Loris SC
WDKD(AM) Newberry SC
WDXY(AM) Sumter SC
KCCR(AM) Pierre SD
WBEJ(AM) Elizabethton TN
WEKR(AM) Fayetteville TN
WIFA(AM) Knoxville TN
WNSG(AM) Nashville TN
WSDT(AM) Soddy-Daisy TN
WENK(AM) Union City TN
KVLF(AM) Alpine TX
KXYL(AM) Brownwood TX
KTAM(AM) Bryan TX
KXIT(AM) Dalhart TX
KPBL(AM) Hemphill TX
KBGE(AM) Kilgore TX
KSOX(AM) Raymondville TX
KXOX(AM) Sweetwater TX
WROU(AM) Petersburg VA
WGMN(AM) Roanoke VA
WTON(AM) Staunton VA
WSKI(AM) Montpelier VT
KCVL(AM) Colville WA
KXLE(AM) Ellensburg WA
KGY(AM) Olympia WA
WOMT(AM) Manitowoc WI
WHFA(AM) Poynette WI
WOBT(AM) Rhinelander WI
WJMC(AM) Rice Lake WI
WKEZ(AM) Bluefield WV
WBES(AM) Dunbar WV
WDNE(AM) Elkins WV
KFBC(AM) Cheyenne WY
KEVA(AM) Evanston WY
KASL(AM) Newcastle WY
KRAL(AM) Rawlins WY
KTHE(AM) Thermopolis WY

1250 khz
WZOB(AM) Fort Payne AL
WAPZ(AM) Wetumpka AL
KOFC(AM) Fayetteville AR
KPZK(AM) Little Rock AR
KBSZ(AM) Wickenburg AZ
KHIL(AM) Willcox AZ
KHOT(AM) Madera CA
KZER(AM) Santa Barbara CA
KNWH(AM) Twentynine Palms CA
KLLK(AM) Willits CA
WQHL(AM) Live Oak FL
WHNZ(AM) Tampa FL
WSRA(AM) Albany GA
WYTH(AM) Madison GA
KDNZ(AM) Cedar Falls IA
WSPL(AM) Streator IL
WGL(AM) Fort Wayne IN
WRAY(AM) Princeton IN
WKHK(AM) Kansas City KS
WWFT(AM) Nicholasville KY
WLCK(AM) Scottsville KY
WARE(AM) Ware MA
WNEM(AM) Bridgeport MI
KBRF(AM) Fergus Falls MN
KCUE(AM) Red Wing MN
KBTC(AM) Houston MO
WHNY(AM) McComb MS
KIKC(AM) Forsyth MT
WGHB(AM) Farmville NC
WKDX(AM) Hamlet NC
WBRM(AM) Marion NC
KTFJ(AM) Dakota City NE
WKBR(AM) Manchester NH
WMTR(AM) Morristown NJ
WIPS(AM) Ticonderoga NY
WCHO(AM) Washington Court House OH
KCST(AM) Florence OR
WLEM(AM) Emporium PA
*WPEL(AM) Montrose PA
WEAE(AM) Pittsburgh PA
WQXA(AM) York PA
WJIT(AM) Sabana PR
WTMA(AM) Charleston SC
WKBL(AM) Covington TN

WRKQ(AM) Madisonville TN
WNTT(AM) Tazewell TN
KPJC(AM) Paris TX
*KDEI(AM) Port Arthur TX
KZDC(AM) San Antonio TX
KIKZ(AM) Seminole TX
KNEU(AM) Roosevelt UT
WDVA(AM) Danville VA
WLQM(AM) Franklin VA
WPRZ(AM) Warrenton VA
*KWSU(AM) Pullman WA
KKDZ(AM) Seattle WA
WSSP(AM) Milwaukee WI
WYKM(AM) Rupert WV

1260 khz
WYDE(AM) Birmingham AL
KCCB(AM) Corning AR
KBHC(AM) Nashville AR
KKGO(AM) Beverly Hills CA
KOIT(AM) San Francisco CA
*WSHU(AM) Westport CT
WWRC(AM) Washington DC
WAMS(AM) Newark DE
WFTW(AM) Fort Walton Beach FL
WSUA(AM) Miami FL
WIYD(AM) Palatka FL
WUFE(AM) Baxley GA
WBBK(AM) Blakely GA
WTJH(AM) East Point GA
*KFFF(AM) Boone IA
KSSL(AM) Idaho Falls ID
KWEI(AM) Weiser ID
WSDZ(AM) Belleville IL
WNDE(AM) Indianapolis IN
KBRH(AM) Baton Rouge LA
WMKI(AM) Boston MA
WPNW(AM) Zeeland MI
KROX(AM) Crookston MN
KDUZ(AM) Hutchinson MN
KSGF(AM) Springfield MO
WGVM(AM) Greenville MS
WCSA(AM) Ripley MS
WKXR(AM) Asheboro NC
WZBO(AM) Edenton NC
KIMB(AM) Kimball NE
WBUD(AM) Trenton NJ
KTRC(AM) Santa Fe NM
WBNR(AM) Beacon NY
WNSS(AM) Syracuse NY
WWMK(AM) Cleveland OH
WNXT(AM) Portsmouth OH
KWSH(AM) Wewoka OK
KLYC(AM) McMinnville OR
WRIE(AM) Erie PA
WPHB(AM) Philipsburg PA
WISO(AM) Ponce PR
WMUU(AM) Greenville SC
WHYM(AM) Lake City SC
KWYR(AM) Winner SD
WNOO(AM) Chattanooga TN
WMCH(AM) Church Hill TN
WDKN(AM) Dickson TN
WCLC(AM) Jamestown TN
KSML(AM) Diboll TX
KLDS(AM) Falfurrias TX
KKSA(AM) San Angelo TX
KWNX(AM) Taylor TX
KTUE(AM) Tulia TX
WCHV(AM) Charlottesville VA
WWVT(AM) Christiansburg VA
WXCE(AM) Amery WI
WWIS(AM) Black River Falls WI
WEKZ(AM) Monroe WI
WOCO(AM) Oconto WI
WTBZ(AM) Grafton WV
KPOW(AM) Powell WY

1270 khz
WGSV(AM) Guntersville AL
WIJD(AM) Prichard AL
KDJI(AM) Holbrook AZ
KXBX(AM) Lakeport CA
KNWT(AM) Thousand Palms CA
KJUG(AM) Tulare CA
WRLZ(AM) Eatonville FL
WNOG(AM) Naples FL
WNLS(AM) Tallahassee FL

WYXC(AM) Cartersville GA
WSHE(AM) Columbus GA
WJJC(AM) Commerce GA
KNDI(AM) Honolulu HI
KTFI(AM) Twin Falls ID
WEIC(AM) Charleston IL
WKBF(AM) Rock Island IL
WFRN(AM) Elkhart IN
WWCA(AM) Gary IN
WXGO(AM) Madison IN
KSCB(AM) Liberal KS
WAIN(AM) Columbia KY
WFUL(AM) Fulton KY
KVCL(AM) Winnfield LA
WSPR(AM) Springfield MA
WCBC(AM) Cumberland MD
WMKT(AM) Charlevoix MI
WXYT(AM) Detroit MI
WWWI(AM) Baxter MN
KWEB(AM) Rochester MN
KGNM(AM) Saint Joseph MO
KOZQ(AM) Waynesville MO
WMLC(AM) Monticello MS
WCGC(AM) Belmont NC
WMPM(AM) Smithfield NC
KLXX(AM) Bismarck-Mandan ND
WTSN(AM) Dover NH
WMIZ(AM) Vineland NJ
KINN(AM) Alamogordo NM
KBZZ(AM) Sparks NV
WHLD(AM) Niagara Falls NY
WDLA(AM) Walton NY
WILE(AM) Cambridge OH
WUCO(AM) Marysville OH
KRVT(AM) Claremore OK
KAJO(AM) Grants Pass OR
WLBR(AM) Lebanon PA
WHGS(AM) Hampton SC
*KNWC(AM) Sioux Falls SD
WLIK(AM) Newport TN
WQKR(AM) Portland TN
KEPS(AM) Eagle Pass TX
KFLC(AM) Fort Worth TX
WTJZ(AM) Newport News VA
WHEO(AM) Stuart VA
KBAM(AM) Longview WA
WRJC(AM) Mauston WI
KIML(AM) Gillette WY

1280 khz
WPID(AM) Piedmont AL
WWPG(AM) Tuscaloosa AL
KNBY(AM) Newport AR
KXEG(AM) Phoenix AZ
KXTK(AM) Arroyo Grande CA
*KFRN(AM) Long Beach CA
KUYL(AM) Stockton CA
KBNO(AM) Denver CO
WJWK(AM) Seaford DE
WGTX(AM) De Funiak Springs FL
WIPC(AM) Lake Wales FL
WTMY(AM) Sarasota FL
WLCG(AM) Macon GA
KCOB(AM) Newton IA
WBIG(AM) Aurora IL
WGBF(AM) Evansville IN
KSOK(AM) Arkansas City KS
WCPM(AM) Cumberland KY
WODT(AM) New Orleans LA
WEIM(AM) Fitchburg MA
WFAU(AM) Gardiner ME
WFYC(AM) Alma MI
WWTC(AM) Minneapolis MN
KVOX(AM) Moorhead MN
KDKD(AM) Clinton MO
KYRO(AM) Potosi MO
WSAT(AM) Salisbury NC
WYAL(AM) Scotland Neck NC
KCNI(AM) Broken Bow NE
KRZE(AM) Farmington NM
KDOX(AM) Henderson NV
WADO(AM) New York NY
WHTK(AM) Rochester NY
WONW(AM) Defiance OH
KPRV(AM) Poteau OK
KRVM(AM) Eugene OR
WFBS(AM) Berwick PA

Broadcasting & Cable Yearbook 2006
D-650

U.S. AM Stations by Frequency

WHVR(AM) Hanover PA
WJST(AM) New Castle PA
WCMN(AM) Arecibo PR
WANS(AM) Anderson SC
WJAY(AM) Mullins SC
WMCP(AM) Columbia TN
WDNT(AM) Dayton TN
KSLI(AM) Abilene TX
KWHI(AM) Brenham TX
KVWG(AM) Pearsall TX
KZNS(AM) Salt Lake City UT
WOWZ(AM) Appomattox VA
WYVE(AM) Wytheville VA
KLDY(AM) Lacey WA
KPTQ(AM) Spokane WA
KIT(AM) Yakima WA
WGLR(AM) Lancaster WI
WNAM(AM) Neenah-Menasha WI

1290 khz
WOPP(AM) Opp AL
WBTG(AM) Sheffield AL
WYEA(AM) Sylacauga AL
KDMS(AM) El Dorado AR
KUOA(AM) Siloam Springs AR
KCUB(AM) Tucson AZ
KPAY(AM) Chico CA
KAZA(AM) Gilroy CA
KKDD(AM) San Bernardino CA
KZSB(AM) Santa Barbara CA
WTMI(AM) West Hartford CT
WWTX(AM) Wilmington DE
WCFI(AM) Ocala FL
WPCF(AM) Panama City Beach FL
WJNO(AM) West Palm Beach FL
WCHK(AM) Canton GA
WTKS(AM) Savannah GA
KOUU(AM) Pocatello ID
WIRL(AM) Peoria IL
KWLS(AM) Pratt KS
WCBL(AM) Benton KY
WKLB(AM) Manchester KY
KJEF(AM) Jennings LA
WNIL(AM) Niles MI
WLBY(AM) Saline MI
KBMO(AM) Benson MN
KALM(AM) Thayer MO
WJBI(AM) Batesville MS
WNBN(AM) Meridian MS
WTYL(AM) Tylertown MS
KGVO(AM) Missoula MT
WHKY(AM) Hickory NC
WJCV(AM) Jacksonville NC
WXKL(AM) Sanford NC
KKAR(AM) Omaha NE
WKBK(AM) Keene NH
WNBF(AM) Binghamton NY
WOMP(AM) Bellaire OH
WHIO(AM) Dayton OH
KKSL(AM) Lake Oswego OR
KUMA(AM) Pendleton OR
WFBG(AM) Altoona PA
WRNI(AM) Providence RI
WQMC(AM) Sumter SC
WATO(AM) Oak Ridge TN
KIVY(AM) Crockett TX
KRGE(AM) Weslaco TX
KWFS(AM) Wichita Falls TX
WDZY(AM) Colonial Heights VA
WRRA(AM) Frederiksted VI
KIKN(AM) Port Angeles WA
WMCS(AM) Greenfield WI
WKLJ(AM) Sparta WI
WVOW(AM) Logan WV
KOWB(AM) Laramie WY

1300 khz
WBSA(AM) Boaz AL
WTLS(AM) Tallassee AL
WKXM(AM) Winfield AL
KWCK(AM) Searcy AR
KROP(AM) Brawley CA
KYNO(AM) Fresno CA
*KPMO(AM) Mendocino CA
KAZN(AM) Pasadena CA
KKML(AM) Colorado Springs CO
WAVZ(AM) New Haven CT
WTIR(AM) Cocoa Beach FL

WFFG(AM) Marathon FL
WQBN(AM) Temple Terrace FL
WMTM(AM) Moultrie GA
WNEA(AM) Newnan GA
WIMO(AM) Winder GA
KGLO(AM) Mason City IA
KLER(AM) Orofino ID
WRDZ(AM) La Grange IL
WFRX(AM) West Frankfort IL
WBZQ(AM) Huntington IN
WBOW(AM) Terre Haute IN
WLXG(AM) Lexington KY
WIBR(AM) Baton Rouge LA
KSYB(AM) Shreveport LA
WJDA(AM) Quincy MA
WJFK(AM) Baltimore MD
WOOD(AM) Grand Rapids MI
WQPM(AM) Princeton MN
KMMO(AM) Marshall MO
WOAD(AM) Jackson MS
WLNC(AM) Laurinburg NC
WSYD(AM) Mount Airy NC
KBRL(AM) McCook NE
WPNH(AM) Plymouth NH
WIMG(AM) Ewing NJ
KPTL(AM) Carson City NV
WAMF(AM) Fulton NY
WXRL(AM) Lancaster NY
WTMM(AM) Rensselaer NY
WRCR(AM) Spring Valley NY
WERE(AM) Cleveland OH
WMVO(AM) Mount Vernon OH
KAKC(AM) Tulsa OK
*KAPL(AM) Phoenix OR
KACI(AM) The Dalles OR
WWCH(AM) Clarion PA
WKZN(AM) West Hazleton PA
WTIL(AM) Mayaguez PR
WCKI(AM) Greer SC
WKSC(AM) Kershaw SC
KOLY(AM) Mobridge SD
WMTN(AM) Morristown TN
WNQM(AM) Nashville TN
KVET(AM) Austin TX
KKUB(AM) Brownfield TX
KLAR(AM) Laredo TX
KSET(AM) Silsbee TX
WKCY(AM) Harrisonburg VA
KKOL(AM) Seattle WA
WCLG(AM) Morgantown WV
WJYP(AM) Saint Albans WV

1310 khz
WHEP(AM) Foley AL
WJUS(AM) Marion AL
WQAH(AM) Priceville AL
KBOK(AM) Malvern AR
KXAM(AM) Mesa AZ
KIQQ(AM) Barstow CA
KFVR(AM) Crescent City CA
KMKY(AM) Oakland CA
KFKA(AM) Greeley CO
WICH(AM) Norwich CT
WYND(AM) De Land FL
WAUC(AM) Wauchula FL
WPBC(AM) Decatur GA
WOKA(AM) Douglas GA
WPLV(AM) West Point GA
KOKX(AM) Keokuk IA
KDLS(AM) Perry IA
KLIX(AM) Twin Falls ID
WTLC(AM) Indianapolis IN
KFLA(AM) Scott City KS
WTTL(AM) Madisonville KY
WDOC(AM) Prestonsburg KY
KEZM(AM) Sulphur LA
KMBS(AM) West Monroe LA
WORC(AM) Worcester MA
WLOB(AM) Portland ME
WDTW(AM) Dearborn MI
WCCW(AM) Traverse City MI
KRBI(AM) Saint Peter MN
KACE(AM) Birch Tree MO
KOCR(AM) Joplin MO
KEIN(AM) Great Falls MT
WISE(AM) Asheville NC
WGSP(AM) Charlotte NC

WTIK(AM) Durham NC
KNOX(AM) Grand Forks ND
KGMT(AM) Fairbury NE
WADB(AM) Asbury Park NJ
WEMG(AM) Camden NJ
WXMC(AM) Parsippany-Troy Hills NJ
KKNS(AM) Corrales NM
WRSB(AM) Canandaigua NY
WVIP(AM) Mount Kisco NY
WTLB(AM) Utica NY
WDPN(AM) Alliance OH
KNPT(AM) Newport OR
WBFD(AM) Bedford PA
WTZN(AM) Troy PA
WNAE(AM) Warren PA
WDKD(AM) Kingstree SC
WDOD(AM) Chattanooga TN
WDXI(AM) Jackson TN
WOCV(AM) Oneida TN
KZIP(AM) Amarillo TX
KTCK(AM) Dallas TX
KAHL(AM) San Antonio TX
WDCT(AM) Fairfax VA
WCMS(AM) Newport News VA
KZXR(AM) Prosser WA
WIBA(AM) Madison WI
WSLW(AM) White Sulphur Springs WV

1320 khz
WZZK(AM) Birmingham AL
WAGF(AM) Dothan AL
KYHN(AM) Fort Smith AR
KRLW(AM) Walnut Ridge AR
*KAWC(AM) Yuma AZ
KSDT(AM) Hemet CA
*KKSM(AM) Oceanside CA
KCTC(AM) Sacramento CA
WATR(AM) Waterbury CT
WLQY(AM) Hollywood FL
WJGR(AM) Jacksonville FL
WDDV(AM) Venice FL
WHIE(AM) Griffin GA
KNIA(AM) Knoxville IA
KMAQ(AM) Maquoketa IA
WKAN(AM) Kankakee IL
KLWN(AM) Lawrence KS
WBRT(AM) Bardstown KY
WCVG(AM) Covington KY
WNGO(AM) Mayfield KY
KNCB(AM) Vivian LA
WARL(AM) Attleboro MA
WICO(AM) Salisbury MD
WILS(AM) Lansing MI
WDMJ(AM) Marquette MI
KOZY(AM) Grand Rapids MN
KSIV(AM) Clayton MO
WRJW(AM) Picayune MS
WCOG(AM) Greensboro NC
WKRK(AM) Murphy NC
KHRT(AM) Minot ND
KOLT(AM) Scottsbluff NE
WDER(AM) Derry NH
KRDD(AM) Roswell NM
WHHO(AM) Hornell NY
WLOH(AM) Lancaster OH
WOBL(AM) Oberlin OH
KCLI(AM) Clinton OK
KSCR(AM) Eugene OR
WTKZ(AM) Allentown PA
WGET(AM) Gettysburg PA
WJAS(AM) Pittsburgh PA
WSKN(AM) San Juan PR
WISW(AM) Columbia SC
KELO(AM) Sioux Falls SD
WKIN(AM) Kingsport TN
WMSR(AM) Manchester TN
KVMC(AM) Colorado City TX
KXYZ(AM) Houston TX
KFNZ(AM) Salt Lake City UT
WVGM(AM) Lynchburg VA
WVNZ(AM) Richmond VA
WWWT(AM) Randolph VT
KXRO(AM) Aberdeen WA
KGDC(AM) Walla Walla WA
WFHR(AM) Wisconsin Rapids WI

1330 khz
WPRN(AM) Butler AL
WZCT(AM) Scottsboro AL
KXXA(AM) Conway AR
KJLL(AM) South Tucson AZ
KWKW(AM) Los Angeles CA
KLBS(AM) Los Banos CA
KJPR(AM) Shasta Lake City CA
WJNX(AM) Fort Pierce FL
WWAB(AM) Lakeland FL
WEBY(AM) Milton FL
WCVC(AM) Tallahassee FL
WLBB(AM) Carrollton GA
WMLT(AM) Dublin GA
WGTJ(AM) Murrayville GA
KWLO(AM) Waterloo IA
WKTA(AM) Evanston IL
WRAM(AM) Monmouth IL
WNTA(AM) Rockford IL
WVHI(AM) Evansville IN
WTRE(AM) Greensburg IN
KNSS(AM) Wichita KS
WKDP(AM) Corbin KY
WMOR(AM) Morehead KY
KVOL(AM) Lafayette LA
WRCA(AM) Waltham MA
WJSS(AM) Havre de Grace MD
WTRX(AM) Flint MI
WLOL(AM) Minneapolis MN
KUKU(AM) Willow Springs MO
WNIX(AM) Greenville MS
WANG(AM) Havelock NC
KGAK(AM) Gallup NM
*WWRV(AM) New York NY
WEBO(AM) Owego NY
WSPQ(AM) Springville NY
WHAZ(AM) Troy NY
WGFT(AM) Campbell OH
WFIN(AM) Findlay OH
WYPC(AM) Wellston OH
WELW(AM) Willoughby-Eastlake OH
KKPZ(AM) Portland OR
WFNN(AM) Erie PA
WBHV(AM) Somerset PA
WENA(AM) Yauco PR
WPJS(AM) Conway SC
WYRD(AM) Greenville SC
WAEW(AM) Crossville TN
KMIL(AM) Cameron TX
KSWA(AM) Graham TX
KINE(AM) Kingsville TX
KLBO(AM) Monahans TX
KGLD(AM) Tyler TX
WBTM(AM) Danville VA
WRAA(AM) Luray VA
WOLD(AM) Marion VA
WESR(AM) Onley-Onancock VA
KENU(AM) Enumclaw WA
*KMBI(AM) Spokane WA
WHBL(AM) Sheboygan WI
WETZ(AM) New Martinsville WV
KOVE(AM) Lander WY

1340 khz
WFMH(AM) Cullman AL
WSBM(AM) Florence AL
WMRK(AM) Selma AL
WFEB(AM) Sylacauga AL
KBTA(AM) Batesville AR
KZNG(AM) Hot Springs AR
*KCAT(AM) Pine Bluff AR
KIKO(AM) Miami AZ
KPGE(AM) Page AZ
KATA(AM) Arcata CA
KWXY(AM) Cathedral City CA
KCBL(AM) Fresno CA
KOMY(AM) La Selva Beach CA
KTPI(AM) Mojave CA
KTOX(AM) Needles CA
KEWE(AM) Oroville CA
KYNS(AM) San Luis Obispo CA
KIST(AM) Santa Barbara CA
*KCFR(AM) Denver CO
KTMM(AM) Grand Junction CO
KVRH(AM) Salida CO
WYBC(AM) New Haven CT
WYCB(AM) Washington DC
WTAN(AM) Clearwater FL

WWFL(AM) Clermont FL
WROD(AM) Daytona Beach FL
WDSR(AM) Lake City FL
WPBR(AM) Lantana FL
WTYS(AM) Marianna FL
WITS(AM) Sebring FL
WFSH(AM) Valparaiso-Niceville FL
WGAU(AM) Athens GA
WALR(AM) Atlanta GA
WSGF(AM) Augusta GA
WGAA(AM) Cedartown GA
WOKS(AM) Columbus GA
WBBT(AM) Lyons GA
WALH(AM) Mountain City GA
WTIF(AM) Tifton GA
KROS(AM) Clinton IA
KACH(AM) Preston ID
WSOY(AM) Decatur IL
WJPF(AM) Herrin IL
WJOL(AM) Joliet IL
WBIW(AM) Bedford IN
WTRC(AM) Elkhart IN
WXFN(AM) Muncie IN
KCKN(AM) Kansas City KS
KSEK(AM) Pittsburg KS
WCMI(AM) Ashland KY
WBGN(AM) Bowling Green KY
WKCB(AM) Hindman KY
WNBS(AM) Murray KY
WEKY(AM) Richmond KY
KRMD(AM) Shreveport LA
WGAW(AM) Gardner MA
WNBH(AM) New Bedford MA
WBRK(AM) Pittsfield MA
*WMDR(AM) Augusta ME
WNZS(AM) Veazie ME
WLEW(AM) Bad Axe MI
WBBL(AM) Grand Rapids MI
WCSR(AM) Hillsdale MI
WMTE(AM) Manistee MI
WAGN(AM) Menominee MI
WMBN(AM) Petoskey MI
WEXL(AM) Royal Oak MI
KVBR(AM) Brainerd MN
KDLM(AM) Detroit Lakes MN
KRBT(AM) Eveleth MN
KROC(AM) Rochester MN
KWLM(AM) Willmar MN
KXEO(AM) Mexico MO
KLID(AM) Poplar Bluff MO
KSMO(AM) Salem MO
KADI(AM) Springfield MO
WKOZ(AM) Kosciusko MS
WAML(AM) Laurel MS
KCAP(AM) Helena MT
KPRK(AM) Livingston MT
KYLT(AM) Missoula MT
WDCR(AM) Hanover NH
WWNH(AM) Madbury NH
WMID(AM) Atlantic City NJ
KCQL(AM) Aztec NM
KSSR(AM) Santa Rosa NM
KVOT(AM) Taos NM
KTSN(AM) Elko NV
KRLV(AM) Las Vegas NV
KXEQ(AM) Reno NV
WWLF(AM) Auburn NY
WENT(AM) Gloversville NY
WKSN(AM) Jamestown NY
WLVL(AM) Lockport NY
WMSA(AM) Massena NY
WALL(AM) Middletown NY
WIRY(AM) Plattsburgh NY
WNCO(AM) Ashland OH
*WOUB(AM) Athens OH
WIZE(AM) Springfield OH

Broadcasting & Cable Yearbook 2006

U.S. AM Stations by Frequency

WSTV(AM) Steubenville OH
KIHN(AM) Hugo OK
KEBC(AM) Midwest City OK
KTFX(AM) Sand Springs OK
KLOO(AM) Corvallis OR
KWVR(AM) Enterprise OR
KIHR(AM) Hood River OR
KBBR(AM) North Bend OR
WPNT(AM) Connellsville PA
*WSAJ(AM) Grove City PA
WOYL(AM) Oil City PA
WHAT(AM) Philadelphia PA
WYCK(AM) Plains PA
WRAW(AM) Reading PA
WTRN(AM) Tyrone PA
WWPA(AM) Williamsport PA
WWNA(AM) Aguadilla PR
WQSC(AM) Charleston SC
WRHI(AM) Rock Hill SC
WSSC(AM) Sumter SC
KIJV(AM) Huron SD
KTOQ(AM) Rapid City SD
WBAC(AM) Cleveland TN
WKRM(AM) Columbia TN
WGRV(AM) Greeneville TN
WKGN(AM) Knoxville TN
WLOK(AM) Memphis TN
WCDT(AM) Winchester TN
KWKC(AM) Abilene TX
KRHC(AM) Burnet TX
KAND(AM) Corsicana TX
KVIV(AM) El Paso TX
KKAM(AM) Lubbock TX
KRBA(AM) Lufkin TX
KOLE(AM) Port Arthur TX
KCRN(AM) San Angelo TX
KVNN(AM) Victoria TX
WKEY(AM) Covington VA
WHAP(AM) Hopewell VA
WVCV(AM) Orange VA
WSTA(AM) Charlotte Amalie VI
WVNR(AM) Poultney VT
WSTJ(AM) Saint Johnsbury VT
KLKI(AM) Anacortes WA
KTCR(AM) Kennewick WA
KVSN(AM) Tumwater WA
KWWX(AM) Wenatchee WA
WLDY(AM) Ladysmith WI
WJYI(AM) Milwaukee WI
WXKX(AM) Clarksburg WV
WEPM(AM) Martinsburg WV
WMON(AM) Montgomery WV
WELA(AM) Welch WV
KSGT(AM) Jackson WY
KYCN(AM) Wheatland WY
KWOR(AM) Worland WY

1350 khz
WELB(AM) Elba AL
WGAD(AM) Gadsden AL
KZTD(AM) Cabot AR
KBID(AM) Bakersfield CA
KTDD(AM) San Bernardino CA
KSRO(AM) Santa Rosa CA
KGHF(AM) Pueblo CO
WNLK(AM) Norwalk CT
WINY(AM) Putnam CT
WMMV(AM) Cocoa FL
WDCF(AM) Dade City FL
WCRM(AM) Fort Myers FL
WFNS(AM) Blackshear GA
WRWH(AM) Cleveland GA
WNNG(AM) Warner Robins GA
KRNT(AM) Des Moines IA
KRLC(AM) Lewiston ID
KTIK(AM) Nampa ID
WOAM(AM) Peoria IL
WJBD(AM) Salem IL
WIOU(AM) Kokomo IN
KMAN(AM) Manhattan KS
WLOU(AM) Louisville KY
WSMB(AM) New Orleans LA
WGDN(AM) Gladwin MI
KCHK(AM) New Prague MN
KDIO(AM) Ortonville MN
WCMP(AM) Pine City MN
KCHR(AM) Charleston MO

KWMO(AM) Washington MO
WKCU(AM) Corinth MS
WQNX(AM) Aberdeen NC
WZNN(AM) Black Mountain NC
WHIP(AM) Mooresville NC
WLLY(AM) Wilson NC
KBRX(AM) O'Neill NE
WEZS(AM) Laconia NH
WHWH(AM) Princeton NJ
KABQ(AM) Albuquerque NM
WCBA(AM) Corning NY
WRNY(AM) Rome NY
WARF(AM) Akron OH
WCSM(AM) Celina OH
WCHI(AM) Chillicothe OH
KPNS(AM) Duncan OK
KTLQ(AM) Tahlequah OK
WOYK(AM) York PA
WEGA(AM) Vega Baja PR
WPFM(AM) Darlington SC
WRKM(AM) Carthage TN
KCAR(AM) Clarksville TX
KCOX(AM) Jasper TX
KCOR(AM) San Antonio TX
WYSK(AM) Fredericksburg VA
WNVA(AM) Norton VA
WGPL(AM) Portsmouth VA
WPDR(AM) Portage WI

1360 khz
WIXI(AM) Jasper AL
WMOB(AM) Mobile AL
WMFC(AM) Monroeville AL
WELR(AM) Roanoke AL
KLYR(AM) Clarksville AR
KFFA(AM) Helena AR
KPXQ(AM) Glendale AZ
KFIV(AM) Modesto CA
KWDJ(AM) Ridgecrest CA
KLSD(AM) San Diego CA
KHNC(AM) Johnstown CO
WDRC(AM) Hartford CT
WHNR(AM) Cypress Gardens FL
WCGL(AM) Jacksonville FL
WKAT(AM) North Miami FL
WHCG(AM) Metter GA
WGJK(AM) Rome GA
KMJM(AM) Cedar Rapids IA
KBKB(AM) Fort Madison IA
KSCJ(AM) Sioux City IA
WLBK(AM) De Kalb IL
WVMC(AM) Mount Carmel IL
WGFA(AM) Watseka IL
KAHS(AM) El Dorado KS
WFLW(AM) Monticello KY
KNIR(AM) New Iberia LA
KBYO(AM) Tallulah LA
WLYN(AM) Lynn MA
WKYO(AM) Caro MI
WKMI(AM) Kalamazoo MI
KKBJ(AM) Bemidji MN
KRWC(AM) Buffalo MN
KMRN(AM) Cameron MO
KELE(AM) Mountain Grove MO
WFFF(AM) Columbia MS
WCHL(AM) Chapel Hill NC
*KNGN(AM) McCook NE
WNNJ(AM) Newton NJ
WNJC(AM) Washington Township NJ
KBUY(AM) Ruidoso NM
WYOS(AM) Binghamton NY
WOEN(AM) Olean NY
WSAI(AM) Cincinnati OH
WOW(AM) Conneaut OH
KOHU(AM) Hermiston OR
KUIK(AM) Hillsboro OR
WPTT(AM) McKeesport PA
WPPA(AM) Pottsville PA
WELP(AM) Easley SC
WBLC(AM) Lenoir City TN
WNAH(AM) Nashville TN
KDJW(AM) Amarillo TX
KACT(AM) Andrews TX
KWWJ(AM) Baytown TX
KKTX(AM) Corpus Christi TX
KMNY(AM) Hurst TX
WWWJ(AM) Galax VA

WHBG(AM) Harrisonburg VA
KKMO(AM) Tacoma WA
WTAQ(AM) Green Bay WI
WVRQ(AM) Viroqua WI
WHJC(AM) Matewan WV
WMOV(AM) Ravenswood WV
KRKK(AM) Rock Springs WY

1370 khz
WBYE(AM) Calera AL
KAWW(AM) Heber Springs AR
KTPA(AM) Prescott AR
KWRM(AM) Corona CA
KPCO(AM) Quincy CA
KZSF(AM) San Jose CA
KGEN(AM) Tulare CA
WOCA(AM) Ocala FL
WCOA(AM) Pensacola FL
WZTA(AM) Vero Beach FL
WGHC(AM) Clayton GA
WLOP(AM) Jesup GA
WFDR(AM) Manchester GA
WLOV(AM) Washington GA
KUPA(AM) Pearl City HI
KDTH(AM) Dubuque IA
WLLM(AM) Lincoln IL
WGCL(AM) Bloomington IN
WLTH(AM) Gary IN
KGNO(AM) Dodge City KS
KALN(AM) Iola KS
WJQI(AM) Fort Campbell KY
WGOH(AM) Grayson KY
WTKY(AM) Tompkinsville KY
WWLG(AM) Pikesville MD
WDEA(AM) Ellsworth ME
WLJW(AM) Cadillac MI
WGHN(AM) Grand Haven MI
KSUM(AM) Fairmont MN
KWRT(AM) Boonville MO
KCRV(AM) Caruthersville MO
WMGO(AM) Canton MS
KXTL(AM) Butte MT
WLTC(AM) Gastonia NC
*WLLN(AM) Lillington NC
WTAB(AM) Tabor City NC
*KWTL(AM) Grand Forks ND
KAWL(AM) York NE
WFEA(AM) Manchester NH
WALK(AM) East Patchogue NY
WRWD(AM) Ellenville NY
*WXXI(AM) Rochester NY
WSPD(AM) Toledo OH
KAST(AM) Astoria OR
WWCB(AM) Corry PA
WPAZ(AM) Pottstown PA
WKMC(AM) Roaring Spring PA
WIVV(AM) Vieques PR
WDEF(AM) Chattanooga TN
WDXE(AM) Lawrenceburg TN
WRGS(AM) Rogersville TN
KFRO(AM) Longview TX
KJCE(AM) Rollingwood TX
KSOP(AM) South Salt Lake UT
WHEE(AM) Martinsville VA
WSHV(AM) South Hill VA
WBTN(AM) Bennington VT
KWNC(AM) Quincy WA
WCCN(AM) Neillsville WI
*WVMR(AM) Frost WV
WVLY(AM) Moundsville WV

1380 khz
WRAB(AM) Arab AL
WGYV(AM) Greenville AL
WVSA(AM) Vernon AL
KDXE(AM) North Little Rock AR
KLPZ(AM) Parker AZ
KWJL(AM) Lancaster CA
KTKZ(AM) Sacramento CA
KZFX(AM) Salinas CA
WFNW(AM) Naugatuck CT
WTMC(AM) Wilmington DE
WWRF(AM) Lake Worth FL
WELE(AM) Ormond Beach FL
WWMI(AM) Saint Petersburg FL
WAOK(AM) Atlanta GA
KCIM(AM) Carroll IA
KCII(AM) Washington IA

WTJK(AM) South Beloit IL
WKJG(AM) Fort Wayne IN
KCNW(AM) Fairway KS
WMTA(AM) Central City KY
WMJR(AM) Winchester KY
WPYR(AM) Baton Rouge LA
WSCG(AM) Greenville MI
WPHM(AM) Port Huron MI
KLIZ(AM) Brainerd MN
KAGE(AM) Winona MN
KSLG(AM) Saint Louis MO
WNLA(AM) Indianola MS
WTOB(AM) Winston-Salem NC
KUVR(AM) Holdrege NE
WMYF(AM) Portsmouth NH
WABH(AM) Bath NY
WKDM(AM) New York NY
WDLW(AM) Lorain OH
KXCA(AM) Lawton OK
KMUS(AM) Sperry OK
KSRV(AM) Ontario OR
WTYM(AM) Kittanning PA
WMLP(AM) Milton PA
WCBG(AM) Waynesboro PA
WOLA(AM) Barranquitas PR
WNRI(AM) Woonsocket RI
WAGS(AM) Bishopville SC
WPCH(AM) North Augusta SC
KOTA(AM) Rapid City SD
KQKD(AM) Redfield SD
WYSH(AM) Clinton TN
WHEW(AM) Franklin TN
WLRM(AM) Millington TN
KRCM(AM) Beaumont TX
KBWD(AM) Brownwood TX
KHEY(AM) El Paso TX
KFNI(AM) Pleasanton TX
WLRV(AM) Lebanon VA
WBTK(AM) Richmond VA
WSYB(AM) Rutland VT
KRKO(AM) Everett WA
WFCL(AM) Clintonville WI
WMTD(AM) Hinton WV
KJUA(AM) Cheyenne WY

1390 khz
WHMA(AM) Anniston AL
KDQN(AM) De Queen AR
KFFK(AM) Rogers AR
KLTX(AM) Long Beach CA
KLOC(AM) Turlock CA
*KGNU(AM) Denver CO
WAVP(AM) Avon Park FL
WAJD(AM) Gainesville FL
WISK(AM) Americus GA
WTNL(AM) Reidsville GA
KCLN(AM) Clinton IA
WGRB(AM) Chicago IL
WFIW(AM) Fairfield IL
WZZB(AM) Seymour IN
KNCK(AM) Concordia KS
WANY(AM) Albany KY
WKIC(AM) Hazard KY
KFRA(AM) Franklin LA
WPLM(AM) Plymouth MA
WEGP(AM) Presque Isle ME
WLCM(AM) Charlotte MI
KRFO(AM) Owatonna MN
KXSS(AM) Waite Park MN
KJPW(AM) Waynesville MO
WROA(AM) Gulfport MS
WMER(AM) Meridian MS
WEED(AM) Rocky Mount NC
WADA(AM) Shelby NC
WJRM(AM) Troy NC
KRRZ(AM) Minot ND
KENN(AM) Farmington NM
KHOB(AM) Hobbs NM
WEOK(AM) Poughkeepsie NY
WRIV(AM) Riverhead NY
WFBL(AM) Syracuse NY
WBLL(AM) Bellefontaine OH
WMPO(AM) Middleport-Pomeroy OH
WNIO(AM) Youngstown OH
KCRC(AM) Enid OK
KSLM(AM) Salem OR
WLAN(AM) Lancaster PA

WRSC(AM) State College PA
WISA(AM) Isabela PR
WLUA(AM) Belton SC
WXTC(AM) Charleston SC
KJAM(AM) Madison SD
WYXI(AM) Athens TN
WTJS(AM) Jackson TN
WMCT(AM) Mountain City TN
KULP(AM) El Campo TX
KBEC(AM) Waxahachie TX
KLGN(AM) Logan UT
WZHF(AM) Arlington VA
WKPA(AM) Lynchburg VA
WVAA(AM) Burlington VT
KJOX(AM) Yakima WA
WRIG(AM) Schofield WI
WKLP(AM) Keyser WV

1400 khz
WWTM(AM) Decatur AL
WXAL(AM) Demopolis AL
WJLD(AM) Fairfield AL
WFPA(AM) Fort Payne AL
WANI(AM) Opelika AL
KELD(AM) El Dorado AR
KCLA(AM) Pine Bluff AR
KWYN(AM) Wynne AR
KSUN(AM) Phoenix AZ
KRVZ(AM) Springerville-Eagar AZ
KTUC(AM) Tucson AZ
KJOK(AM) Yuma AZ
KVTO(AM) Berkeley CA
KESQ(AM) Indio CA
KQMS(AM) Redding CA
KKJL(AM) San Luis Obispo CA
KUNX(AM) Santa Paula CA
KUKI(AM) Ukiah CA
KVBL(AM) Visalia CA
KRLN(AM) Canon City CO
KDTA(AM) Delta CO
KFTM(AM) Fort Morgan CO
KBLJ(AM) La Junta CO
KWUF(AM) Pagosa Springs CO
WSTC(AM) Stamford CT
WILI(AM) Willimantic CT
WFLL(AM) Fort Lauderdale FL
WIRA(AM) Fort Pierce FL
WBAU(AM) Fort Walton Beach FL
WZAZ(AM) Jacksonville FL
WPRY(AM) Perry FL
WSDO(AM) Sanford FL
WZHR(AM) Zephyrhills FL
WAJQ(AM) Alma GA
WLTA(AM) Alpharetta GA
WSGC(AM) Elberton GA
WNEX(AM) Macon GA
WHBS(AM) Moultrie GA
WCOH(AM) Newnan GA
WHGM(AM) Savannah GA
KCOG(AM) Centerville IA
KADR(AM) Elkader IA
KVFD(AM) Fort Dodge IA
KART(AM) Jerome ID
KRPL(AM) Moscow ID
KIGO(AM) Saint Anthony ID
KSPT(AM) Sandpoint ID
WDWS(AM) Champaign IL
WGIL(AM) Galesburg IL
WEOA(AM) Evansville IN
WBAT(AM) Marion IN
KVOE(AM) Emporia KS
KAYS(AM) Hays KS
WCYN(AM) Cynthiana KY
WIEL(AM) Elizabethtown KY
WFTG(AM) London KY
WFPR(AM) Hammond LA
KAOK(AM) Lake Charles LA
KWLA(AM) Many LA
WHTB(AM) Fall River MA
WLLH(AM) Lowell MA
WHMP(AM) Northampton MA
WWIN(AM) Baltimore MD
WJZN(AM) Augusta ME
WVAE(AM) Biddeford ME
WWNZ(AM) Veazie ME
WRCC(AM) Battle Creek MI
WDTK(AM) Detroit MI

U.S. AM Stations by Frequency

*WLJN(AM) Elmwood Township MI
WCCY(AM) Houghton MI
WQXO(AM) Munising MI
WSAM(AM) Saginaw MI
WSJM(AM) Saint Joseph MI
WKNW(AM) Sault Ste. Marie MI
KEYL(AM) Long Prairie MN
KMHL(AM) Marshall MN
KLBB(AM) Saint Paul MN
WEEP(AM) Virginia MN
KFRU(AM) Columbia MO
KJFF(AM) Festus MO
KSIM(AM) Sikeston MO
KGMY(AM) Springfield MO
WBIP(AM) Booneville MS
WJWF(AM) Columbus MS
WYKC(AM) Grenada MS
WFOR(AM) Hattiesburg MS
WKXI(AM) Jackson MS
KBCK(AM) Deer Lodge MT
KXGN(AM) Glendive MT
KXGF(AM) Great Falls MT
WKEW(AM) Greensboro NC
WMFA(AM) Raeford NC
WSIC(AM) Statesville NC
WMXF(AM) Waynesville NC
WSMY(AM) Weldon NC
KQDJ(AM) Jamestown ND
KBRB(AM) Ainsworth NE
KCOW(AM) Alliance NE
KLIN(AM) Lincoln NE
WTSL(AM) Hanover NH
WLTN(AM) Littleton NH
WOND(AM) Pleasantville NJ
KVSF(AM) Santa Fe NM
KCHS(AM) Truth or Consequences NM
KTNM(AM) Tucumcari NM
KSHP(AM) North Las Vegas NV
KBDB(AM) Sparks NV
KWNA(AM) Winnemucca NV
WAMC(AM) Albany NY
WWWS(AM) Buffalo NY
WDNY(AM) Dansville NY
WSLB(AM) Ogdensburg NY
WMAN(AM) Mansfield OH
WPAY(AM) Portsmouth OH
KWON(AM) Bartlesville OK
KTMC(AM) McAlester OK
KREF(AM) Norman OK
KNND(AM) Cottage Grove OR
KJDY(AM) John Day OR
KBCH(AM) Lincoln City OR
WEST(AM) Easton PA
WJET(AM) Erie PA
WTCY(AM) Harrisburg PA
WWGE(AM) Loretto PA
WKBI(AM) Saint Marys PA
WICK(AM) Scranton PA
WRAK(AM) Williamsport PA
WIDA(AM) Carolina PR
WCOS(AM) Columbia SC
WGTN(AM) Georgetown SC
WSPG(AM) Spartanburg SC
KBJM(AM) Lemmon SD
WJZM(AM) Clarksville TN
WHUB(AM) Cookeville TN
WLSB(AM) Copperhill TN
WKPT(AM) Kingsport TN
WGAP(AM) Maryville TN
WZNG(AM) Shelbyville TN
KRUN(AM) Ballinger TX
KBYG(AM) Big Spring TX
KUNO(AM) Corpus Christi TX
*KHCB(AM) Galveston TX
KGVL(AM) Greenville TX
*KHCH(AM) Huntsville TX
KEBE(AM) Jacksonville TX
KIUN(AM) Pecos TX
KEYE(AM) Perryton TX
KREW(AM) Plainview TX
KVRP(AM) Stamford TX
KTEM(AM) Temple TX
KEWL(AM) Texarkana TX
KVOU(AM) Uvalde TX
KENT(AM) Parowan UT
KSRR(AM) Provo UT
WKAV(AM) Charlottesville VA

WHHV(AM) Hillsville VA
WPCE(AM) Portsmouth VA
WINC(AM) Winchester VA
KLCK(AM) Goldendale WA
KEDO(AM) Longview WA
KRSC(AM) Othello WA
KITZ(AM) Silverdale WA
WATW(AM) Ashland WI
WBIZ(AM) Eau Claire WI
WDUZ(AM) Green Bay WI
WRJN(AM) Racine WI
WRDB(AM) Reedsburg WI
WOBG(AM) Clarksburg WV
WRON(AM) Ronceverte WV
WVRC(AM) Spencer WV
WBBD(AM) Wheeling WV
WBTH(AM) Williamson WV
KKTL(AM) Casper WY
KODI(AM) Cody WY

1410 khz
WLVV(AM) Mobile AL
WIQR(AM) Prattville AL
WZZA(AM) Tuscumbia AL
KTCS(AM) Fort Smith AR
KERN(AM) Bakersfield CA
KRML(AM) Carmel CA
KTME(AM) Lompoc CA
KMYC(AM) Marysville CA
KCAL(AM) Redlands CA
KIIX(AM) Fort Collins CO
WPOP(AM) Hartford CT
WDOV(AM) Dover DE
WMYR(AM) Fort Myers FL
WQBQ(AM) Leesburg FL
WHBT(AM) Tallahassee FL
WKKP(AM) McDonough GA
WYIS(AM) McRae GA
WLAQ(AM) Rome GA
KGRN(AM) Grinnell IA
KLEM(AM) Le Mars IA
WRMN(AM) Elgin IL
*WIHM(AM) Taylorville IL
WLAS(AM) Lafayette IN
KKLO(AM) Leavenworth KS
KGSO(AM) Wichita KS
WHLN(AM) Harlan KY
KDBS(AM) Alexandria LA
WMSX(AM) Brockton MA
WHAG(AM) Halfway MD
WNWZ(AM) Grand Rapids MI
KLFD(AM) Litchfield MN
KRWB(AM) Roseau MN
WDSK(AM) Cleveland MS
WEGO(AM) Concord NC
WSRC(AM) Durham NC
WVCB(AM) Shallotte NC
KHOL(AM) Beulah ND
KOOQ(AM) North Platte NE
WHTG(AM) Eatontown NJ
WDOE(AM) Dunkirk NY
WELM(AM) Elmira NY
WENU(AM) South Glens Falls NY
WNER(AM) Watertown NY
WING(AM) Dayton OH
KBNP(AM) Portland OR
WLSH(AM) Lansford PA
KQV(AM) Pittsburgh PA
WRSS(AM) San Sebastian PR
WPCC(AM) Clinton SC
WBBX(AM) Kingston TN
WCMT(AM) Martin TN
WSTN(AM) Somerville TN
KLVQ(AM) Athens TX
KNTX(AM) Bowie TX
KCUL(AM) Marshall TX
KRIL(AM) Odessa TX
KBAL(AM) San Saba TX
KNAL(AM) Victoria TX
WRIS(AM) Roanoke VA
WIZM(AM) La Crosse WI
WSCW(AM) South Charleston WV
KWYO(AM) Sheridan WY

1420 khz
WACT(AM) Tuscaloosa AL
KBHS(AM) Hot Springs AR
KPOC(AM) Pocahontas AR

KMOG(AM) Payson AZ
KTAN(AM) Sierra Vista AZ
KSTN(AM) Stockton CA
WLIS(AM) Old Saybrook CT
WDJA(AM) Delray Beach FL
WBRD(AM) Palmetto FL
WAOC(AM) Saint Augustine FL
WRCG(AM) Columbus GA
WATB(AM) Decatur GA
WPEH(AM) Louisville GA
WLET(AM) Toccoa GA
WKWN(AM) Trenton GA
KKEA(AM) Honolulu HI
WOC(AM) Davenport IA
WINI(AM) Murphysboro IL
WIMS(AM) Michigan City IN
KJCK(AM) Junction City KS
KULY(AM) Ulysses KS
WHBN(AM) Harrodsburg KY
WVJS(AM) Owensboro KY
KPEL(AM) Lafayette LA
WBSM(AM) New Bedford MA
WBEC(AM) Pittsfield MA
WFLT(AM) Flint MI
WKPR(AM) Kalamazoo MI
KTOE(AM) Mankato MN
KRLL(AM) California MO
KBTN(AM) Neosho MO
WQBC(AM) Vicksburg MS
WIGG(AM) Wiggins MS
WMYN(AM) Mayodan NC
*WGAS(AM) South Gastonia NC
WVOT(AM) Wilson NC
KHLP(AM) Omaha NE
WASR(AM) Wolfeboro NH
WNRS(AM) Herkimer NY
WACK(AM) Newark NY
WLNA(AM) Peekskill NY
WHK(AM) Cleveland OH
KTJS(AM) Hobart OK
KMHS(AM) Coos Bay OR
WCOJ(AM) Coatesville PA
WCED(AM) DuBois PA
WUKQ(AM) Ponce PR
WCRE(AM) Cheraw SC
KGIM(AM) Aberdeen SD
WEMB(AM) Erwin TN
WKSR(AM) Pulaski TN
KFYN(AM) Bonham TX
KPIR(AM) Granbury TX
KLFB(AM) Lubbock TX
KGNB(AM) New Braunfels TX
WAMV(AM) Amherst VA
WXGM(AM) Gloucester VA
WKCW(AM) Warrenton VA
WRSA(AM) Saint Albans VT
KITI(AM) Chehalis-Centralia WA
KRIZ(AM) Renton WA
KUJ(AM) Walla Walla WA
WJUB(AM) Plymouth WI
WTCR(AM) Kenova WV

1430 khz
WFHK(AM) Pell City AL
WRMG(AM) Red Bay AL
KHBM(AM) Monticello AR
KWST(AM) El Centro CA
KFIG(AM) Fresno CA
KJAY(AM) Sacramento CA
KMRB(AM) San Gabriel CA
KVVN(AM) Santa Clara CA
KEZW(AM) Aurora CO
WTMN(AM) Gainesville FL
WOIR(AM) Homestead FL
WLKF(AM) Lakeland FL
WLTG(AM) Panama City FL
WGFS(AM) Covington GA
WDAL(AM) Dalton GA
KASI(AM) Ames IA
WEEF(AM) Highland Park IL
WCMY(AM) Ottawa IL
WXNT(AM) Indianapolis IN
WXAM(AM) Buffalo KY
WYMC(AM) Mayfield KY
KMRC(AM) Morgan City LA
WPNI(AM) Amherst MA
WXKS(AM) Everett MA

WNAV(AM) Annapolis MD
WION(AM) Ionia MI
KNSP(AM) Staples MN
KKOZ(AM) Ava MO
KAOL(AM) Carrollton MO
WIL(AM) Saint Louis MO
WDEX(AM) Monroe NC
WMNC(AM) Morganton NC
WDJS(AM) Mount Olive NC
WRXO(AM) Roxboro NC
KRGI(AM) Grand Island NE
WNSW(AM) Newark NJ
KCRX(AM) Roswell NM
WENE(AM) Endicott NY
WFOB(AM) Fostoria OH
WCLT(AM) Newark OH
KALV(AM) Alva OK
KTBZ(AM) Tulsa OK
KYKN(AM) Keizer OR
WVAM(AM) Altoona PA
WNEL(AM) Caguas PR
WBLR(AM) Batesburg SC
WNFO(AM) Ridgeland SC
KBRK(AM) Brookings SD
WOWW(AM) Germantown TN
WPLN(AM) Madison TN
KROO(AM) Breckenridge TX
KEES(AM) Gladewater TX
KCOH(AM) Houston TX
KLO(AM) Ogden UT
WHAN(AM) Ashland VA
WKEX(AM) Blacksburg VA
WDIC(AM) Clinchco VA
KCLK(AM) Asotin WA
KBRC(AM) Mount Vernon WA
WBEV(AM) Beaver Dam WI
WQOQ(AM) Durand WI
WEIR(AM) Weirton WV

1440 khz
WLWI(AM) Montgomery AL
KITA(AM) Little Rock AR
KAZG(AM) Scottsdale AZ
KVON(AM) Napa CA
KDIF(AM) Riverside CA
KUHL(AM) Santa Maria CA
KRDZ(AM) Wray CO
WWCL(AM) Lehigh Acres FL
WPRD(AM) Winter Park FL
WGMI(AM) Bremen GA
WGIG(AM) Brunswick GA
WDXQ(AM) Cochran GA
KCHE(AM) Cherokee IA
KPTO(AM) Pocatello ID
WIBH(AM) Anna IL
WPRS(AM) Paris IL
WGEM(AM) Quincy IL
WROK(AM) Rockford IL
WPGW(AM) Portland IN
KMAJ(AM) Topeka KS
WCDS(AM) Glasgow KY
WYGH(AM) Paris KY
WEZJ(AM) Williamsburg KY
KMLB(AM) Monroe LA
WVEI(AM) Worcester MA
WJAE(AM) Westbrook ME
WMAX(AM) Bay City MI
WDOW(AM) Dowagiac MI
WMKM(AM) Inkster MI
KDIZ(AM) Golden Valley MN
WRBE(AM) Lucedale MS
WSEL(AM) Pontotoc MS
WBLA(AM) Elizabethtown NC
WLXN(AM) Lexington NC
KKXL(AM) Grand Forks ND
WMVB(AM) Millville NJ
WNYG(AM) Babylon NY
WFNY(AM) Gloversville NY
WJJL(AM) Niagara Falls NY
WSGO(AM) Oswego NY
WRGM(AM) Ontario OH
WHKZ(AM) Warren OH
KMED(AM) Medford OR
KODL(AM) The Dalles OR
WCDL(AM) Carbondale PA
WNPV(AM) Lansdale PA
WGLD(AM) Red Lion PA

WGVL(AM) Greenville SC
WJBS(AM) Holly Hill SC
WZYX(AM) Cowan TN
WHDM(AM) McKenzie TN
KPUR(AM) Amarillo TX
KEYS(AM) Corpus Christi TX
KETX(AM) Livingston TX
KELG(AM) Manor TX
KTNO(AM) University Park TX
WKLV(AM) Blackstone VA
WNFL(AM) Green Bay WI
WHIS(AM) Bluefield WV
WAJR(AM) Morgantown WV

1449 khz
V6AH(AM) Pohnpei FM

1450 khz
KLAM(AM) Cordova AK
KIAL(AM) Unalaska AK
WDNG(AM) Anniston AL
WZGX(AM) Bessemer AL
WDLK(AM) Dadeville AL
WWNT(AM) Dothan AL
WTKI(AM) Huntsville AL
WLAY(AM) Muscle Shoals AL
KNHD(AM) Camden AR
KENA(AM) Mena AR
KDAP(AM) Douglas AZ
KNOT(AM) Prescott AZ
KVSL(AM) Show Low AZ
KWFM(AM) Tucson AZ
KCIK(AM) Blue Lake CA
KFSD(AM) Escondido CA
KGAM(AM) Palm Springs CA
KTIP(AM) Porterville CA
KEST(AM) San Francisco CA
KVML(AM) Sonora CA
KVEN(AM) Ventura CA
KOBO(AM) Yuba City CA
KGIW(AM) Alamosa CO
KSKE(AM) Buena Vista CO
KAVP(AM) Colona CO
KGRE(AM) Greeley CO
WCUM(AM) Bridgeport CT
WOL(AM) Washington DC
WILM(AM) Wilmington DE
WWJB(AM) Brooksville FL
WMFJ(AM) Daytona Beach FL
WOCN(AM) Miami FL
WBSR(AM) Pensacola FL
WSRQ(AM) Sarasota FL
WSTU(AM) Stuart FL
WTAL(AM) Tallahassee FL
WGPC(AM) Albany GA
WBHF(AM) Cartersville GA
WCON(AM) Cornelia GA
WKEU(AM) Griffin GA
WMVG(AM) Milledgeville GA
WVLD(AM) Valdosta GA
KMRY(AM) Cedar Rapids IA
KBFI(AM) Bonners Ferry ID
KVSI(AM) Montpelier ID
KIOV(AM) Payette ID
*KEZJ(AM) Twin Falls ID
WCEV(AM) Cicero IL
WVON(AM) Cicero IL
WKEI(AM) Kewanee IL
WFMB(AM) Springfield IL
WLYV(AM) Fort Wayne IN
WAVG(AM) Jeffersonville IN
WASK(AM) Lafayette IN
WAOV(AM) Vincennes IN
KWBW(AM) Hutchinson KS
WTCO(AM) Campbellsville KY
WWXL(AM) Manchester KY
WDXR(AM) Paducah KY
WLKS(AM) West Liberty KY
KSIG(AM) Crowley LA
KNOC(AM) Natchitoches LA
WBYU(AM) New Orleans LA
WNBP(AM) Newburyport MA
WMAS(AM) Springfield MA
WTBO(AM) Cumberland MD
WRKD(AM) Rockland ME
WKTG(AM) South Paris ME
WATZ(AM) Alpena MI
WHTC(AM) Holland MI

U.S. AM Stations by Frequency

WMIQ(AM) Iron Mountain MI
WIBM(AM) Jackson MI
WKLA(AM) Ludington MI
WNBY(AM) Newberry MI
WHLS(AM) Port Huron MI
KATE(AM) Albert Lea MN
KBUN(AM) Bemidji MN
KBMW(AM) Breckenridge MN
WELY(AM) Ely MN
KNSI(AM) Saint Cloud MN
KYLS(AM) Fredericktown MO
KQYX(AM) Joplin MO
KIRX(AM) Kirksville MO
KOKO(AM) Warrensburg MO
KWPM(AM) West Plains MO
WROX(AM) Clarksdale MS
WCJU(AM) Columbia MS
WFFX(AM) Meridian MS
WNAT(AM) Natchez MS
WROB(AM) West Point MS
KMMS(AM) Bozeman MT
KQDI(AM) Great Falls MT
KYLW(AM) Lockwood MT
KGRZ(AM) Missoula MT
KVCK(AM) Wolf Point MT
WATA(AM) Boone NC
WGNC(AM) Gastonia NC
WIZS(AM) Henderson NC
WHKP(AM) Hendersonville NC
WNOS(AM) New Bern NC
WCIE(AM) Spring Lake NC
KZZJ(AM) Rugby ND
KWBE(AM) Beatrice NE
WKXL(AM) Concord NH
WKXW(AM) Atlantic City NJ
WCTC(AM) New Brunswick NJ
KRZY(AM) Albuquerque NM
KLMX(AM) Clayton NM
KOBE(AM) Las Cruces NM
KSEL(AM) Portales NM
KHIT(AM) Reno NV
WENI(AM) Corning NY
WWSC(AM) Glens Falls NY
WHDL(AM) Olean NY
WKIP(AM) Poughkeepsie NY
WYFY(AM) Rome NY
WJER(AM) Dover-New Philadelphia OH
WMOH(AM) Hamilton OH
WLEC(AM) Sandusky OH
KWHW(AM) Altus OK
KGFF(AM) Shawnee OK
KSIW(AM) Woodward OK
KLZS(AM) Eugene OR
KFLS(AM) Klamath Falls OR
KLBM(AM) La Grande OR
*KBPS(AM) Portland OR
WPSE(AM) Erie PA
WFRA(AM) Franklin PA
WDAD(AM) Indiana PA
WPAM(AM) Pottsville PA
WMAJ(AM) State College PA
WJPA(AM) Washington PA
WCPR(AM) Coamo PR
WLKW(AM) West Warwick RI
WQNT(AM) Charleston SC
WCRS(AM) Greenwood SC
WHSC(AM) Hartsville SC
WQJM(AM) Myrtle Beach SC
KBFS(AM) Belle Fourche SD
KSQP(AM) Pierre SD
KYNT(AM) Yankton SD
WLAR(AM) Athens TN
WLMR(AM) Chattanooga TN
WTRO(AM) Dyersburg TN
WSMG(AM) Greeneville TN
WLAF(AM) La Follette TN
WGNS(AM) Murfreesboro TN
KIKR(AM) Beaumont TX
KBEN(AM) Carrizo Springs TX
KCTI(AM) Gonzales TX
KMBL(AM) Junction TX
KCYL(AM) Lampasas TX
KMHT(AM) Marshall TX
KNET(AM) Palestine TX
KSNY(AM) Snyder TX
*KEYY(AM) Provo UT

KZNU(AM) Saint George UT
WBVA(AM) Bayside VA
WFTR(AM) Front Royal VA
WCLM(AM) Highland Springs VA
WREL(AM) Lexington VA
WSNO(AM) Barre VT
WTSA(AM) Brattleboro VT
KBKW(AM) Aberdeen WA
KCLX(AM) Colfax WA
KONP(AM) Port Angeles WA
KSUH(AM) Puyallup WA
KFIZ(AM) Fond du Lac WI
WHRY(AM) Hurley WI
WDLB(AM) Marshfield WI
WRCO(AM) Richland Center WI
WHNK(AM) Parkersburg WV
KBBS(AM) Buffalo WY
KVOW(AM) Riverton WY

1460 khz

WMCJ(AM) Cullman AL
WHAL(AM) Phenix City AL
KTYM(AM) Inglewood CA
KABL(AM) Salinas CA
KRRS(AM) Santa Rosa CA
KCNR(AM) Shasta CA
KZNT(AM) Colorado Springs CO
WQXM(AM) Bartow FL
WZEP(AM) De Funiak Springs FL
WZNZ(AM) Jacksonville FL
WXEM(AM) Buford GA
KHRA(AM) Honolulu HI
KXNO(AM) Des Moines IA
WROY(AM) Carmi IL
WIXN(AM) Dixon IL
WJCI(AM) Rantoul IL
WKAM(AM) Goshen IN
WNVI(AM) North Vernon IN
KKOY(AM) Chanute KS
WEKB(AM) Elkhorn City KY
WRVK(AM) Mt. Vernon KY
WXOK(AM) Baton Rouge LA
KBSF(AM) Springhill LA
WBET(AM) Brockton MA
WEMD(AM) Easton MD
WBRN(AM) Big Rapids MI
WPON(AM) Walled Lake MI
KDWA(AM) Hastings MN
KDMA(AM) Montevideo MN
KKAQ(AM) Thief River Falls MN
KHOJ(AM) Saint Charles MO
WELZ(AM) Belzoni MS
WRKB(AM) Kannapolis NC
WEWO(AM) Laurinburg NC
WHBK(AM) Marshall NC
KLTC(AM) Dickinson ND
KXPN(AM) Kearney NE
WIFI(AM) Florence NJ
KENO(AM) Las Vegas NV
WDDY(AM) Albany NY
WVOX(AM) New Rochelle NY
WHIC(AM) Rochester NY
WBNS(AM) Columbus OH
WBKC(AM) Painesville OH
KZUE(AM) El Reno OK
KCKX(AM) Stayton OR
WMBA(AM) Ambridge PA
WTKT(AM) Harrisburg PA
WEMR(AM) Tunkhannock PA
WRRE(AM) Juncos PR
WLRP(AM) San Sebastian PR
WDOG(AM) Allendale SC
WBCU(AM) Union SC
WJAK(AM) Jackson TN
WEEN(AM) Lafayette TN
WXRQ(AM) Mount Pleasant TN
KTFW(AM) Burleson TX
KBRZ(AM) Freeport TX
KCWM(AM) Hondo TX
KBZO(AM) Lubbock TX
WKDV(AM) Manassas VA
WRAD(AM) Radford VA
*KARR(AM) Kirkland WA
KUTI(AM) Yakima WA
WBJX(AM) Racine WI
WBOG(AM) Tomah WI
WBUC(AM) Buckhannon WV

1470 khz

WIJK(AM) Evergreen AL
KNXN(AM) Sierra Vista AZ
KUTY(AM) Palmdale CA
KIID(AM) Sacramento CA
KEZZ(AM) Estes Park CO
WMMW(AM) Meriden CT
WLVU(AM) Dunedin FL
WWNN(AM) Pompano Beach FL
WXAG(AM) Athens GA
WCLA(AM) Claxton GA
WRGA(AM) Rome GA
KWSL(AM) Sioux City IA
KWAY(AM) Waverly IA
WCFJ(AM) Chicago Heights IL
WMBD(AM) Peoria IL
*WGNR(AM) Anderson IN
KAIR(AM) Atchison KS
KYUU(AM) Liberal KS
WBFC(AM) Stanton KY
KLCL(AM) Lake Charles LA
WAZN(AM) Watertown MA
WJDY(AM) Salisbury MD
WTTR(AM) Westminster MD
WLAM(AM) Lewiston ME
WFNT(AM) Flint MI
WKLZ(AM) Kalamazoo MI
KLBP(AM) Brooklyn Park MN
KFMZ(AM) Brookfield MO
KMAL(AM) Malden MO
WCHJ(AM) Brookhaven MS
WNAU(AM) New Albany MS
WVBS(AM) Burgaw NC
WWBG(AM) Greensboro NC
WTOE(AM) Spruce Pine NC
KHND(AM) Harvey ND
WNYY(AM) Ithaca NY
WPDM(AM) Potsdam NY
WLQR(AM) Toledo OH
KVLH(AM) Pauls Valley OK
KITO(AM) Vinita OK
WKAP(AM) Allentown PA
WLOA(AM) Farrell PA
WQXL(AM) Columbia SC
WLMC(AM) Georgetown SC
WBCR(AM) Alcoa TN
WVOL(AM) Berry Hill TN
KYYW(AM) Abilene TX
KDHN(AM) Dimmitt TX
KWRD(AM) Henderson TX
KUOL(AM) San Marcos TX
KNFL(AM) Tremonton UT
WBTX(AM) Broadway-Timberville VA
WTZE(AM) Tazewell VA
KELA(AM) Centralia-Chehalis WA
KBSN(AM) Moses Lake WA
WBKV(AM) West Bend WI
WEMM(AM) Huntington WV
KKTY(AM) Douglas WY

1480 khz

WYMR(AM) Bridgeport AL
WLPH(AM) Irondale AL
WABB(AM) Mobile AL
KTHS(AM) Berryville AR
KPHX(AM) Phoenix AZ
KABN(AM) Concord CA
KGOE(AM) Eureka CA
KYOS(AM) Merced CA
KVNR(AM) Santa Ana CA
KSBQ(AM) Santa Maria CA
KAVA(AM) Pueblo CO
WNEZ(AM) Windsor CT
WFLN(AM) Arcadia FL
WVOI(AM) Marco Island FL
WUNA(AM) Ocoee FL
*WKGC(AM) Panama City Beach FL
WYZE(AM) Atlanta GA
WGUS(AM) Augusta GA
KLEE(AM) Ottumwa IA
KRXR(AM) Gooding ID
WSPY(AM) Geneva IL
WJBM(AM) Jerseyville IL
WPFR(AM) Terre Haute IN
WRSW(AM) Warsaw IN
KCZZ(AM) Mission KS
KQAM(AM) Wichita KS
WHVO(AM) Hopkinsville KY

WEZC(AM) Neon KY
WTLO(AM) Somerset KY
KIOU(AM) Shreveport LA
WSAR(AM) Fall River MA
*WGVU(AM) Kentwood MI
WSDS(AM) Salem Township MI
WIOS(AM) Tawas City MI
KAUS(AM) Austin MN
KKCQ(AM) Fosston MN
WGFY(AM) Charlotte NC
WZFB(AM) Fair Bluff NC
WPFJ(AM) Franklin NC
WYRN(AM) Louisburg NC
KLMS(AM) Lincoln NE
WLEA(AM) Hornell NY
WZRC(AM) New York NY
WHBC(AM) Canton OH
WCIN(AM) Cincinnati OH
WCNS(AM) Latrobe PA
WDAS(AM) Philadelphia PA
WISL(AM) Shamokin PA
WEEO(AM) Shippensburg PA
WMDD(AM) Fajardo PR
WZJY(AM) Mt. Pleasant SC
KSDR(AM) Watertown SD
WJFC(AM) Jefferson City TN
WBBP(AM) Memphis TN
WJLE(AM) Smithville TN
KNIT(AM) Dallas TX
KLVL(AM) Pasadena TX
KCHL(AM) San Antonio TX
KHQN(AM) Spanish Fork UT
WPWC(AM) Dumfries-Triangle VA
WTOX(AM) Glen Allen VA
WTOY(AM) Salem VA
WNBX(AM) Springfield VT
KNTB(AM) Lakewood WA
KBMS(AM) Vancouver WA
WLMV(AM) Madison WI
KRAE(AM) Cheyenne WY

1490 khz

WANA(AM) Anniston AL
WAJF(AM) Decatur AL
WIRB(AM) Level Plains AL
WHBB(AM) Selma AL
KWXT(AM) Dardanelle AR
KXAR(AM) Hope AR
KDRS(AM) Paragould AR
KOTN(AM) Pine Bluff AR
KZZZ(AM) Bullhead City AZ
KCUZ(AM) Clifton AZ
KYCA(AM) Prescott AZ
KFFN(AM) Tucson AZ
KWAC(AM) Bakersfield CA
KMET(AM) Banning CA
KICO(AM) Calexico CA
KRKC(AM) King City CA
KTOB(AM) Petaluma CA
KBLF(AM) Red Bluff CA
KBKO(AM) Santa Barbara CA
KOWL(AM) South Lake Tahoe CA
*KSYC(AM) Yreka CA
KCFC(AM) Boulder CO
KPKE(AM) Gunnison CO
KXRE(AM) Manitou Springs CO
WGCH(AM) Greenwich CT
WWPR(AM) Bradenton FL
WNDA(AM) De Land FL
WAFZ(AM) Immokalee FL
WMBM(AM) Miami Beach FL
WECM(AM) Milton FL
WTTB(AM) Vero Beach FL
WSIR(AM) Winter Haven FL
WMOG(AM) Brunswick GA
WCHM(AM) Clarkesville GA
WQSY(AM) Cordele GA
WYYZ(AM) Jasper GA
WKUN(AM) Monroe GA
WSFB(AM) Quitman GA
WSNT(AM) Sandersville GA
WSYL(AM) Sylvania GA
WRLA(AM) West Point GA
KBUR(AM) Burlington IA
WDBQ(AM) Dubuque IA
KXLQ(AM) Indianola IA

KRIB(AM) Mason City IA
KCID(AM) Caldwell ID
KRTK(AM) Chubbuck ID
WKRO(AM) Cairo IL
WDAN(AM) Danville IL
WESL(AM) East St. Louis IL
WPNA(AM) Oak Park IL
WZOE(AM) Princeton IL
WKBV(AM) Richmond IN
WNDV(AM) South Bend IN
KKAN(AM) Phillipsburg KS
KTOP(AM) Topeka KS
WFKY(AM) Frankfort KY
WCLU(AM) Glasgow KY
WFXY(AM) Middlesboro KY
WOMI(AM) Owensboro KY
WSIP(AM) Paintsville KY
WIKC(AM) Bogalusa LA
KEUN(AM) Eunice LA
KJIN(AM) Houma LA
KRUS(AM) Ruston LA
WCCM(AM) Haverhill MA
WMRC(AM) Milford MA
WACM(AM) West Springfield MA
WARK(AM) Hagerstown MD
WBAE(AM) Portland ME
WTVL(AM) Waterville ME
WABJ(AM) Adrian MI
WTIQ(AM) Manistique MI
WMPX(AM) Midland MI
WODJ(AM) Whitehall MI
KXRA(AM) Alexandria MN
KQDS(AM) Duluth MN
KLGR(AM) Redwood Falls MN
KDMO(AM) Carthage MO
KTTR(AM) Rolla MO
KDRO(AM) Sedalia MO
WXBD(AM) Biloxi MS
WCLD(AM) Cleveland MS
WHOC(AM) Philadelphia MS
WTUP(AM) Tupelo MS
WRTM(AM) Vicksburg MS
KDBM(AM) Dillon MT
KBSR(AM) Laurel MT
WDUR(AM) Durham NC
WLOE(AM) Eden NC
WAZZ(AM) Fayetteville NC
WWNB(AM) New Bern NC
WRMT(AM) Rocky Mount NC
WSTP(AM) Salisbury NC
WSVM(AM) Valdese NC
WWIL(AM) Wilmington NC
KNDC(AM) Hettinger ND
KOVC(AM) Valley City ND
KOMJ(AM) Omaha NE
WEMJ(AM) Laconia NH
WUVR(AM) Lebanon NH
WUSS(AM) Pleasantville NJ
KRSN(AM) Los Alamos NM
KRTN(AM) Raton NM
KRUI(AM) Ruidoso Downs NM
WCSS(AM) Amsterdam NY
WBTA(AM) Batavia NY
WKNY(AM) Kingston NY
WICY(AM) Malone NY
WDLC(AM) Port Jervis NY
WCDO(AM) Sidney NY
WOLF(AM) Syracuse NY
WTYX(AM) Watkins Glen NY
WBEX(AM) Chillicothe OH
WJMO(AM) Cleveland Heights OH
WOHI(AM) East Liverpool OH
WMOA(AM) Marietta OH
WMRN(AM) Marion OH
KMFS(AM) Guthrie OK
KBIX(AM) Muskogee OK
KBKR(AM) Baker City OR
KRNR(AM) Roseburg OR
KBZY(AM) Salem OR
WESB(AM) Bradford PA
WAZL(AM) Hazleton PA
WPRR(AM) Johnstown PA
WLPA(AM) Lancaster PA
WBCB(AM) Levittown-Fairless Hills PA
WMGW(AM) Meadville PA
WNBT(AM) Wellsboro PA
WDEP(AM) Ponce PR

U.S. AM Stations by Frequency

WVGB(AM) Beaufort SC
WGCD(AM) Chester SC
WPCI(AM) Greenville SC
WJDJ(AM) Hartsville SC
KFCR(AM) Custer SD
KORN(AM) Mitchell SD
WOPI(AM) Bristol TN
WJOC(AM) Chattanooga TN
WCSV(AM) Crossville TN
WITA(AM) Knoxville TN
WCKD(AM) Lebanon TN
WJJM(AM) Lewisburg TN
WDXL(AM) Lexington TN
KFON(AM) Austin TX
KIBL(AM) Beeville TX
KBST(AM) Big Spring TX
KQTY(AM) Borger TX
KNEL(AM) Brady TX
KWMC(AM) Del Rio TX
KHVL(AM) Huntsville TX
KLNT(AM) Laredo TX
KZZN(AM) Littlefield TX
KPLT(AM) Paris TX
KYZS(AM) Tyler TX
KVWC(AM) Vernon TX
KWUD(AM) Woodville TX
*KYFO(AM) Ogden UT
WCVA(AM) Culpeper VA
WPAK(AM) Farmville VA
WLRT(AM) Hampton VA
WKVT(AM) Brattleboro VT
WFAD(AM) Middlebury VT
WIKE(AM) Newport VT
KBRO(AM) Bremerton WA
KBIS(AM) Forks WA
KEYG(AM) Grand Coulee WA
KWOK(AM) Hoquiam WA
KLOG(AM) Kelso WA
KYNR(AM) Toppenish WA
KTEL(AM) Walla Walla WA
WGEZ(AM) Beloit WI
WLFN(AM) La Crosse WI
WIGM(AM) Medford WI
WOSH(AM) Oshkosh WI
WSWW(AM) Charleston WV
WTCS(AM) Fairmont WV
WAEY(AM) Princeton WV
WSGB(AM) Sutton WV
KUGR(AM) Green River WY
KGOS(AM) Torrington WY

1494 khz
*V6AI(AM) Yap FM

1500 khz
WQCR(AM) Alabaster AL
WVSM(AM) Rainsville AL
WKAX(AM) Russellville AL
KIEV(AM) Culver City CA
KSJX(AM) San Jose CA
WFIF(AM) Milford CT
WTOP(AM) Washington DC
WKIZ(AM) Key West FL
WPSO(AM) New Port Richey FL
WDPC(AM) Dallas GA
WSEM(AM) Donalsonville GA
WAYS(AM) Macon GA
KUMU(AM) Honolulu HI
WGEN(AM) Geneseo IL
WPMB(AM) Vandalia IL
WPJX(AM) Zion IL
WBRI(AM) Indianapolis IN
WAKE(AM) Valparaiso IN
WKXO(AM) Berea KY
WMJL(AM) Marion KY
WOLY(AM) Battle Creek MI
WLQV(AM) Detroit MI
WDEE(AM) Reed City MI
KSTP(AM) Saint Paul MN
KDFN(AM) Doniphan MO
WQMS(AM) Quitman MS
WSMX(AM) Winston-Salem NC
WGHT(AM) Pompton Lakes NJ
*KABR(AM) Alamo Community NM
WBZI(AM) Xenia OH
WASN(AM) Youngstown OH
KPGM(AM) Pawhuska OK
WMNT(AM) Manati PR

WEAC(AM) Gaffney SC
WDEB(AM) Jamestown TN
WTNE(AM) Trenton TN
KBRN(AM) Boerne TX
KMXO(AM) Merkel TX
KJIM(AM) Sherman TX
KANI(AM) Wharton TX

1510 khz
KFNN(AM) Mesa AZ
KIRV(AM) Fresno CA
KSPA(AM) Ontario CA
KPIG(AM) Piedmont CA
KCUV(AM) Littleton CO
WWBC(AM) Cocoa FL
KIFG(AM) Iowa Falls IA
WDID(AM) Highland IL
WWHN(AM) Joliet IL
WLRB(AM) Macomb IL
WJOT(AM) Wabash IN
KNNS(AM) Larned KS
KAGY(AM) Port Sulphur LA
WWZN(AM) Boston MA
*WJKN(AM) Jackson MI
KCTE(AM) Independence MO
KMRF(AM) Marshfield MO
WEAL(AM) Greensboro NC
KTTT(AM) Columbus NE
WRNJ(AM) Hackettstown NJ
WFAI(AM) Salem NJ
WPUT(AM) Brewster NY
WLGN(AM) Logan OH
WLKR(AM) Norwalk OH
WWSM(AM) Annville-Cleona PA
WPGR(AM) Monroeville PA
WSQD(AM) Lajas PR
WDRF(AM) Woodruff SC
KMSD(AM) Milbank SD
WLAC(AM) Nashville TN
KAGC(AM) Bryan TX
KVCI(AM) Canton TX
KCTX(AM) Childress TX
KMND(AM) Midland TX
KBED(AM) Nederland TX
KROB(AM) Robstown TX
KSTV(AM) Stephenville TX
KLLB(AM) West Jordan UT
KGA(AM) Spokane WA
WAUK(AM) Waukesha WI

1520 khz
WTLM(AM) Opelika AL
KMPG(AM) Hollister CA
KVTA(AM) Port Hueneme CA
WHIM(AM) Apopka FL
WXYB(AM) Indian Rocks Beach FL
WEXY(AM) Wilton Manors FL
WDCY(AM) Douglasville GA
WKVQ(AM) Eatonton GA
KSIB(AM) Creston IA
WHOW(AM) Clinton IL
WLUV(AM) Loves Park IL
WKVI(AM) Knox IN
WKWH(AM) Shelbyville IN
WLGC(AM) Greenup KY
WRSL(AM) Stanford KY
KFXZ(AM) Lafayette LA
WIZZ(AM) Greenfield MA
WTRI(AM) Brunswick MD
WMLM(AM) Saint Louis MI
WLKM(AM) Three Rivers MI
KOLM(AM) Rochester MN
KRHW(AM) Sikeston MO
WQMA(AM) Marks MS
WDSL(AM) Mocksville NC
WGMA(AM) Spindale NC
WARR(AM) Warrenton NC
KMAV(AM) Mayville ND
WWKB(AM) Buffalo NY
WTHE(AM) Mineola NY
WQCT(AM) Bryan OH
WINW(AM) Canton OH
WJMP(AM) Kent OH
WDMN(AM) Rossford OH
KOKC(AM) Oklahoma City OK
KGDD(AM) Oregon City OR
WCHE(AM) West Chester PA
WVOZ(AM) San Juan PR

WKMG(AM) Newberry SC
KSQB(AM) Sioux Falls SD
WNWS(AM) Brownsville TN
WHHQ(AM) Elizabethton TN
KYND(AM) Cypress TX
KHLT(AM) Hallettsville TX

1530 khz
KVDW(AM) England AR
KHPI(AM) Moreno Valley CA
KFBK(AM) Sacramento CA
KCMN(AM) Colorado Springs CO
WDJZ(AM) Bridgeport CT
WENG(AM) Englewood FL
WYMM(AM) Jacksonville FL
WTTI(AM) Dalton GA
KDSN(AM) Denison IA
WJJG(AM) Elmhurst IL
KPCR(AM) Quincy IL
WJOT(AM) Wabash IN (duplicate?)
WVBF(AM) Middleborough Center MA
WCTR(AM) Chestertown MD
WLSP(AM) Lapeer MI
WYGR(AM) Wyoming MI
KSMM(AM) Shakopee MN
KMAM(AM) Butler MO
WRPM(AM) Poplarville MS
WLLQ(AM) Chapel Hill NC
WOBX(AM) Wanchese NC
WJDM(AM) Elizabeth NJ
WCKY(AM) Cincinnati OH
KXTD(AM) Wagoner OK
WFYL(AM) McConnellsburg PA
WYNE(AM) North East PA
WUPR(AM) Utuado PR
WASC(AM) Spartanburg SC
WDAP(AM) Huntingdon TN
KZNX(AM) Creedmoor TX
KGBT(AM) Harlingen TX
KNBO(AM) New Boston TX
KCLR(AM) Ralls TX
WFIC(AM) Collinsville VA
WMBE(AM) Chilton WI

1540 khz
WRSM(AM) Sumiton AL
KDYN(AM) Ozark AR
KASA(AM) Phoenix AZ
KMPC(AM) Los Angeles CA
KREA(AM) Honolulu HI
KXEL(AM) Waterloo IA
WSMI(AM) Litchfield IL
WBNL(AM) Boonville IN
WADM(AM) Decatur IN
WLOI(AM) La Porte IN
WMCB(AM) Martinsville IN
KNGL(AM) McPherson KS
KLKC(AM) Parsons KS
WAKY(AM) Greensburg KY
KGLA(AM) Gretna LA
WACA(AM) Wheaton MD
*KTGG(AM) Spring Arbor MI
KBOA(AM) Kennett MO
WKXG(AM) Greenwood MS
WOGR(AM) Charlotte NC
WTXY(AM) Whiteville NC
WYNC(AM) Yanceyville NC
WGIP(AM) Exeter NH
WDCD(AM) Albany NY
WSIV(AM) East Syracuse NY
WBCO(AM) Bucyrus OH
WABQ(AM) Cleveland OH
WRTK(AM) Niles OH
WBTC(AM) Uhrichsville OH
WNWR(AM) Philadelphia PA
WECZ(AM) Punxsutawney PA
WIBS(AM) Guayama PR
WADK(AM) Newport RI
WTBI(AM) Pickens SC
WBIN(AM) Benton TN
WJJT(AM) Jellico TN
WBRY(AM) Woodbury TN
KGBC(AM) Galveston TX
KEDA(AM) San Antonio TX
KZMP(AM) University Park TX
WREJ(AM) Richmond VA
KXPA(AM) Bellevue WA
WTKM(AM) Hartford WI

1550 khz
WLOR(AM) Huntsville AL
*KUAZ(AM) Tucson AZ
KWRN(AM) Apple Valley CA
KXEX(AM) Fresno CA
KYCY(AM) San Francisco CA
WDZK(AM) Bloomfield CT
WRHC(AM) Coral Gables FL
WAMA(AM) Tampa FL
WTHB(AM) Augusta GA
WAZX(AM) Smyrna GA
WKTF(AM) Vienna GA
KIWA(AM) Sheldon IA
WJIL(AM) Jacksonville IL
WCSJ(AM) Morris IL
WOCC(AM) Corydon IN
WCVL(AM) Crawfordsville IN
WMDH(AM) New Castle IN
WNDI(AM) Sullivan IN
KDCC(AM) Dodge City KS
KKLE(AM) Winfield KS
WIRV(AM) Irvine KY
WMSK(AM) Morganfield KY
WPFC(AM) Port Allen LA
WNTN(AM) Newton MA
WSRY(AM) Elkton MD
WSHN(AM) Fremont MI
KAPE(AM) Cape Girardeau MO
KSFT(AM) Saint Joseph MO
KLFJ(AM) Springfield MO
WCLY(AM) Raleigh NC
WBFJ(AM) Winston-Salem NC
KICS(AM) Hastings NE
KKJY(AM) Albuquerque NM
KXTO(AM) Reno NV
WCGR(AM) Canandaigua NY
WUTQ(AM) Utica NY
WXOL(AM) Delaware OH
KMAD(AM) Madill OK
KYAL(AM) Sapulpa OK
WURP(AM) Braddock PA
WITK(AM) Pittston PA
WTTC(AM) Towanda PA
WKFE(AM) Yauco PR
WBSC(AM) Bennettsville SC
WIGN(AM) Bristol TN
WCTZ(AM) Clarksville TN
WKJQ(AM) Parsons TN
KZRK(AM) Canyon TX
KCOM(AM) Comanche TX
KWBC(AM) Navasota TX
KMRI(AM) West Valley City UT
WKBA(AM) Vinton VA
WVAB(AM) Virginia Beach VA
KRPI(AM) Ferndale WA
KKAD(AM) Vancouver WA
WZRK(AM) Lake Geneva WI
WTUX(AM) Madison WI
WEVR(AM) River Falls WI
WMRE(AM) Charles Town WV

1560 khz
WZTQ(AM) Centre AL
WCMA(AM) Daleville AL
KNZR(AM) Bakersfield CA
KIQS(AM) Willows CA
WINV(AM) Beverly Hills FL
WINT(AM) Melbourne FL
WPGY(AM) Ellijay GA
KLNG(AM) Council Bluffs IA
WBYS(AM) Canton IL
WSQR(AM) Sycamore IL
WSEZ(AM) Paoli IN
WRIN(AM) Rensselaer IN
KABI(AM) Abilene KS
WQXY(AM) Hazard KY
WKDO(AM) Liberty KY
WPAD(AM) Paducah KY
WSLA(AM) Slidell LA
WKIK(AM) La Plata MD
WNWN(AM) Portage MI
KBEW(AM) Blue Earth MN
WMBH(AM) Joplin MO
KLTI(AM) Macon MO
KTUI(AM) Sullivan MO
WYZD(AM) Dobson NC
WQEW(AM) New York NY
WTNS(AM) Coshocton OH

WCNW(AM) Fairfield OH
WTOD(AM) Toledo OH
KOCY(AM) Del City OK
KKUZ(AM) Sallisaw OK
WRSJ(AM) Bayamon PR
WAHT(AM) Clemson SC
WAGL(AM) Lancaster SC
KKAA(AM) Aberdeen SD
WBOL(AM) Bolivar TN
WMRO(AM) Gallatin TN
KZQQ(AM) Abilene TX
KILE(AM) Bellaire TX
KNGR(AM) Daingerfield TX
KHBR(AM) Hillsboro TX
KTXZ(AM) West Lake Hills TX
WSBV(AM) South Boston VA
KZIZ(AM) Sumner WA
WGLB(AM) Elm Grove WI
WFSP(AM) Kingwood WV

1570 khz
WCRL(AM) Oneonta AL
KBRI(AM) Brinkley AR
KBJT(AM) Fordyce AR
KCVR(AM) Lodi CA
KPRO(AM) Riverside CA
KTGE(AM) Salinas CA
KSXT(AM) Loveland CO
WTWB(AM) Auburndale FL
WVOJ(AM) Fernandina Beach FL
WOKC(AM) Okeechobee FL
WSSA(AM) Morrow GA
KUAU(AM) Haiku HI
KMCD(AM) Fairfield IA
KQWC(AM) Webster City IA
WBGZ(AM) Alton IL
WFRL(AM) Freeport IL
WBGX(AM) Harvey IL
WTAY(AM) Robinson IL
WGLL(AM) Auburn IN
WILO(AM) Frankfort IN
WWSZ(AM) New Albany IN
KNDY(AM) Marysville KS
WLBQ(AM) Morgantown KY
WKKS(AM) Vanceburg KY
WABL(AM) Amite LA
KLLA(AM) Leesville LA
WNSH(AM) Beverly MA
WPEP(AM) Taunton MA
WNST(AM) Towson MD
WWCK(AM) Flint MI
WFUR(AM) Grand Rapids MI
KYCR(AM) Golden Valley MN
KAKK(AM) Walker MN
KBCV(AM) Hollister MO
KLEX(AM) Lexington MO
WIZK(AM) Bay Springs MS
WONA(AM) Winona MS
WNCA(AM) Siler City NC
WTLK(AM) Taylorsville NC
WECU(AM) Winterville NC
WVTL(AM) Amsterdam NY
WFLR(AM) Dundee NY
WFTU(AM) Riverhead NY
WPTW(AM) Piqua OH
WANR(AM) Warren OH
KTAT(AM) Frederick OK
KMUR(AM) Pryor OK
*WPGM(AM) Danville PA
WISP(AM) Doylestown PA
WQTW(AM) Latrobe PA
WPPC(AM) Penuelas PR
KVTK(AM) Vermillion SD
WNKX(AM) Centerville TN
WCLE(AM) Cleveland TN
WTRB(AM) Ripley TN
KVLG(AM) La Grange TX
KPYK(AM) Terrell TX
WSWV(AM) Pennington Gap VA
WYTI(AM) Rocky Mount VA
WSCO(AM) Appleton WI
WKBH(AM) Holmen WI
WLKD(AM) Minocqua WI

1580 khz
WVOK(AM) Oxford AL
KHGG(AM) Van Buren AR
KMIK(AM) Tempe AZ

U.S. AM Stations by Frequency

KBLA(AM) Santa Monica CA
KWYD(AM) Colorado Springs CO
WNTF(AM) Bithlo FL
WTCL(AM) Chattahoochee FL
WSRF(AM) Fort Lauderdale FL
WCCF(AM) Punta Gorda FL
WEAM(AM) Columbus GA
KCHA(AM) Charles City IA
WKKD(AM) Aurora IL
WDQN(AM) Du Quoin IL
WBBA(AM) Pittsfield IL
WBCP(AM) Urbana IL
WCNB(AM) Connersville IN
WDND(AM) South Bend IN
WAMW(AM) Washington IN
WXRA(AM) Georgetown KY
WPKY(AM) Princeton KY
KXZZ(AM) Lake Charles LA
WPGC(AM) Morningside MD
WWSJ(AM) Saint Johns MI
KDOM(AM) Windom MN
KTGR(AM) Columbia MO
KESM(AM) El Dorado Springs MO
KNIM(AM) Maryville MO
WAMY(AM) Amory MS
WORV(AM) Hattiesburg MS
WESY(AM) Leland MS
WPMP(AM) Pascagoula-Moss Point MS
WZKY(AM) Albemarle NC
KAMI(AM) Cozad NE
WGYM(AM) Hammonton NJ
WLIM(AM) Patchogue NY
WVKO(AM) Columbus OH
KOKB(AM) Blackwell OK
KGAL(AM) Lebanon OR
WVZN(AM) Columbia PA
WRDD(AM) Ebensburg PA
WXXP(AM) Waynesburg PA
WEKO(AM) Morovis PR
WWGS(AM) Georgetown SC
WPJK(AM) Orangeburg SC
WNPZ(AM) Knoxville TN
WLIJ(AM) Shelbyville TN
KGAF(AM) Gainesville TX
KIRT(AM) Mission TX
KTLU(AM) Rusk TX
KWED(AM) Seguin TX
KQRL(AM) Waco TX
WILA(AM) Danville VA
WTTN(AM) Watertown WI

1590 khz
WVNA(AM) Tuscumbia AL
KZRA(AM) Springdale AR
KLIV(AM) San Jose CA
KKZZ(AM) Ventura CA
KRSX(AM) Victorville CA
WPSL(AM) Port St. Lucie FL
WRXB(AM) Saint Petersburg Beach FL
WPUL(AM) South Daytona FL
WALG(AM) Albany GA
WQCH(AM) La Fayette GA
WXRS(AM) Swainsboro GA
WTGA(AM) Thomaston GA
KWBG(AM) Boone IA
WONX(AM) Evanston IL
WAIK(AM) Galesburg IL
WNTS(AM) Beech Grove IN
WRCY(AM) Mount Vernon IN
KVGB(AM) Great Bend KS
WLBN(AM) Lebanon KY
KKAY(AM) White Castle LA
WFBR(AM) Glen Burnie MD
WKHZ(AM) Ocean City MD
WTVB(AM) Coldwater MI
WHLX(AM) Marine City MI
KCNN(AM) East Grand Forks MN
KDJS(AM) Willmar MN
KDEX(AM) Dexter MO
KPRT(AM) Kansas City MO
KMOZ(AM) Rolla MO
WZRX(AM) Jackson MS
WBHN(AM) Bryson City NC
WVOE(AM) Chadbourn NC
WCSL(AM) Cherryville NC
WHPY(AM) Clayton NC
WYSR(AM) High Point NC
KTCH(AM) Wayne NE
WSMN(AM) Nashua NH
KQLO(AM) Sun Valley NV
WAUB(AM) Auburn NY
WASB(AM) Brockport NY
WGGO(AM) Salamanca NY
WAKR(AM) Akron OH
WSRW(AM) Hillsboro OH
KWEY(AM) Weatherford OK
KMBD(AM) Tillamook OR
WZUM(AM) Carnegie PA
WHGT(AM) Chambersburg PA
WPWA(AM) Chester PA
WPSN(AM) Honesdale PA
WXRF(AM) Guayama PR
WARV(AM) Warwick RI
WABV(AM) Abbeville SC

1593 khz
V6AK(AM) Truk FM

1600 khz
WEUP(AM) Huntsville AL
WXVI(AM) Montgomery AL
KNWA(AM) Bellefonte AR
KYBC(AM) Cottonwood AZ
KXEW(AM) South Tucson AZ
KGST(AM) Fresno CA
KAHZ(AM) Pomona CA
KTAP(AM) Santa Maria CA
KUBA(AM) Yuba City CA
KCKK(AM) Lakewood CO
WKEN(AM) Dover DE
WQOP(AM) Atlantic Beach FL
WKWF(AM) Key West FL
WMNE(AM) Riviera Beach FL
WOKB(AM) Winter Garden FL
WAOS(AM) Austell GA
WLGA(AM) Algona IA
KCRG(AM) Cedar Rapids IA
WCGO(AM) Chicago Heights IL
WMCW(AM) Harvard IL
WBTO(AM) Linton IN
WARU(AM) Peru IN
KMDO(AM) Fort Scott KS
WAIA(AM) Beaver Dam KY
WTSZ(AM) Eminence KY
KLEB(AM) Golden Meadow LA
WUNR(AM) Brookline MA
WHNP(AM) East Longmeadow MA
WLXE(AM) Rockville MD
WAAM(AM) Ann Arbor MI
WMHG(AM) Muskegon MI
KZGX(AM) Watertown MN

WCAM(AM) Camden SC
WATX(AM) Algood TN
WKTP(AM) Jonesborough TN
WDBL(AM) Springfield TN
KGAS(AM) Carthage TX
KEAS(AM) Eastland TX
KELP(AM) El Paso TX
KMIC(AM) Houston TX
KDAV(AM) Lubbock TX
KRQX(AM) Mexia TX
KDAE(AM) Sinton TX
WFTH(AM) Richmond VA
KLFE(AM) Seattle WA
WIXK(AM) New Richmond WI
WPVL(AM) Platteville WI
WTRW(AM) Two Rivers WI

KATZ(AM) Saint Louis MO
KTTN(AM) Trenton MO
WIDU(AM) Fayetteville NC
WTZQ(AM) Hendersonville NC
KDAK(AM) Carrington ND
KNCY(AM) Nebraska City NE
KRFS(AM) Superior NE
KRKE(AM) Albuquerque NM
WEHH(AM) Elmira Heights-Horseheads NY
WWRL(AM) New York NY
WMCR(AM) Oneida NY
WULM(AM) Springfield OH
WTTF(AM) Tiffin OH
KOPT(AM) Eugene OR
KOHI(AM) Saint Helens OR
WHOL(AM) Allentown PA
WHJB(AM) Bedford PA
WPDC(AM) Elizabethtown PA
WJSA(AM) Jersey Shore PA
WLUZ(AM) Bayamon PR
WFIS(AM) Fountain Inn SC
WKZK(AM) North Augusta SC
WMQM(AM) Lakeland TN
KRVA(AM) Cockrell Hill TX
KOGT(AM) Orange TX
KOKE(AM) Pflugerville TX
KRRD(AM) Centerville UT
WCPK(AM) Chesapeake VA
WXMY(AM) Saltville VA
KVRI(AM) Blaine WA
WRPN(AM) Ripon WI
WZZW(AM) Milton WV
WKKX(AM) Wheeling WV

1610 khz
KALT(AM) Atlanta TX

1620 khz
KSMH(AM) West Sacramento CA
WNRP(AM) Gulf Breeze FL
KBLI(AM) Blackfoot ID
WHLY(AM) South Bend IN
KOZN(AM) Bellevue NE
WTAW(AM) College Station TX
WDHP(AM) Frederiksted VI
KYIZ(AM) Renton WA

1630 khz
WRDW(AM) Augusta GA
KCJJ(AM) Iowa City IA
KKGM(AM) Fort Worth TX
KRND(AM) Fox Farm WY

1640 khz
KDIA(AM) Vallejo CA
WTNI(AM) Biloxi MS
KFXY(AM) Enid OK
KDZR(AM) Lake Oswego OR
KBJA(AM) Sandy UT
WKSH(AM) Sussex WI

1650 khz
KWHN(AM) Fort Smith AR
KFOX(AM) Torrance CA
KBJD(AM) Denver CO
KCNZ(AM) Cedar Falls IA
KHRO(AM) El Paso TX
WHKT(AM) Portsmouth VA

1660 khz
KTIQ(AM) Merced CA
WCNZ(AM) Marco Island FL
KXTR(AM) Kansas City KS
WQSN(AM) Kalamazoo MI
WFNA(AM) Charlotte NC
KQWB(AM) West Fargo ND
WWRU(AM) Jersey City NJ
WGIT(AM) Canovanas PR
KRZI(AM) Waco TX
KXOL(AM) Brigham City UT

1670 khz
KHPY(AM) Moreno Valley CA
KNRO(AM) Redding CA
WMWR(AM) Dry Branch GA
WTDY(AM) Madison WI

1680 khz
KAVT(AM) Fresno CA
WLAA(AM) Winter Garden FL
KRJO(AM) Monroe LA
WDSS(AM) Ada MI
WTTM(AM) Princeton NJ
KTFH(AM) Seattle WA

1690 khz
KFSG(AM) Roseville CA
KDDZ(AM) Arvada CO
WWAA(AM) Avondale Estates GA
WRLL(AM) Johnston City IL
WPTX(AM) Lexington Park MD

1700 khz
WEUV(AM) Huntsville AL
WJCC(AM) Miami Springs FL
KBGG(AM) Des Moines IA
KVNS(AM) Brownsville TX
KKLF(AM) Sherman TX

U.S. FM Stations by Frequency

87.9 mhz
*KSFH(FM) Mountain View CA

88.1 mhz
*KRUA(FM) Anchorage AK
*KCUK(FM) Chevak AK
*KCDS(FM) Deadhorse AK
*WAYH(FM) Harvest AL
*WSJL(FM) Northport AL
*KAPG(FM) Bentonville AR
*KARH(FM) Forrest City AR
*KBPW(FM) Hampton AR
*KUYI(FM) Hotevilla AZ
*KLTU(FM) Mammoth AZ
*KNNB(FM) Whiteriver AZ
*KCFY(FM) Yuma AZ
*KECG(FM) El Cerrito CA
*KFCF(FM) Fresno CA
*KLWG(FM) Lompoc CA
*KKJZ(FM) Long Beach CA
*KCRY(FM) Mojave CA
*KNSQ(FM) Mount Shasta CA
*KQNC(FM) Quincy CA
*KEDR(FM) Sacramento CA
*KSRH(FM) San Rafael CA
*KZSC(FM) Santa Cruz CA
*KFLL(FM) Susanville CA
*KDNK(FM) Glenwood Springs CO
*KAFM(FM) Grand Junction CO
*KFDN(FM) Lakewood CO
*KPGS(FM) Pagosa Springs CO
*WESU(FM) Middletown CT
*WMNR(FM) Monroe CT
*WMHS(FM) Pike Creek DE
*WJIS(FM) Bradenton FL
*WEAZ(FM) Holly Hill FL
*WRGP(FM) Homestead FL
*WCRJ(FM) Jacksonville FL
*WBGY(FM) Naples FL
*WHIJ(FM) Ocala FL
*WUWF(FM) Pensacola FL
*WAYF(FM) West Palm Beach FL
*WLXP(FM) Savannah GA
*WAYT(FM) Thomasville GA
*WJSP-FM Warm Springs GA
*KHMG(FM) Barrigada GU
*KHPR(FM) Honolulu HI
*KICB(FM) Fort Dodge IA
*KBBG(FM) Waterloo IA
*KTFY(FM) Buhl ID
*WESN(FM) Bloomington IL
*WCRX(FM) Chicago IL
*WSSD(FM) Chicago IL
*WBMF(FM) Crete IL
*WAXR(FM) Geneseo IL
*WLTL(FM) La Grange IL
*WAES(FM) Lincolnshire IL
*WLRA(FM) Lockport IL
*WPTH(FM) Olney IL
*WLWJ(FM) Petersburg IL
*WSOG(FM) Spring Valley IL
*WETN(FM) Wheaton IL
*WNTH(FM) Winnetka IL
*WVPE(FM) Elkhart IN
*WHCI(FM) Hartford City IN
*WMBL(FM) Mitchell IN
*WJCF(FM) Morristown IN
*WNAS(FM) New Albany IN
*WKRY(FM) Versailles IN
*KBTL(FM) El Dorado KS
*KBCU(FM) North Newton KS
*KJTY(FM) Topeka KS
*WAYD(FM) Auburn KY
*WTRT(FM) Benton KY
*WDFB-FM Danville KY
*WRFL(FM) Lexington KY
*WAXG(FM) Mt. Sterling KY
*WKVY(FM) Somerset KY
*KAYT(FM) Jena LA
*KPAQ(FM) Plaquemine LA
*WMBR(FM) Cambridge MA
*WFHL(FM) New Bedford MA
*WCHC(FM) Worcester MA
*WYPR(FM) Baltimore MD
*WMUC-FM College Park MD
*WYPF(FM) Frederick MD
*WBFH(FM) Bloomfield Hills MI
*WBLW(FM) Gaylord MI
*WHYT(FM) Goodland Township MI
*WHPR(FM) Highland Park MI
*WKHN(FM) Hubbard Lake MI
*WLGH(FM) Leroy Township MI
*WDTR(FM) Monroe MI
*WPQZ(FM) Muskegon MI
*WSDP(FM) Plymouth MI
*WAQQ(FM) Rogers Heights MI
*WYCE(FM) Wyoming MI
*KRLX(FM) Northfield MN
*KVSC(FM) Saint Cloud MN
*KBOJ(FM) Worthington MN
*KLFC(FM) Branson MO
*KCOU(FM) Columbia MO
*KYRV(FM) Concordia MO
*KDHX(FM) Saint Louis MO
*WURC(FM) Holly Springs MS
*WMAW-FM Meridian MS
*KGVA(FM) Fort Belknap Agency MT
*WCQS(FM) Asheville NC
*WPIR(FM) Hickory NC
*WGHW(FM) Lockwoods Folly Town NC
*WKNC-FM Raleigh NC
*KCNT(FM) Hastings NE
*KMLV(FM) Ralston NE
*WYGG(FM) Asbury Park NJ
*WNJS-FM Berlin NJ
*WJPG(FM) Cape May Court House NJ
*WNJT-FM Trenton NJ
KKNM(FM) Gallup NM
*KNMA(FM) Socorro NM
*KRNM(FM) Chalan Kanoa-Saipan NP
*KCEP(FM) Las Vegas NV
*WXBA(FM) Brentwood NY
*WCWP(FM) Brookville NY
*WUBJ(FM) Jamestown NY
*WGWR(FM) Liberty NY
*WARY(FM) Valhalla NY
*WFRW(FM) Webster NY
*WZIP(FM) Akron OH
*WBGU(FM) Bowling Green OH
*WBCJ(FM) Spencerville OH
*WDPR(FM) West Carrollton OH
*KDIM(FM) Coweta OK
*KMSI(FM) Moore OK
*KKRI(FM) Pocola OK
*KDJC(FM) Baker City OR
*KLBR(FM) Bend OR
*KWVA(FM) Eugene OR
*KLFO(FM) Florence OR
*KGRI(FM) Lebanon OR
*KMPQ(FM) Roseburg OR
*WDIY(FM) Allentown PA
*WEFR(FM) Erie PA
*WTGP(FM) Greenville PA
*WXPH(FM) Harrisburg PA
*WRWJ(FM) Murrysville PA
*WBGM(FM) New Berlin PA
*WPEB(FM) Philadelphia PA
*WRSK(FM) Slippery Rock PA
*WRGN(FM) Sweet Valley PA
*WZZD(FM) Warwick PA
*WPTC(FM) Williamsport PA
*WCRP(FM) Guayama PR
*WELH(FM) Providence RI
*WBLQ(FM) Westerly RI
*WSBF-FM Clemson SC
*WRJA-FM Sumter SC
*KRSD(FM) Sioux Falls SD
*WUTC(FM) Chattanooga TN
*WAMP(FM) Jackson TN
*WFSK(FM) Nashville TN
*WAZD(FM) Savannah TN
*KGNZ(FM) Abilene TX
*KFRT(FM) Bay City TX
*KLBT(FM) Beaumont TX
*KGLF(FM) Doss TX
*KITG(FM) Gonzales TX
*KHOY(FM) Laredo TX
*KTXT-FM Lubbock TX
*KHID(FM) McAllen TX
*KNTU(FM) McKinney TX
*KFTG(FM) Pasadena TX
*KNLE-FM Round Rock TX
*KFRI(FM) Stanton TX
*KVLW(FM) Waco TX
*KWCR-FM Ogden UT
*KPGR(FM) Pleasant Grove UT
*WHOV(FM) Hampton VA
*WRIH(FM) Richmond VA
*WNCH(FM) Norwich VT
*KTRW-FM East Wenatchee WA
*KCWU(FM) Ellensburg WA
*KTCV(FM) Kennewick WA
*KSBC(FM) Nile WA
*KLOP(FM) Ocean Park WA
*KAYB(FM) Sunnyside WA
*WHID(FM) Green Bay WI
*WJTY(FM) Lancaster WI
*WMWK(FM) Milwaukee WI
*WVBC(FM) Bethany WV
*WKJL(FM) Clarksburg WV
*WMUL(FM) Huntington WV
*WPCN(FM) Point Pleasant WV
*KWYH(FM) Cheyenne WY
*KCWW(FM) Evanston WY
*KCWC-FM Riverton WY
*KPRQ(FM) Sheridan WY

88.3 mhz
*WJCK(FM) Piedmont AL
*WAPR(FM) Selma AL
*KBCM(FM) Blytheville AR
*KXUA(FM) Fayetteville AR
*KABF(FM) Little Rock AR
*KNAI(FM) Phoenix AZ
*KPHF(FM) Phoenix AZ
*KDKL(FM) Coalinga CA
*KMUE(FM) Eureka CA
*KAXL(FM) Green Acres CA
*KLVN(FM) Livingston CA
*KLVC(FM) Magalia CA
*KUCR(FM) Riverside CA
*KSDS(FM) San Diego CA
*KCLU(FM) Thousand Oaks CA
*KPYR(FM) Craig CO
*KLHV(FM) Fort Collins CO
*KPRH(FM) Montrose CO
*KTPL(FM) Pueblo CO
*WAVQ(FM) Key West FL
*WBIY(FM) La Belle FL
*WLMS(FM) Lecanto FL
*WJNF(FM) Marianna FL
*WIRP(FM) Pennsuco FL
*WTLG(FM) Starke FL
*WPOZ(FM) Union Park FL
*WPPR(FM) Demorest GA
*WAWH(FM) Dublin GA
*WNEE(FM) Jasper GA
*WLPT(FM) Jesup GA
*KCCK-FM Cedar Rapids IA
*KNNU(FM) Newton IA
*KMSC(FM) Sioux City IA
*KARJ(FM) Kuna ID
*WCLR(FM) Arlington Heights IL
*WZRD(FM) Chicago IL
*WDGC-FM Downers Grove IL
*WAWF(FM) Kankakee IL
*WIUS(FM) Macomb IL
*WHCM(FM) Palatine IL
*WPJC(FM) Pontiac IL
*WPRC(FM) Princeton IL
*WJLY(FM) Ramsey IL
*WFEN(FM) Rockford IL
*WQNA(FM) Springfield IL
*WEAX(FM) Angola IN
*WDSO(FM) Chesterton IN
*WNIN-FM Evansville IN
*WLAB(FM) Fort Wayne IN
*WWMU(FM) Muncie IN
*WSOH(FM) New Washington IN
*KBJQ(FM) Bronson KS
*KVCO(FM) Concordia KS
*KYFW(FM) Wichita KS
*WSGP(FM) Glasgow KY
*WOCS(FM) Lerose KY
*WRBH(FM) New Orleans LA
*KAPI(FM) Ruston LA
*WBMT(FM) Boxford MA
*WIQH(FM) Concord MA
*WGAO(FM) Franklin MA
*WRPS(FM) Rockland MA
*WYAR(FM) Yarmouth ME
*WCBN-FM Ann Arbor MI
*WXOU(FM) Auburn Hills MI
*WICE(FM) Ironwood MI
*WAYK(FM) Kalamazoo MI
*WAAQ(FM) Onsted MI
*WNFA(FM) Port Huron MI
*WSHJ(FM) Southfield MI
*WEJC(FM) White Star MI
*KBPN(FM) Brainerd MN
*KJAB-FM Mexico MO
*KWND(FM) Springfield MO
*WAFR(FM) Tupelo MS
*KFRD(FM) Butte MT
*KPGB(FM) Pryor MT
*WGWG(FM) Boiling Springs NC
*WGPS(FM) Elizabeth City NC
*WUAW(FM) Erwin NC
*KBMK(FM) Bismarck ND
*KLNB(FM) Grand Island NE
*KLJV(FM) Scottsbluff NE
*WEVS(FM) Nashua NH
*WVBH(FM) Beach Haven West NJ
*WBGO(FM) Newark NJ
*KLYT(FM) Albuquerque NM
*KLRH(FM) Sparks NV
*WVCR-FM Loudonville NY
*WFSO(FM) Olivebridge NY
*WXLU(FM) Peru NY
*WSBU(FM) Saint Bonaventure NY
*WLIU(FM) Southampton NY
*WAER(FM) Syracuse NY
*WCOU(FM) Warsaw NY
*WBWC(FM) Berea OH
*WJVS(FM) Cincinnati OH
*WLFC(FM) Findlay OH
*WMRT(FM) Marietta OH
*WOHP(FM) Portsmouth OH
*WAUI(FM) Shelby OH
*WVSO(FM) South Vienna OH
*WXTS-FM Toledo OH
*WXUT(FM) Toledo OH
*KAZC(FM) Tishomingo OK
*KSRG(FM) Ashland OR
*KBVM(FM) Portland OR
*WGEV(FM) Beaver Falls PA
*WDCV-FM Carlisle PA
*WZXQ(FM) Chambersburg PA
*WWEC(FM) Elizabethtown PA
*WRCT(FM) Pittsburgh PA
*WPGP(FM) Tafton PA
*WRUO(FM) Mayaguez PR
*WQRI(FM) Bristol RI
*WAFJ(FM) Belvedere SC
*WMBJ(FM) Murrell's Inlet SC
*KESD(FM) Brookings SD
*KTPT(FM) Rapid City SD
*WQNN(FM) Brownsville TN
*WAYQ(FM) Clarksville TN
*WCQR-FM Kingsport TN
*WOEZ(FM) Maynardville TN
*WMTS-FM Murfreesboro TN
*WBIA(FM) Shelbyville TN
*KJRT(FM) Amarillo TX
*KBNR(FM) Brownsville TX
*WDSO(FM) Chesterton IN
*KAFR(FM) Conroe TX
*KJCR(FM) Keene TX
*KPAC(FM) San Antonio TX
*KCPW-FM Salt Lake City UT
*WOTC(FM) Edinburg VA
*WRVL(FM) Lynchburg VA
*WNUB-FM Northfield VT
*KMLW(FM) Moses Lake WA
*WHWC(FM) Menomonie WI
*KNIL(FM) Jackson WY

88.5 mhz
*KAKL(FM) Anchorage AK
*KTNA(FM) Talkeetna AK
*WLJR(FM) Birmingham AL
*WJIA(FM) Guntersville AL
*WBHY-FM Mobile AL
*KLKA(FM) Globe AZ
*KFLT-FM Tucson AZ
*KWTW(FM) Bishop CA
*KVFR(FM) Laytonville CA
*KSBR(FM) Mission Viejo CA
*KCSN(FM) Northridge CA
*KPSC(FM) Palm Springs CA
*KJCQ(FM) Quincy CA
*KQED-FM San Francisco CA
*KLVH(FM) San Luis Obispo CA
*KQKL(FM) Selma CA
*KHMS(FM) Victorville CA
*KGNU-FM Boulder CO
*KCIC(FM) Grand Junction CO
*KTAH(FM) Steamboat Springs CO
*KTDU(FM) Trimble CO
*WVOF(FM) Fairfield CT
*WEDW-FM Stamford CT
*WAMU(FM) Washington DC
*WJCB(FM) Clewiston FL
*WWLC(FM) Cross City FL
*WMFL(FM) Florida City FL
*WWIA(FM) Palm Bay FL
*WFCF(FM) Saint Augustine FL
*WKPX(FM) Sunrise FL
*WMNF(FM) Tampa FL
*WFRP(FM) Americus GA
*WRAS(FM) Atlanta GA
*WTMQ(FM) Lumpkin GA
*WVDA(FM) Valdosta GA
*KURE(FM) Ames IA
*KALA(FM) Davenport IA
*KIAD(FM) Dubuque IA
*KBDC(FM) Mason City IA
*KDCR(FM) Sioux Center IA
*KBSY(FM) Burley ID
*WBEL(FM) Cairo IL
*WHPK-FM Chicago IL
*WHFH(FM) Flossmoor IL
*WGBK(FM) Glenview IL
*WHSD(FM) Hinsdale IL
*WBNH(FM) Pekin IL
*WGCA-FM Quincy IL
*WTMK(FM) Lowell IN
*WHNI(FM) Rochester IN
*WCRT(FM) Terre Haute IN
*WXVW(FM) Veedersburg IN
*KBQC(FM) Independence KS
*KAKA(FM) Salina KS
*WEKF(FM) Corbin KY
*WBMK(FM) Morehead KY
*WJIE-FM Okolona KY
*WJFM(FM) Baton Rouge LA
*WFCR(FM) Amherst MA
*WWTA(FM) Marion MA
*WHCF(FM) Bangor ME
*WSEW(FM) Sanford ME
*WGVU-FM Allendale MI
*WJOM(FM) Eagle MI
*WJKQ(FM) Jackson MI
*WIAB(FM) Mackinaw City MI
*WOAS(FM) Ontonagon MI
*KNCM(FM) Appleton MN
*KCRB(FM) Bemidji MN
*KBEM-FM Minneapolis MN

Broadcasting & Cable Yearbook 2006

D-657

U.S. FM Stations by Frequency

*KGSF(FM) Anderson MO
*KLJC(FM) Kansas City MO
*KUMR(FM) Rolla MO
*WUSM-FM Hattiesburg MS
*WJSU(FM) Jackson MS
*WXBE(FM) Beaufort NC
*WZNB(FM) New Bern NC
*WRTP(FM) Roanoke Rapids NC
*WHYC(FM) Swanquarter NC
*WFDD-FM Winston-Salem NC
*KEYA(FM) Belcourt ND
*KCJL(FM) Lincoln ND
*KLCV(FM) Lincoln NE
*WNJP(FM) Sussex NJ
*KPKJ(FM) Mentmore NM
*KEKL(FM) Mesquite NV
*WPOB-FM Plainview NY
*WRUR-FM Rochester NY
*WCII(FM) Spencer NY
*WKWZ(FM) Syosset NY
*WMUB(FM) Oxford OH
*WLRY(FM) Rushville OH
*WYSA(FM) Wauseon OH
*WYSU(FM) Youngstown OH
*KTKL(FM) Stigler OK
*KSBA(FM) Coos Bay OR
*KPIJ(FM) Junction City OR
*KLMF(FM) Klamath Falls OR
*KLRF(FM) Milton-Freewater OR
*KMKR(FM) Oakridge OR
*KWRX(FM) Redmond OR
*KAIK(FM) Tillamook OR
*WMCE(FM) Erie PA
*WYFU(FM) Masontown PA
*WXPN(FM) Philadelphia PA
*WRKC(FM) Wilkes-Barre PA
*WTMV(FM) Youngsville PA
*WPLI(FM) Levittown PR
*WEPC(FM) Belton SC
*WFCH(FM) Charleston SC
*WTTU(FM) Cookeville TN
*WVCP(FM) Gallatin TN
*WZXX(FM) Lawrenceburg TN
*WQOX(FM) Memphis TN
*WAUT-FM Tullahoma TN
*KHIB(FM) Bastrop TX
*KPBB(FM) Brownfield TX
*KLRW(FM) Byrne TX
*KCKT(FM) Crockett TX
*KOIR(FM) Edinburg TX
*KTEP(FM) El Paso TX
*KBMD(FM) Marble Falls TX
*KEOM(FM) Mesquite TX
*KPMB(FM) Plainview TX
*KVLT(FM) Temple TX
*KAYK(FM) Victoria TX
*KMQX(FM) Weatherford TX
*WVTW(FM) Charlottesville VA
*WJLZ(FM) Virginia Beach VA
*WPVA(FM) Saint Johnsbury VT
*KRLF(FM) Pullman WA
*KPLU-FM Tacoma WA
*KYVT(FM) Yakima WA
*WGNV(FM) Milladore WI
*WRGX(FM) Sturgeon Bay WI
*WVPN(FM) Charleston WV

88.7 mhz
*KJHA(FM) Houston AK
*WELL-FM Dadeville AL
*WRWA(FM) Dothan AL
*WQPR(FM) Muscle Shoals AL
*KBPU(FM) De Queen AR
*KNAU(FM) Flagstaff AZ
*KISL(FM) Avalon CA
*KUBO(FM) Calexico CA
*KSPC(FM) Claremont CA
*KZLU(FM) Inyokern CA
*KMPO(FM) Modesto CA
*KAIS(FM) Redwood Valley CA
*KQSC(FM) Santa Barbara CA
*KXJS(FM) Sutter CA
*KYLU(FM) Tehachapi CA
*KRZA(FM) Alamosa CO
*KCME(FM) Manitou Springs CO
*WNHU(FM) West Haven CT
*WWKG(FM) Clermont FL

*WKTO(FM) Edgewater FL
*WAYJ(FM) Fort Myers FL
*WJFR(FM) Jacksonville FL
*WMOC(FM) Lumber City GA
*WJDS(FM) Sparta GA
*KLNI(FM) Decorah IA
*KIGC(FM) Oskaloosa IA
*KWDM(FM) West Des Moines IA
*WPCD(FM) Champaign IL
*WLUW(FM) Chicago IL
*WSIE(FM) Edwardsville IL
*WRSE(FM) Elmhurst IL
*WCSF(FM) Joliet IL
*WSRI(FM) Sugar Grove IL
*WGVE(FM) Gary IN
*WICR(FM) Indianapolis IN
*WBHW(FM) Loogootee IN
*WMMT(FM) Whitesburg KY
*KRVS(FM) Lafayette LA
*KBMQ(FM) Monroe LA
*WIAA(FM) Interlochen MI
*WMLS(FM) Grand Marais MN
*KMSE(FM) Rochester MN
*KXMS(FM) Joplin MO
*KTRM(FM) Kirksville MO
*WYTF(FM) Indianola MS
*WJZB(FM) Starkville MS
*KLKM(FM) Kalispell MT
*WXDU(FM) Durham NC
*WRAE(FM) Raeford NC
*WAGO(FM) Snow Hill NC
*WNCW(FM) Spindale NC
*KFBN(FM) Fargo ND
*KLNE-FM Lexington NE
*WRSU-FM New Brunswick NJ
*WXXY-FM Port Republic NJ
*WPSC-FM Wayne NJ
*KWPR(FM) Lund NV
*KUNR(FM) Reno NV
*WBFO(FM) Buffalo NY
*WHCL-FM Clinton NY
*WRHU(FM) Hempstead NY
*WSQA(FM) Hornell NY
*WPKM(FM) Montauk NY
*WNYK(FM) Nyack NY
*WRHV(FM) Poughkeepsie NY
*WFNP(FM) Rosendale NY
*WKYJ(FM) Rouses Point NY
*WOBO(FM) Batavia OH
*WOFN(FM) Beach City OH
*WUFM(FM) Columbus OH
*WJCU(FM) University Heights OH
*KQUJ(FM) Ada OK
*KLVV(FM) Ponca City OK
*KWTU(FM) Tulsa OK
*KLOY(FM) Astoria OR
*KLVP-FM Cherryville OR
*KBVR(FM) Corvallis OR
*KOAP(FM) Lakeview OR
*KJKL(FM) Selma OR
*WWLU(FM) Lincoln University PA
*WWCF(FM) McConnellsburg PA
*WZXM(FM) Middletown PA
*WSYC-FM Shippensburg PA
*WBYX(FM) Stroudsburg PA
*WCYJ-FM Waynesburg PA
*WJMF(FM) Smithfield RI
*WAGP(FM) Beaufort SC
*WYFV(FM) Cayce SC
*WAYM(FM) Columbia TN
*WIGH(FM) Lexington TN
*KAZI-FM Austin TX
*KASV(FM) Borger TX
*KKLM(FM) Corpus Christi TX
*KEPI(FM) Eagle Pass TX
*KTCU-FM Fort Worth TX
*KHFD(FM) Hereford TX
*KUHF(FM) Houston TX
*KKER(FM) Kerrville TX
*KTPB(FM) Kilgore TX
*KLVW(FM) West Odessa TX
*KMCU(FM) Wichita Falls TX
*KNKL(FM) North Ogden UT
*WFOS(FM) Chesapeake VA
*WXJM(FM) Harrisonburg VA
*WWPV-FM Colchester VT
*WRVT(FM) Rutland VT

*KAGU(FM) Spokane WA
*WERN(FM) Madison WI
*WRFW(FM) River Falls WI
*KOHR(FM) Sheridan WY

88.9 mhz
*KEUL(FM) Girdwood AK
*KMJG(FM) Homer AK
*KJLP(FM) Palmer AK
*WMFT(FM) Tuscaloosa AL
*KKDU(FM) El Dorado AR
*KAOW(FM) Fort Smith AR
*KAIC(FM) Tucson AZ
*KAWC-FM Yuma AZ
*KUCI(FM) Irvine CA
*KTLW(FM) Lancaster CA
*KXLU(FM) Los Angeles CA
*KFPR(FM) Redding CA
*KOGR(FM) Rosedale CA
*KXJZ(FM) Sacramento CA
*KUSP(FM) Santa Cruz CA
*KRTM(FM) Temecula CA
*KDUV(FM) Visalia CA
*KCJX(FM) Carbondale CO
*KLCQ(FM) Eaton CO
*KRFC(FM) Fort Collins CO
*WJMJ(FM) Hartford CT
*WQCS(FM) Fort Pierce FL
*WDNA(FM) Miami FL
*WFSU-FM Tallahassee FL
*WYFE(FM) Tarpon Springs FL
*WMSL(FM) Athens GA
*WWIO-FM Brunswick GA
*WBKG(FM) Macon GA
*WGUR(FM) Milledgeville GA
*WKEU-FM The Rock GA
*KHJC(FM) Lihue HI
*KIHS(FM) Adel IA
*KSTM(FM) Indianola IA
*KDMR(FM) Mitchellville IA
*KJIA(FM) Spirit Lake IA
*KLRX(FM) Wapello IA
*KWVI(FM) Waverly IA
*KLHS-FM Lewiston ID
*KEFX(FM) Twin Falls ID
*WEIU(FM) Charleston IL
*WIIT(FM) Chicago IL
*WEPS(FM) Elgin IL
*WMXM(FM) Lake Forest IL
*WLNX(FM) Lincoln IL
*WJCG(FM) Monee IL
*WVSI(FM) Mount Vernon IL
*WWGN(FM) Ottawa IL
*WRRG(FM) River Grove IL
*WARG(FM) Summit IL
*WJCJ(FM) Ladoga IN
*WSND-FM Notre Dame IN
*WMYJ(FM) Oolitic IN
*WJYW(FM) Union City IN
*KPRD(FM) Hays KS
*KTJO-FM Ottawa KS
*WKYU-FM Bowling Green KY
*WEKU(FM) Richmond KY
*WERS(FM) Boston MA
*WEAA(FM) Baltimore MD
*WMDR-FM Oakland ME
*WDBM(FM) East Lansing MI
*WJCE(FM) Elkton MI
*WAKL(FM) Flint MI
*WBLU-FM Grand Rapids MI
*KNSR(FM) Collegeville MN
*KRNW(FM) Chillicothe MO
*KSEF(FM) Farmington MO
*KJLU(FM) Jefferson City MO
*WMAU-FM Bude MS
*WKNA(FM) Senatobia MS
*KNFR(FM) Butte MT
*KGFC(FM) Great Falls MT
*KYWH(FM) Lockwood MT
*WUND-FM Manteo NC
*WSHA(FM) Raleigh NC
*KLJA(FM) Jamestown ND
*KMPR(FM) Minot ND
*KVSS(FM) Omaha NE
*WAJM(FM) Atlantic City NJ
*WMNJ(FM) Madison NJ
*WBZC(FM) Pemberton NJ

*WMCX(FM) West Long Branch NJ
*KHII(FM) Cloudcroft NM
*KNMI(FM) Farmington NM
*KLLU(FM) Gallup NM
*KRUC(FM) Las Cruces NM
*KNPR(FM) Las Vegas NV
*WCIY(FM) Canandaigua NY
*WITC(FM) Cazenovia NY
*WCVF-FM Fredonia NY
*WNYO(FM) Oswego NY
*WRPJ(FM) Port Jervis NY
*WFRS(FM) Smithtown NY
*WSIA(FM) Staten Island NY
*WSLJ(FM) Watertown NY
*WRDL(FM) Ashland OH
*WBJV(FM) Steubenville OH
*WSTB(FM) Streetsboro OH
*WHEI(FM) Tiffin OH
*WCSU-FM Wilberforce OH
*KARU(FM) Cache OK
*KWXC(FM) Grove OK
*KYLV(FM) Oklahoma City OK
*KKLJ(FM) Klamath Falls OR
*KYOR(FM) Newport OR
*KQFE(FM) Springfield OR
*WFSE(FM) Edinboro PA
*WFRJ(FM) Johnstown PA
*WNNW(FM) New Wilmington PA
*WQSU(FM) Selinsgrove PA
*WBYO(FM) Sellersville PA
*WPUC(FM) Ponce PR
*WKVC(FM) North Myrtle Beach SC
*WNSC-FM Rock Hill SC
*WMBW(FM) Chattanooga TN
*WTNN(FM) Union City TN
*KETR(FM) Commerce TX
*KMBH-FM Harlingen TX
*KLDN(FM) Lufkin TX
*KSUR(FM) Mart TX
*WCVE(FM) Richmond VA
*KCSH(FM) Ellensburg WA
*WLSU(FM) La Crosse WI
*WYMS(FM) Milwaukee WI
*WOJB(FM) Reserve WI
*WVPW(FM) Buckhannon WV
*WVEP(FM) Martinsburg WV
*KAIW(FM) Laramie WY
*KWCF(FM) Sheridan WY

89.1 mhz
*WKNG-FM Heflin AL
*WLBF(FM) Montgomery AL
*KUAR(FM) Little Rock AR
*KLVK(FM) Fountain Hills AZ
*KUAZ-FM Tucson AZ
*KCEA(FM) Atherton CA
*KPRX(FM) Bakersfield CA
*KVID(FM) Barstow CA
*KHAP(FM) Chico CA
*KCJH(FM) Livingston CA
*KCRU(FM) Oxnard CA
*KBBF(FM) Santa Rosa CA
*KTLC(FM) Canon City CO
*KRLJ(FM) La Junta CO
*KVMT(FM) Montrose CO
*WNPR(FM) Norwich CT
*WXHL-FM Christiana DE
*WUFT-FM Gainesville FL
*WLAZ(FM) Kissimmee FL
*WFSW(FM) Panama City FL
*WSMR(FM) Sarasota FL
*WBCX(FM) Gainesville GA
*KWOF-FM Hiawatha IA
*KPVL(FM) Postville IA
*KWAR(FM) Waverly IA
*KAWS(FM) Boise ID
*WNIE(FM) Freeport IL
*WVJC(FM) Mount Carmel IL
*WONC(FM) Naperville IL
*WGLT(FM) Normal IL
*WSPM(FM) Cloverdale IN
*WBOI(FM) Fort Wayne IN
*WAUZ(FM) Greensburg IN
*KMUW(FM) Wichita KS
*KOUZ(FM) Blanchard LA
*KVDP(FM) Dry Prong LA
*WBSN-FM New Orleans LA

*KLPI-FM Ruston LA
*KHBQ(FM) Sulphur LA
*WHAB(FM) Acton MA
*WETH(FM) Hagerstown MD
*WTRK(FM) Bay City MI
*WWKM(FM) Imlay City MI
*WIDR(FM) Kalamazoo MI
*WPHS(FM) Warren MI
*WEMU(FM) Ypsilanti MI
*KCLC(FM) Saint Charles MO
*KWFC(FM) Springfield MO
*WMBU(FM) Forest MS
*WPAS(FM) Pascagoula MS
*KUFM(FM) Missoula MT
*KVLQ(FM) Lincoln ND
*KHNE-FM Hastings NE
*KKSB(FM) Scottsbluff NE
*WEVO(FM) Concord NH
*WWCJ(FM) Cape May NJ
*WFDU(FM) Teaneck NJ
*WWFM(FM) Trenton NJ
*KANW(FM) Albuquerque NM
*KRSR(FM) Roswell NM
*WDWN(FM) Auburn NY
*WBSU(FM) Brockport NY
*WCID(FM) Friendship NY
*WNYU-FM New York NY
*WMHT-FM Schenectady NY
*WJPZ-FM Syracuse NY
*WOUC-FM Cambridge OH
*WJJE(FM) Delaware OH
*WOUL-FM Ironton OH
*WNZN(FM) Lorain OH
*WLMH(FM) Morrow OH
*WUSO(FM) Springfield OH
*WKSV(FM) Thompson OH
*KWRI(FM) Bartlesville OK
*KYCU(FM) Clinton OK
*KXTH(FM) Seminole OK
*KSMF(FM) Ashland OR
*KMHD(FM) Gresham OR
*KLFR(FM) Reedsport OR
*WBYH(FM) Hawley PA
*WFNM(FM) Lancaster PA
*WLOG(FM) Markleysburg PA
*WSFX(FM) Nanticoke PA
*WYBF(FM) Radnor Township PA
*WRXV(FM) State College PA
*WXVU(FM) Villanova PA
*WLJK(FM) Aiken SC
*KVFL(FM) Pierre SD
*KAUR(FM) Sioux Falls SD
*KBHU-FM Spearfish SD
*KJBB(FM) Watertown SD
*WYLV(FM) Alcoa TN
*WNAZ-FM Nashville TN
*WDNX(FM) Olive Hill TN
*KXLV(FM) Amarillo TX
*KEOS(FM) College Station TX
*KOHM(FM) Lubbock TX
*KYFP(FM) Palestine TX
*KSTX(FM) San Antonio TX
*KSQX(FM) Springtown TX
*KQXS(FM) Stephenville TX
*KBYU-FM Provo UT
*WWIP(FM) Cheriton VA
*WCNV(FM) Heathsville VA
*WVTF(FM) Roanoke VA
*KFAE-FM Richland WA
*WBSD(FM) Burlington WI
*KLWC(FM) Casper WY
*KURT(FM) Jackson WY

89.3 mhz
*KATB(FM) Anchorage AK
*WALN(FM) Carrollton AL
*WLRH(FM) Huntsville AL
*KAYH(FM) Fayetteville AR
*KKLT(FM) Texarkana AR
*KAIH(FM) Lake Havasu City AZ
*KNAQ(FM) Prescott AZ
*KPFB(FM) Berkeley CA
*KOHL(FM) Fremont CA
*KVPR(FM) Fresno CA
*KPJP(FM) Greenville CA
*KCRI(FM) Indio CA
*KAKX(FM) Mendocino CA

Broadcasting & Cable Yearbook 2006
D-658

U.S. FM Stations by Frequency

*KLSI(FM) Moss Beach CA
*KQEI-FM North Highlands CA
*KPCC(FM) Pasadena CA
*KPDO(FM) Pescadero CA
*KMTG(FM) San Jose CA
*KLFF-FM San Luis Obispo CA
*KUVO(FM) Denver CO
*KLBV(FM) Steamboat Springs CO
*WRTC-FM Hartford CT
*WSGG(FM) Norfolk CT
*WPFW(FM) Washington DC
*WRMB(FM) Boynton Beach FL
*WKFA(FM) Saint Catherine FL
*WPIO(FM) Titusville FL
*WBJY(FM) Americus GA
*WRFG(FM) Atlanta GA
*WECC-FM Folkston GA
*KPRG(FM) Hagatna GU
*KIPO(FM) Honolulu HI
*KJMC(FM) Des Moines IA
*KUOI-FM Moscow ID
*WKKC(FM) Chicago IL
*WDLM-FM East Moline IL
*WNUR-FM Evanston IL
*WZRS(FM) Pana IL
*WIPA(FM) Pittsfield IL
*WGNJ(FM) Saint Joseph IL
*WJEL(FM) Indianapolis IN
*WYTJ(FM) Linton IN
*WRXH(FM) Plymouth IN
*WVXR(FM) Richmond IN
*WNKJ(FM) Hopkinsville KY
*WFPL(FM) Louisville KY
*WGCF(FM) Paducah KY
*WRKF(FM) Baton Rouge LA
*WAMH(FM) Amherst MA
*WHSN(FM) Bangor ME
*WMSJ(FM) Freeport ME
*WTLI(FM) Bear Creek Township MI
*WHFR(FM) Dearborn MI
*WMSQ(FM) Marlette MI
*WBLD(FM) Orchard Lake MI
*WJKN-FM Spring Arbor MI
*WGNB(FM) Zeeland MI
*KCMP(FM) Northfield MN
*KOPJ(FM) Sebeka MN
*KRSW(FM) Worthington MN
*KTBJ(FM) Festus MO
*KCUR-FM Kansas City MO
*WAII(FM) Hattiesburg MS
*WATU(FM) Port Gibson MS
*KLMT(FM) Billings MT
*KRFR(FM) Bozeman MT
*WXYC(FM) Chapel Hill NC
*WSOE(FM) Elon NC
*WTEB(FM) New Bern NC
*WZRI(FM) Spring Lake NC
*WBFJ-FM Winston-Salem NC
*KUND-FM Grand Forks ND
*KZUM(FM) Lincoln NE
*KXNE-FM Norfolk NE
*WNJB(FM) Bridgeton NJ
*WFJS(FM) Hazlet NJ
*KELP-FM Mesquite NM
*WSKG-FM Binghamton NY
*WGSU(FM) Geneseo NY
*WLJP(FM) Monroe NY
*WMHN(FM) Webster NY
*WVXC(FM) Chillicothe OH
*WCSB(FM) Cleveland OH
*WYSM(FM) Lima OH
*WYSZ(FM) Maumee OH
*WMKV(FM) Reading OH
*WKRW(FM) Wooster OH
*KALU(FM) Langston OK
*KCCU(FM) Lawton OK
*KSSO(FM) Norman OK
*KLRB(FM) Stuart OK
*KLOV(FM) Winchester OR
*WJCS(FM) Allentown PA
*WQED(FM) Pittsburgh PA
*WRDV(FM) Warminster PA
*WJVP(FM) Culebra PR
*WSCI(FM) Charleston SC
*WRFE(FM) Chesterfield SC
*WLFJ(FM) Greenville SC
*KBHE-FM Rapid City SD

*WMKW(FM) Crossville TN
*WAJJ(FM) McKenzie TN
*WYPL(FM) Memphis TN
*KPBD(FM) Big Spring TX
*KPBE(FM) Brownwood TX
*KNON(FM) Dallas TX
*KHCP(FM) Paris TX
*KJJN(FM) San Angelo TX
*KXBJ(FM) Victoria TX
*KAER(FM) Saint George UT
*WVTU(FM) Charlottesville VA
*WJYA(FM) Emporia VA
*KASB(FM) Bellevue WA
*KUGS(FM) Bellingham WA
*KAOS(FM) Olympia WA
*KVIX(FM) Port Angeles WA
*KBNO-FM White Salmon WA
*WPNE-FM Green Bay WI
*WWLA(FM) South Charleston WV

89.5 mhz
*KWVK(FM) Kasilof AK
*WBFR(FM) Birmingham AL
*WGTF(FM) Dothan AL
*WRNF(FM) Selma AL
*KCAC(FM) Camden AR
*KBMJ(FM) Heber Springs AR
*KJZA(FM) Drake AZ
*KBAQ-FM Phoenix AZ
*KBES(FM) Ceres CA
*KARQ(FM) East Sonora CA
*KSMC(FM) Moraga CA
*KVMR(FM) Nevada City CA
*KLFH(FM) Ojai CA
*KPBS-FM San Diego CA
*KPOO(FM) San Francisco CA
*KSBX(FM) Santa Barbara CA
*KGLV(FM) Shafter CA
*KPRA(FM) Ukiah CA
*KXRD(FM) Victorville CA
*KBWA(FM) Brush CO
*KTCF(FM) Dolores CO
*KPRN(FM) Grand Junction CO
*KTSC-FM Pueblo CO
*WPKN(FM) Bridgeport CT
*WKSG(FM) Cedar Creek FL
*WGSG(FM) Mayo FL
*WFIT(FM) Melbourne FL
*WSRX(FM) Naples FL
*WPCS(FM) Pensacola FL
*WYFK(FM) Columbus GA
*WNGU(FM) Dahlonega GA
*WYFS(FM) Savannah GA
*WYFW(FM) Winder GA
*KHKE(FM) Cedar Falls IA
*KLCD(FM) Decorah IA
*KEGR(FM) Fort Dodge IA
*KTSY(FM) Caldwell ID
*KLRI(FM) Rigby ID
*WNIJ(FM) De Kalb IL
*WJMU(FM) Decatur IL
*WDRS(FM) Dorsey IL
*WGRN(FM) Greenville IL
*WIUW(FM) Warsaw IL
*WBSB(FM) Anderson IN
*WBEW(FM) Chesterton IN
*WFCI(FM) Franklin IN
*WWTS(FM) Logansport IN
*WBKE-FM North Manchester IN
*KHCD(FM) Salina KS
*WKPB(FM) Henderson KY
*KAHJ(FM) Bunkie LA
*KYFL(FM) Monroe LA
*WNCK(FM) Nantucket MA
*WSKB(FM) Westfield MA
*WSCL(FM) Salisbury MD
*WAHS(FM) Auburn Hills MI
*WCMU-FM Mount Pleasant MI
*WOVI(FM) Novi MI
*WOFR(FM) Schoolcraft MI
*WBHG(FM) Alexandria MN
*WJRF(FM) Duluth MN
*KBPG(FM) Montevideo MN
*KQAL(FM) Winona MN
*KNLH(FM) Cedar Hill MO
*KOPN(FM) Columbia MO

*KCFV(FM) Ferguson MO
*KOKS(FM) Poplar Bluff MO
*WMAE-FM Booneville MS
*WPRG(FM) Columbia MS
*WYAZ(FM) Yazoo City MS
*WTJY(FM) Asheboro NC
*KPPR(FM) Williston ND
*KOSJ(FM) Mitchell NE
*WSJI(FM) Cherry Hill NJ
*WSOU(FM) South Orange NJ
*KENW-FM Portales NM
*KQRI(FM) Socorro NM
*KCNV(FM) Las Vegas NV
*WCOF(FM) Arcade NY
*WSLU(FM) Canton NY
*WSLL(FM) Saranac Lake NY
*WUNY(FM) Utica NY
*WBCY(FM) Archbold OH
*WCVV(FM) Belpre OH
*WDPS(FM) Dayton OH
*WQRP(FM) Dayton OH
*WHSS(FM) Hamilton OH
*WVMS(FM) Sandusky OH
*WVXW(FM) West Union OH
*KJCC(FM) Carnegie OK
*KWGS(FM) Tulsa OK
*KTEC(FM) Klamath Falls OR
*KEFS(FM) North Powder OR
*KPFR(FM) Pine Grove OR
*KTCB(FM) Tillamook OR
*WDNR(FM) Chester PA
*WAWN(FM) Franklin PA
*WITF-FM Harrisburg PA
*WNTE(FM) Mansfield PA
*WWPJ(FM) Pen Argyl PA
*KLND(FM) Little Eagle SD
*WETS(FM) Johnson City TN
*WMOT(FM) Murfreesboro TN
*KMFA(FM) Austin TX
*KZBJ(FM) Bay City TX
*KEPX(FM) Eagle Pass TX
*KXCR(FM) El Paso TX
*KBMM(FM) Odessa TX
*KLUX(FM) Robstown TX
*KTOT(FM) Spearman TX
*KVNE(FM) Tyler TX
*KYQX(FM) Weatherford TX
*KMOC(FM) Wichita Falls TX
*KAGJ(FM) Ephraim UT
*KUSR(FM) Logan UT
*WHRV(FM) Norfolk VA
*WWED(FM) Spotsylvania VA
*WVPR(FM) Windsor VT
*KEWU-FM Cheney WA
*KJVH(FM) Longview WA
*KNHC(FM) Seattle WA
*KSOH(FM) Wapato WA
*WCLQ(FM) Wausau WI
*WAUA(FM) Petersburg WV
*KWRR(FM) Ethete WY

89.7 mhz
*KXKM(FM) McCarthy AK
*KBHN(FM) Booneville AR
*KUAP(FM) Pine Bluff AR
*KRMH(FM) Red Mesa AZ
*KNCA(FM) Burney CA
*KFJC(FM) Los Altos CA
*KLVM(FM) Prunedale CA
*KGBM(FM) Randsburg CA
*KSGN(FM) Riverside CA
*KXHV(FM) Sacramento CA
*KHFR(FM) Santa Maria CA
*KARM(FM) Visalia CA
*KEPC(FM) Colorado Springs CO
*KXWA(FM) Loveland CO
*KTPS(FM) Pagosa Springs CO
*KRYI(FM) Rye CO
*WDJW(FM) Somers CT
*WMCU(FM) Miami FL
*WJLU(FM) New Smyrna Beach FL
*WVFS(FM) Tallahassee FL
*WUSF(FM) Tampa FL
*WDCO-FM Cochran GA
*WTXR(FM) Toccoa Falls GA
*WWBM(FM) Yates GA
*KIWR(FM) Council Bluffs IA

*KRUI-FM Iowa City IA
*KRNL-FM Mount Vernon IA
*WCBW-FM East St. Louis IL
*WONU(FM) Kankakee IL
*WBMV(FM) Mount Vernon IL
*WLUJ(FM) Springfield IL
*WRGF(FM) Greenfield IN
*WHWE(FM) Howe IN
*WUBS(FM) South Bend IN
*WISU(FM) Terre Haute IN
*WTUR(FM) Upland IN
*KNBU(FM) Baldwin City KS
*KANH(FM) Emporia KS
*KBDA(FM) Great Bend KS
*WAAJ(FM) Benton KY
*WNKU(FM) Highland Heights KY
*WDCL-FM Somerset KY
*KAVK(FM) Many LA
*KBIO(FM) Natchitoches LA
*WGBH(FM) Boston MA
*WTMD(FM) Towson MD
*WMED(FM) Calais ME
*WMHB(FM) Waterville ME
*WJOJ(FM) Harrisville MI
*WJCQ(FM) Jackson MI
*WLNZ(FM) Lansing MI
*WOCR(FM) Olivet MI
*KBSB(FM) Bemidji MN
*KCMF(FM) Fergus Falls MN
*WLSN(FM) Grand Marais MN
*KMSU(FM) Mankato MN
*KUMM(FM) Morris MN
*KYMC(FM) Ballwin MO
*KOZO(FM) Branson MO
*KJCV(FM) Country Club MO
*KKTR(FM) Kirksville MO
*KCVQ(FM) Knob Noster MO
*KNLP(FM) Potosi MO
*KMNR(FM) Rolla MO
*WPAE(FM) Centreville MS
*WZKM(FM) Waynesboro MS
*KBIL(FM) Park City MT
*KAIB(FM) Whitehall MT
*WCPE(FM) Raleigh NC
*WDVV(FM) Wilmington NC
*KNRI(FM) Bismarck ND
*WNJN-FM Atlantic City NJ
*WDVR(FM) Delaware Township NJ
*WRDR(FM) Freehold Township NJ
*WGLS-FM Glassboro NJ
*KUSW(FM) Farmington NM
*KMBN(FM) Las Cruces NM
*KTDB(FM) Ramah NM
*WALF(FM) Alfred NY
*WKVJ(FM) Dannemora NY
*WEOS(FM) Geneva NY
*WITR(FM) Henrietta NY
*WNJA(FM) Jamestown NY
*WFGB(FM) Kingston NY
*WRHO(FM) Oneonta NY
*WSSK(FM) Saratoga Springs NY
*WRUC(FM) Schenectady NY
*WOSU-FM Columbus OH
*WTKC(FM) Findlay OH
*WKSU-FM Kent OH
*KJTH(FM) Ponca City OK
*KWYA(FM) Astoria OR
*KLCC(FM) Eugene OR
*WQEJ(FM) Johnstown PA
*WVYA(FM) Williamsport PA
*WRTU(FM) San Juan PR
*WMHK(FM) Columbia SC
*KUSD(FM) Vermillion SD
*WDYN-FM Chattanooga TN
*WAWI(FM) Lawrenceburg TN
*WAUV(FM) Ripley TN
*KACU(FM) Abilene TX
*KACC(FM) Alvin TX
*KTXB(FM) Beaumont TX
*KWCB(FM) Floresville TX
*KVRK(FM) Sanger TX
*KEQX(FM) Stephenville TX
*KZMU(FM) Moab UT
*WAUQ(FM) Charles City VA
*WVLS(FM) Monterey VA
*KWFJ(FM) Roy WA

*WUEC(FM) Eau Claire WI
*WUWM(FM) Milwaukee WI
*WHND(FM) Sister Bay WI
*WSHC(FM) Shepherdstown WV
*KAXG(FM) Gillette WY

89.9 mhz
*KUAC(FM) Fairbanks AK
*WTBB(FM) Gadsden AL
*WAKD(FM) Sheffield AL
*WTSU(FM) Troy AL
*KZIG(FM) Cave City AR
*KCOO(FM) Coolidge AZ
*KJTA(FM) Flagstaff AZ
*KNDL(FM) Angwin CA
*KCRH(FM) Hayward CA
*KJCU(FM) Laytonville CA
*KEFR(FM) Le Grand CA
*KPPN(FM) Pollock Pines CA
*KFER(FM) Santa Cruz CA
*KCRW(FM) Santa Monica CA
*KFRS(FM) Soledad CA
*KTMH(FM) Colona CO
*KFRY(FM) Pueblo CO
*KPRE(FM) Vail CO
*WQTQ(FM) Hartford CT
*WAPJ(FM) Torrington CT
*WWEB(FM) Wallingford CT
*WJCT-FM Jacksonville FL
*WUCF-FM Orlando FL
*WCNO(FM) Palm City FL
*WJTF(FM) Panama City FL
*WTFH(FM) Helen GA
*KAYP(FM) Burlington IA
*KBSK(FM) McCall ID
*KWJT(FM) Rathdrum ID
*KAWZ(FM) Twin Falls ID
*WLCA(FM) Godfrey IL
*WLKL(FM) Mattoon IL
*WCBU(FM) Peoria IL
*WOJC(FM) Crothersville IN
*WHLP(FM) Hanna IN
*WBRO(FM) Marengo IN
*WATI(FM) Vincennes IN
*WHPL(FM) West Lafayette IN
*KAIG(FM) Dodge City KS
*KRPS(FM) Pittsburg KS
*WRVG(FM) Georgetown KY
*WSOF-FM Madisonville KY
*KLXA(FM) Alexandria LA
*WWNO(FM) New Orleans LA
*KSJY(FM) Saint Martinville LA
*KDAQ(FM) Shreveport LA
*WSCB(FM) Springfield MA
*WOEL-FM Elkton MD
*WMTB-FM Emmittsburg MD
*WERU-FM Blue Hill ME
*WAYG(FM) Grand Rapids MI
*WTHS(FM) Holland MI
*WKDS(FM) Kalamazoo MI
*WLJN-FM Traverse City MI
*WHWG(FM) Trout Lake MI
*KMOJ(FM) Minneapolis MN
*KRPR(FM) Rochester MN
*KQRB(FM) Windom MN
*KGNA-FM Arnold MO
*KFFW(FM) Cabool MO
*KMCV(FM) High Point MO
*KAUF(FM) Kennett MO
*KGNV(FM) Washington MO
*WMAB-FM Mississippi State MS
*KGPR(FM) Great Falls MT
*KUKL(FM) Kalispell MT
*KBGA(FM) Missoula MT
*WDAV(FM) Davidson NC
*WRVS-FM Elizabeth City NC
*KDPR(FM) Dickinson ND
*KFLV(FM) Wilber NE
*WNJM(FM) Manahawkin NJ
*WJPH(FM) Woodbine NJ
*KUNM(FM) Albuquerque NM
*WFBF(FM) Buffalo NY
*WKCR-FM New York NY
*WXLG(FM) North Creek NY
*WSUF(FM) Noyack NY
*WRVO(FM) Oswego NY
*WDPG(FM) Greenville OH

Broadcasting & Cable Yearbook 2006

D-659

U.S. FM Stations by Frequency

*WLHS(FM) West Chester OH
*KTGS(FM) Ada OK
*KWKL(FM) Grandfield OK
*KBPS-FM Portland OR
*KKJA(FM) Redmond OR
*WVIA-FM Scranton PA
*WTLR(FM) State College PA
*WJWJ-FM Beaufort SC
*KQFR(FM) Rapid City SD
*WDVX(FM) Clinton TN
*WEVL(FM) Memphis TN
*WAYW(FM) New Johnsonville TN
*KACV-FM Amarillo TX
*KTLZ(FM) Cuero TX
*KBNL(FM) Laredo TX
*KTSW(FM) San Marcos TX
*KBDE(FM) Temple TX
*WPER(FM) Culpeper VA
*WFFC(FM) Ferrum VA
*WMRL(FM) Lexington VA
*WVRU(FM) Radford VA
*WNRS-FM Sweet Briar VA
*WCMD-FM Barre VT
*KGRG(FM) Auburn WA
*KGHP(FM) Gig Harbor WA
*KPLW(FM) Wenatchee WA
*WHSA(FM) Brule WI
*WVFL(FM) Fond du Lac WI
*WORT(FM) Madison WI
*WWSP(FM) Stevens Point WI
*WVRN(FM) Wittenberg WI
*WVWV(FM) Huntington WV
*WVNP(FM) Wheeling WV
*KRWT(FM) West Laramie WY

90.1 mhz

*KRAW(FM) Sterling AK
*WOCG(FM) Huntsville AL
*KBNV(FM) Fayetteville AR
*KLRO(FM) Hot Springs AR
*KRMB(FM) Bisbee AZ
*KWFH(FM) Parker AZ
*KTQX(FM) Bakersfield CA
*KBPK(FM) Buena Park CA
*KZFR(FM) Chico CA
*KCBX(FM) San Luis Obispo CA
*KZSU(FM) Stanford CA
*KYCC(FM) Stockton CA
*KSAK(FM) Walnut CA
*KLRD(FM) Yucaipa CA
*KVOD(FM) Denver CO
*KHCO(FM) Hayden CO
*KUTE(FM) Ignacio CO
*WRXC(FM) Shelton CT
*WGSK(FM) South Kent CT
*WECS(FM) Willimantic CT
*WCSP-FM Washington DC
*WTJT(FM) Baker FL
*WGCU-FM Fort Myers FL
*WJUF(FM) Inverness FL
*WKWR(FM) Key West FL
*WABE(FM) Atlanta GA
*WXVS(FM) Waycross GA
*WOI-FM Ames IA
*KDUB(FM) Dubuque IA
*KNWO(FM) Cottonwood ID
*WTSG(FM) Carlinville IL
*WEFT(FM) Champaign IL
*WMBI-FM Chicago IL
*WAWJ(FM) Marion IL
*WFYI-FM Indianapolis IN
*KXJH(FM) Linton IN
*WRFM(FM) Wadesville IN
*KHCC-FM Hutchinson KS
*WHMR(FM) Ledbetter KY
*WJSO(FM) Pikeville KY
*WJCR-FM Upton KY
*WYCM(FM) Charlton MA
*WCAI(FM) Woods Hole MA
*WMEA(FM) Portland ME
*WUCX-FM Bay City MI
*WNMU-FM Marquette MI
*WLSO(FM) Sault Ste. Marie MI
*KNSE(FM) Austin MN
*KSJR-FM Collegeville MN
*KADU(FM) Hibbing MN
*KSRQ(FM) Thief River Falls MN

*KKFI(FM) Kansas City MO
*KBKC(FM) Moberly MO
*KRHS(FM) Overland MO
*KSCV(FM) Springfield MO
*WMPR(FM) Jackson MS
*KBLW(FM) Billings MT
*KNMC(FM) Havre MT
*KHLV(FM) Helena MT
*WZPE(FM) Bath NC
*WCCE(FM) Buie's Creek NC
*WNAA(FM) Greensboro NC
*WJKA(FM) Jacksonville NC
*WZRU(FM) Roanoke Rapids NC
*KFKX(FM) Hastings NE
*KRDR(FM) Red River NM
*KRLU(FM) Roswell NM
*KQMC(FM) Hawthorne NV
*WIFF(FM) Binghamton NY
*WGMC(FM) Greece NY
*WRCU-FM Hamilton NY
*WMHQ(FM) Malone NY
*WXHD(FM) Mount Hope NY
*WUSB(FM) Stony Brook NY
*WWJS(FM) Watertown NY
*WOHC(FM) Chillicothe OH
*WJYC(FM) Delhi Hills OH
*WXML(FM) Upper Sandusky OH
*WOUZ(FM) Zanesville OH
*KOCU(FM) Altus OK
*KCSC(FM) Edmond OK
*KSOR(FM) Ashland OR
*KQHR(FM) Hood River OR
*KKLP(FM) La Pine OR
*KAJC(FM) Salem OR
*WIUP-FM Indiana PA
*WPSB(FM) Kane PA
*WVMN(FM) New Castle PA
*WRTI(FM) Philadelphia PA
*WCIT(FM) Trout Run PA
*WWQS(FM) Pastillo PR
*WHMC-FM Conway SC
*WEPR(FM) Greenville SC
*KSFS(FM) Sioux Falls SD
*WKNP(FM) Jackson TN
*WKTS(FM) Kingston TN
*WZYZ(FM) Spencer TN
*KERA(FM) Dallas TX
*KPFT(FM) Houston TX
*KTXI(FM) Ingram TX
*KAMY(FM) Lubbock TX
*KPBJ(FM) Midland TX
*KSAU(FM) Nacogdoches TX
*KUTX(FM) San Angelo TX
*KSYM-FM San Antonio TX
*KUER(FM) Salt Lake City UT
*WMVE(FM) Chase City VA
*WJCN(FM) Nassawadox VA
*WDCE(FM) Richmond VA
*WPVA(FM) Waynesboro VA
*WIVH(FM) Christiansted VI
*WRUV(FM) Burlington VT
*KMWS(FM) Mount Vernon WA
*KWGV(FM) Olympia WA
*KQWS(FM) Omak WA
*KOLU(FM) Pasco WA
*KNWP(FM) Port Angeles WA
*KUPS(FM) Tacoma WA
*WORQ(FM) Green Bay WI
*WRPN-FM Ripon WI
*WPWV(FM) Princeton WV
*KUWP(FM) Powell WY

90.3 mhz

*KNBA(FM) Anchorage AK
*WBHM(FM) Birmingham AL
*WDYF(FM) Dothan AL
*KAEN(FM) Melbourne AR
*KLFS(FM) Van Buren AR
*KNAG(FM) Grand Canyon AZ
*KBMH(FM) Holbrook AZ
*KFLR-FM Phoenix AZ
*KMRO(FM) Camarillo CA
*KBXO(FM) Coachella CA
*KDVS(FM) Davis CA
*KFNO(FM) Fresno CA
*KLAI(FM) Laytonville CA
*KAZU(FM) Pacific Grove CA

*KUSF(FM) San Francisco CA
*KBUT(FM) Crested Butte CO
*KLFV(FM) Grand Junction CO
*KTAD(FM) Sterling CO
*WWPT(FM) Westport CT
*WJLH(FM) Flagler Beach FL
*WAFG(FM) Fort Lauderdale FL
*WYJC(FM) Greenville FL
*WLVF-FM Haines City FL
*WEJF(FM) Palm Bay FL
*WAEF(FM) Cordele GA
*WHCJ(FM) Savannah GA
*WCIF(FM) Hilo HI
*KTUH(FM) Honolulu HI
*KWIT(FM) Sioux City IA
*KBSU(FM) Boise ID
*KZJB(FM) Pocatello ID
*WUSI(FM) Olney IL
*WQUB(FM) Quincy IL
*WVIK(FM) Rock Island IL
*WFOF(FM) Covington IN
*WBCL(FM) Fort Wayne IN
*KBUZ(FM) Topeka KS
*WMKY(FM) Morehead KY
*WKWC(FM) Owensboro KY
*WBRH(FM) Baton Rouge LA
*KYLC(FM) Lake Charles LA
*KEDM(FM) Monroe LA
*WCCT-FM Harwich MA
*WZBC(FM) Newton MA
*WAIJ(FM) Grantsville MD
*WDIH(FM) Salisbury MD
*WBLV(FM) Twin Lake MI
*KFAI(FM) Minneapolis MN
*KCCD(FM) Moorhead MN
*KMKL(FM) North Branch MN
*KWUR(FM) Clayton MO
*KGNN-FM Cuba MO
*KNLG(FM) New Bloomfield MO
*KGSP(FM) Parkville MO
*KLUH(FM) Poplar Bluff MO
*KCRL(FM) Sunrise Beach MO
*WMAH-FM Biloxi MS
*WMAV-FM Oxford MS
*KJFT(FM) Arlee MT
*KMZO(FM) Hamilton MT
*WFHE(FM) Hickory NC
*WKNS(FM) Kinston NC
*WBFY(FM) Pinehurst NC
*KMNE-FM Bassett NE
*KRNU(FM) Lincoln NE
*WNJZ(FM) Cape May Court House NJ
*WRPR(FM) Mahwah NJ
*WVPH(FM) Piscataway NJ
*WKNJ-FM Union Township NJ
*WMSC(FM) Upper Montclair NJ
*KKCC(FM) Clovis NM
*KLGQ(FM) Grants NM
*WAMC-FM Albany NY
*WCIH(FM) Elmira NY
*WHPC(FM) Garden City NY
*WJSL(FM) Houghton NY
*WHCR-FM New York NY
*WDFH(FM) Ossining NY
*WAIH(FM) Potsdam NY
*WRVD(FM) Syracuse NY
*WCDR-FM Cedarville OH
*WCPN(FM) Cleveland OH
*WOTL(FM) Toledo OH
*KLCU(FM) Ardmore OK
*KVRS(FM) Lawton OK
*KTVR-FM La Grande OR
*KSLC(FM) McMinnville OR
*KLON(FM) Rockaway Beach OR
*KWBX(FM) Salem OR
*KZRI(FM) Welches OR
*WESS(FM) East Stroudsburg PA
*WJTL(FM) Lancaster PA
*WARC(FM) Meadville PA
*WXLV(FM) Schnecksville PA
*WRIU(FM) Kingston RI
*WSSB-FM Orangeburg SC
*WRBK(FM) Richburg SC
*KASD(FM) Rapid City SD
*WCSK(FM) Kingsport TN
*WUTK(FM) Knoxville TN

*WUTM(FM) Martin TN
*WPLN-FM Nashville TN
*KBUB(FM) Brownwood TX
*KEDT-FM Corpus Christi TX
*KBJS(FM) Jacksonville TX
*KPHS(FM) Plains TX
*WOKG(FM) Galax VA
*WHRO-FM Norfolk VA
*WRXT(FM) Roanoke VA
*KWYQ(FM) Longview WA
*KEXP-FM Seattle WA
*KWRS(FM) Spokane WA
*KNWY(FM) Yakima WA
*WBCR-FM Beloit WI
*WHLA(FM) La Crosse WI
*WJWD(FM) Marshall WI
*WRST-FM Oshkosh WI
*WHBM-FM Park Falls WI
*WVPG(FM) Parkersburg WV
*KCSP-FM Casper WY
*KUWJ(FM) Jackson WY
*KWYC(FM) Orchard Valley WY

90.5 mhz

*KXGA(FM) Glennallen AK
*KWMD(FM) Kasilof AK
*KAOG(FM) Jonesboro AR
*KLRE-FM Little Rock AR
*KUAT-FM Tucson AZ
*KHSU-FM Arcata CA
*KIBC(FM) Burney CA
*KVHS(FM) Concord CA
*KADV(FM) Modesto CA
*KWMR(FM) Point Reyes Station CA
*KSJS(FM) San Jose CA
*KKTO(FM) Tahoe City CA
*KVOV(FM) Carbondale CO
*KTLF(FM) Colorado Springs CO
*KCSU(FM) Fort Collins CO
*WPKT(FM) Meriden CT
*WVUM(FM) Coral Gables FL
*WREH(FM) Cypress Quarters FL
*WYFB(FM) Gainesville FL
*WANM(FM) Tallahassee FL
*WBVM(FM) Tampa FL
*WUOG(FM) Athens GA
*WPWB(FM) Byron GA
*WFRC(FM) Columbus GA
*WTLD(FM) Jesup GA
*WVRI(FM) Pavo GA
*KPHL(FM) Pahala HI
*KHOE(FM) Fairfield IA
*WRTE(FM) Chicago IL
*WAPO(FM) Mount Vernon IL
*WMTH(FM) Park Ridge IL
*WNIU(FM) Rockford IL
*WSCT(FM) Springfield IL
*WIKL(FM) Greencastle IN
*WWDS(FM) Muncie IN
*WPUM(FM) Rensselaer IN
*KBMP(FM) Enterprise KS
*KZNA(FM) Hill City KS
*KRBW(FM) Ottawa KS
*WVHM(FM) Benton KY
*WUOL(FM) Louisville KY
*WTHL(FM) Somerset KY
*KTLN(FM) Thibodaux LA
*WSMA(FM) Scituate MA
*WICN(FM) Worcester MA
*WCRH(FM) Williamsport MD
*WKHS(FM) Worton MD
*WMEP(FM) Camden MI
*WKAR-FM East Lansing MI
*WPHN(FM) Gaylord MI
*KDNI(FM) Duluth MN
*KGAC(FM) Saint Peter MN
*KWWC-FM Columbia MO
*KXCV(FM) Maryville MO
*KSMS-FM Point Lookout MO
*WCSO(FM) Columbus MS
*WQVI(FM) Forest MS
*WAQL(FM) McComb MS
*WASU-FM Boone NC
*WBUX(FM) Buxton NC
*WWCU(FM) Cullowhee NC
*WYQS(FM) Mars Hill NC
*WZRN(FM) Norlina NC

*WDCC(FM) Sanford NC
*WWIL-FM Wilmington NC
*WAJC(FM) Wilson NC
*WSNC(FM) Winston-Salem NC
*KCND(FM) Bismarck ND
*WSPS(FM) Concord NH
*WPEA(FM) Exeter NH
*WVFA(FM) Lebanon NH
*WWFP(FM) Brigantine NJ
*WXGN(FM) Egg Harbor Township NJ
*WCVH(FM) Flemington NJ
*WBJB-FM Lincroft NJ
*WVBV(FM) Medford Lakes NJ
*WJSV(FM) Morristown NJ
*KCIE(FM) Dulce NM
*KSOS(FM) Las Vegas NV
*WBXL(FM) Baldwinsville NY
*WHRW(FM) Binghamton NY
*WSUC-FM Cortland NY
*WXXE(FM) Fenner NY
*WJFF(FM) Jeffersonville NY
*WBER(FM) Rochester NY
*WHVT(FM) Clyde OH
*WCBE(FM) Columbus OH
*WVML(FM) Millersburg OH
*KNYD(FM) Broken Arrow OK
*KSSX(FM) Chickasha OK
*KAYM(FM) Weatherford OK
*KORM(FM) Astoria OR
*KVLB(FM) Bend OR
*KLCO(FM) Newport OR
*WERG(FM) Erie PA
*WVBU-FM Lewisburg PA
*WDUQ(FM) Pittsburgh PA
*WIDA-FM Carolina PR
*WUSC-FM Columbia SC
*WVCF(FM) Freeman SD
*WSMC-FM Collegedale TN
*WUMC(FM) Elizabethton TN
*WSMM(FM) Selmer TN
*KAGT-FM Abilene TX
*KUT(FM) Austin TX
*KZFT(FM) Fannett TX
*KTXG(FM) Greenville TX
*KSHU(FM) Huntsville TX
*KFLB-FM Odessa TX
*KBAH(FM) Plainview TX
*KPDR(FM) Wheeler TX
*KTEO(FM) Wichita Falls TX
*KZCL(FM) Logan UT
*WJYJ(FM) Fredericksburg VA
*WPIM(FM) Martinsville VA
*WISE-FM Wise VA
*WFTF(FM) Rutland VT
*WCKJ(FM) Saint Johnsbury VT
*KACS(FM) Chehalis WA
*KNWV(FM) Clarkston WA
*KWCW(FM) Walla Walla WA
*WVCF(FM) Eau Claire WI
*WSUP(FM) Platteville WI
*WPFF(FM) Sturgeon Bay WI
*WMLJ(FM) Summersville WV
*KBUW(FM) Buffalo WY
*KUWN(FM) Newcastle WY
*KUWZ(FM) Rock Springs WY

90.7 mhz

*WGRW(FM) Anniston AL
*WVAS(FM) Montgomery AL
*WVUA-FM Tuscaloosa AL
*KVRN(FM) Marvell AR
*KNAA(FM) Show Low AZ
*KALX(FM) Berkeley CA
*KFRP(FM) Coalinga CA
*KFSR(FM) Fresno CA
*KHRI(FM) Hollister CA
*KPFK(FM) Los Angeles CA
*KZYX(FM) Philo CA
*KSRI(FM) Santa Cruz CA
*KGDP-FM Santa Maria CA
*KYKL(FM) Tracy CA
*KGUD(FM) Longmont CO
*KTEI(FM) Placerville CO
*KDRE(FM) Sterling CO
*WMFE-FM Orlando FL
*WKGC-FM Panama City FL
*WXEL(FM) West Palm Beach FL

Broadcasting & Cable Yearbook 2006

U.S. FM Stations by Frequency

*WWXC(FM) Albany GA
*WACG-FM Augusta GA
*WAYR-FM Brunswick GA
*WUWG(FM) Carrollton GA
*WMVV(FM) Griffin GA
*WFSL(FM) Thomasville GA
*KKUA(FM) Wailuku HI
*KWOI(FM) Carroll IA
*KOJI(FM) Okoboji IA
*KAIO(FM) Idaho Falls ID
*KBSQ(FM) McCall ID
*KCIR(FM) Twin Falls ID
*WVKC(FM) Galesburg IL
*WBEQ(FM) Morris IL
*WPSR(FM) Evansville IN
*WKPW(FM) Knightstown IN
*WQSG(FM) Lafayette IN
*WMHD-FM Terre Haute IN
*KPOR(FM) Emporia KS
*KJHK(FM) Lawrence KS
*KYWA(FM) Wichita KS
*WCVK(FM) Bowling Green KY
*WPTJ(FM) Paris KY
*KLSA(FM) Alexandria LA
*WWOZ(FM) New Orleans LA
*WTCC(FM) Springfield MA
*WWTE(FM) Wellfleet MA
*WKKL(FM) West Barnstable MA
*WSDL(FM) Ocean City MD
*WAUS(FM) Berrien Springs MI
*WNFR(FM) Sandusky MI
*WNMC-FM Traverse City MI
*KBPR(FM) Brainerd MN
*WTIP(FM) Grand Marais MN
*KZSE(FM) Rochester MN
*KOBC(FM) Joplin MO
*KHGN(FM) Kirksville MO
*KTTK(FM) Lebanon MO
*KWMU(FM) Saint Louis MO
*WATP(FM) Laurel MS
*KGFA(FM) Great Falls MT
*KECC(FM) Miles City MT
*WFAE(FM) Charlotte NC
*WNCU(FM) Durham NC
*WOTJ(FM) Morehead City NC
*KABU(FM) Fort Totten ND
*KFJM(FM) Grand Forks ND
*KNFA(FM) Grand Island NE
*KVNO(FM) Omaha NE
*WEVN(FM) Keene NH
*WLMW(FM) Manchester NH
*WYRS(FM) Manahawkin NJ
*KKCJ(FM) Cannon AFB NM
*KRWG(FM) Las Cruces NM
*KSFR(FM) Santa Fe NM
*WETD(FM) Alfred NY
*WGCC-FM Batavia NY
*WFUV(FM) New York NY
*WPGL(FM) Pattersonville NY
*WPNR-FM Utica NY
*WGLE(FM) Lima OH
*WVMC(FM) Mansfield OH
*WMCO(FM) New Concord OH
*WSNR(FM) Norwalk OH
*WKTL(FM) Struthers OH
*KFXT(FM) Sulphur OK
*KAYE-FM Tonkawa OK
*KJOV(FM) Woodward OK
*KANL(FM) Baker City OR
*KMWR(FM) Brookings OR
*KBOO(FM) Portland OR
*WRTL(FM) Ephrata PA
*WVMM(FM) Grantham PA
*WLGY(FM) Nanty Glo PA
*WKPS(FM) State College PA
*WCLH(FM) Wilkes-Barre PA
*WCRG(FM) Williamsport PA
*WJHD(FM) Portsmouth RI
*WYFH(FM) North Charleston SC
*KSDJ(FM) Brookings SD
*WKNQ(FM) Dyersburg TN
*WAUO(FM) Hohenwald TN
*KAVW(FM) Amarillo TX
*KTAA(FM) Big Sandy TX
*KCWV(FM) Brownfield TX
*KPBN(FM) Freer TX
*KTER(FM) Rudolph TX

*KVRT(FM) Victoria TX
*KSGU(FM) Saint George UT
*WUVT-FM Blacksburg VA
*WAZP(FM) Cape Charles VA
*WEHC(FM) Emory VA
*WMRA(FM) Harrisonburg VA
*WJSC-FM Johnson VT
*WVTC(FM) Randolph Center VT
*KNWR(FM) Ellensburg WA
*KSER(FM) Everett WA
*KZUU(FM) Pullman WA
*WHAD(FM) Delafield WI
*WVSS(FM) Menomonie WI
*WFGH(FM) Fort Gay WV
*WLKV(FM) Ripley WV

90.9 mhz
*WELJ(FM) Brewton AL
*WJAB(FM) Huntsville AL
*KBSA(FM) El Dorado AR
*KLLN(FM) Newark AR
*KWRB(FM) Bisbee AZ
*KGCB(FM) Prescott AZ
*KHDC(FM) Chualar CA
*KPSH(FM) Coachella CA
*KWTM(FM) June Lake CA
*KXPR(FM) Sacramento CA
*KGZO(FM) Shafter CA
*KBDG(FM) Turlock CA
*KASF(FM) Alamosa CO
*KVNF(FM) Paonia CO
*KXWY(FM) Rye CO
*WCNI(FM) New London CT
*WETA(FM) Washington DC
*WAQV(FM) Crystal River FL
*WKTZ-FM Jacksonville FL
*WGES(FM) Key Largo FL
*WJIR(FM) Key West FL
*WSOR(FM) Naples FL
*WJWV(FM) Fort Gaines GA
*WOAK(FM) La Grange GA
*WRAF-FM Toccoa Falls GA
*WVVS(FM) Valdosta GA
*KKCR(FM) Hanalei HI
*KUNI(FM) Cedar Falls IA
*KLOX(FM) Creston IA
*KMDY(FM) Keokuk IA
*WDCB(FM) Glen Ellyn IL
*WILL-FM Urbana IL
*WBDG(FM) Indianapolis IN
*WBSW(FM) Marion IN
*WCJL(FM) Morgantown IN
*KHCT(FM) Great Bend KS
*WKUE(FM) Elizabethtown KY
*WEKH(FM) Hazard KY
*KSLU(FM) Hammond LA
*KIKL(FM) Lafayette LA
*WBUR-FM Boston MA
*WMEH(FM) Bangor ME
*WMPG(FM) Gorham ME
*WQAC(FM) Alma MI
*WTCK(FM) Charlevoix MI
*WRCJ-FM Detroit MI
*WWZP(FM) Freeland MI
*WMSD(FM) Rose Township MI
*WIRR(FM) Virginia-Hibbing MN
*KKLW(FM) Willmar MN
*KRCU(FM) Cape Girardeau MO
*KNLN(FM) Vienna MO
*KTBG(FM) Warrensburg MO
*KSMW(FM) West Plains MO
*WMAO-FM Greenwood MS
*WAQB(FM) Tupelo MS
*KQLU(FM) Belgrade MT
*KLRV(FM) Billings MT
*KDWG(FM) Dillon MT
*KSPL(FM) Kalispell MT
*WQFS(FM) Greensboro NC
*WURI(FM) Manteo NC
*WRQM(FM) Rocky Mount NC
*WSIF(FM) Wilkesboro NC
*KNHA(FM) Hastings NE
*KPNO(FM) Norfolk NE
*WSCS(FM) New London NH
*KVLK(FM) Belen NM
*KSJE(FM) Farmington NM
*KSHI(FM) Zuni NM

*WCDB(FM) Albany NY
*WKRB(FM) Brooklyn NY
*WLJH(FM) Glens Falls NY
*WSQG-FM Ithaca NY
*WCOT(FM) Jamestown NY
*WAMK(FM) Kingston NY
*WSLO(FM) Malone NY
*WONY(FM) Oneonta NY
*WAVX(FM) Schuyler Falls NY
*WJNY(FM) Watertown NY
*WGBE(FM) Bryan OH
*WGUC(FM) Cincinnati OH
*WCVJ(FM) Jefferson OH
*WFCO(FM) Lancaster OH
*WNZR(FM) Mount Vernon OH
*WCWS(FM) Wooster OH
*KKVO(FM) Altus OK
*KOKF(FM) Edmond OK
*KXRT(FM) Idabel OK
*KJCH(FM) Coos Bay OR
*KIDH(FM) Jordan Valley OR
*KSKF(FM) Klamath Falls OR
*KRBM(FM) Pendleton OR
*WITX(FM) Beaver Falls PA
*WZZH(FM) Honesdale PA
*WJRC(FM) Lewistown PA
*WHYY-FM Philadelphia PA
*WLGI(FM) Hemingway SC
*KDSD-FM Pierpont SD
*KWRC(FM) Rapid City SD
*KCSD(FM) Sioux Falls SD
*WWOG(FM) Cookeville TN
*KAMU-FM College Station TX
*KCBI(FM) Dallas TX
*KTSU(FM) Houston TX
*KKLU(FM) Lubbock TX
*KSWP(FM) Lufkin TX
*KAVO(FM) Pampa TX
*KPEB(FM) San Angelo TX
*KYFS(FM) San Antonio TX
*KRCL(FM) Salt Lake City UT
*WWMC(FM) Lynchburg VA
*WCWM(FM) Williamsburg VA
*KVTI(FM) Tacoma WA
*WHRM(FM) Wausau WI
*WPIB(FM) Bluefield WV
*WVPM(FM) Morgantown WV
*KLWV(FM) Chugwater WY
*KUWG(FM) Gillette WY
*KUWX(FM) Pinedale WY

91.1 mhz
*KSKA(FM) Anchorage AK
*WEGL(FM) Auburn AL
*WJSR(FM) Birmingham AL
*WVSU-FM Birmingham AL
*WAQU(FM) Selma AL
*WAXU(FM) Troy AL
*KMTC(FM) Russellville AR
*KANX(FM) Sheridan AR
*KNLB(FM) Lake Havasu City AZ
*KNOG(FM) Nogales AZ
*KFRJ(FM) China Lake CA
*KLVY(FM) Fairmead CA
*KMUD(FM) Garberville CA
*KCSM(FM) San Mateo CA
*KRCB-FM Santa Rosa CA
*KDSC(FM) Thousand Oaks CA
*KWSB-FM Gunnison CO
*KLDV(FM) Morrison CO
*WSHU(FM) Fairfield CT
*WBVC(FM) Pomfret CT
*WJED(FM) Dogwood Lakes Estate FL
*WJFP(FM) Fort Pierce FL
*WPSM(FM) Fort Walton Beach FL
*WKES(FM) Lakeland FL
*WUJC(FM) Saint Marks FL
*WREK(FM) Atlanta GA
*WSVH(FM) Savannah GA
*WABR-FM Tifton GA
*KANO(FM) Hilo HI
*KTPR(FM) Fort Dodge IA
*KUNZ(FM) Ottumwa IA
*KISU-FM Pocatello ID
*KBSS(FM) Sun Valley ID
*WDBX(FM) Carbondale IL
*WIBI(FM) Carlinville IL

*WKCC(FM) Kankakee IL
*WGSL(FM) Loves Park IL
WYGS(FM) Columbus IN
*WGCS(FM) Goshen IN
*WBSH(FM) Hagerstown IN
*WEDM(FM) Indianapolis IN
*WCYT(FM) Lafayette Township IN
*WIRE(FM) Lebanon IN
*WVUB(FM) Vincennes IN
*KANZ(FM) Garden City KS
*KCFN(FM) Wichita KS
*KLSU(FM) Baton Rouge LA
*KOJO(FM) Lake Charles LA
*KXUL(FM) Monroe LA
*WPDD(FM) Norco LA
*WMUA(FM) Amherst MA
*WNAN(FM) Nantucket MA
*WJJW(FM) North Adams MA
*WSMU-FM North Dartmouth MA
*WKMY(FM) Winchendon MA
*WHFC(FM) Bel Air MD
*WBOR(FM) Brunswick ME
XETRA-FM Tijuana MEX
*WOLW(FM) Cadillac MI
*WFUM-FM Flint MI
*WGGL-FM Houghton MI
*WPCJ(FM) Pittsford MI
*KXLC(FM) La Crescent MN
*KNOW-FM Minneapolis-St. Paul MN
*KCCM-FM Moorhead MN
*KBGM(FM) Park Hills MO
*KSMU(FM) Springfield MO
*WASM(FM) Natchez MS
*WMSV(FM) Starkville MS
*KLEU(FM) Lewistown MT
*KMZL(FM) Missoula MT
*WPGT(FM) Roanoke Rapids NC
*WRSH(FM) Rockingham NC
*KTNE-FM Alliance NE
*KDCV-FM Blair NE
*KUCV(FM) Lincoln NE
*WVNH(FM) Concord NH
*WWNJ(FM) Dover Township NJ
*WFMU(FM) East Orange NJ
*KAQF(FM) Clovis NM
*KEDP(FM) Las Vegas NM
*KVKL(FM) Las Vegas NV
*KAIZ(FM) Mesquite NV
*WSQE(FM) Corning NY
*WHVP(FM) Hudson NY
*WOSS(FM) Ossining NY
*WTSC-FM Potsdam NY
*WSPN(FM) Saratoga Springs NY
*WRMU(FM) Alliance OH
*WRUW-FM Cleveland OH
*WOSE(FM) Coshocton OH
*WDUB(FM) Granville OH
*WOSB(FM) Marion OH
*KQPD(FM) Ardmore OK
*KAYC(FM) Durant OK
*KKRD(FM) Enid OK
*KJRF(FM) Lawton OK
*KWAX(FM) Eugene OR
*KAPK(FM) Grants Pass OR
*KTMK(FM) Tillamook OR
*WUFR(FM) Bedford PA
*WBUQ(FM) Bloomsburg PA
*WZBT(FM) Gettysburg PA
*WSAJ-FM Grove City PA
*WRTY(FM) Jackson Township PA
*WMSS(FM) Middletown PA
*WWHW(FM) Dillon SC
*WYFG(FM) Gaffney SC
*KTSD-FM Reliance SD
*KAOR(FM) Vermillion SD
*WTSE(FM) Benton TN
*WKCS(FM) Knoxville TN
*WKNO-FM Memphis TN
*WRVU(FM) Nashville TN
*KWTS(FM) Canyon TX
*KVER(FM) El Paso TX
*KHKV(FM) Kerrville TX
*KTAI(FM) Kingsville TX
*KYBJ(FM) Lake Jackson TX
*KBWC(FM) Marshall TX
*KKXI(FM) Pittsburg TX
*KSGR(FM) Portland TX

*KSUU(FM) Cedar City UT
*WTJU(FM) Charlottesville VA
*WOKD-FM Danville VA
*WHCE(FM) Highland Springs VA
*WNSB(FM) Norfolk VA
*WRMC-FM Middlebury VT
*WGDR(FM) Plainfield VT
*KTJC(FM) Kelso WA
*KPBX-FM Spokane WA
*KYPL(FM) Yakima WA
*WLFM(FM) Appleton WI
*WGTD(FM) Kenosha WI

91.3 mhz
*WVOB(FM) Dothan AL
*WFIX(FM) Florence AL
*WHIL-FM Mobile AL
*WTBJ(FM) Oxford AL
*KUCA(FM) Conway AR
*KUAF(FM) Fayetteville AR
*KXCI(FM) Tucson AZ
*KFRB(FM) Bakersfield CA
*KWTH(FM) Barstow CA
*KIDE(FM) Hoopa CA
*KDRH(FM) King City CA
*KCPR(FM) San Luis Obispo CA
*KSVY(FM) Sonoma CA
*KUOP(FM) Stockton CA
*KNYR(FM) Yreka CA
*KMSA(FM) Grand Junction CO
*KLRY(FM) Gypsum CO
*KSUT(FM) Ignacio CO
*KLZV(FM) Sterling CO
*WWUH(FM) West Hartford CT
*WVUD(FM) Newark DE
*WWKO(FM) Belleview FL
*WAKJ(FM) De Funiak Springs FL
*WSEB(FM) Englewood FL
*WOLR(FM) Lake City FL
*WLRN-FM Miami FL
*WHIF(FM) Palatka FL
*WATY(FM) Folkston GA
*WJTG(FM) Fort Valley GA
*KDFR(FM) Des Moines IA
*WNIW(FM) La Salle IL
*WIUM(FM) Macomb IL
*WJCZ(FM) Milford IL
*WSLE(FM) Salem IL
*WFHB(FM) Bloomington IN
*WHJE(FM) Carmel IN
*WNDY(FM) Crawfordsville IN
*WJCO(FM) Montpelier IN
*WWHI(FM) Muncie IN
*WBNI-FM Orland IN
*KAXR(FM) Arkansas City KS
*KANV(FM) Olsburg KS
*WUKY(FM) Lexington KY
*WKMS-FM Murray KY
*KSCL(FM) Shreveport LA
*WSHL-FM Easton MA
*WXPL(FM) Fitchburg MA
*WDJM-FM Framingham MA
*WCUW(FM) Worcester MA
*WESM-FM Princess Anne MD
*WMEW(FM) Waterville ME
*WCHW-FM Bay City MI
*WJOG(FM) Good Hart MI
*WCSG(FM) Grand Rapids MI
*WOES(FM) Ovid-Elsie MI
*WSGR-FM Port Huron MI
*KRSU(FM) Appleton MN
*KMSK(FM) Austin MN
*KNBJ(FM) Bemidji MN
*KBIA(FM) Columbia MO
*KBIY(FM) Van Buren MO
*WGTC(FM) Hickory MS
*WMPN-FM Jackson MS
*KAPC(FM) Butte MT
*WLFA(FM) Asheville NC
*WFQS(FM) Franklin NC
*WZMB(FM) Greenville NC
*WHQR(FM) Wilmington NC
*WXRI(FM) Winston-Salem NC
*KMHA(FM) Four Bears ND
*KAYA(FM) Hubbard NE
*KLPR(FM) Kearney NE
*WUNH(FM) Durham NH

U.S. FM Stations by Frequency

*WEVH(FM) Hanover NH
*WKNH(FM) Keene NH
*WRTQ(FM) Ocean City NJ
*WTSR(FM) Trenton NJ
*KNIS(FM) Carson City NV
*KBSJ(FM) Jackpot NV
*WXLH(FM) Blue Mountain Lake NY
*WBNY(FM) Buffalo NY
*WOLN(FM) Olean NY
*WVKR-FM Poughkeepsie NY
*WRLI-FM Southampton NY
*WCNY-FM Syracuse NY
*WAPS(FM) Akron OH
*WOUB-FM Athens OH
*WGTE-FM Toledo OH
*WYSO(FM) Yellow Springs OH
*KAKO(FM) Ada OK
*KRSC-FM Claremore OK
*KOAB-FM Bend OR
*WLVR(FM) Bethlehem PA
*WCIG(FM) Carbondale PA
*WQLN-FM Erie PA
*WLCH(FM) Lancaster PA
*WGRC(FM) Lewisburg PA
*WYEP-FM Pittsburgh PA
*WXAC(FM) Reading PA
*WIPR-FM San Juan PR
*WDOM(FM) Providence RI
*WLTR(FM) Columbia SC
*WLMU(FM) Harrogate TN
*WCPI(FM) McMinnville TN
*WUTS(FM) Sewanee TN
*KAQD(FM) Abilene TX
*KVLU(FM) Beaumont TX
*KVFM(FM) Beeville TX
*KYJC(FM) Commerce TX
*KDKR(FM) Decatur TX
*KNCT-FM Killeen TX
*KBKN(FM) Lamesa TX
*KZLV(FM) Lytle TX
*KOCV(FM) Odessa TX
*KPVU(FM) Prairie View TX
*KGLY(FM) Tyler TX
*WMLU(FM) Farmville VA
*WVST-FM Petersburg VA
*WPAR(FM) Salem VA
*WTRM(FM) Winchester VA
*WIUV(FM) Castleton VT
*KBCS(FM) Bellevue WA
*KCED(FM) Centralia WA
*KGTS(FM) College Place WA
*WHEM(FM) Eau Claire WI
*WMVM(FM) Goodman WI
*WHHI(FM) Highland WI
*WSTM(FM) Kiel WI
*KUWS(FM) Superior WI
*WQAB(FM) Philippi WV
*KUWA(FM) Afton WY
*KSUW(FM) Sheridan WY
KUWT(FM) Thermopolis WY

91.5 mhz

*KSUA(FM) Fairbanks AK
*KWJG(FM) Kasilof AK
*WSTF(FM) Andalusia AL
*WSGN(FM) Gadsden AL
*WUAL-FM Tuscaloosa AL
*WEBT(FM) Valley AL
*KOUX(FM) Blytheville AR
*KALR(FM) Hot Springs AR
*KCMH(FM) Mountain Home AR
*KJZZ(FM) Phoenix AZ
*KGHR(FM) Tuba City AZ
*KNHM(FM) Bayside CA
*KKUP(FM) Cupertino CA
*KASK(FM) Fairfield CA
*KSJV(FM) Fresno CA
*KRQZ(FM) Lompoc CA
*KUSC(FM) Los Angeles CA
*KKRO(FM) Redding CA
*KYDS(FM) Sacramento CA
*KZYZ(FM) Willits CA
*KAJX(FM) Aspen CO
*KRCC(FM) Colorado Springs CO
*KSJD(FM) Cortez CO
*KUNC-FM Greeley CO

*WGRS(FM) Guilford CT
*WMIE(FM) Cocoa FL
*WJYO(FM) Fort Myers FL
*WAPN(FM) Holly Hill FL
*WLPJ(FM) New Port Richey FL
*WFSQ(FM) Tallahassee FL
*WPRK(FM) Winter Park FL
*WWEV-FM Cumming GA
*WGPH(FM) Vidalia GA
*KUNY(FM) Mason City IA
*KBSX(FM) Boise ID
*KBYR-FM Rexburg ID
*WLHW(FM) Casey IL
*WBEZ(FM) Chicago IL
*WCIC(FM) Pekin IL
*WNIQ(FM) Sterling IL
*WFWR(FM) Attica IN
*WJCY(FM) Cicero IN
*WJHS(FM) Columbia City IN
*WUEV(FM) Evansville IN
*WGRE(FM) Greencastle IN
*WRFT(FM) Indianapolis IN
*WECI(FM) Richmond IN
*WJLR(FM) Seymour IN
*KANU(FM) Lawrence KS
*KSNS(FM) Medicine Lodge KS
*WVCT(FM) Keavy KY
*WBFI(FM) McDaniels KY
*KBAN(FM) De Ridder LA
*KPAE(FM) Erwinville LA
*KGRM(FM) Grambling LA
*WTUL(FM) New Orleans LA
*KSUL(FM) Port Sulphur LA
*KNSU(FM) Thibodaux LA
*WBIM-FM Bridgewater MA
*WUML(FM) Lowell MA
*WMFO(FM) Medford MA
*WMLN-FM Milton MA
*WNMH(FM) Northfield MA
*WSDH(FM) Sandwich MA
*WMHC(FM) South Hadley MA
*WZLY(FM) Wellesley MA
*WBJC(FM) Baltimore MD
*WRBC(FM) Lewiston ME
*WSJB-FM Standish ME
*WVCM(FM) Iron Mountain MI
*WUPX(FM) Marquette MI
*WMHW-FM Mount Pleasant MI
*WJOH(FM) Raco MI
*WICA(FM) Traverse City MI
*KNWF(FM) Fergus Falls MN
*KCFB(FM) Saint Cloud MN
*KNGA(FM) Saint Peter MN
*KQMN(FM) Thief River Falls MN
*KSIV-FM Saint Louis MO
*WFBI(FM) Greenville MS
*WAVI(FM) Oxford MS
*KAFH(FM) Great Falls MT
*KPLG(FM) Plains MT
*WBJD(FM) Atlantic Beach NC
*WUNC(FM) Chapel Hill NC
*KPRJ(FM) Jamestown ND
*KRNE-FM Merriman NE
*KIOS-FM Omaha NE
*WDBK(FM) Blackwood NJ
*KFLQ(FM) Albuquerque NM
*KRUX(FM) Las Cruces NM
*KNCC(FM) Elko NV
*KUNV(FM) Las Vegas NV
*WSQX-FM Binghamton NY
*WVHC(FM) Herkimer NY
*WNYE(FM) New York NY
*WXXI-FM Rochester NY
*WRPI(FM) Troy NY
*WKHR(FM) Bainbridge OH
*WHKC(FM) Columbus OH
*WBIE(FM) Delphos OH
*WKRJ(FM) New Philadelphia OH
*WOBC-FM Oberlin OH
*WOSP(FM) Portsmouth OH
*KSYE(FM) Frederick OK
*KVAZ(FM) Henryetta OK
*KOBK(FM) Baker City OR
*KWVZ(FM) Florence OR
*KOPB-FM Portland OR
*KSRS(FM) Roseburg OR
*WPSU(FM) State College PA

*WSRN-FM Swarthmore PA
*WCVY(FM) Coventry RI
*WKCL(FM) Ladson SC
*WHCB(FM) Bristol TN
*WNRZ(FM) Dickson TN
*WFHU(FM) Henderson TN
*WFMQ(FM) Lebanon TN
*WAWL-FM Red Bank TN
*WTML(FM) Tullahoma TN
*KBCX(FM) Big Spring TX
*KHVT(FM) Bloomington TX
*KAXH(FM) Borger TX
*KTXP(FM) Bushland TX
*KANJ(FM) Giddings TX
*KHML(FM) Madisonville TX
*KCAS(FM) McCook TX
*KWLD(FM) Plainview TX
*KTXK(FM) Texarkana TX
*KUSU-FM Logan UT
*WARN(FM) Culpeper VA
*WPIN-FM Dublin VA
*WLUR(FM) Lexington VA
*WYCS(FM) Yorktown VA
*WGLY-FM Bolton VT
*WWLR(FM) Lyndonville VT
*KLWS(FM) Moses Lake WA
*KUBS(FM) Newport WA
*WEMY(FM) Green Bay WI
*WRSG(FM) Middlebourne WV
*WGLZ(FM) West Liberty WV
*KUWD(FM) Sundance WY

91.7 mhz

*WYFD(FM) Decatur AL
*WPIL(FM) Heflin AL
*WAQG(FM) Ozark AL
*KBDO(FM) Des Arc AR
*KRMC(FM) Douglas AZ
*KPUB(FM) Flagstaff AZ
*KNAD(FM) Page AZ
*KCHO(FM) Chico CA
*KXSR(FM) Groveland CA
*KHCS(FM) Palm Desert CA
*KBDH(FM) San Ardo CA
*KALW(FM) San Francisco CA
*KFHL(FM) Wasco CA
*KOTO(FM) Telluride CO
*WXCI(FM) Danbury CT
*WHUS(FM) Storrs CT
*WRTX(FM) Dover DE
*WMPH(FM) Wilmington DE
*WNLE(FM) Fernandina Beach FL
*WJLF(FM) Gainesville FL
*WMKL(FM) Key Largo FL
*WAPB(FM) Madison FL
*WMKO(FM) Marco FL
*WEGS(FM) Milton FL
*WFFL(FM) Panama City FL
*WVIJ(FM) Port Charlotte FL
*WFTI-FM Saint Petersburg FL
*WWFR(FM) Stuart FL
*WUNV(FM) Albany GA
*WUGA(FM) Athens GA
*WLPE(FM) Augusta GA
*WCCV(FM) Cartersville GA
*WTJB(FM) Columbus GA
*WWET(FM) Valdosta GA
*KSUI(FM) Iowa City IA
*KBSM(FM) McCall ID
*KRFA-FM Moscow ID
*KBSW(FM) Twin Falls ID
*WBJW(FM) Albion IL
*WBGL(FM) Champaign IL
*WVNL(FM) Vandalia IL
*WKJR(FM) Jasper IN
*WIWC(FM) Kokomo IN
*WEEM(FM) Pendleton IN
*WBSJ(FM) Portland IN
*WETL(FM) South Bend IN
*KZAN(FM) Hays KS
*KCVS(FM) Salina KS
*WWHR(FM) Bowling Green KY
*WAPD(FM) Campbellsville KY
*WJVK(FM) Owensboro KY
*WWJD(FM) Pippa Passes KY
*KAPM(FM) Alexandria LA
*KLSP(FM) Angola LA

*KMSL(FM) Mansfield LA
*KNWD(FM) Natchitoches LA
*WGAJ(FM) Deerfield MA
*WJWT(FM) Gardner MA
*WAVM(FM) Maynard MA
*WNEF(FM) Newburyport MA
*WMWM(FM) Salem MA
*WBSL-FM Sheffield MA
*WSHD(FM) Eastport ME
*WCML-FM Alpena MI
*WUOM(FM) Ann Arbor MI
*WMCQ(FM) Muskegon MI
*KAXE(FM) Grand Rapids MN
*KLSE-FM Rochester MN
*WMCN(FM) Saint Paul MN
*KNSW(FM) Worthington-Marshall MN
*KCVO-FM Camdenton MO
*KJIR(FM) Hannibal MO
*KMVC(FM) Marshall MO
*KNEO(FM) Neosho MO
*KCOZ(FM) Point Lookout MO
*KCVX(FM) Salem MO
*WSQH(FM) Forest MS
*WAOY(FM) Gulfport MS
*WVSD(FM) Itta Bena MS
*WJTA(FM) Kosciusko MS
*WPRL(FM) Lorman MS
*WAJS(FM) Tupelo MS
*KEMC(FM) Billings MT
*KUHM(FM) Helena MT
*WBKU(FM) Ahoskie NC
*WSGE(FM) Dallas NC
*KPNE-FM North Platte NE
*WNEC-FM Henniker NH
*WPCR-FM Plymouth NH
*WLFR(FM) Pomona NJ
*KUPR(FM) Alamogordo NM
*KZPI(FM) Deming NM
*KTGW(FM) Fruitland NM
*KGLP(FM) Gallup NM
*KLNR(FM) Panaca NV
*KTPH(FM) Tonopah NV
*WICB(FM) Ithaca NY
*WFRH(FM) Kingston NY
*WOSR(FM) Middletown NY
*WSQC-FM Oneonta NY
*WRVJ(FM) Watertown NY
*WVXU(FM) Cincinnati OH
*WOSV(FM) Mansfield OH
*WYTN(FM) Youngstown OH
*WJIC(FM) Zanesville OH
*KPSU(FM) Goodwell OK
*KARG(FM) Poteau OK
*KOSU(FM) Stillwater OK
*KEOL(FM) La Grande OR
*KDOV(FM) Medford OR
*WMUH(FM) Allentown PA
*WLBS(FM) Bristol PA
*WCUC-FM Clarion PA
*WIXQ(FM) Millersville PA
*WKDU(FM) Philadelphia PA
*WVMW-FM Scranton PA
*WJAZ(FM) Summerdale PA
*WBMR(FM) Telford PA
*WNJR(FM) Washington PA
*WCUR(FM) West Chester PA
*WRLC(FM) Williamsport PA
*WYTL(FM) Wyomissing PA
*WNNV(FM) San German PR
*WLPG(FM) Florence SC
*WTBI-FM Greenville SC
*WAPX-FM Clarksville TN
*WHRS(FM) Cookeville TN
*WUMR(FM) Memphis TN
*WFCM-FM Murfreesboro TN
*KVRX(FM) Austin TX
*KHPU(FM) Brownwood TX
*KBNJ(FM) Corpus Christi TX
*KVTT(FM) Dallas TX
*KOOP(FM) Hornsby TX
*KTRU(FM) Houston TX
*KRTU(FM) San Antonio TX
*KOHS(FM) Orem UT
*KRDC-FM Saint George UT
*KUFR(FM) Salt Lake City UT
*WEMC(FM) Harrisonburg VA
*WGLV(FM) Woodstock VT

*KZAZ(FM) Bellingham WA
*KBLD(FM) Kennewick WA
*KSVR(FM) Mount Vernon WA
*KXOT(FM) Tacoma WA
*WLWR(FM) Fond du Lac WI
*WSUM(FM) Madison WI
*WMSE(FM) Milwaukee WI
*WXPR(FM) Rhinelander WI
*WSHS(FM) Sheboygan WI
*WSUW(FM) Whitewater WI
*WVPB(FM) Beckley WV
*WVVU-FM Morgantown WV
*KDUW(FM) Douglas WY

91.9 mhz

*KBRW-FM Barrow AK
*KDLL(FM) Kenai AK
*KUHB-FM Saint Paul AK
*KUDU(FM) Tok AK
*WGIB(FM) Birmingham AL
*WMBV(FM) Dixons Mills AL
*WLJS-FM Jacksonville AL
*WJIF(FM) Opp AL
*KBPB(FM) Harrison AR
*KASU(FM) Jonesboro AR
*KXRJ(FM) Russellville AR
*KVJC(FM) Globe AZ
*KOHN(FM) Sells AZ
*KYRM(FM) Yuma AZ
*KHSR(FM) Crescent City CA
*KHKL(FM) Laytonville CA
*KSPB(FM) Pebble Beach CA
*KWTD(FM) Ridgecrest CA
*KVCR(FM) San Bernardino CA
*KCSB-FM Santa Barbara CA
*KLVR(FM) Santa Rosa CA
*KCSS(FM) Turlock CA
*KDUR(FM) Durango CO
*KLXV(FM) Glenwood Springs CO
*KCFP(FM) Pueblo CO
*WSLX(FM) New Canaan CT
*WHGN(FM) Crystal River FL
*WYFO(FM) Lakeland FL
*WKVH(FM) Monticello FL
*WAYL(FM) Saint Augustine FL
*WSCF-FM Vero Beach FL
*WCLK(FM) Atlanta GA
*WLFS(FM) Port Wentworth GA
*WVGS(FM) Statesboro GA
*WASW(FM) Waycross GA
*KSDA-FM Agat GU
*KAQA(FM) Kilauea HI
*KWRV(FM) Sun Valley ID
*WSIU(FM) Carbondale IL
*WJCH(FM) Joliet IL
*WUIS(FM) Springfield IL
*WQKO(FM) Howe IN
*WVSH(FM) Huntington IN
*WJEF(FM) Lafayette IN
*WHOJ(FM) Terre Haute IN
*KTCC(FM) Colby KS
*KONQ(FM) Dodge City KS
*KNGM(FM) Emporia KS
*KWBI(FM) Great Bend KS
*KARF(FM) Independence KS
*KSDB(FM) Manhattan KS
*KBDD(FM) Winfield KS
*WFPK(FM) Louisville KY
*KAXV(FM) Bastrop LA
*KMRL(FM) Buras LA
*WUMB-FM Boston MA
*WFPB-FM Falmouth MA
*WOZQ(FM) Northampton MA
*WAIC(FM) Springfield MA
*WCFM(FM) Williamstown MA
*WBPR(FM) Worcester MA
*WFWM(FM) Frostburg MD
*WGTS(FM) Takoma Park MD
*WYFP(FM) Harpswell ME
*WMEB-FM Orono ME
*WMTU-FM Houghton MI
*WORW(FM) Port Huron MI
*KXBR(FM) International Falls MN
*KBHZ(FM) Willmar MN
*KNLQ(FM) Cuba MO
*KWJC(FM) Liberty MO
*KNLM(FM) Marshfield MO

U.S. FM Stations by Frequency

*KSRD(FM) Saint Joseph MO
*WOWL(FM) Burnsville MS
*WAUM(FM) Duck Hill MS
*KGLT(FM) Bozeman MT
*KFRW(FM) Great Falls MT
*KUFN(FM) Hamilton MT
*WFSS(FM) Fayetteville NC
*WAAE(FM) New Bern NC
*WRCM(FM) Wingate NC
*KBFR(FM) Bismarck ND
*KDSU(FM) Fargo ND
*KCNE-FM Chadron NE
*KTLX(FM) Columbus NE
*KDNE(FM) Crete NE
*KWSC(FM) Wayne NE
*WBGD(FM) Brick Township NJ
*WNTI(FM) Hackettstown NJ
*KNLK(FM) Santa Rosa NM
*WNGN(FM) Argyle NY
*WCEB(FM) Corning NY
*WSHR(FM) Lake Ronkonkoma NY
*WCEL(FM) Plattsburgh NY
*WRVN(FM) Utica NY
*WLKP(FM) Belpre OH
*WOUH-FM Chillicothe OH
*WGDE(FM) Defiance OH
*WKCO(FM) Gambier OH
*WMEJ(FM) Proctorville OH
*KSSU(FM) Durant OK
*KBCW(FM) McAlester OK
*KMUN(FM) Astoria OR
*KRVM(FM) Eugene OR
*KWSO(FM) Warm Springs OR
*WCAL(FM) California PA
*WVME(FM) Meadville PA
*KQSD-FM Lowry SD
*WUOT(FM) Knoxville TN
*KXRI(FM) Amarillo TX
*KPFC(FM) Callisburg TX
*KLOW(FM) Dripping Springs TX
*KAZF(FM) Hebronville TX
*KHCJ(FM) Jefferson TX
*KAVX(FM) Lufkin TX
*KMEO(FM) Mertzon TX
*KPCW(FM) Park City UT
*WNRN(FM) Charlottesville VA
*WVTR(FM) Marion VA
*WCMK(FM) Putney VT
*KSFC(FM) Spokane WA
*KDNA(FM) Yakima WA
*WEMI(FM) Appleton WI
*WHDI(FM) Sister Bay WI
*WLBL-FM Wausau WI
*WXPW(FM) Wausau WI
*WBHZ(FM) Elkins WV
*WPHP(FM) Wheeling WV
*KLWD(FM) Gillette WY
*KUWR(FM) Laramie WY

92.1 mhz
KQEZ(FM) Houston AK
WJJN(FM) Columbia AL
WKUL(FM) Cullman AL
WZEW(FM) Fairhope AL
WERH-FM Hamilton AL
KHPQ(FM) Clinton AR
KDQN-FM De Queen AR
KKEG(FM) Fayetteville AR
KSBS-FM Pago Pago AS
KFMA(FM) Green Valley AZ
KZUA(FM) Holbrook AZ
KSGC(FM) Tusayan AZ
KPSL-FM Bakersfield CA
KOND(FM) Clovis CA
KSOQ-FM Escondido CA
KQCM(FM) Joshua Tree CA
KXCL(FM) Placerville CA
KKDV(FM) Walnut Creek CA
KJMN(FM) Castle Rock CO
KTHN(FM) La Junta CO
WLBW(FM) Fenwick Island DE
WFFY(FM) Destin FL
WAFZ(FM) Immokalee FL
WJXR(FM) Macclenny FL
WNFK(FM) Perry FL
WLTQ(FM) Venice FL
WRLX(FM) West Palm Beach FL

WDDQ(FM) Adel GA
WBTR-FM Carrollton GA
WSGC-FM Elberton GA
WJGA-FM Jackson GA
WPEH-FM Louisville GA
KCHE-FM Cherokee IA
KUEL(FM) Fort Dodge IA
KRLS(FM) Knoxville IA
*KIBX(FM) Bonners Ferry ID
KPPC(FM) Pocatello ID
WQKQ(FM) Carthage IL
WWGO(FM) Charleston IL
WFPS(FM) Freeport IL
*WBST(FM) Muncie IN
WROI(FM) Rochester IN
WZDM(FM) Vincennes IN
KREP(FM) Belleville KS
KMZA(FM) Seneca KS
WBVX(FM) Carlisle KY
WTKY-FM Tompkinsville KY
KSYR(FM) Benton LA
KTSR(FM) De Quincy LA
KLIL(FM) Moreauville LA
KVCL-FM Winnfield LA
*WOMR(FM) Provincetown MA
WUFK(FM) Fort Kent ME
*WUPI(FM) Presque Isle ME
WPHX-FM Sanford ME
WOUF(FM) Beulah MI
WIDL(FM) Caro MI
WDOW-FM Dowagiac MI
WGHN-FM Grand Haven MI
WVXH(FM) Harrison MI
WCSR-FM Hillsdale MI
WTXQ(FM) Saint Johns MI
WWAX(FM) Hermantown MN
WYRQ(FM) Little Falls MN
KLQP(FM) Madison MN
KRUE(FM) Waseca MN
KKOZ-FM Ava MO
KMOE(FM) Butler MO
KMFC(FM) Centralia MO
*KCVZ(FM) Dixon MO
KSDL(FM) Sedalia MO
WBKN(FM) Brookhaven MS
WKXY(FM) Clarksdale MS
WJMG(FM) Hattiesburg MS
WMSU(FM) Starkville MS
WUMS(FM) University MS
WJNS-FM Yazoo City MS
WMNC-FM Morganton NC
WCDG(FM) Moyock NC
WRSV(FM) Rocky Mount NC
KZRX(FM) Dickinson ND
WFEX(FM) Peterborough NH
WVLT(FM) Vineland NJ
KATK-FM Carlsbad NM
KJZS(FM) Sparks NV
WSEN-FM Baldwinsville NY
WCKR(FM) Hornell NY
WVTK(FM) Port Henry NY
WRNQ(FM) Poughkeepsie NY
WLNG(FM) Sag Harbor NY
WDLA-FM Walton NY
WOHF(FM) Bellevue OH
WYVK(FM) Middleport OH
WBIK(FM) Pleasant City OH
WZOQ(FM) Wapakoneta OH
WROU-FM West Carrollton OH
KIZS(FM) Broken Arrow OK
KFXI(FM) Marlow OK
KMZE(FM) Woodward OK
KWVR-FM Enterprise OR
*KAVE(FM) Oakridge OR
KSYD(FM) Reedsport OR
WKPL(FM) Ellwood City PA
WRKW(FM) Johnstown PA
WSNU(FM) Lock Haven PA
WPPT(FM) Mercersburg PA
WQFM(FM) Nanticoke PA
WWKL(FM) Palmyra PA
*WPTS-FM Pittsburgh PA
WZET(FM) Hormigueros PR
WZOL(FM) Luquillo PR
WBHC-FM Hampton SC
WWNU(FM) Irmo SC
WMYB(FM) Myrtle Beach SC

WQQK(FM) Hendersonville TN
WEUZ(FM) Minor Hill TN
KOPY(FM) Alice TX
KCZO(FM) Carrizo Springs TX
KXEZ(FM) Farmersville TX
KTFW-FM Glen Rose TX
KQJZ(FM) Hutto TX
KTNR(FM) Kenedy TX
KNBT(FM) New Braunfels TX
KROI(FM) Seabrook TX
KHOS(FM) Sonora TX
KDOK(FM) Tyler TX
KTCE(FM) Payson UT
WDIC-FM Clinchco VA
*WWHS-FM Hampden-Sydney VA
WCDX(FM) Mechanicsville VA
WMOO(FM) Derby Center VT
KCRK-FM Colville WA
WLTU(FM) Manitowoc WI
WRJC-FM Mauston WI
WMEQ-FM Menomonie WI
WEZY(FM) Racine WI
WXXM(FM) Sun Prairie WI
*WVWC(FM) Buckhannon WV
KFRZ(FM) Green River WY

92.3 mhz
WLWI-FM Montgomery AL
KIPR(FM) Pine Bluff AR
KWCD(FM) Bisbee AZ
KKFR(FM) Glendale AZ
KRED-FM Eureka CA
KHHT(FM) Los Angeles CA
KSJO(FM) San Jose CA
KHJQ(FM) Susanville CA
KJYE(FM) Grand Junction CO
KSTH(FM) Holyoke CO
KVRH-FM Salida CO
WCMQ-FM Hialeah FL
WWKA(FM) Orlando FL
WMOQ(FM) Bostwick GA
WAEG(FM) Evans GA
WSSJ(FM) Hinesville GA
WLZN(FM) Macon GA
WQLI(FM) Pelham GA
KSSK-FM Waipahu HI
KKHQ-FM Oelwein IA
KIZN(FM) Boise ID
KMQS(FM) Victor ID
WZPW(FM) Peoria IL
WTTS(FM) Bloomington IN
WFWI(FM) Fort Wayne IN
WPWX(FM) Hammond IN
KMXW(FM) Newton KS
KCCV-FM Olathe KS
WYGE(FM) London KY
WZAQ(FM) Louisa KY
WDVW(FM) La Place LA
KMYY(FM) Rayville LA
WERQ-FM Baltimore MD
WWHC(FM) Oakland MD
WMME-FM Augusta ME
WZUU(FM) Allegan MI
WMXD(FM) Detroit MI
WJPD(FM) Ishpeming MI
KXRA-FM Alexandria MN
WIL-FM Saint Louis MO
KSAR(FM) Thayer MO
KTTN-FM Trenton MO
WOHT(FM) Grenada MS
KKRY(FM) Miles City MT
KQRK(FM) Ronan MT
WKRR(FM) Asheboro NC
WQSL(FM) Jacksonville NC
WZPR(FM) Nags Head NC
KEZO-FM Omaha NE
WGXL(FM) Hanover NH
KRST(FM) Albuquerque NM
KOMP(FM) Las Vegas NV
KSVL(FM) Smith NV
WXRK(FM) New York NY
WFLY(FM) Troy NY
WXTM(FM) Cleveland Heights OH
WCOL-FM Columbus OH
KREU(FM) Roland OK
KGON(FM) Portland OR
*WKVR-FM Huntingdon PA

WNBQ(FM) Mansfield PA
WLGL(FM) Riverside PA
WRRN(FM) Warren PA
WPRO-FM Providence RI
KQRQ(FM) Rapid City SD
WDEF-FM Chattanooga TN
WYNU(FM) Milan TN
KOFX(FM) El Paso TX
KIJN-FM Farwell TX
KRNH(FM) Kerrville TX
KIIZ-FM Killeen TX
KETX(FM) Livingston TX
KCUL(FM) Marshall TX
KNFM(FM) Midland TX
KNRG(FM) New Ulm TX
KQVT(FM) Victoria TX
WSRV(FM) Deltaville VA
WXLK(FM) Roanoke VA
KULE-FM Ephrata WA
WJMQ(FM) Clintonville WI
WRLS-FM Hayward WI
WOSQ(FM) Spencer WI
WXCR(FM) New Martinsville WV

92.5 mhz
WXJC-FM Cordova AL
WWXQ(FM) Trinity AL
KWYN-FM Wynne AR
KTHQ(FM) Eagar AZ
KMYX-FM Arvin CA
KBRE-FM Atwater CA
KSRW(FM) Independence CA
KKAL(FM) Paso Robles CA
KGBY(FM) Sacramento CA
KDJM(FM) Broomfield CO
KCRT-FM Trinidad CO
WWYZ(FM) Waterbury CT
WNDT(FM) Alachua FL
WRQC(FM) Estero FL
WPAP-FM Panama City FL
WYUU(FM) Safety Harbor FL
WFJO(FM) Folkston GA
WKZZ(FM) Tifton GA
WEKS(FM) Zebulon GA
KJJY(FM) West Des Moines IA
WDEK(FM) De Kalb IL
WKKQ(FM) Rushville IL
WCFF(FM) Urbana IL
WZWZ(FM) Kokomo IN
KQMA-FM Phillipsburg KS
KCVT(FM) Silver Lake KS
WBKR(FM) Owensboro KY
KHCL(FM) Arcadia LA
KVPI-FM Ville Platte LA
WXRV(FM) Haverhill MA
WXMD(FM) Pocomoke City MD
XHRM-FM Tijuana MEX
WJSZ(FM) Ashley MI
WFDX(FM) Atlanta MI
WBGV(FM) Marlette MI
WKOQ(FM) Newaygo MI
*WIRN(FM) Buhl MN
KQRS-FM Golden Valley MN
KXKK(FM) Park Rapids MN
KKWQ(FM) Warroad MN
*KSMR(FM) Winona MN
KSYN(FM) Joplin MO
KELE-FM Mountain Grove MO
KPPL(FM) Poplar Bluff MO
KAYX(FM) Richmond MO
WESE(FM) Baldwyn MS
WQST-FM Forest MS
WQYZ(FM) Ocean Springs MS
KAAR(FM) Butte MT
KPQX(FM) Havre MT
WYFL(FM) Henderson NC
WBEE-FM Rochester NY
WZKL(FM) Alliance OH
WOFX-FM Cincinnati OH
WVKS(FM) Toledo OH
KPRV-FM Heavener OK
KKRE(FM) Hollis OK
KOMA(FM) Oklahoma City OK
KLAD-FM Klamath Falls OR
WQMU(FM) Indiana PA
WJUN-FM Mexico PA
WXTU(FM) Philadelphia PA

WKGB-FM Susquehanna PA
WORO(FM) Corozal PR
WESC-FM Greenville SC
WCSQ-FM Manning SC
KELO-FM Sioux Falls SD
KULL(FM) Abilene TX
KBEY(FM) Burnet TX
KZPS(FM) Dallas TX
KRPT(FM) Devine TX
KKLB(FM) Elgin TX
KCOL-FM Groves TX
KZRC(FM) Markham TX
KHTZ(FM) Navasota TX
KQSI(FM) San Augustine TX
*KHTA(FM) Wake Village TX
KYKM(FM) Yoakum TX
KXFF(FM) Cedar City UT
KCUA(FM) Naples UT
KUUU(FM) South Jordan UT
WINC-FM Winchester VA
KLSY-FM Bellevue WA
KZHR(FM) Dayton WA
WJJQ-FM Tomahawk WI
WBWI-FM West Bend WI
WZAC(FM) Danville WV
KBOG(FM) Douglas WY
KLZY(FM) Powell-Cody WY

92.7 mhz
WAFN-FM Arab AL
WKZJ(FM) Eufaula AL
WJBB-FM Haleyville AL
WTDR-FM Talladega AL
KLYR-FM Clarksville AR
KASR(FM) Conway AR
KRRN(FM) Kingman AZ
KNGY(FM) Alameda CA
KLRS(FM) Chico CA
KLIT(FM) Fountain Valley CA
KKUU(FM) Indio CA
KTOM-FM Marina CA
KMFB(FM) Mendocino CA
KZIQ-FM Ridgecrest CA
KELT(FM) Riverside CA
KZSQ-FM Sonora CA
KMLT(FM) Thousand Oaks CA
KKCH(FM) Glenwood Springs CO
WGMD(FM) Rehoboth Beach DE
WJBT(FM) Green Cove Springs FL
WEOW(FM) Key West FL
WAVW(FM) Stuart FL
WKKZ(FM) Dublin GA
WBGA(FM) Saint Simons Island GA
KHWI(FM) Hilo HI
KLGA-FM Algona IA
KTWA(FM) Ottumwa IA
KORT-FM Grangeville ID
KSRA-FM Salmon ID
WKIE(FM) Arlington Heights IL
WLSR(FM) Galesburg IL
WVZA(FM) Herrin IL
WKIF(FM) Kankakee IL
WQLZ(FM) Taylorville IL
WJCP(FM) Austin IN
WZBD(FM) Berne IN
WSKT(FM) Spencer IN
KANR(FM) Belle Plaine KS
KILS(FM) Minneapolis KS
WRVC-FM Catlettsburg KY
WMIK-FM Middlesboro KY
WHVE(FM) Russell Springs KY
WQCK(FM) Clinton LA
KWJM(FM) Farmerville LA
KLPL-FM Lake Providence LA
KJVC(FM) Mansfield LA
WMVY(FM) Tisbury MA
WBZS-FM Prince Frederick MD
WQDY-FM Calais ME
WOXO-FM Norway ME
WQTX(FM) Charlotte MI
WDZZ-FM Flint MI
WYVN(FM) Saugatuck MI
KLOZ(FM) Eldon MO
KSJQ(FM) Savannah MO
WKRA-FM Holly Springs MS
KVCK-FM Wolf Point MT
WQNC(FM) Harrisburg NC

U.S. FM Stations by Frequency

KFAB-FM Kindred ND
KBRB-FM Ainsworth NE
KUSO(FM) Albion NE
WOBM-FM Toms River NJ
KDSK(FM) Grants NM
KRSY-FM La Luz NM
KQAY-FM Tucumcari NM
KDSS(FM) Ely NV
KHWK(FM) Tonopah NV
KWNA-FM Winnemucca NV
WENY-FM Elmira NY
WZAA(FM) Garden City NY
*WGFR(FM) Glens Falls NY
WXUR(FM) Herkimer NY
WRRV(FM) Middletown NY
WBDB(FM) Ogdensburg NY
WQEL(FM) Bucyrus OH
*WCVZ(FM) South Zanesville OH
KTRX(FM) Dickson OK
KKBS(FM) Guymon OK
KQHC(FM) Burns OR
KGBR(FM) Gold Beach OR
KNCU(FM) Newport OR
KMSW(FM) The Dalles OR
WCCR(FM) Clarion PA
WJSM-FM Martinsburg PA
WSJW(FM) Starview PA
WKSX(FM) Johnston SC
KGFX-FM Pierre SD
WBZH(FM) Harriman TN
KALP(FM) Alpine TX
KIVY-FM Crockett TX
KINL(FM) Eagle Pass TX
KKBA(FM) Kingsville TX
KJBZ(FM) Laredo TX
KJAK(FM) Slaton TX
KESO(FM) South Padre Island TX
KBDX(FM) Blanding UT
WFHG-FM Abingdon VA
WUVA(FM) Charlottesville VA
WKVT-FM Brattleboro VT
KNCW(FM) Omak WA
WAUN(FM) Kewaunee WI
WPKG(FM) Neillsville WI
WDUX-FM Waupaca WI
WGIE(FM) Clarksburg WV
WPMW(FM) Mullens WV
KIQZ(FM) Rawlins WY

92.9 mhz

KFAT(FM) Anchorage AK
WBLX-FM Mobile AL
WTUG-FM Tuscaloosa AL
KVRE(FM) Hot Springs Village AR
KAFF-FM Flagstaff AZ
KWMT-FM Tucson AZ
KFGY(FM) Healdsburg CA
KJEE(FM) Montecito CA
KXFG(FM) Sun City CA
KFSO-FM Visalia CA
KSPZ(FM) Colorado Springs CO
WDSD(FM) Smyrna DE
WIKX(FM) Charlotte Harbor FL
WMFQ(FM) Ocala FL
WZGC(FM) Atlanta GA
WAAC(FM) Valdosta GA
KATF(FM) Dubuque IA
KKIA(FM) Ida Grove IA
WRPW(FM) Colfax IL
WSEI(FM) Olney IL
WNDV-FM South Bend IN
WSKL(FM) Veedersburg IN
KMXN(FM) Osage City KS
WLXX(FM) Lexington KY
KHLA(FM) Jennings LA
KTKC(FM) Springhill LA
WBOX-FM Varnado LA
WBOS(FM) Brookline MA
WEZQ(FM) Bangor ME
WJZQ(FM) Cadillac MI
*WSCD-FM Duluth MN
*KFSI(FM) Rochester MN
KKJM(FM) Saint Joseph MN
KGRC(FM) Hannibal MO
KLSC(FM) Malden MO
KOMG(FM) Ozark MO
KKID(FM) Salem MO

WDTL-FM Cleveland MS
WDXO(FM) Hazlehurst MS
KLFM(FM) Great Falls MT
KEZQ(FM) West Yellowstone MT
KYYY(FM) Bismarck ND
KKXL-FM Grand Forks ND
KTGL(FM) Beatrice NE
KMOR(FM) Scottsbluff NE
KTZA(FM) Artesia NM
KYBR(FM) Espanola NM
KRWN(FM) Farmington NM
KSCQ(FM) Silver City NM
KMXQ(FM) Socorro NM
KURK(FM) Reno NV
WBUF(FM) Buffalo NY
WBPM(FM) Saugerties NY
WEHM(FM) Southampton NY
WGTZ(FM) Eaton OH
KBEZ(FM) Tulsa OK
KAST-FM Astoria OR
WLTJ(FM) Pittsburgh PA
WMGS(FM) Wilkes-Barre PA
WTPM(FM) Aguadilla PR
WYQE(FM) Naguabo PR
WZLA-FM Abbeville SC
WEGX(FM) Dillon SC
KSDR-FM Watertown SD
WMFS(FM) Bartlett TN
WJXA(FM) Nashville TN
WNPC-FM Newport TN
KLRK(FM) Marlin TX
KKBQ-FM Pasadena TX
KDCD(FM) San Angelo TX
KROM(FM) San Antonio TX
KBKH(FM) Shamrock TX
KNIN-FM Wichita Falls TX
KBLQ-FM Logan UT
WVHL(FM) Farmville VA
WFOG(FM) Suffolk VA
WEZF(FM) Burlington VT
KISM(FM) Bellingham WA
KZZU(FM) Spokane WA
KDBL(FM) Toppenish WA
WYNW(FM) Birnamwood WI
WECL(FM) Elk Mound WI
WDHC(FM) Berkeley Springs WV
WCWV(FM) Summersville WV
WLGT(FM) Buffalo WY

93.1 mhz

WGMZ(FM) Glencoe AL
KZLE(FM) Batesville AR
*KHDX(FM) Conway AR
KKHJ(FM) Pago Pago AS
KLJZ(FM) Yuma AZ
KXGO(FM) Arcata CA
KCBS-FM Los Angeles CA
KOSO(FM) Patterson CA
KKXX-FM Shafter CA
KMGJ(FM) Grand Junction CO
WKRO(FM) Edgewater FL
WHDR(FM) Miami FL
WBBK-FM Blakely GA
WEAS-FM Savannah GA
WGAC-FM Warrenton GA
KQMQ-FM Honolulu HI
KWCC(FM) Muscatine IA
KZMG(FM) New Plymouth ID
WXRT-FM Chicago IL
WYDS(FM) Decatur IL
WTFX-FM Clarksville IN
WNOU(FM) Indianapolis IN
KHMY(FM) Pratt KS
WMKZ(FM) Monticello KY
WDHR(FM) Pikeville KY
KQID(FM) Alexandria LA
WHYN-FM Springfield MA
WPOC(FM) Baltimore MD
WMGX(FM) Portland ME
WDRQ(FM) Detroit MI
WIMK(FM) Iron Mountain MI
KXLP(FM) New Ulm MN
KWRT(FM) Boonville MO
KBDZ(FM) Perryville MO
WGDQ(FM) Hattiesburg MS
WYAB(FM) Yazoo City MS
KGCX(FM) Sidney MT

WMQX-FM Winston-Salem NC
KRVN-FM Lexington NE
WPAT-FM Paterson NJ
WDTH(FM) Wildwood Crest NJ
KQOL-FM Las Vegas NV
WNTQ(FM) Syracuse NY
WZAK(FM) Cleveland OH
WFGF(FM) Lima OH
KKNU(FM) Springfield-Eugene OR
WQYX(FM) Clearfield PA
WZMJ(FM) Batesburg SC
KRCS(FM) Sturgis SD
KKYA(FM) Yankton SD
WWGM(FM) Alamo TN
WOCE(FM) Benton TN
WMYU(FM) Karns TN
KQIZ-FM Amarillo TX
KMKT(FM) Bells TX
KSTV-FM Dublin TX
KSII(FM) El Paso TX
KTYL-FM Tyler TX
WJZV(FM) Ettrick VA
WSVO(FM) Staunton VA
WHIT-FM De Forest WI
WJBL(FM) Ladysmith WI
WBVQ(FM) Barrackville WV
WLWF(FM) Ravenswood WV
KTRZ(FM) Riverton WY

93.3 mhz

KXBA(FM) Nikiski AK
KVAK-FM Valdez AK
WPGG(FM) Evergreen AL
KMJI(FM) Ashdown AR
KKZR(FM) Bryant AR
KAGL(FM) El Dorado AR
KDKB(FM) Mesa AZ
KXAZ(FM) Page AZ
KBHR(FM) Big Bear City CA
KRHV(FM) Big Pine CA
KNTO(FM) Chowchilla CA
KHTS-FM El Cajon CA
KRZZ(FM) San Francisco CA
KZOZ(FM) San Luis Obispo CA
KJDX(FM) Susanville CA
KKDC(FM) Dolores CO
KTCL(FM) Fort Collins CO
KLMR-FM Lamar CO
*WFAR(FM) Danbury CT
WPLA(FM) Callahan FL
WGWD(FM) Gretna FL
WFLZ-FM Tampa FL
WVFJ-FM Manchester GA
KIOA(FM) Des Moines IA
WPBG(FM) Peoria IL
WTRH(FM) Ramsey IL
WBTU(FM) Kendallville IN
WQTY(FM) Linton IN
WDNS(FM) Bowling Green KY
WKYQ(FM) Paducah KY
WQUE-FM New Orleans LA
WSNE-FM Taunton MA
WKQZ(FM) Midland MI
KBLB(FM) Nisswa MN
KMXV(FM) Kansas City MO
KIGL(FM) Seligman MO
KNSX(FM) Steelville MO
WSYE(FM) Houston MS
KYYA(FM) Billings MT
KGGL(FM) Missoula MT
WTPT(FM) Forest City NC
*WOGR-FM Salisbury NC
WERO(FM) Washington NC
KSJZ(FM) Jamestown ND
KHUS(FM) Bennington NE
WNHW(FM) Belmont NH
KKOB-FM Albuquerque NM
*WCAN(FM) Canajoharie NY
WFKL(FM) Fairport NY
WWSE(FM) Jamestown NY
WBWZ(FM) New Paltz NY
WCIZ-FM Watertown NY
WLZT(FM) Chillicothe OH
WAKW(FM) Cincinnati OH
WNCD(FM) Youngstown OH
KKNG-FM Newcastle OK
WQZS(FM) Meyersdale PA

WBZD(FM) Muncy PA
WMMR(FM) Philadelphia PA
WZMT(FM) Ponce PR
WWWZ(FM) Summerville SC
KJRV(FM) Wessington Springs SD
WHRP(FM) Tullahoma TN
KDHT(FM) Cedar Park TX
KDBN(FM) Haltom City TX
KBAT(FM) Midland TX
KQBU-FM Port Arthur TX
KITE(FM) Port Lavaca TX
KUBL-FM Salt Lake City UT
WFLS-FM Fredericksburg VA
KUBE(FM) Seattle WA
*KRKL(FM) Walla Walla WA
WBSZ(FM) Ashland WI
WIZM-FM La Crosse WI
WJZI(FM) Milwaukee WI
*WKVW(FM) Marmet WV
KJAX(FM) Jackson WY

93.5 mhz

WMLV(FM) Butler AL
KBKG(FM) Corning AR
KBFC(FM) Forrest City AR
KKTZ(FM) Lakeview AR
KSNX(FM) Show Low AZ
KNAC(FM) Earlimart CA
KXSM(FM) Hollister CA
KDAI(FM) Ontario CA
KDAY(FM) Redondo Beach CA
KLKX(FM) Rosamond CA
KKBN(FM) Twain Harte CA
KMKX(FM) Willits CA
KALQ-FM Alamosa CO
WZBH(FM) Georgetown DE
WBGF(FM) Belle Glade FL
WKEY-FM Key West FL
WEBZ(FM) Port St. Joe FL
WLJA-FM Ellijay GA
WVOH-FM Hazlehurst GA
KPOA(FM) Lahaina HI
KQNG-FM Lihue HI
KQCS(FM) Bettendorf IA
KKMI(FM) Burlington IA
WVIX(FM) Joliet IL
WEBX(FM) Tuscola IL
WLFW(FM) Chandler IN
WHTY(FM) Hartford City IN
WKHY(FM) Lafayette IN
KOTE(FM) Eureka KS
KLKC(FM) Parsons KS
KWME(FM) Wellington KS
WMMG-FM Brandenburg KY
WAIN-FM Columbia KY
KGGM(FM) Delhi LA
KJAE(FM) Leesville LA
WDVT(FM) Harwichport MA
WCTB(FM) Fairfield ME
WBCM(FM) Boyne City MI
WKMJ(FM) Hancock MI
WHMI-FM Howell MI
KSCR-FM Benson MN
KITN(FM) Worthington MN
KRMS-FM Osage Beach MO
*KRSS(FM) Tarkio MO
WHJT(FM) Clinton MS
KLAN(FM) Glasgow MT
WLQB(FM) Ocean Isle Beach NC
*WYFQ-FM Wadesboro NC
KKOT(FM) Columbus NE
WMWV(FM) Conway NH
KWES(FM) Ruidoso NM
KADD(FM) Logandale NV
WZCR(FM) Hudson NY
WVBR-FM Ithaca NY
WRTN(FM) New Rochelle NY
WOKR(FM) Remsen NY
WBNV(FM) Barnesville OH
WRQN(FM) Bowling Green OH
KRKZ(FM) Altus OK
KWFX(FM) Woodward OK
KHAL(FM) Condon OR
KDCQ(FM) Coos Bay OR
KFLY(FM) Lakeview OR
WTPA(FM) Mechanicsburg PA
WHPA(FM) Northern Cambria PA

WSBG(FM) Stroudsburg PA
WDOG(FM) Allendale SC
WARQ(FM) Columbia SC
WKBQ(FM) Covington TN
WKZX-FM Lenoir City TN
WKWX(FM) Savannah TN
KLXK(FM) Breckenridge TX
WBHT(FM) Crockett TX
KIKT(FM) Greenville TX
KOOK(FM) Junction TX
KBAW(FM) Zapata TX
KSNN(FM) Saint George UT
WAXM(FM) Big Stone Gap VA
WBBC-FM Blackstone VA
WSNV(FM) Salem VA
WYAC-FM Christiansted VI
WTSM(FM) Springfield VT
KOZI-FM Chelan WA
WOZZ(FM) New London WI
WBTQ(FM) Buckhannon WV

93.7 mhz

KAFC(FM) Anchorage AK
WDJC-FM Birmingham AL
WRJM-FM Geneva AL
KISR(FM) Fort Smith AR
KJBR(FM) Marked Tree AR
KHBM-FM Monticello AR
KRQQ(FM) Tucson AZ
KCLB-FM Coachella CA
KXZM(FM) Felton CA
KSKS(FM) Fresno CA
KHWD(FM) Roseville CA
KDB(FM) Santa Barbara CA
KJZY(FM) Sebastopol CA
KRAI-FM Craig CO
KSBV(FM) Salida CO
WZMX(FM) Hartford CT
WSTW(FM) Wilmington DE
WTLT(FM) Naples FL
WOGK(FM) Ocala FL
WGYL(FM) Vero Beach FL
WPEZ(FM) Jeffersonville GA
WMPZ(FM) Ringgold GA
KKRL(FM) Carroll IA
KZBQ(FM) Pocatello ID
WTRX-FM Pontiac IL
WQKC(FM) Seymour IN
WFRR(FM) Walton IN
KAIR-FM Horton KS
KYEZ(FM) Salina KS
WDGG(FM) Ashland KY
KRDJ(FM) New Iberia LA
KXKS-FM Shreveport LA
WQSX(FM) Lawrence MA
WRMO(FM) Milbridge ME
WRCL(FM) Frankenmuth MI
WBCT(FM) Grand Rapids MI
WKAD(FM) Harrietta MI
WNBY-FM Newberry MI
KXXR(FM) Minneapolis MN
KTUF(FM) Kirksville MO
KSD(FM) Saint Louis MO
WMJY(FM) Biloxi MS
WQLJ(FM) Oxford MS
KOBB-FM Bozeman MT
KTZZ(FM) Conrad MT
WBNE(FM) Wrightsville Beach NC
WDAY-FM Fargo ND
KIZZ(FM) Minot ND
KXXI(FM) Gallup NM
KLKO(FM) Elko NV
KWNZ(FM) Sun Valley NV
*WCOV-FM Clyde NY
WBLK(FM) Depew NY
WEGQ(FM) Scotia NY
WFCJ(FM) Miamisburg OH
WQIO(FM) Mount Vernon OH
KSPI-FM Stillwater OK
KTMT-FM Medford OR
KPDQ-FM Portland OR
WBUS(FM) Boalsburg PA
WSJR(FM) Dallas PA
WRKZ(FM) Pittsburgh PA
WZNT(FM) San Juan PR
WSIM(FM) Bishopville SC
WXJY(FM) Georgetown SC

U.S. FM Stations by Frequency

WFBC-FM Greenville SC
WALI(FM) Walterboro SC
KBRK-FM Brookings SD
KVAR(FM) Pine Ridge SD
KWYR-FM Winner SD
WTKB-FM Atwood TN
WBXE(FM) Baxter TN
WFFI(FM) Kingston Springs TN
KLBJ-FM Austin TX
KKRW(FM) Houston TX
KNOR(FM) Krum TX
KXTQ-FM Lubbock TX
KLGL(FM) Richfield UT
WPYA(FM) Chesapeake VA
WAZR(FM) Woodstock VA
WXAL-FM Addison VT
KXAA(FM) Cle Elum WA
KGSG(FM) Pasco WA
KDRK-FM Spokane WA
WEKZ-FM Monroe WI
WBFM(FM) Sheboygan WI
WLSL(FM) Three Lakes WI
KSHF(FM) Cheyenne WY
KYTI(FM) Sheridan WY

93.9 mhz
WYTK(FM) Rogersville AL
WQSI(FM) Union Springs AL
KAMJ-FM Gosnell AR
KMGN(FM) Flagstaff AZ
KRIT(FM) Parker AZ
KFMF(FM) Chico CA
KHDV(FM) King City CA
KZLA-FM Los Angeles CA
KBBU(FM) Modesto CA
KRLT(FM) South Lake Tahoe CA
KYSL(FM) Frisco CO
WKYS(FM) Washington DC
WLVE(FM) Miami Beach FL
WKDG(FM) Martinez GA
WMTM-FM Moultrie GA
KUAM-FM Hagatna GU
KIKI-FM Honolulu HI
KLUA(FM) Kailua-Kona HI
KIAI(FM) Mason City IA
KSOU-FM Sioux Center IA
WCEZ(FM) Carthage IL
WLIT-FM Chicago IL
WYEC(FM) Kewanee IL
WABZ(FM) Sherman IL
*WPFR-FM Clinton IN
WISG(FM) Fishers IN
KDGS(FM) Andover KS
KZRD(FM) Dodge City KS
WSEK(FM) Burnside KY
WKTG(FM) Madisonville KY
KMXH(FM) Alexandria LA
WRSI(FM) Turners Falls MA
WCYI(FM) Lewiston ME
WAVC(FM) Mio MI
KKRC(FM) Granite Falls MN
WTBX(FM) Hibbing MN
KSSZ(FM) Fayette MO
KGKS(FM) Scott City MO
KJMK(FM) Webb City MO
KSPQ(FM) West Plains MO
WGRM-FM Greenwood MS
WRXW(FM) Pearl MS
WRSN(FM) Burlington NC
KSWN(FM) McCook NE
KRTN-FM Raton NM
WDNY-FM Dansville NY
*WNYC-FM New York NY
WKXZ(FM) Norwich NY
*WQKE(FM) Plattsburgh NY
WLWD(FM) Columbus Grove OH
KIMY(FM) Watonga OK
WUSE(FM) Fairview PA
WKBI-FM Saint Marys PA
WJXY-FM Conway SC
WIGL(FM) Saint Matthews SC
KKMK(FM) Rapid City SD
WSIB(FM) Selmer TN
WAYA(FM) Spring City TN
KMXR(FM) Corpus Christi TX
KINT-FM El Paso TX
KOYN(FM) Paris TX

KCRN-FM San Angelo TX
KBNU(FM) Uvalde TX
WMEV-FM Marion VA
WLVB(FM) Morrisville VT
WMXR(FM) Woodstock VT
KTAC(FM) Ephrata WA
WMMA(FM) Nekoosa WI
WDOR-FM Sturgeon Bay WI
WRRR-FM Saint Marys WV
KTAK(FM) Riverton WY

94.1 mhz
WZBQ(FM) Carrollton AL
WXQW(FM) Meridianville AL
KKPT(FM) Little Rock AR
KRDE(FM) Globe AZ
KXKQ(FM) Safford AZ
KISV(FM) Bakersfield CA
KNCO-FM Grass Valley CA
KSLG-FM Hydesville CA
KBKY(FM) Merced CA
KLMM(FM) Morro Bay CA
KMYI(FM) San Diego CA
KKXK(FM) Montrose CO
WAKU(FM) Crawfordville FL
WSJT(FM) Lakeland FL
WTYS-FM Marianna FL
WMEZ(FM) Pensacola FL
WSOS-FM Saint Augustine FL
WQBT(FM) Savannah GA
WSTR(FM) Smyrna GA
KRNA(FM) Iowa City IA
KBXL(FM) Caldwell ID
WMIX-FM Mount Vernon IL
WGFA-FM Watseka IL
WCKZ(FM) Roanoke IN
KDNS(FM) Downs KS
KFKF-FM Kansas City KS
WLYE-FM Glasgow KY
WEMX(FM) Kentwood LA
WVIC(FM) Jackson MI
WUPK(FM) Marquette MI
WWKR(FM) Pentwater MI
KKLN(FM) Atwater MN
KFML(FM) Little Falls MN
KPVR(FM) Bowling Green MO
KRKX(FM) Billings MT
KOPR(FM) Butte MT
WKXS-FM Leland NC
WTHZ(FM) Lexington NC
WWHA(FM) Oriental NC
KQCH(FM) Omaha NE
KNEB-FM Scottsbluff NE
WFTN-FM Franklin NH
KZRR(FM) Albuquerque NM
KZOR(FM) Hobbs NM
KMXB(FM) Henderson NV
WZNE(FM) Brighton NY
WNYV(FM) Whitehall NY
WHBC-FM Canton OH
WVMX(FM) Cincinnati OH
KTSO(FM) Glenpool OK
KZCD(FM) Lawton OK
KXIX(FM) Bend OR
*KOOZ(FM) Myrtle Point OR
KTIL-FM Tillamook OR
WYSP(FM) Philadelphia PA
WQKX(FM) Sunbury PA
WNOD(FM) Mayaguez PR
WHJY(FM) Providence RI
WHZQ(FM) Cross Hill SC
WGSS(FM) Kingstree SC
KSDN(FM) Aberdeen SD
WMBZ(FM) Germantown TN
WLZK(FM) Paris TN
WFFH(FM) Smyrna TN
KMXJ-FM Amarillo TX
KQXY-FM Beaumont TX
KULF(FM) Brenham TX
KDLK-FM Del Rio TX
KTFM(FM) Floresville TX
KLNO(FM) Fort Worth TX
KAJI(FM) Point Comfort TX
KODJ(FM) Salt Lake City UT
WXEZ(FM) Yorktown VA
KCLK-FM Clarkston WA

KMPS-FM Seattle WA
WIAL(FM) Eau Claire WI
WJJO(FM) Watertown WI
WQZK-FM Keyser WV
WAXS(FM) Oak Hill WV

94.3 mhz
WIZB(FM) Abbeville AL
WQZX(FM) Greenville AL
KAMO-FM Rogers AR
KFPB(FM) Chino Valley AZ
KBUX(FM) Quartzsite AZ
KDUC(FM) Barstow CA
KCRE-FM Crescent City CA
KEBN(FM) Garden Grove CA
KLMG(FM) Jackson CA
KOKO-FM Kerman CA
KBUA(FM) San Fernando CA
KILO(FM) Colorado Springs CO
KKQZ(FM) Wellington CO
WYBC-FM New Haven CT
WNFB(FM) Lake City FL
WGMX(FM) Marathon FL
WZZR(FM) Riviera Beach FL
KEEI(FM) Hanapepe HI
KDLX(FM) Makawao HI
KADQ-FM Rexburg ID
WRMS-FM Beardstown IL
WPMJ(FM) Chillicothe IL
WJKL(FM) Elgin IL
WLIE-FM Golconda IL
WMKR(FM) Pana IL
WSSQ(FM) Sterling IL
WREB(FM) Greencastle IN
WZOC(FM) Plymouth IN
WKWH-FM Rushville IN
KCVW(FM) Kingman KS
WULF(FM) Hardinsburg KY
WIFX(FM) Jenkins KY
WEGI(FM) Oak Grove KY
KTRY-FM Bastrop LA
WTIX-FM Galliano LA
WZAI(FM) Brewster MA
WINX-FM Cambridge MD
WCYY(FM) Biddeford ME
WFCX(FM) Leland MI
WZNL(FM) Norway MI
KKIN-FM Aitkin MN
KULO(FM) Alexandria MN
KDOM-FM Windom MN
KATI(FM) California MO
WKZW(FM) Bay Springs MS
WXRZ(FM) Corinth MS
WBAD(FM) Leland MS
WWNK(FM) Farmville NC
WJIJ(FM) Norlina NC
WZKB(FM) Wallace NC
WJLK-FM Asbury Park NJ
WILW(FM) Avalon NJ
KYEE(FM) Alamogordo NM
KDEM(FM) Deming NM
WLVY(FM) Elmira NY
WKXP(FM) Kingston NY
WMJC(FM) Smithtown NY
WKKI(FM) Celina OH
WKKJ(FM) Chillicothe OH
WDIF(FM) Marion OH
KXOO(FM) Elk City OK
WNAK-FM Carbondale PA
WBXQ(FM) Cresson PA
WQCM(FM) Greencastle PA
WHUZ(FM) Saegertown PA
WWNQ(FM) Forest Acres SC
WSCC-FM Goose Creek SC
WCMG(FM) Latta SC
WLSQ-FM Dyer TN
WJJM-FM Lewisburg TN
WNFZ(FM) Oak Ridge TN
WJTT(FM) Red Bank TN
KBTS(FM) Big Spring TX
KNVR(FM) Cameron TX
KYOX(FM) Comanche TX
KHER(FM) Crystal City TX
KFST-FM Fort Stockton TX
KRVL(FM) Kerrville TX
KYXX(FM) Ozona TX
KSEY-FM Seymour TX

KXRQ(FM) Roosevelt UT
WTON-FM Staunton VA
WBPS-FM Warrenton VA
WBTN-FM Bennington VT
KAQX(FM) Long Beach WA
WROE(FM) Neenah-Menasha WI
WQPC(FM) Prairie du Chien WI
WRLF(FM) Fairmont WV

94.5 mhz
WYSF(FM) Birmingham AL
WHOD(FM) Jackson AL
KOLX(FM) Barling AR
KJIW-FM Helena AR
KOOL-FM Phoenix AZ
KCNO(FM) Alturas CA
KSEH(FM) Brawley CA
KSPE(FM) Ellwood CA
KBAY(FM) Gilroy CA
KGEN-FM Hanford CA
KMYT(FM) Temecula CA
KWNE(FM) Ukiah CA
KCUV(FM) New Castle CO
*WERB(FM) Berlin CT
WCFB(FM) Daytona Beach FL
WARO(FM) Naples FL
WFBX(FM) Parker FL
WBYZ(FM) Baxley GA
KKEZ(FM) Fort Dodge IA
KHTQ(FM) Hayden ID
WLRW(FM) Champaign IL
WRZR(FM) Loogootee IN
KSKL(FM) Scott City KS
WIBW-FM Topeka KS
WMXL(FM) Lexington KY
KSMB(FM) Lafayette LA
KRUF(FM) Shreveport LA
WJMN(FM) Boston MA
WKSQ(FM) Ellsworth ME
WCEN-FM Hemlock MI
WTNR(FM) Holland MI
WLJZ(FM) Mackinaw City MI
WELY-FM Ely MN
KSTP-FM Saint Paul MN
KRXL(FM) Kirksville MO
KKLR(FM) Poplar Bluff MO
KMON-FM Great Falls MT
WGBT(FM) Eden NC
WWOC(FM) Hatteras NC
KQDY(FM) Bismarck ND
KLIQ(FM) Hastings NE
WPST(FM) Trenton NJ
KKOR(FM) Gallup NM
KOYT(FM) Elko NV
KUUB(FM) Sun Valley NV
*WNED-FM Buffalo NY
WRCZ(FM) Ravena NY
WYYY(FM) Syracuse NY
WDKF(FM) Englewood OH
WXRF(FM) Port Clinton OH
KEMX(FM) Locust Grove OK
KJDY-FM Canyon City OR
KMGE(FM) Eugene OR
WDAC(FM) Lancaster PA
WWSW-FM Pittsburgh PA
WLTS(FM) State College PA
WSPX(FM) Bowman SC
WMUU-FM Greenville SC
WYEZ(FM) Murrell's Inlet SC
KPLO-FM Reliance SD
*KCFS(FM) Sioux Falls SD
WFGZ(FM) Lobelville TN
KSOC(FM) Gainesville TX
KFRQ(FM) Harlingen TX
KTBZ-FM Houston TX
KFMX-FM Lubbock TX
KEMA(FM) Three Rivers TX
KBCT-FM Waco TX
KVFX(FM) Logan UT
WRVQ(FM) Richmond VA
WJEN(FM) Rutland VT
KLYK(FM) Kelso WA
KRXY(FM) Shelton WA
KATS(FM) Yakima WA
WRJO(FM) Eagle River WI
WKTI(FM) Milwaukee WI

WTMB(FM) Tomah WI
WZJO(FM) Dunbar WV
KMLD(FM) Casper WY

94.7 mhz
KADX(FM) Houston AK
WTBF-FM Brundidge AL
KKLV(FM) Turrell AR
KFLG-FM Kingman AZ
KEWB(FM) Anderson CA
KSSJ(FM) Fair Oaks CA
*KAJP(FM) Firebaugh CA
KTWV(FM) Los Angeles CA
KLOB(FM) Thousand Palms CA
KRKS-FM Boulder CO
WRDX(FM) Dover DE
WSYR-FM Gifford FL
WDEC-FM Americus GA
KWXX-FM Hilo HI
KUMU-FM Honolulu HI
KZEG(FM) Clinton IA
KMCH(FM) Manchester IA
WZZN(FM) Chicago IL
WFBQ(FM) Indianapolis IN
WFIA-FM New Albany IN
KGGG(FM) Sterling KS
WQQR(FM) Mayfield KY
WKLW-FM Paintsville KY
WBIO(FM) Philpot KY
WOPR(FM) Lacombe LA
WMAS-FM Springfield MA
WARW(FM) Bethesda MD
WCSX(FM) Birmingham MI
*WCVM(FM) Bronson MI
KCLH(FM) Caledonia MN
KNSG(FM) Springfield MN
KSKK(FM) Staples MN
KSHE(FM) Crestwood MO
KTTS-FM Springfield MO
WWJK(FM) Jackson MS
WQDR(FM) Raleigh NC
KNOX-FM Grand Forks ND
KNEN(FM) Norfolk NE
*WFME(FM) Newark NJ
KBOM(FM) Santa Fe NM
*WMHI(FM) Cape Vincent NY
WYUL(FM) Chateaugay NY
WIYN(FM) Deposit NY
WBAR-FM Lake Luzerne NY
WSNY(FM) Columbus OH
KHBZ-FM Oklahoma City OK
KRRM(FM) Rogue River OR
WFGO(FM) Erie PA
WBRX(FM) Patton PA
WMTT(FM) Tioga PA
WODA(FM) Bayamon PR
WICI(FM) Sumter SC
WAAW(FM) Williston SC
WOJG(FM) Bolivar TN
WGSQ(FM) Cookeville TN
KBSO(FM) Corpus Christi TX
KYSE(FM) El Paso TX
KGRW(FM) Friona TX
KWKQ(FM) Graham TX
KAMX(FM) Luling TX
KIXY-FM San Angelo TX
KVLL-FM Woodville TX
KNRK(FM) Camas WA
WZOR(FM) Mishicot WI
WOFM(FM) Mosinee WI
WELK(FM) Elkins WV

94.9 mhz
WKSJ-FM Mobile AL
KMSX(FM) Maumelle AR
KYNF(FM) Prairie Grove AR
KMXZ-FM Tucson AZ
KHRQ(FM) Baker CA
KPYG(FM) Cambria CA
KBZT(FM) San Diego CA
KYLD(FM) San Francisco CA
KBOS-FM Tulare CA
WMGE-FM Miami Beach FL
WTNT-FM Tallahassee FL
WWRM(FM) Tampa FL
WLTM(FM) Atlanta GA
WHKN(FM) Millen GA
KGGO(FM) Des Moines IA

U.S. FM Stations by Frequency

KRVB(FM) Nampa ID
KPKY(FM) Pocatello ID
WRHK(FM) Danville IL
WDKB(FM) De Kalb IL
WAAG(FM) Galesburg IL
WYNG(FM) Mount Carmel IL
KSBH(FM) Coushatta LA
WPRF(FM) Reserve LA
WSYY-FM Millinocket ME
WCNF(FM) Benton Harbor MI
WMMQ(FM) East Lansing MI
WKJZ(FM) Hillman MI
WKZC(FM) Scottville MI
KCPI(FM) Albert Lea MN
KMXK(FM) Cold Spring MN
KQDS-FM Duluth MN
KLCH(FM) Lake City MN
KCMO-FM Kansas City MO
*WKVF(FM) Byhalia MS
WKOR-FM Columbus MS
KYSS-FM Missoula MT
KTZU(FM) Velva ND
*KJLT-FM North Platte NE
WHOM(FM) Mt. Washington NH
KWYK-FM Aztec NM
KBIM-FM Roswell NM
WKLL(FM) Frankfort NY
*WONB(FM) Ada OH
WMOJ(FM) Fairfield OH
WQMX(FM) Medina OH
WSNA(FM) South Webster OH
KOOS(FM) North Bend OR
*WRSD(FM) Folsom PA
WRBT(FM) Harrisburg PA
WOGG(FM) Oliver PA
WHKS(FM) Port Allegany PA
WVCO(FM) Loris SC
KLRJ(FM) Aberdeen SD
WMSR-FM Collinwood TN
WAEZ(FM) Greeneville TN
WKVZ(FM) Ripley TN
KLTY(FM) Arlington TX
*KOLI(FM) Electra TX
KQUR(FM) Laredo TX
KXBN(FM) Cedar City UT
KHTB(FM) Provo UT
WSLC-FM Roanoke VA
WPTE(FM) Virginia Beach VA
KIOK(FM) Richland WA
*KUOW(FM) Seattle WA
WOLX-FM Baraboo WI
KZWY(FM) Sheridan WY

95.1 mhz
WRTT-FM Huntsville AL
WXFX(FM) Prattville AL
KAMS(FM) Mammoth Spring AR
KVIB(FM) Sun City West AZ
KTTI(FM) Yuma AZ
*KAAX(FM) Avenal CA
KMXI(FM) Chico CA
KHOP(FM) Oakdale CA
KFRG(FM) San Bernardino CA
KBBY-FM Ventura CA
KRDO-FM Colorado Springs CO
KKNN(FM) Delta CO
WRKI(FM) Brookfield CT
WBPC(FM) Ebro FL
WAPE-FM Jacksonville FL
WBVD(FM) Melbourne FL
WCHZ(FM) Harlem GA
WMGB(FM) Montezuma GA
KAOI-FM Wailuku HI
KMAQ-FM Maquoketa IA
KCZE(FM) New Hampton IA
WUEZ(FM) Carterville IL
WDZQ(FM) Decatur IL
WVLI(FM) Kankakee IL
WAJI(FM) Fort Wayne IN
WVNI(FM) Nashville IN
*WVUR-FM Valparaiso IN
KICT-FM Wichita KS
WGGC(FM) Bowling Green KY
WFLE-FM Flemingsburg KY
*WXRB(FM) Dudley MA
WXTK(FM) West Yarmouth MA
WRBS(FM) Baltimore MD

WFBE(FM) Flint MI
KRVI(FM) Detroit Lakes MN
KWOA-FM Worthington MN
KMXL(FM) Carthage MO
KTKS(FM) Versailles MO
WYYW(FM) Marion MS
WQNZ(FM) Natchez MS
WONA-FM Winona MS
KMMS-FM Bozeman MT
*KXEI(FM) Havre MT
KTHC(FM) Sidney MT
WNKS(FM) Charlotte NC
WRNS-FM Kinston NC
KRKR(FM) Lincoln NE
WAYV(FM) Atlantic City NJ
KSYU(FM) Corrales NM
KNYE(FM) Pahrump NV
WFXF(FM) Honeoye Falls NY
WVXG(FM) Mount Gilead OH
KQCV-FM Shawnee OK
KSND(FM) Monmouth OR
KLTW-FM Prineville OR
WZZO(FM) Bethlehem PA
WIKZ(FM) Chambersburg PA
WWGY(FM) Grove City PA
WEGM(FM) San German PR
WSSX-FM Charleston SC
KSQY(FM) Deadwood SD
WCDZ(FM) Dresden TN
KORQ(FM) Baird TX
KYKR(FM) Beaumont TX
KNDE(FM) College Station TX
KCOR-FM Comfort TX
KQRX(FM) Midland TX
KEWL-FM New Boston TX
KVIC(FM) Victoria TX
WQMZ(FM) Charlottesville VA
WJKC(FM) Christiansted VI
WJAN(FM) Sunderland VT
KITI-FM Winlock WA
WQRB(FM) Bloomer WI
WIIL(FM) Kenosha WI
WLST(FM) Marinette WI
WXIL(FM) Parkersburg WV
KCGY(FM) Laramie WY
KYCS(FM) Rock Springs WY

95.3 mhz
WFFN(FM) Cordova AL
WRLD-FM Valley AL
KCXY(FM) East Camden AR
KERX(FM) Paris AR
KCDQ(FM) Douglas AZ
KOZT(FM) Fort Bragg CA
KBHH(FM) Kerman CA
KRTY(FM) Los Gatos CA
KLLY(FM) Oildale CA
KXTZ(FM) Pismo Beach CA
KUIC(FM) Vacaville CA
KSLV-FM Monte Vista CO
WKDB(FM) Laurel DE
WOLZ(FM) Fort Myers FL
WXCV(FM) Homosassa Springs FL
WPYO(FM) Maitland FL
WSRM(FM) Coosa GA
WJYF(FM) Nashville GA
KQMG-FM Independence IA
KIFG-FM Iowa Falls IA
KOKX-FM Keokuk IA
KCSI(FM) Red Oak IA
KCII(FM) Washington IA
KLER-FM Orofino ID
KPND(FM) Sandpoint ID
KECH-FM Sun Valley ID
WRXX(FM) Centralia IL
WRKX(FM) Ottawa IL
WEVX(FM) Rantoul IL
WYHY(FM) Winnebago IL
WLFF(FM) Brookston IN
WUME-FM Paoli IN
WNDI-FM Sullivan IN
KCKS(FM) Concordia KS
KINZ(FM) Humboldt KS
KHCA(FM) Wamego KS
WIKI(FM) Carrollton KY
WMSK-FM Morganfield KY
WVRB(FM) Wilmore KY

KQKI(FM) Bayou Vista LA
WHRB(FM) Cambridge MA
WPVQ(FM) Greenfield MA
WALZ-FM Machias ME
WWWA(FM) Winslow ME
WUBB(FM) York Center ME
WQTE(FM) Adrian MI
WBXX(FM) Battle Creek MI
WCFX(FM) Clare MI
WAOR(FM) Niles MI
WGVS-FM Whitehall MI
WXXZ(FM) Grand Marais MN
KNOF(FM) Saint Paul MN
KDJS-FM Willmar MN
KAGE-FM Winona MN
KDKD-FM Clinton MO
KXMO-FM Owensville MO
WAFM(FM) Amory MS
WVIM-FM Coldwater MS
WADI(FM) Corinth MS
WRKG(FM) Drew MS
WZNF(FM) Lumberton MS
WOBR-FM Wanchese NC
KSEL-FM Portales NM
KNUW(FM) Santa Clara NM
KRJC(FM) Elko NV
WGIX(FM) Gouverneur NY
WBKT(FM) Norwich NY
WHFM(FM) Southampton NY
WKTN(FM) Kenton OH
WKLM(FM) Millersburg OH
WLKR(FM) Norwalk OH
WZLR(FM) Xenia OH
KMGZ(FM) Lawton OK
KKBC-FM Baker City OR
KURY-FM Brookings OR
KUJZ(FM) Creswell OR
KLCR(FM) Lakeview OR
WZWW(FM) Bellefonte PA
WDNH-FM Honesdale PA
WBLJ-FM Shamokin PA
WTTC-FM Towanda PA
WJPA-FM Washington PA
WFMV(FM) South Congaree SC
KLXS-FM Pierre SD
WTBG(FM) Brownsville TN
WALV(FM) Cleveland TN
*WYFC(FM) Clinton TN
KNEL-FM Brady TX
KDDD-FM Dumas TX
KFLP-FM Floydada TX
KFRO-FM Gilmer TX
KHYI(FM) Howe TX
KPBM(FM) McCamey TX
KVWG-FM Pearsall TX
KZSP(FM) South Padre Island TX
WKHK(FM) Colonial Heights VA
WZRV(FM) Front Royal VA
WXBX(FM) Rural Retreat VA
WHLF-FM South Boston VA
WXLF(FM) White River Junction VT
KXLE-FM Ellensburg WA
KXXK(FM) Hoquiam-Aberdeen WA
WXRO(FM) Beaver Dam WI
WGMO(FM) Shell Lake WI
WRLB(FM) Rainelle WV
KZJH(FM) Jackson WY

95.5 mhz
WHMA-FM Ashland AL
WTVY-FM Dothan AL
WFMH-FM Holly Pond AL
WJDB-FM Thomasville AL
KYOT-FM Phoenix AZ
KBOQ(FM) Carmel CA
KLOS(FM) Los Angeles CA
KRVG(FM) Glenwood Springs CO
KPHT(FM) Rocky Ford CO
WLDI(FM) Fort Pierce FL
WNDD(FM) Silver Springs FL
WBTS(FM) Doraville GA
WIXV(FM) Savannah GA
KSTO(FM) Hagatna GU
KAIM-FM Honolulu HI
KZAT-FM Belle Plaine IA
KJCY(FM) Saint Ansgar IA
KGLI(FM) Sioux City IA

WFUN-FM Bethalto IL
WNUA(FM) Chicago IL
WGLO(FM) Pekin IL
WFMS(FM) Indianapolis IN
KOLS(FM) Dodge City KS
KQNS-FM Lindsborg KS
KNDY-FM Marysville KS
WQHY(FM) Prestonsburg KY
KRRQ(FM) Lafayette LA
WPGC-FM Morningside MD
WJJB-FM Topsham ME
WKQI(FM) Detroit MI
WJZJ(FM) Glen Arbor MI
KKZY(FM) Bemidji MN
KBEK(FM) Mora MN
KRDS-FM New Prague MN
KAAN-FM Bethany MO
KTOZ-FM Pleasant Hope MO
KJEZ(FM) Poplar Bluff MO
WHLH(FM) Jackson MS
WOXD(FM) Oxford MS
KMBR(FM) Butte MT
KMHK(FM) Hardin MT
*WHPE-FM High Point NC
WPWZ(FM) Pinetops NC
KXGT(FM) Jamestown ND
KSDZ(FM) Gordon NE
KHFM(FM) Santa Fe NM
KWNR(FM) Henderson NV
KNEV(FM) Reno NV
WYJB(FM) Albany NY
WPLJ(FM) New York NY
WFHM-FM Cleveland OH
WHOK(FM) Lancaster OH
KQMX(FM) Clinton OK
KITX(FM) Hugo OK
KWEN(FM) Tulsa OK
KXJM(FM) Portland OR
WFGI-FM Johnstown PA
WBYL(FM) Salladasburg PA
WBRU(FM) Providence RI
WIBZ(FM) Wedgefield SC
WSM-FM Nashville TN
KKMJ-FM Austin TX
KZFM(FM) Corpus Christi TX
KAFX-FM Diboll TX
KLAQ(FM) El Paso TX
KJKB(FM) Jacksboro TX
KAIQ(FM) Wolfforth TX
*KYFO-FM Ogden UT
WZXI(FM) Buffalo Gap VA
WXXX(FM) South Burlington VT
WIFC(FM) Wausau WI
KWYY(FM) Casper WY

95.7 mhz
WBHJ(FM) Tuscaloosa AL
KSEC(FM) Bentonville AR
KSSN(FM) Little Rock AR
KWKM(FM) Saint Johns AZ
KUSS(FM) Carlsbad CA
KJFX(FM) Fresno CA
KPAT(FM) Orcutt CA
KALF(FM) Red Bluff CA
KZBR(FM) San Francisco CA
KMGG(FM) Denver CO
WKSS(FM) Hartford CT
WBTP(FM) Clearwater FL
WGCX(FM) Navarre FL
WXDJ(FM) North Miami Beach FL
WHOG-FM Ormond-by-the-Sea FL
WIOL(FM) Greenville GA
WATG(FM) Trion GA
WQPW(FM) Valdosta GA
KSWI(FM) Atlantic IA
KQWC-FM Webster City IA
KEZJ-FM Twin Falls ID
WCRC(FM) Effingham IL
WSEY(FM) Oregon IL
WJDK-FM Seneca IL
WSHP(FM) Attica IN
WQMF(FM) Jeffersonville IN
WYPW(FM) Nappanee IN
KCHZ(FM) Ottawa KS
WCCK(FM) Calvert City KY
KLKL(FM) Minden LA
WTKL(FM) New Orleans LA

KROK(FM) South Fort Polk LA
WWMJ(FM) Ellsworth ME
WLHT-FM Grand Rapids MI
*WHWL(FM) Marquette MI
*WCMB-FM Oscoda MI
KDAL-FM Duluth MN
KQYK(FM) Lake Crystal MN
KKOK-FM Morris MN
KWWR(FM) Mexico MO
WTGY(FM) Charleston MS
WHAL-FM Horn Lake MS
KCGM(FM) Scobey MT
WXRC(FM) Hickory NC
WKML(FM) Lumberton NC
KNDK-FM Langdon ND
*KROA(FM) Grand Island NE
WZID(FM) Manchester NH
KPCL(FM) Farmington NM
KPER(FM) Hobbs NM
WAQX-FM Manlius NY
WPIG(FM) Olean NY
WIMX(FM) Gibsonburg OH
WDPT(FM) Piqua OH
WVKF(FM) Shadyside OH
KKAJ-FM Ardmore OK
KXLS(FM) Lahoma OK
KBOY-FM Medford OR
WMRF-FM Lewistown PA
WBHD(FM) Olyphant PA
WBEN-FM Philadelphia PA
WFID(FM) Rio Piedras PR
WWBD(FM) Bamberg SC
KSQB-FM Dell Rapids SD
WAYB-FM Graysville TN
WFKX(FM) Henderson TN
WTXM(FM) Maryville TN
KBST-FM Big Spring TX
KARX(FM) Claude TX
KHJZ-FM Houston TX
KLEY-FM Jourdanton TX
KOTY(FM) Mason TX
KBGO(FM) Waco TX
WFLO-FM Farmville VA
WVKL(FM) Norfolk VA
WDOT(FM) Danville VT
KJR-FM Seattle WA
KNLT(FM) Walla Walla WA
WRQT(FM) La Crosse WI
WRIT-FM Milwaukee WI
KFMR(FM) Marbleton WY

95.9 mhz
KXLR(FM) Fairbanks AK
WKXN(FM) Greenville AL
WTWX-FM Guntersville AL
WTGZ(FM) Tuskegee AL
KWHF(FM) Harrisburg AR
KUUZ(FM) Lake Village AR
KZGL(FM) Cottonwood AZ
KFSH-FM Anaheim CA
KBYN(FM) Arnold CA
KXXZ(FM) Barstow CA
KOCP(FM) Camarillo CA
KRSH(FM) Healdsburg CA
KSKD(FM) Livingston CA
KNLF(FM) Quincy CA
KIDN-FM Hayden CO
WEFX(FM) Norwalk CT
WOSC(FM) Bethany Beach DE
WSJZ-FM Sebastian FL
WRBA(FM) Springfield FL
WQZY(FM) Dublin GA
KPVS(FM) Hilo HI
KSRF(FM) Poipu HI
KCHA-FM Charles City IA
KILR-FM Estherville IA
KIIK-FM Fairfield IA
KCOB-FM Newton IA
KLZX(FM) Weston ID
WERV-FM Aurora IL
*WOLG(FM) Carlinville IL
WHOW-FM Clinton IL
WDQN-FM Du Quoin IL
WNLF(FM) Macomb IL
WIJY(FM) Franklin IN
WEFM(FM) Michigan City IN
WWSY(FM) Seelyville IN

U.S. FM Stations by Frequency

WKID(FM) Vevay IN
WKUZ(FM) Wabash IN
KCAY(FM) Russell KS
KSOK-FM Winfield KS
WFTM-FM Maysville KY
WGKY(FM) Wickliffe KY
KZLG(FM) Mansura LA
KMAR-FM Winnsboro LA
WATD-FM Marshfield MA
WUPE(FM) Pittsfield MA
WWIN-FM Glen Burnie MD
WICL(FM) Williamsport MD
WRED(FM) Saco ME
WLKM-FM Three Rivers MI
KQCL(FM) Faribault MN
WLKX-FM Forest Lake MN
WWWI-FM Pillager MN
KYLS-FM Ironton MO
KTRI-FM Mansfield MO
KKBL(FM) Monett MO
WCNA(FM) Potts Camp MS
WBBN(FM) Taylorsville MS
KKMT(FM) Columbia Falls MT
KLCM(FM) Lewistown MT
WPNC-FM Plymouth NC
WCVP-FM Robbinsville NC
WRAT(FM) Point Pleasant NJ
KZRM(FM) Chama NM
KIVA(FM) Santa Rosa NM
KKTC(FM) Taos NM
WFLR-FM Dundee NY
WCQL(FM) Glens Falls NY
WVOS-FM Liberty NY
WJKW(FM) Athens OH
WNPQ(FM) New Philadelphia OH
WYNT(FM) Upper Sandusky OH
KYBE(FM) Frederick OK
KKBD(FM) Sallisaw OK
KAZY(FM) Woodward OK
WGGI(FM) Benton PA
WAKZ(FM) Sharpsville PA
WCRI(FM) Block Island RI
KZZI(FM) Belle Fourche SD
WRZK(FM) Colonial Heights TN
WLQK(FM) Livingston TN
WMXK(FM) Morristown TN
KBRA(FM) Freer TX
KHMC(FM) Goliad TX
KPWW(FM) Hooks TX
KCKL(FM) Malakoff TX
KFWR(FM) Mineral Wells TX
KSCH(FM) Sulphur Springs TX
KMGR(FM) Delta UT
KZHK(FM) Saint George UT
WGRQ(FM) Colonial Beach VA
KZML(FM) Quincy WA
WKSZ(FM) De Pere WI
WDMO(FM) Durand WI
WMQA-FM Minocqua WI
WBKY(FM) Portage WI
*WDKL(FM) Grafton WV
WSTG(FM) Princeton WV
KVAN(FM) Rock River WY

96.1 mhz

*KNOM-FM Nome AK
WXFL(FM) Florence AL
WRKH(FM) Mobile AL
WQKS-FM Montgomery AL
KMRX(FM) El Dorado AR
KCWD(FM) Harrison AR
KLPX(FM) Tucson AZ
KWRK(FM) Window Rock AZ
KSIQ(FM) Brawley CA
KSQQ(FM) Morgan Hill CA
KYMX(FM) Sacramento CA
KWIE(FM) San Jacinto CA
KSLY-FM San Luis Obispo CA
KKXS(FM) Shingletown CA
KSLK(FM) Visalia CA
KIBT(FM) Fountain CO
KSME(FM) Greeley CO
KSTR-FM Montrose CO
WRXK-FM Bonita Springs FL
WTMP-FM Dade City FL
WEJZ(FM) Jacksonville FL
WHBX(FM) Tallahassee FL

WKLS(FM) Atlanta GA
KMXG(FM) Clinton IA
KCVM(FM) Hudson IA
KNWM(FM) Madrid IA
KID-FM Idaho Falls ID
WQQB(FM) Rantoul IL
WQLK(FM) Richmond IN
KANS(FM) Emporia KS
WKKQ(FM) Barbourville KY
WSTO(FM) Owensboro KY
WLXO(FM) Stamping Ground KY
KRVE(FM) Brusly LA
KYKZ(FM) Lake Charles LA
WSRS(FM) Worcester MA
WQHR(FM) Presque Isle ME
WHNN(FM) Bay City MI
WVTI(FM) Holland MI
KQPR(FM) Albert Lea MN
KGPZ(FM) Coleraine MN
KQHT(FM) Crookston MN
*KLRQ(FM) Clinton MO
WLZA(FM) Eupora MS
WYYL(FM) Tunica MS
WBBB(FM) Raleigh NC
WIBT(FM) Shelby NC
KYYZ(FM) Williston ND
*KINI(FM) Crookston NE
KICX-FM McCook NE
KEFM(FM) Omaha NE
WTTH(FM) Margate City NJ
WJYE(FM) Buffalo NY
WLVG(FM) Center Moriches NY
WVLF(FM) Norwood NY
WPKF(FM) Poughkeepsie NY
WODZ-FM Rome NY
WMTR-FM Archbold OH
WKFM(FM) Huron OH
KXXY-FM Oklahoma City OK
KITO-FM Vinita OK
KZEL-FM Eugene OR
KSRV-FM Ontario OR
KLKY(FM) Stanfield OR
WCTO(FM) Easton PA
WKST-FM Pittsburgh PA
WSOX(FM) Red Lion PA
WPHD(FM) South Waverly PA
WAEL-FM Maricao PR
WAVF(FM) Hanahan SC
KIXX(FM) Watertown SD
KCTX-FM Childress TX
KGUL(FM) Edna TX
KBTQ(FM) Harlingen TX
KKTX-FM Kilgore TX
KAGG(FM) Madisonville TX
KMRK-FM Odessa TX
KEYE-FM Perryton TX
KXXM(FM) San Antonio TX
KNCE(FM) Winters TX
WJDV(FM) Broadway VA
WROX-FM Exmore VA
WIVI(FM) Charlotte Amalie VI
WDEV-FM Warren VT
KXXO(FM) Olympia WA
KIXZ-FM Opportunity WA
WLKG(FM) Lake Geneva WI
WJMC-FM Rice Lake WI
WTCX(FM) Ripon WI
WXYM(FM) Tomah WI
WKWS(FM) Charleston WV
KKLX(FM) Worland WY

96.3 mhz

KRPM(FM) Houston AK
KHLS(FM) Blytheville AR
KTTG(FM) Mena AR
KSWG(FM) Wickenburg AZ
KFMI(FM) Eureka CA
KXOL-FM Los Angeles CA
KUBB(FM) Mariposa CA
KLZN(FM) Susanville CA
KXCM(FM) Twentynine Palms CA
WHUR-FM Washington DC
WXOF(FM) Yankeetown FL
WJIZ(FM) Albany GA
KRTR(FM) Kailua HI
KRNQ(FM) Keokuk IA
WLCN(FM) Atlanta IL

WBBM-FM Chicago IL
WJAA(FM) Austin IN
WNHT(FM) Churubusco IN
WHHH(FM) Indianapolis IN
KZDY(FM) Cawker City KS
KZCH(FM) Derby KS
KSSH(FM) Ingalls KS
KACZ(FM) Riley KS
WIVY(FM) Morehead KY
WXKY-FM Stanford KY
WRZE(FM) Nantucket MA
WLOB-FM Rumford ME
WDVD(FM) Detroit MI
WLXT(FM) Petoskey MI
KTTB(FM) Glencoe MN
KIHT(FM) Saint Louis MO
WUSJ(FM) Jackson MS
KSCY(FM) Big Sky MT
KRZN(FM) Billings MT
KBAZ(FM) Hamilton MT
WRHT(FM) Morehead City NC
WCFR-FM Walpole NH
KBZU(FM) Albuquerque NM
KKLZ(FM) Las Vegas NV
WQXR-FM New York NY
WAJZ(FM) Voorheesville NY
WLVQ(FM) Columbus OH
KIXT(FM) Bay City OR
WJSA-FM Jersey Shore PA
WKQW(FM) Oil City PA
WKSP(FM) Aiken SC
WGOG(FM) Walhalla SC
WCJK(FM) Murfreesboro TN
WJBZ-FM Seymour TN
KXIT-FM Dalhart TX
KTDR(FM) Del Rio TX
KHEY-FM El Paso TX
KSCS(FM) Fort Worth TX
KLSN(FM) Hudson TX
KQBT(FM) Llano TX
KLLL-FM Lubbock TX
KXRK(FM) Provo UT
WROV-FM Martinsville VA
KRCW(FM) Royal City WA
WSFQ(FM) Peshtigo WI
WMAD(FM) Sauk City WI
WOTR(FM) Lost Creek WV

96.5 mhz

KKIS-FM Soldotna AK
WMJJ(FM) Birmingham AL
KHTE-FM England AR
KDAP-FM Douglas AZ
KRFM(FM) Show Low AZ
KBKO-FM Bakersfield CA
KYXY(FM) San Diego CA
KOIT-FM San Francisco CA
KLCA(FM) Tahoe City CA
KFLS-FM Tulelake CA
KXPK(FM) Evergreen CO
KJBL(FM) Julesburg CO
WTIC-FM Hartford CT
WZNS(FM) Fort Walton Beach FL
WPOW(FM) Miami FL
WHTQ(FM) Orlando FL
WYNF(FM) Gray GA
WJCL-FM Savannah GA
KSOM(FM) Audubon IA
WMT-FM Cedar Rapids IA
KOZE-FM Lewiston ID
KLIX-FM Twin Falls ID
WKIB(FM) Anna IL
WWCT(FM) Farmington IL
WKOT(FM) Marseilles IL
WAZY-FM Lafayette IN
WGZB-FM Lanesville IN
WTGG(FM) Amite LA
KFTE(FM) Breaux Bridge LA
KVKI-FM Shreveport LA
WQHH(FM) Dewitt MI
WFAT(FM) Portage MI
WKLK-FM Cloquet MN
KJJK-FM Fergus Falls MN
KWWK(FM) Rochester MN
KRBZ(FM) Kansas City MO
KSPW(FM) Sparta MO
WKDJ-FM Clarksdale MS

WXHB(FM) Richton MS
KDZN(FM) Glendive MT
WOXL-FM Biltmore Forest NC
WFLB(FM) Laurinburg NC
KBYZ(FM) Bismarck ND
KRGI-FM Grand Island NE
WMLL(FM) Bedford NH
KLMA(FM) Hobbs NM
KBKZ(FM) Raton NM
WBKX(FM) Fredonia NY
WVNV(FM) Malone NY
WCMF-FM Rochester NY
WAKS(FM) Akron OH
WYGY(FM) Lebanon OH
KECO(FM) Elk City OK
KRAV(FM) Tulsa OK
KBDN(FM) Bandon OR
KCBZ(FM) Cannon Beach OR
KWLZ-FM Warm Springs OR
WKYE(FM) Johnstown PA
*WPEL-FM Montrose PA
WRDW-FM Philadelphia PA
WCMA-FM Fajardo PR
*KNWC-FM Sioux Falls SD
WDOD-FM Chattanooga TN
WXJB(FM) Harrogate TN
WBFG(FM) Parker's Crossroads TN
KLTG(FM) Corpus Christi TX
KHMX(FM) Houston TX
KNRX(FM) Sterling City TX
WCTG(FM) Chincoteague VA
WKLR(FM) Fort Lee VA
KJAQ(FM) Seattle WA
WKLH(FM) Milwaukee WI
WRKP(FM) Moundsville WV
WXCC(FM) Williamson WV
KQSW(FM) Rock Springs WY

96.7 mhz

WMXA(FM) Opelika AL
WKXK(FM) Pine Hill AL
KYDL(FM) Hot Springs AR
KOKR(FM) Newport AR
KDYN(FM) Ozark AR
KRCY-FM Lake Havasu City AZ
KWMX(FM) Williams AZ
KEZL(FM) Fowler CA
KNOB(FM) Healdsburg CA
KUNA-FM La Quinta CA
KMRQ(FM) Manteca CA
KZAP(FM) Paradise CA
KCAL-FM Redlands CA
KWIZ(FM) Santa Ana CA
KLJR-FM Santa Paula CA
KSYV(FM) Solvang CA
KUUR(FM) Carbondale CO
WKHL-FM Stamford CT
WDXQ-FM Cochran GA
WVVA(FM) Peachtree City GA
WYZK(FM) Valdosta GA
KLBA-FM Albia IA
KKEX(FM) Preston ID
WSSR(FM) Joliet IL
WKGL-FM Loves Park IL
WIHN(FM) Normal IL
WCVS-FM Virden IL
WHTI(FM) Alexandria IN
WBWB(FM) Bloomington IN
WCOE(FM) La Porte IN
WORX-FM Madison IN
WFML(FM) Vincennes IN
KGTR(FM) Larned KS
KBBE(FM) McPherson KS
WBVR-FM Auburn KY
KBZZ(FM) Morgan City LA
KWCL-FM Oak Grove LA
WCEI-FM Easton MD
WDLD(FM) Halfway MD
WCME(FM) Boothbay Harbor ME
*WUFN(FM) Albion MI
WLXV(FM) Cadillac MI
*WVXA(FM) Rogers City MI
KKCQ-FM Bagley MN
KDOG(FM) North Mankato MN
KKSR(FM) Sartell MN
KCMQ(FM) Columbia MO
KAHR(FM) Poplar Bluff MO

WFFF-FM Columbia MS
WUJM(FM) Gulfport MS
WSEL-FM Pontotoc MS
KISN(FM) Belgrade MT
KZIN-FM Shelby MT
WKJX(FM) Elizabeth City NC
WNCC-FM Franklin NC
WKRX(FM) Roxboro NC
KQZZ(FM) Devils Lake ND
WLTN-FM Lisbon NH
WQSO(FM) Rochester NH
KNMB(FM) Cloudcroft NM
KMDZ(FM) Las Vegas NM
KHIX(FM) Carlin NV
WPTR-FM Clifton Park NY
WHBE(FM) East Hampton NY
WYSX(FM) Morristown NY
WOLF-FM Oswego NY
WTSX(FM) Port Jervis NY
WXZO(FM) Willsboro NY
WCMJ(FM) Cambridge OH
WCSM-FM Celina OH
WBVI(FM) Fostoria OH
WKOV-FM Wellston OH
KBEL-FM Idabel OK
KCRF-FM Lincoln City OR
WVNW-FM Burnham PA
WFRM-FM Coudersport PA
*WPGM-FM Danville PA
WLLF(FM) Mercer PA
WLTY(FM) Cayce SC
WBZT-FM Mauldin SC
KZMX-FM Hot Springs SD
WMOD(FM) Bolivar TN
WNKX-FM Centerville TN
KTYS(FM) Flower Mound TX
KOYE(FM) Frankston TX
KHFI-FM Georgetown TX
KXOX-FM Sweetwater TX
KCFM(FM) Levan UT
WWZW(FM) Buena Vista VA
WTSA-FM Brattleboro VT
KZTB(FM) Benton City WA
KWWW-FM Quincy WA
WBDK(FM) Algoma WI
WJJH(FM) Ashland WI
WYTE(FM) Whiting WI
WKMM(FM) Kingwood WV
KMGW(FM) Casper WY
KIMX(FM) Laramie WY

96.9 mhz

KYSC(FM) Fairbanks AK
WRSA-FM Decatur AL
WDJR(FM) Enterprise AL
KWLR(FM) Maumelle AR
KSSW(FM) Nashville AR
KMXP(FM) Phoenix AZ
KHDR(FM) Lenwood CA
KWAV(FM) Monterey CA
KSEG(FM) Sacramento CA
KCCY(FM) Pueblo CO
KBCR-FM Steamboat Springs CO
WINK-FM Fort Myers FL
WJGL(FM) Jacksonville FL
WKEZ-FM Tavenier FL
WRDO(FM) Fitzgerald GA
WAKB(FM) Wrens GA
KFMN(FM) Lihue HI
KIAQ(FM) Clarion IA
KKGL(FM) Nampa ID
WLBH-FM Mattoon IL
WXLP(FM) Moline IL
WWDV(FM) Zion IL
WHPZ(FM) Bremen IN
WKLO(FM) Hardinsburg IN
KKOW-FM Pittsburg KS
KFIX(FM) Plainville KS
WDDJ(FM) Paducah KY
WGKS(FM) Paris KY
KZMZ(FM) Alexandria LA
WTKK(FM) Boston MA
WBPW(FM) Presque Isle ME
WLAV-FM Grand Rapids MI
WBTI(FM) Lexington MI
WWCM(FM) Standish MI
KMFY(FM) Grand Rapids MN

U.S. FM Stations by Frequency

KZBK(FM) Brookfield MO
KUPH(FM) Mountain View MO
WTCD(FM) Indianola MS
WXAB(FM) McLain MS
KQRV(FM) Deer Lodge MT
WYMY(FM) Goldsboro NC
WKKT(FM) Statesville NC
KZKK(FM) Seward NE
KCMI(FM) Terrytown NE
WFPG-FM Atlantic City NJ
KDAG(FM) Farmington NM
WRRB(FM) Arlington NY
WGRF(FM) Buffalo NY
WOUR(FM) Utica NY
*WOKL(FM) Troy OH
WNKL(FM) Wauseon OH
WLRD(FM) Willard OH
KQOB(FM) Enid OK
KROG(FM) Grants Pass OR
WRRK(FM) Braddock PA
WLAN-FM Lancaster PA
WREQ(FM) Ridgebury PA
WNRT(FM) Manati PR
WSUY(FM) Charleston SC
KDLO-FM Watertown SD
WXBQ-FM Bristol TN
KMML(FM) Amarillo TX
KXYL-FM Brownwood TX
KIOX-FM El Campo TX
KVMV(FM) McAllen TX
KMCM(FM) Odessa TX
KSCN(FM) Pittsburg TX
WWUZ(FM) Bowling Green VA
WSIG(FM) Mount Jackson VA
KGY-FM McCleary WA
KZTA(FM) Naches WA
KEZE(FM) Spokane WA
WWWX(FM) Oshkosh WI
WVVV(FM) Williamstown WV
KAML-FM Gillette WY
KMTN(FM) Jackson WY

97.1 mhz
WWMG(FM) Millbrook AL
KEZG(FM) Calico Rock AR
KAMD-FM Camden AR
KTZR-FM Green Valley AZ
KLSX(FM) Los Angeles CA
KTSE-FM Patterson CA
KLRM(FM) San Luis Obispo CA
*KULV(FM) Ukiah CA
KSEQ(FM) Visalia CA
WASH(FM) Washington DC
WSUN-FM Holiday FL
WOSN(FM) Indian River Shores FL
WFOX(FM) Gainesville GA
KNWB(FM) Hilo HI
WDRV(FM) Chicago IL
WLHK(FM) Shelbyville IN
KSKU(FM) Hutchinson KS
WKEQ-FM Somerset KY
WXCM(FM) Whitesville KY
WEZB(FM) New Orleans LA
*WLIC(FM) Frostburg MD
WQJZ(FM) Ocean Pines MD
WWBX(FM) Bangor ME
WKRK-FM Detroit MI
WGLQ(FM) Escanaba MI
KYCK(FM) Crookston MN
KTCZ-FM Minneapolis MN
KFTK(FM) Florissant MO
KNIM-FM Maryville MO
KAYQ(FM) Warsaw MO
WOKK(FM) Meridian MS
KKBR(FM) Billings MT
KALS(FM) Kalispell MT
WQMG-FM Greensboro NC
WYND-FM Hatteras NC
KYYX(FM) Minot ND
KELN(FM) North Platte NE
KBCQ(FM) Roswell NM
KXPT(FM) Las Vegas NV
WQHT(FM) New York NY
WREO-FM Ashtabula OH
WBVB(FM) Coal Grove OH
WBNS-FM Columbus OH
KMMY(FM) Muskogee OK

KYCH-FM Portland OR
WBHT(FM) Mountain Top PA
WOWY(FM) University Park PA
KPSD(FM) Faith SD
WRQQ(FM) Goodlettsville TN
WHRK(FM) Memphis TN
KTHT(FM) Cleveland TX
KEGL(FM) Fort Worth TX
KVRP-FM Haskell TX
KCYN(FM) Moab UT
KZHT(FM) Salt Lake City UT
WZRT(FM) Rutland VT
KXRX(FM) Walla Walla WA
WCOW-FM Sparta WI
WDBS(FM) Sutton WV

97.3 mhz
KEAG(FM) Anchorage AK
WNCB(FM) Homewood AL
KDEW-FM De Witt AR
KNCQ(FM) Redding CA
KSON-FM San Diego CA
KLLC(FM) San Francisco CA
KBCO-FM Boulder CO
WZBG(FM) Litchfield CT
WFLC(FM) Miami FL
WSKY-FM Micanopy FL
WRAK-FM Bainbridge GA
WAEV(FM) Savannah GA
KHKI(FM) Des Moines IA
KGRR(FM) Epworth IA
KKNL(FM) New London IA
KLCE(FM) Blackfoot ID
WRUL(FM) Carmi IL
WFYR(FM) Elmwood IL
WTIM-FM Taylorville IL
WMEE(FM) Fort Wayne IN
KKJQ(FM) Garden City KS
WAQZ(FM) Fort Thomas KY
WRLV-FM Salyersville KY
WJMG(FM) Bastrop LA
KMDL(FM) Kaplan LA
KDBH(FM) Natchitoches LA
WJFD-FM New Bedford MA
WJDF(FM) Orange MA
WMJO(FM) Essexville MI
WDEE-FM Reed City MI
*KDNW(FM) Duluth MN
KRVY-FM Starbuck MN
KZPL(FM) Lee's Summit MO
KYRX(FM) Marble Hill MO
KXUS(FM) Springfield MO
WFMN(FM) Flora MS
WKSO(FM) Natchez MS
WFMM(FM) Sumrall MS
WKBC-FM North Wilkesboro NC
WMNX(FM) Wilmington NC
KRGY(FM) Aurora NE
KBLR-FM Blair NE
WIXM(FM) Millville NJ
KKSS(FM) Santa Fe NM
KZTQ(FM) Carson City NV
WYXL(FM) Ithaca NY
WMYY(FM) Schoharie NY
WZAD(FM) Wurtsboro NY
WJZE(FM) Oak Harbor OH
KWEY(FM) Weatherford OK
KSHR-FM Coquille OR
*WZZE(FM) Glen Mills PA
WRVV(FM) Harrisburg PA
WPCL(FM) Northern Cambria PA
WDGT(FM) Rio Grande PR
KMXC(FM) Sioux Falls SD
WKJQ(FM) Parsons TN
WMAX-FM South Pittsburg TN
KKLY(FM) Pecos TX
KSTQ(FM) Plainview TX
KAJA(FM) San Antonio TX
WGH-FM Newport News VA
*KKRS(FM) Davenport WA
KBSG-FM Tacoma WA
WQBW(FM) Milwaukee WI
WKWK-FM Wheeling WV

97.5 mhz
WABB-FM Mobile AL
WZLM(FM) Talladega AL
KQUS-FM Hot Springs AR

KRZS(FM) Flagstaff AZ
KSZR(FM) Oro Valley AZ
KABX-FM Merced CA
KLYY(FM) Riverside CA
KRUZ(FM) Santa Barbara CA
WPCV(FM) Winter Haven FL
WUFF(FM) Eastman GA
WPZE(FM) Fayetteville GA
WHLJ(FM) Statenville GA
KZGZ(FM) Hagatna GU
KHNR(FM) Honolulu HI
KBVU-FM Alta IA
KFMS(FM) Franklin ID
*KTWD(FM) Wallace ID
WDLJ(FM) Breese IL
WHMS-FM Champaign IL
WBBA-FM Pittsfield IL
WZOK(FM) Rockford IL
KJCK(FM) Junction City KS
WZZP(FM) Hopkinsville KY
WAMZ(FM) Louisville KY
KTJZ(FM) Tallulah LA
WICO-FM Salisbury MD
WIGY(FM) Madison ME
WYTZ(FM) Bridgman MI
WKLT(FM) Kalkaska MI
WJIM-FM Lansing MI
*WYDM(FM) Monroe MI
WEFG-FM Whitehall MI
KDKK-FM Park Rapids MN
KNXR(FM) Rochester MN
KOEA(FM) Doniphan MO
KNMO-FM Nevada MO
KDAA(FM) Rolla MO
WWMS(FM) Oxford MS
KOZB(FM) Livingston MT
KKCT(FM) Bismarck ND
WOKQ(FM) Dover NH
WTHK(FM) Trenton NJ
KVEG(FM) Mesquite NV
WZEC(FM) Hoosick Falls NY
WALK-FM Patchogue NY
WFRY-FM Watertown NY
WONE-FM Akron OH
WVNU(FM) Greenfield OH
WTGR(FM) Union City OH
KPAK(FM) Alva OK
KLAK(FM) Durant OK
KMOD-FM Tulsa OK
KNLR(FM) Bend OR
KSHL(FM) Gleneden Beach OR
WDDH(FM) Saint Marys PA
WIOB(FM) Mayaguez PR
WCOS-FM Columbia SC
WJXB-FM Knoxville TN
WLLX(FM) Lawrenceburg TN
KFNC(FM) Beaumont TX
KBNA-FM El Paso TX
KFTX(FM) Kingsville TX
KGKL-FM San Angelo TX
KWTX-FM Waco TX
KCYQ(FM) Richfield UT
WWWV(FM) Charlottesville VA
WQOK(FM) South Boston VA
KOLW(FM) Othello WA
WHDG(FM) Rhinelander WI
WQBE-FM Charleston WV
WLTF(FM) Martinsburg WV
KDLY(FM) Lander WY

97.7 mhz
WKKR(FM) Auburn AL
WEZZ(FM) Clanton AL
WKLD(FM) Oneonta AL
WSMO(FM) Thomaston AL
WKXM-FM Winfield AL
KABK-FM Augusta AR
KAVV(FM) Benson AZ
KQVO(FM) Calexico CA
KWIN(FM) Lodi CA
KFFG(FM) Los Altos CA
KRCK-FM Mecca CA
KVVS(FM) Mojave CA
KVRV(FM) Monte Rio CA
KHHZ(FM) Oroville CA
KSMJ(FM) Shafter CA

KZYR(FM) Avon CO
WCTY(FM) Norwich CT
WAFL(FM) Milford DE
WYYX(FM) Bonifay FL
WAVK(FM) Marathon FL
WTLQ-FM Punta Rassa FL
WMGZ(FM) Eatonton GA
WDMG-FM Ocilla GA
WKCX(FM) Rome GA
WTCQ(FM) Vidalia GA
WWUF(FM) Waycross GA
KCRR(FM) Grundy Center IA
KHBT(FM) Humboldt IA
KOTM-FM Ottumwa IA
WMOI(FM) Monmouth IL
WYVR(FM) Petersburg IL
WSTQ(FM) Streator IL
WQUL(FM) West Frankfort IL
WSDM-FM Brazil IN
WZOW(FM) Goshen IN
WLQI(FM) Rensselaer IN
KSNP(FM) Burlington KS
WWKY(FM) Providence KY
KPCH(FM) Dubach LA
KAPB(FM) Marksville LA
WBOT(FM) Brockton MA
*WYAJ(FM) Sudbury MA
WOQL(FM) Winchendon MA
WMDM-FM Lexington Park MD
WCXU(FM) Caribou ME
WNSX(FM) Winter Harbor ME
WMRX-FM Beaverton MI
WOLV-FM Houghton MI
*WVXM(FM) Manistee MI
WTGV-FM Sandusky MI
KLGR-FM Redwood Falls MN
KPOW-FM La Monte MO
KHZR(FM) Potosi MO
KQMO(FM) Shell Knob MO
WRJH(FM) Brandon MS
WTYJ(FM) Fayette MS
WTYL-FM Tylertown MS
KGLM-FM Anaconda MT
WWNF(FM) Kinston NC
WURB(FM) Windsor NC
KMTY(FM) Holdrege NE
KBBX-FM Nebraska City NE
KLVO(FM) Belen NM
KPSA-FM Lordsburg NM
WBKK(FM) Amsterdam NY
WENI-FM Big Flats NY
WCZX(FM) Hyde Park NY
WILE-FM Byesville OH
WGGN(FM) Castalia OH
WAXZ(FM) Georgetown OH
WCJO(FM) Jackson OH
*WTGN(FM) Lima OH
WOXY(FM) Oxford OH
KICM(FM) Healdton OK
*KHIM(FM) Mangum OK
KRAT(FM) Altamont OR
KACI-FM The Dalles OR
WLER-FM Butler PA
WVRT(FM) Mill Hall PA
WLKH(FM) Somerset PA
WBRQ(FM) Cidra PR
WWXM(FM) Garden City SC
KNBZ(FM) Redfield SD
WTNE-FM Trenton TN
KATX(FM) Eastland TX
KLTO-FM McQueeney TX
KBMI(FM) Roma TX
KWRW(FM) Rusk TX
KALK(FM) Winfield TX
WMJD(FM) Grundy VA
WGMT(FM) Lyndon VT
KYSN(FM) East Wenatchee WA
KFFR(FM) Pullman WA
KFMY(FM) Raymond WA
WAQE-FM Barron WI
WGLR-FM Lancaster WI
WFDL-FM Lomira WI
WSRG-FM Sturgeon Bay WI
WRON-FM Ronceverte WV

97.9 mhz
WRVX(FM) Eufaula AL
WVOK-FM Oxford AL
WJWZ(FM) Wetumpka AL
KTLO-FM Mountain Home AR
KUPD-FM Tempe AZ
KPOD-FM Crescent City CA
KLAX-FM East Los Angeles CA
KTTA(FM) Esparto CA
KMGV(FM) Fresno CA
KLUK(FM) Needles CA
KEXA(FM) Salinas CA
KISZ-FM Cortez CO
WPKX(FM) Enfield CT
WXTB(FM) Clearwater FL
WFKS(FM) Neptune Beach FL
WRMF(FM) Palm Beach FL
WJZT(FM) Woodville FL
WIBB-FM Fort Valley GA
KKBG(FM) Hilo HI
*KOWI(FM) Lamoni IA
*KCMR(FM) Mason City IA
KSEZ(FM) Sioux City IA
KQFC(FM) Boise ID
WLUP-FM Chicago IL
WXEF(FM) Effingham IL
WVVN(FM) Heyworth IL
*WGNR-FM Anderson IN
WSLM-FM Salem IN
KWGB(FM) Colby KS
KRBB(FM) Wichita KS
WZQQ(FM) Hyden KY
KQLK(FM) De Ridder LA
WIYY(FM) Baltimore MD
WBEY-FM Crisfield MD
WJBQ(FM) Portland ME
WJLB(FM) Detroit MI
WGRD-FM Grand Rapids MI
WIHC(FM) Newberry MI
WEVE-FM Eveleth MN
KICK-FM Palmyra MO
KBXB(FM) Sikeston MO
KFBD-FM Waynesville MO
KXDG(FM) Webb City MO
WCPR-FM D'Iberville MS
WBAQ(FM) Greenville MS
WMSO(FM) Newton MS
KVVR(FM) Dutton MT
WNBB(FM) Bayboro NC
WPEG(FM) Concord NC
WTRG(FM) Gaston NC
*KFNW-FM Fargo ND
KRSI(FM) Garapan-Saipan NP
WSKQ-FM New York NY
WPXY-FM Rochester NY
WSKS(FM) Whitesboro NY
WRIP(FM) Windham NY
WNCI(FM) Columbus OH
KKWD(FM) Edmond OK
KZBB(FM) Poteau OK
KNRQ-FM Eugene OR
KHTO-FM Milton-Freewater OR
*KRRC(FM) Portland OR
WXTA(FM) Edinboro PA
WBSX(FM) Hazleton PA
WIIZ(FM) Blackville SC
KLMP(FM) Rapid City SD
WSIX-FM Nashville TN
KGNC-FM Amarillo TX
KBFB(FM) Dallas TX
KBXX(FM) Houston TX
KODM(FM) Odessa TX
KBZN(FM) Ogden UT
WZZU(FM) Lynchburg VA
WGOD-FM Charlotte Amalie VI
WSPT-FM Stevens Point WI
WKKW(FM) Fairmont WV
WDNQ(FM) Kenova WV
KQLF(FM) Cheyenne WY
KTAG(FM) Cody WY
KZWB(FM) Green River WY

98.1 mhz
KLEF(FM) Anchorage AK
KWLF(FM) Fairbanks AK
WTXT(FM) Fayette AL
*KVIP-FM Redding CA
KIFM(FM) San Diego CA

U.S. FM Stations by Frequency

KISQ(FM) San Francisco CA
KKJG(FM) San Luis Obispo CA
KRXV(FM) Yermo CA
KKFM(FM) Colorado Springs CO
KAYW(FM) Meeker CO
*WQAQ(FM) Hamden CT
WKZE-FM Salisbury CT
WOCM(FM) Selbyville DE
WTKE(FM) Holt FL
WQHL-FM Live Oak FL
WNUE-FM Titusville FL
WMRZ(FM) Dawson GA
WELT(FM) East Dublin GA
WMGP(FM) Hogansville GA
KAWV(FM) Lihue HI
KHAK(FM) Cedar Rapids IA
KGTM(FM) Rexburg ID
WZOE-FM Princeton IL
WIBN(FM) Earl Park IN
WRAY-FM Princeton IN
KSKZ(FM) Copeland KS
KUSN(FM) Dearing KS
KUDL(FM) Kansas City KS
WBUL-FM Lexington KY
WDGL(FM) Baton Rouge LA
WCTK(FM) New Bedford MA
WGFN(FM) Glen Arbor MI
*WEUL(FM) Kingsford MI
WKCQ(FM) Saginaw MI
KBEW-FM Blue Earth MN
WWJO(FM) Saint Cloud MN
KOZX(FM) Cabool MO
KYKY(FM) Saint Louis MO
WMXI(FM) Laurel MS
WQSM(FM) Fayetteville NC
WOBX-FM Manteo NC
KFGE(FM) Milford NE
KBAC(FM) Las Vegas NM
KBUL-FM Carson City NV
WHWK(FM) Binghamton NY
WKDD(FM) Canton OH
*WUDR(FM) Dayton OH
WDFM(FM) Defiance OH
KJMZ(FM) Lawton OK
KVRO(FM) Stillwater OK
KCYS(FM) Seaside OR
WFGY(FM) Altoona PA
WOGL(FM) Philadelphia PA
WYBB(FM) Folly Beach SC
WHZT(FM) Seneca SC
WXMX(FM) Millington TN
WKXJ(FM) Signal Mountain TN
KTLT(FM) Anson TX
KVET-FM Austin TX
KRRG(FM) Laredo TX
KKCL(FM) Lorenzo TX
KTAL-FM Texarkana TX
KREC(FM) Brian Head UT
WBRF(FM) Galax VA
WTVR-FM Richmond VA
WJJR(FM) Rutland VT
KING-FM Seattle WA
KISC(FM) Spokane WA
WISM-FM Altoona WI
WLKN(FM) Cleveland WI
WMGN(FM) Madison WI

98.3 mhz
WDLT-FM Chickasaw AL
WAGH(FM) Fort Mitchell AL
WKEA-FM Scottsboro AL
WTRB-FM Sylacauga AL
KQSM(FM) Bentonville AR
KFCM(FM) Cherokee Village AR
KOHT(FM) Marana AZ
KQSS(FM) Miami AZ
KRDX(FM) Nogales AZ
KKLD(FM) Prescott Valley AZ
KHRN(FM) Huron CA
KXBX-FM Lakeport CA
KDAR(FM) Oxnard CA
KWNN(FM) Turlock CA
KRCV(FM) West Covina CA
KEJJ(FM) Gunnison CO
KATR-FM Otis CO
WDAQ(FM) Danbury CT
WILI-FM Willimantic CT

WWRZ(FM) Fort Meade FL
WRTO-FM Goulds FL
WQXZ(FM) Cordele GA
WGCO(FM) Midway GA
KJMD(FM) Pukalani HI
KWQW(FM) Boone IA
KDZY(FM) McCall ID
KSNQ(FM) Twin Falls ID
WCCQ(FM) Crest Hill IL
WWHP(FM) Farmer City IL
WRIK-FM Metropolis IL
WRAN(FM) Tower Hill IL
WRDZ-FM Plainfield IN
WZZY(FM) Winchester IN
WQXE(FM) Elizabethtown KY
WOKE(FM) Garrison KY
WHAY(FM) Whitley City KY
KZRZ(FM) West Monroe LA
WHAI(FM) Greenfield MA
WSMD-FM Mechanicsville MD
WTWR-FM Monroe MI
WRUP(FM) Munising MI
WLCS(FM) North Muskegon MI
*WCMZ-FM Sault Ste. Marie MI
WCSY-FM South Haven MI
WBJI(FM) Blackduck MN
KQYB(FM) Spring Grove MN
WCKK(FM) Carthage MS
WDFX(FM) Cleveland MS
WJDR(FM) Prentiss MS
KBEV-FM Dillon MT
WDLZ(FM) Murfreesboro NC
WSFM(FM) Oak Island NC
WIST(FM) Thomasville NC
WLGT(FM) Washington NC
KYNU(FM) Carrington ND
KBBN-FM Broken Bow NE
WLNH-FM Laconia NH
WMGQ(FM) New Brunswick NJ
WTKU(FM) Ocean City NJ
WVIN-FM Bath NY
WKJY(FM) Hempstead NY
WSUL(FM) Monticello NY
*WPSA(FM) Paul Smiths NY
WTRY-FM Rotterdam NY
WQRT(FM) Salamanca NY
WYBL(FM) Ashtabula OH
WPKO-FM Bellefontaine OH
WXXR(FM) Fredericktown OH
*WKET(FM) Kettering OH
WLGN-FM Logan OH
WTWS(FM) Bend OR
KLDR(FM) Harbeck-Fruitdale OR
KJNI(FM) Rainier OR
WOGI(FM) Charleroi PA
WWBE(FM) Mifflinburg PA
WTTP(FM) Las Piedras PR
WIDI(FM) Quebradillas PR
WSLT(FM) Clearwater SC
WLJI(FM) Summerton SC
KUQL(FM) Wessington Springs SD
WRJB(FM) Camden TN
WKSR-FM Pulaski TN
WLOD-FM Sweetwater TN
KEEP(FM) Bandera TX
KPDB(FM) Big Lake TX
KFYZ-FM Bonham TX
KBOC(FM) Bridgeport TX
KORA-FM Bryan TX
KULM(FM) Columbus TX
KICA-FM Farwell TX
*KVLZ(FM) Gatesville TX
KLHB(FM) Odem TX
KYYK(FM) Palestine TX
KPTX(FM) Pecos TX
KXDJ(FM) Spearman TX
KCUB-FM Stephenville TX
KARB(FM) Price UT
WLUS-FM Clarksville VA
WKSI-FM Stephens City VA
WMYP(FM) Frederiksted VI
KEYW(FM) Pasco WA
WJMR-FM Menomonee Falls WI
WCQM(FM) Park Falls WI
WCEF(FM) Ripley WV
KGRR(FM) Glenrock WY
KZZS(FM) Story WY

KERM(FM) Torrington WY

98.5 mhz
WINL(FM) Linden AL
KURB(FM) Little Rock AR
KWXY-FM Cathedral City CA
KDFO-FM Delano CA
KSAY(FM) Fort Bragg CA
KRXQ(FM) Sacramento CA
KUFX(FM) San Jose CA
KYGO-FM Denver CO
WGBG(FM) Seaford DE
WKTK(FM) Crystal River FL
WFSY(FM) Panama City FL
WUSV(FM) San Carlos Park FL
WSB-FM Atlanta GA
WLPF(FM) Ocilla GA
KDNN(FM) Honolulu HI
KOEL-FM Cedar Falls IA
KQKQ-FM Council Bluffs IA
KLLP(FM) Chubbuck ID
KZID(FM) Orofino ID
*WAHI-FM Augusta IL
WPIA(FM) Eureka IL
WXXQ(FM) Freeport IL
WACF(FM) Paris IL
WQKZ(FM) Ferdinand IN
WMYK(FM) Peru IN
KSAJ-FM Abilene KS
WYLD-FM New Orleans LA
WBMX(FM) Boston MA
WEBB(FM) Waterville ME
WNWN-FM Coldwater MI
WUPS(FM) Houghton Lake MI
*KTIS-FM Minneapolis MN
KTJJ(FM) Farmington MO
KWKJ(FM) Windsor MO
WZLQ(FM) Tupelo MS
KGHL-FM Billings MT
KBBZ(FM) Kalispell MT
WDWG(FM) Rocky Mount NC
KRKU(FM) McCook NE
WBBO(FM) Ocean Acres NJ
KABG(FM) Los Alamos NM
KLUC-FM Las Vegas NV
WCTW(FM) Catskill NY
WCKM-FM Lake George NY
WKSE(FM) Niagara Falls NY
WNYR-FM Waterloo NY
WBON(FM) Westhampton NY
WRRM(FM) Cincinnati OH
WNCX(FM) Cleveland OH
*WCMO(FM) Marietta OH
KACO(FM) Ardmore OK
KTIJ(FM) Elk City OK
KVOO-FM Tulsa OK
WGYI(FM) Oil City PA
WKRZ(FM) Wilkes-Barre PA
WYCR(FM) York-Hanover PA
WPRM-FM San Juan PR
WBZF(FM) Hartsville SC
WLXC(FM) Lexington SC
WDAI(FM) Pawley's Island SC
WGIC(FM) Cookeville TN
WTFM(FM) Kingsport TN
WGAP(FM) Clarksville TX
KYMI(FM) Los Ybanez TX
KGBT-FM McAllen TX
KTJM(FM) Port Arthur TX
KRXT(FM) Rockdale TX
KBBT(FM) Schertz TX
KIFX(FM) Roosevelt UT
WACL(FM) Elkton VA
KEYG-FM Grand Coulee WA
WQLH(FM) Green Bay WI

98.7 mhz
WBHK(FM) Warrior AL
KLBQ(FM) El Dorado AR
KPKX(FM) Phoenix AZ
KYSR(FM) Los Angeles CA
KSXY(FM) Middletown CA
KLOQ(FM) Winton CA
KRTZ(FM) Cortez CO
WNLC(FM) East Lyme CT
WMZQ-FM Washington DC
WKGR(FM) Fort Pierce FL
WLLD(FM) Holmes Beach FL

WCNK(FM) Key West FL
WYCT(FM) Pensacola FL
WISK-FM Americus GA
WBTY(FM) Homerville GA
KMGO(FM) Centerville IA
KSMA-FM Osage IA
WFMT(FM) Chicago IL
WNNS(FM) Springfield IL
WQME(FM) Anderson IN
WASK-FM Battle Ground IN
KFH-FM Clearwater KS
WHOP-FM Hopkinsville KY
WKDO-FM Liberty KY
KKST(FM) Oakdale LA
WVMV(FM) Detroit MI
WFGR(FM) Grand Rapids MI
WGLI(FM) Hancock MI
KQWB-FM Moorhead MN
KISD(FM) Pipestone MN
KWTO-FM Springfield MO
WJKK(FM) Vicksburg MS
KXDR(FM) Hamilton MT
WSMW(FM) Greensboro NC
WILT(FM) Jacksonville NC
KACL(FM) Bismarck ND
KSID-FM Sidney NE
WBYY(FM) Somersworth NH
WINQ(FM) Winchester NH
WCZT(FM) Villas NJ
*KMTH(FM) Maljamar NM
KKVS(FM) Truth or Consequences NM
WGMM(FM) Corning NY
WRKS(FM) New York NY
WPAC(FM) Ogdensburg NY
WLZW(FM) Utica NY
*WYKL(FM) Crestline OH
*WSLN(FM) Delaware OH
WYRO(FM) McArthur OH
KYTT-FM Coos Bay OR
KUBQ(FM) La Grande OR
KARO(FM) Nyssa OR
KUPL-FM Portland OR
WQWK(FM) Pleasant Gap PA
WXZX(FM) Culebra PR
WYKZ(FM) Beaufort SC
KOUT(FM) Rapid City SD
WAMB-FM Nashville TN
WOKI(FM) Oliver Springs TN
KPRF(FM) Amarillo TX
KLUV-FM Dallas TX
KELI(FM) San Angelo TX
KTXN-FM Victoria TX
KBEE(FM) Salt Lake City UT
WNOR(FM) Norfolk VA
KLES(FM) Mabton WA
WMDC(FM) Mayville WV
WRVZ(FM) Pocatalico WV
WOVK(FM) Wheeling WV
KRSV-FM Afton WY
KHIH(FM) Laramie WY

98.9 mhz
KYMG(FM) Anchorage AK
WBAM-FM Montgomery AL
KBNF(FM) Chester CA
KCVR-FM Columbia CA
KSOF(FM) Dinuba CA
KHWY(FM) Essex CA
KSOL(FM) San Francisco CA
KKMG(FM) Pueblo CO
WGUF(FM) Marco FL
WBCG(FM) Murdock FL
WMMO(FM) Orlando FL
WBZE(FM) Tallahassee FL
WQMT(FM) Chatsworth GA
KITH(FM) Kapaa HI
KGRA(FM) Jefferson IA
KQCR-FM Parkersburg IA
WJEZ(FM) Dwight IL
WISH-FM Galatia IL
WHQQ(FM) Neoga IL
WHTS(FM) Rock Island IL
WZKF(FM) Salem IN
KKRK(FM) Coffeyville KS
KQRC-FM Leavenworth KS
WSIP-FM Paintsville KY
WUUU(FM) Franklinton LA

WORC-FM Webster MA
WSBY-FM Salisbury MD
WCLZ(FM) Brunswick ME
WKLZ-FM Petoskey MI
WOWE(FM) Vassar MI
KTCO(FM) Duluth MN
KZPK(FM) Paynesville MN
KFLW(FM) Saint Robert MO
WAJV(FM) Brooksville MS
WYKK(FM) Quitman MS
KAAK(FM) Great Falls MT
WNBR-FM Windsor NC
KKPR-FM Kearney NE
KBZB(FM) Pioche NV
WBZA(FM) Rochester NY
WXMG(FM) Upper Arlington OH
WBYR(FM) Van Wert OH
WMXY(FM) Youngstown OH
KYIS(FM) Oklahoma City OK
WQKY(FM) Emporium PA
WQLV(FM) Millersburg PA
WUSL(FM) Philadelphia PA
WAZS-FM McClellanville SC
WSPA-FM Spartanburg SC
WANT(FM) Lebanon TN
WMPW(FM) Munford TN
KTUX(FM) Carthage TX
KLMO-FM Dilley TX
KHHL(FM) Leander TX
KLYD(FM) Snyder TX
WCUL(FM) Orange VA
WOKO(FM) Burlington VT
KWJZ(FM) Seattle WA
KKZX(FM) Spokane WA
*WVCX(FM) Tomah WI
WDNE-FM Elkins WV

99.1 mhz
KRUP(FM) Dillingham AK
WDGM(FM) Greensboro AL
WAHR(FM) Huntsville AL
KMAG(FM) Fort Smith AR
KSMD(FM) Pangburn AR
KWDO(FM) Waldo AR
KOFH(FM) Nogales AZ
KTMG(FM) Prescott AZ
KFMM(FM) Thatcher AZ
KAJK-FM Ferndale CA
KGGI(FM) Riverside CA
KSQL(FM) Santa Cruz CA
KXFM(FM) Santa Maria CA
*KARA(FM) Williams CA
KMTS(FM) Glenwood Springs CO
KUAD-FM Windsor CO
WPLR(FM) New Haven CT
WWOJ(FM) Avon Park FL
WQIK-FM Jacksonville FL
WEDR(FM) Miami FL
WDEN-FM Macon GA
KAGB(FM) Waimea HI
KSKB(FM) Brooklyn IA
KUPI-FM Idaho Falls ID
KTPZ(FM) Mountain Home ID
WXTT(FM) Danville IL
*KJIL(FM) Copeland KS
KTLI(FM) El Dorado KS
KSEK-FM Girard KS
WCBL-FM Benton KY
WHSX(FM) Edmonton KY
WJMM-FM Keene KY
KXKC(FM) New Iberia LA
WPLM-FM Plymouth MA
WLZL(FM) Annapolis MD
WLKE(FM) Bar Harbor ME
WSMK(FM) Buchanan MI
WFMK(FM) East Lansing MI
WIKB-FM Iron River MI
KEEZ-FM Mankato MN
KLLZ-FM Walker MN
KFUO-FM Clayton MO
KYOO-FM Halfway MO
WYMX(FM) Greenwood MS
WKNN-FM Pascagoula MS
KCMM(FM) Belgrade MT
WVOD(FM) Manteo NC
WZFX(FM) Whiteville NC
KCAD(FM) Dickinson ND

U.S. FM Stations by Frequency

WNNH(FM) Henniker NH
WAWZ(FM) Zarephath NJ
KKIT(FM) Angel Fire NM
KCLV-FM Clovis NM
KGLX(FM) Gallup NM
KXMT(FM) Taos NM
KCMY(FM) Gardnerville-Minden NV
WAAL(FM) Binghamton NY
WHKO(FM) Dayton OH
WFRO-FM Fremont OH
KODZ(FM) Eugene OR
WYOT(FM) Ebensburg PA
WUKQ-FM Mayaguez PR
WBAW-FM Barnwell SC
KZNC(FM) Huron SD
WNML-FM Loudon TN
KAYG(FM) Camp Wood TX
KRYS-FM Corpus Christi TX
KFZO(FM) Denton TX
KNES(FM) Fairfield TX
KODA(FM) Houston TX
KHKX(FM) Odessa TX
WXGM-FM Gloucester VA
WJNV(FM) Jonesville VA
WSLQ(FM) Roanoke VA
KUJ-FM Walla Walla WA
WMYX(FM) Milwaukee WI
WKFX(FM) Rice Lake WI
WGGE(FM) Parkersburg WV
KNYN(FM) Fort Bridger WY
KWYW(FM) Lost Cabin WY

99.3 mhz
WMFC-FM Monroeville AL
KVLD(FM) Atkins AR
KAPW(FM) Cotton Plant AR
KZYP(FM) Pine Bluff AR
KSXX(FM) Payson AZ
KKBB(FM) Bakersfield CA
KJWL(FM) Fresno CA
*KLVS(FM) Grass Valley CA
KMXX(FM) Imperial CA
KVYN(FM) Saint Helena CA
KNNN(FM) Shasta Lake City CA
KJOY(FM) Stockton CA
WLRQ-FM Cocoa FL
WJBX(FM) Fort Myers Beach FL
WPBH(FM) Mexico Beach FL
WCON-FM Cornelia GA
WKCN(FM) Lumpkin GA
*KFFF-FM Boone IA
KKBZ(FM) Clarinda IA
KDST(FM) Dyersville IA
KWAY-FM Waverly IA
WDUK(FM) Havana IL
WAJK(FM) La Salle IL
WXFM(FM) Mount Zion IL
WSCH(FM) Aurora IN
WKVI-FM Knox IN
WCJC(FM) Van Buren IN
KWIC(FM) Topeka KS
WWKF(FM) Fulton KY
WVLE(FM) Scottsville KY
KNBB(FM) Ruston LA
WLZX(FM) Northampton MA
WKTJ-FM Farmington ME
WBQQ(FM) Kennebunk ME
WATZ-FM Alpena MI
WBNZ(FM) Frankfort MI
WMSH-FM Sturgis MI
WJQK(FM) Zeeland MI
KXRZ(FM) Alexandria MN
KWNO-FM Rushford MN
KKDQ(FM) Thief River Falls MN
KCLR-FM Boonville MO
KCGQ-FM Gordonville MO
KUNQ(FM) Houston MO
WBVV(FM) Booneville MS
WHER(FM) Heidelberg MS
KMXE-FM Red Lodge MT
WQDK(FM) Ahoskie NC
WFRD(FM) Hanover NH
WZBZ(FM) Pleasantville NJ
KVLV-FM Fallon NV
KRGT(FM) Indian Springs NV
WFKP(FM) Ellenville NY
WLLG(FM) Lowville NY

WSNN(FM) Potsdam NY
WLLW(FM) Seneca Falls NY
WTNS-FM Coshocton OH
WNXT-FM Portsmouth OH
KADA-FM Ada OK
KCDL(FM) Cordell OK
KGVE(FM) Grove OK
KLOR-FM Ponca City OK
WOXX(FM) Franklin PA
WHKF(FM) Harrisburg PA
WZXR(FM) South Williamsport PA
WPKL(FM) Uniontown PA
WJZS(FM) Block Island RI
WBT-FM Chester SC
WWKT-FM Kingstree SC
WPBX(FM) Crossville TN
WTZR(FM) Elizabethton TN
WNRX(FM) Jefferson City TN
WZLT(FM) Lexington TN
KPSM(FM) Brownwood TX
KEFH(FM) Clarendon TX
KJAZ(FM) Thorndale TX
KLBL(FM) White Oak TX
WVES(FM) Accomac VA
WFQX(FM) Front Royal VA
WKJM(FM) Petersburg VA
WYSK-FM Spotsylvania VA
KDDS-FM Elma WA
KDRM(FM) Moses Lake WA
KQSN(FM) Naches WA
WDMP-FM Dodgeville WI
WKEB(FM) Medford WI
WOWN(FM) Shawano WI
KKTY-FM Douglas WY
KTGA(FM) Saratoga WY

99.5 mhz
WZRR(FM) Birmingham AL
KBTA-FM Batesville AR
KHMB(FM) Hamburg AR
KAKS(FM) Huntsville AR
KDIS-FM Little Rock AR
KMTB(FM) Murfreesboro AR
KIIM-FM Tucson AZ
KLOK-FM Greenfield CA
KNTI(FM) Lakeport CA
KKLA-FM Los Angeles CA
KHYZ(FM) Mountain Pass CA
KMRJ(FM) Rancho Mirage CA
KQMT(FM) Denver CO
WIHT(FM) Washington DC
WJBR-FM Wilmington DE
WAFC-FM Clewiston FL
WKSM-FM Fort Walton Beach FL
WAIL(FM) Key West FL
WBXY(FM) La Crosse FL
WQYK-FM Saint Petersburg FL
WKAA(FM) Willacoochee GA
KHUI(FM) Honolulu HI
KHAM(FM) Britt IA
KDAO-FM Eldora IA
KKMA(FM) Le Mars IA
KZZQ(FM) Winterset IA
KWEI-FM Fruitland ID
WUSN(FM) Chicago IL
WDQZ(FM) Lexington IL
WCOY(FM) Quincy IL
WZPL(FM) Greenfield IN
KHAZ(FM) Hays KS
WKDP-FM Corbin KY
WKDQ(FM) Henderson KY
KBXG(FM) Lake Charles LA
WRNO-FM New Orleans LA
WKLB-FM Lowell MA
WJCX(FM) Pittsfield ME
WYCD(FM) Detroit MI
WNGE(FM) Negaunee MI
WYSS(FM) Sault Ste. Marie MI
*KBHW(FM) International Falls MN
*KSJN(FM) Minneapolis MN
KPRW(FM) Perham MN
KHCR(FM) Bismarck MO
KADI-FM Republic MO
KMCJ(FM) Colstrip MT
KBLL(FM) Helena MT
WXNR(FM) Grifton NC
WMAG(FM) High Point NC

KUTT(FM) Fairbury NE
WEVJ(FM) Jackson NH
KMGA(FM) Albuquerque NM
KROL-FM Las Cruces NM
*KWFL(FM) Roswell NM
KPXP(FM) Garapan-Saipan NP
WTKW(FM) Bridgeport NY
WDCX(FM) Buffalo NY
*WBAI(FM) New York NY
WRVE(FM) Schenectady NY
WOKN(FM) Southport NY
WGAR-FM Cleveland OH
WAOL(FM) Ripley OH
KXBL(FM) Henryetta OK
KBZQ(FM) Lawton OK
KAGO-FM Klamath Falls OR
KWJJ-FM Portland OR
KJMX(FM) Reedsport OR
WXOT(FM) Mount Union PA
*WUSR(FM) Scranton PA
WKXC-FM Aiken SC
WRNN(FM) Socastee SC
KOLY-FM Mobridge SD
WYGO(FM) Madisonville TN
KKPS(FM) Brownsville TX
KNFX-FM Bryan TX
KPLX(FM) Fort Worth TX
KQBR(FM) Lubbock TX
KISS-FM San Antonio TX
KJMY(FM) Bountiful UT
WYTT(FM) Emporia VA
WVIQ(FM) Christiansted VI
KZZL-FM Pullman WA
KAAP(FM) Rock Island WA
WPKR(FM) Omro WI
WJLS-FM Beckley WV
WYMJ(FM) New Martinsville WV
WBYG(FM) Point Pleasant WV
KCUG(FM) Chugwater WY
KRKI(FM) Newcastle WY

99.7 mhz
KMBQ(FM) Wasilla AK
WOOF-FM Dothan AL
KXTY(FM) Morro Bay CA
KIOO(FM) Porterville CA
KFRC-FM San Francisco CA
KTOR(FM) Westwood CA
KPTE(FM) Durango CO
WGNX(FM) Vero Beach FL
WNNX(FM) Atlanta GA
KBEA-FM Muscatine IA
WXAJ(FM) Hillsboro IL
WSHW(FM) Frankfort IN
WDJX(FM) Louisville KY
KMJJ-FM Shreveport LA
WIMI(FM) Ironwood MI
*WUGN(FM) Midland MI
KXDL(FM) Browerville MN
KKCK(FM) Marshall MN
KMAC(FM) Gainesville MO
KYYS(FM) Kansas City MO
KBTN-FM Neosho MO
KTTR-FM Saint James MO
WJMI(FM) Jackson MS
WRFX(FM) Kannapolis NC
WZAX(FM) Nashville NC
KOGA-FM Ogallala NE
WNTK-FM New London NH
WBHX(FM) Tuckerton NJ
WJUX(FM) Monticello NY
WBGK(FM) Newport Village NY
WZXV(FM) Palmyra NY
WBZX(FM) Columbus OH
WKSD(FM) Paulding OH
KNID(FM) Alva OK
KMTK(FM) Bend OR
WSPI(FM) Mount Carmel PA
WSHH(FM) Pittsburgh PA
*WVYC(FM) York PA
WSKO-FM Wakefield-Peacedale RI
WXST(FM) Hollywood SC
WWTN(FM) Manchester TN
WMC-FM Memphis TN
KBZD(FM) Amarillo TX
KROY(FM) Palacios TX
KBCY(FM) Tye TX

KVST(FM) Willis TX
WVSG(FM) Coeburn VA
WYFI(FM) Norfolk VA
WCYK-FM Staunton VA
KHHK(FM) Yakima WA
WWIS-FM Black River Falls WI
WLYD(FM) Sturgeon Bay WI

99.9 mhz
KFMJ(FM) Ketchikan AK
WRJL-FM Eva AL
WMXC(FM) Mobile AL
WQNR(FM) Tallassee AL
*KSWH(FM) Arkadelphia AR
KTCS-FM Fort Smith AR
KGPQ(FM) Monticello AR
KWCK(FM) Searcy AR
KESZ(FM) Phoenix AZ
KRCX-FM Marysville CA
KCIV(FM) Mount Bullion CA
KOLA(FM) San Bernardino CA
KTYD(FM) Santa Barbara CA
KEKB(FM) Fruita CO
KVUU(FM) Pueblo CO
WEZN-FM Bridgeport CT
WKIS(FM) Boca Raton FL
WEGT(FM) Lafayette FL
WGNE-FM Palatka FL
WSNT-FM Sandersville GA
WQSA(FM) Unadilla GA
KJKS(FM) Kahului HI
KTOH(FM) Kalaheo HI
KCWN(FM) New Sharon IA
KZDX(FM) Burley ID
WIXO(FM) Bartonville IL
WOOZ-FM Harrisburg IL
WRZA(FM) Park Forest IL
WTHI-FM Terre Haute IN
KWKR(FM) Leoti KS
KSKG(FM) Salina KS
WVLC(FM) Mannsville KY
WMTC-FM Vancleve KY
KTDY(FM) Lafayette LA
WNYN-FM Athol MA
WQRC(FM) Barnstable MA
*WHHB(FM) Holliston MA
WFRE(FM) Frederick MD
WWFG(FM) Ocean City MD
WTHT(FM) Auburn ME
WHFB-FM Benton Harbor MI
WPIQ(FM) Manistique MI
WHAK-FM Rogers City MI
KAUS-FM Austin MN
KVOX-FM Moorhead MN
KCML(FM) Saint Joseph MN
WUSZ(FM) Virginia MN
KBFL(FM) Buffalo MO
KIRK(FM) Macon MO
KZMA(FM) Naylor MO
KFAV(FM) Warrenton MO
WSMS(FM) Artesia MS
KBOZ-FM Bozeman MT
WKSF(FM) Asheville NC
WKXB(FM) Burgaw NC
WHDX(FM) Buxton NC
KMXA-FM Minot ND
KGOR(FM) Omaha NE
KTQM-FM Clovis NM
KXTC(FM) Thoreau NM
WIII(FM) Cortland NY
WBTZ(FM) Plattsburgh NY
WLQT(FM) Kettering OH
WKKO(FM) Toledo OH
WTUZ(FM) Uhrichsville OH
KRKT-FM Albany OR
KWRL(FM) La Grande OR
WQBR(FM) Avis PA
WODE-FM Easton PA
WXKC(FM) Erie PA
WIOA(FM) San Juan PR
KTSM-FM El Paso TX
KTXM(FM) Hallettsville TX
KSHN-FM Liberty TX
KMOO(FM) Mineola TX
KGEE(FM) Monahans TX
KTEZ(FM) Mount Enterprise TX
KSAB(FM) Robstown TX

WACO-FM Waco TX
KLUR(FM) Wichita Falls TX
KONY(FM) Saint George UT
WFXQ(FM) Chase City VA
WZBB(FM) Stanleytown VA
KISW(FM) Seattle WA
KXLY-FM Spokane WA
WDRK(FM) Cornell WI
WJVL(FM) Janesville WI
WIZD(FM) Rudolph WI
WVAF(FM) Charleston WV
KKPL(FM) Cheyenne WY

100.1 mhz
KYKD(FM) Bethel AK
KWHQ-FM Kenai AK
*KMXT(FM) Kodiak AK
WGSY(FM) Phenix City AL
WDXX(FM) Selma AL
KVNA-FM Flagstaff AZ
KGMN(FM) Kingman AZ
KNGS(FM) Coalinga CA
KZRO(FM) Dunsmuir CA
KGBA-FM Holtville CA
*KLVJ(FM) Julian CA
KHWZ(FM) Ludlow CA
KZST(FM) Santa Rosa CA
KQOD(FM) Stockton CA
KKZQ(FM) Tehachapi CA
WVVE(FM) Panama City Beach FL
WCKT(FM) Port Charlotte FL
WQMJ(FM) Forsyth GA
WMZD(FM) Statesboro GA
WNSY(FM) Talking Rock GA
WXKT(FM) Washington GA
KDWD(FM) Emmetsburg IA
KCTN(FM) Garnavillo IA
KITT(FM) Soda Springs ID
WKAI(FM) Macomb IL
WGLC-FM Mendota IL
WJBD-FM Salem IL
WNUY(FM) Bluffton IN
WFLQ(FM) French Lick IN
WFRI(FM) Winamac IN
WMDJ-FM Allen KY
WKQQ(FM) Winchester KY
KRVV(FM) Bastrop LA
WMNB(FM) North Adams MA
WWFX(FM) Southbridge MA
*WBRS(FM) Waltham MA
*WUMF-FM Farmington ME
WHOU-FM Houlton ME
WCUZ(FM) Bear Lake MI
WBCH-FM Hastings MI
WVIB(FM) Holton MI
KOLV(FM) Olivia MN
WZFJ(FM) Pequot Lakes MN
KKWK(FM) Cameron MO
KDJR(FM) De Soto MO
KBBM(FM) Jefferson City MO
KOMC-FM Kimberling City MO
WQXB(FM) Grenada MS
KMMR(FM) Malta MT
KZOQ-FM Missoula MT
KATQ-FM Plentywood MT
WBXB(FM) Edenton NC
KBFZ(FM) Kimball NE
WPNH-FM Plymouth NH
WJRZ-FM Manahawkin NJ
KTHX-FM Dayton NV
WDST(FM) Woodstock NY
WNIR(FM) Kent OH
WXZQ(FM) Piketon OH
WSWR(FM) Shelby OH
KYFM(FM) Bartlesville OK
KYKC(FM) Byng OK
WWOT(FM) Altoona PA
WBRR(FM) Bradford PA
WQFN(FM) Forest City PA
WQIC(FM) Lebanon PA
WWFN-FM Lake City SC
WXBT(FM) West Columbia SC
WASL(FM) Dyersburg TN
WRLT(FM) Franklin TN
KNRB(FM) Atlanta TX
KYBI(FM) Lufkin TX
KCLL(FM) San Angelo TX

U.S. FM Stations by Frequency

WYFJ(FM) Ashland VA
WVBE-FM Lynchburg VA
WKQY(FM) Tazewell VA
WPJP(FM) Port Washington WI
WDDC(FM) Portage WI
WRHN(FM) Rhinelander WI
WKBH-FM West Salem WI
WCLG-FM Morgantown WV
WDZN(FM) Romney WV
WDMX(FM) Vienna WV
KYOD(FM) Glendo WY

100.3 mhz
KICY-FM Nome AK
*KJNP-FM North Pole AK
WAOQ(FM) Brantley AL
WKGA(FM) Dadeville AL
WLAY-FM Tuscumbia AL
KDJE(FM) Jacksonville AR
KMRR(FM) Globe AZ
KJMB(FM) Blythe CA
KWPT(FM) Fortuna CA
KRQK(FM) Lompoc CA
KKBT(FM) Los Angeles CA
KMAK(FM) Orange Cove CA
KHGQ(FM) Quincy CA
KBRG(FM) San Jose CA
KIMN(FM) Denver CO
WBIG-FM Washington DC
WNCV(FM) Niceville FL
WRUM(FM) Orlando FL
WCTH(FM) Plantation Key FL
WOBB(FM) Tifton GA
KOKU(FM) Hagatna GU
KAPA(FM) Hilo HI
KCCN-FM Honolulu HI
KMXD(FM) Des Moines IA
KQXR(FM) Payette ID
KATZ-FM Alton IL
WIXY(FM) Champaign IL
WILV(FM) Chicago IL
WCCI(FM) Savanna IL
WLKI(FM) Angola IN
WIFE(FM) Connersville IN
KQLS(FM) Colby KS
KTCM(FM) Kingman KS
KDVV(FM) Topeka KS
*KSWC(FM) Winfield KS
WVVR(FM) Hopkinsville KY
KRRV-FM Alexandria LA
KLRZ(FM) Larose LA
WKIT-FM Brewer ME
WNIC(FM) Dearborn MI
WGRY-FM Grayling MI
KJZI(FM) Minneapolis MN
KSNR(FM) Thief River Falls MN
*KCVJ(FM) Osceola MO
KURM-FM South West City MO
KUKU-FM Willow Springs MO
WNSL(FM) Laurel MS
KLSK(FM) Great Falls MT
WLGP(FM) Harkers Island NC
WVBZ(FM) High Point NC
KZEN(FM) Central City NE
WHEB(FM) Portsmouth NH
WHTZ(FM) Newark NJ
KPEK(FM) Albuquerque NM
KWAW(FM) Garapan-Saipan NP
WDHI(FM) Delhi NY
WBGJ(FM) Sylvan Beach NY
WKBE(FM) Warrensburg NY
WCLT-FM Newark OH
*KJCM(FM) Snyder OK
KCXR(FM) Taft OK
KRWQ(FM) Gold Hill OR
KKRZ(FM) Portland OR
WHGL-FM Canton PA
WGYY(FM) Meadville PA
WPHI-FM Media PA
WIVA-FM Aguadilla PR
WKKB(FM) Middletown RI
WSEA(FM) Atlantic Beach SC
WORG(FM) Elloree SC
KFXS(FM) Rapid City SD
WNOX(FM) Oak Ridge TN
KTEX(FM) Brownsville TX
KJKK(FM) Dallas TX

KILT-FM Houston TX
KOMX(FM) Pampa TX
KCYY(FM) San Antonio TX
KMMX(FM) Tahoka TX
KXAL-FM Tatum TX
KSFI(FM) Salt Lake City UT
WARV-FM Petersburg VA
KWIQ-FM Moses Lake WA
WNCY-FM Neenah-Menasha WI
WAFD(FM) Webster Springs WV
KZMQ-FM Greybull WY

100.5 mhz
KBFX(FM) Anchorage AK
WLDA(FM) Fort Rucker AL
WRAX(FM) Helena AL
KDEZ(FM) Jonesboro AR
KZHE(FM) Stamps AR
KMQA(FM) East Porterville CA
KTDE(FM) Gualala CA
KMEN(FM) Mendota CA
KPSI-FM Palm Springs CA
KZZO(FM) Sacramento CA
KXDZ(FM) Templeton CA
KRSJ(FM) Durango CO
KCUF(FM) El Jebel CO
WRCH(FM) New Britain CT
WOYS(FM) Apalachicola FL
WHHZ(FM) Newberry FL
WWWQ(FM) College Park GA
WXRS-FM Swainsboro GA
KDEC-FM Decorah IA
*KBYI(FM) Rexburg ID
KQZB(FM) Troy ID
WRVY-FM Henry IL
WYMG(FM) Jacksonville IL
WWKI(FM) Kokomo IN
WSJD(FM) Princeton IN
WLUE(FM) Louisville KY
WXQL(FM) Carrollton MI
WTRV(FM) Walker MI
*WSCN(FM) Cloquet MN
KXAC(FM) Saint James MN
KSWF(FM) Aurora MO
KKCA(FM) Fulton MO
KMEM-FM Memphis MO
WBLE(FM) Batesville MS
WRTM-FM Port Gibson MS
KJJM(FM) Baker MT
WXXK(FM) Lebanon NH
KSFX(FM) Roswell NM
KKJI(FM) Henderson NV
WVOR-FM Rochester NY
WOMP-FM Bellaire OH
WKXA(FM) Findlay OH
KATT-FM Oklahoma City OK
KCGR(FM) Cottage Grove OR
KQFM(FM) Hermiston OR
WYGL-FM Elizabethville PA
WJNG(FM) Johnsonburg PA
WCDW(FM) Susquehanna PA
WALC(FM) Charleston SC
WSSL-FM Gray Court SC
WHLZ(FM) Marion SC
KIKN-FM Salem SD
KQBB(FM) Center TX
KNNK(FM) Dimmitt TX
KMVL-FM Madisonville TX
KBDR(FM) Mirando City TX
WZEZ(FM) Goochland VA
WXMM(FM) Norfolk VA
WTLX(FM) Columbus WI
WKEE-FM Huntington WV
WDYK(FM) Ridgeley WV

100.7 mhz
KFMG(FM) Juneau AK
KBBQ-FM Fort Smith AR
KAWW-FM Heber Springs AR
KJIK(FM) Duncan AZ
KSLX-FM Scottsdale AZ
KIBS(FM) Bishop CA
KTHU(FM) Corning CA
KATJ-FM George CA
KPRC-FM Salinas CA
KFMB-FM San Diego CA
KVVZ(FM) San Rafael CA
KHAY(FM) Ventura CA

KMOZ-FM Grand Junction CO
KGFT(FM) Pueblo CO
WHYI-FM Fort Lauderdale FL
WBWT(FM) Midway FL
WJLQ(FM) Pensacola FL
WMTX(FM) Tampa FL
WKQL(FM) Brunswick GA
WEAM-FM Buena Vista GA
WLRR(FM) Milledgeville GA
*KJYL(FM) Eagle Grove IA
KKRQ(FM) Iowa City IA
KISY(FM) Gooding ID
KIBG(FM) Wallace ID
WRXQ(FM) Coal City IL
WVMG(FM) Normal IL
WBYT(FM) Elkhart IN
WMGI(FM) Terre Haute IN
KHOK(FM) Hoisington KS
WKLX(FM) Beaver Dam KY
WCYO(FM) Irvine KY
WYPY(FM) Baton Rouge LA
KZBL(FM) Natchitoches LA
WZLX(FM) Boston MA
WZBA(FM) Westminster MD
WTBM(FM) Mexico ME
WOBE(FM) Crystal Falls MI
WKVK(FM) Honor MI
WITL-FM Lansing MI
WWTH(FM) Oscoda MI
KIKV-FM Sauk Centre MN
KGMO(FM) Cape Girardeau MO
KMZU(FM) Carrollton MO
KBZI(FM) Deerfield MO
KFNS-FM Troy MO
WDMS(FM) Greenville MS
KXLB(FM) Livingston MT
WZJS(FM) Banner Elk NC
WRVA-FM Rocky Mount NC
KDJZ(FM) Harwood ND
*KGBI-FM Omaha NE
WZXL(FM) Wildwood NJ
KLVF(FM) Las Vegas NM
KXXQ(FM) Milan NM
WOTT(FM) Henderson NY
WHUD(FM) Peekskill NY
KRZQ-FM Sparks NV
*WKVU(FM) Utica NY
WMMS(FM) Cleveland OH
*WEEC(FM) Springfield OH
KTFR(FM) Chelsea OK
KMGX(FM) Bend OR
KPPT-FM Toledo OR
WLEV(FM) Allentown PA
*WCOG-FM Galeton PA
WZPT(FM) New Kensington PA
WXYX(FM) Bayamon PR
WGTN-FM Andrews SC
KMLO(FM) Lowry SD
WBGQ(FM) Bulls Gap TN
WUSY(FM) Cleveland TN
WYDL(FM) Middleton TN
KFGL(FM) Abilene TX
KASE-FM Austin TX
KWRD-FM Highland Village TX
KPXI(FM) Overton TX
KKHT-FM Winnie TX
KEGH(FM) Brigham City UT
WFNR-FM Christiansburg VA
WQPO(FM) Harrisonburg VA
WRIC(FM) Richlands VA
WVAY(FM) Wilmington VT
KQBZ(FM) Seattle WA
KHSS(FM) Walla Walla WA
WBIZ-FM Eau Claire WI
WKKV-FM Racine WI
KOLZ(FM) Cheyenne WY
KGWY(FM) Gillette WY

100.9 mhz
KCDV(FM) Cordova AK
KAKN(FM) Naknek AK
*KFSK(FM) Petersburg AK
WALX(FM) Selma AL
KDEL-FM Arkadelphia AR
KTCN(FM) Eureka Springs AR
KWKK(FM) Russellville AR
KHOM(FM) Salem AR
KZMK(FM) Sierra Vista AZ

KQSR(FM) Yuma AZ
KAEH(FM) Beaumont CA
KSSB(FM) Calipatria CA
KXTS(FM) Calistoga CA
KRAJ(FM) Johannesburg CA
KMIX(FM) Tracy CA
KNEC(FM) Yuma CO
WKNL(FM) New London CT
WXJZ(FM) Gainesville FL
WJAQ(FM) Marianna FL
WLYU(FM) Lyons GA
WPGA-FM Perry GA
WTHB-FM Waynesboro GA
WCJM-FM West Point GA
WHPO(FM) Hoopeston IL
WZUS(FM) Macon IL
WBZG(FM) Peru IL
WQFL(FM) Rockford IL
WBDC(FM) Huntingburg IN
WYJZ(FM) Lebanon IN
WPGW-FM Portland IN
KCLY(FM) Clay Center KS
WIZF(FM) Erlanger KY
WLSK(FM) Lebanon KY
KHLL(FM) Richwood LA
WRNX(FM) Amherst MA
WAAI(FM) Hurlock MD
WYNZ(FM) Westbrook ME
WWBR(FM) Big Rapids MI
*WICV(FM) East Jordan MI
WQXC-FM Otsego MI
WYLZ(FM) Pinconning MI
KOWZ-FM Blooming Prairie MN
WCMP-FM Pine City MN
KRRY(FM) Canton MO
KTUI-FM Sullivan MO
WJXN-FM Utica MS
WKBB(FM) West Point MS
WPZS(FM) Albemarle NC
WIFM-FM Elkin NC
WSTS(FM) Fairmont NC
WFMI(FM) Southern Shores NC
KAUJ(FM) Grafton ND
KEJL(FM) Eunice NM
WKLI-FM Albany NY
WPGI(FM) Horseheads NY
WKRL-FM North Syracuse NY
WCDO-FM Sidney NY
WBNO-FM Bryan OH
WMJK(FM) Clyde OH
WJAW-FM McConnelsville OH
WXIZ(FM) Waverly OH
KGLC(FM) Miami OK
KPNC-FM Ponca City OK
KXOJ-FM Sapulpa OK
*KBUG(FM) Malin OR
WAYC(FM) Bedford PA
WVLY-FM Milton PA
WRKT(FM) North East PA
WPAL-FM Ridgeville SC
WVHR(FM) Huntingdon TN
KXGL(FM) Amarillo TX
KIXC-FM Quanah TX
KEPG(FM) Victoria TX
KWSA(FM) Price UT
WIQO-FM Covington VA
WNNT-FM Warsaw VA
WWFY(FM) Berlin VT
KARY-FM Grandview WA
WRCO-FM Richland Center WI
WKOY-FM Princeton WV
WMXE(FM) South Charleston WV
WZST(FM) Westover WV
KTED(FM) Douglas WY

101.1 mhz
KAKQ-FM Fairbanks AK
KRXX(FM) Kodiak AK
WYDE-FM Cullman AL
WZTZ(FM) Elba AL
WFNU(FM) Repton AL
KWBF(FM) North Little Rock AR
*KLRC(FM) Siloam Springs AR
KRRK(FM) Lake Havasu City AZ
KNRJ(FM) Payson AZ
KHYL(FM) Auburn CA

KWYE(FM) Fresno CA
KRTH(FM) Los Angeles CA
KWCA(FM) Weaverville CA
KOSI(FM) Denver CO
WWDC-FM Washington DC
WJRR(FM) Cocoa Beach FL
WAVV(FM) Marco FL
WYOO(FM) Springfield FL
WTGA-FM Thomaston GA
WAFT(FM) Valdosta GA
KLHI(FM) Lahaina HI
KXIA(FM) Marshalltown IA
KMCL-FM McCall ID
WKQX(FM) Chicago IL
WVRV(FM) East St. Louis IL
WVEL-FM Glasford IL
WLZQ(FM) South Whitley IN
KEOJ(FM) Caney KS
KFNF(FM) Oberlin KS
WSGS(FM) Hazard KY
WUBT(FM) Russellville KY
KBON(FM) Mamou LA
WNOE-FM New Orleans LA
KRMD-FM Shreveport LA
WTWV(FM) Mashpee MA
WQMR(FM) Snow Hill MD
WWPN(FM) Westernport MD
WRIF(FM) Detroit MI
WUPY(FM) Ontonagon MI
WQON(FM) Roscommon MI
KBHP(FM) Bemidji MN
KLQL(FM) Luverne MN
KHME(FM) Winona MN
KCFX(FM) Harrisonville MO
WLIN-FM Durant MS
KZMT(FM) Helena MT
WQZL(FM) Belhaven NC
WZTK(FM) Burlington NC
KQDJ-FM Valley City ND
KDSR(FM) Williston ND
KLIR(FM) Columbus NE
WGIR-FM Manchester NH
KVLC(FM) Hatch NM
KSFQ(FM) White Rock NM
KCNM-FM Garapan-Saipan NP
KPKK(FM) Amargosa Valley NV
WBUG-FM Fort Plain NY
WCBS-FM New York NY
WWCD(FM) Grove City OH
WHOT-FM Youngstown OH
KWOX(FM) Woodward OK
KUFO-FM Portland OR
KAVJ(FM) Sutherlin OR
WBEB(FM) Philadelphia PA
WGMR(FM) Tyrone PA
WRIO(FM) Ponce PR
WROQ(FM) Anderson SC
WLVH(FM) Hardeeville SC
KDDX(FM) Spearfish SD
KJMS(FM) Memphis TN
WRR(FM) Dallas TX
KONO-FM Helotes TX
KLOL(FM) Houston TX
KONE(FM) Lubbock TX
KNVO-FM Port Isabel TX
KPLD(FM) Kanab UT
KBER(FM) Ogden UT
WDYL(FM) Chester VA
KEYF-FM Cheney WA
KOHO-FM Leavenworth WA
WVRE(FM) Dickeyville WI
WIXX(FM) Green Bay WI
WHSM-FM Hayward WI
KPIN(FM) Pinedale WY

101.3 mhz
KGOT(FM) Anchorage AK
WAGF-FM Dothan AL
WBFA(FM) Smiths AL
KARV-FM Ola AR
KPBQ-FM Pine Bluff AR
KATY-FM Idyllwild CA
KSTT-FM Los Osos-Baywood Park CA
KIOI(FM) San Francisco CA
KIQX(FM) Durango CO
WKCI-FM Hamden CT
WNCL(FM) Milford DE

U.S. FM Stations by Frequency

WKYZ(FM) Key Colony Beach FL
WHLG(FM) Port St. Lucie FL
WTMG(FM) Williston FL
WQIL(FM) Chauncey GA
KSIB-FM Creston IA
KKYY(FM) Whiting IA
KUUL(FM) East Moline IL
WMCI(FM) Mattoon IL
WVIL(FM) Virginia IL
WFMG(FM) Richmond IN
*WBAA-FM West Lafayette IN
KFDI-FM Wichita KS
WMJM(FM) Jeffersontown KY
WEZG(FM) Sturgis KY
KKGB(FM) Sulphur LA
WKCG(FM) Augusta ME
WBFX(FM) Grand Rapids MI
WSUE(FM) Sault Ste. Marie MI
KDWB-FM Richfield MN
KTXR(FM) Springfield MO
WMUT(FM) Grenada MS
WJDQ(FM) Meridian MS
WBBV(FM) Vicksburg MS
KRYK(FM) Chinook MT
KIKC-FM Forsyth MT
WWQQ-FM Wilmington NC
KOLT-FM Bridgeport NE
KLZA(FM) Falls City NE
WYKR-FM Haverhill NH
KJFA(FM) Albuquerque NM
KRNG(FM) Fallon NV
WBRV-FM Boonville NY
WCPV(FM) Essex NY
WRMM-FM Rochester NY
WQAR(FM) Stillwater NY
WNCO-FM Ashland OH
WAGX(FM) Manchester OH
KLAW(FM) Lawton OK
KMCO(FM) McAlester OK
WROZ(FM) Lancaster PA
WGGY(FM) Scranton PA
WWDM(FM) Sumter SC
WCMT-FM South Fulton TN
WECO-FM Wartburg TN
KOXE(FM) Brownwood TX
KMMZ(FM) Crane TX
KNCN(FM) Sinton TX
WWDE-FM Hampton VA
WWKS(FM) Cruz Bay VI
KGDN(FM) Pasco WA
WBRB(FM) Buckhannon WV

101.5 mhz
WQEM(FM) Columbiana AL
KBGR(FM) Beebe AR
KMLK(FM) El Dorado AR
KAVH(FM) Eudora AR
KLEZ(FM) Malvern AR
KZON(FM) Phoenix AZ
KIXF(FM) Baker CA
KGFM(FM) Bakersfield CA
KEKA-FM Eureka CA
KMJE(FM) Gridley CA
*KAMB(FM) Merced CA
*KRVH(FM) Rio Vista CA
KGB-FM San Diego CA
KTKE(FM) Truckee CA
WLYF(FM) Miami FL
WTKX-FM Pensacola FL
WXSR(FM) Quincy FL
WPOI(FM) Saint Petersburg FL
WSOL-FM Brunswick GA
WKHX-FM Marietta GA
KAOY(FM) Kealakekua HI
KKSI(FM) Eddyville IA
KCVI(FM) Blackfoot ID
KATW(FM) Lewiston ID
WBNQ(FM) Bloomington IL
WCIL-FM Carbondale IL
WKKG(FM) Columbus IN
*WBGW(FM) Fort Branch IN
WNSN(FM) South Bend IN
KIKS-FM Iola KS
KSLS(FM) Liberal KS
KMKF(FM) Manhattan KS
WLRO(FM) Richmond KY
WRZI(FM) Vine Grove KY

WYNK-FM Baton Rouge LA
WMJZ-FM Gaylord MI
WJNR-FM Iron Mountain MI
WMTE-FM Manistee MI
WWBN(FM) Tuscola MI
KFGI(FM) Crosby MN
KRJM(FM) Mahnomen MN
KCGN-FM Ortonville MN
KRRW(FM) Saint James MN
KPLA(FM) Columbia MO
WWUN-FM Clarksdale MS
WHDZ(FM) Buxton NC
WRAL(FM) Raleigh NC
KSSS(FM) Bismarck ND
KROR(FM) Hastings NE
WWHQ(FM) Meredith NH
WKXW-FM Trenton NJ
KRMQ-FM Clovis NM
KWRP(FM) Pecos NM
KIDX(FM) Ruidoso NM
WRCD(FM) Canton NY
WXHC(FM) Homer NY
WMXO(FM) Olean NY
WPDH(FM) Poughkeepsie NY
*WCWT-FM Centerville OH
WRYV(FM) Gallipolis OH
WRVF(FM) Toledo OH
*WOBN(FM) Westerville OH
KTBT(FM) Collinsville OK
KFLY(FM) Corvallis OR
WDKC(FM) Covington PA
WORD-FM Pittsburgh PA
WFYN(FM) Waynesboro PA
WKSA-FM Isabela PR
WWBB(FM) Providence RI
*KVCX(FM) Gregory SD
WVFB(FM) Celina TN
WNWS-FM Jackson TN
WQUT(FM) Johnson City TN
WFTZ(FM) Manchester TN
WTPR-FM McKinnon TN
WJOR-FM Saint Joseph TN
KROX-FM Buda TX
KSTB(FM) Crystal Beach TX
KSNY-FM Snyder TX
KNUE(FM) Tyler TX
KEGA(FM) Oakley UT
WBQB(FM) Fredericksburg VA
WZZI(FM) Vinton VA
WEXP(FM) Brandon VT
WRSY(FM) Marlboro VT
KPLZ(FM) Seattle WA
WIBA-FM Madison WI

101.7 mhz
KPEN-FM Soldotna AK
*KSTK(FM) Wrangell AK
WBEI(FM) Reform AL
WMXN-FM Stevenson AL
KBYB(FM) Hope AR
KVLO(FM) Humnoke AR
KVOM-FM Morrilton AR
KCTT-FM Yellville AR
KKYZ(FM) Sierra Vista AZ
KQAZ(FM) Springerville-Eagar AZ
KXSB(FM) Big Bear Lake CA
KCDU(FM) Carmel CA
KSBL(FM) Carpinteria CA
KRER(FM) Hamilton City CA
KKIQ(FM) Livermore CA
KXFX(FM) Santa Rosa CA
KTUN(FM) Eagle CO
KBRU-FM Fort Morgan CO
WZEB(FM) Ocean View DE
WTOT-FM Graceville FL
WDVH-FM Trenton FL
WCZR(FM) Vero Beach FL
WNUQ(FM) Albany GA
WYUM(FM) Mount Vernon GA
WTHO-FM Thomson GA
WRBV(FM) Warner Robins GA
KBKB-FM Fort Madison IA
KAYL-FM Storm Lake IA
WRCV(FM) Dixon IL
WGEL(FM) Greenville IL
WTYE(FM) Robinson IL
WURK(FM) Elwood IL

WLDE(FM) Fort Wayne IN
WIVR(FM) Kentland IN
KVOE-FM Emporia KS
KREJ(FM) Medicine Lodge KS
WKYM(FM) Monticello KY
WJZO(FM) Shelbyville KY
WFNX(FM) Lynn MA
WBRK-FM Pittsfield MA
WFZX(FM) Searsport ME
*WPRJ(FM) Coleman MI
WHZZ(FM) Lansing MI
WMRR(FM) Muskegon Heights MI
KLDJ(FM) Duluth MN
KRCH(FM) Rochester MN
WHMH-FM Sauk Rapids MN
KGOZ(FM) Gallatin MO
KHST(FM) Lamar MO
KLPW-FM Union MO
WYOY(FM) Gluckstadt MS
KTNY(FM) Libby MT
WVRR(FM) Newport NH
WJKS(FM) Canton NJ
KLEA-FM Lovington NM
KAJZ(FM) Rio Rancho NM
KCLS(FM) Ely NV
WLOF(FM) Attica NY
WFLK(FM) Geneva NY
WENU-FM Hudson Falls NY
WLTB(FM) Johnson City NY
WSCP-FM Pulaski NY
WBEA(FM) Southold NY
WJER-FM Dover OH
WNKO(FM) Newark OH
WKSW(FM) Urbana OH
KEOK(FM) Tahlequah OK
KLRR(FM) Redmond OR
WCCL(FM) Central City PA
WMVL(FM) Linesville PA
WKZQ-FM Myrtle Beach SC
WMGL(FM) Ravenel SC
WJSQ(FM) Athens TN
WKOM(FM) Columbia TN
WORM-FM Savannah TN
WJLE-FM Smithville TN
KTCY(FM) Azle TX
KXGJ(FM) Bay City TX
KEKO(FM) Hebronville TX
KSAM-FM Huntsville TX
KAYD-FM Silsbee TX
KLTD(FM) Temple TX
WLQM-FM Franklin VA
WKWI(FM) Kilmarnock VA
WJJX(FM) Lynchburg VA
WWBU(FM) Radford VA
WEVI(FM) Frederiksted VI
WCVT(FM) Stowe VT
KMNA(FM) Prosser WA
WELD-FM Petersburg WV
KDNO(FM) Thermopolis WY
KZEW(FM) Wheatland WY

101.9 mhz
WHHY-FM Montgomery AL
KIYS(FM) Jonesboro AR
KMXF(FM) Lowell AR
KLXQ(FM) Mountain Pine AR
KOQO-FM Fresno CA
KSCA(FM) Glendale CA
KCCL-FM Shingle Springs CA
KKCS-FM Colorado Springs CO
WJHM(FM) Daytona Beach FL
WWGR(FM) Fort Myers FL
WBGE(FM) Bainbridge GA
WAZX-FM Cleveland GA
WPNG(FM) Pearson GA
WTUN(FM) Ringgold GA
WJFL(FM) Tennille GA
KTKB(FM) Hagatna GU
KUCD(FM) Pearl City HI
*KNWS-FM Waterloo IA
KDBI(FM) Emmett ID
WTMX(FM) Skokie IL
WQQL(FM) Springfield IL
WKLU(FM) Brownsburg IN
WARU-FM Roann IN
KKQY(FM) Hill City KS
WQXQ(FM) Central City KY

KNOE-FM Monroe LA
WLMG(FM) New Orleans LA
WCIB(FM) Falmouth MA
WLIF(FM) Baltimore MD
WPOR(FM) Portland ME
WOZI(FM) Presque Isle ME
*WDET-FM Detroit MI
WKQS-FM Negaunee MI
WLDR-FM Traverse City MI
KQKK(FM) Walker MN
WFTA(FM) Fulton MS
WZYQ(FM) Mound Bayou MS
KRSQ(FM) Laurel MT
WBAV-FM Gastonia NC
WIKS(FM) New Bern NC
KBTO(FM) Bottineau ND
KKBX(FM) Fargo ND
KLTQ(FM) Lincoln NE
KTAO(FM) Taos NM
KWID(FM) Las Vegas NV
WZKZ(FM) Alfred NY
WJIV(FM) Cherry Valley NY
WHUG(FM) Jamestown NY
WQCD(FM) New York NY
WKRQ(FM) Cincinnati OH
WRBP(FM) Hubbard OH
KTST(FM) Oklahoma City OK
KCMX-FM Ashland OR
KINK(FM) Portland OR
KMMG(FM) Weston OR
WAVT-FM Pottsville PA
WZAR(FM) Ponce PR
KTWB(FM) Sioux Falls SD
KATP(FM) Amarillo TX
KZTR(FM) Franklin TX
KSML-FM Huntington TX
KACQ(FM) Lometa TX
KBUS(FM) Paris TX
KWFR(FM) San Angelo TX
KQXT(FM) San Antonio TX
KPQP(FM) Ogden UT
WHTE(FM) Ruckersville VA
WKSK-FM South Hill VA
KTSL(FM) Medical Lake WA
WDEZ(FM) Wausau WI
WVOW-FM Logan WV
WVAQ(FM) Morgantown WV
KIGN(FM) Burns WY

102.1 mhz
KDBZ(FM) Anchorage AK
WQUA(FM) Citronelle AL
WDRM(FM) Decatur AL
KENA-FM Mena AR
KOKY(FM) Sherwood AR
KCMT(FM) Oro Valley AZ
KAHM(FM) Prescott AZ
KPRI(FM) Encinitas CA
KZPE(FM) Ford City CA
KRKC-FM King City CA
KCEZ(FM) Los Molinos CA
KDFC-FM San Francisco CA
KXDC(FM) Estes Park CO
WKLG(FM) Rock Harbor FL
WWAV-FM Santa Rosa Beach FL
WQLC(FM) Watertown FL
WWWD(FM) Bolingbroke GA
WGMG(FM) Crawford GA
WZAT(FM) Savannah GA
WZBN(FM) Sylvester GA
KTBH-FM Kurtistown HI
KUQQ(FM) Milford IA
KCHQ(FM) Driggs ID
WDNL(FM) Danville IL
WQLF(FM) Lena IL
WIBV(FM) Mount Vernon IL
WALS(FM) Oglesby IL
KZSN(FM) Hutchinson KS
WLJC(FM) Beattyville KY
WLLE(FM) Clinton KY
WKYL(FM) Lawrenceburg KY
KQIS(FM) Basile LA
KDKS-FM Blanchard LA
WAQY(FM) Springfield MA
WGUY(FM) Dexter ME
WLEW-FM Bad Axe MI
*WMUK(FM) Kalamazoo MI

KCAJ(FM) Roseau MN
KEEY-FM Saint Paul MN
KQRA(FM) Brookline MO
KSRC(FM) Kansas City MO
KJFM(FM) Louisiana MO
WMMZ(FM) Meridian MS
WRQO(FM) Monticello MS
KBUD(FM) Sardis MS
*KBMC(FM) Bozeman MT
WJMH(FM) Reidsville NC
KPNY(FM) Alliance NE
WSAK(FM) Hampton NH
KTRA-FM Farmington NM
KRNV-FM Reno NV
*WJCA(FM) Albion NY
WDNB(FM) Jeffersonville NY
WZUN(FM) Phoenix NY
WAVR(FM) Waverly NY
WDOK(FM) Cleveland OH
WIMT(FM) Lima OH
WRVB(FM) Marietta OH
KHKC-FM Atoka OK
KTFX-FM Warner OK
WOWQ(FM) DuBois PA
WIOQ(FM) Philadelphia PA
WMXT(FM) Pamplico SC
KFMH(FM) Belle Fourche SD
WLCT(FM) Lafayette TN
WWST(FM) Sevierville TN
KPRR(FM) El Paso TX
KDGE(FM) Fort Worth TX
KMJQ(FM) Houston TX
KFZX(FM) Monahans TX
KBUC(FM) Raymondville TX
WRXL(FM) Richmond VA
WWHV(FM) Virginia Beach VA
WCVR-FM Randolph VT
KSWW(FM) Montesano WA
KPQ-FM Wenatchee WA
WRKU(FM) Forestville WI
WLUM-FM Milwaukee WI

102.3 mhz
*KHNS(FM) Haines AK
WAMI-FM Opp AL
WELR-FM Roanoke AL
KTRQ(FM) Colt AR
KCJC(FM) Dardanelle AR
KQEW(FM) Fordyce AR
KWRQ(FM) Clifton AZ
KJJJ(FM) Lake Havasu City AZ
KZXY-FM Apple Valley CA
KJLH-FM Compton CA
KBLO(FM) Corcoran CA
KJJZ(FM) Indio CA
KJSN(FM) Modesto CA
KYOE(FM) Point Arena CA
KNTK(FM) Weed CA
KSMT(FM) Breckenridge CO
KVLE-FM Gunnison CO
KJEB(FM) Strasburg CO
KSPK(FM) Walsenburg CO
WXLM(FM) Stonington CT
WTRS(FM) Dunnellon FL
WMBX(FM) Jensen Beach FL
WEKL(FM) Augusta GA
WLKQ-FM Buford GA
WWLD(FM) Cairo GA
WKZR(FM) Milledgeville GA
WQTU(FM) Rome GA
KCZQ(FM) Cresco IA
KXGE(FM) Dubuque IA
KZSR(FM) Onawa IA
KICR(FM) Coeur d'Alene ID
WRMJ(FM) Aledo IL
WYCA(FM) Crete IL
WEBQ-FM Eldorado IL
WDQX(FM) Morton IL
WRHL-FM Rochelle IL
WKJT(FM) Teutopolis IL
WXLC(FM) Waukegan IL
WXTW(FM) Auburn IN
WLHM(FM) Logansport IN
WCBK-FM Martinsville IN
WOZW(FM) New Carlisle IN
WBTO-FM Petersburg IN
WCYN-FM Cynthiana KY

U.S. FM Stations by Frequency

WUGO(FM) Grayson KY
WXMA(FM) Louisville KY
WCLU-FM Munfordville KY
WLLK-FM Somerset KY
KBCE(FM) Boyce LA
WCDJ(FM) Truro MA
WMMJ(FM) Bethesda MD
WCXX(FM) Madawaska ME
WYBR(FM) Big Rapids MI
WHKB(FM) Houghton MI
WGRT(FM) Port Huron MI
*WTHN(FM) Sault Ste. Marie MI
KRCQ(FM) Detroit Lakes MN
KBXR(FM) Columbia MO
KDEX-FM Dexter MO
KJPW-FM Waynesville MO
WGCM-FM Gulfport MS
WIQQ(FM) Leland MS
WWSL(FM) Philadelphia MS
WKZU(FM) Ripley MS
WECR-FM Beech Mountain NC
WKIX(FM) Goldsboro NC
WFNC-FM Lumberton NC
WPTM(FM) Roanoke Rapids NC
KRNY(FM) Kearney NE
WWHK(FM) Concord NH
WXXS(FM) Lancaster NH
WAIV(FM) Cape May NJ
WSUS(FM) Franklin NJ
KKYC(FM) Clovis NM
KVUW(FM) Wendover NV
WBAB(FM) Babylon NY
WKKF(FM) Ballston Spa NY
WISY(FM) Canandaigua NY
WRGR(FM) Tupper Lake NY
WFXN-FM Galion OH
WPOS-FM Holland OH
WKLN(FM) Wilmington OH
KKEN(FM) Duncan OK
KRTQ(FM) Sand Springs OK
KWDQ(FM) Woodward OK
KEHK(FM) Brownsville OR
KCRX-FM Seaside OR
WCAT-FM Carlisle PA
WQHZ(FM) Erie PA
WDMT(FM) Pittston PA
WMIO(FM) Cabo Rojo PR
WRML(FM) Pageland SC
WMFX(FM) Saint Andrews SC
KKQQ(FM) Volga SD
WZDQ(FM) Humboldt TN
WGOW-FM Soddy-Daisy TN
KPEZ(FM) Austin TX
KXCT(FM) Coleman TX
KLJT(FM) Jacksonville TX
KKPN(FM) Rockport TX
KUVA(FM) Uvalde TX
KWFS-FM Wichita Falls TX
KDUT(FM) Randolph UT
WSUH(FM) Crozet VA
WDXC(FM) Pound VA
WLFE-FM Saint Albans VT
KYYT(FM) Goldendale WA
WQTC-FM Manitowoc WI
WVRQ-FM Viroqua WI
WAUH(FM) Wautoma WI
WHTL-FM Whitehall WI
WMTD-FM Hinton WV
WFBY(FM) Weston WV

102.5 mhz
KIAK-FM Fairbanks AK
WESP(FM) Dothan AL
WDXB(FM) Jasper AL
KPZK-FM Cabot AR
KAFN(FM) Gould AR
KNIX-FM Phoenix AZ
KCNQ(FM) Kernville CA
KDUQ(FM) Ludlow CA
KDON-FM Salinas CA
KSNI-FM Santa Maria CA
KSFM(FM) Woodland CA
KQZR(FM) Craig CO
KTRR(FM) Loveland CO
WHPT(FM) Sarasota FL
WPIJ(FM) Summerland Key FL
WAMJ(FM) Mableton GA

WEBL(FM) Warner Robins GA
WYNR(FM) Waycross GA
KSTZ(FM) Des Moines IA
KMGI(FM) Pocatello ID
KIBR(FM) Sandpoint ID
*WGNN(FM) Fisher IL
WJRE(FM) Galva IL
WQRJ(FM) Mitchell IN
WMDH-FM New Castle IN
KACY(FM) Arkansas City KS
KKCI(FM) Goodland KS
KBLS(FM) North Fort Riley KS
KKCV(FM) Rozel KS
WLTO(FM) Nicholasville KY
WFMF(FM) Baton Rouge LA
WCRB(FM) Waltham MA
WOLC(FM) Princess Anne MD
WQSS(FM) Camden ME
WIOG(FM) Bay City MI
WCMM(FM) Gulliver MI
WBZV(FM) Hudson MI
KMFX-FM Lake City MN
KQIC(FM) Willmar MN
KIXQ(FM) Joplin MO
KEZK-FM Saint Louis MO
KKDY(FM) West Plains MO
WJKX(FM) Ellisville MS
WAGR-FM Lexington MS
KMSO(FM) Missoula MT
WERX-FM Columbia NC
WMYI(FM) Hendersonville NC
WKXU(FM) Louisburg NC
WIOZ-FM Southern Pines NC
KDVL(FM) Devils Lake ND
KIOT(FM) Los Lunas NM
WBAZ(FM) Bridgehampton NY
WTSS(FM) Buffalo NY
WUMX(FM) Rome NY
WZOO-FM Edgewood OH
WHIZ-FM Zanesville OH
KTNT(FM) Eufaula OK
WDVE(FM) Pittsburgh PA
WRFY-FM Reading PA
WIAC(FM) San Juan PR
WXLY(FM) North Charleston SC
*KZSD-FM Martin SD
WOWF(FM) Crossville TN
WQZQ(FM) Dickson TN
KMKS(FM) Bay City TX
KTCX(FM) Beaumont TX
KBRQ(FM) Hillsboro TX
KZII-FM Lubbock TX
KHLE(FM) Mason TX
KKYR-FM Texarkana TX
KMAD-FM Whitesboro TX
WOLD-FM Marion VA
WUSQ-FM Winchester VA
KRAO-FM Colfax WA
KZOK-FM Seattle WA
*WNWC-FM Madison WI
KRBR(FM) Superior WI
KHOC(FM) Casper WY

102.7 mhz
KSRJ(FM) Juneau AK
WCKS-FM Fruithurst AL
KWLT(FM) North Crossett AR
KLSZ-FM Van Buren AR
KSSI(FM) China Lake CA
KALZ(FM) Fresno CA
KIIS-FM Los Angeles CA
*KLVB(FM) Red Bluff CA
KBIQ(FM) Manitou Springs CO
WPHK(FM) Blountstown FL
WRGO(FM) Cedar Key FL
WXHT(FM) Madison FL
WXBM-FM Milton FL
WMXJ(FM) Pompano Beach FL
WHKR(FM) Rockledge FL
WPMA(FM) Buckhead GA
WYSC(FM) McRae GA
WBDX(FM) Trenton GA
KDDB(FM) Waipahu HI
KYTC(FM) Northwood IA
WJEQ(FM) Macomb IL
WZZT(FM) Morrison IL
WVAZ(FM) Oak Park IL

WLEG(FM) Ligonier IN
WBOW-FM Terre Haute IN
KLDG(FM) Liberal KS
WVEK-FM Cumberland KY
WMJL(FM) Marion KY
WAKY-FM Springfield KY
WKWY(FM) Tompkinsville KY
KJNA-FM Jena LA
WQSR(FM) Baltimore MD
WHTD(FM) Mount Clemens MI
WMOM(FM) Pentwater MI
KQEG(FM) La Crescent MN
KTIG(FM) Pequot Lakes MN
*KNTN(FM) Thief River Falls MN
KQUL(FM) Lake Ozark MO
WCNG(FM) Murphy NC
WGNI(FM) Wilmington NC
KFRX(FM) Lincoln NE
WJSE(FM) Petersburg NJ
KSTJ(FM) Boulder City NV
WBDR(FM) Cape Vincent NY
WNEW(FM) New York NY
WRCI(FM) Webster NY
WEBN(FM) Cincinnati OH
WCPZ(FM) Sandusky OH
KJYO(FM) Oklahoma City OK
KCNA(FM) Cave Junction OR
KYTE(FM) Newport OR
WKSB(FM) Williamsport PA
WAKX(FM) Narragansett Pier RI
WPUB-FM Camden SC
WGOR(FM) New Ellenton SC
KYBB(FM) Canton SD
WEKX(FM) Jellico TN
WEGR(FM) Memphis TN
KTXZ-FM Jasper TX
KHXS(FM) Merkel TX
KSRX(FM) San Antonio TX
KBLZ(FM) Winona TX
KQMB(FM) Midvale UT
WSNZ(FM) Appomattox VA
WEQX(FM) Manchester VT
KORD-FM Richland WA
*WRVM(FM) Suring WI
WVSR-FM Charleston WV
WGYE(FM) Mannington WV

102.9 mhz
WKXX(FM) Attalla AL
WNPT-FM Linden AL
KHOZ-FM Harrison AR
KARN-FM Sheridan AR
KQST(FM) Sedona AZ
KBLX-FM Berkeley CA
KWTY(FM) Cartago CA
KIWI(FM) McFarland CA
KXLM(FM) Oxnard CA
KLQV(FM) San Diego CA
KWYL(FM) South Lake Tahoe CA
WDRC-FM Hartford CT
WMXQ(FM) Jacksonville FL
WJGO(FM) Tice FL
WMJE(FM) Clarkesville GA
WVRK(FM) Columbus GA
WPMX(FM) Statesboro GA
KISH(FM) Hagatna GU
KZIA(FM) Cedar Rapids IA
KTFG(FM) Sioux Rapids IA
KWYS-FM Island Park ID
KMVX(FM) Jerome ID
WSOY-FM Decatur IL
WMKB(FM) Earlville IL
WLME(FM) Cannelton IN
WXXB(FM) Delphi IN
WYGB(FM) Edinburgh IN
WXKE(FM) Huntington IN
KHUT(FM) Hutchinson KS
KIND-FM Independence KS
KQTP(FM) Saint Marys KS
WLKS-FM West Liberty KY
KMEZ(FM) Belle Chasse LA
KAJN-FM Crowley LA
KVMA-FM Shreveport LA
WPXC(FM) Hyannis MA
WKIK-FM California MD
WROG-FM Cumberland MD
WCRQ(FM) Dennysville ME

WBLM(FM) Portland ME
WWWW(FM) Ann Arbor MI
WFUR-FM Grand Rapids MI
WMKC(FM) Saint Ignace MI
WLTE-FM Minneapolis MN
KMFG(FM) Nashwauk MN
KEZS-FM Cape Girardeau MO
KMMO-FM Marshall MO
WMSI(FM) Jackson MS
KCTR-FM Billings MT
WLYT(FM) Hickory NC
WELS-FM Kinston NC
WWMY(FM) Raleigh NC
KWGO(FM) Burlington ND
KADL(FM) Imperial NE
KBRX-FM O'Neill NE
KNFT-FM Bayard NM
KIXN(FM) Hobbs NM
KAZX(FM) Kirtland NM
KLBU(FM) Pecos NM
WNCQ-FM Canton NY
*WMHR(FM) Syracuse NY
WCLX(FM) Westport NY
WDHT(FM) Springfield OH
KQIB(FM) Idabel OK
KYSF(FM) Bonanza OR
KSJJ(FM) Redmond OR
WOKW(FM) Curwensville PA
WMGK(FM) Philadelphia PA
WYFM(FM) Sharon PA
WDIN(FM) Camuy PR
WKQI(FM) Orangeburg SC
WWRK(FM) Scranton SC
KBWS-FM Sisseton SD
WBUZ(FM) La Vergne TN
KNDA(FM) Alice TX
KDMX(FM) Dallas TX
KLTN(FM) Houston TX
KITY(FM) Llano TX
WOWI(FM) Norfolk VA
*WIUJ(FM) Charlotte Amalie VI
KNBQ(FM) Centralia WA
KVAB(FM) Clarkston WA
WHQG(FM) Milwaukee WI
WBDL(FM) Reedsburg WI
WELC-FM Welch WV
KARS(FM) Laramie WY

103.1 mhz
KMXS(FM) Anchorage AK
KSBZ(FM) Sitka AK
WEUP-FM Moulton AL
KXSA-FM Dermott AR
KFFA-FM Helena AR
KRWA-FM Waldron AR
KFTT(FM) Bagdad AZ
KCDX(FM) Florence AZ
KKCY(FM) Colusa CA
KDLE(FM) Newport Beach CA
KAAT(FM) Oakhurst CA
KEZN(FM) Palm Desert CA
KLUN(FM) Paso Robles CA
KDLD(FM) Santa Monica CA
KTPI-FM Tehachapi CA
KVFG(FM) Victorville CA
KHRD(FM) Weaverville CA
KSPN-FM Aspen CO
KAVD(FM) Limon CO
WMXZ(FM) De Funiak Springs FL
WPBZ(FM) Indiantown FL
WFKZ(FM) Plantation Key FL
WAIB(FM) Tallahassee FL
WLOQ(FM) Winter Park FL
WFXA-FM Augusta GA
KDMG(FM) Burlington IA
KCDA(FM) Post Falls ID
WVIV-FM Highland Park IL
WAKO-FM Lawrenceville IL
WCSJ-FM Morris IL
WGFB(FM) Rockton IL
WKZS(FM) Covington IN
WHME(FM) South Bend IN
WXCH(FM) Versailles IN
WPKE-FM Coal Run KY
WGRK-FM Greensburg KY
WGBF-FM Henderson KY

WWLT(FM) Manchester KY
WRKA(FM) Saint Matthews KY
KQLQ(FM) Columbia LA
WRNR-FM Grasonville MD
WAFY-FM Middletown MD
WDME-FM Dover Foxcroft ME
WGDN-FM Gladwin MI
WQUS(FM) Lapeer MI
KFIL-FM Preston MN
WMBC(FM) Columbus MS
WOSM-FM Ocean Springs MS
*KVCM(FM) Helena MT
*WUAG(FM) Greensboro NC
WLHC(FM) Robbins NC
KRVX(FM) Wimbledon ND
KNCY-FM Auburn NE
KKJK(FM) Ravenna NE
KHQT(FM) Las Cruces NM
WHRL(FM) Albany NY
*WCIK(FM) Bath NY
WBZO(FM) Bay Shore NY
WTOJ(FM) Carthage NY
WGNY-FM Newburgh NY
WZOZ(FM) Oneonta NY
WVKO-FM Johnstown OH
WNDH(FM) Napoleon OH
WRAC(FM) West Union OH
KOFM(FM) Enid OK
KRSB-FM Roseburg OR
WFEZ(FM) Avoca PA
WQFX-FM Russell PA
WJHT(FM) State College PA
WANB-FM Waynesburg PA
WOMG(FM) Columbia SC
WRIX-FM Honea Path SC
WGZO(FM) Parris Island SC
WYAK-FM Surfside Beach SC
KJAM-FM Madison SD
WLLJ(FM) Etowah TN
WMXX-FM Jackson TN
WIKQ(FM) Tusculum TN
KRGN(FM) Amarillo TX
KKCN(FM) Ballinger TX
KSSM(FM) Copperas Cove TX
KPAS(FM) Fabens TX
KVJM(FM) Hearne TX
KTXX(FM) Karnes City TX
KMUL-FM Muleshoe TX
KDVE(FM) Pittsburg TX
KVWC-FM Vernon TX
KJQN(FM) Coalville UT
WWDW(FM) Alberta VA
WJMA-FM Culpeper VA
WRJT(FM) Royalton VT
KQBE(FM) Ellensburg WA
WOGB(FM) Kaukauna WI
WKCJ(FM) Lewisburg WV
WHBR-FM Parkersburg WV
KYDT(FM) Sundance WY

103.3 mhz
WMXS(FM) Montgomery AL
KIXB(FM) El Dorado AR
KWOZ(FM) Mountain View AR
KZKE(FM) Seligman AZ
KCEE(FM) Grass Valley CA
KZPO(FM) Lindsay CA
KATM(FM) Modesto CA
KVYB(FM) Santa Barbara CA
*KSCU(FM) Santa Clara CA
KTMQ(FM) Temecula CA
KUKI-FM Ukiah CA
*KPRU(FM) Delta CO
WQQQ(FM) Sharon CT
WVYB(FM) Holly Hill FL
WVEE(FM) Atlanta GA
WWSN(FM) Waycross GA
KSHK(FM) Kekaha HI
WJOD(FM) Asbury IA
KAZR(FM) Pella IA
KTFC(FM) Sioux City IA
KSAS-FM Caldwell ID
KFTZ(FM) Idaho Falls ID
WIVQ(FM) Spring Valley IL
WRZX(FM) Indianapolis IN
WAXL(FM) Santa Claus IN
KJLS(FM) Hays KS

U.S. FM Stations by Frequency

WXZZ(FM) Georgetown KY
WCDV(FM) Hammond LA
KBIU(FM) Lake Charles LA
WODS(FM) Boston MA
WMCM(FM) Rockland ME
WKFR-FM Battle Creek MI
WFXD(FM) Marquette MI
WQLB(FM) Tawas City MI
*KUMD-FM Duluth MN
KZCR(FM) Fergus Falls MN
KPRS(FM) Kansas City MO
KLOU(FM) Saint Louis MO
WZKR(FM) Decatur MS
KDTR(FM) Florence MT
WKVS(FM) Lenoir NC
WMGV(FM) Newport NC
WPRB(FM) Princeton NJ
KDRF(FM) Albuquerque NM
WEDG(FM) Buffalo NY
WMXW(FM) Vestal NY
*WCRF(FM) Cleveland OH
*WDEQ-FM De Graff OH
WMLX(FM) Saint Mary's OH
KJSR(FM) Tulsa OK
KKCW(FM) Beaverton OR
WYTR(FM) Brookville PA
WARM-FM York PA
WVJP-FM Caguas PR
WJMX-FM Cheraw SC
WOLT(FM) Greer SC
WKDF(FM) Nashville TN
KESN(FM) Allen TX
KDFM(FM) Falfurrias TX
KJOJ-FM Freeport TX
KCRS-FM Midland TX
KJCS(FM) Nacogdoches TX
WAKG(FM) Danville VA
WLTK(FM) New Market VA
WESR-FM Onley-Onancock VA
WWMP(FM) Waterbury VT
KWLN(FM) Wilson Creek WA
WGLX-FM Wisconsin Rapids WI
WTCR-FM Huntington WV

103.5 mhz
KWVV-FM Homer AK
WMXV(FM) Russellville AL
KZYQ(FM) Lake Village AR
KLNZ(FM) Glendale AZ
KTEA(FM) Cambria CA
KOST(FM) Los Angeles CA
KHSL-FM Paradise CA
KBMB(FM) Sacramento CA
KRAY-FM Salinas CA
KRFX(FM) Denver CO
WGMS-FM Washington DC
WJKI(FM) Bethany Beach DE
WFUS(FM) Bradenton FL
WAKT-FM Callaway FL
WMIB(FM) Fort Lauderdale FL
WJAD(FM) Leesburg GA
KNEI-FM Waukon IA
WKSC-FM Chicago IL
WXLT(FM) Christopher IL
WIKK(FM) Newton IL
WAWC(FM) Syracuse IN
KQLA(FM) Ogden KS
WASE(FM) Radcliff KY
KLAA(FM) Tioga LA
*WCCH(FM) Holyoke MA
WMUZ(FM) Detroit MI
WTCM-FM Traverse City MI
KUAL-FM Brainerd MN
KYSM-FM Mankato MN
KWXD(FM) Asbury MO
KLUE(FM) Poplar Bluff MO
WRBO(FM) Como MS
KZMY(FM) Bozeman MT
WRCQ(FM) Dunn NC
KZZY(FM) Devils Lake ND
KXNP(FM) North Platte NE
KISF(FM) Las Vegas NV
WQBJ(FM) Cobleskill NY
WKTU(FM) Lake Success NY
WUUF(FM) Sodus NY
WJQZ(FM) Wellsville NY
WGRR(FM) Hamilton OH

WJZA(FM) Lancaster OH
KVSP(FM) Anadarko OK
KLDZ(FM) Medford OR
KWHT(FM) Pendleton OR
WKAB(FM) Berwick PA
WOGH(FM) Burgettstown PA
WLAK(FM) Huntingdon PA
WEZL(FM) Charleston SC
WZSN(FM) Greenwood SC
WIMZ-FM Knoxville TN
KJNZ(FM) Hereford TX
KZRB(FM) New Boston TX
KBPA(FM) San Marcos TX
KAMZ(FM) Tahoka TX
KRSP-FM Salt Lake City UT
*WMRY(FM) Crozet VA
WZVA(FM) Marion VA
WAXJ(FM) Frederiksted VI

103.7 mhz
WAAO-FM Andalusia AL
WQEN(FM) Gadsden AL
KABZ(FM) Little Rock AR
KODS(FM) Carnelian Bay CA
KMLA(FM) El Rio CA
*KLVG(FM) Garberville CA
KRZR(FM) Hanford CA
KIQQ-FM Newberry Springs CA
KPLN(FM) San Diego CA
KKSF(FM) San Francisco CA
KBNG(FM) Ridgway CO
WRUF-FM Gainesville FL
WQOL(FM) Vero Beach FL
WULS(FM) Broxton GA
WVKX(FM) Irwinton GA
WBMZ(FM) Metter GA
WPUP(FM) Royston GA
KNUQ(FM) Paauilo HI
KLKK(FM) Clear Lake IA
WLLR-FM Davenport IA
KXKT(FM) Glenwood IA
KSKI-FM Sun Valley ID
KKTN(FM) Victor ID
WDBR(FM) Springfield IL
*WFIU(FM) Bloomington IN
WHZR(FM) Royal Center IN
KEYN-FM Wichita KS
WCBJ(FM) Campton KY
WPTQ(FM) Cave City KY
WKED-FM Frankfort KY
WFGE(FM) Murray KY
KBTT(FM) Haughton LA
WXCY(FM) Havre de Grace MD
WCZE(FM) Harbor Beach MI
WSPZ-FM Hartford MI
WHYB(FM) Menominee MI
KKBJ-FM Bemidji MN
KLZZ(FM) Waite Park MN
KJEL(FM) Lebanon MO
WUSW(FM) Hattiesburg MS
KBBB(FM) Billings MT
WSOC-FM Charlotte NC
WBNU(FM) Shallotte NC
WRHD(FM) Williamston NC
WKNE(FM) Keene NH
WPKQ(FM) North Conway NH
WMGM(FM) Atlantic City NJ
WNNJ-FM Newton NJ
KNMZ(FM) Alamogordo NM
KYVA-FM Grants NM
KPZA-FM Jal NM
WQNY(FM) Ithaca NY
WCKY-FM Tiffin OH
KESC(FM) Wilburton OK
KXPC(FM) Lebanon OR
WRTS(FM) Erie PA
WCXR(FM) Lewisburg PA
WEEO-FM McConnellsburg PA
WXLX(FM) Lajas PR
WEEI-FM Westerly RI
KGIM-FM Redfield SD
KRRO(FM) Sioux Falls SD
KCDD(FM) Hamlin TX
KVIL-FM Highland Park-Dallas TX
KOUL(FM) Sinton TX
KIOL(FM) Willis TX
WMXB(FM) Richmond VA

KMTT(FM) Tacoma WA
WWIB(FM) Hallie WI
WXSS(FM) Wauwatosa WI
WCIR-FM Beckley WV
WQWV(FM) Fisher WV
KQLT(FM) Casper WY

103.9 mhz
KUWL(FM) College AK
WJRL-FM Ozark AL
KPGG(FM) Ashdown AR
KCJF(FM) Earle AR
KKIX(FM) Fayetteville AR
KEDJ(FM) Gilbert AZ
KRCD(FM) Inglewood CA
KEDD(FM) Johannesburg CA
KCXX(FM) Lake Arrowhead CA
KKFS(FM) Lincoln CA
KDJK(FM) Mariposa CA
KMBY-FM Seaside CA
KBDS(FM) Taft CA
KSYC-FM Yreka CA
KYZX(FM) Pueblo West CO
KSNO-FM Snowmass Village CO
WXKB(FM) Cape Coral FL
WPPL(FM) Blue Ridge GA
WDDK(FM) Greensboro GA
WRPG(FM) Hawkinsville GA
WTYB(FM) Springfield GA
KUOO(FM) Spirit Lake IA
WXAN(FM) Ava IL
WWYW(FM) Dundee IL
WNOI(FM) Flora IL
WQCY(FM) Quincy IL
WRBI(FM) Batesville IN
WIMC(FM) Crawfordsville IN
WXRD(FM) Crown Point IN
WYLT(FM) Fort Wayne IN
WRBR-FM South Bend IN
*KHYM(FM) Copeland KS
KOMB(FM) Fort Scott KS
KNZA(FM) Hiawatha KS
WNTC(FM) Drakesboro KY
WWEL(FM) London KY
WPTI(FM) Louisville KY
WXKQ(FM) Whitesburg KY
WOCN-FM South Yarmouth MA
WOCQ(FM) Berlin MD
WWVZ(FM) Braddock Heights MD
WVOM(FM) Howland ME
WLEN(FM) Adrian MI
*WCMW-FM Harbor Springs MI
WRSR(FM) Owosso MI
KBHL(FM) Osakis MN
KTNX(FM) Arcadia MO
KCHI-FM Chillicothe MO
KRLI(FM) Malta Bend MO
KMCR(FM) Montgomery City MO
WCLD-FM Cleveland MS
WWKZ(FM) Columbus MS
KZMN(FM) Kalispell MT
WNNL(FM) Fuquay-Varina NC
WWTB(FM) Topsail Beach NC
KVMI(FM) Arthur ND
KOZY-FM Gering NE
KNLV-FM Ord NE
KRFS-FM Superior NE
KGRT-FM Las Cruces NM
KZMI(FM) Garapan-Saipan NP
WVOA-FM Mexico NY
WSRK(FM) Oneonta NY
WQBK-FM Rensselaer NY
WRCN-FM Riverhead NY
WDKX(FM) Rochester NY
*WANC(FM) Ticonderoga NY
WFAS-FM White Plains NY
WXEG(FM) Beavercreek OH
WTDA(FM) Westerville OH
KBVL(FM) Pawhuska OK
WALY(FM) Bellwood PA
WPPZ-FM Jenkintown PA
WLMI(FM) Kane PA
WCOZ(FM) Laporte PA
WWIZ(FM) Mercer PA
WLSW(FM) Scottdale PA
WOLI(FM) Easley SC
WHXT(FM) Orangeburg SC

WXIS(FM) Erwin TN
WDEB-FM Jamestown TN
WTRZ-FM McMinnville TN
KXCS(FM) Cameron TX
KTHP(FM) Hemphill TX
KMHT-FM Marshall TX
KQXC-FM Wichita Falls TX
KUDE(FM) Nephi UT
KGNT(FM) Smithfield UT
WXCF-FM Clifton Forge VA
WYFT(FM) Luray VA
KBDB-FM Forks WA
KVAS(FM) Ilwaco WA
KBBD(FM) Spokane WA
WVBO(FM) Winneconne WI
WETZ-FM New Martinsville WV
KXXL(FM) Gillette WY

104.1 mhz
KBRJ(FM) Anchorage AK
WYOK(FM) Atmore AL
KILX(FM) Hatfield AR
KPOC-FM Pocahontas AR
KZPT(FM) Tucson AZ
KBOX(FM) Lompoc CA
KHKK(FM) Modesto CA
KMHX(FM) Windsor CA
KFRR(FM) Woodlake CA
KBVC(FM) Buena Vista CO
KNAB-FM Burlington CO
KFMU-FM Oak Creek CO
WPHH(FM) Waterbury CT
WWUS(FM) Big Pine Key FL
WTKS-FM Cocoa Beach FL
WGLF(FM) Tallahassee FL
WRJY(FM) Brunswick GA
WRBN(FM) Clayton GA
WALR-FM La Grange GA
WRBX(FM) Reidsville GA
KLTI-FM Ames IA
KORR(FM) American Falls ID
WMQZ(FM) Colchester IL
WRDA(FM) Jerseyville IL
WBWN(FM) Le Roy IL
WIKY-FM Evansville IN
WLBC-FM Muncie IN
KGGF-FM Fredonia KS
WCKQ(FM) Campbellsville KY
KHEV(FM) Houma LA
KJLO-FM Monroe LA
WBCN(FM) Boston MA
WWZZ(FM) Waldorf MD
*WVGR(FM) Grand Rapids MI
WSAG(FM) Pinconning MI
KSDM(FM) International Falls MN
KBOT(FM) Pelican Rapids MN
KZJK(FM) Saint Louis Park MN
KSGF-FM Ash Grove MO
KJMO(FM) Jefferson City MO
KMHM(FM) Lutesville MO
WZKS(FM) Union MS
KHKR-FM East Helena MT
WCXL-FM Kill Devil Hills NC
WTQR(FM) Winston-Salem NC
KIBZ(FM) Crete NE
KCDY(FM) Carlsbad NM
KABQ-FM Santa Fe NM
WHTT-FM Buffalo NY
WWYL(FM) Chenango Bridge NY
WQAL(FM) Cleveland OH
WPAY-FM Portsmouth OH
KMGL(FM) Oklahoma City OK
KFIS(FM) Scappoose OR
KWPK-FM Sisters OR
WAEB-FM Allentown PA
WNNK-FM Harrisburg PA
WPXZ-FM Punxsutawney PA
WERR(FM) Utuado PR
WYAV-FM Myrtle Beach SC
KIQK(FM) Rapid City SD
WNAX-FM Yankton SD
WCLE-FM Calhoun TN
WUCZ-FM Carthage TN
WTNV(FM) Jackson TN
KWTR(FM) Big Lake TX
KWOW(FM) Clifton TX
KBFM(FM) Edinburg TX

KRBE(FM) Houston TX
KRIO-FM Pearsall TX
KTDK(FM) Sanger TX
KKUS(FM) Tyler TX
WMNV(FM) Rupert VT
KXDD(FM) Yakima WA
WRLU(FM) Algoma WI
WZEE(FM) Madison WI
WMZK(FM) Merrill WI
WDCI(FM) Bridgeport WV
*WVSB(FM) Romney WV
KANT(FM) Guernsey WY
KCGL(FM) Powell WY

104.3 mhz
*KTOO(FM) Juneau AK
WZYP(FM) Athens AL
WQZZ(FM) Eutaw AL
WHLW(FM) Luverne AL
*KLMZ(FM) Fouke AR
KBCN-FM Marshall AR
KAJM(FM) Payson AZ
KXSE(FM) Davis CA
KHIP(FM) Gonzales CA
KBIG-FM Los Angeles CA
KSHA(FM) Redding CA
KMXY(FM) Grand Junction CO
KJCD(FM) Longmont CO
WIFL(FM) Inglis FL
*WKZM(FM) Sarasota FL
WEAT-FM West Palm Beach FL
WAJQ-FM Alma GA
WBBQ-FM Augusta GA
WKHC(FM) Dahlonega GA
KIJI(FM) Tumon GU
KPHW(FM) Kaneohe HI
KRKN(FM) Eldon IA
KLTB(FM) Boise ID
WCBH(FM) Casey IL
WJMK(FM) Chicago IL
WEGK(FM) Charlestown IN
KCAR-FM Galena KS
KVGB-FM Great Bend KS
WXBC(FM) Hardinsburg KY
WEZJ-FM Williamsburg KY
KEZP(FM) Bunkie LA
WSMJ(FM) Baltimore MD
WABK-FM Gardiner ME
*WVCN(FM) Baraga MI
WOMC(FM) Detroit MI
WCZY-FM Mount Pleasant MI
KLKS(FM) Breezy Point MN
KZLT-FM East Grand Forks MN
KVGO(FM) Spring Valley MN
KZIO(FM) Two Harbors MN
KDBB(FM) Bonne Terre MO
KBEQ(FM) Kansas City MO
KXOQ(FM) Kennett MO
KKAC(FM) Vandalia MO
WMJU(FM) Bude MS
WGNL(FM) Greenwood MS
WQNQ(FM) Fletcher NC
WJSG(FM) Hamlet NC
WFXK(FM) Tarboro NC
KJUL(FM) North Las Vegas NV
WAXQ(FM) New York NY
WFRG-FM Utica NY
WOGF-FM East Liverpool OH
WNLT(FM) Harrison OH
WJZK(FM) Richwood OH
KKMX(FM) Tri City OR
WKNB(FM) Clarendon PA
WSKE(FM) Everett PA
KKSD(FM) Milbank SD
WEYE(FM) Surgoinsville TN
KQFX(FM) Borger TX
KLZK(FM) Brownfield TX
KGAS-FM Carthage TX
KBLT(FM) Leakey TX
KXBT(FM) Taylor TX
KSOP-FM Salt Lake City UT
WKCY-FM Harrisonburg VA
WZIN(FM) Charlotte Amalie VI
WWOD(FM) Hartford VT
KAFE(FM) Bellingham WA
KMNT(FM) Chehalis WA
KZBE(FM) Omak WA

U.S. FM Stations by Frequency

KHTR(FM) Pullman WA
WECB(FM) Seymour WI

104.5 mhz
KMGC(FM) Camden AR
KWXE(FM) Glenwood AR
KTRN(FM) White Hall AR
KZUL-FM Lake Havasu City AZ
KCEC-FM Wellton AZ
KIQO(FM) Atascadero CA
KVLI-FM Lake Isabella CA
KBTW(FM) Lenwood CA
KFOG(FM) San Francisco CA
KSTY(FM) Canon City CO
WFYV-FM Atlantic Beach FL
WKAK(FM) Albany GA
WYYU(FM) Dalton GA
KDAT(FM) Cedar Rapids IA
*WBVN(FM) Carrier Mills IL
WFMB-FM Springfield IL
WJJK(FM) Noblesville IN
KFXJ(FM) Augusta KS
WLKT(FM) Lexington-Fayette KY
KNOU(FM) Empire LA
KBEF(FM) Gibsland LA
WNXX(FM) Jackson LA
KBYO-FM Tallulah LA
WXLO(FM) Fitchburg MA
WKHJ(FM) Mountain Lake Park MD
WSNX-FM Muskegon MI
WILZ(FM) Saginaw MI
KJLY(FM) Blue Earth MN
KSLQ-FM Washington MO
WXRR(FM) Hattiesburg MS
WQJB(FM) State College MS
KKVU(FM) Stevensville MT
WSTK(FM) Aurora NC
WHLC(FM) Highlands NC
WCCG(FM) Hope Mills NC
WRQR(FM) Wilmington NC
*KCVN(FM) Cozad NE
KSRZ(FM) Omaha NE
WVMJ(FM) Conway NH
KKFG(FM) Bloomfield NM
KLBZ(FM) Reserve NM
KDOT(FM) Reno NV
WABT(FM) Mechanicville NY
WLZZ(FM) Montpelier OH
WQKT(FM) Wooster OH
KMYZ-FM Pryor OK
KMCQ(FM) The Dalles OR
WXXO(FM) Cambridge Springs PA
WSNI(FM) Philadelphia PA
WNBT-FM Wellsboro PA
WRFQ(FM) Mt. Pleasant SC
WGFX(FM) Gallatin TN
WKHT(FM) Knoxville TN
WRVR-FM Memphis TN
KKDA-FM Dallas TX
KPUS(FM) Gregory TX
KJTX(FM) Jefferson TX
KKMY(FM) Orange TX
KZEP-FM San Antonio TX
WGRX(FM) Falmouth VA
WNVZ(FM) Norfolk VA
*KMIH(FM) Mercer Island WA
KMJY-FM Newport WA
WAXX(FM) Eau Claire WI
WXER(FM) Plymouth WI
*WCCX(FM) Waukesha WI
WSLD(FM) Whitewater WI
WHAJ(FM) Bluefield WV
KRQU(FM) Laramie WY
KSIT(FM) Rock Springs WY

104.7 mhz
KKED(FM) Fairbanks AK
*KCAW(FM) Sitka AK
WZZK-FM Birmingham AL
KRBK(FM) Booneville AR
KFLI(FM) Des Arc AR
KOOU(FM) Hardy AR
KTOY(FM) Texarkana AR
KNWJ(FM) Leone AS
KZZP(FM) Mesa AZ
KHUM(FM) Garberville CA
KCAQ(FM) Oxnard CA
KDES(FM) Palm Springs CA

KHTN(FM) Planada CA
KNNG(FM) Sterling CO
KSKE-FM Vail CO
WAAZ-FM Crestview FL
WSGL(FM) Naples FL
WRBQ-FM Tampa FL
WFLM(FM) White City FL
WFSH-FM Athens GA
WSGA(FM) Hinesville GA
KONI(FM) Lanai City HI
KIKX(FM) Ketchum ID
WLMD(FM) Bushnell IL
*WCFL(FM) Morris IL
WNSV(FM) Nashville IL
WFRN-FM Elkhart IN
WITZ-FM Jasper IN
*KVCY(FM) Fort Scott KS
KXBZ(FM) Manhattan KS
WJMD(FM) Hazard KY
WJSH(FM) Folsom LA
KORI(FM) Mansfield LA
KNEK-FM Washington LA
WKPE-FM Orleans MA
WAYZ(FM) Hagerstown MD
WQHQ(FM) Ocean City-Salisbury MD
WBFB(FM) Belfast ME
WHXQ(FM) Kennebunkport ME
WYKX(FM) Escanaba MI
WKJC(FM) Tawas City MI
KCLD-FM Saint Cloud MN
KREZ(FM) Chaffee MO
KKLH(FM) Marshfield MO
KRES(FM) Moberly MO
WJIW(FM) Greenville MS
KBZM(FM) Big Sky MT
WKQC(FM) Charlotte NC
WZUP(FM) Rose Hill NC
KDAM(FM) Hope ND
KNDR(FM) Mandan ND
KTEG(FM) Bosque Farms NM
KMOU(FM) Roswell NM
KWLY(FM) Moapa Valley NV
WBBS(FM) Fulton NY
WMOS(FM) Montauk NY
WSPK(FM) Poughkeepsie NY
*WIRQ(FM) Rochester NY
WTUE(FM) Dayton OH
WKKY(FM) Geneva OH
WIOT(FM) Toledo OH
KIXR(FM) Ponca City OK
KSLE(FM) Wewoka OK
KCMB(FM) Baker City OR
KDUK-FM Florence OR
KFEG(FM) Klamath Falls OR
WPGB(FM) Pittsburgh PA
WKAQ-FM San Juan PR
WNOK(FM) Columbia SC
KKLS-FM Sioux Falls SD
WSGM(FM) Coalmont TN
WMUF-FM Henry TN
WLIV-FM Monterey TN
KKYS(FM) Bryan TX
KYYI(FM) Burkburnett TX
KZAM(FM) Ganado TX
KTXC(FM) Lamesa TX
KWNS(FM) Winnsboro TX
WPZZ(FM) Crewe VA
WNCS(FM) Montpelier VT
KDUX-FM Aberdeen WA
KKRV(FM) Wenatchee WA
WBJZ(FM) Berlin WI
WEXT(FM) Sturtevant WI
WVRC-FM Spencer WV
KTRS-FM Casper WY

104.9 mhz
WOAB(FM) Ozark AL
WSLY(FM) York AL
KAGH-FM Crossett AR
KHPA(FM) Hope AR
KDXY(FM) Lake City AR
KXNA(FM) Springdale AR
KCLT(FM) West Helena AR
KWCX(FM) Willcox AZ
KWIM(FM) Window Rock AZ
KLOA-FM Ridgecrest CA
KRPQ(FM) Rohnert Park CA

KYIX(FM) South Oroville CA
KCNL(FM) Sunnyvale CA
KCRZ(FM) Tipton CA
KRYD(FM) Norwood CO
KRYE(FM) Rye CO
*WIHS(FM) Middletown CT
WHTF(FM) Havana FL
WYGC(FM) High Springs FL
WCVU(FM) Solana FL
WFXE(FM) Columbus GA
WMCG(FM) Milan GA
KLMJ(FM) Hampton IA
KBOE-FM Oskaloosa IA
KLLT(FM) Spencer IA
WXRX(FM) Belvidere IL
KMJM-FM Columbia IL
WFIW-FM Fairfield IL
KBOB-FM Geneseo IL
WPXN(FM) Paxton IL
WXCL(FM) Pekin IL
WINN(FM) Columbus IN
WERK(FM) Muncie IN
WAXI(FM) Rockville IN
KFFX(FM) Emporia KS
KSAL-FM Salina KS
WKYW(FM) Frankfort KY
WXLR(FM) Harold KY
WJRS(FM) Jamestown KY
WKHG(FM) Leitchfield KY
WAVJ(FM) Princeton KY
WSKV(FM) Stanton KY
WKKS-FM Vanceburg KY
KNXX(FM) Donaldsonville LA
*KTOC-FM Jonesboro LA
KZWA(FM) Moss Bluff LA
*WRBB(FM) Boston MA
WBOQ(FM) Gloucester MA
WQBX(FM) Alma MI
*WAIR(FM) Lake City MI
WWKN(FM) Marshall MI
KRFO-FM Owatonna MN
KPWB(FM) Piedmont MO
WZFL(FM) Centreville MS
WFXO(FM) Iuka MS
WBUV(FM) Moss Point MS
WCJU-FM Prentiss MS
KIKF(FM) Cascade MT
WYNA(FM) Calabash NC
WFMZ(FM) Hertford NC
WQNS(FM) Waynesville NC
KTCH-FM Wayne NE
KTMX(FM) York NE
WYRY(FM) Hinsdale NH
WLKZ(FM) Wolfeboro NH
WSJO(FM) Egg Harbor City NJ
KMVR(FM) Mesilla Park NM
WZMR(FM) Altamont NY
WMJQ(FM) Brockport NY
WNGZ(FM) Montour Falls NY
WWKC(FM) Caldwell OH
*WCVO(FM) Gahanna OH
WUZZ-FM Lima OH
WCLV(FM) Lorain OH
WWLS-FM Bethany OK
KREK(FM) Bristow OK
KRIG-FM Nowata OK
*WJRH(FM) Easton PA
WRKY-FM Hollidaysburg PA
WWDL-FM Scranton PA
WCCP-FM Clemson SC
WWVV(FM) Ridgeland SC
WDNT-FM Dayton TN
WKOS(FM) Kingsport TN
WQLA-FM La Follette TN
WYVY(FM) Union City TN
WBOZ(FM) Woodbury TN
KJAV(FM) Alamo TX
KXXS(FM) Dripping Springs TX
KBUK(FM) La Grange TX
KYCX-FM Mexia TX
KPTY(FM) Missouri City TX
KZMP-FM Pilot Point TX
KMFM(FM) Premont TX
KMIQ(FM) Robstown TX
KBTE(FM) Tulia TX
KVOU-FM Uvalde TX
KYLZ(FM) Tremonton UT

WZBL(FM) Roanoke VA
WWRT(FM) Strasburg VA
WNDJ(FM) White Stone VA
WMNG(FM) Christiansted VI
KFNK(FM) Eatonville WA
*KEEH(FM) Spokane WA
WLMX-FM Balsam Lake WI
WPCK(FM) Denmark WI
WTKM-FM Hartford WI
WLXR-FM La Crosse WI
WKQH(FM) Marathon WI
WNFM(FM) Reedsburg WI
WPDX-FM Clarksburg WV
KRRR(FM) Cheyenne WY

105.1 mhz
KTKU(FM) Juneau AK
WQSB(FM) Albertville AL
KMJX(FM) Conway AR
KFLX(FM) Kachina Village AZ
KLBN(FM) Auberry CA
KWSZ(FM) Lompoc CA
KMZT(FM) Los Angeles CA
KOCN(FM) Pacific Grove CA
KNCI(FM) Sacramento CA
KXXL-FM Denver CO
WPFL(FM) Century FL
WHQT(FM) Coral Gables FL
WOMX-FM Orlando FL
WASJ(FM) Panama City Beach FL
WKUB(FM) Blackshear GA
WLVX(FM) Elberton GA
WHEL(FM) Helen GA
KGUM-FM Dededo GU
KINE-FM Honolulu HI
KCCQ(FM) Ames IA
KJOT(FM) Boise ID
KVTY(FM) Lewiston ID
WOJO(FM) Evanston IL
WTAO(FM) Murphysboro IL
WGEM-FM Quincy IL
WEJT(FM) Shelbyville IL
WQHK-FM Decatur IN
WHCC(FM) Ellettsville IN
KZQD(FM) Liberal KS
WTUK(FM) Harlan KY
WRNZ(FM) Lancaster KY
WLRS(FM) Shepherdsville KY
KPEL-FM Abbeville LA
KTGV(FM) Jonesville LA
*WAMQ(FM) Great Barrington MA
*WNEK-FM Springfield MA
WTOS-FM Skowhegan ME
WGFM(FM) Cheboygan MI
WMGC-FM Detroit MI
KLTA(FM) Breckenridge MN
KKCB(FM) Duluth MN
WGVX(FM) Lakeville MN
KARL(FM) Tracy MN
KCRV-FM Caruthersville MO
KCJK(FM) Garden City MO
KOSP(FM) Willard MO
WQJQ(FM) Kosciusko MS
KQBL(FM) Billings MT
KWOL-FM Whitefish MT
WDCG(FM) Durham NC
WSSM(FM) Havelock NC
KAOC(FM) Cavalier ND
KWMW(FM) Maljamar NM
KKRG(FM) Santa Fe NM
KQRT(FM) Las Vegas NV
WWDG(FM) DeRuyter NY
WWPR-FM New York NY
WKOL(FM) Plattsburgh NY
WUBE-FM Cincinnati OH
WQXK(FM) Salem OH
KBLP(FM) Lindsay OK
KTMC-FM McAlester OK
KOSB(FM) Perry OK
KRSK(FM) Molalla OR
KAKT(FM) Phoenix OR
WIOV-FM Ephrata PA
WILQ(FM) Williamsport PA
WIOC(FM) Ponce PR
WWLI(FM) Providence RI
WGFG-FM Branchville SC
WPDT(FM) Johnsonville SC

KAWK(FM) Custer SD
KZKK(FM) Huron SD
WCLC-FM Jamestown TN
WVRY(FM) Waverly TN
KEAN-FM Abilene TX
KYKS(FM) Lufkin TX
KMAT(FM) Seadrift TX
KNJQ(FM) Manti UT
WAVA(FM) Arlington VA
WBHB-FM Bridgewater VA
WCHY(FM) Waunakee WI
WKLC-FM Saint Albans WV

105.3 mhz
WDBT(FM) Headland AL
WBFZ(FM) Selma AL
KJLV(FM) Hoxie AR
KAKJ(FM) Marianna AR
KQOR(FM) Mena AR
KZLZ(FM) Kearny AZ
KHOV-FM Wickenburg AZ
KKDJ(FM) Delano CA
KIOZ(FM) San Diego CA
KITS(FM) San Francisco CA
KRDG(FM) Shingletown CA
KRSX-FM Yermo CA
KZKS(FM) Rifle CO
WJSJ(FM) Fernandina Beach FL
WYKS(FM) Gainesville FL
WZSP(FM) Nocatee FL
WBZY(FM) Bowdon GA
WSTI-FM Quitman GA
WRHQ(FM) Richmond Hill GA
KBGX(FM) Keaau HI
KLYV(FM) Dubuque IA
KNOD(FM) Harlan IA
KIWA-FM Sheldon IA
*WTPC(FM) Elsah IL
WKAY(FM) Knoxville IL
WAOX(FM) Staunton IL
WJLT(FM) Evansville IN
WKOA(FM) Lafayette IN
WMPI(FM) Scottsburg IN
KJML(FM) Columbus KS
KFBZ(FM) Haysville KS
WOVO(FM) Glasgow KY
WXKZ-FM Prestonsburg KY
WKBU(FM) Kenner LA
KLIP(FM) Monroe LA
KNCB-FM Vivian LA
WFRB-FM Frostburg MD
WSHK(FM) Kittery ME
WKHM-FM Brooklyn MI
WCXT(FM) Hart MI
WGVY(FM) Cambridge MN
KYBA(FM) Stewartville MN
KYMO-FM East Prairie MO
KZNN(FM) Rolla MO
WACR-FM Aberdeen MS
KMTX-FM Helena MT
WODR(FM) Fair Bluff NC
KZPR(FM) Minot ND
KKUL(FM) Lincoln NE
KIOD(FM) McCook NE
*KGRD(FM) Orchard NE
WDRE(FM) Calverton-Roanoke NY
*WGKR(FM) Grand Gorge NY
WKPQ(FM) Hornell NY
WYHT(FM) Mansfield OH
KJMM(FM) Bixby OK
KDDQ(FM) Comanche OK
KINB(FM) Kingfisher OK
WYCY(FM) Hawley PA
WDAS-FM Philadelphia PA
WAGI-FM Gaffney SC
WLSZ(FM) Humboldt TN
WKVL-FM Loudon TN
KPTI(FM) Crystal Beach TX
KLLI(FM) Dallas TX
KEZB(FM) Hempstead TX
KLVT-FM Levelland TX
KLSR-FM Memphis TX
KSMG(FM) Seguin TX
WBRW(FM) Blacksburg VA
WBNN-FM Dillwyn VA
WKUS(FM) Norfolk VA
WVJZ(FM) Charlotte Amalie VI

U.S. FM Stations by Frequency

WEBK(FM) Killington VT
KCMS(FM) Edmonds WA
KONA-FM Kennewick WA
WRLO-FM Antigo WI
WFZH(FM) Mukwonago WI
KDWY(FM) Diamondville WY
KREO(FM) Pine Bluffs WY

105.5 mhz
WNSP(FM) Bay Minette AL
WENN(FM) Hoover AL
WVNA-FM Muscle Shoals AL
KYEL(FM) Danville AR
KPFM(FM) Mountain Home AR
KNAS(FM) Nashville AR
KBOA-FM Piggott AR
KWAK-FM Stuttgart AR
KWRF-FM Warren AR
*KLVA(FM) Casa Grande AZ
KRVR(FM) Copperopolis CA
KVMG(FM) Dunnigan CA
KKHB(FM) Eureka CA
KIDI(FM) Guadalupe CA
KBUE(FM) Long Beach CA
KFYV(FM) Ojai CA
KOSS(FM) Rosamond CA
KUUS(FM) San Joaquin CA
KSKX(FM) Security CO
KJAC(FM) Timnath CO
WQGN-FM Groton CT
WFCT(FM) Apalachicola FL
WOLL(FM) Hobe Sound FL
WWWK(FM) Marathon FL
WYZB(FM) Mary Esther FL
WBTT(FM) Naples Park FL
WDUV(FM) New Port Richey FL
WSJF(FM) Saint Augustine Beach FL
WQVE(FM) Camilla GA
WIFO-FM Jesup GA
WIFN(FM) Macon GA
WRXR-FM Rossville GA
KPMW(FM) Haliimaile HI
KELR-FM Chariton IA
KILJ-FM Mount Pleasant IA
KDLS-FM Perry IA
KTHK(FM) Idaho Falls ID
WREZ(FM) Metropolis IL
WCZQ(FM) Monticello IL
WJVO(FM) South Jacksonville IL
WYKT(FM) Wilmington IL
WZSR(FM) Woodstock IL
WQRK(FM) Bedford IN
WTHD(FM) Lagrange IN
WLJE(FM) Valparaiso IN
WWVR(FM) West Terre Haute IN
KVSV-FM Beloit KS
KKOY-FM Chanute KS
WLVK(FM) Fort Knox KY
WKYA(FM) Greenville KY
WMKJ(FM) Mt. Sterling KY
KBKK(FM) Ball LA
KEUN-FM Eunice LA
KDDK(FM) Franklin LA
WBEC-FM Pittsfield MA
WDKZ(FM) Salisbury MD
WBYA(FM) Islesboro ME
WWCK-FM Flint MI
WGKL(FM) Gladstone MI
WADW(FM) Pickford MI
WBMI(FM) West Branch MI
KDDG(FM) Albany MN
KBAJ(FM) Deer River MN
KMGM(FM) Montevideo MN
KRBI-FM Saint Peter MN
KESM-FM El Dorado Springs MO
KZZT(FM) Moberly MO
KKJO(FM) Saint Joseph MO
WNLA-FM Indianola MS
WVBG(FM) Redwood MS
WTNM(FM) Water Valley MS
WABO-FM Waynesboro MS
KRQS(FM) Alberton MT
WXQR(FM) Jacksonville NC
WFJA(FM) Sanford NC
KMAV-FM Mayville ND
KFMT(FM) Fremont NE
WJYY(FM) Concord NH

WGBZ(FM) Cape May Court House NJ
WDHA-FM Dover NJ
KZZX(FM) Alamogordo NM
*KQLV(FM) Bosque Farms NM
KWNM(FM) Hurley NM
WLPW(FM) Lake Placid NY
WSKU(FM) Little Falls NY
WTKV(FM) Oswego NY
WDBY(FM) Patterson NY
WXTQ(FM) Athens OH
*WGOJ(FM) Conneaut OH
WMVR-FM Sidney OH
WWWM-FM Sylvania OH
WCHO-FM Washington Court House OH
WCWO-FM Chickasha OK
KKFC(FM) Coalgate OK
KGFY(FM) Stillwater OK
KDEP(FM) Garibaldi OR
KCGB(FM) Hood River OR
KEUG(FM) Veneta OR
WMKX(FM) Brookville PA
WCHX(FM) Lewistown PA
WMGH-FM Tamaqua PA
WFDT(FM) Aguada PR
WDAR-FM Darlington SC
WCOO(FM) Kiawah Island SC
WYTM-FM Fayetteville TN
WSEV-FM Gatlinburg TN
WBNT-FM Oneida TN
WAKQ(FM) Paris TN
WXOQ(FM) Selmer TN
WRKK-FM Sparta TN
KACT-FM Andrews TX
KUSJ-FM Harker Heights TX
KQXX-FM Mission TX
KMJR(FM) Portland TX
WKDE-FM Altavista VA
WWRE(FM) Berryville VA
WHFD(FM) Lawrenceville VA
WOJL(FM) Louisa VA
WSWV-FM Pennington Gap VA
WGTH-FM Richlands VA
WRAR-FM Tappahannock VA
WKXH-FM Saint Johnsbury VT
KUKN(FM) Longview WA
WUSP(FM) Nekoosa WI
WFBZ(FM) Trempealeau WI
WMMM-FM Verona WI
WUKL(FM) Bethlehem WV
WKQV(FM) Richwood WV
KHAD(FM) Mills WY

105.7 mhz
KNIK-FM Anchorage AK
WQAH-FM Addison AL
WCSN-FM Orange Beach AL
WZHT(FM) Troy AL
KRKD(FM) Dermott AR
KMCK-FM Siloam Springs AR
KVRD-FM Cottonwood AZ
KOAS(FM) Dolan Springs AZ
KXRS(FM) Hemet CA
KVVF(FM) Santa Clara CA
KVAY(FM) Lamar CO
KWGL(FM) Ouray CO
KPMX(FM) Sterling CO
WHJX(FM) Baldwin FL
*WFRF-FM Monticello FL
WWLL(FM) Sebring FL
WFFM(FM) Ashburn GA
WIBL(FM) Augusta GA
WWVA-FM Canton GA
KOKZ(FM) Waterloo IA
WXMP(FM) Peoria IL
WUZR(FM) Bicknell IN
WYXB(FM) Indianapolis IN
WTCJ-FM Tell City IN
KJRL(FM) Herington KS
WTSZ-FM Eminence KY
WLGC-FM Greenup KY
WTBK(FM) Manchester KY
KVVP(FM) Leesville LA
WROR-FM Framingham MA
WHFS(FM) Catonsville MD
*WHMX(FM) Lincoln ME
WOOD-FM Grand Rapids MI

WCUP(FM) L'Anse MI
WGVZ(FM) Eden Prairie MN
KRAQ(FM) Jackson MN
KKKX(FM) Knob Noster MO
KPNT(FM) Sainte Genevieve MO
WJXM(FM) De Kalb MS
WAKH(FM) McComb MS
WRSF(FM) Columbia NC
WGQR(FM) Elizabethtown NC
WFMX(FM) Statesville NC
KSUX(FM) Winnebago NE
WLKC(FM) Campton NH
WCHR-FM Manahawkin NJ
KOZZ-FM Reno NV
WMRV-FM Endicott NY
WNYQ(FM) Queensbury NY
WMJI(FM) Cleveland OH
WZOM(FM) Defiance OH
WFJX(FM) Hilliard OH
KTTL(FM) Alva OK
*KROU(FM) Spencer OK
KQAK(FM) Bend OR
WLKJ(FM) Portage PA
WQXA-FM York PA
WCAD(FM) San Juan PR
WOFE-FM Rockwood TN
WQAK(FM) Union City TN
KAEZ(FM) Amarillo TX
KTKO(FM) Beeville TX
KRNB(FM) Decatur TX
KNAF-FM Fredericksburg TX
*KHCB-FM Houston TX
KRBL(FM) Idalou TX
KYKX(FM) Longview TX
KBIC(FM) Raymondville TX
KXRV(FM) Centerville UT
WMXH-FM Luray VA
WKJS(FM) Richmond VA
KJET(FM) South Bend WA
KZBD(FM) Spokane WA
KRSE(FM) Yakima WA
WAPL-FM Appleton WI
WCFW(FM) Chippewa Falls WI
WXCX(FM) Siren WI
WOBG-FM Salem WV

105.9 mhz
*KRBD(FM) Ketchikan AK
KPFN(FM) Seward AK
WNSI-FM Atmore AL
WRTR(FM) Brookwood AL
WRHY(FM) Centre AL
*WTOH(FM) Mobile AL
KLAZ(FM) Hot Springs AR
KHOT-FM Paradise Valley AZ
KKDG(FM) Fresno CA
KPWR(FM) Los Angeles CA
KRAZ(FM) Santa Ynez CA
KQPM(FM) Ukiah CA
KALC(FM) Denver CO
WHCN(FM) Hartford CT
WXJN(FM) Lewes DE
WOCL(FM) De Land FL
WTZB(FM) Englewood FL
WBGG-FM Fort Lauderdale FL
WILN(FM) Panama City FL
WXMK(FM) Dock Junction GA
WVGA(FM) Lakeland GA
KPOI-FM Honolulu HI
KTLB(FM) Twin Lakes IA
KCIX(FM) Garden City ID
WCKG-FM Elmwood Park IL
WOKZ(FM) Fairfield IL
WGKC(FM) Mahomet IL
WMMC(FM) Marshall IL
WJOT-FM Wabash IN
KSSA(FM) Ingalls KS
KLZR(FM) Lawrence KS
WRVI(FM) Valley Station KY
KBZE(FM) Berwick LA
KTSJ(FM) Opelousas LA
WBCI(FM) Bath ME
WKHQ-FM Charlevoix MI
WDMK(FM) Detroit MI
KWNG(FM) Red Wing MN
KKWS(FM) Wadena MN
KZZK(FM) New London MO

KGBX-FM Nixa MO
KULH(FM) Wheeling MO
WXRG(FM) Pascagoula MS
WOAD-FM Pickens MS
KKNS-FM Missoula MT
KAAQ(FM) Alliance NE
KQKY(FM) Kearney NE
KKCD(FM) Omaha NE
WCAA(FM) Newark NJ
KRZY-FM Santa Fe NM
WJZR(FM) Rochester NY
WLTI(FM) Syracuse NY
WPFB-FM Middletown OH
WWJM(FM) New Lexington OH
KQTZ(FM) Hobart OK
KIRC(FM) Seminole OK
KRJT(FM) Elgin OR
WUBZ-FM Philipsburg PA
WXDX-FM Pittsburgh PA
WPZX(FM) Pocono Pines PA
WEZV(FM) North Myrtle Beach SC
KMIT(FM) Mitchell SD
WGKX(FM) Memphis TN
WNRQ(FM) Nashville TN
WCTU(FM) Tazewell TN
KUZN(FM) Centerville TX
KMFR(FM) Hondo TX
KFMK(FM) Round Rock TX
KUKA(FM) San Diego TX
KKJW(FM) Stanton TX
KLCY-FM Vernal UT
WLNI(FM) Lynchburg VA
WJZW(FM) Woodbridge VA
KRVO(FM) Vancouver WA
WKPO(FM) Evansville WI
*WEGZ(FM) Washburn WI
WTNJ(FM) Mount Hope WV
KTYN(FM) Thayne WY

106.1 mhz
WSTH-FM Alexander City AL
WBMH(FM) Grove Hill AL
WTAK-FM Hartselle AL
KFFB(FM) Fairfield Bay AR
KIKO-FM Claypool AZ
*KCFA(FM) Arnold CA
KRRX(FM) Burney CA
KRAB(FM) Green Acres CA
KPLM(FM) Palm Springs CA
KMEL(FM) San Francisco CA
KWWV(FM) Santa Margarita CA
KNFO(FM) Basalt CO
WRRX(FM) Gulf Breeze FL
WUTL(FM) Tallahassee FL
WKTM(FM) Soperton GA
WRXZ(FM) Sylvester GA
WNGC(FM) Toccoa GA
KLEO(FM) Kahaluu HI
KLSS-FM Mason City IA
KIYX(FM) Sageville IA
KZFN(FM) Moscow ID
KKMV(FM) Rupert ID
WSMI-FM Litchfield IL
WYYS(FM) Streator IL
WDKS(FM) Newburgh IN
WWWY(FM) North Vernon IN
KXKU(FM) Lyons KS
WMOR-FM Morehead KY
KXRR(FM) Monroe LA
WCOD-FM Hyannis MA
WKGO(FM) Cumberland MD
*WMEM(FM) Presque Isle ME
WJXQ(FM) Jackson MI
WHST(FM) Tawas City MI
KLCI(FM) Princeton MN
KJOE(FM) Slayton MN
KOQL(FM) Ashland MO
KWKZ(FM) Charleston MO
WKSY(FM) Picayune MS
WMXU(FM) Starkville MS
KQDI-FM Great Falls MT
WMMY(FM) Jefferson NC
WNMX-FM Waxhaw NC
WRDU(FM) Wilson NC
KQLX-FM Lisbon ND
WHDQ(FM) Claremont NH
KPZE-FM Carlsbad NM

KFMQ(FM) Gallup NM
WNKI(FM) Corning NY
WPDA(FM) Jeffersonville NY
WBLI(FM) Patchogue NY
WVNO-FM Mansfield OH
WBBG(FM) Niles OH
KKBI(FM) Broken Bow OK
KQLL-FM Owasso OK
KIXO(FM) Sulphur OK
KLOO-FM Corvallis OR
WLZS(FM) Beaver Springs PA
WJJZ(FM) Philadelphia PA
WRRH(FM) Hormigueros PR
WFXH-FM Hilton Head Island SC
WTUA(FM) Saint Stephen SC
KTTX(FM) Brenham TX
WHKS(FM) Denton TX
KNEX(FM) Laredo TX
KIOC(FM) Orange TX
KTKY(FM) Refugio TX
KMDX(FM) San Angelo TX
KBAL-FM San Saba TX
WZNR(FM) Poquoson VA
WJJS-FM Vinton VA
WBKS-FM Tacoma WA
WDKM(FM) Adams WI
WACD(FM) Antigo WI
WMIL(FM) Waukesha WI
WRZZ(FM) Elizabeth WV
KBMG(FM) Evanston WY

106.3 mhz
KSUP(FM) Juneau AK
WKNU(FM) Brewton AL
WBTG-FM Sheffield AL
KZKZ-FM Greenwood AR
KOLL-FM Lonoke AR
KYGL(FM) Texarkana AR
KRLW-FM Walnut Ridge AR
KGMG(FM) Oracle AZ
KOMR(FM) Sun City AZ
KMGQ(FM) Goleta CA
*KFYE(FM) Kingsburg CA
KGMX(FM) Lancaster CA
KHPO(FM) Merced CA
KALI-FM Santa Ana CA
KMJV(FM) Soledad CA
KCHC(FM) Willows CA
KPRB(FM) Brush CO
KKHI(FM) Kremmling CO
KWUF-FM Pagosa Springs CO
KKLI(FM) Widefield CO
WJPT(FM) Fort Myers Villas FL
WJBW-FM Jupiter FL
WZMQ(FM) Key Largo FL
WCIF(FM) Melbourne FL
WSBZ(FM) Miramar Beach FL
WJQB(FM) Spring Hill FL
WTUF(FM) Boston GA
WGMK(FM) Donalsonville GA
WQBZ(FM) Fort Valley GA
WOAH(FM) Glennville GA
WKBX(FM) Kingsland GA
KDRB(FM) Ankeny IA
KQTA(FM) Homedale ID
KBJX(FM) Shelley ID
WQRL(FM) Benton IL
WYRB(FM) Genoa IL
WGCY(FM) Gibson City IL
WSRB(FM) Lansing IL
WDDB(FM) Columbia City IN
WCDQ(FM) Crawfordsville IN
WUBU(FM) South Bend IN
WANY-FM Albany KY
WXMZ(FM) Hartford KY
WKMO(FM) Hodgenville KY
WRIL(FM) Pineville KY
WCDA(FM) Versailles KY
KKSJ(FM) Maurice LA
KXOR-FM Thibodaux LA
WEIB(FM) Northampton MA
WCEM-FM Cambridge MD
WBQW(FM) Scarborough ME
WSCG-FM Lakeview MI
WKLA-FM Ludington MI
WGER(FM) Saginaw MI
WMXG(FM) Stephenson MI

U.S. FM Stations by Frequency

KRJB(FM) Ada MN
WMFG-FM Hibbing MN
KPHR(FM) Ortonville MN
KRZK(FM) Branson MO
WZLD(FM) Petal MS
WGNG(FM) Tchula MS
KDBR(FM) Kalispell MT
WLTT(FM) Shallotte NC
KLMY(FM) Lincoln NE
WMTK(FM) Littleton NH
WFNQ(FM) Nashua NH
WHCY(FM) Blairstown NJ
WHTG-FM Eatontown NJ
WKOE(FM) Ocean City NJ
KAGM(FM) Los Lunas NM
WFAF(FM) Mount Kisco NY
WMCR-FM Oneida NY
WYZY(FM) Saranac Lake NY
WCDK(FM) Cadiz OH
WJYD(FM) London OH
WBUK(FM) Ottawa OH
*KGOU(FM) Norman OK
KZZE(FM) Eagle Point OR
WLCY(FM) Blairsville PA
WWLY(FM) Huntingdon PA
WQRM(FM) Smethport PA
WCTL(FM) Union City PA
WWKX(FM) Woonsocket RI
WYNN(FM) Florence SC
WJNI(FM) Ladson SC
WGVC(FM) Simpsonville SC
KZLK(FM) Rapid City SD
KVHT(FM) Vermillion SD
KKHR(FM) Abilene TX
KOOC(FM) Belton TX
KPSO-FM Falfurrias TX
KQQT(FM) Gonzales TX
KPAN-FM Hereford TX
KERB-FM Kermit TX
KHKZ(FM) Mercedes TX
KSEM-FM Seminole TX
KBZS(FM) Wichita Falls TX
WHKX(FM) Bluefield VA
WBOP(FM) Churchville VA
WMNA-FM Gretna VA
WNVA-FM Norton VA
KVLR(FM) Twisp WA
WQCC(FM) La Crosse WI
WWQM-FM Middleton WI
WEVR-FM River Falls WI
WPLT(FM) Spooner WI
WAMX(FM) Milton WV
KLEN(FM) Cheyenne WY

106.5 mhz
KWHL(FM) Anchorage AK
WAVH(FM) Daphne AL
WZNJ(FM) Demopolis AL
WJEC(FM) Vernon AL
KBVA(FM) Bella Vista AR
KELD-FM Hampton AR
KKIK(FM) Horseshoe Bend AR
KKMR(FM) Arizona City AZ
KALT-FM Alturas CA
KIXA(FM) Lucerne Valley CA
KMMT(FM) Mammoth Lakes CA
KWOD(FM) Sacramento CA
KLNV(FM) San Diego CA
KEZR(FM) San Jose CA
KFVR-FM La Junta CO
WBMW(FM) Ledyard CT
WOCY(FM) Carrabelle FL
WCJX(FM) Five Points FL
WBGB(FM) Ponte Vedra Beach FL
WCTQ(FM) Sarasota FL
WZIQ(FM) Smithville GA
WZBX(FM) Sylvania GA
KCQQ(FM) Davenport IA
WARH(FM) Granite City IL
WWBL(FM) Washington IN
KYQQ(FM) Arkansas City KS
WKDZ-FM Cadiz KY
WJSN-FM Jackson KY
WNKR(FM) Williamstown KY
KCIJ(FM) Atlanta LA
KQXL-FM New Roads LA
WWMX(FM) Baltimore MD

WKHW(FM) Pocomoke City MD
WQCB(FM) Brewer ME
WMEF(FM) Fort Kent ME
WQLR(FM) Kalamazoo MI
KFMC(FM) Fairmont MN
*KDXL(FM) Saint Louis Park MN
*KUOM-FM Saint Louis Park MN
KLFN(FM) Sunburg MN
WDAF-FM Liberty MO
KTMO(FM) New Madrid MO
WAID(FM) Clarksdale MS
WSFL-FM New Bern NC
WEND(FM) Salisbury NC
KMCX(FM) Ogallala NE
WMEX(FM) Farmington NH
KEND(FM) Roswell NM
KSNE-FM Las Vegas NV
WPYX(FM) Albany NY
WYRK(FM) Buffalo NY
WKRH(FM) Minetto NY
WMVX(FM) Cleveland OH
WRWK(FM) Delta OH
WDSJ(FM) Greenville OH
KTLS-FM Holdenville OK
KYSJ(FM) Coos Bay OR
WFYY(FM) Bloomsburg PA
WDSN(FM) Reynoldsville PA
WNIK-FM Arecibo PR
WSYN(FM) Georgetown SC
WSKZ(FM) Chattanooga TN
WLVS-FM Clifton TN
WJDT(FM) Rogersville TN
KOVE-FM Galveston TX
KOOI-FM Jacksonville TX
KEJS(FM) Lubbock TX
KZZA(FM) Muenster TX
KOSY-FM Spanish Fork UT
WBTJ(FM) Richmond VA
KSPO(FM) Dishman WA
KWPZ(FM) Lynden WA
KEGX(FM) Richland WA
WLJY(FM) Marshfield WI
WHBZ(FM) Sheboygan Falls WI
WKCH(FM) Whitewater WI
WWLW(FM) Clarksburg WV

106.7 mhz
KGTW(FM) Ketchikan AK
WKMX(FM) Enterprise AL
KHKN(FM) Benton AR
KJBX(FM) Trumann AR
KPPV(FM) Prescott Valley AZ
KSMY(FM) Lompoc CA
KRQR(FM) Orland CA
KROQ-FM Pasadena CA
KJUG-FM Tulare CA
KBPI(FM) Denver CO
WRMA-FM Fort Lauderdale FL
WXXL(FM) Tavares FL
WOKA-FM Douglas GA
WYAY(FM) Gainesville GA
KRTI(FM) Grinnell IA
KIKD(FM) Lake City IA
KTPO(FM) Kootenai ID
WPPN(FM) Des Plaines IL
WPWQ(FM) Mount Sterling IL
WZNX(FM) Sullivan IL
WTLC-FM Greenwood IN
WYFX(FM) Mount Vernon IN
WGLM(FM) West Lafayette IN
KFXX-FM Hugoton KS
KQNK-FM Norton KS
WLFX(FM) Berea KY
WHHT(FM) Horse Cave KY
WZZL(FM) Reidland KY
KYLA(FM) Homer LA
KUMX(FM) North Fort Polk LA
KKND(FM) Port Sulphur LA
KBEB-FM Rayne LA
WMJX(FM) Boston MA
WHXR(FM) North Windham ME
WDTW-FM Detroit MI
WKPK(FM) Gaylord MI
WHTO(FM) Iron Mountain MI
KAOD(FM) Babbitt MN
WJJY(FM) Brainerd MN
KAUL(FM) Ellington MO

KZRQ-FM Mount Vernon MO
WWZD-FM New Albany MS
WSTZ-FM Vicksburg MS
KBQQ(FM) Pinesdale MT
WUIN(FM) Carolina Beach NC
WKVE(FM) Semora NC
KYTZ(FM) Walhalla ND
KEXL(FM) Norfolk NE
WDOX(FM) North Cape May NJ
KZNM(FM) Los Alamos NM
WBDI(FM) Copenhagen NY
WKGS(FM) Irondequoit NY
WLTW(FM) New York NY
WFGA(FM) Hicksville NY
WSRW-FM Hillsboro OH
KTUZ-FM Okarche OK
KLTH(FM) Lake Oswego OR
WAMO-FM Beaver Falls PA
WMHX(FM) Hershey PA
WTCB(FM) Orangeburg SC
KBFO(FM) Aberdeen SD
WNFN(FM) Belle Meade TN
WDXE-FM Lawrenceburg TN
WRMX(FM) Norris TN
KQTY-FM Borger TX
KCHX(FM) Midland TX
KELZ-FM Terrell Hills TX
WJFK-FM Manassas VA
WIZN(FM) Vergennes VT
KZPH(FM) Cashmere WA
WJLW(FM) Allouez WI
WATQ(FM) Chetek WI
*WHFI(FM) Lindside WV
WVKM(FM) Matewan WV

106.9 mhz
WBPT(FM) Birmingham AL
KXIO(FM) Clarksville AR
KXFE(FM) Dumas AR
KYXK(FM) Gurdon AR
KDVA(FM) Buckeye AZ
KCEL(FM) California City CA
KQLB(FM) Los Banos CA
*KEAR(FM) San Francisco CA
KDGL(FM) Yucca Valley CA
KNKN(FM) Pueblo CO
WCCC-FM Hartford CT
WKZY(FM) Cross City FL
WZZS(FM) Zolfo Springs FL
KWYI(FM) Kawaihae HI
KOJY(FM) Bloomfield IA
KIHK(FM) Rock Valley IA
KMOK(FM) Lewiston ID
WSWT(FM) Peoria IL
WDML(FM) Woodlawn IL
WMRI(FM) Marion IN
KBGL(FM) Larned KS
KTPK(FM) Topeka KS
WVEZ(FM) Louisville KY
WYMV(FM) Madisonville KY
KEDG(FM) Alexandria LA
WWEG(FM) Hagerstown MD
WRXS(FM) Ocean City MD
WBQX(FM) Thomaston ME
WUPM(FM) Ironwood MI
WMUS(FM) Muskegon MI
*WSAE(FM) Spring Arbor MI
KARP-FM Dassel MN
WMOZ(FM) Moose Lake MN
KROC-FM Rochester MN
KTXY(FM) Jefferson City MO
WHKL(FM) Crenshaw MS
WRBE-FM Lucedale MS
WKZB(FM) Stonewall MS
*KMSM-FM Butte MT
WMIT(FM) Black Mountain NC
WKQB(FM) Southern Pines NC
KHRT-FM Minot ND
KEGK(FM) Wahpeton ND
KCTY-FM Plattsmouth NE
WSCY(FM) Moultonborough NH
*WKDN-FM Camden NJ
KRNO(FM) Incline Village NV
WPHR(FM) Auburn NY
WKZA(FM) Lakewood NY
WRQK(FM) Canton OH
*WWSU(FM) Dayton OH

WMRN-FM Marion OH
KHTT(FM) Muskogee OK
KCST-FM Florence OR
KKRB(FM) Klamath Falls OR
*WRIJ(FM) Masontown PA
WZYY(FM) Renovo PA
WEZX(FM) Scranton PA
WMEG(FM) Guayama PR
WGZR(FM) Bluffton SC
WWYN(FM) McKenzie TN
WKXD(FM) Monterey TN
KMZZ(FM) Bishop TX
KLUB(FM) Bloomington TX
KHLB(FM) Burnet TX
KHPT(FM) Conroe TX
KRVF(FM) Kerens TX
KAZE(FM) Ore City TX
KKYN-FM Plainview TX
KRIA(FM) Plainview TX
KLGD(FM) Stamford TX
KRAR(FM) Brigham City UT
WBWR(FM) Bedford VA
WAFX(FM) Suffolk VA
KRWM(FM) Bremerton WA
WFMR(FM) Brookfield WI
WNNO-FM Wisconsin Dells WI
KASS(FM) Casper WY

107.1 mhz
KCNY(FM) Bald Knob AR
KTHS-FM Berryville AR
KXHT(FM) Marion AR
KDRS-FM Paragould AR
KFYX(FM) Texarkana AR
KVVA-FM Apache Junction AZ
KSSE(FM) Arcadia CA
KCWR(FM) Bakersfield CA
KSRT(FM) Cloverdale CA
KSSD(FM) Fallbrook CA
KMMM(FM) Madera CA
KNKK(FM) Needles CA
KSES-FM Seaside CA
KESR(FM) Shasta Lake City CA
KSSC(FM) Ventura CA
KPVW(FM) Aspen CO
KLJH(FM) Bayfield CO
KSIR-FM Bennett CO
WIIS(FM) Key West FL
WZJZ(FM) Lehigh Acres FL
WAOA-FM Melbourne FL
WFXM(FM) Gordon GA
WTSH-FM Rockmart GA
WTLY-FM Thomasville GA
WYFA(FM) Waynesboro GA
KDSN-FM Denison IA
*KNWI(FM) Osceola IA
KROJ(FM) Vinton IA
KTHI(FM) Caldwell ID
KQEO(FM) Idaho Falls ID
WEAI(FM) Lynnville IL
WSPY-FM Plano IL
WPGU(FM) Urbana IL
WKRV(FM) Vandalia IL
WYXY(FM) Boonville IN
WEDJ(FM) Danville IN
WZVN(FM) Lowell IN
KMOQ(FM) Baxter Springs KS
WHIR-FM Danville KY
WKCB-FM Hindman KY
WUHU(FM) Smiths Grove KY
KFNV-FM Ferriday LA
WHMD(FM) Hammond LA
KWLV(FM) Many LA
KOGM(FM) Opelousas LA
WFHN(FM) Fairhaven MA
WTDK(FM) Federalsburg MD
WQKL(FM) Ann Arbor MI
WCKC(FM) Cadillac MI
WSAQ(FM) Port Huron MI
WTLZ(FM) Saginaw MI
WIRX(FM) Saint Joseph MI
WFMP(FM) Coon Rapids MN
KKEQ(FM) Fosston MN
KMGK(FM) Glenwood MN
KBMV-FM Birch Tree MO
KBHI(FM) Miner MO
WBYP(FM) Belzoni MS

WKNZ(FM) Collins MS
WXYK(FM) Gulfport MS
WLSM-FM Louisville MS
WFXC(FM) Durham NC
KSFT-FM South Sioux City NE
WERZ(FM) Exeter NH
*WEVC(FM) Gorham NH
WWYY(FM) Belvidere NJ
WWZY(FM) Long Branch NJ
KNKT(FM) Armijo NM
KTUM(FM) Tatum NM
WXPK(FM) Briarcliff Manor NY
WFFG-FM Corinth NY
WLIR-FM Hampton Bays NY
WNUS(FM) Belpre OH
WAZU(FM) Circleville OH
WDOH(FM) Delphos OH
WBKS(FM) Ironton OH
WKFS(FM) Milford OH
KLBC(FM) Durant OK
KYNZ(FM) Lone Grove OK
*KLVU(FM) Sweet Home OR
WJJJ(FM) Greensburg PA
WEXC(FM) Greenville PA
*WQJU(FM) Mifflintown PA
WLIH(FM) Whitneyville PA
WQSD(FM) Briarcliff Acres SC
WRHM(FM) Lancaster SC
KDBX(FM) Clear Lake SD
KGSR(FM) Bastrop TX
KRXB(FM) Beeville TX
KDXX(FM) Benbrook TX
KRVA-FM Campbell TX
KPUR(FM) Canyon TX
KAUM(FM) Colorado City TX
*KWBU-FM Waco TX
WTTX-FM Appomattox VA
*WCHG-FM Hot Springs VA
WPSK-FM Pulaski VA
WORK(FM) Barre VT
WZLF(FM) Bellows Falls VT
KRQT(FM) Castle Rock WA
KAZZ(FM) Deer Park WA
WFON(FM) Fond du Lac WI
WOCO-FM Oconto WI
WPVL-FM Platteville WI
WCBC-FM Keyser WV
KROW(FM) Lovell WY

107.3 mhz
WQLT(FM) Florence AL
KQDD(FM) Osceola AR
KFXR(FM) Chinle AZ
KMXM(FM) Colorado City AZ
KURQ(FM) Grover Beach CA
KIXW-FM Lenwood CA
*KNHT(FM) Rio Dell CA
KSTN-FM Stockton CA
KRMR(FM) Hayden CO
KRKV(FM) Las Animas CO
WRQX(FM) Washington DC
WROO(FM) Jacksonville FL
WYCL(FM) Pensacola FL
WXGL(FM) Saint Petersburg FL
WMCD(FM) Claxton GA
WCGQ(FM) Columbus GA
KGRS(FM) Burlington IA
KIOW(FM) Forest City IA
WDDD-FM Marion IL
WDKR(FM) Maroa IL
WRZQ-FM Greensburg IN
WRSW-FM Warsaw IN
KTHR(FM) Wichita KS
WCTT-FM Corbin KY
WTHX(FM) Lebanon Junction KY
WTGE(FM) Baker LA
WAAF(FM) Worcester MA
WBZN(FM) Old Town ME
WKLQ(FM) Greenville MI
KNUJ-FM Sleepy Eye MN
KESY(FM) Cuba MO
KMJK(FM) Lexington MO
WFCG(FM) Tylertown MS
KINX(FM) Great Falls MT
WTKF(FM) Atlantic NC
WCLN-FM Clinton NC
KBBK(FM) Lincoln NE

U.S. FM Stations by Frequency

WPUR(FM) Atlantic City NJ
WRWD-FM Highland NY
WNVE(FM) South Bristol Township NY
WRCK(FM) Utica NY
WYBZ(FM) Crooksville OH
WNWV(FM) Elyria OH
WJUC(FM) Swanton OH
KVRW(FM) Lawton OK
KOMS(FM) Poteau OK
KACW(FM) North Bend OR
WDBA(FM) DuBois PA
WEGH(FM) Northumberland PA
WCMN-FM Arecibo PR
WJMZ-FM Anderson SC
WVSZ(FM) Chesterfield SC
KQRN(FM) Mitchell SD
KSLT(FM) Spearfish SD
WKZP(FM) Spencer TN
KLTR(FM) Caldwell TX
KJKE(FM) Ingleside TX
KJAS(FM) Jasper TX
KLFX(FM) Nolanville TX
KPOS(FM) Post TX
KISX(FM) Whitehouse TX
WXLZ-FM Lebanon VA
WBBT-FM Powhatan VA
WVGN(FM) Charlotte Amalie VI
KFFM(FM) Yakima WA
WSJY(FM) Fort Atkinson WI
WNXR(FM) Iron River WI
WKAZ(FM) Miami WV
KKAW(FM) Albin WY
KAOX(FM) Kemmerer WY

107.5 mhz
KASH-FM Anchorage AK
KOMT(FM) Mountain Home AR
KSED(FM) Sedona AZ
KHYT(FM) Tucson AZ
KQPT(FM) Colusa CA
KXO-FM El Centro CA
KPIG-FM Freedom CA
KVBE(FM) Hanford CA
KLVE(FM) Los Angeles CA
KQKS(FM) Lakewood CO
WAMR-FM Miami FL
WWGF(FM) Donalsonville GA
WTIF-FM Omega GA
WJZZ-FM Roswell GA
WDBN(FM) Wrightsville GA
*KILV(FM) Castana IA
KKDM(FM) Des Moines IA
KYZK(FM) Sun Valley ID

WGCI-FM Chicago IL
WDBQ-FM Galena IL
WABX(FM) Evansville IN
KSCB-FM Liberal KS
WIOK(FM) Falmouth KY
WZLK(FM) Virgie KY
KCIL(FM) Houma LA
KJMH(FM) Lake Arthur LA
KXKZ(FM) Ruston LA
WFCC-FM Chatham MA
WKHI(FM) Fruitland MD
WFNK(FM) Lewiston ME
WGPR(FM) Detroit MI
WCCW-FM Traverse City MI
KLIZ-FM Brainerd MN
KBGY(FM) Faribault MN
KARZ(FM) Marshall MN
KFEB(FM) Campbell MO
KWBZ(FM) Monroe City MO
WMJW(FM) Cleveland MS
WKXI-FM Magee MS
KZRV(FM) Billings MT
KLTC-FM Superior MT
WAZO(FM) Southport NC
WKZL(FM) Winston-Salem NC
KJKJ(FM) Grand Forks ND
KSMX(FM) Clovis NM
KQBA(FM) Los Alamos NM
KXTE(FM) Pahrump NV
WBBI(FM) Endwell NY
WBLS(FM) New York NY
WCKX(FM) Columbus OH
WZRX-FM Fort Shawnee OH
WFXJ-FM North Kingsville OH
WZZZ(FM) Portsmouth OH
*KOSN(FM) Ketchum OK
KIFS(FM) Ashland OR
KVMX(FM) Banks OR
WBVE(FM) Bedford PA
WBYN(FM) Boyertown PA
WNKT(FM) Saint George SC
WHBQ-FM Germantown TN
WRVW(FM) Lebanon TN
KOAI(FM) Fort Worth TX
KLDE(FM) Lake Jackson TX
KQBO(FM) Rio Grande City TX
KSJT-FM San Angelo TX
KXTN-FM San Antonio TX
KENZ(FM) Orem UT
WCJZ(FM) Charlottesville VA
WDUZ-FM Brillion WI
WCCN-FM Neillsville WI
WEGW(FM) Wheeling WV

107.7 mhz
WUHT(FM) Birmingham AL
WFXX(FM) Georgiana AL
WPRN-FM Lisman AL
KLAL(FM) Wrightsville AR
KSRN(FM) Kings Beach CA
KSAN(FM) San Mateo CA
KIST-FM Santa Barbara CA
KCDZ(FM) Twentynine Palms CA
*WFCS(FM) New Britain CT
WWRX(FM) Pawcatuck CT
WMGF(FM) Mount Dora FL
WHFX(FM) Darien GA
WPRW-FM Martinez GA
WEGC(FM) Sasser GA
KKOA(FM) Volcano HI
KICD-FM Spencer IA
WYST(FM) Fairbury IL
WLLT(FM) Polo IL
WSFR(FM) Corydon IN
WMRS(FM) Monticello IN
*KGCR(FM) Goodland KS
KMAJ-FM Topeka KS
WKCA(FM) Owingsville KY
WBQI(FM) Bar Harbor ME
WHSB(FM) Alpena MI
WMQT(FM) Ishpeming MI
WRKR(FM) Portage MI
KBMX(FM) Proctor MN
KLCX(FM) Saint Charles MN
*KCVK(FM) Otterville MO
KSLZ(FM) Saint Louis MO
KRWP(FM) Stockton MO
WAZA(FM) Liberty MS
WUKS(FM) Saint Pauls NC
KSYZ-FM Grand Island NE
WTPL(FM) Hillsboro NH
*WRRC(FM) Lawrenceville NJ
WGNA-FM Albany NY
*WECW(FM) Elmira NY
WLKK(FM) Wethersfield Township NY
WMMX(FM) Dayton OH
WXXF(FM) Loudonville OH
WSEO(FM) Nelsonville OH
WPFX-FM North Baltimore OH
KRXO(FM) Oklahoma City OK
KUMA-FM Pendleton OR
WUUZ(FM) Cooperstown PA
WGTY(FM) Gettysburg PA
WBZR-FM Tunkhannock PA
WVOZ-FM Carolina PR
WHHM-FM Henderson TN
WIVK-FM Knoxville TN

KINV(FM) Georgetown TX
KTBQ(FM) Nacogdoches TX
KPLT-FM Paris TX
WHQX(FM) Cedar Bluff VA
WTOP-FM Warrenton VA
WJCD(FM) Windsor VA
KNDD(FM) Seattle WA
WVCY-FM Milwaukee WI
WFSP-FM Kingwood WV

107.9 mhz
WJAM-FM Orrville AL
KEZA(FM) Fayetteville AR
KFIN(FM) Jonesboro AR
KMLE(FM) Chandler AZ
KUZZ-FM Bakersfield CA
KSEA(FM) Greenfield CA
*KMJC-FM Mount Shasta CA
KLLE(FM) North Fork CA
KDND(FM) Sacramento CA
KWVE(FM) San Clemente CA
KPAW(FM) Fort Collins CO
KBKL(FM) Grand Junction CO
KDZA-FM Pueblo CO
WEBE(FM) Westport CT
WNDN(FM) Chiefland FL
WSRZ-FM Coral Cove FL
WMFM(FM) Key West FL
WPFM-FM Panama City FL
WIRK-FM West Palm Beach FL
WHTA(FM) Hampton GA
WWRQ-FM Valdosta GA
KGMZ-FM Aiea HI
KKRF(FM) Stuart IA
KFMW(FM) Waterloo IA
KXLT-FM Eagle ID
WXET(FM) Arcola IL
WLEY-FM Aurora IL
WCDD(FM) Canton IL
WTPI(FM) Indianapolis IN
WJFX(FM) New Haven IN
WAMW-FM Washington IN
KZLS(FM) Great Bend KS
KSJM(FM) Winfield KS
WKYR-FM Burkesville KY
WCVQ(FM) Fort Campbell KY
WWAG(FM) McKee KY
WBTF(FM) Midway KY
KRKA(FM) Erath LA
KQHN(FM) Oil City LA
WXKS-FM Medford MA
*WFSI(FM) Annapolis MD
WHQO(FM) Skowhegan ME

*WVAC-FM Adrian MI
WCZW(FM) Charlevoix MI
WCRZ(FM) Flint MI
WSHZ(FM) Muskegon MI
KQQL(FM) Anoka MN
KLTE(FM) Kirksville MO
KCLQ(FM) Lebanon MO
WFCA(FM) Ackerman MS
WZKX(FM) Bay St. Louis MS
WLNK(FM) Charlotte NC
WNCT-FM Greenville NC
KPFX(FM) Fargo ND
KWPN-FM West Point NE
WRNB(FM) Pennsauken NJ
*WWPH(FM) Princeton Junction NJ
KKBO(FM) Alamogordo NM
KBQI(FM) Albuquerque NM
KVGS(FM) Laughlin NV
WWHT(FM) Syracuse NY
WENZ(FM) Cleveland OH
WODB(FM) Delaware OH
KEYB(FM) Altus OK
KHPE(FM) Albany OR
*WHHS(FM) Havertown PA
WDSY-FM Pittsburgh PA
WKVB(FM) Port Matilda PA
WKRF(FM) Tobyhanna PA
WRVH(FM) Williamsport PA
WGTR(FM) Bucksport SC
WLOW(FM) Port Royal SC
KWSF(FM) Flandreau SD
WOGT(FM) East Ridge TN
KEYJ-FM Abilene TX
KQQK(FM) Beaumont TX
KZRK-FM Canyon TX
KVLY(FM) Edinburg TX
KFAN-FM Johnson City TX
KESS-FM Lewisville TX
KQLM(FM) Odessa TX
KHCK-FM Robinson TX
KIXS(FM) Victoria TX
KUDD(FM) Roy UT
WYYD(FM) Amherst VA
WTYD(FM) West Point VA
*WVPS(FM) Burlington VT
*KMBI-FM Spokane WA
WLRK(FM) Wausau WI
WEMM-FM Huntington WV
KRVK(FM) Midwest WY

Canadian AM Stations by Frequency

530 khz
CIAO(AM) Brampton ON

540 khz
CBT(AM) Grand Falls-Windsor NF
CBEF(AM) Windsor ON
*CBKF-1(AM) Gravelbourg SK
*CBK(AM) Regina SK

550 khz
CHLN(AM) Trois Rivieres PQ

560 khz
CHTK(AM) Prince Rupert BC
CHVO(AM) Carbonear NF
CFOS(AM) Owen Sound ON

570 khz
CKWL(AM) Williams Lake BC
CFCB(AM) Corner Brook NF
CKGL(AM) Kitchener ON
CKSW(AM) Swift Current SK
*CFWH(AM) Whitehorse YT

580 khz
CKUA(AM) Edmonton AB
CKXR(AM) Salmon Arm BC
CFRA(AM) Ottawa ON
CKPR(AM) Thunder Bay ON
CKWW(AM) Windsor ON

590 khz
CFTK(AM) Terrace BC
CFAR(AM) Flin Flon MB
CJCW(AM) Sussex NB
VOCM(AM) Saint John's NF
CJCL(AM) Toronto ON
CKRS(AM) Saguenay PQ

600 khz
CKBD(AM) Vancouver BC
CFCT(AM) Tuktoyaktuk NT
CKAT(AM) North Bay ON
CJWW(AM) Saskatoon SK

610 khz
CKYL(AM) Peace River AB
CHNL(AM) Kamloops BC
CHTM(AM) Thompson MB
CKTB(AM) Saint Catharines ON
CHNC(AM) New Carlisle PQ
CKRW(AM) Whitehorse YT

620 khz
CKCM(AM) Grand Falls NF
CFRP(AM) Forestville PQ
CKRM(AM) Regina SK

630 khz
CHED(AM) Edmonton AB
CKOV(AM) Kelowna BC
CFCO(AM) Chatham ON
CFCY(AM) Charlottetown PE
CHLT(AM) Sherbrooke PQ

640 khz
*CBN(AM) Saint John's NF
CFMJ(AM) Toronto ON

650 khz
CISL(AM) Richmond BC
CKGA(AM) Gander NF
CKOM(AM) Saskatoon SK

660 khz
CFFR(AM) Calgary AB

680 khz
*CHFA(AM) Edmonton AB
CJOB(AM) Winnipeg MB
CFTR(AM) Toronto ON

690 khz
*CBU(AM) Vancouver BC
CINF(AM) Verdun PQ

710 khz
CKVO(AM) Clarenville NF

720 khz
CHTN(AM) Charlottetown PE

730 khz
CHMJ(AM) Vancouver BC
CKDM(AM) Dauphin MB
CKAC(AM) Montreal PQ

740 khz
CBX(AM) Edmonton AB
CHCM(AM) Marystown NF
CHWO(AM) Toronto ON

750 khz
CBGY(AM) Bonavista Bay NF
CKJH(AM) Melfort SK

760 khz
CFLD(AM) Burns Lake BC

770 khz
CHQR(AM) Calgary AB

780 khz
CFDR(AM) Dartmouth NS

790 khz
CFCW(AM) Camrose AB
CFNW(AM) Port au Choix NF
CIGM(AM) Sudbury ON

800 khz
CKOR(AM) Penticton BC
*VOWR(AM) Saint John's NF
CJBQ(AM) Belleville ON
CKDR(AM) Dryden ON
CKLW(AM) Windsor ON
CJAD(AM) Montreal PQ
CHRC(AM) Quebec PQ
CHAB(AM) Moose Jaw SK

810 khz
CKJS(AM) Winnipeg MB
CJVA(AM) Caraquet NB

820 khz
CHAM(AM) Hamilton ON

830 khz
CKKY(AM) Wainwright AB

840 khz
CKBX(AM) 100 Mile House BC

850 khz
CKBA(AM) Athabasca AB

860 khz
*CFPR(AM) Prince Rupert BC
*CHAK(AM) Inuvik NT
CJBC(AM) Toronto ON
CBKF-2(AM) Saskatoon SK

870 khz
CKIR(AM) Invermere BC
CFBV(AM) Smithers BC
CFSX(AM) Stephenville NF

880 khz
CHQT(AM) Edmonton AB
CKKC(AM) Nelson BC
CKLQ(AM) Brandon MB

890 khz
CJDC(AM) Dawson Creek BC

900 khz
*CKMO(AM) Victoria BC
CKDH(AM) Amherst NS
CHML(AM) Hamilton ON
CKTS(AM) Sherbrooke PQ
CKBI(AM) Prince Albert SK

910 khz
CKDQ(AM) Drumheller AB

920 khz
CFRY(AM) Portage la Prairie MB
CJCH(AM) Halifax NS
CKNX(AM) Wingham ON

930 khz
CJCA(AM) Edmonton AB
CFBC(AM) Saint John NB
CJYQ(AM) Saint John's NF

940 khz
CINW(AM) Montreal PQ
CJGX(AM) Yorkton SK

950 khz
CFAM(AM) Altona MB
CKNB(AM) Campbellton NB
CHER(AM) Sydney NS

960 khz
CFAC(AM) Calgary AB
CHNS(AM) Halifax NS
CFFX(AM) Kingston ON

970 khz
CJYR(AM) Edson AB

980 khz
CKNW(AM) New Westminster BC
CFPL(AM) London ON
CKRU(AM) Peterborough ON
CJME(AM) Regina SK

990 khz
CBW(AM) Winnipeg MB
*CBY(AM) Corner Brook NF
CBOF-1(AM) Maniwaki PQ
CKGM(AM) Montreal PQ

1010 khz
*CBR(AM) Calgary AB
CFRB(AM) Toronto ON

1020 khz
CKVH(AM) High Prairie AB

1040 khz
CKST(AM) Vancouver BC
CJMS(AM) Saint Constant PQ

1050 khz
*CKSB(AM) Saint Boniface MB
CHUM(AM) Toronto ON
CJNB(AM) North Battleford SK

1060 khz
CKMX(AM) Calgary AB

1070 khz
CFAX(AM) Victoria BC
CBA(AM) Moncton NB
CHOK(AM) Sarnia ON

1090 khz
CKKW(AM) Kitchener ON

1130 khz
CKWX(AM) Vancouver BC

1140 khz
CHRB(AM) High River AB
CBI(AM) Sydney NS

1150 khz
CKFR(AM) Kelowna BC
CKOC(AM) Hamilton ON
CJRC(AM) Gatineau PQ

1190 khz
CFSL(AM) Weyburn SK

1200 khz
CFGO(AM) Ottawa ON

1210 khz
CKWA(AM) Slave Lake AB
*VOAR(AM) Mount Pearl NF
CFYM(AM) Kindersley SK

1220 khz
CJRB(AM) Boissevain MB
CJUL(AM) Cornwall ON
CHSC(AM) Saint Catharines ON
CKSM(AM) Shawinigan PQ

1230 khz
CJNL(AM) Merritt BC
CHFC(AM) Churchill MB
CFLN(AM) Goose Bay NF
CFFB(AM) Iqaluit NU

1240 khz
CJOR(AM) Osoyoos BC
CJAV(AM) Port Alberni BC
CFNI(AM) Port Hardy BC
CJAR(AM) The Pas MB
CKIM(AM) Baie Verte NF
CKDR-6(AM) Atikokan ON
CJCS(AM) Stratford ON
CJMD(AM) Chibougamau PQ
CFLM(AM) La Tuque PQ
CJNS(AM) Meadow Lake SK

1250 khz
CHSM(AM) Steinbach MB
CJYE(AM) Oakville ON

1260 khz
CFRN(AM) Edmonton AB
CKHJ(AM) Fredericton NB

1270 khz
CHAT(AM) Medicine Hat AB
CJCB(AM) Sydney NS
CFGT(AM) Alma PQ

1280 khz
CHQB(AM) Powell River BC
CFMB(AM) Montreal PQ
CJSL(AM) Estevan SK

1290 khz
CFRW(AM) Winnipeg MB
CJBK(AM) London ON

1310 khz
CHLW(AM) Saint Paul AB
CIWW(AM) Ottawa ON

1320 khz
CHMB(AM) Vancouver BC
CKEC(AM) New Glasgow NS
CJMR(AM) Mississauga ON

1330 khz
CJYM(AM) Rosetown SK

1340 khz
CIBQ(AM) Brooks AB
CFKC(AM) Creston BC
CKCR(AM) Revelstoke BC
CIVH(AM) Vanderhoof BC
CFLW(AM) Wabush NF
*CFYK(AM) Yellowknife NT
CKDR-5(AM) Red Lake ON
CFED(AM) Chapais PQ
CBGN(AM) Sainte Anne des Monts PQ

1350 khz
CKAD(AM) Middleton NS
CKDO(AM) Oshawa ON

1370 khz
CFOK(AM) Westlock AB

1380 khz
CKPC(AM) Brantford ON
CKLC(AM) Kingston ON

1400 khz
CKSQ(AM) Stettler AB
CHNL-1(AM) Clearwater BC
CKGR(AM) Golden BC
CIOR(AM) Princeton BC
*CBG(AM) Gander NF

1410 khz
CFUN(AM) Vancouver BC
CKSL(AM) London ON

1420 khz
CKDY(AM) Digby NS
CKPT(AM) Peterborough ON

1430 khz
CHKT(AM) Toronto ON

1440 khz
CKJR(AM) Wetaskiwin AB

1450 khz
CHOR(AM) Summerland BC
CFAB(AM) Windsor NS
CHUC(AM) Cobourg ON
*CHMO(AM) Moosonee ON

1460 khz
CJOY(AM) Guelph ON

1470 khz
CJVB(AM) Vancouver BC

1490 khz
CFWB(AM) Campbell River BC
CFNC(AM) Cross Lake MB
CJSN(AM) Shaunavon SK

1510 khz
CKOT(AM) Tillsonburg ON

1540 khz
CHIN(AM) Toronto ON

1550 khz
*CBE(AM) Windsor ON

1570 khz
CKMW(AM) Winkler-Morden MB
CFAV(AM) Laval PQ

1610 khz
CHEV Toronto ON
CHHA(AM) Toronto ON
CJWI(AM) Montreal PQ

Canadian FM Stations by Frequency

88.1 mhz
*CFRH-FM Penetanguishene ON
*CKLN-FM Toronto ON

88.3 mhz
CJIQ-FM Kitchener/Paris ON
*CBQT-FM Thunder Bay ON
CKIA-FM Quebec PQ
CFAK-FM Sherbrooke PQ

88.5 mhz
CJSR-FM Edmonton AB
CIBH-FM Parksville BC
*CBAF-FM Moncton NB
CKDX-FM Newmarket ON
CBME-FM Montreal PQ

88.7 mhz
CFUR-FM Prince George BC
CIMX-FM Windsor ON
CHIC-FM Rouyn-Noranda PQ

88.9 mhz
CJSI-FM Calgary AB
*CBTK-FM Kelowna BC
CHNI-FM Saint John NB
CIRV-FM Toronto ON
*CJMQ-FM Lennoxville PQ

89.1 mhz
*CHUO-FM Ottawa ON
*CKRL-FM Quebec PQ
CJBR-FM Rimouski PQ
CFOU-FM Trois Rivieres PQ

89.3 mhz
*CISM-FM Montreal PQ

89.5 mhz
CJSE-FM Shediac NB
*CFGB-FM Happy Valley NF
CJRL-FM Kenora ON
*CIUT-FM Toronto ON

89.7 mhz
CBCX-FM Calgary AB
CJSU-FM Duncan BC
CKGN-FM Kapuskasing ON

89.9 mhz
CFWE-FM Lac La Biche AB
CBTE-FM Crawford Bay BC
CIHT-FM Ottawa ON
*CBE-FM Windsor ON
CFBS-FM Lourdes-de-Blanc-Sablon PQ
CJCF-FM Cumberland House SK
CJLR-FM La Ronge SK
CFNK-FM Pinehouse Lake SK

90.1 mhz
*CJSF-FM Burnaby BC
CJMP-FM Powell River BC
*CFJU-FM Kedgwick NB
CBBS-FM Sudbury ON
CJBE-FM Port-Menier PQ

90.3 mhz
CBEG-FM Sarnia ON
CJBC-FM Toronto ON
*CKUT-FM Montreal PQ

90.5 mhz
*CBCV-FM Victoria BC
CJPN-FM Fredericton NB
CBHA-FM Halifax NS
CFCR-FM Saskatoon SK

90.7 mhz
*CBOF-FM Ottawa ON

90.9 mhz
*CJSW-FM Calgary AB
CBX-FM Edmonton AB
CBUX-FM Vancouver BC
CBBX-FM Sudbury ON
*CION-FM Quebec PQ

91.1 mhz
CKXL-FM Saint Boniface MB
*CINN-FM Hearst ON
*CJRT-FM Toronto ON
CFUT-FM Shawinigan PQ

91.3 mhz
CJZN-FM Victoria BC
CBD-FM Saint John NB
CJLX-FM Belleville ON
CFBW-FM Hanover ON
CIRA-FM Montreal PQ
*CJTR-FM Regina SK

91.5 mhz
CBYG-FM Prince George BC
CBAX-FM Halifax NS
CKBT-FM Kitchener-Waterloo ON
*CBO-FM Ottawa ON
*CJAM-FM Windsor ON

91.7 mhz
CHBN-FM Edmonton AB
CIXL-FM Welland ON

91.9 mhz
CKNI-FM Moncton NB
CKVI-FM Kingston ON
CKLY-FM Lindsay (city of Kawartha Lakes) ON
CKLX-FM Montreal PQ
CJEC-FM Quebec PQ

92.1 mhz
CJAY-FM Calgary AB
CFNR-FM Terrace BC
CITI-FM Winnipeg MB
CJOZ-FM Bonavista Bay NF
CKPC-FM Brantford ON
CHOD-FM Cornwall ON
CJQQ-FM Timmins ON
CJDM-FM Drummondville PQ
CFVD-FM-2 Pohenegamook PQ
CHMX-FM Regina SK

92.3 mhz
CFRK-FM Fredericton NB
CKOZ-FM Corner Brook NF
CJET-FM Smiths Falls ON

92.5 mhz
CKNG-FM Edmonton AB
CFBX-FM Kamloops BC
CFMH-FM Saint John NB
CJAQ-FM Toronto ON
CKAJ-FM Jonquiere PQ
CFQR-FM Montreal PQ

92.7 mhz
CIAM-FM Fort Vermilion AB
CJEM-FM Edmundston NB
CJBX-FM London ON
*CFFF-FM Peterborough ON
CJRQ-FM Sudbury ON
CFIM-FM Iles-de-la-Madeleine PQ
CJOS-FM Caronport SK

92.9 mhz
CIBW-FM Drayton Valley AB
CKIC-FM Winnipeg MB
CKLE-FM Bathurst NB
CHOH-FM Hearst ON
CBBK-FM Kingston ON
CFQC-FM Saskatoon SK

93.1 mhz
CJXX-FM Grande Prairie AB
CFRY-FM Portage la Prairie MB
CKBW-FM-2 Shelburne NS
CHAY-FM Barrie ON
CFOB-FM Fort Frances ON
CFNO-FM Marathon ON
CKCU-FM Ottawa ON
CHMT-FM Timmins ON
CHLQ-FM Charlottetown PE

93.3 mhz
CJOK-FM Fort McMurray AB
CJBZ-FM Taber AB
CKSG-FM Cobourg ON
CFRU-FM Guelph ON
CJMF-FM Quebec PQ

93.5 mhz
CIHS-FM Wetaskiwin AB
CJLY-FM Nelson BC
CKZX-FM New Denver BC
CJEL-FM Winkler MB
CIKX-FM Grand Falls NB
CKUM-FM Moncton NB
*CHMR-FM Saint John's NF
CJLS-FM-2 New Tusket NS
CBCL-FM London ON
CFXJ-FM Toronto ON
CBM-FM Montreal PQ
CJAS-FM Saint Augustin PQ

93.7 mhz
CKWY-FM Wainwright AB
CJJR-FM Vancouver BC
CIFX-FM Lewisporte NF
CKOL-FM Campbellford ON
CKYC-FM Owen Sound ON
CBMI-FM Baie Comeau PQ
CBJ-FM Chicoutimi PQ
CFGE-FM Sherbrooke PQ

93.9 mhz
CFWC-FM Brantford ON
CKKL-FM Ottawa ON
CIDR-FM Windsor ON

94.1 mhz
CHSJ-FM Saint John NB
CICU-FM Eskasoni Indian Reserve NS
CKNR-FM Elliot Lake ON
CBL-FM Toronto ON
CKCN-FM Sept-Iles PQ
CIMG-FM Swift Current SK
CFGW-FM Yorkton SK

94.3 mhz
CIRX-FM Prince George BC
CHIQ-FM Winnipeg MB
CKSY-FM Chatham ON
CJTW-FM Kitchener-Waterloo ON
CJSD-FM Thunder Bay ON
CJFH-FM Woodstock ON
CKMF-FM Montreal PQ
*CHYZ-FM Sainte Foy PQ

94.5 mhz
CHBW-FM Rocky Mountain House AB
CHET-FM Chetwynd BC
CFBT-FM Vancouver BC
CKCW-FM Moncton NB
CKBW-FM-1 Liverpool NS
CJRG-FM Gaspe PQ
CJAB-FM Saguenay PQ
CKCK-FM Regina SK

94.7 mhz
CHKF-FM Calgary AB
CKLF-FM Brandon MB
CHOZ-FM Saint John's NF
CFEP-FM Eastern Passage NS
CIWV-FM Hamilton ON
CJDS-FM Saint Pamphile PQ
CHEY-FM Trois Rivieres PQ
CJNE-FM Nipawin SK

94.9 mhz
CJPR-FM Blairmore AB
*CKUA-FM Edmonton AB
CKWM-FM Kentville NS
CKPE-FM Sydney NS
*CHRW-FM London ON

95.1 mhz
CHVN-FM Winnipeg MB
CKMV-FM Grand Falls NB
*CFMU-FM Hamilton ON
CKUE-FM Chatham ON
CKCB-FM Collingwood ON
*CJOA-FM Thunder Bay ON
CILE-FM Havre-Saint-Pierre PQ
CBF-FM Montreal PQ
CFMC-FM Saskatoon SK

95.3 mhz
CJXK-FM Grand Centre (Cold Lake) AB
CKZZ-FM Vancouver BC
CING-FM Hamilton ON
CHUT-FM Lac-Simon (Louvicourt) PQ
CHOE-FM Matane PQ
*CBVX-FM Quebec PQ

95.5 mhz
CHLB-FM Lethbridge AB
CKGY-FM Red Deer AB
CBA-FM Moncton NB
CJLS-FM Yarmouth NS
CJOJ-FM Belleville ON
CJTK-FM Sudbury ON
CFVD-FM Degelis PQ
CFLX-FM Sherbrooke PQ

95.7 mhz
*CKRP-FM Falher AB
CJAT-FM Trail BC
CKTP-FM Fredericton Centre NB
CJNI-FM Halifax NS
CFJB-FM Barrie ON
CBQS-FM Sioux Narrows ON
CKYK-FM Alma PQ
CKYQ-FM Plessisville PQ

95.9 mhz
CHFM-FM Calgary AB
CKSA-FM Lloydminster AB
*CKUW-FM Winnipeg MB
CHOS-FM Rattling Brook NF
CJKX-FM Ajax ON
CFPL-FM London ON
CJFM-FM Montreal PQ

96.1 mhz
CFMY-FM Medicine Hat AB
CILZ-FM Greenville BC
CHKG-FM Vancouver BC
CKX-FM Brandon MB
CINB-FM Saint John NB
CHMY-FM Renfrew ON
*CBCT-FM Charlottetown PE

96.3 mhz
CKRA-FM Edmonton AB
CINC-FM Thompson MB
CBDQ-FM Labrador City NF
CIOZ-FM Marystown NF
CJLS-FM-1 Barrington NS
CFMK-FM Kingston ON
CFMX-FM-1 Toronto ON
CIHO-FM Saint Hilarion PQ

96.5 mhz
CJPG-FM Portage la Prairie MB
CIXN-FM Fredericton NB
CKUL-FM Halifax NS
CKMN-FM Rimouski-Mont Joli PQ
CHOA-FM Rouyn-Noranda PQ

96.7 mhz
CKGF-FM-2 Greenwood BC
CILT-FM Steinbach MB
CHYM-FM Kitchener ON
CHYR-FM Leamington ON
CHVR-FM Pembroke ON

96.9 mhz
CKIS-FM Calgary AB
CKLG-FM Vancouver BC
CJXL-FM Moncton NB
CKSS-FM Red Rocks NF
CFIX-FM Chicoutimi PQ
CKOI-FM Verdun PQ
*CBK-FM Regina SK

97.1 mhz
CJTS-FM Lethbridge AB
CJMG-FM Penticton BC
CKRO-FM Pokemouche NB
CIGL-FM Belleville ON
CHLC-FM Baie Comeau PQ
CHLX-FM Gatineau PQ
CKFI-FM Swift Current SK

97.3 mhz
CIRK-FM Edmonton AB
CKLR-FM Courtenay BC
CJCI-FM Prince George BC
CHWV-FM Saint John NB
CJRM-FM Labrador City NF
CKON-FM Akwesasne ON
*CJIV-FM Dryden ON
CJEZ-FM Toronto ON
CKUJ-FM Kuujjuaq PQ
CHGA-FM Maniwaki PQ
CFJO-FM Thetford Mines PQ

97.5 mhz
CIYR-FM Hinton AB
CKRV-FM Kamloops BC
CFFM-FM Williams Lake BC
CJKR-FM Winnipeg MB
VOCM-FM Saint John's NF
*CKDU-FM Halifax NS
CIQM-FM London ON
CHOX-FM La Pocatiere PQ

97.7 mhz
CFGP-FM Grande Prairie AB
CKLJ-FM Olds AB
CHDH-FM Siksika AB
CKTK-FM Kitimat BC
CBUF-FM Vancouver BC
CFCV-FM Saint Andrews NF
CKEN-FM Kentville NS
CHMS-FM Bancroft ON
CHTZ-FM Saint Catharines ON
*CFTH-FM-1 Harrington Harbour PQ
CHOM-FM Montreal PQ
CBKF-FM Regina SK
CIDD-FM White Bear Lake Resort SK

97.9 mhz
CKYX-FM Fort McMurray AB
CHSR-FM Fredericton NB
CFLC-FM Churchill Falls NF
CJLL-FM Ottawa ON
CFPS-FM Port Elgin ON
CJRE-FM Riviere au Renard PQ
CJCQ-FM North Battleford SK

98.1 mhz
CHTD-FM Saint Stephen NB
CKBW-FM Bridgewater NS
CHPB-FM Cochrane ON
*CBON-FM Sudbury ON
CHFI-FM Toronto ON
CHOI-FM Quebec PQ
*CBSI-FM Sept-Iles PQ
CFMQ-FM Hudson Bay SK
CHON-FM Whitehorse YT

98.3 mhz
CKSR-FM Chilliwack BC
CIFM-FM Kamloops BC
CFPX-FM Pukatawagan MB
CBW-FM Winnipeg MB
CBAL-FM Moncton NB

Canadian FM Stations by Frequency

CFLY-FM Kingston ON
CFWP-FM Wahta Mohawk Territory near Bala ON
CIAX-FM Windsor PQ
CJMK-FM Saskatoon SK

98.5 mhz
CIBK-FM Calgary AB
CHRX-FM Fort St. John BC
CIOC-FM Victoria BC
CIOS-FM Stephenville NF
CINU-FM Truro NS
CKWR-FM Kitchener ON
CFTH-FM-2 La Tabatiere PQ
CHMP-FM Longueuil PQ

98.7 mhz
CKXD-FM Gander NF
CBQX-FM Kenora ON
CIKI-FM Rimouski PQ

98.9 mhz
CIZZ-FM Red Deer AB
CFCP-FM Courtenay BC
CJYC-FM Saint John NB
CJFX-FM Antigonish NS
CHCD-FM Simcoe ON
CHYC-FM Sudbury ON
CHIK-FM Quebec PQ
CIZL-FM Regina SK

99.1 mhz
CJDR-FM Fernie BC
CJZZ-FM Winnipeg MB
CKIX-FM Saint John's NF
CHRI-FM Ottawa ON
CBLA-FM Toronto ON
CIDI-FM Lac-Brome PQ
CIPC-FM Port-Cartier PQ
CJMM-FM Rouyn-Noranda PQ
CFNJ-FM Saint Gabriel-de-Brandon PQ
CFMM-FM Prince Albert SK

99.3 mhz
CKQR-FM Castlegar BC
CKDV-FM Prince George BC
CFOX-FM Vancouver BC
CFAN-FM Miramichi City NB
CKQN-FM Baker Lake NU
CJBC-FM-4 London ON
CFSF-FM Sturgeon Falls ON
CKGB-FM Timmins ON
CJAN-FM Asbestos PQ
*CBV-FM-6 La Malbaie PQ
CFOR-FM Maniwaki PQ

99.5 mhz
CJLT-FM Medicine Hat AB
CBZF-FM Fredericton NB
CKTY-FM Truro NS
CFBG-FM Bracebridge ON
CKKK-FM Peterborough ON
CJPX-FM Montreal PQ
CHRL-FM Roberval PQ

99.7 mhz
CHJM-FM Saint Georges PQ

99.9 mhz
CHSU-FM Kelowna BC
CFWM-FM Winnipeg MB
CHOY-FM Moncton NB
CJIJ-FM Sydney NS
CKIQ-FM Iqaluit NU
CFGX-FM Sarnia ON
*CBCS-FM Sudbury ON
CJUK-FM Thunder Bay ON
CKFM-FM Toronto ON
CFVM-FM Amqui PQ
CHEF-FM Matagami PQ

100.1 mhz
CKFU-FM Fort St. John BC
CKBZ-FM Kamloops BC
CIOO-FM Halifax NS
CJCD-FM-1 Hay River NT
CJCD-FM Yellowknife NT
CHCQ-FM Belleville ON

CHFN-FM Cape Croker (Neyaashiinigmiing) ON
CKAG-FM Pikogan PQ
CJEB-FM Trois Rivieres PQ

100.3 mhz
CFBR-FM Edmonton AB
CKCQ-FM Quesnel BC
CKKQ-FM Victoria BC
CFOZ-FM Argentia NF
CJLF-FM Barrie ON
*CKRZ-FM Ohsweken ON
CJMJ-FM Ottawa ON
*CKMS-FM Waterloo ON
CHVD-FM Dolbeau-Mistassini PQ
CJMC-FM Sainte Anne des Monts PQ

100.5 mhz
CFSR-FM Hope BC
CHLS-FM Lillooet BC
CIOK-FM Saint John NB
CBBL-FM London ON
CHUR-FM North Bay ON
CHAS-FM Sault Ste. Marie ON
*CFIN-FM Lac-Etchemin PQ
CIBO-FM Senneterre PQ

100.7 mhz
CIGV-FM Penticton BC
CIAJ-FM Prince Rupert BC
CHNR-FM Winnipeg MB
CHIN-FM Toronto ON
CBFX-FM Montreal PQ
CILG-FM Moose Jaw SK
CIAY-FM Whitehorse YT

100.9 mhz
CFXL-FM High River-Okotoks AB
*CBWK-FM Thompson MB
CKTO-FM Truro NS
CKHA-FM Haliburton ON
CKAP-FM Kapuskasing ON
*CBJX-FM Chicoutimi PQ
CKNU-FM Donnacona PQ

101.1 mhz
CFMI-FM New Westminster BC
CKXA-FM Brandon MB
CFAI-FM Edmundston NB
CKSJ-FM Saint John's NF
CIQB-FM Barrie ON
CKEY-FM Fort Erie ON
CJWL-FM Iroquois Falls ON
CFRM-FM Little Current ON
CKBY-FM Smiths Falls ON

101.3 mhz
CKKN-FM Prince George BC
CKUN-FM Christian Island ON
CKOT-FM Tillsonburg ON
CJSA-FM Toronto ON
CKII-FM Dolbeau-Mistassini PQ
CHEQ-FM Sainte-Marie-de-Beauce PQ

101.5 mhz
CKNL-FM Fort St. John BC
CILK-FM Kelowna BC
CJUM-FM Winnipeg MB
*CBZ-FM Fredericton NB
CIGO-FM Port Hawkesbury NS
*CIOI-FM Hamilton ON
CJKL-FM Kirkland Lake ON
CKWF-FM Peterborough ON
*CIBL-FM Montreal PQ
*CBRX-FM Rimouski PQ
CHQX-FM Prince Albert SK

101.7 mhz
CHLY-FM Nanaimo BC
*CBQ-FM Thunder Bay ON
CKNX-FM Wingham ON
CHIP-FM Fort Coulonge PQ
CHRG-FM Maria (Reserve) PQ
CJSO-FM Sorel PQ

101.9 mhz
CKER-FM Edmonton AB
CKKC-FM Crawford Bay BC
*CITR-FM Vancouver BC

*CFUV-FM Victoria BC
CHFX-FM Halifax NS
CKLB-FM Yellowknife NT
CJSS-FM Cornwall ON
*CFRC-FM Kingston ON
CKFX-FM North Bay ON
CHAI-FM Chateauguay PQ
CFDA-FM Victoriaville PQ

102.1 mhz
*CBR-FM Calgary AB
CKHL-FM High Level AB
CISW-FM Whistler BC
CFNY-FM Brampton ON
CHPR-FM Hawkesbury ON
CJRW-FM Summerside PE
CBGA-FM Matane PQ
CFEL-FM Montmagny PQ
CJDJ-FM Saskatoon SK

102.3 mhz
CKRX-FM Fort Nelson BC
CKWV-FM Nanaimo BC
CKY-FM Winnipeg MB
CKXG-FM Grand Falls-Windsor NF
CKJJ-FM Belleville ON
CHST-FM London ON
*CHIM-FM Timmins ON
CINQ-FM Montreal PQ
CIGB-FM Trois Rivieres PQ
CHSN-FM Estevan SK
CJNS-FM Meadow Lake SK

102.5 mhz
*CBOX-FM Ottawa ON

102.7 mhz
*CFRO-FM Vancouver BC
*CBH-FM Halifax NS
CFGI-FM Georgina Island ON
CBJE-FM Chicoutimi PQ
CITE-FM-1 Sherbrooke PQ
CJMV-FM Val d'Or PQ
CKZP-FM Zenon Park SK

102.9 mhz
CHDI-FM Edmonton AB
CHDR-FM Cranbrook BC
CKLH-FM Hamilton ON
CHCR-FM Killaloe ON
CFOM-FM Levis PQ
CJOI-FM Rimouski PQ

103.1 mhz
CIQX-FM Calgary AB
CJFW-FM Terrace BC
CHTT-FM Victoria BC
CKMM-FM Winnipeg MB
CJMO-FM Moncton NB
CFMX-FM Cobourg ON
CJBB-FM Englehart ON
CFHK-FM St. Thomas ON
CFMF-FM Fermont PQ
CIAU-FM Radisson PQ
CKOD-FM Valleyfield PQ

103.3 mhz
*CBOQ-FM Ottawa ON
CKLP-FM Parry Sound ON
CHAA-FM Longueuil PQ

103.5 mhz
CHMM-FM MacKenzie BC
CHQM-FM Vancouver BC
CFHA-FM Saint John NB
CKHZ-FM Halifax NS
CIVR-FM Yellowknife NT
CIDC-FM Orangeville ON
CJLM-FM Joliette PQ
CKRB-FM Saint Georges-de-Beauce PQ

103.7 mhz
CBRF-FM Calgary AB
CJPT-FM Brockville ON
CFBU-FM Saint Catharines ON
CFID-FM Acton Vale PQ
CIMI-FM Charlesbourg PQ
*CKRK-FM Kahnawake PQ

CIEL-FM Riviere du Loup PQ

103.9 mhz
CISN-FM Edmonton AB
CIMS-FM Balmoral NB
CFQM-FM Moncton NB
CKXX-FM Corner Brook NF
CHNO-FM Sudbury ON
CKDK-FM Woodstock ON
CKWE-FM Maniwaki (Kitigan Zibi Anishinabeg Reserve) PQ
CIME-FM Saint Jerome PQ

104.1 mhz
CHAD-FM Dawson Creek BC
CFQX-FM Selkirk MB
CJCJ-FM Woodstock NB
CIFA-FM Yarmouth NS
CICZ-FM Midland ON
CHYK-FM Timmins ON
CKTF-FM Gatineau PQ
CKNA-FM Natashquan PQ
CFZZ-FM Saint Jean-Iberville PQ
CIOT-FM Nipawin SK

104.3 mhz
CFRQ-FM Dartmouth NS
CJQM-FM Sault Ste. Marie ON
CBF-FM-1 Trois Rivieres PQ
CHGO-FM Val d'Or PQ

104.5 mhz
CISP-FM Pemberton BC
CFLG-FM Cornwall ON
CFQK-FM Kaministiquia ON
CJTT-FM New Liskeard ON
CHUM-FM Toronto ON
CKAU-FM Maliotenam PQ
CIGR-FM Sherbrooke PQ

104.7 mhz
CHBZ-FM Cranbrook BC
CKLZ-FM Kelowna BC
CIPN-FM Pender Harbour BC
CKKS-FM Sechelt BC
CFLO-FM Mont-Laurier PQ
CBVE-FM Quebec PQ

104.9 mhz
CFMG-FM Saint Albert AB
CKBC-FM Bathurst NB
CFJR-FM Brockville ON
CBQL-FM Savant Lake ON
CJLA-FM Lachute PQ
*CHOC-FM Saint Remi PQ
CKVX-FM Kindersley SK
CFWF-FM Regina SK

105.1 mhz
CKRY-FM Calgary AB
CHAL-FM Halifax NS
CBI-FM Sydney NS
CBQR-FM Rankin Inlet NU
CFLZ-FM Niagara Falls ON
CKQM-FM Peterborough ON
CKIE-FM Toronto ON
CBMR-FM Fermont PQ
CFIC-FM Listuguj PQ
CKDG-FM Montreal PQ
CJVR-FM Melfort SK

105.3 mhz
CFXY-FM Fredericton NB
CJKK-FM Clarenville NF
CFCA-FM Kitchener ON
CISS-FM Ottawa ON
CJMX-FM Sudbury ON
CKTG-FM Thunder Bay ON
CHRD-FM Drummondville PQ
CHRM-FM Matane PQ

105.5 mhz
CHUB-FM Red Deer AB
CICY-FM Selkirk MB
CFBK-FM Huntsville ON
CHRY-FM Toronto ON
CKLD-FM Thetford Mines PQ
*CBKS-FM Saskatoon SK

105.7 mhz
CBU-FM Vancouver BC
CICF-FM Vernon BC
CIKR-FM Kingston ON
CHRE-FM Saint Catharines ON
CFGL-FM Laval PQ
CFDM-FM Meadow Lake SK

105.9 mhz
CJRY-FM Edmonton AB
CITA-FM Moncton NB
CHPD-FM Aylmer ON
CHJX-FM London ON
CICX-FM Orillia ON
*CBKA-FM La Ronge SK

106.1 mhz
CKLM-FM Lloydminster AB
CKKX-FM Peace River AB
CKGO-FM-1 Boston Bar BC
*CKJM-FM Cheticamp NS
CIMJ-FM Guelph ON
CHEZ-FM Ottawa ON
CIMO-FM Magog PQ

106.3 mhz
CHKS-FM Sarnia ON
*CBV-FM Quebec PQ

106.5 mhz
CHMN-FM Canmore AB
CJJJ-FM Brandon MB
CIXK-FM Owen Sound ON
CFIE-FM Toronto ON
CFEI-FM Saint Hyacinthe PQ

106.7 mhz
CJRX-FM Lethbridge AB
CFDV-FM Red Deer AB
CIKZ-FM Kitchener-Waterloo ON
CJIT-FM Lac Megantic PQ
CFET-FM Tagish YT

106.9 mhz
CHWF-FM Nanaimo BC
CIBX-FM Fredericton NB
*CHMA-FM Sackville NB
*CBN-FM Saint John's NF
*CIXX-FM London ON
CKQB-FM Ottawa ON
CHRQ-FM Restigouche PQ

107.1 mhz
CKQC-FM Abbotsford BC
CISQ-FM Squamish BC
CFEQ-FM Winnipeg MB
CILQ-FM North York ON
CJTN-FM Quinte West ON
CJWA-FM Wawa ON
CIBM-FM Riviere du Loup PQ

107.3 mhz
CFGQ-FM Calgary AB
CHBE-FM Victoria BC
CKOE-FM Moncton NB
CKHR-FM Hay River NT
CFRT-FM Iqaluit NU
CHUK-FM Mashteuiatsh (Pointe-Bleue) PQ
CITE-FM Montreal PQ

107.5 mhz
CKCL-FM Chilliwack BC
CIEG-FM Egmont BC
CISC-FM Gibsons BC
CKIZ-FM Vernon BC
CJFY-FM Blackville NB
CJDV-FM Cambridge ON
CITF-FM Quebec PQ

107.7 mhz
CFRV-FM Lethbridge AB
CKMB-FM Barrie ON
CKTI-FM Kettle Point ON
CHGK-FM Stratford ON

107.9 mhz
CJWV-FM Winnipeg MB
CJXY-FM Burlington ON
*CKDJ-FM Ottawa ON

Radio Formats Defined

AAA (or Triple A)—Adult Album Alternative. Eclectic choice of music ranging from hard rock to folk music.

Adult Contemporary—Recent popular songs, with a few oldies. The songs tend to be upbeat and soft. News and talk segments are prominent during rush hour "drive times." Also known as **Light Rock**.

Agriculture & Farm—News, weather and features of interest to farmers and others involved in agriculture.

Albanian.

Album-Oriented Rock—Popular rock music from past and present rock albums. Also see **Rock/AOR**.

Alternative—Rock music first popularized in the late 80s and early 90s. Also known as **Progressive**.

American Indian—Programming for North American Indians; includes native language (i.e. Navajo) broadcasts.

Arabic.

Armenian.

Beautiful Music—Uninterrupted, instrumental soft music. There is usually very little talk and few commercials. Also known as **Easy Listening**.

Big Band—Popular music from the 30s and 40s. Primarily instrumental works by bands such as Glen Miller's Orchestra and Tommy Dorsey. Also see **Nostalgia**.

Black—Music, talk and news targeted at Black listeners. Music at these stations is similar to **Urban Contemporary** stations, but this format caters more directly to the interests and tastes of Black audiences.

Bluegrass—Related formats are **Country** and **Folk**.

Blues—Some **Jazz** and **Progressive** stations also program blues music.

Children—Programming for children, usually for educational purposes. Includes music, informational programming, and news presented for young people.

Chinese.

Christian.

Classic Rock—Popular rock music of the 60s, 70s and 80s. Also see **Rock/AOR**.

Classical—Classical music, often long pieces played without interruption. Announcers provide extended commentary and criticism on the pieces. Special features, such as live concerts, are common. Primarily a noncommercial FM format.

Comedy—Recorded stand-up comics and/or old radio comedy series. A rare format.

Contemporary Hit/Top-40—Current hot selling records. Usually a playlist of 20 to 40 songs continuously played throughout the day. DJs are often upbeat "personalities." News and information are given light coverage.

Country—Country music, ranging from older traditional country and western to today's "Hit Country" sounds. The amount of news and talk on country stations varies widely from station to station.

Croatian.

Czech.

Disco—High-energy dance music first popular in the 70s. Also see **Black** and **Urban Contemporary**.

Discussion.

Diversified—See **Variety/Diverse**.

Drama/Literature—Dramatic readings, poetry, and broadcasts of live dramatic performances. A rare format in the U.S. and Canada.

Easy Listening—Similar to **Beautiful Music**, but may include some soft rock.

Educational—Informative and instructional programming, such as over-the-air college courses. Primarily a noncommercial format.

Eskimo.

Ethnic—Programming for ethnic minorities, mostly in foreign languages.

Farsi.

Filipino.

Finnish.

Folk—Played full-time on very few stations, American folk music is also heard on noncommercial **Variety** stations. Also see **Bluegrass**.

Foreign Language/Ethnic—In addition to the specific language categories (i.e. French, German), this format denotes multilingual stations and others catering to ethnic minorities.

French.

Full Service—Mixture of music, news and talk with a general target audience.

German.

Golden Oldies—Hit songs of the 50s. Also see **Oldies**.

Gospel—Especially popular in the South, evangelical music is programmed on many **Religious** format stations.

Greek.

Hardcore.

Hebrew.

Hindi.

Hungarian.

Inspirational.

Irish.

Italian.

Japanese.

Jazz—Primarily a noncommercial FM format. Some Classical stations program jazz music features.

Jewish.

Korean.

Light Rock—See **Adult Contemporary**.

Lithuanian.

MOR (Middle-of-the-Road)—Traditional AM format featuring a balanced mix of music, news and talk. Songs are usually popular standards. Announcers are often personalities who try to keep the listener interested and informed. News, both local and national, plays an important role at most MOR stations; coverage of sporting events and other features of interest to the community is common.

Native American.

New Age—Soft "fusion" (a form mixing elements of jazz and rock), often played as background entertainment. As the name implies, this format is a recent development.

New Wave—A type of rock music which gained popularity in the early 80s, often performed by United Kingdom musicians.

News—Continous coverage of local, national and international news, including sports, weather forecasts and features.

News/Talk—Combination of news and talk formats. One of these elements may receive more emphasis. Also see **News** and **Talk**.

Nostalgia—Popular tunes from the 30s, 40s and 50s. Nostalgia stations often feature on-air personalities, and usually have heavy news and information coverage.

Oldies—Hit songs from the 50s, 60s and 70s. Usually played by upbeat DJs, with news, talk and special features (chart countdowns, trivia contests, etc.) playing an important role.

Other—Programming which falls outside the categories listed here.

Polish.

Polka—Music for the traditional dance. Most polka format stations are located in Wisconsin.

Portuguese.

Progressive—Progressive stations play many types of music, often including avant-garde music not played on conventional stations. Primarily a noncommercial format, common among college radio stations. Also known as **Alternative**.

Public Affairs—Community interest programming (ie: broadcasts of city council meetings.) Many noncommercial, **News**, and **Talk** stations cover local issues on news features or talk shows.

Reggae—Jamaican music. Often played on **Progressive** stations.

Religious—Inspirational/spiritual talk and music. Most religious stations air Christian sermons or songs. Also see **Gospel**.

Rock/AOR—Rock music from the 60s to the present. Album-oriented rock features music "sweeps" or uninterrupted sets. News plays a secondary role. Also see **Classic Rock**.

Russian.

Sacred.

Scottish.

Serbian.

Slovak.

Slovenian.

Spanish.

Sports— Play-by-play and taped coverage, sports news, interviews, discussion.

Talk—Topical programs on various subjects. Includes health, finance, and community issues. Listener call-in and interview shows are common, and the host's personality tends to be an important element.

Many talk stations air national satellite-delivered talk programs. News, sports and weather are usually emphasized during "drive times." Also see **News** and **News/Talk.**

Tejano—Bicultural programming including Spanish programming, popular in Texas, particularly near the Mexican border. Interest surged in this type of Spanish music during the early 90s.

Ukranian.

Top-40—See **Contemporary Hit/Top-40**.

Underground—The opposite of mainstream, this music is produced and appreciated by those outside the establishment.

Urban Contemporary—Dance music, often from a variety of genres (i.e. rhythm & blues, rap). Most Urban Contemporary stations emphasize music by Black artists. Also see **Black** and **Disco**.

Variety/Diverse—A station listing four or more formats. Typical of noncommerical stations.

Vietnamese.

Women—Programming for women. Emphasis on news and information, pertaining to women's issues.

U.S. and Canada Radio Programming Formats

	United States					Canada				
Format	Total	AM	FM	Com	Non	Total	AM	FM	Com	Non
Adult Contemp	1758	281	1477	1648	110	220	32	188	213	7
Agriculture	59	47	12	59	0	3	3	0	3	0
Albanian	0	0	0	0	0	0	0	0	0	0
Album-Oriented Rock	88	0	88	77	11	7	1	6	7	0
Alternative	260	3	257	121	139	12	0	12	5	7
American Indian	4	2	2	2	2	3	0	3	3	0
Arabic	1	1	0	1	0	0	0	0	0	0
Armenian	0	0	0	0	0	0	0	0	0	0
Beautiful Music	76	34	42	56	20	2	0	2	1	1
Big Band	87	64	23	75	12	1	0	1	1	0
Black	89	58	31	74	15	1	0	1	1	0
Bluegrass	33	24	9	27	6	0	0	0	0	0
Blues	103	29	74	69	34	3	0	3	1	2
Children	55	47	8	50	5	0	0	0	0	0
Chinese	4	4	0	4	0	3	2	1	3	0
Christian	1209	297	912	488	721	32	3	29	29	3
Classic Rock	637	21	616	594	43	67	2	65	66	1
Classical	511	14	497	51	460	32	3	29	16	16
Comedy	1	1	0	1	0	1	0	1	1	0
Contemporary Hit/Top-40	634	36	598	540	94	73	14	59	71	2
Country	2126	635	1491	2095	31	139	66	73	132	7
Croation	0	0	0	0	0	0	0	0	0	0
Czech	0	0	0	0	0	0	0	0	0	0
Disco	1	0	1	1	0	0	0	0	0	0
Discussion	0	0	0	0	0	0	0	0	0	0
Diversified	287	28	259	28	259	85	16	69	54	31
Drama/Literature	0	0	0	0	0	1	0	1	1	0
Easy Listening	52	20	32	43	9	6	1	5	6	0
Educational	252	21	231	21	231	8	3	5	3	5
Eskimo	0	0	0	0	0	1	0	1	1	0
Ethnic	73	43	30	62	11	19	7	12	17	2
Farsi	1	1	0	1	0	0	0	0	0	0
Filipino	2	1	1	2	0	1	0	1	1	0
Finnish	0	0	0	0	0	0	0	0	0	0
Folk	16	1	15	1	15	1	1	0	0	1
Foreign/Ethnic	63	29	34	55	8	9	4	5	9	0
French	3	3	0	3	0	43	1	42	36	7
Full Service	67	55	12	62	5	0	0	0	0	0
German	0	0	0	0	0	1	0	1	1	0
Golden Oldies	19	9	10	19	0	2	1	1	2	0
Gospel	627	434	193	532	95	2	1	1	1	1
Greek	4	4	0	4	0	0	0	0	0	0
Hardcore	0	0	0	0	0	0	0	0	0	0
Hebrew	0	0	0	0	0	0	0	0	0	0
Hindi	0	0	0	0	0	1	0	1	1	0
Hungarian	0	0	0	0	0	0	0	0	0	0
Inspirational	102	15	87	24	78	2	1	1	2	0
Irish	1	1	0	1	0	0	0	0	0	0
Italian	2	2	0	2	0	0	0	0	0	0

Broadcasting & Cable Yearbook 2006

U.S. and Canada Radio Programming Formats

Format	United States Total	AM	FM	Com	Non	Canada Total	AM	FM	Com	Non
Japanese	1	1	0	1	0	0	0	0	0	0
Jazz	365	18	347	60	305	18	2	16	7	11
Jewish	0	0	0	0	0	0	0	0	0	0
Korean	10	10	0	10	0	0	0	0	0	0
Light Rock	41	5	36	39	2	13	1	12	13	0
Lithuanian	0	0	0	0	0	0	0	0	0	0
MOR	219	162	57	195	24	49	18	31	47	2
Native American	8	2	6	2	6	3	0	3	3	0
New Age	25	3	22	10	15	0	0	0	0	0
New Wave	0	0	0	0	0	0	0	0	0	0
News	753	283	470	339	414	31	11	20	25	6
News/talk	1279	1036	243	1098	181	60	38	22	41	19
Nostalgia	115	81	34	107	8	5	4	1	4	1
Oldies	1113	467	646	1083	30	52	37	15	50	2
Other	220	90	130	182	38	14	2	12	12	2
Polish	5	5	0	5	0	0	0	0	0	0
Polka	5	3	2	4	1	0	0	0	0	0
Portugese	3	1	2	2	1	0	0	0	0	0
Progressive	156	7	149	15	141	4	0	4	3	1
Public Affairs	70	19	51	19	51	21	4	17	13	8
Reggae	4	2	2	3	1	0	0	0	0	0
Religious	834	391	443	442	392	6	3	3	4	2
Rock/AOR	546	12	534	396	150	63	6	57	61	2
Russian	2	2	0	2	0	0	0	0	0	0
Sacred	0	0	0	0	0	0	0	0	0	0
Scottish	0	0	0	0	0	0	0	0	0	0
Serbian	0	0	0	0	0	0	0	0	0	0
Slovak	0	0	0	0	0	0	0	0	0	0
Slovenian	0	0	0	0	0	0	0	0	0	0
Smooth Jazz	40	1	39	35	5	3	0	3	3	0
Soul	7	2	5	7	0	0	0	0	0	0
Spanish	698	376	322	633	65	1	1	0	1	0
Sports	944	838	106	931	13	16	15	1	16	0
Talk	767	605	162	691	76	23	8	15	15	8
Tejano	25	6	19	25	0	0	0	0	0	0
Top-40	67	8	59	64	3	12	0	12	12	0
Triple A	87	1	86	47	40	0	0	0	0	0
Ukranian	0	0	0	0	0	0	0	0	0	0
Underground	1	0	1	0	1	0	0	0	0	0
Urban Contemporary	361	62	299	298	63	6	0	6	4	2
Variety/Diverse	297	71	226	101	196	55	4	51	40	15
Vietnamese	5	5	0	5	0	0	0	0	0	0
Women	0	0	0	0	0	0	0	0	0	0

Programming on Radio Stations in the U.S.

Adult Contemp

KDBZ(FM) Anchorage AK
KMXS(FM) Anchorage AK
KYMG(FM) Anchorage AK
*KBRW-FM Barrow AK
KCDV(FM) Cordova AK
*KDLG(AM) Dillingham AK
KAKQ-FM Fairbanks AK
KYSC(FM) Fairbanks AK
*KEUL(FM) Girdwood AK
*KHNS(FM) Haines AK
KWVV-FM Homer AK
KQEZ(FM) Houston AK
KFMG(FM) Juneau AK
KINY(AM) Juneau AK
KSRJ(FM) Juneau AK
KTKN(AM) Ketchikan AK
KRXX(FM) Kodiak AK
KAKN(FM) Naknek AK
KPFN(FM) Seward AK
KIFW(AM) Sitka AK
KKIS-FM Soldotna AK
KVAK(AM) Valdez AK
KMBQ(FM) Wasilla AK
WRFS(AM) Alexander City AL
WYOK(FM) Atmore AL
WKXX(FM) Attalla AL
WMJJ(FM) Birmingham AL
WYSF(FM) Birmingham AL
WDLT-FM Chickasaw AL
WKGA(FM) Dadeville AL
WRSA-FM Decatur AL
WAGF-FM Dothan AL
WOOF-FM Dothan AL
WKMX(FM) Enterprise AL
WKZJ(FM) Eufaula AL
WQLT(FM) Florence AL
WCKS-FM Fruithurst AL
WFXX(FM) Georgiana AL
WAHR(FM) Huntsville AL
WHOD(FM) Jackson AL
WWMG(FM) Millbrook AL
*WBHY-FM Mobile AL
WMXC(FM) Mobile AL
WMXS(FM) Montgomery AL
WMXA(FM) Opelika AL
WCSN-FM Orange Beach AL
WVOK-FM Oxford AL
WOAB(FM) Ozark AL
WGSY(FM) Phenix City AL
WPID(AM) Piedmont AL
WBEI(FM) Reform AL
WALX(FM) Selma AL
WTRB-FM Sylacauga AL
WTUG(FM) Tuscaloosa AL
KDEL-FM Arkadelphia AR
KMJI(FM) Ashdown AR
KCNY(FM) Bald Knob AR
KBTA-FM Batesville AR
KZLE(FM) Batesville AR
KAMD-FM Camden AR
KCON(AM) Conway AR
*KUCA(FM) Conway AR
KBKG(FM) Corning AR
KDMS(FM) El Dorado AR
KLBQ(FM) El Dorado AR
KMRX(FM) El Dorado AR
KEZA(FM) Fayetteville AR
KHMB(FM) Hamburg AR
KOOU(FM) Hardy AR
KHOZ(AM) Harrison AR
KILX(FM) Hatfield AR
KAWW-FM Heber Springs AR
KFFA-FM Helena AR
KBHS(AM) Hot Springs AR
KLAZ(FM) Hot Springs AR
KYDL(FM) Hot Springs AR
KKTZ(FM) Lakeview AR
KURB(FM) Little Rock AR
KMSX(FM) Maumelle AR
KSSW(FM) Nashville AR

KDRS-FM Paragould AR
KBOA-FM Piggott AR
KOTN(AM) Pine Bluff AR
KPOC(AM) Pocahontas AR
KPOC-FM Pocahontas AR
KYNF(FM) Prairie Grove AR
KWKK(FM) Russellville AR
KOKY(FM) Sherwood AR
KJBX(FM) Trumann AR
KWDO(FM) Waldo AR
KLAL(FM) Wrightsville AR
KSBS-FM Pago Pago AS
KVVA-FM Apache Junction AZ
KDVA(FM) Buckeye AZ
KIKO-FM Claypool AZ
KWRQ(FM) Clifton AZ
KMXM(FM) Colorado City AZ
KJIK(FM) Duncan AZ
KVNA-FM Flagstaff AZ
KMRR(FM) Globe AZ
KFLX(FM) Kachina Village AZ
KZUL-FM Lake Havasu City AZ
KSZR(FM) Oro Valley AZ
KXAZ(FM) Page AZ
KESZ(FM) Phoenix AZ
KMXP(FM) Phoenix AZ
KPKX(FM) Phoenix AZ
KSUN(AM) Phoenix AZ
*KGCB(FM) Prescott AZ
KNOT(AM) Prescott AZ
KPPV(FM) Prescott Valley AZ
KQST(FM) Sedona AZ
KRFM(FM) Show Low AZ
KZMK(FM) Sierra Vista AZ
KOMR(FM) Sun City AZ
KTBA(AM) Tuba City AZ
KMXZ-FM Tucson AZ
KZPT(FM) Tucson AZ
KSGC(FM) Tusayan AZ
KWIM(FM) Window Rock AZ
KLJZ(FM) Yuma AZ
KZXY-FM Apple Valley CA
KHYL(FM) Auburn CA
KBLX-FM Berkeley CA
KJMB(FM) Blythe CA
*KBPK(FM) Buena Park CA
KCDU(FM) Carmel CA
KSBL(FM) Carpinteria CA
KMXI(FM) Chico CA
KOND(FM) Clovis CA
KQPT(FM) Colusa CA
KCRE-FM Crescent City CA
KPOD(AM) Crescent City CA
KXSE(FM) Davis CA
KXO-FM El Centro CA
KHWY(FM) Essex CA
KFMI(FM) Eureka CA
KAJK-FM Ferndale CA
KSAY(FM) Fort Bragg CA
KLIT(FM) Fountain Valley CA
KALZ(FM) Fresno CA
KJWL(FM) Fresno CA
KKDG(FM) Fresno CA
KMGQ(FM) Goleta CA
KNCO-FM Grass Valley CA
KMJE(FM) Gridley CA
KTDE(FM) Gualala CA
KATY-FM Idyllwild CA
KSRW(FM) Independence CA
KRCD(FM) Inglewood CA
KRAJ(FM) Johannesburg CA
KRKC(FM) King City CA
KXBX-FM Lakeport CA
KGMX(FM) Lancaster CA
KKIQ(FM) Livermore CA
*KCJH(FM) Livingston CA
KSKD(FM) Livingston CA
KBOX(FM) Lompoc CA
KBIG-FM Los Angeles CA
KCBS-FM Los Angeles CA

KLVE(FM) Los Angeles CA
KOST(FM) Los Angeles CA
KYSR(FM) Los Angeles CA
KSTT-FM Los Osos-Baywood Park CA
KMMT(FM) Mammoth Lakes CA
KJSN(FM) Modesto CA
KIDD(AM) Monterey CA
KWAV(FM) Monterey CA
KLMM(FM) Morro Bay CA
KHYZ(FM) Mountain Pass CA
KTNS(AM) Oakhurst CA
KLLY(FM) Oildale CA
KFYV(FM) Ojai CA
KXLM(FM) Oxnard CA
KEZN(FM) Palm Desert CA
KLUN(FM) Paso Robles CA
KOSO(FM) Patterson CA
*KLVM(FM) Prunedale CA
KLXR(AM) Redding CA
KSHA(FM) Redding CA
KZIQ-FM Ridgecrest CA
KELT(FM) Riverside CA
KOSS(FM) Rosamond CA
KYMX(FM) Sacramento CA
KZZO(FM) Sacramento CA
KVYN(FM) Saint Helena CA
KFMB-FM San Diego CA
KMYI(FM) San Diego CA
KIOI(FM) San Francisco CA
KKSF(FM) San Francisco CA
KLLC(FM) San Francisco CA
KOIT(AM) San Francisco CA
KOIT-FM San Francisco CA
KEZR(FM) San Jose CA
KKJL(AM) San Luis Obispo CA
KVYB(FM) Santa Barbara CA
KSBQ(AM) Santa Maria CA
KLJR-FM Santa Paula CA
KZST(FM) Santa Rosa CA
KESR(FM) Shasta Lake City CA
KIRN(AM) Simi Valley CA
KSYV(FM) Solvang CA
KZSQ-FM Sonora CA
KRLT(FM) South Lake Tahoe CA
KJOY(FM) Stockton CA
*KYCC(FM) Stockton CA
KHJQ(FM) Susanville CA
KLCA(FM) Tahoe City CA
KMLT(FM) Thousand Oaks CA
KLOB(FM) Thousand Palms CA
KCRZ(FM) Tipton CA
KTKE(FM) Truckee CA
KCDZ(FM) Twentynine Palms CA
KWNE(FM) Ukiah CA
KUIC(FM) Vacaville CA
KBBY(FM) Ventura CA
KKZZ(AM) Ventura CA
*KHMS(FM) Victorville CA
KKDV(FM) Walnut Creek CA
KRXV(FM) Yermo CA
KMHX(FM) Windsor CA
KPRB(FM) Brush CO
KRDO-FM Colorado Springs CO
KRTZ(FM) Cortez CO
KRAI-FM Craig CO
KALC(FM) Crested Butte CO
KIMN(FM) Denver CO
KMGG(FM) Denver CO
KOSI(FM) Denver CO
KIQX(FM) Durango CO
KPTE(FM) Durango CO
KEZZ(AM) Estes Park CO
KFTM(AM) Fort Morgan CO
KKCH(FM) Glenwood Springs CO
KJYE(FM) Grand Junction CO
KMXY(FM) Grand Junction CO
KSTH(FM) Holyoke CO
KTRR(FM) Loveland CO
KBIQ(FM) Manitou Springs CO
KSLV-FM Monte Vista CO
KWUF-FM Pagosa Springs CO

KJMP(AM) Pierce CO
KVUU(FM) Pueblo CO
KBNG(FM) Ridgway CO
KPHT(FM) Rocky Ford CO
KVRH-FM Salida CO
KPMX(FM) Sterling CO
KKLI(FM) Widefield CO
WEZN-FM Bridgeport CT
WDAQ(FM) Danbury CT
WNLC(FM) East Lyme CT
WTIC-FM Hartford CT
WBMW(FM) Ledyard CT
WZBG(FM) Litchfield CT
WRCH(FM) New Britain CT
WINY(AM) Putnam CT
WQQQ(FM) Sharon CT
*WAPJ(FM) Torrington CT
WEBE(FM) Westport CT
WILI(AM) Willimantic CT
WASH(FM) Washington DC
WRQX(FM) Washington DC
*WXHL-FM Christiana DE
WRDX(FM) Dover DE
WJWL(AM) Georgetown DE
WKDB(FM) Laurel DE
WAFL(FM) Milford DE
WJBR-FM Wilmington DE
WSTW(FM) Wilmington DE
WOYS(FM) Apalachicola FL
WWUS(FM) Big Pine Key FL
*WJIS(FM) Bradenton FL
*WKSG(FM) Cedar Creek FL
WLQH(AM) Chiefland FL
WBTP(FM) Clearwater FL
WHQT(FM) Coral Gables FL
*WAQV(FM) Crystal River FL
WKTK(FM) Crystal River FL
WCFB(FM) Daytona Beach FL
WROD(AM) Daytona Beach FL
WBPC(FM) Ebro FL
WRMA(FM) Fort Lauderdale FL
WWRZ(FM) Fort Meade FL
WINK-FM Fort Myers FL
WJPT(FM) Fort Myers Villas FL
WSYR-FM Gifford FL
WCMQ-FM Hialeah FL
WVYB(FM) Holly Hill FL
WXCV(FM) Homosassa Springs FL
WIFL(FM) Inglis FL
WEJZ(FM) Jacksonville FL
WMXQ(FM) Jacksonville FL
WMBX(FM) Jensen Beach FL
WZMQ(FM) Key Largo FL
WKEY-FM Key West FL
WNFB(FM) Lake City FL
WAVK(FM) Marathon FL
WGMX(FM) Marathon FL
WAVV(FM) Marco FL
*WJNF(FM) Marianna FL
WMMB(AM) Melbourne FL
WAMR-FM Miami FL
WFLC(FM) Miami FL
WLYF(FM) Miami FL
WSBZ(FM) Miramar Beach FL
WMGF(FM) Mount Dora FL
WBCG(FM) Murdock FL
WSGL(FM) Naples FL
WTLT(FM) Naples FL
WDUV(FM) New Port Richey FL
*WLPJ(FM) New Port Richey FL
WNCV(FM) Niceville FL
*WHIJ(FM) Ocala FL
WMMO(FM) Orlando FL
WOMX-FM Orlando FL
*WHIF(FM) Palatka FL
WRMF(FM) Palm Beach FL
*WCNO(FM) Palm City FL
WFSY(FM) Panama City FL
WVVE(FM) Panama City Beach FL
WBSR(AM) Pensacola FL
WJLQ(FM) Pensacola FL

WHLG(FM) Port St. Lucie FL
WKLG(FM) Rock Harbor FL
WSOS-FM Saint Augustine FL
WRXB(AM) Saint Petersburg Beach FL
WWLL(FM) Sebring FL
WCVU(FM) Solana FL
WPIK(FM) Summerland Key FL
WBZE(FM) Tallahassee FL
WMTX(FM) Tampa FL
WWRM(FM) Tampa FL
WGNX(FM) Vero Beach FL
WGYL(FM) Vero Beach FL
WEAT-FM West Palm Beach FL
WRLX(FM) West Palm Beach FL
WDDQ(FM) Adel GA
WDEC-FM Americus GA
WLTM(FM) Atlanta GA
WSB-FM Atlanta GA
WBBQ-FM Augusta GA
WBGE(FM) Bainbridge GA
WRAK-FM Bainbridge GA
WSOL-FM Brunswick GA
WMCD(FM) Claxton GA
WRBN(FM) Clayton GA
WGMG(FM) Crawford GA
WYYU(FM) Dalton GA
WXMK(FM) Dock Junction GA
WGMK(FM) Donalsonville GA
WMLT(AM) Dublin GA
WMGZ(FM) Eatonton GA
WRDO(FM) Fitzgerald GA
WSGA(FM) Hinesville GA
WJGA-FM Jackson GA
WALR-FM La Grange GA
*WBKG(FM) Macon GA
WJYF(FM) Nashville GA
WPNG(FM) Pearson GA
WQLI(FM) Pelham GA
WPGA-FM Perry GA
WSTI-FM Quitman GA
WRHQ(FM) Richmond Hill GA
WKCX(FM) Rome GA
WQTU(FM) Rome GA
WEGC(FM) Sasser GA
WMZD(FM) Statesboro GA
WPMX(FM) Statesboro GA
WJFL(FM) Tennille GA
WTLY(FM) Thomasville GA
WTWA(AM) Thomson GA
WKZZ(FM) Tifton GA
WBDX(FM) Trenton GA
WQPW(FM) Valdosta GA
WTCQ(FM) Vidalia GA
WWSN(FM) Waycross GA
KSTO(FM) Hagatna GU
KUAM(AM) Hagatna GU
KUAI(AM) Eleele HI
KHBC(AM) Hilo HI
KKBG(FM) Hilo HI
KPVS(FM) Hilo HI
KWXX-FM Hilo HI
KINE-FM Honolulu HI
KSSK(AM) Honolulu HI
KUMU-FM Honolulu HI
KLEO(FM) Kahaluu HI
KJKS(FM) Kahului HI
KRTR-FM Kailua HI
KLUA(FM) Kailua-Kona HI
KWYI(FM) Kawaihae HI
KAOY(FM) Kealakekua HI
KFMN(FM) Lihue HI
KQNG-FM Lihue HI
KAOI-FM Wailuku HI
KSSK-FM Waipahu HI
KLGA(AM) Algona IA
KLGA-FM Algona IA
KLTI-FM Ames IA
KJAN(AM) Atlantic IA
KSKB(FM) Brooklyn IA
KBUR(AM) Burlington IA
KGRS(FM) Burlington IA

Broadcasting & Cable Yearbook 2006

D-686

Programming on Radio Stations in the U.S.

KKMI(FM) Burlington IA
KCIM(AM) Carroll IA
KKRL(FM) Carroll IA
KMRY(AM) Cedar Rapids IA
WMT-FM Cedar Rapids IA
KCOG(AM) Centerville IA
KELR-FM Chariton IA
KCHE-FM Cherokee IA
KKBZ(FM) Clarinda IA
KMXG(FM) Clinton IA
KCZQ(FM) Cresco IA
*KLOX(FM) Creston IA
KDEC-FM Decorah IA
KDSN(AM) Denison IA
KDSN-FM Denison IA
KMXD(FM) Des Moines IA
KSTZ(FM) Des Moines IA
KATF(FM) Dubuque IA
KDAO-FM Eldora IA
KADR(AM) Elkader IA
KIIK-FM Fairfield IA
KIOW(FM) Forest City IA
KUEL(FM) Fort Dodge IA
KGRN(AM) Grinnell IA
KLMJ(FM) Hampton IA
KCVM(FM) Hudson IA
KHBT(FM) Humboldt IA
KQMG(AM) Independence IA
KQMG-FM Independence IA
KIFG(AM) Iowa Falls IA
KOKX(AM) Keokuk IA
KRLS(FM) Knoxville IA
KLEM(AM) Le Mars IA
KMCH(FM) Manchester IA
*KBDC(FM) Mason City IA
KLSS-FM Mason City IA
KWPC(AM) Muscatine IA
KKNL(FM) New London IA
KCWN(FM) New Sharon IA
KZSR(FM) Onawa IA
KSMA-FM Osage IA
KTWA(FM) Ottumwa IA
KQCR-FM Parkersburg IA
KIYX(FM) Sageville IA
KSOU-FM Sioux Center IA
KGLI(FM) Sioux City IA
KUOO(FM) Spirit Lake IA
KAYL-FM Storm Lake IA
KCII(AM) Washington IA
KWAY-FM Waverly IA
KQWC-FM Webster City IA
KORR(FM) American Falls ID
KLCE(FM) Blackfoot ID
KTHI(FM) Caldwell ID
KLLP(FM) Chubbuck ID
KMCL(AM) Donnelly ID
KXLT-FM Eagle ID
KCIX(FM) Garden City ID
KISY(FM) Gooding ID
KMVX(FM) Jerome ID
KATW(FM) Lewiston ID
KMCL-FM McCall ID
KLER-FM Orofino ID
KSRA(AM) Salmon ID
KSRA-FM Salmon ID
KBJX(FM) Shelley ID
WKIB(FM) Anna IL
WXET(FM) Arcola IL
WUEZ(FM) Carterville IL
WHMS-FM Champaign IL
WLRW(FM) Champaign IL
WILV(FM) Chicago IL
WLIT-FM Chicago IL
WNUA(FM) Chicago IL
KMJM-FM Columbia IL
WDNL(FM) Danville IL
WDEK(FM) De Kalb IL
WDKB(FM) De Kalb IL
WLBK(AM) De Kalb IL
WDQN(AM) Du Quoin IL
WJEZ(FM) Dwight IL
WVRV(FM) East St. Louis IL
WXEF(FM) Effingham IL
WEBQ-FM Eldorado IL
WYST(FM) Fairbury IL
WFIW-FM Fairfield IL
WNOI(FM) Flora IL

WISH-FM Galatia IL
WJRE(FM) Galva IL
WSPY(AM) Geneva IL
WLDS(AM) Jacksonville IL
WSSR(FM) Joliet IL
WVIX(FM) Joliet IL
WYEC(FM) Kewanee IL
WKAY(FM) Knoxville IL
WAJK(FM) La Salle IL
WAKO(AM) Lawrenceville IL
WAKO-FM Lawrenceville IL
WKAI(FM) Macomb IL
WMMC(FM) Marshall IL
WLBH-FM Mattoon IL
WREZ(FM) Metropolis IL
WRIK-FM Metropolis IL
WMOI(FM) Monmouth IL
*WCFL(FM) Morris IL
WVMC(AM) Mount Carmel IL
*WBMV(FM) Mount Vernon IL
WXFM(FM) Mount Zion IL
WNSV(FM) Nashville IL
WVMG(FM) Normal IL
WVAZ(FM) Oak Park IL
WCMY(AM) Ottawa IL
WRKX(FM) Ottawa IL
WPXN(FM) Paxton IL
*WCIC(FM) Pekin IL
WSWT(FM) Peoria IL
WXMP(FM) Peoria IL
WLLT(FM) Polo IL
*WGCA-FM Quincy IL
WTAY(AM) Robinson IL
WTYE(FM) Robinson IL
WRHL-FM Rochelle IL
WGFB(FM) Rockton IL
WJBD-FM Salem IL
WJDK-FM Seneca IL
WEJT(FM) Shelbyville IL
WABZ(FM) Sherman IL
WTMX(FM) Skokie IL
WIVQ(FM) Spring Valley IL
WNNS(FM) Springfield IL
WAOX(FM) Staunton IL
WSSQ(FM) Sterling IL
WRAN(FM) Tower Hill IL
WKRV(FM) Vandalia IL
WPMB(AM) Vandalia IL
WGFA-FM Watseka IL
WXLC(FM) Waukegan IL
WZSR(FM) Woodstock IL
WQME(FM) Anderson IN
WLKI(FM) Angola IN
WZBD(FM) Berne IN
WNUY(FM) Bluffton IN
WBNL(AM) Boonville IN
WDDB(FM) Columbia City IN
WCDQ(FM) Crawfordsville IN
WADM(AM) Decatur IN
WIKY-FM Evansville IN
WVHI(AM) Evansville IN
WAJI(FM) Fort Wayne IN
WMEE(FM) Fort Wayne IN
WYLT(FM) Fort Wayne IN
WSHW(FM) Frankfort IN
WKAM(AM) Goshen IN
WZPL(FM) Greenfield IN
WRZQ-FM Greensburg IN
WPWX(FM) Hammond IN
WKLO(FM) Hardinsburg IN
WXKE(FM) Huntington IN
WTPI(FM) Indianapolis IN
WITZ(AM) Jasper IN
WITZ-FM Jasper IN
WKVI(FM) Knox IN
WKVI-FM Knox IN
WZWZ(FM) Kokomo IN
*WIRE(FM) Lebanon IN
WYJZ(FM) Lebanon IN
WLEG(FM) Ligonier IN
WSAL(AM) Logansport IN
WZVN(FM) Lowell IN
WORX-FM Madison IN
WMRI(FM) Marion IN
WEFM(FM) Michigan City IN
WMRS(FM) Monticello IN
*WWDS(FM) Muncie IN

WYPW(FM) Nappanee IN
WMDH(AM) New Castle IN
WPGW(AM) Portland IN
WLQI(FM) Rensselaer IN
WFMG(FM) Richmond IN
WAXL(FM) Santa Claus IN
WWSY(FM) Seelyville IN
WZZB(AM) Seymour IN
WLHK(FM) Shelbyville IN
WNSN(FM) South Bend IN
WLZQ(FM) South Whitley IN
WAWC(FM) Syracuse IN
WTCJ(AM) Tell City IN
WBOW-FM Terre Haute IN
WAKE(AM) Valparaiso IN
*WVUB(FM) Vincennes IN
WZDM(FM) Vincennes IN
*WRFM(FM) Wadesville IN
WAMW-FM Washington IN
WGLM(FM) West Lafayette IN
WZZY(FM) Winchester IN
KABI(AM) Abilene KS
KKOY-FM Chanute KS
KCLY(FM) Clay Center KS
KQLS(FM) Colby KS
KSKZ(FM) Copeland KS
KOLS(FM) Dodge City KS
KAHS(AM) El Dorado KS
KTLI(FM) El Dorado KS
KANS(AM) Emporia KS
KFFX(FM) Emporia KS
KVOE(AM) Emporia KS
KGGF-FM Fredonia KS
KKJQ(FM) Garden City KS
KZLS(FM) Great Bend KS
KJLS(FM) Hays KS
KFBZ(FM) Haysville KS
KSKU(FM) Hutchinson KS
*KARF(FM) Independence KS
KIND-FM Independence KS
KIKS-FM Iola KS
KUDL(FM) Kansas City KS
KSCB-FM Liberal KS
KQNS-FM Lindsborg KS
KBBE(FM) McPherson KS
KMXW(FM) Newton KS
KBLS(FM) North Fort Riley KS
KQNK(AM) Norton KS
KQNK-FM Norton KS
KQLA(FM) Ogden KS
KLKC(AM) Parsons KS
KLKC-FM Parsons KS
KHMY(FM) Pratt KS
KCAY(FM) Russell KS
KRSL(AM) Russell KS
KMAJ-FM Topeka KS
KTOP(AM) Topeka KS
KHCA(FM) Wamego KS
KRBB(FM) Wichita KS
WKLX(FM) Beaver Dam KY
WSEK(FM) Burnside KY
WCKQ(FM) Campbellsville KY
WBVX(FM) Carlisle KY
WQXQ(FM) Central City KY
WCTT-FM Corbin KY
WQXE(FM) Elizabethtown KY
WCVQ(FM) Fort Campbell KY
WJQI(AM) Fort Campbell KY
WKED-FM Frankfort KY
WUGO(FM) Grayson KY
WHOP-FM Hopkinsville KY
WHHT(FM) Horse Cave KY
WZQQ(FM) Hyden KY
WRNZ(FM) Lancaster KY
WKYL(FM) Lawrenceburg KY
WTHX(FM) Lebanon Junction KY
WKHG(FM) Leitchfield KY
WMXL(FM) Lexington KY
WLUE(FM) Louisville KY
WXMA(FM) Louisville KY
WYMV(FM) Madisonville KY
WWLT(FM) Manchester KY
WFXY(FM) Middlesboro KY
WMOR-FM Morehead KY
WCLU-FM Munfordville KY
*WGCF(FM) Paducah KY
*WPAD(AM) Paducah KY

WKLW-FM Paintsville KY
WGKS(FM) Paris KY
*WWJD(FM) Pippa Passes KY
WQHY(FM) Prestonsburg KY
WHVE(FM) Russell Springs KY
WLLK-FM Somerset KY
WCDA(FM) Versailles KY
KRVE(FM) Brusly LA
KWJM(FM) Farmerville LA
KFNV-FM Ferriday LA
WCDV(FM) Hammond LA
WKBU(FM) Kenner LA
WDVW(FM) La Place LA
KTDY(FM) Lafayette LA
KBIU(FM) Lake Charles LA
KASO(AM) Minden LA
KBZZ-FM Morgan City LA
KDBH(FM) Natchitoches LA
WEZB(FM) New Orleans LA
WLMG(FM) New Orleans LA
KKST(FM) Oakdale LA
KNBB(FM) Ruston LA
KVKI-FM Shreveport LA
KNEK-FM Washington LA
KZRZ(FM) West Monroe LA
KVCL(AM) Winnfield LA
WQRC(FM) Barnstable MA
WBMX(FM) Boston MA
WMJX(FM) Boston MA
WJIB(AM) Cambridge MA
WEIM(AM) Fitchburg MA
WXLO(FM) Fitchburg MA
WSBS(AM) Great Barrington MA
WHAI(FM) Greenfield MA
WXRV(FM) Haverhill MA
WCOD-FM Hyannis MA
WATD-FM Marshfield MA
WMRC(AM) Milford MA
*WMLN-FM Milton MA
WNAW(AM) North Adams MA
WJDF(FM) Orange MA
WBEC-FM Pittsfield MA
WBRK-FM Pittsfield MA
WPLM(AM) Plymouth MA
WPLM-FM Plymouth MA
*WRPS(FM) Rockland MA
WESX(AM) Salem MA
WOCN-FM South Yarmouth MA
WHYN-FM Springfield MA
WMAS(AM) Springfield MA
WMAS-FM Springfield MA
WSNE-FM Taunton MA
WSRS(FM) Worcester MA
WNAV(AM) Annapolis MD
WLIF(FM) Baltimore MD
WWMX(FM) Baltimore MD
WMMJ(FM) Bethesda MD
WWVZ(FM) Braddock Heights MD
WTRI(AM) Brunswick MD
WCEM-FM Cambridge MD
WCTR(AM) Chestertown MD
WKGO(FM) Cumberland MD
WCEI-FM Easton MD
WSRY(AM) Elkton MD
WFRB(FM) Frostburg MD
WKHI(FM) Fruitland MD
WWEG(FM) Hagerstown MD
WILC(AM) Laurel MD
WAFY(FM) Middletown MD
WKHJ(FM) Mountain Lake Park MD
WMSG(AM) Oakland MD
WQHQ(FM) Ocean City-Salisbury MD
WXMD(FM) Pocomoke City MD
WCTN(FM) Potomac-Cabin John MD
WWZZ(FM) Waldorf MD
WKCG(AM) Augusta ME
WQDY-FM Calais ME
WCXU(FM) Caribou ME
WCRQ(FM) Dennysville ME
WDME-FM Dover Foxcroft ME
WKSQ(FM) Ellsworth ME
WKTJ-FM Farmington ME
WFAU(AM) Gardiner ME
WHOU-FM Houlton ME
WALZ-FM Machias ME
WCXX(FM) Madawaska ME
WMGX(FM) Portland ME

WQHR(FM) Presque Isle ME
XHRM-FM Tijuana MEX
WLEN(FM) Adrian MI
WQBX(FM) Alma MI
WHSB(FM) Alpena MI
WQKL(FM) Ann Arbor MI
WLEW-FM Bad Axe MI
WBXX(FM) Battle Creek MI
WIOG(FM) Bay City MI
WCUZ(FM) Bear Lake MI
WCNF(FM) Benton Harbor MI
WOUF(FM) Beulah MI
WWBR(FM) Big Rapids MI
WYBR(FM) Big Rapids MI
WKHM-FM Brooklyn MI
WLXV(FM) Cadillac MI
WIDL(FM) Caro MI
*WPRJ(FM) Coleman MI
WDVD(FM) Detroit MI
WMGC-FM Detroit MI
WFMK(FM) East Lansing MI
WGLQ(FM) Escanaba MI
WCRZ(FM) Flint MI
WKPK(FM) Gaylord MI
WGHN(AM) Grand Haven MI
WGHN-FM Grand Haven MI
WLHT-FM Grand Rapids MI
WOOD-FM Grand Rapids MI
WCXT(FM) Hart MI
WCSR(FM) Hillsdale MI
WKVK(FM) Honor MI
WBZV(FM) Hudson MI
WIMI(FM) Ironwood MI
WUPM(FM) Ironwood MI
WMQT(FM) Ishpeming MI
WQLR(FM) Kalamazoo MI
WBTI(FM) Lexington MI
WKLA(AM) Ludington MI
WKLA-FM Ludington MI
WHTD(FM) Mount Clemens MI
WCZY-FM Mount Pleasant MI
WSHZ(FM) Muskegon MI
WKQS-FM Negaunee MI
WNBY-FM Newberry MI
WZNL(FM) Norway MI
WWTH(FM) Oscoda MI
WGRT(FM) Port Huron MI
WPHM(AM) Port Huron MI
WQON(FM) Roscommon MI
WTGV-FM Sandusky MI
WSOO(AM) Sault Ste. Marie MI
WMXG(FM) Stephenson MI
WLKM-FM Three Rivers MI
WLDR-FM Traverse City MI
WTRV(FM) Walker MI
WTRV(FM) Walker MI
WBMI(FM) West Branch MI
KDDG(FM) Albany MN
KAUS(AM) Austin MN
KKBJ-FM Bemidji MN
KKZY(FM) Bemidji MN
KSCR-FM Benson MN
WJJY-FM Brainerd MN
KLTA(FM) Breckenridge MN
KLKS(FM) Breezy Point MN
KXDL(FM) Browerville MN
KRWC(AM) Buffalo MN
WKLK-FM Cloquet MN
KMXK(FM) Cold Spring MN
KROX(AM) Crookston MN
KDLM(AM) Detroit Lakes MN
KDAL-FM Duluth MN
KZLT-FM East Grand Forks MN
WEVE-FM Eveleth MN
KFMC(FM) Fairmont MN
WLKX-FM Forest Lake MN
KMGK(FM) Glenwood MN
*WTIP(FM) Grand Marais MN
KMFY(FM) Grand Rapids MN
WWAX(FM) Hermantown MN
KGHS(AM) International Falls MN
KLCH(FM) Lake City MN
KFML(FM) Little Falls MN
KLTF(AM) Little Falls MN
KQAD(AM) Luverne MN
KEEZ-FM Mankato MN
KKCK(FM) Marshall MN

Broadcasting & Cable Yearbook 2006
D-687

Programming on Radio Stations in the U.S.

KJZI(FM) Minneapolis MN	WWSL(FM) Philadelphia MS	KYTZ(FM) Walhalla ND	KKVV(AM) Las Vegas NV	WJKW(FM) Athens OH
KTCZ-FM Minneapolis MN	WKSY(FM) Picayune MS	KPNY(FM) Alliance NE	KSNE-FM Las Vegas NV	*WOUB-FM Athens OH
WLTE(FM) Minneapolis MN	WRTM-FM Port Gibson MS	KWBE(AM) Beatrice NE	*KSOS(FM) Las Vegas NV	WXTQ(FM) Athens OH
KMGM(FM) Montevideo MN	WKZB(FM) Stonewall MS	KLIR(FM) Columbus NE	KADD(AM) Logandale NV	WBNV(FM) Barnesville OH
KDOG(FM) North Mankato MN	WZLQ(FM) Tupelo MS	*KINI(FM) Crookston NE	KWLY(FM) Moapa Valley NV	WPKO-FM Bellefontaine OH
KYMN(AM) Northfield MN	WJKK(FM) Vicksburg MS	KRGI(AM) Grand Island NE	KNEV(FM) Reno NV	WCMJ(FM) Cambridge OH
KTIG(FM) Pequot Lakes MN	KGLM-FM Anaconda MT	KSYZ-FM Grand Island NE	KJZS(FM) Sparks NV	WHBC-FM Canton OH
KPRW(FM) Perham MN	KISN(FM) Belgrade MT	KHAS(AM) Hastings NE	WYJB(FM) Albany NY	WKDD(FM) Canton OH
KBMX(FM) Proctor MN	KBBB(FM) Billings MT	KLIQ(FM) Hastings NE	*WBXL(FM) Baldwinsville NY	WCSM-FM Celina OH
*KCFB(FM) Saint Cloud MN	KYYA(FM) Billings MT	KMTY(FM) Holdrege NE	WVIN-FM Bath NY	WKKI(FM) Celina OH
KCML(FM) Saint Joseph MN	KZRV(FM) Billings MT	KBBK(FM) Lincoln NE	WBAZ(FM) Bridgehampton NY	WLZT(FM) Chillicothe OH
KSTP-FM Saint Paul MN	KOBB(AM) Bozeman MT	KICX-FM McCook NE	WJYE(FM) Buffalo NY	WAKW(FM) Cincinnati OH
KKSR(FM) Sartell MN	KZMY(FM) Bozeman MT	KSWN(FM) McCook NE	WTSS(FM) Buffalo NY	*WJVS(FM) Cincinnati OH
KNUJ-FM Sleepy Eye MN	KOPR(FM) Butte MT	KEXL(FM) Norfolk NE	WISY(FM) Canandaigua NY	WKRQ(FM) Cincinnati OH
KNSG(FM) Springfield MN	KRYK(FM) Chinook MT	KNEN(FM) Norfolk NE	WTOJ(FM) Carthage NY	WLW(AM) Cincinnati OH
KSKK(FM) Staples MN	KVVR(FM) Dutton MT	KELN(FM) North Platte NE	WCTW(FM) Catskill NY	WRRM(FM) Cincinnati OH
KRVY-FM Starbuck MN	KLAN(FM) Glasgow MT	KEFM(FM) Omaha NE	WLVG(FM) Center Moriches NY	WVMX(FM) Cincinnati OH
KYBA(FM) Stewartville MN	KXGN(FM) Glendive MT	KOMJ(AM) Omaha NE	WGMM(FM) Corning NY	WFHM-FM Cleveland OH
KQKK(FM) Walker MN	KAAK(FM) Great Falls MT	KQCH(FM) Omaha NE	WNKI(FM) Corning NY	WMVX(FM) Cleveland OH
KQIC(FM) Willmar MN	KXDR(FM) Hamilton MT	KSRZ(FM) Omaha NE	WDNY-FM Dansville NY	WQAL(FM) Cleveland OH
KAGE-FM Winona MN	KOJM(AM) Havre MT	KSID-FM Sidney NE	WFLR-FM Dundee NY	WBNS-FM Columbus OH
KWOA-FM Worthington MN	KMTX(AM) Helena MT	KWPN-FM West Point NE	WFKP(FM) Ellenville NY	WNCI(FM) Columbus OH
KBMV-FM Birch Tree MO	KMTX-FM Helena MT	KTMX(FM) York NE	WENY-FM Elmira NY	WSNY(FM) Columbus OH
KFMZ(AM) Brookfield MO	KALS(FM) Kalispell MT	WBNC(AM) Conway NH	WLVY(FM) Elmira NY	WTNS-FM Coshocton OH
KZBK(FM) Brookfield MO	KBSR(AM) Laurel MT	WVMJ(FM) Conway NH	WBKX(FM) Fredonia NY	WMMX(FM) Dayton OH
KKWK(FM) Cameron MO	KTNY(FM) Libby MT	WFTN-FM Franklin NH	*WHPC(FM) Garden City NY	WDFM(FM) Defiance OH
KRRY(FM) Canton MO	KATL(AM) Miles City MT	WGXL(FM) Hanover NH	WENT(AM) Gloversville NY	WXOL(FM) Delaware OH
KMXL(FM) Carthage MO	KMSO(FM) Missoula MT	*WNEC-FM Henniker NH	WHLI(FM) Hempstead NY	WJER-FM Dover OH
*KNLH(FM) Cedar Hill MO	KQRK(FM) Ronan MT	WKNE(FM) Keene NH	WKJY(FM) Hempstead NY	WZOO-FM Edgewood OH
KREZ(FM) Chaffee MO	KTHC(FM) Sidney MT	WLNH-FM Laconia NH	WZEC(FM) Hoosick Falls NY	WKXA-FM Findlay OH
KPLA(FM) Columbia MO	KKVU(FM) Stevensville MT	WLTN-FM Lisbon NH	WKPQ(FM) Hornell NY	WBVI(FM) Fostoria OH
KBZI(FM) Deerfield MO	WECR-FM Beech Mountain NC	WZID(FM) Manchester NH	WCZX(FM) Hyde Park NY	WFOB(AM) Fostoria OH
KLOZ(FM) Eldon MO	WSQL(AM) Brevard NC	WHOM(FM) Mt. Washington NH	WYXL(FM) Ithaca NY	WFRO-FM Fremont OH
KAUL(FM) Ellington MO	*WCCE(FM) Buie's Creek NC	WFNQ(FM) Nashua NH	WWSE(FM) Jamestown NY	*WCVO(FM) Gahanna OH
KMAC(FM) Gainesville MO	WRSN(FM) Burlington NC	WBYY(FM) Somersworth NH	WLTB(FM) Johnson City NY	WVNU(FM) Greenfield OH
KCJK(FM) Garden City MO	WYNA(FM) Calabash NC	WASR(AM) Wolfeboro NH	WIZR(FM) Johnstown NY	WNLT(FM) Harrison OH
KYOO-FM Halfway MO	WKQC(FM) Charlotte NC	WJLK-FM Asbury Park NJ	WKNY(AM) Kingston NY	WRBP(FM) Hubbard OH
KGRC(FM) Hannibal MO	WLNK(FM) Charlotte NC	WAYV(FM) Atlantic City NJ	WVOS-FM Liberty NY	WKTN(FM) Kenton OH
KUGT(AM) Jackson MO	*WWCU(FM) Cullowhee NC	WFPG-FM Atlantic City NJ	WSKU(FM) Little Falls NY	WLQT(FM) Kettering OH
KTXY(FM) Jefferson City MO	WFXC(FM) Durham NC	WHCY(FM) Blairstown NJ	WMSA(AM) Massena NY	WAGX(FM) Manchester OH
KSRC(FM) Kansas City MO	WZBO(AM) Edenton NC	WAIV(FM) Cape May NJ	WSUL(FM) Monticello NY	WVNO-FM Mansfield OH
KIRK(FM) Macon MO	WKJX(FM) Elizabeth City NC	WHTG-FM Eatontown NJ	WBWZ(FM) New Paltz NY	WYHT(FM) Mansfield OH
KLSC(FM) Malden MO	WIFM(FM) Elkin NC	WSJO(FM) Egg Harbor City NJ	WLTW(FM) New York NY	WMOA(AM) Marietta OH
KTRI(FM) Mansfield MO	WTRG(FM) Gaston NC	WIMG(AM) Ewing NJ	WPLJ(FM) New York NY	WKLM(FM) Millersburg OH
KXEO(AM) Mexico MO	WBAV-FM Gastonia NC	WSUS(FM) Franklin NJ	WGNY-FM Newburgh NY	WQIO(FM) Mount Vernon OH
KMCR(FM) Montgomery City MO	WSMW(FM) Greensboro NC	WWZY(FM) Long Branch NJ	WKKZ(FM) Norwich NY	WNDH(FM) Napoleon OH
KUPH(FM) Mountain View MO	WYND-FM Hatteras NC	WMGQ(FM) New Brunswick NJ	WVLF(FM) Norwood NY	WWJM(FM) New Lexington OH
KGBX-FM Nixa MO	WANG(AM) Havelock NC	WBBO(FM) Ocean Acres NJ	WMXO(FM) Olean NY	WLKR-FM Norwalk OH
KTOZ-FM Pleasant Hope MO	WSSM(FM) Havelock NC	WIBG(AM) Ocean City NJ	WMCR(AM) Oneida NY	WKSD(FM) Paulding OH
KAHR(FM) Poplar Bluff MO	WHKP(AM) Hendersonville NC	WPAT-FM Paterson NJ	WMCR-FM Oneida NY	WNXT-FM Portsmouth OH
*KNLP(FM) Potosi MO	WMYI(FM) Hendersonville NC	WOBM-FM Toms River NJ	WSRK(FM) Oneonta NY	WMLX(FM) Saint Mary's OH
KADI-FM Republic MO	WTZQ(AM) Hendersonville NC	WCZT(FM) Villas NJ	WALK-FM Patchogue NY	WCPZ(FM) Sandusky OH
KDAA(FM) Rolla MO	WLYT(FM) Hickory NC	WMIZ(AM) Vineland NJ	WHUD(FM) Peekskill NY	WMVR-FM Sidney OH
KGNM(AM) Saint Joseph MO	WMAG(FM) High Point NC	WVLT(FM) Vineland NJ	WYLF(AM) Penn Yan NY	*WCVZ(FM) South Zanesville OH
KKJO(FM) Saint Joseph MO	WCXL(FM) Kill Devil Hills NC	WAWZ(FM) Zarephath NJ	WZUN(FM) Phoenix NY	*WKTL(FM) Struthers OH
KEZK-FM Saint Louis MO	WLNC(AM) Laurinburg NC	KKOB-FM Albuquerque NM	WIRY(AM) Plattsburgh NY	WWWM-FM Sylvania OH
KYKY(FM) Saint Louis MO	WZAX(FM) Nashville NC	KMGA(FM) Albuquerque NM	WPDM(FM) Potsdam NY	WTTF(AM) Tiffin OH
KGKS(FM) Scott City MO	*WAAE(FM) New Bern NC	KPEK(FM) Albuquerque NM	WSNN(FM) Potsdam NY	WRVF(FM) Toledo OH
KSDL(FM) Sedalia MO	WNNC(AM) Newton NC	KWYK-FM Aztec NM	WRNQ(FM) Poughkeepsie NY	WYNT(FM) Upper Sandusky OH
*KWND(FM) Springfield MO	WPNC-FM Plymouth NC	KAMQ(AM) Carlsbad NM	WNYQ(FM) Queensbury NY	WERT(AM) Van Wert OH
KTTN(AM) Trenton MO	WRAL(FM) Raleigh NC	KCDY(FM) Carlsbad NM	WOKR(FM) Remsen NY	WKOV-FM Wellston OH
*KBIY(FM) Van Buren MO	*WZRU(FM) Roanoke Rapids NC	KSMX(FM) Clovis NM	WLGZ(AM) Rochester NY	*WYSO(FM) Yellow Springs OH
KSLQ-FM Washington MO	WAYN(AM) Rockingham NC	KTQM-FM Clovis NM	WRMM-FM Rochester NY	WMXY(FM) Youngstown OH
KJPW(FM) Waynesville MO	WEND(FM) Salisbury NC	KSYU(FM) Corrales NM	WVOR-FM Rochester NY	WHIZ-FM Zanesville OH
KJMK(FM) Webb City MO	WIOZ-FM Southern Pines NC	KDEM(FM) Deming NM	WGGO(AM) Salamanca NY	KTTL(FM) Alva OK
KULH(FM) Wheeling MO	WRGC(AM) Sylva NC	KKOR(FM) Gallup NM	WNBZ(AM) Saranac Lake NY	KYFM(FM) Bartlesville OK
WKZW(FM) Bay Springs MS	WFXK(FM) Tarboro NC	KZOR(FM) Hobbs NM	WYZY(FM) Saranac Lake NY	KQMX(FM) Clinton OK
WMJY(FM) Biloxi MS	WADE(AM) Wadesboro NC	KBAC(FM) Las Vegas NM	WRVE(FM) Schenectady NY	KLAK(FM) Durant OK
WMJU(FM) Bude MS	WERO(AM) Washington NC	KLVF(FM) Las Vegas NM	WCDO(AM) Sidney NY	KSEO(AM) Durant OK
*WOWL(FM) Burnsville MS	WLGT(FM) Washington NC	KMVR(FM) Mesilla Park NM	WCDO-FM Sidney NY	KQOB(FM) Enid OK
*WKVF(FM) Byhalia MS	WGNI(FM) Wilmington NC	KLBU(FM) Pecos NM	WMJC(FM) Smithtown NY	KQTZ(FM) Hobart OK
WMGO(AM) Canton MS	*WWIL-FM Wilmington NC	KRTN(AM) Raton NM	WHFM(FM) Southampton NY	KTLS-FM Holdenville OK
WAID(FM) Clarksdale MS	*WRCM(FM) Wingate NC	KAJZ(FM) Rio Rancho NM	WRCR(FM) Spring Valley NY	KQIB(FM) Idabel OK
WFFF-FM Columbia MS	*WSNC(FM) Winston-Salem NC	KBIM-FM Roswell NM	WSPQ(AM) Springville NY	KXLS(FM) Lahoma OK
WLIN-FM Durant MS	KVMI(FM) Arthur ND	KINF(AM) Roswell NM	WQAR(FM) Stillwater NY	KBZQ(FM) Lawton OK
WLZA(FM) Eupora MS	KHOL(AM) Beulah ND	KSSR(AM) Santa Rosa NM	WLTI(FM) Syracuse NY	KYNZ(FM) Lone Grove OK
WFTA(FM) Fulton MS	KFYR(AM) Bismarck ND	KSCQ(FM) Silver City NM	WYYY(FM) Syracuse NY	KMGL(FM) Oklahoma City OK
WGNL(FM) Greenwood MS	KYYY(FM) Bismarck ND	KHAC(AM) Tse Bonito NM	WRGR(FM) Tupper Lake NY	KYIS(FM) Oklahoma City OK
WUJM(FM) Gulfport MS	KLXX(AM) Bismarck-Mandan ND	KQAY-FM Tucumcari NM	WLZW(FM) Utica NY	KPRV(FM) Poteau OK
WSYE(FM) Houston MS	KDIX(AM) Dickinson ND	KZMI(FM) Garapan-Saipan NP	WMXW(FM) Vestal NY	*KXTH(FM) Seminole OK
WNLA-FM Indianola MS	KKXL(AM) Grand Forks ND	KHIX(FM) Carlin NV	WNYR-FM Waterloo NY	KGFF(AM) Shawnee OK
WIQQ(FM) Leland MS	KHND(AM) Harvey ND	KELK(AM) Elko NV	WAVR(FM) Waverly NY	*KJCM(FM) Snyder OK
WJDQ(FM) Meridian MS	KQDJ(AM) Jamestown ND	KCLS(FM) Ely NV	WFAS-FM White Plains NY	KSPI-FM Stillwater OK
WKSO(FM) Natchez MS	KNDK-FM Langdon ND	KVLV(FM) Fallon NV	WNYV(FM) Whitehall NY	KBEZ(FM) Tulsa OK
WOXD(FM) Oxford MS	KIZZ(FM) Minot ND	KKJJ(FM) Henderson NV	WRIP(FM) Windham NY	KRAV(FM) Tulsa OK
WQLJ(FM) Oxford MS	KMXA-FM Minot ND	KMXB(FM) Henderson NV	WZKL(AM) Alliance OH	KESC(FM) Wilburton OK
WRXW(FM) Pearl MS	KQDJ(FM) Valley City ND	KRNO(FM) Incline Village NV	WREO-FM Ashtabula OH	KMZE(FM) Woodward OK

Broadcasting & Cable Yearbook 2006

D-688

Programming on Radio Stations in the U.S.

KCMX-FM Ashland OR	WBEB(FM) Philadelphia PA	KZLK(FM) Rapid City SD	KSHN(FM) Liberty TX	WEZF(FM) Burlington VT
KAST-FM Astoria OR	WBEN-FM Philadelphia PA	KNBZ(FM) Redfield SD	KONE(FM) Lubbock TX	WMOO(FM) Derby Center VT
KVMX(FM) Banks OR	WDAS-FM Philadelphia PA	KELO-FM Sioux Falls SD	KYBI(FM) Lufkin TX	WGMT(FM) Lyndon VT
KKCW(FM) Beaverton OR	WPEN(AM) Philadelphia PA	KMXC(FM) Sioux Falls SD	KAMX(FM) Luling TX	WVNR(AM) Poultney VT
KMGX(FM) Bend OR	WSNI(FM) Philadelphia PA	KVHT(FM) Vermillion SD	*KZLV(FM) Lytle TX	WJJR(FM) Rutland VT
KYSF(FM) Bonanza OR	*WPTS-FM Pittsburgh PA	KIXX(FM) Watertown SD	KZRC(FM) Markham TX	WZRT(FM) Rutland VT
KURY-FM Brookings OR	WSHH(FM) Pittsburgh PA	KWYR-FM Winner SD	KLRK(FM) Marlin TX	WWMP(FM) Waterbury VT
KCBZ(FM) Cannon Beach OR	WHKS(FM) Port Allegany PA	KYNT(AM) Yankton SD	KLSR-FM Memphis TX	KLKI(AM) Anacortes WA
KFLY(FM) Corvallis OR	WPPA(AM) Pottsville PA	WBGQ(FM) Bulls Gap TN	KHKZ(FM) Mercedes TX	KLSY-FM Bellevue WA
KCGR(FM) Cottage Grove OR	WPXZ-FM Punxsutawney PA	WCLE-FM Calhoun TN	KCHX(FM) Midland TX	KAFE(FM) Bellingham WA
*KLCC(FM) Eugene OR	WZYY(FM) Renovo PA	WRJB(FM) Camden TN	KCRS-FM Midland TX	KBAI(AM) Bellingham WA
KMGE(FM) Eugene OR	WDSN(FM) Reynoldsville PA	WALV(FM) Cleveland TN	KTEZ(FM) Mount Enterprise TX	KRWM(FM) Bremerton WA
KCST-FM Florence OR	WKMC(AM) Roaring Spring PA	WKRM(AM) Columbia TN	KHTZ(FM) Navasota TX	KOZI(AM) Chelan WA
KGBR(FM) Gold Beach OR	WKBI(AM) Saint Marys PA	WGIC(FM) Cookeville TN	KZRB(FM) New Boston TX	KOZI-FM Chelan WA
KLDR(FM) Harbeck-Fruitdale OR	WKBI-FM Saint Marys PA	WKBQ(FM) Covington TN	KODM(FM) Odessa TX	KCRK-FM Colville WA
KQFM(FM) Hermiston OR	WATS(AM) Sayre PA	WASL(FM) Dyersburg TN	KKMY(FM) Orange TX	KCMS(FM) Edmonds WA
KCGB(FM) Hood River OR	WLSW(FM) Scottdale PA	WLLJ(FM) Etowah TN	KAZE(FM) Ore City TX	KQBE(FM) Ellensburg WA
KKRB(FM) Klamath Falls OR	WWDL-FM Scranton PA	*WVCP(FM) Gallatin TN	KGRO(AM) Pampa TX	KLOG(AM) Kelso WA
KWRL(FM) La Grande OR	*WBYO(FM) Sellersville PA	WSEV-FM Gatlinburg TN	KPLT-FM Paris TX	KLYK(FM) Kelso WA
KLTH(FM) Lake Oswego OR	WEEO(AM) Shippensburg PA	WMBZ(FM) Germantown TN	KPTX(FM) Pecos TX	KONA(AM) Kennewick WA
KQIK-FM Lakeview OR	WQRM(FM) Smethport PA	WBZH(FM) Harriman TN	KRIA(FM) Plainview TX	KONA-FM Kennewick WA
KLYC(AM) McMinnville OR	*WBYX(FM) Stroudsburg PA	*WLMU(FM) Harrogate TN	*KPVU(FM) Prairie View TX	KTSL(FM) Medical Lake WA
KSND(FM) Monmouth OR	WSBG(FM) Stroudsburg PA	WHHM-FM Henderson TN	KFMK(FM) Round Rock TX	KIXI(AM) Mercer Island-Seattle WA
KYTE(FM) Newport OR	WMGH-FM Tamaqua PA	WEKX(FM) Jellico TN	*KNLE(FM) Round Rock TX	KSWW(FM) Montesano WA
KACW(FM) North Bend OR	WBZR(FM) Tunkhannock PA	WKTP(AM) Jonesborough TN	KIXY-FM San Angelo TX	KDRM(FM) Moses Lake WA
KUMA-FM Pendleton OR	WEMR(AM) Tunkhannock PA	WMYU(FM) Karns TN	KQXT(FM) San Antonio TX	KWDB(AM) Oak Harbor WA
KYCH-FM Portland OR	WTRN(AM) Tyrone PA	WTFM(FM) Kingsport TN	KBAL(AM) San Saba TX	KGY(AM) Olympia WA
KLTW-FM Prineville OR	WCTL(FM) Union City PA	*WKTS(FM) Kingston TN	KSMG(FM) Seguin TX	KXXO(FM) Olympia WA
KLRR(FM) Redmond OR	WNAE(AM) Warren PA	WJXB-FM Knoxville TN	KBKH(FM) Shamrock TX	KEYW(FM) Pasco WA
KJMX(FM) Reedsport OR	*WCYJ-FM Waynesburg PA	WDXE-FM Lawrenceburg TN	KJIM(AM) Sherman TX	*KRLF(FM) Pullman WA
*KLFR(FM) Reedsport OR	WNBT-FM Wellsboro PA	WKZX-FM Lenoir City TN	*KSQX(FM) Springtown TX	KAAP(FM) Rock Island WA
*KMPQ(FM) Roseburg OR	WKSB(FM) Williamsport PA	WZLT(FM) Lexington TN	KMMX(FM) Tahoka TX	KPLZ(FM) Seattle WA
KWPK-FM Sisters OR	WRVH(FM) Williamsport PA	WYGO(FM) Madisonville TN	KTYL-FM Tyler TX	KUBE(FM) Seattle WA
KMCQ(FM) The Dalles OR	WARM-FM York PA	WFTZ(FM) Manchester TN	KBNU(FM) Uvalde TX	KWJZ(FM) Seattle WA
KODL(AM) The Dalles OR	WFDT(FM) Aguada PR	WKCE(FM) Maryville TN	KQVT(FM) Victoria TX	KMAS(AM) Shelton WA
KKMX(FM) Tri City OR	WABA(AM) Aguadilla PR	WMC-FM Memphis TN	KVIC(FM) Victoria TX	*KAGU(FM) Spokane WA
KEUG(FM) Veneta OR	WTPM(FM) Aguadilla PR	*WQOX(FM) Memphis TN	KBZS(FM) Wichita Falls TX	KEZE(FM) Spokane WA
*KWSO(FM) Warm Springs OR	WMIA(FM) Arecibo PR	WRVR-FM Memphis TN	KALK(FM) Winfield TX	KISC(FM) Spokane WA
WLEV(FM) Allentown PA	WLUZ(AM) Bayamon PR	WYDL(FM) Middleton TN	KREC(FM) Brian Head UT	KXLY-FM Spokane WA
WFEZ(FM) Avoca PA	WMIO(FM) Cabo Rojo PR	WCRK(AM) Morristown TN	KBLQ(FM) Logan UT	KITI-FM Winlock WA
WAYC(FM) Bedford PA	WNEL(FM) Caguas PR	WMPW(FM) Munford TN	*KPCW(FM) Park City UT	KJOX(AM) Yakima WA
WZWW(FM) Bellefonte PA	WVJP(AM) Caguas PR	WCJK(FM) Murfreesboro TN	KWSA(FM) Price UT	KRSE(FM) Yakima WA
WLCY(FM) Blairsville PA	WVOZ-FM Carolina PR	WJXA(FM) Nashville TN	KSRR(AM) Provo UT	WISM-FM Altoona WI
WFYY(FM) Bloomsburg PA	WCPR(FM) Coamo PR	WNRQ(FM) Nashville TN	KIFX(FM) Roosevelt UT	WACD(FM) Antigo WI
WESB(AM) Bradford PA	WXRF(AM) Guayama PR	WBNT-FM Oneida TN	KXRQ(FM) Roosevelt UT	WATK(AM) Antigo WI
WXXO(FM) Cambridge Springs PA	WOIZ(AM) Guayanilla PR	WOCV(AM) Oneida TN	KSNN(FM) Saint George UT	WLMX-FM Balsam Lake WI
WIKZ(FM) Chambersburg PA	WIOB(FM) Mayaguez PR	WLZK(FM) Paris TN	KBEE(FM) Salt Lake City UT	WRPQ(AM) Baraboo WI
*WZXQ(FM) Chambersburg PA	WTIL(AM) Mayaguez PR	WSEV(AM) Sevierville TN	KBEE-FM Salt Lake City UT	WBEV(AM) Beaver Dam WI
WCCR(FM) Clarion PA	WEXS(AM) Patillas PR	WCMT-FM South Fulton TN	KSFI(FM) Salt Lake City UT	WWIS-FM Black River Falls WI
WQYX(FM) Clearfield PA	WIOC(FM) Ponce PR	WAYA(FM) Spring City TN	KOSY-FM Spanish Fork UT	WCFW(FM) Chippewa Falls WI
WWCB(AM) Corry PA	*WPUC-FM Ponce PR	WTNE(AM) Trenton TN	WAVA(FM) Arlington VA	WLKN(FM) Cleveland WI
WFRM-FM Coudersport PA	WZAR(FM) Ponce PR	*KACU(FM) Abilene TX	WCJZ(FM) Charlottesville VA	WKSZ(FM) De Pere WI
WOKW(FM) Curwensville PA	WFID(FM) Rio Piedras PR	*KGNZ(FM) Abilene TX	WQMZ(FM) Charlottesville VA	WDMO(FM) Durand WI
WQKY(FM) Emporium PA	WIOA(FM) San Juan PR	KNDA(FM) Alice TX	WNLR(AM) Churchville VA	WIAL(FM) Eau Claire WI
WXKC(FM) Erie PA	WLRP(AM) San Sebastian PR	KMXJ-FM Amarillo TX	WXCF(AM) Clifton Forge VA	WFON(FM) Fond du Lac WI
*WRSD(FM) Folsom PA	WRSS(AM) San Sebastian PR	KKMJ-FM Austin TX	WXCF-FM Clifton Forge VA	WSJY(FM) Fort Atkinson WI
WOXX(FM) Franklin PA	WERR(FM) Utuado PR	KNUZ(AM) Bellville TX	*WPIN-FM Dublin VA	WQLH(FM) Green Bay WI
WGET(AM) Gettysburg PA	WENA(FM) Yauco PR	KULF(FM) Brenham TX	WEVA(AM) Emporia VA	WHSM-FM Hayward WI
WGRP(AM) Greenville PA	WWLI(FM) Providence RI	KLZK(FM) Brownfield TX	WFLO-FM Farmville VA	WRLS-FM Hayward WI
WRVV(FM) Harrisburg PA	*WBLQ(FM) Westerly RI	KBWD(AM) Brownwood TX	WBQB(FM) Fredericksburg VA	WLFN(AM) La Crosse WI
WMHX(FM) Hershey PA	WYKZ(FM) Beaufort SC	KKYS(FM) Bryan TX	WXGM(AM) Gloucester VA	WLXR-FM La Crosse WI
WRKY-FM Hollidaysburg PA	WCAM(AM) Camden SC	KRHC(FM) Burnet TX	WXGM-FM Gloucester VA	WLKG(FM) Lake Geneva WI
WCCS(AM) Homer City PA	WLTY(FM) Cayce SC	KLTR(FM) Caldwell TX	WMJD(FM) Grundy VA	*WJTY(FM) Lancaster WI
WDNH-FM Honesdale PA	WALC(FM) Charleston SC	*KETR(FM) Commerce TX	WWDE-FM Hampton VA	WFDL-FM Lomira WI
WLAK(FM) Huntingdon PA	WSSX-FM Charleston SC	KLTG(FM) Corpus Christi TX	WKWI(FM) Kilmarnock VA	WMGN(FM) Madison WI
WFGI-FM Johnstown PA	WCRE(AM) Cheraw SC	KDMX(FM) Dallas TX	WOLD-FM Marion VA	WZEE(FM) Madison WI
WLAN-FM Lancaster PA	WSLT(FM) Cheraw SC	KRNB(FM) Decatur TX	WZVA(FM) Marion VA	WOMT(AM) Manitowoc WI
WROZ(FM) Lancaster PA	WORG(FM) Elloree SC	KTDR(FM) Del Rio TX	WNVA(FM) Norton VA	WLST(FM) Marinette WI
WCOZ(FM) Laporte PA	WZSN(FM) Greenwood SC	KAFX-FM Diboll TX	WESR-FM Onley-Onancock VA	WLJY(FM) Marshfield WI
WQTW(AM) Latrobe PA	WCSQ(FM) Manning SC	KVLY(FM) Edinburg TX	WSWV(AM) Pennington Gap VA	WRJC(FM) Mauston WI
WQIC(FM) Lebanon PA	WMYB(FM) Myrtle Beach SC	KINT-FM El Paso TX	WSWV-FM Pennington Gap VA	WKEB(FM) Medford WI
*WGRC(FM) Lewisburg PA	WKDK(AM) Newberry SC	KSII(FM) El Paso TX	WRIC(FM) Richlands VA	WJMT(FM) Merrill WI
WMRF-FM Lewistown PA	WTCB(FM) Orangeburg SC	KTSM-FM El Paso TX	WMXB(FM) Richmond VA	*WGNV(FM) Milladore WI
WSNU(FM) Lock Haven PA	WMGL(FM) Ravenel SC	KFST(AM) Fort Stockton TX	WTVR-FM Richmond VA	WKTI(FM) Milwaukee WI
WNBQ(FM) Mansfield PA	WWVV(FM) Ridgeland SC	KZTR(FM) Franklin TX	WSLQ(FM) Roanoke VA	WMYX(FM) Milwaukee WI
*WRIJ(FM) Masontown PA	WIGL(FM) Saint Matthews SC	KSOC(FM) Gainesville TX	WZBL(FM) Roanoke VA	WOKY(AM) Milwaukee WI
WPPT(FM) Mercersburg PA	WSPA-FM Spartanburg SC	KPUS(FM) Gregory TX	*WPAR(FM) Salem VA	WQBW(FM) Milwaukee WI
*WMSS(FM) Middletown PA	KBFO(FM) Aberdeen SD	KEZB(FM) Hempstead TX	WSNV(FM) Salem VA	WEKZ-FM Monroe WI
WVRT(FM) Mill Hall PA	KBRK-FM Brookings SD	KHMX(FM) Houston TX	WHLF(FM) South Boston VA	WROE(FM) Neenah-Menasha WI
WQLV(FM) Millersburg PA	KFCR(AM) Custer SD	KODA(FM) Houston TX	WRAR-FM Tappahannock VA	WPKG(FM) Neillsville WI
WVLY-FM Milton PA	KZKK(FM) Huron SD	KSML-FM Huntington TX	WPTE(FM) Virginia Beach VA	WXER(FM) Plymouth WI
WSPI(FM) Mount Carmel PA	KMSD(AM) Milbank SD	KLJT(FM) Jacksonville TX	WNDJ(FM) White Stone VA	WPDR(AM) Portage WI
*WRWJ(FM) Murrysville PA	KQRN(FM) Mitchell SD	KOOI(FM) Jacksonville TX	WINC-FM Winchester VA	WJMC(AM) Rice Lake WI
WZPT(FM) New Kensington PA	KOLY(AM) Mobridge SD	KJAS(FM) Jasper TX	*WIUJ(FM) Charlotte Amalie VI	WEVR(AM) River Falls WI
*WWNW(FM) New Wilmington PA	KGFX(FM) Pierre SD	KKBA(FM) Kingsville TX	WVIQ(FM) Christiansted VI	WEVR-FM River Falls WI
WNCC(AM) Northern Cambria PA	KLXS-FM Pierre SD	*KHOY(FM) Laredo TX	WYAC(FM) Christiansted VI	WECB(FM) Seymour WI
WKQW(AM) Oil City PA	KKMK(FM) Rapid City SD	KRRG(FM) Laredo TX	WTSA-FM Brattleboro VT	*WSHS(FM) Sheboygan WI

Broadcasting & Cable Yearbook 2006

D-689

Programming on Radio Stations in the U.S.

WSPT-FM Stevens Point WI
WDOR(AM) Sturgeon Bay WI
WDOR-FM Sturgeon Bay WI
WSRG(FM) Sturgeon Bay WI
WXXM(FM) Sun Prairie WI
WXYM(FM) Tomah WI
WDUX-FM Waupaca WI
WNNO-FM Wisconsin Dells WI
WHAJ(FM) Bluefield WV
*WPIB(FM) Bluefield WV
WDCI(FM) Bridgeport WV
WVAF(FM) Charleston WV
*WKJL(FM) Clarksburg WV
WOBG(AM) Clarksburg WV
WWLW(FM) Clarksburg WV
WZJO(FM) Dunbar WV
WDNE(AM) Elkins WV
WELK(FM) Elkins WV
WTBZ(AM) Grafton WV
WFSP-FM Kingwood WV
WVOW(AM) Logan WV
WVOW-FM Logan WV
WLTF(FM) Martinsburg WV
WHJC(AM) Matewan WV
WVKM(FM) Matewan WV
WYMJ(FM) New Martinsville WV
WXIL(FM) Parkersburg WV
*WQAB(FM) Philippi WV
WRON(AM) Ronceverte WV
WRRR-FM Saint Marys WV
WMXE(FM) South Charleston WV
WCWV(FM) Summersville WV
WSGB(AM) Sutton WV
WELC(AM) Welch WV
WELC-FM Welch WV
WBTH(AM) Williamson WV
KHOC(FM) Casper WY
KMGW(FM) Casper WY
KJUA(AM) Cheyenne WY
KQLF(FM) Cheyenne WY
KTAG(FM) Cody WY
KNYN(FM) Fort Bridger WY
KYOD(FM) Glendo WY
KAOX(FM) Kemmerer WY
KIMX(FM) Laramie WY
KWYW(FM) Lost Cabin WY
KIQZ(FM) Rawlins WY
KRAL(AM) Rawlins WY
KTHE(AM) Thermopolis WY
KZEW(FM) Wheatland WY
KKLX(FM) Worland WY

Agriculture

KSIR(AM) Brush CO
KNAB(AM) Burlington CO
KNAB-FM Burlington CO
KSPK(FM) Walsenburg CO
KDSN(AM) Denison IA
KAYL(AM) Storm Lake IA
WSMI(AM) Litchfield IL
WLBH(AM) Mattoon IL
WMCL(AM) McLeansboro IL
WSLM(AM) Salem IN
WSLM-FM Salem IN
KLOE(AM) Goodland KS
KNDY(AM) Marysville KS
KFRM(AM) Salina KS
KDHL(AM) Faribault MN
WYRQ(FM) Little Falls MN
KMHL(AM) Marshall MN
KOLV(FM) Olivia MN
KLOH(AM) Pipestone MN
KCUE(AM) Red Wing MN
KKOZ(AM) Ava MO
KKOZ-FM Ava MO
KAOL(AM) Carrollton MO
KMZU(FM) Carrollton MO
KCRV(AM) Caruthersville MO
KRES(FM) Moberly MO
WNIX(AM) Greenville MS
KGLE(AM) Glendive MT
KMON(AM) Great Falls MT
WDAY(AM) Fargo ND
KNOX(AM) Grand Forks ND
KZZJ(AM) Rugby ND
KCSR(AM) Chadron NE

KJSK(AM) Columbus NE
KRVN(AM) Lexington NE
KNEB-FM Scottsbluff NE
KTIC(AM) West Point NE
WRFD(AM) Columbus-Worthington OH
WEDI(AM) Eaton OH
KWHW(AM) Altus OK
KOKK(AM) Huron SD
KBJM(AM) Lemmon SD
KGFX(AM) Pierre SD
KXRB(AM) Sioux Falls SD
KBHB(AM) Sturgis SD
KWAT(AM) Watertown SD
WNAX(AM) Yankton SD
KRUN(AM) Ballinger TX
KVWG(AM) Pearsall TX
KVWG-FM Pearsall TX
KVWC(AM) Vernon TX
KVWC-FM Vernon TX
KBSN(AM) Moses Lake WA
KWNC(AM) Quincy WA
WRDB(AM) Reedsburg WI
WJMC(AM) Rice Lake WI
WCUB(AM) Two Rivers WI
WTTN(AM) Watertown WI
WELD-FM Petersburg WV

Album-Oriented Rock

KDJE(FM) Jacksonville AR
KWBF-FM North Little Rock AR
KERX(FM) Paris AR
KRAB(FM) Green Acres CA
KHDR(FM) Lenwood CA
KHWZ(FM) Ludlow CA
KIST-FM Santa Barbara CA
KTYD(FM) Santa Barbara CA
*KASF(FM) Alamosa CO
KILO(FM) Colorado Springs CO
KBPI(FM) Denver CO
WYYX(FM) Bonifay FL
WFBX(FM) Parker FL
WTKX-FM Pensacola FL
WNDD(FM) Silver Springs FL
WVRK(FM) Columbus GA
WYNF(FM) Gray GA
WPEZ(FM) Jeffersonville GA
KGUM-FM Dededo GU
KFMW(FM) Waterloo IA
KRVB(FM) Nampa ID
WXRX(FM) Belvidere IL
*WARG(FM) Summit IL
KACY(FM) Arkansas City KS
KQRC-FM Leavenworth KS
WZZP(FM) Hopkinsville KY
WZAQ(FM) Louisa KY
WLRS(FM) Shepherdsville KY
WMVY(FM) Tisbury MA
WAAF(FM) Worcester MA
WIYY(FM) Baltimore MD
WDLD(FM) Halfway MD
WBLM(FM) Portland ME
WIMK(FM) Iron Mountain MI
WJXQ(FM) Jackson MI
WUPK(FM) Marquette MI
WRKR(FM) Portage MI
KQDS-FM Duluth MN
KQRA(FM) Brookline MO
KCMQ(FM) Columbia MO
KSHE(FM) Crestwood MO
KZRQ-FM Mount Vernon MO
WFXO(FM) Iuka MS
WXQR(FM) Jacksonville NC
WSFL-FM New Bern NC
KSSS(FM) Bismarck ND
KQZZ(FM) Devils Lake ND
KJKJ(FM) Grand Forks ND
KDAM(FM) Hope ND
WFRD(FM) Hanover NH
WHOM(FM) Mt. Washington NH
*WMNJ(FM) Madison NJ
KZRR(FM) Albuquerque NM
KEND(FM) Roswell NM
KLKO(FM) Elko NV
*WDWN(FM) Auburn NY

*WGCC-FM Batavia NY
*WBSU(FM) Brockport NY
*WCWP(FM) Brookville NY
WEDG(FM) Buffalo NY
WFXF(FM) Honeoye Falls NY
*WNYU-FM New York NY
WCMF-FM Rochester NY
*WARY(FM) Valhalla NY
WRQK(FM) Canton OH
WEBN(FM) Cincinnati OH
WDOK(FM) Cleveland OH
WTUE(FM) Dayton OH
WBYR(FM) Van Wert OH
KATT-FM Oklahoma City OK
KHBZ-FM Oklahoma City OK
KLRR(FM) Redmond OR
WLLF(FM) Mercer PA
WMMR(FM) Philadelphia PA
*WQSU(FM) Selinsgrove PA
WQSD(FM) Briarcliff Acres SC
WFXH-FM Hilton Head Island SC
WMFX(FM) Saint Andrews SC
WWRK(FM) Scranton SC
KRRO(FM) Sioux Falls SD
WLQK(FM) Livingston TN
WOKI(FM) Oliver Springs TN
KQQK(FM) Beaumont TX
KJKE(FM) Ingleside TX
KFMX-FM Lubbock TX
KISS-FM San Antonio TX
KBZS(FM) Wichita Falls TX
*KWCR-FM Ogden UT

Alternative

*KRUA(FM) Anchorage AK
KUWL(FM) College AK
*WEGL(FM) Auburn AL
WUHT(FM) Birmingham AL
WZEW(FM) Fairhope AL
WXRP(AM) Hanceville AL
WRAX(FM) Helena AL
*WVUA-FM Tuscaloosa AL
*KCAC(FM) Camden AR
KVDW(AM) England AR
*KXUA(FM) Fayetteville AR
KXNA(FM) Springdale AR
KEDJ(FM) Gilbert AZ
KFMA(FM) Green Valley AZ
KOHT(FM) Marana AZ
KZON(FM) Phoenix AZ
KQAZ(FM) Springerville-Eagar AZ
KWMT-FM Tucson AZ
*KSPC(FM) Claremont CA
*KVHS(FM) Concord CA
*KKUP(FM) Cupertino CA
*KFSR(FM) Fresno CA
KSLG-FM Hydesville CA
KDLE(FM) Newport Beach CA
KROQ-FM Pasadena CA
KMRJ(FM) Rancho Mirage CA
*KUCR(FM) Riverside CA
KHWD(FM) Roseville CA
KWOD(FM) Sacramento CA
KBZT(FM) San Diego CA
*KUSF(FM) San Francisco CA
*KSCU(FM) Santa Clara CA
KDLD(FM) Santa Monica CA
KMBY-FM Seaside CA
KCNL(FM) Sunnyvale CA
KKZQ(FM) Tehachapi CA
KFRR(FM) Woodlake CA
*KLRD(FM) Yucaipa CA
KSMT(FM) Breckenridge CO
*KSJD(FM) Cortez CO
KTCL(FM) Fort Collins CO
*KMSA(FM) Grand Junction CO
*WQAQ(FM) Hamden CT
*WFCS(FM) New Britain CT
*WNHU(FM) West Haven CT
WPLA(FM) Callahan FL
WJRR(FM) Cocoa Beach FL
*WVUM(FM) Coral Gables FL
WOCL(FM) De Land FL
WSUN-FM Holiday FL
WPBZ(FM) Indiantown FL
WIIS(FM) Key West FL

*WXSR(FM) Quincy FL
*WKPX(FM) Sunrise FL
*WUOG(FM) Athens GA
WNNX(FM) Atlanta GA
*WRFG(FM) Atlanta GA
WAEG(FM) Evans GA
*WGUR(FM) Milledgeville GA
*WVGS(FM) Statesboro GA
KLHI-FM Lahaina HI
KUCD(FM) Pearl City HI
KBVU-FM Alta IA
*KICB(FM) Fort Dodge IA
*KSTM(FM) Indianola IA
*KIGC(FM) Oskaloosa IA
KMSC(FM) Sioux City IA
*KWDM(FM) West Des Moines IA
KQXR(FM) Payette ID
KCDA(FM) Post Falls ID
KSKI-FM Sun Valley ID
WKQX(FM) Chicago IL
WXRT-FM Chicago IL
WZZN(FM) Chicago IL
*WRSE(FM) Elmhurst IL
*WGBK(FM) Glenview IL
*WLCA(FM) Godfrey IL
*WIUS(FM) Macomb IL
WIBV(FM) Mount Vernon IL
*WRRG(FM) River Grove IL
*WARG(FM) Summit IL
*WHJE(FM) Carmel IN
*WJHS(FM) Columbia City IN
*WGRE(FM) Greencastle IN
*WCYT(FM) Lafayette Township IN
WAQZ(FM) Fort Thomas KY
*WRFL(FM) Lexington KY
KFTE(FM) Breaux Bridge LA
KNXX(FM) Donaldsonville LA
WNXX(FM) Jackson LA
*KXUL(FM) Monroe LA
*KNWD(FM) Natchitoches LA
*KLPI-FM Ruston LA
*KSCL(FM) Shreveport LA
*WAMH(FM) Amherst MA
WBCN(FM) Boston MA
*WRBB(FM) Boston MA
WBOS(FM) Brookline MA
*WFPB-FM Falmouth MA
*WDJM-FM Framingham MA
WFNX(FM) Lynn MA
*WSMU-FM North Dartmouth MA
*WKKL(FM) West Barnstable MA
*WSKB(FM) Westfield MA
WMTB-FM Emmittsburg MD
WFWM(FM) Frostburg MD
WRXS(FM) Ocean City MD
WTMD(FM) Towson MD
WHSN(FM) Bangor ME
WCLZ(FM) Brunswick ME
WPHX-FM Sanford ME
XETRA-FM Tijuana MEX
WQAC-FM Alma MI
*WHFR(FM) Dearborn MI
WDET-FM Detroit MI
*WDBM(FM) East Lansing MI
WGRD-FM Grand Rapids MI
*WTHS(FM) Holland MI
*WUPX(FM) Marquette MI
*WOVI(FM) Novi MI
*WPHS(FM) Warren MI
*WYCE(FM) Wyoming MI
*KUOM-FM Saint Louis Park MN
*KSRQ(FM) Thief River Falls MN
KCFV(FM) Ferguson MO
*KTRM(FM) Kirksville MO
*KMVC(FM) Marshall MO
KZZK(FM) New London MO
*KGSP(FM) Parkville MO
KNSX(FM) Steelville MO
WHOC(AM) Philadelphia MS
*WMSV(FM) Starkville MS
WUMS(FM) University MS
*WGLT(FM) Bozeman MT
KBAZ(FM) Hamilton MT
*KBGA(FM) Missoula MT
*WZMB(FM) Greenville NC
*WKNC-FM Raleigh NC

WEND(FM) Salisbury NC
*WDCC(FM) Sanford NC
*KFJM(FM) Grand Forks ND
*KRNU(FM) Lincoln NE
KCTY-FM Plattsmouth NE
*KWSC(FM) Wayne NE
WFEX(FM) Peterborough NH
WPNH-FM Plymouth NH
WHTG-FM Eatontown NJ
*WMNJ(FM) Madison NJ
WDOX(FM) North Cape May NJ
WBBO(FM) Ocean Acres NJ
WJSE(FM) Petersburg NJ
*WLFR(FM) Pomona NJ
*WTSR(FM) Trenton NJ
*WMSC(FM) Upper Montclair NJ
*WPSC-FM Wayne NJ
KDRF(FM) Albuquerque NM
KTEG(FM) Bosque Farms NM
*KXTE(FM) Pahrump NV
KRZQ-FM Sparks NV
WHRL(FM) Albany NY
WXPK(FM) Briarcliff Manor NY
WZNE(FM) Brighton NY
*WBSU(FM) Brockport NY
*WBNY(FM) Buffalo NY
WEDG(FM) Buffalo NY
*WITC(FM) Cazenovia NY
*WGSU(FM) Geneseo NY
WLIR-FM Hampton Bays NY
WXRK(FM) New York NY
*WNYK(FM) Nyack NY
WDFH(FM) Ossining NY
WBTZ(FM) Plattsburgh NY
*WQKE(FM) Plattsburgh NY
*WTSC-FM Potsdam NY
WQBK-FM Rensselaer NY
*WBER(FM) Rochester NY
*WIRQ(FM) Rochester NY
*WSIA(FM) Staten Island NY
WXEG-FM Beavercreek OH
*WCSB(FM) Cleveland OH
WRWK(FM) Delta OH
WOXY(FM) Oxford OH
*WXUT(FM) Toledo OH
*WOBN(FM) Westerville OH
*KRSC-FM Claremore OK
KMYZ-FM Pryor OK
KAZY(FM) Woodward OK
*KSBA(FM) Coos Bay OR
*KBVR(FM) Corvallis OR
KNRQ-FM Eugene OR
KROG(FM) Grants Pass OR
*KSLC(FM) McMinnville OR
*KWBX(FM) Salem OR
*WBUQ(FM) Bloomsburg PA
*WESS(FM) East Stroudsburg PA
*WFSE(FM) Edinboro PA
*WWEC(FM) Elizabethtown PA
*WXPH(FM) Harrisburg PA
*WARC(FM) Meadville PA
*WXPN(FM) Philadelphia PA
WUBZ-FM Philipsburg PA
*WXDX-FM Pittsburgh PA
WDMT(FM) Pittston PA
*WUSR(FM) Scranton PA
*WVMW-FM Scranton PA
*WRSK(FM) Slippery Rock PA
WBRU(FM) Providence RI
*WJMF(FM) Smithfield RI
WAVF(FM) Hanahan SC
*KAUR(FM) Sioux Falls SD
*KBHU-FM Spearfish SD
WMFS(FM) Bartlett TN
*WTTU(FM) Cookeville TN
WTZR(FM) Elizabethton TN
WNFZ(FM) Oak Ridge TN
*WAWL-FM Red Bank TN
KEYJ-FM Abilene TX
*KACV-FM Amarillo TX
*KVRX(FM) Austin TX
KGSR(FM) Bastrop TX
*KHPU(FM) Brownwood TX
KROX-FM Buda TX
KXCS(FM) Cameron TX
KDGE(FM) Fort Worth TX
KQRX(FM) Midland TX

Programming on Radio Stations in the U.S.

*KTSW(FM) San Marcos TX
KESO(FM) South Padre Island TX
KNRX(FM) Sterling City TX
KJMY(FM) Bountiful UT
KJQN(FM) Coalville UT
KPLD(FM) Kanab UT
KNJQ(FM) Manti UT
KENZ(FM) Orem UT
*KOHS(FM) Orem UT
KXRK(FM) Provo UT
*KRDC-FM Saint George UT
*WNRN(FM) Charlottesville VA
WYSK-FM Spotsylvania VA
*WCWM(FM) Williamsburg VA
WZIN(FM) Charlotte Amalie VI
*WJSC-FM Johnson VT
WEQX(FM) Manchester VT
*WVTC(FM) Randolph Center VT
WRJT(FM) Royalton VT
*KASB(FM) Bellevue WA
KFNK(FM) Eatonville WA
*KCWU(FM) Ellensburg WA
*KTCV(FM) Kennewick WA
*KEXP-FM Seattle WA
KNDD(FM) Seattle WA
*KXOT(FM) Tacoma WA
*KYVT(FM) Yakima WA
*WBSD(FM) Burlington WI
WMAD(FM) Sauk City WI
*WSUW(FM) Whitewater WI
WQZK-FM Keyser WV
*WSHC(FM) Shepherdstown WV
*WGLZ(FM) West Liberty WV
KKPL(FM) Cheyenne WY

American Indian

KNDN(AM) Farmington NM
KHAC(AM) Tse Bonito NM
*KWSO(FM) Warm Springs OR

Beautiful Music

*KJNP-FM North Pole AK
WJRD(AM) Tuscaloosa AL
KFLG(AM) Bullhead City AZ
KBUX(FM) Quartzsite AZ
KWXY(AM) Cathedral City CA
KWXY-FM Cathedral City CA
KCVR-FM Columbia CA
KLXR(AM) Redding CA
KIRN(AM) Simi Valley CA
*KGUD(FM) Longmont CO
*WJMJ(FM) Hartford CT
WVOI(AM) Marco Island FL
WTOT(AM) Marianna FL
WECM(AM) Milton FL
WNCV(FM) Niceville FL
*WNEE(FM) Jasper GA
WNNG(AM) Warner Robins GA
KWLO(AM) Waterloo IA
KQWC(AM) Webster City IA
KXLT-FM Eagle ID
WJIL(AM) Jacksonville IL
WAXI(FM) Rockville IN
KVSV-FM Beloit KS
WMST(AM) Mt. Sterling KY
KSIG(AM) Crowley LA
WNBH(AM) New Bedford MA
*WYAR(FM) Yarmouth ME
WMUZ(FM) Detroit MI
WMPX(AM) Midland MI
KLKS(FM) Breezy Point MN
WKLK(AM) Cloquet MN
*KGNA-FM Arnold MO
KWRT-FM Boonville MO
*KGNN-FM Cuba MO
KTXR(FM) Springfield MO
WBAQ(FM) Greenville MS
WROA(AM) Gulfport MS
WELO(AM) Tupelo MS
WNMX(FM) Waxhaw NC
*KMTH(FM) Maljamar NM
*KENW-FM Portales NM
WYOS(AM) Binghamton NY
WCBA(AM) Corning NY

*WHPC(FM) Garden City NY
WTLB(AM) Utica NY
WSRW(AM) Hillsboro OH
WSRW(AM) Hillsboro OH
*WFCO(FM) Lancaster OH
KCST(AM) Florence OR
WNAK-FM Carbondale PA
*WPGM(AM) Danville PA
*WPGM-FM Danville PA
*WPEL-FM Montrose PA
WNAK(AM) Nanticoke PA
WNIK-FM Arecibo PR
WVJP(AM) Caguas PR
WVJP-FM Caguas PR
WORO(AM) Corozal PR
WKSA-FM Isabela PR
WIAC-FM San Juan PR
WIOA(FM) San Juan PR
WMUU-FM Greenville SC
WDOD(AM) Chattanooga TN
*WOEZ(FM) Maynardville TN
KXYL(AM) Brownwood TX
KNNK(FM) Dimmitt TX
*KNCT-FM Killeen TX
KBBT(FM) Schertz TX
KPYK(AM) Terrell TX
*KTXK(FM) Texarkana TX
*WIUJ(FM) Charlotte Amalie VI
WDHP(AM) Frederiksted VI
WBTN(AM) Bennington VT
WSTJ(AM) Saint Johnsbury VT
*KBCS(FM) Bellevue WA
*KSOH(FM) Wapato WA
WHSM(AM) Hayward WI

Big Band

KGOT(FM) Anchorage AK
*KBRW-FM Barrow AK
WAUD(AM) Auburn AL
KFPW(AM) Fort Smith AR
KOMT(FM) Mountain Home AR
KFLG(AM) Bullhead City AZ
KTUC(AM) Tucson AZ
*KCEA(FM) Atherton CA
KTEA(FM) Cambria CA
KIDD(AM) Monterey CA
KEZW(AM) Aurora CO
KNAB(AM) Burlington CO
*WNHU(FM) West Haven CT
WJWK(AM) Seaford DE
WTOT(AM) Marianna FL
WMMB(AM) Melbourne FL
WECM(AM) Milton FL
WJNA(AM) Royal Palm Beach FL
WKII(AM) Solana FL
WMLB(AM) East Point GA
KCLN(AM) Clinton IA
KWLO(AM) Waterloo IA
KQWC(AM) Webster City IA
KRPL(AM) Moscow ID
WFRL(AM) Freeport IL
WAIK(AM) Galesburg IL
WPMB(AM) Vandalia IL
WGFA(AM) Watseka IL
WFRX(AM) West Frankfort IL
KABI(AM) Abilene KS
KSGL(AM) Wichita KS
WQSX(FM) Lawrence MA
*WICN(FM) Worcester MA
WWLG(AM) Pikesville MD
*WYAR(FM) Yarmouth ME
WRCC(AM) Battle Creek MI
WMRX-FM Beaverton MI
WCBY(AM) Cheboygan MI
WMPX(AM) Midland MI
WQXO(AM) Munising MI
WOAP(AM) Owosso MI
WODJ(AM) Whitehall MI
KLKS(FM) Breezy Point MN
KWLK(AM) Cleveland MS
KWRT-FM Boonville MO
KAPE(AM) Cape Girardeau MO
KOMC-FM Kimberling City MO
KRLI(FM) Malta Bend MO
KTOZ(AM) Springfield MO
WELO(AM) Tupelo MS

WPAQ(AM) Mount Airy NC
WNOS(AM) New Bern NC
WBLO(AM) Thomasville NC
WPNH(AM) Plymouth NH
WOBM(AM) Lakewood NJ
*KNCC(FM) Elko NV
KHIT(AM) Reno NV
KBDB(AM) Sparks NV
WPTR(AM) Clifton Park NY
WCBA(AM) Corning NY
WALK(AM) East Patchogue NY
WRWD(AM) Ellenville NY
WHUC(AM) Hudson NY
WABY(AM) Mechanicville NY
WSGO(AM) Oswego NY
WKIP(AM) Poughkeepsie NY
WUAM(AM) Saratoga Springs NY
WNCO(AM) Ashland OH
*WKHR(FM) Bainbridge OH
*WLBS(FM) Bristol PA
WRIE(AM) Erie PA
WPEN(AM) Philadelphia PA
WJAS(AM) Pittsburgh PA
*WRDV(FM) Warminster PA
WLOW(FM) Port Royal SC
WDOD(AM) Chattanooga TN
*WOEZ(FM) Maynardville TN
KPYK(AM) Terrell TX
*WFOS(FM) Chesapeake VA
WSVG(AM) Mount Jackson VA
*WIUJ(FM) Charlotte Amalie VI
WSTJ(AM) Saint Johnsbury VT
KLKI(AM) Anacortes WA
KBRD(AM) Lacey WA
KWDB(AM) Oak Harbor WA
WCCN(AM) Neillsville WI
WBBD(FM) Wheeling WV

Black

WANA(AM) Anniston AL
WATV(AM) Birmingham AL
WXAL(AM) Demopolis AL
WMGJ(AM) Gadsden AL
WHOG(AM) Hobson City AL
WLOR(AM) Huntsville AL
WMFC(AM) Monroeville AL
WZZA(AM) Tuscumbia AL
WAPZ(AM) Wetumpka AL
*KABF(FM) Little Rock AR
KAKJ(FM) Marianna AR
KCLT(FM) West Helena AR
KTYM(AM) Inglewood CA
*KSRH(FM) San Rafael CA
*WNHU(FM) West Haven CT
WZAZ(AM) Jacksonville FL
WWAB(AM) Lakeland FL
WYZE(AM) Atlanta GA
WFXA-FM Augusta GA
WWLD(FM) Cairo GA
WOKS(AM) Columbus GA
WJGA-FM Jackson GA
WBBT(FM) Lyons GA
WLCG(AM) Macon GA
*KIGC(FM) Oskaloosa IA
*WIIT(FM) Chicago IL
WVAZ(AM) Oak Park IL
WVEL(AM) Pekin IL
WCVG(AM) Covington KY
WLOU(AM) Louisville KY
KSLO(AM) Opelousas LA
KRUS(AM) Ruston LA
KOKA(AM) Shreveport LA
KBSF(AM) Springhill LA
KTKC(AM) Springhill LA
KVCL-FM Winnfield LA
WBGR(AM) Baltimore MD
WFBR(AM) Glen Burnie MD
WEFG-FM Whitehall MI
WCHJ(AM) Brookhaven MS
WCLD(AM) Cleveland MS
WKRA-FM Holly Springs MS
WCPC(AM) Houston MS
WXTN(AM) Lexington MS
WMIS(AM) Natchez MS
WKOR(AM) Starkville MS
WFMO(AM) Fairmont NC

WIDU(AM) Fayetteville NC
WFMC(AM) Goldsboro NC
*WNAA(FM) Greensboro NC
WHNC(AM) Henderson NC
WEGG(AM) Rose Hill NC
WWIL(AM) Wilmington NC
KBLR-FM Blair NE
WDCR(AM) Hanover NH
*WNEC-FM Henniker NH
*KCEP(FM) Las Vegas NV
WSIV(AM) East Syracuse NY
WTHE(AM) Mineola NY
WBLS(FM) New York NY
*WHCR-FM New York NY
WLIB(AM) New York NY
*WBGU(FM) Bowling Green OH
WGFT(AM) Campbell OH
WCIN(AM) Cincinnati OH
*WSLN(FM) Delaware OH
WASN(AM) Youngstown OH
*WIXQ(FM) Millersville PA
WNAP(AM) Norristown PA
WDAS(AM) Philadelphia PA
WDAS-FM Philadelphia PA
WDOG(AM) Allendale SC
WDOG-FM Allendale SC
WPJS(AM) Conway SC
WPFM(AM) Darlington SC
WEAC(AM) Gaffney SC
WBZF(FM) Hartsville SC
*WLGI(FM) Hemingway SC
WASC(AM) Spartanburg SC
WMRB(AM) Columbia TN
*WVCP(FM) Gallatin TN
WFKX(FM) Henderson TN
WDIA(AM) Memphis TN
*WMTS-FM Murfreesboro TN
KGGR(AM) Dallas TX
KCOH(AM) Houston TX
WKBY(AM) Chatham VA
WILA(AM) Danville VA
WSHV(AM) South Hill VA

Bluegrass

*WPIL(FM) Heflin AL
WRMG(AM) Red Bay AL
*WAMU(FM) Washington DC
WCHK(AM) Canton GA
WALH(AM) Mountain City GA
WYHG(AM) Young Harris GA
WGOH(AM) Grayson KY
WMTL(AM) Leitchfield KY
WTWZ(AM) Clinton MS
WPYB(AM) Benson NC
WKGX(AM) Lenoir NC
WDSL(AM) Mocksville NC
WPAQ(AM) Mount Airy NC
WMPM(AM) Smithfield NC
WADV(AM) Lebanon PA
WJDJ(AM) Hartsville SC
WGOC(AM) Blountville TN
*WDVX(FM) Clinton TN
WLSB(AM) Copperhill TN
WSDQ(AM) Dunlap TN
*WPLN-FM Nashville TN
WUAT(AM) Pikeville TN
WLIJ(AM) Shelbyville TN
WLOD-FM Sweetwater TN
*WTML(FM) Tullahoma TN
*KAMU-FM College Station TX
WDUF(AM) Duffield VA
WGFC(AM) Floyd VA
WLRV(AM) Lebanon VA
WYTI(AM) Rocky Mount VA
WXMY(AM) Saltville VA
KOHO-FM Leavenworth WA
WDBS(FM) Sutton WV

Blues

WDLK(AM) Dadeville AL
WQZZ(AM) Eutaw AL
WKXN(AM) Greenville AL
*WJAB(FM) Huntsville AL
WKXK(FM) Pine Hill AL

WAPZ(AM) Wetumpka AL
KCLT(FM) West Helena AR
KOHT(FM) Marana AZ
KAJM(FM) Payson AZ
KRML(AM) Carmel CA
KJLH-FM Compton CA
*KKUP(FM) Cupertino CA
*KSDS(FM) San Diego CA
*KCSS(FM) Turlock CA
KQKS(FM) Lakewood CO
WTMP-FM Dade City FL
WKIQ(AM) Eustis FL
WVKX(FM) Irwinton GA
WLZN(FM) Macon GA
WTYB(FM) Springfield GA
WRXZ(FM) Sylvester GA
WZBN(FM) Sylvester GA
KUAM-FM Hagatna GU
KATZ-FM Alton IL
*WSSD(FM) Chicago IL
WESL(AM) East St. Louis IL
*WDCB(FM) Glen Ellyn IL
*WGLT(FM) Normal IL
WTLC-FM Greenwood IN
WHHH(FM) Indianapolis IN
WTLO(AM) Somerset KY
KTRY-FM Bastrop LA
KBRH(AM) Baton Rouge LA
*KLSU(FM) Baton Rouge LA
KMEZ(FM) Belle Chasse LA
KNOU(FM) Empire LA
KJMH(FM) Lake Arthur LA
KRUS(AM) Ruston LA
KNEK(FM) Washington LA
WILD(AM) Boston MA
*WUMB-FM Boston MA
WBOT(FM) Brockton MA
*WFPB-FM Falmouth MA
WATD-FM Marshfield MA
*WNEF(FM) Newburyport MA
*WBPR(FM) Worcester MA
*WESM(FM) Princess Anne MD
WRED(FM) Saco ME
WDMK(FM) Detroit MI
WSPZ-FM Hartford MI
WJNZ(FM) Kentwood MI
*WLNZ(FM) Lansing MI
*WNMC-FM Traverse City MI
*WEMU(FM) Ypsilanti MI
*KJLU(FM) Jefferson City MO
*KMVC(FM) Marshall MO
*KCOZ(FM) Point Lookout MO
WBSL(AM) Bay St. Louis MS
WONG(AM) Canton MS
WROX(AM) Clarksdale MS
WTYJ(FM) Fayette MS
*WVSD(FM) Itta Bena MS
WKXI(AM) Jackson MS
*WMPR(FM) Jackson MS
WEEZ(AM) Laurel MS
WESY(AM) Leland MS
*WPRL(FM) Lorman MS
WNBN(AM) Meridian MS
WMIS(AM) Natchez MS
WZLD(FM) Petal MS
WABO(AM) Waynesboro MS
WQZL(FM) Belhaven NC
WQMG-FM Greensboro NC
WQNC(FM) Harrisburg NC
WARR(AM) Warrenton NC
WENC(AM) Whiteville NC
KBLR-FM Blair NE
*WBZC(FM) Pemberton NJ
*WFDU(FM) Teaneck NJ
*KCEP(FM) Las Vegas NV
WRKS(FM) New York NY
WJZR(FM) Rochester NY
*WXXI(FM) Rochester NY
*WSPN(FM) Saratoga Springs NY
WDAO(AM) Dayton OH
WXMG(FM) Upper Arlington OH
*KRVM(FM) Eugene OR
*KMHD(FM) Gresham OR
WKSP(FM) Aiken SC
WYNN(AM) Florence SC
WALD(AM) Walterboro SC
WVOL(AM) Berry Hill TN

Programming on Radio Stations in the U.S.

WBOL(AM) Bolivar TN
*WUTC(FM) Chattanooga TN
*WEVL(FM) Memphis TN
*KAZI-FM Austin TX
KBFB(FM) Dallas TX
KTXN-FM Victoria TX
*WFOS(FM) Chesapeake VA
*WMRY(FM) Crozet VA
WVKL(FM) Norfolk VA
KRIZ(AM) Renton WA
WKKV-FM Racine WI

Children

WQUA(FM) Citronelle AL
KDIS-FM Little Rock AR
KMIK(AM) Tempe AZ
KAVT(AM) Fresno CA
KMKY(AM) Oakland CA
KDIS(AM) Pasadena CA
KIID(AM) Sacramento CA
KKDD(AM) San Bernardino CA
KDDZ(AM) Arvada CO
WDZK(AM) Bloomfield CT
WAJD(AM) Gainesville FL
WBWL(AM) Jacksonville FL
WMYM(AM) Miami FL
WDYZ(AM) Orlando FL
WDWD(AM) Atlanta GA
WNEX(AM) Macon GA
WPGA(AM) Perry GA
WSDZ(AM) Belleville IL
WRDZ(AM) La Grange IL
WPJX(AM) Zion IL
WRDZ-FM Plainfield IN
KQAM(AM) Wichita KS
WDRD(AM) Newburg KY
WBYU(AM) New Orleans LA
*WMDR(AM) Augusta ME
WFDF(AM) Flint MI
KDIZ(AM) Golden Valley MN
WBHR(AM) Sauk Rapids MN
KPHN(AM) Kansas City MO
WGFY(AM) Charlotte NC
WCOG(AM) Greensboro NC
KYDZ(AM) Bellevue NE
*WVBH(FM) Beach Haven West NJ
KALY(AM) Los Ranchos de Albuquerque NM
WWLF(AM) Auburn NY
WQEW(AM) New York NY
WOLF-FM Oswego NY
WOLF(AM) Syracuse NY
WWMK(AM) Cleveland OH
KOCY(AM) Del City OK
KDZR(AM) Lake Oswego OR
WWCS(AM) Canonsburg PA
*WWCF(FM) McConnellsburg PA
WDDZ(AM) Pawtucket RI
KMKI(AM) Plano TX
KRDY(AM) San Antonio TX
*KTEO(FM) Wichita Falls TX
KKAT(AM) Salt Lake City UT
KWDZ(AM) Salt Lake City UT
WDZY(AM) Colonial Heights VA
KKDZ(AM) Seattle WA
WGEE(AM) Superior WI
*WMLJ(FM) Summersville WV

Chinese

KAZN(AM) Pasadena CA
KAHZ(AM) Pomona CA
KSON(AM) San Diego CA
WZRC(AM) New York NY

Christian

KAFC(FM) Anchorage AK
*KAKL(FM) Anchorage AK
KYKD(FM) Bethel AK
KAGV(AM) Big Lake AK
KAKN(FM) Naknek AK
KICY-FM Nome AK
*KJLP(FM) Palmer AK
WIZB(FM) Abbeville AL

WAVU(AM) Albertville AL
*WGRW(FM) Anniston AL
WASG(AM) Atmore AL
WDJC-FM Birmingham AL
*WGIB(FM) Birmingham AL
*WELJ(FM) Brewton AL
WALN(FM) Carrollton AL
*WELL-FM Dadeville AL
WGZS(AM) Dothan AL
WKWL(AM) Florala AL
*WTBB(FM) Gadsden AL
*WJIA(FM) Guntersville AL
*WAYH(FM) Harvest AL
WBXR(AM) Hazel Green AL
*WOCG(FM) Huntsville AL
WIXI(AM) Jasper AL
WLYJ(AM) Jasper AL
*WBHY(AM) Mobile AL
*WBHY-FM Mobile AL
WXVI(AM) Montgomery AL
*WAQG(FM) Ozark AL
WIJD(AM) Prichard AL
WJBY(AM) Rainbow City AL
*WAQU(FM) Selma AL
*WAKD(FM) Sheffield AL
WBTG(AM) Sheffield AL
*WAXU(FM) Troy AL
KABK-FM Augusta AR
KBGR(FM) Beebe AR
*KAPG(FM) Bentonville AR
*KBCM(FM) Blytheville AR
*KBHN(FM) Booneville AR
KWXT(AM) Dardanelle AR
*KBPU(FM) De Queen AR
*KBNV(FM) Fayetteville AR
KOFC(AM) Fayetteville AR
*KLMZ(FM) Fouke AR
KZKZ-FM Greenwood AR
*KBPW(FM) Hampton AR
*KBPB(FM) Harrison AR
*KBMJ(FM) Heber Springs AR
KJIW-FM Helena AR
*KALR(FM) Hot Springs AR
*KLRO(FM) Hot Springs AR
KJLV(FM) Hoxie AR
KJBR(FM) Marked Tree AR
KCGS(AM) Marshall AR
*KVRN(FM) Marvell AR
*KMTC(FM) Russellville AR
*KLRC(FM) Siloam Springs AR
*KKLT(FM) Texarkana AR
KKLV(AM) Turrell AR
*KLFS(FM) Van Buren AR
KNWJ(AM) Leone AS
*KWRB(FM) Bisbee AZ
*KLVA(FM) Casa Grande AZ
KCKY(AM) Coolidge AZ
KAPR(AM) Douglas AZ
*KRMC(FM) Douglas AZ
*KJZA(FM) Drake AZ
*KLVK(FM) Fountain Hills AZ
KJAA(AM) Globe AZ
*KVJC(FM) Globe AZ
*KNLB(FM) Lake Havasu City AZ
*KNOG(FM) Nogales AZ
*KFLR-FM Phoenix AZ
KXEG(AM) Phoenix AZ
*KGCB(FM) Prescott AZ
KQTL(AM) Sahuarita AZ
KNXN(AM) Sierra Vista AZ
KTBA(AM) Tuba City AZ
*KFLT(AM) Tucson AZ
KGMS(AM) Tucson AZ
KWIM(FM) Window Rock AZ
*KCFY(FM) Yuma AZ
*KYRM(FM) Yuma AZ
KFSH-FM Anaheim CA
*KWTW(FM) Bishop CA
KBNF(FM) Chester CA
*KDKL(FM) Coalinga CA
KVMG(FM) Dunnigan CA
*KARQ(FM) East Sonora CA
*KLVY(FM) Fairmead CA
KIRV(AM) Fresno CA
KWRU(AM) Fresno CA
*KLVG(FM) Garberville CA
KKMC(AM) Gonzales CA

*KLVS(FM) Grass Valley CA
*KHRI(FM) Hollister CA
*KLVJ(FM) Julian CA
*KWTM(FM) June Lake CA
*KDRH(FM) King City CA
*KFYE(FM) Kingsburg CA
*KTLW(FM) Lancaster CA
*KHKL(FM) Laytonville CA
KKFS(FM) Lincoln CA
*KLVN(FM) Livingston CA
*KRQZ(FM) Lompoc CA
*KFRN(AM) Long Beach CA
KKLA-FM Los Angeles CA
*KLVC(FM) Magalia CA
*KAMB(FM) Merced CA
KCIV(FM) Mount Bullion CA
*KMJC-FM Mount Shasta CA
*KLFH(FM) Ojai CA
KGDP(AM) Orcutt CA
KDAR(FM) Oxnard CA
*KHCS(FM) Palm Desert CA
*KLVM(FM) Prunedale CA
*KJCQ(FM) Quincy CA
KNLF(FM) Quincy CA
*KGBM(FM) Randsburg CA
*KLVB(FM) Red Bluff CA
*KKRO(FM) Redding CA
*KVIP(AM) Redding CA
KVIP-FM Redding CA
*KWTD(FM) Ridgecrest CA
*KSGN(FM) Riverside CA
KFSG(AM) Roseville CA
KDBV(AM) Salinas CA
KWVE(FM) San Clemente CA
*KLFF-FM San Luis Obispo CA
*KLVH(FM) San Luis Obispo CA
KPRZ(AM) San Marcos-Poway CA
*KSRI(FM) Santa Cruz CA
*KGDP-FM Santa Maria CA
KSBQ(AM) Santa Maria CA
*KLVR(FM) Santa Rosa CA
*KQKL(FM) Selma CA
KYIX(FM) South Oroville CA
KUYL(AM) Stockton CA
*KRTM(FM) Temecula CA
*KYKL(FM) Tracy CA
*KULV(FM) Ukiah CA
*KHMS(FM) Victorville CA
*KXRD(FM) Victorville CA
*KARM(FM) Visalia CA
*KSAK(FM) Walnut CA
KALI(AM) West Covina CA
*KARA(FM) Williams CA
KLJH(FM) Bayfield CO
*KTLC(FM) Canon City CO
*KTMH(FM) Colona CO
*KTLF(FM) Colorado Springs CO
KWYD(AM) Colorado Springs CO
KLTT(AM) Commerce City CO
KDTA(AM) Delta CO
*KPOF(AM) Denver CO
*KTCF(FM) Dolores CO
*KLCQ(FM) Eaton CO
*KLHV(FM) Fort Collins CO
*KLXV(FM) Glenwood Springs CO
KJOL(AM) Grand Junction CO
*KLFV(FM) Grand Junction CO
*KLRY(FM) Gypsum CO
*KFDN(FM) Lakewood CO
*KXWA(FM) Loveland CO
KBIQ(FM) Manitou Springs CO
*KCBR(AM) Monument CO
*KLDV(FM) Morrison CO
*KTPS(FM) Pagosa Springs CO
KGFT(FM) Pueblo CO
*KTPL(FM) Pueblo CO
*KLBV(FM) Steamboat Springs CO
*KLZV(FM) Sterling CO
*KTDU(FM) Trimble CO
*WIHS(FM) Middletown CT
*WSGG(FM) Norfolk CT
*WXHL-FM Christiana DE
WYBT(AM) Blountstown FL
*WKSG(FM) Cedar Creek FL
WAKU(FM) Crawfordville FL
*WWLC(FM) Cross City FL
*WAQV(FM) Crystal River FL

*WHGN(FM) Crystal River FL
WREH(FM) Cypress Quarters FL
*WAKJ(FM) De Funiak Springs FL
*WSEB(FM) Englewood FL
*WNLE(FM) Fernandina Beach FL
*WJLH(FM) Flagler Beach FL
*WMFL(FM) Florida City FL
*WAFG(FM) Fort Lauderdale FL
*WAYJ(FM) Fort Myers FL
WCRM(AM) Fort Myers FL
*WJYO(FM) Fort Myers FL
*WPSM(FM) Fort Walton Beach FL
*WJLF(FM) Gainesville FL
*WYJC(FM) Greenville FL
*WEAZ(FM) Holly Hill FL
*WCRJ(FM) Jacksonville FL
WROS(AM) Jacksonville FL
WIOJ(AM) Jacksonville Beach FL
*WGES(FM) Key Largo FL
*WMKL(FM) Key Largo FL
*WJIR(FM) Key West FL
*WLAZ(FM) Kissimmee FL
*WBIY(FM) La Belle FL
WOLR(FM) Lake City FL
*WJNF(FM) Marianna FL
*WMCU(FM) Miami FL
*WEGS(FM) Milton FL
*WKVH(FM) Monticello FL
*WSRX(FM) Naples FL
WGCX(FM) Navarre FL
*WLPJ(FM) New Port Richey FL
*WHIJ(FM) Ocala FL
WTLN(AM) Orlando FL
*WHIF(FM) Palatka FL
*WWIA(FM) Palm Bay FL
*WCNO(FM) Palm City FL
*WIRP(FM) Pennsuco FL
WTBN(AM) Pinellas Park FL
WBGB(FM) Ponte Vedra Beach FL
*WAYL(FM) Saint Augustine FL
*WSMR(FM) Sarasota FL
WCVC(AM) Tallahassee FL
*WFRF(FM) Tallahassee FL
WTAL(AM) Tallahassee FL
*WBVM(FM) Tampa FL
*WPOZ(FM) Union Park FL
*WSCF-FM Vero Beach FL
*WAYF(FM) West Palm Beach FL
*WBJY(FM) Americus GA
*WMSL(FM) Athens GA
WAEC(AM) Atlanta GA
WNIV(AM) Atlanta GA
*WLPE(FM) Augusta GA
WGMI(AM) Bremen GA
WAYR-FM Brunswick GA
WPMA(FM) Buckhead GA
*WPWB(FM) Byron GA
WCHM(AM) Clarkesville GA
WAEF(FM) Cordele GA
WWGF(FM) Donalsonville GA
*WAWH(FM) Dublin GA
WECC-FM Folkston GA
*WMVV(FM) Griffin GA
*WTFH(FM) Helen GA
*WNEE(FM) Jasper GA
*WLPT(FM) Jesup GA
WVFJ-FM Manchester GA
WSSA(AM) Morrow GA
WGTJ(AM) Murrayville GA
WNEA(AM) Newnan GA
WJEP(AM) Ochlocknee GA
WLPF(FM) Ocilla GA
*WVRI(FM) Pavo GA
*WLFS(FM) Port Wentworth GA
*WLXP(FM) Savannah GA
*WYFS(FM) Savannah GA
WZIQ(FM) Smithville GA
*WAYT(FM) Thomasville GA
*WTXR(FM) Toccoa Falls GA
WBDX(FM) Trenton GA
*WGPH(FM) Vidalia GA
*WASW(FM) Waycross GA
*KSDA-FM Agat GU
*KHMG(FM) Barrigada GU
*KCIF(FM) Hilo HI
KAIM-FM Honolulu HI
KGU(AM) Honolulu HI

*KIHS(FM) Adel IA
KSKB(FM) Brooklyn IA
*KAYP(FM) Burlington IA
*KILV(FM) Castana IA
KLNG(AM) Council Bluffs IA
KPSZ(AM) Des Moines IA
*KJYL(FM) Eagle Grove IA
*KWOF-FM Hiawatha IA
KMDY(FM) Keokuk IA
KNWM(FM) Madrid IA
KCWN(FM) New Sharon IA
*KNWI(FM) Osceola IA
KJCY(FM) Saint Ansgar IA
*KYFR(AM) Shenandoah IA
KSOU(AM) Sioux Center IA
KTFC(FM) Sioux City IA
KTFG(FM) Sioux Rapids IA
*KJIA(FM) Spirit Lake IA
*KLRX(FM) Wapello IA
*KNWS(FM) Waterloo IA
KWOF(AM) Waterloo IA
KZZQ(FM) Winterset IA
KSPD(AM) Boise ID
*KTFY(FM) Buhl ID
KBGN(AM) Caldwell ID
KBXL(FM) Caldwell ID
*KTSY(FM) Caldwell ID
KRTK(FM) Chubbuck ID
*KARJ(FM) Kuna ID
*KZJB(FM) Pocatello ID
*KLRI(FM) Rigby ID
*KAWZ(FM) Twin Falls ID
*KCIR(FM) Twin Falls ID
*KEFX(FM) Twin Falls ID
*WCLR(FM) Arlington Heights IL
WRMS(AM) Beardstown IL
*WBEL(FM) Cairo IL
*WIBI(FM) Carlinville IL
*WBVN(FM) Carrier Mills IL
*WCBH(FM) Casey IL
WKZI(AM) Casey IL
*WMBI-FM Chicago IL
*WBMF(FM) Crete IL
WYCA(FM) Crete IL
WDQN-FM Du Quoin IL
*WRYT(AM) Edwardsville IL
WJKL(FM) Elgin IL
WPIA(FM) Eureka IL
*WAXR(FM) Geneseo IL
*WYRB(FM) Genoa IL
*WGRN(FM) Greenville IL
WCBW(AM) Highland IL
WDID(AM) Highland IL
*WAWF(FM) Kankakee IL
*WONU(FM) Kankakee IL
WSRB(FM) Lansing IL
WLLM(AM) Lincoln IL
*WAWJ(FM) Marion IL
*WJCZ(FM) Milford IL
*WJCG(FM) Monee IL
*WCFL(FM) Morris IL
*WAPO(FM) Mount Vernon IL
*WBMV(FM) Mount Vernon IL
WIBV(FM) Mount Vernon IL
*WPTH(FM) Olney IL
*WWGN(FM) Ottawa IL
*WZRS(FM) Pana IL
*WCIC(FM) Pekin IL
*WLWJ(FM) Petersburg IL
*WPJC(FM) Pontiac IL
*WPRC(FM) Princeton IL
*WGCA-FM Quincy IL
*WJLY(FM) Ramsey IL
*WFEN(FM) Rockford IL
WQFL(FM) Rockford IL
*WGNJ(FM) Saint Joseph IL
*WSLE(FM) Salem IL
*WLUJ(FM) Springfield IL
*WSCT(FM) Springfield IL
*WSRI(FM) Sugar Grove IL
*WIHM(FM) Taylorville IL
*WETN(FM) Wheaton IL
*WGNR(AM) Anderson IN
*WGNR-FM Anderson IN
WQME(FM) Anderson IN
WYXY(FM) Boonville IN
WHPZ(FM) Bremen IN

Broadcasting & Cable Yearbook 2006

D-692

Programming on Radio Stations in the U.S.

*WPFR-FM Clinton IN
WFRN(AM) Elkhart IN
WFRN-FM Elkhart IN
*WBCL(FM) Fort Wayne IN
WFCV(AM) Fort Wayne IN
*WLAB(FM) Fort Wayne IN
WLYV(AM) Fort Wayne IN
WIJY(FM) Franklin IN
*WIKL(FM) Greencastle IN
*WAUZ(FM) Greensburg IN
*WQKO(FM) Howe IN
WBRI(AM) Indianapolis IN
*KXJH(FM) Linton IN
WVNI(FM) Nashville IN
WFIA-FM New Albany IN
*WSOH(FM) New Washington IN
WGAB(AM) Newburgh IN
*WRXH(FM) Plymouth IN
*WJLR(FM) Seymour IN
WHME(FM) South Bend IN
*WHOJ(FM) Terre Haute IN
WPFR(AM) Terre Haute IN
*WJYW(FM) Union City IN
*WTUR(FM) Upland IN
*WATI(FM) Vincennes IN
*WRFM(FM) Wadesville IN
WFRR(FM) Walton IN
WAMW(AM) Washington IN
*KAXR(FM) Arkansas City KS
KEOJ(FM) Caney KS
*KHYM(FM) Copeland KS
*KJIL(FM) Copeland KS
KTLI(FM) El Dorado KS
*KNGM(FM) Emporia KS
*KBMP(FM) Enterprise KS
*KVCY(FM) Fort Scott KS
*KBDA(FM) Great Bend KS
*KWBI(FM) Great Bend KS
KJRL(FM) Herington KS
*KBQC(FM) Independence KS
KCVW(FM) Kingman KS
KKLO(AM) Leavenworth KS
KZQD(FM) Liberal KS
*KSNS(FM) Medicine Lodge KS
KCCV-FM Olathe KS
*KRBW(FM) Ottawa KS
*KTJO-FM Ottawa KS
KCCV(AM) Overland Park KS
*KCVS(FM) Salina KS
KCVT(FM) Silver Lake KS
KHCA(FM) Wamego KS
*KCFN(FM) Wichita KS
*KYFW(FM) Wichita KS
*KBDD(FM) Winfield KS
*WAYD(FM) Auburn KY
*WAAJ(FM) Benton KY
*WCVK(FM) Bowling Green KY
*WAPD(FM) Campbellsville KY
WMTA(AM) Central City KY
WCVG(AM) Covington KY
*WDFB-FM Danville KY
*WRVG(FM) Georgetown KY
*WSGP(FM) Glasgow KY
WKCB(AM) Hindman KY
*WNKJ(FM) Hopkinsville KY
WFIA(AM) Louisville KY
*WWLT(FM) Manchester KY
*WBMK(FM) Morehead KY
*WJVK(FM) Owensboro KY
*WGCF(FM) Paducah KY
*WWJD(FM) Pippa Passes KY
*WKVY(FM) Somerset KY
WXKY-FM Stanford KY
WRVI(FM) Valley Station KY
WMTC(AM) Vancleve KY
WMTC(FM) Vancleve KY
WVRB(FM) Wilmore KY
WMJR(FM) Winchester KY
*KAPM(FM) Alexandria LA
KJMJ(AM) Alexandria LA
*KLXA-FM Alexandria LA
KHCL(FM) Arcadia LA
*KAXV(FM) Bastrop LA
KBCL(AM) Bossier City LA
*KBAN(FM) De Ridder LA
KVDP(FM) Dry Prong LA
KBEF(FM) Gibsland LA

KKNO(AM) Gretna LA
*KIKL(FM) Lafayette LA
*KOJO(FM) Lake Charles LA
*KYLC(FM) Lake Charles LA
*KAVK(FM) Many LA
*KBMQ(FM) Monroe LA
KLIC(AM) Monroe LA
*KYFL(FM) Monroe LA
*KBIO(FM) Natchitoches LA
KNIR(AM) New Iberia LA
*WBSN-FM New Orleans LA
WLNO(AM) New Orleans LA
WVOG(AM) New Orleans LA
KUMX(FM) North Fort Polk LA
*KSUL(FM) Port Sulphur LA
KHLL(FM) Richwood LA
*KAPI(FM) Ruston LA
*KSJY(FM) Saint Martinville LA
KIOU(AM) Shreveport LA
KSYB(AM) Shreveport LA
*WYCM(FM) Charlton MA
WFGL(FM) Fitchburg MA
WCMX(AM) Leominster MA
WJOE(AM) Orange-Athol MA
WRBS(FM) Baltimore MD
WKDI(AM) Denton MD
WSRY(AM) Elkton MD
*WYPF(FM) Frederick MD
*WLIC(FM) Frostburg MD
*WAIJ(FM) Grantsville MD
WJSS(AM) Havre de Grace MD
WWGB(AM) Indian Head MD
WCTN(AM) Potomac-Cabin John MD
*WDIH(FM) Salisbury MD
WWPN(FM) Westernport MD
*WMDR(AM) Augusta ME
*WHCF(FM) Bangor ME
WBCI(FM) Bath ME
*WFST(AM) Caribou ME
*WMSJ(FM) Freeport ME
*WHMX(FM) Lincoln ME
WJCX(FM) Pittsfield ME
WWWA(FM) Winslow ME
*WUFN(FM) Albion MI
*WVCN(FM) Baraga MI
WOLY(AM) Battle Creek MI
*WTRK(FM) Bay City MI
*WTLI(FM) Bear Creek Township MI
*WCVM(FM) Bronson MI
*WLJW(FM) Cadillac MI
WLCM(AM) Charlotte MI
*WPRJ(FM) Coleman MI
WLQV(AM) Detroit MI
WMUZ(FM) Detroit MI
WDOW-FM Dowagiac MI
*WLJN(AM) Elmwood Township MI
*WAKL(FM) Flint MI
WSNL(AM) Flint MI
*WBLW(FM) Gaylord MI
*WAYG(FM) Grand Rapids MI
*WCSG(FM) Grand Rapids MI
*WCZE(FM) Harbor Beach MI
*WJOJ(FM) Harrisville MI
*WWKM(FM) Imlay City MI
*WVCM(FM) Iron Mountain MI
*WAYK(FM) Kalamazoo MI
*WLGH(FM) Leroy Township MI
WCAR(AM) Livonia MI
*WUGN(FM) Midland MI
*WDTR(FM) Monroe MI
*WMCQ(FM) Muskegon MI
*WPCJ(FM) Pittsford MI
*WJKN-FM Spring Arbor MI
*WSAE(FM) Spring Arbor MI
*WUFL(FM) Sterling Heights MI
*WLJN-FM Traverse City MI
*WEJC(FM) White Star MI
WDEO(AM) Ypsilanti MI
WJQK(FM) Zeeland MI
WPNW(AM) Zeeland MI
*KBHG(FM) Alexandria MN
*KDNW(FM) Duluth MN
*WJRF(FM) Duluth MN
KBGY(FM) Faribault MN
WLKX-FM Forest Lake MN
KKEQ(FM) Fosston MN
*KADU(FM) Hibbing MN

*KBHW(FM) International Falls MN
*KXBR(FM) International Falls MN
WCTS(AM) Maplewood MN
*KTIS(AM) Minneapolis MN
WLOL(FM) Minneapolis MN
*KMKL(FM) North Branch MN
KCGN-FM Ortonville MN
KBHL(FM) Osakis MN
KTIG(FM) Pequot Lakes MN
WZFJ(FM) Pequot Lakes MN
KKMS(AM) Richfield MN
*KFSI(FM) Rochester MN
*KCFB(FM) Saint Cloud MN
*KKJM(FM) Saint Joseph MN
KSMM(AM) Shakopee MN
*KKLW(FM) Willmar MN
KQRB(FM) Windom MN
*KBOJ(FM) Worthington MN
*KGNA-FM Arnold MO
KPVR(FM) Bowling Green MO
*KLFC(FM) Branson MO
KOMC(FM) Branson MO
*KOZO(FM) Branson MO
*KFFW(FM) Caboool MO
KCVO-FM Camdenton MO
KMFC(FM) Centralia MO
KSIV(AM) Clayton MO
*KLRQ(FM) Clinton MO
*KGNN-FM Cuba MO
*KCVZ(FM) Dixon MO
*KTBJ(FM) Festus MO
*KOBC(FM) Joplin MO
KOCR(AM) Joplin MO
KWAS(AM) Joplin MO
*KAUF(FM) Kennett MO
KLTE(FM) Kirksville MO
*KCVQ(FM) Knob Noster MO
*KTTK(FM) Lebanon MO
*KNLM(FM) Marshfield MO
*KBKC(FM) Moberly MO
KELE(AM) Mountain Grove MO
*KCVJ(FM) Osceola MO
*KCVK(FM) Otterville MO
*KBGM(FM) Park Hills MO
*KOKS(FM) Poplar Bluff MO
KHZR(FM) Potosi MO
KADI-FM Republic MO
KAYX(FM) Richmond MO
KGNM(AM) Saint Joseph MO
*KSRD(FM) Saint Joseph MO
KJSL(FM) Saint Louis MO
*KSIV-FM Saint Louis MO
KXEN(AM) Saint Louis MO
*KCVX(FM) Salem MO
*KSCV(FM) Springfield MO
*KWFC(FM) Springfield MO
*KWND(FM) Springfield MO
*KCRL(FM) Sunrise Beach MO
*KRSS(FM) Tarkio MO
*KGNV(FM) Washington MO
KKLL(AM) Webb City MO
KULH(FM) Wheeling MO
*WKVF(FM) Byhalia MS
WWUN-FM Clarksdale MS
WDFX(FM) Cleveland MS
WHJT(FM) Clinton MS
WKNZ(FM) Collins MS
*WPRG(FM) Columbia MS
*WMBU(FM) Forest MS
WQST-FM Forest MS
*WQVI(FM) Forest MS
*WSQH(FM) Forest MS
WJIW(FM) Greenville MS
*WAOY(FM) Gulfport MS
WCPC(AM) Houston MS
*WYTF(FM) Indianola MS
WSJC(AM) Magee MS
WMER(AM) Meridian MS
*WAVI(FM) Oxford MS
*WPAS(FM) Pascagoula MS
WPMP(FM) Pascagoula-Moss Point MS
WSAO(AM) Senatobia MS
*WAFR(FM) Tupelo MS
*WAJS(AM) Tupelo MS
WLRC(AM) Walnut MS
*KLMT(FM) Billings MT

*KLRV(FM) Billings MT
KMZK(AM) Billings MT
*KFRD(FM) Butte MT
*KMZO(FM) Hamilton MT
*KHLV(FM) Helena MT
KALS(FM) Kalispell MT
*KLEU(FM) Lewistown MT
*KMZL(FM) Missoula MT
*WBKU(FM) Ahoskie NC
*WLFA(FM) Asheville NC
WZJS(FM) Banner Elk NC
*WXBE(FM) Beaufort NC
WMIT(FM) Black Mountain NC
WVBS(AM) Burgaw NC
WOGR(AM) Charlotte NC
*WKKLW(FM) Charlotte NC
*WYFQ(AM) Charlotte NC
WHPY(AM) Clayton NC
WCLN-FM Clinton NC
WTIK(AM) Durham NC
WPFJ(AM) Franklin NC
WLTC(AM) Gastonia NC
WJSG(FM) Hamlet NC
WKDX(FM) Hamlet NC
WLGP(FM) Harkers Island NC
WJCV(AM) Jacksonville NC
WTRU(AM) Kernersville NC
WDJS(AM) Mount Olive NC
WECR(AM) Newland NC
*WBFY(FM) Pinehurst NC
WPJL(AM) Raleigh NC
*WPGT(FM) Roanoke Rapids NC
*WRTP(FM) Roanoke Rapids NC
WKVE(FM) Semora NC
*WAGO(FM) Snow Hill NC
*WGAS(AM) South Gastonia NC
*WZRI(FM) Spring Lake NC
WJRM(AM) Troy NC
WJFJ(FM) Tryon NC
WADE(AM) Wadesboro NC
WDRU(AM) Wake Forest NC
WZKB(FM) Wallace NC
*WDVV(FM) Wilmington NC
*WWIL-FM Wilmington NC
*WAJC(FM) Wilson NC
WVOT(AM) Wilson NC
*WRCM(FM) Wingate NC
WBFJ(AM) Winston-Salem NC
*WBFJ-FM Winston-Salem NC
WPIP(AM) Winston-Salem NC
*KNRI(FM) Bismarck ND
*KFBN(FM) Fargo ND
*KFNW-FM Fargo ND
*KWTL(AM) Grand Forks ND
KDJZ(FM) Harwood ND
*KVLQ(FM) Lincoln ND
KNDR(FM) Mandan ND
KHRT-FM Minot ND
KTGO(FM) Tioga ND
KAMI(AM) Cozad NE
*KCVN(FM) Cozad NE
*KLNB(FM) Grand Island NE
*KROA(FM) Grand Island NE
*KAYA(FM) Hubbard NE
*KLCV(FM) Lincoln NE
*KJLT(AM) North Platte NE
KCRO(AM) Omaha NE
*KGBI-FM Omaha NE
*KVSS(FM) Omaha NE
*KGRD(FM) Orchard NE
*KMLV(FM) Ralston NE
*KLJV(FM) Scottsbluff NE
*KFLV(FM) Wilber NE
*WVNH(FM) Concord NH
*WVFA(FM) Lebanon NH
*WLMW(FM) Manchester NH
*WJPG(FM) Cape May Court House NJ
*WXGN(FM) Egg Harbor Township NJ
*WRDR(FM) Freehold Township NJ
*WYRS(FM) Manahawkin NJ
*WVBV(FM) Medford Lakes NJ
*WFME(FM) Newark NJ
WIBG(AM) Ocean City NJ
WXMC(AM) Parsippany-Troy Hills NJ
WKMB(AM) Stirling NJ
WAWZ(FM) Zarephath NJ
KKIM(AM) Albuquerque NM

*KLYT(FM) Albuquerque NM
KSVA(AM) Albuquerque NM
*KVLK(FM) Belen NM
*KQLV(FM) Bosque Farms NM
KAMQ(AM) Carlsbad NM
*KAQF(FM) Clovis NM
*KZPI(FM) Deming NM
KNMI(FM) Farmington NM
KPCL(FM) Farmington NM
*KTGW(FM) Fruitland NM
*KMBN(FM) Las Cruces NM
KROL(FM) Las Cruces NM
KELP-FM Mesquite NM
*KRLU(FM) Roswell NM
KHAC(AM) Tse Bonito NM
*KNIS(FM) Carson City NV
KRNG(FM) Fallon NV
KKVV(AM) Las Vegas NV
*KAIZ(FM) Mesquite NV
*KIHM(AM) Reno NV
*KLRH(FM) Sparks NV
WDCD(AM) Albany NY
*WJCA(FM) Albion NY
*WCOF(FM) Arcade NY
*WNGN(FM) Argyle NY
WNYG(AM) Babylon NY
*WCIK(FM) Bath NY
*WIFF(FM) Binghamton NY
WASB(AM) Brockport NY
*WMJQ(FM) Brockport NY
WDCX(FM) Buffalo NY
*WFBF(FM) Buffalo NY
*WCIY(FM) Canandaigua NY
WRSB(FM) Canandaigua NY
*WMHI(FM) Cape Vincent NY
*WCOV-FM Clyde NY
*WKVJ(FM) Dannemora NY
WSIV(AM) East Syracuse NY
*WCIH(FM) Elmira NY
*WCID(FM) Friendship NY
*WLJH(FM) Glens Falls NY
*WGKR(FM) Grand Gorge NY
*WHVP(FM) Hudson NY
*WCOT(FM) Jamestown NY
*WFGB(FM) Kingston NY
*WGWR(FM) Liberty NY
*WMHQ(FM) Malone NY
*WLJP(FM) Monroe NY
WVIP(FM) Mount Kisco NY
*WWRV(AM) New York NY
WNYK(FM) Nyack NY
WZXV(FM) Palmyra NY
*WPGL(FM) Pattersonville NY
*WRPJ(FM) Port Jervis NY
*WSSK(FM) Saratoga Springs NY
WMYY(FM) Schoharie NY
*WAVX(FM) Schuyler Falls NY
*WFRS(FM) Smithtown NY
*WCII(FM) Spencer NY
*WMHR(FM) Syracuse NY
WHAZ(FM) Troy NY
*WKVU(FM) Utica NY
*WCOU(FM) Warsaw NY
*WWJS(FM) Watertown NY
*WMHN(FM) Webster NY
WRCI(FM) Webster NY
*WBCY(FM) Archbold OH
WJKW(FM) Athens OH
*WCVV(FM) Belpre OH
*WLKP(FM) Belpre OH
WCER(AM) Canton OH
WAKW(FM) Cincinnati OH
*WCRF(FM) Cleveland OH
WFHM-FM Cleveland OH
*WGOJ(FM) Conneaut OH
*WYKL(FM) Crestline OH
*WQRP(FM) Dayton OH
*WJYC(FM) Delhi Hills OH
*WBIE(FM) Delphos OH
*WCVO(FM) Gahanna OH
WPOS-FM Holland OH
WIRO(AM) Ironton OH
*WCVJ(FM) Jefferson OH
*WFCO(FM) Lancaster OH
*WTGN(FM) Lima OH
*WYSM(FM) Lima OH
*WVMC-FM Mansfield OH

Broadcasting & Cable Yearbook 2006
D-693

Programming on Radio Stations in the U.S.

*WYSZ(FM) Maumee OH	WDBA(FM) DuBois PA	*WCQR-FM Kingsport TN	*KSWP(FM) Lufkin TX	WMNV(FM) Rupert VT
WFCJ(FM) Miamisburg OH	WLOA(AM) Farrell PA	WHGG(AM) Kingsport TN	*KZLV(FM) Lytle TX	*WFTF(FM) Rutland VT
*WVML(FM) Millersburg OH	*WAWN(FM) Franklin PA	WFFI(FM) Kingston Springs TN	*KBMD(FM) Marble Falls TX	KGNW(AM) Burien-Seattle WA
*WNZR(FM) Mount Vernon OH	*WCOG-FM Galeton PA	WIFA(AM) Knoxville TN	KVMV(FM) McAllen TX	*KGTS(FM) College Place WA
WNPQ(AM) New Philadelphia OH	*WVMM(FM) Grantham PA	WITA(AM) Knoxville TN	KMXO(AM) Merkel TX	*KKRS(FM) Davenport WA
*WMEJ(FM) Proctorville OH	*WKBO(FM) Harrisburg PA	WNPZ(AM) Knoxville TN	KRQX(AM) Mexia TX	KCIS(AM) Edmonds WA
WDMN(AM) Rossford OH	*WBYH(FM) Hawley PA	WRJZ(AM) Knoxville TN	KYCX-FM Mexia TX	KCMS(FM) Edmonds WA
*WLRY(FM) Rushville OH	*WFRJ(FM) Johnstown PA	WBLC(AM) Lenoir City TN	KGEE(FM) Monahans TX	*KTJC(FM) Kelso WA
*WVMS(FM) Sandusky OH	WDAC(FM) Lancaster PA	*WIGH(FM) Lexington TN	KNBO(AM) New Boston TX	*KBLD(FM) Kennewick WA
*WAUI(FM) Shelby OH	*WJTL(FM) Lancaster PA	WFGZ(FM) Lobelville TN	*KBMM(FM) Odessa TX	*KJVH(FM) Longview WA
*WBCJ(FM) Spencerville OH	WGRC(FM) Lewisburg PA	*WAJJ(FM) McKenzie TN	KFLB(AM) Odessa TX	*KWYQ(FM) Longview WA
*WEEC(FM) Springfield OH	*WJRC(FM) Lewistown PA	WENO(AM) Nashville TN	*KFLB-FM Odessa TX	KWPZ(FM) Lynden WA
*WBJV(FM) Steubenville OH	*WRIJ(FM) Masontown PA	*WNAZ-FM Nashville TN	KPXI(FM) Overton TX	KTSL(FM) Medical Lake WA
*WOKL(FM) Troy OH	*WYFU(FM) Masontown PA	*WAYW(FM) New Johnsonville TN	KAVO(FM) Pampa TX	*KSBC(FM) Nile WA
*WYSA(FM) Wauseon OH	*WVME(FM) Meadville PA	WKVZ(FM) Ripley TN	*KHCP(FM) Paris TX	*KLOP(FM) Ocean Park WA
*KQPD(FM) Ardmore OK	*WZXM(FM) Middletown PA	WDTM(AM) Selmer TN	*KKXI(FM) Pittsburg TX	KGDN(FM) Pasco WA
*KWRI(FM) Bartlesville OK	*WQJU(FM) Mifflintown PA	*WBIA(FM) Shelbyville TN	KBAH(AM) Plainview TX	KFFR(FM) Pullman WA
*KARU(FM) Cache OK	*WRWJ(FM) Murrysville PA	WFFH(FM) Smyrna TN	*KWLD(FM) Plainview TX	*KRLF(FM) Pullman WA
*KJCC(FM) Carnegie OK	*WBGM(FM) New Berlin PA	WDBL(AM) Springfield TN	KFNI(FM) Pleasanton TX	*KWFJ(FM) Roy WA
KTFR(FM) Chelsea OK	*WVMN(FM) New Castle PA	WVRY(FM) Waverly TN	*KSGR(FM) Portland TX	KLFE(AM) Seattle WA
*KDIM(FM) Coweta OK	WPCL(FM) Northern Cambria PA	WBOZ(FM) Woodbury TN	KPOS(FM) Post TX	*KEEH(FM) Spokane WA
*KAYC(FM) Durant OK	WWKL(FM) Palmyra PA	*KAQD(FM) Abilene TX	KCLR(AM) Ralls TX	*KAYB(FM) Sunnyside WA
*KOKF(FM) Edmond OK	WORD-FM Pittsburgh PA	*KGNZ(FM) Abilene TX	KBIC(FM) Raymondville TX	KVSN(FM) Tumwater WA
KXOO(FM) Elk City OK	WPIT(AM) Pittsburgh PA	KTEK(AM) Alvin TX	*KTER(FM) Rudolph TX	*KRKL(FM) Walla Walla WA
*KWKL(FM) Grandfield OK	WWNL(AM) Pittsburgh PA	KAEZ(FM) Amarillo TX	KCRN(AM) San Angelo TX	*KPLW(FM) Wenatchee WA
*KXRT(FM) Idabel OK	WREQ(FM) Ridgebury PA	*KAVW(FM) Amarillo TX	KCRN-FM San Angelo TX	KJOX(AM) Yakima WA
*KJRF(FM) Lawton OK	*WBYO(FM) Sellersville PA	KTNZ(AM) Amarillo TX	KCRN-FM San Angelo TX	KYAK(AM) Yakima WA
*KVRS(FM) Lawton OK	WWII(AM) Shiremanstown PA	*KXLV(FM) Amarillo TX	KSLR(AM) San Antonio TX	*WHEM(FM) Eau Claire WI
KEMX(FM) Locust Grove OK	*WRXV(FM) State College PA	*KXRI(FM) Amarillo TX	*KYFS(FM) San Antonio TX	*WVCF(FM) Eau Claire WI
KGLC(FM) Miami OK	*WTLR(FM) State College PA	KTLT(FM) Anson TX	KUBR(AM) San Juan TX	*WLWR(FM) Fond du Lac WI
KTLV(AM) Midwest City OK	*WBYX(FM) Stroudsburg PA	KLTY(FM) Arlington TX	KUOL(AM) San Marcos TX	*WORQ(FM) Green Bay WI
*KMSI(FM) Moore OK	*WPGP(FM) Tafton PA	*KHIB(FM) Bastrop TX	*KVRK(FM) Sanger TX	WWIB(FM) Hallie WI
*KYLV(FM) Oklahoma City OK	*WCIT(FM) Trout Run PA	*KZBJ(FM) Bay City TX	KMAT(FM) Seadrift TX	WRRD(AM) Jackson WI
*KKRI(FM) Pocola OK	WCTL(FM) Union City PA	*KTXB(FM) Beaumont TX	KDAE(AM) Sinton TX	WJOK(AM) Kaukauna WI
*KJTH(FM) Ponca City OK	*WZZD(FM) Warwick PA	KIBL(AM) Beeville TX	KJAK(FM) Slaton TX	*WSTM(FM) Kiel WI
*KLVV(FM) Ponca City OK	WLIH(FM) Whitneyville TN	KPDB(FM) Big Lake TX	KSNY(AM) Snyder TX	WZRK(AM) Lake Geneva WI
*KARG(FM) Poteau OK	WCRG(FM) Williamsport PA	*KTAA(FM) Big Sandy TX	KHOS(AM) Sonora TX	*WNWC-FM Madison WI
KTFX(AM) Sand Springs OK	*WYTL(FM) Wyomissing PA	*KBCX(FM) Big Spring TX	*KFRI(FM) Stanton TX	*WGNV(FM) Milladore WI
*KXTH(FM) Seminole OK	*WTMV(FM) Youngsville PA	*KAXH(FM) Borger TX	*KBDE(FM) Temple TX	WJYI(AM) Milwaukee WI
KQCV-FM Shawnee OK	WBRQ(FM) Cidra PR	*KPBB(FM) Brownfield TX	*KVLT(FM) Temple TX	*WMWK(FM) Milwaukee WI
*KTKL(FM) Stigler OK	WXZX(FM) Culebra PR	*KBUB(FM) Brownwood TX	KTNO(AM) University Park TX	WSSP(AM) Milwaukee WI
*KAYM(FM) Weatherford OK	*WCRP(FM) Guayama PR	*KHPU(FM) Brownwood TX	KBNU(FM) Uvalde TX	WVCY-FM Milwaukee WI
*KJOV(FM) Woodward OK	WRRH(FM) Hormigueros PR	*KPBE(FM) Brownwood TX	*KAYK(FM) Victoria TX	WFZH(FM) Mukwonago WI
KHPE(FM) Albany OR	WNRT(FM) Manati PR	KPSM(FM) Brownwood TX	*KXBJ(FM) Victoria TX	*WPPF(FM) Sturgeon Bay WI
KWIL(AM) Albany OR	WZNA(AM) Moca PR	*KLRW(FM) Byrne TX	KBBW(AM) Waco TX	*WRGX(FM) Sturgeon Bay WI
*KWYA(FM) Astoria OR	WPPC(AM) Penuelas PR	KAYG(FM) Camp Wood TX	*KVLW(FM) Waco TX	*WVCX(FM) Tomah WI
*KANL(FM) Baker City OR	*WNNV(FM) San German PR	KVCI(AM) Canton TX	*KHTA(FM) Wake Village TX	*WEGZ(FM) Washburn WI
KNLR(FM) Bend OR	WERR(FM) Utuado PR	*KCZO(FM) Carrizo Springs TX	KRGE(AM) Weslaco TX	*WPIB(FM) Bluefield WV
*KVLB(FM) Bend OR	WLUA(AM) Belton SC	*KAFR(FM) Conroe TX	*KLVW(FM) West Odessa TX	*WKJL(FM) Clarksburg WV
*KMWR(FM) Brookings OR	*WAFJ(FM) Belvedere SC	*KKLM(FM) Corpus Christi TX	*KMOC(FM) Wichita Falls TX	*WBHZ(FM) Elkins WV
*KLVP-FM Cherryville OR	WBAJ(AM) Blythwood SC	*KCKT(FM) Crockett TX	KKHT-FM Winnie TX	WTCS(AM) Fairmont WV
KYSJ(FM) Coos Bay OR	WQXL(AM) Columbia SC	*KCBI(FM) Dallas TX	KBAW(FM) Zapata TX	*WDKL(FM) Grafton WV
KYTT-FM Coos Bay OR	WOLI(FM) Easley SC	KIXL(AM) Del Valle TX	*KNKL(FM) North Ogden UT	WEMM(AM) Huntington WV
*KAPK(FM) Grants Pass OR	*WLPG(FM) Florence SC	*KEPI(FM) Eagle Pass TX	*KYFO-FM Ogden UT	WEMM-FM Huntington WV
*KIDH(FM) Jordan Valley OR	WLMC(AM) Georgetown SC	*KEPX(FM) Eagle Pass TX	*KEYY(AM) Provo UT	WOKU(FM) Hurricane WV
*KKLJ(FM) Klamath Falls OR	WLFJ(AM) Greenville SC	KELP(AM) El Paso TX	*KANN(AM) Roy UT	WTCR(AM) Kenova WV
*KKLP(FM) La Pine OR	*WLFJ-FM Greenville SC	*KXCR(FM) El Paso TX	*KAER(FM) Saint George UT	WFSP(AM) Kingwood WV
KKSL(AM) Lake Oswego OR	WCKI(AM) Greer SC	KPAS(FM) Fabens TX	*KUFR(FM) Salt Lake City UT	*WKVW(FM) Marmet WV
*KGRI(FM) Lebanon OR	WOLT(FM) Greer SC	KLDS(AM) Falfurrias TX	KMRI(AM) West Valley City UT	WZZW(AM) Milton WV
*KBUG(FM) Malin OR	*WMBJ(FM) Murrell's Inlet SC	*KZFT(FM) Fannett TX	WABS(AM) Arlington VA	WMON(AM) Montgomery WV
*KLRF(FM) Milton-Freewater OR	WTBI(FM) Pickens SC	KIJN(AM) Farwell TX	WAVA(FM) Arlington VA	*WRKP(FM) Moundsville WV
KARO(FM) Nyssa OR	WQMC(AM) Sumter SC	KIJN-FM Farwell TX	WYFJ(FM) Ashland VA	*WPWV(FM) Princeton WV
*KAPL(AM) Phoenix OR	WSSC(AM) Sumter SC	KDFT(AM) Ferris TX	*WAZP(FM) Cape Charles VA	WRLB(FM) Rainelle WV
*KPFR(FM) Pine Grove OR	WBZK(AM) York SC	*KWCB(FM) Floresville TX	WYRV(AM) Cedar Bluff VA	WRRL(AM) Rainelle WV
KKPZ(AM) Portland OR	KLRJ(AM) Aberdeen SD	KBRZ(AM) Freeport TX	*WAUQ(FM) Charles City VA	*WLKV(FM) Ripley WV
KPDQ(AM) Portland OR	*KVCF(FM) Freeman SD	*KPBN(FM) Freer TX	WPMH(AM) Claremont VA	WJYP(AM) Saint Albans WV
KPDQ-FM Portland OR	KVCX(FM) Gregory SD	*KVLZ(FM) Gatesville TX	*WARN(FM) Culpeper VA	*KCSP-FM Casper WY
*KLON(FM) Rockaway Beach OR	*KTPT(FM) Rapid City SD	KANJ(FM) Giddings TX	*WPER(FM) Casper WY...	*KLWC(FM) Casper WY
KCCS(AM) Salem OR	*KNWC-FM Sioux Falls SD	*KAZF(FM) Hebronville TX	*WOKD-FM Danville VA	*KLWV(FM) Chugwater WY
*KWBX(FM) Salem OR	KSLT(FM) Spearfish SD	KEKO(FM) Hebronville TX	*WPIN-FM Dublin VA	KUYO(AM) Evansville WY
KFIS(FM) Scappoose OR	*KJBB(FM) Watertown SD	KWRD-FM Highland Village TX	*WJYA(FM) Emporia VA	*KAXG(FM) Gillette WY
*KJKL(FM) Selma OR	*WYLV(FM) Alcoa TN	*KHCB-FM Houston TX	*WJYJ(FM) Fredericksburg VA	*KWYC(FM) Orchard Valley WY
KORE(AM) Springfield-Eugene OR	WATX(AM) Algood TN	*KSBJ(FM) Humble TX	*WWMC(FM) Lynchburg VA	*KRWT(FM) West Laramie WY
*KLVU(FM) Sweet Home OR	*WTKB-FM Atwood TN	*KHCH(FM) Huntsville TX	*WPIM(FM) Martinsville VA	
*KLVP(AM) Tigard OR	WBIN(AM) Benton TN	*KBJS(FM) Jacksonville TX	WNRV(AM) Narrows-Pearisburg VA	**Classic Rock**
*KAIK(FM) Tillamook OR	*WHCB(FM) Bristol TN	*KHCJ(FM) Jefferson TX	WLTK(FM) New Market VA	
KLWJ(AM) Umatilla OR	WNKX(AM) Centerville TN	KERB(AM) Kermit TX	WBTK(AM) Richmond VA	KBFX(FM) Anchorage AK
*KZRI(FM) Welches OR	WJOC(AM) Chattanooga TN	KERB-FM Kermit TX	*WRXT(FM) Roanoke VA	KLAM(AM) Cordova AK
*KLOV(FM) Winchester OR	WLMR(AM) Chattanooga TN	*KHKV(FM) Kerrville TX	*WPAR(FM) Salem VA	KXLR(FM) Fairbanks AK
KGRV(AM) Winston OR	*WAYQ(FM) Clarksville TN	*KKER(FM) Kerrville TX	WSBV(AM) South Boston VA	KRPM(FM) Houston AK
WAVL(AM) Apollo PA	*WKFN(AM) Clarksville TN	*KYBJ(FM) Lake Jackson TX	*WJLZ(FM) Virginia Beach VA	KSUP(FM) Juneau AK
*WGEV(FM) Beaver Falls PA	*WNRZ(FM) Dickson TN	*KBKN(FM) Lamesa TX	WPRZ(AM) Warrenton VA	KRXX(FM) Kodiak AK
WBYN(FM) Boyertown PA	*WUMC(FM) Elizabethton TN	KLAR(AM) Laredo TX	*WPVA(FM) Waynesboro VA	KSLD(AM) Soldotna AK
*WCIG(FM) Carbondale PA	WLLJ(AM) Etowah TN	KBLT(FM) Leakey TX	WTFX(AM) Winchester VA	*WJSR(FM) Birmingham AL
*WZXQ(FM) Chambersburg PA	*WPLX(AM) Germantown TN	KYMI(FM) Los Ybanez TX	*WYCS(FM) Yorktown VA	WZRR(FM) Birmingham AL
WPWA(AM) Chester PA	WAYB-FM Graysville TN	*KAMY(FM) Lubbock TX	WEVI(FM) Frederiksted VI	WERH-FM Hamilton AL
WVCH(AM) Chester PA	*WAMP(FM) Jackson TN	*KKLU(FM) Lubbock TX	*WCMK(FM) Putney VT	WTAK-FM Hartselle AL

Programming on Radio Stations in the U.S.

WRKH(FM) Mobile AL
WQKS-FM Montgomery AL
WVNA-FM Muscle Shoals AL
WXFX(FM) Prattville AL
WMXN-FM Stevenson AL
*KSWH(FM) Arkadelphia AR
KLCN(AM) Blytheville AR
KMJX(FM) Conway AR
KRKD(FM) Dermott AR
KAGL(FM) El Dorado AR
KKEG(FM) Fayetteville AR
KXJK(AM) Forrest City AR
KCWD(FM) Harrison AR
KDEZ(FM) Jonesboro AR
KKPT(FM) Little Rock AR
KHBM-FM Monticello AR
KLXQ(FM) Mountain Pine AR
KYGL(FM) Texarkana AR
KLSZ-FM Van Buren AR
KMGN(FM) Flagstaff AZ
KCDX(FM) Florence AZ
KFLX(FM) Kachina Village AZ
KRRK(FM) Lake Havasu City AZ
KWKM(FM) Saint Johns AZ
KSLX-FM Scottsdale AZ
KHYT(FM) Tucson AZ
KLPX(FM) Tucson AZ
KQSR(FM) Yuma AZ
KALT-FM Alturas CA
KXGO(FM) Arcata CA
KHRQ(FM) Baker CA
KRHV(FM) Big Pine CA
KOCP(FM) Camarillo CA
KWTY(FM) Cartago CA
KTHU(FM) Corning CA
KDFO-FM Delano CA
KZRO(FM) Dunsmuir CA
KJFX(FM) Fresno CA
KBAY(FM) Gilroy CA
KHIP(FM) Gonzales CA
KVLI-FM Lake Isabella CA
KHDR(FM) Lenwood CA
KCBS-FM Los Angeles CA
KDJK(FM) Mariposa CA
KHKK(FM) Modesto CA
KVRV(FM) Monte Rio CA
KLUK(FM) Needles CA
KIOO(FM) Porterville CA
KLKX(FM) Rosamond CA
KSEG(FM) Sacramento CA
KGB-FM San Diego CA
KPLN(FM) San Diego CA
KUFX(FM) San Jose CA
KZOZ(FM) San Luis Obispo CA
KSAN(FM) San Mateo CA
KXFM(FM) Santa Maria CA
KXFX(FM) Santa Rosa CA
KTMQ(FM) Temecula CA
KHRD(FM) Weaverville CA
KTOR(FM) Westwood CA
KDGL(FM) Yucca Valley CA
KAVP(AM) Colona CO
KKFM(FM) Colorado Springs CO
KQZR(FM) Craig CO
KKNN(FM) Delta CO
KQMT(FM) Denver CO
KRFX(FM) Denver CO
KTUN(FM) Eagle CO
KPAW(FM) Fort Collins CO
KRVG(FM) Glenwood Springs CO
KVLE-FM Gunnison CO
KWGL(FM) Ouray CO
KYZX(FM) Pueblo West CO
KSBV(FM) Salida CO
KCRT-FM Trinidad CO
KKQZ(FM) Wellington CO
WRKI(FM) Brookfield CT
WEFX(FM) Norwalk CT
WGBG(FM) Seaford DE
WNDT(FM) Alachua FL
WFYV-FM Atlantic Beach FL
WWUS(FM) Big Pine Key FL
WRXK-FM Bonita Springs FL
WFFY(FM) Destin FL
WCJX(FM) Five Points FL
WBGG-FM Fort Lauderdale FL
WKGR(FM) Fort Pierce FL
*WJUF(FM) Inverness FL
WKYZ(FM) Key Colony Beach FL
WAIL(FM) Key West FL
WAIL(FM) Key West FL
WARO(FM) Naples FL
WHTQ(FM) Orlando FL
WHOG-FM Ormond-by-the-Sea FL
WXGL(FM) Saint Petersburg FL
WWAV-FM Santa Rosa Beach FL
WHPT(FM) Sarasota FL
WNDD(FM) Silver Springs FL
WRBA(FM) Springfield FL
WGLF(FM) Tallahassee FL
WUTL(FM) Tallahassee FL
WKLS(FM) Atlanta GA
WZGC(FM) Atlanta GA
WEKL(FM) Augusta GA
WVRK(FM) Columbus GA
WQBZ(FM) Fort Valley GA
WIOL(FM) Greenville GA
WMGP(FM) Hogansville GA
WBBT(AM) Lyons GA
WBMZ(FM) Metter GA
WTUN(FM) Ringgold GA
WIXV(FM) Savannah GA
*WKEU-FM The Rock GA
WWRQ-FM Valdosta GA
WYZK(FM) Valdosta GA
KPOI-FM Honolulu HI
KLKK(FM) Clear Lake IA
KCQQ(FM) Davenport IA
KGGO(FM) Des Moines IA
KXGE(FM) Dubuque IA
KKSI(FM) Eddyville IA
KGRR(FM) Epworth IA
KCRR(FM) Grundy Center IA
KKRQ(FM) Iowa City IA
KRNA(FM) Iowa City IA
KRNQ(FM) Keokuk IA
KKMA(FM) Le Mars IA
*KUNY(FM) Mason City IA
KUQQ(FM) Milford IA
KSEZ(FM) Sioux City IA
KJOT(FM) Boise ID
KQEO(FM) Idaho Falls ID
KWYS-FM Island Park ID
KIKX(FM) Ketchum ID
KKGL(FM) Nampa ID
KMGI(FM) Pocatello ID
KECH-FM Sun Valley ID
KSNQ(FM) Twin Falls ID
WDLJ(FM) Breese IL
*WPCD(FM) Champaign IL
WDRV(FM) Chicago IL
WRXQ(FM) Coal City IL
WRHK(FM) Danville IL
WXTT(FM) Danville IL
WMKB(FM) Earlville IL
KUUL(FM) East Moline IL
WRVY-FM Henry IL
WYMG(FM) Jacksonville IL
*WMXM(FM) Lake Forest IL
WQLF(FM) Lena IL
WKGL-FM Loves Park IL
WJEQ(FM) Macomb IL
WGKC(FM) Mahomet IL
WXLP(FM) Moline IL
WZZT(FM) Morrison IL
WIKK(FM) Newton IL
WGLO(FM) Pekin IL
WBZG(FM) Peru IL
WTRX-FM Pontiac IL
WZNX(FM) Sullivan IL
WCVS-FM Virden IL
WQUL(FM) West Frankfort IL
WWDV(FM) Zion IL
WHTI(FM) Alexandria IN
*WEAX(FM) Angola IN
WSHP(FM) Attica IN
WJAA(FM) Austin IN
WKLU(FM) Brownsburg IN
*WHJE(FM) Carmel IN
WSFR(FM) Corydon IN
WXRD(FM) Crown Point IN
WABX(FM) Evansville IN
WFWI(FM) Fort Wayne IN
WZOW(FM) Goshen IN
WHTY(FM) Hartford City IN
WFBQ(FM) Indianapolis IN
WQMF(FM) Jeffersonville IN
WKHY(FM) Lafayette IN
WRZR(FM) Loogootee IN
WOZW(FM) New Carlisle IN
WWWY(FM) North Vernon IN
WMYK(FM) Peru IN
WSJD(FM) Princeton IN
WCKZ(FM) Roanoke IN
WRSW-FM Warsaw IN
*WBAA-FM West Lafayette IN
WWVR(FM) West Terre Haute IN
KFXJ(FM) Augusta KS
KKRK(FM) Coffeyville KS
KZRD(FM) Dodge City KS
KOTE(FM) Eureka KS
KCAR-FM Galena KS
KSEK-FM Girard KS
KVGB-FM Great Bend KS
KINZ(FM) Humboldt KS
KWKR(FM) Leoti KS
KILS(FM) Minneapolis KS
KDVV(FM) Topeka KS
KWIC(FM) Topeka KS
KTHR(FM) Wichita KS
WLFX(FM) Berea KY
WDNS(FM) Bowling Green KY
WCBJ(FM) Campton KY
WPTQ(FM) Cave City KY
WXLR(FM) Harold KY
WXMZ(FM) Hartford KY
WKTG(FM) Madisonville KY
WTBK(FM) Manchester KY
WKYM(FM) Monticello KY
WLRO(FM) Richmond KY
WRZI(FM) Vine Grove KY
WKQQ(FM) Winchester KY
KZMZ(FM) Alexandria LA
KCIJ(FM) Atlanta LA
WDGL(FM) Baton Rouge LA
KLIP(FM) Monroe LA
KRDJ(FM) New Iberia LA
WRNO-FM New Orleans LA
KKGB(FM) Sulphur LA
KXOR-FM Thibodaux LA
WNYN-FM Athol MA
WZLX(FM) Boston MA
WCIB(FM) Falmouth MA
WROR-FM Framingham MA
*WGAO(FM) Franklin MA
WKPE-FM Orleans MA
*WSDH(FM) Sandwich MA
WAQY(FM) Springfield MA
*WYAJ(FM) Sudbury MA
WARW(FM) Bethesda MD
*WMTB-FM Emmittsburg MD
WDLD(FM) Halfway MD
WSMD-FM Mechanicsville MD
WZBA(FM) Westminster MD
WBQI(FM) Bar Harbor ME
WKIT-FM Brewer ME
WQDY-FM Calais ME
WQSS(FM) Camden ME
*WSHD(FM) Eastport ME
WWMJ(FM) Ellsworth ME
WHXQ(FM) Kennebunkport ME
WSHK(FM) Kittery ME
WFNK(FM) Lewiston ME
WFZX(FM) Searsport ME
WZUU(FM) Allegan MI
WJSZ(FM) Ashley MI
WFDX(FM) Atlanta MI
WLEW-FM Bad Axe MI
WCSX(FM) Birmingham MI
WCKC(FM) Cadillac MI
WGFM(FM) Cheboygan MI
WDTW-FM Detroit MI
WMMQ(FM) East Lansing MI
WBFX(FM) Grand Rapids MI
WLAV-FM Grand Rapids MI
WKJZ(FM) Hillman MI
WOLV(FM) Houghton MI
WIMK(FM) Iron Mountain MI
WFCX(FM) Leland MI
WUPK(FM) Marquette MI
WKQZ(FM) Midland MI
WMRR(FM) Muskegon Heights MI
WIHC(FM) Newberry MI
WAOR(FM) Niles MI
*WOVI(FM) Novi MI
WRSR(FM) Owosso MI
WWKR(FM) Pentwater MI
WYLZ(FM) Pinconning MI
WRKR(FM) Portage MI
WILZ(FM) Saginaw MI
WYVN(FM) Saugatuck MI
WSUE(FM) Sault Ste. Marie MI
WQLB(FM) Tawas City MI
KQPR-FM Albert Lea MN
KXRA-FM Alexandria MN
KKLN(FM) Atwater MN
KLIZ-FM Brainerd MN
KQDS(AM) Duluth MN
KQDS-FM Duluth MN
KQCL(FM) Faribault MN
KQRS-FM Golden Valley MN
WXXZ(FM) Grand Marais MN
KRAQ(FM) Jackson MN
KARZ(FM) Marshall MN
KKCK(FM) Marshall MN
KMFG(FM) Nashwauk MN
KXLP(FM) New Ulm MN
KWNG(FM) Red Wing MN
KRCH(FM) Rochester MN
*KRPR(FM) Rochester MN
KRWB(AM) Roseau MN
KLFN(FM) Sunburg MN
KLZZ(FM) Waite Park MN
KLLZ-FM Walker MN
KGMO(FM) Cape Girardeau MO
KSHE(FM) Crestwood MO
KDFN(AM) Doniphan MO
KCGQ-FM Gordonville MO
KCFX(FM) Harrisonville MO
KRXL(FM) Kirksville MO
KPOW-FM La Monte MO
KKLH(FM) Marshfield MO
KNIM-FM Maryville MO
KWBZ(FM) Monroe City MO
KZZK(FM) New London MO
KRMS-FM Osage Beach MO
KJEZ(FM) Poplar Bluff MO
KIHT(FM) Saint Louis MO
KIGL(FM) Seligman MO
KXUS(FM) Springfield MO
KFBD-FM Waynesville MO
KXDG(FM) Webb City MO
KSPQ(FM) West Plains MO
WSMS(FM) Artesia MS
WZKR(FM) Decatur MS
WRKG(FM) Drew MS
WYMX(FM) Greenwood MS
WMUT(FM) Grenada MS
WXRR(FM) Hattiesburg MS
WWJK(FM) Jackson MS
WZNF(FM) Lumberton MS
WXRG(FM) Pascagoula MS
WCNA(FM) Potts Camp MS
WSTZ-FM Vicksburg MS
KJJM(FM) Baker MT
KRKX(FM) Billings MT
KMBR(FM) Butte MT
KTZZ(FM) Conrad MT
KQDI-FM Great Falls MT
KZMT(FM) Helena MT
KBBZ(FM) Kalispell MT
KZMN(FM) Kalispell MT
KXLO(AM) Lewistown MT
KMTA(AM) Miles City MT
KZOQ-FM Missoula MT
KMXE-FM Red Lodge MT
KGCX(FM) Sidney MT
KWYS(AM) West Yellowstone MT
WKRR(FM) Asheboro NC
*WZPE(FM) Bath NC
WCLN(AM) Clinton NC
WRFX-FM Kannapolis NC
WSFL-FM New Bern NC
WBNU(FM) Shallotte NC
WQNS(FM) Waynesville NC
*WSIF(FM) Wilkesboro NC
WRDU(FM) Wilson NC
WBNE(FM) Wrightsville Beach NC
KBYZ(FM) Bismarck ND
KZRX(FM) Dickinson ND
KPFX(FM) Fargo ND
KTGL(FM) Beatrice NE
KBBN-FM Broken Bow NE
KKOT(FM) Columbus NE
KFMT(FM) Fremont NE
KROR(FM) Hastings NE
KRKR(FM) Lincoln NE
KRKU(FM) McCook NE
KBRX(AM) O'Neill NE
KMOR(FM) Scottsbluff NE
WMLL(FM) Bedford NH
WWHK(FM) Concord NH
WSAK(FM) Hampton NH
WMTK(FM) Littleton NH
WWHQ(FM) Meredith NH
WMGM(FM) Atlantic City NJ
WCHR-FM Manahawkin NJ
WNNJ-FM Newton NJ
WTHK(FM) Trenton NJ
WZXL(FM) Wildwood NJ
KNMZ(FM) Alamogordo NM
KBZU(FM) Albuquerque NM
KKIT(FM) Angel Fire NM
KZRM(FM) Chama NM
KEJL(FM) Eunice NM
KDAG(FM) Farmington NM
KXXI(FM) Gallup NM
KMDZ(FM) Las Vegas NM
KIOT(FM) Los Lunas NM
KSFX(FM) Roswell NM
KIDX(FM) Ruidoso NM
KABQ-FM Santa Fe NM
KSCQ(FM) Silver City NM
KTUM(FM) Tatum NM
KRSI(FM) Garapan-Saipan NP
KKLZ(FM) Las Vegas NV
KOZZ-FM Reno NV
KURK(FM) Reno NV
WPYX(FM) Albany NY
*WGCC-FM Batavia NY
WAAL(FM) Binghamton NY
WTKW(FM) Bridgeport NY
WGRF(FM) Buffalo NY
WIII(FM) Cortland NY
*WECW(FM) Elmira NY
WBBI(FM) Endwell NY
WCPV(FM) Essex NY
WCQL(FM) Glens Falls NY
WLPW(FM) Lake Placid NY
WMOS(FM) Montauk NY
WNGZ(FM) Montour Falls NY
WFAF(FM) Mount Kisco NY
WAXQ(FM) New York NY
WJJL(AM) Niagara Falls NY
*WRHO(FM) Oneonta NY
WTKV(FM) Oswego NY
WPDH(FM) Poughkeepsie NY
WRCZ(FM) Ravena NY
WRCN-FM Riverhead NY
WQRT(FM) Salamanca NY
WRVE(FM) Schenectady NY
WLLW(FM) Seneca Falls NY
WRGR(FM) Tupper Lake NY
WRCK(FM) Utica NY
WBON-FM Westhampton NY
WLKK(FM) Wethersfield Township NY
WOHF(FM) Bellevue OH
WQEL(FM) Bucyrus OH
*WCWT-FM Centerville OH
WOFX-FM Cincinnati OH
WNCX(FM) Cleveland OH
WLVQ(FM) Columbus OH
WXXR(FM) Fredericktown OH
WFXN-FM Galion OH
*WDUB(FM) Granville OH
WFJX(FM) Hilliard OH
WRBP(FM) Hubbard OH
*WKET(FM) Kettering OH
WUZZ-FM Lima OH
WXXF(FM) Loudonville OH
WAGX(FM) Manchester OH
WYRO(FM) McArthur OH
*WLMH(FM) Morrow OH
WPFX-FM North Baltimore OH
WFXJ-FM North Kingsville OH

Broadcasting & Cable Yearbook 2006

D-695

Programming on Radio Stations in the U.S.

WBIK(FM) Pleasant City OH
WXKR(FM) Port Clinton OH
WZZZ(FM) Portsmouth OH
WSNA(FM) South Webster OH
*WKTL(FM) Struthers OH
WZLR(FM) Xenia OH
KRKZ(FM) Altus OK
KWCO-FM Chickasha OK
KDDQ(FM) Comanche OK
KCDL(FM) Cordell OK
KTRX(FM) Dickson OK
*KHIM(FM) Mangum OK
KTMC-FM McAlester OK
KRXO(FM) Oklahoma City OK
KLOR-FM Ponca City OK
WBBZ(AM) Ponca City OK
KPRV(AM) Poteau OK
KKBD(FM) Sallisaw OK
KJSR(FM) Tulsa OK
KWDQ(FM) Woodward OK
KBDN(FM) Bandon OR
KTWS(FM) Bend OR
KEHK(FM) Brownsville OR
KLOO-FM Corvallis OR
KZEL-FM Eugene OR
KAGO-FM Klamath Falls OR
KFEG(FM) Klamath Falls OR
KUBQ(FM) La Grande OR
KLCR(FM) Lakeview OR
KCRF-FM Lincoln City OR
KBOY-FM Medford OR
KGON(FM) Portland OR
KCRX-FM Seaside OR
KMSW(FM) The Dalles OR
KPPT-FM Toledo OR
WBVE(FM) Bedford PA
*WBUQ(FM) Bloomsburg PA
WBUS(FM) Boalsburg PA
WRRK(FM) Braddock PA
WMKX(FM) Brookville PA
*WCAL(FM) California PA
WUUZ(FM) Cooperstown PA
WWCB(AM) Corry PA
WBXQ(FM) Cresson PA
WODE-FM Easton PA
WQHZ(FM) Erie PA
WQCM(FM) Greencastle PA
*WKVR-FM Huntingdon PA
WJNG(FM) Johnsonburg PA
WCXR(FM) Lewisburg PA
WCHX(FM) Lewistown PA
WRKT(FM) North East PA
WBRX(FM) Patton PA
WMGK(FM) Philadelphia PA
WPZX(FM) Pocono Pines PA
WQFX-FM Russell PA
WEZX(FM) Scranton PA
WYFM(FM) Sharon PA
*WRSK(FM) Slippery Rock PA
WZXR(FM) South Williamsport PA
WKGB-FM Susquehanna PA
WMTT(FM) Tioga PA
*WNJR(FM) Washington PA
*WRLC(FM) Williamsport PA
WQXA-FM York PA
*WRIU(FM) Kingston RI
WROQ(FM) Anderson SC
WWBD(FM) Bamberg SC
WYBB(FM) Folly Beach SC
WBZT-FM Mauldin SC
WRFQ(FM) Mt. Pleasant SC
WYAV(FM) Myrtle Beach SC
WQKI-FM Orangeburg SC
WMXT(FM) Pamplico SC
WMFX(FM) Saint Andrews SC
KSDN-FM Aberdeen SD
KYBB(FM) Canton SD
KDBX(FM) Clear Lake SD
KFXS(FM) Rapid City SD
KRRO(FM) Sioux Falls SD
WBXE(FM) Baxter TN
*WAPX-FM Clarksville TN
*WFHU(FM) Henderson TN
WQUT(FM) Johnson City TN
WIMZ-FM Knoxville TN
WKHT(FM) Knoxville TN
WEGR(FM) Memphis TN

WYNU(FM) Milan TN
WRKK-FM Sparta TN
KFGL(FM) Abilene TX
KPEZ(FM) Austin TX
KRXB(FM) Beeville TX
KBTS(FM) Big Spring TX
KLUB(FM) Bloomington TX
KNFX-FM Bryan TX
KYYI(FM) Burkburnett TX
KARX(FM) Claude TX
KXIT-FM Dalhart TX
KZPS(FM) Dallas TX
KWMC(AM) Del Rio TX
KICA(FM) Farwell TX
KDBN(FM) Haltom City TX
KBRQ(FM) Hillsboro TX
KMFR(FM) Hondo TX
KKRW(FM) Houston TX
*KSHU(FM) Huntsville TX
KBGE(AM) Kilgore TX
KKTX-FM Kilgore TX
KONE(FM) Lubbock TX
KZRC(FM) Markham TX
KHXS(FM) Merkel TX
KFZX(FM) Monahans TX
KTBQ(FM) Nacogdoches TX
KNRG(FM) New Ulm TX
KIOC(FM) Orange TX
KBUS(FM) Paris TX
*KKXI(FM) Pittsburg TX
KAJI(FM) Point Comfort TX
KWFR(FM) San Angelo TX
KZEP-FM San Antonio TX
KLTD(FM) Temple TX
KTAL-FM Texarkana TX
KNAL(AM) Victoria TX
KTXN-FM Victoria TX
KMAD-FM Whitesboro TX
KBDX(FM) Blanding UT
*KAGJ(FM) Ephraim UT
KCUA(FM) Naples UT
KZHK(FM) Saint George UT
KRSP-FM Salt Lake City UT
WWRE(FM) Berryville VA
WBRW(FM) Blacksburg VA
WWUZ(FM) Bowling Green VA
WWWV(FM) Charlottesville VA
WCTG(FM) Chincoteague VA
WBOP(FM) Churchville VA
WKLR(FM) Fort Lee VA
WWRT(FM) Strasburg VA
WAFX(FM) Suffolk VA
WKVT-FM Brattleboro VT
WCVR-FM Randolph VT
*WVTC(FM) Randolph Center VT
WVAY(FM) Wilmington VT
KDUX-FM Aberdeen WA
KISM(FM) Bellingham WA
KZPH(FM) Cashmere WA
KRQT(FM) Castle Rock WA
KVAB(FM) Clarkston WA
KRAO-FM Colfax WA
*KGHP(FM) Gig Harbor WA
KQSN(FM) Naches WA
KFMY(FM) Raymond WA
KJR-FM Seattle WA
KZOK(FM) Seattle WA
KKZX(FM) Spokane WA
KZBD(FM) Spokane WA
KYNR(AM) Toppenish WA
KRVO(FM) Vancouver WA
KPQ-FM Wenatchee WA
WJLW(FM) Allouez WI
WRLO-FM Antigo WI
WJJH(FM) Ashland WI
WQOQ(AM) Durand WI
WRJO(FM) Eagle River WI
WECL(FM) Elk Mound WI
WQTC(FM) Manitowoc WI
WMEQ-FM Menomonie WI
WKLH(FM) Milwaukee WI
WOZZ(FM) New London WI
WTCX(FM) Ripon WI
WGMO(FM) Shell Lake WI
WAUH(FM) Wautoma WI
WKBH-FM West Salem WI
WGLX-FM Wisconsin Rapids WI

*WVVC(FM) Buckhannon WV
WRZZ(FM) Elizabeth WV
WQZK-FM Keyser WV
WCLG-FM Morgantown WV
WPMW(FM) Mullens WV
WXCR(FM) New Martinsville WV
WKOY-FM Princeton WV
WOBG-FM Salem WV
WFBY(FM) Weston WV
KASS(FM) Casper WY
KXXL(FM) Gillette WY
KZJH(FM) Jackson WY
KARS-FM Laramie WY
KRQU(FM) Laramie WY
KRVK(FM) Midwest WY
KCGL(FM) Powell WY
KTRZ(FM) Riverton WY
KSIT(FM) Rock Springs WY
KZWY(FM) Sheridan WY

Classical

KLEF(FM) Anchorage AK
*KBRW-FM Barrow AK
*KUAC(FM) Fairbanks AK
*WBHM(FM) Birmingham AL
*WRWA(FM) Dothan AL
*WSGN(FM) Gadsden AL
*WLRH(FM) Huntsville AL
*WLJS-FM Jacksonville AL
*WHIL-FM Mobile AL
*WQPR(FM) Muscle Shoals AL
*WAPR(FM) Selma AL
*WTSU(FM) Troy AL
*WUAL-FM Tuscaloosa AL
*KBSA(FM) El Dorado AR
*KUAF(FM) Fayetteville AR
*KASU(FM) Jonesboro AR
*KLRE-FM Little Rock AR
*KXRJ(FM) Russellville AR
*KNAU(FM) Flagstaff AZ
*KNAG(FM) Grand Canyon AZ
*KNAD(FM) Page AZ
*KBAQ-FM Phoenix AZ
*KNAQ(FM) Prescott AZ
*KNAA(FM) Show Low AZ
*KUAT-FM Tucson AZ
*KAWC(FM) Yuma AZ
*KPRX(FM) Bakersfield CA
KQVO(FM) Calexico CA
KBOQ(FM) Carmel CA
*KCHO(FM) Chico CA
*KHSR(FM) Crescent City CA
KFSD(AM) Escondido CA
*KVPR(FM) Fresno CA
*KXSR(FM) Groveland CA
KMZT-FM Los Angeles CA
*KUSC(FM) Los Angeles CA
*KCSN(FM) Northridge CA
*KPSC(FM) Palm Springs CA
*KNHT(FM) Rio Dell CA
*KXPR(FM) Sacramento CA
KPBS-FM San Diego CA
KDFC-FM San Francisco CA
*KCBX(FM) San Luis Obispo CA
KDB(FM) Santa Barbara CA
*KQSC(FM) Santa Barbara CA
*KSBX(FM) Santa Barbara CA
*KRCB-FM Santa Rosa CA
*KUOP(FM) Stockton CA
*KKTO(FM) Tahoe City CA
*KDSC(FM) Thousand Oaks CA
KVEN(AM) Ventura CA
*KNYR(FM) Yreka CA
*KAJX(FM) Aspen CO
*KVOV(FM) Carbondale CO
*KPRU(FM) Delta CO
*KVOD(FM) Denver CO
*KCME(FM) Manitou Springs CO
*KCFP(FM) Pueblo CO
*KPRE(FM) Vail CO
*WSHU(FM) Fairfield CT
*WGRS(FM) Guilford CT
*WJMJ(FM) Hartford CT
*WPKT(FM) Meriden CT
*WMNR(FM) Monroe CT
*WSLX(FM) New Canaan CT

*WNPR(FM) Norwich CT
*WRXC(FM) Shelton CT
*WGSK(FM) South Kent CT
*WEDW-FM Stamford CT
WTMI(AM) West Hartford CT
WGMS-FM Washington DC
*WRTX(FM) Dover DE
WTMP-FM Dade City FL
*WGCU-FM Fort Myers FL
*WQCS(FM) Fort Pierce FL
*WUFT-FM Gainesville FL
*WJCT-FM Jacksonville FL
*WMKO(FM) Marco FL
WKAT(AM) North Miami FL
WMFE-FM Orlando FL
*WUWF(FM) Pensacola FL
*WFSQ(FM) Tallahassee FL
*WUSF(FM) Tampa FL
*WXEL(FM) West Palm Beach FL
*WPRK(FM) Winter Park FL
WXOF(FM) Yankeetown FL
*WUNV(FM) Albany GA
*WUGA(FM) Athens GA
*WABE(FM) Atlanta GA
*WACG-FM Augusta GA
*WWIO-FM Brunswick GA
*WUWG(FM) Carrollton GA
*WDCO-FM Cochran GA
*WTJB(FM) Columbus GA
*WNGU(FM) Dahlonega GA
*WPPR(FM) Demorest GA
*WJWV(FM) Fort Gaines GA
*WSVH(FM) Savannah GA
*WFSL(FM) Thomasville GA
*WABR-FM Tifton GA
*WWET(FM) Valdosta GA
*WJSP-FM Warm Springs GA
*WXVS(FM) Waycross GA
*KPRG(FM) Hagatna GU
*KANO(FM) Hilo HI
*KHPR(FM) Honolulu HI
*KKUA(FM) Wailuku HI
*WOI-FM Ames IA
*KWOI(FM) Carroll IA
*KHKE(FM) Cedar Falls IA
*KLCD(FM) Decorah IA
*KHOE(FM) Fairfield IA
*KTPR(FM) Fort Dodge IA
*KSUI(FM) Iowa City IA
*KOWI(FM) Lamoni IA
*KRNI(AM) Mason City IA
*KOJI(FM) Okoboji IA
*KWIT(FM) Sioux City IA
*KBSU(AM) Boise ID
*KBSU-FM Boise ID
*KIBX(FM) Bonners Ferry ID
*KNWO(FM) Cottonwood ID
*KBSM(FM) McCall ID
*KRFA-FM Moscow ID
*KBYI(FM) Rexburg ID
*KWRV(FM) Sun Valley ID
*KBSW(FM) Twin Falls ID
*WSIU(FM) Carbondale IL
WFMT(FM) Chicago IL
*WNIE(FM) Freeport IL
*WNIW(FM) La Salle IL
*WLNX(FM) Lincoln IL
*WIUM(FM) Macomb IL
*WUSI(FM) Olney IL
*WCBU(FM) Peoria IL
*WIPA(FM) Pittsfield IL
*WQUB(FM) Quincy IL
*WVIK(FM) Rock Island IL
*WNIU(FM) Rockford IL
*WUIS(FM) Springfield IL
*WNIQ(FM) Sterling IL
*WILL-FM Urbana IL
*WIUW(FM) Warsaw IL
*WETN(FM) Wheaton IL
WYHY(FM) Winnebago IL
*WBSB(FM) Anderson IN
*WFIU(FM) Bloomington IN
*WNIN-FM Evansville IN
*WBSH(FM) Hagerstown IN
*WFYI-FM Indianapolis IN
*WICR(FM) Indianapolis IN
*WBSW(FM) Marion IN

*WBST(FM) Muncie IN
*WSND-FM Notre Dame IN
*WBNI-FM Orland IN
*WBSJ(FM) Portland IN
*WECI(FM) Richmond IN
*KANH(FM) Emporia KS
*KANZ(FM) Garden City KS
*KHCT(FM) Great Bend KS
*KZNA(FM) Hill City KS
*KHCC-FM Hutchinson KS
KXTR(AM) Kansas City KS
*KANU(FM) Lawrence KS
*KANV(FM) Olsburg KS
*KRPS(FM) Pittsburg KS
*KHCD(FM) Salina KS
*KMUW(FM) Wichita KS
*WKYU-FM Bowling Green KY
*WEKF(FM) Corbin KY
*WKUE(FM) Elizabethtown KY
*WEKH(FM) Hazard KY
*WKPB(FM) Henderson KY
*WUOL(FM) Louisville KY
*WMKY(FM) Morehead KY
*WKMS-FM Murray KY
*WEKU(FM) Richmond KY
*WDCL-FM Somerset KY
WSKV(FM) Stanton KY
*KLSA(FM) Alexandria LA
*WRKF(FM) Baton Rouge LA
*KEDM(FM) Monroe LA
*WWNO(FM) New Orleans LA
*KDAQ(FM) Shreveport LA
*KTLN(FM) Thibodaux LA
*WFCR(FM) Amherst MA
*WGBH(FM) Boston MA
WHRB(FM) Cambridge MA
WFCC-FM Chatham MA
WCRB(FM) Waltham MA
*WBJC(FM) Baltimore MD
*WFWM(FM) Frostburg MD
*WSCL(FM) Salisbury MD
*WMEH(FM) Bangor ME
*WMED(FM) Calais ME
*WMEP(FM) Camden ME
WMEF(FM) Fort Kent ME
WBQQ(FM) Kennebunk ME
*WMEA(FM) Portland ME
*WMEM(FM) Presque Isle ME
WBQW(FM) Scarborough ME
WBQX(FM) Thomaston ME
*WMEW(FM) Waterville ME
*WYAR(FM) Yarmouth ME
*WCML-FM Alpena MI
*WUCX-FM Bay City MI
*WAUS(FM) Berrien Springs MI
*WICV(FM) East Jordan MI
*WKAR-FM East Lansing MI
*WBLU-FM Grand Rapids MI
*WGGL-FM Houghton MI
*WIAA(FM) Interlochen MI
*WMUK(FM) Kalamazoo MI
*WIAB(FM) Mackinaw City MI
*WNMU-FM Marquette MI
*WCMU-FM Mount Pleasant MI
*WCMB-FM Oscoda MI
WKLZ-FM Petoskey MI
*WCMZ-FM Sault Ste. Marie MI
WWCM(FM) Standish MI
*WBLV(FM) Twin Lake MI
*KRSU(FM) Appleton MN
*KCRB-FM Bemidji MN
*KBPR(FM) Brainerd MN
*KSJR-FM Collegeville MN
*KSJR-FM Collegeville MN
*WSCD-FM Duluth MN
*KCMF-FM Fergus Falls MN
*WMLS(FM) Grand Marais MN
*KSJN(FM) Minneapolis MN
*KCCM-FM Moorhead MN
*KLSE-FM Rochester MN
*KGAC(FM) Saint Peter MN
*KQMN(FM) Thief River Falls MN
*WIRR(FM) Virginia-Hibbing MN
*KRSW(FM) Worthington MN
*KRCU(FM) Cape Girardeau MO
*KRNW(FM) Chillicothe MO
KFUO-FM Clayton MO

Broadcasting & Cable Yearbook 2006

D-696

Programming on Radio Stations in the U.S.

*KBIA(FM) Columbia MO
*KXMS(FM) Joplin MO
*KKTR(FM) Kirksville MO
*KWJC(FM) Liberty MO
*KXCV(FM) Maryville MO
*KSMS-FM Point Lookout MO
*KUMR(FM) Rolla MO
*KSMU(FM) Springfield MO
*KSMW(FM) West Plains MO
*WMAH-FM Biloxi MS
*WMAE-FM Booneville MS
*WMAU-FM Bude MS
*WMAO-FM Greenwood MS
*WUSM-FM Hattiesburg MS
*WMPN-FM Jackson MS
*WMAW-FM Meridian MS
*WMAB-FM Mississippi State MS
*WMAV-FM Oxford MS
*KEMC(FM) Billings MT
*KBMC(FM) Bozeman MT
*KAPC(FM) Butte MT
*KUFN(FM) Hamilton MT
*KNMC(FM) Havre MT
*KUHM(FM) Helena MT
*KUKL(FM) Kalispell MT
KPRK(AM) Livingston MT
*KUFM(FM) Missoula MT
*WCQS(FM) Asheville NC
*WDAV(FM) Davidson NC
*WFQS(FM) Franklin NC
*WKNS(FM) Kinston NC
*WTEB(FM) New Bern NC
*WZRN(FM) Norlina NC
*WCPE(FM) Raleigh NC
*WHQR(FM) Wilmington NC
*WFDD-FM Winston-Salem NC
*KCND(FM) Bismarck ND
*KDPR(FM) Dickinson ND
*KUND-FM Grand Forks ND
*KPRJ(FM) Jamestown ND
*KMPR(FM) Minot ND
*KPPR(FM) Williston ND
*KTNE-FM Alliance NE
*KMNE-FM Bassett NE
*KCNE-FM Chadron NE
*KHNE-FM Hastings NE
*KLNE-FM Lexington NE
*KUCV(FM) Lincoln NE
*KRNE-FM Merriman NE
*KXNE-FM Norfolk NE
*KPNE-FM North Platte NE
*KIOS-FM Omaha NE
*KVNO(FM) Omaha NE
*WWCJ(FM) Cape May NJ
*WWNJ(FM) Dover Township NJ
*WRTQ(FM) Ocean City NJ
WPRB(FM) Princeton NJ
*WWFM(FM) Trenton NJ
KNMB(FM) Cloudcroft NM
*KSJE(FM) Farmington NM
*KRWG(FM) Las Cruces NM
*KMTH(FM) Maljamar NM
*KENW-FM Portales NM
KHFM(FM) Santa Fe NM
*KSFR(FM) Santa Fe NM
*KRNM(FM) Chalan Kanoa-Saipan NP
*KNCC(FM) Elko NV
*KCNV(FM) Las Vegas NV
*KXPT(FM) Las Vegas NV
*KUNR(FM) Reno NV
KSVL(FM) Smith NV
*KTPH(FM) Tonopah NV
WBKK(FM) Amsterdam NY
*WSKG-FM Binghamton NY
*WNED-FM Buffalo NY
*WSQE(FM) Corning NY
*WJSL(FM) Houghton NY
*WSQG-FM Ithaca NY
*WNJA(FM) Jamestown NY
*WKCR-FM New York NY
*WNYC-FM New York NY
WQXR-FM New York NY
*WSQC-FM Oneonta NY
*WRHV(FM) Poughkeepsie NY
*WXXI-FM Rochester NY
*WMHT-FM Schenectady NY
*WRLI-FM Southampton NY

*WCNY-FM Syracuse NY
*WUNY(FM) Utica NY
*WJNY(FM) Watertown NY
*WGBE(FM) Bryan OH
*WOUH-FM Chillicothe OH
*WGUC(FM) Cincinnati OH
WMJK(FM) Clyde OH
*WOSU-FM Columbus OH
*WOSE(FM) Coshocton OH
*WGDE(FM) Defiance OH
*WDPG(FM) Greenville OH
*WKSU-FM Kent OH
*WGLE(FM) Lima OH
WCLV(FM) Lorain OH
*WOSV(FM) Mansfield OH
*WMRT(FM) Marietta OH
*WOSB(FM) Marion OH
*WKRJ(FM) New Philadelphia OH
*WNRK(FM) Norwalk OH
WBKC(AM) Painesville OH
*WOSP(FM) Portsmouth OH
*WKSV(FM) Thompson OH
*WGTE-FM Toledo OH
*WDPR(FM) West Carrollton OH
*WKRW(FM) Wooster OH
*WYSU(FM) Youngstown OH
*WOUZ(FM) Zanesville OH
*KOCU(FM) Altus OK
*KLCU(FM) Ardmore OK
*KYCU(FM) Clinton OK
*KCSC(FM) Edmond OK
*KCCU(FM) Lawton OK
*KBCW(FM) McAlester OK
*KOSU(FM) Stillwater OK
*KWTU(FM) Tulsa OK
*KSOR(FM) Ashland OR
*KSRG(FM) Ashland OR
*KWAX(FM) Eugene OR
*KWVZ(FM) Florence OR
*KQHR(FM) Hood River OR
*KLMF(FM) Klamath Falls OR
*KOAP(FM) Lakeview OR
*KOOZ(FM) Myrtle Point OR
*KBPS-FM Portland OR
KCMD(FM) Portland OR
*KWRX(FM) Redmond OR
*KSRS(FM) Roseburg OR
*WDIY(FM) Allentown PA
*WMCE(FM) Erie PA
*WQLN-FM Erie PA
*WSAJ(AM) Grove City PA
*WSAJ-FM Grove City PA
*WITF-FM Harrisburg PA
*WRTY(FM) Jackson Township PA
*WQEJ(FM) Johnstown PA
*WPSB(FM) Kane PA
WYNE(AM) North East PA
*WWPJ(FM) Pen Argyl PA
*WRTI(FM) Philadelphia PA
*WQED-FM Pittsburgh PA
*WVIA-FM Scranton PA
*WJAZ(FM) Summerdale PA
*WVYA(FM) Williamsport PA
*WRUO(FM) Mayaguez PR
*WIPR-FM San Juan PR
*WRTU(FM) San Juan PR
WCRI(FM) Block Island RI
*WSCI(FM) Charleston SC
*WLTR(FM) Columbia SC
*WHMC-FM Conway SC
*WEPR(FM) Greenville SC
*KESD(FM) Brookings SD
KPSD(FM) Faith SD
*KQSD-FM Lowry SD
*KDSD-FM Pierpont SD
*KBHE-FM Rapid City SD
*KTSD-FM Reliance SD
*KCSD(FM) Sioux Falls SD
*KRSD(FM) Sioux Falls SD
*KUSD(FM) Vermillion SD
*WSMC-FM Collegedale TN
*WHRS(FM) Cookeville TN
*WFHU-FM Henderson TN
*WKNP(FM) Jackson TN
*WETS-FM Johnson City TN
*WETS(FM) Johnson City TN
*WCSK(FM) Kingsport TN

*WUOT(FM) Knoxville TN
*WFMQ(FM) Lebanon TN
*WKNO-FM Memphis TN
*WPLN-FM Nashville TN
*WTML(FM) Tullahoma TN
*KACU(FM) Abilene TX
*KMFA(FM) Austin TX
*KVLU(FM) Beaumont TX
*KAMU-FM College Station TX
*KEDT-FM Corpus Christi TX
WRR(FM) Dallas TX
*KTEP(FM) El Paso TX
*KTCU-FM Fort Worth TX
*KMBH-FM Harlingen TX
*KUHF(FM) Houston TX
*KSHU(FM) Huntsville TX
*KTXI(FM) Ingram TX
*KTPB(FM) Kilgore TX
*KNCT-FM Killeen TX
*KOHM(FM) Lubbock TX
*KLDN(FM) Lufkin TX
*KHID(FM) McAllen TX
*KOCV(FM) Odessa TX
*KPAC(FM) San Antonio TX
*KTOT(FM) Spearman TX
*KTXK(FM) Texarkana TX
*KVRT(FM) Victoria TX
*KWBU-FM Waco TX
*KMCU(FM) Wichita Falls TX
*KUSR(FM) Logan UT
*KUSU-FM Logan UT
*KPCW(FM) Park City UT
*KBYU-FM Provo UT
*KUER(FM) Salt Lake City UT
*WVTU(FM) Charlottesville VA
*WVTW(FM) Charlottesville VA
*WFOS(FM) Chesapeake VA
*WFFC(FM) Ferrum VA
*WEMC(FM) Harrisonburg VA
*WMRA(FM) Harrisonburg VA
*WMRL(FM) Lexington VA
*WVTR(FM) Marion VA
*WHRO-FM Norfolk VA
*WCVE(FM) Richmond VA
*WVTF(FM) Roanoke VA
WNDJ(FM) White Stone VA
*WISE-FM Wise VA
WBTN-FM Bennington VT
*WVPS(FM) Burlington VT
*WNCH(FM) Norwich VT
*WRVT(FM) Rutland VT
*WVPA(FM) Saint Johnsbury VT
WCVT(FM) Stowe VT
*WVPR(FM) Windsor VT
*KZAZ(FM) Bellingham WA
*KNWV(FM) Clarkston WA
*KNWR(FM) Ellensburg WA
KLDY(AM) Lacey WA
KOHO-FM Leavenworth WA
*KQWS(FM) Omak WA
*KNWP(FM) Port Angeles WA
*KWSU(AM) Pullman WA
*KFAE-FM Richland WA
KING-FM Seattle WA
*KPBX-FM Spokane WA
*KNWY(FM) Yakima WA
WFMR(FM) Brookfield WI
*WHSA(FM) Brule WI
*WUEC-FM Eau Claire WI
*WPNE-FM Green Bay WI
*WGTD(FM) Kenosha WI
*WHLA-FM La Crosse WI
*WLSU-FM La Crosse WI
*WERN(FM) Madison WI
*WORT-FM Madison WI
*WVSS(FM) Menomonie WI
*WXPR(FM) Rhinelander WI
*WHND(FM) Sister Bay WI
*WHRM(FM) Wausau WI
*WVPB(FM) Beckley WV
*WVPW(FM) Buckhannon WV
*WVPN(FM) Charleston WV
*WVVW(FM) Huntington WV
*WVEP(FM) Martinsburg WV
*WVPM(FM) Morgantown WV
*WVPG(FM) Parkersburg WV
*WAUA(FM) Petersburg WV

*WVNP(FM) Wheeling WV
*KUWA(FM) Afton WY
*KDUW(FM) Douglas WY
*KUWG(FM) Gillette WY
*KUWJ(FM) Jackson WY
*KUWR(FM) Laramie WY
*KUWN(FM) Newcastle WY
*KUWX(FM) Pinedale WY
*KUWP(FM) Powell WY
*KUWZ(FM) Rock Springs WY
*KSUW(FM) Sheridan WY
*KUWD(FM) Sundance WY
KUWT(FM) Thermopolis WY

Comedy
KPHX(AM) Phoenix AZ
KFXY(AM) Enid OK

Contemporary Hit/Top-40
KGOT(FM) Anchorage AK
KWLF(FM) Fairbanks AK
*KHNS(FM) Haines AK
KKIS-FM Soldotna AK
WZYP(FM) Athens AL
WZBQ(FM) Carrollton AL
WAGF-FM Dothan AL
WKZJ(FM) Eufaula AL
WLDA(FM) Fort Rucker AL
WQEN(FM) Gadsden AL
WABB-FM Mobile AL
WHHY-FM Montgomery AL
WBFA(FM) Smiths AL
WBHJ(FM) Tuscaloosa AL
*KSWH(FM) Arkadelphia AR
KMRX(FM) El Dorado AR
KHTE-FM England AR
KISR(FM) Fort Smith AR
KIYS(FM) Jonesboro AR
KMXF(FM) Lowell AR
*KVRN(FM) Marvell AR
KGPQ(FM) Monticello AR
KMCK(FM) Siloam Springs AR
KKHJ(FM) Pago Pago AS
KCDQ(FM) Douglas AZ
KGVY(AM) Green Valley AZ
KOHT(FM) Marana AZ
KZZP(FM) Mesa AZ
KIKO(AM) Miami AZ
KIDR(AM) Phoenix AZ
KRQQ(FM) Tucson AZ
KZPT(FM) Tucson AZ
KLJZ(FM) Yuma AZ
KEWB(FM) Anderson CA
KBKO-FM Bakersfield CA
KISV(FM) Bakersfield CA
KDUC(FM) Barstow CA
KXSB-FM Big Bear Lake CA
KSIQ(FM) Brawley CA
KKDJ(FM) Delano CA
KHTS-FM El Cajon CA
KFMI(FM) Eureka CA
KSSD(FM) Fallbrook CA
KWPT(FM) Fortuna CA
*KOHL(FM) Fremont CA
KQCM(FM) Joshua Tree CA
KOKO(FM) Kerman CA
KWIN(FM) Lodi CA
KIIS-FM Los Angeles CA
KPWR(FM) Los Angeles CA
KDUQ(FM) Ludlow CA
KSXY(FM) Middletown CA
KVVS(FM) Mojave CA
*KSMC(FM) Moraga CA
*KSFH(FM) Mountain View CA
*KLFH(FM) Ojai CA
KCAQ(FM) Oxnard CA
KPSI(FM) Palm Springs CA
KHTN(FM) Planada CA
KNLF(FM) Quincy CA
*KRVH(FM) Rio Vista CA
KGGI(FM) Riverside CA
KDND(FM) Sacramento CA
KRAY-FM Salinas CA

KMEL(FM) San Francisco CA
KYLD(FM) San Francisco CA
KWWV(FM) Santa Margarita CA
KDLD(FM) Santa Monica CA
KLJR-FM Santa Paula CA
KNNN(FM) Shasta Lake City CA
KBOS-FM Tulare CA
KWNN(FM) Turlock CA
KCDZ(FM) Twentynine Palms CA
KWNE(FM) Ukiah CA
*KDUV(FM) Visalia CA
KSEQ(FM) Visalia CA
*KASF(FM) Alamosa CO
KMGJ(FM) Grand Junction CO
*KTSC-FM Pueblo CO
WQGN-FM Groton CT
WKCI-FM Hamden CT
WKSS(FM) Hartford CT
WWRX(FM) Pawcatuck CT
WILI-FM Willimantic CT
WIHT(FM) Washington DC
WZEB(FM) Ocean View DE
*WMPH(FM) Wilmington DE
WFCT(FM) Apalachicola FL
WXKB(FM) Cape Coral FL
WJHM(FM) Daytona Beach FL
WRLZ(AM) Eatonville FL
WHYI-FM Fort Lauderdale FL
WLDI(FM) Fort Pierce FL
WZNS(FM) Fort Walton Beach FL
WHTF(FM) Havana FL
WVYB(FM) Holly Hill FL
WLLD(FM) Holmes Beach FL
WIFL(FM) Inglis FL
WAPE-FM Jacksonville FL
WEOW(FM) Key West FL
WXHT(FM) Madison FL
WAOA-FM Melbourne FL
WBVD(FM) Melbourne FL
WEDR(FM) Miami FL
WMYM(AM) Miami FL
WPOW(FM) Miami FL
WBTT(FM) Naples Park FL
WILN(FM) Panama City FL
WPFM-FM Panama City FL
WPRY(AM) Perry FL
WWMI(AM) Saint Petersburg FL
WFLZ-FM Tampa FL
WXXL(FM) Tavares FL
WNUE-FM Titusville FL
V6AH(FM) Pohnpei FM
*V6AI(AM) Yap FM
WNUQ(FM) Albany GA
WFSH-FM Athens GA
WCGQ(FM) Columbus GA
WXMK(FM) Dock Junction GA
WKKZ(FM) Dublin GA
WELT(FM) East Dublin GA
WVFJ-FM Manchester GA
WMGB(FM) Montezuma GA
WAEV(FM) Savannah GA
WZAT(FM) Savannah GA
WSTR(FM) Smyrna GA
KOKU(FM) Hagatna GU
KPMW(FM) Haliimaile HI
KNWB(FM) Hilo HI
KIKI-FM Honolulu HI
KPHW(FM) Kaneohe HI
KNUQ(FM) Paauilo HI
KSRF(FM) Poipu HI
KJMD(FM) Pukalani HI
KDDB(FM) Waipahu HI
KCCQ(FM) Ames IA
KSWI(FM) Atlantic IA
KZAT-FM Belle Plaine IA
KZIA(FM) Cedar Rapids IA
KQKQ-FM Council Bluffs IA
KKDM(FM) Des Moines IA
KLYV(FM) Dubuque IA
KDWD(FM) Emmetsburg IA
KRTI(FM) Grinnell IA
KCJJ(AM) Iowa City IA
KBEA-FM Muscatine IA
KSMA-FM Osage IA
KOTM-FM Ottumwa IA
KFTZ(FM) Idaho Falls ID
KVTY(FM) Lewiston ID

Broadcasting & Cable Yearbook 2006

D-697

Programming on Radio Stations in the U.S.

KZFN(FM) Moscow ID	KSMB(FM) Lafayette LA	WKBC-FM North Wilkesboro NC	WNKL(FM) Wauseon OH	KKLS-FM Sioux Falls SD
KZMG(FM) New Plymouth ID	KZLG(FM) Mansura LA	WSFM(FM) Oak Island NC	*WYSA(FM) Wauseon OH	KMXC(FM) Sioux Falls SD
WERV-FM Aurora IL	KNOE-FM Monroe LA	WRHD(FM) Williamston NC	WTDA(FM) Westerville OH	KRCS(FM) Sturgis SD
WBNQ(FM) Bloomington IL	KMRC(AM) Morgan City LA	WKZL(FM) Winston-Salem NC	*WCWS(FM) Wooster OH	*KAOR(FM) Vermillion SD
WCDD(FM) Canton IL	WEZB(FM) New Orleans LA	KKXL-FM Grand Forks ND	WHOT-FM Youngstown OH	KWYR-FM Winner SD
WCIL-FM Carbondale IL	KRUF(FM) Shreveport LA	*KCNT(FM) Hastings NE	KIZS(FM) Broken Arrow OK	WPBX(FM) Crossville TN
WQKQ(FM) Carthage IL	*KNSU(FM) Thibodaux LA	KFRX(FM) Lincoln NE	*KSSU(FM) Durant OK	WQZQ(FM) Dickson TN
WLRW(FM) Champaign IL	*WGAJ(FM) Deerfield MA	WJYY(FM) Concord NH	KKWD(FM) Edmond OK	WLSQ-FM Dyer TN
WBBM-FM Chicago IL	WFHN(FM) Fairhaven MA	WKNE(FM) Keene NH	KTIJ(FM) Elk City OK	*WUMC(FM) Elizabethton TN
WKSC-FM Chicago IL	*WGAO(FM) Franklin MA	WXXS(FM) Lancaster NH	KMGZ(FM) Lawton OK	*WVCP(FM) Gallatin TN
WRPW(FM) Colfax IL	WBOQ(FM) Gloucester MA	*WDBK(FM) Blackwood NJ	KHTT(FM) Muskogee OK	WAEZ(FM) Greeneville TN
WSOY-FM Decatur IL	WXKS-FM Medford MA	WGBZ(FM) Cape May Court House NJ	KJYO(FM) Oklahoma City OK	*WLMU(FM) Harrogate TN
WYDS(FM) Decatur IL	WRZE(FM) Nantucket MA	WNSW(AM) Newark NJ	KZBB(FM) Poteau OK	WLSZ(FM) Humboldt TN
WOJO(FM) Evanston IL	*WSDH(FM) Sandwich MA	WZBZ(FM) Pleasantville NJ	KMUS(AM) Sperry OK	WNRX(FM) Jefferson City TN
WISH-FM Galatia IL	*WYAJ(FM) Sudbury MA	WPST(FM) Trenton NJ	KIFS(FM) Ashland OR	WRVW(FM) Lebanon TN
WVZA(FM) Herrin IL	WTRI(AM) Brunswick MD	KYEE(FM) Alamogordo NM	KXIX(FM) Bend OR	*WUTM(FM) Martin TN
WXAJ(FM) Hillsboro IL	WPGC-FM Morningside MD	*KNMI(FM) Farmington NM	KQHC(FM) Burns OR	WYDL(FM) Middleton TN
WVLI(FM) Kankakee IL	WMME-FM Augusta ME	KAZX(FM) Kirtland NM	KDUK-FM Florence OR	WAKQ(FM) Paris TN
WEAI(FM) Lynnville IL	WWBX(FM) Bangor ME	KHQT(FM) Las Cruces NM	KLDR(FM) Harbeck-Fruitdale OR	WWST(FM) Sevierville TN
*WLKL(FM) Mattoon IL	WBZN(FM) Old Town ME	KBCQ(FM) Roswell NM	KKRB(FM) Klamath Falls OR	WKXJ(FM) Signal Mountain TN
WZPW(FM) Peoria IL	WJBQ(FM) Portland ME	KKSS(FM) Santa Fe NM	*KEOL(FM) La Grande OR	WKZP(FM) Spencer TN
WYVR(FM) Petersburg IL	WRED(FM) Saco ME	KPXP(FM) Garapan-Saipan NP	KTMT-FM Medford OR	KPRF(FM) Amarillo TX
*WGCA-FM Quincy IL	*WSJB-FM Standish ME	KZTQ(FM) Carson City NV	KHTO(FM) Milton-Freewater OR	KQIZ-FM Amarillo TX
WQQB(FM) Rantoul IL	WDSS(AM) Ada MI	KLUC-FM Las Vegas NV	KRSK(FM) Molalla OR	KXGL(FM) Amarillo TX
*WRRG(FM) River Grove IL	*WAHS(FM) Auburn Hills MI	KQRT(FM) Las Vegas NV	KOOS(FM) North Bend OR	KORQ(FM) Baird TX
WHTS(FM) Rock Island IL	WKFR-FM Battle Creek MI	KWID(FM) Las Vegas NV	*KAVE(FM) Oakridge OR	KQXY-FM Beaumont TX
WZOK(FM) Rockford IL	*WTRK(FM) Bay City MI	KVEG(FM) Mesquite NV	KKRZ(FM) Portland OR	*KPFC(FM) Callisburg TX
WIVQ(FM) Spring Valley IL	WYBR(FM) Big Rapids MI	KWNZ(FM) Sun Valley NV	KXJM(FM) Portland OR	KDHT(FM) Cedar Park TX
WDBR(FM) Springfield IL	*WBFH(FM) Bloomfield Hills MI	*WBXL(FM) Baldwinsville NY	KEUG(FM) Veneta OR	KZFM(FM) Corpus Christi TX
WSTQ(FM) Streator IL	WSMK(FM) Buchanan MI	WKKF(FM) Ballston Spa NY	WAEB-FM Allentown PA	KMMZ(FM) Crane TX
WKRV(FM) Vandalia IL	WKHQ-FM Charlevoix MI	*WXBA(FM) Brentwood NY	WHOL(AM) Allentown PA	KJKK(FM) Dallas TX
WXTW(FM) Auburn IN	WCFX(FM) Clare MI	*WBSU(FM) Brockport NY	WWOT(FM) Altoona PA	KHKS(FM) Denton TX
WBWB(FM) Bloomington IN	*WPRJ(FM) Coleman MI	*WKRB(FM) Brooklyn NY	*WCUC-FM Clarion PA	KBFM(FM) Edinburg TX
WEGK(FM) Charlestown IN	WWCK(AM) Flint MI	WTSS(FM) Buffalo NY	WYOT(FM) Ebensburg PA	KPRR(FM) El Paso TX
WNHT(FM) Churubusco IN	WWCK-FM Flint MI	*WCIY(FM) Canandaigua NY	WRTS(FM) Erie PA	KWKQ(FM) Graham TX
WIMC(FM) Crawfordsville IN	WRCL(FM) Frankenmuth MI	WBDR(FM) Cape Vincent NY	*WZZE(FM) Glen Mills PA	KCDD(FM) Hamlin TX
WXXB(FM) Delphi IN	WKMJ-FM Hancock MI	WYUL(FM) Chateaugay NY	WNNK-FM Harrisburg PA	KPWW(FM) Hooks TX
*WFCI(FM) Franklin IN	*WHPR(FM) Highland Park MI	WWYL(FM) Chenango Bridge NY	WLAN-FM Lancaster PA	KMIC(AM) Houston TX
*WHWE(FM) Howe IN	WVTI(FM) Holland MI	WBDI(FM) Copenhagen NY	*WNTE(FM) Mansfield PA	KRBE(FM) Houston TX
*WVSH(FM) Huntington IN	WUPS(FM) Houghton Lake MI	WNKI(FM) Corning NY	WXOT(FM) Mount Union PA	KNEX(FM) Laredo TX
*WBDG(FM) Indianapolis IN	WHMI(FM) Howell MI	WDHI(FM) Delhi NY	WBHT(FM) Mountain Top PA	KQUR(FM) Laredo TX
*WEDM(FM) Indianapolis IN	WUPM(FM) Ironwood MI	WLVY(FM) Elmira NY	WBHD(FM) Olyphant PA	KRRG(FM) Laredo TX
WHHH(FM) Indianapolis IN	WVIC(FM) Jackson MI	WMRV-FM Endicott NY	WIOQ(FM) Philadelphia PA	KZII-FM Lubbock TX
WNOU(FM) Indianapolis IN	WHZZ(FM) Lansing MI	*WCID(FM) Friendship NY	WRDW-FM Philadelphia PA	KBAT(FM) Midland TX
WAZY-FM Lafayette IN	WBTI(FM) Lexington MI	WFNY(AM) Gloversville NY	WKST-FM Pittsburgh PA	KZZA(FM) Muenster TX
*WCYT(FM) Lafayette Township IN	WTWR-FM Monroe MI	WKGS(FM) Irondequoit NY	WRKZ(FM) Pittsburgh PA	KMRK-FM Odessa TX
WLHM(FM) Logansport IN	WSNX-FM Muskegon MI	WKTU(FM) Lake Success NY	WKVB(FM) Port Matilda PA	KAZE(FM) Ore City TX
*WNAS(FM) New Albany IN	WKQS-FM Negaunee MI	WKZA(FM) Lakewood NY	WAVT-FM Pottsville PA	*KWLD(FM) Plainview TX
WJFX(FM) New Haven IN	WMOM(FM) Pentwater MI	WSKU(FM) Little Falls NY	*WYBF(FM) Radnor Township PA	KMKI(AM) Plano TX
WDKS(FM) Newburgh IN	*WORW(FM) Port Huron MI	*WVCR-FM Loudonville NY	WRFY-FM Reading PA	KKPN(FM) Rockport TX
WUME-FM Paoli IN	WYSS(FM) Sault Ste. Marie MI	WYSX(FM) Morristown NY	WAKZ(FM) Sharpsville PA	*KNLE-FM Round Rock TX
WZKF(FM) Salem IN	KXRZ(FM) Alexandria MN	WQHT(FM) New York NY	WJHT(FM) State College PA	KIXY-FM San Angelo TX
WNDV(AM) South Bend IN	*KBSB(FM) Bemidji MN	WKSE(FM) Niagara Falls NY	WQKX(FM) Sunbury PA	KMDX(FM) San Angelo TX
WNDV-FM South Bend IN	KCLH(FM) Caledonia MN	WBDB(FM) Ogdensburg NY	WKRF(FM) Tobyhanna PA	KSRX(FM) San Antonio TX
WTCJ-FM Tell City IN	WKLK(AM) Cloquet MN	*WOSS(FM) Ossining NY	WGMR(FM) Tyrone PA	KXXM(FM) San Antonio TX
WMGI(FM) Terre Haute IN	KTTB(FM) Glencoe MN	WBLI(FM) Patchogue NY	*WXVU(FM) Villanova PA	KSCH(FM) Sulphur Springs TX
*WVUB(FM) Vincennes IN	WTBX(FM) Hibbing MN	WVTK(FM) Port Henry NY	WNBT-FM Wellsboro PA	KXBT(FM) Taylor TX
KDGS(FM) Andover KS	KDWB-FM Richfield MN	WPKF(FM) Poughkeepsie NY	WKRZ-FM Wilkes-Barre PA	KELZ-FM Terrell Hills TX
KMOQ(FM) Baxter Springs KS	KROC-FM Rochester MN	WSPK(FM) Poughkeepsie NY	WKSB(FM) Williamsport PA	KEPG(FM) Victoria TX
*KTCC(FM) Colby KS	KCLD-FM Saint Cloud MN	WPXY-FM Rochester NY	WQXA-FM York PA	KVIC(FM) Victoria TX
KZCH(FM) Derby KS	KSYN(FM) Joplin MO	WENU(AM) South Glens Falls NY	WYCR(FM) York-Hanover PA	KWTX-FM Waco TX
KLZR(FM) Lawrence KS	KMXV(FM) Kansas City MO	*WJPZ-FM Syracuse NY	WCMN-FM Arecibo PR	KISX(FM) Whitehouse TX
KMXN(FM) Osage City KS	*KWJC(FM) Liberty MO	WNTQ(FM) Syracuse NY	WMIA(AM) Arecibo PR	KNIN-FM Wichita Falls TX
KCHZ(FM) Ottawa KS	KKBL(FM) Monett MO	WWHT(FM) Syracuse NY	WBQN(AM) Barceloneta-Manati PR	KQXC-FM Wichita Falls TX
*KTJO-FM Ottawa KS	*KCLC(FM) Saint Charles MO	WFLY(FM) Troy NY	WODA(FM) Bayamon PR	KRAR(FM) Brigham City UT
KACZ(FM) Riley KS	KSLZ(FM) Saint Louis MO	WKBE(FM) Warrensburg NY	WXLX(FM) Lajas PR	*KSUU(FM) Cedar City UT
KSAL-FM Salina KS	KSPW(FM) Sparta MO	WCIZ(FM) Watertown NY	WAEL-FM Maricao PR	KXBN(FM) Cedar City UT
*KYWA(FM) Wichita KS	KWKJ(FM) Windsor MO	WSKS(FM) Whitesboro NY	WPRA(AM) Mayaguez PR	KVFX(FM) Logan UT
WWKF(FM) Fulton KY	WACR-FM Aberdeen MS	*WONB(FM) Ada OH	WUKQ-FM Mayaguez PR	*KWCR-FM Ogden UT
WKIC(AM) Hazard KY	WMBC(FM) Columbus MS	*WZIP(FM) Akron OH	WEKO(AM) Morovis PR	KTCE(FM) Payson UT
WZQQ(FM) Hyden KY	WYOY(FM) Gluckstadt MS	WOMP-FM Bellaire OH	WEXS(AM) Patillas PR	KHTB(FM) Provo UT
WRNZ(FM) Lancaster KY	WXYK(FM) Gulfport MS	WWMK(AM) Cleveland OH	WEGM(FM) San German PR	KCYQ(FM) Richfield UT
WLSK(FM) Lebanon KY	WNSL(FM) Laurel MS	*WUFM(FM) Columbus OH	WENA(AM) Yauco PR	KXRQ(FM) Roosevelt UT
WLKT(FM) Lexington-Fayette KY	WZYQ(FM) Mound Bayou MS	WLWD(FM) Columbus Grove OH	*WCVY(FM) Coventry RI	KUDD(FM) Roy UT
WDJX(FM) Louisville KY	WQYZ(FM) Ocean Springs MS	WGTZ(FM) Eaton OH	WPRO-FM Providence RI	KZHT(FM) Salt Lake City UT
WFTM-FM Maysville KY	KMZK(AM) Billings MT	WFRO-FM Fremont OH	WWKX(FM) Woonsocket RI	KUUU(FM) South Jordan UT
WBTF(FM) Midway KY	KBEV-FM Dillon MT	WBKS(FM) Ironton OH	WGTN-FM Andrews SC	*WEHC(FM) Emory VA
WEGI(FM) Oak Grove KY	KIKC(AM) Forsyth MT	*WVMC-FM Mansfield OH	WSEA(FM) Atlantic Beach SC	*WWHS-FM Hampden-Sydney VA
WSTO(FM) Owensboro KY	KOFI(AM) Kalispell MT	WRVB(FM) Marietta OH	WSSX-FM Charleston SC	WQPO(FM) Harrisonburg VA
WDDJ(FM) Paducah KY	KRSQ(FM) Laurel MT	WDIF(FM) Marion OH	WJMX-FM Cheraw SC	*WHCE(FM) Highland Springs VA
*WGCF(FM) Paducah KY	WNKS(FM) Charlotte NC	WYSZ(FM) Maumee OH	WNOK(FM) Columbia SC	WJJX(FM) Lynchburg VA
WZLK(FM) Virgie KY	WDCG(FM) Durham NC	WYVK(FM) Middleport OH	WWXM(FM) Garden City SC	WZVA(FM) Marion VA
KQID(FM) Alexandria LA	WQSM(FM) Fayetteville NC	WKFS(FM) Milford OH	WFBC-FM Greenville SC	WNVZ(FM) Norfolk VA
WFMF(FM) Baton Rouge LA	WJCV(FM) Jacksonville NC	WXZQ(FM) Piketon OH	WHSC(AM) Hartsville SC	WNVA-FM Norton VA
KQLK(FM) De Ridder LA	WQSL(FM) Jacksonville NC	WVKF(FM) Shadyside OH	WHZT(FM) Seneca SC	WZNR(FM) Poquoson VA
KRKA(FM) Erath LA	WRHT(FM) Morehead City NC	WVKS(FM) Toledo OH	KQRN(FM) Mitchell SD	WXLK(FM) Roanoke VA
KHEV(FM) Houma LA	WZPR(FM) Nags Head NC	WZOQ(FM) Wapakoneta OH	KQRQ(FM) Rapid City SD	WHTE-FM Ruckersville VA

Programming on Radio Stations in the U.S.

WHLF(FM) South Boston VA
WJJS-FM Vinton VA
WAZR(FM) Woodstock VA
WORK(FM) Barre VT
*WWLR(FM) Lyndonville VT
*WVTC(FM) Randolph Center VT
WXXX(FM) South Burlington VT
KBDB-FM Forks WA
KBIS(AM) Forks WA
KAQX(FM) Long Beach WA
*KMIH(FM) Mercer Island WA
*KUBS(FM) Newport WA
KZBE(FM) Omak WA
KOLW(FM) Othello WA
KHTR(FM) Pullman WA
KWWW-FM Quincy WA
*KNHC(FM) Seattle WA
KUBE(FM) Seattle WA
KJET(FM) South Bend WA
*KWRS(FM) Spokane WA
KZZU-FM Spokane WA
KBKS-FM Tacoma WA
*KVTI(FM) Tacoma WA
KUJ-FM Walla Walla WA
KPQ-FM Wenatchee WA
KFFM(FM) Yakima WA
WBIZ-FM Eau Claire WI
WKPO(FM) Evansville WI
WIXX(FM) Green Bay WI
WZEE(FM) Madison WI
WRHN(FM) Rhinelander WI
WLYD(FM) Sturgeon Bay WI
*WPFF(FM) Sturgeon Bay WI
WKSH(AM) Sussex WI
*WCLQ(FM) Wausau WI
WIFC(FM) Wausau WI
WLRK(FM) Wausau WI
WXSS(FM) Wauwatosa WI
WCIR-FM Beckley WV
WVSR-FM Charleston WV
WQWV(FM) Fisher WV
WKEE-FM Huntington WV
WVKM(FM) Matewan WV
WVAQ(FM) Morgantown WV
WRVZ(FM) Pocatalico WV
WSTG(FM) Princeton WV
*WPHP(FM) Wheeling WV
KTRS-FM Casper WY
KAML-FM Gillette WY
KDLY(FM) Lander WY
KYCS(FM) Rock Springs WY
KZZS(FM) Story WY

Country

KASH-FM Anchorage AK
KBRJ(FM) Anchorage AK
*KCUK(FM) Chevak AK
KLAM(AM) Cordova AK
*KDLG(AM) Dillingham AK
KIAK-FM Fairbanks AK
*KIYU(AM) Galena AK
*KJHA(FM) Houston AK
KTKU(FM) Juneau AK
KWHQ-FM Kenai AK
KGTW(FM) Ketchikan AK
KVOK(AM) Kodiak AK
*KJNP(AM) North Pole AK
*KJNP-FM North Pole AK
KRSA(AM) Petersburg AK
*KUHB-FM Saint Paul AK
KSBZ(FM) Sitka AK
KPEN-FM Soldotna AK
KVAK(AM) Valdez AK
WQAH-FM Addison AL
WQSB(FM) Albertville AL
WSTH-FM Alexander City AL
WAAO-FM Andalusia AL
WRAB(AM) Arab AL
WHMA-FM Ashland AL
WKAC(AM) Athens AL
WNSI-FM Atmore AL
WKKR(FM) Auburn AL
WZZK(AM) Birmingham AL
WZZK-FM Birmingham AL
WAOQ(FM) Brantley AL
WKNU(FM) Brewton AL

WYMR(AM) Bridgeport AL
WPRN(AM) Butler AL
WEIS(AM) Centre AL
WRHY(FM) Centre AL
WBIB(AM) Centreville AL
WEZZ(FM) Clanton AL
WKUL(FM) Cullman AL
WDRM(FM) Decatur AL
WTVY-FM Dothan AL
WELB(AM) Elba AL
WZTZ(FM) Elba AL
WDJR(FM) Enterprise AL
WPGG(FM) Evergreen AL
WLDX(AM) Fayette AL
WTXT(FM) Fayette AL
WKWL(AM) Florala AL
WXFL(FM) Florence AL
WZOB(AM) Fort Payne AL
WGEA(AM) Geneva AL
WQZX(FM) Greenville AL
WBMH(FM) Grove Hill AL
WTWX-FM Guntersville AL
WJBB-FM Haleyville AL
WERH(AM) Hamilton AL
*WPIL(FM) Heflin AL
WFMH-FM Holly Pond AL
WNCB(FM) Homewood AL
WBHP(AM) Huntsville AL
WCKS(AM) Jacksonville AL
WDXB(FM) Jasper AL
WINL(FM) Linden AL
WNPT-FM Linden AL
WZZX(AM) Lineville AL
WPRN-FM Lisman AL
WKSJ-FM Mobile AL
WBAM-FM Montgomery AL
WLWI-FM Montgomery AL
WKLD(FM) Oneonta AL
WAMI(AM) Opp AL
WAMI-FM Opp AL
WOPP(AM) Opp AL
WJRL-FM Ozark AL
WOAB(FM) Ozark AL
WFHK(AM) Pell City AL
WRMG(AM) Red Bay AL
WELR-FM Roanoke AL
WKEA-FM Scottsboro AL
WWIC(AM) Scottsboro AL
WDXX(FM) Selma AL
WTDR(FM) Talladega AL
WLAY-FM Tuscumbia AL
WQSI(FM) Union Springs AL
WKXM(AM) Winfield AL
WYLS(AM) York AL
KPGG(FM) Ashdown AR
KOLX(FM) Barling AR
KEWI(AM) Benton AR
KHKN(FM) Benton AR
KQSM-FM Bentonville AR
KTHS(AM) Berryville AR
KTHS-FM Berryville AR
KHLS(FM) Blytheville AR
KLYR(AM) Clarksville AR
KLYR-FM Clarksville AR
KXIO(FM) Clarksville AR
KHPQ(FM) Clinton AR
KAGH(AM) Crossett AR
KAGH-FM Crossett AR
KYEL(FM) Danville AR
KCJC(FM) Dardanelle AR
KWXT(FM) Dardanelle AR
KDQN-FM De Queen AR
KDEW-FM De Witt AR
KXSA-FM Dermott AR
KXFE(FM) Dumas AR
KCXY(FM) East Camden AR
KIXB(FM) El Dorado AR
KKIX(FM) Fayetteville AR
KQEW(FM) Fordyce AR
KBFC(FM) Forrest City AR
KMAG(FM) Fort Smith AR
KTCS-FM Fort Smith AR
KWXE(FM) Glenwood AR
KWXI(FM) Glenwood AR
KYXK(FM) Gurdon AR
KWHF(FM) Harrisburg AR
KHOZ-FM Harrison AR

KFFA(AM) Helena AR
KHPA(FM) Hope AR
KKIK(FM) Horseshoe Bend AR
KQUS-FM Hot Springs AR
KFIN(FM) Jonesboro AR
KDXY(FM) Lake City AR
KSSN(FM) Little Rock AR
KVMA(AM) Magnolia AR
KBOK(AM) Malvern AR
KAMS(AM) Mammoth Spring AR
KBCN-FM Marshall AR
KENA(AM) Mena AR
KVOM-FM Morrilton AR
KPFM(FM) Mountain Home AR
KTLO(AM) Mountain Home AR
KWOZ(FM) Mountain View AR
KMTB(FM) Murfreesboro AR
KOKR(FM) Newport AR
KARV-FM Ola AR
KDYN(AM) Ozark AR
KDYN-FM Ozark AR
KPBQ-FM Pine Bluff AR
KHOM(FM) Salem AR
KWCK-FM Searcy AR
KZHE(FM) Stamps AR
KWAK(FM) Stuttgart AR
KFYX(FM) Texarkana AR
KOSY(AM) Texarkana AR
KRLW-FM Walnut Ridge AR
KWRF(AM) Warren AR
KWRF-FM Warren AR
KWYN(AM) Wynne AR
KWYN-FM Wynne AR
KAVV(FM) Benson AZ
KWCD(FM) Bisbee AZ
KMLE(FM) Chandler AZ
KFXR-FM Chinle AZ
KFPB(FM) Chino Valley AZ
KCUZ(AM) Clifton AZ
KVRD-FM Cottonwood AZ
KDAP-FM Douglas AZ
KTHQ(FM) Eagar AZ
KAFF(AM) Flagstaff AZ
KAFF-FM Flagstaff AZ
KRDE(FM) Globe AZ
KZUA(FM) Holbrook AZ
KFLG-FM Kingman AZ
KGMN(FM) Kingman AZ
KJJJ(FM) Lake Havasu City AZ
KQSS(FM) Miami AZ
KPGE(FM) Page AZ
KLPZ(AM) Parker AZ
KMOG(AM) Payson AZ
KNIX-FM Phoenix AZ
KTMG(FM) Prescott AZ
KBUX(FM) Quartzsite AZ
KXKQ(FM) Safford AZ
KSED(FM) Sedona AZ
KFMM(FM) Thatcher AZ
*KGHR(FM) Tuba City AZ
KIIM-FM Tucson AZ
KSWG(FM) Wickenburg AZ
KHIL(AM) Willcox AZ
KWCX(FM) Willcox AZ
KTNN(AM) Window Rock AZ
KINO(AM) Winslow AZ
*KAWC(AM) Yuma AZ
KTTI(FM) Yuma AZ
KCNO(FM) Alturas CA
KBYN(FM) Arnold CA
KIXF(FM) Baker CA
KCWR(FM) Bakersfield CA
KUZZ(AM) Bakersfield CA
KUZZ-FM Bakersfield CA
KIBS(FM) Bishop CA
KROP(AM) Brawley CA
KUSS(FM) Carlsbad CA
KKCY(FM) Colusa CA
KPOD-FM Crescent City CA
KWST(AM) El Centro CA
KSOQ-FM Escondido CA
KEKA-FM Eureka CA
KRED-FM Eureka CA
KQEQ(AM) Fowler CA
KSKS(FM) Fresno CA
KATJ(AM) George CA
KFGY(FM) Healdsburg CA

*KIDE(FM) Hoopa CA
KCNQ(FM) Kernville CA
KRKC(AM) King City CA
KIXW-FM Lenwood CA
KCAA(AM) Loma Linda CA
KZLA-FM Los Angeles CA
KRTY(FM) Los Gatos CA
KTOM-FM Marina CA
KUBB(FM) Mariposa CA
KATM(FM) Modesto CA
*KSMC(FM) Moraga CA
KPLM(FM) Palm Springs CA
KHSL-FM Paradise CA
KKAL(FM) Paso Robles CA
KYOE(FM) Point Arena CA
KALF(FM) Red Bluff CA
KNCQ(FM) Redding CA
KLOA-FM Ridgecrest CA
KWDJ(AM) Ridgecrest CA
KRPQ(FM) Rohnert Park CA
KNCI(FM) Sacramento CA
KPRC-FM Salinas CA
KFRG(FM) San Bernardino CA
KTDD(AM) San Bernardino CA
KSON-FM San Diego CA
KUUS(FM) San Joaquin CA
KKJG(FM) San Luis Obispo CA
KSNI-FM Santa Maria CA
KRAZ(FM) Santa Ynez CA
KXFG(FM) Sun City CA
KJDX(FM) Susanville CA
KTPI-FM Tehachapi CA
KJUG(AM) Tulare CA
KJUG-FM Tulare CA
KFLS-FM Tulelake CA
KKBN(FM) Twain Harte CA
KXCM(FM) Twentynine Palms CA
KQPM(FM) Ukiah CA
KUKI(FM) Ukiah CA
KHAY(FM) Ventura CA
KVFG(FM) Victorville CA
KSYC-FM Yreka CA
KALQ-FM Alamosa CO
KBVC(FM) Buena Vista CO
KNAB-FM Burlington CO
KSTY(FM) Canon City CO
KKCS-FM Colorado Springs CO
KISZ-FM Cortez CO
*KSJD(FM) Cortez CO
KRAI(AM) Craig CO
KYGO-FM Denver CO
KRSJ(FM) Durango CO
KXDC(FM) Estes Park CO
KEKB(FM) Fruita CO
KMTS(FM) Glenwood Springs CO
KRKY(AM) Granby CO
KMOZ-FM Grand Junction CO
KPKE(FM) Gunnison CO
KJBL(FM) Julesburg CO
KTHN(FM) La Junta CO
KCKK(AM) Lakewood CO
KLMR(FM) Lamar CO
KVAY(FM) Lamar CO
KAVD(FM) Limon CO
KAYW(FM) Meeker CO
KSLV(FM) Monte Vista CO
KKXK(FM) Montrose CO
KUBC(AM) Montrose CO
KRYD(FM) Norwood CO
KATR-FM Otis CO
KWUF(FM) Pagosa Springs CO
KCCY(FM) Pueblo CO
KZKS(FM) Rifle CO
KBCR(AM) Steamboat Springs CO
KBCR-FM Steamboat Springs CO
KNNG(FM) Sterling CO
KJEB(FM) Strasburg CO
KCRT(FM) Trinidad CO
KSKE-FM Vail CO
KSPK(FM) Walsenburg CO
KUAD-FM Windsor CO
WPKX(FM) Enfield CT
WCTY(FM) Norwich CT
WWYZ(FM) Waterbury CT
WMZQ-FM Washington DC
WXJN(FM) Lewes DE
WDSD(FM) Smyrna DE

WWOJ(FM) Avon Park FL
WQXM(FM) Bartow FL
WBGF(FM) Belle Glade FL
WPHK(FM) Blountstown FL
WYBT(FM) Blountstown FL
WKIS(FM) Boca Raton FL
WFUS(FM) Bradenton FL
WAKT-FM Callaway FL
WOCY(FM) Carrabelle FL
WIKX(FM) Charlotte Harbor FL
WAFC-FM Clewiston FL
WAAZ-FM Crestview FL
WJSB(AM) Crestview FL
WYNY(AM) Cross City FL
WZEP(AM) De Funiak Springs FL
WTRS(FM) Dunnellon FL
WKRO-FM Edgewater FL
WWGR(FM) Fort Myers FL
WDVH(AM) Gainesville FL
WGWD(FM) Gretna FL
WNRP(FM) Gulf Breeze FL
WYGC(FM) High Springs FL
WQIK-FM Jacksonville FL
WROO(FM) Jacksonville FL
WQHL-FM Live Oak FL
WMAF(AM) Madison FL
WJAQ(FM) Marianna FL
WTYS(AM) Marianna FL
WYZB(FM) Mary Esther FL
WXBM-FM Milton FL
*WBGY(FM) Naples FL
WOGK(FM) Ocala FL
WOKC(AM) Okeechobee FL
WWKA(FM) Orlando FL
WGNE-FM Palatka FL
WIYD(AM) Palatka FL
WPAP-FM Panama City FL
WYCT(FM) Pensacola FL
WNFK(FM) Perry FL
WCTH(FM) Plantation Key FL
WCKT(FM) Port Charlotte FL
WHKR(FM) Rockledge FL
WAOC(AM) Saint Augustine FL
WQYK-FM Saint Petersburg FL
WUSV(FM) San Carlos Park FL
WCTQ(FM) Sarasota FL
WAVW(FM) Stuart FL
WAIB(FM) Tallahassee FL
WTNT-FM Tallahassee FL
WDVH-FM Trenton FL
WQLC(FM) Watertown FL
WIRK-FM West Palm Beach FL
WPCV(FM) Winter Haven FL
WZZS(FM) Zolfo Springs FL
*V6AI(AM) Yap FM
WKAK(FM) Albany GA
WAJQ-FM Alma GA
WISK-FM Americus GA
WIBL(FM) Augusta GA
WBAF(AM) Barnesville GA
WBYZ(FM) Baxley GA
WKUB(FM) Blackshear GA
WBBK(AM) Blakely GA
WBBK-FM Blakely GA
WPPL(FM) Blue Ridge GA
WTUF(FM) Boston GA
WMOQ(FM) Bostwick GA
WRJY(FM) Brunswick GA
WJTH(AM) Calhoun GA
WCHK(FM) Canton GA
WBTR-FM Carrollton GA
WQMT(FM) Chatsworth GA
WRWH(AM) Cleveland GA
WDXQ(AM) Cochran GA
WDXQ-FM Cochran GA
WJJC(AM) Commerce GA
WCON(AM) Cornelia GA
WCON-FM Cornelia GA
WCUG(AM) Cuthbert GA
WKHC(FM) Dahlonega GA
WSEM(AM) Donalsonville GA
WOKA-FM Douglas GA
WQZY(FM) Dublin GA
WXLI(AM) Dublin GA
WUFF(AM) Eastman GA
WUFF-FM Eastman GA
WSGC-FM Elberton GA

Programming on Radio Stations in the U.S.

WPGY(AM) Ellijay GA	KBOE(AM) Oskaloosa IA	WACF(FM) Paris IL	KZSN(FM) Hutchinson KS	WLBQ(AM) Morgantown KY
*WATY(FM) Folkston GA	KLEE(AM) Ottumwa IA	WXCL(FM) Pekin IL	KJCK(AM) Junction City KS	WRVK(AM) Mt. Vernon KY
WYAY(FM) Gainesville GA	KCSI(FM) Red Oak IA	WBBA-FM Pittsfield IL	KFKF-FM Kansas City KS	WLOC(AM) Munfordville KY
WHIE(AM) Griffin GA	KOAK(AM) Red Oak IA	KPCR(AM) Quincy IL	KLDG(FM) Liberal KS	WFGE(FM) Murray KY
WKLY(AM) Hartwell GA	KIHK(FM) Rock Valley IA	WCOY(FM) Quincy IL	KSLS(FM) Liberal KS	WLTO(FM) Nicholasville KY
WVOH-FM Hazlehurst GA	KIWA(AM) Sheldon IA	WJBD(AM) Salem IL	KXKU(FM) Lyons KS	WBKR(FM) Owensboro KY
WIFO-FM Jesup GA	KIWA-FM Sheldon IA	WCCI(FM) Savanna IL	KXBZ(FM) Manhattan KS	WKCA(FM) Owingsville KY
WKBX(FM) Kingsland GA	KICD-FM Spencer IA	WJVO(FM) South Jacksonville IL	KNDY(AM) Marysville KS	WKYQ(FM) Paducah KY
WQCH(AM) La Fayette GA	KKRF(FM) Stuart IA	WFMB-FM Springfield IL	KNDY-FM Marysville KS	WSIP-FM Paintsville KY
WPEH(AM) Louisville GA	KNEI-FM Waukon IA	WKJT(FM) Teutopolis IL	KFNF(FM) Oberlin KS	WBIO(FM) Philpot KY
WPEH-FM Louisville GA	KWAY(AM) Waverly IA	WSCH(FM) Aurora IN	KOFO(AM) Ottawa KS	WDHR(FM) Pikeville KY
WKCN(FM) Lumpkin GA	KJJY(FM) West Des Moines IA	WJCP(FM) Austin IN	KKOW(AM) Pittsburg KS	WLSI(AM) Pikeville KY
WLYU(FM) Lyons GA	KKYY(FM) Whiting IA	WRBI(FM) Batesville IN	KKOW-FM Pittsburg KS	WRIL(FM) Pineville KY
WAYS(AM) Macon GA	KFXD(AM) Boise ID	WLFF(FM) Brookston IN	KQTP(FM) Saint Marys KS	WDOC(AM) Prestonsburg KY
WDEN-FM Macon GA	KIZN(FM) Boise ID	WLFW(FM) Chandler IN	KSKG(FM) Salina KS	WRUS(AM) Russellville KY
WKHX-FM Marietta GA	KQFC(FM) Boise ID	WKKG(FM) Columbus IN	KYEZ(FM) Salina KS	WRLV-FM Salyersville KY
WKDG(FM) Martinez GA	KICR(FM) Coeur d'Alene ID	WCNB(AM) Connersville IN	KMZA(FM) Seneca KS	WVLE(FM) Scottsville KY
WMCG(FM) Milan GA	KORT(AM) Grangeville ID	WIFE(FM) Connersville IN	KTPK(FM) Topeka KS	WKEQ-FM Somerset KY
WKZR(FM) Milledgeville GA	KORT-FM Grangeville ID	WKZS(FM) Covington IN	WIBW-FM Topeka KS	WRSL(AM) Stanford KY
WHKN(FM) Millen GA	KID-FM Idaho Falls ID	WQHK-FM Decatur IN	KULY(AM) Ulysses KS	WSKV(FM) Stanton KY
WYUM(FM) Mount Vernon GA	KTHK(FM) Idaho Falls ID	WYGB(FM) Edinburgh IN	KFDI-FM Wichita KS	WKWY(FM) Tompkinsville KY
WALH(AM) Mountain City GA	KUPI-FM Idaho Falls ID	WBYT(FM) Elkhart IN	KFTI(AM) Wichita KS	WTKY(AM) Tompkinsville KY
WCOH(AM) Newnan GA	KART(AM) Jerome ID	WHCC(FM) Ellettsville IN	KSOK-FM Winfield KS	WTKY-FM Tompkinsville KY
WTIF-FM Omega GA	KMOK(AM) Lewiston ID	WQKZ(FM) Ferdinand IN	WANY(AM) Albany KY	WKKS(AM) Vanceburg KY
WTSH-FM Rockmart GA	KRLC(AM) Lewiston ID	WFLQ(FM) French Lick IN	WANY-FM Albany KY	WLKS-FM West Liberty KY
WGJK(AM) Rome GA	KDZY(FM) McCall ID	WREB(FM) Greencastle IN	WMDJ-FM Allen KY	WXKQ(FM) Whitesburg KY
WSNT-FM Sandersville GA	KVSI(AM) Montpelier ID	WTRE(AM) Greensburg IN	WDGG(FM) Ashland KY	WHAY(FM) Whitley City KY
WJCL-FM Savannah GA	KMHI(AM) Mountain Home ID	WBDC(FM) Huntingburg IN	WBVR-FM Auburn KY	WGKY(FM) Wickliffe KY
WXRS-FM Swainsboro GA	KLER(AM) Orofino ID	WFMS(FM) Indianapolis IN	WKKQ(FM) Barbourville KY	WEZJ(AM) Williamsburg KY
WSYL(AM) Sylvania GA	KOUU(AM) Pocatello ID	WAVG(AM) Jeffersonville IN	WBRT(AM) Bardstown KY	WEZJ-FM Williamsburg KY
WZBX(FM) Sylvania GA	KZBQ(FM) Pocatello ID	WBTU(FM) Kendallville IN	WCBL(AM) Benton KY	WNKR(FM) Williamstown KY
WKNG(AM) Tallapoosa GA	KKEX(FM) Preston ID	WIVR(FM) Kentland IN	WGGC(FM) Bowling Green KY	KROF(AM) Abbeville LA
WTHO-FM Thomson GA	KKMV(FM) Rupert ID	*WKPW(FM) Knightstown IN	WMMG(AM) Brandenburg KY	KRRV-FM Alexandria LA
WOBB(FM) Tifton GA	KIGO(AM) Saint Anthony ID	WWKI(FM) Kokomo IN	WMMG-FM Brandenburg KY	WABL(AM) Amite LA
WTIF(AM) Tifton GA	KOFE(AM) Saint Maries ID	WCOE(FM) La Porte IN	WXAM(AM) Buffalo KY	WTGE(FM) Baker LA
WNGC(FM) Toccoa GA	KSRA(AM) Salmon ID	WKOA(FM) Lafayette IN	WKYR-FM Burkesville KY	KBKK(FM) Ball LA
WAAC(AM) Valdosta GA	KSRA-FM Salmon ID	WLAS(AM) Lafayette IN	WKDZ-FM Cadiz KY	WYNK-FM Baton Rouge LA
WEBL(AM) Warner Robins GA	KIBR(FM) Sandpoint ID	WTHD(FM) Lagrange IN	WCCK(FM) Calvert City KY	WYPY(FM) Baton Rouge LA
WXKT(FM) Washington GA	KBRV(AM) Soda Springs ID	WBTO(AM) Linton IN	WIKI(FM) Carrollton KY	KQKI(FM) Bayou Vista LA
WYNR(FM) Waycross GA	KITT(FM) Soda Springs ID	WQTY(FM) Linton IN	WLLE(FM) Clinton KY	WBOX(AM) Bogalusa LA
WCJM-FM West Point GA	KEZJ-FM Twin Falls ID	WCBK-FM Martinsville IN	WAIN-FM Columbia KY	KSBH(FM) Coushatta LA
WKAA(FM) Willacoochee GA	KMQS(FM) Victor ID	WMCB(AM) Martinsville IN	WKDP(FM) Corbin KY	KEUN(AM) Eunice LA
WYHG(FM) Young Harris GA	KWAL(AM) Wallace ID	WQRJ(FM) Mitchell IN	WCPM(AM) Cumberland KY	KEUN-FM Eunice LA
WEKS(FM) Zebulon GA	WRMJ(FM) Aledo IL	WRCY(AM) Mount Vernon IN	WVEK-FM Cumberland KY	WUUU(FM) Franklinton LA
KUAI(AM) Eleele HI	WIBH(AM) Anna IL	WYFX(FM) Mount Vernon IN	WCYN-FM Cynthiana KY	KLEB(AM) Golden Meadow LA
KHCM(FM) Honolulu HI	WLCN(FM) Atlanta IL	WMDH-FM New Castle IN	WHSX(FM) Edmonton KY	WFPR(AM) Hammond LA
KDLX(FM) Makawao HI	WRMS-FM Beardstown IL	WPGW(FM) Portland IN	WFLE(AM) Flemingsburg KY	WHMD(FM) Hammond LA
KKOA(FM) Volcano HI	WLMD(AM) Bushnell IL	WRAY-FM Princeton IN	WFLE-FM Flemingsburg KY	KYLA(FM) Homer LA
KKNE(AM) Waipahu HI	WRUL(FM) Carmi IL	*WECI(FM) Richmond IN	WLVK(FM) Fort Knox KY	KCIL(FM) Houma LA
KLBA-FM Albia IA	WIXY(FM) Champaign IL	WQLK(FM) Richmond IN	WFKN(AM) Franklin KY	KJNA-FM Jena LA
WJOD(AM) Asbury IA	KSGM(AM) Chester IL	WHZR(FM) Royal Center IN	WFUL(AM) Fulton KY	KJEF(AM) Jennings LA
KSOM(FM) Audubon IA	WUSN(FM) Chicago IL	WKWH-FM Rushville IN	WLYE-FM Glasgow KY	KMDL(FM) Kaplan LA
KDMG(FM) Burlington IA	WCCQ(FM) Crest Hill IL	WSLM(AM) Salem IN	WGOH(AM) Grayson KY	KBXG(FM) Lake Charles LA
KOEL-FM Cedar Falls IA	WDZQ(FM) Decatur IL	WMPI(FM) Scottsburg IN	WAKY(AM) Greensburg KY	KYKZ(FM) Lake Charles LA
KHAK(FM) Cedar Rapids IA	WRCV(FM) Dixon IL	WQKC(FM) Seymour IN	WGRK-FM Greensburg KY	KJAE(FM) Leesville LA
KMGO(FM) Centerville IA	WDQN(AM) Du Quoin IL	WSKT(FM) Spencer IN	WLGC(AM) Greenup KY	KVVP(FM) Leesville LA
KIAQ(FM) Clarion IA	WCRC(FM) Effingham IL	WNDI(AM) Sullivan IN	WLGC-FM Greenup KY	KORI(FM) Mansfield LA
KZEG(FM) Clinton IA	WFYR(FM) Elmwood IL	WNDI-FM Sullivan IN	WULF(FM) Hardinsburg KY	KWLV(FM) Many LA
KSIB(AM) Creston IA	WOKZ(FM) Fairfield IL	WTHI-FM Terre Haute IN	WXBC(FM) Hardinsburg KY	KAPB-FM Marksville LA
KSIB-FM Creston IA	WFPS(FM) Freeport IL	WLJE(FM) Valparaiso IN	WTUK(FM) Harlan KY	KJLO-FM Monroe LA
WLLR-FM Davenport IA	WXXQ(FM) Freeport IL	WCJC(FM) Van Buren IN	WHBN(AM) Harrodsburg KY	KXKC(FM) New Iberia LA
KDSN(AM) Denison IA	WAAG(FM) Galesburg IL	WXCH(FM) Versailles IN	WKCM(AM) Hawesville KY	WNOE-FM New Orleans LA
KHKI(FM) Des Moines IA	KBOB-FM Geneseo IL	WKID(FM) Vevay IN	WSGS(FM) Hazard KY	KOGM(FM) Opelousas LA
KDST(FM) Dyersville IA	WLIE-FM Golconda IL	WFML(FM) Vincennes IN	WKDQ(FM) Henderson KY	KSLO(AM) Opelousas LA
KRKN(FM) Eldon IA	WGEL(FM) Greenville IL	WKUZ(FM) Wabash IN	WKMO(FM) Hodgenville KY	KMYY(FM) Rayville LA
KILR-FM Estherville IA	WEBQ(AM) Harrisburg IL	WWBL(FM) Washington IN	WVVR(FM) Hopkinsville KY	KXKZ(FM) Ruston LA
KIOW(FM) Forest City IA	WOOZ-FM Harrisburg IL	KSOK(AM) Arkansas City KS	WCYO(FM) Irvine KY	KRMD-FM Shreveport LA
KWMT(AM) Fort Dodge IA	WDUK(FM) Havana IL	KAIR(AM) Atchison KS	WEKG(AM) Jackson KY	KWKH(AM) Shreveport LA
KBKB-FM Fort Madison IA	WHPO(FM) Hoopeston IL	KREP(FM) Belleville KS	WJSN(FM) Jackson KY	KXKS-FM Shreveport LA
KCTN(FM) Garnavillo IA	WAKO(AM) Lawrenceville IL	KSNP(FM) Burlington KS	WJKY(AM) Jamestown KY	KLAA(FM) Tioga LA
KXKT(FM) Glenwood IA	WAKO-FM Lawrenceville IL	KCLY(FM) Clay Center KS	WJRS(FM) Jamestown KY	WBOX-FM Varnado LA
KLMJ(FM) Hampton IA	WBWN(FM) Le Roy IL	KWGB(FM) Colby KS	WBUL-FM Lexington KY	KNCB(AM) Vivian LA
KKIA(FM) Ida Grove IA	WSMI(AM) Litchfield IL	KXXX(AM) Colby KS	WLXX(FM) Lexington KY	KNCB-FM Vivian LA
KGRA(FM) Jefferson IA	WSMI-FM Litchfield IL	KNCK(FM) Concordia KS	WKDO(AM) Liberty KY	KVCL-FM Winnfield LA
KNIA(AM) Knoxville IA	WLUV(FM) Loves Park IL	KUSN(FM) Dearing KS	WKDO-FM Liberty KY	KMAR-FM Winnsboro LA
KIKD(FM) Lake City IA	WZUS(FM) Macon IL	KDNS(FM) Downs KS	WWEL(FM) London KY	WPVQ(FM) Greenfield MA
KMCH(FM) Manchester IA	WDDD-FM Marion IL	KVOE-FM Emporia KS	WAMZ(FM) Louisville KY	WKLB-FM Lowell MA
KMAQ(FM) Maquoketa IA	WMCI(FM) Mattoon IL	KOTE(FM) Eureka KS	WPTI(FM) Louisville KY	WCTK(FM) New Bedford MA
KXIA(FM) Marshalltown IA	WMCL(AM) McLeansboro IL	KKJQ(FM) Garden City KS	WFMW(AM) Madisonville KY	WUHN(AM) Pittsfield MA
KIAI(FM) Mason City IA	WGLC(FM) Mendota IL	KLOE(AM) Goodland KS	WKLB(FM) Manchester KY	WESO(AM) Southbridge MA
KILJ-FM Mount Pleasant IA	WMOK(AM) Metropolis IL	KHAZ(FM) Hays KS	WVLC(FM) Mannsville KY	WARE(AM) Ware MA
KWCC(FM) Muscatine IA	WFXN(AM) Moline IL	KNZA(FM) Hiawatha KS	WQQR(FM) Mayfield KY	WGFP(AM) Webster MA
KCZE(FM) New Hampton IA	WRAM(AM) Monmouth IL	KKQY(FM) Hill City KS	WWAG(FM) McKee KY	WOQL(FM) Winchendon MA
KCOB(AM) Newton IA	WMIX-FM Mount Vernon IL	KHOK(FM) Hoisington KS	WMKZ(FM) Monticello KY	WPOC(FM) Baltimore MD
KCOB-FM Newton IA	WALS(FM) Oglesby IL	KBUF(FM) Holcomb KS	WMOR(AM) Morehead KY	WKIK-FM California MD
KYTC(FM) Northwood IA	WSEI(FM) Olney IL	KAIR-FM Horton KS	WMSK(AM) Morganfield KY	WINX-FM Cambridge MD
KKHQ(FM) Oelwein IA	WMKR(FM) Pana IL	KHUT(FM) Hutchinson KS	WMSK-FM Morganfield KY	WBEY-FM Crisfield MD

Broadcasting & Cable Yearbook 2006

D-700

Programming on Radio Stations in the U.S.

WROG(FM) Cumberland MD	KTCO(FM) Duluth MN	KESM-FM El Dorado Springs MO	WAKH(FM) McComb MS	WKBC(AM) North Wilkesboro NC
WFRE(FM) Frederick MD	WELY(AM) Ely MN	KTJJ(FM) Farmington MO	WOKK(FM) Meridian MS	WLQB(FM) Ocean Isle Beach NC
WFRB-FM Frostburg MD	KSUM(AM) Fairmont MN	KFAL(AM) Fulton MO	WRQO(FM) Monticello MS	WWHA(FM) Oriental NC
WAYZ(FM) Hagerstown MD	KBRF(FM) Fergus Falls MN	KGOZ(FM) Gallatin MO	WBUV(FM) Moss Point MS	WQDR(FM) Raleigh NC
WXCY(FM) Havre de Grace MD	KJJK-FM Fergus Falls MN	KBTC(AM) Houston MO	WQNZ(FM) Natchez MS	WCBT(AM) Roanoke Rapids NC
WAAI(FM) Hurlock MD	KSDM(FM) International Falls MN	KUNQ(FM) Houston MO	WWZD-FM New Albany MS	WPTM(FM) Roanoke Rapids NC
WKIK(AM) La Plata MD	KKOJ(AM) Jackson MN	KYLS-FM Ironton MO	WWMS(FM) Oxford MS	WCVP-FM Robbinsville NC
WWHC(FM) Oakland MD	KMFX-FM Lake City MN	KIXQ(FM) Joplin MO	WKNN-FM Pascagoula MS	WDWG(FM) Rocky Mount NC
WWFG(FM) Ocean City MD	KLTF(FM) Little Falls MN	KBEQ-FM Kansas City MO	WRJW(AM) Picayune MS	WKRX(FM) Roxboro NC
WICO-FM Salisbury MD	WYRQ(FM) Little Falls MN	KOTC(AM) Kennett MO	WJDR(FM) Prentiss MS	WCAB(AM) Rutherfordton NC
WTHT(FM) Auburn ME	KEYL(AM) Long Prairie MN	KTUF(FM) Kirksville MO	WYKK(FM) Quitman MS	WWGP(AM) Sanford NC
WLKE(FM) Bar Harbor ME	KLQL(FM) Luverne MN	KXKX(FM) Knob Noster MO	WKZU(FM) Ripley MS	WADA(AM) Shelby NC
WBFB(FM) Belfast ME	KLQP(FM) Madison MN	KCLQ(FM) Lebanon MO	WQJB(FM) State College MS	WMPM(FM) Smithfield NC
WQCB(FM) Brewer ME	KYSM-FM Mankato MN	KJEL(FM) Lebanon MO	WBBN(FM) Taylorsville MS	WKQB(FM) Southern Pines NC
WCTB(FM) Fairfield ME	KDMA(AM) Montevideo MN	KLWT(AM) Lebanon MO	WTYL(AM) Tylertown MS	WCOK(AM) Sparta NC
WTBM(FM) Mexico ME	KVOX-FM Moorhead MN	KJFM(FM) Louisiana MO	WTYL-FM Tylertown MS	WFMX(FM) Statesville NC
WSYY-FM Millinocket ME	KKOK-FM Morris MN	KLTI(FM) Macon MO	WBBV(FM) Vicksburg MS	WKKT(FM) Statesville NC
WOXO-FM Norway ME	KCHK(AM) New Prague MN	KMMO(AM) Marshall MO	WABO(AM) Waynesboro MS	WTAB(AM) Tabor City NC
WPOR(FM) Portland ME	KNUJ(AM) New Ulm MN	KMMO(FM) Marshall MO	WABO-FM Waynesboro MS	WACB(AM) Taylorsville NC
WBPW(FM) Presque Isle ME	KBLB(FM) Nisswa MN	KMEM-FM Memphis MO	WIGG(AM) Wiggins MS	WKSK(AM) West Jefferson NC
WMCM(FM) Rockland ME	KOLV(FM) Olivia MN	KWWR(FM) Mexico MO	WONA(AM) Winona MS	WWQQ-FM Wilmington NC
WEBB(FM) Waterville ME	KDIO(AM) Ortonville MN	KRES(FM) Moberly MO	WONA-FM Winona MS	WTQR(FM) Winston-Salem NC
WTVL(AM) Waterville ME	KRFO-FM Owatonna MN	KELE(AM) Mountain Grove MO	KFLN(AM) Baker MT	*KEYA(FM) Belcourt ND
WUBB(FM) York Center ME	KPRM(AM) Park Rapids MN	KELE-FM Mountain Grove MO	KCTR-FM Billings MT	KBMR(AM) Bismarck ND
WQTE(FM) Adrian MI	KXKK(FM) Park Rapids MN	KBTN(AM) Neosho MO	KGHL(AM) Billings MT	KKCT(FM) Bismarck ND
WATZ-FM Alpena MI	KZPK(FM) Paynesville MN	KBTN-FM Neosho MO	KGHL-FM Billings MT	KQDY(FM) Bismarck ND
WWWW(FM) Ann Arbor MI	KBOT(FM) Pelican Rapids MN	KNEM(AM) Nevada MO	KBOZ-FM Bozeman MT	KBTO(FM) Bottineau ND
WLEW(AM) Bad Axe MI	WWWI-FM Pillager MN	KNMO(FM) Nevada MO	KAAR(FM) Butte MT	KPOK(AM) Bowman ND
WHFB-FM Benton Harbor MI	WCMP-FM Pine City MN	KTMO(FM) New Madrid MO	*KMSM-FM Butte MT	KDAK(AM) Carrington ND
WBCM(FM) Boyne City MI	KLOH(AM) Pipestone MN	KOMG(FM) Ozark MO	KIKF(FM) Cascade MT	KYNU(FM) Carrington ND
WYTZ(FM) Bridgman MI	KFIL(AM) Preston MN	KICK-FM Palmyra MO	KBCK(AM) Deer Lodge MT	KAOC(FM) Cavalier ND
WKYO(AM) Caro MI	KFIL-FM Preston MN	KBDZ(FM) Perryville MO	KQRV(FM) Deer Lodge MT	KDLR(AM) Devils Lake ND
WNWN-FM Coldwater MI	KLCI(FM) Princeton MN	KPWB(FM) Piedmont MO	KDBM(FM) Dillon MT	KZZY(FM) Devils Lake ND
WYCD(FM) Detroit MI	WQPM(AM) Princeton MN	KKLR(FM) Poplar Bluff MO	KHKR-FM East Helena MT	KCAD(FM) Dickinson ND
WYKX(FM) Escanaba MI	KLGR(FM) Redwood Falls MN	KPPL(FM) Poplar Bluff MO	KIKC-FM Forsyth MT	KLTC(AM) Dickinson ND
WCXI(AM) Fenton MI	KWWK(FM) Rochester MN	KYRO(AM) Potosi MO	KLTZ(AM) Glasgow MT	KKBX(FM) Fargo ND
WFBE(FM) Flint MI	KWNO-FM Rushford MN	KMOZ(AM) Rolla MO	KDZN(FM) Glendive MT	KXPO(AM) Grafton ND
WGDN-FM Gladwin MI	WWJO(FM) Saint Cloud MN	KZNN(FM) Rolla MO	KMON(AM) Great Falls MT	KNOX-FM Grand Forks ND
WBCT(FM) Grand Rapids MI	KRRW(FM) Saint James MN	KSD(FM) Saint Louis MO	KMON-FM Great Falls MT	KNDC(AM) Hettinger ND
WGRY-FM Grayling MI	KEEY-FM Saint Paul MN	WIL(AM) Saint Louis MO	KPQX(FM) Havre MT	KSJB(AM) Jamestown ND
WCMM(FM) Gulliver MI	KRBI(AM) Saint Peter MN	WIL-FM Saint Louis MO	KBLL-FM Helena MT	KNDK(AM) Langdon ND
WBCH(AM) Hastings MI	KIKV-FM Sauk Centre MN	KKID(FM) Salem MO	KDBR(FM) Kalispell MT	KQLX-FM Lisbon ND
WBCH-FM Hastings MI	WVAL(AM) Sauk Rapids MN	KSMO(AM) Salem MO	KLCM(FM) Lewistown MT	KMAV(AM) Mayville ND
WCEN-FM Hemlock MI	KJOE(FM) Slayton MN	KSJQ(FM) Savannah MO	KLCB(AM) Libby MT	KMAV-FM Mayville ND
WTNR(FM) Holland MI	KQYB(FM) Spring Grove MN	KDRO(AM) Sedalia MO	KMMR(FM) Malta MT	KCJB(AM) Minot ND
WVIB(FM) Holton MI	KNSP(AM) Staples MN	KQMO(FM) Shell Knob MO	KKRY(FM) Miles City MT	KYYX(FM) Minot ND
WHKB(FM) Houghton MI	KKAQ(AM) Thief River Falls MN	KBXB(FM) Sikeston MO	KGGL(FM) Missoula MT	KDDR(AM) Oakes ND
WJNR-FM Iron Mountain MI	KKDQ(FM) Thief River Falls MN	KRHW(AM) Sikeston MO	KYSS-FM Missoula MT	KZZJ(AM) Rugby ND
WJMS(AM) Ironwood MI	KARL(FM) Tracy MN	KTTS-FM Springfield MO	KATQ(AM) Plentywood MT	KTGO(AM) Tioga ND
WJPD(FM) Ishpeming MI	KVKK(FM) Verndale MN	KRWP(FM) Stockton MO	KATQ-FM Plentywood MT	KOVC(AM) Valley City ND
WSCG(FM) Lakeview MI	WUSZ(FM) Virginia MN	KTUI-FM Sullivan MO	KERR(AM) Polson MT	KDSR(FM) Williston ND
WCUP(FM) L'Anse MI	KMFX(AM) Wabasha MN	KSAR(FM) Thayer MO	KCGM(FM) Scobey MT	KEYZ(AM) Williston ND
WITL-FM Lansing MI	KKWS(FM) Wadena MN	KTTN-FM Trenton MO	KZIN-FM Shelby MT	KYYZ(FM) Williston ND
WBGV(FM) Marlette MI	KWAD(AM) Wadena MN	KLPW(FM) Union MO	KLTC-FM Superior MT	KBRB(AM) Ainsworth NE
WFXD(FM) Marquette MI	KXSS(AM) Waite Park MN	KKAC(FM) Vandalia MO	KVCK-FM Wolf Point MT	KUSO(FM) Albion NE
WHYB(FM) Menominee MI	KKWQ(FM) Warroad MN	KTKS(FM) Versailles MO	WQDK(FM) Ahoskie NC	KAAQ(FM) Alliance NE
WAVC(FM) Mio MI	KRUE(FM) Waseca MN	KFAV(FM) Warrenton MO	WKXR(AM) Asheboro NC	KNCY-FM Auburn NE
WKBZ(AM) Muskegon MI	KDJS-FM Willmar MN	KWRE(AM) Warrenton MO	WKSF(FM) Asheville NC	KRGY(FM) Aurora NE
WMUS(FM) Muskegon MI	KDOM(AM) Windom MN	KAYQ(FM) Warsaw MO	WNBB(FM) Bayboro NC	KOLT-FM Bridgeport NE
WNBY(AM) Newberry MI	KDOM-FM Windom MN	KKDY(FM) West Plains MO	WPYB(AM) Benson NC	KCNI(AM) Broken Bow NE
WUPY(FM) Ontonagon MI	KAGE(FM) Winona MN	WBLE(FM) Batesville MS	WKYK(FM) Burnsville NC	KZEN(FM) Central City NE
WSAQ(FM) Port Huron MI	KWXD(FM) Asbury MO	WIZK(AM) Bay Springs MS	WSME(FM) Camp Lejeune NC	KCSR(AM) Chadron NE
WKCQ(FM) Saginaw MI	KSWF(FM) Aurora MO	WZKX(FM) Bay St. Louis MS	WPTL(AM) Canton NC	KQSK(FM) Chadron NE
WMKC(FM) Saint Ignace MI	KKOZ(AM) Ava MO	WBYP(FM) Belzoni MS	WSOC-FM Charlotte NC	KUTT(FM) Fairbury NE
WMLM(AM) Saint Louis MI	KAAN(AM) Bethany MO	WBIP(AM) Booneville MS	WRSF(FM) Columbia NC	KSDZ(FM) Gordon NE
WSDS(AM) Salem Township MI	KAAN-FM Bethany MO	WBKN(FM) Brookhaven MS	WWNK(FM) Farmville NC	KRGI-FM Grand Island NE
WMIC(FM) Sandusky MI	KYOO(AM) Bolivar MO	WCKK(FM) Carthage MS	WNCC-FM Franklin NC	KRNY(FM) Kearney NE
WKZC(FM) Scottville MI	KCLR-FM Boonville MO	WZFL-FM Centreville MS	WKIX(FM) Goldsboro NC	KIMB(AM) Kimball NE
WKJC(FM) Tawas City MI	KWRT(AM) Boonville MO	WKDJ-FM Clarksdale MS	WJSG(FM) Hamlet NC	KRVN(AM) Lexington NE
WLKM(AM) Three Rivers MI	KRZK(FM) Branson MO	WDTL-FM Cleveland MS	WWOC(FM) Hatteras NC	KRVN-FM Lexington NE
WTCM-FM Traverse City MI	KMAM(AM) Butler MO	WMJW(FM) Cleveland MS	WIZS(AM) Henderson NC	KIOD(FM) McCook NE
KRJB(FM) Ada MN	KMOE(FM) Butler MO	WFFF(AM) Columbia MS	WMMY(FM) Jefferson NC	KFGE(FM) Milford NE
KKIN-FM Aitkin MN	KATI(FM) California MO	WKOR-FM Columbus MS	WRNS-FM Kinston NC	KNCY(AM) Nebraska City NE
KASM(AM) Albany MN	KRLL(AM) California MO	WADI(FM) Corinth MS	WKGX(FM) Lenoir NC	KXNP(FM) North Platte NE
KAUS-FM Austin MN	KEZS-FM Cape Girardeau MO	WDMS(FM) Greenville MS	WKVS(FM) Lenoir NC	KMCX(FM) Ogallala NE
KKCQ-FM Bagley MN	KAOL(AM) Carrollton MO	WABG(AM) Greenwood MS	WKXU(FM) Louisburg NC	KBRX-FM O'Neill NE
KBHP(FM) Bemidji MN	KMZU(FM) Carrollton MO	WQBX(FM) Grenada MS	WYRN(AM) Louisburg NC	KOIL(AM) Plattsmouth NE
WBJI(FM) Blackduck MN	KCRV(FM) Caruthersville MO	WYKC(FM) Grenada MS	WKML(FM) Lumberton NC	KNEB(AM) Scottsbluff NE
KBEW-FM Blue Earth MN	KRMO(AM) Cassville MO	WGCM(FM) Gulfport MS	WBRM(AM) Marion NC	KNEB-FM Scottsbluff NE
KUAL-FM Brainerd MN	KCHR(AM) Charleston MO	WCPC(AM) Houston MS	WDSL(AM) Mocksville NC	KZKX(FM) Seward NE
KBMW(AM) Breckenridge MN	KWKZ(FM) Charleston MO	WFXO(FM) Iuka MS	WIXE(AM) Monroe NC	KSID(AM) Sidney NE
KRWC(AM) Buffalo MN	KDKD-FM Clinton MO	WMSI(FM) Jackson MS	WMNC(AM) Morganton NC	KRFS-FM Superior NE
KGPZ(FM) Coleraine MN	KESY(FM) Cuba MO	WUSJ(FM) Jackson MS	WMNC-FM Morganton NC	KVSH(AM) Valentine NE
KROX(AM) Crookston MN	KDEX(AM) Dexter MO	WAGR-FM Lexington MS	WPAQ(AM) Mount Airy NC	KTCH(AM) Wayne NE
KARP-FM Dassel MN	KDEX-FM Dexter MO	WLSM-FM Louisville MS	WSYD(FM) Mount Airy NC	KTIC(AM) West Point NE
KRCQ(FM) Detroit Lakes MN	KOEA(FM) Doniphan MO	WRBE(FM) Lucedale MS	WKRK(FM) Murphy NC	KSUX(FM) Winnebago NE
KKCB(FM) Duluth MN	KESM(AM) El Dorado Springs MO	WYYW(FM) Marion MS	WECR(FM) Newland NC	WNHW(FM) Belmont NH

Broadcasting & Cable Yearbook 2006

D-701

Programming on Radio Stations in the U.S.

WOKQ(FM) Dover NH	WDLA-FM Walton NY	KKNG-FM Newcastle OK	WHVR(AM) Hanover PA	WNAX(AM) Yankton SD
WYKR-FM Haverhill NH	WCJW(AM) Warsaw NY	KRIG-FM Nowata OK	WRBT(AM) Harrisburg PA	WNAX-FM Yankton SD
WYRY(FM) Hinsdale NH	WFRY-FM Watertown NY	KTST(FM) Oklahoma City OK	WPSN(AM) Honesdale PA	WSLV(AM) Ardmore TN
WXXK(FM) Lebanon NH	WTYX(AM) Watkins Glen NY	KXXY-FM Oklahoma City OK	WHUN(AM) Huntingdon PA	WQSV(AM) Ashland City TN
WSCY(FM) Moultonborough NH	WLSV(AM) Wellsville NY	KPNC-FM Ponca City OK	WKYE(FM) Johnstown PA	WJSQ(FM) Athens TN
WNTK(AM) Newport NH	WNYV(AM) Whitehall NY	KOMS(FM) Poteau OK	WNTJ(AM) Johnstown PA	WLAR(AM) Athens TN
WPKQ(FM) North Conway NH	WNCO-FM Ashland OH	KMUR(AM) Pryor OK	WLMI(FM) Kane PA	WGOC(AM) Blountville TN
WINQ(FM) Winchester NH	WNUS(FM) Belpre OH	KIRC(AM) Seminole OK	WADV(AM) Lebanon PA	WMOD(FM) Bolivar TN
WOF(AM) Andover NJ	WAIS(AM) Buchtel OH	KGFY(FM) Stillwater OK	WYNS(AM) Lehighton PA	WXBQ-FM Bristol TN
WPUR(FM) Atlantic City NJ	WWKC(FM) Caldwell OH	*KLRB(FM) Stuart OK	WGYY(FM) Meadville PA	WTBG(FM) Brownsville TN
KZZX(FM) Alamogordo NM	WKKJ(FM) Chillicothe OH	KIXO(FM) Sulphur OK	WJUN-FM Mexico PA	WFWL(AM) Camden TN
KBQI(FM) Albuquerque NM	WUBE-FM Cincinnati OH	KEOK(FM) Tahlequah OK	WWBE(AM) Mifflinburg PA	WUCZ-FM Carthage TN
KRST(FM) Albuquerque NM	WGAR-FM Cleveland OH	KVOO-FM Tulsa OK	WGYI(FM) Oil City PA	WVFB(FM) Celina TN
KTZA(FM) Artesia NM	WCOL-FM Columbus OH	KWEN(FM) Tulsa OK	WOGG(FM) Oliver PA	WNKX(AM) Centerville TN
KNFT-FM Bayard NM	WTNS(AM) Coshocton OH	KITO(AM) Vinita OK	WXTU(FM) Philadelphia PA	WNKX-FM Centerville TN
KARS(AM) Belen NM	WHKO(FM) Dayton OH	KITO-FM Vinita OK	WPHB(AM) Philipsburg PA	WUSY(FM) Cleveland TN
KATK-FM Carlsbad NM	WZOM(FM) Defiance OH	KTFX-FM Warner OK	WDSY-FM Pittsburgh PA	WLVS-FM Clifton TN
KLMX(AM) Clayton NM	WOGF(FM) East Liverpool OH	KWEY(AM) Weatherford OK	WLGL(FM) Riverside PA	*WDVX(FM) Clinton TN
KCLV-FM Clovis NM	WEDI(AM) Eaton OH	KWEY-FM Weatherford OK	WDDH(FM) Saint Marys PA	WYSH(AM) Clinton TN
KKYC(FM) Clovis NM	WKKY(FM) Geneva OH	KWSH(AM) Wewoka OK	WBYL(FM) Salladasburg PA	WMCP(AM) Columbia TN
KOTS(AM) Deming NM	WAXZ(FM) Georgetown OH	KWFX(FM) Woodward OK	WGGY(FM) Scranton PA	WGSQ(FM) Cookeville TN
KTRA-FM Farmington NM	WSRW-FM Hillsboro OH	KWOX(FM) Woodward OK	WYGL(FM) Selinsgrove PA	WHUB(AM) Cookeville TN
KGLX(FM) Gallup NM	WKFM(FM) Huron OH	KRKT-FM Albany OR	WBLJ-FM Shamokin PA	WLSB(AM) Copperhill TN
KYVA(AM) Gallup NM	WCJO(FM) Jackson OH	KTHH(AM) Albany OR	*WRSK(FM) Slippery Rock PA	WKBL(AM) Covington TN
KIXN(FM) Hobbs NM	WHOK(FM) Lancaster OH	KCMB(FM) Baker City OR	WNTW(AM) Somerset PA	WZYX(AM) Cowan TN
KPER(FM) Hobbs NM	WYGY(FM) Lebanon OH	KMTK(FM) Bend OR	WKZV(FM) Washington PA	WOWF(FM) Crossville TN
KWNM(FM) Hurley NM	WFGF(FM) Lima OH	KURY(AM) Brookings OR	WCBG(AM) Waynesboro PA	WDKN(AM) Dickson TN
KRSY-FM La Luz NM	WIMT(FM) Lima OH	KZZR(AM) Burns OR	WANB-FM Waynesburg PA	WSDQ(AM) Dunlap TN
KGRT-FM Las Cruces NM	WLGN(AM) Logan OH	KJDY-FM Canyon City OR	WXXP(FM) Waynesburg PA	WOGT(FM) East Ridge TN
KFUN(AM) Las Vegas NM	WLGN-FM Logan OH	KSHR-FM Coquille OR	WILQ(FM) Williamsport PA	WBEJ(AM) Elizabethton TN
KWMW(FM) Maljamar NM	WMRN-FM Marion OH	KNND(AM) Cottage Grove OR	WQXA(AM) York PA	WEMB(AM) Erwin TN
KSEL-FM Portales NM	WUCO(AM) Marysville OH	KUJZ(FM) Creswell OR	WCNX(AM) Hope Valley RI	WPFD(AM) Fairview TN
*KTDB(FM) Ramah NM	WQMX(FM) Medina OH	KWVR-FM Enterprise OR	WKXC-FM Aiken SC	WEKR(AM) Fayetteville TN
KBKZ(FM) Raton NM	WPFB-FM Middletown OH	KCST-FM Florence OR	WDOG(AM) Allendale SC	WYTM-FM Fayetteville TN
KMOU(FM) Roswell NM	WLZZ(FM) Montpelier OH	KSHL(FM) Gleneden Beach OR	WDOG-FM Allendale SC	WAKM(AM) Franklin TN
KWES(FM) Ruidoso NM	WSEO(FM) Nelsonville OH	KGBR(FM) Gold Beach OR	WAGS(AM) Bishopville SC	WHIN(AM) Gallatin TN
KKRG(FM) Santa Fe NM	WCLT-FM Newark OH	KRWQ(FM) Gold Hill OR	WGZR(FM) Bluffton SC	WGRV(AM) Greeneville TN
KSSR(AM) Santa Rosa NM	WOBL(AM) Oberlin OH	KOHU(AM) Hermiston OR	WGTR(FM) Bucksport SC	WXJB(FM) Harrogate TN
KMXQ(FM) Socorro NM	WNXT(AM) Portsmouth OH	KIHR(AM) Hood River OR	WEZL(FM) Charleston SC	WTNK(AM) Hartsville TN
KCHS(AM) Truth or Consequences NM	WPAY-FM Portsmouth OH	KJDY(AM) John Day OR	WVSZ(FM) Chesterfield SC	WMUF-FM Henry TN
KTNM(AM) Tucumcari NM	WAOL(FM) Ripley OH	KLAD-FM Klamath Falls OR	WCOS-FM Columbia SC	WMLR(FM) Hohenwald TN
KBUL-FM Carson City NV	WQXK(FM) Salem OH	KQIK(AM) Lakeview OR	WHZQ(FM) Cross Hill SC	WVHR(FM) Huntingdon TN
KRJC(FM) Elko NV	WCKY-FM Tiffin OH	KXPC(FM) Lebanon OR	WWNQ(FM) Forest Acres SC	WTNV(FM) Jackson TN
KDSS(FM) Ely NV	WKKO(FM) Toledo OH	*KBUG(FM) Malin OR	WAGI(FM) Gaffney SC	WDEB(AM) Jamestown TN
KVLV(AM) Fallon NV	WTOD(FM) Toledo OH	KNCU(FM) Newport OR	WSSL-FM Gray Court SC	WDEB-FM Jamestown TN
KCMY(FM) Gardnerville-Minden NV	WTUZ(FM) Uhrichsville OH	KSRV-FM Ontario OR	WESC-FM Greenville SC	WJFC(AM) Jefferson City TN
KWNR(FM) Henderson NV	WTGR(FM) Union City OH	KWHT(FM) Pendleton OR	WBHC-FM Hampton SC	WIVK-FM Knoxville TN
KWLY(FM) Moapa Valley NV	WYNT(FM) Upper Sandusky OH	KAKT(FM) Phoenix OR	WHGS(AM) Hampton SC	WQLA-FM La Follette TN
KUUB(FM) Sun Valley NV	WKSW(FM) Urbana OH	KCMD(FM) Portland OR	WJDJ(AM) Hartsville SC	WEEN(AM) Lafayette TN
KWNA-FM Winnemucca NV	WCHO-FM Washington Court House OH	KUPL-FM Portland OR	WHYM(AM) Lake City SC	WLCT(FM) Lafayette TN
WGNA-FM Albany NY	WXIZ(FM) Waverly OH	KWJJ-FM Portland OR	WRHM(FM) Lancaster SC	WDXE(AM) Lawrenceburg TN
WZKZ(FM) Alfred NY	WRAC(FM) West Union OH	KRCO(AM) Prineville OR	WYMB(AM) Manning SC	WLLX(FM) Lawrenceburg TN
WZMR(FM) Altamont NY	WKLN(FM) Wilmington OH	KSJJ(FM) Redmond OR	WHLZ(FM) Marion SC	WWLX(FM) Lawrenceburg TN
WHWK(FM) Binghamton NY	WQKT(FM) Wooster OH	KDUN(AM) Reedsport OR	WPCH(AM) North Augusta SC	WANT(FM) Lebanon TN
WBRV(AM) Boonville NY	WBZI(AM) Xenia OH	KRRM(FM) Rogue River OR	WNKT(FM) Saint George SC	WCOR(AM) Lebanon TN
WBRV-FM Boonville NY	KADA-FM Ada OK	KRNR(AM) Roseburg OR	WYAK-FM Surfside Beach SC	WLIL(AM) Lenoir City TN
WYRK(FM) Buffalo NY	KEYB(FM) Altus OK	KRSB-FM Roseburg OR	WBCU(AM) Union SC	WAXO(FM) Lewisburg TN
WNCQ-FM Canton NY	KWHW(AM) Altus OK	KOHI(AM) Saint Helens OR	WGOG(FM) Walhalla SC	WJJM(AM) Lewisburg TN
WFFG-FM Corinth NY	KNID(FM) Alva OK	KCYS(FM) Seaside OR	WALI(FM) Walterboro SC	WJJM-FM Lewisburg TN
WFLR(AM) Dundee NY	KKAJ-FM Ardmore OK	KKNU(FM) Springfield-Eugene OR	KGIM(AM) Aberdeen SD	WLIV(AM) Livingston TN
WBUG-FM Fort Plain NY	KHKC-FM Atoka OK	KCKX(FM) Stayton OR	KBFS(AM) Belle Fourche SD	WGAP(AM) Maryville TN
WAMF(FM) Fulton NY	KREK(FM) Bristow OK	KFIR(AM) Sweet Home OR	KZZI(FM) Belle Fourche SD	WWYN(FM) McKenzie TN
WBBS(FM) Fulton NY	KKBI(AM) Broken Bow OK	WFGY(FM) Altoona PA	KWSF(FM) Flandreau SD	WBMC(AM) McMinnville TN
WFLK(FM) Geneva NY	KYKC(FM) Byng OK	WWSM(AM) Annville-Cleona PA	KZMX(AM) Hot Springs SD	WTRZ-FM McMinnville TN
WRWD-FM Highland NY	KKFC(FM) Coalgate OK	WQBR(FM) Avis PA	KZMX-FM Hot Springs SD	WGKX-FM Memphis TN
WCKR(FM) Hornell NY	KKEN(FM) Duncan OK	WGGI(FM) Benton PA	KOKK(AM) Huron SD	WLIV-FM Monterey TN
WPGI(FM) Horseheads NY	KLBC(FM) Durant OK	WOGH(FM) Burgettstown PA	KZNC(FM) Huron SD	WMCT(AM) Mountain City TN
WQNY(FM) Ithaca NY	KECO(FM) Elk City OK	WVNW(FM) Burnham PA	KBJM(AM) Lemmon SD	WKDF(FM) Nashville TN
WHUG(FM) Jamestown NY	KOFM(FM) Enid OK	WHGL-FM Canton PA	KMLO(FM) Lowry SD	WSIX-FM Nashville TN
WDNB(FM) Jeffersonville NY	KTNT(FM) Eufaula OK	WCAT-FM Carlisle PA	KJAM(AM) Madison SD	WSM(AM) Nashville TN
WKXP(FM) Kingston NY	KYBE(FM) Frederick OK	WIOO(AM) Carlisle PA	KJAM-FM Madison SD	WSM-FM Nashville TN
WXRL(AM) Lancaster NY	KGVE(FM) Grove OK	WFGI(AM) Charleroi PA	KMIT(FM) Mitchell SD	WNPC(AM) Newport TN
WVOS(AM) Liberty NY	KGYN(FM) Guymon OK	WOGI(FM) Charleroi PA	KGFX(FM) Pierre SD	WNPC-FM Newport TN
WLLG(FM) Lowville NY	KICM(FM) Healdton OK	WKNB(FM) Clarendon PA	KIMM(AM) Rapid City SD	WBNT-FM Oneida TN
WVNV(FM) Malone NY	KPRV-FM Heavener OK	WWCH(AM) Clarion PA	KIQK(FM) Rapid City SD	WOCV(AM) Oneida TN
WBGK(FM) Newport Village NY	KXBL(FM) Henryetta OK	WFRM(AM) Coudersport PA	KOUT(FM) Rapid City SD	WMUF(AM) Paris TN
WBKT(FM) Norwich NY	KTJS(AM) Hobart OK	WDKC(FM) Covington PA	KGIM-FM Redfield SD	WKJQ(FM) Parsons TN
WPIG(FM) Olean NY	KITX(FM) Hugo OK	WOWQ(FM) DuBois PA	KPLO-FM Reliance SD	WUAT(AM) Pikeville TN
WDOS(AM) Oneonta NY	KBEL-FM Idabel OK	WCTO(FM) Easton PA	KIKN-FM Salem SD	WKSR-FM Pulaski TN
WSCP-FM Pulaski NY	KLAW(AM) Lawton OK	WXTA(FM) Edinboro PA	KTWB(AM) Sioux Falls SD	WTRB(AM) Ripley TN
WBEE-FM Rochester NY	KBLP(FM) Lindsay OK	WYGL-FM Elizabethville PA	KXRB(AM) Sioux Falls SD	WOFE-FM Rockwood TN
WUMX(FM) Rome NY	KMAD(AM) Madill OK	WLEM(FM) Emporium PA	KBWS-FM Sisseton SD	WJDT(FM) Rogersville TN
WSCP(AM) Sandy Creek-Pulaski NY	KFXI(FM) Marlow OK	WIOV-FM Ephrata PA	KKQQ(FM) Volga SD	WRGS(AM) Rogersville TN
WUUF(FM) Sodus NY	KMCO(FM) McAlester OK	WSKE(FM) Everett PA	KDLO-FM Watertown SD	WJOR-FM Saint Joseph TN
WOKN(FM) Southport NY	KNED(AM) McAlester OK	WUSE(FM) Fairview PA	KSDR-FM Watertown SD	WKWX(FM) Savannah TN
WSPQ(AM) Springville NY	KMMY(FM) Muskogee OK	WGTY(FM) Gettysburg PA	KWYR(AM) Winner SD	WORM-FM Savannah TN
WFRG-FM Utica NY		WWGY(FM) Grove City PA	KKYA(FM) Yankton SD	WXOQ(FM) Selmer TN

Broadcasting & Cable Yearbook 2006

D-702

Programming on Radio Stations in the U.S.

WLIJ(AM) Shelbyville TN	KSCS(FM) Fort Worth TX	KGKL-FM San Angelo TX	WSIG(FM) Mount Jackson VA	WEKZ(AM) Monroe WI
WJLE(AM) Smithville TN	KNAF(AM) Fredericksburg TX	KAJA(FM) San Antonio TX	WGH-FM Newport News VA	WNCY-FM Neenah-Menasha WI
WJLE-FM Smithville TN	KNAF-FM Fredericksburg TX	KCYY(FM) San Antonio TX	WXMM(FM) Norfolk VA	WIXK(AM) New Richmond WI
WEPG(AM) South Pittsburg TN	KGAF(FM) Gainesville TX	KKYX(AM) San Antonio TX	WNVA-FM Norton VA	WOCO(AM) Oconto WI
WTZX(AM) Sparta TN	KZAM(AM) Ganado TX	KQSI(FM) San Augustine TX	WESR(AM) Onley-Onancock VA	WPKR(FM) Omro WI
WSBI(AM) Static TN	KTFW-FM Glen Rose TX	KBAL(FM) San Saba TX	WCUL(FM) Orange VA	WCQM(FM) Park Falls WI
WCTU(FM) Tazewell TN	KCTI(AM) Gonzales TX	KWED(AM) Seguin TX	WDXC(FM) Pound VA	WBKY(FM) Portage WI
WNTT(AM) Tazewell TN	KSWA(AM) Graham TX	KIKZ(AM) Seminole TX	WPSK-FM Pulaski VA	WDDC(FM) Portage WI
WTNE-FM Trenton TN	KPIR(AM) Granbury TX	KSEM-FM Seminole TX	WWBU(FM) Radford VA	WQPC(FM) Prairie du Chien WI
WHRP(FM) Tullahoma TN	KGVL(AM) Greenville TX	KAYD-FM Silsbee TX	WSLC-FM Roanoke VA	WNFM(FM) Reedsburg WI
WIKQ(FM) Tusculum TN	KIKT(FM) Greenville TX	KOUL(FM) Sinton TX	WYTI(AM) Rocky Mount VA	WHDG(FM) Rhinelander WI
WYVY(AM) Union City TN	KHLT(AM) Hallettsville TX	KSNY-FM Snyder TX	WCRR(AM) Rural Retreat VA	WAQE(AM) Rice Lake WI
WECO-FM Wartburg TN	KTXM(AM) Hallettsville TX	KHOS-FM Sonora TX	WXMY(AM) Saltville VA	WJMC-FM Rice Lake WI
WCDT(AM) Winchester TN	KCLW(AM) Hamilton TX	KLGD(FM) Stamford TX	WKSK-FM South Hill VA	WRCO-FM Richland Center WI
WBRY(AM) Woodbury TN	KUSJ(FM) Harker Heights TX	KVRP(AM) Stamford TX	WZBB(FM) Stanleytown VA	WTCH(FM) Shawano WI
KEAN-FM Abilene TX	KVRP-FM Haskell TX	KKJW(FM) Stanton VA	WCYK-FM Staunton VA	WBFM(FM) Sheboygan WI
KYYW(AM) Abilene TX	KTHP(FM) Hemphill TX	KCUB-FM Stephenville TX	WKDW(AM) Staunton VA	WCOW-FM Sparta WI
KOPY(AM) Alice TX	KWRD(AM) Henderson TX	KXOX(AM) Sweetwater TX	WKSI-FM Stephens City VA	WOSQ(FM) Spencer WI
KALP(FM) Alpine TX	KPAN(AM) Hereford TX	KXOX-FM Sweetwater TX	WHEO(AM) Stuart VA	WPLT(FM) Spooner WI
KATP(FM) Amarillo TX	KHBR(AM) Hillsboro TX	KKYR-FM Texarkana TX	WNNT-FM Warsaw VA	WEXT(FM) Sturtevant WI
KDJW(AM) Amarillo TX	KCWM(AM) Hondo TX	KBCY(FM) Tye TX	WUSQ-FM Winchester VA	WCUB(AM) Two Rivers WI
KGNC-FM Amarillo TX	KILT-FM Houston TX	KKUS(FM) Tyler TX	WYVE(AM) Wytheville VA	WVRQ-FM Viroqua WI
KMML-FM Amarillo TX	KHYI(FM) Howe TX	KNUE(FM) Tyler TX	WXAL-FM Addison VT	WTTN(AM) Watertown WI
KACT(AM) Andrews TX	KLSN(FM) Hudson TX	KVOU-FM Uvalde TX	WZLF(FM) Bellows Falls VT	WMIL(FM) Waukesha WI
KACT-FM Andrews TX	KSAM-FM Huntsville TX	KVWC(AM) Vernon TX	WWFY(FM) Berlin VT	WDUX(AM) Waupaca WI
KASE-FM Austin TX	KRBL(FM) Idalou TX	KIXS(FM) Victoria TX	WOKO(FM) Burlington VT	WDEZ(FM) Wausau WI
KVET-FM Austin TX	KEBE(AM) Jacksonville TX	KVNN(AM) Victoria TX	WLVB(FM) Morrisville VT	WBKV(AM) West Bend WI
KKCN(FM) Ballinger TX	KTXJ-FM Jasper TX	KBCT-FM Waco TX	WIKE(AM) Newport VT	WBWI-FM West Bend WI
KRUN(AM) Ballinger TX	KMBL(AM) Junction TX	WACO-FM Waco TX	WVNR(FM) Poultney VT	WSLD(FM) Whitewater WI
KMKS(FM) Bay City TX	KOOK(FM) Junction TX	KBEC(AM) Waxahachie TX	WJEN(FM) Rutland VT	WYTE(FM) Whiting WI
KYKR(FM) Beaumont TX	KAML(AM) Kenedy-Karnes City TX	KLBL(FM) White Oak TX	WLFE-FM Saint Albans VT	WJLS-FM Beckley WV
KTKO(FM) Beeville TX	KRNH(FM) Kerrville TX	KLUR(FM) Wichita Falls TX	WKXH(FM) Saint Johnsbury VT	WCST(AM) Berkeley Springs WV
KMKT-FM Bells TX	KRVL(FM) Kerrville TX	KWFS-FM Wichita Falls TX	WJAN(FM) Sunderland VT	WDHC(FM) Berkeley Springs WV
KTON(AM) Belton TX	KFTX(FM) Kingsville TX	KVST(FM) Willis TX	WXLF(FM) White River Junction VT	WBRB(FM) Buckhannon WV
KFYN(AM) Bonham TX	KNOR(FM) Krum TX	KNCE(FM) Winters TX	KNBQ(FM) Centralia WA	WCAW(AM) Charleston WV
KFYZ-FM Bonham TX	KBUK(FM) La Grange TX	KVLL-FM Woodville TX	KMNT(FM) Chehalis WA	WKWS(FM) Charleston WV
KQTY(AM) Borger TX	KVLG(AM) La Grange TX	KWUD(AM) Woodville TX	KCLK-FM Clarkston WA	WGIE(FM) Clarksburg WV
KQTY-FM Borger TX	KPET(AM) Lamesa TX	KYKM(FM) Yoakum TX	KCLX(AM) Colfax WA	WPDX-FM Clarksburg WV
KNEL-FM Brady TX	KTXC(FM) Lamesa TX	KMTI(AM) Manti UT	KCVL(AM) Colville WA	WZAC(FM) Danville WV
KLXK(FM) Breckenridge TX	KCYL(AM) Lampasas TX	KCYN(FM) Moab UT	KYSN(FM) East Wenatchee WA	WDNE-FM Elkins WV
KTTX(AM) Brenham TX	KLVT-FM Levelland TX	KEGA(FM) Oakley UT	KXLE-FM Ellensburg WA	WKKW(FM) Fairmont WV
KWHI(AM) Brenham TX	KSHN-FM Liberty TX	KPQP(FM) Ogden UT	KXLE-FM Ellensburg WA	*WFGH(FM) Fort Gay WV
KBOC(FM) Bridgeport TX	KZZN(AM) Littlefield TX	KARB(FM) Price UT	KULE-FM Ephrata WA	*WVMR(AM) Frost WV
KTEX(FM) Brownsville TX	KETX-FM Livingston TX	KSLL(AM) Price UT	KYYT(FM) Goldendale WA	WTCR-FM Huntington WV
KOXE(FM) Brownwood TX	KACQ(FM) Lometa TX	KLGL(FM) Richfield UT	KEYG(FM) Grand Coulee WA	WKMM(FM) Kingwood WV
KORA-FM Bryan TX	KYKX(FM) Longview TX	KNEU(AM) Roosevelt UT	KXXK(FM) Hoquiam-Aberdeen WA	WKCJ(FM) Lewisburg WV
KTFW(AM) Burleson TX	KLLL-FM Lubbock TX	KONY(FM) Saint George UT	KVAS(FM) Ilwaco WA	WGYE(FM) Mannington WV
KBEY(FM) Burnet TX	KQBR(AM) Lubbock TX	KSOP-FM Salt Lake City UT	KBRD(AM) Lacey WA	WTNJ(FM) Mount Hope WV
KHLB(FM) Burnet TX	KYKS(FM) Lufkin TX	KUBL-FM Salt Lake City UT	KBAM(AM) Longview WA	WGGE(FM) Parkersburg WV
KMIL(AM) Cameron TX	KAGG(FM) Madisonville TX	KSOP(FM) South Salt Lake UT	KUKN(FM) Longview WA	WHNK(FM) Parkersburg WV
KGAS-FM Carthage TX	KMVL-FM Madisonville TX	KYLZ(FM) Tremonton UT	KGY-FM McCleary WA	WELD-FM Petersburg WV
KDET(AM) Center TX	KCKL(FM) Malakoff TX	KLCY-FM Vernal UT	KWIQ-FM Moses Lake WA	WWYO(AM) Pineville WV
KQBB(FM) Center TX	KMHT(AM) Marshall TX	WVES(FM) Accomac VA	KAPS(AM) Mount Vernon WA	WBYG(FM) Point Pleasant WV
KCTX-FM Childress TX	KMHT-FM Marshall TX	WKDE-FM Altavista VA	KNCW(FM) Omak WA	WLWF(FM) Ravenswood WV
KCAR(AM) Clarksville TX	KLSR-FM Memphis TX	WYYD(FM) Amherst VA	KIXZ-FM Opportunity WA	WVAR(AM) Richwood WV
KCLE(AM) Cleburne TX	KRQX(AM) Mexia TX	WAXM(FM) Big Stone Gap VA	KZZL-FM Pullman WA	WCEF(FM) Ripley WV
KTHT(FM) Cleveland TX	KYCX-FM Mexia TX	WBBC-FM Blackstone VA	KIOK(FM) Richland WA	*WVSB(FM) Romney WV
KSTA(AM) Coleman TX	KNFM(FM) Midland TX	WHKX-FM Bluefield VA	KORD-FM Richland WA	WYKM(AM) Rupert WV
KAUM(FM) Colorado City TX	KMOO-FM Mineola TX	WWZW(FM) Buena Vista VA	KMPS-FM Seattle WA	WVRC-FM Spencer WV
KVMC(AM) Colorado City TX	KFWR(FM) Mineral Wells TX	WHQX(FM) Cedar Bluff VA	KDRK-FM Spokane WA	WDBS(FM) Sutton WV
KULM(FM) Columbus TX	KJSA(AM) Mineral Wells TX	WLUS-FM Clarksville VA	KDBL(FM) Toppenish WA	WHAW(AM) Weston WV
KCOM(AM) Comanche TX	KIMP(AM) Mount Pleasant TX	WDIC(AM) Clinchco VA	KYNR(AM) Toppenish WA	WZST(FM) Westover WV
KYOX(FM) Comanche TX	KMUL(FM) Muleshoe TX	WKHK(FM) Colonial Heights VA	KVLR(FM) Twisp WA	WOVK(FM) Wheeling WV
KRYS-FM Corpus Christi TX	KJCS(FM) Nacogdoches TX	WIQO-FM Covington VA	KKRV(FM) Wenatchee WA	WXCC(FM) Williamson WV
KAND(AM) Corsicana TX	KHKX(FM) Odessa TX	WSVS(AM) Crewe VA	KUTI(AM) Yakima WA	KRSV(AM) Afton WY
KBHT(FM) Crockett TX	KOGT(AM) Orange TX	WJMA-FM Culpeper VA	KXDD(FM) Yakima WA	KRSV-FM Afton WY
KIVY-FM Crockett TX	KYXX(FM) Ozona TX	WAKG-FM Danville VA	WRLU(FM) Algoma WI	KKAW(FM) Albin WY
KSTB(FM) Crystal Beach TX	KROY(FM) Palacios TX	WBNN-FM Dillwyn VA	WBSZ(FM) Ashland WI	KLGT(FM) Buffalo WY
KXIT(AM) Dalhart TX	KNET(FM) Palestine TX	WDUF(FM) Duffield VA	WXRO(FM) Beaver Dam WI	KIGN(FM) Burns WY
KDLK-FM Del Rio TX	KYYK(FM) Palestine TX	WJZV(FM) Ettrick VA	WISS(AM) Berlin WI	KQLT(FM) Casper WY
KDHN(AM) Dimmitt TX	KOMX(FM) Pampa TX	WGRX(FM) Falmouth VA	WQRB(FM) Bloomer WI	KWYY(FM) Casper WY
KSTV-FM Dublin TX	KOYN(FM) Paris TX	WFLO(AM) Farmville VA	WATQ(FM) Chetek WI	KOLZ(FM) Cheyenne WY
KDDD(AM) Dumas TX	KPLT(AM) Paris TX	WVHL(FM) Farmville VA	WJMQ(FM) Clintonville WI	KDWY(FM) Diamondville WY
KATX(FM) Eastland TX	KKBQ-FM Pasadena TX	WLQM-FM Franklin VA	WPCK(FM) Denmark WI	KKTY-FM Douglas WY
KEAS(AM) Eastland TX	KVWG(FM) Pearsall TX	WFLS-FM Fredericksburg VA	WVRE(FM) Dickeyville WI	KEVA(AM) Evanston WY
KGUL(FM) Edna TX	KVWG-FM Pearsall TX	WFTR(AM) Front Royal VA	WDMP(AM) Dodgeville WI	KRND(AM) Fox Farm WY
KIOX-FM El Campo TX	KREH(FM) Pecan Grove TX	WBRF(FM) Galax VA	WDMP-FM Dodgeville WI	KGWY(FM) Gillette WY
KULP(AM) El Campo TX	KIUN(AM) Pecos TX	WMNA(AM) Gretna VA	WAXX(FM) Eau Claire WI	KFRZ(FM) Green River WY
KHEY-FM El Paso TX	KKLY(FM) Pecos TX	WNRG(AM) Grundy VA	WTKM(AM) Hartford WI	KZMQ(AM) Greybull WY
KHRO(AM) El Paso TX	KEYE(AM) Perryton TX	WKCY-FM Harrisonburg VA	WTKM-FM Hartford WI	KZMQ-FM Greybull WY
*KOLI(FM) Electra TX	KVJY(AM) Pharr TX	*WCHG(FM) Hot Springs VA	WJVL(FM) Janesville WI	KJAX(FM) Jackson WY
KNES(FM) Fairfield TX	KSCN(FM) Pittsburg TX	WJNV(FM) Jonesville VA	WQCC(FM) La Crosse WI	KSGT(AM) Jackson WY
KPSO-FM Falfurrias TX	KKYN-FM Plainview TX	WXLZ-FM Lebanon VA	WLDY(AM) Ladysmith WI	KOVE(AM) Lander WY
KTYS(FM) Flower Mound TX	KIXC-FM Quanah TX	WOJL(FM) Louisa VA	WGLR(FM) Lancaster WI	KCGY(FM) Laramie WY
KFLP-FM Floydada TX	KREL(FM) Quanah TX	WRAA(AM) Luray VA	WGLR-FM Lancaster WI	KHAT(FM) Laramie WY
KFST-FM Fort Stockton TX	KRXT(FM) Rockdale TX	WMEV-FM Marion VA	WIGM(AM) Medford WI	KASL(AM) Newcastle WY
KPLX(FM) Fort Worth TX	KDCD(FM) San Angelo TX	*WVLS(FM) Monterey VA	WWQM(FM) Middleton WI	KPIN(FM) Pinedale WY

Broadcasting & Cable Yearbook 2006

D-703

Programming on Radio Stations in the U.S.

KLZY(FM) Powell-Cody WY
KTAK(FM) Riverton WY
KQSW(FM) Rock Springs WY
KYTI(FM) Sheridan WY
KYDT(FM) Sundance WY
KDNO(FM) Thermopolis WY
KERM(FM) Torrington WY
KGOS(AM) Torrington WY
KYCN(AM) Wheatland WY

Disco

KNRJ(FM) Payson AZ

Diversified

*KSKA(FM) Anchorage AK
*KUAC(FM) Fairbanks AK
KCAM(AM) Glennallen AK
*KXGA(FM) Glennallen AK
*KHNS(FM) Haines AK
*KTOO(FM) Juneau AK
*KRBD(FM) Ketchikan AK
*KMXT(FM) Kodiak AK
*KOTZ(FM) Kotzebue AK
*KXKM(FM) McCarthy AK
*KNOM(AM) Nome AK
*KNOM-FM Nome AK
*KSDP(AM) Sand Point AK
*KCAW(FM) Sitka AK
*KTNA(FM) Talkeetna AK
*KCHU(FM) Valdez AK
*KSTK(FM) Wrangell AK
*WLJR(FM) Birmingham AL
*KZIG(FM) Cave City AR
*KKDU(FM) El Dorado AR
*KABF(FM) Little Rock AR
KVSA(AM) McGehee AR
*KNNB(FM) Whiteriver AZ
*KALX(FM) Berkeley CA
*KPFA(FM) Berkeley CA
*KPFB(FM) Berkeley CA
*KZFR(FM) Chico CA
*KSPC(FM) Claremont CA
*KECG(FM) El Cerrito CA
*KMUE(FM) Eureka CA
*KFSR(FM) Fresno CA
*KMUD(FM) Garberville CA
KNOB(FM) Healdsburg CA
*KCRI(FM) Indio CA
*KUCI(FM) Irvine CA
*KLAI(FM) Laytonville CA
*KCRY(FM) Mojave CA
KHPY(AM) Moreno Valley CA
*KKSM(AM) Oceanside CA
*KCRU(FM) Oxnard CA
*KUCR(FM) Riverside CA
*KXHV(FM) Sacramento CA
*KBDH(FM) San Ardo CA
*KALW(FM) San Francisco CA
KPOO(FM) San Francisco CA
*KUSF(FM) San Francisco CA
*KCPR(FM) San Luis Obispo CA
*KUSP(FM) Santa Cruz CA
*KZSC(FM) Santa Cruz CA
*KCRW(FM) Santa Monica CA
*KZSU(FM) Stanford CA
*KCSS(FM) Turlock CA
*KZYZ(FM) Willits CA
*KLRD(FM) Yucaipa CA
*KCJX(FM) Carbondale CO
*KRCC(FM) Colorado Springs CO
*KBUT(FM) Crested Butte CO
*KDUR(FM) Durango CO
*KUNC-FM Greeley CO
*WPKN(FM) Bridgeport CT
*WRTC-FM Hartford CT
*WFCS(FM) New Britain CT
*WSLX(FM) New Canaan CT
*WHUS(FM) Storrs CT
*WVUD(FM) Newark DE
*WFCF(FM) Saint Augustine FL
*WVFS(FM) Tallahassee FL
*WMNF(FM) Tampa FL
*WREK(FM) Atlanta GA
*KPRG(FM) Hagatna GU

*KKCR(FM) Hanalei HI
*KAQA(FM) Kilauea HI
*KWLC(AM) Decorah IA
*KRUI-FM Iowa City IA
*KRNI(AM) Mason City IA
KIWA(AM) Sheldon IA
*KWAR(FM) Waverly IA
*KBSQ(FM) McCall ID
*KEZJ(FM) Twin Falls ID
*WESN(FM) Bloomington IL
*WDBX(FM) Carbondale IL
*WHPK-FM Chicago IL
*WDGC-FM Downers Grove IL
*WEPS(FM) Elgin IL
*WTPC(FM) Elsah IL
*WMXM(FM) Lake Forest IL
*WLRA(FM) Lockport IL
*WHCM(FM) Palatine IL
*WQNA(FM) Springfield IL
*WILL(AM) Urbana IL
*WNTH(FM) Winnetka IL
*WFHB(FM) Bloomington IN
*WPSR(FM) Evansville IN
*WUEV(FM) Evansville IN
*WHWE(FM) Howe IN
*WRFT(FM) Indianapolis IN
WMRS(FM) Monticello IN
*WBKE-FM North Manchester IN
*WVUR-FM Valparaiso IN
*KBTL(FM) El Dorado KS
*KANZ(FM) Garden City KS
*KTJO-FM Ottawa KS
KKAN(AM) Phillipsburg KS
*WOCS(FM) Lerose KY
*WMMT(FM) Whitesburg KY
*KLSP(FM) Angola LA
*KLSU(FM) Baton Rouge LA
WOMN(AM) Franklinton LA
*KSCL(FM) Shreveport LA
*WHAB(FM) Acton MA
*WAMH(FM) Amherst MA
*WERS(FM) Boston MA
*WBIM-FM Bridgewater MA
*WSHL-FM Easton MA
*WCCT-FM Harwich MA
*WHHB(FM) Holliston MA
*WUML(FM) Lowell MA
*WMLN-FM Milton MA
*WOZQ(FM) Northampton MA
*WNMH(FM) Northfield MA
*WMWM(FM) Salem MA
*WBSL-FM Sheffield MA
*WAIC(FM) Springfield MA
*WNEK-FM Springfield MA
*WTCC(FM) Springfield MA
*WSKB(FM) Westfield MA
*WCHC(FM) Worcester MA
*WCUW(FM) Worcester MA
*WKHS(FM) Worton MD
*WERU-FM Blue Hill ME
*WBOR(FM) Brunswick ME
*WMPG(FM) Gorham ME
*WRBC(FM) Lewiston ME
*WMEB-FM Orono ME
*WUPI(FM) Presque Isle ME
*WMHB(FM) Waterville ME
*WYAR(FM) Yarmouth ME
*WVAC-FM Adrian MI
*WCBN-FM Ann Arbor MI
*WBFH(FM) Bloomfield Hills MI
*WKDS(FM) Kalamazoo MI
*WOCR(FM) Olivet MI
*WNMC-FM Traverse City MI
KDAL(AM) Duluth MN
*KFAI(FM) Minneapolis MN
KOLV(FM) Olivia MN
*KCVO-FM Camdenton MO
*KWUR(FM) Clayton MO
*KOPN(FM) Columbia MO
*KCVZ(FM) Dixon MO
*KCVQ(FM) Knob Noster MO
*KCVJ(FM) Osceola MO
*KCVK(FM) Otterville MO
KLUE(FM) Poplar Bluff MO
*KMNR(FM) Rolla MO
*KUMR(FM) Rolla MO
*KDHX(FM) Saint Louis MO

*KCVX(FM) Salem MO
*KGLT(FM) Bozeman MT
*KECC(FM) Miles City MT
*WXYC(FM) Chapel Hill NC
*WXDU(FM) Durham NC
*WSOE(FM) Elon NC
*WUAG(FM) Greensboro NC
WLHC(FM) Robbins NC
*WSIF(FM) Wilkesboro NC
*KMHA(FM) Four Bears ND
*WFKX(FM) Hastings NE
*KZUM(FM) Lincoln NE
*WSPS(FM) Concord NH
WDCR(AM) Hanover NH
WAJM(FM) Atlantic City NJ
*WDVR(FM) Delaware Township NJ
*WFMU(FM) East Orange NJ
*WCVH(FM) Flemington NJ
*WGLS-FM Glassboro NJ
*WNTI(FM) Hackettstown NJ
*KUNM(FM) Albuquerque NM
*KCIE(FM) Dulce NM
*KWPR(FM) Lund NV
KBZB(FM) Pioche NV
*WCDB(FM) Albany NY
*WALF(FM) Alfred NY
*WKRB(FM) Brooklyn NY
*WCVF-FM Fredonia NY
*WRCU-FM Hamilton NY
*WPKM(FM) Montauk NY
*WXHD(FM) Mount Hope NY
*WFUV(FM) New York NY
*WONY(FM) Oneonta NY
*WNYO(FM) Oswego NY
*WVKR-FM Poughkeepsie NY
WFTU(AM) Riverhead NY
*WRUR-FM Rochester NY
*WUSB(FM) Stony Brook NY
*WKWZ(FM) Syosset NY
*WPNR-FM Utica NY
*WMCO(FM) New Concord OH
*WOBC-FM Oberlin OH
*WJCU(FM) University Heights OH
*WCWS(FM) Wooster OH
*KPSU(FM) Goodwell OK
*KMUN(FM) Astoria OR
*KWVA(FM) Eugene OR
*KTEC(FM) Klamath Falls OR
*KLCO(FM) Newport OR
*KBOO(FM) Portland OR
*KRRC(FM) Portland OR
*WMUH(FM) Allentown PA
*WDCV-FM Carlisle PA
*WESS(FM) East Stroudsburg PA
*WMCE(FM) Erie PA
*WRSD(FM) Folsom PA
*WTGP(FM) Greenville PA
*WHHS(FM) Havertown PA
*WPSB(FM) Kane PA
*WLCH(FM) Lancaster PA
*WIXQ(FM) Millersville PA
*WSFX(FM) Nanticoke PA
*WPEB(FM) Philadelphia PA
WPHE(AM) Phoenixville PA
*WRCT(FM) Pittsburgh PA
*WYBF(FM) Radnor Township PA
*WXLV(FM) Schnecksville PA
*WSRN-FM Swarthmore PA
*WCUR(FM) West Chester PA
*WCLH(FM) Wilkes-Barre PA
*WRLC(FM) Williamsport PA
WNIK(AM) Arecibo PR
WQBS(FM) San Juan PR
*WRIU(FM) Kingston RI
*WJHD(FM) Portsmouth RI
*WELH(FM) Providence RI
*WJWJ-FM Beaufort SC
*KCFS(FM) Sioux Falls SD
*WAPX-FM Clarksville TN
*WAPX-FM Clarksville TN
WSGM(FM) Coalmont TN
*WMTS-FM Murfreesboro TN
*WRVU(FM) Nashville TN
*KUT(FM) Austin TX
*KTXP(FM) Bushland TX
*KPFT(FM) Houston TX
*KTRU(FM) Houston TX

*KTSU(FM) Houston TX
*KOHM(FM) Lubbock TX
*KTXT-FM Lubbock TX
KLSR-FM Memphis TX
*KEOM(FM) Mesquite TX
*KUTX(FM) San Angelo TX
*KWBU-FM Waco TX
*KRCL(FM) Salt Lake City UT
*WUVT-FM Blacksburg VA
*WEHC(FM) Emory VA
*WMLU(FM) Farmville VA
*WWHS-FM Hampden-Sydney VA
*WLUR(FM) Lexington VA
*WVST-FM Petersburg VA
*WDCE(FM) Richmond VA
*WCWM(FM) Williamsburg VA
WSTA(AM) Charlotte Amalie VI
WAXJ(FM) Frederiksted VI
WDHP(AM) Frederiksted VI
*WRUV(FM) Burlington VT
*WJSC-FM Johnson VT
*WWLR(FM) Lyndonville VT
*WRMC-FM Middlebury VT
*WGDR(FM) Plainfield VT
WDEV(AM) Waterbury VT
KXPA(AM) Bellevue WA
*KCED(FM) Centralia WA
*KCWU(FM) Ellensburg WA
*KSER(FM) Everett WA
*KAOS(FM) Olympia WA
*KZUU(FM) Pullman WA
*KEXP-FM Seattle WA
KYNR(AM) Toppenish WA
*KWCW(FM) Walla Walla WA
*WRST-FM Oshkosh WI
*WOJB(FM) Reserve WI
*KUWS(FM) Superior WI
*WVBC(FM) Bethany WV
*WWVC(FM) Buckhannon WV
*WVMR(AM) Frost WV
*WMUL(FM) Huntington WV
*WWVU-FM Morgantown WV
*WQAB(FM) Philippi WV
KROE(AM) Sheridan WY

Easy Listening

KHAR(AM) Anchorage AK
*WVAS(FM) Montgomery AL
KLEZ(FM) Malvern AR
KTLO-FM Mountain Home AR
KNAI(FM) Phoenix AZ
KAHM(FM) Prescott AZ
KGFM(FM) Bakersfield CA
WAVV(FM) Marco FL
*WKGC(AM) Panama City Beach FL
WKEZ-FM Tavenier FL
WGPC(AM) Albany GA
KCHA-FM Charles City IA
*KCMR(FM) Mason City IA
KAYL(AM) Storm Lake IA
WGCY(FM) Gibson City IL
WSPY-FM Plano IL
WYYS(FM) Streator IL
WGFA(FM) Watseka IL
KVSV-FM Beloit KS
WJEJ(AM) Hagerstown MD
WEZQ(FM) Bangor ME
WNIC(FM) Dearborn MI
WCCY(AM) Houghton MI
WCZY-FM Mount Pleasant MI
WMBN(AM) Petoskey MI
WIOS(FM) Tawas City MI
KYMO(AM) East Prairie MO
WBAQ(FM) Greenville MS
WGCM-FM Gulfport MS
KHDN(AM) Hardin MT
WHLC(FM) Highlands NC
WEZS(AM) Laconia NH
KLEA(AM) Lovington NM
*WMEJ(FM) Proctorville OH
*KEZX(FM) Medford OR
KORC(AM) Waldport OR
WLTS(AM) State College PA
WFDT(FM) Aguada PR
WFID(FM) Rio Piedras PR
WDAR-FM Darlington SC

WYEZ(FM) Murrell's Inlet SC
WEZV(FM) North Myrtle Beach SC
WCPH(AM) Etowah TN
*WDNX(FM) Olive Hill TN
*KHCH(AM) Huntsville TX
KETX(AM) Livingston TX
KRFE(AM) Lubbock TX
*KLUX(FM) Robstown TX
WXEZ(FM) Yorktown VA
WNAM(AM) Neenah-Menasha WI
WOCO-FM Oconto WI
WEZY(FM) Racine WI

Educational

*KXKM(FM) McCarthy AK
*WSTF(FM) Andalusia AL
*WLJR(FM) Birmingham AL
WQEM(FM) Columbiana AL
*WYFD(FM) Decatur AL
*WDYF(FM) Dothan AL
*WVOB(FM) Dothan AL
*WLBF(FM) Montgomery AL
*WTBJ(FM) Oxford AL
*KZIG(FM) Cave City AR
KOFC(AM) Fayetteville AR
KJBN(AM) Little Rock AR
*KCMH(FM) Mountain Home AR
*KWRB(FM) Bisbee AZ
*KRMC(FM) Douglas AZ
*KJTA(FM) Flagstaff AZ
*KPUB(FM) Flagstaff AZ
*KNOG(FM) Nogales AZ
*KNNB(FM) Whiteriver AZ
*KALX(FM) Berkeley CA
*KIBC(FM) Burney CA
*KHAP(FM) Chico CA
*KVHS(FM) Concord CA
*KECR(AM) El Cajon CA
*KECG(FM) El Cerrito CA
*KMUE(FM) Eureka CA
*KMUD(FM) Garberville CA
*KEFR(FM) Le Grand CA
*KFRN(AM) Long Beach CA
*KAKX(FM) Mendocino CA
*KADV(FM) Modesto CA
*KSMC(FM) Moraga CA
*KSGN(FM) Riverside CA
*KUSF(FM) San Francisco CA
*KBBF(FM) Santa Rosa CA
*KZSU(FM) Stanford CA
*KCLU(FM) Thousand Oaks CA
*KBUT(FM) Crested Butte CO
*KICC(FM) Grand Junction CO
WADS(AM) Ansonia CT
*WERB(FM) Berlin CT
*WFAR(FM) Danbury CT
*WQTQ(FM) Hartford CT
WYBC(AM) New Haven CT
*WAPJ(FM) Torrington CT
*WVUD(FM) Newark DE
*WTJT(FM) Baker FL
*WJED(FM) Dogwood Lakes Estate FL
*WJFP(FM) Fort Pierce FL
WXYB(AM) Indian Rocks Beach FL
*WJIR(FM) Key West FL
*WKES(FM) Lakeland FL
*WYFO(FM) Lakeland FL
*WMCU(FM) Miami FL
*WHIJ(FM) Ocala FL
*WPCS(FM) Pensacola FL
*WVIJ(FM) Port Charlotte FL
*WKZM(FM) Sarasota FL
WATB(AM) Decatur GA
*WOAK(FM) La Grange GA
*WYFS(FM) Savannah GA
*WVGS(FM) Statesboro GA
*KKCR(FM) Hanalei HI
*KCIF(FM) Hilo HI
*KAQA(FM) Kilauea HI
*KHJC(FM) Lihue HI
*KHOE(FM) Fairfield IA
*KRUI-FM Iowa City IA
*KPVL(FM) Postville IA
*KBBG(FM) Waterloo IA
*KWAR(FM) Waverly IA
*KCIR(FM) Twin Falls ID

Programming on Radio Stations in the U.S.

*KEFX(FM) Twin Falls ID
*WBGL(FM) Champaign IL
*WHPK-FM Chicago IL
*WKKC(FM) Chicago IL
*WMBI-FM Chicago IL
*WZRD(FM) Chicago IL
*WEPS(FM) Elgin IL
*WGNN(FM) Fisher IL
*WGBK(FM) Glenview IL
*WKCC(FM) Kankakee IL
*WLRA(FM) Lockport IL
*WVJC(FM) Mount Carmel IL
*WWGN(FM) Ottawa IL
*WHCM(FM) Palatine IL
*WPSR(FM) Evansville IN
*WGVE(FM) Gary IN
*WHWE(FM) Howe IN
*WQKO(FM) Howe IN
*WRFT(FM) Indianapolis IN
*WWHI(FM) Muncie IN
*WNAS(FM) New Albany IN
*WEEM(FM) Pendleton IN
*WJLR(FM) Seymour IN
*WETL(FM) South Bend IN
KDCC(AM) Dodge City KS
*KONQ(FM) Dodge City KS
*KANZ(FM) Garden City KS
*KZNA(FM) Hill City KS
*WDFB-FM Danville KY
*WVCT(FM) Keavy KY
*WSOF-FM Madisonville KY
*WBFI(FM) McDaniels KY
*WTHL(FM) Somerset KY
*KVDP(FM) Dry Prong LA
*KPAE(FM) Erwinville LA
*WRBH(FM) New Orleans LA
WBNW(AM) Concord MA
*WCCT-FM Harwich MA
*WOZQ(FM) Northampton MA
*WRPS(FM) Rockland MA
*WSDH(FM) Sandwich MA
*WFSI(FM) Annapolis MD
*WOEL-FM Elkton MD
*WGTS(FM) Takoma Park MD
*WMDR(AM) Augusta ME
*WERU-FM Blue Hill ME
*WYAR(FM) Yarmouth ME
*WBFH(FM) Bloomfield Hills MI
*WRCJ-FM Detroit MI
*WIDR(FM) Kalamazoo MI
*WKDS(FM) Kalamazoo MI
*WPCJ(FM) Pittsford MI
*KMSK(FM) Austin MN
*KMSU(FM) Mankato MN
KTIG(FM) Pequot Lakes MN
*KCFB(FM) Saint Cloud MN
*KVSC(FM) Saint Cloud MN
*KGNA-FM Arnold MO
*KRHS(FM) Overland MO
*KMNR(FM) Rolla MO
*WPAE(FM) Centreville MS
*KGLT(FM) Bozeman MT
*KMSM-FM Butte MT
*KDWG(FM) Dillon MT
*KGPR(FM) Great Falls MT
*KBGA(FM) Missoula MT
*WPIR(FM) Hickory NC
*WRSH(FM) Rockingham NC
WBFJ(AM) Winston-Salem NC
*KABU(FM) Fort Totten ND
*KMNE-FM Bassett NE
*KTLX(FM) Columbus NE
*KCNT(FM) Hastings NE
*KIOS-FM Omaha NE
*WVFA(FM) Lebanon NH
*WSCS(FM) New London NH
*WSJI(FM) Cherry Hill NJ
*WGLS(FM) Glassboro NJ
*WYRS(FM) Manahawkin NJ
*WFME(FM) Newark NJ
*WVPH(FM) Piscataway NJ
*KTDB(FM) Ramah NM
*KSHI(FM) Zuni NM
*KNIS(FM) Carson City NV
*KNCC(FM) Elko NV
*WXBA(FM) Brentwood NY
*WFBF(FM) Buffalo NY

*WHPC(FM) Garden City NY
*WBAI(FM) New York NY
*WNYE(FM) New York NY
*WONY(FM) Oneonta NY
*WOSS(FM) Ossining NY
*WPSA(FM) Paul Smiths NY
*WPOB-FM Plainview NY
*WFRS(FM) Smithtown NY
*WCII(FM) Spencer NY
*WWJS(FM) Watertown NY
*WFRW(FM) Webster NY
*WRDL(FM) Ashland OH
*WHVT(FM) Clyde OH
*WDEQ-FM De Graff OH
*WHSS(FM) Hamilton OH
*WKET(FM) Kettering OH
*WLMH(FM) Morrow OH
*WMCO(FM) New Concord OH
*WOBC-FM Oberlin OH
*WLHS(FM) West Chester OH
*KKVO(FM) Altus OK
*KOSN(FM) Ketchum OK
KQCV(AM) Oklahoma City OK
*KOSU(FM) Stillwater OK
KBNP(AM) Portland OR
*KBPS(AM) Portland OR
*WLCH(FM) Lancaster PA
*WMSS(FM) Middletown PA
*WRCT(FM) Pittsburgh PA
WREQ(FM) Ridgebury PA
*WCLH(FM) Wilkes-Barre PA
*WVYC(FM) York PA
*WIDA-FM Carolina PR
*WJVP(FM) Culebra PR
*WCRP(FM) Guayama PR
*WEPC(FM) Belton SC
*WYFV(FM) Cayce SC
*WTBI-FM Greenville SC
*WMBJ(FM) Murrell's Inlet SC
*KJBB(FM) Watertown SD
*WHCB(FM) Bristol TN
*WMBW(FM) Chattanooga TN
*WWOG(FM) Cookeville TN
*WMKW(FM) Crossville TN
*WCSK(FM) Kingsport TN
*WCPI(FM) McMinnville TN
*WEVL(FM) Memphis TN
*WQOX(FM) Memphis TN
*WFCM-FM Murfreesboro TN
*WDNX(FM) Olive Hill TN
*WAWL-FM Red Bank TN
*WFCM(AM) Smyrna TN
*KJRT(FM) Amarillo TX
*KRGN(FM) Amarillo TX
*KASV(FM) Borger TX
*KBNR(FM) Brownsville TX
*KEOS(FM) College Station TX
*KBNJ(FM) Corpus Christi TX
*KVTT(FM) Dallas TX
*KOIR(FM) Edinburg TX
*KVER(FM) El Paso TX
*KTSU(FM) Houston TX
*KAVX(FM) Lufkin TX
KRIO(AM) McAllen TX
*KPHS(FM) Plains TX
*KTER(FM) Rudolph TX
KSLR(AM) San Antonio TX
KHOS(AM) Sonora TX
*KPDR(FM) Wheeler TX
*KRCL(FM) Salt Lake City UT
*WFOS(FM) Chesapeake VA
WPER(FM) Culpeper VA
WOTC(FM) Edinburg VA
*WEMC(FM) Harrisonburg VA
*WRVL(FM) Lynchburg VA
*WISE-FM Wise VA
WGOD-FM Charlotte Amalie VI
*WRUV(FM) Burlington VT
*KKRS(FM) Davenport WA
*KNHC(FM) Seattle WA
*WBCR-FM Beloit WI
*WHHI(FM) Highland WI
*WHLA(FM) La Crosse WI
*WHA(AM) Madison WI
*WSUM(FM) Madison WI
*WHWC(FM) Menomonie WI
*WYMS(FM) Milwaukee WI

*KUWS(FM) Superior WI
*WHRM(FM) Wausau WI
*WVBC(FM) Bethany WV
WQBE-FM Charleston WV
*WWVU-FM Morgantown WV
KVOW(AM) Riverton WY

Farsi
KIRN(AM) Simi Valley CA

Filipino
KTKB(FM) Hagatna GU
KNDI(AM) Honolulu HI

Folk
*WDJW(FM) Somers CT
*WGCS(FM) Goshen IN
*WUMB-FM Boston MA
*WFPB-FM Falmouth MA
*WNEF(FM) Newburyport MA
WFPB(AM) Orleans MA
*WBPR(FM) Worcester MA
*WICN(FM) Worcester MA
*KGPR(FM) Great Falls MT
*WPSU(FM) State College PA
*KZSD-FM Martin SD
*WETS(FM) Johnson City TN
*KRCL(FM) Salt Lake City UT
*WMRY(FM) Crozet VA
*KBCS(FM) Bellevue WA
*WXPR(FM) Rhinelander WI

Foreign/Ethnic
KVTO(AM) Berkeley CA
*KBES(FM) Ceres CA
KCVR-FM Columbia CA
KBIF(AM) Fresno CA
KOQO-FM Fresno CA
KLOK-FM Greenfield CA
KIGS(AM) Hanford CA
KHDV(FM) King City CA
KSQQ(FM) Morgan Hill CA
KLYY(FM) Riverside CA
KEST(AM) San Francisco CA
KEST(AM) San Francisco CA
KSOL(FM) San Francisco CA
KMRB(AM) San Gabriel CA
KSJX(AM) San Jose CA
KALI-FM Santa Ana CA
KUKI(AM) Ukiah CA
WDJZ(AM) Bridgeport CT
*WPFW(FM) Washington DC
WUST(AM) Washington DC
WAFC(FM) Clewiston FL
WAVS(AM) Davie FL
WRMA(FM) Fort Lauderdale FL
WSRF(AM) Fort Lauderdale FL
WRTO-FM Goulds FL
WWRF(AM) Lake Worth FL
WAMR-FM Miami FL
WPGS(AM) Mims FL
WHSR(AM) Pompano Beach FL
WAZX-FM Cleveland GA
WATB(AM) Decatur GA
KISH(AM) Hagatna GU
KCCN(FM) Honolulu HI
*KIPO(FM) Honolulu HI
KZOO(AM) Honolulu HI
KPOA(FM) Lahaina HI
WCEV(AM) Cicero IL
WOJO(FM) Evanston IL
WONX(AM) Evanston IL
WNWI(AM) Oak Lawn IL
WPNA(AM) Oak Park IL
KTCM(FM) Kingman KS
WUMB-FM Boston MA
WUNR(AM) Brookline MA
WLYN(AM) Lynn MA
WJFD-FM New Bedford MA
*WNEF(FM) Newburyport MA
*WTCC(FM) Springfield MA
*WBPR(FM) Worcester MA

WNSW(AM) Newark NJ
WKTX(AM) Cortland OH
WVJP-FM Caguas PR
WMDD(AM) Fajardo PR
WZET(FM) Hormigueros PR
WSOL(AM) San German PR
WPRM-FM San Juan PR
WVOZ(AM) San Juan PR
KHER(AM) Crystal City TX
KFZO(FM) Denton TX
*KEPX(FM) Eagle Pass TX
KGRW(FM) Friona TX
KGOL(AM) Humble TX
KQLM(FM) Odessa TX
KMFM(AM) Premont TX

French
KROF(AM) Abbeville LA
KEUN(AM) Eunice LA
KLEB(AM) Golden Meadow LA

Full Service
WTLS(AM) Tallassee AL
*KHDX(FM) Conway AR
KHTS(AM) Canyon Country CA
KVCU(AM) Boulder CO
KIUP(AM) Durango CO
KVRH-FM Salida CO
WLAD(AM) Danbury CT
WTIC(AM) Hartford CT
WICH(AM) Norwich CT
WILI(AM) Willimantic CT
WDEL(AM) Wilmington DE
KNUI(AM) Kahului HI
WMT(AM) Cedar Rapids IA
KROS(AM) Clinton IA
KDTH(AM) Dubuque IA
WJBC(AM) Bloomington IL
WSQR(AM) Sycamore IL
WIMS(AM) Michigan City IN
WZZB(AM) Seymour IN
WZZY(FM) Winchester IN
WFKY(AM) Frankfort KY
WCLU(AM) Glasgow KY
WQRC(FM) Barnstable MA
WNAW(AM) North Adams MA
WBRK(AM) Pittsfield MA
WNAV(AM) Annapolis MD
WTVB(AM) Coldwater MI
WDBC(AM) Escanaba MI
WHTC(AM) Holland MI
WION(AM) Ionia MI
WSAM(AM) Saginaw MI
WSJM(AM) Saint Joseph MI
KLFD(AM) Litchfield MN
KCAJ-FM Roseau MN
WJON(AM) Saint Cloud MN
KQRV(FM) Deer Lodge MT
KUSO(FM) Albion NE
KBRL(AM) McCook NE
KELK(AM) Elko NV
WENT(AM) Gloversville NY
WSYR(AM) Syracuse NY
WRIP(FM) Windham NY
WATH(AM) Athens OH
WHBC(AM) Canton OH
*WCDR-FM Cedarville OH
WBEX(AM) Chillicothe OH
*WOHC(FM) Chillicothe OH
WLW(AM) Cincinnati OH
WHIO(AM) Dayton OH
*WOHP(FM) Portsmouth OH
KBCH(AM) Lincoln City OR
KEX(AM) Portland OR
WBVP(AM) Beaver Falls PA
WEEU(AM) Reading PA
*WBLQ(FM) Westerly RI
WLSC(AM) Loris SC
WOPI(AM) Bristol TN
KNAF(AM) Fredericksburg TX
KSEY-FM Seymour TX
KSST(AM) Sulphur Springs TX
KTBB(AM) Tyler TX
WAGE(AM) Leesburg VA

WFAD(AM) Middlebury VT
WOMT(AM) Manitowoc WI
WFHR(AM) Wisconsin Rapids WI
WMOV(AM) Ravenswood WV
KFBC(AM) Cheyenne WY

Golden Oldies
WGOL(AM) Russellville AL
KBBQ-FM Fort Smith AR
WRZN(AM) Hernando FL
WOKA(AM) Douglas GA
WDQX(FM) Morton IL
WQCY(FM) Quincy IL
WSDM-FM Brazil IN
WGOP(AM) Pocomoke City MD
WGTO(AM) Cassopolis MI
WWKN(FM) Marshall MI
KOZY(AM) Grand Rapids MN
KBEK(FM) Mora MN
WWMY(FM) Raleigh NC
WIBT(FM) Shelby NC
WCHN(AM) Norwich NY
WLOH(AM) Lancaster OH
KSEO(AM) Durant OK
WIBZ(FM) Wedgefield SC
KMCM(FM) Odessa TX
WEIR(AM) Weirton WV

Gospel
KAKN(FM) Naknek AK
KICY(AM) Nome AK
WAVU(AM) Albertville AL
WANA(AM) Anniston AL
WRAB(AM) Arab AL
WBCA(AM) Bay Minette AL
WAGG(AM) Birmingham AL
WAYE(AM) Birmingham AL
WXJC(AM) Birmingham AL
*WELJ(FM) Brewton AL
WBYE(AM) Calera AL
WEIS(AM) Centre AL
WZTQ(AM) Centre AL
WBIB(AM) Centreville AL
WQEM(FM) Columbiana AL
WXJC-FM Cordova AL
WDLK(AM) Dadeville AL
WCMA(AM) Daleville AL
WXAL(AM) Demopolis AL
WAGF(AM) Dothan AL
WRJL-FM Eva AL
WJLD(AM) Fairfield AL
WKWL(AM) Florala AL
WGEA(AM) Geneva AL
WJBB(AM) Haleyville AL
WERH(AM) Hamilton AL
*WKNG-FM Heflin AL
WENN(FM) Hoover AL
WDJL(AM) Huntsville AL
WEUP(AM) Huntsville AL
WEUV(AM) Huntsville AL
*WJAB(AM) Huntsville AL
WLOR(AM) Huntsville AL
*WOCG(FM) Huntsville AL
WLPH(AM) Irondale AL
WRJX(AM) Jackson AL
WIXI(AM) Jasper AL
WGOK(AM) Mobile AL
WLVV(AM) Mobile AL
WMFC(AM) Monroeville AL
WMGY(AM) Montgomery AL
WURL(AM) Moody AL
WHIY(AM) Moulton AL
*WJIF(FM) Opp AL
WHAL(AM) Phenix City AL
WKXK(FM) Pine Hill AL
WQAH(AM) Priceville AL
WLPR(AM) Prichard AL
WVSM(AM) Rainsville AL
WRMG(AM) Red Bay AL
WKAX(AM) Russellville AL
WZCT(AM) Scottsboro AL
WBTG-FM Sheffield AL
WNUZ(AM) Talladega AL
WTSK(AM) Tuscaloosa AL

Programming on Radio Stations in the U.S.

WWPG(AM) Tuscaloosa AL	*WJTG(FM) Fort Valley GA	WBFC(AM) Stanton KY	WHLH(FM) Jackson MS	WGTM(AM) Wilson NC
WBIL(AM) Tuskegee AL	WXKO(AM) Fort Valley GA	*WJCR-FM Upton KY	*WMPR(FM) Jackson MS	WLLY(AM) Wilson NC
*WEBT(FM) Valley AL	WXJO(AM) Gordon GA	KWDF(AM) Ball LA	WOAD(AM) Jackson MS	WBTE(AM) Windsor NC
WJEC(FM) Vernon AL	WTHV(AM) Hahira GA	*WJFM(FM) Baton Rouge LA	WZRX(AM) Jackson MS	WNBR-FM Windsor NC
KNWA(AM) Bellefonte AR	WKLY(AM) Hartwell GA	WNDC(AM) Baton Rouge LA	*WJTA(FM) Kosciusko MS	WURB(AM) Windsor NC
KBRI(AM) Brinkley AR	WVOH(AM) Hazlehurst GA	WXOK(AM) Baton Rouge LA	WAML(AM) Laurel MS	WAAA(AM) Winston-Salem NC
KPZK-FM Cabot AR	WGML(AM) Hinesville GA	WIKC(AM) Bogalusa LA	WESY(AM) Leland MS	WPOL(AM) Winston-Salem NC
KNHD(AM) Camden AR	WVKX(AM) Irwinton GA	*KMRL(AM) Buras LA	WXTN(AM) Lexington MS	WSMX(AM) Winston-Salem NC
KWXT(AM) Dardanelle AR	*WTLD(FM) Jesup GA	KDLA(AM) De Ridder LA	*WPRL(FM) Lorman MS	*WXRI(FM) Winston-Salem NC
*KAYH(FM) Fayetteville AR	*WMOC(AM) Lumber City GA	KGGM(FM) Delhi LA	WRBE(AM) Lucedale MS	WYNC(AM) Yanceyville NC
KFSA(AM) Fort Smith AR	WDDO(AM) Macon GA	WCKW(AM) Garyville LA	WAPF(AM) McComb MS	KHRT(AM) Minot ND
KTCS(AM) Fort Smith AR	WLCG(AM) Macon GA	KKNO(AM) Gretna LA	WMER(AM) Meridian MS	KTFJ(AM) Dakota City NE
*KBPB(AM) Harrison AR	WKKP(AM) McDonough GA	WOPR(FM) Lacombe LA	WNBN(AM) Meridian MS	*KJLT-FM North Platte NE
KJIW-FM Helena AR	WHCG(AM) Metter GA	KFXZ(AM) Lafayette LA	WMIS(AM) Natchez MS	WIMG(AM) Ewing NJ
KVLO(FM) Humnoke AR	WKGQ(AM) Milledgeville GA	KXZZ(AM) Lake Charles LA	WOSM(FM) Ocean Springs MS	WNSW(AM) Newark NJ
KAAY(AM) Little Rock AR	WKUN(AM) Monroe GA	KJVC(FM) Mansfield LA	WRJW(AM) Picayune MS	*WXXY-FM Port Republic NJ
*KABF(FM) Little Rock AR	WMNZ(AM) Montezuma GA	KRJO(AM) Monroe LA	WSEL(AM) Pontotoc MS	WFAI(AM) Salem NJ
KITA(AM) Little Rock AR	WSSA(AM) Morrow GA	WYLD(AM) New Orleans LA	WSEL-FM Pontotoc MS	*WFDU(FM) Teaneck NJ
KJBN(AM) Little Rock AR	WMTM(AM) Moultrie GA	KTTP(AM) Pineville LA	WRPM(AM) Poplarville MS	WNJC(AM) Washington Township NJ
KPZK(AM) Little Rock AR	WALH(AM) Mountain City GA	WPRF(FM) Reserve LA	WXHB(FM) Richton MS	*KUPR(FM) Alamogordo NM
KENA(AM) Mena AR	WRBX(FM) Reidsville GA	KRUS(AM) Ruston LA	WSAO(AM) Senatobia MS	*KHII(FM) Cloudcroft NM
*KLLN(FM) Newark AR	WTNL(AM) Reidsville GA	KNCB(AM) Vivian LA	WAVN(AM) Southaven MS	WUFO(AM) Amherst NY
*KCAT(AM) Pine Bluff AR	WZOT(AM) Rockmart GA	WCMX(AM) Leominster MA	*WAQB(FM) Tupelo MS	WBBF(AM) Buffalo NY
KTPA(AM) Prescott AR	WROM(AM) Rome GA	WBGR(AM) Baltimore MD	WRTM(AM) Vicksburg MS	WTHE(AM) Mineola NY
KOSE(AM) Wilson AR	WBIC(AM) Royston GA	WCAO(AM) Baltimore MD	WROB(AM) West Point MS	*WOFN(FM) Beach City OH
*KCJH(FM) Livingston CA	WSNT(AM) Sandersville GA	WWIN(AM) Baltimore MD	*KPGB(FM) Pryor MT	WGFT(AM) Campbell OH
*KYCC(FM) Stockton CA	WHGM(AM) Savannah GA	*WLIC(FM) Frostburg MD	WRCS(AM) Ahoskie NC	WINW(AM) Canton OH
KDYA(AM) Vallejo CA	WJLG(AM) Savannah GA	WFBR(AM) Glen Burnie MD	*WTJY(FM) Asheboro NC	WJMO(AM) Cleveland Heights OH
KLDC(AM) Brighton CO	WSOK(AM) Savannah GA	*WAIJ(FM) Grantsville MD	WSKY(AM) Asheville NC	WVKO(AM) Columbus OH
WDJZ(AM) Bridgeport CT	WTYB(FM) Springfield GA	WPGC(AM) Morningside MD	WPYB(AM) Benson NC	WCNW(AM) Fairfield OH
WNEZ(AM) Windsor CT	WJAT(AM) Swainsboro GA	WJDY(AM) Salisbury MD	WFGW(AM) Black Mountain NC	WJYD(AM) London OH
WYCB(AM) Washington DC	WHGH(AM) Thomasville GA	*WHCF(FM) Bangor ME	WVOE(AM) Chadbourn NC	WJTB(AM) North Ridgeville OH
WKEN(AM) Dover DE	WSTT(AM) Thomasville GA	*WFST(FM) Caribou ME	WRNA(AM) China Grove NC	WXIC(AM) Waverly OH
WAMS(AM) Newark DE	WLET(AM) Toccoa GA	WFLT(AM) Flint MI	WYZD(AM) Dobson NC	*WCSU-FM Wilberforce OH
WHIM(AM) Apopka FL	WTHB-FM Waynesboro GA	WMKM(AM) Inkster MI	WCKB(AM) Dunn NC	WLRD(FM) Willard OH
WAVP(AM) Avon Park FL	WIMO(AM) Winder GA	*WUNN(AM) Mason MI	WDUR(AM) Durham NC	WKFI(AM) Wilmington OH
WSWN(AM) Belle Glade FL	WYHG(AM) Young Harris GA	WEXL(AM) Royal Oak MI	WTIK(AM) Durham NC	*KQUJ(FM) Ada OK
*WWKO(FM) Belleview FL	KOJY(FM) Bloomfield IA	WWSJ(AM) Saint Johns MI	WCLW(AM) Eden NC	*KTGS(FM) Ada OK
WNVY(AM) Cantonment FL	KTFC(FM) Sioux City IA	WCHB(AM) Taylor MI	WBXB(FM) Edenton NC	*KNYD(FM) Broken Arrow OK
*WWKG(FM) Clermont FL	KTFG(FM) Sioux Rapids IA	WWJC(AM) Duluth MN	WFMO(AM) Fairmont NC	*KVAZ(FM) Henryetta OK
*WJED(FM) Dogwood Lakes Estate FL	*KBBG(FM) Waterloo IA	KNOF(FM) Saint Paul MN	WSTS(FM) Fairmont NC	KKRX(AM) Lawton OK
WKIQ(AM) Eustis FL	WXAN(FM) Ava IL	*KOZO(FM) Branson MO	WIDU(AM) Fayetteville NC	KVIS(AM) Miami OK
*WNLE(FM) Fernandina Beach FL	*WTSG(FM) Carlinville IL	KCRV(AM) Caruthersville MO	WWOL(AM) Forest City NC	KTLV(AM) Midwest City OK
WIRA(AM) Fort Pierce FL	WEIC(AM) Charleston IL	*KNLH(FM) Cedar Hill MO	WNNL(FM) Fuquay-Varina NC	KPGM(AM) Pawhuska OK
WTMN(AM) Gainesville FL	WGRB(AM) Chicago IL	*KYRV(FM) Concordia MO	WFMC(AM) Goldsboro NC	*KLRB(FM) Stuart OK
WLVF(AM) Haines City FL	*WSSD(FM) Chicago IL	*KNLQ(FM) Cuba MO	WYCV(AM) Granite Falls NC	*KFXT(FM) Sulphur OK
*WLVF-FM Haines City FL	WESL(AM) East St. Louis IL	KAUL(FM) Ellington MO	WEAL(AM) Greensboro NC	KTLQ(AM) Tahlequah OK
*WAPN(FM) Holly Hill FL	WYRB(FM) Genoa IL	KGGN(AM) Gladstone MO	WKEW(AM) Greensboro NC	*KAZC(FM) Tishomingo OK
WZAZ(AM) Jacksonville FL	WVEL-FM Glasford IL	*KJIR(FM) Hannibal MO	*WNAA(FM) Greensboro NC	KIMY(FM) Watonga OK
WWAB(AM) Lakeland FL	WBGX(AM) Harvey IL	*KJLU(FM) Jefferson City MO	WPET(AM) Greensboro NC	WPWA(AM) Chester PA
WTYS-FM Marianna FL	WDID(AM) Highland IL	KPRT(AM) Kansas City MO	WKDX(AM) Hamlet NC	WADV(AM) Lebanon PA
WMBM(AM) Miami Beach FL	WWHN(AM) Joliet IL	KMHM(AM) Lutesville MO	WHNC(AM) Henderson NC	WJSM-FM Martinsburg PA
*WWIA(FM) Palm Bay FL	WSRB(FM) Lansing IL	KMRF(AM) Marshfield MO	*WPIR(FM) Hickory NC	*WRIJ(FM) Masontown PA
WBRD(AM) Palmetto FL	WGGH(AM) Marion IL	*KJAB-FM Mexico MO	WJCV(AM) Jacksonville NC	WPGR(AM) Monroeville PA
WRNE(AM) Pensacola FL	WINU(AM) Shelbyville IL	*KNEO(FM) Neosho MO	WRKB(AM) Kannapolis NC	*WRWJ(FM) Murrysville PA
WZNO(AM) Pensacola FL	WBCP(AM) Urbana IL	*KNLG(FM) New Bloomfield MO	WKTE(AM) King NC	WGBN(AM) New Kensington PA
*WTLG(FM) Starke FL	WNTS(AM) Beech Grove IN	KPWB(AM) Piedmont MO	WELS(AM) Kinston NC	WNAP(AM) Norristown PA
WHBT(AM) Tallahassee FL	WYGS(FM) Columbus IN	*KOKS(FM) Poplar Bluff MO	WELS-FM Kinston NC	WANS(AM) Anderson SC
WEXY(AM) Wilton Manors FL	WPWX(FM) Hammond IN	*KNLP(FM) Potosi MO	WEWO(AM) Laurinburg NC	WBAW-FM Barnwell SC
WOKB(AM) Winter Garden FL	WTLC(AM) Indianapolis IN	KATZ(AM) Saint Louis MO	WAGR(AM) Lumberton NC	WVGB(AM) Beaufort SC
WSIR(AM) Winter Haven FL	WLHN(AM) Muncie IN	KSTL(AM) Saint Louis MO	WHBK(AM) Marshall NC	WBSC(AM) Bennettsville SC
WJYZ(AM) Albany GA	WFIA-FM New Albany IN	*KBIY(FM) Van Buren MO	WDSL(AM) Mocksville NC	WSPX(FM) Bowman SC
WAJQ(AM) Alma GA	WSLM(AM) Salem IN	WFCA(FM) Ackerman MS	WDEX(AM) Monroe NC	WGCV(AM) Cayce SC
WXAG(AM) Athens GA	WFRI(AM) Winamac IN	WIZK(AM) Bay Springs MS	WIXE(AM) Monroe NC	WXTC(AM) Charleston SC
WAFS(AM) Atlanta GA	*WVHM(FM) Benton KY	WBYP(FM) Belzoni MS	WCIS(AM) Morganton NC	WGCD(AM) Chester SC
WYZE(AM) Atlanta GA	WSFE(AM) Burnside KY	WELZ(AM) Belzoni MS	WCVP(AM) Murphy NC	WPFM(AM) Darlington SC
WGUS(AM) Augusta GA	WCVG(AM) Covington KY	WCHJ(AM) Brookhaven MS	WWNB(AM) New Bern NC	WDSC(AM) Dillon SC
WTHB(AM) Augusta GA	WEKT(AM) Elkton KY	WAJV(FM) Brooksville MS	WAUG(AM) New Hope NC	WEGX(FM) Dillon SC
WGMI(AM) Bremen GA	WIOK(FM) Falmouth KY	WMGO(AM) Canton MS	WCBQ(AM) Oxford NC	WYNN(AM) Florence SC
WULS(FM) Broxton GA	WFUL(AM) Fulton KY	WONG(AM) Canton MS	WDEX(AM) Monroe NC	WAGI-FM Gaffney SC
WEAM-FM Buena Vista GA	WOKE(FM) Garrison KY	WCLD(AM) Cleveland MS	WTEL(AM) Red Springs NC	WLMC(AM) Georgetown SC
WQIL(FM) Chauncey GA	WFSR(AM) Harlan KY	WFFF(AM) Columbia MS	WEGG(AM) Rose Hill NC	*WTBI-FM Greenville SC
WCLA(AM) Claxton GA	WKVG(AM) Jenkins KY	WTWG(AM) Columbus MS	*WOGR-FM Salisbury NC	WPJM(AM) Greer SC
WRWH(AM) Cleveland GA	*WHMR(FM) Ledbetter KY	WTYJ(FM) Fayette MS	WXKL(AM) Sanford NC	WJDJ(AM) Hartsville SC
WOKS(AM) Columbus GA	WGWM(AM) London KY	WJIW(FM) Greenville MS	WVCB(AM) Shallotte NC	*WLGI(FM) Hemingway SC
WSHE(AM) Columbus GA	WLLV(AM) Louisville KY	WGRM(AM) Greenwood MS	WMPM(AM) Smithfield NC	WJBS(AM) Holly Hill SC
WCON(AM) Cornelia GA	WMIK(AM) Middlesboro KY	WGRM-FM Greenwood MS	WGMA(AM) Spindale NC	WPDT(FM) Johnsonville SC
WCUG(AM) Cuthbert GA	WMIK-FM Middlesboro KY	WKXG(AM) Greenwood MS	WTAB(AM) Tabor City NC	WGSS(FM) Kingstree SC
WDPC(AM) Dallas GA	WFLW(AM) Monticello KY	WQFX(FM) Gulfport MS	WCPS(AM) Tarboro NC	*WKCL(FM) Ladson SC
WTTI(AM) Dalton GA	WRVK(AM) Mt. Vernon KY	WORV(AM) Hattiesburg MS	WTLK(AM) Taylorsville NC	WAGL(AM) Lancaster SC
WSEM(AM) Donalsonville GA	WCGW(AM) Nicholasville KY	WOEG(AM) Hazlehurst MS	WJRM(AM) Troy NC	WJAY(AM) Mullins SC
WDCY(AM) Douglasville GA	WWFT(AM) Nicholasville KY	WKRA(AM) Holly Springs MS	WOBX(AM) Wanchese NC	WKZK(AM) North Augusta SC
WTJH(AM) East Point GA	WSIP(AM) Paintsville KY	WKRA-FM Holly Springs MS	WENC(AM) Whiteville NC	WPJK(AM) Orangeburg SC
WLJA-FM Ellijay GA	WSIP-FM Paintsville KY	WHAL-FM Horn Lake MS	WWWC(AM) Wilkesboro NC	*WSSB-FM Orangeburg SC
WPZE(FM) Fayetteville GA	WCBR(AM) Richmond KY	WCPC(AM) Houston MS	WIAM(AM) Williamston NC	WRML(FM) Pageland SC
WBHB(AM) Fitzgerald GA	WIDS(AM) Russell Springs KY	WNLA(AM) Indianola MS	WLSG(AM) Wilmington NC	WQKI(AM) Saint Matthews SC
WQMJ(FM) Forsyth GA	WRLV(AM) Salyersville KY	*WVSD(FM) Itta Bena MS	WWIL(AM) Wilmington NC	WTUA(FM) Saint Stephen SC

Broadcasting & Cable Yearbook 2006

Programming on Radio Stations in the U.S.

WCSZ(AM) Sans Souci SC
WQMC(AM) Sumter SC
WALD(AM) Walterboro SC
WAAW(FM) Williston SC
WWGM(FM) Alamo TN
WOJG(FM) Bolivar TN
WJOC(AM) Chattanooga TN
WMCH(AM) Church Hill TN
WCTZ(AM) Clarksville TN
WCLE(AM) Cleveland TN
WSGM(FM) Coalmont TN
WMRB(AM) Columbia TN
WHUB(AM) Cookeville TN
WEMB(AM) Erwin TN
WEKR(AM) Fayetteville TN
WTNK(AM) Hartsville TN
WJAK(AM) Jackson TN
WDEB(FM) Jamestown TN
WWAM(AM) Jasper TN
WJJT(AM) Jellico TN
WETB(AM) Johnson City TN
WBBX(AM) Kingston TN
WKGN(AM) Knoxville TN
WKXV(AM) Knoxville TN
WGLH(FM) La Follette TN
WEEN(AM) Lafayette TN
WDXL(AM) Lexington TN
WRKQ(AM) Madisonville TN
WBMC(AM) McMinnville TN
WBBP(FM) Memphis TN
WLOK(AM) Memphis TN
WXRQ(AM) Mount Pleasant TN
WNAH(AM) Nashville TN
WNSG(AM) Nashville TN
WUAT(AM) Pikeville TN
WOFE(AM) Rockwood TN
WJOR-FM Saint Joseph TN
WSIB(FM) Selmer TN
WJBZ-FM Seymour TN
WLIJ(AM) Shelbyville TN
WSMT(AM) Sparta TN
WEYE(FM) Surgoinsville TN
WDEH(AM) Sweetwater TN
WJIG(AM) Tullahoma TN
WECO(AM) Wartburg TN
WVRY(FM) Waverly TN
WQSE(AM) White Bluff TN
WBOZ(FM) Woodbury TN
*KAGT-FM Abilene TX
KLVQ(AM) Athens TX
KNRB(FM) Atlanta TX
KPYN(AM) Atlanta TX
*KAZI-FM Austin TX
KWWJ(AM) Baytown TX
KZZB(AM) Beaumont TX
*KHVT(FM) Bloomington TX
KGAS(AM) Carthage TX
KDET(AM) Center TX
KYOK(AM) Conroe TX
KNGR(AM) Daingerfield TX
KNIT(AM) Dallas TX
*KDKR(FM) Decatur TX
KNNK(FM) Dimmitt TX
*KWCB(FM) Floresville TX
KHVN(AM) Fort Worth TX
KKGM(AM) Fort Worth TX
KWRD(AM) Henderson TX
KJTX(FM) Jefferson TX
KRMY(AM) Killeen TX
KLVT(AM) Levelland TX
KZZN(AM) Littlefield TX
KFIT(AM) Lockhart TX
*KFTG(FM) Pasadena TX
*KPVU(FM) Prairie View TX
KBIC(FM) Raymondville TX
KCHL(AM) San Antonio TX
KFIT EXP STN San Antonio TX
KZEE(AM) Weatherford TX
KWNS(FM) Winnsboro TX
KLLB(AM) West Jordan UT
WWDW(FM) Alberta VA
WTTX-FM Appomattox VA
WBTX(AM) Broadway-Timberville VA
WKBY(AM) Chatham VA
WCPK(AM) Chesapeake VA
WVSG(FM) Coeburn VA
WFIC(AM) Collinsville VA

WPZZ(FM) Crewe VA
WDVA(AM) Danville VA
WILA(AM) Danville VA
WDUF(AM) Duffield VA
WGFC(AM) Floyd VA
WLQM(AM) Franklin VA
WWWJ(AM) Galax VA
WHHV(AM) Hillsville VA
WHFD(FM) Lawrenceville VA
WLRV(AM) Lebanon VA
WLLL(AM) Lynchburg VA
WMEV(AM) Marion VA
WTJZ(AM) Newport News VA
WROU(AM) Petersburg VA
WGPL(AM) Portsmouth VA
WGTH(AM) Richlands VA
WGTH-FM Richlands VA
WFTH(AM) Richmond VA
WWWR(AM) Roanoke VA
WYTI(AM) Rocky Mount VA
WXMY(AM) Saltville VA
WRAR(AM) Tappahannock VA
*WTRM(FM) Winchester VA
*WYCS(FM) Yorktown VA
WGOD(AM) Charlotte Amalie VI
KGSG(FM) Pasco WA
KZIZ(AM) Sumner WA
WGLB(AM) Elm Grove WI
WJLS(AM) Beckley WV
*WKJL(FM) Clarksburg WV
WPDX(AM) Clarksburg WV
*WFGH(FM) Fort Gay WV
WAMN(AM) Green Valley WV
WEMM-FM Huntington WV
WOTR(FM) Lost Creek WV
WWYO(AM) Pineville WV
WBGS(AM) Point Pleasant WV
*WPCN(FM) Point Pleasant WV
WAEY(AM) Princeton WV
WRRL(AM) Rainelle WV
WYKM(AM) Rupert WV
WSCW(AM) South Charleston WV
WVRC(AM) Spencer WV
*WMLJ(FM) Summersville WV
WAFD(FM) Webster Springs WV

Greek

WXYB(AM) Indian Rocks Beach FL
WPSO(AM) New Port Richey FL
WEEF(AM) Highland Park IL
WNTN(AM) Newton MA

Inspirational

*KUDU(FM) Tok AK
*WOCG(FM) Huntsville AL
*KFLR-FM Phoenix AZ
*KFLT(AM) Tucson AZ
*KAXL(FM) Green Acres CA
*KTLW(FM) Lancaster CA
*KCJH(FM) Livingston CA
*KHCS(FM) Palm Desert CA
*KVIP(AM) Redding CA
*KVIP-FM Redding CA
*KYCC(FM) Stockton CA
*KARM(FM) Visalia CA
*KTCF(FM) Dolores CO
*KTPL(FM) Pueblo CO
*WKZM(FM) Sarasota FL
WTJH(AM) East Point GA
*KSDA-FM Agat GU
*KCMR(FM) Mason City IA
*KNWS-FM Waterloo IA
KBGN(AM) Caldwell ID
WRMS(AM) Beardstown IL
*WZRS(FM) Pana IL
*WLWJ(FM) Petersburg IL
*WIHM(FM) Taylorville IL
*WGNR-FM Anderson IN
*KXJH(FM) Linton IN
*WRXH(FM) Plymouth IN
*WUBS(FM) South Bend IN
*WATI(AM) Vincennes IN
*WTRT(FM) Benton KY
*KMRL(FM) Buras LA

*KBAN(FM) De Ridder LA
*KYLC(FM) Lake Charles LA
WPRF(FM) Reserve LA
*WHCF(FM) Bangor ME
*WUFN(FM) Albion MI
*WNFA(FM) Port Huron MI
*WNFR(FM) Sandusky MI
*WTHN(FM) Sault Ste. Marie MI
*KTGG(AM) Spring Arbor MI
*KDNI(FM) Duluth MN
*KTIS-FM Minneapolis MN
*KBPG(FM) Montevideo MN
*KBHZ(FM) Willmar MN
KOCR(AM) Joplin MO
WBVV(FM) Booneville MS
*WURC(FM) Holly Springs MS
*KBLW(FM) Billings MT
KMCJ(FM) Colstrip MT
*KGFC(FM) Great Falls MT
*KXEI(FM) Havre MT
*KVCM(FM) Helena MT
WPZS(FM) Albemarle NC
WCLN-FM Clinton NC
*WGPS(FM) Elizabeth City NC
WNNL(FM) Fuquay-Varina NC
*KAYA(FM) Hubbard NE
*KPNO(FM) Norfolk NE
*KJLT-FM North Platte NE
*KGRD(FM) Orchard NE
*WSJI(FM) Cherry Hill NJ
WIBG(AM) Ocean City NJ
*KFLQ(FM) Albuquerque NM
*WNGN(FM) Argyle NY
*WCII(FM) Spencer NY
*WCRF(FM) Cleveland OH
*WVMC-FM Mansfield OH
*WVML(FM) Millersburg OH
*WVMS(FM) Sandusky OH
*KSYE(FM) Frederick OK
KGLC(FM) Miami OK
*KLVV(FM) Ponca City OK
*KWYA(FM) Astoria OR
*KMWR(FM) Brookings OR
WDBA(FM) DuBois PA
*WAWN(FM) Franklin PA
*WVMN(FM) New Castle PA
WLMC(AM) Georgetown SC
WJNI(FM) Ladson SC
WFMV(FM) South Congaree SC
*WLJI(FM) Summerton SC
KLMP(FM) Rapid City SD
WLRM(AM) Millington TN
*KCBI(FM) Dallas TX
*KHCH(FM) Huntsville TX
KCRN-FM San Angelo TX
*KHTA(FM) Wake Village TX
*WAUQ(FM) Charles City VA
*WARN(FM) Culpeper VA
WTJZ(AM) Newport News VA
WRIS(AM) Roanoke VA
*WCMD-FM Barre VT
*WGLY-FM Bolton VT
*WCKJ(FM) Saint Johnsbury VT
*WGLV(FM) Woodstock VT
KCIS(AM) Edmonds WA
*KCSH(FM) Ellensburg WA
*KAYB(FM) Sunnyside WA
*KYPL(FM) Yakima WA
WRLB(AM) Rainelle WV
*KOHR(FM) Sheridan WY

Irish

WROL(AM) Boston MA

Italian

WDZK(AM) Bloomfield CT
WEEF(AM) Highland Park IL

Japanese

KZOO(AM) Honolulu HI

Jazz

*KSKA(FM) Anchorage AK
WAUD(AM) Auburn AL
*WVSU-FM Birmingham AL
*WJAB(FM) Huntsville AL
*WQPR(FM) Muscle Shoals AL
*WAPR(FM) Selma AL
*WUAL-FM Tuscaloosa AL
*KBSA(FM) El Dorado AR
*KUAF(FM) Fayetteville AR
*KASU(FM) Jonesboro AR
*KABF(FM) Little Rock AR
*KUAR(FM) Little Rock AR
*KJZZ(FM) Phoenix AZ
KYOT-FM Phoenix AZ
*KUAZ(AM) Tucson AZ
*KUAZ-FM Tucson AZ
KWRK(FM) Window Rock AZ
*KAWC-FM Yuma AZ
*KNCA(FM) Burney CA
KRML(FM) Carmel CA
KVIN(AM) Ceres CA
*KCHO(FM) Chico CA
*KSPC(FM) Claremont CA
KRVR(FM) Copperopolis CA
*KECG(FM) El Cerrito CA
*KFSR(FM) Fresno CA
KMGQ(FM) Goleta CA
*KKJZ(FM) Long Beach CA
KTWV(FM) Los Angeles CA
*KSBR(FM) Mission Viejo CA
*KNSQ(FM) Mount Shasta CA
*KQNC(FM) Quincy CA
*KXJZ(FM) Sacramento CA
*KSDS(FM) San Diego CA
KKSF(FM) San Francisco CA
*KSJS(FM) San Jose CA
*KCBX(FM) San Luis Obispo CA
*KCSM(FM) San Mateo CA
KRUZ(FM) Santa Barbara CA
*KSBX(FM) Santa Barbara CA
KSMJ(FM) Shafter CA
*KZSU(FM) Stanford CA
*KXJS(FM) Sutter CA
*KCLU(FM) Thousand Oaks CA
*KRZA(FM) Alamosa CO
*KAJX(FM) Aspen CO
*KUVO(FM) Denver CO
*KCME(FM) Manitou Springs CO
*WDJW(FM) Somers CT
*WPFW(FM) Washington DC
*WRTX(FM) Dover DE
WJSJ(FM) Fernandina Beach FL
*WGCU-FM Fort Myers FL
*WUFT-FM Gainesville FL
WXJZ(FM) Gainesville FL
*WJUF(FM) Inverness FL
WCNK(FM) Key West FL
WSJT(FM) Lakeland FL
*WMKO(FM) Marco FL
*WDNA(FM) Miami FL
WLVE(FM) Miami Beach FL
*WUCF(FM) Orlando FL
WASJ(FM) Panama City Beach FL
WSJF(FM) Saint Augustine Beach FL
*WUSF(FM) Tampa FL
WGYL(FM) Vero Beach FL
WLOQ(FM) Winter Park FL
*WCLK(FM) Atlanta GA
WJZZ-FM Roswell GA
*WSVH(FM) Savannah GA
*KIPO(FM) Honolulu HI
*WOI-FM Ames IA
KDRB(AM) Ankeny IA
*KCPS(AM) Burlington IA
*KCCK-FM Cedar Rapids IA
*KALA(FM) Davenport IA
*KJMC(FM) Des Moines IA
*KTPR(FM) Fort Dodge IA
*KBBG(FM) Waterloo IA
*KIBX(FM) Bonners Ferry ID
*KBSK(FM) McCall ID
*KISU-FM Pocatello ID
*KEZJ(FM) Twin Falls ID
*WBEZ(FM) Chicago IL
*WHPK-FM Chicago IL

WNUA(FM) Chicago IL
WPMJ(FM) Chillicothe IL
*WNIJ(FM) De Kalb IL
*WSIE(FM) Edwardsville IL
*WNUR-FM Evanston IL
*WDCB(FM) Glen Ellyn IL
*WBEQ(FM) Morris IL
*WGLT(FM) Normal IL
*WCBU(FM) Peoria IL
*WIPA(FM) Pittsfield IL
*WQUB(FM) Quincy IL
*WUIS(FM) Springfield IL
WBCP(AM) Urbana IL
*WFIU(FM) Bloomington IN
*WBEW(FM) Chesterton IN
*WVPE(FM) Elkhart IN
*WUEV(FM) Evansville IN
*WBOI(FM) Fort Wayne IN
*WICR(FM) Indianapolis IN
*WBAA(AM) West Lafayette IN
*KANH(FM) Emporia KS
KKCI(FM) Goodland KS
*KANU(FM) Lawrence KS
*KJHK(FM) Lawrence KS
*KANV(FM) Olsburg KS
*KRPS(FM) Pittsburg KS
*KMUW(FM) Wichita KS
*WKYL(FM) Lawrenceburg KY
*WFPK(FM) Louisville KY
*WKMS-FM Murray KY
*KLSU(FM) Baton Rouge LA
*WBRH(FM) Baton Rouge LA
*KEDM(FM) Monroe LA
*WWOZ(FM) New Orleans LA
KVCL(AM) Winnfield LA
*WFCR(FM) Amherst MA
*WMUA(FM) Amherst MA
*WGBH(FM) Boston MA
WHRB(FM) Cambridge MA
*WOMR(FM) Provincetown MA
*WICN(FM) Worcester MA
*WEAA(FM) Baltimore MD
WSMJ(FM) Baltimore MD
*WYPR(FM) Baltimore MD
*WFWM(FM) Frostburg MD
WQJZ(FM) Ocean Pines MD
*WESM(FM) Princess Anne MD
WBQI(FM) Bar Harbor ME
*WYAR(FM) Yarmouth ME
*WGVU-FM Allendale MI
*WCML-FM Alpena MI
*WUCX-FM Bay City MI
*WDET-FM Detroit MI
WGPR(FM) Detroit MI
*WBLU-FM Grand Rapids MI
*WCMW-FM Harbor Springs MI
*WMUK-FM Kalamazoo MI
*WLNZ-FM Lansing MI
*WNMU-FM Marquette MI
*WCMU-FM Mount Pleasant MI
*WCMB-FM Oscoda MI
*WSGR-FM Port Huron MI
*WCMZ-FM Sault Ste. Marie MI
*WWCM(FM) Standish MI
*WNMC-FM Traverse City MI
*WBLV-FM Twin Lake MI
WGVS-FM Whitehall MI
*WEMU(FM) Ypsilanti MI
*KBEM-FM Minneapolis MN
*WMCN(FM) Saint Paul MN
*KQAL(FM) Winona MN
*KRCU(FM) Cape Girardeau MO
*KRNW(FM) Chillicothe MO
*KWWC-FM Columbia MO
*KJLU(FM) Jefferson City MO
*KRLI(FM) Malta Bend MO
*KXCV(FM) Maryville MO
*KCOZ(FM) Point Lookout MO
*KCLC(FM) Saint Charles MO
*WMAH-FM Biloxi MS
*WMAE-FM Booneville MS
*WMAU-FM Bude MS
*WMAO-FM Greenwood MS
*WURC(FM) Holly Springs MS
*WVSD-FM Itta Bena MS
*WJSU-FM Jackson MS
*WMPN-FM Jackson MS

Broadcasting & Cable Yearbook 2006
D-707

Programming on Radio Stations in the U.S.

*WPRL(FM) Lorman MS
*WMAW-FM Meridian MS
*WMAB-FM Mississippi State MS
*WMAV-FM Oxford MS
WKBB(FM) West Point MS
*KEMC(FM) Billings MT
*KBMC(FM) Bozeman MT
*KAPC(FM) Butte MT
*KGPR(FM) Great Falls MT
*KUFN(FM) Hamilton MT
*KNMC(FM) Havre MT
*KUHM(FM) Helena MT
*KUKL(FM) Kalispell MT
*KUFM(FM) Missoula MT
*WCQS(FM) Asheville NC
*WASU-FM Boone NC
WVOE(AM) Chadbourn NC
*WNCU(FM) Durham NC
*WFSS(FM) Fayetteville NC
*WFQS(FM) Franklin NC
*WNAA(FM) Greensboro NC
*WUAG(FM) Greensboro NC
*WSHA(FM) Raleigh NC
*WDCC(FM) Sanford NC
WARR(AM) Warrenton NC
*WHQR(FM) Wilmington NC
*WSNC(FM) Winston-Salem NC
*KCND(FM) Bismarck ND
*KDPR(FM) Dickinson ND
*KFJM(FM) Grand Forks ND
*KPRJ(FM) Jamestown ND
*KMPR(FM) Minot ND
*KPPR(FM) Williston ND
*KLPR(FM) Kearney NE
*KZUM(FM) Lincoln NE
*KIOS-FM Omaha NE
*WNEC-FM Henniker NH
WEZS(AM) Laconia NH
*WBGO(FM) Newark NJ
*WRTQ(FM) Ocean City NJ
WPRB(FM) Princeton NJ
*KGLP(FM) Gallup NM
*KRWG(FM) Las Cruces NM
*KSFR(FM) Santa Fe NM
*KRNM(FM) Chalan Kanoa-Saipan NP
*KNCC(FM) Elko NV
*KBSJ(FM) Jackpot NV
*KUNR(FM) Reno NV
KJZS(FM) Sparks NV
*WSQX-FM Binghamton NY
*WCWP(FM) Brookville NY
*WBFO(FM) Buffalo NY
*WEOS(FM) Geneva NY
*WGMC(FM) Greece NY
*WRCU-FM Hamilton NY
*WVHC(FM) Herkimer NY
*WSQA(FM) Hornell NY
*WICB(FM) Ithaca NY
*WUBJ(FM) Jamestown NY
*WHCR-FM New York NY
*WKCR-FM New York NY
*WOLN(FM) Olean NY
WJZR(FM) Rochester NY
*WSPN(FM) Saratoga Springs NY
*WLIU(FM) Southampton NY
*WAER(FM) Syracuse NY
*WBGU(FM) Bowling Green OH
*WOUH-FM Chillicothe OH
*WCPN(FM) Cleveland OH
*WDPS(FM) Dayton OH
*WSLN(FM) Delaware OH
WDSJ(FM) Greenville OH
WJZA(FM) Lancaster OH
*WMRT(FM) Marietta OH
*WMUB(FM) Oxford OH
WJZK(FM) Richwood OH
*WXTS-FM Toledo OH
*WCSU-FM Wilberforce OH
*WOUZ(FM) Zanesville OH
*KALU(FM) Langston OK
*KGOU(FM) Norman OK
*KROU(FM) Spencer OK
*KSMF(FM) Ashland OR
*KSBA(FM) Coos Bay OR
*KBVR(FM) Corvallis OR
*KMHD(FM) Gresham OR
*KSKF(FM) Klamath Falls OR

*KOAP(FM) Lakeview OR
*KEZX(AM) Medford OR
*KLCO(FM) Newport OR
*WBUQ(FM) Bloomsburg PA
*WQLN-FM Erie PA
*WRTY(FM) Jackson Township PA
WJJZ(FM) Philadelphia PA
*WRTI(FM) Philadelphia PA
*WDUQ(FM) Pittsburgh PA
*WXAC(FM) Reading PA
*WUSR(FM) Scranton PA
*WVIA-FM Scranton PA
*WPSU(FM) State College PA
*WJAZ(FM) Summerdale PA
*WRKC(FM) Wilkes-Barre PA
*WPTC(FM) Williamsport PA
*WVYA(FM) Williamsport PA
WIBS(AM) Guayama PR
*WRUO(FM) Mayaguez PR
*WRTU(FM) San Juan PR
WJZS(FM) Block Island RI
*WELH(FM) Providence RI
*WSCI(FM) Charleston SC
*WSSB-FM Orangeburg SC
*WNSC-FM Rock Hill SC
WAZS(AM) Summerville SC
*WRJA-FM Sumter SC
KPSD(FM) Faith SD
*KQSD-FM Lowry SD
*KZSD-FM Martin SD
*KDSD-FM Pierpont SD
*KBHE-FM Rapid City SD
*KTSD-FM Reliance SD
*KAUR(FM) Sioux Falls SD
*KUSD(FM) Vermillion SD
WBOL(AM) Bolivar TN
*WUTC(FM) Chattanooga TN
*WFHU(FM) Henderson TN
*WUOT(FM) Knoxville TN
*WOEZ(FM) Maynardville TN
*WUMR(FM) Memphis TN
*WMOT(FM) Murfreesboro TN
*WFSK(FM) Nashville TN
*WRVU(FM) Nashville TN
*KUT(FM) Austin TX
*KVLU(FM) Beaumont TX
*KAMU-FM College Station TX
*KETR(FM) Commerce TX
*KEDT-FM Corpus Christi TX
*KTEP(FM) El Paso TX
*KTCU-FM Fort Worth TX
*KMBH-FM Harlingen TX
KHJZ-FM Houston TX
*KTSU(FM) Houston TX
*KSHU(FM) Huntsville TX
*KLDN(FM) Lufkin TX
*KHID(FM) McAllen TX
*KNTU(FM) McKinney TX
*KSAU(FM) Nacogdoches TX
KPJC(AM) Paris TX
*KWLD(FM) Plainview TX
*KUTX(FM) San Angelo TX
*KRTU(FM) San Antonio TX
KZSP(FM) South Padre Island TX
*KVRT(FM) Victoria TX
*KMCU(FM) Wichita Falls TX
*KUSR(FM) Logan UT
KBZN(FM) Ogden UT
*KUER(FM) Salt Lake City UT
*WVTU(FM) Charlottesville VA
*WVTW(FM) Charlottesville VA
*WVTR(FM) Marion VA
*WHRV(FM) Norfolk VA
*WVST-FM Petersburg VA
*WVRU(FM) Radford VA
*WVTF(FM) Roanoke VA
WJCD(FM) Windsor VA
*WIUJ(FM) Charlotte Amalie VI
*WRUV(FM) Burlington VT
*WVPS(FM) Burlington VT
*WRVT(FM) Rutland VT
*WVPA(FM) Saint Johnsbury VT
*WVPR(FM) Windsor VT
*KBCS(FM) Bellevue WA
*KZAZ(FM) Bellingham WA
*KEWU-FM Cheney WA
KOHO(FM) Leavenworth WA

*KVIX(FM) Port Angeles WA
*KZUU(FM) Pullman WA
*KPBX-FM Spokane WA
*KPLU-FM Tacoma WA
KYNR(FM) Toppenish WA
*WUEC(FM) Eau Claire WI
*WLSU(FM) La Crosse WI
*WYMS(FM) Milwaukee WI
*WWSP(FM) Stevens Point WI
*WSUW(FM) Whitewater WI
*WVPB(FM) Beckley WV
*WVPW(FM) Buckhannon WV
*WVPN(FM) Charleston WV
*WVWV(FM) Huntington WV
*WVEP(FM) Martinsburg WV
*WVPM(FM) Morgantown WV
*WVPG(FM) Parkersburg WV
*WVNP(FM) Wheeling WV
*KCWC-FM Riverton WY

Korean

KXMX(AM) Anaheim CA
KYPA(AM) Los Angeles CA
KFOX(AM) Torrance CA
KHRA(AM) Honolulu HI
KREA(AM) Honolulu HI
WKTA(AM) Evanston IL
WWRU(AM) Jersey City NJ
WDCT(AM) Fairfax VA
KWYZ(AM) Everett WA
KSUH(AM) Puyallup WA

Light Rock

WYNI(AM) Monroeville AL
WFNU(FM) Repton AL
KNEC(FM) Yuma CO
WJKI(FM) Bethany Beach DE
WLRQ-FM Cocoa FL
WMEZ(FM) Pensacola FL
WEGC(FM) Sasser GA
WTGA(AM) Thomaston GA
WTGA-FM Thomaston GA
KDAT(FM) Cedar Rapids IA
KLLT(FM) Spencer IA
WHOW-FM Clinton IL
WVEZ(FM) Louisville KY
WAVJ(FM) Princeton KY
WPKY(FM) Princeton KY
KSYR(FM) Benton LA
WGER(FM) Saginaw MI
KBEK(FM) Mora MN
KRVY-FM Starbuck MN
KHME(FM) Winona MN
WCNG(FM) Murphy NC
KZPR(FM) Minot ND
WLTQ(FM) Lincoln NE
KSFT-FM South Sioux City NE
WFPG-FM Atlantic City NJ
WWYY(FM) Belvidere NJ
WBHX(FM) Tuckerton NJ
WBTA(AM) Batavia NY
WDOH(FM) Delphos OH
KCGR(FM) Cottage Grove OR
KDEP(FM) Garibaldi OR
WLTJ(FM) Pittsburgh PA
KOLY(AM) Mobridge SD
KXCT(FM) Coleman TX
KVIL-FM Highland Park-Dallas TX
KLFX(FM) Nolanville TX
KODM(FM) Odessa TX
*KYQX(FM) Weatherford TX
WJDV(FM) Broadway VA
WTSM(FM) Springfield VT
*KTCV(FM) Kennewick WA

MOR

KGTL(AM) Homer AK
KIFW(AM) Sitka AK
*WSTF(FM) Andalusia AL
*WDYF(FM) Dothan AL
WHEP(AM) Foley AL
WLVV(AM) Mobile AL
*WLBF(FM) Montgomery AL

WNZZ(AM) Montgomery AL
WTLM(AM) Opelika AL
KFFB(AM) Fairfield Bay AR
KVRE(FM) Hot Springs Village AR
KTLO-FM Mountain Home AR
KBHC(AM) Nashville AR
KFLG(AM) Bullhead City AZ
KYBC(AM) Cottonwood AZ
KGVY(AM) Green Valley AZ
KSAZ(AM) Marana AZ
KNOT(AM) Prescott AZ
KNTI(FM) Lakeport CA
KXBX(AM) Lakeport CA
KESP(AM) Modesto CA
KABL(AM) Salinas CA
KIRN(AM) Simi Valley CA
KEZW(AM) Aurora CO
KIUP(AM) Durango CO
KLMR-FM Lamar CO
KRDZ(AM) Wray CO
WMRD(AM) Middletown CT
*WAPJ(FM) Torrington CT
WWFL(AM) Clermont FL
WAAZ-FM Crestview FL
WJSB(AM) Crestview FL
WOSN(FM) Indian River Shores FL
WONN(AM) Lakeland FL
*WSOR(FM) Naples FL
*WJTF(FM) Panama City FL
WITS(AM) Sebring FL
WGHC(AM) Clayton GA
WCON(AM) Cornelia GA
WPGY(AM) Ellijay GA
WLRR(FM) Milledgeville GA
WMNZ(AM) Montezuma GA
WPAX(AM) Thomasville GA
WNEG(AM) Toccoa GA
*WRAF-FM Toccoa Falls GA
WLOV(AM) Washington GA
*WYFW(FM) Winder GA
KUAM(AM) Hagatna GU
KJAN(AM) Atlantic IA
KBUR(AM) Burlington IA
KDEC(AM) Decorah IA
KRNT(AM) Des Moines IA
KMAQ-FM Maquoketa IA
KPTO(AM) Pocatello ID
WAIK(AM) Galesburg IL
WRDA(FM) Jerseyville IL
WLRB(AM) Macomb IL
WLBH(AM) Mattoon IL
WCSJ-FM Morris IL
WOAM(AM) Peoria IL
WNTA(AM) Rockford IL
WBNL(AM) Boonville IN
WLOI(AM) La Porte IN
WDND(AM) South Bend IN
KABI(AM) Abilene KS
*KONQ(FM) Dodge City KS
KIND(AM) Independence KS
*WCVK(FM) Bowling Green KY
WCTT(AM) Corbin KY
WSON(AM) Henderson KY
WLBN(AM) Lebanon KY
WYMC(AM) Mayfield KY
KQIS(AM) Basile LA
KJIN(AM) Houma LA
WOCN-FM South Yarmouth MA
WEMD(AM) Easton MD
*WYPF(FM) Frederick MD
WWLG(AM) Pikesville MD
WVAE(AM) Biddeford ME
XETRA(AM) Tijuana MEX
WAAM(AM) Ann Arbor MI
WMHG(AM) Muskegon MI
WOAP(AM) Owosso MI
WMJH(AM) Rockford MI
WSAM(AM) Saginaw MI
WCSY-FM South Haven MI
WODJ(AM) Whitehall MI
KATE(AM) Albert Lea MN
*KMSK(FM) Austin MN
KLBP(AM) Brooklyn Park MN
KROX(AM) Crookston MN
KMRS(AM) Morris MN
WCMP(AM) Pine City MN
KTRF(AM) Thief River Falls MN

KITN(FM) Worthington MN
KWAS(AM) Joplin MO
KCXL(AM) Liberty MO
KTOZ(AM) Springfield MO
*KGNV(FM) Washington MO
KBZM(FM) Big Sky MT
*KDWG(FM) Dillon MT
KXGF(AM) Great Falls MT
KTNY(FM) Libby MT
KMMR(FM) Malta MT
WSQL(AM) Brevard NC
WBAG(AM) Burlington-Graham NC
WCNC(AM) Elizabeth City NC
WAZZ(AM) Fayetteville NC
WFSC(AM) Franklin NC
WTZQ(AM) Hendersonville NC
WJCV(AM) Jacksonville NC
WCVP(AM) Murphy NC
WNOS(AM) New Bern NC
WIOZ(AM) Pinehurst NC
WSAT(AM) Salisbury NC
KBRB(AM) Ainsworth NE
WWNH(AM) Madbury NH
WFEA(AM) Manchester NH
WOF(AM) Andover NJ
WADB(AM) Asbury Park NJ
WVNJ(AM) Oakland NJ
WBUD(AM) Trenton NJ
*WMCX(FM) West Long Branch NJ
WCMC(AM) Wildwood NJ
KKJY(AM) Albuquerque NM
KATK(AM) Carlsbad NM
KSNM(AM) Las Cruces NM
KKOB Exp Stn Santa Fe NM
KBET(AM) Winchester NV
WINR(AM) Binghamton NY
WCGR(AM) Canandaigua NY
WECK(AM) Cheektowaga NY
WCBA(AM) Corning NY
WRWD(AM) Ellenville NY
WWSC(AM) Glens Falls NY
*WITR(FM) Henrietta NY
WHUC(AM) Hudson NY
WRTN(FM) New Rochelle NY
WVOX(AM) New Rochelle NY
WNEW(FM) New York NY
WOEN(AM) Olean NY
*WPSA(FM) Paul Smiths NY
WLNA(AM) Peekskill NY
WKIP(AM) Poughkeepsie NY
WTLB(AM) Utica NY
WFAS(AM) White Plains NY
WAKR(AM) Akron OH
WNCO(AM) Ashland OH
WATH(AM) Athens OH
WBNO-FM Bryan OH
WILE-FM Byesville OH
WMNI(AM) Columbus OH
WONW(AM) Defiance OH
WOHI(AM) East Liverpool OH
WJMP(AM) Kent OH
*WVMC-FM Mansfield OH
WLKR-FM Norwalk OH
WCHO(AM) Washington Court House OH
WHIZ(AM) Zanesville OH
KSHO(AM) Lebanon OR
KBCH(AM) Lincoln City OR
KTIL-FM Tillamook OR
WNAK-FM Carbondale PA
WEST(AM) Easton PA
WFRA(AM) Franklin PA
WQMU(FM) Indiana PA
WCRO(AM) Johnstown PA
WLSH(AM) Lansford PA
WNAK(AM) Nanticoke PA
WEGH(FM) Northumberland PA
WOYL(AM) Oil City PA
WJAS(AM) Pittsburgh PA
WTIV(AM) Titusville PA
WNBT(AM) Wellsboro PA
WMSW(AM) Hatillo PR
WISA(AM) Isabela PR
WPPC(AM) Penuelas PR
WBMJ(AM) San Juan PR
WIVV(AM) Vieques PR
WXEW(AM) Yabucoa PR

Programming on Radio Stations in the U.S.

*WEPC(FM) Belton SC
WCRS(AM) Greenwood SC
*WKCL(FM) Ladson SC
WLOW(FM) Port Royal SC
WSNW(AM) Seneca SC
KWAT(AM) Watertown SD
WKTP(AM) Jonesborough TN
WKPT(AM) Kingsport TN
WAMB(AM) Nashville TN
WAMB-FM Nashville TN
KFON(AM) Austin TX
KAAM(AM) Garland TX
KMVL(FM) Madisonville TX
KNBO(AM) New Boston TX
KDAE(AM) Sinton TX
KLGN(AM) Logan UT
*KYFO(AM) Ogden UT
WAMV(AM) Amherst VA
WPYA(FM) Chesapeake VA
WFVA(AM) Fredericksburg VA
WMXH-FM Luray VA
WRVQ(FM) Richmond VA
WTON-FM Staunton VA
WAMM(AM) Woodstock VA
WJOY(AM) Burlington VT
KAZZ(FM) Deer Park WA
KKAD(AM) Vancouver WA
*WLBL(AM) Auburndale WI
WFCL(AM) Clintonville WI
*WJTY(FM) Lancaster WI
WOMT(AM) Manitowoc WI
WRJC(AM) Mauston WI
WJMT(AM) Merrill WI
WJUB(AM) Plymouth WI
WXCX(AM) Siren WI
WLSL(FM) Three Lakes WI
WKLP(AM) Keyser WV
*WHFI(FM) Lindside WV
WWYO(AM) Pineville WV
WSLW(AM) White Sulphur Springs WV
KWYO(AM) Sheridan WY

Native American

*KUYI(FM) Hotevilla AZ
*KRMH(FM) Red Mesa AZ
*KOHN(FM) Sells AZ
*KGHR(FM) Tuba City AZ
*KSUT(FM) Ignacio CO
WKAM(AM) Goshen IN
*KINI(FM) Crookston NE
KGAK(AM) Gallup NM

New Age

KFLX(FM) Kachina Village AZ
*KFJC(FM) Los Altos CA
KLLY(FM) Oildale CA
KMRJ(FM) Rancho Mirage CA
KEST(AM) San Francisco CA
KKSF(FM) San Francisco CA
KCPS(AM) Burlington IA
*KBSM(FM) McCall ID
*WNUR-FM Evanston IL
*KHCT(FM) Great Bend KS
*KHCC-FM Hutchinson KS
*KHCD(FM) Salina KS
*WYAJ(FM) Sudbury MA
*WMTB-FM Emmittsburg MD
*WMHW-FM Mount Pleasant MI
WELY-FM Ely MN
*KCOZ(FM) Point Lookout MO
*KLPR(FM) Kearney NE
*WNEC-FM Henniker NH
WBUZ(FM) La Vergne TN
*KSAU(FM) Nacogdoches TX
KBZN(FM) Ogden UT
KHQN(AM) Spanish Fork UT
*KGHP(FM) Gig Harbor WA
*KCWC-FM Riverton WY

News

*KSKA(FM) Anchorage AK
*KLAM(AM) Cordova AK
KFBX(AM) Fairbanks AK

*KTOO(FM) Juneau AK
*KDLL(FM) Kenai AK
*KMXT(FM) Kodiak AK
KAKN(FM) Naknek AK
*KFSK(FM) Petersburg AK
*KCAW(FM) Sitka AK
*WBHM(FM) Birmingham AL
WFMH(FM) Cullman AL
WHOS(AM) Decatur AL
*WRWA(FM) Dothan AL
WULA(AM) Eufaula AL
WDLT(AM) Fairhope AL
WHEP(AM) Foley AL
*WSGN(FM) Gadsden AL
WJBB(AM) Haleyville AL
*WLRH(FM) Huntsville AL
WNZZ(AM) Montgomery AL
*WQPR(FM) Muscle Shoals AL
WAPR(FM) Selma AL
*WTSU(FM) Troy AL
KEWI(AM) Benton AR
*KUCA(FM) Conway AR
KCAB(AM) Dardanelle AR
*KBSA(FM) El Dorado AR
*KUAF(FM) Fayetteville AR
KXJK(AM) Forrest City AR
KAFN(FM) Gould AR
*KASU(AM) Jonesboro AR
KBOK(AM) Malvern AR
KARN-FM Sheridan AR
KWAK(AM) Stuttgart AR
KHGG(AM) Van Buren AR
KFNX(AM) Cave Creek AZ
*KNAU(FM) Flagstaff AZ
*KPUB(FM) Flagstaff AZ
*KNAD(FM) Page AZ
*KBAQ-FM Phoenix AZ
KIDR(AM) Phoenix AZ
*KJZZ(FM) Phoenix AZ
*KNAQ(FM) Prescott AZ
*KNAA(FM) Show Low AZ
*KUAZ(FM) Tucson AZ
KVOI(AM) Tucson AZ
*KAWC(FM) Yuma AZ
*KHSU-FM Arcata CA
*KPRX(FM) Bakersfield CA
KSZL(AM) Barstow CA
KBLX-FM Berkeley CA
*KNCA(FM) Burney CA
*KCHO(FM) Chico CA
KABN(AM) Concord CA
*KHSR(FM) Crescent City CA
*KVPR(FM) Fresno CA
*KFRN(FM) Long Beach CA
KFWB(AM) Los Angeles CA
KNX(AM) Los Angeles CA
*KNSQ(FM) Mount Shasta CA
KTOX(AM) Needles CA
*KAZU(FM) Pacific Grove CA
KPSI(FM) Palm Springs CA
KNTS(AM) Palo Alto CA
*KZYX(FM) Philo CA
KAHZ(AM) Pomona CA
*KQNC(FM) Quincy CA
KQMS(AM) Redding CA
*KNHT(FM) Rio Dell CA
*KXJZ(FM) Sacramento CA
KVCR(FM) San Bernardino CA
KCBQ(AM) San Diego CA
KCBS(AM) San Francisco CA
KGO(AM) San Francisco CA
KSFO(AM) San Francisco CA
KLIV(AM) San Jose CA
*KCBX(FM) San Luis Obispo CA
KUHL(AM) Santa Maria CA
KJPR(AM) Shasta Lake City CA
KSYV(FM) Solvang CA
*KUOP(FM) Stockton CA
KSUE(AM) Susanville CA
*KXJS(FM) Sutter CA
*KKTO(FM) Tahoe City CA
*KZYZ(FM) Willits CA
*KNYR(FM) Yreka CA
KUBA(AM) Yuba City CA
*KRZA(FM) Alamosa CO
KNFO(FM) Basalt CO
KCFC(FM) Boulder CO

*KRCC(FM) Colorado Springs CO
*KCFR(AM) Denver CO
*KDNK(FM) Glenwood Springs CO
*KPRN(FM) Grand Junction CO
*KUNC-FM Greeley CO
KPKE(AM) Gunnison CO
*KPRH(FM) Montrose CO
*KVMT(FM) Montrose CO
*KVNF(FM) Paonia CO
*KCFP(FM) Pueblo CO
KKPC(AM) Pueblo CO
KBCR(AM) Steamboat Springs CO
KBCR-FM Steamboat Springs CO
KJEB(AM) Strasburg CO
*KPRE(FM) Vail CO
WGCH(AM) Greenwich CT
WQUN(AM) Hamden CT
*WPKT(FM) Meriden CT
WNPR(FM) Norwich CT
*WEDW-FM Stamford CT
WXLM(AM) Stonington CT
*WETA(FM) Washington DC
WTOP(AM) Washington DC
WILM(AM) Wilmington DE
WTAN(AM) Clearwater FL
*WGCU-FM Fort Myers FL
*WQCS(FM) Fort Pierce FL
WTOT-FM Graceville FL
*WMKO(FM) Marco FL
*WFIT(FM) Melbourne FL
WMFE-FM Orlando FL
*WFSW(FM) Panama City FL
*WKGC-FM Panama City FL
WPNN(AM) Pensacola FL
*WUWF(FM) Pensacola FL
*WANM(FM) Tallahassee FL
*WUSF(FM) Tampa FL
*WXEL(FM) West Palm Beach FL
V6AK(AM) Truk FM
V6AI(AM) Yap FM
*WUNV(FM) Albany GA
*WUGA(FM) Athens GA
*WACG-FM Augusta GA
WBBQ-FM Augusta GA
*WWIO-FM Brunswick GA
*WUWG(FM) Carrollton GA
WBHF(AM) Cartersville GA
WYXC(AM) Cartersville GA
*WDCO-FM Cochran GA
WDAK(AM) Columbus GA
*WTJB(FM) Columbus GA
*WNGU(FM) Dahlonega GA
WATB(AM) Decatur GA
*WPPR(FM) Demorest GA
*WJWV(FM) Fort Gaines GA
WKEU(AM) Griffin GA
WQCH(AM) La Fayette GA
WMVG(AM) Milledgeville GA
WCNN(AM) North Atlanta GA
*WSVH(FM) Savannah GA
WXRS(AM) Swainsboro GA
WPAX(AM) Thomasville GA
*WABR-FM Tifton GA
WNEG(AM) Toccoa GA
*WWET(FM) Valdosta GA
WVOP(AM) Vidalia GA
*WJSP-FM Warm Springs GA
*WXVS(FM) Waycross GA
*KPRG(FM) Hagatna GU
KRTR(AM) Honolulu HI
KJAN(AM) Atlantic IA
*KWOI(FM) Carroll IA
*KUNI(FM) Cedar Falls IA
KCHA(AM) Charles City IA
*KLNI(FM) Decorah IA
KILR-FM Estherville IA
KIOW(FM) Forest City IA
*KTPR(FM) Fort Dodge IA
KVFD(AM) Fort Dodge IA
KXIC(AM) Iowa City IA
KIFG-FM Iowa Falls IA
*KOWI(FM) Lamoni IA
KLEM(AM) Le Mars IA
*KRNI(AM) Mason City IA
KCOB(AM) Newton IA
KAYL-FM Storm Lake IA

KCII-FM Washington IA
*KBSU-FM Boise ID
*KBSX(FM) Boise ID
*KIBX(FM) Bonners Ferry ID
*KBSY(FM) Burley ID
KVNI(AM) Coeur d'Alene ID
*KNWO(FM) Cottonwood ID
*KBSM(FM) McCall ID
*KBSQ(FM) McCall ID
*KRFA-FM Moscow ID
KIDO(AM) Nampa ID
*KBYI(FM) Rexburg ID
*KBSS(FM) Sun Valley ID
WRMJ(AM) Aledo IL
*WSIU(FM) Carbondale IL
WBBM(AM) Chicago IL
*WCRX(FM) Chicago IL
*WNIJ(FM) De Kalb IL
WIXN(AM) Dixon IL
*WNIE(FM) Freeport IL
*WDCB(FM) Glen Ellyn IL
WKIF(FM) Kankakee IL
*WNIW(FM) La Salle IL
*WIUM(FM) Macomb IL
*WUSI(FM) Olney IL
WPRS(AM) Paris IL
*WIPA(FM) Pittsfield IL
WGEM-FM Quincy IL
*WQUB(FM) Quincy IL
*WVIK(FM) Rock Island IL
WNTA(AM) Rockford IL
WJBD-FM Salem IL
WCCI(FM) Savanna IL
*WUIS(FM) Springfield IL
WSDR(AM) Sterling IL
WSQR(AM) Sycamore IL
*WIUW(FM) Warsaw IL
WFRX(AM) West Frankfort IL
*WBSB(FM) Anderson IN
WBIW(AM) Bedford IN
WZBD(FM) Berne IN
*WFHB(FM) Bloomington IN
*WFIU(FM) Bloomington IN
*WREB(FM) Greencastle IN
*WBSH(FM) Hagerstown IN
WXGO(AM) Madison IN
*WBSW(FM) Marion IN
*WBST(FM) Muncie IN
WLBC-FM Muncie IN
*WBSJ(FM) Portland IN
WRAY(AM) Princeton IN
WSLM-FM Salem IN
WZZB(AM) Seymour IN
KDCC(FM) Dodge City KS
KGNO(AM) Dodge City KS
KVOE(AM) Emporia KS
*KHCT(FM) Great Bend KS
KVGB(AM) Great Bend KS
*KHCC-FM Hutchinson KS
KWBW(AM) Hutchinson KS
KKAN(AM) Phillipsburg KS
*KRPS(FM) Pittsburg KS
*KHCD(FM) Salina KS
KMZA(FM) Seneca KS
KMUW(FM) Wichita KS
WBRT(AM) Bardstown KY
*WKYU-FM Bowling Green KY
WEKF(FM) Corbin KY
WKUE(FM) Elizabethtown KY
WKYW(FM) Frankfort KY
WGOH(AM) Grayson KY
WEKH(FM) Hazard KY
*WKPB(FM) Henderson KY
*WNKU(FM) Highland Heights KY
WLAP(AM) Lexington KY
*WUKY(FM) Lexington KY
WKJK(AM) Louisville KY
WTTL(AM) Madisonville KY
*WMKY(FM) Morehead KY
*WKMS-FM Murray KY
WNBS(AM) Murray KY
*WEKU(FM) Richmond KY
*WDCL-FM Somerset KY
WAKY-FM Springfield KY
*KLSA(FM) Alexandria LA
WIBR(AM) Baton Rouge LA
WJBO(AM) Baton Rouge LA

KEUN(AM) Eunice LA
*KGRM(FM) Grambling LA
KASO(AM) Minden LA
*KEDM(FM) Monroe LA
*WRBH(FM) New Orleans LA
WSMB(AM) New Orleans LA
*WWNO(FM) New Orleans LA
*KDAQ(FM) Shreveport LA
KRMD(AM) Shreveport LA
KSYB(AM) Shreveport LA
KTIB(AM) Thibodaux LA
*KTLN(FM) Thibodaux LA
*WHAB(FM) Acton MA
*WFCR(FM) Amherst MA
WPNI(AM) Amherst MA
*WBUR-FM Boston MA
*WGBH(FM) Boston MA
WCAP(AM) Lowell MA
WPLM(AM) Plymouth MA
WESO(AM) Southbridge MA
WARE(AM) Ware MA
WXTR(FM) Frederick MD
*WETH(FM) Hagerstown MD
WILC(AM) Laurel MD
*WSCL(FM) Salisbury MD
WFED(AM) Silver Spring MD
*WMEH(FM) Bangor ME
*WMED(FM) Calais ME
WCXU(FM) Caribou ME
WLVP(AM) Gorham ME
WCNM(AM) Lewiston ME
WLAM(AM) Lewiston ME
WCXX(FM) Madawaska ME
WHXR(FM) North Windham ME
WEGP(AM) Presque Isle ME
WTME(AM) Rumford ME
WKTQ(AM) South Paris ME
WNZS(AM) Veazie ME
*WGVU-FM Allendale MI
*WCML-FM Alpena MI
WTKA(AM) Ann Arbor MI
WMAX(AM) Bay City MI
WHFB(AM) Benton Harbor-St. Joseph MI
WNEM(AM) Bridgeport MI
WNZK(AM) Dearborn Heights MI
*WDET-FM Detroit MI
WJR(AM) Detroit MI
WWJ(AM) Detroit MI
*WKAR-FM East Lansing MI
WSHN(AM) Fremont MI
WMJZ-FM Gaylord MI
*WBLU-FM Grand Rapids MI
WSCG(AM) Greenville MI
*WCMW-FM Harbor Springs MI
*WGGL-FM Houghton MI
*WIAA(FM) Interlochen MI
WZAM(AM) Ishpeming MI
WJIM(AM) Lansing MI
*WIAB(FM) Mackinaw City MI
*WNMU-FM Marquette MI
*WCMU-FM Mount Pleasant MI
WCMB(AM) Oscoda MI
WWKK(AM) Petoskey MI
*WCMZ-FM Sault Ste. Marie MI
WWCM(AM) Standish MI
WMSH(AM) Sturgis MI
*WICA(FM) Traverse City MI
*WBLV(FM) Twin Lake MI
WGVS-FM Whitehall MI
*WEMU(FM) Ypsilanti MI
KASM(AM) Albany MN
*KNCM(FM) Appleton MN
*KNSE(FM) Austin MN
*KNBJ(FM) Bemidji MN
*KBPN(FM) Brainerd MN
*WIRN(FM) Buhl MN
*WSCN(FM) Cloquet MN
*KNSR(FM) Collegeville MN
KDHL(AM) Faribault MN
*KNWF(FM) Fergus Falls MN
*WLSN(FM) Grand Marais MN
KDWA(AM) Hastings MN
KDUZ(AM) Hutchinson MN
*KXLC(FM) La Crescent MN
*KMSU(FM) Mankato MN
*KTIS(AM) Minneapolis MN

Broadcasting & Cable Yearbook 2006

D-709

Programming on Radio Stations in the U.S.

*KNOW-FM Minneapolis-St. Paul MN	*KHNE-FM Hastings NE	KIHN(AM) Hugo OK	WDXI(AM) Jackson TN	KWNC(AM) Quincy WA
*KCCD(FM) Moorhead MN	KRVN(AM) Lexington NE	KITX(AM) Hugo OK	*WKNP(FM) Jackson TN	KOMO(AM) Seattle WA
WCMP(AM) Pine City MN	KRVN-FM Lexington NE	*KOSN(FM) Ketchum OK	WKTP(AM) Jonesborough TN	KTTH(AM) Seattle WA
WCMP-FM Pine City MN	*KUCV(FM) Lincoln NE	KCCU(FM) Lawton OK	WKPT(AM) Kingsport TN	*KUOW(FM) Seattle WA
KLOH(AM) Pipestone MN	*KRNE-FM Merriman NE	*KOSU(FM) Stillwater OK	*WUOT(FM) Knoxville TN	KBBO(AM) Selah WA
*KZSE(FM) Rochester MN	*KPNE-FM North Platte NE	*KWGS(FM) Tulsa OK	*WKNO-FM Memphis TN	*KPBX-FM Spokane WA
*KNGA(FM) Saint Peter MN	KOIL(AM) Plattsmouth NE	KSMF(FM) Ashland OR	*WYPL(FM) Memphis TN	KSBN(AM) Spokane WA
*KNTN(FM) Thief River Falls MN	KOLT(AM) Scottsbluff NE	*KSOR(FM) Ashland OR	WPLN-FM Nashville TN	*KSFC(FM) Spokane WA
KTRF(AM) Thief River Falls MN	KWPN-FM West Point NE	*KOAB-FM Bend OR	WNTT(AM) Tazewell TN	*KPLU-FM Tacoma WA
KOWZ(AM) Waseca MN	WKBK(AM) Keene NH	KZZR(AM) Burns OR	*WTML(FM) Tullahoma TN	KYNR(AM) Toppenish WA
KSGF-FM Ash Grove MO	WASR(AM) Wolfeboro NH	*KSBA(FM) Coos Bay OR	WQMV(AM) Waverly TN	*KNWY(FM) Yakima WA
KAAN(AM) Bethany MO	WSUS(FM) Franklin NJ	*KLFO(FM) Florence OR	*KACU(FM) Abilene TX	WATW(AM) Ashland WI
KAAN-FM Bethany MO	*WBJB-FM Lincroft NJ	KAGI(AM) Grants Pass OR	*KUT(FM) Austin TX	*WUEC(FM) Eau Claire WI
KYOO(AM) Bolivar MO	KKNS(AM) Corrales NM	*KLMF(FM) Klamath Falls OR	KSKY(AM) Balch Springs TX	*WPNE-FM Green Bay WI
*KRCU(FM) Cape Girardeau MO	*KGLP(FM) Gallup NM	*KSKF(FM) Klamath Falls OR	*KVLU(FM) Beaumont TX	*WGTD(FM) Kenosha WI
KRMO(AM) Cassville MO	*KMTH(FM) Maljamar NM	*KTVR-FM La Grande OR	KBST-FM Big Spring TX	*WLSU(FM) La Crosse WI
*KRNW(FM) Chillicothe MO	*KTDB(FM) Ramah NM	*KOAP(FM) Lakeview OR	KRHC(AM) Burnet TX	*WERN(FM) Madison WI
KDKD-FM Clinton MO	*KLBZ(FM) Reserve NM	KGAL(AM) Lebanon OR	*KTXP(FM) Bushland TX	*WHA(AM) Madison WI
*KBIA(FM) Columbia MO	KRUI(AM) Ruidoso Downs NM	*KOOZ(FM) Myrtle Point OR	*KAMU-FM College Station TX	WISN(AM) Milwaukee WI
*KCUR-FM Kansas City MO	KCHS(AM) Truth or Consequences NM	*KLCO(FM) Newport OR	*KETR(FM) Commerce TX	*WUWM(FM) Milwaukee WI
*KKFI(FM) Kansas City MO	*KNCC(FM) Elko NV	*KRBM(FM) Pendleton OR	*KEDT-FM Corpus Christi TX	WRDB(AM) Reedsburg WI
KMBZ(AM) Kansas City MO	KTSN(AM) Elko NV	KUMA(AM) Pendleton OR	KAND(AM) Corsicana TX	WRCO-FM Richland Center WI
*KKTR(FM) Kirksville MO	*KNPR(FM) Las Vegas NV	KCMX(AM) Phoenix OR	KRLD(AM) Dallas TX	WEVR-FM River Falls WI
KNIM(AM) Maryville MO	KRLV(AM) Las Vegas NV	KEX(AM) Portland OR	*KTEP(FM) El Paso TX	*WHND(FM) Sister Bay WI
*KXCV(FM) Maryville MO	*KWPR(FM) Lund NV	*KOPB-FM Portland OR	*KMBH-FM Harlingen TX	WJJQ(FM) Tomahawk WI
KBTN(AM) Neosho MO	*KLNR(FM) Panaca NV	*KSRS(FM) Roseburg OR	*KPFT(FM) Houston TX	WXCO(AM) Wausau WI
KBDZ(FM) Perryville MO	KUNR(FM) Reno NV	*KTBR(AM) Roseburg OR	KTRH(AM) Houston TX	*WXPW(FM) Wausau WI
*KSMS-FM Point Lookout MO	*KTPH(FM) Tonopah NV	*KSJK(AM) Talent OR	*KUHF(FM) Houston TX	*WVPB(FM) Beckley WV
KMIS(AM) Portageville MO	*WAMC-FM Albany NY	*WDIY(FM) Allentown PA	*KSHU(FM) Huntsville TX	*WVPW(FM) Buckhannon WV
KYRO(AM) Potosi MO	WVTL(AM) Amsterdam NY	WBVP(AM) Beaver Falls PA	*KTXI(FM) Ingram TX	*WVPN(FM) Charleston WV
*KUMR(FM) Rolla MO	WYSL(AM) Avon NY	WBLF(AM) Bellefonte PA	KAML(AM) Kenedy-Karnes City TX	*WVVV(FM) Huntington WV
*KWMU(FM) Saint Louis MO	*WSKG-FM Binghamton NY	WZUM(AM) Carnegie PA	*KLDN(FM) Lufkin TX	*WVEP(FM) Martinsburg WV
KLFJ(AM) Springfield MO	*WSQX-FM Binghamton NY	*WFSE(FM) Edinboro PA	KCUL(AM) Marshall TX	*WVPM(FM) Morgantown WV
*KSMU(FM) Springfield MO	*WCWP(FM) Brookville NY	*WQLN-FM Erie PA	KCUL-FM Marshall TX	*WVPG(FM) Parkersburg WV
KSAR(FM) Thayer MO	*WBFO(FM) Buffalo NY	WFRA(AM) Franklin PA	*KHID(FM) McAllen TX	*WAUA(FM) Petersburg WV
KTTN-FM Trenton MO	*WCAN(FM) Canajoharie NY	WGET(AM) Gettysburg PA	KWEL(AM) Midland TX	*WVNP(FM) Wheeling WV
*KSMW(FM) West Plains MO	*WSQE(FM) Corning NY	WJSM(FM) Martinsburg PA	KGNB(AM) New Braunfels TX	KRSV(AM) Afton WY
WHSY(AM) Hattiesburg MS	*WGSU(FM) Geneseo NY	KYW(AM) Philadelphia PA	*KOCV(FM) Odessa TX	KRSV-FM Afton WY
*WURC(FM) Holly Springs MS	*WSQA(FM) Hornell NY	*WHYY-FM Philadelphia PA	KOGT(AM) Orange TX	*KBUW(FM) Buffalo WY
*WJSU(FM) Jackson MS	*WSQG-FM Ithaca NY	KQV(AM) Pittsburgh PA	KBUS(FM) Paris TX	*KUWC(FM) Casper WY
*WMPN-FM Jackson MS	WJTN(AM) Jamestown NY	*WDUQ(FM) Pittsburgh PA	KOKE(FM) Pflugerville TX	*KDUW(FM) Douglas WY
*WMAB-FM Mississippi State MS	*WUBJ(FM) Jamestown NY	WECZ(AM) Punxsutawney PA	KGKL(AM) San Angelo TX	KIML(AM) Gillette WY
*WMAV-FM Oxford MS	WLLG(FM) Lowville NY	*WVIA-FM Scranton PA	*KUTX(FM) San Angelo TX	*KUWG(FM) Gillette WY
KBUL(AM) Billings MT	*WOSR(FM) Middletown NY	WQRM(FM) Smethport PA	*KSTX(FM) San Antonio TX	*KUWJ(FM) Jackson WY
*KEMC(FM) Billings MT	WBBR(AM) New York NY	*WPSU(FM) State College PA	KJIM(AM) Sherman TX	KHAT(AM) Laramie WY
*KBMC(FM) Bozeman MT	WCBS(AM) New York NY	WLIH(FM) Whitneyville PA	*KTOT(FM) Spearman TX	*KUWR(FM) Laramie WY
*KAPC(FM) Butte MT	WINS(AM) New York NY	*WVYA(FM) Williamsport PA	KVRT(FM) Victoria TX	*KUWN(FM) Newcastle WY
*KGPR(FM) Great Falls MT	*WNYC-FM New York NY	WORA(AM) Mayaguez PR	*KMCU(FM) Wichita Falls TX	*KUWX(FM) Pinedale WY
*KUFN(FM) Hamilton MT	*WOLN(FM) Olean NY	*WRUO(FM) Mayaguez PR	KNNZ(AM) Cedar City UT	KPOW(AM) Powell WY
KHDN(AM) Hardin MT	*WSQC-FM Oneonta NY	WEKO(AM) Morovis PR	KMTI(AM) Manti UT	*KUWZ(FM) Rock Springs WY
*KUHM(FM) Helena MT	*WDFH(FM) Ossining NY	WEXS(AM) Patillas PR	*KPCW(FM) Park City UT	*KSUW(FM) Sheridan WY
*KUKL(FM) Kalispell MT	WEBO(AM) Owego NY	WSOL(AM) San German PR	KENT(AM) Parowan UT	*KUWD(FM) Sundance WY
*WCQS(FM) Asheville NC	*WCEL(FM) Plattsburgh NY	WCNX(AM) Hope Valley RI	*KUER(FM) Salt Lake City UT	KYDT(FM) Sundance WY
WGCR(AM) Brevard NC	*WRLI-FM Southampton NY	WXNI(AM) Westerly RI	WKDE(AM) Altavista VA	KUWT(FM) Thermopolis WY
WLOE(AM) Eden NC	WRCR(AM) Spring Valley NY	*WLJK(AM) Aiken SC	WOWZ(AM) Appomattox VA	
*WFSS(FM) Fayetteville NC	*WAER(FM) Syracuse NY	*WJWJ-FM Beaufort SC	WDIC-FM Clinchco VA	**News/talk**
*WFQS(FM) Franklin NC	*WANC(FM) Ticonderoga NY	WQNT(AM) Charleston SC	*WOTC(FM) Edinburg VA	
WTRU(AM) Kernersville NC	WTNY(AM) Watertown NY	*WSCI(FM) Charleston SC	WLRT(AM) Hampton VA	KBYR(AM) Anchorage AK
*WKNS(FM) Kinston NC	WAKR(AM) Akron OH	*WLTR(FM) Columbia SC	*WEMC(FM) Harrisonburg VA	KFQD(AM) Anchorage AK
WMYN(AM) Mayodan NC	WFUN(AM) Ashtabula OH	*WHMC-FM Conway SC	*WMRA(FM) Harrisonburg VA	KUDO(AM) Anchorage AK
WCVP(AM) Murphy NC	WYBL(FM) Ashtabula OH	*WEPR(FM) Greenville SC	WAGE(AM) Leesburg VA	KFAR(AM) Fairbanks AK
*WTEB(FM) New Bern NC	*WCVV(FM) Belpre OH	WRHM(FM) Lancaster SC	*WMRL(FM) Lexington VA	*KUAC(FM) Fairbanks AK
*WZNB(FM) New Bern NC	*WGBE(FM) Bryan OH	WSNW(AM) Seneca SC	WLVA(AM) Lynchburg VA	KTKN(AM) Ketchikan AK
*WZRN(FM) Norlina NC	WAIS(AM) Buchtel OH	WBCU(AM) Union SC	*WCVE(FM) Richmond VA	*KXKM(FM) McCarthy AK
WAYN(AM) Rockingham NC	WILE(AM) Cambridge OH	KGIM(AM) Aberdeen SD	*WVTF(FM) Roanoke VA	*KNOM(AM) Nome AK
WEED(AM) Rocky Mount NC	WCSM-FM Celina OH	KSDN(AM) Aberdeen SD	WVAB(AM) Virginia Beach VA	*KNOM-FM Nome AK
WNCA(AM) Siler City NC	*WOUH-FM Chillicothe OH	KBFS(AM) Belle Fourche SD	WTOP-FM Warrenton VA	KIFW(AM) Sitka AK
*WNCW(FM) Spindale NC	*WCPN(FM) Cleveland OH	*KESD(FM) Brookings SD	*WISE-FM Wise VA	KSRM(AM) Soldotna AK
WCIE(FM) Spring Lake NC	*WCBE(FM) Columbus OH	KDSJ(AM) Deadwood SD	WYVE(AM) Wytheville VA	*KTNA(FM) Talkeetna AK
WSIC(AM) Statesville NC	*WGDE(FM) Defiance OH	KPSD(FM) Faith SD	WJOY(AM) Burlington VT	WDNG(AM) Anniston AL
WWTB(FM) Topsail Beach NC	*WKSU-FM Kent OH	KOKK(AM) Huron SD	*WVPS(FM) Burlington VT	WVNN(AM) Athens AL
*WHQR(FM) Wilmington NC	*WFCO(FM) Lancaster OH	*KQSD-FM Lowry SD	WRVT(AM) Rutland VT	WAPI(AM) Birmingham AL
*WFDD-FM Winston-Salem NC	*WGLE(FM) Lima OH	KJAM-FM Madison SD	*WVPA(FM) Saint Johnsbury VT	WERC(AM) Birmingham AL
*KCND(FM) Bismarck ND	WLTP(AM) Marietta OH	*KZSD(FM) Martin SD	WDEV(AM) Waterbury VT	WYDE-FM Cullman AL
KDLR(AM) Devils Lake ND	WMOA(AM) Marietta OH	*KDSD(FM) Pierpont SD	*WVPR(FM) Windsor VT	WXAL(AM) Demopolis AL
*KDPR(FM) Dickinson ND	*WOSB(FM) Marion OH	*KTSD-FM Reliance SD	KLKI(AM) Anacortes WA	WWNT(AM) Dothan AL
*KFBN(FM) Fargo ND	*WKRJ(FM) New Philadelphia OH	*KNWC(FM) Sioux Falls SD	*KASB(FM) Bellevue WA	WBCF(AM) Florence AL
KKXL(AM) Grand Forks ND	*WNRK(FM) Norwalk OH	*KNWC-FM Sioux Falls SD	*KZAZ(FM) Bellingham WA	WAAX(AM) Gadsden AL
*KPRJ(FM) Jamestown ND	WNXT(AM) Portsmouth OH	*KRSD(FM) Sioux Falls SD	KOZI-FM Chelan WA	WGEA(AM) Geneva AL
*KMPR(FM) Minot ND	*WKSV(FM) Thompson OH	*KUSD(FM) Vermillion SD	*KNWV(FM) Clarkston WA	WRJM-FM Geneva AL
KDDR(AM) Oakes ND	*WGTE-FM Toledo OH	KJJQ(FM) Volga SD	*KGHP(FM) Gig Harbor WA	WGYV(AM) Greenville AL
KOVC(AM) Valley City ND	*WKRW(FM) Wooster OH	KWAT(AM) Watertown SD	KEDO(AM) Longview WA	WGSV(AM) Guntersville AL
*KPPR(FM) Williston ND	*WYSU(FM) Youngstown OH	WCTA(AM) Alamo TN	*KLWS(FM) Moses Lake WA	WABB(AM) Mobile AL
*KTNE-FM Alliance NE	*WOUZ(FM) Zanesville OH	WOPI(AM) Bristol TN	KQWS(FM) Omak WA	WPMI(AM) Mobile AL
KNCY-FM Auburn NE	*KOCU(FM) Altus OK	WJZM(AM) Clarksville TN	*KNWP(FM) Port Angeles WA	*WACV(AM) Montgomery AL
*KCNE-FM Chadron NE	*KYCU(FM) Clinton OK	*WSMC-FM Collegedale TN	*KVIX(FM) Port Angeles WA	WLWI(AM) Montgomery AL
KGMT(AM) Fairbury NE	KCRC(AM) Enid OK	*WHRS(FM) Cookeville TN	*KWSU(AM) Pullman WA	WANI(AM) Opelika AL

Programming on Radio Stations in the U.S.

WQLS(AM) Ozark AL
WHBB(AM) Selma AL
WFEB(AM) Sylacauga AL
WTBC(AM) Tuscaloosa AL
*WUAL-FM Tuscaloosa AL
WVNA(AM) Tuscumbia AL
WAPZ(AM) Wetumpka AL
KAPZ(AM) Bald Knob AR
KELD(AM) El Dorado AR
KFAY(AM) Farmington AR
KBJT(AM) Fordyce AR
KWHN(AM) Fort Smith AR
KYHN(AM) Fort Smith AR
KELD-FM Hampton AR
KAWW(AM) Heber Springs AR
KZNG(AM) Hot Springs AR
KBTM(AM) Jonesboro AR
KARN(AM) Little Rock AR
*KUAR(FM) Little Rock AR
KVOM(AM) Morrilton AR
KNBY(AM) Newport AR
KSMD(FM) Pangburn AR
KDRS(AM) Paragould AR
KCLA(AM) Pine Bluff AR
KOTN(AM) Pine Bluff AR
KARV(AM) Russellville AR
KWYN(AM) Wynne AR
KFNX(AM) Cave Creek AZ
KVNA(AM) Flagstaff AZ
KDJI(AM) Holbrook AZ
KAAA(AM) Kingman AZ
KNTR(AM) Lake Havasu City AZ
KFNN(AM) Mesa AZ
KLPZ(AM) Parker AZ
KFYI(AM) Phoenix AZ
KKNT(AM) Phoenix AZ
KTAR(AM) Phoenix AZ
KYCA(AM) Prescott AZ
KQNA(AM) Prescott Valley AZ
KATO(AM) Safford AZ
KQTL(AM) Sahuarita AZ
KAZM(AM) Sedona AZ
KVWM(AM) Show Low AZ
KTAN(AM) Sierra Vista AZ
KJLL(AM) South Tucson AZ
KXXT(AM) Tolleson AZ
KNST(AM) Tucson AZ
KTUC(AM) Tucson AZ
KYET(AM) Williams AZ
KBLU(AM) Yuma AZ
KJOK(AM) Yuma AZ
KCFJ(AM) Alturas CA
KERN(AM) Bakersfield CA
KGET(AM) Bakersfield CA
KNZR(AM) Bakersfield CA
KQVO(AM) Calexico CA
KPAY(AM) Chico CA
*KZFR(FM) Chico CA
KGOE(AM) Eureka CA
KINS(AM) Eureka CA
KMJ(AM) Fresno CA
KRLA(AM) Glendale CA
KNCO(AM) Grass Valley CA
KOMY(AM) La Selva Beach CA
KQAB(AM) Lake Isabella CA
KCAA(AM) Loma Linda CA
KTME(AM) Lompoc CA
*KPFK(FM) Los Angeles CA
KTNQ(AM) Los Angeles CA
KWKW(AM) Los Angeles CA
*KPMO(AM) Mendocino CA
KTIQ(AM) Merced CA
KYOS(AM) Merced CA
KFIV(AM) Modesto CA
KNRY(AM) Monterey CA
KXTY(FM) Morro Bay CA
KMJC(AM) Mount Shasta CA
KVON(AM) Napa CA
*KQEI-FM North Highlands CA
KNEW(AM) Oakland CA
KGAM(AM) Palm Springs CA
KNWQ(AM) Palm Springs CA
KUTY(AM) Palmdale CA
KKXX(AM) Paradise CA
*KPCC(AM) Pasadena CA
KLUN(AM) Paso Robles CA
KPRL(AM) Paso Robles CA

KWKU(AM) Pomona CA
KVTA(AM) Port Hueneme CA
KTIP(AM) Porterville CA
KHGQ(FM) Quincy CA
KPCO(AM) Quincy CA
KFBK(AM) Sacramento CA
KSAC(AM) Sacramento CA
KTIE(AM) San Bernardino CA
KCBQ(AM) San Diego CA
KFMB(AM) San Diego CA
KOGO(AM) San Diego CA
*KPBS-FM San Diego CA
KIQI(AM) San Francisco CA
*KQED-FM San Francisco CA
KZSF(AM) San Jose CA
KVEC(AM) San Luis Obispo CA
KYNS(AM) San Luis Obispo CA
KZSB(AM) Santa Barbara CA
KSCO(AM) Santa Cruz CA
KSMA(AM) Santa Maria CA
*KRCB-FM Santa Rosa CA
KSRO(AM) Santa Rosa CA
KIRN(AM) Simi Valley CA
KVML(AM) Sonora CA
KOWL(AM) South Lake Tahoe CA
KTHO(AM) South Lake Tahoe CA
*KCLU(FM) Thousand Oaks CA
KIIS(AM) Thousand Oaks CA
KNWH(AM) Twentynine Palms CA
KNTK(FM) Weed CA
*KAJX(FM) Aspen CO
KSKE(AM) Buena Vista CO
KRLN(AM) Canon City CO
KVOR(AM) Colorado Springs CO
KZNT(AM) Colorado Springs CO
KVFC(AM) Cortez CO
*KBUT(FM) Crested Butte CO
KBJD(AM) Denver CO
KBNO(AM) Denver CO
KNUS(AM) Denver CO
KOA(AM) Denver CO
KDGO(AM) Durango CO
KIUP(AM) Durango CO
KFTM(AM) Fort Morgan CO
KGLN(AM) Glenwood Springs CO
KNZZ(AM) Grand Junction CO
KFKA(AM) Greeley CO
KRMR(FM) Hayden CO
KHNC(AM) Johnstown CO
KSXT(AM) Loveland CO
KWUF(AM) Pagosa Springs CO
KCSJ(AM) Pueblo CO
KGFT(AM) Pueblo CO
KVRH(AM) Salida CO
KCOL(AM) Wellington CO
WPRX(AM) Bristol CT
*WQAQ(FM) Hamden CT
WDRC(AM) Hartford CT
WTIC(AM) Hartford CT
WZBG(FM) Litchfield CT
WMMW(AM) Meriden CT
WMRD(AM) Middletown CT
WELI(AM) New Haven CT
WNLK(AM) Norwalk CT
WSTC(AM) Stamford CT
WATR(AM) Waterbury CT
WWCO(AM) Waterbury CT
*WSHU(AM) Westport CT
WILI(AM) Willimantic CT
*WAMU(FM) Washington DC
WMAL(AM) Washington DC
WOL(AM) Washington DC
*WPFW(FM) Washington DC
WDOV(AM) Dover DE
WGMD(FM) Rehoboth Beach DE
WDEL(AM) Wilmington DE
WFLN(AM) Arcadia FL
WTWB(AM) Auburndale FL
WINV(AM) Beverly Hills FL
WWJB(AM) Brooksville FL
WKFL(AM) Bushnell FL
WMMV(AM) Cocoa FL
WTIR(AM) Cocoa Beach FL
WRHC(AM) Coral Gables FL
WDCF(AM) Dade City FL
WNDB(AM) Daytona Beach FL
WGTX(AM) De Funiak Springs FL

WZEP(AM) De Funiak Springs FL
WNDA(AM) De Land FL
WYND(AM) De Land FL
WNWF(AM) Destin FL
WNTR(AM) Dunedin FL
WENG(AM) Englewood FL
*WAFG(FM) Fort Lauderdale FL
WINK(AM) Fort Myers FL
WJNX(AM) Fort Pierce FL
WFTW(AM) Fort Walton Beach FL
WRUF(AM) Gainesville FL
WXYB(AM) Indian Rocks Beach FL
*WJCT-FM Jacksonville FL
WJGR(AM) Jacksonville FL
WOKV(AM) Jacksonville FL
WJBW(AM) Jupiter FL
WKIZ(AM) Key West FL
WLKF(AM) Lakeland FL
WPBR(AM) Lantana FL
WFFG(AM) Marathon FL
WGUF(FM) Marco FL
WCNZ(AM) Marco Island FL
WMEL(AM) Melbourne FL
WAQI(AM) Miami FL
WIOD(AM) Miami FL
*WLRN-FM Miami FL
WOCN(AM) Miami FL
WQBA(AM) Miami FL
WSUA(AM) Miami FL
WSKY-FM Micanopy FL
WNOG(AM) Naples FL
WPSO(AM) New Port Richey FL
WCFI(AM) Ocala FL
WOCA(AM) Ocala FL
WDBO(AM) Orlando FL
WELE(AM) Ormond Beach FL
WLTG(AM) Panama City FL
WCOA(AM) Pensacola FL
WAMT(AM) Pine Castle-Sky Lake FL
WFLF(AM) Pine Hills FL
WPTK(AM) Pine Island Center FL
WWBA(AM) Pinellas Park FL
WPSL(AM) Port St. Lucie FL
WCCF(AM) Punta Gorda FL
WFOY(AM) Saint Augustine FL
WSDO(AM) Sanford FL
WIBQ(AM) Sarasota FL
WLSS(AM) Sarasota FL
WSRQ(AM) Sarasota FL
WSTU(AM) Stuart FL
*WFSU-FM Tallahassee FL
WNLS(AM) Tallahassee FL
WTAL(AM) Tallahassee FL
WFLA(AM) Tampa FL
WHNZ(AM) Tampa FL
WFTL(AM) West Palm Beach FL
WJNO(AM) West Palm Beach FL
WPRD(AM) Winter Park FL
WZHR(AM) Zephyrhills FL
WALG(AM) Albany GA
WLTA(AM) Alpharetta GA
WGAU(AM) Athens GA
*WABE(FM) Atlanta GA
WAOK(AM) Atlanta GA
WGKA(AM) Atlanta GA
WGST(AM) Atlanta GA
WSB(AM) Atlanta GA
WGAC(AM) Augusta GA
WRDW(AM) Augusta GA
WGIG(AM) Brunswick GA
WMOG(AM) Brunswick GA
WGRA(AM) Cairo GA
WJTH(AM) Calhoun GA
WLBB(AM) Carrollton GA
WRCG(AM) Columbus GA
WSRM(FM) Coosa GA
WBLJ(AM) Dalton GA
WMWR(AM) Dry Branch GA
WMLT(AM) Dublin GA
WDUN(AM) Gainesville GA
WHIE(AM) Griffin GA
WRPG(FM) Hawkinsville GA
WVCC(AM) Hogansville GA
WLOP(AM) Jesup GA
WVGA(AM) Lakeland GA
WMAC(AM) Macon GA
WYTH(AM) Madison GA

WLAQ(AM) Rome GA
WRGA(AM) Rome GA
WWIO(AM) Saint Mary's GA
WBMQ(AM) Savannah GA
WWNS(AM) Statesboro GA
WKWN(AM) Trenton GA
WFVR(AM) Valdosta GA
WGAC-FM Warrenton GA
WWGA(AM) Waycross GA
WCGA(AM) Woodbine GA
KGUM(AM) Hagatna GU
KPUA(AM) Hilo HI
KHBZ(AM) Honolulu HI
KHNR-FM Honolulu HI
*KHPR(FM) Honolulu HI
KHVH(AM) Honolulu HI
*KIPO(FM) Honolulu HI
KWAI(AM) Honolulu HI
KAOI(AM) Kihei HI
KQNG(AM) Lihue HI
*KKUA(FM) Wailuku HI
KASI(AM) Ames IA
*WOI(AM) Ames IA
KWBG(AM) Boone IA
KBUR(AM) Burlington IA
WMT(AM) Cedar Rapids IA
WOC(AM) Davenport IA
WHO(AM) Des Moines IA
WDBQ(AM) Dubuque IA
KILR(AM) Estherville IA
KMCD(AM) Fairfield IA
KBKB(AM) Fort Madison IA
*WSUI(AM) Iowa City IA
KOKX(AM) Keokuk IA
KFJB(AM) Marshalltown IA
KWPC(AM) Muscatine IA
KOEL(AM) Oelwein IA
*KOJI(AM) Okoboji IA
KBOE-FM Oskaloosa IA
KLEE(AM) Ottumwa IA
KMA(AM) Shenandoah IA
KMNS(AM) Sioux City IA
KSCJ(AM) Sioux City IA
*KWIT(FM) Sioux City IA
KXEL(AM) Waterloo IA
KQWC-FM Webster City IA
KBOI(AM) Boise ID
KBFI(AM) Bonners Ferry ID
KFMS(FM) Franklin ID
KID(AM) Idaho Falls ID
KRLC(AM) Lewiston ID
KSEI(AM) Pocatello ID
KWIK(AM) Pocatello ID
KSPT(AM) Sandpoint ID
KLIX(AM) Twin Falls ID
KWEI(AM) Weiser ID
WBGZ(AM) Alton IL
WBIG(AM) Aurora IL
WCIL(AM) Carbondale IL
WDWS(AM) Champaign IL
KSGM(AM) Chester IL
*WBEZ(FM) Chicago IL
WGN(AM) Chicago IL
WIND(AM) Chicago IL
WLS(AM) Chicago IL
WDAN(AM) Danville IL
WLBK(AM) De Kalb IL
WSOY(AM) Decatur IL
WWYW(FM) Dundee IL
WCRA(AM) Effingham IL
WRMN(AM) Elgin IL
WJJG(AM) Elmhurst IL
WFIW(AM) Fairfield IL
*WGNN(FM) Fisher IL
WGIL(AM) Galesburg IL
WGEN(AM) Geneseo IL
WJPF(AM) Herrin IL
WJIL(AM) Jacksonville IL
WLDS(AM) Jacksonville IL
WKEI(AM) Kewanee IL
WLPO(AM) La Salle IL
WSMI(AM) Litchfield IL
WLBH(AM) Mattoon IL
*WBEQ(FM) Morris IL
WCSJ-FM Morris IL
WINI(AM) Murphysboro IL
WVLN(AM) Olney IL

WCMY(AM) Ottawa IL
WMBD(AM) Peoria IL
WZOE(AM) Princeton IL
WTAD(AM) Quincy IL
WRHL(AM) Rochelle IL
WROK(AM) Rockford IL
WHCO(AM) Sparta IL
WMAY(AM) Springfield IL
WTAX(AM) Springfield IL
*WNIQ(FM) Sterling IL
WSPL(AM) Streator IL
WTIM-FM Taylorville IL
*WILL(AM) Urbana IL
WKRS(AM) Waukegan IL
WHBU(AM) Anderson IN
WGCL(AM) Bloomington IN
WHON(AM) Centerville IN
*WBEW(FM) Chesterton IN
WCSI(AM) Columbus IN
WTRC(AM) Elkhart IN
*WVPE(FM) Elkhart IN
WGBF(AM) Evansville IN
*WNIN-FM Evansville IN
*WBOI(FM) Fort Wayne IN
WFCV(AM) Fort Wayne IN
WOWO(AM) Fort Wayne IN
WLTH(AM) Gary IN
WTRE(AM) Greensburg IN
WJOB(AM) Hammond IN
*WFYI-FM Indianapolis IN
WIBC(AM) Indianapolis IN
WXNT(AM) Indianapolis IN
WIOU(AM) Kokomo IN
WSAL(AM) Logansport IN
WBAT(AM) Marion IN
WKBV(AM) Richmond IN
*WVXR(FM) Richmond IN
WSBT(AM) South Bend IN
WAOV(AM) Vincennes IN
*WBAA(AM) West Lafayette IN
KKOY(AM) Chanute KS
KGGF(AM) Coffeyville KS
KCNW(AM) Fairway KS
KIUL(AM) Garden City KS
KLOE(AM) Goodland KS
*KZNA(FM) Hill City KS
KLWN(AM) Lawrence KS
KSCB(AM) Liberal KS
KMAN(AM) Manhattan KS
KCCV(AM) Overland Park KS
KQMA-FM Phillipsburg KS
KINA(AM) Salina KS
KSAL(AM) Salina KS
KCVT(FM) Silver Lake KS
KMAJ(AM) Topeka KS
WIBW(AM) Topeka KS
KLEY(AM) Wellington KS
KNSS(AM) Wichita KS
KKLE(AM) Winfield KS
WAIA(AM) Beaver Dam KY
WKCT(AM) Bowling Green KY
WKDZ(AM) Cadiz KY
WCTT(AM) Corbin KY
WKDP(AM) Corbin KY
WHIR(AM) Danville KY
WBOB(AM) Florence KY
WHOP(AM) Hopkinsville KY
WVLK(AM) Lexington KY
*WFPL(FM) Louisville KY
WGTK(AM) Louisville KY
WHAS(AM) Louisville KY
WNGO(AM) Mayfield KY
*WBFI(FM) McDaniels KY
WMST(AM) Mt. Sterling KY
WOMI(AM) Owensboro KY
WKYX(AM) Paducah KY
WKYH(AM) Paintsville KY
WEKY(AM) Richmond KY
WRUS(AM) Russellville KY
WTLO(AM) Somerset KY
WTCW(AM) Whitesburg KY
KSYL(AM) Alexandria LA
WABL(AM) Amite LA
*WRKF(FM) Baton Rouge LA
WIKC(AM) Bogalusa LA
WASO(AM) Covington LA
KAOK(AM) Lake Charles LA

Broadcasting & Cable Yearbook 2006

D-711

Programming on Radio Stations in the U.S.

KLCL(AM) Lake Charles LA
KMLB(AM) Monroe LA
KNOE(AM) Monroe LA
KNOC(AM) Natchitoches LA
WGSO(AM) New Orleans LA
WTIX(AM) New Orleans LA
WWL(AM) New Orleans LA
KSLO(AM) Opelousas LA
KEEL(AM) Shreveport LA
WARL(AM) Attleboro MA
WNSH(AM) Beverly MA
WBZ(AM) Boston MA
WBET(AM) Brockton MA
WMSX(AM) Brockton MA
WBNW(AM) Concord MA
WHNP(AM) East Longmeadow MA
WSAR(AM) Fall River MA
WEIM(AM) Fitchburg MA
WGAW(AM) Gardner MA
*WAMQ(FM) Great Barrington MA
WHMQ(AM) Greenfield MA
WCCM(AM) Haverhill MA
*WMLN-FM Milton MA
*WNAN(FM) Nantucket MA
WBSM(AM) New Bedford MA
WDIS(AM) Norfolk MA
WHMP(AM) Northampton MA
WBEC(AM) Pittsfield MA
WESX(AM) Salem MA
WHYN(AM) Springfield MA
WPEP(AM) Taunton MA
*WBUR(AM) West Yarmouth MA
WXTK(FM) West Yarmouth MA
*WCAI(FM) Woods Hole MA
WORC(AM) Worcester MA
WTAG(AM) Worcester MA
WBAL(AM) Baltimore MD
*WEAA(FM) Baltimore MD
WITH(AM) Baltimore MD
WOLB(AM) Baltimore MD
*WYPR(FM) Baltimore MD
WCBC(AM) Cumberland MD
WFMD(AM) Frederick MD
WFRB(AM) Frostburg MD
WMET(AM) Gaithersburg MD
WHAG(AM) Halfway MD
WPTX(AM) Lexington Park MD
WKHZ(AM) Ocean City MD
*WSDL(FM) Ocean City MD
WICO(AM) Salisbury MD
WQMR(AM) Snow Hill MD
WCME(FM) Boothbay Harbor ME
*WMEP(AM) Camden ME
WMEF(FM) Fort Kent ME
WFAU(AM) Gardiner ME
WLVP(AM) Gorham ME
WVOM(FM) Howland ME
WLAM(AM) Lewiston ME
WJCX(FM) Pittsfield ME
WGAN(AM) Portland ME
WLOB(AM) Portland ME
*WMEA(FM) Portland ME
*WMEM(FM) Presque Isle ME
WRKD(AM) Rockland ME
WLOB-FM Rumford ME
WPHX(AM) Sanford ME
WWNZ(AM) Veazie ME
*WMEW(FM) Waterville ME
WABJ(AM) Adrian MI
WAAM(AM) Ann Arbor MI
*WUOM(FM) Ann Arbor MI
WBCK(AM) Battle Creek MI
*WUCX-FM Bay City MI
WBRN(AM) Big Rapids MI
WATT(AM) Cadillac MI
WMKT(AM) Charlevoix MI
WDTK(AM) Detroit MI
*WKAR(AM) East Lansing MI
WCHT(AM) Escanaba MI
*WFUM-FM Flint MI
WOOD(AM) Grand Rapids MI
*WVGR(FM) Grand Rapids MI
WMPL(AM) Hancock MI
WVXH(AM) Harrison MI
WBCH(AM) Hastings MI
WHTC(AM) Holland MI
WMIQ(AM) Iron Mountain MI

WIAN(AM) Ishpeming MI
WKHM(AM) Jackson MI
WKMI(AM) Kalamazoo MI
WKZO(AM) Kalamazoo MI
WKZO(AM) Kalamazoo MI
*WMUK(AM) Kalamazoo MI
*WGVU(AM) Kentwood MI
WLDR(AM) Kingsley MI
WKLA(AM) Ludington MI
WMTE(AM) Manistee MI
*WVXM(FM) Manistee MI
WDMJ(AM) Marquette MI
WGVS(AM) Muskegon MI
WJML(AM) Petoskey MI
WPHM(AM) Port Huron MI
*WVXA(FM) Rogers City MI
WSGW(AM) Saginaw MI
WSJM(AM) Saint Joseph MI
WMIC(AM) Sandusky MI
WKNW(AM) Sault Ste. Marie MI
WMMI(AM) Shepherd MI
WCHB(AM) Taylor MI
WTCM(AM) Traverse City MI
WMFN(AM) Zeeland MI
KATE(AM) Albert Lea MN
KXRA(AM) Alexandria MN
KAUS(AM) Austin MN
WWWI(AM) Baxter MN
KBEW(AM) Blue Earth MN
KRWC(AM) Buffalo MN
KDLM(AM) Detroit Lakes MN
KDAL(AM) Duluth MN
WEBC(AM) Duluth MN
KCNN(AM) East Grand Forks MN
KRBT(AM) Eveleth MN
KBRF(AM) Fergus Falls MN
KLTF(AM) Little Falls MN
WYRQ(FM) Little Falls MN
KMHL(AM) Marshall MN
WCCO(AM) Minneapolis MN
WWTC(AM) Minneapolis MN
KMRS(AM) Morris MN
WNMT(AM) Nashwauk MN
KCUE(AM) Red Wing MN
KROC(AM) Rochester MN
KNSI(AM) Saint Cloud MN
WJON(AM) Saint Cloud MN
*KNGA(FM) Saint Peter MN
KRBI(AM) Saint Peter MN
KWLM(AM) Willmar MN
KDOM(AM) Windom MN
KDOM-FM Windom MN
KWNO(AM) Winona MN
KWOA(AM) Worthington MN
*KNSW(FM) Worthington-Marshall MN
KSWM(AM) Aurora MO
KKOZ(AM) Ava MO
KKOZ-FM Ava MO
KBFL(FM) Buffalo MO
KMRN(AM) Cameron MO
KZIM(AM) Cape Girardeau MO
KFRU(AM) Columbia MO
*KOPN(FM) Columbia MO
*KGNN-FM Cuba MO
KREI(AM) Farmington MO
KSSZ(FM) Fayette MO
KJFF(AM) Festus MO
KHMO(AM) Hannibal MO
KLIK(AM) Jefferson City MO
KWOS(AM) Jefferson City MO
KQYX(AM) Joplin MO
KLWT(AM) Lebanon MO
KMAL(AM) Malden MO
KRMS(AM) Osage Beach MO
KFMO(AM) Park Hills MO
*KCOZ(FM) Point Lookout MO
KWOC(AM) Poplar Bluff MO
KTTR(AM) Rolla MO
KTTR-FM Saint James MO
KFEQ(AM) Saint Joseph MO
KMOX(AM) Saint Louis MO
KTRS(AM) Saint Louis MO
KSMO(AM) Salem MO
KSIS(AM) Sedalia MO
KSIM(AM) Sikeston MO
KURM-FM South West City MO
KSGF(AM) Springfield MO

KWTO(AM) Springfield MO
KTUI(AM) Sullivan MO
KALM(AM) Thayer MO
*KGNV(FM) Washington MO
KOZQ(AM) Waynesville MO
KWPM(AM) West Plains MO
KUKU(AM) Willow Springs MO
WAMY(AM) Amory MS
*WMAH-FM Biloxi MS
WTNI(AM) Biloxi MS
*WMAU-FM Bude MS
WDSK(AM) Cleveland MS
WCJU(AM) Columbia MS
WJWF(AM) Columbus MS
WPBQ(AM) Flowood MS
*WMAO-FM Greenwood MS
WTCD(FM) Indianola MS
WKOZ(AM) Kosciusko MS
WMXI(FM) Laurel MS
WJZD(FM) Long Beach MS
*WPRL(FM) Lorman MS
WAKK(AM) McComb MS
WHNY(AM) McComb MS
*WMAW-FM Meridian MS
WMOX(AM) Meridian MS
WNAT(AM) Natchez MS
WJNT(AM) Pearl MS
*WKNA(FM) Senatobia MS
WQBC(AM) Vicksburg MS
WKBB(FM) West Point MS
KGVW(AM) Belgrade MT
KBLG(AM) Billings MT
KMMS(AM) Bozeman MT
*KGVA(FM) Fort Belknap Agency MT
KQDI(AM) Great Falls MT
KLYQ(AM) Hamilton MT
KOJM(AM) Havre MT
KBLL(AM) Helena MT
KCAP(AM) Helena MT
KOFI(AM) Kalispell MT
KGVO(AM) Missoula MT
KKNS-FM Missoula MT
KJJR(AM) Whitefish MT
WQNX(AM) Aberdeen NC
WSPC(AM) Albemarle NC
WWNC(AM) Asheville NC
WTKF(FM) Atlantic NC
*WBJD(FM) Atlantic Beach NC
WZNN(AM) Black Mountain NC
WXIT(AM) Blowing Rock NC
WATA(AM) Boone NC
*WBUX(FM) Buxton NC
WCHL(AM) Chapel Hill NC
*WUNC(FM) Chapel Hill NC
WBT(AM) Charlotte NC
*WFAE(FM) Charlotte NC
WDNC(AM) Durham NC
*WNCU(FM) Durham NC
WGAI(AM) Elizabeth City NC
WFNC(AM) Fayetteville NC
WIDU(AM) Fayetteville NC
WGBR(AM) Goldsboro NC
WSML(AM) Graham NC
*WFHE(FM) Hickory NC
WHKY(AM) Hickory NC
WMFR(AM) High Point NC
WJNC(AM) Jacksonville NC
WAAV(AM) Leland NC
WJRI(AM) Lenoir NC
WLXN(AM) Lexington NC
WFNC-FM Lumberton NC
*WUND-FM Manteo NC
WURI(FM) Manteo NC
WKRK(AM) Murphy NC
WAUG(AM) New Hope NC
WDNZ(AM) Raleigh NC
WPTF(AM) Raleigh NC
WRBZ(AM) Raleigh NC
*WRQM(FM) Rocky Mount NC
WCAB(AM) Rutherfordton NC
WSTP(AM) Salisbury NC
WLTT(FM) Shallotte NC
WNCA(AM) Siler City NC
WNCA(AM) Siler NC
WEEB(AM) Southern Pines NC
WTXY(AM) Whiteville NC
WSJS(AM) Winston-Salem NC

KFYR(AM) Bismarck ND
KXMR(AM) Bismarck ND
WDAY(AM) Fargo ND
KNOX(AM) Grand Forks ND
KQDJ(AM) Jamestown ND
KNDK(AM) Langdon ND
KQLX(AM) Lisbon ND
KHRT(AM) Minot ND
KEYZ(AM) Williston ND
KCOW(AM) Alliance NE
*KMNE-FM Bassett NE
KWBE(AM) Beatrice NE
KJSK(AM) Columbus NE
KHUB(AM) Fremont NE
KRGI(AM) Grand Island NE
KGFW(AM) Kearney NE
*KLNE-FM Lexington NE
KFOR(AM) Lincoln NE
KLIN(AM) Lincoln NE
KSWN(FM) McCook NE
WJAG(AM) Norfolk NE
KODY(AM) North Platte NE
KFAB(AM) Omaha NE
KKAR(AM) Omaha NE
KNEB(AM) Scottsbluff NE
*WEVO(FM) Concord NH
WKXL(AM) Concord NH
WTSN(AM) Dover NH
WGIP(AM) Exeter NH
*WEVC(FM) Gorham NH
*WEVH(FM) Hanover NH
WQTH(AM) Hanover NH
WTSL(AM) Hanover NH
WTPL(FM) Hillsboro NH
WEVJ(FM) Jackson NH
WEVN(FM) Keene NH
WUVR(AM) Lebanon NH
WGIR(AM) Manchester NH
WKBR(AM) Manchester NH
WEVS(FM) Nashua NH
WSMN(AM) Nashua NH
WNTK-FM New London NH
WGIN(AM) Rochester NH
*WNJN-FM Atlantic City NJ
*WNJS-FM Berlin NJ
*WNJB(FM) Bridgeton NJ
*WNJZ(FM) Cape May Court House NJ
WIFI(AM) Florence NJ
WRNJ(AM) Hackettstown NJ
WGYM(AM) Hammonton NJ
*WFJS(FM) Hazlet NJ
*WNJM(FM) Manahawkin NJ
WCTC(AM) New Brunswick NJ
WOND(AM) Pleasantville NJ
WHWH(AM) Princeton NJ
*WNJP(FM) Sussex NJ
*WNJT-FM Trenton NJ
KINN(AM) Alamogordo NM
KKOB(AM) Albuquerque NM
*KUNM(FM) Albuquerque NM
KENN(AM) Farmington NM
KYKK(AM) Hobbs NM
KOBE(AM) Las Cruces NM
KNMX(AM) Las Vegas NM
KTBL(AM) Los Ranchos de Albuquerque NM
*KENW-FM Portales NM
KSEL(AM) Portales NM
KBIM(AM) Roswell NM
KINF(AM) Roswell NM
*KSFR(FM) Santa Fe NM
*KRNM(FM) Chalan Kanoa-Saipan NP
KCNM(AM) Garapan-Saipan NP
KDWN(AM) Las Vegas NV
KXNT(AM) North Las Vegas NV
KNUU(AM) Paradise NV
KKOH(AM) Reno NV
KBZZ(AM) Sparks NV
WAMC(AM) Albany NY
WROW(AM) Albany NY
WCSS(AM) Amsterdam NY
WBTA(AM) Batavia NY
WINR(AM) Binghamton NY
WNBF(AM) Binghamton NY
WBEN(AM) Buffalo NY

WNED(AM) Buffalo NY
WCGR(AM) Canandaigua NY
WENI(AM) Corning NY
WWLE(AM) Cornwall NY
WKRT(AM) Cortland NY
WFLR(AM) Dundee NY
WFLR-FM Dundee NY
WDOE(AM) Dunkirk NY
WHBE(FM) East Hampton NY
WENY(AM) Elmira NY
*WEOS(FM) Geneva NY
WGVA(AM) Geneva NY
WWSC(AM) Glens Falls NY
WLEA(AM) Hornell NY
WWLZ(AM) Horseheads NY
WHCU(AM) Ithaca NY
*WJFF(FM) Jeffersonville NY
*WAMK(FM) Kingston NY
WGHQ(AM) Kingston NY
WLVL(AM) Lockport NY
WYBG(AM) Massena NY
WALL(AM) Middletown NY
WVOX(AM) New Rochelle NY
WADO(AM) New York NY
*WBAI(FM) New York NY
WLIB(AM) New York NY
*WNYC(AM) New York NY
WOR(AM) New York NY
WACK(AM) Newark NY
*WSUF(FM) Noyack NY
*WRVO(FM) Oswego NY
WTWK(AM) Plattsburgh NY
WHAM(AM) Rochester NY
WROC(AM) Rochester NY
*WXXI(AM) Rochester NY
WGY(AM) Schenectady NY
*WUSB(FM) Stony Brook NY
*WRVD(FM) Syracuse NY
WSYR(AM) Syracuse NY
WIBX(AM) Utica NY
WRUN(AM) Utica NY
*WRVN(FM) Utica NY
*WRVJ(FM) Watertown NY
WHLO(AM) Akron OH
WATH(AM) Athens OH
*WOUB(AM) Athens OH
WOMP(AM) Bellaire OH
WBLL(AM) Bellefontaine OH
*WOUC-FM Cambridge OH
WCER(AM) Canton OH
WBEX(AM) Chillicothe OH
*WVXC(FM) Chillicothe OH
WLW(AM) Cincinnati OH
*WVXU(AM) Cincinnati OH
*WCSB(FM) Cleveland OH
WERE(AM) Cleveland OH
WHK(AM) Cleveland OH
WTAM(AM) Cleveland OH
*WOSU(AM) Columbus OH
WTVN(AM) Columbus OH
*WOSE(FM) Coshocton OH
WHIO(AM) Dayton OH
WING(AM) Dayton OH
WEOL(AM) Elyria OH
WFIN(AM) Findlay OH
WMOH(AM) Hamilton OH
*WOUL-FM Ironton OH
WIMA(AM) Lima OH
WMAN(AM) Mansfield OH
*WMRT(FM) Marietta OH
WMRN(AM) Marion OH
WUCO(AM) Marysville OH
WMVO(AM) Mount Vernon OH
WCLT(AM) Newark OH
*WMUB(FM) Oxford OH
WBKC(AM) Painesville OH
WULM(AM) Springfield OH
WSTV(AM) Steubenville OH
WCWA(AM) Toledo OH
WSPD(AM) Toledo OH
WBTC(AM) Uhrichsville OH
WANR(AM) Warren OH
WHKZ(AM) Warren OH
*WVXW(FM) West Union OH
*WYSO(FM) Yellow Springs OH
WKBN(AM) Youngstown OH
WHIZ(AM) Zanesville OH

Broadcasting & Cable Yearbook 2006

D-712

Programming on Radio Stations in the U.S.

KWHW(AM) Altus OK	WARM(AM) Scranton PA	WETR(AM) Knoxville TN	KVEL(AM) Vernal UT	WPDR(AM) Portage WI
KWON(AM) Bartlesville OK	WBZU(AM) Scranton PA	WNML(AM) Knoxville TN	WFHG-FM Abingdon VA	WRJN(AM) Racine WI
KCLI(AM) Clinton OK	WBHV(AM) Somerset PA	WCKD(AM) Lebanon TN	WFNR(AM) Blacksburg VA	WJMC(AM) Rice Lake WI
KGWA(AM) Enid OK	WRSC(AM) State College PA	WLOD(AM) Loudon TN	WFHG(AM) Bristol VA	WRPN(AM) Ripon WI
KTJS(AM) Hobart OK	WKOK(AM) Sunbury PA	WPLN(AM) Madison TN	WCHV(AM) Charlottesville VA	*WRPN-FM Ripon WI
KEBC(AM) Midwest City OK	*WNJR(FM) Washington PA	WWTN(FM) Manchester TN	WINA(AM) Charlottesville VA	*WRFW(FM) River Falls WI
*KGOU(FM) Norman OK	WCHE(AM) West Chester PA	WCMT(AM) Martin TN	WFNR-FM Christiansburg VA	WHBL(AM) Sheboygan WI
KOKC(AM) Oklahoma City OK	WKZN(AM) West Hazleton PA	WAKI(AM) McMinnville TN	WFLO(AM) Farmville VA	WKLJ(AM) Sparta WI
KQCV(AM) Oklahoma City OK	WILK(AM) Wilkes-Barre PA	WKAM(AM) Memphis TN	WSVA(AM) Harrisonburg VA	WSPT(AM) Stevens Point WI
KTOK(AM) Oklahoma City OK	WRAK(AM) Williamsport PA	WREC(AM) Memphis TN	WREL(AM) Lexington VA	*KUWS(FM) Superior WI
WKY(AM) Oklahoma City OK	*WRLC(FM) Williamsport PA	WGNS(AM) Murfreesboro TN	WBRG(AM) Lynchburg VA	WTTN(AM) Watertown WI
*KROU(FM) Spencer OK	WWPA(AM) Williamsport PA	WLAC(AM) Nashville TN	*WHRV(FM) Norfolk VA	WFDL(AM) Waupun WI
KSPI(AM) Stillwater OK	WSBA(AM) York PA	WNOX(FM) Oak Ridge TN	WNIS(AM) Norfolk VA	WSAU(AM) Wausau WI
KFAQ(AM) Tulsa OK	WCMN(AM) Arecibo PR	*WFCM(AM) Smyrna TN	WTAR(AM) Norfolk VA	WFHR(AM) Wisconsin Rapids WI
KRMG(AM) Tulsa OK	WMIA(AM) Arecibo PR	WGOW-FM Soddy-Daisy TN	WRJR(AM) Portsmouth VA	WWNR(AM) Beckley WV
KAST(AM) Astoria OR	WYAC(AM) Cabo Rojo PR	WXQK(AM) Spring City TN	WRVA(AM) Richmond VA	WHIS(AM) Bluefield WV
KBKR(AM) Baker City OR	WNEL(AM) Caguas PR	KWKC(AM) Abilene TX	WRVA(AM) Richmond VA	WCHS(AM) Charleston WV
KWRO(AM) Coquille OR	WOIZ(AM) Guayanilla PR	KGNC(AM) Amarillo TX	WFIR(AM) Roanoke VA	WTBZ(AM) Grafton WV
KLOO(AM) Corvallis OR	WMSW(AM) Hatillo PR	KIXZ(AM) Amarillo TX	WTZE(AM) Tazewell VA	WMTD(AM) Hinton WV
*KOAC(AM) Corvallis OR	WSQD(AM) Lajas PR	KRGN(FM) Amarillo TX	WKCI(AM) Waynesboro VA	WRVC(AM) Huntington WV
KNND(AM) Cottage Grove OR	WMNT(AM) Manati PR	KLBJ(AM) Austin TX	WINC(AM) Winchester VA	WVHU(AM) Huntington WV
KWVR(AM) Enterprise OR	WKJB(AM) Mayaguez PR	KFNC(FM) Beaumont TX	WVGN(FM) Charlotte Amalie VI	WEPM(AM) Martinsburg WV
*KLCC(FM) Eugene OR	WDEP(AM) Ponce PR	KLVI(AM) Beaumont TX	WVWI(AM) Charlotte Amalie VI	WRNR(AM) Martinsburg WV
KPNW(AM) Eugene OR	WISO(AM) Ponce PR	KRCM(AM) Beaumont TX	WSNO(AM) Barre VT	WAJR(AM) Morgantown WV
KUGN(AM) Eugene OR	WPAB(AM) Ponce PR	KWHI(AM) Brenham TX	WBTN(AM) Bennington VT	WVLY(AM) Moundsville WV
KAJO(AM) Grants Pass OR	WPRP(AM) Ponce PR	KVNS(AM) Brownsville TX	WKVT(AM) Brattleboro VT	WVNT(AM) Parkersburg WV
KUIK(AM) Hillsboro OR	WUKQ(AM) Ponce PR	KXYL-FM Brownwood TX	WVMT(AM) Burlington VT	WRRL(AM) Rainelle WV
KYKN(AM) Keizer OR	WAPA(AM) San Juan PR	*KEOS(FM) College Station TX	WWWT(AM) Randolph VT	WJYP(AM) Saint Albans WV
KAGO(AM) Klamath Falls OR	*WIPR(AM) San Juan PR	WTAW(AM) College Station TX	WSYB(AM) Rutland VT	WWVA(AM) Wheeling WV
KFLS(AM) Klamath Falls OR	WKAQ(AM) San Juan PR	KEYS(AM) Corpus Christi TX	WDEV-FM Warren VT	*KUWA(FM) Afton WY
KLBM(AM) La Grande OR	WOSO(AM) San Juan PR	KKTX(AM) Corpus Christi TX	KBKW(AM) Aberdeen WA	KBBS(AM) Buffalo WY
*KDOV(FM) Medford OR	WUNO(AM) San Juan PR	KHER(FM) Crystal City TX	KXRO(AM) Aberdeen WA	KFBC(AM) Cheyenne WY
KMED(AM) Medford OR	WUPR(AM) Utuado PR	*KERA(FM) Dallas TX	KGMI(AM) Bellingham WA	KLEN(FM) Cheyenne WY
KNPT(AM) Newport OR	WENA(AM) Yauco PR	KLIF(AM) Dallas TX	*KUGS(FM) Bellingham WA	KRAE(AM) Cheyenne WY
KBBR(AM) North Bend OR	WKFE(AM) Yauco PR	KRLD(AM) Dallas TX	KARI(AM) Blaine WA	KODI(AM) Cody WY
KSRV(AM) Ontario OR	WADK(AM) Newport RI	KURV(AM) Edinburg TX	KELA(AM) Centralia-Chehalis WA	KUGR(AM) Green River WY
*KAPL(AM) Phoenix OR	WHJJ(AM) Providence RI	KULP(AM) El Campo TX	KOZI(AM) Chelan WA	KOWB(AM) Laramie WY
KBNP(AM) Portland OR	WPRO(AM) Providence RI	KROD(AM) El Paso TX	*KNWR(FM) Ellensburg WA	KGAB(AM) Orchard Valley WY
KPOJ(AM) Portland OR	WRNI(AM) Providence RI	KTSM(AM) El Paso TX	KXLE(AM) Ellensburg WA	KROE(AM) Sheridan WY
KXL(AM) Portland OR	WNRI(AM) Woonsocket RI	*KWCB(FM) Floresville TX	KULE(AM) Ephrata WA	
KRDM(AM) Redmond OR	WOON(AM) Woonsocket RI	KFLC(AM) Fort Worth TX	KONA(AM) Kennewick WA	
*KLFR(FM) Reedsport OR	WOON(AM) Woonsocket RI	WBAP(AM) Fort Worth TX	KTCR(AM) Kennewick WA	**Nostalgia**
*KMPQ(FM) Roseburg OR	WAIM(AM) Anderson SC	KBRA(AM) Freer TX	KBSN(AM) Moses Lake WA	WGMZ(FM) Glencoe AL
KQEN(AM) Roseburg OR	WTMA(AM) Charleston SC	KGAF(AM) Gainesville TX	*KMWS(FM) Mount Vernon WA	KVRC(AM) Arkadelphia AR
KRNR(AM) Roseburg OR	WBT-FM Chester SC	KLAT(AM) Houston TX	*KSVR(FM) Mount Vernon WA	KHBM(AM) Monticello AR
KOHI(AM) Saint Helens OR	WVOC(AM) Columbia SC	KNTH(AM) Houston TX	KONP(AM) Port Angeles WA	KFTT(FM) Bagdad AZ
KACI(AM) The Dalles OR	WFIS(AM) Fountain Inn SC	KPRC(AM) Houston TX	KZXR(AM) Prosser WA	*KCEA(FM) Atherton CA
KMBD(AM) Tillamook OR	WEAC(AM) Gaffney SC	KCOX(AM) Jasper TX	KQQQ(AM) Pullman WA	KXBX(AM) Lakeport CA
KPAM(AM) Troutdale OR	WGTN(AM) Georgetown SC	KLNT(AM) Laredo TX	*KFAE-FM Richland WA	KZPO(FM) Lindsay CA
KLWJ(AM) Umatilla OR	WYRD(AM) Greenville SC	KFRO(AM) Longview TX	KIRO(AM) Seattle WA	KIDD(AM) Monterey CA
WAEB(AM) Allentown PA	WCRS(AM) Greenwood SC	KFYO(AM) Lubbock TX	KKNW(AM) Seattle WA	KPAT(FM) Orcutt CA
WRTA(AM) Altoona PA	WRIX-FM Honea Path SC	KJTV(AM) Lubbock TX	KKOL(AM) Seattle WA	KBLF(AM) Red Bluff CA
WBFD(AM) Bedford PA	WQJM(AM) Myrtle Beach SC	KRFE(AM) Lubbock TX	KQBZ(FM) Seattle WA	KCTC(AM) Sacramento CA
WGPA(AM) Bethlehem PA	WRHI(AM) Rock Hill SC	KCRS(AM) Midland TX	KGA(AM) Spokane WA	KXDZ(FM) Templeton CA
*WBUQ(FM) Bloomsburg PA	WORD(AM) Spartanburg SC	KSFA(AM) Nacogdoches TX	KQNT(AM) Spokane WA	KEZW(AM) Aurora CO
WISR(AM) Butler PA	WSPA(AM) Spartanburg SC	KWBC(AM) Navasota TX	KXLY(AM) Spokane WA	WNLC(FM) East Lyme CT
WHYL(AM) Carlisle PA	WSPG(AM) Spartanburg SC	KOLE(AM) Port Arthur TX	KGDC(AM) Walla Walla WA	WQUN(AM) Hamden CT
WCHA(AM) Chambersburg PA	WDXY(AM) Sumter SC	KKSA(AM) San Angelo TX	KUJ(AM) Walla Walla WA	WFCT(AM) Apalachicola FL
WWCH(AM) Clarion PA	*WRJA-FM Sumter SC	KCOR(AM) San Antonio TX	*KWWS(FM) Walla Walla WA	WROD(AM) Daytona Beach FL
WCOJ(AM) Coatesville PA	KJAM(AM) Madison SD	KTSA(AM) San Antonio TX	KPQ(AM) Wenatchee WA	WBAU(AM) Fort Walton Beach FL
WVZN(AM) Columbia PA	KMSD(AM) Milbank SD	WOAI(AM) San Antonio TX	KDNA(FM) Yakima WA	WGRO(AM) Lake City FL
WFRM(AM) Coudersport PA	KORN(AM) Mitchell SD	*KTSW(FM) San Marcos TX	KIT(AM) Yakima WA	WINT(AM) Melbourne FL
WJET(AM) Erie PA	KCCR(AM) Pierre SD	KWED(AM) Seguin TX	WXCE(AM) Amery WI	WDIZ(AM) Panama City FL
WPSE(AM) Erie PA	KOTA(AM) Rapid City SD	KBKH(AM) Shamrock TX	*WLBL(AM) Auburndale WI	WJNA(AM) Royal Palm Beach FL
WZSK(AM) Everett PA	KELO(AM) Sioux Falls SD	KWNX(AM) Taylor TX	WBEV(AM) Beaver Dam WI	WMOG(AM) Brunswick GA
WHP(AM) Harrisburg PA	KSOO(AM) Sioux Falls SD	KTEM(AM) Temple TX	WISS(AM) Berlin WI	KUPI(AM) Ammon ID
*WITF-FM Harrisburg PA	WNAX(AM) Yankton SD	KLUP(AM) Terrell Hills TX	*WHSA(FM) Brule WI	WCGO(AM) Chicago Heights IL
WRKK(AM) Hughesville PA	WBCR(AM) Alcoa TN	KTFS(AM) Texarkana TX	*WHAD(FM) Delafield WI	WAIK(AM) Galesburg IL
WPRR(AM) Johnstown PA	WBIN(AM) Benton TN	KSEV(AM) Tomball TX	WAYY(AM) Eau Claire WI	WMIX(AM) Mount Vernon IL
WNPV(AM) Lansdale PA	WTBG(FM) Brownsville TN	KTBB(AM) Tyler TX	KFIZ(AM) Fond du Lac WI	WCVL(AM) Crawfordsville IN
WLBR(AM) Lebanon PA	WDEF(AM) Chattanooga TN	KWTX(AM) Waco TX	WFAW(AM) Fort Atkinson WI	WILO(AM) Frankfort IN
WIEZ(AM) Lewistown PA	WGOW(AM) Chattanooga TN	KWFS(AM) Wichita Falls TX	WDUZ(AM) Green Bay WI	KAHS(AM) El Dorado KS
WWGE(AM) Loretto PA	WBAC(AM) Cleveland TN	KVLL-FM Woodville TX	WTAQ(AM) Green Bay WI	WIVY(FM) Morehead KY
WJSM-FM Martinsburg PA	WCRV(AM) Collierville TN	KSUB(AM) Cedar City UT	WOGO(AM) Hallie WI	WVJS(AM) Owensboro KY
WPTT(AM) McKeesport PA	WPTN(AM) Cookeville TN	*KUSU-FM Logan UT	*WHHI(FM) Highland WI	KSIG(AM) Crowley LA
WMGW(AM) Meadville PA	*WMKW(FM) Crossville TN	KVNU(AM) Logan UT	WCLO(AM) Janesville WI	KJIN(AM) Houma LA
WPPT(AM) Mercersburg PA	WDNT(AM) Dayton TN	KQMB(FM) Midvale UT	WHBY(AM) Kimberly WI	WIZZ(AM) Greenfield MA
WKST(AM) New Castle PA	WDKN(AM) Dickson TN	KOAL(AM) Price UT	WIZM(AM) La Crosse WI	WTBO(AM) Cumberland MD
WOYL(AM) Oil City PA	*WKNQ(FM) Dyersburg TN	*KBYU-FM Provo UT	WLDY(AM) Ladysmith WI	WWLG(AM) Pikesville MD
WNTP(AM) Philadelphia PA	WCPH(AM) Etowah TN	KSVC(AM) Richfield UT	WIBA(AM) Madison WI	WJZN(AM) Augusta ME
WPHB(AM) Philipsburg PA	WAKM(AM) Franklin TN	KDXU(AM) Saint George UT	WTDY(AM) Madison WI	WABI(AM) Bangor ME
KDKA(AM) Pittsburgh PA	WHEW(AM) Franklin TN	KZNU(AM) Saint George UT	WDLB(AM) Marshfield WI	WDEA(AM) Ellsworth ME
WDVE(FM) Pittsburgh PA	WNWS-FM Jackson TN	*KCPW-FM Salt Lake City UT	WMEQ(AM) Menomonie WI	WBAE(AM) Portland ME
WPGB(FM) Pittsburgh PA	WTJS(AM) Jackson TN	KNRS(AM) Salt Lake City UT	*WVSS(FM) Menomonie WI	*WYAR(FM) Yarmouth ME
WPAZ(AM) Pottstown PA	*WETS(FM) Johnson City TN	KSL(AM) Salt Lake City UT	WTMJ(AM) Milwaukee WI	WCBY(AM) Cheboygan MI
*WYBF(AM) Radnor Township PA	WJCW(AM) Johnson City TN	KBJA(AM) Sandy UT	WOSH(AM) Oshkosh WI	WDBC(AM) Escanaba MI
WEEU(AM) Reading PA	WKIN(AM) Kingsport TN	KCPW(AM) Tooele UT	*WHBM-FM Park Falls WI	WFNT(AM) Flint MI

Broadcasting & Cable Yearbook 2006

D-713

Programming on Radio Stations in the U.S.

WGRY(AM) Grayling MI
WILS(AM) Lansing MI
WOAP(AM) Owosso MI
WLXT(FM) Petoskey MI
WMJH(AM) Rockford MI
WSPZ(AM) South Haven MI
KKIN(AM) Aitkin MN
KBMO(AM) Benson MN
KDKK-FM Park Rapids MN
KBFL(FM) Buffalo MO
KTOZ(AM) Springfield MO
WJBI(AM) Batesville MS
WIIN(AM) Ridgeland MS
KMTX(AM) Helena MT
KVCK(AM) Wolf Point MT
WIST(FM) Thomasville NC
WMXF(AM) Waynesville NC
*KFBN(FM) Fargo ND
WMYF(AM) Portsmouth NH
KVSF(AM) Santa Fe NM
WKLI-FM Albany NY
WDNY(AM) Dansville NY
WTLA(AM) North Syracuse NY
WZOZ(FM) Oneonta NY
*WRVO(FM) Oswego NY
WSGO(AM) Oswego NY
WBZA(FM) Rochester NY
*WRVD(FM) Syracuse NY
*WRVN(FM) Utica NY
*WRVJ(FM) Watertown NY
WNCO(AM) Ashland OH
WQCT(AM) Bryan OH
WCDK(FM) Cadiz OH
WCHI(AM) Chillicothe OH
WJEH(FM) Gallipolis OH
*WMKV(FM) Reading OH
WSOM(AM) Salem OH
WYPC(AM) Wellston OH
WNIO(AM) Youngstown OH
KTIL-FM Tillamook OR
KRAM(AM) West Klamath OR
WKAP(AM) Allentown PA
WNAK-FM Carbondale PA
WRIE(AM) Erie PA
WNAK(AM) Nanticoke PA
WPEN(AM) Philadelphia PA
WJAS(AM) Pittsburgh PA
WLKJ(AM) Portage PA
WPIC(AM) Sharon PA
WLKH(FM) Somerset PA
WTIV(AM) Titusville PA
WLKW(AM) West Warwick RI
WGTN-FM Andrews SC
WCAM(AM) Camden SC
WLOW(FM) Port Royal SC
WAMB(AM) Nashville TN
WAMB-FM Nashville TN
KSLI(AM) Abilene TX
KBST(AM) Big Spring TX
KRHC(AM) Burnet TX
KERV(AM) Kerrville TX
WSNZ(AM) Appomattox VA
WCVA(AM) Culpeper VA
WZEZ(FM) Goochland VA
WRAD(AM) Radford VA
KBRD(AM) Lacey WA
KOMW(AM) Omak WA
WCCN(AM) Neillsville WI
WETZ(AM) New Martinsville WV
WETZ-FM New Martinsville WV

Oldies

KEAG(FM) Anchorage AK
*KIYU(AM) Galena AK
*KMJG(FM) Homer AK
*KWJG(FM) Kasilof AK
KFMJ(FM) Ketchikan AK
KXBA(FM) Nikiski AK
*KUHB-FM Saint Paul AK
KIFW(AM) Sitka AK
WAFN-FM Arab AL
WKAC(AM) Athens AL
WATV(AM) Birmingham AL
WBPT(FM) Birmingham AL
WEBJ(AM) Brewton AL
WTBF-FM Brundidge AL

WACQ(AM) Carrville AL
WAVH(FM) Daphne AL
WZNJ(FM) Demopolis AL
WFPA(AM) Fort Payne AL
WGAD(AM) Gadsden AL
WDGM(FM) Greensboro AL
WGYV(AM) Greenville AL
WXQW(FM) Meridianville AL
WMFC-FM Monroeville AL
WOPP(AM) Opp AL
WVOK(AM) Oxford AL
WPID(AM) Piedmont AL
WMXV(FM) Russellville AL
WMRK(AM) Selma AL
WZLM(FM) Talladega AL
WJDB(AM) Thomasville AL
WXWQ(FM) Trinity AL
WRLD-FM Valley AL
WKXM-FM Winfield AL
KVLD(FM) Atkins AR
KEWI(AM) Benton AR
KSEC(FM) Bentonville AR
KRBK(FM) Booneville AR
KFCM(FM) Cherokee Village AR
KGFL(AM) Clinton AR
KTRQ(FM) Colt AR
KBKG(FM) Corning AR
KFLI(FM) Des Arc AR
KBBQ-FM Fort Smith AR
KFPW(AM) Fort Smith AR
KBYB(FM) Hope AR
KKIK(FM) Horseshoe Bend AR
KZYQ(FM) Lake Village AR
KOLL-FM Lonoke AR
KQOR(FM) Mena AR
KNAS(FM) Nashville AR
KWLT(FM) North Crossett AR
KQDD(FM) Osceola AR
KAMO-FM Rogers AR
KWAK(FM) Stuttgart AR
KRLW(AM) Walnut Ridge AR
KCLT(FM) West Helena AR
KCTT-FM Yellville AR
KRDE(FM) Globe AZ
KGVY(AM) Green Valley AZ
KRRN(FM) Kingman AZ
KRCY-FM Lake Havasu City AZ
KIKO(AM) Miami AZ
KGMG(FM) Oracle AZ
KOOL-FM Phoenix AZ
KOY(AM) Phoenix AZ
KKLD(FM) Prescott Valley AZ
KBUX(FM) Quartzsite AZ
KAZG(FM) Scottsdale AZ
KZKE(FM) Seligman AZ
KSNX(FM) Show Low AZ
KVSL(AM) Show Low AZ
KKYZ(FM) Sierra Vista AZ
KRVZ(FM) Springerville-Eagar AZ
KTKT(AM) Tucson AZ
KWFM(AM) Tucson AZ
KWMX(FM) Williams AZ
KJOK(AM) Yuma AZ
KQSR(FM) Yuma AZ
KIQO(FM) Atascadero CA
KBRE(FM) Atwater CA
KHYL(FM) Auburn CA
KBID(AM) Bakersfield CA
KKBB(FM) Bakersfield CA
KKGO(FM) Beverly Hills CA
KBOV(AM) Bishop CA
KODS(FM) Carnelian Bay CA
KZRO(FM) Dunsmuir CA
KXO(AM) El Centro CA
KKHB(FM) Eureka CA
KMGV(FM) Fresno CA
KAZA(AM) Gilroy CA
KCEE(FM) Grass Valley CA
KRAK(FM) Hesperia CA
KHRN(FM) Huron CA
KOKO(FM) Kerman CA
KVLI-FM Lake Isabella CA
KWSZ(FM) Lompoc CA
KRTH(FM) Los Angeles CA
KCEZ(FM) Los Molinos CA
KABX-FM Merced CA
KHPO(FM) Merced CA

KNKK(FM) Needles CA
KHOP(FM) Oakdale CA
KOCN(FM) Pacific Grove CA
KDES-FM Palm Springs CA
KNWQ(AM) Palm Springs CA
KOLA(FM) San Bernardino CA
KURS(AM) San Diego CA
KFRC(AM) San Francisco CA
KFRC-FM San Francisco CA
KISQ(FM) San Francisco CA
KZBR(FM) San Francisco CA
KCCL-FM Shingle Springs CA
KRDG(FM) Shingletown CA
KQOD(FM) Stockton CA
KSTN(AM) Stockton CA
KFSO-FM Visalia CA
KRCV(FM) West Covina CA
KRSX-FM Yermo CA
KGIW(AM) Alamosa CO
KRLN(AM) Canon City CO
KCMN(AM) Colorado Springs CO
KSPZ(FM) Colorado Springs CO
KXKL-FM Denver CO
KBKL(FM) Grand Junction CO
KEJJ(FM) Gunnison CO
KKHI(FM) Kremmling CO
KBLJ(AM) La Junta CO
KLIM(FM) Limon CO
KDZA-FM Pueblo CO
KBCR(FM) Steamboat Springs CO
KSTC(AM) Sterling CO
WDRC-FM Hartford CT
WKNL(FM) New London CT
WREF(FM) Ridgefield CT
WKZE(FM) Sharon CT
WKHL(FM) Stamford CT
WBIG-FM Washington DC
WLBW(FM) Fenwick Island DE
WNCL(FM) Milford DE
*WMHS(FM) Pike Creek DE
WWBF(AM) Bartow FL
WRGO(FM) Cedar Key FL
WPFL(FM) Century FL
WMMV(AM) Cocoa FL
WSRZ-FM Coral Cove FL
WKZY(FM) Cross City FL
WGTX(FM) De Funiak Springs FL
WZEP(AM) De Funiak Springs FL
WOLZ(FM) Fort Myers FL
WOLL(FM) Hobe Sound FL
WJGL(FM) Jacksonville FL
WBXY(FM) La Crosse FL
WEGT(FM) Lafayette FL
WWWK(FM) Marathon FL
WVOI(AM) Marco Island FL
WTOT(AM) Marianna FL
WPBH(FM) Mexico Beach FL
WECM(FM) Milton FL
WSBB(AM) New Smyrna Beach FL
WMFQ(FM) Ocala FL
WPLK(AM) Palatka FL
WYCL(FM) Pensacola FL
WMXJ(FM) Pompano Beach FL
WSOS(AM) Saint Augustine Beach FL
WPOI(FM) Saint Petersburg FL
WJCM(FM) Sebring FL
WJQB(FM) Spring Hill FL
WRBQ-FM Tampa FL
WJGO(FM) Tice FL
WQOL(FM) Vero Beach FL
WTTB(FM) Vero Beach FL
WDDQ(AM) Adel GA
WISK(AM) Americus GA
WMGR(AM) Bainbridge GA
WKQL(FM) Brunswick GA
WEBS(AM) Calhoun GA
WBHF(AM) Cartersville GA
WGAA(AM) Cedartown GA
WMJE(FM) Clarkesville GA
WQXZ(FM) Cordele GA
WGFS(AM) Covington GA
WCUG(AM) Cuthbert GA
WHFX(FM) Darien GA
WKVQ(AM) Eatonton GA
WFJO(FM) Folkston GA
WDDK(FM) Greensboro GA
WKEU(AM) Griffin GA

WCEH(AM) Hawkinsville GA
WTRP(AM) La Grange GA
WIFN(FM) Macon GA
WYTH(AM) Madison GA
WYIS(AM) McRae GA
WYSC(FM) McRae GA
WGCO(FM) Midway GA
WMNZ(AM) Montezuma GA
WMTM-FM Moultrie GA
WDMG-FM Ocilla GA
WSFB(AM) Quitman GA
WTYB(FM) Springfield GA
WNSY(FM) Talking Rock GA
WATG(FM) Trion GA
WZQZ(AM) Trion GA
WVOP(AM) Vidalia GA
WWUF(FM) Waycross GA
WRLA(AM) West Point GA
KGMZ-FM Aiea HI
KHUI(FM) Honolulu HI
KQMQ-FM Honolulu HI
KTOH(FM) Kalaheo HI
KBGX(FM) Keaau HI
KONI(FM) Lanai City HI
KLBA-FM Albia IA
KASI(AM) Ames IA
KCHE(AM) Cherokee IA
KCLN(AM) Clinton IA
KIOA(FM) Des Moines IA
*KJMC(FM) Des Moines IA
KGRR(FM) Epworth IA
KIOW(FM) Forest City IA
KVFD(FM) Fort Dodge IA
KLMJ(FM) Hampton IA
KNOD(FM) Harlan IA
KKMA(FM) Le Mars IA
KDAO(AM) Marshalltown IA
KRIB(AM) Mason City IA
KILJ(AM) Mount Pleasant IA
*KIGC(FM) Oskaloosa IA
KBIZ(AM) Ottumwa IA
KTLB(FM) Twin Lakes IA
KCII(AM) Washington IA
KCII-FM Washington IA
KOKZ(FM) Waterloo IA
KGEM(AM) Boise ID
KLTB(FM) Boise ID
KBAR(FM) Burley ID
KCID(AM) Caldwell ID
KVNI(AM) Coeur d'Alene ID
KRPL(AM) Moscow ID
KPKY(FM) Pocatello ID
KACH(AM) Preston ID
KGTM(FM) Rexburg ID
KLIX-FM Twin Falls ID
KTFI(AM) Twin Falls ID
WQRL(FM) Benton IL
WBYS(AM) Canton IL
WROY(AM) Carmi IL
WILY(AM) Centralia IL
WJMK(FM) Chicago IL
WMQZ(FM) Colchester IL
WIXN(AM) Dixon IL
KUUL(FM) East Moline IL
WDBQ-FM Galena IL
WMCW(AM) Harvard IL
WJBM(AM) Jerseyville IL
WRLL(AM) Johnston City IL
WEAI(FM) Lynnville IL
WDKR(FM) Maroa IL
WKOT(FM) Marseilles IL
WPWQ(FM) Mount Sterling IL
WHQQ(FM) Neoga IL
WSEY(FM) Oregon IL
WPBG(FM) Peoria IL
WZOE-FM Princeton IL
WTRH(FM) Ramsey IL
WKXQ(FM) Rushville IL
WQQL(FM) Springfield IL
WCFF(FM) Urbana IL
WYKT(FM) Wilmington IL
WASK-FM Battle Ground IN
WQRK(FM) Bedford IN
WUZR(FM) Bicknell IN
WLME(FM) Cannelton IN
WINN(FM) Columbus IN
WOCC(AM) Corydon IN

WIBN(FM) Earl Park IN
WURK(FM) Elwood IN
WJLT(FM) Evansville IN
WISG(FM) Fishers IN
WLDE(FM) Fort Wayne IN
WTLC-FM Greenwood IN
WBZQ(AM) Huntington IN
WAWK(AM) Kendallville IN
WASK(AM) Lafayette IN
*WJEF(FM) Lafayette IN
WXGO(AM) Madison IN
WBAT(AM) Marion IN
WEFM(FM) Michigan City IN
WERK(FM) Muncie IN
WJJK(FM) Noblesville IN
WSEZ(FM) Paoli IN
*WEEM(FM) Pendleton IN
WTCA(AM) Plymouth IN
WZOC(FM) Plymouth IN
WRIN(AM) Rensselaer IN
WROI(FM) Rochester IN
WZZB(AM) Seymour IN
WDND(AM) South Bend IN
WSKL(FM) Veedersburg IN
WJOT(AM) Wabash IN
WJOT-FM Wabash IN
WRSW-FM Warsaw IN
KSAJ-FM Abilene KS
KZDY(FM) Cawker City KS
KCKS(FM) Concordia KS
KVOE(AM) Emporia KS
KMDO(FM) Fort Scott KS
KOMB(FM) Fort Scott KS
KCAR-FM Galena KS
KKCI(FM) Goodland KS
KAYS(AM) Hays KS
KALN(AM) Iola KS
KBGL(FM) Larned KS
KGTR(FM) Larned KS
KNGL(AM) McPherson KS
KLKC(AM) Parsons KS
KLKC-FM Parsons KS
KWLS(AM) Pratt KS
KSKL(FM) Scott City KS
KGGG(FM) Sterling KS
KWME(FM) Wellington KS
KEYN-FM Wichita KS
KFTI(AM) Wichita KS
WMDJ-FM Allen KY
WCBL-FM Benton KY
WKXO(AM) Berea KY
WAIN(AM) Columbia KY
WCTT(AM) Corbin KY
WCYN(AM) Cynthiana KY
WEKB(FM) Elkhorn City KY
WFKY(FM) Frankfort KY
WOVO(FM) Glasgow KY
WUGO(FM) Grayson KY
WKYA(FM) Greenville KY
WHLN(AM) Harlan KY
WXLR(FM) Harold KY
WQXY(AM) Hazard KY
WHVO(AM) Hopkinsville KY
WIRV(AM) Irvine KY
WKDO-FM Liberty KY
WWXL(AM) Manchester KY
WMJL(AM) Marion KY
WMJL-FM Marion KY
WFTM(FM) Maysville KY
WMKJ(FM) Mt. Sterling KY
WRKY(AM) Murray KY
WVJS(AM) Owensboro KY
WPAD(AM) Paducah KY
WPKE(FM) Pikeville KY
WANO(AM) Pineville KY
WPRT(AM) Prestonsburg KY
WXKZ-FM Prestonsburg KY
WWKY(FM) Providence KY
WASE(FM) Radcliff KY
WRKA(FM) Saint Matthews KY
WCND(FM) Shelbyville KY
WTLO(AM) Somerset KY
WAKY-FM Springfield KY
WLKS(FM) West Liberty KY
KPEL-FM Abbeville LA
WTGG(FM) Amite LA
KMEZ(FM) Belle Chasse LA

Programming on Radio Stations in the U.S.

KEZP(FM) Bunkie LA	KCPI(FM) Albert Lea MN	KKGR(AM) East Helena MT	WRNJ(AM) Hackettstown NJ	WJER(AM) Dover-New Philadelphia OH
KPCH(FM) Dubach LA	KULO(FM) Alexandria MN	KLCY(AM) East Missoula MT	WOBM(AM) Lakewood NJ	WMOJ(FM) Fairfield OH
WTIX-FM Galliano LA	KQQL(FM) Anoka MN	KIKC(AM) Forsyth MT	WJRZ-FM Manahawkin NJ	WZRX-FM Fort Shawnee OH
KLEB(AM) Golden Meadow LA	KAUS(AM) Austin MN	KXGN(AM) Glendive MT	WMTR(AM) Morristown NJ	WRYV(FM) Gallipolis OH
WFPR(AM) Hammond LA	KBEW(AM) Blue Earth MN	KEIN(AM) Great Falls MT	WNNJ(AM) Newton NJ	WGRR(FM) Hamilton OH
KHLA(FM) Jennings LA	KRWC(AM) Buffalo MN	KLFM(FM) Great Falls MT	WTKU(FM) Ocean City NJ	WRBP(FM) Hubbard OH
KLLA(AM) Leesville LA	KFGI(FM) Crosby MN	KOFI(AM) Kalispell MT	WUSS(AM) Pleasantville NJ	WDLW(AM) Lorain OH
KLKL(FM) Minden LA	KDAL-FM Duluth MN	KTNY(FM) Libby MT	WGHT(AM) Pompton Lakes NJ	WAGX(FM) Manchester OH
KLIL(FM) Moreauville LA	KLDJ(FM) Duluth MN	KYLT(AM) Missoula MT	KRKE(AM) Albuquerque NM	WMRN(AM) Marion OH
KZBL(FM) Natchitoches LA	KJJK(AM) Fergus Falls MN	KBQQ(FM) Pinesdale MT	KKFG(FM) Bloomfield NM	WUCO(AM) Marysville OH
WTKL(AM) New Orleans LA	KKCQ(AM) Fosston MN	KSEN(AM) Shelby MT	KCCC(AM) Carlsbad NM	*WLMH(FM) Morrow OH
KWCL-FM Oak Grove LA	KKRC(FM) Granite Falls MN	KEZQ(FM) West Yellowstone MT	KWKA(AM) Clovis NM	WIOI(FM) New Boston OH
KBEB-FM Rayne LA	WMFG-FM Hibbing MN	WZKY(AM) Albemarle NC	KDSK(FM) Grants NM	WNKO(FM) Newark OH
KTIB(AM) Thibodaux LA	KDUZ(AM) Hutchinson MN	WOXL-FM Biltmore Forest NC	KMIN(AM) Grants NM	WBBG(FM) Niles OH
KVPI(AM) Ville Platte LA	KRAQ(AM) Jackson MN	WBHN(AM) Bryson City NC	KYVA-FM Grants NM	WLKR(AM) Norwalk OH
KVPI-FM Ville Platte LA	KQEG(FM) La Crescent MN	WKXB(FM) Burgaw NC	KVLC(FM) Hatch NM	WBUK(FM) Ottawa OH
WODS(FM) Boston MA	KFML(FM) Little Falls MN	WPCM(AM) Burlington NC	KHOB(AM) Hobbs NM	WDPT(FM) Piqua OH
WDVT(FM) Harwichport MA	KLQP(FM) Madison MN	WLZR(AM) Canton NC	KABG(FM) Los Alamos NM	WPTW(AM) Piqua OH
WATD-FM Marshfield MA	KRJM(FM) Mahnomen MN	WCSL(AM) Cherryville NC	KLEA-FM Lovington NM	WMLX(FM) Saint Mary's OH
WTWV(FM) Mashpee MA	KYSM(AM) Mankato MN	WCLN(AM) Clinton NC	KRTN-FM Raton NM	WSWR(FM) Shelby OH
WMNB(FM) North Adams MA	WMOZ(FM) Moose Lake MN	WERX-FM Columbia NC	*KRDR(FM) Red River NM	WULM(AM) Springfield OH
WUPE(FM) Pittsfield MA	KCHK(AM) New Prague MN	WEGO(AM) Concord NC	KCRX(FM) Roswell NM	WDIG(AM) Steubenville OH
WJDA(AM) Quincy MA	KRDS-FM New Prague MN	WBLA(AM) Elizabethtown NC	KBUY(FM) Ruidoso NM	WWWM-FM Sylvania OH
WORC-FM Webster MA	KRFO(AM) Owatonna MN	WGQR(FM) Elizabethtown NC	KSCQ(FM) Silver City NM	WTTF(FM) Tiffin OH
WCRN(AM) Worcester MA	KISD(FM) Pipestone MN	WODR(FM) Fair Bluff NC	KCHS(AM) Truth or Consequences NM	WELW(FM) Willoughby-Eastlake OH
WAMD(AM) Aberdeen MD	KWNG(FM) Red Wing MN	WGNC(AM) Gastonia NC	KSFQ(FM) White Rock NM	WKVX(AM) Wooster OH
WCMD(AM) Cumberland MD	KLGR-FM Redwood Falls MN	WNCT-FM Greenville NC	KSTJ(FM) Boulder City NV	WNCD(FM) Youngstown OH
WTBO(AM) Cumberland MD	KNXR(FM) Rochester MN	WFMZ(FM) Hertford NC	KELY(AM) Ely NV	KALV(AM) Alva OK
WTDK(FM) Federalsburg MD	KLCX(FM) Saint Charles MN	WAIZ(AM) Hickory NC	KQOL-FM Las Vegas NV	KACO(FM) Ardmore OK
WARK(AM) Hagerstown MD	KXAC(FM) Saint James MN	WCCG(FM) Hope Mills NC	KNYE(FM) Pahrump NV	KRVT(AM) Claremore OK
WMDM-FM Lexington Park MD	KZJK(FM) Saint Louis Park MN	WILT(FM) Jacksonville NC	KWNA(FM) Winnemucca NV	KTAT(AM) Frederick OK
WKHW(FM) Pocomoke City MD	KVGO(FM) Spring Valley MN	WWNF(FM) Kinston NC	WSEN-FM Baldwinsville NY	KTSO(FM) Glenpool OK
WTTR(FM) Westminster MD	KSNR(FM) Thief River Falls MN	WFLB(AM) Laurinburg NC	WABH(AM) Bath NY	KVRW(FM) Lawton OK
WJTO(AM) Bath ME	KAKK(AM) Walker MN	WTHZ(FM) Lexington NC	WBZO(FM) Bay Shore NY	KTMC(AM) McAlester OK
WCXU(FM) Caribou ME	KZGX(FM) Watertown MN	WLON(AM) Lincolnton NC	WENI-FM Big Flats NY	KOMA(FM) Oklahoma City OK
WGUY(FM) Dexter MI	KDJS(AM) Willmar MN	WHIP(FM) Mooresville NC	WHTT-FM Buffalo NY	KOKL(FM) Okmulgee OK
WABK-FM Gardiner ME	KWNO(AM) Winona MN	WCDG(FM) Moyock NC	WWKB(AM) Buffalo NY	KQLL-FM Owasso OK
WBYA(FM) Islesboro ME	KOZX(FM) Cabool MO	WLWL(AM) Rockingham NC	WPTR(AM) Clifton Park NY	KVLH(AM) Pauls Valley OK
WOZI(FM) Presque Isle ME	KAPE(AM) Cape Girardeau MO	WRXO(AM) Roxboro NC	WIYN(FM) Deposit NY	KOSB(FM) Perry OK
WYNZ(FM) Westbrook ME	KCRV-FM Caruthersville MO	WFJA(AM) Sanford NC	WDOE(AM) Dunkirk NY	KLOR-FM Ponca City OK
*WYAR(FM) Yarmouth ME	KWKZ(FM) Charleston MO	WOHS(AM) Shelby NC	WALK(AM) East Patchogue NY	KVRO(FM) Stillwater OK
XHRM-FM Tijuana MEX	KCHI(AM) Chillicothe MO	WTOE(AM) Spruce Pine NC	WFKL(FM) Fairport NY	KSLE(FM) Wewoka OK
WRCC(AM) Battle Creek MI	KCHI-FM Chillicothe MO	WACB(AM) Taylorsville NC	WGIX-FM Gouverneur NY	KSIW(AM) Woodward OK
WHNN(FM) Bay City MI	KDKD(AM) Clinton MO	WBLO(AM) Thomasville NC	WXUR(FM) Herkimer NY	KRAT(FM) Altamont OR
WMRX-FM Beaverton MI	KYMO-FM East Prairie MO	WIST(FM) Thomasville NC	WXHC(FM) Homer NY	KQAK(FM) Bend OR
WXQL(FM) Carrollton MI	KESM(AM) El Dorado Springs MO	WSVM(AM) Valdese NC	WLEA(AM) Hornell NY	KURY(AM) Brookings OR
WCZW(FM) Charlevoix MI	KYLS(FM) Fredericktown MO	WMQX-FM Winston-Salem NC	WZCR(FM) Hudson NY	KCNA(FM) Cave Junction OR
WTVB(FM) Coldwater MI	KKCA(FM) Fulton MO	*KEYA(FM) Belcourt ND	WENU-FM Hudson Falls NY	KDCQ(FM) Coos Bay OR
WOBE(FM) Crystal Falls MI	KJMO(FM) Jefferson City MO	KACL(FM) Bismarck ND	WHVW(FM) Hyde Park NY	KKNX(FM) Eugene OR
WOMC(FM) Detroit MI	KCMO-FM Kansas City MO	KDVL(FM) Devils Lake ND	WKSN(AM) Jamestown NY	KODZ(FM) Eugene OR
WMJO(FM) Essexville MI	KBOA(AM) Kennett MO	KDIX(AM) Dickinson ND	WCKM-FM Lake George NY	KCST-FM Florence OR
WMJZ-FM Gaylord MI	KXOQ(FM) Kennett MO	KAUJ(FM) Grafton ND	WICY(AM) Malone NY	KLYC(AM) McMinnville OR
WGKL(FM) Gladstone MI	KOMC-FM Kimberling City MO	KKXL(AM) Grand Forks ND	WABT(FM) Mechanicville NY	KLDZ(FM) Medford OR
WFGR(FM) Grand Rapids MI	KIRX(AM) Kirksville MO	KXGT(FM) Jamestown ND	WCBS-FM New York NY	KBZY(AM) Salem OR
WKAD(AM) Harrietta MI	KQUL(FM) Lake Ozark MO	KFAB-FM Kindred ND	WGNY(AM) Newburgh NY	KSWB(AM) Seaside OR
WSPZ-FM Hartford MI	KRLI(FM) Malta Bend MO	KRRZ(AM) Minot ND	WPAC(FM) Ogdensburg NY	KAVJ(FM) Sutherlin OR
*WHPR(FM) Highland Park MI	KYRX(FM) Marble Hill MO	KEGK(FM) Wahpeton ND	WHDL(AM) Olean NY	KACI-FM The Dalles OR
*WKHN(FM) Hubbard Lake MI	KZZT(FM) Moberly MO	KCOW(AM) Alliance NE	WMCR(AM) Oneida NY	KCUP(AM) Toledo OR
WIKB(AM) Iron River MI	KXMO-FM Owensville MO	KGMT(AM) Fairbury NE	WMCR-FM Oneida NY	KPPT-FM Toledo OR
WIKB-FM Iron River MI	KLID(AM) Poplar Bluff MO	KTNC(AM) Falls City NE	WDBY(FM) Patterson NY	WKAP(AM) Allentown PA
*WJCQ(FM) Jackson MI	KSFT(AM) Saint Joseph MO	KFMT(FM) Fremont NE	WKOL(FM) Plattsburgh NY	WFBG(AM) Altoona PA
*WJKQ(FM) Jackson MI	KOKO(AM) Warrensburg MO	KSDZ(FM) Gordon NE	WDLC(AM) Port Jervis NY	WLZS(FM) Beaver Springs PA
WJIM-FM Lansing MI	KWMO(AM) Washington MO	KUVR(AM) Holdrege NE	WTSX(FM) Port Jervis NY	WBFD(AM) Bedford PA
WMTE-FM Manistee MI	KOSP(FM) Willard MO	KADL(FM) Imperial NE	WRIV(AM) Riverhead NY	WALY(FM) Bellwood PA
WTIQ(AM) Manistique MI	KUKU-FM Willow Springs MO	KKPR-FM Kearney NE	WODZ-FM Rome NY	WFBS(AM) Berwick PA
WHLX(AM) Marine City MI	WWZQ(AM) Aberdeen MS	KBFZ(FM) Kimball NE	WTRY-FM Rotterdam NY	WKAB(AM) Berwick PA
WAGN(AM) Menominee MI	WAFM(AM) Amory MS	KKUL(AM) Lincoln NE	WLNG(FM) Sag Harbor NY	WBRR(FM) Bradford PA
WQXO(AM) Munising MI	WIZK(AM) Bay Springs MS	KBRL(AM) McCook NE	WGGO(AM) Salamanca NY	*WLBS(FM) Bristol PA
*WPQZ(FM) Muskegon MI	WVIM-FM Coldwater MS	KOOQ(AM) North Platte NE	WBPM(FM) Saugerties NY	WYTR(FM) Brookville PA
WNGE(FM) Negaunee MI	WHKL(FM) Crenshaw MS	KOGA(AM) Ogallala NE	WVKZ(AM) Schenectady NY	WASP(AM) Brownsville PA
WNIL(FM) Niles MI	WOHT(FM) Grenada MS	KGOR(FM) Omaha NE	WCDO-FM Sidney NY	WBUT(AM) Butler PA
WLCS(FM) North Muskegon MI	WDXO(FM) Hazlehurst MS	KRFS(AM) Superior NE	WNVE(FM) South Bristol Township NY	WCCL(AM) Central City PA
*WAAQ(FM) Onsted MI	WHER(FM) Heidelberg MS	KOAQ(AM) Terrytown NE	WIPS(AM) Ticonderoga NY	WCPA(AM) Clearfield PA
WAKV(FM) Otsego MI	WQJQ(FM) Kosciusko MS	KTCH-FM Wayne NE	WDLA(AM) Walton NY	WPNT(FM) Connellsville PA
WQXC-FM Otsego MI	WAGR(FM) Lexington MS	KAWL(AM) York NE	WTBQ(AM) Warwick NY	WCED(FM) DuBois PA
WLXT(FM) Petoskey MI	WAZA(FM) Liberty MS	WMOU(AM) Berlin NH	WJQZ(FM) Wellsville NY	WRDD(AM) Ebensburg PA
WSAG(FM) Pinconning MI	WQMA(AM) Marks MS	WMEX(FM) Farmington NH	WNYV(FM) Whitehall NY	WKPL(FM) Ellwood City PA
WHLS(AM) Port Huron MI	WNAU(AM) New Albany MS	WNNH(FM) Henniker NH	WZAD(FM) Wurtsboro NY	WFGO(FM) Erie PA
WDEE-FM Reed City MI	WMSO(FM) Newton MS	WZBK(AM) Keene NH	*WRMU(FM) Alliance OH	WQFN(FM) Forest City PA
WHAK-FM Rogers City MI	WOAD-FM Pickens MS	WLTN(AM) Littleton NH	WRQN(FM) Bowling Green OH	WHKF(FM) Harrisburg PA
*WAQQ(FM) Rogers Heights MI	WCJU-FM Prentiss MS	WQSO(FM) Rochester NH	WBCO(AM) Bucyrus OH	WTKT(AM) Harrisburg PA
WYVN(FM) Saugatuck MI	WVBG(FM) Redwood MS	WCFR-FM Walpole NH	WHBC(AM) Canton OH	WYCY(FM) Hawley PA
*WSHJ(FM) Southfield MI	WYAB(FM) Yazoo City MS	WLKZ(FM) Wolfeboro NH	WMJI(FM) Cleveland OH	WAZL(AM) Hazleton PA
WMSH(FM) Sturgis MI	KANA(AM) Anaconda MT	WMID(AM) Atlantic City NJ	WVBV(FM) Coal Grove OH	WWLY(FM) Huntingdon PA
WCCW-FM Traverse City MI	KKBR(FM) Billings MT	WILW(FM) Avalon NJ	WYBZ(FM) Crooksville OH	WDAD(AM) Indiana PA
WPON(AM) Walled Lake MI	KOBB-FM Bozeman MT	WWTR(FM) Bridgewater NJ	WODB(FM) Delaware OH	WTYM(AM) Kittanning PA
WEFG-FM Whitehall MI	KXTL(AM) Butte MT	WIFI(AM) Florence NJ		

Broadcasting & Cable Yearbook 2006

D-715

Programming on Radio Stations in the U.S.

WCNS(AM) Latrobe PA	KUQL(FM) Wessington Springs SD	KWRW(FM) Rusk TX	WHRY(AM) Hurley WI	KWIZ(FM) Santa Ana CA
WKVA(AM) Lewistown PA	WVOL(AM) Berry Hill TN	KELI(FM) San Angelo TX	WNXR(AM) Iron River WI	KKXX-FM Shafter CA
WMVL(FM) Linesville PA	WBOL(AM) Bolivar TN	KONO(AM) San Antonio TX	WOGB(FM) Kaukauna WI	KYAA(AM) Soquel CA
WBPZ(AM) Lock Haven PA	WKOM(FM) Columbia TN	KBPA(FM) San Marcos TX	WJBL(FM) Ladysmith WI	KGEN(AM) Tulare CA
WQZS(FM) Meyersdale PA	WPTN(AM) Cookeville TN	KBKH(FM) Shamrock TX	WLTU(FM) Manitowoc WI	KRSX(AM) Victorville CA
WAMO(AM) Millvale PA	WZYX(AM) Cowan TN	KJIM(AM) Sherman TX	WMDC(FM) Mayville WI	KWCA(FM) Weaverville CA
WPLY(AM) Mount Pocono PA	WAEW(FM) Crossville TN	KSST(AM) Sulphur Springs TX	WRIT-FM Milwaukee WI	KSFM(FM) Woodland CA
WBZD-FM Muncy PA	WDNT-FM Dayton TN	KEWL(AM) Texarkana TX	WOFM(FM) Mosinee WI	KUBA(AM) Yuba City CA
WQFM(FM) Nanticoke PA	WCDZ(FM) Dresden TN	KDOK(FM) Tyler TX	WSFQ(FM) Peshtigo WI	KZYR(FM) Avon CO
WJST(AM) New Castle PA	WTRO(AM) Dyersburg TN	KGLD(FM) Tyler TX	WPVL-FM Platteville WI	KLVZ(AM) Denver CO
WHPA(FM) Northern Cambria PA	WMRO(AM) Gallatin TN	KVOU(AM) Uvalde TX	WPRE(AM) Prairie du Chien WI	KQKS(FM) Lakewood CO
WNCC(AM) Northern Cambria PA	*WVCP(FM) Gallatin TN	KVWC(AM) Vernon TX	WRDB(AM) Reedsburg WI	*KVMT(FM) Montrose CO
WKQW(AM) Oil City PA	WRQQ(FM) Goodlettsville TN	KVWC-FM Vernon TX	WIZD(FM) Rudolph WI	*KVNF(FM) Paonia CO
WKQW-FM Oil City PA	WSMG(AM) Greeneville TN	KNAL(AM) Victoria TX	WOWN(FM) Shawano WI	KVRH(AM) Salida CO
WOGL(FM) Philadelphia PA	*WLMU(FM) Harrogate TN	KBGO(FM) Waco TX	WBOG(AM) Tomah WI	KJJD(AM) Windsor CO
WWSW-FM Pittsburgh PA	WIRJ(AM) Humboldt TN	KWUD(AM) Woodville TX	WTMB(FM) Tomah WI	WCUM(AM) Bridgeport CT
WITK(AM) Pittston PA	WMXX-FM Jackson TN	KXOL(AM) Brigham City UT	WJJQ-FM Tomahawk WI	WZMX(FM) Hartford CT
WYCK(AM) Plains PA	WKOS(FM) Kingsport TN	KXFF(FM) Cedar City UT	WTRW(AM) Two Rivers WI	WFNW(AM) Naugatuck CT
WQWK(FM) Pleasant Gap PA	*WKCS(FM) Knoxville TN	KLGN(AM) Logan UT	WVRQ(AM) Viroqua WI	WTMP(AM) Egypt Lake FL
WPAM(AM) Pottsville PA	WMSR(AM) Manchester TN	KODJ(FM) Salt Lake City UT	WTTN(AM) Watertown WI	WTZB(FM) Englewood FL
WSOX(FM) Red Lion PA	WCMT(AM) Martin TN	KGNT(FM) Smithfield UT	WHTL-FM Whitehall WI	WMIB(FM) Fort Lauderdale FL
WHUZ(FM) Saegertown PA	WTXM(FM) Maryville TN	KUNF(AM) Washington UT	WKCH(FM) Whitewater WI	WMIB(FM) Fort Lauderdale FL
WKBI(AM) Saint Marys PA	WHDM(AM) McKenzie TN	WBWR(FM) Bedford VA	WVBO(FM) Winneconne WI	WJAX(FM) Jacksonville FL
WLSW(FM) Scottsdale PA	WTPR-FM McKinnon TN	WBHB-FM Bridgewater VA	WBVQ(FM) Barrackville WV	WWAB(AM) Lakeland FL
WICK(AM) Scranton PA	WXMX(FM) Millington TN	WODI(AM) Brookneal VA	WIWS(AM) Beckley WV	WLBE(AM) Leesburg FL
WYFM(FM) Sharon PA	WCRK(AM) Morristown TN	WFXQ(FM) Chase City VA	WUKL(FM) Bethlehem WV	WPYO(FM) Maitland FL
WPHD(FM) South Waverly PA	WMTN(AM) Morristown TN	*WFOS(FM) Chesapeake VA	WKEZ(AM) Bluefield WV	WBWT(FM) Midway FL
WCDW(FM) Susquehanna PA	WLIK(AM) Newport TN	WCTG(FM) Chincoteague VA	WBTQ(FM) Buckhannon WV	WBWT(FM) Midway FL
WTTC(AM) Towanda PA	WRMX-FM Norris TN	WDIC-FM Clinchco VA	WMRE(AM) Charles Town WV	WONQ(AM) Oviedo FL
WTTC-FM Towanda PA	WATO(AM) Oak Ridge TN	WGRQ(FM) Colonial Beach VA	WELD(AM) Fisher WV	WONQ(AM) Oviedo FL
WPKL(FM) Uniontown PA	WTPR(AM) Paris TN	WKEY(AM) Covington VA	*WFGH(FM) Fort Gay WV	WRNE(AM) Pensacola FL
*WRDV(FM) Warminster PA	WQKR(AM) Portland TN	WSUH(FM) Crozet VA	WMTD(AM) Hinton WV	WMNE(AM) Riviera Beach FL
WRRN(FM) Warren PA	WKSR(AM) Pulaski TN	WBTM(FM) Danville VA	WMTD-FM Hinton WV	WFLM(FM) White City FL
WJPA(AM) Washington PA	WKSR-FM Pulaski TN	WILA(AM) Danville VA	WCBC-FM Keyser WV	WSIR(AM) Winter Haven FL
WJPA-FM Washington PA	WORM(AM) Savannah TN	WYTT(FM) Emporia VA	WKAZ(FM) Miami WV	WLVX(FM) Elberton GA
WMIA(AM) Arecibo PR	WNTT(AM) Tazewell TN	WZRV(FM) Front Royal VA	WCLG(FM) Morgantown WV	WPLO(AM) Grayson GA
WLUZ(AM) Bayamon PR	WENK(AM) Union City TN	WMJD(FM) Grundy VA	WAXS(FM) Oak Hill WV	WMPZ(FM) Ringgold GA
WLUZ(FM) Bayamon PR	WWON(AM) Waynesboro TN	WLES(FM) Lawrenceville VA	WADC(AM) Parkersburg WV	WMPZ(FM) Ringgold GA
WCMA-FM Fajardo PR	KULL(FM) Abilene TX	WZZU(FM) Lynchburg VA	WRON-FM Ronceverte WV	WHLJ(FM) Statenville GA
WOIZ(AM) Guayanilla PR	KBYG(AM) Big Spring TX	WVCV(AM) Orange VA	WDMX(FM) Vienna WV	WHGH(AM) Thomasville GA
WTTP(FM) Las Piedras PR	KNTX(AM) Bowie TX	WARV-FM Petersburg VA	WHAW(AM) Weston WV	WLET(AM) Toccoa GA
WAEL(AM) Mayaguez PR	KNEL(AM) Brady TX	WBBT-FM Powhatan VA	WBBD(AM) Wheeling WV	*WWBM(FM) Yates GA
WTIL(AM) Mayaguez PR	KROO(AM) Breckenridge TX	WBTJ(FM) Richmond VA	WBTH(AM) Williamson WV	KUAI(AM) Eleele HI
WLEO(FM) Ponce PR	KRVA-FM Campbell TX	WRXL(FM) Richmond VA	KBBS(AM) Buffalo WY	KHWI(FM) Hilo HI
WZAR(FM) Ponce PR	KPUR-FM Canyon TX	WXBX(FM) Rural Retreat VA	KMLD(FM) Casper WY	KIPA(AM) Hilo HI
WIDI(FM) Quebradillas PR	KCTX(AM) Childress TX	WSVO(FM) Staunton VA	KRRR(FM) Cheyenne WY	KSSK(FM) Honolulu HI
WKVM(AM) San Juan PR	KEFH(FM) Clarendon TX	WFOG(FM) Suffolk VA	KKTY(AM) Douglas WY	KUPA(AM) Pearl City HI
WRSS(FM) San Sebastian PR	KGAP(FM) Clarksville TX	WKQY(FM) Tazewell VA	KMER(AM) Kemmerer WY	*KJMC(FM) Des Moines IA
WWBB(FM) Providence RI	KCCT(AM) Corpus Christi TX	WZZI(FM) Vinton VA	KREO(FM) Pine Bluffs WY	*KSUI(FM) Iowa City IA
WZLA-FM Abbeville SC	KMXR(FM) Corpus Christi TX	WMBG(FM) Williamsburg VA	KPIN(AM) Pinedale WY	KRIB(AM) Mason City IA
WZLA-FM Abbeville SC	KIVY(AM) Crockett TX	WSTA(FM) Charlotte Amalie VI	KVOW(AM) Riverton WY	*KBBG(FM) Waterloo IA
WKSP(FM) Dalhart TX	KXIT(FM) Dalhart TX	WMNG(FM) Christiansted VI	KRKK(AM) Rock Springs WY	KYZK(FM) Sun Valley ID
WBSC(AM) Bennettsville SC	KBFB(FM) Dallas TX	WWOD(FM) Hartford VT	KROE(AM) Sheridan WY	WKKD(AM) Aurora IL
WSIM(FM) Bishopville SC	KLUV-FM Dallas TX	WFAD(AM) Middlebury VT	KTHE(AM) Thermopolis WY	WFUN-FM Bethalto IL
WGFG(FM) Branchville SC	KWMC(AM) Del Rio TX	WSKI(AM) Montpelier VT	KWOR(AM) Worland WY	WGCI-FM Chicago IL
WPUB(FM) Camden SC	KDDD-FM Dumas TX	WVNR(FM) Poultney VT		WWHP(FM) Farmer City IL
WLTQ(AM) Charleston SC	KINL(FM) Eagle Pass TX	WNBX(FM) Springfield VT	**Other**	*WKCC(FM) Kankakee IL
WCRE(AM) Cheraw SC	KAMA(AM) El Paso TX	KLKI(AM) Anacortes WA		WSRB(FM) Lansing IL
WAHT(AM) Clemson SC	KOFX(FM) El Paso TX	KBRO(AM) Bremerton WA	*KBBI(AM) Homer AK	*WVJC(FM) Mount Carmel IL
WOMG(FM) Columbia SC	KSVE(AM) El Paso TX	KRQT(FM) Castle Rock WA	*KBBI(AM) Homer AK	WKBF(FM) Rock Island IL
WYNN(AM) Florence SC	KXEZ(FM) Farmersville TX	KITI(AM) Chehalis-Centralia WA	WDBT(FM) Headland AL	WBCP(AM) Urbana IL
WSYN(FM) Georgetown SC	KFRO-FM Gilmer TX	KEYF-FM Cheney WA	WOZK(AM) Ozark AL	WXTW(FM) Auburn IN
WPCI(AM) Greenville SC	KKDA(AM) Grand Prairie TX	KEYF(AM) Dishman WA	WTBF(AM) Troy AL	WNHT(FM) Churubusco IN
WCZZ(AM) Greenwood SC	KCOL-FM Groves TX	KLCK(AM) Goldendale WA	KXHT(FM) Marion AR	*WSWI(AM) Evansville IN
WWNU(FM) Irmo SC	KONO-FM Helotes TX	KEYG-FM Grand Coulee WA	KSUD(AM) West Memphis AR	WLOI(AM) La Porte IN
WJES(AM) Johnston SC	KTBZ-FM Houston TX	KARY-FM Grandview WA	KVVA-FM Apache Junction AZ	WARU(AM) Peru IN
WKSX(FM) Johnston SC	KHVL(AM) Huntsville TX	KNTB(AM) Lakewood WA	KKFR(FM) Glendale AZ	WARU-FM Roann IN
WKSC(AM) Kershaw SC	KRVF(FM) Kerens TX	KEDO(AM) Longview WA	KLNZ(FM) Glendale AZ	WKWH(AM) Shelbyville IN
WCOO(FM) Kiawah Island SC	KLDE(FM) Lake Jackson TX	KBRC(AM) Mount Vernon WA	KTZR-FM Green Valley AZ	KSJM(FM) Winfield KS
WDKD(AM) Kingstree SC	KSHN-FM Liberty TX	KMJY(FM) Newport WA	KAZM(AM) Sedona AZ	KSJM(FM) Winfield KS
WWKT-FM Kingstree SC	KITY(FM) Llano TX	KWDB(AM) Oak Harbor WA	*KOHN(FM) Sells AZ	WTSZ-FM Eminence KY
WAGL(AM) Lancaster SC	KKCL(FM) Lorenzo TX	KRIZ(AM) Renton WA	KNCR(AM) Fortuna CA	*WMKY(FM) Morehead KY
WGOR(FM) New Ellenton SC	KDAV(AM) Lubbock TX	KBSG-FM Tacoma WA	KQEQ(AM) Fowler CA	KQLQ(FM) Columbia LA
WKDK(AM) Newberry SC	KCUL(AM) Marshall TX	KYNR(AM) Toppenish WA	KBIF(AM) Fresno CA	*KRVS(FM) Lafayette LA
WXLY(FM) North Charleston SC	KCUL-FM Marshall TX	KKSN(AM) Vancouver WA	KVBE(FM) Hanford CA	KLRZ(FM) Larose LA
*WRBK(FM) Richburg SC	KYCX-FM Mexia TX	KRVO(FM) Longview WA	KGBA-FM Holtville CA	KAGY(AM) Port Sulphur LA
WGVC(FM) Simpsonville SC	KQXX-FM Mission TX	KNLT(AM) Walla Walla WA	KBRC(FM) Mount Vernon WA	WMKI(AM) Boston MA
WICI(FM) Sumter SC	KLBO(AM) Monahans TX	KTEL(AM) Walla Walla WA	KZAP(FM) Paradise CA	WSBS(AM) Great Barrington MA
WWOF(AM) Walhalla SC	KEWL-FM New Boston TX	WDKM(AM) Adams WI	KZAP(FM) Paradise CA	WVBF(AM) Middleborough Center MA
KAWK(FM) Custer SD	KZRB(FM) New Boston TX	WBDK(FM) Algoma WI	KXTZ(FM) Pismo Beach CA	WNTN(AM) Newton MA
KDSJ(AM) Deadwood SD	KMCM(FM) Odessa TX	WATW(AM) Ashland WI	KXCL(AM) Placerville CA	*WSMU-FM North Dartmouth MA
KSQB-FM Dell Rapids SD	KREH(AM) Pecan Grove TX	WOLX-FM Baraboo WI	KLOA(AM) Ridgecrest CA	*WESM(FM) Princess Anne MD
KBJM(AM) Lemmon SD	KEYE-FM Perryton TX	WAQE-FM Barron WI	KGBY(FM) Sacramento CA	WICL(FM) Williamsport MD
KKSD(FM) Milbank SD	KPLX(AM) Port Lavaca TX	WGEZ(FM) Beloit WI	KJAY(AM) Sacramento CA	XHRM(FM) Tijuana MEX
KCCR(AM) Pierre SD	KREW(AM) Plainview TX	WWIS(AM) Black River Falls WI	KWIE(FM) San Jacinto CA	WWBR(FM) Big Rapids MI
KKLS(FM) Rapid City SD	KITE(FM) Port Lavaca TX	WRJO(FM) Eagle River WI	KWIE(FM) San Jacinto CA	WBCH-FM Hastings MI
KSQB(AM) Sioux Falls SD	KROB(AM) Robstown TX	WRKU(FM) Forestville WI	KLOK(AM) San Jose CA	WFAT(AM) Portage MI
	KTLU(AM) Rusk TX			

Broadcasting & Cable Yearbook 2006

*WSHJ(FM) Southfield MI
WMFN(AM) Zeeland MI
KZCR(FM) Fergus Falls MN
*KMSU(FM) Mankato MN
*KCCM-FM Moorhead MN
*KRLX(FM) Northfield MN
KLBB(AM) Saint Paul MN
*KGAC(FM) Saint Peter MN
KRBI-FM Saint Peter MN
*KSMR(FM) Winona MN
*KSMR(FM) Winona MN
KWRT-FM Boonville MO
KBXR(FM) Columbia MO
WKCU(AM) Corinth MS
*WURC(FM) Holly Springs MS
WQMS(AM) Quitman MS
KBSR(AM) Laurel MT
WGQR(FM) Elizabethtown NC
WQNQ(FM) Fletcher NC
WWNF(FM) Kinston NC
WDLZ(FM) Murfreesboro NC
WWDR(AM) Murfreesboro NC
*WZNB(FM) New Bern NC
*WDCC(FM) Sanford NC
WOHS(AM) Shelby NC
*KABU(FM) Fort Totten ND
KSJZ(FM) Jamestown ND
WFTN(AM) Franklin NH
WNTK(AM) Newport NH
WHTG(AM) Eatontown NJ
*KGLP(FM) Gallup NM
KAGM(FM) Los Lunas NM
KBOM(FM) Santa Fe NM
KSHP(AM) North Las Vegas NV
WDDY(AM) Albany NY
WCSS(AM) Amsterdam NY
WBNR(AM) Beacon NY
WEHH(AM) Elmira Heights-Horseheads NY
WLVL(AM) Lockport NY
WKDM(AM) New York NY
WBEA(FM) Southold NY
WTOR(AM) Youngstown NY
WLEC(AM) Sandusky OH
KTBT(FM) Collinsville OK
KKBC-FM Baker City OR
KVMX(FM) Banks OR
KQFM(FM) Hermiston OR
WLER-FM Butler PA
WZUM(AM) Carnegie PA
*WRTL(FM) Ephrata PA
WPPZ-FM Jenkintown PA
WBCB(AM) Levittown-Fairless Hills PA
WEDO(AM) McKeesport PA
WPHI-FM Media PA
WVPO(AM) Stroudsburg PA
*WRKC(FM) Wilkes-Barre PA
WGIT(AM) Canovanas PR
WXZX(FM) Culebra PR
WGDL(AM) Lares PR
WTTP(FM) Las Piedras PR
WTTP(FM) Las Piedras PR
WZMT(FM) Ponce PR
WIDI(FM) Quebradillas PR
WAKX(FM) Narragansett Pier RI
WAKX(FM) Narragansett Pier RI
WVCO(FM) Loris SC
WGZO(FM) Parris Island SC
WXBT(FM) West Columbia SC
KBRK(AM) Brookings SD
WXIS(FM) Erwin TN
WOWW(AM) Germantown TN
WDAP(AM) Huntingdon TN
WMAX-FM South Pittsburg TN
*KACV-FM Amarillo TX
KBZD(FM) Amarillo TX
KOOC(FM) Belton TX
KQFX(FM) Borger TX
KNEL(AM) Brady TX
KBSO(FM) Corpus Christi TX
KPTI(FM) Crystal Beach TX
*KVTT(FM) Dallas TX
KBXX(FM) Houston TX
KIKK(AM) Pasadena TX
KMJR(FM) Portland TX
KROM(FM) San Antonio TX
*KSYM-FM San Antonio TX
*KSYM-FM San Antonio TX
KPYK(AM) Terrell TX
KBTE(FM) Tulia TX
KBTE(FM) Tulia TX
KTXN-FM Victoria TX
KWUD(AM) Woodville TX
*KZMU(FM) Moab UT
*KRDC-FM Saint George UT
KMRI(AM) West Valley City UT
WMXH-FM Luray VA
*WHRO-FM Norfolk VA
WJOI(AM) Norfolk VA
WHKT(AM) Portsmouth VA
WIVI(FM) Charlotte Amalie VI
WJKC(FM) Christiansted VI
WJKC(FM) Christiansted VI
*WWPV-FM Colchester VT
WDEV-FM Warren VT
KXAA(FM) Cle Elum WA
KENU(AM) Enumclaw WA
KSBN(AM) Spokane WA
WERL(AM) Eagle River WI
WHSM-FM Hayward WI
WTUX(AM) Madison WI
*WMSE(FM) Milwaukee WI
WKFX(FM) Rice Lake WI
WRCO(AM) Richland Center WI
WMMM-FM Verona WI
*WXPW(FM) Wausau WI
WDZN(FM) Romney WV
KAML-FM Gillette WY

Polish

WNWI(AM) Oak Lawn IL
WPNA(AM) Oak Park IL
WNVR(AM) Vernon Hills IL
WRKL(AM) New City NY
WLIM(AM) Patchogue NY

Polka

*WOES(FM) Ovid-Elsie MI
KASM(AM) Albany MN
WKTX(AM) Cortland OH
WTKM(AM) Hartford WI
WTKM-FM Hartford WI

Portugese

KLBS(AM) Los Banos CA
*WFAR(FM) Danbury CT
WAKX(FM) Narragansett Pier RI

Progressive

*KRUA(FM) Anchorage AK
*KSUA(FM) Fairbanks AK
*WTOH(FM) Mobile AL
*KXRJ(FM) Russellville AR
*KXCI(FM) Tucson AZ
KLLY(FM) Oildale CA
*KSPB(FM) Pebble Beach CA
*KRCB-FM Santa Rosa CA
*KCSU-FM Fort Collins CO
KFMU-FM Oak Creek CO
*WXCI(FM) Danbury CT
*WVOF(FM) Fairfield CT
*WDJW(FM) Somers CT
*WVUD(FM) Newark DE
*WKPX(FM) Sunrise FL
*WPRK(FM) Winter Park FL
*WREK(FM) Atlanta GA
*WVGS(FM) Statesboro GA
*KIWR(FM) Council Bluffs IA
*KALA(FM) Davenport IA
*KWLC(AM) Decorah IA
*KRUI-FM Iowa City IA
*KRNI(AM) Mason City IA
*KRNL-FM Mount Vernon IA
*WLUW(FM) Chicago IL
*WJMU(FM) Decatur IL
*WNUR-FM Evanston IL
*WLCA(FM) Godfrey IL
*WMXM(FM) Lake Forest IL
*WIUS(FM) Macomb IL
*KSDB-FM Manhattan KS
*WWHR(FM) Bowling Green KY
*WTUL(FM) New Orleans LA
*WBIM-FM Bridgewater MA
*WMBR(FM) Cambridge MA
*WIQH(FM) Concord MA
*WXPL(FM) Fitchburg MA
*WCCH(FM) Holyoke MA
*WUML(FM) Lowell MA
*WJJW(FM) North Adams MA
*WSMU-FM North Dartmouth MA
*WZLY(FM) Wellesley MA
*WCHC(FM) Worcester MA
WRNR-FM Grasonville MD
*WUMF-FM Farmington ME
*WMEB-FM Orono ME
*WMEW(FM) Waterville ME
*WYAR(FM) Yarmouth ME
WGRD-FM Grand Rapids MI
*WIDR(FM) Kalamazoo MI
*WMHW-FM Mount Pleasant MI
*WSDP(FM) Plymouth MI
*KUOM(AM) Minneapolis MN
*KUMM(FM) Morris MN
*KVSC(FM) Saint Cloud MN
*WMCN(FM) Saint Paul MN
*KWUR(FM) Clayton MO
*KCOU(FM) Columbia MO
*WUAG(FM) Greensboro NC
*WDCC(FM) Sanford NC
*WSIF(FM) Wilkesboro NC
*KDNE(FM) Crete NE
KIBZ(FM) Crete NE
*WUNH(FM) Durham NH
WDCR(AM) Hanover NH
*WNEC-FM Henniker NH
*WKNH(FM) Keene NH
*WPCR-FM Plymouth NH
*WRPR(FM) Mahwah NJ
*WJSV(FM) Morristown NJ
*WVPH(FM) Piscataway NJ
WPRB(FM) Princeton NJ
*WTSR(FM) Trenton NJ
*WKNJ-FM Union Township NJ
WNJC(AM) Washington Township NJ
WRRB(FM) Arlington NY
*WHCL-FM Clinton NY
*WCVF-FM Fredonia NY
*WEOS(FM) Geneva NY
*WGFR(FM) Glens Falls NY
*WRCU-FM Hamilton NY
*WRHO(FM) Oneonta NY
*WIRQ(FM) Rochester NY
*WFNP(FM) Rosendale NY
*WSPN(FM) Saratoga Springs NY
*WRUC(FM) Schenectady NY
WEHM(FM) Southampton NY
*WUSB(FM) Stony Brook NY
WCLX(FM) Westport NY
WLKK(FM) Wethersfield Township NY
WDST(FM) Woodstock NY
*WOUB(AM) Athens OH
*WUFM(FM) Columbus OH
*WDUB(FM) Granville OH
*WMCO(FM) New Concord OH
*WUSO(FM) Springfield OH
*WHEI(FM) Tiffin OH
*WJCU(FM) University Heights OH
*WOBN(FM) Westerville OH
*WYSO(FM) Yellow Springs OH
*KWVA(FM) Eugene OR
*KEOL(FM) La Grande OR
*WWEC(FM) Elizabethtown PA
*WZBT(FM) Gettysburg PA
*WTGP(FM) Greenville PA
*WKVR-FM Huntingdon PA
*WARC(FM) Meadville PA
*WMSS(FM) Middletown PA
*WIXQ(FM) Millersville PA
*WKDU(FM) Philadelphia PA
*WPTS-FM Pittsburgh PA
*WXAC(FM) Reading PA
*WRSK(FM) Slippery Rock PA
*WCLH(FM) Wilkes-Barre PA
*WRLC(FM) Williamsport PA
*WVYC(FM) York PA
*WDOM(FM) Providence RI
*WDOM(FM) Providence RI
*WSBF-FM Clemson SC
*KAOR(FM) Vermillion SD
*WNRZ(FM) Dickson TN
*WRVU(FM) Nashville TN
*WUTS(FM) Sewanee TN
*KERA(FM) Dallas TX
*KSAU(FM) Nacogdoches TX
KHQN(AM) Spanish Fork UT
*WEHC(FM) Emory VA
*WMLU(FM) Farmville VA
*WFFC(FM) Ferrum VA
*WWHS-FM Hampden-Sydney VA
*WXJM(FM) Harrisonburg VA
*WDCE(FM) Richmond VA
*WCWM(FM) Williamsburg VA
*WIUV(FM) Castleton VT
*WRMC-FM Middlebury VT
*KUGS(FM) Bellingham WA
*KSVR(FM) Mount Vernon WA
*KEXP-FM Seattle WA
*KWRS(FM) Spokane WA
*KUPS(FM) Tacoma WA
*WBSD(FM) Burlington WI
*WWSP(FM) Stevens Point WI
*WVBC(FM) Bethany WV
*WVWC(FM) Buckhannon WV
*WWVU-FM Morgantown WV
*KUWA(FM) Afton WY
*KDUW(FM) Douglas WY
*KUWG(FM) Gillette WY
*KUWJ(FM) Jackson WY
*KUWR(FM) Laramie WY
*KUWN(FM) Newcastle WY
*KUWX(FM) Pinedale WY
*KCWC-FM Riverton WY
*KUWZ(FM) Rock Springs WY
*KSUW(FM) Sheridan WY
*KUWD(FM) Sundance WY
KUWT(FM) Thermopolis WY

Public Affairs

*KYUK(AM) Bethel AK
*KFSK(FM) Petersburg AK
KIAL(AM) Unalaska AK
*KCHU(AM) Valdez AK
WYDE-FM Cullman AL
KFNN(AM) Mesa AZ
*KNAI(FM) Phoenix AZ
*KUAZ-FM Tucson AZ
*KPFA(FM) Berkeley CA
*KPFB(FM) Berkeley CA
KLTX(AM) Long Beach CA
*KAFM(FM) Grand Junction CO
WQUN(AM) Hamden CT
*WCSP-FM Washington DC
*WETA(FM) Washington DC
WNDA(AM) De Land FL
*WUFT-FM Gainesville FL
*WJUF(FM) Inverness FL
WPBR(AM) Lantana FL
*WKFA(FM) Saint Catherine FL
*WPIO(FM) Titusville FL
*WGLT(FM) Normal IL
*WFHB(FM) Bloomington IN
WILO(AM) Frankfort IN
*WGVE(FM) Gary IN
*WJCF(FM) Morristown IN
WKCT(AM) Bowling Green KY
*WRPS(FM) Rockland MA
*WETH(FM) Hagerstown MD
*WDIH(FM) Salisbury MD
*WMEH(FM) Bangor ME
*WMED(FM) Calais ME
*WMEP(FM) Camden ME
WMEF(FM) Fort Kent ME
*WMEA(FM) Portland ME
*WMEM(FM) Presque Isle ME
WMPL(AM) Hancock MI
*KMSK(FM) Austin MN
*KMSU(FM) Mankato MN
KAUL(FM) Ellington MO
*KCUR-FM Kansas City MO
*KBIY(FM) Van Buren MO
*WJSU(FM) Jackson MS
*WRVS-FM Elizabeth City NC
WNCA(AM) Siler City NC
WSMX(AM) Winston-Salem NC
*KABU(FM) Fort Totten ND
KSWV(AM) Santa Fe NM
*WNYC(AM) New York NY
WOR(AM) New York NY
*WPSA(FM) Paul Smiths NY
*WGBE(FM) Bryan OH
*WOSU(AM) Columbus OH
*WGDE(FM) Defiance OH
*WGLE(FM) Lima OH
*WGTE-FM Toledo OH
KIXR(FM) Ponca City OK
*KTCB(FM) Tillamook OR
*WDIY(FM) Allentown PA
*WDUQ(FM) Pittsburgh PA
WIAC(AM) San Juan PR
*WJWJ-FM Beaufort SC
*KQSD-FM Lowry SD
*KUSD(FM) Vermillion SD
*WQOX(FM) Memphis TN
*WYPL(FM) Memphis TN
*KUSR(FM) Logan UT
*WHRV(FM) Norfolk VA
WFHR(AM) Wisconsin Rapids WI
*WAUA(FM) Petersburg WV

Reggae

*KJLU(FM) Jefferson City MO
WARR(AM) Warrenton NC
WLIB(AM) New York NY
WJKC(FM) Christiansted VI

Religious

*KATB(FM) Anchorage AK
*KJHA(FM) Houston AK
KIAM(AM) Nenana AK
*KNOM(AM) Nome AK
*KNOM-FM Nome AK
*KJNP(AM) North Pole AK
KRSA(AM) Petersburg AK
*KUDU(FM) Tok AK
*WSTF(FM) Andalusia AL
WRAB(AM) Arab AL
WATV(AM) Birmingham AL
*WBFR(FM) Birmingham AL
*WLJR(FM) Birmingham AL
WBSA(AM) Boaz AL
WMCJ(AM) Cullman AL
*WYFD(FM) Decatur AL
*WMBV(FM) Dixons Mills AL
*WDYF(FM) Dothan AL
*WGTF(FM) Dothan AL
*WVOB(FM) Dothan AL
*WFIX(FM) Florence AL
*WTBB(FM) Gadsden AL
WGEA(AM) Geneva AL
WBXR(AM) Hazel Green AL
*WBHY-FM Mobile AL
WMOB(AM) Mobile AL
*WLBF(FM) Montgomery AL
*WTBJ(FM) Oxford AL
*WJCK(FM) Piedmont AL
WBTG(AM) Sheffield AL
WYEA(AM) Sylacauga AL
WZZA(AM) Tuscumbia AL
WAPZ(AM) Wetumpka AL
WKXM(AM) Winfield AL
*KZIG(FM) Cave City AR
*KBDO(FM) Des Arc AR
KTCN(FM) Eureka Springs AR
*KARH(FM) Forrest City AR
*KAOW(FM) Fort Smith AR
*KALR(FM) Hot Springs AR
*KLRO(FM) Hot Springs AR
*KAOG(FM) Jonesboro AR
KUUZ(FM) Lake Village AR
KAAY(AM) Little Rock AR
KWLR(FM) Maumelle AR
*KCMH(FM) Mountain Home AR
*KANX(FM) Sheridan AR
KMTL(AM) Sherwood AR
*KLRC(FM) Siloam Springs AR
*KRMB(FM) Bisbee AZ

Programming on Radio Stations in the U.S.

*KWRB(FM) Bisbee AZ	*WMFL(FM) Florida City FL	*WBJW(FM) Albion IL	WEZC(AM) Neon KY	*WGNB(FM) Zeeland MI
*KJTA(FM) Flagstaff AZ	*WAFG(FM) Fort Lauderdale FL	WXAN(AM) Ava IL	WNOP(AM) Newport KY	KJLY(FM) Blue Earth MN
KPXQ(AM) Glendale AZ	*WJYO(FM) Fort Myers FL	WRMS(AM) Beardstown IL	WWFT(AM) Nicholasville KY	KYCR(AM) Golden Valley MN
*KNLB(FM) Lake Havasu City AZ	WMYR(AM) Fort Myers FL	*WOLG(FM) Carlinville IL	*WJIE-FM Okolona KY	WCTS(AM) Maplewood MN
*KWFH(FM) Parker AZ	*WJFP(FM) Fort Pierce FL	*WTSG(FM) Carlinville IL	*WKWC(FM) Owensboro KY	*KTIS(AM) Minneapolis MN
KASA(AM) Phoenix AZ	*WYFB(FM) Gainesville FL	*WBGL(FM) Champaign IL	*WPTJ(FM) Paris KY	KCGN-FM Ortonville MN
*KPHF(FM) Phoenix AZ	WACC(AM) Hialeah FL	WAIT(AM) Chicago IL	WYGH(AM) Paris KY	KCUE(AM) Red Wing MN
*KGCB(FM) Prescott AZ	WOIR(AM) Homestead FL	*WMBI-FM Chicago IL	*WJSO(FM) Pikeville KY	KCWJ(AM) Blue Springs MO
KTBA(AM) Tuba City AZ	WCGL(AM) Jacksonville FL	WYLL(AM) Chicago IL	WRLV(AM) Salyersville KY	KOMC(AM) Branson MO
KWIM(FM) Window Rock AZ	*WJFR(FM) Jacksonville FL	*WDLM(AM) East Moline IL	WLCK(AM) Scottsville KY	KMFC(FM) Centralia MO
*KYRM(FM) Yuma AZ	*WJIR(FM) Key West FL	*WDLM-FM East Moline IL	*WTHL(FM) Somerset KY	*KFUO(AM) Clayton MO
*KNDL(FM) Angwin CA	WOTS(AM) Kissimmee FL	*WCBW-FM East St. Louis IL	WMTC(AM) Vancleve KY	*KJCV(FM) Country Club MO
KLFF(AM) Arroyo Grande CA	*WKES(FM) Lakeland FL	*WRYT(AM) Edwardsville IL	WMTC-FM Vancleve KY	KEXS(AM) Excelsior Springs MO
KBRT(AM) Avalon CA	*WYFO(FM) Lakeland FL	*WGNN(FM) Fisher IL	WBCE(AM) Wickliffe KY	*KMCV(FM) High Point MO
*KFRB(FM) Bakersfield CA	*WLMS(FM) Lecanto FL	WBGX(AM) Harvey IL	WEKC(AM) Williamsburg KY	KBCV(FM) Hollister MO
*KWTH(FM) Barstow CA	*WAPB(FM) Madison FL	*WJCH(FM) Joliet IL	KJMJ(AM) Alexandria LA	KUGT(AM) Jackson MO
*KWTW(FM) Bishop CA	*WJNF(FM) Marianna FL	*WGSL(FM) Loves Park IL	KWDF(AM) Ball LA	*KHGN(FM) Kirksville MO
KCIK(AM) Blue Lake CA	*WGSG(FM) Mayo FL	WGGH(AM) Marion IL	KBZE(FM) Berwick LA	KLEX(AM) Lexington MO
*KIBC(FM) Burney CA	WCIF(FM) Melbourne FL	*WJCG(FM) Monee IL	WIKC(AM) Bogalusa LA	KMRF(FM) Marshfield MO
*KMRO(FM) Camarillo CA	*WMCU(FM) Miami FL	*WBNH(FM) Pekin IL	*WQCK(FM) Clinton LA	KELE(AM) Mountain Grove MO
KFIA(AM) Carmichael CA	WJCC(AM) Miami Springs FL	*WCIC(FM) Pekin IL	KAJN-FM Crowley LA	*KLUH(FM) Poplar Bluff MO
*KHAP(FM) Chico CA	*WFRF-FM Monticello FL	WVEL(AM) Pekin IL	*KVDP(FM) Dry Prong LA	*KOKS(FM) Poplar Bluff MO
*KFRJ(FM) China Lake CA	WSOR(FM) Naples FL	WPEO(AM) Peoria IL	*KPAE(FM) Erwinville LA	*KSIV-FM Saint Louis MO
*KBXO(FM) Coachella CA	*WJLU(FM) New Smyrna Beach FL	*WGNJ(FM) Saint Joseph IL	WCKW(AM) Garyville LA	KXEN(AM) Saint Louis MO
*KFRP(FM) Coalinga CA	*WAYR(AM) Orange Park FL	WAUR(AM) Sandwich IL	KKNO(AM) Gretna LA	KRHW(AM) Sikeston MO
KRDU(AM) Dinuba CA	*WJTF(FM) Panama City FL	*WSOG(FM) Spring Valley IL	*KAYT(FM) Jena LA	*KWFC(FM) Springfield MO
*KECR(AM) El Cajon CA	*WPCS(FM) Pensacola FL	WIHM(AM) Taylorville IL	*KTOC-FM Jonesboro LA	*KNLN(FM) Vienna MO
*KASK(FM) Fairfield CA	WVTJ(AM) Pensacola FL	WGLL(AM) Auburn IN	*WBOK(AM) New Orleans LA	*WPAE(FM) Centreville MS
KJPG(AM) Frazier Park CA	*WVIJ(FM) Port Charlotte FL	WNTS(AM) Beech Grove IN	WLNO(AM) New Orleans LA	WTGY(FM) Charleston MS
KBIF(AM) Fresno CA	*WKFA(FM) Saint Catherine FL	*WSPM(FM) Cloverdale IN	WSHO(AM) New Orleans LA	WWUN-FM Clarksdale MS
*KEYQ(AM) Fresno CA	*WFTI-FM Saint Petersburg FL	*WFOF(FM) Covington IN	WPFC(AM) Port Allen LA	*WAUM(FM) Duck Hill MS
*KFNO(FM) Fresno CA	*WTLG(FM) Starke FL	WVHI(AM) Evansville IN	KOKA(AM) Shreveport LA	*WAII(FM) Hattiesburg MS
KYNO(AM) Fresno CA	*WWFR(FM) Stuart FL	*WBGW(FM) Fort Branch IN	KBSF(AM) Springhill LA	WAML(AM) Laurel MS
KKMC(AM) Gonzales CA	WTAL(AM) Tallahassee FL	WLYV(AM) Fort Wayne IN	KTKC(FM) Springhill LA	*WATP(FM) Laurel MS
*KPJP(FM) Greenville CA	WTIS(AM) Tampa FL	WPWX(FM) Hammond IN	KBYO(AM) Tallulah LA	WESY(AM) Leland MS
KESQ(AM) Indio CA	*WYFE(FM) Tarpon Springs FL	*WHLP(FM) Hanna IN	KVCL-FM Winnfield LA	WAKK(AM) McComb MS
KTYM(AM) Inglewood CA	WPIO(FM) Titusville FL	WBRI(AM) Indianapolis IN	WSRO(AM) Ashland MA	*WAQL(FM) McComb MS
*KJCU(FM) Laytonville CA	*WWXC(FM) Albany GA	*WIWC(FM) Kokomo IN	WEZE(AM) Boston MA	*WASM(FM) Natchez MS
*KEFM(FM) Le Grand CA	WLTA(AM) Alpharetta GA	*WYTJ(FM) Linton IN	WROL(AM) Boston MA	*WATU(FM) Port Gibson MS
KJOP(AM) Lemoore CA	*WFRP(FM) Americus GA	*WBHW(FM) Loogootee IN	WACE(AM) Chicopee MA	*WJZB(FM) Starkville MS
KLTX(AM) Long Beach CA	WAEC(AM) Atlanta GA	*WMBL(FM) Mitchell IN	WVNE(AM) Leicester MA	WKOR(FM) Starkville MS
KHOT(AM) Madera CA	WGUN(AM) Atlanta GA	WNDZ(AM) Portage IN	WNEB(AM) Worcester MA	*WZKM(FM) Waynesboro MS
*KADV(FM) Modesto CA	WFAM(AM) Augusta GA	*WCRT(FM) Terre Haute IN	*WFSI(FM) Annapolis MD	WJNS-FM Yazoo City MS
KKXX(AM) Paradise CA	WBAF(AM) Barnesville GA	*WHOJ(FM) Terre Haute IN	WBMD(AM) Baltimore MD	KGVW(AM) Belgrade MT
KCBC(AM) Riverbank CA	WUFE(AM) Baxley GA	*WKRY(FM) Versailles IN	*WOEL-FM Elkton MD	KURL(AM) Billings MT
KPRO(AM) Riverside CA	WGMI(AM) Bremen GA	*WATI(FM) Vincennes IN	WFRB(AM) Frostburg MD	*KFRD(FM) Butte MT
*KSGN(FM) Riverside CA	*WCCV(FM) Cartersville GA	*WHPL(FM) West Lafayette IN	*WLIC(FM) Frostburg MD	KGLE(AM) Glendive MT
*KEBR(FM) Rocklin CA	*WFRC(FM) Columbus GA	*KBJQ(FM) Bronson KS	*WAIJ(FM) Grantsville MD	*KSPL(FM) Kalispell MT
*KEDR(FM) Sacramento CA	*WYFK(FM) Columbus GA	KCLY(FM) Clay Center KS	WJSS(AM) Havre de Grace MD	*KPLG(FM) Plains MT
KEZY(AM) San Bernardino CA	*WWEV-FM Cumming GA	*KHYM(FM) Copeland KS	WOLC(FM) Princess Anne MD	WCGC(AM) Belmont NC
KWVE(FM) San Clemente CA	WDPC(AM) Dallas GA	*KJIL(FM) Copeland KS	*WGTS(FM) Takoma Park MD	WGCR(AM) Brevard NC
KSDO(AM) San Diego CA	WATB(AM) Decatur GA	*KPOR(FM) Emporia KS	WWPN(AM) Westernport MD	*WCCE(FM) Buie's Creek NC
*KEAR(FM) San Francisco CA	WDCY(AM) Douglasville GA	*KVCY(FM) Fort Scott KS	*WCRH(FM) Williamsport MD	WPTL(AM) Canton NC
KFAX(AM) San Francisco CA	WMVV(FM) Griffin GA	*KGCR(FM) Goodland KS	*WFST(AM) Caribou ME	WMYT(AM) Carolina Beach NC
*KHFR(FM) Santa Maria CA	WWWE(AM) Hapeville GA	*KPRD(FM) Hays KS	*WYFP(FM) Harpswell ME	WHVN(AM) Charlotte NC
*KGZO(FM) Shafter CA	WGML(AM) Hinesville GA	KREJ(FM) Medicine Lodge KS	WTME(AM) Rumford ME	*WCKB(AM) Dunn NC
*KFRS(FM) Soledad CA	*WOAK(FM) La Grange GA	KJRG(AM) Newton KS	*WSEW(FM) Sanford ME	WSRC(AM) Durham NC
*KWG(FM) Stockton CA	WBML(AM) Macon GA	KCCV-FM Olathe KS	WKTQ(AM) South Paris ME	WLOE(AM) Eden NC
*KPRA(FM) Ukiah CA	*WYFS(FM) Savannah GA	KCCV(AM) Overland Park KS	WMAX(AM) Bay City MI	WFMO(AM) Fairmont NC
KDIA(AM) Vallejo CA	*WRAF-FM Toccoa Falls GA	*KAKA(AM) Salina KS	*WTRK(FM) Bay City MI	WWOL(AM) Forest City NC
KERI(AM) Wasco-Greenacres CA	WAFT(AM) Valdosta GA	KFLA(AM) Scott City KS	WLJW(AM) Cadillac MI	WFMC(AM) Goldsboro NC
KSMH(AM) West Sacramento CA	WYFA(FM) Waynesboro GA	KCVT(FM) Silver Lake KS	*WOLW(FM) Cadillac MI	WYCV(AM) Granite Falls NC
KRKS-FM Boulder CO	*WYFW(FM) Winder GA	*KBUZ(FM) Topeka KS	WLCM(AM) Charlotte MI	WYFL(FM) Henderson NC
KLTT(AM) Commerce City CO	*KHMG(FM) Barrigada GU	*KJTY(FM) Topeka KS	WLQV(AM) Detroit MI	*WHPE-FM High Point NC
KRKS(AM) Denver CO	KTWG(AM) Hagatna GU	KSGL(AM) Wichita KS	*WLJN(AM) Elmwood Township MI	WRNS(AM) Kinston NC
*KCIC(FM) Grand Junction CO	KUAU(AM) Haiku HI	*KYWA(FM) Wichita KS	*WPHN(FM) Gaylord MI	WMYN(AM) Mayodan NC
KFEL(AM) Pueblo CO	*KCIF(FM) Hilo HI	WYWY(AM) Barbourville KY	WGDN(AM) Gladwin MI	*WOTJ(FM) Morehead City NC
KGFT(FM) Pueblo CO	KHNR(AM) Honolulu HI	WLJC(FM) Beattyville KY	WFUR(AM) Grand Rapids MI	WDJS(AM) Mount Olive NC
KJEB(FM) Strasburg CO	KLHT(AM) Honolulu HI	*WCVK(FM) Bowling Green KY	WFUR-FM Grand Rapids MI	WKRK(AM) Murphy NC
WADS(AM) Ansonia CT	*KFFF(AM) Boone IA	WKDP(AM) Corbin KY	WKPR(AM) Kalamazoo MI	*WAAE(FM) New Bern NC
*WFAR(FM) Danbury CT	*KFFF-FM Boone IA	WCVG(AM) Covington KY	WEUL(FM) Kingsford MI	WAUG(AM) New Hope NC
*WJMJ(FM) Hartford CT	KLNG(AM) Council Bluffs IA	WCPM(AM) Cumberland KY	*WMPC(AM) Lapeer MI	WECR(AM) Newland NC
WFIF(AM) Milford CT	*KDFR(FM) Des Moines IA	WHIR-FM Danville KY	*WHWL(FM) Marquette MI	WJIJ(FM) Norlina NC
*WCTF(AM) Vernon CT	KWKY(AM) Des Moines IA	WIOK(FM) Falmouth KY	WRDT(AM) Monroe MI	WCLY(AM) Raleigh NC
WHIM(AM) Apopka FL	*KEGR(FM) Fort Dodge IA	WHBN(AM) Harrodsburg KY	WOAP(AM) Owosso MI	WEED(AM) Rocky Mount NC
WQOP(AM) Atlantic Beach FL	*KDCR(FM) Sioux Center IA	*WJMD(FM) Hazard KY	WADW(FM) Pickford MI	WEGG(AM) Rose Hill NC
WSWN(AM) Belle Glade FL	KTFC(FM) Sioux City IA	WKVG(AM) Jenkins KY	*WPCJ(FM) Pittsford MI	WYAL(AM) Scotland Neck NC
WLVJ(AM) Boynton Beach FL	KTFG(FM) Sioux Rapids IA	WDFB(AM) Junction City KY	*WNFA(FM) Port Huron MI	WVCB(AM) Shallotte NC
*WRMB(FM) Boynton Beach FL	*KNWS(AM) Waterloo IA	*WVCT(FM) Keavy KY	*WMSD(FM) Rose Township MI	*WAGO(FM) Snow Hill NC
WTCL(AM) Chattahoochee FL	*KNWS-FM Waterloo IA	WJMM-FM Keene KY	*WNFR(FM) Sandusky MI	WCOK(AM) Sparta NC
*WMIE(FM) Cocoa FL	KNJY(AM) Boise ID	WKDO(AM) Liberty KY	*WOFR(FM) Schoolcraft MI	WGMA(AM) Spindale NC
WWBC(AM) Cocoa FL	KBXL(FM) Caldwell ID	WYGE(FM) London KY	*KTGG(AM) Spring Arbor MI	*WYFQ-FM Wadesboro NC
WMFJ(AM) Daytona Beach FL	*KWJT(FM) Rathdrum ID	*WSOF(FM) Madisonville KY	*WSAE(FM) Spring Arbor MI	WOBX(AM) Wanchese NC
WYND(AM) De Land FL	*KBYR-FM Rexburg ID	*WBFI(FM) McDaniels KY	*WUFL(FM) Sterling Heights MI	WSMY(AM) Weldon NC
*WJED(FM) Dogwood Lakes Estate FL	*KAWZ(FM) Twin Falls ID	WMSK(AM) Morganfield KY	WHST(FM) Tawas City MI	WIAM(AM) Williamston NC
*WKTO(FM) Edgewater FL	*KEFX(FM) Twin Falls ID	*WAXG(FM) Mt. Sterling KY	*WLJN-FM Traverse City MI	WLSG(FM) Wilmington NC
*WNLE(FM) Fernandina Beach FL	*KTWD(FM) Wallace ID	WLCR(AM) Mt. Washington KY	*WHWG(FM) Trout Lake MI	WBTE(AM) Windsor NC

Programming on Radio Stations in the U.S.

WURB(FM) Windsor NC
WPOL(AM) Winston-Salem NC
*WSNC(FM) Winston-Salem NC
*KBFR(FM) Bismarck ND
*KCJL(FM) Lincoln ND
KHRT(AM) Minot ND
*KFNW(AM) West Fargo ND
*KTLX(FM) Columbus NE
*KAYA(FM) Hubbard NE
*KNGN(AM) McCook NE
*KPNO(FM) Norfolk NE
*KVSS(FM) Omaha NE
KCMI(FM) Terrytown NE
WDER(AM) Derry NH
*WVFA(FM) Lebanon NH
*WKDN-FM Camden NJ
WTMR(AM) Camden NJ
*WSJI(FM) Cherry Hill NJ
WCHR(AM) Flemington NJ
WWDJ(AM) Hackensack NJ
*WYRS(FM) Manahawkin NJ
WXMC(AM) Parsippany-Troy Hills NJ
*WJPH(FM) Woodbine NJ
*KFLQ(FM) Albuquerque NM
KNKT(FM) Armijo NM
*KZPI(FM) Deming NM
*KRUC(FM) Las Cruces NM
KINF(AM) Roswell NM
*KWFL(FM) Roswell NM
KHAC(AM) Tse Bonito NM
KKVV(AM) Las Vegas NV
*KSOS(FM) Las Vegas NV
*KIHM(FM) Reno NV
KXTO(AM) Reno NV
WLOF(FM) Attica NY
WDCX(FM) Buffalo NY
*WMHI(FM) Cape Vincent NY
WCHP(AM) Champlain NY
WJIV(FM) Cherry Valley NY
WSIV(AM) East Syracuse NY
WRWD(FM) Ellenville NY
WLNL(AM) Horseheads NY
*WFRH(FM) Kingston NY
WBAR-FM Lake Luzerne NY
*WMHQ(FM) Malone NY
WVOA-FM Mexico NY
WTHE(AM) Mineola NY
WJUX(FM) Monticello NY
WMCA(AM) New York NY
*WWRV(AM) New York NY
WHLD(AM) Niagara Falls NY
*WFSO(FM) Oliverbridge NY
WZXV(FM) Palmyra NY
WHIC(AM) Rochester NY
WYFY(AM) Rome NY
*WFRS(FM) Smithtown NY
*WFRW(FM) Webster NY
*WOFN(FM) Beach City OH
WJYM(AM) Bowling Green OH
WILB(AM) Canton OH
WGGN(FM) Castalia OH
*WCDR-FM Cedarville OH
*WOHC(FM) Chillicothe OH
WTSJ(AM) Cincinnati OH
WABQ(AM) Cleveland OH
*WCRF(FM) Cleveland OH
*WHVT(FM) Clyde OH
WRFD(AM) Columbus-Worthington OH
*WCUE(FM) Cuyahoga Falls OH
*WJJE(FM) Delaware OH
WGNZ(AM) Fairborn OH
WNLT(FM) Harrison OH
*WVML(FM) Millersburg OH
WCCD(AM) Parma OH
*WOHP(FM) Portsmouth OH
*WLRY(FM) Rushville OH
*WVMS(FM) Sandusky OH
*WCVZ(FM) South Zanesville OH
*WEEC(FM) Springfield OH
*WOTL(FM) Toledo OH
*WXML(FM) Upper Sandusky OH
WASN(AM) Youngstown OH
*WYTN(FM) Youngstown OH
*WJIC(FM) Zanesville OH
*KKVO(FM) Altus OK
KEOR(AM) Atoka OK
*KNYD(FM) Broken Arrow OK

*KKRD(FM) Enid OK
KMFS(AM) Guthrie OK
*KALU(FM) Langston OK
KQCV(AM) Oklahoma City OK
KXOJ-FM Sapulpa OK
KCFO(AM) Tulsa OK
*KORM(FM) Astoria OR
*KJCH(FM) Coos Bay OR
*KDOV(FM) Medford OR
*KLRF(FM) Milton-Freewater OR
*KBVM(FM) Portland OR
*KAJC(FM) Salem OR
*KQFE(FM) Springfield OR
KLWJ(AM) Umatilla OR
KGRV(AM) Winston OR
*WITX(FM) Beaver Falls PA
WHJB(AM) Bedford PA
*WFKJ(AM) Cashtown PA
*WZXQ(FM) Chambersburg PA
WPWA(AM) Chester PA
WVCH(AM) Chester PA
*WPGM(AM) Danville PA
*WPGM-FM Danville PA
WISP(AM) Doylestown PA
*WEFR(FM) Erie PA
WJSA(AM) Jersey Shore PA
WJSA-FM Jersey Shore PA
WJSM(AM) Martinsburg PA
WJSM-FM Martinsburg PA
*WRIJ(FM) Masontown PA
*WVME(FM) Meadville PA
*WPEL(FM) Montrose PA
*WPEL-FM Montrose PA
*WRWJ(FM) Murrysville PA
*WBGM(FM) New Berlin PA
*WVMN(FM) New Castle PA
WPCL(FM) Northern Cambria PA
WQOR(AM) Olyphant PA
WDAS(AM) Philadelphia PA
WFIL(AM) Philadelphia PA
WPHE(AM) Phoenixville PA
WGLD(FM) Red Lion PA
*WBYO(FM) Sellersville PA
*WBYX(FM) Stroudsburg PA
WRGN(FM) Sweet Valley PA
*WBMR(FM) Telford PA
*WRDV(FM) Warminster PA
WLIH(FM) Whitneyville PA
WMIA(AM) Arecibo PR
WFAB(AM) Ceiba PR
*WJVP(FM) Culebra PR
WCGB(AM) Juana Diaz PR
WRRE(AM) Juncos PR
*WPLI(FM) Levittown PR
WZOL(FM) Luquillo PR
WCHQ(AM) Quebradillas PR
WBMJ(AM) San Juan PR
WKVM(AM) San Juan PR
WIVV(AM) Vieques PR
WRIB(AM) Providence RI
WARV(AM) Warwick RI
WMIR(AM) Atlantic Beach SC
WVCD(AM) Bamberg-Denmark SC
*WAGP(FM) Beaufort SC
WVGB(AM) Beaufort SC
*WEPC(FM) Belton SC
*WYFV(FM) Cayce SC
*WFCH(FM) Charleston SC
*WMHK(FM) Columbia SC
WQXL(AM) Columbia SC
WELP(AM) Easley SC
WFGN(AM) Gaffney SC
*WYFG(FM) Gaffney SC
WMUU(AM) Greenville SC
*WTBI-FM Greenville SC
WBZF(FM) Hartsville SC
WRIX(AM) Homeland Park SC
WZJY(AM) Mt. Pleasant SC
WKZK(AM) North Augusta SC
*WYFH(FM) North Charleston SC
*WKVC(FM) North Myrtle Beach SC
WNMB(AM) North Myrtle Beach SC
WPJK(AM) Orangeburg SC
WAVO(AM) Rock Hill SC
WQIZ(AM) Saint George SC
WDRF(AM) Woodruff SC
KKAA(AM) Aberdeen SD

*KVCF(FM) Freeman SD
*KVCX(FM) Gregory SD
*KQFR(FM) Rapid City SD
KQKD(AM) Redfield SD
*KNWC(AM) Sioux Falls SD
*KJBB(FM) Watertown SD
WWGM(FM) Alamo TN
WQSV(AM) Ashland City TN
WBIN(AM) Benton TN
WIGN(AM) Bristol TN
*WDYN-FM Chattanooga TN
*WMBW(FM) Chattanooga TN
*WYFC(FM) Clinton TN
WSGM(FM) Coalmont TN
WCRV(AM) Collierville TN
*WAYM(FM) Columbia TN
WMRB(AM) Columbia TN
*WWOG(FM) Cookeville TN
*WMKW(FM) Crossville TN
*WAUO(FM) Hohenwald TN
WCLC(AM) Jamestown TN
WCLC-FM Jamestown TN
WDEB(AM) Jamestown TN
WKXV(AM) Knoxville TN
*WLAF(AM) La Follette TN
WMQM(AM) Lakeland TN
*WAWI(FM) Lawrenceburg TN
WBLC(AM) Lenoir City TN
WFLI(AM) Lookout Mountain TN
WBBP(AM) Memphis TN
WMCT(AM) Mountain City TN
*WFCM-FM Murfreesboro TN
WENO(AM) Nashville TN
WLAC(AM) Nashville TN
WNQM(AM) Nashville TN
WYFN(AM) Nashville TN
WDNX(FM) Olive Hill TN
WKJQ(AM) Parsons TN
*WAUV(FM) Ripley TN
*WAZD(FM) Savannah TN
*WFCM(AM) Smyrna TN
WSTN(AM) Somerville TN
*WZYZ(FM) Spencer TN
WCTU(FM) Tazewell TN
*WAUT(FM) Tullahoma TN
*KAGT-FM Abilene TX
KDRY(AM) Alamo Heights TX
*KJRT(FM) Amarillo TX
KRGN(FM) Amarillo TX
KWWJ(AM) Baytown TX
KPDB(FM) Big Lake TX
KMZZ(FM) Bishop TX
*KASV(FM) Borger TX
*KBNR(FM) Brownsville TX
KAGC(AM) Bryan TX
KBEN(AM) Carrizo Springs TX
*KBNJ(FM) Corpus Christi TX
KCTA(AM) Corpus Christi TX
KGGR(AM) Dallas TX
*KDKR(FM) Decatur TX
KVOZ(AM) Del Mar Hills TX
KDHN(AM) Dimmitt TX
*KOIR(FM) Edinburg TX
*KVER(FM) El Paso TX
KIVI(AM) El Paso TX
KIJN(AM) Farwell TX
KIJN-FM Farwell TX
KFST(AM) Fort Stockton TX
KGBC(AM) Galveston TX
*KHCB(AM) Galveston TX
*KBJS(FM) Jacksonville TX
*KJCR(FM) Keene TX
KRMY(AM) Killeen TX
KINE(AM) Kingsville TX
*KBNL(FM) Laredo TX
KYMI(FM) Los Ybanez TX
*KAMY(FM) Lubbock TX
*KBIB(AM) Marion TX
KRIO(AM) McAllen TX
*KCAS(FM) McCook TX
KRQX(AM) Mexia TX
KJBC(AM) Midland TX
*KFLB(AM) Odessa TX
*KFLB-FM Odessa TX
*KYFP(FM) Palestine TX
*KPMB(FM) Plainview TX
*KDEI(FM) Port Arthur TX

KMFM(FM) Premont TX
KBMI(AM) Roma TX
KCRN(AM) San Angelo TX
KCRN-FM San Angelo TX
KTUE(AM) Tulia TX
*KGLY(FM) Tyler TX
*KVNE(FM) Tyler TX
*KXBJ(FM) Victoria TX
KANI(AM) Wharton TX
*KPDR(FM) Wheeler TX
KNAK(AM) Delta UT
KHQN(AM) Spanish Fork UT
WABN(AM) Abingdon VA
WYFJ(AM) Ashland VA
WLSD(AM) Big Stone Gap VA
WZAP(AM) Bristol VA
WGGM(AM) Chester VA
WNLR(AM) Churchville VA
*WPER(FM) Culpeper VA
WKTR(AM) Earlysville VA
*WOTC(FM) Edinburg VA
WKNV(AM) Fairlawn VA
WFAX(AM) Falls Church VA
WPAK(AM) Farmville VA
WYFT(FM) Luray VA
*WKPA(AM) Lynchburg VA
*WRVL(FM) Lynchburg VA
WNRV(AM) Narrows-Pearisburg VA
WYFI(FM) Norfolk VA
WYRM(AM) Norfolk VA
WSWV(AM) Pennington Gap VA
WPCE(AM) Portsmouth VA
WRJR(AM) Portsmouth VA
WGTH-FM Richlands VA
WREJ(AM) Richmond VA
WRIS(AM) Roanoke VA
WCRR(AM) Rural Retreat VA
WXLZ(AM) Saint Paul VA
WKGM(AM) Smithfield VA
WKBA(AM) Vinton VA
WGOD-FM Charlotte Amalie VI
*WIVH(FM) Christiansted VI
WTWN(AM) Wells River VT
KARI(AM) Blaine WA
*KACS(FM) Chehalis WA
KSPO(FM) Dishman WA
*KCSH(FM) Ellensburg WA
KTAC(FM) Ephrata WA
KTBI(AM) Ephrata WA
*KARR(AM) Kirkland WA
KWPZ(FM) Lynden WA
*KMLW(FM) Moses Lake WA
KXLI(AM) Opportunity WA
KOLU(FM) Pasco WA
*KRLF(FM) Pullman WA
*KBLE(AM) Seattle WA
*KMBI(AM) Spokane WA
KMBI-FM Spokane WA
KTRW(AM) Spokane WA
KVSN(AM) Tumwater WA
KHSS(FM) Walla Walla WA
*KSOH(FM) Wapato WA
*KPLW(FM) Wenatchee WA
*KBNO-FM White Salmon WA
*WEMI(FM) Appleton WI
WYNW(FM) Birnamwood WI
*WDVM(AM) Eau Claire WI
*WVCF(FM) Eau Claire WI
*WEMY(FM) Green Bay WI
*WJTY(FM) Lancaster WI
*WJWD(FM) Marshall WI
WVCY-FM Milwaukee WI
WMMA(FM) Nekoosa WI
*WVCY(FM) Oshkosh WI
WHFA(FM) Poynette WI
WKLJ(AM) Sparta WI
*WNWC(AM) Sun Prairie WI
*WRVM(FM) Suring WI
*WVCX(FM) Tomah WI
*WEGZ(FM) Washburn WI
WJLS(AM) Beckley WV
*WKJL(FM) Clarksburg WV
WEMM(AM) Huntington WV
WFSP(AM) Kingwood WV
WOTR(FM) Lost Creek WV
WOAY(AM) Oak Hill WV
WELD(FM) Petersburg WV

WBGS(AM) Point Pleasant WV
WMXE(FM) South Charleston WV
KUYO(AM) Evansville WY
*KLWD(FM) Gillette WY

Rock/AOR

KWHL(FM) Anchorage AK
*KCUK(FM) Chevak AK
*KCDS(FM) Deadhorse AK
*KDLG(FM) Dillingham AK
KKED(FM) Fairbanks AK
KKED(FM) Fairbanks AK
*KIYU(FM) Galena AK
KSUP(FM) Juneau AK
*KUHB-FM Saint Paul AK
KNSA(AM) Unalakleet AK
WYSF(FM) Birmingham AL
WRTR(FM) Brookwood AL
WMLV(FM) Butler AL
WESP(FM) Dothan AL
WRTT-FM Huntsville AL
WQNR(FM) Tallassee AL
WTGZ(FM) Tuskegee AL
KKZR(FM) Bryant AR
KCCB(AM) Corning AR
KVDW(FM) England AR
KKEG(FM) Fayetteville AR
KTRN(FM) White Hall AR
KZGL(FM) Cottonwood AZ
KDKB(AM) Mesa AZ
KUPD-FM Tempe AZ
KMXZ-FM Tucson AZ
*KAWC(AM) Yuma AZ
KBRE(FM) Atwater CA
KRRX(FM) Burney CA
KWTY(FM) Cartago CA
KFMF(FM) Chico CA
KSSI(FM) China Lake CA
KCLB-FM Coachella CA
*KVHS(FM) Concord CA
*KDVS(FM) Davis CA
KSOF(FM) Dinuba CA
KHUM(FM) Garberville CA
KRAB(FM) Green Acres CA
KURQ(FM) Grover Beach CA
KRZR(FM) Hanford CA
KCXX(FM) Lake Arrowhead CA
*KRQZ(FM) Lompoc CA
KFFG(FM) Los Altos CA
KLOS(FM) Los Angeles CA
*KXLU(FM) Los Angeles CA
KIXA(FM) Lucerne Valley CA
KMRQ(FM) Manteca CA
KRCK-FM Mecca CA
*KAKX(FM) Mendocino CA
KMFB(FM) Mendocino CA
KHKK(FM) Modesto CA
KJEE(FM) Montecito CA
*KSFH(FM) Mountain View CA
KRQR(FM) Orland CA
KMRJ(FM) Rancho Mirage CA
KCAL-FM Redlands CA
KRXQ(FM) Sacramento CA
*KXHV(FM) Sacramento CA
KIOZ(FM) San Diego CA
KYXY(FM) San Diego CA
KFOG(FM) San Francisco CA
KITS(FM) San Francisco CA
*KSJS(FM) San Jose CA
KZOZ(FM) San Luis Obispo CA
*KSCU(FM) Santa Clara CA
KXFX(FM) Santa Rosa CA
*KCSS(FM) Turlock CA
*KSAK(FM) Walnut CA
KMKX(FM) Willits CA
*KLRD(FM) Yucaipa CA
KSMT(FM) Breckenridge CO
*KSJD(FM) Cortez CO
KEZZ(AM) Estes Park CO
KIDN-FM Hayden CO
KSTR-FM Montrose CO
KFMU-FM Oak Creek CO
*WERB(FM) Berlin CT
*WQAQ(FM) Hamden CT
WCCC-FM Hartford CT
WHCN(FM) Hartford CT

Programming on Radio Stations in the U.S.

WPLR(FM) New Haven CT	*WCYT(FM) Lafayette Township IN	*KDXL(FM) Saint Louis Park MN	WRRB(FM) Arlington NY	WYSP(FM) Philadelphia PA
WPHH(FM) Waterbury CT	WBTO-FM Petersburg IN	WHMH-FM Sauk Rapids MN	WBAB(FM) Babylon NY	WUBZ-FM Philipsburg PA
*WECS(FM) Willimantic CT	*WPUM(FM) Rensselaer IN	KZIO(FM) Two Harbors MN	*WGCC-FM Batavia NY	WDVE(FM) Pittsburgh PA
WWDC-FM Washington DC	WRBR-FM South Bend IN	*KQAL(FM) Winona MN	WRCD(FM) Canton NY	*WXAC(FM) Reading PA
WOSC(FM) Bethany Beach DE	*WISU(FM) Terre Haute IN	*KSMR(FM) Winona MN	*WHCL-FM Clinton NY	*WUSR(FM) Scranton PA
WZBH(FM) Georgetown DE	KANR(FM) Belle Plaine KS	KDBB(FM) Bonne Terre MO	WQBJ(FM) Cobleskill NY	*WSYC-FM Shippensburg PA
WYYX(FM) Bonifay FL	KJML(FM) Columbus KS	KFEB(FM) Campbell MO	*WCEB(FM) Corning NY	WZXR(FM) South Williamsport PA
WNDN(FM) Chiefland FL	KMDO(AM) Fort Scott KS	*KCOU(FM) Columbia MO	*WSUC-FM Cortland NY	WSBG(FM) Stroudsburg PA
WXTB(FM) Clearwater FL	*KJHK(FM) Lawrence KS	KCGQ-FM Gordonville MO	WWDG(FM) DeRuyter NY	WKGB-FM Susquehanna PA
WJRR(FM) Cocoa Beach FL	KQRC-FM Leavenworth KS	KBBM(FM) Jefferson City MO	WKLL(FM) Frankfort NY	WMTT(FM) Tioga PA
WRQC(FM) Estero FL	KMKF(FM) Manhattan KS	KRBZ(FM) Kansas City MO	*WGFR(FM) Glens Falls NY	WOWY(FM) University Park PA
WJBX(FM) Fort Myers Beach FL	*KSDB-FM Manhattan KS	KYYS(FM) Kansas City MO	WOTT(FM) Henderson NY	WFYN(FM) Waynesboro PA
WJBX(FM) Fort Myers Beach FL	KFIX(FM) Plainville KS	*KWJC(FM) Liberty MO	WFXF(FM) Honeoye Falls NY	*WRKC(FM) Wilkes-Barre PA
WKSM(FM) Fort Walton Beach FL	KICT-FM Wichita KS	KBHI(FM) Miner MO	*WICB(FM) Ithaca NY	*WPTC(FM) Williamsport PA
WRUF-FM Gainesville FL	*KSWC(FM) Winfield KS	KRMS-FM Osage Beach MO	WVBR-FM Ithaca NY	*WVYC(FM) York PA
WHDR(FM) Miami FL	WRVC-FM Catlettsburg KY	KJEZ(FM) Poplar Bluff MO	WPDA(FM) Jeffersonville NY	WMEG(FM) Guayama PR
WHHZ(FM) Newberry FL	WPKE-FM Coal Run KY	KFLW(FM) Saint Robert MO	WAQX-FM Manlius NY	WCAD(FM) San Juan PR
WMMO(FM) Orlando FL	WAQZ(FM) Fort Thomas KY	KPNT(FM) Sainte Genevieve MO	WRRV(FM) Middletown NY	WIAC-FM San Juan PR
WHOG-FM Ormond-by-the-Sea FL	WXZZ(FM) Georgetown KY	WCPR-FM D'Iberville MS	WKRH(FM) Minetto NY	*WQRI(FM) Bristol RI
WFKZ(FM) Plantation Key FL	WXMZ(FM) Hartford KY	WUSW(FM) Hattiesburg MS	WXRK(FM) New York NY	WHJY(FM) Providence RI
WXSR(FM) Quincy FL	WGBF-FM Henderson KY	WRXW(FM) Pearl MS	WKRL-FM North Syracuse NY	WSUY(FM) Charleston SC
WSJZ-FM Sebastian FL	WKCB-FM Hindman KY	KQBL(FM) Billings MT	*WRHO(FM) Oneonta NY	WARQ(FM) Columbia SC
WGLF(FM) Tallahassee FL	WIFX-FM Jenkins KY	KRZN(FM) Billings MT	*WDFH(FM) Ossining NY	WKZQ-FM Myrtle Beach SC
WLTQ-FM Venice FL	WKTG(FM) Madisonville KY	KKMT(FM) Columbia Falls MT	*WNYO(FM) Oswego NY	*KAUR(FM) Sioux Falls SD
*WRAS(FM) Atlanta GA	WZZL(FM) Reidland KY	*KDWG(FM) Dillon MT	*WPOB-FM Plainview NY	KDDX(FM) Spearfish SD
WCHZ(FM) Harlem GA	WJZO(FM) Shelbyville KY	KINX(FM) Great Falls MT	WRCN-FM Riverhead NY	*KAOR(FM) Vermillion SD
WJAD(FM) Leesburg GA	WXCM(FM) Whitesville KY	KQDI-FM Great Falls MT	*WSBU(FM) Saint Bonaventure NY	WBXE(FM) Baxter TN
WVVA(FM) Peachtree City GA	*KLSU(FM) Baton Rouge LA	KMHK(FM) Hardin MT	WEGQ(FM) Scotia NY	WDEF-FM Chattanooga TN
WRHQ(FM) Richmond Hill GA	KFTE(FM) Breaux Bridge LA	KBBZ(FM) Kalispell MT	WEHM(FM) Southampton NY	WDOD-FM Chattanooga TN
WRXR-FM Rossville GA	KNXX(FM) Donaldsonville LA	KOZB(FM) Livingston MT	WHFM(FM) Southampton NY	WSKZ(FM) Chattanooga TN
WPUP(FM) Royston GA	WNXX(FM) Jackson LA	*KBGA(FM) Missoula MT	WOUR(FM) Utica NY	WRZK(FM) Colonial Heights TN
*WVVS(FM) Valdosta GA	KXRR(FM) Monroe LA	*WASU-FM Boone NC	*WPNR(FM) Utica NY	WZDQ(FM) Humboldt TN
WWRQ-FM Valdosta GA	*KXUL(FM) Monroe LA	*WWCU(FM) Cullowhee NC	WDST(FM) Woodstock NY	*WUTK-FM Knoxville TN
WDBN(FM) Wrightsville GA	*KNWD(FM) Natchitoches LA	WRCQ(FM) Dunn NC	WONE-FM Akron OH	WKXD(FM) Monterey TN
KUMU-FM Honolulu HI	KKND(FM) Port Sulphur LA	WTPT(FM) Forest City NC	*WZIP(FM) Akron OH	WMXK(FM) Morristown TN
KLHI-FM Lahaina HI	KBYO(FM) Tallulah LA	WXNR(FM) Grifton NC	*WRMU(FM) Alliance OH	WQAK(FM) Union City TN
KQCS(FM) Bettendorf IA	*WMUA(FM) Amherst MA	WXRC(FM) Hickory NC	*WRDL(FM) Ashland OH	*KACC(FM) Alvin TX
KKEZ(FM) Fort Dodge IA	WRNX(FM) Amherst MA	WVBZ(FM) High Point NC	*WBWC(FM) Berea OH	KLBJ-FM Austin TX
KAZR(FM) Pella IA	WMJX(FM) Boston MA	WXQR(FM) Jacksonville NC	WAZU(FM) Circleville OH	KROX-FM Buda TX
KSEZ(FM) Sioux City IA	*WBMT(FM) Boxford MA	WRFX(FM) Kannapolis NC	WMMS(FM) Cleveland OH	KXCS(FM) Cameron TX
KCVI-FM Blackfoot ID	WHRB(FM) Cambridge MA	WOBX-FM Manteo NC	WXTM(FM) Cleveland Heights OH	*KWTS(FM) Canyon TX
KZDX(FM) Burley ID	*WMBR(FM) Cambridge MA	WMGV-FM Newport NC	WBZX(FM) Columbus OH	KZRK-FM Canyon TX
KHTQ(FM) Hayden ID	*WIQH(FM) Concord MA	WBBB(FM) Raleigh NC	*WUFM(FM) Columbus OH	KTUX(FM) Carthage TX
KOZE-FM Lewiston ID	*WGAJ(FM) Deerfield MA	*WKNC-FM Raleigh NC	WTUE(FM) Dayton OH	KLAQ(FM) El Paso TX
KTPZ(FM) Mountain Home ID	WPXC(FM) Hyannis MA	WEND(FM) Salisbury NC	*WSLN(FM) Delaware OH	*KTCU-FM Fort Worth TX
KQXR(FM) Payette ID	WLZX(FM) Northampton MA	*WDCC(FM) Sanford NC	WKXA-FM Findlay OH	KHFI-FM Georgetown TX
KADQ-FM Rexburg ID	*WOMR(FM) Provincetown MA	WAZO(FM) Southport NC	*WLFC(FM) Findlay OH	KHLT(AM) Hallettsville TX
KKTN(FM) Victor ID	*WMHC(FM) South Hadley MA	WOBR(FM) Wanchese NC	WZRX-FM Fort Shawnee OH	KTXM(FM) Hallettsville TX
KLZX(FM) Weston ID	WWFX(FM) Southbridge MA	WRQR(FM) Wilmington NC	WWCD(FM) Grove City OH	KFRQ(FM) Harlingen TX
WXRX(FM) Belvidere IL	*WZLY(FM) Wellesley MA	*KEYA(FM) Belcourt ND	*WHSS(FM) Hamilton OH	*KTAI(FM) Kingsville TX
WRXX(FM) Centralia IL	WXMD(FM) Pocomoke City MD	KHUS(FM) Bennington NE	*WKET(FM) Kettering OH	KFMX-FM Lubbock TX
*WPCD(FM) Champaign IL	WCYY(FM) Biddeford ME	*KINI(FM) Crookston NE	*WCMO(FM) Marietta OH	KZRC(FM) Markham TX
WWGO(FM) Charleston IL	*WUMF-FM Farmington ME	KLZA(FM) Falls City NE	*WYSZ(FM) Maumee OH	*KKXI(FM) Pittsburg TX
WKQX(FM) Chicago IL	WCYI(FM) Lewiston ME	KOZY-FM Gering NE	WJZE(FM) Oak Harbor OH	KMJR(FM) Portland TX
WLUP-FM Chicago IL	*WRBC(FM) Lewiston ME	*KFKX(FM) Hastings NE	*WUSO(FM) Springfield OH	KMDX(FM) San Angelo TX
*WLUW(FM) Chicago IL	WMEB-FM Orono ME	*KLPR(FM) Kearney NE	*WSTB(FM) Streetsboro OH	KISS-FM San Antonio TX
WXRT-FM Chicago IL	WTOS-FM Skowhegan ME	KLMY(FM) Lincoln NE	WIOT(FM) Toledo OH	*KVRK(FM) Sanger TX
WXLT(FM) Christopher IL	*WQAC-FM Alma MI	KOGA-FM Ogallala NE	*WYSA(FM) Wauseon OH	KNCN(FM) Sinton TX
*WRSE(FM) Elmhurst IL	*WCHW-FM Bay City MI	KEZO-FM Omaha NE	*WLHS(FM) West Chester OH	KLYD(FM) Snyder TX
WKTA(AM) Evanston IL	WCUZ(FM) Bear Lake MI	KKCD(FM) Omaha NE	*WOBN(FM) Westerville OH	KIOL(FM) Willis TX
WWCT(FM) Farmington IL	WRIF(FM) Detroit MI	*KWSC(FM) Wayne NE	*WCWS(FM) Wooster OH	KEGH(FM) Brigham City UT
*WHFH(FM) Flossmoor IL	WBNZ(FM) Frankfort MI	WHDQ(FM) Claremont NH	KACO(FM) Ardmore OK	KXRV(FM) Centerville UT
WLSR(FM) Galesburg IL	WGFN(FM) Glen Arbor MI	WFRD(FM) Hanover NH	KKBS(FM) Guymon OK	KBER(FM) Ogden UT
*WLCA(FM) Godfrey IL	WJZJ(FM) Glen Arbor MI	WGIR-FM Manchester NH	KZCD(FM) Lawton OK	WCJZ(FM) Charlottesville VA
*WCSF(FM) Joliet IL	WKLQ(FM) Greenville MI	WVRR(FM) Newport NH	KMYZ-FM Pryor OK	WDYL(FM) Chester VA
*WLTL(FM) La Grange IL	WGLI(FM) Hancock MI	*WPCR-FM Plymouth NH	KRTQ(FM) Sand Springs OK	WBOP(FM) Churchville VA
WDQZ(FM) Lexington IL	WKLT(FM) Kalkaska MI	WHEB(FM) Portsmouth NH	KCXR(FM) Taft OK	WACL(FM) Elkton VA
WNLF(FM) Macomb IL	WQUS(FM) Lapeer MI	WDHA-FM Dover NJ	KMOD-FM Tulsa OK	WROX-FM Exmore VA
*WLKL(FM) Mattoon IL	WLJZ(FM) Mackinaw City MI	*WNTI(FM) Hackettstown NJ	KZZE(FM) Eagle Point OR	WFQX(FM) Front Royal VA
WTAO-FM Murphysboro IL	WKQZ(FM) Midland MI	*WJSV(FM) Morristown NJ	KUFO(FM) Portland OR	WROV-FM Martinsville VA
*WONC(FM) Naperville IL	WAOR(FM) Niles MI	WDOX(FM) North Cape May NJ	KWLZ(FM) Warm Springs OR	WNOR(FM) Norfolk VA
WIHN(FM) Normal IL	*WBLD(FM) Orchard Lake MI	*WBZC(FM) Pemberton NJ	WZZO(FM) Bethlehem PA	WRXL(FM) Richmond VA
WEVX(FM) Rantoul IL	WKLZ-FM Petoskey MI	WRAT(FM) Point Pleasant NJ	*WBUQ(FM) Bloomsburg PA	WYSK-FM Spotsylvania VA
WQLZ(FM) Taylorville IL	WRKR(FM) Portage MI	*WSOU(FM) South Orange NJ	WSJR(FM) Dallas PA	*WNRS-FM Sweet Briar VA
WEBX(FM) Tuscola IL	WIRX(FM) Saint Joseph MI	KRWN(FM) Farmington NM	*WFSE(FM) Edinboro PA	WEXP(FM) Brandon VT
WPGU(FM) Urbana IL	WSUE(FM) Sault Ste. Marie MI	KFMQ(FM) Gallup NM	WEXC(FM) Greenville PA	*WWLR(FM) Lyndonville VT
WDML(FM) Woodlawn IL	*WNMC-FM Traverse City MI	KPSA-FM Lordsburg NM	WRVV(FM) Harrisburg PA	*WNUB-FM Northfield VT
*WEAX(FM) Angola IN	WWBN(FM) Tuscola MI	KQBA(FM) Los Alamos NM	WBSX(FM) Hazleton PA	*WVTC(FM) Randolph Center VT
WXTW(FM) Auburn IN	KAOD(FM) Babbitt MN	*KRDR(FM) Red River NM	WRKY-FM Hollidaysburg PA	WIZN(FM) Vergennes VT
*WDSO(FM) Chesterton IN	KLIZ(FM) Brainerd MN	KSFX(FM) Roswell NM	*WKVR-FM Huntingdon PA	WMXR(FM) Woodstock VT
WNHT(FM) Churubusco IN	KQHT(FM) Crookston MN	KRSI(FM) Garapan-Saipan NP	WRKW(FM) Johnstown PA	*KGRG(FM) Auburn WA
WTFX-FM Clarksville IN	KBAJ(FM) Deer River MN	KRNO(FM) Incline Village NV	*WVBU-FM Lewisburg PA	KNRK(FM) Camas WA
*WRGF(FM) Greenfield IN	KRVI(FM) Detroit Lakes MN	KOMP(FM) Las Vegas NV	*WNTE(FM) Mansfield PA	*KCWU(FM) Ellensburg WA
*WBDG(FM) Indianapolis IN	KQDS(AM) Duluth MN	KDOT(FM) Reno NV	WEEO-FM McConnellsburg PA	KBIS(AM) Forks WA
WRZX(FM) Indianapolis IN	KXXR(FM) Minneapolis MN	KRZQ(FM) Sparks NV	WTPA(FM) Mechanicsburg PA	*KZUU(FM) Pullman WA
WYXB(FM) Indianapolis IN	KQWB-FM Moorhead MN	*WCDB(FM) Albany NY	WWIZ(FM) Mercer PA	KEGX(FM) Richland WA
WKHY(FM) Lafayette IN	KPHR(FM) Ortonville MN	*WETD(FM) Alfred NY	*WKDU(FM) Philadelphia PA	KISW(FM) Seattle WA

Broadcasting & Cable Yearbook 2006

D-720

Programming on Radio Stations in the U.S.

KJAQ(FM) Seattle WA
*KWRS(FM) Spokane WA
*KWCW(FM) Walla Walla WA
KXRX(FM) Walla Walla WA
KATS(FM) Yakima WA
WAPL-FM Appleton WI
WDRK(FM) Cornell WI
WIIL(FM) Kenosha WI
WRQT(FM) La Crosse WI
WIBA-FM Madison WI
WKQH(FM) Marathon WI
WMZK(FM) Merrill WI
WHQG(FM) Milwaukee WI
WLUM-FM Milwaukee WI
WMQA-FM Minocqua WI
WZOR(FM) Mishicot WI
WCCN-FM Neillsville WI
WWWX(FM) Oshkosh WI
*WSUP(FM) Platteville WI
WBDL(FM) Reedsburg WI
*WRFW(FM) River Falls WI
*WSHS(FM) Sheboygan WI
WHBZ(FM) Sheboygan Falls WI
*WRGX(FM) Sturgeon Bay WI
KRBR(FM) Superior WI
WJJO(FM) Watertown WI
*WSUW(FM) Whitewater WI
WRLF(FM) Fairmont WV
WAMX(FM) Milton WV
WHBR-FM Parkersburg WV
WKLC-FM Saint Albans WV
WEGW(FM) Wheeling WV
KMTN(FM) Jackson WY

Russian

KICY(AM) Nome AK
WKTA(AM) Evanston IL

Smooth Jazz

KNIK-FM Anchorage AK
*WVAS(FM) Montgomery AL
KOAS(FM) Dolan Springs AZ
KMET(AM) Banning CA
KSSJ(FM) Fair Oaks CA
KEZL(FM) Fowler CA
KJJZ(FM) Indio CA
KIFM(FM) San Diego CA
KJZY(FM) Sebastopol CA
KKXS(FM) Shingletown CA
KMYT(FM) Temecula CA
KJCD(FM) Longmont CO
KSKX(FM) Security CO
*WKTZ(FM) Jacksonville FL
WZJZ(FM) Lehigh Acres FL
WSBZ(FM) Miramar Beach FL
WJZT(FM) Woodville FL
WSSJ(FM) Hinesville GA
WARH(FM) Granite City IL
WYJZ(FM) Lebanon IN
WUBU(FM) South Bend IN
WJSH(FM) Folsom LA
KKSJ(FM) Maurice LA
KTSJ(FM) Opelousas LA
WEIB(FM) Northampton MA
WJZQ(FM) Cadillac MI
WVMV(FM) Detroit MI
KJZI(FM) Minneapolis MN
WDAF-FM Liberty MO
*WCCE(FM) Buie's Creek NC
*WRMU(FM) Alliance OH
WNWV(FM) Elyria OH
WFGA(FM) Hicksville OH
WSJW(FM) Starview PA
KOAI(FM) Fort Worth TX
*KPVU(FM) Prairie View TX
WCJZ(FM) Charlottesville VA
WJZW(FM) Woodbridge VA
KWJZ(FM) Seattle WA
WBJZ(FM) Berlin WI
WJZI(FM) Milwaukee WI

Soul

KDJM(FM) Broomfield CO
KMXH(FM) Alexandria LA
WILD(AM) Boston MA
WRBO(FM) Como MS
WQMG-FM Greensboro NC
WRKS(FM) New York NY
WWRL(AM) New York NY

Spanish

WQCR(AM) Alabaster AL
WWGC(AM) Albertville AL
WKAC(AM) Athens AL
WZGX(AM) Bessemer AL
WCOC(AM) Dora AL
WYAM(AM) Hartselle AL
WCRL(AM) Oneonta AL
WKAX(AM) Russellville AL
WQRX(AM) Valley Head AL
KZTD(FM) Cabot AR
KDQN(AM) De Queen AR
KPZA(AM) Hot Springs AR
KAKS(AM) Huntsville AR
KFFK(AM) Rogers AR
KZRA(AM) Springdale AR
KAYR(AM) Van Buren AR
KVVA-FM Apache Junction AZ
KKMR(FM) Arizona City AZ
*KRMB(FM) Bisbee AZ
KMIA(AM) Black Canyon City AZ
KCKY(AM) Coolidge AZ
KEVT(AM) Cortaro AZ
KDAP(AM) Douglas AZ
*KRMC(FM) Douglas AZ
KLNZ(FM) Glendale AZ
KZLZ(FM) Kearny AZ
*KNOG(FM) Nogales AZ
KOFH(FM) Nogales AZ
KCMT(FM) Oro Valley AZ
KHOT-FM Paradise Valley AZ
KRIT(FM) Parker AZ
KIDR(AM) Phoenix AZ
*KNAI(FM) Phoenix AZ
KSUN(AM) Phoenix AZ
KXEW(AM) South Tucson AZ
KTKT(AM) Tucson AZ
KCEC-FM Wellton AZ
KHOV-FM Wickenburg AZ
*KYRM(FM) Yuma AZ
KWRN(AM) Apple Valley CA
KSSE(FM) Arcadia CA
KBYN(FM) Arnold CA
*KCFA(FM) Arnold CA
KMYX-FM Arvin CA
KLBN(FM) Auberry CA
KAFY(AM) Bakersfield CA
KPSL-FM Bakersfield CA
*KTQX(FM) Bakersfield CA
KWAC(AM) Bakersfield CA
KIQQ(FM) Barstow CA
KXXZ(FM) Barstow CA
KAEH(FM) Beaumont CA
KXSB(FM) Big Bear Lake CA
KSEH(FM) Brawley CA
KICO(AM) Calexico CA
*KUBO(FM) Calexico CA
KCEL(FM) California City CA
KXTS(FM) Calistoga CA
*KMRO(FM) Camarillo CA
KNTO(FM) Chowchilla CA
*KHDC(FM) Chualar CA
KFPT(AM) Clovis CA
KOND(FM) Clovis CA
KCVR-FM Columbia CA
KBLO(FM) Corcoran CA
KFVR(AM) Crescent City CA
KXSE(FM) Davis CA
KCHJ(AM) Delano CA
KCHJ(FM) Delano CA
KLAX-FM East Los Angeles CA
KMQA(FM) East Porterville CA
KMLA(FM) El Rio CA
KSPE-FM Ellwood CA
KTTA(FM) Esparto CA
KSSD(FM) Fallbrook CA

KXZM(FM) Felton CA
KDAC(AM) Fort Bragg CA
KQEQ(AM) Fowler CA
*KEYQ(AM) Fresno CA
KGST(AM) Fresno CA
KKDG(FM) Fresno CA
KOQO-FM Fresno CA
*KSJV(FM) Fresno CA
KWRU(AM) Fresno CA
KYNO(AM) Fresno CA
KEBN(FM) Garden Grove CA
KAZA(AM) Gilroy CA
KSCA(FM) Glendale CA
KLOK-FM Greenfield CA
KSEA(FM) Greenfield CA
KIDI(FM) Guadalupe CA
KGEN-FM Hanford CA
KXRS(FM) Hemet CA
KMPG(AM) Hollister CA
KXSM(FM) Hollister CA
KMXX(FM) Imperial CA
KESQ(AM) Indio CA
KRCD(FM) Inglewood CA
KLMG(AM) Jackson CA
KEDD(FM) Johannesburg CA
KBHH(FM) Kerman CA
KHDV(FM) King City CA
KSRN(FM) Kings Beach CA
KUNA-FM La Quinta CA
KWJL(AM) Lancaster CA
*KVFR(FM) Laytonville CA
KBTW(FM) Lenwood CA
KSKD(FM) Livingston CA
KCVR(AM) Lodi CA
KRQK(FM) Lompoc CA
KSMY(FM) Lompoc CA
KBUE(FM) Long Beach CA
KLTX(AM) Long Beach CA
KHJ(AM) Los Angeles CA
KLVE(FM) Los Angeles CA
KTNQ(AM) Los Angeles CA
KWKW(AM) Los Angeles CA
KXOL(FM) Los Angeles CA
KQLB(FM) Los Banos CA
KMMM(FM) Madera CA
KRCX-FM Marysville CA
KIWI(FM) McFarland CA
KTIQ(AM) Merced CA
KBBU(FM) Modesto CA
KLMM(FM) Morro Bay CA
KIQQ-FM Newberry Springs CA
KLLE(FM) North Fork CA
KAAT(AM) Oakhurst CA
KMAK(FM) Orange Cove CA
KHHZ(FM) Oroville CA
KOXR(AM) Oxnard CA
KXLM(FM) Oxnard CA
KLUN(FM) Paso Robles CA
KTSE-FM Patterson CA
KTOB(AM) Petaluma CA
KATD(AM) Pittsburg CA
KWKU(AM) Pomona CA
KCAL(AM) Redlands CA
KDIF(AM) Riverside CA
KFSG(AM) Roseville CA
KDBV(AM) Salinas CA
KRAY-FM Salinas CA
KTGE(AM) Salinas CA
KEZY(AM) San Bernardino CA
KLNV(FM) San Diego CA
KLQV(FM) San Diego CA
KSDO(AM) San Diego CA
KBUA(FM) San Fernando CA
KIQI(AM) San Francisco CA
KSOL(FM) San Francisco CA
KBRG(FM) San Jose CA
KSJO(FM) San Jose CA
KZSF(AM) San Jose CA
KJDJ(FM) San Luis Obispo CA
KLRM(FM) San Luis Obispo CA
KVVZ(FM) San Rafael CA
KWIZ(FM) Santa Ana CA
KBKO(AM) Santa Barbara CA
KZER(AM) Santa Barbara CA
KVVF(FM) Santa Clara CA
KSQL(FM) Santa Cruz CA
*KGDP-FM Santa Maria CA

KSBQ(AM) Santa Maria CA
KTAP(AM) Santa Maria CA
KBLA(AM) Santa Monica CA
KLJR-FM Santa Paula CA
KUNX(AM) Santa Paula CA
*KBBF(FM) Santa Rosa CA
KRRS(AM) Santa Rosa CA
KSES-FM Seaside CA
*KGZO(FM) Shafter CA
KMBX(AM) Soledad CA
KMJV(FM) Soledad CA
KSTN-FM Stockton CA
KBDS(FM) Taft CA
KMIX(FM) Tracy CA
KGEN(AM) Tulare CA
KLOC(AM) Turlock CA
KSSC(FM) Ventura CA
KRSX(FM) Victorville CA
KSLK(FM) Visalia CA
KALI(AM) West Covina CA
KLLK(FM) Willits CA
KLOQ-FM Winton CA
KOBO(AM) Yuba City CA
KPVW(FM) Aspen CO
KMXA(AM) Aurora CO
KJMN(FM) Castle Rock CO
KBNO(AM) Denver CO
*KGNU(AM) Denver CO
KXPK(FM) Evergreen CO
KFTM(AM) Fort Morgan CO
KEXO(AM) Grand Junction CO
KGRE(AM) Greeley CO
KXRE(AM) Manitou Springs CO
KAVA(AM) Pueblo CO
KNKN(FM) Pueblo CO
KRMX(AM) Pueblo CO
KJJD(AM) Windsor CO
WADS(AM) Ansonia CT
WCUM(AM) Bridgeport CT
WPRX(AM) Bristol CT
WFNW(AM) Naugatuck CT
WLAT(AM) New Britain CT
WRYM(AM) New Britain CT
WXCT(AM) Southington CT
WYUS(AM) Milford DE
WNTF(AM) Bithlo FL
WWPR(AM) Bradenton FL
WLCC(AM) Brandon FL
WEWC(AM) Callahan FL
WRHC(AM) Coral Gables FL
WRLZ(AM) Eatonville FL
WVOJ(AM) Fernandina Beach FL
WRMA(FM) Fort Lauderdale FL
WCRM(FM) Fort Myers FL
WJNX(AM) Fort Pierce FL
WRTO-FM Goulds FL
WACC(AM) Hialeah FL
WCMQ-FM Hialeah FL
WOIR(AM) Homestead FL
WAFZ(AM) Immokalee FL
WAFZ-FM Immokalee FL
*WGES(FM) Key Largo FL
WZMQ(FM) Key Largo FL
WMFM(FM) Key West FL
*WLAZ(FM) Kissimmee FL
WOTS(AM) Kissimmee FL
WIPC(AM) Lake Wales FL
WWRF(AM) Lake Worth FL
WMGG(AM) Largo FL
WQBQ(FM) Leesburg FL
WWCL(AM) Lehigh Acres FL
WAMR-FM Miami FL
WAQI(AM) Miami FL
*WDNA(FM) Miami FL
WOCN(AM) Miami FL
WQBA(AM) Miami FL
WSUA(AM) Miami FL
WWFE(AM) Miami FL
WJCC(AM) Miami Springs FL
WNMA(AM) Miami Springs FL
WZSP(FM) Nocatee FL
WXDJ(FM) North Miami Beach FL
WUNA(AM) Ocoee FL
WRMQ(FM) Orlando FL
WRUM(FM) Orlando FL
*WIRP(FM) Pennsuco FL
WTLQ-FM Punta Rassa FL

WPSP(AM) Royal Palm Beach FL
WYUU(FM) Safety Harbor FL
WOYE(AM) Saint Cloud FL
WRMD(AM) Saint Petersburg FL
WSDO(AM) Sanford FL
WAMA(AM) Tampa FL
WQBN(AM) Temple Terrace FL
WNUE-FM Titusville FL
WAUC(AM) Wauchula FL
WLAA(AM) Winter Garden FL
WPRD(AM) Winter Park FL
WAOS(AM) Austell GA
WBZY(FM) Bowdon GA
WLKQ-FM Buford GA
WXEM(AM) Buford GA
WWVA-FM Canton GA
WDAL(AM) Dalton GA
WLBA(AM) Gainesville GA
WPLO(AM) Grayson GA
WWWE(AM) Hapeville GA
WHEL(FM) Helen GA
WFTD(AM) Marietta GA
WAZX(FM) Smyrna GA
WKTM(FM) Soperton GA
*WJDS(FM) Sparta GA
WGTA(FM) Summerville GA
WKTF(AM) Vienna GA
KDNZ(AM) Cedar Falls IA
KBGG(FM) Des Moines IA
*KOJI(FM) Okoboji IA
*KWIT(FM) Sioux City IA
KWSL(AM) Sioux City IA
KDBI(FM) Emmett ID
KWEI-FM Fruitland ID
KRXR(AM) Gooding ID
KDJQ(AM) Meridian ID
KFTA(AM) Rupert ID
*WMBI(AM) Chicago IL
WNTD(AM) Chicago IL
WRTO(AM) Chicago IL
WPPN(FM) Des Plaines IL
WOJO(FM) Evanston IL
WONX(AM) Evanston IL
WVIV-FM Highland Park IL
WEDJ(FM) Danville IN
WSYW(AM) Indianapolis IN
WRSW-FM Warsaw IN
KYQQ(FM) Arkansas City KS
KDCC(AM) Dodge City KS
KFXX-FM Hugoton KS
KSSA(FM) Ingalls KS
KKHK(AM) Kansas City KS
KTCM(FM) Kingman KS
KYUU(AM) Liberal KS
KCZZ(AM) Mission KS
*KYWA(FM) Wichita KS
WNTC(AM) Drakesboro KY
KGLA(AM) Gretna LA
WFNO(AM) Norco LA
WUNR(AM) Brookline MA
WNNW(AM) Lawrence MA
*WFHL(FM) New Bedford MA
WJOE(AM) Orange-Athol MA
WSPR(AM) Springfield MA
WRCA(AM) Waltham MA
WACM(AM) West Springfield MA
WLZL(FM) Annapolis MD
WYRE(AM) Annapolis MD
WTRI(AM) Brunswick MD
WWGB(AM) Indian Head MD
WILC(AM) Laurel MD
WBZS-FM Prince Frederick MD
WLXE(FM) Rockville MD
WACA(AM) Wheaton MD
WNWZ(AM) Grand Rapids MI
WYGR(AM) Wyoming MI
*KKFI(FM) Kansas City MO
KQMO(FM) Shell Knob MO
WMYT(AM) Carolina Beach NC
WLLQ(AM) Chapel Hill NC
WGSP(AM) Charlotte NC
WCXN(AM) Claremont NC
WRRZ(AM) Clinton NC
WRTG(AM) Garner NC
WYMY(FM) Goldsboro NC
WWBG(AM) Greensboro NC
WNCT(AM) Greenville NC

Programming on Radio Stations in the U.S.

WGOS(AM) High Point NC	KWBY(AM) Woodburn OR	WAMB(AM) Nashville TN	KNEX(FM) Laredo TX	*KSVR(FM) Mount Vernon WA
WSRP(AM) Jacksonville NC	WHOL(AM) Allentown PA	WKDA(AM) Nashville TN	KHHL(FM) Leander TX	KZTA(FM) Naches WA
WLNR(AM) Kinston NC	*WLCH(FM) Lancaster PA	WNQM(AM) Nashville TN	KESS-FM Lewisville TX	KRSC(AM) Othello WA
WSGH(AM) Lewisville NC	WPHE(AM) Phoenixville PA	KKHR(FM) Abilene TX	KYMI(FM) Los Ybanez TX	KMNA(FM) Prosser WA
*WLLN(AM) Lillington NC	*WXAC(FM) Reading PA	KJAV(FM) Alamo TX	KBZO(AM) Lubbock TX	KZML(FM) Quincy WA
WGSB(AM) Mebane NC	WOQI(AM) Adjuntas PR	KTCY(FM) Azle TX	KLFB(AM) Lubbock TX	KRCW(AM) Royal City WA
WNOW(AM) Mint Hill NC	WABA(AM) Aguadilla PR	KXGJ(FM) Bay City TX	KXTQ(AM) Lubbock TX	KZTS(AM) Sunnyside WA
WREV(AM) Reidsville NC	WIVA-FM Aguadilla PR	KQQK(FM) Beaumont TX	KELG(AM) Manor TX	KKMO(AM) Tacoma WA
WZUP(FM) Rose Hill NC	WTPM(FM) Aguadilla PR	KIBL(AM) Beeville TX	*KBIB(AM) Marion TX	KYXE(AM) Union Gap WA
WWGP(AM) Sanford NC	WWNA(AM) Aguadilla PR	KDXX(FM) Benbrook TX	KGBT-FM McAllen TX	KWWX(AM) Wenatchee WA
WNCA(AM) Siler City NC	WCMN(AM) Arecibo PR	KPDB(AM) Big Lake TX	KRIO(AM) McAllen TX	*KBNO-FM White Salmon WA
WCIE(AM) Spring Lake NC	WCMN-FM Arecibo PR	KBYG(AM) Big Spring TX	*KPBJ(FM) Midland TX	KWLN(FM) Wilson Creek WA
WETC(AM) Wendell-Zebulon NC	WMIA(AM) Arecibo PR	KBRN(AM) Boerne TX	KBDR(FM) Mirando City TX	*KDNA(FM) Yakima WA
WTOB(AM) Winston-Salem NC	WNIK(AM) Arecibo PR	KKUB(AM) Brownfield TX	KIRT(AM) Mission TX	WDGY(AM) Hudson WI
KBBX-FM Nebraska City NE	WBQN(AM) Barceloneta-Manati PR	*KPBB(FM) Brownfield TX	KIMP(AM) Mount Pleasant TX	WLMV(AM) Madison WI
WCEC(AM) Salem NH	WOLA(AM) Barranquitas PR	*KBNR(FM) Brownsville TX	KLHB(AM) Odem TX	WBJX(AM) Racine WI
WEMG(AM) Camden NJ	WLUZ(AM) Bayamon PR	KKPS(FM) Brownsville TX	KOZA(AM) Odessa TX	KBMG(AM) Evanston WY
WJDM(AM) Elizabeth NJ	WODA(FM) Bayamon PR	*KPBE(FM) Brownwood TX	KQLM(FM) Odessa TX	
WCAA(FM) Newark NJ	WRSJ(AM) Bayamon PR	KXYL(AM) Brownwood TX	KLVL(AM) Pasadena TX	**Sports**
WXMC(AM) Parsippany-Troy Hills NJ	WYAC(AM) Cabo Rojo PR	KTAM(AM) Bryan TX	KRIO-FM Pearsall TX	
WPAT(AM) Paterson NJ	WNEL(AM) Caguas PR	KMIL(AM) Cameron TX	KOKE(FM) Pflugerville TX	KTZN(AM) Anchorage AK
WPAT-FM Paterson NJ	WVJP(AM) Caguas PR	KAYG(FM) Camp Wood TX	KZMP-FM Pilot Point TX	KCBF(AM) Fairbanks AK
WMIZ(AM) Vineland NJ	WVJP-FM Caguas PR	KBEN(AM) Carrizo Springs TX	*KPMB(FM) Plainview TX	WAUD(AM) Auburn AL
*KUPR(FM) Alamogordo NM	WDIN(FM) Camuy PR	KCZO(FM) Carrizo Springs TX	KREW(AM) Plainview TX	WNSP(FM) Bay Minette AL
*KANW(FM) Albuquerque NM	WGIT(FM) Canovanas PR	KJON(AM) Carrollton TX	KRIA(FM) Plainview TX	WJOX(FM) Birmingham AL
KJFA(FM) Albuquerque NM	WIDA(FM) Carolina PR	KDET(AM) Center TX	KFNI(AM) Pleasanton TX	WFMH(AM) Cullman AL
KRZY(AM) Albuquerque NM	WBRQ(FM) Cidra PR	KWOW(FM) Clifton TX	KQBU-FM Port Arthur TX	WKUL(FM) Cullman AL
*KUNM(FM) Albuquerque NM	WXZX(FM) Culebra PR	KCOR-FM Comfort TX	KTJM(FM) Port Arthur TX	WWTM(AM) Decatur AL
KLVO(FM) Belen NM	WIBS(AM) Guayama PR	KUNO(AM) Corpus Christi TX	KNVO-FM Port Isabel TX	WZNJ(FM) Demopolis AL
KPZE-FM Carlsbad NM	WZET(FM) Hormigueros PR	KMMZ(FM) Crane TX	KUHD(AM) Port Neches TX	WOOF(AM) Dothan AL
*KZPI(FM) Deming NM	WALO(AM) Humacao PR	KXOI(AM) Crane TX	KMFM(FM) Premont TX	WIJK(AM) Evergreen AL
KDCE(AM) Espanola NM	WCGB(AM) Juana Diaz PR	KHER(FM) Crystal City TX	KCLR(AM) Ralls TX	WHEP(AM) Foley AL
KYBR(FM) Espanola NM	WSQD(AM) Lajas PR	KFZO(FM) Denton TX	KBUC(FM) Raymondville TX	WTKI(AM) Huntsville AL
KRZE(AM) Farmington NM	WGDL(AM) Lares PR	KSML(AM) Diboll TX	KQBO(FM) Rio Grande City TX	WUMP(AM) Madison AL
KLMA(FM) Hobbs NM	WMNT(AM) Manati PR	KLMO-FM Dilley TX	KHCK-AM Robinson TX	WPMI(AM) Mobile AL
KPZA-FM Jal NM	WIOB(FM) Mayaguez PR	KDHN(AM) Dimmitt TX	KSAB(AM) Robstown TX	WACV(AM) Montgomery AL
*KRUC(FM) Las Cruces NM	WPRA(AM) Mayaguez PR	KXXS(FM) Dripping Springs TX	KBMI(FM) Roma TX	WMSP(AM) Montgomery AL
*KRWG(FM) Las Cruces NM	WTIL(AM) Mayaguez PR	KEPS(AM) Eagle Pass TX	KRTX(FM) Rosenberg-Richmond TX	WLAY(AM) Muscle Shoals AL
KFUN(AM) Las Vegas NM	WEKO(AM) Morovis PR	*KEPX(FM) Eagle Pass TX	*KTER(FM) Rudolph TX	WIQR(AM) Prattville AL
KNMX(AM) Las Vegas NM	WYQE(FM) Naguabo PR	*KOIR(FM) Edinburg TX	KSJT-FM San Angelo TX	WELR(AM) Roanoke AL
KQBA(FM) Los Alamos NM	WPPC(AM) Penuelas PR	KVLY(FM) Edinburg TX	KAHL(AM) San Antonio TX	WNSI(AM) Robertsdale AL
KZNM(FM) Los Alamos NM	WDEP(AM) Ponce PR	KAMA(AM) El Paso TX	KCOR(AM) San Antonio TX	WYTK(FM) Rogersville AL
KINF(AM) Roswell NM	WPAB(AM) Ponce PR	KBNA(AM) El Paso TX	KROM(FM) San Antonio TX	WFEB(AM) Sylacauga AL
KRDD(AM) Roswell NM	WPRP(AM) Ponce PR	KBNA-FM El Paso TX	KXTN-FM San Antonio TX	WACT(AM) Tuscaloosa AL
KNUW(FM) Santa Clara NM	WRIO(FM) Ponce PR	KINT-FM El Paso TX	KZDC(AM) San Antonio TX	WTBC(AM) Tuscaloosa AL
KRZY-FM Santa Fe NM	WZAR(FM) Ponce PR	KSVE(AM) El Paso TX	KQSI(FM) San Augustine TX	WVNA(AM) Tuscumbia AL
KSWV(AM) Santa Fe NM	WZMT(FM) Ponce PR	*KVER(FM) El Paso TX	KUKA(FM) San Diego TX	WVSA(AM) Vernon AL
*KNLK(FM) Santa Rosa NM	WCHQ(AM) Quebradillas PR	KVIV(AM) El Paso TX	KUBR(AM) San Juan TX	WAPZ(AM) Wetumpka AL
KSSR(AM) Santa Rosa NM	WIDI(FM) Quebradillas PR	KXPL(AM) El Paso TX	KUOL(AM) San Marcos TX	KBTA(AM) Batesville AR
KXMT(FM) Taos NM	WHOY(AM) Salinas PR	KYSE(FM) El Paso TX	KIKZ(AM) Seminole TX	KEWI(AM) Benton AR
KKVS(FM) Truth or Consequences NM	WSOL(AM) San German PR	KKLB(AM) Elgin TX	KSEY(AM) Seymour TX	KREB(AM) Bentonville-Bella Vista AR
KDOX(AM) Henderson NV	WAPA(AM) San Juan PR	KDFM(FM) Falfurrias TX	KDAE(AM) Sinton TX	KASR(FM) Conway AR
KRGT(FM) Indian Springs NV	WIAC(AM) San Juan PR	KPSO-FM Falfurrias TX	KHOS(AM) Sonora TX	KXXA(AM) Conway AR
KISF(FM) Las Vegas NV	WIOA(AM) San Juan PR	KMUL(AM) Farwell TX	KSTV(AM) Stephenville TX	KCAB(AM) Dardanelle AR
KKVV(AM) Las Vegas NV	WQBS(AM) San Juan PR	KDFT(AM) Ferris TX	KSCH(AM) Sulphur Springs TX	KNEA(AM) Jonesboro AR
KQRT(FM) Las Vegas NV	*WRTU(FM) San Juan PR	KFST-FM Fort Stockton TX	KAMZ(FM) Tahoka TX	KTTG(FM) Mena AR
KRLV(AM) Las Vegas NV	WSKN(AM) San Juan PR	KEGL(FM) Fort Worth TX	KXAL-FM Tatum TX	KVOM(AM) Morrilton AR
KRNV-FM Reno NV	WZNT(FM) San Juan PR	KFLC(AM) Fort Worth TX	KYST(AM) Texas City TX	KDXE(AM) North Little Rock AR
KXEQ(AM) Reno NV	WRSS(AM) San Sebastian PR	KLNO(FM) Frankston TX	KTUE(AM) Tulia TX	KDRS(AM) Paragould AR
KXTO(AM) Reno NV	WRSS(AM) San Sebastian PR	KOYE(FM) Frankston TX	KSAH(AM) Universal City TX	KOTN(AM) Pine Bluff AR
KQLO(AM) Sun Valley NV	WERR(FM) Utuado PR	KBRZ(AM) Freeport TX	KTNO(AM) University Park TX	KARV(AM) Russellville AR
KLSQ(AM) Whitney NV	WUPR(AM) Utuado PR	KJOJ-FM Freeport TX	KZMP(AM) University Park TX	KHGG(AM) Van Buren AR
WZAA(FM) Garden City NY	WIVV(AM) Vieques PR	*KPBN(FM) Freer TX	KUVA(FM) Uvalde TX	KRWA-FM Waldron AR
WALL(AM) Middletown NY	WIVV(AM) Vieques PR	KGRW(FM) Friona TX	KRGE(AM) Weslaco TX	KVNA(AM) Flagstaff AZ
WADO(AM) New York NY	WIVV(AM) Vieques PR	KXEB(AM) Frisco TX	KTXZ(AM) West Lake Hills TX	KIKO(AM) Miami AZ
*WHCR-FM New York NY	WXEW(AM) Yabucoa PR	*KHCB(AM) Galveston TX	KBAW(AM) Zapata TX	KGME(AM) Phoenix AZ
WSKQ-FM New York NY	WKFE(AM) Yauco PR	KOVE-FM Galveston TX	KRRD(AM) Centerville UT	KIDR(AM) Phoenix AZ
*WWRV(AM) New York NY	WALE(AM) Greenville RI	KINV(FM) Georgetown TX	KSVN(AM) Ogden UT	KMVP(AM) Phoenix AZ
WEOK(AM) Poughkeepsie NY	WKKB(FM) Middletown RI	KOFY(FM) Gilmer TX	KDUT(FM) Randolph UT	KTAR(AM) Phoenix AZ
WVKO-FM Johnstown OH	*WELH(FM) Providence RI	KGBT(AM) Harlingen TX	KBJA(AM) Sandy UT	KQNA(AM) Prescott Valley AZ
*WNZN(FM) Lorain OH	WPMZ(AM) Providence RI	KEKO(AM) Hebronville TX	WKDL(AM) Alexandria VA	KATO(AM) Safford AZ
KZUE(AM) El Reno OK	WRIB(AM) Providence RI	KJNZ(FM) Hereford TX	WZHF(AM) Arlington VA	KAZM(AM) Sedona AZ
KTAT(AM) Frederick OK	WBLR(AM) Batesburg SC	KEYH(AM) Houston TX	WPWC(AM) Dumfries-Triangle VA	KTAN(AM) Sierra Vista AZ
KINB(FM) Kingfisher OK	WCEO(AM) Columbia SC	KLAT(AM) Houston TX	WKDV(AM) Manassas VA	KDUS(AM) Tempe AZ
KTUZ-FM Okarche OK	WGVL(FM) Greenville SC	KLOL(AM) Houston TX	WVXX(AM) Norfolk VA	KCUB(AM) Tucson AZ
KREU(FM) Roland OK	WQVA(AM) Lexington SC	KLTN(FM) Houston TX	WVNZ(AM) Richmond VA	KFFN(AM) Tucson AZ
KXTD(AM) Wagoner OK	WAZS-FM McClellanville SC	KQUE(AM) Houston TX	WBPS-FM Warrenton VA	KNST(AM) Tucson AZ
*KORM(FM) Astoria OR	WKMG(AM) Newberry SC	KXYZ(AM) Houston TX	WKCW(AM) Warrenton VA	KTUC(AM) Tucson AZ
KCGR(FM) Cottage Grove OR	WNFO(AM) Ridgeland SC	KMNY(AM) Hurst TX	*WIUJ(FM) Charlotte Amalie VI	KJOK(AM) Yuma AZ
KMUZ(AM) Gresham OR	WBZK(AM) York SC	KLEY-FM Jourdanton TX	WMYP(FM) Frederiksted VI	KATA(AM) Arcata CA
KUIK(AM) Hillsboro OR	WMPS(AM) Bartlett TN	KERB(AM) Kermit TX	KBKW(AM) Aberdeen WA	KXTK(AM) Arroyo Grande CA
KXOR(FM) Junction City OR	WOCE(AM) Benton TN	KERB-FM Kermit TX	KXPA(AM) Bellevue WA	KDFO(FM) Bakersfield CA
KRTA(AM) Medford OR	WNWS(AM) Brownsville TN	*KHKV(FM) Kerrville TX	KZTB(FM) Benton City WA	KGEO(AM) Bakersfield CA
KZNY(AM) Milwaukie OR	WHEW(AM) Franklin TN	KINE(AM) Kingsville TX	*KCED(AM) Centralia WA	KMET(AM) Banning CA
KGDD(AM) Oregon City OR	WGSF(AM) Memphis TN	*KBNL(FM) Laredo TX	KZHR(FM) Dayton WA	KFPT(AM) Clovis CA
KXMG(AM) Portland OR	*WMTS-FM Murfreesboro TN	*KHOY(FM) Laredo TX	KDDS-FM Elma WA	KWRM(AM) Corona CA
KMMG(FM) Weston OR	WAMB(AM) Nashville TN	KLAR(AM) Laredo TX	KLES(FM) Mabton WA	KCBL(AM) Fresno CA

Broadcasting & Cable Yearbook 2006

Programming on Radio Stations in the U.S.

KFIG(AM) Fresno CA	WPCF(AM) Panama City Beach FL	WDWS(AM) Champaign IL	KSYL(AM) Alexandria LA	KBUN(AM) Bemidji MN
KXEX(AM) Fresno CA	WPSL(AM) Port St. Lucie FL	*WCRX(FM) Chicago IL	WJBO(AM) Baton Rouge LA	KVBR(AM) Brainerd MN
KAVL(AM) Lancaster CA	WFOY(AM) Saint Augustine FL	WGN(AM) Chicago IL	KRRP(AM) Coushatta LA	KDLM(AM) Detroit Lakes MN
KLAC(AM) Los Angeles CA	WDAE(AM) Saint Petersburg FL	WMVP(AM) Chicago IL	WASO(AM) Covington LA	WEBC(AM) Duluth MN
KMPC(AM) Los Angeles CA	WBZZ(AM) Seffner FL	WSCR(AM) Chicago IL	WSKR(AM) Denham Springs LA	KDHL(AM) Faribault MN
KSPN(AM) Los Angeles CA	WAXY(AM) South Miami FL	WDAN(AM) Danville IL	KPCH(FM) Dubach LA	KDWA(AM) Hastings MN
KWKW(AM) Los Angeles CA	WSTU(AM) Stuart FL	WSOY(AM) Decatur IL	*KGRM(FM) Grambling LA	WMFG(AM) Hibbing MN
KMFB(AM) Mendocino CA	*WANM(AM) Tallahassee FL	WGIL(AM) Galesburg IL	KPEL(AM) Lafayette LA	KDUZ(AM) Hutchinson MN
KBKY(FM) Merced CA	WHBT(AM) Tallahassee FL	*WGBK(FM) Glenview IL	KVOL(AM) Lafayette LA	KFAN(AM) Minneapolis MN
KESP(AM) Modesto CA	WHNZ(AM) Tampa FL	WJPF(AM) Herrin IL	KAOK(AM) Lake Charles LA	KFXN(AM) Minneapolis MN
KXTY(FM) Morro Bay CA	WEFL(AM) Tequesta FL	WDDD(AM) Johnston City IL	KLCL(AM) Lake Charles LA	KVOX(AM) Moorhead MN
KEWE(AM) Oroville CA	WIXC(AM) Titusville FL	WLPO(AM) La Salle IL	KNOE(AM) Monroe LA	WCMP-FM Pine City MN
KNTS(AM) Palo Alto CA	WDDV(AM) Venice FL	WLUV(AM) Loves Park IL	WODT(AM) New Orleans LA	KWEB(AM) Rochester MN
KPRL(AM) Paso Robles CA	WJNO(AM) West Palm Beach FL	WZZT(AM) Morrison IL	WSMB(AM) New Orleans LA	KRBI(AM) Saint Peter MN
KWKU(AM) Pomona CA	WZHR(AM) Zephyrhills FL	WYNG(FM) Mount Carmel IL	WWL(AM) New Orleans LA	KDOM(AM) Windom MN
KNLF(FM) Quincy CA	WSRA(AM) Albany GA	WPRS(AM) Paris IL	KEEL(AM) Shreveport LA	KWNO(AM) Winona MN
KNRO(AM) Redding CA	WRFC(AM) Athens GA	WIRL(AM) Peoria IL	KRMD(AM) Shreveport LA	KBFL(FM) Buffalo MO
KHTK(AM) Sacramento CA	WQXI(AM) Atlanta GA	WZOE(AM) Princeton IL	KSYB(AM) Shreveport LA	KGIR(AM) Cape Girardeau MO
KSAC(AM) Sacramento CA	WGAC(AM) Augusta GA	WGEM(AM) Quincy IL	WSLA(AM) Slidell LA	KDKD-FM Clinton MO
KZFX(AM) Salinas CA	WNRR(AM) Augusta GA	WJCI(AM) Rantoul IL	KEZM(AM) Sulphur LA	KTGR(AM) Columbia MO
KNBR(AM) San Francisco CA	WRDW(AM) Augusta GA	WTJK(AM) South Beloit IL	KMBS(AM) West Monroe LA	KRFT(AM) De Soto MO
KKJL(AM) San Luis Obispo CA	WSGF(AM) Augusta GA	WHCO(AM) Sparta IL	WARL(AM) Attleboro MA	KHMO(AM) Hannibal MO
KVEC(AM) San Luis Obispo CA	WFNS(AM) Blackshear GA	WFMB(AM) Springfield IL	WEEI(AM) Boston MA	KCTE(AM) Independence MO
KTCT(AM) San Mateo CA	WPPL(FM) Blue Ridge GA	WTAX(AM) Springfield IL	WWZN(AM) Boston MA	WMBH(AM) Joplin MO
KIST(AM) Santa Barbara CA	WMOG(AM) Brunswick GA	WSDR(AM) Sterling IL	WBET(AM) Brockton MA	KCSP(AM) Kansas City MO
KIRN(AM) Simi Valley CA	WSFN(AM) Brunswick GA	WSPL(AM) Streator IL	WAMG(AM) Dedham MA	WHB(AM) Kansas City MO
KIRN(AM) Simi Valley CA	WBHF(AM) Cartersville GA	WVIL(FM) Virginia IL	WSAR(AM) Fall River MA	KLWT(AM) Lebanon MO
KOWL(AM) South Lake Tahoe CA	WYXC(AM) Cartersville GA	KFNS(AM) Wood River IL	WEIM(AM) Fitchburg MA	KNIM(AM) Maryville MO
KTHO(AM) South Lake Tahoe CA	WEAM(AM) Columbus GA	WHBU(AM) Anderson IN	WCAP(AM) Lowell MA	KFMO(AM) Park Hills MO
KXPS(AM) Thousand Palms CA	WRCG(AM) Columbus GA	WBIW(AM) Bedford IN	WLLH(AM) Lowell MA	KLID(AM) Poplar Bluff MO
KVBL(AM) Visalia CA	WSHE(AM) Columbus GA	WSDX(AM) Brazil IN	WBSM(AM) New Bedford MA	KMIS(AM) Portageville MO
KNFO(FM) Basalt CO	WSHE(AM) Columbus GA	WKLU(FM) Brownsburg IN	WHMP(AM) Northampton MA	KTTR(AM) Rolla MO
KSIR(AM) Brush CO	WDMG(AM) Douglas GA	WCSI(AM) Columbus IN	WBEC(AM) Pittsfield MA	KFEQ(AM) Saint Joseph MO
KRDO(AM) Colorado Springs CO	WMLT(AM) Dublin GA	WGL(AM) Fort Wayne IN	WESX(AM) Salem MA	KMOX(AM) Saint Louis MO
KVOR(AM) Colorado Springs CO	WDUN(AM) Gainesville GA	WKJG(AM) Fort Wayne IN	WARE(AM) Ware MA	KSLG(AM) Saint Louis MO
KBNO(AM) Denver CO	WGGA(AM) Gainesville GA	WOWO(AM) Fort Wayne IN	WNNZ(AM) Westfield MA	KTRS(AM) Saint Louis MO
KKFN(AM) Denver CO	WHIE(AM) Griffin GA	WIJY(FM) Franklin IN	WVEI(AM) Worcester MA	KSMO(AM) Salem MO
KLZ(AM) Denver CO	WCEH(AM) Hawkinsville GA	WLTH(AM) Gary IN	WBAL(AM) Baltimore MD	KLTK(AM) South West City MO
KOA(AM) Denver CO	WLOP(AM) Jesup GA	WREB(FM) Greencastle IN	WJFK(AM) Baltimore MD	KGMY(AM) Springfield MO
KDGO(AM) Durango CO	WLAG(AM) La Grange GA	WIBC(AM) Indianapolis IN	WCEM(AM) Cambridge MD	KWTO(AM) Springfield MO
KIIX(AM) Fort Collins CO	WMAC(AM) Macon GA	WNDE(AM) Indianapolis IN	WFMD(AM) Frederick MD	KWTO-FM Springfield MO
KTMM(AM) Grand Junction CO	WMVG(AM) Milledgeville GA	WXLW(AM) Indianapolis IN	WICO(AM) Salisbury MD	KTUI-FM Sullivan MO
KWUF(AM) Pagosa Springs CO	WCNN(AM) North Atlanta GA	WIOU(AM) Kokomo IN	WTGM(AM) Salisbury MD	KTTN-FM Trenton MO
KCSJ(AM) Pueblo CO	WLAQ(AM) Rome GA	WBAT(AM) Marion IN	WQMR(FM) Snow Hill MD	KFNS-FM Troy MO
KGHF(AM) Pueblo CO	WUUS(AM) Rossville GA	WGOM(AM) Marion IN	WNST(AM) Towson MD	KOKO(AM) Warrensburg MO
KRGS(AM) Rifle CO	WHGM(AM) Savannah GA	WLBC-FM Muncie IN	WABI(AM) Bangor ME	WAMY(AM) Amory MS
KBCR(AM) Steamboat Springs CO	WTKS(AM) Savannah GA	WXFN(AM) Muncie IN	WZON(AM) Bangor ME	WXBD(AM) Biloxi MS
KKZN(AM) Thornton CO	WPTB(AM) Statesboro GA	WWSZ(AM) New Albany IN	WBQI(FM) Bar Harbor ME	WCJU(AM) Columbia MS
KSPK(FM) Walsenburg CO	WWNS(AM) Statesboro GA	WNVI(AM) North Vernon IN	WJJB(AM) Brunswick ME	WJWF(AM) Columbus MS
WINE(AM) Brookfield CT	WXRS(AM) Swainsboro GA	WZZB(AM) Seymour IN	WLVP(AM) Gorham ME	WPBQ(AM) Flowood MS
WGCH(AM) Greenwich CT	WVLD(AM) Valdosta GA	WHLY(AM) South Bend IN	WIGY(FM) Madison ME	WGVM(AM) Greenville MS
WSUB(AM) Groton CT	WVOP(AM) Vidalia GA	WSBT(AM) South Bend IN	WTBM(FM) Mexico ME	WFOR(AM) Hattiesburg MS
WPOP(AM) Hartford CT	KUAU(AM) Haiku HI	WBOW(AM) Terre Haute IN	WSYY(AM) Millinocket ME	WHSY(AM) Hattiesburg MS
WMMW(AM) Meriden CT	KHLO(AM) Hilo HI	WAOV(AM) Vincennes IN	WOXO-FM Norway ME	WJDX(AM) Jackson MS
WAVZ(AM) New Haven CT	KPUA(AM) Hilo HI	WRSW(AM) Warsaw IN	WSKW(AM) Skowhegan ME	WSFZ(AM) Jackson MS
WXLM(AM) Stonington CT	KKEA(AM) Honolulu HI	KFH-FM Clearwater KS	WJJB-FM Topsham ME	*WPRL(FM) Lorman MS
WTEM(AM) Washington DC	KKON(AM) Kealakekua HI	KGNO(AM) Dodge City KS	WJAE(AM) Westbrook ME	WHNY(AM) McComb MS
WWTX(AM) Wilmington DE	KAOI(AM) Kihei HI	KIUL(AM) Garden City KS	WNSX(FM) Winter Harbor ME	WFFX(AM) Meridian MS
WBGF(FM) Belle Glade FL	KQNG(AM) Lihue HI	KKCI(AM) Goodland KS	WFYC(AM) Alma MI	WMOX(AM) Meridian MS
WWPR(AM) Bradenton FL	KMVI(AM) Wailuku HI	KVGB(AM) Great Bend KS	WTKA(AM) Ann Arbor MI	WMLC(AM) Monticello MS
WWJB(AM) Brooksville FL	KCNZ(AM) Cedar Falls IA	KCKN(AM) Kansas City KS	WBRN(AM) Big Rapids MI	WNAT(AM) Natchez MS
WKFL(AM) Bushnell FL	KCRG(AM) Cedar Rapids IA	KNNS(AM) Larned KS	WQTX(FM) Charlotte MI	WTUP(AM) Tupelo MS
WRHC(AM) Coral Gables FL	KMJM(AM) Cedar Rapids IA	KLWN(AM) Lawrence KS	WDTW(AM) Dearborn MI	WQBC(AM) Vicksburg MS
WNDB(AM) Daytona Beach FL	KJOC(AM) Davenport IA	KMAN(AM) Manhattan KS	WDFN(AM) Detroit MI	KBLG(AM) Billings MT
WNDA(AM) De Land FL	KWKY(AM) Des Moines IA	KSEK(AM) Pittsburg KS	WXYT(AM) Detroit MI	KMMS(AM) Bozeman MT
WLVU(AM) Dunedin FL	KXNO(AM) Des Moines IA	KINA(AM) Salina KS	WDOW(AM) Dowagiac MI	KBOW(AM) Butte MT
WFLL(AM) Fort Lauderdale FL	WDBQ(AM) Dubuque IA	KMAJ(AM) Topeka KS	WVFN(AM) East Lansing MI	KGEZ(AM) Kalispell MT
WGGG(AM) Gainesville FL	KILR-FM Estherville IA	KTOP(AM) Topeka KS	WTRX(AM) Flint MI	KGRZ(AM) Missoula MT
WRUF(AM) Gainesville FL	KVFD(AM) Fort Dodge IA	WIBW(AM) Topeka KS	WMJZ-FM Gaylord MI	WISE(AM) Asheville NC
WTKE(FM) Holt FL	KXLQ(AM) Indianola IA	KGSO(AM) Wichita KS	WBBL(AM) Grand Rapids MI	WTKF(FM) Atlantic NC
WFXJ(AM) Jacksonville FL	KIFG-FM Iowa Falls IA	KKLE(AM) Winfield KS	WTKG(AM) Grand Rapids MI	WZNN(AM) Black Mountain NC
WNNR(AM) Jacksonville FL	KOKX(AM) Keokuk IA	WCMI(AM) Ashland KY	WSCG(AM) Greenville MI	WATA(AM) Boone NC
WZNZ(AM) Jacksonville FL	KLEM(AM) Le Mars IA	WAIA(AM) Beaver Dam KY	WMPL(AM) Hancock MI	WFNA(AM) Charlotte NC
WKWF(AM) Key West FL	KOEL(AM) Oelwein IA	WBGN(AM) Bowling Green KY	WIBM(AM) Jackson MI	WFNZ(AM) Charlotte NC
WHOO(AM) Kissimmee FL	KSCJ(AM) Sioux City IA	WTCO(AM) Campbellsville KY	WQSN(AM) Kalamazoo MI	WCSL(AM) Cherryville NC
WDSR(AM) Lake City FL	KAYL(AM) Storm Lake IA	WOKT(AM) Cannonsburg KY	WLSP(AM) Lapeer MI	*WWCU(FM) Cullowhee NC
WQHL(AM) Live Oak FL	KHPP(AM) Waukon IA	WNES(AM) Central City KY	WKKK(AM) Petoskey MI	WDNC(AM) Durham NC
WFFG(AM) Marathon FL	KBLI(AM) Blackfoot ID	WTSZ(AM) Eminence KY	WPHM(AM) Port Huron MI	WGAI(AM) Elizabeth City NC
WMEL(AM) Melbourne FL	KBFI(AM) Bonners Ferry ID	WXRA(AM) Georgetown KY	WIDG(AM) Saint Ignace MI	WGHB(AM) Farmville NC
WQAM(AM) Miami FL	KRLC(AM) Lewiston ID	WCDS(AM) Glasgow KY	WTXQ(AM) Saint Johns MI	WFAY(AM) Fayetteville NC
WQAM(AM) Miami FL	KTIK(AM) Nampa ID	WUGO(FM) Grayson KY	WSJM(AM) Saint Joseph MI	WGNC(AM) Gastonia NC
WNMA(AM) Miami Springs FL	KIOV(AM) Payette ID	WLXG(AM) Lexington KY	WLBY(AM) Saline MI	WYSR(AM) High Point NC
WWCN(AM) North Fort Myers FL	KWIK(AM) Pocatello ID	WVLK(AM) Lexington KY	WKNW(AM) Sault Ste. Marie MI	WJNC(AM) Jacksonville NC
WMOP(AM) Ocala FL	KRXK(AM) Rexburg ID	WKRD(AM) Louisville KY	WMSH(AM) Sturgis MI	WLXN(AM) Lexington NC
WQTM(AM) Orlando FL	KSPT(AM) Sandpoint ID	WTTL(AM) Madisonville KY	WCCW(AM) Traverse City MI	WLON(AM) Lincolnton NC
WELE(AM) Ormond Beach FL	WBIG(AM) Aurora IL	WKYX(AM) Paducah KY	WMFN(AM) Zeeland MI	WRBZ(AM) Raleigh NC
WLTG(AM) Panama City FL	WCIL(AM) Carbondale IL	KDBS(AM) Alexandria LA	KNFX(AM) Austin MN	WRMT(AM) Rocky Mount NC

Broadcasting & Cable Yearbook 2006

D-723

Programming on Radio Stations in the U.S.

WCAB(AM) Rutherfordton NC	WFUN(AM) Ashtabula OH	WWGE(AM) Loretto PA	WMC(AM) Memphis TN	WREL(AM) Lexington VA
WTSB(AM) Selma NC	WBLL(AM) Bellefontaine OH	WMGW(AM) Meadville PA	WREC(AM) Memphis TN	WBRG(AM) Lynchburg VA
WOHS(AM) Shelby NC	WQEL(FM) Bucyrus OH	WJUN(AM) Mexico PA	*WUMR(FM) Memphis TN	WLNI(FM) Lynchburg VA
WNCA(AM) Siler City NC	WILE(AM) Cambridge OH	WKST(AM) New Castle PA	WGNS(AM) Murfreesboro TN	WVGM(AM) Lynchburg VA
WSIC(AM) Statesville NC	WCER(AM) Canton OH	WIP(AM) Philadelphia PA	WBFG(FM) Parker's Crossroads TN	*WWMC(FM) Lynchburg VA
WMFD(AM) Wilmington NC	WCSM-FM Celina OH	WPHB(AM) Philipsburg PA	WQBB(AM) Powell TN	WJFK-FM Manassas VA
WVOT(AM) Wilson NC	WLW(AM) Cincinnati OH	WBGG(AM) Pittsburgh PA	WTNE-FM Trenton TN	WNRV(AM) Narrows-Pearisburg VA
KFYR(AM) Bismarck ND	WSAI(AM) Cincinnati OH	WEAE(AM) Pittsburgh PA	WQMV(AM) Waverly TN	WCMS(AM) Newport News VA
WDAY(AM) Fargo ND	WERE(AM) Cleveland OH	WEEU(AM) Reading PA	KZQQ(AM) Abilene TX	WRAD(AM) Radford VA
KQDJ(AM) Jamestown ND	WKNR(AM) Cleveland OH	WIOV(AM) Reading PA	KESN(FM) Allen TX	WRNL(AM) Richmond VA
KOVC(AM) Valley City ND	WTAM(AM) Cleveland OH	WKBI(AM) Saint Marys PA	KGNC(AM) Amarillo TX	WXGI(AM) Richmond VA
KOZN(AM) Bellevue NE	WBNS(AM) Columbus OH	WARM(AM) Scranton PA	KPUR(AM) Amarillo TX	WGMN(AM) Roanoke VA
KICS(AM) Hastings NE	WING(AM) Dayton OH	WEJL(AM) Scranton PA	KVET(AM) Austin TX	WINC(AM) Winchester VA
KXPN(AM) Kearney NE	WONE(AM) Dayton OH	WMAJ(AM) State College PA	KRUN(AM) Ballinger TX	WYVE(AM) Wytheville VA
KLMS(AM) Lincoln NE	WEOL(AM) Elyria OH	WKOK(AM) Sunbury PA	KIKR(AM) Beaumont TX	WVWI(AM) Charlotte Amalie VI
KSWN(AM) McCook NE	WMOH(AM) Hamilton OH	WTZN(AM) Troy PA	KBST(AM) Big Spring TX	WSNO(AM) Barre VT
KXSP(AM) Omaha NE	WIMA(AM) Lima OH	WBAX(AM) Wilkes-Barre PA	KZRK(AM) Canyon TX	WTSA(AM) Brattleboro VT
KOLT(AM) Scottsbluff NE	WMAN(AM) Mansfield OH	WLYC(AM) Williamsport PA	KZNE(AM) College Station TX	WVMT(AM) Burlington VT
KWPN-FM West Point NE	WMOA(AM) Marietta OH	WRAK(AM) Williamsport PA	KEYS(AM) Corpus Christi TX	WDEV-FM Warren VT
WTSV(AM) Claremont NH	WUCO(AM) Marysville OH	WOYK(AM) York PA	KSIX(AM) Corpus Christi TX	WDEV(AM) Waterbury VT
WTSN(AM) Dover NH	WTIG(AM) Massillon OH	WGIT(AM) Canovanas PR	KZNX(AM) Creedmoor TX	WNHV(AM) White River Junction VT
WGIP(AM) Exeter NH	WJAW-FM McConnelsville OH	WXRF(AM) Guayama PR	KRLD(AM) Dallas TX	KXLX(AM) Airway Heights WA
WTSL(AM) Hanover NH	WMPO(AM) Middleport-Pomeroy OH	WMNT(AM) Manati PR	KTCK(AM) Dallas TX	KLKI(AM) Anacortes WA
WTPL(FM) Hillsboro NH	WRGM(AM) Ontario OH	WAEL(AM) Mayaguez PR	KURV(AM) Edinburg TX	KCLK(AM) Asotin WA
WLTN(AM) Littleton NH	WIZE(AM) Springfield OH	WVOZ(AM) San Juan PR	KULP(AM) El Campo TX	KPUG(AM) Bellingham WA
WGIR(AM) Manchester NH	WLQR(AM) Toledo OH	WADK(AM) Newport RI	KHEY(AM) El Paso TX	KELA(AM) Centralia-Chehalis WA
WKBR(AM) Manchester NH	WBTC(AM) Uhrichsville OH	WPRO(AM) Providence RI	KROD(AM) El Paso TX	KXLE(AM) Ellensburg WA
WSMN(AM) Nashua NH	WHKZ(AM) Warren OH	WSKO(AM) Providence RI	KFLC(AM) Fort Worth TX	KULE(AM) Ephrata WA
WSNH(AM) Nashua NH	WELW(AM) Willoughby-Eastlake OH	WSKO-FM Wakefield-Peacedale RI	KKGM(AM) Fort Worth TX	KRKO(AM) Everett WA
WGIN(AM) Rochester NH	WQKT(FM) Wooster OH	WEEI-FM Westerly RI	KBRA(FM) Freer TX	KWOK(AM) Hoquiam WA
WPAT(AM) Paterson NJ	WBBW(AM) Youngstown OH	WZMJ(FM) Batesburg SC	KXEB(AM) Frisco TX	KBSN(AM) Moses Lake WA
WPHY(AM) Trenton NJ	WKBN(AM) Youngstown OH	WQIS(AM) Camden SC	KVRP-FM Haskell TX	KWIQ(AM) Moses Lake North WA
KRSY(AM) Alamogordo NM	KADA(AM) Ada OK	WCCP-FM Clemson SC	KBME(AM) Houston TX	KRSC(AM) Othello WA
KABQ(AM) Albuquerque NM	KVSO(AM) Ardmore OK	WPCC(AM) Clinton SC	KILT(AM) Houston TX	KFLD(AM) Pasco WA
KDEF(AM) Albuquerque NM	WWLS-FM Bethany OK	WCOS(AM) Columbia SC	KTRH(AM) Houston TX	KZXR(AM) Prosser WA
KNML(AM) Albuquerque NM	KOKB(AM) Blackwell OK	WOIC(AM) Columbia SC	*KSHU(FM) Huntsville TX	KALE(AM) Richland WA
KCQL(AM) Aztec NM	KPNS(AM) Duncan OK	WVOC(AM) Columbia SC	KAML(AM) Kenedy-Karnes City TX	KIRO(AM) Seattle WA
KNFT(AM) Bayard NM	KADS(AM) Elk City OK	WIQB(AM) Conway SC	KFRO(AM) Longview TX	KJR(AM) Seattle WA
KCLV(AM) Clovis NM	KBEL(AM) Idabel OK	WJXY-FM Conway SC	KKAM(AM) Lubbock TX	KBBO(AM) Selah WA
KENN(AM) Farmington NM	KXCA(AM) Lawton OK	WTMZ(AM) Dorchester Terrace-Brentwood SC	KCUL(AM) Marshall TX	KJRB(AM) Spokane WA
KYKK(AM) Hobbs NM	WWLS(AM) Moore OK	WOLS(AM) Florence SC	KCUL-FM Marshall TX	KHHO(AM) Tacoma WA
KOBE(AM) Las Cruces NM	KBIX(AM) Muskogee OK	WFIS(AM) Fountain Inn SC	KMND(AM) Midland TX	KYNR(AM) Toppenish WA
KRSN(AM) Los Alamos NM	KREF(AM) Norman OK	WXJY(FM) Georgetown SC	KBED(AM) Nederland TX	KUJ(AM) Walla Walla WA
KRUI(AM) Ruidoso Downs NM	KOKP(AM) Perry OK	WFXH(AM) Hilton Head Island SC	KGNB(AM) New Braunfels TX	KKRT(AM) Wenatchee WA
KTRC(AM) Santa Fe NM	KYAL(AM) Sapulpa OK	WWFN-FM Lake City SC	KRIL(AM) Odessa TX	WSCO(AM) Appleton WI
KTSN(AM) Elko NV	KSPI(AM) Stillwater OK	WRHM(FM) Lancaster SC	KOGT(AM) Orange TX	WISS(AM) Berlin WI
KBAD(AM) Las Vegas NV	KEOK(FM) Tahlequah OK	WQTK(AM) Moncks Corner SC	KSOX(AM) Raymondville TX	WDUZ-FM Brillion WI
KENO(AM) Las Vegas NV	KTLQ(AM) Tahlequah OK	WRHI(AM) Rock Hill SC	KGKL(AM) San Angelo TX	WMBE(AM) Chilton WI
KLAV(AM) Las Vegas NV	KCFO(AM) Tulsa OK	WSPA(AM) Spartanburg SC	KKSA(AM) San Angelo TX	WEAQ(AM) Chippewa Falls WI
KRLV(AM) Las Vegas NV	KTBZ(AM) Tulsa OK	WSPG(AM) Spartanburg SC	KTKR(AM) San Antonio TX	WTLX(FM) Columbus WI
KSHP(AM) North Las Vegas NV	KTMT(AM) Ashland OR	WALI(FM) Walterboro SC	*KTSW(FM) San Marcos TX	WBIZ(AM) Eau Claire WI
KPLY(AM) Reno NV	KAST(AM) Astoria OR	KGIM(AM) Aberdeen SD	KTDK(FM) Sanger TX	KFIZ(AM) Fond du Lac WI
KBZZ(AM) Sparks NV	KKEE(AM) Astoria OR	KSDN(AM) Aberdeen SD	KJIM(AM) Sherman TX	WFAW(AM) Fort Atkinson WI
WVTL(AM) Amsterdam NY	KBND(AM) Bend OR	KBFS(AM) Belle Fourche SD	KKLF(AM) Sherman TX	WKTY(AM) La Crosse WI
WYSL(AM) Avon NY	KICE(AM) Bend OR	KIJV(AM) Huron SD	KSET(AM) Silsbee TX	WTSO(AM) Madison WI
WPUT(AM) Brewster NY	KHSN(AM) Coos Bay OR	KORN(AM) Mitchell SD	KWNX(AM) Taylor TX	WMAM(AM) Marinette WI
WBEN(AM) Buffalo NY	KLOO(AM) Corvallis OR	KSOO(AM) Sioux Falls SD	KTEM(AM) Temple TX	WDLB(AM) Marshfield WI
WGR(AM) Buffalo NY	KRVM(AM) Eugene OR	KWSN(AM) Sioux Falls SD	KCMC(AM) Texarkana TX	WIGM(AM) Medford WI
WELM(AM) Elmira NY	KSCR(AM) Eugene OR	KVTK(AM) Vermillion SD	KTBB(AM) Tyler TX	WMEQ(AM) Menomonie WI
WENE(AM) Endicott NY	KUIK(AM) Hillsboro OR	WNFN(FM) Belle Meade TN	KYZS(AM) Tyler TX	WTMJ(AM) Milwaukee WI
WMML(AM) Glens Falls NY	KFLS(AM) Klamath Falls OR	WNSR(AM) Brentwood TN	KQRL(AM) Waco TX	WLKD(AM) Minocqua WI
WWSC(AM) Glens Falls NY	KKJX(AM) Klamath Falls OR	WOPI(AM) Bristol TN	KRZI(AM) Waco TX	WOSH(AM) Oshkosh WI
WNRS(AM) Herkimer NY	KGAL(AM) Lebanon OR	WRKM(AM) Carthage TN	KQMB(FM) Midvale UT	WNBI(AM) Park Falls WI
WHCU(AM) Ithaca NY	KNPT(AM) Newport OR	WDEF(AM) Chattanooga TN	KJQS(AM) Murray UT	WPVL(AM) Platteville WI
WJTN(AM) Jamestown NY	KTIX(AM) Pendleton OR	WJZM(AM) Clarksville TN	KALL(AM) North Salt Lake City UT	WOBT(AM) Rhinelander WI
WIRD(AM) Lake Placid NY	KQEN(AM) Roseburg OR	WCSV(AM) Crossville TN	KENT(AM) Parowan UT	WRCO-FM Richland Center WI
WIXT(AM) Little Falls NY	KSLM(AM) Salem OR	WEMB(AM) Erwin TN	KOAL(AM) Price UT	WEVR(AM) River Falls WI
WLVL(AM) Lockport NY	KMBD(AM) Tillamook OR	WCPH(AM) Etowah TN	KOVO(AM) Provo UT	WEVR-FM River Falls WI
WADO(AM) New York NY	WTKZ(AM) Allentown PA	WEKR(AM) Fayetteville TN	KSVC(AM) Richfield UT	WCLB(AM) Sheboygan WI
WEPN(AM) New York NY	WVAM(AM) Altoona PA	WHEW(AM) Franklin TN	KFNZ(AM) Salt Lake City UT	WDOR-FM Sturgeon Bay WI
WFAN(AM) New York NY	WMBA(AM) Ambridge PA	WGFX(FM) Gallatin TN	KSL(AM) Salt Lake City UT	WJJQ(AM) Tomahawk WI
WACK(AM) Newark NY	WBVP(AM) Beaver Falls PA	WMLR(AM) Hohenwald TN	KZNS(AM) Salt Lake City UT	WJJQ-FM Tomahawk WI
WLNA(AM) Peekskill NY	WBLF(AM) Bellefonte PA	WHMT(AM) Humboldt TN	KVEL(AM) Vernal UT	WFBZ(FM) Trempealeau WI
WEAV(AM) Plattsburgh NY	*WBUQ(FM) Bloomsburg PA	WJCW(AM) Johnson City TN	WCBX(AM) Bassett VA	WAUK(AM) Waukesha WI
WADR(AM) Remsen NY	WISR(AM) Butler PA	WKTP(AM) Jonesborough TN	WBVA(AM) Bayside VA	WCHS(AM) Charleston WV
WTMM(AM) Rensselaer NY	WWCB(AM) Corry PA	WKIN(AM) Kingsport TN	WKEX(AM) Blacksburg VA	WSWW(AM) Charleston WV
WRNY(AM) Rome NY	*WESS(FM) East Stroudsburg PA	WKPT(AM) Kingsport TN	WKLV(AM) Blackstone VA	WXKX(AM) Clarksburg WV
WSPQ(AM) Springville NY	WEEX(AM) Easton PA	WNML(AM) Knoxville TN	WBDY(AM) Bluefield VA	WBES(AM) Dunbar WV
*WAER(FM) Syracuse NY	WPDC(AM) Elizabethtown PA	WVLZ(AM) Knoxville TN	WFHG(AM) Bristol VA	WMMN(AM) Fairmont WV
WHEN(AM) Syracuse NY	WFNN(AM) Erie PA	WINA(AM) Charlottesville VA	WRVC(AM) Huntington WV
WNSS(AM) Syracuse NY	WPSE(AM) Erie PA	WQLA-FM La Follette TN	WKAV(AM) Charlottesville VA	WEPM(AM) Martinsburg WV
WOFX(AM) Troy NY	WFRA(AM) Franklin PA	WCKD(AM) Lebanon TN	WDIC-FM Clinchco VA	WRNR(AM) Martinsburg WV
WPIE(AM) Trumansburg NY	WGET(AM) Gettysburg PA	WNML-FM Loudon TN	WPIN(AM) Dublin VA	WVLY(AM) Moundsville WV
WIBX(AM) Utica NY	WTKT(AM) Harrisburg PA	WMSR(AM) Manchester TN	WODY(AM) Fieldale VA	WJYP(AM) Saint Albans WV
WUTQ(AM) Utica NY	WTYM(AM) Kittanning PA	WWTN(FM) Manchester TN	WGAT(AM) Gate City VA	WJAW(AM) Saint Marys WV
WNER(AM) Watertown NY	WLPA(AM) Lancaster PA	WAKI(AM) McMinnville TN	WLRT(AM) Hampton VA	WKKX(AM) Wheeling WV
WARF(AM) Akron OH	WCNS(AM) Latrobe PA	WHBQ(AM) Memphis TN	WHBG(AM) Harrisonburg VA	KRSV(AM) Afton WY

Broadcasting & Cable Yearbook 2006

D-724

Programming on Radio Stations in the U.S.

KRSV-FM Afton WY
KBBS(AM) Buffalo WY
KKTL(AM) Casper WY
KVOC(AM) Casper WY
KFBC(AM) Cheyenne WY
KRAE(AM) Cheyenne WY
KODI(AM) Cody WY
KIML(AM) Gillette WY
KOWB(AM) Laramie WY
KYDT(FM) Sundance WY

Talk

KENI(AM) Anchorage AK
*KYUK(AM) Bethel AK
KRUP(FM) Dillingham AK
KFBX(AM) Fairbanks AK
KADX(FM) Houston AK
KJNO(AM) Juneau AK
KVOK(AM) Kodiak AK
*KUDU(FM) Tok AK
KVAK(AM) Valdez AK
WHMA(AM) Anniston AL
WASG(AM) Atmore AL
WYDE(AM) Birmingham AL
WEBJ(AM) Brewton AL
WFMH(AM) Cullman AL
WKUL(FM) Cullman AL
WAJF(AM) Decatur AL
WOOF(AM) Dothan AL
WULA(AM) Eufaula AL
WIJK(AM) Evergreen AL
WJLD(AM) Fairfield AL
WABF(AM) Fairhope AL
WHEP(AM) Foley AL
WTKI(AM) Huntsville AL
WNSI(AM) Robertsdale AL
WBTG(AM) Sheffield AL
WTBF(AM) Troy AL
WVSA(AM) Vernon AL
KOLX(FM) Barling AR
KEWI(AM) Benton AR
KREB(AM) Bentonville-Bella Vista AR
KXJK(AM) Forrest City AR
KHOZ(AM) Harrison AR
KXAR(AM) Hope AR
KNEA(AM) Jonesboro AR
KABZ(FM) Little Rock AR
KTTG(FM) Mena AR
KWCK(AM) Searcy AR
KARN-FM Sheridan AR
KWAK(AM) Stuttgart AR
KZZZ(AM) Bullhead City AZ
KFNX(AM) Cave Creek AZ
KXAM(AM) Mesa AZ
KGME(AM) Phoenix AZ
KIDR(AM) Phoenix AZ
KNXN(AM) Sierra Vista AZ
KVOI(AM) Tucson AZ
KXMX(AM) Anaheim CA
KIXW(AM) Apple Valley CA
KBRT(AM) Avalon CA
KAFY(AM) Bakersfield CA
KGEO(AM) Bakersfield CA
KRXA(AM) Carmel Valley CA
KNWZ(AM) Coachella CA
*KMUE(FM) Eureka CA
KWSW(AM) Eureka CA
KIRV(AM) Fresno CA
*KMUD(FM) Garberville CA
KCEE(FM) Grass Valley CA
KGBA-FM Holtville CA
KABC(AM) Los Angeles CA
KFI(AM) Los Angeles CA
KLSX(FM) Los Angeles CA
KTLK(AM) Los Angeles CA
KMYC(AM) Marysville CA
KTRB(AM) Modesto CA
KTOX(AM) Needles CA
KQKE(AM) Oakland CA
KMXE(AM) Orange CA
KGDP(AM) Orcutt CA
KDAR(AM) Oxnard CA
KGAM(AM) Palm Springs CA
KPSI(AM) Palm Springs CA
KNTS(AM) Palo Alto CA
*KZYX(FM) Philo CA

KAHZ(AM) Pomona CA
KNLF(FM) Quincy CA
KSTE(AM) Rancho Cordova CA
KQMS(AM) Redding CA
*KVIP(AM) Redding CA
KTKZ(AM) Sacramento CA
*KVCR(FM) San Bernardino CA
KCBQ(AM) San Diego CA
KLSD(AM) San Diego CA
KEST(AM) San Francisco CA
KFAX(AM) San Francisco CA
KGO(AM) San Francisco CA
KSFO(AM) San Francisco CA
KYCY(AM) San Francisco CA
KPRZ(AM) San Marcos-Poway CA
KIST(AM) Santa Barbara CA
KTMS(AM) Santa Barbara CA
*KGDP-FM Santa Maria CA
KUHL(AM) Santa Maria CA
KIRN(AM) Simi Valley CA
KNWT(AM) Thousand Palms CA
KXPS(AM) Thousand Palms CA
KCEO(AM) Vista CA
KERI(AM) Wasco-Greenacres CA
*KZYZ(FM) Willits CA
KNFO(FM) Basalt CO
KSIR(AM) Brush CO
KKML(AM) Colorado Springs CO
KWYD(AM) Colorado Springs CO
KLTT(AM) Commerce City CO
KHOW(AM) Denver CO
KKFN(AM) Denver CO
KJOL(AM) Grand Junction CO
*KUTE(FM) Ignacio CO
KRCN(AM) Longmont CO
KJEB(FM) Strasburg CO
KKZN(AM) Thornton CO
KVLE(AM) Vail CO
WICC(AM) Bridgeport CT
WGCH(AM) Greenwich CT
WMMW(AM) Meriden CT
WMRD(AM) Middletown CT
WLIS(AM) Old Saybrook CT
WXLM(AM) Stonington CT
*WAPJ(FM) Torrington CT
WSNG(AM) Torrington CT
WTEM(AM) Washington DC
WWRC(AM) Washington DC
WILM(AM) Wilmington DE
WTMC(AM) Wilmington DE
WORL(AM) Altamonte Springs FL
WHIM(AM) Apopka FL
WFLN(AM) Arcadia FL
WQOP(AM) Atlantic Beach FL
WSBR(AM) Boca Raton FL
WTAN(AM) Clearwater FL
WTKS-FM Cocoa Beach FL
WDJA(AM) Delray Beach FL
WSRF(AM) Fort Lauderdale FL
WTOT-FM Graceville FL
WACC(AM) Hialeah FL
WTKE(FM) Holt FL
WYMM(AM) Jacksonville FL
WIOJ(AM) Jacksonville Beach FL
WWTK(AM) Lake Placid FL
WWAB(AM) Lakeland FL
WJXR(FM) Macclenny FL
WINZ(AM) Miami FL
WMBM(AM) Miami Beach FL
WNMA(AM) Miami Springs FL
WEBY(AM) Milton FL
*WEGS(FM) Milton FL
WWCN(AM) North Fort Myers FL
WMOP(AM) Ocala FL
WQTM(AM) Orlando FL
WRMQ(AM) Orlando FL
WTLN(AM) Orlando FL
*WFSW(FM) Panama City FL
*WJTF(FM) Panama City FL
WPTK(AM) Pine Island Center FL
WTBN(AM) Pinellas Park FL
WTWD(AM) Plant City FL
WHSR(AM) Pompano Beach FL
WWNN(AM) Pompano Beach FL
WZZR(AM) Riviera Beach FL
WTMY(AM) Sarasota FL
WPUL(AM) South Daytona FL

WYOO(FM) Springfield FL
WCZR(FM) Vero Beach FL
WTTB(AM) Vero Beach FL
WZTA(AM) Vero Beach FL
WBZT(AM) West Palm Beach FL
WRFC(AM) Athens GA
WALR(AM) Atlanta GA
WGUN(AM) Atlanta GA
WNIV(AM) Atlanta GA
WQXI(AM) Atlanta GA
WNRR(AM) Augusta GA
WAAA(AM) Avondale Estates GA
WBBK(AM) Blakely GA
WYXC(AM) Cartersville GA
WGHC(AM) Clayton GA
WSEM(AM) Donalsonville GA
WDDK(FM) Greensboro GA
WKLY(AM) Hartwell GA
WFOM(AM) Marietta GA
WTNL(AM) Reidsville GA
WXRS(AM) Swainsboro GA
WQSA(FM) Unadilla GA
*WJSP-FM Warm Springs GA
WPLV(AM) West Point GA
WIMO(AM) Winder GA
KUAU(AM) Haiku HI
KKEA(AM) Honolulu HI
KORL(AM) Honolulu HI
KRTR(AM) Honolulu HI
KUMU(AM) Honolulu HI
KWQW(FM) Boone IA
KCPS(AM) Burlington IA
KCNZ(AM) Cedar Falls IA
*KUNI(FM) Cedar Falls IA
KCHA(AM) Charles City IA
KJOC(AM) Davenport IA
KPSZ(AM) Des Moines IA
KWKY(AM) Des Moines IA
KCJJ(AM) Iowa City IA
KGLO(AM) Mason City IA
KICD(AM) Spencer IA
*KNWS(AM) Waterloo IA
KSLJ(AM) Blackfoot ID
KSPD(AM) Boise ID
KBAR(AM) Burley ID
KBGN(AM) Caldwell ID
KSSL(AM) Idaho Falls ID
KOZE(AM) Lewiston ID
KIDO(AM) Nampa ID
KTIK(AM) Nampa ID
*KBSW(FM) Twin Falls ID
WNTX(AM) Brookport IL
WCAZ(AM) Carthage IL
WMVP(AM) Chicago IL
*WSSD(FM) Chicago IL
WYLL(AM) Chicago IL
WVON(AM) Cicero IL
WHOW(AM) Clinton IL
WCPT(AM) Crystal Lake IL
WCKG(FM) Elmwood Park IL
WGNU(AM) Granite City IL
WDDD(AM) Johnston City IL
WJOL(AM) Joliet IL
WKAN(AM) Kankakee IL
WGGH(AM) Marion IL
WFXN(AM) Moline IL
WMIX(AM) Mount Vernon IL
*WPTH(FM) Olney IL
WPRS(AM) Paris IL
WPEO(AM) Peoria IL
WTRH(FM) Ramsey IL
WNTA(AM) Rockford IL
*WGNJ(FM) Saint Joseph IL
WAUR(AM) Sandwich IL
WFMB(AM) Springfield IL
WSDR(AM) Sterling IL
*WGNR(AM) Anderson IN
WBIW(AM) Bedford IN
WFRN(AM) Elkhart IN
WIJY(FM) Franklin IN
WWCA(AM) Gary IN
WBRI(AM) Indianapolis IN
WNDE(AM) Indianapolis IN
WTLC(AM) Indianapolis IN
WGOM(AM) Marion IN
WMRS(AM) Monticello IN
WFIA-FM New Albany IN

WRAY(AM) Princeton IN
WSLM-FM Salem IN
*WHOJ(FM) Terre Haute IN
KFH-FM Clearwater KS
KGNO(AM) Dodge City KS
KCNW(AM) Fairway KS
KVGB(AM) Great Bend KS
KBUF(AM) Holcomb KS
KBWB(AM) Hutchinson KS
KCVW(FM) Kingman KS
KCCV-FM Olathe KS
KFRM(AM) Salina KS
KTOP(AM) Topeka KS
KFH(AM) Wichita KS
*KYWA(FM) Wichita KS
KKLE(AM) Winfield KS
KKXO(AM) Berea KY
WNES(AM) Central City KY
WFTG(AM) London KY
WFIA(AM) Louisville KY
WKJK(AM) Louisville KY
WTTL(AM) Madisonville KY
WNBS(AM) Murray KY
WWFT(AM) Nicholasville KY
WDOC(AM) Prestonsburg KY
WSFC(AM) Somerset KY
WLXO(FM) Stamping Ground KY
KJMJ(AM) Alexandria LA
WJBO(AM) Baton Rouge LA
WPYR(AM) Baton Rouge LA
KBCL(AM) Bossier City LA
*KGRM(FM) Grambling LA
KVOL(AM) Lafayette LA
KWLA(AM) Many LA
KLIC(AM) Monroe LA
KMRC(AM) Morgan City LA
WSHO(AM) New Orleans LA
KRMD(AM) Shreveport LA
KVCL(AM) Winnfield LA
WSRO(AM) Ashland MA
*WBUR-FM Boston MA
WEEI(AM) Boston MA
WEZE(AM) Boston MA
WRKO(AM) Boston MA
WROL(AM) Boston MA
WTKK(FM) Boston MA
WTTT(AM) Boston MA
WACE(AM) Chicopee MA
WXKS(AM) Everett MA
WHTB(AM) Fall River MA
WKOX(AM) Framingham MA
WCAP(AM) Lowell MA
WNNZ(AM) Westfield MA
*WSKB(FM) Westfield MA
WBIS(AM) Annapolis MD
WCBM(AM) Baltimore MD
WJFK(AM) Baltimore MD
WTNT(AM) Bethesda MD
WHFS(FM) Catonsville MD
WKDI(AM) Denton MD
*WYPF(FM) Frederick MD
WARK(AM) Hagerstown MD
WDMV(AM) Poolesville MD
WZON(AM) Bangor ME
WBCI(FM) Bath ME
WJJB(AM) Brunswick ME
WREM(AM) Monticello ME
WZAN(AM) Portland ME
WEGP(AM) Presque Isle ME
WHQO(FM) Skowhegan ME
WJJB-FM Topsham ME
WJAE(AM) Westbrook ME
WNSX(FM) Winter Harbor ME
WATZ(AM) Alpena MI
WTKA(AM) Ann Arbor MI
WMAX(AM) Bay City MI
WHFB(AM) Benton Harbor-St. Joseph MI
WDTW(AM) Dearborn MI
WNZK(AM) Dearborn Heights MI
WDFN(AM) Detroit MI
WKRK-FM Detroit MI
WLQV(AM) Detroit MI
WVFN(AM) East Lansing MI
*WLJN(AM) Elmwood Township MI
WTRX(AM) Flint MI
WSHN(AM) Fremont MI

WTKG(AM) Grand Rapids MI
WSCG(AM) Greenville MI
*WHPR(FM) Highland Park MI
WJMS(AM) Ironwood MI
WKLZ(AM) Kalamazoo MI
WJIM(AM) Lansing MI
WKLA(AM) Ludington MI
WPIQ(FM) Manistique MI
WWKK(AM) Petoskey MI
WHAK(AM) Rogers City MI
WSDS(AM) Salem Township MI
WLBY(AM) Saline MI
WIOS(AM) Tawas City MI
WCCW(AM) Traverse City MI
*WICA(FM) Traverse City MI
*WLJN-FM Traverse City MI
WPON(AM) Walled Lake MI
WDEO(AM) Ypsilanti MI
WPNW(AM) Zeeland MI
KNFX(AM) Austin MN
KBUN(AM) Bemidji MN
KKBJ(AM) Bemidji MN
KLIZ(AM) Brainerd MN
WFMP(FM) Coon Rapids MN
KROX(AM) Crookston MN
*KDNI(FM) Duluth MN
WWJC(AM) Duluth MN
WELY(AM) Ely MN
KKCQ(AM) Fosston MN
KYCR(AM) Golden Valley MN
KDWA(AM) Hastings MN
WMFG(AM) Hibbing MN
KTOE(AM) Mankato MN
KFAN(AM) Minneapolis MN
KFXN(AM) Minneapolis MN
KLOH(AM) Pipestone MN
KKMS(AM) Richfield MN
KOLM(AM) Rochester MN
KWEB(AM) Rochester MN
KTNF(AM) Saint Louis Park MN
KSTP(AM) Saint Paul MN
WMGT(AM) Stillwater MN
KOWZ(AM) Waseca MN
*KGNA-FM Arnold MO
KSGF-FM Ash Grove MO
KGIR(AM) Cape Girardeau MO
*KNLH(FM) Cedar Hill MO
KCHR(AM) Charleston MO
*KFUO(AM) Clayton MO
KFTK(FM) Florissant MO
KCMO(AM) Kansas City MO
*KKFI(FM) Kansas City MO
*KKTR(FM) Kirksville MO
KBNN(AM) Lebanon MO
KCXL(AM) Liberty MO
KWIX(AM) Moberly MO
KELE(AM) Mountain Grove MO
KLID(AM) Poplar Bluff MO
*KNLP(FM) Potosi MO
KJSL(AM) Saint Louis MO
KLTK(AM) South West City MO
KADI(AM) Springfield MO
KLFJ(AM) Springfield MO
*KSCV(FM) Springfield MO
KWTO-FM Springfield MO
KSAR(FM) Thayer MO
KLPW(AM) Union MO
KJPW(AM) Waynesville MO
WBSL(AM) Bay St. Louis MS
WXRZ(AM) Corinth MS
WFMN(FM) Flora MS
WABG(AM) Greenwood MS
WFOR(AM) Hattiesburg MS
WHSY(AM) Hattiesburg MS
WJDX(AM) Jackson MS
WALT(AM) Meridian MS
WNBN(AM) Meridian MS
WHOC(AM) Philadelphia MS
WSSO(AM) Starkville MS
WFMM(FM) Sumrall MS
WKMQ(AM) Tupelo MS
WTNM(AM) Water Valley MS
KURL(AM) Billings MT
KBOZ(AM) Bozeman MT
KGEZ(AM) Kalispell MT
KGRZ(AM) Missoula MT
*KUFM(FM) Missoula MT

Programming on Radio Stations in the U.S.

WCGC(AM) Belmont NC	WFAN(AM) New York NY	WPYT(AM) Wilkinsburg PA	WAVA(FM) Arlington VA	**Tejano**
WFGW(AM) Black Mountain NC	WMCA(AM) New York NY	WLUZ(AM) Bayamon PR	WHAN(AM) Ashland VA	KXEW(AM) South Tucson AZ
WATA(AM) Boone NC	WNEW(FM) New York NY	WTIL(AM) Mayaguez PR	WBVA(AM) Bayside VA	KOQO-FM Fresno CA
WSQL(AM) Brevard NC	WHLD(AM) Niagara Falls NY	WBMJ(AM) San Juan PR	WODI(AM) Brookneal VA	WAFZ(AM) Immokalee FL
WZTK(AM) Burlington NC	WSLB(AM) Ogdensburg NY	WQII(AM) San Juan PR	WZXI(FM) Buffalo Gap VA	KOPY-FM Alice TX
WBAG(AM) Burlington-Graham NC	WEBO(AM) Owego NY	WRSS(AM) San Sebastian PR	WWVT(AM) Christiansburg VA	KFON(AM) Austin TX
WOGR(AM) Charlotte NC	*WCEL(FM) Plattsburgh NY	WIVV(AM) Vieques PR	WEVA(AM) Emporia VA	KKPS(AM) Brownsville TX
WZRH(AM) Dallas NC	WEAV(AM) Plattsburgh NY	WXEW(AM) Yabucoa PR	WFVA(AM) Fredericksburg VA	KTJK(AM) Del Rio TX
WLOE(AM) Eden NC	*WAIH(FM) Potsdam NY	WEEI-FM Westerly RI	WGAT(AM) Gate City VA	KFZO(AM) Denton TX
WPEK(AM) Fairview NC	WHTK(AM) Rochester NY	WXNI(AM) Westerly RI	WMNA-FM Gretna VA	KTMR(AM) Edna TX
WGHB(AM) Farmville NC	WSFW(AM) Seneca Falls NY	*WLJK(FM) Aiken SC	WKCY(AM) Harrisonburg VA	KKLB(AM) Elgin TX
WNCT(AM) Greenville NC	WFBL(AM) Syracuse NY	WQSC(AM) Charleston SC	WHAP(AM) Hopewell VA	KPSO-FM Falfurrias TX
WHKP(AM) Hendersonville NC	WNSS(AM) Syracuse NY	WISW(AM) Columbia SC	WAGE(AM) Leesburg VA	KTFM(FM) Floresville TX
WGOS(AM) High Point NC	*WANC(FM) Ticonderoga NY	WJMX(AM) Florence SC	WLNI(FM) Lynchburg VA	KGRW(FM) Friona TX
WYSR(AM) High Point NC	WTBQ(AM) Warwick NY	WOLS(AM) Florence SC	WJFK-FM Manassas VA	KHMC(FM) Goliad TX
WKMT(AM) Kings Mountain NC	WATN(AM) Watertown NY	WAGI-FM Gaffney SC	WHEE(AM) Martinsville VA	KBTQ(FM) Harlingen TX
WKXU(FM) Louisburg NC	WRCI(FM) Webster NY	WSCC-FM Goose Creek SC	WCMS(AM) Newport News VA	KJBZ(FM) Laredo TX
WYRN(AM) Louisburg NC	WXZO(FM) Willsboro NY	WCKI(AM) Greer SC	WESR(AM) Onley-Onancock VA	KEJS(FM) Lubbock TX
WIXE(AM) Monroe NC	WFUN(AM) Ashtabula OH	WFXH(FM) Hilton Head Island SC	WVCV(AM) Orange VA	KLTO-FM McQueeney TX
WXNC(AM) Monroe NC	*WOFN(FM) Beach City OH	*WMBJ(FM) Murrell's Inlet SC	WLEE(AM) Richmond VA	KHCK(FM) Robinson TX
*WAAE(FM) New Bern NC	WAIS(AM) Buchtel OH	WAVO(AM) Rock Hill SC	WNDJ(FM) White Stone VA	KMIQ(FM) Robstown TX
WWNB(AM) New Bern NC	WGFT(AM) Campbell OH	WRNN(FM) Socastee SC	WDHP(FM) Frederiksted VI	KSAB(FM) Robstown TX
*WZRN(FM) Norlina NC	WCIN(AM) Cincinnati OH	WQMC(AM) Sumter SC	WVAA(AM) Burlington VT	KRTX(AM) Rosenberg-Richmond TX
WEED(AM) Rocky Mount NC	WCKY(AM) Cincinnati OH	WWOF(AM) Walhalla SC	WRSA(AM) Saint Albans VT	KCLL(FM) San Angelo TX
WNCA(AM) Siler City NC	WDBZ(AM) Cincinnati OH	KBFS(AM) Belle Fourche SD	KCLK(AM) Asotin WA	KXTN-FM San Antonio TX
WFMI(FM) Southern Shores NC	WKRC(AM) Cincinnati OH	KIJV(AM) Huron SD	KWMG(AM) Auburn-Federal Way WA	KUVA(FM) Uvalde TX
WWTB(AM) Topsail Beach NC	WTSJ(AM) Cincinnati OH	KORN(AM) Mitchell SD	KPUG(AM) Bellingham WA	
WDLX(AM) Washington NC	WHKW(AM) Cleveland OH	KSQP(AM) Pierre SD	KGNW(FM) Burien-Seattle WA	**Top-40**
WBFJ(FM) Winston-Salem NC	WTPG(AM) Columbus OH	KTOQ(FM) Rapid City SD	KOZI-FM Chelan WA	
KFGO(AM) Fargo ND	WOW(AM) Conneaut OH	KSDR(AM) Watertown SD	KMAX(AM) Colfax WA	KFAT(FM) Anchorage AK
KTGO(AM) Tioga ND	WFOB(AM) Fostoria OH	WCTA(AM) Alamo TN	KSPO(AM) Dishman WA	WJDB-FM Thomasville AL
KQWB(AM) West Fargo ND	WHTH(AM) Heath OH	WYXI(AM) Athens TN	KTAC(FM) Ephrata WA	KLBQ(FM) El Dorado AR
KTTT(AM) Columbus NE	WNIR(FM) Kent OH	*WHCB(FM) Bristol TN	KTBI(AM) Ephrata WA	KOFH(FM) Nogales AZ
KHLP(AM) Omaha NE	WLTP(AM) Marietta OH	WNKX(AM) Centerville TN	KRKO(AM) Everett WA	KQST(FM) Sedona AZ
KOLT(AM) Scottsbluff NE	WPFB(AM) Middletown OH	WDOD(AM) Chattanooga TN	KLAY(AM) Lakewood WA	KWRN(AM) Apple Valley CA
KAWL(AM) York NE	WCCD(AM) Parma OH	WLMR(AM) Chattanooga TN	KGTK(AM) Olympia WA	KLRS(FM) Chico CA
WDER(AM) Derry NH	WPAY(AM) Portsmouth OH	WCTZ(AM) Clarksville TN	KOMW(AM) Omak WA	KSRT(FM) Cloverdale CA
WQTH(AM) Hanover NH	*WLRY(FM) Rushville OH	WJZM(AM) Clarksville TN	KRSC(AM) Othello WA	KSLY-FM San Luis Obispo CA
WKBK(AM) Keene NH	*WCVZ(FM) South Zanesville OH	WPWT(AM) Colonial Heights TN	KIKN(AM) Port Angeles WA	KSME(FM) Greeley CO
WEMJ(AM) Laconia NH	WASN(AM) Youngstown OH	WZYX(AM) Cowan TN	KPTK(AM) Seattle WA	KKMG(FM) Pueblo CO
WCEC(AM) Salem NH	KOKB(AM) Blackwell OK	WRWB(AM) Harrogate TN	*KUOW(FM) Seattle WA	WKCI-FM Hamden CT
WKXW(AM) Atlantic City NJ	*KNYD(FM) Broken Arrow OK	WIRJ(AM) Humboldt TN	KVI(AM) Seattle WA	WMXZ(FM) De Funiak Springs FL
WOBM(AM) Lakewood NJ	KPNS(AM) Duncan OK	WKVL(AM) Knoxville TN	KBBO(AM) Selah WA	WYKS(FM) Gainesville FL
WIXM(FM) Millville NJ	KXCA(AM) Lawton OK	WRJZ(AM) Knoxville TN	KITZ(AM) Silverdale WA	WFKS(FM) Neptune Beach FL
WVNJ(AM) Oakland NJ	KTLR(AM) Oklahoma City OK	WLOK(AM) Memphis TN	KJRB(AM) Spokane WA	WMTX(FM) Tampa FL
*WVPH(FM) Piscataway NJ	KAKC(AM) Tulsa OK	WWTQ(AM) Memphis TN	KPTQ(AM) Spokane WA	WWWQ(FM) College Park GA
WGHT(AM) Pompton Lakes NJ	KCFO(AM) Tulsa OK	WAMB(AM) Nashville TN	KSBN(AM) Spokane WA	WBTS(FM) Doraville GA
WKXW-FM Trenton NJ	KWFX(FM) Woodward OK	WAMB-FM Nashville TN	*KSOH(FM) Wapato WA	WBTY(FM) Homerville GA
WNJC(AM) Washington Township NJ	KZZR(AM) Burns OR	WQBB(AM) Powell TN	*WLFM(FM) Appleton WI	KSHK(FM) Kekaha HI
KRSY(AM) Alamogordo NM	KEJO(AM) Corvallis OR	WZNG(AM) Shelbyville TN	WEAQ(AM) Chippewa Falls WI	KSAS-FM Caldwell ID
KKIM(AM) Albuquerque NM	KLZS(AM) Eugene OR	WQMV(AM) Waverly TN	WTLX(FM) Columbus WI	WAZY-FM Lafayette IN
KSVP(AM) Artesia NM	KOPT(AM) Eugene OR	KZQQ(AM) Abilene TX	*WDVM(AM) Eau Claire WI	KVSV(AM) Beloit KS
KNFT(AM) Bayard NM	KRVM(AM) Eugene OR	KPUR(AM) Amarillo TX	*WHID(FM) Green Bay WI	KJCK-FM Junction City KS
KICA(AM) Clovis NM	KKSL(AM) Lake Oswego OR	KZIP(AM) Amarillo TX	WNFL(AM) Green Bay WI	KLZR(FM) Lawrence KS
KKNS(AM) Corrales NM	KGAL(AM) Lebanon OR	KVET(AM) Austin TX	WMCS(AM) Greenfield WI	WUHU(FM) Smiths Grove KY
*KNMI(FM) Farmington NM	KUMA(AM) Pendleton OR	KSKY(AM) Balch Springs TX	WKBH(AM) Holmen WI	WKKS-FM Vanceburg KY
KLBZ(FM) Reserve NM	KCMX(AM) Phoenix OR	KBST(AM) Big Spring TX	WMIN(AM) Hudson WI	KSMB(FM) Lafayette LA
KRUI(AM) Ruidoso Downs NM	KEX(AM) Portland OR	KBYG(AM) Big Spring TX	WAUN(FM) Kewaunee WI	WJMN(FM) Boston MA
*KNIS(FM) Carson City NV	KFXX(AM) Portland OR	KZNX(AM) Creedmoor TX	*WHLA(FM) La Crosse WI	WDKZ(FM) Salisbury MD
KPTL(AM) Carson City NV	KKPZ(AM) Portland OR	KGGR(AM) Dallas TX	WKTY(AM) La Crosse WI	WKQI(FM) Detroit MI
KTSN(AM) Elko NV	KPDQ(AM) Portland OR	KLLI(FM) Dallas TX	WMAM(AM) Marinette WI	KOQL(FM) Ashland MO
KKVV(AM) Las Vegas NV	KPDQ-FM Portland OR	KTCK(AM) Dallas TX	*WHWC(FM) Menomonie WI	KBUD(FM) Sardis MS
KLAV(AM) Las Vegas NV	KSLM(AM) Salem OR	*KVTT(FM) Dallas TX	WJMT(AM) Merrill WI	WDAY-FM Fargo ND
KSFN(AM) North Las Vegas NV	WMBA(AM) Ambridge PA	KIXL(AM) Del Valle TX	WISN(AM) Milwaukee WI	KQKY(FM) Kearney NE
KXTE(FM) Pahrump NV	WBVP(AM) Beaver Falls PA	KRPT(FM) Devine TX	WCSW(AM) Shell Lake WI	WERZ(FM) Exeter NH
KBZB(FM) Pioche NV	WHJB(FM) Bedford PA	KATX(FM) Eastland TX	KNAF(FM) Fredericksburg TX	WWJZ(AM) Mount Holly NJ
KJFK(AM) Reno NV	*WBUQ(FM) Bloomsburg PA	KEAS(AM) Eastland TX	*WHDI(FM) Sister Bay WI	WHTZ(FM) Newark NJ
KBDB(AM) Sparks NV	WBYN(FM) Boyertown PA	KFCD(AM) Farmersville TX	*WNWC(AM) Sun Prairie WI	KXTC(FM) Thoreau NM
KRZQ-FM Sparks NV	WURP(AM) Braddock PA	KNAF(FM) Fredericksburg TX	WDSM(AM) Superior WI	WDRE(FM) Calverton-Roanoke NY
*WAMC-FM Albany NY	WDAC(FM) Lancaster PA	KEES(AM) Gladewater TX	*WVCX(FM) Tomah WI	*WECW(FM) Elmira NY
WVTL(AM) Amsterdam NY	WJSM(AM) Martinsburg PA	KCOH(AM) Houston TX	WJJQ(AM) Tomahawk WI	WMCR(AM) Oneida NY
WAUB(AM) Auburn NY	WFYL(AM) McConnellsburg PA	KILT(AM) Houston TX	*WEGZ(FM) Washburn WI	WMCR-FM Oneida NY
WSEN(AM) Baldwinsville NY	WEDO(AM) McKeesport PA	KXYZ(AM) Houston TX	*WLBL-FM Wausau WI	WLNG(FM) Sag Harbor NY
WBUF(FM) Buffalo NY	WMLP(AM) Milton PA	KTXX(FM) Karnes City TX	WBUC(AM) Buckhannon WV	WAKS(FM) Akron OH
*WCAN(FM) Canajoharie NY	WKQW(AM) Oil City PA	*KAVX(FM) Lufkin TX	WVTS(AM) Charleston WV	WMTR-FM Archbold OH
WCKL(AM) Catskill NY	WDAS(AM) Philadelphia PA	KWEL(AM) Midland TX	WBES(AM) Dunbar WV	WDKF(FM) Englewood OH
WCHP(AM) Champlain NY	WFIL(AM) Philadelphia PA	KOKE(AM) Pflugerville TX	WRKP(FM) Moundsville WV	KBVL(FM) Pawhuska OK
WJIV(FM) Cherry Valley NY	WHAT(AM) Philadelphia PA	KDVE(FM) Pittsburg TX	WRON(AM) Ronceverte WV	*KAYE-FM Tonkawa OK
WSDE(AM) Cobleskill NY	*WHYY-FM Philadelphia PA	KVOP(AM) Plainview TX	WEIR(AM) Weirton WV	WXYX(FM) Bayamon PR
WENE(AM) Endicott NY	WIP(AM) Philadelphia PA	KJCE(AM) Rollingwood TX	WHAW(AM) Weston WV	WNOD(FM) Mayaguez PR
WHHO(AM) Hornell NY	WPHT(AM) Philadelphia PA	KGKL(AM) San Angelo TX	WTWO(AM) Casper WY	WKAQ-FM San Juan PR
WLIE(AM) Islip NY	WURD(AM) Philadelphia PA	KSLR(AM) San Antonio TX	KUYO(AM) Evansville WY	WSSX-FM Charleston SC
WNYY(AM) Ithaca NY	WWDB(AM) Philadelphia PA	KTNO(AM) University Park TX	KIML(AM) Gillette WY	KDSJ(AM) Deadwood SD
WJTN(AM) Jamestown NY	WBGG(AM) Pittsburgh PA	KALL(AM) North Salt Lake City UT	KPOW(AM) Powell WY	WMSR-FM Collinwood TN
*WOSR(FM) Middletown NY	WEAE(AM) Pittsburgh PA	KLO(AM) Ogden UT		WHBQ-FM Germantown TN
WABC(AM) New York NY	WECZ(AM) Punxsutawney PA	KTKK(AM) Sandy UT		WBMC(AM) McMinnville TN
WEPN(AM) New York NY	*WNJR(FM) Washington PA	WABS(AM) Arlington VA		

Broadcasting & Cable Yearbook 2006

Programming on Radio Stations in the U.S.

WYDL(FM) Middleton TN
KNDE(FM) College Station TX
KMIC(AM) Houston TX
WZNR(FM) Poquoson VA
KRXY(FM) Shelton WA
WIZM-FM La Crosse WI
WELK(FM) Elkins WV
*WQAB(FM) Philippi WV

Triple A

*KGHR(FM) Tuba City AZ
KBHR(FM) Big Bear City CA
*KNCA(FM) Burney CA
KPYG(FM) Cambria CA
KPRI(FM) Encinitas CA
KOZT(FM) Fort Bragg CA
KPIG-FM Freedom CA
KHUM(FM) Garberville CA
KRSH(FM) Healdsburg CA
*KNSQ(FM) Mount Shasta CA
KPIG(AM) Piedmont CA
KSPN-FM Aspen CO
KBCO-FM Boulder CO
KYSL(FM) Frisco CO
KSNO-FM Snowmass Village CO
WKZE-FM Salisbury CT
WOCM(FM) Selbyville DE
*WUWF(FM) Pensacola FL
*KISU-FM Pocatello ID
KPND(FM) Sandpoint ID
WTTS(FM) Bloomington IN
KACY(FM) Arkansas City KS
*WNKU(FM) Highland Heights KY
*WUKY(FM) Lexington KY
*WFPK(FM) Louisville KY
*KSLU(FM) Hammond LA
KROK(FM) South Fort Polk LA
WXRV(FM) Haverhill MA
WRSI(FM) Turners Falls MA
WUFK(FM) Fort Kent ME
*WLNZ(FM) Lansing MI
WGVY(FM) Cambridge MN
*KUMD-FM Duluth MN
WGVZ(FM) Eden Prairie MN
*WTIP(FM) Grand Marais MN
WGVX(FM) Lakeville MN
*KCMP(FM) Northfield MN
*KMSE(FM) Rochester MN
*KSRQ(FM) Thief River Falls MN
KZPL(FM) Lee's Summit MO
*KTBG(FM) Warrensburg MO
*WUSM-FM Hattiesburg MS
KMMS-FM Bozeman MT
KDTR(FM) Florence MT
*WGWG(FM) Boiling Springs NC
WUIN(FM) Carolina Beach NC
*WSGE(FM) Dallas NC
WVOD(FM) Manteo NC
*WNCW(FM) Spindale NC
WLKC(FM) Campton NH
WMWV(FM) Conway NH
*WBJB-FM Lincroft NJ
KBAC(FM) Las Vegas NM
KTAO(FM) Taos NM
*WGFR(FM) Glens Falls NY
*WFUV(FM) New York NY
*WAPS(FM) Akron OH
*WDPS(FM) Dayton OH
*WYSO(FM) Yellow Springs OH
*KRSC-FM Claremore OK
*KSMF(FM) Ashland OR
*KSKF(FM) Klamath Falls OR
KINK(FM) Portland OR
KSYD(FM) Reedsport OR
*WYEP-FM Pittsburgh PA
*KSDJ(FM) Brookings SD
KSQY(FM) Deadwood SD
*WUTC(FM) Chattanooga TN
WRLT(FM) Franklin TN
WKVL-FM Loudon TN
KEEP(FM) Bandera TX
KFAN-FM Johnson City TX
*KSYM-FM San Antonio TX
*WNRN(FM) Charlottesville VA
WSRV(FM) Deltaville VA
*WVRU(FM) Radford VA

WTYD(FM) West Point VA
WDOT(FM) Danville VT
WEBK(FM) Killington VT
WRSY(FM) Marlboro VT
WNCS(FM) Montpelier VT
*WNUB-FM Northfield VT
*KGHP(FM) Gig Harbor WA
KMTT(FM) Tacoma WA
*WUWM(FM) Milwaukee WI
*KBUW(FM) Buffalo WY
*KUWC(FM) Casper WY

Underground

*WZBC(FM) Newton MA

Urban Contemporary

WANA(AM) Anniston AL
WDLT-FM Chickasaw AL
WJJN(FM) Columbia AL
WQZZ(FM) Eutaw AL
WJLD(AM) Fairfield AL
WSBM(AM) Florence AL
WAGH(FM) Fort Mitchell AL
WMGJ(AM) Gadsden AL
WKXN(FM) Greenville AL
WHOG(AM) Hobson City AL
WLOR(AM) Huntsville AL
WJUS(AM) Marion AL
WBLX-FM Mobile AL
WEUP-FM Moulton AL
WJAM-FM Orrville AL
WZMG(FM) Pepperell AL
WKXK(FM) Pine Hill AL
WBFZ(FM) Selma AL
WZHT(FM) Troy AL
WZZA(AM) Tuscumbia AL
WBHK(FM) Warrior AL
WJWZ(FM) Wetumpka AL
WSLY(FM) York AL
*KSWH(FM) Arkadelphia AR
KMGC(AM) Camden AR
KMLK(FM) El Dorado AR
KAMJ-FM Gosnell AR
KAKJ(FM) Marianna AR
KIPR(FM) Pine Bluff AR
*KUAP(FM) Pine Bluff AR
KZYP(FM) Pine Bluff AR
KTOY(FM) Texarkana AR
KKFR(FM) Glendale AZ
KLJZ(FM) Yuma AZ
KNGY(FM) Alameda CA
KJLH(FM) Compton CA
*KCRH(FM) Hayward CA
KKUU(FM) Indio CA
KHDV(FM) King City CA
KHHT(FM) Los Angeles CA
KKBT(FM) Los Angeles CA
*KSFH(FM) Mountain View CA
KDAI(FM) Ontario CA
KDAY(FM) Redondo Beach CA
KBMB(FM) Sacramento CA
KDON-FM Salinas CA
KEXA(FM) Salinas CA
KYLD(FM) San Francisco CA
*KSJS(FM) San Jose CA
KWYL(FM) South Lake Tahoe CA
*KSAK(FM) Walnut CA
*KASF(FM) Alamosa CO
KIBT(FM) Fountain CO
*WQTQ(FM) Hartford CT
WKND(FM) Manchester CT
WYBC-FM New Haven CT
*WECS(FM) Willimantic CT
WHUR-FM Washington DC
WKYS(FM) Washington DC
WHJX(FM) Baldwin FL
WBTP(FM) Clearwater FL
WHQT(FM) Coral Gables FL
WVCG(FM) Coral Gables FL
WHNR(AM) Cypress Gardens FL
WCFB(FM) Daytona Beach FL
*WJFP(FM) Fort Pierce FL
WJBT(FM) Green Cove Springs FL
WRRX(FM) Gulf Breeze FL

WJBW-FM Jupiter FL
WRNE(AM) Pensacola FL
WEBZ(FM) Port St. Joe FL
WRXB(AM) Saint Petersburg Beach FL
WBZE(AM) Tallahassee FL
WHBX(FM) Tallahassee FL
WTMG(FM) Williston FL
*WPRK(FM) Winter Park FL
WJIZ-FM Albany GA
WFFM(FM) Ashburn GA
WVEE(FM) Atlanta GA
WFXA-FM Augusta GA
WSOL-FM Brunswick GA
WWLD(FM) Cairo GA
WQVE(FM) Camilla GA
WFXE(FM) Columbus GA
WQMJ(FM) Forsyth GA
WIBB-FM Fort Valley GA
WFOX(FM) Gainesville GA
WOAH(FM) Glennville GA
WFXM(FM) Gordon GA
WHTA(FM) Hampton GA
WVKX(FM) Irwinton GA
WALR-FM La Grange GA
WAMJ(FM) Mableton GA
WLZN(FM) Macon GA
WPRW-FM Martinez GA
WBGA(FM) Saint Simons Island GA
WEAS-FM Savannah GA
WQBT(FM) Savannah GA
WHLJ(FM) Statenville GA
WRXZ(FM) Sylvester GA
WZBN(FM) Sylvester GA
WGOV(AM) Valdosta GA
WRBV(FM) Warner Robins GA
WAKB(FM) Wrens GA
KUAM-FM Hagatna GU
KZGZ(FM) Hagatna GU
*KALA(FM) Davenport IA
*KJMC(FM) Des Moines IA
KATZ-FM Alton IL
WKRO(AM) Cairo IL
*WPCD(FM) Champaign IL
*WKKC(FM) Chicago IL
*WMBI(AM) Chicago IL
WDZ(AM) Decatur IL
*WIUS(FM) Macomb IL
WCZQ(FM) Monticello IL
WHTS(FM) Rock Island IL
WEOA(AM) Evansville IN
*WBDG(FM) Indianapolis IN
WHHH(FM) Indianapolis IN
WGZB-FM Lanesville IN
*WISU(FM) Terre Haute IN
*KSDB-FM Manhattan KS
*KYWA(FM) Wichita KS
WIZF(FM) Erlanger KY
WMJM(FM) Jeffersontown KY
WLOU(AM) Louisville KY
WBTF(FM) Midway KY
WDXR(AM) Paducah KY
WUBT(FM) Russellville KY
KEDG(FM) Alexandria LA
KJMG(FM) Bastrop LA
KRVV(FM) Bastrop LA
KBZE(FM) Berwick LA
KDKS-FM Blanchard LA
KBCE(FM) Boyce LA
KTSR(FM) De Quincy LA
KNOU(FM) Empire LA
KDDK(FM) Franklin LA
*KGRM(FM) Grambling LA
KBTT(FM) Haughton LA
KTGV(FM) Jonesville LA
WEMX(FM) Kentwood LA
KJCB(AM) Lafayette LA
KRRQ(FM) Lafayette LA
KJMH(FM) Lake Arthur LA
KZWA(FM) Moss Bluff LA
*KNWD(FM) Natchitoches LA
WQUE-FM New Orleans LA
*WWOZ(FM) New Orleans LA
WYLD(FM) New Orleans LA
KQXL-FM New Roads LA
KMJJ-FM Shreveport LA
KVMA-FM Shreveport LA
KBYO(AM) Tallulah LA

*WRBB(FM) Boston MA
WBOT(FM) Brockton MA
*WOZQ(FM) Northampton MA
*WMHC(FM) South Hadley MA
WERQ-FM Baltimore MD
WOCQ(FM) Berlin MD
WMMJ(FM) Bethesda MD
WWIN-FM Glen Burnie MD
WSBY-FM Salisbury MD
WRED(FM) Saco ME
WDMK(FM) Detroit MI
WJLB(FM) Detroit MI
WMXD(FM) Detroit MI
WQHH(FM) Dewitt MI
WXLA(AM) Dimondale MI
WDZZ-FM Flint MI
WJNZ(AM) Kentwood MI
WHTD(FM) Mount Clemens MI
WSNX-FM Muskegon MI
WNWN(AM) Portage MI
WTLZ(FM) Saginaw MI
WOWE(FM) Vassar MI
*KMOJ(FM) Minneapolis MN
KDMO(AM) Carthage MO
*KJLU(FM) Jefferson City MO
KPRS(FM) Kansas City MO
KMJK(FM) Lexington MO
WESE(FM) Baldwyn MS
WRJH(FM) Brandon MS
WAJV(FM) Brooksville MS
WMGO(FM) Canton MS
WCLD-FM Cleveland MS
WWKZ(FM) Columbus MS
WJXM(FM) De Kalb MS
WJKX(FM) Ellisville MS
WNIX(FM) Greenville MS
WJMG(FM) Hattiesburg MS
WKRA-FM Holly Springs MS
WJMI(FM) Jackson MS
*WMPR(FM) Jackson MS
WBAD(FM) Leland MS
WJZD(FM) Long Beach MS
*WPRL(FM) Lorman MS
WKXI-FM Magee MS
WZLD(FM) Petal MS
WMSU(FM) Starkville MS
WMXU(FM) Starkville MS
WGNG(FM) Tchula MS
WZKS(FM) Union MS
WJXN-FM Utica MS
KMZK(AM) Billings MT
KLSK(FM) Great Falls MT
WVOE(AM) Chadbourn NC
WPEG(FM) Concord NC
WFXC(FM) Durham NC
WGBT(FM) Eden NC
*WRVS-FM Elizabeth City NC
WTRG(FM) Gaston NC
WKXS(FM) Leland NC
WIKS(FM) New Bern NC
WPWZ(FM) Pinetops NC
WJMH(FM) Reidsville NC
WRSV(FM) Rocky Mount NC
WUKS(FM) Saint Pauls NC
WFXK(FM) Tarboro NC
WSMY(AM) Weldon NC
WENC(AM) Whiteville NC
WZFX(FM) Whiteville NC
WMNX(FM) Wilmington NC
WAAA(AM) Winston-Salem NC
KBLR-FM Blair NE
*KZUM(FM) Lincoln NE
*WSPS(FM) Concord NH
*WNEC-FM Henniker NH
*WDBK(FM) Blackwood NJ
WJKS(FM) Canton NJ
WIMG(AM) Ewing NJ
WTTH(FM) Margate City NJ
WRNB(FM) Pennsauken NJ
WDTH(FM) Wildwood Crest NJ
*KCEP(FM) Las Vegas NV
KVGS(FM) Laughlin NV
*WCDB(FM) Albany NY
WPHR(FM) Auburn NY
*WCWP(FM) Brookville NY
WWWS(AM) Buffalo NY
WBLK(FM) Depew NY

*WRCU-FM Hamilton NY
*WVHC(FM) Herkimer NY
*WICB(FM) Ithaca NY
WBLS(FM) New York NY
WWPR-FM New York NY
*WOSS(FM) Ossining NY
*WNYO(FM) Oswego NY
WDKX(FM) Rochester NY
*WFNP(FM) Rosendale NY
*WPNR-FM Utica NY
WAJZ(FM) Voorheesville NY
WENZ(FM) Cleveland OH
WZAK(FM) Cleveland OH
WCKX(FM) Columbus OH
WIMX(FM) Gibsonburg OH
WRBP(FM) Hubbard OH
WLJM(AM) Lima OH
WRTK(AM) Niles OH
WJTB(AM) North Ridgeville OH
WDHT(FM) Springfield OH
WDIG(AM) Steubenville OH
WJUC(FM) Swanton OH
WROU-FM West Carrollton OH
*WCSU-FM Wilberforce OH
KVSP(FM) Anadarko OK
KJMM(FM) Bixby OK
*KALU(FM) Langston OK
KJMZ(FM) Lawton OK
KRMP(AM) Oklahoma City OK
KGTO(AM) Tulsa OK
*KBVR(FM) Corvallis OR
*KWVA(FM) Eugene OR
WAMO-FM Beaver Falls PA
WJJJ(FM) Greensburg PA
WTCY(AM) Harrisburg PA
WPPZ-FM Jenkintown PA
WLAN(AM) Lancaster PA
*WWLU(FM) Lincoln University PA
WAMO(AM) Millvale PA
WHAT(AM) Philadelphia PA
WUSL(FM) Philadelphia PA
WKVB(FM) Port Matilda PA
*WUSR(FM) Scranton PA
*WRLC(FM) Williamsport PA
WBRU(FM) Providence RI
*WJMF(FM) Smithfield RI
WJMZ-FM Anderson SC
WIIZ(FM) Blackville SC
WYNN-FM Florence SC
WLVH(FM) Hardeeville SC
*WLGI(FM) Hemingway SC
WXST(FM) Hollywood SC
WJNI(FM) Ladson SC
WCMG(FM) Latta SC
WLXC(FM) Lexington SC
WHXT(FM) Orangeburg SC
WPJK(AM) Orangeburg SC
*WSSB-FM Orangeburg SC
WDAI(FM) Pawley's Island SC
WPAL-FM Ridgeville SC
WASC(AM) Spartanburg SC
WWWZ(FM) Summerville SC
WWDM(FM) Sumter SC
WXBT(FM) West Columbia SC
WNOO(AM) Chattanooga TN
WFKX(FM) Henderson TN
WQQK(FM) Hendersonville TN
WKGN(AM) Knoxville TN
*WFMQ(FM) Lebanon TN
KJMS(FM) Memphis TN
WDIA(AM) Memphis TN
WHRK(FM) Memphis TN
WEUZ(FM) Minor Hill TN
WJTT(FM) Red Bank TN
*KAZI-FM Austin TX
KTCX(FM) Beaumont TX
KHPT(FM) Conroe TX
KSSM(FM) Copperas Cove TX
KBFB(FM) Dallas TX
KKDA-FM Dallas TX
KEPS(AM) Eagle Pass TX
KSOC(FM) Gainesville TX
KVJM(FM) Hearne TX
KCOH(AM) Houston TX
KMJQ(FM) Houston TX
KIIZ-FM Killeen TX
*KBWC(FM) Marshall TX

Broadcasting & Cable Yearbook 2006
D-727

Programming on Radio Stations in the U.S.

KPTY(FM) Missouri City TX
KZRB(FM) New Boston TX
KSJL(AM) Somerset TX
KZEY(AM) Tyler TX
KBLZ(FM) Winona TX
*KRDC-FM Saint George UT
*WNRN(FM) Charlottesville VA
WUVA(FM) Charlottesville VA
WVBE-FM Lynchburg VA
WCDX(FM) Mechanicsville VA
WKUS(FM) Norfolk VA
*WNSB(FM) Norfolk VA
WOWI(FM) Norfolk VA
WKJM(FM) Petersburg VA
WBTJ(FM) Richmond VA
WKJS(FM) Richmond VA
WVBE(FM) Roanoke VA
WTOY(AM) Salem VA
WQOK(FM) South Boston VA
WWHV(FM) Virginia Beach VA
WSTA(AM) Charlotte Amalie VI
WVJZ(FM) Charlotte Amalie VI
WWKS(FM) Cruz Bay VI
WWKS(FM) Cruz Bay VI
*WVTC(FM) Randolph Center VT
KYIZ(AM) Renton WA
KBBD(FM) Spokane WA
KYNR(AM) Toppenish WA
KBMS(AM) Vancouver WA
KHHK(FM) Yakima WA
WJMR-FM Menomonee Falls WI
WNOV(AM) Milwaukee WI
WLYD(FM) Sturgeon Bay WI

Variety/Diverse

*KNBA(FM) Anchorage AK
*KBRW(AM) Barrow AK
*KYUK(AM) Bethel AK
*KCUK(FM) Chevak AK
KZPA(AM) Fort Yukon AK
*KEUL(FM) Girdwood AK
*KMJG(FM) Homer AK
*KWJG(FM) Kasilof AK
*KDLL(FM) Kenai AK
*KCAW(FM) Sitka AK
WRVX(FM) Eufaula AL
*WLRH(FM) Huntsville AL
*WLJS-FM Jacksonville AL
WHLW(FM) Luverne AL
KBVA(FM) Bella Vista AR
KAVH(FM) Eudora AR
KURM(AM) Rogers AR
*KXRJ(FM) Russellville AR
KUOA(AM) Siloam Springs AR
*KRMH(FM) Red Mesa AZ
KSED(FM) Sedona AZ
*KXCI(FM) Tucson AZ
KBSZ(AM) Wickenburg AZ
*KAWC(AM) Yuma AZ
*KHSU-FM Arcata CA
KAHI(AM) Auburn CA
*KISL(FM) Avalon CA
KWRM(AM) Corona CA
*KKUP(FM) Cupertino CA
*KDVS(FM) Davis CA
*KFCF(FM) Fresno CA
KTDE(FM) Gualala CA
*KCRH(FM) Hayward CA

KTYM(AM) Inglewood CA
*KFJC(FM) Los Altos CA
*KPFK(FM) Los Angeles CA
KAKX(FM) Mendocino CA
KVMR(FM) Nevada City CA
*KCSN(FM) Northridge CA
*KZYX(FM) Philo CA
*KWMR(FM) Point Reyes Station CA
KMRJ(FM) Rancho Mirage CA
*KFPR(FM) Redding CA
*KYDS(FM) Sacramento CA
*KSRH(FM) San Rafael CA
*KCSB-FM Santa Barbara CA
*KFER(FM) Santa Cruz CA
*KSVY(FM) Sonoma CA
*KRZA(FM) Alamosa CO
*KGNU-FM Boulder CO
*KEPC(FM) Colorado Springs CO
*KRFC(FM) Fort Collins CO
*KWSB-FM Gunnison CO
*KUTE(FM) Ignacio CO
*KOTO(FM) Telluride CO
KJAC(FM) Timnath CO
*WVOF(FM) Fairfield CT
*WESU(FM) Middletown CT
*WCNI(FM) New London CT
*WBVC(FM) Pomfret CT
*WWEB(FM) Wallingford CT
*WWUH(FM) West Hartford CT
*WWPT(FM) Westport CT
WBGC(AM) Chipley FL
*WRGP(FM) Homestead FL
WIOJ(AM) Jacksonville Beach FL
WWFE(AM) Miami FL
WVLG(AM) Wildwood FL
*WRFG(FM) Atlanta GA
*WBCX(FM) Gainesville GA
WYYZ(AM) Jasper GA
WBKZ(AM) Jefferson GA
*WHCJ(FM) Savannah GA
WZAT(FM) Savannah GA
*WPLH(FM) Tifton GA
*KURE(FM) Ames IA
*KHOE(FM) Fairfield IA
KOKX-FM Keokuk IA
*KRNL-FM Mount Vernon IA
KDLS(AM) Perry IA
KDLS-FM Perry IA
*KLHS-FM Lewiston ID
*KUOI-FM Moscow ID
WKIE(FM) Arlington Heights IL
*WEFT(FM) Champaign IL
*WEIU(FM) Charleston IL
*WIIT(FM) Chicago IL
*WKKC(FM) Chicago IL
*WLUW(FM) Chicago IL
*WRTE(FM) Chicago IL
WSBC(AM) Chicago IL
*WZRD(FM) Chicago IL
WCFJ(AM) Chicago Heights IL
*WVKC(FM) Galesburg IL
WDUK(FM) Havana IL
*WHSD(FM) Hinsdale IL
*WLTL(FM) La Grange IL
*WAES(FM) Lincolnshire IL
WRZA(FM) Park Forest IL
*WMTH(FM) Park Ridge IL
*WFWR(FM) Attica IN
*WNDY(FM) Crawfordsville IN

*WPSR(FM) Evansville IN
WTRE(AM) Greensburg IN
*WHCI(FM) Hartford City IN
*WJEL(FM) Indianapolis IN
WAWK(AM) Kendallville IN
*WBRO(FM) Marengo IN
*WECI(FM) Richmond IN
*KVCO(FM) Concordia KS
*KONQ(FM) Dodge City KS
*KZAN(FM) Hays KS
*KBCU(FM) North Newton KS
KQMA-FM Phillipsburg KS
WHBN(AM) Harrodsburg KY
KBON(FM) Mamou LA
KKAY(AM) White Castle LA
*WMUA(FM) Amherst MA
*WMUA(FM) Amherst MA
WBMX(FM) Boston MA
*WMBR(FM) Cambridge MA
*WXRB(FM) Dudley MA
*WWTA(FM) Marion MA
*WAVM(FM) Maynard MA
*WMFO(FM) Medford MA
WMRC(AM) Milford MA
WNBP(AM) Newburyport MA
WNTN(AM) Newton MA
*WMHC(FM) South Hadley MA
*WSCB(FM) Springfield MA
*WZLY(FM) Wellesley MA
WQSR(FM) Baltimore MD
*WHFC(FM) Bel Air MD
*WMUC-FM College Park MD
*WUMF-FM Farmington ME
*WXOU(FM) Auburn Hills MI
*WHFR(FM) Dearborn MI
*WRCJ-FM Detroit MI
*WMTU-FM Houghton MI
*WIDR(FM) Kalamazoo MI
*WYDM(FM) Monroe MI
*WOAS(FM) Ontonagon MI
*WBLD(FM) Orchard Lake MI
*WLSO(FM) Sault Ste. Marie MI
*WYCE(FM) Wyoming MI
WYGR(AM) Wyoming MI
KOWZ-FM Blooming Prairie MN
WELY(AM) Ely MN
WELY-FM Ely MN
*WTIP(FM) Grand Marais MN
*KAXE(FM) Grand Rapids MN
*KVSC(FM) Saint Cloud MN
WMGT(AM) Stillwater MN
*KSMR(FM) Winona MN
*KYMC(AM) Ballwin MO
KRMO(AM) Cassville MO
*KLJC(FM) Kansas City MO
KCXL(AM) Liberty MO
*KGSP(FM) Parkville MO
*WUSM-FM Hattiesburg MS
WAPF(AM) McComb MS
*KGVA(FM) Fort Belknap Agency MT
*KGPR(FM) Great Falls MT
*WSGE(FM) Dallas NC
*WRVS-FM Elizabeth City NC
*WUAW(FM) Erwin NC
*WQFS(FM) Greensboro NC
WHKP(AM) Hendersonville NC
*WYQS(FM) Mars Hill NC
WAME(AM) Statesville NC
*WHYC(FM) Swanquarter NC

*KDSU(FM) Fargo ND
*KDCV-FM Blair NE
*WPEA(FM) Exeter NH
*WBGD(FM) Brick Township NJ
WSNJ(AM) Bridgeton NJ
*WRRC(FM) Lawrenceville NJ
WMVB(AM) Millville NJ
*WRSU-FM New Brunswick NJ
*WLFR(FM) Pomona NJ
*WWPH(FM) Princeton Junction NJ
KDAZ(AM) Albuquerque NM
*KRUX(FM) Las Cruces NM
KWRP(FM) Pecos NM
KRSI(FM) Garapan-Saipan NP
*KUNV(FM) Las Vegas NV
*WALF(FM) Alfred NY
*WHRW(FM) Binghamton NY
*WXLH(FM) Blue Mountain Lake NY
*WSLU(FM) Canton NY
*WHCL-FM Clinton NY
*WSUC-FM Cortland NY
*WXXE(FM) Fenner NY
*WCVF-FM Fredonia NY
WGBB(AM) Freeport NY
*WHPC(FM) Garden City NY
*WRHU(FM) Hempstead NY
WJGK(AM) Kingston NY
*WSHR(FM) Lake Ronkonkoma NY
*WSLO(FM) Malone NY
*WBAI(FM) New York NY
*WKCR-FM New York NY
*WXLG(FM) North Creek NY
*WXLU(FM) Peru NY
*WAIH(FM) Potsdam NY
*WSLL(FM) Saranac Lake NY
WSPQ(AM) Springville NY
WBGJ(FM) Sylvan Beach NY
*WRPI(FM) Troy NY
*WSLJ(FM) Watertown NY
*WAPS(FM) Akron OH
*WOBO(FM) Batavia OH
*WBGU(FM) Bowling Green OH
*WRUW-FM Cleveland OH
*WCBE(FM) Columbus OH
WKTX(AM) Cortland OH
*WUDR(FM) Dayton OH
*WWSU(FM) Dayton OH
*WKCO(FM) Gambier OH
*WDUB(FM) Granville OH
WMVO(AM) Mount Vernon OH
KIHN(AM) Hugo OK
*KSRG(FM) Ashland OR
KMHS(AM) Coos Bay OR
*KLFO(FM) Florence OR
*KEOL(FM) La Grande OR
*KWSO(FM) Warm Springs OR
*WJCS(FM) Allentown PA
WGPA(AM) Bethlehem PA
*WLVR(FM) Bethlehem PA
WHLM(AM) Bloomsburg PA
WZUM(AM) Carnegie PA
*WDNR(FM) Chester PA
*WJRH(FM) Easton PA
*WERG(FM) Erie PA
*WIUP-FM Indiana PA
WKHB(AM) Irwin PA
WKFB(AM) Jeannette PA
*WFNM(FM) Lancaster PA
WEDO(AM) McKeesport PA

*WKDU(FM) Philadelphia PA
WNWR(AM) Philadelphia PA
WRAW(AM) Reading PA
*WKPS(FM) State College PA
WMBS(AM) Uniontown PA
WOQI(AM) Adjuntas PR
WCGB(AM) Juana Diaz PR
WDEP(AM) Ponce PR
WJIT(AM) Sabana PR
WEGA(AM) Vega Baja PR
*WUSC-FM Columbia SC
WLBG(AM) Laurens SC
*KLND(FM) Little Eagle SD
*WAPX-FM Clarksville TN
WHHM-FM Henderson TN
*WCSK(FM) Kingsport TN
WYGO(FM) Madisonville TN
*WEVL(FM) Memphis TN
*WUTS(FM) Sewanee TN
WSGI(AM) Springfield TN
KVLF(AM) Alpine TX
KILE(AM) Bellaire TX
*KNON(FM) Dallas TX
*KOOP(FM) Hornsby TX
KRBA(AM) Lufkin TX
*KEOM(FM) Mesquite TX
KNBT(FM) New Braunfels TX
KREH(AM) Pecan Grove TX
KRTX(AM) Rosenberg-Richmond TX
KCFM(FM) Levan UT
*KZMU(FM) Moab UT
*KPGR(FM) Pleasant Grove UT
*WTJU(FM) Charlottesville VA
*WVTW(FM) Charlottesville VA
WDUF(AM) Duffield VA
*WHOV(FM) Hampton VA
WCLM(AM) Highland Springs VA
*WWMC(FM) Lynchburg VA
*WVTR(FM) Marion VA
*WIUV(FM) Castleton VT
*KBLD(FM) Kennewick WA
KBRD(AM) Lacey WA
KSUH(AM) Puyallup WA
KZML(FM) Quincy WA
*WLFM(FM) Appleton WI
*WBCR-FM Beloit WI
WHIT-FM De Forest WI
*WORT(FM) Madison WI
WOCO(AM) Oconto WI
*WXPR(FM) Rhinelander WI
*WRFW(FM) River Falls WI
*WCCX(FM) Waukesha WI
WDLS(AM) Wisconsin Dells WI
WQWV(FM) Fisher WV
*WRSG(FM) Middlebourne WV
WKWK-FM Wheeling WV
WVVV(FM) Williamstown WV
*KWRR(FM) Ethete WY

Vietnamese

KZSJ(AM) San Martin CA
KVNR(AM) Santa Ana CA
KVVN(FM) Santa Clara CA
KJOJ(AM) Conroe TX
KYND(AM) Cypress TX

Programming on Radio Stations in Canada

Adult Contemp

CHFM-FM Calgary AB
CIQX-FM Calgary AB
CKMX(AM) Calgary AB
CHMN-FM Canmore AB
CKRA-FM Edmonton AB
CJYR(AM) Edson AB
*CKRP-FM Falher AB
CFGP-FM Grande Prairie AB
CIYR-FM Hinton AB
CFRV-FM Lethbridge AB
CFMY-FM Medicine Hat AB
CKKX-FM Peace River AB
CHUB-FM Red Deer AB
CIZZ-FM Red Deer AB
CFMG-FM Saint Albert AB
CKWY-FM Wainwright AB
CKGO-FM-1 Boston Bar BC
CFLD(AM) Burns Lake BC
CKSR-FM Chilliwack BC
CHNL-1(AM) Clearwater BC
CFCP-FM Courtenay BC
CKLR-FM Courtenay BC
CJSU-FM Duncan BC
CIEG-FM Egmont BC
CISC-FM Gibsons BC
CFSR-FM Hope BC
CHNL(AM) Kamloops BC
CKBZ-FM Kamloops BC
CHSU-FM Kelowna BC
CILK-FM Kelowna BC
CJNL(AM) Merritt BC
CKWV-FM Nanaimo BC
CKZX-FM New Denver BC
CJOR(AM) Osoyoos BC
CIBH-FM Parksville BC
CISP-FM Pemberton BC
CIPN-FM Pender Harbour BC
CIGV-FM Penticton BC
CJAV(AM) Port Alberni BC
CFNI(AM) Port Hardy BC
CIOR(AM) Princeton BC
CKXR(AM) Salmon Arm BC
CFBV(AM) Smithers BC
CISQ-FM Squamish BC
CJAT-FM Trail BC
CHQM-FM Vancouver BC
CKLG-FM Vancouver BC
CKZZ-FM Vancouver BC
CICF-FM Vernon BC
CKIZ-FM Vernon BC
CIOC-FM Victoria BC
CISW-FM Whistler BC
CKLF-FM Brandon MB
CKDM(AM) Dauphin MB
CILT-FM Steinbach MB
CJAR(AM) The Pas MB
CHTM(AM) Thompson MB
CJEL-FM Winkler MB
CFWM-FM Winnipeg MB
CHNR-FM Winnipeg MB
CKY-FM Winnipeg MB
CKBC-FM Bathurst NB
CKNB(AM) Campbellton NB
CJVA(AM) Caraquet NB
CJEM-FM Edmundston NB
CJPN-FM Fredericton NB
CIKX-FM Grand Falls NB
CKMV-FM Grand Falls NB
CFAN-FM Miramichi City NB
CFQM-FM Moncton NB
CIOK-FM Saint John NB
CJCW(AM) Sussex NB
CJCJ-FM Woodstock NB
CFOZ-FM Argentia NF
CJOZ-FM Bonavista Bay NF
CJKK-FM Clarenville NF
CKOZ-FM Corner Brook NF
CFLN(AM) Goose Bay NF
CIFX-FM Lewisporte NF
CIOZ-FM Marystown NF

CHOS-FM Rattling Brook NF
CKSS-FM Red Rocks NF
CHOZ-FM Saint John's NF
CKSJ-FM Saint John's NF
VOCM(AM) Saint John's NF
CIOS-FM Stephenville NF
CJLS-FM-1 Barrington NS
CIOO-FM Halifax NS
CKWM-FM Kentville NS
CKEC(AM) New Glasgow NS
CJLS-FM-2 New Tusket NS
CIGO-FM Port Hawkesbury NS
CBI-FM Sydney NS
CKPE-FM Sydney NS
CKTO-FM Truro NS
CJLS-FM Yarmouth NS
CJCD-FM-1 Hay River NT
CJCD-FM Yellowknife NT
CBQR-FM Rankin Inlet NU
CHMS-FM Bancroft ON
CHAY-FM Barrie ON
CIQB-FM Barrie ON
CIGL-FM Belleville ON
CJOJ-FM Belleville ON
CFBG-FM Bracebridge ON
CKPC-FM Brantford ON
CFJR-FM Brockville ON
CJPT-FM Brockville ON
CJXY-FM Burlington ON
CJDV-FM Cambridge ON
CKSY-FM Chatham ON
CHUC(AM) Cobourg ON
CKSG-FM Cobourg ON
CHPB-FM Cochrane ON
CKCB-FM Collingwood ON
CFLG-FM Cornwall ON
CKNR-FM Elliot Lake ON
CJBB-FM Englehart ON
CFOB-FM Fort Frances ON
CIMJ-FM Guelph ON
CKLH-FM Hamilton ON
CHPR-FM Hawkesbury ON
CHOH-FM Hearst ON
*CINN-FM Hearst ON
CFBK-FM Huntsville ON
CKGN-FM Kapuskasing ON
CJRL-FM Kenora ON
CFLY-FM Kingston ON
CJKL-FM Kirkland Lake ON
CKWR-FM Kitchener ON
CHYR-FM Leamington ON
CKLY-FM Lindsay (city of Kawartha Lakes) ON
CFPL(AM) London ON
CIQM-FM London ON
CFNO-FM Marathon ON
CKDX-FM Newmarket ON
CFLZ-FM Niagara Falls ON
CHUR-FM North Bay ON
CICX-FM Orillia ON
CISS-FM Ottawa ON
CJMJ-FM Ottawa ON
CKLP-FM Parry Sound ON
*CFRH-FM Penetanguishene ON
CHMY-FM Renfrew ON
CHSC(AM) Saint Catharines ON
CFGX-FM Sarnia ON
CHAS-FM Sault Ste. Marie ON
CHCD-FM Simcoe ON
CHGK-FM Stratford ON
CFSF-FM Sturgeon Falls ON
CHYC-FM Sudbury ON
CJMX-FM Sudbury ON
CJUK-FM Thunder Bay ON
CJUK-FM Thunder Bay ON
CKPR(AM) Thunder Bay ON
CHYK-FM Timmins ON
CHFI-FM Toronto ON
CHUM-FM Toronto ON
CJWA-FM Wawa ON
CIDR-FM Windsor ON
CKNX-FM Wingham ON

CFVM-FM Amqui PQ
CJAN-FM Asbestos PQ
CHLC-FM Baie Comeau PQ
CIEU-FM Carleton PQ
CHAI-FM Chateauguay PQ
CBJ-FM Chicoutimi PQ
CFVD-FM Degelis PQ
CHRD-FM Drummondville PQ
CJDM-FM Drummondville PQ
CFMF-FM Fermont PQ
CFRP(AM) Forestville PQ
*CFTH-FM-1 Harrington Harbour PQ
*CKRK-FM Kahnawake PQ
CFLM(AM) La Tuque PQ
CJLA-FM Lachute PQ
CFGL-FM Laval PQ
CFOM-FM Levis PQ
CHAA-FM Longueuil PQ
CHGA-FM Maniwaki PQ
CFLO-FM Mont-Laurier PQ
CFEL-FM Montmagny PQ
CITE-FM Montreal PQ
CJFM-FM Montreal PQ
CHNC(AM) New Carlisle PQ
CHIK-FM Quebec PQ
*CION-FM Quebec PQ
CITF-FM Quebec PQ
CJEC-FM Quebec PQ
CJMF-FM Quebec PQ
*CKRL-FM Quebec PQ
CJBR-FM Rimouski PQ
CKMN-FM Rimouski-Mont Joli PQ
CIEL-FM Riviere du Loup PQ
CHOA-FM Rouyn-Noranda PQ
CJMM-FM Rouyn-Noranda PQ
CJAB-FM Saguenay PQ
CJAS-FM Saint Augustin PQ
CKRB-FM Saint Georges-de-Beauce PQ
CFZZ-FM Saint Jean-Iberville PQ
CIME-FM Saint Jerome PQ
CHEQ-FM Sainte-Marie-de-Beauce PQ
CKCN-FM Sept-Iles PQ
CKSM(AM) Shawinigan PQ
CFGE-FM Sherbrooke PQ
CITE-FM-1 Sherbrooke PQ
CKLD-FM Thetford Mines PQ
CJEB-FM Trois Rivieres PQ
CKOD-FM Valleyfield PQ
CFDA-FM Victoriaville PQ
CKVM-FM Ville-Marie PQ
CFYM(AM) Kindersley SK
CFNK-FM Pinehouse Lake SK
CKBI(AM) Prince Albert SK
CHMX-FM Regina SK
CIZL-FM Regina SK
CJYM(AM) Rosetown SK
CFMC-FM Saskatoon SK
CJMK-FM Saskatoon SK
CFGW-FM Yorkton SK
CIAY-FM Whitehorse YT

Agriculture

CFAM(AM) Altona MB
CJRB-FM Boissevain MB
CKRM(AM) Regina SK

Album-Oriented Rock

CKLZ-FM Kelowna BC
CJAR-FM The Pas MB
CHRE-FM Saint Catharines ON
CJMX-FM Sudbury ON
CJQQ-FM Timmins ON
CJEZ-FM Toronto ON
CHOI-FM Quebec PQ
CIZL-FM Regina SK

Alternative

*CJSW-FM Calgary AB
CJSR-FM Edmonton AB
CFEQ-FM Winnipeg MB
*CHMR-FM Saint John's NF
CKHZ-FM Halifax NS
*CIOI-FM Hamilton ON
CHRW-FM London ON
*CKDJ-FM Ottawa ON
CHRY-FM Toronto ON
*CKLN-FM Toronto ON
CIMI-FM Charlesbourg PQ
*CISM-FM Montreal PQ

American Indian

CHDH-FM Siksika AB
CHFN-FM Cape Croker (Neyaashiinigmiing) ON
CFNK-FM Pinehouse Lake SK

Beautiful Music

CBX-FM Edmonton AB
*CION-FM Quebec PQ

Big Band

CFEP-FM Eastern Passage NS

Black

CHRY-FM Toronto ON

Blues

*CBR-FM Calgary AB
*CHRW-FM London ON
CKLX-FM Montreal PQ

Chinese

CKER-FM Edmonton AB
CHMB(AM) Vancouver BC
CJVB(AM) Vancouver BC

Christian

CJSI-FM Calgary AB
CJCA(AM) Edmonton AB
CJRY-FM Edmonton AB
CJTS-FM Lethbridge AB
CJLT-FM Medicine Hat AB
CIAJ-FM Prince Rupert BC
CHVN-FM Winnipeg MB
CKJS(AM) Winnipeg MB
CJFY-FM Blackville NB
CIXN-FM Fredericton NB
CITA-FM Moncton NB
CKOE-FM Moncton NB
CINB-FM Saint John NB
CINU-FM Truro NS
CHPD-FM Aylmer ON
CJLF-FM Barrie ON
CKJJ-FM Belleville ON
CFWC-FM Brantford ON
*CJIV-FM Dryden ON
CJTW-FM Kitchener-Waterloo ON
CHJX-FM London ON
CJYE(AM) Oakville ON
CHRI-FM Ottawa ON
CKKK-FM Peterborough ON
CJTK-FM Sudbury ON
*CJOA-FM Thunder Bay ON
*CHIM-FM Timmins ON
CJFH-FM Woodstock ON
CHIC-FM Rouyn-Noranda PQ
CJOS-FM Caronport SK
CIOT-FM Nipawin SK

CIAY-FM Whitehorse YT

Classic Rock

CFGQ-FM Calgary AB
CKIS-FM Calgary AB
CFBR-FM Edmonton AB
CIRK-FM Edmonton AB
CKYX-FM Fort McMurray AB
CJXK-FM Grand Centre (Cold Lake) AB
CFRV-FM Lethbridge AB
CFDV-FM Red Deer AB
CJBZ-FM Taber AB
CKNL-FM Fort St. John BC
CFMI-FM New Westminster BC
CKDV-FM Prince George BC
CFNR-FM Terrace BC
CKX-FM Brandon MB
CHTM(AM) Thompson MB
CITI-FM Winnipeg MB
CFAI-FM Edmundston NB
CFRK-FM Fredericton NB
CIBX-FM Fredericton NB
CJMO-FM Moncton NB
CJYC-FM Saint John NB
CFOZ-FM Argentia NF
CJOZ-FM Bonavista Bay NF
CJKK-FM Clarenville NF
CKOZ-FM Corner Brook NF
CKXD-FM Gander NF
CKXG-FM Grand Falls-Windsor NF
CIOZ-FM Marystown NF
CHOS-FM Rattling Brook NF
CKSS-FM Red Rocks NF
CHOZ-FM Saint John's NF
VOCM-FM Saint John's NF
CIOS-FM Stephenville NF
CKBW-FM Bridgewater NS
CFRQ-FM Dartmouth NS
CKBW-FM-1 Liverpool NS
CKEC-FM New Glasgow NS
CKBW-FM-2 Shelburne NS
CJIJ-FM Sydney NS
CKIQ-FM Iqaluit NU
CFJB-FM Barrie ON
CJXY-FM Burlington ON
CKTI-FM Kettle Point ON
CFCA-FM Kitchener ON
CFRM-FM Little Current ON
CILQ-FM North York ON
*CKRZ-FM Ohsweken ON
CKGE-FM Oshawa ON
CHEZ-FM Ottawa ON
CKQB-FM Ottawa ON
CKWF-FM Peterborough ON
CKTG-FM Thunder Bay ON
CKDK-FM Woodstock ON
CFVM-FM Amqui PQ
CKAJ-FM Jonquiere PQ
CFOM-FM Levis PQ
CHOI-FM Quebec PQ
CJMF-FM Quebec PQ
CKIA-FM Quebec PQ
CFJO-FM Thetford Mines PQ
CHGO-FM Val d'Or PQ
CJNE-FM Nipawin SK
CFMM-FM Prince Albert SK
CFWF-FM Regina SK
CIZL-FM Regina SK
CKCK-FM Regina SK
CFET-FM Tagish YT
CHON-FM Whitehorse YT

Classical

*CBR-FM Calgary AB
CBX-FM Edmonton AB
CKUA(AM) Edmonton AB
*CKUA-FM Edmonton AB
*CBU(AM) Vancouver BC

Programming on Radio Stations in Canada

CBU-FM Vancouver BC
CBW-FM Winnipeg MB
*CBZ-FM Fredericton NB
CBA-FM Moncton NB
*CBN-FM Saint John's NF
*VOWR(AM) Saint John's NF
CBAX-FM Halifax NS
*CBH-FM Halifax NS
CFMX-FM Cobourg ON
*CBOQ-FM Ottawa ON
*CBOX-FM Ottawa ON
CIXK-FM Owen Sound ON
CBL-FM Toronto ON
CFMX-FM-1 Toronto ON
CJBC-FM Toronto ON
*CBE-FM Windsor ON
*CBJX-FM Chicoutimi PQ
CHLX-FM Gatineau PQ
CBF-FM Montreal PQ
CBM-FM Montreal PQ
CJPX-FM Montreal PQ
*CBVX-FM Quebec PQ
*CKRL-FM Quebec PQ
*CBRX-FM Rimouski PQ
CBF-FM-1 Trois Rivieres PQ
*CBK-FM Regina SK
*CBKS-FM Saskatoon SK

Comedy

CFHA-FM Saint John NB

Contemporary Hit/Top-40

CIBQ(AM) Brooks AB
CKNG-FM Edmonton AB
CJYR-FM Edson AB
CFRV-FM Lethbridge AB
CIZZ-FM Red Deer AB
CKRX-FM Fort Nelson BC
CKRV-FM Kamloops BC
CKTK-FM Kitimat BC
CKKN-FM Prince George BC
CHTK(AM) Prince Rupert BC
CKDM(AM) Dauphin MB
CJPG-FM Portage la Prairie MB
CICY-FM Selkirk MB
CHIQ-FM Winnipeg MB
CKMM-FM Winnipeg MB
CKLE-FM Bathurst NB
CKNB(AM) Campbellton NB
CJEM-FM Edmundston NB
CKMV-FM Grand Falls NB
CHWV-FM Saint John NB
CFOZ-FM Argentia NF
CJOZ-FM Bonavista Bay NF
CJKK-FM Clarenville NF
CKOZ-FM Corner Brook NF
CIFX-FM Lewisporte NF
CIOZ-FM Marystown NF
CHOS-FM Rattling Brook NF
CKSS-FM Red Rocks NF
CHOZ-FM Saint John's NF
CKIX-FM Saint John's NF
CIOS-FM Stephenville NF
CJFX-FM Antigonish NS
CKBW-FM Bridgewater NS
CKBW-FM-1 Liverpool NS
CKBW-FM-2 Shelburne NS
CJIJ-FM Sydney NS
CKDR-6(AM) Atikokan ON
CKMB-FM Barrie ON
CJOJ-FM Belleville ON
CKPC(AM) Brantford ON
CKDR(AM) Dryden ON
CKEY-FM Fort Erie ON
CKAP-FM Kapuskasing ON
CKBT-FM Kitchener-Waterloo ON
CHST-FM London ON
*CHMO(AM) Moosonee ON
CIDC-FM Orangeville ON
CHRI-FM Ottawa ON
CIHT-FM Ottawa ON
CIXK-FM Owen Sound ON
CKDR-5(AM) Red Lake ON

CFHK-FM St. Thomas ON
CHYC-FM Sudbury ON
CIXL-FM Welland ON
CKYK-FM Alma PQ
CFVM-FM Amqui PQ
CIEU-FM Carleton PQ
CHAI-FM Chateauguay PQ
CFVD-FM Degelis PQ
*CKRK-FM Kahnawake PQ
CHOX-FM La Pocatiere PQ
CFLM(AM) La Tuque PQ
CBGA-FM Matane PQ
CKMF-FM Montreal PQ
CHNC(AM) New Carlisle PQ
CFVD-FM-2 Pohenegamook PQ
CIPC-FM Port-Cartier PQ
CKMN-FM Rimouski-Mont Joli PQ
CHLN(AM) Trois Rivieres PQ
CIGB-FM Trois Rivieres PQ
CKOI-FM Verdun PQ
CKJH(AM) Melfort SK
CFMM-FM Prince Albert SK
CKRW(AM) Whitehorse YT

Country

CKBA(AM) Athabasca AB
CJPR-FM Blairmore AB
CIBQ(AM) Brooks AB
CKRY-FM Calgary AB
CFCW(AM) Camrose AB
CIBW-FM Drayton Valley AB
CKDQ(AM) Drumheller AB
CISN-FM Edmonton AB
CJOK-FM Fort McMurray AB
CJXX-FM Grande Prairie AB
CKHL-FM High Level AB
CKVH(AM) High Prairie AB
CHRB(AM) High River AB
CFWE-FM Lac La Biche AB
CHLB-FM Lethbridge AB
CKSA-FM Lloydminster AB
CHAT(AM) Medicine Hat AB
CKLJ-FM Olds AB
CKYL(AM) Peace River AB
CKGY-FM Red Deer AB
CHBW-FM Rocky Mountain House AB
CHLW(AM) Saint Paul AB
CKWA(AM) Slave Lake AB
CKSQ(AM) Stettler AB
CKKY(AM) Wainwright AB
CFOK(AM) Westlock AB
CIHS-FM Wetaskiwin AB
CKJR(AM) Wetaskiwin AB
CKBX(AM) 100 Mile House BC
CKQC-FM Abbotsford BC
CFWB(AM) Campbell River BC
CHBZ-FM Cranbrook BC
CJDC(AM) Dawson Creek BC
CILZ-FM Greenville BC
CIGV-FM Penticton BC
CJAV(AM) Port Alberni BC
CHQB-FM Powell River BC
CJCI-FM Prince George BC
CKCQ-FM Quesnel BC
CJFW-FM Terrace BC
CJJR-FM Vancouver BC
CIVH(AM) Vanderhoof BC
CKWL(AM) Williams Lake BC
CKLQ(AM) Brandon MB
CKXA(AM) Brandon MB
CFRY(AM) Portage la Prairie MB
CFRY-FM Portage la Prairie MB
CFPX-FM Pukatawagan MB
CFQX-FM Selkirk MB
CICY-FM Selkirk MB
CJAR(AM) The Pas MB
CHTM(AM) Thompson MB
CKMW(AM) Winkler-Morden MB
CKNB-FM Campbellton NB
CFXY-FM Fredericton NB
CKHJ(AM) Fredericton NB
CJXL-FM Moncton NB
CHSJ-FM Saint John NB
CHTD-FM Saint Stephen NB
CHVO-FM Carbonear NF
CFLC-FM Churchill Falls NF

CKVO(AM) Clarenville NF
CFCB(AM) Corner Brook NF
CKGA(AM) Gander NF
CKCM(AM) Grand Falls NF
CHCM(AM) Marystown NF
CFNW(AM) Port au Choix NF
CFCV-FM Saint Andrews NF
CJYQ(AM) Saint John's NF
VOCM(AM) Saint John's NF
*VOWR(AM) Saint John's NF
CFSX-FM Stephenville NF
CFLW(AM) Wabush NF
*CKJM-FM Cheticamp NS
CFDR(AM) Dartmouth NS
CKDY(AM) Digby NS
CHFX-FM Halifax NS
CKEN-FM Kentville NS
CKAD(AM) Middleton NS
CKEC(AM) New Glasgow NS
CJCB(AM) Sydney NS
CKTY-FM Truro NS
CFAB(AM) Windsor NS
CKLB-FM Yellowknife NT
CJKX-FM Ajax ON
CHCQ-FM Belleville ON
CJBQ(AM) Belleville ON
CHUC-FM Cobourg ON
CHAM(AM) Hamilton ON
CING-FM Hamilton ON
CFQK-FM Kaministiquia ON
CKTI-FM Kettle Point ON
CIKZ-FM Kitchener-Waterloo ON
CJBX-FM London ON
CICZ-FM Midland ON
*CHMO(AM) Moosonee ON
CKAT(AM) North Bay ON
*CKRZ-FM Ohsweken ON
CKYC-FM Owen Sound ON
CHVR-FM Pembroke ON
CKQM-FM Peterborough ON
CJQM-FM Sault Ste. Marie ON
CKBY-FM Smiths Falls ON
CIGM-FM Sudbury ON
CKOT(AM) Tillsonburg ON
CHMT-FM Timmins ON
CKNX(AM) Wingham ON
CFCY-FM Charlottetown PE
CJRW-FM Summerside PE
CFGT(AM) Alma PQ
CHIP-FM Fort Coulonge PQ
*CFTH-FM-1 Harrington Harbour PQ
CKAJ-FM Jonquiere PQ
*CKRK-FM Kahnawake PQ
*CFIN-FM Lac-Etchemin PQ
CFIC-FM Listuguj PQ
CHRG-FM Maria (Reserve) PQ
CKIA-FM Quebec PQ
CKMN-FM Rimouski-Mont Joli PQ
CJMS(AM) Saint Constant PQ
CJSL-FM Estevan SK
CFMQ-FM Hudson Bay SK
CKVX-FM Kindersley SK
CJLR-FM La Ronge SK
CFDM-FM Meadow Lake SK
CJNS(AM) Meadow Lake SK
CJNS-FM Meadow Lake SK
CJVR-FM Melfort SK
CILG-FM Moose Jaw SK
CJNB-FM North Battleford SK
CKRM-FM Regina SK
CFQC-FM Saskatoon SK
CJWW(AM) Saskatoon SK
CJSN-FM Shaunavon SK
CKSW-FM Swift Current SK
CFSL(AM) Weyburn SK
CJGX(AM) Yorkton SK
CHON-FM Whitehorse YT

Diversified

*CBR(AM) Calgary AB
*CHFA-FM Edmonton AB
CKUA(AM) Edmonton AB
*CKUA-FM Edmonton AB
CHET-FM Chetwynd BC
CHAD-FM Dawson Creek BC

CFBX-FM Kamloops BC
CHLY-FM Nanaimo BC
CJLY-FM Nelson BC
CFUR-FM Prince George BC
CBUF-FM Prince George BC
*CITR-FM Vancouver BC
*CFUV-FM Victoria BC
*CKSB(AM) Saint Boniface MB
CKXL-FM Saint Boniface MB
CICY-FM Selkirk MB
*CBWK-FM Thompson MB
CBW(AM) Winnipeg MB
CBW-FM Winnipeg MB
*CKUW-FM Winnipeg MB
CJVA(AM) Caraquet NB
CBZF-FM Fredericton NB
CHSR-FM Fredericton NB
*CFJU-FM Kedgwick NB
*CHMA-FM Sackville NB
CJRM-FM Labrador City NF
CIFX-FM Lewisporte NF
*CBN-FM Saint John's NF
*CHMR-FM Saint John's NF
*VOWR(AM) Saint John's NF
CBHA-FM Halifax NS
*CBH-FM Halifax NS
*CKDU-FM Halifax NS
CIFA-FM Yarmouth NS
CFCT(AM) Tuktoyaktuk NT
*CFYK(AM) Yellowknife NT
CKON-FM Akwesasne ON
CKOL-FM Campbellford ON
CKUN-FM Christian Island ON
CFRU-FM Guelph ON
*CFMU-FM Hamilton ON
CFBW-FM Hanover ON
CHCR-FM Killaloe ON
CBBK-FM Kingston ON
*CFRC-FM Kingston ON
CKVI-FM Kingston ON
CKWR-FM Kitchener ON
CJIQ-FM Kitchener/Paris ON
CBBL-FM London ON
CJBC-FM-4 London ON
*CKRZ-FM Ohsweken ON
*CBOQ-FM Ottawa ON
*CBOX-FM Ottawa ON
CKCU-FM Ottawa ON
CKQB-FM Ottawa ON
*CFFF-FM Peterborough ON
CHRY-FM Toronto ON
*CKMS-FM Waterloo ON
*CBE(AM) Windsor ON
CBEF-FM Windsor ON
*CBE-FM Windsor ON
CFMF-FM Fermont PQ
CFIM-FM Iles-de-la-Madeleine PQ
CKAJ-FM Jonquiere PQ
CBOF-1(AM) Maniwaki PQ
CBGA-FM Matane PQ
CIRA-FM Montreal PQ
*CKUT-FM Montreal PQ
CFVD-FM-2 Pohenegamook PQ
CBVE-FM Quebec PQ
CKIA-FM Quebec PQ
CHRL-FM Roberval PQ
*CBSI-FM Sept-Iles PQ
CFLX-FM Sherbrooke PQ
CFOU-FM Trois Rivieres PQ
CIAX-FM Windsor PQ
*CBKF-1(AM) Gravelbourg SK
CFMQ-FM Hudson Bay SK
CJLR-FM La Ronge SK
*CBK(AM) Regina SK
CBKF-FM Regina SK
*CJTR-FM Regina SK
CBKF-2(AM) Saskatoon SK
*CBKS-FM Saskatoon SK
CIDD-FM White Bear Lake Resort SK

Drama/Literature

CBF-FM-1 Trois Rivieres PQ

Easy Listening

CJRB(AM) Boissevain MB
CFEP-FM Eastern Passage NS
CHAL-FM Halifax NS
CKOT-FM Tillsonburg ON
CJEZ-FM Toronto ON
CFMQ-FM Hudson Bay SK

Educational

CHDH-FM Siksika AB
*CBG(AM) Gander NF
CBT(AM) Grand Falls-Windsor NF
*CFGB-FM Happy Valley NF
*CBCS-FM Sudbury ON
CJBC(AM) Toronto ON
*CHYZ-FM Sainte Foy PQ
*CBSI-FM Sept-Iles PQ

Eskimo

CKQN-FM Baker Lake NU

Ethnic

CHKF-FM Calgary AB
CKER-FM Edmonton AB
CFWE-FM Lac La Biche AB
CHKG-FM Vancouver BC
CJVB(AM) Vancouver BC
CKJS-FM Winnipeg MB
CFRU-FM Guelph ON
*CFMU-FM Hamilton ON
CJMR-FM Mississauga ON
CJLL-FM Ottawa ON
CHHA(AM) Toronto ON
CHKT(AM) Toronto ON
CJSA-FM Toronto ON
*CJAM-FM Windsor ON
CHUK-FM Mashteuiatsh (Pointe-Bleue) PQ
CFMB(AM) Montreal PQ
CJWI(AM) Montreal PQ
CKDG-FM Montreal PQ
CJLR-FM La Ronge SK

Filipino

CJSA-FM Toronto ON

Folk

*VOWR(AM) Saint John's NF

Foreign/Ethnic

CHMB(AM) Vancouver BC
CKQN-FM Baker Lake NU
CIAO(AM) Brampton ON
CHIN(AM) Toronto ON
CHIN-FM Toronto ON
CIRV-FM Toronto ON
CFMB(AM) Montreal PQ
CINQ-FM Montreal PQ
CJCF-FM Cumberland House SK

French

CBCX-FM Calgary AB
CBRF-FM Calgary AB
*CKRP-FM Falher AB
CBUX-FM Vancouver BC
*CKSB(AM) Saint Boniface MB
CKXL-FM Saint Boniface MB
*CFJU-FM Kedgwick NB
CHOY-FM Moncton NB
CKUM-FM Moncton NB
CKRO-FM Pokemouche NB
CJRM-FM Labrador City NF
*CKJM-FM Cheticamp NS
CBAX-FM Halifax NS
CIVR-FM Yellowknife NT
CFRT-FM Iqaluit NU
CHOD-FM Cornwall ON

Programming on Radio Stations in Canada

CHOH-FM Hearst ON
CKGN-FM Kapuskasing ON
CJBC-FM-4 London ON
*CHUO-FM Ottawa ON
*CFRH-FM Penetanguishene ON
CFSF-FM Sturgeon Falls ON
CHYK-FM Timmins ON
CKIE-FM Toronto ON
CFID-FM Acton Vale PQ
CBJ-FM Chicoutimi PQ
CKII-FM Dolbeau-Mistassini PQ
CJDM-FM Drummondville PQ
CFMF-FM Fermont PQ
CHIP-FM Fort Coulonge PQ
CHLX-FM Gatineau PQ
CHME-FM Les Escoumins PQ
CHUK-FM Mashteuiatsh (Pointe-Bleue) PQ
CHEF-FM Matagami PQ
CFLO-FM Mont-Laurier PQ
CINQ-FM Montreal PQ
CHIC-FM Rouyn-Noranda PQ
*CHYZ-FM Sainte Foy PQ
CFAK-FM Sherbrooke PQ
CFLX-FM Sherbrooke PQ
CIGR-FM Sherbrooke PQ
CJEB-FM Trois Rivieres PQ
CFRG-FM Gravelbourg SK

German

CHPD-FM Aylmer ON

Golden Oldies

CHAB(AM) Moose Jaw SK
CJNE-FM Nipawin SK

Gospel

CIHS-FM Wetaskiwin AB
*VOAR(AM) Mount Pearl NF

Hindi

CJSA-FM Toronto ON

Inspirational

CKER-FM Edmonton AB
CJRB(AM) Boissevain MB

Jazz

*CJSW-FM Calgary AB
CKUA(AM) Edmonton AB
*CKUA-FM Edmonton AB
*CBU(AM) Vancouver BC
CBU-FM Vancouver BC
CBHA-FM Halifax NS
CBBL-FM London ON
*CHRW-FM London ON
CBBS-FM Sudbury ON
*CKLU-FM Sudbury ON
*CJRT-FM Toronto ON
*CBJX-FM Chicoutimi PQ
CHLX-FM Gatineau PQ
CKLX-FM Montreal PQ
*CKRL-FM Quebec PQ
*CBRX-FM Rimouski PQ
*CBK-FM Regina SK
*CBKS-FM Saskatoon SK

Light Rock

CKFU-FM Fort St. John BC
CKGF-FM-2 Greenwood BC
CIOC-FM Victoria BC
CKXL-FM Saint Boniface MB
CKDH(AM) Amherst NS
CJTN-FM Quinte West ON
CKGB-FM Timmins ON
CHLQ-FM Charlottetown PE
CIMF-FM Gatineau PQ
CHOE-FM Matane PQ

CFQR-FM Montreal PQ
CHEY-FM Trois Rivieres PQ
CHSN-FM Estevan SK

MOR

*CHFA(AM) Edmonton AB
CHET-FM Chetwynd BC
CKCL-FM Chilliwack BC
CKKC-FM Crawford Bay BC
CFKC(AM) Creston BC
CHAD-FM Dawson Creek BC
CKKC(AM) Nelson BC
CKNW(AM) New Westminster BC
CFTK(AM) Terrace BC
CKBD-FM Vancouver BC
CHBE-FM Victoria BC
CFAM(AM) Altona MB
CHSM(AM) Steinbach MB
CHNR-FM Winnipeg MB
CJVA-FM Caraquet NB
CKRO-FM Pokemouche NB
CKEC-FM New Glasgow NS
CKHR-FM Hay River NT
CFCO(AM) Chatham ON
CHOD-FM Cornwall ON
CHWO(AM) Toronto ON
CKWW(AM) Windsor ON
CJAN-FM Asbestos PQ
CHLC-FM Baie Comeau PQ
CFIX-FM Chicoutimi PQ
CHVD-FM Dolbeau-Mistassini PQ
CHRD-FM Drummondville PQ
CFRP(AM) Forestville PQ
CJRG-FM Gaspe PQ
CILE-FM Havre-Saint-Pierre PQ
CJLM-FM Joliette PQ
CJIT-FM Lac Megantic PQ
*CFIN-FM Lac-Etchemin PQ
CHEF-FM Matagami PQ
CHRM-FM Matane PQ
CKAC(AM) Montreal PQ
CKNA-FM Natashquan PQ
CKYQ-FM Plessisville PQ
CJBR-FM Rimouski PQ
CJRE-FM Riviere au Renard PQ
CFNJ-FM Saint Gabriel-de-Brandon PQ
CIHO-FM Saint Hilarion PQ
CJDS-FM Saint Pamphile PQ
CJMC-FM Sainte Anne des Monts PQ
CHEQ-FM Sainte-Marie-de-Beauce PQ
CHLN-FM Trois Rivieres PQ
CKBI(AM) Prince Albert SK
CJSN(AM) Shaunavon SK
CIMG-FM Swift Current SK

Native American

CICU-FM Eskasoni Indian Reserve NS
CFIE-FM Toronto ON
CKUJ-FM Kuujjuaq PQ

News

*CJSW-FM Calgary AB
CBX-FM Edmonton AB
CBTE-FM Crawford Bay BC
*CBTK-FM Kelowna BC
CJNL(AM) Merritt BC
*CFPR(AM) Prince Rupert BC
CHMJ(AM) Vancouver BC
CKWX(AM) Vancouver BC
CKIZ-FM Vernon BC
CBA(AM) Moncton NB
CBD-FM Saint John NB
CBGY(AM) Bonavista Bay NF
CBHA-FM Halifax NS
CIFA-FM Yarmouth NS
CBQX-FM Kenora ON
CKGE-FM Oshawa ON
CHSC-FM Saint Catharines ON
CBEG-FM Sarnia ON
*CBQT-FM Thunder Bay ON
CFTR(AM) Toronto ON
CBMI-FM Baie Comeau PQ

CHRD-FM Drummondville PQ
*CBV-FM-6 La Malbaie PQ
CFBS-FM Lourdes-de-Blanc-Sablon PQ
CKWE-FM Maniwaki (Kitigan Zibi Anishinabeg Reserve) PQ
CBME-FM Montreal PQ
CINW(AM) Montreal PQ
CINF-FM Verdun PQ
CJOS-FM Caronport SK
CFMM-FM Prince Albert SK
*CBK(AM) Regina SK

News/talk

*CBR(AM) Calgary AB
CHQR(AM) Calgary AB
CBX(AM) Edmonton AB
*CHFA(AM) Edmonton AB
CHDH-FM Siksika AB
CKOV(AM) Kelowna BC
CKNW(AM) New Westminster BC
*CFPR(AM) Prince Rupert BC
*CBU(AM) Vancouver BC
*CFRO-FM Vancouver BC
*CBCV-FM Victoria BC
CFAX(AM) Victoria BC
CJOB(AM) Winnipeg MB
*CKUW-FM Winnipeg MB
*CBZ-FM Fredericton NB
*CBAF-FM Moncton NB
CKNI-FM Moncton NB
CHNI-FM Saint John NB
*CBY-FM Corner Brook NF
*CBG(AM) Gander NF
*CBN-FM Saint John's NF
VOCM(AM) Saint John's NF
CJNI-FM Halifax NS
*CHAK(AM) Inuvik NT
*CFYK(AM) Yellowknife NT
CFFB(AM) Iqaluit NU
CHML(AM) Hamilton ON
CKGL-FM Kitchener ON
CFPL(AM) London ON
CJBK(AM) London ON
CFRA(AM) Ottawa ON
CFOS(AM) Owen Sound ON
CKTB-FM Saint Catharines ON
*CBCS-FM Sudbury ON
*CKLU-FM Sudbury ON
*CBQ-FM Thunder Bay ON
CFMJ(AM) Toronto ON
CFRB(AM) Toronto ON
*CBE-FM Windsor ON
CKLW(AM) Windsor ON
CBJ-FM Chicoutimi PQ
CKNU-FM Donnacona PQ
CJRC-FM Gatineau PQ
CFIM-FM Iles-de-la-Madeleine PQ
CBGA-FM Matane PQ
CJAD(AM) Montreal PQ
CKAC(AM) Montreal PQ
CBVE-FM Quebec PQ
*CBV-FM Quebec PQ
CJBR-FM Rimouski PQ
CKRS(AM) Saguenay PQ
CBGN-FM Sainte Anne des Monts PQ
CKCN-FM Sept-Iles PQ
CKSM-FM Shawinigan PQ
CFLX-FM Sherbrooke PQ
CHLT(AM) Sherbrooke PQ
CHLN-FM Trois Rivieres PQ
CJME-FM Regina SK
CJWW-FM Saskatoon SK
CKOM-FM Saskatoon SK

Nostalgia

CJCH-FM Halifax NS
CKPT(AM) Peterborough ON
CKWW(AM) Windsor ON
*CFIN-FM Lac-Etchemin PQ
CFAV(AM) Laval PQ

Oldies

CFFR(AM) Calgary AB
CHQT(AM) Edmonton AB
CHNL-1(AM) Clearwater BC
CHAD-FM Dawson Creek BC
CHNL(AM) Kamloops BC
CKFR(AM) Kelowna BC
CJNL(AM) Merritt BC
CIBH-FM Parksville BC
CKOR(AM) Penticton BC
CISL(AM) Richmond BC
CKKS-FM Sechelt BC
CHOR(AM) Summerland BC
CFAR(AM) Flin Flon MB
CFRW(AM) Winnipeg MB
CFBC(AM) Saint John NB
CFCV-FM Saint Andrews NF
*VOWR(AM) Saint John's NF
CHNS(AM) Halifax NS
CBI-FM Sydney NS
CHER(AM) Sydney NS
CKDR-6(AM) Atikokan ON
CKPC(AM) Brantford ON
CHUC(AM) Cobourg ON
CJUL(AM) Cornwall ON
CKDR(AM) Dryden ON
CJOY(AM) Guelph ON
CKOC(AM) Hamilton ON
CFFX(AM) Kingston ON
CFMK-FM Kingston ON
CKLC(AM) Kingston ON
CKKW(AM) Kitchener ON
CKSL(AM) London ON
CKDO(AM) Oshawa ON
CIWW(AM) Ottawa ON
CJMJ-FM Ottawa ON
CKKL-FM Ottawa ON
CFOS(AM) Owen Sound ON
CKRU(AM) Peterborough ON
CFPS-FM Port Elgin ON
CHOK(AM) Sarnia ON
CJCS(AM) Stratford ON
CHUM(AM) Toronto ON
CKFM-FM Toronto ON
CHTN(AM) Charlottetown PE
*CFTH-FM-1 Harrington Harbour PQ
CFOM-FM Levis PQ
CHRG-FM Maria (Reserve) PQ
CFEI-FM Saint Hyacinthe PQ
CFYM(AM) Kindersley SK
CFNK-FM Pinehouse Lake SK
CKBI(AM) Prince Albert SK
CJYM(AM) Rosetown SK

Other

*CBR(AM) Calgary AB
CHET-FM Chetwynd BC
CKCW-FM Moncton NB
CJFX-FM Antigonish NS
CKUL-FM Halifax NS
CFFB(AM) Iqaluit NU
CHOH-FM Hearst ON
CJTT-FM New Liskeard ON
CBQS-FM Sioux Narrows ON
CJET-FM Smiths Falls ON
CHIP-FM Fort Coulonge PQ
*CBV-FM-6 La Malbaie PQ
CHUT-FM Lac-Simon (Louvicourt) PQ
CINQ-FM Montreal PQ

Progressive

CBU-FM Vancouver BC
CFNY-FM Brampton ON
CKCU-FM Ottawa ON
*CJAM-FM Windsor ON
CHOI-FM Quebec PQ

Public Affairs

*CKRP-FM Falher AB
CBTE-FM Crawford Bay BC
*CBTK-FM Kelowna BC

CBYG-FM Prince George BC
*CFRO-FM Vancouver BC
*CFRO-FM Vancouver BC
CFNC(AM) Cross Lake MB
CBA(AM) Moncton NB
CBGY-FM Bonavista Bay NF
CBI(AM) Sydney NS
CJLX-FM Belleville ON
*CFMU-FM Hamilton ON
CBQX-FM Kenora ON
CKCU-FM Ottawa ON
CBQL-FM Savant Lake ON
*CBQ-FM Thunder Bay ON
CBLA-FM Toronto ON
CBL-FM Toronto ON
*CKMS-FM Waterloo ON
CBMI-FM Baie Comeau PQ
*CHOC-FM Saint Remi PQ
*CBKA-FM La Ronge SK

Religious

CHRB(AM) High River AB
*VOAR(AM) Mount Pearl NF
CJTK-FM Sudbury ON
CIRA-FM Montreal PQ
*CION-FM Quebec PQ
CKSW(AM) Swift Current SK

Rock/AOR

CJAY-FM Calgary AB
CFBR-FM Edmonton AB
CHDI-FM Edmonton AB
CJRX-FM Lethbridge AB
CKLM-FM Lloydminster AB
CKQR-FM Castlegar BC
CHDR-FM Cranbrook BC
CJDR-FM Fernie BC
CHRX-FM Fort St. John BC
CKGR-FM Golden BC
CKIR(AM) Invermere BC
CIFM-FM Kamloops BC
CHWF-FM Nanaimo BC
CJMG-FM Penticton BC
CIRX-FM Prince George BC
CJCI-FM Prince George BC
CKCQ-FM Quesnel BC
CKCR(AM) Revelstoke BC
CFOX-FM Vancouver BC
CIVH-FM Vanderhoof BC
CJZN-FM Victoria BC
CKKQ-FM Victoria BC
CFFM-FM Williams Lake BC
CKWL-FM Williams Lake BC
CFPX-FM Pukatawagan MB
CJKR-FM Winnipeg MB
*CKUW-FM Winnipeg MB
CFXY-FM Fredericton NB
CKIM-FM Baie Verte NF
CKXX-FM Corner Brook NF
CKBW-FM Bridgewater NS
CKTO-FM Truro NS
CFJB-FM Barrie ON
CJLX-FM Belleville ON
CFNY-FM Brampton ON
CJXY-FM Burlington ON
CKUE-FM Chatham ON
CJSS-FM Cornwall ON
CJBB-FM Englehart ON
CIKR-FM Kingston ON
CHYM-FM Kitchener ON
CFPL-FM London ON
CKFX-FM North Bay ON
CKQB-FM Ottawa ON
CHTZ-FM Saint Catharines ON
CHKS-FM Sarnia ON
CJRQ-FM Sudbury ON
CJSD-FM Thunder Bay ON
CIMX-FM Windsor ON
CKTF-FM Gatineau PQ
CFOR-FM Maniwaki PQ
CHOM-FM Montreal PQ
*CKRL-FM Quebec PQ
CIKI-FM Rimouski PQ
CIBM-FM Riviere du Loup PQ

Broadcasting & Cable Yearbook 2006

Programming on Radio Stations in Canada

CHJM-FM Saint Georges PQ
CIGR-FM Sherbrooke PQ
CJSO-FM Sorel PQ
CFJO-FM Thetford Mines PQ
CJCQ-FM North Battleford SK
CHQX-FM Prince Albert SK
CJDJ-FM Saskatoon SK
CKFI-FM Swift Current SK

Smooth Jazz

CIQX-FM Calgary AB
CJZZ-FM Winnipeg MB
CIWV-FM Hamilton ON

Spanish

CHHA(AM) Toronto ON

Sports

CFAC(AM) Calgary AB
CHQR(AM) Calgary AB
CFRN(AM) Edmonton AB
CHED(AM) Edmonton AB
CKNW(AM) New Westminster BC
CFNR-FM Terrace BC
CKST(AM) Vancouver BC
CHML(AM) Hamilton ON

CFPL(AM) London ON
CFGO(AM) Ottawa ON
CHEV Toronto ON
CJCL(AM) Toronto ON
CKGM(AM) Montreal PQ
CHRC(AM) Quebec PQ
CKSM(AM) Shawinigan PQ
CHLN(AM) Trois Rivieres PQ

Talk

CHED(AM) Edmonton AB
CFNR-FM Terrace BC
CFUN(AM) Vancouver BC
*CBWK-FM Thompson MB
CKTP-FM Fredericton Centre NB
CBD-FM Saint John NB
CBDQ-FM Labrador City NF
CBQR-FM Rankin Inlet NU
CFGO(AM) Ottawa ON
CBLA-FM Toronto ON
CJCL(AM) Toronto ON
*CJAM-FM Windsor ON
*CBCT-FM Charlottetown PE
CFGT(AM) Alma PQ
CBJE-FM Chicoutimi PQ
CHMP-FM Longueuil PQ
CKWE-FM Maniwaki (Kitigan Zibi Anishinabeg Reserve) PQ
*CIBL-FM Montreal PQ

*CBRX-FM Rimouski PQ
*CBSI-FM Sept-Iles PQ
CKTS(AM) Sherbrooke PQ
*CBK(AM) Regina SK
*CFWH(AM) Whitehorse YT

Top-40

CFBT-FM Vancouver BC
CKHZ-FM Halifax NS
CIDC-FM Orangeville ON
CISS-FM Ottawa ON
CFSF-FM Sturgeon Falls ON
CHNO-FM Sudbury ON
CJAQ-FM Toronto ON
CKTF-FM Gatineau PQ
CJIT-FM Lac Megantic PQ
CIMO-FM Magog PQ
CJMV-FM Val d'Or PQ
CFDM-FM Meadow Lake SK

Urban Contemporary

CIBK-FM Calgary AB
CHBN-FM Edmonton AB
*CKUW-FM Winnipeg MB
CKHZ-FM Halifax NS
*CIXX-FM London ON
CFXJ-FM Toronto ON

Variety/Diverse

CIAM-FM Fort Vermilion AB
*CJSF-FM Burnaby BC
*CBTK-FM Kelowna BC
CHLS-FM Lillooet BC
CHMM-FM MacKenzie BC
CJMP-FM Powell River BC
CBUX-FM Vancouver BC
*CBCV-FM Victoria BC
CJJJ-FM Brandon MB
CHFC(AM) Churchill MB
CINC-FM Thompson MB
CJUM-FM Winnipeg MB
CKIC-FM Winnipeg MB
CIMS-FM Balmoral NB
*CBAF-FM Moncton NB
CBAL-FM Moncton NB
CKUM-FM Moncton NB
CFMH-FM Saint John NB
CJSE-FM Shediac NB
*CBY(AM) Corner Brook NF
*CKJM-FM Cheticamp NS
CKHR-FM Hay River NT
CBQR-FM Rankin Inlet NU
CFGI-FM Georgina Island ON
CKHA-FM Haliburton ON
CJWL-FM Iroquois Falls ON
CKGN-FM Kapuskasing ON
*CBOF-FM Ottawa ON

*CBO-FM Ottawa ON
CFBU-FM Saint Catharines ON
CBBX-FM Sudbury ON
*CBON-FM Sudbury ON
*CKLU-FM Sudbury ON
*CIUT-FM Toronto ON
CJBC(AM) Toronto ON
CKIE-FM Toronto ON
CFWP-FM Wahta Mohawk Territory near Bala ON
CFID-FM Acton Vale PQ
CFTH-FM-2 La Tabatiere PQ
CFLM(AM) La Tuque PQ
*CJMQ-FM Lennoxville PQ
CKAU-FM Maliotenam PQ
CHGA-FM Maniwaki PQ
CKWE-FM Maniwaki (Kitigan Zibi Anishinabeg Reserve) PQ
CHRG-FM Maria (Reserve) PQ
CBFX-FM Montreal PQ
CJBE-FM Port-Menier PQ
*CBV-FM Quebec PQ
CIAU-FM Radisson PQ
*CHYZ-FM Sainte Foy PQ
CIBO-FM Senneterre PQ
*CBK-FM Regina SK
CFCR-FM Saskatoon SK
CKZP-FM Zenon Park SK
CFET-FM Tagish YT

Special Programming on Radio Stations in the U.S.

Adult Contemp

KNTI(FM) Lakeport CA 3 hrs
KOLV(FM) Olivia MN
WKBO(AM) Harrisburg PA
WRDW-FM Philadelphia PA 11 hrs

Agriculture

WANA(AM) Anniston AL 1 hr
WKAC(AM) Athens AL 5 hrs
WVNN(AM) Athens AL 2 hrs
WNSI-FM Atmore AL 5 hrs
WBYE(AM) Calera AL 2 hr
WACQ(AM) Carrville AL 1 hr
WZTQ(AM) Centre AL 1 hr
WFMH(AM) Cullman AL 2 hrs
WKUL(FM) Cullman AL 15 hrs
WTVY-FM Dothan AL 5 hrs
WKMX(FM) Enterprise AL 2 hrs
WULA(AM) Eufaula AL 2 hrs
WABF(AM) Fairhope AL 1 hr
WKWL(AM) Florala AL 1 hr
WHEP(AM) Foley AL 2 hrs
WZOB(AM) Fort Payne AL 2 hrs
WJBB(AM) Haleyville AL 3 hrs
WERH(AM) Hamilton AL
WBHP(AM) Huntsville AL 6 hrs
WINL(FM) Linden AL 10 hrs
WACV(AM) Montgomery AL 5 hrs
WOPP(AM) Opp AL 2 hrs
WKEA-FM Scottsboro AL 1 hr
WHBB(AM) Selma AL 10 hrs
WBTG-FM Sheffield AL 1 hr
WTLS(AM) Tallassee AL 6 hrs
WTBF(AM) Troy AL 17 hrs
KAPZ(AM) Bald Knob AR 3 hrs
KAAB(AM) Batesville AR 5 hrs
KEWI(AM) Benton AR 4 hrs
KTHS(AM) Berryville AR 15 hrs
KTHS-FM Berryville AR 15 hrs
KXXA(AM) Conway AR 6 hrs
KHTE-FM England AR 5 hrs
KVDW(AM) England AR 5 hrs
KXJK(AM) Forrest City AR 16 hrs
KFFA(AM) Helena AR 16 hrs
KFIN(FM) Jonesboro AR 13 hrs
KNEA(AM) Jonesboro AR 6 hrs
KVMA(AM) Magnolia AR 2 hrs
KVSA(AM) McGehee AR 5 hrs
KBOA-FM Piggott AR 5 hrs
KPBQ-FM Pine Bluff AR 2 hrs
KPOC(AM) Pocahontas AR 10 hrs
KPOC-FM Pocahontas AR 10 hrs
KURM(AM) Rogers AR 10 hrs
KARV(AM) Russellville AR 5 hrs
KWCK(AM) Searcy AR 10 hrs
KWCK-FM Searcy AR 3 hrs
KUOA(AM) Siloam Springs AR 1 hr
KWAK(AM) Stuttgart AR 6 hrs
KFYX(FM) Texarkana AR 2 hrs
KOSE(AM) Wilson AR 5 hrs
KWYN(AM) Wynne AR 6 hrs
KDJI(AM) Holbrook AZ 8 hrs
KLPZ(AM) Parker AZ 1 hr
KVSL(AM) Show Low AZ 2 hrs
KJOK(AM) Yuma AZ 2 hrs
KCFJ(AM) Alturas CA 1 hr
KERN(AM) Bakersfield CA 1 hr
KISV(FM) Bakersfield CA 1 hr
KJMB(FM) Blythe CA 5 hrs
KXO(AM) El Centro CA 7 hrs
KRKC(AM) King City CA 10 hrs
KUBB(FM) Mariposa CA 2 hrs
KYOS(AM) Merced CA 5 hrs
KESP(AM) Modesto CA 3 hrs
KBLF(AM) Red Bluff CA 5 hrs
KHTK(AM) Sacramento CA 4 hrs
KSTN(AM) Stockton CA 3 hrs
KJUG(AM) Tulare CA 5 hrs
KJUG-FM Tulare CA 5 hrs
KWNE(FM) Ukiah CA 1 hr

KUBA(AM) Yuba City CA 4 hrs
KGIW(AM) Alamosa CO 6 hrs
KRAI(AM) Craig CO 1 hr
KFTM(AM) Fort Morgan CO 6 hrs
KRKY(AM) Granby CO 1 hr
KFKA(AM) Greeley CO 15 hrs
KRCN(AM) Longmont CO 1 hr
KSLV(AM) Monte Vista CO 1 hr
KSTC(AM) Sterling CO 15 hrs
KCRT(AM) Trinidad CO 2 hrs
KCOL(AM) Wellington CO 2 hrs
KRDZ(AM) Wray CO 10 hrs
WGMD(FM) Rehoboth Beach DE 2 hrs
WGBG(FM) Seaford DE 1 hr
WBGF(FM) Belle Glade FL 5 hrs
WDCF(AM) Dade City FL 2 hrs
WLBE(AM) Leesburg FL 3 hrs
WTYS(AM) Marianna FL 1 hr
WCFI(AM) Ocala FL 5 hrs
WDVH-FM Trenton FL 2 hrs
WZZS(FM) Zolfo Springs FL 1 hr
V6AH(AM) Pohnpei FM 20 hrs
WAJQ(AM) Alma GA 2 hrs
WAJQ-FM Alma GA 2 hrs
WDEC-FM Americus GA 1 hr
WGAC(AM) Augusta GA 1 hr
WMGR(AM) Bainbridge GA 3 hrs
WFNS(AM) Blackshear GA 10 hrs
WJTH(AM) Calhoun GA 1 hr
WDXQ(AM) Cochran GA 3 hrs
WDXQ-FM Cochran GA 3 hrs
WRCG(AM) Columbus GA 3 hrs
WJJC(AM) Commerce GA 2 hrs
WCUG(AM) Cuthbert GA 8 hrs
WDMG(AM) Douglas GA 4 hrs
WMLT(AM) Dublin GA 6 hrs
WBHB(AM) Fitzgerald GA 6 hrs
WKLY(AM) Hartwell GA 1 hr
WCEH(AM) Hawkinsville GA 5 hrs
WVOH(AM) Hazlehurst GA 2 hrs
WIFO-FM Jesup GA 5 hrs
WLOP(AM) Jesup GA 10 hrs
WQCH(AM) La Fayette GA 2 hrs
WYTH(AM) Madison GA 15 hrs
WMCG(FM) Milan GA 1 hr
WHKN(FM) Millen GA 10 hrs
WMTM(AM) Moultrie GA 16 hrs
WALH(AM) Mountain City GA 2 hrs
WSTI-FM Quitman GA 5 hrs
WWNS(AM) Statesboro GA 12 hrs
WJAT(AM) Swainsboro GA 5 hrs
WSYL(AM) Sylvania GA 5 hrs
WPAX(AM) Thomasville GA 2 hrs
WTHO-FM Thomson GA 3 hrs
WTIF(AM) Tifton GA 5 hrs
KLGA(AM) Algona IA
KLGA-FM Algona IA
KJAN(AM) Atlantic IA 12 hrs
KWBG(AM) Boone IA 15 hrs
KBUR(AM) Burlington IA 19 hrs
KCPS(AM) Burlington IA 10 hrs
WMT(AM) Cedar Rapids IA 19 hrs
KCHA(AM) Charles City IA 12 hrs
KCHA-FM Charles City IA 12 hrs
KCHE(AM) Cherokee IA 12 hrs
KCLN(AM) Clinton IA 10 hrs
KROS(AM) Clinton IA 5 hrs
KCZQ(AM) Cresco IA 12 hrs
WOC(AM) Davenport IA 10 hrs
KDSN(AM) Denison IA 12 hrs
KDSN-FM Denison IA 7 hrs
WHO(AM) Des Moines IA 15 hrs
KDTH(AM) Dubuque IA 17 hrs
KDST(AM) Dyersville IA
KDWD(FM) Emmetsburg IA 10 hrs
KILR(AM) Estherville IA 9 hrs
KILR-FM Estherville IA 4 hrs
KMCD(AM) Fairfield IA 10 hrs
KIOW(FM) Forest City IA 15 hrs
KWMT(AM) Fort Dodge IA
KCTN(FM) Garnavillo IA

KGRN(AM) Grinnell IA 12 hrs
KLMJ(FM) Hampton IA 8 hrs
KNOD(FM) Harlan IA 3 hrs
KHBT(FM) Humboldt IA 10 hrs
KKIA(FM) Ida Grove IA 10 hrs
KIFG(AM) Iowa Falls IA 5 hrs
KGRA(FM) Jefferson IA 2 hrs
KOKX(AM) Keokuk IA 6 hrs
KOKX-FM Keokuk IA 3 hrs
KLEM(AM) Le Mars IA 18 hrs
KMCH(FM) Manchester IA 7 hrs
KMAQ(AM) Maquoketa IA 10 hrs
KGLO(AM) Mason City IA 15 hrs
KCZE(FM) New Hampton IA 12 hrs
KCOB(AM) Newton IA 2 hrs
KCOB-FM Newton IA 4 hrs
KOEL(AM) Oelwein IA 16 hrs
*KNWI(FM) Osceola IA 8 hrs
KBIZ(AM) Ottumwa IA 12 hrs
KMA(AM) Shenandoah IA
*KDCR(AM) Sioux Center IA 2 hrs
KMNS(AM) Sioux City IA 20 hrs
KSCJ(AM) Sioux City IA 5 hrs
KTFC(FM) Sioux City IA 1 hr
KAYL(AM) Storm Lake IA 5 hrs
KKRF(FM) Stuart IA 5 hrs
KTLB(FM) Twin Lakes IA 15 hrs
KCII-FM Washington IA
KQWC(AM) Webster City IA 8 hrs
KNJY(AM) Boise ID 5 hrs
KCID(AM) Caldwell ID 16 hrs
KTHI(FM) Caldwell ID 4 hrs
KORT(AM) Grangeville ID 2 hrs
KID(AM) Idaho Falls ID 18 hrs
KOZE(AM) Lewiston ID 2 hrs
KRLC(AM) Lewiston ID 5 hrs
KVSI(AM) Montpelier ID 2 hrs
KRPL(AM) Moscow ID 4 hrs
KZFN(FM) Moscow ID 4 hrs
KWIK(AM) Pocatello ID 3 hrs
KACH(AM) Preston ID 3 hrs
KSRA(AM) Salmon ID 4 hrs
KSRA-FM Salmon ID 4 hrs
KLIX(AM) Twin Falls ID 2 hrs
KTFI(AM) Twin Falls ID 3 hrs
WSDZ(AM) Belleville IL 3 hrs
WQRL(FM) Benton IL 3 hrs
WBNQ(FM) Bloomington IL 1 hr
WJBC(AM) Bloomington IL 13 hrs
WLMD(FM) Bushnell IL 3 hrs
WKRO(AM) Cairo IL 12 hrs
WBYS(AM) Canton IL 10 hrs
WCIL(AM) Carbondale IL 1 hr
WROY(AM) Carmi IL 6 hrs
WDWS(AM) Champaign IL 10 hrs
WEIC(AM) Charleston IL 8 hrs
KSGM(AM) Chester IL 2 hrs
WDAN(AM) Danville IL 20 hrs
WLBK(AM) De Kalb IL 12 hrs
WSOY(AM) Decatur IL 10 hrs
WIXN(AM) Dixon IL 11 hrs
WDQN(AM) Du Quoin IL 3 hrs
KUUL(FM) East Moline IL 1 hr
WFIW(AM) Fairfield IL 16 hrs
WFIW-FM Fairfield IL 12 hrs
WFRL(AM) Freeport IL 15 hrs
WAAG(FM) Galesburg IL 5 hrs
WGIL(AM) Galesburg IL 10 hrs
WGEL(FM) Greenville IL 19 hrs
WEBQ(AM) Harrisburg IL 6 hrs
WDUK(FM) Havana IL 4 hrs
WRVY-FM Henry IL 4 hrs
WCBW(AM) Highland IL 3 hrs
WJIL(AM) Jacksonville IL 8 hrs
WLDS(AM) Jacksonville IL 20 hrs
WJBM(AM) Jerseyville IL 18 hrs
WJOL(AM) Joliet IL 3 hrs
WKAN(AM) Kankakee IL 10 hrs
WKEI(AM) Kewanee IL 20 hrs
WSMI(AM) Litchfield IL 18 hrs
WSMI-FM Litchfield IL 18 hrs

WLUV(AM) Loves Park IL 6 hrs
WJEQ(FM) Macomb IL 1 hr
WLRB(AM) Macomb IL 1.25 hrs
WZUS(FM) Macon IL 5 hrs
WLBH-FM Mattoon IL 9 hrs
WMCI(FM) Mattoon IL 5 hrs
WFXN(AM) Moline IL 1 hr
WMOI(FM) Monmouth IL 8 hrs
WRAM(AM) Monmouth IL 18 hrs
WCZQ(FM) Monticello IL 11 hrs
WCSJ-FM Morris IL 10 hrs
WVMC(AM) Mount Carmel IL 5 hrs
WMIX(AM) Mount Vernon IL 18 hrs
WMIX-FM Mount Vernon IL 12 hrs
WHQQ(FM) Neoga IL 7 hrs
WVLN(AM) Olney IL 10 hrs
WCMY(AM) Ottawa IL 9 hrs
WPXN(FM) Paxton IL 1 hr
WMBD(AM) Peoria IL 15 hrs
WBBA-FM Pittsfield IL 10 hrs
WSPY-FM Plano IL 18 hrs
WZOE(AM) Princeton IL 15 hrs
KPCR(AM) Quincy IL 9 hrs
WGEM-FM Quincy IL 10 hrs
WTAY(AM) Robinson IL 3 hrs
WTYE(FM) Robinson IL 6 hrs
WKXQ(FM) Rushville IL 6 hrs
WJBD(AM) Salem IL 4 hrs
WJBD-FM Salem IL 4 hrs
WAUR(AM) Sandwich IL 15 hrs
WINU(AM) Shelbyville IL 5 hrs
WHCO(AM) Sparta IL 20 hrs
WTAX(AM) Springfield IL 16 hrs
WSDR(AM) Sterling IL 16 hrs
WSQR(AM) Sycamore IL 6 hrs
WTIM-FM Taylorville IL 20 hrs
WRAN(AM) Tower Hill IL 6 hrs
*WILL(AM) Urbana IL 7 hrs
WPMB(AM) Vandalia IL 4 hrs
WGFA-FM Watseka IL 18 hrs
WSCH(AM) Aurora IN 3 hrs
WRBI(FM) Batesville IN 5 hrs
WBIW(AM) Bedford IN 3 hrs
WINN(FM) Columbus IN 2 hrs
WCVL(AM) Crawfordsville IN 5 hrs
WADM(AM) Decatur IN 2 hrs
WIKY-FM Evansville IN 17 hrs
WILO(AM) Frankfort IN 12 hrs
WSHW(FM) Frankfort IN 8 hrs
WFLQ(FM) French Lick IN 3 hrs
WREB(FM) Greencastle IN 5 hrs
WTRE(AM) Greensburg IN 10 hrs
WBDC(FM) Huntingburg IN 5 hrs
WAWK(AM) Kendallville IN 1 hr
WLOI(AM) La Porte IN 8 hrs
WASK(AM) Lafayette IN 2 hrs
WKOA(AM) Lafayette IN 3 hrs
WSAL(AM) Logansport IN 10 hrs
WRZR(FM) Loogootee IN 2 hrs
WORX-FM Madison IN 3 hrs
WXGO(AM) Madison IN 3 hrs
WCBK-FM Martinsville IN 1 hr
WMCB(AM) Martinsville IN 1 hr
WEFM(FM) Michigan City IN
WRCY(AM) Mount Vernon IN 5 hrs
WMDH(AM) New Castle IN 1 hr
WMDH-FM New Castle IN 1 hr
WSEZ(AM) Paoli IN 7 hrs
WTCA(AM) Plymouth IN 11 hrs
WLQI(FM) Rensselaer IN 15 hrs
WRIN(AM) Rensselaer IN 6 hrs
WKBV(AM) Richmond IN 4 hrs
WROI(FM) Rochester IN 10 hrs
WKWH-FM Rushville IN 18 hrs
WAXL(AM) Santa Claus IN 3 hrs
WZZB(AM) Seymour IN 2 hrs
WNDI(AM) Sullivan IN 6 hrs
WKUZ(AM) Wabash IN 5 hrs
WRSW(AM) Warsaw IN 11 hrs
WRSW-FM Warsaw IN 2 hrs
WWBL(FM) Washington IN 15 hrs

KSOK(AM) Arkansas City KS 10 hrs
KAIR(AM) Atchison KS 7 hrs
KVSV(AM) Beloit KS 9 hrs
KSNP(FM) Burlington KS 8 hrs
KGNO(AM) Dodge City KS 15 hrs
KDNS(FM) Downs KS 6 hrs
KIUL(AM) Garden City KS 5 hrs
*KGCR(FM) Goodland KS 2 hrs
KVGB(AM) Great Bend KS 7 hrs
KHAZ(FM) Hays KS 10 hrs
KNZA(FM) Hiawatha KS 14 hrs
KBUF(AM) Holcomb KS 15 hrs
KNNS(AM) Larned KS 10 hrs
KSCB(AM) Liberal KS 6 hrs
KSLS(FM) Liberal KS 12 hrs
KOFO(AM) Ottawa KS 2 hrs
KLKC(AM) Parsons KS 2 hrs
KKAN(AM) Phillipsburg KS 10 hrs
KRSL(AM) Russell KS 2 hrs
KFRM(AM) Salina KS 5 hrs
KSAL(AM) Salina KS 6 hrs
KFLA(AM) Scott City KS 5 hrs
KMZA(FM) Seneca KS 7 hrs
KULY(AM) Ulysses KS 12 hrs
KLEY(AM) Wellington KS 10 hrs
WANY(AM) Albany KY 2 hrs
WBRT(AM) Bardstown KY 10 hrs
WKDZ(AM) Cadiz KY 2 hrs
WNES(AM) Central City KY 7 hrs
WAIN(AM) Columbia KY 2 hrs
WCPM(AM) Cumberland KY 1 hr
WCYN(AM) Cynthiana KY 15 hrs
WHIR(AM) Danville KY 1 hr
WHSX(FM) Edmonton KY 15 hrs
WFKN(AM) Franklin KY 6 hrs
WAKY(AM) Greensburg KY 15 hrs
WXBC(AM) Hardinsburg KY 5 hrs
WKCM(AM) Hawesville KY 3 hrs
WSON(AM) Henderson KY 2 hrs
WKMO(FM) Hodgenville KY 2 hrs
WHOP-FM Hopkinsville KY 15 hrs
WVLK(AM) Lexington KY 1 hr
WHAS(AM) Louisville KY 1 hr
WKLB(AM) Manchester KY 1 hr
WMJL(AM) Marion KY 3 hrs
WMJL-FM Marion KY 3 hrs
WNGO(AM) Mayfield KY 4 hrs
WQQR(FM) Mayfield KY 4 hrs
WFTM(AM) Maysville KY 6 hrs
WFTM-FM Maysville KY 6 hrs
WMIK(AM) Middlesboro KY 1 hr
WFLW(AM) Monticello KY 5 hrs
WLBQ(AM) Morgantown KY 3 hrs
WMST(AM) Mt. Sterling KY 2 hrs
WLOC(AM) Munfordville KY 2 hrs
WNBS(AM) Murray KY 6 hrs
WBKR(AM) Owensboro KY 2 hrs
WVJS(AM) Owensboro KY 1 hr
WKCA(FM) Owingsville KY 3 hrs
WBIO(FM) Philpot KY 5 hrs
WLCK(AM) Scottsville KY 3 hrs
WVLE(FM) Scottsville KY 3 hrs
WCND(AM) Shelbyville KY 6 hrs
WKEQ-FM Somerset KY 1 hr
WSFC(AM) Somerset KY 2 hrs
WTLO(AM) Somerset KY 1 hr
WAKY-FM Springfield KY 10 hrs
WRSL(AM) Stanford KY 4 hrs
WMTC(AM) Vancleve KY 1 hr
WMTC-FM Vancleve KY 2 hrs
WLKS(AM) West Liberty KY 5 hrs
KQLQ(FM) Columbia LA 3 hrs
KRRP(AM) Coushatta LA 3 hrs
KSIG(AM) Crowley LA 5 hrs
KFNV-FM Ferriday LA 2 hrs
WFPR(AM) Hammond LA 1 hr
KJNA-FM Jena LA 3 hrs
KNEK(AM) Washington LA 4 hrs
KMAR-FM Winnsboro LA 5 hrs
WSBS(AM) Great Barrington MA 1 hr
WTRI(AM) Brunswick MD 2 hrs

Special Programming on Radio Stations in the U.S.

WSRY(AM) Elkton MD 1 hr
WJEJ(AM) Hagerstown MD 1 hr
WICO(AM) Salisbury MD 1 hr
WTTR(AM) Westminster MD 4 hrs
WABJ(AM) Adrian MI 7 hrs
WFYC(AM) Alma MI 4 hrs
WQBX(FM) Alma MI 4 hrs
WATZ(AM) Alpena MI 3 hrs
WTKA(AM) Ann Arbor MI 9 hrs
WLEW(AM) Bad Axe MI 4 hrs
WBCM(FM) Boyne City MI 1 hr
WKYO(AM) Caro MI 18 hrs
WTVB(AM) Coldwater MI 6 hrs
WDOW(AM) Dowagiac MI 7 hrs
WCHT(AM) Escanaba MI 1 hr
WGHN(AM) Grand Haven MI 5 hrs
WCSR(AM) Hillsdale MI 3 hrs
WION(AM) Ionia MI 8 hrs
WKZO(AM) Kalamazoo MI 10 hrs
WOAP(AM) Owosso MI 2 hrs
WPHM(AM) Port Huron MI 1 hr
WSGW(AM) Saginaw MI 10 hrs
WMLM(AM) Saint Louis MI 5 hrs
WMIC(AM) Sandusky MI 12 hrs
WSPZ(AM) South Haven MI 3 hrs
WTCM(AM) Traverse City MI 5 hrs
WPNW(AM) Zeeland MI 1 hr
KASM(AM) Albany MN 6 hrs
KATE(AM) Albert Lea MN 18 hrs
KXRA(AM) Alexandria MN 5 hrs
KKCQ-FM Bagley MN 10 hrs
KBMO(AM) Benson MN 10 hrs
KSCR-FM Benson MN 10 hrs
KBEW(AM) Blue Earth MN 15 hrs
KJLY(FM) Blue Earth MN 5 hrs
WGVY(FM) Cambridge MN 8 hrs
WFMP(FM) Coon Rapids MN
KROX(AM) Crookston MN 10 hrs
KDLM(AM) Detroit Lakes MN 1 hr
KCNN(AM) East Grand Forks MN 6 hrs
KFMC(FM) Fairmont MN 6 hrs
KSUM(AM) Fairmont MN 18 hrs
KBRF(AM) Fergus Falls MN 15 hrs
KKCQ(AM) Fosston MN 5 hrs
*KAXE(FM) Grand Rapids MN 1 hr
KDUZ(AM) Hutchinson MN 18 hrs
KKOJ(AM) Jackson MN 15 hrs
KLFD(AM) Litchfield MN 20 hrs
KLTF(AM) Little Falls MN 8 hrs
KEYL(AM) Long Prairie MN 5 hrs
KQKL(FM) Luverne MN 10 hrs
KLQP(FM) Madison MN 5 hrs
KDMA(AM) Montevideo MN 7 hrs
KMGM(FM) Montevideo MN 1 hr
KYMN(AM) Northfield MN 6 hrs
KDIO(AM) Ortonville MN 18 hrs
WCMP(AM) Pine City MN 6 hrs
WQPM(AM) Princeton MN 2 hrs
KOLM(AM) Rochester MN 3 hrs
KROC(AM) Rochester MN 12 hrs
KIKV-FM Sauk Centre MN 20 hrs
KNSG(FM) Springfield MN 15 hrs
KNSP(AM) Staples MN 6 hrs
KSNR(FM) Thief River Falls MN 1 hr
KTRF(AM) Thief River Falls MN 12 hrs
KARL(FM) Tracy MN 15 hrs
KWAD(AM) Wadena MN 10 hrs
KDJS(AM) Willmar MN 5 hrs
KDJS-FM Willmar MN
KWLM(AM) Willmar MN 8 hrs
KAGE(AM) Winona MN
KWOA(AM) Worthington MN
KAAN(AM) Bethany MO 10 hrs
KWRT(AM) Boonville MO 5 hrs
KMAM(AM) Butler MO 15 hrs
KMOE(FM) Butler MO 15 hrs
KOZX(FM) Cabool MO 2 hrs
KATI(FM) California MO 5 hrs
KRLL(AM) California MO 5 hrs
KMRN(AM) Cameron MO 5 hrs
KZIM(AM) Cape Girardeau MO 5 hrs
KDMO(AM) Carthage MO 12 hrs
KRMO(AM) Cassville MO 10 hrs
KWKZ(FM) Charleston MO 1 hr
KDFN(AM) Doniphan MO 5 hrs
KREI(AM) Farmington MO 5 hrs

KTJJ(FM) Farmington MO 6 hrs
KUNQ(FM) Houston MO 2 hrs
KWOS(AM) Jefferson City MO 12 hrs
KBOA(AM) Kennett MO 5 hrs
KIRX(AM) Kirksville MO 10 hrs
KBNN(AM) Lebanon MO 8 hrs
KMMO(AM) Marshall MO 6 hrs
KMMO-FM Marshall MO 6 hrs
KNIM(AM) Maryville MO 5 hrs
KMEM-FM Memphis MO 8 hrs
KWWR(AM) Mexico MO 4 hrs
KXEO(AM) Mexico MO 3 hrs
KMCR(FM) Montgomery City MO 2 hrs
KBTN(AM) Neosho MO 6 hrs
KNEM(AM) Nevada MO 1 hr
KNMO(FM) Nevada MO 1 hr
KBDZ(FM) Perryville MO 2 hrs
KZNN(FM) Rolla MO 3 hrs
KFEQ(AM) Saint Joseph MO 20 hrs
KSMO(AM) Salem MO 18 hrs
KDRO(AM) Sedalia MO 6 hrs
KBXB(FM) Sikeston MO 3 hrs
KRHW(AM) Sikeston MO 6 hrs
KSIM(AM) Sikeston MO 12 hrs
KSGF(AM) Springfield MO 5 hrs
KTTS-FM Springfield MO 5 hrs
KWTO(AM) Springfield MO 20 hrs
KRWP(FM) Stockton MO 8 hrs
KSAR(FM) Thayer MO 4 hrs
KTKS(FM) Versailles MO 5 hrs
KOKO(AM) Warrensburg MO 4 hrs
KWRE(AM) Warrenton MO 10 hrs
KUKU-FM Willow Springs MO 6 hrs
WCKK(FM) Carthage MS
WBAQ(FM) Greenville MS 1 hr
WNIX(AM) Greenville MS 10 hrs
WROA(AM) Gulfport MS 1 hr
WCPC(AM) Houston MS 5 hrs
WTCD(FM) Indianola MS 5 hrs
WJDX(AM) Jackson MS 2 hrs
WMSI(FM) Jackson MS 1 hr
WIQQ(FM) Leland MS 6 hrs
WRQO(FM) Monticello MS 1 hr
WMIS(AM) Natchez MS 6 hrs
WWMS(FM) Oxford MS 2 hrs
WHOC(AM) Philadelphia MS 2 hrs
WRJW(AM) Picayune MS 6 hrs
WQMS(AM) Quitman MS 2 hrs
WELO(AM) Tupelo MS 1 hr
WTYL(AM) Tylertown MS 6 hrs
WJNS-FM Yazoo City MS 16 hrs
KFLN(AM) Baker MT 10 hrs
KBOW(AM) Butte MT 5 hrs
KBCK(AM) Deer Lodge MT 2 hrs
KXGN(AM) Glendive MT 2 hrs
KXGF(AM) Great Falls MT 2 hrs
KOJM(AM) Havre MT 4 hrs
KPQX(FM) Havre MT 10 hrs
*KXEI(FM) Havre MT 1 hr
KXLO(AM) Lewistown MT
KKRY(FM) Miles City MT 1 hr
KMTA(AM) Miles City MT 8 hrs
KATQ(AM) Plentywood MT 5 hrs
KATQ-FM Plentywood MT 5 hrs
KCGM(FM) Scobey MT 6 hrs
KSEN(AM) Shelby MT 8 hrs
KZIN-FM Shelby MT 4 hrs
KVCK(AM) Wolf Point MT 6 hrs
KVCK-FM Wolf Point MT 1 hr
WQDK(FM) Ahoskie NC 7 hrs
WKXR(AM) Asheboro NC 1 hr
WWNC(AM) Asheville NC 1 hr
WGAI(AM) Elizabeth City NC 3 hrs
WFMO(AM) Fairmont NC 5 hrs
WNCT(AM) Greenville NC 10 hrs
WCXL(FM) Kill Devil Hills NC 2 hrs
WKTE(AM) King NC 2 hrs
WHBK(AM) Marshall NC 3 hrs
WMNC(AM) Morganton NC 2 hrs
WPAQ(AM) Mount Airy NC 1 hr
WWDR(AM) Murfreesboro NC 10 hrs
WCVP(AM) Murphy NC 3 hrs
WCBQ(AM) Oxford NC
WPTF(AM) Raleigh NC 10 hrs
WTEL(AM) Red Springs NC 5 hrs
WPTM(FM) Roanoke Rapids NC 15

WEGG(AM) Rose Hill NC 9 hrs
WKRX(FM) Roxboro NC 5 hrs
WRXO(AM) Roxboro NC 5 hrs
WWGP(AM) Sanford NC 7 hrs
WYAL(AM) Scotland Neck NC 2 hrs
WMPM(AM) Smithfield NC 2 hrs
WTAB(AM) Tabor City NC 12 hrs
WADE(AM) Wadesboro NC 1 hr
WETC(AM) Wendell-Zebulon NC 5 hrs
WKSK(AM) West Jefferson NC 3 hrs
WENC(AM) Whiteville NC 5 hrs
WTXY(AM) Whiteville NC 2 hrs
WBMR(AM) Bismarck ND 4 hrs
KPOK(AM) Bowman ND 2 hrs
KFGO(AM) Fargo ND 20 hrs
*KMHA(FM) Four Bears ND 1 hr
KAUJ(AM) Grafton ND 18 hrs
KXPO(AM) Grafton ND 18 hrs
KNDC(AM) Hettinger ND
KQDJ(AM) Jamestown ND 6 hrs
KSJB(AM) Jamestown ND 12 hrs
KFAB-FM Kindred ND 15 hrs
KNDK(AM) Langdon ND 12 hrs
KQLX(AM) Lisbon ND 14 hrs
KCJB(AM) Minot ND 4 hrs
KHRT(AM) Minot ND 1 hr
KZPR(FM) Minot ND 4 hrs
KDDR(AM) Oakes ND 15 hrs
KUSO(FM) Albion NE 10 hrs
KAAQ(FM) Alliance NE 4 hrs
KCOW(AM) Alliance NE 18 hrs
KWBE(AM) Beatrice NE 14 hrs
KCNI(AM) Broken Bow NE
KZEN(FM) Central City NE 20 hrs
KCSR(AM) Chadron NE 6 hrs
KQSK(FM) Chadron NE 4 hrs
KKOT(FM) Columbus NE 8 hrs
KTTT(AM) Columbus NE 5 hrs
KGMT(AM) Fairbury NE 18 hrs
KHUB(AM) Fremont NE 6 hrs
KHAS(AM) Hastings NE 2 hrs
KMTY(FM) Holdrege NE 5 hrs
KUVR(AM) Holdrege NE 5 hrs
KGFW(AM) Kearney NE 8 hrs
KRVN-FM Lexington NE 10 hrs
KICX-FM McCook NE 6 hrs
KIOD(FM) McCook NE 6 hrs
KSWN(FM) McCook NE 6 hrs
KNCY(AM) Nebraska City NE 3 hrs
KNEN(FM) Norfolk NE 10 hrs
KMCX(FM) Ogallala NE 2 hrs
KOGA(AM) Ogallala NE 10 hrs
KFAB(AM) Omaha NE 5 hrs
KBRX(AM) O'Neill NE 12 hrs
KOIL(AM) Plattsmouth NE 6 hrs
KNEB(AM) Scottsbluff NE 18 hrs
KNEB-FM Scottsbluff NE 18 hrs
KOLT(AM) Scottsbluff NE 5 hrs
KSID(AM) Sidney NE 5 hrs
KRFS(AM) Superior NE 5 hrs
KRFS-FM Superior NE
KOAQ(AM) Terrytown NE
KTCH(AM) Wayne NE 20 hrs
KWPN-FM West Point NE 10 hrs
KAWL(AM) York NE 7 hrs
*WNEC-FM Henniker NH 4 hrs
WSNJ(AM) Bridgeton NJ 10 hrs
WFAI(AM) Salem NJ 8 hrs
KRSY(AM) Alamogordo NM 1 hr
KCLV-FM Clovis NM 6 hrs
KICA(AM) Clovis NM 5 hrs
KOTS(AM) Deming NM 5 hrs
KSEL-FM Portales NM 1 hr
KEND(FM) Roswell NM 1 hr
KMXQ(FM) Socorro NM 2 hrs
KWNA(AM) Winnemucca NV 2 hrs
WBTA(AM) Batavia NY 1 hr
WABH(AM) Bath NY 1 hr
WVIN-FM Bath NY 1 hr
WBRV-FM Boonville NY 3 hrs
WWLE(AM) Cornwall NY 1 hr
WRWD-FM Highland NY 1 hr
WXHC(FM) Homer NY 1 hr
WHHO(AM) Hornell NY
WJTN(AM) Jamestown NY 1 hr
WIXT(AM) Little Falls NY 1 hr
WLVL(AM) Lockport NY 6 hrs

WLLG(FM) Lowville NY 3 hrs
WICY(AM) Malone NY 1 hr
WYBG(AM) Massena NY
WALL(AM) Middletown NY 1 hr
WACK(AM) Newark NY 5 hrs
WEOK(AM) Poughkeepsie NY 2 hrs
WRIV(AM) Riverhead NY 8 hrs
WUAM(AM) Saratoga Springs NY 1 hr
WSPQ(AM) Springville NY 1 hr
WIPS(AM) Ticonderoga NY 6 hrs
WIBX(AM) Utica NY 14 hrs
WDLA(AM) Walton NY 2 hrs
WCJW(AM) Warsaw NY 11 hrs
WTNY(AM) Watertown NY 3 hrs
WNCO(AM) Ashland OH 3 hrs
WAIS(AM) Buchtel OH 5 hrs
WBCO(AM) Bucyrus OH 4 hrs
WCER(AM) Canton OH 6 hrs
WHBC(AM) Canton OH 1 hr
WMNI(AM) Columbus OH 2 hrs
WWOW(AM) Conneaut OH 1 hr
WDOH(FM) Delphos OH 8 hrs
WJER-FM Dover OH 2 hrs
WJER(AM) Dover-New Philadelphia OH 2 hrs
WFIN(AM) Findlay OH 7 hrs
WFRO-FM Fremont OH 4 hrs
WAXZ(FM) Georgetown OH 10 hrs
WKTN(FM) Kenton OH 4 hrs
WLOH(AM) Lancaster OH 1 hr
WIMA(AM) Lima OH 3 hrs
WIMT(FM) Lima OH 10 hrs
WMOA(AM) Marietta OH 1 hr
WMRN(AM) Marion OH 5 hrs
WUCO(AM) Marysville OH 10 hrs
WMPO(FM) Middleport-Pomeroy OH 1 hr
WSEO(FM) Nelsonville OH
WLKR-FM Norwalk OH 3 hrs
WOBL(AM) Oberlin OH 5 hrs
WBUK(FM) Ottawa OH 5 hrs
WPTW(AM) Piqua OH 6 hrs
WSOM(AM) Salem OH 2 hrs
WLEC(AM) Sandusky OH 2 hrs
WSWR(FM) Shelby OH 12 hrs
WMVR-FM Sidney OH 10 hrs
WCKY-FM Tiffin OH 3 hrs
WTTF(AM) Tiffin OH 3 hrs
WSPD(AM) Toledo OH 3 hrs
WTUZ(AM) Uhrichsville OH 1 hr
WYNT(FM) Upper Sandusky OH 3 hrs
WCHO(AM) Washington Court House OH 5 hrs
WRAC(FM) West Union OH 10 hrs
WQKT(FM) Wooster OH 2 hrs
WBZI(AM) Xenia OH 5 hrs
WHIZ(FM) Zanesville OH 2 hrs
KEYB(FM) Altus OK 2 hrs
KKBI(FM) Broken Bow OK 5 hrs
KZUE(AM) El Reno OK 7 hrs
KGWA(AM) Enid OK 3 hrs
KTAT(AM) Frederick OK 2 hrs
KIHN(AM) Hugo OK 1 hr
KITX(FM) Hugo OK 2 hrs
KMAD(AM) Madill OK 2 hrs
KMMY(FM) Muskogee OK 5 hrs
KPNC-FM Ponca City OK 5 hrs
KCXR(AM) Taft OK 1 hr
KFAQ(AM) Tulsa OK 5 hrs
KIMY(FM) Watonga OK 1 hr
KSIW(AM) Woodward OK
KWOX(FM) Woodward OK 10 hrs
KBKR(AM) Baker City OR 2 hrs
KZZR(AM) Burns OR 6 hrs
KWVR(AM) Enterprise OR 4 hrs
KWVR-FM Enterprise OR 4 hrs
KAGO(AM) Klamath Falls OR 3 hrs
KKJX(FM) Klamath Falls OR 1 hr
KLBM(AM) La Grande OR 2 hrs
KSRV(AM) Ontario OR 15 hrs
KSRV-FM Ontario OR 15 hrs
KUMA(AM) Pendleton OR 10 hrs
KCKX(AM) Stayton OR 15 hrs
KACI(AM) The Dalles OR 1 hr
KODL(AM) The Dalles OR 4 hrs
KLWJ(AM) Umatilla OR 1 hr

WHLM(AM) Bloomsburg PA 1 hr
WCOJ(AM) Coatesville PA 2 hrs
WFRM(AM) Coudersport PA 2 hrs
WDAC(FM) Lancaster PA 4 hrs
WJSM(AM) Martinsburg PA 4 hrs
WJUN-FM Mexico PA 1 hr
*WPEL(AM) Montrose PA 1 hr
WEEU(AM) Reading PA 2 hrs
WATS(AM) Sayre PA 1 hr
WKGB-FM Susquehanna PA 1 hr
WSBA(AM) York PA 4 hrs
WSOL(AM) San German PR 2 hrs
WVCD(AM) Bamberg-Denmark SC 1 hr
WOLS(AM) Florence SC 1 hr
WBZF(AM) Hartsville SC 3 hrs
WHSC(AM) Hartsville SC 3 hrs
WJBS(AM) Holly Hill SC 2 hrs
WJAY(AM) Mullins SC 10 hrs
WQMC(AM) Sumter SC 2 hrs
KGIM(AM) Aberdeen SD 12 hrs
KSDN(AM) Aberdeen SD 15 hrs
KBFS(AM) Belle Fourche SD 20 hrs
KBRK(AM) Brookings SD 9 hrs
KZMX(AM) Hot Springs SD 6 hrs
KJAM(AM) Madison SD 11 hrs
KMSD(AM) Milbank SD 6 hrs
KMIT(FM) Mitchell SD 18 hrs
KORN(AM) Mitchell SD 10 hrs
KOLY(AM) Mobridge SD
KIMM(AM) Rapid City SD 1 hr
KTOQ(AM) Rapid City SD 2 hrs
KPLO-FM Reliance SD 1 hr
KSDR-FM Watertown SD 8 hrs
KKYA(FM) Yankton SD 5 hrs
KYNT(AM) Yankton SD 5 hrs
WNAX(AM) Yankton SD 35 hrs
WLAR(AM) Athens TN 2 hrs
*WHCB(FM) Bristol TN 1 hr
WNKX(FM) Centerville TN 1 hr
WNKX-FM Centerville TN
WMCP(AM) Columbia TN 4 hrs
WZYX(AM) Cowan TN 2 hrs
WEKR(AM) Fayetteville TN 1 hr
WHIN(AM) Gallatin TN 5 hrs
WXJB(AM) Harrogate TN 2 hrs
WDXI(AM) Jackson TN 12 hrs
WCLC(AM) Jamestown TN 2 hrs
WDEB(AM) Jamestown TN 3 hrs
WJFC(AM) Jefferson City TN 1 hr
WBUZ(FM) La Vergne TN 1 hr
WEEN(AM) Lafayette TN 5 hrs
WKZX-FM Lenoir City TN 5 hrs
WLIL(AM) Lenoir City TN 4 hrs
WLIV(AM) Livingston TN 2 hrs
WMSR(AM) Manchester TN
WAKI(AM) McMinnville TN 2 hrs
WBMC(AM) McMinnville TN 5 hrs
WREC(AM) Memphis TN 3 hrs
WSM(AM) Nashville TN 6 hrs
*WDNX(FM) Olive Hill TN 1 hr
WMUF(AM) Paris TN 2 hrs
WUAT(AM) Pikeville TN 5 hrs
WLIJ(AM) Shelbyville TN 3 hrs
WDBL(AM) Springfield TN 10 hrs
WYVY(FM) Union City TN 5 hrs
WCDT(AM) Winchester TN 15 hrs
KYYW(AM) Abilene TX 3 hrs
KGNC(AM) Amarillo TX 11 hrs
KFYN(AM) Bonham TX 5 hrs
KNTX(AM) Bowie TX 4 hrs
KNEL-FM Brady TX 4 hrs
KWHI(AM) Brenham TX 3 hrs
KBOC(AM) Bridgeport TX 5 hrs
KOXE(FM) Brownwood TX 3 hrs
KCAR(AM) Clarksville TX 2 hrs
KSTA(AM) Coleman TX 14 hrs
KXCT(AM) Coleman TX 14 hrs
KZNE(AM) College Station TX 10 hrs
KVMC(AM) Colorado City TX 8 hrs
KXIT(AM) Dalhart TX 7 hrs
KDDD-FM Dumas TX 5 hrs
KURV(AM) Edinburg TX 10 hrs
KNES(FM) Fairfield TX 3 hrs
KIJN(AM) Farwell TX 3 hrs
KMUL(AM) Farwell TX 3 hrs
KFLP-FM Floydada TX 8 hrs

Special Programming on Radio Stations in the U.S.

WBAP(AM) Fort Worth TX 6 hrs
KNAF(AM) Fredericksburg TX 5 hrs
KGAF(AM) Gainesville TX 2 hrs
KCTI(AM) Gonzales TX 5 hrs
KPIR(AM) Granbury TX 1 hr
KGVL(AM) Greenville TX 5 hrs
KHLT(AM) Hallettsville TX 6 hrs
KVRP-FM Haskell TX 8 hrs
KWRD(AM) Henderson TX 5 hrs
KPAN(AM) Hereford TX 12 hrs
KEBE(AM) Jacksonville TX 9 hrs
KOOI-FM Jacksonville TX 9 hrs
KCOX(AM) Jasper TX 5 hrs
KMBL(AM) Junction TX 6 hrs
KVLG(AM) La Grange TX 4 hrs
KCYL(AM) Lampasas TX 5 hrs
KZZN(AM) Littlefield TX 7 hrs
KFYO(AM) Lubbock TX 15 hrs
KCUL(AM) Marshall TX 3 hrs
KCUL-FM Marshall TX 3 hrs
KRQX(AM) Mexia TX 12 hrs
KSFA(AM) Nacogdoches TX 7 hrs
KNET(AM) Palestine TX 6 hrs
KOMX(FM) Pampa TX 10 hrs
KBUS(FM) Paris TX 6 hrs
KIUN(AM) Pecos TX 3 hrs
KEYE(AM) Perryton TX 2 hrs
KEYE-FM Perryton TX 2 hrs
KKYN-FM Plainview TX 12 hrs
KVOP(AM) Plainview TX 12 hrs
KFNI(AM) Pleasanton TX 3 hrs
KITE(FM) Port Lavaca TX 1 hr
KIXC-FM Quanah TX 3 hrs
KGKL(AM) San Angelo TX 6 hrs
KBAL(AM) San Saba TX 2 hrs
KBAL-FM San Saba TX 2 hrs
KWED(AM) Seguin TX 6 hrs
KIKZ(AM) Seminole TX 5 hrs
KSEM-FM Seminole TX 5 hrs
KBKH(FM) Shamrock TX 25 hrs
KDAE(AM) Sinton TX 6 hrs
KSTV(AM) Stephenville TX 5 hrs
KXOX(AM) Sweetwater TX 5 hrs
KVOU(AM) Uvalde TX 12 hrs
KBEC(AM) Waxahachie TX 5 hrs
KWUD(AM) Woodville TX 02 hrs
KSUB(AM) Cedar City UT 6 hrs
KNAK(AM) Delta UT 5 hrs
KVNU(AM) Logan UT 2 hrs
KMTI(AM) Manti UT 5 hrs
KOAL(AM) Price UT 5 hrs
KSVC(AM) Richfield UT 1 hr
KHQN(AM) Spanish Fork UT 4 hrs
KVEL(AM) Vernal UT 2 hrs
WBTX(AM) Broadway-Timberville VA 1 hr
WWZW(FM) Buena Vista VA 3 hrs
WDIC(AM) Clinchco VA 1 hr
WPZZ(FM) Crewe VA 10 hrs
WDUF(AM) Duffield VA 5 hrs
WEVA(AM) Emporia VA one hr
WPAK(AM) Farmville VA 1 hr
WWWJ(AM) Galax VA 1 hr
WXGM(AM) Gloucester VA 2 hrs
WXGM-FM Gloucester VA 2 hrs
WMNA(AM) Gretna VA 8 hrs
WNRG(AM) Grundy VA 5 hrs
WSVA(AM) Harrisonburg VA 8 hrs
WHHV(AM) Hillsville VA 1 hr
WKWI(FM) Kilmarnock VA 2 hrs
WOJL(AM) Louisa VA 2 hrs
WRVA(AM) Richmond VA 3 hrs
WXLZ(AM) Saint Paul VA 3 hrs
WKGM(AM) Smithfield VA 02 hrs
WSBV(AM) South Boston VA 1 hr
WKDW(AM) Staunton VA 1 hr
WHEO(AM) Stuart VA 4 hrs
WRAR-FM Tappahannock VA 5 hrs
WKCW(AM) Warrenton VA 1 hr
WKCI(AM) Waynesboro VA 2 hrs
WZLF(FM) Bellows Falls VT 1 hr
WFAD(AM) Middlebury VT 1 hr
*WGDR(FM) Plainfield VT 1 hr
KNBQ(FM) Centralia WA 1 hr
KOZI(AM) Chelan WA 3 hrs
KOZI(AM) Chelan WA 3 hrs
KCLX(AM) Colfax WA 5 hrs

KYSN(FM) East Wenatchee WA 1 hr
KTBI(AM) Ephrata WA 15 hrs
KULE(AM) Ephrata WA 1 hr
KULE-FM Ephrata WA 5 hrs
KONA(AM) Kennewick WA 3 hrs
KBRC(AM) Mount Vernon WA 5 hrs
KNCW(FM) Omak WA 1 hr
KOMW(AM) Omak WA 2 hrs
KQQQ(AM) Pullman WA 3 hrs
KWNC(AM) Quincy WA 5 hrs
KGA(AM) Spokane WA 1 hr
KQNT(AM) Spokane WA 6 hrs
KTEL(AM) Walla Walla WA 5 hrs
KPQ(AM) Wenatchee WA 3 hrs
KIT(AM) Yakima WA 6 hrs
WBEV(AM) Beaver Dam WI 8 hrs
WXRO(FM) Beaver Dam WI 6 hrs
WFCL(AM) Clintonville WI 8 hrs
WAXX(FM) Eau Claire WI 15 hrs
WAYY(AM) Eau Claire WI 5 hrs
KFIZ(AM) Fond du Lac WI 10 hrs
WTAQ(AM) Green Bay WI 5 hrs
WAUN(FM) Kewaunee WI 10 hrs
WKTY(AM) La Crosse WI 10 hrs
WGLR(AM) Lancaster WI 10 hrs
WTSO(AM) Madison WI 20 hrs
WMAM(AM) Marinette WI 3 hrs
WDLB(AM) Marshfield WI 14 hrs
WIGM(AM) Medford WI 10 hrs
WMEQ(FM) Menomonie WI 15 hrs
WJMT(AM) Merrill WI 7 hrs
WCCN(AM) Neillsville WI 19 hrs
WPKR(FM) Omro WI 4 hrs
WPVL(AM) Platteville WI 12 hrs
WJUB(AM) Plymouth WI 5 hrs
WPDR(AM) Portage WI 6 hrs
WNFM(FM) Reedsburg WI 18 hrs
WRCO(AM) Richland Center WI 2 hrs
WRCO-FM Richland Center WI 18 hrs
WEVR(AM) River Falls WI 18 hrs
*WRFW(FM) River Falls WI 10 hrs
WTCH(AM) Shawano WI 21 hrs
WHBL(AM) Sheboygan WI 10 hrs
WCSW(AM) Shell Lake WI 3 hrs
WOSQ(FM) Spencer WI 8 hrs
WDOR-FM Sturgeon Bay WI 5 hrs
WVRQ(AM) Viroqua WI 2 hrs
WVRQ-FM Viroqua WI 5 hrs
WDUX(AM) Waupaca WI 4 hrs
WFDL(AM) Waupun WI 5 hrs
WDEZ(AM) Wausau WI 4 hrs
WSAU(AM) Wausau WI 5 hrs
WHTL-FM Whitehall WI 5 hrs
WELD(AM) Fisher WV 3 hrs
*WVMR(AM) Frost WV 5 hrs
WTBZ(AM) Grafton WV 1 hr
WKCJ(FM) Lewisburg WV 3 hrs
WGGE(FM) Parkersburg WV 2 hrs
WLWF(AM) Ravenswood WV 1 hr
WWVA(AM) Wheeling WV 2 hrs
KFBC(AM) Cheyenne WY 1 hr
KMER(AM) Kemmerer WY 3 hrs
KCGY(FM) Laramie WY 1 hr
KHAT(AM) Laramie WY 1 hr
KASL(AM) Newcastle WY 5 hrs
KPOW(AM) Powell WY 19 hrs
KTAK(FM) Riverton WY 5 hrs
KVOW(AM) Riverton WY 5 hrs
KGOS(AM) Torrington WY 20 hrs
KYCN(AM) Wheatland WY 3 hrs
KZEW(FM) Wheatland WY 7 hrs

Alternative

KWKM(FM) Saint Johns AZ 3 hrs
*KALW(FM) San Francisco CA 4 hrs
KFMU-FM Oak Creek CO 4 hrs
WRUF-FM Gainesville FL 6 hrs
WXXL(FM) Tavares FL 6 hrs
KECH-FM Sun Valley ID 5 hrs
*WPCD(FM) Champaign IL 4 hrs
*WQUB(FM) Quincy IL 2 hrs
KIND-FM Independence KS 4 hrs
WFNX(FM) Lynn MA 3 hrs
*WRCJ-FM Detroit MI 6 hrs
WFRD(FM) Hanover NH 1 hr
KAGM(FM) Los Lunas NM 18 hrs

KRNG(FM) Fallon NV
*WGCC-FM Batavia NY
*WDPS(FM) Dayton OH 3 hrs
*WHSS(FM) Hamilton OH 1 hr
KSPI-FM Stillwater OK
WFBC-FM Greenville SC 2 hrs
KWKQ(FM) Graham TX 10 hrs
*KRTU(FM) San Antonio TX 21 hrs
*KYVT(FM) Yakima WA 3 hrs
*KUWS(FM) Superior WI 16 hrs

American Indian

*KRUA(FM) Anchorage AK 3 hrs
*KDLG(AM) Dillingham AK 1 hr
*KIYU(AM) Galena AK 2 hrs
KCAM(AM) Glennallen AK 1 hr
*KTOO(FM) Juneau AK 1 hr
*KDLL(FM) Kenai AK 10 hrs
KIAM(AM) Nenana AK 3 hrs
*KJNP(AM) North Pole AK 2 hrs
WNSI-FM Atmore AL 1 hr
*KABF(FM) Little Rock AR 2 hrs
KRDE(FM) Globe AZ 6 hrs
*KUAZ(AM) Tucson AZ 1 hr
*KXCI(FM) Tucson AZ 2 hrs
*KNNB(FM) Whiteriver AZ 8 hrs
KTNN(AM) Window Rock AZ
*KZFR(FM) Chico CA 2 hrs
*KFCF(FM) Fresno CA 2 hrs
*KMUD(FM) Garberville CA 1 hr
*KIDE(FM) Hoopa CA 20 hrs
*KCSB-FM Santa Barbara CA 3 hrs
KRTZ(FM) Cortez CO 1 hr
*KAFM(FM) Grand Junction CO 3 hrs
*KSUT(FM) Ignacio CO 7 hrs
*WUCF-FM Orlando FL 2 hrs
WKHC(FM) Dahlonega GA 1 hr
*WBCX(FM) Gainesville GA 4 hrs
*KISU-FM Pocatello ID 4 hrs
KWIK(AM) Pocatello ID 1 hr
*WUEV(FM) Evansville IN 1 hr
*WMMT(FM) Whitesburg KY 45 hrs
*WMFO(FM) Medford MA 6 hrs
*WHFC(FM) Bel Air MD 3 hrs
*WUPI(FM) Presque Isle ME 2 hrs
WCUP(FM) L'Anse MI 2 hrs
*WLNZ(FM) Lansing MI 3. hrs
*WNMC-FM Traverse City MI 1 hr
*KBSB(FM) Bemidji MN 3 hrs
*KAXE(FM) Grand Rapids MN 3 hrs
*KVSC(FM) Saint Cloud MN 4 hrs
*KKFI(FM) Kansas City MO 2 hrs
KVCK-FM Wolf Point MT 1 hr
*WWCU(FM) Cullowhee NC 5. hrs
*WFSS(FM) Fayetteville NC 3 hrs
*KEYA(FM) Belcourt ND 9 hrs
*KCND(FM) Bismarck ND 2 hrs
*KDPR(FM) Dickinson ND 2 hrs
*KABU(FM) Fort Totten ND 19 hrs
*KMHA(FM) Four Bears ND 4 hrs
*KPRJ(FM) Jamestown ND 2 hrs
*KMPR(FM) Minot ND 2 hrs
*KPPR(FM) Williston ND 2 hrs
*KINI(FM) Crookston NE 15 hrs
*WNEC-FM Henniker NH 18 hrs
*KABR(FM) Alamo Community NM 10 hrs
KPCL(FM) Farmington NM 7 hrs
*KGLP(FM) Gallup NM 1 hr
KGLX(FM) Gallup NM 3 hrs
KYVA-FM Grants NM 10 hrs
*KTDB(FM) Ramah NM 8 hrs
*KSFR(FM) Santa Fe NM 4 hrs
KXTC(FM) Thoreau NM 1 hr
*KSHI(FM) Zuni NM 20 hrs
WYBG(AM) Massena NY
*WBAI(FM) New York NY 1 hr
*WCWS(FM) Wooster OH 2 hrs
KVSP(FM) Anadarko OK 1 hr
KZUE(AM) El Reno OK 1 hr
*KOSN(FM) Ketchum OK 1 hr
KIRC(FM) Seminole OK 1 hr
*KOSU(FM) Stillwater OK 1 hr
KWSH(FM) Wewoka OK 1 hr
*KMUN(FM) Astoria OR 2 hrs
*KTEC(FM) Klamath Falls OR 1 hr

KOLY(AM) Mobridge SD
KOLY-FM Mobridge SD
*KBHE-FM Rapid City SD 1 hr
*KTSD-FM Reliance SD 1 hr
*KBHB(AM) Sturgis SD 2 hrs
*KAOR(FM) Vermillion SD 2 hrs
*KUSD(AM) Vermillion SD 1 hr
WLIL(AM) Lenoir City TN 1 hr
*WRVU(FM) Nashville TN 2 hrs
*KOOP(FM) Hornsby TX 1 hr
*KZMU(FM) Moab UT 5 hrs
*KRCL(FM) Salt Lake City UT 4 hrs
*WUVT-FM Blacksburg VA 4 hrs
*WGDR(FM) Plainfield VT 1 hr
*KSER(FM) Everett WA 2 hrs
*KAOS(FM) Olympia WA 3 hrs
*KSFC(FM) Spokane WA 5 hrs
KYNR(FM) Toppenish WA 20 hrs
*WPNE-FM Green Bay WI 2. hrs
*WOJB(FM) Reserve WI 15 hrs
*WHND(FM) Sister Bay WI 2 hrs
WLWF(AM) Ravenswood WV 1 hr

Arabic

WCEV(AM) Cicero IL 2 hrs
WPNA(AM) Oak Park IL 2 hrs
KLAV(AM) Las Vegas NV 7 hrs
*WDIY(FM) Allentown PA 1 hr
*WMUH(FM) Allentown PA 2 hrs
KARI(AM) Blaine WA 1 hr

Armenian

KTYM(AM) Inglewood CA 2 hrs
*KUSF(FM) San Francisco CA 1 hr
*WJCU(FM) University Heights OH 2 hrs
WRIB(AM) Providence RI 1 hr

Beautiful Music

*KNOG(FM) Nogales AZ 5 hrs
WMDJ-FM Allen KY
WMRX-FM Beaverton MI 2 hrs
*KUMM(FM) Morris MN 2 hrs
KHND(AM) Harvey ND 3 hrs
WALK-FM Patchogue NY
KNNK(FM) Dimmitt TX 20 hrs
*KZAZ(FM) Bellingham WA 7 hrs

Big Band

*KASU(FM) Jonesboro AR 2 hrs
KQST(FM) Sedona AZ 4 hrs
*WGRS(FM) Guilford CT 8 hrs
*WMNR(FM) Monroe CT 4 hrs
*WRXC(FM) Shelton CT 8 hrs
*WGSK(FM) South Kent CT 8 hrs
WTAN(AM) Clearwater FL 2 hrs
WPGS(AM) Mims FL 4 hrs
KROS(AM) Clinton IA 3 hrs
*WSIU(FM) Carbondale IL 4 hrs
WLBK(AM) De Kalb IL 5 hrs
WHPO(FM) Hoopeston IL 1 hr
WTAY(AM) Robinson IL 10 hrs
WTYE(FM) Robinson IL 10 hrs
WINU(AM) Shelbyville IL 2 hrs
WMAY(AM) Springfield IL 5 hrs
WXNT(AM) Indianapolis IN 2 hrs
WAWK(AM) Kendallville IN 2 hrs
KIND(AM) Independence KS 2 hrs
KLKC(AM) Parsons KS 3 hrs
*WKMS-FM Murray KY 2 hrs
KVCL(AM) Winnfield LA 4 hrs
WDIS(AM) Norfolk MA 1 hr
*WESM(FM) Princess Anne MD 10 hrs
*WKHS(FM) Worton MD 2 hrs
*WHFR(FM) Dearborn MI 5 hrs
WBNZ(FM) Frankfort MI 2 hrs
*WLNZ(FM) Lansing MI 1 hr
WMLM(AM) Saint Louis MI 4 hrs
WIOS(FM) Tawas City MI 6 hrs
KLTF(AM) Little Falls MN 5 hrs
KYMN(AM) Northfield MN 3 hrs
KOLV(FM) Olivia MN

*KRCU(FM) Cape Girardeau MO 1 hr
*KXMS(FM) Joplin MO 2 hrs
KPRK(AM) Livingston MT 4 hrs
KMTA(AM) Miles City MT 2 hrs
WXIT(AM) Blowing Rock NC 4 hrs
*WCCE(FM) Buie's Creek NC 4 hrs
*WZRU(FM) Roanoke Rapids NC 4 hrs
WLHC(FM) Robbins NC 4 hrs
KMTY(FM) Holdrege NE 5 hrs
KUVR(AM) Holdrege NE 5 hrs
WSNJ(AM) Bridgeton NJ
*WNTI(FM) Hackettstown NJ 4 hrs
KRSY(AM) Alamogordo NM 6 hrs
KRSN(AM) Los Alamos NM 8 hrs
WDNY(AM) Dansville NY 3 hrs
WDNY-FM Dansville NY 3 hrs
*WHPC(FM) Garden City NY 4 hrs
WWSC(AM) Glens Falls NY
*WNYC(AM) New York NY 2 hrs
WDOS(AM) Oneonta NY 7 hrs
WRGR(FM) Tupper Lake NY 2 hrs
WNYV(FM) Whitehall NY 3 hrs
WATH(AM) Athens OH 15 hrs
WOHI(AM) East Liverpool OH 4 hrs
WKFI(AM) Wilmington OH 5 hrs
WBBZ(AM) Ponca City OK 3 hrs
KBEZ(FM) Tulsa OK 5 hrs
WNPV(AM) Lansdale PA 3 hrs
WLSH(AM) Lansford PA 4 hrs
WPHB(AM) Philipsburg PA 5 hrs
WRAW(AM) Reading PA 5 hrs
WCRI(FM) Block Island RI 4 hrs
WJMX(FM) Florence SC 3 hrs
WBZF(FM) Hartsville SC 3 hrs
WHSC(AM) Hartsville SC 3 hrs
WMYB(FM) Myrtle Beach SC
*KTPB(FM) Kilgore TX 4 hrs
*KNCT-FM Killeen TX 6 hrs
WKSI-FM Stephens City VA 2 hrs
WFAD(AM) Middlebury VT 21 hrs
WVNR(AM) Poultney VT 3 hrs
KELA(AM) Centralia-Chehalis WA 3 hrs
KEYG(AM) Grand Coulee WA 4 hrs
WATW(AM) Ashland WI
WBOG(AM) Tomah WI 3 hrs
*WVMR(AM) Frost WV 3 hrs
*WWVU-FM Morgantown WV 2 hrs

Black

*KSKA(FM) Anchorage AK 8 hrs
*KSUA(FM) Fairbanks AK 8 hrs
*KHNS(FM) Haines AK 4 hrs
KIAL(AM) Unalaska AK 04 hrs
WANA(AM) Anniston AL 12 hrs
WHMA-FM Ashland AL 6 hrs
WNSI-FM Atmore AL 1 hr
WQUA(FM) Citronelle AL 18 hrs
WEZZ(FM) Clanton AL 5 hrs
WULA(AM) Eufaula AL 3 hrs
WGYV(AM) Greenville AL 6 hrs
*WJAB(FM) Huntsville AL 3 hrs
WMGY(AM) Montgomery AL 15 hrs
*WVAS(FM) Montgomery AL 5 hrs
WOPP(AM) Opp AL 4 hrs
WKAX(AM) Russellville AL 4 hrs
WHBB(AM) Selma AL 18 hrs
WTRB-FM Sylacauga AL 6 hrs
KAMD-FM Camden AR 5 hrs
*KUAF(FM) Fayetteville AR 5 hrs
KFFA(AM) Helena AR 10 hrs
KITA(AM) Little Rock AR 19 hrs
KOSE(AM) Wilson AR 6 hrs
KDVA(FM) Buckeye AZ 6 hrs
KTKT(AM) Tucson AZ 1 hr
*KXCI(FM) Tucson AZ 4 hrs
KPFA(FM) Berkeley CA 18 hrs
*KMUD(FM) Garberville CA 3 hrs
*KXLU(FM) Los Angeles CA 10 hrs
KMPO(FM) Modesto CA 3 hrs
*KVMR(FM) Nevada City CA 4 hrs
*KSPB(FM) Pebble Beach CA 18 hrs
KZYX(FM) Philo CA 6 hrs
*KUCR(FM) Riverside CA 18 hrs
*KCRW(FM) Santa Monica CA

Broadcasting & Cable Yearbook 2006
D-735

Special Programming on Radio Stations in the U.S.

KMBY-FM Seaside CA 4 hrs
*KYCC(FM) Stockton CA 6 hrs
KDIA(AM) Vallejo CA 2 hrs
KDYA(AM) Vallejo CA 2 hrs
*KGNU-FM Boulder CO 7 hrs
KLDC(AM) Brighton CO 2 hrs
*KCSU-FM Fort Collins CO 3 hrs
*KAFM(FM) Grand Junction CO 3 hrs
*KMSA(FM) Grand Junction CO 6 hrs
*WPKN(FM) Bridgeport CT 4 hrs
WFIF(AM) Milford CT 6 hrs
*WCNI(FM) New London CT 3 hrs
*WVUD(FM) Newark DE 10 hrs
WPHK(FM) Blountstown FL 12 hrs
*WVUM(FM) Coral Gables FL 7 hrs
WAVS(AM) Davie FL
WRUF(AM) Gainesville FL 4 hrs
*WUFT-FM Gainesville FL 4 hrs
WGWD(FM) Gretna FL 20 hrs
WIOJ(AM) Jacksonville Beach FL 3 hrs
WLBE(AM) Leesburg FL 3 hrs
WMEL(AM) Melbourne FL 2 hrs
WMFQ(FM) Ocala FL 2 hrs
WOCA(AM) Ocala FL 2 hrs
*WKGC-FM Panama City FL 6 hrs
WPRY(AM) Perry FL 2 hrs
WJNA(AM) Royal Palm Beach FL 2 hrs
*WKPX(FM) Sunrise FL 3 hrs
*WVFS(FM) Tallahassee FL 8 hrs
*WBVM(FM) Tampa FL 4 hrs
WDEC-FM Americus GA 5 hrs
WRFC(AM) Athens GA 15 hrs
WFNS(AM) Blackshear GA 10 hrs
WMOG(AM) Brunswick GA 8 hrs
WGRA(AM) Cairo GA 6 hrs
WEBS(AM) Calhoun GA 2 hrs
WBTR-FM Carrollton GA 5 hrs
WDXQ(AM) Cochran GA 6 hrs
WDXQ-FM Cochran GA 6 hrs
WCUG(AM) Cuthbert GA 4 hrs
WUFF(AM) Eastman GA 5 hrs
WBHB(AM) Fitzgerald GA 4 hrs
*WBCX(FM) Gainesville GA 12 hrs
WLAG(AM) La Grange GA 1 hr
WYTH(AM) Madison GA 13 hrs
WYIS(AM) McRae GA 4 hrs
WMVG(AM) Milledgeville GA 4 hrs
WJEP(AM) Ochlocknee GA 2 hrs
WWIO(AM) Saint Mary's GA 4 hrs
WTGA(AM) Thomaston GA 4 hrs
WLET(AM) Toccoa GA
KLNG(AM) Council Bluffs IA 6 hrs
*KTPR(FM) Fort Dodge IA 4 hrs
*KRUI-FM Iowa City IA 12 hrs
*KUOI-FM Moscow ID 3 hrs
KATZ-FM Alton IL
*WESN(FM) Bloomington IL 18 hrs
*WEFT(FM) Champaign IL 8 hrs
WCEV(AM) Cicero IL 7 hrs
*WVKC(FM) Galesburg IL 6 hrs
*WCSF(FM) Joliet IL 2 hrs
WJOL(AM) Joliet IL 1 hr
*WMXM(FM) Lake Forest IL 6 hrs
*WLRA(FM) Lockport IL 15 hrs
*WQNA(FM) Springfield IL 9 hrs
*WEAX(FM) Angola IN 2 hrs
WPWX(FM) Hammond IN
*WFYI-FM Indianapolis IN 5 hrs
WXFN(AM) Muncie IN 3 hrs
*WBAA(AM) West Lafayette IN 1 hr
WWVR(FM) West Terre Haute IN 6 hrs
*KONQ(FM) Dodge City KS 10 hrs
KWBW(AM) Hutchinson KS 2 hrs
*KSDB-FM Manhattan KS 4 hrs
*WCVK(FM) Bowling Green KY 2 hrs
*WWHR(FM) Bowling Green KY 2 hrs
WCPM(AM) Cumberland KY 3 hrs
WHBN(AM) Harrodsburg KY 1 hr
*WNKJ(FM) Hopkinsville KY 7 hrs
WFXY(AM) Middlesboro KY 2 hrs
WEKY(AM) Richmond KY 12 hrs
*KLSP(FM) Angola LA 10 hrs
KAJN-FM Crowley LA 2 hrs
KFNV-FM Ferriday LA 3 hrs
WOMN(AM) Franklinton LA 5 hrs
*KLPI-FM Ruston LA 6 hrs
*KSCL(FM) Shreveport LA 3 hrs
*KNSU(FM) Thibodaux LA 8 hrs
KVPI-FM Ville Platte LA 10 hrs
KVCL(AM) Winnfield LA 3 hrs
KVCL-FM Winnfield LA 20 hrs
*WAMH(FM) Amherst MA 12 hrs
*WERS(FM) Boston MA 15 hrs
WMKI(AM) Boston MA 2 hrs
WUNR(AM) Brookline MA 20 hrs
WHRB(FM) Cambridge MA 18 hrs
*WMBR(FM) Cambridge MA 15 hrs
*WGAJ(FM) Deerfield MA 5 hrs
*WUML(FM) Lowell MA 2 hrs
*WMFO(FM) Medford MA 12 hrs
*WMLN-FM Milton MA 4 hrs
*WZBC(FM) Newton MA 2 hrs
*WOZQ(FM) Northampton MA 20 hrs
*WNMH(FM) Northfield MA 8 hrs
*WOMR(FM) Provincetown MA 3 hrs
*WMWM(FM) Salem MA 16 hrs
*WBSL-FM Sheffield MA 2 hrs
*WMHC(FM) South Hadley MA 1 hr
WMAS(AM) Springfield MA 1 hr
*WNEK-FM Springfield MA 8 hrs
*WYAJ(FM) Sudbury MA 6 hrs
*WCHC(FM) Worcester MA 8 hrs
WKHI(FM) Fruitland MD 5 hrs
WJSS(AM) Havre de Grace MD
*WERU-FM Blue Hill ME 4 hrs
*WUPI(FM) Presque Isle ME 2 hrs
*WMHB(FM) Waterville ME 8 hrs
WLQV(AM) Detroit MI 10 hrs
*WRCJ-FM Detroit MI 4 hrs
WVIB(FM) Holton MI 3 hrs
*WIDR(FM) Kalamazoo MI 18 hrs
*WUPX(FM) Marquette MI 6 hrs
WHLS(AM) Port Huron MI 1 hr
WSJM(AM) Saint Joseph MI 5 hrs
*WNMC-FM Traverse City MI 20 hrs
WMFN(AM) Zeeland MI 2hrs hrs
*KAXE(FM) Grand Rapids MN 2 hrs
*KFAI(FM) Minneapolis MN 10 hrs
*KVSC(FM) Saint Cloud MN 6 hrs
KNOF(FM) Saint Paul MN 5 hrs
KMFC(FM) Centralia MO 3 hrs
*KOPN(FM) Columbia MO 10 hrs
*KCFV(FM) Ferguson MO 4 hrs
KLSC(FM) Malden MO 6 hrs
*KMVC(FM) Marshall MO 10 hrs
KLID(AM) Poplar Bluff MO 2 hrs
KDRO(AM) Sedalia MO 1 hr
WBLE(FM) Batesville MS 3 hrs
WELZ(AM) Belzoni MS 20 hrs
WCJU(AM) Columbia MS 112 hrs
WKCU(AM) Corinth MS 2 hrs
WGVM(AM) Greenville MS 5 hrs
WABG(AM) Greenwood MS 4 hrs
WGRM(AM) Greenwood MS 2 hrs
WCPC(AM) Houston MS 10 hrs
WNBN(AM) Meridian MS
WPMP(AM) Pascagoula-Moss Point MS 3 hrs
WRJW(AM) Picayune MS 8 hrs
WJDR(FM) Prentiss MS 5 hrs
WSSO(AM) Starkville MS 12 hrs
*KGLT(FM) Bozeman MT 1 hr
WFGW(AM) Black Mountain NC 1 hr
WRRZ(AM) Clinton NC 5 hrs
*WNCU(FM) Durham NC
WGAI(AM) Elizabeth City NC 4 hrs
*WRVS-FM Elizabeth City NC 15 hrs
*WUAW(FM) Erwin NC
WSML(AM) Graham NC 18 hrs
WKEW(AM) Greensboro NC 10 hrs
*WQFS(FM) Greensboro NC 20 hrs
*WZMB(FM) Greenville NC 9 hrs
WYRN(AM) Louisburg NC
WHIP(AM) Mooresville NC 6 hrs
WDJS(AM) Mount Olive NC 5 hrs
WNNC(AM) Newton NC 2 hrs
*WKNC-FM Raleigh NC 10 hrs
WRXO(AM) Roxboro NC 4 hrs
WTSB(AM) Selma NC 6 hrs
*KRNU(FM) Lincoln NE 2 hrs
*KZUM(FM) Lincoln NE 13 hrs
*KIOS-FM Omaha NE 2 hrs
*KWSC(FM) Wayne NE 4 hrs
*WUNH(FM) Durham NH 4 hrs
*WGLS-FM Glassboro NJ 10 hrs
*WFJS(FM) Hazlet NJ 12 hrs
*WRRC(FM) Lawrenceville NJ 10 hrs
*WMNJ(FM) Madison NJ 6 hrs
*WSOU(FM) South Orange NJ 2 hrs
*WKNJ-FM Union Township NJ 2 hrs
*WMSC(FM) Upper Montclair NJ 4 hrs
KKIM(AM) Albuquerque NM 2 hrs
*WXBA(FM) Brentwood NY 5 hrs
*WBSU(FM) Brockport NY 1 hr
*WBNY(FM) Buffalo NY 12 hrs
*WSLU(FM) Canton NY
WSIV(AM) East Syracuse NY 20 hrs
*WCVF-FM Fredonia NY 8 hrs
*WRCU-FM Hamilton NY 10 hrs
WHLI(AM) Hempstead NY 1 hr
WKJY(FM) Hempstead NY 1 hr
WLNL(AM) Horseheads NY 1 hr
WVOX(AM) New Rochelle NY 1 hr
*WBAI(FM) New York NY 10 hrs
*WKCR-FM New York NY 12 hrs
*WNYU-FM New York NY 5 hrs
WHLD(AM) Niagara Falls NY 2 hrs
WJJL(AM) Niagara Falls NY 2 hrs
*WNYK(FM) Nyack NY 6 hrs
*WONY(FM) Oneonta NY 3 hrs
*WOSS(FM) Ossining NY 2 hrs
*WQKE(FM) Plattsburgh NY 9 hrs
WRNY(AM) Rome NY 3 hrs
*WFNP(FM) Rosendale NY 14 hrs
*WUSB(FM) Stony Brook NY 12 hrs
*WJPZ-FM Syracuse NY 12 hrs
*WRPI(FM) Troy NY 8 hrs
*WOUB(AM) Athens OH 8 hrs
*WCDR-FM Cedarville OH 2 hrs
*WOHC(FM) Chillicothe OH 2 hrs
*WCSB(FM) Cleveland OH 20 hrs
WERE(AM) Cleveland OH 6 hrs
*WOSU(AM) Columbus OH 1 hr
*WWSU(FM) Dayton OH 12 hrs
*WDUB(FM) Granville OH 9 hrs
WRBP(FM) Hubbard OH
WMAN(AM) Mansfield OH 1 hr
WFCJ(FM) Miamisburg OH 4 hrs
WNPQ(FM) New Philadelphia OH 4 hrs
WCCD(AM) Parma OH 3 hrs
*WOHP(FM) Portsmouth OH 2 hrs
WLEC(AM) Sandusky OH 6 hrs
*WEEC(FM) Springfield OH 1 hr
*WXUT(FM) Toledo OH 8 hrs
*WOBN(FM) Westerville OH 2 hrs
KZBB(FM) Poteau OK 2 hrs
*KMUN(FM) Astoria OR 2 hrs
KKNX(AM) Eugene OR 3 hrs
*KLCC(FM) Eugene OR 3 hrs
*KRVM-FM Eugene OR 2 hrs
*KWVA(FM) Eugene OR 4 hrs
*KTEC(FM) Klamath Falls OR 3 hrs
*KEOL(FM) La Grande OR 12 hrs
*KSLC(FM) McMinnville OR 2 hrs
*KLCO(FM) Newport OR 3 hrs
*KRRC(FM) Portland OR 10 hrs
KXMG(AM) Portland OR 1 hr
KAVJ(FM) Sutherlin OR 1 hr
WBVP(AM) Beaver Falls PA 6 hrs
*WLVR(FM) Bethlehem PA 12 hrs
*WCAL(FM) California PA 4 hrs
*WCUC-FM Clarion PA 6 hrs
*WFSE(FM) Edinboro PA 15 hrs
*WKVR-FM Huntingdon PA 10 hrs
*WIUP-FM Indiana PA 14 hrs
*WFNM(FM) Lancaster PA 6 hrs
*WNTE(FM) Mansfield PA 5 hrs
*WARC(FM) Meadville PA 8 hrs
WJST(AM) New Castle PA 1 hr
*WKDU(FM) Philadelphia PA 8 hrs
*WRCT(FM) Pittsburgh PA 12 hrs
*WVMW-FM Scranton PA 2 hrs
*WSYC-FM Shippensburg PA 9 hrs
*WXVU(FM) Villanova PA 10 hrs
WSBA(AM) York PA 3 hrs
WBRU(FM) Providence RI 20 hrs
WARV(AM) Warwick RI 2 hrs
WOON(AM) Woonsocket RI 1 hr
WLUA(AM) Belton SC 8 hrs
WBSC(AM) Bennettsville SC 15 hrs
*WSCI(FM) Charleston SC 5 hrs
WCRE(AM) Cheraw SC 5 hrs
WFIS(AM) Fountain Inn SC 4 hrs
WJBS(AM) Holly Hill SC 17 hrs
WRIX(AM) Homeland Park SC 7 hrs
WRML(FM) Pageland SC 2 hrs
*KSDJ(FM) Brookings SD 8 hrs
WYXI(AM) Athens TN 1 hr
*WHCB(FM) Bristol TN 1 hr
*WMBW(FM) Chattanooga TN 1 hr
*WAPX-FM Clarksville TN 6 hrs
WKBL(AM) Covington TN 12 hrs
*WMKW(FM) Crossville TN 3 hrs
WHIN(AM) Gallatin TN 2 hrs
WMRO(AM) Gallatin TN 7 hrs
*WVCP(FM) Gallatin TN 8 hrs
WITA(AM) Knoxville TN 8 hrs
WKZX-FM Lenoir City TN 1 hr
WLIL(AM) Lenoir City TN 1 hr
WDXL(AM) Lexington TN 4 hrs
*WEVL(FM) Memphis TN 10 hrs
*WQOX(FM) Memphis TN 5 hrs
WXRQ(AM) Mount Pleasant TN 4 hrs
WGNS(AM) Murfreesboro TN 9 hrs
WLAC(AM) Nashville TN 20 hrs
*WRVU(FM) Nashville TN 3 hrs
WOFE(AM) Rockwood TN 1 hr
*WUTS(FM) Sewanee TN 2 hrs
WLIJ(AM) Shelbyville TN 1 hr
WYVY(FM) Union City TN 5 hrs
*KGNZ(FM) Abilene TX 2 hrs
KZQQ(AM) Abilene TX 4 hrs
*KACV-FM Amarillo TX 8 hrs
KLVQ(AM) Athens TX 1 hr
KAGC(AM) Bryan TX 2 hrs
*KWTS(FM) Canyon TX 3 hrs
KIXL(AM) Del Valle TX 6 hrs
KTMR(AM) Edna TX 3 hrs
KNES(FM) Fairfield TX 3 hrs
KGVL(AM) Greenville TX 1 hr
*KOOP(FM) Hornsby TX 2 hrs
*KPFT(FM) Houston TX 15 hrs
KHVL(AM) Huntsville TX 5 hrs
*KBJS(FM) Jacksonville TX 1 hr
*KTAI(FM) Kingsville TX 8 hrs
KVLG(AM) La Grange TX 1 hr
KSHN-FM Liberty TX 3 hrs
KFRO(AM) Longview TX 3 hrs
*KTXT-FM Lubbock TX 6 hrs
KZRC(FM) Markham TX 4 hrs
KLRK(FM) Marlin TX 4 hrs
KHKZ(FM) Mercedes TX 3 hrs
KLVL(AM) Pasadena TX 4 hrs
*KPVU(FM) Prairie View TX 6 hrs
KPYK(AM) Terrell TX 5 hrs
KQRL(AM) Waco TX 4 hrs
*KZMU(FM) Moab UT 3 hrs
*KRCL(FM) Salt Lake City UT 20 hrs
*WTJU(FM) Charlottesville VA 8 hrs
WKEY(AM) Covington VA 1 hr
WFAX(AM) Falls Church VA 15 hrs
WMNA(AM) Gretna VA 2 hrs
WKWI(FM) Kilmarnock VA 6 hrs
*WVRU(FM) Radford VA 6 hrs
WKBA(AM) Vinton VA 10 hrs
WKCI(AM) Waynesboro VA 3 hrs
*WGDR(FM) Plainfield VT 8 hrs
*KUGS(FM) Bellingham WA 10 hrs
*KRLF(FM) Pullman WA 1 hr
*KZUU(FM) Pullman WA 12 hrs
*KNHC(FM) Seattle WA
*KSFC(FM) Spokane WA 2 hrs
*KWRS(FM) Spokane WA 12 hrs
*KUPS(FM) Tacoma WA 18 hrs
KJOX(AM) Yakima WA 2 hrs
*WORT(FM) Madison WI 3 hrs
*WMSE(FM) Milwaukee WI 13 hrs
*KUWS(FM) Superior WI 4 hrs
*WCCX(FM) Waukesha WI 3 hrs
*WVWC(FM) Buckhannon WV 4 hrs
*WWVU-FM Morgantown WV 9 hrs
*WQAB(FM) Philippi WV 2 hrs
WLWF(FM) Ravenswood WV 1 hr
*WPHP(FM) Wheeling WV 4 hrs

Bluegrass

*WQPR(FM) Muscle Shoals AL
WNUZ(AM) Talladega AL 6 hrs
*WUAL-FM Tuscaloosa AL
*KABF(FM) Little Rock AR 6 hrs
*KFJC(FM) Los Altos CA 8 hrs
*KCSN(FM) Northridge CA 5 hrs
*KDUR(FM) Durango CO 6 hrs
WOCM(FM) Selbyville DE 1 hr
WWOJ(FM) Avon Park FL 2 hrs
*WUCF-FM Orlando FL 3 hrs
WTUF(FM) Boston GA 5 hrs
*WUWG(FM) Carrollton GA 2 hrs
WJJC(AM) Commerce GA 13 hrs
*WQNA(FM) Springfield IL 6 hrs
*WUIS(FM) Springfield IL 2 hrs
WAWK(AM) Kendallville IN 2 hrs
*WPUM(FM) Rensselaer IN 3 hrs
*WECI(FM) Richmond IN 19 hrs
*KANU(FM) Lawrence KS 4 hrs
WEKT(AM) Elkton KY
WGOH(AM) Grayson KY 13 hrs
*WNKU(FM) Highland Heights KY 3 hrs
WWAG(FM) McKee KY 9 hrs
*WMKY(FM) Morehead KY 3 hrs
WKCA(FM) Owingsville KY 3 hrs
WKWY(FM) Tompkinsville KY 6 hrs
WTKY(AM) Tompkinsville KY 6 hrs
WTKY-FM Tompkinsville KY 6 hrs
*WMMT(FM) Whitesburg KY 10 hrs
*WMMT(FM) Whitesburg KY 39 hrs
WTCW(AM) Whitesburg KY 10 hrs
WGKY(FM) Wickliffe KY 6 hrs
*WOMR(FM) Provincetown MA 3 hrs
WKHW(FM) Pocomoke City MD 4 hrs
*WDET-FM Detroit MI 3 hrs
*WMUK(FM) Kalamazoo MI 4 hrs
*KBEM-FM Minneapolis MN 4 hrs
*KOPN(FM) Columbia MO 6 hrs
KTJJ(FM) Farmington MO 2 hrs
*KUMR(FM) Rolla MO 5 hrs
*KCLC(FM) Saint Charles MO 12 hrs
*KDHX(FM) Saint Louis MO 8 hrs
WKZU(FM) Ripley MS 2 hrs
WZJS(FM) Banner Elk NC 3 hrs
*WCCE(FM) Buie's Creek NC 3 hrs
*WQFS(FM) Greensboro NC 3 hrs
WECR(AM) Newland NC 2 hrs
WQDR(FM) Raleigh NC
WLHC(FM) Robbins NC 3 hrs
WEGG(AM) Rose Hill NC 10 hrs
WTQR(FM) Winston-Salem NC 2 hrs
*WDVR(FM) Delaware Township NJ 6 hrs
*WBJB-FM Lincroft NJ 3 hrs
*WBZC(FM) Pemberton NJ 4 hrs
*WFDU(FM) Teaneck NJ 18 hrs
*KGLP(FM) Gallup NM 12 hrs
*KRWG(FM) Las Cruces NM 8 hrs
*WBFO(FM) Buffalo NY 3 hrs
WXHC(FM) Homer NY 2 hrs
*WSQG-FM Ithaca NY 5 hrs
*WUBJ(FM) Jamestown NY 3 hrs
*WOLN(FM) Olean NY 3 hrs
*WVKR-FM Poughkeepsie NY 5 hrs
*WCNY-FM Syracuse NY 3 hrs
*WUNY(FM) Utica NY 3 hrs
*WJNY(FM) Watertown NY 3 hrs
*WOSU(AM) Columbus OH 12 hrs
*WYSO(FM) Yellow Springs OH 6 hrs
KVSP(FM) Anadarko OK 2 hrs
KTNT(FM) Eufaula OK 3 hrs
WWSM(AM) Annville-Cleona PA 3 hrs
WDKC(FM) Covington PA 1 hr
WSKE(FM) Everett PA 3 hrs
*WVMM(FM) Grantham PA 2 hrs
WLMI(FM) Kane PA 1 hr
WPHB(AM) Philipsburg PA 4 hrs
*WYEP-FM Pittsburgh PA 4 hrs
*WQSU(FM) Selinsgrove PA 7 hrs
*WBYO(FM) Sellersville PA 2 hrs
*WBYX(FM) Stroudsburg PA 3. hrs
*WZZD(FM) Warwick PA 3 hrs
WCRI(FM) Block Island RI 4 hrs
WOPI(AM) Bristol TN 9 hrs
WVFB(FM) Celina TN 6 hrs

Broadcasting & Cable Yearbook 2006

D-736

Special Programming on Radio Stations in the U.S.

*WHRS(FM) Cookeville TN 1 hr
WEMB(AM) Erwin TN 2 hrs
*WVCP(FM) Gallatin TN 2 hrs
WCLC(AM) Jamestown TN 3 hrs
WWAM(AM) Jasper TN 1 hr
*WLAF(AM) La Follette TN 7 hrs
*WRVU(FM) Nashville TN 3 hrs
*WUTS(FM) Sewanee TN 2 hrs
WSBI(AM) Static TN 1 hr
WNTT(AM) Tazewell TN
*KETR(FM) Commerce TX 3 hrs
KSWA(AM) Graham TX 2 hrs
KSHN-FM Liberty TX 2 hrs
*KOCV(AM) Odessa TX 2 hrs
WKDE-FM Altavista VA 10 hrs
WWZW(FM) Buena Vista VA 1 hr
*WFTR(AM) Front Royal VA 2 hrs
WMNA(AM) Gretna VA 20 hrs
WMNA-FM Gretna VA 4 hrs
*WEMC(FM) Harrisonburg VA 12 hrs
WOJL(FM) Louisa VA 14 hrs
WSIG(FM) Mount Jackson VA 6 hrs
WCUL(FM) Orange VA
WKDW(AM) Staunton VA 1 hr
WKCW(AM) Warrenton VA
*KBCS(FM) Bellevue WA
*WOJB(FM) Reserve WI 2 hrs
WVRQ-FM Viroqua WI 2 hrs
*WVMR(AM) Frost WV 5 hrs
*WWVU-FM Morgantown WV 1 hr
WMOV(AM) Ravenswood WV 10 hrs
KKTY-FM Douglas WY 1 hr

Blues

*KUAC(FM) Fairbanks AK 4 hrs
*KTNA(FM) Talkeetna AK 5 hrs
WDLT-FM Chickasaw AL 18 hrs
WLDA(FM) Fort Rucker AL 5 hrs
*WVAS(FM) Montgomery AL 6 hrs
*WQPR(FM) Muscle Shoals AL
*WUAL-FM Tuscaloosa AL
*WVUA-FM Tuscaloosa AL 3 hrs
KFFA(AM) Helena AR 8 hrs
*KASU(FM) Jonesboro AR
KERX(FM) Paris AR 3 hrs
KWKM(FM) Saint Johns AZ 1 hr
*KNCA(FM) Burney CA 6 hrs
*KSPC(FM) Claremont CA 4 hrs
*KFSR(FM) Fresno CA 6 hrs
*KKJZ(FM) Long Beach CA 15 hrs
*KSBR(FM) Mission Viejo CA 3 hrs
*KNSQ(FM) Mount Shasta CA 6 hrs
*KVMR(FM) Nevada City CA 7 hrs
KHOP(FM) Oakdale CA 2 hrs
KZAP(FM) Paradise CA 4 hrs
*KZYX(FM) Philo CA 3 hrs
KRXQ(FM) Sacramento CA 1 hr
*KXJZ(FM) Sacramento CA 7 hrs
*KCPR(FM) San Luis Obispo CA 3 hrs
*KCSM(FM) San Mateo CA 5 hrs
*KSCU(FM) Santa Clara CA 3 hrs
*KCLU(FM) Thousand Oaks CA 5 hrs
*KRCC(FM) Colorado Springs CO 5 hrs
*KDUR(FM) Durango CO 6 hrs
*KIBT(FM) Fountain CO 3 hrs
*KWSB(FM) Gunnison CO 3 hrs
KWUF(FM) Pagosa Springs CO 10 hrs
*KVNF(FM) Paonia CO 3 hrs
*KOTO(FM) Telluride CO 7 hrs
*WESU(FM) Middletown CT 10 hrs
*WFCS(FM) New Britain CT 12 hrs
*WUCF(FM) Orlando FL 2 hrs
*WFCF(FM) Saint Augustine FL 4 hrs
*WKPX(FM) Sunrise FL 3 hrs
*WCLK(FM) Atlanta GA 3 hrs
WQVE(FM) Camilla GA 5 hrs
*WOI(AM) Ames IA 3 hrs
*KUNI(FM) Cedar Falls IA 8 hrs
KROS(AM) Clinton IA 1 hr
*KRUI-FM Iowa City IA 3 hrs
*KRNI(AM) Mason City IA 8 hrs
*KUNY(FM) Mason City IA 8 hrs
*KOJI(FM) Okoboji IA 2 hrs
*KWIT(FM) Sioux City IA 2 hrs
KECH-FM Sun Valley ID 8. hrs

*WEFT(FM) Champaign IL 10 hrs
WMKB(FM) Earlville IL 5 hrs
WVRV(FM) East St. Louis IL 1 hr
*WIUM(FM) Macomb IL 7 hrs
*WIUS(FM) Macomb IL 4 hrs
*WQUB(FM) Quincy IL 2 hrs
*WNIU(FM) Rockford IL 4 hrs
*WQNA(FM) Springfield IL 3 hrs
*WARG(FM) Summit IL 6 hrs
WTTS(FM) Bloomington IN 2 hrs
*WVPE(FM) Elkhart IN 15 hrs
*WFYI-FM Indianapolis IN 4 hrs
*WCYT(FM) Lafayette Township IN 2 hrs
*KTCC(FM) Colby KS 3 hrs
KOTE(FM) Eureka KS 2 hrs
*KANU(FM) Lawrence KS 4 hrs
*KJHK(FM) Lawrence KS 2 hrs
*WNKU(FM) Highland Heights KY 6 hrs
*WRFL(FM) Lexington KY 3 hrs
*WMKY(FM) Morehead KY 3 hrs
*WKMS-FM Murray KY 2 hrs
*WMMT(FM) Whitesburg KY 2 hrs
*WMMT(FM) Whitesburg KY 5 hrs
*KLSU(FM) Baton Rouge LA 3 hrs
KBCE(FM) Boyce LA 1 hr
*KSLU(FM) Hammond LA 6 hrs
*KEDM(FM) Monroe LA 4 hrs
*KNWD(FM) Natchitoches LA 6 hrs
*KSCL(FM) Shreveport LA 1 hr
*WMUA(FM) Amherst MA 15 hrs
*WERS(FM) Boston MA 15 hrs
*WGBH(FM) Boston MA 8 hrs
WHRB(FM) Cambridge MA 4 hrs
*WCCH(FM) Holyoke MA 6 hrs
*WSMU-FM North Dartmouth MA 7 hrs
*WESM(FM) Princess Anne MD 5 hrs
*WTMD(FM) Towson MD 3 hrs
WBQI(FM) Bar Harbor ME 15 hrs
*WERU-FM Blue Hill ME 5 hrs
*WMEB-FM Orono ME 7 hrs
WPHX-FM Sanford ME 3 hrs
*WQAC-FM Alma MI 7 hrs
*WCBN-FM Ann Arbor MI 3 hrs hrs
WGTO(AM) Cassopolis MI 4 hrs
*WHFR(FM) Dearborn MI 6 hrs
*WDET-FM Detroit MI 10 hrs
*WRCJ-FM Detroit MI 6 hrs
*WDBM(FM) East Lansing MI 4 hrs
WKLT(FM) Kalkaska MI 2 hrs
WNWN(AM) Shiremanstown PA 4 hrs
WRKR(FM) Portage MI 4 hrs
*WPHS(FM) Warren MI 3 hrs
*WTIP(FM) Grand Marais MN 15 hrs
*KUMM(FM) Morris MN 2 hrs
*KVSC(FM) Saint Cloud MN 6 hrs
*KCOU(FM) Columbia MO 2 hrs
*KOPN(FM) Columbia MO 13 hrs
*KJLU(FM) Jefferson City MO
*KKFI(FM) Kansas City MO 9 hrs
KPOW-FM La Monte MO 6 hrs
*KGSP(FM) Parkville MO 12 hrs
*KCLC(FM) Saint Charles MO 7 hrs
*KDHX(FM) Saint Louis MO 12 hrs
KTOZ(FM) Springfield MO 4 hrs
WESE(FM) Baldwyn MS 6 hrs
*WUSM-FM Hattiesburg MS 10 hrs
WKRA-FM Holly Springs MS 12 hrs
*WJSU(FM) Jackson MS 2 hrs
WJZD(FM) Long Beach MS 20 hrs
WASU-FM Boone NC 2 hrs
*WNAA(FM) Greensboro NC 3 hrs
*WQFS(FM) Greensboro NC 2 hrs
*WZMB(FM) Greenville NC 3 hrs
WVOD(FM) Manteo NC 2 hrs
*WSHA(FM) Raleigh NC 8 hrs
*WNCW(FM) Spindale NC 4 hrs
*KCND(FM) Bismarck ND 2 hrs
*KFJM(FM) Grand Forks ND 3 hrs
KRNU(FM) Lincoln NE 4 hrs
*KUCV(FM) Lincoln NE 1 hr
*KZUM(FM) Lincoln NE 13 hrs
KKCD(FM) Omaha NE 1 hr
*KWSC(FM) Wayne NE 2 hrs
WHDQ(FM) Claremont NH 1 hr
*WUNH(FM) Durham NH 3 hrs

WFRD(FM) Hanover NH 1 hr
*WNEC-FM Henniker NH 4 hrs
*WKNH(FM) Keene NH 3 hrs
*WPCR-FM Plymouth NH 3 hrs
*WNTI(FM) Hackettstown NJ 11 hrs
*WBJB-FM Lincroft NJ 4 hrs
*WMNJ(FM) Madison NJ 4 hrs
KBAC(FM) Las Vegas NM 2 hrs
KRSI(FM) Garapan-Saipan NP 6 hrs
*WBFO(FM) Buffalo NY 8 hrs
*WGMC(FM) Greece NY 3 hrs
*WRHU(FM) Hempstead NY 2 hrs
*WICB(FM) Ithaca NY 2 hrs
WVBR-FM Ithaca NY 5 hrs
*WUBJ(FM) Jamestown NY 8 hrs
*WOLN(FM) Olean NY 8 hrs
WZOZ(FM) Oneonta NY 2 hrs
WTKV(FM) Oswego NY 1 hr
WPDH(FM) Poughkeepsie NY
*WSPN(FM) Saratoga Springs NY 9 hrs
*WUSB(FM) Stony Brook NY 10 hrs
*WAER(FM) Syracuse NY 3 hrs
*WONB(FM) Ada OH 6 hrs
*WCBE(FM) Columbus OH 3 hrs
*WDPS(FM) Dayton OH 6 hrs
WJZE(FM) Oak Harbor OH
*WUSO(FM) Springfield OH 3 hrs
WJUC(FM) Swanton OH 5 hrs wkly
*WXTS-FM Toledo OH 5 hrs
*WXUT(FM) Toledo OH 2 hrs
*WYSO(FM) Yellow Springs OH 4 hrs
*KRSC-FM Claremore OK 6 hrs
*KGOU(FM) Norman OK 8 hrs
*KROU(FM) Spencer OK 8 hrs
*KSMF(FM) Ashland OR 6 hrs
*KSBA(FM) Coos Bay OR 6 hrs
KUJZ(FM) Creswell OR 2 hrs
*KLCC(FM) Eugene OR 3 hrs
*KMHD(FM) Gresham OR 15 hrs
*KSKF(FM) Klamath Falls OR 6 hrs
*KLCO(FM) Newport OR 4 hrs
KYTE(FM) Newport OR 2 hrs
KMCQ(FM) The Dalles OR 4 hrs
*WDCV-FM Carlisle PA 6 hrs
*WDNR(FM) Chester PA 2 hrs
*WPSB(FM) Kane PA 3 hrs
*WKDU(FM) Philadelphia PA 3 hrs
*WYEP-FM Pittsburgh PA 7 hrs
*WSYC-FM Shippensburg PA 2 hrs
WWII(AM) Shiremanstown PA 4 hrs
*WPSU(FM) State College PA 3 hrs
*WRDV(FM) Warminster PA 3 hrs
*WRLC(FM) Williamsport PA 3 hrs
*WRIU(FM) Kingston RI 3 hrs
*WSSB-FM Orangeburg SC 2 hrs
*KAUR(FM) Sioux Falls SD 3 hrs
*WTTU(FM) Cookeville TN 3 hrs
WRLT(FM) Franklin TN 2 hrs
*WETS(FM) Johnson City TN 12 hrs
*WQOX(FM) Memphis TN 5 hrs
*WRVU(FM) Nashville TN 3 hrs
*WUTS(FM) Sewanee TN 5 hrs
*KAZI-FM Austin TX 6 hrs
*KUT(FM) Austin TX 6 hrs
KLUB(FM) Bloomington TX 1 hr
KVJM(FM) Hearne TX 4 hrs
*KSAU(FM) Nacogdoches TX 2 hrs
*KOCV(FM) Odessa TX 4 hrs
*KUTX(FM) San Angelo TX 6 hrs
*KSTX(FM) San Antonio TX 6 hrs
KNCN(FM) Sinton TX 2 hrs
*KSUU(FM) Cedar City UT 4 hrs
*KZMU(FM) Moab UT 19 hrs
*WMRY(FM) Crozet VA 4 hrs
*WWHS-FM Hampden-Sydney VA 2 hrs
*WHOV(FM) Hampton VA 3 hrs
*WMRA(FM) Harrisonburg VA 4 hrs
*WMRL(FM) Lexington VA 4 hrs
*WVRU(FM) Radford VA 2 hrs
WCVE(FM) Richmond VA 5 hrs
*WCWM(FM) Williamsburg VA 3 hrs
WRMC-FM Middlebury VT 10 hrs
WIZN(FM) Vergennes VT 3 hrs
*KSER(FM) Everett WA 6 hrs

*KKZX(FM) Spokane WA 2 hrs
*KPLU-FM Tacoma WA 12 hrs
*KUPS(FM) Tacoma WA 6 hrs
*WBSD(FM) Burlington WI 3 hrs
*WUEC(FM) Eau Claire WI 3 hrs
WMCS(AM) Greenfield WI 6 hrs
*WHND(FM) Sister Bay WI 2 hrs
*WWSP(FM) Stevens Point WI 4 hrs
*WVWC(FM) Buckhannon WV 2 hrs

Children

KLEF(FM) Anchorage AK 1 hr
*KTOO(FM) Juneau AK 1 hr
*KMXT(FM) Kodiak AK 1 hr
KAKN(FM) Naknek AK 3 hrs
*KRSA(AM) Petersburg AK 10 hrs
*WMBV(FM) Dixons Mills AL 3 hrs
*WRWA(FM) Dothan AL 1 hr
*WTSU(FM) Troy AL 1 hr
KFMM(FM) Thatcher AZ 2 hrs
*KCFY(FM) Yuma AZ 7 hrs wkly
*KYRM(FM) Yuma AZ 6 hrs
KZRO(FM) Dunsmuir CA 2 hrs
KGBA-FM Holtville CA 4 hrs
KSPN(AM) Los Angeles CA 24 hrs
*KXLU(FM) Los Angeles CA 1 hr
KWVE(FM) San Clemente CA 3 hrs
KFAX(AM) San Francisco CA 1 hr
*WIHS(FM) Middletown CT 9 hrs
*WAPJ(FM) Torrington CT 1 hr
*WAFG(FM) Fort Lauderdale FL 4 hrs
*WJYO(FM) Fort Myers FL 5 hrs
*WJLF(FM) Gainesville FL 1 hr
WMEL(AM) Melbourne FL one hr
WZSP(FM) Nocatee FL
*WIRP(FM) Pennsuco FL 6 hrs
*WBVM(FM) Tampa FL 4 hrs
WDWD(AM) Atlanta GA
*WTJB(FM) Columbus GA 1 hr
*KHMG(FM) Barrigada GU 2 hrs
*KHOE(FM) Fairfield IA 3 hrs
KTFC(FM) Sioux City IA 5 hrs
KTFG(FM) Sioux Rapids IA 5 hrs
*KCIR(FM) Twin Falls ID 2 hrs
*WLUW(FM) Chicago IL 2 hrs
WCEV(AM) Cicero IL 6 hrs
*WUEV(FM) Evansville IN 5 hrs
WSYW(AM) Indianapolis IN 5 hrs
*KJTY(FM) Topeka KS 5 hrs
*KPAE(FM) Erwinville LA 5 hrs
WMKI(AM) Boston MA 18 hrs
WFCC-FM Chatham MA 1 hr
WJSS(AM) Havre de Grace MD 1 hr
*WKHS(FM) Worton MD 5 hrs
*WHCF(FM) Bangor ME 6 hrs
*WBOR(FM) Brunswick ME 3 hrs
WBQX(FM) Thomaston ME 1 hr
WDBC(AM) Escanaba MI 1 hr
*WLNZ(FM) Lansing MI 1 hr
*WSAE(FM) Spring Arbor MI 2 hrs
KJLY(FM) Blue Earth MN 4 hrs
*WTIP(FM) Grand Marais MN
*KGNA-FM Arnold MO 7 hrs
*KYMC(FM) Ballwin MO 1 hr
*KGNN-FM Cuba MO 7 hrs
*KKBL(FM) Monett MO 2 hrs
*KGNV(FM) Washington MO 6 hrs
*WPAE(FM) Centreville MS 5 hrs
*WMBU(FM) Forest MS 5 hrs
*WUSM-FM Hattiesburg MS 2 hrs
WLRC(AM) Walnut MS
*KLMT(FM) Billings MT 2 hrs
*WMIT(FM) Black Mountain NC 2.5 hrs
*KABU(FM) Fort Totten ND 12 hrs
WMVB(AM) Millville NJ 3 hrs
*WMHI(FM) Cape Vincent NY 11 hrs
*WMHQ(FM) Malone NY 11 hrs
WYBG(AM) Massena NY
*WRHO(FM) Oneonta NY 2 hrs
*WMHR(FM) Syracuse NY 11 hrs
*WMHN(FM) Webster NY 11 hrs
WFCJ(FM) Miamisburg OH 2 hrs
KIHN(AM) Hugo OK 1 hr
*KMUN(FM) Astoria OR 6 hrs
*KWVA(FM) Eugene OR 4 hrs

*WFKJ(AM) Cashtown PA 12 hrs
*WDNR(FM) Chester PA 2 hrs
WCOJ(AM) Coatesville PA 2 hrs
WDBA(FM) DuBois PA 2 hrs
*WXPN(FM) Philadelphia PA 5 hrs
WCTL(FM) Union City PA 1 hr
*WTMV(FM) Youngsville PA 10 hrs
*KLND(FM) Little Eagle SD 4 hrs
*WHCB(FM) Bristol TN 10 hrs
KESN(FM) Allen TX 2 hrs
KBYG(AM) Big Spring TX 1 hr
KPSM(FM) Brownwood TX 3 hrs
WRR(FM) Dallas TX 2 hrs
KMIC(AM) Houston TX 10 hrs
*KTPB(FM) Kilgore TX 1 hr
*KNLE-FM Round Rock TX 4 hrs
*KTER(FM) Rudolph TX 4 hrs
KPYK(AM) Terrell TX 1 hr
*KVNE(FM) Tyler TX 4 hrs
*WTJU(FM) Charlottesville VA 2 hrs
WPRZ(AM) Warrenton VA 7 hrs
*WVPS(FM) Burlington VT .5 hrs
*WWOD(FM) Hartford VT 3 hrs
WCVT(FM) Stowe VT 1 hr
*WWMP(FM) Waterbury VT 3 hrs
WTWN(AM) Wells River VT
*KRLF(FM) Pullman WA 5 hrs
*KDNA(FM) Yakima WA 5. hrs
*WLWR(FM) Fond du Lac WI 8 hrs
*WGNV(FM) Milladore WI 4 hrs
*WVPG(FM) Parkersburg WV 1 hr
*WQAB(FM) Philippi WV 2 hrs

Chinese

KGBA-FM Holtville CA 14 hrs
KKLA-FM Los Angeles CA 2 hrs
KEST(AM) San Francisco CA
*KUSF(FM) San Francisco CA 9 hrs
KSJX(AM) San Jose CA 10 hrs
WXYB(AM) Indian Rocks Beach FL 1 hr
*KSDA-FM Agat GU 1 hr
*WMBR(FM) Cambridge MA 2 hrs
WJDA(AM) Quincy MA 3 hrs
*WZLY(FM) Wellesley MA 1 hr
*WDBM(FM) East Lansing MI 4 hrs
WSDS(FM) Salem Township MI 4 hrs
*KRNM(FM) Chalan Kanoa-Saipan NP 1 hr
*WUSB(FM) Stony Brook NY 1 hr
*WRPI(FM) Troy NY 2 hrs
WBZK(AM) York SC 10 hrs
*KHCB(AM) Galveston TX 13 hrs
*KHCB-FM Houston TX 1 hr
*KHCH(AM) Huntsville TX 1 hr
*WUVT-FM Blacksburg VA 2 hrs

Christian

KCAM(AM) Glennallen AK 8 hrs
KJLH-FM Compton CA 6 hrs
KNCO(FM) Grass Valley CA 4 hrs
KFTM(FM) Fort Morgan CO 6 hrs
WEBY(AM) Milton FL 7 hrs
WMGF(FM) Mount Dora FL 20 hrs
WROM(AM) Rome GA
WDML(FM) Woodlawn IL 3 hrs
KIND-FM Independence KS 2 hrs
*WRFL(FM) Lexington KY 3 hrs
*WHFC(FM) Bel Air MD 6 hrs
KCPI(FM) Albert Lea MN 3 hrs
*KYMC(FM) Ballwin MO 1 hr
*KWJC(FM) Liberty MO 10 hrs
KNEM(FM) Nevada MO 5 hrs
KNMO(FM) Nevada MO 5 hrs
KAYX(FM) Richmond MO
KKDY(FM) West Plains MO 3 hrs
*WASU-FM Boone NC 3 hrs
*WSGE(FM) Dallas NC
*WYQS(FM) Mars Hill NC 15 hrs
*WKNC-FM Raleigh NC 4 hrs
WLHC(FM) Robbins NC 7 hrs
KTNC(AM) Falls City NE 1 hr
*WKNH(FM) Keene NH 3 hrs
*WITR(FM) Henrietta NY 10 hrs

Special Programming on Radio Stations in the U.S.

*WRIP(FM) Windham NY 2 hrs
*WRDL(FM) Ashland OH 7 hrs
KGFY(FM) Stillwater OK 4 hrs
KLDR(FM) Harbeck-Fruitdale OR 2 hrs wkly hrs
*WCYJ-FM Waynesburg PA 3 hrs
WFIS(AM) Fountain Inn SC 3 hrs
KSLT(FM) Spearfish SD 10 hrs
WNRQ(FM) Nashville TN 6 hrs
KQTY(AM) Borger TX 5 hrs
KQTY-FM Borger TX 5 hrs
KPSO-FM Falfurrias TX 3 hrs
KWEL(AM) Midland TX 2.5 hrs
*KSAU(FM) Nacogdoches TX 2 hrs
KMAS(AM) Shelton WA 4 hrs

Classic Rock

KEDD(FM) Johannesburg CA 4 hrs
KMMT(FM) Mammoth Lakes CA 4 hrs
KVAY(FM) Lamar CO 4 hrs
*WXCI(FM) Danbury CT 3 hrs
WSGL(FM) Naples FL 5 hrs
*KWLC(AM) Decorah IA
*WCSF(FM) Joliet IL 4 hrs
*WRRG(FM) River Grove IL 2 hrs
*WBKE-FM North Manchester IN 6 hrs
*WECI(FM) Richmond IN 16 hrs
*WVUR-FM Valparaiso IN 3 hrs
*KTCC(FM) Colby KS 3 hrs
*WKMS-FM Murray KY 2 hrs
*WBIM-FM Bridgewater MA 6 hrs
*WRBC(FM) Lewiston ME 11 hrs
WKLT(FM) Kalkaska MI
*KUMM(FM) Morris MN 2 hrs
*KVSC(FM) Saint Cloud MN 8 hrs
*KMVC(FM) Marshall MO 4 hrs
WERX-FM Columbia NC
*WPSC-FM Wayne NJ 12 hrs
*WCWP(FM) Brookville NY 2 hrs
*WHPC(FM) Garden City NY 2 hrs
*WQKE(FM) Plattsburgh NY 12 hrs
WMKX(FM) Brookville PA 6 hrs
*WJRH(FM) Easton PA 4 hrs
*WCYJ-FM Waynesburg PA 3 hrs
*WCLH(FM) Wilkes-Barre PA 9 hrs
*WDOM(FM) Providence RI 3 hrs
*KSAU(FM) Nacogdoches TX 14 hrs
KNCN(FM) Sinton TX 2 hrs
*WVBC(FM) Bethany WV 8 hrs
KKTY-FM Douglas WY 3 hrs

Classical

*KBRW(AM) Barrow AK 2 hrs
*KYUK(AM) Bethel AK 4 hrs
KCAM(AM) Glennallen AK 10 hrs
*KHNS(FM) Haines AK 14 hrs
*KRBD(FM) Ketchikan AK 11 hrs
*KOTZ(FM) Kotzebue AK 4 hrs
KIAM(AM) Nenana AK 1 hr
KICY-FM Nome AK 2 hrs
*KNOM(AM) Nome AK 5 hrs
*KNOM-FM Nome AK 5 hrs
KRSA(FM) Petersburg AK 5 hrs
*KCAW(FM) Sitka AK 15 hrs
*KSTK(FM) Wrangell AK 4 hrs
KQSM-FM Bentonville AR 2 hrs
KTCN(FM) Eureka Springs AR 5 hrs
*KSMC(FM) Moraga CA 4 hrs
*KAZU(FM) Pacific Grove CA 3 hrs
*KZYX(FM) Philo CA 14 hrs
*KUCR(FM) Riverside CA 14 hrs
*KUSF(FM) San Francisco CA 6 hrs
KHJQ(FM) Susanville CA 5 hrs
*KCSS(FM) Turlock CA 3 hrs
*KGNU-FM Boulder CO 13 hrs
*KDUR(FM) Durango CO 6 hrs
KIUP(AM) Durango CO 2 hrs
*KCIC(FM) Grand Junction CO 14 hrs
*KSUT(FM) Ignacio CO 8 hrs
*KVNF(FM) Paonia CO 15 hrs
KVRH(AM) Salida CO 3 hrs
KVRH(AM) Salida CO 3 hrs
*KOTO(FM) Telluride CO 9 hrs
*WPKN(FM) Bridgeport CT 2 hrs

*WRTC-FM Hartford CT 4 hrs
*WCNI(FM) New London CT 6 hrs
*WGSK(FM) South Kent CT 1 hr
*WWEB(FM) Wallingford CT 2 hrs
*WNHU(FM) West Haven CT 9 hrs
*WVUD(FM) Newark DE 10 hrs
WKEY-FM Key West FL 4 hrs
*WFIT(FM) Melbourne FL 3 hrs
*WRAS(FM) Atlanta GA 3 hrs
*WREK(FM) Atlanta GA 15 hrs
WMOG(AM) Brunswick GA 1 hr
WYTH(AM) Madison GA 1 hr
*WGUR(FM) Milledgeville GA 7 hrs
*KWLC(FM) Decorah IA
*KDFR(FM) Des Moines IA 2 hrs
*KCMR(FM) Mason City IA 5 hrs
KSAS-FM Caldwell ID 2 hrs
KSRA(AM) Salmon ID 1 hr
KSRA-FM Salmon ID 1 hr
*WESN(FM) Bloomington IL 6 hrs
*WHPK-FM Chicago IL 10 hrs
*WEPS(FM) Elgin IL 3 hrs
*WTPC(FM) Elsah IL 3 hrs
*WVKC(FM) Galesburg IL 18 hrs
*WJCH(FM) Joliet IL 3 hrs
*WMXM(FM) Lake Forest IL 3 hrs
*WLRA(FM) Lockport IL 6 hrs
*WMTH(FM) Park Ridge IL 4 hrs
*WEAX(FM) Angola IN 4 hrs
*WDSO(FM) Chesterton IN 1 hr
*WBKE-FM North Manchester IN 10 hrs
*WPUM(FM) Rensselaer IN 3 hrs
*WVUR-FM Valparaiso IN 3 hrs
*WVUB(FM) Vincennes IN 6 hrs
KIND(AM) Independence KS 3 hrs
*KLSU(FM) Baton Rouge LA 3 hrs
*WTUL(FM) New Orleans LA 15 hrs
*KLPI-FM Ruston LA 3 hrs
*WAMH(FM) Amherst MA 3 hrs
WPNI(AM) Amherst MA 2 hrs
*WXPL(FM) Fitchburg MA 2 hrs
WPVQ(FM) Greenfield MA 6 hrs
*WCCH(FM) Holyoke MA 2 hrs
*WUML(FM) Lowell MA 4 hrs
*WZBC(FM) Newton MA 3 hrs
*WJJW(FM) North Adams MA 3 hrs
*WOZQ(FM) Northampton MA 2 hrs
*WNMH(FM) Northfield MA 2 hrs
*WOMR(FM) Provincetown MA 16 hrs
*WYAJ(FM) Sudbury MA 3 hrs
WMVY(FM) Tisbury MA 4 hrs
WCRB(FM) Waltham MA
*WSKB(FM) Westfield MA 3 hrs
*WCHC(FM) Worcester MA 6 hrs
*WHFC(FM) Bel Air MD 18 hrs
WERU-FM Blue Hill ME 4 hrs
*WBOR(FM) Brunswick ME 8 hrs
*WSJB-FM Standish ME 2 hrs
*WOES(FM) Ovid-Elsie MI 1 hr
WRSR(FM) Owosso MI 1 hr
WELY(AM) Ely MN 6 hrs
*KAXE(FM) Grand Rapids MN 2 hrs
*KUMM(FM) Morris MN 3 hrs
KNXR(FM) Rochester MN 4 hrs
*WMCN(FM) Saint Paul MN 4 hrs
*KQAL(FM) Winona MN 14 hrs
KIXQ(FM) Joplin MO 3 hrs
*WJJC(FM) Liberty MO 10 hrs
*KGNV(FM) Washington MO 5 hrs
*KGLT(FM) Bozeman MT 11 hrs
KMSM-FM Butte MT 2 hrs
*KNMC(FM) Havre MT 10 hrs
KALS(AM) Kalispell MT 1 hr
*WFSS(FM) Fayetteville NC 3 hrs
*WQFS(FM) Greensboro NC 3 hrs
*WZMB(FM) Greenville NC 3 hrs
WVOD(FM) Manteo NC 6 hrs
*WYQS(FM) Mars Hill NC 7 hrs
WCVP(FM) Murphy NC 20 hrs
*WSNC(FM) Winston-Salem NC 4 hrs
KHAS(AM) Hastings NE 4 hrs
*KLPR(FM) Kearney NE 18 hrs
KCMI(FM) Terrytown NE 4 hrs
WDCR(AM) Hanover NH 8 hrs
*WKNH(FM) Keene NH 4 hrs
*WPCR-FM Plymouth NH 3 hrs

*WKDN-FM Camden NJ 2 hrs
*WCVH(FM) Flemington NJ 10 hrs
*WMNJ(FM) Madison NJ 2 hrs
WDOX(FM) North Cape May NJ 3 hrs
*WLFR(FM) Pomona NJ 4 hrs
*KUNM(FM) Albuquerque NM 12 hrs
KPCL(FM) Farmington NM 1 hr
*KGLP(FM) Gallup NM 8 hrs
*WXLH(FM) Blue Mountain Lake NY
WBFO(FM) Buffalo NY 1 hr
*WSLU(FM) Canton NY
*WHCL(FM) Clinton NY 9 hrs
*WRCU-FM Hamilton NY 4 hrs
*WJSL(FM) Houghton NY 5 hrs
WHVW(AM) Hyde Park NY 16 hrs
*WBAI(FM) New York NY 5 hrs
*WONY(FM) Oneonta NY 3 hrs
*WSRK(FM) Oneonta NY 2 hrs
*WLIM(AM) Patchogue NY 7 hrs
*WVKR-FM Poughkeepsie NY 3 hrs
*WUSB(FM) Stony Brook NY 14 hrs
*WKWZ(FM) Syosset NY 6 hrs
*WPNR-FM Utica NY 10 hrs
*WFRW(FM) Webster NY 2 hrs
*WOBO(FM) Batavia OH 1 hr
*WBGU(FM) Bowling Green OH 3 hrs
*WCUE(FM) Cuyahoga Falls OH 2 hrs
*WLFC(FM) Findlay OH 3 hrs
*WMCO(FM) New Concord OH 4 hrs
*WUSO(FM) Springfield OH 3 hrs
*WYTN(FM) Youngstown OH 2 hrs
WBBZ(AM) Ponca City OK 5 hrs
*KBVR(FM) Corvallis OR 6 hrs
*KEOL(FM) La Grande OR 4 hrs
*KRRC(FM) Portland OR 4 hrs
*WLVR(FM) Bethlehem PA 8 hrs
*WESS(FM) East Stroudsburg PA 4 hrs
*WZBT(FM) Gettysburg PA 3 hrs
*WIUP-FM Indiana PA 15 hrs
WJSA(AM) Jersey Shore PA 1 hr
WJSA-FM Jersey Shore PA 1 hr
*WFNM(FM) Lancaster PA 2 hrs
*WARC(FM) Meadville PA 10 hrs
*WPEL(FM) Montrose PA 1 hr
*WJST(AM) New Castle PA 1 hr
*WHYY-FM Philadelphia PA 4 hrs
*WRCT(FM) Pittsburgh PA 3 hrs
WRAW(AM) Reading PA 1 hr
*WXLV(FM) Schnecksville PA 13 hrs
*WUSR(FM) Scranton PA 5 hrs
*WVMW-FM Scranton PA 7 hrs
*WSYC-FM Shippensburg PA 2 hrs
WRSC(AM) State College PA 3 hrs
*WRLC(FM) Williamsport PA 1 hr
*WVYC(FM) York PA 8 hrs
*WTMV(FM) Youngsville PA 2.5 hrs
WTPM(FM) Aguadilla PR 7 hrs
*WMUU-FM Greenville SC 14 hrs
WMYB(FM) Myrtle Beach SC
WQMC(AM) Sumter SC 15 hrs
*WHCB(FM) Bristol TN 1 hr
*WFHU(FM) Henderson TN 7 hrs
*WRVU(FM) Nashville TN 5 hrs
*WDNX(FM) Olive Hill TN 5 hrs
*WUTS(FM) Sewanee TN 4 hrs
*KWTS(FM) Canyon TX 4 hrs
*KTRU(FM) Houston TX 5 hrs
*KNTU(FM) McKinney TX 6 hrs
KSUU(FM) Cedar City UT 3 hrs
KPCW(FM) Park City UT 17 hrs
*KRDC-FM Saint George UT 15 hrs
*WWHS-FM Hampden-Sydney VA 2 hrs
*WVRU(FM) Radford VA 15 hrs
WDCE(FM) Richmond VA 3 hrs
*WCWM(FM) Williamsburg VA 11 hrs
*WIUJ(FM) Charlotte Amalie VI 5 hrs
*WIUV(FM) Castleton VT 3 hrs
*WJSC-FM Johnson VT 1 hr
*WWLR(FM) Lyndonville VT 2 hrs
*WRMC-FM Middlebury VT 15 hrs
*WGDR(FM) Plainfield VT 3 hrs
WDEV(AM) Waterbury VT 1 hr
KELA(AM) Centralia-Chehalis WA 2 hrs
KULE(AM) Ephrata WA 5 hrs

KEYG(AM) Grand Coulee WA 4 hrs
*KMLW(FM) Moses Lake WA 1 hr
KAGU(FM) Spokane WA 2 hrs
*WLFM(FM) Appleton WI 10 hrs
*WMSE(FM) Milwaukee WI 3 hrs
*WSUP(FM) Platteville WI 4 hrs
WRJN(FM) Racine WI 2 hrs
*WVBC(FM) Bethany WV 2 hrs
*WWVC(FM) Buckhannon WV 2 hrs
*WZJO(FM) Dunbar WV 2 hrs
*WWVU-FM Morgantown WV 4 hrs
KMTN(FM) Jackson WY

Comedy

KTCL(FM) Fort Collins CO 1 hr
KEYN-FM Wichita KS 2 hrs
*WAMH(FM) Amherst MA 3 hrs
*WVSD(FM) Itta Bena MS 2 hrs
*WPCR-FM Plymouth NH 3 hrs
*WITR(FM) Henrietta NY 2 hrs
WLUZ(AM) Bayamon PR 19 hrs

Contemporary Hit/Top-40

*KNOM(AM) Nome AK 12 hrs
*KNOM-FM Nome AK 12 hrs
*KCRW(FM) Santa Monica CA
*KCSS(FM) Turlock CA 10 hrs
*WXCI(FM) Danbury CT 3 hrs
WZHR(AM) Zephyrhills FL 10 hrs
KIOW(FM) Forest City IA 19 hrs
*WBKE-FM North Manchester IN 10 hrs
WCOQ(FM) Berlin MD 6 hrs
*WRCJ-FM Detroit MI 10 hrs
*KUMM(FM) Morris MN 2 hrs
KLOZ(FM) Eldon MO 6 hrs
WTNM(FM) Water Valley MS 4 hrs
KATQ-FM Plentywood MT
*WIRQ(FM) Rochester NY 3 hrs
WQIO(FM) Mount Vernon OH 4 hrs
*WKVR-FM Huntingdon PA 15 hrs
WVOZ(FM) San Juan PR 15 hrs
KILE(AM) Bellaire TX
*KVTI(FM) Tacoma WA 3 hrs
*WRFW(FM) River Falls WI

Country

*KBRW(AM) Barrow AK 7 hrs
*KYUK(AM) Bethel AK 4 hrs
*KHNS(FM) Haines AK 17 hrs
*KRBD(FM) Ketchikan AK 14 hrs
KIAL(AM) Unalaska AK 04 hrs
*KSTK(FM) Wrangell AK 16 hrs
WKAC(AM) Athens AL 13 hrs
*KPFA(FM) Berkeley CA 18 hrs
*KFJC(FM) Los Altos CA 8 hrs
*KVMR(FM) Nevada City CA 7 hrs
*KAZU(FM) Pacific Grove CA 6 hrs
*KVNF(FM) Paonia CO 5 hrs
*KOTO(FM) Telluride CO 12 hrs
WQQQ(FM) Sharon CT 3 hrs
*WAPJ(FM) Torrington CT 3 hrs
*WWEB(FM) Wallingford CT 2 hrs
*WAMU(FM) Washington DC 4 hrs
WPIK(FM) Summerland Key FL 1 hr
WBTS(FM) Doraville GA 5 hrs
KSTO(FM) Hagatna GU 12 hrs
KROS(AM) Clinton IA 6 hrs
KGRN(AM) Grinnell IA 12 hrs
WTAY(AM) Robinson IL 12 hrs
WTYE(FM) Robinson IL 12 hrs
*WPUM(FM) Rensselaer IN 3 hrs
*KLSP(FM) Angola LA 6 hrs
*WTUL(FM) New Orleans LA 3 hrs
WHRB(FM) Cambridge MA 4 hrs
WPVQ(FM) Greenfield MA 6 hrs
*WZBC(FM) Newton MA 3 hrs
*WOZQ(FM) Northampton MA 2 hrs
*WTCC(FM) Springfield MA 4 hrs
*WKHS(FM) Worton MD 2 hrs
*WSJB-FM Standish ME 3 hrs
*WCBN-FM Ann Arbor MI 3 hrs

*WDBM(FM) East Lansing MI 4 hrs
WSDS(AM) Salem Township MI 12 hrs
*WPHS(FM) Warren MI 4 hrs
WELY(AM) Ely MN 6 hrs
*KAXE(FM) Grand Rapids MN 3 hrs
*WMCN(FM) Saint Paul MN 2 hrs
*KSRQ(FM) Thief River Falls MN 5 hrs
*KCFV(FM) Ferguson MO 4 hrs
*KDHX(FM) Saint Louis MO 10 hrs
WLRC(FM) Walnut MS
*KXEI(FM) Havre MT 1 hr
*WASU-FM Boone NC 8 hrs
*WUAW(FM) Erwin NC
*WZMB(FM) Greenville NC 3 hrs
WCVP(FM) Murphy NC 12 hrs
WSMX(AM) Winston-Salem NC 3 hrs
*KMHA(FM) Four Bears ND 8 hrs
KCNI(FM) Broken Bow NE
KRVN(AM) Lexington NE 8 hrs
*WNEC-FM Henniker NH 3 hrs
*WRHU(FM) Hempstead NY 2 hrs
WLNL(AM) Horseheads NY 1 hr
WVBR-FM Ithaca NY 4 hrs
*WKCR-FM New York NY 6 hrs
WGGO(AM) Salamanca NY 5 hrs
*WKWZ(FM) Syosset NY 6 hrs
*WRPI(FM) Troy NY 2 hrs
*WBGU(FM) Bowling Green OH 4 hrs
*KRSC-FM Claremore OK 5 hrs
*KRVM-FM Eugene OR 1 hr
*KWVA(FM) Eugene OR 3 hrs
*KRRC(FM) Portland OR 2 hrs
*WFKJ(AM) Cashtown PA 4 hrs
*WCUC-FM Clarion PA 6 hrs
WSKE(FM) Everett PA 2 hrs
*WRCT(FM) Pittsburgh PA 3 hrs
*WQSU(FM) Selinsgrove PA 6 hrs
WMBS(AM) Uniontown PA 4 hrs
*WRDV(FM) Warminster PA 4 hrs
*WCYJ-FM Waynesburg PA 3 hrs
*WCHE(AM) West Chester PA 2 hrs
*WDOM(FM) Providence RI 2 hrs
WOPI(AM) Bristol TN 9 hrs
WWLX(FM) Lawrenceburg TN 8 hrs
*WEVL(FM) Memphis TN 15 hrs
*WSM(AM) Nashville TN 12 hrs
*WUTS(FM) Sewanee TN 2 hrs
*KPCW(FM) Park City UT 18 hrs
*WJSC-FM Johnson VT 3 hrs
*WBSD(FM) Burlington WI 4 hrs
*WOJB(FM) Reserve WI 15 hrs
*WRFW(FM) River Falls WI

Croation

*WKTL(FM) Struthers OH 1 hr
WKBN(AM) Youngstown OH 2 hrs
WFGI(FM) Charleroi PA 1 hr
WOGI(FM) Charleroi PA 1 hr
WEDO(AM) McKeesport PA 1 hr
WKZV(FM) Washington PA 1 hr
WRRD(AM) Jackson WI 2 hrs

Czech

KMRY(AM) Cedar Rapids IA 3 hrs
WCEV(AM) Cicero IL 2 hrs
*WOES(FM) Ovid-Elsie MI 1 hr
WAAL(FM) Binghamton NY 1 hr
WYOS(AM) Binghamton NY 1 hr
WOMP(AM) Bellaire OH 2 hrs
WERE(AM) Cleveland OH 1 hr
KMIL(AM) Cameron TX 8 hrs
KULP(AM) El Campo TX 5 hrs
KHLT(AM) Hallettsville TX 3 hrs
KHBR(AM) Hillsboro TX 2 hrs
KVLG(AM) La Grange TX 6 hrs
KTEM(AM) Temple TX 3 hrs
WAUN(FM) Kewaunee WI 1 hr

Disco

*WBIM-FM Bridgewater MA 9 hrs
*WOZQ(FM) Northampton MA 2 hrs
*WTMD(FM) Towson MD 3 hrs
*WVBU-FM Lewisburg PA 6 hrs

Broadcasting & Cable Yearbook 2006

Special Programming on Radio Stations in the U.S.

Discussion
WNDN(FM) Chiefland FL

Diversified
*KALW(FM) San Francisco CA 1 1/2 hrs
WUMS(FM) University MS 2 hrs
*WNAA(FM) Greensboro NC 7 hrs
WRSS(AM) San Sebastian PR

Drama/Literature
*KUAR(FM) Little Rock AR 2 hrs
*KZYX(FM) Philo CA 3 hrs
*KCRW(FM) Santa Monica CA
*KOTO(FM) Telluride CO 3 hrs
*WGLT(FM) Normal IL 2 hrs
*WOES(FM) Ovid-Elsie MI 1 hr
*KMSK(FM) Austin MN 3 hrs
*KMSU(FM) Mankato MN 3 hrs
*WNCW(FM) Spindale NC 3 hrs
*WRHU(FM) Hempstead NY 1 hr
*WNYC-FM New York NY 5 hrs
*WQED-FM Pittsburgh PA 1 hr
KPYK(AM) Terrell TX 7 hrs
*KAGU(FM) Spokane WA 2 hrs
*WQAB(FM) Philippi WV 2 hrs

Educational
*KXRJ(FM) Russellville AR
*KCRH(FM) Hayward CA 1 hr
KVEC(AM) San Luis Obispo CA
*KYCC(FM) Stockton CA 1 hr
WGCH(AM) Greenwich CT 2 hrs
*WJMJ(FM) Hartford CT
*WHIF(FM) Palatka FL 10 hrs
*WKGC(AM) Panama City Beach FL 8 hrs
KGUM(AM) Hagatna GU 1 hr
*KWLC(AM) Decorah IA
*WEPS(FM) Elgin IL 13 hrs
*WDCB(FM) Glen Ellyn IL 12 hrs
*WOMR(FM) Provincetown MA 10 hrs
*WFWM(FM) Frostburg MD 5 hrs
*WNMU-FM Marquette MI
*WSGE(FM) Dallas NC 4 hrs
*WBAI(FM) New York NY
*WDPS(FM) Dayton OH 2 hrs
KBNP(AM) Portland OR
*WESS(FM) East Stroudsburg PA 7 hrs
*WPUC-FM Ponce PR
WPWT(AM) Colonial Heights TN 1 hr
*KMFA(FM) Austin TX 2 hrs
WRVA(AM) Richmond VA 2 hrs
*WRFW(FM) River Falls WI
WWYO(AM) Pineville WV 2 hrs

Farsi
WUST(AM) Washington DC 5 hrs

Filipino
*KBRW(AM) Barrow AK 2 hrs
*KMXT(FM) Kodiak AK 2 hrs
KCHJ(AM) Delano CA 3 hrs
*KECG(FM) El Cerrito CA 2 hrs
KKLA-FM Los Angeles CA 1 hr
*KMPO(FM) Modesto CA 1 hr
KSJX(AM) San Jose CA 2 hrs
WXYB(AM) Indian Rocks Beach FL 1 hr
WPSO(AM) New Port Richey FL 1 hr
*V6AI(AM) Yap FM 5 hrs
KWAI(AM) Honolulu HI 7 hrs
KNUI(AM) Kahului HI 12 hrs
KLAV(AM) Las Vegas NV 5 hrs
KBRO(AM) Bremerton WA 4 hrs

Finnish
*KUSF(FM) San Francisco CA 1 hr
*WFHB(FM) Bloomington IN 3 hrs
WEIM(AM) Fitchburg MA 25 hrs
KRBT(AM) Eveleth MN 1 hr
*KAXE(FM) Grand Rapids MN 2 hrs
*WBXL(FM) Baldwinsville NY 2 hrs

Folk
*KSKA(FM) Anchorage AK 4 hrs
*KUAC(FM) Fairbanks AK 10 hrs
*KHNS(FM) Haines AK 6 hrs
*KRBD(FM) Ketchikan AK 10 hrs
*WSGN(FM) Gadsden AL 2 hrs
*WQPR(FM) Muscle Shoals AL 5 hrs
*WUAL-FM Tuscaloosa AL 5 hrs
*KUAF(FM) Fayetteville AR 5 hrs
*KASU(FM) Jonesboro AR 4 hrs
*KABF(FM) Little Rock AR 10 hrs
*KUAR(FM) Little Rock AR 3 hrs
KCTT-FM Yellville AR 10 hrs
KVNA(AM) Flagstaff AZ 4hrs hrs
*KXCI(FM) Tucson AZ 2 hrs
*KPFA(FM) Berkeley CA 10 hrs
*KNCA(FM) Burney CA 3 hrs
*KFSR(FM) Fresno CA 3 hrs
*KPFK(FM) Los Angeles CA 5 hrs
*KXLU(FM) Los Angeles CA 1 hr
*KSBR(FM) Mission Viejo CA 2 hrs
*KMPO(FM) Modesto CA 4 hrs
*KNSQ(FM) Mount Shasta CA 3 hrs
*KVMR(FM) Nevada City CA 13 hrs
*KAZU(FM) Pacific Grove CA 6 hrs
*KZYX(FM) Philo CA 8 hrs
KVYN(AM) Saint Helena CA 2 hrs
*KCBX(FM) San Luis Obispo CA 15 hrs
*KRCB-FM Santa Rosa CA 6 hrs
*KAJX(FM) Aspen CO 4 hrs
*KGNU-FM Boulder CO 20 hrs
*KAFM(FM) Grand Junction CO 10 hrs
*KMSA(FM) Grand Junction CO 2 hrs
*WSHU(FM) Fairfield CT 5 hrs
*WGRS(FM) Guilford CT 2 hrs
*WMNR(FM) Monroe CT 2 hrs
WYBC-FM New Haven CT 3 hrs
*WCNI(FM) New London CT 9 hrs
*WRXC(FM) Shelton CT 2 hrs
*WGSK(FM) South Kent CT 2 hrs
*WNHU(FM) West Haven CT 6 hrs
*WVUD(FM) Newark DE 15 hrs
*WUFT-FM Gainesville FL 1 hr
*WFIT(FM) Melbourne FL 5 hrs
*WKGC(AM) Panama City Beach FL 2 hrs
*WFCF(FM) Saint Augustine FL 3 hrs
*WVFS(FM) Tallahassee FL 3 hrs
V6AH(AM) Pohnpei FM 20 hrs
*WUGA(FM) Athens GA 4 hrs
*WUWG(FM) Carrollton GA 2 hrs
*KUNI(FM) Cedar Falls IA 15 hrs
KROS(AM) Clinton IA 2 hrs
*KIWR(FM) Council Bluffs IA 2 hrs
*KWLC(AM) Decorah IA
*KHOE(FM) Fairfield IA 6 hrs
*KRNI(AM) Mason City IA 15 hrs
*KUNY(FM) Mason City IA 15 hrs
*KRNL-FM Mount Vernon IA 2 hrs
*KWAR(FM) Waverly IA 3 hrs
*KBSU(FM) Boise ID
*KRFA-FM Moscow ID
*KUOI-FM Moscow ID 3 hrs
*KISU-FM Pocatello ID 2 hrs
*WSIU(FM) Carbondale IL 3 hrs
*WEFT(FM) Champaign IL 10 hrs
*WEIU(FM) Charleston IL 4 hrs
WFMT(FM) Chicago IL 4 hrs
*WLUW(FM) Chicago IL 2 hrs
*WNIJ(FM) De Kalb IL 4 hrs
*WNUR-FM Evanston IL 3 hrs
*WDCB(FM) Glen Ellyn IL 12 hrs
*WIUM(FM) Macomb IL 7 hrs
*WGLT(FM) Normal IL 4 hrs
*WQUB(FM) Quincy IL 2 hrs
*WQNA(FM) Springfield IL 8 hrs
*WFHB(FM) Bloomington IN 10 hrs
*WVPE(FM) Elkhart IN 9 hrs
*WICR(FM) Indianapolis IN 1 hr
*WBAA(AM) West Lafayette IN 5 hrs
*KANZ(FM) Garden City KS 6 hrs
*KZNA(FM) Hill City KS 6 hrs
*KRPS(FM) Pittsburg KS 3 hrs
*KMUW(FM) Wichita KS 6 hrs
*WKYU-FM Bowling Green KY 5 hrs
*WKUE(FM) Elizabethtown KY 5 hrs
*WKPB(FM) Henderson KY 5 hrs
*WNKU(FM) Highland Heights KY 3 hrs
*WRFL(FM) Lexington KY 3 hrs
*WMKY(FM) Morehead KY 2 hrs
*WDCL-FM Somerset KY 5 hrs
*KSCL(FM) Shreveport LA 6 hrs
WSLA(AM) Slidell LA 5 hrs
*WFCR(FM) Amherst MA 4 hrs
*WMUA(FM) Amherst MA 15 hrs
*WGBH(FM) Boston MA 10 hrs
*WAMQ(FM) Great Barrington MA 7 hrs
*WUML(FM) Lowell MA 4 hrs
*WSMU-FM North Dartmouth MA 11 hrs
*WOZQ(FM) Northampton MA 4 hrs
*WOMR(FM) Provincetown MA 17 hrs
*WBSL-FM Sheffield MA 2 hrs
*WMHC(FM) South Hadley MA 3 hrs
*WSKB(FM) Westfield MA 3 hrs
*WMTB-FM Emmittsburg MD 1 hr
*WTMD(FM) Towson MD 3 hrs
*WERU-FM Blue Hill ME 15 hrs
*WBOR(FM) Brunswick ME 12 hrs
*WRBC(FM) Lewiston ME 4 hrs
*WMEB-FM Orono ME 4 hrs
*WMHB(FM) Waterville ME 12 hrs
*WCBN-FM Ann Arbor MI 3 hrs
*WDET-FM Detroit MI 3 hrs
WBNZ(FM) Frankfort MI 2 hrs
*WBLU-FM Grand Rapids MI 5 hrs
*WCMW-FM Harbor Springs MI 3 hrs
*WIAA(FM) Interlochen MI 3 hrs
*WLNZ(FM) Lansing MI 3 hrs
*WNMC-FM Traverse City MI 11 hrs
*WBLV-FM Twin Lake MI 5 hrs
*WYCE(FM) Wyoming MI 1 hr
*KMSK(FM) Austin MN 5 hrs
*KBSB(FM) Bemidji MN 3 hrs
*KAXE(FM) Grand Rapids MN 6 hrs
WMFG(AM) Hibbing MN
*KMSU(FM) Mankato MN 5 hrs
*KFAI(FM) Minneapolis MN 6 hrs
*KUMM(FM) Morris MN 1 hr
*KVSC(FM) Saint Cloud MN 8 hrs
*WMCN(FM) Saint Paul MN 2 hrs
*KGAC(FM) Saint Peter MN 9 hrs
*KRCU(FM) Cape Girardeau MO
*KOPN(FM) Columbia MO 2 hrs
*KKFI(FM) Kansas City MO 4 hrs
*KCOZ(FM) Point Lookout MO 10 hrs
*KUMR(FM) Rolla MO 5 hrs
*KDHX(FM) Saint Louis MO 10 hrs
*WUSM-FM Hattiesburg MS 2 hrs
*KEMC(FM) Billings MT 5 hrs
*KGLT(FM) Bozeman MT 12 hrs
*WCQS(FM) Asheville NC 9 hrs
*WBUX(FM) Buxton NC 20 hrs
*WUNC-FM Chapel Hill NC 20 hrs
*WWCU(FM) Cullowhee NC 4. hrs
*WFSS(FM) Fayetteville NC 3 hrs
*WFQS(FM) Franklin NC 9 hrs
*WQFS(FM) Greensboro NC 6 hrs
*WUND-FM Manteo NC 20 hrs
*WURI(FM) Manteo NC 20 hrs
*WZRU(FM) Roanoke Rapids NC 5 hrs
WLHC(FM) Robbins NC 3 hrs
*WNCW(FM) Spindale NC 12 hrs
*WHQR(FM) Wilmington NC 1 hr
*KEYA(FM) Belcourt ND 4 hrs
*KCND(FM) Bismarck ND 6 hrs
*KDPR(FM) Dickinson ND 6 hrs
*KPRJ(FM) Jamestown ND 6 hrs
*KMPR(FM) Minot ND 6 hrs
*KPPR(FM) Williston ND 6 hrs
*KRNU(FM) Lincoln NE 2 hrs
*KUCV(FM) Lincoln NE 1 hr
*KZUM(FM) Lincoln NE 8 hrs
*WEVO(FM) Concord NH 3 hrs
*WUNH(FM) Durham NH 4 hrs
*WEVC(FM) Gorham NH 3 hrs
*WEVH(FM) Hanover NH 3 hrs
*WNEC-FM Henniker NH 18 hrs
WEVJ(FM) Jackson NH 3 hrs wklly hrs
*WEVN(FM) Keene NH 3 hrs
*WKNH(FM) Keene NH 6 hrs
*WDVR(FM) Delaware Township NJ 6 hrs
*WBZC(FM) Pemberton NJ 4 hrs
*WLFR(FM) Pomona NJ 3 hrs
*WFDU(FM) Teaneck NJ 18 hrs
*WTSR(FM) Trenton NJ 4 hrs
*KUNM(FM) Albuquerque NM 5 hrs
*KSJE(FM) Farmington NM 15 hrs
*KGLP(FM) Gallup NM 10 hrs
*KRWG(FM) Las Cruces NM 8 hrs
*KUNR(FM) Reno NV 2 hrs
*WAMC-FM Albany NY 7 hrs
*WSKG-FM Binghamton NY 5 hrs
*WXLH(FM) Blue Mountain Lake NY
*WBNY(FM) Buffalo NY 3 hrs
*WCAN(FM) Canajoharie NY 7 hrs
*WSLU(FM) Canton NY
*WSQE(FM) Corning NY 5 hrs
*WCVF(FM) Fredonia NY 3 hrs
*WICB(FM) Ithaca NY 2 hrs
*WSQG-FM Ithaca NY 5 hrs
WVBR-FM Ithaca NY 8 hrs
*WJFF(FM) Jeffersonville NY 10 hrs
*WAMK(FM) Kingston NY 7 hrs
WYBG(AM) Massena NY 1
*WOSR(FM) Middletown NY 7 hrs
*WBAI(FM) New York NY 2 hrs
*WSUF(FM) Noyack NY 5 hrs
*WRHO(FM) Oneonta NY 5 hrs
*WSQC-FM Oneonta NY 5 hrs
WTKV(FM) Oswego NY 3 hrs
*WCEL(FM) Plattsburgh NY 7 hrs
*WRUR-FM Rochester NY 2 hrs
*WSPN(FM) Saratoga Springs NY 6 hrs
*WUSB(FM) Stony Brook NY 15 hrs
*WANC(FM) Ticonderoga NY 6 hrs
*WRPI(FM) Troy NY 2 hrs
WTBQ(AM) Warwick NY
*WBGU(FM) Bowling Green OH 4 hrs
*WRUW-FM Cleveland OH 18 hrs
*WDPS(FM) Dayton OH 2 hrs
*WLFC(FM) Findlay OH 3 hrs
*WKSU(FM) Kent OH 12 hrs
*WOBC-FM Oberlin OH 12 hrs
*WMUB(FM) Oxford OH 5 hrs
*WJCU(FM) University Heights OH 2 hrs
*WKRW(FM) Wooster OH 12 hrs
*WYSO(FM) Yellow Springs OH 2 hrs
*WYSU(FM) Youngstown OH 3 hrs
*KRSC-FM Claremore OK 5 hrs
*KSMF(FM) Ashland OR 3 hrs
*KMUN(FM) Astoria OR 18 hrs
*KSBA(FM) Coos Bay OR 3 hrs
*KBVR(FM) Corvallis OR 4 hrs
*KLCC(FM) Eugene OR 12 hrs
*KRVM-FM Eugene OR 3 hrs
*KSKF(FM) Klamath Falls OR 3 hrs
*KTEC(FM) Klamath Falls OR 3 hrs
*KLCO(FM) Newport OR 12 hrs
*WDIY(FM) Allentown PA 12 hrs
WWCS(AM) Canonsburg PA 2 hrs
*WZBT(FM) Gettysburg PA 6 hrs
*WIUP-FM Indiana PA 4 hrs
*WPSB(FM) Kane PA 10 hrs
*WHYY-FM Philadelphia PA 4 hrs
*WXPN(FM) Philadelphia PA 5 hrs
*WRCT(FM) Pittsburgh PA 3 hrs
*WYEP-FM Pittsburgh PA 9 hrs
WEEU(AM) Reading PA 1 hr
*WPSU(FM) State College PA 12 hrs
*WRDV(FM) Warminster PA 4 hrs
*WRIU(FM) Kingston RI 15 hrs
*WJMF(FM) Smithfield RI 4 hrs
*KAUR(FM) Sioux Falls SD 2 hrs
*KCSD(FM) Sioux Falls SD 5 hrs
*WHCB(FM) Bristol TN 1 hr
*WTTU(FM) Cookeville TN 3 hrs
*WQOX(FM) Memphis TN 3 hrs
*WRVU(FM) Nashville TN 3 hrs
*KUT(FM) Austin TX 4 hrs
*KAMU-FM College Station TX 3 hrs
*KEOS(FM) College Station TX 10 hrs
*KTEP(FM) El Paso TX 3 hrs
*KOOP(FM) Hornsby TX 7 hrs
*KTRU(FM) Houston TX 3 hrs
*KOCV(FM) Odessa TX 4 hrs
*KUTX(FM) San Angelo TX 4 hrs
*KSTX(FM) San Antonio TX 5 hrs
*KZMU(FM) Moab UT 6 hrs
*WNRN(FM) Charlottesville VA 19 hrs
*WTJU(FM) Charlottesville VA 20 hrs
*WMRY(FM) Crozet VA 8 hrs
*WMRA(FM) Harrisonburg VA 8 hrs
*WMRL(FM) Lexington VA 8 hrs
*WHRV(FM) Norfolk VA 7 hrs
*WVRU(FM) Radford VA 1 hr
*WCVE(FM) Richmond VA 6 hrs
*WVPS(FM) Burlington VT 4 hrs
*WIUV(FM) Castleton VT 4 hrs
*WRMC-FM Middlebury VT 15 hrs
WNCS(FM) Montpelier VT 4 hrs
*WGDR(FM) Plainfield VT 10 hrs
*WRVT(FM) Rutland VT 4 hrs
*WVPR(FM) Windsor VT 6 hrs
*KUGS(FM) Bellingham WA 6 hrs wkly hrs
*KZAZ(FM) Bellingham WA 8 hrs
*KNWR(FM) Ellensburg WA
*KSER(FM) Everett WA 2 hrs
*KAOS(FM) Olympia WA 16 hrs
*KZUU(FM) Pullman WA 4 hrs
*KFAE-FM Richland WA
*KAGU(FM) Spokane WA 2 hrs
*KPBX-FM Spokane WA
*KWRS(FM) Spokane WA 8 hrs
*WHSA(FM) Brule WI 3 hrs
*WBSD(FM) Burlington WI 5 hrs
*WUEC(FM) Eau Claire WI 3 hrs
*WPNE-FM Green Bay WI 8 hrs
*WVSS(FM) Menomonie WI 6 hrs
*WHND(FM) Sister Bay WI 3 hrs
*WLBL-FM Wausau WI 3 hrs
*WVBC(FM) Bethany WV 2 hrs
WWYO(AM) Pineville WV 1 hr
WLWF(FM) Ravenswood WV 2 hrs
MMOV(AM) Ravenswood WV 2 hrs
WHAW(AM) Weston WV 4 hrs
*KUWA(FM) Afton WY 5 hrs
*KUWJ(FM) Jackson WY 10 hrs
*KUWR(FM) Laramie WY 10 hrs
*KUWZ(FM) Rock Springs WY 10 hrs

Foreign/Ethnic
*KJHA(FM) Houston AK 3 hrs
*KJNP(AM) North Pole AK 1 hr
*KCAW(FM) Sitka AK 3 hrs
KSAZ(AM) Marana AZ 2 hrs
*KKUP(FM) Cupertino CA 19 hrs
KBIF(AM) Fresno CA 56 hrs
*KFCF(FM) Fresno CA 1 hr
*KMUD(FM) Garberville CA 1 hr
KMYC(AM) Marysville CA 2 hrs
*KVMR(FM) Nevada City CA 20 hrs
*KAZU(FM) Pacific Grove CA 6 hrs
*KXJZ(FM) Sacramento CA 2 hrs
KEST(AM) San Francisco CA
*KUSF(FM) San Francisco CA 2 hrs
KMRB(AM) San Gabriel CA 4 hrs
*KCSB-FM Santa Barbara CA 2 hrs
*KCRW(FM) Santa Monica CA
KOBO(AM) Yuba City CA 3 hrs
KUBA(AM) Yuba City CA 4 hrs
*KRZA(AM) Alamosa CO 3 hrs
*KCME(FM) Manitou Springs CO
*WFAR(FM) Danbury CT 1 hr
*WJMJ(FM) Hartford CT 1 hr
*WWUH(FM) West Hartford CT 14 hrs
WHUR-FM Washington DC 6 hrs
WYUS(AM) Milford DE 3 hrs

Special Programming on Radio Stations in the U.S.

WXYB(AM) Indian Rocks Beach FL 5 hrs
WHOO(AM) Kissimmee FL 2 hrs
*WDNA(FM) Miami FL 10 hrs
*WLRN(FM) Miami FL 3 hrs
WTMY(AM) Sarasota FL 4 hrs
*WRFG(FM) Atlanta GA 9 hrs
WWWE(AM) Hapeville GA 6 hrs
*WWET(FM) Valdosta GA 3 hrs
*KSDA-FM Agat GU 4 hrs
KUAM(AM) Hagatna GU 10 hrs
KUAI(AM) Eleele HI 5 hrs
KWAI(AM) Honolulu HI 2 hrs
KKON(AM) Kealakekua HI
*KDCR(FM) Sioux Center IA 1 hr
*WHPK-FM Chicago IL 4 hrs
*WLUW(FM) Chicago IL 8 hrs
WONX(AM) Evanston IL 28 hrs
WEEF(AM) Highland Park IL
WVIV-FM Highland Park IL
*WQNA(FM) Springfield IL 3 hrs
*WFHB(FM) Bloomington IN 3 hrs
WNDZ(AM) Portage IN 4 hrs
*WBAA(AM) West Lafayette IN 2 hrs
*WMMT(FM) Whitesburg KY 1 hr
*KLSU(FM) Baton Rouge LA 3 hrs
WCDV(FM) Hammond LA 3 hrs
*KSCL(FM) Shreveport LA 3 hrs
*KNSU(FM) Thibodaux LA 2 hrs
*WMUA(FM) Amherst MA 12 hrs
WSRO(AM) Ashland MA 2 hrs
*WRBB(FM) Boston MA 5 hrs
*WMBR(FM) Cambridge MA 4 hrs
*WMFO(FM) Medford MA 13 hrs
*WZBC(FM) Newton MA 4 hrs
WRCA(AM) Waltham MA 16 hrs
*WCUW(FM) Worcester MA 10 hrs
*WEAA(FM) Baltimore MD 7 hrs
WMET(AM) Gaithersburg MD 4 hrs
*WMEB-FM Orono ME 3 hrs
*WUPI(FM) Presque Isle ME 2 hrs
*WMHB(FM) Waterville ME 10 hrs
*WHFR(FM) Dearborn MI 2 hrs
*WIDR(FM) Kalamazoo MI 6 hrs
KOLM(AM) Rochester MN 1 hr
KNOF(FM) Saint Paul MN 1 hr
*WMCN(FM) Saint Paul MN 16 hrs
*KDHX(FM) Saint Louis MO 2 hrs
*WSHA(FM) Raleigh NC 7 hrs
KMTY(AM) Holdrege NE 1 hr
*WFMU(FM) East Orange NJ 15 hrs
*WBJB-FM Lincroft NJ 3 hrs
WPRB(FM) Princeton NJ 6 hrs
*KUNM(FM) Albuquerque NM 9 hrs
KTAO(FM) Taos NM 5 hrs
*KUNR(FM) Reno NV 9 hrs
*WCVF-FM Fredonia NY 10 hrs
*WGMC(FM) Greece NY 1 hr
*WICB(FM) Ithaca NY 2 hrs
WJTN(AM) Jamestown NY 1 hr
WKSN(AM) Jamestown NY 1 hr
WTHE(AM) Mineola NY 5 hrs
*WRHO(FM) Oneonta NY 2 hrs
*WRHV(FM) Poughkeepsie NY 1 hr
*WSPN(FM) Saratoga Springs NY 3 hrs
*WAER(FM) Syracuse NY 4 hrs
*WRPI(FM) Troy NY 1 hr
*WAPS(FM) Akron OH 3 hrs
*WCSB(FM) Cleveland OH 8 hrs
*WDPS(FM) Dayton OH 2 hrs
WIMX(FM) Gibsonburg OH 8 hrs
*WDUB(FM) Granville OH 2 hrs
*KLCO(FM) Newport OR 3 hrs
*KBOO(FM) Portland OR 4 hrs
KXMG(AM) Portland OR 1 hr
WWCS(AM) Canonsburg PA 2 hrs
WZUM(AM) Carnegie PA 2 hrs
*WKDU(FM) Philadelphia PA 12 hrs
WTPM(FM) Aguadilla PR 1 hr
*KDEI(FM) Port Arthur TX 0.5 hrs
KEDA(AM) San Antonio TX 4 hrs
*KZMU(FM) Moab UT 1 hr
*KRCL(FM) Salt Lake City UT 5 hrs
*WUVT-FM Blacksburg VA 8 hrs
WREJ(AM) Richmond VA 1 hr
*KAOS(FM) Olympia WA 1 hr

*KPBX-FM Spokane WA
*WHID(FM) Green Bay WI 2. hrs
WEKZ(AM) Monroe WI 3 hrs
KBBS(AM) Buffalo WY 1 hr

French

*KTOO(FM) Juneau AK 2 hrs
*KUSF(FM) San Francisco CA 2 hrs
*KSRH(FM) San Rafael CA 1 hr
*WPKN(FM) Bridgeport CT 2 hrs
WUST(AM) Washington DC 15 hrs
*WUCF-FM Orlando FL 1 hr
WOKB(AM) Winter Garden FL 7 hrs
KQIS(FM) Basile LA 5 hrs
KQKI(FM) Bayou Vista LA 4 hrs
KSIG(AM) Crowley LA 18 hrs
KLEB(AM) Golden Meadow LA 13 hrs
WCDV(FM) Hammond LA 4 hrs
KHLA(FM) Jennings LA 12 hrs
KJEF(AM) Jennings LA 12 hrs
KLIL(FM) Moreauville LA 5 hrs
KSLO(AM) Opelousas LA 18 hrs
*KSCL(FM) Shreveport LA 2 hrs
KEZM(AM) Sulphur LA 5 hrs
KVPI-FM Ville Platte LA 18 hrs
WROL(AM) Boston MA 15 hrs
WJIB(AM) Cambridge MA 10 hrs
*WMBR(FM) Cambridge MA 2 hrs
WHTB(AM) Fall River MA 1 hr
*WNMH(FM) Northfield MA 2 hrs
*WCUW(FM) Worcester MA 2 hrs
WLAM(AM) Lewiston ME 2 hrs
*WRBC(FM) Lewiston ME 2 hrs
*WMEB-FM Orono ME 4 hrs
*WCBN-FM Ann Arbor MI 1 hr
*KFAI(FM) Minneapolis MN 2 hrs
WMOU(AM) Berlin NH 3 hrs
WFEA(AM) Manchester NH 3 hrs
WSMN(AM) Nashua NH 3 hrs
WCHP(AM) Champlain NY
*WOBC-FM Oberlin OH 1 hr
*KRRC(FM) Portland OR 2 hrs
WWCS(AM) Canonsburg PA 2 hrs
WNRI(AM) Woonsocket RI 4 hrs
WOON(AM) Woonsocket RI 1 hr
*WEVL(FM) Memphis TN 1 hr
*WRVU(FM) Nashville TN 1 hr
*WUTS(FM) Sewanee TN 2 hrs
*WIUJ(FM) Charlotte Amalie VI 4 hrs

Full Service

WTMY(AM) Sarasota FL 2 hrs

German

KTYM(AM) Inglewood CA 1 hr
*KCSN(FM) Northridge CA 3 hrs
KFKA(AM) Greeley CO 1 hr
*WVOF(FM) Fairfield CT 2 hrs
WUST(AM) Washington DC 7 hrs
*WKTO(FM) Edgewater FL 1.5 hrs
WXYB(AM) Indian Rocks Beach FL 2 hrs
KSKB(FM) Brooklyn IA 1 hr
*KRNL-FM Mount Vernon IA 2 hrs
WIIT(FM) Chicago IL 3 hrs
WKTA(FM) Evanston IL 5 hrs
WGNU(AM) Granite City IL 2 hrs
WCBW(AM) Highland IL 1 hr
WVIV-FM Highland Park IL
*WICR(FM) Indianapolis IN 1 hr
WNDZ(AM) Portage IN 2 hrs
*WCUW(FM) Worcester MA 2 hrs
WBMD(AM) Baltimore MD 1 hr
WATZ(AM) Alpena MI 2 hrs
WKCQ(AM) Saginaw MI 3 hrs
KASM(AM) Albany MN 2 hrs
WEW(AM) Saint Louis MO 3 hrs
KTTT(AM) Columbus NE 5 hrs
KBRX(AM) O'Neill NE 6 hrs
*KUNV(FM) Las Vegas NV 1 hr
*WBXL(FM) Baldwinsville NY 3 hrs
WHVW(AM) Hyde Park NY 1 hr
WKNY(AM) Kingston NY 1 hr

WXRL(AM) Lancaster NY 1 hr
WVOA-FM Mexico NY 2 hrs
WTHE(AM) Mineola NY 1 hr
WTLA(AM) North Syracuse NY 2 hrs
WSGO(AM) Oswego NY 2 hrs
*WAPS(FM) Akron OH 2 hrs
*WOBO(FM) Batavia OH 5 hrs
*WCPN(FM) Cleveland OH 1 hr
*WCSB(FM) Cleveland OH 1 hr
WKTX(AM) Cortland OH 5 hrs
*WQRP(FM) Dayton OH 3 hrs
WONW(AM) Defiance OH 4 hrs
WDLW(AM) Lorain OH one hrs
WCWA(AM) Toledo OH 1 hr
WELW(AM) Willoughby-Eastlake OH 1 hr
KKRX(AM) Lawton OK 1 hr
*WMUH(FM) Allentown PA 2 hrs
WGPA(AM) Bethlehem PA 2 hrs
*WWCS(AM) Canonsburg PA 2 hrs
*WDCV-FM Carlisle PA 1 hr
*WMCE(FM) Erie PA 4 hrs
WEEU(AM) Reading PA 2 hrs
*WCLH(FM) Wilkes-Barre PA 3 hrs
*WRVU(FM) Nashville TN 1 hr
KHLT(AM) Hallettsville TX 3 hrs
*KOOP(FM) Hornsby TX .5 hrs
KVLG(AM) La Grange TX 1 hr
KIKZ(AM) Seminole TX 1 hr
KSEM-FM Seminole TX 1 hr
WKGM(AM) Smithfield VA 1 hr
KARI(AM) Blaine WA 2 hrs
WSSP(AM) Milwaukee WI 8 hrs
WEKZ(AM) Monroe WI 3 hrs
WXER(AM) Plymouth WI 3 hrs

Golden Oldies

KGFT(FM) Pueblo CO 11 hrs
WSYY(FM) Millinocket ME

Gospel

KFAR(AM) Fairbanks AK 2 hrs
*KHNS(FM) Haines AK 3 hrs
*KSDP(AM) Sand Point AK 3 hrs
KIAL(AM) Unalaska AK 02 hrs
WVNN(AM) Athens AL 3 hrs
WNSI-FM Atmore AL 1 hr
WAUD(AM) Auburn AL 2 hrs
WJOX(AM) Birmingham AL 5 hrs
WBSA(AM) Boaz AL
WAOQ(FM) Brantley AL 14. hrs
WEBJ(AM) Brewton AL 3 hrs
WKNU(FM) Brewton AL 2 hrs
WBYE(AM) Calera AL 11 hrs
WACQ(AM) Carrville AL 5 hrs
WQUA(FM) Citronelle AL 6 hrs
WKGA(FM) Dadeville AL 3 hrs
WOOF(AM) Dothan AL 17 hrs
WTVY-FM Dothan AL 4 hrs
WELB(AM) Elba AL 12 hrs
WZOB(AM) Fort Payne AL 5 hrs
WGAD(AM) Gadsden AL 5 hrs
WHOG(AM) Hobson City AL 7 hrs
WDJL(AM) Huntsville AL 6 hrs
*WJAB(FM) Huntsville AL 5 hrs
WCKS(AM) Jacksonville AL 2 hrs
WIXI(AM) Jasper AL 5 hrs
WINL(AM) Linden AL 5 hrs
WLWI-FM Montgomery AL 4 hrs
*WVAS(FM) Montgomery AL 5 hrs
WAMI(AM) Opp AL 15 hrs
WAMI-FM Opp AL 15 hrs
WOPP(AM) Opp AL 19 hrs
WJRL-FM Ozark AL 8 hrs
WQLS(AM) Ozark AL 5 hrs
WJBY(AM) Rainbow City AL 60 hrs wkly
WGOL(AM) Russellville AL 4 hrs
WFEB(AM) Sylacauga AL 6 hrs
WNUZ(AM) Talladega AL 7 hrs
*WEBT(FM) Valley AL
KEWI(AM) Benton AR 10 hrs
KAMD-FM Camden AR 19 hrs
KBJT(AM) Fordyce AR 11 hrs

KHOZ(AM) Harrison AR 10 hrs
KFFA(AM) Helena AR 4 hrs
KFFA-FM Helena AR 2 hrs
KBOK(AM) Malvern AR 8 hrs
KUOA(AM) Siloam Springs AR 2 hrs
KZHE(FM) Stamps AR 8 hrs
KFYX(AM) Texarkana AR 2 hrs
KWRF(AM) Warren AR 8 hrs
KWRF-FM Warren AR 8 hrs
KCLT(FM) West Helena AR 15 hrs
KDVA(AM) Buckeye AZ 7 hrs
*KXCI(FM) Tucson AZ 2 hrs
KXMX(AM) Anaheim CA
KCEL(FM) California City CA 3 hrs
KRML(AM) Carmel CA 6 hrs
KJLH-FM Compton CA 6 hrs
*KECG(FM) El Cerrito CA 5 hrs
KTDE(FM) Gualala CA 1 hr
KGBA-FM Holtville CA 7 hrs
KSRN(FM) Kings Beach CA 1 hr
*KPFK(FM) Los Angeles CA 2.5 hrs
KYOS(AM) Merced CA 1 hr
*KAZU(FM) Pacific Grove CA 4 hrs
*KZYX(FM) Philo CA 2 hrs
KTIP(AM) Porterville CA 16 hrs
KEST(AM) San Francisco CA
KISQ(FM) San Francisco CA 3 hrs
KDIA(AM) Vallejo CA 7 hrs
KDYA(AM) Vallejo CA 7 hrs
KUBA(AM) Yuba City CA 2 hrs
*KASF(FM) Alamosa CO 4 hrs
KRTZ(FM) Cortez CO 1 hr
KSLV(AM) Monte Vista CO 4 hrs
*KVNF(FM) Paonia CO 3 hrs
KGFT(FM) Pueblo CO 3 3 hrs
*WQTQ(FM) Hartford CT 12 hrs
*WRTC-FM Hartford CT 6 hrs
*WESU(FM) Middletown CT 6 hrs
WYBC(FM) New Haven CT 8 hrs
*WCNI(FM) New London CT 3 hrs
*WAPJ(FM) Torrington CT 1 hr
*WNHU(FM) West Haven CT 4 hrs
WNEZ(AM) Windsor CT 5 hrs
WHUR-FM Washington DC 14 hrs
WAFL(FM) Milford DE 6 hrs
WYBT(AM) Blountstown FL 15 hrs
WWPR(AM) Bradenton FL 6 hrs
WDCF(AM) Dade City FL 6 hrs
WTMP-FM Dade City FL 20 hrs
WZEP(AM) De Funiak Springs FL 10 hrs
WTMP(AM) Egypt Lake FL 20 hrs
WENG(AM) Englewood FL 2 hrs
WBAU(AM) Fort Walton Beach FL 2 hrs
*WUFT-FM Gainesville FL 1 hr
*WJUF(FM) Inverness FL 1 hr
WWAB(AM) Lakeland FL 12 hrs
WLBE(AM) Leesburg FL 4 hrs
WQHL(AM) Live Oak FL 7 hrs
WQHL-FM Live Oak FL 7 hrs
WMAF(AM) Madison FL
WTYS(AM) Marianna FL 11 hrs
WPGS(AM) Mims FL 4 hrs
WLTG-FM Panama City FL 7 hrs
WRNE(AM) Pensacola FL
WTMY(AM) Sarasota FL 6 hrs
WPUL(AM) South Daytona FL
WCVC(AM) Tallahassee FL 17 hrs
WIXC(AM) Titusville FL 2 hrs
WQLC(FM) Watertown FL 4 hrs
WFLM(FM) White City FL 5 hrs
WOKB(AM) Winter Garden FL 12 hrs
WZZS(FM) Zolfo Springs FL 2 hrs
V6AH(AM) Pohnpei FM 2 hrs
WFSH-FM Athens GA 2 hrs
*WCLK(FM) Atlanta GA 17 hrs
WTUF(AM) Boston GA 7 hrs
WJTH(AM) Calhoun GA 2 hrs
WQVE(FM) Camilla GA 16 hrs
WLBB(AM) Carrollton GA 7 hrs
WDXQ(AM) Cochran GA 6 hrs
WDXQ-FM Cochran GA 6 hrs
WCON-FM Cornelia GA 10 hrs
WTTI(AM) Dalton GA 1 hr
WOKA(AM) Douglas GA 4 hrs

WQZY(FM) Dublin GA 3 hrs
WBHB(AM) Fitzgerald GA 10 hrs
WRDO(FM) Fitzgerald GA 6 hrs
WFJO(FM) Folkston GA 5 hrs
*WBCX(FM) Gainesville GA 6 hrs
WJGA-FM Jackson GA 15 hrs
WLOP(AM) Jesup GA 10 hrs
WLAG(AM) La Grange GA 3 hrs
WHCG(AM) Metter GA 4 hrs
*WGUR(FM) Milledgeville GA 10 hrs
WNEA(AM) Newnan GA 15 hrs
WJEP(AM) Ochlocknee GA 3 hrs
WRBX(FM) Reidsville GA 161 hrs
WGJK(AM) Rome GA 19 hrs
WPTB(AM) Statesboro GA 6 hrs
WJAT(AM) Swainsboro GA 2 hrs
WPAX(AM) Thomasville GA 7 hrs
WTHO-FM Thomson GA 1 hr
WLET(AM) Toccoa GA
WNGC(FM) Toccoa GA
WKWN(AM) Trenton GA 12 hrs
WAAC(AM) Valdosta GA 4 hrs
WGOV(AM) Valdosta GA 14 hrs
WVLD(AM) Valdosta GA 2 hrs
*WVVS(FM) Valdosta GA 2 hrs
KSTO(FM) Hagatna GU 6 hrs
KELR-FM Chariton IA 5 hrs
KROS(AM) Clinton IA 1 hr
*KALA(AM) Davenport IA 13 hrs
*KHOE(FM) Fairfield IA 3 hrs
KYTC(FM) Northwood IA 1 hr
KBOE(FM) Oskaloosa IA 9 hrs
*KIGC(FM) Oskaloosa IA 12 hrs
KLEE(FM) Ottumwa IA 6 hrs
KIHK(FM) Rock Valley IA 3 hrs
KTLB(FM) Twin Lakes IA 2 hrs
*KBBG(FM) Waterloo IA
KWIK(FM) Pocatello ID 2 hrs
WBGZ(AM) Alton IL 4 hrs
WKRO(FM) Cairo IL 12 hrs
*WLUW(FM) Chicago IL 4 hrs
*WSSD(FM) Chicago IL
WCEV(AM) Cicero IL 7 hrs
WWHP(FM) Farmer City IL 3 hrs
*WDCB(FM) Glen Ellyn IL 2 hrs
WHPO(FM) Hoopeston IL 7 hrs
WJOL(AM) Joliet IL 1 hr
*WMXM(FM) Lake Forest IL 3 hrs
WPNA(AM) Oak Park IL 2 hrs
WVAZ(FM) Oak Park IL 4 hrs
WBBA-FM Pittsfield IL 3 hrs
WNTA(AM) Rockford IL 20 hrs
WPMB(AM) Vandalia IL 1 hr
WYKT(FM) Wilmington IL 4 hrs
WBNL(AM) Boonville IN 5 hrs
WIFE(FM) Connersville IN 6 hrs
WURK(FM) Elwood IN 4 hrs
WFLQ(FM) French Lick IN 4 hrs
WKAM(AM) Goshen IN 6 hrs
WXLW(AM) Indianapolis IN 5 hrs
WYXB(FM) Indianapolis IN 10 hrs
*WKPW(FM) Knightstown IN
WMRS(FM) Monticello IN 5 hrs
WNDZ(AM) Portage IN 2 hrs
WRIN(AM) Rensselaer IN 2 hrs
WAXI(FM) Rockville IN 2 hrs
WTCJ(AM) Tell City IN 6 hrs
WWVR(FM) West Terre Haute IN
KDNS(FM) Downs KS 5 hrs
KHAZ(FM) Hays KS 3 hrs
KINZ(FM) Humboldt KS 3 hrs
KHUT(FM) Hutchinson KS 5 hrs
KWBW(AM) Hutchinson KS 11 hrs
KNNS(AM) Larned KS 6 hrs
*KSDB-FM Manhattan KS 3 hrs
KFNF(FM) Oberlin KS 2 hrs
KKAN(AM) Phillipsburg KS 12 hrs
KFRM(AM) Salina KS 5 hrs
KSKG(FM) Salina KS 3 hrs
*KMUW(FM) Wichita KS 3 hrs
WANY(AM) Albany KY 6 hrs
WMDJ-FM Allen KY
WKXO(AM) Berea KY 12 hrs
WLFX(FM) Berea KY 12 hrs
WAIN-FM Columbia KY 15 hrs
WEKT(AM) Elkton KY
WJQI(AM) Fort Campbell KY 10 hrs

Special Programming on Radio Stations in the U.S.

WGOH(AM) Grayson KY 8 hrs
WHVO(AM) Hopkinsville KY 3 hrs
WLBN(AM) Lebanon KY 5 hrs
WKLB(AM) Manchester KY 4 hrs
WFTM(AM) Maysville KY 5 hrs
WFTM-FM Maysville KY 5 hrs
WFXY(AM) Middlesboro KY 3 hrs
WMIK(AM) Middlesboro KY 2 hrs
WLBQ(AM) Morgantown KY 3 hrs
WLOC(AM) Munfordville KY 20 hrs
WKCA(FM) Owingsville KY 4 hrs
WKYQ(FM) Paducah KY 2 hrs
WKYX(FM) Paducah KY 2 hrs
WRLV-FM Salyersville KY 4 hrs
WKWY(FM) Tompkinsville KY 7 hrs
WTKY(FM) Tompkinsville KY 8 hrs
WTKY-FM Tompkinsville KY 8 hrs
WKKS(AM) Vanceburg KY 16 hrs
WBCE(AM) Wickliffe KY
WGKY(FM) Wickliffe KY 5 hrs
KJMG(FM) Bastrop LA 24 hrs
KRVV(FM) Bastrop LA 4 hrs
KBCE(AM) Boyce LA 19 hrs
*KPAE(FM) Erwinville LA 15 hrs
KFNV-FM Ferriday LA 4 hrs
WOMN(AM) Franklinton LA 10 hrs
*KGRM(FM) Grambling LA 17 hrs
WFPR(AM) Hammond LA 12 hrs
WHMD(FM) Hammond LA 4 hrs
KJIN(AM) Houma LA
KHLA(FM) Jennings LA 6 hrs
KJEF(AM) Jennings LA 6 hrs
KJCB(AM) Lafayette LA 20 hrs
KJLO-FM Monroe LA 4 hrs
KBZZ-FM Morgan City LA 6 hrs
KMRC(AM) Morgan City LA 10 hrs
*KNWD(FM) Natchitoches LA 3 hrs
*KLPI-FM Ruston LA 3 hrs
KSYB(AM) Shreveport LA 8 hrs
KBSF(FM) Springhill LA 15 hrs
KEZM(AM) Sulphur LA 5 hrs
*KNSU(FM) Thibodaux LA 4 hrs
KVCL(AM) Winnfield LA 5 hrs
KVCL-FM Winnfield LA 20 hrs
KMAR-FM Winnsboro LA 20 hrs
*WMUA(FM) Amherst MA 9 hrs
*WRBB(FM) Boston MA 8 hrs
WBET(AM) Brockton MA 1 hr
WJIB(AM) Cambridge MA 4 hrs
*WMLN-FM Milton MA 3 hrs
*WSMU-FM North Dartmouth MA 2 hrs
*WMHC(FM) South Hadley MA 1 hr
*WAIC(FM) Springfield MA
WPEP(AM) Taunton MA 12 hrs
*WEAA(FM) Baltimore MD 13 hrs
*WMTB-FM Emmittsburg MD 1 hr
WKHI(FM) Fruitland MD 5 hrs
WJSS(AM) Havre de Grace MD
WAAI(FM) Hurlock MD 3 hrs
WKHW(FM) Pocomoke City MD 5 hrs
*WESM(FM) Princess Anne MD 20 hrs
*WMDR(FM) Augusta ME
WQTE(FM) Adrian MI 2 hrs
*WCBN-FM Ann Arbor MI 1 hr
WGTO(AM) Cassopolis MI 10 hrs
WLCM(FM) Charlotte MI 3 hrs
*WRCJ-FM Detroit MI 4 hrs
WXLA(AM) Dimondale MI 5 hrs
WDZZ-FM Flint MI 8 hrs
*WIDR(FM) Kalamazoo MI 3 hrs
WJNZ(AM) Kentwood MI 4 hrs
WTLZ(FM) Saginaw MI 6 hrs
WMLM(AM) Saint Louis MI 2 hrs
KDUZ(AM) Hutchinson MN 3 hrs
KLQL(FM) Luverne MN 4 hrs
KYOO(AM) Bolivar MO 2 hrs
KBFL(FM) Buffalo MO 3 hrs
KATI(FM) California MO 3 hrs
KRLL(AM) California MO 3 hrs
KRMO(AM) Cassville MO 2 hrs
KMFC(FM) Centralia MO 2 hrs
KCHR(AM) Charleston MO 10 hrs
KWKZ(FM) Charleston MO 6 hrs
*KOPN(FM) Columbia MO 3 hrs
KUNQ(FM) Houston MO 10 hrs
*KJLU(FM) Jefferson City MO
*KTTK(FM) Lebanon MO 7 hrs

*KTTK(FM) Lebanon MO 80 hrs
*KJAB-FM Mexico MO 20 hrs
KWBZ(FM) Monroe City MO 4 hrs
*KGSP(FM) Parkville MO 3 hrs
*KCLC(FM) Saint Charles MO 9 hrs
KDRO(AM) Sedalia MO 6 hrs
*KWND(FM) Springfield MO 3 hrs
KTTN-FM Trenton MO 6 hrs
KSPQ(FM) West Plains MO 5 hrs
WWZQ(AM) Aberdeen MS 8 hrs
WAMY(AM) Amory MS 6 hrs
WESE(FM) Baldwyn MS 6 hrs
WJBI(AM) Batesville MS
WBSL(FM) Bay St. Louis MS 13 hrs
WBKN(FM) Brookhaven MS 3 hrs
*WPAE(FM) Centreville MS 15 hrs
WKRA(FM) Holly Springs MS 12 hrs
WCPC(AM) Houston MS 40 hrs
*WJSU(FM) Jackson MS 18 hrs
*WPRL(FM) Lorman MS 16 hrs
WNAT(AM) Natchez MS 18 hrs
WNAU(AM) New Albany MS
WWZD-FM New Albany MS 4 hrs
WOXD(FM) Oxford MS 4 hrs
WPMP(AM) Pascagoula-Moss Point MS
WKZU(FM) Ripley MS 6 hrs
WSAO(AM) Senatobia MS
WAVN(FM) Southaven MS 19 hrs
WLRC(AM) Walnut MS
WROB(AM) West Point MS 2 hrs
WIGG(AM) Wiggins MS
WKXR(FM) Asheboro NC 10 hrs
WSKY(FM) Asheville NC 6 hrs
WWNC(AM) Asheville NC 3 hrs
WZJS(FM) Banner Elk NC 1 hr
*WGWG(FM) Boiling Springs NC 15 hrs
WATA(AM) Boone NC 5 hrs
WGCR(FM) Brevard NC
WSQL(FM) Brevard NC 8 hrs
*WCCE(FM) Buie's Creek NC 11 hrs
WKYK(FM) Burnsville NC 12 hrs
WCLN(AM) Clinton NC 7.5 hrs
WPEG(FM) Concord NC 4 hrs
WFXC(FM) Durham NC 4 hrs
*WNCU(FM) Durham NC
WCNC(AM) Elizabeth City NC 7 hrs
*WRVS-FM Elizabeth City NC 19 hrs
WBLA(AM) Elizabethtown NC 8 hrs
WGQR(FM) Elizabethtown NC 8 hrs
*WFSS(FM) Fayetteville NC 4 hrs
WKIX(FM) Goldsboro NC 4 hrs
WYCV(AM) Granite Falls NC
WLNC(AM) Laurinburg NC 4 hrs
WLON(AM) Lincolnton NC 5 hrs
WBRM(AM) Marion NC 5 hrs
WDJS(AM) Mount Olive NC 5 hrs
WIKS(FM) New Bern NC 4 hrs
WECR(AM) Newland NC 10 hrs
WPJL(AM) Raleigh NC
*WSHA(FM) Raleigh NC 20 hrs
*WZRU(FM) Roanoke Rapids NC 6 hrs
WRSV(FM) Rocky Mount NC 20 hrs
WKRX(FM) Roxboro NC 4 hrs
WKRX(FM) Roxboro NC 4 hrs
WRXO(FM) Roxboro NC 5 hrs
WADA(AM) Shelby NC 5 hrs
WNCA(AM) Siler City NC 15 hrs
WEEB(AM) Southern Pines NC 6 hrs
*WNCW(FM) Spindale NC 2 hrs
WAME(AM) Statesville NC 5 hrs
WFXK(FM) Tarboro NC 3 hrs
WACB(AM) Taylorsville NC 12 hrs
WSVM(AM) Valdese NC 4 hrs
WZKB(FM) Wallace NC 3 hrs
WKSK(FM) West Jefferson NC 5 hrs
WYNC(AM) Yanceyville NC
*KABU(FM) Fort Totten ND 7 hrs
KAUJ(AM) Grafton ND 4 hrs
KXPO(AM) Grafton ND 5 hrs
KQLX(AM) Lisbon ND 6 hrs
KTGO(AM) Tioga ND 11 hrs
*KINI(FM) Crookston NE 6 hrs
KMTY(FM) Holdrege NE 5 hrs
KUVR(AM) Holdrege NE 5 hrs

*KRNU(FM) Lincoln NE 2 hrs
KRFS(AM) Superior NE 3 hrs
WTMR(AM) Camden NJ 20 hrs
*WFJS(FM) Hazlet NJ 12 hrs
WTTH(AM) Margate City NJ 5 hrs
WMVB(AM) Millville NJ 8 hrs
*WTSR(FM) Trenton NJ 6 hrs
*WMSC(FM) Upper Montclair NJ 2 hrs
*WMCX(FM) West Long Branch NJ 6 hrs
*WJPH(FM) Woodbine NJ 1 hr
KRSY(AM) Alamogordo NM 8 hrs
KATK(AM) Carlsbad NM 2 hrs
*KCEP(FM) Las Vegas NV 19 hrs
*WCDB(FM) Albany NY 3 hrs
WROW(AM) Albany NY 3 hrs
*WXLH(FM) Blue Mountain Lake NY
*WSLU(FM) Canton NY
WSIV(AM) East Syracuse NY 1 hr
*WEOS(FM) Geneva NY 3 hrs
*WITR(FM) Henrietta NY 8 hrs
WHVW(FM) Hyde Park NY 1.5 hrs
WXRL(AM) Lancaster NY 2 hrs
*WVCR-FM Loudonville NY 3 hrs
WVOX(AM) New Rochelle NY 1 hr
WJJL(AM) Niagara Falls NY 1 hr
WLIM(FM) Patchogue NY 2 hrs
WDKX(FM) Rochester NY 7 hrs
*WRUR-FM Rochester NY 3 hrs
WMYY(FM) Schoharie NY
*WAER(FM) Syracuse NY 3 hrs
*WONB(FM) Ada OH 3 hrs
*WRMU(FM) Alliance OH 2 hrs
*WOBO(FM) Batavia OH 3 hrs
WAIS(AM) Buchtel OH 3 hrs
WCER(AM) Canton OH 4 hrs
WTSJ(FM) Cincinnati OH 15 hrs
WABQ(AM) Cleveland OH
*WWSU(FM) Dayton OH 3 hrs
WOHI(AM) East Liverpool OH 1 hr
*WCVO(FM) Gahanna OH 6 hrs
*WHSS(FM) Hamilton OH 2 hrs
WPOS-FM Holland OH 20 hrs
WJYD(FM) London OH 10 hrs
WTIG(AM) Massillon OH 6 hrs wkly. hrs
WMPO(AM) Middleport-Pomeroy OH 18 hrs
WQIO(FM) Mount Vernon OH 2 hrs
WNPQ(FM) New Philadelphia OH 4 hrs
WPAY(AM) Portsmouth OH 6 hrs
WULM(AM) Springfield OH 6 hrs
WJUC(FM) Swanton OH 12 hrs wkly hrs
WERT(AM) Van Wert OH 3 hrs
WBZI(AM) Xenia OH 6 hrs
KADA(AM) Ada OK 5 hrs
KADA-FM Ada OK 5 hrs
KKAJ-FM Ardmore OK 6 hrs
KYFM(FM) Bartlesville OK 4 hrs
KOKB(AM) Blackwell OK 11 hrs
KKBI(FM) Broken Bow OK 4 hrs
*KRSC-FM Claremore OK 4 hrs
KDDQ(AM) Comanche OK 2 hrs
KTNT(FM) Eufaula OK 3 hrs
KPRV-FM Heavener OK 12 hrs
KIHN(AM) Hugo OK 5 hrs
KITX(FM) Hugo OK 3 hrs
KFXI(FM) Marlow OK 8 hrs
KTMC(AM) McAlester OK 5 hrs
KTMC-FM McAlester OK 2 hrs
KKNG-FM Newcastle OK 8 hrs
KRIG-FM Nowata OK 4 hrs
KPRV(AM) Poteau OK 5 hrs
KFAQ(AM) Tulsa OK 2 hrs
KIMY(FM) Watonga OK 4 hrs
KAJO(AM) Grants Pass OR 1 hr
KYKN(AM) Keizer OR 6 hrs
KKSL(AM) Lake Oswego OR 15 hrs
KWBY(AM) Woodburn OR 3 hrs
WWSM(AM) Annville-Cleona PA 3 hrs
WCHA(AM) Chambersburg PA 4 hrs
WCOJ(AM) Coatesville PA 2 hrs
*WERG(FM) Erie PA 3 hrs
WSKE(FM) Everett PA 1 hr
*WZBT(FM) Gettysburg PA 1 hr
WVMM(FM) Grantham PA 2 hrs

WTCY(AM) Harrisburg PA
WTKT(AM) Harrisburg PA 2 hrs
*WIUP-FM Indiana PA 1 hr
WJSA(AM) Jersey Shore PA 2 hrs
WJSA-FM Jersey Shore PA 2 hrs
WJUN(AM) Mexico PA 3 hrs
WQZS(FM) Meyersdale PA 5 hrs
WWBE(FM) Mifflinburg PA 3 hrs
WHAT(AM) Philadelphia PA 12 hrs
*WKDU(FM) Philadelphia PA 4 hrs
WURD(AM) Philadelphia PA 9 hrs
WUSL(FM) Philadelphia PA 4 hrs
WPHB(AM) Philipsburg PA 6 hrs
WRAW(AM) Reading PA 1 hr
*WXLV(FM) Schnecksville PA 4 hrs
*WBYO(FM) Sellersville PA 3 hrs
WWII(AM) Shiremanstown PA 2 hrs
*WZZD(FM) Warwick PA 3 hrs
WKZV(AM) Washington PA 1 hr
*WRLC(FM) Williamsport PA 6 hrs
WTMV(FM) Youngsville PA 2 hrs
*WJMF(FM) Smithfield RI 2 hrs
WOON(AM) Woonsocket RI 1 hr
*WZLA-FM Abbeville SC 8 hrs
WGTN-FM Andrews SC 5 hrs
WBT-FM Chester SC 6 hrs
WOLS(AM) Florence SC 4 hrs
WFIS(AM) Fountain Inn SC 4 hrs
WBZF(FM) Hartsville SC 3 hrs
WHSC(AM) Hartsville SC 3 hrs
WWKT-FM Kingstree SC 4 hrs
WZJY(AM) Mt. Pleasant SC
WKMG(AM) Newberry SC 3 hrs
WRHI(AM) Rock Hill SC 5 hrs
WALI(FM) Walterboro SC 5 hrs
*KLND(FM) Little Eagle SD 3 hrs
KSQB(AM) Sioux Falls SD 4 hrs
KBHB(AM) Sturgis SD 3 hrs
WATX(AM) Algood TN
WVOL(AM) Berry Hill TN 6 hrs
*WHCB(FM) Bristol TN 15 hrs
WFWL(AM) Camden TN 8 hrs
WRJB(FM) Camden TN 4 hrs
WVFB(FM) Celina TN 7 hrs
WNKX(AM) Centerville TN 5 hrs
WNKX-FM Centerville TN
WMSR-FM Collinwood TN
WHUB(AM) Cookeville TN 11 hrs
WZYX(FM) Cowan TN 10 hrs
WCDZ(FM) Dresden TN 1 hr
WSDQ(AM) Dunlap TN 7 hrs
WEMB(AM) Erwin TN 10 hrs
WMRO(AM) Gallatin TN 13 hrs
*WVCP(FM) Gallatin TN 6 hrs
WXJB(FM) Harrogate TN 2 hrs
*WFHU(FM) Henderson TN 9 hrs
WFKX(FM) Henderson TN 4 hrs
WHHM-FM Henderson TN 10 hrs
WQQK(FM) Hendersonville TN 6 hrs
WMLR(AM) Hohenwald TN 4 hrs
WDXI(AM) Jackson TN 16 hrs
WNRX(FM) Jefferson City TN 4 hrs
*WKTS(FM) Kingston TN 8 hrs
WKZX-FM Lenoir City TN 18 hrs
WLIL(AM) Lenoir City TN 18 hrs
WAXO(AM) Lewisburg TN 12 hrs
WDXL(AM) Lexington TN 10 hrs
WLIV(AM) Livingston TN 18 hrs
WDIA(AM) Memphis TN
WTRB(AM) Ripley TN 6 hrs
WJLE(FM) Smithville TN 15 hrs
WJLE-FM Smithville TN 15 hrs
WEPG(AM) South Pittsburg TN 10 hrs
WTZX(AM) Sparta TN 6 hrs
WDBL(AM) Springfield TN 10 hrs
WSBI(AM) Static TN 10 hrs
WCTU(FM) Tazewell TN
WNTT(AM) Tazewell TN
WYVY(FM) Union City TN 7 hrs
*KGNZ(FM) Abilene TX 2 hrs
KDRY(AM) Alamo Heights TX 5 hrs
KIXZ(AM) Amarillo TX 6 hrs
*KAZI-FM Austin TX 18 hrs
KORQ(FM) Baird TX 3 hrs
KBYG(AM) Big Spring TX 6 hrs
KQTY(AM) Borger TX 3 hrs
KQTY-FM Borger TX 3 hrs

KNTX(AM) Bowie TX 4 hrs
KULF(FM) Brenham TX 10 hrs
KBOC(FM) Bridgeport TX 9 hrs
*KHPU(FM) Brownwood TX 4 hrs
KPSM(FM) Brownwood TX 2 hrs
KMIL(AM) Cameron TX 6 hrs
KCAR(FM) Clarksville TX 6 hrs
KSTA(AM) Coleman TX 7 hrs
KXCT(AM) Coleman TX 7 hrs
*KEOS(FM) College Station TX 3 hrs
KCOM(AM) Comanche TX 5 hrs
KSSM(FM) Copperas Cove TX
KBHT(FM) Crockett TX 5 hrs
KDDD(AM) Dumas TX 5 hrs
KATX(FM) Eastland TX 5 hrs
KEAS(AM) Eastland TX 5 hrs
*KTEP(FM) El Paso TX 4 hrs
KNES(FM) Fairfield TX 3 hrs
KSWA(AM) Graham TX 2 hrs
KVJM(FM) Hearne TX 5 hrs
KHBR(AM) Hillsboro TX 6 hrs
KCOX(FM) Jasper TX 6 hrs
KOOK(FM) Junction TX 2 hrs
KERV(AM) Kerrville TX 3 hrs
KRNH(FM) Kerrville TX 3 hrs
KRVL(FM) Kerrville TX 2 hrs
*KTAI(FM) Kingsville TX 6 hrs
KYMI(FM) Los Ybanez TX 16 hrs
KZRC(FM) Markham TX 4 hrs
KHKZ(FM) Mercedes TX 2 hrs
KRQX(AM) Mexia TX 3 hrs
KYCX-FM Mexia TX 3 hrs
KLBO(AM) Monahans TX 3 hrs
KJCS(FM) Nacogdoches TX 3 hrs
KHTZ(FM) Navasota TX 4 hrs
KPLT(AM) Paris TX 4 hrs
KRXT(FM) Rockdale TX 2 hrs
KBAL(AM) San Saba TX 7 hrs
KBAL-FM San Saba TX 7 hrs
KBKH(FM) Shamrock TX 6 hrs
KXOX(AM) Sweetwater TX 4 hrs
KTFS(AM) Texarkana TX 2 hrs
KTBB(AM) Tyler TX 5 hrs
*KVNE(FM) Tyler TX 4 hrs
KZEY(FM) Tyler TX 16 hrs
KVWC(AM) Vernon TX 16 hrs
KALK(FM) Winfield TX 1 hr
KWUD(AM) Woodville TX 6 hrs
KBLQ-FM Logan UT 8 hrs
*KWCR-FM Ogden UT 3 hrs
*KUER(FM) Salt Lake City UT 3 hrs
WKDE(AM) Altavista VA 5 hrs
WKDE-FM Altavista VA 5 hrs
WKEX(FM) Blacksburg VA 5 hrs
*WTJU(FM) Charlottesville VA 1 hr
WKEY(AM) Covington VA 2 hrs
WEVA(AM) Emporia VA 3 hrs
WPAK(AM) Farmville VA 12 hrs
WLQM(FM) Franklin VA 12 hrs
WGAT(AM) Gate City VA 20 hrs
WMNA(AM) Gretna VA 15 hrs
WCLM(AM) Highland Springs VA 5 wkly hrs
WKWI(FM) Kilmarnock VA 5 hrs
WOJL(AM) Louisa VA 3 hrs
WVGM(AM) Lynchburg VA 19 hrs
WMEV(AM) Marion VA 2 hrs
WSIG(FM) Mount Jackson VA 4 hrs
WNVA(AM) Norton VA 15 hrs
WCUL(FM) Orange VA 2 hrs
WVCV(AM) Orange VA 2 hrs
*WVST-FM Petersburg VA 13 hrs
WREJ(AM) Richmond VA 1 hr
WXLZ(AM) Saint Paul VA 15 hrs
WKGM(AM) Smithfield VA 5 hrs
WHLF(FM) South Boston VA 6 hrs
WQOK(FM) South Boston VA 9 hrs
WTZE(AM) Tazewell VA 5 hrs
WKCW(AM) Warrenton VA 6 hrs
WMBG(AM) Williamsburg VA 5 hrs
WYVE(AM) Wytheville VA 4 hrs
WWOD(AM) Hartford VT 2 hrs
WMNV(FM) Rupert VT
WTWN(AM) Wells River VT
KBDB-FM Forks WA 4 hrs
KBIS(AM) Forks WA 6.5 hrs
KWDB(AM) Oak Harbor WA 6 hrs

Broadcasting & Cable Yearbook 2006

Special Programming on Radio Stations in the U.S.

*KNHC(FM) Seattle WA 6 hrs
KITZ(AM) Silverdale WA 2 hrs
KJOX(AM) Yakima WA 2 hrs
WATK(AM) Antigo WI 2 hrs
WMCS(AM) Greenfield WI 5 hrs
WBJX(AM) Racine WI 8 hrs
WKKV-FM Racine WI 4 hrs
WRCO(AM) Richland Center WI 6 hrs
WKCJ(AM) Lewisburg WV 6 hrs
WVNT(AM) Parkersburg WV 4 hrs
WELD-FM Petersburg WV 3 hrs
WLWF(FM) Ravenswood WV 7 hrs
WCWV(FM) Summersville WV 15 hrs
WHAW(AM) Weston WV 18 hrs
WXCC(FM) Williamson WV 8 hrs
KJUA(AM) Cheyenne WY 1 hr
KKTY-FM Douglas WY 1 hr

Greek

*WBVM(FM) Tampa FL 1 hr
WONX(AM) Evanston IL 2 hrs
WVIV-FM Highland Park IL
WJOB(AM) Hammond IN 1 hr
WUNR(AM) Brookline MA 2 hrs
WLYN(AM) Lynn MA 4 hrs
*WTCC(FM) Springfield MA 2 hrs
WGFP(AM) Webster MA 1 hr
WBMD(AM) Baltimore MD 2 hrs
WSDS(AM) Salem Township MI 4 hrs
WKBR(AM) Manchester NH 8 hrs
WAAL(FM) Binghamton NY 1 hr
WTHE(AM) Mineola NY 5 hrs
*WRPI(FM) Troy NY 2 hrs
WKTX(AM) Cortland OH 2 hrs
WCCD(AM) Parma OH 2 hrs
*WKTL(FM) Struthers OH 1 hr
WEDO(AM) McKeesport PA 1 hr
WKST(AM) New Castle PA 1 hr
WBZK(AM) York SC 10 hrs
*WUVT-FM Blacksburg VA 2 hrs
WEIR(AM) Weirton WV 1 hr

Hardcore

*WZBC(FM) Newton MA 3 hrs
*WQFS(FM) Greensboro NC 4 hrs
*WITR(FM) Henrietta NY 2 hrs
*WNRN(FM) Charlottesville VA 4 hrs
*WWHS-FM Hampden-Sydney VA 4 hrs

Hebrew

*WHPK-FM Chicago IL 1 hr
KLAV(AM) Las Vegas NV 1 hr
*WKDU(FM) Philadelphia PA 3 hrs

Hindi

WCEV(AM) Cicero IL 1 hr
WEEF(AM) Highland Park IL
KLAV(AM) Las Vegas NV 1 hr
*KBOO(FM) Portland OR 1 hr
KXMG(AM) Portland OR 1 hr
WWII(AM) Shiremanstown PA 1 hr
*WEVL(FM) Memphis TN 1 hr
KTEK(AM) Alvin TX 3 hrs
KGOL(AM) Humble TX 15 hrs
*KTAI(FM) Kingsville TX 3 hrs

Hungarian

KTYM(AM) Inglewood CA 1 hr
*WVOF(FM) Fairfield CT 2 hrs
*WAPS(FM) Akron OH 1 hr
*WCPN(FM) Cleveland OH 1 hr
WKTX(AM) Cortland OH 7 hrs
*WQRP(FM) Dayton OH 3 hrs
*WKTL(FM) Struthers OH 1 hr
*WJCU(FM) University Heights OH 3 hrs
WEDO(AM) McKeesport PA 1 hr

Inspirational

*WGTS(FM) Takoma Park MD
WNBN(AM) Meridian MS
*WCID(FM) Friendship NY

Irish

KRLA(AM) Glendale CA 1 hr
*KUSF(FM) San Francisco CA 1 hr
*KRCC(FM) Colorado Springs CO 5 hrs
WQUN(AM) Hamden CT 2 hrs
WMRD(AM) Middletown CT 1 hr
*WNHU(FM) West Haven CT 5 hrs
*WUCF-FM Orlando FL 1 hr
*WHPK-FM Chicago IL 1 hr
WCEV(AM) Cicero IL 2 hrs
WPNA(AM) Oak Park IL 7 hrs
*KANU(FM) Lawrence KS 2 hrs
*WNKU(FM) Highland Heights KY 3 hrs
*WGBH(FM) Boston MA 2 hrs
WBET(AM) Brockton MA 2 hrs
WUNR(AM) Brookline MA 2 hrs
WACE(AM) Chicopee MA 2 hrs
WATD-FM Marshfield MA 6 hrs
WNBP(AM) Newburyport MA 4 hrs
WNTN(AM) Newton MA 6 hrs
*WZBC(FM) Newton MA 2 hrs
WBRK(AM) Pittsfield MA 1 hr
*WTMD(FM) Towson MD 2 hrs
WUFK(FM) Fort Kent ME 3 hrs
*WUNH(FM) Durham NH 2 hrs
WAAL(FM) Binghamton NY 2 hrs
WYOS(AM) Binghamton NY 2 hrs
*WHPC(FM) Garden City NY 3 hrs
*WRHU(FM) Hempstead NY 5 hrs
WHVW(AM) Hyde Park NY 1 hr
WKNY(AM) Kingston NY 1 hr
*WVCR-FM Loudonville NY 3 hrs
*WFUV(FM) New York NY 10 hrs
WLIM(AM) Patchogue NY 1 hr
WLLW(FM) Seneca Falls NY 2 hrs
WSFW(AM) Seneca Falls NY 2 hrs
WTBQ(FM) Warwick NY 1 hr
WTBQ(AM) Warwick NY 2 hrs
*WCBE(FM) Columbus OH 4 hrs
*WKTL(FM) Struthers OH 1 hr
*WJCU(FM) University Heights OH 2 hrs
WGBN(AM) New Kensington PA 2 hrs
*WYEP-FM Pittsburgh PA 2 hrs
*WEVL(FM) Memphis TN 4 hrs

Italian

KTYM(AM) Inglewood CA 3 hrs
*KUSF(FM) San Francisco CA 1 hr
WICC(AM) Bridgeport CT 5 hrs
*WFAR(AM) Danbury CT 1 hr
*WVOF(FM) Fairfield CT 1 hr
WGCH(AM) Greenwich CT 1 hr
WMRD(AM) Middletown CT 2 hrs
WXCT(AM) Southington CT 4.5 hrs
WATR(AM) Waterbury CT 3 hrs
*WWUH(FM) West Hartford CT 3 hrs
WXYB(AM) Indian Rocks Beach FL 2 hrs
WMEL(FM) Melbourne FL 2 hrs
WDUV(FM) New Port Richey FL 1 hr
WPSO(AM) New Port Richey FL 2 hrs
*WUCF-FM Orlando FL 1 hr
WBET(AM) Brockton MA 2 hrs
WUNR(AM) Brookline MA 1 hr
WKOX(AM) Framingham MA 1 hr
WNNW(AM) Lawrence MA 2 hrs
WLYN(AM) Lynn MA 4 hrs
WNTN(AM) Newton MA 2 hrs
*WTCC(FM) Springfield MA 2 hrs
*WZLY(FM) Wellesley MA 1 hr
*WHRW(FM) Binghamton NY 3 hrs
*WCVF-FM Fredonia NY 3 hrs
WAMF(AM) Fulton NY 2 hrs
*WHPC(FM) Garden City NY 2 hrs
*WRHU(FM) Hempstead NY 4 hrs
WHVW(AM) Hyde Park NY 1 hr

WJTN(AM) Jamestown NY 1 hr
WIZR(AM) Johnstown NY 1 hr
WLVL(AM) Lockport NY 2 hrs
WVOA(AM) Mexico NY 2 hrs
WJJL(AM) Niagara Falls NY 4 hrs
WLIM(AM) Patchogue NY 4 hrs
*WRUC(FM) Schenectady NY 1 hr
WLLW(FM) Seneca Falls NY 2 hrs
WSFW(AM) Seneca Falls NY 2 hrs
WUTQ(AM) Utica NY 2 hrs
*WAPS(FM) Akron OH 2 hrs
WERE(AM) Cleveland OH 1 hr
WRTK(AM) Niles OH 1 hr
*WJCU(FM) University Heights OH 2 hrs
WELW(AM) Willoughby-Eastlake OH 1 hr
WNIO(AM) Youngstown OH 3 hrs
KXMG(AM) Portland OR 1 hr
*WMUH(FM) Allentown PA 1 hr
WBVP(AM) Beaver Falls PA 1 hr
WWCS(AM) Canonsburg PA 2 hrs
*WERG(FM) Erie PA 3 hrs
WEDO(AM) McKeesport PA 1 hr
WGBN(AM) New Kensington PA 2 hrs
WURD(AM) Philadelphia PA 3 hrs
WPIC(AM) Sharon PA 2 hrs
WRIB(AM) Providence RI 5 hrs
WFAX(AM) Falls Church VA 1 hr
WREJ(AM) Richmond VA 1 hr
*WMSE(FM) Milwaukee WI 3 hrs
WRJN(AM) Racine WI 2.5 hrs
WOBG(AM) Clarksburg WV 1 hr
WRLF(FM) Fairmont WV 3 hrs
WTCS(AM) Fairmont WV 3 hrs
WEIR(AM) Weirton WV 3 hrs

Japanese

KTYM(AM) Inglewood CA 1 hr
KEST(AM) San Francisco CA
*KCSB-FM Santa Barbara CA 1 hr
*V6AI(FM) Yap FM 5 hrs
*KSDA-FM Agat GU 1 hr
KUAM(AM) Hagatna GU 3 hrs
KPUA(AM) Hilo HI 6 hrs
*WAMH(FM) Amherst MA 2 hrs
*WZLY(FM) Wellesley MA 1 hr
*WBXL(FM) Baldwinsville NY 1 hr
*KWVA(FM) Eugene OR 2 hrs
*WRVU(FM) Nashville TN 2 hrs

Jazz

*KSKA(FM) Anchorage AK 5 hrs
*KBRW(FM) Barrow AK 6 hrs
KAKQ-FM Fairbanks AK 3 hrs
*KUAC(FM) Fairbanks AK 15 hrs
*KIYU(FM) Galena AK 4 hrs
*KHNS(FM) Haines AK 5 hrs
*KBBI(FM) Homer AK 5 hrs
*KTOO(FM) Juneau AK 14 hrs
*KRBD(FM) Ketchikan AK 10 hrs
*KSTK(FM) Wrangell AK 8 hrs
WDLT-FM Chickasaw AL 5 hrs
WZEW(FM) Fairhope AL 6 hrs
WEUP(AM) Huntsville AL 2 hrs
WJRL-FM Ozark AL 4 hrs
WWPG(AM) Tuscaloosa AL 2 hrs
KEZA(FM) Fayetteville AR
*KXRJ(FM) Russellville AR 15 hrs
KGVY(AM) Green Valley AZ
KNOT(AM) Prescott AZ 2 hrs
KQST(FM) Sedona AZ 15 hrs
*KXCI(FM) Tucson AZ 2 hrs
KHOV-FM Wickenburg AZ 2 hrs
*KHSU-FM Arcata CA 10 hrs
*KPFA(FM) Berkeley CA 15 hrs
KRML(AM) Carmel CA 140 hrs
*KHSR(FM) Crescent City CA 10 hrs
KMUD(FM) Garberville CA 6 hrs
KFGY(FM) Healdsburg CA 5 hrs
*KFJC(FM) Los Altos CA 7 hrs
*KPFK(FM) Los Angeles CA 14 hrs
KMMT(FM) Mammoth Lakes CA 2 hrs
*KSMC(FM) Moraga CA 5 hrs
KHOP(FM) Oakdale CA 2 hrs

*KZYX(FM) Philo CA 11 hrs
KLXR(AM) Redding CA 2 hrs
*KUCR(FM) Riverside CA 6 hrs
*KUSF(FM) San Francisco CA 3 hrs
KYCY(AM) San Francisco CA
*KCRW(FM) Santa Monica CA
*KRCB-FM Santa Rosa CA 6 hrs
KNNN(FM) Shasta Lake City CA 3 hrs
KZSQ-FM Sonora CA 3 hrs
*KCSS(FM) Turlock CA 4 hrs
*KASF(FM) Alamosa CO 6 hrs
*KGNU-FM Boulder CO 15 hrs
KVCU(AM) Boulder CO 3 hrs
*KRCC(FM) Colorado Springs CO 15 hrs
*KDUR(FM) Durango CO 9 hrs
KIQX(FM) Durango CO 7 hrs
*KIUP(AM) Durango CO 4 hrs
*KCSU-FM Fort Collins CO 3 hrs
*KMSA(FM) Grand Junction CO 12 hrs
*KWSB-FM Gunnison CO 3 hrs
*KSUT(FM) Ignacio CO 15 hrs
KFMU-FM Oak Creek CO 4 hrs
*KWUF-FM Pagosa Springs CO 10 hrs
*KVNF(FM) Paonia CO 17 hrs
*KOTO(FM) Telluride CO 9 hrs
*WPKN(FM) Bridgeport CT 16 hrs
*WXCI(FM) Danbury CT 1 hr
*WQTQ(FM) Hartford CT 12 hrs
WZBG(FM) Litchfield CT 2 hrs
WMRD(AM) Middletown CT 4 hrs. weekly
WYBC-FM New Haven CT 8 hrs
*WCNI(FM) New London CT 9 hrs
WLIS(AM) Old Saybrook CT 4 hrs
WQQQ(FM) Sharon CT 3 hrs
WXLM(FM) Stonington CT 2 hrs
*WNHU(FM) West Haven CT 12 hrs
*WECS(FM) Willimantic CT 16 hrs
WNEZ(AM) Windsor CT 3 hrs
*WAMU(FM) Washington DC 5 hrs
*WVUD(FM) Newark DE 15 hrs
WGMD(FM) Rehoboth Beach DE 2 hrs
*WKTO(FM) Edgewater FL 2 hrs
*WJLF(FM) Gainesville FL 2 hrs
WLLD(FM) Holmes Beach FL 3 hrs
WXCV(FM) Homosassa Springs FL 7 hrs
WMXQ(FM) Jacksonville FL 4 hrs
WKEY-FM Key West FL 4 hrs
WAVV(FM) Marco FL 4 hrs
*WFIT(FM) Melbourne FL 20 hrs
WRXB(AM) Saint Petersburg Beach FL 15 hrs
*WFSU-FM Tallahassee FL 8 hrs
WFLM(FM) White City FL 5 hrs
*WPRK(FM) Winter Park FL 3 hrs
*WUGA(FM) Athens GA 4 hrs
*WABE(FM) Atlanta GA 7 hrs
*WREK(FM) Atlanta GA 15 hrs
*WACG-FM Augusta GA 18 hrs
*WDCO-FM Cochran GA 4 hrs
*WNGU(FM) Dahlonega GA 4 hrs
*WPPR(FM) Demorest GA 4 hrs
*WJWV(FM) Fort Gaines GA 4 hrs
WFXM(FM) Gordon GA 3 hrs
*WGUR(FM) Milledgeville GA 12 hrs
WWIO(AM) Saint Mary's GA 4 hrs
*WSVH(FM) Savannah GA 4 hrs
*WVGS(FM) Statesboro GA 5 hrs
*WABR-FM Tifton GA 4 hrs
*WVVS(FM) Valdosta GA 2 hrs
*WWET(FM) Valdosta GA 4 hrs
*WWSN(FM) Waycross GA 5 hrs
*WXVS(FM) Waycross GA 4 hrs
KUAI(AM) Eleele HI 4 hrs
*WOI(AM) Ames IA 7 hrs
KMXG(FM) Clinton IA 3 hrs
KROS(AM) Clinton IA 1 hr
*KWLC(AM) Decorah IA
*KHOE(AM) Fairfield IA 2 hrs
*KRUI-FM Iowa City IA 3 hrs
*KRNL-FM Mount Vernon IA 2 hrs
*KOJI(FM) Okoboji IA 17 hrs
*KIGC(FM) Oskaloosa IA 12 hrs
KAZR(FM) Pella IA 6 hrs
*KWIT(FM) Sioux City IA 17 hrs

KSAS-FM Caldwell ID 4 hrs
*KBSM(FM) McCall ID
*KRFA-FM Moscow ID
*KUOI-FM Moscow ID 4 hrs
KECH-FM Sun Valley ID 6. hrs
*WESN(FM) Bloomington IL 6 hrs
*WEIU(FM) Charleston IL 4 hrs
*WFMT(FM) Chicago IL 5 hrs
*WIIT(FM) Chicago IL 9 hrs
*WLUW(FM) Chicago IL 2 hrs
*WSSD(FM) Chicago IL
*WEPS(FM) Elgin IL 6 hrs
*WRSE-FM Elmhurst IL 6 hrs
*WTPC(FM) Elsah IL 3 hrs
*WVKC(FM) Galesburg IL 15 hrs
WYMG(FM) Jacksonville IL 2 hrs
*WCSF(FM) Joliet IL 2 hrs
*WMXM(FM) Lake Forest IL 6 hrs
*WLRA(FM) Lockport IL 15 hrs
*WIUM(FM) Macomb IL 5 hrs
*WIUS(FM) Macomb IL 5 hrs
WPNA(AM) Oak Park IL 4 hrs
*WMTH(FM) Park Ridge IL 2 hrs
WOAM(AM) Peoria IL 2 hrs
*WRRG(FM) River Grove IL 5 hrs
*WVIK(FM) Rock Island IL 9 hrs
WNNS(FM) Springfield IL 6 hrs
*WARG(FM) Summit IL 6 hrs
*WEAX(FM) Angola IN 2 hrs
WIJY(FM) Franklin IN 10 hrs
*WGRE(FM) Greencastle IN 3 hrs
WTPI(FM) Indianapolis IN 6 hrs
*WVUR-FM Valparaiso IN 3 hrs
KAHS(AM) El Dorado KS 2 hrs
*KANZ(FM) Garden City KS 15 hrs
*KZNA(FM) Hill City KS 15 hrs
*KSDB-FM Manhattan KS 3 hrs
KRBB(FM) Wichita KS 2 hrs
*WKYU-FM Bowling Green KY 15 hrs
*WKUE(FM) Elizabethtown KY 15 hrs
WRNZ(FM) Lancaster KY 2 hrs
*WRFL(FM) Lexington KY 3 hrs
WWXL(AM) Manchester KY 2 hrs wkly hrs
*WMKY(FM) Morehead KY 3 hrs
*WDCL-FM Somerset KY 15 hrs
*KLSP(FM) Angola LA 7 hrs
KBCE(FM) Boyce LA 3 hrs
*KGRM(FM) Grambling LA 15 hrs
KJCB(AM) Lafayette LA 2 hrs
*WWNO(FM) New Orleans LA 6 hrs
*KSCL(FM) Shreveport LA 3 hrs
*KNSU(FM) Thibodaux LA 1 hr
*KTLN(FM) Thibodaux LA 6 hrs
*WAMH(FM) Amherst MA 8 hrs
*WERS(FM) Boston MA 15 hrs
*WRBB(FM) Boston MA 8 hrs
*WGAJ(FM) Deerfield MA 2 hrs
*WXPL(FM) Fitchburg MA 4 hrs
*WDJM-FM Framingham MA 3 hrs
*WAMQ(FM) Great Barrington MA 13 hrs
WPVQ(FM) Greenfield MA 6 hrs
*WCCH(FM) Holyoke MA 2 hrs
WFNX(FM) Lynn MA 8 hrs
*WMLN-FM Milton MA 3 hrs
*WZBC(FM) Newton MA 6 hrs
*WJJW(FM) North Adams MA 4 hrs
*WSMU-FM North Dartmouth MA 10 hrs
*WOZQ(FM) Northampton MA 6 hrs
*WNMH(FM) Northfield MA 10 hrs
*WMMM(FM) Salem MA 3 hrs
*WBSL-FM Sheffield MA 15 hrs
*WYAJ(FM) Sudbury MA 5 hrs
WMVY(FM) Tisbury MA 4 hrs
*WSKB(FM) Westfield MA 6 hrs
*WCHC(FM) Worcester MA 6 hrs
WLIF(FM) Baltimore MD 8 hrs
*WHFC(FM) Bel Air MD 18 hrs
*WKHS(FM) Worton MD 2 hrs
*WERU-FM Blue Hill ME 18 hrs
WBOR(FM) Brunswick ME 20 hrs
*WUMF-FM Farmington ME 15 hrs
*WRBC(FM) Lewiston ME 4 hrs
WBQW(FM) Scarborough ME 5 hrs
*WSJB-FM Standish ME 3 hrs

Special Programming on Radio Stations in the U.S.

*WBQX(FM) Thomaston ME 2 hrs
*WMHB(FM) Waterville ME 8 hrs
*WQAC-FM Alma MI 2 hrs
*WCBN-FM Ann Arbor MI 17 hrs
*WHFR(FM) Dearborn MI 16 hrs
*WRCJ-FM Detroit MI 4 hrs
WXLA(AM) Dimondale MI 3 hrs
*WDBM(FM) East Lansing MI 5 hrs
*WKAR-FM East Lansing MI 7 hrs
WGFN(FM) Glen Arbor MI 4 hrs
*WTHS(FM) Holland MI 6 hrs
*WIAA(FM) Interlochen MI 3 hrs
WJNZ(AM) Kentwood MI 6 hrs
*WUPX(FM) Marquette MI 2 hrs
WRKR(FM) Portage MI
*KAXE(FM) Grand Rapids MN 6 hrs
*KFAI(FM) Minneapolis MN 12 hrs
*KUMM(FM) Morris MN 3 hrs
*KVSC(FM) Saint Cloud MN 15 hrs
*WMCN(FM) Saint Paul MN 4 hrs
*KYMC(FM) Ballwin MO 6 hrs
*KCOU(FM) Columbia MO 10 hrs
*KOPN(FM) Columbia MO 4 hrs
*KCFV(FM) Ferguson MO 4 hrs
*KKFI(FM) Kansas City MO 10 hrs
*KGSP(FM) Parkville MO 14 hrs
*KMNR(FM) Rolla MO 3 hrs
*KUMR(FM) Rolla MO 9 hrs
*KDHX(FM) Saint Louis MO 12 hrs
KMOX(AM) Saint Louis MO 4 hrs
*KSMU(FM) Springfield MO 10 hrs
KTOZ(AM) Springfield MO 12 hrs
WGNL(FM) Greenwood MS 6 hrs
*WUSM-FM Hattiesburg MS 18 hrs
*KMSM-FM Butte MT 5 hrs
WECR-FM Beech Mountain NC
WSQL(AM) Brevard NC 10 hrs
*WSGE(FM) Dallas NC 3 hrs
*WXDU(FM) Durham NC 18 hrs
*WRVS-FM Elizabeth City NC 19 hrs
*WQFS(FM) Greensboro NC 3 hrs
*WZMB(FM) Greenville NC 4 hrs
*WKNS(FM) Kinston NC 6 hrs
*WYQS(FM) Mars Hill NC 7 hrs
WIKS(FM) New Bern NC 2 hrs
WNOS(AM) New Bern NC 12 hrs
*WTEB(FM) New Bern NC 4 hrs
WNNC(AM) Newton NC 3 hrs
*WZRU(FM) Roanoke Rapids NC 6 hrs
WLHC(FM) Robbins NC 15 hrs
*WNCW(FM) Spindale NC 5 hrs
WFXK(FM) Tarboro NC 4 hrs
WOBR-FM Wanchese NC 3 hrs
*WHQR(FM) Wilmington NC 15 hrs
*WFDD-FM Winston-Salem NC 16 hrs
*KFKX(FM) Hastings NE 3 hrs
*KRNU(FM) Lincoln NE 2 hrs
*KUCV(FM) Lincoln NE 5 hrs
KEZO-FM Omaha NE 3 hrs
*KIOS-FM Omaha NE 10 hrs
KKCD(FM) Omaha NE 4 hrs
KCTY-FM Plattsmouth NE 4 hrs
*KWSC(FM) Wayne NE 2 hrs
*WUNH(FM) Durham NH 5 hrs
WDCR(AM) Hanover NH 6 hrs
*WKNH(FM) Keene NH 3 hrs
WFEX(FM) Peterborough NH 6 hrs
*WPCR-FM Plymouth NH 3 hrs
*WDVR(FM) Delaware Township NJ 11 hrs
*WNTI(FM) Hackettstown NJ 9 hrs
*WMNJ(FM) Madison NJ 2 hrs
*WBZC(FM) Pemberton NJ 4 hrs
*WLFR(FM) Pomona NJ 10 hrs
*WFDU(FM) Teaneck NJ 3 hrs
*WTSR(FM) Trenton NJ 4 hrs
*WKNJ-FM Union Township NJ 8 hrs
*WMSC(FM) Upper Montclair NJ 2 hrs
*WPSC(FM) Wayne NJ 12 hrs
*WMCX(FM) West Long Branch NJ 3 hrs
KKIT(FM) Angel Fire NM 4 hrs
KWYK-FM Aztec NM 3 hrs
*KSJE(FM) Farmington NM 15 hrs
KRSN(FM) Los Alamos NM 2 hrs
KTAO(FM) Taos NM 5 hrs

*KRSI(FM) Garapan-Saipan NP 1 hr
*KCEP(FM) Las Vegas NV 12 hrs
KNEV(FM) Reno NV 2 hrs
*WAMC-FM Albany NY 18 hrs
*WCDB(FM) Albany NY 10 hrs
WVIN-FM Bath NY 2 hrs
*WHRW(FM) Binghamton NY 9 hrs
*WSKG-FM Binghamton NY
*WXLH(FM) Blue Mountain Lake NY
*WBNY(FM) Buffalo NY 3 hrs
*WCAN(FM) Canajoharie NY 17 hrs
*WSLU(FM) Canton NY
*WHCL-FM Clinton NY 9 hrs
*WSQE(FM) Corning NY
*WHPC(FM) Garden City NY 5 hrs
*WRCU-FM Hamilton NY 12 hrs
*WRHU(FM) Hempstead NY 20 hrs
*WITR(FM) Henrietta NY 8 hrs
*WICB(FM) Ithaca NY 13 hrs
*WSQG-FM Ithaca NY 7 hrs
*WJFF(FM) Jeffersonville NY 10 hrs
*WAMK(FM) Kingston NY 13 hrs
*WOSR(FM) Middletown NY 13 hrs
*WBAI(FM) New York NY 5 hrs
*WNYC-FM New York NY 4 hrs
WQXR-FM New York NY 2 hrs
*WONY(FM) Oneonta NY 6 hrs
*WRHO(FM) Oneonta NY 4 hrs
*WSQC-FM Oneonta NY
WZOZ(FM) Oneonta NY 2 hrs
*WOSS(FM) Ossining NY 2 hrs
*WLIM(AM) Patchogue NY 4 hrs
*WCEL(FM) Plattsburgh NY 13 hrs
*WRHV(FM) Poughkeepsie NY 2 hrs
*WQBK-FM Rensselaer NY 2 hrs
*WDKX(FM) Rochester NY 4 hrs
*WRUR-FM Rochester NY
*WFNP(FM) Rosendale NY 4 hrs
*WMHT-FM Schenectady NY 1 hr
*WRUC(FM) Schenectady NY 15 hrs
WLLW(FM) Seneca Falls NY 1 hr
WSFW(AM) Seneca Falls NY 1 hr
*WKWZ(FM) Syosset NY 12 hrs
*WCNY-FM Syracuse NY 7 hrs
*WANC(FM) Ticonderoga NY 17 hrs
*WPNR(FM) Utica NY 14 hrs
*WUNY(FM) Utica NY 7 hrs
*WJNY(FM) Watertown NY 5 hrs
WRIP(FM) Windham NY 3 hrs
*WRDL(FM) Ashland OH 5 hrs
*WOBO(FM) Batavia OH 5 hrs
*WGBE(FM) Bryan OH
*WCSB(FM) Cleveland OH 12 hrs
*WRUW-FM Cleveland OH 11 hrs
*WCBE(FM) Columbus OH 4 hrs
*WWSU(FM) Dayton OH 3 hrs
*WGDE(FM) Defiance OH 16 hrs
WBVI(FM) Fostoria OH 3 hrs
WFRO-FM Fremont OH 10 hrs
*WWCD(FM) Grove City OH 3 hrs
WRBP(FM) Hubbard OH 12 hrs
WVKO-FM Johnstown OH 10 hrs
*WGLE(FM) Lima OH 16 hrs
WLJM(AM) Lima OH 2 hrs
WCLV(FM) Lorain OH 5 hrs
*WMCO(FM) New Concord OH 10 hrs
*WOBC(FM) Oberlin OH 15 hrs
*WUSO(FM) Springfield OH 6 hrs
*WGTE-FM Toledo OH 16 hrs
WRVF(FM) Toledo OH 6 hrs
*WOBN(FM) Westerville OH 1 hr
*WYSO(FM) Yellow Springs OH 12 hrs
*KRSC-FM Claremore OK 5 hrs
KBZQ(FM) Lawton OK 4 hrs
*KCCU(FM) Lawton OK
*KZBB(FM) Poteau OK 2 hrs
*KOAC(AM) Corvallis OR 12 hrs
*KWVA(FM) Eugene OR 6 hrs
*KEOL(FM) La Grande OR 6 hrs
KYTE(FM) Newport OR 4 hrs
*KRRC(FM) Portland OR 10 hrs
KLRR(FM) Redmond OR 5 hrs
KAVJ(FM) Sutherlin OR 2 hrs
*WDIY(FM) Allentown PA 10 hrs
*WLVR(FM) Bethlehem PA 12 hrs
*WBUQ(FM) Bloomsburg PA 2 hrs
WMKX(FM) Brookville PA 3 hrs

*WDCV-FM Carlisle PA 6 hrs
*WDNR(FM) Chester PA 2 hrs
*WCUC-FM Clarion PA 3 hrs
*WESS(FM) East Stroudsburg PA 6 hrs
*WJRH(FM) Easton PA 9 hrs
*WMCE(FM) Erie PA 4 hrs
*WZBT(FM) Gettysburg PA 4 hrs
*WVMM(FM) Grantham PA 4 hrs
*WKVR(FM) Huntingdon PA 3 hrs
*WIUP-FM Indiana PA 15 hrs
*WPSB(FM) Kane PA 3 hrs
*WFNM(FM) Lancaster PA 8 hrs
*WVBU-FM Lewisburg PA 3 hrs
*WNTE(FM) Mansfield PA 2 hrs
*WARC(FM) Meadville PA 4 hrs
*WIXQ(FM) Millersville PA 2 hrs
WVLY-FM Milton PA 3 hrs
*WHYY-FM Philadelphia PA 4 hrs
*WRCT(FM) Pittsburgh PA 18 hrs
*WXLV(FM) Schnecksville PA 6 hrs
*WVMW-FM Scranton PA 10 hrs
*WSYC-FM Shippensburg PA 3 hrs
*WPSU(FM) State College PA 4 hrs
WKGB-FM Susquehanna PA 2 hrs
*WRDV(FM) Warminster PA 3 hrs
*WNJR(FM) Washington PA 3 hrs
*WCLH(FM) Wilkes-Barre PA 3 hrs
*WRLC(FM) Williamsport PA 8 hrs
*WVYC(FM) York PA 8 hrs
WWNA(AM) Aguadilla PR 3 hrs
WOLA(AM) Barranquitas PR 5 hrs
WUKQ-FM Mayaguez PR 6 hrs
WADK(AM) Newport RI 4 hrs
WBRU(FM) Providence RI 18 hrs
WEGX(FM) Dillon SC 1 hr
WOLS(AM) Florence SC 4 hrs
WYNN(AM) Florence SC
*WLGI(FM) Hemingway SC 18 hrs
*WSSB-FM Orangeburg SC 10 hrs
WSPA-FM Spartanburg SC 6 hrs
*KSDJ(FM) Brookings SD 2 hrs
*KCSD(FM) Sioux Falls SD 10 hrs
KELO-FM Sioux Falls SD 6 hrs
*WAPX-FM Clarksville TN 6 hrs
*WTTU(FM) Cookeville TN 3 hrs
WRLT(FM) Franklin TN 2 hrs
*WFHU(FM) Henderson TN 45 hrs
*WFMQ(FM) Lebanon TN 4 hrs
*WEVL(FM) Memphis TN 15 hrs
*WQOX(FM) Memphis TN 5 hrs
*WMTS-FM Murfreesboro TN 4 hrs
WAMB(AM) Nashville TN 3 hrs
*WAMB-FM Nashville TN 3 hrs
*WRVU(FM) Nashville TN 18 hrs
WJTT(FM) Red Bank TN 2 hrs
*WUTS(FM) Sewanee TN 4 hrs
*KACU(FM) Abilene TX 3 hrs
*KACV-FM Amarillo TX 12 hrs
KGSR(FM) Bastrop TX 6 hrs
*KWTS(FM) Canyon TX 3 hrs
*KEOS(FM) College Station TX 3 hrs
KFRO-FM Gilmer TX 5 hrs
*KOOP(FM) Hornsby TX 3 hrs
KODA(FM) Houston TX 4 hrs
*KTRU(FM) Houston TX 14 hrs
KFAN-FM Johnson City TX
*KTPB(FM) Kilgore TX 4 hrs
*KNCT-FM Killeen TX 15 hrs
KMND(AM) Midland TX 1 hr
*KOCV(FM) Odessa TX 4 hrs
KQXT(FM) San Antonio TX 4 hrs
*KSTX(FM) San Antonio TX 6 hrs
*KTXK(FM) Texarkana TX 15 hrs
*KWBU-FM Waco TX 10 hrs
KBLQ-FM Logan UT 4 hrs
*KPCW(FM) Park City UT 12 hrs
*KRDC(FM) Saint George UT 10 hrs
*WWHS-FM Hampden-Sydney VA 6 hrs
*WXJM(FM) Harrisonburg VA 14 hrs
*WVRU(FM) Radford VA 19 hrs
*WCVE-FM Richmond VA 13 hrs
*WDCE(FM) Richmond VA 9 hrs
*WCWM(FM) Williamsburg VA 13 hrs
*WISE-FM Wise VA 9 hrs
*WIUJ(FM) Charlotte Amalie VI 6 hrs

*WIUV(FM) Castleton VT 10 hrs
*WWLR(FM) Lyndonville VT 3 hrs
WEQX(FM) Manchester VT 4 hrs
*WRMC-FM Middlebury VT 10 hrs
WNCS(FM) Montpelier VT 5 hrs
*WGDR(FM) Plainfield VT 6 hrs
*WXLF(FM) White River Junction VT 4 hrs
*KUGS(FM) Bellingham WA 10 hrs wkly hrs
*KNWR(FM) Ellensburg WA
*KSER(FM) Everett WA 2 hrs
KBRD(AM) Lacey WA 1 hr
*KWSU(FM) Pullman WA 14 hrs
*KZUU(FM) Pullman WA 12 hrs
*KFAE-FM Richland WA 15 hrs
*KUOW(FM) Seattle WA 5 hrs
*KAGU(FM) Spokane WA 2 hrs
*KPBX-FM Spokane WA
*KUPS(FM) Tacoma WA 12 hrs
*WHSA(FM) Brule WI 6 hrs
*WBSD(FM) Burlington WI 4 hrs
*WPNE-FM Green Bay WI 10 hrs
*WORT(FM) Madison WI 15 hrs
*WHWC(FM) Menomonie WI 3 hrs
*WVSS(FM) Menomonie WI 5 hrs
*WMSE(FM) Milwaukee WI 15 hrs
*WSUP(FM) Platteville WI 3 hrs
*WOJB(FM) Reserve WI 10 hrs
*WXPR(FM) Rhinelander WI 8 hrs
*WRFW(FM) River Falls WI
*WHND(FM) Sister Bay WI 10 hrs
*KUWS(FM) Superior WI 15 hrs
*WSUW(FM) Whitewater WI 6 hrs
*WVVC(FM) Buckhannon WV 8 hrs
*WQZK-FM Keyser WV 2 hrs
*WWVU-FM Morgantown WV 9 hrs
*WQAB(FM) Philippi WV 4 hrs
WMOV(AM) Ravenswood WV 2 hrs
*WPHP(FM) Wheeling WV 1 hr
*KUWA(FM) Afton WY 5 hrs
KMTN(FM) Jackson WY
*KUWJ(FM) Jackson WY 6 hrs
*KUWR(FM) Laramie WY 6 hrs
*KUWZ(FM) Rock Springs WY 6 hrs

Jewish
KRLA(AM) Glendale CA 1 hr
*KCSN(FM) Northridge CA 3 hrs
WMRD(AM) Middletown CT 1 hr
WILI(AM) Willimantic CT 1 hr
WPBR(AM) Lantana FL 3 hrs
WMEL(AM) Melbourne FL 2 hrs
WEEF(AM) Highland Park IL
*WCBN-FM Ann Arbor MI 1 hr
*WBZC(FM) Pemberton NJ 4 hrs
WMCA(AM) New York NY 9 hrs
*WDIY(FM) Allentown PA 1 hr
*WHCB(FM) Bristol TN 1 hr
*KACV-FM Amarillo TX 16 hrs
*KEOS(FM) College Station TX 2 hrs

Korean
*KSDA-FM Agat GU 1 hr
*WLUW(FM) Chicago IL 6 hrs
WONX(AM) Evanston IL 20 hrs
*WNKJ(FM) Hopkinsville KY 1 hr
*KRNM(FM) Chalan Kanoa-Saipan NP 1 hr
*WUSB(FM) Stony Brook NY 1 hr

Light Rock
*KTNA(FM) Talkeetna AK 5 hrs

Lithuanian
WXCT(AM) Southington CT 1.5 hrs
WCEV(AM) Cicero IL 4 hrs
WONX(AM) Evanston IL 1 hr
WNDZ(AM) Portage IN 1 hr
WBMD(AM) Baltimore MD 1 hr
*WGMC(FM) Greece NY 1 hr

*WKTL(FM) Struthers OH 1 hr
*WJCU(FM) University Heights OH 2 hrs
WEDO(AM) McKeesport PA 1 hr

MOR
WFRB(FM) Frostburg MD
WSNJ(AM) Bridgeton NJ
WBUK(FM) Ottawa OH 4 hrs

Native American
*KMXT(FM) Kodiak AK 1 hr
*KDUR(FM) Durango CO 3 hrs
KIXR(FM) Ponca City OK 3 hrs

New Age
*KUAC(FM) Fairbanks AK 3 hrs
*WBHM(FM) Birmingham AL 8 hrs
*WSGN(FM) Gadsden AL 10 hrs
*WQPR(FM) Muscle Shoals AL 20 hrs
*WUAL-FM Tuscaloosa AL 20 hrs
*KASU(FM) Jonesboro AR
KQST(FM) Sedona AZ 10 hrs
KEST(AM) San Francisco CA
*KVNF(FM) Paonia CO 6 hrs
*WXCI(FM) Danbury CT 3 hrs
*WSHU(FM) Fairfield CT 6 hrs
*WGRS(FM) Guilford CT 1 hr
*WMNR(FM) Monroe CT 1 hr
*WRXC(FM) Shelton CT 1 hr
*WGSK(FM) South Kent CT 1 hr
*WMFE-FM Orlando FL 4 hrs
*WFCF(FM) Saint Augustine FL 4 hrs
*WRAS(FM) Atlanta GA 3 hrs
*WUWG(FM) Carrollton GA 3 hrs
*KCCK(FM) Cedar Rapids IA 7 hrs
*KTPR(FM) Fort Dodge IA 10 hrs
*KUNY(FM) Mason City IA 10 hrs
*WSIU(FM) Carbondale IL 4 hrs
*WSIE(FM) Edwardsville IL 10 hrs
*WTPC(FM) Elsah IL 3 hrs
*WNIU(FM) Rockford IL 2 hrs
WINN(FM) Columbus IN 3 hrs
*WKMS-FM Murray KY 3 hrs
*KEDM(FM) Monroe LA 7 hrs
*KNWD(FM) Natchitoches LA 12 hrs
*WMEB-FM Orono ME 3 hrs
*KMSK(FM) Austin MN 5 hrs
*KMSU(FM) Mankato MN 5 hrs
*KCOZ(FM) Point Lookout MO 10 hrs
*KDHX(FM) Saint Louis MO 6 hrs
*WUSM-FM Hattiesburg MS 10 hrs
*WYQS(FM) Mars Hill NC 6 hrs
*WZRU(FM) Roanoke Rapids NC 10 hrs
*KUND-FM Grand Forks ND 4 hrs
*KZUM(FM) Lincoln NE 8 hrs
*WKNH(FM) Keene NH 4 hrs
*WKNJ-FM Union Township NJ 8 hrs
*WHPC(FM) Garden City NY 1 hr
*WSUF(FM) Noyack NY 6 hrs
*WVKR-FM Poughkeepsie NY 9 hrs
*WAER(FM) Syracuse NY 3 hrs
*WOBO(FM) Batavia OH 2 hrs
*WGDE(FM) Defiance OH 4 hrs
WJZA(FM) Lancaster OH 2 hrs
*WGLE(FM) Lima OH
WJZK(FM) Richwood OH 2 hrs
*WGTE(FM) Toledo OH 4 hrs
*WYSO(FM) Yellow Springs OH 4 hrs
*KGOU(FM) Norman OK 4 hrs
*KROU(FM) Spencer OK 4 hrs
*WQLN-FM Erie PA 2 hrs
*WIUP-FM Indiana PA 4 hrs
*WVBU-FM Lewisburg PA 1 hr
*WKDU(FM) Philadelphia PA 2 hrs
*WQED-FM Pittsburgh PA 1 hr
*WRDV(FM) Warminster PA 3 hrs
WCRI(FM) Block Island RI 4 hrs
WRLT(FM) Franklin TN 2 hrs
*WUTS(FM) Sewanee TN 4 hrs
*KAMU-FM College Station TX 5 hrs
*KTRU(FM) Houston TX 1 hr

Broadcasting & Cable Yearbook 2006

D-743

Special Programming on Radio Stations in the U.S.

*KTPB(FM) Kilgore TX 6 hrs
*KNTU(FM) McKinney TX 3 hrs
WSNZ(FM) Appomattox VA 8 hrs
*WVRU(FM) Radford VA 3 hrs
*KPBX-FM Spokane WA
*WRFW(FM) River Falls WI
*WWVU-FM Morgantown WV 6 hrs
KMTN(FM) Jackson WY
KHAT(AM) Laramie WY 3 hrs

New Wave

*WVUA-FM Tuscaloosa AL 4 hrs

News

KIAL(AM) Unalaska AK 14 hrs
WEBJ(AM) Brewton AL 8 hrs
WBCF(AM) Florence AL 5 hrs
KJBN(AM) Little Rock AR
KWBF-FM North Little Rock AR 15 hrs
KGVY(AM) Green Valley AZ
KBHR(FM) Big Bear City CA 8 hrs
KWXY(AM) Cathedral City CA 2 hrs
KWXY-FM Cathedral City CA 2 hrs
KNTS(AM) Palo Alto CA
*KRZA(FM) Alamosa CO 4 hrs
WILI-FM Willimantic CT 1 hr
WRZN(AM) Hernando FL 4 hrs
*WRGP(FM) Homestead FL 3 hrs
WCNK(FM) Key West FL 1 hr
WAZX(AM) Smyrna GA
KLGA(AM) Algona IA
KLGA-FM Algona IA
KTFC(FM) Sioux City IA 10 hrs
WXET(FM) Arcola IL
*WPCD(FM) Champaign IL 8 hrs
WUZR(FM) Bicknell IN
*WGCS(FM) Goshen IN 8 hrs
WXBC(FM) Hardinsburg KY 15 hrs
WMJL(AM) Marion KY
WMJL-FM Marion KY
WGKY(FM) Wickliffe KY 5 hrs
*WBPR(FM) Worcester MA
WKIK(AM) La Plata MD
WSMD-FM Mechanicsville MD
*WPHS(FM) Warren MI 5 hrs
KBNN(AM) Lebanon MO
KCXL(AM) Liberty MO 4 hrs
KSIM(AM) Sikeston MO
KRWP(FM) Stockton MO
WKXU(FM) Louisburg NC
*KZUM(FM) Lincoln NE 11 hrs
KDSS(FM) Ely NV
WBAZ(FM) Bridgehampton NY
WFXF(FM) Honeoye Falls NY 1 hr
*WKCR-FM New York NY 3 hrs
*WOSS(FM) Ossining NY 7 hrs
WJZR(FM) Rochester NY 1 hr
WBEA(FM) Southold NY
*WCII(FM) Spencer NY 14 hrs
WCLV(FM) Lorain OH 1 hr
KSPI(AM) Stillwater OK
*KMHD(FM) Gresham OR 5 hrs
KMUZ(AM) Gresham OR 3 hrs
*WRTU(FM) San Juan PR 7 hrs
WIVV(AM) Vieques PR 7 hrs
WHYM(AM) Lake City SC
WAMB(AM) Nashville TN 6 hrs
WAMB-FM Nashville TN 6 hrs
KCYL(AM) Lampasas TX 14 hrs
*KSUU(FM) Cedar City UT
WEVA(AM) Emporia VA 14 hrs
WVCV(AM) Orange VA 18 hrs
WHEO(FM) Stuart VA 10 hrs
*KASB(FM) Bellevue WA 3 hrs
KQQQ(AM) Pullman WA 10 hrs
WOMT(AM) Manitowoc WI 18 hrs
*KUWJ(FM) Jackson WY 3 hrs
*KUWR(FM) Laramie WY 3 hrs

News/talk

*WVAS(FM) Montgomery AL 4 hrs
KWKM(FM) Saint Johns AZ 2 hrs
WCCC-FM Hartford CT 10 hrs

WWWE(AM) Hapeville GA 14 hrs
*WHFH(FM) Flossmoor IL 1 hr
WRDA(FM) Jerseyville IL 3 hrs
*WLTL(FM) La Grange IL 10 hrs
*WLRA(FM) Lockport IL 10 hrs
WITZ-FM Jasper IN 3 hrs
WWVR(FM) West Terre Haute IN
*KCFN(FM) Wichita KS
WFLW(AM) Monticello KY 10 hrs
WCBR(AM) Richmond KY
KUGT(AM) Jackson MO
WQNQ(FM) Fletcher NC 5 hrs
WCBQ(AM) Oxford NC
WLHC(FM) Robbins NC 10 hrs
WMPM(AM) Smithfield NC 12 hrs
KLIQ(FM) Hastings NE
WSNJ(AM) Bridgeton NJ
*WJSV(FM) Morristown NJ 3 hrs
*WFDU(FM) Teaneck NJ 6 hrs
KSNE-FM Las Vegas NV 1 hr
*WCDB(FM) Albany NY 1 hr
*WITC(FM) Cazenovia NY 3 hrs
WCKM-FM Lake George NY
WJJL(AM) Niagara Falls NY 5 hrs
*WOSS(FM) Ossining NY 3 hrs
*WNYO(FM) Oswego NY 4 hrs
*WFNP(FM) Rosendale NY 5 hrs
*WRMU(FM) Alliance OH 5 hrs
WRBP(FM) Hubbard OH
KIMY(FM) Watonga OK 7 hrs
*WESS(FM) East Stroudsburg PA 6 hrs
*WFSE(FM) Edinboro PA 3 hrs
*WQLN-FM Erie PA 3 hrs
WBCU(AM) Union SC 10 hrs
*KLND(FM) Little Eagle SD 5 hrs
KYMI(FM) Los Ybanez TX 10 hrs
KRFE(AM) Lubbock TX 15 hrs
KTFS(AM) Texarkana TX
KMER(AM) Kemmerer WY 7 hrs
*KUWZ(FM) Rock Springs WY 3 hrs

Nostalgia

KNTK(FM) Weed CA 2 hrs
*WAMU(FM) Washington DC 4 hrs
*KCMR(FM) Mason City IA 10 hrs
WAAM(AM) Ann Arbor MI 6 hrs
KCHK(AM) New Prague MN 18 hrs
KRDS-FM New Prague MN 18 hrs
WDOS(AM) Oneonta NY 2 hrs
WZKL(FM) Alliance OH
*WFSE(FM) Edinboro PA 2 hrs
WLXC(FM) Lexington SC
KLSR-FM Memphis TX 10 hrs
KEYG(AM) Grand Coulee WA 4 hrs
KARS-FM Laramie WY 6 hrs
KHAT(AM) Laramie WY 6 hrs

Oldies

KRSA(AM) Petersburg AK 5 hrs
*WJAB(FM) Huntsville AL 3 hrs
WJRL-FM Ozark AL 6 hrs
KTCN(FM) Eureka Springs AR 2 hrs
KEZA(FM) Fayetteville AR
*KAZU(FM) Pacific Grove CA 5 hrs
*KSPB(FM) Pebble Beach CA 4 hrs
KRAI-FM Craig CO 9 hrs
*KWSB-FM Gunnison CO 3 hrs
*WPFW(FM) Washington DC 3 hrs
*WVUM(FM) Coral Gables FL 5 hrs
WXCV(FM) Homosassa Springs FL 6 hrs
WMAF(FM) Madison FL
WYTH(AM) Madison GA 10 hrs
WGOV(AM) Valdosta GA 10 hrs
*WRSE(FM) Elmhurst IL 9 hrs
*WQUB(FM) Quincy IL 2 hrs
*WRRG(FM) River Grove IL 11 hrs
WJVO(FM) South Jacksonville IL 5 hrs
WBIW(AM) Bedford IN
*WCYT(FM) Lafayette Township IN 2 hrs
KOTE(FM) Eureka KS 6 hrs
WIFX-FM Jenkins KY
WKKS(AM) Vanceburg KY 7 hrs

*WMMT(FM) Whitesburg KY 8 hrs
*KLPI-FM Ruston LA 12 hrs
WXLO(FM) Fitchburg MA 5 hrs
WHAI(FM) Greenfield MA 13 hrs
WHMQ(AM) Greenfield MA 13 hrs
WPVQ(FM) Greenfield MA 5 hrs
*WAVM(FM) Maynard MA 1 hr
WOMR(FM) Provincetown MA 9 hrs
*WEAA(FM) Baltimore MD 5 hrs
*WKHS(FM) Worton MD 6 hrs
WDME-FM Dover Foxcroft ME 6 hrs
WCFX(FM) Clare MI 3 hrs
*WRCJ-FM Detroit MI 3 hrs
*WHKB(FM) Houghton MI 16 hrs
WMPX(AM) Midland MI 2 hrs
WUPY(FM) Ontonagon MI 4 hrs
KASM(AM) Albany MN
KEYL(AM) Long Prairie MN 3 hrs
KNUJ(AM) New Ulm MN 8 hrs
KXLP(FM) New Ulm MN 15 hrs
KOLV(FM) Olivia MN
KKAQ(AM) Thief River Falls MN 6 hrs
KKDQ(FM) Thief River Falls MN 6 hrs
*KJLU(FM) Jefferson City MO
KTOZ(AM) Springfield MO 4 hrs
*WVSD(FM) Itta Bena MS 10 hrs
KBAZ(FM) Hamilton MT 3 hrs
KPRK(AM) Livingston MT 5 hrs
*WNAA(FM) Greensboro NC 5 hrs
WIXE(AM) Monroe NC 5 hrs
*WZRU(FM) Roanoke Rapids NC 4 hrs
WLTT(FM) Shallotte NC 6 hrs
KAUJ(FM) Grafton ND 4 hrs
KLIR(FM) Columbus NE 12 hrs
*WDVR(FM) Delaware Township NJ 13 hrs
*WNTI(FM) Hackettstown NJ 3 hrs
*WTSR(FM) Trenton NJ 6 hrs
*WGCC-FM Batavia NY
*WCEB(FM) Corning NY 6 hrs
WWSC(AM) Glens Falls NY
WVBR-FM Ithaca NY 5 hrs
WLVL(AM) Lockport NY 5 hrs
*WNYU(FM) New York NY 3 hrs
WZOZ(FM) Oneonta NY 2 hrs
WHUD(FM) Peekskill NY 5 hrs
WPDH(FM) Poughkeepsie NY 4 hrs
WSFW(AM) Seneca Falls NY 3 hrs
*WRDL(FM) Ashland OH 4 hrs
KBZQ(AM) Lawton OK 6 hrs
KKNG-FM Newcastle OK 12 hrs
WMBA(AM) Ambridge PA 3 hrs
WMKX(FM) Brookville PA 8 hrs
WWCS(AM) Canonsburg PA 4 hrs
*WDNR(FM) Chester PA 2 hrs
WOKW(FM) Curwensville PA 2 hrs
*WESS(FM) East Stroudsburg PA 8 hrs
*WVMM(FM) Grantham PA 4 hrs
WCCS(AM) Homer City PA 9 hrs
WLSH(AM) Lansford PA 3 hrs
WPTT(AM) McKeesport PA 9 hrs
WMGH-FM Tamaqua PA 14 hrs
*WNJR(FM) Washington PA 3 hrs
*WCYJ-FM Waynesburg PA 3 hrs
WMIA(AM) Arecibo PR
*WBLQ(FM) Westerly RI 8 hrs
WYKZ(FM) Beaufort SC 5 hrs
WHSC(AM) Hartsville SC 5 hrs
WSPA-FM Spartanburg SC 10 hrs
WMXX-FM Jackson TN 15 hrs
WWLX(AM) Lawrenceburg TN 8 hrs
KFGL(AM) Abilene TX 2 hrs
KFYN(AM) Bonham TX 6 hrs
KFYZ-FM Bonham TX 6 hrs
*KTRU(FM) Houston TX 3 hrs
KJAS(FM) Jasper TX 3 hrs
*WVRU(FM) Radford VA 5 hrs
WTSA-FM Brattleboro VT 16 hrs
WIZN(FM) Vergennes VT 3 hrs
WLKG(FM) Lake Geneva WI 10 hrs
WLST(FM) Marinette WI
*WRFW(FM) River Falls WI
*WFGH(FM) Fort Gay WV 19 hrs
*WWVU-FM Morgantown WV 8 hrs

Other

*KRUA(FM) Anchorage AK 20 hrs
*KSUA(FM) Fairbanks AK 19 hrs
*KTOO(FM) Juneau AK 1 hr
*KNOM(AM) Nome AK 14 hrs
*KNOM-FM Nome AK 14 hrs
KIFW(AM) Sitka AK 3 hrs
*WMBV(FM) Dixons Mills AL 3 hrs
WABF(AM) Fairhope AL 6 hrs
WBCF(AM) Florence AL 5 hrs
*WVUA-FM Tuscaloosa AL 3 hrs
*KUAR(FM) Little Rock AR 4 hrs
KNAU(FM) Flagstaff AZ
*KHSU-FM Arcata CA 14 hrs
KIXF(FM) Baker CA
*KSPC(FM) Claremont CA 6 hrs
*KHSR(FM) Crescent City CA 14 hrs
*KFSR(FM) Fresno CA 1 hr
*KFSR(FM) Fresno CA 9 hrs
*KSBR(FM) Mission Viejo CA 9 hrs
KTRB(AM) Modesto CA 1 hr
KNTS(AM) Palo Alto CA
*KZYX(FM) Philo CA 8 hrs
KTIP(AM) Porterville CA 1 hr
KNBR(FM) San Francisco CA
KVEC(AM) San Luis Obispo CA
*KSCU(FM) Santa Clara CA 1 hr
*KSCU(FM) Santa Clara CA 6 hrs
KLCA(FM) Tahoe City CA 2 hrs
KIUP(AM) Durango CO 4 hrs
KTCL(FM) Fort Collins CO 1 hr
KRDZ(AM) Wray CO 3 hrs
*WGRS(FM) Guilford CT 1 hr
WCCC-FM Hartford CT 10 hrs
*WRTC-FM Hartford CT 6 hrs
WZBG(FM) Litchfield CT
*WESU(FM) Middletown CT 5 hrs
*WMNR(FM) Monroe CT 1 hr
WQQQ(FM) Sharon CT 2 hrs
WQQQ(FM) Sharon CT 3 hrs
WQQQ(FM) Sharon CT 5 hrs
*WRXC(FM) Shelton CT 1 hr
*WAPJ(FM) Torrington CT 4 hrs
*WPFW(FM) Washington DC 1 hr
WWUS(FM) Big Pine Key FL 4 hrs
WAKU(FM) Crawfordville FL 3 hrs
*WJLF(FM) Gainesville FL 5 hrs
WXYB(AM) Indian Rocks Beach FL
WIIS(FM) Key West FL 4 hrs
WPBR(AM) Lantana FL 17 hrs
WVOI(AM) Marco Island FL 6.5 hr
WOCN(AM) Miami FL 84 hrs
WPSO(FM) New Port Richey FL
WCTH(FM) Plantation Key FL 3 hrs
WHKR(FM) Rockledge FL 1 hr
*WFCF(FM) Saint Augustine FL 4 hrs
*WCLK(FM) Atlanta GA 12 hrs
*WRAS(FM) Atlanta GA 3 hrs
*WRAS(FM) Atlanta GA 6 hrs
*WREK(FM) Atlanta GA 18 hrs
WGAC(AM) Augusta GA 3 hrs
WBTS(FM) Doraville GA 2 hrs
WWIO(AM) Saint Mary's GA 1 hr
WWIO(AM) Saint Mary's GA 3 hrs
KGUM(AM) Hagatna GU 7 hrs
KHBC(AM) Hilo HI
KWXX-FM Hilo HI 20 hrs
KKEA(AM) Honolulu HI 10 hrs
KNDI(AM) Honolulu HI 2 hrs
KNDI(AM) Honolulu HI 7 hrs
KWAI(AM) Honolulu HI 5 hrs
*KKUA(FM) Wailuku HI 3 hrs
KLGA(AM) Algona IA
KLGA-FM Algona IA
*KIWR(FM) Council Bluffs IA 4 hrs
*KMSC(FM) Sioux City IA 4 hrs
*KWAR(FM) Waverly IA 3 hrs
*KWAR(FM) Waverly IA 5 hrs
KRLC(AM) Lewiston ID 2 hrs
KIGO(AM) Saint Anthony ID 2hrs wkly
WILY(AM) Centralia IL
WCEV(AM) Cicero IL 1 hr
WCEV(AM) Cicero IL 2 hrs
*WTPC(FM) Elsah IL 9 hrs
WGNU(AM) Granite City IL 2 hrs

*WYMG(FM) Jacksonville IL 1 hr
*WLRA(FM) Lockport IL 15 hrs
*WRRG(FM) River Grove IL 11 hrs
*WUIS(FM) Springfield IL 19 hrs
WGFA-FM Watseka IL 2 hrs
*WETN(FM) Wheaton IL 2 hrs
*WGRE(FM) Greencastle IN 2 hrs
WNDV-FM South Bend IN 4 hrs
*WWHR(FM) Bowling Green KY 2 hrs
*WNKU(FM) Highland Heights KY 2 hrs
*WFPK(FM) Louisville KY 3 hrs
*WVLC(FM) Mannsville KY 5 hrs
WRLV-FM Salyersville KY 6 1/2 hrs
WAKY-FM Springfield KY 12 hrs
*WTKY(AM) Tompkinsville KY 1 hr
*WTKY-FM Tompkinsville KY 1 hr
WEKC(AM) Williamsburg KY
*KLSP(FM) Angola LA 4 hrs
KEUN(AM) Eunice LA 6 hrs
*KSLU(FM) Hammond LA 10 hrs
*WERS(FM) Boston MA 4 hrs
*WGBH(FM) Boston MA 3 hrs
WRKO(AM) Boston MA 8 hrs
*WBIM-FM Bridgewater MA 3 hrs
WHTB(AM) Fall River MA 11 hrs
*WXPL(FM) Fitchburg MA 2 hrs
*WDJM-FM Framingham MA 2 hrs
*WDJM-FM Framingham MA 4 hrs
WXRV(FM) Haverhill MA
*WUML(FM) Lowell MA 4 hrs
*WFNX(FM) Lynn MA 4 hrs
WATD-FM Marshfield MA
WNTN(AM) Newton MA 2 hrs
*WZBC(FM) Newton MA 2 hrs
WESX(AM) Salem MA 8 hrs
*WMHC(FM) South Hadley MA 2 hrs
*WCHC(FM) Worcester MA 9 hrs
*WEAA(FM) Baltimore MD 5 hrs
*WHFC(FM) Bel Air MD 15 hrs
*WTMD(FM) Towson MD 1 hr
*WBOR(FM) Brunswick ME 10 hrs
*WUMF-FM Farmington ME 15 hrs
*WMPG(FM) Gorham ME 18 hrs
*WYFP(FM) Harpswell ME 3 hrs
*WMEB-FM Orono ME 10 hrs
*WDBM(FM) East Lansing MI 4 hrs
WCHT(AM) Escanaba MI 1 hr
WMJO(FM) Essexville MI 8 hrs
WKPK(FM) Gaylord MI 5. hrs
WILS(AM) Lansing MI 5 hrs
WSPZ(AM) South Haven MI
WMFN(AM) Zeeland MI 1 hr
WKLK(FM) Cloquet MN 2 hrs
WLKX-FM Forest Lake MN 9 hrs
KCHK(AM) New Prague MN 40 hrs
*WMCN(FM) Saint Paul MN 4 hrs
*KSRQ(FM) Thief River Falls MN 5 hrs
KYOO(AM) Bolivar MO 3 hrs
*KRCU(FM) Cape Girardeau MO 6 hrs
*KCOU(FM) Columbia MO 4 hrs
KLOZ(FM) Eldon MO
*KCFV(FM) Ferguson MO 4 hrs
*KCFV(FM) Ferguson MO 8 hrs
KFAL(AM) Fulton MO 6 hrs
KCXL(AM) Liberty MO 12 hrs
KRWP(FM) Stockton MO
*KGNV(FM) Washington MO 5 hrs
*WUSM-FM Hattiesburg MS 3 hrs
WUMS(FM) University MS 2 hrs
WLRC(AM) Walnut MS
WJNS-FM Yazoo City MS 16 hrs
KXGN(AM) Glendive MT 5 hrs
WERX-FM Columbia NC
*WWCU(FM) Cullowhee NC 5. hrs
*WSGE(FM) Dallas NC 8 hrs
WCKB(AM) Dunn NC 9 hrs
*WFSS(FM) Fayetteville NC 3 hrs
WBAV-FM Gastonia NC 8 hrs
*WUAG(FM) Greensboro NC 14 hrs
*WZMB(FM) Greenville NC 9 hrs
WKGX(AM) Lenoir NC 16 hrs
WPAQ(AM) Mount Airy NC 15 hrs
WSTP(AM) Salisbury NC 5 hrs
WTAB(AM) Tabor City NC
*WHQR(FM) Wilmington NC 1 hr

Special Programming on Radio Stations in the U.S.

KBTO(FM) Bottineau ND 5 hrs wkly hrs
*KUCV(FM) Lincoln NE 1 hr
KEFM(FM) Omaha NE 2 hrs
WMOU(AM) Berlin NH 3 hrs
WDCR(AM) Hanover NH 3 hrs
WFRD(FM) Hanover NH 2 hrs
*WKNH(FM) Keene NH 7 hrs
WWNH(AM) Madbury NH 24 hrs
WFEX(FM) Peterborough NH 2 hrs
WPNH(AM) Plymouth NH 6 hrs
*WMNJ(FM) Madison NJ 6 hrs
WXMC(AM) Parsippany-Troy Hills NJ 1 hr
*WPSC-FM Wayne NJ 18 hrs
*WPSC-FM Wayne NJ 3 hrs
KBAC(FM) Las Vegas NM 4 hrs
KCNM(AM) Garapan-Saipan NP
KDSS(FM) Ely NV
KELY(AM) Ely NV 8 hrs
KLAV(AM) Las Vegas NV 4 hrs
*KUNV(FM) Las Vegas NV 2 hrs
*WCDB(FM) Albany NY 10 hrs
*WCDB(FM) Albany NY 3 hrs
WCSS(AM) Amsterdam NY 12 hrs
*WBNY(FM) Buffalo NY 3 hrs
WDNY(AM) Dansville NY 4 hrs
*WEOS(FM) Geneva NY 10 hrs
*WITR(FM) Henrietta NY 2 hrs
WVBR-FM Ithaca NY 6 hrs
WLVL(AM) Lockport NY 5 hrs
WABC(AM) New York NY 3 hrs
*WKCR(FM) New York NY 6 hrs
*WKCR(FM) New York NY 8 hrs
*WNYU-FM New York NY 13 hrs
*WONY(FM) Oneonta NY 3 hrs
WEBO(AM) Owego NY 16 hrs
WEOK(AM) Poughkeepsie NY 2 hrs
*WVKR(FM) Poughkeepsie NY 8 hrs
WTMM(AM) Rensselaer NY 5 hrs
*WRUR-FM Rochester NY 26 hrs
WBEA(FM) Southold NY
*WRUW-FM Cleveland OH 16 hrs
WWCD(FM) Grove City OH 4 hrs
WPFB(AM) Middletown OH 2 hrs
*WOBC-FM Oberlin OH 20 hrs
*WOBC-FM Oberlin OH 8 hrs
WBKC(AM) Painesville OH
WSTV(AM) Steubenville OH 2 hrs
*WXUT(FM) Toledo OH 2 hrs
*WOBN(FM) Westerville OH 2 hrs
*WYSO(FM) Yellow Springs OH 3 hrs
*KOKF(FM) Edmond OK 12 hrs
KKBS(FM) Guymon OK 5 hrs
KSPI(AM) Stillwater OK
KUJZ(FM) Creswell OR 4 hrs
*KLCC(FM) Eugene OR 9 hrs
*KTEC(FM) Klamath Falls OR 15 hrs
*KLCO(FM) Newport OR 6 hrs
KACI(AM) The Dalles OR 3 hrs
KMCQ(FM) The Dalles OR 3 hrs
WMBA(AM) Ambridge PA 5 hrs
*WDCV-FM Carlisle PA 1 hr
WCCR(FM) Clarion PA
WKHB(AM) Irwin PA 14 hrs
*WVBU-FM Lewisburg PA 2 hrs
WRKT(FM) North East PA 1 hr
*WKDU(FM) Philadelphia PA 4 hrs
WJAS(AM) Pittsburgh PA 2 hrs
*WRCT(FM) Pittsburgh PA 12 hrs
*WXLV(FM) Schnecksville PA 6 hrs
*WUSR(FM) Scranton PA 10 hrs
WPIC(AM) Sharon PA 12 hrs
WMBS(AM) Uniontown PA 3 hrs
*WCYJ-FM Waynesburg PA 3 hrs
*WPTC(FM) Williamsport PA 10 hrs
WMNT(AM) Manati PR
WUKQ(AM) Ponce PR
*WRIU(FM) Kingston RI 6 hrs
WVGB(AM) Beaufort SC
WJBS(AM) Holly Hill SC 2 hrs
WMXT(FM) Pamplico SC 5 hrs
KGIM(AM) Aberdeen SD
*KLND(FM) Little Eagle SD 2 hrs
*KAUR(FM) Sioux Falls SD 6 hrs
WNAX(AM) Yankton SD 15 hrs
*WHCB(FM) Bristol TN 2 hrs

*WHRS(FM) Cookeville TN 1 hr
*WTTU(FM) Cookeville TN 6 hrs
WWAM(AM) Jasper TN 1 hr
WKGN(AM) Knoxville TN 1 hr
WEGR(FM) Memphis TN
*WMTS-FM Murfreesboro TN 2 hrs
*WRVU(FM) Nashville TN 11 hrs
KNRB(FM) Atlanta TX 18 hrs
KBYG(AM) Big Spring TX 12 hrs
KPSM(FM) Brownwood TX 5 hrs
KAGC(AM) Bryan TX 2 hrs
KAGC(AM) Bryan TX 4 hrs
*KWTS(AM) Canyon TX 11 hrs
*KAMU-FM College Station TX 5 hrs
KTSM(AM) El Paso TX 1 hr
KSWA(AM) Graham TX 2 hrs
KPRC(AM) Houston TX 16 hrs
KRVL(FM) Kerrville TX 1 hr
*KTPB(FM) Kilgore TX 2 hrs
KHKZ(FM) Mercedes TX 3 hrs
KYCX-FM Mexia TX 1 hr
KYCX-FM Mexia TX 12 hrs
KYCX-FM Mexia TX 6 hrs
KWEL(AM) Midland TX 1 hr
*KOCV(FM) Odessa TX 4 hrs
KRXT(FM) Rockdale TX 10 hrs
*KRTU(FM) San Antonio TX 2 hrs
KNCN(FM) Sinton TX 1 hr
WKEX(AM) Blacksburg VA 3 hrs
*WNRN(FM) Charlottesville VA 6 hrs
WEVA(AM) Emporia VA 3 hrs
*WEMC(FM) Harrisonburg VA 1 hr
WRVA(AM) Richmond VA 2 hrs
WFOG(AM) Suffolk VA 1 hr
*WISE-FM Wise VA 2 hrs
*WVPS(FM) Burlington VT 8 hrs
WEQX(FM) Manchester VT 5 hrs
WIKE(AM) Newport VT 5 hrs
WVNR(AM) Poultney VT 3 hrs
*WRVT(FM) Rutland VT 3 hrs
*WVPR(FM) Windsor VT 3 hrs
*KGRG(FM) Auburn WA 9 hrs
*KUGS(FM) Bellingham WA 17 hrs wkly hrs
*KUGS(FM) Bellingham WA 2 hrs wkly hrs
KBRO(AM) Bremerton WA 4 hrs
KGNW(AM) Burien-Seattle WA
*KSER(AM) Everett WA 2 hrs
*KZUU(FM) Pullman WA 2 hrs
KLFE(AM) Seattle WA 2 hrs
KLFE(AM) Seattle WA 4 hrs
*KNHC(FM) Seattle WA 6 hrs
*KPBX-FM Spokane WA
*KPLU-FM Tacoma WA 2 hrs
*KUPS(FM) Tacoma WA 4 hrs
*WBSD(FM) Burlington WI 5 hrs
*WWSP(FM) Stevens Point WI 1 hr
*WCCX(FM) Waukesha WI 3 hrs
WDLS(AM) Wisconsin Dells WI 5 hrs
WGGE(FM) Parkersburg WV 5 hrs
*WVPG(FM) Parkersburg WV 2 hrs
*WVSB(FM) Romney WV

Polish

KXMX(AM) Anaheim CA
*KSPC(FM) Claremont CA 3 hrs
*KUSF(FM) San Francisco CA 1 hr
WPRX(AM) Bristol CT 2 hrs
*WVOF(FM) Fairfield CT 3 hrs
WGCH(AM) Greenwich CT 1 hr
*WRTC-FM Hartford CT 3 hrs
WMMW(AM) Meriden CT 1 hr
WMRD(AM) Middletown CT 2 hrs
WRYM(AM) New Britain CT 5 hrs
*WCNI(FM) New London CT 3 hrs
WICH(AM) Norwich CT 1 hr
WXCT(AM) Southington CT 1 hr
WATR(AM) Waterbury CT 2 hrs
*WWUH(FM) West Hartford CT 3 hrs
*WKTO(FM) Edgewater FL 1.5 hr
WXYB(AM) Indian Rocks Beach FL 2 hrs
WLBE(AM) Leesburg FL 2 hrs
WPSO(FM) New Port Richey FL 1 hr

WSBB(AM) New Smyrna Beach FL 1 hr
WTMY(AM) Sarasota FL 1 hr
KSKB(AM) Brooklyn IA 1 hr
WCEV(AM) Cicero IL 11 hrs
WVIV-FM Highland Park IL
WJOL(AM) Joliet IL 1 hr
WHCO(AM) Sparta IL 2 hrs
WJOB(AM) Hammond IN 2 hrs
WIMS(AM) Michigan City IN 3 hrs
WDND(AM) South Bend IN 1 hr
*WMUA(FM) Amherst MA 5 hrs
WBET(AM) Brockton MA 2 hrs
WUNR(AM) Brookline MA 2 hrs
WACE(AM) Chicopee MA 1 hr
WHTB(AM) Fall River MA 1 hr
WNNW(AM) Lawrence MA 1 hr
WLYN(AM) Lynn MA 2 hrs
WNBH(AM) New Bedford MA 2 hrs
*WJJW(FM) North Adams MA 3 hrs
WHMP(AM) Northampton MA 2 hrs
WBRK(AM) Pittsfield MA 2 hrs
WESX(AM) Salem MA 2 hrs
*WBSL-FM Sheffield MA 1 hr
WESO(AM) Southbridge MA 3 hrs
*WTCC(FM) Springfield MA 2 hrs
WARE(AM) Ware MA 4 hrs
WGFP(AM) Webster MA 1 hr
*WCUW(FM) Worcester MA 6 hrs
WORC(AM) Worcester MA 4 hrs
WBMD(AM) Baltimore MD 2 hrs
WATZ(AM) Alpena MI 2 hrs
WATZ-FM Alpena MI 2 hrs
WLEW(AM) Bad Axe MI 2 hrs
WIBM(AM) Jackson MI 1.5 hrs
WMTE-FM Manistee MI 6 hrs
*WOES(FM) Ovid-Elsie MI 1 hr
WMIC(AM) Sandusky MI 5 hrs
*WPHS(FM) Warren MI 2 hrs
WBMI(FM) West Branch MI 6 hrs
WNMT(AM) Nashwauk MN 2 hrs
KRDS-FM New Prague MN 18 hrs
WEW(AM) Saint Louis MO 2 hrs
KJSK(AM) Columbus NE 2 hrs
KTTT(AM) Columbus NE 5 hrs
KOIL(AM) Plattsmouth NE 1 hr
KOIL(AM) Plattsmouth NE 2 hrs
*WUNH(FM) Durham NH 1 hr
WSMN(AM) Nashua NH 1 hr
WWTR(AM) Bridgewater NJ 3 hrs
*WFJS(FM) Hazlet NJ 2 hrs
*WSOU(FM) South Orange NJ 2 hrs
WAAL(FM) Binghamton NY 3 hrs
*WHRW(FM) Binghamton NY 3 hrs
WYOS(AM) Binghamton NY 3 hrs
*WBFO(FM) Buffalo NY 3 hrs
WECK(AM) Cheektowaga NY 2 hrs
WDOE(AM) Dunkirk NY 6 hrs
WAMF(AM) Fulton NY 5 hrs
*WHPC(FM) Garden City NY 1 hr
*WGMC(FM) Greece NY 2 hrs
*WRHU(FM) Hempstead NY 3 hrs
*WUBJ(FM) Jamestown NY 3 hrs
WIZR(AM) Johnstown NY 1 hr
WKNY(AM) Kingston NY 1 hr
WXRL(AM) Lancaster NY 8 hrs
WLVL(AM) Lockport NY 1 hr
*WVCR-FM Loudonville NY 3 hrs
WVOA-FM Mexico NY 4 hrs
WHLD(AM) Niagara Falls NY 17 hrs
WJJL(AM) Niagara Falls NY 2 hrs
WTLA(AM) North Syracuse NY 2 hrs
*WOLN(FM) Olean NY 5 hrs
WSGO(AM) Oswego NY 2 hrs
WEOK(AM) Poughkeepsie NY 1 hr
*WVKR(FM) Poughkeepsie NY 5 hrs
WRIV(AM) Riverhead NY 4 hrs
WGGO(AM) Salamanca NY 1 hr
*WSPN(FM) Saratoga Springs NY 3 hrs
WLLW(FM) Seneca Falls NY 2 hrs
WSFW(AM) Seneca Falls NY 2 hrs
*WUSB(FM) Stony Brook NY 1 hr
WIBX(AM) Utica NY 3 hrs
WUTQ(AM) Utica NY 4 hrs
WTBQ(AM) Warwick NY
WNYV(FM) Whitehall NY 1 hr

*WOBO(FM) Batavia OH 3 hrs
WOMP(AM) Bellaire OH 2 hrs
*WCPN(FM) Cleveland OH 1 hr
WERE(AM) Cleveland OH 2 hrs
WKTX(AM) Cortland OH 1 hr
WDLW(AM) Lorain OH 3 hrs
WRTK(AM) Niles OH 1 hr
WSTV(AM) Steubenville OH 2 hrs
*WKTL(FM) Struthers OH 14 hrs
WCWA(AM) Toledo OH 1 hr
WTOD(AM) Toledo OH 4 hrs
*WJCU(FM) University Heights OH 2 hrs
WELW(AM) Willoughby-Eastlake OH 1 hr
WKAP(AM) Allentown PA 3 hrs
*WMUH(FM) Allentown PA 2 hrs
WVAM(AM) Altoona PA 1 hr
WMBA(AM) Ambridge PA 2 hrs
WWSM(AM) Annville-Cleona PA 2 hrs
WBVP(AM) Beaver Falls PA 1 hr
WWCS(AM) Canonsburg PA 2 hrs
WFGI(AM) Charleroi PA 2 hrs
WOGI(FM) Charleroi PA 2 hrs
*WERG(FM) Erie PA 3 hrs
*WMCE(FM) Erie PA 3 hrs
WRIE(AM) Erie PA 1 hr
WCCS(AM) Homer City PA 3 hrs
WKHB(AM) Irwin PA 2 hrs
WNTJ(AM) Johnstown PA 5 hrs
WEDO(AM) McKeesport PA 1 hr
WQFM(FM) Nanticoke PA 1 hr
WKST(AM) New Castle PA 1 hr
WGBN(AM) New Kensington PA 3 hrs
WYCK(AM) Plains PA 3 hrs
WPAZ(AM) Pottstown PA 1 hr
WECZ(AM) Punxsutawney PA 3 hrs
WRAW(AM) Reading PA 2 hrs
*WXLV(FM) Schnecksville PA 6 hrs
WICK(AM) Scranton PA 2 hrs
WPIC(AM) Sharon PA 6 hrs
WCDW(FM) Susquehanna PA 5 hrs
WKZV(AM) Washington PA 3 hrs
WLKW(AM) West Warwick RI 2 hrs
WNRI(AM) Woonsocket RI 2 hrs
WOON(AM) Woonsocket RI 3 hrs
KYNT(AM) Yankton SD 1 hr
*KOOP(FM) Hornsby TX .5 hrs
KVLG(AM) La Grange TX 6 hrs
KBEC(AM) Waxahachie TX 2 hrs
KANI(AM) Wharton TX 6 hrs
WVNR(AM) Poultney VT 1 hr
WJMT(AM) Merrill WI 3 hrs
WRPN(AM) Ripon WI 2 hrs
*WRPN-FM Ripon WI 2 hrs
WSPT(AM) Stevens Point WI 1 hr
WSAU(AM) Wausau WI 3 hrs
WMOV(AM) Ravenswood WV 1 hr
WBBD(AM) Wheeling WV 2 hrs

Polka

KZAT-FM Belle Plaine IA 2 hrs
KDSN(AM) Denison IA 4 hrs
KMAQ(AM) Maquoketa IA 3 hrs
KLEE(AM) Ottumwa IA 1 hr
WLUV(AM) Loves Park IL 6 hrs
WPNA(AM) Oak Park IL 15 hrs
WTAY(AM) Robinson IL 3 hrs
KCAY(FM) Russell KS
KRSL(AM) Russell KS 4 hrs
*WTMD(FM) Towson MD 2 hrs
WNBY(AM) Newberry MI 2 hrs
WUPY(FM) Ontonagon MI 2 hrs
WOAP(AM) Owosso MI 4 hrs
WYGR(AM) Wyoming MI 3 hrs
WKLK(AM) Cloquet MN 2 hrs
KRBT(AM) Eveleth MN 3 hrs
*KAXE(FM) Grand Rapids MN 2 hrs
WMFG(AM) Hibbing MN 4 hrs
KDUZ(AM) Hutchinson MN 8 hrs
KWNO(AM) Winona MN 5 hrs
KHND(AM) Harvey ND 3 hrs
KTTT(AM) Columbus NE
WGHT(AM) Pompton Lakes NJ 1 hr
WAAL(FM) Binghamton NY 4 hrs
WYOS(AM) Binghamton NY 4 hrs

WTHE(AM) Mineola NY 1 hr
*WZIP(FM) Akron OH 4 hrs
WNDH(AM) Napoleon OH 2 hrs
WELW(AM) Willoughby-Eastlake OH 15 hrs
WKBN(AM) Youngstown OH 2 hrs
KCRC(AM) Enid OK 1 hr
WMBA(AM) Ambridge PA 2 hrs
WGPA(AM) Bethlehem PA 12 hrs
WHYL(AM) Carlisle PA 2 hrs
WLMI(FM) Kane PA 1 hr
WPTT(AM) McKeesport PA 2 hrs
WPHB(AM) Philipsburg PA 6 hrs
WWII(AM) Shiremanstown PA 7 hrs
WMGH-FM Tamaqua PA 3 hrs
WKZV(AM) Washington PA 2 hrs
KYNT(AM) Yankton SD 1 hr
*WMTS-FM Murfreesboro TN 2 hrs
KWHI(AM) Brenham TX 2 hrs
KULM(FM) Columbus TX 12 hrs
KNAF(AM) Fredericksburg TX 4.5 hrs
KCTI(AM) Gonzales TX 5 hrs
KRXT(FM) Rockdale TX 2 hrs hrs
KYKM(FM) Yoakum TX 9 hrs
WDKM(FM) Adams WI 14 hrs
WATW(AM) Ashland WI 1 hr
WLDY(AM) Ladysmith WI 3 hrs
WOFM(FM) Mosinee WI 3 hrs
WCCN(AM) Neillsville WI 2 hrs
WIZD(FM) Rudolph WI 3 hrs
WBOG(AM) Tomah WI 2 hrs
WVRQ(FM) Viroqua WI 6 hrs

Portugese

KSTN-FM Stockton CA 4 hrs
*WRTC-FM Hartford CT 8 hrs
*WWUH(FM) West Hartford CT 3 hrs
WMKI(FM) Boston MA 1 hr
WACE(AM) Chicopee MA 1 hr
WSAR(AM) Fall River MA 3 hrs
*WMFO(FM) Medford MA 3 hrs
WMRC(AM) Milford MA 2 hrs
WPEP(AM) Taunton MA 10 hrs
WPHE(AM) Phoenixville PA 3 hrs
WRIB(AM) Providence RI 3 hrs
WNRI(AM) Woonsocket RI 2 hrs
*WRVU(FM) Nashville TN 2 hrs

Progressive

*KFJC(FM) Los Altos CA 4 hrs
*WONC(FM) Naperville IL 14 hrs
WTTS(FM) Bloomington IN 4 hrs
*WDSO(FM) Chesterton IN 8 hrs
*WBKE-FM North Manchester IN 7 hrs
*WECI(FM) Richmond IN 18 hrs
*WBIM-FM Bridgewater MA 3 hrs
KMVC(FM) Marshall MO 10 hrs
*KCLC(FM) Saint Charles MO 7 hrs
*WKNC-FM Raleigh NC 12 hrs
*KZUM(FM) Lincoln NE 15 hrs
*WFDU(FM) Teaneck NJ
*WHPC(FM) Garden City NY 4 hrs
WRRV(AM) Middletown NY 2 hrs
*WONY(FM) Oneonta NY 3 hrs
*WIRQ(FM) Rochester NY 3 hrs
WIOT(FM) Toledo OH 2 hrs
*KRSC-FM Claremore OK 12 hrs
*WCAL(FM) California PA 6 hrs
*WCUC-FM Clarion PA 9 hrs
*WHRV(FM) Norfolk VA 14 hrs
WIZN(FM) Vergennes VT 1 hr
*KZUU(FM) Pullman WA 10 hrs
*WSUP(FM) Platteville WI 6 hrs

Public Affairs

WDLT-FM Chickasaw AL 4 hrs
WEUP(AM) Huntsville AL 1 hr
KMLE(FM) Chandler AZ 1 hr
*KGHR(FM) Tuba City AZ 5 hrs
*KPFA(FM) Berkeley CA 18 hrs
*KNCA(FM) Burney CA 7 hrs
*KSPC(FM) Claremont CA 3 hrs
*KCRH(FM) Hayward CA 5 hrs

Special Programming on Radio Stations in the U.S.

KYSR(FM) Los Angeles CA 2 hrs
KTRB(AM) Modesto CA 2 hrs
*KNSQ(FM) Mount Shasta CA 7 hrs
KTYD(FM) Santa Barbara CA 1 hr
KIMN(FM) Denver CO 2 hrs
KJJD(AM) Windsor CO
WSTW(FM) Wilmington DE 1 hr
WXTB(FM) Clearwater FL 4 hrs
WIRA(FM) Fort Pierce FL 1 hr
WVOP(AM) Vidalia GA 2 hrs
*WEFT(FM) Champaign IL 5 hrs
*WDGC-FM Downers Grove IL 6 hrs
KUUL(AM) East Moline IL 6 hrs
*WEPS(FM) Elgin IL 3 hrs
WFXN(AM) Moline IL 4 hrs
WPNA(AM) Oak Park IL 5 hrs
WVAZ(FM) Oak Park IL 2 hrs
WYKT(FM) Wilmington IL 4 hrs
WVEZ(FM) Louisville KY 4 hrs
WMJL(AM) Marion KY 1 hr
WMJL-FM Marion KY 1 hr
*WMMT(FM) Whitesburg KY 3 hrs
WNSH(FM) Beverly MA 2 hrs
WJMN(FM) Boston MA 2 hrs
WCCM(AM) Haverhill MA 2 hrs
WXRV(FM) Haverhill MA 1 hr
*WMLN-FM Milton MA 2 hrs
WSNE-FM Taunton MA 4 hrs
*WERU-FM Blue Hill ME 9 hrs
*WCBN-FM Ann Arbor MI 5 hrs
WDMK(FM) Detroit MI 2 hrs
WCCY(AM) Houghton MI 1 hr
*KQAL(FM) Winona MN 10 hrs
*KJLU(FM) Jefferson City MO
KCMO(AM) Kansas City MO 1 1/2 hrs
KCMO-FM Kansas City MO 1 1/2 hrs
*KDHX(FM) Saint Louis MO 5 hrs
*WUSM-FM Hattiesburg MS 10 hrs
WCLN(AM) Clinton NC
WPAQ(AM) Mount Airy NC 1 hr
WKRK(AM) Murphy NC 3 hrs
*KABU(FM) Fort Totten ND 5 hrs
KLIQ(FM) Hastings NE
*KZUM(FM) Lincoln NE 11 hrs
*WBJB-FM Lincroft NJ 5 hrs
*WRPR(FM) Mahwah NJ 12 hrs
WMTR(AM) Morristown NJ 5 hrs
WNNJ(AM) Newton NJ 1 hr
*WTSR(FM) Trenton NJ 8 hrs
*KUNV(FM) Las Vegas NV 4 hrs
*WXLH(FM) Blue Mountain Lake NY
*WBSU(FM) Brockport NY 8 hrs
*WCWP(FM) Brookville NY 5 hrs
WJYE(FM) Buffalo NY 2 hrs
*WNED(FM) Buffalo NY
*WSLU(FM) Canton NY
*WRHU(FM) Hempstead NY 4 hrs
WAQX-FM Manlius NY 1 hr
*WKDM(AM) New York NY
*WDFH(FM) Ossining NY 20 hrs
WUMX(FM) Rome NY 1 hr
WQAR(AM) Stillwater NY
*WJPZ-FM Syracuse NY 13 hrs
*WARY(FM) Valhalla NY 10 hrs
WNYV(FM) Whitehall NY 5 hrs
*WZIP(FM) Akron OH 11 hrs
WRQN(FM) Bowling Green OH 1 hr
*WRUW-FM Cleveland OH 8 hrs
*WDPS(FM) Dayton OH 2 hrs
WKKY(FM) Geneva OH 2 hrs
*WHSS(FM) Hamilton OH 5 hrs
KJSR(FM) Tulsa OK 2 hrs
*KSMF(FM) Ashland OR 7 hrs
*KSOR(FM) Ashland OR 7 hrs
*KSBA(FM) Coos Bay OR 7 hrs
*KSKF(FM) Klamath Falls OR 7 hrs
KBNP(AM) Portland OR
KACI(AM) The Dalles OR 1 hr
WWCH(AM) Clarion PA
WSJR(FM) Dallas PA 1 hr
*WQLN-FM Erie PA 5 hrs
WRTS(FM) Erie PA 1 hr
WTKT(AM) Harrisburg PA 2 hrs
WIOQ(FM) Philadelphia PA
WSHH(FM) Pittsburgh PA 1 hr
*WRSK(FM) Slippery Rock PA 1 hr
*WRLC(FM) Williamsport PA 2 hrs

WAGS(AM) Bishopville SC 2 hrs
WOCE(FM) Benton TN 2 hrs
WKHT(FM) Knoxville TN 2 hrs
WQBB(AM) Powell TN 2 hrs
KDHT(FM) Cedar Park TX 2 hrs
KBFM(FM) Edinburg TX
KTSM(FM) El Paso TX 1 hr
KTBZ-FM Houston TX 1 hr
*KSWP(FM) Lufkin TX 2 hrs
KAMX(FM) Luling TX 2 hrs
*KNTU(FM) McKinney TX 2 hrs
KCYY(FM) San Antonio TX 2 hrs
KKYX(AM) San Antonio TX 2 hrs
KQXT(FM) San Antonio TX 1 hr
KNCN(FM) Sinton TX 1 hr
KVEL(AM) Vernal UT 1 hr
WBRF(FM) Galax VA 1 hr
*WVRU(FM) Radford VA 6 hrs
WMOO(FM) Derby Center VT 8 hrs
WJJR(FM) Rutland VT 1 hr
KEDO(AM) Longview WA 2 hrs
WNBI(AM) Park Falls WI 5 hrs
*WWSP(FM) Stevens Point WI 5 hrs
WWYO(AM) Pineville WV 8 hrs

Reggae

*KBBI(AM) Homer AK 3 hrs
*WJAB(FM) Huntsville AL 4 hrs
*WVUA-FM Tuscaloosa AL 3 hrs
*KABF(FM) Little Rock AR 4 hrs
*KSPC(FM) Claremont CA 8 hrs
KFSR(FM) Fresno CA 6 hrs
*KSBR(FM) Mission Viejo CA 3 hrs
*KSPB(FM) Pebble Beach CA 2 hrs
*KZYX(FM) Philo CA 5 hrs
*KCSB-FM Santa Barbara CA 6 hrs
*KCSS(FM) Turlock CA
*KASF(FM) Alamosa CO 5 hrs
KSMT(FM) Breckenridge CO 2 hrs
*KRCC(FM) Colorado Springs CO 6 hrs
KTCL(FM) Fort Collins CO 2 hrs
*KWSB-FM Gunnison CO 6 hrs
*WXCI(FM) Danbury CT 2 hrs
*WQTQ(FM) Hartford CT 4 hrs
*WESU(FM) Middletown CT 10 hrs
WMRD(AM) Middletown CT 1 hr
*WRGP(FM) Homestead FL 3 hrs
WIIS(FM) Key West FL 1 hr
*WFIT(FM) Melbourne FL 2 hrs
*WFCF(FM) Saint Augustine FL 4 hrs
*WANM(FM) Tallahassee FL 3 hrs
WFLM(FM) White City FL 5 hrs
*WCLK(FM) Atlanta GA 3 hrs
*WRAS(FM) Atlanta GA 4 hrs
*WVGS(FM) Statesboro GA 3 hrs
KWXX-FM Hilo HI 20 hrs
KAOY(FM) Kealakekua HI 4 hrs
*KRUI-FM Iowa City IA 3 hrs
*WTPC(FM) Elsah IL 6 hrs
*WNUR-FM Evanston IL 4 hrs
*KJHK(FM) Lawrence KS 3 hrs
*KLSU(FM) Baton Rouge LA 3 hrs
*WTUL(FM) New Orleans LA 4 hrs
*KLPI-FM Ruston LA 6 hrs
*KSCL(FM) Shreveport LA 4 hrs
*WUML(FM) Lowell MA 4 hrs
*WMLN-FM Milton MA 8 hrs
*WZBC(FM) Newton MA 4 hrs
*WSMU-FM North Dartmouth MA 10 hrs
*WZLY(FM) Wellesley MA 2 hrs
*WSKB(FM) Westfield MA 3 hrs
*WESM-FM Princess Anne MD 2 hrs
*WTMD(FM) Towson MD 2 hrs
*WERU-FM Blue Hill ME 4 hrs
*WBOR(FM) Brunswick ME 10 hrs
WPHX-FM Sanford ME 2 hrs
*WCBN-FM Ann Arbor MI 4 hrs 6 hrs
*WDET-FM Detroit MI 2 hrs
*WLNZ(FM) Lansing MI 4 hrs
*KUMM(FM) Morris MN 2 hrs
*KCOU(FM) Columbia MO 2 hrs
*KJLU(FM) Jefferson City MO
*WVSD(FM) Itta Bena MS 3 hrs
*WJSU(FM) Jackson MS 2 hrs

*WFSS(FM) Fayetteville NC 3 hrs
*WNAA(FM) Greensboro NC 7 hrs
*WZMB(FM) Greenville NC 7 hrs
WVOD(FM) Manteo NC 2 hrs
*WKNC-FM Raleigh NC 5 hrs
*WHQR(FM) Wilmington NC 3 hrs
KKCD(FM) Omaha NE 1 hr
WDCR(AM) Hanover NH 9 hrs
*WKNH(FM) Keene NH 3 hrs
*WPCR-FM Plymouth NH 3 hrs
*WNTI(FM) Hackettstown NJ 3 hrs
*WBZC(FM) Pemberton NJ 4 hrs
KRSI(FM) Garapan-Saipan NP 22 hrs
*WBNY(FM) Buffalo NY 3 hrs
*WHCL-FM Clinton NY 2 hrs
*WCVF-FM Fredonia NY 3 hrs
*WEOS(FM) Geneva NY 3 hrs
*WITR(FM) Henrietta NY 5 hrs
*WICB(FM) Ithaca NY 2 hrs
*WVCR-FM Loudonville NY 3 hrs
*WNYU-FM New York NY 2 hrs
*WPNR-FM Utica NY 5 hrs
*WRUW-FM Cleveland OH 7 hrs
*WDUB(FM) Granville OH 2 hrs
*WVKO-FM Johnstown OH 5 hrs
*WCWS(FM) Wooster OH 3 hrs
*KEOL(FM) La Grande OR 7 hrs
*KBOO(FM) Portland OR 10 hrs
*WLVR(FM) Bethlehem PA 6 hrs
*WWCS(AM) Canonsburg PA 2 hrs
*WJRH(FM) Easton PA 6 hrs
*WERG(FM) Erie PA 4 hrs
*WKVR-FM Huntingdon PA 3 hrs
*WRIU(FM) Kingston RI 7 hrs
*WSSB-FM Orangeburg SC 4 hrs
*WRVU(FM) Nashville TN 3 hrs
*WUTS(FM) Sewanee TN 5 hrs
*KAZI-FM Austin TX 6 hrs
*KTRU(FM) Houston TX 6 hrs
*KTSU(FM) Houston TX 8 hrs
*KSAU(FM) Nacogdoches TX 2 hrs
*WWHS-FM Hampden-Sydney VA 4 hrs
*WHOV(FM) Hampton VA 4 hrs
*WCWM(FM) Williamsburg VA 6 hrs
WIZN(FM) Vergennes VT 1 hr
*KGRG(FM) Auburn WA 4 hrs
*KSER(FM) Everett WA 2 hrs
*KUPS(FM) Tacoma WA 6 hrs
*WBSD(FM) Burlington WI 3 hrs
*WWVU-FM Morgantown WV 5 hrs

Religious

KYMG(FM) Anchorage AK 1 hr
*KBRW(AM) Barrow AK 1 hr
*KNOM(AM) Nome AK 20 hrs
*KNOM-FM Nome AK 20 hrs
KIAL(AM) Unalaska AK 04 hrs
WKNU(FM) Brewton AL 2 hrs
WTVY-FM Dothan AL 3 hrs
WKMX(FM) Enterprise AL 8 hrs
WIJK(AM) Evergreen AL
WABF(AM) Fairhope AL 6 hrs
WKWL(AM) Florala AL 12 hrs
WAGH(FM) Fort Mitchell AL 6 hrs
WZOB(AM) Fort Payne AL 5 hrs
WLDA(FM) Fort Rucker AL 5 hrs
WRTT-FM Huntsville AL
WTKI(AM) Huntsville AL 4 hrs
*WLJS-FM Jacksonville AL 3 hrs
WEUP-FM Moulton AL 1 hr
WNSI(AM) Robertsdale AL 6 hrs
WGOL(AM) Russellville AL 10 hrs
WKEA-FM Scottsboro AL 4 hrs
WBHJ(FM) Tuscaloosa AL 5 hrs
WTBC(AM) Tuscaloosa AL 3 hrs
*WVUA-FM Tuscaloosa AL 3 hrs
KMJI(FM) Ashdown AR 4 hrs
KEWI(AM) Benton AR 5 hrs
KLYR(FM) Clarksville AR 8 hrs
KAVV(FM) Benson AZ 3 hrs
KCUZ(AM) Clifton AZ 2 hrs
KFYI(FM) Phoenix AZ 2 hrs
KQST(FM) Sedona AZ 5 hrs
KTKT(AM) Tucson AZ 2 hrs
KHOV-FM Wickenburg AZ 1 hr

KXMX(AM) Anaheim CA
KERN(AM) Bakersfield CA 1 hr
KISV(FM) Bakersfield CA 1 hr
KMET(AM) Banning CA 4 hrs
KJLH-FM Compton CA 3 hrs
KCNQ(FM) Kernville CA 1 hr
KLBS(AM) Los Banos CA 8 hrs
KDUQ(AM) Ludlow CA 1 hr
*KSMC(FM) Moraga CA 2 hrs
KAAT(AM) Oakhurst CA 2 hrs
KWKU(AM) Pomona CA 15 hrs
*KUSF(FM) San Francisco CA 5 hrs
KVML(AM) Sonora CA 3 hrs
KSTN(AM) Stockton CA 5 hrs
KSUE(AM) Susanville CA 3 hrs
KXPS(FM) Thousand Palms CA 17 hrs
KDIA(AM) Vallejo CA 5 hrs
KDYA(AM) Vallejo CA 5 hrs
KUBA(AM) Yuba City CA 2 hrs
KCMN(AM) Colorado Springs CO 3 hrs
*KSJD(FM) Cortez CO 1 hr
KFKA(AM) Greeley CO 4 hrs
KUBC(AM) Montrose CO 3 hrs
KVRH(AM) Salida CO 2 hrs
KVRH-FM Salida CO 2 hrs
KCRT(AM) Trinidad CO 5 hrs
KSPK(FM) Walsenburg CO 2 hrs
KCOL(AM) Wellington CO 1 hr
WGCH(AM) Greenwich CT 3 hrs
WMMW(AM) Meriden CT 4 hrs
*WECS(FM) Willimantic CT 3 hrs
WILI(AM) Willimantic CT 2 hrs
WJWL(FM) Georgetown DE 6 hrs
WYUS(AM) Milford DE 10 hrs
WGMD(FM) Rehoboth Beach DE 2 hrs
WSTW(FM) Wilmington DE 1 hr
WYBT(AM) Blountstown FL
WWPR(AM) Bradenton FL 2 hrs
WLQH(FM) Chiefland FL 9 hrs
*WVUM(FM) Coral Gables FL 6 hrs
WKZY(FM) Cross City FL 5 hrs
WYNY(AM) Cross City FL 5 hrs
WHNR(AM) Cypress Gardens FL 10 hrs
WDCF(AM) Dade City FL 6 hrs
WNDB(AM) Daytona Beach FL 5 hrs
WLVU(AM) Dunedin FL 2 hrs
WIRA(AM) Fort Pierce FL 1 hr
WXYB(AM) Indian Rocks Beach FL 8 hrs
WROO(FM) Jacksonville FL 2 hrs
WWRF(AM) Lake Worth FL 4 hrs
WONN(AM) Lakeland FL 2 hrs
WQHL(AM) Live Oak FL 6 hrs
WMEL(AM) Melbourne FL 6 hrs
WQAM(AM) Miami FL 4 hrs
WARO(FM) Naples FL 2 hrs
WPSO(FM) New Port Richey FL 8 hrs
WSBB(AM) New Smyrna Beach FL 5 hrs
*WHIF(FM) Palatka FL 10 hrs
WIYD(AM) Palatka FL 5 hrs
WFBX(FM) Parker FL 5 hrs
WCOA(AM) Pensacola FL 6 hrs
WPSL(AM) Port St. Lucie FL 6 hrs
WSDO(AM) Sanford FL 3 hrs
WKII(AM) Solana FL 4 hrs
WPIK(AM) Summerland Key FL 1 hr
WIXC(AM) Titusville FL 6 hrs
WSIR(AM) Winter Haven FL 14 hrs
V6AH(AM) Pohnpei FM 2 hrs
V6AI(AM) Yap FM 4 hrs
WSB(AM) Atlanta GA 3 hrs
WMGR(AM) Bainbridge GA 12 hrs
WJTH(AM) Calhoun GA 16 hrs
WGFS(AM) Covington GA 14 hrs
WBLJ(AM) Dalton GA
WDMG(AM) Douglas GA 6 hrs
WMLB(AM) East Point GA 4 hrs
WDDK(FM) Greensboro GA 6 hrs
WWWE(AM) Hapeville GA 12 hrs
WCEH(AM) Hawkinsville GA 1 hr
WLAG(AM) La Grange GA 2 hrs
WMAC(AM) Macon GA 4 hrs
WHKN(FM) Millen GA 2 hrs
WROM(AM) Rome GA

WGTA(AM) Summerville GA 12 hrs
WPAX(AM) Thomasville GA 3 hrs
WTHO-FM Thomson GA 6 hrs
WLET(AM) Toccoa GA
WKWN(AM) Trenton GA 6 hrs
*WVVS(FM) Valdosta GA 2 hrs
WVOP(AM) Vidalia GA 8 hrs
KCHE-FM Cherokee IA 4 hrs
KROS(AM) Clinton IA 4 hrs
KCQQ(AM) Davenport IA 1 hr
*KWLC(AM) Decorah IA
KILR(AM) Estherville IA 11 hrs
KILR-FM Estherville IA 11 hrs
KNOD(AM) Harlan IA 2 hrs
KNIA(AM) Knoxville IA 18 hrs
KMCH(FM) Manchester IA 4 hrs
KRIB(AM) Mason City IA 5 hrs
KYTC(AM) Northwood IA 2 hrs
KBIZ(AM) Ottumwa IA 4 hrs
KSCJ(AM) Sioux City IA 5 hrs
KLLT(FM) Spencer IA 2 hrs
KXTLB(AM) Twin Lakes IA 2 hrs
KXEL(AM) Waterloo IA 20 hrs
KVNI(AM) Coeur d'Alene ID 3 hrs
KMCL-FM McCall ID 1 hr
KVSI(AM) Montpelier ID 2 hrs
KRPL(AM) Moscow ID 2 hrs
KZFN(FM) Moscow ID 2 hrs
KWIK(AM) Pocatello ID 1 hr
KSPT(AM) Sandpoint ID 2 hrs
KTFI(AM) Twin Falls ID 5 hrs
WRMJ(AM) Aledo IL 3 hrs
KATZ-FM Alton IL 2 hrs
WBGZ(AM) Alton IL 3 hrs
WBIG(AM) Aurora IL 6 hrs
WDWS(AM) Champaign IL 4 hrs
KSGM(AM) Chester IL 6 hrs
*WIIT(FM) Chicago IL 2 hrs
WDKB(AM) De Kalb IL 1 hr
WLBK(AM) De Kalb IL 6 hrs
WDQN(AM) Du Quoin IL 5 hrs
WAIK(AM) Galesburg IL 6 hrs
WGIL(AM) Galesburg IL 4 hrs
WLSR(AM) Galesburg IL 2 hrs
WLIE-FM Golconda IL 1 hr
WJBM(AM) Jerseyville IL 3 hrs
WKEI(AM) Kewanee IL 6 hrs
WLBH(AM) Mattoon IL 5 hrs
WMOK(AM) Metropolis IL 5 hrs
WRAM(AM) Monmouth IL 3 hrs
WDQX(FM) Morton IL 1 hr
WINI(AM) Murphysboro IL 6 hrs
*WONC(FM) Naperville IL 4 hrs
WPNA(AM) Oak Park IL 4 hrs
WYVR(FM) Petersburg IL 5 hrs
WBBA-FM Pittsfield IL 3 hrs
WKBF(AM) Rock Island IL 1 hr
WKXQ(AM) Rushville IL 6 hrs
WJBD(AM) Salem IL 6 hrs
WHCO(AM) Sparta IL 10 hrs
WTIM-FM Taylorville IL 4 hrs
WRAN(AM) Tower Hill IL 3 hrs
*WETN(FM) Wheaton IL 3 hrs
WZSR(FM) Woodstock IL 1 hr
WQME(FM) Anderson IN 9 hrs
WNUY(FM) Bluffton IN 4 hrs
WCNB(AM) Connersville IN 12 hrs
WBYT(FM) Elkhart IN 2 hrs
WISG(FM) Fishers IN 3 hrs
WFLQ(FM) French Lick IN 6 hrs
*WGRE(FM) Greencastle IN 2 hrs
WTRE(AM) Greensburg IN 3 hrs
WJOB(AM) Hammond IN 2 hrs
WBDC(FM) Huntingburg IN 5 hrs
WORX-FM Madison IN 6 hrs
WEFM(FM) Michigan City IN 4 hrs
WMDH(AM) New Castle IN 2 hrs
WRIN(AM) Rensselaer IN 10 hrs
WFMG(FM) Richmond IN 4 hrs
WROI(FM) Rochester IN 6 hrs
WQKC(AM) Seymour IN 3 hrs
WZZB(AM) Seymour IN 6 hrs
WDND(AM) South Bend IN 2 hrs
WSBT(AM) South Bend IN 2 hrs
WSKT(FM) Spencer IN 6 hrs
WAWC(FM) Syracuse IN 4 hrs

Broadcasting & Cable Yearbook 2006

Special Programming on Radio Stations in the U.S.

WCJC(FM) Van Buren IN 3 hrs
KABI(AM) Abilene KS 4 hrs
KSOK(AM) Arkansas City KS 5 hrs
KSNP(FM) Burlington KS 3 hrs
KDCC(AM) Dodge City KS
KVGB(AM) Great Bend KS 2 hrs
KFBZ(FM) Haysville KS 2 hrs
KHOK(FM) Hoisington KS 8 hrs
KJCK(AM) Junction City KS 4 hrs
KNNS(AM) Larned KS 5 hrs
KLWN(AM) Lawrence KS 4 hrs
KNGL(AM) McPherson KS 5 hrs
KLKC(AM) Parsons KS 2 hrs
WIBW(AM) Topeka KS 6 hrs
KLEY(AM) Wellington KS 4 hrs
*KCFN(FM) Wichita KS
WKXO(AM) Berea KY 12 hrs
WMMG(AM) Brandenburg KY 8 hrs
WKDP-FM Corbin KY 5 hrs
WCYN(AM) Cynthiana KY 10 hrs
WHIR(AM) Danville KY 8 hrs
WJQI(AM) Fort Campbell KY 4 hrs
WFKY(AM) Frankfort KY 6 hrs
WFKN(AM) Franklin KY
WXBC(FM) Hardinsburg KY 7 hrs
WHVO(AM) Hopkinsville KY 6 hrs
WRNZ(FM) Lancaster KY 4 hrs
WKYL(FM) Lawrenceburg KY 2 hrs
WGWM(AM) London KY 6 hrs
WHAS(AM) Louisville KY 2 hrs
WVEZ(FM) Louisville KY 4 hrs
WNGO(AM) Mayfield KY 10 hrs
WQQR(FM) Mayfield KY 10 hrs
WFTM(AM) Maysville KY 5 hrs
WFXY(AM) Middlesboro KY 3 hrs
WLBQ(AM) Morgantown KY 9 hrs
WPAD(AM) Paducah KY 7 hrs
WCBR(AM) Richmond KY 35 hrs
WEKY(AM) Richmond KY 6 hrs
WTLO(AM) Somerset KY 4 hrs
WEKC(AM) Williamsburg KY 7 hrs
KQIS(FM) Basile LA 1 hr
KFNV-FM Ferriday LA 4 hrs
KLCL(AM) Lake Charles LA 2 hrs
KVVP(AM) Leesville LA 9 hrs
WSLA(AM) Slidell LA 5 hrs
KVCL(AM) Winnfield LA 15 hrs
WBZ(AM) Boston MA 4 hrs
*WERS(FM) Boston MA 1 hr
*WRBB(FM) Boston MA 4 hrs
WRKO(AM) Boston MA 1 hr
*WGAO(FM) Franklin MA 8 hrs
WSBS(AM) Great Barrington MA 1 hr
WBEC(AM) Pittsfield MA 3 hrs
WBRK(AM) Pittsfield MA 2 hrs
*WMWM(FM) Salem MA 3 hrs
WMAS(AM) Springfield MA 2 hrs
WITH(AM) Baltimore MD 4 hrs
WOLB(AM) Baltimore MD 2 hrs
WCEM(AM) Cambridge MD 5 hrs
WCEM-FM Cambridge MD 6 hrs
WSRY(AM) Elkton MD 3 hrs
*WMTB-FM Emmittsburg MD 4 hrs
WAYZ(FM) Hagerstown MD 3 hrs
WXCY(FM) Havre de Grace MD 2 hrs
*WMDR(AM) Augusta ME
WVAE(AM) Biddeford ME 2 hrs
WSKW(AM) Skowhegan ME
WABJ(AM) Adrian MI 3 hrs
*WQAC-FM Alma MI 2 hrs
WATZ(AM) Alpena MI 3 hrs
WATZ-FM Alpena MI 1 hr
WAAM(AM) Ann Arbor MI 4 hrs
*WAUS(FM) Berrien Springs MI 10 hrs
WYBR(FM) Big Rapids MI 1 hr
WCFX(FM) Clare MI 1 hr
WXLA(AM) Dimondale MI 5 hrs
WDBC(AM) Escanaba MI 4 hrs
WDZZ-FM Flint MI 1 hr
WCSR(FM) Hillsdale MI 10 hrs
*WTHS(FM) Holland MI 14 hrs
WCCY(AM) Houghton MI 1 hr
WKHM(AM) Jackson MI 4 hrs
*WIDR(FM) Kalamazoo MI 3 hrs
WKZO(AM) Kalamazoo MI 5 hrs
WFCX(FM) Leland MI 1 hr
WMTE-FM Manistee MI 2 hrs

WMPX(AM) Midland MI 3 hrs
WTWR-FM Monroe MI 3 hrs
WNIL(AM) Niles MI 6 hrs
WUPY(AM) Ontonagon MI 3 hrs
WOAP(AM) Owosso MI 4 hrs
WRSR(FM) Owosso MI 1 hr
WWKR(FM) Pentwater MI 3 hrs
WJML(AM) Petoskey MI 8 hrs
KXRA(AM) Alexandria MN 2 hrs
KXRZ(AM) Alexandria MN 3 hrs
KKCQ-FM Bagley MN 9 hrs
WKLK(AM) Cloquet MN 5 hrs
KDLM(AM) Detroit Lakes MN 8 hrs
WELY(AM) Ely MN 6 hrs
KBRF(AM) Fergus Falls MN 7 hrs
KJJK(AM) Fergus Falls MN 3 hrs
WLKX-FM Forest Lake MN 6 hrs
KKCQ(AM) Fosston MN 4 hrs
WMFG(AM) Hibbing MN 4 hrs
KLFD(AM) Litchfield MN 3 hrs
KLTF(AM) Little Falls MN 1 hr
KEYL(AM) Long Prairie MN 4 hrs
KQAD(AM) Luverne MN 5 hrs
KMHL(AM) Marshall MN 7 hrs
KYMN(AM) Northfield MN 2 hrs
KDIO(AM) Ortonville MN 5 hrs
KLOH(AM) Pipestone MN 5 hrs
KQIC(FM) Willmar MN 2 hrs
KAGE(AM) Winona MN
KAAN(AM) Bethany MO 1 hr
KMRN(AM) Cameron MO 4 hrs
KCRV(AM) Caruthersville MO 20 hrs
KCXL(AM) Liberty MO 3 hrs
*KMVC(FM) Marshall MO 16 hrs
KMEM-FM Memphis MO 4 hrs
*KJAB-FM Mexico MO 20 hrs
KMCR(FM) Montgomery City MO 2 hrs
KELE-FM Mountain Grove MO 3 hrs
KBDZ(FM) Perryville MO 5 hrs
KLID(AM) Poplar Bluff MO 2 hrs
KMIS(AM) Portageville MO 4 hrs
*KCLC(FM) Saint Charles MO 7 hrs
KMOX(AM) Saint Louis MO 1 hr
KDRO(AM) Sedalia MO 3 hrs
KWTO(AM) Springfield MO 1 hr
KLPW(AM) Union MO 6 hrs
KTKS(FM) Versailles MO 3 hrs
KOKO(AM) Warrensburg MO 6 hrs
KJPW(AM) Waynesville MO 3 hrs
KSPQ(FM) West Plains MO 10 hrs
WAFM(FM) Amory MS 2 hrs
WAMY(AM) Amory MS 6 hrs
WHJT(FM) Clinton MS 5 hrs
WBAQ(FM) Greenville MS 4 hrs
WDMS(FM) Greenville MS 1 hr
WNIX(AM) Greenville MS 5 hrs
WFOR(AM) Hattiesburg MS 8 hrs
WTCD(AM) Indianola MS 11 hrs
WIQQ(FM) Leland MS 6 hrs
WQMA(AM) Marks MS 4 hrs
WMOX(AM) Meridian MS 8 hrs
WRQO(AM) Monticello MS 10 hrs
WRJW(AM) Picayune MS 16 hrs
WKZU(FM) Ripley MS 2 hrs
KBOW(AM) Butte MT 2 hrs
*KMSM-FM Butte MT 3 hrs
KXTL(AM) Butte MT 1 hr
KMTA(AM) Miles City MT 1 hr
KMSO(FM) Missoula MT 1 hr
KATQ(AM) Plentywood MT 6 hrs
KATQ-FM Plentywood MT 6 hrs
WWNC(AM) Asheville NC 3 hrs
WXIT(FM) Blowing Rock NC 8 hrs
WSQL(AM) Brevard NC 4 hrs
WBAG(AM) Burlington-Graham NC 5 hrs
WLZR(AM) Canton NC 7 hrs
WRRZ(AM) Clinton NC 6 hrs
WGAI(AM) Elizabeth City NC 4 hrs
WQNQ(FM) Fletcher NC 2 hrs
*WQFS(FM) Greensboro NC 1 hr
WBRM(AM) Marion NC 7 hrs
WHIP(FM) Mooresville NC 6 hrs
WECR(AM) Newland NC 5 hrs
WPTM(FM) Roanoke Rapids NC 3 hrs
WNCA(AM) Siler City NC 12 hrs
WMPM(AM) Smithfield NC 8 hrs

WTOE(AM) Spruce Pine NC 8 hrs
WMXF(AM) Waynesville NC 3 hrs
WENC(AM) Whiteville NC 4 hrs
WTXY(AM) Whiteville NC 10 hrs
*KEYA(FM) Belcourt ND 10 hrs
KAUJ(FM) Grafton ND 3 hrs
KXPO(AM) Grafton ND 3 hrs
KNDK(AM) Langdon ND 4 hrs
KDDR(AM) Oakes ND 3 hrs
KEYZ(AM) Williston ND 5 hrs
KZEN(FM) Central City NE 5 hrs
KJSK(AM) Columbus NE 20 hrs
KLIR(FM) Columbus NE 4 hrs
*KINI(FM) Crookston NE 6 hrs
*KFKX(FM) Hastings NE 3 hrs
KRVN(AM) Lexington NE 12 hrs
KRFS(AM) Superior NE 3 hrs
WHCY(FM) Blairstown NJ 1 hr
*WDVR(FM) Delaware Township NJ 6 hrs
WSJO(FM) Egg Harbor City NJ 4 hrs
WIFI(AM) Florence NJ 12 hrs
*WRDR(FM) Freehold Township NJ 6 hrs
*WNTI(FM) Hackettstown NJ 4 hrs
*WFJS(FM) Hazlet NJ 5 hrs
*WMNJ(FM) Madison NJ 2 hrs
WTTH(AM) Margate City NJ 1 hr
WNNJ(AM) Newton NJ 1 hr
WGHT(AM) Pompton Lakes NJ 2 hrs
WNJC(AM) Washington Township NJ 6 hrs
KRSY(AM) Alamogordo NM 4 hrs
KKIT(FM) Angel Fire NM 8 hrs
KARS(AM) Belen NM
KWNM(AM) Hurley NM
KLEA(AM) Lovington NM 3 hrs
KINF(AM) Roswell NM 15 hrs
KLAV(AM) Las Vegas NV 3 hrs
KSNE-FM Las Vegas NV 1 hr
KNEV(FM) Reno NV 1 hr
WYSL(AM) Avon NY 4 hrs
WBNR(AM) Beacon NY 5 hrs
WAAL(AM) Binghamton NY 3 hrs
*WHRW(FM) Binghamton NY 6 hrs
WYOS(AM) Binghamton NY 3 hrs
WBRV-FM Boonville NY 3 hrs
*WCWP(FM) Brookville NY 4 hrs
*WHCL-FM Clinton NY 2 hrs
WDNY(AM) Dansville NY 1 hr
WDNY-FM Dansville NY 1 hr
WFLR(AM) Dundee NY 5 hrs
WFLR-FM Dundee NY 5 hrs
WELM(AM) Elmira NY 1 hr
WGBB(AM) Freeport NY 6 hrs
WMML(AM) Glens Falls NY 3 hrs
WXHC(FM) Homer NY 1 hr
WLIE(AM) Islip NY 3 hrs
WKSN(AM) Jamestown NY 2 hrs
WGHQ(AM) Kingston NY 3 hrs
WXRL(AM) Lancaster NY 5 hrs
WIXT(AM) Little Falls NY 1 hr
WLVL(AM) Lockport NY 3 hrs
WLLG(FM) Lowville NY 2 hrs
WVOX(AM) New Rochelle NY 3 hrs
WOR(AM) New York NY 4 hrs
WGNY(AM) Newburgh NY 4 hrs
WTLA(AM) North Syracuse NY 2 hrs
*WNYK(FM) Nyack NY 2 hrs
WDOS(AM) Oneonta NY 7 hrs
WEBO(AM) Owego NY 6 hrs
*WQKE(FM) Plattsburgh NY 3 hrs
WEOK(AM) Poughkeepsie NY 2 hrs
*WRUR-FM Rochester NY 1 hr
WMYY(FM) Schoharie NY
WSPQ(AM) Springville NY 2 hrs
WRGR(FM) Tupper Lake NY 1 hr
WAJZ(FM) Voorheesville NY 1 hr
WTBQ(AM) Warwick NY
WNYV(FM) Whitehall NY 2 hrs
*WONB(FM) Ada OH 1 hr
*WOBO(FM) Batavia OH 2 hrs
WBLL(AM) Bellefontaine OH 6 hrs
WBCO(AM) Bucyrus OH 4 hrs
WQEL(FM) Bucyrus OH 5 hrs
WCER(AM) Canton OH 5 hrs
WKKI(FM) Celina OH 2 hrs

WERE(AM) Cleveland OH 2 hrs
WMNI(AM) Columbus OH 2 hrs
WHIO(AM) Dayton OH 2 hrs
*WWSU(FM) Dayton OH 11 hrs
WDFM(FM) Defiance OH 3 hrs
WZOM(FM) Defiance OH 6 hrs
*WLFC(FM) Findlay OH 3 hrs
WRBP(FM) Hubbard OH 6 hrs
WBKS(FM) Ironton OH 3 hrs
WIRO(AM) Ironton OH 7 hrs
WVKO-FM Johnstown OH 13 hrs
WLJM(AM) Lima OH 11 hrs
WMOA(AM) Marietta OH 1 hr
WYVK(FM) Middleport OH 6 hrs
WMPO(AM) Middleport-Pomeroy OH 6 hrs
WMVO(AM) Mount Vernon OH 7 hrs
*WMCO(FM) New Concord OH 2 hrs
WOBL(AM) Oberlin OH 1 hr
WDMN(AM) Rossford OH
WLEC(AM) Sandusky OH 6 hrs
WCWA(AM) Toledo OH 3 hrs
WSPD(AM) Toledo OH 5 hrs
WBTC(AM) Uhrichsville OH 2 hrs
WTUZ(AM) Uhrichsville OH 1 hr
*WOBN(FM) Westerville OH 4 hrs
WHIZ-FM Zanesville OH 1 hr
KVSP(FM) Anadarko OK 1 hr
KWON(AM) Bartlesville OK 5 hrs
WWLS-FM Bethany OK
KKWD(FM) Edmond OK 2 hrs
KTNT(FM) Eufaula OK 5 hrs
KGYN(AM) Guymon OK 8 hrs
KICM(AM) Healdton OK 6 hrs
KTJS(AM) Hobart OK 15 hrs
KTMC-FM McAlester OK 5 hrs
WBBZ(AM) Ponca City OK 5 hrs
KZBB(FM) Poteau OK 1 hr
KGFF(AM) Shawnee OK 4 hrs
KSIW(AM) Woodward OK
KWIL(AM) Albany OR 168 hrs
KNND(AM) Cottage Grove OR 3 hrs
KAJO(AM) Grants Pass OR 8 hrs
KMUZ(AM) Gresham OR 1 hr
KUIK(AM) Hillsboro OR 2 hrs
KQIK(AM) Lakeview OR 2 hrs
KQIK-FM Lakeview OR 2 hrs
*KSLC(FM) McMinnville OR 2 hrs
KNPT(AM) Newport OR 2 hrs
KACI(AM) The Dalles OR 1 hr
KWBY(AM) Woodburn OR 5 hrs
WBVP(AM) Beaver Falls PA 6 hrs
WBLF(AM) Bellefonte PA 2 hrs
WHLM(FM) Bloomsburg PA 2 hrs
WISR(AM) Butler PA 6 hrs
*WCAL(FM) California PA 6 hrs
WWCS(AM) Canonsburg PA 2 hrs
WIOO(AM) Carlisle PA 5 hrs
WCCL(FM) Central City PA 4 hrs
WCHA(AM) Chambersburg PA 8 hrs
WCCR(AM) Clarion PA 5 hrs
WWCH(AM) Clarion PA 8 hrs
WCOJ(AM) Coatesville PA 8 hrs
*WFSE(FM) Edinboro PA 4 hrs
*WWEC(FM) Elizabethtown PA 4 hrs
*WTGP(FM) Greenville PA 1 hr
WHUN(AM) Huntingdon PA 2 hrs
WKVR-FM Huntingdon PA 3 hrs
WDAD(AM) Indiana PA 2 hrs
WTYM(AM) Kittanning PA 4 hrs
WNPV(AM) Lansdale PA 5 hrs
WCNS(AM) Latrobe PA 3 hrs
WEDO(AM) McKeesport PA 1 hr
WJUN(AM) Mexico PA 6 hrs
*WMSS(FM) Middletown PA 10 hrs
WPGR(AM) Monroeville PA 5 hrs
WNAK(AM) Nanticoke PA 8 hrs
WGBN(AM) New Kensington PA 2 hrs
*WWNW(FM) New Wilmington PA 3 hrs
WWKL(FM) Palmyra PA 6 hrs
WHKS(FM) Port Allegany PA 2 hrs
WPAZ(AM) Pottstown PA 12 hrs
WRAW(AM) Reading PA 1 hr
WKBI-FM Saint Marys PA 2 hrs
WBZU(AM) Scranton PA 1 hr
WICK(AM) Scranton PA 3 hrs

*WUSR(FM) Scranton PA 4 hrs
WPIC(AM) Sharon PA 2 hrs
*WRSK(FM) Slippery Rock PA 1 hr
WQRM(FM) Smethport PA 2 hrs
WTRN(AM) Tyrone PA 4 hrs
*WXVU(FM) Villanova PA 2 hrs
WKZV(AM) Washington PA 1 hr
WCHE(AM) West Chester PA 8 hrs
WKZN(AM) West Hazleton PA 1 hr
WILK(AM) Wilkes-Barre PA 1 hr
*WRLC(FM) Williamsport PA 3 hrs
WMIA(AM) Arecibo PR 3 hrs
WALO(AM) Humacao PR 2 hrs
WEXS(AM) Patillas PR 2 hrs
WKVM(AM) San Juan PR 40 hrs wkly
WCRI(FM) Block Island RI 2 hrs
*WJMF(FM) Smithfield RI 2 hrs
WGTN-FM Andrews SC 2 hrs
WAGS(AM) Bishopville SC 7 hrs
WQNT(AM) Charleston SC 1 hr
WQSC(AM) Charleston SC 1 hr
WMUU-FM Greenville SC 20 hrs
WYRD(AM) Greenville SC 3 hrs
WBHC-FM Hampton SC 11 hrs
WHSC(AM) Hartsville SC 6 hrs
WHSC(FM) Hartsville SC 6 hrs
WKMG(AM) Newberry SC 2 hrs
WQKI-FM Orangeburg SC 6 hrs
WRML(FM) Pageland SC 5 hrs
WORD(AM) Spartanburg SC 4 hrs
WSPA(AM) Spartanburg SC 5 hrs
WSPA-FM Spartanburg SC 3 hrs
KBFS(AM) Belle Fourche SD 2 hrs
WNAX(AM) Yankton SD 16 hrs
WCTA(AM) Alamo TN 9 hrs
WYXI(AM) Athens TN 8 hrs
WMPS(AM) Bartlett TN 7 hrs
WGOC(AM) Blountville TN 16 hrs
WJZM(AM) Clarksville TN
WCLE(AM) Cleveland TN 6 hrs
WYSH(AM) Clinton TN 15 hrs
WKRM(AM) Columbia TN 4 hrs
WZYX(AM) Cowan TN 12 hrs
WDKN(AM) Dickson TN 12 hrs
WAKM(AM) Franklin TN 6 hrs
WXJB(AM) Harrogate TN 2 hrs
WJFC(AM) Jefferson City TN 4 hrs
WNRX(AM) Jefferson City TN 2 hrs
WJCW(AM) Johnson City TN 4 hrs
WKGN(AM) Knoxville TN 5 hrs
WLIV(AM) Livingston TN 15 hrs
WREC(AM) Memphis TN 4 hrs
WNSG(AM) Nashville TN 2 hrs
WLIK(AM) Newport TN 18 hrs
WUAT(AM) Pikeville TN 15 hrs
WJTT(FM) Red Bank TN 4 hrs
WLIJ(AM) Shelbyville TN 11 hrs
WCMT-FM South Fulton TN 6 hrs
WSMT(AM) Sparta TN 10 hrs
WCDT(AM) Winchester TN 6 hrs
KYYW(AM) Abilene TX 5 hrs
KGNC(AM) Amarillo TX 4 hrs
KQIZ-FM Amarillo TX 2 hrs
KLVQ(AM) Athens TX 8 hrs
KFYN(AM) Bonham TX 6 hrs
KQTY(AM) Borger TX 1 hr
KLXK(FM) Breckenridge TX 3 hrs
KWHI(AM) Brenham TX 3 hrs
*KWTS(FM) Canyon TX 3 hrs
KGAS(AM) Carthage TX 10 hrs
KGAS-FM Carthage TX 10 hrs
KCTX-FM Childress TX 5 hrs
KHER(FM) Crystal City TX 2 hrs
KTDR(FM) Del Rio TX 3 hrs
KWMC(AM) Del Rio TX 5 hrs
KTSM(AM) El Paso TX 3 hrs
KFLP-FM Floydada TX 10 hrs
KGVL(AM) Greenville TX 6 hrs
KIKT(FM) Greenville TX 6 hrs
KCLW(AM) Hamilton TX 6 hrs
KVRP-FM Haskell TX 6 hrs
KTBZ-FM Houston TX 1 hr
KERV(AM) Kerrville TX 2 hrs
KVLG(AM) La Grange TX 5 hrs
KCYL(AM) Lampasas TX 10 hrs
KSHN-FM Liberty TX 5 hrs

Broadcasting & Cable Yearbook 2006

D-747

Special Programming on Radio Stations in the U.S.

KZZN(AM) Littlefield TX 5 hrs
KFYO(AM) Lubbock TX 6 hrs
KCKL(FM) Malakoff TX 7 hrs
KLRK(FM) Marlin TX 2 hrs
KLSR-FM Memphis TX 5 hrs
KBED(AM) Nederland TX 4 hrs
KNBT(FM) New Braunfels TX 3 hrs
KNET(AM) Palestine TX 7 hrs
KEYE(AM) Perryton TX 3 hrs
KEYE-FM Perryton TX 3 hrs
KIXC-FM Quanah TX 2 hrs
KMIQ(FM) Robstown TX 6 hrs
KDCD(FM) San Angelo TX 2 hrs
KELI(FM) San Angelo TX 6 hrs
KQXT(AM) San Antonio TX 2 hrs
KIKZ(AM) Seminole TX 6 hrs
KSEM(FM) Seminole TX 6 hrs
KSTV(AM) Stephenville TX 6 hrs
KPYK(AM) Terrell TX 11 hrs
KBCY(FM) Tye TX 5 hrs
KTXZ(AM) West Lake Hills TX 6 hrs
KWUD(AM) Woodville TX 03 hrs
KSUB(AM) Cedar City UT
KVNU(AM) Logan UT 3 hrs
*KWCR-FM Ogden UT 3 hrs
*KBYU-FM Provo UT 2 hrs
KXRQ(FM) Roosevelt UT 6 hrs
KDXU(AM) Saint George UT 4 hrs
KVEL(AM) Vernal UT
WKEX(AM) Blacksburg VA 3 hrs
WDIC(AM) Clinchco VA 12 hrs
WBNN-FM Dillwyn VA
WFLO(AM) Farmville VA 10 hrs
WFLO-FM Farmville VA 1 hr
WBQB(FM) Fredericksburg VA 2 hrs
WXGM(AM) Gloucester VA 2 hrs
WXGM-FM Gloucester VA 2 hrs
WKCY(AM) Harrisonburg VA 2 hrs
*WXJM(FM) Harrisonburg VA 2 hrs
WOJL(FM) Louisa VA 3 hrs
WMXH-FM Luray VA 3 hrs
WRAA(AM) Luray VA 7 hrs
WZZU(FM) Lynchburg VA 1 hr
WMEV(AM) Marion VA 8 hrs
WNIS(AM) Norfolk VA 2 hrs
WNVA(AM) Norton VA 2 hrs
WCUL(FM) Orange VA 1 hr
WVCV(AM) Orange VA 1 hr
*WDCE(FM) Richmond VA 3 hrs
WRVA(AM) Richmond VA 10 hrs
WYTI(FM) Rocky Mount VA 10 hrs
WHEO(AM) Stuart VA 10 hrs
WFOG(FM) Suffolk VA 2 hrs
WKCW(AM) Warrenton VA 6 hrs
WVVI(AM) Charlotte Amalie VI 6 hrs
WYAC-FM Christiansted VI 3 hrs
*WRMC-FM Middlebury VT 1 hr
WVNR(AM) Poultney VT 2 hrs
WMNV(FM) Rupert VT
KLKI(AM) Anacortes WA 1 hr
KYSN(FM) East Wenatchee WA 1 hr
KARY-FM Grandview WA 8 hrs
KIKN(AM) Port Angeles WA 1 hr
KRIZ(AM) Renton WA 18 hrs
*KWRS(FM) Spokane WA 6 hrs
KZIZ(AM) Sumner WA 18 hrs
KHSS(AM) Walla Walla WA 3 hrs
*KDNA(FM) Yakima WA 4. hrs
WATW(AM) Ashland WI 5 hrs
WRPQ(AM) Baraboo WI 4 hrs
WCFW(FM) Chippewa Falls WI 2 hrs
WPCK(FM) Denmark WI 3 hrs
WMCS(AM) Greenfield WI 3.25 hrs
WJOK(FM) Kaukauna WI 3 hrs
WAUN(FM) Kewaunee WI 3 hrs
WLJY(FM) Marshfield WI 2 hrs
WJMT(AM) Merrill WI 3 hrs
WMYX(FM) Milwaukee WI 1 hr
WSSP(AM) Milwaukee WI 3 hrs
WTMJ(AM) Milwaukee WI 2 hrs
WLKD(AM) Minocqua WI 3 hrs
WMQA-FM Minocqua WI 3 hrs
WNBI(FM) Park Falls WI 1 hr
*WRFW(FM) River Falls WI
WVRQ(AM) Viroqua WI 6 hrs
WTTN(AM) Watertown WI 4 hrs
WSAU(AM) Wausau WI 3 hrs

*WVBC(FM) Bethany WV 4 hrs
WKEZ(AM) Bluefield WV 5 hrs
WBUC(AM) Buckhannon WV 7 hrs
*WVWC(FM) Buckhannon WV 4 hrs
WMRE(AM) Charles Town WV
WELD(AM) Fisher WV 10 hrs
*WVMR(FM) Frost WV 10 hrs
WTBZ(AM) Grafton WV 8 hrs
WRVC(AM) Huntington WV 3 hrs
WKCJ(FM) Lewisburg WV 4 hrs
WEPM(AM) Martinsburg WV 6 hrs
WADC(AM) Parkersburg WV 3 hrs
WLWF(FM) Ravenswood WV 7 hrs
WRON(AM) Ronceverte WV 5 hrs
WCWV(FM) Summersville WV 18 hrs
WELC(AM) Welch WV 15 hrs
WZST(FM) Westover WV
KLGT(FM) Buffalo WY 1 hr
KASL(AM) Newcastle WY 2 hrs

Rock/AOR

KIAL(AM) Unalaska AK 08 hrs
*KSPB(FM) Pebble Beach CA 2 hrs
*KZYX(FM) Philo CA 6 hrs
*WXCI(FM) Danbury CT 3 hrs
*WNHU(FM) West Haven CT 9 hrs
*KWLC(FM) Decorah IA
*KRUI-FM Iowa City IA 3 hrs
*KMSC(FM) Sioux City IA 4 hrs
*WRSE(FM) Elmhurst IL 9 hrs
*WARG(FM) Summit IL
*WBKE-FM North Manchester IN 6 hrs
*WVUR-FM Valparaiso IN 3 hrs
*KTCC(FM) Colby KS 7 hrs
*WSMU-FM North Dartmouth MA 4 hrs
*WYAJ(FM) Sudbury MA 3 hrs
WDME-FM Dover Foxcroft ME 1 hr
*WYFP(FM) Harpswell ME 4 hrs
*WQAC-FM Alma MI 2 hrs
*WQAC-FM Alma MI 5 hrs
*WRCJ-FM Detroit MI 2 hrs
*WSDP(FM) Plymouth MI 2 hrs
*WSGR-FM Port Huron MI 12 hrs
KMGK(FM) Glenwood MN 8 hrs
*WTIP(FM) Grand Marais MN 15 hrs
*KUMM(FM) Morris MN 2 hrs
*KOPN(FM) Columbia MO 6 hrs
KYYA(FM) Billings MT
*WUAW(FM) Erwin NC
*WZMB(FM) Greenville NC 9 hrs
*KWSC(FM) Wayne NE 2 hrs
*WNTI(FM) Hackettstown NJ 6 hrs
*WRRC(FM) Lawrenceville NJ 10 hrs
KRNG(FM) Fallon NV
*WGCC-FM Batavia NY
*WHPC(FM) Garden City NY 2 hrs
*WEOS(FM) Geneva NY 6 hrs
*WONY(FM) Oneonta NY 3 hrs
*WOSS(FM) Ossining NY 2 hrs
*WQKE(FM) Plattsburgh NY 10 hrs
*WFNP(FM) Rosendale NY 7 hrs
*WOBO(FM) Batavia OH 5 hrs
*WRUW-FM Cleveland OH 10 hrs
*WHSS(FM) Hamilton OH 1 hr
WIOT(FM) Toledo OH 2 hrs
*WXUT(FM) Toledo OH 4 hrs
*WCWS(FM) Wooster OH 4 hrs
KOKF(FM) Edmond OK 2 hrs
*KSLC(FM) McMinnville OR 7 hrs
*WCAL(FM) California PA 5 hrs
*WJRH(FM) Easton PA 6 hrs
*WUSR(FM) Scranton PA 8 hrs
WSBG(FM) Stroudsburg PA 3 hrs
*WNJR(FM) Washington PA 10 hrs
*WCLH(FM) Wilkes-Barre PA 18 hrs
WPTC(FM) Williamsport PA 5 hrs
*WDOM(FM) Providence RI 6 hrs
*WTTU(FM) Cookeville TN 3 hrs
WVCP(FM) Gallatin TN 15 hrs
WHHM-FM Henderson TN 6 hrs
*KRTU(FM) San Antonio TX 2 hrs
KNCN(FM) Sinton TX 2 hrs
*KSUU(FM) Cedar City UT 4 hrs
WIVI(FM) Charlotte Amalie VI
*KUPS(FM) Tacoma WA 8 hrs
*WSUP(FM) Platteville WI 6 hrs

*WRFW(FM) River Falls WI
*WSUW(FM) Whitewater WI 14 hrs
*WVVU-FM Morgantown WV 3 hrs
KYOD(FM) Glendo WY 2 hrs

Russian

*KJNP(AM) North Pole AK 11 hrs
WUST(AM) Washington DC 5 hrs
WEEF(AM) Highland Park IL
*WZLY(FM) Wellesley MA 1 hr
*WUPI(FM) Presque Isle ME 2 hrs
*WDCV-FM Carlisle PA 1 hr
*WRVU(FM) Nashville TN 1 hr
*KUGS(FM) Bellingham WA 2 hrs wkly
KKNW(AM) Seattle WA 5 hrs
KLFE(AM) Seattle WA 12 hrs

Sacred

WHOU-FM Houlton ME 1 hr

Scottish

*KBCS(FM) Bellevue WA 5 hrs

Serbian

WXYB(AM) Indian Rocks Beach FL 3 hrs
WNDZ(AM) Portage IN 2 hrs
WEDO(AM) McKeesport PA 1 hr
WRJN(AM) Racine WI 2 hrs

Slovak

*WWPT(FM) Westport CT 3 hrs
WPNA(AM) Oak Park IL
*WCPN(FM) Cleveland OH 1 hr
WERE(AM) Cleveland OH 1 hr
*WKTL(FM) Struthers OH 2 hrs
WEDO(AM) McKeesport PA 1 hr

Slovenian

*WAPS(FM) Akron OH 2 hrs
WKTX(AM) Cortland OH 2 hrs
WEDO(AM) McKeesport PA 1 hr

Smooth Jazz

*WONB(FM) Ada OH 12 hrs

Soul

KBAC(FM) Las Vegas NM 2 hrs
*WYEP-FM Pittsburgh PA 3 hrs

Spanish

*KSKA(FM) Anchorage AK 8 hrs
*KSUA(FM) Fairbanks AK 3 hrs
*KTOO(FM) Juneau AK 2 hrs
*KMXT(FM) Kodiak AK 1 hr
WKAC(AM) Athens AL 24 hrs
WBYE(AM) Calera AL 1 hr
WLDA(FM) Fort Rucker AL 4 hrs
*WTBB(FM) Gadsden AL 1 hr
WFMH-FM Holly Pond AL 24 hrs wkly
*WJAB(FM) Huntsville AL 2 hrs
*WTBJ(FM) Oxford AL 1 hr
WQRX(AM) Valley Head AL
KBBQ-FM Fort Smith AR 6 hrs
KFPW(AM) Fort Smith AR 6 hrs
KAAY(AM) Little Rock AR 2 hrs
*KABF(FM) Little Rock AR 10 hrs
*KRMC(FM) Douglas AZ 24 hrs
KVNA(FM) Flagstaff AZ 3 hrs
KXEG(AM) Phoenix AZ 2 hrs
*KUAZ(FM) Tucson AZ 5 hrs
*KUAZ(AM) Tucson AZ 3 hrs
*KXCI(FM) Tucson AZ 4 hrs

KINO(AM) Winslow AZ 3 hrs
*KAWC(FM) Yuma AZ 15 hrs
KXMX(AM) Anaheim CA
*KZFR(FM) Chico CA 6 hrs
KKCY(AM) Colusa CA 1 hr
KTHU(FM) Corning CA 1 hr
*KKUP(FM) Cupertino CA 3 hrs
*KECG(FM) El Cerrito CA 3 hrs
KBIF(AM) Fresno CA 6 hrs
*KFCF(FM) Fresno CA 5 hrs
*KMUD(FM) Garberville CA 2 hrs
KAZA(FM) Gilroy CA 133 hrs
KKMC(AM) Gonzales CA 5 hrs
KTYM(AM) Inglewood CA 1 hr
KNTI(FM) Lakeport CA 3 hrs
KXBX(AM) Lakeport CA 3 hrs
*KPFK(FM) Los Angeles CA 2.5 hrs
*KADV(AM) Modesto CA 1 hr
*KSMC(FM) Moraga CA 3 hrs
KVON(AM) Napa CA 5 hrs
KBLF(AM) Red Bluff CA 4 hrs
*KFPR(FM) Redding CA 4 hrs
KDIF(AM) Riverside CA 168 hrs
*KCPR(FM) San Luis Obispo CA 3 hrs
KPRZ(AM) San Marcos-Poway CA 22 hrs
*KCSB-FM Santa Barbara CA 12 hrs
KSTN-FM Stockton CA
KWNE(FM) Ukiah CA 4 hrs
KGIW(AM) Alamosa CO 6 hrs
*KRZA(FM) Alamosa CO 14 hrs
*KGNU-FM Boulder CO 3 hrs
KSMT(FM) Breckenridge CO 2 hrs
*KUVO(FM) Denver CO 15 hrs
KRKY(AM) Granby CO 1 hr
*KAFM(FM) Grand Junction CO 3 hrs
*KLFV(FM) Grand Junction CO 2 hrs
*KWSB-FM Gunnison CO 1 hr
KRCN(AM) Longmont CO 1 hr
KSLV(AM) Monte Vista CO 10 hrs
*KVNF(FM) Paonia CO 2 hrs
*WPKN(FM) Bridgeport CT 4 hrs
*WVOF(FM) Fairfield CT 12 hrs
*WRTC-FM Hartford CT 5 hrs
*WFCS(FM) New Britain CT 2 hrs
WYBC(AM) New Haven CT 1 hr
*WCNI(FM) New London CT 3 hrs
*WHUS(FM) Storrs CT 3 hrs
*WWUH(FM) West Hartford CT 3 hrs
*WECS(FM) Willimantic CT 9 hrs
WILI(AM) Willimantic CT 1 hr
WUST(AM) Washington DC 15 hrs
*WVUD(FM) Newark DE 2 hrs
WDEL(AM) Wilmington DE 2 hrs
WWPR(AM) Bradenton FL 15 hrs
*WVUM(FM) Coral Gables FL 2 hrs
WDCF(AM) Dade City FL 3 hrs
*WKTO(FM) Edgewater FL 2 hrs
*WJFP(FM) Fort Pierce FL 2 hrs
*WAPN(FM) Holly Hill FL 4 hrs
*WRGP(FM) Homestead FL 3 hrs
WXYB(AM) Indian Rocks Beach FL 2 hrs
WKEY-FM Key West FL 3 hrs
*WJNF(FM) Marianna FL 1 1/4 hrs
WMNE(AM) Riviera Beach FL
WJNA(AM) Royal Palm Beach FL 2 hrs
*WFCF(FM) Saint Augustine FL 4 hrs
WJCM(AM) Sebring FL 1 hr
*WVFS(FM) Tallahassee FL 2 hrs
*WBVM(FM) Tampa FL 4 hrs
WTIS(AM) Tampa FL 1 hr
WSIR(AM) Winter Haven FL 10 hrs
*WRFG(FM) Atlanta GA 5 hrs
WTHV(AM) Hahira GA 5 hrs
WGML(AM) Hinesville GA 1 hr
KWAI(AM) Honolulu HI 3 hrs
KZAT-FM Belle Plaine IA 2 hrs
KOJY(FM) Bloomfield IA 1wkly hrs
KCHE(AM) Cherokee IA 1 hr
KLNG(AM) Council Bluffs IA 10 hrs
*KALA(FM) Davenport IA 15 hrs
KDSN(AM) Denison IA 4 hrs
*KHOE(FM) Fairfield IA 2 hrs
*KRUI(FM) Iowa City IA 3 hrs
*KRNL-FM Mount Vernon IA 1 hr

KAYL(AM) Storm Lake IA 3 hrs
KBGN(AM) Caldwell ID 5 hrs
KLLP(FM) Chubbuck ID 4 hrs
KART(AM) Jerome ID 9 hrs
KMHI(AM) Mountain Home ID 7 hrs
KFTA(AM) Rupert ID
*WEFT(FM) Champaign IL 3 hrs
*WIIT(FM) Chicago IL 5 hrs
*WLUW(FM) Chicago IL 5 hrs
*WMBI(AM) Chicago IL 12 hrs
WRMN(AM) Elgin IL 10 hrs
WWHN(AM) Joliet IL 1 hr
*WIUS(FM) Macomb IL 3 hrs
*WFEN(FM) Rockford IL 1 hr
WSDR(AM) Sterling IL 4 hrs
WLYV(AM) Fort Wayne IN 1 hr
*WGCS(FM) Goshen IN 8 hrs
WBDC(FM) Huntingburg IN .5 hrs
*WBKE-FM North Manchester IN 1 hr
*WEEM(FM) Pendleton IN 5 hrs
WRSW(AM) Warsaw IN 2 hrs
WRSW-FM Warsaw IN 2 hrs
KDCC(AM) Dodge City KS
KFFX(FM) Emporia KS 2 hrs
KVOE(AM) Emporia KS 3 hrs
*KANZ(FM) Garden City KS 6 hrs
KKCI(FM) Goodland KS 1 hr
*KZNA(FM) Hill City KS 6 hrs
KWKR(FM) Leoti KS 3 hrs
KSLS(FM) Liberal KS 5 hrs
*KBCU(FM) North Newton KS 2 hrs
KULY(AM) Ulysses KS 3 hrs
*KMUW(FM) Wichita KS 2 hrs
KRBB(FM) Wichita KS 3 hrs
*WNKJ(FM) Hopkinsville KY 1 hr
WCND(AM) Shelbyville KY 2 hrs
*WAMH(FM) Amherst MA 4 hrs
*WFCR(FM) Amherst MA 4 hrs
*WMUA(FM) Amherst MA 9 hrs
*WBUR-FM Boston MA 5 hrs
WMKI(AM) Boston MA 2 hrs
*WRBB(FM) Boston MA 4 hrs
WROL(AM) Boston MA 10 hrs
*WDJM-FM Framingham MA 8 hrs
*WCCH(FM) Holyoke MA 2 hrs
WNNW(AM) Lawrence MA 10 hrs
*WMFO(FM) Medford MA 3 hrs
*WMLN-FM Milton MA 7 hrs
*WOZQ(FM) Northampton MA 2 hrs
*WNMH(FM) Northfield MA 4 hrs
*WMWM(FM) Salem MA 3 hrs
*WBSL-FM Sheffield MA 2 hrs
*WTCC(FM) Springfield MA 14 hrs
WORC-FM Webster MA 1 hr
*WZLY(FM) Wellesley MA 1 hr
*WBUR(AM) West Yarmouth MA 5 hrs
*WSKB(FM) Westfield MA 3 hrs
*WCUW(FM) Worcester MA 19 hrs
WOLB(AM) Baltimore MD 2 hrs
*WMPG(FM) Gorham ME 2 hrs
WLEN(FM) Adrian MI 4 hrs
WQTE(FM) Adrian MI 3 hrs
*WCBN-FM Ann Arbor MI 3 hrs
*WRCJ-FM Detroit MI 2 hrs
*WKAR(AM) East Lansing MI 3 hrs
WHTC(AM) Holland MI 3 hrs
*WTHS(FM) Holland MI 8 hrs
WIBM(AM) Jackson MI 2 hrs
*WIDR(FM) Kalamazoo MI 3 hrs
WLNZ(FM) Lansing MI 4 hrs
*WOAS(FM) Ontonagon MI 1 hr
WOAP(AM) Owosso MI 6 hrs
WHLS(AM) Port Huron MI 1 hr
*WNMC-FM Traverse City MI 2 hrs
*WYCE(FM) Wyoming MI 10 hrs
WPNW(AM) Zeeland MI 1 hr
KATE(AM) Albert Lea MN 2 hrs
KYCR(AM) Golden Valley MN 14 hrs
KDUZ(AM) Hutchinson MN 1 hr
KYSM(FM) Mankato MN 1 hr
*KBEM-FM Minneapolis MN 4 hrs
*KFAI(FM) Minneapolis MN 8 hrs
KCHK(AM) New Prague MN 6 hrs
KYMN(AM) Northfield MN 2 hrs
KRFO(AM) Owatonna MN 2 hrs
KLOH(AM) Pipestone MN 2 hrs
KOLM(AM) Rochester MN 2 hrs

Special Programming on Radio Stations in the U.S.

KRRW(FM) Saint James MN 1 hr
KNOF(FM) Saint Paul MN 1 hr
*KSRQ(FM) Thief River Falls MN 1 hr
KAOL(AM) Carrollton MO 2 hrs
KMZU(FM) Carrollton MO 3 hrs
KDMO(AM) Carthage MO 6 hrs
KMFC(FM) Centralia MO 1 hr
*KCUR-FM Kansas City MO 2 hrs
*KKFI(FM) Kansas City MO 16 hrs
WHB(AM) Kansas City MO 2 hrs
KCXL(AM) Liberty MO 5 hrs
*KDHX(FM) Saint Louis MO 4 hrs
WEW(AM) Saint Louis MO 10 hrs
WRRZ(AM) Clinton NC 5 hrs
*WSGE(FM) Dallas NC 1 hr
WCLW(AM) Eden NC 6 hrs
*WUAG(FM) Greensboro NC 2 hrs
WDJS(AM) Mount Olive NC 5 hrs
WMFA(AM) Raeford NC 6 hrs
*WSHA(FM) Raleigh NC 3 hrs
WTSB(AM) Selma NC 5 hrs
WNCA(AM) Siler City NC 25 hrs
WKSK(AM) West Jefferson NC 1 hr
*WHQR(FM) Wilmington NC 1 hr
KAUJ(FM) Grafton ND 2 hrs
KJSK(AM) Columbus NE 6 hrs
*KRNU(FM) Lincoln NE 2 hrs
*KZUM(FM) Lincoln NE 4 hrs
*KJLT(AM) North Platte NE 1 hr
KCTY-FM Plattsmouth NE 2 hrs
KNEB(AM) Scottsbluff NE 5 hrs
WFEA(AM) Manchester NH 2 hrs
WOF(AM) Andover NJ 3 hrs
*WBJB-FM Lincroft NJ 4 hrs
WMVB(AM) Millville NJ 2 hrs
*WSOU(FM) South Orange NJ 1 hr
*WFDU(FM) Teaneck NJ 3 hrs
*WMSC(FM) Upper Montclair NJ 2 hrs
*KFLQ(FM) Albuquerque NM 3 hrs
KSVA(AM) Albuquerque NM 4 hrs
*KUNM(FM) Albuquerque NM 9 hrs
KCQL(AM) Aztec NM 6 hrs
KATK-FM Carlsbad NM
KLMX(AM) Clayton NM 2 hrs
KOTS(AM) Deming NM 8 hrs
*KGLP(FM) Gallup NM 10 hrs
KMIN(AM) Grants NM 2'hrs hrs
KYVA-FM Grants NM 4 hrs
KVLC(AM) Hatch NM 6 hrs
*KRWG(FM) Las Cruces NM 10 hrs
KBUY(AM) Ruidoso NM 4 hrs
*KSFR(FM) Santa Fe NM 4 hrs
KXTC(AM) Thoreau NM 8 hrs
KCHS(AM) Truth or Consequences NM 12 hrs
KTNM(AM) Tucumcari NM 18 hrs
KKVV(AM) Las Vegas NV 20 hrs
*KUNV(FM) Las Vegas NV 5 hrs
KKOH(AM) Reno NV 2 hrs
*WCDB(FM) Albany NY 3 hrs
*WHRW(FM) Binghamton NY 9 hrs
*WCWP(FM) Brookville NY 1 hr
WCHP(AM) Champlain NY
WDOE(AM) Dunkirk NY 2 hrs
WGBB(AM) Freeport NY 2 hrs
*WHPC(FM) Garden City NY 1 hr
*WGMC(FM) Greece NY 10 hrs
WJTN(AM) Jamestown NY 1 hr
WIZR(FM) Johnstown NY 1 hr
*WVCR-FM Loudonville NY 3 hrs
WVOA-FM Mexico NY 15 hrs
WTHE(AM) Mineola NY 1 hr
*WBAI(FM) New York NY 3 hrs
*WKCR-FM New York NY 10 hrs
*WNYU-FM New York NY 2 hrs
WGNY(AM) Newburgh NY 1 hr
WHLD(AM) Niagara Falls NY 19 hrs
*WRHO(FM) Oneonta NY 2 hrs
*WNYO(FM) Oswego NY 6 hrs
*WVKR-FM Poughkeepsie NY 3 hrs
*WRUR-FM Rochester NY 6 hrs
*WFNP(FM) Rosendale NY 3 hrs
*WSPN(FM) Saratoga Springs NY 3 hrs
*WRUC(FM) Schenectady NY 3 hrs
*WUSB(FM) Stony Brook NY 3 hrs
*WBGU(FM) Bowling Green OH 4 hrs

WTSJ(AM) Cincinnati OH 3 hrs
*WCSB(FM) Cleveland OH 12 hrs
*WWSU(FM) Dayton OH 3 hrs
WEOL(AM) Elyria OH 2 hrs
*WLFC(FM) Findlay OH 4 hrs
WFOB(AM) Fostoria OH 3 hrs
*WDUB(FM) Granville OH 2 hrs
WRBP(FM) Hubbard OH 2 hrs
WDLW(AM) Lorain OH 7 hrs
WXKR(FM) Port Clinton OH 1 hr
*WKTL(FM) Struthers OH 1 hr
WERT(AM) Van Wert OH 1 hr
KWHW(AM) Altus OK 16 hrs
KGYN(AM) Guymon OK 8 hrs
KBZQ(FM) Lawton OK 4 hrs
KTLV(AM) Midwest City OK 4 hrs
KTLR(AM) Oklahoma City OK 3 hrs
KTFX(FM) Sand Springs OK 12 hrs
*KMUN(FM) Astoria OR 3 hrs
*KBVR(FM) Corvallis OR 4 hrs
*KLCC(FM) Eugene OR 5 hrs
*KWVA(FM) Eugene OR 6 hrs
*KAGI(FM) Grants Pass OR 6 hrs
KOHU(AM) Hermiston OR 6 hrs
KUIK(AM) Hillsboro OR 21 hrs
KCGB(FM) Hood River OR 4 hrs
KIHR(AM) Hood River OR 14 hrs
KAGO(AM) Klamath Falls OR 5 hrs
*KTEC(FM) Klamath Falls OR 3 hrs
KLYC(AM) McMinnville OR 8 hrs
*KLCO(FM) Newport OR 5 hrs
*KBOO(FM) Portland OR 10 hrs
*KBPS(FM) Portland OR 1 hr
*KBVM(FM) Portland OR 14 hrs
KKPZ(AM) Portland OR 20 hrs
*KRRC(FM) Portland OR 2 hrs
KRCO(AM) Prineville OR 4 hrs
KACI-FM The Dalles OR 1 hr
KODL(AM) The Dalles OR 2 hrs
KLWJ(AM) Umatilla OR 1 hr
*WDIY(FM) Allentown PA 3 hrs
*WMUH(FM) Allentown PA 4 hrs
WGPA(AM) Bethlehem PA 2-4 hrs
WWCS(AM) Canonsburg PA 2 hrs
*WDCV-FM Carlisle PA 1 hr
*WJRH(FM) Easton PA 6 hrs
*WERG(FM) Erie PA 3 hrs
*WMCE(FM) Erie PA 3 hrs
*WQLN-FM Erie PA 1 hr
*WZBT(FM) Gettysburg PA 4 hrs
WEDO(AM) McKeesport PA 1 hr
WWKL(AM) Palmyra PA 14 hrs
WNTP(AM) Philadelphia PA 2 hrs
WRAW(AM) Reading PA 3 hrs
*WXAC(FM) Reading PA 8 hrs
*WCLH(FM) Wilkes-Barre PA 3 hrs
*WVYC(FM) York PA 1 hr
WMIA(AM) Arecibo PR 16 hrs
WKJB(AM) Mayaguez PR 1 hr
*WRIU(FM) Kingston RI 3 hrs
WXNI(FM) Westerly RI
WKMG(AM) Newberry SC 10 hrs
*KLND(FM) Little Eagle SD 1 hr
*WHCB(FM) Bristol TN 1 hr
*WETS(FM) Johnson City TN 1 hr
*WFMQ(FM) Lebanon TN 3 hrs
*WYPL(FM) Memphis TN 1 hr
*WFSK(FM) Nashville TN 15 hrs
WNQM(AM) Nashville TN
*WRVU(FM) Nashville TN 2 hrs
KVLF(AM) Alpine TX 10 hrs
KKCN(FM) Ballinger TX 4 hrs
KRUN(AM) Ballinger TX 4 hrs
*KVLU(FM) Beaumont TX 5 hrs
KNEL-FM Brady TX 6 hrs
KXYL(AM) Brownwood TX 36 hrs
*KWTS(FM) Canyon TX 3 hrs
KDHT(FM) Cedar Park TX 2 hrs
KSTA(AM) Coleman TX 5 hrs
KXCT(FM) Coleman TX 5 hrs
KCTA(AM) Corpus Christi TX 6 hrs
*KEDT-FM Corpus Christi TX 4 hrs
KDHN(AM) Dimmitt TX 17 hrs
KTMR(AM) Edna TX 12 hrs
KULP(AM) El Campo TX 14 hrs
KELP(AM) El Paso TX 12 hrs
*KTEP(FM) El Paso TX 2 hrs

KCTI(AM) Gonzales TX 6 hrs
KCLW(AM) Hamilton TX 12 hrs
*KMBH-FM Harlingen TX 3 hrs
*KOOP(FM) Hornsby TX 10 hrs
KHCB-FM Houston TX 10 hrs
*KHCH(FM) Huntsville TX 8 hrs
*KSHU(FM) Huntsville TX 4 hrs
*KBJS(FM) Jacksonville TX 1 hr
KRNH(FM) Kerrville TX 4 hrs
*KTAI(FM) Kingsville TX 3 hrs
*KNTU(FM) McKinney TX 6 hrs
KLSR-FM Memphis TX 6 hrs
KIMP(AM) Mount Pleasant TX 25 hrs
*KLUX(FM) Robstown TX 3 hrs
KTLU(AM) Rusk TX 10 hrs
KWRW(FM) Rusk TX 10 hrs
KSLR(AM) San Antonio TX 18 hrs
KXOX(AM) Sweetwater TX 8 hrs
KPYK(AM) Terrell TX 1 hr
*KVNE(FM) Tyler TX 2 hrs
KQRL(AM) Waco TX 14 hrs
KANI(AM) Wharton TX 3 hrs
*KPDR(FM) Wheeler TX 5 hrs
KWFS(FM) Wichita Falls TX 4 hrs
*KWCR-FM Ogden UT 16 hrs
*KEYY(AM) Provo UT 5 hrs
*KRCL(FM) Salt Lake City UT 9 hrs
KVEL(AM) Vernal UT
*WTJU(FM) Charlottesville VA 2 hrs
WWWJ(AM) Galax VA 20 hrs
*WHOV(FM) Hampton VA 12 hrs
*WXJM(FM) Harrisonburg VA 3 hrs
WKGM(AM) Smithfield VA 01 hrs
*WIUJ(FM) Charlotte Amalie VI 4 hrs
*WIUV(FM) Castleton VT 1 hr
*WRMC-FM Middlebury VT 1 hr
KLKI(AM) Anacortes WA 6 hrs
KOZI(AM) Chelan WA 5 hrs
KOZI-FM Chelan WA 4 hrs
KBSN(AM) Moses Lake WA 9 hrs
KBRC(AM) Mount Vernon WA 3 hrs
*KAOS(FM) Olympia WA 6 hrs
KOMW(AM) Omak WA 2 hrs
*KZUU(FM) Pullman WA 3 hrs
KUOW(FM) Seattle WA 2 hrs
KMAS(AM) Shelton WA 2.5 hrs
*KWRS(FM) Spokane WA 2 hrs
*KDNA(AM) Yakima WA 106 hrs
*WEMI(FM) Appleton WI 1 hr
WDUZ-FM Brillion WI 2 hrs
*WEMY(FM) Green Bay WI 1 hr
*WHID(FM) Green Bay WI 3 hrs
WMCS(AM) Greenfield WI 5 hrs
WRRD(AM) Jackson WI 2 hrs
*WMSE(FM) Milwaukee WI 3 hrs
WSSP(AM) Milwaukee WI 1 hrs
*WSHS(FM) Sheboygan WI 3. hrs
*WCCX(FM) Waukesha WI 8 hrs
*WMLJ(FM) Summersville WV 1 hr
KRAE(AM) Cheyenne WY 2 hrs
KUGR(AM) Green River WY 5 hrs
KGOS(AM) Torrington WY 1 hr

Sports

*KRUA(FM) Anchorage AK 1 hr
WATV(AM) Birmingham AL 10 hrs
*WVSU-FM Birmingham AL
*WMBV(FM) Dixons Mills AL 1 hr
WUMP(AM) Madison AL
WMGY(AM) Montgomery AL 6 hrs
WKLD(FM) Oneonta AL
WZCT(AM) Scottsboro AL 19 hrs
WVNA(AM) Tuscumbia AL
WQRX(AM) Valley Head AL
WKXM(AM) Winfield AL 3 hrs
WKXM-FM Winfield AL 10 hrs
KFFA(AM) Helena AR 15 hrs
KFFA-FM Helena AR
KJBN(AM) Little Rock AR
*KLVA(FM) Casa Grande AZ 7 hrs
KDJI(AM) Holbrook AZ 10 hrs
KAAA(AM) Kingman AZ
KNOT(AM) Prescott AZ 8 hrs
KQST(FM) Sedona AZ
KMET(AM) Banning CA 3 hrs
KRKC(AM) King City CA 9 hrs

KMXE(AM) Orange CA
KTIP(AM) Porterville CA 6 hrs
KLIB(AM) Roseville CA
KNBR(AM) San Francisco CA
KLIV(AM) San Jose CA
KKJL(AM) San Luis Obispo CA
KVEC(AM) San Luis Obispo CA
KVML(AM) Sonora CA 15 hrs
KIUP(AM) Durango CO 4 hrs
KRSJ(FM) Durango CO 4 hrs
KFTM(AM) Fort Morgan CO 10 hrs
KUBC(AM) Montrose CO 5 hrs
KCOL(AM) Wellington CO 7 hrs
WGCH(AM) Greenwich CT 6 hrs
*WAPJ(FM) Torrington CT 2-8 hrs
WWCO(AM) Waterbury CT varies hrs
WXJN(FM) Lewes DE
WWBF(AM) Bartow FL
WSWN(AM) Belle Glade FL
*WVUM(FM) Coral Gables FL 5 hrs
WNDB(AM) Daytona Beach FL
WACC(AM) Hialeah FL
WFLF(AM) Pine Hills FL
WTBN(AM) Pinellas Park FL varies hrs
WAOC(AM) Saint Augustine FL
WFOY(AM) Saint Augustine FL
WKII(FM) Solana FL
WNLS(FM) Tallahassee FL
WGAU(AM) Athens GA
WALR(AM) Atlanta GA
WMGR(AM) Bainbridge GA 15 hrs
WGAA(AM) Cedartown GA
WGFS(AM) Covington GA varies hrs
WBTS(FM) Doraville GA
WDDK(FM) Greensboro GA
WCEH(AM) Hawkinsville GA
WFOM(AM) Marietta GA fall hrs
WAZX(AM) Smyrna GA
WKWN(AM) Trenton GA 10 hrs
KPUA(AM) Hilo HI
KCPS(AM) Burlington IA 10 hrs
*KWLC(FM) Decorah IA 6 hrs
KDWD(FM) Emmetsburg IA 1 hr
KLMJ(FM) Hampton IA
KGRA(FM) Jefferson IA 3 hrs
KIKD(FM) Lake City IA
KMCH(FM) Manchester IA 7 hrs
*KWDM(FM) West Des Moines IA 3 hrs
KMCL-FM McCall ID 1 hr
KIGO(AM) Saint Anthony ID 10 hrs wkly hrs
KOFE(AM) Saint Maries ID 3 hrs
KTFI(AM) Twin Falls ID 3 hrs
WXET(FM) Arcola IL
WSDZ(AM) Belleville IL 13 hrs
WRXX(AM) Centralia IL
WGN(AM) Chicago IL
WXEF(FM) Effingham IL
WWHP(FM) Farmer City IL 5 hrs
*WHFH(FM) Flossmoor IL 4 hrs
WAIK(AM) Galesburg IL 10 hrs
WGIL(AM) Galesburg IL 15 hrs
*WGBK(FM) Glenview IL 9 hrs
WJBM(AM) Jerseyville IL 13 hrs
WVLI(FM) Kankakee IL
*WLTL(FM) La Grange IL 5 hrs
WFXN(AM) Moline IL 8 hrs
WBBA-FM Pittsfield IL 6 hrs
WGFA-FM Watseka IL 18 hrs
*WETN(FM) Wheaton IL 5 hrs
*WYKT(FM) Wilmington IL 12 hrs
WHBU(AM) Anderson IN
WBIW(AM) Bedford IN
WQRK(FM) Bedford IN
WUZR(FM) Bicknell IN
WKLU(FM) Brownsburg IN
WLME(FM) Cannelton IN 6 hrs
*WJHS(FM) Columbia City IN
*WGCS(FM) Goshen IN 10 hrs
WJOB(AM) Hammond IN
WBDC(FM) Huntingburg IN 6 hrs
WIVR(FM) Kentland IN
*WEEM(FM) Pendleton IN 10 hrs
WAXI(FM) Rockville IN
WNDV(AM) South Bend IN
WNDV-FM South Bend IN

WAMW-FM Washington IN
*KTCC(FM) Colby KS 3 hrs
*KONQ(FM) Dodge City KS 5 hrs
KAYS(AM) Hays KS
KSEK(AM) Pittsburg KS
WHIR(AM) Danville KY 20 hrs
WUGO(AM) Grayson KY
WKCM(AM) Hawesville KY 6 hrs
WLXG(AM) Lexington KY
WFTG(AM) London KY
WLBQ(AM) Morgantown KY 3 hrs
WKYX(AM) Paducah KY 8 hrs
WCBR(AM) Richmond KY
WEZJ(AM) Williamsburg KY
WEZJ-FM Williamsburg KY
KJIN(AM) Houma LA
WSLA(AM) Slidell LA
KEZM(AM) Sulphur LA 12 hrs
KXOR-FM Thibodaux LA
WORC(AM) Worcester MA 6 hrs
WTAG(AM) Worcester MA
WNAV(AM) Annapolis MD
WTRI(AM) Brunswick MD 5 hrs
WXCY(FM) Havre de Grace MD 6 hrs
WKIK(AM) La Plata MD
WMCM(FM) Rockland ME
WRKD(AM) Rockland ME
WSKW(AM) Skowhegan ME
*WBFH(FM) Bloomfield Hills MI 6 hrs
WDMK(FM) Detroit MI 2 hrs
WKMI(AM) Kalamazoo MI
WAGN(AM) Menominee MI 12 hrs
WNBY-FM Newberry MI
WRSR(FM) Owosso MI 4 hrs
WJML(FM) Petoskey MI
WWWI(AM) Baxter MN
WBJI(FM) Blackduck MN 4 hrs
KXDL(FM) Browerville MN 2 hrs
*WTIP(FM) Grand Marais MN 2 hrs
KEYL(AM) Long Prairie MN 10 hrs
KZIM(AM) Cape Girardeau MO 10 hrs
KWAS(AM) Joplin MO
KBDZ(FM) Perryville MO 5 hrs
KSIM(AM) Sikeston MO
KURM-FM South West City MO
KRWP(AM) Stockton MO
WZLD(FM) Petal MS 3 hrs
WRJW(AM) Picayune MS 4 hrs
WIGG(AM) Wiggins MS
KMON(AM) Great Falls MT 5 hrs
KPRK(AM) Livingston MT
KMTA(AM) Miles City MT 3 hrs
WECR-FM Beech Mountain NC
WCGC(AM) Belmont NC
WCSL(AM) Cherryville NC 3 hrs
WZBO(AM) Edenton NC
WAZZ(AM) Fayetteville NC
WGOS(AM) High Point NC 10 hrs
WELS-FM Kinston NC
WRNS-FM Kinston NC 6 hrs
WFLB(FM) Laurinburg NC
WKXU(FM) Louisburg NC
WECR(AM) Newland NC
WCBQ(AM) Oxford NC
WQDR(FM) Raleigh NC
WNCA(AM) Siler City NC 6 hrs
WEEB(AM) Southern Pines NC
WAME(AM) Statesville NC
WSVM(AM) Valdese NC 15 hrs
WTQR(FM) Winston-Salem NC
KLXX(AM) Bismarck-Mandan ND 6 hrs
KDLR(AM) Devils Lake ND
KDIX(AM) Dickinson ND
KFGO(AM) Fargo ND 20 hrs
KMAV(AM) Mayville ND
KMAV-FM Mayville ND
KRRZ(AM) Minot ND
KGFW(AM) Kearney NE 10 hrs
*KRNU(FM) Lincoln NE 2 hrs
KIOD(FM) McCook NE 10 hrs
KSWN(FM) McCook NE 10 hrs
KNCY(AM) Nebraska City NE 6 hrs
KOIL(AM) Plattsmouth NE
WHTG(AM) Eatontown NJ 29 hrs
*WJSV(AM) Morristown NJ 3 hrs
WCTC(AM) New Brunswick NJ
WGHT(AM) Pompton Lakes NJ 2 hrs

Special Programming on Radio Stations in the U.S.

WHWH(AM) Princeton NJ
*WSOU(FM) South Orange NJ 10 hrs
*WMSC(FM) Upper Montclair NJ 3 hrs
*WMCX(FM) West Long Branch NJ 11 hrs
KICA(AM) Clovis NM 4 hrs
KBIM-FM Roswell NM
KKOH(AM) Reno NV
WBTA(AM) Batavia NY 9 hrs
WBAZ(FM) Bridgehampton NY
*WCWP(FM) Brookville NY 3 hrs
WBEN(AM) Buffalo NY
*WHCL-FM Clinton NY 6 hrs
WDNY-FM Dansville NY 4 hrs
*WKCR-FM New York NY 3 hrs
WODZ-FM Rome NY
*WRUC(FM) Schenectady NY 4 hrs
WUUF(FM) Sodus NY 5 hrs
WFAS(AM) White Plains NY 8 hrs
*WZIP(FM) Akron OH 3 hrs
WBNO-FM Bryan OH
WQCT(AM) Bryan OH
WCDK(FM) Cadiz OH
WBVB(FM) Coal Grove OH
WING(AM) Dayton OH
WFIN(AM) Findlay OH 12 hrs
WMOH(AM) Hamilton OH
WLOH(AM) Lancaster OH 8 hrs
WFGF(FM) Lima OH
WMOA(AM) Marietta OH 15 hrs
WKLM(FM) Millersburg OH
WBUK(FM) Ottawa OH 2 hrs
WBKC(FM) Painesville OH
WPTW(AM) Piqua OH 8 hrs
WCWA(AM) Toledo OH 15 hrs
WHIZ-FM Zanesville OH 3 hrs
KADA-FM Ada OK 3 hrs
KCLI(AM) Clinton OK
KOCY(AM) Del City OK
KXXY-FM Oklahoma City OK
KOKL(AM) Okmulgee OK 10 hrs
KSPI(AM) Stillwater OK
KURY-FM Brookings OR
KPNW(AM) Eugene OR
KYKN(AM) Keizer OR
KRTA(AM) Medford OR
KBBR(AM) North Bend OR
KEX(AM) Portland OR
KFXX(AM) Portland OR
KQEN(AM) Roseburg OR
KCKX(AM) Stayton OR
WRTA(AM) Altoona PA
WBVE(FM) Bedford PA
WZWW(FM) Bellefonte PA 3 hrs
*WBUQ(FM) Bloomsburg PA 4 hrs
*WFSE(FM) Edinboro PA
WTCY(AM) Harrisburg PA
WNTJ(AM) Johnstown PA 20 hrs
*WFNM(FM) Lancaster PA 2 hrs
WLAN-FM Lancaster PA
WNPV(AM) Lansdale PA 6 hrs
WBPZ(AM) Lock Haven PA
*WMSS(FM) Middletown PA 5 hrs
WQLV(FM) Millersburg PA 6 hrs
WWKL(FM) Palmyra PA
WNTP(AM) Philadelphia PA 5 hrs
KQV(AM) Pittsburgh PA
WEAE(AM) Pittsburgh PA
WDMT(FM) Pittston PA
WARM(AM) Scranton PA
*WQSU(FM) Selinsgrove PA 4 hrs
*WRSK(FM) Slippery Rock PA 1 hr
WQRM(AM) Smethport PA 3 hrs
WBHV(AM) Somerset PA 12 hrs
WKZV(AM) Washington PA 1 hr
WBAX(AM) Wilkes-Barre PA
*WPTC(FM) Williamsport PA 2 hrs
WQXA(AM) York PA
WEXS(AM) Patillas PR 6 hrs
WLEO(AM) Ponce PR
*WDOM(FM) Providence RI 2 hrs
*WBLQ(FM) Westerly RI 2 hrs
WVGB(AM) Beaufort SC
WGTR(FM) Bucksport SC 8 hrs
WISW(AM) Columbia SC

WAGI-FM Gaffney SC
WYRD(AM) Greenville SC
WAVO(AM) Rock Hill SC
WORD(AM) Spartanburg SC
WSPA(AM) Spartanburg SC 12 hrs
WBCU(AM) Union SC 10 hrs
KZKK(FM) Huron SD
KKSD(AM) Milbank SD 5 hrs
KIMM(AM) Rapid City SD
KSDR-FM Watertown SD 8 hrs
WNAX(AM) Yankton SD 10 hrs
WOCE(FM) Benton TN
WHUB(AM) Cookeville TN 10 hrs
WAKM(AM) Franklin TN 6 hrs
WAEZ(FM) Greeneville TN
WTNK(AM) Hartsville TN
WDXI(AM) Jackson TN 16 hrs
WFLI(AM) Lookout Mountain TN
WMSR(AM) Manchester TN
*WQOX(FM) Memphis TN 6 hrs
WTNE-FM Trenton TN 20 hrs
WBOZ(FM) Woodbury TN 5 hrs
KSKY(AM) Balch Springs TX
KCAR(AM) Clarksville TX 10 hrs
KRLD(AM) Dallas TX
KROD(AM) El Paso TX
KFLP-FM Floydada TX
WBAP(AM) Fort Worth TX
KGAF(AM) Gainesville TX 3 hrs
KCOH(AM) Houston TX
KCYL(AM) Lampasas TX 8 hrs
KJTV(AM) Lubbock TX
KSFA(AM) Nacogdoches TX
KJAK(FM) Slaton TX 5 hrs
KBTE(FM) Tulia TX
KGLD(AM) Tyler TX
KVOU-FM Uvalde TX
*KPGR(FM) Pleasant Grove UT 4 hrs
WKEX(AM) Blacksburg VA 4 hrs
WLQM(FM) Franklin VA
WFVA(AM) Fredericksburg VA
WMNA(AM) Gretna VA 10 hrs
*WRVL(FM) Lynchburg VA
WNIS(AM) Norfolk VA
WVBE(FM) Roanoke VA
WYTI(AM) Rocky Mount VA
WTFX(AM) Winchester VA
WKVT-FM Brattleboro VT 6 hrs
WVAA(AM) Burlington VT 10 hrs
WFAD(AM) Middlebury VT 10 hrs
WVNR(FM) Poultney VT 10 hrs
WJEN(FM) Rutland VT 4 hrs
*KASB(FM) Bellevue WA 6 hrs
*KCED(FM) Centralia WA 4 hrs
KCLX(AM) Colfax WA 7 hrs
KBDB-FM Forks WA 20 hrs
KBIS(AM) Forks WA 20 hrs
KONA(AM) Kennewick WA 8 hrs
KTCR(AM) Kennewick WA
KEGX(FM) Richland WA
KKNW(AM) Seattle WA 15 hrs
KOMO(AM) Seattle WA
KJRB(AM) Spokane WA
KXLY(AM) Spokane WA 20 hrs
KKAD(AM) Vancouver WA 18 hrs
WBEV(AM) Beaver Dam WI 18 hrs
WNFL(AM) Green Bay WI 15 hrs
WLKG(FM) Lake Geneva WI 2 hrs
WLST(FM) Marinette WI
WMAM(AM) Marinette WI
WPVL(AM) Platteville WI 15 hrs
WRPN(AM) Ripon WI 15 hrs
*WRPN-FM Ripon WI 15 hrs
WCOW-FM Sparta WI
WOSQ(FM) Spencer WI
*WWSP(FM) Stevens Point WI 3 hrs
WDOR(FM) Sturgeon Bay WI
*KUWS(FM) Superior WI 6 hrs
WAUK(AM) Waukesha WI
WDUX-FM Waupaca WI 15 hrs
WJLS(AM) Beckley WV 3 hrs
WXKX(AM) Clarksburg WV
WAJR(AM) Morgantown WV
WTNJ(AM) Mount Hope WV
WWYO(FM) Pineville WV 18 hrs

Talk

WEBJ(AM) Brewton AL 15 hrs
WBCF(AM) Florence AL 12 hrs
WNUZ(AM) Talladega AL 5 hrs
WVNA(AM) Tuscumbia AL
KRBK(AM) Booneville AR 9 hrs
KHTE-FM England AR 10 hrs
KVDW(AM) England AR 10 hrs
KBOK(AM) Malvern AR 6 hrs
KCGS(AM) Marshall AR 7 hrs
KCUZ(AM) Clifton AZ 8 hrs
KJLH-FM Compton CA 8.5 hrs
KXBX(AM) Lakeport CA 5 hrs
KXTZ(FM) Pismo Beach CA 1 hr
*KASF(FM) Alamosa CO 6 hrs
KFTM(AM) Fort Morgan CO 5 hrs
KGRE(AM) Greeley CO 1 hr
WICH(AM) Norwich CT 15 hrs
WINY(AM) Putnam CT 10 hrs
WEBE(FM) Westport CT 1 hr
WWPR(AM) Bradenton FL 10 hrs
WDCF(AM) Dade City FL 16 hrs
WOTS(AM) Kissimmee FL 20 hrs
WPGS(AM) Mims FL 1 hr
WCFI(AM) Ocala FL 13 hrs
WRNE(AM) Pensacola FL
*WWFR(FM) Stuart FL 1 hr
WBAF(AM) Barnesville GA 5 hrs
*WFRC(FM) Columbus GA 8 hrs
WDDK(FM) Greensboro GA
WYTH(AM) Madison GA 15 hrs
KXEL(AM) Waterloo IA 15 hrs
KOFE(AM) Saint Maries ID
WSDZ(AM) Belleville IL
*WSSD(FM) Chicago IL 6 hrs
*WHFH(FM) Flossmoor IL 1 hr
WAIK(AM) Galesburg IL 10 hrs
WEEF(AM) Highland Park IL 5 hrs
*WCSF(FM) Joliet IL 4 hrs
WGFA(AM) Watseka IL 5 hrs
WKLU(FM) Brownsburg IN
WISG(FM) Fishers IN 1 hr
*WPUM(FM) Rensselaer IN 1 hr
WLBN(AM) Lebanon KY 5 hrs
WTBK(FM) Manchester KY 8 hrs
WRVK(AM) Mt. Vernon KY 15 hrs
KBCE(FM) Boyce LA 1 hr
*WAMH(FM) Amherst MA 2 hrs
WTRI(AM) Brunswick MD 2 hrs
WJEJ(AM) Hagerstown MD 8 hrs
WDZZ-FM Flint MI 1 hr
WDEO(AM) Ypsilanti MI
WKLK(FM) Cloquet MN 1 hr
*KUMM(FM) Morris MN 3 hrs
KNXR(FM) Rochester MN 2 hrs
*KOZO(FM) Branson MO 5 hrs
KAYX(FM) Richmond MO
KSIM(AM) Sikeston MO
WTCD(FM) Indianola MS 10 hrs
WATA(AM) Boone NC 20 hrs
WRFX-FM Kannapolis NC 3 hrs
WENC(AM) Whiteville NC 5 hrs
WHND(AM) Harvey ND 8 hrs
KOIL(AM) Plattsmouth NE
WMOU(AM) Berlin NH 2 hrs
*WCVH(FM) Flemington NJ 2 hrs
WRNJ(AM) Hackettstown NJ 10 hrs
WOBM(AM) Lakewood NJ 12 hrs
KPSA(AM) Roswell NM 15 hrs
KMXQ(FM) Socorro NM 1 hr
WUFO(AM) Amherst NY 8 hrs
*WSQX-FM Binghamton NY 10 hrs
WENT(AM) Gloversville NY 1 hr
*WNYC(AM) New York NY 3 hrs
WEOK(AM) Poughkeepsie NY 5 hrs
WBEA(FM) Southold NY
WONW(AM) Defiance OH 3 hrs
WUZZ-FM Lima OH 16 hrs
WNXT(AM) Portsmouth OH
*WLRY(FM) Rushville OH 16 hrs
*WKOF(FM) Edmond OK 5 hrs
KCRC(AM) Enid OK 5 hrs
KGFF(AM) Shawnee OK
KWIP(AM) Dallas OR 5 hrs
KWVR(AM) Enterprise OR 15 hrs

KQEN(AM) Roseburg OR
*KSJK(AM) Talent OR 6 hrs
KACI(AM) The Dalles OR 10 hrs
*WBUQ(FM) Bloomsburg PA 10 hrs
WKHB(AM) Irwin PA
WBHD(FM) Olyphant PA
WMBS(AM) Uniontown PA
WZAR(FM) Ponce PR 15 hrs
*WRTU(FM) San Juan PR 2 hrs
*WBLQ(FM) Westerly RI 15 hrs
WOLS(AM) Florence SC 16 hrs
WAGI(FM) Gaffney SC 10 hrs
WLMC(AM) Georgetown SC 4 hrs
WRIX-FM Honea Path SC 20 hrs
WOCE(FM) Benton TN
WZYX(AM) Cowan TN
KIXZ(AM) Amarillo TX 2 hrs
*KAZI-FM Austin TX 10 hrs
KNES(AM) Fairfield TX 15 hrs
KMJQ(FM) Houston TX 3 hrs
KTBZ-FM Houston TX 2 hrs
KKCL(FM) Lorenzo TX 17 hrs
*KSTX(FM) San Antonio TX 6 hrs
KSUB(AM) Cedar City UT
WFVA(AM) Fredericksburg VA
WRVA(AM) Richmond VA 1 hr
WJCD(FM) Windsor VA 5 hrs
WFAD(AM) Middlebury VT 10 hrs
KBKW(AM) Aberdeen WA
KGNW(AM) Burien-Seattle WA
KXLY(AM) Spokane WA 15 hrs
KXLY(AM) Spokane WA 5 hrs
*KVTI(FM) Tacoma WA 4 hrs
*WRFW(FM) River Falls WI
WAJR(AM) Morgantown WV
WMOV(AM) Ravenswood WV 2 hrs
KOVE(AM) Lander WY 15 hrs

Tejano

KPAN(AM) Hereford TX 15 hrs

Top-40

KOLV(FM) Olivia MN
KATQ(AM) Plentywood MT
WGFY(FM) Charlotte NC

Triple A

*KOJI(FM) Okoboji IA 14 hrs
*KWIT(FM) Sioux City IA 12 hrs
*KMUW(FM) Wichita KS 14 hrs
*KOPN(FM) Columbia MO 10 hrs
*WEOS(FM) Geneva NY 12 hrs
WEQX(FM) Manchester VT 4 hrs

Ukrainan

WILI(AM) Willimantic CT 1 hr
WPNA(AM) Oak Park IL
WHLD(AM) Niagara Falls NY 1 hr
WCCD(AM) Parma OH 1 hr
*WKTL(FM) Struthers OH 1 hr
KARI(AM) Blaine WA 1 hr

Underground

*WMTS-FM Murfreesboro TN 10 hrs

Urban Contemporary

*KSCU(FM) Santa Clara CA 15 hrs
*KCSU-FM Fort Collins CO 3 hrs
*WQTQ(FM) Hartford CT 19 hrs
WRGP(FM) Homestead FL 12 hrs
*KICB(FM) Fort Dodge IA 2 hrs
*KRUI(FM) Iowa City IA 3 hrs
*KMSC(FM) Sioux City IA 4 hrs
WTPC(FM) Elsah IL 3 hrs
*WQUB(FM) Quincy IL 2 hrs
*WVUR-FM Valparaiso IN 3 hrs
*KTCC(FM) Colby KS 4 hrs

*WKMS-FM Murray KY 3 hrs
*WBIM-FM Bridgewater MA 9 hrs
*WZBC(FM) Newton MA 3 hrs
*WSMU-FM North Dartmouth MA 14 hrs
*WKHS(FM) Worton MD 2 hrs
*WBOR(FM) Brunswick ME 15 hrs
*WMEB-FM Orono ME 5 hrs
*WSGR-FM Port Huron MI 6 hrs
*KMVC(FM) Marshall MO 20 hrs
*WASU-FM Boone NC 6 hrs
*WXDU(FM) Durham NC 12 hrs
*KFKX(FM) Hastings NE 8 hrs
*WKNH(FM) Keene NH 4 hrs
*WPSC-FM Wayne NJ 18 hrs
KRNG(FM) Fallon NV
*WIRQ(FM) Rochester NY 3 hrs
*WHSS(FM) Hamilton OH 1 hr
*WUSO(FM) Springfield OH 9 hrs
*WCWS(FM) Wooster OH 3 hrs
*KOKF(FM) Edmond OK 3 hrs
*WBUQ(FM) Bloomsburg PA 10 hrs
*WCAL(FM) California PA 12 hrs
*WDCV-FM Carlisle PA 15 hrs
*WUSR(FM) Scranton PA 6 hrs
WBRU(FM) Providence RI 20 hrs
*WDOM(FM) Providence RI 16 hrs
*KCFS(FM) Sioux Falls SD 5 hrs
*WTTU(FM) Cookeville TN 3 hrs
*KSAU(FM) Nacogdoches TX 4 hrs
*WIUV(FM) Castleton VT 5 hrs
*WRMC-FM Middlebury VT 12 hrs
*KGRG(FM) Auburn WA 2 hrs
*WSUP(FM) Platteville WI 4 hrs
*WSUW(FM) Whitewater WI 14 hrs

Variety/Diverse

*WEGL(FM) Auburn AL
KBHR(FM) Big Bear City CA 2 hrs
WAZX(AM) Smyrna GA
*WVVS(FM) Valdosta GA 16 hrs
*KIWR(FM) Council Bluffs IA 16 hrs
*WNUR-FM Evanston IL 12 hrs
*WDCB(FM) Glen Ellyn IL 7 hrs
*WWNO(FM) New Orleans LA 4 hrs
*KTLN(FM) Thibodaux LA 4 hrs
*KGAC(FM) Saint Peter MN 8 hrs
WPEG(FM) Concord NC 8 hrs
WHKP(FM) Hendersonville NC 18 hrs
*WSHA(FM) Raleigh NC 4 hrs
*WITC(FM) Cazenovia NY 10 hrs
*WBAI(FM) New York NY
*KOKF(FM) Edmond OK 5 hrs
WEZY(FM) Racine WI

Vietnamese

KXMX(AM) Anaheim CA 2 hrs
*WLUW(FM) Chicago IL 1 hr
*KHCB(AM) Galveston TX 4 hrs
*WSHS(FM) Sheboygan WI 3 hrs

Women

*KPFA(FM) Berkeley CA 10 hrs
*KAZU(FM) Pacific Grove CA 6 hrs
*WCNI(FM) New London CT 3 hrs
*WPFW(FM) Washington DC 3 hrs
KROS(AM) Clinton IA 5 hrs
*KMSC(FM) Sioux City IA 5 hrs
*WMMT(FM) Whitesburg KY 2 hrs
KNSG(FM) Springfield MN 3 hrs
WNBN(AM) Meridian MS
WUMS(FM) University MS 1 hr
KAWL(AM) York NE 3 hrs
*WRPI(FM) Troy NY 2 hrs
*WXUT(FM) Toledo OH 2 hrs
KUJZ(FM) Creswell OR 2 hrs
*WFSK(FM) Nashville TN 3 hrs
KGNW(AM) Burien-Seattle WA

Special Programming on Radio Stations in Canada

Agriculture
CFAC(AM) Calgary, AB 10 hrs
CFCW(AM) Camrose, AB 5 hrs
CKDQ(AM) Drumheller, AB 8 hrs
CJYR(AM) Edson, AB 2 hrs
CHRB(AM) High River, AB 5 hrs
CHLW(AM) Saint Paul, AB 5 hrs
CKKY(AM) Wainwright, AB 10 hrs
CFOK(AM) Westlock, AB 5 hrs
CKSR-FM Chilliwack, BC 2 hrs
CIGV-FM Penticton, BC 1 hr
CKLQ(AM) Brandon, MB 18 hrs
CFRY(AM) Portage la Prairie, MB 4 hrs
CHSM(AM) Steinbach, MB
CBW(AM) Winnipeg, MB 6 hrs
CKDH(AM) Amherst, NS 2 hrs
CKDY(AM) Digby, NS 7 hrs
CKEN-FM Kentville, NS 5 hrs
CKAD(AM) Middleton, NS 3 hrs
CJBQ(AM) Belleville, ON 3 hrs
CFCO(AM) Chatham, ON 5 hrs
CHCD-FM Simcoe, ON 5 hrs
CFRB(AM) Toronto, ON 2 hrs
CJSL(AM) Estevan, SK 4 hrs
CFYM(AM) Kindersley, SK
CJNB(AM) North Battleford, SK 7 hrs
CKBI(AM) Prince Albert, SK 2 hrs
*CBK(AM) Regina, SK 5 hrs
CKSW(AM) Swift Current, SK 5 hrs
CFSL(AM) Weyburn, SK 3 hrs

American Indian
CJSR-FM Edmonton, AB 2 hrs
CFNR-FM Terrace, BC 9 hrs
CHMB(AM) Vancouver, BC 1 hr
*CFUV-FM Victoria, BC 1 hr
CFAR(AM) Flin Flon, MB
CHTM(AM) Thompson, MB 10 hrs
CHSR-FM Fredericton, NB 1 hr
CKON-FM Akwesasne, ON
*CHMO(AM) Moosonee, ON 5 hrs
CKCU-FM Ottawa, ON 2 hrs
CKLP-FM Parry Sound, ON 1 hr
CFBU-FM Saint Catharines, ON 1 hr
CBQS-FM Sioux Narrows, ON 1 hr
CHNO-FM Sudbury, ON 1 hr
*CIUT-FM Toronto, ON 2 hrs
*CKRK-FM Kahnawake, PQ 10 hrs
*CBKA-FM La Ronge, SK 20 hrs
*CJTR-FM Regina, SK 4 hrs

Big Band
CFBG-FM Bracebridge, ON 1 hr

Black
CJSR-FM Edmonton, AB 7 hrs
*CFRO-FM Vancouver, BC 14 hrs
*CITR-FM Vancouver, BC 18 hrs
CHSR-FM Fredericton, NB 3 hrs
CKLB-FM Yellowknife, NT 1 hr
*CFMU-FM Hamilton, ON 4 hrs
CKCU-FM Ottawa, ON 12 hrs
CHRY-FM Toronto, ON
*CJAM-FM Windsor, ON 10 hrs
*CIBL-FM Montreal, PQ 13 hrs
*CKUT-FM Montreal, PQ 20 hrs
*CKRL-FM Quebec, PQ 6 hrs
CFNJ-FM Saint Gabriel-de-Brandon, PQ 1 hr
*CJTR-FM Regina, SK 2 hrs

Bluegrass
CKOL-FM Campbellford, ON 3 hrs
CHCR-FM Killaloe, ON 6 hrs

Blues
CKXL-FM Saint Boniface, MB 2 hrs
*CHMR-FM Saint John's, NF 6 hrs
*CFMU-FM Hamilton, ON 5 hrs
CFRM-FM Little Current, ON 2 hrs
CKFM-FM Toronto, ON 1 hr
CIEU-FM Carleton, PQ 5 hrs

Children
CHVN-FM Winnipeg, MB 1 hr
*CKUW-FM Winnipeg, MB 2 hrs
CKGN-FM Kapuskasing, ON 2 hrs
CHRI-FM Ottawa, ON 2 hrs

Chinese
*CFRO-FM Vancouver, BC 2 hrs
CHSR-FM Fredericton, NB 3 hrs
*CHUO-FM Ottawa, ON 2 hrs
CHRY-FM Toronto, ON
CINQ-FM Montreal, PQ 5 hrs
*CJTR-FM Regina, SK 1 hr

Christian
*CIXX-FM London, ON 3 hrs

Classic Rock
CKWA(AM) Slave Lake, AB 5 hrs

Classical
CHQT(AM) Edmonton, AB 12 hrs
CJSR-FM Edmonton, AB 2 hrs
CKBX(AM) 100 Mile House, BC 1 hr
CIGV-FM Penticton, BC 2 hrs
CHOR(AM) Summerland, BC 3 hrs
CIOC-FM Victoria, BC 5 hrs
CFAM(AM) Altona, MB 15 hrs
CBW(AM) Winnipeg, MB 8 hrs
*CKUW-FM Winnipeg, MB 4 hrs
CHSR-FM Fredericton, NB 6 hrs
*CHMR-FM Saint John's, NF 10 hrs
CHOD-FM Cornwall, ON 4 hrs
*CFMU-FM Hamilton, ON 5 hrs
CHAS-FM Sault Ste. Marie, ON 5 hrs
CFRB(AM) Toronto, ON 7 hrs
*CBE(AM) Windsor, ON 4 hrs
*CJAM-FM Windsor, ON 4 hrs
CIEU-FM Carleton, PQ 3 hrs
CHIP-FM Fort Coulonge, PQ 2 hrs
CJRG-FM Gaspe, PQ 2 hrs
*CFIN-FM Lac-Etchemin, PQ 4 hrs
CHGA-FM Maniwaki, PQ 1 hr
*CIBL-FM Montreal, PQ 4 hrs
CKIA-FM Quebec, PQ 3 hrs
CKMN-FM Rimouski-Mont Joli, PQ 3 hrs
CFNJ-FM Saint Gabriel-de-Brandon, PQ 2 hrs
CIHO-FM Saint Hilarion, PQ 2 hrs
CJMC-FM Sainte Anne des Monts, PQ 2 hrs
CFLX-FM Sherbrooke, PQ 7 hrs
CJSO-FM Sorel, PQ 2 hrs
CFMC-FM Saskatoon, SK 2 hrs

Ethnic
CKER-FM Edmonton, AB 10 hrs
*CITR-FM Vancouver, BC 2 hrs
*CIOI-FM Hamilton, ON 2 hrs
*CHUO-FM Ottawa, ON 6 hrs

Filipino
CKJS(AM) Winnipeg, MB 20 hrs

Finnish
CKTG-FM Thunder Bay, ON 1 hr

Folk
CJSR-FM Edmonton, AB 16 hrs
CKXL-FM Saint Boniface, MB 2 hrs
*CKUW-FM Winnipeg, MB 10 hrs
CFAN-FM Miramichi City, NB 2 hrs
*CHMR-FM Saint John's, NF 6 hrs
*VOWR(AM) Saint John's, NF 15 hrs
CJLX-FM Belleville, ON 1 hr
CKPC-FM Brantford, ON 1 hr
CKCU-FM Ottawa, ON 12 hrs
*CJAM-FM Windsor, ON 4 hrs
CIEU-FM Carleton, PQ 3 hrs
CHGA-FM Maniwaki, PQ 5 hrs
*CKUT-FM Montreal, PQ 3 hrs

Foreign/Ethnic
*CJSF-FM Burnaby, BC 2 hrs
CFKC(AM) Creston, BC 2 hrs
CJAV(AM) Port Alberni, BC 1 hr
CJAT-FM Trail, BC 2 hrs
*CFRO-FM Vancouver, BC 8 hrs
CHSR-FM Fredericton, NB 5 hrs
*CKJM-FM Cheticamp, NS 1 hr
CHAK(AM) Inuvik, NT 18 hrs
CFCT-FM Tuktoyaktuk, NT 5 hrs
*CFYK-FM Yellowknife, NT 16 hrs
CBQR-FM Rankin Inlet, NU 10 hrs
CJLX-FM Belleville, ON 2 hrs
CKWR-FM Kitchener, ON 4 hrs
*CBQT-FM Thunder Bay, ON 1 hr
CKOT(AM) Tillsonburg, ON 2 hrs
CHRY-FM Toronto, ON
CINQ-FM Montreal, PQ 18 hrs
CKIA-FM Quebec, PQ 3 hrs
CHON-FM Whitehorse, YT 15 hrs

French
*CJSW-FM Calgary, AB 1 hr
CJSR-FM Edmonton, AB 1 hr
*CFUV-FM Victoria, BC 2 hrs
CKXL-FM Saint Boniface, MB 120 hrs wkly hrs
CKBC-FM Bathurst, NB 9 hrs
CKNB(AM) Campbellton, NB 18 hrs
CHSR-FM Fredericton, NB 2 hrs
CKHJ(AM) Fredericton, NB 1 hr
*CHMR-FM Saint John's, NF 2 hrs
CJLX-FM Belleville, ON 1 hr
*CFMU-FM Hamilton, ON 1 hr
CHCR-FM Killaloe, ON 8 hrs
CKCU-FM Ottawa, ON 2 hrs
*CKLU-FM Sudbury, ON 19 hrs
CHRY-FM Toronto, ON
*CIUT-FM Toronto, ON 2 hrs
CKAJ-FM Jonquiere, PQ
*CFIN-FM Lac-Etchemin, PQ
CHAA-FM Longueuil, PQ 18 hrs
*CKUT-FM Montreal, PQ 9 hrs
CJBR-FM Rimouski, PQ
CFCR-FM Saskatoon, SK 1 hr

German
*CJSW-FM Calgary, AB 2 hrs
CKJS(AM) Winnipeg, MB 6 hrs
CKPC-FM Brantford, ON 4 hrs
CKWR-FM Kitchener, ON 3 hrs
*CHUO-FM Ottawa, ON 2 hrs
*CKLU-FM Sudbury, ON 1 hr
CKOT(AM) Tillsonburg, ON 1 hr
CFCR-FM Saskatoon, SK 2 hrs

Gospel
CJSR-FM Edmonton, AB 2 hrs
CILK-FM Kelowna, BC 3 hrs
CFNR-FM Terrace, BC 1 hr
CFFM-FM Williams Lake, BC 4 hrs
CHVN-FM Winnipeg, MB 4 hrs
CKOL-FM Campbellford, ON 3 hrs
CFCO(AM) Chatham, ON 2 hrs
CKSY-FM Chatham, ON 2 hrs
CFBW-FM Hanover, ON 7 hrs
CKGN-FM Kapuskasing, ON 2 hrs
CFRM-FM Little Current, ON 3 hrs
CKLP-FM Parry Sound, ON 1 hr
CKOT-FM Tillsonburg, ON 1 hr
CHRY-FM Toronto, ON
CHIP-FM Fort Coulonge, PQ 7 hrs
*CKUT-FM Montreal, PQ 2 hrs
CJWW(AM) Saskatoon, SK 3 hrs

Greek
CKJR(AM) Wetaskiwin, AB 2 hrs
*CFRO-FM Vancouver, BC 1 hr
*CITR-FM Vancouver, BC 1 hr
CKJS(AM) Winnipeg, MB 1 hr
CJLX-FM Belleville, ON 1 hr
CKWR-FM Kitchener, ON 2 hrs
CHAA-FM Longueuil, PQ 5 hrs
CINQ-FM Montreal, PQ 13 hrs

Hebrew
CHRY-FM Toronto, ON

Hindi
*CHMR-FM Saint John's, NF 1 hr
CHWO(AM) Toronto, ON 8 hrs

Hungarian
CKOT(AM) Tillsonburg, ON 1 hr

Irish
CHVO(AM) Carbonear, NF 8 hrs
CKXD-FM Gander, NF 12 hrs
CIGO-FM Port Hawkesbury, NS 1 hr

Italian
*CJSW-FM Calgary, AB 1 hr
CKER-FM Edmonton, AB 3 hrs
CHMB(AM) Vancouver, BC 1 hr
*CFUV-FM Victoria, BC 2 hrs
CKJS(AM) Winnipeg, MB 5 hrs
CFRU-FM Guelph, ON 1 hr
*CFMU-FM Hamilton, ON 1 hr
CHYR-FM Leamington, ON 3 hrs
CKCU-FM Ottawa, ON 1 hr
CHAS-FM Sault Ste. Marie, ON 2 hrs
CJQM-FM Sault Ste. Marie, ON 4 hrs
*CKLU-FM Sudbury, ON 1 hr
CKTG-FM Thunder Bay, ON
CHWO(AM) Toronto, ON 4 hrs
*CKRL-FM Quebec, PQ 2 hrs
*CJTR-FM Regina, SK 1 hr
CFCR-FM Saskatoon, SK 1 hr

Japanese
CHMB(AM) Vancouver, BC 7 hrs

Jazz
CKMX(AM) Calgary, AB 5 hrs
CHOR(AM) Summerland, BC 3 hrs
CFOX-FM Vancouver, BC 2 hrs

*CFRO-FM Vancouver, BC 16 hrs
CKXL-FM Saint Boniface, MB 4 hrs
CBW-FM Winnipeg, MB 3 hrs
*CKUW-FM Winnipeg, MB 10 hrs
CKLE-FM Bathurst, NB 2 hrs
CFAI-FM Edmundston, NB 3 hrs
CHSR-FM Fredericton, NB 6 hrs
CJMO-FM Moncton, NB 2 hrs
CKUM-FM Moncton, NB 4 hrs
*CHMR-FM Saint John's, NF 6 hrs
*CKJM-FM Cheticamp, NS 3 hrs
CFRQ-FM Dartmouth, NS 3 hrs
CIVR-FM Yellowknife, NT 4 hrs
CJLX-FM Belleville, ON 4 hrs
CFBG-FM Bracebridge, ON 2 hrs
CHOD-FM Cornwall, ON 4 hrs
*CFMU-FM Hamilton, ON 10 hrs
CKGE-FM Oshawa, ON 2 hrs
*CHUO-FM Ottawa, ON 5 hrs
CKCU-FM Ottawa, ON 15 hrs
CKWF-FM Peterborough, ON 12 hrs
CFBU-FM Saint Catharines, ON 4 hrs
CHAS-FM Sault Ste. Marie, ON 2 hrs
CHRY-FM Toronto, ON
*CBE(AM) Windsor, ON
*CJAM-FM Windsor, ON 6 hrs
CIEU-FM Carleton, PQ 3 hrs
CFMF-FM Fermont, PQ 1 hr
CJRG-FM Gaspe, PQ 2 hrs
*CFIN-FM Lac-Etchemin, PQ 6 hrs
CHGA-FM Maniwaki, PQ 3 hrs
*CIBL-FM Montreal, PQ 14 hrs
*CBVX-FM Quebec, PQ 16 hrs
CKIA-FM Quebec, PQ 4 hrs
CFNJ-FM Saint Gabriel-de-Brandon, PQ 2 hrs
CIHO-FM Saint Hilarion, PQ 2 hrs
CFLX-FM Sherbrooke, PQ 8 hrs
CFMC-FM Saskatoon, SK 2 hrs

New Age
CFGX-FM Sarnia, ON 7 hrs

News
*CFPR(AM) Prince Rupert, BC
CHKT(AM) Toronto, ON 18 hrs
*CBVX-FM Quebec, PQ 7 hrs

News/talk
CKPR(AM) Thunder Bay, ON 10 hrs
*CFTH-FM-1 Harrington Harbour, PQ

Nostalgia
CFRN(AM) Edmonton, AB

Oldies
CFRN(AM) Edmonton, AB
CJSU-FM Duncan, BC 12 hrs
CKXX-FM Corner Brook, NF 3 hrs
CHIP-FM Fort Coulonge, PQ
CJLM-FM Joliette, PQ 6 hrs
CHAA-FM Longueuil, PQ 9 hrs
CKMN-FM Rimouski-Mont Joli, PQ 3 hrs
CFDA-FM Victoriaville, PQ 3 hrs

Other
CKUA(AM) Edmonton, AB
CISC-FM Gibsons, BC 3 hrs
CKFR(AM) Kelowna, BC 2 hrs
CHLS-FM Lillooet, BC 16 hrs
CKKS-FM Sechelt, BC 3 hrs
CKXL-FM Saint Boniface, MB 4 hrs
CJAR(AM) The Pas, MB 5 hrs

Special Programming on Radio Stations in Canada

CHVN-FM Winnipeg, MB 6 hrs
CIOK-FM Saint John, NB 4 hrs
*CBN(AM) Saint John's, NF 3 hrs
CIVR-FM Yellowknife, NT 3 hrs
CJLX-FM Belleville, ON 1 hr
CFBG-FM Bracebridge, ON 1 hr
CFMJ(AM) Toronto, ON
*CIBL-FM Montreal, PQ 8 hrs
CINQ-FM Montreal, PQ 16 hrs

Polish

CJSR-FM Edmonton, AB 2 hrs
CKER-FM Edmonton, AB 6 hrs
*CFRO-FM Vancouver, BC 5 hrs
*CFUV-FM Victoria, BC 1 hr
CKJS(AM) Winnipeg, MB 7 hrs
CHCR-FM Killaloe, ON 1 hr
CKWR-FM Kitchener, ON 4 hrs
CKCU-FM Ottawa, ON 1 hr
*CKLU-FM Sudbury, ON 1 hr
CHWO(AM) Toronto, ON 2 hrs
*CJAM-FM Windsor, ON 1 hr
CFCR-FM Saskatoon, SK 1 hr

Portugese

CKER-FM Edmonton, AB 2 hrs
CFOK(AM) Westlock, AB 5 hrs
*CJSF-FM Burnaby, BC 2 hrs
CJOR(AM) Osoyoos, BC 3 hrs
CKJS(AM) Winnipeg, MB 8 hrs

CJDV-FM Cambridge, ON 2 hrs
CKWR-FM Kitchener, ON 5 hrs
CFBU-FM Saint Catharines, ON 2 hrs
CHWO(AM) Toronto, ON 11 hrs
CINQ-FM Montreal, PQ 12 hrs
*CJTR-FM Regina, SK 1 hr

Public Affairs

*CFPR(AM) Prince Rupert, BC
CHLN(AM) Trois Rivieres, PQ 8 hrs

Reggae

CKXL-FM Saint Boniface, MB 2 hrs
*CHMR-FM Saint John's, NF 2 hrs
*CFMU-FM Hamilton, ON 4 hrs
CKFM-FM Toronto, ON 1 hr
*CIBL-FM Montreal, PQ 4 hrs

Religious

CKDQ(AM) Drumheller, AB 2 hrs
CHLW(AM) Saint Paul, AB 5 hrs
CFOK(AM) Westlock, AB 6 hrs
CIVH(AM) Vanderhoof, BC 5 hrs
CHTM(AM) Thompson, MB 12 hrs
CFAN-FM Miramichi City, NB 4 hrs
CJCW(AM) Sussex, NB 4 hrs
*CHMR-FM Saint John's, NF 4 hrs
*VOWR(AM) Saint John's, NF 10 hrs

CFSX(AM) Stephenville, NF 1 hr
CHMS-FM Bancroft, ON 1 hr
CJSS-FM Cornwall, ON 1 hr
CFRU-FM Guelph, ON 1 hr
CHYR-FM Leamington, ON 3 hrs
CKDO(AM) Oshawa, ON 1 hr
CKGE-FM Oshawa, ON 1 hr
*CHUO-FM Ottawa, ON 2 hrs
CKCU-FM Ottawa, ON 3 hrs
CKTG-FM Thunder Bay, ON
CKNX(AM) Wingham, ON 6 hrs
CHRD-FM Drummondville, PQ 1 hr
*CFIN-FM Lac-Etchemin, PQ 1 hr
CJSL(AM) Estevan, SK 10 hrs
CKJH-FM Melfort, SK 9 hrs
CJNB(AM) North Battleford, SK 10 hrs
CJDJ-FM Saskatoon, SK 6 hrs
CFSL(AM) Weyburn, SK 9 hrs

Rock/AOR

CJDC(AM) Dawson Creek, BC 4 hrs
CKXL-FM Saint Boniface, MB 10 hrs wkly hrs
CHIP-FM Fort Coulonge, PQ

Scottish

CKEC(AM) New Glasgow, NS
CIGO-FM Port Hawkesbury, NS 2 hrs
CFBW-FM Hanover, ON 2 hrs
CJTN-FM Quinte West, ON 1 hr

Spanish

*CJSW-FM Calgary, AB 1 hr
CJSR-FM Edmonton, AB 2 hrs
CKER-FM Edmonton, AB 8 hrs
*CJSF-FM Burnaby, BC 4 hrs
CHMB(AM) Vancouver, BC 1 hr
*CITR-FM Vancouver, BC 2 hrs
*CFUV-FM Victoria, BC 2 hrs
CKXL-FM Saint Boniface, MB 2 hrs
CKJS(AM) Winnipeg, MB 3 hrs
CFRU-FM Guelph, ON
*CFMU-FM Hamilton, ON 1 hr
*CIOI-FM Hamilton, ON 3 hrs
CHOH-FM Hearst, ON 1 hr
CKWR-FM Kitchener, ON 4 hrs
*CHUO-FM Ottawa, ON 3 hrs
CFBU-FM Saint Catharines, ON 4 hrs
*CKLU-FM Sudbury, ON 1 hr
CHRY-FM Toronto, ON
CHWO(AM) Toronto, ON 3 hrs
*CIUT-FM Toronto, ON 4 hrs
*CJAM-FM Windsor, ON 1 hr
*CFIN-FM Lac-Etchemin, PQ
CHAA-FM Longueuil, PQ 3 hrs
CINQ-FM Montreal, PQ 16 hrs
*CKUT-FM Montreal, PQ 6 hrs
CKIA-FM Quebec, PQ 4 hrs
*CKRL-FM Quebec, PQ 2 hrs
CFLX-FM Sherbrooke, PQ 3 hrs
CFCR-FM Saskatoon, SK 2 hrs

Sports

CFFR(AM) Calgary, AB 15 hrs
CFCW(AM) Camrose, AB
CKFR(AM) Kelowna, BC 10 hrs
CHMS-FM Bancroft, ON 2 hrs
CFFX(AM) Kingston, ON
CJBX-FM London, ON
CHOK(AM) Sarnia, ON
CFMJ(AM) Toronto, ON

Talk

CISQ-FM Squamish, BC 5 hrs
CHMS-FM Bancroft, ON 5 hrs
CFMQ-FM Hudson Bay, SK

Ukranian

CKER-FM Edmonton, AB 10 hrs
CJRL-FM Kenora, ON 1 hr

Urban Contemporary

*CHYZ-FM Sainte Foy, PQ 15 hrs

Vietnamese

CHMB(AM) Vancouver, BC 2 hrs
CKCU-FM Ottawa, ON 1 hr
CHAA-FM Longueuil, PQ 5 hrs

U.S. Radio Markets

Abilene, TX: Rank 244
MSA: 132,400 TSA: 263,200
American Family Radio: KAQD(FM)
Clear Channel Communications Inc.: KEYJ-FM, KFGL(FM), KSLI(AM), KULL-FM, KYYW(AM)
Cumulus Media Inc.: KBCY(FM), KCDD(FM), KHXS-FM, KTLT(FM)

Akron, OH: Rank 73
MSA: 597,200 TSA: 1,301,600
Clear Channel Communications Inc.: WARF(AM), WHLO
Family Stations Inc.: WCUE
Rubber City Radio Group Inc.: WAKR, WQMX-FM

Albany, GA: Rank 269
MSA: 104,300 TSA: 485,400
Clear Channel Communications Inc.: WJYZ, WOBB-FM, WRAK-FM
Cumulus Media Inc.: WALG, WEGC-FM, WGPC, WJAD-FM, WQVE-FM
Good News Network: WZIQ-FM
On Top Communications Inc.: WFFM(FM), WRXZ(FM)

Albany-Schenectady-Troy, NY: Rank 62
MSA: 777,900 TSA: 1,348,400
ABC Inc.: WDDY(AM)
Anastos Media Group Inc.: WABY(AM), WQAR-FM, WUAM(AM), WVKZ
Capital Media Corp.: WHAZ, WMYY-FM, WZEC-FM
Clear Channel Communications Inc.: WGY, WHRL-FM, WKKF(FM), WOFX(AM), WPYX-FM, WTRY-FM
Crawford Broadcasting Co.: WDCD(AM), WPTR(FM)
Galaxy Communications L.P.: WEGQ(FM), WRCZ(FM)
Pamal Broadcasting Ltd.: WAJZ-FM, WENU(AM), WFLY-FM, WIZR, WKLI-FM, WROW, WZMR-FM
Regent Communications Inc.: WABT-FM, WGNA-FM, WQBJ-FM, WTMM
Vox Radio Group L.P.: WNYQ-FM, WUHN
WAMC/Northeast Public Radio: WAMC(AM), WAMC-FM, WCAN-FM

Albuquerque, NM: Rank 70
MSA: 654,200 TSA: 1,016,900
ABC Inc.: KALY
American General Media: KAGM(FM), KARS, KKIM, KLVO-FM
Citadel Broadcasting Corp.: KBZU(FM), KDRF(FM), KKOB, KKOB-FM, KNML(AM), KRST-FM, KTBL(AM)
Clear Channel Communications Inc.: KABQ, KABQ-FM, KBQI(FM), KPEK-FM, KTEG(FM), KZRR-FM
Entravision Communications Corp.: KRZY, KRZY-FM
Family Life Communications Inc.: KFLQ(FM)
Simmons Media Group: KKNS(AM)
Univision Radio: KAJZ(FM), KIOT-FM, KJFA(FM), KKRG(FM), KKSS-FM
Wilkins Communications Network Inc.: KXKS

Alexandria, LA: Rank 221
MSA: 157,900 TSA: 405,500
American Family Radio: KAPM(FM)
Clear Channel Communications Inc.: KDBS, KKST-FM, KZMZ-FM
EMF Broadcasting: KLXA-FM, KWDF
Opus Media Holdings LLC: KBKK(FM), KEZP-FM, KLAA(FM)
Radio Maria Inc.: KJMJ(AM)
The Radio Group: KAPB-FM

Allentown-Bethlehem, PA: Rank 68
MSA: 682,500 TSA: 938,400
Citadel Broadcasting Corp.: WCTO-FM, WLEV-FM
Clear Channel Communications Inc.: WAEB, WKAP, WZZO-FM
J-Systems Franchising Corp.: WLSH
Nassau Broadcasting Partners L.P.: WEEX, WTKZ, WWYY-FM, WYNS

Altoona, PA: Rank 265
MSA: 110,000 TSA: 523,200
Allegheny Mountain Network Stations: WKMC, WTRN
Forever Broadcasting: WALY-FM, WFBG, WRKY-FM, WVAM, WWOT(FM)

Amarillo, TX: Rank 195
MSA: 191,200 TSA: 332,300
American Family Radio: KAVW(FM)
Clear Channel Communications Inc.: KATP(FM), KIXZ, KMML-FM, KMXJ-FM
Cumulus Media Inc.: KARX(FM), KPUR, KPUR-FM, KQIZ-FM, KZRK-FM
EMF Broadcasting: KXLV(FM), KXRI(FM)
Family Life Communications Inc.: KRGN-FM
Morris Radio LLC: KGNC
Tejas Broadcasting Ltd. LLP: KBZD(FM), KQFX-FM, KTNZ

Anchorage, AK: Rank 172
MSA: 228,900 TSA: 330,200
American Radio Brokers Inc./SFO: KADX(FM), KAXX
Clear Channel Communications Inc.: KASH-FM, KBFX(FM), KENI, KGOT-FM, KTZN, KYMG-FM
EMF Broadcasting: KAKL(FM)
Morris Radio LLC: KBRJ(FM), KEAG-FM, KFQD, KHAR, KMXS-FM, KWHL-FM
New Northwest Broadcasters LLC: KDBZ(FM), KFAT(FM), KQEZ-FM

Ann Arbor, MI: Rank 147
MSA: 295,400 TSA: 295,000
WDEO(AM)
Birach Broadcasting Corp.: WSDS(AM)
Clear Channel Communications Inc.: WLBY(AM), WTKA, WWWW(FM)
First Broadcasting Investment Partners LLC: WAAM

Appleton-Oshkosh, WI: Rank 134
MSA: 320,300 TSA: 884,200
Cumulus Media Inc.: WNAM, WOGB-FM, WOSH, WPKR-FM, WWWX-FM
Midwest Communications Inc.: WNCY-FM, WOZZ-FM, WROE-FM
Mountain Dog Media: WFON(FM)
Relevant Radio: WJOK
Results Broadcasting: WFCL, WJMQ(FM)
VCY America Inc.: WVCY
Woodward Communications Inc.: WAPL-FM, WHBY(AM), WSCO(AM)

Asheville, NC: Rank 161
MSA: 255,600 TSA: 502,600
Clear Channel Communications Inc.: WPEK(AM), WQNQ(FM), WWNC
Wilkins Communications Network Inc.: WSKY(AM)

Atlanta, GA: Rank 10
MSA: 3,860,100 TSA: 5,183,700
ABC Inc.: WDWD, WYAY-FM
Beasley Broadcast Group Inc.: WAEC, WWWE(AM)
Clear Channel Communications Inc.: WBZY(FM), WCOH, WGST, WKLS(FM), WVVA(FM), WWVA-FM
Cox Enterprises Inc.: WALR-FM, WBTS(FM), WFOX(FM), WSB, WSB-FM
Davis Broadcasting Inc.: WLKQ-FM
Dickey Broadcasting Co.: WALR, WCNN, WFOM
GHB Radio Group: WYZE
Infinity Broadcasting Corp.: WAOK, WZGC-FM
Jacobs Media Corp.: WGGA
Jefferson-Pilot Communications Co.: WQXI, WSTR-FM
La Favorita Inc.: WAOS(AM), WXEM
Multicultural Radio Broadcasting Inc.: WGFS
Radio One Inc.: WAMJ(FM), WHTA(FM), WPZE(FM)
Salem Communications Corp.: WAFS(AM), WFSH-FM, WGKA(AM), WLTA, WNIV
Susquehanna Radio Corp.: WNNX-FM, WWWQ(FM)
Willis Broadcasting Corp.: WTJH

Atlantic City-Cape May, NJ: Rank 135
MSA: 318,100 TSA: 537,600
Access.1 Communications Corp.: WGYM(AM), WMGM-FM, WOND, WTKU-FM, WUSS(AM)
Equity Communications LP: WAIV(FM), WAYV(FM), WCMC(AM), WDTH(FM), WGBZ(FM), WMID(AM), WTTH(FM), WZBZ(FM), WZXL(FM)
Millennium Radio Group LLC: WFPG-FM, WIXM(FM), WKXW(AM), WPUR-FM, WSJO(FM)
Press Communications L.L.C.: WKOE-FM

Augusta, GA: Rank 112
MSA: 414,400 TSA: 601,600
Beasley Broadcast Group Inc.: WCHZ-FM, WGAC, WGAC-FM, WGOR(FM), WGUS(AM), WKDG-FM, WKXC-FM, WRDW(AM), WSLT-FM
Bible Broadcasting Network: WYFA-FM
Clear Channel Communications Inc.: WBBQ-FM, WIBL(FM), WKSP(FM), WPCH(AM)
Cumulus Media Inc.: WPRW-FM
Eastern Broadcasting Group Inc.: WNRR(AM)
Radio One Inc.: WAEG-FM, WAKB-FM, WFXA-FM, WTHB-FM
Wilkins Communications Network Inc.: WFAM(AM)

Augusta-Waterville, ME: Rank 267
MSA: 106,400 TSA: 433,500
Atlantic Coast Radio L.L.C.: WLOB-FM
Citadel Broadcasting Corp.: WEBB-FM, WJZN(AM), WMME-FM, WTVL(AM)
Clear Channel Communications Inc.: WFAU, WKCG-FM, WTOS-FM
Mountain Wireless Inc.: WCTB-FM, WHQO-FM, WSKW

Austin, TX: Rank 42
MSA: 1,204,800 TSA: 1,800,400
KHHL(FM), KKLB-FM
Border Media Partners LLC: KELG(AM), KFON, KTXZ, KXXS(FM)
Clear Channel Communications Inc.: KASE-FM, KFMK-FM, KHFI-FM, KPEZ-FM, KVET-FM
Emmis Communications Corp.: KBPA(FM), KDHT(FM), KGSR-FM, KLBJ, KROX-FM
Houston Christian Broadcasters Inc.: KHIB(FM)
Infinity Broadcasting Corp.: KAMX(FM), KJCE, KKMJ-FM
Simmons Media Group: KWNX(AM), KZNX(AM)
Univision Radio: KINV(FM)

Bakersfield, CA: Rank 81
MSA: 542,500 TSA: 584,600
American General Media: KBID, KERI(AM), KERN, KGEO, KISV-FM, KKXX-FM
Buck Owens Productions Inc.: KUZZ
Buckley Broadcasting Corp.: KKBB-FM, KLLY-FM, KNZR, KSMJ(FM)
Clear Channel Communications Inc.: KDFO(AM), KDFO-FM, KGET(AM)
Family Stations Inc.: KFRB-FM
IHR Educational Broadcasting: KJPG(AM)
Lotus Communications Corp.: KCHJ, KIWI(FM), KPSL-FM, KWAC

Baltimore, MD: Rank 21
MSA: 2,249,900 TSA: 3,020,000
WFBR(AM), WTTR(AM)
Clear Channel Communications Inc.: WCAO, WPOC-FM, WSMJ(FM)
Family Stations Inc.: WBGR, WBMD
First Broadcasting Investment Partners LLC: WAMD
Infinity Broadcasting Corp.: WHFS(FM), WJFK, WQSR(FM), WWMX-FM
Radio One Inc.: WERQ-FM, WWIN, WWIN-FM
Salem Communications Corp.: WITH(AM)
Shamrock Communications Inc.: WZBA(FM)

Bangor, ME: Rank 216
MSA: 163,900 TSA: 428,600
WNSX(FM)
Clear Channel Communications Inc.: WABI, WBFB-FM, WGUY-FM, WKSQ-FM, WVOM-FM
Cumulus Media Inc.: WBZN-FM, WEZQ-FM, WQCB-FM
Daniel F. Priestley Stns: WNZS(AM)
The Zone Corp.: WKIT-FM, WZON

Baton Rouge, LA: Rank 83
MSA: 529,100 TSA: 1,350,200
Citadel Broadcasting Corp.: KQXL-FM, KRDJ(FM), WCDV(FM), WEMX-FM, WIBR, WXOK
Clear Channel Communications Inc.: KRVE-FM, WJBO, WPYR(AM), WSKR, WYNK-FM
EMF Broadcasting: WQCK-FM
Family Worship Center Church Inc.: WJFM-FM
Guaranty Broadcasting Co.: KNXX(FM), WDGL-FM, WNXX(FM), WTGE-FM, WYPY(FM)

Battle Creek, MI: Rank 259
MSA: 117,100 TSA: 117,000
WOLY
Clear Channel Communications Inc.: WBCK, WRCC, WWKN-FM
Family Life Communications Inc.: WUFN(FM)

Beaumont-Port Arthur, TX: Rank 133
MSA: 321,800 TSA: 564,200
Clear Channel Communications Inc.: KCOL-FM, KIOC-FM, KKMY-FM, KLVI, KYKR-FM
Cumulus Media Inc.: KAYD-FM, KBED(AM), KIKR, KQXY-FM, KTCX-FM
Family Stations Inc.: KTXB-FM
Radio Maria Inc.: KDEI(AM)

Beckley, WV: Rank 294
MSA: 68,700 TSA: 284,000
First Media Radio LLC: WJLS-FM
Southern Communications Corp.: WAXS-FM, WCIR-FM, WIWS, WMTD, WMTD-FM, WTNJ-FM, WWNR

Bend, OR: Rank 224
MSA: 156,500 TSA: 151,700

Billings, MT: Rank 261
MSA: 115,800 TSA: 192,900
Clear Channel Communications Inc.: KBBB(FM), KBUL, KCTR-FM, KKBR-FM, KMHK-FM
EMF Broadcasting: KLRV(FM)
Fisher Broadcasting Company: KBLG, KRKX(FM), KRZN(FM), KYYA-FM

Broadcasting & Cable Yearbook 2006

U.S. Radio Markets

New Northwest Broadcasters LLC: KGHL, KGHL-FM, KQBL(FM), KRSQ-FM, KZRV(FM)
Sun Mountain Inc.: KBSR

Biloxi-Gulfport-Pascagoula, MS: Rank 138
MSA: 314,500 TSA: 501,000
American Family Radio: WAOY-FM
Clear Channel Communications Inc.: WKNN-FM, WMJY-FM, WQYZ-FM
Triad Broadcasting Co. L.L.C.: WCPR-FM, WTNI(AM), WUJM(FM), WXBD, WXRG-FM, WXYK-FM

Binghamton, NY: Rank 179
MSA: 214,900 TSA: 294,200
Citadel Broadcasting Corp.: WNBF, WWYL(FM), WYOS(AM)
Clear Channel Communications Inc.: WBBI(FM), WENE(AM), WINR, WKGB-FM, WMXW-FM
CSN International: WIFF(FM)
Double O Radio Corp.: WIYN-FM

Birmingham, AL: Rank 57
MSA: 865,600 TSA: 1,863,300
Citadel Broadcasting Corp.: WAPI, WFFN-FM, WJOX, WRAX(FM), WUHT(FM), WYSF-FM, WZRR-FM
Clear Channel Communications Inc.: WDXB(FM), WENN(FM), WMJJ-FM, WQEN(FM)
Cox Enterprises Inc.: WAGG(AM), WBHJ-FM, WBHK-FM, WBPT(FM), WNCB(FM), WZZK(FM), WZZK-FM
Crawford Broadcasting Co.: WDJC-FM, WXJC(AM), WXJC-FM, WYDE(AM), WYDE-FM
Family Stations Inc.: WBFR-FM
Joy Christian Communications Inc.: WLYJ(AM)
MCL/MCM-Inc.: WATV
Willis Broadcasting Corp.: WAYE

Bismarck, ND: Rank 286
MSA: 85,000 TSA: 202,500
Clear Channel Communications Inc.: KBMR, KFYR, KQDY(FM), KSSS-FM, KXMR
Cumulus Media Inc.: KACL(FM), KKCT-FM, KLXX
EMF Broadcasting: KNRI(FM)
Family Stations Inc.: KBFR(FM)

Bloomington, IL: Rank 242
MSA: 136,100 TSA: 240,600
Back Bay Broadcasters Inc.: WIHN-FM, WYST(FM)
Regent Communications Inc.: WBWN-FM, WJBC

Bluefield, WV: Rank 280
MSA: 92,300 TSA: 218,000
Baker Family Stations: WAMN
Peggy Sue Broadcasting Corp.: WRIC-FM
Triad Broadcasting Co. L.L.C.: WBDY, WHIS, WHQX-FM, WKEZ, WKOY-FM, WTZE

Boise, ID: Rank 108
MSA: 416,100 TSA: 631,700
Citadel Broadcasting Corp.: KBOI, KIZN-FM, KKGL-FM, KQFC-FM, KTIK, KZMG(FM)
Clear Channel Communications Inc.: KCIX(FM), KFXD(FM), KIDO(AM), KSAS-FM, KXLT-FM
Journal Communications Inc.: KCID, KGEM, KQXR-FM, KRVB(FM)
KSPD Inc.: KBXL(FM), KSPD
Locally Owned Radio LLC: KISY(FM), KTPZ(FM)

Boston: Rank 11
MSA: 3,841,100 TSA: 6,619,400
WAMG(AM), WBIX(AM), WLLH
ABC Inc.: WMKI(AM)
Beasley Broadcast Group Inc.: WRCA
Bob Bittner Broadcasting Inc.: WJIB
Clear Channel Communications Inc.: WJMN-FM, WKOX, WXKS
Costa-Eagle Radio Ventures L.P.: WCCM(AM), WNNW(AM)
Entercom Communications Corp.: WEEI, WQSX(FM), WRKO
Greater Media Inc.: WBOS-FM, WKLB-FM, WMJX-FM, WROR-FM, WTKK(FM)
Infinity Broadcasting Corp.: WBCN-FM, WBMX-FM, WBZ, WODS-FM, WZLX-FM
Langer Broadcasting Group L.L.C.: WSRO(AM)
Multicultural Radio Broadcasting Inc.: WAZN(AM), WLYN
Northeast Broadcasting Company Inc.: WXRV-FM
Phoenix Media Communications Group: WFEX(FM), WFNX(FM)
Radio One Inc.: WBOT(FM), WILD
Rose City Radio Corp.: WWZN(AM)
Salem Communications Corp.: WEZE, WROL, WTTT(AM)

Bowling Green, KY: Rank 211
MSA: 168,800 TSA: 279,400
Commonwealth Broadcasting Corp.: WCDS(AM), WHHT(FM), WOVO(FM), WPTQ(FM)
Forever Communications Inc.: WBGN(AM), WBVR-FM, WLYE-FM, WUHU(FM)

Bridgeport, CT: Rank 120
MSA: 395,600 TSA: 389,200
Blount Communications Group: WFIF
Cox Enterprises Inc.: WEZN-FM
Cumulus Media Inc.: WICC

Brunswick, GA: Rank 297
MSA: 61,200 TSA: 186,100
Qantum Communications Corp.: WBGA(FM), WGIG(AM), WHFX(FM), WMOG, WWSN-FM, WYNR(FM)

Bryan-College Station, TX: Rank 239
MSA: 138,300 TSA: 243,700
Bryan Broadcasting Corp.: KZNE(AM), WTAW(AM)
Clear Channel Communications Inc.: KAGG(FM), KKYS-FM, KNFX-FM
Equicom Inc.: KTAM, KXCS(FM), KZTR-FM
Fort Bend Broadcasting Co.: KHTZ(FM)

Buffalo-Niagara Falls, NY: Rank 52
MSA: 989,000 TSA: 1,403,500
Citadel Broadcasting Corp.: WBBF(AM), WEDG-FM, WGRF-FM, WHLD, WHTT-FM
Corus Entertainment Inc.: CFNY-FM
Crawford Broadcasting Co.: WDCX-FM
Entercom Communications Corp.: WBEN, WGR, WKSE-FM, WLKK(FM), WWKB, WWWS
Family Stations Inc.: WFBF-FM
Infinity Broadcasting Corp.: WBLK(FM), WBUF(FM), WECK, WJYE-FM, WYRK-FM

Burlington, VT: Rank 136
MSA: 317,100 TSA: 508,200
Clear Channel Communications Inc.: WCPV-FM, WEAV, WEZF-FM, WVTK(FM), WXZO(FM)
Deer Creek Broadcasting LLC: WIZN-FM
Hall Communications Inc.: WJOY, WKOL-FM, WOKO-FM
Northeast Broadcasting Company Inc.: WNCS-FM, WTWK(AM), WWMP(FM)
Radio Vermont Group Inc.: WCVT-FM, WDEV-FM, WVAA(AM)

Canton, OH: Rank 129
MSA: 350,000 TSA: 435,400
Clear Channel Communications Inc.: WKDD(FM)
Cumulus Media Inc.: WRQK-FM
NextMedia Group Inc.: WHBC

Cape Cod, MA: Rank 185
MSA: 203,400 TSA: 230,200
WDVT(FM), WPXC-FM, WTWV(FM)
Qantum Communications Corp.: WCIB-FM, WCOD-FM, WRZE-FM, WXTK-FM
Sandab Communications L.P. II: WOCN-FM, WQRC(FM)

Casper, WY: Rank 298
MSA: 59,100 TSA: 138,000
Clear Channel Communications Inc.: KKTL, KRVK(FM), KTRS-FM, KTWO, KWYY-FM
Mt. Rushmore Broadcasting Inc.: KASS(FM), KHOC-FM, KMLD(FM), KQLT-FM, KVOC

Cedar Rapids, IA: Rank 214
MSA: 166,300 TSA: 665,800
Clear Channel Communications Inc.: KKRQ-FM, KMJM(AM), KXIC, WMT, WMT-FM
Cumulus Media Inc.: KDAT(FM), KHAK-FM, KRNA-FM

Champaign, IL: Rank 220
MSA: 160,200 TSA: 489,500
Back Bay Broadcasters Inc.: WEBX-FM, WEVX(FM), WGKC-FM, WQQB(FM)
Illinois Bible Institute Inc.: WBGL-FM
Saga Communications Inc.: WCFF(FM), WIXY-FM, WLRW-FM, WXTT(FM)

Charleston, SC: Rank 88
MSA: 500,500 TSA: 729,100
Apex Broadcasting Inc.: WAVF-FM, WXST(FM)
Bible Broadcasting Network: WYFH-FM
Citadel Broadcasting Corp.: WMGL-FM, WNKT-FM, WSSX-FM, WSUY-FM, WTMA, WWWZ-FM, WXTC
Clear Channel Communications Inc.: WALC-FM, WEZL-FM, WLTQ(AM), WRFQ-FM, WSCC-FM, WXLY-FM
Family Stations Inc.: WFCH-FM
Glory Communications Inc.: WTUA-FM
Jabar Communications Inc.: WAZS(AM), WAZS-FM
Kirkman Communications Inc.: WQNT(FM), WQSC, WQTK(AM), WTMZ
L M Communications Inc.: WCOO(FM), WYBB-FM

Charleston, WV: Rank 181
MSA: 214,100 TSA: 561,500
Baker Family Stations: WOKU
Bristol Broadcasting Co. Inc.: WBES(AM), WVTS(AM), WZJO(FM)
L M Communications Inc.: WJYP(AM), WSCW
West Virginia Radio Corp.: WKAZ-FM, WRVZ-FM, WSWW

Charlotte-Gastonia-Rock Hill, NC-SC: Rank 35
MSA: 1,409,800 TSA: 2,909,500
ABC Inc.: WGFY
Bible Broadcasting Network: WYFQ(AM)
Clear Channel Communications Inc.: WEND-FM, WIBT(FM), WKKT-FM, WLYT-FM, WRFX-FM
Davidson Media Group LLC: WBZK, WNOW
Ford Broadcasting Inc.: WRKB, WRNA
GHB Radio Group: WAVO, WCGC, WEGO, WHVN, WNMX-FM
Infinity Broadcasting Corp.: WBAV-FM, WFNA(AM), WFNZ, WKQC(FM), WPEG-FM, WSOC-FM
Jefferson-Pilot Communications Co.: WBT, WBT-FM
Neely Enterprises: WLTC
Norsan Consulting and Management Inc.: WGSP, WXNC(AM)
Our Three Sons Broadcasting L.L.P.: WRHI
Radio One Inc.: WQNC(FM)
Truth Broadcasting Corp.: WZRH(AM)

Charlottesville, VA: Rank 231
MSA: 147,200 TSA: 331,300
Baker Family Stations: WKTR
Clear Channel Communications Inc.: WCHV, WCJZ(FM), WCYK-FM, WHTE-FM, WKAV, WSUH(FM)
Piedmont Communications Inc.: WOJL(FM)
Saga Communications Inc.: WINA, WQMZ(FM), WWWV-FM

Chattanooga, TN: Rank 106
MSA: 420,900 TSA: 1,024,900
WNOO
Bahakel Communications: WDEF-FM, WDOD
Citadel Broadcasting Corp.: WGOW, WGOW-FM, WOGT-FM
Clear Channel Communications Inc.: WKXJ(FM), WMAX-FM, WRXR-FM, WTUN(FM), WUSY-FM, WUUS(AM)
The Moody Bible Institute of Chicago: WMBW-FM
Wilkins Communications Network Inc.: WLMR(AM)
Willis Broadcasting Corp.: WSDT

Cheyenne, WY: Rank 291
MSA: 72,900 TSA: 122,000
American Family Radio: KWYH(FM)
Clear Channel Communications Inc.: KCGY(FM), KGAB, KIGN(FM), KLEN-FM, KQLF(FM)
Northeast Broadcasting Company Inc.: KHAT(AM), KRAE, KSHF(FM)
Regent Communications Inc.: KARS-FM, KKPL(FM)

Chicago: Rank 3
MSA: 7,698,300 TSA: 9,111,600
ABC Inc.: WLS, WMVP, WPJX(AM), WRDZ, WZZN(FM)
Birach Broadcasting Corp.: WNWI
Bonneville International Corporation: WDRV(FM), WILV(FM), WTMX-FM, WWDV(FM)
Clear Channel Communications Inc.: WGCI-FM, WGRB(AM), WKSC-FM, WLIT-FM, WNUA-FM, WVAZ-FM
Crawford Broadcasting Co.: WPWX(FM), WSRB(FM), WYCA(FM)
EMF Broadcasting: WCLR(FM), WSRI(FM)
Emmis Communications Corp.: WKQX-FM, WLUP-FM
Family Stations Inc.: WJCH-FM
Infinity Broadcasting Corp.: WBBM, WCKG-FM, WJMK-FM, WSCR(AM), WUSN-FM, WXRT-FM
Kovas Communications of Indiana Inc.: WCGO, WKKD
McNaughton-Jakle Stations: WBIG, WJKL-FM, WRMN
Multicultural Radio Broadcasting Inc.: WNTD
Newsweb Corp.: WAIT(AM), WCFJ, WCPT(AM), WKIE-FM, WNDZ, WRZA(FM), WSBC(AM)
NextMedia Group Inc.: WERV-FM, WJOL, WKRS, WLIP, WRXQ(FM), WWYW(FM), WXLC-FM, WZSR-FM
Polnet Communications Ltd.: WEEF, WKTA, WNVR
Porter County Broadcasting Corp.: WAKE, WLJE-FM, WXRD-FM, WZVN-FM
Relevant Radio: WAUR, WWCA
Salem Communications Corp.: WIND, WYLL(FM)
Spanish Broadcasting System Inc.: WLEY-FM
STARadio Corp.: WYKT-FM
The Moody Bible Institute of Chicago: WMBI(AM), WMBI-FM
Three Eagles Communications: WCCQ-FM
Tribune Broadcasting Co.: WGN(AM)
Univision Radio: WOJO-FM, WPPN(FM), WRTO(AM), WVIV-FM, WVIX(FM)

Chico, CA: Rank 199
MSA: 186,000 TSA: 407,600
Deer Creek Broadcasting LLC: KHHZ(FM), KHSL-FM, KMXI-FM, KPAY
Family Stations Inc.: KHAP(FM)
Fritz Communications Inc.: KCEZ(FM), KKCY-FM, KLRS-FM, KMJE-FM, KRQR-FM, KTHU(FM)

Broadcasting & Cable Yearbook 2006

U.S. Radio Markets

Regent Communications Inc.: KALF(FM), KFMF-FM, KQPT(FM), KZAP-FM

Cincinnati, OH: Rank 28
MSA: 1,705,200 TSA: 2,478,700
Clear Channel Communications Inc.: WCKY(AM), WKFS-FM, WKRC, WLW, WSAI(AM), WVMX-FM
EMF Broadcasting: WJYC(FM)
First Broadcasting Investment Partners LLC: WAOL-FM, WAXZ-FM, WOXY-FM
Infinity Broadcasting Corp.: WAQZ(FM), WGRR-FM, WKRQ-FM, WUBE-FM
Pillar of Fire Inc.: WAKW-FM
Plessinger Radio Group: WCVG
Radio One Inc.: WIZF-FM
Salem Communications Corp.: WBOB, WTSJ
Susquehanna Radio Corp.: WMOJ-FM, WRRM-FM, WYGY(FM)
Vernon R Baldwin Inc.: WCNW, WMOH, WNLT-FM

Clarksville-Hopkinsville, TN-KY: Rank 206
MSA: 171,900 TSA: 221,900
Key Broadcasting Inc.: WHOP(AM), WHOP-FM
Saga Communications Inc.: WEGI(FM), WVVR(FM)

Cleveland, OH: Rank 25
MSA: 1,799,900 TSA: 3,294,300
WCCD(AM)
ABC Inc.: WWMK
Clear Channel Communications Inc.: WGAR-FM, WMJI-FM, WMMS-FM, WTAM
Elyria-Lorain Broadcasting Co.: WEOL
Infinity Broadcasting Corp.: WDOK-FM, WNCX(FM), WQAL-FM, WXTM(FM)
Radio One Inc.: WENZ-FM, WERE, WJMO, WZAK-FM
Salem Communications Corp.: WFHM-FM, WHK(AM), WHKW(AM), WKNR(AM)
The Moody Bible Institute of Chicago: WCRF-FM

Colorado Springs, CO: Rank 97
MSA: 460,400 TSA: 771,600
Bahakel Communications: KILO-FM
Citadel Broadcasting Corp.: KKFM-FM, KKMG-FM, KKML(AM), KVOR
Clear Channel Communications Inc.: KIBT(FM), KKLI-FM, KVUU-FM
Crawford Broadcasting Co.: KCBR, KCMN
Latino Communications LLC: KXRE
Pikes Peak Broadcasting Co.: KRDO(AM)
Salem Communications Corp.: KBIQ(FM), KGFT-FM, KZNT(AM)
Superior Broadcasting of Denver LLC: KKCS-FM

Columbia, MO: Rank 258
MSA: 122,400 TSA: 590,500
Best Broadcast Group: KZZT-FM
Cumulus Media Inc.: KBXR(FM), KFRU, KOQL-FM, KPLA(FM)
The Curators of the University of Missouri: KBIA(FM)
Zimmer Radio Group: KATI(FM), KFAL, KTXY-FM

Columbia, SC: Rank 90
MSA: 485,400 TSA: 855,000
WQKI(AM)
Bible Broadcasting Network: WYFV-FM
Citadel Broadcasting Corp.: WISW, WLXC-FM, WTCB-FM
Clear Channel Communications Inc.: WCOS, WLTY-FM, WNOK(FM), WVOC, WXBT(FM)
Double O Radio Corp.: WWNQ(FM), WWNU(FM)
Eastern Broadcasting Group Inc.: WCEO(AM)
Glory Communications Inc.: WFMV(FM), WGCV(AM)
Good News Network: WBLR
Inner City Broadcasting: WARQ(AM), WHXT-FM, WMFX(FM), WOIC(AM), WWDM(FM), WZMJ-FM
Miller Communications Inc.: WIGL(FM)

Columbus, GA: Rank 187
MSA: 201,000 TSA: 560,300
Archway Broadcasting Group: WCGQ-FM, WKCN-FM, WRCG, WRLD-FM
Bible Broadcasting Network: WYFK-FM
Clear Channel Communications Inc.: WAGH-FM, WDAK, WGSY-FM, WHAL(AM), WSHE-FM, WSTH-FM, WVRK-FM
Davis Broadcasting Inc.: WEAM, WEAM-FM, WIOL(FM), WKZJ(FM), WOKS
Family Stations Inc.: WFRC-FM

Columbus, OH: Rank 38
MSA: 1,401,300 TSA: 2,122,200
Clear Channel Communications Inc.: WCOL-FM, WFJX-FM, WLZT-FM, WNCI-FM, WQIO-FM, WTVN(AM)
Dispatch Broadcast Group: WBNS, WBNS-FM
Infinity Broadcasting Corp.: WAZU-FM, WHOK-FM, WLVQ-FM
North American Broadcasting Co. Inc.: WBZX-FM, WMNI, WTDA(FM)
Radio One Inc.: WCKX-FM, WJYD(FM), WXMG-FM
Saga Communications Inc.: WJZA-FM, WJZK(FM), WODB(FM), WSNY-FM
Salem Communications Corp.: WRFD(AM)

Columbus-Starkville-West Point, MS: Rank 271
MSA: 102,200 TSA: 223,500
WTWG(AM)
Air South Radio Inc.: WLZA(FM)
American Family Radio: WCSO(FM), WJZB(FM)
Cumulus Media Inc.: WJWF(AM), WKOR(AM), WKOR-FM, WSMS(FM), WSSO(AM)
TeleSouth Communications Inc.: WROB(AM)
Urban Radio Licenses LLC: WMSU(FM)

Concord (Lake Regions), NH: Rank 169
MSA: 233,400 TSA: 409,100

Cookeville, TN: Rank 285
MSA: 85,400 TSA: 286,200
Clear Channel Communications Inc.: WHUB, WPTN
JWC Broadcasting: WKXD-FM

Corpus Christi, TX: Rank 139
MSA: 313,600 TSA: 465,200
Clear Channel Communications Inc.: KMXR-FM, KNCN-FM, KRYS-FM, KSAB-FM, KUNO
Convergent Broadcasting LLC: KJKE(FM), KKPN(FM)
EMF Broadcasting: KKLM(FM)
Malkan Broadcast Associates: KEYS, KKBA(FM), KZFM(FM)
Tejas Broadcasting Ltd. LLP: KLHB(FM), KLTG-FM, KMJR(FM), KOUL-FM
World Radio Network Inc.: KBNJ(FM)

Dallas-Fort Worth: Rank 5
MSA: 4,730,200 TSA: 6,104,000
ABC Inc.: KESN(FM), KMKI, KTYS(FM), WBAP
Border Media Partners LLC: KFJZ, KJON(AM), KXEB(AM)
Clear Channel Communications Inc.: KDGE(FM), KDMX(FM), KEGL-FM, KFXR(AM), KHKS-FM, KZPS-FM
Crawford Broadcasting Co.: KAAM(AM)
Criswell Communications: KCBI(FM)
Entravision Communications Corp.: KTCY(FM), KZMP(AM), KZMP-FM
First Broadcasting Investment Partners LLC: KCLE(AM), KJSA, KMGS(AM)
Infinity Broadcasting Corp.: KJKK(FM), KLLI(FM), KLUV-FM, KOAI-FM, KRLD, KVIL-FM
LKCM Radio Group L.P.: KFWR(FM), KRVA-FM, KRVF(FM)
M&M Broadcasters Ltd.: KTFW(AM)
Mortenson Broadcasting Co.: KGGR, KHVN, KKGM(AM), KRVA, KTNO(AM)
Multicultural Radio Broadcasting Inc.: KMNY(AM)
Radio One Inc.: KBFB(FM), KSOC(FM)
Salem Communications Corp.: KLTY(FM), KNIT(AM), KSKY(AM)
Susquehanna Radio Corp.: KDBN(FM), KLIF(AM), KPLX(FM), KTCK, KTDK(FM)
Univision Radio: KDXX(FM), KFLC(AM), KFZO(FM), KLNO(FM)

Danbury, CT: Rank 196
MSA: 188,000 TSA: 184,900
Berkshire Broadcasting Corp.: WLAD, WREF
Cumulus Media Inc.: WDBY(FM), WINE

Dayton, OH: Rank 58
MSA: 835,400 TSA: 1,706,600
Clear Channel Communications Inc.: WDKF(FM), WIZE, WLQT-FM, WMMX-FM, WONE, WTUE-FM, WXEG-FM
Cox Enterprises Inc.: WDPT(FM), WHIO, WHKO-FM, WZLR(FM)
EMF Broadcasting: WOKL(FM)
Radio One Inc.: WDHT(FM), WGTZ-FM, WING, WKSW-FM, WROU-FM
WPAY/WPFB Inc.: WPFB, WPFB-FM

Daytona Beach, FL: Rank 89
MSA: 500,300 TSA: 481,800
Black Crow Media Group LLC: WHOG-FM, WKRO-FM, WNDA(AM), WNDB, WVYB-FM
Gore-Overgaard Broadcasting Inc.: WROD
Mega Communications Inc.: WNUE-FM
Renda Broadcasting Corp.: WGNE-FM

Decatur, IL: Rank 279
MSA: 93,000 TSA: 182,200
NextMedia Group Inc.: WDZ(AM), WSOY-FM
The Cromwell Group Inc.: WZNX(FM), WZUS(FM)

Denver-Boulder, CO: Rank 22
MSA: 2,157,700 TSA: 3,296,900
KNRV(AM)
Clear Channel Communications Inc.: KBCO-FM, KBPI(FM), KHOW, KKZN(AM), KMGG(FM), KOA, KRFX-FM, KTCL-FM
Crawford Broadcasting Co.: KLDC, KLTT, KLVZ(AM), KLZ
EMF Broadcasting: KLDV(FM)
Entercom Communications Corp.: KALC(FM), KEZW, KOSI-FM, KQMT(FM)
Entravision Communications Corp.: KJMN-FM, KMXA, KXPK-FM
Infinity Broadcasting Corp.: KDJM(FM), KIMN-FM, KXKL-FM
Jefferson-Pilot Communications Co.: KCKK, KJCD(FM), KKFN
Latino Communications LLC: KBNO(AM)
NRC Broadcasting Inc.: KCUV(AM)
Pillar of Fire Inc.: KPOF
Salem Communications Corp.: KBJD, KNUS, KRKS(AM), KRKS-FM

Des Moines, IA: Rank 91
MSA: 483,600 TSA: 982,800
Citadel Broadcasting Corp.: KGGO-FM, KHKI-FM, KJJY(FM), KWQW(FM)
Clear Channel Communications Inc.: KASI, KCCQ(FM), KDRB(FM), KKDM-FM, KXNO(AM), WHO(AM)
Family Stations Inc.: KDFR(FM)
Northwestern College & Radio: KNWI(FM), KNWM(FM)
Saga Communications Inc.: KAZR(FM), KIOA(FM), KLTI-FM, KSTZ(FM)

Detroit: Rank 9
MSA: 3,892,600 TSA: 5,233,800
ABC Inc.: WDRQ-FM, WJR
Birach Broadcasting Corp.: WNZK, WPON
Christian Broadcasting System Ltd.: WLQV
CHUM Ltd.: CKLW, CKWW
Clear Channel Communications Inc.: WDFN, WDTW(AM), WDTW-FM, WJLB-FM, WKQI-FM, WMXD-FM, WNIC-FM
Crawford Broadcasting Co.: WEXL, WMUZ-FM, WRDT(AM)
Davidson Media Group LLC: WMKM
Family Life Communications Inc.: WUFL
Greater Media Inc.: WCSX-FM, WMGC-FM, WRIF(FM)
Infinity Broadcasting Corp.: WOMC-FM, WVMV-FM, WWJ, WXYT, WYCD-FM
Liggett Communications L.L.C.: WHLX(AM), WPHM
Radio One Inc.: WCHB, WDMK(FM), WHTD(FM)
Salem Communications Corp.: WDTK(AM)

Dothan, AL: Rank 193
MSA: 195,200 TSA: 479,100
Styles Media Group LLC: WKMX-FM, WLDA(FM), WQLS-FM, WTVY-FM
Wilson Broadcasting Inc.: WAGF, WAGF-FM, WJJN-FM

Dubuque, IA: Rank 235
MSA: 141,200 TSA: 217,000
American Family Radio: KIAD(FM)
Cumulus Media Inc.: KLYV-FM, KXGE-FM, WDBQ, WDBQ-FM, WJOD-FM
Morgan Murphy Stations (Evening Telegram Co): WGLR, WPVL, WPVL-FM
Radio Dubuque Inc.: KDTH, KGRR-FM

Duluth-Superior, MN-WI: Rank 204
MSA: 174,000 TSA: 395,600
Clear Channel Communications Inc.: KBMX(FM), KLDJ-FM, WEBC
Heartland Communications Group LLC: WNXR(FM)
Midwest Communications Inc.: KDAL, KTCO-FM, WDSM, WGEE(AM), WUSZ-FM
Northwestern College & Radio: KDNI(FM), KDNW(FM)
Red Rock Radio Corp.: KQDS-FM, KZIO-FM, WWAX-FM

Eau Claire, WI: Rank 243
MSA: 134,000 TSA: 353,000
Clear Channel Communications Inc.: WATQ(FM), WBIZ, WISM-FM, WMEQ(AM), WQRB-FM
Maverick Media LLC: WAXX-FM, WAYY(AM), WDRK(FM), WEAQ, WECL-FM, WIAL-FM
Relevant Radio: WDVM(AM)
VCY America Inc.: WVCF-FM

El Paso, TX: Rank 76
MSA: 573,600 TSA: 825,800
Clear Channel Communications Inc.: KHEY(AM), KPRR-FM, KTSM(AM)
EMF Broadcasting: KXCR-FM
Entravision Communications Corp.: KHRO(AM), KINT-FM, KOFX-FM, KYSE(FM)
Regent Communications Inc.: KROD, KSII-FM
Univision Radio: KAMA, KBNA(AM), KBNA-FM
World Radio Network Inc.: KVER-FM

Elizabeth City-Nags Head, NC: Rank 245
MSA: 132,100 TSA: 174,200
Convergent Broadcasting LLC: WFMZ(FM), WVOD(FM), WYND-FM, WZPR(FM)
CSN International: WGPS(FM)
East Carolina Radio Group: WCNC(AM), WERX-FM, WKJX-FM, WOBX(AM), WRSF(FM), WZBO(AM)
MAX Media L.L.C.: WCXL(FM), WGAI(AM), WWOC(FM)
Willis Broadcasting Corp.: WBXB(FM)

Elkins-Buckhannon-Weston, WV: Rank 272
MSA: 102,100 TSA:

Broadcasting & Cable Yearbook 2006

U.S. Radio Markets

Elmira-Corning, NY: Rank 218
MSA: 161,500 TSA: 283,500
Backyard Broadcasting LLC: WNKI-FM, WPGI-FM, WWLZ
CSN International: WREQ-FM
Family Life Network: WCIH-FM, WCIK-FM
Pembrook Pines Media Group: WABH, WEHH, WELM, WOKN-FM
Route 81 Radio LLC: WCBA, WENI(AM), WENI-FM, WENY, WENY-FM, WGMM(FM)

Erie, PA: Rank 165
MSA: 240,400 TSA: 437,700
Citadel Broadcasting Corp.: WQHZ(FM), WRIE, WXTA-FM
Family Stations Inc.: WEFR-FM
NextMedia Group Inc.: WFGO-FM, WFNN(AM), WJET(AM), WRKT-FM, WRTS-FM

Eugene-Springfield, OR: Rank 150
MSA: 290,900 TSA: 692,300
Churchill Communications LLC: KLZS(AM), KOPT(AM), KXOR(AM)
Clear Channel Communications Inc.: KDUK-FM, KPNW
Cumulus Media Inc.: KEHK-FM, KSCR(AM), KUGN, KUJZ(FM), KZEL-FM
Family Stations Inc.: KQFE-FM
McKenzie River Broadcasting Company, Inc.: KKNU(FM), KMGE-FM

Evansville, IN: Rank 160
MSA: 256,500 TSA: 724,700
Regent Communications Inc.: WDKS-FM, WGBF, WGBF-FM, WJLT(FM), WKDQ-FM, WYNG(FM)
South Central Communications Corp.: WABX-FM, WEOA, WLFW(FM), WSTO-FM, WYXY(FM)
The Original Company Inc.: WRCY(AM), WYFX(FM)
Word Broadcasting Network: WVHI

Fargo-Moorhead, ND-MN: Rank 223
MSA: 157,100 TSA: 432,400
Clear Channel Communications Inc.: KFAB-FM, KFGO, KRVI(FM), KVOX, WDAY-FM
Forum Communications Co.: WDAY
Leighton Enterprises Inc.: KBOQ(FM)
Northwestern College & Radio: KFNW(AM)
Triad Broadcasting Co. L.L.C.: KLTA(FM), KPFX-FM, KQWB-FM, KVOX-FM

Fayetteville (Northwest Arkansas), AR: Rank 141
MSA: 305,400 TSA: 437,200
American Family Radio: KBNV(FM)
Clear Channel Communications Inc.: KEZA-FM, KIGL(FM), KKIX-FM, KMXF-FM
Cumulus Media Inc.: KAMO-FM, KFAY, KKEG-FM, KMCK-FM, KQSM-FM, KYNF(FM), KZRA
Davidson Media Group LLC: KAKS(FM)
KERM Inc.: KURM

Fayetteville, NC: Rank 128
MSA: 353,600 TSA: 846,600
WFMO
Beasley Broadcast Group Inc.: WAZZ, WFLB-FM, WKML-FM, WTEL(AM), WUKS-FM, WZFX-FM
Cumulus Media Inc.: WFNC, WFNC-FM, WKQB-FM, WRCQ-FM
Davidson Media Group LLC: WSTS-FM

Flagstaff-Prescott, AZ: Rank 153
MSA: 280,700 TSA: 401,800
KAHM(FM), KPPV(FM), KQNA(AM), KRZS(FM), KYCA(AM)
3 Point Media: KKLD(FM)
Yavapai Broadcasting Corp.: KVNA(AM), KVNA-FM, KVRD-FM, KYBC(AM), KZGL(FM)

Flint, MI: Rank 125
MSA: 370,000 TSA: 557,300
ABC Inc.: WFDF
Birach Broadcasting Corp.: WCXI(AM)
Christian Broadcasting System Ltd.: WSNL(AM)
Citadel Broadcasting Corp.: WFBE-FM, WTRX
Cumulus Media Inc.: WDZZ-FM, WRSR-FM, WWCK
EMF Broadcasting: WAKL(FM)
Regent Communications Inc.: WFNT, WLSP, WWBN-FM

Florence, SC: Rank 215
MSA: 166,100 TSA: 513,300
Apex Broadcasting Inc.: WCSQ(FM)
Cumulus Media Inc.: WCMG-FM, WHLZ(FM), WHSC, WMXT-FM, WWFN-FM, WYNN
GHB Radio Group: WHYM(AM), WOLS
Glory Communications Inc.: WPDT-FM
Qantum Communications Corp.: WDAR-FM, WJMX, WJMX-FM, WWRK(FM)

Florence-Muscle Shoals, AL: Rank 257
MSA: 122,500 TSA: 264,300
Big River Broadcasting Corp.: WQLT(FM), WXFL(FM)
Urban Radio Licenses LLC: WMXV(FM)

Fort Collins-Greeley, CO: Rank 126
MSA: 369,700 TSA: 362,600
Clear Channel Communications Inc.: KIIX(AM), KSME(FM)
EMF Broadcasting: KLHV(FM)
NRC Broadcasting Inc.: KJAC(FM)
Superior Broadcasting of Denver LLC: KXDC(FM)

Fort Myers-Naples-Marco Island, FL: Rank 64
MSA: 744,800 TSA: 925,900
Beasley Broadcast Group Inc.: WJBX-FM, WJPT(FM), WRXK-FM, WWCN, WXKB-FM
Clear Channel Communications Inc.: WBTT(FM), WCKT(FM), WOLZ-FM, WZJZ(FM)
Fort Myers Broadcasting Co.: WINK(AM), WINK-FM, WPTK(AM), WTLQ-FM
Meridian Broadcasting Inc.: WNOG, WRQC(FM), WTLT-FM
Relevant Radio: WCNZ(AM), WMYR, WVOI(AM)
Renda Broadcasting Corp.: WGUF-FM, WJGO(FM), WSGL-FM, WWGR-FM
WAY-FM Media Group Inc.: WAYJ-FM

Fort Pierce-Stuart-Vero Beach, FL: Rank 100
MSA: 445,000 TSA: 454,500
Black Media Works Inc.: WJFP-FM
Clear Channel Communications Inc.: WAVW(FM), WCZR(FM), WQOL-FM, WSYR-FM, WZTA(AM)
Vero Beach Broadcasters LLC: WGNX(FM), WGYL-FM, WOSN-FM, WTTB

Fort Smith, AR: Rank 177
MSA: 221,100 TSA: 509,100
American Family Radio: KAOW(FM)
Clear Channel Communications Inc.: KKBD(FM), KMAG-FM, KWHN(AM), KZBB-FM
Cumulus Media Inc.: KBBQ-FM, KLSZ-FM, KOMS-FM
Pearson Broadcasting: KERX(FM), KTTG-FM
Pharis Broadcasting: KFPW, KHGG(AM), KOLX-FM, KRBK(FM)

Fort Walton Beach, FL: Rank 205
MSA: 157,300 TSA: 196,600
WTKE(FM)
Cumulus Media Inc.: WFTW, WNCV-FM, WYZB-FM, WZNS-FM
Qantum Communications Corp.: WMXZ-FM, WWAV-FM

Fort Wayne, IN: Rank 105
MSA: 425,700 TSA: 842,200
Artistic Media Partners Inc.: WDDB(FM)
Bott Radio Network: WFCV
Christian Broadcasting System Ltd.: WLYV
Federated Media: WBYR-FM, WFWI-FM, WKJG(AM), WMEE-FM, WOWO, WQHK-FM
Sarkes Tarzian Inc.: WAJI(FM), WLDE-FM
Summit City Radio Group: WCKZ(FM), WGL, WNHT(FM), WXKE(FM), WXTW(FM), WYLT(FM)

Frederick, MD: Rank 197
MSA: 186,900 TSA: 183,800
Clear Channel Communications Inc.: WFMD(AM), WFRE(FM)

Fredericksburg, VA: Rank 154
MSA: 280,300 TSA: 336,300

Fresno, CA: Rank 66
MSA: 711,700 TSA: 1,435,100
Clear Channel Communications Inc.: KALZ(FM), KBOS-FM, KCBL, KEZL-FM, KFSO-FM, KRDU, KRZR-FM
Family Stations Inc.: KFNO-FM
Gore-Overgaard Broadcasting Inc.: KBIF
Infinity Broadcasting Corp.: KFPT(AM), KKDG(FM), KMGV-FM, KMJ, KOQO-FM, KSKS-FM, KWYE(FM)
Lotus Communications Corp.: KGST, KLBN-FM, KMMM(FM)
Mapleton Communications LLC: KFYE(FM)
Moon Broadcasting: KAAT(FM)
Multicultural Radio Broadcasting Inc.: KWRU(FM)
Pappas Telecasting Companies: KVBE(FM)
Univision Radio: KLLE(FM), KOND(FM)
Wilks Broadcast Group LLC: KFRR-FM, KJFX-FM, KUUS(FM)

Gainesville-Ocala, FL: Rank 86
MSA: 513,700 TSA: 873,700
Asterisk Inc.: WMFQ-FM, WXJZ(FM), WYGC(FM)
Bible Broadcasting Network: WYFB-FM
Entercom Communications Corp.: WKTK-FM, WSKY-FM
Jablamo LLC: WDVH(AM), WHHZ(FM), WTMG-FM, WTMN(AM)
Pamal Broadcasting Ltd.: WDVH-FM

Wooster Republican Printing Co.: WNDD-FM, WNDT(FM), WOGK(FM)

Grand Forks, ND-MN: Rank 288
MSA: 82,300 TSA: 151,800
Clear Channel Communications Inc.: KJKJ-FM, KKXL, KQHT-FM, KSNR-FM
Leighton Enterprises Inc.: KCNN, KNOX, KYCK-FM

Grand Junction, CO: Rank 264
MSA: 110,600 TSA: 250,000
Cherry Creek Radio LLC: KKXK-FM, KUBC(AM)
Cumulus Media Inc.: KBKL(FM), KEKB-FM, KEXO, KKNN-FM, KMXY-FM
EMF Broadcasting: KLFV(FM)
MBC Grand Broadcasting Inc.: KMGJ(FM), KMOZ-FM, KNZZ(AM)
United Ministries: KJOL(AM)

Grand Rapids, MI: Rank 67
MSA: 703,400 TSA: 1,606,900
Birach Broadcasting Corp.: WMFN, WMJH
Citadel Broadcasting Corp.: WKLQ-FM, WLAV-FM, WTNR(FM)
Clear Channel Communications Inc.: WBCT-FM, WMRR-FM, WOOD, WSNX-FM, WTKG, WVTI-FM
Kuiper Stns: WFUR
Midwest Communications Inc.: WHTC(AM)
Regent Communications Inc.: WFGR-FM, WGRD-FM, WNWZ, WTRV-FM

Great Falls, MT: Rank 295
MSA: 67,500 TSA: 117,000
American Family Radio: KAFH(FM), KGFA(FM)
Cherry Creek Radio LLC: KLFM-FM, KMON, KMON-FM, KVVR(FM)
Family Stations Inc.: KFRW(FM)
Fisher Broadcasting Company: KAAK(FM), KINX(FM), KQDI, KQDI-FM, KXGF

Green Bay, WI: Rank 186
MSA: 201,900 TSA: 930,800
Cumulus Media Inc.: WDUZ(AM), WDUZ-FM, WJLW-FM, WPCK(FM), WQLH-FM
Evangel Ministries Inc.: WEMY-FM
Midwest Communications Inc.: WLYD(FM), WNFL, WTAQ(AM)
Results Broadcasting: WOWN-FM, WTCH
Woodward Communications Inc.: WKSZ(FM), WZOR(FM)

Greensboro-Winston Salem-High Point, NC: Rank 45
MSA: 1,113,300 TSA: 2,281,400
Baker Family Stations: WXRI-FM
Clear Channel Communications Inc.: WGBT(FM), WMAG(FM), WTQR-FM, WVBZ(FM)
Curtis Media Group: WPCM
Davidson Media Group LLC: WSGH, WTOB, WWBG
Eastern Broadcasting Group Inc.: WYSR(AM)
Entercom Communications Corp.: WJMH-FM, WMQX-FM, WPET, WQMG-FM, WSMW(FM)
GHB Radio Group: WBLO(AM), WIST(FM)
Infinity Broadcasting Corp.: WMFR, WSJS, WSML
Truth Broadcasting Corp.: WCOG, WKEW, WPOL, WTRU(AM)

Greenville-New Bern-Jacksonville, NC: Rank 87
MSA: 501,800 TSA: 1,113,300
WDLX
American Family Radio: WAAE-FM, WJKA(FM)
Archway Broadcasting Group: WLGT(FM), WRHD(FM), WRHT-FM, WWHA(FM), WWNK(FM)
Beasley Broadcast Group Inc.: WIKS-FM, WMGV-FM, WNCT, WNCT-FM, WSFL-FM, WXNR-FM
CTC Media Group Inc.: WNOS, WSME(AM), WWNB
Curtis Media Group: WWNF(FM)
Estuardo Valdemar Rodriguez and Leonor Rodriguez Stns: WLNR
NextMedia Group Inc.: WANG, WERO(FM), WILT(FM), WQSL-FM, WQZL(FM), WRNS-FM, WSSM(FM), WXQR-FM

Greenville-Spartanburg, SC: Rank 60
MSA: 813,700 TSA: 1,864,800
Barnstable Broadcasting Inc.: WGVC(FM), WROQ-FM, WTPT-FM
Clear Channel Communications Inc.: WESC-FM, WGVL, WLFJ(AM), WMYI(FM)
Cox Enterprises Inc.: WHZT(FM), WJMZ-FM
Entercom Communications Corp.: WOLI-FM, WOLT-FM, WORD(AM), WSPA(AM), WYRD
Wilkins Communications Network Inc.: WELP(AM)

Hagerstown-Chambersburg-Waynesboro, MD-PA: Rank 166
MSA: 239,500 TSA: 377,800
Allegheny Mountain Network Stations: WEEO-FM
Main Line Broadcasting LLC: WCHA, WDLD(FM), WHAG, WIKZ-FM, WQCM(FM)
Nassau Broadcasting Partners L.P.: WARK, WWEG(FM)
Prettyman Broadcasting Co.: WICL(FM), WLTF(FM)
VerStandig Broadcasting: WAYZ(FM), WCBG(AM), WFYN(FM), WPPT(FM)

Broadcasting & Cable Yearbook 2006

U.S. Radio Markets

Hamptons-Riverhead, NY: Rank 260
MSA: 116,400 TSA: 114,500

Harrisburg-Lebanon-Carlisle, PA: Rank 78
MSA: 558,400 TSA: 1,571,900
Citadel Broadcasting Corp.: WCAT-FM, WMHX(FM)
Clear Channel Communications Inc.: WHP, WKBO, WRBT-FM, WTKT(AM)
Cumulus Media Inc.: WTCY, WTPA-FM, WWKL(FM)
MAX Media L.L.C.: WYGL-FM
Route 81 Radio LLC: WHYL

Harrisonburg, VA: Rank 276
MSA: 98,200 TSA: 287,400
WBOP-FM
Clear Channel Communications Inc.: WACL-FM, WKCY
VerStandig Broadcasting: WBHB-FM, WHBG, WJDV(FM), WQPO-FM, WSVA

Hartford-New Britain-Middletown, CT: Rank 50
MSA: 1,043,700 TSA: 2,743,100
ABC Inc.: WDZK
Buckley Broadcasting Corp.: WDRC(AM), WDRC-FM
Clear Channel Communications Inc.: WHCN-FM, WKSS-FM, WPHH(FM), WWYZ-FM
Davidson Media Group LLC: WXCT(AM)
Family Stations Inc.: WCTF
Freedom Communications of Connecticut Inc.: WKND(AM), WLAT(AM), WNEZ(AM)
Infinity Broadcasting Corp.: WRCH-FM, WTIC, WZMX-FM

Hilton Head, SC: Rank 217
MSA: 162,300 TSA: 180,600

Honolulu, HI: Rank 63
MSA: 766,800 TSA: 996,000
Clear Channel Communications Inc.: KDNN(FM), KHBZ(AM), KHVH, KSSK(AM), KSSK-FM, KUCD(FM)
Cox Enterprises Inc.: KCCN-FM, KINE-FM, KKNE(AM), KPHW(FM), KRTR(AM), KRTR-FM
Salem Communications Inc.: KAIM-FM, KGMZ-FM, KGU, KHCM(AM), KHNR(AM), KHNR-FM, KHUI(FM)
Visionary Related Entertainment L.L.C.: KDDB(FM), KPOI-FM, KQMQ-FM, KUMU-FM

Houston-Galveston: Rank 7
MSA: 4,353,000 TSA: 5,135,200
ABC Inc.: KMIC(AM)
Clear Channel Communications Inc.: KBME, KHMX-FM, KKRW-FM, KODA-FM, KPRC, KTBZ-FM, KTRH
Convergent Broadcasting LLC: KPUS(FM)
Cox Enterprises Inc.: KHPT(FM), KKBQ-FM, KLDE(FM), KTHT(FM)
Cumulus Media Inc.: KFNC(FM), KIOL(FM), KSTB-FM
Entravision Communications Corp.: KGOL
Houston Christian Broadcasters Inc.: KHCB
Infinity Broadcasting Corp.: KHJZ-FM, KIKK, KILT
Liberman Broadcasting Inc.: KEYH, KJOJ, KJOJ-FM, KQQK(FM), KQUE, KSEV, KTJM-FM
Multicultural Radio Broadcasting Inc.: KXYZ
Pacifica Foundation Inc.: KPFT-FM
Radio One Inc.: KBXX(FM), KMJQ-FM, KROI(FM)
Salem Communications Inc.: KKHT-FM, KNTH(AM), KTEK
SIGA Broadcasting Corp.: KGBC, KLVL
Susquehanna Radio Corp.: KRBE(FM)
The RAFTT Corp.: KILE
Univision Radio: KLAT, KLTN-FM, KOVE-FM, KPTI(FM), KPTY(FM), KQBU-FM, KRTX

Huntington-Ashland, WV-KY: Rank 156
MSA: 270,900 TSA: 596,700
WLGC, WLGC-FM
Baker Family Stations: WOKT
Clear Channel Communications Inc.: WAMX-FM, WBKS(FM), WBVB-FM, WIRO, WTCR, WTCR-FM, WVHU(AM), WZZW
Connoisseur Media LLC: WDNQ(FM)
Kindred Communications Inc.: WCMI, WDGG-FM, WRVC, WRVC-FM
Mortenson Broadcasting Co.: WEMM(AM), WEMM-FM

Huntsville, AL: Rank 115
MSA: 407,600 TSA: 967,900
Black Crow Media Group LLC: WAHR-FM, WLOR, WRTT-FM
Clear Channel Communications Inc.: WBHP, WDRM-FM, WHOS, WTAK-FM, WWXQ-FM, WXQW-FM
Cumulus Media Inc.: WHRP(FM), WUMP, WVNN
Wilkins Communications Network Inc.: WBXR

Indianapolis, IN: Rank 41
MSA: 1,312,200 TSA: 2,273,700
ABC Inc.: WRDZ-FM
Clear Channel Communications Inc.: WFBQ-FM, WNDE, WRZX-FM
Emmis Communications Corp.: WIBC(AM), WLHK(FM), WYXB(FM)
Entercom Communications Corp.: WTPI-FM
Mid-America Radio Group Inc.: WMCB
Radio One Inc.: WHHH-FM, WTLC, WTLC-FM, WYJZ(FM)
Rodgers Broadcasting Corp.: WCNB(AM)
Sarkes Tarzian Inc.: WTTS-FM
Susquehanna Radio Corp.: WFMS-FM, WISG(FM), WJJK(FM)
The Moody Bible Institute of Chicago: WGNR-FM
Wilkins Communications Network Inc.: WBRI

Ithaca, NY: Rank 282
MSA: 91,000 TSA: 151,400
Citadel Broadcasting Corp.: WKRT
Pembrook Pines Media Group: WPIE
Saga Communications Inc.: WHCU, WNYY(AM), WQNY-FM, WYXL-FM

Jackson, MS: Rank 122
MSA: 386,400 TSA: 804,300
Backyard Broadcasting LLC: WRXW(FM), WWJK(FM)
Clear Channel Communications Inc.: WHLH(FM), WJDX, WMSI-FM, WQJQ-FM, WSTZ-FM, WZRX
Inner City Broadcasting: WJMI-FM, WKXI, WKXI-FM, WOAD, WOAD-FM
New South Communications Inc.: WIIN, WJKK-FM, WUSJ(FM), WYOY-FM
On Top Communications Inc.: WRJH-FM
TeleSouth Communications Inc.: WFMN-FM

Jackson, TN: Rank 289
MSA: 79,600 TSA: 489,000
Black Crow Media Group LLC: WFKX(FM), WHHM-FM, WWYN(FM), WZDQ(FM)
Clear Channel Communications Inc.: WTJS, WYNU-FM
Grace Broadcasting Services Inc.: WWGM(FM)

Jacksonville, FL: Rank 48
MSA: 1,057,600 TSA: 1,410,700
3 Point Media: WSOS(AM)
ABC Inc.: WBWL
Clear Channel Communications Inc.: WFKS(FM), WFXJ(AM), WJBT-FM, WPLA-FM, WQIK-FM, WROO-FM, WSOL-FM
Cox Enterprises Inc.: WAPE-FM, WFYV-FM, WJGL(FM), WMXQ-FM, WOKV
Norsan Consulting and Management Inc.: WNNR(AM), WVOJ(AM)
Renda Broadcasting Corp.: WEJZ-FM, WKQL(FM), WSOS-FM
Salem Communications Corp.: WBGB-FM, WJGR, WZAZ, WZNZ
Tama Broadcasting Inc.: WHJX(FM), WJSJ(FM), WSJF(FM)
Word Broadcasting Network Inc.: WYMM(AM)

Johnson City-Kingsport-Bristol, TN-VA: Rank 99
MSA: 452,000 TSA: 886,000
Baker Family Stations: WCQR-FM
Bristol Broadcasting Co. Inc.: WAEZ(FM), WFHG(AM), WFHG-FM, WTZR(FM), WXBQ-FM
Citadel Broadcasting Corp.: WGOC, WJCW, WKIN
Glenwood Communications Corp.: WKPT, WKTP, WMEV, WOPI

Johnstown, PA: Rank 190
MSA: 198,700 TSA: 320,600
2510 Licenses LLC: WBHV(AM), WCCL(FM)
Family Stations Inc.: WFRJ-FM
Forever Broadcasting: WFGI-FM, WKYE(FM), WLKH(FM), WLKJ(FM), WNTJ(AM), WNTW(AM), WPRR(AM), WRKW(FM), WYOT(FM)
He's Alive Inc.: WPCL(FM)
Renda Broadcasting Corp.: WYTR(FM)
Vernal Enterprises Inc.: WHPA(FM), WNCC(AM), WRDD

Jonesboro, AR: Rank 290
MSA: 73,700 TSA: 330,200
American Family Radio: KAOG(FM)
Clear Channel Communications Inc.: KFIN(FM), KIYS(FM), KNEA(AM)
EMF Broadcasting: KJLV(FM)
Saga Communications Inc.: KDEZ(FM), KJBX(FM)

Joplin, MO: Rank 237
MSA: 138,500 TSA: 398,700
KHST(FM), KWXD-FM, WMBH(AM)
Textron Financial Corp.: KBTN, KCAR-FM, KJML-FM, KMOQ-FM, KQYX(AM)
Zimmer Radio Group: KIXQ(FM), KJMK-FM, KSYN-FM, KXDG-FM

Kalamazoo, MI: Rank 184
MSA: 204,000 TSA: 666,100
Cumulus Media Inc.: WKFR-FM, WKMI, WRKR-FM
Forum Communications Co.: WZUU-FM
Kuiper Stns: WKPR
Midwest Communications Inc.: WNWN, WNWN-FM

Kansas City, MO-KS: Rank 29
MSA: 1,553,300 TSA: 2,316,600
ABC Inc.: KPHN

Bick Broadcasting Co.: KSIS(AM)
Bott Radio Network: KAYX(FM), KCCV, KCCV-FM, KLEX
Carter Broadcast Group Inc.: KPRT
Cumulus Media Inc.: KMJK(FM)
Davidson Media Group LLC: KCZZ(AM)
Entercom Communications Corp.: KCSP(AM), KKHK(AM), KMBZ, KQRC-FM, KRBZ(FM), KUDL-FM, KXTR(AM), KYYS-FM, WDAF-FM
Infinity Broadcasting Corp.: KBEQ-FM, KFKF-FM, KMXV-FM, KSRC-FM
Susquehanna Radio Corp.: KCFX(FM), KCJK(FM), KCMO, KCMO-FM
The Curators of the University of Missouri: KCUR-FM
Wilkins Communications Network Inc.: KCNW(AM)

Killeen-Temple, TX: Rank 158
MSA: 262,700 TSA: 315,500
Clear Channel Communications Inc.: KIIZ-FM, KLFX-FM
Cumulus Media Inc.: KLTD-FM, KOOC(FM), KSSM(FM), KTEM, KUSJ(FM)
EMF Broadcasting: KVLZ(FM)
Infinity Broadcasting Corp.: KXBT(FM)
M&M Broadcasters Ltd.: KTON
Martin Broadcasting Inc.: KRMY

Knoxville, TN: Rank 71
MSA: 633,300 TSA: 1,324,200
WIFA(AM), WITA
Citadel Broadcasting Corp.: WIVK-FM, WNML(AM), WNML-FM, WOKI(FM)
Horne Radio Group: WATO, WGAP, WKVL(AM), WKVL-FM, WLOD, WMTY(AM)
Journal Communications Inc.: WKHT(FM), WMYU(FM), WQBB, WWST(FM)
Peg Broadcasting Crossville LLC: WPBX(FM)
South Central Communications Corp.: WIMZ-FM, WJXB-FM, WTXM-FM
Southern Media Group Inc.: WBZH(FM)

La Crosse, WI: Rank 228
MSA: 154,500 TSA: 192,500

Lafayette, IN: Rank 246
MSA: 131,600 MSA: 348,100
American Family Radio: WQSG(FM)
Artistic Media Partners Inc.: WAZY-FM, WLAS(AM), WLFF(FM), WSHP(FM)
Kaspar Broadcasting Group: WSHW-FM
RadioWorks Inc.: WKHY(FM), WXXB(FM)
Schurz Communications Inc.: WASK, WASK-FM, WKOA-FM
The Moody Bible Institute of Chicago: WHPL-FM

Lafayette, LA: Rank 103
MSA: 435,100 TSA: 604,700
KEUN, KEUN-FM
Citadel Broadcasting Corp.: KNEK, KRRQ-FM, KSMB-FM, KXKC(FM)
EMF Broadcasting: KIKL(FM)
Pittman Broadcasting Services LLC: KFXZ(AM), KKSJ(FM), KTSJ(FM), KVOL
Radio Maria Inc.: KNIR
Regent Communications Inc.: KFTE-FM, KMDL-FM, KPEL, KRKA(FM), KROF

Lake Charles, LA: Rank 229
MSA: 154,200 TSA: 248,500
American Family Radio: KYLC(FM)
Apex Broadcasting Inc.: KLCL, KNGT(FM), KTSR(FM)
Cumulus Media Inc.: KAOK, KBIU(FM), KKGB-FM, KQLK(FM), KYKZ-FM
Radio Maria Inc.: KOJO-FM

Lakeland-Winter Haven, FL: Rank 98
MSA: 452,300 TSA: 541,000
Bible Broadcasting Network: WYFO-FM
Hall Communications Inc.: WLKF, WONN, WPCV-FM, WWRZ-FM
Infinity Broadcasting Corp.: WSJT-FM
The Moody Bible Institute of Chicago: WKES-FM

Lancaster, PA: Rank 113
MSA: 411,800 TSA: 856,600
Citadel Broadcasting Corp.: WIOV-FM
Clear Channel Communications Inc.: WLAN
Hall Communications Inc.: WLPA, WROZ-FM

Lansing-East Lansing, MI: Rank 121
MSA: 390,200 TSA: 1,027,900
Christian Broadcasting System Ltd.: WLCM
Citadel Broadcasting Corp.: WFMK(FM), WITL-FM, WJIM(AM), WVFN(AM)
Family Life Communications Inc.: WUNN(AM)
MacDonald Broadcasting Co.: WHZZ-FM, WILS
Rubber City Radio Group Inc.: WJXQ-FM, WQTX(FM), WTXQ(FM), WVIC(FM)

Laredo, TX: Rank 208
MSA: 170,800 TSA: 188,200
Border Media Partners LLC: KBDR(FM), KLNT, KNEX-FM

Broadcasting & Cable Yearbook 2006

U.S. Radio Markets

Las Vegas, NV: Rank 32
MSA: 1,438,600 TSA: 1,648,100
Beasley Broadcast Group Inc.: KJUL-FM, KKLZ-FM, KSTJ-FM
Clear Channel Communications Inc.: KQOL-FM, KSNE-FM, KWID(FM), KWNR-FM
Entravision Communications Corp.: KQRT(FM)
Infinity Broadcasting Corp.: KKJJ(FM), KLUC-FM, KMXB-FM, KXNT, KXTE-FM
Kemp Communications Inc.: KBTB(AM), KVEG(FM)
Lotus Communications Corp.: KBAD, KENO, KOMP-FM, KWWN(AM), KXPT-FM
McNaughton-Jakle Stations: KSHP
Univision Radio: KISF-FM, KLSQ(AM)

LaSalle-Peru, IL: Rank 247
MSA: 131,100 TSA: 141,700

Laurel-Hattiesburg, MS: Rank 227
MSA: 154,800 TSA: 295,500
American Family Radio: WAII-FM, WATP-FM
Blakeney Communications Inc.: WBBN(FM), WKZW-FM, WXHB-FM, WXRR-FM
Clear Channel Communications Inc.: WEEZ, WFOR, WHER-FM, WJKX-FM, WNSL-FM, WUSW-FM, WZLD(FM)
EMF Broadcasting: WKNZ-FM

Lawton, OK: Rank 283
MSA: 89,800 TSA: 220,400
American Family Radio: KVRS-FM
Clear Channel Communications Inc.: KLAW(FM), KVRW-FM, KZCD(FM)
Monarch Broadcasting Inc.: KQTZ-FM
Perry Publishing & Broadcasting Co.: KKRX, KVSP(FM), KXCA(AM)

Lebanon-Rutland-White River Junction, NH-VT: Rank 180
MSA: 214,800 TSA: 284,700

Lewiston-Auburn, ME: Rank 278
MSA: 93,100 TSA: 93,200
Gleason Radio Group: WCNM(AM)
Nassau Broadcasting Partners L.P.: WLAM(AM)

Lexington-Fayette, KY: Rank 104
MSA: 430,300 TSA: 877,300
Clear Channel Communications Inc.: WBUL-FM, WKQQ-FM, WLKT-FM, WMXL-FM, WXRA(AM)
Cumulus Media Inc.: WLRO-FM, WLTO-FM, WVLK, WXZZ-FM
EMF Broadcasting: WRVG(FM)
L M Communications Inc.: WBTF-FM, WBVX(FM), WCDA-FM, WLXG
Mortenson Broadcasting Co.: WCGW, WWFT(AM)
Vernon R Baldwin Inc.: WVRB-FM
Wallingford Broadcasting Co.: WEKY, WKXO, WLFX(FM)

Lima, OH: Rank 250
MSA: 128,500 TSA: 339,500
Clear Channel Communications Inc.: WIMA, WZRX-FM
Maverick Media LLC: WDOH-FM, WFGF(FM), WLJM, WUZZ-FM, WZOQ(FM)

Lincoln, NE: Rank 176
MSA: 222,800 TSA: 392,500
Clear Channel Communications Inc.: KIBZ(FM), KLMY(FM), KTGL-FM, KZKX-FM
Three Eagles Communications: KFRX(FM), KRKR(FM)
Triad Broadcasting Co. L.L.C.: KLIN, KLNC(FM)

Little Rock, AR: Rank 85
MSA: 515,500 TSA: 1,093,600
KASR(FM)
ABC Inc.: KDIS-FM
Archway Broadcasting Group: KOLL-FM
Citadel Broadcasting Corp.: KAAY, KARN, KARN-FM, KIPR-FM, KLAL-FM, KOKY-FM, KPZK(AM), KPZK-FM, KURB-FM
Clear Channel Communications Inc.: KDJE(FM), KHKN(FM), KMJX-FM, KMSX(FM), KSSN-FM
Metropolitan Radio Group Inc.: KGHT
Noalmark Broadcasting Corp.: KBOK(AM)
Searcy Broadcasting Inc.: KZTD(AM)
US Stations LLC: KQUS-FM

Los Angeles: Rank 2 TSA: 15,218,200
ABC Inc.: KABC, KDIS(AM), KLOS-FM, KSPN(AM)
Amaturo Groups: KLIT(FM)
Clear Channel Communications Inc.: KAVL, KBIG-FM, KFI, KHHT(FM), KIIS-FM, KLAC, KOSS-FM, KOST-FM, KTLK(AM), KTPI-FM, KYSR-FM
Crawford Broadcasting Co.: KBRT
Emmis Communications Corp.: KPWR-FM, KZLA-FM
Entravision Communications Corp.: KDLD(FM), KDLE(FM), KLYY(FM), KSSE(FM)
Family Stations Inc.: KFRN

Hi-Favor Broadcasting LLC: KLTX
High Desert Broadcasting LLC: KGMX-FM, KUTY, KWJL(AM)
Infinity Broadcasting Corp.: KFWB, KLSX-FM, KNX, KROQ-FM, KRTH-FM, KTWV-FM
Liberman Broadcasting Inc.: KBUA(FM), KBUE(FM), KEBN(FM), KHJ(AM), KWIZ-FM
Lotus Communications Corp.: KIRN(AM), KWKU(AM), KWKW
Multicultural Radio Broadcasting Inc.: KAHZ(AM), KALI, KAZN, KBLA, KYPA
Pacifica Foundation Inc.: KPFK-FM
Radio One Inc.: KKBT(FM)
Rose City Radio Corp.: KMPC(AM)
Salem Communications Corp.: KFSH-FM, KKLA-FM, KRLA(AM), KXMX(AM)
Spanish Broadcasting System Inc.: KLAX-FM, KXOL-FM
Styles Media Group LLC: KDAY(FM)
Univision Radio: KLVE-FM, KRCD(FM), KRCV(FM), KSCA-FM, KTNQ

Louisville, KY: Rank 55
MSA: 923,000 TSA: 1,423,700
WWSZ(AM)
ABC Inc.: WDRD(AM)
Clear Channel Communications Inc.: WCND, WJZO(FM), WKJK, WKRD(AM), WLUE(FM), WQMF-FM, WTFX-FM, WZKF(FM)
Commonwealth Broadcasting Corp.: WTSZ(AM), WTSZ-FM
Cox Enterprises Inc.: WPTI(FM), WRKA-FM, WSFR-FM, WVEZ(FM)
EMF Broadcasting: WSOH(FM)
Mortenson Broadcasting Co.: WLLV, WLOU
Radio One Inc.: WDJX-FM, WEGK(FM), WGZB-FM, WLRS(FM), WMJM-FM, WXMA(FM)
Salem Communications Corp.: WFIA, WFIA-FM, WGTK(AM), WRVI-FM
Susquehanna Radio Corp.: WAVG(AM)

Lubbock, TX: Rank 182
MSA: 211,300 TSA: 370,200
Clear Channel Communications Inc.: KFYO, KKAM, KKCL-FM, KQBR(FM)
EMF Broadcasting: KKLU(FM)
Entravision Communications Corp.: KAIQ(FM), KBZO
Family Life Communications Inc.: KAMY(FM)
Ramar Communications II Ltd.: KJTV(AM), KXTQ-FM
Wilks Broadcast Group LLC: KLLL-FM, KMMX(FM), KONE(FM)

Macon, GA: Rank 155
MSA: 278,000 TSA: 610,400
American Family Radio: WBKG-FM
Clear Channel Communications Inc.: WEBL(FM), WIBB-FM, WLCG, WMWR(AM), WQBZ-FM, WRBV-FM, WYNF(FM)
Cumulus Media Inc.: WAYS(AM), WDDO, WDEN-FM, WIFN(FM), WLZN(FM), WMAC, WMGB(FM), WPEZ(FM)
Roberts Communications Inc.: WQMJ(FM), WXJO(AM), WXKO
Rodgers Broadcasting Corp.: WBML

Madison, WI: Rank 96
MSA: 461,700 TSA: 1,079,400
Clear Channel Communications Inc.: WIBA, WMAD(FM), WTSO, WXXM(FM)
Entercom Communications Corp.: WCHY(FM), WMMM-FM, WOLX-FM
Family Stations Inc.: WJJO-FM
Northwestern College & Radio: WNWC(AM), WNWC-FM
Relevant Radio: WHFA(AM)
The Mid-West Family Broadcast Group: WLMV(AM), WTDY, WTUX(AM), WWQM-FM

Manchester, NH: Rank 191
MSA: 197,600 TSA: 566,600
Northeast Broadcasting Company Inc.: WKBR
Saga Communications Inc.: WFEA, WMLL(FM), WZID(FM)

Mankato-New Ulm-St. Peter, MN: Rank 274
MSA: 100,700 TSA: 218,300
Clear Channel Communications Inc.: KXLP(FM)
Ingstad Brothers Broadcasting LLC: KNUJ(AM)
Linder Broadcasting Group: KTOE(AM)
Three Eagles Communications: KEEZ-FM, KRBI(AM)

Marion-Carbondale (Southern Illinois): Rank 236
MSA: 140,200 TSA: 270,000
American Family Radio: WAWJ(FM)
Clear Channel Communications Inc.: WDDD, WDDD-FM, WFRX, WQUL-FM, WTAO-FM, WVZA-FM
MAX Media L.L.C.: WCIL, WJPF, WOOZ-FM, WUEZ(FM), WXLT(FM)

Mason City, IA: Rank 239
MSA: 68,800 TSA: 148,200
American Family Radio: KBDC(FM)
Clear Channel Communications Inc.: KGLO(AM), KIAI(FM), KSMA-FM
Three Eagles Communications: KRIB(AM)

McAllen-Brownsville-Harlingen, TX: Rank 59
MSA: 817,800 TSA: 885,000

Border Media Partners LLC: KBUC(FM), KESO-FM, KJAV-FM, KSOX, KURV, KZSP-FM
Clear Channel Communications Inc.: KBFM(FM), KHKZ(FM), KQXX-FM, KTEX-FM, KVNS(AM)
Entravision Communications Corp.: KFRQ-FM, KKPS-FM, KNVO-FM, KVLY-FM
Multicultural Radio Broadcasting Inc.: KVJY
Univision Radio: KGBT, KGBT-FM
World Radio Network Inc.: KVMV-FM

Meadville-Franklin, PA: Rank 255
MSA: 125,300 TSA: 125,200

Medford-Ashland, OR: Rank 212
MSA: 168,300 TSA: 275,700
Clear Channel Communications Inc.: KIFS(FM), KLDZ(FM), KMED, KRWQ-FM, KZZE-FM
Mapleton Communications LLC: KAKT(FM), KBOY-FM, KCMX, KTMT
Opus Broadcasting Systems Inc.: KCNA(FM), KEZX(AM), KROG-FM, KRTA

Melbourne-Titusville-Cocoa, FL: Rank 94
MSA: 465,500 TSA: 451,200
Clear Channel Communications Inc.: WMMB, WMMV
Cumulus Media Inc.: WHKR-FM, WINT(AM), WSJZ-FM
Genesis Communications Inc.: WIXC(AM)
Rama Communications Inc.: WTIR(AM)

Memphis, TN: Rank 49
MSA: 1,047,900 TSA: 1,788,400
Bott Radio Network: WCRV
Citadel Broadcasting Corp.: WGKX-FM, WRBO(FM), WXMX(FM)
Clear Channel Communications Inc.: KJMS-FM, WDIA, WEGR(FM), WHAL-FM, WREC(AM)
EMF Broadcasting: KKLV(FM), WPLX(AM)
Entercom Communications Corp.: WMBZ(FM), WRVR-FM, WWTQ(AM)
F W Robbert Broadcasting Co. Inc.: WMQM(AM)
First Broadcasting Investment Partners LLC: WVIM-FM
Infinity Broadcasting Corp.: WMC(AM), WMC-FM, WMFS(FM)
Simmons Media Group: KSUD
Sudbury Services Inc.: KLCN

Merced, CA: Rank 183
MSA: 208,700 TSA: 202,300
Bott Radio Network: KCIV
Buckley Broadcasting Corp.: KHTN(FM), KUBB-FM
Citadel Broadcasting Corp.: KDJK(FM)
EMF Broadcasting: KLVN(FM)
Mapleton Communications LLC: KHPO(FM), KLOQ-FM, KTIQ(AM), KYOS

Meridian, MS: Rank 296
MSA: 63,800 TSA: 231,000
Clear Channel Communications Inc.: WFFX, WJDQ-FM, WYYW-FM
Mississippi Broadcasters L.L.C.: WJXM(FM), WKZB(FM), WMMZ-FM
New South Communications Inc.: WALT

Miami-Fort Lauderdale-Hollywood, FL: Rank 12
MSA: 3,505,100 TSA: 4,616,100
ABC Inc.: WMYM(AM)
Beasley Broadcast Group Inc.: WHSR, WKIS-FM, WPOW-FM, WQAM, WWNN
Clear Channel Communications Inc.: WBGG-FM, WHYI-FM, WINZ(AM), WIOD, WLVE-FM, WMGE(FM), WMIB(FM)
Cox Enterprises Inc.: WEDR-FM, WFLC-FM, WHDR(FM), WHQT-FM
Entravision Communications Corp.: WLQY
Inner City Broadcasting: WSRF
James Crystal Inc.: WFLL(AM)
Jefferson-Pilot Communications Co.: WAXY, WLYF(FM), WMXJ-FM
Multicultural Radio Broadcasting Inc.: WEXY, WJCC(AM), WNMA
Radio One Inc.: WVCG
Salem Communications Corp.: WKAT
Spanish Broadcasting System Inc.: WCMQ-FM, WRMA-FM, WXDJ-FM
Univision Radio: WAMR-FM, WAQI, WQBA, WRTO-FM

Middlesex-Somerset-Union, NJ: Rank 39
MSA: 1,383,100 TSA: 1,373,400

Milwaukee-Racine, WI: Rank 33
MSA: 1,429,200 TSA: 2,040,500
ABC Inc.: WKSH(AM)
Bliss Communications Inc.: WBKV, WBWI-FM, WRJN
Clear Channel Communications Inc.: WISN, WKKV-FM, WMIL-FM, WOKY, WQBW(FM), WRIT-FM
Entercom Communications Corp.: WMYX-FM, WSSP(AM), WXSS-FM
Family Stations Inc.: WMWK-FM
Good Karma Broadcasting L.L.C.: WAUK
Journal Communications Inc.: WTMJ
Milwaukee Radio Alliance L.L.C.: WJZI-FM, WMCS
NextMedia Group Inc.: WEXT-FM

U.S. Radio Markets

Relevant Radio: WPJP(FM), WZRK(AM)
Saga Communications Inc.: WHQG(FM), WJMR-FM, WJYI, WKLH-FM
Salem Communications Corp.: WFZH(FM), WRRD(AM)
VCY America Inc.: WVCY-FM

Minneapolis-St. Paul, MN: Rank 16
MSA: 2,632,400 TSA: 3,683,000
KTNF(AM)
ABC Inc.: KQRS-FM, KXXR-FM, WGVY(FM), WGVZ(FM)
Clear Channel Communications Inc.: KDWB-FM, KEEY-FM, KFAN, KFXN, KJZI(FM), KQQL-FM, KTCZ-FM
Davidson Media Group LLC: KLBB, KLBP(AM)
EMF Broadcasting: KMKL(FM)
Hubbard Broadcasting Inc.: KSTP, KSTP-FM, WFMP(FM), WIXK(AM)
Infinity Broadcasting Corp.: KZJK(FM), WCCO
Ingstad Brothers Broadcasting LLC: KCHK
Northwestern College & Radio: KTIS, KTIS-FM
Relevant Radio: KSMM, WLOL(AM)
Salem Communications Corp.: KKMS, KYCR, WWTC

Mobile, AL: Rank 93
MSA: 470,300 TSA: 1,076,000
WABB, WABB-FM
Clear Channel Communications Inc.: WBUV(FM), WKSJ-FM, WPMI(AM), WRKH-FM
Cumulus Media Inc.: WBLX-FM, WDLT, WDLT-FM, WGOK, WYOK-FM
Family Worship Center Church Inc.: WQUA-FM
Goforth Media Inc.: WBHY-FM
Martin Broadcasting Inc.: WLVV

Modesto, CA: Rank 111
MSA: 414,500 TSA: 1,386,200
Bustos Media LLC: KBBU(FM)
Citadel Broadcasting Corp.: KATM(FM), KESP(AM), KHKK-FM, KHOP-FM, KWNN-FM
Clear Channel Communications Inc.: KFIV, KJSN-FM, KMRQ(FM), KOSO-FM
Entravision Communications Corp.: KTSE-FM
Pappas Telecasting Companies: KPMP(AM), KTRB

Monmouth-Ocean, NJ: Rank 51
MSA: 1,021,400 TSA: 1,013,200

Monroe, LA: Rank 256
MSA: 123,300 TSA: 514,200
Bible Broadcasting Network: KYFL-FM
Communications Capital Managers LLC: KPCH-FM
Holladay Broadcasting of Louisiana LLC: KJMG-FM, KLIP-FM, KMLB, KRJO(AM), KRVV-FM
New South Communications Inc.: KJLO-FM
Opus Media Holdings LLC: KMYY(FM), KXRR(FM), KZRZ(FM)

Monterey-Salinas-Santa Cruz, CA: Rank 79
MSA: 555,100 TSA: 603,200
KNRY, KRXA(AM), KYAA(AM)
Buckley Broadcasting Corp.: KWAV-FM
Bustos Media LLC: KZSJ(AM)
Clear Channel Communications Inc.: KABL(AM), KDON-FM, KOCN-FM, KPRC-FM, KTOM-FM, KZFX(AM)
Entravision Communications Corp.: KMBX(AM), KSES-FM
Latin Entertainment Network Inc.: KEXA(FM), KHDV(FM), KMJV(FM), KRAY-FM, KTGE
Lazer Broadcasting Corp.: KXSM(FM)
Mapleton Communications LLC: KBOQ(FM), KCDU(FM), KHIP-FM, KMBY-FM, KPIG-FM
Univision Radio: KSQL(FM)

Montgomery, AL: Rank 151
MSA: 287,500 TSA: 696,800
Bluewater Broadcasting Co. LLC: WACV, WBAM-FM, WJWZ-FM, WQKS-FM
Clear Channel Communications Inc.: WHLW(FM), WWMG(FM), WZHT-FM
Cumulus Media Inc.: WHHY-FM, WMSP, WNZZ, WXFX-FM
GHB Radio Group: WMGY

Montpelier-Barre-St. Johnsbury, VT: Rank 266
MSA: 108,600 TSA: 283,400

Morgantown-Clarksburg-Fairmont, WV: Rank 175
MSA: 223,300 TSA: 398,700
Burbach Broadcasting Group: WGIE(FM), WGYE(FM), WOBG, WOBG-FM, WXKK(AM)
McGraw/Elliott Group Stations: WBVQ(FM)
Tschudy Broadcast Group: WPDX(FM), WZST-FM

Morristown, NJ: Rank 109
MSA: 415,000 TSA: 410,100

Muncie-Marion, IN: Rank 205
MSA: 172,400 TSA: 194,300

Muskegon, MI: Rank 233
MSA: 146,800 TSA: 211,400
American Family Radio: WMCQ(FM)
Clear Channel Communications Inc.: WKBZ(AM), WMUS(FM), WSHZ(FM)
Cumulus Media Inc.: WMHG(AM)
Unity Broadcasting Inc.: WVIB(FM)

Myrtle Beach, SC: Rank 164
MSA: 245,700 TSA: 417,400
Cumulus Media Inc.: WDAI-FM, WIQB(AM), WSEA(FM), WSYN-FM, WXJY-FM, WYAK-FM
NextMedia Group Inc.: WKZQ-FM, WMYB(FM), WQJM(AM), WRNN(FM), WYAV(FM)
Qantum Communications Corp.: WGTR-FM, WQSD(FM), WWXM(FM)

Nashville, TN: Rank 44
MSA: 1,125,000 TSA: 2,099,600
Bible Broadcasting Network: WYFN
Citadel Broadcasting Corp.: WGFX-FM, WKDF-FM
Clear Channel Communications Inc.: WLAC, WRVW-FM, WSIX-FM, WUBT(FM)
Cumulus Media Inc.: WQQK-FM, WRQQ(FM), WSM-FM, WWTN-FM
Davidson Media Group LLC: WMDB, WNSG
F W Robbert Broadcasting Co. Inc.: WNQM
Grace Broadcasting Services Inc.: WFGZ-FM
Salem Communications Corp.: WBOZ-FM, WFFH(FM), WFFI(FM), WVRY-FM
South Central Communications Corp.: WCJK(FM), WJXA-FM
Southern Wabash Communications Corp.: WMGC, WNSR
The Cromwell Group Inc.: WBUZ(FM), WQZQ-FM
WAY-FM Media Group Inc.: WAYM(FM)

Nassau-Suffolk, NY (Long Island): Rank 18
MSA: 2,393,800 TSA: 2,379,200

New Bedford-Fall River, MA: Rank 174
MSA: 225,500 TSA: 226,700

New Haven, CT: Rank 107
MSA: 420,800 TSA: 761,000
Buckley Broadcasting Corp.: WMMW
Clear Channel Communications Inc.: WAVZ, WELI
Cox Enterprises Inc.: WPLR-FM

New London, CT: Rank 171
MSA: 230,000 TSA: 470,200
Citadel Broadcasting Corp.: WSUB, WXLM(FM)
Hall Communications Inc.: WCTY-FM, WICH, WILI-FM, WKNL(FM), WNLC-FM

New Orleans, LA: Rank 47
MSA: 1,079,200 TSA: 1,935,400
WOPR(FM), WPRF(FM)
ABC Inc.: WBYU
Citadel Broadcasting Corp.: WKND-FM, WLRZ-FM, WMEZ-FM, WDVW(FM), WKSY-FM
Clear Channel Communications Inc.: WHEV(FM), WNOE-FM, WODT, WRNO-FM, WYLD
Entercom Communications Corp.: WEZB-FM, WKBU(FM), WSMB, WTKL-FM, WWL(AM)
F W Robbert Broadcasting Co. Inc.: WVOG
GHB Radio Group: WTIX
Southwest Broadcasting Inc.: WJSH(FM)
Spotlight Broadcasting LLC: KAGY
Willis Broadcasting Corp.: WBOK

New River Valley, NY: Rank 232
MSA: 147,000 TSA: 197,300

New York: Rank 1 TSA: 18,785,400
ABC Inc.: WABC(AM), WEPN(AM), WPLJ(FM)
Access.1 Communications Corp.: WWRL
Back Bay Broadcasters Inc.: WBAZ(FM), WBEA(FM), WHBE(FM)
Barnstable Broadcasting Inc.: WBZO-FM, WHLI, WMJC(FM), WRCN-FM
Buckley Broadcasting Inc.: WOR
Citadel Broadcasting Corp.: WMOS(FM)
Clear Channel Communications Inc.: WALK(AM), WAXQ-FM, WHTZ-FM, WKTU(FM), WLTW-FM, WWPR-FM
Cox Enterprises Inc.: WBAB(FM), WBLI-FM, WEFX-FM, WGBB, WHFM-FM, WKHL-FM, WNLK(AM)
Cumulus Media Inc.: WEBE-FM
Emmis Communications Corp.: WQCD(FM), WQHT-FM, WRKS(FM)
Family Stations Inc.: WFME-FM
Greater Media Inc.: WCTC(AM), WDHA-FM, WMGQ(FM), WMTR, WWTR(AM)
Infinity Broadcasting Corp.: WCBS, WFAN, WINS, WNEW-FM, WXRK-FM
Inner City Broadcasting: WBLS-FM, WLIB
Millennium Radio Group LLC: WADB, WJLK-FM
Multicultural Radio Broadcasting Inc.: WJDM, WKDM(AM), WNSW, WNYG, WPAT, WZRC
Pacifica Foundation Inc.: WBAI-FM
Pamal Broadcasting Ltd.: WLNA(AM), WXPK(FM)
Pillar of Fire Inc.: WAWZ(FM)
Polnet Communications Ltd.: WLIM, WRKL
Press Communications L.L.C.: WHTG, WHTG-FM, WWZY-FM
Rose City Radio Corp.: WSNR(FM)
Salem Communications Corp.: WMCA, WWDJ
Spanish Broadcasting System Inc.: WPAT-FM, WSKQ-FM
The Morey Organization Inc.: WBON-FM, WDRE(FM), WLIR-FM
The New York Times Co.: WQXR-FM
Universal Broadcasting of New York Inc.: WTHE, WVNJ
Univision Radio: WADO, WCAA-FM, WZAA(FM)

Newburgh-Middletown, NY (Mid-Hudson Valley): Rank 137
MSA: 315,900 TSA: 420,700
Clear Channel Communications Inc.: WFKP(FM)
Cumulus Media Inc.: WALL, WZAD-FM
Sunrise Broadcasting Corp.: WGNY
WAMC/Northeast Public Radio: WOSR-FM

Norfolk-Virginia Beach-Newport News, VA: Rank 40
MSA: 1,314,600 TSA: 1,687,600
ABC Inc.: WHKT, WRJR(AM)
Baker Family Stations: WKGM
Bible Broadcasting Network: WYFI-FM
Clear Channel Communications Inc.: WCDG(FM), WJCD(FM), WKUS(FM), WOWI-FM
Davidson Media Group LLC: WVXX(AM)
Entercom Communications Corp.: WNVZ-FM, WPTE-FM, WVKL-FM, WWDE-FM
MAX Media L.L.C.: WCMS(AM), WFOG(FM), WGH-FM, WXEZ-FM, WXMM(FM)
On Top Communications Inc.: WWHV(FM)
Saga Communications Inc.: WAFX-FM, WJOI
Sinclair Communications Inc.: WNIS, WPYA(FM), WROX-FM, WTAR(AM), WZNR(FM)
Willis Broadcasting Corp.: WCPK, WGPL, WPCE
Word Broadcasting Network Inc.: WYRM(AM)

Odessa-Midland, TX: Rank 188
MSA: 200,800 TSA: 324,000
American Family Radio: KBMM(FM)
Clear Channel Communications Inc.: KCHX(FM), KCRS(AM), KFZX-FM, KMRK-FM
Cumulus Media Inc.: KBAT(FM), KGEE-FM, KMND, KODM-FM, KRIL
EMF Broadcasting: KLVW(FM)
Encore Broadcasting L.L.C.: KHKX(FM), KMCM-FM, KQRX-FM
Family Life Communications Inc.: KFLB(AM), KFLB-FM
La Promesa Foundation: KJBC(AM)

Oklahoma City, OK: Rank 53
MSA: 985,100 TSA: 1,450,900
Bott Radio Network: KQCV, KQCV-FM
Citadel Broadcasting Corp.: KATT-FM, KKWD(FM), KYIS-FM, WKY, WWLS, WWLS-FM
Clear Channel Communications Inc.: KHBZ-FM, KTOK(AM), KTST-FM, KXXY-FM
EMF Broadcasting: KYLV-FM
Family Worship Center Church Inc.: KMFS(AM)
One Ten Broadcast Group Inc.: KIRC-FM
Perry Publishing & Broadcasting Co.: KRMP(AM)
Renda Broadcasting Corp.: KMGL-FM, KOKC(AM), KOMA(FM), KRXO-FM
Tyler Media Broadcasting Corp.: KOCY(AM), KTLR(AM), KTUZ-FM

Olean, NY: Rank 210
MSA: 169,000 TSA: 170,100

Omaha-Council Bluffs, NE-IA: Rank 72
MSA: 610,000 TSA: 1,238,400
Clear Channel Communications Inc.: KEFM-FM, KFAB, KGOR-FM, KHUS(FM), KXKT(FM)
EMF Broadcasting: KMLV(FM)
Journal Communications Inc.: KEZO-FM, KHLP(AM), KKCD-FM, KOMJ(AM), KQCH(FM), KXSP(AM)
Nebraska Rural Radio Association: KWPN-FM
Salem Communications Corp.: KCRO, KGBI-FM
Waitt Radio Inc.: KCTY-FM, KKAR, KLTQ(FM), KOIL(AM), KOZN(AM), KQKQ-FM, KYDZ(AM)
Wilkins Communications Network Inc.: KLNG(AM)

Orlando, FL: Rank 37
MSA: 1,402,300 TSA: 3,327,000
ABC Inc.: WDYZ(AM)
Clear Channel Communications Inc.: WFLF(FM), WJRR-FM, WMGF-FM, WQTM(AM), WRUM(FM), WTKS-FM, WXXL-FM
Cox Enterprises Inc.: WCFB-FM, WDBO, WHTQ-FM, WMMO-FM, WPYO(FM)
Genesis Communications Inc.: WAMT(AM), WHOO(AM)

U.S. Radio Markets

Infinity Broadcasting Corp.: WJHM-FM, WOCL-FM, WOMX-FM
J&V Communications Inc.: WOTS, WPRD
Rama Communications Inc.: WLAA(AM), WNTF, WOKB

Oxnard-Ventura, CA: Rank 117
MSA: 403,500 TSA: 837,800
Cumulus Media Inc.: KBBY-FM, KHAY-FM, KVEN
Entravision Communications Corp.: KSSC(FM)
Gold Coast Broadcasting LLC: KCAQ(FM), KFYV(FM), KKZZ(AM), KOCP-FM, KUNX(AM), KVTA
Lazer Broadcasting Corp.: KOXR
Salem Communications Corp.: KDAR(FM)

Palm Springs, CA: Rank 144
MSA: 302,200 TSA: 287,100
Entravision Communications Corp.: KLOB-FM
Infinity Broadcasting Corp.: KEZN-FM
Morris Radio LLC: KDGL(FM), KKUU(FM), KNWQ(AM), KNWT(AM), KNWZ(AM), KXPS(AM)
News-Press & Gazette Co.: KESQ, KUNA-FM
RR Broadcasting: KGAM, KPSI

Panama City, FL: Rank 241
MSA: 136,600 TSA: 294,400
American Family Radio: WFFL(FM)
Clear Channel Communications Inc.: WDIZ, WEBZ-FM, WFBX(FM), WPAP-FM
Double O Radio Corp.: WAKT-FM, WASJ(FM), WPFM-FM, WRBA(FM)
Styles Media Group LLC: WILN-FM, WPCF(AM), WVVE(FM), WYOO-FM, WYYX-FM
Williams Communications Inc.: WLTG

Parkersburg-Marietta, WV-OH: Rank 250
MSA: 128,500 TSA: 302,200
Burbach Broadcasting Group: WADC, WGGE(FM), WHBR-FM, WRZZ-FM, WVNT(AM), WXIL-FM
Clear Channel Communications Inc.: WDMX-FM, WHNK(AM), WLTP(AM), WNUS-FM, WRVB-FM

Pensacola, FL: Rank 123
MSA: 378,600 TSA: 721,700
Clear Channel Communications Inc.: WTKX-FM, WYCL-FM
Cumulus Media Inc.: WCOA
Parnal Broadcasting Ltd.: WMEZ-FM, WXBM-FM

Peoria, IL: Rank 148
MSA: 294,800 TSA: 615,700
Back Bay Broadcasters Inc.: WDQX(FM), WXCL(FM), WXMP(FM), WZPW(FM)
Illinois Bible Institute Inc.: WCIC-FM
Regent Communications Inc.: WFYR-FM, WGLO-FM, WIXO(FM), WPIA(FM), WVEL, WVEL-FM
Triad Broadcasting Co. L.L.C.: WIRL(AM), WMBD, WPBG-FM, WSWT-FM

Philadelphia: Rank 6
MSA: 4,354,900 TSA: 7,684,100
WURD(AM)
ABC Inc.: WWJZ
Beasley Broadcast Group Inc.: WRDW-FM, WTMR, WWDB(AM), WXTU-FM
Clear Channel Communications Inc.: WDAS, WIOQ-FM, WJJZ-FM, WSNI(FM), WUSL-FM
Family Stations Inc.: WKDN-FM
GHB Radio Group: WNAP
Great Scott Broadcasting: WPAZ
Greater Media Inc.: WBEN-FM, WMMR-FM, WPEN
Infinity Broadcasting Corp.: KYW, WIP, WPHT
Inner City Broadcasting: WHAT
Mega Communications Inc.: WEMG(AM)
Radio One Inc.: WPHI-FM, WPPZ-FM, WRNB(FM)
Route 81 Radio LLC: WCOJ(AM)
Salem Communications Corp.: WFIL(AM), WNTP(AM)

Phoenix, AZ: Rank 15
MSA: 2,938,500 TSA: 3,450,000
KASA
ABC Inc.: KMIK
Bonneville International Corporation: KMVP, KPKX(FM), KTAR(AM)
Clear Channel Communications Inc.: KESZ-FM, KGME(AM), KMXP-FM, KNIX-FM, KOY, KYOT-FM, KZZP-FM
EMF Broadcasting: KLVK(FM)
Emmis Communications Corp.: KKFR-FM
Entravision Communications Corp.: KDVA(FM), KLNZ-FM, KMIA(FM), KVVA-FM
Family Life Communications Inc.: KFLR-FM
Family Stations Inc.: KPHF-FM
Infinity Broadcasting Corp.: KMLE-FM, KOOL-FM, KZON(FM)
James Crystal Inc.: KXEG(AM), KXXT(AM)
Multicultural Radio Broadcasting Inc.: KIDR
Salem Communications Corp.: KKNT(AM), KPXQ(AM)
Sandusky Radio: KAZG(AM), KDKB(FM), KDUS

Univision Radio: KHOT-FM, KHOV-FM, KMRR(FM), KOMR(FM)

Pittsburg, KS (Southeast Kansas): Rank 240
MSA: 136,700 TSA: 160,500

Pittsburgh, PA: Rank 23
MSA: 2,015,100 TSA: 3,041,000
ABC Inc.: WEAE
Birach Broadcasting Corp.: WWCS
Broadcast Communications Inc.: WKFB(AM), WKHB(AM)
Butler County Radio Network Inc.: WBUT, WISR, WLER-FM
Clear Channel Communications Inc.: WBGG(AM), WDVE-FM, WKST-FM, WPGB(FM), WXDX-FM
Infinity Broadcasting Corp.: KDKA, WDSY-FM, WRKZ(FM), WZPT-FM
Inner City Broadcasting: WURP(AM)
Keymarket Communications LLC: WASP, WFGI(AM), WOGF(FM), WOGG(FM), WPKL(FM), WPNT(AM)
Langer Broadcasting Group L.L.C.: WPYT(AM)
MCL/MCM-Inc.: WAMO-FM, WJJJ(FM), WPGR(FM)
Renda Broadcasting Corp.: WJAS
Salem Communications Corp.: WORD-FM
Wilkins Communications Network Inc.: WWNL(AM)

Portland, ME: Rank 167
MSA: 283,700 TSA: 858,300
Atlantic Coast Radio L.L.C.: WJAE, WJJB(AM), WLOB, WRED-FM
Blount Communications Group: WBCI-FM
Bob Bittner Broadcasting Inc.: WJTO
Citadel Broadcasting Corp.: WBLM-FM, WCLZ(FM), WCYI(FM), WCYY-FM, WHOM-FM, WJBQ-FM
Nassau Broadcasting Partners L.P.: WBQW-FM, WFNK(FM), WHXR(FM), WLVP(AM), WTHT(FM)
Saga Communications Inc.: WBAE, WGAN(AM), WMGX(FM), WPOR(FM), WYNZ-FM, WZAN

Portland, OR: Rank 24
MSA: 1,963,400 TSA: 2,515,500
ABC Inc.: KDZR(AM), KKSL(AM)
Bustos Media LLC: KGDD(AM), KMUZ, KXMG(AM), KZNY(AM)
Clear Channel Communications Inc.: KEX, KKCW-FM, KPOJ(AM)
Crawford Broadcasting Co.: KKPZ(AM)
EMF Broadcasting: KLVP(AM), KLVP-FM, KZRI(FM)
Entercom Communications Corp.: KFXX(AM), KGON-FM, KKSN(AM), KNRK-FM, KRSK(FM), KSLM, KYCH-FM
Infinity Broadcasting Corp.: KCMD(AM), KINK(FM), KLTH(FM), KUFO-FM, KUPL-FM, KVMX(FM)
Pamplin Broadcasting: KKAD(AM), KPAM
Rose City Radio Corp.: KXL
Salem Communications Corp.: KPDQ-FM

Portsmouth-Dover-Rochester, NH: Rank 114
MSA: 408,500 TSA: 405,900
Blount Communications Group: WDER
Citadel Broadcasting Corp.: WOKQ-FM, WSAK(FM), WSHK(FM)
Clear Channel Communications Inc.: WERZ-FM, WGIP, WHEB-FM, WQSO-FM, WUBB-FM
Costa-Eagle Radio Ventures L.P.: WCEC(AM)

Poughkeepsie, NY: Rank 162
MSA: 254,900 TSA: 783,500
Clear Channel Communications Inc.: WBPM(FM), WBWZ-FM, WKIP, WPKF(FM), WRNQ-FM, WRWD-FM
Cumulus Media Inc.: WCZX-FM, WEOK, WRRB(FM)
Parnal Broadcasting Ltd.: WBNR, WSPK-FM

Providence-Warwick-Pawtucket, RI: Rank 36
MSA: 1,404,000 TSA: 2,014,100
WNRI
ABC Inc.: WDDZ(AM)
Anastos Media Group Inc.: WPEP
Astro Tele-Communications Corp. Rhode Island: WADK, WJZS(FM)
Blount Communications Group: WARV
Citadel Broadcasting Corp.: WBSM, WFHN-FM, WPRO, WSKO, WSKO-FM, WWKX-FM
Clear Channel Communications Inc.: WHJJ, WHJY-FM, WSNE-FM, WWBB-FM
Davidson Media Group LLC: WAKX-FM, WKKB(FM)
Entercom Communications Corp.: WEEI-FM
Hall Communications Inc.: WCTK(FM), WLKW(AM), WNBH

Pueblo, CO: Rank 253
MSA: 127,300 TSA: 226,900
Bahakel Communications: KYZX(FM)
Clear Channel Communications Inc.: KCCY(FM), KCSJ, KDZA-FM, KGHF
Family Stations Inc.: KFRY(FM)
Latino Communications Corp.: KAVA
Metropolitan Radio Group Inc.: KNKN-FM, KRMX

Puerto Rico: Rank 13
MSA: 3,250,400 TSA: 3,236,900
WNIK, WNIK-FM, WQBS
Calvary Evangelistic Mission Inc.: WBMJ, WCGB, WIVV
International Broadcasting Corp.: WCHQ(AM), WEKO(AM), WIBS, WRSJ(AM), WTIL, WVOZ-FM, WXRF
Media Power Group Inc.: WDEP(AM), WKFE, WLEY, WSKN(AM)
Spanish Broadcasting System Inc.: WCMA-FM, WEGM(FM), WIOA(FM), WIOB-FM, WIOC-FM, WMEG-FM, WNOD(FM), WODA(FM), WZET(FM), WZMT-FM, WZNT-FM
Univision Radio: WKAQ, WUKQ(AM), WUKQ-FM
Uno Radio Group: WCMN, WFDT(FM), WFID-FM, WIVA-FM, WLEO(AM), WNEL, WORA, WPRM-FM, WPRP, WRIO-FM, WUNO(AM)

Quad Cities, IA-IL (Davenport-Rock Island-Moline): Rank 143
MSA: 303,400 TSA: 706,500
Clear Channel Communications Inc.: KCQQ(FM), KMXG(FM), KUUL(FM), WFXN(AM), WLLR-FM, WOC
Cumulus Media Inc.: KBEA-FM, KBOB-FM, KJOC, KQCS(FM), WXLP-FM
Mercury Broadcasting Co. Inc.: WKBF
Miller Media Group: WKEI(AM)

Raleigh-Durham, NC: Rank 43
MSA: 1,143,700 TSA: 2,717,100
WDUR
Capitol Broadcasting Co. Inc.: WRAL(FM)
Clear Channel Communications Inc.: WDCG-FM, WRDU-FM, WRSN-FM, WRVA-FM
Curtis Media Group: WBBB-FM, WCLY, WDNC(AM), WDNZ(AM), WFMC, WWMY(FM), WYRN(AM)
Davidson Media Group LLC: WTIK
Estuardo Valdemar Rodriguez and Leonor Rodriguez Stns: WGSB, WLLQ(AM), WRTG
Radio One Inc.: WFXC-FM, WFXK-FM, WNNL-FM, WQOK-FM
Truth Broadcasting Corp.: WDRU(AM)
Willis Broadcasting Corp.: WSRC

Rapid City, SD: Rank 275
MSA: 99,000 TSA: 223,500
American Family Radio: KASD(FM)
Bethesda Christian Broadcasting: KLMP-FM
CSN International: KWRC(FM)
Duhamel Broadcasting Enterprises: KDDX(FM), KOTA
Family Stations Inc.: KQFR-FM
Haugo Broadcasting Inc.: KSQY-FM, KTOQ
Triad Broadcasting Co. L.L.C.: KBHB, KFXS-FM, KKLS, KOUT-FM

Reading, PA: Rank 131
MSA: 339,200 TSA: 332,300
Citadel Broadcasting Corp.: WIOV
Clear Channel Communications Inc.: WRAW

Redding, CA: Rank 226
MSA: 155,700 TSA: 253,200
EMF Broadcasting: KKRO(FM), KLVB(FM)
Fritz Communications Inc.: KESR(FM), KEWB-FM, KHRD(FM), KNCQ-FM
Regent Communications Inc.: KNNN(FM), KNRO(AM), KQMS, KRRX-FM, KSHA-FM

Reno, NV: Rank 124
MSA: 378,000 TSA: 620,300
Americom: KBZZ(AM), KJFK(AM), KLCA-FM, KRNO(FM), KZTQ(FM)
Azteca Broadcasting Corp.: KXEQ
Citadel Broadcasting Corp.: KBUL-FM, KKOH, KNEV-FM
Entravision Communications Corp.: KRNV-FM
IHR Educational Broadcasting: KIHM(AM)
Lotus Communications Corp.: KDOT-FM, KHIT, KOZZ-FM, KPLY(AM), KUUB(FM)
NextMedia Group Inc.: KJZS(FM), KRZQ-FM, KTHX-FM, KURK(FM)

Richmond, VA: Rank 56
MSA: 898,600 TSA: 1,386,800
4M Communications Inc.: WLEE(AM), WVNZ(AM)
ABC Inc.: WDZY
American Family Radio:
Clear Channel Communications Inc.: WBTJ(FM), WRNL, WRVA, WRVQ-FM, WTVR-FM
Cox Enterprises Inc.: WDYL-FM, WKHK-FM, WKLR-FM, WMXB-FM
Radio One Inc.: WCDX-FM, WKJM(FM), WKJS(FM), WPZZ(FM), WROU(AM)
Salem Communications Corp.: WBTK(AM)
The MainQuad Group: WARV-FM, WBBT-FM, WHAP

Riverside-San Bernardino, CA: Rank 27
MSA: 1,756,600 TSA: 2,687,000
Amaturo Groups: KELT-FM
Anaheim Broadcasting Corp.: KCAL-FM, KOLA(FM)
Clear Channel Communications Inc.: KDIF, KGGI-FM, KKDD, KTDD(AM)
Hi-Favor Broadcasting LLC: KEZY(AM)
Infinity Broadcasting Corp.: KFRG-FM
Lazer Broadcasting Corp.: KCAL, KXRS-FM, KXSB-FM

Broadcasting & Cable Yearbook 2006

U.S. Radio Markets

Salem Communications Corp.: KTIE(AM)

Roanoke-Lynchburg, VA: Rank 116
MSA: 404,000 TSA: 1,028,700
Baker Family Stations: WPAR-FM, WRXT-FM, WTTX-FM
Centennial Broadcasting LLC: WLEQ(FM), WLNI-FM, WZZI-FM, WZZU(FM)
Clear Channel Communications Inc.: WGMN, WJJS-FM, WROV-FM, WSNV(FM), WSNZ(FM), WVGM, WYYD-FM, WZBL(FM)
Kovas Communications of Indiana Inc.: WLVA
Mel Wheeler Inc.: WFIR(AM), WSLQ-FM, WVBE(AM), WVBE-FM, WXLK-FM
Perception Media Group Inc.: WCQV(AM), WWWR

Rochester, MN: Rank 230
MSA: 150,100 TSA: 431,400
Clear Channel Communications Inc.: KRCH(FM), KWEB(AM)
Cumulus Media Inc.: KOLM(AM), KROC(AM)

Rochester, NY: Rank 54
MSA: 941,600 TSA: 1,181,400
WACK(AM), WASB
Clear Channel Communications Inc.: WFXF(FM), WHAM, WHTK, WISY-FM, WKGS-FM
Crawford Broadcasting Co.: WLGZ(AM), WRCI(FM)
Entercom Communications Corp.: WBEE-FM, WBZA(FM), WFKL(FM)
Holy Family Communications: WHIC(AM)
Infinity Broadcasting Corp.: WCMF-FM, WPXY-FM, WRMM-FM

Rockford, IL: Rank 152
MSA: 283,500 TSA: 607,900
Cumulus Media Inc.: WKGL-FM, WROK, WXXQ-FM, WZOK-FM
Good Karma Broadcasting L.L.C.: WTJK
Maverick Media LLC: WGFB(FM), WNTA, WXRX-FM, WYHY(FM)

Rocky Mount-Wilson, NC: Rank 200
MSA: 185,800

Sacramento, CA: Rank 26
MSA: 1,758,100 TSA: 3,140,900
KSAC(AM)
ABC Inc.: KIID(AM)
Bustos Media LLC: KTTA-FM
Cherry Creek Radio LLC: KRLT-FM
Citadel Broadcasting Corp.: KWYL(FM)
Clear Channel Communications Inc.: KFBK, KGBY-FM, KHYL-FM, KSTE
EMF Broadcasting: KLVS(FM)
Entercom Communications Corp.: KCTC, KDND(FM), KRXQ-FM, KSEG-FM, KSSJ-FM, KWOD-FM
Entravision Communications Corp.: KBMB(FM), KCCL-FM, KRCX-FM, KXSE(FM)
Family Stations Inc.: KEDR-FM
First Broadcasting Investment Partners LLC: KXCL(FM)
IHR Educational Broadcasting: KAHI, KSMH(AM)
Infinity Broadcasting Corp.: KHTK, KHWD(FM), KNCI-FM, KSFM-FM, KYMX-FM, KZZO-FM
Lazer Broadcasting Corp.: KSRN(FM)
Salem Communications Corp.: KFIA, KTKZ

Saginaw-Bay City-Midland, MI: Rank 130
MSA: 340,800 TSA: 1,269,700
Citadel Broadcasting Corp.: WHNN-FM, WILZ-FM, WIOG(FM), WKQZ-FM, WYLZ-FM
MacDonald Broadcasting Co.: WKCQ-FM, WMJO(FM), WSAM
Meredith Broadcasting Group, Meredith Corp.: WNEM(AM)
NextMedia Group Inc.: WCEN-FM, WSGW, WTLZ-FM, WXQL(FM)

Salisbury-Ocean City, MD: Rank 146
MSA: 296,100 TSA: 526,000
Birach Broadcasting Corp.: WGOP(AM)
Clear Channel Communications Inc.: WDKZ(FM), WLBW-FM, WOSC-FM, WSBY-FM, WTGM, WWFG-FM
Delmarva Broadcasting Co.: WAFL-FM, WICO(AM), WNCL(FM), WQJZ-FM, WXJN-FM, WXMD(FM)
Great Scott Broadcasting: WGBG-FM, WJWL, WKDB(FM), WKHW-FM, WOCQ-FM, WZEB(FM)

Salt Lake City-Ogden-Provo, UT: Rank 31
MSA: 1,485,600 TSA: 1,832,200
3 Point Media: KHTB(FM)
ABC Inc.: KWDZ(FM)
Azteca Broadcasting Corp.: KSVN
Bible Broadcasting Network: KYFO-FM
Bonneville International Corporation: KQMB(FM), KRSP-FM, KSFI-FM, KSL
Bustos Media LLC: KDUT(FM), KRRD(AM)
Carlson Communications International: KDYL(AM)
Citadel Broadcasting Corp.: KBEE(FM), KBER-FM, KENZ-FM, KJQS(AM), KKAT(AM), KPQP(FM)

Clear Channel Communications Inc.: KALL(AM), KJMY(FM), KNRS, KODJ-FM, KOSY-FM, KXRV(FM), KZHT(FM)
Family Stations Inc.: KUFR-FM
Legacy Communications Corp.: KYFO(AM)
Millcreek Broadcasting L.L.C.: KUDD(FM), KUUU(FM)
Simmons Media Group: KEGH(FM), KOVO, KRAR-FM, KXOL, KXRK-FM, KZNS(AM)

San Angelo, TX: Rank 284
MSA: 86,300 TSA: 125,500
Criswell Communications: KCRN, KCRN-FM
EMF Broadcasting: KLRW(FM)
Encore Broadcasting L.L.C.: KELI-FM, KGKL, KGKL-FM, KKCN(FM), KNRX(FM)
Foster Communications Co. Inc.: KCLL(FM), KIXY-FM, KKSA, KWFR-FM

San Antonio, TX: Rank 30
MSA: 1,552,100 TSA: 1,997,000
KSJL
ABC Inc.: KRDY(AM)
Bible Broadcasting Network: KYFS-FM
Border Media Partners LLC: KFNI, KSAH(AM), KTFM(FM)
Clear Channel Communications Inc.: KIXS-FM, KQXT-FM, KTKR, KXXM-FM, WOAI
Cox Enterprises Inc.: KCYY(FM), KELZ-FM, KISS-FM, KKYX, KONO, KONO-FM, KSMG(FM)
Infinity Broadcasting Corp.: KSRX(FM), KTSA
Lotus Communications Corp.: KZEP-FM
Martin Broadcasting Inc.: KCHL
Multicultural Radio Broadcasting Inc.: KZDC
Salem Communications Corp.: KLUP(AM), KSLR
SIGA Broadcasting Corp.: KTMR
Univision Radio: KAHL(AM), KBBT(FM), KCOR(AM), KCOR-FM, KLTO-FM, KXTN-FM
Victoria RadioWorks Ltd.: KEPG-FM, KNAL(AM)

San Diego, CA: Rank 17
MSA: 2,484,900 TSA: 2,674,700
KFMB
Astor Broadcast Group: KCEO, KFSD(AM)
Clear Channel Communications Inc.: KGB-FM, KHTS-FM, KIOZ-FM, KLSD(AM), KMYI(FM), KOGO(AM), KUSS(FM), XETRA
EMF Broadcasting: KLVJ-FM
Entravision Communications Corp.: KSSD(FM)
Hi-Favor Broadcasting LLC: KSDO
Infinity Broadcasting Corp.: KPLN-FM, KYXY-FM
Jefferson-Pilot Communications Co.: KBZT(FM), KIFM-FM, KSON-FM, KSOQ-FM
Multicultural Radio Broadcasting Inc.: KSON
Salem Communications Corp.: KCBQ, KPRZ
Univision Radio: KLNV-FM, KLQV-FM

San Francisco: Rank 4
MSA: 5,829,700 TSA: 7,309,700
KBAY(FM), KEZR-FM
ABC Inc.: KGO, KMKY
American Radio Brokers Inc./SFO: KABN(AM)
Bonneville International Corporation: KDFC-FM, KOIT, KOIT-FM, KZBR(FM)
Clear Channel Communications Inc.: KCNL(FM), KIOI-FM, KISQ-FM, KKSF-FM, KMEL-FM, KNEW, KQKE(AM), KSJO-FM, KYLD-FM
Coast Radio Company Inc.: KKDV(FM), KKIQ-FM, KUIC-FM
EMF Broadcasting: KLVR-FM
Entravision Communications Corp.: KBRG(FM), KLOK
Family Stations Inc.: KFRC
Fritz Communications Inc.: KRPQ-FM
Infinity Broadcasting Corp.: KCBS, KEAR-FM, KFRC-FM, KITS-FM, KLLC-FM, KYCY
Inner City Broadcasting: KBLX-FM, KVTO, KVVN
Mapleton Communications LLC: KPIG(AM)
Maverick Media LLC: KSRO, KVRV(FM), KXFX-FM
Moon Broadcasting: KLLK, KRRS, KTOB(AM)
Multicultural Radio Broadcasting Inc.: KATD, KEST, KIQI
Pacifica Foundation Inc.: KPFA-FM
Salem Communications Corp.: KFAX, KNTS(AM)
Sinclair Communications Inc.: KSXY(FM)
Spanish Broadcasting System Inc.: KRZZ(FM)
Susquehanna Radio Corp.: KFFG-FM, KFOG-FM, KNBR, KSAN-FM, KTCT
Univision Radio: KSOL(FM), KVVF(FM), KVVZ(FM)

San Jose, CA: Rank 34
MSA: 1,413,100 TSA: 1,677,300
Multicultural Radio Broadcasting Inc.: KSJX(AM)

San Luis Obispo, CA: Rank 173
MSA: 226,500 TSA: 393,300
American General Media: KIQO-FM, KKAL(FM), KKJG-FM, KLRM(FM), KZOZ-FM
Clear Channel Communications Inc.: KSLY-FM, KSTT-FM, KURQ(FM), KVEC
EMF Broadcasting: KLVH(FM)
Lazer Broadcasting Corp.: KLMM(FM)
Mapleton Communications LLC: KPYG(FM), KXTZ-FM, KYNS(AM)

Santa Barbara, CA: Rank 207
MSA: 171,300 TSA: 342,800
Clear Channel Communications Inc.: KBKO, KIST(AM), KIST-FM, KSBL-FM, KSPE-FM, KTYD-FM
Cumulus Media Inc.: KMGQ(FM), KRUZ(FM), KVYB(FM)
Lazer Broadcasting Corp.: KZER(AM)

Santa Fe, NM: Rank 237
MSA: 138,500 TSA: 197,400
American General Media: KTRC(AM), KVSF(AM), KZNM(FM)
Clear Channel Communications Inc.: KBAC(FM), KSFQ-FM

Santa Maria-Lompoc, CA: Rank 209
MSA: 170,700 TSA: 168,000
American General Media: KBOX(FM), KPAT-FM, KRQK-FM
Clear Channel Communications Inc.: KSMY(FM)
Family Stations Inc.: KHFR(FM)
Lazer Broadcasting Corp.: KSBQ
Mapleton Communications LLC: KTME, KUHL, KWSZ(FM)

Santa Rosa, CA: Rank 118
MSA: 402,200 TSA: 402,100

Sarasota-Bradenton, FL: Rank 74
MSA: 591,500 TSA: 746,500
Clear Channel Communications Inc.: WDDV(AM), WFUS(FM), WLTQ-FM, WSRQ(AM), WSRZ-FM, WTZB(FM)
Cox Enterprises Inc.: WHPT(FM)
Infinity Broadcasting Corp.: WLLD-FM
Metropolitan Radio Group Inc.: WBRD, WTMY
Northwestern College & Radio: WSMR-FM
Salem Communications Corp.: WLSS(AM)
The Moody Bible Institute of Chicago: WKZM-FM
Viper Communications Broadcast Group: WENG

Savannah, GA: Rank 157
MSA: 263,100 TSA: 728,000
WRHQ-FM
Bible Broadcasting Network: WYFS-FM
Clear Channel Communications Inc.: WAEV-FM, WLVH-FM, WSOK, WTKS(AM), WYKZ(FM)
Cumulus Media Inc.: WBMQ, WEAS-FM, WIXV-FM, WJCL-FM, WJLG, WTYB(FM), WZAT-FM
Tama Broadcasting Inc.: WSGA(FM)
Triad Broadcasting Co. L.L.C.: WFXH(AM), WGCO(FM), WGZR(FM), WLOW(FM), WWVV(FM)

Seattle-Tacoma, WA: Rank 14
MSA: 3,204,800 TSA: 3,763,000
ABC Inc.: KKDZ
Bustos Media LLC: KWMG(AM)
Clear Channel Communications Inc.: KFNK(FM), KHHO, KJR, KUBE-FM
CRISTA Broadcasting: KCIS(AM), KCMS(FM)
Entercom Communications Corp.: KBSG-FM, KIRO, KISW-FM, KMTT-FM, KNDD-FM, KQBZ-FM, KTTH(AM)
Family Stations Inc.: KARR
Fisher Broadcasting Company: KOMO, KPLZ-FM
Infinity Broadcasting Corp.: KBKS-FM, KJAQ(FM), KMPS-FM, KPTK(AM), KZOK-FM
Multicultural Radio Broadcasting Inc.: KXPA
Premier Broadcasters: KRXY-FM
Salem Communications Corp.: KGNW, KKMO, KKOL, KLFE, KTFH(AM)
Sandusky Radio: KIXI, KLSY-FM, KRWM-FM, KWJZ(FM)
Seattle Streaming Radio LLC: KBRO, KNTB

Sebring, FL: Rank 287
MSA: 82,500 TSA: 80,600
Cohan Radio Group Inc.: WITS(AM), WJCM(AM), WWLL(FM), WWOJ(FM), WWTK(AM)

Sheboygan, WI: Rank 276
MSA: 98,200 TSA: 98,300
Midwest Communications Inc.: WHBL(AM), WHBZ(FM)
Mountain Dog Media: WCLB(AM), WXER(FM)

Shreveport, LA: Rank 132
MSA: 332,200 TSA: 892,800
Access.1 Communications Corp.: KBTT(FM), KLKL(FM), KOKA, KSYR(FM), KTAL-FM
Amistad Communications Inc.: KASO, KSYB(AM)
Clear Channel Communications Inc.: KEEL(AM), KTUX-FM, KVKI-FM, KWKH(AM)
Cumulus Media Inc.: KMJJ-FM, KQHN(FM), KRMD-FM, KVMA-FM
Metropolitan Radio Group Inc.: KIOU, KORI-FM, KTKC-FM

Sioux City, IA: Rank 273
MSA: 101,400 TSA: 284,000
Clear Channel Communications Inc.: KGLI-FM, KMNS, KSEZ-FM, KSFT-FM, KWSL

Broadcasting & Cable Yearbook 2006

U.S. Radio Markets

Waitt Broadcasting Inc.: KKYY(FM)

South Bend, IN: Rank 178
MSA: 220,800 TSA: 879,500
Artistic Media Partners Inc.: WNDV, WNDV-FM, WOZW(FM)
Federated Media: WAOR-FM, WBYT-FM
Le Sea Broadcasting: WHME-FM
Progressive Broadcasting System Inc.: WFRN-FM
Schurz Communications Inc.: WNSN-FM, WSBT

Spokane, WA: Rank 92
MSA: 480,800 TSA: 738,900
KXLI(AM)
Citadel Broadcasting Corp.: KBBD(FM), KEYF(AM), KEYF-FM, KGA, KJRB
Clear Channel Communications Inc.: KCDA(FM), KIXZ-FM, KKZX-FM, KPTQ(AM), KQNT(AM)
First Broadcasting Investment Partners LLC: KAZZ(FM)
Morgan Murphy Stations (Evening Telegram Co): KEZE-FM, KXLY, KZZU-FM
Morris Radio LLC: KWIQ(AM)
Pamplin Broadcasting: KTSL-FM
The Moody Bible Institute of Chicago: KMBI-FM

Springfield, MA: Rank 82
MSA: 529,500 TSA: 597,400
Citadel Broadcasting Corp.: WMAS
Clear Channel Communications Inc.: WHYN, WNNZ, WPKX-FM
Davidson Media Group LLC: WACM, WSPR
Pamal Broadcasting Ltd.: WPNI(AM), WRNX-FM
Saga Communications Inc.: WAQY-FM, WHMP, WHNP(AM), WLZX(FM), WRSI(FM)

Springfield, MO: Rank 145
MSA: 300,800 TSA: 655,000
Bott Radio Network: KSCV(FM)
Clear Channel Communications Inc.: KGMY, KSWF(FM), KTOZ-FM, KXUS-FM
Journal Communications Inc.: KSGF(AM), KSGF-FM, KSPW(FM)
Meyer Communications Inc.: KTXR-FM, KWTO, KWTO-FM
The Mid-West Family Broadcast Group: KKLH(FM), KOMG(FM), KOSP(FM), KQRA(FM)

St. Cloud, MN: Rank 219
MSA: 161,100 TSA: 482,600
Leighton Enterprises Inc.: KCML(FM), KNSI, KZPK-FM
Regent Communications Inc.: KKSR(FM), KLZZ-FM, KMXK-FM, KXSS(AM), WJON
Tri-County Broadcasting Inc.: WBHR, WHMH-FM

St. Louis, MO: Rank 20
MSA: 2,262,000 TSA: 2,737,800
ABC Inc.: WSDZ
Big League Broadcasting LLC: KFNS(AM), KFNS-FM, KRFT(AM)
Birach Broadcasting Corp.: WEW
Bonneville International Corporation: WARH(FM), WIL(AM), WIL-FM, WVRV-FM
Bott Radio Network: KSIV(AM), KSIV-FM
Clear Channel Communications Inc.: KATZ, KATZ-FM, KLOU-FM, KMJM-FM, KSD-FM, KSLZ-FM
Crawford Broadcasting Co.: KJSL, KSTL
Emmis Communications Corp.: KFTK(FM), KIHT-FM, KPNT-FM, KSHE(FM), WRDA(FM)
Infinity Broadcasting Corp.: KEZK-FM, KMOX, KYKY-FM
Kaspar Broadcasting Group: KWRE
Radio One Inc.: WFUN-FM
Shepherd Group: KJFF(AM)
Simmons Media Group: KSLG(AM), WESL
The Curators of the University of Missouri: KWMU-FM

Stamford-Norwalk, CT: Rank 142
MSA: 304,800 TSA: 300,900

State College, PA: Rank 254
MSA: 127,100 TSA: 312,700
2510 Licenses LLC: WBUS(FM), WOWY(FM), WRSC
Family Stations Inc.: WXFR(FM)
First Media Radio LLC: WZWW-FM
Forever Broadcasting: WJHT(FM), WLTS(FM), WMAJ, WQWK(FM)
Magnum Broadcasting Inc.: WBLF, WPHB, WUBZ-FM

Stockton, CA: Rank 80
MSA: 542,600 TSA: 526,100
Citadel Broadcasting Corp.: KJOY-FM, KWIN-FM
Clear Channel Communications Inc.: KQOD-FM, KUYL(AM)
Entravision Communications Corp.: KCVR, KMIX-FM
IHR Educational Broadcasting: KWG(AM)

Sunbury-Selingrove-Lewisburg, PA: Rank 213
MSA: 167,400 TSA: 245,100

Sussex, NJ: Rank 248
MSA: 130,400 TSA: 176,900
Clear Channel Communications Inc.: WNNJ, WSUS-FM

Syracuse, NY: Rank 77
MSA: 558,500 TSA: 991,900
Buckley Broadcasting Corp.: WFBL(AM), WSEN(AM)
Citadel Broadcasting Corp.: WAQX-FM, WLTI(FM), WNTQ(FM)
Clear Channel Communications Inc.: WBBS-FM, WHEN, WPHR(FM), WSYR, WWDG(FM), WYYY-FM
Galaxy Communications L.P.: WSCP, WSCP-FM, WSGO, WTKW-FM, WTLA, WZUN(FM)
Mars Hill Network: WMHR-FM
WOLF Radio Inc.: WOLF, WOLF-FM

Tallahassee, FL: Rank 163
MSA: 246,400 TSA: 563,000
Clear Channel Communications Inc.: WTLY(FM), WTNT-FM, WXSR-FM
Cumulus Media Inc.: WGLF(FM), WHBT(AM), WHBX(FM), WWLD(FM)
Opus Media Holdings LLC: WAIB-FM, WEGT(FM), WHTF-FM, WUTL(FM)

Tampa-St. Petersburg-Clearwater, FL: Rank 19
MSA: 2,262,900 TSA: 3,667,000
ABC Inc.: WWMI
Bible Broadcasting Network: WYFE-FM
Clear Channel Communications Inc.: WBTP(FM), WFLA(AM), WHNZ(AM), WXTB-FM
Cox Enterprises Inc.: WDUV-FM, WPOI(FM), WSUN-FM, WWRM(FM), WXGL(FM)
Family Stations Inc.: WFTI-FM
Genesis Communications Inc.: WLVU(AM), WWBA
Infinity Broadcasting Corp.: WBZZ(AM), WQYK-FM, WRBQ-FM, WYUU(FM)
Mega Communications Inc.: WLCC, WMGG(AM)
Metropolitan Radio Group Inc.: WRXB
Salem Communications Corp.: WNTR(AM), WTBN(AM), WTWD(AM)
Tama Broadcasting Corp.: WTMP, WTMP-FM
Wagenvoord Advertising Group Inc.: WDCF, WTAN, WZHR(AM)

Terre Haute, IN: Rank 203
MSA: 174,300 TSA: 350,200
Crossroads Communications Inc.: WAXI-FM, WBOW(AM), WSDM-FM, WSDX(AM)
Emmis Communications Corp.: WTHI-FM, WWVR-FM
Key Broadcasting Inc.: WACF-FM, WPRS
The Cromwell Group Inc.: WCBH-FM
The Original Company Inc.: WQTY-FM

Texarkana, TX-AR: Rank 263
MSA: 112,900 TSA: 286,400
Arklatex LLC: KBYB(FM), KCMC, KFYX(FM), KTFS(AM), KTOY(FM)
Clear Channel Communications Inc.: KKYR-FM, KOSY(AM), KPWW-FM, KYGL-FM
EMF Broadcasting: KKLT(FM)
Family Worship Center Church Inc.: KNRB(FM)
Textron Financial Corp.: KEWL(AM), KEWL-FM, KPGG(FM)

The Florida Keys, FL: Rank 292
MSA: 70,800

Toledo, OH: Rank 84
MSA: 517,400 TSA: 1,137,700
Clear Channel Communications Inc.: WCWA, WIOT(FM), WPFX-FM, WRVF(FM), WSPD, WVKS-FM
Cumulus Media Inc.: WLQR, WRQN-FM, WRWK(FM), WTOD, WTWR-FM, WWWM-FM, WXKR-FM
Family Stations Inc.: WOTL-FM
Family Worship Center Church Inc.: WJYM
Urban Radio Licenses LLC: WIMX-FM, WJZE-FM

Topeka, KS: Rank 194
MSA: 192,900 TSA: 500,900
American Family Radio: KBUZ(FM)
Bott Radio Network: KCVT(FM)
Cumulus Media Inc.: KCHZ(FM), KMAJ, KTOP, KWIC-FM
Morris Radio LLC: WIBW

Traverse City-Petoskey, MI: Rank 192
MSA: 196,100 TSA: 482,500
Fort Bend Broadcasting Co.: WBNZ(FM), WLDR-FM, WOUF(FM)
Good News Media Inc.: WLJN-FM
MacDonald Garber Broadcasting Co.: WKHQ-FM, WMBN(AM)
Midwestern Broadcasting Co.: WBCM(FM), WCCW(AM), WJZQ(FM), WTCM(AM)
Northern Star Broadcasting L.L.C.: WGFM(FM), WGFN(FM), WJZJ(FM), WLJZ(FM)

Trenton, NJ: Rank 140
MSA: 313,400 TSA: 836,700
Millennium Radio Group LLC: WBUD, WKXW-FM, WTTM
Multicultural Radio Broadcasting Inc.: WHWH, WTTM
Nassau Broadcasting Partners L.P.: WPHY(AM), WPST(FM), WTHK(FM)

Tri-Cities, WA (Richland-Kennewick-Pasco): Rank 202
MSA: 181,600 TSA: 400,300
Bustos Media LLC: KZTB(FM)
Cherry Creek Radio LLC: KONA, KONA-FM
Clear Channel Communications Inc.: KEYW-FM, KFLD
CSN International: KBLD(FM)
EMF Broadcasting: KRKL(FM)
Moon Broadcasting: KMNA(FM), KZXR
New Northwest Broadcasters LLC: KALE, KIOK-FM, KNLT-FM, KTCR

Tucson, AZ: Rank 61
MSA: 783,300 TSA: 1,086,000
Citadel Broadcasting Corp.: KCUB, KHYT-FM, KIIM-FM, KSZR(FM), KTUC
Clear Channel Communications Inc.: KNST, KOHT-FM, KRQQ-FM, KTZR-FM, KWFM(AM), KWMT-FM, KXEW
EMF Broadcasting: KAIC(FM)
Family Life Communications Inc.: KFLT, KFLT-FM
Good News Communications Inc.: KGMS(AM), KVOI
Journal Communications Inc.: KGMG-FM, KMXZ-FM, KZPT-FM
Lotus Communications Corp.: KFMA-FM, KLPX-FM, KTKT
Multicultural Radio Broadcasting Inc.: KQTL

Tulsa, OK: Rank 65
MSA: 722,000 TSA: 1,338,200
KMUR(AM), KRVT(AM)
ABC Inc.: KMUS(AM)
Adonai Radio Group: KCXR(FM), KEMX-FM, KMMY-FM, KXOJ-FM, KYAL(AM)
Clear Channel Communications Inc.: KAKC(AM), KIZS(FM), KMOD-FM, KQLL-FM, KTBT(FM), KTBZ(AM)
Cox Enterprises Inc.: KJSR-FM, KRAV-FM, KRMG, KRTQ-FM, KWEN-FM
Journal Communications Inc.: KFAQ(AM), KXBL(FM)
K95.5 Inc.: KTFX, KTFX-FM
Perry Publishing & Broadcasting Co.: KGTO, KJMM-FM
Renda Broadcasting Corp.: KBEZ(FM), KHTT-FM
Shamrock Communications Inc.: KMYZ-FM, KTSO(FM)

Tupelo, MS: Rank 189
MSA: 200,000 TSA: 461,900
Air South Radio Inc.: WFTA-FM
American Family Radio: WAQB-FM
Clear Channel Communications Inc.: WBVV(FM), WESE-FM, WKMQ(AM), WTUP, WWKZ(FM), WWZD-FM
Stanford Communications Inc.: WAMY, WWZQ
Urban Radio Licenses LLC: WACR-FM

Tuscaloosa, AL: Rank 234
MSA: 142,500 TSA: 327,400
Citadel Broadcasting Corp.: WBEI(FM), WJRD(AM), WTSK, WTUG-FM
Clear Channel Communications Inc.: WACT, WRTR(FM), WTXT-FM, WZBQ-FM
The Moody Bible Institute of Chicago: WMFT(FM)

Tyler-Longview, TX: Rank 149
MSA: 292,900 TSA: 821,300
Access.1 Communications Corp.: KFRO, KKUS(FM), KOOI-FM, KYKX-FM
Clear Channel Communications Inc.: KBGE(AM), KISX-FM, KKTX-FM, KNUE(FM), KTYL-FM
Gleiser Communications LLC: KDOK-FM, KEES, KTBB, KYZS
Reynolds Radio Inc.: KLBL(FM)
Salem Communications Corp.: KPXI-FM
Waller Broadcasting: KEBE, KFRO-FM, KLJT-FM, KXAL-FM

Utica-Rome, NY: Rank 159
MSA: 259,600 TSA: 400,900
Bible Broadcasting Network: WYFY
Clear Channel Communications Inc.: WADR, WIXT(AM), WOKR(FM), WRNY, WSKS(FM), WSKU(FM), WUTQ
EMF Broadcasting: WKVU(FM)
Galaxy Communications L.P.: WKLL-FM, WRCK-FM, WTLB
Regent Communications Inc.: WFRG-FM, WIBX, WODZ-FM
WAMC/Northeast Public Radio: WRUN

Valdosta, GA: Rank 268
MSA: 104,500 TSA: 169,900

Victor Valley, CA: Rank 127
MSA: 357,800 TSA: 343,200

Visalia-Tulare-Hanford, CA: Rank 101
MSA: 444,300 TSA: 428,500
Azteca Broadcasting Corp.: KGEN, KGEN-FM

U.S. Radio Markets

Buckley Broadcasting Corp.: KIOO-FM, KSEQ-FM
Clear Channel Communications Inc.: KVBL
IHR Educational Broadcasting: KJOP
Moon Broadcasting: KMQA-FM

Waco, TX: Rank 198
MSA: 186,700 TSA: 605,200
Border Media Partners LLC: KWOW-FM
Clear Channel Communications Inc.: KBGO(FM), KBRQ(FM), KWTX, KWTX-FM, WACO-FM
Simmons Media Group: KLRK(FM), KQRL(FM), KRZI(AM)
Univision Radio: KHCK-FM

Washington, DC: Rank 8
MSA: 4,132,800 TSA: 7,040,000
WKDV
ABC Inc.: WJZW-FM, WMAL
Bonneville International Corporation: WFED(AM), WGMS-FM, WTOP, WTOP-FM, WWVZ-FM, WWZZ(FM), WXTR
Clear Channel Communications Inc.: WASH-FM, WBIG-FM, WIHT(FM), WMZQ-FM, WTEM, WTNT(AM), WWDC-FM, WWRC(AM)
Entravision Communications Corp.: WACA
Infinity Broadcasting Corp.: WARW-FM, WJFK-FM, WLZL(FM), WPGC, WPGC-FM
Mega Communications Inc.: WBPS-FM, WBZS-FM, WKDL(AM)
Multicultural Radio Broadcasting Inc.: WLXE(AM), WZHF
Nassau Broadcasting Partners L.P.: WAFY-FM
Pacifica Foundation Inc.: WPFW-FM
Radio One Inc.: WKYS-FM, WMMJ-FM, WYCB
Salem Communications Corp.: WABS, WAVA(FM)
Somar Communications Inc.: WKIK, WMDM-FM

Waterloo-Cedar Falls, IA: Rank 252
MSA: 128,400 TSA: 543,200
Bahakel Communications: KFMW-FM, KOKZ-FM, KWLO, KXEL
Cumulus Media Inc.: KCRR(FM), KKHQ-FM, KOEL-FM
KM Communications Inc.: KQMG, KQMG-FM
Northwestern College & Radio: KNWS

Watertown, NY: Rank 281
MSA: 92,100 TSA: 216,200
Clancy-Mance Communications: WATN, WBDI(FM), WBDR(FM), WTOJ(FM)
Mars Hill Network: WMHI-FM
Regent Communications Inc.: WNER(AM), WTNY

Wausau-Stevens Point, WI (Central Wisconsin): Rank 168
MSA: 233,900 TSA: 543,000
Badger Communications L.L.C.: WXCO
Midwest Communications Inc.: WDEZ-FM, WIZD-FM, WOFM-FM, WRIG, WSAU
Muzzy Broadcasting L.L.C.: WKQH-FM, WSPT
NewRadio Group LLC: WDLB, WFHR, WOSQ-FM, WYTE-FM

West Palm Beach-Boca Raton, FL: Rank 46
MSA: 1,098,000 TSA: 3,040,300

ABC Inc.: WMNE(AM)
Beasley Broadcast Group Inc.: WSBR
Clear Channel Communications Inc.: WBZT(AM), WJNO(AM), WKGR-FM, WLDI-FM, WOLL-FM, WRLX-FM, WZZR(FM)
Infinity Broadcasting Corp.: WEAT-FM, WIRK-FM, WJBW-FM, WMBX-FM, WPBZ-FM
James Crystal Inc.: WDJA(AM), WFTL(AM), WJBW(AM), WJNA(AM), WLVJ(AM)
WAY-FM Media Group Inc.: WAYF(FM)

Wheeling, WV: Rank 249
MSA: 129,900 TSA: 338,600
Clear Channel Communications Inc.: WBBD, WEGW-FM, WVKF(FM), WWVA(AM)
Keymarket Communications LLC: WOMP, WOMP-FM, WUKL(FM)

Wichita Falls, TX: Rank 262
MSA: 114,600 TSA: 338,700
Clear Channel Communications Inc.: KBZS(FM), KNIN-FM, KWFS
Cumulus Media Inc.: KLUR-FM, KOLI-FM, KQXC-FM, KYYI-FM

Wichita, KS: Rank 95
MSA: 462,600 TSA: 675,500
KAHS(AM)
ABC Inc.: KQAM
American Family Radio: KCFN(FM)
Bible Broadcasting Network: KYFW-FM
Clear Channel Communications Inc.: KRBB(FM), KTHR(FM), KZCH(FM), KZSN-FM
EMF Broadcasting: KTLI-FM
Entercom Communications Corp.: KDGS(FM), KEYN-FM, KFBZ(FM), KFH(AM), KFH-FM, KNSS(AM)
Journal Communications Inc.: KFTI(AM), KFXJ(FM), KICT-FM, KMXW(FM), KYQQ-FM
Robert Ingstad Broadcast Properties: KBUF(AM)
WAY-FM Media Group Inc.: KYWA(FM)

Wilkes Barre-Scranton, PA: Rank 69
MSA: 681,400 TSA: 1,174,900
WITK(AM)
Citadel Broadcasting Corp.: WARM, WBHD(FM), WBHT-FM, WBSX(FM), WMGS-FM, WSJR(FM)
Clear Channel Communications Inc.: WHCY-FM
Entercom Communications Corp.: WBZU(AM), WDMT(FM), WFEZ(FM), WGGI-FM, WGGY-FM, WILK, WKRF(FM), WKRZ-FM, WKZN(AM)
Holy Family Communications: WQOR(AM)
MAX Media L.L.C.: WFYY(FM)
Nassau Broadcasting Partners L.P.: WVPO
Route 81 Radio LLC: WAZL, WCDL(AM), WNAK, WNAK-FM
Shamrock Communications Inc.: WBAX, WEJL, WEZX-FM, WQFM-FM, WQFN(FM)

Williamsport, PA: Rank 270
MSA: 102,600 TSA: 311,200
Backyard Broadcasting LLC: WBZD-FM, WILQ-FM, WRVH(FM), WWPA

Clear Channel Communications Inc.: WBYL(FM), WRAK, WRKK, WVRT(FM)

Wilmington, DE: Rank 75
MSA: 581,800 TSA: 711,100
Clear Channel Communications Inc.: WILM, WWTX(AM)
Delmarva Broadcasting Co.: WDEL, WSTW-FM, WXCY(FM)
NextMedia Group Inc.: WJBR-FM
Priority Radio Inc.: WSRY(AM)

Wilmington, NC: Rank 170
MSA: 230,400 TSA: 376,000
Cumulus Media Inc.: WAAV, WGNI-FM, WMNX-FM, WWQQ-FM
Family Radio Network Inc.: WDVV-FM, WLSG(AM), WMYT, WWIL
NextMedia Group Inc.: WAZO(FM), WKXB-FM, WMFD, WRQR-FM
Sea-Comm Inc.: WBNE(FM), WBNU(FM), WLTT(FM)

Winchester, VA: Rank 225
MSA: 155,900 TSA: 361,900
WSVG(FM)
Clear Channel Communications Inc.: WAZR-FM, WFQX-FM, WTFX(FM)
Mid Atlantic Network: WINC, WWRE(FM), WWRT(FM)
Vox Radio Group L.P.: WSIG(FM)

Worcester, MA: Rank 110
MSA: 414,700 TSA: 763,800
WORC
Blount Communications Group: WNEB, WVNE(AM)
Citadel Broadcasting Corp.: WORC-FM, WWFX(FM), WXLO-FM
Clear Channel Communications Inc.: WTAG
Entercom Communications Corp.: WVEI(AM)
Northeast Broadcasting Company Inc.: WJOE(AM), WNYN-FM

Yakima, WA: Rank 201
MSA: 184,400 TSA: 207,700
Bustos Media LLC: KYXE(AM), KZTA-FM, KZTS(AM)
Clear Channel Communications Inc.: KDBL(FM), KIT, KUTI(AM)
New Northwest Broadcasters LLC: KARY-FM, KBBO(AM), KHHK-FM, KJOX(AM)

York, PA: Rank 102
MSA: 436,900 TSA: 1,351,600
WQXA
Citadel Broadcasting Corp.: WQXA-FM
Hall Communications Inc.: WSJW(FM)
Susquehanna Radio Corp.: WARM-FM, WGLD(AM), WSBA, WSOX-FM

Youngstown-Warren, OH: Rank 119
MSA: 399,100 TSA: 917,800
Beacon Broadcasting Inc.: WANR
Clear Channel Communications Inc.: WAKZ(FM), WBBG(FM), WKBN, WNIO(AM)
Cumulus Media Inc.: WBBW, WLLF-FM, WPIC, WSOM, WWIZ-FM
Family Stations Inc.: WYTN-FM
Forever Broadcasting: WWGY(FM)
Holy Family Communications: WLOA(AM)
Salem Communications Corp.: WHKZ(AM)

U.S. Radio Markets: Arbitron Metro Survey Area Ranking

This chart ranks the 298 radio markets by Metro Survey Area population. Figures include all persons aged 12 or older and are based on 2000 U.S. Bureau of Census estimates updated and projected to January 1, 2006. Data reflects the Fall 2005 Arbitron market definitions. A single asterisk (*) following a market name indicates that the market is embedded in a larger nearby market. See U.S. Radio Markets beginning on pg. D-753 for details. The double asterisk (**) following the Monmouth-Ocean, NJ, market indicates that Monmouth County is included in both the Monmouth-Ocean, NJ, and New York Metro markets. The triple asterisk (***) following the Manchester, NH, market indicates that a portion of Rockingham County is included in both the Manchester, NH, and Portsmouth-Dover-Rochester, NH, markets.

Rank	Market	Population
1	New York, NY	15,332,000
2	Los Angeles, CA	10,790,100
3	Chicago, IL	7,698,300
4	San Francisco, CA	5,829,700
5	Dallas-Ft. Worth, TX	4,730,200
6	Philadelphia, PA	4,354,900
7	Houston-Galveston, TX	4,353,000
8	Washington, DC	4,132,800
9	Detroit, MI	3,892,600
10	Atlanta, GA	3,860,100
11	Boston, MA	3,841,100
12	Miami-Ft. Lauderdale-Hollywood, FL	3,505,100
13	Puerto Rico	3,250,400
14	Seattle-Tacoma, WA	3,204,800
15	Phoenix, AZ	2,938,500
16	Minneapolis-St. Paul, MN	2,632,400
17	San Diego, CA	2,484,900
18	Nassau-Suffolk (Long Island), NY	2,393,800
19	Tampa-St. Petersburg-Clearwater, FL	2,262,900
20	St. Louis, MO	2,262,000
21	Baltimore, MD	2,249,900
22	Denver-Boulder, CO	2,157,700
23	Pittsburgh, PA	2,015,100
24	Portland, OR	1,963,400
25	Cleveland, OH	1,799,900
26	Sacramento, CA	1,758,100
27	Riverside-San Bernardino, CA	1,756,600
28	Cincinnati, OH	1,705,200
29	Kansas City, MO-KS	1,553,300
30	San Antonio, TX	1,552,100
31	Salt Lake City-Ogden-Provo, UT	1,485,600
32	Las Vegas, NV	1,438,600
33	Milwaukee-Racine, WI	1,429,200
34	San Jose, CA	1,413,100
35	Charlotte-Gastonia-Rock Hill, NC-SC	1,409,800
36	Providence-Warwick-Pawtucket, RI	1,404,000
37	Orlando, FL	1,402,300
38	Columbus, OH	1,401,300
39	Middlesex-Somerset-Union, NJ	1,383,100
40	Norfolk-Virginia Beach-Newport News, VA	1,314,600
41	Indianapolis, IN	1,312,200
42	Austin, TX	1,204,800
43	Raleigh-Durham, NC	1,143,700
44	Nashville, TN	1,125,000
45	Greensboro-Winston Salem-High Point, NC	1,113,300
46	West Palm Beach-Boca Raton, FL	1,098,000
47	New Orleans, LA	1,079,200
48	Jacksonville, FL	1,057,600
49	Memphis, TN	1,047,900
50	Hartford-New Britain-Middletown, CT	1,043,700
51	Monmouth-Ocean, NJ**	1,021,400
52	Buffalo-Niagara Falls, NY	989,000
53	Oklahoma City, OK	958,100
54	Rochester, NY	941,600
55	Louisville, KY	923,000
56	Richmond, VA	898,600
57	Birmingham, AL	865,600
58	Dayton, OH	835,400
59	McAllen-Brownsville-Harlingen, TX	817,500
60	Greenville-Spartanburg, SC	813,700
61	Tucson, AZ	783,300
62	Albany-Schenectady-Troy, NY	777,900
63	Honolulu, HI	766,800
64	Ft. Myers-Naples-Marco Island, FL	744,800
65	Tulsa, OK	722,000
66	Fresno, CA	711,700
67	Grand Rapids, MI	703,400
68	Allentown-Bethlehem, PA	682,500
69	Wilkes Barre-Scranton, PA	681,400
70	Albuquerque, NM	654,200
71	Knoxville, TN	633,300
72	Omaha-Council Bluffs, NE-IA	610,000
73	Akron, OH	597,200
74	Sarasota-Bradenton, FL	591,500
75	Wilmington, DE	581,800
76	El Paso, TX	573,600
77	Syracuse, NY	558,500
78	Harrisburg-Lebanon-Carlisle, PA	558,400
79	Monterey-Salinas-Santa Cruz, CA	555,100
80	Stockton, CA	542,600
81	Bakersfield, CA	542,500
82	Springfield, MA	529,500
83	Baton Rouge, LA	529,100
84	Toledo, OH	517,400
85	Little Rock, AR	515,500
86	Gainesville-Ocala, FL	513,700
87	Greenville-New Bern-Jacksonville, NC	501,800
88	Charleston, SC	500,500
89	Daytona Beach, FL	500,300
90	Columbia, SC	485,400
91	Des Moines, IA	483,600
92	Spokane, WA	480,800
93	Mobile, AL	470,300
94	Melbourne-Titusville-Cocoa, FL	465,500
95	Wichita, KS	462,600
96	Madison, WI	461,700
97	Colorado Springs, CO	460,400
98	Lakeland-Winter Haven, FL	452,300
99	Johnson City-Kingsport-Bristol, TN-VA	452,000
100	Ft. Pierce-Stuart-Vero Beach, FL	445,000
101	Visalia-Tulare-Hanford, CA	444,300
102	York, PA	436,900
103	Lafayette, LA	435,100
104	Lexington-Fayette, KY	430,300
105	Ft. Wayne, IN	425,700
106	Chattanooga, TN	420,900
107	New Haven, CT	420,800
108	Boise, ID	416,100
109	Morristown, NJ	415,000
110	Worcester, MA	414,700
111	Modesto, CA	414,500
112	Augusta, GA	414,400
113	Lancaster, PA	411,800
114	Portsmouth-Dover-Rochester, NH	408,500
115	Huntsville, AL	407,600
116	Roanoke-Lynchburg, VA	404,000
117	Oxnard-Ventura, CA	403,500
118	Santa Rosa, CA	402,200
119	Youngstown-Warren, OH	399,100
120	Bridgeport, CT	395,600
121	Lansing-East Lansing, MI	390,200
122	Jackson, MS	386,400
123	Pensacola, FL	378,600
124	Reno, NV	378,000
125	Flint, MI	370,000
126	Ft. Collins-Greeley, CO	369,700
127	Victor Valley, CA	357,800
128	Fayetteville, NC	353,600
129	Canton, OH	350,000
130	Saginaw-Bay City-Midland, MI	340,800
131	Reading, PA	339,200
132	Shreveport, LA	332,200
133	Beaumont-Port Arthur, TX	321,800
134	Appleton-Oshkosh, WI	320,300
135	Atlantic City-Cape May, NJ	318,100
136	Burlington-Plattsburgh, VT-NY	317,100
137	Newburgh-Middletown (Mid-Hudson Valley), NY	315,900
138	Biloxi-Gulfport-Pascagoula, MS	314,500
139	Corpus Christi, TX	313,600
140	Trenton, NJ	313,400

# U.S. Radio Markets: Arbitron Metro Survey Area Ranking

#	Market	Population
141	Fayetteville (Northwest Arkansas), AR	305,400
142	Stamford-Norwalk, CT	304,800
143	Quad Cities (Davenport-Rock Island-Moline), IA-IL	303,400
144	Palm Springs, CA	302,200
145	Springfield, MO	300,800
146	Salisbury-Ocean City, MD	296,100
147	Ann Arbor, MI	295,400
148	Peoria, IL	294,800
149	Tyler-Longview, TX	292,900
150	Eugene-Springfield, OR	290,900
151	Montgomery, AL	287,500
152	Rockford, IL	283,500
153	Flagstaff-Prescott, AZ	280,700
154	Fredericksburg, VA	280,300
155	Macon, GA	278,000
156	Huntington-Ashland, WV-KY	270,900
157	Savannah, GA	263,100
158	Killeen-Temple, TX	262,700
159	Utica-Rome, NY	259,600
160	Evansville, IN	256,500
161	Asheville, NC	255,600
162	Poughkeepsie, NY	254,900
163	Tallahassee, FL	246,400
164	Myrtle Beach, SC	245,700
165	Erie, PA	240,400
166	Hagerstown-Chambersburg-Waynesboro, MD-PA	239,500
167	Portland, ME	238,700
168	Wausau-Stevens Point (Central Wisconsin), WI	233,900
169	Concord (Lake Regions), NH	233,400
170	Wilmington, NC	230,400
171	New London, CT	230,000
172	Anchorage, AK	228,900
173	San Luis Obispo, CA	226,500
174	New Bedford-Fall River, MA	225,500
175	Morgantown-Clarksburg-Fairmont, WV	223,300
176	Lincoln, NE	222,800
177	Ft. Smith, AR	221,100
178	South Bend, IN	220,800
179	Binghamton, NY	214,900
180	Lebanon-Rutland-White River Junction, NH-VT	214,800
181	Charleston, WV	214,100
182	Lubbock, TX	211,300
183	Merced, CA	208,700
184	Kalamazoo, MI	204,000
185	Cape Cod, MA	203,400
186	Green Bay, WI	201,900
187	Columbus, GA	201,000
188	Odessa-Midland, TX	200,800
189	Tupelo, MS	200,000
190	Johnstown, PA	198,700
191	Manchester, NH***	197,600
192	Traverse City-Petoskey, MI	196,100
193	Dothan, AL	195,200
194	Topeka, KS	192,900
195	Amarillo, TX	191,200
196	Danbury, CT	188,000
197	Frederick, MD	186,900
198	Waco, TX	186,700
199	Chico, CA	186,000
200	Rocky Mount-Wilson, NC	185,800
201	Yakima, WA	184,400
202	Tri-Cities (Richland-Kennewick-Pasco), WA	181,600
203	Terre Haute, IN	174,300
204	Duluth-Superior, MN-WI	174,000
205	Muncie-Marion, IN	172,400
206	Clarksville-Hopkinsville, TN-KY	171,900
207	Santa Barbara, CA	171,300
208	Laredo, TX	170,800
209	Santa Maria-Lompoc, CA	170,700
210	Olean, NY	169,000
211	Bowling Green, KY	168,800
212	Medford-Ashland, OR	168,300
213	Sunbury-Selinsgrove-Lewisburg, PA	167,400
214	Cedar Rapids, IA	166,300
215	Florence, SC	166,100
216	Bangor, ME	163,900
217	Hilton Head, SC	162,300
218	Elmira-Corning, NY	161,500
219	St. Cloud, MN	161,100
220	Champaign, IL	160,200
221	Alexandria, LA	157,900
222	Ft. Walton Beach, FL	157,300
223	Fargo-Moorhead, ND-MN	157,100
224	Bend, OR	156,500
225	Winchester, VA	155,900
226	Redding, CA	155,700
227	Laurel-Hattiesburg, MS	154,800
228	La Crosse, WI	154,500
229	Lake Charles, LA	154,200
230	Rochester, MN	150,100
231	Charlottesville, VA	147,200
232	New River Valley, VA	147,000
233	Muskegon, MI	146,800
234	Tuscaloosa, AL	142,500
235	Dubuque, IA	141,200
236	Marion-Carbondale (Southern Illinois), IL	140,200
237	Joplin, MO	138,500
237	Santa Fe, NM	138,500
239	Bryan-College Station, TX	138,300
240	Pittsburg, KS (Southeast Kansas)	136,700
241	Panama City, FL	136,600
242	Bloomington, IL	136,100
243	Eau Claire, WI	134,000
244	Abilene, TX	132,400
245	Elizabeth City-Nags Head, NC	132,100
246	Lafayette, IN	131,600
247	LaSalle-Peru, IL	131,100
248	Sussex, NJ	130,400
249	Wheeling, WV	129,900
250	Parkersburg-Marietta, WV-OH	128,500
250	Lima, OH	128,500
252	Waterloo-Cedar Falls, IA	128,400
253	Pueblo, CO	127,300
254	State College, PA	127,100
255	Meadville-Franklin, PA	125,300
256	Monroe, LA	123,300
257	Florence-Muscle Shoals, AL	122,500
258	Columbia, MO	122,400
259	Battle Creek, MI	117,100
260	Hamptons-Riverhead, NY	116,400
261	Billings, MT	115,800
262	Wichita Falls, TX	114,600
263	Texarkana, TX-AR	112,900
264	Grand Junction, CO	110,600
265	Altoona, PA	110,000
266	Montpelier-Barre-St. Johnsbury, VT	108,600
267	Augusta-Waterville, ME	106,400
268	Valdosta, GA	104,500
269	Albany, GA	104,300
270	Williamsport, PA	102,600
271	Columbus-Starkville-West Point, MS	102,200
272	Elkins-Buckhannon-Weston, WV	102,100
273	Sioux City, IA	101,400
274	Mankato-New Ulm-St. Peter, MN	100,700
275	Rapid City, SD	99,000
276	Sheboygan, WI	98,200
276	Harrisonburg, VA	98,200
278	Lewiston-Auburn, ME	93,100
279	Decatur, IL	93,000
280	Bluefield, WV	92,300
281	Watertown, NY	92,100
282	Ithaca, NY	91,000
283	Lawton, OK	89,800
284	San Angelo, TX	86,300
285	Cookeville, TN	85,400
286	Bismarck, ND	85,000
287	Sebring, FL	82,500
288	Grand Forks, ND-MN	82,300
289	Jackson, TN	79,600
290	Jonesboro, AR	73,700
291	Cheyenne, WY	72,900
292	The Florida Keys, FL	70,800
293	Mason City, IA	68,800
294	Beckley, WV	68,700
295	Great Falls, MT	67,500
296	Meridian, MS	63,800
297	Brunswick, GA	61,200
298	Casper, WY	59,100

Broadcasting & Cable Yearbook 2006

Section E
Programming

Broadcast TV Programming Services
- Major Broadcast TV Networks E-2
- Major TV Program Syndicators/Distributors E-3
- Regional Broadcast TV Networks E-4

Cable TV Programming Services
- National Cable Networks..E-5
- Regional Cable News Networks E-12
- Regional Cable Sports Networks..................................E-14
- Cable Audio Services...E-16

TV News Programming Services
- Major National TV News Organizations E-17
- TV News Services E-19

Radio Programming Services
- National Radio Programming Services............................E-21
- Regional Radio Programming Services E-25
- Radio News Services...E-27
- Radio Format Providers.......................................E-30
- Music Licensing..E-32

Canadian Programming Services
- Canadian Broadcast Networks...................................E-33
- Canadian Cable Networks E-34
- Canadian Radio Networks and Services E-37
- Producers, Distributors, and Production Services Alphabetical Index ..E-38
- Producers, Distributors, and Production Services Subject Index E-68

Broadcasting & Cable Yearbook 2006

Major Broadcast TV Networks

ABC

ABC Inc., 500 S. Buena Vista St., Burbank, CA 91521. Phone: 818-460-7477; Web site: abc.go.com.

77 W. 66th St., New York, NY 10023. Phone: 212-456-7777.

Anne Sweeney, pres, Disney-ABC Television Group; Julia Franz, exec VP; James L. Hedges, CFO; Stephen McPherson, pres, ABC Primetime Entertainment; Mark Pedowitz, pres, Touchstone Television; Morgan Wandell, sr VP; Michael Shaw, pres, sls and mktg; John Rouse, pres, affil rel; Michael T. Mellon, sr VP, rsch; Brain Frons, pres, ABC Daytime; George Bodenheimer, pres, ABC Sports and ESPN Inc.; Walter Liss, pres, ABC TV Stations Group.

Ownership: The Walt Disney Co., 500 S. Buena Vista St., Burbank, CA 91521-9722. Phone: 818-560-1000; Web site: www.disney.com.

George Mitchell, chmn; Michael Eisner, CEO; Robert Iger, pres and COO; Thomas O. Staggs, sr exec VP and CFO; Alan Braveman, sr exec VP/gen counsel; Zenia Mucha, sr VP corporate communication; Preston Padden, exec VP/govt rel.

CBS

51 W. 52nd St., New York, NY 10019. Phone: 212-975-4321; Web site: www.cbs.com.

7800 Beverly Blvd., Los Angeles, CA 90036. Phone: 323-575-2345.

Leslie Moonves, chmn, CBS, co-pres and co-CEO of Viacom Inc.; Nancy Tellem, pres, CBS Paramount Network Television Entertainment Group; Nina Tassler, pres, CBS Entertainment; David Stapf, pres, Paramount Network Television; Jo Ann Ross, pres, network sls; George Schweitzer, pres, CBS mktg group; Gil Schwartz, exec VP, communications; Martin Shea, exec VP, investor rel; Robert Rose, sr VP, opns and engrg; Fred Reynolds, pres and CEO, Viacom stns; Michael Dolan, exec VP/CFO, Viacom.

Ownership: Viacom Inc., 1515 Broadway, New York, NY 10036. Phone: 212-258-6000; Web site: www.viacom.com.

Sumner Redstone, chmn and CEO; Leslie Moonves, co-pres and co-COO; Tom Freston, co-pres and co-COO; Carol A. Melton, exec VP and govt rel; George S. Abrams; David R. Andelman, bd of directors.

FOX

10201 W. Pico Blvd., Los Angeles, CA 90064. Phone: 310-369-1000; Web site: www.fox.com.

1211 Ave. of the Americas, New York, NY 10036. Phone: 212-852-7000.

Gail Berman, pres, Entertainment, Fox Broadcasting Co.; Anthony Vinciquera, pres and CEO, Fox Networks Group; Ed Wilson, pres, Fox Television Network; Andy Setos, pres, engineering, Fox Networks Group; Robert Quicksilver, pres, network distribution, Fox Television Network; Jon Nesvig, pres, sales, Fox Broadcasting Co.; Joseph Earley, exec VP, publicity and corporate communications, Fox Broadcasting Co.; Brian Lewis, sr VP, Fox News; David Hill, chmn and CEO, Fox Sports Television Group; Lou D'Ermilio, sr VP and corporate communications, Fox Sports; Lachlan Murdoch, chmn, Fox TV Stations; Ivery Van Allen, VP media rel, Fox TV Stations.

Ownership: News Corp., 1211 Ave. of the Americas, New York, NY 10036. Phone: 212-852-7000; Web site: wwww.newscorp.com.

Rupert Murdoch, chmn and CEO; Peter Chernin, pres and COO; Lachlan Murdoch, deputy COO; David DeVoe, CFO.

NBC

30 Rockefeller Plaza, 25th Fl., New York, NY 10112. Phone: 212-664-4444; Web site: www.nbc.com.

3000 W. Alameda Ave., Burbank, CA 91523.

Barry Wallach, exec VP sls; Bob Wright, chmn and CEO, NBC Universal; Randy Falco, pres, NBC Universal Television Networks Group; Jeff Zucker, pres, NBC Universal Television Group; John Damiano, exec VP, affil rel; Keith Turner, pres, NBC Universal sls and mktg; Alan Wurtzel, pres, NBC Universal Research; Arthur Hasson, exec VP sls and new business; Marc Graboff, exec VP, NBC Universal Television Group; Kevin Reilly, pres, NBC Entertainment; Angela Bromstad, co-pres, NBC Universal Television; Rebecca Marks, VP, publicity; Dick Ebersol, chmn, NBC & olympics; Jay Ireland, pres, NBC Universal Television Stations.

Ownership: NBC Universal, a subsidiary of General Electric; NBC Universal, 30 Rockefeller Plaza, New York, NY 10112. Phone: 212-664-4444; Web site: www.nbcuni.com.

Bob Wright, chmn and CEO; Deborah M. Reif, pres, NBC Universal Digital Media; Lynn Calpeter, exec VP and CFO; David Overbeeke, exec VP and CIO, NBC Universal; Rick Cotton, exec VP and general counsel; Anna Perez, exec VP, communications; Marc Saperstein, sr exec VP, human resources and communications.

General Electric, 3135 Eastern Tpke., Fairfield, CT 06828. Phone: 203-373-2211; Web site: www.ge.com.

Jeffrey Immelt, chmn and CEO.

PAX

601 Clearwater Park Rd., West Palm Beach FL 33401. Phone: 561-659-4122; Web site: www.pax.tv.

Bill Scott, pres, PAX Television Network; Doug Baker, pres PAX Television Station Group; Stephen P. Appel, pres, sales and marketing, PAX Television Network.

Ownership: Paxson Communications Corp., 601 Clearwater Park Rd., West Palm Beach FL 33401. Phone: 561-659-4122; Web site: www.pax.tv.

Lowell Paxson, chmn and CEO; Dean Goodman, COO and pres; Thomas E. Severson, sr VP and CFO.

UPN

Like CBS, UPN is owned by Viacom. The two network share resources and personnel. Some senior UPN executives report to executives at CBS.

11800 Wilshire Blvd., Los Angeles, CA 90025. Phone: 310-575-7000; Web site: www.upn.com.

Leslie Moonves, co-pres and co-COO, Viacom Inc.; Dawn Ostroff, pres, UPN Entertainment; Michael Mandelker, exec VP, network sls; Kim Fleary, sr VP, comedy dev; Maggie Murphy, sr VP, drama dev; Sandy Pastoor, sr VP, affil rel.

Ownership: Viacom Inc., 1515 Broadway, New York, NY 10036. Phone: 212-258-6000; Web site: www.viacom.com.

Sumner Redstone, chmn and CEO; Leslie Moonves, co-pres and co-COO; Tom Freston, co-pres and co-COO.

The WB

4000 Warner Blvd., Burbank, CA 91522. Phone: 818-977-5000; Web site: www.thewb.com.

Garth Ancier, chmn; David Janollari, pres, entertainment; Bob Bibb, co-pres, marketing; Lewis Goldstein, co-pres, marketing; Michael Ross, exec VP, business affairs; Brad Turell, exec VP, network communications; Ken Werner, exec VP, network distribution.

Ownership: Time Warner Inc., One Time Warner Center, New York, NY 10019. Phone: 212-484-8000; Web site: www.timewarner.com.

Richard Parsons, chmn and CEO; Jeffrey Bewkes, chmn, entertainment and networks group (includes The WB); Don Logan, chmn, media and communications group.

Major TV Program Syndicators/Distributors

Buena Vista Television

Head Office: 500 S. Buena Vista St., Burbank, CA 91521; Tel: 818-560-1000.

Management: Janice Marinelli, pres; Jennie Born, VP, natl promotions; Sandra Brewer, VP, affiliate relations; John Bryan, exec VP and gen sls mgr; Blake Bryant, VP, creative svcs; Dan Cohen, sr VP, gen mgr, Buena Vista Pay TV & Distribution; Kim Harbin, VP, publicity; Mary Kellogg, exec VP, current progmg, Buena Vista Prodns; Lloyd Komesar, exec VP, strategic research; Rob Morhaim, VP, development, Buena Vista Prodns; Sal Sardo, exec VP, mktg.

New York Office: 7 W. 66th St., New York, NY 10023; Tel: 212-456-1740; Fax: 212-456-0396.

Management: Howard Levy, exec VP, adv sales.

Major first-run programming: Live with Regis and Kelly, The Tony Danza Show, Who Wants to be a Millionaire, Ebert & Roeper.

Major off-network programming: Alias, According to Jim, Home Improvement, My Wife and Kids.

King World Productions

Head Office: 2401 Colorado Ave., Suite 110, Santa Monica, CA 90404; Tel: 310-264-3300; Fax: 310-264-3301.

Management: Roger King, CEO, CBS Enterprises and King World Productions, Inc.; Robert Madden, COO; Delilah Loud, sr VP, adv & promotion; Arthur Sando, sr VP, communications, CBS Enterprises; Mike Stornello, sr VP, dev.

New York Office: 1700 Broadway, 32nd & 33rd Fl., New York, NY 10019; Tel: 212-315-4000; Fax: 212-582-9255. Management: Joe DiSalvo, pres, domestic television sales; Steve Hirsch, pres, King World media sales; Michael Auerbach, sr VP, King World media sls; Jonathan Birkhahn, sr VP, business affrs.

New Jersey Office: 830 Morris Tpke., Short Hills, NJ 07078; Tel: 973-376-1313; Fax: 973-376-7787.

Management: Steve LoCascio, sr VP and CFO, CBS Enterprises and King World Productions, Inc.; Moira Coffey, exec VP, rsch.

Major first-run programming: The Oprah Winfrey Show, Dr. Phil, Wheel of Fortune, Jeopardy!, Inside Edition, Mr. Food, CBS MarketWatch, Bob Vila's Home Again.

Major off-network programming: Everybody Loves Raymond, CSI: Crime Scene Investigation, CSI: Miami.

NBC Universal Television Distribution

Head Office: NBC Enterprises. 3400 W. Olive Ave., Suite 6th Fl., Burbank, CA 91505; Tel: 818-526-6900; Fax: 818-526-6922.

Management: Ed Wilson, pres; Jon Hookstratten, exec VP, admin and opns; Jerry Petry, exec VP; Linda Finnell, sr VP progmg; Steve Badeau, VP rsch; Regina Thomas, VP progmg; Mary Beth McAdaragh, VP mktg; Mara jacobberger, dir mktg.

Major first-run programming: Access Hollywood, Blind Date, The Chris Matthews Show, The Jane Pauley Show, Jerry Springer Show, Maury, The Wall Street Journal Report.

Major off-network programming: Fear Factor, Law & Order, Law & Order: SVU, Law & Order: Criminal Intent, Providence, Crossing Jordan.

Paramount Worldwide Television Distribution

Head Office: 5555 Melrose Ave., Hollywood, CA 90038-3197; Tel: 323-956-5000.

Management: Joel Berman, president, Paramount Worldwide Television Distribution; John Nogawski, pres; Greg Meidel, pres, progmg; Terry Wood, exec VP, progmg; Mark Dvornik, exec VP, gen sls mgr; Michael Mischler, EVP, mktg; John Wentworth, EVP, mktg and media rel; Dawn Abel, sr VP, rsch; Dennis Emerson, SVP, off-net sales manager; John Kohler, SVP, creative affairs; David LaFountaine, SVP, advertising & promotion; Phil Murphy, SVP, group operations; Bill Weber, SVP, TV systems & archive services.

New York Office: 1515 Broadway, 33rd Fl., New York, NY 10036; Tel: (212) 258-6000.

Scott Koondel, SVP, natl sls mgr.

CBS Paramount International Television

Armando Nunez, president, CBS Paramount International Television

Major first-run programming: Entertainment Tonight, ET Weekend, The Insider, Insider Weekend, Judge Joe Brown, Judge Judy, Maximum Exposure, The Montel Williams Show, Unexplained Mysteries.

Major off-network programming: Becker, Cheers, Frasier, Star Trek Next Generation, Girlfriends, The Parkers.

Sony Pictures Television

Head Office: 10202 W. Washington Blvd., Culver City, CA 90232; Tel: 310-244-4000.

Management: Steve Mosko, pres; Russ Krasnoff, pres, progmg and production; John Weiser, pres distribution; Jeannie Bradley, exec VP, current progmg; Gregory Boone, exec VP, legal affrs; Richard Frankie, exec VP, business opns; Ed Lammi, exec VP, production; Don Loughery, exec VP, business affrs; David Mumford, exec VP, planning and opns; Robert Oswaks, exec VP, mktg; Helen Verno, exec VP, movies for television and miniseries.

New York Office: 550 Madison Ave., New York, NY 10022; Tel: 212-833-8500.

Management: Barbara "Bo" Argentino, exec VP, adv sales; John J. Rohrs, exec VP, cable sales.

Major broadcast network: Joan of Arcadia, The King of Queens, The Young and the Restless, Days of our Lives.

Major cable network: Huff, Rescue Me, The Shield, Strong Medicine.

Major first-run syndication: Life & Style, Pat Croce: Moving In, Wheel of Fortune, Jeopardy! (latter two distributed by King World).

Major off-network syndication: Seinfeld, The King of Queens.

Twentieth Television

Head Office: 10201 W. Pico Blvd., Los Angeles, CA 90035. Tel: 310-369-1000; Fax: 310-369-3899. Web site: www.fox.com.

Office: Fox Television PO Box 900, Beverly Hills, CA. Tel: 310-369-1000.

Management: Les Eisner, VP, media rel; Bob Cook, pres and COO; Robb Dalton, pres, progmg and development; Paul Franklin, exec VP, gen sales mgr, bcst; Marisa Fermin, exec VP, business and legal affrs; Joanne Burns, sr VP, mktg, research and new media; Steve MacDonald, sr VP, gen sales mgr, basic cable; Susan Kantor, sr VP, mktg and creative; Elaine Bauer-Brooks, sr VP, progmg and development; Daniel Tibbets, VP, Foxlab, Inc. and VP, prodn.

New York Office: 1211 Ave. of the Americas, 3rd Fl., New York, NY 10036; Tel: 212-556-2400.

Management: Andrew Butcher, VP, corporate affrs and communication; Bob Cesa, exec VP, adv sls and basic cable sales; Dave Barrington, sr VP, adv sls; Bob Riordan, sr VP, adv sls, DIRECTV.

Major first run programming: Ambush Makeover, Good Day Live, Divorce Court, Texas Justice.

Major off-network programming: The Simpsons, Malcolm in the Middle, Yes, Dear, 24, Reba, The Bernie Mac Show, Dharma & Greg and King of the Hill.

Warner Bros. Domestic Cable Distribution

Head Office: 4000 Warner Blvd., Bldg. 160, Burbank, CA 91522; Tel: 818-977-4340; Fax: 818-977-4474.

Management: Eric Frankel, pres; Gus Lucas, exec VP; Ron Sunderland, sr VP, legal and business affrs; Linda Abrams, VP, mktg; Mark DeVitre, VP, sales; Donald Putrimas, VP, finance; Pam Ritchie, VP, sls planning & program inventory; Mike Russo, VP, sls.

Major off-network programming: Third Watch, The West Wing, The Gilmore Girls, Smallville, Without a Trace (sold to Turner for a fall 2006 debut).

Warner Bros. Domestic Television Distribution

Head Office: 4001 Olive Ave., 4th Fl., Burbank, CA 91522; Tel: 818-954-5652; Fax: 818-954-5697.

Management: Dick Robertson, pres; Jim Paratore, exec VP; Bruce K. Rosenblum, exec VP, media rsch; Lenny Bart, sr VP, admin; Bill Marcus, sr VP, sales; Rick Meril, sr VP, sls; Liz Huszarik, sr VP, media rsch; Peter Roth, pres, Warner Bros. Television; Len Goldstein, exec VP dev, Warner Bros. Television; Scott Rowe, VP, corporate communications, Warner Bros. Entertainment.

New York Office: 1325 Ave. of the Americas, 31st Fl., New York, NY 10019; Tel: 212-636-5102; Fax: 212-636-5380.

Management: Michael Teicher, exec VP, media sales; Roseann Cacciola, sr VP, gen sls mgr and media sls.

Major first-run programming: The Ellen DeGeneres Show, Extra, The People's Court, Judge Mathis, The Larry Elder Show.

Major off-network programming: Friends, The Drew Carey Show, Will & Grace.

Regional Broadcast TV Networks

ALIN-TV, 149 Madison Ave., Suite 602, New York, NY 10016. Phone: (212) 889-1327. Fax: (212) 213-6968. Alan Steinberg, chmn; Alan Cohen, pres.

ALIN-TV offers locally originated progmg on a line-up of leading ind stns providing natl participation on a daily basis. Specific networks are provided to zero in on target audience progmg: prime, prime access, teen/young adult, late night entertainment, daytime, weekend entertainment, news, & kids.

American Public Television, 55 Summer St. 4th Fl., Boston, MA 02110. Phone: (617) 338-4455. Fax: (617) 338-5369. Web Site: www.aptonline.org. Cynthia Fennerman, pres; Chris Funkhauser, VP/exch & distr svs; Eric Luskin, VP/premium svs & syndication.

Comprises WETA-TV, WHMM, both Washington, DC; WEDW(TV) Bridgeport, WEDY(TV) New Haven, WEDH(TV) Hartford, WEDN(TV) Norwich, all Connecticut; WCBB Augusta, WMED-TV Calais, WMEB-TV Orono, WMEM-TV Presque Isle, all Maine; WGBH-TV Boston, WGBX-TV Boston, WGBY-TV Springfield, all Massachusetts; WENH-TV Durham, WEKW-TV Keene, WLED-TV Littleton, all New Hampshire; WNJT-TV Trenton, New Jersey; WSKG(TV) Binghamton, WNED-TV Buffalo, WNET(TV) New York, WLIW-TV Plainview, WXXI(TV) Rochester, WMHT(TV) Schenectady, WCNY-TV Syracuse, WNPE-TV Watertown, all New York; WCET-TV Cincinnati, WVIZ-TV Cleveland, WPTD-TV Dayton, all Ohio; WLVT-TV Bethlehem-Allentown, WPSX-TV Clearfield, WITF-TV Harrisburg, WHYY-TV Philadelphia, WQED(TV) Pittsburgh, WVIA(TV) Scranton-Wilkes Barre, WQLN Erie, all Pennsylvania; WSBE-TV Providence, Rhode Island; WMPT-TV Annapolis, WMPB(TV) Baltimore, WWPB(TV) Hagerstown, WCPB-TV Salisbury, all Maryland. Service virtually all Public Television stations in the U.S.

California Farm Network, 2300 River Plaza Dr., Sacramento, CA 95833. Phone: (916) 561-5550. Fax: (916) 561-5695. E-mail: rmiller@cfbf.com. Web Site: www.cfbf.com. Bob Krauter, exec dir; Ron Miller, opns mgr.

Comprises KUVI-TV Bakersfield, KAEF-TV Eureka, KSEE-TV Fresno, KIXE-TV Redding, KRCR-TV Redding, KSBW-TV Salinas, KSBY-TV San Luis Obispo, K26AY Lakeport, KXTV-TV Sacramento, KPXN-TV Los Angeles, KFTY-TV Santa Rosa, KBHAA-TV San Francisco, all California; KYMA(TV) Yuma, Arizona; RFD-TV dish nestwork direct TV.

California-Oregon Broadcasting Inc., Box 1489, Medford, OR 97501. Phone: (541) 779-5555. Fax: (541) 779-1151. E-mail: kobi@kobi5.com. Web Site: www.localnewscomesfirst.com. Patricia C. Smullin, pres.

Eugene, OR 97408. KEVU-KISR-TV, 2940 Chad Dr. Phone: (541) 682-2525. Mark Mitzger, gen mgr.

Medford, OR 91501. KOBI-TV, 125 S.Fir St. Phone: (541) 779-5555. Fax: (541) 779-1151. Pat Sumllin, owner.

Comprises KLSR-TV & KEVU-TV Eugene, KOTI(TV) Klamath Falls, KOBI(TV) Medford, all Oregon. Represented by John Blair & Co., Northwest.

4X Network, Box 1686, 3425 S. Broadway, Minot, ND 58701. Phone: (701) 852-2104. Fax: (701) 838-9360. E-mail: jolson@kxmcnews.com. Web Site: www.kxmc.com. Tim Reiten, pres; David Reiten, gen mgr.

Comprises KXMB-TV Bismarck, KXMA-TV Dickinson, KXMC-TV Minot, KXMD-TV Williston, all North Dakota. Represented by Katz Continental.

KMWB, (Sinclair Communication Inc.). 1640 Como Ave., St. Paul, MN 55108. Phone: (651) 646-2300. Fax: (651) 646-1220. E-mail: jongstad@kmwb. Web Site: www.kmwb23.com. Art Lanham, pres & gen mgr; Miles Kennedy, VP & controller; Bob Weinstein, natl sls mgr; Jeff Ongstad, creative svcs dir.

Minnesota, Wisconsin. Represented by Millenium.

KSN Television Group, Box 333, 833 N. Main St., Wichita, KS 67201. Phone: (316) 265-3333. Fax: (316) 292-1197. Web Site: www.ksn.com. Shawn Oswald, gen mgr.

Comprises KSNG Garden City, KSNC Great Bend, KSNT Topeka, KSNW Wichita, KSNK Oberlin, all Kansas.

Represented by Katz. Above TV stns affiliated with NBC Television Network. Owned by Lee Enterprises, Davenport, IA.

KWCH-TV, Media General Broadcast Group, Box 12, Wichita, KS 67201. Phone: (316) 838-1212. Fax: (316) 831-6198. Web Site: www.kwch.com. Joan Barrett, VP/gen mgr.

Comprises KBSD-TV Ensign-Dodge City, KBSL-TV Goodland, KBSH-TV Hays, KWCH-TV Wichita-Hutchinson, all Kansas. Represented by HRP.

Kansas Television Network, 1500 N. West St., Wichita, KS 67203. Phone: (316) 943-4221. Fax: (316) 943-5493. Web Site: www.kake.com. Terry Cole Trabert, pres/gen mgr.

Comprises KLBY-TV Colby, KUPK-TV Garden City, KAKE-TV Wichita, all Kansas. Represented by Katz.

Keloland TV Young Broadcasting of Sioux Falls Inc., KELO TV Bldg., 501 S. Phillips Ave., Sioux Falls, SD 57104. Phone: (605) 336-1100. Fax: (605) 334-3447. Web Site: www.keloland.com. Vincent Young, chmn; Mark Millage, news dir.

Comprises KDLO-TV Florence, KPLO-TV Reliance, KELO-TV Sioux Falls, KCLO-TV Rapid City, all South Dakota. Represented by Adam Young Inc.

National Educational Telecommunications Association, Box 50008, Columbia, SC 29250. Phone: (803) 799-5517. Fax: (803) 771-4831. E-mail: skip@netaonline.org. Web Site: www.netaonline.org. Skip Hinton, pres.

Comprises Alabama PTV Birmingham, Alabama; KAKM Anchorage, KUAC Fairbanks, KYUK Bethel, Alaska; KUAT Tuscon, Arizona; Arkansas ETV Conway, Arkansas; KOCE Hunting Beach, KTEH San Jose, KVCR San Bernardino, KLCS Los Angeles, all California; WBCC Cocoa, WCEU Daytona Beach, WFSU Tallahassee, WGCU Fort Myers, WJCT Jacksonville, WLRN Miami, WSRE Pensacola, WUFT Gainesville, WUSF Tampa, WXEL West Palm Beach, all Florida; Georgia Public Broadcasting Atlanta, WPBA Atlanta, both Georgia; Idaho PTV Boise, Idaho; WSIU/WUSI Cardondale, Illinois; WTBU Indianapolis, WYIN Merrillville, Indiana; KOOD Bunker Hill, Kansas; Kentucky ETV Lexington, WKYU Bowling Green, both Kentucky; LA Public Broadcasting Baton Rouge, WLAE New Orleans, both Louisiana; Maryland Public Broadcasting Owings Mills, Maryland; WGVU Grand Rapids, Michigan; Mississippi EB Jackson, Mississippi; KCPT Kansas City, KETC St. Louis, KMOS Warrensburg, KOZK Ozarks Public TV Springfield, all Missouri; Montana PTV Bozeman, Montana; Nebraska ETV Lincoln, Nebraska; KLVX Las Vegas, Nevada; New Hampshire PTV Durham, New Hampshire; NJN Trenton, New Jersey; KENW Portales, KNME Albuquerque, KRWG Las Cruces, all New Mexico; WLIW Long Island, WMHT Schenectady, WNET New York, WPBS Watertown, all New York; UNC-TV Research Triangle Park, North Carolina; Prairie Public Television Fargo, North Dakota; WOUB Athens, WPTD Dayton, Ohio; KRSC Claremore, Oklahoma ETV Oklahoma City, both Oklahoma; Oregon Public Broadcasting Portland, Oregon; WLVT Allentown, WPSX University Park, WYBE Philadelphia, all Pennsylvania; WSBE Providence, Rhode Island; South Carolina ETV Columbia, South Carolina; South Dakota Public Television Vermillion, South Dakota, WCTE Cookeville, WNPT Nashville, WKNO Memphis, WLJT Martin, WSJK Knoxville, WTCI Chattanooga, all Tennessee; KAMU College Station, KWBU Waco, KEDT Corpus Christi, KERA Dallas, KLRN San Antonio, KLRU Austin, KMBH Harlingen, KNCT Killeen, KOCV Odessa, KTXT Lubbock, all Texas; KBYU Provo, KUED Salt Lake City, Utah; Vermont PTV Colchester, Vermont; WTJX St. Thomas, Virgin Islands; WBRA Roanoke, WCVE Richmond, WHRO Norfolk, WVPT Harrisonburg, all Virginia; KSPS Spokane, Washington; West Virginia Public Broadcasting Charleston, West Virginia; Wisconsin ETV Madison, Wisconsin, Wyoming PTV Riverton, Wyoming.

Nebraska Television Network (NTV), Box 220, Kearney, NE 68848. Phone: (308) 743-2494. Fax: (308) 743-2644. E-mail: news@nebraskatv.net. Web Site: www.nebraska.tv. Janet Noll, gen mgr.

Comprises KTVG(TV) Grand Island; KHGI-TV13, Kearney,

Hastings, Grand Island; KWNB-TV North Platte & KSNB-TV Superior and the translators of K02HB, K17CI, K11KV, K12KW, K13OM, K13NP, K13VO, K06EY. Represented by Petry.

North Dakota Television, 200 N. 4th St., Bismarck, ND 58501. Phone: (701) 255-5757. Fax: (701) 255-8220. Web Site: www.kfyrtv.com. Holly Stewart, gen mgr; Julie Jensen, natl sls mgr; Jim Sande, mgr opns & progmg; Barry Shumaier, loc sls mgr; Dick Heidt, news dir.

Comprises KFYR-TV Bismarck, KQCD-TV Dickinson, KMOT-TV Minot, KUMV-TV Williston, all North Dakota; KVLY-TV, serving North Dakota, South Dakota & Montana. Represented by Blair.

Ohio Educational Telecommunications Network Commission, 2470 North Star Rd., Columbus, OH 43221. Phone: (614) 644-1714. Fax: (614) 644-3112. E-mail: christofi@oet.state.oh.us. Web Site: www.oet.edu. Denos Christofi, exec dir.

Comprises WEAO Akron, WNEO-TV Alliance, WOUB-TV Athens, WBGU-TV Bowling Green, WOUC-TV Cambridge, WCET Cincinnati, WVIZ-TV Cleveland, WOSU-TV Columbus, WPTD Dayton, WPTO Oxford, WPBO-TV Portsmouth, WGTE-TV Toledo, all Ohio.

Pacific Mountain Network, 1550 Park Ave., Denver, CO 80218-1661. Phone: (303) 837-8000. Fax: (303) 837-9797. Joseph P. Zesbaugh, pres; Dana J. Rouse, VP progmg; Mary Lou Ray, VP learning svcs.

Comprises KAKM Anchorage, KYUK-TV Bethel, KUAC-TV Fairbanks, KTOO-TV Juneau, all Alaska; KAET Phoenix, KUAT-TV Tucson, both Arizona; KEET Eureka, KVPT Fresno, KOCE-TV Huntington Beach, KCET Los Angeles, KIXE-TV Redding, KRCB-TV Rohnert Park, KVIE Sacramento, KMTP-TV San Francisco, KVCR-TV San Bernardino, KPBS-TV San Diego, KQED/KQEC San Francisco, KTEH San Jose, KCSM-TV San Mateo, all California; KBDI-TV Denver, KRMA-TV Denver, KTSC Pueblo, all Colorado; KHET Honolulu, KMEB Wailuku, both Hawaii; KAID/KUID-TV/KISU-TV Boise, Idaho; KUSM, Bozeman, Montana; KLVX Las Vegas, KNPB Reno, both Nevada; KNME-TV Albuquerque, KRWG-TV Las Cruces, KENW Portales, all New Mexico; KOAC-TV/KTVR/KOAP-TV, Portland, KSYS Medford, all Oregon; KBYU-TV Provo, KUED Salt Lake City, both Utah; KWSU-TV Pullman, KCTS-TV Seattle, KSPS-TV Spokane, KTPS/KCKA Tacoma, KYVE-TV Yakima, all Washington; KCWC-TV Cheyenne, Wyoming.

Pennsylvania Public Television Network, Box 397, 24 Northeast Dr., Hershey, PA 17033. Phone: (717) 533-6010. Fax: (717) 533-4236. E-mail: sparker@pptn.org. Web Site: www.pptn.org. Larry Miller, gen mgr.

Comprises WLVT-TV Bethlehem, WQLN-TV Erie, WITF-TV Harrisburg, WHYY-TV Philadelphia, WQED-TV Pittsburgh, WVIA-TV Scranton, WPSX-TV University Park, WYBE-TV, Philadelphia, all Pennsylvania.

SJL Broadcast Management Corp., 3203 3rd Ave. N., Suite 300, Billings, MT 59101. Phone: (406) 256-0705. Fax: (406) 252-9144. Dave McCurdy.

Montecito, CA 93108, 633 Picacho Ln. Phone: (805) 969-9278. Fax: (805) 969-2399. George D. Lilly, pres.

Comprises WICU-TV and WSEE-TV Erie, WTAJ-TV, Altoona, all Pennsylvania; WBNG-TV, Binghamton, NY. KSBY-TV

Wisconsin Educational Communications Board, 3319 W. Beltline Hwy., Madison, WI 53713-4296. Phone: (608) 264-9600. Fax: (608) 264-9664. Web Site: www.ecb.org. Wendy Wink, exec dir.

Comprises WPNE(TV) Green Bay, WHLA-TV La Crosse, WHWC-TV Menomonie/Eau Claire, WLEF-TV Park Falls, WHRM-TV Wausau, all Wisconsin. Affils: Wisconsin WMVS(TV) Milwaukee; WDSE-TV Duluth, Minnesota.

National Cable Networks

A&E Network, 235 E. 45th St., New York, NY 10017. Phone: (212) 210-1400. Fax: (212) 210-9755. Web Site: www.aetv.com. Abbe Raven, pres/CEO; Whitney Goit II, exec VP; David Zagin, sr VP; Mel Berning, exec VP; Bob DeBitetto, gen mgr.

A&E Network offers discerning viewers a unique blend of original progmg featuring its signature series BIOGRAPHY, original movies, dramas, series & documentaries. A&E Network also administers The History Channel (see listing).

Serving 88 million subs in the United States & Canada. On 10,000 cable systems. Satellite: Galaxy V, transponder 23.

ABC Family Channel, 500 S. Buena Vista St., Burbank, CA 91521. Phone: (818) 560-1000. Web Site: www.abcfamily.com. Ben Pyne, sr VP; Laura Nathanson, exec VP; Nicole Nochols, VP; Anne Sweeney, chmn.

Newport Beach, CA 92660, 660 Newport Center Dr, Suite 770. Phone: (714) 759-7685. Fax: (714) 759-9491. Janice Slipp, dir western rgn.

Englewood, CO 80111, 5445 DCT Pkwy, Suite 525. Phone: (303) 220-8901. Fax: (303) 220-9102. Tracy Jenkins, J.D., dir Rocky Mountain rgn.

Atlanta, GA 30349, Box 492347. Phone: (770) 461-4929. Fax: (770) 461-8678. Russell A. Breault, VP eastern division.

Oakbrook, IL 60523, 1301 W. 22nd St, Suite 902. Phone: (630) 990-0437. Fax: (630) 990-0463. Ralph Trentadue, natl dir lcl adv sls; Shirley Hill, VP western division.

New York, NY 10036, 1133 Ave. of the Americas, 36th Fl. Phone: (212) 782-1860. Fax: (212) 782-1865. Steve Israelsky, VP Northeast rgn.

Lewisville, TX 75067, 1422 W. Main St, Suite 201. Phone: (972) 436-2217. Fax: (972) 436-0209. Mark Solow, dir Southwest rgn.

Virginia Beach, VA 23450-2050, Box 2050, 2877 Guardian Ln. Phone: (757) 459-6281. Fax: (757) 459-6429. Craig Sherwood, sr VP/mgng dir. (Hqtrs affil sls & rel).

Basic cable network available in over 87 million homes nationwide 24 hours; delivers a dynamic mix of quality entertainment with original series & movies, classics fron Disney. Satellite: Galaxy V, transponder 11.

ABS-CBN (The Flilipino Channel), 859 Cowan Rd., Burlingame, CA 94010. Phone: (650) 697-3700. Fax: (650) 697-3500. Rafael Lopez, mgng dir; Michael Scott, VP.

A 24-hour all Filipino premium svc ch delivered via satellite from the Philippines.

Serving 35,000 subs on 11 systems. Satellite: Galaxy 11, transponder 24.

ANA Television Network, 1510 H St. N.W., Suite 400, Washington, DC 20005. Phone: (202) 898-8222. Fax: (202) 898-8088. Angelyn Adams, CFO.

Arabic-language TV net bcstg to the Arab-American community 24 hours via cable, wireless cable, satellite.

Satellite: DIRECTV Plus. Satellite: Galaxy V, transponder 11.

ART (Arab Radio & Television), 315 Arden Ave., Suite 26, Glendale 91203. Phone: (818) 243-0278. Fax: (818) 243-9278. Web Site: www.art.tv.net. Michael Scott, VP.

ART's foundation is based on the largest gen entertainment library in the Middle East. Available 24 hours a day in North America, has progmg targeted to second generation Arab Americans. Satellite: Galaxy 11, transponder 24.

AYM Sports, Avenida Chapultepac 405, Colonia Juarez, Delegacion Cuauhtemoc, Mexico 06600. Web Site: www.aymsports.tv. Benjamin Hinojosa, pres; Carlos Carrillo, progmg VP.

Available 24 hours a day, 100% Mexican network consisting of soccer, basketball, rodeo charreadas, horse racing, boxing, kick boxing, jujitsu, karate, tae kwon do, swimming, driving, truck series, rallies and much more. Satellite: Telestar 7, transponder 12.

Access Television Network Inc., 2600 Michelson Dr., Suite 1650, Irvine, CA 92612. Phone: (949) 263-9900. Fax: (949) 757-1526. Web Site: www.accesstv.com. George Henry, CEO; Robert T. Tyler, CFO; Mark R. Russo, engrg VP.

Organized natl marketplace for paid progmg on loc cable systems. On 300 cable systems.26 million subs. Satellite: Galaxy VII, transponder 16.0, 16.5.

African Independent Television (AIT), One AIT Rd., PMB 1309, Apapa, Alagbado-Lagos Nigeria. Phone: (212) 213-2070. Chief Raymond Dokesi, chmn/CEO.

AIT is a Pan-African gen entertainment ch offering news, talk show, soap opera, sports, Afician culture & music 24 hours a day. Areas: United States & Afica. Satellite: Telstar 5, transponder 5.

American Movie Classics (AMC), (Rainbow Programming Service Holdings Inc.). 200 Jericho Quadrangle, Jericho, NY 11753. Phone: (516) 803-4300. Fax: (516) 803-4426. Web Site: www.amctv.com. David Sehring, sr VP; Kathleen Dore, pres.

AMC is a 24 hour, movie-based mix or original series, documentaries & specials. 85 million subs. Satellite: Satcom C-4, transponder 1.

America's Collectibles Network (ACNTV), 10001 Kingston Park, Suite 57, Knoxville 37922. Phone: (865) 693-8471. Fax: (865) 560-3298. Web Site: www.acntv.com. F. Robert Hall, pres; Harris Bagley, VP.

ACNT offers a wide var of jewelry & gemstones at reduced prices, 24 hours a day home shopping, in the United States & Canada. Serving more than 63 million subs. Satellite: Telstar7, Transponder 21, Galaxy 11, Transponder 19.

America's Store, (A Division of Home Shopping Network). One HSN Dr., St. Petersburg, FL 33729. Phone: (727) 872-1000. Fax: (727) 872-7356. Web Site: www.americasstore.com. Peter Ruben, exec VP; Tom McInerney, CEO; Barry Diller, chmn/CEO; Will Keller, VP/gen mgr; Mike McMahon, opns VP.

America's Store offers live, 24 hour video retail nework featuring merchandise with proven appeal in an upbeat, spontaneous style. 18 million subs. Satellite: Satcom C-3, transponder 10.

Anime Network, 10114 West Sam Houston Pkwy. S., Suite 200, Houston 77099. Phone: (713) 341-7200. Fax: (713) 341-7199. Web Site: www.theanimenetwork.com. John Ledford, chmn/CEO; Kevin Corcoran, pres.

Anime is an exploration of Western pop culture. Anime reaches males 18-35 demographic with foru different genres, including martial arts, comedy, science fiction & drama 24 hours a day, basic ad-supported. Serving more than 84 million subs.

The Anti-Aging Network, Inc., Box 3485, Beverly Hills, CA 90212. Phone: (805) 379-2373. Fax: (805) 373-6595. Web Site: www.antiagenet.tv. Elysa Henley-Frerer, pres/CEO.

Progmg is informational, educ, & motivational, designed to empower viewer's to "live better longer" & "get an edge on aging." Slated to launch as a cable net in fall 2004.

BBC America, 7475 Wisconsin Ave., Suite 1100, Bethesda, MD 20814. Phone: (301) 347-2222. Web Site: www.bbcamerica.com. Parule Basu-Barua, sr VP; Jo Petherbridge, sr VP; Mary Pratt Henaghan, opns VP; Chris Carr, CFO; Sarah Barnett, VP; Jennifer Lewi, mktg VP; David Bernath, progmg VP; Scott Langerman, VP.

BBC America is a 24 hour award-winning TV featuring razor-sharp comedies, provocative dramas & life changing makeovers. Digital, Analog & DBS. Satellite: Satcom C3. 37 million. Satellite: Galaxy VII, transponder 22.

BET (Black Entertainment Television), One BET Plaza, 1235 W. St. N.E., Washington, DC 20018. Phone: (202) 608-2200. Fax: (202) 608-2631. Web Site: www.bet.com. Robert L. Johnson, chmn; Debra Lee, pres/CEO; Byron Marchant, exec VP & gen counsel; Keli Lawson, mktg VP.

Burbank, CA 91505. BET/Los Angeles - Production, 2801 W. Olive Ave. Phone: (818) 566-9940. Fax: (818) 566-1655.

Washington, DC 20018. Network Operations, 1899 Ninth St. N.E. Phone: (202) 608-2800.

Washington, DC 20018. BET Film Production Facility, 2000 West Pl. N.E. Phone: (202) 608-2800. Fax: (202) 608-2629.

Chicago, IL 60607. BET/Chicago, 180 N. Stetson Ct, Suite 4350. Phone: (312) 819-8600.

New York, NY 10017. BET/New York, 380 Madison Ave, 20th Fl. Phone: (212) 716-5600. Fax: (212) 697-2050.

BET is the nation's leading TV network providing 24 hour for African-American audience in the United States, Canada & the Caribbean. BET Digital Networks-BET jazz, BET Gospel & BET Hip-Hop. 78 million subs. Satellite: Galaxy V, transponder 20.

BET Jazz: The Jazz Channel, 1235 W St. N. E., Washington, DC 20018. Phone: (202) 608-2000. Fax: (202) 608-2631. Web Site: www.bet.com. Robert L. Johnson, chmn/CEO; Debra L. Lee, pres/COO.

The Jazz Channel is a 24-hour TV progmg svc dedicated exclusively to jazz through in-studio performances, documentaries,concert coverage & celebrity interviews. 9 million subs. Satellite: Galaxy VII, transponder 21.

Bandamax, 5999 Center Dr., Los Angeles 90045. Phone: (301) 348-3371. Web Site: www.tutv.tv. Mark Feldman, pres/CEO; Carlos Madrazo, CFO; Chris Fager, exec VP; Ariela Nerobay, VP sls.

Bandamax features a 24-hour a day country music video, including best artists in Tex-Mex, Norteno, Banda & Manachi genres. De Pelicula Sp-language films, De Pelicula Clasico films of Mexico's golden era.

Behavior Communications, 777 DeLaCommune W., Montreal, PQ H3C 1Y1. Canada. Phone: (514) 879-3339. Fax: (514) 954-5577.

Integrated entertainment technology, content creation company that designs & develops characters & svcs to deliver to young, design conscious and technologically savy audiences.

Black Belt TV, The Martial Arts Network, Box 3215, San Dimas, CA 91773. Phone: (909) 971-9300. Fax: (909) 394-0791. Web Site: www.blackbelttv.com. Erik D. Jones, chmn/CEO.

Based on the popularity & participation in martial arts, we have created a 24 hours / 7 days a week cable television network that targets demographics highly desired by advertisers. Our appeal focuses on all income level individuals & families. BLACK BELT TV provides programming for advertisers seeking to attract martial arts practitioners/enthusiasts, health/fitness-minded individuals, as well as sports enthusiasts, suppliers of exercise equipment, & other companies & product manufacturers that can directly reach their target audience. Our programming includes martial arts movies, martial arts training/self-defense, self-improvement programs, sports-, women-, & children-oriented programs, martial arts news, & much more.

Bloomberg Television, 499 Park Ave., New York 10022. Phone: (212) 893-3331. Fax: (202) 522-2400. Web Site: www.bloomberg.com/media/tv. Kenneth Kohn, editor; Betsy Alekman, mktg.

A sophisticated 24-hour business & financial news ch. Serving over 200 million subs worldwide, United States, Canada, Central & South America, Europe,& Asia/Pacific. Satellite: Galaxy 11, HITS, C3.

The Boating Channel (TBC), 60 Bay St., Sag Harbor, NY 11963-2022. Phone: (631) 725-4440. Fax: (631) 725-0748. Web Site: www.boatingchannel.com. Barbara-Jo London, CEO; Daniel E. London, COO; Phillip J. Kassel, Esq & legal counsel; Gregory Hahn, exec producer.

Marine news & weather, entertainment, info & educ for the recreational, professional boater & cruise vacationer.

Boston Kids & Family TV, 43 Hawkins St., Suite 1B, Boston 02114. Phone: (617) 635-3112. Fax: (617) 635-4475. E-mail: cable@ci.boston.ma.us. Web Site: www.cityofboston.gov/cable. Michael Lynch, dir; David Burt, stn mgr.

A partnership between the City of Boston & WGBH. Available 24 hour a day , edu TV progmg. PBS Kids from WGBH in Boston.

Bravo, (NBC Cable Network). 30 Rockefeller Plaza, 14th Fl. East, New York, NY 10112. Phone: (212) 664-4444. E-mail: programming@bravotv.com. Web Site: www.bravotv.com. Frances Berwick, progmg VP; Jeff Gaspin, pres.

Bravo offers innovative arts & entertainment progmg with a unique point of view featuring original series, theater, dance, music & documentaries 24 hour.

Serving 75 million subs. Satellite: Satcom C-4, transponder 7.

Buzztime Entertainment, Inc., 5966 La Place Ct., Suite 100, Carlsbad 92008. Phone: (760) 476-1976. Fax: (760) 438-3505. Web Site: www.buzztime.com. Stanley Kinsey, chmn/CEO; Tyrone Lam, pres/COO; Dan Sweeney, sr VP; Pat Ruble, VP.

Buzztime is the only 24-hour interactive entertainment bcst created exclusively for TV audiences. Featuring play-along trivia games for players of all interests & ability levels.

CCTV 4, 11 Fuxing Rd., Beijing 100859. China. Phone: (310) 414-2110. Fax: (310) 141-2101. Michael Scott, VP.

China Central TV (CCTV) China's only national bcstg network. Provide Info about China's politics, economy, society, culture, science, edu & history, also Chinese viewers, living outside of China, 24 hours a day. Serving more than 100 million subs. Satellite: Galaxy 11, transponder 24.

Broadcasting & Cable Yearbook 2006

E-5

CMT: Country Music Television, 330 Commerce St., Nashville, TN 37201. Phone: (615) 335-8400. Fax: (615) 335-8615. Web Site: www.cmt.com. Brian Philips, VP/gen mgr.

CMT, America's # one country music network, 24 hours a day. CMT, owned & operated by MTV networks. Serving 73.5 million subs. Satellite: Satcom C-4, transponder 24, Satcom C3, transponder 18 west coast.

CNBC, 900 Sylvan Ave., One CNBC Plaza, Englewood Cliffs, NJ 07632. Phone: (201) 735-2622. E-mail: info@cnbc.com. Web Site: www.cnbc.com. Mark Hoffman, pres.

CNBC set the standard for up-to-the-minute business news & incisive analysis of global financial markets. During primetime, the network presents broad-base news, talk, interview & entertainment progmg.

Serving 86 million subs. Satellite: Galaxy 5, transponder 13.

CNN-Cable News Network, One CNN Ctr., Atlanta, GA 30303. Phone: (404) 827-1500. Web Site: www.cnn.com. Jim Walton, pres; Eason Jordan, exec VP; Sue Bunda, sr VP.

CNN provides coverage of major breaking stories, business, weather, sports & special reports, worldwide audience, 24 hour.

Serving over 75.1 million subs. Satellite: Galaxy 5, transponder 5.

CNN en Espanol, One CNN Ctr., Atlanta, GA 30303. Phone: (404) 878-1515. Fax: (404) 878-0050. Web Site: www.cnnenespanol.com. Christopher Crommett, sr VP; Chris Cramer, pres; Caroline Rittenberry, VP.

A 24-hour Sp-language news network in the United States & Latin America. The network keeps its loyal viewers connected with the events, issues trends that matter most to them & their families.

Serving more than 13 million subs.

CNNfn, 5 Penn Plaza, New York, NY 10001. Phone: (212) 714-7800. Fax: (212) 714-6925. Web Site: www.money.com. Ken Jautz, exec VP & gen mgr.

CNN/fn provides up-to-the-minute mkt & industry news coverage from Wall Street and throughout the world, United States, Latin America & Asia. The network also offers viewers in-depth personal finance progmg, interview & call-in, eleven hours a day.

CNN Headline News, One CNN Ctr., Atlanta, GA 30348-5366. Phone: (404) 827-1500. Web Site: www.cnn.com/hln. Roland Santo, exec VP & gen mgr.

Provides viewers with a 30-minute news, 24 hours a day. Each half-hour covers major news stories as well as business, sports, medicine, entertainment, weather & human interest topics. Areas: United States, Canada, Mexico & Caribbean.

Serving over 86 million subs. Satellite: Galaxy 5, transponder 22.

CNNI (CNN International), One CNN Ctr., 3rd Flr., Atlanta, GA 30348. Phone: (404) 827-1500. Web Site: www.cnn.com/cnni. Rena Golden, VP/gen mgr; Eric Ludgood, VP; Chris Cramer, mgng dir.

A 24-hour global news & info, with live, breaking world news, sports, features & weather. Serving 170 million worldwide.

c/net: the computer network, 235 Second St., San Francisco, CA 94105. Phone: (415) 344-2000. Phone: (415) 344-2910. Fax: (415) 274-3750. Web Site: www.cnet.com. Shelby Bonnie, CEO.

The current line up is CNET news.com, airs weekly on CNBC- every Sat. & Sun., 4 pm(eastern) & CNET tv.com airs on syndication.

C-SPAN (Cable Satellite Public Affairs Network), 400 N. Capitol St. N.W., Suite 650, Washington, DC 20001. Phone: (202) 737-3220. Fax: (202) 737-3323. Web Site: www.c-span.org. Brian P. Lamb, chmn/CEO; Robert Kennedy, exec VP; Susan Swain, CEO; Bruce Collins, exec VP.

C-SPAN progmg includes live coverage of the House of Representatives, National Pres Club speeches & congressional hearings. C-SPAN 2 live coverage of the U.S. Senate & C-SPAN 3 pub affrs TV. 87 million subs. Satellite: Satcom C-3, transponder 7.

CSTV: College Sports Television, Chelsea Piers, Pier 62, Suite 316, New York 10011. Phone: (212) 342-8700. Fax: (212) 342-8899. Web Site: www.cstv.com. Brian Bedol, pres/CEO; Chris Bevilacqua, exec VP.

The network televises regular season & championship events coverage from every major collegiate athletic conference & televises nine NCAA Championships available 24-hour, ad-supported. 15 million subs. Satellite: Galaxy IR, transponder 22.

CTI Zhong Tian Channel, 1255 Corporate Center Dr., Suite 212, Monterey Park 91754. Phone: (323) 415-0068. Andy Chung, gen mgr.

A 24-hour Mandarin-Chinese ch, consists of progmg derived from Chinese TV Int'l reputable Zhong Tian news. Satelite: Galaxy 11, transponder 24.

The California Channel, 1121 L St., Suite 110, Sacramento, CA 95814. Phone: (916) 444-9792. Fax: (916) 444-9812. E-mail: calchannel@calchannel.com. Web Site: www.calchannel.com. John Hancock, pres; James Gualtieri, opns mgr.

Televised coverage of California state legislature & govt agency proceedings. M-F, 9 AM-3:30 PM. On 174 cable systems.5.2 million subs. Satellite: Satcom C-4, transponder 5.

Canal 24 Horas, 1100 Ponce de Leon Blvd., Coral Gables 33134. Phone: (305) 444-4402. Fax: (305) 444-6301. E-mail: aragon@tveamerica.com. Web Site: www.rtve.es. Mariano Aragon, mgr.

A 24 hour news network from TVE which offers a Headline News fromat with 30 minute blocks. The network also produces 17 different 30 minutes daily & wkly news magazines. Areas: United States, Mexico, Caribbean, Central & South America & Europe. 250,000 subs. Satellite: Telstar 5, transponder 1.

Cartoon Network, 1050 Techwood Dr. N.W., Altanta, GA 30318. Phone: (404) 827-4700. Fax: (404) 827-1700. Web Site: www.cartoonnetwork.com. Jim Samples, gen mgr; Dennis Adamovich, mktg VP; Gary Albright, sr VP; Bob Higgins, progmg VP.

A Turner Broadcasting System. Inc.'s 24-hour Cartoon Network offers the best in animated entertainment. Drawing from the world's largest cartoon library, also showcases unique original ventures such as "Johnny Bravo,' "Cow and Chicken," "Dexter's Laboratory," "Ed, Edd n Eddy," and "Cartoon Cartoon." Serving 86 million subs around the world. Satellite: Galaxy 1, transponder 15 (West). Satellite: Galaxy IR, transponder 8 (East).

Cartoon Network Latin America, 1030 Techwood Dr., Atlanta, GA 30318. Phone: (404) 885-2434. Fax: (404) 885-2157. E-mail: ruthie.stephenson@turner.com. Web Site: www.cartoonnetworkla.com. Barry Koch, VP/gen mgr.

The first global 24-hour cable ch programmed entirely with cartoons. Available in Sp, Portuguese or English.

Serving more than 10.9 million subs. Satellite: PanAmSat 3R.

CelticVision, 179 Amory St., Brookline, MA 02446. Phone: (617) 566-4844. Fax: (617) 566-7536. E-mail: celtictv@aol.com. Lawrence Baker, pres.

Serving 140,000 subs on 2 cable systems.

Celticvision: The Irish Channel, 95 Wexford St., Needham, MA 02494. Phone: (781) 444-2080. Fax: (781) 449-7074.

Material drawn from RTE, UTV & the BBC, with original material creating a 24-hour ch of alt English-language progmg with a distinctly Irish flavor. Serving 200,000 subs on 3 multiple systems.

Channel One Russia Worldwide Network, 20 Frunzenskaya Daberezhmaya, Suite D, Moscow 119146. Phone: (310) 414-2110. Fax: (310) 414-2101. Web Site: www.firstchannel.tv. David Quinn, dir.

A 24-hour Russian language ch for Russian communities throughout the United States. The ch consists of dramas, movies, news, children progmg, sports, talk show and more. Satellite: Galaxy 11, transponder 24.

Children's Cable Network, (A division of Olympic Entertainment Group). 2001 E. Flamingo Rd., Las Vegas, NV 89119. Phone: (702) 369-2588. Fax: (702) 369-8284. Web Site: www.oeg-ccn.com.

Non-violent, educ children's progmg. Progmg hours 6 AM-12 noon.

Chronicle DTV, 53 W. 36th St., Suite 203, New York 10018. Phone: (212) 337-9700 ext.105. Fax: (212) 352-1190. Web Site: www.chronicledtv.com. David Peipers, chmn; Richard Blume, pres/CEO.

A 24-hour digital TV progmg network offering diverse selection of feature length non-fiction & documentary programs. Chronicle is seen in 35 cities in the United States, Los Angeles, Miami, West Palm Beach & Orlando. one million subs. Satellite: Telstar 5, transponder 22.

Cinemax, (Home Box Office). 1100 Ave. of the Americas, New York, NY 10036. Phone: (212) 512-1000. Fax: (212) 512-1166. Web Site: www.cinemax.com. Chris Albrecht, chmn/CEO.

Cinemax is a 24-hour digital pay-TV svc designed to provide viewers with the most movies & fewest repeats. Multiplex chs: Cinemax, MoreMAX, ActionMAX, ThrillerMAX, WMAX, @MAX, 5StarMAX, OuterMAX. Cinemax is seen in the United States & Puerto Rico. 39 million subs. Satellite: Galaxy IR, transponder 23.

Classic Arts Showcase, Box 828, Burbank, CA 91503. Phone: (323) 878-0283. Fax: (323) 878-0329. E-mail: casmail@earthlink.net. Web Site: www.classicartsshowcase.org. Charlie Mount, gen mgr; James D. Rigler, pres & progmg dir.

CAS is a non-profit arts progmg svc that include 16 art disciplines. The svc also features classic video from independent producers with the right to show clips. We require copies from masters on BetaCam-SP Tap. Available 24 hour.

Serving 60 million subs. Satellite: Galaxy 1R, transponder 5.

Collectors Channel Inc., Box 702, 67 River St., Hudson, MA 01749-0702. Phone: (508) 788-5474. E-mail: allcollectors@aol.com. Web Site: www.allcollectors.com. Gary Sohmers, pres; Roy Thompson, VP; Fred Sherman, VP; Joel Shames, VP; Joyce Dostale, CEO.

Basic svc, 24-hour progmg targeted to collectors of various merchandise & memorabilia. Educ & entertaining progmg with a shopping element.

College Entertainment Network, 6255 Sunset Blvd., Suite 611, Hollywood 90028. Phone: (323) 465-9880. Fax: (323) 465-9881. Web Site: www.collegeentertainment.com. Robert Artura, pres/CEO; Georgina Montalvan, VP mktg.

College Entertainment Network is a world of college TV stn on one network, it features block of programs, from extreme sports to entertainment. 10 million subs.

Comedy Central, 1775 Broadway, New York, NY 10019. Phone: (212) 767-8600. Fax: (212) 767-8592. Web Site: www.comedycentral.com. Hank Close, exec VP; Tony Fox, exec VP; Doug Herzog, pres; Bill Hilary, VP/gen mgr; Cathy Tankosic, sr VP.

Los Angeles, CA 90067, 2049 Century Park E, Suite 4250. Phone: (310) 201-9500. Fax: (310) 201-9488.

A 24-hour all comedy TV network that covers stand-up, sketch comedy, movies, talk shows, sitcoms, specials & classics TV shows.

Serving 84.8 million subs. Satellites: Satcom C-3, transponder 21 (east), Galaxy 1R, transponder 1 (west).

Courtroom Television Network (Court TV), 600 3rd Ave., 2nd Fl., New York, NY 10016. Phone: (212) 973-2800. Fax: (212) 973-3210. Web Site: www.courttv.com. Henry Schlieff, chmn/CEO; Robert Rose, exec VP; Mary Silverman, VP progmg; Ira Fields, CFO; Art Bell, pres/COO.

Court TV telecast trails day by day & high profile original programs 24-hour. Serving 80 million subs.

The Crime Channel, 42335 Washington St., Palm Desert, CA 92211. Phone: (760) 360-6151. Fax: (760) 360-3258. E-mail: crimechannel@dc.rr.com. Arnie Frank, pres.

The Crime Channel offers series, movies, documentaries, original productions, on the spot crime news & foreign programs. Satellite: Satcom C-1, transponder 11.

DIY (Do It Yourself Network), 9721 Sherrill Blvd., Knoxville, TN 37932. Phone: (865) 694-2700. Fax: (865) 690-9281. Web Site: www.diynet.com. Bob Baskerville, pres; Robyn Ulrich, VP mktg; Jeff Sears, VP.

DIY cable TV network operated by Scripps Networks, providing in depth demonstrations & tips for categories such as home improvement, home bldg, tools, products, gardening, landscaping, automotive, boating, decorating, design, arts, crafts, cooking, hobby & recreations, 24-hour a day. 25 million subs. Satellite: Galaxy IR, transponder 4.

Daystar Television Network, 4201 Pool Rd., Colleyville 76034. Phone: (817) 571-1229. Fax: (817) 571-7458. E-mail: comments@daystar.com. Web Site: www.daystar.com. Janice Smith, VP progmg; David Troxel, VP.

Daystar TV Network is a Christian TV network, is available from DirectTV, Dish Network 24-hours a day. Our progmg is multi-ch & interdenominational.

De Pelicula, 5999 Center Dr., Los Angeles 90045. Phone: (301) 348-3371. Web Site: www.tutv.tv. Mark Feldman, pres/CEO; Carlos Madrazo, CFO.

A 24-hour contemporary & classic movie ch featuring the best Sp language films.

Multiplex ch: De Pelicula Clasico is a 24-hour movie ch featuring the best films of Mexico's golden era.

TeleHit is a young, hip & cutting-edge, trend setting lite-style & music ch. 750,000 subs.

Deep Dish TV, 339 Lafayette St., New York, NY 10012. Phone: (212) 473-8933. Fax: (212) 420-8223. Web Site: www.igc.org/deepdish. Ron Davis, chmn; Tom Pool, exec dir; Victoria Macdonado, VP.

Educational progmg (one hour a wk) distributed to PBS & pub access chs. Satellite: Galaxy IR, transponder 15.

Discovery Channel, (Discovery Communications). One Discover Pl., Silver Spring, MD 20910. Phone: (240) 662-0000. Fax: (240) 662-1854. Web Site: www.discovery.com. John S. Hendricks, chmn; Annie Howell, sls VP; Bill Campbell, pres; Judith McHale, pres/CEO; Bill McGowan, sr VP; Clark Buntint, sr VP; Jane Root, VP/gen mgr.

Discovery Channel is the largest cable TV in the United States & nation's premier provider of real world entertainment, offering a signature mix of compelling high ebd productions value & vivid cinematography worldwide, ad-supported. Multiplex chs: Discovery en Espansol, Discovery HD Theater, Discovery Health Channel, Discovery Home Channel, Discovery Network, US, Discovery Times Channel, Discovery Wings Channel, The Science Channel & Animal Planet.

Serving over 88 million subs. Satellites: Satcom C-4, transponder 21 east, Galaxy 5, transponder 12 west.

Discovery Kids Channel, (Discovery Communications). One Discovery Pl., Silver Spring, MD 20910. Phone: (240) 662-2000. Fax: (240) 662-1854. Web Site: www.discovery.com. John Hendricks, chmn; Judith McHale, pres/CEO; W. Clark Bunting II, exec VP; Mark Kozaki, sr VP; Marjorie Kaplan, VP/gen mgr.

Discovery Kids Channel is a place where kids can explore the world, from space stns to shark infested waters for the preschoolers to older kids, 24-hour a day. Serving 30 million subs. Satellite: Satcom C3, transponder 22, HITS: G4-R, transponder 11.

The Disney Channel, 3800 W. Alameda Ave., Burbank, CA 91505. Phone: (818) 569-7500. Fax: (818) 566-1358. Web Site: www.disneychannel.com. Rich Ross, pres.

A 24-hour gen entertainment network for kids & families through original series, movies & contempary acquired progmg. Serving over 25 million subs. Satellite: Galaxy 5, transponder 1 east, Galaxy 1-R, transponder 7 west.

The Dream Network, 9300 Georgia Ave., Suite 206, Silver Springs 20910. Phone: (301) 587-0000. Fax: (301) 587-7464. Web Site: www.thedreamnetwork.com. Alvin Augustus Jones, pres/CEO.

The Dream Network is the urban family choice for news, talk, sports & gospel music. Seen in the United States, Canada, Caribbean, Europe, Africa & Asia. Serving 25 million subs on 10 million cable systems. Satellite: DirecTV.

E! Entertainment Television, 5750 Wilshire Blvd., Los Angeles, CA 90036-3709. Phone: (323) 954-2400. Fax: (323) 954-2500. Web Site: www.eonline.com. Neil Baker, sr VP; Mark Sonnenberg, exec VP; Mindy Herman, pres/CEO; David T. Cassaro, exec VP; Ken Bettsteller, CEO.

New York, NY 10036, 11 W. 42nd St. Phone: (212) 852-5100. (212) 852-5151. Dave Cassaro, exec VP.

A 24-hour progmg network covering celebrities, entertainment news, gossip & pop-culture, feature behind the scenes with today's biggest stars. 84 million subs. Satellite: Satcom C-3, transponder 23.

ESPN, ESPN Plaza, Bristol, CT 06010-9454. Phone: (860) 766-2000. Fax: (860) 766-2400. Web Site: www.espn.com. George Bodenheimer, pres; Edwin M. Durso, exec VP; Lee Ann Daly, VP mktg; Chris Driessen, CFO.

New York, NY 10158-0180, 605 3rd Ave. Phone: (212) 916-9200.

A 24-hour svc covering sports events, news, info, & lifestyle progmg.

ESPN CLASSIC is a 24-hour, all sports network devoted to telecasting the greatest games, stories, heroes & memories in the history of sports. Serving 50 millon subs. Satellite: Galaxy 10R, transponder 20.

ESPN DEPORTE offers a wide var of domestic & intl sports progmg 24-hour. Serving 14 million subs. Satellite: Galaxy 10R, transponder 20.

ESPN HD offers a 24-hour high definition TV svc from ESPN, features high profile telecast. Satellite: Galaxy 10R, transponder 22.

ESPNEWS , the nation's only 24-hour TV sports news svc, provides an expanded window for news & highlights,as well as live coverage of beaking news. Serving 50 million subs. Satellite: Galaxy 10R, transponder 21. 88 million subs. Satellite: Galaxy V, transponder 9.

ESPN2, ESPN Plaza, Bristol, CT 06010-9454. Phone: (860) 766-2000. Fax: (860) 766-2400. Web Site: www.espn.com. George Bodenheimer, pres.

A 24-hour sports network features a progmg line-up on par with ESPN. 86 million subs. Satellite: Galaxy V, transponder 14.

ESPNU, c/o ESPN Regional Television, 11001 Rushmore Dr., Charlotte, NC 28277. Phone: (704) 973-5000. Burke Magnus, VP/gen mgr.

EWTN, The Global Catholic Network. 5817 Old Leeds Rd., Irondale, AL 35210. Phone: (205) 271-2900. Fax: (205) 271-2925. Web Site: www.ewtn.com. R. William Steltemeier, chmn/CEO; Michael P. Warsaw, pres; Chris Wegemer, VP mktg; Scott Hults, dir; Doug Keck, VP.

America's largest relg cable network offers coml-free family-oriented progmg in English & Sp. EWTN features documentaries, music, drama, live talk shows, animated children shows & special church events from around the world. 53 million subs. Satellite: Galaxy IR, transponder 11.

Ecology Communications, 9171 Victoria Dr., Ellicott City 21042. Phone: (410) 465-0480. Fax: (410) 461-5152. Web Site: www.ecology.com. Shelley Duvall, chmn/CEO; Eric McLamb, pres.

Ecology Communications focuse on ecology & enviroment in a var of entertainment-driven formats wkly. 10 million subs.

Encore Media Corp., 8900 Liberty Cir., Englewood, CO 80112. Phone: (720) 852-7700. Fax: (720) 852-3067. Web Site: www.starzsuperpak.com. John J. Sie, chmn/CEO; Mark Bauman, pres/CEO; Robert B. Clasen, pres.

Los Angeles, CA 90025. International Channel, 11766 Wilshire Blvd, Suite 710. Phone: (310) 477-9922. Fax: (310) 477-4544. Victoria Kent, rgnl VP.

Englewood, CO 80111. Founders, 5445 DTC Pkwy, Suite 600. Phone: (303) 771-7700. Fax: (303) 267-4001. Robin Feller, rgnl VP.

Englewood, CO 80111. New Media, 5445 DTC Pkwy, Suite 600. Phone: (303) 771-7700. Fax: (303) 267-4098. Leslie Nittler, VP sls & mktg.

Atlanta, GA 30342. southeast region, 5775 Peachtree Dunwoody Rd, Suite D-620. Phone: (404) 531-7060. Fax: (404) 531-7075. Cindy Feinberg, rgnl VP.

Chicago, IL 60601. central region, 111 E. Wacker Dr, Suite 1300. Phone: (312) 938-8900. Fax: (312) 938-8902. Susan LeVarsky, rgnl VP.

Hoboken, NJ 07030. eastern region, 70 Hudson St. Phone: (201) 239-9020. Fax: (201) 239-2290. Shanita Evans, rgnl VP.

Carrollton, TX 75006. Time Warner & Central region office, 2340 E. Trinity Mills Rd, Suite 300. Phone: (972) 417-2866. Fax: (972) 417-2806. Paige Holmes.

Encore Media Corp. offers the following premium cable progmg svcs:

ENCORE presents hit movies from the 1960s, 1970s & 1980s, coml-free, 24-hours per day. Serves 6 millions subs. Satellite: Galaxy 1-R, transponder, 3.

STARZ!-encore 8 features first-run releases from leading distributors 24-hours per day. Serves 2 million subs. Satellite: Satcom C-4, transponder 2.

MOVIEPLEX is a STARZ! ch, never shows R-rated progmg and is offered as an analog feed only. Serves 5.4 million subs. Satellite: Satcom C 4, transponder 5 east & west.

MYSTERY features great coml-free mystery movies, 24-hours a day.

STARZ ON DEMAND is an enchancement to STARZ!. Satellite: Galaxy 1R, transponder 13 east & west.

STARZ! CINEMA features movies for everyone who is passionate about movies. Satellite: Galaxy 1R, transponder 13 east, Satcom C4, transponder 5 west.

STARZ! FAMILY is the first and only coml-free ch showing family movies. Satellite: Galaxy 1R, transponder 13 east, Satcom C4, transponder 5 west.

STARZ! SUPER PAK features new hit movies. Serves 12 million subs. Satellite: Galaxy 1R, transponder 13 east & west.

STARZ KIDS is a 24-hour ch for kids ages 2-8. Satellite: Galaxy 1R, transponder 13 east, Satcom C4, transponder 5 west.

STARZ! THEATER is programme like a movie theater. Satellite: Galaxy 1R, transponder 13 east, Satcom C4, transponder 5 west.

TRUE STORIES tell is like it is, presenting real life dramas. Satellite: Galaxy 1R, transponder 13 east & west.

WESTERN ch features Hollywood's most popular past & contemporary western films.

ENCORE THEMATIC MULTIPLEX offers six, genre-specific movie svcs 24-hours per day.

Satellite: Galaxy 1-R, transponder 13.

ENCORE THEME BY DAY offers hit movies from the 1960s, 1970s & 1980s. Genres are determined by the day of the week.

ENCORE HD is the high definition version of the flagship Encore movies svc, 24-hour. Serves over 63,699 subs. Satellite: Galaxy 13, transponder 7 west, transponder 9 east, Digital Digicipher II.

ACTION offers non-stop excitement, action movies featured nightly.

LOVE STORIES is the place for movie romance. Satellite: Galaxy 1R, transponder 3, east & west.

eSignal, 3955 Point Eden Way, Hayward, CA 94545. Phone: (510) 266-6000. Fax: (510) 266-6100. Web Site: www.esignal.com. Chuck Thompson, pres; Grant Mader, VP net ops & telecommunications.

Real-time stock, option, commodity quotation service & sports service delivered via cable TV, FM frequency & bcst VBI to end user PC.

Serving more than 20,000 subs on more than 850 systems. Satellites: Satcom F3, transponder 11; Galaxy 3, transponder 24.

EUROCINEMA, European Movies on TV. 387 Park Ave., 3rd Fl., New York, NY 10016. E-mail: eurocinema @envrocinema.com. Web Site: www.eurocinema.com.

Non-Hollywood movies service for Broadband & Digital TV

FX Networks Inc., (A subsidiary of Fox, Inc.). 1440 S. Sepulveda Blvd., Los Angeles, CA 90025. Phone: (310) 444-8135. Fax: (310) 235-2853. Web Site: www.fxnetworks.com. John Landgraf, pres; Chuck Saftler, VP progmg; Christy Dees, dev dir; Michael Sakin, sr VP; Mark DeVitre, sr VP; Chris Carlisle, sr VP; Lindsay Gardner, exec VP; Steve LeBlang, rsch dir; John Solberg, VP; Steve Webster, VP; Eric Shiu, VP.

An entertainment basic cable net from Fox Television involving hit series, daily films, original programs & sports.

Serving more than 53 million subs on 3,293 cable systems. Satellite: Hughes Communications Galaxy 7, transponder 4 & 5.

FamilyNet, 6350 West Fwy., Fort Worth, TX 76116. Phone: (800) 832-6638. Phone: (817)737-4011. Fax: (817) 298-3388. E-mail: info@familynet.com. Web Site: www.familynet.com. Martin Coleman, COO; R. Chip Turner, VP mktg; Bob Sutton, pres/CEO; Ray Raley, engrg VP.

FamilyNet is a full-time cable network with 50+ hours of original values-based programs weekly. Reliable, safe television for today's family. Satellite Intersat Americas 13, transponder 20.

The Filipino Channel, (ABS-CBN International). 859 Cowan Rd., Burlingame, CA 94010. Phone: (650) 697-3700. Fax: (650) 697-3500. E-mail: tfc@abs-cbni. Web Site: www.tfc-na.com. Rene Encarnacioni, sr VP; Rafael Lopez, VP; Lyla Paniagua, mgr.

A 24-hour svc for Filipinos worldwide. Progmg originates at ABS-CBN, the Philippines top-rated net. Time-shifted for North America.

Satellite: PAS-2 for Pacific delivery, Telstar 5 (ku) transponder 22 for North America. On 17 cable systems.100,000 subs.

Food Network, 1180 Sixth Ave., 12th Fl., New York, NY 10036. Phone: (212) 398-8836. Web Site: www.foodtv.com. Eric Ober, pres/CEO.

A 24-hour cable & satellite delivered net devoted to food & good living.

Serving 33 million subs.

Food Network, 1180 6th Ave., 12th Fl., New York, NY 10036. Phone: (212) 398-8836. Fax: (212) 736-7716. Web Site: www.foodnetwork.com. Judy Girard, pres; Brooke Johnson, VP/gen mgr; Adam Rockmore, VP mktg; Mark O'Connor, dir.

A 24-hour network committed to exploring new, different & interesting ways to approach food. 82 million subs. Satellite: Galaxy IR, transponder 4.

Fox Movie Channel, (FX Networks Inc.). 10000 Santa Monica Blvd., Los Angeles, CA 90065. Phone: (310) 789-4667. Fax: (310) 789-4687. Web Site: www.fxnetworks.com. Mark P. DeVitre, VP/gen mgr; Chuck Saftler, gen mgr; Billy Hall, VP progmg; Peter Liguori, pres/CEO.

The network is dedicated to preserving Hollywood history through original series & specials. Satellite: Galaxy GE7, transponder 7.

FX (FOX BASIC CABLE) is a flagship gen entertainment basic cable network from Fox, 19 hours a day. Serving 84 million subs.

Fox Net, 10201 W. Pico Blvd., 4th Fl., Bldg. 89, Los Angeles, CA 90035. Phone: (310) 369-1000. Fax: (310) 969-1360. Susan Kiel, VP; Dwayne Bright, progmg dir; Wendy Chambers, dir; Betty Wang, dir mktg; Keith Goldberg, dir; Mark Handwerger, natl sls mgr; Julie Allen, natl sls mgr; Steve Nazar, opns mgr.

Los Angeles, CA 90035. FOX Broadcasting Co, 10201 W. Pico Blvd. Phone: (310) 369-5153. Fax: (310) 969-0316. Susan Kiel, VP, Network Distribution & Cable Operations.

A 24-hour basic cable affil to Fox Broadcasting Co.

Serving 2 million subs on 1,350 cable systems. Satellite: Satcom C-1, transponder 19.

Fox News Channel

See listing in Major National TV News Organizations, this section.

Free Speech TV, Box 6060, Boulder, CO 80306. Phone: (303) 442-8445. Fax: (303) 442-6472. Web Site: www.freespeech.org. John Schwartz, pres; Jon Stout, gen mgr.

FSTV airs primarily social, political, cultural & environmental documentaries & news progms, 24-hours a day. Serving 25 million subs on cable & DISH Network. 130.15,500,000.

Fuel, 1440 S. Sepulveda Blvd., Suite 1900, Los Angeles 90025. Fax: (310) 444-8559. E-mail: hookup@fuel.tv. Web Site: www.fuel.tv. Cj Olivares, VP progmg; David Sternberg, gen mgr; Kelsey Martinez, dir.

A 24-hour sports network featuring snowboarding, wakeboarding, surfing, BMX, motorcross & skateboarding. Serving 5 million subs. Satellite: Galaxy II, transponder 5.

Broadcasting & Cable Yearbook 2006

E-7

Fuse, 11 Penn Plaza, 15th Fl., New York, NY 10001. Phone: (212) 324-3400. Fax: (212) 324-3445. Web Site: www.fuse.tv. Marc Juris, pres; Norman Schoenfeld, VP progmg; Michael Goldstein, VP; Kim Martin, exec VP; Theano Apostolou, VP.

Santa Monica, CA 90404. The Water Garden, 2425 W. Olympic Blvd, Suite 5050. Phone: (310) 998-9300. John Pezzini, VP.

Chicago, IL 60601. Chicago Office, 205 N. Michigan, Suite 803A. Phone: (312) 938-4222. Joseph Glennon, Sr. VP.

Fuse is the only all-music, viewer-influenced TV network, featuring music videos, exclusive artist interviews, live concerts & specials. Serving 35 million subs. Satellite; Loral Skynet Telstar 7, transponder 14.

Galavision, 605 3rd Ave., 12th Fl., New York, NY 10158. Phone: (212) 455-5300. Fax: (212) 986-4731. Web Site: www.univisionnetworks.com. Tim Krass, exec VP; Steve Males, VP mktg; Timothy Spillane, VP.

Los Angeles, CA 90045, 6701 Center Dr. W, Suite 650. Phone: (310) 348-3600.

Chicago, IL 60611, 541 N. Fairbanks Ct, Suite 1240. Phone: (312) 494-5101.

Dallas, TX 75201, 2323 Bryan St, Suite 1900. Phone: (214) 758-2300.

A 24-hr Sp language cable network for united states hispanics in distribution & viewership. 37 million subs. Satellite: Satcom C-4, transponder 4.

Game Show Network, 2150 Colorado Ave., Santa Monica, CA 90404. Phone: (310) 255-6800. Fax: (310) 255-6810. Web Site: www.gameshownetwork.com. Rich Cronin, CEO & pres; Dena Kaplan, mktg VP; Bob Boden, progmg VP; Ann Droste, sls dir.

Chicago, IL 60610, 515 N. State St. Suite 2120. Phone: (312) 261-4500. Fax: (312) 261-4521.

New York, NY 10019, 680 Fifth Ave. 11th Fl. Phone: (212) 333-2510. Fax: (646) 557-2996.

Dallas, TX 75201, The Republic Center, 325 N. St. Paul St. Suite 1500. Phone: (214) 965-8500. Fax: (214) 965-8576.

Game Show Network (GSN) is the only U.S. television network dedicated to game programming and interactive game playing, featuring over 65 hours per week of original programming and enhanced classics.

Reaching 50 million subs.

Global Television Network, 289 Great Rd., Acton, MA 01720. Phone: (978) 264-9921. Fax: (978) 264-9547. Web Site: www.globaltelevision.com.

Automotive entertainment & info via video on demand, worldwide web & dir mktg.

Serving 200,000 subs on 1 cable system.

The Golf Channel, 7580 Commerce Center Dr., Orlando, FL 32819. Phone: (407) 363-4653. Fax: (407) 363-7976. Web Site: www.thegolfchannel.com. David Manougian, pres; Justin Smith, sr VP; Bill O'Donnell, sr VP; Robert Greenway, VP progmg.

A 24-hour ch offering a blend of tournament coverage from the PGA, LPGA, Sr Tour, Nike, EPGA Tours, as well as instruction, interactive talk, news, profiles, classics, travel & more.

Serving 30 million subs on 2,200 cable systems. Satellite: Galaxy VI, Transponder 7.

GoodLife TV Network, 650 Massachusetts Ave. N.W., Washington, DC 20001. Phone: (202) 289-6633. Fax: (202) 289-6632. Web Site: www.goodtv.com. Mark Ringwald, VP progmg; Lawrence R. Meli, pres/CEO.

GoodLife TV Network is the nation's only full-time cable ch dedicated to improving the quality of American life through info & entertainment programs. Satellite: Galaxy IR, transponder 22.

Great American Country, 9697 E. Mineral Ave., Centennial, CO 80112. Phone: (303) 792-3111. Fax: (303) 784-8518. Web Site: www.countrystars.com. Jeffrey Wayne, pres/CEO; Kenneth O. Street, sr VP; Anthony M. Aiello, VP; Scott Durand, VP mktg; Glenn Jones, chmn.

GAC is a country music video network, features national & loc advertising, also featuring a broad var of videos programs for ages 25-54, 24 hours a day. 24 million subs. Satellite: Satcom C-3, transponder 20.

Guthy-Renker Television, 41-550 Eclectic St., Suite 200, Palm Desert, CA 92260. Phone: (760) 773-9022. Fax: (310) 234-3601. Web Site: www.guthy-renker.com. Bill Guthy, CEO; Greg Renker, CEO.

Direct-response TV

HDNET, 2400 N. Ulster St., Denver 80238. Phone: (303) 388-8500. Fax: (303) 388-9600. E-mail: info@hd.net. Web Site: www.hd.net. Mark Cuban, chmn/pres; Philip Garvin, gen mgr.

HDNET, the leader in high-indefinition bcstg, produces & televises 24-hour a day. Satellite: Galaxy 9, transponder 19C.

HDNET Movies is a 24-hour coml-free schedule of full-length feature films. Satellite: Galaxy 9, transponder 19C.

HSN, The Home Shopping Network, One HSN Dr., St. Petersburg, FL 33729. Phone: (727) 872-1000. Fax: (727) 872-7356. Web Site: www.hsn.com. Bob Rosenblatt, pres; Peter Ruben, exec VP; Tom McInerney, CEO.

HSN offers live, 24-hour video retailing. 81 million subs. Satellite: Satcom C-4, transponder 10.

Hallmark Channel, 12700 Ventura Blvd., Suite 200, Studio City, CA 91604-2463. Phone: (818) 755-2400. Fax: (818) 755-2564. Web Site: www.hallmarkchannel.com. David Evans, pres/CEO; David Kenin, VP progmg; Chris Moseley, exec VP; Charles Stanford, VP business affrs.

A 24-hour basic cable ch that provides high quality entertainment progmg to a national audience. 56 million subs. Satellite: Satcom C-3, transponder 5.

The History Channel, (A&E Television Networks). 235 E. 45th St., New York, NY 10017. Phone: (212) 210-1375. Fax: (212) 907-9409. Web Site: www.historychannel.com. Nickolas Davatzes, pres/CEO; Dan Davids, VP/gen mgr; Charles Maday, sr VP.

A 24-hour progmg svc featuring historical documentaries, specials & mini-series. 86 million subs. Satellite: Satcom C-3, transponder 12.

Home & Garden Television Network (HGTV), 9721 Sherrill Blvd., Knoxville, TN 37932. Phone: (865) 694-2700. Fax: (865) 694-4392. Web Site: www.hgtv.com. Mike Boyd, VP mktg; Burton Jablin, pres.

HGTV is a 24-hour network that provide practical info & creative ideas to help the viewers to make the most of their lives at home & is designed to appeal to all ages & lifestyles. Satellite: Galaxy IR, transponder 4.

Home Box Office (HBO), 1100 Ave. of the Americas, New York, NY 10036. Phone: (212) 512-1000. Fax: (212) 512-1166. Web Site: www.hbo.com. Chris Albrecht, chmn/CEO.

Features 24-hour var progmg including theatrical films, original movies, specials, documentaries, sports, & series.

Multiplex chs. HBO, HBO 2, HBO Latino, HBO Signature, HBO Family, HBO Comedy, HBO Zone - known collectively as HBO The Works. MoreMAX.

Serving 39 million subs. Satellites: Analog, Galaxy 1R, transponder 23; Galaxy 1R, transponder 18; Analog: Galaxy 5, transponder 8; Galaxy 3R, transponder 16; Galaxy 3R, transponder 20; Galaxy 3R, transponder 19.

Home Improvement Television Network, 3441 Baker St., San Diego, CA 92117. Phone: (858) 273-0572. Fax: (858) 273-8410. E-mail: homefix@hometvnet.com. Web Site: www.hometvnet.com. Bruce Lamb, pres.

Providers of home improvement progmg & 90-second video vignettes.

ICF Film, 11 Penn Plaza, New York, NY 10001. Phone: (516) 803-4500. Fax: (516) 803-4506. Web Site: www.ifctv.com. Jonathan Sehring, pres; Ed Carroll, VP/gen mgr; Greg Hill, exec VP; Cynthia Burnell, sr VP. Satellite: Galaxy VII,

The Idea Channel, 1502 Powell Ave., Erie, PA 16455. Phone: (814) 464-9068. Fax: (814) 464-9069. E-mail: cca@erie.net. Web Site: www.ideachannel.com. Bob Chitester, chmn; Rick Platt, dir.

Educ progmg.

The Independent Film Channel (IFC), (A division of Rainbow Media Programming Holdings). 200 Jericho Quadrangle, Jericho, NY 11753. Phone: (516) 803-3000. Fax: (516) 803-4616. Web Site: www.ifctv.com. Jonathan D. Sehring, pres; Edward Carroll, VP/gen mgr; Greg Hill, exec VP; Cynthia Burnell, VP/gen mgr.

A 24-hour uncut coml-free ch, capturing the true spirit of independent film, original series, live events & enchanced new media progmg. Serving 29 million subs. Satellite: Galaxy 7, transponder 14.

The Inspiration Network INSP, 7910 Crescent Executive Dr., 5th Fl., Charlotte, NC 28217. Phone: (704) 525-9800. Fax: (704) 525-9899. Web Site: www.inspnets.com. David Cerullo, pres/CEO; Rod Tapp, exec VP; Tom Hohman, sr VP; Larry Simms, VP sls; Ron Shuping, VP progmg.

INSP blends ministry programs with family-oriented movies, dramas, music & children's programs along with concerts & specials. 21 million subs. Satellite: Galaxy IR, transponder 17.

Inspirational Life Television, (I-Lifetv). 7910 Crescent Executive Dr., 5th Fl., Charlotte, NC 28217. Phone: (704) 525-9800. Fax: (704) 527-9899. Web Site: www.inspnets.com. David Cerullo, pres/CEO; Tom Hohman, sr VP; Larry Sims, VP sls.

Ilifetv is a 24-hour a day programmer & digital TV network which distributes life-enriching, edu entertainment progmg. 6 million subs. Satellite: Galaxy IR, transponder 7.

International Channel, 8900 Liberty Circle, Englewood, CO 80112. Phone: (720) 853-2933. Fax: (720) 853-2901. Web Site: www.internationalchannel.com. John J. Sie, chmn/CEO; Scott Wheeler, sr VP; Steve Smith, exec VP; Jim Honiotes, mktg VP & VP; Billo Georges, VP adv; Kent Rice, pres/CEO; Rod Shanks, VP finance; Lane E. Hammond, VP business affrs.

El Segundo, CA 90245, 2250 E. Imperial Hwy, Suite 630. Phone: (310) 414-2100. Fax: (310) 414-2101.

Des Plaines, IL 60018, 2700 River Road, Suite 108. Phone: (847) 298-9152. Fax: (847) 298-9491.

New York, NY 10022, 570 Lexington Ave, 36th Floor. Phone: (212) 527-9917. Fax: (212) 527-9915.

Seattle, WA 98119, 18 W. Mercer, Suite 110. Phone: (206) 282-2762. Fax: (206) 282-2763.

International Channel is the only cable ch serving multiple ethnic audiences 24-hour a day nationwide. On 1400.12.5 million subs. Satellite: Galaxy IX, transponder 24.

International Networks/AZN Television, 4100 E. Dry Creek Rd., Suite A 300, Centennial, CO 80122. Phone: (303) 712-5400. Phone: (303) 712-5454 (customer svc). Fax: (303) 712-5401. Web Site: www.azntv.com. Steve Smith, mgng dir.

In-language premium cable channels & Asign American basic cable channel. Full satellite info: www.internationalnetworkscom/24hrpaychannels/education/satellite_faq.aspx Over 1,000.Over 12,000,000. 24.

Jewelry Television By ACN, 10001 Kingston Pike, Suite 57, Knoxville, TN 37922. Phone: (865) 692-6000. Fax: (865) 693-3688. Web Site: www.acntv.com. Patsy Harris, dir; Mike Mason, VP; Harry Bagley, sr VP.

ACN is the only network that focuses exclusively on the sls of fine jewelry & gemstones, 24-hours a day. On 11 million cable systems.32 milion subs. Satellite: Telstar 5, transponder 19.

Jewish Television Network, 13743 Ventura Blvd., Suite 200, Sherman Oaks, CA 91423. Phone: (818) 789-5891. E-mail: jewishtv@earthlink.net. Web Site: www.jewishtvnetwork.com. Jay Sanderson, CEO.

Production & cablecasting of net-quality Jewish progmg in news, pub affrs, education, arts, PBS & entertainment.

Serving 6 million subs on 15 cable systems.

The Jones Companies, 9697 E. Mineral Ave., Englewood, CO 80112. Phone: (303) 792-3111. Fax: (303) 784-8549. Web Site: www.jones.com. Glenn Jones, pres/CEO.

A 24-hour revenue providing svc that features full-length product demonstrations & introduction of new products in a hands-on demonstration format.

Serving 26 million subs. Satellite: GE Satcom C3, transponder 20.

KTLA, United Video (a company of the United Video Satellite Group). 5800 Sunset Blvd., Los Angeles, CA 90028. Phone: (323) 460-5500. Fax: (323) 962-1691. John Reardon, VP/gen mgr.

Los Angeles WB stn offers movies, news, specials & live sporting events, featuring the Los Angeles Clippers basketball . Services offered: Ind satellite carrier serving CATV, SMATV & MMDS distributing WGN, WPIX, KTLA & WFMT (FM) Network Svcs.

Satellite: Spacenet 6E. On 220 cable systems.1 million subs. transponder 15.

The Learning Channel (TLC), (Discovery Communications). One Discovery Pl., Silver Spring, MD 20910. Phone: (240) 662-2000. Fax: (240) 662-1854. Web Site: www.discovery.com. John J. Hendricks, chmn; John B. Ford, sr VP; Bill Goodwyn, exec VP.

The network features dynamic non-fiction progmg about science, history, real life adventure, human behavior & lifestyle, 24-hour a day.

Serving 87 million subs.

Satellite: Satcom C-3, transponder 2 east, Satcom C4, transponder 14 west.

Lifetime Movie Network, 309 W. 49th St., New York, NY 10019. Phone: (212) 424-7000. Web Site: www.lifetimetv.com. Carole Black, pres/CEO; James Wesley, CFO; Rick Haskins, VP/gen mgr; Tim Brooks, VP rsch.

Lifetime is committed to offering the highest quality entertainment & info progmg 24-hours a day. Serving more than 36 million subs. Satellite: Telstar 7, transponder 14, Galaxy XR, transponder 20.

LIFETIME Television, 309 W. 49th St., New York, NY 10019. Phone: (212) 424-7000. Web Site: www.lifetimetv.com. Betty Cohen, pres/CEO; Barbara Fisher, exec VP; James Wesley, CFO; Lynn Picard, exec VP; Rick Haskins, exec VP; Louise Henry Bryson, exec VP; Patricia Langer, VP business affrs; Meredith Wagner, exec VP; Tim Brooks, VP rsch; Richard Basso, sr VP; Gwynne McConkey, opns VP.

Lifetime is committed to offering the highest quality entertainment, info progmg & advocating a wide range of issues affecting women & their families, 24 hours a day nationwide . Launched in 1984. Serving over 87 million subs. Lifetime Movie Network in 1998 & a second sister svc, Lifetime Real Women, launched in August 2001. On the web, Lifetime Online (www.lifetimetv.com) features informational resources & interactive entertainment. All four svcs, Lifetime TV, Lifetime Movie Network, Lifetime Real Women Online, are part of Lifetime Entertainment svcs, a 50/50 joint venture of The Hearst Corp & The Walt Disney Co. Satellite: GAlaxy V, transponder 21 east, Satcom, C3, tansponder 4 west. Satellite: Galaxy V, transponder 21.

The Locomotion Channel, 404 Washington Ave., Penthouse, Miami Beach, FL 33139. Phone: (786) 276-1140. Fax: (305) 894-3609. E-mail: locomotion@cisnerostv.com. Rodrigo Piza, gen mgr; Elizabeth Blanco, VP sls; Walter Zamora, dir; Javiera Balmaceda, mgr.

The Locomotion features the best intl productions created specifically for viewers ages 18-35, combining electronic music & digital culture 24-hours a day. On 1.2 milion cable systems. Satellite: Pan-Am Satcom 5.

MGA Communications, 4140 N. 41st St., ., Arlington, VA 22207. Phone: (703) 522-1185. Fax: (703) 522-8015. Web Site: www.MGA-co.com. Max Gratzl, CEO.

Direct-response TV. Production, media placement, & fulfillment mgmt.

Serving 2.2 million subs on 4 cable systems. Satellite: SATCOM 4.24.

MSNBC, One MSNBC Plaza, Secaucus, NJ 07094. Phone: (201) 583-5000. Fax: (201) 583-5179. Web Site: www.msnbc.com. Erik Sorenson, pres; Val Nicholas, VP mktg.

MSNBC is an all news network 24-hours a day. 82 million subs. Satellite: Galaxy IR, transponder 10.

MTV Latino, 1111 Lincoln Rd., 6th Fl., Miami Beach, FL 33139. Phone: (305) 535-3700. Fax: (305) 672-5204. Web Site: www.mtvla.com.

MTV's sixth global network, 24-hour progmg, advertiser supported and available in Latin America & the United States.

Serving over 8.5 million subs. Satellite: Satcom C3, transponder 19 (USA); PanAm Sat 3, transponder 5C & 6C (Latin America).

MTV: Music Television, MTV Networks Inc. 1515 Broadway, New York, NY 10036. Phone: (212) 258-8000. Fax: (212) 258-8100. Web Site: www.mtv.com. Brian Garden, pres; Judy McGrath, pres.

A 24-hour music video ch in stereo.

Serving 88.7 million subs. Satellites: Satcom C-4, transponder 17 east, Satcom C-3, transponder 16 west.

Multiplex chs: MTV Espanol is a 24-hour music network featuring ground-breaking Latin pop, rock en Espanol, & Latin alternative music for the new Latino generation in the united states. Serving 13 million subs. Satellite: GE 3, transponder 15.

MTV Hits offers the best in pop, rock & hip hop music videos for ages 12-24. Serving 18 million subs. Satellite: GE 3, transponder 15.

MTV Jam is the home of hip hop, R&B, soul & everything urban. Serves under 10 million subs. Satellite: GE 3, transponder 15. MTV2 is a full svc music ch. Serves 55 million subs. Satellite: GE 3, transponder 15.

Nickelodeon Gas-Games & Sports For Kids, is part of MTV Network's Digital Suite. Serves 15.6 million subs. Satellite: C-3, transponder 15.

M2: Music Television, 1633 Broadway, 32nd Fl., New York, NY 10036. Phone: (212) 654-6177. Fax: (212) 654-6179. Web Site: www.mtv.com. Dan Shatner, gen mgr.

Twenty-four hours of freeform mus video with loc mus info.

Serving 10 million subs. Satellite: Satcom C3, transponder 16.

The Movie Channel (TMC), (Showtime Networks Inc.). 1633 Broadway, New York, NY 10019. Phone: (212) 708-1600. Fax: (212) 654-1212. Web Site: www.showtimeonline.com. Matthew C. Blank, chmn/CEO; Robert Greenblatt, pres.

TMC features daily movie marathons, overnight & double vision weekends, 24-hours a day. Serving 34.8 million subs. Satellites: Satcom C-3, transponder 19 east; Satcom G-9, transponder 5 west.

Movie Channel Xtra, The offers more of viewers favorite movies 24-hour.

NFL Network, 280 Park Ave., 17th Fl., New York, NY 10017. Phone: (212) 450-2000. Fax: (212) 681-7599. E-mail: palanskys@nfl.com. Web Site: www.nfl.com/nflnetwork. Steve Bornstein, pres/CEO; Adam Shaw, sr VP.

A national cable & satellite ch telecasting NFL content 24 hrs a day. Satellites: Galaxy 11, Transponder 9. Serving 30 million subs on more than 60 cable systems.

National & International Singles Television Network, 505 S. Beverly Dr., Suite 364, Beverly Hills, CA 90212. Phone: (213) 467-1543. Fax: (213) 962-8768. E-mail: rbuck12550@aol.com.

Interactive dating svcs with variety entertainment for upscale professional singles earning high incomes. Business & international chs in Southern California.

Serving 15 million subs on 2 cable systems.

National Geographic Channel, 1145 17th St. N.W., Washington, DC 20036-4688. Phone: (202) 912-6500. Fax: (202) 912-6603. E-mail: comments@natgeochannel.com. Web Site: www.nationalgeographic.com/channel. Laureen Ong, pres; John Ford, exec VP; Kiera Hynnien, sr VP.

NGC provides viewers with direct connection to adventures all over the world & unique access to the most repected scientists, journalists & filmmakers, 24-hours a day. 47 million subs. Satellite: Satcom C-3, transponder 1.

National Jewish Television Network, Box 480, Wilton, CT 06897. Phone: (203) 834-3799. E-mail: nj@jewishmail.com. Joel A. Levitch, pres/CEO.

NJT offers documentaries, children's programs, news magazines, Info, cultural & relg progmg for the Jewish community, presented 3 hours every Sunday.

Serving 10 million subs. Satellite: C-Band.

Nationality Broadcasting Network, (Radio-WKTX 830 AM/NBN TV). 11906 Madison Ave., Lakewood, OH 44107. Phone: (216) 221-0330. Fax: (216) 221-3638. Jim Georgiades, opns mgr.

Provides internationally & locally-produced nationality TV & radio progmg, special programs & comls; also full-svc production house.

Serving one cable system and the scola tv network.

Newsworld International, (North American Television Inc.). 1230 Ave. of the America, New York, NY 10020. Phone: (212) 413-5000. Fax: (212) 413-6546. Web Site: www.nwitv.com. Lou Cooper, VP progmg; John Bernbach, chmn; Patrick Vien, pres/CEO; Doug Halloway, pres.

Intl progmg covering top stories from around the world plus current affrs, documentaries, the latest business, financial & sports news, 24-hours a day.

Serving 18 million subs. Satellite: Galaxy 1R, GE3, transponder 22, MPEG2.

NICK at NITE

See Nickelodeon.

Nickelodeon, (MTV Networks Inc.). 1515 Broadway, New York, NY 10036. Phone: (212) 258-8000. Fax: (212) 258-6284. Tom Freston, chmn/CEO; Cyma Zarghami, VP/gen mgr; Jeff Dunn, CEO.

Nickelodeon cable network targets kids. NICK at NITE provides entertainment svc for the TV generation.

Serving 87.9 million subs. Satellite: Satcom C-4, transponder 3 east. NICK at NITE is on 4,381 cable systems. Satellites: Satcom C-3, transponder 18 west. NICKTOONS is the 24-hour digital destination for the next generation of animation. Serving 13 million subs. Satellite: C-3, transponder 15. NICK2 gives viewers the convenience of watching their favorite Nickelodeon & NICK at NITE shows at different times of the day.

Noah's World International, 11448 Kanapali Ln., Boynton Beach 33437. Phone: (561) 732-2108. Fax: (516) 732-5108. Web Site: www.noahsworldtv.com. Ken Klein, pres; Ilan Klein, exec VP.

Noah's World Internation profiles & present enlightened countries around the globe, 24-hours a day.

Noggin/The N, 1633 Broadway, 7th Fl., New York, NY 10019. Phone: (212) 654-3000. Web Site: www.noggin.com. Tom Ascheim, VP/gen mgr; Kenny Miller, VP progmg.

The N, the nighttime network for teens, 24-hours a day. Satellite: Satcom C-3, transponder 15.

Oasis TV, Inc., 9887 Santa Monica Blvd., Suite 200, Beverly Hills, CA 90212-1604. Phone: (310) 553-4300. Fax: (310) 553-1159. Web Site: www.oasistv.com. Robert Schnitzer, chmn/CEO; Anthony Bevacqua, VP; Victoria Overton, pres.

Oasis TV is a global TV programmer of cutting-edge body-mind-spirit news, inspiration & entertainment, 24-hours a day. On 250,000 cable systems.1.4 million subs.

Open TV, 233 Park Ave. S., 10th Fl., New York, NY 10003. Phone: (212) 497-7000. Fax: (212) 497-7001. E-mail: info@actv.com. Web Site: www.actv.com. David Reese, pres/CEO.

Branchburg, NJ 08876, 3040 Rte 22 W., Suite 210. Phone: (908) 252-3800. David Reese.

Individualized TV progmg for educ & entertainment.

The Outdoor Channel, 43445 Business Park Dr., Suite 103, Temecula, CA 92590. Phone: (800) 770-5750. Fax: (909) 699-6313. Web Site: www.outdoorchannel.com. Jake Hartwidk, exec VP; Andrew Dale, pres/CEO; Wade Sherman, sr VP; Amy Hendrickson, VP mktg; Greg Harrigan, VP sls.

Outdoor Channel offers progmg such as fishing, hunting, hiking , competitive shooting & motor sports, 24-hours a day.

Serving 26 million subs. Satellite: Galaxy 10R, Transponder 24, Digital.

Outdoor Life Network, 281 Tresser Blvd., 9th Fl., Stamford, CT 06901. Phone: (203) 406-2500. Fax: (203) 406-2530. Web Site: www.olntv.com. Peter Sumpf, VP; Becky Ruthven, sr VP; Peter Englehart, sr VP; John West, sr VP; Wendy McCoy, VP mktg; Susan Panisch, VP progmg.

Los Angeles, CA 90064, 11835 W. Olympic Blvd, Suite 980. Phone: (310) 473-5404. Fax: (310) 473-6525.

New York, NY 10016, 90 Park Ave., 2nd Fl. Phone: (212) 883-4000. Fax: (212) 687-1819.

OLN provides viewers with non-stop action, 24-hours a day.

Serving 58 million subs. Satellite: Galaxy II, transponder 21. On 4,893 cable systems.

OVATION-The Arts Network, 5801 Duke St., Suite D-112, Alexandria, VA 22304. Phone: (703) 813-6310. Fax: (703) 813-6336. E-mail: info@ovationtv.com. Web Site: www.ovationtv.com. Edward J. Mathias, chmn; Harold E. Morse, pres/CEO; Susan Wittenberg, VP progmg; Lee J. Lindbloom, VP.

The network covers arts news from around the world & children's arts programs, 20 hours a day. 6.6 million subs. Satellite: Galaxy VII, transponder 13.

Oxygen Media Inc., 75 9th Ave., New York, NY 10011. Phone: (212) 651-2070. Fax: (212) 651-2099. E-mail: webmaster@oxygen.com. Web Site: www.oxygen.com. Geraldine B. Laybourne, chmn/CEO; Lisa G. Hall, COO; Mary G. Murano, exec VP; Daniel H. Taitz, gen counsel.

Oxygen Media is a 24-hour cable network TV for women. Serving 49 million subs. Satellite: Satcom C3, transponder east Analog, Galaxy II, transponder 13 west Digital.

Pennsylvania Cable Network, 401 Fallowfield Rd, Camp Hill, PA 17011. Phone: (717) 730-6000. Fax: (717) 730-6009. E-mail: pcntv@pcntv.com. Web Site: www.pcntv.com. Brian Lockman, pres/CEO; William J. Bova, VP progmg; Debra Kohr Sheppard, opns VP.

Philadelphia, PA 19101, 400 N. Broad St. Phone: (215) 854-4455. Corey Clarke, bureau chief.

Pittsburgh, PA 15222, Pittsburgh Post Gazette Bldg, 34 Blvd. Phone: (412) 263-1300. Doug Sicchitano, bureau chief.

The nation's preeminent state pub affrs net, with live & same-day coverage of the Pennsylvania General Assembly. PCN also covers significant state events, such as high school sports finals.

Serving 3.3 million subs on 150 cable systems. Satellite: AMC-6, transponder 15.

Pentagon Channel, 601 North Fairfax St., Alexandria 22314. Phone: (703) 428-0265. Fax: (703) 428-0466. E-mail: pentagonchannel@hq.afis.osd.mil. Gene Brink, gen mgr.

Pentagon Channel is a gov owned TV of the Department of Defense, providing internal communications to service members, families, the National Guard, the Reserve & military retirees, available 24-hour. 5.3 million subs.

Plato Learning Inc., 10801 Nesbitt Ave. South, Bloomington, MN 55437. Phone: (800) 447-5286. Web Site: www.plato.com. John Kernan, chmn/CEO; Carl Zeiger, pres/COO; Sandy Fivecoat, VP sls.

Interactive TV progmg for children.

Playboy TV, (Playboy Entertainment Group). 2706 Media Center Dr., Los Angeles, CA 90065. Phone: (323) 276-4000. Fax: (323) 276-4500. Web Site: www.playboytv.com. James English, pres; Sol Weisel, exec VP; Jeff Jenest, exec VP; Craig Simon, sr VP.

Entertainment targeted to adults. Schedule consists of nearly 100% original Playboy programs with the balance comprised of acquired programs & feature films. Serving 4.5 under PPV svc. Satellite: Galaxy 5, transponder 2.

Hot Zone is a 24-hour Pay-Per-View ch for adults. Satellite: Telstar 7, transponder 5.

Hot Networks is a 24-hour Pay-Per-View ch for adults. Satellite: Telstar 7, transponder 5.

Praise Television, 28059 US Hwy. 19 N., Suite 300, Clearwater 33761. Phone: (800) 921-9692. Fax: (727) 530-0671. Dustin Rubeck, pres.

A 24-hour, Christian music for family entertainment. Satellite: GE-1, transponder 7.

Product Information Network (PIN), 9697 East Mineral Ave., Englewood 80155-3309. Phone: (303) 784-8321. Fax: (303) 784-8549. Jon Shaver, COO; Richard Steele, VP sls; Tom Cahill, VP mktg.

A 24-hour info network, ad-supported. 35 million subs. Satellite: Satcom C-3, transponder 20.

Puma TV, 2029 S.W. 105th Ct., Miami 33165-7937. Phone: (305) 554-1876. Fax: (305) 554-6776. Jose Luis Rodriguez, pres; Osvaldo Rodriguez, VP.

Puma TV offers a wide var of info programs on fashion, modeling & entertainment, music ch by Hispanic for Hispanic, 24-hours. 2.7 million subs. Satellite: Telstar 5,

QVC, Studio Park, West Chester, PA 19380. Phone: (484) 701-1000. Web Site: www.qvc.com. Douglas S. Briggs, pres; William F. Costello, pres/COO; Tim Megaw, sr VP; Randy Ronning, exec VP.

QVC, Inc. is the world's preeminent electronic retailer mktg a wide var of brand name products, categories as home furnishings, licensed products, fashions, beauty, electronics & fine jewelry. The company's other divisions/subsidiaries include, Loc, on Q Music, QVC International. 85.4 million subs. Satellite: Satcom C-4, transponder 9.

The Real Estate Network-TREN, 325 Sharon Park Dr., Suite 512, Menlo Park, CA 94025. Phone: (650) 361-1000. Fax: (650) 361-1880. E-mail: kevintren@yahoo.com. Kevin L. Keithley, CEO; Ronald D. Keithley, COO.

Niche advertiser-supported entertainment progmg & interactive svc focusing on merchandising real estate listings & related products & svcs throughout America.

Recovery Network, 1411 5th St., Suite 250, Santa Monica, CA 90401. Phone: (310) 393-3979. Fax: (310) 393-5749. E-mail: info@recoverynetwork.com.

Progmg addresses behavioral & alternative health care issues & treatments for eating disorders, addictions, depression, sexual addictions, substance abuse, etc.

Serving 5 million subs on 36 systems. Satellite: Galaxy 7. Launched Spring 1996.

SCOLA, Box 619, McClelland, IA 51548-0619. Phone: (712) 566-2202. Fax: (712) 566-2502. Francis Lajba, pres; John Millar, VP; Dan Pike, mgr.

Foreign language news & educ progmg, 24-hours a day. Satellite: Telstar 5,

STARNET, 1332 Enterprise Dr., Suite 200, West Chester, PA 19380. Phone: (610) 692-5900. Fax: (610) 692-6487. Jerry Lenfest, pres/CEO; Joy Tartar, CFO.

Automatic cross-ch tune-in promotion service for basic, pay, & pay-per-view delivered via satellite. Nu-Star - automatic cross ch tune-in promotion service for basic pay, and pay-per-view delivered via satellite. The Promoter - individualized tune-in promotion for PPV delivered via satellite.

Serving 23 million subs on 960 cable systems for STARNET. Satellite: Satcom C-4, transponder 12.

Sci-Fi Channel, (USA Networks). 1230 Ave. of the Americas, New York, NY 10020. Fax: (212) 413-5000. Fax: (212) 413-6509. Web Site: www.scifi.com. Bonnie Hammer, pres; David Howe, sr VP; Mark Stern, exec VP.

Dedicated to a broad range of science fiction & fact, fantasy, & horror programs, 24-hours a day.

Serving 83 million subs. Satellite: Galaxy 5, transponder 4 east, Galaxy 1R, transponder 24 west.

Shop at Home Network, (A Scripps Media Company). Box 305249, Nashville, TN 37932. Phone: (615) 263-8000. Fax: (615) 263-8084. Judy Girard, pres; Bennett S. Smith, exec VP; Teresa H. Wells, VP.

Sells merchandise such as jewelry, housewares, fitness, cookware, beauty products & more, 24-hours. 47 million subs. Satellite: Galaxy IX, transponder 10.

ShopNBC, 6740 Shady Oak Rd., Eden Prairie 55344. Phone: (952) 943-6000. Fax: (952) 943-6011. E-mail: shopnbc@shopnbc.com. Web Site: www.shopnbc.com. Will Lansing, pres/CEO; Richard Barnes, COO.

ShopNBC provides 24-hours of home shopping. 56 million subs. Satellite: Galaxy IR, transponder 12.

Short TV, 580 Broadway, Suite 1104, New York 10012. Phone: (212) 226-6258. Fax: (212) 925-5802. E-mail: info@shorttv.com. Web Site: www.shorttv.com. Roland Dib, pres.

Short films, available 24-hours, ad-supported. 2.5 million subs.

Showtime Networks Inc., 1633 Broadway, New York, NY 10019. Phone: (212) 708-1600. Fax: (212) 708-1212. Web Site: www.showtimeonline.com. Matthew C. Blank, chmn/CEO.

Showtime Networks Inc. (SNI), which is a wholly owned subsidiary of Viacom Inc., owns the premium TV nets SHOWTIME, THE MOVIE CHANNEL & FLIX. SNI also operates & manages the premium TV net SUNDANCE CHANNEL which is owned by SNI, Robert Redford & Polygram Filmed Entertainment. SHOWTIME on Espanol, a separate audio feed of SHOWTIME, is available for the Spanish-speaking audience. SNI also markets & distributes sports & entertainment events for exhibition to subscribers on a pay-per-view basis. Multiplex chs: SHOWTIME BEYOND features sci-fi, horror & fantasy. SHOWTIME PAY-PER-VIEW. SHOWTIME EXTREME is comprised exclusively of action movies. SHOWTIME FAMILY ZONE is a ch for the entire family. SHOWTIME NEXT is SHOWTIME'S interactive playground targeting gen young adults 18-24. SHOWTIME SHOWCASE offers great progmg with Showtime originals airing. SHOWTIME TOO is a multi-feed ch. SHOWTIME WOMEN highlights women who are instrumental in moving the story ahead, in front of & behind the camera. THE MOVIE CHANNEL HD is a all movie svc., 34.8 million subs. Satellite: Satcom C-3, transponder 19 (east).

Si TV, 3030 Andrita St., Bldg. A, Los Angeles 90065. Phone: (323) 256-8900. Fax: (323) 256-9888. Web Site: www.sitv.com. Jeff Valdez, chmn/CEO; Leo Perez, COO; Rita Morales, VP progmg.

SiTV is a Latino-themed network in English that features original progmg, comedy, drama, var shows, talk-format strips, music & style shows, available 24-hours.

SingleVision Entertainment Television Network, 760 Skipper Dr., Atlanta, GA 30318. Phone: (678) 596-5909. E-mail: singlevisiontv@netscape.net. Web Site: www.singlevisiontv.com. Michael Wilson, CEO; Nina Rich, pres/COO.

Entertainment & info for unmarried people. Progmg targeted to Generation X & includes interactive televised personals. Advertiser supported. 4 million subs. Satellite: Galaxy VI,

Skyview World Media, Two Executive Dr., Suite 6000, Fort Lee 07024. Phone: (201) 242-3000. Fax: (201) 944-5961. E-mail: info@kskyviewmedia.com. Web Site: www.skyviewmedia.com. John Lunsford, pres/CEO; James Helfott, sr VP.

Skyview World Media is North America's leading provider of foreign ethnic progmg. 100,000 subs.

Soapnet, 3800 West Alameda Ave., Burbank 91505. Phone: (818) 569-7500. Fax: (818) 566-1358. Web Site: www.soapnet.com. Deborah Blackwell, sr VP; Mary Ellen DiPrisco, VP progmg; Sherri York, VP mktg.

Soapnet features today's soaps tonight, classic soaps, news & info from the world of soaps, 24-hours. Serving 35.7 million subs. Satellite: Galaxy 10 R.

Sorpresa, 6125 Airport Fwy., Suite 200, Fort Worth 76117. Phone: (817) 222-1234. Fax: (817) 222-9809. Web Site: www.sorpresatv.net. Leonard Firestone, chmn/CEO; Michael Fletcher, pres.

The nation's first network dedicated to America's Hispanic children, available 24-hours, ad-supported, Digital Premium. Satellite: Telstar 5, transponder 24.

SourceSuite, LLC, 5601 MacArthur Blvd., Suite 201, Irving 75038. Phone: (469) 524-0116. Fax: (469) 417-0314. Web Site: www.intchan.com. Charlie Barnes, gen mgr.

SourceSuite is a leading provider of interactive TV products, available 24-hours. 400,000 subs.

Speed Channel, 9711 Southern Pines Blvd., Charlotte, NC 28277. Phone: (704) 731-2222. Jim Liberatore, pres.

Speed Channel is among the fastest growing sports cable network in the country, 24-hours a day. 57.1 million subs. Satellite: Satcom C-4, transponder 11.

Spice 1, 2706 Media Center Dr., Los Angeles 90065. Phone: (323) 276-4000. Fax: (323) 276-4500. Web Site: www.spicetv.com. James English, pres.

An erotic adult-theme movie network, Premium, Pay-Per-View, available 24-hours. Multiplex ch: Spice 2. 11,000 subs. Satellite: Telstar 5,

Spike TV, (division of MTV Networks). 1515 Broadway, 37th Fl., New York, NY 10036. Phone: (212) 846-4095. Fax: (212) 846-1926. Web Site: www.spiketv.com. Kevin Kaye, exec VP; Jim Burns, sr VP.

Nashville, TN 37214, 2806 Opryland Dr. Phone: (615) 457-7230.

Network for men. 87.2 million subs. Satellite: Satcom C-3, transponder 18.

The Sportsman Channel, W236 S7050 Big Bend Dr., Suite 6, Big Bend 53103. Phone: (262) 662-3800. Fax: (262) 662-3890. Web Site: www.thesportsmanchannel.com. C Michael Cooley, pres/CEO; Todd D. Hansen, sr VP; Jim Seley, progmg dir; Darrell Lake, VP sls.

The Sportsman Channel provides continuos hunting & fishing progmg 24-hours a day. 10.7 million subs. Satellite: Telstar 5, Transponder 1.

Starz!, See Encore Media Corp.

The Style Network, 5750 Wilshire Blvd., Los Angeles, CA 90036-3709. Phone: (323) 954-2400. Fax: (323) 954-2500. Web Site: www.eonline.com. Mark Sonnenberg, exec VP; Mindy Herman, pres/CEO; Kenneth Bettsteller, COO.

Style Network covers the gamut of the lifestyle genre. 34 million subs.

Sun TV, 2245 Godby Rd., Atlanta 30349. Phone: (404) 766-9197. Fax: (404) 767-5264. David C. Simon, pres/CEO; Virgil Scott, VP.

Sun TV network features news, sports, entertainment, sitcoms, soaps, talk shows from 6:30 AM-midnight Saturday-Sunday (EST). Original progmg from the Caribbean, Central & South America. Serving 700,000 subs. Satellite: Galaxy 4-13.

Sundance Channel, 1633 Broadway, 8th Fl., New York, NY 10019. Phone: (212) 654-1500. Fax: (212) 654-4738. Web Site: www.sundancechannel.com. Larry Aidem, pres/CEO.

Sundance Channel is a 24-hours a day ch, featuring uncut coml-free programs, providing TV viewers daring & engaging feature films, short, documentaries, world cinema & animation. 17 million subs. Satellite: Satcom C-4, transponder 20.

TBN-Trinity Broadcasting Network, (TBN Cable Network). 2823 W. Irving Blvd., Irving, TX 75061. Phone: (972) 313-9500. Fax: (972) 313-1010. Web Site: www.tbn.org. Paul Crouch, pres; Robert Higley, VP mktg.

TBN is America's most watched relg network, offering 24-hours of coml-free inspiritional original programs, that appeal to viewers in many denominations. Progmg includes Nashville gospel concerts, health & fitness, talk shows & svcs from America's largest Churches. Multiplex ch: TBN Enlace USA is a 24-hour multi-faith Hispanic ch from Trinity Broadcasting Network. The Church Channel is a new digital network from TBN features church svc program from Protestant, Catholic & Jewish faith groups, 24-hours. On 43.4 million cable systems.49 million subs. Satellite: Galaxy V, transponder 3.

TBS Superstation, 1050 Techwood Dr. N.W., Atlanta, GA 30318. Phone: (404) 827-1700. Web Site: www.tbssuperstation.com. Christy Kresiberg, VP; Ken Schwab, sr VP; Steve Koonin, exec VP & COO.

TBS is a 24-hour ad-supported cable network that is home to top off-network comtemp comedies, high-profile original reality series, blockbuster movies & action-packed sports, Major League Baseball, Pac 10 & Big 12 college football. 88.1 million subs. Satellite: Galaxy V, transponder 6.

TEN-The Erotic Network, 7007 Winchester Cir., Suite 200, Boulder 80301. Phone: (303) 786-8700. Fax: (303) 938-8388. Web Site: www.noof.com. Ken Boenish, pres; Michael Weiner, CEO; William Mossa, VP mktg.

TEN is a network that uses the "un-inhibited" editing standard, 24-hours a day. Multiplex chs: TEN On Demand, TENBlox, TENBlue, TENClips & TENXtsy, PLEASURE. Serving 13.7 million subs. Satellite: Telstar 7-24, TUN, G10R-7.

TNT Latin America, 1030 Techwood Dr., Atlanta, GA 30318. Phone: (404) 885-2434. Fax: (404) 885-2157. E-mail: tnta_la@turner.com. Web Site: www.tntla.turner.com. Rick Perez, VP/gen mgr.

24-hour cable network bcst in Sp, Portuguese, English featuring contemp, original movies, NBA coverage & exclusive premieres.

Serving more than 8.5 million subs in 39 countries in the region. Satellite: PanAmSat 1, transponder 3.

TNT (Turner Network Television), 1050 Techwood Dr. N.W., Atlanta, GA 30318. Phone: (404) 885-4339. Fax: (404) 885-4318. Mark Lazarus, pres; Ken Schwab, sr VP; Steve Koonin, exec VP; Karen Cassell, sr VP; Michael Borza, sr VP; Michael Wright, sr VP; Jon Marks, sr VP; Tom Carr, mktg VP.

TNT, the destination for drama, is cable's only network combining award-winning original films. 88.2 million subs. Satellite: Galaxy V, transponder 17.

TR!O, 1230 Ave. of the Americas, New York 10020. Phone: (212) 413-5000. Fax: (212) 413-6552. Web Site: www.triotv.com. Lauren Zalaznick, pres.

TR!O is an entertainment cable TV ch reflecting pop culture, 24-hours a day. Serving 20 million subs. Satellite: Galaxy 1R, transponder 24, Satcom C3, transponder 8.

TV Asia, (Asian Star Broadcasting Network Inc.). 76 National Rd., Edison, NJ 08817. Phone: (732) 650-1100. Fax: (732) 650-1112. Michael Scott, VP.

TV Asia provides a wide range of prgmg produced for South Asian Americans, 24-hours.

Satellite: Galaxy II, transponder 24.

National Cable Networks

TV Asia, 76 National Rd., Edison, NJ 08817. Phone: (732) 650-1100. Fax: (732) 650-1112. Web Site: www.tvasiausa.com. Rohit Vyas, dir.

Asian movies, serials, news & other South Asian entertainment programs.

Serving 15,000 subs on 3 cable systems. Satellite: Echostar.

TV Games (TVG) Network, 6701 Center Dr. W., Los Angeles 90045. Phone: (310) 242-9500. Web Site: www.tvgnetwork.com. Ryan O'Hara, COO. 12 million subs. Satellite: GE-1, transponder 23.

TV Guide Channel, 6922 Hollywood Blvd., Los Angeles, CA 90028. Phone: (323) 817-4600. Web Site: www.tvguide.com. Jeff Shell, CEO; Ian Aaron, pres; Ray Hopkins, exec VP.

New York, NY 10017, 708 Third Ave., 21st Fl. Phone: (212) 370-1799. Fax: (212) 370-7575. Chris Manning, eastern sls mgr.

The network combines original etertaining long-form progmg with comprehensive listing info 24-hours a day. 70 million subs. Satellite: Satcom C-4,

TV Japan, (Japan Network Group Inc.). 100 Broadway, 15th Fl., New York, NY 10005. Phone: (212) 262-3377. Fax: (212) 262-5577. E-mail: tatsumi@tvjapan.net. Web Site: www.tvjapan.net. Mitsuo Sekino, pres/CEO; Masao Watari, sr VP; Hidehiko Fujikawa, sr VP.

TV Japan is a Japanese language ch, available 24-hours a day. Satellite: Galaxy II, transponder 24.

TV Land, 1515 Broadway, New York 10036. Phone: (212) 258-8000. Fax: (212) 846-1775. Larry W. Jones, VP/gen mgr.

TV Land is the only network dedicated to the best of everything TV from the past 50 years, available 24-hours. 82.1 million subs. Satellite: Satcom C-3, transponder 18.

Talk Internetwork, Inc., 9662 E. Volture Dr., Scottsdale, AZ 85260. Phone: (480) 551-9774. E-mail: info@talkinternet@aol.com. Web Site: www.talkinternet.com. Edwin Cooperstein, pres; Pat McMahon, VP; Ken Colburn, VP; Paul Hermanson, CFO; Hugh Downs, dir.

A 24-hour, live, all-talk progmg internet site.

Talkline Communications Television Network, Box 20108, Park West Stn., New York, NY 10025-1510. Phone: (212) 769-1925. Fax: (212) 799-4195. Web Site: www.talklinecommunication.com. Zev J. Brenner, pres.

Jewish programs with newsmaker guests, celebrity interviews as well as informational progmg. Presented Sundays 11 AM-6 PM EST nationally & Sundays 2-5 PM EST & 9-11 PM EST in the New York area.

Serving more than 18 million subs on 825 cable systems.

TechTV, 650 Townsend St., 3rd Fl., San Francisco 94103. Phone: (415) 355-4000. Fax: (415) 355-4670. E-mail: techtvinfo@techtv.com. Joseph Gillespie, exec VP; Greg Brannan, sr VP; Peter Gochis, VP sls.

TechTV intrigues viewers with everything from help & info to cutting-edge factual progmg to outrageous late-night fun. 43 milion subs. Satellite: Satcom C-4, transponder 12.

Telemundo, 2290 W. 8th Ave., Hialeah 10019. Phone: (305) 889-7200. Fax: (305) 889-7205. Jim McNamara, pres/CEO; Don Brown, CFO; Ramon Escobar, exec VP.

Telemundo, a United States Sp-language TV network, available 24-hours. Multiplex ch: Telemundo Internacional. Serving 32 million subs. Satellite: Satcom, transponder 20 east, AMC-4, transponder 8 west.

The Tennis Channel Inc., 2850 Ocean Park Blvd., Suite 150, Santa Monica, CA 90405. Phone: (310) 656-9400. Fax: (310) 656-9433. Web Site: www.thetennischannel.com. David Safran, VP adv; Faye Walker, VP mktg; John Morse, VP rsch; Frank Garland, sr VP.

The Tennis Channel, 2850 Ocean Park Blvd., Santa Monica 90405. Phone: (310) 314-9400. Fax: (310) 314-9433. Web Site: www.thetennischannel.com. Steve Bellamy, pres; Ken Solomon, chmn/CEO; John Brady, CFO; Keith Manasco, VP opns.

The Tennis Channel is the 24-hour cable TV network devoted to tennis & other racquet sports, ad-supported. 3 million subs. Satellite: Telstar 3, transponder 15.

The Theatre Channel, Box 2676, Venice, CA 90294. Phone: (310) 823-6508. Fax: (310) 823-3431. E-mail: info@theatrechannel.com. Web Site: www.theatrechannel.com. Cheryl Beach, CEO.

Traditional & alternative live theatre dance, opera, children's theatre in a videotape format.

Time Warner Cable, 120 E. 23rd St., New York, NY 10010. Phone: (212) 598-7200. Web Site: www.timewarner.com. Howard Szarfarc, gen mgr; Barbara Kelly, gen mgr.

Flushing, NY 11355, 41-61 Kissena Blvd.

Cable service.

Satellite: 1.3 million subs.

Toon Disney, 3800 W. Alameda Ave., Burbank, CA 91505. Phone: (818) 569-7500. Fax: (818) 566-1358. Web Site: www.toondisney.com. Ann Sweeney, pres.

Toon Disney is a var of acquired animated programs, 24-hours a day. Serving more than 43 million subs. Satellite: Galaxy 10R.

Travel Channel, 8516 Georgia Ave., Silver Spring, MD 20910. Phone: (240) 662-0000. Fax: (240) 662-1854. Web Site: www.travelchannel.com. John S. Hendricks, chmn; Judith McHale, pres/CEO.

Travel Channel is the only TV network devoted to travel entertainment, 24-hours a day. 74.9 million subs. Satellite: Satcom C-4, Transponder 13.

Tribune Media Services, TMS TV Listings. 435 N. Michigan Ave., Suite 1500, Chicago, IL 60611. Phone: (312) 222-8668. Fax: (312) 222-1360. E-mail: bneedleman@tribune.com. Web Site: www.biz.zap2it.com. Barbara S. Needleman, VP; Dana Gage, exec dir; Kathy Tolstrup, sls & mkt gen mgr & TV products; John Kelleher, gen mgr of Electronic Program Guides.

Glens Falls, NY 12801, One Apollo Dr. Phone: (800) 424-4747. Brian Ward, opns dir.

Content leader in print television program guides, program guide/local community channel video products, TV program schedules/cable lineups for digital & advanced analog IPG set-top box applications, movie showtimes & weather info.

Turner Classic Movies (TCM), 1050 Techwood Dr. N.W., Atlanta, GA 30318. Phone: (404) 885-5535. Web Site: www.turnerclassicmovies.com. Tom Karsch, VP/gen mgr; Mark Lazarus, pres.

Features Hollywood's greatest movies of all time, presented 24-hours, coml-free. 63.9 million subs.

U.S.A. Networks, 1230 Ave. of the Americas, New York, NY 10020. Phone: (212) 413-5000. Fax: (212) 413-6509. Douglas Holloway, pres; Michele Ganeless, exec VP.

Gen entertainment network featuring movies, original series, sports specials, teen & children's progmg, 24-hours a day.

Serving 88.1 million subs. Satellites: Galaxy 5 transponder 19 east, Galaxy 1R, transponder 21 west.

Univision Television Group, 5999 Center Dr., Los Angeles, CA 90045. Phone: (310) 348-4865. Fax: (310) 348-3643. E-mail: tkrass@univision.net. Web Site: www.univisionnetworks.com. Ray Rodriguez, pres/COO; Mario Rodriguez, chmn/CEO; Carlos Bardasano, VP progmg; Robert V. Cahill, sec; Jeffrey T. Hinson, exec VP; Andrew W. Hobson, sr VP; C. Douglas Kranwinkle, exec VP.

New York, NY 10158. East, 605 Third Ave, 26 Fl. Phone: (212) 455-5342. Fax: (212) 986-4731. John Heffron, VP affll rels.

Dallas, TX 75201. Central, 2323 Bryan St, Suite 1900. Phone: (214) 758-2405. Fax: (214) 758-2395. Deanna Andaverde, VP affll rel.

A 24-hour most watched TV network (Sp or English) among the nation's growing Hispanic population, featuring movies, novellas, sports, children progmg, musical special, national & loc newscasts.

Serving 34.5 million subs. Satellite: Galaxy 1R.

Telefutura is the newest 24-hour gen-interest Sp language bcstg network. Serves 7.2 million subs. Satellite: Galaxy 1. Satellite: Galaxy IR,

Urban Television Network Corp., 18505 South Hwy. 377, Fort Worth, TX 76126. Phone: (817) 512-3033. Fax: (817) 512-3034. Web Site: www.uatvn.com. Fred Hutton, pres.

VH1 (Music First), (MTV Networks Inc.). 1515 Broadway, New York, NY 10036. Phone: (212) 846-7840. Web Site: www.vh1.com. Christina Norman, pres.

VH1 is a 24-hour ch that features new, current & classic music video, for viewers ages 18-49 who grew up with music videos.

Multiplex chs: VH1 Classic, VH1 Country, VH1 Megahits, VH1 Soul & VH Uno. 86.3 million subs. Satellite: Satcom C-4, transponder 23.

ValueVision, ValueVision International Inc., 6740 Shady Oak Rd., Eden Prairie, MN 55344. Phone: (952) 943-6000. Fax: (952) 943-6011. Web Site: www.shopnbc.com. Gene C McCaffery, pres/CEO; Richard Barnes, CFO; Nathan Fagre, gen counsel; Liz Haesler, exec VP; John Ryan, exec VP; Anthony Giombetti, dir.

ValueVision Media (Nasdaq:VVTV) operates in the rapidly growing converged world of TV, the Internet & e-commerce. In an effort to capitalize on this industry, ValueVision Media owns & operates a number of assets and is organized in five synergistic entities: ShopNBC, ShopNBC.com, Enhanced Broadcast Technologies, ValueVision Direct, & FanBuzz. The company flagship media property, ShopNBC, the nation's fasting growing shopping network, is bcst into 55 million homes 24 hrs a D. GE Equity & NBC own approximately 40% of ValueVision Media.

Viewer's Choice, 909 3rd Ave., 21st Fl., New York, NY 10022. Phone: (212) 486-6600. Fax: (212) 688-9497. E-mail: webmaster@ppv.com. Web Site: www.ppv.com.

Los Angeles, CA 90067, 1888 Century Park E. Phone: (310) 785-9094. (310) 785-9194. Fax: (310) 785-9195. (310) 785-9769.

Atlanta, GA 30338, 1117 Perimeter Ctr. W, Suite 500 E. Phone: (404) 399-3119. Fax: (404) 399-3014.

Southfield, MI 48034, 26677 W. Twelve Mile Rd. Phone: (810) 354-3375. Fax: (810) 358-9693.

Leading pay-per-view network, offering top box office titles, sports, & entertainment events through 35 plus digital chs of NVOD svc.

Serving 28 million addressable households & 100 million sub units on 1,700 cable systems. Satellites: Satcom C-3, transponder 3; Satcom C-4, transponder 18.

WSBK-TV, (Boscom). 83 Leo M. Birmingham Pkwy., Brighton, MA 02135. Phone: (617) 783-3838. Betsy Bianco, dir mktg.

WSBK-TV is a 24-hour ind ch from Boston featuring sports, movies, news & specials.

Satellite: GE 3, transponder 3. WSBK is a UPN (United Paramount Network).

The Weather Channel, 300 Interstate North Pkwy., Atlanta, GA 30339. Phone: (770) 226-0000. Fax: (770) 226-2950. Web Site: www.weather.com. Patrick Scott, pres; Terry Connelly, VP/gen mgr; Lyn Andrews, pres.

New York, NY 10022, 845 Third Ave, 11th Floor. Phone: (212) 893-2245. Lyn Andrews, Pres. TWC Media Solutions.

All-weather progmg 24-hours a day; natl, international, rgnl & loc weather forecasts & features. Multiplex ch: WeatherScan.

Serving 87.5 million subs. Satellite: GE Satcom C-3, transponder 13.

WE-Women's Entertainment, 200 Jericho Quadrangle, Jericho, NY 11753. Phone: (516) 803-4400. Fax: (516) 803-4398. Kathleen Dore, pres; Josh Sapan, CEO; Andrea Greenburg, exec VP.

A 24-hour cable network featuring classic movies & TV progmg devoted entirely to romance.

Serving 51.4 million subs. Satellite: Galaxy 7, transponder 12.

Wisdom Television, Box 1546, 2481 John Nash Blvd., Bluefield, WV 24701. Phone: (304) 323-8000. Fax: (304) 323-2975. Web Site: www.wisdommedia.com. Cindy Sheets, CEO; Jack Howard, VP opns.

Wisdom Television is a 24-hour TV network, offering info & entertainment to the expanding worldwide community interested in personal & professional growth, health, wellness, global issues & intellectual viewpoints. Satellite progmg for the C-band & cable industry.

Serving 6.5 million subs. Satellite: AMC 1, transponder 12.

Worship Network, 28059 US Hwy. 19 N., Suite 300, Clearwater, FL 33761-2643. Phone: (727) 536-0036. Fax: (727) 530-0671. Don Anderson, pres; Len Van Noord, VP; Tim Brown, VP progmg.

Worship Network features, scenery from around the world with words of wisdom from scriptures & inspirational music. Available 24 hours a day. 66 million subs. transponder 7.

Regional Cable News Networks

The Arizona News Channel, 5555 N 7th Ave., Phoenix, AZ 85013. Phone: (602) 379-2401. Fax: (602) 379-2459. Web Site: www.azfamily.com.

Arizona's first and only 24-hour local news service built on a unique partnership; live local breaking coverage gives viewers the latest news from around the Valley; NewsChannel 3's "Good Morning Arizona," "Good Day Arizona," "Good Evening Arizona" and "The News Show" replay throughout the day on the AZ News Channel, Cox Cable Channel 14; programming also includes local productions exclusive to cable, such as "Project Parenting."

Bay News 9, 7901 66th St. N., Pinellas Park, FL 33781. Phone: (727) 437-2000. Fax: (727) 437-2031. Fax: (727) 437-2034 (newsroom). E-mail: viewer@baynews9.com. Web Site: www.baynews9.com. Elliott Wiser, VP & gen mgr; Steve Weitekamp, opns mgr; Terry Zurowski, prom mgr; Sylvia Sethares, gen sls mgr; Linda Levy, news dir.

Bay News 9 is a 24-hour ch owned & operated by Advance Newhouse. The ch serves over 940,000 cable customers in Pinellas, Hillsborough, Polk, Manatee, Hernando, Citrus & Pasco counties.

Bay TV, 1001 Van Ness Ave., San Francisco, CA 94109. Phone: (415) 441-4444. Fax: (415) 561-8745. E-mail: frounfelter-@baytv.com. Web Site: www.baytv.com. Paul Dinovitz, VP & gen mgr.

A 24-hour loc news, sports & info cable ch.

CLTV News (ChicagoLand Television News), 2000 York Rd., Suite 114, Oak Brook, IL 60523. Phone: (630) 368-4000. Fax: (630) 571-0489. Web Site: www.cltv.com. Judy Juds; Cris Wyatt, opns supvr; Cathy Ornburn, production mgr; Steve Farber, mngn editor; Rick Kramer, assignment mgr.

Covers Chicago loc & rgnl news, sports, news, weather & traf info, serving 1.8 million subs.

CN8 - The Comcast Network, 1500 Market St., 28th Fl., W. Tower, Philadelphia, PA 19102. Phone: (215) 981-7750. Fax: (215) 981-8420. Michael A. Doyle, pres & founder; Melissa Kennedy, dir mktg communications.

CN8, The Comcast Network, is an award-winning, 24-hour news, talk, sports and entertainment cable network created by Comcast Cable Communications, that has steadily won viewers, awards and accolades since its inception in 1996. CN8 provides quality locally-produced programming in four main areas-live, interactive television; regional news; entertainment; and coverage of high school, college and professional sports. CN8 continues to expand its compelling mix of news, talk, sports and entertainment programming through the Eastern seaboard, from Washington DC, to the new England area, broadcasting to 6.2 million viewers everyday.

CablePulse24, 299 Queen St. W., Toronto, ON M5V 2Z5. Canada. Phone: (416) 591-5757. Fax: (416) 593-6397. E-mail: info@cp24.com. Web Site: www.pulse24.com. Stephen Hurlbut, VP/gen mgr; Dan Hamilton, VP sls; Tina Cortese, dir of news progmg; Keith Wilson, opns dir; Karen Reid, news dir; David Kirkwood, VP; Jenny Norush, adv dir; Bev Nenson, dir of publicity; Allan Schwebel, VP mktg & VP sls.

Rgnl 24-hour a day English language news & information channel.

The California Channel, 1121 L St, Suite 110, Sacramento, CA 95814. Phone: (916) 444-9792. Fax: (916) 444-9812. Web Site: www.calchannel.com. John Hancock, pres; Linda Robertson, dir finance & admin.

The California Channel is an independent, nonprofit, public affairs cable television network. Programming includes coverage of California Assembly and Senate floor sessions and committee meetings, capitol press conferences, and proceedings of regulatory boards and state commissions. 33.5 hours/week, serving 5,800,000 subs.

CBS News 4, 8900 N.W. 18th Terrace, Miami, FL 33172. Phone: (305) 591-4444. Web Site: www.cbs4news.com.

Central Florida News 13, 64 E. Concord St., Orlando, FL 32801. Phone: (407) 513-1300. Fax: (407) 513-1310. E-mail: newsdesk@cfnews13.com. Robin Smythe, gen mgr; Stephen Chavarie, news dir; Jerry Carstens, business mgr.

24 hour cable news channel serving Orlando & the Central Florida Region.

Country Television Network San Diego, 1600 Pacific Hwy., MS A359, San Diego, CA 92101-2481. Phone: (619) 595-4600. Fax: (619)557-4027. E-mail: video1is@co.san-diego.ca.us. Web Site: www.co.san-diego.ca.us/ctn. Michael Workman, dir; Janice McGee, owner; Barry Fraser, cable franchise admin.

Country Television Network San Diego makes country government more accessible and understandable to the citizens of San Diego County through informational programming focusing on the services, programs and current issues of county government. 24/day serving 708,700 subs.

Florida's News Channel, 1801 Halstead Blvd., Tallahassee, FL 32309. Phone: (850) 222-6397. Fax: (850) 894-5202. Web Site: www.flnews.com. Bob Brillante, CEO; Frank Watson, VP/gen mgr.

Provides news to cable systems in Florida. Spot inventory, half hour progrms, digital production facilities are available.

Las Vegas One, 3228 Channel 8 Drive, Las Vegas, NV 89109. Phone: (702) 696-7111. Fax: (702) 696-7222. Robert Stoldal, gen mgr & news dir.

Las Vegas One is a 24-hour local news channel serving the Las Vegas area.

Local News on Cable (LNC), 103 Third St., Norfolk, VA 23510. Phone: (757) 664-5400. Fax: (757) 664-5420. Web Site: www.pilotonline.com. Shelley Chevalier, gen mgr; Dick Splitstone, exec producer; Cindy Willett, news dir.

Michigan Government Television, 4th Fl., Romney Bldg., 111 S. Capitol Ave., Lansing, MI 48909. Phone: (517) 373-4250. Fax: (517) 335-7342. E-mail: mgtv@mgtv.org. Web Site: www.mgtv.org. Bill Trevarthen, exec dir.

Cable network covering all branches of Michigan's state government.

Neighborhood News 12, 111 New South Rd., Hicksville, NY 11801. Phone: (516) 393-3378. Fax: (516)393-0021. Web Site: www.new12.com. Barry J. Romanski, gen mgr.

Neighborhood News 12 is a 24-hour news channel for individual communities, as defined by a single zip code. Literally "Neighborhood News," the format is sometimes described as an electronic community newspaper combining traditional video packages, voiceovers, music tracks, animation and still digital images. 24/7 serving 209,000 subs.

New England Cable News, 160 Wells Ave., Newton, MA 02459. Phone: (617) 630-5000. Fax: (617) 630-5057. Fax: (617) 630-5055. Web Site: www.necnews.com. Philip Balboni, pres; Charles Kravetz, stn mgr & news dir.

A 24-hour rgnl news net.

New York 1 News, 75 9th Ave., 6th Fl., New York, NY 10011. Phone: (212) 691-6397. Fax: (212) 563-7154. E-mail: ny/news@ny1.com. Web Site: www.ny1.com. Steve Paulus, sr VP news; Peter Landis, news dir; Tom Farkas, exec editor; Bernie Han, VP; Joe Truncale, VP; Dan Jacobson, mngn editor.

A 24-hour, all-news cable ch devoted primarily to coverage of New York City & its neighborhoods.

News 12 Bronx, 930 Soundview Ave., Bronx, NY 10473. Phone: (718) 861-6800. Ralph Cerenzio, sr VP & ad sls.

News 12 Bronx is a 24-hour regional news programming service (a News 12 Regional Network). 24/day serving 250,000 subs.

News 14 Carolina, 316 East Morehead St., Suite 100, Charlotte, NC 28202. Phone: (704) 973-5700. Fax: (704) 973-2770. Web Site: www.news14.com. Ron Miller, VP & gen mgr; Jim Newman, dir & news.

New 14 Carolina offers 24-hour local news; and weather every ten minutes on the Ones.

News Channel 8, 1100 Wilson Blvd., 6th Fl., Arlington, VA 22209. Phone: (703) 236-9628. Web Site: www.news8.net. Chris Pike; Amy Woods, gen sls mgr; Alex Likowski, news dir.

News Channel 8 is a regional news service for the Washington, DC, metropolitan area, featuring, localized programming and advertising for subscribers in three separate regions - Maryland, Northern Virginia and the District of Columbia. 24/day serving 1,200,000 subs.

News Now 53, 777 Northwest Grand Blvd., Suite 600, Oklahoma City, OK 73118. Phone: (405) 600-6600. Fax: (405) 600-0670. Mark Kanter, VP & gen mgr & Cox Media.

News Now 53 is a rebroadcast of KWTV-CBS newscasts in Oklahoma City and KOTV-CBS in Tulsa, OK. 24/day serving 430,000 subs.

News On One, 3501 Farnam, Omaha, NE 68131. Phone: (402) 346-6666. Fax: (402) 233-7888. Web Site: www.wowt.com.

News 10 Now, 815 Erie Blvd. E., Syracuse, NY 13210. Phone: (315) 234-1000. Web Site: www.news10now.com. Ron Lombard, gen mgr.

News 12 Connecticut, 28 Cross St., Norwalk, CT 06851. Phone: (203) 849-1321. Fax: (203) 849-1327. E-mail: news12.ct@news12.com. Web Site: www.news12.com. Tom Appleby, news dir.

24 hour, 7 day week reg news ch featuring hyper-loc news coverage including sports & weather.

News 12 Long Island, One Media Crossways, Woodbury, NY 11797. Phone: (516) 393-1242. Fax: (516) 393-1456. Web Site: www.news12.com. E-mail: new12li@news12.com. Patrick Dolan, news dir.

A 24-hour rgnl news service.

News 12 New Jersey, 450 Raritan Ctr. Pkwy., Edison, NJ 08837. Phone: (732) 346-3210. Fax: (732) 346-3364. E-mail: news12nj@news12.com. Web Site: www.news12.com. Jonathan Knopf, news dir & gen mgr; Allison Gibson, asst news dir; Rick Young, dir adv prom; Larry Meyrowitz, dir opns; Laura Johnson, rgnl sls mgr; Regina Schittig, business mgr; Eric Bloomberg, chief engr.

24-hour news from six news bureaus throughout New Jersey & reaching 1,700,000 cable homes.

News 12 Westchester, 6 Executive Plaza, Yonkers, NY 10701. Phone: (914) 378-8916. Fax: (914) 378-8938. Web Site: www.news12.com. Janine Rose, news dir; Don Dudley, exec producer.

24-hour news organization covering Westchester County.

Newschannel 5+, 474 James Robertson Pkwy., Nashville, TN 37219. Phone: (615) 248-5233. Fax: (615) 248-5269. Web Site: www.newschannel5.com. Lem Lewis, pres & gen mgr.

Newschannel 5+ is a provider of local news and information in its entirety to the immediate Nashville area. 24/4 serving 300,000.

Newswatch 15, 474 James Robertson Pkwy., New Orleans, LA 70116. Phone: (504) 529-4444. Fax: (504) 529-6471. Web Site: www.wwltv.com. Gary Teaney, opns dir; Sandy Breland, news dir.

Newswatch 15 offers a rebroadcast of WWL-TV, the number one CBS metered affiliate morning and evening news in the United States. 24/day serving 325,559 subs.

NorthWest Cable News, 333 Dexter Ave. N., Seattle, WA 98109. Phone: (206) 448-3600. Fax: (206) 448-3797. Web Site: www.nwcn.com. Paul Fin, VP; Dave Lougee, gen mgr; Don Jacobs, dir opns; Rollin Wood, gen sls mgr; Bill Kaczaraba, news dir.

24-hour news for the Northwest.

Ohio News Network, 770 Twin Rivers Dr., Columbus, OH 43215. Phone: (614) 280-3600. Fax: (614) 280-6305. Web Site: www.ohionewsnow.com. Tom Griesdorn, VP/gen mgr; Frank Willson, mktg dir; Barb Geller, affil rel mgr; Greg Fisher, news dir; Jason Pheister, progmg dir; Vince Jones, opns mgr; Chuck DeVendra, sls dir.

Regional Cable News Networks

24/7 cable news channel featuring local news, weather, and sports for the people of Ohio. Currently seen in 1.5 million homes.

Orange County Newschannel, 625 North Grand Avenue, Santa Ana, CA 92701. Phone: (714) 565-3800. Fax: (714) 565-3650. Mike Sweeney, gen mgr; Don Engelhardt, chief engr; Mya Bulwa, exec producer; Susanne Lysak, news dir.

Orange County Newschannel features exclusive coverage of local news, sports, weather and traffic in southern California's Orange County. 24 hours serving 575,000 subs.

Pennsylvania Cable Network, 401 Fallowfield Rd., Camp Hill, PA 17011. Phone: (717) 730-6000. Fax: (717) 730-6005. E-mail: pctv@pctv.com. Web Site: www.pcntv.com. Brian Lockman, pres/CEO; William J. Bova, progmg VP; Debra Kohr Sheppard, VP opns.

PCN is the nation's pre-eminent state public affairs network, with live and same day coverage of the Pennsylvania Senate and House, and other government activities. PCN televises significant state events (such as high school sports championships), tours museums and manufacturing facilities in the state, and distributes educational programming.

Pittsburgh Cable News Channel (PCNC), 11 Television Hill, Pittsburgh, PA 15214. Phone: (412) 237-1190. Fax: (412) 237-1286. Web Site: www.realpittsburgh.com. E-mail: burgnews@wpix.com. John Howell, gen mgr & VP; Mark W. Barash, stn mgr; Jennifer Rigby, news dir.

Loc & rgnl news, talk & info.

R News/Time Warner Communications, 71 Mt. Hope Ave., Rochester, NY 14620. Phone: (585) 756-2424. Fax: (585) 756-1673. Web Site: www.rnews.com. Ed Buttaccio, opns dir; Jim Aroune, opns mgr.

Loc news 24-hours 7 days per week. Interactive daily call-in show. Nightly loc Sp newscast.

Regional News Network, 721 Broadway, Kingston, NY 12401. Phone: (914) 339-6200. Fax: (914) 339-6264. Richard French, gen mgr; James Sweeny, news dir.

RNN is a 24 hour provider of news and public information targeted to suburban New York, Connecticut, and New Jersey serving 250,000.

Rhode Island News Channel, 10 Orms St., Providence, RI 02904. Phone: (401) 453-8000. Fax: (401) 331-4431. Web Site: www.abc6.com. Ingrid Johansen, news dir.

Rhode Island News Channel is a simulcast and rebroadcast of WLNE newscasts for Rhode Island.

San Antonio News Channel, c.b.a. News 9 San Antonio, 600 E. Euclid Ave., San Antonio, TX 78212. Phone: (210) 581-9000. Web Site: www.news9sanantonio.com.

San Diego's Newschannel 15, Box 85347, San Diego, CA 92186. Phone: (619) 237-1010. Fax: (619) 527-0369. Web Site: www.kgtv.com. Mike Stutz, news dir.

San Diego's Newchannel 15 provides original newscasts, repeats of KGTV-10 newscasts, and live break-ins 24 hours.

Six News Now, Box 66, Sarasota, FL 34230. Phone: (941) 957-5466. Fax: (941) 957-5276. Web Site: www.snn6.com. Frank Verdel, gen mgr & news dir.

A 24-hour cable news ch with focus on loc news & info.

Texas Cable News, 570 Young St., Dallas, TX 75202. Phone: (214) 977-4500. Fax: (214) 977-4610. Web Site: www.txcn.com. James T. Aitken, VP/gen mgr; Steve Ackermann, exec news dir.

24-hour loc/rgnl news ch covering the state of Texas.

Tri-State Media News (TSM news), 2215 DuPont Pkwy., New Castle, DE 19770. Phone: (877) TSM-NEWS. Web Site: www.tsmnews.com. Stanley H. Green, pres/CEO.

WJLA-TV/Newschannel 8, 1100 Wilson Blvd., 6th Fl., Arlington, VA 22209. Phone: (703) 236-9628. Fax: (703) 236-2336. Web Site: www.newschannel8.net. James Killen, sr VP.

A 24-hour rgnl news service for Washington, DC, suburban Maryland & northern Virginia. On 15 cable systems serving 1,125,000 subs.

Regional Cable Sports Networks

College Sports Television, Chelsea Piers, Pier 62, Suite 316, New York, NY 10011. Phone: (212) 342-8700. Fax: (212) 342-8899. E-mail: fans@cstv.com. Web Site: www.cstv.com.

Comcast SportsNet, 3601 South Broad St., Philadelphia, PA 19148. Phone: (215) 336-3500. Fax: (215) 952-5996. E-mail: mbcasey@comcastsportsnet.com. Web Site: www.comcastsportsnet.com. Jack Williams, pres; Sam Schroeder, VP progmg; Stephanie Smith, VP mktg.

Rgnl TV progmg svcs includes live coverage of Philadelphia Flyers ice hockey, Philadelphia '76ers basketball, Philadelphia Phillies baseball, pro boxing, college basketball, football, indoor lacross, ABL, loc sports news & sports talk programs.

Serving 3 million subs on MSOS(16).

Comcast SportsNet Mid-Atlantic, 7700 Wisconsin Ave., Suite 200, Bethesda, MD 20814. Phone: (301) 718-3200. Fax: (301) 718-3300. Web Site: midatlantic.comcast sportsnet.com. Jeff Wagner, gen sls mgr; Steve Weber, engrg dir.

Rgnl sports net serving mid-Atlantic. Progmg includes Orioles baseball, Capitals, hockey, Wizards, basketball, ACC & CAA.

Serving 4.4 million subs on over 200 cable systems.

Satellite: Spacenet III, transponder 12-H, channel 23 (scrambled).

Cox Sports AZ, 20401 N. 29th Ave., Phoenix, AZ 85027. Phone: (623) 322-8001. Fax: (623) 322-7424. Steve Rizley, VP/gen mgr; Ivan Johnson, VP; Fran Mallace, gen mgr.

Phoenix Suns basketball, sports specials, high school sports & high school championships, etc. Phoenix metropolitan area serving over 500,000 subs. Loc microwave/fiber distributed regionally to additional operators.

Cox Sports San Diego, 5159 Federal Blvd., San Diego, CA 92105. Phone: (619) 263-9251. Fax: (619) 266-5540. Marty Youngman, mgr.

San Diego Padres baseball, etc.

Cox Sports Television, 800 W. Commerce Rd., Suite 400, Harahan, LA 70123. E-mail: coxsportstv@cox.com.

CSS - Comcast/Charter Sports Southeast, 2995 Courtyards Dr., Norcross, GA 30071. Phone: (770) 559-7800. Phone: (770) 559-2742 (Jeff Miller). Fax: (770) 559-2329. Michael Sheehey, VP/gen mgr; Steve White, sr VP; Jeff Miller, mktg.

ESPN Inc., ESPN Plaza, Bristol, CT 06010. Phone: (860) 766-2000. Fax: (860) 766-2400. Web Site: www.espn.com. George Bodenheimer, pres/CEO.

ESPN offers a var of professional & amateur sports, including NFL, college basketball, NHL major league baseball, the woman's NCAA tournament.

On 28,000 affiliating cable systems serving over 77 million subs.

ESPNews, ESPN Plaza, Bristol, CT 06010-9454. Phone: (860) 585-2000. Fax: (860) 766-2400. Web Site: www.espn.com. Rob Tobias, mgr; Judy Murron, office mgr.

Empire Sports Network, 795 Indian Church Rd., West Seneca, NY 14224. Phone: (716) 558-8444. Fax: (716) 558-8430. Web Site: www.empiresports.com. Bob Koshinski, VP/gen mgr; Joe DelBalso, progmg dir; Dean Giopulos, dir mktg; Paul Martello, dir; John Demerle, exec producer; Mark Ewart, engrg dir; Kenny Atkinson, dir.

Rgnl sports net servicing upstate New York. Buffalo Bills progmg, Buffalo Sabres, AAA baseball, Syracuse University, collegiate events.

Serving 1.1 million subs on 50 cable systems.

Satellite: GE5, T4 (digital ku).

ESPN Classic, ESPN Plaza, Bristol, CT 06010. Phone: (860) 766-2000. Fax: (860) 766-2400. Web Site: www.espn.com.

Classic sporting events, sports series, documentaries & movies; home shopping for sports merchandise & interactive sports games.

Serving 20 million subs on 400 plus cable systems.

Satellite: Galaxy 7, transponder 13 (compressed).

FSN Florida, 1550 Sawgrass Corporate Pkwy., Suite 350, Sunrise, FL 33323. Phone: (954) 845-9994. Fax: (954) 845-0923. Web Site: www.fsnflorida.com. Brad Heard, VP progmg; Jeff Genthner, VP/gen mgr; Larry Hoepfner, VP mktg.

FSN Florida progmg includes Major League Baseball's Marlins, Tampa Bay Devil Rays & National Hockey League's Florida Panthers. Serving 5 million subs on 150 cable systems.

Satellite: GE 1, transponder 4, channel 230.

Fox Sports en Espanol, 1000 Santa Monica Blvd., Los Angeles, CA 90067. Phone: (310) 286-3800. Fax: (310) 286-6389. E-mail: valvarez@foxsportsintl.com. Web Site: www.fse.terra.com. Robert L. Thompson, pres; David Sternberg, gen mgr; Tom Maney, sr VP; Raul De Quesada, mktg VP; Veronica Alvarez, mktg mgr; Dermot McQuarrie, VP progmg.

Los Angeles, CA 90067, 10000 Santa Monica Blvd, Suite 333. Phone: (310) 286-6300. Fax: (310) 286-6375.

Live, exclusive coverage in Spanish of the Copa Toyota Libertadores & Major League Baseball's postseason, boxing & nightly sports news. Serving 6 million subs on 1,321 cable systems. Satellite: Satcom C1, Transponder 1, channel 8 (SA Power VU IRD D9225).

Fox Sports Net, 1440 S. Sepulveda Blvd., Los Angeles, CA 90025. Phone: (310) 444-8123. Fax: (310) 479-8856. Web Site: www.foxsports.com. David Hill, pres/CEO; Tracy Dolgin, exec VP; Bob Thompson, exec VP; Arthur Smith, VP progmg; Jim Martin, exec VP; Jeff Shell, CFO.

A natl, rgnl & loc supplier of sports progmg.

Serves 68 million subs through 22 rgnl sports nets.

FOX Sports Net Arizona, 2 North Central, Suite 1700, One Renaissance Sq., Phoenix, AZ 85004. Phone: (602) 257-9500. Fax: (602) 257-0848. Web Site: www.foxsports.com. Rebecca O'Sullivan, gen mgr.

Provides rgnl coverage of loc interest sports progmg.

Serving 1 million subs on 32 cable systems. Satellite: C-1/16.

Fox Sports Net Bay Area, 77 Geary St., 5th Fl., San Francisco, CA 94108. Phone: (415) 296-8900. Fax: (415) 296-9198. Jeff Krolik, VP/gen mgr; Chris Geer, dir; Jay Dela Cruz, mgr; Ted Griggs, VP progmg; Michael McCright, gen sls mgr.

Rgnl & natl sports progmg including San Francisco Giants, Oakland Athletics, Golden State Warriors, Sacramento Kings, San Jose Sharks, San Jose Clash, Pac-10 football & basketball.

On 150 cable systems serving more than 3 million subs.

Satellite: Compressed, GE-1, T 18 Channel 110.

Fox Sports Net Chicago, 350 N. Orleans, Suite S1-100, Chicago, IL 60654. Phone: (312) 396-9800. Fax: (312) 396-5808. Web Site: www.fsnchicago.com. Julie Johnson, VP; Don Graham, VP progmg.

Rgnl all-sports cable net serving Illinois, Indiana & Iowa, featuring Chicago Bulls, Blackhawks & Cubs/White Sox games, collegiate & high school sports.

Serving 3.8 million subs on over 160 cable systems.

Satellite: GE-1, transponder 13.

Fox Sports Net Detroit, 26555 Evergreen Rd., Suite 90, Southfield, MI 480276. Phone: (248) 226-9700. Web Site: www.foxsports.com. E-mail: detroit@foxsports.net. Lisa Giles, progmg mgr; Helena Rogers, mgr; John Tuohey, exec producer; Tim Bryant, dir; Karen Kanigowski, dir.

Cable sports net featuring Detroit Pistons, Red Wings, Tigers, Fury, Shock, CCHA hockey & Michigan High School Association championship contests.

Serving 2.8 million subs on more than 70 cable systems.

Satellite: G7, transponder 23 digital.

Fox Sports Net Midwest, 700 St. Louis Union Station, Suite 300, St. Louis, MO Phone: (314) 206-7020. Fax: (314) 206-7070. E-mail: midwest@foxsports.net. Web Site: www.foxsports.com. Jack Donovan, VP/gen mgr; Matt Riordan, natl sls mgr; Mark Hulsey, exec producer; Ken Allgeyer, gen sls mgr; Alex Tevlin, progmg mgr; David Pokorny, mktg dir.

Fox Sports Net Midwest reaches more than 4.2 million cable and satellite television homes in six Midwest states. It telecasts more that 1,700 hours of local programming each year, including coverage of St. Louis Cardinals baseball, St. Louis Blues hockey, Indian Pacers basketball, Indiana Fever basketball, Kansas City Royals baseball, Big 12 football, Big 12 women's basketball, Big 12 showcase, University of Missouri athletics, Kansas State University athletics, Missouri Valley Conference basketball and championship events, Gateway Conference football, Mid-Continent Conference basketball, Horizon League basketball, and local high school sports programs, including collegiate coaches shows, and the "Midwest Sports Report," the only nightly 30 minute show covering sports in the Midwest.

Fox Sports Net New England, 42 3rd Ave., Burlington, MA 01803-4414. Phone: (781) 270-7200. Web Site: www.foxsports.com. Steven Reagan, VP progmg; David Woodman, gen mgr; Nancy Larkin, VP mktg; Gregg Sanders, VP.

Boston Celtics basketball, New York Mets (Connecticut only), college basketball, golf, football, hockey, professional tennis, soccer & auto racing.

On 215 cable systems serving 2.9 million subs.

Satellite: GE1, transponder 14.

Fox Sports Net New York, 4 Penn Plaza, 4th Fl., New York, NY 10001. Phone: (212) 465-6000. Fax: (212) 465-6024.

A two-ch rgnl sports network that delivers approximately 300 live games of the New York Islanders, Mets, New Jersey Nets & Devils, in addition to horse racing, college football, basketball & variety of sports specials.

On 128 affil cable systems serving more than 2.7 million subs.

Satellite: GE SpaceNet 2, transponders 1.

Fox Sports Net North, 90 S. 11th St., Minneapolis, MN 55403. Phone: (612) 330-2468. Fax: (612) 330-9010. Web Site: www.foxcable.com. Steve Woelfel, VP/gen mgr; Jim Denn, dir; Greg Phillips, dir.

Rgnl Sports Network: Minnesota, Iowa, Wisconsin, South Dakota & North Dakota. MLB & Brewers, NBA Timberwolves & Bucks, University of Minnesota hockey, & women's athletics, University of Wisconsin men's & women's athletics, Marquette University athletics.

Serving 3 million subs.

Satellite: GE 3, transponder 6.

Fox Sports Net Northwest, 3626 156th Ave. S.E., Bellevue, WA 98006. Phone: (425) 641-0104. Fax: (425) 641-9811. Web Site: www.foxsports.com. Mark Shuken, VP/gen mgr; Amy Affeld, progmg dir; Mike Smith, controller; Liz Serrette, opns mgr; Julie McCormack, mgr; Brett Bibby, gen sls mgr.

Coverage of PAC-10, Big Sky, other collegiate conference athletic events; Mariners, SuperSonics & other professional & high school events in the Pacific Northwest rgn.

Serving 2.4 million subs on 100 cable systems.

Satellite: G7, transponder 4.

Fox Sports Net Ohio, 9200 S. Hills Blvd., Suite 200, Broadview Heights, OH 44147. Phone: (440) 746-8000. Fax: (440) 746-9480. Web Site: www.foxsports.com. Steve Liverani, VP/gen mgr; Jim Cook, VP sls; Charlie Knudson, gen sls mgr; Jeanmarie Fucci, dir mktg; Steve Pawlowski, mgr.

Cincinnati, OH 45242, 11311 Cornell Park Dr, Suite 406. Phone: (513) 469-2006. Fax: (513) 469-2007. Web Site: www.foxsports.net.

Live sports progmg: Cleveland Indians, Cleveland Cavaliers, Cincinnati Reds, Columbus Blue Jackets, college football, basketball & sports news.

Serving 4.5 million subs on 206 cable systems.

Satellite: Satcom GE1, transponder T4. Alternate: GE1 T17.

Fox Sports Net Pittsburgh, 2 Allegheny Ctr., Suite 1000, Pittsburgh, PA 15212. Phone: (412) 322-9500. Fax: (412) 237-8439. Web Site: www.foxsports.com. Steve Tello, VP/gen mgr; Sharon Dowdell, mgr; Dwight McCune, gen sls mgr.

Rgnl sports network available to cable companies in Pennsylvania, Ohio, West Virginia, western New York & Maryland. Progmg includes Pittsburgh Pirates, Penguins & collegiate sports featuring Pitt men's basketball, West Virginia, Penn State, Mid America, conference events, nightly show "Sovranon Sports Beat," Pittsburgh Steeler wkly press conference, loc high school football championships, WPIAC football championships.

Serving 2.9 million subs on 64 cable systems.

Satellite: Galaxy XI.

Fox Sports Net Rocky Mountain, 2300 15th St., Suite 300, Denver, CO 80202. Phone: (720) 898-2700. Fax: (720) 898-2735. Steven Gravlin, dir; Tim Giggs, gen mgr; Amy Turner, dir.

Rgnl sports network serving 8 states. Progmg includes Denver Nuggets, Utah Jazz, Colorado Avalanche, Colorado Rockies, Univ of Denver & Big 12 conference. Serving 2.2 million subs on 300 cable systems.

Satellites: G7.

Broadcasting & Cable Yearbook 2006

Regional Cable Sports Networks

Fox Sports Net South, 1175 Peachtree St. N.E., Bldg. 100, Suite 200, Atlanta, GA 30361. Phone: (404) 230-7300. Fax: (404) 230-7399. Web Site: www.foxsports.com. Hunter Nickell, VP/gen mgr; Steve Craddock, exec producer & VP; Chris Killebrew, VP; Jim Claussen, VP; Bill Irish, VP progmg; Cheryl Raiford, VP; Jamie Kimbrough, dir; Brian Hogan, gen sls mgr; Jon Cohen, natl sls mgr; Vaughn Morrison, news dir; Chelsea Baskin, dir mktg; Brandon Howell, rgnl sls mgr.

NCAA sports, Atlanta Hawks, Memphis Grizzlies basketball, Atlanta Braves, Baltimore Orioles baseball, Carolina Hurricanes & Nashville Predators hockey, NASCAR, golf, tennis & much more.

Serving 10.5 million subs on more than 1,100 cable systems.

Satellite: Galaxy 11, transponder 4, channel 2.

Fox Sports Net Southwest, 100 E. Royal Ln., Suite 200, Irving, TX 75039. Phone: (972) 868-1800. Fax: (972) 868-1678. Web Site: www.foxsports.com. Jon Heidtke, VP/gen mgr; Max Robinson, gen sls mgr; Mike Anastassiou, exec producer; Tom Garnier, program dir; Mike Ibanez, mktg dir; Ramon Alvarez, dir.

Rgnl sports net serving Texas, Oklahoma, Arkansas, Louisiana & parts of New Mexico.

Serving 8 million subs on 1,300 cable and satellite systems.

Satellite: Galaxy 11, transponder 4 (digitally compressed).

Fox Sports Net West, 10000 Santa Monica Blvd., Los Angeles, CA 90067. Phone: (310) 286-3800. Richard Bastista, VP.

Los Angeles Lakers basketball, Kings hockey, Lazers indoor soccer, Strings tennis; San Diego Soccers soccer & collegiate sports, etc.

Fox Sports Net West 2, 10000 Santa Monica Blvd., Los Angeles, CA 90067. Phone: (310) 286-3800. Fax: (310) 286-3875. E-mail: swebster@foxsports.net. Web Site: www.foxsports.com. Kitty Cohen, gen mgr; Lisa Laky, VP sls; Gary Garcia, VP; Steve Webster, dir; Allyson Davis, dir mktg; Matt Cacciato, VP; Brian Decker, dir.

Rgnl sports net featuring the Los Angeles Dodgers, Los Angeles Clippers, Los Angeles Galaxy, Mighty Ducks of Anaheim, USC & UCLA athletic events & other sports.

Serving 3 million subs.

Satellite: G7, transponder 5.

Fox Sports World, 10000 Santa Monica Blvd., Los Angeles, CA 90067. Phone: (310) 286-3800. Fax: (310) 286-6389. E-mail: valvarez@foxsportsintl.com. Robert L. Thompson, pres; Dermot McQuarrie, VP progmg; Tom Maney, sr VP; Sean Riley, sr VP; David Sternberg, gen mgr; Raul De Quesada, VP.

America's top TV destination for intl first division soccer, Major League Soccer, championship rugby & round-the-clock global sports reporting. Serving 20 million subs on 5,015 cable systems. Satellite: Satcom C1, transponder 1, channel 8 (SA Power VU IRD D9225).

Madison Square Garden Network, 4 Penn Plaza, 4th Fl., New York, NY 10001. Phone: (212) 465-6000. Fax: (212) 465-6024. Web Site: www.msgnetwork.com. Mike McCarthy, exec producer; Jerry Passaro, VP progmg; Joe Cohen, exec VP.

New York Knicks, Rangers & Yankees; college football & basketball games; boxing. Exclusive Garden events as well as original series progmg.

Serving more than 6.1 million subs on more than 250 cable systems.

Satellite: Satcom 4, transponder 6.

New England Sports Network (NESN), Fenway Park, 70 Brookline Ave., Boston, MA 02215. Phone: (617) 536-9233. Fax: (617) 536-7814. Web Site: www.nesn.com. John O'Leary, VP; Raymond J. Guilbault, CFO; Sean P. McGrail, gen mgr & pres; Peter Plaehn, VP mktg.

NESN is a cable sports svc that delivers Boston Bruins, Red Sox, New England college sports as well as boxing, tennis, fishing, bowling & wrestling.

Serving 3.5 million subs on 28 cable systems.

Satellites: Satcom F-4, transponder 13; GE C-3, transponder 14.

The Sports Network, 2200 Byberry Rd., Hatboro, PA 19040. Phone: (215) 441-8444. Fax: (215) 441-5767. E-mail: kzajac@sportsnetwork.com. Web Site: www.sportsnetwork.com. Mickey Charles, pres/CEO; Phil Sokol, dir opns; Bruce Michaels, dir in technology; Jim Gillis, mng editor; Ken Zajac, sls dir; Kevin Spiegel, dir Internet content; Rob Dougherty, dir info svcs.

International real-time sports wire svc providing content, branded web pages, satellite and/or computer feeds directly to broadcasters (radio & TV), print, Internet sites, wireless with state of the art technology.

Sunshine Network, 1000 Legion Place, Suite 1600, Orlando, FL 32801-1060. Phone: (407) 648-1150. Fax: (407) 245-2571. E-mail: asksunshine@sunshinenetwork.com. Web Site: www.sunshinenetwork.com. Amy Pempel, dir; Cathy Weeden, VP/gen mgr.

Rgnl sports cable network. Progmg includes Orlando Magic & Miami Heat NBA basketball, Tampa Bay Lightning NHL hockey, Miami Dolphins, Florida State, University of Florida, UCF, Atlantic Sun, ACC, SEC, & SSC, athletics, as well as a wide variety of loc & rgnl sports events plus Sports Talk Live & Tailgate Saturday. Serving 5.9 million subs on 60 plus cable systems.

Satellites: Galaxy II, transponder 4.

Victory Sports One, 60 S. 6th St., Suite 3700, Minneapolis, MN 55403. Phone: (612) 661-3778. E-mail: info@victorysports.com. Web Site: www.victorysports.com.

VideoSeat Pay-Per-View, (A division of Host Communications Inc.). 546 E. Main St., Lexington, KY 40508. Phone: (859) 226-4678. Fax: (859) 226-4391. E-mail: dossd@hcionline.com. Web Site: www.hostcommunications.com. W. James Host, CEO.

VideoSeat handles turnkey pay-per-view syndication of several top schools in college football, including: Kentucky, Mississippi State, South Carolina, & Tennessee. Systems in Kentucky, Georgia, Mississippi, South Carolina & Tennessee.

Yankees Entertainment and Sports Network LLC, The Chrysler Bldg., 405 Lexington Ave., 36th Fl., New York, NY 10174-3699. Phone: (646) 487-3600. Fax: (646) 487-3612. E-mail: info@yesnetwork.com. Web Site: www.yesnetwork.com.

Cable Audio Services

CRN Networks, 10487 Sunland Blvd., Sunland, CA 91040. Phone: (818) 352-7152. Fax: (818) 352-3229. E-mail: CRN@crni.net. Web Site: www.crni.net.

Used on the cable system's alphanumeric/text ch, part of the FM service package & on the cable system's music-on-hold. Provides 24-hour talk service with adult contemp, oldies, sports talk & specials.

On 125 cable systems nationwide serving 26 million subs.

Satellite: Galaxy 11, transponder 6, audio 8.0. Digital service available. CRNI 1-6 with 6 talk networks on Galaxy 10, transponder 13, virtual channels 521-526.

The Classical Station, WCPE, Box 897, Wake Forest, NC 27588. Phone: (919) 556-5178. Fax: (919) 556-9273. E-mail: wcpe@wcpe.org. Web Site: theclassicalstation.org. Deborah S. Proctor, pres/CEO; Richard A. Storck, progmg dir; Rae Weaver, distribution mgr.

Free 24-hour classical music progmg with live announcers for radio, cable, other distributors. Weekly request programs, opera and features. Galaxy 5 satellite (Tr 7, Dual Fmt, 5.58/6.12MHz) or 4DTV G5 958.

DMX Music Inc., 11400 W. Olympic Blvd., Suite 1100, Los Angeles, CA 90064-1507. Phone: (310) 444-1744. Fax: (310) 444-1717. Web Site: www.dmxmusic.com. Lon A. Troxel, pres/CEO; Frank Pet, sr VP; Doug Talley, CTO; Christy Noel, sr VP.

Offers uninterrupted premium digital audio mus progmg via satellite & cable to residential & coml subs, currently offering 90 different formats.

Moody Broadcasting Network, 820 N. LaSalle Blvd., Chicago, IL 60610. Phone: (800) 621-7031. Phone: (312) 329-4433. Fax: (312) 329-4339. E-mail: mbn@moody.edu. Web Site: www.mbn.org. Douglas Hastings, progmg mgr & opns mgr; Perry Straw, mgr.

Provides 24-hour format of relg & educ progmg; mus, drama, talk, news & pub affrs.

On 426 radio stns nationwide.

Satellites: AMC-3, transponder 7D (13-Digital Stereo); Satcom AMC-5, transponder 10 (Alaska beam only-SCPC-MONO).

Music Choice, 110 Gibraltar Rd., Suite 200, Horsham, PA 19044. Phone: (215) 784-5840. Fax: (215) 784-5869. Web Site: www.musicchoice.com. David J. Del Beccaro, pres/CEO; Paula Calhoun, sr VP & gen counsel; Jeremy Rosenberg, sr VP; Christina Tancredi, sr VP, mktg & adv.

Music Choice is the premier music television network, reaching US households through digital cable and satellite television. Music Choice programs interruption-free music for homes and businesses and distributes televised concerts and music shows. The MUSIC CHOICE music channels reach 33 million households and the Music Choice Concert Series airs in 44 million homes nationally. Headquartered in Horsham, Pa, Music Choice is a partnership among subsidiaries of Microsoft Corporation, Motorola, Inc., Sony Corporation of America, Warner Music Group, Inc., EMI Music and several leading US cable providers: Adelphia Cable Communications, Comcast Cable Communications, Cox Communications and Time Warner Cable. MUSIC CHOICE is a registered trademark of Music Choice.

WFMT Radio Network, 5400 N. St. Louis Ave., Chicago, IL 60625. Phone: (773) 279-2000. Fax: (773) 279-2199. Web Site: www.wfmt.com. Steve Robinson, sr VP; Daniel Schmidt, pres/CEO.

Classical music, spoken arts & fine arts program series & specials. Satellite- & tape-delivered. Major symphony orchestras, opera, jazz, exclusive BBC & Radio Deutsche Welle progmg, WFMT-produced archival & spoken-word progmg, live studio performances, folk music. Since 1976.

Serving more than 900 radio outlets worldwide.

Satellite: Galaxy 4, digital frequeney B72.0.

"The Weather Center", (a broadcast service of Aviation Weather Inc.). 701 Gervais St., Suite 150-224, Columbia, SC 29201. Phone: (803) 739-2827. E-mail: wxcenter@aol.com. Web Site: www.aviationweatherinc.com. L.R. Ferguson, pres.

"Regional Radio Broadcast/Weathercast Network" across the Carolinas and Georgia in over 20 broadcast markets. Weather forecasting, site-specific broadcast services for stations all across America. 100% barter.

Yesterday U.S.A., 2001 Plymouth Rock, Richardson, TX 75081. Phone: (972) 889-8255. Fax: (972) 889-2329. E-mail: bill@yesterdayusa.com. Web Site: www.yesterdayusa.com. William J. Bragg, gen mgr.

A 24-hour natl radio voice of the National Museum of Communication of Irving, TX. Presenting public domain old-time radio shows & vintage music free of charge & without comls.

Satellites: G5, transponder 7 (6.8 narrow bands, audio subcarrier of WGN).

Major National TV News Organizations

ABC News

Ownership: Walt Disney Company

7 W. 66th St., New York, NY 10023; Tel: 212-456-7777

Executives: David Westin, pres (reports to Alex Wallau, pres, ABC Network Operations and Administration); Paul Slavin, sr VP; Phyllis McGrady, sr VP, exec producer, special progmg, 20/20, GMA, specials; Bob Murphy, sr VP, multimedia; Amy Entelis, sr VP, talent recruitment and business affairs; Kerry Marash, VP, editorial quality; Dawn Porter, dir of news practices; Barbara Fedida, dir of news practices; Dan Renaldo, sr VP, finance and operations; Andrea Cohen, VP, business affairs; Jeffrey Schneider, VP, news media; Derek Medina, VP, business development; Dick Wald, sr VP, consultant; Roger Goodman, VP, special projects; Paul Mason, sr VP.

Domestic Bureaus (fully staffed)

Atlanta: 2580 Cumberland Pkwy. S.E., Suite 160, Atlanta, GA 30339; Tel: 770-431-2380; Fax: 770-431-7800

Kate O'Brian, bureau chief; David Herndon, deputy bureau chief; John Boswell, assignment editor.

Chicago: 190 N. State St., Chicago, IL 60601; Tel: 312-899-4015; Fax: 312-899-4050

Ron Schofield, bureau chief; Susan Caraher, assignment editor.

Los Angeles: 4151 Prospect Ave., Los Angeles, CA 90027; Tel: 323-671-5261, Fax: 323-671-5210

David Eaton, bureau chief; Charlie Herman, deputy bureau chief; Michael Ray Gammon, assignment editor; Derick Yanehiro, assignment editor; Marilyn Heck, assignment editor; Roger Scott, assignment editor, weekend; Chris Cahan, assignment editor, weekend.

New York: 47 W. 66th St., 3rd Fl., New York, NY 10023; Tel: 212-456-2700, 212-456-7777; Fax: 212-456-2214

Mimi Gurbst, VP, news coverage; Kris Sebastian, VP, Northeast bureau chief; Chuck Lustig, dir of foreign news; Patrick Sullivan, assignment mgr; Justin Anderson, assignment editor; Ed Bailey, assignment editor; Wendy Fisher, assignment editor; Ursula Fahy, assignment editor; Barbara Chen, assignment editor; Michael Kreisel, assignment editor; Barbara Garcia, assignment editor; Clem Lane, assignment editor; Eva Price, assignment editor; Shepard Boucher, assignment editor.

Washington: 1717 DeSales St., N.W., Washington, DC 20036; Tel: 202-222-7700 / 8560-7700; Fax: 202-222-7684 / 7686

Robin Sproul, bureau chief; Dennis Dunleavey, deputy bureau chief; Diane Boozer, assignment editor; Dee Carden, assignment editor; George Sanchez, assignment editor; Zack Wolf, assignment editor; Julianne Donofrio, assignment editor.

Domestic Bureaus (stringers)

Boston: 175 N. Highland Ave., 4th Fl., Needham, MA 02494; Tel: 781-455-6002; Fax: 781-449-6694; 781-449-6037 (medical unit)

Dallas: 508 Young St., Dallas, TX 75202; Tel: 214-749-7013; Fax: 214-741-3421

Denver: Diamond Hill Office Complex, Bldg. C, 2460 W. 26th Ave., Suit 130-C, Denver, CO 80211; Tel: 303-458-0700; Fax: 303-455-8326

Miami: 2801 Ponce de Leon Blvd., Suite 422, Coral Gables, FL 33134; Tel: 305-448-9036; Fax: 305-446-8529

Seattle: 557 Roy St., Seattle, Washington 98109; Tel: 206-404-9110; Fax: 206-404-9117

International Bureaus

Beijing: 4-1-71 Jian Guo Men Wai Compound, Beijing, China; Tel: 861 06532 2671; Fax: 861 06532 2668

Josh Gerstein; Chito Romana.

Havana: Tel: 537 8793 650; Fax: 537 8730 087

Mara Valdes.

Hong Kong: 21/F Shell Tower, Times Square, One Matheson St., Causeway Bay, Hong Kong; Tel: 852 2203 2000; Fax: 852 2203 1400

Mark Litke; Andrew Morse.

Jerusalem: 206 Jaffa Rd., Jerusalem, Israel; Tel: 9722 500 5911; Fax: 9722 500 2051.

John Yang; Simon McGregor-Wood; Bruno Nota.

Kenya: Tel: 2542 522 624

Martin Seemungal.

London: 3 Queen Caroline St., London W6 9PE, United Kingdom; Tel: 44 208 222 5500 / 8309-5500; Fax: 44 208 222 5020

Marcus Wilford; Robin Wiener.

Mexico City: Reforma 350 Piso 12, Colonia Juarez, C. P. 06600 Mexico D.F.; Tel: 525 55 511 2790; Fax: 525 55 511 2785

Jose Cohen.

Moscow: Bolshoi Afanieveskay, Per 7, Moscow, CIS, Russia; Tel: 7095 232 3737 / 7095 291 1987 / 8590-2500; Fax: 7095 202 5827

Tomek Rolski.

Paris: 155 Rue du Faubourg St. Honore, 75008 Paris, France; Tel: 33 1 58 56 35 00; Fax: 33 1 43 59 38 28

Bruno Silvestre.

Rome: Piazza Grazioli, 5, Rome 00186, Italy; Tel: 3906 679 7715; Fax: 3906 679 7704

Phoebe Natanson.

Tokyo: NHK Hoso Center East Bldg., 7F, Jinnan 2-2-1, Shibuya-Ku, Tokyo, 150-8001, Japan; Tel: 813 3485 2631; Fax: 813 3485 2641

Chika Nakayama.

Primetime Shows: 20/20: David Sloan, exec producer; Good Morning America: Shelley Ross, exec producer; Nightline: Leroy Sievers, exec producer; Primetime Thursday: David Doss, exec producer; This Week with George Stephanopoulos: Tom Bettag, exec producer; World News Now: vacant; World News Tonight with Peter Jennings: Jon Banner, exec producer; World News Tonight Saturday and World News Tonight Sunday: Craig Bengtson, exec producer.

Affiliate News Service: ABSAT, 47 W. 66th St., New York, NY 10023; Tel: 212-456-4134 Mike Huitt, dir; Chris Myers, opns mgr.

CBS News

Ownership: Viacom

51 W. 52nd St., New York, NY 10019; Tel: 212-975-4321; Fax: 212-975-3285; national desk: 212-975-4114; Fax: 212-975-1893; foreign desk: 212-975-3019; Fax: 212-245-7560

Executives: Andrew Heyward, pres (reports to Leslie Moonves, pres, CBS Television); Marcy McGinnis, sr VP, news coverage; John Frazee, VP, news services; Betsey West, sr VP, primetime; Sandra Genelius, VP, communications; Frank Governale, VP, news operations; Linda Mason, VP, public affairs; James McKenna, VP, finance and admin; Janet Leissner, VP, DC bureau mgr; John Paxson, VP, London bureau chief.

Domestic Bureaus

Atlanta: 535 Plasamour Dr. N.E., Atlanta, GA 30309; Tel: 404-872-8301

Dallas: 1011 N. Central Expressway, Dallas, TX 75231; Tel: 214-739-1199; Fax: 214-696-9011

Michael Pool, bureau chief.

Los Angeles: 7800 Beverly Blvd., Los Angeles, CA 90036; Tel: 323-575-2345

Jennifer Siebens, bureau chief

Miami: 4770 Biscayne Blvd., Miami, FL 33101; Tel: 305-571-4400

San Francisco: 825 Battery St., San Francisco, CA 94111; Tel: 415-362-8177

Washington: 2020 M St., N.W., Washington, DC 20036; Tel: 202-457-4321; Fax: 202-331-1765 (newsroom)

Janet Leissner, bureau chief.

International Bureaus

Amman, Jordan; Baghdad, Iraq; Beijing, China; Bonn, German; Hong Kong; Johannesburg, South Africa; London, England; Moscow, Russia; Paris, France; Rome, Italy; Tel Aviv, Israel; Tokyo, Japan.

Primetime Shows: CBS Evening News: Jim Murphy, exec producer; The Early Show: Michael Bass, sr exec producer; CBS Morning New: Michael Bass, exec producer; Up to the Minute: Karen Sacks, exec producer; 60 Minutes (Sunday Edition): Jeff Fager, exec producer; 60 Minutes (Weekday Edition): Josh Howard, exec producer; 48 Hours Mystery: Susan Zirinsky, exec producer; The Saturday Early Show: Michael Bass, exec producer; CBS News Sunday Morning: Rand Morrison, exec producer.

Affiliate News Service: CBS News Service, 524 W. 57th St., New York, NY 10019; Tel: 212-975-5641 John Frazee, sr VP.

CNBC

1 CNBC Plaza, Englewood Cliffs, NJ 07632; Tel: 201-735-2622; assignment desk: 201-735-3000; assignment desk fax: 201-735-3200

Executives: Pamela Thomas-Graham, pres and CEO (reports to Jeff Zucker, pres, NBC Entertainment); Lilach Asofsky, sr VP, mktg and rsch; Judith H. Dobrzynski, mgng editor, business news; Lauren Donovan, sr VP and gen counsel; Scott Drake, VP, management information technology; David Friend, sr VP, business news; Cheryl Gould, primetime and weekend progmg; Kari Joaquin, VP, human resources; John Kelly, sr VP, adv sales; Bob Meyers, gen mgr, CNBC Enterprises; Kevin Egan, VP and CFO; Steve Fastook, VP, engineering and operations; Amy Zelvin, VP, public relations.

Domestic Bureaus

New York: 30 Rockefeller Plaza, New York, NY 10112; Tel: 212-664-4444; Fax: 212-664-2994

Washington: 1025 Connecticut Ave., N.W., Suite 800, Washington, DC 20036; Tel: 202-467-5400; Fax: 202-737-4985

Alan Murray, bureau chief.

Los Angeles: 3000 W. Alameda Ave., Burbank, CA 91523; Tel: 818-840-3214; Fax: 818-840-4181

Heather Allen, bureau chief.

International Bureaus: London; Singapore.

Primetime Shows: Wake Up Call: Gary Kanofsky, exec producer; Squawk Box: Bill McCandles, exec producer; Morning Call: Rich Fisherman, exec producer; Power Lunch: Bob Fasbender, exec producer; Street Signs: Andy Hoffman, exec producer; Closing Bell: Alex Crippen, exec producer; Kudlow & Cramer: Matt Quayle, exec producer; Bullseye: Matt Quayle, exec producer; Capital Report: Steve Lewis, exec producer; Special Report: Diane Galligan, exec producer; Dennis Miller: Eddie Feldman, exec producer; Louis Rukeyser's Wall Street: Rich Carolan, exec producer; Suze Orman: Amy Fellar, exec producer.

CNN

1 CNN Center, Atlanta, GA 30303; Tel: 404-827-1700; national desk: 404-827-1511; international desk: 404-827-1519

Executives: Jim Walton, pres, news group (reports to Philip Kent, chmn and CEO, Turner Broadcasting); Sid Bedingfield, exec VP and gen mgr; Sue Bunda, sr VP;

Chris Cramer, exec VP, CNN International; Rick Davis, exec VP, news standards and practices; Princell Hair, exec VP and gen mgr; Eason Jordan, exec VP and chief news exec; Rolando Santos, exec VP and gen mgr, HLN; Ken Jautz, exec VP and gen mgr, CNNfn.

Domestic Bureaus

New York: 1 Time Warner Center, New York, NY 10019; Tel: 212-275-7800; Fax: 212-275-9520

Karen Curry, bureau chief.

Boston: 637 Washington St., #208, Brookline, MA 02446; Tel: 617-264-9905

Dan Lothian, bureau chief.

Chicago: 435 N. Michigan Ave., Chicago, IL 60611; Tel: 312-645-8555

Los Angeles: 6430 W. Sunset Blvd., Los Angeles, CA 90028; Tel: 323-993-5000

Pete Janows, bureau chief.

Miami: 12000 Biscayne Blvd. N., Miami, FL 33181; Tel: 305-895-4885

John Zarrella, bureau chief.

Washington: 820 First St. N.E., Washington, DC 20022; Tel: 202-898-7900

David Bohrman, bureau chief.

International Bureaus

Hong Kong: 30 F Oxford House, 979 Kings Rd., Taikoo Pl., Quarry Bay, Hong Kong

London: CNN, Turner House, 16 Great Marlborough, London WIS7HS, United Kingdom

Primetime Shows: NewsNight with Aaron Brown: Sharon van Zwieten, exec producer; Anderson Cooper - Anderson Cooper 360: Terry Baker, sr exec producer; Lou Dobbs Tonight: Bill Dorman, exec producer; American Morning with Soledad O'Brien and Bill Hemmer: Wil Surrat, exec producer; Paula Zahn Now: Mark Nelson, sr exec producer; Larry King Live: Wendy Walker Whitworth, sr exec producer.

Fox News Channel

Ownership: News Corp.

1211 Ave. of the Americas, New York, NY 10036; Tel: 212-301-3000; Fax: 212-301-4224

Executives: Rupert Murdoch, chmn and CEO; Peter Chemin, pres and COO, Martin Pompadur, exec VP; David DeVoe, sr VP, and CFO; Andrew Butcher, VP corporate affrs and communications, News Corp;

Dianne Brandi, VP, legal and business affairs; Kim Hume, VP, DC bureau chief; Brian Lewis, sr VP, corporate communications; Kevin Magee, VP, progmg; John Moody, sr VP, news editorial; Paul Rittenberg, sr VP, adv sales; Bill Shine, VP, production; John Stack, VP, newsgathering.

Domestic Bureaus

Atlanta: 260 14th St., N.W., Atlanta, GA 30318; Tel: 404-685-2280

Todd Ciganek, bureau chief.

Denver: Total Bldg N. Tower, 999 18th St., Suite 1665, Denver, CO 80202; Tel: 303-383-1170; Fax: 303-383-1171

Denis King, bureau chief.

Dallas: 301 N. Market St., Suite 450, Dallas, TX 75202: Tel: 214-742-5005: Fax: 214-742-1067

Russ Cosby, bureau chief.

Los Angeles: 2044 Armocast Ave., Los Angeles, CA 90025; Tel: 310-571-2000/5/7; Fax: 310-571-2013

John Brady, bureau chief.

Miami: 1440 79th St. Causeway, Suite 208, North Bay Village, FL 33141; Tel: 305-866-8007; Fax: 305-866-5444

Nancy Harmeyer, bureau chief.

San Francisco: 901 Battery St., Suite 308, San Francisco, CA 94111; Tel: 415-951-8550; Fax: 415-951-8645

Washington: 2201 C St., N.W., Washington, DC 20520; Tel: 202-496-0109; Fax: 202-824-6426

Kim Hume, bureau chief.

International Bureaus

Hong Kong: One Harbour Front, 18 Tak Fung St., 15th Fl. Hunghan, Kkowloon, Hong Kong; Tel: 011-852-2821-8853; Fax: 011-852-2621-8658

Jerusalem: 206 Jaffa Rd., PO Box 13172, Jerusalem 91131, Israel; Tel: 011-972-2500-1421; Fax: 011-972-3642-2226

London: Grant Way, Isleworth, Middlesex TW7 500, United Kingdom; Tel: 011-44-171-805-7146; Fax: 011-44-171-805-7140

Moscow: 3 Gruzinsky Pereulok, KV. 311-312, Moskow 123056, Russia; Tel: 011-7502-221-3221; Fax: 011-7095-254-5828

Primetime Shows: Special Report with Brit Hume: Jim Eldridge, sr producer; Fox Report with Shepard Smith: Jay Wallace, sr producer; The O'Reilly Factor:

Amy Sohnen, exec producer; Hannity and Colmes: Meade Cooper, sr producer; On the Record with Greta Van Susteren: Suzanne Scott, sr producer.

MSNBC

1 MSNBC Plaza, Seacaucus, NJ 07094; Tel: 201-583-5000

Executives: Rick Kaplan, pres and gen mgr (reports to Neal Shapiro, pres of NBC News); Phil Griffin, VP, primetime progmg; Mark Effron, VP, news, daytime progmg; Robin Garfield, VP, strategic opns; Val Nicholas, VP, mktg; Jeremy Gaines, VP, communications; Nick Tzanis, VP, technical operations.

Primetime Shows: The Abrams Report: Meghan Shaefer, exec producer; Hardball: Tammy Haddad, exec producer; Lester Holt live; Countdown with Keith Olbermann: Izzy Povich, exec producer; Deborah Norville Tonight: Bruce Perlmutter, exec producer; Scarborough Country: Lia Macko, exec producer.

NBC News

Ownership: NBC Universal

30 Rockefeller Plaza, New York, NY 10112; Tel: 212-664-4444

Executives: Bob Wright, chm and CEO; Lynn Calpeter, exec VP and CFO; David Overbeeke, exec VP CIO; John Eck, pres info technology and opns; Anna Perez, exec VP communications; Rick Cotton, exec VP gen counsel; Neal Shapiro, pres (reports to Jeff Zucker, pres, NBC Entertainment); Lisa Hsia, VP; Bill Wheatley, VP; Elena Nachmanoff, VP, talent development; David McCormick, dir, standards and practices; Lloyd Siegel, dir, news partnerships; Jocelyn Cordova, dir, talent recruitment.

Domestic Bureaus

Midwest Bureau: 454 N. Columbus Dr., 1st Fl., Chicago, IL 60611

Stewart Dan, bureau chief.

Primetime Shows: Nightly News: Steve Capus, exec producer; TODAY: Tom Touchet, exec producer; Dateline: David Corvo, exec producer; Meet the Press: Betsy Fischer, exec producer; Weekend Today: Don Nash, exec producer; Weekend Nightly News: Bob Epstein, exec producer; Chris Matthews Show: Nancy Nathan, exec producer.

Affiliate News Service: NBC News Channel, 925 Woodridge Center Dr., Charlotte, NC 28217, Tel: 704-329-8700 Bob Horner, pres; Sharon Houston, exec producer.

TV News Services

ABC News
See ABC listing in Major National TV News Organizations, this section.

APTN Productions, The Interchange, Oval Rd., Camden Lock, London NW1 7DZ. United Kingdom. Phone: (0) 20 7482 7400. Fax: (0) 20 7413 8312. E-mail: aptn_productions@ap.org. Web Site: www.aptn.com.
New York, NY 10023, 1995 Broadway. Phone: (212) 362-4440.
International TV svcs company, daily satellite news feeds to bcstrs worldwide, tech facilities, camera crew hire worldwide.
Serves TV.

AccuWeather Inc., 385 Science Park Rd., State College, PA 16803. Phone: (814) 235-8600. Fax: (814) 235-8609. E-mail: info@accuwx.com. Web Site: www.accuweather.com. Joel N. Myers, pres; Gary Kemp, sls VP.
Proven ratings power with ULTRA-local exclusive and non-exclusive weather systems & svcs for bcst and Internet. Your complete weather source.

Africa News Service Inc., 920 M Street S.E., Washington, DC 20002. Phone: (202) 546-0777. Fax: (202) 546-0676. Web Site: www.allafrica.com. Reed Kramer, CEO; Akwe Amosu, exec producer.
A news & info service on African affrs for TV, radio & print news svcs.

Agence France-Presse, 1015 15th St. N.W., Suite 500, Washington, DC 20005. Phone: (202) 289-0700. Fax: (202) 414-0525. Web Site: www.afp.com. E-mail: afp-usa@afp.com. George Biannic, dir; Francis Kohn, editor.
Produces a variety of international news svcs for radio & TV, including text wires in six languages, photo wires, graphics & financial wires (plus multimedia svcs).

American Academy of Dermatology, Communications Dept., American Academy of Dermatology. Box 4014, Schaumburg, IL 60168-4014. Phone: (847) 330-0230. Fax: (847) 330-0050. Web Site: www.aad.org. Donna Stein, exec dir.
Washington, DC 20005-4355, 1350 I Street NW, Suite 870. Phone: (202) 842-3555. Fax: (202) 842-4355.
Expert physicians available for TV & radio interviews, audio & video tapes on skin cancer detection, as well as information on skin, hair and nail conditioning.

American Heart Association National Center, 7272 Greenville Ave., Dallas, TX 75231. Phone: (214) 706-1330. Phone: (800) 242-8721. Fax: (214) 706-5243. Web Site: www.americanheart.org. M. Cass Wheeler, CEO.
Periodic satellite news feeds of medical rsch stories.

The Associated Press, AP Broadcast News Center, 1825 K St. N.W., Suite 800, Washington, DC 20006-1202. Phone: (202) 736-1100. Phone: (800) 821-4747. Fax: (202) 736-1124. Web Site: www.apbroadcast.com. James R. Williams III, VP.
AP Services for TV: Video: APTV. Wires: APTV Wire, AP Megastream, AP NewsPower, AP specialty wires. Graphics: AP GraphicsBank, AP PhotoStream. Software: AP NewsCenter; AP NewsDesk; AP NewsDesk (LAN). New media: Fax svcs, AP Online, AP Audiotex Data Delivery: AP Express.

Audio-Video News, 3622 Stanford Cir., Falls Church, VA 22041. Phone: (703) 354-6795. E-mail: connielawn@aol.com.
Covers major natl, international & specialty stories for radio & TV stns in the U.S. & around the world. Also do live talk-back features.
Serves radio & TV.

Bloomberg L.P., 499 Park Ave., New York, NY 10022. Phone: (212) 318-2200, EXT. 2201. Fax: (917) 369-5000. Web Site: www.bloomberg.com. John Meehan, editor.
24-hour TV ch. Business & news reports for radio & TV stns. Full news service.

British Information Services, 845 3rd Ave., New York, NY 10022. Phone: (212) 745-0277. Fax: (212) 745-0359. Web Site: www.britainusa.org. Mark Hopkinson, Head Radio/TV div; Sarah Kendall, mktg.
Assists radio & TV crews visiting the United Kingdom.
Serves radio & TV.

Broadcast Interview Source, 2233 Wisconsin Ave. N.W., Washington, DC 20007. Phone: (202) 333-5000. Phone: (202) 333-5000. Fax: (202) 342-5411. E-mail: editor@yearbook.com. Web Site: www.expertclick.com. Mitchell P. Davis, editor.
Free source of interview contacts

Broadcast News Ltd., 36 King St. E., Toronto, ON M5C 2L9. Canada. Phone: (416) 364-3172. Fax: (416) 364-1325. E-mail: tscott@broadcastnews.ca. Web Site: www.cp.org. Eric Morrison, pres; Scott White, Editor in chief.
Full wire & audio svcs (news agency), satellite delivery for radio program syndicators.
Serves radio & TV.

CBS News
See CBS listing in Major National TV News Organizations, this section.

CNN and CNN Headline News
See listing in Major National TV News Organizations, this section.

Camera Planet, 253 Fifth Ave., New York, NY 10016. Phone: (212) 779-0500. Web Site: www.cameraplanet.com. E-mail: archive@cameraplanet.com. Steven Rosenbaum, exec producer.
TV production & dev company specializing in documentaries (A&E, Investigative Reports and Inside Story; (CNN, Perspectives); (CBS Eye on People, I Witness); and specials (ABC Entertainment, Next: Life in the 21st Century; VH1, Crunch to the Beat). The History channel, MSNBC.

Canada NewsWire Limited Broadcast Services, 20 Bay St. Waterpark Pl., Suite 1500, Toronto, ON M5J 2N8. Canada. Phone: (416) 863-9350. Fax: (416) 863-4825. E-mail: cnw@newswire.ca. Web Site: www.newswire.ca. Brian MacDonald, mgr.
Calgary, AB T2P 3C5 Canada, Gulf Canada Sq, 401 Ninth Ave. S.W., Suite 835. Phone: (403) 269-7605. Fax: (403) 263-7888. TWX: 03-824872. E-mail: Michle.dauphine@newswire.ca. Krista Wightman, mgr.
Vancouver, BC V6B 4NB Canada, 650 West Georgia St, Suite 1103. Phone: (604) 669-7764. Fax: (604) 669-4356. TWX: 04-508529. Larry Cardy, VP western Canada.
Halifax, NS B4A 1E6 Canada, Sun Tower, 1550 Bedford Hwy., Suite 410. Phone: (902) 422-1411. Fax: (902) 422-3507. TWX: 019-21534. E-mail: jgallant@newswire.ca. Robert Moffatt, mgr Atlantic Canada.
Ottawa, ON K1P 6A9 Canada, 255 Albert St, Suite 460. Phone: (613) 563-4465. Fax: (613) 563-0548. TWX: 053-3292. Hugh Johnson, VP natl capital rgn.
Montreal, PQ H3B 2J6 Canada, 1155 Rene Levesque Blvd. W, Suite 3310. Phone: (514) 878-2520. Fax: (514) 878-4451. TWX: 505-60936. E-mail: scmtl@newswire.ca. Elaire Carr, VP Quebec.
Distributor of video & radio news releases, features, PSA & corporate productions via satellite & hard copy.

Capitol Television News Service, 1629 S St., Sacramento, CA 95814. Phone: (916) 446-7890. Phone: (800) 672-2728. Fax: (916) 446-7893. E-mail: sabrina@pacsat.com. Web Site: www.pacsat.com. Steve Mallory, pres; Sabrina Demayo, reporter.
A video wire svc providing daily news coverage, via satellite, of California's capitol for radio & TV stns throughout the state.
Serves radio & TV.

The Church of Jesus Christ of Latter-day Saints (Mormons), 15 E. South Temple St., 2nd Fl., Salt Lake City, UT 84150. Phone: (801) 240-2205. Fax: (801) 240-1167. E-mail: purdyrm@ldschurch.org. Web Site: www.lds.org. Michael Purdy, mgr; Dale Bills, mgr; Kim Farah, mgr.
Offers free pub affrs, news & feature progmg; also guests for talk shows. Pub affrs progmg is not church-oriented.
Serves radio & TV.

Compu-Weather Inc., 2566 Rt. 52, Hopewell Junction, NY 12533. Phone: (800) 825-4445. Fax: (800) 825-4441. E-mail: sales@compu-weather.com. Web Site: www.compu-weather.com. Jeff Wimmer, pres; Todd Gross, VP.
TV & radio svc providing weather forecasts, features, info & actualities.

Congressional Quarterly Inc., 1255 22nd St. NW, Washington, DC 20037. Phone: (202) 419-8500. Phone: (800) 432-2250. Fax: (800) 380-3810. E-mail: kwhite@cq.com. Web Site: www.cq.com. Keith White, gen mgr; Robert Merry, pres.
Congressional Quarterly Weekly Report & News Service, editorial rsch reports, newsletters, seminars, rsch, reference volumes, paperbacks; daily & wkly congressional info publications.

Connecticut Weather Center Inc., 18 Woodside Ave., Danbury, CT 06810-7123. Phone: (203) 730-2899. Fax: (203) 730-2839. E-mail: weatherlab@ctweather.com. Web Site: www.ctweather.com. William Jacquemin, pres.
Weather forecasts for all media. Custom intros/outros/lives. Accurate forecasts. Barter or cash arrangement available.

Fairchild Broadcast News, 405 E 42nd St, Suite 310, New York, NY 10012. Phone: (212) 593-3294. Fax: (212) 686-7308. Jay Levy, pres.
Gathers & disseminates news around the world.

Feature Story News, 1730 Rhode Island Ave., Suite 405, Washington, DC 20036. Phone: (202) 296-9012. Fax: (202) 296-9205. E-mail: markss@featurestory.com. Web Site: www.featurestory.com. Simon Marks, pres.
New York, NY 10036, 226 W. 47th St, 2nd floor. Phone: (212) 764-5848. Nathan King, correspondent.
Ind supplier of radio & TV news to English-language bcstrs worldwide. Bureaus in Washington, Moscow, London, New York, Tehran & Beijing.
Radio Only.

Fox News Channel
See listing in Major National TV News Organizations, this section.

Golden Lamb Productions, Box 47, Schoolhouse Rd., Nassau, NY 12123. Phone: (866) 457-2739. Phone: (518) 422-6772 (pager). Fax: (518) 766-4558. Web Site: www.glpvideoproduction.com. Dow Haynor, pres; Clinton Whittlemore, VP.
ENG, EFP crews, HD and SD; SNG available. Serves the Northeast; 24-hour call; packages, live remotes, camera crane news & sports.

Hollywood News Service, 15030 Ventura Blvd., Suite 742, Sherman Oaks, CA 91403. Phone: (818) 986-8168. Phone: (818) 990-5945. Fax: (818) 789-8047. E-mail: subscribe@newscalender.com. Web Site: www.newscalendar.com.
A wire service to the entertainment media. Publisher of Hollywood News Calendar in Los Angeles; Entertainment News Calendar in New York.

Independent Television News of London Ltd., 400 N. Capital St., Suite 899, Washington, DC 20001. Phone: (202) 429-9080. Fax: (202) 429-8948. Web Site: www.itn.co.uk. Robert Moore; David Smith, correspondent; Al Ansfey, producer; Zoe Conway, producer.
London WC1X 8XV, ITN House, 200 Grays Inn Rd. Phone: 011-441-637-2424. 017-833-3000. Stewart Purvis, editor.
Other branches: South Africa, Moscow, London. Hong Kong. British TV news, Washington bureau.

Israel Broadcasting Service, 800 2nd Ave., New York, NY 10017. Phone: (212) 499-5402. Fax: (212) 499-5425. E-mail: newyork@israel.org. Web Site: www.israel.org. David Nakhirtman, dir.
Free radio & TV programs & footage about Israel.

Kyodo News International, Inc., 747 Third Ave., Suite 1803, New York, NY 10017. Phone: (212) 508-5440. Fax: (212) 508-5441. E-mail: kno@kyodonews.com. Web Site: www.kyodo.co.jp.
Kyodo's Japanese-language news svc is distributed to almost all newspapers & radio, TV in Japan. The combined circulation of newspaper subscribers is about 50 million.

LANS (Los Angeles News Service), 1247 Lincoln Blvd., Suite 262, Santa Monica, CA 90401. Phone: (310) 345-1437. Fax: (310) 230-0817. E-mail: lans@highdefinition.net. Web Site: www.highdefinition.net. Marika Gerrard, mgr.
Provides helicopter reporting & video svcs for KNX Newsradio (CBS) and KCBS TV; videotape library available. Gyrostabilized helicopter aerials a specialty.
Serves radio & TV.

Medialink, 708 Third Ave., New York, NY 10017. Phone: (212) 682-8300. Phone: (800) 843-0677. Fax: (212) 682-5260. Web Site: www.medialink.com. E-mail: info@medialink.com. Monica Jennings, sr VP.
London W1P 5AH, 7 Fitzroy Sq. Phone: 44-207 554 2700. Fax: 44-207 554 2710.
Los Angeles, CA 90028, 6430 Sunset Blvd, Suite 1100. Phone: (323) 465-0111. Fax: (323) 465-9230.

TV News Services

San Francisco, CA 94111, One Maritime Plaza, Suite 1670. Phone: (415) 296-8877. Fax: (415) 296-9929.
Washington, DC 20045, Natl. Press Bldg., 529 14th St. N.W., Suite 1230-A. Phone: (202) 628-3800. Fax: (202) 628-2377.
Chicago, IL 60611, The Time & Life Bldg, 541 N. Fairbanks Ct, Suite 1910. Phone: (312) 222-9850. Fax: (312) 222-9810.
Dallas, TX 75248, 16000 Dallas Pkwy, Suite 275. Phone: (972) 774-0200. Fax: (972) 774-0222.
International video & audio PR, satellite feed & news advisory service. Accessible by computer/newswire in U.S. & European newsrooms.
Serves radio & TV.

MediaOne Services, 901 Battery St., Suite 220, San Francisco, CA 94111. Phone: (415) 262-4222. Fax: (415) 693-5005. E-mail: info@mediaoneservices.com. Web Site: www.mediaoneservices.com. Andy Orgel, pres.
Satellite uplinking & fiber-optic transmission capabilities. 20'x 40'& 30' x 30' studios for production of cable progmg, teleconferences, live interviews, satellite press tours.
Serves radio & TV.

Metro Weather Service Inc., 71 S. Central Ave., Valley Stream, NY 11580. Phone: (800) 488-7866. Fax: (516) 568-8853. E-mail: metrowx@aol.com. Web Site: www.metrowx.com. Pat Pagano, pres.
Tailored weather forecasts for TV & briefings to weathercasters.
Serves radio & TV.

Miami News Net, 2641 S.W. 27th St., Miami, FL 33133. Phone: (305) 285-0044. Fax: (305) 285-0074. E-mail: mnn@bellsouth.net. Web Site: www.miaminewsnet.com. Catherine A. Scull, pres.
A 24-hour TV news, sports & entertainment svc that provides crews, video archive, avid, beta edit & feed facilities. Live talkback studio facilities, dual path digital KU uplink trunk.

Mountain News Corporation, 50 Vashell Way, Suite 200, Orinda, CA 94563. Phone: (925) 254-4456. Fax: (925) 254-7923. E-mail: info@mountainnews.com. Web Site: www.mountainnews.com. Rob Brown, pres; Chad Dyer, VP.
Mountain News Corporation, formally AMI News, is the largest & oldest producer of winter & summer progmg for media. We deliver the most accurate & timing news & info covering mountain activities.

NBC News
See NBC listing in Major National TV News Organizations, this section.

NOAA/National Weather Service Headquarters, 1325 East-West Hwy., Silver Spring, MD 20910. Phone: (301) 713-0700. Fax: (301) 713-1598. Web Site: www.nws.noaa.gov. Gregory A. Mandt, dir.
Anchorage, AK 99513-7575, 222 W. Seventh Ave, 23, Rm. 517. Phone: (907) 271-5136.
Honolulu, HI 96813, Grosvenor Ctr. Mauka Tower, 737 Bishop St., Suite 2200. Phone: (808) 532-6416. Fax: (808) 532-5569. James Weyman, dir Pacific rgn.
Kansas City, MO 64153-2371, 7220 N.W. 101 Terr. Phone: (816) 891-8914. Sandy Boyse, dir central rgn.
Bohemia, NY 11716-2626, 630 Johnson Ave. Phone: (516) 244-0101. Dean Gulezian, dir eastern rgn.
Fort Worth, TX 76102-6171, 819 Taylor St, Rm. 10A03. Phone: (817) 978-1000. Erma Nations, dir southern rgn.
Salt Lake City, UT 84147-1102, Federal Bldg, 125 S. State St., Rm. 1311. Phone: (801) 524-5122. Vickie L. Nadolski, dir western rgn.
Weather & flood warnings, forecasts & related info for the media & gen public.

The Nasdaq Stock Market, 1 Liberty Plaza, New York, NY 10006. Phone: (212) 858-5211. Fax: (646) 625-6548. E-mail: petersos@nasdaq.com. Web Site: www.nasdaq.com. Robert Greifeld, pres/CEO.
Customized loc data for the stock market.
Serves radio & TV.

Nemo News Service, 7179 Via Maria, San Jose, CA 95139. Phone: (408) 226-6339. Phone: (800) 243-8433. Fax: (408) 226-6403. E-mail: dickreizner@worldnet.att.net. Dick Reizner, owner.
On-assignment coverage of news & sporting events for radio & TV stns worldwide.
Serves radio & TV.

Potomac Television, 529 14th St., N.W., Suite 480, National Press Bldg., Washington, DC 20045. Phone: (202) 783-5030. Fax: (202) 628-7228. E-mail: jnorins@ptpngroup.com. Web Site: www.ptpngroup.com. Nicholas J. Chiaia Jr., pres; Tiina Murasev, opns mgr.
Washington, DC, news coverage, studios, editing facilities, live shots, crews, satellite capability & duplications.

Nippon TV Network Corp., 50 Rockefeller Plaza, Suite 940, New York, NY 10020. Phone: (212) 765-5076. Fax: (212) 489-8395. Web Site: www.tvic.com. Atsushi Hatayama, bureau chief; Vivian Lam, Senior account executive.
Localized TV news svc.

NorthStar Studios Inc., 3201 Dickerson Pike, Nashville, TN 37207. Phone: (615) 650-6000. Fax: (615) 650-6300. E-mail: grant.barbre@northstarstudios.tv. Web Site: www.northstarstudios.tv. Grant Barbre, VP/gen mgr.
Complete television production services: 7 stages, mobile production/uplink trucks, network origination, transmissions, digital archiving, Avid/DS, linear editing, graphics/animations, ENG crews.

Presson Perspectives, 600 Druid Rd. E., Clearwater, FL 33756. Phone: (727) 461-1885. Phone: (800) 249-4521. Fax: (727) 443-1984. E-mail: gpresson@tampabayrr.com. Gina Presson, producer & pres; Cheri Fazioli, producer.
Specializing in TV news & documentary production & electronic publishing. Svcs include rsch, field production, videography, postproduction, & satellite feeds for radio & TV.
Serves radio & TV.

Radio Press News Service, 8633 Arbor Dr., El Cerrito, CA 94530-2728. Phone: (510) 524-9559. Fax: (510) 459-0000. E-mail: jag4jl@aol.com. J.L. Levit, CEO; R.M. Master, VP.
Natl coverage, with special unit for northern California, Bay Area of California & adjacent states, photographer on staff. Multimedia news, *Travellands* & *Vacationland*. Special features, articles, transcriptions, video features.

Reuters America, 3 Times Sq., New York, NY 10036. Phone: (964) 223-4000. Web Site: www.reuters.com. E-mail: stephen.naru@reuters.com. Tom Glocer, CEO.
Worldwide TV news production & transmission svcs for loc TV stns/producers. Camera crews, production facilities, news bureaus, satellite svcs, video/slide archives.

The Seattle Video Bureau, Box 99218, Seattle, WA 98199. Phone: (206) 448-2500. Fax: (206) 378-1700. E-mail: sub@seattlevideo.com. Web Site: www.seattlevideo.com. David Oglevie, pres.
ENG/EFP crews with BETACAM SP kits. Net experienced.

Skywatch Weather Center, 347 Prestley Rd., Bridgeville, PA 15017. Phone: (412) 221-6000. Phone: (800) 759-9282. Fax: (412) 221-3160. E-mail: airscl@skywatchweather.com. Web Site: www.skywatchweather.com. Dr. Stanley J. Penkala PhD., pres.
Weather forecasts targeted to the lstng area, & comprehensive briefings for on-air talent.
Serves radio & TV.

Skyways Communications, L.L.C., 89 Access Rd., Suite 20, Norwood, MA 02062. Phone: (781) 551-9960. Fax: (781) 551-5956. Web Site: www.skyways.net. LuAnn Reeb, pres; Scott R. Hess, VP.
Custom TV news gathering, producing & mobile satellite uplinking svcs. Provides bcst-experienced crews, producers, reporters & technicians for breaking news, live-event coverage & webcasting.

The Sports Network, 2200 Byberry Rd., Suite 200, Hatboro, PA 19040. Phone: (215) 441-8444. Fax: (215) 441-5767. E-mail: kzajac@sportsnetwork.com. Web Site: www.sportsnetwork.com. Mickey Charles, pres; Jim Gillis, editor; Phil Sokol, dir opns; Bruce Michaels, dir opns; Ken Zajac, sls dir; Rob Dougherty, dir.
International real-time sports wire svc providing content, branded web pages, satellite and/or computer feeds directly to broadcasters (radio & TV), print, Internet sites, wireless with state of the art technology.

Tankersley Productions, Inc., St. Louis, 8022 Venetian Dr., St. Louis, MO 63105. Phone: (314) 725-0116. Fax: (314) 725-5709. E-mail: randy@tankersleyproductions.com. Web Site: www.tankersleyproductions.com. Randy Tankersley, pres.
Full-bcst svcs. ENG/EFP Beta SP crews with/without producers, avid nonlinear editing.

U.S. Conference of Catholic Bishops, Department of Communication, Film/TV Review Svcs. 3211 Fourth St. NE, Washington, DC 20017. Phone: (202) 541-3000. E-mail: ofb@email.msn.com. Web Site: www.usccb.org. Gerri Pare, dir; David DiCerto, media reviews off.
Publishes wkly reviews of movies & TV with moral observations for concerned parents.

VNU Entertainment News Wire, 100 Boylston St., Suite 210, Boston, MA 02116. Phone: (617) 482-9447. Fax: (617) 482-9562. E-mail: dgallagher@nuemedia.com. Web Site: www.vnuenw.com. John Lerner, VP; Don Gallagher, editor; Sam Bell, sls.
Advance news from BPI-owned publications serving radio, TV & nwsprs.

WB11.com WPIX-TV New York, 220 E. 42nd St., New York, NY 10017. Phone: (212) 949-1100. Fax: (212) 210-2591. Web Site: wb11.trb.com.

WSI (Weather Services International), 400 Minuteman Rd., Andover, MA 01810. Phone: (978) 983-6300. Fax: (978) 983-6400. Web Site: www.wsi.com. Mark Gildersleeve, pres; Steve Ward, VP/gen mgr; Linda Maynard, mktg.
WSI is the leading source of professional on-air weather systems, solutions & forecasting svc for TV, including TrueView, the most innovative weather storytelling tool available.

The Washington Bureau, 400 N. Capitol St. N.W., Suite 775, Washington, DC 20001. Phone: (202) 347-6396. Fax: (202) 628-6295. E-mail: rtillery@twbnews.com. Web Site: www.twbnews.com. Richard Tillery, Bureau chief; Julia Rockler, CEO.
Custom TV news coverage: ENG crews, producers & talent. Prod svcs: editing, studio, remote & satellite capabilities. Two live studios. Teleconference capability. Fiber Optic connectivity with Capital, White House & other locations.

Washington News Network, 400 N. Capitol St. N.W., Suite G-50, Washington, DC 20001. Phone: (202) 628-4000. Fax: (202) 628-4015. David Oziel, bureau chief.
Washington news bureau for more than 100 TV stns, rgnl nets & news programs nationwide. Provides reporter packages & vo/sots, crew hires & hearing video transcripts. Full editing, studio & satellite facilities on Capitol Hill.

"The Weather Center", (a broadcast service of Aviation Weather Inc.). 701 Gervais St., Suite 150-224, Columbia, SC 29201. Phone: (803) 739-2827. E-mail: wxcenter@aol.com. Web Site: www.aviationweatherinc.com. L.R. Ferguson, pres.
"Regional Radio Broadcast/Weathercast Network" across the Carolinas and Georgia in over 20 broadcast markets. Weather forecasting, site-specific broadcast services for stations all across America. 100% barter.

WeatherData Inc., 245 N. Waco St., Suite 310, Wichita, KS 67202. Phone: (316) 265-9127. Fax: (316) 265-1949. Web Site: www.weatherdata.com. E-mail: ceo@weatherdata.com. Mike Smith, CEO.
Forecasts for radio & TV, meteorology training, slides & videotape of weather & related phenomena. Nexrad radar interpretation seminar; distributor of Nexrad weather display systems. Meteorologist 24/7, storm monitoring & customer svc.

Weathermean, 1390 Oak Ct., Boulder, CO 80304. Phone: (303) 443-7443. E-mail: danielniemeyer@colorado.edu. Daniel Niemeyer, pres.
Visual weather statistic for TV comparing current weather & forecasts to typical weather.

WeatherVision Inc., 916 Foley St., Jackson, MS 39202-3406. Phone: (601) 352-6673. Fax: (601) 948-6052. E-mail: edward@weathervision.com. Web Site: www.weathervision.com. Edward St. Pe, pres; Jason McCleave, VP.
Customized, localized TV weathercasts with or without meteorologists. Barter/cash via Ku-band satellite. Complete studio teleport for use by news media on site. Avid editing available on site.
Serves radio & TV.

National Radio Programming Services

ABC Radio Networks

ABC Inc. Executives: George Bodenheimer, pres ABC Sports - ABC TV Network & pres ESPN; Lloyd Braun, chmn ABC Entertainment TV Group; Alan Braverman, exec VP/gen counsel The Walt Disney Co.; John Hare, pres ABC Radio Division; Larry Hyams, VP primetime audience analysis; Traug Keller, pres ABC Radio Networks; Walter C. Liss Jr., pres ABC Owned TV Stations-ABC Broadcasting; Zenia Mucha, sr VP corporate communications The Walt Disney Co; Angela Shapiro, pres ABC Family Channel-ABC TV Group; Carmen J. Smith, VP community initiatives ABC Inc. & VP talent dev programs ABC Entertainment TV Group; Alex Wallau, pres ABC TV Network; John E. McConnell, progmg/comments ABC Radio Network; David Westin, pres ABC News; Laurie Younger, pres Buena Vista Worldwide TV Distribution.

ABC Radio Networks Executives: John Hare, pres ABC Radio Division; Darryl Brown, exec VP/gen mgr ABC Radio Networks; JP Colaco, pres/gen mgr Radio Disney; Mitch Dolan, pres ABC Radio Station Group 1; Anne Gatoff, VP/dir finance ABC Radio; Traug Keller, pres ABC Radio Networks; Kevin Miller, VP mktg.

ABC 24-Hour Formats: ABC AC, Classic R & B (Urban Oldies),Today's Hits & Yesterdays Favorites (Best of the 70s through today), Classic Rock (Classic AOR), Country Coast-to-Coast (Contemporary Country), Hot AC (Young AC), Memories (Adult Soft Oldies), Oldies Radio, Real Country, Rejoice! (Gospel), Stardust (MOR), The Touch (Urban AC).

Music & Sports: *American Country Countdown with Bob Kingsley; American Gold; ESPN Radio; Flashback; Radio Disney; Rock & Roll's Greatest Hits with Dick Bartley; The Ride.*

Urban Programming: *DeDe McGuire's Word on the Street; The Doug Banks Morning Show; The Smiley Report with Tavis Smiley; The Tom Joyner Morning Show.*

News & Talk Programming: *ABC News; ABC Sports; America's Most Wanted; Batchelor and Alexander; Business Week Business Reports; Focus on the Family; MoneyTalk with Bob Brinker; Paul Harvey News & Comment; Satellite Sisters; The Larry Elder Show; The Mark Davis Show; The Mitch Albom Show; The Sam Donaldson Show; The Sean Hannity Show.*

East Region

77 W. 66th St., New York, NY 10023. (212) 456-7777.

Departments: Advertising Sales, Affiliate Marketing East, Finance, Research, MIS.

Executives: Traug Keller, sr VP adv sls & mktg; Geoff Rich, VP progmg exec.

125 West End Ave., New York 10023. (212) 441-4368.

Departments: ABC News Radio, Engineering, Network Programming, International.

Executives: Robert Donnelly, VP engrg; Chris Berry, VP news radio.

West Region

13725 Montfort Dr., Dallas, TX 75240. (972) 991-9200.

Departments: Affiliate Marketing West; Entertainment Programming; Marketing & Promotion; ABC 24-Hour Formats; Advertising Sales (Southwest); Engineering; Finance; MIS; Research; Clearance; International.

Executives: James Robinson, pres; Phil Hall, sr VP progmg; Jennifer Purtan, sr VP ad sls; Darryl Brown, exec VP affil mktg; Ralph Modugno, VP finance; Kevin Miller, sr VP business dev and govt rel.

American Urban Radio Networks

Executive/Sales Offices: 655 Third Ave., 24th Fl., New York, NY 10017. (212) 883-2100. FAX: (212) 297-2571. Web site: www.aurnol.com. E-mail: information@aurnol.com.

Program Headquarters: 960 Penn Ave., Suite 200, Pittsburgh, PA 15222-3811. (412) 456-4000. FAX: (412) 456-4040 (progmg). FAX: (412) 456-4077 (admin). Contact: Ty Miller, (412) 456-4036.

Officers: Ronald Davenport, co-chmn; E.J. "Jay" Williams Jr, pres; Vernon Wright, sr VP sls; Howard Eisen, rgnl dir sls; Jerry Lopes, pres progmg opns & affiliations; Ron Atkins, VP entertainment progmg; Glenn Bryant, sr VP opns; Jerry Boulding, sr VP entertainment progmg.

AP Radio Networks

The AP Radio Networks are **AP All News Radio (ANR)** and **AP Network News (APNN)**, both administered by the Radio Division of the AP Broadcast organization. ANR is a live news network that taps AP's worldwide resources to deliver the latest audio news from around the globe 24 hours a day. APNN provides newscasts, sportscasts, business reports, entertainment reports and features plus actuality feeds. APNN provides regularly scheduled programming on the Main Channel and live, long-form coverage of special events and major breaking news on the Hotline channel.

AP (Associated Press)

AP is a not-for-profit cooperative owned by 1,550 members. Any newspaper, radio or TV stn can become a member.

International Headquarters: 450 W. 33rd St., New York, NY 10001. (212) 621-1500. General/National Desk: (212) 621-1600. International Desk: (212) 621-1750. FAX: (212) 621-5469, arts and entertainment; (212) 621-1587 business news. Web site: www.ap.org. E-mail: info@ap.org (no attachments).

AP Broadcast

AP Broadcast News Center: 1825 K St. N.W., Suite 800, Washington, DC 20006-1253. (800) 821-4747 (TV). FAX: (202) 736-1199, news; (202) 736-1124, admin; (202) 736-1107, VP office. Web site: www.apbroadcast.com.

Advisory Board Officers: President: Ed Christian, CEO SAGA Communications, Gross Pointe Farms, MI; VP for Radio: Jim Farley, VP news & progmg WTOP AM/FM, Washington, DC; VP for TV: Ed Quinn, pres Broadcasting Group KGTV-TV, San Diego, CA; Jim Williams, VP; Greg Groce, dir.

Advisory Board for Radio: Clark Brown, pres radio div Jefferson-Pilot Communications, Atlanta, GA; John Dickey, exec VP Cumulus Media Inc., Atlanta, GA; Dick Ferguson, co-COO Cox Radio, Milford, CT; Dan Halyburton, sr VP/gen mgr Susquehanna Radio Corp., Dallas, TX; Gabe Hobbs, natl dir news/talk Clear Channel Communications, Tampa, FL; Zemira Jones, pres/gen mgr ABC Radio - Chicago, Chicago, IL; Laura Morris, VP/mkt mgr Infinity Broadcasting Inc., Houston, TX; Jim Russell, sr VP Minnesota Public Radio, Los Angeles, CA; Thomas Callahan, gen mgr.

Senior Management: James R. Williams III, VP/dir; Thomas Callahan, gen mgr AP Radio; George Galt, dir business affrs; Greg Groce, dir business opns and dev; Brad Kalbfeld, deputy dir and mgr editor; Jim Kathman, dir mkt strategy; Roger Lockhart, dir mkt and communications; Mike Palmer, dir Broadcast Digital Distribution Systems and Strategy; Lee Perryman, deputy dir bcst div and dir bcst tech; John Phillips, dir financial planning; Christine Sloan, dir HR.

Sales Management: Bill Burke, product mgr for bcst tech; Carol Robinson, rgnl sls mgr Medium Markets; Cushmeer Singleton, rgnl sls mgr, Division II; Susan Spaulding, dir Radio Groups and Internet Sales; Richard Turkheimer, rgnl sls mgr Large Markets.

Newsroom Management: Denise Vance, international mgr of the Americas for APTN; Wally Hindes, asst managing ed Radio; Ed Tobias, asst managing ed Broadcast News; Barbara Worth, asst managing ed News; Ken Ericson, asst mngg ed/domestic TV; Phillip Whiteacre, dir sls/mktg bsct technology; Larry Price, dir TV groups & stns; Dave Gwizdowski, dir TV networks/syndications.

AP Broadcast: Radio Division

(800) 527-7234. E-mail: apradio@ap.org.

Executives: Thomas Callahan, gen mgr, (202)736-1105, tcallahan@ap.org; Susan Spaulding, dir Radio Group and Internet Sales, (202) 736-9622, sspaulding@ap.org.

CBS

Headquarters: 51 W. 52nd St., New York, NY 10019; (212) 975-4321; Fax: (212) 975-4516; 7800 Beverly Blvd., Los Angeles, CA 90036; (213) 852-2345.

CBS

Leslie Moonves, pres/chmn/CEO; Andrew Heyward, pres CBS News; Sean McManus, pres CBS Sports; Bill Korn, exec VP strategic planning, business dev & bcst opns; Fred Reynolds, exec VP & CFO; Jack Bergen, sr VP corporate rels; Martin Franks, sr VP CBS & pres CBS Foundation; Helene Blieberg, VP exec dir CBS Foundation; Dean Daniels, VP/gen mgr CBS New Media; Matthew Margo, VP program practices East Coast; Carol Altieri, VP program practices West Coast; Gil Schwartz, sr VP communications; Lisa Caputo, VP corporate communications; Peter K. Schruth, sr VP/gen mgr affil rel; Jay Gold, VP finance; Gary McCarthy, VP finance West Coast; Kenneth Cooper, VP facilities opns; Bruce Taub, VP financial planning; Donald W. Janson, VP business process analysis; Tom Gentile, VP strategic planning; Derek Reisfeld, VP business dev.

David Zemelman, sr VP human resources; Karen Beldegreen, VP compensation & policy; Anthony Ambrosio, VP per benefits; James Sirmons, exec VP industrial rel; Ed Yergeau, VP industrial rel; Leon Schulzinger, VP industrial rel East Coast; John McLean, VP industrial rel West Coast; Nan Tepper, VP human resources West Coast; Joseph A. Flaherty, sr VP tech; Jay Fine, sr VP/gen mgr East Coast bcst opns; Darcy Antonellis, VP tech & Olympics opns; Brent Stranathan, VP bcst distribution; Raymond W. Potter, VP field opns; Robert Seidel, VP engrg & advanced technology; Charles Cappleman, sr VP West Coast & engrg; Michael Klausman, pres studio center; Steve Schifrin, VP program production svcs; Harvey Holt, VP stage opns; Barry Zegal, VP tech opns; David Zink, VP chief info officer; John Difronzo, VP info svcs; Michael Vinyard, VP info systems West Coast; Thomas Maile, VP telecommunications; Dennis D'Oca, VP risk mgmt; Elliott Matz, VP/dir real estate; Ellen Kaden, exec VP/gen counsel/sec; Martin P. Messinger, sr VP/deputy gen counsel; Susan J. Holliday, sr VP deputy gen counsel; Howard F. Jaeckel, assoc gen counsel licensing; Susanna M. Lowy, assoc gen counsel litigation; Mark W. Engstrom, assoc gen counsel labor; Sanford I. Kryle, assoc gen counsel contracts/rights dev; Mark W. Johnson, assoc gen counsel Washington DC; Jane R. Cottrell, assoc gen counsel GWSC; Derk Zimmerman, sr VP new ventures & business dev.

CBS News

Andrew Heyward, pres; Jonathan C. Klein, exec VP; Linda Mason, VP pub affrs; Lane Venardos, VP hard news & special events; Ted Savaglio, VP program planning; Al Ortiz, VP/bureau mgr Washington; Scott Herman, sr VP news CBS radio; Harvey Nagler, gen mgr news CBS radio; Marcy McGinnis, VP London bureau chief; John Frazee, VP news svcs; Frank Governale, VP opns; James McKenna, VP finance & admin; Josie Thomas, sr VP diversity.

CBS Sports

SportsLine.com. Inc.: 2200 W. Cypress Creek Rd., Ft. Lauderdale, FL 333309. (954) 489-4000 ext 5026. Fax: (954) 771-2807. Web Site: www.sportsline.com

Management: Michael Levy, pres/CEO; Mark J. Mariani, pres sls/mktg; Kenneth W. Sanders, ecec VP strategic/financial planning; Stephen E. Snyder, exec VP, product dev/opns.

Board of Directors: Michael Levy, chmn; Thomas Cullen; Gerry Hogan; Richard B. Horrow; Sherrill W. Hudson; Joseph Lacob; Sean McManus; Andrew Nibley; Russell I. Pillar; Michael P. Schulhof.

CBS Affiliate Relations

Peter K. Schruth, sr VP/gen mgr affil rel; Preston Farr, VP/dir affil rel; Frances Eigendorff, VP/dir affil rel; Jeffrey McIntyre, VP mktg/affil rel.

CBS Enterprises

Roger King, chmn/CEO; Ed Wilson, pres; Bob Cook, Marvin Shirley & Rainer Siek, exec VPs.

East Coast

1700 Broadway, 32nd & 33rd Fl., New York, NY 10019. (212) 315-4000; FAX: (212) 582-9255.

Infinity Station Group

Dan Mason, pres; Farid Suleman, sr VP/CFO; Wes Spencer, VP/controller; Stephen A. Hildebrandt, VP/gen counsel; Scott Herman, VP news; Harvey Nagler, gen mgr news; Anthony Masiello, VP tech opns.

Infinity-Owned Radio Stations

Rick Caffey, VP/gen mgr WVEE-FM Atlanta; Michael Hughes VP/gen mgr WZGC-FM Atlanta; Jim Dolan, VP/gen mgr WCAO Baltimore; Bob Phillips, VP/gen mgr WLIF-FM Baltimore; Tony Berardini, VP/gen mgr WBCN-FM Boston; Ted Jordan, gen mgr WBZ/WODS-FM Boston; Mark Hannon, VP/gen mgr WZLX-FM Boston; Rod Zimmerman, VP/gen mgr WBBM Chicago; Dave Robbins, VP/gen mgr WBBM-FM Chicago; Michael Disny, VP/gen mgr WCKG-FM Chicago (Elmwood Park, IL); Mike Fowler, VP/gen mgr WJMK-FM Chicago); Weezie Kramer, VP/gen mgr WMAQ Chicago; Rob Zimmerman, VP/gen mgr WSCR/WXRT-FM Chicago; Jack Mortenson, VP/gen mgr KHVN Dallas; Dave Presher, KOAI-FM Dallas; Dave Siebert, VP/gen mgr KLUV-FM Dallas; Jerry Bobo, VP/gen mgr KRLD Dallas; Dave Siebert, VP/gen mgr KVIL-FM Dallas; Stephen Schram, VP/gen mgr WOMC-FM & WVMV-FM Detroit; Rich Homberg, VP/gen mgr WWJ/WKRK-FM, VP/gen mgr WXYT Detroit; Joe Armao, VP/gen mgr WYCD-FM Detroit; Laura Morris, VP/gen mgr KILT-AM-FM Houston/KIKK-AM-FM Houston (Pasadena, TX); Joshua Mednick, VP/gen mgr KXYZ Houston; Pat Duffy, VP/gen mgr KNX Los Angeles; Dave Van Dyke, VP/gen mgr KCBS-FM Los Angeles; Pat Duffy, VP/gen mgr KFWB Los Angeles; Dave Armstrong, VP/gen mgr KRLA Los Angeles (Pasadena); Bob Moore, gen mgr KLSX-FM Los Angeles; Trip Reeb, VP/gen mgr KROQ-FM Los Angeles (Pasadena); Pat Duffy, VP/gen mgr KRTH-FM Los Angeles; Bob Moore, VP/gen mgr KTWV-FM Los Angeles; Brian Whittemore, VP/gen mgr WCCO Minneapolis; Dick Carlson, VP/gen mgr WLTE-FM Minneapolis; Chad Brown, VP/gen mgr WCBS New, VP/gen mgr WCBS-FM New York; Lee Davis, VP/gen mgr WFAN New York; Greg Janoff, VP/gen mgr WINS New York; Scott Herman, VP/gen mgr WNEW-FM New York; Tom Chiusano, VP/gen mgr WXRK-FM/WZRC New York; David Yadgaroff, VP/gen mgr KYW Philadelphia; Sil Scaglione, VP/gen mgr WPHT Philadelphia; Butch Forster, VP/gen mgr WIP Philadelphia; Sil Scaglione, VP/gen mgr WOGL-FM Philadelphia; Michael Young, VP/gen mgr KDKA Pittsburgh; Jim Hardy, VP/gen mgr KOME-FM San Jose; Steve DiNardo, VP/gen mgr KCBS San Francisco; Earnest L. James, VP/gen mgr KFRC-AM-FM/KYCY-AM-FM; Steve DiNardo, VP/gen mgr KITS-FM & KLLC-FM San Francisco; Ron Longinotti, VP/gen mgr KPIX-AM-FM San Francisco; Tom Langmyer, VP/gen mgr KMOX; Lee Clear, KLOU-FM St. Louis; Charlie Ochs, VP/gen mgr WQYK-AM-FM Tampa (Seffner/St. Petersburg); Melissa Huston, VP/gen mgr WARW-FM Washington, DC (Bethesda, MD); Sam Rogers, VP/gen mgr WHFS-FM Washington, DC (Annapolis); Alan Leinward, VP/gen mgr WJFK-AM-FM Washington, DC (Baltimore); Sam Rogers, VP/gen mgr WPGC-AM-FM Washington, DC (Morningside, MD).

CNN Radio Networks

Headquarters: One CNN Ctr. N.W., Atlanta, GA 30303-2762. (404) 827-2750. Web Site: www.cnnradionet.com.

CNN Radio: Natl & International radio news network, features web accessible sound bites.

Parent Company: Time Warner

Principal Executives: Jim Walton, pres CNN USA; Rick Davis, exe VP, News Standards & practices; Princell Hair, exec VP/gen mgr CNN/US; Eason Jordan, chief news exec; Nancy Lane, VP/exec dir CNN Newsgathering; Cindy Patrick, exec VP opns; Jack Womack, exec VP CNN Newsource; Robert Garcia, VP CNN Radio; Harley Hotchkiss, dir opns CNN Radio; Richard Benson, exec producer CNN Radio.

Bureaus: Atlanta; Chicago; Dallas; Denver; Los Angeles; Miami; New York; San Francisco; Seattle; Washington D.C.; Baghdad; Bangkok; Beijing; Beirut; Berlin; Buenos Aires, Cairo; Dubai, Frankfurt; Havana; Hong Kong, Islamabad; Istanbul; Jakarta; Jerusalem; Johannesburg; Lagos; London; Madrid; Mexico City; Moscow; Nairobi; New Delhi; Paris; Rome; Tokyo; Seoul; Sidney.

Eastern Public Radio

Mailing Address: Georgette Bronfman, exec dir, Eastern Public Radio, Box 615, Kensington, MD 20895. Phone: (301) 943-2930. E-mail: info@easternpublicradio.org. Web Site: http://www.easternpublicradio.org.

Executive: Georgette Bronfman, exec dir.

Board of Directors: Jeanne Fisher (co-chmn); Lee Ferraro (vice-chmn) WYEP-FM Pittsburgh, PA; John Kraus (at-large) WRVO Oswego, NY; Michael Black (sec) WEOS Geneva, NY; Scott Hanley (at-large) WDUQ-FM Pittsburgh, PA; Quyen Shanahan (at-large) WXPN-FM Philadelphia, PA; Ellen Rocco (at-large) Canton, NY; Maxie Jackson (at-large) WETA Baltimore, MD.

Family Stations Inc.

Headquarters: 290 Hegenberger Rd., Oakland, CA 94621. (510) 568-6200. (800) 543-1495. E-Mail: info@familyradio.com; Web site: www.familyradio.com.

Executives: Harold Camping, pres/gen mgr; David Hoff, progmg mgr; Dan Elyea, engrg mgr.

Conservative Christian mus & progmg. Some talk, limited news six days per week. Nonprofit, educational with 40 O & Os, one affil. International shortwave with 10 languages. Two TV & several trans. Satellite: GE Americom GE-1, transponder #2.

Jones Radio Networks

Headquarters: 8200 S. Akron St., Suite 103, Centennial, CO 80112 (303) 784-8700; (800) 609-5663 (Denver); (800) 426-9082 (Seattle); (800) 611-5663 (Washington D.C.); (888) 644-8255. FAX: (303) 784-8612. Web site: www.jonesradio.com.

Executives: Jeffrey C. Wayne, pres; Ron Hartenbaum, CEO; Phil Barry, VP/gen mgr; Frank De Santis, VP/gen mgr; James LaMarca, exec VP/COO.

Sales & Marketing: Patrick Crocker, sls dir; Kim Ketchel, mktg mgr.

24-Hour Formats: U.S. Country, CD Country, Classic Hit Country, Adult Contemporary, Adult Hit Radio, Rock Classics, Good Time Oldies, Music of Your Life, Smooth Jazz, Branding Power.

News & Talk Programming: Neal Boortz, Fight Back with David Horowitz, Handel on the Law, Clark Howard, The Clark Howard Minute, Nick Michaels Outside the Box, Making Money with Doug Fabian, Newsweek On-Air, Wall Street Wake-Up with Chris Byron, Newsweek on Air, The Ed Schultz Show.

Personalities: Bill Cody Classic Country Weekend, Delilah, Alan Kabel, Lia, Dave Wingert, Danny Wright All Night.

Research & Prep: American Comedy Network, BDSradio.com, Jimmy Carter Entertainment Report, Gossip To Go With Flo, Jones Research Network, Jones Prep Country, Jones Prep AC, Jones Prep CHR, Jones Preo Rock, Jones Prep Oldies, RadioVoodoo.

Moody Broadcasting Network

Headquarters: 820 N. LaSalle Blvd., Chicago, IL 60610. (800) 621-7031; (312) 329-4271. FAX: (312) 329-4368. Web Site: http://www.mbn.org; E-mail: mbn@moody.edu.

Executives: Doug Hastings, div mgr, broadcast & progmg & opns; David Woodworth, admin tech dev; Tony Rufo, satellite dept mgr.

Relg & educ stereo audio progmg; mus, talk, news & pub affrs 24 hours a day. Services 370 radio affils in 50 states, Washington, DC, Puerto Rico & the Virgin Islands & on 7 cable systems serving 66,22 subs. Also provides ACCUWatch, an automatic transmitter monitoring svcs to radio stns for unattended opns. Satellites: AMC-3, transponder 17 (digital FM-quad, aka DVB, stereo audio), & AMC-8 (Aurora III), transponder 10 (SCPC mono audio).

National Public Radio (NPR)

Headquarters: 635 Massachusetts Ave. N.W., Washington, DC 20001. (202) 513-2000. FAX: (202) 513-3329. Web Site: http://www.npr.org.

Corporate Team: Kevin Klose, pres/CEO; Ken Stern exec VP; Bruce Drake, VP news and info; Jeffrey Dvorkin, ombudsman; Jim Elder, CFO/treas and VP finance; Barbara Hall, VP devexec dir; Kathleen Jackson, VP HR; Neal Jackson, VP legal affrs; Jay Kernis, sr VP progmg; Peter Loewenstein, VP distribution; Jackie Nixon, dir audience and corp rsch; Dana Davis Rehm, VP member and program svcs; Margaret Low Smith, VP progmg; Mike Starling, VP engrg; Maria C. Thomas, VP/gen mgr NPR Online; Michael Riksen, VP, govt rel; Walt Swanston, dir diversity mgmt.

Board of Directors: Mark Handley, (chmn of bd), pres/gen mgr NH Public Radio; Bruce Haines, (vice-chmn), gen mgr, Northwest Indian Public radio; John A. Hermann Jr., (chair NPR Foundation), mng dir, J.P. Morgan Securities Inc.; Paul Delaney, (member), dir Initiative on Racial mythology of the Gene Media Forum; Carol Cartwright, (member), pres, Kent State Univ.; Howard H. Stevenson, (member), Sarofirm-Rock professor business admin at Harvard Univ.: Lyle Logan, (member), sr. VP personal financial svcs; Judith Winston, (member) principal Winston Withers & Associates LLC.

Member Station Managers: Ron Gordon, pres/gen mgr WPLN; Cephas Bowles, gen mgr WBGO-FM; Tim Eby, radio mgr WOSU-FM; John Stark, gen mgr KNAN; Bruce Haines, gen mgr Northeast IN Public Radio; Scott Hanley, dir/gen mgr WDUQ-FM; Michael Lazar, pres/gen mgr Capital Public Radio Inc.; Ellen Rocco, stn mgr North Country Radio; JoAnn Urofsky, gen mgr WUSF; Mark Vogelzang, pres/gen mgr VT Public Radio; Jo Anne Wallace, VP/gen mgr KQED.

This noncommercial, satellite-delivered radio system serves a growing audience of more than 15 million Americans each week via 620 public radio stations and the Internet. NPR also serves: Europe, Asia, Australia and Africa via NPR Worldwide; military installations overseas via American Forces Network; and Japan via cable.

NPR provides member stns with progmg, professional dev, promotional support, program distribution & representation in Washington on issues affecting bcstg. Programs include *All Things Considered, Morning Edition, Weekend Edition, Talk of the Nation, Justice Talking, Car Talk, Fresh Air, The Motley Fool Radio Show, JazzSet, Living on Earth,* & *The Thistle & Shamrock.*

Public Radio International

Headquarters: 100 N. 6th St., Suite 900A, Minneapolis, MN 55403. (612) 338-5000. FAX: (612) 330-9222. Web Site: http://www.pri.org.

Management Staff: Stephen Salyer, pres/CEO; Timothy J. Engel, sr VP/CFO; Melinda Ward, sr VP production, Alisa Miller, sr VP and head PRI content; Eleanor Harris, sr VP and head, mktg/distribution; Elinor Gould Zimmerman, VP/resource dev.

Background Information: PRI is a Minneapolis-based public radio network and audio publisher that provides over 400 hours each week of original programming broadcast by over 715 pub radio stn affiliates. Its progmg also is available on locally-branded publ radio stn Web sites, internationally through the World Radio Network, and nationwide via Sirius Satellite Radio. PRI was founded in 1983 as American Public Radio by five leading public radio stations to develop distinctive radio programs and to diversify the public radio offerings available to American listeners. The Network's leading programming includes *A Prairie Home Companion,* with Garrison Keillor, *Marketplace, This American Life,* PRI's *The World,* and *Studio 360,* as well as 24-hour program services *Classical 24,* and BBC World Service.

Superadio Network

Headquarters: 56 Central St., Southborough, MA 01745. (508) 480-9000. FAX: (508) 480-9288. Web Site: http://www.superadio.com; E-mail: mixes@superadio.com.

Executives: John Garabedian, CEO; Jack Bryant, COO; Gary Bernstein, pres; Rich O'Brien, sr VP radio progmg/dir affil rel; Sean Drasher, VP progmg; Steve McVie Solomon, VP progmg; Rich Rapiti, VP affil rel; John Campanario, mgr affil rel; Alexis Coble, mgr CD distrib; Chris Hebert, mgr opns; Joan Brooks, business mgr; Wesley Stafford, sls support.

All Night Cafe: CHR, weeknights 5 hrs. Host: Matthew Reid of Z95.7 San Francisco. Deliv: interactive digital satellite. Listener requests, mixing, contests and celebrity gossip. Interfaces with local production system.

Behind the Scenes Gospel: Gospel, wkly 2 hrs. Hosts: Eric Faison; Tracy Foye-Green. Deliv: CD. "Praise Party" with contemporary and classic gospel; "The Gos-Pill" with minister Dr. Val.

City Jam: Dance, wkly 4 hrs. Deliv: CD. Dance and rhythm classics.

Classic Jam: Urban, wkly 4 hrs. Deliv: CD. 80s, 90s Hip-Hop and R&B.

Classic Jam Mini-Mixx: Urban, wkly 7.5 mins. Deliv: CD. Core artists include Run-DMC, The Notorious BIG, Zhane, Mary J. Blige, Soul II Soul, New Edition, Snoop Dogg, LL Cool J, Salt 'n Pepa, En Vogue, and Guy, etc.

Elvis Only: Oldies, wkly one hr. Host: Jay Gordon. Deliv: CD, MP2, MP3.

Hip-Hop Comedy Kut: Urban, 10 min daily. Mixed by DJ Kut and DJ Rated R. Deliv: CD. Comedy bits mixed in with song hooks.

Hit AC Mix: Hot AC, 4 hrs wkly. Mixed by Aaron Scofield. Deliv: CD, MP2, MP3. Incorporates the playlist of the station, remixed and then beat-mixed.

Howie Carr Show: Talk, 3 hrs daily. Host: Howie Carr. Unique talk with his own take on the world.

Inspiration Jam: Gospel, 2 hrs wkly. Deliv: CD. Gospel and inspirational secular mus mixed, beat-to-beat.

Jump Off: Hip-Hop, 3 hrs wkly. Host: Ed Lover and Doctor Dre. The hottest Hip-Hop and R&B joints and the who's who in Hip-Hop.

Kool Jam: Urban, 4 hrs wkly. Deliv: CD. Funky old school R&B classics with no rap.

Lost in the 80's: Urban AC, 2 hrs wkly. Hosts: Derrick Jonzun; Stephanie Williams. Deliv: CD. Restrospective of R&B favorites. Features include "80's Club Jam", "One-Hit Wonder", "80's Timeline", and actualities and bytes from artists.

New Skool Mini-Mixx: Urban, 5 min wkly. Deliv: CD. Core artists include Missy Elliot, Snoop Dogg, LL Cool J, 112, P-Diddy, Jagged Edge, Dr. Dre, Ashanti, Mary J. Blige, Ludacris, etc.

Old Skool Mini-Mixx: Urban AC, 7.5 min wkly. Deliv: CD. Core artists include Parliament, Stevie Wonder, Prince, Zapp, Kool & The Gang, Rick James, Teena Marie, Shalamar, Michael Jackson, The Commodores, Gap Band, etc.

Oldies Jam: R&B Oldies, 4 hrs wkly. Hit-intensive 70s, 80s R&B. Core artists include Earth Wind & Fire, Barry White, Prince, Rick James, Parliament, Tavares, and Kool & The Gang.

On the Air: R&B, 3 hrs wkly. Host: Russ Parr. Features celebrity interviews, "Horror-Scopes", "The Wrong Songs Mix" by DJ 6th Sense, and "The Fat Five", counting down the top five songs on the Urban charts.

Open House Party: CHR, S-Su 5 hrs. Hosted by John Garabedian. Deliv: satellite. Live request call-ins, live celebrity interviews, great giveaways.

Paul Oakenfold Presents: Alternative rock, 2 or 3 hrs wkly. Mixed by Paul Oakenfold.

Pecos Pero Locos: Latin, 2 hrs wkly. Deliv: CD. Hip-Hop served up by Khool Aid and Johnny Cuervo.

Rap Jam: Urban, 4 hrs wkly. Deliv: CD. Aggressive, cutting-edge, all-rap/Hip-Hop mix.

Retro Country USA: Country, 2 hrs wkly. Host: Ken Cooper. Deliv: CD, MP2, MP3. Greatest country hits 1980-1989.

Retro Pop Reunion: Hot AC, 4 hrs wkly. Host: Joe Cortese. Deliv: CD, MP2, MP3. Hits of the video music era 1980-1992.

Retro Pop: The 90's: Hot AC, 2 hrs wkly. Host: Joe Cortese. Deliv: CD. 90s favorites to one-hit-wonders. Artists like Goo Goo Dolls, Smash Mouth, Alanis Morrisette.

Slam Jam: Urban, 4 hrs wkly. Deliv: CD. Today's hottest Hip-Hop and R&B mixed by high-profile major-market radio DJ's.

Smooth Jam: Urban, 4 hrs wkly. Deliv: CD. Contemporary and classic R&B with no Rap.

The Soul Lounge: Urban, 4 hrs wkly. Host: Terry Bello. Deliv: CD. Urban Vibe/neo-soul format and lifestyle. Features include "The Happs" entertainment report, "Tongue & Groove", a poem/spoken word segment, Artist of the Week, artist interview, and "The Vibe Session", an hour mix.

Spin Cycle: Talk, 2 hrs wkly. Deliv: CD. DJ Spinderella Keeps drivetime hot with mixing and miscellaneous skills plus old school Black spin.

Supermixx 80's: 80s, 4 hrs wkly. Deliv: CD. Beat-mixed retro.

Supermixx Mainstream: CHR dance, 4 hrs wkly. Deliv: CD. Beat-mixed Top 40.

Supermixx Rhythmic: CHR rhythmic, 4 hrs wkly. Deliv: CD. Beat-mixed Urban.

Supermixx Rock: Alternative, 4 hrs wkly. Deliv: CD. Beat-mixed Alternative (or Modern) Rock.

Tony's Trippin': Urban, 2 min daily. Deliv: CD. Two minute vignettes through topical humor, Halle Berry, P-Diddy, Bobby & Whitney etc.

United Press International

Headquarters: 1510 H St. N.W., Washington, DC 20005. (202) 898-8000. FAX: (202) 898-8057. E-mail: tips@upi.com (news); sales@upi.com (general); support@upi.com (cust svc). Web site: www.upi.com.

Executives: Nicholas Chiaia, sr VP; Christopher Ching, VP of finance; Larry Moffitt, VP of planning/dev; Steven Sweet, CIO.

Executives Editors: Arnand de Borchgrave, (editor at large); Michael Marshall, editor in chief; Dalal Saoud; middle east bureau chief; Martin Walker, editor English language opns. Editorial Staffs: Alejandra Aguirre; Mohamad Assaf; Phil Berardelli; John Hendel; T.K. Maloy; Martin Sieff; Steve Mitchell; Shaun Waterman.

Broadcast History: In 1935, UPI became the first news svc to supply news to broadcasters. Ten years later, UPI started the first sports wire. In 1958, UPI began the first wire service radio network, providing radio stns with voice reports from correspondents all over the globe.

USA Radio Networks

Headquarters: 2290 Springlake Rd., Suite 107, Dallas, TX 75234. (972) 484-3900; (800) 829-8111; (972) 241-6826, Sales/Syndication; (972) 243-3489, News; (972) 243-3498, Talk Programming. Web site: www.usaradio.com.

Executives: Mark Maddoux, pres/CEO; Tim Maddoux, VP/COO; David Maddoux, IS technology.

Affiliate Relations: Tim Lee, affil sls; Robert Jimenez, affil sls; Tracy Maddoux, affil rel.

Advertiser Sales Division: Buddy Vaughn, adv sls; Tiffany Forney, madv sls.

Correspondents: Andrew Adams, Tokyo; Anya Ardayeva and Guy Chazan, Moscow; Susan Lackey, London; Ellen Ratner, DC; Connie Lawn, Washington; Laurence Frost, Paris; Nathan Morley, Cyprus; Ronnie Nathaniels, Manila; David Bendo, Jerusalem.

Directors: Bob Morrison, news and sports; Judy Hydock, asst news.

Editors/Producers: Charlie Butts, relg; Quentin Campbell; John Hansen; Chris Leuba; Andy McCall; Judy Siegel; Melanie Smith; Curt Lewis; Robert McReynolds, Richard Curtis, Lindsay Hooker.

Anchors: Russ Rossman, sr anchor; John Scott; Jason Walker; Allen Stone; Ray Canevari.

Weekend News Anchors: Cynthia King; David Palmer; Melanie Smith; Bill Jackson; Jack Dereat.

Weekend Sports Anchor: Will Patterson.

Broadcast Operations & Engineering: Tom King, engr; Andrew Hydock, opns.

Service available via Satcom C-5 & through other nets & outlets. The USA Radio Network includes over 1,500 affiliated radio stns.

Programs

Daily:

DayBreak USA: weekdays, ET. National news, dollars & sense financial info, entertainment, movies music & TV shows. Tips on recreation, getting in shape and adding some Fun to Life and much more!

Point of View: weekdays, ET. Marlin Maddoux hosts America's original daily political roundtable with top-name guests & solid values.

The Roth Show: weekdays 1 pm-2 pm, ET. Host Laurie Roth is a talk show standing on principles and leading the charge for the legions of Americans who aare saying "Enough Already!"

The Judicial Watch Report: From behind the scenes and inside the beltway in Washington D.C. Can be described as "no holds barred" radio.

Wize Trade Live A "live" call-in-talk show that determines with accuracy that action of an investors stock is based on supply and demand.

International News Hour: A "Live" from Jersualem bureau brings the latest news from around the world.

Weekends:

Outdoors, The Weekend: Host, Alex Langer covers virtually every aspect of outdoor and recreational topics.

Cruise control: Enjoy working on your own automobile? Perftect for the weekend mechanic as well as the seasonal professional

Life Matters in the 21st Century: With today's fast paced life styles and increasing levels of stress, it is harder than ever to maintain good mental and physical health. Greg Meadows explores these issues from traditional and non traditional ways of improving your health.

ApParently: Radio for Parents with Susan Sierra is for and about Parents and Parenting from infancy to the teenage years.

The Ron Seggi Show Live from Universal Studios Florida: The show is two hours of the hottest stars, entertainers and celebrities.

Mick William's Cyber Line: Mick Williams answers listeners questions on a wide range of topics from the internet, software, hardware, and what's new in technology.

News Products

USA News: five-minute top-of-the-hour, two-minute bottom-of-the-hour NewsBreaks; special reports; coverage of national & world news via USA's worldwide team of news professionals.

USA Sports: delivered on the 45 minutes mark with breaking news, pro coverage, & all college scores in a fast-paced delivery.

USA Business Reports: latest stock closings, corporate news, as well as developments in personal finance to help listeners stretch their dollars.

The Wall Street Journal Radio Network

Headquarters: 1155 Avenue of the Americas, 8th Fl., New York, NY 10036. (212) 416-2375. FAX: (800) 828-6397. E-Mail: wsjradio@dowjones.com. Web site: www.wsjradio.com.

Executives: Paul Bell, exec dir, (212) 597-5606; Nancy Abramson, dir affil rels, (914) 244-0655 ; Arthur Krielmelman, adv sls dir, (212) 597-6072; Debra Adamski, mgr affil radio sls, (212) 597-5605; Bryan Mitchell, Eastern rgnl sls mgr, (212) 597-5934; Ken Alandt, Mid-West-Western sls mgr, (313) 226-1226; Ken Martin, affil mkt rep, (212) 597-5610; Janie Edwards, traf dir, (212) 597-5609; Jay Colon, network coord affidavits and commercials, (212) 597-5608; Patrice Sikora, mgr editor, (609) 520-4477; Pat O'Neill, afternoon newsrom editor and news inquiries, (609) 520-4356; Jeff Bellinger, morning news ed and news inquiries, (609) 520-4389; Chuck Fishman, producer (The Wall Street Journal This Morning), (609) 520-7904; Newsroom, technical issues, (609) 520-4100.

Provides *The Wall Street Journal Report*, 18 two-minute hourly business & financial newscasts each weekday & six weekend reports. *The Dow Jones Money Report* provides 16 one-minute newsbriefs focusing on money news & consumer trends. The net also provides six weekend reports. Progmg is satellite-delivered on Satcom C5, Transponder 23. Business news script svcs also available.

Westwood One

Headquarters: 40 W. 57th St. 5th Fl., New York, NY 10019. (212) 641-2000. FAX: (212) 247-0393. Web site: www.westwoodone.com.

Principal Executives: Shane Coppola, pres/CEO; Chuck Bortnick, COO; Peter Kosann, co-COO; Gary Worobow, exec VP business affrs/dev; Andrew Zaref, CFO; Paul Gregrey, exec VP/dir sls; Shawn Pastor, sr VP affil sls/business dev; Dennis Green, sr VP affil sls; James Starace, VP affil info & compliance; Tina Haut, exec VP/gen counsel; Carolyn Jones, VP human res; Paul Bronstein, VP rsch; Luis Rodriguez, VP info tech; Conrad Trautman, sr VP oper & engrg.

Westwood One Programming

News

News Networks: CBS Radio News, CNBC Business Radio, CNNRadio News, Marketwatch.com, NBC News Radio, Westwood One News.

News Features: CBS Healthwatch, Dr. Emily Senay, Dave Ross, Entertainment Report, In the Marketplace, Osgood File, Raising our Kids, What's in the News, World News Roundup, Christopher Glenn.

Talk

Talk Programs: America in the Morning, America this Week, The Jim Bonhannon Show, The Don & Mike Show, First Light, G. Gordon Liddy Show, Imus in the Morning, Larry King Live, Loveline, The Tom Leykis Show, On the Garden Line with Jerry Baker, The Radio Factor with Bill O'Reilly, Troubleshooter Tom Martino, The Week in Review.

Sports

Football: Monday Night Football, Sunday Night Football, NFL Playoffs, NFL Championships, Super Bowl, Pro Bowl, Sunday & Saturday Doubleheaders, NCAA Football, NFL Insider, NFL Preview, In the Huddle, The NFL Today.

Basketball: NCAA Basketball, March To Madness, National Invitational Tournament.

Golf: British Open Championship, Masters, PGA Championship, US Open.

Other Sports: Olympics, Focus on Racing Radio, Wimbledon, HBO Boxing.

Sports Features: John Madden Sports Quiz, The Madden Minute, Scoreboard, Sports Central USA, Sports Time, Sports World Roundup, Sportsfeed, Today in Auto Racing, Today in Golf, Today in Sports, Westwood One Sports Report, 3rd & Long with Howie Long.

Entertainment

Features: *Daily Show with John Stewart, ET Radio Minute, Late Show with David Letterman, Late Late Show with Craig Kilborn.*

Music

Alt/Modern Rock: *Absolutely Live, The Fax Prep Service, Loveline, MTV Radio Network, Out of Order.*

Contemporary/CHR: *The E! Radio Network Prep Service, MTV Radio Network, MTV's Total Request Live Weekend Countdown, Night Flight, Saturday Night All Request 80s, VH1 Behind the Music, Storytellers and Concerts, VH1 Radio Network.*

Classic Rock: *The Beatle Brunch, The Beatle Years, Off the Record, Superstar Concert Series, VH1 Behind the Music, Storytellers and Concerts, VH1 Radio Network.*

Country: *CMT Radio Network, Country's Cutting Edge, Country Gold, Country's Inside Trak, Country Six Pack, CMT's Country Countdown USA with Lon Helton, Grand Ole Opry, Stars of Country, The Weekly Country Music Countdown, Young and Verna.*

Oldies: *The Beatle Brunch, The Beatle Years, Doo Wop Heaven, The Motown Show, Oldies Six Pack.*

Urban/Hip Hop: *BET Radio Network, MTV Radio Network, MTV's TRL Weekend Countdown (Rhythmic).*

Urban/Hip Hop: *The Academy Of Country Music Awards, The BET Awards, Country Artist Album Premieres and Specials, The GRAMMY Awards, MTV Concerts and Specials, Music Events and Concerts, NFL Kickoff, VH1 Concerts and Specials.*

Prep Services

BET Radio Network, The CBS Morning Resource, The E! Radio Network, CMT Radio Morning Facts, MTV, VH1 Morning Prep, Westwood One Prep, BET Prep, Entertainment Newsfeed, Westwood One One-on-One.

24-Hour Formats

Adult Rock & Roll, Adult Standards, Bright AC, CNN Headline News, Hot Country, Mainstream Country, The Oldies Channel, Soft AC.

WFMT Radio Network

Headquarters: 5400 N. St. Louis Ave., Chicago, IL. (773) 583-5000. Web Site: http://www.wfmt.com

Executives: Daniel Schmidt, pres/CEO; Steve Robinson, sr VP/WFMT; Reese P. Marcusson, exec VP/CFO; Sandra P. Guthman, chmn; Farrell Frentress, exec VP dev; V.J. McAleer, sr VP production; Joanie Bayhack, sr VP corporate communication/direct mktg.

Satellite-delivered performing arts, jazz & spoken word progmg to over 1500 coml & pub radio stns domestically & 40 countries abroad. Among the feature progms are concerts by major symphony orchestras; productions by opera companies; concerts from Europe; concerts & spoken word from the BBC; mus & verbal documentaries; folk mus; *BSN Around the Clock*, a customized classical mus format svc; the WFMT Jazz Satellite Network, a customized jazz format svc & periodic specials.

Regional Radio Programming Services

Agrinet News Network, 104 Radio Rd., Powells Point, NC 27966. Phone: (252) 491-2414. Fax: (252) 491-2939. Web Site: www.agrinetradio.com. E-mail: info@agrinetradio.com. Bill Ray, pres.

Comprises 150 stns in Virginia, Maryland, Pennsylvania, New Jersey, West Virginia, North Carolina, South Carolina, Delaware, Alabama, Florida, Georgia, New York, Illinois, Indiana. Nationally distributed Agrinet news program.

Alaska Public Radio Network, 810 E. Ninth Ave., Anchorage, AK 99501- 3826. Phone: (907) 277-2776. Fax: (907) 263-7450. E-mail: aprn@alaska.net. Web Site: www.aprn.org.

Juneau, AK 99801. Juneau Alaska News Bureau, 530 Park St. Phone: (907) 586-6948. Dave Donaldson, state capitol bureau chief.

Washington, DC 20008. Washington, DC News Bureau, 2801 Quebec St. N.W, Suite 505. Phone: (202) 488-1961. Joel Southern, capitol bureau chief.

Satellite-delivered news/info programs to 26 member stations across Alaska from state-of-the-art studios, headquartered in Anchorage.

Allegheny Mountain Network, Box 247, Tyrone, PA 16686. Phone: (814) 684-3200. Fax: (814) 684-1220. E-mail: amnnet@aol.com.

Comprises 12 stns in Pennsylvania. Represented by Dome & Associates.

American Ag Network, 214 W. Pleasant Dr., Pierre, SD 57501-2472. Phone: (605) 224-9911. Fax: (605) 224-8984. E-mail: markswendsen@amfmradio.biz. Mark Swendsen, pres & gen mgr.

Comprises 40 stns: 16 in South Dakota, 22 in North Dakota & 2 in Montana.

Arkansas Radio Network, 700 Wellington Hills Rd., Little Rock, AR 72211. Phone: (501) 401-0228. Phone: (800) 839.4610. Fax: (501) 401-0362. Web Site: www.arkansasradionetwork.com.

Comprises 63 interconnected stns, all in Arkansas. Represented by StateNets & McGauren Guild.

Beasley Broadcast Group, 3033 Riviera Dr., Suite 200, Naples, FL 34103. Phone: (239) 263-5000. Fax: (239) 263-8191. Web Site: www.bbgi.com. George G. Beasley, chmn/CEO; Bruce Beasley, pres/COO.

Comprises 20 stns in seven states: one in Arkansas, five in Florida, four in North Carolina, four in Pennsylvania, two in Georgia, three in South Carolina, & one in New Jersey.

Berkshire Broadcasting Co. Inc., 466 Curran Hwy., North Adams, MA 01247. Phone: (413) 663-6567. Fax: (413) 662-2143. E-mail: wnaw@wnaw.com. Web Site: www.wnaw.com. Corydon Thurston, pres.

Comprises three stns in western Massachusetts. Serving Berkshire County, MA-southwestern, Vermont-eastern, NY-northwestern, CT. Represented by Kettell-Carter (Boston).

Brownfield Network, (A division of Learfield Communications Inc.). 505 Hobbs Rd., Jefferson City, MO 65109-6829. Phone: (573) 893-5700. Fax: (573) 893-8094. E-mail: cyoung@learfield.com. Web Site: www.brownfieldnetwork.com. Bruce Beasley, pres.

Comprises 205 stns in Illinois, Iowa, Missouri, Nebraska, Indiana, South Dakota & Wisconsin. Represented by In-House.

Paul Bunyan Network, Paul Bunyan Bldg., 314 E. Front, Traverse City, MI 49684. Phone: (231) 947-7675. Fax: (231) 929-3988. E-mail: wtcm@wtcmradio.com. Ross Biederman, pres & gen mgr; Jim Sofonia, chief engr; Jon Patrick, natl sls mgr; Jack O'Malley, progmg dir.

Comprises five stns in Michigan. Represented by Katz Radio.

CRN International Inc., One Circular Ave., Hamden, CT 06514. Phone: (203) 288-2002. Fax: (203) 281-3291. Web Site: www.crnradio.com. Barry Berman, pres; S. Richard Kalt, exec VP; Patrick Kane, sr VP.

Features include *Ski Watch®*, a 60-second daily ski conditions update. Summer-oriented progmg includes *Beach Watch®* & *Summer Watch®*. Small business programs include the *Small Business Report* & *Small Business Profile*. All programs available on a barter basis.

California News Radio, 14605 N. Airport Dr., Suite 370, Scottsdale, AZ 85260. Phone: (480) 483-8415. Fax: (480) 922-3120. Web Site: www.skyviewsatellite.com. Jeanne-Marie Condo, gen mgr.

Compu-Weather Inc., 2566 Rt. 52, Hopewell Junction, NY 12533. Phone: (800) 825-4445. Fax: (800) 825-4441. E-mail: sales@compu-weather.com. Web Site: www.compu-weather.com. Jeff Wimmer, pres; Todd Gross, VP.

Florida Public Radio Network, 1600 Red Barber Plaza, Tallahassee, FL 32310. Phone: (850) 487-3194. Fax: (850) 487-3293. E-mail: fpr@wfsy.org. Web Site: www.fsu.edu.

Serves 13 FM public radio stns in Florida. Represented by Susan Gage & Buzz Conover, reporters.

Florida's Radio Networks, 2500 Maitland Ctr. Pkwy., Suite 407, Maitland, FL 32751. Phone: (407) 916-7810. Phone: (407) 916-7800. Fax: (407) 916-7425. E-mail: help@frn.com. Web Site: www.frn.com. Jim Poling, opns mgr; Rick Green, gen mgr; Jim Underwood, gen sls mgr.

Comprises 58 stns in Florida. Represented by StateNets Inc.

Georgia News Network, 1819 Peachtree Rd., Suite 700, Atlanta, GA 30309. Phone: (404) 607-9045. Phone: (800) 776-4638. E-mail: robmaynard@clearchannel.com. Web Site: www.georgianewsnetwork.com. Linda Kent, sls; Rob Maynard, opns mgr.

Comprises 108 in Georgia. Represented by Statnets.

Hawkeye Network, 505 Hobbs Rd., Jefferson City, MO 65109. Phone: (573) 893-7200. Fax: (573) 893-2321. Web Site: www.learfield.com. Clyde G. Lear, pres; Greg Brown, VP; Keith Sampson, exec producer; Eric Buchanan, gen mgr; Aaron Worsham, opns VP.

Comprises 50 stns in Iowa.

Hispanic Radio Network Inc., 1126 16th St. N.W., Suite 350, Washington, DC 20036. Phone: (202) 637-8800. Fax: (202) 637-8801. E-mail: news@hrn.org. Web Site: www.hrn.org. Jeff Kline, chmn/CEO; Carlos Alcazar, pres.

Comprises 80 stns in Arizona, California, Florida, Georgia, Idaho, Illinois, Louisiana, Massachusetts, Missouri, Nevada, New Mexico, New York, Oklahoma, Oregon, Pennsylvania, Rhode Island, Texas, Utah, Washington, & Washington, DC.

Hometown Radio Network, 1100 Chester Ave., Suite 100, Cleveland, OH 44115. Phone: (216) 781-4070. Fax: (216) 348-8408. Web Site: www.regionalreps.com.

Comprises over 1000 affils in Delaware, Florida, Georgia, Iowa, Illinois, Indiana, Kansas, Kentucky, Maryland, Nebraska, North Carolina, Ohio, Oklahoma, Pennsylvania, South Carolina, Virginia, & West Virginia. Represented by: Regional Reps Corp.

ION Radio Network, Box 1223, Airport Rd., Morristown, NJ 07960. Phone: (973) 983-8222. Fax: (973) 983-1390. E-mail: steve@ionweather.com. Web Site: www.ionweather.com. Stephen Pellettiere, pres.

Comprises 19 stns: five in New Jersey, six in New York, three in Pennsylvania, two in Maryland, two in Connecticut & one in Rhode Island.

Illinois Radio Network, 430 W. Erie, Suite 325, Chicago, IL 60610. Phone: (312) 943-6363. Fax: (312) 943-5109. Web Site: www.illinoisradionetwork.com. Ben Kiningham, Bureau Chief; Dennis Mellott, gen mgr; James R. Anderson, news dir.

A statewide satellite-delivered net providing news, sports, business & special progmg. IRN 67 affils. Representative: StateNets.

KEDA Radio, 510 S. Flores, San Antonio, TX 78204. Phone: (210) 226-5254. Fax: (210) 227-7937. E-mail: kedakid@aol.com. Web Site: www.ontheradio.net/radiostations/kedaam.aspx.

Comprises three stns in Texas, three affiliates. Represented by Caballero Spanish Media.

Kansas Agriculture Network, Box 1818, Topeka, KS 66601-1818. Phone: (785) 272-2199. Fax: (785) 272-3536. Web Site: www.radionetworks.com. Craig Colbach, gen mgr; Ed O'Donnell, opns mgr; Jason Weil, sls mgr.

Comprises 37 stns in Kansas. Represented by Katz Radio.

Kansas Information Network, Box 1818, Topeka, KS 66601-1818. Phone: (785) 272-2199. Fax: (785) 272-3536. Web Site: www.radionetworks.com. Craig Colbach, gen mgr; Ed O'Donnell, opns mgr; Liz Montano, news dir.

Comprises 45 stns in Kansas. Represented by StateNets.

Kansas State Sports Network, 1632 S. Maze Rd., Wichita 67209. Phone: (316) 721-8484.

Kentucky News Network, (A subsidiary of Clear Channel Radio Inc.). One Radio Dr., Louisville, KY 40218. Phone: (502) 479-2240. Fax: (502) 479-2229. Ed Huckleberry, editor; Doug Wethington, gen sls mgr; Price Allen, dir; Jack Crowner, dir.

Comprises 93 stns: 92 in Kentucky, one in West Virginia. Represented by StatesNets. Live via satellite.

La Super Kadena, 117 Eleanor Roosevelt, Suite 1, San Juan, PR 00918. Phone: (787) 833-1610. E-mail: superkadena@spiderlink.net. Reinaldo Royo, gen mgr.

Comprises eight stns in Puerto Rico.

Linder Farm Network, 1929 Cedar Ave. S., Owatonna, MN 55060. Phone: (507) 444-9224. Fax: (507) 444-9080. E-mail: farm@linderradio.com. Web Site: www.linderfarmnetwork.com. Jeff Stewart, mktg.

Comprises 22 stns in Minnesota. Represented by Katz Radio.

Louisiana Agri-News Network, 263 Third St., 5th Fl., Baton Rouge, LA 70801. Phone: (225) 383-8695. Fax: (225) 383-5020. E-mail: bill-rigell@la-net.net. Web Site: www.la-net.net. Bill Rigell, pres/CEO; Michael Hudson, VP sls & VP mktg.

Comprises 66 stns in Louisiana & Mississippi. Represented by McGavren Guild.

Louisiana Network Inc., 263 Third St., 5th Fl., Baton Rouge, LA 70801. Phone: (225) 383-8695. Fax: (225) 383-5020. E-mail: bill.rigell@la-net.net. Web Site: www.la-net.net. Bill Rigell, pres/CEO; Michael Hudson, VP sls & VP mktg.

Comprises 84 stns in Louisiana. Represented by news net: State Nets, Agri-News Network: McGavren Guild.

The MNN Radio Networks Inc., 331 11th St. S., Minneapolis, MN 55404-1009. Phone: (612) 321-7200. Fax: (612) 321-7202. Timothy Shears, pres; James Rasmussen, VP progmg.

Comprises 93 stns in Minnesota, North Dakota, South Dakota, Iowa. Represented by State Networks Inc. (retail) & self represented (agricultural).

Michigan Farm Radio Network, 325 South Walnut, Lansing, MI 48933. Phone: (517) 484-4888. Fax: (517) 484-5015. E-mail: skpaul@mfrn.com. Web Site: www.mfrn.com. Dennis Mellott, gen mgr & pres; Karen Tremble, adv.

Comprises 26 stns in Michigan. Represented by J.L. Farmakis.

Michigan Radio Network, 325 S. Walnut, Lansing, MI 48933. Phone: (517) 484-4888. Fax: (517) 484-1389. Web Site: www.michiganradionetwork.com. Dennis Mellott, pres & gen mgr; Rob Baykian, news dir.

A statewide satellite-delivered net providing news, sports, business & special progmg. MRN 70 affils. Representative: StateNets.

Mid-America Ag Network, 1632 S. Maze Rd., Wichita, KS 67209. Phone: (316) 721-8484. Fax: (316) 721-8276. Web Site: www.maanradio.com. Larry Steckline, pres & owner; Greg Steckline, VP.

Comprises 44 stns in Colorado, Kansas, Nebraska & Oklahoma. Represented by Torbet Radio.

Mississippi Agri Network, 6311 Ridgewood Rd., Jackson, MS 39211. Phone: (601) 957-1700. Fax: (601) 956-5228. Web Site: www.telesouth.com; www.supertalkms.com.

Comprises 35 affils in Mississippi. Represented by McGavren/Guild.

Mississippi News Network, 6311 Ridgewood Rd., Jackson, MS 39211. Phone: (601) 957-1700. Fax: (601) 956-5228. E-mail: kdillon@telesouth.com. Web Site: www.telesouth.com. Kim Dillon, mktg dir; Steve Davenport, pres/CEO.

Comprises 82 affils in Mississippi. Represented by StateNets.

Mississippi State Basketball Network, 6311 Ricgewood Rd., Jackson, MS 39211. Phone: (601) 957-1700. Fax: (601) 956-5228. Steve Davenport, pres/CEO; Kim Dillon, mktg dir.

Comprises 28 affils in Mississippi & one in Tennessee.

Regional Radio Programming Services

Mississippi State Football Network, 6311 Ridgewood Rd., Jackson, MS 39211. Phone: (601) 957-1700. Fax: (601) 956-5228. E-mail: kdillon@telesouth.com. Web Site: www.telesouth.com. Kim Dillon, mktg dir; Steve Davenport, pres/CEO.

Comprises 30 affils in Mississippi & one in Alabama. Represented by Kim Dillon.

Missourinet, (A division of Learfield Communications Inc.). 505 Hobbs Rd., Jefferson City, MO 65109. Phone: (573) 893-2829. Fax: (573) 893-8094. E-mail: bpriddy@learfield.com. Web Site: www.missourinet.com. Bob Priddy, news dir; Scott Brandon, opns dir.

Serves Missouri - 70 affils.

Mountain News Network, 50 Vashell Way, Suite 200, Orinda, CA 94563. Phone: (925) 254-4456. Phone: Eastern Bureau: (800) 736-0370. Fax: (925) 254-6135. Robert B. Brown, pres; Martha Baer, VP progmg.

Comprises 1,537 stns nationwide.

NRG Media, LLC, , Fort Atkinson, WI 53538. Phone: (920) 563-2667. Fax: (920) 563-0315. E-mail: jvriezen@nrgbroadcast.com. Jim Vriezen, gen mgr.

Comprises 182 stns in Wisconsin, Illinois & Michigan.

National Educational Telecommunications Association, Box 50008, Columbia, SC 29250. Phone: (803) 799-5517. Fax: (803) 771-4831. Web Site: www.netaonline.org. Skip Hinton, pres.

Eighty-four members in 38 states & the U.S. Virgin Islands.

New South Communications Inc., Box 5797, Meridian, MS 39302. Phone: (601) 693-2661. Fax: (601) 483-0826. Ed Holladau, pres.

Comprises 18 stns: five in Louisiana, ten in Mississippi & three in Alabama. Represented by McGavren Guild.

North Carolina News Network, 711 Hillsborough St., Raleigh, NC 27603. Phone: (919) 890-6030. Fax: (919) 890-6024. Web Site: www.ncnn.com. Bob Hankin, gen mgr; Joe Wade Formicola, opns mgr; Ellen Reinhardt, news dir.

Comprises 90 stns in North Carolina. Represented by StateNets.

North Dakota News Network, Box 1197, Pierre, SD 57501. Phone: (605) 224-9911. Fax: (605) 224-8984. E-mail: markswendsen@amfmradio.biz. Mark Swendsen, pres & gen mgr.

Comprises 24 stns in North Dakota. Represented by StateNets.

Ohio Educational Telecommunications Network Commission, 2470 North Star Rd., Columbus, OH 43221. Phone: (614) 644-1714. Fax: (614) 644-3112. Web Site: www.oet.edu.

Comprising 12 TV stns & 32 radio stns, 10 radio reading svcs, & eight educ technology.

Oklahoma News Network, (Oklahoma Agrinet). Box 1000, Oklahoma City, OK 73101. Phone: (405) 858-1400, Ext. 278. Fax: (405) 840-5808. E-mail: waynegriggs@clearchannel.com. Derrick Nance, gen sls mgr; Ron Hays, farm dir; Larry J. Rhodes, opns dir; Beth Myers, news dir; Wayne Griggs, affil rel dir; Bill Hurley, VP/gen mgr.

Comprises 55 stns in Oklahoma. Represented by StateNets.

Pittsburgh Country Network, 1831 Murray Ave. #216, Pittsburgh, PA 15217. Phone: (412) 421-2600. Fax: (412) 421-6001. E-mail: rafson@cmsradio.com. Web Site: www.cmsradio.com. Roger Rafson, pres.

Comprises three stns in Pennsylvania. Represented by Commercial Media Sales.

Radio Iowa, (A division of Learfield Communications Inc.). 2700 Grand Ave., Suite 103, Des Moines, IA 50312. Phone: (515) 282-1984. Fax: (515) 282-1879. E-mail: radioiowa@learfield.com. Web Site: www.radioiowa.com. Clyde G. Lear, pres/CEO; Travis Ford, gen mgr; O. Kay Henderson, news dir.

Comprises 55 affils in Iowa.

Radio Pennsylvania Network, (A Division of WITF Inc.). 1982 Locust Ln., Harrisburg, PA 17109. Phone: (717) 232-8400. Phone: (717) 236-6000. Fax: (717) 232-7612. E-mail: radiopa@radiopa.org. Web Site: www.radiopa.org.

Bcsts state news, sports & features to affils in Pennsylvania. Comprises 80 stns. Represented by NASRN.

South Carolina News Network, (A division of Telesouth Communications Inc.). 3710 Landmark Dr., Suite 100, Columbia, SC 29204. Phone: (803) 790-4300. Fax: (803) 790-4309. Stacy Long, sls dir; Tom Jackson, gen mgr; William Christopher, news dir; Phil Kornblut, Sports dir.

Comprises 40 affils in South Carolina.

South Dakota News Network, Box 1197, Pierre, SD 57501. Phone: (605) 224-9911. Fax: (605) 224-8984. E-mail: markswendsen@amfmradio.biz. Mark Swendsen, pres & gen mgr.

Comprises 20 stns in South Dakota. Represented by StateNets.

Southeast AgNet, Box 130, Kenansville, FL 34739. Phone: (407) 436-1909. Fax: (407) 436-1364. E-mail: gary@southeastagnet.com. Web Site: www.southeastagnet.com. Gary Cooper, pres; Robin Loftin, VP.

Stns interconnected via Internet. Comprises 65 affils in Florida, Georgia & the Alabama rgn.

Southern Farm Network, 3012 Highwoods Blvd., Suite 200, Raleigh, NC 27604. Phone: (919) 876-0674. Fax: (919) 790-8369. E-mail: bpprice@southernfarmnetwork.com. Web Site: www.southernfarmnetwork.com. Barbara G. Price, opns mgr.

Comprises 20 affils in North Carolina & South Carolina.

Temple University Public Radio, WRTI-FM, 1509 Cecil B. Moore, 3rd Fl., Philadelphia, PA 19122-6080. Phone: (215) 204-8405. Fax: (215) 204-7027. Rick Torpey, gen sls mgr; Tobias Poole, opns dir; Jeffrey DePolo, engrg dir.

Comprises four stns in Pennsylvania, one in New Jersey & one in Delaware.

Tennessee Agri-Net, (Subsidiary of Clear Channel Communications Inc.). 55 Music Square West, Nashville, TN 37203. Phone: (615) 774-4785. Fax: (615) 687-9797. E-mail: janetpatterson@clearchannel.com. Web Site: www.tennesseeradionetwork.com. Janet Patterson, gen sls mgr; Chris Romer, opns dir.

Comprises 48 stns in Tennessee.

Tennessee Radio Network, (A subsidiary of Clear Channel Broadcasting Inc.). 55 Music Sq. W., Nashville, TN 37203. Phone: (615) 664-2400. Fax: (615) 687-9797. E-mail: janetpatterson@clearchannel.com. Web Site: www.tennesseeradionetwork.com. Chris Romer, opns mgr; Janet Patterson, gen sls mgr.

Comprises 76 stns in Tennessee. Representative Buddy Sadler, affil rel dir.

Texas State Network, 1080 Ballpark Way, Arlington, TX 76011. Phone: (817) 543-5400. Fax: (817) 543-5570. E-mail: tbishop@cbs.com. Web Site: www.tsnradio.com. Jerry Bobo, pres & gen mgr; Tony Bishop, gen sls mgr; Julius Graw, opns mgr; Dan Bell, dir.

Austin, TX 78701, 502 E. 11th St, Suite 320. Phone: (512) 474-5275. Fax: 512 476 9232. Candy Schmidt: Regional Sales Director.

Provides newscasts, sportscasts, agriculture reports, longform programs to 165 stns in Texas & the Texas Rangers Radio Network. The oldest & largest state radio network owned by CBS Radio. Represented by StateNets.

Tiger Network, (A division of Learfield Communications Inc.). 505 Hobbs Rd., Jefferson City, MO 65109. Phone: (314) 893-7200. Fax: (314) 893-2321. Web Site: www.learfield.com. Clyde G. Lear, pres; Greg Brown, VP; Keith Sampson, exec producer; Laird Veatch, gen mgr; Aaron Worsham, VP—Sports.

Comprises 55 stns in Missouri.

Tribune Radio Networks, 435 N. Michigan Ave., Chicago, IL 60611. Phone: (312) 222-3342. Fax: (312) 222-4876. E-mail: tribuneradio@tribune.com. Web Site: www.tribuneradio.com. Barbra Pabst, network opns.

Network comprised of: Chicago Cubs Network (50 stns), National Farm Report (260 stns), Farming America (200 stns), Agri-Voice Network (95 stns), Samuelson's Soapbox (150 stns). Represented by Eastman.

University of Mississippi Baseball Network, 6311 Ridgewood Rd., Jackson, MS 39211. Phone: (601) 957-1700. Fax: (601) 956-5228. E-mail: kdillon@telesouth.com. Web Site: www. telesouth.com; www.supertalkms.com. Steve Davenport, pres; Kim Dillon, VP.

Comprises 30 affils in Mississippi & one in Tennessee. Represented by Kim Dillon.

University of Mississippi Basketball Network, 6311 Ridgewood Rd., Jackson, MS 39211. Phone: (601) 957-1700. Fax: (601) 956-5228. E-mail: kdillon@telesouth.com. Web Site: www.telesouth.com; www.supertalkms.com. Steve Davenport, pres; Kim Dillon, mktg dir.

Comprises 30 affils in Mississippi & one in Tennessee. Represented by Kim Dillon.

University of Mississippi Football Network, 6311 Ridgewood Rd., Jackson, MS 39211. Phone: (601) 957-1700. Fax: (601) 956-5228. Steve Davenport, pres; Kim Dillon, mktg dir.

Comprises 30 affils in Mississippi & one in Tennessee. Represented by Tim Fritts.

Univision Radio, 3102 Oak Lawn Ave., Suite 215, Dallas, TX 75219. Phone: (214) 525-7700. Fax: (214) 525-7750. Web Site: www.univision.net.

Comprises 42 stns: seven in California, four in Florida, three in Illinois, two in Nevada, two in New York, 22 in Texas & two in Arizona. Represented by Katz Radio.

Virginia Radio Networks, 200 N. 22nd St., Richmond, VA 23223. Phone: (804) 474-6600. Fax: (804) 474-0168. Web Site: www.varadionetworks.com.

Serving Virginia News Network; Lawn & Garden Network (in Pennsylvania, North Carolina, South Carolina, Tennessee, Ohio, Kentucky, Virginia & West Virginia); Washington Redskins (in Pennsylvania, North Carolina, South Carolina, Virginia & West Virginia); VA AG Net.

WV Radio Corp. and Metronews Radio Network, Greer Bldg., 1251 Earl L. Core Rd., Morgantown, WV 26505. Phone: (304) 296-0029. Fax: (304) 296-3876. Web Site: www.wvmetronews.com.

Comprises West Virginia News (58 stns in West Virginia) & Mountaineer Sports Network (72 stns in West Virginia).

"The Weather Center", (A broadcast service of Aviation Weather Inc.). 701 Gervais St., Suite 150-224, Columbia, SC 29201. Phone: (803) 739-2827. E-mail: wxcenter@aviationweatherinc.com. Web Site: www.aviationweatherinc.com.

"Regional Radio Broadcast/Weathercast Network" across the Carolinas and Georgia in over 20 broadcast markets. Weather forecasting, site-specific broadcast services for stations all across America. 100% barter.

Western Agri-Radio Networks, (dba California Agri-Radio Network & Southwest Agri-Radio Network). 1700 S. 1st Ave., Suite 214, Yuma, AZ 85364. Phone: (928) 782-1440. Fax: (928) 782-1474. E-mail: ggatley@sprynet.com. Web Site: www.westernagri-radio.net.

Yuma, AZ 85364. Southwest Agri-Radio Network, 1700 S. 1st Ave, Suite 214. Phone: (800) 944-6077. Fax: (520) 782-1474. E-mail: ggatley@sprynet.com. Web Site: www.home.com/sprynet/ggatley.

Yuma, AZ 85364. California Agri-Radio Network, 1700 S. 1st Ave, Suite 214. Phone: (800) 944-6077. (520) 782-1440. Fax: (520) 782-1474. E-mail: ggatley@sprynet.com. Web Site: www.home.com/sprynet/ggatley.

Fifteen radio stations in California & two in Arizona. Represented by J.L. Famarkis.

Wisconsin Radio Network, 222 State St., Suite 401, Madison, WI 53703. Phone: (608) 251-3900. Fax: (608) 251-7233. E-mail: dforbis@learfield.com. Web Site: www.wrn.com. Dale Forbis, gen mgr.

Statewide satellite-delivered net providing Wisconsin news & sports.

Yancey AG Network, Box 1000, Oklahoma City, OK 73101. Phone: (405) 858-1400, ext. 267. Phone: (800) 327-6638. Web Site: www.farmnews.net. E-mail: waynegriggs@clearchannel.com. Ron Hays, progmg dir.

Comprises 54 stns: 11 in Arkansas, 13 in Louisiana, 17 in Mississippi, eight in Missouri, & five in Tennessee. Representative J.L. Farmakis

Radio News Services

ABC News
See ABC listing in National Radio Programming Services, this section.

AMI News, 50 Vashell Way, Suite 200, Orinda, CA 94563. Phone: (925) 254-4456. Fax: (925) 254-6135. E-mail: info@mountainviewnews.com. Web Site: www.theamigroup.com. Chad Dyer, VP/internet news svcs., Eastern Bureau. Phone: (800) 736-0370.

MP3 Wave phone- & tape-supplied features focusing on skiing, fishing, camping, travel & beach conditions with related news & information. Offered seasonally. Available on the Internet.

AccuWeather Inc., 385 Science Park Rd., State College, PA 16803. Phone: (814) 235-8600. Fax: (814) 235-8609. E-mail: info@accuwx.com. Web Site: www.accuweather.com. Dr. Joel N. Myers, pres; Gary Kemp, sls VP.

Coml weather service providing exclusive AccuWeather forecasts, top personalities & studio digital sound for radio plus internet content. Cash/barter.

Africa News Service Inc., 920 M St. S.E., Washington, DC 20003. Phone: (202) 546-0777. Fax: (202) 546-0676. Web Site: www.allafrica.com. Reed Kramer, CEO; Tamela Hultman, chief strategy off; Amrada Mahtar Ba, pres; Akwe Amosu, exec editor.

A news & info service on African affrs.

Agence France-Presse, 1015 15th St. N.W., Washington, DC 20005. Phone: (202) 289-0700. Fax: (202) 414-0525. E-mail: afp-usa@afp.com. Web Site: www.afp.com. Georges Biannic; Francis Kohn, chief editor; Gerry Aziakou, deputy editor; Mary Ann Carter, editor asst.

Produces a var of international news svcs, including text wires in six languages, photo wires, graphics & financial wires.

Alaska Public Radio Network, 810 E. Ninth Ave., Anchorage, AK 99501- 3826. Phone: (907) 277-2776. Fax: (907) 263-7450. E-mail: aprn@alaska.net. Web Site: www.aprn.org. Juneau, AK 99801. Juneau Alaska News Bureau, 530 Park St. Phone: (907) 586-6948. Dave Donaldson, state capitol bureau chief.

Washington, DC 20008. Washington, DC News Bureau, 2801 Quebec St. N.W, Suite 505. Phone: (202) 488-1961. Joel Southern, capitol bureau chief.

Satellite-delivered news/info programs to 26 member stations across Alaska from state-of-the-art studios, headquartered in Anchorage.

American Academy of Dermatology, Communications Dept., American Academy of Dermatology. Box 4014, Schaumburg, IL 60168-4014. Phone: (847) 330-0230. Fax: (847) 330-0050. Web Site: www.aad.org. Donna Stein, exec dir.

Washington, DC 20005-4355, 1350 I Street NW, Suite 870. Phone: (202) 842-3555. Fax: (202) 842-4355.

Expert physicians available for TV & radio interviews, audio & video tapes on skin cancer detection, as well as information on skin, hair and nail conditioning.

American Heart Association, 7272 Greenville Ave., Dallas, TX 75231-4596. Phone: (214) 373-6300. Fax: (214) 706-5243. Web Site: www.americanheart.org. Tim Elsner, dir.

Rsch & lifestyle reports, distributed by tape & live copy.

American Urban Radio Networks, 960 Penn Ave., Suite 200, Pittsburgh, PA 15222. Phone: (412) 456-4000. Fax: (412) 456-4040. Ronald R. Davenport, chmn; Jerry Lopes, pres; Glen Bryant, opns VP; Sydney Small, co chmn.

Chicago, IL 60601, 75 E. Wacker Dr, Suite 2600. Phone: (312) 558-9090. Fax: (312) 558-9280. Mike Davis, VP sls.

Gross Pointe, MI 48230, 1133 Whittier Rd. Phone: (313) 885-4243. Fax: (313) 885-2192. J.D. Mackay, dir. sls.

New York, NY 10017, 655 3rd Ave. Phone: (212) 883-2100. Fax: (212) 297-2571. Leon Cleveland, sr VP sls; Tom White, vp sls.

Info, news, sports & entertainment of special interest to Blacks & other minorities.

Associated Press Broadcast Services, 1825 K St. N.W., Washington, DC 20006-1202. Phone: (202) 736-1100. Fax: (202) 736-1199 (news). Fax: (202) 736-1124 (admin). Web Site: www.apbroadcast.com.

Real-time state, natl & international high-speed news wires; full-svc, coml-free radio nets; news mgmt software for TV & radio.

Radio Only.

Associated Press Network News
See Associated Press listing in Major National Radio Networks, this section.

Audio-Video News, 3622 Stanford Cir., Falls Church, VA 22041. Phone: (703) 354-6795. E-mail: connielawn@aol.com. Web Site: www.dcski.com. Connie Lawn,.

Covers major natl, international & specialty stories for radio & TV stns in the United States & around the world. Also live "inserts" into radio & TV shows.

The Berns Bureau, Box 2939, Washington, DC 20013-2939. Phone: (202) 314-5165. Fax: (202) 628-1432. Matt Kaye,.

Complete "localized" coverage of Washington, DC. Satellite ISDN & telephone transmission. Audio news releases. Govt, politics, farm, relg & other progmg for radio. Audio services for TV.

Black Radio Network Inc. (BRN), 166 Madison Ave., New York, NY 10016. Phone: (212) 686-6850. Fax: (212) 686-7308. Diane Levy, pres; Roy Thompson, VP/news dir; Bill Baldwin, bureau mgr New York; Peter Knight, sls VP; Sam Tucker, bureau mgr Washington; Sam Clark, bureau mgr Los Angeles.

Provides a daily actuality news service emphasizing minority-oriented items.

British Information Services, 845 Third Ave., New York, NY 10022. Phone: (212) 745-0395. Fax: (212) 758-5395. Web Site: www.britfm.com.

Provides daily audio news feed service filed by digital line from London at no cost to stns. Assists radio & TV crews visiting the United Kingdom.

Broadcast News Ltd., 36 King St. E., Toronto, ON M5C 2L9. Canada. Phone: (416) 364-3172. Fax: (416) 364-8896. Web Site: www.broadcastnews.ca. E-mail: info@broadcastnews.ca.

Full wire & audio svcs (news agency), satellite delivery for radio program syndicators.

Radio Only.

CBS News
See CBS listing in National Radio Programming Services, this section.

CNN Radio News, Westwood One Radio Networks, 40 W. 57th St., New York, NY 10019. Phone: (212) 641-2000. Fax: (212) 641-2185. Web Site: www.westwoodone.com. Fred Bennett, sr VP.

Top- & bottom-of-the-hour radio newscasts 24-hours a day plus business, sports & lifestyle updates.

Canada NewsWire Limited Broadcast Services, 20 Bay St. Waterpark Pl., Suite 1500, Toronto, ON M5J 2N8. Canada. Phone: (416) 863-9350. Fax: (416) 863-4825. E-mail: cnw@newswire.ca. Web Site: www.newswire.ca. Brian MacDonald, mgr.

Calgary, AB T2P 3C5 Canada, Gulf Canada Sq, 401 Ninth Ave. S.W., Suite 835. Phone: (403) 269-7605. Fax: (403) 263-7888. TWX: 03-824872. E-mail: Michle.dauphine@newswire.ca. Krista Wightman, mgr.

Vancouver, BC V6B 4NB Canada, 650 West Georgia St, Suite 1103. Phone: (604) 669-7764. Fax: (604) 669-4356. TWX: 04-508529. Larry Cardy, VP western Canada.

Halifax, NS B4A 1E6 Canada, Sun Tower, 1550 Bedford Hwy., Suite 420. Phone: (902) 422-1411. Fax: (902) 422-3507. TWX: 019-21534. E-mail: jgallant@newswire.ca. Robert Moffatt, mgr Atlantic Canada.

Ottawa, ON K1P 6A9 Canada, 255 Albert St, Suite 460. Phone: (613) 563-4465. Fax: (613) 563-0548. TWX: 053-3292. Hugh Johnson, VP natl capital rgn.

Montreal, PQ H3B 2J6 Canada, 1155 Rene Levesque Blvd. W, Suite 3310. Phone: (514) 878-2520. Fax: (514) 878-4451. TWX: 055-60936. E-mail: scmtl@newswire.ca. Elaire Carr, VP Quebec.

Distributor of video & radio news releases, features, PSA & corporate productions via satellite & hard copy.

Capital Television News Service (CTNS), 1629 S. St., Sacramento, CA 95814. Phone: (916) 446-7890. Fax: (916) 446-7893. E-mail: pacsat@pacsat.com. Web Site: www.pacsat.com. Steve Mallory, pres; Sabrina Demayo, reporter.

TV & radio service providing daily news coverage, via satellite, of California's capitol for TV & radio stns throughout the state.

Radio Only.

The Church of Jesus Christ of Latter-day Saints (Mormons), 50 East North Temple, Salt Lake City, UT 84150. Phone: (801) 240-4612. Fax: (801) 240-5449. E-mail: russelldg@chq.byu.edu. Web Site: www.lds.org. David S. Porter, radio rel mgr; R. Michael Purdy, TV rel mgr; Donald G. Russell, media rel.

Offers free pub affrs, news & feature progmg for TV & radio; also guests for talk shows. Pub affrs progmg is not church-oriented.

Compu-Weather Inc., 2566 Rt. 52, Hopewell Junction, NY 12533. Phone: (800) 284-7246. Fax: (845) 226-1918. E-mail: sales@compu-weather.com. Web Site: www.compu-weather.com. Jeff Wimmer, pres; Tore Jakobsen, VP.

Weather forecasts, features, info & actualities for TV & radio.

Congressional Quarterly Inc., 1255 22nd St. N.W., Washington, DC 20037. Phone: (202) 419-8500. Fax: (202) 728-1863. E-mail: clientservices@cq.com. Web Site: www.cq.com. Andrew Barnes, chmn; Andrew P. Corty, vice-chmn; Robert Merry, pres; David Rapp, exec editor.

Print & Web-based info products & svcs on govt, politics & current interest topics. Daily & wkly publications, reference books & newsletters.

Connecticut Weather Center Inc., 18 Woodside Ave., Danbury, CT 06810-7123. Phone: (203) 730-2899. Fax: (203) 730-2839. E-mail: weatherlab@ctweather.com. Web Site: www.ctweather.com. William Jacquemin, pres.

Weather forecasts for all media. Custom intros/outros/lives. Accurate forecasts. Barter or cash arrangement available.

Corus Radio Network, 700 W. Georgia St., Suite 2000, Vancouver, BC V7Y 1K9. Canada. Phone: (604) 331-2830. Fax: (604) 331-2722. E-mail: akrueger@cknw.com. Web Site: www.corusradio.network.com. Ray Dagg, sls; Allan Krueger, opns mgr; Gord MacDonarld, news dir; Mark Friesen, chief engr; Tom Plasteras, mgr.

Live & pre-recorded info & entertainment program production & satellite delivery to rgnl & natl Canadian radio stations.

Dairyline Radio, 1843 Front St., Suite A, Lynden, WA 98264. Phone: (360) 354-5596, EXT. 101. Fax: (360) 354-7517. E-mail: bbaker@dairyline.com. Web Site: www.dairyline.com. Lee Mielke, pres; Bill Baker, mktg dir. Wilmington, NC 28403-7224. DairyBusiness Communications, 7225 Wrightsville Ave, 204.

Lynden, WA 98264

Five minute & 9 1/2 minute Dairy Report- weekdays. Daily updates of news affecting the dairy industry.

ESPN/SportsTicker, 19 East 34th St.-7th Fl., New York, NY 10016. Phone: (212) 515-1298. Fax: (212) 515-1211. E-mail: newsroom@sportsticker.com. Web Site: www.sportsticker.com. John Mastroberardino, gen mgr; Lou Monaco, dir; Jim Morgantheler, gen mgr; Vin Bagnaturo, sls dir.

Boston, MA 02210, Boston Fish Pier, West Bldg. #1, Suite 302. Phone: (617) 951-0070. Fax: (617) 737-9960.

New York, NY 10158, 19 E 34th St. Phone: (212) 515-1000. Fax: (212) 515-1211.

24-hour sports news & information provider, instant scores & complete sports news coverage on all professional & major college events.

Earth Reports Environmental News Science, 18600 Queen Anne Rd, Upper Marlboro, MD 20774. Phone: (301) 249-8200. Fax: (301) 249-3613. E-mail: info@earthreports.org. Web Site: www.earthreports.org. Fred Tutman, pres.

Environmental news service offering actualities & specials.

Entertainment News Calendar, 250 W. 57th St., Suite #1431, New York, NY 10107. Phone: (212) 421-1370. Fax: (212) 563-3488. E-mail: editor@newscalendar.com. Web Site: www.newscalendar.com. Evelyn Heyward, editor.

Sherman Oaks, CA 91403. Hollywood News Calender, 15030 Ventura Blvd., Ste 742. Phone: (818) 990-5945. Carolyn Fox, publisher.

Daily entertainment news svc.

Fairchild Broadcast News, 405 E 42nd St, Suite 310, New York, NY 10012. Phone: (212) 593-3294. Fax: (212) 686-7308. Jay Levy, pres.

Gathers & disseminates news around the world.

Feature Story News, 1730 Rhode Island Ave., Suite 405, Washington, DC 20036. Phone: (202) 296-9012. Fax: (202) 296-9205. E-mail: markss@featurestory.com. Web Site: www.featurestory.com. Simon Marks, pres.

New York, NY 10036, 226 W. 47th St, 2nd floor. Phone: (212) 764-5848. Nathan King, correspondent.

Ind supplier of radio & TV news to English-language bcstrs worldwide. Bureaus in Washington, Moscow, London, New York, Tehran & Beijing.

Radio Only.

Hollywood News Calendar, 15030 Ventura Blvd., Suite 742, Sherman Oaks, CA 91403. Phone: (818) 990-5945. Phone: (818) 986-8186. Fax: (818) 789-8047. Web Site: www.newscalendar.com. Carolyn Fox, publisher; Susan Fox-Davis, editor.

New York, NY 10107. Entertainment News Calender, 250 W. 57th St, #1431. Phone: (212) 421-1370. Fax: (212) 563-3488. Carolyn Fox, publisher.

Daily entertainment news service.

Israel Broadcasting Service, 800 Second Ave., New York, NY 10017. Phone: (212) 499-5402. Fax: (212) 499-5425. E-mail: newyork@israel.org.

Free radio & TV programs, features from & about Israel.

Kyodo News International, 50 Rockefeller Plaza, 8th Fl., New York, NY 10020. Phone: (212) 397-3723. Fax: (212) 397-3721. E-mail: tmitsudome@kyodonews.com. Web Site: www.kyodo.co.jp. Toshi Mitsudome, VP.

Real time news service, emphasizing economic, business, sports & political coverage of Japan & Asia.

Medialink, 708 3rd Ave., New York, NY 10017. Phone: (212) 682-8300. Fax: (212) 682-5260. Web Site: www.medialink.com. E-mail: info@medialink.com. Lawrence Moskowitz, pres; Michele Wallace, opns VP.

London W1R 3AA, 37/38 Golden Sq. Phone: 44-71-240-3923. Jim Gold.

Los Angeles, CA 90028, 6430 Sunset Blvd, Suite 1100. Phone: (323) 465-0111.

San Francisco, CA 94111, One Maritime Plaza. Phone: (415) 296-8877. Fax: (415) 296-9929.

Washington, DC 20005, 1401 New York Ave. N.W, Suite 520. Phone: (202) 628-3800.

Atlanta, GA 30326, 3340 Peachtree Rd. N.E, Suite 1520. Phone: (404) 848-7500.

Chicago, IL 60611, The Time & Life Bldg., 541 N. Fairbanks Ct., Suite 1910. Phone: (312) 222-9850.

Dallas, TX 75244, 4851 LBJ Fwy, Suite 605. Phone: (972) 774-0200.

International video & audio PR, satellite feed and news advisory service. Advisories accessible by computer/newswire in United States & Europe.

Metro Networks/Shadow Broadcast Services, a Westwood One Co., 2800 Post Oak, Suite 4000, Houston, TX 77056. Phone: (713) 407-6000. Fax: (713) 407-6049. Web Site: www.westwoodone.com. Chuck Bortnick, pres; Scott Cody, mgr.

Los Angeles, CA 90048, 6420 Wilshire Blvd, 4th Fl. Phone: (323) 782-6150. Fax: (323) 782-6199. David Piper, news bureau chief.

San Diego, CA 92108, 591 Camino de la Reina, Suite 525. Phone: (619) 298-4300. Fax: (619) 298-1865. Gayle Newman, news bureau chief.

San Francisco, CA 94107, 185 Berry St, Suite 5503. Phone: (415) 974-1890. Fax: (415) 974-1171. Joe McConnell, news bureau chief.

Denver, CO 80211, 2460 W. 26th Ave, Suite 140-C. Phone: (303) 455-4355. Fax: (303) 455-1248. Robin Commons, news bureau chief.

Miami, FL 33169, 1111 Parkcentre Blvd, Suite 400. Phone: (305) 621-6387. Fax: (305) 621-6767. John Levitt, news bureau chief.

Atlanta, GA 30329, 2970 Clairmont Rd. N.E, Suite 780. Phone: (770) 290-1365. Fax: (770) 290-1371. Jim Ribble, news bureau chief.

Chicago, IL 60654, Merchandise Mart Plaza, Suite 1547. Phone: (312) 467-2900. Fax: (312) 467-2956. John Tomlinson, VP/gen mgr news.

Boston, MA 02114, 7 Bulfinch Pl, 4th Fl. Phone: (617) 742-2266. Fax: (617) 742-8464. Bob MacNeil, news bureau chief.

Philadelphia, PA 19127, 3901 Main St. Phone: (215) 509-7800. Fax: (215) 509-7680. Bill Yeager, VP news, sports & weather.

Houston, TX 77056, 2800 Post Oak Blvd, Suite 4000. Phone: (713) 407-6000. Fax: (713) 407-6749. Brian Hill, news bureau chief.

Provider of traf reporting svcs & leading supplier of loc news, sports, weather & video news svcs to the TV & radio bcst industries.

Metro Weather Service Inc., 71 So. Central Ave., Ste. 102, Valley Stream, NY 11580. Phone: (516) 568-8844. Fax: (516) 568-8853. E-mail: metrowx@aol.com. Web Site: www.metroweather.com. Pat Pagano, pres.

Tailored weather forecasts for radio & TV. Feature reports—farming, marine, ski, long-range forecasts—via phone, computer, fax, switched 56.

Mutual Broadcasting System/Mutual Radio News

See Mutual Broadcasting System listing under Westwood Radio Network in Major National Radio Networks, this section.

NOAA/National Weather Service, 1325 East-West Hwy., Silver Spring, MD 20910. Phone: (301) 713-0622. Fax: (301) 713-1292. Web Site: www.noaa.gov. Jack F. Kelly, dir NWS; Curtis Carey, dir pub aff.

Anchorage, AK 99513-7575, 222 W. Seventh Ave, Suite 23. Phone: (907) 271-5136. Fax: (907) 271-3711.

Honolulu, HI 96813, Mauka Tower, 737 Bishop St, Suite 2200. Phone: (808) 532-6416. Fax: (808) 532-5569. Richard H. Hagemeyer, dir Pacific rgn.

Kansas City, MO 64106-2897, 601 E. 12th St. Phone: (816) 426-5400. Fax: (816) 426-3270. Richard P. Augulis, dir central rgn.

Bohemia, NY 11716, 630 Johnson Ave. Phone: (516) 244-0100. Fax: (516) 244-0109. John T. Forsing, dir eastern rgn.

Fort Worth, TX 76102, 819 Taylor St. Phone: (978) 334-2668. (978) 334-2651. Fax: (978) 334-4187. X. William Proenza, dir southern rgn.

Salt Lake City, UT 84138-1102, NOAA Federal Bldg, 125 S. State St, Rm. 1210. Phone: (801) 524-5122. Fax: (801) 524-5270. Vickie Nadolski, dir western rgn.

Weather & flood warnings, forecasts & related info for the media & general pub.

Nemo News Service, 7179 Via Maria, San Jose, CA 95139. Phone: (408) 226-6339. Phone: (800) 243-8433. Fax: (408) 226-6403. E-mail: dickreizner@worldnet.att.net. Dick Reizner,.

On-assignment coverage of news & sporting events for radio & TV stns worldwide.

News Broadcast Network, 451 Park Ave S., New York, NY 10016. Phone: (212) 684-8919. Fax: (212) 684-9650. E-mail: info@newbroadcastnetwork.com. Web Site: www.newsbroadcastnetwork.com. Robert R. Hill, exec VP; Michael Hill, pres.

Washington Phone: (703) 893-4577. (202) 638-1603. Fax: (703) 893-6967. (202) 638-1607.

Los Angeles, CA Phone: (909) 621-6903. Fax: (909) 621-9492.

Chicago, IL Phone: (603) 963-4455. Fax: (603) 963-4487.

Seattle, WA Phone: (206) 624-7505. Fax: (206) 624-7556.

Milwaukee, WI Phone: (414) 321-6210. Fax: (414) 321-3608.

Production & distribution of electronic news releases, actualities & pub affrs programs distributed by satellite, telephone & tape.

North American Network, 7910 Woodmont Ave., Suite 1400, Bethesda, MD 20814. Phone: (301) 654-9810. Fax: (301) 654-9828. Web Site: www.radiospace.com. Tom Sweeney, pres; Tammy Van Don Sellaar, VP.

Audio news releases & talk show interviews. On-site coverage for corps, govt agencies & assns.

RWN Communications Inc., Box 15688, Baton Rouge, LA 70895-5688. Phone: (225) 928-4302. Fax: (225) 928-2102. E-mail: radioweather@cox.net. Web Site: www.radioweather.com. Tony Doherty, pres.

Specialized weather forecasts, weather info service bcst to radio stns; barter.

Radio America, 1030 15th St. N.W., Ste 1040, Washington, DC 20005. Phone: (202) 408-0944. Fax: (202) 408-1087. E-mail: radioa@radioamerica.org. Web Site: www.radioamerica.org. James C. Roberts, pres; Rich McFadden, news dir.

Short & long-form programs, special series, documentaries, daily one-hour news show.

Radio Press News Service, 8633 Arbor Dr., El Cerrito, CA 94530-2728. Phone: (510) 524-9559. Fax: (510) 459-0000. E-mail: jag4jl@aol.com. J.L. Levit, CEO; R.M. Master, VP.

Natl coverage, with special unit for northern California, Bay Area of California & adjacent states, photographer on staff. Multimedia news, *Travellands* & *Vacationland*. Special features, articles, transcriptions, video features.

Radio Pulsebeat News, Box 418, Hewlett, NY 11557. Phone: (212) 686-6850. Fax: (212) 686-7308. Jay R. Levy,.

Gen actuality news service.

RadioTour.com, 2233 Wisconsin Ave. N.W., Washington, DC 20007. Phone: (202) 333-4904. Fax: (202) 342-5411. Web Site: www.expertclick.com.

Publisher of free *Yearbook of Experts, Authorities & Spokespersons*.

Reuters America Inc., 1333 H St. N.W., Washington, DC 20005. Phone: (202) 898-8300. Fax: (202) 898-8383. Web Site: www.reuters.com. Steve Ginsburg, editor-in-charge (bcst svcs & online); Rob Doherty, bureau chief; Mitch Koppelman, VP; David Weissler, assignment editor.

The Reuter Broadcast Report & Reuter Broadcast PLUS, features natl & international news, sports, business news, entertainment & weather.

Skywatch Weather Center, 347 Prestley Rd., Bridgeville, PA 15017. Phone: (800) SKY-WATCH. Fax: (412) 221-3160. E-mail: airsci@skywatchweather.com. Web Site: www.skywatchweather.com. Dr. Stanley Penkala, pres.

Taped, live & MP3 weathercasts targeted to the listing area, in stn-specified formats. Featuring accuracy, clarity & mature voices.

The Sports Network, 2200 Byberry Rd., Hatboro, PA 19040. Phone: (215) 441-8444. Fax: (215) 441-5767. Web Site: www.sportsnetwork.com. Mickey Charles, pres/CEO; Phil Sokol, dir opns; Bruce Michaels, dir in technology; Jim Gillis, mgng editor; Ken Zajac, sls dir; Kevin Spiegel, dir Internet content; Rob Dougherty, dir information svcs.

International real-time sports wire svc providing content, branded web pages, satellite and/or computer feeds directly to broadcasters (radio & TV), print, Internet sites, wireless with state of the art technology.

Studio M Productions, 4032 Wilshire Blvd., Ste 403, Los Angeles, CA 90010. Phone: (888) 389-7372. Fax: (213) 389-3299. E-mail: senator@sound4film-tv.com. Web Site: www.sound4film-tv.com. Mike Michaels, gen mgr.

Honolulu, HI 96830, 8715 Waikiki Stn. Phone: (888) 389-7372. Fax: (213) 389-3299. E-mail: senator@sound4film-tv.com. Web Site: www.sound4film-tv.com.

Stringers, crew news, sports, features, remote bcsts, engrs, announcers, reporters & equipment for radio, TV, film & video.

Texas State Networks, 1080 Ballpark Way, Arlington, TX 76011. Phone: (817) 543-5400. Fax: (817) 543-5572. E-mail: tsnnews@cbs.com. Web Site: www.tsnradio.com. Jerry Bobo, pres; Tony Bishop, gen sls mgr; Julius Graw, dir news & opns; Kirk Kinder, satellite distro; Dan Bell, affil rel.

Austin, TX 78701. Austin News Bureau, 502 E. 11th, Suite 320. Phone: (512) 474-5264 (NEWS). (512) 474-5275 (SALES). Robert Wood, dir.

News service of the Texas State Networks. Provides Texas news, sports, agriculture, business & weather, Texas Rangers Radio Network & special features & long form programs.

The Nasdaq Stock Market, 9513 Key West Ave., Rockville, MD 20850. Phone: (202) 728-8884. Fax: (202) 728-6993. Web Site: www.nasdaqnews.com. E-mail: nasdaqnew@nasdaq.com. Scott Peterson, dir media rel.

Free daily stock market reports tailored for loc & rgnl audiences. Voicers with Nasdaq market data & financial analysis.

Trans World Communications Inc., Box 418, Hewlett, NY 11557. Phone: (212) 686-6850. Fax: (212) 686-7308. Jay Levy, pres.

Produces audio news svcs for radio & TV bcstg.

United Press International Inc., 1510 H St. N.W., Washington, DC 20005. Phone: (202) 898-8000. Fax: (202) 898-8057. Web Site: www.upi.com. John O'Sullivan,.

Full global text, audio, photo news & info svcs 24-hours a day. Morning drive progmg. 24-hours world, natl news, sports, weather, features, financial reports.

VNU Entertainment News Wire, 100 Boylston St., Suite 210, Boston, MA 02116. Phone: (617) 482-9447. Fax: (617) 482-9562. Web Site: www.vnuenw.com.

Advance news from VNU owned publications.

Views and People in the News (VP News), 1212 Fifth Ave., New York, NY 10029. Phone: (212) 876-6503. Fax: (212) 876-6503. Arthur Gary, editor.

Other offices located in Chicago, Los Angeles & San Francisco. News svcs to radio stns currently serving more than 100,000 subs; sells syndicated less than half-hour radio shows.

TV-CATV only.

WINGS: Women's International News Gathering Service, Box 95090, Vancouver, BC BC V5T 4T8. Canada. Phone: (604) 876-6994. Web Site: www.wings.org. E-mail: wings@wings.org. Frieda Werden, producer.

Austin, TX 78764, Box 33220. Stacy Pettigrew, bureau mgr.

Syndicate audio news & current affrs program, both produced in-house & acquired, focus on women & hard news. Distribution CD, satellite, & FTP.

Radio News Services

The Wall Street Journal Radio Network, 1155 Avenue of the Americas, 8th Fl., New York, NY 10036. Phone: (800) 828-6397. E-mail: wsjradio@dowjones.com. Web Site: www.wsjradio.com.

Hourly business & financial news reports transmitted live via satellite 18 times daily from the Journal's New York newsroom. Dow Jones Money Report also transmitted 18 times daily.

"The Weather Center", (a broadcast service of Aviation Weather Inc.). 701 Gervais St., Suite 150-224, Columbia, SC 29201. Phone: (803) 739-2827. E-mail: wxcenter@aol.com. Web Site: www.aviationweatherinc.com. L.R. Ferguson, pres.

"Regional Radio Broadcast/Weathercast Network" across the Carolinas and Georgia in over 20 broadcast markets. Weather forecasting, site-specific broadcast services for stations all across America. 100% barter.

Weather-One, (A wholly-owned division of Liberty Hill Broadcasting). 31800 Northwestern Hwy., Suite 100, Farmington Hills, MI 48334. Phone: (248) 737-3000. Fax: (248) 737-3555. E-mail: barryzate@aol.com. Barry Zate, sr VP.

Provides weather forecasting svcs, advanced storm warnings, agricultural & ski info to radio stns.

WeatherData Inc., 245 N. Waco, Suite 310, Wichita, KS 67202. Phone: (316) 265-9127. Fax: (316) 265-1949. Web Site: www.weatherdata.com. Mike Smith, CEO.

Weather radar, graphic & info display systems, training, on air forecast & storm warning svcs. Select Warn, Storm Hawk, 24/7 storm monitoring, & customer svc. Complete system integration & training.

Evan Weiner Productions, 370 Claremont Ave., Mount Vernon, NY 10552. Phone: (914) 667-9070. Phone: (203) 288-2597 (producer). Fax: (914) 667-3043. E-mail: evan4256@aol.com. Web Site: www.bickley.com/evan_weiner.html. Evan Weiner, exec producer; Gary Chester, on-air talent & legal department; Don Barberino, producer.

Sports commentaries & reporting. Current program: The Business of Sports, commentaries on Metro Source.

Westwood One Producers, Radio New Services. 40 W. 57th St., New York, NY 10019. Phone: (212) 641-2000. Fax: (212) 641-2185. Web Site: www.westwoodone.com. Shane Cappola, CEO; Jacque Tortoroli, CFO; Paul Bronstein, sr VP; Gary Yusko, sr VP; Peter Kosann, exec VP.

Culver City, CA 90232-2689, 9540 Washington Blvd. Phone: (310) 204-5000. Fax: (310) 840-4380.

Valencia, CA 91355, 25060 W. Ave. Stanford, Suite 100. Phone: (805) 294-9000. Fax: (805) 294-9380.

Atlanta, GA 30361, 1201 Peachtree St. N.W., 400 Colony Sq., Suite 200. Phone: (404) 870-9084. Fax: (404) 870-9085. Susan Bravman, AE.

Chicago, IL 60601, 111 E. Wacker Dr, Suite 2900. Phone: (312) 938-0222. Fax: (312) 616-8140. Ted S. Jakubiak, VP Midwest sls.

Troy, MI 48084, 3250 W. Big Beaver, Suite 139. Phone: (248) 649-0960. Fax: (248) 649-1584. Dave A. Gneiser, VP Detroit sls.

Dallas, TX 75231, 7577 Ramblin Rd, Suite 1462. Phone: (214) 373-0022. Fax: (214) 373-0511.

Arlington, VA 22202, 1755 S. Jefferson Davis Hwy. Phone: (703) 413-8300. Fax: (703) 413-8445.

Producer & distributor of radio progmg including CNN, NBC, Mutual, CNBC Business Radio, 24-hour music formats, long-short-form talk, music & news programs.

World Radio Network, Box 1212, London SW8 2ZF. United Kingdom. Phone: 44-20-7896-9000. Fax: 44-20-7896-9008. E-mail: email@wrn.org. Web Site: www.wrn.org. Karl Miosga, mngg dir; Tim Ashburner, dir tech opns; Jeff Cohen, dev dir.

Boston, MA 02125, 11 Rockmere St. Phone: (617) 436-9024. Sue Schardt, North American rep.

WRN Network One (via Galaxy 5) news & features ch, comprises live progmg segments in English & languages from more than 20 international bcstrs. Also supplies many customized progmg feeds to radio stns.

Radio Format Providers

ABC Radio Networks, 13725 Montfort Dr., Dallas, TX 75240. Phone: (972) 991-9200. Fax: (972) 776-4640. Web Site: www.abcradionetwork.com. John Hare, pres; Julie Atherton, dir mktg.

Los Angeles, CA 90068, 3575 Cahuenga Blvd, Suite 555. Phone: (213) 845-1050. Fax: (213) 851-0341.

San Francisco, CA 94111, 900 Front St. Phone: (415) 954-8675. Fax: (415) 956-2983.

Atlanta, GA 30305, 3060 Peachtree Rd. N.W, Suite 1470. Phone: (404) 841-1055. Fax: (404) 841-1066.

Chicago, IL 60601, 333 N. Michigan, Suite 1615. Phone: (312) 899-4058. Fax: (312) 899-4089.

Southfield, MI 48075, 3000 Town Ctr, Suite 2910. Phone: (248) 304-4393. Fax: (248) 304-4390. (Detroit office).

New York, NY 10019, 825 Seventh Ave., 4th Fl. Phone: (212) 456-1777. Fax: (212) 456-1899. Linda Ruggiero, affil mktg.

Dallas, TX 75240, 13725 Montfort Dr. Phone: (972) 991-9200. Fax: (972) 448-3395.

Kingstowne, VA 22315, 7687 Lavenham Landing. Phone: (703) 922-5400. Fax: (703) 922-5402. (Washington office).

Bcsts five full-service line nets, Paul Harvey News & Comment, ESPN Radio, long-form progmg, 24-hour formats, ABC News, ABC Sports, & d/wkly features.

Alternative Programming, 4215 Brendenwood Rd., Rockford, IL 61107. Phone: (800) 231-2818. Fax: (815) 229-5043. E-mail: altprog@aol.com. Gary A. Knoll, pres.

Complete music formats for radio - current music for various formats - custom CD service.

American Blues Network, Box 6216, Gulfport, MS 39506. Phone: (800) 896-5307, ext 117.

American Comedy Network & Onion Radio News, 91 River St., Milford, CT 06460. Phone: (203) 877-8210. Fax: (203) 877-8242. E-mail: acn@americancomedynetwork.com. Web Site: www.americancomedynetwork.com. Adrienne Munos, sls; Kurt Luchs, gen mgr; Ben Churchill, producer.

Comedy service providing daily topical audio sound bites, song parodies, fake commercials. Comedy CD, email prep and gold library. Onion Radio News 10 features every week via web and more.

Toby Arnold & Associates, 3234 Commander Dr., Carrollton, TX 75006. Phone: (972) 661-8200. Phone: (800) 527-5335. Fax: (972) 250-6014. E-mail: toby@taamusic.com. Web Site: www.taamusic.com. Toby Arnold, pres/CEO; Dolly Arnold, VP & COO; Lawrence Mangiameli, VP & dir.

Audio Production libraries for radio. Station Imaging, Morning show promo sweeper, stager packages for all formats. Cash or Barter.

Bailey Broadcasting Services, 655 N. Central Ave, 17th Fl., Glendale, CA 91203. Phone: (818) 649-7865. Fax: (818) 649-7501. E-mail: bbsradio@leebailey.com. Web Site: www.leebailey.com. Lee Bailey, pres.

Produces & syndicates d/wkly urban oriented entertainment: music info programs & specials.

The Beethoven Satellite Network, (BSN Around the Clock). 5400 N. St. Louis Ave., Chicago, IL 60625. Phone: (773) 279-2112. Fax: (773) 279-7199. Web Site: www.wfmt.com. Carol Martinez, mgr; Terry Medina, mgr; Steve Robinson, sr VP.

Satellite-delivered classical mus format service 24-hours daily serving over 300 outlets nationwide. Produced by WFMT-FM Chicago. Since 1986.

Satellite: Galaxy 6, Digital frequency B72.4.

CBS Radio Networks, 524 West 57th St., New York, NY 10019. Phone: (212) 975-2044. Fax: (212) 974-0615. E-mail: barobinson@cbs.com. Web Site: www.westwoodone.com. Beth Robinson, VP progmg.

This division currently offers NFL Football, NCAA Basketball & College Football. Also syndicates David Letterman's Top Ten List.

CRN International Inc., One Circular Ave., Hamden, CT 06514. Phone: (203) 288-2002. Fax: (203) 281-3291. E-mail: crn1995@aol.com. Web Site: www.crnradio.com. Barry Berman, pres; S. Richard Kalt, exec VP; Patrick Kane, sr VP; Doug Harris, dir.

Features include Ski Watch®, a 60-second, daily ski conditions update. Summer-oriented progmg includes Beach Watch® & Summer Watch.® Small business programs include the Small Business Report & Small Business Profile. All programs available on a barter basis.

Christmas Music Networks, 11000 W. 96th Terr., Overland Park, KS 66214-2258. Fax: (913) 492-7941. E-mail: xmasnet@sbcglobal.net. Ross Reagan, pres; John Jessup, VP.

"The best Christmas music progmg available." 36-hours of digitally-produced Christmas Eve & Christmas Day progmg. Four different formats: Adult contemp, news/talk, oldies & country.

The Classical Station, WCPE, Box 897, Wake Forest, NC 27588. Phone: (919) 556-5178. Fax: (919) 556-9273. E-mail: wcpe@wcpe.org. Web Site: theclassicalstation.org. Deborah S. Proctor, gen mgr.

Free 24-hour classical music progmg with live announcers for radio, cable, other distributors. Weekly request programs, opera and features.

Creative Radio Network, Box 7749, Thousand Oaks, CA 91359. Phone: (818) 991-3892. Fax: (818) 991-3894. Darwin Lamm, pres.

Radio music program for A/C—country & modern. Elvis international form magazine.

Dialogue, One Woodrow Wilson Plaza, 1300 Pennsylvania Ave., N.W., Washington, DC 20004-3027. Phone: (202) 691-4146. Fax: (202) 691-4141. E-mail: dialogue@wwic.si.edu. Web Site: www.wilsoncenter.org/dialogue. Rachel Edmonds, producer; John Tyler, dir; George Liston Seay, exec producer.

Wkly half-hour program of conversations on natl, internatl affrs, history & culture. Available to pub & coml stns free of charge on CD. Progmg produced by the Woodrow Wilson International Center for Scholars.

Eagle Media Productions Ltd., Box 580, Northford, CT 06472. Phone: (203) 294-1190. Fax: (203) 294-9512. E-mail: louadler@ix.netcom.com. Web Site: www.louadler.com. Louis Adler, pres; Thalia Adler, VP/gen mgr.

Offers Medical Journal, 90-second feature-barter; CD delivery.

Excelsior Radio Networks, 116 E. 27th St., New York, NY 10016. Phone: (212) 679-3200. Fax: (212) 681-1952. E-mail: robscolaro@aol.com. Michael R. Ewing, pres/COO; Jonathan Goldman, exec VP.

Las Vegas, NV 89119, 1445 E. Tropicana Ave. Phil Hall, gen mgr.

Sports talk 24-hours a day. Sports analysis & commentary on AOL & the internet.

Executive Broadcast Services, 5015 Farthing Dr., Colorado Springs, CO 80906. Phone: (719) 579-6676. Fax: (719) 579-6664. E-mail: skip@executivebroadcast.com. Web Site: www.executivebroadcast.com. Skip Joeckel, pres.

Markets & sells a select line of programs, products & svcs to U.S. radio stns.

Far West Communications Inc., 2401 Rockdell St., La Crescenta, CA 91214-1738. Phone: (818) 248-2400. Fax: (818) 248-2596. E-mail: farwestinc@aol.com. Paul J. Ward, gen mgr; Skip Joeckel, mktg dir; Paul J. Ward, pres; Ron Blassnig, chief engr.

Formats: Gold Plus, 30 Plus, True Country, True Country II, Modern MOR. Svcs: MASTERDISC, custom song libraries on CD; delivery on analog tape, CD, DAT.

Fischer Broadcast Services, 10841 Bittersweet Lane, Fishers, IN 46038-2203. Phone: 317-514-5757. Fax: (317) 578-3884. E-mail: superfisch@mindspring.com. Web Site: www.superfisch.com. Scott Fischer, pres.

SUPERFISCH—THE PROMO VOICE SUPERHERO. Scott Fischer, signature voice artist for DirecTV Sports, Fox Sports Net Networks, and other fine affiliates. Myriad reads—always right! ISDN/MP3.

Ghostwriters/Radio Mall, 2412 Unity Ave. N., Dept BR, Minneapolis, MN 55422-3450. Phone: 763-522-6256. Fax: 763-522-6256. E-mail: info@radiomall.com. Web Site: www.radiomall.com. David Dworkin, owner.

Over 18 years experience with products sold to more than 6,500 radio stations worldwide as well as TV stations, audio-video producers, and cable operators. If you have a finished product that you'd like to market to radio stations, contact us. We offer a 60-day money-back guarantee.

Globe Productions, Box 20465, Roanoke, VA 24018. Phone: (540) 344-3283. E-mail: recordial@yahoo.com. J.W. Sheperd, pres & owner.

Audio restoration & preservation services.

Hispanic Radio Network Inc., 740 National Press Bldg., Washington, DC 20045. Phone: (202) 637-8800. Fax: (202) 637-8801. E-mail: jeff@hrn.org. Web Site: www.hrn.org. Jeff Kline, chmn/CEO.

Washington, DC 20005, 1030 50th St, Suite 400. Phone: (202) 637-8800. Sebastian Puente, bureau chief.

Melbourne, FL 32901, 909 E. New Haven Ave. Ilia Leon, dir affil communications.

Produces & syndicates five daily Spanish radio programs, news with natl, rgnl & statewide adv available free to stns.

J.N. Productions, 902-1790 Bayshore Dr., Vancouver, BC V6G 3G5. Canada. Phone: 604-331-0690. E-mail: info@jnproductions.bc.ca. Web Site: www.jnproductions.bc.ca. Jakob Nortman, pres.

For all your voiceover needs, including narration, corporate videos, on-hold telephone messages and announcements for GPS systems. Radio production facilities available.

Jameson Broadcast Inc., 1644 Hawthorne St., Sarasota, FL 34239. Phone: (941) 906-8800. Fax: (941) 906-8801. E-mail: jamie@jamesonbcast.com. Web Site: www.jamesonbroadcast.com/radio.

Specializes in short-form entertainment, info programs & promotions.

Jones MediaAmerica Inc., 11 W. 42nd St., 28th Fl., New York, NY 10036. Phone: (212) 302-1100. Fax: (212) 556-9402.

Los Angeles, CA 91403, 15233 Ventura Blvd, Penthouse 8. Phone: (818) 986-8500. Brenda Holland, mgng dir western rgn; Daniel Depercin, natl account mgr.

Marathon Shores, FL 33050, 11399 Overseas Hwy. Phone: (305) 289-4524. Judy Langley, natl account mgr S.E.

Chicago, IL 60611, 401 N. Michigan Ave, Suite 1200. Phone: (312) 840-8260. Michael Soifer natl account mgr; Dave Simon, natl acc mgr.

Nashville, TN 37212, 1110 16th Ave. S. John Alexander, mus mktg mgr.

MediaAmerica is the largest independent marketer of natl radio programs in the United States. MAI represents over 70 radio programs servicing the following formats: AOR, modern rock, CHR, urban, country, AC, news info, class, jazz/new age, talk, 24-hour satellite delivered & sports progmg.

Jones Radio Networks, (A Jones Media Networks Company). 8200 S. Akron St., Suite 103, Centennial, CO 80112. Phone: (303) 784-8700. Web Site: www.jonesradio.com. Bob Hampton, pres; Phil Barry, gen mgr; Susan Stephens, dir; Patrick Crocker, dir; Amy Bolton, dir; Jim LaMarca, VP.

New York, NY 10036. New York office, 11 W. 42nd St, 28th Fl. Phone: (888) 644-8255.

Seattle, WA 98121. Seattle office, 2211 5th Ave. Phone: (800) 426-9082.

Premiere producer of 24-hr. format progmg, daypart personality programs & various music svcs to radio stns.

Launch Radio Networks, (a division of United Stations Radio Network). 58 W. 40th St., 4th Fl, New York, NY 10018. Phone: (212) 536-3600. Fax: (212) 536-6801. Web Site: www.launchradionetworks.com. E-mail: programming@launchradionetworks.com. Dave Ankers, pres; Charlie Colombo, exec VP; Dia Stein, progmg dir; Dan Brassem, dir.

Launch Radio Networks produces, distributes music, entertainment news & svcs for radio stns as well as other media worldwide.

Liberty Works Radio Network, 12 Carroll St., Reisterstown, MD 21136. Phone: (410) 876-0002. Fax: (410) 857-2854. E-mail: info@libertyworksradio.com. Web Site: www.libertyworksradio.com.

24 hours, seven days a week, total network serving radio stns nationwide. News on the hour & half-hour available to stns at no charge.

MRN Radio (Motor Racing Network), 1801 W. International Speedway Blvd., Daytona Beach, FL 32114. Phone: (386) 947-6400. Fax: (386) 947-6716. E-mail: mrn-radio@mrnnet.com. Web Site: www.mrnradio.com.

Live bcsts of NASCAR stock car racing & related programs via satellite.

J J McKay Productions Inc., 3240 S. Newcombe St., Denver, CO 80227. Phone: (303) 980-1948. J.J. McKay, pres.

Maximum-impact production and versatile voice-over talent. All formats. Choose the voice for today AND tomorrow! Delivered via analog tape, DAT, ISDN/Zephyr, MP3, DCI.

Broadcasting & Cable Yearbook 2006

Radio Format Providers

Miller Broadcast Management, 616 W. Fulton St., Suite 516, Chicago, IL 60661. Phone: (312) 454-1111. Fax: (312) 454-0044. Web Site: info@millerbroadcast.com. Lisa Miller, pres; Matt Miller, VP.

Music & Entertainment News, 4775 Durham Rd., Guilford, CT 06437-3607. Phone: (203) 457-1039. E-mail: mlund@snet.net. Michael Paul Lund, pres.

Featurette licensed to big band, nostalgia & easy lstng stns across the country includes audio trivia incorporated into questions about radio & TV, music personalities & nostalgia of all kinds. Music entertainment news.

Musical Starstreams, Box 12685, LaJolla, CA 92037-2685. Phone: (619) 276-8989. Fax: (619) 276-0918. E-mail: forest@starstreams.com. Web Site: www.starstreams.com.

Musical Starstreams is a wkly two-hour program of "exotic electronica" targeted to adults age 25-54.

Orange Productions, 523 Righters Ferry Rd., 1st Fl., Bala Cynwyd, PA 19004. Phone: (610) 667-8620. Fax: (610) 667-8939. E-mail: orange@snip.net. Web Site: www.soundsofsinatra.com. Sid Mark, pres; Jon Harmelin, VP/gen mgr; Brian Mark, opns mgr.

Production & distribution of a wkly two-hour program *Sounds of Sinatra*.

Premiere Radio Networks Inc., 15260 Ventura Blvd., Fifth Floor, Sherman Oaks, CA 91403-5339. Phone: (818) 377-5300. Fax: (818) 377-5333. E-mail: webmaster@premrad.com. Web Site: www.premrad.com. Kraig T. Kitchin, pres/COO; Larry Morgan Sr., sr VP; Jennifer Leimgruber, sr VP; Lark Hadley, exec VP; Greg Noack, exec VP; Gary Krantz, VP opns.

Sherman Oaks, CA 91403, 15260 Ventura Blvd. Phone: (818) 377-5300. Theresa Gage, sr VP/western sls.

San Francisco, CA 94105, 100 Spear St, Suite 300. Phone: (415) 281-2421. John Breen, mgr/northwest sls.

Troy, MI 48083, 100 E. Big Beaver Rd, Suite 900. Phone: (248) 526-4100. Michael Berman, VP/Detroit sls.

Atlanta, GA 30309, 1819 Peachtree Rd. N.E, Suite 427. Phone: (404) 367-8493. Alex Coessens, VP/southern sls.

Chicago, IL 60611, 875 N. Michigan Ave, Suite 1450. Phone: (312) 266-3870. Jon Viola, VP/Midwest sls.

New York, NY 10020, 1270 Ave. of the Americas. Phone: (212) 445-3900. Catherine Mongarella, sr VP/eastern sls.

Dallas, TX 75243, 12655 N. Central Expwy, Suite 800. Phone: (972) 239-6220. Kim Hunter, sr VP/southwest sls.

Premiere Radio features the following personalities: Rush Limbaugh, Dr. Laura Schlessinger, Jim Rome, Rick Dees, Casey Kasem, Dr. Dean Edell, Bob (Kevoian) & Tom (Griswold), Phil Hendrie, Leeza Gibbons, Michael Reagan, George Noory, Blair Garner, Carson Daly, John Boy & Billy, Matt Drudge, Kidd Kraddick, Glenn Beck & others.

RPM Radio Programming and Management Inc., 1133 West Long Lake Rd., Bloomfield Hills, MI 48302. Phone: (800) 521-2537. Phone: (248) 647-1068. Fax: (248) 647-3936. E-mail: rpmorlk@aol.com. Web Site: www.tophitsusa.com. Thomas M. Krikorian, pres.

Top Hits USA wkly CD svc & CD libraries including Solid Gold, Spectrum A/C & Country One. Classic rock, CD Christmas library.

Radio Center for People with Disabilities (RCPD), 680 N. Lake Shore Dr., Suite 1230, Chicago, IL 60611. Phone: (312) 640-5000. Fax: (312) 640-5010. Brad Saul, CEO.

New City, NY 10956, 2 Settlers Ct. Phone: (914) 634-9140. Susan Null-Berman, VP sls.

Produce & syndicate shows:*CyberReports, Real Estate USA, Furniture Guys, Home Ranger, The Group Room, Real Estate Minute*. We also place adv on ATM's across the country, on Norwegian Cruise Lines & on Northwest Airlines.

Radio Express Inc., 1415 W. Magnolia Blvd., Suite 201, Burbank, CA 91506. Phone: (818) 295-5800. Fax: (818) 295-5801. Web Site: www.radioexpress.com. Tom Rounds, CEO; John Fleck, pres.

Distributors outside the United States: *The World Chart Show, Rick Dees Weekly Top 40, Country Countdown, Hot Mix, Hitdisc, Golddisc, Supercharger Production tool kit & Production libraries by firstcom music*. Programs available by cash or barter, libraries & products cash only.

Radio Spirits, 2 Ridgedale Ave., Cedar Knolls, NJ 07927. Phone: (973) 539-7557. Fax: (847) 524-8245. Web Site: www.radiospirits.com. Hakan Lindskog, pres.

Radio producers of the nationally-syndicated old time radio program *When Radio Was*. Complete digital recording studio features Sonic Solutions Digital Work Station with No-Noise.

SFX Radio Network, Clear Channel Entertainment, 220 W. 42nd St., New York, NY 10036. Phone: (917) 421-4000. Web Site: www.sfxnet.com.

Offers both wkly & mthy shows featuring classic rock, country, urban contemp & live concerts in addition to stn prep svcs.

Salem Music Network Inc., (A division of Salem Music Networks/Salem Radio Network). 402 BNA Dr., Suite 400, Nashville, TN 37217. Phone: (615) 367-2210. Fax: (615) 367-0758. E-mail: info@salemmusicnetwork.com. Web Site: www.salemmusicnetwork.com. Michael S. Miller, gen mgr; Greg Anderson, pres.

Dickson, TN 37055. Dickson, 204 N. Main St, Suite 10. Phone: (615) 740-9879. Fax: (615) 740-7799. E-mail: terry@solidgospel.com. Web Site: www.solidgospel.com. Carl Campbell, stn mgr; Michael S. Miller, gen mgr.

Murfreesboro, TN 37130. Murfreesboro, 312 S. Church St. Phone: (615) 890-3233. Fax: (615) 890-2990. E-mail: kevin@solidgospel.com. Web Site: www.solidgospel105.com. Kevin R. Anderson, stn mgr; Michael S. Miller, gen mgr.

Irving, TX 75063. Texas, Salem Radio Nework, 6400 Beltline Rd. Phone: (972) 831-1920. Fax: (972) 831-8626. Greg Anderson, gen mgr.

Provider of three different 24-hour Christian music formats via digital satellite to 230+ radio stations throughout the US and Canada, and operator of two greater Nashville (TN) radio stations.

Semaphore Entertainment Group (SEG), 32 E. 57th St., 7th Fl., New York, NY 10022. Phone: (212) 371-6850. Fax: (212) 888-8650. Web Site: www.seg.com.

Produces & distributes cable progmg.

Sheridan Broadcasting Corp., 960 Penn Ave., Suite 200, Pittsburgh, PA 15222. Phone: (412) 456-4008. Phone: (800) 456-4211. Fax: (412) 456-4040 (progmg). Fax: (412) 457-4077 (admin). Ronald Davenport, chmn.

Provides hourly news & sports, longform talk & mus progmg as well as *USA Music Magazine*. Other alternative progmg includes *Coming Soon* movie review, *Straight Up* with Bev Smith & *White House Report* with White House correspondent April Ryan.

Sirius Satellite Radio, 1221 Ave. of the Americas, 36th Fl., New York, NY 10020. Phone: (212) 584-5100. Fax: (212) 584-5200. Web Site: www.sirius.com.

Southcott Productions, Box 33185, Granada Hills, CA 91343. Phone: (818) 368-4938. Fax: (818) 368-4938. E-mail: mylradio@aol.com. Web Site: www.musicofyourlife.com. Chuck Southcott, owner.

North Hollywood, CA 91602, 4605 Lankershim Blvd, Suite 702. Phone: (818) 755-9952. Chuck Southcott, program dir.

Adult pop standards, progmg hqtrs for *Music of Your Life Radio Network*. Talent includes: Gary Owens, Wink Martindale, Peter Marshall, Pat Boone, Johnny Magnus, Ken Young & Les Brown Jr.

TM Century Inc., 2002 Academy, Dallas, TX 75234. Phone: (972) 406-6800. Fax: (972) 406-6890. E-mail: tmci@tmcentury.com. Web Site: www.tmcentury.com. David Graupner, pres/CEO; Eve Mayer Orsburn, VP Sales & Marketing.

GoldDisc music libraries, HitDisc wkly mus service, mus on hard drive, jingles, mus libraries production, special programs, CD-ROM.

Talkline Communications Network, Box 20108, Park West Station, New York, NY 10025-1510. Phone: (212) 769-1925. Fax: (212) 799-4195. E-mail: tcntalk@aol.com. Web Site: www.talkline communication.com. Zev J. Brenner, pres.

National Jewish radio network featuring news, interviews with newsmaker guests & celebrities; live call-in format; live segments from Israel; satellite delivered. Available on barter.

24 Karat Productions Inc., 1717 W. Sanderling Ln., Port St. Lucie, FL 34982. Phone: (772) 465-5511. Fax: (772) 465-5511. Web Site: www.markprichard1@msn.com. Mark Prichard, pres/CEO; Gloria Prichard, exec VP.

Music 1, classic pop, over 10,000 stereo selections w/mthy updates for radio, offices; on tape or CD, consultant svcs.

United Press International, 1510 H St. N.W., Washington, DC 20005. Phone: (202) 898-8111. Phone: (202) 898-8100. Fax: (202) 898-8057. Web Site: www.upi.com. Tobin C. Beck, news dir.

Full-svc company offers a number of short-form info features to its affil radio stns.

Virtual Radio, Box 579, 4521 Campus Dr., Irvine, CA 92612. Phone: (949) 752-9237. Fax: (949)752-9456. E-mail: joel@virtualradio.com. Web Site: www.virtualradio.com. Joel Easton, mng dir.

Virtual Radio is the oldest music website providing a new radio format, content & internet expertise to bcstrs world wide.

WFMT Fine Arts Radio, 5400 N. St. Louis Ave., Chicago, IL 60625. Phone: (773) 279-2000. Fax: (773) 279-2199. Web Site: www.wfmt.com. Daniel Schmidt, pres/CEO; Peter Whorf, progmg dir; Steve Robinson, sr VP.

Classical, opera & folk mus, news & fine art progmg 24-hours per day through United Video Inc. Serving 200 cable systems in 30 states with 850,000 subs.

WFMT Radio Network/BSN Around the Clock, 5400 N. St. Louis Ave., Chicago, IL 60625. Phone: (773) 279-2000. Fax: (773) 279-2199. E-mail: finearts@wfmt.com. Web Site: www.wfmt.com. Steve Robinson, sr VP.

Provides 24-hour-a-week classical music program format svc via satellite to more than 500 stns; programs in one-hour modules with program host & loc sound.

"The Weather Center", (a broadcast service of Aviation Weather Inc.). 701 Gervais St., Suite 150-224, Columbia, SC 29201. Phone: (803) 739-2827. E-mail: wxcenter@aol.com. Web Site: www.aviationweatherinc.com. L.R. Ferguson, pres.

"Regional Radio Broadcast/Weathercast Network" across the Carolinas and Georgia in over 20 broadcast markets. Weather forecasting, site-specific broadcast services for stations all across America. 100% barter.

Westwood One Producers, Radio New Services. 40 W. 57th St., New York, NY 10019. Phone: (212) 641-2000. Fax: (212) 641-2185. Web Site: www.westwoodone.com. Shane Cappola, CEO; Jacque Tortoroli, CFO; Paul Bronstein, sr VP; Gary Yusko, sr VP; Peter Kosann, exec VP.

Culver CA 90232-2689, 9540 Washington Blvd. Phone: (310) 204-5000. Fax: (310) 840-4380.

Valencia, CA 91355, 25060 W. Ave. Stanford, Suite 100. Phone: (805) 294-9000. Fax: (805) 294-9380.

Atlanta, GA 30361, 1201 Peachtree St. N.W., 400 Colony Sq., Suite 200. Phone: (404) 870-9084. Fax: (404) 870-9085. Susan Bravman, AE.

Chicago, IL 60601, 111 E. Wacker Dr, Suite 2900. Phone: (312) 938-0222. Fax: (312) 616-8140. Ted S. Jakubiak, VP Midwest sls.

Troy, MI 48084, 3250 W. Big Beaver, Suite 139. Phone: (248) 649-0960. Fax: (248) 649-1584. Dave A. Gneiser, VP Detroit sls.

Dallas, TX 75231, 7577 Ramblin Rd, Suite 1462. Phone: (214) 373-0022. Fax: (214) 373-0511.

Arlington, VA 22202, 1755 S. Jefferson Davis Hwy. Phone: (703) 413-8300. Fax: (703) 413-8445.

Producer & distributor of radio progmg including CNN, NBC, Mutual, CNBC Business Radio, 24-hour music formats, long-short-form talk, music & news programs.

World Radio Network, Box 1212, London SW8 2ZF. United Kingdom. Phone: 44-20-7896-9000. Fax: 44-20-7896-9008. E-mail: email@wrn.org. Web Site: www.wrn.org. Karl Miosga, mng dir; Tim Ashburner, dir tech opns; Jeff Cohen, dev dir.

Boston, MA 02125, 11 Rockmere St. Phone: (617) 436-9024. Sue Schardt, North American rep.

WRN Network One (via Galaxy 5) news & features ch, comprises live progmg segments in English & languages from more than 20 international bcstrs. Also supplies many customized progmg feeds to radio stns.

Music Licensing

APM/Associated Production Music, 6255 Sunset Blvd., Suite 820, Hollywood, CA 90028. Phone: (323) 461-3211. Fax: (323) 461-9102. E-mail: sales@apmmusic.com. Web Site: www.apmmusic.com. Connie Red, sls dir.

New York, NY 10016, 240 Madison Ave., 11th Fl. Phone: (800) 276-6874. (212) 856-9800. Fax: (212) 856-9807. George Macisa, natl sls mgr.

Sixteen libraries: KPM, Bruton, Sonoton, Carlin, Castle, NFL. Over 3,000 CDs, personalized packages, music search, 15-20 new CD releases mthy.

American Society of Composers, Authors & Publishers (ASCAP), One Lincoln Plaza, New York, NY 10023. Phone: (212) 621-6000. Fax: (212) 621-6446. E-mail: info@ascap.com. Web Site: www.ascap.com. Marilyn Bergman, chmn/pres.

London W1S3LJ. ASCAP - London, 8 Cork St. Phone: 011-44-207-439-0907. Fax: 011-44-207-434-0073.

Los Angeles, CA 90046. ASCAP - Los Angeles, 7920 W. Sunset Blvd, Suite 300. Phone: (323) 883-1000. Fax: (323) 883-1049.

Miami Beach, FL 33139. ASCAP - Miami, 420 Lincoln Rd, Suite 385. Phone: (305) 673-3446. Fax: (305) 673-2446.

Atlanta, GA 30339. ASCAP - Atlanta, 2690 Cumberland Pkwy, Suite 490. Phone: (770) 805-3470. Fax: (770) 805-3470. (Not a membership office).

Chicago, IL 60647. ASCAP - Midwest, 1608 N. Milwaukee Ave, Suite 1007. Phone: (773) 394-4286. Fax: (773) 394-5639.

Nashville, TN 37203. ASCAP - Nashville, 2 Music Sq. W. Phone: (615) 742-5000. Fax: (615) 742-5060.

A membership assn of more than 200,000 composers, lyricists, & music publishers, ASCAP licenses the pub performances of its members' works. ASCAP has reciprocal agreements with foreign societies representing virtually every country that has laws protecting copyright.

BMI-Broadcast Music Inc. 320 W. 57th St., New York, NY 10019. Phone: (212) 586-2000. Fax: (212) 489-2368. Web Site: www.bmi.com. Del R. Bryant, pres/CEO; John Cody, CFO.

Miami, FL 33126, 5201 Blue Lagoon Dr, Suite 310. Phone: (305) 266-3636.

Atlanta, GA 30326, Tower Pl. 100, 3340 Peachtree Rd. N.E., Suite 570. Phone: (404) 261-5151.

Hato Rey, PR 00917, Bank Trust Plaza, 255 Ponce de leon Ave, East Wing, Suite A-262. Phone: (787) 754-6490.

London, NO NWISHN United Kingdom, 84 Harley House, Marlebone Rd. Phone: 0114420 7486 2036.

Los Angeles, CA 90069, 8730 Sunset Blvd. Phone: (310) 659-9109.

Nashville, TN 37203, 10 Music Sq. E. Phone: (615) 401-2000.

Licenses the pub performance rights of musical compositions for more than 300,000 songwriters, composers & music publishers; maintains reciprocal arrangements with more than 40 licensing organizations worldwide.

European American Music Distributors L.L.C., P.O. Box 4340, 15800 NW 48th Ave., Miami, FL 33014. Phone: (305) 521-1604. Fax: (305) 521-1638. E-mail: eamdc@eamdc.com. Web Site: www.eamdc.com. Sue Sinclair, dir.

Music publisher & distributor.

The Harry Fox Agency Inc., 711 3rd Ave., New York, NY 10017. Phone: (212) 370-5330. Fax: (212) 953-2384. Web Site: www.harryfox.com. Jacqueline Charlesworth, VP; Gary Churgin, pres/CEO.

Music licensing.

SESAC Inc., 55 Music Sq. E., Nashville, TN 37203. Phone: (615) 320-0055. Fax: (615) 329-9627. E-mail: dhoughton@sesac.com. Web Site: www.sesac.com. Pat Collins, pres/COO; Deborah Houghton, VP.

London W1H 3FF, 6 Kenrick Pl. Phone: 020-7486-9994. Fax: 020-7486-9929. Wayne Bickerton.

New York, NY 10019, 152 W. 57th St., 57th Fl. Phone: (212) 586-3450. Fax: (212) 489-5699. Deb Houghton, VP bcst licensing.

Performing rights organization representing a diversity of copyrighted music.

Society of Composers, Authors & Music Publishers of Canada (SOCAN), Societe Canadienne des auteurs, compositeurs et editeurs de musique. 41 Valleybrook Dr., Toronto, ON M3B 2S6. Canada. Phone: (416) 445-8700. Fax: (416) 445-7108. E-mail: socan@socan.ca. Web Site: www.socan.ca.

Dartmouth B2Y 2N6, Queen Sq., 45 Alderney Dr., Suite 802. Phone: (902) 464-7000. Fax: (902) 464-9696.

Edmonton T6H 5P9, 1145 Weber Centre, 5555 Calgary Tr. Phone: (780) 439-9049. Fax: (780) 432-1555.

Montreal H3A 3J2, 600, boul. de Maisonneuve Ouest, Bureau 500. Phone: (514) 844-8377. Fax: (514) 849-8446.

Vancouver V6E 2V2, 1201 W. Pender St, Suite 400. Phone: (604) 669-5569. Fax: (604) 688-1142.

SOCAN licenses the public performance of music in Canada & distributes performance royalties to copyright holders worldwide.

Warner Bros. Publications, 15800 N.W. 48th Ave., Miami, FL 33014. Phone: (305) 620-1500. Fax: (305) 621-4869. Fax: (305) 621-1094. Web Site: www.warnerbrospublications.com.

Full-line music publishers of popular, standard & educ music as well as instructional videos from influential musicians. International market.

Canadian Broadcast Networks

Astral Television Networks

Head Office: Astral Media Inc., 2100, rue Sainte-Catherine Ouest, Bureau 1000, Montréal PQ H3H 2T3. (514) 939-5000. Fax: (514) 939-1515. Web site: www.astralmedia.com.

Television Division (English): BCE Place, 181 Bay St., Suite 2100, Box 787, Toronto, ON M5J 2T3. (416) 956-2010. Fax: (416) 956-2035.

Television Division (French): 200 rue Sainte-Catherine Ouest, Bureau 1000, Montreal, PQ H3H 2T3. (514) 939-5090. Fax: (514) 939-5098.

Principal Officers: Ian Greenberg, pres/CEO; Andre Bureau, chmn of bd; Louis Ryan, VP strategic planning; Alain Bergaron, VP communications, Astra Media Inc.; Claude Gagnon, VP/CFO, Astra Media Inc.; Sidney Greenberg, VP; Louis Ryan, VP strategic planning; Sophie Emond, VP reg/govt affairs; Gaetan Ayotte, asst VP hum res; Louis Marcotte, asst VP finance; Monique Ryan, VP legal affairs; Michael Arpin, sr advisor reg/govt affairs; Claude Gagnon, VP finance/CEO; Arnold Chiasson, VP hum res; Louis Ryan, VP strategic planning & business; Sidney Greenberg, VP.

Television: The Movie Network; Super Ecran; Moviepix; Canal Vie; Vrak.TV; Z; Canal D; Family; Tele Annonces; Viewer's Choice; Historia; Series+; MusiMax; Musique Plus; Teletoon; Canal Indigo.

CTV Inc., a division of Bell Globemedia

Head Office: 9 Channel Nine Ct., Scarborough, ON, Canada M1S 4B5. (416) 332-5000. Fax: (416) 332-5283. Web site: www.ctv.ca.

CTV Executives: Ivan Fecan, CEO; Rick Brace, pres; Roger Dunbar, VP adv sls; Joe Carter, sr VP sports sls; Sally Basmajian, VP sls/mktg; Lino Bramucci, sr VP/gen mgr RDS sls; Bill Mustos, sr VP dramatic progmg; Andrew Saunders, VP, integrated sls/mktg Bell Globemedia; Robin Fillingham, CFO/chief admin off; Phillip Crawley, publisher/CEO; Paul Sparke, sr VP corporate/public affrs.

CTV Sales Offices

Montreal, PQ H2K 4R2: 1010 Sherbrooke St., Suite 1803. (514) 529-2105. Fax: (514) 521-0102.

Vancouver, BC V6Z 1X5: 750 Burrard St., (604) 608-2868. Fax: (604) 609-5796.

New York, NY 10017: Telerep, One Dag Hammarskjold Plaza, 25th Fl. (212) 759-8787. Fax: (212) 486-8746.

Canadian Broadcasting Corp.

The Canadian Broadcasting Corp. (CBC) is a publicly owned corporation established by the Broadcasting Act (1936) of the Canadian Parliament to provide the natl bcstg svc in Canada in the two official languages English & French. Under this legislation, the CBC is subject to regulations of the Canadian Radio-Television & Telecommunications Commission (CRTC).

Program Services: The progmg on CBC networks is nearly all Canadian and virtually free of coml adv. Newsworld is a 24-hour natl satellite to cable English-language news & info svc. Le Réeseau de l'information (RDI) is a 24-hour natl satellite-to-cable French-language news & info svc. The heart of CBC's natl distribution system is Canada's Anik E2 satellite, carrying progmg through six different time zones.

Head Office: 181 Queen St., Ottawa, ON K1P 1K9. (613) 724-1200. TDD: (613) 288-6455. Web Site: www.cbc.ca.

CBC Board of Directors: Carole Taylor, chairwoman; Robert Rabinovitch, pres/CEO; John Kim Bell; Helene Fortin; Marie Giguere; Roy L. Heenan; Jane Heffelfinger; Robert Lantos; Clarence LeBreton; Howard McNutt; L. Richard O'Hagan; James S. Palmer.

Principal Officers: Robert Rabinovitch, pres/CEO; Harold Redekopp, exec VP, English Television; Daniel Gourd, exec VP, French Television; Jane Chalmers, VP English Radio; Sylvain Lafrance, VP French Radio and New Media; Pierre Nollet, VP/gen counsel/corporate sec; George C.B. Smith, sr VP human resources and organization; Johanne Charbonneau, VP/CFO; Raymond Carnovale, VP/CTO; Michel Tremblay, VP strategy and bus devel; William B. Chambers, VP communications; Michel Saint-Cyr, pres Real Estate div.

CBC Ombudsmen: David Bazay, English svcs, Box 500, Station A, Toronto, ON M5W 1E6; E-mail: ombudsman@cbc.ca. Web Site: www.cbc.ca/obusdman. Renaud Gilbert, French svcs, Box 6000, Montreal, PQ H3C 3A8; E-mail: ombudsman@radio-canada.ca. Web Site: www.radio-canada-ca/obudsman.

English Networks: Box 500, 250 Front St. W., Station A, Toronto, ON M5W 1E6. (866) 306-4636. TDD: (416) 205-6688; E-mail: cbcinput@cbc.ca.

French Networks: Box 6000, 1400 Rene-Levesque Blvd. E., Montreal, PQ H3C 3A8. (514) 597-6000. TDD: (514) 597-6013; E-mail: auditoire@radio-canada.ca.

Newfoundland Region (English): Box 12010, Station A, St. John's, NF A1B 3T8. (709) 576-5000.

Maritime Region (English): Box 3000, Halifax, NS B3J 3E9. (902) 420-8311.

Atlantic Provinces (French): Box 950, Moncton, NB E1C 8N8. (506) 853-6666.

Quebec Region (English): Box 6000, Montreal, PQ H3C 3A8. (514) 597-6000.

Quebec City & Eastern Quebec Region (French): Box 18800, Ste. Foy, PQ G1V 9L4. (418) 654-1341.

Ontario Region (English): Box 500, Station A, Toronto, ON M5W 1E6. (416) 205-3311.

Ontario Region (French): Box 3220, Station C, Ottawa, ON K1Y 1E4. (613) 724-1200.

Manitoba Region (English & French): Box 160, Winnipeg, MB R3C 2H1. (204) 788-3222.

Saskatchewan Region (English & French): 2440 Broad St., Box 540, Regina, SK S4P 4A1. (306) 347-9540.

Alberta Region (English & French): Box 555, Edmonton, AB T5J 2P4. (780) 468-7500.

British Columbia Region (English & French): Box 4600, Vancouver, BC V6B 4A2. (604) 662-6000.

CBC North: 5129 49th St., Box 160, Yellowknife, NT X1A 1P8. (867) 920-5400.

Global Television Network

Head Office: 81 Barber Greene Rd., Don Mills, ON M3C 2A2. (416) 446-5311. (800) 387-8001 (Toll-Free). Fax: (416) 446-5449. Web site: www.canada.com/globaltv.

Principal Officers: L.H. Asper, chmn/CEO Canwest Global Communications Corp.; Gerry Noble, pres/CEO Global Communications Ltd.; Loren Mawhinney, VP Canadian production Global Communications Ltd.; Doug Bonar, VP Global Communications Ltd.; Doug Hoover, VP progmg Global Communications Ltd.; Ken Johnson, VP mktg Global Communications Ltd.; John Burgis, VP finance Global Communications Ltd.; Cam Johnson, treas Global Communications Ltd.

CanWest Global Officers and Management: Leonard Asper, pres/CEO; Frank Mc Kenna, chmn bd; David Asper, exec VP/chmn; Gail Asper, gen counsel/sec; Tom Strike, COO; Richard Leipsic, VP/gen counsel; John Cunningham, VP corporate dev; Geoffry Elliot, VP corporate affrs; John E. Maguire, VP finance/CEO; Gary A. Maavara, VP corporate dev.

TVA

Head Office: 1600 de Maisonneuve Blvd. E., Montreal Qurbec H2L 4P2. (514) 526-2951; Fax: (514) 598-6086. Web site: www.tva.ca.

Affiliates: CFCM Sainte-Foy; CHLT Sherbrooke; CHEM Trois-Rivieres; CFER Pointe-au-Pere; CJPM Saguenay; CHAU Carleton; CIMT Riv.-du-Loup; CFEM Rouyn; CHOT Hull.

Television Quatre Saisons

Head Office: 612 rue Saint-Jacques, Montreal, PQ H3C 5R1. (514) 390-6035.

Principal Officers: Michel Carter, pres/CEO; Rene Guimond, pres/COO; Jean-Marc Fortier, VP corp serv; Therese David, VP comm; Luc Doyon, VP progmg; Richard Gauthier, VP human resources; Monique Lacharite, VP finance & admin.

Affiliates: CFJP Montreal, PQ; CFAP Quebec, PQ; CFRS Saguenay, PQ; CFKS Sherbrooke, PQ; CFKM Trois Rivieres, PQ; CFTF Riviere Du Loup, PQ; CFVS Val d'Or, PQ; CFGS Gatineau, PQ.

Canadian Cable Networks

ARTV, 1400 boul. Rene-Levesque Est, Bureau A-53-1, Montreal, PQ H2L 2M2. Canada. Phone: (514) 597-3636. Fax: (514) 597-3633. Web Site: www.artv.ca.

Aboriginal Peoples Television Network, 339 Portage Ave., Winnipeg, MB R3B 2C3. Canada. Phone: (204) 947-9331. Fax: (204) 947-9307. E-mail: info@aptn.ca. Web Site: www.aptn.ca.

Alliance Broadcasting, (dba Showcase TV & History TV). 121 Bloor St. E., Toronto, ON M4W 3M5. Canada. Phone: (416) 967-1174. Fax: (416) 960-0971. Web Site: www.allianceatlantis.com. Phyllis Yaffe, pres/CEO.

Best of Canadian & international TV series & movies. Serving 5 million subs on 100 cable systems. Satellite: ANIK-E2.

Atlantic Satellite Network (ASN), Box 1653, Halifax, NS B3J 2Z6. Canada. Phone: (902) 453-4000. Fax: (902) 454-3302. E-mail: bt@ctv.ca. Web Site: www.ctv.ca. Mike Elgie, VP/gen mgr; Rich Marchand, gen sls mgr; Jane Hefler, production mgr; L. Wartman, opns dir; Laird White, prom dir.

Movies & news, educ programs weekend mornings. Serves 51 cable systems. Satellite: Anik C-1.

BookTelevision: The Channel, 299 Queen St. W., Toronto, ON M5V 2Z5. Canada. Phone: (416) 591-5757. Web Site: www.booktelevision.com. Dr. Ron Keast, pres/CEO; Daniel Richler, editor-in-chief/supervising producer; Jill Bonenfant, progmg dir; Joel Goldberg, mgng dir & creative/production svcs; Richard Hiron, mgng dir & sls & mktg; Pam Hnytka, publicist.

BookTelevision: The Channel spotlights all the writing that informs & entertains us in our daily lives.

Bravo!, 299 Queen St. W., Toronto, ON M5V 2Z5. Canada. Phone: (416) 591-5757. Fax: (416) 591-8497. E-mail: bravomail@bravo.ca. Web Site: www.bravo.ca. Paul Gratton, VP; John Gunn, production dir; Isme Bennie, dir progmg & acquistions; Jennifer C.S. Lo, dir communications; David Kirkwood, VP; Allan Schwebel, VP, VP & affil sls & mktg.

Bravo! NewStyle Arts Channel is dedicated to entertaining, stimulating and enlightening veiwers who have a taste for more complex television. Bravo! delivers a wide array of fine arts programming, balancing longer-form structured shows and shorter pieces that appear in a more random way as "flow" to create a fluid mix of distinctive music, dance, opera, drama, literature, cinema, visual art, the art of television and the art of talk. Serving 5.8 million subs on 700 cable systems.

CBC Newsworld, Box 500, Station A, Toronto, ON M5W 1E6. Canada. Phone: (416) 205-2409. Fax: (416) 205-8684. Web Site: www.newsworld.com. E-mail: maria_mirowicz@cbc.ca. Maria Mirowicz, program dir.

Live 24-hour news & info network on basic cable, satellite & wireless in Canada.

On 1500 cable systems serving 8 million subs. Satellite: Anik E2 (Ku-band).

CPAC-Cable Public Affairs Channel, (A subsidiary of Consortium of Canadian Cable Companies). 1750-45 O'Connor St., Ottawa, ON K1P 1A4. Canada. Phone: (613) 567-2722. Fax: (613) 567-2741. E-mail: comments@cpac.ca. Web Site: www.cpac.ca. Kenneth C. Stein, chmn; Colette Watson, gen mgr; Ray Skaff, progmg dir; Daniel Perras, production mgr; David Carroll, tech opns; Ian Mitchell, tech opns.

Uncut, unfiltered coverage of Canadian pub affrs issues including LIVE bcsts of the House of Commons & its Standing Committees. Serving 7.2 million subs.

CTV Newsnet, Box 9, Station "O", Toronto, ON M4A 2M9. Canada. Phone: (416) 332-5000. E-mail: news@ctv.ca. Web Site: www.ctv.ca.

Continually updated headline news, business, sports, weather & entertainment, every 15 minutes.

CTV Pay-Per-View Sports, Box 9, Station "O", Toronto, ON M4A 2M9. Canada. Phone: (416) 332-5000. Web Site: www.ctvpayperviewsports.com. Suzanne Steeves, VP/gen mgr; Doug Beeforth, VP/mgng dir & CTV sports group; Nikki Moffat, VP/controller & CTV sports group.

Pay-per-view sports packages & special events coverage. Coverage area: national.

Canadian Learning Television (CLT), 299 Queen St. W., Toronto, ON M5V 2Z5. Canada. Phone: (416) 591-5757. Phone: (780) 440-7777. Fax: (780) 440-8899. Web Site: www.clt.ca. Ron Keast, pres/CEO; Peter Palframan, VP finance; Jill Bonenfant, progmg dir; Richard Hiron, mgng dir & sls & mktg; Joel Goldberg, mgng dir & creative/production svcs; Allan Schwebel, VP & affil sls & mktg.

Adult education stn offering access to accredited learning opportunities, including university & college credit courses, personal development, training & job opportunities.

Canadian Satellite Communications Inc. (CANCOM), 2055 Flavelle Blvd., Mississauga, ON L5K 1Z8. Canada. Phone: (905) 403-2020. Fax: (905) 403-2022. Web Site: www.cancom.ca. Louise Cyr, office mgr.

Expert in evaluating, selecting, integrating & implementing satellite-based solutions for business. Cancom operates in four main lines of business: broadcast solutions, tracking solutions, learning solutions & data solutions.

Le Canal Nouvelles, 1600 boul. de Maisonneuve est, Montreal, PQ H2L 4P2. Canada. Phone: (514) 790-6688. Fax: (514) 598-6037. Web Site: www.tva.canoe.ca.

Les Chaines Tele Astral, Les Chaines Tele Astral, Une division d'Astra Media, 2100, Ste-Catherine St. W., Rm. 700, Montreal, PQ H3H 2T3. Canada. Phone: (514) 939-3150. Fax: (514) 939-3151. Web Site: www.astral.com. Pierre Roy, pres/ceo; Johanne Saint-Laurent, sr VP financees/opns & business affrs; Judith Brosseau, sr VP progmg Canal D Historia Series; Marie Collin, sr VP progmg Canal Vie Vraktv Z; Sylvie Shapiro, VP rsch & dev; Gaetan Ayotte, VP human resources.

Progmg includes Super cran, the Fr pay-TV stn; Canal Famille, children's progmg stn devoted to children from ages 3 to 14; Canal D, a specialty ch featuring mainly documentaries.

Serving 245,000 subs (Super Ecran); 2,110,000 subs (Canal Famille), &1,705,000 subs (Canal D).

Serving 370 cable systems.

Satellite: Anik E-2, transponder 11-A.

The Comedy Network, Box 1000, Station "O", Toronto, ON M4A 2W3. Canada. Phone: (416) 332-5300. Fax: (416) 332-5283. Susanne Boyce, Pres of Progmg & Chairman of Media Group; Ed Robinson, Pres & Gen Mgr; Jon Hales, mktg mgr; Rick Brace, pres; Brent Haynes, program dir; Patrick Patterson, sls dir; Nikki Moffat, Sr VP financee.

A 24-hour service featuring Canadian & international programs devoted exclusively to comedy sketches, standup comedy, & ongoing comedy series. Coverage area: national.

Country Music Television (Canada), 64 Jefferson Ave, Unit 18, Toronto, ON M6K 3H4. Canada. Phone: (416) 534-1191. E-mail: info@cmt.ca. Web Site: www.cmtcanada.ca. John Cassaday, CEO.

A 24-hour mus & entertainment net that combines mus videos with programs and features that focus on the artists and their mus.

Serving 7 million subs on 1,487 cable systems in Canada.

Satellite: Anik E2 (Ku-Band), transponder T4.

CourtTV Canada, 3720-76th Ave., Edmonton, AB T6B 2N9. Canada. Phone: (780) 440-7777. Fax: (780) 440-8899. E-mail: courttv@incentre.net. Web Site: www.courttvcanada.ca. Dr. Ron Keast, pres/CEO; Joel Goldberg, mgng dir.

CourtTV Canada, in partnership with the U.S. based CourtTV, combines CourtTV's compelling daytime live trial coverage and legal analysis from inside U.S. courts with legal and police dramas, movies, documentaries and series from Canada and abroad.

DMX Music-Canada, 7260 12th St. S.E., Suite 120, Calgary, AB T2H 2S5. Canada. Phone: (403) 640-8527. Fax: (403) 253-2788. E-mail: brad.trumble@dmxmusic.com. Web Site: www.dmx.ca. Brad Trumble, opns VP.

Formerly a residential service, now a commercial service exclusively. Considering a return to the Canadian market. DMX commercial audio svc; 102 formats digital audio.

Serving 8000 subs. Satellites: C3 Bank, TBA (Ku-band) delivered by satellite ant.

Discovery Channel, #9 Channel 9 Ct., Toronto, ON M1S 4B5. Canada. Phone: (416) 332-5000. Web Site: www.ctv.ca. Meg Pinto, consultant.

Non-fiction documentary TV progmg focusing on the themes of nature, science & technology, adventure.

On 385 cable systems serving 5.6 million subs. Satellite: Anik E2, Channel 210.

Drive-In Classics, 299 Queen St. W., Toronto, ON M5V 2Z5. Canada. Phone: (416) 591-5757. E-mail: driveinclassics@driveinclassics.ca. Web Site: www.driveinclassics.ca. Paul Gratton, VP/gen mgr; Isme Bennie, dir progmg & acquistions; Jim Shutsa, dir production; Gord McWatters, creative dir; David Kirkwood, VP & sls & mktg; Jennifer C.S. Lo, dir communications; Allan Schwebel, VP & affil sls & mktg.

Fairchild Television Ltd., B8-525 W. Broadway, Vancouver, BC V5Z 4K5. Canada. Phone: (604) 708-1313. Fax: (604) 708-1300. E-mail: info@fairchildtv.com. Web Site: www.fairchildtv.com. Joseph Chan, pres.

The only Chinese language specialty TV across Canada. Serving 330,000 subs on 8 cable systems.

Family Channel Inc., Box 787, BCE Place, 181 Bay St., Toronto, ON M5J 2T3. Canada. Phone: (416) 956-2030. Fax: (416) 956-2035. E-mail: info@family.ca. Web Site: www.family.ca. Len Cochrane, pres/CEO; Kevin Wright, VP progmg; Darrel Atherley, VP sls & mktg; John Pow, VP finance.

Premium TV net offering family entertainment based on 60% from the Disney Channel, 25% Canadian & 15% international progmg.

Serving 3 million subs on 300 cable systems.

Satellite: Anik E1, Ku-band, DVC GI DigiCipher I. Western Feed: transponder T-22.6 IRD ch 359 (stereo) 559 (mono). Eastern Feed: transponder T-22.5 IRD ch 358 (stereo) 558 (mono). Orbital Position: 111.1 degrees west longitude. DVC: general instrument DigiCipher I.

FashionTelevisionChannel, 299 Queen St. W., Toronto, ON M5V 2Z5. Canada. Phone: (416) 591-5757. Web Site: www.ftchannel.com. Marcia Martin, VP/gen mgr; David Kirkwood, VP sls; Ellen Baine, VP progmg; Scott Greig, creative dir; Jay Levine, production supvr; Bev Nenson, dir publicity; Allan Schwebel, VP-affil sls & mktg.

Food Network Canada, 121 Bloor St. E., Toronto, ON M4W 3M5. Canada. Phone: (416) 967-1174. E-mail: info@allianceatlantis.com. Web Site: www.foodtv.ca. Eileen Morrison,.

HGTV Canada, 121 Bloor St. E., Suite 200, Toronto, ON M4W 3M5. Canada. Phone: (866) 967-4488 (viewer relations). Phone: (416) 967-0022 (main reception). Fax: (416) 960-0971. E-mail: feedback@hgtv.ca. Web Site: www.hgtv.ca. Phyllis Yaffee, pres.

A 24-hour Canadian home & garden progmg resource. Serving 5.2 million subs.

Satellite: F1, transponder T19.

History Television, 121 Bloor St. E., Suite B1, Toronto, ON M4W 3M5. Canada. Phone: (416) 967-1174. Fax: (416) 960-0971. Web Site: www.allianceatlantis.com. Phyllis Yaffe,.

A 24-hour program svc featuring current & world history told in documentaries, mini-series & feature films.

Satellite: Launching September 1997. On 350 cable systems serving 4 million subs.

Satellite: Anik e-2, transponder 19.

Life Network, 121 Bloor St. E., Suite 200, Toronto, ON M4W 3M5. Canada. Phone: (416) 967-0022. E-mail: info@lifenetwork.ca. Web Site: www.lifenetwork.ca. Phyllis Yaffe,.

Offers lifestyle entertainment progmg about the people, places & experiences that make the journey of life worthwhile & interesting.

Serving 26 million English & Fr subs on 100 cable systems.

Satellite: Anik E2 (Ku-band), transponder T19 (horizontal).

La Magnetotheque, 1055 Rene Levesque E., Suite 501, Montreal, PQ H2L 4S5. Canada. Phone: (514) 282-1999. Fax: (514) 282-1676. Web Site: www.lamagnetheque.qc.ca. E-mail: info@lamagnetheque.qc.ca. Majorie Theodore, dir.

French-language reading svc for persons who are blind, visually impaired, or print-handicapped.

Movie Central, 5324 Calgary Tr., Suite 200, Edmonton, AB T6H 4J8. Canada. Phone: (780) 430-2800. Fax: (780) 437-3188. Web Site: www.moviecentral.com. Paul Robertson, pres; Andrew Eddy, VP/gen mgr.

Coml-free premium pay TV svc including movies, mus &

Broadcasting & Cable Yearbook 2006

comedy specials, major sports events & boxing (Superchannel, Movie Max!, Viewers Choice, Pay-Per-View).

Serving 300,000 subs on 170 cable systems.

Satellite: Anik E2.

MuchLOUD, 299 Queen St. W., Toronto, ON M5V 2Z5. Canada. Phone: (416) 591-5757. E-mail: muchloud@muchmusic.com. Web Site: www.muchloud.com. David Kines, VP/gen mgr; Sheila Sullivan, dir of progmg; David Johnson, sr creative dir; Neil Staite, opns dir; David Kirkwood, VP-sls & mktg; Sandra Puglielli, dir publicity; Allan Schwebel, VP-affil sls & mktg.

For fans of hard music everywhere - MuchLOUD delivers. Alternative, metal and punk music videos, featured alongside exclusive artist interviews, specials, classic archival material and up-to-the-minute concert info.

MuchMoreMusic, 299 Queen St. W., Toronto, ON M5V 2Z5. Canada. Phone: (416) 591-5757. E-mail: muchmoremail@muchmoremusic.com. Web Site: www.muchmoremusic.com. David Kines, VP/gen mgr; Sheila Sullivan, program dir; David Johnson, sr creative dir; Neil Staite, opns dir; David Kirkwood, VP; Sandra Puglielli, dir of publicity; Allan Schwebel, VP.

Brings music fans Hot AC MusicVideo, top international specials, documentaries, movies and a growing roster of exclusive, original programming they can't find anywhere else.

MuchMoreRetro, 299 Queen St. W., Toronto, ON M5V 2Z5. Canada. Phone: (416) 591-5757. E-mail: request@muchmoreretro.com. Web Site: www.muchmoreretro.com. David Kines, VP/gen mgr; Sheila Sullivan, dir of progmg; David Johnson, sr creative dir; Neil Staite, dir of opns; David Kirkwood, VP-sls & mktg; Allan Schwebel, VP-affil sls & mktg; Sandra Puglielli, dir of publicity.

Source for 24/7 classic videoflow from artists including The Police, Madonna, Bon Jovi, Corey Hart, Prince, Aerosmith, Duran Duran, Janet Jackson, Rush, Nirvana and Alanis Morissette and more.

MuchMusic, 299 Queen St. W., Toronto, ON M5V 2Z5. Canada. Phone: (416) 591-5757. E-mail: muchmail@muchmusic.com. Web Site: www.muchmusic.com. Sheila Sullivan, progmg dir; David Johnson, sr creative dir; Neil Staite, opns dir; David Kines, VP/gen mgr; Sandra Puglielli, dir of publicity; Allan Schwebel, VP; David Kirkwood, VP.

Live to air approximately 8 hours daily from streetfront headquarters in downtown Toronto, with videoflow showcasing live performance & interviews from musical artists & celebrity guests.

Serving 7,063,468 subs.

Satellite: Anik F1, transponder 17, L-Band Frequency 977.75 mhz.

MuchVibe, 299 Queen St. W., Toronto, ON M5V 2Z5. Canada. Phone: (416) 591-5757. E-mail: muchvibe@muchmusic.com. Web Site: www.muchvibe.ca. David Kines, VP/gen mgr; Sheila Sullivan, progmg dir; David Johnson, sr creative dir; Neil Staite, opns dir; David Kirkwood, VP-sls & mktg; Sandra Puglielli, dir of publicity; Allan Schwebel, VP-affil sls & mktg.

The source for top music videos, interviews, concert specials, concert listings and classic clips from the CHUM music video archive. Hip Hop, Rap, R&B, Old School, Reggae and more.

MusiMax & MusiquePlus, 355 rue Ste- Catherine O., Montreal, PQ H3B 1A5. Canada. Phone: (514) 284-7587. Fax: (514) 284-1889. Web Site: www.musiqueplus.com. Pierre Marchand, VP/gen mgr; Louis Panneton, VP mktg.

Musimax is a French-language speciality svc owned equally by Astral Media Inc. of Montreal and CHUM Ltd. of Toronto. MusiquePlus is MuchMusic's French-language counterpart in Quebec. Serving 2.078 million subs on approximately 120 cable systems . Satellite: Anik F1, transponder 9B.

Omni Television, (Multilingual Television Ltd.). 545 Lakeshore Blvd. W., Toronto, ON M5V 1A3. Canada. Phone: (416) 260-0047. Fax: (416) 260-3621. E-mail: info@omnitv.ca. Web Site: www.omnitv.ca. Tony Viner, pres; Leslie Sole, VP/gen mgr; Tom Ayley, VP finance; Madeline Ziniak, VP production/exec producer; J.H. Nelles, VP mktg; K. Colasanti, VP opns.

Canada's first multicultural TV stn with 60 percent of progmg dedicated to the growing multicultural market & 40 percent of progmg in English. Coverage area reaches 90 percent of Ontario including Toronto/Hamilton, Kitchener, London & Ottawa.

Serving 2,862,877 subs on 145 cable systems.

Outdoor Life Network, Box 9, Station "O", Toronto, ON M4A 2M9. Canada. Phone: (416) 332-5640. Fax: (416) 332-5283. Rick Brace, pres; Joe Carter, sr VP; Bart Yabsley, exec VP; Nikki Moffat, Sr VP Finance; Adam Ashton, mktg VP; Anna Stambolic, dir; Andrea Goldstein, Communications Mgr.

A 24-hour service featuring programs that deal exclusively with outdoor recreation, conservation, wilderness & adventure. Coverage area: national.

Prime TV, 2100 One Lombard Pl., Winnipeg, MB R3B-OX3. Canada. Phone: (204) 926-4800. Web Site: www.globaltv.com. Bill Hunt, VP/gen mgr.

The best of TV. Classy & classic entertainment & informational progmg for those moving on from youth-skewed traditional TV fare. 5 million subs.

RDI-Le Reseau de l'information, 1400 Blvd. Rene-Levesque E., Montreal, PQ H2L 2M2. Canada. Phone: (514) 597-7224. Fax: (514) 597-5226. E-mail: gilles_desjardins@radio-canada.ca. Web Site: www.radio-canada.ca/rdi. Martin Cloutier, exec dir; Robert Nadeau, progmg.

RDI-Le Resean de info is Canada's French-language news network. RDI provide live coverage major events, newscasters every half hour, sports, financial news, as well as info programs on a wide range of topics. 9.2 million subs.

Report on Business Television, 720 King St. W., 10th Fl., Toronto, ON M5V 2T3. Canada. Phone: (416) 957-8100. Web Site: www.robtv.com.

Le Reseau des sports, 1755 Blvd. Rene-Levesque Est, Suite 300, Montreal, PQ H2K 4P6. Canada. Phone: (514) 599-2244. Fax: (514) 599-2299. E-mail: webmaster@rds.ca. Web Site: www.rds.ca. Gerry Frappier, gen mgr & pres; Michel Gagnon, mktg VP; Francois Messier, progmg VP.

Provides 24-hour sports TV in Fr.

Satellite: ANIK E-2, transponder T-18.

The Score Television Network, 370 King St. W., Suite 304, Toronto, ON M5V 1J9. Canada. Phone: (416) 977-6787. Fax: (416) 977-0238. E-mail: info@thescore.ca. Web Site: www.thescore.ca. John Levy, chmn & CEO; David Errington, VP/gen mgr; Rob Macornson, pres.

Delivers the most comprehensive svc of professional & amateur sports news & info from Canada & around the world & is in every major Canadian cable market. Available in more than 5 million cable homes.

Serving 5.4 million subs on 370 cable systems.

Satellite: Anik F1, transponder 19.

Sex TV: The Channel, 299 Queen St. W., Toronto, ON M5V 2Z5. Canada. Phone: (416) 591-5757. Web Site: www.sextvthechannel.com. Marcia Martin, VP/gen mgr; David Kirkwood, VP sls; Ellen Baine, VP progmg; Brad Brough, creative dir; Allan Schwebel, VP-affil sls & mktg; Bev Nenson, dir of publicity.

The Shopping Channel, 59 Ambassador Dr., Mississauga, ON L5T 2P9. Canada. Phone: (905) 565-3500. Phone: (905) 565-2600 (voicemail attendant). Fax: (905) 565-2641. Web Site: www.theshoppingchannel.ca. Marg Grimes, gen mgr; Barbara Mallon, opns VP.

Live, shop-at-home televised retail svc, offering a var of consumer products.

Serving 5.7 million subs across Canada via cable & satellite.

Satellite: Anik E2, transponder 5.

Space: The Imagination Station, 299 Queen St. W., Toronto, ON M5V 2Z5. Canada. Phone: (416) 591-5757. Web Site: www.spacecast.com. Jim Shutsa, dir production; Paul Gratton, VP/gen mgr; Isme Bennie, dir of progmg & acquisitions; Gord McWatters, creative dir; Jennifer C.S. Lo, dir communications; Allan Schwebel, VP & affil sls & mktg; David Kirkwood, VP-sls & mktg.

Cable-delivered, national, 24 hour, English-language Science Fiction, Science Fact, Speculation and Fantasy channel. The program mix includes memorable sci-fi classics and current popular series, plus feature films, documentaries, specials and daily original productions with a tilt to information and new age speculation.

Sportsnet, Box 9, Station "O", Toronto, ON M4A-2M9. Canada. Phone: (416) 332-5000. Web Site: www.sportsnet.ca. Suzanne Steeves, VP/gen mgr; Roman Melnyk, VP business affrs; Scott Moore, VP production; Frank Abels, dir affil rel & mktg.

From big league to small town, CTV Sportsnet spans the sports spectrum, offering a wide variety of professional & amateur sports. Coverage area: national.

Star! The Entertainment Information Station, 299 Queen St. W., Toronto, ON M5V 2Z5. Canada. Phone: (416) 591-7400. E-mail: info@star-tv.com. Web Site: www.star-tv.com. Marcia Martin, VP/gen mgr; David Kirkwood, VP sls; Ellen Baine, VP progmg; Susan Arthur, mktg dir; Scott Greig, creative dir; James Wood, production supvr; Bev Nenson, dir of publicity; Allan Schwebel, VP & affil sls & mktg.

Canada's only 24-hour national specialty service dedicated to the world of showbiz news and information. Programming includes in-depth specials and events, detailed behind-the scene features on major movies, exclusive interviews with the world's biggest celebrities and extensive live coverage of award shows, premieres and galas.

TMN—The Movie Network/MOVIEPIX, Box 787, BCE Place, Suite 100, 181 Bay St., Toronto, ON M5J 2T3. Canada. Phone: (416) 956-2010. Fax: (416) 956-2018. Web Site: www.movienetwork.ca. Joe Tedesco, VP finance business affrs & MIS.

Two English-language, gen interest, pay TV nets featuring recent movie titles on the multi-channeled TMN, & new classics on MOVIEPIX.

Serving 350,000 subs on 200 cable systems.

Satellite: Anik E1 (Ku-band), transponder T31 (TMN); Anik E2 (Ku-band), transponder T27 (MOVIEPIX).

TSN—The Sports Network, # 9 Channel 9 Ct., Toronto, ON M1S 4B5. Canada. Phone: (416) 332-5000. Web Site: www.ctv.ca. Phil King, pres.

A 24-hour sports ch distributed on cable in Canada. Covers all major professional & amateur sports.

On more than 2,000 systems serving 6.1 million subs.

Satellite: Anik E1, transponder 18 KU-H.

TVOntario, 2180 Yonge St., Toronto, ON M4T 2T1. Canada. Phone: (416) 484-2600. Fax: (416) 484-6285. E-mail: acochrane@tvontario.org. Web Site: www.tvontario.org.

Provides educ progmg in English & Fr off air & via cable systems throughout Ontario.

TVO network (English) serves 98% of Ontario households. (Fr) serves 75% of Ontario households & 300,000 households in Quebec. Together the nets are on 327 cable systems.

Satellites: Anik F1, transponder 21.

Talk TV, Box 9, Station "O", Toronto, ON M4A 2M9. Canada. Phone: (416) 332-5030. Fax: (416) 332-5283. Rick Brace, pres; Susanne Boyce, Programming Pres. & Chairman & CTV Media Group; Ed Robinson, gen mgr; Nikki Moffat, Sr. VP Finance; Scott Henderson, mgr.

TELETOON, Box 787, 181 Bay St., Toronto, ON M5J 2T3. Canada. Phone: (416) 956-2060. Fax: (416) 956-2070. E-mail: info@teletoon.com. Web Site: www.teletoon.com. Len Cochrane; Hillary Firestone, net mktg & proms; Carole Bonneay, progmg VP.

This specialty net shows the best in animation from Canada & around the planet.

Serving 6 million subs on 1,000 cable systems.

Satellite: Anik E2, transponder 20. 1000.6 Million.

Treehouse TV, 64 Jefferson Ave., Unit 18, Toronto, ON M6K-3H4. Canada. Phone: (416) 534-1191. Web Site: www.treehousetv.ca. Susan Ross, VP/gen mgr; Peter Moss, VP progmg; John Cvecich, mktg mgr.

Treehouse TV is a specialty net dedicated to providing a variety of imaginative, stimulating and coml-free progmg for preschoolers from morning until bedtime.

Serving 4 million subs on 180 cable systems.

Satellite: Anik E-2, transponder 5.

Viewer's Choice Canada, Box 787, BCE Place, Suite 100, 181 Bay St., Toronto, ON M5J 2T3. Canada. Phone: (416) 956-2010. Fax: (416) 956-2055. Web Site: www.viewerschoice.com. John Riley, pres/CEO; Vash Ramnarace, dir financial & admin; Mark Waschulzik, affil sls mgr.

Eastern Canada's pay-per-view network.

On 50 cable systems serving 600,000 addressable subs.

Satellites: Anik E1; Anik E2.

Vision TV: (Canada's Multi Faith Network), 80 Bond St., Toronto, ON M5B 1X2. Canada. Phone: (416) 368-3194. Fax: (416) 368-9774. Web Site: www.visiontv.ca. E-mail: estella@visiontv.ca. Bill Roberts, pres/CEO; Chris Johnson, progmg VP; Mark Prasuhn, COO.

Programs presented by 30 plus faith groups, British comedies, movies dramas, documentaries, pub affrs, music & performance.

Serving 7.8 million subs on 12 cable systems. Satellite: Anik F1, transponder 5.

VoicePrint(TM), (A division of The National Broadcast Reading Service Inc.). 150 Laird Dr. Annex, Toronto, ON M4G 3V7. Canada. Phone: (416) 422-4222. Fax: (416) 422-1633. E-mail: nbrs@nbrscanada.com. Web Site: www.voiceprintcanada.com. Robert S. Trimbee, pres; Heather Lusignan, dir; John Stubbs, dir.

Read published news in audio format for blind, vision-restricted & sr Canadians.

Canadian Cable Networks

W Network, 64 Jefferson Ave., Unit 18, Toronto, ON M6K 3H4. Canada. Phone: (416) 534-1191. Web Site: www.wnetwork.ca.

The Weather Network/MeteoMedia Inc., (A division of Pelmorex Communications Inc.). 1755 Rene-Levesque Blvd. E., Suite 251, Montreal, PQ H2K 4P6. Canada. Phone: (514) 597-1700. Fax: (514) 597-2981. Web Site: www.theweathernetwork.com. Pierre L. Morrissette, pres/CEO; Luc Perreault, VP affil rel.

Natl satellite-to-cable TV network bcstg in Fr (MétéoMédia) & English (The Weather Network) offering weather & environmental info 24-hours a day, 7 days a week.

Serving 8.2 million subs on 752 headends.

Satellite: Anik E2, transponder 1A.

YTV Canada Inc., 64 Jefferson Ave., Unit 18, Toronto, ON M6K 3H4. Canada. Phone: (416) 534-1191. Fax: (416) 533-0346. E-mail: info@ytv.ca. Web Site: www.ytv.ca. Peter Moss, VP progmg & production; Susan Schaefer, mktg VP; Jamie Hagerty, VP finance communications; Suzanne Carpenter, VP sls.

English language basic cable specialty svc dedicated to children, teens & their families.

On approximately 1,200 cable systems serving an estimated 8.1 million subs.

Satellite: ANIK E1 East/West-DVC, transponder 7 (nationwide), 111 degrees (Ku-band), vert polarization, 11900 MHZ.

Canadian Radio Networks and Services

Astral Radio and Énergie

Head Office: Astral Media Inc., Bureaux de la direction, 2100, rue Sainte-Catherine Ouest, Bureau 1000, Montréal PQ H3H 2T3. (514) 939-5000. Fax: (514) 939-1515. Web site: www.astralmedia.com.

Radio Division: 1717 boul. Rene-Levesque E., Bureau 120, Montreal, PQ H2L 4T9. (514) 529-3210. FAX: (514) 529-9308. Web site: www.radioenergie.com.

Principal Officers: Ian Greenberg, pres/CEO; Andre Bureau, chmn of bd; Louis Ryan, VP strategic planning; Alain Bergaron, VP communications; Sophie Emond, VP reg/govt affairs; Gaetan Ayotte, asst VP hum res; Louis Marcotte, asst VP finance; Monique Ryan, VP legal affairs; Michael Arpin, sr advisor reg/govt affairs; Claude Gagnon, VP finance; Arnold Chiasson, VP hum res; Jacques Parisien, pres; John Eddy, VP astra Media Radio Atlantic; Denis Rozen, VP Astral Media Radio; Luc Sabbatini, exec VP Atral Media Quebec; Robert Trempe, VP sls/mktg.

Affiliates: FM Stations: 94.3 (Montréal); 98.9 (Québec); 99.1 (Rouyn-Noranda); 102.3 (Mauricie); 102.7 (Val d'Or); 104.1 (Outaouais); 106.1 (Estrie); CITÉ (Montréal); CITF (Québec); CIMF (Hull); CFIX (Chicoutimi); CITÉ (Sherbrooke); CHEY (Trois-Rivières); CFEI 106.5 (Saint-Hyacinthe); CIKX (Grand Falls, New-Brunswick); CJCJ (Woodstock, New-Brunswick); CFXY (Fredericton, New-Brunswick); CIBX (Fredericton, New-Brunswick); CKTO (Truro, Nova Scotia); CKTY (Truro, Nova Scotia); AM Stations: CKHJ (Fredericton, New-Brunswick); CKBC (Bathurst, New-Brunswick).

Canadian Broadcasting Corp.

The Canadian Broadcasting Corp. (CBC) is a publicly owned corporation established by the Broadcasting Act (1936) of the Canadian Parliament to provide the natl bcstg svc in Canada in the two official languages, English & French. Under this legislation, the CBC is governed by the 1991 Broadcasting Act and subject to regulations of the Canadian Radio-Television and Telecommunications Commission (CRTC).

Program Services: The CBC operates English and French AM & FM stereo networks. The progmg on these networks is nearly all Canadian and virtually free of coml adv. CBC North bcsts radio programs to Canada's north in English, French and eight native languages, serving the special needs of native & non-native groups in the Yukon, the Northwest Territories and northern Quebec. Radio Canada International is Canada's voice abroad. Bcstg on shortwave in seven languages, RCI's progmg reflects Canada's political, economic, social & cultural spectrum to an international audience. Newsworld is a 24-hour natl satellite to cable English-language news & info svc. Le Réeseau de l'information (RDI) is a 24-hour natl satellite to cable French-language news & info svc. The heart of CBC's natl distribution system is Canada's Anik E2 satellite, carrying progmg through six different time zones. CBC's progmg is bcst over 684 AM & FM stns.

Head Office: 181 Queen St., Box 3220, Station C, Ottawa, ON K1P 1K9. (613) 724-1200. TDD: (613) 724-5173. Web site: www.cbc.ca; E-mail: commho@cbc.ca.

CBC Board of Directors: Carole Taylor, chairwoman; Robert Rabinovitch, pres/CEO; Helene Fortin; Marie Giguere; Roy L. Heenan; Jane Heffelfinger; Clarence LeBreton; Howard McNutt; L. Richard O'Hagan; James S. Palmer.

Principal Officers: Robert Rabinovitch, pres/CEO; Harold Redekopp, exec VP, English Television; Daniel Gourd, exec VP, French Television; Jane Chalmers, VP English Radio; Sylvain Lafrance, VP French Radio and New Media; Pierre Nollet, VP/gen counsel/corporate sec; George C.B. Smith, sr VP human resources and organization; Johanne Charbonneau, VP/CFO; Raymond Carnovale, VP/CTO; Michel Tremblay, VP strategy and bus devel; William B. Chambers, VP communications; Michel Saint-Cyr, pres Real Estate div.

CBC Ombudsmen: David Bazay, English svcs, Box 500, Station A, Toronto, ON M5W 1E6; E-mail: ombudsman@cbc.ca. Web site: www.cbc.ca/ombudsman. Renaud Gilbert, French svcs, Box 6000, Montreal, PQ H3C 3A8; E-mail ombudsman@radio-canada.ca. Web Site: www.radio-canda-ca/ombudsman.

English Networks: 250 Front St. W., Box 500, Station A, Toronto, ON M5W 1E6. (866) 306-4636. TDD: (416) 205-6688; E-mail: cbcinput@cbc.ca.

French Networks: Box 6000, Montreal, PQ H3C 3A8. (514) 597-6000. TDD: (514) 597-6013; E-mail: auditoire@radio-canada.ca.

Newfoundland Region (English): Box 12010, Station A, St. John's, NF A1B 3T8. (709) 576-5000.

Maritime Region (English): Box 3000, Halifax, NS B3J 3E9. (902) 420-8311.

Atlantic Provinces (French): Box 950, Moncton, NB E1C 8N8. (506) 853-6666.

Quebec Region (English): Box 6000, Montreal, PQ H3C 3A8. (514) 597-6000.

Quebec City & Eastern Quebec Region (French): Box 18800, Ste. Foy, PQ G1V 9L4. (418) 654-1341.

Ontario Region (English): Box 500, Station A, Toronto, ON M5W 1E6. (416) 205-3311.

Ontario Region (French): Box 3220, Station C, Ottawa, ON K1Y 1E4. (613) 724-1200.

Manitoba Region (English & French): Box 160, Winnipeg, MB R3C 2H1. (204) 788-3222.

Saskatchewan Region (English & French): 2440 Broad St., Box 540, Regina, SK S4P 4A1. (306) 347-9540.

Alberta Region (English & French): Box 555, Edmonton, AB T5J 2P4. (780) 468-7500.

British Columbia Region (English & French): Box 4600, Vancouver, BC V6B 4A2. (604) 662-6000.

CBC North: 5129 49th St., Box 160, Yellowknife, NT X1A 1P8. (867) 920-5400.

Producers, Distributors, and Production Services Alphabetical Index

A

ABC Family Channel, 500 S. Buena Vista St., Burbank, CA 91521. Phone: (818) 560-1000. Web Site: www.abcfamily.com.
TV-CATV only.
ABC Family features quality, contemporary entertainment for all members of the family including original series, movies & specials. Available in over 87 million homes via basic cable.

ABC Radio Networks, 444 Madison Ave., 9th Fl., New York, NY 10022. Phone: (212) 735-1700. Fax: (212) 735-1799. Web Site: www.abcradio.com. John McConnell, sr VP; Tom Powell, VP; Dave Kaufman, VP; Dan Formento, VP.
Radio Only.
Producers of natl & international radio features, such as *Flashback, Flashback Pop Quiz* & *Rock Slides*.

ABC Radio Networks, 13725 Montfort Dr., Dallas, TX 75240. Phone: (972) 991-9200. Fax: (972) 991-9890. Web Site: www.abcradio.com. Traug Keller, pres; Darryl Brown, exec VP; Robert Hall, progmg VP; John Russo, VP affil rel west; T.J. Lambert, VP sports.
Radio Only.
Live 24-hour-a-day premium progmg available featuring 10 radio formats. Also includes SMN PRIZM rsch clustering.

ACC Entertainment, Bavariafilmplatz 7, 82031 Grünwald, Munich Phone: 49-89 64981-332. Phone: 49-89 64981-232. E-mail: accficm@acc.com.
TV-CATV only.
Film & TV producers, distributors.

ACTV Inc., 233 Park Ave., 10th Floor, New York, NY 10020. Phone: (212) 497-7000. Fax: (212) 497-7001. Web Site: www.actv.com. E-mail: info@actv.com. William C. Samuels, chmn; Christopher Cline, CFO; David Reese, CEO.
TV-CATV only.
Interactive TV progmg for educ & entertainment.

ADM—International Film & TV Distribution, Drienerwolde House, Drienerwoldeweg, Hengelo, IL 7552 PC. Netherlands. Phone: 31 74 250 6843. Fax: 31 74 250 1874. Carole K. Hodson, mgng dir; Herman Melzer, chmn acquisitions; Sarah J. Mydlak, dir sales & mktg.
TV-CATV only.
International distributor of film & TV programs including features, classics, documentaries, children's, plus much more.

ALIN TV, 149 Madison Ave., Suite 602, New York, NY 10016. Phone: (212) 889-1327. Fax: (212) 213-6968. Alan Cohen, pres.
TV-CATV only.
Unwired TV natl network.

ANA Television Network, 1510 H St. N.W., Suite 400, Washington, DC 20005. Phone: (202) 898-8222. Fax: (202) 898-8088. Angelyn Adams, CFO.
TV-CATV only.
Arabic-language TV net bcstg to the Arab-American community 24 hours via cable, wireless cable, satellite.
Satellite: DIRECTV Plus.

APA International Film Distributors Inc., 14260 S.W. 136th, Suite 16, Miami, FL 33186. Phone: (305) 234-4321. Fax: (305) 234-7565. E-mail: apafilm@bellsouth.net.
TV-CATV only.
TV program production & distribution.

APM/Associated Production Music, 6255 Sunset Blvd., Suite 820, Hollywood, CA 90028. Phone: (323) 461-3211. Phone: (800) 543-4276. Fax: (323) 461-9102. E-mail: sales@apmmusic.com. Web Site: www.apmmusic.com.
New York, NY 10173, 342 Madison Ave, Suite 1200. Phone: (800) 276-6874. Craig Giummarra, sls mgr.
TV-CATV only.
Sixteen Libraries: KPM, Bruton, Sonoton, Carlin, Castle, NFL. Over 3,000 CDs, Personalized Packages, Music Search, 15-20 New CD releases mthy.

ATA Trading Corp., Box 307, Massapequa Park, NY 11762. Phone: (516) 541-5336. Fax: (516) 541-5336. E-mail: atat@verizon.net. Harold G. Lewis, pres; Susan Lewis, VP.
TV-CATV only.
Worldwide distributors for ind producers in all areas of feature films, made-for-TV productions, series, documentaries & children's programs.

Academy Entertainment, 59 Westminster Ave., Bergenfield, NJ 07621. Phone: (201) 385-8139. Phone: (201) 394-1849. Fax: (201) 385-8196. E-mail: mlrfilms@aol.com. Alan Miller, pres; Al Leifer, co-pres.
TV-CATV only.
Distribution of film, TV & video progmg worldwide.

Accuracy in Media Inc., 4455 Connecticut Ave. N.W., Suite 330, Washington, DC 20008. Phone: (202) 364-4401. Fax: (202) 364-4098. E-mail: info@aim.org. Web Site: www.aim.org. Don Irvine, chmn.
Radio Only.
Nationwide media monitoring organization produces documentary TV films, one-minute weekday radioo commentaries, bi-monthly publications, and programs that critique media coverage.

Acme, 9976 W. Wanda Dr., Beverly Hills, CA 90210. Phone: (310) 276-5509. Fax: (310) 276-1183. Bradley Friedman, pres; David Temianka, dir; Fred Wietzchz, CEO.
TV-CATV only.
Feature film & TV production, music videos, childrens progmg, commercials, robotics, scripting, tin ton props, rock music stock footage, space stock footage.

Adler Media Inc., 6849 Old Dominion Dr., Suite 420, McLean, VA 22101. Phone: (703) 556-8880. Fax: (703) 556-9288. E-mail: sales@adlermediatv.com. Web Site: www.adlermediatv.com. Larry Adler, pres; Ingrid Enzelsberger, sls dir.
TV-CATV only.
Program distributor to TV, cable & home video mkts worldwide. Handles series, documentaries, music & children's features completed or in dev.

Advanced Digital Services, Inc., 948 N. Cahuenga Blvd., Hollywood, CA 90038. Phone: (323) 468-2200. Fax: (323) 468-2211. Web Site: www.adshollywood.com. Andrew McIntyre, pres; Kevin Yates, COO.
TV-CATV only.
Video duplication, standard conversion.

Adventist Media, 101 W. Cochran, Simi Valley, CA 93065. Phone: (805) 955-7777. Fax: (805) 522-1082. E-mail: info@faithfortoday.tv. Marshall Chase, gen mgr.
TV-CATV only.
TV program production & distribution.

African Family Film Foundation, Box 630, Santa Cruz, CA 95061-0630. Phone: (831) 426-3133. E-mail: taale@africanfamily.org. Web Site: www.africanfamily.org. Taale Laafi Rosellini, dir.
TV-CATV only.
Production & distribution of films & videotapes promoting African family life & culture.

Agency for Instructional Technology (AIT), Box A, Bloomington, IN 47402-0120. Phone: (800) 457-4509. Phone: (812) 339-2203. Fax: (812) 333-4218. E-mail: info@ait.net. Web Site: www.ait.net.
Bloomington, IN 47404, 1800 N. Stonelake Dr. (Shipping address).
TV-CATV only.
Produces, acquires & distributes technology-based learning resources—including video, videodisc, software & print—for all K-12 curricular areas, vocational educ/tech prep, early childhood, & professional dev.

Agora TV, 195 Hicks Dr. S.E., Marietta, GA 30060. Phone: (404) 226-4503. Fax: (678) 581-3750. E-mail: joe@agoratv.tv. Web Site: www.agoratv.tv. Joseph Gora, pres.
TV-CATV only.
TV production & equipment rental.

Agrinet Farm Radio Network, 104 Radio Rd., Powell's Point, NC 27966. Phone: (252) 491-2414. Fax: (252) 491-2939. Web Site: www.agrinetradio.com. Bill Ray, dir; Gary Gross, dir opns; Lisa Ray, natl sls mgr.
TV-CATV only.
State, rgnl & natl agricultural news, mkts & weather.

Airwaves Audio Inc., 150 Mutual St., Toronto, ON M5B 2M1. Canada. Phone: (416) 977-1098. James Kennedy, pres.
TV-CATV only.
Audiovisual & industrial postproduction. Audio recording & mixing for radio & TV.

Alden Films, Box 449, Clarksburg, NJ 08510. Phone: (732) 462-3522. Fax: (732) 294-0330. E-mail: info@aldenfilms.com. Web Site: www.aldenfilms.com. Paul Weinberg, pres; Fran Fried, admin asst.
TV-CATV only.
Distributes nearly 600 films & videos on Israel & Judaica. Official distributor for state of Israel.

All Media Productions Inc., 12259-A Cleveland Ave., Nunica, MI 49448. Phone: (616) 837-0776. Fax: (616) 837-0897. Web Site: www.allmediaproductions.com. E-mail: linda@allmediaproductions.com. Linda Langs, pres.
TV-CATV only.
Web dev, internet mktg & film distribution.

All My Features Inc., 9190 Clearstream Terr., Mechanicsville, VA 23111. Phone: (804) 730-1534. Fax: (804) 559-4809.
TV-CATV only.
Provides daily entertainment news, entertainment-related features via audio & computer feeds.

All Productions, 7025 Regner Rd., Suite 5, San Diego, CA 92119. Phone: (619) 284-2566. Fax: (619) 460-6160. E-mail: mikeall@eudoramail.com. Web Site: www.allproductions.com. Michael J. All, CEO; Stephen A. All, CFO; Jean M. All, pres.
San Diego, CA 92119-1941, 7025 Regner Rd. Phone: (619) 460-4837. (619) 286-7733. Fax: (619) 460-6160.
TV-CATV only.
TV & radio program production & distribution; cable-ready TV progmg; promotion film production, production svcs; TV & radio spots; coml announcers.

Allegro Productions Inc., 1000 Clint Moore Rd., Suite 211, Boca Raton, FL 33487. Phone: (800) 275-4636. Fax: (888) 329-3737. E-mail: allegro@ssrvideo.com. Web Site: www.ssrvideo.com. Jerome G. Forman, pres.
TV-CATV only.
Educational & corporate progmg, including documentary/bcst. From concept to completion, offering full service video post production, CD-ROM/DVD authoring, multi-format duplication, 3D animation & effects.

Allied Production and Distribution Services, 135 W. Hancock St., Decatur, GA 30030. Phone: (404) 373-1227. Fax: (404) 373-1227. Edwin Clark, pres.
TV-CATV only.
TV program production & distribution.

Aloha Productions, Box 33648, San Diego, CA 92163. Phone: (619) 275-7357. Phone: (800) 223-2564. Fax: (858) 490-3397. E-mail: aloharn@portparadise.com. Hal Hodgson, exec producer.
Original coml music production, scoring, jingles, long-form; movie & TV scores.

Alternative Programming, 4215 Brendenwood Rd., Rockford, IL 61107. Phone: (800) 231-2818. Fax: (815) 229-5043. E-mail: altprog@aol.com. Gary A. Knoll, pres.
Radio Only.
Complete music formats for radio - current music for various formats - custom CD service.

Altman Productions, 3401 Macomb St. N.W., Washington, DC 20016. Phone: (202) 362-3088. Fax: (202) 362-0234. E-mail: itsacademicquiz@aol.com. Sophie B. Altman, exec producer; Susan Altman, producer; Susan Lechner, editor.
TV-CATV only.

Broadcasting & Cable Yearbook 2006

Producers, Distributors, and Production Services Alphabetical Index

TV & radio program production. Producers of It's Academic, the high school quiz program.

Americ Disc, 11 Oval Dr., Islandia, NY 11788. Phone: (631) 234-0200. Fax: (631) 232-4430.
TV-CATV only.
Film processing, film-to-tape transfers, video editing, videocassette, audiocassette duplication, CD-ROM & CD-Audio duplication packaging & fulfillment.

America On The Road, 4038 Exultant Dr., Rancho Palos Verdes, CA 90275. Phone: (310) 265-9873. Fax: (310) 544-4318. E-mail: aotrradio@cox.net. Web Site: www.americaontheroad.com. Ed Yelin, producer; Al Herskovitz, ptnr.
TV-CATV only.
One hour wkly, 2.5-minute daily automotive consumer show.

America One Television, 100 E. Royal Ln., Suite 100, Irving, TX 75039. Phone: (972) 969-1900. Fax: (972) 969-1915. E-mail: amy@americaone.com. Web Site: www.americaone.com.
TV-CATV only.
24 hour-a-day gen entertainment bcst network.

American Blues Network, Box 6216, Gulfport, MS 39506. Phone: (800) 896-5307, ext 117.
Radio Only.

American Chiropractic Association Inc., 1701 Clarendon Blvd., Arlington, VA 22209. Phone: (703) 276-8800. Fax: (703) 243-2593. Web Site: www.acatoday.com.
TV-CATV only.
Professional membership organization.

American Farm Bureau Federation, 225 Touhy Ave., Park Ridge, IL 60068. Phone: (847) 685-8752. Fax: (847) 685-8950. E-mail: stut@fb.org. Web Site: www.fb.org. Stewart Truelsen, dir.
TV-CATV only.
AGFeed, mthy video feed of news stories about food & agriculture, Newsline radio svc, Focus on Agriculture commentary, stock footage.

American Foundation for the Blind, 11 Penn Plaza, Suite 300, New York, NY 10001. Phone: (212) 502-7600. Phone: (800) 232-5463. Fax: (212) 502-7777. E-mail: afbinfo@afb.net. Web Site: www.afb.org. Carl Augusto, pres; Liz Greco-Rocks, dir.
San Francisco, CA 94111. AFB National Employment Center, 111 Pine Street, Suite 725. Phone: (415) 392-4845. Fax: (415) 392-0383. E-mail: sanfran@afb.net.
Washington, DC 20002. Governmental Relations, 820 First Street, NE, Suite 400. Phone: (202) 408-0200. Fax: (202) 289-7880. E-mail: afbgov@afb.net.
Atlanta, GA 30303. AFB National Literacy Center, 100 Peachtree Street, Suite 620. Phone: (404) 525-2303. Fax: (404) 659-6957. E-mail: atlanta@afb.net.
Chicago, IL 60611. AFB Midwest, 401 N. Michigan Avenue, Suite 350. Phone: (312) 396-4420. Fax: (312) 527-4660. E-mail: chicago@afb.net.
Dallas, TX 75235. AFB Southwest, 260 Treadway Plaza, Exchange Park. Phone: (214) 352-7222. Fax: (214) 352-3214. E-mail: dallas@afb.net.
Huntington, WV 25701. AFB Technology and Employment Center at Huntington, West Virginia, 949 Third Avenue, Suite 200. Phone: (304) 523-8651. Fax: (304) 523-8656. E-mail: WV@afb.net.
TV-CATV only.
Provides consultation & referrals, social & technological rsch, publications, info svcs, public educ, govt rel & talking books.

American Heart Association, 7272 Greenville Ave., Dallas, TX 75231-4596. Phone: (214) 706-1330. Fax: (214) 706-5243. Karen Hunter, dir; Karen Astle, mgr.
TV-CATV only.
Video news releases, stock footage related to heart & disease for news programs.

American Public Television, 55 Summer St., Boston, MA 02110. Phone: (617) 338-4455. Fax: (617) 338-5369. Web Site: www.aptonline.org. Cynthia Fenneman, pres/COO.
TV-CATV only.
Major distributor of high quality TV programs to all U.S. public TV stns. Also distributor of programs to international media.

American Stock Exchange, 86 Trinity Pl., New York, NY 10006. Phone: (212) 306-1229. Fax: (212) 306-5489. E-mail: kenneth.meyer@amex.com. Web Site: www.amex.com. Kimberly Zapien, dir.
TV-CATV only.
TV studio location on a trading floor, teleprompters,

access to industry analysts, production and postproduction svcs.

American TelNet, 855 SW 78th Ave., Plantation, FL 33324. Phone: (954) 453-7000. Fax: (954) 453-7809. E-mail: success@americantelnet.com.
An 800/900 Interactive svc bureau offering a wide var of turnkey pay-per-call entertainment & business programs.

AmericaNurse TV Productions, Box 7717, Romeoville Plainfield, IL 60446. Phone: (815) 773-4497. Web Site: www.americianurse.com. Karen Gibson, R.N., producer.
Palm Beach, FL 33480, Box 83.
TV-CATV only.
Consumer educ shows on health, safety & other self-help titles. Entertaining introduction to optional alternative & mainstream medicine & Rx.

America's Most Wanted, 5151 Wisconsin Ave. N.W., Washington, DC 20016. Phone: (202) 205-2600. Fax: (202) 204-2604.
TV-CATV only.
Wkly reality-based program for Fox TV.

Anderson Productions Ltd. (APL), 37 W. 20th St., Loft #904, New York, NY 10011. Phone: (212) 414-9220. Fax: (212) 206-0279. E-mail: andersontv@aol.com. Steven C. F. Anderson, exec producer & pres; Brian Peter Falk, dir.
TV-CATV only.
Reality-based TV program production for bcst & cable TV.

Angel Films Co., 967 Hwy. 40, New Franklin, MO 65274-9778. Phone: (573) 698-3900. Fax: (573) 698-3900. E-mail: phoeenix@phoeenix.org. William H. Hoehne Jr., chmn; Joyce L. Chow, CEO; Arlene Hulse, pres; Leana Le Gee, VP mktg & adv VP; Matthew P. Eastman, VP production.
TV-CATV only.
Production, distribution, syndication of progmg for adults & children.

Animated Production Services, 321 W. 44th St., New York, NY 10036. Phone: (212) 265-2942. Fax: (212) 265-2944. Web Site: www.digitaltofilm.com.
TV-CATV only.
TV program, coml, promotional film production, distribution & production svcs, digital film.

Antenne 2 - French TV 2, 1290 Ave. of the Americas, Suite 3410, New York, NY 10104. Phone: (212) 581-1771. Fax: (212) 541-4309.
TV-CATV only.
TV program production.

The Arabic Channel, 366 86 St., 1st Fl., Brooklyn, NY 11209-5002. Phone: (718) 238-2450. Fax: (718) 238-2465. Gamil Tawfol, pres/CEO; Marguerite M. Moore, VP; Dr. Saleh El-Ahwal, VP.
TV-CATV only.
Arabic language progmg bcst Time Warner/Comcast Cablevision.

Archive Films/Archive Photos, 75 Varick St., 5th Floor, New York, NY 10013. Phone: (646) 613-4000. Phone: (800) 876-5115. Fax: (646) 613-4140. E-mail: sales@archivefilms.com. Web Site: www.archivefilms.com.
111 45 Stockholm. Archive Films/Archive Photos Scandinavia, Birger Jarlsgatan 55. Phone: 46 8 20 89 20. Fax: 46 8 20 89 33. Contact: Lennert Karlsson.
Cologne 50969. Archive Films GMBH, Bremstrasse 12. Phone: 49 221 936 4080. Fax: 49 221 360 4112. Contact: Craig Burns.
London W1P 6EE. Archive Films/Archive Photos, 17 Conway St. Phone: 44 171 312 0300. Fax: 44 171 391 9123. Contact: Chris Blakeston.
Milan 20123. Archive Films/Archive Photos Italy, Via Terraggio 17. Phone: 39 2 874 693. Fax: 39 2 805 7739. Contact: Guido Rossi.
Paris Ducaud 75009. Archive Films/Archive Photos, 4 Boulevard Poissonniere. Phone: 33 1 55 77 00 00. Fax: 33 1 55 77 00 66. Contact: Sylvie Ducaud.
TV-CATV only.
Stock footage/photo library providing all types of historical footage & photos for use in products for TV/CATV.

Ardustry Home Entertainment LLC, 21250 Califa St., Woodland Hills, CA 91367. Phone: (818) 712-9070. Fax: (818) 712-9000. Web Site: www.ardustry.com. Cheryl Freeman, CEO.
TV-CATV only.
Distribution, dev, production documentaries, TV series, kids, specials.

Arkadia Entertainment Corp., 34 E. 23rd St., 3rd Fl., New York, NY 10010. Phone: (212) 533-0007. Fax: (212) 979-0266. E-mail: arkadian@aol.com. Web Site: www.arkadiarecords.com. Bob Karcy, CEO.
Radio Only.
CD, DVD, video production & distribution worldwide. A broad range of exclusive progmg.

Armedia Communications, 307-3219 Young St., Toronto, ON M4N 2L3. Canada. Phone: (905) 889-0076. Fax: (905) 889-0078. David Mazmanian, owner.
TV-CATV only.
Audio, video, music production & bcst svcs.

J. Arnold Productions, 363 Massachusetts Ave., Lexington, MA 02420. Phone: (781) 674-2277. Fax: (781) 674-0272. E-mail: jarpro@aol.com. James Arnold, pres; Lori Arnold, production mgr; Eric Fisher, production mgr.
Charlotte, NC 28117, 147 Cove Creek Rd. Phone: (704) 663-4444. Fax: (704) 663-6696. James Arnold, pres.
TV-CATV only.
Full-svc on location video production. ENG-EFP crews & Betacam equipment packages.

The Kay Arnold Group, 34 Kramer Dr., Paramus, NJ 07652. Phone: (201) 652-6037. Fax: (201) 612-8578. Kay Arnold, pres.
TV-CATV only.
Production & distribution of film & tape programs for TV, satellite, cable, home video & non-theatrical.

Toby Arnold and Associates Inc., 3234 Commander Dr., Carrollton, TX 75006. Phone: (800) 527-5335. Phone: (972) 661-8200. Fax: (972) 250-6014. E-mail: toby@taamusic.com. Web Site: www.taamusic.com. Toby Arnold, pres; Dolly Arnold, VP/COO; Lawrence Mangiameli, VP/creative dir.
TV-CATV only.
Audio production libraries for TV & radio. Station Imaging, Morning show promo sweeper, stager packages for all formats.

Artisan PictureWorks Ltd., 800 Forrest St. N.W., Atlanta, GA 30318. Phone: (404) 355-3398. Fax: (404) 350-0302. E-mail: info@artisanpicture.com. Web Site: www.artisanpictureworks.com. Bryan Gartman, pres; Amy Thompson, production mgr; Dan Valdes, mgr.
TV-CATV only.
Studio facilities feature Ultimatte, fiber optics to satellite uplink. Live multicam specialists. Remote & in-house production facilities.

Artist View Entertainment Inc., 12500 Riverside Dr., Suite 201B, North Hollywood, CA 91607. Phone: (818) 752-2480. Fax: (818) 752-9339. E-mail: artistview@earthlink.net. Web Site: artistviewent.com. Scott J. Jones, pres; Jay E. Joyce, VP.
TV-CATV only.
Worldwide distribution in all media specializing in feature films.

Ascent Entertainment Group Inc., 1225 17th St., Suite 1800, Denver, CO 80202. Phone: (303) 308-7000. Fax: (303) 308-0485.
San Jose, CA 95119. On Command Corp., 6331 San Ignacio Ave.
Palm Bay, FL 32905. Ascent Network Services, 2330 Commerce Park Dr. N.E. Phone: (800) 327-2818. Larry Tennant, VP distribution & customer service.
Memphis, TN 38118, 2600 Thousand Oaks, Suite 1400. Phone: (901) 367-1444. Ric Swift, VP natl sls.
TV-CATV-Radio.
Hotel entertainment & info svcs, videoconferencing, satellite bcst distribution, & network construction & maintenance.

Ascent Media Management East, 235 Pegasus Ave., Northvale, NJ 07647. Phone: (201) 767-3800. Fax: (201) 784-2769. E-mail: agavin@apvi.com. Web Site: www.apvi.com. Don Buck, pres; Al Gavin, sls VP; Tony Beswick, VP/gen mgr.
Burbank, CA 91502. Audio Plus Video - West, 200 S. Flower St. Phone: (818) 841-7100. Larry Kingen, VP/gen mgr.
TV-CATV only.
Standards & aspect ratio conversion, international duplication, PAL/NTSC editing, film-to-tape transfers, 16 X 9 audio layback, restoration & satellite svcs, dud authoring, compression, streaming.

Ascent Media Network Services, 2901 W. Alameda Ave., Burbank, CA 91505. Phone: (818) 840-7174. Fax: (818) 567-1131. Web Site: www.ascentmedia.com. Sharon Pyne, opns dir; Lennis Schwartz, VP opns; Jodynne Wood, sls dir.

Broadcasting & Cable Yearbook 2006

E-39

Producers, Distributors, and Production Services Alphabetical Index

London, NO WIT 2NS United Kingdom, 48 Charlotte St.
TV-CATV only.
AM NS powers the broadcast-cable networks around the world. We distribute programming content over our integrated fiber and satellite network.

Ascent Media Network Services, 250 Harbor Dr., Stamford, CT 06902. Phone: (203) 965-6000. Fax: (203) 965-6405. Web Site: www.ascentmedia.com. Francis G. Luperella, sr VP; Matt Armstrong, VP mktg.
Singapore. Asia Bcst Centre Phone: (612) 330-2639. E-mail: vhendra@abc.gwns.com. Vincent Helseth.
Minneapolis, MN 55038. GWNS Minneapolis, 6845 20th Ave. Phone: (612) 330-2639. Joel Helseth, sls & mktg.
TV-CATV only.
Video transmission, origination; technical consulting, new media products; private networks, post production, studio, graphics; bcst event svcs & satellite svcs.

Asia Pacific Productions, 19698 S.E. Cottonwood St., Portland, OR 97267. Phone: (503) 723-6456. Fax: (503) 723-6456. E-mail: info@approd.com. Web Site: www.approd.com. Thomas F. Hopkins, pres; Miyuki Shigeji, VP.
Kobe 653-088 Japan, 3-17 Higashi Maruyomo Cho. Phone: 81 78 691 2450 Telephone/Fax.
TV-CATV only.
Provides news, documentary & program production; coml production; business/promotional film & video production; production svcs for TV/CATV.

Associated Press Television News, 1825 K St., N.W., Suite 800, Washington, DC 20036. Phone: (202) 736-9595. Fax: (202) 736-9619. Web Site: www.ap.org.
TV-CATV only.
TV news production, news library, video editing & ENG production.

Associated Television International, 4401 Wilshire Blvd., Los Angeles, CA 90010. Phone: (323) 556-5600. Fax: (323) 556-5610. Fax: www.associatedtelevision.com. E-mail: atiwest@aol.com.
TV-CATV only.
Full-svc production, distribution & syndication company in business for over 20 years.

Association of Islamic Charitable Projects, 4431 Walnut St., Philadelphia, PA 19104. Phone: (215) 387-8888. Fax: (215) 387-3815. Web Site: www.aicp.org.
TV-CATV only.
Islamic progmg. Educational micro-bcst network service for metro Philadelphia.

At a Glance, 6350 W. Freeway, Fort Worth, TX 76116. Phone: (817) 570-1400. Phone: (800) 266-1837. Fax: (817) 737-9436. E-mail: info@familynet.com. Web Site: www.familynetradio.com. Lisa Bratton, radio mktg & distribution; Donna Senn, radio Distribution; Chuck Ries, producer.
Radio Only.
Variety of topics: health, fitness, character, parenting, etc. 60 second spots, 10 per month, on CD.

Atlantic Video Inc., 650 Massachusetts Ave. N.W., Washington, DC 20001. Phone: (202) 408-0900. Fax: (202) 408-8496. Web Site: www.atlanticvideo.com. Doug Moon Joo, pres; John Sommers, VP/gen mgr; Amy Schwab, mktg dir.
Alexandria, VA 22304, 150 S. Gordon St. Phone: (703) 823-2800.
TV-CATV only.
Soundstages, postproduction, graphics, duplication, remote, satellite uplink, videoconferencing, film-to-tape, D-2, digital 110 pathways & audio sweetening.

Auburn Television, (A division of Telecommunications). Auburn University, Admin. Bldg., Corner of Samford & Donahue, Auburn, AL 36849-5423. Phone: (334) 844-5707. Fax: (334) 844-5708. Web Site: www.auburn.edu. Richard Burnett, exec dir; Larry Shaw, chief engr; Deborah Howard, opns mgr.
Montgomery, AL 36104. Broadview Mall, 401 Adams St, Box 7. Phone: (344) 223-5708. Rich Michaelson, dir.
TV-CATV only.
TV/studio/remote production, Tape/CD/DVD production, satellite uplink/downlink & avid edit suite, CATV

Audible Advertising Productions Inc., Desota Bldg., 215 W. 91st St., Suite 25, New York, NY 10024. Phone: (212) 873-1238. Mary Hurt, exec producer.
Radio Only.
Musical comls for radio; syndicated orchestrations with original lyrics for each client.

The Audio Department Inc., 119 W. 57th St., 4th Fl., New York, NY 10019. Phone: (212) 586-3503. Fax: (212) 245-1675. Web Site: www.theaudiodepartment.com. Aimee Mitchaud, mgr; Lola Norarevian, mgr.
TV-CATV only.
Audio & audio for video, adv & media promotion.

Audio Production Services, University of Colorado, Campus Box 379, 312 Stadium Bldg., Boulder, CO 80309. Phone: (303) 492-2675. Fax: (303) 492-7017.
Radio Only.
Radio program production.

Auritt Communications Group, 729 Seventh Ave., 5th Fl., New York, NY 10019. Phone: (212) 302-6230. Fax: (212) 302-2969. Web Site: www.auritt.com. Joan Auritt, pres.
TV-CATV only.
Satellite media tours, event coverage, video news releases, B-roll packages, radio tours, audio new releases, sls/corporate videos, web casting, print tours

Australian Tourist Commission, 2049 Century Park E. Ste 1920, Los Angeles, CA 90067-3121. Phone: (310) 229-4871. Fax: (310) 552-1215. E-mail: rmonfrini@atc.australia.com. Web Site: www.australia.com. Robert Monfrini, dir.
TV-CATV only.
TV program distribution.

Avid Technology Inc. Avid Technology Park, One Park W., Tewksbury, MA 01876. Phone: (800) 949-2843. Phone: (978) 640-6789. Fax: (978) 640-1366. E-mail: info@avid.com. Web Site: www.avid.com.
TV-CATV only.
Avid Technology is a leading supplier of newsroom computer, editing, playback & effects systems. Implemented as stand-alone or networked systems, Avid solutions provide speed, creativity & operating efficiencies throughout the newsroom.

Axcess Broadcast Services Inc., 4801 Spring Valley, Suite 105-B, Dallas, TX 75244. Phone: (972) 386-6847. Fax: (972) 386-5207.
TV-CATV only.
Sls consulting for new businesses in the top 100 markets. CD production library, radio, TV promotions & IDs.

B

BBC Worldwide Americas Inc., 747 3rd Ave., 7th Fl., New York, NY 10017. Phone: (212) 705-9300. Fax: (212) 888-0576.
TV-CATV only.
TV program production & distribution, home video, library sls, licensing.

BBC Worldwide Television Ltd., 80 Woodlands, London W12 0TT. Fax: (181) 749-0538. Fax: (181) 576-2000. E-mail: webguide@bbc.co.uk. Web Site: www.bbc.co.uk.
TV-CATV-Radio.
Program licensing to international bcstrs & generation of co-production business. Dev of BBC branded satellite & cable channels worldwide.

BKN Kids Network, 41 Madison Ave., New York, NY 10010. Phone: (212) 213-2700. Fax: (212) 685-8332. Web Site: www.amazin.com.
Entertainment & media company specializing in the youth market. Hqtrs in New York & offices in Chicago, Los Angeles & Paris, France.

S. Banks Group Inc., 174 Johnston Ave., Toronto, ON M2N 1H3. Canada. Phone: (416) 224-0296. Fax: (416) 224-8542. Sydney Banks, pres.
TV-CATV only.
Feature film and TV program production.

Bardel Entertainment Inc., 548 Beatty St., Vancouver, BC V6B 2L3. Canada. Phone: (604) 669-5589. Fax: (604) 669-9079. E-mail: bardel@bardelanimation.com. Web Site: www.bardelentertainment.com or www.bardelanimation.com. Barry Ward, pres; Delna Bhesania, CEO; Cathy Schoch, producer.
TV-CATV only.
High quality 3D, Maya & hybrids of digital & traditional animation svcs for feature film, television, interactive media, internet & commercials.

Bavaria Film GmbH, Bavariafilmplatz 7, 82031Geiselgasteig/Munich Phone: 49 89 6499 0. Fax: 49 89 6492 507. E-mail: presse@bavaria-film.de. Web Site: www.bavaria-film.de. Dieter Frank, pres; Thilo Kleine, pres; Peter Kussius, sls mgr.
TV-CATV only.
Dubbing, film laboratories, film & tape transfers, film & TV production, production svcs, multimedia svcs.

Bayliss, (Formerly Gene Bayliss). 208 Good Hill Rd., Weston, CT 06883-2326. Phone: (203) 227-7521. Fax: (203) 454-1032. Web Site: www.genebayliss.com. Gene Bayliss, producer & consultant.
Produces, directs video conferences, videotapes for corporations & industries, meetings & special events.

Beach Associates, 2601A Wilson Blvd., Arlington, VA 22201. Phone: (703) 812-8813. Fax: (703) 812-9710. E-mail: thebeach@beachassociates.com. Web Site: www.beachassociates.com.
TV-CATV only.
A full-svc visual communications firm. Staff producers, writers & dirs provide full creative direction & project mgmt from concept dev, treatment, scripting & graphics design to production & delivery. Offers videotape, live event production, consulting svcs for organizational communications. Provides comprehensive production svcs for videotape, special event & live business TV-video conference progmg. Also offers media training, VNR production, video press tours, consulting for private networks, new media svcs including distributed multimedia, WWW design & CD rom dev.

Beckmann International, Meadow Ct., West St., Ramsey, Isle of Man IM8 1AE. Phone: 44 01624 816585. Fax: 44 01624 816589. E-mail: beckmann@enterprise.net. Web Site: www.beckmanngroup.co.uk.
TV-CATV only.
International sls distributor specializing in non-fiction progmg.

Beethoven Satellite Network, (Classical Music Format Service). c/o WFMT Fine Arts Radio, 5400 N. St. Louis Ave., Chicago, IL 60625. Phone: (773) 279-2000. Phone: (800) USA-WFMT. Fax: (773) 279-2199. Web Site: www.wfmt.com. Steve Robinson, VP; Peter Vandegraaff, progmg dir; Carol Martinez, stn mgr.
Radio Only.
Program production & distribution; 168 hour-a-week classical music format with program hosts in one-hour modules, loc sound included.

Dave Bell Associates Inc., 3211 Cahuenga Blvd. W., Hollywood, CA 90068. Phone: (323) 851-7801. Fax: (323) 851-9349. E-mail: dbmovies@aol.com. Dave Bell, pres; Ted Weiant, VP; Fred Putman, VP; Kitty Stallings, Associate.
TV-CATV only.
Dev & production of TV movies, reality series, feature films, documentaries & game shows.

Bell Foto Art Productions, 375 C Josephine St., Denver, CO 80206. Phone: (303) 377-4606. Fax: (303) 322-2443. E-mail: bellfoto@att.net. Web Site: www.bellfoto.tv. Chris Bell, owner.
TV-CATV only.
Award winning video production: VNR, corporate, news sports, medical, training & legal. Story tellers in Beta SP, DV-cam, 24 & high Definition-Varicam.

Bellon Entertainment, 250 W. 57th St., Suite 1414, New York, NY 10107. Phone: (212) 265-1222. Fax: (212) 265-7318. E-mail: bellonent@aol.com. Gregory P. Bellon, pres.
TV-CATV only.
Represent and develop TV formats for worldwide distribution.

Best Film & Video Corp., 108 New South Rd., Hicksville, NY 11801. Phone: (516) 931-6969. Fax: (516) 931-5959. Roy B. Winnick, pres; Dana Miller, dir mktg.
Beverly Hills, CA 90210, 242 N. Canon Dr. Phone: (310) 274-9944. Fax: (310) 274-9960.
TV program production & distribution of home video.

Big Ticket Television, Bldg. 45, Sunset Gower Studios, 1438 N. Gower St., Hollywood, CA 90028-8362. Phone: (323) 860-7400. Fax: (323) 468-4176. E-mail: bigticket@segi-mail.com.
TV-CATV only.
Syndication, sitcom dev & program dev.

Black Audio Devices, Box 106, Ventura, CA 93002-0106. Phone: (805) 653-5557. Fax: (805) 653-5557. Web Site: www.blackaudio.com.
TV-CATV only.

Producers, Distributors, and Production Services Alphabetical Index

Blackbird Productions, 535 King's Rd., Suite 115, The Plaza, London SWIO 0SZ. Phone: +44 (0171) 352-4882. Fax: +44 (0171) 351-3728.
TV-CATV only.
Program production & distribution.

Blackstone Stock Footage, 509 Upsall Drive, Antioch, TN 37013. Phone: (615) 731-5310. Fax: (615) 731-5232. E-mail: g.clifford@worldnet.att.net. Web Site: www.blackstonestockfootage.com. Glenda Clifford, pres.
TV-CATV only.
We offer: Archival newsreel footage, medical, extreme sports, landmarks from around the wopld, food, people, animals, underwater, timelapse cities and nature.

Blanc Communications Corp., 171 Pier Ave., Suite 517, Santa Monica, CA 90405. Phone: (310) 278-2600. Fax: (310) 396-8434.
TV program production; TV & radio coml production & distribution.

The Chuck Blore Co., 17428 Tarzana St., Encino, CA 91316. Phone: (818) 784-5104. Fax: (818) 986-1196. E-mail: bloregroup@aol.com. Web Site: www.chuckblore.com. Chuck Blore, CEO.
TV-CATV only.
TV programs & coml production svcs. Radio coml production svcs. TV programs consultation.

Blue Canyon Productions, Box 6622, Santa Fe, NM 87502. Phone: (505) 989-9298. Web Site: www.bluecanyonproductions.com. Jim Terr, pres.
TV-CATV only.
Award-winning, nationally-bcst jingle, PSA & radio spot production, voice-overs & video production, as well as music production & scoring, scripting.

Blue Heaven Productions, 11 Glenwood Rd., Toms River, NJ 08753-4117. Phone: (732) 349-8569. E-mail: raynorman3@juno.com. Ray Norman, pres.
Radio Only.
Nostalgia music production library, CD masters made

Blue Sky Studios, 44 S. Broadway, White Plains, NY 10601. Phone: (914) 259-6500. Fax: (914) 259-6499. E-mail: query@blueskystudios.com. Web Site: www.blueskystudios.com. Brian Keane, gen mgr.
TV-CATV only.
Dev & production of CG animated films.

Robert L. Bocchino, 264 Montgomery Ave., Haverford, PA 19041-1531. Phone: (610) 649-0993. Fax: (610) 649-0895. Robert L. Bocchino, owner.
TV-CATV only.
Voice over artist, coml spokesperson.

Bonneville Communications, 5 Triad Ctr., Suite 700, Salt Lake City, UT 84180-1121. Phone: (801) 237-2600. Fax: (801) 237-2614. E-mail: bonneville@bonneville.com. Web Site: www.bonneville.com. Gregg D. Garber, gen mgr; Marc Lee, dir; Paul Yates, controller & VP.
TV-CATV only.
A values-driven adv agency engaged in communications for quality life.

Boston Symphony Orchestra, Symphony Hall, 301 Massachusetts Ave., Boston, MA 02115. Phone: (617) 266-1492. Fax: (617) 638-9367. Web Site: www.bso.org. Mark Volpe, mngg dir.
TV-CATV only.
Evening at Pops TV series & other special TV productions. Originates regular radio bcst of BSO concerts.

Dick Brescia Associates, 164 Garfield St., Haworth, NJ 07641. Phone: (201) 385-6566. Fax: (201) 385-6449. E-mail: dbasyndicators@prodigy.net. Web Site: www.ictx.com/dba.
Radio Only.
Radio shows: *When Radio Was*, *Stan Freberg Here*. Radio movie classics, radio super heroes.

Brillig Productions Inc., 770 Amalfi Dr., Pacific Palisades, CA 90272. Phone: (310) 459-4450. Fax: (310) 459-4456. E-mail: brilligprod@cooliwk.net. Barry Brown, pres; Joy Brown, VP.
TV-CATV only.
Feature films, TV features, TV comls, documentaries.

British Broadcasting Corp., (Fine Arts Programs.). c/o WFMT Radio Network, 5400 N. St. Louis Ave., Chicago, IL 60625. Phone: (773) 279-2000. Fax: (773) 279-2199. E-mail: finearts@wfmt.com. Web Site: www.wfmt.com. Carol Martinez, mgr; Steve Robinson, sr VP.
Radio Only.
Distribute wkly series *My Music*, & *My Word* for coml & public stns in the United States by WFMT Fine Arts Network.

Broadcast News Service, Box 919, Norwood, MA 02062-0919. Phone: (781) 344-6988. Fax: (781) 344-8928. P. J. Romano, dir.
TV-CATV only.
Radio, TV features & productions, audio news & features.

Broadcast Programming, 2211 5th Ave., Seattle, WA 98121. Phone: (206) 728-2741. Phone: (800) 426-9082. Fax: (206) 441-6582. E-mail: experts@jmseattle.com. Web Site: www.jonesradio.com.
Radio Only.
Daypart personality progmg, music log & consulting services.

Broadview Media, 4455 W. 77th St., Minneapolis, MN 55435. Phone: (952) 835-4455. Fax: (952) 835-0971. E-mail: michaels@broadviewmedia.com. Michaael Smith, VP progmg.
TV-CATV only.
Full-svc production, postproduction & creative svcs for the production of TV programs.

Himan Brown-Radio Drama Network, 285 Central Park W., New York, NY 10024. Phone: (212) 724-4333. Himan Brown, owner.
Radio Only.
Radio program production; TV & film program production; CD-ROM production.

Bruder Releasing Inc. (BRI), 2020 Broadway, Santa Monica, CA 90404. Phone: (310) 829-2222. Fax: (310) 829-0202. E-mail: bruder@brivideo.net. Web Site: www.46ri.net. Marc Bruder, pres.
TV-CATV only.
Supplies ind films to pay-per-view, cable, bcst & video markets worldwide.

Bulbeck & Mas SL, Quinones, 2, 28015 Madrid Phone: 34 91 594 2709. Fax: 34 91 445 7212. E-mail: bymfilms@bulbeckymas.com.
TV-CATV only.
Specialists in libraries of Spanish features.

Burrud Productions Inc., 16351 Gothard St., Unit D, Huntington Beach, CA 92647. Phone: (714) 842-8422. Fax: (714) 842-0433. E-mail: burrudprod@aol.com. Web Site: www.burrud.com. John Burrund, pres/CEO; Linda Karabin, VP; Drew Horton, VP; Valerie Chow, VP; Shannon Mead, exec dir & CEO.
TV-CATV only.
Feature film & TV production of reality, wildlife, oceanic, human adventure, documentary & world exploration progmg.

Buzzco Associates Inc., 33 Bleecker St., Suite 5A, New York, NY 10012. Phone: (212) 473-8800. Fax: (212) 473-8891. E-mail: info@buzzzco.com. Web Site: www.buzzzco.com.
TV-CATV only.
A full range of animation from traditional to innovative computer 2-D.

C

CABLEready Corp., 98 East Avenue, Norwalk, CT 06851-5029. Phone: (203) 855-7979. Fax: (203) 855-8370. E-mail: info@cableready.net. Web Site: www.cableready.net. Gary Lico, pres; Lou Occhicone, VP progmg; Sabrina Sanchez, dir; Kerry Novick, VP sls.
TV-CATV only.
Dev & sls of programs to U.S. cable TV networks & systems & all international telecasters.

CA Media Development, Box 1141, 1415 Hooper Ave., Suite 203, Toms River, NJ 08754. Phone: (732) 797-1965. Fax: (732) 797-1260. E-mail: ca.media@comcast.net. Greg Koziar, pres.
TV-CATV only.
Full svc adv agency, as well as coml production, for radio & cable TV.

CBC International Sales, Box 500, Stn. A, Toronto, ON M5W 1E6. Canada. Phone: (416) 205-3500. Fax: (416) 205-3482. E-mail: cbcis@toronto.cbc.ca. Christina Criss Hajek; Susan Hewitt, head international sls (London) & new business dev; Sandra Sarciada-Naughton,.
London W1P 8DD, 43/51 Great Titchfield St.
Los Angeles, CA 90025, 1950 Sawtelle Blvd, Suite 333.
TV-CATV only.
CBC is Canada's natl bcstr. Produces & distributes TV progmg in both English & French.

CCI Entertainment Ltd., 18 Dupont St., Toronto, ON MSR 1V2. Canada. Phone: (416) 964-8750. Fax: (416) 964-1980. Arnie Zipursky, pres/CEO; Annette Frymer, COO.
TV-CATV only.
Distributor & co-producer, producer

CCM Media Services, 104 Woodmont Blvd., Suite 300, Nashville, TN 37205. Phone: (615) 386-3011. Fax: (615) 312-4266. E-mail: bengland@ccmcom.com. Web Site: www.ccmmagazine.com.
Radio Only.
Nationally syndicated radio programs, as well as spot and radio special production. "ccm radio magazine" is the flagship show

CDC United Network, 40 Rue Souveraine, 1050 Brussels Phone: (322) 502-6640. Fax: (322) 502-6656. E-mail: alexandre@cdc.skynet.be MOBILE: 3275713057.
TV-CATV only.
TV distribution & merchandising in Latin America.

C.D. Media Inc., 1776 Broadway, 4th Fl., New York, NY 10019. Phone: (212) 735-1111. Fax: (212) 459-9343.
Radio Only.
Offers *Rick Dees Weekly Top 40*, a four-hour CHR countdown wkly; *Satellite Comedy Network*, daily comedy vignettes & parody songs via satellite.

CDR Communications Inc., 9310-B Old Keene Mill Rd., Burke, VA 22015. Phone: (703) 569-3400. Fax: (703) 569-3448. E-mail: chris@cdrcommunications.com. Web Site: www.communications.com. Christopher D. Rogers, pres; Nancy B. Rogers, VP.
TV-CATV only.
Film, TV, video & radio production: teleconferences, documentaries, adv campaigns, PSAs; graphics / animation, syndication / promotion, publishing / distribution, postproduction & mktg.

CFP Video Productions, Box 86, Caldwell, NJ 07006-0086. Phone: (973) 226-2481. Fax: (973) 226-2480. E-mail: don.spitzmiller@verizon.net. Donald Spitzmiller, pres; Richard A. Schwarz, producer.
Full video and audio services for television and industrial productions. Avid edit service/post production.

CIFEX International Inc., One Peconic Hills Ct., Southampton, NY 11968-1618. Phone: (631) 283-9454. Fax: (631) 283-4210. E-mail: cifex@prodigy.net. Gerald J. Rappoport, pres; Beulah Rappoport, VP business affrs; Shirley Clarke, VP mktg.
TV-CATV only.
Distributor of foreign-language feature films, animated & live-action short films & documentaries.

CMT, 330 Commerce St., Nashville, TN 37201. Phone: (615) 335-8400. Fax: (615) 335-8615. Web Site: www.cmt.com. Brian Philips, sr VP; Judy McGrath, pres; Jama Bowen, VP; Martin Clayton, VP/Gen Mgr & CMT.com; Mary Beth Cunin, VP/Program Planning & scheduling; James Hitchcock, VP/ Creative & Marketing; Nick Loria, VP/ Ad Sls; Chris Parr, VP/ Music & Talent.
TV-CATV only.
America's #1 country music network, provides original programming, live concerts, events, & music videos by established and cutting edge artists, news and info.

CNBC Syndication, 900 Sylvan Ave., Englewood Cliffs, NJ 07632. Phone: (201) 735-2622. Fax: (201) 585-3365. Howard Homonoff, VP/gen mgr; Steve Blechman, mgr; Margaret Agsteribbe, mgr; Pamela Thomas Graham, CEO.
TV-CATV only.
Syndicated TV program, *Wall Street Journal Report*, business events.

CNDP—Centre National de Documentation Pedagogique, 29, rue D'Ulm, 75005 Paris Phone: 330146349310. Phone: 33146329308. Fax: 330-14-40-72-789. Web Site: www.cndp.fr.
TV-CATV-Radio.
Production & distribution of educational TV & multimedia programs.

CN8, The Comcast Network, Penns Landing Studio, 1351 S. Columbus Blvd., Philadelphia, PA 19147. Phone: (215) 468-2222. Fax: (215) 468-3812. Web Site: www.cn8.tv. Jonathan Gorchow; David Shane, dir of progmg & CN8; Cheryl Flamini, VP of business dev & Eastern division; Peggy Giordano, mgr & CN8 progmg; Denise Pettyfordy, dir of network adv sls & CN8; Larry Watzman, creative svcs dir & CN8; Alex Soumbenioits, mktg & PR mgr & CN8; Brian McLendon, dir of network productions & CN8; Scott Clark, dir of engrg & CN8; Stephanie Millagranna, admin

Producers, Distributors, and Production Services Alphabetical Index

coord; Mark Dudzinski, stn mgr; Rich Frantz, mgr engr; Jon Gurevitch, VP sports; Buck Dopp, VP.

New Castle, DE 19720. New Castle Studio, 2215 N. Dupont Hwy. Phone: (302) 661-4202. Fax: (302) 661-4201. Assignment desk: (302) 661-4290. Fax: (302) 661-4291.

TV-CATV only.

CN8, The Comcast Network, is a rgnl cable network offering news, sports, & entertainment progmg to 3.9 million cable homes.

CNN Newsource Sales Inc., One CNN Center, 12 North, Atlanta, GA 30303. Phone: (404) 827-5032. Fax: (404) 827-4466. Jerry DeMink, VP/news dev; John Lee, sr VP sls; Ed Stephen, VP mktg.

Los Angeles, CA 90028, 6430 Sunset Blvd, Suite 300. Phone: (323) 993-5160. Bob Morris, VP sls & affil rel.

Chicago, IL 60601, 180 N. Stetson Ave, Suite 2700. Phone: (312) 729-5925. Gary Butterfield, VP sls & affil rel.

New York, NY 10018, 420 Fifth Ave., 4th Fl. Phone: (212)852-6734. (212) 852-6688. Joe Middleburg, VP sls & affil rel; Doug Jones, VP sls & affil rel.

TV-CATV only.

Provider of news & information content to the local bcst news industry.

C N R Radio, Box 22246, Minneapolis, MN 55422-0246. Phone: (763) 537-5868. E-mail: cnradio@aol.com. Web Site: http://members.aol.com/cnradio/home.html. George Carden, pres & producer.

Radio Only.

News interviews, soundbites and features with newsmakers for primarily Christian radio stations and networks.

COMPRO Productions Inc., 2080 Peachtree Industrial Ct., Suite 115, Atlanta, GA 30341. Phone: (770) 455-1943. Fax: (770) 455-3356. E-mail: compro@compro-atl.com. Web Site: www.compro-atl.com. Nels Anderson, pres; Steve Brinson, VP; Kim Anderson, VP.

TV-CATV only.

Full-svc company specializing in film & video production for corporate & bcst communications. Features a fully component Betacam SP on-line editing system, 16mm film editing, studio facilities, 3/4-inch off-line editing, video duplication & distribution, & location vehicles.

CRM Learning, 2215 Faraday Ave., Carlsbad, CA 92008-7295. Phone: (800) 421-0833. Fax: (760) 931-5792. Web Site: www.crmlearning.com. Peter J. Jordan, pres/CEO.

TV-CATV only.

Production & distribution of business training films.

CRN International, One Circular Ave., Hamden, CT 06514. Phone: (203) 288-2002. Fax: (203) 281-3291. Web Site: www.crnradio.com. Barry Berman, pres; S. Richard Kalt, exec VP.

Radio Only.

Short-form customized radio progms & promotions; *SkiWatch® BeachWatch* & small business reports.

CS Associates, 200 Dexter Ave, Watertown, MA 02472-4236. Phone: (617) 923-0077. Fax: (617) 923-0025. E-mail: programs@csassociates.com. Charles Schuerhoff, pres; Brian Gilbert, aquisitions; Lisa Carey, VP intl sales; Jason Redmond, Mgr of Acquisitions.

TV-CATV only.

Program distribution, specializing in documentaries, foreign & domestic TV & cable; broker co-productions.

CTVC Hillside Studios, Merry Hill Rd., Bushey, Watford, Herts WD23 1DR. Phone: 020 8950 4426. Fax: 020 8950 1437. E-mail: barrie.allcott@ctvc.co.uk. Web Site: www.ctvc.co.uk. Barrie Allcott, mgng dir; Ray Bruce, producer.

TV-CATV only.

Producers of programs with humanitarian values, especially relg. Also full bcst facilities available for hire.

CTV Television Inc., Box 9, Stn. O, Toronto, ON M4A 2M9. Canada. Phone: (416) 332-5000. Fax: (416) 332-5065. Web Site: www.ctv.ca. Susanne Boyce, pres CTV progmg.

TV-CATV only.

TV bcstg, program production & distribution.

C 2 Productions Inc., 15430 Catalpa Cove Ln., Fort Myers, FL 33908. Phone: (239) 437-4222. Fax: (239) 437-2042. E-mail: C2Productions@earthlink.net. Web Site: chriscorley.com.

TV-CATV only.

Voiceovers delivered digitally or in person.

Cable Films & Video, Box 7171, Country Club Station, Kansas City, MO 64113. Phone: (913) 362-2804. Phone: (800) 514-2804. Fax: (913) 362-2804. E-mail: cablefilms@msn.com. Web Site: www.onlineworld.com/movies. Herbert Miller, CEO.

TV-CATV only.

Classic films, all formats: one inch BETA SP, CD-ROM, U-Matic, PAL, NTSC, SECAM, DVD. Over 300 motion pictures & classic cartoons, clips available.

Call For Action Inc., 5272 River Rd., Suite 300, Bethesda, MD 20816. Phone: (301) 657-8260. Fax: (301) 657-2914. Web Site: www.callforaction.org. Shirley L. Rooker, pres & pres.

TV-CATV only.

International hotline service, affiliated with the bcst media, that provides info, assistance to individuals & small businesses with consumer problems.

Camera Group, 3920 N. 29th Ave., Hollywood, FL 33022. Phone: (305) 945-2020. Fax: (305) 945-1117. E-mail: cameragrp@aol.com. Web Site: www.cameragroup.com. Eileen Garcia-Di Rosa, pres.

TV-CATV only.

Rental, sls, svc & maintenance of motion picture, TV & video production equipment.

CamMate Studios, 425 E. Comstock, Chandler, AZ 85225. Phone: (480) 813-9500. Fax: (480) 813-9292. E-mail: cammate@cammate.com. Web Site: www.cammate.com. Ron Mitchell, CEO.

TV-CATV only.

CamMate camera, steady shot.

Campbell-Ewald Advertising, 30400 Van Dyke, Warren, MI 48093. Phone: (586) 574-3400. Fax: (586) 558-5891. Web Site: www.campbell-ewald.com. Anthony J. Hopp, CEO/chmn/pres; S.H. Gilbert, exec VP/CFO; D.A. Karnowsky, VP; W.J. Ludwig, VP; L.M. Schultz, VP; J.T. Seregny, VP.

Los Angeles, CA 90025, 11100 Santa Monica Blvd, 6th Fl. Phone: (213) 914-2200.

Chicago, IL 60611, One Magnificent Mile, 930 N. Michigan Ave, Suite 1060. Phone: (312) 587-2650.

New York, NY 10017, One Dag Hammarskjold Plaza. Phone: (212) 605-8000.

TV-CATV only.

TV programs, TV radio coml, promotion film production.

Canamedia Productions Ltd., 1670 Bayview Ave., Suite 408, Toronto, ON M4G 3C2. Canada. Phone: (416) 483-7446. Fax: (416) 483-7529. E-mail: canamed@canamedia.com. Web Site: www.canamedia.com. Les Harris, pres; Patrick Perdue, North American sls mgr; Paul Hutchson, international sls exec; Warren Campbell, North American Sales & Aquisitions; Andrea Stokes, International Sales & Acquisitions; Anne-Marie Leger, Archive Sales & Business Affairs.

TV-CATV only.

Canamedia offers production & international distribution services. It also exclusively represents in Canada the ITN Archive & Natural History New Zealand Archives.

CanLib Inc., 4819 Galendo St., Woodland Hills, CA 91364-4326. Phone: (818) 888-6005. Fax: (818) 888-2505. E-mail: canlibinc@adelphia.net. Gene Accas, pres; Carol Stevens, exec VP & sec/treas.

TV-CATV only.

Bcstg & media consulting: rsch for producers, distributors, advertisers, agencies & law firms (legal expert witness).

Cannell Studios, 7083 Hollywood Blvd., Suite 600, Hollywood, CA 90028. Phone: (323) 465-5800. Fax: (323) 856-7390. Web Site: www.cannell.com. Stephen J. Cannell, chmn/CEO.

TV-CATV only.

Capital Communications, 2357-3 South Tamiami Trl., Venice, FL 34293. Phone: (941) 492-4688. Fax: (941) 492-4923. E-mail: cap5678@isp.com. Web Site: www.isp.com. James Springer, pres/COO.

TV-CATV only.

International distributor of pre-packaged TV programs.

Carden & Cherry Syndication Inc., 1220 McGavock St., Nashville, TN 37203. Phone: (615) 255-6694. Fax: (615) 255-8345.

TV-CATV only.

TV & radio coml production & distribution; production svcs.

Careco Television Productions, 5717 N.W. Pkwy., Suite 104, San Antonio, TX 78249. Phone: (800) 668-8081. Fax: (210) 697-0150. Web Site: www.outdooraction.com. Charles Goodloe, pres; Lavonne Kacalek, VP.

TV-CATV only.

Producer of *American Outdoors* & *Fishing Texas*, weekly half hour series.

Caridi Entertainment, 250 W. 57th St., Suite 1326, New York, NY 10107. Phone: (212) 581-2277. Fax: (212) 581-2278. E-mail: c.caridi@att.net.

TV-CATV only.

Full-svc international distributor & production company.

Carleton Productions International Inc., 1500 Merivale Rd., 5th Fl., Nepean, ON K2E 6Z5. Canada. Phone: (613) 224-9666. Fax: (613) 224-9074. E-mail: cpi@magi.com. Web Site: www.carletonproductions.com. Mark Ross, pres.

TV & radio programs, coml production & distribution & production svcs.

George Carlson & Associates, 323 First Ave. W., Seattle, WA 98119. Phone: (206) 213-0562. Fax: (206) 213-0562. George Carlson, producer.

TV-CATV only.

Producers/distributors of 1/2-hour color, true life, travel adventure series to all parts of the world called *The Traveler & Northwest Traveler*.

Carlton International Media Inc., 11145 N.W. 1st Pl., Coral Springs, FL 33071. Phone: (954) 345-1620. Fax: (954) 345-1490. E-mail: clarea@msn.com. Web Site: www.carltonint.co.uk. Claire Alter, VP; Rupert Dillnot-Cooper, CEO; Louise Pedersen, mgr.

Studio City, CA 91604 Phone: (818) 753-6363. Jeri Sacks, VP/US sls.

TV-CATV only.

British TV distributor, licenses a wide range of programs worldwide.

Carpel Video Inc., 429 E. Patrick St., Frederick, MD 21701. Phone: (800) 238-4300. Fax: (301) 694-3500. Fax: (301) 694-9510. Web Site: www.carpelvideo.com. Andy Carpel, pres.

TV-CATV only.

Videotape recyclers; production svcs, video tape to DVD duplication.

Carriage House Studios, 119 Westhill Rd., Stamford, CT 06902. Phone: (203) 358-0065. Fax: (203) 964-4988. E-mail: chstudios@aol.com. John Montagnese, pres & Studio mgr.

TV-CATV only.

Recording studio.

Carsey-Werner Distribution, 4024 Radford Ave., Administration Building, Suite 460, Studio City, CA 91604. Phone: (818) 655-5957. Fax: (818) 655-5930. Web Site: www.cwm.com. Bob Dubelko, co-pres/COO; Herbert Lazarus, pres/international; Dirk van de Bunt, co-pres/head of prodn; James Kraus, exec VP/gen sls mgr.

TV-CATV only.

TV program distribution.

Sandra Carter Productions Inc., 230 W. 79th St., Suite 102, New York, NY 10024. Phone: (212) 875-1811. Fax: (212) 875-0088. E-mail: sales@sandra-carter.com. Web Site: www.sandra-carter.com. Sandra Carter, pres; Sal Ayvazoglu, dir worldwide sls.

TV-CATV only.

Distribution to all media, co-production deals, production, principle product in factual series.

Castle Hill Productions Inc., 36 W. 25th St., 2nd Fl., New York, NY 10010. Phone: (212) 242-1500. Fax: (212) 414-5737. E-mail: mm@castlehillproductions.com. Web Site: www.castlehillproductions.com. Julian Schlossberg, chmn; Mel Maron, pres; Barbara Karmel, VP TV sls.

Boca Raton, FL 33431, 2385 Executive Center Dr, Suite 100.

TV-CATV only.

Movie distribution for theater, TV, cable, and video.

Catholic Communication Campaign, 3211 4th St. N.E., Washington, DC 20017. Phone: (202) 541-3204. Phone: (202) 541-3129. E-mail: pgarcia@usccb.org. Web Site: www.usccb.org/ccc. Michael Graziano, pres; Michael A. Graziano, chief engr; Pat Ryan Garcia, dir distribution.

TV-CATV only.

TV & radio production & distribution.

Catholic Communications Corp., 65 Elliot St., Springfield, MA 01101. Phone: (413) 452-0645. Fax: (413) 747-0273. E-mail: m.graziano@diospringfield.org. Michael A. Graziano, pres.

TV-CATV only.

TV & radio production svcs.

Producers, Distributors, and Production Services Alphabetical Index

Catholic Television Network, Box 430, 9531 Akron-Canfield Rd., Canfield, OH 44406-0430. Phone: (330) 533-2243. Fax: (330) 533-1907. E-mail: judyctny@aol.com. Web Site: www.doy.org. Bob Gavalier, gen mgr.
TV-CATV only.
24-hour ecumenical TV ch.

Celebrities Productions, 7777 Bonhomme Ave.-Suite 900, St. Louis, MO 63105. Phone: (314) 862-7800. Fax: (314) 721-5171. I.J. Davis, pres; David Dovich, VP; Walt Williams, VP.
TV-CATV only.
Creation & production of radio & TV spots, programs & audio visuals; arrangement for celebrity talent, music, syndication & video conference production.

CelebrityFootage, 320 S. Almont Dr., Beverly Hills, CA 90211. Phone: (310) 360-9600. Fax: (310) 360-9696. E-mail: michael@celebrityfootage.com. Web Site: www.celebrityfootage.com. Michael Goldberg, pres.
TV-CATV only.
Provides broadcasters with celebrity entertainment news from the Los Angeles area, including movie premieres, award shows & charity benefits.

Celluloid Dreams, 24 rue Lamartine 75009, Paris Phone: (33) 1 49 70 83 20. Fax: (33) 1 49 70 03 71. Web Site: www.celluloid-dreams.com.
TV-CATV only.
International distribution of ind features, documentaries & animation films.

Center City Film & Video, 1503-05 Walnut St., Philadelphia, PA 19102. Phone: (215) 568-4134. Fax: (215) 568-6011. E-mail: centercity@ccfv.com. Web Site: www.ccfv.com. Jordan M. Schwartz, chmn/pres; Brian Isely, VP/gen mgr; John Gillespie, exec producer.
TV-CATV only.
Award winning production staff, video; film production, studio; remote camera packages including ultimatte, digital audio suite, flint, complete post production.

Central City Productions, Inc., 401 N. Wabash St., Suite 608, Chicago, IL 60611. Phone: (312) 321-9491. Fax: (312) 321-9921. Web Site: www.ccptv.com. Don Jackson, chmn; Erma Gray David, pres; Rosemary Jackson, VP; Rhonda Jackson, syndication mgr; Jennifer J. Jackson, gen mgr; Heather Davis, sls VP.
TV-CATV only.
Production & mktg of bcst & cable TV progmg targeted towards minority viewers.

Central Park Media, 250 W. 57th St., Suite 317, New York, NY 10107. Phone: (212) 977-7456 (X-201). Fax: (212) 977-8709. E-mail: jod@teamcpm.com. Web Site: www.centralparkmedia.com. John O'Donnell, mgng dir.
TV-CATV only.
Over 200 Japanese Anime titles available for TV & cable.

Century III at Universal Studios Florida, 2000 Universal Studios Plaza, Orlando, FL 32819-7606. Phone: (407) 354-1000. Fax: (407) 352-8662. E-mail: rcibella@century3.com. Web Site: www.century3.com.
TV-CATV-Radio.
Full-svc production & postproduction facility, audio department, custom graphics, digital editing capabilities, film transfers, interactive department, satellite uplink svcs.

Channel Four Television, 124 Horseferry Rd., London SW1 2TX. Phone: 44 20 7396 4444. E-mail: righttoreply@channel.4.com. Web Site: www.channel4.com.
TV-CATV only.
UK bcstr.

Chicago Radio Syndicate Inc., 15003 Lemay St., Van Nuys, CA 91405. Phone: (800) 621-6949. Fax: (818) 376-8529. Web Site: www.sandyorkin-crs.com. E-mail: sandyo@earthlink.net. Sandy Orkin, pres.
Radio Only.
Syndication of Dick Orkin comedy features—*Chickenman, Tooth Fairy & Mini-People* & commercial camgaigns.

Children's Media Productions, Box 40400, Pasadena, CA 91114-7400. Phone: (626) 797-5462. Fax: (626) 797-7524. E-mail: childrensmedia@yahoo.com. Web Site: www.childrensmedia.com. C. Ray Carlson, pres; Joy Carlson, PR.
TV-CATV only.
Producer & distributor of children's progmg, videos & feature films, worldwide.

Christian Children's Associates Inc., Box 446, Toms River, NJ 08754. Phone: (732) 240-3003. Fax: (732) 286-4244. E-mail: adventurepals@juno.com. Web Site: www.adventurepals.com. Jean Donaldson, pres; Frank Troilo, VP; Reverend William Cook, Ass't Director.
TV-CATV only.
Production & distribution of radio & TV progmg for children.

Christian Media Network, Box 448, Jacksonville, OR 97530. Phone: (541) 899-8888. Web Site: www.christianmedianetwork.com. James Lloyd, owner.
Radio Only.

The Christian Science Sentinel - Radio Edition, One Norway St., C4-20, Boston, MA 02115-3122. Phone: (617) 450-2000. Fax: (617) 450-3997. E-mail: sentinelradio@csps.com. Web Site: www.sentinelradio.com. Susan Kerr, sr producer.
Radio Only.
Radio news programs.

Christian TV Services of Ellicottville Inc., P. O. Box 209, Ellicottville, NY 14731-0209. Phone: (716) 699-2549. Fax: (716) 699-2590. E-mail: geothayer@yahoo.com. Web Site: www.christiantvservices.com.net&.org. Rev. George A. Thayer, pres/CEO.
TV-CATV only.
Christian, media consultants "Ministering to ministries around the world"; locally linked area worship places, internet listing places; svcs.

The Christophers Inc., 12 E. 48th St., New York, NY 10017. Phone: (212) 759-4050. Fax: (212) 838-5073. E-mail: mail@christophers.org. Web Site: www.christophers.org. Tony Rossi, producer; Sally Potenza, assoc producer.
TV-CATV only.
TV & radio production & distribution.

Chrysalis Distribution, 13 Bramley Rd., London WI0 6SP. Phone: (44) 207 4674. Fax: (44) 207 221 6286. E-mail: distribution@chrysalis.co.uk. Christina Willoughby, mgng dir.
TV-CATV only.
International sale of TV programs to all media worldwide.

Cimarron Group, 6855 Santa Monica Blvd., Hollywood, CA 90038. Phone: (323) 337-0300. Fax: (323) 337-0333. Web Site: www.cimarrongroup.com. Cheryl Savala, sr art dir; Bob Farina, owner.
TV-CATV only.
TV promotions, spec shoots, graphics, sls presentations, trade & consumer print design, title treatment & image campaigns.

Cinecraft Productions Inc., 2515 Franklin Blvd., Cleveland, OH 44113. Phone: (216) 781-2300. Fax: (216) 781-1067. E-mail: info@cinecraft.com. Web Site: www.cinecraft.com. Neil G. McCormick, chmn; Neil G. MCCormick, mgr; Maria E. Keckan, pres.
TV-CATV only.
Betacam field production; 60' x 70' sound stage with hard cyc; AVID MC1000NT; Animation with Soft Image; interactive DVD & CD-R development.

CineFilm/CineTransfer, 2156 Faulkner Rd. N.E., Atlanta, GA 30324. Phone: (404) 633-1448. Phone: (800) 633-1448. Fax: (404) 633-3867. E-mail: csr@cinefilmlab.com. Web Site: www.cinefilmlab.com. William G. Thorton, pres; Jim Ogburn, gen mgr.
TV-CATV only.
16mm, super 16mm, 35mm color negative processing & printing. Dailies thru release prints. State-of-the-art video dailies & scene-to-scene transfers. Spirit Data Cini, all HD Formats

CineGroupe, 1151 Alexandre-DeSeve St., Montreal, PQ H2L 2T7. Canada. Phone: (514) 524-7567. Fax: (514) 524-7344. E-mail: mdalein@cinegroupe.ca. Web Site: www.cinegroupe.com. Jacques Pettigrew, pres/CEO; Michel Lemire, VP production; Hubert Gariepy, VP/opns & exec producer; Andre-Gilles Gagne, postproduction dir; Michel Poisson, dir Toontech (paint & trace studio).
TV-CATV only.
Animation, TV production, postproduction, paint & trace studio, distribution of animation TV series for children.

Cinema Concepts Animation Studio, 2030 Powers Ferry Rd., #214, Atlanta, GA 30339. Phone: (770) 956-7460. Fax: (770) 956-8358. E-mail: cctsc@mindspring.com. Web Site: www.cinemaconcepts.com. Stewart D. Harnell, CEO; Sharron A. Harnell, VP; John Price, studio dir; Theresa Dickey, gen mgr.
TV-CATV-Radio.

Animated corporate IDs, presentation/policy trailers for TV, cable & motion picture theatres, theatrical trailer fulfillment.

The Cinema Guild Inc., 130 Madison Ave., 2nd Fl., New York, NY 10016-7038. Phone: (212) 685-6242. Fax: (212) 685-4717. E-mail: info@cinemaguild.com. Web Site: www.cinemaguild.com. Gary Crowdus, gen mgr; Philip Hobel, chmn/CEO; Mary Ann Hobel, co-chmn.
TV-CATV only.
Film & video distribution to theatrical, non-theatrical, TV & home video mkts, worldwide.

Cinema Sound Ltd., 311 W. 75th St., New York, NY 10023. Phone: (212) 799-4800. Fax: (212) 799-2057. Joan S. Franklin, pres; John S. Rockwell, production dir.
Radio Only.
State of the art recording studio.

Circle Oak Productions Inc., 33 N. Birch Hill Rd., Patterson, NY 12563. Phone: (845) 878-9017. Fax: (845) 878-9018.
Educ film production.

Tim Cissell Music, 1120 Grassmere Dr., Richardson, TX 75080-2909. Phone: (972) 680-0817. Fax: (972) 680-0866. E-mail: tcissell@wtd.net. Tim Cissell, owner.
TV-CATV only.
Offers music composition & production for all media (TV/CATV & radio)—jingles, IDs, film & video.

The Dick Clark Productions, 3003 W. Olive Ave., Burbank, CA 91505. Phone: (818) 841-3003. Fax: (818) 954-8609. Web Site: www.dickclarkproductions.com. Dick Clark, chmn/CEO; Francis C. La Maina, pres/COO; Bill Simon, CFO.
TV-CATV only.
TV production for networks, cable & syndication. Produces series, specials & movies for TV.

Classic Media, 860 Broadway, 6th Fl., New York, NY 10003. Phone: (212) 659-3011. Fax: (212) 659-1958. Douglas Schwalbe, head of international; Bob Higgins, head of creative affrs & production.
Beverly Hills, CA 90211, 8640 Wilshire Blvd. Phone: (310) 659-6004. Fax: (310) 659-4599. Leslie Levine, Dorothy Schecter.
TV-CATV only.
Classic Media is a New York-based entertainment company that manages some of the most recognizable family oriented properties across all media including feature film, television, home video & consumer products.

The Classical Station, WCPE, Box 897, Wake Forest, NC 27588. Phone: (919) 556-5178. Fax: (919) 556-9273. E-mail: wcpe@wcpe.org. Web Site: theclassicalstation.org. Deborah S. Proctor, gen mgr.
TV-CATV only.
Free 24-hour classical music progmg with live announcers for radio, cable, other distributors. Weekly request programs, opera and features.

Claster Television Inc., 9630 Deereco Rd., Timonium, MD 21093. Phone: (410) 561-5500. Fax: (410) 561-5511.
TV-CATV only.
TV program distribution.

Clausen Communications Inc., 575 Dunmar Cir., Winter Springs, FL 32708-3905. Phone: (407) 696-9095. Fax: (407) 696-3119. Henry Barentz, CEO; C. Clausen, pres; Chris Clausen, VP.
TV-CATV only.
Network quality voice-overs for TV & radio stns. Same day service on internet, switched 56/ISDN, CD, DAT or analog delivery.

Clayton-Davis & Associates Inc., 7777 Bonhomme Ave.—Suite 900, St. Louis, MO 63105. Phone: (314) 862-7800. Fax: (314) 721-5171. Web Site: www.claytondavis.com. Jennifer A. Davis, pres; Steve Pezold, VP.
TV-CATV only.
Program production, syndication & barter.

Clear Channel Broadcasting Inc., 55 Music Sq. West, Nashville, TN 37203. Phone: (615) 664-2400. Fax: (615) 664-2457. E-mail: davealpert@clearchannel.com. Dave Alpert, pres; Kevin Moore, VP sls; Tom Stevens, opns dir.
TV-CATV-Radio.
State radio networking, collegiate radio & TV networking.

Producers, Distributors, and Production Services Alphabetical Index

Clear Channel Entertainment Television, 220 W. 42nd St., 9th Fl., New York, NY 10036. Phone: (917) 421-5206. Fax: (917) 421-5239. Web Site: www.clearchannelentertainment.com. Steve Stern, exec producer; Joe Townley, pres; Marc Forest, progmg VP; Dawn Olejar, opns VP.
TV-CATV only.
Produces TV programs & promotion films, documentary film production, sports event television production.

Clever Cleaver Productions, 5369 Blackberry Way, Oceanside, CA 92057. Phone: (858) 695-3991. Fax: (858) 695-3992. E-mail: clevercook@cox.net. Web Site: www.clevercleaver.com. Lee N. Gerovitz, pres; Steve Cassarino, VP.
TV-CATV only.
260 3-minute cooking vignettes & 27 30-minute cooking shows (cash or barter); 2-minute tailgate cooking vignettes (free licensing fee).

Coe Film Associates Inc., 70 E. 96th St., New York, NY 10128. Phone: (212) 831-5355. Fax: (212) 996-6728. E-mail: cfainc@juno.com.
TV-CATV only.
TV program distribution.

Colon & Associates Inc., 7100 Blvd. East, Guttenberg, NJ 07093. Phone: (201) 869-4615. Fax: (201) 869-6217. E-mail: rei616@aol.com. Web Site: www.saptv.com. Reinaldo Colon, pres & CEO.
TV-CATV-Radio.
Program distribution, production, Spanish language dubbing.

ComBridges, 70 Irwin St., San Rafael, CA 94901. Phone: (415) 454-5505. Fax: (415) 454-1941. Web Site: www.combridges.com. E-mail: info@combridges.com. Jon Leland, pres & creative dir; Donna Nieddu, mgr; John Kraus, exec producer.
TV-CATV only.
Source of videos, seminars & interactive media. Producer, websites.

Combs Music, 421 Cedar Trail, Winston-Salem, NC 27104. Phone: (336) 760-3905. Fax: (336) 760-3855. E-mail: dave@combsmusic.com. Web Site: www.combsmusic.com.
TV-CATV only.
Composes, produces, publishes & distributes easy lstng instrumental music, e.g., *Rachel's Song*.

Comcast Media Center, 4100 E. Dry Creek Rd., Littleton, CO 80122. Phone: (303) 486-3800. Fax: (303) 486-3891. Web Site: www.comcast.com.
TV-CATV only.
Network origination, production, postproduction, uplinking, compression, remote production, audio production.

Command Productions, Box 3000, Sausalito, CA 94966-3000. Phone: (415) 332-3161. Fax: (415) 332-1901. E-mail: audio@commandproductions.com. Web Site: www.commandproductions.com. Warren Weagant, pres; Kitt Weagant, VP.
TV-CATV only.
Radio-TV, CATV audio voice identification and promotion production.

Communications III Inc., 1156 Dublin Rd., Suite 101, Columbus, OH 43215. Phone: (614) 485-4500. Fax: (614) 485-4512. E-mail: shalliday@comiii.com. Web Site: www.comIII.com. Scott Halliday, pres; Saundra Smith, chief engr.
TV-CATV only.
Central Ohio C-band satellite and Teleport services. with access to studio, edit suites and at Ohio State University and various downtown locations.

Compu-Weather Inc., 2566 Rt. 52, Hopewell Junction, NY 12533. Phone: (800) 825-4445. Fax: (800) 825-4441. E-mail: sales@compuweather.com. Web Site: www.compuweather.com. Jeff Wimmer, pres; Todd Gross, VP.
TV-CATV only.
Weather & environmental features, actualities, forecasts & info.

Concept Videos, 5371 Punta Alta, Apt.1E, Laguna Hills, CA 92653. Phone: (800) 333-8252. Fax: (877) 523-5592. E-mail: wjconnell@preschoolpower.com. Web Site: www.preschoolpower.com. William Connell, pres.
TV-CATV only.
Gold medal winning children's series, *Pre-School Power*, (13 x 30) recently telecast on 190 public TV stns.

Consolidated Film Industries (CFI), 959 N. Seward St., Hollywood, CA 90038. Phone: (323) 960-7444. Fax: (323) 960-7573. Web Site: www.technicolor.com.
TV-CATV only.
Film processing; titles & opticals; videotape transfers; office rentals.

CONTACT Radio, 3900 Westminster Pl., St. Louis, MO 63108. Phone: (314) 533-0320. Phone: (888) 7-contact. Fax: (314) 533-0335. E-mail: gkolarcik@contractradio.org. Web Site: www.contactradio.org. Gary Kolarcik, exec dir; Trish Muyco-Tobin, production mgr.
Radio Only.
Producer of "Contact", a pub affairs radio program of 29 & 15 minute lengths, wkly & free to radio stations; and Contact minutes", a one minute spot addressing human needs and family values.

Continental Recordings Inc., 23 Mirimichi Street, Plainville, MA 02762-1710. Phone: (508) 699- 0003. Fax: (617) 699-0005. E-mail: danf31@earthlink.net. Web Site: www.creativemarketingandcommunications.com. Terry Dean, pres.
TV-CATV only.
Coml jingles, stn IDs, original music creation & production, cassette duplication & bcstg adv consultation, CD duplicator.

William F. Cooke Television Programs, 890 Yonge St., Suite 800, Toronto, ON M4W 3P4. Canada. Phone: (416) 967-6141. Fax: (416) 967-5133. E-mail: cooketv@canada.com. William F. Cooke, pres/CEO; Alex McWilliams, pres TV distribution.
TV-CATV only.
TV program production & distribution.

Cookie Jar Group, 1055 Rene Levesque E., 9th Floor, Montreal, PQ H2L 4S5. Canada. Phone: (514) 843-7070. Fax: (514) 843-6773. E-mail: info@cinar.com. Web Site: www.cinar.com. Steward Syder, CEO; Peter Moss, pres; David Ferguson, pres; Steve Carson, Cinar Education.
TV-CATV only.
Dev, production, postproduction & distribution of non-violent, quality kids & family live action animated progmg, & educational products.

Coote Communications, 568 Carver Hill, Milton, ON LQT 5K5. Canada. Phone: (905) 203-0065. E-mail: amcoote@hotmail.com. Morgan Coote, pres; Donald Coote, VP.
TV-CATV only.
Complete film & videotape production from script to screen.

Cornell University Educational Television Center, 126 CCCGarden Avenue, Ithaca, NY 14853-6601. Phone: (607) 255-8162. Fax: (607) 255-1563. E-mail: grp2@cornell.edu. Web Site: www.DLS.cornell.edu. David O. Watkins; Glen Palmer, mgr business/production svcs.
TV-CATV only.
Satellite uplinks, Betacam DvcPro video production & postproduction, audio production

Country Crossroads FamilyNet Radio, 6350 W. Freeway, Fort Worth, TX 76116. Phone: (817) 570-1400. Phone: (800) 266-1837. Fax: (817) 737-9436. E-mail: info@familynet.com. Web Site: www.familynetradio.com. Lisa Bratton, radio mktg & distribution; Donna Senn, radio distribution; Kirk Teegarden, producer.
Radio Only.
Country music with interviews. Program hosted by Grammy Award winner Bill Mack. 30 minute wkly on CD.

Cramer Productions Center, 425 University Ave., Norwood, MA 02062. Phone: (781) 278-2300. Fax: (781) 255-0721. E-mail: info@crameronline.com. Web Site: www.crameronline.com. Tom Martin, pres; Rich Sturchio, VP.
TV-CATV only.
Film & video production svcs from design to presentation; staging svcs; video duplications. Web-casting, interactive media.

Thomas Craven Film Corp., 5 W. 19th St., New York, NY 10011-4216. Phone: (212) 463-7190. Fax: (212) 627-4761. E-mail: tcfc@aol.com. Michael Craven, pres; Ernest Barbieri, VP.
TV-CATV-Radio.
Complete film & video production svcs from scripting through shooting & editing to distribution.

Crawford Communications, 3845 Pleasantdale Rd., Atlanta, GA 30340. Phone: (404) 876-7149. Fax: (678) 421-6717. Web Site: www.crawford.com. Jesse C. Crawford, owner; Paul Hansel, pres; Bill Thompson, sls dir; Jessica Moore, mktg dir.
TV-CATV-Radio.
Computer graphics, animation, production & postproduction svcs domestic & international teleport.

Creative International Activities Ltd., 372 Central Park W., New York, NY 10025. Phone: (212) 663-8944. Fax: (212) 865-8486. E-mail: ciaklaus@aol.com. Klaud J. Lehmann, pres.
International TV program syndication & consultation.

Creative Marketing & Communications Corp., 7633 Athenia Dr., Cincinnati, OH 45244. Phone: (513) 624-8301. Phone: (800) 845-8477. Fax: (513) 624-8302. Web Site: www.cmcideas.com. Terry Dean, pres; Susan Dean, VP.
Radio Only.
Syndicated 30- to 60-second coml wraparounds.

Creative Radio Network, Box 7749, Thousand Oaks, CA 91359. Phone: (818) 991-3892. Fax: (818) 991-3894. Darwin Lamm, pres.
Radio Only.
Radio program production & syndication—all formats; holiday & artist specials.

Crest National Digital Media Complex, 1000 N. Highland Ave., Hollywood, CA 90038. Phone: (323) 466-0624. Fax: (323) 461-8901. Web Site: www.crestnational.com. E-mail: info@crestnational.com. Ron Stein, pres; John Walker, exec sls mgr.
TV-CATV only.
Full videotape postproduction including film transfer, processing, sweetening & duplication.

The Crime Channel, PMB 371, 42335 Washington St., Suite F, Palm Desert, CA 92211. Phone: (760) 360-6151, EXT. 4. Fax: (760) 360-3258. Arnold Frank, pres.
TV-CATV only.
TV program distribution & bcstg.

Critical Mass Releasing Inc., 77 Mowat Ave., Suite 110, Toronto, ON M6K 3E3. Canada. Phone: (416) 538-2535. Fax: (416) 538-3367. E-mail: cmass@netcom.ca. William Alexander, pres; Lisa-Marie Doorey, Dir of International sls.
TV-CATV only.
International TV & domestic distribution, TV & film, film & series production, theatrical & video releasing.

Ben Cromer Communications, Box 526, Round Hill, VA 20142. Phone: (540) 338-5486. Fax: (540) 338-5486. E-mail: info@bencromer.com. Ben Cromer, pres.
TV-CATV-Radio.
Feature writing & script preparation for print & bcst media; specializing in the music & entertainment industry; telecommunications; business/economics & travel/history.

Crossroads Christian Communications Inc., Box 5100, Burlington, ON L7R 4M2. Canada. Phone: (905) 335-7100.
TV-CATV only.
Produces 100 Huntley Street program.

Crown International Pictures Inc., 8701 Wilshire Blvd., Beverly Hills, CA 90211. Phone: (310) 657-6700. Fax: (310) 657-4489. E-mail: crown@crownintlpictures.com. Web Site: www.crownintlpictures.com. Scott E. Schwimer, sr VP; Mark Tenser, pres/CEO; Lisa Agay, dir publ & adv.
TV-CATV only.
Film production & distribution.

Crystal Pictures Inc., 9 Pack Sq., #204, Asheville, NC 28801. Phone: (828) 285-9995. Fax: (828) 285-9997. E-mail: cryspic@aol.com. Joshua Tager, pres; Jane Anne Rolston, gen sls mgr.
Ashville, NC 28801, 9 S.W. Pack Sq. Phone: (828) 285-9996. Fax: (828) 285-9997.
TV-CATV only.
Distribution of feature film & svcs to all TV outlets in United States & abroad.

Cube International, 1863 Pamela Ct., Suite 50, Simi Valley, CA 9365. Phone: (661) 255-1945. Fax: (805) 527-1160. E-mail: phill@cubeinternational.com. Web Site: www.cubeinternational.com. Olivier de Courson, mgng dir; Phillip G. Catherall, mgng dir.
TV-CATV only.
Film & TV distribution to all worldwide markets & media.

Curb Entertainment International Corp., 3907 W. Alameda Ave., Burbank, CA 91505. Phone: (818) 843-8580. Fax: (818) 566-1719. E-mail: info@curbentertainment.com. Web Site: www.curbentertainment.com. Carole Curb, pres; Mike Curb, chmn; Ilda Toth, exec dir; Aaron Rogers, dir mktg.
TV-CATV only.

Producers, Distributors, and Production Services Alphabetical Index

International production & distribution co.

Custom Productions Inc., 1334 3rd St. Promenade, Suite 300, Santa Monica, CA 90401. Phone: (310) 393-4144. Fax: (310) 393-1143. Web Site: www.customproductions.TV. Steve Stockman, pres.

TV-CATV only.

Creation & production of custom TV campaigns for radio stns and TV news stns in the top 25 markets.

D

DC Audio, (Dryden Clarke Audio & Daily Feed). 1783 Lanier Pl. N.W., Suite B, Washington, DC 20009. Phone: (202) 667-1234. Fax: (202) 667-5578. E-mail: dfeed@dailyfeed.com. Web Site: www.dailyfeed.com. John Dryden, pres.

Radio Only.

Produces The Daily Feed, a 90-second political, social satire radio commentary. Markets cash and bartered radio inventory to 18 + demos.

DG Systems, 750 W. John Carpenter Fwy., Irving, TX 75039. Phone: (972) 581-2000. Fax: (972) 581-2001. Web Site: www.dgsystems.com. Marty Melody, VP sls.

North Hollywood, CA 91601, 10545 Burbank Blvd. Phone: (818) 753-3000. Fax: (818) 985-0614.

Chicago, IL 60610, 110 W. Hubbard St. Phone: (312) 828-1146. Fax: (312) 828-0498.

Louisville, KY 40213, 100 High Rise Dr., Ste. 124. Phone: (502) 962-8676. Fax: (502) 962-8571.

Southfield, MI 48075, 21725 Melrose Ave. Phone: (248) 386-0400.

New York, NY 10017, 219 E. 44th St. Phone: (212) 547-3966. Fax: (212) 547-3987.

New York, NY 10016, 600 Third Ave. Phone: (212) 953-9300.

Wilmington, OH 45177, 1175 Airport Rd., Bldg. #2. Phone: (937) 382-7110.

TV-CATV-Radio.

Duplication & distribution of corporate training & educ, TV & radio programs. Distribution of syndicated TV programs via satellite & videotape.

DIC Entertainment, 4100 W. Alameda Ave., Burbank, CA 91505. Phone: (818) 955-5400. Fax: (818) 955-5696. Web Site: www.dicentertainment.com. Andy Heyward, chmn/CEO; Brad Brooks, pres; Jedd Gold, mktg VP.

TV-CATV only.

DIC Entertainment, a leading children's entertainment company, is a full-service studio dedicated to creating, developing, producing, distributing, marketing and merchandising children's and family-based intellectual properties.

DLT Entertainment Ltd., 31 W. 56th St., New York, NY 10019. Phone: (212) 245-4680. Fax: (212) 315-1132. Web Site: www.dltentertainment.com. Donald L. Taffner, owner; John Fitzgerald, CEO; Donald Taffner Jr., VP; Jeff Cotugno, VP.

TV-CATV only.

TV program production & distribution.

DMX Music, 900 E. Pine St., Seattle, WA 98122. Phone: (800) 831-8001. Fax: (206) 329-9952. Web Site: www.dmxmusic.com. Liberty Media, owner.

TV-CATV-Radio.

Programmer & supplier of satellite-delivered music svcs for business & cable TV. Available satellite direct or through FM subcarrier.

D-Squared Media, 30 E. 20th St., 7th Fl., New York, NY 10003. Phone: (212) 478-1005. Fax: (212) 254-3489. E-mail: solutions@dsquaredmedia.com. Web Site: www.dsquaredmedia.com. Adriana E. Davis, exec producer; Bryan S. Durr, dir/videographer.

TV-CATV only.

Film, video, & radio production svcs from script to screen.

D-V-X International, (A division of Demo-Vox Sound Studio Inc.). 1038 Bay Ridge Ave., Brooklyn, NY 11219. Phone: (718) 680-7234. Fax: (718) 680-7234.

TV-CATV only.

Video recording, creative production & postproduction svcs.

DWJ Television, One Robinson Ln., Ridgewood, NJ 07450. Phone: (201) 445-1711. Fax: (201) 445-8352. E-mail: dwjinfo@dwjtv.com. Web Site: www.dwjtv.com. Daniel G. Johnson, pres; Michael L. Friedman, exec VP; Cynthia Boseski, sr VP.

TV-CATV only.

Provides TV & radio progmg & production; promotional video production & production svcs.

Daley Video, 4095 Hitchcock Rd., Concord, CA 94518. Phone: (925) 676-7260. Fax: (413) 541-8354. E-mail: gadaley@aol.com. Greg Daley, owner/CEO.

TV-CATV only.

Betacam SP, D1 digital betacom editing & 3/4-inch postproduction; TV production.

Dallas Cowboys Broadcasting, Dallas Cowboys Football Club, One Cowboys Pkwy., Irving, TX 75063. Phone: (972) 556-9345. Fax: (972) 556-9339. Scott Purcel, dir opns.

TV-CATV only.

Dandelion Distribution Ltd., Unit 5 Churchill Court, Station Rd., North Harrow, Middlesex HA2 7SA. Fax: 44(0)181 863 0463. Phone: 44(0)181 863 1888.

TV-CATV only.

International distribution & production company producing drama, documentaries, animation & movies.

Dargaud-Marina, 15-27 rue Moussorgski, Paris 75018. France. Phone: 331-5326-3100. Fax: 331-5326-3113. E-mail: sales@dargaudmarina.fr. Gaspard De Chavagnac, mgng dir; Claude De Saint Vincent, pres; Patrick Desiev, VP finance; G. Guillot, sls.

TV-CATV only.

Distribution & production company specialized in children's progmg, mainly animation.

Darino Films/Library of Special Effects, 222 Park Ave. S., New York, NY 10003. Phone: (212) 228-4024. E-mail: edarino@hotmail.com. Ed Darino, owner.

TV-CATV only.

Distributors of TV programs, video, CD, animation, educationals, effects libraries, stock footage libraries, production CD & DVD.

Daro Film Distribution, Le Victoria, 13 Blvd. Princess Charlotte, MC 98000. Phone: (377) 979-1600. Fax: (377) 979-1590. E-mail: daro@meditnet.com.

TV-CATV only.

International distribution, co-production, co-financing of TV programs & films.

Jeff Davis Productions Inc., 6166 Mulholland Hwy., Los Angeles, CA 90068. Phone: (323) 464-3500. Fax: (323) 464-1414. Web Site: www.jeffdavis.com.

TV-CATV only.

Voiceover & production.

DaviSound, Box 521, 1504 Sunset, Newberry, SC 29108. Phone: (803) 276-0639. E-mail: davisound@hotmail.com. Web Site: www.davisound.com. Hayne Davis; Annette Davis, opns mgr.

TV-CATV only.

Coml & promotional writing & producing for radio, jingles & program production & distribution. Also provides DaviSound "Tool Boxes," custom fabricated pro audio equipment.

De Wolfe Music Library Inc., 25 W. 45th St., New York, NY 10036. Phone: (212) 382-0220. Fax: (212) 382-0278. E-mail: info@dewolfmusic.com. Web Site: www.dewolfemusic.com. Andrew M. Jacobs, pres; Jamie Gillespie, Mgr Music Sls.

TV-CATV-Radio.

The largest independant production music library in the world!

DeLuxe Laboratories, 1377 N. Serrano Ave., Hollywood, CA 90027. Phone: (323) 462-6171. Fax: (323) 461-0608. Web Site: www.bydeluxe.com. Cyril Drabinsky, pres; Steve Van Anda, sls VP.

TV-CATV only.

Full svc motion picture processing lab with labs in Toronto, London, Rome.

Design Partners Inc., 1438 N. Gower St., Hollywood, CA 90028. Phone: (323) 856-9191. Fax: (323) 856-9258. E-mail: linda@dpi-ld.com. Web Site: www.dpi-ld.com. Greg Brunton, pres; Linda Korbel, mgng ptnr.

TV-CATV only.

TV, lighting design, industrial production & TV production & tech supervision svcs.

Devillier Donegan Enterprises L.P., 4401 Connecticut Ave. N.W., 6th Floor, Washington, DC 20008. Phone: (202) 686-3980. Fax: (202) 686-3999. Web Site: www.ddegroup.com. Ronald J. Devillier, pres/CEO; Brian Donegan, exec VP; Joan Lanigan, VP business legal affrs; Linda Ekizian, VP mktg; Gregory Diefenbach, production & dev; John Esteban, VP finance/admin.

TV-CATV only.

Worldwide distribution of progmg: international & ind documentaries, Hollywood profiles, science series, drama, natural history progmg & the performing arts.

Devlin Design Group Inc., 12526 High Bluff, # 300, San Diego, CA 92130. Phone: (760) 634-6515. Fax: (760) 634-6929. E-mail: creative@ddgtv.com. Web Site: www.ddgtv.com. Dan Devlin,.

TV-CATV only.

Designs, builds & installs news sets & newsrooms. Facility planning, broadcast consulting, tech & lighting direction. Virtual Reality Rsch & Dev Ctr. Virtual sets, soft sets.

Dialing for Dollars, (A division of Newhoff Blumberg Inc.). 111 Hamlet Hill Rd. (1413), Baltimore, MD 21210. Phone: (410) 433-4141. Fax: (410) 433-4403. Theodore Newhoff Jr., chmn.

TV-CATV only.

TV program production & distribution.

Digital Brewery L.L.C., 3820 Packard, Suite 150, Ann Arbor, MI 48108. Phone: (800) 572-0098. Phone: (734) 975-8880. Fax: (734) 975-8915. Web Site: www.digitalbrewery.com. Terry Dollhoff, co-pres; Sal Calabrese, co-pres.

TV-CATV only.

Packaged animations include backgrounds, holidays, corporate, adv & globes, maps & flags.

Digital Force, 149 Madison Ave., 12th Fl., New York, NY 10016. Phone: (212) 252-9300. Fax: (212) 252-7377. E-mail: info@digitalforce.com. Web Site: www.digitalforce.com. Jerome Bunke, pres; Neil Poynter, production mgr.

TV-CATV only.

Compact disc, CD-ROM & cassette production service to meet the needs of bcstrs, cable networks, & small labels/ind artists. Clients include the National Football League (NFL) & National Hockey League (NHL) on Fox TV as well as PSAs & promotional discs from bcstrs nationwide, ABC TV & CNBC.

Dimension 3 Corp, 5240 Medina Rd., Woodland Hills, CA 91364-1913. Phone: (818) 592-0999. Fax: (818) 592-0987. E-mail: info@d3.com. Web Site: www.d3.com. Daniel L. Symmes, pres.

TV-CATV only.

Supplies 3-D bcst TV process & 3-D film; equipment, consultation & 3-D glasses.

Disney Channel, 3800 W. Alameda Ave., Burbank, CA 91505. Phone: (818) 569-7700. Fax: (818) 845-8249. Web Site: www.disneychannel.com. Anne M. Sweeney, pres.

TV-CATV only.

Original TV program production & distribution.

Walt Disney Company, 500 S. Buena Vista St., Burbank, CA 91521-0990. Phone: (818) 560-1000. Fax: (818) 560-1930. Zenia Mucha, corporate comm.

TV-CATV only.

The Walt Disney Company subsidiary; develops & syndicates first-run adult & children's progmg, off-network progmg & feature film packages.

The Walt Disney Company, 500 S. Buena Vista St., Burbank, CA 91521. Phone: (818) 560-1000. Fax: (818) 560-1930. Web Site: www.disney.com. Michael Eisner, chmn/CEO.

TV-CATV only.

Diversified Communications Inc., 2000 M St. N.W., Suite 340, Washington, DC 20036. Phone: (202) 775-4300. Fax: (202) 775-4363. Web Site: www.dciteleport.com. Al Levin, pres; Nelson Crumling, VP.

TV-CATV only.

Complete mobile facilities, Ku-band uplink trucks, extensive loc & global connectivity; internationally compliant, fully redundant Ku-band air transportable uplink.

D'Ocon Films Productions, c/ Calaf.3 Bajos, Barcelona 08021. Phone: 34-93-240-41-22. Fax: 34-93-240-41-24. E-mail: docon@docon.es.

TV-CATV only.

Principally an animation company offering full range of pre-production, production & postproduction svcs either developing our own concepts or co-producing.

The Dolmatch Group Ltd., Box 3298, 19697 Glen Brae Dr., Saratoga, CA 95070. Phone: (408) 741-8620. Fax: (408) 741-8620. E-mail: tdgdolmatch@yahoo.com. Murray Dolmatch, pres; Sandra Dolmatch, VP.

TV-CATV only.

Represents producers in the United States, United Kingdom, Germany, France & Italy; distributes feature films,

Producers, Distributors, and Production Services Alphabetical Index

documentaries & animation; active in co-production & co-financing.

Domain Communications L.L.C., 289 S. Main Pl., Carol Stream, IL 60188-2425. Phone: (630) 668-5300. Fax: (630) 668-0158. E-mail: dmorris@domaincommuications.com. Web Site: www.domaincommunications.com. David Morris, pres; Jim Draper, VP sls.
Radio Only.
Recording audio studios, production, CD replication, high-speed cassette duplicating, fulfillment.

DOME PRODUCTIONS, 1 Blue Jays Way, Suite #3400, Toronto, ON M5V1J3. Canada. Phone: (416) 341-2001. Phone: (514) 731-3663. Fax: (416) 341-2020. Fax: (514) 731-4646. E-mail: mcarlylee@domeprod.com. Web Site: www.domeproductions.com. Mary Ellen Carlyle, sr VP & gen mgr.
Mont-Royal, PQ Canada, 5647 Ferrier.
TV-CATV-Radio.
Mobile production trucks (High Definition, Digital, Analog), telecommunications (Fibre/Satellite transmission, satellite media tours, playouts), Host broadcast (Design, production, engineering, operations).

Donnelly & Associates, 7507 Sunset Blvd., Suite 202, Los Angeles, CA 90046. Phone: (323) 850-5861. Fax: (323) 850-5866. E-mail: wpdonnelly@earthlink.net. W.P. Donnelly, pres.
TV-CATV only.
Mktg & licensing films to pay-TV, network & syndication packages.

Dorling Kindersley Vision, 80 Strand, London WC2R 0RL. Phone: 0044 207 010 3000. Fax: 0044 207 010 6536. E-mail: dkvision@dk-uk.com. Web Site: www.dk-uk.com.
TV-CATV only.
Produces programs for the international TV & video markets, incorporating visual design with universally appealing subjects.

John Driscoll/VoiceOver America, Box 744, Mill Valley, CA 94941. Phone: (888) 766-2049. Phone: (415) 388-8701. Fax: (415) 388-8719. E-mail: johndriscoll @voiceoveramerica.com. Web Site: www.johndriscoll.com. John Moore, pres/CEO. VoiceOverPeople.com, c/o AT&A. Phone: (818) 760-6688.
TV-CATV only.
The new millenium's premiere voice talent for stn branding available instantly via ISDN & web download.

Mark Druck Productions Inc., 300 E. 40th St., New York, NY 10016. Phone: (212) 682-5980. Fax: (212) 682-5981. E-mail: markdruck@aol.com. Mark Druck, pres; Lisa Dodenhoff, producer.
TV-CATV only.
TV & video tape industrial progmg, prom film production & distribution.

Duke International, Box 46, Douglas, Isle of Man IM99 1DD. Phone: (+44) 1624 640020. Fax: (+44) 1624 640001. E-mail: info@dukesales.com. Web Site: www.dukesales.com. Jon Quayle, sls dir.
TV-CATV only.
A wide range of powersport progmg, documentaries, clips; also production & editing facilities.

The D.L. Dykes Jr. Foundation, 305 E. Capitol St., Jackson, MS 39201. Phone: (601) 354-0767. Joe Todaro, production mgr; David R. Dyker, CEO.
TV-CATV only.
Program production, Collage® non-linear post suite, digital audio capable. Non-profit.

E

E! Entertainment Television, 5750 Wilshire Blvd., Los Angeles, CA 90036-3709. Phone: (323) 954-2400. Fax: (323) 954-2500. Web Site: www.eonline.com. Neil Baker, sr VP; Mark Sonnenberg, exec VP; Mindy Herman, pres/CEO; David T. Cassaro, exec VP; Ken Bettsteller, CEO.
New York, NY 10036, 11 W. 42nd St. Phone: (212) 852-5100. (212) 852-5151. Dave Cassaro, exec VP.
TV-CATV only.
A 24-hour progmg network covering celebrities, entertainment news, gossip & pop-culture, feature behind the scenes with today's biggest stars.

ESPI Video, 8144 Walnut Hill Lane, Suite 850, Dallas, TX 75219. Phone: (214) 522-6699. Fax: (214) 522-7699. E-mail: gsleeper@espivideo.com. Web Site: www.espivideo.com. Gary Sleeper, pres; Scott Anderson, sr producer.

TV-CATV only.
Full-svc production company specializing in corporate video production. Postproduction facilities & on-location svcs also available.

ESPN Radio Network, ESPN Plaza, Bristol, CT 06010. Phone: (860) 766-2661. Fax: (860) 860-5523. Web Site: www.espnradio.com. John A. Walsh, exec editor; Len Weiner, progmg dir; John Martin, exec producer.
Radio Only.
NBA On ESPN Radio; College Game Day (Sat); ESPN Radio weekends; Brent Musburger afternoon drive sportscasts; AM & PM drive commentaries; *NFL Gameday* (Sun)

ESPN Regional Television, 11001 Rushmore Dr., Charlotte, NC 28277. Phone: (704) 973-5000. Fax: (704) 973-5090. Web Site: www.espn.com. Chuck Gerber, exec VP/gen mgr.
TV-CATV only.
Producer & distributor of TV sports events including college & professional basketball, boxing & auto racing for over-the-air & cable.

ETN—Educational Telecommunications Network, (An ETV service of the Los Angeles County Office of Education). 9300 Imperial Hwy., Rm. 126, Los Angeles County Office of Education, Downey, CA 90242-2890. Phone: (562) 401-5622. Fax: (562) 922-8841. E-mail: etn@lacoe.edu. Web Site: www.lacoe.edu. Richard Quinones PhD., division dir.
TV-CATV only.
ETN develops & transmits educ programs in the major K-12 curriculum areas as well as adult educ & parent educ programs (via satellite over Ku-band) to schools, homes & offices nationwide.

EUE Screen Gems Studios, 222 E. 44th St., New York, NY 10017. Phone: (212) 450-1600. Fax: (212) 450-1610. Bill Vassar, VP; Larry Coatto, technical officer.
Wilmington, NC 28405, 1223 N. 23rd St. Phone: (910) 343-3500.
TV program, coml production & distribution.

Eagle Eye Film Company, 824 N. Victory Blvd., Burbank, CA 91502. Phone: (818) 506-6100. Fax: (818) 506-4313. Web Site: www.eagleyepost.com. James Tucci, chief tech off; Joel Minnich, opns coord.
Editing facility, editing rentals, RAID storage solutions.

Eagle Media Productions Ltd., Box 580, Northford, CT 06472. Phone: (203) 294-1190. Fax: (203) 294-9512. E-mail: louadler@ix.netcom.com. Louis C. Adler, pres; Thalia Adler, VP.
Radio Only.
Radio program syndication, program & news consultant. Producers of *Medical Journal.*

Earthwatch Radio, 10 Science Hall, 550 N. Park St., Madison, WI 53706. Phone: (608) 263-3063. Fax: (608) 262-2273. E-mail: spomplun@wise.edu. Web Site: ewradio.org. Steve Pomplun, producer; Richard Hoops, producer.
Radio Only.
Daily two-minute radio feature on environment & science. Ten progms distributed mthy on compact disc. Programs distruted monthly on compact disc.

Eaton Films Ltd., 10 Holbein Mews, London SW1W 8NN. Phone: (44) 207-823-6173. Fax: (44) 207-823-6017. E-mail: eaton.films@talk21.com. Judith Bland, dir; Liz Cook, dir internatonal sls.
TV & video distribution.

Ebbets Field Productions Ltd., Box 42, Wykagyl Stn, New Rochelle, NY 10804. Phone: (914) 636-1281. E-mail: zap@cloud9.net. David Saperstein, pres.
TV-CATV only.
Writers, dirs & producers of film (features, TV, cable) & video.

Echo Radio Productions Inc., 44895 Hwy. 82, Aspen, CO 81611. Phone: (800) 385-4612. Fax: (970) 925-2640. Fax: (970) 925-9369. E-mail: kayla@echoradio.com. Web Site: www.echoradio.com. Kayla Hoffman-Cook, VP; Rodney H. Jacobs, CEO.
Radio Only.
Syndicator & producer of radio vignette programming.

Ecumedia News Service, Box 358, Ridgefield, CT 06877. Phone: (203) 431-6092. Fax: (212) 870-2030. E-mail: roy.lloyd@ecunet.org. Roy T. Lloyd, dir.
Radio Only.
News stories, features & actualities about ethics & relg produced for radio.

Ecumenical Communications, 48 Eastview Rd., Terryville, CT 06786. Phone: (860) 585-5090. Robert J. Geckler, owner.
Radio Only.
Radio program production & distribution; production & restoration svcs; produce wkly half hour old-time radio program *Tune Back To Yesterday.*

Elliot and Friends, Inc., 1020 Brewer Pl., Sarasota, FL 34236. E-mail: elliotone@aol.com. Web Site: www.elliotandfriends.com. Debi McNabb, creator & pres.
TV-CATV only.

Ellis Entertainment, 1300 Yonge St., Suite 300, Toronto, ON M4T 1X3. Canada. Phone: (416) 924-2186. Fax: (416) 924-6115. E-mail: sales@ellisent.com. Web Site: www.ellisent.com. R. Stephen Ellis, pres; Caroline Godin, mgr progmg sls.
TV-CATV only.
Full-svc TV & CATV domestic & foreign program distribution & production house.

Ellis Entertainment, 1300 Yonge St., Suite 300, Toronto, ON M4T 1X3. Canada. Phone: (416) 924-2186. Fax: (416) 924-6115. E-mail: sales@ellisent.com. Caroline Godin, natl sls mgr; Stephen Ellis, pres; Kip Spidell, production mgr.
TV-CATV only.
Producers and distributors of 1000+ hrs of non-fiction and family entertainment for TV and video for four decades.

Empire Burbank Studio, 1845 Empire Ave., Burbank, CA 91504. Phone: (818) 840-1400. Fax: (818) 567-1062.
TV-CATV only.
Sound stage studio rental, audience rated TV studios, full-svc production facilities & equipment, ultimate stage.

Encore Video Productions Inc., 811 Main St., Myrtle Beach, SC 29577. Phone: (843) 448-9900. Fax: (843) 448-9235. E-mail: frank@encorevideo.biz. Web Site: www.encorevideo.biz. Rik Dickinson, pres; Frank Payne, VP.
TV-CATV only.
Location & studio production, specializing in EFP/ENG 1-Camera productions, full script to screen svc, VNR, EPK satellite media tours, teleconferences, & magazine TV production. Betagami SP, non-linear editing.

Enoki Films U.S.A. Inc., 16430 Ventura Blvd., Suite 308, Encino, CA 91436. Phone: (818) 907-6503. Fax: (818) 907-6506. E-mail: info@enokifilmsusa.com. Web Site: www.enokifilmsusa.com. Yoshi Enoki, pres; Ricki Ames, VP worldwide distribution.
TV-CATV only.
Producer & distributor of children's animation for TV & video.

Envoy Productions, 660 Mason RIdge Ctr. Dr., St. Louis, MO 63141-8557. Phone: (314) 317-4216. Fax: (314) 317-4299. E-mail: sandi.clement@lhm.org. Web Site: www.envoyproductions.com. Sandi Clement, Manager; Kurt R. Klaus, pres.
TV-CATV only.
TV & radio production & distribution (English & Sp). Syndicates 30-minute wkly radio shows, *The Lutheran Hour* & *Woman to Woman*, & 30-minute wkly TV show *On Main Street* and TV holiday specials.

Episcopal Church Center, 815 2nd Ave., New York, NY 10017. Phone: (212) 716-6102. Fax: (212) 949-8059. Web Site: www.episcopalchurch.org.
Spokespersons for church & society issues.

Essence Television Productions Inc., 1500 Broadway, New York, NY 10036. Phone: (212) 642-0600. Fax: (212) 921-5173. Web Site: www.essence.com. Edward Lewis, chmn/CEO.
TV-CATV only.
TV program production.

Ethnic-American Broadcasting Co., Two Executive Drive, Fort Lee, NJ 07024. Phone: (201) 242-3000. Fax: (201) 944-5961. E-mail: info@skyview.
Fort Lee, NJ 07024, 2 Executive Dr, Suite 600. Phone: (201) 242-3000.
TV-CATV-Radio.
Provides ethnic radio & TV language svcs via DBS & through cable systems throughout North America.

Eurocine, 33 Ave. Des Champs Elysees, Paris 75008. Phone: 33.1.42.25.6492. Fax: 33.1.42.25.7338. E-mail: eurocine@club-internet.fr. Web Site: www.eurocine.net.
TV-CATV only.
Production & distribution in all media.

Producers, Distributors, and Production Services Alphabetical Index

Europe Images International, 1 Rond-Point Victor Hugo, F-92130, Issy-Les-Moulineaux France. Phone: (33) 1 55 95 58 00. Fax: (33) 1 55 95 58 10. E-mail: Europe-Images@europeimages.com. Web Site: www.europeimages.com. John Rouilly, CEO.
TV-CATV only.
Acquires, distributes & invests in international TV progmg. Catalog close to 5 hours broken into three categories, drama, children's documentaries.

Evangelical Lutheran Church in America, 8765 W. Higgins Rd., Chicago, IL 60631. Phone: (773) 380-2941. Fax: (773) 380-2406. E-mail: ava.martin@elca.org. Web Site: www.elca.org.
TV-CATV-Radio.
TV & radio progmg, promotional film production & distribution; production svcs., news.

Evergreen Entertainment Group, 1825 Ponce De Leon Blvd., Suite 450, Coral Gables, FL 33134-3626. Phone: (305) 460-4448. E-mail: evergreenenter@juno.com. Migdalia Inocencio, pres.
TV-CATV only.
Worldwide programs distribution; international co-production liaison; marketing and programming cable/satellite.

Expand Images, 7 Rue Taylor, Paris 75010. Phone: (33) 0148-0305-44. Fax: (33) 0148-0345-04. E-mail: communication@expand.fr. Web Site: www.expand.fr.
TV-CATV only.
Production & distribution company.

Eye in the Woods, Box 89, Brewton, AL 36427. Phone: (251) 809-1909. Fax: (251) 809-0729. Web Site: www.eyeinthewoods.com. Dale Faust, pres/exec producer.
TV-CATV only.
Produce a weekly show viewed on The Outdoor Channel.

Eyewitness Kids News, LLC, Box 116, 182 Sound Beach Ave., Old Greenwich, CT 06870-0116. Phone: (203) 637-3653. Fax: (203) 698-0812. E-mail: primonews@aol.com. Web Site: www.Kidsnewsnet.com. A.T. Primo, pres.
TV-CATV only.
Coaching of TV news & program talent;Strategic planning; production svcs.

F

FTC/Orlando, 503 W. Robinson St., Orlando, FL 32801. Phone: (407) 422-8246. Fax: (407) 843-0738. E-mail: ftcorlando@aol.com. Web Site: www.ftcorlando.com. A.J. Foresta, pres.
TV-CATV only.
Full-svc film & TV production company, specializing in coml & feature production. Area specialty: steadicam.

Faith for Today, 101 W. Cochran St., Simi Valley, CA 93065. Phone: (888) 940-0062. Fax: (805) 522-2114. E-mail: info@faithfortoday.tv. Web Site: www.faithfortoday.tv. Michael Tucker, Speaker/Director.
TV-CATV only.
Producer & distributor of *Lifestyle Magazine*, *McDougall M.D.* & *The Evidence*.

Family Stations Inc., 290 Hegenberger Rd., Oakland, CA 94621. Phone: (510) 568-6200. Phone: (800) 543-1495. Fax: (510) 633-7983. E-mail: famradio@familyradio.com. Web Site: www.familyradio.com. Harold E. Camping, pres/gen mgr; Rick Prime, tech dir; W. Craig Hulsebos, progmg mgr; William Thornton, VP.
Radio Only.
Radio program production & distribution.

FamilyNet, 6350 W. Freeway, Fort Worth, TX 76116. Phone: (817) 737-4011. Fax: (817) 377-4372. E-mail: ddavis@familynet.com. Web Site: www.familynet.com. David Clark, pres; Glenn McEowen, VP tech opns; Martin Coleman, VP production team; Chip Turner, VP mktg; Darin Davis, VP sls & traffic.
TV-CATV only.
FamilyNet is a 24/7 cable network. In addition, FamilyNet produces 5 syndicated radio progms. Values based, family oriented progmg.

FamilyNet Radio, 6350 W. Freeway, Fort Worth, TX 76116-4511. Phone: (817) 570-1400. Phone: (800) 266-1837. Fax: (817) 737-9436. E-mail: lbratton@familynet.com. Web Site: www.familynetradio.com. Lisa Young; Donna Senn, radio distribution.
Radio Only.
FamilyNet Radio produces 5 radio programs: *Powerline*, *Country Crossroads*, *MasterControl*, *Strength for Living*, *On Track* & "At a Glance" PSAs.

Faraone Communications Inc., 75 West End Ave., R-9A, New York, NY 10023. Phone: (212) 489-1313. Fax: (212) 489-8978. E-mail: tedfaraone@verizon.net. Web Site: www.pr-agency.com.
Valley Village, CA 91607. Valley Village, 4804 Laurel Canyon Blvd., Ste 516.
TV-CATV only.
Media rel svcs to producers & distributors of radio & TV programs, talent & home video.

Federal Citizen Information Center, 1800 F St. N.W., Rm. G-142, Washington, DC 20405. Phone: (202) 501-1794. Fax: (202) 501-4281. E-mail: nancy.tyler@gsa.gov. Web Site: www.pueblo.gsa.gov. Teresa Nasif, dir; Nancy Gregory Tyler, bcst mgr.
TV-CATV-Radio.
TV & radio PSAs promoting FirstGov.gov, the official web portal of the federal government.

Festival de Television de Monte-Carlo, 4, Boulevard du Jardin Exotique, Monte Carlo 98000. Phone: 377 93 10 40 60. Fax: 377 93 50 70 14. E-mail: info@tvfestival.com. Web Site: www.tvfestival.com.
TV-CATV only.
Competition of TV films & miniseries; news programs; producers. Conferences, panels & other market-related activities.

Film House Inc., 810 Dominican Dr., Nashville, TN 37228. Phone: (615) 255-4000. Fax: (615) 255-4111. E-mail: results@filmhouse.com. Curt Hahn, CEO; Ron Routson, pres/COO; Wayne Campbell, VP mktg; Andy Cohen, CFO; Edith Johnson, VP.
TV-CATV only.
Creates & produces TV mktg campaigns for radio & TV stns worldwide.

Film Roman Inc., 12020 Chandler Blvd., Suite 200, North Hollywood, CA 91607. Phone: (818) 761-2544. Fax: (818) 985-2973. Web Site: www.filmroman.com. John Hyde, pres/CEO.
TV-CATV only.
Animation production studio.

Filmoption International Inc., 3401 St. Antoine St., Westmount, PQ H3Z 1X1. Canada. Phone: (416) 598-1557. Fax: (416) 593-0013. E-mail: mrosilo@filmoption.com. Web Site: www.filmoption.com. Maryse Rouillard, pres; Lizanne Rouillard, VP; Muriel Rosilio, sr exec sls & co-productions; Evangelia Ozek, sls exec.
Toronto, ON M5J 2L7 Canada, 144 Front St. West, Suite 760. Phone: (416) 598-1557. Fax: (416) 593-0013. E-mail: mrosilio@filmoption.com. Muriel rosilio, sr exec sls co-productions.
Westmount, PQ H3Z 1X1 Canada, 3401 St-Antoine. Phone: (215) 931-6180. Fax: (514) 939-2034. E-mail: mrouilla@filmoption.com. Maryse Rouillard, pres.
TV-CATV only.
International distribution of TV programs.

Films Five Inc., 42 Overlook Rd., Great Neck, NY 11020. Phone: (516) 487-5865. Walter Bergman, pres.
TV-CATV only.
Pre- & postproduction; film & video comls, documentaries, sls films.

Films for the Humanities & Sciences Inc./FFH Video, Box 2053, Princeton, NJ 08543-2053. Phone: (609) 275-1400. Phone: (800) 257-5126. Fax: (609) 275-3767. E-mail: custserv@films.com. Web Site: www.films.com. Betsy Sherer, pres/CEO; Diane Bilello, VP sls.
TV-CATV only.
Distributes programs for bcst & cable industries to non-theatrical, educ, institutional, home video & business markets.

Films of the Nations, Box 449, Clarksburg, NJ 08510. Phone: (732) 462-3522. Fax: (732) 294-0330. E-mail: aldfilms@bellatlantic.net. Web Site: www.aldenfilms.com. Paul Weinberg, pres.
TV-CATV only.
TV program, promotion & educ film distribution.

Financial Media Services, Inc., Box 870928, Stone Mountain, GA 30087. Phone: (770) 413-2258. Fax: (770) 465-0180. E-mail: charles@charlesross.com.
TV-CATV-Radio.
Produces & syndicates nationally syndicated radio show *Your Personal Finance*.

David Finch Distribution Ltd., Box 264, Walton-on-Thames KT12 3YR. United Kingdom. Phone: 44-1932-882733. Fax: 44-1932-882108. E-mail: sales@david-finch.com. David Finch, chief exec.
TV-CATV only.
Supply of programs for home video & TV worldwide. Acquisition for United Kingdom home video.

Finger Lakes Productions International, 119 S. Cayuga St., Ithaca, NY 14850. Phone: (607) 275-9400. E-mail: world@flpradio.com. Web Site: www.flpradio.com. Paul Bartishevich, pres/CEO.
Radio Only.
Full-svc radio mktg, production & syndication of short-form radio features. International marketing, sales & consulting.

First Marketing, 3300 Gateway Dr., Pompano Beach, FL 33069. Phone: (954) 979-0700. Phone: (800) 641-9251. Fax: (954) 971-4707. Web Site: www.first-marketing.com. Ronald Drenning, pres; Neil Rosenbaum, VP/business dev.
TV-CATV only.
First Marketing offers 30 yrs of experience partnering with marketing professionals to dev custom communications programs designed to enhance custom relationships & profitability.

1st Miracle Productions, 3439 W. Cahuenga Blvd., Hollywood, CA 90068. Phone: (323) 874-6000. Fax: (323) 874-4252. E-mail: sales@1stmiracleproductions.com. Web Site: www.1stmiracleproductions.com. Moshe Bibiyan, CEO; Simon Bibiyan, pres.
TV-CATV only.
International distribution, co-production, postproduction finance.

First Run/Icarus Films, 32 Court St., 21st Fl., Brooklyn, NY 10201. Phone: (718) 488-8900. Fax: (718) 488-8642. E-mail: info@frif.com. Web Site: www.frif.com. Jonathan Miller, pres.
TV-CATV only.
International TV program distribution: documentaries, current affrs, music, arts, cultural programs.

FirstCom Music, 1325 Capital Pkwy., Suite 109, Carrollton, TX 75006. Phone: (800) 858-8880. Fax: (972) 242-6526. E-mail: info@firstcom.com. Web Site: www.firstcom.com. Ken Nelson, sr VP/exec producer; Carol Riffert, exec VP.
TV-CATV-Radio.
FirstCom Music offers the highest quality, most professionally produced, best sounding, easiest-to-use music libraries in the industry. Guaranteed.

Fischer Broadcast Services 10841 Bittersweet Lane, Fishers, IN 46038-2203. Phone: 317-514-5757. Fax: (317) 578-3884. E-mail: superfisch@mindspring.com. Web Site: www.superfisch.com. Scott Fischer, pres.
TV-CATV-Radio.
SUPERFISCH—THE PROMO VOICE SUPERHERO. Scott Fischer, signature voice artist for DirecTV Sports, Fox Sports Net Networks, and other fine affiliates. Myriad reads—always right! ISDN/MP3.

Broadcasting & Cable Yearbook 2006

Producers, Distributors, and Production Services Alphabetical Index

Forde Motion Picture Labs, 306 Fairview Ave. N., Seattle, WA 98109. Phone: (206) 682-2510. Phone: (800) 682-2510. Fax: (206) 682-2560. Web Site: www.fordelabs.com. Richard E. Vedvick, pres.
TV-CATV only.
Overnight processing of 35mm/16mm Eastman color negative dailies; release printing.

Four Star Media, 201 E. 15th St., New York, NY 10003. Phone: (212) 533-5994.
Radio Only.
Radio progmg production, distribution & mktg.

Fox Digital, Fox Network Ctr., 10201 W. Pico Blvd., Los Angeles, CA 90035. Phone: (310) 369-6622. Fax: (310) 969-6125. Web Site: www.fox.com.
TV-CATV only.
Videotape production facilities, stages & equipment.

Fox 17 Studio Productions, 631 Mainstream Dr., Nashville, TN 37228. Phone: (615) 244-1717. Fax: (615) 259-3962. Web Site: www.wztv.com. E-mail: production@fox17.com. Bill Zuckerman, prom dir.
TV-CATV only.
Full range video & film production facility; 25 x 40 studio & 60 x 60 studio soundstage; betacams & a variety of tape formats for TV/CATV.

Fox Sports West, 1100 S. Flower St., Los Angeles, CA 90015. Phone: (213) 743-7800. Fax: (213) 743-7835. Web Site: www.foxsports.com. Steve Simpson, gen mgr; Dennis Johnson, public relations dir.
TV-CATV only.
TV program production & distribution.

Fox 29 WUTV Sinclair, 951 Whitehaven Rd., Grand Island, NY 14072. Phone: (716) 773-7531. Fax: (716) 773-5753. Web Site: www.wutv.com. Don Moran, gen mgr; Jon May, progmg coord.
TV-CATV only.
TV coml production; U.S. rep, KATZ; Canadian rep, Airtime.

France TV Distribution, Immeuble Le Barjac, 1, blvd. Victor, Paris 75015. Phone: 01-44-2501-18. Fax: 01-44-2501-01. Web Site: www.francetv.com.
TV-CATV only.
Marketing & sls of French progmg.

Sandy Frank Entertainment Inc., 954 Lexington Ave., Suite 255, New York, NY 10021. Phone: (212) 772-1889. Fax: (212) 772-2297. E-mail: filmsfe@aol.com. Web Site: www.sandyfrankent.com. Sandy Frank, chmn/CEO; Damaso V. Santana, exec VP; Rosalie Perrone, controller; Sandi Spidell, VP opns; Maury Shields, VP business affrs; Barbara Kalicinska, sls; Sophia Evans, sls; Susan Piscitello, sls.
TV-CATV only.
TV production & syndication.

Free Speech TV (FSTV), Box 6060, Boulder, CO 80306. Phone: (303) 442-8445. Fax: (303) 442-6472. Web Site: www.freespeech.org. E-mail: info@freespeech.org. John Schwartz, pres/CEO; Jon Stout, gen mgr; Nathaniel Reeder, opns dir.
TV-CATV only.
Acquires works from activists, independent film/video artists & community based media; providing exposure to progressive ideas; FSTV's "Mobile-Eyes" series connects viewers with social change organizations.

Freewheelin' Films Ltd., Box 599, Aspen, CO 81612. Phone: (970) 925-2640. Fax: (970) 925-9369. Web Site: www.fwf.com. Rodney H. Jacobs, CEO; Kayla Hoffman-Cook, VP.
TV-CATV only.
25-yr old production company specializing in entertainment, sports & lifestyle specials.

The Fremantle Corp., 660 Madison Ave., 21 Floor, New York, NY 10021. Phone: (212) 421-4530. Fax: (212) 207-8357. Web Site: www.fremantlecorp.com. Paul Talbot, pres; Diane Tripp, co-managing dir; Blanca Oca Pertierra, VP Latin America & home video; Keith Talbot, co-managing dir.
TV-CATV only.
International TV program distribution & co-production.

Fremantle Media Ltd., 1 Stephen St., London W1T 1AL. United Kingdom. Phone: 44 (0)20 7691-6000. Fax: 44 (0)20 7691-6100. E-mail: feedback@freemantlemedia.com. Web Site: www.pearsontv.com. Greg Dyke, CEO; Tony Cohen, mng dir; James Bennet, CEO.
TV production & distribution.

FremantleMedia North America Inc., 2700 Colorado Ave., Suite 450, Santa Monica, CA 90404. Phone: (310) 255-4700. Fax: (310) 255-4800. Web Site: www.fremantlemedia.com. David Lyle, pres; Cecile Frot Coutaz, COO.
New York, NY 10036, 1540 Broadway. Catherine V, MacKay, Deputy CEO.
TV-CATV only.
TV production.

Chuck Fries Productions Inc., 6922 Hollywood Blvd., 12th Fl., Hollywood, CA 90028. Phone: (310) 203-9520. Fax: (323) 466-2266. E-mail: chuckfries@aol.com.
TV-CATV only.
Domestic & international TV, home video, & feature film production & distribution.

G

GLL TV Enterprises Inc., 8009 Via Fiore, Sarasota, FL 34238. Phone: (941) 925-4339. Fax: (941) 925-3976. E-mail: glltv@pobox.com. Gunther L. Less, pres; Ellen G. Less, sec/treas.
TV-CATV only.
TV program, coml, promotional film production & distribution. Journey to Adventure, the longest-running syndicated travel show on TV.

GMI Media L.L.C., 2211 5th Ave., Seattle, WA 98121. Phone: (206) 374-8889. Fax: (206) 374-2150. E-mail: moreinfo@gmimedia.com. Web Site: www.gmimedia.com. Ron Erak, pres; Richard Germaine, VP/gen mgr.
TV-CATV only.
Custom ID jingle packages for all radio & TV formats. CD production libraries. Voice overs & production for promotions & spots.

GRB Entertainment, 13400 Riverside Dr., 3rd Fl., Studio City, CA 91423. Phone: (818) 728-7697. Fax: (818) 728-7601. E-mail: gbenz@grbtv.com. Web Site: www.grbtv.com. Gary R. Benz, pres/CEO.
TV-CATV only.
Production & distribution (TV).

GTN, 13320 Northend Ave., Oak Park, MI 48237. Phone: (248) 548-2500. Fax: (248) 548-1916. Web Site: www.gtninc.com. Doug Cheek, pres.
TV-CATV only.
Studios, remote equipment, multi-format editing, film transfer, audio & duplication svcs, on-site satellite svcs & graphics.

GVI, 1775 K St. N.W., Suite 220, Washington, DC 20006. Phone: (202) 293-4488. Fax: (202) 293-3293. E-mail: andy@gvimail.com. Web Site: www.g-v-i.com. Andy Hemmindinger, pres; Bob Burnett, VP.
Full creative script-to-screen production, Beta SP fieldcrews, computer graphics. Avid editing, equipment rental & DVD authoring.

Galavision, 605 Third Ave., 12th Fl., New York, NY 10158-0180. Phone: (212) 455-5300. Fax: (212) 953-0198. Web Site: www.univision.com. Ray Rodriguez, pres/COO.
Los Angeles, CA 90045, 6701 Center Dr. W, Suite 650. Phone: (310) 348-3640. Fax: (310) 348-3643.
Dallas, TX 75201, 2323 Bryan St, Suite 1900. Phone: (214) 758-2392. Fax: (214) 758-2395.
TV-CATV only.
Spanish TV program distribution, cable.

Gedeon Programmes, 44-50 av du Capitaine Glarner, Saint-Quen 93585. Fax: 33 01 49 48 65 03. Phone: 33 01 49 48 65 00. Web Site: www.gedeonprogrammes.com.
TV-CATV only.
Films, TV movies, TV series, interactive fiction.

General Broadcasting Co. Inc., 8 N. Bothwell St., Suite 103, Palatine, IL 60067. Phone: (847) 202-8804. Fax: (847) 202-8834. Robert E. Potter, pres; Charles E. Maples, VP; Dean Mulchaey, production mgr; Eric Edgerton, gen mgr.
Background music, environmental music progmg.

General Conference of Seventh-day Adventists, 12501 Old Columbia Pike, Silver Spring, MD 20904-6600. Phone: (301) 680-6000. Phone: (301) 680-6300. Fax: (301) 680-6312. E-mail: news@adventist.org. Web Site: www.adventist.org. Ray Dabrowski, dir; Benjamin Schoun, dir.
TV-CATV only.
Radio & TV program production & distribution.

Georgia Film, Video & Music Office, 285 Peachtree Ctr. Ave., Suite 1000, Atlanta, GA 30303. Phone: (404) 656-3591. Fax: (404) 656-3565. E-mail: film@georgia.org. Web Site: www.filmgeorgia.org. Greg Torre, dir.
TV-CATV only.
Mailing address: Box 1776, Atlanta, GA 30301-1776.
Location scouting & preproduction svcs provided to feature film, TV movie, coml & multimedia production companies.

Getty Images, 601 N. 34th St., Seattle, WA 98103. Phone: (206) 925-5000. Fax: (206) 925-5001. E-mail: sales@gettyimages.com. Web Site: www.gettyimages.com.
TV-CATV only.
Getty Images is an imagery company creating and providing still and moving images to communications professionals around the globe.

Ghostwriters/Radio Mall, 2412 Unity Ave. N., Dept BR, Minneapolis, MN 55422-3450. Phone: 763-522-6256. Fax: 763-522-6256. E-mail: radio@radiomall.com. Web Site: www.radiomall.com. David Dworkin, owner.
TV-CATV only.
Over 18 years experience with products sold to more than 6,500 radio stations worldwide as well as TV stations, audio-video producers, and cable operators. If you have a finished product that you'd like to market to radio stations, contact us. We offer a 60-day money-back guarantee.

Lon Gibby Productions, Inc./ Gibby Media Group, E. 113 Magnesium Rd., Spokane, WA 99208. Phone: (509) 467-1113. Phone: (800) 200-1113. Fax: (509) 467-4763. E-mail: lon@longibby.com. Web Site: www.longibby.com. Lon Gibby, pres/CEO.
Multimedia productions, video, CD-Rom, CD-I, producers of bcst TV programs, commercials, infomercials, corporate videos & webcasting

Gladney Communications Ltd., 101 Reni Rd., Manhasset, NY 11030. Phone: (516) 627-3016. Fax: (516) 767-1957. Norman Gladney, pres; Marion Gladney, exec VP.
TV-CATV only.
TV & radio production & distribution.

Glenray Productions Inc., Box 40400, Pasadena, CA 91114-7400. Phone: (626) 797-5462. Fax: (626) 797-7524. E-mail: glenray@pacbell.net. Web Site: www.familymedia.net. C. Ray Carlson, pres; Joy Carlson, pub rel.
TV-CATV only.
Films, TV series, video distribution & production, primarily for family & children.

Global Entertainment Media, 1645 S. Rancho Santa Fe Rd., Suite 208, San Marcos, CA 92069. Phone: (760) 752-4407. Fax: (760) 752-4427. E-mail: sales@gem-media.com. Web Site: www.gem-media.com. Alexander A. Fiore, dir; Mercedes M. Fiore, pres & CFO; Damaris Ghourdjian, VP mktg.
TV-CATV only.
Production & distribution company.

Global Telemedia Inc., 98 E. Ave., Norwalk, CT 06851. Phone: (203) 854-9985. Fax: (203) 855-8370. E-mail: gt@globaltelemedia.com. Web Site: www.globaltelemedia.com. Greg Kimmelman, pres/CEO; Anne Gulledge, dir.
TV-CATV only.
Production & distribution of bcst TV & DVD progmg worldwide.

Globe Productions, Box 20465, Roanoke, VA 24018. Phone: (540) 344-3283. E-mail: recordial@yahoo.com. J.W. Sheperd, pres & owner.
Radio Only.
Audio restoration & preservation services.

GlobeCast, 1270 Avenue of the Americas, Ste 2800, New York, NY 10020. Phone: (212) 373-5140. Fax: (212) 399-1949. E-mail: info@globecastna.com. Web Site: www.globecast.com. David Sprechman, pres/CEO; Mary Frost, Sr sls VP; Jonathan Feldman, VP business affrs; Keven Cahoon, VP mktg.
Culver City, CA 90232. GlobeCast Los Angeles/California, 10525 W. Washington Blvd. Phone: 1-310-845-3900. Fax: 1-310-845-3904.
Washington, DC 20005. GlobeCast Washington/DC, 1120 G Street, NW - 2nd Floor. Phone: 1-202-383-2745. Fax: 1-202-393-4914.
Miami, FL 33166. GlobeCast Miami Headquarters America/Florida, 7291 NW 74th St. Phone: 1-310-687-1600. Fax: 1-305-341-4424.
Salt Lake City, UT 84119. GlobeCast Salt Lake City/Utah, 1193 West 2400 South, Suite A. Phone: 1-801-908-1100. Fax: 1-801-954-0991.
TV-CATV only.

Producers, Distributors, and Production Services Alphabetical Index

Globecast Audio division supports a comprehensive package of audio transmission svcs:

ABC/Keystone Ventures provides Satcom C5 DATS/SEDAT distribution svcs to 7,000 radio stns.

3D2, a high-quality digital net designed to service the entertainment industry, connections post-production facilities, recording studios & voice-over talent worldwide.

A/FX Network utilizing Telos Zephyr code located at venues for sports backhauls & special events.

"Hybrid" bridging svcs to simplify a digital world full of different flavored audio codecs.

Remote Production Packages for single or multi-station remote broadcasts.

GlobeCast North America, 10525 W. Washington Blvd., Culver City, CA 90230. Phone: (310) 845-3900. Fax: (310) 845-3904. Web Site: www.globecast.com. Ken Drake, dir opns.

TV-CATV only.

In the center of Hollywood, GlobeCast North America's Sunset facility provides studio production second audio progmg (SAP), & related client facility svcs on an as-scheduled or contractual basis. GlobeCast's studio is completely integrated w/GlobeCast's network of global, end-to-end connectivity via satellite, fiber optics & microwave.

GlobeCast North America, provides the bcstg industry with a unique combination of both recognized expertise & extensive inter-continental svcs. Through GlobeCast's vast global infrastructure of over 100 transponders, 30 teleports & interconnect facilities, the company provides instant access to the world's major media markets. GlobeCast North America is part of France Telecom, one of the worlds largest telecommunications companies.

Jeff Gold Productions Inc., 13900 Panay Way, M-307, Marina del Rey, CA 90292. Phone: (310) 827-9165. Jeff Gold, dir.

TV-CATV only.

Production svcs, film & coml production.

Golden Gate Studios, (KTLN TV 68). 400 Tamal Plaza, Corte Madera, CA 94925. Phone: (415) 945-7642. Fax: (415) 924-0264. E-mail: bavery@tln.com. Web Site: www.goldengatestudios.com. Brian Avery, stn mgr.

TV-CATV only.

2 Studios, Green Screen Options, Full Production Packages

The Samuel Goldwyn Films, 9570 W. Pico Blvd., Suite 400, Los Angeles, CA 90035-6405. Phone: (310) 860-3100. Fax: (310) 860-3195. Samuel Goldwyn Jr., chmn/CEO; Meyer Gottlieb, COO.

Movie acquisition & distribution.

Good Life Associates, Box 81803, Lincoln, NE 68501. Phone: (402) 464-6440. Fax: (402) 464-6880. E-mail: martinj@backtothebible.org. Web Site: www.goodlifeassociates.org. Thomas C. Schindler, pres; Martin Jones, dir.

Radio Only.

Radio program, coml production & distribution svcs.

Good News Broadcasting Association Inc., 6400 Cornhusker Hwy., Lincoln, NE 68501. Phone: (402) 464-7200. Fax: (402) 464-7474. E-mail: info@backtothebible/backtothebible.com. Web Site: www.backtothebible.org. Woodrow Kroll, pres.

TV-CATV only.

Radio & TV program production & distribution.

Gordon Productions, Box 640549, San Francisco, CA 94164. Phone: (415) 776-7484. Fax: (415) 776-7822. E-mail: john@gpvideo.com. Web Site: www.gpvideo.com. John Gordon, pres; Les Lieurance, VP; Jerry Gordon, CEO.

TV-CATV only.

Production/distribution of video news releases, TV pub svc announcements, audio news releases. Distribution via satellite path fire & cassette

Gould Entertainment Corp., 101 W. 57th St., Suite 10B, New York, NY 10019. Phone: (212) 586-5760. Michael J. Gould, pres.

TV-CATV only.

Consultants, packagers, distributors of progmg; specialists in mktg foreign programs

Grace Digital Media, 1919 M St. N.W., Suite 200, Washington, DC 20036. Phone: (202) 775-0894. Fax: (202) 775-1288. Web Site: www.gracedigitalmedia.com. Cheryl Reagan, pres.

TV-CATV only.

Full-svc production/postproduction facility, camera crews, equipment rental, TV studios & satellite facilities.

Billy Graham Evangelistic Association, Radio Department, Box 1270, Charlotte, NC 28201. Phone: (704) 401-2432. Fax: (704) 401-3028. E-mail: had@bgea.org. Franklin Graham, pres; Roger Flessing, dir.

Radio Only.

Granada America, 15303 Ventura Blvd., Suite 800, Sherman Oaks, CA 91403. Phone: (818) 783-7474. Fax: (818) 753-6388. E-mail: stephen@hamdon.com. Stephen J. Davis, CEO; Gary G. Goldberger, exec VP; Linda Ross, sr VP/finance & admin.

TV-CATV only.

Worldwide distribution & production of made-for-TV movies.

Great Chefs Television/Publishing, (A division of G.C.I., Inc.). Box 56757, New Orleans, LA 70156. Phone: (504) 581-5000. Fax: (504) 581-1188. E-mail: info@greatchefs.com. Web Site: www.greatchefs.com. John Shoup, pres/CEO; Linda Nix, dir.

TV-CATV only.

Production & distribution of cooking & jazz TV programs, videos, CDs, CD-ROMs, books.

Great North Productions, 3720-76 Ave., Edmonton, AB T6B 2N9. Canada. Phone: (780) 440-2022. Fax: (403) 440-3400. Web Site: www.greatnorth.ab.ca. Penny Ritco, VP.

TV-CATV only.

A full-svc international production & distribution company, providing worldwide distribution for bcst home video, non-theatrical markets & co-production opportunities.

Great Plains National (GPN), Box 80669, Lincoln, NE 68501. Phone: (800) 228-4630. Fax: (800) 306-2330. E-mail: gpn@unl.edu. Web Site: www.gpn.unl.edu. Stephen C. Lenzen, dir.

TV-CATV only.

Acquires, produces, promotes & distributes videotaped instructional videos for bcst, cablecast & audiovisual use.

The Griffin Group, 130 S. El Camino Dr., Beverly Hills, CA 90212. Phone: (310) 385-2700. Fax: (310) 358-2701. Web Site: www.merv.com. Larry Cohen, pres/CEO.

TV-CATV only.

Full-svc dev & production company; slate includes series, specials & films. Also real estate & hotel ownership.

Grinberg Film Libraries Inc., 21011 Itasca St., Unit D, Chatworth, CA 91311. Phone: (818) 709-2450. Fax: (818) 709-8540. Web Site: www.grinberg.com. W. "Bill" Brewington, CEO.

TV-CATV only.

Stock footage & news library.

Groove Addicts, 12211 West Washington Blvd., Los Angeles, CA 90066. Phone: (310) 572-4646. Fax: (310) 572-4647. E-mail: info@grooveaddicts.com. Web Site: www.grooveaddicts.com. Dain Eric Blair, CEO; Cindy Rosmann, VP/gen mgr.

TV-CATV only.

Custom, syndicated news, image, promotion music for bcst & entertainment projects worldwide. Standout jingle & I.D. packages. Barter & Cash opportunities.

Grove Television Enterprises Inc., 46216 Dry Creek Dr., Badger, CA 93603. Phone: (559) 337-2595. Fax: (559) 337-1334. John W. Hyde, pres/CEO.

TV-CATV only.

TV production & distribution international & domestic.

H

HAVE Inc., 309 Power Ave., Hudson, NY 12534-2448. Phone: (518) 828-2000. Phone: (800) 999-4283. Fax: (518) 828-2008. E-mail: have@haveinc.com. Web Site: www.haveinc.com. Nancy Gordon, pres; Paul Swedenburg, VP.

TV-CATV only.

Distribution of audio & videotape, equipment, accessories & supplies, featuring BELDEN, CANARE & MOGAMI cable. Duplication, postproduction svcs & international standards conversion svcs. CD-Audio & CD-ROM, DVD replication & duplication. DVD authoring.

HEA Productions, 313 Gahbauer Rd., Hudson, NY 12534. Phone: (518) 822-1717. Fax: (518) 822-1042. E-mail: susan@susanhamilton.com. Susan Hamilton, pres.

TV-CATV only.

Radio & TV music production.

HIT Entertainment P.L.C., Maple House, 149-150 Tottenham Ct. Rd., 5th Fl., London W1T 7NF. United Kingdom. Phone: 20-7554-2500. Fax: 20-7388-9321. E-mail: contactus@hitentertainment.com. Web Site: www.hitentertainment.com. Rob Lawes, CEO; Peter Orton, chmn; Charles Caminada, sls dir; Steve Ruffini, CFO.

Beverly Hills, CA 90212, 9300 Wilshire Blvd., 2nd Fl. Phone: (301) 724-8979.

Allen, TX 7500-3320, 830 Greenville Ave. Phone: (972) 390-6000.

TV-CATV only.

Distributor, co-producer & financier of quality animiation, children's & natural history progmg.

Alfred Haber Distribution Inc., 111 Grand Ave., Palisades Park, NJ 07650. Phone: (201) 224-8000. Fax: (201) 947-4500. E-mail: info@haberinc.com. Web Site: www.alfredhaber.com. Robert Kennedy, exec VP; Alfred Haber, pres.

TV-CATV only.

TV program distribution.

Halland Broadcast Services Inc., 2412 Unity Ave. N., Minneapolis, MN 55422. Phone: (763) 522-6256. Fax: (763) 522-6256. E-mail: info@h-b-s.com. Web Site: www.h-b-s.com. Dave Dworkin, mgr.

Radio Only.

Rock 'n' Roll Graffiti oldies library on compact disc, The Eighties Plus AC/CHR library on compact disc & The Seventies AC/CHR gold library on compact disc. Country music libraries on compact disc. All is available on hard drive.

Hamilton Productions Inc., 7732 Georgetown Pike, McLean, VA 22102. Phone: (703) 734-5444. Fax: (703) 734-5449. E-mail: jah@dgsys.net. John Hamilton, pres; Jay Hamilton, VP; Anne H. Deger, VP.

TV-CATV only.

Ind TV production firm.

Handel Film Corp., 8787 Shoreham Dr., Apt. 609, West Hollywood, CA 90069. Phone: (310) 652-3887. Fax: (310) 657-2746.

TV-CATV only.

TV program production & distribution.

Hanna-Barbera Productions Inc., 15303 Ventura Blvd., Suite 1400, Sherman Oaks, CA 91403. Phone: (818) 977-7500. Fax: (818) 977-7510. Web Site: www.hanna-barbera.com. William Hanna; Joseph Barbera, co-chmn.

TV program production.

Happi Associates, Box 110892, Nashville, TN 37222. Phone: (615) 220-6050. Phone: (615) 604-1981. E-mail: doddrace@aol.com. Skeeter Dodd, gen mgr.

Radio Only.

Radio program & mgmt; country formats; motivational speaking, jingles ID & coml, production music, features, customized productions.

Larry Harmon Pictures Corp., 7080 Hollywood Blvd., Suite 202, Hollywood, CA 90028. Phone: (323) 463-2331. Fax: (323) 463-7219. E-mail: tellbozo@aol.com. Web Site: www.bozo.com. Larry Harmon, pres; Susan Harmon, exec VP; Jerry Digney, VP/mktg.

TV-CATV only.

Owner & distributor of Bozo cartoons & live show franchise, & Laurel & Hardy cartoons.

Harmony Gold U.S.A. Inc., 7655 Sunset Blvd., Los Angeles, CA 90046. Phone: (323) 851-4900. Fax: (323) 851-5599. E-mail: aletz @harmonygold.com. Web Site: www.harmonygold.com. Frank Agrama, chmn/CEO; Colleen Morris, pres; Alan Letz, exec VP.

TV-CATV only.

TV production, international TV distribution.

Harpo Productions, 110 N. Carpenter St., Chicago, IL 60607. Phone: (312) 633-1000. Web Site: www.oprah.com.

Produces "The Oprah Winfrey Show."

Health Net Productions & Pet Talk, 185 N. New Ballas Rd., St. Louis, MO 63141. Phone: (314) 997-5422. Fax: (314) 997-5422. E-mail: judyleven@aol.com. Judy Leventhal, pres; Chuck LeRoi, VP.

TV-CATV only.

Distributes 90-second pharmacy vignettes, 45 to 60-second pet care vignettes & 90-second sports medicine vignettes.

Hearst Entertainment, Inc., 888 Seventh Ave., New York, NY 10019. Phone: (212) 455-4000. Phone: (800) 526-5464. Fax: (212) 455-4310. Web Site: www.hearstent.com. Bruce L. Palsner, pres; Robert Corona, sr VP; Tom Devlin, sr VP; Stacey Valenza, VP mktg; Glenda Grant, pres.

Producers, Distributors, and Production Services Alphabetical Index

London SW1X 9AY. London (Sales), 136 Sloane St, 9th Fl. Phone: (44) 20 7565 6675. Fax: (44) 20 7565 6675.
Los Angeles, CA 90025. Hearst Entertainment Productions, 1640 S. Sepulveda Blvd. Phone: (310) 478-1700. Fax: (310) 478-2202.
New York, NY 10017, 235 E 45th St. Phone: (212) 455-4000. Fax: (212) 983-6379.
TV-CATV only.
Leading producer and distributor of made-for-television movies, first-run entertainment, animated series, reality and documentary progmg for the global marketplace.

Hearts of Space Inc., Box 5916, Sausalito, CA 94966-5916. Phone: (415) 331-3200. Fax: (415) 331-3280. E-mail: info@hos.com. Web site: www.hos.com. Stephen M. Hill, pres & producer; Leyla Rael Hill, VP/gen mgr.
Radio Only.
Syndicated one-hour progmg of ambient, electronic, multi-cultural & contemplative spacemusic via NPR satellite transmission.

Heil Enterprises, Box 1372, Lancaster, PA 17608-1372. Phone: (717) 898-9100. Fax: (717) 898-6600. E-mail: info@thegospelgreats.com. Web Site: www.thegospelgreats.com.
Radio Only.
Radio program, production & distribution.

Arthur Henley Productions, 101 W. 23rd St., #2462, New York, NY 10011. Phone: (718) 263-0136. E-mail: ah55@webtv.net. Arthur Henley, pres.
TV-CATV only.
TV & radio program production; radio program distribution.

Henninger Media Services, Inc., 2601-A Wilson Blvd., Arlington, VA 22201. Phone: (703) 243-3444. Phone: (888) 243-3444. Fax: (703) 243-5697. Fax: (703) 243-4023. Web Site: www.henninger.com. Rob Henninger, CEO; Doug Miller, sls dir & dir mktg; Brian J. Kelly, gen mgr; Adam Kranitz, mktg mgr.
Los Angeles, CA 90404. Tribeca Henninger Editing Tools-CA (T.H.E. Tools), 3000 W. Olympic Blvd, Ste. 1350. Phone: (310) 264-4192. Fax: (310) 264-4194. Jon Tronowski, facility mgr.
Washington, DC 20007. Henninger Capitol, 2121 Wisconsin Ave. N.W. Phone: (202) 965-7800. Fax: (202) 965-7815. Bobby Wright, gen mgr.
Washington, DC 20036. Henninger 1150 Post, 1150 17th St, Suite 401. Phone: (202) 833-3444. Fax: (202) 833-3995. Peggy Polito, facility mgr.
New York, NY 10013. Tribeca Henninger Editing Tools-NY (T.H.E. Tools), Tribeca Media Center, 65 North Moore St. Phone: (212) 226-7770. Fax: (212) 226-8157. Jon Miles, gen mgr.
Nashville, TN 37228. Henninger Elite, Metro Center, 50 Vantage Way, Suite 100. Phone: (615) 256-7678. Fax: (615) 255-7212. Roy Giorgio, gen mgr.
Arlington, VA 22201. Henninger Media Development, 2601-A Wilson Blvd. Phone: (703) 243-3444. Fax: (703) 243-5697. Steven Schupak, gen mgr.
Richmond, VA 23220. Commonwealth Film Labs, 1500 Brook Rd. Phone: (804) 649-8611. Fax: (804) 648-7715. Roger Robison, gen mgr.
Richmond, VA 23223. Henninger Richmond, 1901 E. Franklin St, Suite 103. Phone: (804) 644-5006. Fax: (804) 783-0820. Scott Witthaus, gen mgr.
TV-CATV only.
TV postproduction, film & video, film processing, 2-D & 3-D graphics, TV progmg dev, distribution; multi-media & DVDs.

Heritage/Baruch Television Distribution, 1025 Connecticut Ave. N.W., Suite 1012, Washington, DC 20036-5417. Phone: (202) 833-1777. Fax: (202) 496-0162. Ed Baruch, pres; Steve Smallwood, VP; Valerie Cooley-Elliott, dir mktg.
TV-CATV only.
Mktg, syndication & production/distribution of progmg to network syndication international.

Highland Laboratories, Administration Bldg., Pier 96, San Francisco, CA 94124. Phone: (415) 981-5010. Fax: (415) 981-5019. Web Site: www.highlandlab.com. B.J. Brose, pres.
TV-CATV only.
Video, audio, film duplication, film transfers: D-2, Betacam, 2 inches, 1 inch, 3/4 inch, 1/2 inch.

Jack Hilton Inc., 230 Park Ave., Suite 1530, New York, NY 10169. Phone: (212) 687-2002. Fax: (212) 697-9008.
TV-CATV only.
TV & video productions.

The History Makers, 1900 S. Michigan Ave., Chicago, IL 60616. Phone: (312) 674-1900. Fax: (312) 674-1915. Web Site: www.thehistorymakers.com. Julieanna L. Richardson,.
TV-CATV only.
Video production,

Holigan Investment Group Ltd., 15950 N. Dallas Pkwy., Suite 750, Dallas, TX 75248. Phone: (972) 387-7999. Fax: (972) 387-1685. Web Site: www.michael.holigan.com. Michael Holigan, exec producer; Tim Dickey, exec producer.
Dallas, TX 75240, 6029 Beltline, Suite 110.
TV-CATV only.
Production & syndication of YOUR NEW HOUSE and THE REALITY OF SPEED; 30 minute TV programs.

Home Improvement Television Network, 3441 Baker St., San Diego, CA 92117. Phone: (858) 273-0572. Fax: (858) 273-8410. E-mail: homefix@hometvnet.com. Web Site: www.hometvnet.com. Bruce Lamb, pres.
TV-CATV only.
Providers of home improvement progmg & 90-second video vignettes.

Hometown Illinois Radio Network, Box 169, 918 E. Park, Taylorville, IL 62568-0169. Phone: (217) 824-3395. Fax: (217) 824-3301. Web Site: www.randyradio.com. Randal J. Miller, pres.
Radio Only.
Wired network providing loc reports from Illinois State Fair, Illinois Farm Bureau Convention & Commodity Classic.

Horizon Audio Creations, Box 486, 74 Chemin De Lanse, Hudson Heights-Rigaud, PQ J0P 1J0. Canada. Phone: (450) 451-4549. Fax: (450) 451-4549. E-mail: reachcraigcutler@videotron.ca. Craig W. Cutler, pres; Marguerite Blais, progmg mgr; Mary-Lou Dodd, opns mgr.
Radio Only.
Radio program, coml production; production svcs; inflight audio progmg & adv.

Horizons Television Inc., 9305 Monalaine Ct., Great Falls, VA 22066. Phone: (703) 759-7500. Fax: (703) 759-1620. E-mail: admin@horizonstv.com. Web Site: www.horizonstv.com. Timothy E. Donner, exec dir.
TV-CATV only.
Creative dev & full-svc production of reality-based TV programs & commissioned videos for diverse organizations & assns. Avid media composer.

Thomas Horton Associates Inc., 408 Bryant Cir., Suite K, Ojai, CA 93023. Phone: (805) 646-7866. Fax: (805) 646-3600. E-mail: tha@sharktv.com. Web Site: www.sharktv.com. Thomas F. Horton, pres; Jean Horton Garner, sr VP; Garry R. Garner, dir mktg.
TV-CATV only.
TV program full-svc production, postproduction, international & domestic distribution, specializing in award-winning documentaries.

Host Communications Inc., 546 E. Main St., Lexington, KY 40508-2300. Phone: (859) 226-4678. Fax: (859) 226-4419. Web Site: www.hostcommunications.com. James Host, CEO; Gordon Whitner, pres/COO.
TV-CATV only.
TV & radio production & syndication.

Hot Box Digital, 367 N. Hwy. 101, Solana Beach, CA 92075. Phone: (858) 292-8520. Fax: (858) 292-8520. Cam MacMillan, exec producer.
TV-CATV only.
Design & production of bcst 3-D computer graphics. Logo animation, stn packages. All tape formats supported. Productions of Subito Studio Video Graphics Volumes.

Marie Hoy Film & TV, 18 Bruton Pl. Berkeley Sq., Mayfair, London W1X 7AA. Phone: 020-7851-6666. Fax: 017-1493-3997. E-mail: mariehoy@cocoon.co.uk.
TV-CATV only.
Coproduction Funding & Financial Packaging.

Huntridge Video Productions Inc., Box 3813, Greenville, SC 29608-3813. Phone: (864) 271-3348. Fax: (864) 232-4462. E-mail: mat@huntridge.com. Web Site: www.huntridge.com.
TV-CATV only.
TV production & postproduction.

I

ISL Television Ltd., Seymour News House, Seymour News, London W1H 9PE. Phone: (44) 171 616 11 11. Fax: (44) 171 616-1110. Web Site: www.islworld.com.
TV-CATV only.
TV program sls & distribution, bcst sponsorship, events & TV program production & TV consultancy.

The Idea Channel, 1502 Powell Ave., Erie, PA 16505. Phone: (814) 464-9068. Fax: (814) 464-9069. E-mail: info@ideachannel.com. Web Site: www.ideachannel.com. Bob Chitester, pres/CEO; Rick Platt, VP/COO.
TV-CATV only.
Discussions 20-40 minutes in length, featuring two or three leading scholars on a wide variety of subjects. Internet offerings also.

The Image Generators, 18156 Darnell Dr., Olney, MD 20832. Phone: (301) 924-5700. Fax: (301) 570-8916. E-mail: mweiner@imagegenerators.com. Web Site: www.imagegenerators.com. Michael J. Weiner, pres/CEO.
TV-CATV only.
Voice-overs, radio spot & program production; media training, progmg concept to completion; ISDN-equipped (TELOS).

The Image Group, 305 E. 46th St., 3rd Fl., New York, NY 10017. Phone: (212) 548-4400. Fax: (212) 752-3745. Mike Buckner, gen mgr; Warren Fredericks, engrg dir.
TV-CATV only.
Complete postproduction svcs; film-to-tape, editing & graphics.

Imagers Inc., 1575 Northside Dr., Suite 490, Atlanta, GA 30318. Phone: (404) 351-5800. Fax: (404) 351-9020. Web Site: www.imagers.com.
TV coml production & distribution; production svcs.

Images Communication Arts Corp., 366 N. Broadway, Suite 410, Jericho, NY 11753. Phone: (516) 939-2990. Robert Braverman, pres.
TV-CATV only.
Syndication & co-production of TV & radio program series & specials. Syndication of "old-time radio" dramas.

In-Motion Pictures, 5 Percy St., London W1T 1DG. United Kingdom. Phone: (207) 467-6880. Fax: (207) 467-6890. E-mail: Sales@jment.com. Web Site: www.jment.com. Dr. Hilmar Siebert, chmn; Julian Freeston, CFO.
Beverly Hills, CA 90212, 412 S. Beverly dr., 5th Fl. Phone: (301) 789-4500.
TV-CATV only.
Film & TV production & distribution.

Independent Artists, (A Division of Screen Gems Ltd). 16 W. 56th St., New York, NY 10019. Phone: (212) 765-4640. Fax: (212) 765-4686. E-mail: indartists@mindspring.com. Herb Sidel, exec producer & gen mgr.
TV-CATV only.
TV coml production.

Independent Edge Films, 719 52nd St. N., St. Petersburg, FL 33710. Phone: (727) 321-2898. E-mail: michaelfox@indi-edge.com. Web Site: www.indi-edge.com. Michael D. Fox,.
TV-CATV only.
Ind motion picture/TV/web production & distribution.

Integrity Media, 401 E. Corpoorate Dr., #222, Lewisville, TX 75057. Phone: (214) 222-7878. Fax: (214) 222-7838. E-mail: schalupka@integritymedia.net. Douglas Neece, pres; Sandy Chalupka, VP.
TV-CATV only.
TV & radio program distribution, time buying & media planning.

International Broadcasting Network, Box 691111, 5206 FM 1960 W., Suite 105, Houston, TX 77269. Phone: (281) 587-8900. Fax: (281) 774-9923. E-mail: ibn@ev1.net. Paul Broyles, pres.
TV-CATV only.
Network of ten low power stns; including loc produced progmg.

International Program Consultants Inc., 52 E. End Ave., New York, NY 10028. Phone: (212) 734-9096. Fax: (212) 734-6495. Russell J. Kagan, mgng dir.
TV-CATV only.
International TV distribution, TV progmg & home video acquisition consultation, co-production consultation.

International Tele-Film, 41 Horner Ave., Unit #3, Toronto, ON M8Z 4X4. Canada. Phone: (416) 252-1173. Fax: (416) 252-1676. E-mail: info@itf.ca. Web Site: www.itf.ca.
TV-CATV only.
Distributor for documentaries, features, series & specials, in Canada & worldwide.

Producers, Distributors, and Production Services Alphabetical Index

International Television Broadcasting Inc., 36-01 36th Ave., 2nd Fl., Long Island City, NY 11106. Phone: (718) 784-8555. Fax: (718) 784-8901. E-mail: info@itvgold.com. Web Site: www.itvgold.com. Dr. Sathya Viswanath, pres.
TV-CATV only.
Full time Indian TV program for cable & bcst TV.

International Television Corp., 4380 N.W. 128th St., Miami, FL 33054. Phone: (305) 688-7475. Fax: (305) 685-5697. Web Site: www.coralintl.com. Jose Escalante, VP/gen mgr; Guadalupe D'Agostino, VP international sls.
TV-CATV only.
TV progmg distribution & production. Worldwide distribution, co-productions.

Ion Weather Network, 13 B East Main St., Denville, NJ 07834. Phone: (973) 983-8222. Fax: (973) 983-1390. Web Site: www.ionweather.com. E-mail: steve@ionweather.com. Stephen Pellettiere Sr., pres; Stephen Pellettiere Jr., consultant.
Radio Only.
Gen weather forecasts, science info.

Irving Productions Inc., 3202 E. 21st, Tulsa, OK 74114. Phone: (918) 744-1221. Fax: (918) 744-1223. E-mail: irving@irvingproductions.com. Web Site: www.irvingproductions.com. Dick Schmitz, pres.
TV-CATV only.
Audio recording & production svcs for all media.

It Is Written Television, Box O, Thousand Oaks, CA 91360. Phone: (805) 955-7733. Fax: (805) 955-7734. E-mail: iiw@iiw.org. Web Site: www.iiw.org. Mark Finley, dir; Shawn Boonstra, assoc speaker.
TV-CATV only.
TV & radio program production & distribution; internet.

Italtoons Corp., 32 W. 40th St., New York, NY 10018. Phone: (212) 730-0280. Fax: (212) 730-0313. E-mail: salesinfo@italtoons.com. Web Site: www.italtoons.com. Giuliana Nicodemi, pres; Luisa Rivosecchi, sls; Ken Priester, gen mgr.
TV-CATV only.
TV program production & distribution. Children's animation.

Ivanhoe Broadcast News Inc., 2745 W. Fairbanks Ave., Winter Park, FL 32789. Phone: (407) 740-0789. Fax: (407) 740-5320. E-mail: mthomas@ivanhoe.com. Web Site: www.ivanhoe.com. Majorie BeKaert Thomas, pres; Bette Bon Fleur, CEO; John Cherry, pres.
TV-CATV only.
Producer & syndicator of targeted new series. Medical breakthrough, Prescription Health & Smart Woman.

J

JAM Creative Productions Inc., 5454 Parkdale Dr., Dallas, TX 75227. Phone: (214) 388-5454. Fax: (214) 381-4647. E-mail: sales@jingles.com. Web Site: www.jingles.com. Jonathan M. Wolfert, pres; Mary Lyn Wolfert, sr VP; Tom Parma, sls; Cary Bass, sls; Randy Bell, sls.
TV-CATV only.
ID jingle & coml production for radio & TV, custom music & production svcs.

J&H Music Programming, 5814 Fleming Terr. Rd., Greensboro, NC 27410. Phone: (336) 218-8052. Fax: (336) 218-8052. Joseph V. Gelo, pres; Helen J. Gelo, VP.
Radio Only.
Radio program distribution.

JC Productions Inc., 1851 Murray Hill Station, New York, NY 10016. Phone: (212) 532-2820 phone/fax. E-mail: jcpro@bellatlantic.net. Web Site: www.jc-productions.com. Joe Conforti, dir.
TV-CATV only.
Live action coml production; CD-ROM multimedia production; 3D animation & graphic design.

JGT Media Productions, 12408 86th Pl., N.E., Kirkland, WA 98034-2601. Phone: (425) 820-4523. Fax: (425) 820-4523. J. Graley Taylor,.
TV program, promotion film production & distribution; production svcs; rgnl award program, ARBY Awards; film & video production.

J.N. Productions, 902-1790 Bayshore Dr., Vancouver, BC V6G 3G5. Canada. Phone: 604-331-0690. E-mail: info@jnproductions.bc.ca. Web Site: www.jnproductions.bc.ca. Jakob Nortman, pres.
Radio Only.
For all your voiceover needs, including narration, corporate videos, on-hold telephone messages and announcements for GPS systems. Radio production facilities available.

James & Associates Inc., (formerly J & A Sound). 63 Christopher St., New York, NY 10014-4246. Phone: (212) 331-0186. Fax: (212) 505-0959. E-mail: tom@jandasound.com. Thomas S. James, pres.
TV-CATV only.
Original scoring for film & TV.

Jameson Broadcast Inc., 1644 Hawthorne St., Sarasota, FL 34239. Phone: (941) 906-8800. Fax: (941) 906-8801. E-mail: radio@jamesonbcast.com. Web Site: www.jamesonbroadcast.com. Jamie G. Jameson, pres; Trulee C. Jameson, VP.
Radio Only.
Radio program production, syndication & special projects.

Jams Productions Inc., 1262 Don Mills Rd., Suite 203, Toronto, ON M3B 2W7. Canada. Phone: (416) 449-4844. Fax: (416) 449-4843. E-mail: alan@jamsproductions.ca. Marion Schwarz, pres; Alan Schwarz, VP & producer; Susan Schwarz, producer & producer.
TV-CATV only.
TV program production.

Janson Media, 88 Semmens Rd., Harrington Park, NJ 07640. Phone: (201) 784-8488. Fax: (201) 784-3993. E-mail: info@janson.com. Web Site: www.janson.com. Stephen Janson, pres; Zara Janson, VP; Betsy Van Ost, dir; Lynne Warshavsky, office mgr.
TV-CATV only.
International TV & video/ DVD program distribution & production; video/DVD publishing.

Jefferson-Pilot Sports, 1900 W. Morehead St., Charlotte, NC 28208. Phone: (704) 374-3669. Fax: (704) 374-3859. E-mail: jweber@jpsports.com. Web Site: www.jpsports.com. Edward M. Hull, pres & gen mgr; Pam Hawthorne, gen sls mgr & VP; Powell Kidd, VP opns; Jimmy Rayburn, opns mgr, VP & opns mgr; Jeff Tennant, VP sls & VP mktg.
Atlanta, GA 30326, 3390 Peachtree Rd, NE, Suite 1000. Phone: (404) 364-6556. Fax: (404) 364-6557. Jim Weilbaecher, dir sls.
Rutherford, NJ 07070, Meadows Office Complex, 201 Rt. 17 N, Suite 300. Phone: (201) 438-2088. Fax: (201) 939-0224. Adam J. Moore, dir sls.
TV-CATV only.
TV & CATV sports production & syndication.

Jerusalem Radio Productions, 545 W. 111th St., Suite 8-I, New York, NY 10025. Phone: (212) 666-2144.
Radio program production & distribution; production svcs.

The Johnson Group, 6800 Fleetwood Rd, Suite 100, McLean, VA 22101. Phone: (703) 356-4004. Fax: (703) 356-6969. E-mail: rmjcameron@aol.com. Web Site: www.thejgroup.com. Robert M. Johnson, pres; Joe Fab, VP.
Radio Only.
Video, film, multimedia & radio creative svcs & production.

Joe Jones Productions, 10556 Arnwood Rd., Lake View Terrace, CA 91342. Phone: (818) 899-4457. Fax: (818) 899-4457. E-mail: jojones@jojonesnetcom.com. Joe Jones, exec producer; Marion Jones, VP opns.
TV-CATV only.
TV, radio coml & program production; jingle production & production svcs.

Jones Radio Networks (a Jones Media Networks company). 8200 S. Akron St., Suite 103, Centennial, CO 80112. Phone: (303) 784-8700. E-mail: betterservice@jonesradio.net. Web Site: www.jonesradio.com. Bob Hampton, pres; Jim LaMarca, exec VP; Phil Barry, gen mgr; Susan Stephens, dir; Patrick Crocker, dir; Amy Bolton, dir; Kim Ketchel, mktg dir.
New York, NY 10036. New York office, 11 W. 42nd St., 28th Fl. Phone: (888) 644-8255.
Seattle, WA 98121. Seattle office, 2211 5th Ave. Phone: (800) 426-9082.
Radio Only.
Premier producer of 24-hr. format progmg, daypart personality programs & various music svcs to radio stns.

Tom Jones Recording Studios, 1620 Greenview Dr. S.W., Rochester, MN 55902-1034. Phone: (507) 288-7711. Fax: (507) 288-4531. Thomas H. Jones, pres; Aaron Manthei, chief engr.
TV-CATV only.
Recording studio, cassette duplication, compact disc duplication recording svcs. Radio program & coml production.

Jordan Klein Film & Video, 10197 S.E. 144th Pl., Summerfield, FL 34491. Phone: (352) 288-3999. Fax: (352) 288-5538. E-mail: jkfv01@gate.net. Web Site: www.jordy.com. Jordan Klein Jr., pres.
TV-CATV only.
Underwater, on-the-water production; rental film, video housing & crews; Bahamas specialist.

Nicole Jouve, 54 Avenue du Roule, Neuilly Sur Seine 92200. France. Phone: 33 1 47 22 43 27. Fax: 33 1 47 22 43 27. E-mail: interamany@aol.com. Nicole Jouve, pres.
TV-CATV only.
Distribution of French films (non-theatrical, TV & video), documentaries (Jean Rouch) childrens programs.

Juravic Entertainment, 620 Glenridge Dr., Glenview, IL 60025. Phone: (847) 998-5998. Fax: (847) 998-6013. E-mail: dljuravic@aol.com.
TV-CATV only.
TV program syndication.

K

KCRA-TV, (Hearst-Argyle Television Inc). 3 Television Cir., Sacramento, CA 95814-0794. Phone: (916) 446-3333. Fax: (916) 325-3731. Web Site: www.thekcrachannel.com. Elliott Troshinsky, pres & gen mgr.
TV-CATV only.
TV program & coml production; production svcs.

KCSN 88.5 FM, California State University, Northridge, 18111 Nordhoff St., Northridge, CA 91330-8312. Phone: (818) 677-3090. E-mail: frederick.d.johnson@csun.edu. Web Site: www.kcsn.org. Michael Worrall, chief engr; Fred Johnson, gen mgr; Martin Perlich, progmg dir; Laura Kelly, dev dir.
Radio Only.
Public radio serving parts of Los Angeles, CA—classical weekdays, eclectic weeknights & weekends. PRI, AP affil. The best of public radio.

KJD Teleproductions, 30 Whyte Dr., Voorhees, NJ 08043. Phone: (856) 751-3500. Fax: (856) 751-7729. E-mail: mactoday@earthlink.net. Web Site: www.kjdteleproductions.com. Larry Scott, pres/CEO.
TV-CATV only.
TV, radio program, coml, promotion film production & distribution; production svcs; TV processing lab.

KPTS-TV, 320 West 21st St. N., Wichita, KS 67203-2499. Phone: (316) 838-3090. Fax: (316) 838-8586. E-mail: dchecots@kpts.org. Web Site: www.kpts.org. Don Checots, gen mgr; Dave McClintock, dir opns & engrg dir.
TV-CATV only.
Industrial video production for corporate training & mktg communications.

KTOO-TV & Radio Station, 360 Egan Dr., Juneau, AK 99801. Phone: (907) 586-1670. Fax: (907) 586-3612. E-mail: info@ktoo.org. Web Site: www.ktoo.org. Jeff Brown, dir.
TV-CATV only.
A radio program highlighting diversified music & stories for children.

KUSA Television, 500 Speer Blvd., Denver, CO 80203. Phone: (303) 871-9999. Fax: (303) 698-4700. E-mail: kusa@9news.com. Web Site: www.9news.com. Asa Darrow, production mgr.
TV-CATV only.
News production only.

David Kaye Productions Inc., 9160 Beverly Blvd., Suite 302, Beverly Hills, CA 90210. Phone: (800) 843-3933. Phone: (310) 362-8722. Fax: (604) 921-1926. E-mail: kayeman@shawbiz.ca. Web Site: www.davidkaye.com. David Kaye, pres; Stephan J. Sisk, opns.
TV-CATV only.

Broadcasting & Cable Yearbook 2006

Producers, Distributors, and Production Services Alphabetical Index

Full svc voice-over production company, providing radio & TV imaging & branding around the world.

Kazmark Entertainment Group, 14320 Ventura Blvd., Suite 601, Sherman Oaks, CA 91423. Phone: (818) 981-4410. Fax: (818) 501-2211. E-mail: jkaz@earthlink.net. Web Site: paulae@earthlink.net.
TV-CATV only.
Pay-per-view productions & distributors for cable TV.

The Kenwood Group, 75 Varney Pl., San Francisco, CA 94107-1922. Phone: (415) 957-5333. Fax: (415) 957-5311. Web Site: www.kenwoodgroup.com. Christina Crowley, pres.
Creative svcs & production of comls & corporate communications, film, video, multimedia, meetings & events.

Killer Tracks, 6534 W. Sunset Blvd., Hollywood, CA 90028-7202. Phone: (323) 957-4455. Fax: (323) 957-4470. E-mail: sales@killertracks.com. Web Site: www.killertracks.com.
TV-CATV only.
Provides production music library & sound effects.

King World Media Sales, 1700 Broadway, 32nd Fl., New York, NY 10019. Phone: (212) 315-4000. Fax: (212) 459-9255. Web Site: www.kingworld.com. Steven R. Hirsch, pres; Michael Auerbach, sr VP; Robin King, VP; Scott Trupchak, account exec; Robert Cole, account exec; Kim Wright, account exec.
TV-CATV only.
Barter syndication sls for King World Productions, Don Cornelius Productions, Western International & others.

King World Productions, 2401 Colorado Ave., Santa Monica, CA 90404. Phone: (310) 264-3405. Fax: (310) 264-3366. Web Site: www.kingworld.com. Bob Madden, exec VP; Arthur Sando, sr VP.
Atlanta, GA 30338, 1050 Crown Pointe Pkwy., Suite 1800. Phone: (770) 392-9044. Fax: (770) 671-1607. John Holdridge, sr VP Southern sls.
Chicago, IL 60611, 455 Cityfront Plaza Dr. Phone: (312) 245-4820. Fax: (312) 245-4826. Sean O'Boyle, VP midwestern sls.
New York, NY 10019, 51 West 52nd Street. Phone: (310) 975-4920. Fax: (212) 975-9685. Joe DiSalvo, sr VP & gen sls mgr; Sid Beighley, VP eastern sls; F. Manfred, VP cable sls.
Dallas, TX 75248, 17060 Dallas Pkwy, Suite 209. Phone: (972) 733-3777. Fax: (972) 733-1156.
TV-CATV only.
TV program production, distribution, mktg to domestic syndication & other TV venues.

Kipany Productions Ltd., 32 E. 39th St., New York, NY 10016. Phone: (212) 883-8300. Fax: (212) 883-0409. E-mail: share82308@aol.com. T. Hendry, pres; K. Colligan, CEO.
TV-CATV only.
Video production, bcst progmg, mktg, sale and communications experts/web designers specializing in Telcom, event management.

Klein &, 20530 Pacific Coast Hwy., Malibu, CA 90265. Phone: (310) 317-9599. Fax: (310) 456-7701. E-mail: imagedoctor@kleinand.com. Web Site: www.kleinand.com. Bob Klein, owner.
TV-CATV only.
Mktg & promotion for the electronic media.

Knowledge In A Nutshell Inc., Box 597, Pittsburgh, PA 15230. Fax: (412) 765-3672. E-mail: audrey@knowledgeinanutshell.com. Web Site: www.knowledgeinanutshell.com. Charles Reichblum, pres.
TV-CATV only.
Syndicates radio/TV program, Knowledge in a Nutshell. Distributes "The Edible Game Smart Cooke".

Kultur/White Star Video, 195 Hwy. 36, West Long Branch, NJ 07764. Phone: (732) 229-2343. Phone: (800) 458-5887. Fax: (732) 229-0066. E-mail: info@kultur.com. Web Site: www.kultur.com. Dennis M. Hedlund, pres; Pearl Lee, VP; John Winfrey, sls; Ronald Davis, mgng dir; Maryann Mills, mgr.
TV-CATV only.
Suppliers of programs on home video cassette in North America. Selection includes documentaries, opera, ballet, classical music, profiles, theater, comedy, fitness, country music, rock & roll.

L

Lakeside Television Co. Inc., 300 Highpoint Dr., Unit #712, Hartsdale, NY 10530. Phone: (914) 946-7806. Fax: (914) 946-7806 (fax/phone). Bernard Schulman, pres; Diane Ross, VP.
TV-CATV only.

TV program distribution & production & syndication.

Lambert Television, 100 N. Crescent Dr., 2nd Flr., Beverly Hills, CA 90210. Phone: (310) 551-1900. Fax: (310) 385-4004. E-mail: jones@lamberttv.com. Web Site: www.lamberttv.com. Michael Jones, exec VP.
TV-CATV only.
Lambert Television owns and operates a television station group.

Lapco Communications, 437 E. Beil Ave., Nazareth, PA 18064. Phone: (610) 759-9444. Fax: (610) 759-8589. E-mail: sales@lapcocom.com. Web Site: www.lapcocom.com. P. Pagilaro, pres; L. Van Winkle, VP.
TV-CATV only.
TV progmg & production, computer graphics, producers of original progmg, TV comls, TV promotion production, production mgmt, computer stock background library.

Launch Radio Networks, (a division of United Stations Radio Network). 58 W. 40th St., 4th Fl., New York, NY 10018. Phone: (212) 536-3600. Fax: (212) 536-6801. Web Site: www.launchradionetworks.com. E-mail: programming@launchradionetworks.com. Dave Ankers, pres; Charlie Colombo, exec VP; Dia Stein, progmg dir; Dan Brassem, dir.
Radio Only.
Launch Radio Networks produces, distributes music, entertainment news & svcs for radio stns as well as other media worldwide.

Leadem to Water Production Inc., Box 279, Oregon City, OR 97045. Phone: (503) 631-7661. Fax: (503) 631-7672. E-mail: info@horsemansworld.com. Web Site: www.horsemansworld.com. Jeff Tracy,.
TV-CATV only.
Produces syndicated radio show *Horseman's World*, coml video narrations, produces World bcst for A.Q.H.A. on 250+ stn, cable TV houses northwest & cowboy cooking.

John Lemmon Films, 1325 Rock Point Rd., Charlotte, NC 28270. Phone: (704) 532-1944. Fax: (704) 566-1984. E-mail: jlemmon@jlf.com. Web Site: www.jlf.com. Mike Rosinski, head animator.
TV-CATV only.
Clay, cel & stop-motion animation for TV specials, comls, program openings & on-air IDs.

Leo Productions, 1 Rond Point Victor Hugo, 92130-Issy-Les-Moulineaux France. Phone: (331) 55 95 57 00. Fax: (331) 55 95 57 01. E-mail: leo@leoproductions.com. Web Site: www.leoproductions.com. Jean-Louis Brugat, mgng dir.
TV-CATV only.
TV production, progmg consultants, live bcsts.

Leukemia & Lymphoma Society, 1311 Mamaroneck Ave., White Plains, NY 10605. Phone: (914) 949-5213. Fax: (914) 949-6691. E-mail: lanereg@lls.org. Web Site: www.leukemia-lymphoma.org. Nancy Klein, VP mktg; Geralyn Laneve, VP.
TV-CATV only.
Produces & distributes educational ideas to inform & educate viewers about leukemia & related diseases & available treatment.

Liberty Studios Inc., 238 E. 26th St., New York, NY 10010. Phone: (212) 532-1865. Fax: (212) 779-2207. E-mail: email@libertystudios.us. Anthony Lover, pres; John Sawyer, VP.
TV-CATV only.
TV program, commercial, film & video production.

Lifestyle Magazine/The Evidence, 101 W. Cochran St., Simi Valley, CA 93065. Phone: (888) 940-0062. Fax: (805) 522-2114. E-mail: info@ffttv.org. Web Site: www.faithfortoday.tv. Michael Tucker, dir.
TV-CATV only.
TV program production & distribution.

Lifetime Television Network, 34-12 36th St., Astoria, NY 11106. Phone: (800) 706-3606. Phone: (718) 706-3600. Fax: (718) 706-3500. Web Site: www.lifetimetv.com. Gwynne McConkey, sr VP; Mitchell Brill, dir studio opns.
TV-CATV only.
Provides 16,000 sq feet of three fully equipped, acoustically engineered studios in New York City. Fiber optics & satellite linkups provide worldwide connectivity. Inventory of cameras, lighting & grip complements, motorized grid systems, audio/video gear & support facilities.

Lightbridge Production & Distribution, 1051 Broadway, Sonoma, CA 95476. Phone: (707) 939-4920. Fax: (707) 939-4919. Roy Walkenhorst, CEO; Judy Brooks, founder.
TV-CATV only.
TV & video progmg.

Lighthouse Productions, 118 S. Main St., Goshen 46526. Phone: (574) 533-1400. Fax: (661) 760-8775. E-mail: audicolabels@audicolabels.com. Web Site: www.audicolabels.com. Bill Landow, owner.
TV-CATV only.
Audio, video full production svc, documentaries, training, audio & video recording svcs.

Lightyear Entertainment L.P., 434 Ave of the Americas, 6th flr., New York, NY 10111. Phone: (212) 353-5084. Fax: (212) 353-5083. E-mail: mail@lightyear.com. Web Site: www.lightyear.com. Arnold Holland, pres/CEO.
TV-CATV only.
TV program production & distribution. Audio & video distribution.

Limelight Communications Inc., 2532 W. Meredith Dr., Vienna, VA 22181. Phone: (703) 242-4596. Phone: Cell (703) 626-3167. Fax: (703) 242-0324. E-mail: moreinfo@limelight.com. Web Site: www.limelight.com. Kenneth Reff, pres; Linda Falkerson, VP.
TV-CATV only.
Writing, producing & editing svcs for bcst & industrial clients. Available as sub-contractors for specific svcs, or to fully produce complete shows.

Lindberg Productions Inc., 24 Mulford Ave., East Hampton, NY 11937. Phone: (212) 599-1239. Phone: (917) 696-1826. E-mail: ctimany@aol.com. Larry Lindberg, pres; Erika Shapeero, producer.
TV-CATV only.
Video production for business & industry.

Lion and Fox Recording Studios, 6100 Lincolnia Rd., Alexandria, VA 22312. Phone: (703) 941-6100. E-mail: mail@lionfox.com. Web Site: www.lionfox.com. Harold Lion, chmn; James Fox, pres; Sally Lion, VP.
TV-CATV only.
Digital audio production for TV & radio; music & EFX libraries; CD and CD-ROM & cassette duplication; location audio.

Lions Gate Entertainment, (A division of Trimark Holdings). 2700 Colorado Ave., Suite 200, Santa Monica, CA 90404. Phone: (310) 449-9200. Fax: (310) 392-0252. Web Site: www.lionsgatefilms.com. Don Feltheimer, pres/CEO.
TV-CATV only.
Domestic & international TV, film, video distribution & adv sls firm. Builds, manages, invests in domestic & foreign bcst networks.

Litton Syndications Inc., Litton Towers, 2213 Middle St., 2nd Fl., Sullivan's Island, SC 29482. Phone: (843) 883-5060. Fax: (843) 883-9957. E-mail: tim@litton.tv. Web Site: www.litton.tv. David L. Morgan, pres/CEO; Tim Voit, VP/dir sls.
TV-CATV only.
TV distribution (TV program sls & mktg).

London Weekend Television International, South Bank TV Ctr., Upper ground, London SE1 9LT. United Kingdom. Phone: (020) 7620-1620. E-mail: images@lwt.co.uk. Web Site: www.lwt.co.uk. Charles Allen, mgng dir; Steve Morrison, head admin.
New York, NY 10110, 500 Fifth Ave, Suite 1710. Phone: (212) 682-3055. Fax: (212) 869-3693. Ellis Bell, CPA.
TV-CATV only.
TV program production & distribution.

Longhorn Radio Network, 1 University Station, (A0704) University of Texas, Austin, TX 78712-1090. Phone: (512) 471-1631. Fax: (512) 471-3700. Web Site: www.kut.org. J. Stewart Vanderwilt, dir; Hawk Mendenhall, progmg dir.
Radio Only.

Lookout Productions/Extreme Footage, 250 W. 57th St., Suite 1830, New York, NY 10107. Phone: (212) 974-1020. Fax: (212) 245-7204.
TV-CATV only.
We provide original stock on all subjects: from our film collections; by shooting custom stock; & by scouring the earth.

Loral Skynet, (A subsidiary of Loral Cyberstar). 2440 Research Blvd. #200, Rockville, MD 20850. Phone: (301) 258-8101. Fax: (301) 258-8119. Web Site: www.loralskynet.com. Terry Hart, pres/CEO; Gayle Armstrong, VP mktg.

Broadcasting & Cable Yearbook 2006

Producers, Distributors, and Production Services Alphabetical Index

London W1P 8AE. Loral Cyberstar-Europe, Inc., 131-151 Great Titchfield St. Phone: +44 171 892 3700.
TV-CATV-Radio.
International satellite communications company that leases capacity for video transmissions for TV & other program distributors. Also provides Internet access & private network svcs directly to Internet Service Providers & multinational businesses worldwide. Svcs include data networking, voice, video, teleconferencing & news distribution to multiple points worldwide.

Luna Television Network, 246 5th Ave., Suite 600, New York, NY 10001. Phone: (212) 213-4100. Fax: (212) 213-2898.
TV-CATV only.
Syndicate Spanish, bilingual, & English-language programming to U.S. Hispanic TV stns plus international sls.

M

MAKWDE Productions, 10556 Arnwood Rd., Lake View Terrace, CA 91342. Phone: (818) 899-4457. Fax: (818) 890-4050. E-mail: feetrell@ix.netcom.com. Marion Jones, pres/CEO; Dwayne Jones, dir sls & mktg; Keith Jones, adv mgr; Detra Jones, opns mgr; Joe Jones, international.
TV-CATV only.
TV coml producers, radio programs, coml & jingle producers.

MAN QC Creations, 123 E. Dania Beach Blvd., Dania, FL 33004. Phone: (954) 921-1111.
TV-CATV only.
Worldwide on-location production; complete digital production & postproduction svcs; studio facility; TV progmg.

MGM Inc., 2500 Broadway, Santa Monica, CA 90404. Phone: (310) 449-3000. Fax: (310) 264-1244. Web Site: www.mgm.com.
TV-CATV only.
TV program distribution.

MGM TV Canada, 20 Queen St. West #3500, Toronto, ON H5H 3R3. Canada. Phone: (416) 260-9680. Fax: (416) 260-9993. Web Site: www.mgm.com.
TV-CATV only.
Film distribution for all UA, Polygram & Orion film library (features, series & animated).

MG/Perin Inc., 110 Green St. Suite 304, New York, NY 10012. Phone: (212) 941-9750. Fax: (212) 941-9122. E-mail: mgperin@aol.com. Richard Perin, pres.
TV-CATV only.
TV program production & distribution.

MPL Media, 621 Mainstream Dr., Ste 260, Nashville, TN 37228. Phone: (615) 256-1675. Fax: (615) 256-0757. E-mail: pshedlock@mplmedia.com. Web Site: www.mplmedia.com. Peggy Shedlock, VP.
16/35 color negative processing, rank cintel & ursagold transfer, video edit, graphics, VHS duplication, DVD authoring & fulfillment.

MRC Films, Box 697, Plainview, NY 11803. Phone: (516) 796-7568. E-mail: jlmollot@worldnet.att.net. Larry Mollot, exec producer.
TV-CATV only.
Producers of original progmg for bcst, cablecast, TV comls & PSAs.

MRN Radio, 1801 International Speedway Blvd., Daytona Beach, FL 32114. Phone: (386) 947-6400. Fax: (386) 947-6716. Web Site: www.mrnradio.com. Cheryl Knight, dir affil; Steve Harrison, natl sls mgr.
Radio Only.
Live coverage of NASCAR stock car racing plus *NASCAR LIVE* wkly telephone talk, *NASCAR Today* daily news program, via satellite.

MSE, 540 Toby Hill Rd., Westbrook, CT 06498. Phone: (860) 399-0191. Fax: (860) 399-0196. E-mail: marcia@mseusa.com. Web Site: www.mseusa.com. Marcia Simon, pres.
TV-CATV only.
Bcst & promotional writing & production; specialists in health & medical progmg.

MTI The Image Group, 885 2nd Ave., Level C, New York, NY 10017. Phone: (212) 548-7700. Fax: (212) 759-7465. E-mail: jromano@image-group.com. Web Site: www.image-group.com.
New York, NY 10019, 727 11th Ave. Phone: (212) 649-6333. Jerry Romano, dir business dev.
New York, NY 10016, 401 Fifth Ave. Phone: (212) 592-0600.
TV-CATV only.
Nine studios, 25 Digital online suites, 10 Avids, four infernos, 63 D platforms, NIT/MAC platforms, URSA Diamond/c-Reality, Digital Sound mixing Duplication.

MTM Entertainment Inc., 12700 Ventura Blvd., Suite 200, Studio City, CA 91604. Phone: (310) 235-9700.
TV-CATV only.
TV program production & distribution.

MVI Post, 6320 Castle Pl., Falls Church, VA 22044. Phone: (703) 536-7678. Fax: (703) 536-9490. E-mail: mailbox@mvipost.com. Web Site: www.mvipost.com. Frank Maniglia Jr., pres; Craig Maniglia, VP.
TV-CATV-Radio.
Full-svc video, audio & graphics postproduction; features screensound digital audio system 601 component digital video suite, high definition digital postproduction facility.

MacNeil/Lehrer Productions, 2700 S. Quincy St., Suite 250, Arlington, VA 22206. Phone: (703) 998-2170. Fax: (703) 998-5707. Web Site: www.pbs.org/newshour. E-mail: pbs@newshour.org. Dan Werner, pres; David Sit, VP; Harold Crawford, controller; Susan Mills, dir program dev; Pam Wyatt, dir admin.
TV-CATV only.
Produces news & info programs for public TV & other coml & cable networks. Production of *The News Hour with Jim Lehrer*.

Madison Square Garden Network, 4 Penn Plaza, 4th Floor, New York, NY 10001. Phone: (212) 465-5926. Fax: (212) 465-6024. E-mail: msgnetpr@thegarden.com. Web Site: www.msgnetwork.com. Mike McCarthy, exec SP MSG; Neil Davis, exec VP adv sls; Leon Schwier, exec production sports design.
TV-CATV only.
NY Knicks, NY Rangers & NY Mets, NY MetroStars, NY Power, NY Islanders & NY Liberty; boxing, college football & basketball; exclusive Garden events; original series.

Magno Sound & Video, 729 7th Ave., New York, NY 10019. Phone: (212) 302-2505. Fax: (212) 819-1282. E-mail: david@magnosound.com. Web Site: www.magnosound.com. Robert Friedman, pres; David Friedman, VP.
TV-CATV only.
Complete film, TV & radio production & postproduction svcs for agency, feature, network, corporate & industrial clients.

Make It Happen Productions Inc., 5925 Troost Ave., No. Hollywood, CA 91601. Phone: (323) 851-6444. Fax: (323) 851-6465. E-mail: bfrank@mihpitv. Billy Frank, pres.
TV-CATV only.
Ind & co-productions, dev of projects, package projects, production svcs, post production.

Man From Mars Productions, 159 Orange St., Manchester, NH 03104-4217. Phone: (603) 668-0652. Fax: (603) 666-4878. E-mail: brouder@juno.com. Web Site: www.manfrommars.com. Ed Brouder, owner.
Radio Only.
Aircheck sls for radio collectors; coml production.

Manhattan Production Music, 355 W. 52nd St., 6th Fl., New York, NY 10019. Phone: (212) 333-5766. Phone: (800) 227-1954. Fax: (212) 262-0814. E-mail: info@mpmmusic.com. Web Site: www.mpmmusic.com. Ron Goldberg,.
TV-CATV only.
Five libraries containing over 300 CDs, including the Audiophile Sound effects series, and the Chesky Classical Library.

Manhattan Transfer Miami, 2850 Tiger Tail, Coconut Grove, FL 33133. Phone: (800) 826-8864. Phone: (305) 857-0350. Fax: (305) 857-0175. Web Site: www.bvinet.com.
Coconut Grove, FL 33133, 2850 Tigertail Ave. Phone: (305) 857-0350. Rick Legow, pres.
Miami Beach, FL 33139, 605 Lincoln Rd, 5th Fl. Rick Legow, pres.
Full-svc video post-production including film transfer, on-line, off-line editing, audio, graphics, progmg, voice dubbing translation, sound stage & new media dev.

Ben Manilla Productions, 576 Sacramento St., 4th Fl., San Francisco, CA 94111. Phone: (415) 421-1220. Fax: (415) 421-4749. E-mail: info@bmpaudio.com. Web Site: www.bmpaudio.com. J. Ben Manilla, pres; Monica Blakely, gen mgr.
Radio Only.
Audio production & progmg for a variety of formats.

Mar Vista Entertainment, 12519 Venice Blvd., Los Angeles, CA 90066. Phone: (310) 737-0950. Fax: (310) 737-9115. E-mail: info@marvista.net. Web Site: www.marvista.com. Ferdando Szew, COO; Michael Jacobs, pres; George Port, exec VP.
Sharon, MA 02067, 210 N. Main St. Phone: (781) 784-2480.
TV-CATV only.
Domestic & international distribution of children's animation & live action features & series, films & documentaries.

Marathon International, 74 rue Bonaparte, 75006 Paris Phone: 331-53-1091-00. Fax: 331-43-2504-66. E-mail: marathon@marathon.fr. Web Site: www.marathon.fr.
TV-CATV only.
Distributor of TV programs worldwide; series, documentaries, animation, wildlife, TV movies.

Maryknoll Productions, 75 Ryder Rd., Maryknoll, NY 10545-0308. Fax: (914) 762-6567. E-mail: nkeel@maryknoll.com. Web Site: www.maryknollmall.org. Lawrence M. Rich, exec producer.
TV-CATV only.
Offers a library of video & film productions featuring Third World countries; radio & TV programs also available.

Maryland Public Television, 11767 Owings Mills Blvd., Owings Mills, MD 21117. Phone: (410) 356-5600. Fax: (410) 581-4338. Web Site: www.mpt.org. Robert Shuman, pres/CEO; Larry Unger, exec VP; Eric Eggleton, sr VP.
TV-CATV only.
TV program production & distribution.

Masai Films Inc., 6922 Hollywood Blvd., Suite 401, Hollywood, CA 90028. Phone: (323) 466-5451. Fax: (323) 466-2440. Fritz Goode,.
TV-CATV only.
TV & radio program & coml producers; production svcs.

Maslow Media Group Inc., 2134 Wisconsin Ave., N.W., Washington, DC 20007. Phone: (202) 965-1100. Fax: (202) 965-6171. E-mail: lmaslow@maslowmedia.com. Web Site: www.maslowmedia.com. Linda Maslow, CEO.
TV-CATV only.
Staffing & recruitment (freelance & fulltime), for best camera crews, cable, film, multimedia, payroll & paymaster svcs nationwide for bcst film & new media industries.

Mason Video, 9632 N. 34th St., Omaha, NE 68112. Phone: (402) 455-9422. Fax: (402) 455-0707. E-mail: melemason@aol.com. Web Site: www.masonvideo.com. Mele Mason, owner.
TV-CATV only.
Offers complete Betacam SP productions. Equipment includes Ikigami HLV55 Betacam.

MasterControl FamilyNet Radio, The Broadcast Communications Group, NAMB. 6350 W. Freeway, Fort Worth, TX 76116. Phone: (817) 570-1400. Phone: (800) 266-1837. Fax: (817) 737-9436. E-mail: lbratton@familynet.com. Web Site: www.familynetradio.com. Lisa Young, radio mktg & distribution; Donna Senn, radio distribution; Chuck Ries, producer.
Radio Only.
Total health program featuring interviews with experts on physical, mental, financial, and spiritual health, hosts Ralph Baker & Terri Barrett.

Matchframe Video, 610 N. Hollywood Way, Suite 101, Burbank, CA 91505. Phone: (818) 840-6800. Fax: (818) 840-2726. George Francisco, CEO; Rand Gladden, pres; Pam Hollander, exec VP; Michael Levy, VP/gen mgr.
TV-CATV only.
In-house editing suites; audio sweetening; portable on-line/off-line (AVID/HD and SD) editing systems; graphics; telecine; tape to tape color connection.

William Mauldin Productions Inc., 1737 Blue Ridge Pkwy., Box 767, Meadow of Dan, VA 24120-0767. Phone: (336) 632-9801. Fax: (336) 632-9494. E-mail: productions@mauldin.net. Web Site: www.mauldin.net. William D. Mauldin, pres/CEO.
TV-CATV only.
Major market talent for narrations & voice overs, documentaries, station IDs, program intros for small market radio. Digital audio & video.

Maximum Marketing Services Inc., 833 W. Jackson, Ste 300, Chicago, IL 60607. Phone: (312) 226-4111. Fax: (312) 226-5765. Web Site: www.maxmarketing.com. John McGowan, pres.
TV-CATV only.
TV & radio program, production & distribution; public relation services.

Broadcasting & Cable Yearbook 2006

E-53

Producers, Distributors, and Production Services Alphabetical Index

Maysles Films, Inc., 250 W. 54th St., New York, NY 10019. Phone: (212) 582-6050. Fax: (212) 586-2057. E-mail: info@mayslesfilms.com. Web Site: www.mayslesfilms.com. Albert Maysles, pres.
TV-CATV only.
Full production svcs for theatrical & TV non-fiction films; adv comls; industrial films, including pre- & postproduction.

Lynn McAfee Photography, 11324 1/2 Hatteras St., North Hollywood, CA 91601. Phone: (818) 761-1317. Lynn McAfee,.
TV-CATV only.
Unit production stills, special photography, all photographic svcs.

McClain Enterprises Inc., 4405-B Belmont Park Terrace, Nashville, TN 37215-3609. Phone: (615) 269-6517. Fax: (615) 269-6648. E-mail: carolyn@mcclaintv.com. Web Site: www.mcclaintv.com. Carolyn McClain, pres.
TV-CATV only.
Custom & syndicated TV mktg for radio, sls consulting, sls & promotional projects for radio & TV stns.

Media Access Group at WGBH, 125 Western Ave., Boston, MA 02134. Phone: (617) 300-3600. Fax: (617) 300-1020. E-mail: access@wgbh.org. Web Site: main.wgbh.org/wgbh/pages/access. Larry Goldberg, dir; Lori Kay, admin dir.
Burbank, CA 91505, 610 N. Hollywood Way, Suite 350. Phone: (818) 562-3344.
New York, NY 10016, 475 Park Ave. S, 10th Fl. Phone: (212) 545-0854.
TV-CATV only.
Provides real-time & off-line captioning, subtitling, descriptive narration & consulting.

The Media Group of Connecticut Inc., 17 Maple St., Weston, CT 06883-1026. Phone: (203) 544-0018. E-mail: mediagr@aol.com. Harvey F. Bellin, pres.
TV-CATV only.
TV, video production, writing, directing & editing; digital animation; dramatization & documentary; TV, corporate & govt svcs offered.

Media Planning Group (MPG), 195 Broadway, 12th Fl., New York, NY 10007. Phone: (646) 587-5000. Fax: (646) 587-5005. Web Site: www.mpgsite.com. Bob Riordan, mgr.
TV-CATV-Radio.
Producers, distributors & TV program packagers; videocassette producer/distributor. Full svc media buying & planning company.

Media Visions, 8430 Terminal Rd., Newington, VA 22079. Phone: (703) 550-1500. Phone: (800) 628-3556. Fax: (703) 550-9711. E-mail: mrock@mediavisions.net. Web Site: www.mediavisions.net. Mike Rock,.
Provides full-svc video duplication, packaging, warehousing & complete order fulfillment. CD, DVD.

Medialink, 708 3rd Ave., 8th Fl., New York, NY 10017. Phone: (212) 682-8300. Fax: (212) 682-2370. E-mail: mwallace@medialink.com. Web Site: www.medialink.com. Mary Buhay, sr VP; Monica Jennings, sr VP.
London EC1 MSQL, 1 Benjamin St. Phone: (011-44-171) 439-1774. Fax: (011-44-171) 689-2110.
Los Angeles, CA 90028, 6430 Sunset Blvd, Suite 1100. Phone: (213) 465-0111. Fax: (213) 465-9230. (213) 465-9231.
Norwalk, CT 06856, 15 Oakwood Ave. Phone: (203) 847-0777. (800) 227-7409. Fax: (203) 847-5899.
Washington, DC 20005, 1401 New York Ave. N.W, Suite 520. Phone: (202) 628-3800. Fax: (202) 628-2377.
Atlanta, GA 70326, 3310 Peach Tree Rd. N.E, Suite 1520. Phone: (404) 848-7500. Fax: (404) 848-7525.
Chicago, IL 60601, The Time & Life Bldg, 541 N. Fairbanks Ct, Suite 1910. Phone: (312) 222-9850. Fax: (312) 222-9810.
Dallas, TX 75244, 4851 LBJ Fwy, Suite 605. Phone: (972) 774-0200. Fax: (972) 774-0321.
TV-CATV only.
Video & audio news release distributor & producer to TV & radio stns throughout the United States & Europe.

MediaTracks Inc., 2250 E. Devon Ave., Suite 150, Des Plaines, IL 60018-4507. Phone: (847) 299-9500. Fax: (847) 299-9501. E-mail: slustig@mediatracks.com. Web Site: www.mediatracks.com. Shel Lustig, pres; Reed Pence, VP.
Radio Only.
Produces, syndicate & distribute radio progmg, news, comls & PSAs. Specialists in health & medicine, news & pub affrs.

Medstar Television Inc., 5920 Hamilton Blvd., Allentown, PA 18106. Phone: (610) 395-1300. Fax: (610) 391-1556. Web Site: www.medstar.com. William P. Ferretti, CEO; Paul Dowling, pres; Ron Petrovich, VP.
TV-CATV only.
Health & medical news progmg includes one-hour specials, Health Matters TV series, MedstarSource & MedstarAdvances news svcs.

Megatrax Production Music Inc., 7629 Fulton Ave., North Hollywood, CA 91605. Phone: (818) 503-5240. Phone: (888) 634-2555. Fax: (818) 503-5244. E-mail: megatrax@megatrax.com. Web Site: www.megatrax.com. John Dwyer, owner; Ron Mendelsohn, owner.
TV-CATV only.
Production music for bcst promotion & adv. Custom scoring & news music packages available.

Bill Melendez Productions Inc., 13400 Riverside Dr., Suite 201, Sherman Oaks, CA 91423. Phone: (818) 382-7382. Fax: (818) 382-7377. E-mail: bmpi@aol.com. Bill Melendez, pres.
TV program, coml animation production.

Message on Hold, Box 747, Hendersonville, NC 28793-0747. Phone: (828) 692-7200. Phone: (800) 223-1930. Fax: (828) 693-1662. E-mail: molton.ad@bellsouth.net. Web Site: www.moltonad.com. J. Ellis Molton, owner; Randy Molton, opns mgr.
Radio Only.
Producers of high-quality comls for telephone "hold" lines. Specializing in automotive, financial, morticians & pharmacies.

Metro Music Productions Inc., 37 W. 20th St., Suite 906, New York, NY 10011. Phone: (212) 229-1700. Phone: (800) 697-7392. Fax: (212) 229-9063. E-mail: info@metromusicinc.com. Web Site: www.metromusicinc.com. Mitch Coodley, pres; Katrina Haskell, office mgr.
TV-CATV only.
Original music scoring for TV progmg, prom, news, sports, comls. Production music library geared toward bcst.

Metro Networks, A Westwood One Co. 300 Bridge St., New Cumberland, PA 17070. Phone: (717) 774-8150. Fax: (717) 774-8160. E-mail: elaine.konkle@metronetworks.com. Web Site: www.metronetworks.com. Elaine Konkle, gen mgr.
TV-CATV-Radio.
TV & radio network; radio production/distribution.

Metro Weather Service Inc., 571 So. Central Ave., Ste 102, Valley Stream, NY 11580. Phone: (516) 568-8844. Phone: (800) 488-7866. Fax: (516) 568-8853. Fax: (800) 768-7998. E-mail: metrowx@aol.com. Web Site: www.metrowx.com. Pat Pagano, pres.
TV-CATV only.
Provides accurate & understandable weather forecasts. Serves any part of the nation; live consultations.

Robert Michelson Inc., 508 3rd Ave., San Francisco, CA 94118. Phone: (415) 386-6862. Fax: (415) 386-2714. E-mail: rm@rmitv.com. Robert Michelson, pres; David Alexander, dir production.
Radio Only.
TV coml production; custom and syndicated TV spots for radio stations. Leading producer of TV spots for rock radio.

Midwest Video Communications Inc., Box 11627, Omaha, NE 68111. Phone: (402) 453-2450. Fax: (402) 933-8990. E-mail: midwestvideo@qwest.net. John S. Turner, pres; John Lott, producer/dir; Artes Johnson, dir.
TV-CATV only.
TV program & distribution; coml production, satellite teleconference productions; business & promotion film productions; production svcs, TV news features production.

Miller Broadcast Management, 616 W. Fulton St., Suite 516, Chicago, IL 60661. Phone: (312) 454-4111. Fax: (312) 454-0044. E-mail: info@millerbroadcast.com. Web Site: www.millerbroadcast.com. Matt Miller, VP; Lisa Miller, pres.
Radio Only.
Produces & syndicates natl progmg including *KidsRadio*.

Robin Miller, Filmaker Inc., 606 W. Broad St., Bethlehem, PA 18018. Phone: (610) 691-0900. Fax: (610) 691-0952. E-mail: mail@filmaker.com. Web Site: www.filmaker.com.
TV-CATV only.
TV program, promotion film production; production svcs.

Warren Miller Entertainment, 2540 Frontier Ave., Suite 104, Boulder, CO 80301. Phone: (303) 442-3430. Fax: (303) 442-3402. E-mail: davidp@warrenmiller.com. Web Site: www.warrenmiller.com. Josh Haskins, producer; David Perry, dir of natl sponsorships.
TV-CATV only.
Second unit feature, coml, TV program, promotion; film production & distribution specializing in snow & outdoor adventure sports.

Miss Universe, L.P., 4121 Radford Ave., Studio City, CA 91604. Phone: (818) 505-6600. Fax: (818) 505-6606. Web Site: www.missuniverse.com. Paula M. Shugart, pres; Tony Santomauro, VP business dev.
TV-CATV only.
TV program production.

Mobile Video Services Ltd., 1620 I St. N.W., Washington, DC 20006. Phone: (202) 331-8882. Fax: (202) 331-9064. E-mail: Bookfeed@mobilevideo.net. Web Site: www.mobilevideo.net. Lawrence J. VanderVeen, pres; Peter Rosenbaum, sls.
TV-CATV only.
Bcst production svcs, best "Official Washington", live shot, remote crews, studio svcs, editing & graphics suites, satellite & fiber transmission svcs.

Modern Entertainment, 16255 Ventura Blvd., Suite1100, Encino, CA 91436. Phone: (818) 386-0444. Fax: (818) 728-3677. Michael Weiser, pres/CEO; Ken Du Bow, sr VP worldwide sls; Allyson Hall, VP international sls.
TV-CATV only.
Distribution of movies world wide, CD, DVD.

Modern Sound Pictures Inc., 1402 Howard St., Omaha, NE 68102. Phone: (402) 341-8476. Fax: (402) 341-8487. E-mail: mspi1@att.net. Web Site: www.modernsoundpictures.com. Sandra L. Smith, pres.
Non-theatrical 16mm film, video rental library & retail audiovisual equipment for rental & sls.

Ellis Molton Advertising, Box 747, Hendersonville, NC 28793-0747. Phone: (828) 692-7200. Phone: (800) 223-1930. Fax: (828) 693-1662. E-mail: molton@bellsouth.net. Web Site: www.moltonad.com. Ellis Molton, owner; Randy Molton, opns mgr.
Radio Only.
Syndicated radio & nwspr series for loc use.

Mondo TV, Via G. Gatti 8/A, 00162 Rome Italy. Phone: 39-6-86320364. Phone: 39-06-86323293. Fax: 39-06-86209836. E-mail: mondotv@mondotv.it. Orlando Corradi, pres/CEO; Gian Claudio Galatoli, dir; Roberto Farina, head international sls.
TV-CATV only.
Animated TV series.

Montgomery Community Television Inc., 7548 Standish Pl., Rockville, MD 20855. Phone: (301) 424-1730. Fax: (301) 294-7476. Web Site: www.montgomerycommunitytv.com. Don Katzen, mktg dir.
TV-CATV only.
Full-svc video production & postproduction, 2,400 sq ft. studio including complete control room, GVG200 switcher, DVE, on- & off-line editing. Also, operation of two cable chs reaching 220,000 subs.

Moody Broadcasting Network, 820 N. LaSalle Blvd., Chicago, IL 60610-3284. Phone: (312) 329-4433. Phone: (800) 621-7031. Fax: (312) 329-4339. E-mail: mbn@moody.edu. Web Site: www.mbn.org. Douglas Hastings, opns mgr & progmg mgr; David Woodworth, administrator tech dev; Robert Neff, VP; Tony Rufo, satellite dept mgr; Wayne Shepherd, progmg mgr.
Radio Only.
Radio program production, full-svc religious digital stereo audio progmg via, satellite internet file download & syndicated tape distribution & ACCUWatch radio transmitter monitoring.

Moonstone Entertainment, Box 7400, Studio City, CA 91614-7400. Phone: (818) 985-3003. Fax: (818) 985-3009. Ernst "Etchie" Stroh, CEO; Yael Stroh, pres.
TV-CATV only.
International distribution and production.

The Charles Morrow Associates Company LLC, 307 7th Ave., Suite 1402, New York, NY 10001. Phone: (212) 989-2400. Fax: (212) 989-2697. E-mail: cmorrow@cmorrow.com. Web Site: www.cmorrow.com. Charlie Morrow, pres.
Radio Only.
Sound design, audio production, music production, audio/visual service, music composition, multimedia producers, surround sound studio, public service announcements.

Producers, Distributors, and Production Services Alphabetical Index

MotorNet, Box 69, Farmingdale, NJ 07727-0069. Phone: (732) 751-1020. Fax: (732) 751-1038. E-mail: motornet@iop.com. Web Site: www.motorsportsreport.com. Charlie Roberts, pres; Ken Stout, producer; Jack Schultz, dir mktg.
Radio Only.
Radio program production & distribution.

Mountain News Corporation, 50 Vashell Way, Suite 200, Orinda, CA 94563-3020. Phone: (925) 254-4456. Fax: (925) 254-7923. E-mail: admin@aminews.com. Web Site: www.theamigroup.com. Rob Brown, pres; Chad Dyen, VP. Eastern Bureau Phone: (800) 736-0370.
Radio Only.
Produce & package outdoor recreation reports of 30, 60 & 90-seconds in length. Also deliver ski reports via phone, computer, facsimilie for on-air, phone lines & web sites.

The Multimedia Group of Canada, 261 St. Sacrement, Montreal, PQ H2Y 3V2. Canada. Phone: (514) 844-3636. Fax: (514) 844-4990. E-mail: mgc@the-mgc.com. Jacques Bouchard, pres/CEO; Sari Buksner, sr VP international sls & acqusition; David Seeler, VP dev & acquisitions.
TV-CATV only.
Participates in the development and distribution of programming in the international market.

Munhwa Broadcasting Corp. (MBC), National Press Bldg., Suite 1131, 529 14th St. N.W., Washington, DC 20045. Phone: (202) 347-0078. Fax: (202) 347-0079. E-mail: mgchoi@imbc.com. Web Site: www.imbc.com. Chang-Young Choi, bureau chief.
TV-CATV only.
Korean natl TV network news.

Munz, 2470 W. 8th Ave., Hialeah, FL 33010. Phone: (305) 884-8200. Fax: (305) 889-7212. Web Site: www.mun2television.com. Don Browne, COO; Yolanda Foster, progmg VP; Tracy McDonough, Dir of Business Operations; Joe Bernard, sls dir; Alvaro Krupkin, Dir of Creative Services+; Maria Acosta, dir opns; Laura Dergal, dir mktg.
TV-CATV only.
English language cable network targeting young U.S. Hispanics.

The Music of Your Life, 350 Fifth Ave., Suite 7307, New York, NY 10118. Phone: (212) 947-0049. Fax: (212) 947-5008. E-mail: info@musicofyourlife.com. Web Site: www.musicofyourlife.com. Kerry Fink, CEO.
North Hollywood, CA 91602. North Hollywood, CA, 4605 Lankeilshim Blvd, Suite 702. Phone: (818) 755-9952. Chuck Southcott, VP programming.
Radio Only.
Music of Your Life satellite radio network for coml radio affil stns, featuring adult standard format

Musical Starstreams, Box 12685, La Jolla, CA 92039-2685. Phone: (619) 276-8989. Fax: (619) 276-0918. E-mail: forest@starstreams.com. Web Site: www.starstreams.com. Radio Only.
Two-hour wkly syndicated exotic electronica mus progmg also available as a full-time format; radio adv production.

Musivision, 185 E. 85th St., New York, NY 10028. Phone: (212) 860-4420.
TV-CATV-Radio.
Design & production of computer graphics & animation for stn IDs, promotions, show openings & coml applications.

Muzak, 3318 Lakemont Blvd., Fort Mill, SC 29708. Phone: (803) 396-3000. Phone: (800) 331-3340. Fax: (803) 396-3136. Web Site: www.muzak.com. E-mail: feedback@muzak.com. Bill Boyd, CEO.
Bcsts 60 chs of business mus, adv parting audio messages, ZNET data bcstg & video via direct bcst satellite.

Myriad Pictures, 405 S. Beverly Dr., 5th Fl., Beverly Hills, CA 90212. Phone: (310) 279-4000. Fax: (310) 279-4001. E-mail: info@myriadpictures.com. Web Site: www.myriadpictures.com. Kirk D'Amico, pres; Philip vonAlbensleben, VP.
TV-CATV only.
An ind TV co-production & distribution company specializing in music series, features, documentaries & drama for the international market.

N

NASA Broadcast & Imaging Branch, NASA Headquarters (PMD), 300 E. St. S.W., Rm. CL78, Washington, DC 20546. Phone: (202) 358-0000. Fax: (202) 358-4333. Mike Crnkovic, chief printing & design.
TV-CATV-Radio.

Aeronautics & Space Report, an hour magazine quarterly (Betacam SP) to media & producers only.

NBD Television Ltd., 2, Royalty Studios, 105 Lancaster Rd., London W11 1QF. United Kingdom. Phone: 44 (0) 20 7243 3646. Fax: 44 (0) 7243 3656. E-mail: distribution@nbdtv.com. Web Site: www.nbdtv.com. Nicky Davies Williams, CEO; Andrew Winter, gen sls mgr.
International TV progmg sls distribution.

NCAA, Box 6222, Indianapolis, IN 46206-6222. Phone: (317) 917-6222. Fax: (317) 917-6807. Fax: (317) 917-6856. E-mail: jrinebold@ncaa.org. Web Site: www.ncaasports.com. Chris Farrow, dir; Ron Schwartz, dir; Jeramy Michiaels, mgr; Frank Rhodes, mgr; Greg Weitekamp, mgr.
New York, NY 10019, 19 West 57th St. Phone: (212) 541-8840. Fax: (212) 262-4647. Ron Schwartz, dir NCAA TV new svcs.
TV-CATV only.
NCAA championship progmg, distribution & footage requests.

NDR Media, Rothenbaumchaussee 159+161, Hamburg 20149. Germany. Phone: (040) 44 1920. E-mail: info@ndrtv.de. Web Site: www.ndrtv.de. Horst Bennit, mngg dir; Hans-Stefan Heyne, head international acquisition; Ulla Lamas-Torres, sls.
TV-CATV only.
Distribution of TV plays, dramas, wildlife, educ, children's & documentary programs.

NFL Films, 1 NFL Plaza, Mt. Laurel, NJ 08054. Phone: (856) 222-3500. Fax: (856) 722-6779. Web Site: www.nflfilms.com. Steve Sabol, pres; William Driber, VP production; Rick Angeli, dir facilities; Barry Wolper, COO; Phil Tuckett, VP entertainment videos; Jeff Howard, VP video opns.
TV-CATV only.
Teleproduction facility: digital editing suites, 16mm & 35mm film processing, film-to-tape transfer, studio & remote production, sound studios, animation & flame.

NHK Japan Broadcasting Corp., 2030 M St. N.W., Suite 706, Washington, DC 20036. Phone: (202) 828-5180. Fax: (202) 828-4571. Web Site: www.nhk.or.jp/englishtop/. Ryuichi Teshima, bureau chief.
TV-CATV only.
TV & radio program distribution.

NRS Group PTY Ltd., 9-13 Lawry Pl., Macquarie, Canberra Act 2614. Australia. Phone: (61) 2-6251-6333. Fax: 61 2-6251-6240. E-mail: grahampatrick@nrsgroup.com.au. Graham Patrick, mngg dir.
TV-CATV only.
Produces range of quality TV series & documentaries, full TV & audio production facility with qualified personnel, international program distributor.

NTN Communications Inc., 5966 La Place Ct., Suite 100, Carlsbad, CA 92008-8830. Phone: (888) PLAYNTN. Fax: (760) 438-3505. Web Site: www.ntn.com. Stanley B. Kinsey, chmn/CEO; Mark deGorter, pres/CEO; James B. Frakes, CFO; Tyrone Lam, pres Buzztime Entertainment Inc.
TV-CATV only.
NTN Communications, Inc.®, a leading producer & distributor of live interactive TV entertainment, broadcasts exciting multi-player games to hospitality venues.

NTV International Corp., 50 Rockefeller Plaza, Suite 940, New York, NY 10020. Phone: (212) 489-8390. Fax: (212) 489-8395. Web Site: www.ntvic.com. Yoichi Shimada, pres.
TV-CATV only.
Complete video production & postproduction facility; satellite transmission capabilities worldwide; ENG package international TV coord, program sls & acquisitions.

NVC Arts, The Forum, 74-80 Camden St., London NW1 0EG. United Kingdom. Phone: 44 (0) 7388 3833. Fax: 44 (0)20 7388 7174. E-mail: mia_fjox-non@nvcarts.com. Web Site: www.nvcarts-tv.com. John Kelleher, mngg dir; Elfyn Morris, stn mgr.
TV-CATV only.
Producers & distributors of opera, ballet & performing arts programs for world TV.

N W Media, 106 SE 11th Avenue, Portland, OR 97214. Phone: (503) 223-5010. Fax: (503) 223-4737. Web Site: www.nwmedia.com. E-mail: info@nwmedia.com. Jeanne Alldredge, pres; Mitchell Harris, sls dir.
TV-CATV-Radio.
Audio/videotape duplication; CD/DVD Duplication, multimedia authoring, graphic design, mastering services; Messaging

NAHB Production Group, (National Association of Home Builders). 1201 15th St. N.W., 5th Fl., Washington, DC 20005. Phone: (202) 822-0200 ext 8543. Fax: (202) 266-8054. E-mail: cgoldweber@nahb.com. Cary Goldweber, exec producer; Joyce Pearson, sr supevrg producer.
Radio Only.
Complete video production/editing facility with large stock library. Productions include weekly HGTV series, political spots, PSA, & instructional/mktg progmgs.

National Church Broadcasting, Box 8263, Haledon, NJ 07508. Phone: (973) 956-2900. Fax: (973) 956-0600. Samuel Cummings, pres; June Young, VP.
TV-CATV only.
Distributor of church & children's religious progmg to radio stns.

National Collegiate Athletic Association, Box 6222, Indianapolis, IN 46206-6222. Phone: (317) 917-6222. Fax: (317) 917-6888. Web Site: www.ncaa.org. Miles Brand, pres; JoJo H. Rinebold, dir.
TV-CATV only.
Producers of selected NCAA championships.

National Council of Churches Communications Unit, 475 Riverside Dr., Rm. 850, New York, NY 10115. Phone: (212) 870-2227. Fax: (212) 870-2030. E-mail: news@ncccusa.org. Web Site: www.ncccusa.org. Shirley . Struchen, dir media resources; Wesley T. Pettillo, dir communications; Carol J. Fouke, dir news svcs.
TV-CATV only.
Bcst production, distribution & assistance to reporters, networks, stns; prepared radio reports & actualities without charge from bcst news professionals.

National Film Board of Canada, 350 Fifth Ave., Suite 4820, New York, NY 10118. Phone: (212) 629-8890. Fax: (212) 629-8502. E-mail: newyork@nfb.ca. Web Site: www.nfb.ca. Christina Rogers, US mktg mgr TV.
TV-CATV only.
TV program distribution.

National Mobile Television, 2740 California St., Torrance, CA 90503. Phone: (310) 782-9945. Phone: (800) 242-0642. Fax: (310) 782-9949. Web Site: www.nmtv.com. Kevin Sublette, gen mgr; Stephanie Hampton, opns dir.
Seattle, WA 98168, 12698 Gateway Dr. Phone: (206)-242-0642.
TV-CATV only.
Mobile TV facilities for remote production of multi-camera events.

National Public Radio, 635 Massachusetts Ave. N.W., Washington, DC 20001-3753. Phone: (513) 414-2000. Fax: (513) 414-3329. Web Site: www.npr.org. Bill Davis; Kevin Klose, pres/CEO; Peter J. Loewenstein, VP distribution; Barbara Hall, dev VP; Kathleen D. Jackson, VP human resources; Mike Starling, engrg VP; Jim Elder, VP/CFO; Celeste James, VP communications; Ken Stern, exec VP; Jeffrey Dvorkin, omsbudman; Jay Kernis, sr VP progmg; Margaret Low-Smith, VP progmg; Maria Thomas, VP online; Dana Davis Rehm, member/progm svcs.
Radio Only.
Radio program production & distribution.

Native American Public Telecommunications Inc., Box 83111, Lincoln, NE 68501. Phone: (402) 472-3522. Fax: (402) 472-8675. Web Site: www.nativetelecom.org. Frank Blythe, exec dir; Mary Ann Koehler, business mgr; Carol Cornsilk, progm/production dir.
TV-CATV only.
Producing & developing educ telecommunication programs for all media including TV & pub radio.

Nemo News, 7179 Via Maria, San Jose, CA 95139. Phone: (408) 226-6339. Fax: (408) 226-6403. E-mail: dickreizner@worldnet.att.net. Dick Reizner,.
TV-CATV only.
ENG unit (all formats) covering assignments worldwide.

Network Music L.L.C., 8750 Wilshire Blvd., Beverly Hills, CA 90211. Phone: (858) 451-6400. Fax: (858) 451-6409. E-mail: feedback@networkmusic.com. Web Site: www.networkmusic.com. Gary Gross, pres; Chuck Ansel, VP opns; Dennis Dunn, VP sls; Todd Kern, dir mktg.
TV-CATV only.
Produces music, sound effects & production elements libraries.

New City Releasing Inc., 20700 Ventura Blvd., Suite 350, Woodland Hills, CA 91364. Phone: (818) 348-2500. Fax: (818) 348-3022. Web Site: www.newcityreleasing.com. Alan B. Burnsteen, pres; David Burstein, VP.
TV-CATV only.

Broadcasting & Cable Yearbook 2006

Producers, Distributors, and Production Services Alphabetical Index

Producer & distributor of motion pictures to cable TV.

New Dimensions Radio, Box 569, Ukiah, CA 95482. Phone: (800) 935-8273. Phone: (707) 468-5215. E-mail: info@newdimensions.org. Web Site: www.newdimensions.org. Michael A. Toms, co-pres; Justine Toms, co-pres.
Radio Only.
Radio program production & distribution.

New Films International, 8484 Wilshire Blvd., Suite 510, Beverly Hills, CA 90211. Phone: (323) 655-1050. Fax: (323) 655-1070. E-mail: newfilms@newfilmsint.com. Web Site: www.newfilmsint.com. Nesin Hason, pres; Sezin Sonar, VP.
TV-CATV-Radio.
U.S.-based distribution company specialized in Romania, Bulgaria, & Turkey.

New Line Television, 888 Seventh Ave., 20th Fl., New York, NY 10106. Phone: (212) 649-4900. Fax: (212) 956-1936. Web Site: www.newline.com. Jim Rosenthal, pres; David Spiegelman, exec VP; Robin Seidner, sr VP.
Los Angeles, CA 90048, 116 N. Robetson.
TV-CATV only.
TV program production & distribution.

New Visions Syndication Inc., 44895 Hwy. 82, Aspen, CO 81611. Phone: (970) 925-2640. Fax: (970) 925-9369. Web Site: www.newvisionssyndication.com. E-mail: kayla@nvs.com. Kayla Hoffman-Cook, VP.
TV-CATV only.
International & domestic syndicator of specials & series; sports, lifestyle & entertainment.

New York Communications, 450 N. Narberth Ave., Suite 105, Narberth, PA 19072. Phone: (610) 668-1771. Fax: (610) 668-2287. E-mail: midandeo1@comcast.net. Michael Davis, pres.
TV-CATV only.
Creates, produces & distributes syndicated TV & radio promotional campaigns.

New Zoo Revue, 6399 Wilshire Blvd., Suite 816, Los Angeles, CA 90048. Phone: (323) 782-3525. Fax: (323) 782-3530. E-mail: newzoo@aol.com. Web Site: www.newzoorevue.com. Barbara Atlas, pres.
TV-CATV only.
TV program production & distribution.

News Broadcast Network, 451 Park Ave. S., 7th Fl., New York, NY 10016. Phone: (212) 684-8910. Fax: (212) 684-9650. Web Site: www.newsbroadcastnetwork.com. Mike Hill, pres; Jill Hill, sr chmn.
TV-CATV-Radio.
Produce & distribute news & feature material to TV & radio stns.

Nightingale-Conant Corp., 6245 W. Howard St., Niles, IL 60714. Phone: (847) 647-0300. Fax: (847) 647-7145. Web Site: www.nightingale.com. Vic Conant, pres.
Radio Only.
Radio program production & distribution.

Nine Network Australia, 6255 Sunset Blvd., Suite 1500, Los Angeles, CA 90028. Phone: (323) 461-3853. Fax: (323) 462-4849.
TV-CATV only.
Studio production facility, standard conversion & all format tape facilities.

No Soap Productions, 936 Broadway, 4th Fl., New York, NY 10010. Phone: (212) 581-5572. Fax: (212) 586-0045. E-mail: dan@nosoap.net. Web Site: www.nosoap.net. Dan Aron, pres.
TV-CATV only.
Radio comls, sound design for radio & TV, voicecasting, production studio-digital.

North American Network, Inc., 7910 Woodmont Ave., Suite 1400, Bethesda, MD 20814. Phone: (301) 654-9810. Fax: (301) 654-9828. E-mail: info@nan.com. Web Site: www.radiospace.com. Thomas P. Sweeney, pres; Tammy Lemley, VP.
Radio Only.
Full-svc radio P.R. providing progmg, news PSAs, promotional campaigns & sls opportunities to stns nationwide in English & Spanish.

North by Northwest Productions, 903 W. Broadway, Spokane, WA 99201. Phone: (509) 324-2949. Fax: (509) 324-2959. E-mail: marcdahlstrom@nxnw.net. Web Site: www.nxnw.net. Marc Dahlstrom, mngng ptnr.
Boise, ID 83702, 601 W. Broad St. Phone: (208) 345-7870. Shane Jibben, opns mgr.

TV-CATV only.
High end video & film production; D1/D2 postproduction; Paint/3D animation; sound design/production; HD ediiting.

North Shore Productions, 746 N. Shore Dr., Detroit Lakes, MN 56501. Phone: (218) 846-1936. Fax: (218) 846-1936. E-mail: nspsfrm@tekstar.com. Web Site: www.agriculture.com/sfradio.
Radio Only.
Produces & distributes "The Career Clinic®" & the "Successful Farming® Radio Magazine", two-minute features with affil sharing natl revenues.

North Star Music, 22 London St., East Greenwich, RI 02818. Phone: (401) 886-8888. Fax: (401) 886-8886. E-mail: info@northstarmusic.com. Web Site: www.northstarmusic.com. Richard R. Waterman, pres.
Radio Only.
Production, distribution, mktg & promotion of recorded music.

Northwest Imaging & FX, 2339 Columbia St., Suite 100, Vancouver, BC V5Y 3Y3. Canada. Phone: (604) 873-9330. Fax: (604) 873-9339. E-mail: nwfx@nwfx.com. Alex Tkach, VP.
TV-CATV only.
Shooting, visual effects, animation, digital editing suites, audio sweetening, Digital Betacam Sp. D-1, 1 inch, duplication Cintel Diamond Film transfer.

O

OASIS TV Inc., 9887 Santa Monica Blvd., Suite 200, Beverly Hills, CA 90212. Phone: (310) 553-4300. Fax: (310) 553-1159. Web Site: www.oasistv.com.
TV-CATV only.
24-hour cable/satellite network providing a broad, well-branded var of new age/human potential progmg.

O. Atlas Enterprises Inc., (New Zoo Review). 6399 Wilshire Blvd., Suite 816, Los Angeles, CA 90048. Phone: (323) 782-3525. Fax: (323) 782-3530. E-mail: newzoo@aol.com. Web Site: www.newzoorevue.com.
TV-CATV only.
International licensing, distribution of progmg for TV, all media.

O'Grady & Associates, 8431 Sabal Palm Ct., Vero Beach, FL 32963-4296. Phone: (772) 234-4177. Fax: (772) 231-9819. E-mail: jfogjr@juno.com. James F. O'Grady Jr., pres.
TV-CATV only.
Brokerage/consulting.

OGM Production Music, 6464 Sunset Blvd., Suite 790, Hollywood, CA 90028. Phone: (323) 461-2701. Phone: (800) 421-4163 (Sales). Fax: (323) 461-1543. E-mail: ogmmusic@ogmmusic.com. Web Site: www.ogmmusic.com. Ole Georg, pres.
TV-CATV only.
Video, cable, films, CD-ROM, bcst, multimedia, infomercials, satellite program, interactive TV, electronic publishing, theatrical features.

Oasis International, 6 Pardee Ave., Suite 103, Toronto, ON M6K 3H5. Canada. Phone: (416) 588-6821. Fax: (416) 588-7276. E-mail: info@oasisinternational.com. Web Site: www.oasisinternational.com. Peter Emerson, pres; Valerie Cabrera, exec VP; Steven Murphy, VP sls.
Santa Monica, CA 90402, 512 11th St.
TV-CATV only.
Worldwide distribution.

Omnimusic 52 Main St., Port Wshington, NY 11050. Phone: (800) 828-6664. Phone: (516) 883-0121. Fax: (516) 883-0271. E-mail: omni@omnimusic.com. Web Site: www.omnimusic.com. Doug Wood, pres; Patti Wood, natl sls mgr; Barbara Ring, mktg dir.
TV-CATV only.
Digitally produced music & sound effect libraries for TV, radio & cable featuring real instruments in various styles & orchestrations.

On Track, 6350 W. Freeway, Fort Worth, TX 76116. Phone: (817) 570-1400. Phone: (800) 266-1837. Fax: (817) 737-9436. E-mail: info@familynet.com. Web Site: www.familynetradio.com. Lisa Bratton, radio mktg & distribution; Donna Senn, radio distribution; Chuck Ries, producer.
Radio Only.
Contemporary Christian music with artist interviews, 30 min. wkly, on CD.

One Hundred Biblemen & Women of the U.S.A., Box 8263, Haledon, NJ 07508. Phone: (973) 956-2900. Fax: (973) 956-0600. Sam Cummings, pres.
TV-CATV only.
Low-cost bcstg & buying network for churches.

Oppix Productions Inc., 1501 Lee Hwy., Suite 203, Arlington, VA 22209. Phone: (703) 524-3000. Fax: (703) 522-3347. E-mail: jim@oppix.com. Web Site: www.oppix.com. James Oppenheimer, pres.
TV-CATV only.
Full-svc video production and post, serving bcst, corporate assns, nonprofit & govt. Avid editing; Beta & DV production.

Orange Productions Inc., 523 Righters Ferry Rd., 1st floor, Bala Cynwyd, PA 19004. Phone: (610) 667-8620. Fax: (610) 667-8939. E-mail: orange@snip.net. Web Site: www.soundsofsinatra.com. Sid Mark, pres; Brian Mark, opns mgr.
Radio Only.
Production & distribution of a wkly two-hour program *Sounds of Sinatra*.

Dick Orkin's Amazing Radio, 15003 Lemay St., Van Nuys, CA 91405. Phone: (800) 621-6949. Fax: (818) 376-8529. E-mail: sandyo@earthlink.net. Web Site: www.sandyorkin-crs.com. Sandy Orkin, pres.
Radio Only.
Syndicated packages of Dick Orkin comls customized for loc advertisers. Available in six categories.

Outdoor Media Group, Box 2151, Lake Oswego, OR 97035. Phone: (503) 675-7345. Fax: (503) 675-7820. E-mail: omg@aojtv.com. Web Site: www.aojtv.com. Russell Cameron, pres.
TV-CATV only.
TV program, coml production & distribution; production svcs.

Jim Owens Entertainment, 624 Grassmere Park, Suite 16, Nashville, TN 37211. Phone: (615) 256-7700. Fax: (615) 242-9735. Web Site: www.crookandchase.com. Jim Owens, pres; Jennifer Anderson, producer.
TV-CATV only.
Radio program production company for syndication. TV production for cable & home video.

P

PACSAT, 1629 S St., Sacramento, CA 95814. Phone: (916) 446-7890. Fax: (916) 446-7893. E-mail: pacsat@pacsat.com. Web Site: www.pacsat.com. Steve Mallory, pres; Marcia Calvin, opns mgr.
TV-CATV only.
Video, audio & satellite professionals. Ku-HD satellite trucks. Ku-/C international flyaways. ENG crews. Fly pack with CCU'S. Post production & graphics.

PAULAR Entertainment L.L.C., 13700 Marina Pointe Dr., Suite 901, Marina del Rey, CA 90292. Phone: (310) 821-0430. Fax: (310) 821-3793. E-mail: thirdwayv@aol.com. Larry Friedricks, ptnr; Paula Fierman, ptnr.
TV-CATV only.
World-wide distribution of feature films, video & TV including movies, series & mini-series.

PBS Video, 1320 Braddock Pl., Alexandria, VA 22314. Phone: (703) 739-5000, EXT. 8614. Fax: (703) 739-8487. Web Site: www.pbs.org. Pat Mitchell, pres/CEO.
Handles videocassette, DVD's sls, rental & licensing of selected PBS programs to schools, colleges, libraries, hospitals & other institutions.

PMTV Producers Management Television, 800 N. Henderson Rd., King of Prussia, PA 19406-3207. Phone: (610) 768-1770. Fax: (610) 768-1773. E-mail: mailto.pmtv@pmtv.com. Web Site: www.pmtv.com. Brian Powers, pres; Rob Schmoll, VP/gen mgr.
TV-CATV only.
Full-svc mobile TV production company, providing mobile units, crews, satellite svcs, lighting, staging, etc. for sports, entertainment & teleconferences worldwide.

PPM Multimedia, Brezo 4 - URB Los Robles, Torrelodones, Madrid 28250. Spain. Phone: (34) 91 859 1913. Fax: (34) 91 859 0932. E-mail: multimedia@ppmm.es. Web Site: www.ppmm.es. Paco Rodriguez, mngng dir.
TV-CATV only.
Distribution of animation, feature films, documentaries, co-production setting.

Producers, Distributors, and Production Services Alphabetical Index

(PSSI) Production & Satellite Services Inc., 11860 Mississippi Ave., Los Angeles, CA 90025. Phone: (310) 575-4400. Fax: (310) 575-4451. E-mail: pssi@pssi-usa.com. Web Site: www.pssi-usa.com. Robert C. Lamb, pres; Brian Nelles, sr VP; Melissa D. Meek, mktg.
TV-CATV only.
Full service production and satellite transmission company with 19 fully redundant C- and Ku-band satellite trucks located nationwide. Available for news, sports, corporate and entertainment events, media tours, video conferencing, webcasting, and downlinks. Additional services include Standard and High Definition digital transmission, encryption, multiple camera productions, event coordination, and a C/Ku Flyaway system for international transmission. skIP Broadband also available for internet, voice connectivity, and webcasting via satellite, ideal in remote areas with little or no connectivity.

Palace Digital Studios, 29 N. Main St., South Norwalk, CT 06854. Phone: (203) 853-1740. Fax: (203) 855-9608. E-mail: wendy@palacedigital.com. Web Site: www.palacedigital.com. Wendy Lambert, pres.
New York, NY 10036. Servi Digital Studios, 35 W. 45th St. Phone: (212) 921-0555. Carol McCoy, VP opns.
TV-CATV only.
On-air promotion design & animation; program opns; identity packages; sls tape creation longform editorial, CD-ROM, & Website design.

Palace Digital Studios, 29 N. Main St., South Norwalk, CT 06854. Phone: (203) 853-1740. Fax: (203) 855-9608. E-mail: wendy@palacedigital.com. Christopher Campbell, CEO; Wendy Lambert, pres/COO.
New York, NY 10036. Palace Studios, 35 W. 45th St. Phone: (212) 921-0555. Al Weiss, pres.
New York, NY 10036. RS Digital Studios, 35 W. 45th St. Phone: (212) 221-3966. Amparo Lizzarazo, pres.
TV-CATV only.
TV program, coml promotional film production & production svcs.

Shelly Palmer Productions, P. O. Box 1877, New York, NY 10156-1877. Phone: (212) 532-3880. E-mail: info@shellypalmer.com. Web Site: www.shellypalmer.com. Shelly Palmer, pres.
TV-CATV only.
Music, video, television, and film production and creative services. Advertising and marketing. Music libraries, sound design, sales videos and post-production.

Pan American Video, 3144 Broadway, Suite 4, Eureka, CA 95501. Phone: (707) 822-3800. Fax: (707) 822-0800. E-mail: panam@panamvideo.com. Web Site: www.panamvideo.com. Teri Lane, pres; Sheila McQuillen, VP.
TV-CATV only.
Public domain movies & TV shows, bcst quality & stock footage.

Pantomime Pictures Inc., 12144 Riverside Dr., North Hollywood, CA 91607. Phone: (818) 980-5555. Fax: (818) 984-3470. Fred Crippen, dir; Matt Crippen, producer.
TV-CATV only.
Animation production & design for TV comls, educ & industrial use. Animation camera for 35 mm & 16 mm.

Paramount Worldwide Television Distribution, 5555 Melrose Ave., Hollywood, CA 90038. Phone: (323) 956-5000. Fax: (323) 862-5555. Web Site: www.paramount.com. Garry Hart, pres; Joel Berman, pres; John Nogawski, pres; Gary Marenzi, pres; Jack Waterman, pres.
TV-CATV only.
TV program production/ distribution.

Parrot Communications International Inc., 2917 N. Ontario St., Burbank, CA 91504. Phone: (818) 567-4700. Fax: (818) 567-4600. E-mail: info@parrotmedia.com. Web Site: www.parrotmedia.com. Robert W. Mertz, pres/CEO; Rae Ann Mertz, exec VP; Michael Norris, VP.
TV-CATV only.
Data base mgmt, direct mail svcs, promotional fulfillment, warehousing, contest fulfillment, bcst faxing, high speed duplication & videotape duplication.

Parrot Productions Ltd., 69 Skyland Dr., Roswell, GA 30075. Phone: (770) 572-1910. Fax: (770) 518-5831. E-mail: admin@positivetv.com. Web Site: www.positivetv.com. Kambiz Azordegan, CEO.
TV-CATV only.
Positive children's progmg with the name of "Tootee" series of 15 shows ready for bcst & books of stories from each individual show, cover children 3-9 yrs old. Stories good for radio on tape.

Pathe International, 21 rue Francois 1 er, 75008 Paris France. Fax: 33-1-40-76-9194. Fax: 33-1-40-76-9169. E-mail: christine.hayet@pathe.com. Web Site: www.pathe.fr. Jerome Seydoux; Eduardo Malone, co-chmn/CEO; Emma Rami, VP finance; Michel Crepon, COO.
TV-CATV only.
Production & distribution of TV films & documentaries. Production of multimedia programs.

Paulist Media Works, 3055 4th St. N.E., Washington, DC 20017. Phone: (202) 269-6064. Fax: (202) 269-4304. E-mail: info@paulist.org. Web Site: www.paulist.org/pmw. Sue Donovan, pres.
TV-CATV only.
Support for non-profit organization in internet svcs/website/web design distribution of relg radio programs, video/documentary production

Paulist Productions, Box 1057, Pacific Palisades, CA 90272. Phone: (310) 454-0688. Fax: (310) 459-6549. E-mail: paulistmail@paulistproductions.org. Web Site: www.paulistproductions.org. Frank Desiderio, CSP, pres; Enid Sevilla, gen mgr & finacial off; Barbara Gangi, producer; Joseph Kim, VP business affrs.
TV-CATV only.
TV program production.

Peckham Productions, 50 S. Buckhout St., Irvington, NY 10533. Phone: (914) 591-4140. Fax: (914) 591-4149. Web Site: www.peckhampix.com. Peter H. Peckham, pres.
TV-CATV only.
Full-svc film & video producer of TV comls, TV programs & TV network promos, industrial films.

Perception Media Group, 1848 Clay St., Roanoke, VA 24013. Phone: (540) 563-5225. Fax: (540) 563-0117. Ben Peyton, pres.
TV-CATV only.
TV & radio coml program production, distribution & jingles. Religious programs & distribution.

Peters Communications, 1555 Berenda Pl., El Cajon, CA 92020. Phone: (858) 565-8511. Fax: (619) 440-1481. E-mail: ppiep@cox.net. Edward J. Peters, pres.
TV-CATV only.
Media mktg consultants, providing rsch, concept, mktg plan, music, graphics & animation.

Philadelphia Flyers Hockey Club, 3601 S. Broad St., Philadelphia, PA 19148. Phone: (215) 465-4500. Fax: (215) 952-4103. E-mail: rryan@comcast-spectacor.com. Web Site: www.philadelphiaflyers.com. Ed Snider, chmn; Bob Clarke, pres; Shawn Tilger, VP mktg.
TV-CATV only.
TV & radio program production.

Phoebus Communications Inc., 10905 Ft. Washington Rd., Suite 300, Fort Washington, MD 20744. Phone: (301) 292-9800. Fax: (301) 292-0829. E-mail: phoebuscom@aol.com. Web Site: www.phoebusinc.net. Gail C. Arnall, Ph.D., pres.
TV-CATV only.
Full scale distance learning network mgmt.

Phoenix Communications Group, 3 Empire Blvd., South Hackensack, NJ 07606. Phone: (201) 807-0888. Fax: (201) 807-0272. Web Site: www.phoenixcomm.com. Joe Podesta, chmn; Jim Holland, pres; Rich Domich, sls VP & mktg; Geoff Belinfante, exec producer & sr VP; Trish Ferreri, mgr.
TV-CATV only.
Major League Sports Newsatellite; TV & video production & distribution; stock footage licensing.

Pied Piper Films Ltd., 825941 Mel-Nott TL, R. R. 2, Shelburne, ON L0N 1S6. Canada. Phone: (519) 925-6558. Fax: (519) 925-6558. Allan Wargon; Lee Israelski, producer.
TV-CATV only.
Motion picture production.

Pike Productions Inc., Box 300, 11 Clarke St., Newport, RI 02840. Phone: (401) 846-8890. Fax: (401) 847-0070. E-mail: info@pikefilmtrailers.com. James A. Pike, pres; Cornelia M. Pike, sls mgr.
Custom ads & special announcement trailers produced & distributed in all formats—35mm, 185x1, Scope, stereo, 70mm stereo.

Planet Pictures Ltd., 4764 Park Granada, Suite 208, Calabasas, CA 91302. Phone: (818) 222-9000. Fax: (818) 222-4370. E-mail: info@planetpictures.com. Web Site: www.planetpictures.com. Jim Hayden, pres; Jennifer Hayden, mgng dir; Peter Torvik, business affrs.
TV-CATV only.
Production & distribution for documentary, informational, reality-based TV programs.

Playboy Entertainment Group Inc., 2706 Media Center Dr., Los Angeles, CA 90065. Phone: (323) 276-4000. Fax: (323) 276-4500. Jim English, pres; James Griffith, sr VP.
Los Angeles, CA 90065. Andrita Studios, 3030 Andrita St. Sol Weisel, VP production.
TV-CATV only.
TV program production, distribution & video.

Playhouse Pictures, Box 2089, Los Angeles, CA 90078-2089. Phone: (323) 851-2112. Fax: (323) 851-2117. E-mail: playpix@aol.com. Ted Woolery, producer; Gerry Woolery, dir; Todd Shalter, dir.
TV-CATV only.
Animated TV coml production & short films.

Point 360, 1133 North Hollywood Way, Burbank, CA 91505. Phone: (818) 556-5700. Fax: (818) 556-5753. Web Site: www.point360.com. Dennis Imbler, gen mgr; Paul Ponzio, VP sls/producer.
Hollywood, CA 90038, 1220 N. Highland Ave. Phone: (323) 957-5500. Rich Appel, gen mgr; Brian Grant, VP business dev.
Hollywood, CA 90038, 712 N. Seward St. Phone: (323) 462-5330. Yvonne Parker, gen mgr; Brian Grant, VP business dev.
Hollywood, CA 90038, 1025 N. McCadden Pl. Phone: (323) 461-8383. Fabian Sanchez, gen mgr; Brian Grant, VP business dev.
Los Angeles, CA 90064, 12421 W. Olympic Blvd. Phone: (310) 207-7079. Carl Segal, gen mgr; Brian Grant, VP business dev.
Postproduction & duplication, film-to-tape transfers, audio svcs. Digital editing, distribution & syndication.

PorchLight Entertainment Inc., 11777 Mississippi Ave., Los Angeles, CA 90025. Phone: (310) 477-8400. Fax: (310) 477-7555. Web Site: www.porchlight.com. Bruce D. Johnson, pres/CEO; William T. Baumann, exec VP & CFO.
TV-CATV only.
Produces & distributes family entertainment progmg including animation, TV movies & interactive multimedia progmg, licensing & merchandising.

Ports of Paradise, Box 33648, San Diego, CA 92163. Phone: (619) 275-7357. Phone: (800) 223-2564. Fax: (858) 490-3397. E-mail: aloharn@portparadise.com. Web Site: www.portparadise.com. J. Hal Hodgson, exec producer.
Radio Only.
Hour-long radio program with Hawaiian music & info. Available on a barter basis.

Positive Children's Programming (PCP), 69 Skyland Dr., Roswell, GA 30075. Phone: (770) 572-1910. Fax: (770) 518-5831. E-mail: admin@positivetv.com. Web Site: www.positivetv.com. Kambiz Azordegan, CEO & creator.
TV-CATV only.
TV progms, 15 shows, books published as series, CD-ROMs, all positive & live action & animation.

Post LLC/The Image Group, 305 E 46th St., 2nt Fl., New York, NY 10017. Phone: (212) 548-4400. Fax: (212) 752-3745. Web Site: www.image-group.com. Charles Pontillo, pres.
Twelve on-line suites, six Avid/EMC2, 2D/3D graphics, two SSL Scenarias, three film transfer, four stages, one remote unit, duplication.

PostWorks, New York, 100 Ave. of the Americas, New York, NY 10013. Phone: (212) 557-4949. Fax: (212) 983-4083. Web Site: www.pwny.com.
TV-CATV only.
Film-to-tape or data in standard or Hi-Definition; editing; digital, Hi-Definition & non-linear; duplication & conversion, and satellite & fibre transmissions.

Potomac TV/Communications, 529 14th St. N.W., Suite 480, Washington, DC 20045. Phone: (202) 783-8000. Fax: (202) 783-1861. E-mail: nkelly@newsworldtv.com. Nick Chiaia, pres.
TV-CATV only.
Full-svc TV production facility. C- & Ku-band satellite transmitters/receive svcs.

Power Play Music Video L.L.C., 223-225 Washington St., Newark, NJ 07102. Phone: (973) 642-5132. Fax: (973) 642-5747. Web Site: www.powerplay-mvtv.com. E-mail: powerplaytv@cs.com. Greg Ferguson, pres.
TV-CATV only.
TV & radio program; coml production & distribution; production svcs.

Broadcasting & Cable Yearbook 2006

Producers, Distributors, and Production Services Alphabetical Index

Powerline, 6350 W. Freeway, Fort Worth, TX 76116. Phone: (817) 570-1400. Phone: (800) 266-1837. Fax: (817) 737-9436. E-mail: info@familynet.com. Web Site: www. familynetradio.com. Lisa Bratton, radio mktg & distribution; Donna Senn, radio distribution; Kirk Teegarden, producer.
Radio Only.
Adult contemp music blended with brief commentaries about life by host Brother Jon Rivers, 30 min wkly on CD.

Powersports/Millenium International, 18226 Ventura Blvd., Suite 102, Tarzana, CA 91356. Phone: (818) 708-9995. Fax: (818) 708-0598. E-mail: intl@ps-mill.com. Web Site: www.ps-mill.com. William McAbian, pres; Tal Dean McAbian, exec VP.
TV-CATV only.
Production & distribution of special interest & documentaries for TV, cable & home video.

Prairie Dog Entertainment, Box 28700, San Diego, CA 92198. Phone: (800) 448-7664. Web Site: www.buckhowdy.com. Steve Vaus, CEO.
Radio Only.
Exclusively offering Buck Howdy's Cow Pie Radio, the fastest growing wkly kids radio program.

Praxis Media Inc., 9 Twilight Pl., South Norwalk, CT 06854. Phone: (203) 866-6666. Fax: (203) 853-8299. E-mail: praxiscc@aol.com. Christopher Campbell, pres & dir; Deborah Weingrad, VP & dir.
TV-CATV only.
TV program, coml, promotional film production; production svcs.

Premiere Radio Networks Inc., 15260 Ventura Blvd., 5th Fl., Sherman Oaks, CA 91403-5339. Phone: (818) 377-5300. Fax: (818) 377-5333. E-mail: webmaster@premrad.com. Web Site: www.premrad.com. Kraig Kitchin, pres; Dan Yukelson, VP finance; Eileen Thorgusen, VP; Rich Meyer, pres; Nancy Deitemeyer, VP opns.
Radio Only.
Line-up includes Bcst Results Group (BRG) features, Olympia, Premiere Comedy Networks Formats, Long-form features, Mediabase rsch formats, music svcs, online, plain-wrap formats, prep & short-form. All features & svcs offered on a barter basis are available via satellite, disc, tape, script or phone, depending on the program.

Presbyterian Church (U.S.A.), 100 Witherspoon St., Louisville, KY 40202-1396. Phone: (502) 569-5211. Phone: (502) 569-5493. Fax: (502) 569-8845. Jerry Van Marter, news dir.
TV-CATV only.
Radio & TV production, video, audio production, distribution, mktg & Internet svcs.

Presson Perspectives, 600 Druid Rd. E., Clearwater, FL 33756. Phone: (727) 461-1885. Fax: (727) 443-1984. E-mail: gpresson@tampabay.rr.com. Web Site: www.medforum.com. Gina Presson, pres & exec producer.
TV-CATV only.
News, documentary & internet production ranging from turnkey pieces to any segment.

Prime Cut Productions Inc., 11909 E. Trail, San Fernando, CA 91342. Phone: (818) 897-7321. Fax: (818) 834-9889. E-mail: janicekaplan@primecutproductions.com. Web Site: www.primecutproductions.com. Edward Flaherty, pres; Jan Kaplan, VP.
Paris 75005, 3 des Ecoles.
TV-CATV only.
NTSC Betacam European producers for American TV; bilingual location professionals; distribution, co-production & stock footage.

Primedia Workplace Learning, 4101 International Pkwy., Carrollton, TX 75007. Phone: (800) 848-1717. Fax: (972) 309-5666. Web Site: www.pwpl.com. Josh Karin, pres/CEO; Gina Valencia, dir mktg.
TV-CATV only.
Video-based, interactive tech training programs for industry, utilities, govt relating to maintenance, opns & safety.

Primo Newservice Inc., Box 116, 182 Sound Beach Ave., Old Greenwich, CT 06870-0116. Phone: (203) 637-0044. Fax: (203) 698-0812. E-mail: primonews@aol.com. Web Site: www.kidsnewsnet.com. Albert T. Primo, pres/CEO.
TV-CATV only.
TV news consulting, strategic news positioning talent & management, coaching. Cable news training; Internet Broadband Service.

Pro Video, 2904-A Colorado Ave., Santa Monica, CA 90404. Phone: (310) 828-2292. E-mail: provideo1@earthlink.net. Joel Webb, pres.
TV-CATV only.
Commercials mastered to DVD & 3/4 inches.

Producers Group, Ltd., 713 S. Pacific Coast Hwy., Suite B, Redondo Beach, CA 90277-4233. Phone: (310) 316-0481. Fax: (310) 316-1482. E-mail: lee.gluckman@producers-group.tv. Lee Gluckman Jr., pres.
TV-CATV only.
Dev & production of theatrical & TV films & series.

Production Garden Music Libraries, 510 E. Ramsey Rd., Suite 4, San Antonio, TX 78216. Phone: (800) 247-5317. Fax: (210) 530-5230. E-mail: sales@productiongarden.com. Web Site: www.productiongarden.com.
TV-CATV only.
Ten distinct music libraries featuring production music, including production elements & sound effects; both lease & buy-out options available.

Productions La Fete, 387 St. Paul W., Montreal, PQ H2Y 2A7. Canada. Phone: (514) 848-0417. Fax: (514) 848-0064. E-mail: info@lafete.com. Rock Demers, pres; Xiao Juan Zhou, VP distribution; Daniel Proulx, VP finance.
TV-CATV only.
Production & distribution, import & export of all kinds of audio-visual products (feature films, drama series, documentaries, multimedia, etc.).

The Program Exchange, 375 Hudson St., New York, NY 10014. Phone: (212) 463-3500. Fax: (212) 463-2662. E-mail: info@programexchange.com. Web Site: www.programexchange.com. Allen Banks, pres; Chris Hallowell, sr VP/mgmg dir.
TV-CATV only.
TV program distribution.

Promark Television, 500 S. Palm Canyon Dr., Suite 220, Palm Springs, CA 92264. Phone: (760) 322-7776. Fax: (760) 322-5149. E-mail: kbeasanski@promarktv.com. Web Site: www.promarktv.com. David Levine, pres/CEO; Karen Beasanski, opns dir; Doug Swartz, comptroller.
TV-CATV only.
TV program production & distribution.

Promusic, 941-A Clint Moore Rd., Boca Raton, FL 33487. Phone: (561) 995-0331. Phone: (800) 322-7879. Fax: (561) 995-8434. E-mail: mail@promusiclibrary.com. Web Site: www.promusiclibrary.com. Alain Leroux, pres; Mike Spitz, sls dir.
Studio City, CA 91604, 11846 Ventura Blvd, Suite 304. Phone: (818) 506-1588. (888) 600-8988. Fax: (818) 506-8580. Dana Ferandelli, Music consultant.
TV-CATV only.
Production music for film, TV & more. Vast CD catalog to choose from with extensive classical & opera.

Protestant Hour Inc., 644 W. Peachtree St., Suite 300, Atlanta, GA 30309-1925. Phone: (404) 815-9110. Fax: (404) 815-0258. E-mail: info@day1.net. Web Site: www.day1.net. Peter Wallace, pres & exec producer.
Radio Only.
Radio program production & distribution; religious ecumenical media.

Public Media Incorporated, 4423 N. Ravenswood Ave., Chicago, IL 60640-1199. Phone: (773) 878-2600. Fax: (773) 878-8406. E-mail: webmasters@homevision.com. Web Site: www.homevision.net. Adrianne Furniss, pres/CEO; Carole Little, VP.
TV-CATV only.
Sls to all TV outlets in North America, foreign & classic cinema distribution.

Purple Grape Post, 2330 Pontius Ave., West Los Angeles 90064. Phone: (310) 479-3877. Fax: (310) 479-9588. E-mail: dillard@grapegroup.com. Web Site: www.grapegroup.com. Valerie Schadt, exec producer; Victoria Quasar, dir; Dillard Sholes, sls.
TV-CATV only.
Full service post; computer graphic, digital compositing, visual effects on-line.

Q

Quality Film & Video, 232 Cockeysville Rd., Hunt Valley, MD 21030. Phone: (410) 785-1920. E-mail: qfv@qualityfilmvideo.com. Web Site: www.qualityfilmvideo.com. Peter A. Garey, pres; Guy G. Garey, VP.
TV-CATV only.
Video production, postproduction svcs, videotape, CD-ROM & DVD duplication.

Questar, 680 N. Lake Shore Dr., Suite 900, Chicago, IL 60611. Phone: (312) 266-9400. Fax: (312) 266-9523. Web Site: www.questar1.com. Jason Nader, pres.
TV-CATV only.
Producer, distributor of travel documentaries, children's cultural historical & natural history.

R

RAD Marketing & Cabletowns, 167 Crary-on-the-Park, Mount Vernon, NY 10550. Phone: (914) 668-3563. Fax: (914) 668-4247. Bob Dadarria, pres; Tom Lockley, VP; Kathy Kruver, account exec; Jaclyn Tucker, account exec.
TV-CATV only.
Consumer list, individuals & household lifestyles. Svcs include: cable TV subs with addressable box direct TV buyers with Tel # scrubbed mailing lists, loc area mkts, —rgnl/natl, sweepstakes entrants list, children lists.

RAI Corp., (Italian Radio TV System). 1350 Ave. of the Americas, 21st Fl., New York, NY 10019. Phone: (212) 468-2500. Fax: (212) 765-1956. Web Site: www.raicorp.net. Mario Bona, CEO; Guido Corso, pres.
TV-CATV only.
Italian natl radio & TV.

RBC Ministries, Box 2222, Grand Rapids, MI 49501-2222. Phone: (616) 942-6770. Fax: (616) 957-5741. E-mail: rbc@rbc.org. Web Site: www.rbc.net. Martin De Haan II, pres.
TV-CATV only.
TV & radio production & distribution. Programs: TV Day of Discovery, Radio-Discover the Word, Words To Live By, Our Daily Bread, Sports Spectrum, My Utmost for His Highest & Walk In The Wood.

RBC Ministries/Midwest Media Managers, Box 2606, Grand Rapids, MI 49501-2606. Phone: (877) 245-0550. Phone: (616) 942-6360. Fax: (616) 957-5741. E-mail: mmm@rbc.net. Web Site: www.rbc.net/mmm. Martin De Haan II, pres; John Nasby, dir; Rod McNany, dir.
TV-CATV only.
In-house agency for RBC Ministries; providing TV/Radio placement & promotional support of RBC resources including the devotional, Our Daily Bread.

RDF Media, 48-49 Princes Pl., London W11 4QA. United Kingdom. Phone: 44 (0)20 7908-1200. Fax: 44 (0)20 7908-1234. E-mail: sales@rdfmedia.com. Web Site: www.rdfmedia.com. David Frank, chief exec; Joely Fether, production dir; Stephen Lambert, progmg dir.
TV-CATV only.
Production & distribution of TV & radio programs.

RMD & Assoc. Inc., 534 Rosemary Cir., Media, PA 19063. Phone: (610) 566-3799. Fax: (610) 566-3799. E-mail: rmdassociates@yahoo.com. Dick D'Anjolell, pres & exec producer; Hank Shaw, tech support svcs; Celeste Walsh, production mgr.
TV-CATV only.
Program creative svcs, production & distribution, specializing in promotion & business info.

ROZON, 2101 Blvd St. Laurent, Montreal H2X 2T5. Phone: (514) 845-3155. Fax: (514) 845-4140. Web Site: www.hahaha.com. Nathalie Bourdon, dir tv sls; Bruce Hills, COO; Gilbert Rozon, pres; Isabelle Begin, dir international TV; Christos Sourligas, international TV sls, publicity, mktg & tv sls.
TV-CATV only.
Producer/distributor of comedy programs, standup comedy & nonverbal light entertainment.

RPM Media Enterprises-The Relic Rack Preview, 108 Holmes Oval, New Providence, NJ 07974-1425. Phone: (908) 464-2222. E-mail: richardjlorenzo@relicrack.com. Web Site: www.relic-rack.com. Richard J. Lorenzo, pres/CEO; Margaret P. Lorenzo, CFO; Jack Kratoville, VP.
Radio Only.
Four-hour wkly rock & roll oldies syndicated entertainment program called the Relic Rack Review, music, news & entertainment show. Prep svcs including Relic Rack Fast Facts. Multi format radio program consulting svcs.

RPM-Radio Programming & Management Inc., 1133 W. Long Lake Rd., Ste 200, Bloomfield Hills, MI 48302. Phone: (248) 647-1068. Phone: (800) 521-2537. Fax: (888) 776-0006. E-mail: rpmorlk@aol.com. Web Site: www.tophitsusa.com. Thomas M. Kirkorian, pres.

Producers, Distributors, and Production Services Alphabetical Index

Radio Only.
Wkly CD service top hits U.S. & CD music libraries. Full CD format svcs & progmg consultation.

The Radio Almanac, 107 Jensen Cir., West Springfield, MA 01089-4451. Phone: (413) 737-7600. Fax: (413) 737-7600. E-mail: cspencer@mail.map.com. Charles G. Spencer,.
TV-CATV only.
Lifestyle info; special rsch; writing, voice & production projects. Monthly filler material publication, featuring events, sports, biographical sketches & other info.

Radio America, 1030 15th St. N.W., Suite 1040, Washington, DC 20005. Phone: (202) 408-0944. Fax: (202) 408-1087. E-mail: radioa@radioamerica.org. Web Site: www.radioamerica.org. James C. Roberts, pres; Mike Paradiso, COO; Rich McFadden, producer; Greg Corombos, producer; Griff Jenkins, producer.
Radio Only.
News & feature svc providing daily, wkly & special programs (90 seconds to one hr) & multi-part documentaries.

Radio & TV Roundup Productions, 653 Sunhaven Dr., Clayton, NJ 08312-1955. Phone: (856) 881-2570. Fax: (856) 307-9506. E-mail: delfon@att.net. Web Site: www.nanes.com. Bill Bertenshaw, CEO; Bobbi Cherrelle, exec producer; B.C. Slachofsky, mgr; Richard Nanes, dir.
Cape May, NJ 08204-0108, Box 108. Bobbi Cherrelle, exec producer.
TV-CATV only.
Production & placement of TV & radio progmg including comls & PSAs. Distribute free classical cds & tv progmg.

Radio Canada International/Canadian Broadcasting Corp., Box 6000, Montreal, PQ H3C 3A8. Canada. Phone: (514) 597-7639. Fax: (514) 597-6607. E-mail: rci@montreal.src.ca. Web Site: www.rcinet.ca. Jean Larin, dir.
Radio Only.
Daily shortwave & internet, seven languages, 24-hour eutelsat F6 Europe, intelsat 707 Africa, asiasat 2. Recorded & live program placement on foreign stns.

Radio City Entertainmement, 2 Penn Plaza, New York, NY 10021. Phone: (212) 465-6000. Phone: (212) 485-7000. Web Site: www.thegarden.com. Katie Schroeder, dir pub affrs.
Los Angeles, CA 90067, 2049 Century Park E, Suite 1200. Phone: (310) 551-2721.
TV-CATV only.
TV program producers; production svcs.

Radio Express Inc., 1415 W. Magnolia Blvd., Burbank, CA 91506. Phone: (818) 295-5800. Fax: (818) 295-5801. E-mail: radioinfo@radioexpress.com. Web Site: radioinfo@radio e. Tom Rounds, CEO; John Fleck, pres; Anita Antonio, gen mgr; Christopher DiMatteo, VP mktg.
Radio Only.
Radio Express exports Radioplay, the best music service for radio, production music and progmg to enhance any music format, worldwide.

Radio Production Services Inc., 201 Lena Dr., Easley, SC 29640-9647. Phone: (864) 855-7191. Fax: (803) 855-7191, EXT. 2. E-mail: kenroy2@aol.com. R. Kenneth Rogers, pres; G. Leighton Grantham III, CFO & VP; Ron Rackley, engrg dir; Nan Cohen, mgr; Jason Gold, sls.
Salem, MA 01970. Radio Production Services Inc., 27 Congress Street. Phone: (978)-740-0990. Fax: (978)-740-0660.
Cold Spring Harbor, NY 11724. Radio Production Services Inc., Box 26. Phone: (516) 246-9182. Alex Silvers, A&R dir.
Nashville, TN 37201. Radio Production Services Inc., 206 Union St, Ext. Phone: (615) 227-1947. Fred James, VP.
TV-CATV only.
Radio program production specializing in early R&B & oldies formats. Radio, TV coml production & distribution. Stn ID packages, jingles, consultation svcs in sls & progmg.

Radio Sound Network, 770 Twin Rivers Dr., Columbus, OH 43215. Phone: (614) 621-5600. Fax: (614) 621-5620. E-mail: sclawson@radiohio.com. Web Site: www.radiohio.com. Steve Clawson, engrg dir; Tony Miller, dir.
Columbus, OH 43215, 175 S. 3rd St. Phone: (614) 460-3850.
Radio Only.
Full-svc digital satellite audio & data distribution, including affil rel & network bldg for new & existing sports, news/talk, music & specialty networks.

Radio Spirits, 2 Ridgedale Ave., Cedar Knolls, NJ 07927. Phone: (800) 359-0570, ext.236. Phone: (973) 539-7557. Fax: (973) 539-1273. E-mail: wholesale@radiospirits.com. Web Site: www.radiospirits.com. Hakan Lindskog, pres; David Carroll, VP sls.
Radio Only.
Syndicated radio production specializing in "Golden Age of Radio." Production of *When Radio Was* with Stan Freberg, bartered to 300 affls.

Radio Television Espanola (RTVE), Edificio Prado Del Rey/ Desp. 3/023, Prado Del Rey, Madrid 28223. Phone: (34 91) 581-54 91. Fax: (34 91) 581-77 41. E-mail: contratos_canales_inter.ep@rtve.es. Web Site: www.rtve.es.
TV-CATV-Radio.
Production & distribution of its own productions as well as some 250 feature films in co-production with independent Spanish & Latin American film producers.

Radioguide People Inc., (Vuolo Video). Box 880, Novi, MI 48376. Phone: (248) 960-9607. Fax: (248) 926-9090. E-mail: artvuolo@aol.com. Web Site: www.vuolovideo.com. Arthur R. Vuolo Jr., pres.
Radio Only.
Publishers of radio stn guides for the gen public; co-sponsored by loc stns & natl advertisers. Produces videos of radio stns, radio events for educational & entertainment purposes.

The Radio-Studio Network, Box 683, Times Square Station, New York, NY 10108-0683. Phone: (800) 608-5835. Fax: (212) 868-5663. E-mail: programming@radio-studio.net. Web Site: www.radio-studio.net. Steve Warren, pres.
Radio Only.
Multi-Format Network Programming by MP3 download. Music, News, Talk, Infomercials.

Rampion Visual Productions L.L.C., 125 Walnut St., Watertown, MA 02472. Phone: (617) 972-1777. Fax: (617) 972-9157. E-mail: info@rampion.com. Web Site: www.rampion.com. Steven V. Tringali, ptnr; Michael R. Garneau, ptnr.
TV-CATV only.
Full Digital Component Editing (BetaSP & DigiBeta), Computer Graphics (2D & 3D), Green Screen Studio, Digital Compositing and DVD creation.

Ray Sports Network, 104 Radio Rd., Powell's Point, NC 27966. Phone: (252) 491-2414. Fax: (252) 491-2939. Web Site: www.agribetradio.com/raysports.htm. Bill Ray, pres; Jody O'Donnell, sports dir.
Radio Only.
TV & radio program & coml production, distribution. Sports syndication.

Raycom Sports, 2815 Coliseum Ctr. Dr., Suite 200, Charlotte, NC 28217. Phone: (704) 378-4400. Fax: (704) 378-4401. E-mail: khaines@raycomsports.com. Web Site: www.raycomsports.com. Ken Haines, pres/CEO; Colin Smith, VP station relations; De Cordell, VP sls; Peter Rolfe, Production.
Mobile, AL 36602. Mobile, 200 Government St., Ste 302. Phone: (251) 432-9340. Steve Haraleson, Dir.
Sacramento, CA 95814. Sacramento, 1107 Second St., Ste 210. Phone: (916) 443-2503. Brian Flojola, VP.
TV-CATV only.
Grant mgmt, sls distribution, produce, market, distribute sports, entertainment progmg nationally & internationally.

The Real Estate Network, 19925 Stevens Creek Blvd., Cupertino, CA 95014. Phone: (408) 725-7530.
TV-CATV only.
Multimedia computer, interactive TV networks for mdse, mktg real estate listings, related goods & svcs.

Redwood Entertainment Inc., 71 Ayers Ct., Suite 3A, Teaneck, NJ 07666. Phone: (201) 833-4368. Fax: (201) 833-4072. E-mail: jcastiel@aol.com. Janet E. Castiel, pres.
TV-CATV only.
TV program, film production, music videos.

Reel Media International Inc., 4516 Lovers Ln., # 178, Dallas, TX 75225-6925. Phone: (214) 521-3301. Fax: (214) 522-3448. E-mail: reelmedia@aol.com. Web Site: www.reelmediaintl.com. Tom T. Moore, pres.
TV-CATV only.
Worldwide distributor of motion pictures, Public Library of 2,000 movies, series & documentaries. Servicing all rights.

Reid/Land Productions Inc., 425 E. 58th St., Suite 46H, New York, NY 10022. Phone: (212) 754-3348. Fax: (212) 754-7034. E-mail: reidland@rcn.com. Allen Reid, pres; Mady Land, exec VP.
TV-CATV only.

Packaging, creation & production of TV programs—variety, entertainment, music, games, sports how-to & cooking.

Russ Reid Company, 2 N. Lake Ave., Suite 600, Pasadena, CA 91101. Phone: (626) 449-6100. Fax: (626) 449-4756. Web Site: www.russreid.com. Carol Philips, VP.
TV-CATV only.
Specializes in fund-raising, direct response adv, direct mail, TV, radio program production, placement & PR for nonprofit organizations.

Reizner & Reizner Film & Video, 7179 Via Maria, San Jose, CA 95139. Phone: (408) 226-6339. Fax: (408) 226-6403. E-mail: dickreizner@worldnet.att.net. Dick Reizner, owner.
TV-CATV only.
Bcst & industrial production in all formats. Certified Legal Video Specialist. Gyrozoom rental.

Reliance Audio Visual Corp., 575 Lexington Ave., New York, NY 10022. Phone: (212) 586-5000. Fax: (914) 237-1004. E-mail: rav@aol.com. Gil M. Meyer, pres; Norma E. Matthews, exec VP.
TV-CATV only.
Audio & video permanent installations, design, video & teleconferencing, consultation, rentals, staging multimedia & video projection, dealerships, leasing, display design.

Response Reward Systems L.C., 1850 Bay Rd., 2-C, Vero Beach, FL 32963. Phone: (772) 234-5449. Fax: (772) 234-5949. E-mail: marcyuk@mpinet.net. Henry Von Kohorn, MBA, Ph.D., CEO.
TV-CATV only.
Patented technology enablling TV viewers in the United States to legally bet, cost-free and risk-free, on the outcome of sports events, from their homes via the Internet.

Reuters Media, 3 Times Sq., 18th Fl., New York, NY 10036. Phone: (646) 223-4300. Fax: (646) 223-4390. Fax: (646) 223-4370. Web Site: www.reuters.com. Richard Sabreen, exec VP.
TV-CATV only.
International news for interactive multimedia news archive for CD-ROM & on-demand applications. Stock photos & film footage.

Reuters Television, 1333 H St. N.W., Washington, DC 20005. Phone: (202) 898-0056. Fax: (202) 898-1236. Web Site: www.reuters.com. John Clarke, editor.
TV-CATV only.
Reuters news & sports svcs include 128 Reuters bureaus, camera crews & a comprehensive satellite network. It serves more than 200 bctrs & their affils in 84 countries. Satellite & news production svcs feature satellite delivery networks. International bcst centers in Moscow, Washington, DC & London. Offers live positions, studio facilities & direct access to the satellite network. Library & program packages cover major news & sporting events.

Rex Recording & Video Post, 1931 S.E. Morrison, Portland, OR 97214. Phone: (503) 238-4525. Fax: (503) 236-8347. E-mail: info@rexpost.com. Web Site: www.rexpost.com. Russell E. Gorsline, pres; Greg Branson, VP/studio mgr.
TV-CATV only.
TV & radio production; audio recording. Video production. CD-ROM, DVD, website.

Richter Productions Inc., 330 W. 42nd St., Suite 2410, New York, NY 10036. Phone: (212) 947-1395. Fax: (212) 643-1208. E-mail: richter330@aol.com. Web Site: www.richtervideos.com. Robert Richter, pres; Amy Kessler, production mgr.
TV-CATV only.
TV program, promotion film production, distribution, film & video.

Riden International Inc., 6024 Paseo Palmilla, Goleta, CA 93117. Phone: (805) 964-7041. Fax: (805) 964-1338. E-mail: rideninc@aol.com. Web Site: www.rideninc.com. Richard Dennison, pres.
TV-CATV only.
TV program production & distribution.

Rigel Entertainment, 4201 Wilshire Blvd., Suite 555, Los Angeles, CA 90010. Phone: (323) 954-8555. Fax: (323) 954-8592. E-mail: info@rigel.tv. John Laing, pres/CEO; Kristie Smith, sls.
TV-CATV only.
Offers international TV, video rights to TV series, MOWs, specials & feature films.

Producers, Distributors, and Production Services Alphabetical Index

River City Video Productions, Box 310601, New Braunfels, TX 78131-0601. Phone: (830) 625-3474. Fax: (830) 625-3710. Web Site: www.fishingandoutdoor.com. Deborah J. Dougherty, pres.
TV-CATV only.
Mktg, instructional & promotional videos & TV commercials.

Roberts Communications Network Inc., 4175 Cameron St., Suite B-10, Las Vegas, NV 89103. Phone: (702) 227-7500. Fax: (702) 227-7501. Tommy Roberts, chmn; Todd Roberts, pres/CEO.
TV-CATV only.
C-Bond satellite transponder capacity, uplinking, encoding & decoding. 50 Channel "Direct To Home" Platform

Rockey Hill and Knowlton, (A division of the Rockey Co.) 2121 Fifth Ave., Seattle, WA 98121. Phone: (206) 728-1100. Fax: (206) 728-1106. Web Site: www.rockey-seattle.com.
Corporate & financial film production. Public relations.

Peter Rodgers Organization, 1800 N. Highland Ave., #412, Hollywood, CA 90028. Phone: (323) 962-1778. Fax: (323) 962-7174. E-mail: profilms@ixpres.com. Web Site: www.profilms.com. Stephen Rodgers, CEO; Teresa Rouse, CFO; Roaul Peter Mongilardi, dir opns.
TV-CATV only.
Celebrating its 26th year representing over 30 productions, companies & independent producers. Consultants, distributors, reps. Over 2,000 hours of progmg.

Romano & Associates Inc., 5094 Dorsey Hall Dr., Suite 104, Ellicott City, MD 21042. Phone: (410) 730-4133. Fax: (410) 730-2219. Web Site: www.racommunications.com. Jim Carroll, VP; Neil Romano, dir & producer.
TV-CATV only.
Full-svc production company specializing in issue-oriented short-feature films & documentaries, PSAs; professional of children's educ videos & comls.

Rose Entertainment, 5529 McLennan Ave., Encino, CA 91436. Phone: (818) 817-7554. Fax: (818) 817-7585. E-mail: rosenter@pacbell.net. Rosamaria Gonzalez, pres; Flory Quiroa, opns mgr.
TV-CATV only.
TV progmg distribution company for Latin America.

Rosler Creative, 88 Howard St., # 2307, San Francisco, CA 94105. Phone: (415) 896-1414. Fax: (415) 896-1616. E-mail: Peter@RoslerCreative.com. Web Site: www.roslercreative.com. Peter Rosler, owner.
San Francisco, CA 94105. San Francisco, CA, 88 Howard St, 2307. Phone: (415) 896-1414. Peter Resler. (Owner).
Radio Only.
TV comls, creative dev & production.
TV-CATV only.

Rosnay International, 6 Rue Robert Estienne, Paris 75008. France. Phone: 01.42.89.18.54. Fax: 01.42.25.34.39. E-mail: fronet3038@aol.com.
TV-CATV only.
Distribution & production company.

Steve Rotfeld Productions Inc., 610 Old Lancaster Rd., Suite 210, Bryn Mawr, PA 19010. Phone: (610) 520-0671. Fax: (610) 520-0681. Web Site: www.rotfeldproductions.com. Steve Rotfeld, pres/exec producer.
TV-CATV only.
A TV production company that produces & syndicates TV shows.

Jack Rourke Productions, Box 1705, Burbank, CA 91507. Phone: (818) 843-4839.
TV-CATV only.
TV & radio program production.

Rysher Entertainment, 2401 Colorado Ave., Suite 200, Santa Monica, CA 90404. Phone: (310) 309-5200. Web Site: www.rysher.com.
Chicago, IL 60611, 625 N. Michigan Ave, Suite 500. Phone: (312) 751-5425. Fax: (312) 644-5179. Cynthia Irving, VP Midwest adv sls.
New York, NY 10017, One Dag Hammarskjold Plaza, 885 2nd Ave, 30th Fl. Phone: (212) 750-9190. Fax: (212) 838-4696. Ira Bernstein, exec VP; Rick Meril, sr VP syndication.
Irving, TX 75039, 6311 N. O'Connor Blvd, Suite N32, LB 121. Phone: (214) 869-7672. Fax: (214) 869-7657. Mark Lipps, VP Southwest sls; Chris Weis, dir Southwest sls.
TV-CATV only.
Producer & distributor of first-run programs.

S

SATVIEW PLUS, 723 Richmond Ave., Staten Island, NY 10302. Phone: (718) 876-7929. Fax: (718) 876-7928.
TV-CATV only.
Satellite-delivered video distribution svcs for both corporations & nonprofit institutions.

SCOLA, 21557 270th St, McClelland, IA 51548. Phone: (712) 566-2202. Fax: (712) 566-2502. E-mail: scola@scola.org. Web Site: www.scola.org. Francis Lajba, pres; John Millar, VP; Dan Pike, telecommunications mgr; Steve Van Outry, chief engr; Rosalie Soloth, coord/accounting.
TV-CATV only.
Satellite retransmission of TV news & educ progmg from 76 countries in original languages for schools & cables.

SESAC Inc., 55 Music Sq. E., Nashville, TN 37203. Phone: (615) 320-0055. Fax: (615) 329-9627. Web Site: www.sesac.com. William Valez, COO.
London W1H 3FF, 6 Kenrick Pl. Phone: (020) 7486-9994. Fax: (020) 7486-9929. Dr. Wayne Bickerton.
Santa Monica, CA 90401, 501 Santa Monica Blvd, Suite 450. Phone: (310) 393-9671. Fax: (310) 393-6497. Pat Rogers, Sr VP - Writer /Publisher Relations.
New York, NY 10019, 152 W. 57th St., 5th Fl. Phone: (212) 484-0600. Fax: (212) 489-5699. Stephen Swid, Freddie Gershon, Ira Smith, Co-Chmn.
Music rights organization representing the performance rights of affil composers, authors & publishers.

SFP Productions, 2 Ave. de L' Europe, 94360 Bry-Sur-Marne Cedex France. Phone: 3316 9833 602. Fax: 0033 11498 33604. E-mail: distribution@sfr.fr. Web Site: www.sfp.fr. Roland Fiszel, CEO; Sophie Vtueite, sls dir.
Distribution worldwide rights (TV movies, series, mini-series documentaries).

SPI International, 55 White St., Suite 1A, New York, NY 10013. Phone: (212) 673-5103. Fax: (212) 673-5183. Web Site: www.spiintl.com. Loni Farhi, pres; Stacey Sobel, VP.
TV-CATV only.
SPI International is an independent distribution company, supplying a wide variety of quality progmg worldwide. SPI specializes in programs with broad global appeal: light entertainment, game shows & animation.

SWTV Production Services Inc., Box 63370, Phoenix, AZ 85082-2013. Phone: (480) 707-1000. Fax: (480) 707-1010. E-mail: jtaylor@swtv.net. Web Site: www.coredigitaltech.com. Scott Barler, pres/CEO.
TV-CATV only.
Mobile TV production.

Sak Entertainment, 398 W. Amelia St., Orlando, FL 32801. Phone: (407) 648-0001. Fax: (407) 648-1333. E-mail: info@sak.com. Web Site: www.sak.com. David Russell, mgng & artistic dir.
TV-CATV only.
Professional comedy actors, dirs, producers & writers. Entertainment consultants for WDW, Universal Studio, Harrahs Corp. & Busch Gardens.

Salter Street Films International Ltd., 1668 Barrington St., Suite 500, Halifax, NS B3J 2A2. Canada. Phone: (902) 420-1577. Fax: (902) 425-8260. Web Site: www.salter.com. Paul Donovan, pres.
International distribution of film, video & TV progmg.

Sanctuary Records Group Ltd., Sanctuary House, 45-53 Sinclair Rd., London W14 0NS. United Kingdom. Phone: 44-020-7602-6351. Fax: 44-020-7603-5941. E-mail: info@sanctuarygroup.com. Web Site: www.sanctuarygroup.com. Brian Leafe,.
TV-CATV only.
Program production & sale.

Edward Sarson Productions, 30 Duke St., Suite 511, Kitchener, ON N2H 3W5. Canada. Phone: (519) 576-1824. Fax: (519) 740-6766. George Sarson, pres.
Producers for the *Toad Patrol* TV series.

The Saturday Evening Post Television Department, (Benjamin Franklin Literary & Medical Society). 1100 Waterway Blvd., Indianapolis, IN 46202. Phone: (317) 634-1100. Fax: (317) 637-0126. E-mail: q.lee@satevepost.com. Web Site: www.satevepost.org. Quinton Lee, dir TV.
TV-CATV only.
Producers & distributors of health shows for radio & TV; commercial production.

SB Management, 890 Monterey, Box 12837, San Luis Obispo, CA 93406. Phone: (805) 543-9214. Fax: (805) 543-9243. E-mail: michael@mikehesser.com. Web Site: www.mikehesser.com. Mike Hesser, pres.
Radio Only.
Consulting & coaching for sls & mgmt.

Scottish Television Ltd., 200 Renfield St., Glasgow G2 3PR. Phone: 011-44-141-300-3000. Fax: 011-44-141-300-3030. Web Site: www.scottishtv.co.uk.
TV-CATV only.
Bcstr & production company.

The Seattle Video Bureau, Box 99218, Seattle, WA 98199. Phone: (206) 448-2500. Fax: (206) 378-1700. E-mail: dave@seattlevideo.com. Web Site: www.seattlevideo.com. David Oglevie, pres.
TV-CATV only.
Location video production for bcst news, corporate & industrial, mktg, & medical. BETACAM SP, & DVCAM, NTSC or PAL formats.

Semaphore Entertainment Group, 32 E. 57th St., New York, NY 10022. Phone: (212) 371-8650. Fax: (212) 888-8650. Web Site: www.seg.com.
TV-CATV-Radio.
TV program production, radio program production & distribution.

SeniorVision Productions, Inc., 418 North Central St., East Bridgewater, MA 02333. Phone: (508) 350-9700. Web Site: www.seniorvision.com. Steve Brown, co-owner; Noah Brookoff, co-owner.
TV-CATV only.
Full-svc video production company offering all aspects of program dev, creation & implementation bcst, S.I.V., corporate.

Seraphim Communications Inc., 1568 Eustis St., St. Paul, MN 55108. Phone: (651) 645-9173. Fax: (651) 645-3515. E-mail: info@seracomm.com. Web Site: www.seracomm.com. Hal Dragseth, pres; Kristin Wiersma, VP.
TV-CATV only.
Full-svc video & AV capabilities. Emphasis on video production from concept through final product. In-house grahics, interactive Web, CD-ROM/DVD.

Sesame Workshop, One Lincoln Plaza, New York, NY 10023. Phone: (212) 595-3456. Fax: (212) 875-6111. Web Site: www.sesameworkshop.org. Gary Knell, pres.
TV-CATV only.
TV program production.

Seven Network Australia Inc., 10100 Santa Monica Blvd., Suite 2060, Los Angeles, CA 90067. Phone: (310)-553-3345. Fax: (310) 553-4812. Zane Bair, gen mgr; Mike Amor, bureau chief.
TV-CATV only.
U.S. office & news bureau of Channel 7, Australia—a major coml TV network of Australia.

1776 Productions, 5 Sparrow Dr., Livingston, NJ 07039. Phone: (973) 533-0762. Fax: (973) 992-1010. E-mail: nce@rcn.com. Ralph Weisinger, pres.
Promotional film production.

Seville Pictures, (division of Behaviour Entertainment Inc.). 150 Eglington Ave. E., Suite 804, Toronto, ON M4P 1E8. Canada. Phone: (416) 480-0453. Fax: (416) 480-0501. E-mail: 1ufor@seville.com. Web Site: www.seville.com. Pierre Brousseau, pres; Andrew Austin, sr VP; David Reckziegel, pres.
Seville pictures is involved in production and distribution of multimedia content for film, TV, video & on-line communication marketplace.

Sam Shad Productions, Box 10853, Reno, NV 89510. Phone: (775) 857-2244. Fax: (775) 857-2272. E-mail: sam@shad.reno.nv.us. Web Site: www.bestofreno.tv. Sam Shad, pres; Bonnie McCorkle, program dev.
TV-CATV only.
Radio progmg & coml production, TV progmg & coml production, TV & radio progmg concepts dev from start to finish, internet design & adv, public relations.

Shadow Broadcast Services, (dba Traffic Scan Network, Inc.). 7707 Waco Ave., Baton Rouge, LA 70806-1440. Phone: (225) 926-7152. Fax: (225) 923-0704. E-mail: johnny@shadowbroadcast.com. Johnny Ahysian, gen mgr.
TV-CATV only.
Traf, news, sports & weather reports for radio, TV & cable systems.

Producers, Distributors, and Production Services Alphabetical Index

Harvey Sheldon Productions, 7855 E. Horizon View Dr., Anaheim Hills, CA 92808. Phone: (714) 281-5929. Fax: (714) 281-5929. Harvey Sheldon, pres.
TV-CATV only.
Daily or wkly classic rock/swing video format for TV & cable stns. On Century Cable available for syndication serving 150,000 TV/cable households in Los Angeles/Orange county.

Shield Productions Inc., 11964 N Lake Dr., Boynton Beach, FL 33436. Phone: (561) 734-5599. Fax: (561) 734-8176. James C. Dolan, pres.
TV-CATV only.
Creation & production of radio & TV comls.

Shukovsky English Entertainment, 4605 Lankershim Blvd., Suite 510, North Hollywood, CA 91602. Phone: (818) 763-9191. Fax: (818) 763-9878. Joel Shukovsky, pres; Diane English, producer.
TV-CATV only.
Producer & distributor of TV progmg, especially half-hour comedy.

Sidewater Enterprises Inc., 2647 Laurel Pass, Los Angeles, CA 90046. Phone: (310) 358-4960. Fax: (323) 656-7853. E-mail: fredericsid@aol.com. Frederic M. Sidewater, pres; Rosalyn G. Sidewater, exec VP.
TV-CATV only.
Consulting regarding financing & distribution for independent productions.

Silverline Pictures, 22837 Ventura Blvd., Ste. 205, Woodland Hills, CA 91364. Phone: (818) 225-9032. Fax: (818) 225-9053. E-mail: silverline@earthlink.net. Web Site: www.silverlinepictures.com. Leman Cetiner, CEO; Axel Munch, pres.
TV-CATV only.
Full-svc production & distribution company producing theatrical, TV & kids series.

Silverman Productions Inc., 106 E. Cary St., Richmond, VA 23219. Phone: (804) 343-1934. Fax: (804) 343-1938. E-mail: donald@silvermstockfootage.com. Web Site: www.silvermanstockfootage.com. Donald Silverman, pres.
TV-CATV-Radio.
Cityscase, arch val, nature & stock footage.

Sing for Joy/WCAL, Saint Olaf College, 1520 Saint Olaf Ave, Northfield, MN 55057. Phone: (612) 798-9225. Fax: (612) 798-8614. E-mail: wcal@stolaf.edu. Web Site: www.singforjoy.com. Rev. W. Bruce Benson, host/producer.
Radio Only.
Sacred choral works with host comments relating the texts to the current scriptural lessons of the ecumenical church year.

Skywatch Weather Center, 347 Prestley Rd., Bridgeville, PA 15017. Phone: (412) 221-6000. Phone: (800)-SKYWATCH. Fax: (412) 221-3160. E-mail: airsci@skyweather.com. Web Site: www.skywatchweather.com. Stanley J. Penkala, pres; Daniel Krzywiecki, VP.
TV-CATV only.
Specially formatted weathercasts produced in the Skywatch Weather Center®.

Smith/Lee Productions, Inc., 7420 Manchester Rd., St. Louis, MO 63143. Phone: (314) 647-3900. Fax: (314) 647-3959. E-mail: global@smithlee.com. Web Site: www.smithlee.com. David Smith, pres; Barry Lee, VP.
TV-CATV only.
TV & radio coml promotional film production; production svcs; studio specializing in Audio Post; music production, voice recording & multimedia.

P. Allen Smith Gardens, Box 7347, Little Rock, AR 72217. Phone: (501) 376-1894. Fax: (501) 376-1896. Web Site: www.pallensmith.com. P. Allen Smith, pres.
TV-CATV only.
Nationally syndicated gardening & lifestyle news inserts reported by professional garden designer Allen Smith.

Soldiers Radio & Television, U.S. Army Public Affairs, 2320 Mill Rd., Suite 100, Alexandria, VA 22314. Phone: (703) 325-5535. Fax: (703) 325-5806. E-mail: srtv@us.army.mil. Web Site: www.army.mil/srtv. Clark Taylor, dir; Jose Velazquez, opns mgr; Gene Gunderson, chief engr; Carolyn Pitt, opns mgr; Melody Day, mktg.
TV-CATV only.
Radio & TV news bureau, soldiers radio network. *Army Newswatch*, a biweekly TV newscast.

Solid Gospel Network (Reach Satellite Network, Inc.), 402 BNA Drive, Suite 400, Nashville, TN 37217. Phone: (615) 367-2210. E-mail: info@SalemMusicNetwork.com. Web Site: www.SalemMusicNetwork.com. Michael S. Miller, gen mgr; Don Burns, progmg dir; Wade Schoenemann, opns mgr; Ed Evensen, Local Traffic Manager; Jim Black, director of Affiliate Relations; Rick Shelton, mgr.
Radio Only.
24-hour, satellite delivered, Christian country and southern gospel network, featuring artists like Gold City, Jeff & Sheri Easter, and the Martins, live from Nashville, the Christian music capital of the world.

Sony Pictures Entertainment, Sony Pictures Plaza, 10202 W. Washington Blvd., Culver City, CA 90232. Phone: (310) 244-4000. Fax: (310) 244-2626. Web Site: www.spesony.com. John Calley, pres.
Atlanta, GA 30309, 1201 W. Peachtree St, 4820. Phone: (404) 892-2725. Susan Grant, VP, southeastern rgn.
Chicago, IL 60611, 455 N. Cityfront Plaza Dr, Suite 3120. Phone: (312) 644-0770. Fax: (312) 644-0781. Stuart Walker, div mgr midwestern rgnl; Tom Cauldo, acct exec.
New York, NY 10022, 711 Fifth Ave. Phone: (212) 702-2920. Fax: (212) 702-6239. Terry Mackin, VP/syndication, eastern rgn.
Dallas, TX 75225, 8117 Preston Rd, Suite 510. Phone: (214) 987-3671. Joe Kissack, mgr syndication southwestern rgn.
TV-CATV only.

SoperSound Music Library, Box 869, Ashland, OR 97520. Phone: (800) 227-9980. Fax: (541) 552-0832. E-mail: info@sopersound.com. Web Site: www.sopersound.com. Dennis Reed, pres.
TV-CATV only.
Contemp music library for all production needs. Available on CDs & direct digital down load online.

Sound*Bytes, 1425 Hopkins St. N.W., Suite 401, Washington, DC 20036. Phone: (202) 296-2022. E-mail: press@soundbytesradio.com. Web Site: www.soundbytesradio.com. Jan Ziff, pres.
Radio Only.
Computer audio show production & syndication.

Sound Idea Productions, 417 Nursery St., Nevada City, CA 95959. Phone: (510) 832-5178. Fax: (510) 832-4829. E-mail: soundidea@oro.net. Glenn Davidson, pres.
Oakland, CA 94612, 405 14th St, Suite 612. Phone: (530) 478-9770.
Radio Only.
Archival Service. Radio production & syndication.

Sound Ideas, 105 W. Beaver Creek Rd., Suite 4, Richmond Hill, ON L4B 1C6. Canada. Phone: (905) 886-5000. Phone: (800) 387-3030. Fax: (905) 886-6800. E-mail: info@sound-ideas.com. Web Site: www.sound-ideas.com. Brian Nimens, pres/CEO; Mike Bell, VP.
TV-CATV only.
Royalty free sound effects, imaging elements & music for the professional audio industry; including bcst, cable, film, multimedia & internet applications.

Sound of Birmingham Productions, 3625 5th Ave. S., Birmingham, AL 35222. Phone: (205) 595-8497. Don Mosley, pres; Betty Mosley, VP/off mgr.
TV-CATV only.
Radio & TV voice-overs, jingles, video sweetening, custom music, recording studios, full-svc studios, ISDN.

Sound Source Networks, 2 St. Clair Ave. W., 11th Fl., Toronto, ON M4V 1L6. Canada. Phone: (416) 922-1290. Fax: (416) 323-6819. E-mail: info@soundsource.ca. Web Site: www.soundsource.ca. Jean Marie Heimrath, pres & gen mgr; Lesley Soldat, VP opns.
Radio Only.
Radio net that produces, markets & distributes radio programs nationally.

Soundshop Recording Studio LLC, 1307 Division St., Nashville, TN 37203. Phone: (615) 244-4149. Fax: (615) 242-8759. E-mail: soundshopstudio@aol.com. Mike bradley, owner; Don Cook, owner.
TV-CATV only.
Music production, recording studios, 2-48 track digital or 24 track analog studios.

Soundtrack, 162 Columbus Ave., Boston, MA 02116-5222. Phone: (617) 303-7500. Fax: (617) 303-7555. Web Site: www.soundtrackboston.com. Jeanne Priest, mgr.
New York, NY 10010, 936 Broadway. Phone: (212) 420-6010. Chris Rich, opns mgr.
Production, postproduction & custom music of all kinds; specializing in sound designs.

Southcott Productions, Box 33185, Granada Hills, CA 91394. Phone: (818) 368-4938. Fax: (818) 368-4938. E-mail: csouthcott@aol.com. Web Site: www.musicofyourlife.com. Chuck Southscott, owner.
Radio Only.
Radio program, coml production & distribution.

Southern STAR, Phone: 612 9519 2677. Fax: 612 9517 2530. E-mail: info@duplitek.com.au. Web Site: www.southern-star.com.au. Neil Balnaves; Errol Sullivan, chief exec entertainment; Robyn Watts, chief exec sls.
TV-CATV only.
Southern Star is an integrated film & TV production distribution & manufacturing group. Southern Star is a public listed company.

Spanish Broadcasting System, 26 W. 56th St., New York, NY 10019. Phone: (212) 541-9200. Fax: (212) 541-6904. Web Site: www.lamusica.com. Raul Alarcon, CEO; Carey Davis, VP/gen mgr; Joseph A. Garcia, CFO.
Radio Only.
Spanish progmg syndication.

Spelling Television Inc., 5700 Wilshire Blvd., Suite 575, Los Angeles, CA 90036. Phone: (323) 965-5700. Fax: (323) 965-5895. Aaron Spelling, chmn of bd; E. Duke Vincent, Vice-chmn; Jonathan Levin, pres.
TV-CATV only.
TV program production.

Charlie Spencer Productions, 107 Jensen Cir., West Springfield, MA 01089-4451. Phone: (413) 737-7600. Fax: (413) 737-7600 (Voice First). E-mail: cspencer@mail.map.com. Charlie Spencer, producer & dir.
TV-CATV only.
Specializes in nature & environmental progmg, as well as outdoor recreation & nature travel. Svcs include consulting, producing, directing, rsch, writing & narration. Progms include *Gardening with Wildflowers*, *The Urban Canoeist* & *American Waste*.

Sport International Inc., Villa del Mar East, 14 J Ave. Isla Verde, Carolina, PR 00979. Phone: (787) 268-8751. Fax: (787) 726-7683. E-mail: hector@hjfsport.com. Web Site: www.hjfsport.com. Hector Figueroa, chmn of bd; Juliet Giamartino, co-chmn; Jennifer Marin, VP event sls & production.
TV-CATV only.
Global mktg, distribution, bcstg, sports events, Pay-Per-View & special entertainment progmg. Current properties include: *This Day in Sports*, *Wide World of Bloopers*, live buying & buying documentaries.

Sports Byline U.S.A., 300 Broadway, Suite 8, San Francisco, CA 94133. Phone: (415) 434-8300. Fax: (415) 391-2569. E-mail: byline@pacbell.net. Web Site: www.sportsbyline.com. Ron Barr, chmn; Darren Peck, pres; Alex Murillo, exec producer.
Radio Only.
Satellite-delivered nationwide radio sports talk network, listener 800 number, 7days (West Coast), barter.

StarDate/Universo, University of Texas at Austin, 2609 University Ave., Suite 3118, Austin, TX 78712. Phone: (512) 471-5285. Fax: (512) 471-5060. E-mail: perez@stardate.org. Web Site: www.stardate.org. Sandra Preston, exec producer; Damond Benningfield, producer.
Radio Only.
Syndicated two-minute radio programs on stars & planets visible in the night sky. Each program is date-specific. English/Spanish.

Charles H Stern Agency Inc., 1999 Ave. of the Stars, Suite 1400, Los Angeles, CA 90267. Phone: (310) 788-4570.
TV-CATV-Radio.
Radio coml production & distribution. Represents a variety of TV & radio personalities.

Steven B. Stevens, 7400 Sweetwater Branch, West Chester, OH 45069. Phone: (513) 755-7300. Fax: (513) 755-7507. E-mail: sbstevens@aol.com. Steven B. Stevens, pres.
TV-CATV only.
Accomplished narrator/voice talent with deep warm authoratative voice.

Marty Stouffer Productions Ltd., 44190 Hwy. 82 E., Aspen, CO 81611. Phone: (970) 925-5536. Fax: (970) 920-3820. E-mail: mary@stoufferoffice.com.
TV-CATV only.
TV program production.

Producers, Distributors, and Production Services Alphabetical Index

Strand Media Group Inc., 12240 Venice Blvd., Suite 23, Los Angeles, CA 90066. Phone: (310) 390-2248. Fax: (310) 390-2857. E-mail: strandmg@aol.com. Web Site: www.somethingyoushouldknow.net. Mike Carruthers, pres.
Radio Only.
Radio programs, coml production & distribution; media buying agent.

Strength for Living, 6350 W. Freeway, Fort Worth, TX 76116. Phone: (817) 570-1400. Phone: (800) 266-1837. Fax: (817) 737-9436. E-mail: info@familynet.org. Web Site: www.familynetradio.com. Lisa Bratton, radio mkktg & distribution; Donna Senn, radio distribution; Chuck Ries, producer.
Radio Only.
Offers audiences relevant messages of hope & spiritual encouragement in their search to find strength for living. Host Bob Reccord.

M C Stuart & Associates Pty Ltd., 2/34 Power St., Balwyn Victoria 03103. Phone: 61 3 9888 5835. Phone: 61 409 885 831 (mobile). Fax: 61 3 9888 5831. Max Stuart, mgng dir & sec.
TV-CATV only.
Worldwide TV & feature film distributors.

Studio Babelsberg GmbH, August-Bebel-St. 26-53, 14482 Potsdam Germany. Phone: 49 (0) 331-72 -13151. Fax: 49 (0) 331-72-12525. E-mail: info@studiobabelsberg.com. Web Site: www.studiobabelsberg.de. Gerhard Bergfried, CEO.
TV-CATV only.
Studio area, studio technology, set design & construction, film laboratory, postproduction, dubbing theatres for films, TV & video.

Studio Center Corp., 200 W. 22nd St., Norfolk, VA 23517. Phone: (757) 622-2111. Fax: (757) 623-5512. E-mail: info@studiocenter.com. Web Site: www.studiocenter.com. Warren Miller, CEO & exec producer.
Las Vegas, CA 89103, 3875 S. Jones Blvd. Phone: (702) 248-2777. Fax: (702) 248-5400. John McClain, Gen Mgr.
Memphis, TN 38112, 2693 Union Ave. Ext. Phone: (901)323-7060. Fax: (901) 320-0003. Sheldon Borgelt.
TV-CATV only.
Radio comls, stn promotions, TV voice-over svcs.

Studio M Productions Unlimited, 4032 Wilshire Blvd., Suite 403, Los Angeles, CA 90010. Phone: (213) 389-7372. Fax: (213) 389-3299. E-mail: soundmxr@earthlink.net. Web Site: www.mandy.com/stu001.html. Mike Michaels, owner/sr engr/producer; Hugo Buehring, progmg mgr.
Los Angeles, CA 90038, 4032 Wilshire Blvd Suite 403. Phone: (213) 389-7372. (888) 389-7372. Fax: (213) 389-3299.
TV-CATV only.
TV & radio program production, tape, film & live production svcs. Live remotes for TV, radio, news & sports.

Suite Audio, 21 Stone Wall Ln., Clinton, CT 06413. Phone: (860) 664-9499. E-mail: info@suiteaudio.com. Web Site: www.suiteaudio.com. Bob Nary, owner/pres.
Clinton, CT 06413. Clinton, CT, 21 Stonewall Ln. Bob Nary, owner.
TV-CATV only.
Facility: ProTools HDII/TDM, Waves restoration & Platinum, Sonic Solutions. Commercial - Program - surround production. CD mastering - authoring - duplication. Cassette duplication.

Sullivan Entertainment Inc./Sullivan Entertainment International, 110 Davenport Rd., Toronto, ON M5R 3R3. Canada. Phone: (416) 921-7177. Fax: (416) 921-7538. Web Site: www.sullivan-ent.com.
London United Kingdom. Sullivan Entertainment Europe Ltd, Savant House, 63-65 Camden High St. Phone: (207) 383-5192. Muriel Thomas, sr VP intl sls.
TV-CATV only.
Production, distribution, home video, dev series & feature film.

Sullivan Video Services Inc., 7 Pickman Dr., Bedford, MA 01730. Phone: (781) 271-1720. Fax: (781) 271-1740. E-mail: johnsul@sull. Web Site: www.sullivanvideo.com. John M. Sullivan, pres.
TV-CATV only.
Full-svc video production company. Provides ENG/EFP news crews & Ku-band satellite svcs, Fiber Optic Studio Tape feeding capabilities.

Pat Summerall Productions, 2105 Waterview Pkwy, Richardson, TX 75080. Phone: (972) 907-2525. Fax: (972) 669-0677. Robert B May Jr., pres/CEO.
TV-CATV only.
Ind video production company offering Beta SP shooting, creative, video conferencing, video editing & duping svcs. Producer of natl cable TV programming.

The Summit Media Group Inc. (Sub 4 Kids Entertainment), 1414 Ave. of the Americas, New York, NY 10019. Phone: (212) 754-4900. Fax: (212) 754-5480. E-mail: shirsch@4kidsent.com. Alfred Kahn, chmn.
TV-CATV only.
Distribution of programs in the United States with emphasis on programs for children.

Sunbow Entertainment, 100 5th Ave., Fl. 3, New York, NY 10011. Phone: (212) 893-1600. Fax: (212) 893-1630. Web Site: www.tvloonland.com. Suzanne Berman, dir creative affrs; Rebecca Gallivan, opns dir.
TV-CATV only.
Developers, producers & distributors of quality children's & family programs, licensors & merchandise.

Sundial Productions, 275 Huyler St., S. Hackensack, NJ 07606. Phone: (201) 525-5100. Fax: (201) 525-5111. Jack Kreismer, Principal; David Lapidus, Principal.
Radio Only.
Voice production company; radio & telephone feature production.

SunGard Output Solutions, 350 Automation Way, Irondale, AL 35210. Phone: (205) 307-6713. Fax: (205) 307-6813. E-mail: jamey.vella@sungard.com. Web Site: www.sungard.com. Joseph Harper, pres; Jamey Vella, natl sls exec.
TV-CATV-Radio.
SunGard's document distribution output channels include: paper, electronic (ebill/email), optical and/ or magnetic media.

Swell Pictures Inc., 455 N. City Front Plaza, 18th Fl., Chicago, IL 60611. Phone: (312) 464-8000. Fax: (312) 464-8020. Web Site: www.swellinc.com. Michael Topel, pres; Joe Flores, sr VP/chief engr; Brian Clark, exec VP; Dave Mueller, VP client svcs; Radi Akel, opns mgr.
TV-CATV only.
Film-to-tape transfer, videotape editing, digital sound editing & original music. Avid, 3-D graphics & compositing, audio & new media.

System TV, 45/47 rue Paul Bert, 92100 Boulogne, Paris France. Phone: (33)-1-55-38-2020. Fax: (33)-1-55-38-20-30. E-mail: daniel@systemtv.fr. Web Site: www.systemtv.fr. Daniel Renoug, pres.
TV-CATV only.
TV program production, press agency, produce weather & info svcs.

T

TM Century Inc., 2002 Academy Ln., Dallas, TX 75234. Phone: (972) 406-6800. Fax: (972) 406-6890. E-mail: tmci@tmcentury.com. Web Site: www.tmcentury.com. David Graupner, pres/CEO.
TV-CATV only.
TMC creates, produces & distributes music-based products for broadcast, including compilation libraries, production music, I.D. packages & commercial jingles.

TRF Production Music Libraries, 747 Chestnut Ridge Rd., Chestnut Ridge, NY 10977. Phone: (800) 899-MUSIC. Phone: (845) 356-0800. Fax: (845) 356-0895. E-mail: info@trfmusic.com. Web Site: www.trfmusic.com. Michael Nurko, pres/CEO.
TV-CATV only.
More than 50,000 selections (4,000 discs) of both contemporary & traditional music. Includes Dennis Music, MP PAN, PowerSound, Pyramid, Supraphon, TRF Alpha, Cobra, Kool Kat, Spain is Music, Adrenalin, Bravo & Stock Music libraries. Also includes complete classical series, sound effects & authentic International Ethnic series.

TR Productions, 209 W. Central St., Suite 108, Natick, MA 01760. Phone: (508) 650-3400. Fax: (508) 650-3455. Web Site: www.trprod.com. Cary M. Benjamin, principal.
TV-CATV only.
Production svcs.

TVOntario, (TVO network, TFO network). Box 200, Stn Q, Toronto, ON M4T 2T1. Canada. Phone: (416) 484-2600. Fax: (416) 484-2662. Web Site: www.tvo.org. Lee Robock, COO; Yuonne Carey-Le, dir.
Educ production, educ bcst international program sls, coproduction.

Talco Productions, 279 E. 44th St., New York, NY 10017. Phone: (212) 697-4015. Fax: (212) 697-4827. E-mail: alaw1@mindspring.com. Alan Lawrence, pres; Marty Holberton, VP.
TV-CATV only.
TV & radio progmg, documentaries, ind & educ production, PR consultation & production.

Talk America Radio Networks, 520 Broad St., Newark, NJ 07102. Phone: (973) 438-3026. Fax: (973) 438-1637. Web Site: www.talkamerica.com. Trang Nguyen, COO; Maurice Bortz, opns VP.
Radio Only.
24-hour talk seven days a week offering live call-in programs. All programs barter & every minute is covered.

Talk Radio Network, (a subsidiary of Premiere Radio Networks). Box 3755, Central Point, OR 97502. Phone: (541) 664-8827. Fax: (541) 664-6250. Web Site: www.talkradionetwork.com. Mark Masters, pres.
Radio Only.
Full-svc live talk radio format 24 hours daily. Serving more than 400 affils nationwide.

Talkline Communications Radio Network, Box 20108, Park West Station, New York, NY 10025-1510. Phone: (212) 769-1925. Fax: (212) 799-4195. E-mail: tcntalk@aol.com. Web Site: www.talklinecommunications.com. Zev J. Brenner, exec producer.
Radio Only.
Natl Jewish radio net. Carried in over 2,500 markets. Contemp Jewish progmg; interview & call-in format with newsmaker guests from politics, entertainment & Israel. Live segments from Israel. Available on barter. Satellite delivered.

Tamouz Media, 37 W. 20th, Suite 1007, New York, NY 10011. Phone: (212) 463-7437. Fax: (212) 463-7409. E-mail: tamouzmedia@aol.com. Web Site: www.tamouz.com. Ilan Ziv, producer.
TV-CATV only.
TV program & documentary production.

Tankersley Productions, Inc., St. Louis, 8022 Venetian Dr., St. Louis, MO 63105. Phone: (314) 725-0116. Fax: (314) 725-5709. E-mail: randy@tankersleyproductions.com. Web Site: www.tankersleyproductions.com. Randy Tankersley, pres.
Full-bcst svcs. ENG/EFP Beta SP crews with/without producers, avid nonlinear editing.

Tapestry International, Ltd., 11 Hanover Sq., 14th Fl., New York, NY 10005. Phone: (212) 505-2288. Fax: (212) 505-5059. E-mail: tunein@tapestry.tv. Nancy L. Walzog, pres; Karen Carlson, dir; Laura Ibanez, sls exec.
TV-CATV only.
Production & distribution company working in the international TV marketplace.

Target Sports Video, 400 E. Lancaster Ave., Wayne, PA 19087. Phone: (610) 688-9233. Fax: (610) 688-2879. E-mail: target@targetsports.com. Web Site: www.targetsports.com. W.W. Orr, pres; Marie Teeters, production coord; David Moore, editor; Steve Pack, editor; Bob Sass, comptroller.
TV-CATV only.
TV & radio coml & promotional film & video production; production svcs.

Technisonic Studios, 500 S. Ewing Ave., Suite G, St. Louis, MO 63103. Phone: (314) 533-1777. Fax: (314) 533-6527. E-mail: mstroot@technisonic.com. Web Site: www.technisonic.com. Mike Stroot,.
TV-CATV only.
16 & 35 mm film production, full-sound studios, video production, film & video editing.

Tel-A-Cast Productions, 1016 Everee Inn Rd., Griffin, GA 30224. Phone: (770) 233-4200. Fax: (770) 233-4247. E-mail: mrenew@osmose.com. Michael Renew, production mgr.
TV-CATV only.
From concept to execution, produces TV & radio comls, training videos, mktg videos & other projects quickly & efficiently.

Tel-Air Interests Inc., 2040 Sherman St., Hollywood, FL 33020. Phone: (954) 924-4949. Fax: (954) 924-4980. E-mail: telair@aol.com. Web Site: www.telairint.com. Grant H. Gravitt Jr., pres; M. L. Gravitt, sec/treas.
TV-CATV only.
Syndicated TV specials (sports & music), contract production, theatrical short subjects & documentary TV & films, infomercials. Digital recording studio, digital & linear editing.

Broadcasting & Cable Yearbook 2006

Producers, Distributors, and Production Services Alphabetical Index

TeleCom Productions Inc., 30 Perimeter Park Dr., Suite 101, Chamblee, Atlanta, GA 30341. Phone: (770) 455-3569. Fax: (770) 455-3938. Web Site: www.tcpatlanta.com. Budd O. Libby, pres; Roger B. Clark, co-chmn; Dan Bower, co-chmn.
TV-CATV-Radio.
Production & syndicator of *Let's Go to the Races, Free Cash Lotto, Daily Race Game* & *Post Time* retail prize promotions; random animated digital drawing systems (RADDS).

Telegenic Programs Inc., 161 Forest Hill Rd., Toronto, ON MSP 2N3. Canada. Phone: (416) 484-8000. Fax: (416) 484-8001. E-mail: telegenic@aol.com. Web Site: www.telegenic.com. H. Lawrence Fein, chmn/CEO; Rhonda Taylor, dir opns.
TV-CATV only.
One of Canada's leading TV distribution & production companies now in its 25th successful year.

Telenium Studios, 525 Mildred Ave., Primos, PA 19018. Phone: (610) 626-6500. Fax: (610) 626-2638. Web Site: www.telenium.com. Todd Strine, CEO; Peter Hayes, mgr; Cathie Hunt, mobile sls.
Philadelphia, PA 19123. Telenium Post, 520 N. Columbus Blvd, Suite 204. Phone: (215) 629-2000. Fax: (219) 625-8353. Mark Reidenaver, dir of post prod.
TV-CATV only.
Studio & location production & postproduction for networks, syndication & cable. Full facilities, production mgmt & creative svcs.

Telepros, Box 1116, Belmont, CA 94002. Phone: (650) 345-0505. E-mail: telepros@comcast.net. Niels Melo, pres.
TV-CATV only.
Producers of live entertainment, sports, news, performing arts, corporate videos and webcasts.

Televents Ltd., 2450 Virginia Ave. N.W., Washington, DC 20037. Phone: (202) 296-0541. Fax: (202) 296-0541. James Avis, mgr.
TV-CATV only.
TV program production & distribution.

Television & Radio Features Inc., 1020 Milwaukee Ave., Deerfield, IL 60015. Phone: (847) 541-7600. Fax: (847) 541-2600. Morton A. Small, pres.
TV-CATV only.
Promotions, prize svcs; mktg.

Television Representatives Inc., 9720 Wilshire Blvd., Suite 202, Beverly Hills, CA 90212-2006. Phone: (310) 278-4050. Fax: (310) 278-3350. Alan Silverbach, pres.
TV-CATV only.
TV program distribution, United States & international.

The Television Syndication Company, Inc., 501 Sabal Lake Dr., Suite 105, Longwood, FL 32779. Phone: (407) 788-6407. Fax: (407) 788-4397. E-mail: tvsco@prodigy.net. Web Site: www.tvsco.com. Cassie M. Yde, pres; Robert E. Yde, dir mktg.
TV-CATV only.
A full-svc TV syndication & distribution organization offering TV progmg to bcstrs worldwide.

Televix Entertainment Inc., 449 S. Beverly Dr., 3rd Fl., Suite 300, Beverly Hills, CA 90212. Phone: (310) 788-5500. Fax: (310) 286-0207. E-mail: postmaster@televix.com. Web Site: www.televix.com. Hugo Rose, CEO; Pamela Popp, sr VP.
TV-CATV only.
Distribution of TV programs in the Latin American & Spanish U.S. markets.

Telfax Inc., 3305 Pleasant Valley Ln., Arlington, TX 76015. Phone: (817) 468-0070. Fax: (817) 468-0111. E-mail: ts4telfax@aol.com. Tony Symanovich, pres.
TV-CATV only.
Remote TV production svcs.

Tepuy, 2745 Ponce de Leon Blvd., Coral Gables, FL 33134. Phone: (305) 774-0033. Fax: (305) 774-7372. Web Site: www.tepuy.com. Marcos Santana, chmn/CEO; Esperanza Garay, VP; Fernando Espejo, dir; Igancio Barrera, exec VP.
Pozuelo de Alarcon 28224 Spain, Via Dos Castillas 9C-P2, 2B. Phone: (3491) 351-7107. Fernando Espeto.
Caracas 1060 Venezuela, Ave. Libertador Torre E, EXA PH-1. Phone: (58212) 953-3363.
TV-CATV only.
Program Distribution.

Danny Thomas Productions, 10100 Santa Monica Blvd., Suite 950, Los Angeles, CA 90067. Phone: (310) 277-4866. Fax: (310) 286-1963. E-mail: anita@dethomasbobo.com. Anita De Thomas, pres.
TV-CATV only.
TV programs, features, coml production.

Thompson Creative, 4631 Insurance Ln., Dallas, TX 75205. Phone: (214) 559-4000. Fax: (214) 521-8578. E-mail: info@thompsoncreative.com. Web Site: www.thompsoncreative.com. J. Larry Thompson, CEO; Susan Price Thompson, pres.
TV-CATV only.
Contemp radio ID jingles for all formats.

Time Capsule Inc., 124 Cottonwood Ln., Centerville, MA 02632. Phone: (800) 822-7785. Fax: (508) 778-5590. E-mail: tc@tcapsule.com. Web Site: www.tcapsule.com. Richard T. Teimer, pres & sls dir; Nancy Q. Proctor, VP affl rel; Bill Stephens, VP special projects.
Radio Only.
System to bring 1,000 more cash ads per year; daily quizzes fit all formats.

Today Video, 475 10th Ave. 10th Fl., New York, NY 11024. Phone: (212) 239-3999. Fax: (212) 239-2999. David Seeger, CEO.
TV-CATV only.
Production svcs.

Toes Production Inc., 22 Hickory Dr., Maplewood, NJ 07040. Phone: (973) 793-5440. Fax: (973) 363-7798. E-mail: phonepatch@aol.com. Brad Abelle, pres.
TV-CATV-Radio.
Brad is a radio talk show host and voice artist.

Tomwil Inc., 4905 Gentry Ave., Valley Village, CA 91607. Phone: (818) 769-0883. Fax: (818) 769-0887. E-mail: tomwil@earthlink.net. James R. Rokos, pres; Wilda A. Rokos, VP.
TV-CATV only.
Distributors of features, light entertainment, sports, series & documentaries to all media in the world market.

Toucan Productions, 315 W. End Ave., Suite 2C, New York, NY 10023. Phone: (212) 580-4882.
TV-CATV only.
Corporate video productions from conception to completion.

Traffic Pulse Networks (A Unit of Mobility Technologies), Moblity Technology - Traffic Pluse Network, 851 Duportail Rd., Suite 220, Wayne, PA 19087. Phone: (610) 725-9700. Fax: (610) 725-0530. E-mail: info@mobility technologies.com. Web Site: www.mobilitytechnologies.com. Doug Alexander, CEO; Jim Brown, VP; Al McGowan, sr VP; Robert Pollan, COO/CFO.
TV-CATV only.
Traffic Pulse Networks provides digital & traditional traffic data to radio, TV & CATV. It also provides an inventory rep service.

The Transcription Company, 4100 W. Burbank Blvd., 3rd Flr., Burbank, CA 91505. Phone: (818) 848-6500. Fax: (818) 556-4150. Web Site: www.transcripts.net. E-mail: customerservice@transcripts.net. Michele Bartmon, dir of admin; Samantha Somers, mgr entertainment transcription.
Newport Beach, CA 92660. Rapidtext Inc., 1801 Dove St, Suite 101. Phone: (949) 399-9200. Glory Johnson, COO & VP.
TV-CATV only.
Transcribe all media: TV shows, films, news, sports, documentaries, meetings interviews. Provide closed captioning. Provide translations. Sell ABC News transcripts.

The Transfer Zone, 13251 Northend, Oak Park, MI 48237-3261. Phone: (248) 548-7580. Fax: (248) 548-0924. E-mail: transferzone@juno.com. Web Site: thetransferzone.com. Roxane B. Newhouse, dir mktg.
TV-CATV only.
International video standard conversions, duplication, film/slide transfers: A-B roll editing, video slide/film. Video to CD & DVD & duplication.

Triage Entertainment Inc., 15260 Ventura Blvd., Suite 700, Sherman Oaks, CA 91403. Phone: (818) 386-6800. Fax: (818) 386-9889. Web Site: www.triageinc.com. Stu Schreiberg, pres; Chris Greenleaf, dev VP; John Bravakis, business mgr; Steve Kroonpnick, exec dev.
TV-CATV only.
Independent, full-svc production company with extensive experience in the production of TV & film; post-production facilities & motion control/graphics department.

Tribune Entertainment Co., 5800 Sunset Blvd., Los Angeles, CA 90028. Phone: (323) 460-5800. Fax: (323) 460-3858. Web Site: www.tribtv.com. Richard H. Askin, pres/CEO; David Berson, sr VP business affairs; Karen Corbin, sr VP progmg & dev; Larry Hutchings, VP; Richard Inouye, VP; Henry Urick, VP mktg; Gina Brittle-Mackey, dir; Taylor Fuller, dir; Seth Howard, dir; Debra McCormick, dir mktg; George NeJame, dir; Natalie Sackin, creative dir & mktg; Jon Krobot, account exec.
Roswell, GA 30076, 1580 Warsaw Rd, Suite 210. Phone: (770) 643-4504. Fax: (770) 643-2549. Samuel K. Fuller, dir, SE rgnl sls.
Chicago, IL 60611, 435 N. Michigan Ave, Suite 1800. Phone: (312) 222-4000. Fax: (312) 222-3815. Michael Adinamis, VP bcst opns; Dick Bailey, dir midwest adviser sls; Jennifer Dreyer, acc exec midwest rgnl sls; Jeff McElheney, acc exec midwest rgnl sls.
New York, NY 10017, 220 E. 42nd St, Suite 400. Phone: (212) 210-1000. Fax: (212) 210-1056. Liz Koman, sr VP adv sls; Steve Mulderrig, sr VP/gen sls mgr.
TV-CATV only.
Acquires, develops, produces & distributes progmg for TV including "Gene Roddenberry's Andromeda," "Gene Roddenberry's Earth: Final Conflict," "BeastMaster," Malibu, CA," "Soul Train," "U.S. Farm Report," "Soul Train Music Awards," "Soul Train Lady of Soul Awards," "Soul Train Christmas Starfest," & "Live from the Academy Awards."

Tribune Radio Networks, 435 N. Michigan Ave., Chicago, IL 60611. Phone: (312) 222-3342. Fax: (312) 222-4876. Web Site: www.tribuneradio.com. Mark Krieschen, gen mgr; Barbara Pabst, mgr opns & sports; Jeff Brummel, mgr agriculture sls.
Radio Only.
Tape & internet digital delivered farm, sports & specialty programs including: *Chicago Cubs Network, Agri-Voice, National Farm Report, Farming America, Samuelson's Sez.*

TRI-COMM Productions, (A First Vision Group Co). 11 Palmetto Pkwy., Suite 201, Hilton Head Island, SC 29926-3703. Phone: (843) 681-5000. Fax: (843) 681-2945. Web Site: www.tri-comm.tv. William J. Robinson, pres/CEO.
TV-CATV only.
A full-svc production company specializing in film HD & digital betacam production, sound design, graphics/animation. Also offers sugar sand beaches & the best golf courses around.

Trident Releasing, 8401 Melrose Pl., 2nd Fl., Los Angeles, CA 90069. Phone: (323) 655-8818. Fax: (323) 655-0515. E-mail: tridents@aol.com. Jean Ovrum, chmn; Victoria Plummer, pres; Kristi Mailing, sls VP.
TV-CATV only.
Acquire feature films in the postproduction & completed stages.

Troma Entertainment, Inc., 733 Ninth Ave., New York, NY 10019. Phone: (212) 757-4555. Fax: (212) 399-9885. Web Site: www.troma.com.
TV-CATV only.
Troma is one of the oldest ind film companies in the world. We produce & distribute films & offer stock footage.

Turner Entertainment Co., 1888 Century Park E., 10th Fl., Los Angeles, CA 90067. Phone: (310) 788-6801. Fax: (310) 788-6810. E-mail: roger.mayer@turner.com. Robert L. Mayer, pres/COO.
TV-CATV only.
Sls, licensing & servicing of major film & TV library.

20th Century Fox/Incendo Television Distribution Ltd., 101 Bloor St. W., Suite 400, Toronto, ON M5S 2Z7. Canada. Phone: (416) 643-3897. Fax: (416) 643-3898. Michael Murphy, sr VP; Kimberley Ball, dir mktg; David Heaph, sls dir.
TV-CATV only.
TV program distribution.

Twentieth Century Fox Television Distribution, Box 900, Beverly Hills, CA 90213-0900. Phone: (310) 369-1000. Fax: (310) 369-8892. Web Site: www.foxfast.com. Mark Kaner, pres; Peter Levinshon, pres; Marion Edwards, exec VP.
London WID 3AP. Twentieth Century Fox Television Distribution, 31-32 Soho Square.. Phone: 44-20-7437-7766. Fax: 44-20-7439-1806.
Moore Park, NO 1363 Australia. Fox Studios Australia, Driver Avenue. Phone: 61-8353-2200. Fax: 61-2-8325-2205.
Sao Paulo 04543-121 Brazil. Fox Film Do Brasil Ltda., Rua Dr. EDuardo De Souza Arrrranha, 387-3o Andar. Phone: 5511-3365-5205. Fax: (5511) 3365-5177.
Toronto, ON M5S 2Z7 Canada. Fox/Incendo, 101 Bloor Street West, Suite #400. Phone: 416-643-3897. Fax: 416-643-3907.
Paris 75008 France. Twentieth Century Fox France,

Broadcasting & Cable Yearbook 2006

E-63

Producers, Distributors, and Production Services Alphabetical Index

Inc., TV Division, 21 bis rue Lord Byron. Phone: 33-1-5393-9398. Fax: 33-1-5393-9397.

Pembroke Pines, FL 33028-2867. Twentieth Century Fox Television Distribution, 2000 N.W. 150th Avenue, Suite 1110. Phone: 954-322-5000. Fax: 954-322-5275.
TV-CATV only.
Production & distribution.

Twentieth Television, 2121 Ave. of the Stars, Suite 2100, Los Angeles, CA 90067. Phone: (310) 369-3924. Fax: (310) 369-1506. Web Site: www.fox.com. Bob Cook, pres/COO; David Shall, exec VP; Mark Kaner, pres; Robb Dalton, pres; Bob Cesa, exec VP.

New York, NY 10036. Twentieth Television, 1211 Avenue of the Americas 16th Fl. Bob Cesa, exec VP adv sls & cable progmg sls.
TV-CATV only.
Produces & distributes progmg for network TV & domestic & international TV markets.

Two Oceans Entertainment Group, 15250 Ventura Blvd., Suite 800, Sherman Oaks, CA 91403. Phone: (818) 501-6550. Fax: (818) 501-6558. E-mail: twoceans@aol.com. Meryl Marshall, pres; Susan Whittaker, dev VP.
TV-CATV only.
Domestic & international TV production. Most recent—*When Danger Follows You Home, Baby Monitor, Sound of Fear, Happily Ever After, Fairy Tales For Every Child*.

U

UBC Radio, 230 Ohio St., Suite 101, Chicago, IL 60611. Phone: (312) 640-5000. Phone: (312) 751-0135. Fax: (312) 640-5010. Bradley Saul, CEO; Ron Gleason, pres.
Radio Only.
Talk radio long form progmg plus short form features.

U.S. Plan B Inc., 466 Orange St., Suite 280, Redlands, CA 92374. Phone: (818) 998-8833. Phone: (888) 877-5262. Fax: (702) 926-2532. E-mail: office@usplanb.com. Web Site: www.usplanb.com. Marc Curtis, producer.
TV-CATV only.
TV news gathering & production crews, stock footage, rsch.

Ukrainian Melody Hour, Box 2257, Washington, DC 20013. Phone: (202) 529-7606. Phone: (202) 269-1824. Fax: (202) 638-5995. Roman V. Marynowych, producer & dir; Odile E. Marynowych, exec sec.
TV-CATV only.
Ukrainian radio, TV & cable program productions.

United Learning Co., 1560 Sherman Ave., Suite 100, Evanston, IL 60201. Phone: (847) 328-9084. Fax: (847) 328-6706. E-mail: joel.altschul@unitedlearning.com. Web Site: www.unitedlearning.com. Joel Altschul, chmn.
TV-CATV only.
Educ programs, series & documentaries, videos & curriculums, streaming.

United Methodist Communications, 810 - 12th Ave. S., Nashville, TN 37203. Phone: (615) 742-5400. Fax: (615) 742-5125. E-mail: lalexander@umcom.org. Web Site: www.umcom.org. Larry Hollon, sec; Jeneane Jones, dir TV progmg.
TV-CATV only.
TV & radio production & distribution.

United Sound Systems Inc., 15849 Wyoming St., Detroit, MI 42838. Phone: (313) 340-4200. Fax: (313) 832-5666.
TV-CATV-Radio.
Audio & duplicating recording, postproduction audio facilities & svcs, & music production.

U.S. Air Force Recruiting Service, Randolph AFB, 550 D Street W., Suite 1, Universal City, TX 78150-5421. Phone: (210) 652-3937. Fax: (210) 652-4892. E-mail: rspsa@rs.af.mil. Web Site: www.airforce.com. Gary Quesenberry, supt bcstg; Ted Northrup, producer & dir.
TV-CATV only.
Custom production of radio & TV PSAs for Air Force recruiting for local communities.

United Stations Radio Network, 25 W. 45 St., New York, NY 10036. Phone: (212) 869-1111. Fax: (212) 869-1115. E-mail: info@unitedstations.com. Web Site: www.unitedstations.com. Nick Verbitsky, CEO.
Los Angeles, CA 90064, 11400 W. Olympic Blvd., # 200. Phone: (310) 914-0188. Anne Martinez, mgr.
Chicago, IL 60606, 333 W. Weeker Dr, # 700. Phone: (312) 444-2034. Rich Baum, VP midwest.
Dallas, TX Phone: (972) 506-8776. Rob Ellis, mgr.

Radio Only.
Entertainment & comedy. Programming for radio stations, news & business & weather features.

University of Colorado Television, Campus Box 379, Boulder, CO 80309. Phone: (303) 492-1857. Fax: (303) 492-7017. E-mail: kathleen.albers@colorado.edu. Kate Albers, producer & dir.
TV-CATV only.
TV & radio program production & distribution; production svcs.

University of Detroit Mercy, Box 19900, Communication Studies Dept., 4001 W. McNichols, Detroit, MI 48219-0900. Phone: (313) 578-0311. Phone: (313) 993-2005. Fax: (313) 993-1166. Web Site: www.udmercy.edu. Michael Jayson, engr.
TV-CATV only.
Radio program syndication.

University of Kentucky Public Relations & Radio-TV News Bureau, Mathews Bldg., Rm. 4, Lexington, KY 40506. Phone: (859) 257-1754. Fax: (859) 257-4017. E-mail: cnath1@email.uky.edu. Web Site: www.uky.edu. Carl Nathe, dir radio/TV news bureau.
TV-CATV only.
TV & radio program & coml, promotional film production & distribution.

Univision Communications Inc., 5999 Center Drive, Los Angeles, CA 90045. Phone: (310) 556-7676. Fax: (310) 556-7615. Web Site: www.univision.net. A. Jerrold Perenchio, chmn/CEO; Ray Rodriguez, pres/COO.
TV-CATV only.
Spanish-language broadcast & cable television networks, radio stations, music record labels and an internet destination.

V

VA-Tech Video/Broadcast Services, 285 Whittemore Hall, Blacksburg, VA 24061. Phone: (540) 231-5930. Fax: (540) 231-4622. Web Site: www.vbs.vt.edu. Mark Harden, mgr.
TV-CATV only.
Complete video & audio production & postproduction svcs. Uplink, downlink & CATV opn. Telephone & data communication.

V I E W Video Inc., 34 E. 23rd St., New York, NY 10010. Phone: (212) 674-5550. Fax: (212) 979-0266. E-mail: viewvid@aol.com. Web Site: www.view.com. Bob Karcy, pres; Stephen R. Kates, dir mktg.
TV-CATV only.
International home video production & distribution of special interest progms in the areas of art, jazz, pop music, opera, dance, children's interactive sports & modern lifestyle progms.

VRI (Video Rentals Inc.), 100 Stonehurst Ct., Northvale, NJ 07647. Phone: (800) 255-2874. Phone: (201) 750-3200. Fax: (201) 784-2795. E-mail: info@rentvri.com. Web Site: www.rentvri.com. Tom Canavan, VP/gen mgr.
TV-CATV only.
Full-svc rental facility with a complete inventory of bcst & industrial video equipment.

VTTV Videothek Electronic TV-Production GmbH + Co Kopier KG, Havelchaussee 161, Berlin 14055. Germany. Phone: (030) 300 95-3. Fax: (030) 300 95-500. E-mail: info@vttv.de. Web Site: www.vttv.de. Paul Bielicki, pres; Friedel Lux, head dev/rsch; Herbert Bauermeister, head creative dept.
TV-CATV only.
Complete production service: studios (600/225 m2), professional equipment for production & postproduction, high definition production units. Commercials, documentaries, features, pop promos, TV.

Valentino Music & Sound Effect Libraries, 500 Executive Blvd., Elmsford, NY 10523. Phone: (914) 347-7878. Phone: (800) 223-6278. Fax: (914) 347-4764. E-mail: tvmusic@ibm.net. Web Site: www.tvmusic.com. Thomas J. Valention, pres; Francis T. Valentino, VP.
TV-CATV only.
Compact disc music & sound effects libraries.

Van Vliet Media, 420 E. 55th St., Suite 6L, New York, NY 10022. Phone: (212) 486-6577. Fax: (212) 980-9826. E-mail: vanvlietmedia@att.net. Web Site: vanvlietmedia.com. Rochelle Bebell, pres.
TV-CATV only.
Digital transfers, dup cardiac angiography.

Venevision International, 550 Biltmore Way, Suite 1180, Coral Gables, FL 33134. Phone: (305) 442-3411. Fax: (305) 448-4762. E-mail: info@venevisionintl.com. Web Site: www.venevisionintl.com. Luis A. Villanueva, pres; Benjamin F. Perez, exec VP; Cristobal Ponte, VP; Mario Castro, mktg & creative svc dir/sls dir Central America; Miguel Somoza, sls.
TV-CATV only.
Distribution of progmg.

Venice Media Services, 299 W. Houston, 10th Fl., New York, NY 10014-3620. Phone: (212) 859-5100. Fax: (212) 727-9495. Peggy Green, pres/Natl Bcstg of Venice U.S.
TV-CATV only.
TV program distribution.

Viacom Inc., 1515 Broadway, New York, NY 10036. Phone: (212) 258-6000. Fax: (212) 258-6465. Web Site: www.viacom.com. Summer M. Redstone, chmn/CEO; Matthew Blank, CEO; Martin Shea, sr VP; Al Weber, pres; Jonathan L. Dolgen, chmn; John Antioco, chmn/CEO; Carl D. Folta, sr VP; Thomas E. Freston, chmn/CEO; Michael D. Fricklas, exec VP; Sherry Lansing, chmn; Herb Scannell, pres; Jack Ramanos, pres; William A. Roskin, sr VP; Carol Melton, sr VP; Mel Karmazin, pres/COO; Richard Bressler, sr VP/CFO.
Hollywood, CA 90038. Paramount Pictures, 5555 Melrose Ave.
Charlotte, NC 28217. Paramount Parks, 8720 Red Oak Blvd, Suite 375.
New York, NY 10019. Showtime Networks Inc., 1633 Broadway.
New York, NY 10020. Simon & Schuster, 1230 Ave. of the Americas.
New York, NY 10036. MTV Networks, 1515 Broadway.
Dallas, TX 75270. Blockbuster Entertainment, 1201 Elm St.
TV-CATV only.
TV program production & distribution, motion pictures production & distribution, book publishing, video production & distribution, theme parks.

Viacom Video Services, 524 W. 57th St., New York, NY 10019-2924. Phone: (212) 975-8139. Fax: (212) 975-7272. E-mail: mjeffers@cbs.com. Web Site: www.viacom.com. Mark Jeffers, dir distribution & opns.
Los Angeles, CA 90024, 10877 Wilshire Blvd. Phone: (310) 446-6051. Fax: (310) 446-6066. Lee Salas, VP & natl sls mgr.
TV-CATV only.
Duplicate & distribute syndicated TV progmg via tape & satellite, coml integration, international standards conversion, uplink/downlink, tape duplication, space segment; high definition.

Video-Cinema Films Inc., 510 E. 86th St., New York, NY 10028. Phone: (212) 734-1632. Fax: (212) 734-1632. Larry Stern, pres.
TV-CATV only.
Distribution/licensor of motion pictures & excerpts for all forms of TV & allied media in US and worldwide.

Video Enterprises Inc., 575 29th St., Manhattan Beach, CA 90266-3430. Phone: (310) 796-5555. Fax: (310) 546-2921. E-mail: hambrose@earthlink.net. Heidi Lane-Ambrose, pres; Renska Somers, office mgr.
TV-CATV-Radio.
Natl placement of ten-second promotional spots on game shows, talk, var & sports programs.

Video I-D Teleproductions Inc., 105 Muller Rd., Washington, IL 61571. Phone: (800) 333-9123. Fax: (309) 444-4333. E-mail: videoid@videoid.com. Web Site: www.videoid.com. Sam B. Wagner, pres; Gwen Wagner, mktg mgr; Larry Strantz, sls consultant.
TV-CATV only.
Full teleproduction svcs, DVD & CD-ROM capabilities, location production, linear & nonlinear editing, 3D graphics, specializing in corporate image, safety, training, sls & mktg.

Video/Media Distribution Inc., 1050 N. State St., Chicago, IL 60610. Phone: (312) 944-4700. Fax: (312) 944-1582. E-mail: shelvm@aol.com. Shel Beugen, pres.
TV-CATV only.
Program sls & syndication svcs to bcst, cable stns & networks.

Video One Inc., 4952 Nagle Ave., Sherman Oaks, CA 91423. Phone: (818) 781-9824. Fax: (818) 753-4704. Robert G. Kaufmann, pres; Kevin E. Hamburger, VP.
Remote TV production facilities.

Broadcasting & Cable Yearbook 2006

Producers, Distributors, and Production Services Alphabetical Index

Video Services, 802 Ewing Ave., Nashville, TN 37203. Phone: (800) 251-1009. Fax: (615) 244-5712. E-mail: info@siffordvideoservices.com. Web Site: www.siffordvideoservices.com. Joel Covington, owner.
TV-CATV only.
CD, DVD, videotape duplication, standard conversions.

Video Techniques Inc., Box 9649, Bradenton, FL 34206-9649. Phone: (941) 758-3077. Fax: (941) 758-4896. E-mail: vti@videotechniques.com. Web Site: www.videotechniques.com. Bob Lorentzen, pres.
TV-CATV only.
Beta SP & MII field & postproduction facilities. CD, DVD authoring & duplication, VHS duplication, streaming video hosting.

VideoActive Productions, 1780 Broadway, Suite 804, New York, NY 10019. Phone: (212) 541-6592. Web Site: www.videoactiveprod.com. Steven Garrin, pres.
TV-CATV only.
Radio, TV, film production/post production.

Videographic West, Box 1093, 30 Benchmark Rd., Suite 203, Avon, CO 81620. Phone: (970) 949-5593. Fax: (970) 949-6331. E-mail: video@colorado.net. Web Site: www.skitv.com. Michael Billingsley, principal; Stephanie Billingsley, principal.
TV-CATV only.
Specializing in cable sports programming and distribution, extensive stock footage of action sports, mountain lifestyle, skiing, golf, family and travel. Full-svc production house, field crews, two SD/component pinnacle Liquid uncompressed NLE workstations, complete multimedia suite with DVD authoring/encoding, 2D animation suite with talented artists.

Videomedia, C/Jose Isbert, 2, Ciudad de la Imagen, Pozuelo De Alarcon, Madrid 28223. Spain. Phone: 34-91-512.8000. Fax: 34-91-518.8017. E-mail: videomedia@videomedia.es. Web Site: www.videomedia.es. Jorge Arque, CEO & pres; Mireia Acosta, fiction mgr; Daniel Acuna, entertainment mgr; Fernanda Montoro, intnl div.
TV-CATV only.
Independent production company. Entertainment formats & programs, documentaries, fiction.

Videosmith Inc., 100 Spring Garden St., Philadelphia, PA 19123. Phone: (215) 238-5070. Fax: (215) 238-5075. E-mail: info@videosmith.com. Web Site: www.videosmith.com. Steven T. Smith, pres.
TV-CATV only.
TV progmg, equipment rentals & production mgmt.

Virginia Tech, CNS (Communications Network Services), 1770 Forecast Dr., Blacksburg, VA 24061-0506. Phone: (540) 231-6460. Fax: (540) 231-8418. Web Site: www.cns.vt.edu. Judy Lilly, dir communications network svcs.
TV-CATV only.
Video & Audio Service to campus - faculty staff & students.

Vision Broadcasting - KVBA TV 19, 1017 New York Ave., Alamogordo, NM 88310-6921. Phone: (505) 437-1919. E-mail: kvba@kvbatv.com. William J. Oeschsner Jr., gen mgr.
TV-CATV only.
Broadcast of Christian & local television, sports, public interest TV.

Vuolo Video Air-Chex, Box 880, Novi, MI 48376. Phone: (248) 960-9607. Fax: (248) 926-9090. E-mail: artvuolo@aol.com. Web Site: www.vuolovideo.com. Arthur Vuolo, Jr., producer.
Radio Only.
Video air checks of American radio stns & *An Inside Look*.

Vyvx, a Division of WillTel Communications, One Technology Center, Tulsa, OK 74103. Phone: (866) WilTel1. Fax: (918) 547-2989. Web Site: www.wiltelcommunications.com. Jeff Storey, pres/CEO.
TV-CATV only.
Distributor of TV comls/traf via satellite by remote VTR control to 600 stns; radio coml distribution; production, postproduction. Multi-format duplication.

W

WKMG Productions, 4466 N. John Young Pkwy., Orlando, FL 32804. Phone: (407) 291-6000. Fax: (407) 521-1204. Web Site: www.local6.com. Henry Maldonado, gen mgr; Jim Murphy, production.
TV program, coml, promotional film production; production svcs, post production & field production. WKMG production resources primarily dedicated to station use.

WCTD AM 1620, 244 Post Rd., Westerly, RI 02891. Phone: (401) 322-1743. Phone: (401) 322-9091. Fax: (401) 322-1645. Web Site: www.wblq.org/htm.wctd. J.J. MacDade Nunez, gen mgr; Chris DiPaola, pres.
Radio Only.
Traveler information.

WFMT Radio Network, 5400 N. St. Louis Ave., Chicago, IL 60625. Phone: (773) 279-2112. Phone: (773) 279-2114. Fax: (773) 279-2119. Web Site: www.wfmt.com. Steve Robinson, sr VP.
Radio Only.
Produces wkly series including Chicago Symphony retrospective & the New York Philharmonic this week for coml & pub stns. Broad range of symphonic, opera & classical music documentary progmg, jazz & folk music, including exclusive features from BBC & Radio Deutsche Welle, Germany.

WGN Television, 2501 W. Bradley Pl., Chicago, IL 60618. Phone: (773) 528-2311. Fax: (773) 528-6857. Web Site: www.wgntv.com. E-mail: wgnttvnews@tribune.com. John Vitanovec, VP/gen mgr; Dominick Mancuso, stn mgr; Merri Dee, community rel dir; Marty Wilke, sls dir; JoAnn Stern, svcs dir; Rob Salerno, dir finance & admin; Greg Caputo, news dir.
TV-CATV only.
TV programs & comls, promotional film production & distribution, production svcs.

WMAQ-TV, NBC Tower, 454 N. Columbus Dr., Chicago, IL 60611-5555. Phone: (312) 836-5555. Fax: (312) 527-4290. Web Site: www.nbc5.com. Larry Wert, pres/gen mgr; Patricia Golden, VP sls.
TV-CATV only.
TV program production; production svcs.

WNN Health and Wealth Motivation, 6699 N. Federal Hwy., Boca Raton, FL 33487. Phone: (561) 997-0074. Fax: (561) 997-0476. Web Site: www.wnnhealthtalkradio.com. Robert Morency, VP/gen mgr.
Radio Only.
Worldwide 24-hour format of motivational speakers & self-help info.

The WPA Film Library, 16101 S. 108th Ave., Orland Park, IL 60467. Phone: (708) 460-0555. Fax: (708) 460-0187. E-mail: sales@wpafilmlibrary.com. Web Site: www.wpafilmlibrary.com. Diane Paradiso, sls.
TV-CATV only.
One of the largest stock footage libraries in the U.S. WPA offers holdings in newsreels, music, pop culture & stock shots.

WQED Multimedia, (The Metropolitan Pittsburgh Public Broadcasting Station). 4802 5th Ave., Pittsburgh, PA 15213. Phone: (412) 622-1300. Fax: (412) 622-6413. E-mail: info@wqed.org. Web Site: www.wqed.org. George L. Miles Jr., pres; Robert Petrilli, sr VP/COO; B.J. Leber, sr VP/stn mgr; Deborah Acklin, sr VP of production & technology.
TV-CATV only.
TV & radio program production & distribution; production svcs.

WQXR, 122 5th Ave., 3rd Fl., New York, NY 10011. Phone: (212) 633-7600. Fax: (212) 633-7666. E-mail: wqxr963fm@aol.com. Web Site: www.wqxr.com. Penny Gaffney, sls VP.
Radio Only.
Radio program production. The classical Radio Station of the New York Times.

WRS/Channel One, (A division of WRS Inc.). 1000 Napor Blvd., Pittsburgh, PA 15205. Phone: (412) 937-7700. Fax: (412) 922-1020. E-mail: jackn@wrslabs.com. Web Site: www.wrslabs.com. F. Jack Napor, pres.
TV-CATV only.
Complete syndication & distribution svcs via satellite & tape. Integration, AMOL encoding, duplication, uplink/downlink fulfillment, audio, film-to-tape transfer; replication of CD/DVD.

WSI Corp., 400 Minuteman Rd., Andover, MA 01810. Phone: (978) 983-6300. Fax: (978) 983-6400. Web Site: www.wsi.com.
TV-CATV only.
World leader in providing real-time weather data, imagery, forecasting & weather programming for bcst stns, cable operators and cable nets.

WTOB Channel 2—Public/Government Access TV, 300 S. Main St., Blacksburg, VA 24062. Phone: (540) 961-1199. Fax: (540) 961-1875. E-mail: wtob@blacksburg.gov. Web Site: www.blacksburg.gov. Derley Aguilar, stn mgr.
TV-CATV only.
Locally originated progmg, live town meetings, equipment training & loan svcs in inch, S-VHS & VHS formats.

WWE Entertainment Inc., Titan Tower, 1241 E. Main St., Stamford, CT 06902. Phone: (203) 352-8600. Fax: (203) 352-8699. Web Site: www.wwe.com. Vincent K. McMahon, chmn; Linda E. McMahon, CEO; James Rothschild, sr VP; Donna Goldsmith, sr VP/licensing & merchandising; Phil Livingston, CFO.
TV-CATV-Radio.
Exclusive worldwide distributor of WWF events, TV programs (bcst network/syndication, PPV & basic cable) & other sports/entertainment properties.

Wade Productions Inc., 493 High Cliffe Lane, Tarrytown, NY 10591. Phone: (212) 286-9111. E-mail: wade@1cj@aol.com. Carolyn J. Wade, pres.
TV-CATV only.
Meetings, video, entertainment, staging & teleconferencing for corporations & assns.

Warner Bros. International Distribution Inc. (Canada), 4576 Yonge St., 2nd Fl., North York, ON M2N 6P1. Canada. Phone: (416) 250-8384. Fax: (416) 250-8598. Web Site: www.wbitv.com. Robert Blair, VP/gen mgr; Leslie Hibbins, prom dir & publicity.
TV-CATV only.
TV progm distribution & promotions for Canada.

Warner Bros., Bldg. 140, 300 Television Plaza, Burbank, CA 91505. Phone: (818) 954-7500. Fax: (818) 954-7322. Peter Ross, pres.
TV-CATV only.
TV program production & distribution.

Warner Bros. Animation, 15301 Ventura Blvd., Suite 115301, Unit E, Sherman Oaks, CA 91403. Phone: (818) 977-8700. Fax: (818) 382-6056. Web Site: www.warnerbros.com. Sander Schwartz, pres.
TV-CATV only.
Develops & produces animated comls & programs; animated theatrical films, episodic television.

Warner Bros. Domestic Television Distribution, 4000 Warner Blvd., Burbank, CA 91522. Phone: (818) 954-5877. Fax: (818) 954-5820. Web Site: www.warnerbros.com. Dick Robertson, pres; Jim Paratore, exec VP; Jacqueline Hartley, VP; Jeff Hufford, VP; Mark O'Brien, sr VP.
Print Department—Burbank: Bud Rowe, foreign TV print administrator. (818) 954-3731.TV program syndication.

Warner Bros. International Television, 4000 Warner Blvd., Burbank, CA 91522. Phone: (818) 954-4040. Jeffrey R. Schlesinger, pres; Mauro Sardi, sls VP; James P. Marrinan, sr VP; Josh Berger, VP; David Camp, VP finance; Lisa Gregorian, VP; Ron Miele, VP; John Whitesell, VP; Catherine Malatesta, sr VP; Susan Kroll, sr VP; Malcolm Dudley-Smith, sr VP; Marsha Armstrong, VP; Monica Dodi, VP; Sal LoCurto, VP mktg; Kelley Nichols, VP; Robert Nitkin, VP; Matthew Robinson, VP.
Acapulco 37 06140. Warner Bros. (Mexico) S.A., Colonea Codesa. Phone: 011-525-211-3353-211-0293. 211-0298-211-0466. Fax: 011-525-553-2822-553-2002. Jorge Sanchez, VP Latin America.
London W1V 4AP. Warner Bros. International TV, 135 Wardour St. Phone: 011-44-171-494-3710. Fax: 011-44-171-287-9086. Richard Milnes, VP UK territories, Turkey, Israel.
Madrid 28033. Warner Bros. International TV, Artuto Soria, 336 1. Phone: 011-34-1-384-06-40. Fax: 011-34-1-384-06-41. Jose Abad, sls exec Sp territories.
Minato-ku, Tokyo 105. Time Warner Entertainment Japan, 1-2-4 Hamamatsu-cho. Phone: 011-81-3-5472-8341. Fax: 011-81-3-5472-6343. Teruji Mochimaru, mgng dir Japan.
North Sydney NSW 2060. Warner Bros. PTY. Ltd., 8-20 Napier St. Phone: 011-61-2-9957-3899. Fax: 011-61-2-9956-7788. Wayne Brown, VP mgng dir Australia, Asia Pacific; Greg Robertson, VP Asia.
Paris 75017. Warner Bros. International TV, 67 Avenue Dewagram. Phone: 011-33-1-5537-5933. Fax: 011-33-1-5537-4968. Michel Lecourt, VP Fr territories.
Rome 00195. Warner Bros. Italia S.R.L., Via Giuseppe Avezzana, 51. Phone: 011-39-6-321-7779. Fax: 011-39-6-321-7278. Rosario Ponzio, mgng dir It-speaking Europe.
North York, ON M2N 6P1 Canada. Warner Bros. International TV, 4576 Yonge St, 2nd Fl. Phone: (416)250-8384. Fax: 416-250-8598. Kevin Byles, VP & gen mgr, Canadian opns.
TV program production & distribution.

Producers, Distributors, and Production Services Alphabetical Index

Warner Bros. Television Production, 4000 Warner Blvd., Burbank, CA 91522. Phone: (818) 954-6000. Fax: (818) 954-7048. Web Site: www.warnerbros.com. Greg Maday, sr VP movies & mini-series; Mary Buck, sr VP talent & casting; Steve Pearlman, sr VP current programs; Robert Rosenbaum, sr VP net prodction; David Sacks, sr VP current progmg; Paul Stager, sr VP studio gen counsel; Julie Waxman, sr VP business affrs.
TV-CATV only.
TV program production.

Warren Only Media Group, Box 2372, Times Square Station, New York, NY 10036. Phone: (585) 507-9368. E-mail: warrenonly@90.com. Web Site: www.warrenonly.com.
TV-CATV only.
Satellite program distribution, syndication, playout and back hauling, film and video production.

Washington Korean Broadcasting Co., 7004-K Little River Tpke, Annandale, VA 22003. Phone: (703) 354-4900. Fax: (703) 354-6078. E-mail: wkbc@wkbc.biz. Web Site: www.wkbc.biz. Yong C. Pak, pres; Yong S. Lee, gen mgr.
Radio Only.
All ethnic progmg in Korean language, news, music, drama & talk show.

Wawatay Native Communication Society, Box 1180, 16 Fifth Ave., Sioux Lookout, ON P8T 1B7. Canada. Phone: (807) 737-2951. Fax: (807) 737-3224. Web Site: www.wawatay.on.ca. Mike Metatawabin, pres; Christine Chisel, exec dir.
TV-CATV only.
Radio & TV (Cree, Ojibway & English) net, bilingual nwspr, aboriginal language translations, multi-track audio recording.

M.D. Wax Courier Films, 1560 Broadway, New York, NY 10036. Phone: (212) 302-5360. Fax: (212) 302-5364. E-mail: mortwax@worldnet.att.net. Mort Wax, pres.
TV-CATV only.
Supplier of foreign films & progmg to all markets.

Wax Music & Sound Design, 18 W. 21st St., 10th Fl., New York, NY 10010-6903. Phone: (212) 989-9292. Fax: (212) 989-5195. E-mail: julia@waxnyc.com. Web Site: www.waxnyc.com. James Wolcott, composer/sound designer; Chris Arbisi, chief engr/head of production; Julia Frodahl, dir mktg & sls.
TV-CATV only.
Original music & sound design for all media. Three digital studios.

"The Weather Center", (a broadcast service of Aviation Weather Inc.). 701 Gervais St., Suite 150-224, Columbia, SC 29201. Phone: (803) 739-2827. E-mail: wxcenter@aol.com. Web Site: www.aviationweatherinc.com. L.R. Ferguson, pres.
"Regional Radio Broadcast/Weathercast Network" across the Carolinas and Georgia in over 20 broadcast markets. Weather forecasting, site-specific broadcast services for stations all across America. 100% barter.

WeatherVision Inc., 916 Foley St., Jackson, MS 39202-3406. Phone: (601) 352-6673. Fax: (601) 948-6052. E-mail: edward@weathervision.com. Web Site: www.weathervision.com. Edward St. Pe, pres; Jason McCleave, VP.
Customized, localized TV weathercasts with or without meteorologists. Barter/cash via Ku-band satellite. Complete studio teleport for use by news media on site. Avid editing available on site.
Serves radio & TV.

Alan Weiss Productions, 355 W. 52nd St., New York, NY 10019. Phone: (212) 974-0606. Fax: (212) 974-0976. Web Site: www.alanweissproductions.com. Alan J. Weiss, pres; Tania Wilk, VP.
TV-CATV only.
Fourteen Emmys for video production. We handle any broadcast, PR or corporate from concept to distribution.

Wellspring, (formerly Fox Lorber Associates, Inc.). 419 Park Ave. S., 20th Fl., New York, NY 10016. Phone: (212) 686-6777. Fax: (212) 685-2625. Web Site: www.wellspring.com. Sheri Levine, sr VP international distribution; Marie Therese Guirgis, dir acquisitions.
TV-CATV only.
Worldwide distributors of film & video properties for home video, standard & non-standard TV.

Welwood International Film Production, 160 Washington S.E., Suite 138, Albuquerque, NM 87108-2731. Phone: (505) 265-1899. E-mail: welwoodint@aol.com. Bill Swortwood, pres/creative dir; Barbara Ferrel, VP/CEO.
TV-CATV only.

Works with consultants, rsch companies & client stns to create effective TV campaigns since 1986.

Westar Music, 105 West Beaver Creek Road, Suite 3, Richmond Hill, ON L4B 1C6. Canada. Phone: (905) 886-3100. Fax: (905) 886-6800. E-mail: info@westarmusic.com. Web Site: www.westarmusic.com. Brian Nimens, pres/CEO.
TV-CATV only.
High caliber production music in a wide variety of categories for broadcast, cable, film, corporate videoand multimedia applications.

Western International Syndication, 12100 Wilshire Blvd., Suite 1050, Los Angeles, CA 90025. Phone: (310) 820-8485. Fax: (310) 820-8376. Web Site: www.wistelevision.com. E-mail: info@wistelevision.com. Chris Lancey, pres/CEO; Dan Zifkin, exec VP/worldwide.
TV-CATV only.
Distributes wkly & special progmg nationwide as well as internationally.

Westwood One Producers, Radio New Services. 40 W. 57th St., New York, NY 10019. Phone: (212) 641-2000. Fax: (212) 641-2185. Web Site: www.westwoodone.com. Shane Cappola, CEO; Jacque Tortoroli, CFO; Paul Bronstein, sr VP; Gary Yusko, sr VP; Peter Kosann, exec VP.
Culver City, CA 90232-2689, 9540 Washington Blvd. Phone: (310) 204-5000. Fax: (310) 840-4380.
Valencia, CA 91355, 25060 W. Ave. Stanford, Suite 100. Phone: (805) 294-9000. Fax: (805) 294-9380.
Atlanta, GA 30361, 1201 Peachtree St. N.W., 400 Colony Sq., Suite 200. Phone: (404) 870-9084. Fax: (404) 870-9085. Susan Bravman, AE.
Chicago, IL 60601, 111 E. Wacker Dr, Suite 2900. Phone: (312) 938-0222. Fax: (312) 616-8140. Ted S. Jakubiak, VP Midwest sls.
Troy, MI 48084, 3250 W. Big Beaver, Suite 139. Phone: (248) 649-0960. Fax: (248) 649-1584. Dave A. Gneiser, VP Detroit sls.
Dallas, TX 75231, 7577 Ramblin Rd, Suite 1462. Phone: (214) 373-0022. Fax: (214) 373-0511.
Arlington, VA 22202, 1755 S. Jefferson Davis Hwy. Phone: (703) 413-8300. Fax: (703) 413-8445.
Producer & distributor of radio progmg including CNN, NBC, Mutual, CNBC Business Radio, 24-hour music formats, long-short-form talk, music & news programs.

White Rabbit Productions, 1587 S. Main St., Salt Lake City, UT 84115. Phone: (800) 549-3115. Phone: (801) 463-9292. Fax: (801) 463-7226. E-mail: info@whiterabbitproductions.com. Web Site: www.whiterabbitproductions.com. Sam Prigg, pres/dir photography.
TV-CATV only.
Complete film & video production svcs; two Ikegami HL-V55 Beta Sp camera packages, digital video point-of-view cam, non-linear editing.

Who Did That Music?, 12211 West Washington Blvd., Los Angeles, CA 90066. Phone: (310) 572-4644. Fax: (310) 572-4647. E-mail: cindy@groveaddicts.com. Web Site: www.grooveaddicts.com. Cindy Rosmann, VP/gen mgr.
TV-CATV only.
Our catalog is growing! We now have 12 libraries, all continuously updated, sound design & SFX. Annual blanket license & custom music packages.

Wide Eye Productions, Inc., 686 N. 9th, Boise, ID 83702. Phone: (208) 336-0391. Fax: (208) 336-6644. E-mail: info@wideeye.tv. Web Site: www.wideeye.tv. Tom Hadzor, dir; Jennifer Isenhart, producer.
TV-CATV only.
Full-service bcst & industrial video production. ENG/EFP. High definition & Sony B-600.

Daniel Wilson Productions Inc., 300 W. 55th St. Ste 8V, New York, NY 10019. Phone: (212) 765-7148. Fax: (212) 765-7916. E-mail: wilprod@verizon.net. Daniel Wilson, pres.
TV & theatrical film production & distribution.

Witt/Thomas Productions, 11901 Santa Monica Blvd., Suite 596, W. Los Angeles, CA 90025. Phone: (310) 472-6004. Fax: (310) 476-5015. Paul Junger Witt; Tony Thomas, partner; Susan Harris, partner.
TV-CATV only.
TV & film production company.

Robert Wold Co., 88 Three Vines Ct., Ladera Ranch, CA 92694. Phone: (949) 363-0993. Fax: (949) 363-2093. E-mail: robertnwold@cox.net. Robert N. Wold, owner.
TV-CATV only.
Special-interest & entertainment progmg for bcst & cable TV. Production, mktg & distribution of syndicated programs.

Fred Wolf Films, 4222 W. Burbank Blvd., Burbank, CA 91505. Phone: (818) 846-0611. Fax: (818) 846-0979. E-mail: administration@fredwolffilms.com. Web Site: www.fredwolffilms.com. Fred Wolf, pres.
TV-CATV only.
TV program production & distribution.

Work Edit, 270 W. 39th St., 11th Floor, New York, NY 10018. Phone: (212) 719-4577. Fax: (212) 719-4380. Web Site: www.workedit.com. Dalton Helms, owner; Ken Sackheim, owner.
TV-CATV only.
Post production services, DVD authoring.

World Events Productions Ltd., One Memorial Dr., St. Louis, MO 63102. Phone: (314) 345-1000. Fax: (314) 345-1091. E-mail: wep@wep.com. Web Site: www.wep.com. Edward J. Koplar, pres; Tiffany Ilardi, mngg dir.
TV-CATV only.
TV program production & distribution.

World Radio Network, Box 1212, London SW8 2ZF. United Kingdom. Phone: 44-20-7896-9000. Fax: 44-20-7896-9008. E-mail: email@wrn.org. Web Site: www.wrn.org. Karl Miosga, mngg dir; Tim Ashburner, dir tech opns; Jeff Cohen, dev dir.
Boston, MA 02125, 11 Rockmere St. Phone: (617) 436-9024. Sue Schardt, North American rep.
WRN Network One (via Galaxy 5) news & features ch, comprises live progmg segments in English & languages from more than 20 international bcstrs. Also supplies many customized progmg feeds to radio stns.

Worldview Entertainment Inc., The Killiam Collection. 145 W. 55th St., Suite 7-D, New York, NY 10019. Phone: (212) 582-6997. Fax: (212) 925-2314. E-mail: birnhardt@aol.com. Sandra J. Birnhak, CEO; Glenn E. Shealey, pres.
TV-CATV only.
Archival stock footage library, distribution to international bcstrs.

Worldvision NY, 143 W. 29th St., New York, NY 10001. Phone: (212) 736-2997. Fax: (212) 736-9755. Web Site: www.worldvision.org. John Claus, exec dir.
London SW1X OAE, Worldvision Enterprises U.K. Ltd, 54 Pont St. Phone: 011-441-71-584-5357. Fax: 011-441-71-581-3483. Bill Peck, Janice Wilson, Zsuzsanna Jung.
Paris 75008, Worldvision Enterprises S.A.R.L, 28, Rue Bayard. Phone: 011-33-1-4723-3995. Fax: 011-33-1-4070-9269. Mary Jane Fourniel, Catherine Molinier, John Hernan.
Rio de Janeiro CEP 22270, 22270 Rua Voluntarios Da Patria N, Gr.604. Phone: 011-55-21-539-2992. Fax: 011-55-21-266-4737. Raymundo Rodriguez, Maria Alice Freire.
Rome 00186, Adalia Anstalt, Via del Corso, 22/Int 10. Phone: 011-39-6-322-5190. Fax: 011-39-6-322-6450. Michael Kiwe, Dorothy Shaw.
Sydney, Milsons Point 02061. Worldvision Enterprises of Australia PTY Ltd., 5-13 Northcliff St. Phone: 011-61-2-9922-4722. Fax: 011-61-2-9955-8207. TWX: (790) 70474. Brian Rhys-Jones, Paul Stuart, Karen Zylstra.
Tokyo 104, Tsukiji Matsurikyu Bldg, 7th Fl, 5-3-3 Tsukiji, Chou-ku. Phone: 011-81-3-3545-3978. Fax: 011-81-3-5550-8316. Mie Horasawa, Yukie Kumagai.
Toronto, ON M5R 2A5 Canada, Worldvision Enterprises of Canada, 1200 Bay St, Suite 802. Phone: (416) 967-1200. Fax: (416) 967-0521. Bruce Swanson, Kathy Fraser.
Los Angeles, CA 90036, 5700 Wilshire Blvd, 5th Fl. Phone: (213) 965-5910. Fax: (213) 965-5915. David McNaney, VP western division.
Coconut Grove, FL 33133. Tele-UNO, Grand Bay Plaza, 2665 S. Bayshore Dr. Phone: (305) 285-4307. Fax: (305) 285-4308. Hilary Hattler, John McDonald.
Atlanta, GA 30346. Worldvision Enterprises Inc. Latin America, 400 Perimeter Ctr. Terr, Suite 185. Phone: (770) 394-3967. Fax: (770) 394-9002. Mary Ann Pasante, Leticia Estrada, Carla Araya.
Atlanta, GA 30346, 400 Perimeter Center Terr, Suite 150. Phone: (404) 394-3967. Fax: (404) 394-9002. John Barrett, VP southern division.
Chicago, IL 60610, 515 N. State St, Suite 2305. Phone: (312) 527-0461. Fax: (312) 527-0688. Tony Bauer, VP central division.
New York, NY 10019, 1700 Broadway. Phone: (212) 261-2700. Fax: (212) 261-2724. Bill Baffi, VP cable & new technologies; Frank L. Browne, VP eastern division.
TV-CATV only.
TV program distribution for ind productions.

The Worship Network, 28059 U.S. Hwy. 19 N., Suite 300, Clearwater, FL 33761. Phone: (727) 536-0036. Fax: (727) 530-0671. E-mail: ken@worship.net. Web Site: www.worship.net. Bruce Koblish, pres/CEO; Bob Shreffler, VP finance; Tim Brown, VP.

Producers, Distributors, and Production Services Alphabetical Index

TV-CATV only.
Inspirational music set to nature scenes, overlaid with scripture 24 hours a day. Progmg is interspersed with short devotional teachings.

Larry John Wright Inc., 1045 E. University Dr., Suite 1, Mesa, AZ 85203. Phone: (480) 833-8111. Fax: (480) 969-2895. E-mail: jessica@ljohnw.com. Web Site: www.larryjohnwright.com. Larry F. John, CEO; John N. Wright, pres.
TV-CATV only.
Own & operate production studios; produce film & video comls, radio comls & jingles, TV shows & industrial videos.

The Wyland Group, 101 W. Cochran St., Simi Valley, CA 93065. Phone: (805) 955-7680. Fax: (805) 522-1082. Web Site: www.lifestyle.org. Chauncey Smith, Account Executive.
TV-CATV only.
Production of health related, family values progmg.

Doug Wyles Productions Inc., 630 9th Ave., New York, NY 10036-3708. Phone: (212) 248-4800. Doug Wyles, pres; John Rokosny, production mgr.
TV-CATV-Radio.
TV Production.

X

XL Media Solutions, 110 N. Ditmar St., Oceanside, CA 92054. Phone: (760) 722-8284. Fax: (888) 722-8234. E-mail: staff@exxelaudio.com. Web Site: www.exxelaudio.com. William Kottcamp, mgr.
Radio Only.
Radio program, coml production & distribution.

Y

Yada/Levine Video Productions, 606 N. Larchmont Blvd., Suite 100, Los Angeles, CA 90004. Phone: (323) 461-1616. Fax: (323) 461-2288. E-mail: video@yadalevine.com. Web Site: www.yadalevine.com. Michael Yada, pres/CEO.
TV-CATV only.
Betacam SP, Digital Betacam and HD production. Camera crews with equipment package. Avid editing.

Yale Video Inc., 1360 N. Hancock St., Anaheim, CA 92807. Phone: (714) 693-5300. Fax: (714) 693-5395. E-mail: yaleinfo@yalevideo.com. Web Site: www.webcastingtv.com. Burton A. Yale, pres.
Offers the latest in editing technology; from D-2 to Hi8.

Yorkshire Television, (A division of Granada Media Group). Television Centre, 104 Kirkstall Rd., Leeds LS3 IJS. United Kingdom. Phone: 0113-243-8283. Fax: 0113-244-5107. E-mail: communications@granadamedia.com. Web Site: www.granada.co.uk. David M.B. Croft; Charles Allen CBE, chmn.
TV-CATV only.
Independent TV program maker & bcstr.

Z

ZBS Foundation, 174 N. River Rd., Fort Edward, NY 12828. Phone: (518) 695-6406. Fax: (518) 695-4041. E-mail: zbs@global2000.net. Web Site: www.zbs.org. Thomas Lopez, pres.
Radio Only.
Producer of audio drama.

Zachry Associates, 500 Chestnut, Suite 2000, Abilene, TX 79602. Phone: (325) 677-1342. Fax: (325) 672-2001. H.C. Zachry, pres.
TV-CATV only.
Produces & distributes TV & radio programs & comls as well as promotional films & production svcs.

Sandy Zimmerman Productions, 4800 Black Bear Rd., Suite 204, Las Vegas, NV 89149. Phone: (702) 731-6491. E-mail: sandyzimm@go.com. Sandy Zimmerman, producer & owner; Robert Gonzales, production mgr.
TV-CATV only.
Develops, produces & distributes TV programs, documentaries, infomercials, travel specials, TV comls, & industrial & corporate videos. Syndicates one-, two- & five-minute program fillers.

Producers, Distributors, and Production Services Subject Index

3-D Films
Blue Sky Studios
Dimension 3 Corp

3-D TV Systems
Dimension 3 Corp
Pro Video

Agricultural Programming, Radio
Agrinet Farm Radio Network
American Farm Bureau Federation
Clear Channel Broadcasting Inc.
Cookie Jar Group
Leadem to Water Production Inc.
Modern Sound Pictures Inc.
Montgomery Community Television Inc.
North Shore Productions
Tribune Entertainment Co.
Tribune Radio Networks

Animation
Angel Films Co.
The Kay Arnold Group
Bardel Entertainment Inc.
Blue Sky Studios
Central Park Media
CineGroupe
Cinema Concepts Animation Studio
Classic Media
Clayton-Davis & Associates Inc.
Crawford Communications
Dargaud-Marina
Walt Disney Company
Enoki Films U.S.A. Inc.
Film House Inc.
Italtoons Corp.
JC Productions Inc.
John Lemmon Films
Magno Sound & Video
Mar Vista Entertainment
The Media Group of Connecticut Inc.
Bill Melendez Productions Inc.
Modern Sound Pictures Inc.
Mondo TV
North by Northwest Productions
Northwest Imaging & FX
PPM Multimedia
Pantomime Pictures Inc.
Pike Productions Inc.
Playhouse Pictures
PorchLight Entertainment Inc.
PostWorks, New York
Productions La Fete
The Program Exchange
Rampion Visual Productions L.L.C.
Romano & Associates Inc.
Edward Sarson Productions
Silverline Pictures
Southern STAR
The Summit Media Group Inc. (Sub 4 Kids Entertainment)
Sunbow Entertainment
Two Oceans Entertainment Group
Videographic West
Warner Bros. Animation
Fred Wolf Films
World Events Productions Ltd.

Audio Production
American TelNet
Armedia Communications
Broadcast News Service
Himan Brown-Radio Drama Network
CA Media Development
CCM Media Services
C N R Radio
CRN International
Clayton-Davis & Associates Inc.
Command Productions

CONTACT Radio
Continental Recordings Inc.
Creative Marketing & Communications Corp.
DaviSound
Domain Communications L.L.C.
John Driscoll/VoiceOver America
Eagle Media Productions Ltd.
Ecumenical Communications
Evangelical Lutheran Church in America
Finger Lakes Productions International
GMI Media L.L.C.
Good Life Associates
Good News Broadcasting Association Inc.
Heil Enterprises
Horizon Audio Creations
Host Communications Inc.
Irving Productions Inc.
The Johnson Group
KJD Teleproductions
David Kaye Productions Inc.
Lion and Fox Recording Studios
Man From Mars Productions
Ben Manilla Productions
William Mauldin Productions Inc.
MediaTracks Inc.
Metro Networks
MotorNet
N W Media
National Public Radio
New Dimensions Radio
No Soap Productions
North Star Music
Dick Orkin's Amazing Radio
Paulist Media Works
Perception Media Group
Presbyterian Church (U.S.A.)
Protestant Hour Inc.
Radio Spirits
Rex Recording & Video Post
Shield Productions Inc.
Smith/Lee Productions, Inc.
Sound of Birmingham Productions
Soundshop Recording Studio LLC
Soundtrack
Studio M Productions Unlimited
Suite Audio
TR Productions
Talco Productions
Technisonic Studios
Thompson Creative
University of Colorado Television
University of Detroit Mercy
University of Kentucky Public Relations & Radio-TV News Bureau
VideoActive Productions
WQXR
ZBS Foundation

Audio Production Library
American TelNet
Blue Heaven Productions
Himan Brown-Radio Drama Network
Clayton-Davis & Associates Inc.
Ghostwriters/Radio Mall
J&H Music Programming
Network Music L.L.C.
OGM Production Music
Radio America
TM Century Inc.
Who Did That Music?

Audio Recording Services
American TelNet
The Audio Department Inc.
Bruder Releasing Inc. (BRI)
Cinema Sound Ltd.
Command Productions
Continental Recordings Inc.
Domain Communications L.L.C.
John Driscoll/VoiceOver America
Horizon Audio Creations
The Image Generators
Irving Productions Inc.

Tom Jones Recording Studios
David Kaye Productions Inc.
Lion and Fox Recording Studios
MVI Post
Matchframe Video
Metro Networks
MotorNet
New Dimensions Radio
No Soap Productions
Omnimusic
Paulist Media Works
Protestant Hour Inc.
Radio Production Services Inc.
Radio Spirits
Reizner & Reizner Film & Video
Rex Recording & Video Post
Sound of Birmingham Productions
Soundshop Recording Studio LLC
Studio M Productions Unlimited
Suite Audio
UBC Radio
VideoActive Productions
WQXR
WRS/Channel One
Washington Korean Broadcasting Co.
WeatherVision Inc.

Audio/Visual Services
American TelNet
Capital Communications
Coote Communications
DG Systems
Great Plains National (GPN)
Host Communications Inc.
Kipany Productions Ltd.
Reliance Audio Visual Corp.
TR Productions
Talco Productions
Videosmith Inc.
Wade Productions Inc.

Background Music
American TelNet
FirstCom Music
Horizon Audio Creations
Joe Jones Productions
Message on Hold
Muzak
OGM Production Music
Omnimusic
Promusic
RPM-Radio Programming & Management Inc.
Westar Music
Who Did That Music?

Camera Operators
J. Arnold Productions
Asia Pacific Productions
Bell Foto Art Productions
CamMate Studios
D-V-X International
Daley Video
FTC/Orlando
Maslow Media Group Inc.
Nemo News
PACSAT
PMTV Producers Management Television
Reizner & Reizner Film & Video
Tankersley Productions, Inc., St. Louis
Telepros
Videosmith Inc.
WKMG Productions
WTOB Channel 2—Public/Government Access TV
White Rabbit Productions
Yada/Levine Video Productions

Broadcasting & Cable Yearbook 2006

Producers, Distributors, and Production Services Subject Index

Cassette Duplicating
Command Productions
Continental Recordings Inc.
Digital Force
Domain Communications L.L.C.
Jeff Gold Productions Inc.
Man From Mars Productions
N W Media
Paulist Media Works
The Transfer Zone

CD Production Library
Toby Arnold and Associates Inc.
Broadcast Programming
Bruder Releasing Inc. (BRI)
Digital Force
Eurocine
FirstCom Music
GMI Media L.L.C.
Ghostwriters/Radio Mall
J&H Music Programming
Metro Music Productions Inc.
OGM Production Music
Primedia Workplace Learning
Production Garden Music Libraries
Promusic
SoperSound Music Library
Who Did That Music?

Children's Programming, Radio
The Walt Disney Company
Miller Broadcast Management
Moody Broadcasting Network
National Church Broadcasting
Parrot Productions Ltd.
Prairie Dog Entertainment
RAD Marketing & Cabletowns
StarDate/Universo
Toes Production Inc.

Children's Programming, Radio & TV
The Dolmatch Group Ltd.
Larry Harmon Pictures Corp.
Bill Melendez Productions Inc.
The Multimedia Group of Canada
Presson Perspectives
Warren Only Media Group
The Worship Network

Children's Programming, TV
Academy Entertainment
The Kay Arnold Group
Bardel Entertainment Inc.
Burrud Productions Inc.
CABLEready Corp.
Canamedia Productions Ltd.
Capital Communications
Sandra Carter Productions Inc.
Central Park Media
Children's Media Productions
Chrysalis Distribution
The Dick Clark Productions
Classic Media
Concept Videos
Cookie Jar Group
Crystal Pictures Inc.
DLT Entertainment Ltd.
Disney Channel
Walt Disney Company
The Walt Disney Company
Dorling Kindersley Vision
Elliot and Friends, Inc.
Ellis Entertainment
Enoki Films U.S.A. Inc.
Eurocine
Filmoption International Inc.
Sandy Frank Entertainment Inc.
Glenray Productions Inc.
Great North Productions
Great Plains National (GPN)
Alfred Haber Distribution Inc.
Larry Harmon Pictures Corp.
International Television Corp.
Jams Productions Inc.
Juravic Entertainment
KJD Teleproductions

Lakeside Television Co. Inc.
Litton Syndications Inc.
MGM TV Canada
Mar Vista Entertainment
Maryland Public Television
Bill Melendez Productions Inc.
Mondo TV
Moonstone Entertainment
New Zoo Revue
O. Atlas Enterprises Inc.
Oasis International
Pantomime Pictures Inc.
Parrot Productions Ltd.
Pied Piper Films Ltd.
PorchLight Entertainment Inc.
Positive Children's Programming (PCP)
PostWorks, New York
Producers Group, Ltd.
Productions La Fete
The Program Exchange
Promark Television
RAD Marketing & Cabletowns
Redwood Entertainment Inc.
Peter Rodgers Organization
Steve Rotfeld Productions Inc.
Salter Street Films International Ltd.
Sanctuary Records Group Ltd.
Edward Sarson Productions
The Saturday Evening Post Television Department
M C Stuart & Associates Pty Ltd.
The Summit Media Group Inc. (Sub 4 Kids Entertainment)
Sunbow Entertainment
Television Representatives Inc.
The Television Syndication Company, Inc.
Toes Production Inc.
The Transcription Company
Triage Entertainment Inc.
Two Oceans Entertainment Group
V I E W Video Inc.
Venevision International
Viacom Inc.
WQED Multimedia
WTOB Channel 2—Public/Government Access TV
Western International Syndication
Daniel Wilson Productions Inc.
Fred Wolf Films
World Events Productions Ltd.
Yorkshire Television

Commercial Distribution, Radio
Campbell-Ewald Advertising
KTOO-TV & Radio Station
MAKWDE Productions
Metro Networks
MotorNet
Dick Orkin's Amazing Radio
Radio America
Washington Korean Broadcasting Co.

Commercial Distribution, Radio & TV
The Chuck Blore Co.
DG Systems
Evergreen Entertainment Group
Robert Michelson Inc.
RAD Marketing & Cabletowns
RDF Media

Commercial Distribution, TV
ADM—International Film & TV Distribution
ATA Trading Corp.
Academy Entertainment
The Kay Arnold Group
Broadview Media
CFP Video Productions
Campbell-Ewald Advertising
Capital Communications
Carlton International Media Inc.
Central Park Media
Duke International
David Finch Distribution Ltd.
Sandy Frank Entertainment Inc.
GLL TV Enterprises Inc.
Global Entertainment Media
Great Chefs Television/Publishing
International Tele-Film
King World Media Sales
Knowledge In A Nutshell Inc.

MAKWDE Productions
Midwest Video Communications Inc.
Oasis International
PPM Multimedia
ROZON
SFP Productions
Harvey Sheldon Productions
Sport International Inc.
Viacom Video Services
Video-Cinema Films Inc.
Yorkshire Television

Commercial Production, Radio
ABC Radio Networks
Toby Arnold and Associates Inc.
The Audio Department Inc.
CCM Media Services
CRN International
Campbell-Ewald Advertising
Carleton Productions International Inc.
Thomas Craven Film Corp.
Creative Marketing & Communications Corp.
DaviSound
Eagle Media Productions Ltd.
Happi Associates
Heil Enterprises
The Image Generators
Irving Productions Inc.
Joe Jones Productions
MAKWDE Productions
Man From Mars Productions
Robert Michelson Inc.
Perception Media Group
Radio Production Services Inc.
Suite Audio
Time Capsule Inc.
UBC Radio
Washington Korean Broadcasting Co.
Larry John Wright Inc.

Commercial Production, Radio & TV
Aloha Productions
Robert L. Bocchino
CA Media Development
Clayton-Davis & Associates Inc.
Continental Recordings Inc.
Coote Communications
John Driscoll/VoiceOver America
Jeff Gold Productions Inc.
JAM Creative Productions Inc.
The Johnson Group
KUSA Television
McClain Enterprises Inc.
Bill Melendez Productions Inc.
No Soap Productions
North by Northwest Productions
RDF Media
RMD & Assoc. Inc.
Radio & TV Roundup Productions
Romano & Associates Inc.
Sam Shad Productions
Shield Productions Inc.
Sound of Birmingham Productions
Strand Media Group Inc.
TM Century Inc.
Video/Media Distribution Inc.
Vyvx, a Division of WillTel Communications

Commercial Production, TV
Agora TV
J. Arnold Productions
The Kay Arnold Group
Asia Pacific Productions
The Audio Department Inc.
Bardel Entertainment Inc.
Brillig Productions Inc.
CMT
Campbell-Ewald Advertising
Carleton Productions International Inc.
Center City Film & Video
Thomas Craven Film Corp.
Custom Productions Inc.
Daley Video
EUE Screen Gems Studios
Encore Video Productions Inc.
FTC/Orlando
Film House Inc.
Fox 17 Studio Productions
Fox 29 WUTV Sinclair
Sandy Frank Entertainment Inc.

Producers, Distributors, and Production Services Subject Index

Jeff Gold Productions Inc.
Golden Gate Studios
The Image Generators
Independent Artists
JC Productions Inc.
Jordan Klein Film & Video
The Kenwood Group
King World Media Sales
Lapco Communications
MAKWDE Productions
MRC Films
Mason Video
Maysles Films, Inc.
McClain Enterprises Inc.
Midwest Video Communications Inc.
Warren Miller Entertainment
New York Communications
Pantomime Pictures Inc.
Peckham Productions
Pied Piper Films Ltd.
Playhouse Pictures
Prime Cut Productions Inc.
Producers Group, Ltd.
ROZON
Reuters Television
River City Video Productions
Rosler Creative
Sanctuary Records Group Ltd.
Sport International Inc.
Sullivan Video Services Inc.
Pat Summerall Productions
Technisonic Studios
Tel-A-Cast Productions
Triage Entertainment Inc.
Video Techniques Inc.
Videosmith Inc.
WKMG Productions
Welwood International Film Production
White Rabbit Productions
Fred Wolf Films
Larry John Wright Inc.
Yada/Levine Video Productions

Computer Graphics

CA Media Development
Center City Film & Video
CineGroupe
Cinema Concepts Animation Studio
Crest National Digital Media Complex
Daley Video
Darino Films/Library of Special Effects
ETN—Educational Telecommunications Network
Film House Inc.
Grace Digital Media
Henninger Media Services, Inc.
The History Makers
The Image Group
JC Productions Inc.
Kipany Productions Ltd.
Magno Sound & Video
Warren Miller Entertainment
Northwest Imaging & FX
PACSAT
Palace Digital Studios
Pike Productions Inc.
Playhouse Pictures
PostWorks, New York
Purple Grape Post
RMD & Assoc. Inc.
Rampion Visual Productions L.L.C.
TR Productions
Traffic Pulse Networks (A Unit of Mobility Technologies)
VA-Tech Video/Broadcast Services
WRS/Channel One

Creative Services

Aloha Productions
American TelNet
Ascent Media Network Services
Bayliss
The Chuck Blore Co.
COMPRO Productions Inc.
Campbell-Ewald Advertising
Center City Film & Video
Cimarron Group
ComBridges
DWJ Television
Devlin Design Group Inc.
ESPI Video
ETN—Educational Telecommunications Network
Ebbets Field Productions Ltd.

Elliot and Friends, Inc.
Film House Inc.
First Marketing
Fox 29 WUTV Sinclair
Jeff Gold Productions Inc.
Independent Artists
JC Productions Inc.
The Johnson Group
The Kenwood Group
Kipany Productions Ltd.
Klein &
Make It Happen Productions Inc.
N W Media
No Soap Productions
Palace Digital Studios
Peters Communications
Praxis Media Inc.
RMD & Assoc. Inc.
Radioguide People Inc.
Redwood Entertainment Inc.
Rosler Creative
Sak Entertainment
Edward Sarson Productions
SeniorVision Productions, Inc.
Strand Media Group Inc.
Talco Productions
TeleCom Productions Inc.
Video I-D Teleproductions Inc.
Wade Productions Inc.
Warren Only Media Group
Larry John Wright Inc.
Sandy Zimmerman Productions

Development, Films

Ardustry Home Entertainment LLC
CIFEX International Inc.
Carsey-Werner Distribution
Curb Entertainment International Corp.
The Walt Disney Company
The Dolmatch Group Ltd.
ETN—Educational Telecommunications Network
Ebbets Field Productions Ltd.
1st Miracle Productions
JC Productions Inc.
Lions Gate Entertainment
Make It Happen Productions Inc.
Richter Productions Inc.
Rosler Creative
Studio Babelsberg GmbH
Tamouz Media
Triage Entertainment Inc.

Development, Films, TV Series & Video

Angel Films Co.
Burrud Productions Inc.
CABLEready Corp.
CDR Communications Inc.
Children's Media Productions
Clayton-Davis & Associates Inc.
ComBridges
Critical Mass Releasing Inc.
DLT Entertainment Ltd.
Devillier Donegan Enterprises L.P.
Duke International
ETN—Educational Telecommunications Network
Film Roman Inc.
Jeff Gold Productions Inc.
Independent Edge Films
Make It Happen Productions Inc.
Oasis International
Pied Piper Films Ltd.
Producers Group, Ltd.
Redwood Entertainment Inc.
Reel Media International Inc.
Sak Entertainment
SeniorVision Productions, Inc.
Silverline Pictures
Pat Summerall Productions
Two Oceans Entertainment Group
Warren Only Media Group
M.D. Wax Courier Films

Development, TV Films, Series

Adler Media Inc.
Dave Bell Associates Inc.
The Chuck Blore Co.
CanLib Inc.
Walt Disney Company

The Walt Disney Company
The Dolmatch Group Ltd.
ETN—Educational Telecommunications Network
Ebbets Field Productions Ltd.
Elliot and Friends, Inc.
Essence Television Productions Inc.
Eurocine
1st Miracle Productions
Freewheelin' Films Ltd.
The Fremantle Corp.
FremantleMedia North America Inc.
Glenray Productions Inc.
The Griffin Group
Thomas Horton Associates Inc.
JC Productions Inc.
Nicole Jouve
Lakeside Television Co. Inc.
MacNeil/Lehrer Productions
Make It Happen Productions Inc.
New Line Television
Pantomime Pictures Inc.
Planet Pictures Ltd.
Questar
Reuters Media
Richter Productions Inc.
Peter Rodgers Organization
SPI International
Sullivan Entertainment Inc./Sullivan Entertainment International
Sunbow Entertainment
Tamouz Media
Tapestry International, Ltd.
Triage Entertainment Inc.
Twentieth Television

Development, Video

AmericaNurse TV Productions
Clayton-Davis & Associates Inc.
ComBridges
The Walt Disney Company
The Dolmatch Group Ltd.
ETN—Educational Telecommunications Network
Essence Television Productions Inc.
Eurocine
Glenray Productions Inc.
Global Telemedia Inc.
The Griffin Group
JC Productions Inc.
Kipany Productions Ltd.
Lions Gate Entertainment
Make It Happen Productions Inc.
Midwest Video Communications Inc.
Questar
Richter Productions Inc.
Tapestry International, Ltd.
Triage Entertainment Inc.
V I E W Video Inc.

Distribution, Audio

DaviSound
Digital Force
Domain Communications L.L.C.
Good Life Associates
The Image Generators
Irving Productions Inc.
North Star Music
Dick Orkin's Amazing Radio
Paulist Media Works

Distribution, Cable

ATA Trading Corp.
Academy Entertainment
Adler Media Inc.
The Kay Arnold Group
Bruder Releasing Inc. (BRI)
Castle Hill Productions Inc.
Central Park Media
DLT Entertainment Ltd.
The Walt Disney Company
FamilyNet
GLL TV Enterprises Inc.
Galavision
Granada America
Great Plains National (GPN)
Grove Television Enterprises Inc.
HAVE Inc.
Janson Media
Kazmark Entertainment Group
Loral Skynet
Mar Vista Entertainment

Broadcasting & Cable Yearbook 2006

Producers, Distributors, and Production Services Subject Index

Media Planning Group (MPG)
Modern Entertainment
Moonstone Entertainment
New City Releasing Inc.
O. Atlas Enterprises Inc.
Oasis International
Playboy Entertainment Group Inc.
Powersports/Millenium International
Rigel Entertainment
Peter Rodgers Organization
Harvey Sheldon Productions
Video-Cinema Films Inc.
M.D. Wax Courier Films
Worldview Entertainment Inc.

Distribution, Cartoons

ATA Trading Corp.
Academy Entertainment
Central Park Media
CineGroupe
Classic Media
Dargaud-Marina
Walt Disney Company
The Dolmatch Group Ltd.
Film Roman Inc.
The Fremantle Corp.
Larry Harmon Pictures Corp.
Italtoons Corp.
Mondo TV
Pan American Video
The Summit Media Group Inc. (Sub 4 Kids Entertainment)
World Events Productions Ltd.

Distribution, Film and Video

ADM—International Film & TV Distribution
ATA Trading Corp.
Academy Entertainment
Accuracy in Media Inc.
Adler Media Inc.
Angel Films Co.
Ardustry Home Entertainment LLC
Arkadia Entertainment Corp.
Ascent Media Network Services
Ascent Media Network Services
CDR Communications Inc.
CIFEX International Inc.
CRM Learning
Canamedia Productions Ltd.
Castle Hill Productions Inc.
Children's Media Productions
The Cinema Guild Inc.
Crystal Pictures Inc.
Cube International
Curb Entertainment International Corp.
Donnelly & Associates
Duke International
Filmoption International Inc.
Films for the Humanities & Sciences Inc./FFH Video
Films of the Nations
David Finch Distribution Ltd.
1st Miracle Productions
First Run/Icarus Films
Free Speech TV (FSTV)
Glenray Productions Inc.
Granada America
Great Plains National (GPN)
Grove Television Enterprises Inc.
Alfred Haber Distribution Inc.
Hearst Entertainment, Inc.
Independent Edge Films
International Tele-Film
JGT Media Productions
Nicole Jouve
Kazmark Entertainment Group
Kultur/White Star Video
Lions Gate Entertainment
Mar Vista Entertainment
Maryknoll Productions
Maysles Films, Inc.
Modern Entertainment
Moonstone Entertainment
Myriad Pictures
New City Releasing Inc.
New Line Television
O. Atlas Enterprises Inc.
PAULAR Entertainment L.L.C.
PPM Multimedia
Pike Productions Inc.
Planet Pictures Ltd.
Playboy Entertainment Group Inc.
Producers Group, Ltd.

Public Media Incorporated
RMD & Assoc. Inc.
Reel Media International Inc.
Richter Productions Inc.
Rigel Entertainment
Peter Rodgers Organization
Salter Street Films International Ltd.
Sanctuary Records Group Ltd.
SeniorVision Productions, Inc.
Seville Pictures
Silverline Pictures
Southern STAR
Marty Stouffer Productions Ltd.
M C Stuart & Associates Pty Ltd.
Television Representatives Inc.
Trident Releasing
V I E W Video Inc.
Video/Media Distribution Inc.
M.D. Wax Courier Films
Worldview Entertainment Inc.

Distribution, Music

ADM—International Film & TV Distribution
Arkadia Entertainment Corp.
Cube International
Joe Jones Productions
Kultur/White Star Video
Loral Skynet
North Star Music

Distribution, Radio & TV Programming

Accuracy in Media Inc.
AmericaNurse TV Productions
CDR Communications Inc.
Catholic Communication Campaign
The Christophers Inc.
The Crime Channel
DG Systems
Dialing for Dollars
Evergreen Entertainment Group
FamilyNet
Gordon Productions
Medialink
National Council of Churches Communications Unit
New Visions Syndication Inc.
News Broadcast Network
Outdoor Media Group
Prairie Dog Entertainment
RAD Marketing & Cabletowns
RBC Ministries/Midwest Media Managers
The Radio-Studio Network
Viacom Video Services
Warren Only Media Group
The Worship Network

Distribution, Radio Programming

Agrinet Farm Radio Network
At a Glance
The Classical Station, WCPE
Clear Channel Broadcasting Inc.
Country Crossroads FamilyNet Radio
The Walt Disney Company
Domain Communications L.L.C.
Eagle Media Productions Ltd.
Good Life Associates
Happi Associates
It Is Written Television
J&H Music Programming
Jameson Broadcast Inc.
The Johnson Group
Jones Radio Networks
Knowledge In A Nutshell Inc.
Leadem to Water Production Inc.
Longhorn Radio Network
Loral Skynet
MAKWDE Productions
MRN Radio
MasterControl FamilyNet Radio
Media Planning Group (MPG)
Metro Networks
Moody Broadcasting Network
MotorNet
Musical Starstreams
National Public Radio
New Dimensions Radio
North American Network, Inc.
North Shore Productions
On Track

Ports of Paradise
Powerline
Premiere Radio Networks Inc.
Protestant Hour Inc.
RPM-Radio Programming & Management Inc.
Radio Canada International/Canadian Broadcasting Corp.
Radio Express Inc.
Radio Spirits
The Radio-Studio Network
Ray Sports Network
Solid Gospel Network (Reach Satellite Network, Inc.)
Sound Source Networks
Sports Byline U.S.A.
Talk America Radio Networks
Talk Radio Network
UBC Radio
United Stations Radio Network
WFMT Radio Network
Washington Korean Broadcasting Co.

Distribution, TV Programming

ADM—International Film & TV Distribution
ATA Trading Corp.
Academy Entertainment
Adler Media Inc.
American Public Television
The Kay Arnold Group
Ascent Media Management East
Ascent Media Network Services
Bellon Entertainment
CABLEready Corp.
CCI Entertainment Ltd.
CNBC Syndication
CS Associates
CTV Television Inc.
CanLib Inc.
Carleton Productions International Inc.
Carsey-Werner Distribution
Sandra Carter Productions Inc.
Castle Hill Productions Inc.
Central Park Media
Chrysalis Distribution
Classic Media
Clever Cleaver Productions
Concept Videos
William F. Cooke Television Programs
The Crime Channel
Critical Mass Releasing Inc.
Cube International
DLT Entertainment Ltd.
Dargaud-Marina
Devillier Donegan Enterprises L.P.
Walt Disney Company
The Walt Disney Company
The Dolmatch Group Ltd.
Donnelly & Associates
Dorling Kindersley Vision
Duke International
Eaton Films Ltd.
Ellis Entertainment
Enoki Films U.S.A. Inc.
Europe Images International
FamilyNet
Film Roman Inc.
Filmoption International Inc.
1st Miracle Productions
First Run/Icarus Films
Fox Sports West
Free Speech TV (FSTV)
The Fremantle Corp.
GRB Entertainment
Galavision
Global Entertainment Media
Granada America
Grove Television Enterprises Inc.
Alfred Haber Distribution Inc.
Harmony Gold U.S.A. Inc.
Hearst Entertainment, Inc.
Henninger Media Services, Inc.
Holigan Investment Group Ltd.
Thomas Horton Associates Inc.
International Tele-Film
International Television Corp.
It Is Written Television
Italtoons Corp.
Ivanhoe Broadcast News Inc.
Jams Productions Inc.
Janson Media
Jefferson-Pilot Sports
Nicole Jouve
Juravic Entertainment
Kazmark Entertainment Group

Broadcasting & Cable Yearbook 2006

Producers, Distributors, and Production Services Subject Index

King World Media Sales
King World Productions
Knowledge In A Nutshell Inc.
Kultur/White Star Video
Lakeside Television Co. Inc.
Lambert Television
Litton Syndications Inc.
Loral Skynet
MAKWDE Productions
MGM TV Canada
MG/Perin Inc.
Mar Vista Entertainment
Media Planning Group (MPG)
Metro Networks
Modern Entertainment
Mondo TV
Moonstone Entertainment
The Multimedia Group of Canada
Myriad Pictures
NRS Group PTY Ltd.
NTN Communications Inc.
National Collegiate Athletic Association
New Films International
O. Atlas Enterprises Inc.
PAULAR Entertainment L.L.C.
PPM Multimedia
Pan American Video
Paramount Worldwide Television Distribution
Parrot Communications International Inc.
Planet Pictures Ltd.
Playboy Entertainment Group Inc.
PorchLight Entertainment Inc.
Power Play Music Video L.L.C.
Powersports/Millenium International
Productions La Fete
Promark Television
Questar
ROZON
Raycom Sports
The Real Estate Network
Reel Media International Inc.
Riden International Inc.
Rigel Entertainment
Peter Rodgers Organization
Rose Entertainment
Rosnay International
Steve Rotfeld Productions Inc.
SPI International
Salter Street Films International Ltd.
Seville Pictures
Harvey Sheldon Productions
Silverline Pictures
Southern STAR
Sport International Inc.
M C Stuart & Associates Pty Ltd.
Sullivan Entertainment Inc./Sullivan Entertainment International
The Summit Media Group Inc. (Sub 4 Kids Entertainment)
Sunbow Entertainment
Telegenic Programs Inc.
Television Representatives Inc.
The Television Syndication Company, Inc.
Televix Entertainment Inc.
Tribune Entertainment Co.
20th Century Fox/Incendo Television Distribution Ltd.
Twentieth Century Fox Television Distribution
Twentieth Television
Univision Communications Inc.
Venevision International
Viacom Inc.
Viacom Video Services
Video-Cinema Films Inc.
Video/Media Distribution Inc.
WRS/Channel One
Warner Bros. International Distribution Inc. (Canada)
M.D. Wax Courier Films
WeatherVision Inc.
Western International Syndication
Robert Wold Co.
World Events Productions Ltd.
Worldview Entertainment Inc.
Worldvision NY

Dubbing Services

Carpel Video Inc.
CineGroupe
D-V-X International
HAVE Inc.
KPTS-TV
Man From Mars Productions
Mondo TV
Studio Babelsberg GmbH
VTTV Videothek Electronic TV-Production GmbH + Co Kopier KG
Video Services
WRS/Channel One

Duplication Services

Advanced Digital Services, Inc.
Agora TV
Ascent Media Management East
Cable Films & Video
Carleton Productions International Inc.
Carpel Video Inc.
Cramer Productions Center
Crest National Digital Media Complex
DG Systems
Duke International
ETN—Educational Telecommunications Network
Great Plains National (GPN)
HAVE Inc.
Heil Enterprises
Highland Laboratories
The Image Group
Tom Jones Recording Studios
Lion and Fox Recording Studios
Media Visions
N W Media
Parrot Communications International Inc.
Point 360
PostWorks, New York
Pro Video
Quality Film & Video
RAD Marketing & Cabletowns
Pat Summerall Productions
The Transfer Zone
TRI-COMM Productions
Viacom Video Services
Video/Media Distribution Inc.
Video Services
Video Techniques Inc.
Vyvx, a Division of WillTel Communications
Work Edit

Editing Services

Agora TV
Ascent Media Management East
Asia Pacific Productions
CMT
COMPRO Productions Inc.
CamMate Studios
Catholic Communications Corp.
Crest National Digital Media Complex
D-V-X International
DWJ Television
Duke International
Fox 29 WUTV Sinclair
Grace Digital Media
Henninger Media Services, Inc.
Highland Laboratories
The History Makers
Host Communications Inc.
The Image Group
MVI Post
Masai Films Inc.
Matchframe Video
Warren Miller Entertainment
N W Media
Northwest Imaging & FX
PACSAT
Perception Media Group
Point 360
Pro Video
Purple Grape Post
Redwood Entertainment Inc.
Reuters Television
Rex Recording & Video Post
River City Video Productions
Romano & Associates Inc.
Seraphim Communications Inc.
Suite Audio
Tankersley Productions, Inc., St. Louis
Technisonic Studios
The Transfer Zone
U.S. Plan B Inc.
Videographic West
Work Edit
Yada/Levine Video Productions

Educational Programming, Radio

At a Glance
Call For Action Inc.
The Classical Station, WCPE
ETN—Educational Telecommunications Network
Ecumenical Communications
FamilyNet Radio
Globe Productions
The Idea Channel
Leadem to Water Production Inc.
Longhorn Radio Network
Moody Broadcasting Network
New Dimensions Radio
Powerline
Prairie Dog Entertainment
Presbyterian Church (U.S.A.)
Radio America
Radio Canada International/Canadian Broadcasting Corp.
The Saturday Evening Post Television Department
StarDate/Universo
WCTD AM 1620
Washington Korean Broadcasting Co.

Educational Programming, Radio & TV

Accuracy in Media Inc.
AmericaNurse TV Productions
Arkadia Entertainment Corp.
Earthwatch Radio
Arthur Henley Productions
Joe Jones Productions
Bill Melendez Productions Inc.
Presson Perspectives
The Radio Almanac
Charlie Spencer Productions
Ukrainian Melody Hour
VA-Tech Video/Broadcast Services
WQED Multimedia

Educational Programming, TV

Ardustry Home Entertainment LLC
Bellon Entertainment
Brillig Productions Inc.
Broadview Media
Burrud Productions Inc.
Call For Action Inc.
Sandra Carter Productions Inc.
Catholic Communication Campaign
Catholic Television Network
Central City Productions, Inc.
Clever Cleaver Productions
The Crime Channel
Cube International
Darino Films/Library of Special Effects
Disney Channel
The D.L. Dykes Jr. Foundation
Elliot and Friends, Inc.
Ellis Entertainment
Enoki Films U.S.A. Inc.
Evergreen Entertainment Group
Filmoption International Inc.
David Finch Distribution Ltd.
First Run/Icarus Films
Freewheelin' Films Ltd.
FremantleMedia North America Inc.
General Conference of Seventh-day Adventists
Global Entertainment Media
Global Telemedia Inc.
Great Plains National (GPN)
Hamilton Productions Inc.
Heritage/Baruch Television Distribution
Home Improvement Television Network
International Broadcasting Network
International Tele-Film
Janson Media
Juravic Entertainment
KPTS-TV
Litton Syndications Inc.
MacNeil/Lehrer Productions
Mar Vista Entertainment
Masai Films Inc.
Mason Video
The Media Group of Connecticut Inc.
Modern Entertainment
Mondo TV
New Zoo Revue
O. Atlas Enterprises Inc.
Pantomime Pictures Inc.
Phoebus Communications Inc.

Pied Piper Films Ltd.
Planet Pictures Ltd.
Powersports/Millenium International
Presbyterian Church (U.S.A.)
SCOLA
The Saturday Evening Post Television Department
M C Stuart & Associates Pty Ltd.
TVOntario
Tamouz Media
Television Representatives Inc.
V I E W Video Inc.
Vision Broadcasting - KVBA TV 19
Daniel Wilson Productions Inc.
Yorkshire Television

Entertainment Programming, Radio

ABC Radio Networks
Agrinet Farm Radio Network
Broadcast Programming
C N R Radio
CRN International
The Dick Clark Productions
Creative Marketing & Communications Corp.
DC Audio
The Walt Disney Company
Ecumenical Communications
Essence Television Productions Inc.
FamilyNet Radio
Jameson Broadcast Inc.
Jones Radio Networks
Launch Radio Networks
Leadem to Water Production Inc.
Ben Manilla Productions
MasterControl FamilyNet Radio
Media Planning Group (MPG)
North American Network, Inc.
On Track
Powerline
Prairie Dog Entertainment
Premiere Radio Networks Inc.
Radio America
Radio Spirits
The Radio-Studio Network
Sam Shad Productions
StarDate/Universo
Talk Radio Network
UBC Radio
United Stations Radio Network
WCTD AM 1620
"The Weather Center"
Larry John Wright Inc.
ZBS Foundation

Entertainment Programming, Radio & TV

Arkadia Entertainment Corp.
The Chuck Blore Co.
Arthur Henley Productions
KJD Teleproductions
Bill Melendez Productions Inc.
New Visions Syndication Inc.
Jim Owens Entertainment
Ukrainian Melody Hour
University of Colorado Television
WQED Multimedia
WWE Entertainment Inc.
M.D. Wax Courier Films

Entertainment Programming, TV

ATA Trading Corp.
J. Arnold Productions
Bell Foto Art Productions
Burrud Productions Inc.
CN8, The Comcast Network
CanLib Inc.
Carsey-Werner Distribution
Sandra Carter Productions Inc.
Central City Productions, Inc.
Chrysalis Distribution
The Dick Clark Productions
Clear Channel Broadcasting Inc.
Clever Cleaver Productions
Country Crossroads FamilyNet Radio
The Crime Channel
Crystal Pictures Inc.
Cube International
The Walt Disney Company
E! Entertainment Television
Ellis Entertainment

Essence Television Productions Inc.
Evergreen Entertainment Group
Faraone Communications Inc.
First Run/Icarus Films
GLL TV Enterprises Inc.
GRB Entertainment
Glenray Productions Inc.
Global Entertainment Media
Global Telemedia Inc.
Gould Entertainment Corp.
Great North Productions
The Griffin Group
Alfred Haber Distribution Inc.
International Tele-Film
International Television Corp.
Janson Media
Jefferson-Pilot Sports
Juravic Entertainment
KPTS-TV
KUSA Television
King World Productions
Kultur/White Star Video
Lakeside Television Co. Inc.
Lapco Communications
Litton Syndications Inc.
Media Planning Group (MPG)
Myriad Pictures
NTN Communications Inc.
New Zoo Revue
Paramount Worldwide Television Distribution
Planet Pictures Ltd.
PorchLight Entertainment Inc.
Powersports/Millenium International
Prime Cut Productions Inc.
Promark Television
Questar
ROZON
Raycom Sports
The Real Estate Network
Reid/Land Productions Inc.
Salter Street Films International Ltd.
Sam Shad Productions
Harvey Sheldon Productions
Sullivan Entertainment Inc./Sullivan Entertainment International
Tel-Air Interests Inc.
The Television Syndication Company, Inc.
Tomwil Inc.
Triage Entertainment Inc.
Turner Entertainment Co.
Twentieth Television
Viacom Inc.
Video-Cinema Films Inc.
Videographic West
Vision Broadcasting - KVBA TV 19
Warner Bros.
Wide Eye Productions, Inc.
Daniel Wilson Productions Inc.
Robert Wold Co.
World Events Productions Ltd.
The Wyland Group
Yorkshire Television

Film and Tape Transfers (Film-to-Tape)

Ascent Media Management East
Carpel Video Inc.
Crawford Communications
Crest Digital National Media Complex
Highland Laboratories
The Image Group
Magno Sound & Video
Matchframe Video
Northwest Imaging & FX
Point 360
PostWorks, New York
Quality Film & Video
The Transfer Zone
VTTV Videothek Electronic TV-Production GmbH + Co Kopier KG
Van Vliet Media

Film Laboratories

Crawford Communications
Crest National Digital Media Complex
DeLuxe Laboratories
Forde Motion Picture Labs
Henninger Media Services, Inc.
Media Visions
Point 360
Studio Babelsberg GmbH

Film Preservation/Restoration

Worldview Entertainment Inc.

Graphic Effects Library

Darino Films/Library of Special Effects

Graphics

Cimarron Group
Devlin Design Group Inc.
Elliot and Friends, Inc.
The Image Group
MVI Post
Matchframe Video
Mobile Video Services Ltd.
Peters Communications
Pro Video
Radioguide People Inc.
River City Video Productions
Technisonic Studios
TRI-COMM Productions

Industrial Films

COMPRO Productions Inc.
CRM Learning
DWJ Television
ESPI Video
Encore Video Productions Inc.
FTC/Orlando
The Kenwood Group
Limelight Communications Inc.
Lindberg Productions Inc.
MRC Films
Make It Happen Productions Inc.
Pantomime Pictures Inc.
Peckham Productions
Primedia Workplace Learning
Tel-Air Interests Inc.
Telepros
Video/Media Distribution Inc.
Wade Productions Inc.
Work Edit

Inflight Audio Progamming

Ellis Entertainment
Horizon Audio Creations
Ports of Paradise
Prairie Dog Entertainment
RDF Media
Redwood Entertainment Inc.
Time Capsule Inc.

Interactive Television

Ascent Media Network Services
NTN Communications Inc.
Parrot Communications International Inc.
PostWorks, New York
The Real Estate Network
SPI International
Video I-D Teleproductions Inc.

Interactive Television Programming

Elliot and Friends, Inc.
Eurocine
Ivanhoe Broadcast News Inc.
NTN Communications Inc.
Phoebus Communications Inc.
Presson Perspectives
Producers Group, Ltd.
The Real Estate Network
Reuters Media
Sunbow Entertainment
University of Colorado Television

Jingles

Aloha Productions
Blue Heaven Productions
CA Media Development
Continental Recordings Inc.
GMI Media L.L.C.
Groove Addicts
JAM Creative Productions Inc.
Joe Jones Productions
MAKWDE Productions

Producers, Distributors, and Production Services Subject Index

Radio Express Inc.
Radio Production Services Inc.
Shield Productions Inc.
Sound of Birmingham Productions
TM Century Inc.
Thompson Creative

Libraries, Film

Getty Images
Granada America
Grinberg Film Libraries Inc.
Grove Television Enterprises Inc.
MGM TV Canada
Modern Entertainment
Pan American Video
Paramount Worldwide Television Distribution
Reel Media International Inc.
Peter Rodgers Organization
Televix Entertainment Inc.
Turner Entertainment Co.
Video-Cinema Films Inc.
The WPA Film Library
Worldview Entertainment Inc.

Libraries, TV

ADM—International Film & TV Distribution
CelebrityFootage
Cube International
Film Roman Inc.
Getty Images
Granada America
Grinberg Film Libraries Inc.
Grove Television Enterprises Inc.
King World Productions
Modern Entertainment
NRS Group PTY Ltd.
New Films International
New Zoo Revue
Pan American Video
Paramount Worldwide Television Distribution
Sanctuary Records Group Ltd.
Televix Entertainment Inc.
Turner Entertainment Co.
Twentieth Century Fox Television Distribution
Viacom Video Services
WWE Entertainment Inc.

Libraries, Video

CelebrityFootage
Children's Media Productions
The Dick Clark Productions
First Run/Icarus Films
Getty Images
Grinberg Film Libraries Inc.
Grove Television Enterprises Inc.
The Idea Channel
National Collegiate Athletic Association
New Zoo Revue
Public Media Incorporated
Reuters Television
River City Video Productions
WWE Entertainment Inc.

Licensing Services

Classic Media
Film Roman Inc.
Getty Images
Grinberg Film Libraries Inc.
Larry Harmon Pictures Corp.
Harmony Gold U.S.A. Inc.
Southern STAR
The Summit Media Group Inc. (Sub 4 Kids Entertainment)
Sunbow Entertainment
TRF Production Music Libraries
Televix Entertainment Inc.
Turner Entertainment Co.
WWE Entertainment Inc.

Location Services

American Stock Exchange
Georgia Film, Video & Music Office
Lion and Fox Recording Studios
Maslow Media Group Inc.
U.S. Plan B Inc.

Medical Programming, Radio

AmericaNurse TV Productions
Creative Marketing & Communications Corp.
Essence Television Productions Inc.
Jameson Broadcast Inc.
MSE
MasterControl FamilyNet Radio
MediaTracks Inc.
Powerline
RPM-Radio Programming & Management Inc.
Radio Production Services Inc.
The Saturday Evening Post Television Department
Talk America Radio Networks
Talk Radio Network

Medical Programming, Radio & TV

AmericaNurse TV Productions
CDR Communications Inc.
Faith for Today
Arthur Henley Productions
Lifestyle Magazine/The Evidence
MSE
Presson Perspectives
Radio & TV Roundup Productions

Medical Programming, TV

J. Arnold Productions
Bell Foto Art Productions
CABLEready Corp.
The D.L. Dykes Jr. Foundation
Hamilton Productions Inc.
Ivanhoe Broadcast News Inc.
Limelight Communications Inc.
Mason Video
Medstar Television Inc.
The Multimedia Group of Canada
The Saturday Evening Post Television Department
The Wyland Group
Sandy Zimmerman Productions

Mobile Production Units

CMT
Cinecraft Productions Inc.
DOME PRODUCTIONS
KUSA Television
Nemo News
PMTV Producers Management Television
(PSSI) Production & Satellite Services Inc.
SWTV Production Services Inc.
Telenium Studios
Telfax Inc.
VTTV Videothek Electronic TV-Production GmbH + Co Kopier KG
Videosmith Inc.
WKMG Productions

Music and Sound Effects

Blue Heaven Productions
FirstCom Music
GMI Media L.L.C.
Ghostwriters/Radio Mall
Manhattan Production Music
Megatrax Production Music Inc.
Network Music L.L.C.
OGM Production Music
Omnimusic
Production Garden Music Libraries
Promusic
SoperSound Music Library
Sound Ideas
TRF Production Music Libraries
Who Did That Music?

Music Composition

Carriage House Studios
Tim Cissell Music
Groove Addicts
Megatrax Production Music Inc.
Metro Music Productions Inc.
Peters Communications
SoperSound Music Library
Valentino Music & Sound Effect Libraries
Wax Music & Sound Design

Music Libraries

Alternative Programming
Broadcast Programming
FirstCom Music
Ghostwriters/Radio Mall
Halland Broadcast Services Inc.
Killer Tracks
MVI Post
Megatrax Production Music Inc.
Metro Music Productions Inc.
Network Music L.L.C.
New Zoo Revue
OGM Production Music
Omnimusic
Production Garden Music Libraries
Promusic
RPM Media Enterprises-The Relic Rack Preview
RPM-Radio Programming & Management Inc.
Radio & TV Roundup Productions
Radio Express Inc.
Smith/Lee Productions, Inc.
Sound Ideas
TM Century Inc.
TRF Production Music Libraries
Valentino Music & Sound Effect Libraries
Westar Music
Who Did That Music?

Music Lyrics

Globe Productions
Wax Music & Sound Design

Music Production

Aloha Productions
Arkadia Entertainment Corp.
Armedia Communications
Carriage House Studios
Tim Cissell Music
Groove Addicts
Joe Jones Productions
Megatrax Production Music Inc.
North Star Music
Shelly Palmer Productions
Peters Communications
Ports of Paradise
Prairie Dog Entertainment
Smith/Lee Productions, Inc.
Soundshop Recording Studio LLC
Valentino Music & Sound Effect Libraries

Music Production, Film and Video

Carriage House Studios
Tim Cissell Music
James & Associates Inc.
Valentino Music & Sound Effect Libraries
Warren Only Media Group
Wax Music & Sound Design

Music Production, Radio

ABC Radio Networks
Toby Arnold and Associates Inc.
Blue Heaven Productions
Carriage House Studios
Halland Broadcast Services Inc.
Happi Associates
RPM Media Enterprises-The Relic Rack Preview
Spanish Broadcasting System
Valentino Music & Sound Effect Libraries
WCTD AM 1620

Music Production, Radio & TV

Aloha Productions
Tim Cissell Music
Continental Recordings Inc.
JAM Creative Productions Inc.
Shield Productions Inc.
SoperSound Music Library
Sound of Birmingham Productions
TM Century Inc.
Ukrainian Melody Hour
Valentino Music & Sound Effect Libraries
Warren Only Media Group
Wax Music & Sound Design

Producers, Distributors, and Production Services Subject Index

Music Production, TV
Toby Arnold and Associates Inc.
Boston Symphony Orchestra
CMT
Central City Productions, Inc.
Tim Cissell Music
James & Associates Inc.
WWE Entertainment Inc.
The Worship Network

Music Programming, Radio
Alternative Programming
The Classical Station, WCPE
Country Crossroads FamilyNet Radio
FamilyNet Radio
Globe Productions
Hearts of Space Inc.
Heil Enterprises
Horizon Audio Creations
J&H Music Programming
Jones Radio Networks
Longhorn Radio Network
Ben Manilla Productions
Musical Starstreams
Muzak
Powerline
RPM Media Enterprises-The Relic Rack Preview
Radio Express Inc.
The Radio-Studio Network
Sing for Joy/WCAL
Soldiers Radio & Television, U.S. Army Public Affairs
Solid Gospel Network (Reach Satellite Network, Inc.)
Sound Source Networks
Spanish Broadcasting System
WCTD AM 1620

Music Scoring
Aloha Productions
Tim Cissell Music
GMI Media L.L.C.
Groove Addicts
James & Associates Inc.
Megatrax Production Music Inc.
Metro Music Productions Inc.
Wax Music & Sound Design

Music Services
Alternative Programming
Broadcast Programming
The Classical Station, WCPE
Groove Addicts
Halland Broadcast Services Inc.
Megatrax Production Music Inc.
Muzak
N W Media
Radio Express Inc.
Radio Production Services Inc.
TM Century Inc.

Music Video Production
Masai Films Inc.
Peckham Productions
Power Play Music Video L.L.C.
Redwood Entertainment Inc.
Sanctuary Records Group Ltd.
Tel-Air Interests Inc.

Nature Programming, TV
CABLEready Corp.
CNBC Syndication
Canamedia Productions Ltd.
Capital Communications
Devillier Donegan Enterprises L.P.
Dorling Kindersley Vision
Earthwatch Radio
Ellis Entertainment
First Run/Icarus Films
GRB Entertainment
Global Entertainment Media
Thomas Horton Associates Inc.
International Television Corp.
Juravic Entertainment
Lakeside Television Co. Inc.
Limelight Communications Inc.
MacNeil/Lehrer Productions
William Mauldin Productions Inc.

Montgomery Community Television Inc.
Oppix Productions Inc.
Southern STAR
Charlie Spencer Productions
Marty Stouffer Productions Ltd.
Tapestry International, Ltd.
Tomwil Inc.
Wide Eye Productions, Inc.
The Worship Network

News Programming, Radio
C N R Radio
Call For Action Inc.
The Christian Science Sentinel - Radio Edition
Clear Channel Broadcasting Inc.
Ecumedia News Service
Hometown Illinois Radio Network
The Image Generators
KCSN 88.5 FM
Launch Radio Networks
Maryknoll Productions
MediaTracks Inc.
Moody Broadcasting Network
National Council of Churches Communications Unit
National Public Radio
North American Network, Inc.
North Shore Productions
RPM Media Enterprises-The Relic Rack Preview
Radio America
Radio Canada International/Canadian Broadcasting Corp.
Ray Sports Network
Shadow Broadcast Services
Sound Source Networks
Talk America Radio Networks
United Stations Radio Network
WCTD AM 1620
Washington Korean Broadcasting Co.

News Programming, Radio & TV
American Farm Bureau Federation
Compu-Weather Inc.
John Driscoll/VoiceOver America
Evangelical Lutheran Church in America
GlobeCast
Gordon Productions
Medialink
Nemo News
News Broadcast Network
Presson Perspectives
Shadow Broadcast Services
Soldiers Radio & Television, U.S. Army Public Affairs
Ukrainian Melody Hour
University of Kentucky Public Relations & Radio-TV News Bureau
Warren Only Media Group

News Programming, TV
J. Arnold Productions
Asia Pacific Productions
Bell Foto Art Productions
Call For Action Inc.
CelebrityFootage
Daley Video
Devillier Donegan Enterprises L.P.
E! Entertainment Television
Evergreen Entertainment Group
Faraone Communications Inc.
Hamilton Productions Inc.
Health Net Productions & Pet Talk
Ivanhoe Broadcast News Inc.
KCRA-TV
Litton Syndications Inc.
Medstar Television Inc.
Midwest Video Communications Inc.
Mobile Video Services Ltd.
PACSAT
Parrot Communications International Inc.
Planet Pictures Ltd.
Potomac TV/Communications
Prime Cut Productions Inc.
Reuters Media
SCOLA
Seven Network Australia Inc.
P. Allen Smith Gardens
Sullivan Video Services Inc.
Telepros
U.S. Plan B Inc.
Video Techniques Inc.

Wide Eye Productions, Inc.
Yorkshire Television

Original Music Scoring
Carriage House Studios
Continental Recordings Inc.
Groove Addicts
JAM Creative Productions Inc.
James & Associates Inc.
Metro Music Productions Inc.
Shelly Palmer Productions
Smith/Lee Productions, Inc.
SoperSound Music Library

Performing Arts Programming, Radio
KCSN 88.5 FM
National Public Radio
RPM Media Enterprises-The Relic Rack Preview
WFMT Radio Network
WQED Multimedia
WQXR

Performing Arts Programming, Radio & TV
The Classical Station, WCPE
Arthur Henley Productions

Performing Arts Programming, TV
Arkadia Entertainment Corp.
Crystal Pictures Inc.
E! Entertainment Television
Faraone Communications Inc.
Free Speech TV (FSTV)
Global Entertainment Media
Kultur/White Star Video
MacNeil/Lehrer Productions
The Multimedia Group of Canada
Myriad Pictures
Reid/Land Productions Inc.
M C Stuart & Associates Pty Ltd.
Tapestry International, Ltd.
Telepros
V I E W Video Inc.
Video-Cinema Films Inc.
WTOB Channel 2—Public/Government Access TV
Yorkshire Television

Photographic Services
Lynn McAfee Photography
Videosmith Inc.
White Rabbit Productions
Sandy Zimmerman Productions

Postproduction Facilities
Agora TV
Ascent Media Network Services
The Audio Department Inc.
CFP Video Productions
CN8, The Comcast Network
Catholic Communications Corp.
Center City Film & Video
Cinecraft Productions Inc.
Crawford Communications
Daley Video
The D.L. Dykes Jr. Foundation
ESPI Video
Eagle Eye Film Company
Films Five Inc.
GVI
Grace Digital Media
Great Plains National (GPN)
Highland Laboratories
Horizons Television Inc.
Thomas Horton Associates Inc.
MVI Post
Matchframe Video
Mobile Video Services Ltd.
NRS Group PTY Ltd.
North by Northwest Productions
Northwest Imaging & FX
Oppix Productions Inc.
Palace Digital Studios
Point 360

Producers, Distributors, and Production Services Subject Index

Power Play Music Video L.L.C.
Purple Grape Post
Rampion Visual Productions L.L.C.
The Saturday Evening Post Television Department
Seraphim Communications Inc.
Soldiers Radio & Television, U.S. Army Public Affairs
Studio Babelsberg GmbH
Tankersley Productions, Inc., St. Louis
Telenium Studios
The Transfer Zone
University of Colorado Television
Video I-D Teleproductions Inc.
Video Techniques Inc.
VideoActive Productions
Videographic West
Vyvx, a Division of WillTel Communications
WKMG Productions
Work Edit

Postproduction Services

Agora TV
American Stock Exchange
CFP Video Productions
CN8, The Comcast Network
Carleton Productions International Inc.
Cookie Jar Group
Cornell University Educational Television Center
Darino Films/Library of Special Effects
DeLuxe Laboratories
Eagle Eye Film Company
GTN
Getty Images
Gordon Productions
Grace Digital Media
HAVE Inc.
KJD Teleproductions
Limelight Communications Inc.
MVI Post
Magno Sound & Video
Masai Films Inc.
Maysles Films, Inc.
Media Access Group at WGBH
Montgomery Community Television Inc.
NTV International Corp.
National Collegiate Athletic Association
Northwest Imaging & FX
PostWorks, New York
Purple Grape Post
Quality Film & Video
RAD Marketing & Cabletowns
Rex Recording & Video Post
Seraphim Communications Inc.
Soundtrack
The Transcription Company
TRI-COMM Productions
VA-Tech Video/Broadcast Services
VTTV Videothek Electronic TV-Production GmbH + Co Kopier KG
VideoActive Productions
WKMG Productions
The WPA Film Library
White Rabbit Productions
ZBS Foundation

Processing Labs

DeLuxe Laboratories

Producers, Documentaries

Adler Media Inc.
American Farm Bureau Federation
Robert L. Bocchino
Brillig Productions Inc.
Broadview Media
Himan Brown-Radio Drama Network
Canamedia Productions Ltd.
Catholic Communication Campaign
CONTACT Radio
Thomas Craven Film Corp.
The Dolmatch Group Ltd.
Ecumedia News Service
FamilyNet
Films Five Inc.
David Finch Distribution Ltd.
Free Speech TV (FSTV)
GRB Entertainment
GVI
Great North Productions
Horizons Television Inc.

Thomas Horton Associates Inc.
Images Communication Arts Corp.
International Television Corp.
Jams Productions Inc.
Janson Media
The Johnson Group
Jordan Klein Film & Video
MRC Films
MacNeil/Lehrer Productions
Make It Happen Productions Inc.
Maryknoll Productions
Maryland Public Television
Maslow Media Group Inc.
William Mauldin Productions Inc.
Maysles Films, Inc.
The Media Group of Connecticut Inc.
Myriad Pictures
O'Grady & Associates
Oppix Productions Inc.
Pied Piper Films Ltd.
Planet Pictures Ltd.
Presbyterian Church (U.S.A.)
Presson Perspectives
Prime Cut Productions Inc.
Productions La Fete
RDF Media
Richter Productions Inc.
SFP Productions
Charlie Spencer Productions
System TV
Talco Productions
Tamouz Media
Tapestry International, Ltd.
Tel-Air Interests Inc.
Toucan Productions
Two Oceans Entertainment Group
The WPA Film Library
Warren Only Media Group
Welwood International Film Production
White Rabbit Productions
Daniel Wilson Productions Inc.

Producers, Film

Angel Films Co.
Ardustry Home Entertainment LLC
S. Banks Group Inc.
Brillig Productions Inc.
Bruder Releasing Inc. (BRI)
CIFEX International Inc.
Cinema Concepts Animation Studio
Classic Media
Coote Communications
Cramer Productions Center
Thomas Craven Film Corp.
Critical Mass Releasing Inc.
Ebbets Field Productions Ltd.
Eurocine
FTC/Orlando
Films Five Inc.
1st Miracle Productions
The Griffin Group
Images Communication Arts Corp.
Independent Artists
Independent Edge Films
JGT Media Productions
The Johnson Group
Jordan Klein Film & Video
Kazmark Entertainment Group
Kultur/White Star Video
Lindberg Productions Inc.
Lions Gate Entertainment
MRC Films
Make It Happen Productions Inc.
Masai Films Inc.
Moonstone Entertainment
Myriad Pictures
O. Atlas Enterprises Inc.
O'Grady & Associates
Paulist Productions
Peckham Productions
Pied Piper Films Ltd.
Pike Productions Inc.
Productions La Fete
Richter Productions Inc.
Rigel Entertainment
Romano & Associates Inc.
Rosler Creative
SFP Productions
Seville Pictures
Silverline Pictures
Charlie Spencer Productions
Studio Babelsberg GmbH

Sullivan Entertainment Inc./Sullivan Entertainment International
Tamouz Media
Toucan Productions
TRI-COMM Productions
Viacom Inc.
Welwood International Film Production
Daniel Wilson Productions Inc.

Producers, Multimedia

Brillig Productions Inc.
ComBridges
Cramer Productions Center
DaviSound
Faraone Communications Inc.
Free Speech TV (FSTV)
Lon Gibby Productions, Inc./ Gibby Media Group
Independent Edge Films
The Johnson Group
Kipany Productions Ltd.
Ben Manilla Productions
Mobile Video Services Ltd.
O'Grady & Associates
Palace Digital Studios
Paulist Productions
PorchLight Entertainment Inc.
Productions La Fete
Rampion Visual Productions L.L.C.
The Real Estate Network
TR Productions
Technisonic Studios
Toucan Productions
Video I-D Teleproductions Inc.
Video/Media Distribution Inc.
Vuolo Video Air-Chex
Warren Only Media Group

Producers, Radio Programming

ABC Radio Networks
Armedia Communications
At a Glance
Blue Heaven Productions
Broadcast News Service
Himan Brown-Radio Drama Network
CCM Media Services
C N R Radio
Call For Action Inc.
Catholic Communication Campaign
The Christian Science Sentinel - Radio Edition
The Christophers Inc.
The Classical Station, WCPE
CONTACT Radio
Country Crossroads FamilyNet Radio
Creative Marketing & Communications Corp.
DC Audio
ESPN Radio Network
Ecumedia News Service
Ecumenical Communications
Envoy Productions
Essence Television Productions Inc.
Evangelical Lutheran Church in America
FamilyNet
Finger Lakes Productions International
General Conference of Seventh-day Adventists
Good Life Associates
Billy Graham Evangelistic Association
Heil Enterprises
The Image Generators
Images Communication Arts Corp.
J&H Music Programming
Jameson Broadcast Inc.
Jones Radio Networks
MAKWDE Productions
MRN Radio
Ben Manilla Productions
Maryknoll Productions
MasterControl FamilyNet Radio
MediaTracks Inc.
Moody Broadcasting Network
MotorNet
Musical Starstreams
National Council of Churches Communications Unit
New Dimensions Radio
North American Network, Inc.
North Shore Productions
O'Grady & Associates
Jim Owens Entertainment
Ports of Paradise
Powerline

Broadcasting & Cable Yearbook 2006

Producers, Distributors, and Production Services Subject Index

Premiere Radio Networks Inc.
Protestant Hour Inc.
Questar
RBC Ministries
RPM Media Enterprises-The Relic Rack Preview
Radio & TV Roundup Productions
Radio Express Inc.
Radio Production Services Inc.
Radio Spirits
The Radio-Studio Network
Ray Sports Network
Sam Shad Productions
Sound Source Networks
Sports Byline U.S.A.
StarDate/Universo
Talco Productions
Talk Radio Network
Time Capsule Inc.
United Stations Radio Network
WFMT Radio Network
WQXR
Wawatay Native Communication Society
"The Weather Center"

Producers, TV Programming

Accuracy in Media Inc.
Adler Media Inc.
Agora TV
AmericaNurse TV Productions
Anderson Productions Ltd. (APL)
Angel Films Co.
Armedia Communications
Ascent Media Network Services
S. Banks Group Inc.
Bardel Entertainment Inc.
Dave Bell Associates Inc.
Bellon Entertainment
Brillig Productions Inc.
Broadcast News Service
Himan Brown-Radio Drama Network
Bruder Releasing Inc. (BRI)
CCI Entertainment Ltd.
CDR Communications Inc.
CFP Video Productions
Call For Action Inc.
Canamedia Productions Ltd.
CanLib Inc.
George Carlson & Associates
Carlton International Media Inc.
Carsey-Werner Distribution
Sandra Carter Productions Inc.
Catholic Communication Campaign
Catholic Communications Corp.
Central City Productions, Inc.
Children's Media Productions
The Christophers Inc.
The Dick Clark Productions
Classic Media
Clever Cleaver Productions
William F. Cooke Television Programs
Cookie Jar Group
Cornell University Educational Television Center
Critical Mass Releasing Inc.
Crystal Pictures Inc.
Curb Entertainment International Corp.
DLT Entertainment Ltd.
D-Squared Media
Dargaud-Marina
Walt Disney Company
Dorling Kindersley Vision
E! Entertainment Television
Ebbets Field Productions Ltd.
Ellis Entertainment
Enoki Films U.S.A. Inc.
Envoy Productions
Evangelical Lutheran Church in America
Faith for Today
FamilyNet
Faraone Communications Inc.
Film Roman Inc.
David Finch Distribution Ltd.
Fox 17 Studio Productions
Fox Sports West
Fox 29 WUTV Sinclair
Sandy Frank Entertainment Inc.
Free Speech TV (FSTV)
Freewheelin' Films Ltd.
The Fremantle Corp.
GLL TV Enterprises Inc.
GRB Entertainment
Lon Gibby Productions, Inc./ Gibby Media Group
Glenray Productions Inc.

Global Telemedia Inc.
Great Chefs Television/Publishing
Great North Productions
Great Plains National (GPN)
The Griffin Group
Hamilton Productions Inc.
Larry Harmon Pictures Corp.
Health Net Productions & Pet Talk
Hearst Entertainment, Inc.
Heritage/Baruch Television Distribution
Jack Hilton Inc.
The History Makers
Holigan Investment Group Ltd.
Home Improvement Television Network
The Idea Channel
Independent Edge Films
International Broadcasting Network
It Is Written Television
Italtoons Corp.
Ivanhoe Broadcast News Inc.
Jams Productions Inc.
KPTS-TV
KUSA Television
King World Productions
Lapco Communications
Lifestyle Magazine/The Evidence
Lightbridge Production & Distribution
MAKWDE Productions
MG/Perin Inc.
MacNeil/Lehrer Productions
Madison Square Garden Network
Maryknoll Productions
Maryland Public Television
Maysles Films, Inc.
The Media Group of Connecticut Inc.
Media Planning Group (MPG)
Montgomery Community Television Inc.
NRS Group PTY Ltd.
NAHB Production Group
National Collegiate Athletic Association
National Council of Churches Communications Unit
New York Communications
News Broadcast Network
North by Northwest Productions
O. Atlas Enterprises Inc.
O'Grady & Associates
Oppix Productions Inc.
Jim Owens Entertainment
PAULAR Entertainment L.L.C.
Palace Digital Studios
Shelly Palmer Productions
Paramount Worldwide Television Distribution
Paulist Productions
Peckham Productions
Pied Piper Films Ltd.
PorchLight Entertainment Inc.
Power Play Music Video L.L.C.
Powersports/Millenium International
Presbyterian Church (U.S.A.)
Prime Cut Productions Inc.
Questar
RBC Ministries
ROZON
Rampion Visual Productions L.L.C.
Raycom Sports
The Real Estate Network
Reel Media International Inc.
Reid/Land Productions Inc.
Reuters Media
Rex Recording & Video Post
Rigel Entertainment
Steve Rotfeld Productions Inc.
SWTV Production Services Inc.
Sanctuary Records Group Ltd.
The Saturday Evening Post Television Department
SeniorVision Productions, Inc.
Seville Pictures
Sam Shad Productions
Silverline Pictures
Southern STAR
Charlie Spencer Productions
Sport International Inc.
Marty Stouffer Productions Ltd.
Sullivan Entertainment Inc./Sullivan Entertainment International
Pat Summerall Productions
Sunbow Entertainment
System TV
Talco Productions
Tamouz Media
Tapestry International, Ltd.
Tel-A-Cast Productions
Tel-Air Interests Inc.
The Television Syndication Company, Inc.
Triage Entertainment Inc.

Tribune Entertainment Co.
Twentieth Century Fox Television Distribution
Twentieth Television
Two Oceans Entertainment Group
Viacom Inc.
Videographic West
Vision Broadcasting - KVBA TV 19
WQED Multimedia
WTOB Channel 2—Public/Government Access TV
Warren Only Media Group
Wawatay Native Communication Society
Wide Eye Productions, Inc.
Daniel Wilson Productions Inc.
Robert Wold Co.
The Wyland Group

Producers, Video

American Farm Bureau Federation
Armedia Communications
J. Arnold Productions
Asia Pacific Productions
Bayliss
Bell Foto Art Productions
Himan Brown-Radio Drama Network
Bruder Releasing Inc. (BRI)
CFP Video Productions
CRM Learning
Sandra Carter Productions Inc.
Catholic Communications Corp.
Children's Media Productions
Cinecraft Productions Inc.
Clever Cleaver Productions
Concept Videos
Coote Communications
Cramer Productions Center
Thomas Craven Film Corp.
Custom Productions Inc.
D-Squared Media
D-V-X International
DWJ Television
ESPI Video
Ebbets Field Productions Ltd.
Encore Video Productions Inc.
Envoy Productions
Evangelical Lutheran Church in America
Faith for Today
Films Five Inc.
David Finch Distribution Ltd.
GLL TV Enterprises Inc.
GVI
General Conference of Seventh-day Adventists
Lon Gibby Productions, Inc./ Gibby Media Group
Good News Broadcasting Association Inc.
Great Chefs Television/Publishing
Health Net Productions & Pet Talk
Jack Hilton Inc.
The History Makers
Home Improvement Television Network
Horizons Television Inc.
The Idea Channel
Independent Artists
JGT Media Productions
The Johnson Group
Jordan Klein Film & Video
Kipany Productions Ltd.
Lapco Communications
Lifestyle Magazine/The Evidence
Lightbridge Production & Distribution
Limelight Communications Inc.
Lindberg Productions Inc.
MRC Films
MSE
Maslow Media Group Inc.
Mason Video
William Mauldin Productions Inc.
McClain Enterprises Inc.
Medialink
Montgomery Community Television Inc.
NAHB Production Group
Nemo News
New York Communications
News Broadcast Network
North by Northwest Productions
O. Atlas Enterprises Inc.
O'Grady & Associates
Oppix Productions Inc.
Palace Digital Studios
Shelly Palmer Productions
Peckham Productions
Pike Productions Inc.
Playboy Entertainment Group Inc.
Potomac TV/Communications

Producers, Distributors, and Production Services Subject Index

Powersports/Millenium International
Praxis Media Inc.
Prime Cut Productions Inc.
Primedia Workplace Learning
Quality Film & Video
RMD & Assoc. Inc.
Reizner & Reizner Film & Video
River City Video Productions
Rosler Creative
Steve Rotfeld Productions Inc.
Sak Entertainment
SeniorVision Productions, Inc.
Seraphim Communications Inc.
Charlie Spencer Productions
Marty Stouffer Productions Ltd.
Sullivan Video Services Inc.
Pat Summerall Productions
TR Productions
Tankersley Productions, Inc., St. Louis
Tel-A-Cast Productions
Telepros
The Television Syndication Company, Inc.
Toucan Productions
Triage Entertainment Inc.
TRI-COMM Productions
U.S. Plan B Inc.
V I E W Video Inc.
Video I-D Teleproductions Inc.
Video/Media Distribution Inc.
Video Techniques Inc.
Vision Broadcasting - KVBA TV 19
Vuolo Video Air-Chex
WTOB Channel 2—Public/Government Access TV
Welwood International Film Production
White Rabbit Productions
Wide Eye Productions, Inc.
Work Edit
Larry John Wright Inc.
The Wyland Group
Yada/Levine Video Productions
Sandy Zimmerman Productions

Production Music Libraries

Toby Arnold and Associates Inc.
The Audio Department Inc.
FirstCom Music
Good News Broadcasting Association Inc.
Manhattan Production Music
Metro Music Productions Inc.
Network Music L.L.C.
OGM Production Music
Omnimusic
Shelly Palmer Productions
Production Garden Music Libraries
Promusic
SeniorVision Productions, Inc.
SoperSound Music Library
Sound Ideas
TRF Production Music Libraries
Westar Music
Who Did That Music?

Production Services

Asia Pacific Productions
Bardel Entertainment Inc.
The Chuck Blore Co.
CFP Video Productions
CNBC Syndication
CTV Television Inc.
Carleton Productions International Inc.
Catholic Communications Corp.
CelebrityFootage
ComBridges
Cornell University Educational Television Center
Cramer Productions Center
D-Squared Media
DWJ Television
Jeff Davis Productions Inc.
De Wolfe Music Library Inc.
Design Partners Inc.
Devlin Design Group Inc.
Dimension 3 Corp
The D.L. Dykes Jr. Foundation
ETN—Educational Telecommunications Network
Encore Video Productions Inc.
Eyewitness Kids News, LLC
FTC/Orlando
Faith for Today
Fox Digital

Fox 17 Studio Productions
Fox 29 WUTV Sinclair
Freewheelin' Films Ltd.
GVI
Georgia Film, Video & Music Office
Gordon Productions
Great Plains National (GPN)
The History Makers
Horizons Television Inc.
JGT Media Productions
J.N. Productions
KJD Teleproductions
KPTS-TV
KUSA Television
Lighthouse Productions
Maryland Public Television
Maslow Media Group Inc.
Warren Miller Entertainment
Mobile Video Services Ltd.
Nemo News
Dick Orkin's Amazing Radio
Outdoor Media Group
(PSSI) Production & Satellite Services Inc.
Palace Digital Studios
Palace Digital Studios
Praxis Media Inc.
RDF Media
Rampion Visual Productions L.L.C.
Raycom Sports
Reizner & Reizner Film & Video
Reuters Television
Romano & Associates Inc.
Seraphim Communications Inc.
Soundtrack
Studio M Productions Unlimited
Tankersley Productions, Inc., St. Louis
Telepros
Toes Production Inc.
Troma Entertainment, Inc.
U.S. Plan B Inc.
Ukrainian Melody Hour
University of Colorado Television
VA-Tech Video/Broadcast Services
VTTV Videothek Electronic TV-Production GmbH + Co Kopier KG
Van Vliet Media
Video I-D Teleproductions Inc.
Video One Inc.
Wade Productions Inc.
Warren Only Media Group
White Rabbit Productions
Yada/Levine Video Productions

Promotion Design

CRN International
Cimarron Group
Design Partners Inc.
First Marketing
Peters Communications
TeleCom Productions Inc.

Promotion Film Distribution/Production

CelebrityFootage
Crown International Pictures Inc.
Film Roman Inc.
Larry Harmon Pictures Corp.
Maryland Public Television
Warren Miller Entertainment
Praxis Media Inc.

Promotion Production, Radio

CRN International
Custom Productions Inc.
DaviSound
Jameson Broadcast Inc.
Palace Digital Studios
Premiere Radio Networks Inc.
RAD Marketing & Cabletowns
Redwood Entertainment Inc.
Toes Production Inc.
UBC Radio
University of Kentucky Public Relations & Radio-TV News Bureau
Vuolo Video Air-Chex
WQXR
Larry John Wright Inc.

Promotion Production, Radio & TV

The Chuck Blore Co.
Command Productions
John Driscoll/VoiceOver America
Film House Inc.
McClain Enterprises Inc.
National Collegiate Athletic Association
New Visions Syndication Inc.
Palace Digital Studios
Shelly Palmer Productions
Radio & TV Roundup Productions
Rosler Creative
Soldiers Radio & Television, U.S. Army Public Affairs
Strand Media Group Inc.
University of Kentucky Public Relations & Radio-TV News Bureau

Promotion Production, TV

CRN International
Custom Productions Inc.
Darino Films/Library of Special Effects
Jeff Gold Productions Inc.
The Media Group of Connecticut Inc.
NTV International Corp.
New York Communications
Palace Digital Studios
Peters Communications
SPI International
Sport International Inc.
TeleCom Productions Inc.
Toes Production Inc.
University of Kentucky Public Relations & Radio-TV News Bureau
Welwood International Film Production
Larry John Wright Inc.

Public Service Announcements

American Farm Bureau Federation
At a Glance
Robert L. Bocchino
Catholic Communication Campaign
The Christophers Inc.
CONTACT Radio
Thomas Craven Film Corp.
Ecumedia News Service
Ecumenical Communications
Envoy Productions
FamilyNet Radio
Finger Lakes Productions International
GVI
KCSN 88.5 FM
Leukemia & Lymphoma Society
Limelight Communications Inc.
MRC Films
Masai Films Inc.
Media Visions
MediaTracks Inc.
NCAA
N W Media
NAHB Production Group
National Council of Churches Communications Unit
News Broadcast Network
North American Network, Inc.
Potomac TV/Communications
Presbyterian Church (U.S.A.)
Romano & Associates Inc.
Soldiers Radio & Television, U.S. Army Public Affairs
StarDate/Universo
U.S. Air Force Recruiting Service
University of Kentucky Public Relations & Radio-TV News Bureau
WCTD AM 1620
WTOB Channel 2—Public/Government Access TV

Publishing, Video and Print

CRM Learning
Essence Television Productions Inc.
First Marketing
Great Chefs Television/Publishing
Playboy Entertainment Group Inc.
Public Media Incorporated
The Radio Almanac
Radioguide People Inc.
Seraphim Communications Inc.
Vuolo Video Air-Chex
Wawatay Native Communication Society

Producers, Distributors, and Production Services Subject Index

Recording Studios
The Audio Department Inc.
Cinema Sound Ltd.
Command Productions
Continental Recordings Inc.
Country Crossroads FamilyNet Radio
Horizon Audio Creations
Irving Productions Inc.
Tom Jones Recording Studios
Lighthouse Productions
Lion and Fox Recording Studios
Magno Sound & Video
No Soap Productions
Smith/Lee Productions, Inc.
Sound of Birmingham Productions
Soundshop Recording Studio LLC
Studio M Productions Unlimited
University of Detroit Mercy
VideoActive Productions
WFMT Radio Network

Religious Programming, Radio
At a Glance
Broadcast News Service
C N R Radio
Domain Communications L.L.C.
Ecumedia News Service
Ecumenical Communications
Evangelical Lutheran Church in America
FamilyNet Radio
Good Life Associates
Heil Enterprises
Integrity Media
International Broadcasting Network
It Is Written Television
MasterControl FamilyNet Radio
Moody Broadcasting Network
On Track
Perception Media Group
Powerline
Presbyterian Church (U.S.A.)
Protestant Hour Inc.
Sing for Joy/WCAL
Solid Gospel Network (Reach Satellite Network, Inc.)
Strength for Living

Religious Programming, Radio & TV
Broadcast News Service
CDR Communications Inc.
Catholic Communication Campaign
Catholic Communications Corp.
Christian TV Services of Ellicottville Inc.
Envoy Productions
Episcopal Church Center
Faith for Today
Family Stations Inc.
General Conference of Seventh-day Adventists
Good Life Associates
Good News Broadcasting Association Inc.
Integrity Media
JGT Media Productions
Maryknoll Productions
National Council of Churches Communications Unit
One Hundred Biblemen & Women of the U.S.A.
RBC Ministries
RBC Ministries/Midwest Media Managers
The Worship Network

Religious Programming, TV
Catholic Television Network
Crossroads Christian Communications Inc.
Ellis Entertainment
Episcopal Church Center
Golden Gate Studios
Good News Broadcasting Association Inc.
Horizons Television Inc.
Integrity Media
It Is Written Television
Jams Productions Inc.
The Media Group of Connecticut Inc.
Presbyterian Church (U.S.A.)
Tel-Air Interests Inc.
Vision Broadcasting - KVBA TV 19

Remote Facilities
Agrinet Farm Radio Network
American Stock Exchange
Continental Recordings Inc.
Cornell University Educational Television Center
DOME PRODUCTIONS
Grace Digital Media
Medialink
National Mobile Television
PMTV Producers Management Television
Ray Sports Network
Reizner & Reizner Film & Video
SWTV Production Services Inc.
Studio M Productions Unlimited
Sullivan Video Services Inc.
Video One Inc.

Satellite Uplink Services
Agrinet Farm Radio Network
American Stock Exchange
Ascent Media Management East
Ascent Media Network Services
The Christian Science Sentinel - Radio Edition
Communications III Inc.
Crawford Communications
DG Systems
DOME PRODUCTIONS
GlobeCast
Longhorn Radio Network
Loral Skynet
Maslow Media Group Inc.
Medialink
NTV International Corp.
PMTV Producers Management Television
(PSSI) Production & Satellite Services Inc.
Potomac TV/Communications
Power Play Music Video L.L.C.
RAD Marketing & Cabletowns
Ray Sports Network
Reuters Television
Roberts Communications Network Inc.
SCOLA
Sullivan Video Services Inc.
Talk America Radio Networks
Talk Radio Network
Telenium Studios
VA-Tech Video/Broadcast Services
Viacom Video Services
Vyvx, a Division of WillTel Communications
WKMG Productions
WFMT Radio Network
WRS/Channel One
Warren Only Media Group
WeatherVision Inc.

Scriptwriters
Coote Communications
Custom Productions Inc.
Ebbets Field Productions Ltd.
Pied Piper Films Ltd.
Praxis Media Inc.
RMD & Assoc. Inc.
Redwood Entertainment Inc.
Sak Entertainment
The Transcription Company
ZBS Foundation
Sandy Zimmerman Productions

Set Design
Devlin Design Group Inc.
Reliance Audio Visual Corp.
Studio Babelsberg GmbH

Sound Design
DaviSound
Ben Manilla Productions
No Soap Productions
The Radio Almanac
Shield Productions Inc.
Smith/Lee Productions, Inc.
Toes Production Inc.
Wax Music & Sound Design

Sound Effects/Sound Effect Libraries
Cinema Sound Ltd.
Films for the Humanities & Sciences Inc./FFH Video
FirstCom Music
Network Music L.L.C.
Omnimusic
Promusic
Sound Ideas
TRF Production Music Libraries

Sound Recording
Continental Recordings Inc.
Highland Laboratories
Irving Productions Inc.
Lion and Fox Recording Studios
Man From Mars Productions
National Public Radio
Soundshop Recording Studio LLC
Studio M Productions Unlimited
TR Productions

Sound Stages
Fox Digital
Telenium Studios

Special Effect Libraries
Network Music L.L.C.
TRF Production Music Libraries

Special Effects
Broadview Media
Dimension 3 Corp
Purple Grape Post

Sports Programming, Radio
Agrinet Farm Radio Network
Ascent Media Network Services
Clear Channel Broadcasting Inc.
ESPN Radio Network
Hometown Illinois Radio Network
MRN Radio
Philadelphia Flyers Hockey Club
Premiere Radio Networks Inc.
Shadow Broadcast Services
Sports Byline U.S.A.
Talk America Radio Networks
Tribune Radio Networks

Sports Programming, Radio & TV
GlobeCast
NCAA
National Collegiate Athletic Association
Philadelphia Flyers Hockey Club
RAD Marketing & Cabletowns
Shadow Broadcast Services
Warren Only Media Group

Sports Programming, TV
CN8, The Comcast Network
Chrysalis Distribution
Clear Channel Broadcasting Inc.
Dallas Cowboys Broadcasting
Fox Sports West
Freewheelin' Films Ltd.
Global Telemedia Inc.
Hamilton Productions Inc.
Jefferson-Pilot Sports
Lindberg Productions Inc.
Madison Square Garden Network
Mason Video
NRS Group PTY Ltd.
National Collegiate Athletic Association
National Mobile Television
Philadelphia Flyers Hockey Club
Raycom Sports
Reid/Land Productions Inc.
Response Reward Systems L.C.
Reuters Media
SWTV Production Services Inc.

Broadcasting & Cable Yearbook 2006

Producers, Distributors, and Production Services Subject Index

Sport International Inc.
M C Stuart & Associates Pty Ltd.
Technisonic Studios
TeleCom Productions Inc.
The Television Syndication Company, Inc.
Tomwil Inc.
Videographic West
Vision Broadcasting - KVBA TV 19

Stage and Studio Rental

CMT
Cinecraft Productions Inc.
Fox Digital
Fox 17 Studio Productions
Golden Gate Studios
Independent Artists
KUSA Television
Sak Entertainment

Standards Conversion

Advanced Digital Services, Inc.
HAVE Inc.
Media Visions
Point 360
The Transfer Zone
Viacom Video Services
Video Services

Stock Footage/Tape

American Farm Bureau Federation
Burrud Productions Inc.
Carpel Video Inc.
CelebrityFootage
Cinema Sound Ltd.
Darino Films/Library of Special Effects
Freewheelin' Films Ltd.
Lon Gibby Productions, Inc./ Gibby Media Group
Thomas Horton Associates Inc.
Media Planning Group (MPG)
Warren Miller Entertainment
National Collegiate Athletic Association
Pan American Video
System TV
The WPA Film Library
Worldview Entertainment Inc.

Studio Facilities

ABC Radio Networks
Ascent Media Network Services
Bardel Entertainment Inc.
CamMate Studios
The Christian Science Sentinel - Radio Edition
Continental Recordings Inc.
D-V-X International
Devlin Design Group Inc.
DOME PRODUCTIONS
ETN—Educational Telecommunications Network
Fox Digital
Fox 17 Studio Productions
Fox 29 WUTV Sinclair
Golden Gate Studios
Independent Artists
MTI The Image Group
Man From Mars Productions
Maryland Public Television
National Public Radio
Reuters Television
Soundshop Recording Studio LLC
Suite Audio
Telenium Studios
University of Colorado Television
University of Detroit Mercy
VTTV Videothek Electronic TV-Production GmbH + Co Kopier KG

Syndication, Cable

Accuracy in Media Inc.
CABLEready Corp.
Crystal Pictures Inc.
Evergreen Entertainment Group
Sandy Frank Entertainment Inc.

GLL TV Enterprises Inc.
Gould Entertainment Corp.
Great Chefs Television/Publishing
Images Communication Arts Corp.
Jefferson-Pilot Sports
King World Productions
Lakeside Television Co. Inc.
Lifestyle Magazine/The Evidence
Lions Gate Entertainment
Media Planning Group (MPG)
Parrot Communications International Inc.
Playboy Entertainment Group Inc.
Power Play Music Video L.L.C.
Raycom Sports
Harvey Sheldon Productions
The Summit Media Group Inc. (Sub 4 Kids Entertainment)
Twentieth Television
University of Detroit Mercy
Video/Media Distribution Inc.

Syndication, Radio

ABC Radio Networks
Accuracy in Media Inc.
Armedia Communications
At a Glance
CONTACT Radio
Country Crossroads FamilyNet Radio
ESPN Radio Network
Eagle Media Productions Ltd.
Envoy Productions
Good News Broadcasting Association Inc.
Happi Associates
Hometown Illinois Radio Network
Images Communication Arts Corp.
Jameson Broadcast Inc.
Jones Radio Networks
Knowledge In A Nutshell Inc.
Longhorn Radio Network
MRN Radio
MasterControl FamilyNet Radio
MediaTracks Inc.
Miller Broadcast Management
Ellis Molton Advertising
The Music of Your Life
Musical Starstreams
NCAA
New Dimensions Radio
North Shore Productions
On Track
Orange Productions Inc.
Dick Orkin's Amazing Radio
Jim Owens Entertainment
Ports of Paradise
Powerline
Premiere Radio Networks Inc.
RPM Media Enterprises-The Relic Rack Preview
RPM-Radio Programming & Management Inc.
Radio America
The Radio-Studio Network
Ray Sports Network
Sing for Joy/WCAL
Solid Gospel Network (Reach Satellite Network, Inc.)
Sound Source Networks
Sports Byline U.S.A.
Strand Media Group Inc.
Strength for Living
Talk America Radio Networks
Talk Radio Network
Time Capsule Inc.
Tribune Radio Networks
UBC Radio
United Stations Radio Network
University of Detroit Mercy
WFMT Radio Network
"The Weather Center"
Larry John Wright Inc.
ZBS Foundation

Syndication, TV

Angel Films Co.
CNBC Syndication
CanLib Inc.
George Carlson & Associates
Carsey-Werner Distribution
William F. Cooke Television Programs
DG Systems
DLT Entertainment Ltd.
Envoy Productions

Faraone Communications Inc.
Sandy Frank Entertainment Inc.
GRB Entertainment
Golden Gate Studios
Gould Entertainment Corp.
Great Chefs Television/Publishing
Hearst Entertainment, Inc.
Heritage/Baruch Television Distribution
Holigan Investment Group Ltd.
Jefferson-Pilot Sports
Juravic Entertainment
KJD Teleproductions
King World Productions
Lakeside Television Co. Inc.
Lifestyle Magazine/The Evidence
Lions Gate Entertainment
MGM TV Canada
MG/Perin Inc.
McClain Enterprises Inc.
The Music of Your Life
NCAA
National Collegiate Athletic Association
New Visions Syndication Inc.
New York Communications
Pan American Video
Paramount Worldwide Television Distribution
Parrot Communications International Inc.
Planet Pictures Ltd.
Potomac TV/Communications
The Program Exchange
Promark Television
Peter Rodgers Organization
Steve Rotfeld Productions Inc.
Harvey Sheldon Productions
P. Allen Smith Gardens
TeleCom Productions Inc.
Television Representatives Inc.
The Television Syndication Company, Inc.
The Transcription Company
Tribune Entertainment Co.
Twentieth Century Fox Television Distribution
Twentieth Television
Viacom Inc.
Video/Media Distribution Inc.
Warren Only Media Group
M.D. Wax Courier Films
WeatherVision Inc.
Welwood International Film Production
Western International Syndication
Robert Wold Co.
Worldvision NY
The Wyland Group

Teleconferences

Ascent Media Network Services
Broadview Media
DOME PRODUCTIONS
Encore Video Productions Inc.
Episcopal Church Center
Grace Digital Media
KPTS-TV
National Mobile Television
PMTV Producers Management Television (PSSI) Production & Satellite Services Inc.
Reizner & Reizner Film & Video
SWTV Production Services Inc.
Vyvx, a Division of WillTel Communications
Wade Productions Inc.

Traffic Reporting

Metro Networks
Shadow Broadcast Services
Traffic Pulse Networks (A Unit of Mobility Technologies)

Training Film Productions

Bell Foto Art Productions
Cinecraft Productions Inc.
ComBridges
Encore Video Productions Inc.
Gordon Productions
Jams Productions Inc.
MSE
Mason Video
National Collegiate Athletic Association
News Broadcast Network
Potomac TV/Communications
Primedia Workplace Learning

Broadcasting & Cable Yearbook 2006

Producers, Distributors, and Production Services Subject Index

Strand Media Group Inc.
Toucan Productions

Training Films

CRM Learning
Coote Communications
Thomas Craven Film Corp.
D-Squared Media
Films for the Humanities & Sciences Inc./FFH Video
International Tele-Film
Primedia Workplace Learning
Toucan Productions

Travel Programming, TV

Burrud Productions Inc.
Capital Communications
George Carlson & Associates
Janson Media
William Mauldin Productions Inc.
NRS Group PTY Ltd.
Promark Television
Questar
M C Stuart & Associates Pty Ltd.
System TV
TRI-COMM Productions
U.S. Plan B Inc.
Videosmith Inc.

Travelogues

George Carlson & Associates
Promark Television
Sandy Zimmerman Productions

Video Conferences

Bayliss
Communications III Inc.
Cornell University Educational Television Center
DWJ Television
DOME PRODUCTIONS
ESPI Video
ETN—Educational Telecommunications Network
Episcopal Church Center
The Idea Channel
Medialink
National Collegiate Athletic Association

Nemo News
PMTV Producers Management Television
(PSSI) Production & Satellite Services Inc.
Reliance Audio Visual Corp.
VA-Tech Video/Broadcast Services
Vyvx, a Division of WillTel Communications
Wade Productions Inc.
WeatherVision Inc.

Videotape Editing

Ascent Media Management East
Broadview Media
Carpel Video Inc.
Daley Video
The D.L. Dykes Jr. Foundation
ESPI Video
Films Five Inc.
Fox 17 Studio Productions
GVI
Highland Laboratories
The History Makers
The Image Group
Independent Edge Films
Limelight Communications Inc.
Matchframe Video
Montgomery Community Television Inc.
North by Northwest Productions
Palace Digital Studios
PostWorks, New York
Rex Recording & Video Post
The Saturday Evening Post Television Department
Sullivan Video Services Inc.
Tel-A-Cast Productions
Telenium Studios
The Transfer Zone
Video Techniques Inc.
VideoActive Productions
Vuolo Video Air-Chex
Wide Eye Productions, Inc.
Yada/Levine Video Productions

Voice-Overs

Robert L. Bocchino
Broadcast News Service
CA Media Development
Cinema Sound Ltd.
Clausen Communications Inc.
Command Productions
D-Squared Media

Jeff Davis Productions Inc.
DaviSound
John Driscoll/VoiceOver America
Eagle Media Productions Ltd.
Ecumedia News Service
Fischer Broadcast Services
GMI Media L.L.C.
Globe Productions
The Image Generators
Irving Productions Inc.
J.N. Productions
David Kaye Productions Inc.
MSE
Magno Sound & Video
William Mauldin Productions Inc.
N W Media
Perception Media Group
RDF Media
The Radio Almanac
Radio & TV Roundup Productions
Shield Productions Inc.
Strand Media Group Inc.
Time Capsule Inc.
Toes Production Inc.
VideoActive Productions
Warren Only Media Group
"The Weather Center"
Work Edit
ZBS Foundation

Weather Programming

Compu-Weather Inc.
Metro Weather Service Inc.
Shadow Broadcast Services
Skywatch Weather Center
System TV
WSI Corp.
"The Weather Center"
WeatherVision Inc.

Weather Programming, Radio

Compu-Weather Inc.
Ion Weather Network
Metro Weather Service Inc.
Sam Shad Productions
Skywatch Weather Center
Sound Source Networks
"The Weather Center"

Section F
Technology

Equipment Manufacturers and Distributors Alphabetical Index F-2
Equipment Manufacturers and Distributors Subject Index..........F-33
Satellite Owners and Operators F-54
Teleports...F-57

Equipment Manufacturers and Distributors Alphabetical Index

A

A & S Case Co. Inc., 5260 Vineland Ave., N. Hollywood, CA 91601. Phone: (818) 509-5920. Fax: (818) 509-1397. E-mail: ascase@earthlink.net. Web Site: www.ascase.com. Kenneth E. Berry, pres.

Reusable shipping cases; computer, musical instrument cases.

A.C.C. Electronix, Inc., 1845 W. Hovey Ave., Normal, IL 61761-4315. Phone: (309) 888-9990. Fax: (309) 452-0893. E-mail: acc@accelectronix.com. Web Site: www.accelectronix.com. Andrew M. Rector, pres.

Repair cartridge tape recorders & reproducers.

ADC, Box 1101, Minneapolis, MN 55440-1101. Phone: (952) 938-8080. Fax: (952) 917-1717. Web Site: www.adc.com. Mike Day, VP; Gokul Hemmady, VP & CFO; Robert E. Switz, pres & chmn.

ADC provides the connections for wireline, wireless, cable, broadcast, and enterprise networks around the world. ADC's equipment & svcs enable high-speed Internet, data, video, and voice svcs.

ADCOUR, 623 Main St., Woburn, MA 01801. Phone: (781) 935-9944. Fax: (781) 937-3499. Richard Jacobs, pres.

Batteries, chargers, power supplies & power conditioning.

ADSCO Line Products Inc., 3500 Washington Ave., Houston, TX 77007. Phone: (713) 880-2424. Fax: (713) 880-2456. Linda Schmuck, pres.

Outside plant line hardware for CATV: guy strand, messengers, lashing wire/rods, formed grips/dead-ends & related line hardware. Stainless steel poleline hardware.

ADTEC Inc., 408 Russell St., Nashville, TN 37206. Phone: (615) 256-6619. Fax: (615) 256-6593. E-mail: sales@adtecinc.com. Web Site: www.adtecinc.com. Ron Johnson, VP.

Jacksonville, FL 32216, 2231 Corporate Square Blvd. Phone: (904) 720-2003. Kevin Ancelin, pres.

Products offered: Loc origination controllers & systems, coml insertion controllers & systems, network delay recording.

aeco Ltd., Offa's Business Park, Welshpool, Powys SY21 8JF. United Kingdom. Phone: 01938 556644. Fax: 01938 556645. E-mail: enquiry@aecgroup.com. Web Site: www.aecogroup.com.

Irvine, CA 92714. Aerosonic USA, 1681 Langley Ave, Bldg. A. Phone: (949) 474-2264. Fax: (949) 474-2259. E-mail: cckev@msn.com. Roger Nicholson.

Videotape quality assurance equipment including open reel VHS testers plus helical scan evaluators & dropout counters (all helical scan formats). CD quality assurance systems for all CD formats; stamper evaluator, bit verifier & birefringence tester available.

AKG Acoustics, U.S., 914 Airpark Center Dr., Nashville, TN 37217. Phone: (615) 620-3800. Fax: (615) 620-3875. E-mail: akgusa@harman.com. Web Site: www.akg-acoustics.com. Doug Mac Callum, VP/gen mgr.

Microphones, headphones, wireless microphones, in-ear monitoring systems, wireless loudspeakers, conferencing products.

AMCO Engineering Co., 3801 Rose St., Schiller Park, IL 60176. Phone: (847) 671-6670. Fax: (847) 671-9469. Web Site: www.amcoengineering.com. Thomas Anderson, pres; Tom Ligman, natl sls mgr; James Walenda, dir mktg.

Data/Communications, monitoring & EMI cabinets, single or multiple bay. Inline or curved configurations, standard or custom.

AMS Neve P.L.C., Billington Rd., Burnley, Lancashire BB11 SUB. United Kingdom. Phone: 44(0)-1282-457011. Fax: 44(0)1282-417282. E-mail: enquiry@ams-neve.com. Web Site: www.ams-neve.com.

North Hollywood, CA 91602, 4220 Lankershim Blvd, 2nd Fl. Phone: (818) 753-8789. Fax: (818) 623-4839. E-mail: enquiry@ams-neve.com. Nigel Toates.

New York, NY 10013, 100 Ave. of the Americas, 5th Fl. Phone: (212) 965-9306. (888)388-6383. Fax: (212) 965-1400. E-mail: enquiry@ams-neve.com. Adrian Weidman.

Distributors of AMS-NEVE analog & digital audio equipment for the bcst, video postproduction, film, mus recording & mastering industries.

AMS Neve Inc., 100 Ave. of the Americas, 5th Fl., New York, NY 10013. Phone: (212) 965-1400. Fax: (212) 965-9306. Web Site: www.amsneve.com. John Hart, pres.

North Hollywood, CA 91602, 4220 Lankershim Blvd., 2nd Fl. Phone: (818) 753-8789. John Hart.

Distributors of AMS-NEVE analog & digital audio equipment for the bcst, video postproduction, film, music recording & mastering industries.

APM/Associated Production Music, 6255 Sunset Blvd., Suite 820, Hollywood, CA 90028. Phone: (323) 461-3211. Phone: (800) 543-4276. Fax: (323) 461-9102. E-mail: sales@apmmusic.com. Web Site: www.apmmusic.com. Connie Red, account exec; Tia Sommer, sls dir.

New York, NY 10016, 240 Madison Ave. Phone: (800) 276-6874. (212) 856-9800. Fax: (212) 856-9807. George Macias, natl sls mgr. (East Coast).

Sixteen production music libraries, over 3,000 CD's, personalized packages, music search svc, 15-20 new CD releases mthy.

APW Enclosure Products, 403 Degner Ave., Mayville, WI 53050-0028. Fax: (920) 387-7196. Web Site: www.apw.com. Carol Flack, mktg.

Modular video center desks, consoles, cabinets, racks for video production, postproduction dubbing & editing.

ARRIS Telewire Supply, 9800 E. Geddes Ave., Englewood, CO 80112. Phone: (720) 895-7000. Fax: (720) 895-7106. Web Site: www.arrisi.com. Bob Puccini, pres.

Full-line, full-svc stocking distributor of products needed to build & svc a broadband communications network with warehouses nationwide.

A R T Applied Research and Technology, 215 Tremont St., Rochester, NY 14608. Phone: (585) 436-2720. Fax: (585) 436-3942. Web Site: www.artproaudoio.com. Philip Betette, pres.

Digital audio signal processors & enhancement devices.

ATCI/Antenna Technology Communications Inc., 450 N. McKemy, Chandler, AZ 85226. Phone: (480) 844-8501. Fax: (480) 898-7667. Web Site: www.atci.com. Gary Hatch, CEO; Ron Kahle, COO/CFO.

Simpson, PA 18407, 289 Atlas St. Phone: (570) 282-3590. William Pryle, area mgr.

Simulsat multibeam earth stns; parabolic antennas from 1.8 m to 32 m. Headend electronics, design & maintenance, used/refurbished equipment.

ATI-Audio Technologies Inc., 328 W. Maple Ave., Horsham, PA 19044. Web Site: www.atiaudio.com. David V. Day, pres.

Bcst audio, mic, line, distribution, interface & turntable amplifiers, power amps, on-air consoles & audio processors.

AVAB America Inc., 434 Payran Street, Petaluma, CA 94952. Phone: (707)778-8990. E-mail: sales@avab.com. Web Site: www.avab.com. Hans J. Lau, pres.

Manufacturer of studio & theatrical lighting equipment; lighting controllers, dimmers, fixtures.

AVCOM of Virginia Inc., 500 Southlake Blvd., Richmond, VA 23236. Phone: (804) 794-2500. Fax: (804) 794-8284. E-mail: sales@avcomofva.com. Web Site: www.avcomofva.com. Ken Parks, pres.

Manufacturer of portable analyzers, network analyzers, microwave sweep generators, satellite receivers, microwave video links & microwave accessories.

AVI Systems, 6271 Bury Dr., Eden Prairie, MN 55346. Phone: (952) 949-3700. Fax: (952) 949-6000. E-mail: info@avisys.com. Web Site: www.avisystems.com. Joe Stoebner, CEO.

Urbandale, IA 50322, 3001 104th St. Phone: (515) 254-9850. Fax: (515) 254-9981. Steve Riley, rgnl mgr.

Bensenville, IL 60106, 621 Busse Rd. Phone: (630) 447-2300. Fax: (630) 477-2301.

Lenexa, KS 66214, 8052 Flint St. Phone: (913) 495-9494. Fax: (913) 495-9479. Tom Madsen, rgnl mgr.

Kentwood, MI 49512, 4575 44th St. S.E., Suite C. Phone: (616) 977-6990. Fax: (616) 977-6991.

Brentwood, MO 63144, 8140 Brentwood Industrial Dr. Phone: (314) 781-5590. Fax: (314) 781-5596.

Bismarck, ND 58503, 1930 E. Century Ave. Phone: (701) 258-6360. Fax: (701) 258-2015. Glenn Bosch, rgnl mgr.

Omaha, NE 68137, 5055 S. 111th St. Phone: (402) 593-6500. Fax: (402) 593-8500. Roland Schlegel, rgnl mgr.

Madison, WI 53716, 21375 Stoughton Rd. Phone: (608) 221-8888. Fax: (608) 221-9252.

New Berlin, WI 53151, 5300. Emmer Dr. Phone: (262) 207-1300. Fax: (262) 207-1301.

Cameras, consoles, monitors, speakers, microphones, remote control, transmitters, exciters, video-conferencing systems & TV bcstg equipment.

AVS Graphics & Media Inc., 3451 S. 11320 W., # A, Salt Lake City, UT 84119. Phone: (801) 975-9799. Fax: (801) 975-0970. E-mail: sales@avsgmedia.com. Web Site: www.avsgmedia.com. Gavin Hunter, CEO.

Bcst & production character generators & Still stores.

AVX Corp., 3900 Electronics Dr., Raleigh, NC 27604. Phone: (919) 878-6200. Fax: (919) 878-6470. Web Site: www.avxcorp.com. Jimmy White, sls dir; Craig Hunter, mktg dir.

Electronic component.

AZCAR U.S.A. Inc., 121 Hillpointe Dr., Suite 700, Canonsburgh, PA 15317. Phone: (724) 873-0800. Fax: (724) 873-4770. E-mail: info@azcar.com. Web Site: www.azcar.com. Stephen Pumple, pres/CEO; John Luff, sr VP business dev; Karl Paulsen, sr VP engrg; Marv Nolan, dire business dev.

Markham, ON L3R 0H3 Canada, 3235 14th Ave. Phone: (905) 470-2545. Fax: (905)470-2556. S. Pumple, pres/CEO.

Cambridge CB1 3HD United Kingdom, #1 College Business Park, Coldhams Lane. Phone: 44 1223 414101. Fax: 44 123 414102. F. Jarvis, dir.

Bcst engrg, systems integration.

Abroyd Communications Ltd., 50 Goebel Unit 5, Cambridge, ON N3C 1Z1. Canada. Phone: (519) 220-0420. Fax: (519) 658-1094. Web Site: www.abroyd.com.

Designers, manufacturers & installers of communication towers; manufacturer for Lightning Dissipation Arrays Chem-Rod from LEC.

Accom Inc., 1490 O'Brien Dr., Menlo Park, CA 94025. Phone: (650) 328-3818. Fax: (650) 327-2511. E-mail: info@accom.com. Web Site: www.accom.com. Junaid Sheikh, chmn/CEO; Phil Bennett, exec VP; Bill Ludwig, VP sls.

Accom designs, manufactures, sell, support a complete line of digital video production, disk recording & editing tools for use in the worldwide professional TV marketplace-encompassing the production, post production, bcstg & computer video markets.

Accurate Sound Corp., 3475A Edison Way, Menlo Park, CA 94025. Phone: (650) 365-2843. Fax: (650) 365-3057. E-mail: ron@accuratesound.com. Web Site: www.accuratesound.com. Ronald M. Newdoll, pres.

High-speed tape duplicating & recording equipment, digital audio logging recorders, audio & videotape conditioners, audio recorders. CD-R recorders for audio & ROM.

AccuWeather Inc., 385 Science Park Rd., State College, PA 16803-2215. Phone: (814) 235-8600. Fax: (814) 235-8609. E-mail: sales@accuux.com. Web Site: www.accuweather.com. Dr. Joel N. Myers, founder & pres; Evan Myers, sr VP/COO; Barry Lee Myers, exec VP/ gen counsel; Elliot Abrams, sr VP/ chief meteorologist; Dr. Joe Sobel, sr VP/dir forensics.

Bensalem, PA 19020, Two Greenwood Sq., Suite 440, 3331 Streal Rd. Phone: (888) 438-9847. Fax: (215) 244-5329. Dave Wrieden, exec dir ad sls.

AccuWeather, Inc. offers a broad new menu of powerful integrated, muturally supporting weather content and weather brand-building solutions.

Acme Electric Corp., Aerospace Division, 528 W. 21st St., Tempe, AZ 85282. Phone: (480) 894-6864. Fax: (480) 921-0470. Web Site: www.acme-electric.com/aerospace. Kevin Kriegel, dir mktg.

Sealed fiber nickel-cadmium batteries, battery chargers, battery control units, & AC/DC & DC/OC converters.

Acoustic Systems, a div. of ETS-LINDEREN, Box 3610, Austin, TX 78764. Phone: (800) 749-1460. Fax: (512) 444-2282. E-mail: info@acousticsystems.com. Web Site: www.acousticsystems.com. Steve Dutton, dev mgr; Charles Roe, sls dir.

Prefabricated & custom-made sound-isolating modular

Equipment Manufacturers and Distributors Alphabetical Index

enclosures for bcst & recording studios, voiceover & folio rooms.

Acoustical Solutions Inc., 2852 East Parham Rd., Richmond, VA 23228. Phone: (800) 782-5742. Fax: (804) 346-8808. E-mail: info@accousticalsolutions.com. Web Site: www.acousticalsolutions.com. Michael Binns, pres; Don Strahle, sales & mktg.

Sound & noise control materials including products for the bcst/recordingindustry, telecommunications industry, architectural acoustics & industrial noise control.

Acrodyne Industries Inc., 10706 Beaver Dam Rd., Cockeysville, PA 21030. Phone: (410) 568-2105. Web Site: www.acrodyne.com. Nat Ostroff, chmn; Mark Polovick, natl sls mgr; Ellen Rainey, mktg mgr.

Phoenixville, PA 19460, 200 Schell Ln. Phone: (610) 917-1300. Fax: (610) 917-8148.

Television transmitters - IOT equipped Quantum Line; solid-state Rohde & Schwarz medium-high power, supported by Acrodyne in North America.

Acterna, Cable Networks Division, 5808 Churchman Bypass, Indianapolis, IN 46203. Phone: (317) 788-9351. Fax: (317) 614-8308. Web Site: www.acterna.com.

Test equipment for video nets, including broadband RF & fiber optics. (SLMs, system analyzers, leakage, sweeps & OTDRs) software.

Adcom, 310 Judson St., Unit 5, Toronto, ON M8Z 5T6. Canada. Phone: (416) 251-3355. Fax: (416) 251-3977.

"Night Suite" DI, non-linear editing systems, bcst control systems, video conferencing. Room control systems "1 room".

Adrienne Electronics Corp., 7225 Bermuda Rd., Unit G, Las Vegas, NV 89119. Phone: (702) 896-1858. Fax: (702) 896-3034. E-mail: info@adrielec.com. Web Site: www.adrielec.com.

Small routing switchers, time code products, machine control products.

Advance Products Co. Inc., 1199 E. Central, Wichita, KS 67214. Phone: (316) 263-4231. Fax: (316) 263-4245. Harold Knapp, gen mgr.

Mobile projector, TV & video, tables & cabinets, wall & ceiling mount brackets.

Advanced Designs Corp., 1169 W. 2nd St., Bloomington, IN 47403. Phone: (812) 333-1922. Fax: (812) 333-2030. E-mail: adc@doprad.com. Web Site: www.doprad.com. Matt McGrath, pres; James Sawtelle, mktg mgr.

DOPRAD® 32 doppler radar system, weather data display system, storm path analyzer, street-level maps, lightning, low-cost remoting & composite live doppler.

Advanced Media Inc., 80 Orville Dr., Bohemia, NY 11716. Phone: (631) 244-1616. Fax: (631) 244-1415. E-mail: team@advancedmedia.com. Web Site: www.advancemedia.com.

Kiosk-interactive technology.

Advanced Media Technologies, Inc., 1520 S. Powerline Rd., Suite F, Deerfield Beach, FL 33442. Phone: (888) 293-5856. Fax: (954) 427-9688. E-mail: sales@advancedmediatech.com. Web Site: www.advancedmediatech.com. Ken Mosca, pres.

AMT supplies high performance products from well-known manufacturers including R, fiber distribution, video, data & IP.

Advanced Research Technology Inc., 404 Apollo Ct., Richardson, TX 75081. Phone: (972) 699-0737. Fax: (972) 644-1313. E-mail: r.edenson@attbi.com.

TV bcst, TV, HDTV Consultation, systems, instrumentation & consulting svcs.

Advent Communications Ltd., Preston Hill House, Nashleigh Hill, Chesham, Buckinghamshire HP5 3HE. United Kingdom. Phone: 44 (0)1494-774400. Fax: 44 (0)1494-791127. E-mail: sales@advent-comm.co.uk. Web Site: www.advent-comm.co.uk.

Satellite systems—flyaway, transportable & fixed. Satellite communications products, equipment for TV, radio & communications.

Aeroflex, 35 South Service Rd., Plainview, NY 11803. Phone: (516) 694-6700. Fax: (516) 694-2562. Web Site: www.aeroflex.com. Jeff Bloomer, pres/CEO.

Trophy Club, TX 76262, 49 Trophy Club Rd. Phone: (817) 430-5842. Carlos Blanco, sls mgr - South America.

Test & measurement instrumentation.

AheadTek, 6410 Via Del Oro, San Jose, CA 95119. Phone: (408) 226-9800. Phone: (408) 226-9991. Fax: (408) 226-9195. Fax: (408) 226-9194. E-mail: patj@drs-ahead.com. Web Site: www.aheadtek.com. Art Hoegger, pres; Pat Johnston, product mgr.

Cost effective solutions for your specialty magnetic head applications.

Peter Albrecht Company Inc., 6250 Industrial Ct., Greendale, WI 53129-2432. Phone: (414) 421-6630. Fax: (414) 421-9091. E-mail: sales@peteralbrecht.com. Web Site: www.peteralbrecht.com. T.C. Ziolkowski, pres.

Motorized studio battens, plaks & other rigging systems. Cyclorama track & curtain systems designed & installed.

Alesis, 12555 Jefferson Blvd., Los Angles, CA 90066. Phone: (310) 821-5000. Fax: (310) 306-2650. Web Site: www.alesis.com.

Digital tape recording system, mixing consoles, digital & analogue signal processing, amplification, drum machines, keyboards.

Alexander Technology, 1938 University, Lisle, IL 60532. Phone: (800) 247-1821. Phone: (641) 423-8955. Fax: (641) 423-1644. John Casey, pres/CEO.

Rechargeable nicad in-board, on-board & battery belts; nicad battery chargers & analyzer/conditioners; portable radio & pager batteries.

Alias/WaveFront Inc., 210 King St. E., Toronto, ON M5A 1J7. Canada. Phone: (416) 362-9181. Fax: (416) 369-6140. Web Site: www.aliaswavefront.com.

Agrate Brianza (MI) 20041. Wavefront Technologies srl, Centro Direzionale Colleoni, Palazzo Cassiopea, Ingresso 1. Phone: 39 39-6-5-7824. Fax: 39 39-654-195.

Bucks HP12 3PR. Wavefront Technologies Ltd., Oakridge House, Wellington Rd., High Wycombe. Phone: 44 494-441273. Fax: 44 494-464904.

Ghent B-9000. Wavefront Technologies N.V., Guldenspoorstraat 21-23. Phone: 32 9-225-45-55. Fax: 32 9-223-44-56.

Paris 75018. Wavefront Technologies, 22, rue Hegesippe Moreau. Phone: 33 1-44-90-11-30. Fax: 33 1-44-90-11-31.

Shinjuku-ku, Tokyo 163. Wavefront Japan, Ltd., 17F Shumitomo Bldg, 2-6-1 Nishi Shinjuku. Phone: 81 3-3342-7300. Fax: 81 3-3342-7353.

Tokyo 102. Nihon I-TEC K.K., Gloria Bldg. 1F, 7 Rijybab-Cho, Chiyoda-Ku. Phone: 81 33-2370690. Fax: 81 33-2885522.

San Ramon, CA 94583, 111 Deerwood Rd, Suite 200. Phone: (510) 831-4830. Fax: (510) 838-8530. (San Francisco office).

Seal Beach, CA 90740, 3020 Old Ranch Pwky, Suite 150. Phone: (310) 799-0011. Fax: (310) 799-1092. (Los Angeles office).

Atlanta, GA 30350, 400 Northridge Rd, Suite 510. Phone: (404) 993-1226. Fax: (404) 993-1859.

Schaumburg, IL 60173, 1930 N. Thoreau Dr, Suite 169. Phone: (708) 397-1092. Fax: (708) 397-1095. (Chicago office).

New York, NY 10016, 475 Park Ave. S., 7th Fl. Phone: (212) 725-7300. Fax: (212) 725-7338.

Springfield, VA 22150, 7420 Alban Station Ct, Suite 200. Phone: (703) 644-2100. Fax: (703) 644-2103. (Washington office).

2D & 3D computer graphic imaging & animation software for professionals in entertainment & industrial markets.

All Mobile Video Inc., 221 W. 26th St., New York, NY 10001. Phone: (212) 727-1234. Fax: (212) 255-6644. Web Site: www.allmobilevideo.com. Anton Duke, CEO; Eric Duke, pres.

San Diego, CA 92123, 9670 Aero Dr. Phone: (619) 569-8451. N. Tabkum, dir West Coast opns.

Saint Petersburg, FL 33742, 10490 Gandy Blvd. Phone: (813) 579-8902. Bary Spencer, dir teleport opns.

Bcst video equipment rental including truck remotes & total carry-in packages, complete studio facilities.

Allen & Heath USA, Agoura Business Center, E. 5304 Derry Ave., Suite C, Agoura Hills, CA 91301. Web Site: www.allen-heath.com. Al Nickols, sls dir.

Audio mixing consoles for recording & live sound applications including automated consoles.

Allen Avionics, Inc., 224 E. Second St., Mineola, NY 11501. Phone: (516) 248-8080. Fax: (516) 747-6724. E-mail: sales@allenavionics.com. Web Site: www.allenavionics.com. Jim Lyons, VP.

All passive components, video filters & delay lines, hum eliminators, LC filters & electromagnetic delay lines.

Allied Electronics Inc., 7410 Pebble Dr., Fort Worth, TX 76118. Fax: (817) 595-6444. Web Site: www.alliedelec.com. Lee Davidson, VP; Robert Pfleg, pres; Bob Whetson, sls dir; Rob Birse, dir.

Rocklin, CA 95765-3705, 590 Menlo Dr, Suite 8. Phone: (916) 435-9370. Fax: (916) 435-9380.

Englewood, CO 80112, 10 Inverness Dr. E, Suite 120. Phone: (303) 790-1664. Fax: (303) 790-8938.

Seminole, FL 33772, 7895 113th St, Suite 300. Phone: (727)579-4660. Fax: (727)-579-1422.

Brooklyn Center, MN 55430, 6120 Earle Brown Dr, Suite 400. Phone: (763) 560-9760. Fax: (763) 560-9744.

Broad line distributor of electronic components.

Allied Tower Co. Inc., 4646 Mandale, Alvin, TX 77511. Phone: (281) 331-9627. Fax: (281) 331-9822. Max Bowen, CEO; Jeff Bowen, pres; Doug W. Moore, VP.

Design, fabrication & erection of FM, AM, TV & communication towers.

Allison Payments Systems L.L.C., 2200 Production Dr., Indianapolis, IN 46241. Phone: (317) 808-2400. Fax: (317) 808-2477. Web Site: www.apsllc.com.

Coupon payment billing systems.

Allsop Inc., Box 23, Bellingham, WA 98227. Phone: (360) 734-9090. Fax: (360) 734-9858. Web Site: www.allsop.com. Jim Allsop, pres; Mike Allsop, co-pres.

Cleaning accessories for audio & video, record care products & compact discs, computer accessories.

Alpack Associates, Inc., 10 Commerce Rd., Unit D, Fairfield, NJ 07004. Phone: (973) 244-4414. Fax: (973) 244-4483. E-mail: info@alpack-pic.com. Les Weinstock, pres.

Standard & custom carrying & shipping cases for all bcst equipment. Both hard & soft case styles.

Alpha Technologies Inc., 3767 Alpha Way, Bellingham, WA 98226. Phone: (360) 647-2360. Fax: (360) 671-4936. E-mail: alpha@alpha.com. Web Site: www.alpha.com. Paul Humphreys, VP mktg; Warren Johnson, pres/COO.

Manufacturer of power systems for coaxial & fiber optic networks. UPS systems, DC products, batteries & surge suppression.

Alpha Video & Electronics Co. (AVEC), 200 Keystone Dr., Carnegie, PA 15106. Phone: (412) 429-2000. Fax: (412) 429-2015. E-mail: avec@aveceng.com. Web Site: www.aveceng.com.

O.B. vans, eng vans, DSNG vans, ENG mast safety device, turnkey systems, camera transporter.

Alpine Optics Inc., 9913 N.W. 20th St., Coral Springs, FL 33071. Phone: (954) 344-9871. Fax: (954) 344-3665. E-mail: toalpine_optics@bellsouth.net. Web Site: www.alpine-optics.com. Horst Stahl, pres.

Repair, maintenance of all Canon, Fujinon, Nikon, Schneider & JVC lenses.

Altronic Research Inc. Box 249, Yellville, AR 72687. Phone: (800) 482-5623. Fax: (870) 449-6000. E-mail: altronic@mtnhome.com. Web Site: www.altronic.com. John Dyess, pres.

Omegaline RF coaxial load resistors (dummy loads).

Aluma Tower Company Inc., Box 2806-BC, Vero Beach, FL 32961-2806. Phone: (772) 567-3423. Fax: (772) 567-3432. E-mail: atc@alumatower.com. Web Site: www.alumatower.com. Theodore E. Gottry, VP.

Aluminum telescoping towers combined with trailers & optional shelters provides mobile units. Vehicle mounted towers for installation on customer's vehicle.

Broadcasting & Cable Yearbook 2006

Amek U.S.A., 8500 Balboa Blvd., Northridge, CA 91329. Phone: (818) 920-3212. Fax: (818) 920-3208. E-mail: amekusa@harman.com.

Amek, TAC (Total Audio Concepts) & Langley audio consoles for production, postproduction, audio recording, sound reinforcement & Medici signal processing equipment.

American Antenna Inc., 4707 Roosevelt St., Glen Park, IN 46408. Phone: (219) 985-4000. Fax: (219) 985-4001. E-mail: sales@americanantenna.com. Web Site: www.americanantenna.com. Nick Michels, pres; Chuck Forsyth, VP sls; Rick Gard, sec.

Distributor, installer of Earth Station Antennas from .45cm to 6.1m motorized actuators, receivers, controllers, LNB's & accessories.

American Eurocopter Corp., 2701 Forum Dr., Grand Prairie, TX 75052-7099. Phone: (972) 641-0000. Fax: (972) 641-3550. Web Site: www.eurocopterusa.com. Marc Paganini, pres; Brenda Revland, dir.

Servicing North American market; manufactures & sells complete line of single- & twin-engine turbine helicopters.

Amerivox Corp., 2208 N.W. Market St., Suite 4, Seattle, WA 98107. Phone: (206) 784-0081. Fax: (808) 982-6849.

Listener info lines, loyal listener lines, interactive voice response systems, all sizes: 2-36 lines.

Ampex Data Systems Corp., 1228 Douglas Ave., Redwood City, CA 94063-3199. Phone: (650) 367-2011. Fax: (650) 367-2444. E-mail: info@ampexdata.com. Web Site: www.ampexdata.com. Ed Bramson, pres/CEO; Bob Atchison, VP; Joel Talcott, VP.

Data recorders, data systems, mass data storage, instrumentation recorder products; 19 mm scanning recorders, library systems (DST & DIS products), related tape, after-market parts & video recorder support.

Amplifier Technologies, Inc., 1749 Chapin Rd., Montebello, CA 90640. Phone: (323) 278-0001. Fax: (310) 323-0083. E-mail: sales@bgw.com. Web Site: www.ati-amp.com. Barbara Wachner, pres; Jeff Wachner, gen sls mgr.

Professional, bcst & coml audio power amplifiers, rack mount accessories, racks, self-powered subwoofer systems & rack mount computer systems.

Amplivox Portable Sound Systems, 3149 MacArthur Blvd., Northbrook, IL 60062. Phone: (847) 498-9000. Fax: (800) 267-5489. E-mail: info@ampli.com. Web Site: www.ampli.com. Don Roth, CEO.

Portable sound systems/lecterns/wireless/indoor-outdoor, made in USA, UL, CSA, CE, 3 year warranty.

Amtel Network, 431 Myrtle St., Suite 6, Glendale, CA 91203. Phone: (818) 551-4995. Fax: (818) 551-4999. Web Site: www.amtelsystems.com. Mike Takamatsu, pres.

Text-visual intercom system.

Analog Digital International Inc., 20 E. 49th St., 2nd Fl., New York, NY 10017-1023. Phone: (212) 688-5110. Fax: (212) 688-5405. E-mail: info@analogdigitalinc.com. Web Site: www.analogdigitalinc.com.

Sls & Rentals of professional /bcst NTSC/PA equipment, post production, DVD authoring, AVID editing , final cut pro editing & training.

Anchor Audio Inc., 3415 W. Lomita Blvd., Torrance, CA 90505. Phone: (310) 784-2300. Fax: (310) 784-0066. E-mail: sales@anchoraudio.com. Web Site: www.anchoraudio.com. David Jacobs, pres; Darren Stanley, VP sls.

Bcst intercom equipment, 2-ch high performance & low cost.

Andrew Corp., 10500 W. 153rd St., Orland Park, IL 60462. Phone: (708) 349-3300. Phone: (800) 255-1479. Fax: (708) 349-5943. Web Site: www.andrew.com. Paul Cox, pres; Barry Cohen, sls dir; George Tong, mgr.

Orland Park, IL 60462, 10500 W. 153rd St. Phone: (708) 349-3300. Paul Cox, group pres; Bary Cohen, sls; George Tong, govt Antennas & ESAs.

VHF & UHF-TV transmitting, microwave & ESA's; coaxial cable; waveguides; towers; equipment shelters; instal svcs, combiners & pressurization equipment.

Antenna Concepts Inc., 6626 Merchandise Way, Diamond Springs, CA 95619. Phone: (530) 621-2015. Fax: (530) 622-3274. E-mail: sales@antennaconcepts.com. Web Site: www.antennaconcepts.com. Mark A. Cunningham, pres/CEO.

Custom & standard low-, medium- and high-power omni or directional digital & analog UHF, VHF, FM, & MMDS bcst antennas. Full power Broadcast antennas. TV: UHF/VHF analog/digital antennas including full-UHF band CP panel. Fm: Ultra Tracker single-lobe.

Anton/Bauer Inc., 14 Progress Dr., Shelton, CT 06484. Phone: (203) 929-1100. Fax: (203) 929-9935. Web Site: www.antonbauer.com.

NiCad, silver zinc & NIMH camera/VTR batteries, chargers, lighting & diagnostic accessories for the professional video industry.

Anvil Cases, 15730 Salt Lake Ave., City of Industry, CA 91745. Phone: (626) 968-4100. Fax: (626) 968-1703. Web Site: www.anvilcase.com. E-mail: info@anvilcase.com.

Heavy-duty reuseable, custom, standard shipping cases & containers for all bcst equipment.

Aphex Systems Ltd., 11068 Randall St., Sun Valley, CA 91352. Phone: (818) 767-2929. Fax: (818) 767-2641. E-mail: sales@aphex.com. Web Site: www.aphex.com. Marvin Caesar, pres; Allen Steelgrave, gen sls mgr; Wayne La Farr, product specialist.

Model 2020 MKIII, Compellor-intelligent AGC, Dominator II precision multi-band peak limiter, Aural Exciter, Expressor, remote controlled mic preams, TVGS MIC/instrument, preamplifiers, analog to digital converters.

Argraph Corp., 111 Asia Pl., Carlstadt, NJ 07072. Phone: (201) 939-7722. Fax: (201) 939-7782. Mark Roth, pres; Martin Lipton, sls.

Hayward, CA 94545. Argraph West, 2710 McCone. Phone: (510) 298-0575.

Anti-stat cleaning cloths, samigron video tripods.

Aries Industries Inc., N63 W22641 Main St., Sussex, WI 53089. Phone: (262) 246-3900. Fax: (262) 246-7099. E-mail: sales@ariesind.com. Web Site: www.ariesind.com. Jim Lenahan, pres/CEO.

Fresno, CA 93727, 5748 E. Shields. Phone: (800) 671-0383. Fax: (559) 291-0463. J. Lenahan, CEO.

Manufacture pipeline inspection televising test & seal equipment.

Arista Information Systems, 2150 Boggs Rd., Suite 430, Duluth, GA 30096. Phone: (678) 473-1885. Fax: (678) 473-1051. E-mail: sales@aristainfo.com. Web Site: www.aristainfo.com. Scott Ford, sls dir.

Cable TV subscriber & statement printing.

Arrakis Systems Inc., 6604 Powell St., Loveland, CO 80538. Phone: (970) 461-0730. Fax: (970) 663-1010. E-mail: sales@arrakis-systems.com. Web Site: www.arrakis-systems.com. Michael C. Palmer, pres; Jon Young, VP sls; Roderic M. Graham, VP.

Audio consoles, digital audio, satellite, live-assist, music-on, hard drive automation & production systems, studio furniture.

Arri Canada Ltd., 415 Horner Ave., Unit 11, Etobicoke, ON M8W 4W3. Canada. Phone: (416) 255-3335. Fax: (416) 255-3399. E-mail: david@arrican.com. Web Site: www.arri.com. David Rosengarten, pres.

ARRI camera, lightning equipment & all professional accessories, sales & service.

Arri, Inc., 617 Rt. 303, Blauvelt, NY 10913-1109. Phone: (845) 353-1400. Fax: (845) 425-1250. E-mail: arriflex@arri.com. Web Site: www.arri.com. Juergen Schwinzer, VP; John Gresch, VP; Volker Bahnemann, pres.

Burbank, CA 91502, 600 N. Victory Blvd. Phone: (818) 841-7070. Bill Russell, western sls mgr.

Professional 16 mm, 35 mm & 65 mm film cameras, ARRI HMI, fresnel, studio fresnel & kit lighting, Zeiss lenses.

Arris, 11450 Technology Circle, Duluth, GA 30097. Phone: (678) 473-2000. Fax: (678) 473-8182. Web Site: www.arrisi.com. Bob Stanzione, pres/CEO; Jim Lakiu, pres; Connie Walters, dir mktg.

Santa Ana, CA 92705, 1936 Deere Ave, 219, Bldg. F. Phone: (800) 854-0443. (714) 757-1630. Fax: (714) 757-1203.

Englewood, CO 80111, 94 Inverness Terrace E. Phone: (303) 799-4343. Fax: (303) 643-4797.

Tinton Falls, NJ 07724, 56 Park Road. Phone: (908) 389-8800. Fax: (908) 389-3746.

CMTS, cable modems, telephony voice ports & modems, oss/provisioning systems, HFC infrastructure products.

Artel Video Systems, a division of Newfound Technology Inc. 330 Codman Hill Rd., Boxborough, MA 01719. Phone: (978) 263-5775. Fax: (978) 263-9755. E-mail: sales@artel.com. Web Site: www.Artel.com. Richard Dellacanoica, pres/CEO.

Coral Springs, FL 33071. Latin America:, 1406 NW 127th Way. Phone: (954) 914-1606. Fax: (954) 757-9201. E-mail: pfalci@artel.com.

Lemont, IL 60439. Western Regional Sales Mgr:, 1258 Cronin Ct. Phone: (630) 257-9190. Fax: (630) 240-9696. E-mail: tks@newfoundtech.com.

Manassas, VA 20110. Eastern Regional Sales Mgr:, 9956 Mallow St. Phone: (703) 393-7431. Fax: (703) 393-7436. E-mail: jfc@newfoundtech.com.

Wanchai, NO Hongkong. Asia/Pacific:, 2/F Shui On Centre, 8 Harbor Rd. Phone: (852) 2868-1993. Fax: (852) 2525-8297. E-mail: rwong@newfoundtech.com.

London E14 3DT United Kingdom. EMEA Regional Sales:, 36 Ferry St. Phone: +44 (0) 207-536-7686. Fax: +44 (0) 774-701-4422. E-mail: jfj@newfoundtech.com.

Artel Video Systems is a leading worldwide supplier of video networking solutions. Artel products sit at the core of mission critical video networks in the world's major sports venues, news organizations, and broadcast facilities. Artel's equipment has linked many of the world's premier events to the worldwide broadcast infrastructure—from the Democratic and Republican National Conventions to the Olympic games.

Artesia Technologies, 700 King Farm Blvd., Suite 400, Rockville, MD 20850. Phone: 301-548-7850. Fax: 301-548-4015. Web Site: www.artesia.com. Brian Hedquist, dir mktg.

Did you know that Digital Asset Management typically has a return on investment of 9 to 18 months? Learn more at Artesia's Seminar Series presented with The Gartner Group & Frank Gilbane.

Ascent Media Management Services, 2901 W. Alameda Ave., Burbank, CA 91505. Phone: (818) 840-7000. Fax: (818) 840-7129. Web Site: www.4mc.com. William Humphrey, pres; Beth Simon, sls VP & sr VP; Andre Macaluso, opns VP.

Northvale, NJ 07647, 235 Pegasus Ave. Phone: (201) 767-3800. Fax: (201) 767-4568. Beth Simon, sr VP sls/mktg.

Postproduction video & film svcs: editing, telecine, sound, duplication, satellite svcs, film lab, standard conversion tape to film transfers & digital asset mgmt.

Ascent Media Services, (Formerly Waterfront Communications Corp.). 545 5th Ave., New York, NY 10017. Phone: (212) 907-1208. Fax: (212) 599-4172.

A transmission company specializing in video switching, quality control, last mile connections, remote transmissions, production & audiovisual svcs to the bcst, cable & corporate TV industries.

Ascent Media Services, 6344 Fountain Ave., Hollywood, CA 90028. Phone: (323) 988-6520. Web Site: www.ascentmedia.com. Edward Olson, VP engrg & techhnology; Lou DiMauro, dir video sls; David Lostracco, dir opns & client svcs., Asia Broadcast Centre. Phone: (65) 548-0388. Jim Crowe, mgng dir.

Minneapolis, MN 55403. GWNS Phone: (612) 330-2639. Joel Helseth, dir sls & mktg.

Video transmission, origination, tech consulting, new media products, private networks, post-production, studio, graphics, bcst event svcs and satellite svcs.

Associated Press Broadcast Services, 1825 K St. N.W., Suite 800, Washington, DC 20006-1202. Phone: (202) 736-1100. Fax: (202) 736-1124. Fax: (202) 736-1199. Web Site: www.apbroadcasting.com. James R. Williams, VP; Lee Perryman, dir.

AP NewsDesk: Newsroom computer software program for mgng TV, radio news & info resources.

Atlantic Inc., 12801 Busch Pl., Sante Fe Springs, CA 90670-3023. Phone: (562) 903-9550. Fax: (562) 903-9053. E-mail: atlantic@atlantic-inc.com. Web Site: www.atlantic-inc.com. Leo Dardashti, pres; Don Dolliver, VP sls.

Manufacturer of metal storage systems for DVDs, CDs, & VHS.

Atlantic Sound Systems, R.R. 2, New Glasgow, Pictou County, NS B2H 5C5. Canada. Phone: (902) 752-8527. E-mail: plann@wisic.com.

Professional bcstg, sound & lighting equipment. Rental & PA Installations.

Atlantic Video Inc., 650 Massachusetts Ave. N.W., Washington, DC 20001. Phone: (202) 408-0900. Fax: (202) 408-8496. E-mail: aschwab@atlanticvideo.com. Web Site: www.atlanticvideo.com. Dong Moon Joo, CEO; Todd Mason, pres; John Summers, VP/gen mgr.

Postproduction, graphics, duplication, remote, satellite uplink/downlink, videoconferencing, film-to-tape transfer, master control for net & digital editing.

Atlas Case Corp., 1380 So. Cherokee St., Denver, CO 80223. Phone: (888) 325-2199. Fax: (877) 525-2339. Web Site: www.atlascases.com. Randy Sabey, pres.

Airline-approved shipping & carrying cases. Local transport cases, custom or from stock.

Equipment Manufacturers and Distributors Alphabetical Index

Atlas Sound, 4545 E. Baseline Rd., Phoenix, AZ 85042. Phone: (800) 876-3332. Phone: (602) 438-4545. Fax: (800) 765-3435. E-mail: atlascustser@atlassound.com. Web Site: www.atlassound.com.

Atlas Sound brand microphone & equipment stands, accessories; equipment consoles, racks & cabinets; loudspeaker systems; a/v monitoring devices.

Audico Labels, 118 South Main St., Goshen, IN 46526. Phone: (574) 533-6688. Phone: (800) 252-5667. Fax: (661) 760-8775. E-mail: audicolabels@audicolabels.com. Web Site: www.audicolabels.com. Bill Landow, owner; Claudia Landow, owner.

Media pressure sensitive labels.

Audio Accessories Inc., 25 Mill St., Marlow, NH 03456. Phone: (603) 446-3335. Fax: (603) 446-7543. E-mail: audioacc@patchbays.com. Web Site: www.patchbays.com. M.B. Hall, pres; T.J. Symonds, opns mgr.

Jack panels, (audio & video patchbays) patch cords, telephone jacks & plugs, pre-wired jack panels (miniature & full-size) & video panels.

Audio Implements/GKC, 1703 Pearl St., Waukesha, WI 53186-5626. Phone: (262) 524-2424. Fax: (262) 524-7898. E-mail: info@audioimplements.com. Web Site: www.audioimplements.com. Walter L. Kolb, owner; Anita Brown, sec.

Acoustic coiled earpiece, receivers & cords, microphone line & monitor amplifiers, used in conjunction with IFB system.

Audio Precision Inc., 5750 S.W. Arctic Dr., Beaverton, OR 97005. Phone: (503) 627-0832. Fax: (503) 641-8906. E-mail: sales@audioprecision.com. Web Site: www.audioprecision.com. David Solomon, sls dir; Al Miksch, CEO.

2700 Series, Portable One & ATS-1, ATS-2 audio test sets for bcst & satellite use.

Audio Processing Technology Ltd., Edgewater Rd., Belfast BT3 9JQ. Phone: (44) 28 9037 1110. Fax: (44) 28 9037 1137. E-mail: aptmarketing@aptx.com. Web Site: www.aptx.com. Noel McKenna, mgng dir; Jon McClintock, dir.

Los Angeles, CA 90028, 6255 Sunset Blvd, Suite 1025. Phone: (323) 463-2963. Fax: (323) 463-8878. Simav Factor.

Digital (apt-X) audio compression system for professional applications such as storage & transmission of audio over low capacity digital circuits such as ISDN.

Audio-Technica U.S., Inc., 1221 Commerce Dr., Stow, OH 44224. Phone: (330) 686-2600. Fax: (330) 688-3752. E-mail: pro@atus.com. Web Site: www.audio-technica.com. Phil Cajka, pres/CEO; Fred Nichols, sr VP; Richard Strungle, VP opns; Jackie Green, VP; Steven Lefkowitz, CFO.

Microphones, wireless microphones, headphones, automatic microphone mixers, phono cartridges, turntables, audio & video accessories.

Audio-Video Engineering Co., One Pineapple Ln., Stuart, FL 34996. Phone: (772) 219-3623. Fax: (772) 219-3624. Olga M. Drucker, pres.

Video hum stop coil (hum bucker).

Audio Video Systems International, 28254 Bakerton Ave., Santa Clarita, CA 91351. Phone: (661) 251-6333. Fax: (661) 251-6802. E-mail: sales@usedvideo.net. Web Site: www.usedvideo.net. Dean Hasse, owner.

Used TV equipment brokers specializing in bcst & industrial VTRs, cameras & editing equipment.

Audioarts Engineering, 600 Industrial Dr., New Bern, NC 28562. Phone: (252) 638-7000. Fax: (252) 635-4857. E-mail: sales@wheatstone.com. Web Site: www.audioarts.net. Gary C. Snow, pres; Andrew Calvanese, VP; Jay Tyler, sls dir.

Manufacturer of digital, analog bcst audio mixing consoles & processing equipment.

Audiolab Electronics Inc., 620 Commerce Dr., Suite C, Roseville, CA 95678. Phone: (916) 784-0200. Fax: (916) 784-1425. E-mail: info@audiolabelectronics.com. Web Site: www.audiolabelectronics.com. Ronald A. Stofan, pres/CEO.

Professional line of bulk tape degaussers for all formats of tape including: Beta SP, DAT 2" reels up to 16" diameters, hard drives, DLT media & degaussing svc.

Auernheimer Labs Corp., 4561 E. Florence Ave., Fresno, CA 93725. Phone: (559) 442-1048. Curley Auernheimer, pres.

Loudspeaker systems; studio, monitor, control room & auditorium.

Auratone Corp., Box 180698, Coronado, CA 92178-0698. Phone: (619) 297-2820. Phone: (619) 758-0817. Fax: (619) 296-8734. Fax: (617) 758-0936. Jack Wilson, pres/ceo/sec.

Recording, bcst, monitor & reference loudspeaker systems. Sound reinforcement, background, foreground & sound distribution loudspeaker systems. Raw loudspeakers (woofers, tweeters).

Austin Insulators Inc., 7510 Airport Rd., Mississauga, ON L4T 2H5. Canada. Phone: (905) 405-1144. Fax: (905) 405-1150. Web Site: www.austin-insulators.com. Patrick Warr, pres; Beverly O'Brien, exec VP.

Base/guyline insulators, static drain devices, tower lighting transformers, replacements for obsolete insulators.

Autogram Corp., Box 456, 1500 Capital Ave., Plano, TX 75074-8113. Phone: (972) 424-8585. Phone: (800) 327-6901. Fax: (972) 423-6334. E-mail: info@autogramcorp.com. Web Site: www.autogramcorp.com. Ernest T. Ankele Jr., pres/CEO; Delores Ankele, comptroller; John A. Stanley Jr., dir mktg.

Pacemaker IIk audio consoles, Pacemaker 6, 8, 10 Slide Pot, Mini-Mix 8 & Mini-Mix 12 Economy Consoles.Solution 20 audio systems, CYA-4 emergency switchers. Autoclock clock/timer/thermometer.

Automatic Devices Company, 2121 S. 12th St., Allentown, PA 18103. Phone: (610) 797-6000. Fax: (610) 797-4088. Web Site: www.automaticdevices.com.

Cyclorama tracks, lighting tracks, lift & draw machines, electronic limit switches.

AVerMedia Technologies Inc., 423 Dixon Landing Rd., Milpitas, CA 95035. Phone: (800) 863-2332. Phone: (408) 263-3828. Web Site: www.aver.com. Arthur Pait, pres.

Aside from TV Turner/Desktop TV Personal Video Recorder products, AVerMeida also provides digital camera picture TV display devices, Document Camera & PC-to-TV Converters.

Avid Broadcast, 1925 Andover St., Tewksbury, MA 01876. Phone: (978) 640-6789. Fax: (978) 640-1366. Web Site: www.avid.com. David Schleifer, dir bcstg & workgroups; Adam Taylor, VP sls & customer svc.

Burbank, CA 91502, 115 N. First St. Phone: (818) 557-2520. Fax: (818) 557-2558. John Steinhauer, dir bcst group sls.

New York, NY 10022, 575 Lexington Ave., 14th Fl. Phone: (212) 983-2424. Fax: (212) 983-8718. Michael Wright, dir sls.

Madison, WI 53719, 6400 Enterprise Ln, Suite 200. Phone: (608) 274-8686. Fax: (608) 273-5876. Robert Long, CTO.

Automated bcst newsroom systems. Non-linear video editing systems, media storage & networking systems, video server, content mgmt systems & asset mgmt systems.

Avid Technology Inc. Metropolitan Technology Park, One Park W., Tewksbury, MA 01876. Phone: (800) 949-AVID. Phone: (978) 640-3669. Fax: (978) 851-0418. Fax: (978) 640-1366. E-mail: info@avid.com. Web Site: www.avid.com. David Krall, pres/CEO; Paul Milbury, CFO; Joe Bentivegna, VP; Chas Smith, VP sls.

Burbank, CA 91502, 115 N. 1st St, Suite 100. Phone: (818) 557-2520. John Steinhauer, dir strategic sls America.

New York, NY 10017, 317 Madison Ave., Suite 521, 5th Fl. Phone: (212) 983-2424. Michael Wright, dir strategic sls.

Avid's networked bcst news productions are designed to facilitate the process of digital news gathering (DNG).

Avtech Systems Inc., 141 Ayers Ct., Teaneck, NJ 07666. Phone: (201) 833-8777. Fax: (201) 833-4995. E-mail: disamuel@aol.com. Fred M. Samuel, pres.

Closed circuit video equipment, components & accessories.

Axcera, Box 525, 103 Freedom Dr., Lawrence, PA 15055. Phone: (724) 873-8100. Fax: (724) 873-8105. E-mail: info@axcera.com. Web Site: www.axcera.com.

High and low power digital, analog, UHF and VHF transmitters and translators; exciter retrofits; MMDS systems and Broadband wireless access technology.

B

B&B Systems, 1840 Flower St., Glendale, CA 91201. Phone: (818) 551-5871. Fax: (818) 247-3487. E-mail: info@b-bsystems.com. Web Site: www.b-bsystems.com.

Design & instal of production & postproduction systems, vans & mobile units, manufacturer of audio monitoring products.

BBE Sound Inc., 5381 Production Dr., Huntington Beach, CA 92649. Phone: (714) 897-6766. Fax: (714) 896-0736. Web Site: www.bbesound.com. Rob Rizzuto, VP sls.

Audio/video signal processors to eliminate phase & amplitude distortion.

BDL-Autoscript, A8 Poplar Business Park, 10 Prestons Rd., London E14 9RL. Phone: +44(0)171538 1427. Fax: +44(0)171515 9529. E-mail: sales@gdlautoscript.com. Chris Lambert, mgng dir; Jill Babington, finincial dir; Giles Dickinson, opns dir.

Wantagh, NY 11793-4024, 3280 Sunrise Hwy, PMB 294. Phone: (516) 799-3869. Lisa Grunert, mgr.

Design & manufacture of digital teleprompt systems, news, studio & location; sale or rental.

BEI Duncan, (Electronics Division). 15771 Red Hill Ave., Tustin, CA 92780. Phone: (714) 258-7500. Fax: (714) 258-8120. Web Site: www.beiduncan.com. Roger Wells, gen mgr; Cory Visser, comptroller.

Faders & attenuators: slide type with linear & audio output, single & dual channel.

BEXT Inc., 1045 10th Ave., San Diego, CA 92101. Phone: (619) 239-8462. Fax: (619) 239-8474. E-mail: mail@bext.com. Web Site: www.bext.com. Dennis Piere, CEO; Claudio Tilesi, CFO.

Radio & Digital TV Transmitters, Antennas, Amplifiers, Boosters, STLs, RF Combiners, RF Filters, Stereo, Generators, XD Radio Encoders and Receivers.

BHP Inc., 4700 Chase Ave., Lincolnwood, IL 60712. Phone: (847) 677-3000. Fax: (847) 677-1311. E-mail: sales@bhpinc.com. Web Site: www.bhpinc.com. Jonathan Banks, pres.

Motion picture laboratory equipment, film printers & accessories.

BMG, 1540 Broadway, New York, NY 10036. Phone: (212) 930-4000. Fax: (212) 930-4015. Web Site: www.bmg.com. Rolf Schmidt Hotz, chmn.

Produce, market & distribute recorded music.

Bald Mountain Laboratory, 222 Bellevue Rd., Troy, NY 12180. Phone: (518) 279-9753. E-mail: hambob@highstream.net. Robert S. Henry, owner.

Frequency readings.

Band Pro Film/Video Inc., 3403 W. Pacific Ave., Burbank, CA 91505. Phone: (818) 841-9655. Fax: (818) 841-7649. E-mail: sales@bandpro.com. Web Site: www.bandpro.com. Amnon Band, owner; Renee Contreras, exec VP.

Tel Aviv 52495, 22 Jabotinski St, Ramat-Gan. Phone: (972) 3-547-0482. Fax: (972) 3-673-1894. Ofer Menashe, dir international sls.

Heimstetten 85551 Germany, Klausnerring 6. Phone: 49 172-823-0365. Gerhard Baieir, mktg dir.

Dealer of professional production equipment for video, motion picture, & high definition, including top makers like Sony, Zeiss, Sachtler, Anton Bauer

Barco Visual Solutions, LLC, 3240 Town Point Dr., Suite 100, Kennesaw, GA 30144. Phone: (770) 218-3200. Fax: (770) 218-3250. E-mail: bpsmarketing@barco.com. Web Site: www.barco.com/projection_systems. Larry Steelman, sls dir; Tom Ray, exec VP & gen mgr; Jim Durant, mktg mgr; Ellyce Kelly, mgr.

BARCO offers complete monitoring solutions for control rooms in telecom traffic, surveillance, public utilities, process control & financing.

Baron Telecom, 2355 Industrial Park Blvd., Cumming, GA 30041. Phone: (678) 455-6298. Phone: 9670 513-1501. Fax: 96780 455-1153. Ran Bukshpan, CEO; Ron Raviv, CFO; Ross Kruchten, pres.

Frederick, MD 21703, 4640 Wedgewood Blvd. Phone: (301) 663-9300. Fax: (301) 663-9584. Tom Cureton.

Houston, TX 77070, 10430 Rogers Rd. Phone: (713) 973-6904. Fax: (713) 973-0205. Ross Kruchten.

Kirkland, WA 98033, 11112 117th Pl. N.E. Phone: (425) 739-9342. Fax: (425) 739-9314. Russ Stromberg.

Project mgmt & turn-key construction of communications towers, including erection, maintenance & inspection of tall towers.

Russ Bassett, 8189 Byron Rd., Whittier, CA 90606. Phone: (562) 945-2445. Fax: (562) 698-8972. E-mail: E-mail@russbassett.com. Web Site: www.russbassett.com. Maurice Heaton, VP mktg; Joe Malerba, VP sls.

High density storage cabinets for video tape, audio tape & CD's.

Equipment Manufacturers and Distributors Alphabetical Index

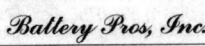

Battery Pros, Inc.
Battery Sales and Assembly Services
PATTI NOVAK
Sr. Sales Rep.

5659 Blackjack Road
Flowery Branch, GA 30542

Telephone (770) 271•8801
(800) 451•7171
Fax (770) 271•9714

Battery Pros Inc. 5659 BlackJack Rd., Flowery Branch, GA 30542-5402. Phone: (770) 271-8801. Phone: (800) 451-7171. Fax: (770) 271-9714. E-mail: sales@batteryprosinc.com. Web Site: www.batteryprosinc.com. Patti Novak, pres; Maria Arce, sec.

Battery recelling/rebuilding for Bricks & Belts, primary & secondary batteries, custom battery pack design & manufacture.

Bauer Transmitters, 10870 Pellicano, #252, El Paso, TX 79935. Phone: (915) 595-1048. Fax: (915) 595-1840. E-mail: paul@bauertx.com. Web Site: www.bauertx.com. Paul E. Gregg, pres.

Remanufactured Bauer-Sparta & Elcom Bauer AM/FM transmitters, AM combining and antenna coupling equipment.

Belar Electronics Laboratory Inc., Box 76, 119 Lancaster Ave., Devon, PA 19333. Phone: (610) 687-5550. Fax: (610) 687-2686. E-mail: sales@belar.com. Web Site: www.belar.com. Arno Meyer, pres.

AM, FM, FM stereo, SCA, RDS/RBDS, shortwave, TV, TV stereo modulation & frequency monitors.

Belden Electronics Divison, Box 1980, Richmond, IN 47375. Phone: (765) 983-5200. Phone: (800) 235-3361. Fax: (765) 983-5294. E-mail: info@belden.com. Web Site: www.belden.com. C. Baker Cunningham, pres/CEO; Peter Wickman, pres; Brian O'Connell, VP sls; Brain O'Connell, mktg VP.

Precision video coaxial, triaxial cables, professional music cables, ENG cables, audio snakes, RGB cables, 50 ohm transmission cables.

Bencher Inc., 831 N. Central Ave., Wood Dale, IL 60191. Phone: (630) 238-1183. Fax: (630) 238-1186. E-mail: bencher@bencher.com. Web Site: www.bencher.com.

Photographic & video vertical camera copystands & accessories, including Motion Picture Maker movable copy stage.

Benchmark Media Systems Inc., 5925 Court St. Rd., Syracuse, NY 13206-1707. Phone: (315) 437-6300. Fax: (315) 437-8119. E-mail: info@benchmarkmedia.com. Web Site: www.benchmarkmedia.com. Allen H. Burdick, pres; R. Rory Rall, sls mgr.

Audio processing & distribution systems, VU/PPM meters, interface/headphone amplifiers, microphone pre-amplifiers; digital to analog & analog to digital converters.

Bend-A-Lite Flexible Neon, 905 G St., Hampton, VA 23661. Phone: (757) 245-7675. Fax: (757) 244-4819. Web Site: www.bendalite.com. E-mail: info@bendalite.com. Hugh Jones, pres; Ron Koppel, mktg dir.

Flexible neon that can be cut with scissors, cut section can be re-electrified. 110v, 12v, 220v, 24v, indoor/outdoor. Lengths up to 300 ft., brilliant neon colors.

Benner-Nawman Inc., 3450 Sabin Brown Rd., Wickenburg, AZ 85390. Phone: (800) 992-3833. Fax: (928) 684-7041. E-mail: mail@bnproducts.com. Web Site: www.bnproducts.com. Edward R. Kientz, pres.

Specialty tools for CATV, cable termination & distribution boxes (cabinets).

Bexel Corp., 801 S. Main St., Burbank, CA 91506. Phone: (818) 841-5051. Fax: (818) 841-1572. E-mail: askburbank@bexel.com. Web Site: www.bexel.com. John Badovinac, mgr; Andy Crist, pres/CEO; Jackie Blake, mktg.

Irvine, CA 92614, 1821 Kaiser Ave. Phone: (949) 955-2222. Fax: (949) 955-2294. Debbie White, rental mgr.

Miami, FL 33179, 20239 N.E. 15th Ct. Phone: (305) 653-5051. Fax: (305) 655-6209. Rick Simpson, rental mgr.

Atlanta, GA 30093, 5555 Oak Brook Pkwy, Suite 160. Phone: (770) 448-3000. Fax: (770) 449-5747. Frank Zamor, rental mgr.

New York, NY 10019, 625 W. 55th St. Phone: (212) 246-5051. Fax: (212) 246-6373. Mke King.

Irving, TX 75061, 1001 N. Union Bower, Suite 130. Phone: (214) 946-5051. Fax: (972) 831-9860. Ashlyn Winfree, rental mgr.

Herndon, VA 20170, 465 Herndon Pkwy. Phone: (703) 437-5559. Fax: (703) 471-2853. Jimmy Brandt, rental.

Seattle, WA 98134, 3314 4th Ave. S. Phone: (206) 628-7000. Fax: (206) 628-7003. Paul Marrocco, rental mgr.

Rental of video equipment & ancillary items to the video & audio production community. Used equipment sls.

Bexel, Inc., 5555 Oak Brook Pkwy., Suite 160, Norcross, GA 30093. Phone: (770) 448-3000. E-mail: info@charterabs.com. Web Site: www.bexel.com.

Orlando, FL 32811, 4201 Vineland Rd, Suite I-12. Phone: (407) 872-0054. Joan Hagle, natl sls mgr.

Chicago, IL 60622, 870 W. Division St, Unit E. Russell Roberts, lead rental coord.

Irving, TX 75038, 3251 W. Story Rd. Phone: (972) 869-9100. Alan McDonald, natl sls mgr.

Leading provider of rental equipment to the bcst & corporate video markets. Cameras, VTRs, digital edit systems, specialty gear.

Beyerdynamic, 56 Central Ave., Farmingdale, NY 11735. Phone: (631) 293-3200. Phone: (800) 293-4463. Fax: (631) 293-3288. E-mail: salesusa@beyerdynamic.com. Web Site: www.beyerdynamic.com. Nel Keinz, mgr; Bob Lowig, sls; Alan Feckanin, natl sls mgr.

Microphones, headsets, monitor headphones, studio & on-location UHF & VHF wireless systems.

Bird Electronic Corp., 30303 Aurora Rd., Solon, OH 44139-2794. Phone: (866) 695-4569. Fax: (866) 546-4306. E-mail: sales@bird-electronic.com. Web Site: www.bird-electronic.com. Buck DeFrance, pres.

RF directional wattmeters; power monitors; VSWR alarms; self, air & water-cooled loads; attenuators. Quality instruments for RF power measurement.

Birns and Sawyer Inc., 1026 N. Highland Ave., Hollywood, CA 90038. Phone: (323) 466-8211. Fax: (323) 466-7049. E-mail: info@birnsandsawyer.com. Web Site: www.birnsandsawyer.com. William Meurer, pres; Peter Anway, sls; John Jacks, mgr; Jim Martin, sls.

North Hollywood, CA 91601. Gunner Lighting Rentals, 5275 Craner Ave. Phone: (818) 766-2525. Robert Rivera, lighting rental mgr.

Professional motion picture equipment such as Arriflex, Aaton, Tiffen, Lowell, LTM, Ronford, O'Connor, Harrison & Harrison, tech books & transvideo monitors; Canon XL-1 with Matte Box. Panasonic 720P HD, Sony 24P HD.

BitCentral Inc., (formerly Miralite Communications Inc. 18872 Bardeen Ave., Irvine, CA 92612. Phone: (949) 253-9003. Fax: (949) 474-1885. E-mail: sales@bitcentral.com. Web Site: www.bitcentral.com. Fred Fourcher, CEO.

Digital broadcasting solutions providers.

Black Audio, Box 106, Ventura, CA 93002. Phone: (805) 653-5557. E-mail: sales@blackaudio.com. Web Site: www.blackaudio.com. Bruce Black, pres.

We provide parts, tools & accessories to all areas of pro audio.

Blimpy Floating Signs/Bend-A-Lite, 905 G St., Hampton, VA 23661. Phone: (757) 245-7675. Phone: (800) 448-2014. Fax: (757) 244-4819. E-mail: info@blimpy.com. Web Site: www.blimpy.com. Hugh Jones, pres; Ron Koppel, mktg dir.

Giant blimps, hot air balloons & rooftop balloons. Complete custom department for any shape or size, flexible neon in seven brilliant colors.

Blonder Tongue Laboratories Inc., Box 1000, One Jake Brown Rd., Old Bridge, NJ 08857-1000. Phone: (732) 679-4000. Fax: (732) 679-4353. Web Site: www.blondertongue.com.

Manufacturer of private cable equipment, including satellite receivers, modulators, processors, amplifiers, combiners, passives.

Bogen Communications Inc., Box 575, 50 Spring St., Ramsey, NJ 07446. Phone: (201) 934-8500. Fax: (201) 934-9832. E-mail: info@bogen.com. Web Site: www.bogen.com. Michael Fleischer, pres; David Chambers, sls VP; Maureen Flotard, CFO.

Audio amplifiers, mixer-preamplifiers, power amplifiers; FM/AM tuners & receivers; intercom systems; public address & sound reinforcement systems; digital repeater products; speakers.

Bogen Imaging Inc., 565 E. Crescent Ave., Ramsey, NJ 07446. Phone: (201) 818-9500. Fax: (201) 818-9177. E-mail: info@bogenimaging.com. Web Site: www.bogenimaging.us. Paul Wagner, sls dir; Mark Bender, sls dir.

Professional video products including tripods, fluid heads, dollies, stands & accessories. Grip equipment & lighting filters.

Boonton Electronics Corp., Box 465, 25 Eastmans Rd., Parsippany, NJ 07054-0465. Phone: (973) 386-9696. Fax: (973) 386-1053. E-mail: boonton@boonton.com. Edward Garcia, pres/CEO; John Kenneally, VP sls; Marc Wolfsohn, CFO; Brent Hessen-Schmidt, mktg dir; Richard Blackwell, engrg VP.

Electronic test & measuring equipment: microwave/RF power, RF voltmeters, capacitance/inductance & modulation meters.

Bradley Broadcast Sales, 7313 Grove Rd., Frederick, MD 21704. Phone: (800) 732-7665. Phone: (301) 682-8700. Fax: (301) 682-8377. E-mail: info@bradleybroadcast.com. Web Site: www.bradleybroadcast. Art Reed, gen mgr; Joellen Reed, mktg mgr.

Radio control room & transmission equipment, professional sound equipment, telephone interface devices.

Broadcast Data Consultants, 51 S. Main Ave., Suite 312, Clearwater, FL 33765. Phone: (727) 442-5566. Phone: (800) 275-6204. E-mail: bdc@broadcastdata.com. Web Site: www.broadcastdata.com. Neil Edwards, VP; Scott Wachtler, pres.

The Traffic C.O.P. for windows traffic billing progm. Free CD Rom demo available.

Broadcast Electronic Services, 4825 Trawler Ct., Jacksonville, FL 32225. Phone: (904) 646-1630. Fax: (904) 641-1443.

Betabox/GPI net 410, video-editing interface products for E.N.G. & postproduction; T.B.C. remote devices.

Broadcast Electronics Inc., 4100 N. 24th St., Quincy, IL 62305. Phone: (217) 224-9600. Fax: (217) 224-9607. E-mail: bdcast@bdcast.com. Web Site: www.bdcast.com. Neil Glassman, VP mktg; Ray Miklius, VP; Tim Bealor, VP.

Radio bcst equipment including digital studio systems, AM, FM transmitters, RPUs & STLs.

Broadcast Engineering, 9800 Metcalf Ave., Overland Park, KS 66212. Phone: (913) 341-1300. Fax: (913) 967-1905. Web Site: www.broadcastengineering.com. E-mail: dtriola@primediabusiness.com. Brad Dick, editor.

Banbury, Oxon OX16 8YJ. Intertec Publishing Corp., Box 250. Phone: +44-129-527-8407. Fax: +44-129-527-8408. Richard Woolley; Tony Chapman.

Shinjuku-ku, Tokyo 162-0822. Orient Echo Inc., 1101 Grand Maison, Shimomiyabi-cho 2-18. Phone: (03) 3235-5961. Fax: (03) 3235-5852. Mashy Yoshikawa.

San Clemente, CA 92672, 127 Avenida del Mar, Suite 2A. Phone: (949) 366-9089. Fax: (949) 366-9289. E-mail: ayercomm@earthlink.net. Rick Ayer.

Reno, NV 89511, 4750 townsite Rd. Phone: (775) 849-8404. Fax: (775) 849-8403. Chuck Bolkcom.

Brooklyn, NY 11231, 335 Court St., 9. Phone: (718) 802-0488. Fax: (718) 522-4751. Josh Gordon.

New York, NY 10011, 249 W. 17th St., 3rd Fl. Phone: (212) 462-3344. Fax: (212) 206-3618. E-mail: jmelton@primediabusiness.com. Joanne Melton.

Broadcast Engineering: Published for mgmt & engrg personnel working in bcst, production, postproduction, cable facilities in North America.

Broadcast Equipment Surplus Inc., Box 1300, Raymond, MS 39154. Phone: (601) 857-8573. Fax: (601) 857-2346. E-mail: jcorkren@ucmail.com. Jeffrey Corkren, VP.

Represents bcst equipment manufacturers; sls, svc, instal, turnkey designs, engrg; new & used equipment.

Broadcast International Group, 10458 N.W. 31st Terr., Miami, FL 33172. Phone: (305) 599-2112. Fax: (305) 599-1133. E-mail: anamaria@bigmiami.com. Web Site: www.bigmiami.com. Ana Maria Sagastegui, pres.

Bcst TV equipment.

Broadcast Microwave Services Inc., 12367 Crosthwaite Cir., Dock 10, Poway, CA 92064. Phone: (858) 391-3050. Phone: (800) 669-9667. Fax: (858) 391-3049. E-mail: dept111@bms-inc.com. Web Site: www.bms-inc.com. Graham Bunney, pres & gen mgr.

Atlanta, GA 30040, 7210 Hunters Path Ln. Phone: (770) 889-7470. Fax: (770) 889-2975. Russell Murphy, sls engr.

Los Angeles, CA 93065, 293 Sycamore Grove. Phone: (805) 581-4566. Fax: (805) 527-8263. Jim Kubit , sls engr.

COFDM wireless microwave, transmitters, receivers & antenna systems for ENG vehicles, helicopters, autotrackers, central receive sites.

Broadcast Sports Technologies, 1360 Blair Dr., Suite A, Odenton, MD 21113. Phone: (410) 672-3900. Fax: (410) 672-3906. Peter Larsson, gen mgr.

Supply microwave, camera & cable equipment for large sporting events. Supply remote control cameras & communication systems.

Broadcasting & Cable Yearbook 2006

F-6

Broadcast Store Inc., 1840 Flower, Glendale, CA 91201. Phone: (818) 551-5858. Fax: (818) 551-0686. E-mail: bcssales@broadcaststore.com. Web Site: www.broadcaststore.com. Lou Claude, pres.

Miami, FL 33179, 1031 Ives Dairy Rd. Phone: 305-266-2112. Fax: 305-266-2113.

New York, NY 10018, 500 W. 37th St. Phone: (212) 268-8800. Fax: (212) 268-1858.

Buy, sell, consign new & preowned Audio/Video bcst equiptment for production & post-production needs.

Broadcast Supply Worldwide, 7012 27th St. W., Tacoma, WA 98466. Phone: (800) 426-8434. Fax: (800) 231-7055. E-mail: sales@bswusa.com. Web Site: www.bswusa.com. Irv Law, chmn; Tim Schwieger, pres.

Audio bcst equipment distributor. Representing over 200 manufacturers worldwide.

Broadcast Video Systems Corp., 40 W. Wilmot St., Richmond Hill, ON L4B 1H8. Canada. Phone: (905) 764-1584. Fax: (905) 764-7438. E-mail: bvs@bvs.ca. Web Site: www.bvs.ca. Bert Verwey, pres.

SDI, analog video keyers, chroma keyers, closed captioning, encoders/decoders, positioner, bridge, V-chip encoders/decoders, data transmission, encoders & transcoders.

Broadcasters General Store Inc., 2480 S.E. 52nd St., Ocala, FL 34480. Phone: (352) 622-7700. Fax: (352) 629-7000. E-mail: info@bgs.cc. Web Site: www.bgs.cc.

Professional audio, video & RF equipment. Telco interfaces, digital codecs, 400 vendor line card.

Bryston Ltd., Box 2170, 677 Neal Dr., Peterborough, ON K9J 7Y4. Canada. Phone: (705) 742-5325. Fax: (705) 742-0882. Web Site: www.bryston.ca.

Audio amplifiers, pre-amplifiers, crossovers, & microphone pre-amps.

Bud Industries Inc., 4605 E. 355 St., Willoughby, OH 44094. Phone: (440) 946-3200. Fax: (440) 951-4015. E-mail: saleseast@budind.com. Web Site: www.budind.com. Blair K. Haas, VP mktg.

Phoenix, AZ 85080, Box 41190. Phone: (623) 516-9494.

Open & welded racks; cabinets & accessories.

Burk Technology, 7 Beaver Brook Rd., Littleton, MA 01460. Phone: (978) 486-0086. Fax: (978) 486-0081. E-mail: sales@burk.com. Web Site: www.burk.com. Peter C. Burk, pres; Anita Russell, gen mgr.

Transmitter remote control systems including multi-site, unattended units & automatic transmitter control system. LX-1 six input stereo selector.

Burle Industries Inc., 1000 New Holland Ave., Lancaster, PA 17601-5688. Phone: (717) 295-6000. Fax: (717) 295-6096. E-mail: burlesls@burle.com. Web Site: www.burle.com. E. Burlefinger, pres/CEO; Carl Rintz, exec VP; Kirk Jenne, gen counsel.

VHF/FM power tubes, photomultipliers & imaging devices.

Burlington A/V Recording Media Inc., 106 Mott St., Oceanside, NY 11572. Phone: (516) 678-4414. Phone: (800) 331-3191. Fax: (516) 678-8959. E-mail: sales@burlington-av.com. Web Site: www.burlington-av.com. Ruth Schwartz, VP; Jan Alan, pres.

Wholesale distributor for all formats of recording media, blank audio/video tape, CD-R, DVD-RR, diskettes, data media, A/V recording equipment.

Burst Electronics Inc., Box 1468, Corrales, NM 87048. Phone: (505) 898-1455. Fax: (505) 898-0159. E-mail: sales@burstelectronics.com. Web Site: www.burstelectronics.com. William J. Kent, pres.

CG, black burst generators, DA's, video switchers, time code, video mixers, decoders, color bar generators.

C

CADCO Systems Inc., 2363 Merritt Dr., Garland, TX 75041. Phone: (972) 271-3651. Phone: (800) 877-2288. Fax: (972) 271-3654. E-mail: carmen@cadcosystems.com. Web Site: www.cadcosystems.com. Steven G. Johnson, chmn/CEO; Carmen Howard, stn mgr.

Manufacturer of CATV & broadband communication products such as modulators, demodulators, signal processors, channel converters, translators & special application headend equipment, fixed-channel & frequency agile.

CATV Services Inc., 15771 N.W. 16th Ct., Miami, FL 33169. Phone: (305) 474-0409. Fax: (305) 474-0947. E-mail: sales@catvservices.com. Web Site: www.catvservices.com. Richard C. Richmond, pres.

Excess inventory professionals, buy & sell.

CBT Systems, 10115 Carroll Canyon Rd., San Diego, CA 92131. Phone: (858) 536-2927. Fax: (858) 536-2354. Darrell Wendhardt, pres.

TV bcst studio systems & mobile unit design, engrg & integration.

C-COR, 60 Decibel Rd., State College, PA 16801. Phone: (814) 238-2461. Fax: (814) 238-4065. Web Site: www.c-cor.net. David Woodle, chmn/CEO.

Pleasanton, CA 94588. Broadband Management Soultions, Software Divison Headquarters, 5673 Gibraltar Dr., Suite 100. Phone: (925) 251-3000. Fax: (925) 467-0600. Douglas W. Engerman.

Lakewood, CO 80228. Broadband Network Services, Services Division, 300 Union Blvd., Suite 515. Phone: (303) 980-8058. Paul E. Janson.

Meriden, CT 06450. Broadband Communication Products, Product Division Headquarters, 999 Research Pkwy. Phone: (203) 630-5700. Fax: (203) 630-5701. John O. Caezza.

Globally-tailored fiber optic, RF & digital video transport telecommunications products, OSS mgmt solutions & high-end tech field svcs for broadband networks.

CEA-Computer Engineering Associates, 8227 Cloverleaf Dr., Suite 308, Millersville, MD 21108. Phone: (410) 987-7003. Fax: (410) 987-6710. E-mail: ceanews@erols.com. Web Site: www.ceanews.com. Paul Keys, pres.

Bridgeport, NJ 08014, 600 Heron Dr. Phone: (800) 888-3922. Steve McKemy, VP.

Gibsonia, PA 15044, 5465 Rt. 8. Phone: (412) 443-2600. Bill Interthal, mgr.

CEA newsroom system—complete automation systems for radio & TV newsrooms.

CECO International Corp., 440 W. 15th St., New York, NY 10011. Phone: (212) 206-8280. Fax: (212) 727-2144. Web Site: www.cecostudios.com. Donald Kline, owner & pres.

Motion picture & TV equipment; sound stages; location trucks with generators.

CED, 3590 N.W. 34th St., Miami, FL 33142. Phone: (305) 635-5361. Fax: (305) 635-5366. David Levy, mgr.

MMDS, wireless cable, UHF, VHF quality transmission systems. Electrical Distributors.

C I S Inc., 3360 Martin Farm Rd., Suwanee, GA 30024. Phone: (678) 482-2000. Fax: (678) 482-2007. E-mail: sales@cisfocus.com. Web Site: www.cisfocus.com. Jeffery Eichler, pres; Lynn Hamlin, VP sls.

Integrated broadband & fiber design software products. Software solutions for network mapping, planning, design, & management of the outside plant.

CMP Enclosures Inc., 3901 Grove Ave., Gurnee, IL 60031. Phone: (847) 244-3230. Fax: (847) 244-3257. E-mail: cmpencl@aol.com. Web Site: www.enclosures.com. Mike Gober, pres; Terry Pullega, VP.

Manufacturers of electronic enclosures for rack mounting equipment.

COASTCOM, 1151 Harbor Bay Pkwy., Alameda, CA 94502. Phone: (510) 523-6000. Fax: (510) 523-6150. E-mail: info@coastcom.com. Web Site: www.coastcom.com. E. M. "Ted" Buttner, pres.

Alameda, CA 94502, 1151 Harbor Bay Pkwy. Phone: (510) 523-6000. Mark Packwood, rgnl sls mgr.

Charlotte, NC 28210, 5000 Sharonwoods Ln. Phone: (704) 643-7221. Duane Hardie, rgnl sls mgr.

Lewisville, TX 75067, 562 Continental Dr. Phone: (972) 316-3611. Mike Walsh, rgnl sls mgr.

Pearl River, WY 10965, 19 Harding St. Phone: (914) 980-3703. Tom McCafferty, rgnl sls mgr.

Manufacturer of T1 voice data network systems specializing in T3 cross connecting, T1 multiplexing & digital program channels for audio bcstg.

COMTEK Inc., 357 W. 2700 S., Salt Lake City, UT 84115. Phone: (801) 466-3463. Phone: (800) 496-3463. Fax: (801) 484-6906. E-mail: sales@comtek.com. Web Site: www.comtek.com. Ralph Belgique, chief engr; Laurel Robertson, sls dir; Jon Belgique, Communication Director.

COMTEK manufactures synthesized & fixed frequency wireless communication equipment & accessories, including cuing systems (IFB) & wireless microphones.

CONTEC Corp., 1023 State St., Schenectady, NY 12307-1511. Phone: (518) 382-8000. Fax: (518) 382-8452. Richard Kielb, sr VP; Steve Knuth, pres/CEO.

Phoenix, AZ 85040, 4114 E. Wood St, Suite 103. Phone: (602) 437-2890. Paul Hagert, mgr.

Tampa, FL 33610, 5906 Breckenridge Rd, Suite A. Phone: (813) 623-1721. Dick Lawton, mgr.

Bloomington, IN 47404, 2480 N. Curry Pike. Phone: (812) 330-8727. Jeff Van Horne, mgr.

Seattle, WA 98148, 1250 S. 192nd St. Phone: (206) 244-5770. Bob Vick, mgr.

Motorola , Pace, Phillips & Scientific Atlanta Authorized Warranty Digital Repair Svc Ct. Manufactor of universal remote controls for digital terminals.

CORPLEX Inc., 203 Northfield Rd., Northfield, IL 60093-3311. Phone: (847) 784-9700. Fax: (847) 784-9701. E-mail: carter730@aol.com. Web Site: www.corplextv.com. Carter Ruehrdaz, pres.

Video production equipment, postproduction equipment, rental & mobile TV.

CPC-Computer Prompting & Captioning Co., 1010 Rockville Pike, Suite 306, Rockville, MD 20852. Phone: (301) 738-8487. Phone: (800) 977-6678. Fax: (301) 738-8488. Web Site: www.cpcweb.com. Dr. Dilip Som, pres; Sidney Hoffman, VP.

Closed captioning, subtitling, DVD, V-Chip, teleprompting systems & svcs, Crossover Links for WebTV.

CS Communications Inc., 9825 Bridleridge Ct., Vienna, VA 22181. Phone: (703) 938-5365. Fax: (703) 938-5823. E-mail: chazsamp@aol.com. Charles E. Sampson, pres.

Engrg & consulting svcs for wireless and satellite systems. System design, feasibility & economic analysis.

CSG Systems, 7887 E. Belleview, Suite 1000, Englewood, CO 80111. Phone: (303) 796-2850. Fax: (303) 804-4088. Web Site: www.csgsystems.com. Jack Pogge, pres/COO; Neal Hansen, CEO; Peter Kalan, CFO; Randall Cardinal; Kurt Silverman, CTO; Willliam Fisher, pres GSS; Ed Nafus, pres BSD; Ed Mangold, sr VP global sls; Sally Else, sr VP product mgmt; Liz Bauer, sr VP investor rel & corp communications; Darren Walsh, sr VP global professional svcs; Alan Michels, VP/gen mgr., MA 038986 Singapore, 6 Temasek Blvd. Phone: 65 6883 1900. 65 6883 1990.

London WC2N6HT United Kingdom, 1-11 John Adams St. Phone: 44 20 7004 1840. 44 20 7004 1841.

Miami, FL 33126, 6303 Blue Lagoon Dr. Phone: (305) 421-8900. (305) 421-8934.

Complete sub info mgmt & data processing systems for the cable TV & telephone industries.

CSI-Camera Support International, Box 681, Woodland Hills, CA 91365. Phone: (818) 224-4850. Fax: (818) 887-5727. E-mail: markintash@aol.com. Web Site: www.csitripods.com.

Camera support dollies, tripods, pan/tilt heads & accessories ENG EFP & studio application for bcst & industrial application.

Cable Leakage Technologies, 903 N. Bowser, Suite 150, Richardson, TX 75081-2375. Phone: (972) 907-8100. Fax: (972) 907-2950. Web Site: www.wavetracker.com. Perry Havens, pres.

Digital RF tracking/mapping system used in CLI monitoring.

Cable Prep, (Ben Hughes Communication Products Co.). Box 373, 207 Middlesex Ave, Chester, CT 06412-0373. Phone: (860) 526-4337. Fax: (860) 526-2291. Web Site: www.cableprep.com. E-mail: toolmaker@cableprep.com. Deborah Morrow, pres; David Morrow, VP.

Cable Prep® TerminX, hex crimp, coring & stripping, drop wire stripping, jacket strippers, messenger removal & tools.

Cable Serv Inc., 4560 Eastgate Pkwy., Mississauga, ON L4W 3W6. Canada. Phone: (905) 629-1111. Fax: (905) 629-1115. Web Site: www.cableserv.com.

TV Exciters, 5-10-20 watt LPTV trans & transmitters, TV modulators, demodulators, processors, & satellite receivers.

Cable Services Company Inc., 2113 Marydale Ave., Williamsport, PA 17701. Phone: (570) 323-8518. Fax: (570) 322-5373. Web Site: www.cable-services.com.

Turnkey fiber-optic & coaxial construction; distributor of CATV products.

Cable Technologies International, 460 Oakdale Ave., Hatboro, PA 19040. Phone: (215) 672-5400. Fax: (215) 672-0440. E-mail: sales@cabletechnologies.com. Web Site: www.cabletechnologies.com. Peter Morse, CEO; Jamie Doughty, office mgr; Frank Pino, opns mgr.

Hand held remotes, converter parts, cosmetic & electronic; test equipment, headend & linegear.

Cable Yellow Pages, 20917 Higging Court, Torrance, CA 90501. Phone: (800) 777-4320. Fax: (310) 212-5392.

Phone directory for cable TV systems.

CablePro, (A division of ICM Corp.). 6260 Downing St., Denver, CO 80216. Phone: (303) 288-8107. Fax: (303) 288-4769. E-mail: sales@icmcorp.net. Web Site: www.icmcorp.net. Randy Holiday, pres; Gary Williams, sls VP.

CablePro's attention to design, material & workmanship produces the highest quality for instal tools.

CableReady Inc., (A division of ICM Corp). 6260 Downing St., Denver, CO 80216. Phone: (303) 288-8107. Fax: (303) 288-4769. E-mail: sales@icmcorp.net. Web Site: www.icmcorp.net. Randy Holliday, pres; Gary Williams, VP sls.

Painted galvolume molding with custom fittings backed by a 15-year warranty, U.L. listed and Class A fire rated.

CableTek Wiring Products Inc., 1150 Taylor St., Elyria, OH 44035. Phone: (440) 365-2487. Fax: (440) 322-0321. E-mail: treilly@apk.net. Web Site: www.cable-tek.com. Tim Reilly, gen mgr.

Interior & exterior surface wiring products; terminal enclosures, residential enclosures, security products.

Cablynx, Inc., (Formerly Nova Systems/Shintron). 24 Tower Office Pk., Woburn, MA 01801. Phone: (781) 933-2000. Fax: (781) 933-4641. E-mail: sales@nova-sys.com. Sam Asano, pres.

Routing switchers, distribution amplifiers, time code, component video, PC accessories, compugraphics to video, frame synchronizer.

Cadix International Inc., 2-11-5 Sakura Shinmachi Setagaya-K4, Suite 210, Tokyo, CA 154-0015. Japan. Phone: 81 3 3427 8901. Fax: 81 3 3427 0201. E-mail: webmaster@cadix.com. Web Site: www.cadix.com.

Manufacturer of fiber & cable design software to speed the dev & mgmt of the cable plant operation.

Calculated Industries Inc., 4840 Hytech Dr., Carson City, NV 89706. Phone: (775) 885-4900. Fax: (775) 885-4949. E-mail: info@calculated.com. Web Site: www.calculated.com. Mark Paulsen,.

Time code calculators work in & convert between all time formats; drop/non-drop, multiple EPS rates for all SMPTE/PAL equations.

California Amplifier, 1401 N. Rice Ave., Oxnard, CA 93030. Phone: (805) 987-9000. Fax: (805) 987-8359. Web Site: www.calamp.com. E-mail: sales@calcamp.som. Tom Prochnow, sls VP; Rick Wheeler, VP; Philip Cox, VP.

Manufacturer of mesh & offset satellite antennas ranging in size from 18" to 16'.

Calumet Photographic, 900 W. Bliss St., Chicago, IL 60622. Phone: (630) 860-7458. Phone: (800) CAL-UMET (225-8638). Fax: (312) 944-4035. Web Site: www.calumetphoto.com. Peter Biasotti, pres.

Calzone Case Co., 225 Black Rock Ave., Bridgeport, CT 06605. Phone: (203) 367-5766. Fax: (203) 336-4406. E-mail: vin.calzone@calzonecase.com. Web Site: www.calzonecase.com. Joseph E. Calzone, pres; Vincent J. Calzone, sls VP.

City of Industry, CA 91745, 15730 Salt Lake Ave. Phone: (626) 968-4100. Fax: (626) 968-1703. Mike Herman, VP admin/sls.

Carrollton, TX 75007, 75006 Luna Rd, Suite 126. Phone: (972) 241-3900. Fax: (972) 241-3998. Tom Mackno, VP.

Manufacturers of custom & standard shipping cases for all industries featuring Escort, LD-ATA, Military, X series, Titan

Camera Service Center, (A division of Arri, Inc.). 619 W. 54th St., New York, NY 10019. Phone: (212) 757-0906. Fax: (212) 713-0075. Web Site: www.cameraservice.com. Hardwrick Johnson, VP opns; Simon Broad, mktg VP.

Fort Lauderdale, FL 33312, 2385 Stirling Rd. Phone: (954) 322-4545. Fax: (954) 322-4188. Ed Stamm.

The largest full-svc film equipment rental company, carrying a complete line of camera & lighting products.

CamMate Studios/Systems, 425 E. Comstock, Chandler, AZ 85225. Phone: (480) 813-9500. Fax: (480) 813-9292. E-mail: cammate@cammate.com. Web Site: www.cammate.com. Ron Mitchell, CEO.

Exclusive sls & rental of the CamMate, a single operator remote camera crane in various configurations for video & film.

Camplex Corporation, 3302 W. 6th Ave., Emporia, KS 66801. Phone: (620) 342-7743. Fax: (620) 342-7405. E-mail: jtwebb@camplex.com. Web Site: www.camplex.com. J. Thomas Webb, CEO; C. Duane Woodmas, pres.

CAMPLEX is a universally adaptable video/audio signals multiplexing system for ENG/EFP/SNG Prosamer cameras, camcorders used in remote applications.

Canare Corp., 531 5th St., Unit A, San Fernando, CA 91340. Phone: (818) 365-2446. Fax: (818) 365-0479. E-mail: berry5@optonline.net. Web Site: www.canare.com. Josh Mayberry, pres; Carol G. Mayberry, VP.

"Star Quad" mic cable, quad-speaker cable, modular snake systems, cable reels, component video cable, video coaxial cable, 75 OHM BNC connectors, digital video patch bays, crimp tools & dies.

Canon U.S.A. Inc., (Broadcast Equipment Division Headquarters). 400 Sylvan Ave., Englewood Cliffs, NJ 07632. Phone: (201) 816-2900. Fax: (201) 816-2909. E-mail: bctv@cusa.canon.com. Web Site: www.canonbroadcast.com. Tom Yamasaki,.

Mississauga, ON L5T 1P7 Canada. Canon Canada Inc., 6390 Dixie Rd. Phone: (905) 795-2012. Fax: (905) 795-2140.

Irvine, CA 92618, 15955 Alton Pkwy. Phone: (949) 753-4330. Fax: (949) 753-4337.

Norcross, GA 30093, 5625 Oakbrook Pkwy. Phone: (770) 849-7895. Fax: (770) 849-7888.

Itasca, IL 60143, 100 Park Blvd. Phone: (630) 250-6231. Fax: (630) 250-0399.

Irvine, TX 75063, 3200 Regent Blvd. Phone: (972) 409-8871. Fax: (972) 409-8869.

Studio, field & ENG lenses & svc, (HDTV/SDTV) video, audio, data optical beam transmission, remote control P/T/Z camera system.

Capstone Communications Inc., 8 Shadow Rd., Upper Saddle River, NJ 07458. Phone: (201) 934-5990. Fax: (201) 934-0192. E-mail: berry@nis.net. Web Site: www.cadacny.com.

Brokerage, rsch consultation & bcst equipment brokerge.

Carpel Video Inc., 429 E. Patrick St., Frederick, MD 21701. Phone: (800) 238-4300. Phone: (301) 694-3500. Fax: (301) 694-9510. Web Site: www.carpelvideo.com. Andy Carpel, pres.

Videotape wholesalers. Mail order post production in MD; store: DVD production and duplication. Lowest prices on 6 blank video tapes. 800-238-4300.

Celco, 8660 Red Oak Ave., Rancho Cucamonga, CA 91730. Phone: (909) 481-4648. Fax: (909) 481-6899. E-mail: info@celco.com. Web Site: www.celco.com.

Design & manufacture of motion picture film recorders.

Center City Film & Video, 1503-05 Walnut St., Philadelphia, PA 19102. Phone: (215) 568-4134. Fax: (215) 568-6011. Web Site: www.ccfv.com. Jordan Schwartz, chmn; Brian Tsely, VP/gen mgr.

Studio/remote/postproduction D-2, D-3, 1" - Beta - 3/4" - ADO - Paint Box/Abekas 62/GV300 with E-Mem; film/tape DaVinci color correction, ADO repositioning & interactive motion control; D-s, D-3; AVID, Digital Betacam.

Central Tower, (A Dielectric Company). 2855 Hwy. 261, Newburgh, IN 47630-8642. Phone: (812) 853-0595. Fax: (812) 853-6652. E-mail: central@centraltower.com. Web Site: www.centraltower.com. Ray Ryan, pres; Tim Ryan, VP sls/mktg.

Manufacture towers for bcst, cellular & two-way, design & engrg of support structures, structural analysis, turnkey systems, antenna rebuilding & tower inspections.

Century Precision Optics, 7701 Haskell Ave., Van Nuys, CA 91406. Phone: (818) 766-3715. Fax: (818) 505-9865. E-mail: info@centuryoptics.com. Web Site: www.centuryoptics.com. Bill Turner, VP.

Wide angle & telephoto lens for video & motion picture cameras; lens accessories; lens service; schneider filters.

Channel Master L.L.C., 1315 Industrial Park Dr., Smithfield, NC 27577. Phone: (919) 934-9711. Fax: (919) 989-2200. Web Site: www.channelmaster.com. Bill Currer, pres; George Jusaites, dir.

Manufacturer of Satellite Broadband, DBS & Off-Air Antenna sysstems, Electronics & Accessories, and Point-to-Point Microwave equipment.

Channel One Lighting Systems Inc., 1522 E. 6th St., Tulsa, OK 74120-4026. Phone: (918) 587-2663. W. Blair Powell, pres.

Complete line of lighting equipment for TV, theatre & industrial applications; specializes in the design & manufacture of electrical distribution, grid & cyclorama systems, curtain & track.

Channell Commercial Corp., Box 9022, 26040 Ynez Rd., Temecula, CA 92589-9022. Phone: (909) 719-2600. Fax: (909) 296-2322. E-mail: info@channellcorp.com. Web Site: www.channellcomm.com. William H. Channell Jr., pres; Andrew M. Zogby, VP global mktg; John Kaiser, VP N America sls.

Global designer & manufacturer of equipment, offers a complete line of enclosures for CATV & telecommunication

Charles Industries Ltd., 5600 Apollo Dr., Rolling Meadows, IL 60008. Phone: (847) 806-6300. Fax: (847) 806-6231. Web Site: www.charlesindustries.com. Joseph T. Charles, pres.

Pedestals, custom security boxes, amplifier & TAP brackets-hardware, splicing vaults, taps, splitters & couplers.

Cheetah International, 8120 Sheridan Blvd., Suite C-206, Westminister, CO 80003. Phone: (520) 751-8681. Fax: (520) 722-1699. E-mail: sales@caption.com. Web Site: www.caption.com. Donald Miller, pres.

Closed captioning software on-line & postproduction & related hardware.

Chicago Condenser Corp., (A division of Capacitor Industries). 6455 N. Avondale Ave., Chicago, IL 60631. Phone: (773) 774-6666. Fax: (773) 774-6690. E-mail: info@capacitorindustries.com. Web Site: www.capacitorindustries.com. Terry Noone, pres.

High Voltage Filter Capacitors for radio & TV bcst transmission.

Chrono-Log Corp., 2 W. Park Rd., Havertown, PA 19083. Phone: (610) 853-1130. Fax: (610) 853-3972. E-mail: chronlog@chronolog.com. Web Site: www.chronolog.com. Paula Freilich, pres.

GPS Receiver (time only), WWV synchronizer, digital clocks & time display systems, time code generators.

Chyron Corp., 5 Hub Dr., Melville, NY 11747. Phone: (631) 845-2000. Fax: (631) 845-3895. Web Site: www.chyron.com. Alec Shapiro, Vp sls & mktg; Ed Grebow, pres/CEO; Steve Sloane, VP international sls; Patricia Lampe, VP/treas; David Buckler, client dev.

Cupertino, CA 95014. Chryon Corp. West, 10121 Miller Ave, Suite 201. Phone: (408) 873-3800. Fax: (408) 986-0452. Denise Gallant, product mgr.

Atlanta, GA 30303, One CNN Ctr., South Towers, Suite 558. Phone: (404) 880-9004. Fax: (404) 880-9104. Ryad Kahale, Chyron rgnl sls.

A leading providor of broadcast hardware, software & services spanning television & the Internet. Provides a broad range of leading edge hardware & software products, including paint & animation systems, character generators, master control switches, & bcst, automation & media mgmt packages.

Cine 60 Inc., 630 9th Ave., New York, NY 10036. Phone: (212) 586-8782. Fax: (212) 459-9556. E-mail: cine60@aol.com. Paul Wildum, pres.

Nickel-Cadmium battery belts, battery packs, chargers, sun-guns & kits.

Cintel Inc., 25020 Ave. Stanford, Suite 190, Valencia, CA 91355. Phone: (661) 294-2310. Fax: (661) 294-1019. E-mail: sales@cintelinc.com. Web Site: www.cintelinc.com. Adam Welsh, mgng dir; Curtis Christianson, opns mgr; David Saville, sls dir.

Chestnut Ridge, NY 10977, 80 Red Schoolhouse Rd, Suite 103. Phone: (914) 371-7220. Fax: (914) 371-6896. David Saville, sls dir.

Flying spot telecines, DVE system, keycode system, high-resolution scanner, color correctors.

Circuit Research Labs Inc. (CRL Systems, Inc.), 1302 W. Drivers WAy, Tempe, AZ 85284-1025. Phone: (480) 403-8300. Fax: (480) 403-8301. E-mail: crl@crlsystems.com. Web Site: www.crlsystems.com. Robert McMartin, CEO; Jay Brentlinger, pres; Robert Orban, VP; Greg Ogonowski, VP new prod dev; Gary Clarkson, VP/sec; Phillip Zeni, COO/VP.

Multiband audio AGCs, compressors & limiters for AM/FM; MTS processors, stereo generators, shortwave, AES/EBU digital audio tester.

Clark Wire & Cable Co. Inc., 1355 Armour Blvd., Mundelein, IL 60060-4401. Phone: (847) 949-9944. Fax: (847) 949-9595. E-mail: sales@clarkwire.com. Web Site: www.clarkwire.com. Susan Clark, pres & owner.

Audio, video, camera & speciality cable products for bcst industry, available in bulk or assembled harnesses, connectors, panels, reels, & boxes.

Clear-Com Communication Systems, 4065 Hollis St., Emeryville, CA 94608-3505. Phone: (510) 496-6666. Fax: (510) 496-6699. E-mail: sales@clearcom.com. Web Site: www.clearcom.com. Michael Wang, gen mgr; Ed Fitzgerald, natl sls mgr. Eastleigh, England, Eastleigh, England. Phone: 44-23-8090-7000. Patrick Woolcocks, EMEA Direct Sales.

Walnut Creek, CA 94596, Box 302. Phone: (925) 932-8134. Peter Giddings, Asia/Pacific dir of sls. (Export division office).

Single & multi-ch hardwire intercom systems for use in teleproduction. Wired & wireless partyline & digital matrix intercom systems.

Clearone Communications Corp., 1825 Research Way, Salt Lake City, UT 84119. Phone: (801) 975-7200. Phone: (800) 945-7730. Fax: (801) 977-0087. Web Site: www.clearone.com. Fran Flood, CEO; Randy Wichinski, CFO.

Professional audio & teleconferencing.

Equipment Manufacturers and Distributors Alphabetical Index

CoarcVideo, Box 2, Rt. 217, Mellenville, NY 12544. Phone: (800) 888-4451. Phone: (518) 672-4451. Fax: (518) 672-4048. E-mail: coarc@aol.com. Bob Spiewak, dir mktg; Alva Stalker, production mgr.

Used by bcstrs, cable systems, duplicating houses, production companies for environmentally-designed videotape reloaded products & standard video tape products; provides Umatic & Betacam VHS tape, program fulfillment svcs. CoarcVideo is part of the Coarc organization, which trains employees & provides various programs for the disabled.

Coaxial Dynamics 6800 Lake Abram Dr., Middleburg Hts., OH 44130. Phone: (440) 243-1100. Fax: (440) 243-1101. E-mail: coaxial@apk.net. Web Site: www.coaxial.com. Joe Kluha, gen mgr.

RF wattmeters, terminations, RF load resistors, RF couplers & accessories.

Cohu Inc., (Electronics Division). Box 85623, San Diego, CA 92186-5623. Phone: (858) 277-6700. Fax: (858) 277-0221. E-mail: info@cohu.com. Web Site: www.cohu.com/cctv. Joe Olmstead Jr., natl sls mgr; Jeff Tyler, mktg mgr.

CCTV cameras & camera control systems, color, CCD, B/W.

Cole Stages, 6670 Lexington Ave., Hollywood, CA 90038. Phone: (323) 467-7870. Fax: (323) 467-7832. Web Site: www.jcband.com/jcsoundstages.html. J.C. Belanger, owner; Anthony Belanger, owner.

Cable-controlled camera booms equipped for film or video, rehearsal pre-production recording all in classiest vibe avail anywhere

Colorado Video Inc., Box 928, Boulder, CO 80306. Phone: (303) 530-9580. Fax: (303) 530-9569. E-mail: kirk@colorado-video.com. Web Site: www.colorado-video.com. Kirk Fowler, pres.

Image transmission for UBI system; time-division video multiplexing/demultiplexing system.

Columbine JDS Systems Inc (CJDS),
See Encoda Systems Inc.

Comex Worldwide Corp., Box 8, Aldie, VA 20105-0008. Phone: (703) 327-1520. Fax: (703) 327-1540. E-mail: cwcmmds@hotmail.com. Web Site: www.comexworldwide.com. Jack A. Rickel, pres/CEO; Susan Rose, gen mgr.

CWC develops bcst & pay TV systems, VHF/UHF bcsts, satellite communications, MMDS & cable systems & turnkey communication systems.

Comm Scope Inc., 1100 Comm Scope Pl. S.E., Hickory, NC 28602. Phone: (800) 982-1708. Phone: (828) 324-2200. Fax: (828) 328-3400. Web Site: www.commscope.com. Frank Drendel, CEO.

Coaxial & fiber-optic cables including CRD & NEC approved drop cables, QR, P3 & CableGuard.

Commercial Electronics Ltd., 1335 Burrard St., Vancouver, BC V6Z 1Z7. Canada. Phone: (604) 669-5525. Fax: (604) 669-6347. E-mail: pro@cemail.ca. Web Site: www.commercialelectronics.ca. H.H. von Tiesenhausen, pres.

Nanaimo, BC V9X-1A5 Canada, 1678 Extension Rd, Unit 2. Phone: (250) 754-7612. Mark Arleft, video sls.

Audio video equipment, systems designs

Commercial Radio Monitoring Co., 103 S.W. Market St., Lee's Summit, MO 64063. Phone: (816) 524-3777. Fax: (816) 524-3777. Web Site: www.commercialradio.us. W. R. Thorsen, pres; Ronald Thorsen, VP.

Frequency measurements & equipment calibration.

Communication & Power Industries, 811 Hansen Way, Palo Alto, CA 94304. Phone: (650) 846-2800. Fax: (650) 846-3706. Web Site: www.cpii.com. Joseph Caldarelli, CEO.

Georgetown, ON L7G-2J4 Canada, 45 River Dr. Phone: (905) 877-0161. Joseph Caldarelli, pres communications & medical products.

Palo Alto, CA 94304, 607 Hansen Way. Phone: (415) 846-2900. Al Ferriera, pres traveling wave tube products.

Palo Alto, CA 94304, 811 Hansen Way. Phone: (415) 846-2800. (415) 846-3700. Armand Staprans, pres microwave products; Jim Commendatore, pres Satcom.

San Carlos, CA 94070, 301 Industrial Way. Phone: (415) 592-1221. H. Frederick Koehler, pres Eimac Div.

Beverly, MA 01915. Beverly Microwave Division, 150 Sohier Rd. Phone: (978) 922-6000. Dennis Gleason, division pres.

Manufactures a complete line of power grid tubes, klystrons & klystrode IOTs, traveling wave tubes, satellite communication transmitters, microwave components.

Communication & Power Industries, EIMAC Division, 301 Industrial Rd., San Carlos, CA 94070. Phone: (650) 592-1221. Phone: (800) 414-8823. Fax: (650) 592-9988. E-mail: powergrid@eimac.cpii.com. Web Site: www.eimac.com. Michael Chen, pres; John Allan, VP mktg.

Power grid tubes, cavity amplifiers, IOT (UHF TV).

Communication Graphics, Inc., 1765 N. Juniper, Broken Arrow, OK 74012. Phone: (800) 331-4438. Phone: (918) 258-6502 (Okla). Fax: (918) 251-8223. Web Site: www.cglink.com. Dave Cleveland, pres.

Choose the company MORE radio stations have selected for printing decals, event stickers, statics, concert patches, magnets, media kits and more!

Communications General Corp., 2685 Alta Vista Dr., Fallbrook, CA 92028-9739. Phone: (760) 723-2700. Robert Gonsett, pres.

Monthly AM, FM & TV frequency measurements in the Southern California area, and spectral measurements.

Communications Specialties Inc., 55 Cabot Ct., Hauppauge, NY 11788. Phone: (631) 273-0404. Fax: (631) 273-1638. E-mail: info@commspecial.com. Web Site: www.commspecial.com. Paul Seiden, sls dir.

Shaw Tower 189702 Singapore, 100 Bencoolen Rd., # 22-09. Phone: (+665) 656 391-8790. Fax: (+656) 656 396-0138. Jeohan Tohkingkeo, rgnl mgr Asia Pacific.

Manufacturer of fiber-optic transmission sytems, including the Pure Digital Fiberlink line for professional quality video, audio and data.

Communications Structures & Services, 645 C. E. Renfro St., Burleson, TX 76028. Phone: (817) 295-8183. Fax: (817) 295-8075. Keith Cendrick, pres.

Tower mf, Erection, maintenance, true turn-key installation, foundations, emergency svcs, antenna & transmission line replacement, site acqustion.

Comprehensive Video Group, 55 Ruta Ct., South Hackensack, NJ 07606. Phone: (201) 229-0025. Phone: (800) 526-0242. Fax: (201) 814-0510. Web Site: www.compvideo.com. Scott Schaefer, VP.

Digital HDTV UpConverter, High Resolution bulk cable, Video/Audio Multi media & Data Cable assemblies (lifetime warranty), connectors, adaptors, wallplates, distribution amps, switches, convertors, etc.

Comprompter Inc., 1707 Main St., Suite 113, La Crosse, WI 54601. Phone: (800) 785-7766. Fax: (608) 784-5013. E-mail: enrnews@enrnews.com. Web Site: www.enrnews.com. Ralph King, pres.

Offers PC-compatible prompting & networked computerized newsroom & newsroom automation systems for radio, TV, corporate & industrial use.

Computer Concepts Corp., 13375 Stemmons Fwy., Suite 400, Dallas, TX 75234. Phone: (800) 255-6350. Phone: (913) 541-0900. Fax: (913) 541-0169. Web Site: www.ccc-dcs.com. Greg L. Dean, chmn.

Total digital integration improves sound, progmg production & scheduling. Business software includes traf & billing for radio.

Computer Resolutions, 35 Benham Ave., Bridgeport, CT 06605. Phone: (203) 384-0742. Fax: (203) 384-0473. Web Site: www.cri1.com. Carl Palmieri, CEO.

PC- & mainframe-based traf systems; both offer multistation capability.

Comrex Corp., 19 Pine Rd., Devens, MA 01434. Phone: (978) 784-1776. Fax: (978) 784-1717. E-mail: info@comrex.com. Web Site: www.comrex.com. Lynn Cheney, pres.

Plain telephone line (POTS), ISDN & wireless audio codecs for high quality remote bcsts.

Comsearch, 19700 Janelia Farm Blvd., Ashburn, VA 20147. Phone: (703) 726-5500. Fax: (703) 726-5600. E-mail: info@comsearch.com. Web Site: www.comsearch.com.

Communication engrg svcs for mobile, microwave & satellite systems, including frequency, propagation & integrations svcs.

ComSonics Inc., 1350 Port Republic Rd., Harrisonburg, VA 22801. Phone: (540) 434-5965. Fax: (540) 432-9794. Web Site: www.comsonics.com. Dennis A. Zimmerman, pres/CEO; Dale Lann, CFO; Donn E. Meyerhoeffer, COO; Donald J. Sommerville, dir sls/mktg.

Manufacture RF signal level meter & RF leakage detector, CATV repair facility.

Comtech Antenna Systems Inc., 3100 Communications Rd., St. Cloud, FL 34769. Phone: (407) 892-6111. Fax: (407) 892-0994. E-mail: info@comtechantenna.com. Web Site: www.comtechantenna.com. Thomas Christy, pres; William Parker, dir mktg.

Satellite antenna systems, sizes 1.8-7.3 meters; Offsat(tm), 2 degree spacing antenna; 3.8, 5.0m & Offsat(tm) transportables.

Concerto Software, 5051 Peachtree Corners Cir., Norcross, GA 30092. Phone: (770) 446-7800. Fax: (770) 239-4725. Web Site: www.concerto.com. Andrew Philipowski, pres.

Newport Beach, CA 92660, 1300 Bristol St. N, Suite 100. Phone: (714) 261-9330. Roy Rich, sls rep.

Great Neck, NY 11021, 1010 Northern Blvd, Suite 208. Phone: (516) 829-0390. Rich Bogner, sls rep.

Dallas, TX 75244, 5001 LBJ Fwy, Suite 727. Phone: (214) 387-5210. Nick Pollard, western rgnl sls mgr.

Dallas, TX 75238, 3778 Realty Rd. Phone: (609) 235-1771. Randy Pugh, natl acct exec.

Automated telephone call processing products for inbound & outbound call ctrs.

Condor D C Power Supplies Inc., (A subsidiary of SL Industries). 2311 Statham Pkwy., Oxnard, CA 93033. Phone: (805) 486-4565. Phone: (800) 235-5929. Fax: (805) 487-8911. Web Site: www.condorpower.com. Owen Farren, owner; Sal Ronchetti, pres.

Multiple outlet strips, surge & noise suppressors, & uninterruptible power supplies.

Condux International, Box 247, 154 Kingswood Rd., Mankato, MN 56001. Phone: (800) 533-2077. Phone: (507) 387-6576. Fax: (507) 387-1442. E-mail: cndxinfo@condux.com. Web Site: www.condux.com. Brad Radichel, pres.

Underground & aerial construction tools & equipment for coaxial cable, telephone & fiber.

Connectronics Corp., Box 3355, 2745 Avondale Ave., Toledo, OH 43607. Phone: (419) 537-0020. Fax: (419) 537-0007. Tom Ricketts, pres; Al Mocek, VP.

Morgan Hill, CA 95037. California, Box 2047′. Phone: (408) 779-8888. Fax: (408) 778-0722.

Audio wire & cable, special wire & cable assys. Interconnect products for audio, video, data & telephone.

Conrac Systems Inc., 5124 Commerce Dr., Baldwin Park, CA 91706. Phone: (626) 480-0095. Fax: (626) 480-0077. Web Site: www.conrac.com. Bill Moeller, pres.

Manufacturer of a var of color & monochrome video monitors for bcst & computer graphic display.

Control Concepts Corp., (A subsidiary of Liebert Corp). Box 1380, 328 Water St., Binghamton, NY 13902-1380. Phone: (607) 724-2484. Phone: (800) 288-6169. Fax: (607) 722-8713. E-mail: info@control-concepts.com. Web Site: www.control-concepts.com. Robert Daniel, pres; Sarah Beadle, dir mktg.

Power protection products for transmitters, studios & CATVs from transients & lightning induced voltages.

Convergent Media Systems Corp., 3490 Piedmont Rd., Suite 800, Atlanta, GA 30305. Phone: (404) 262-1555. Fax: (404) 262-2055. Web Site: www.convergent.com. Murray Holland, owner; Bryan Allen, pres.

Transportable satellite uplinking & downlinking svcs. Includes facilities & transponder time for Ku- & C-band applications.

Convergys Inc., 1551 Sawgrass Corporate Pkwy., Suite 300, Sunrise, FL 33323. Phone: (954) 851-9200. Fax: (954) 851-9224. Web Site: www.convergys.com. Mike Bauza, VP; Kurt Champion, product mgmt.

Atlanta, GA 30319, 4170 Ashford Dunwoody Rd, Suite 525. Phone: (404) 845-4400.

"Cablemaster/Icoms" customer mgmt & billing system running on IBM as/400 platform; solution for the convergent cable TV/Telephone industry.

Cooper Sound Systems Inc., 645 Main St., Suite C, Morro Bay, CA 93442-2273. Phone: (805) 772-1007. Fax: (805) 772-1098. Web Site: www.coopersound.com. E-mail: coopersound@charterinternet.com. Andrew Cooper, pres; Janet Cooper, VP.

Film & video location mixers & accessories, microphone preamplifiers & time code resolvers.

Copperweld Fayetteville Division, 254 Cotton Mill Rd., Fayetteville, TN 37334. Phone: (931) 433-7177. Fax: (931) 433-0419. John D. Turner, pres/CEO; Steve Levy, VP mktg & sls.

Copper-clad aluminium wire, copper-clad steel wire, & aluminum-clad steel wire.

Coptervision, 7625 Hayvenhurst Ave., Suite 41, Van Nuys, CA 91406. Phone: (818) 781-3003. Fax: (818) 782-4070. E-mail: coptervision@pacificnet.net. Web Site: www.coptervision.com. Sarita Spiwak, pres/CEO; Daniel Meltzer, VP/COO.

Coptervision state-of-art remote control helicopters with cameras in all formats. Rollvision 3-axes, wireless, lightweight camera system for various platforms

Corning Cable Systems, 800 17th St. N.W., Hickory, NC 28601. Phone: (828) 327-5000. Fax: (828) 325-5060. Web Site: www.corning.com/cablesystems. Larry Aiello, pres; John D Rockett, sr VP/gen sls mgr.

Manufacturer of optical fiber cables & accessories for video, data, voice communications applications.

Corning Gilbert Inc., 5310 W. Camelback, Glendale, AZ 85301. Phone: (623) 845-5613. Fax: (623) 845-5160. Kathy Murphy, CEO.

Trunk, distribution & "F" connectors for CATV.

Corning Inc., (Telecommunications Products Division). One Riverfront Plaza, Corning, NY 14831. Phone: (800) 525-2524/539-3632 (US & Canada). Phone: (607) 986-8125/3344 (International). E-mail: cofic@corning.com. Web Site: www.corning.com/opticalfiber. Eric Musser, gen mgr; Eric musser, VP.

Single-mode & multimode optical fibers including: InfiniCor laser-optimized multimode fibers, NexCor fiber, SMF-28e fiber, MetroCor fiber, LEAF fiber, & Vascade submarine fibers.

Cortana Corp., Box 2548, Farmington, NM 87499-2548. Phone: (888) 325-5336. Fax: (505) 326-2337. E-mail: cortana@cyberport.com. Evelyn Nott, pres; Henry Bond, VP.

Stati-Cat Lightning Prevention System.

Cortland Cable Co. Inc., Box 330, 44 River St., Cortland, NY 13045-0330. Phone: (607) 753-8276. Fax: (607) 753-3183. E-mail: cortlandcable@cortlandcable.com. Web Site: www.cortlandcable.com. John Stidd, pres; Rick Nye, VP.

Kevlar fiber antenna guys & ropes, including eye splice end terminations-potted sockets.

Costume Armour Inc./Christo Vac, Box 85, 2 Mill St., Cornwall, NY 12518. Phone: (845) 534-9120. Fax: (845) 534-8602. Web Site: www.costumearmour.com. Nino Novellino, pres.

Period armor & weapons, vacuum-formed background panels, custom made props & sculpture.

Countryman Associates Inc., 417 Stanford Ave., Redwood City, CA 94063. Phone: (800) 669-1422. Phone: (650) 364-9988. Fax: (650) 364-2794. E-mail: sales@countryman.com. Carl Countryman, res/chief engr.

Very small precision electret condenser microphones for wide applications & the Type-85 Direct Box.

Crouse-Kimzey Co., 1320 Post & Paddock Rd., Suite 200, Grand Prairie, TX 75050. Phone: (972) 343-9231. Fax: (972) 623-2800. E-mail: sales@proaudio.com. Web Site: www.proaudio.com. John Paul Kimzey, pres.

Colorado Springs, CO 80911. Crouse-Kimzey of Colorado, 4125 Novia Dr. Phone: (800) 257-6233. Fax: (719) 392-8876. Lee Edwards, gen mgr.

Lynn, IN 47355. Crouse Kimzey/Mid-America, 9170 South U.S. Hwy. 27. Phone: (877) 223-2221. Fax: (765) 874-2540. Barry Pike, gen mgr.

Bcst equipment sls.

Crown Broadcast IREC, (division of Crown International Inc). Box 2000, 25166 Leer Dr., Elkhart, IN 46515-2000. Phone: (574) 262-8900. Fax: (574) 262-5399. E-mail: fmsaes@irecl.com. Web Site: www.crownbroadcast.com. Clyde Moore, pres/CEO; Beryl Loomis, exec VP; Gary Beckett, sls dir.

Bcst RF equipment, FM radio transmitters. Supplier to the National weather service for emergency weather radio transmitters.

Cygnal Technology, (formerly Normex Telecom Incorp.). 70 Valleywood Dr., Markham, ON L3R 4T5. Canada. Phone: (905) 944-6500. Fax: (905) 944-6520. E-mail: normex@normex.com. Web Site: www.cygnal.ca.

Mgmt, instal & maintenance svcs for studios, radio-TV transmitters, satellite systems & CATV.

D

DBS Direct, 2815 E. Lake Ave., E., Suite 325, Seattle, WA 98102. Phone: (206) 709-0100. Fax: (206) 709-1588.

Amplifiers, headend equipment, cable, drop material, connectors, passives, tools, traps, enclosures, test equipment, power supplies, etc.

DBX Professional Products, 8760 S. Sandy Pkwy., Sandy, UT 84070. Phone: (801) 568-7660. Fax: (801) 568-7662. E-mail: customer@dbxpro.com. Web Site: www.dbxpro.com. Robert Benson, sls VP.

Audio signal processing devices: compressor/limiters, De-essers, equalizers, gates & noise reduction.

DEDOTEC USA Inc., 216 Little Falls Rd., Cedar Grove, NJ 07009. Phone: (973) 857-8118. Fax: (973) 857-3756. Web Site: www.dedolight.com. E-mail: info@dedeolight.com.

Dedolight low voltage, high intensity lighting fixtures for film, video, ENG & EFP applications. Battery or AC operation.

D.H. Satellite, Box 239, 600 N. Marquette Rd., Prairie du Chien, WI 53821. Phone: (608) 326-6041. Fax: (608) 326-4233. E-mail: mdoll@mhtc.net. Web Site: www.dhsatellite.com. Mike Doll, VP; Cindy Willie, sls.

Manufacturer of solid spun aluminum antennas & mounts. Antennas range from .6m (24") to 5m (16') with various mounting options. Delivery & instal is available from DH for all of our antenna equipment.

DPA Microphones, Inc., 691 Gray Mountain Dr., Lyons, CO 80540. Phone: (303) 823-8878. Fax: (303) 823-5830. E-mail: info-usa@dpamicrophones.com. Web Site: www.dpamicrophones.com. Bill Calma, COO; Mark Bertrand, sls mgr; Clivia Schiebel, mktg & media coord; Barry Fox, mktg mgr; Paul Gonsalves, natl sls mgr.

DPA Microphones features a complete line of cardioid & omnidirectional microphones & accessories for all applicants.

DRS Technologies, 128 S. Industrial Blvd., Enterprise, AL 36330. Phone: (334) 347-3478. Fax: (334) 393-4556. Web Site: www.drs.com. Larry Sabourin, pres; Frank Sloan, dir mktg; Gary Bruce, sls dir.

Doppler weather radar systems (rain & wind measurements) with PC-based graphics display & control.

DSC Laboratories, 3565 Nashua Dr., Mississauga, ON L4V 1R1. Canada. Phone: (905) 673-3211. Fax: (905) 673-0929. E-mail: dsc@dsclabs.com. Web Site: www.dsclabs.com. D. Corley, pres; S. Corley, mktg.

Combi Optical Signal Generators (OSGs) & CamAlign chip charts for camera alignment & matching-deal for studio, shop & stadium.

DST Innovis, 1104 Investment Blvd., Eldorado Hills, CA 95762. Phone: (800) 835-8389. Fax: (916) 934-7054. Web Site: www.dstinnovis.com. Michael McGrail, pres; Robert McKenzie, VP mktg.

North Sydney NSW 2061. CableData (Asia Pacific), Level 4, 44 Miller St, Suite 404. Phone: +61 29.460.2250. Fax: +61 29.460.2238.

Sao Paulo 04571-010. CableData (Latin America), Andar, Suite 81, Ave. Eng Luis Carlos Berrini, 1297. Phone: +55 11.5505.6799. Fax: +55 11.5505.8691.

Customer mgmt & billing solutions for communications & utilities industries. Clients include providers of CATV, telephony, DBS, wireless, electricity, water, gas, waste mgmt, utility & multi-services in over 20 countries.

Dage-MTI Inc., 701 N. Roeske Ave., Michigan City, IN 46360. Phone: (219) 872-5514. Fax: (219) 872-5559. E-mail: dagemti@dagemti.com. Web Site: www.dagemti.com. Arthur D. Sterling, pres; Peggy Moore, dir mktg.

Closed circuit TV cameras & accessories.

Peter W. Dahl Co. Inc., 5869 Waycross, El Paso, TX 79924. Phone: (915) 751-2300. Fax: (915) 751-0768. E-mail: pwdco@pwdahl.com. Web Site: www.pwdahl.com. Peter W. Dahl, pres; Gary L. Komassa, VP.

Heavy duty plate, power, filament, modulation transformers & reactor; single- & three-phase rectifiers, vacuum & oil filled capacitors.

Daily Electronics Corp., 10914 N.E. 39th St., Ste #6, Vancouver, WA 98682. Phone: (360) 896-8856. Phone: (800) 346-6667. Fax: (360) 896-5476. E-mail: daily@worldaccessnet.com. Web Site: www.worldaccessnet.com/~daily/daily.html. Jim Grimes, pres.

Produces vacuum tubes—transmitting, camera, industrial & receiving. Tube rebuilding.

Dalet Digital Media Systems, 50 Broadway, Suite 1500, New York, NY 10004. Phone: (212) 825-3322. Fax: (212) 825-0182. E-mail: sales@dalet.com. Web Site: www.dalet.com. Stephane Guez, CEO; Anna Mae Sokuski, pres.

London SW179SH, Trident Business Centre, 89, Bickersteth Rd. Phone: +44 181 516 7750.

Madrid 28036, Calle Dr. Fleming 16. Phone: +34 914 581 988.

Paris 75010, 251, rue du Fbg St. Martin. Phone: +33 1 40 38 01 39.

Singapore 088449, FBC Singapore, 89 Neil Rd. Phone: +65 3260 672.

Digital automation work stn, network, and Internet solutions for radio stns & groups.

Data Security Inc., 729 Q St., Lincoln, NE 68508. Phone: (800) 225-7554. Phone: (402) 434-5959. Fax: (402) 434-3291. E-mail: eschafer@telesis-inc.com. Web Site: www.datasecurityinc.com. Brian Boles, CEO; Eric Schafer, VP.

Tape Enhancement Series features bulk tape deguassers & videotape cleaner/evaluators.

Datatek Corp., 1121 Bristol Rd., Mountainside, NJ 07092. Phone: (908) 654-8100. Fax: (908) 232-6381. Web Site: www.datateknj.com. Rick Rainey, sls.

Video/audio routing switchers, monitor switchers, machine control system, video/audio amplifiers, transmitter input equalizers.

Delta Electronics Inc., Box 11268, 5730 General Washington Dr., Alexandria, VA 22312. Phone: (703) 354-3350. Fax: (703) 354-0216. Web Site: www.deltaelectronics.com. John Wright, pres; William R. Fox, VP engrg; Joseph S. Novak, VP mktg.

RF instrumentation including ammeters, operating impedance bridges, receiver generators, AM stereo exciters, monitors & audio processors.

DeSisti Lighting, 1109 Grand Ave., North Bergen, NJ 07047-1628. Phone: (201) 319-1100. Fax: (201) 319-1104. E-mail: frank-kosuda@desistiusa.com. Frank Kosuda, pres.

Rome, NO Italy. World Headquarters (Desisti Lighting, Spa), Via Cancelliera 10/A, 00040 Cecchina, Albano Laziale. Phone: 01139-06934991. Fax: 01139-069343489. Fabio Desisti, gen mgr.

Complete professional lighting equipment & svcs. Quartz fresnels, softlights & cyc lights; HMI fresnels, softlights & sunguns; motorized studio lighting.

Devlin Design Group Inc., 12526 High Bluff Dr., Suite 300, San Diego, CA 92130. Phone: (760) 634-6514. E-mail: ddgemail@ddgtv.com. Web Site: www.ddgtv.com. Dan Devlin, CEO; Judy Parker, dir mktg.

Specializes in bcst news productions. News sets, newsrooms, turnkey & design only. Set design, virtual sets, hard set construction, consultation.

Dialogic Communications Corp., 730 Cool Springs Blvd., Franklin, TN 37067. Phone: (615) 790-2882. Fax: (615) 790-1329. Gene Kirby, pres; Charles Smith, VP engrg.

Interactive audio response voice processing equipment & software for pay-per-view, appointment confirmation, outage reporting, etc.

Dictaphone Corp., 3191 Broadbridge Ave., Stratford, CT 06614. Phone: (203) 381-7000. Fax: (203) 386-8597. Web Site: www.dictaphone.com. Rob Schwager, chmn/pres.

Multi-ch voice communications tape recorders (loggers).

Dielectric Communications, Box 949, 22 Tower Rd., Raymond, ME 04071. Phone: (207) 655-4555. Fax: (207) 655-7120. E-mail: dcsales@dielectric.spx.com. Web Site: www.dielectric.com. David White, pres; Dan Ozley, VP sls; Kerry Cozad, VP adv.

Antennas, inside equipment, waveguide, transmission line, switches, loads, pressurization, lighting, TV, Radio, Wireless towers, combiners.

DiGi Co. U.K. LTD., (Formerly Soundtracs, P.L.C.). The School House, 4 Dorking Rd., Epsom, Surrey KT18 7LX. United Kingdom. Phone: 44 01372 845 600. Fax: (44) 01372-845-656. E-mail: info@digiconsoles.com. Web Site: www.digiconsoles.com. David Webster, mktg dir; Robert Doyle, mgng dir.

Glenrothes, Fife KY7 4PA, Baird Rd, Eastfield IND.EST, Unit 0 (East). Phone: 01592-630499. Fax: 01592-630236.

Digital audio mixing consoles

Digidesign, 2001 Junipero Serra Blvd., Daly City, CA 94014-3886. Phone: (650) 731-6300. Fax: (650) 731-6399. E-mail: prodinfo@digidesign.com. Web Site: www.digidesign.com. David Lebolt, gen mgr; Christopher Bock, VP sls. France. France Office, 44 Ave. Georges Pompidou, 92300 Levallois-Perret. Phone: 33 1 41 49 40 10. Fax: 33 1 47 49 40 10. France. France Office, 44 Ave. Georges Pompidou, 92300 Levallois-Perret.

Tokyo 107-0052 Japan. Japan Office, 4F ATT Bldg, 2-11-7 Akasaka, Minato-ku. Phone: 81-3-3505-7963. Fax: 81-3-3505-3417.

Iver Heath, Bucks SLO ONH United Kingdom. UK Office, West Complex, Pinewood Studios, Pinewood Rd. Phone: 44 1753 653322. Fax: 44 1753 658501.

New York, NY 10019. New York Office, 1650 Broadway, Suite 1113. Phone: (212)664-7627.

Equipment Manufacturers and Distributors Alphabetical Index

Digitel Corp., 2719 Piedmont Ave., Duluth, MN 55811. Phone: (218) 727-0202. Jeffrey Stromquist, owner.

Bcst remote control & automation control equipment.

Dimension 3, 5240 Medina Rd., Woodland Hills, CA 91364. Phone: (818) 592-0999. Fax: (818) 592-0987. Web Site: www.d3.com.

Provides 3-D bcst TV processes. Supplies equipment, consultation & 3-D glasses.

Direct Broadcast Services Inc., 612 Corporate Way, Suite 8, Valley Cottage, NY 10989. Phone: (845) 267-2800. Fax: (845) 267-2123. E-mail: lrosengerg @directbroadcast.com. Web Site: www.directbroadcast.com. Leo Rosenberg, pres.

Transmission svcs & rentals: Ku-band uplinking/downlinking, portable microwave, fiber-optic systems, newsvan opns.

Discreet, 10 Duke St., Old Montreal, PQ H3C 2L7. Canada. Phone: (514) 393-1616. Fax: (514) 393-0110. E-mail: product-info@discreet.com. Web Site: www.discreet.com. Paul Lypaczewski, exec VP.

London W1V 5FJ, 22 Soho Sq. Phone: 44 71 734 4224. Simon Shaw, gen mgr.

Santa Monica, CA 90405, 2110 Main St, Suite 207. Phone: (310) 396-1167. Brian Gaffney, gen mgr.

Discreet products solutions for creating, mgng & distributing digital content, so artists can create once and use anywhere.

The Display & Exhibit Source, 4715 McEwen St., Dallas, TX 75244. Phone: (972) 239-0061. Fax: (972) 239-0089. E-mail: sales@displaysource.com. Web Site: www.displaysource.com. Dan South, sls.

Designs, manufactures modular, portable backdrops, displays, signal & graphic systems.

Display Devices Inc., 5880 N. Sheridan Blvd., Arvada, CO 80003. Phone: (303) 412-0399. Fax: (303) 412-9346. Web Site: www.displaydevices.com. Merv Perkins, pres; Ruth Perkins, VP.

CRT, LCD, slide projector motorized lifts & stationary mounts. Custom applications.

Display Systems International Inc., 2214 Hanselman Ave., Saskatoon, SK S7L 6A4. Canada. Phone: (306) 934-6884. Fax: (306) 934-6447. E-mail: sales@displaysystemsintl.com. Web Site: www.displaysystemsintl.com. Dale Lemke, pres.

Low-cost, high-performance IBM compatible character generators/product titlers with off-line editing, remote communications, internet capable, text animation with Windows XP.

Ditch Witch, Box 66, 1959 W. Firr Ave., Perry, OK 73077. Phone: (580) 336-4402. Fax: (580) 572-3523. E-mail: info@ditchwitch.com. Web Site: www.ditchwitch.com.

Manufacturer of trenching, vibratory plow & trenchless technology equipment, electronic locating & tracking equipment, mini-skid steers, excavators & escavator tool-carriers.

DMT USA, Inc., 1224 Forest Pkwy., Unit 140, West Deptford, NJ 08066. Phone: (856) 423-0010. Fax: (856) 423-7002. E-mail: sales@dmtonline.us. Web Site: www.dmtonline.us. Alberto Giorgini, exec VP; Tom Newman, dir mktg.

TV transmitters and translators, DAB, FM, microwaves & stems, antennas, system integration, and scientific applications.

Dolby Laboratories Inc., 100 Potrero Ave., San Francisco, CA 94103. Phone: (415) 558-0200. Fax: (415) 863-1373. Web Site: www.dolby.com. Ray M. Dolby, chmn; Bill Jasper, pres.

Wootton Bassett, Wiltshire SN4 8QJ Phone: 1793 842 100. Tony Spath, bcst projects mgr.

Audio noise reduction & signal processing equipment; digital audio coding for ISDN, cable, satellite & other applications; dolby surround equipment.

Dorrough Electronics, 5221 Collier Pl., Woodland Hills, CA 91364. Phone: (818) 998-2824. Fax: (818) 998-1507. E-mail: dorroughel@aol.com. Web Site: www.dorrough.com. Mike Dorrough, owner.

Chatsworth, CA 91311, 20434 Corisco St. Phone: (818) 998-4886.

Dorrough Electronics manufactures Audio Loudness Meters featuring Peak and Average signals ballistically set for a highly accurate reading.

Doty-Moore Tower Services, 1570 W. Beltline Rd., Cedar Hill, TX 75104. Phone: (972) 637-5000. Fax: (972) 293-1255. Web Site: www.stainlessinc.com. J. Patrick Moore, pres.

Full spectrum of tower maintenance & erection/inspection, construction & inspection svcs. RF svcs include RF mapping of the tower & facilities. 24-hr emergency svc.

Dove Systems, 3563 Sueldo St., Suite E, San Luis Obispo, CA 93401-7590. Phone: (805) 541-8292. Fax: (805) 541-8293. E-mail: dove@dovesystems.com. Web Site: www.dovesystems.com. Gary Dove, owner.

Studio & stage lighting control equipment.

Dow-Key Microwave Corp., 4822 McGrath, Ventura, CA 93003. Phone: (805) 650-0260. Fax: (805) 650-1734. E-mail: askdk@dowkey.com. Web Site: www.dowkey.com. Mark Mandrell, pres.

Microwave switches, coaxial RF relays & switches, 75 ohm & 50 ohm styles available.

R.L. Drake Co., 230 Industrial Dr., Franklin, OH 45005-4496. Phone: (937) 746-4556. Fax: (937) 743-4510. E-mail: catv@rldrake.com. Web Site: www.rldrake.com. Ron Wysong, pres/CEO; Mike Brubakerr, sls VP; Andy Ruffin, sls dir.

Peterborough, ON K9J 7M1 Canada, 655 The Queensway. Phone: (705) 742-3122. Steve Roe, sls mgr.

Analog, digital cable headend equipment including receivers, modulators, processors, accessories for reception & distribution of progmg.

DRS Broadcast Technology, 4212 S. Buckner Blvd., Dallas, TX 75227. Phone: (214) 381-7161. Fax: (214) 381-3250. E-mail: info@drs-bt.com. Web Site: www.contelec.com. Adil Mina, VP Business Development; John Uvodich, VP/gen mgr; Bret Brewer, broadcast mktg mgr.

Birmingham, AL 35226, 2280 Rockcreek Trail. Phone: (205) 822-1078. Dave Hultsman, Regional Sales Manager.

Specialists in AM, FM & SW transmitters, antenna systems & other RF equipment.

Dubner International Inc., 13 Westervelt Pl., Westwood, NJ 07675. Phone: (201) 664-6434. Fax: (201) 358-9377. E-mail: rdubner@compuserve.com. Web Site: www.dubner.com. Robert Dubner, pres.

Manufacturers PC bcst & production equipment. Products include VideoALERT for on-air signal monitoring & response & SCENE STEALER for videotape logging & archiving.

M. Ducommun Co., 58 Main St., Warwick, NY 10990. Phone: (845) 986-5757. Fax: (845) 986-7720. M. Ducommun Jr., pres.

Stopwatches for radio & TV; sls & service.

Dynamic Solutions 2000, 527 Carey Ave., Wilkes-Barre, PA 18702. Phone: (570) 824-7626. Fax: (570) 824-0556. E-mail: jpgibbons@prodigy.net. Web Site: www.ds2000.net. John P. Gibbons, pres.

Convergent billing solutions for the communications & utility industries.

E

e2v technologies Inc., 4 Westchester Plaza, Elmsford, NY 10523. Phone: (914) 592-6050. Fax: (914) 592-5148. E-mail: enquiries@e2v.com. Web Site: www.e2v.com. Mike Kirk, VP.

Mississauga, ON L5A 4H2 Canada, Box 29667. Phone: (905) 848-6430. Fax: (905) 848-9343. Ann Au-Yong.

Buffalo, NY 14221, 80 Post Rd. Phone: (716) 626-9055. Fax: (716) 631-5117. Rick Bossert, natl sls mgr.

Manufacturer of Digital & Analog IOTs, ESCs, Klystrons for UHF TV transmitters; Stellar range of satellite uplink Amplifiers.

EDX Wireless LLC, Box 1547, Eugene, OR 97440-1547. Phone: (541) 345-0019. Fax: (541) 345-8145. E-mail: info@edx.com. Web Site: www.edx.com.

Engrg software & svcs for AM, TV, FM bcst & communication svcs.

EEG Enterprises Inc., 586 Main St., Farmingdale, NY 11735. Phone: (516) 293-7472. Fax: (516) 293-7417. E-mail: sales@eegent.com. Web Site: www.eegent.com. Philip McLaughlin, pres; Eric McErlain, sls mgr.

TV closed captioning technology; HDTV & SDTV, closes caption encoders, decoders; V-chip encoders, decoders & systems; affil communications.

EFI Electronics Corp., 1751 S. 4800 W., Salt Lake City, UT 84104. Phone: (800) 877-1174. Fax: (801) 977-0200. Web Site: www.efinet.com. Terry O'Neal, pres/CEO; Steve Wallace, CFO.

Manufactures a complete line of power protection systems for industrial, coml & computer applications.

ENCO Systems Inc., 29444 Northwestern Hwy., Southfield, MI 48034. Phone: (248) 827-4440. Fax: (248) 827-4441. E-mail: sales@enco.com. Web Site: www.enco.com. Gene Novacek, pres; Don Backus, sls VP.

DADpro32 digital audio delivery systems, custom software engrg for the bcst industry.

E-N-G Mobile Systems Inc., 2245 Via De Mercados, Concord, CA 94520. Phone: (925) 798-4060. Fax: (925) 798-0152. E-mail: sales@e-n-g.com. Web Site: www.e-n-g.com. Dick A. Glass, pres; Ted Kendrick, VP; Ray Iddon, sls.

West Grove, PA 19390, 119 Lloyd Rd. Phone: (610) 659-2640. John Watkins, opns mgr.

Custom-designed ENG & EFP vehicles, rack-ready & turnkey systems. Other mobile electronic systems. ENG system components.

EON Corp., 360 Herndon Pkwy., Herndon, VA 20170. Phone: (703) 467-0230.

Dev & mfg of wireless two-way interactive technology for consumers & businesses which operate via radio frequency.

ERI-Installations Inc., 7777 Gardner Rd., Chandler, IN 47610. Phone: (812) 925-6000. Fax: (812) 925-4030. E-mail: sbeeler@eriinc.com. Web Site: www.eriinc.com. Thomas B. Silliman, pres; Bart Wenderoth, mgr; Todd Forbes, controller.

Antenna, tower instal svc; antenna rebuilding, stand-by antennas, tower up-grades, reinforcing; fully bonded & insured.

ESE, 142 Sierra St., El Segundo, CA 90245. Phone: (310) 322-2136. Fax: (310) 322-8127. E-mail: ese@ese-web.com. Web Site: www.ese-web.com. Brian Way, VP; William Kaiser, pres.

Master clocks, digital clocks, programmable timers, time code generators & readers, distribution amplifiers, programmable clocks.

ETS-Lindgren, 1301 Arrow Point Dr., Cedar Park, TX 78613. Phone: (512) 531-6400. Fax: (512) 531-6500. E-mail: sales@ets-lindgren.com. Web Site: www.ets-lindgren.com. Dave Baron, sls; Bruce Butler, pres; Mark Mawdsley, VP sls.

Non-ionizing radiation test equipment; low frequency survey meters; RF/microwave broadband field strength meters; calibration svcs, software & training.

E-Z Trench Manufacturing Co. Inc., 2315 S. Hwy. 701, Loris, SC 29569. Phone: (843) 756-6444. Fax: (843) 756-6442. Web Site: www.eztrench.com. Roger Porter, pres.

Lightweight trenchers—digs trench, lays cables & covers all in one pass.

Eagle Comtronics Inc., 4562 Waterhouse Rd., Clay, NY 13041. Phone: (315) 622-3402. Fax: (315) 622-3800. E-mail: sales@eaglecomtronics.com. Web Site: www.eaglefilters.com. Bill Devendorf, pres; Alan Devendorf, CEO; Tim Devendorf, exec VP.

CATV manufacturer & designer of security traps, decoders, & tier traps. Custom OEM filter designs.

Eastman Kodak Co., 343 State St., Rochester, NY 14650. Phone: (585) 724-4000. Fax: (585) 724-0663. Web Site: www.kodak.com. Daniel Carp, chmn/CEO; Michael Morley, exec VP.

Cameras, projectors, graphic & motion picture products.

Echostar Communications Corp., 9601 S. Meridian Blvd., Englewood, CO 80211. Phone: (303) 723-1000. Fax: (303) 723-1046. Web Site: www.echostar.com. Charles Ergen, CEO; Michael Dugan, pres/COO; Mark Jackson, sr VP.

Littleton, CO 80120, 5701 S. Santa Fe Rd. Phone: (303) 723-1000. Fax: (303) 723-1099. Charles Ergen, CEO/chman of bd; Brent Gale, dir bcst engrg.

Satellite TV reception systems.

Edcor Electronics Corp., 7130 National Parks Hwy., Carlsbad, NM 88220. Phone: (800) 854-0259. Fax: (505) 887-6880. E-mail: sales@edcorusa.com. Web Site: www.edcorusa.com.

Audio mic/line mixers, headphone amplifiers, line amplifiers, audio mixers & audio transformers; custom transformers.

Eddie Egan & Associates, 6136 W. Washington Blvd., Culver City, CA 90048. Phone: (310) 278-0370. Fax: (310) 275-6412. E-mail: eganfloor@aol.com. Daniel Egan, pres; Armand Egan, VP.

Floor coverings for video stages including wood, vinyl & carpeting.

Equipment Manufacturers and Distributors Alphabetical Index

Eigen, 13366 Grass Valley Ave., Grass Valley, CA 95945. Phone: (530) 265-2020. Fax: (530) 265-2792.
Digital image processors with optional floppy or Winchester disc storage. High-resolution video disc recorders.

Elan Enterprises Ltd., 506 E. St. Charles Rd., Carol Stream, IL 60188. Phone: (800) 331-8382. Fax: (630) 690-6618. E-mail: eeljim8720@aol.com. Web Site: www.generator-inverter.com. Jim Johnsen, pres & sls dir; Joe Johnsen Jr., VP.
Redi-line electric generators. Tripp Lite inverters & sure power isolators.

Elcom Systems Inc., PMB 255, 20423 State Rd. 7 #F6, Boca Raton, FL 33498-6797. Phone: (561) 883-1945. Fax: (561) 883-1945. E-mail: sales@elcomsystems.com. Web Site: www.elcomsystems.com. Leonard Pollachek, pres.
RF coaxial attenuators, terminations, couplers, double balanced mixers, detectors, DC-4.2 Ghz, impedance transformers.

Electro Impulse Laboratory Inc., Box 278, 1805 Rt. 33, Neptune, NJ 07754-0278. Phone: (732) 776-5800. Fax: (732) 776-6793. E-mail: sales@electroimpulse.com. Web Site: www.electroimpulse.com. Mark Rubin, pres.
Manufacturer of dry, forced, air-cooled FM dummy loads & RF calorimeters.

Electro Rent Corp., (Instrument Rental Division). 6060 Sepulveda Blvd., Van Nuys, CA 91411. Phone: (818) 787-2100. Fax: (818) 787-4354. Web Site: www.electrorent.com. Craig Birgi, rgnl mgr.
Duluth, GA 30096, 3500 Corporate Way. Phone: (770) 813-7000. (800) 688-1111. Rich Curry, eastern rgnl sls mgr.
Test rental equipment including CATV sweep analyzers, signal level meters, video generators/monitors, & cable fault locators.

Electroline Equipment Inc., 8265 Blvd. St. Michel, Montreal, PQ H1Z 3E4. Canada. Phone: (514) 374 6335. Fax: (514) 374-9370. E-mail: info@electroline.com. Web Site: www.electroline.com. John Vincent, pres/CEO; Winston Rodrigues, VP opns; Luc Oliver, VP finance; Jay Staiger, dir mktg; Alain Servant, VP.
Cable TV equipment, off-premises addressable systems, passive devices, filters, amplifiers, headend RF signal mgnt equipment & transponders.

Electronic Script Prompting, 6129 Western Ave., Clarendon Hills, IL 60514. Phone: (630) 887-0346. Fax: (630) 887-0389. Web Site: www.prompting.com.
Teleprompting rental & sale.

Electronic Theatre Controls Inc., 3031 Pleasant View Rd., Middleton, WI 53562. Phone: (608) 831-4116. Fax: (608) 836-1736. Web Site: www.etcconnect.com. Fred Foster, pres.
Orlando, FL 32811, 4201 Vineland Rd, Suite I-1. Phone: (407) 843-7770. Rob Raff, southeast rgnl mgr. (Southeast rgnl office).
New York, NY 10036, Film Center Bldg., 630 Ninth Ave., Suite 1001. Phone: (212) 397-8080. Joe DiNardo, northeast rgnl mgr. (Northeast rgnl office).
Entertainment lighting systems, including control consoles, dimming equipment & interface products.

Electronology, Inc., 508 Lakeland Blvd., Mattoon, IL 61938. Phone: (800) 278-2050. Fax: (217) 258-5558. E-mail: info@einc.com. Web Site: www.einc.com. Jay Martin, mgr; John Sullivan, consultant; Jim Renkel, consultant.
Distributor of ITC digicenter digital audio systems, ITC cart machines & products, other audio equipment to bcstrs.

EMCOR Enclosures, 1600 4th Ave. N.W., Rochester, MN 55901. Phone: (507) 287-3535. Fax: (507) 287-3405. Web Site: www.emcorenclosures.com. Tom Ryan, sls dir; Nick Allen, mktg mgr.
Conventional & Flat Panel Display Consoles, modification/custom capabilities, EMI/RFI shielded & Seismic qualified enclosures, a full range of component accessories.

Encoda Systems Inc., (formerly Columbine JDS, Enterprise and DAL/Brake Automation). 1999 Broadway, Suite 4000, Denver, CO 80202-3050. Phone: (303) 237-4000. Fax: (303) 237-0085. E-mail: info@encodasystems.com. Web Site: www.encodasystems.com. Barry Goldsmith, CEO; Rob McConnell, COO.
Chineharn, Basingstole RG24 8WD, 14 Cedarwood, Chineham Business Park. Phone: 44-1256-3790-00. Fax: 44-1256-7073-59.
Colorado Springs, CO 80920, 8415 Explorer Dr. Phone: (719) 548-7416. Fax: (719) 548-1818.
Grand Rapids, MI 49509, 5293-B Clyde Park Ave. S.W. Phone: (616) 532-1446. Fax: (616) 532-8147.
Montreal, PQ H2Y 1Y3 Canada, 390 rue Le Moyne. Phone: (514) 842-0101. Fax: (514) 842-0111.
Bedfordshire, NO LU7 1DD United Kingdom, Arden House, Leighton Buzzard. Phone: 44-1525-8525-99. Fax: 44-1525-8525-98.
New York, NY 10016, 99 Madison Ave., 17th Floor. Phone: (212) 303-4200. Fax: (212) 779-8719.
Encoda is the authority in seamless automation for the business of media. Encoda is the only company offering end-to-end technological solutions to buyers & sellers of adv time within the electronic media marketplace (bcst, cable, wireless, & DBS).

Energy-Onix Broadcast Equipment Co. Inc., Box 801, 1306 River St., Valatie, NY 12184. Phone: (518) 758-1690. Fax: (518) 758-1476. E-mail: energy@energy-onix.com. Web Site: www.energy-onix.com. Bernard Wise, pres.
Transmitters: FM solid state to 10 kw, grounded grid triode to 50 kw & AM & SW to 100 kw. STL, Translator and remote pick up.

Enghouse Systems Limited, 80 Tiverton Ct., Suite 800, Markham, ON L3R 0G4. Canada. Phone: (905) 946-3200. Fax: (905) 946-3201. E-mail: info@enghouse.com. Web Site: www.enghouse.com. Michael Ford, CEO; Tony Murphy, pres; Andrew Nellestyn, pres; Jerry Diakow, VP sls.
CableCad®—automated mapping/facilities mgmt software with integrated design capabilities for Cable TV companies.

Ensat Broadcast Services Inc., 1350 Thornton Rd. S., Oshawa, ON L1J 8C4. Canada. Phone: (519) 648-3613. E-mail: dmacleod@ensatbroadcast.com. Web Site: www.ensatbroadcast.com. Michael J. Martin, pres; Dwane Williams, dir opns; Debbie MacLeod, dir mktg & sls dir.
Oshawa, ON L1J 8C4 Canada. Ensat Broadcast Service Inc., 1350 Thornton Rd. S. Phone: (800) 327-1463.
Ku-Bank uplinking/downlinking, microwave newsvan svcs, production svcs, production services and transmission svcs and rentals.

Ensemble Designs, Box 993, Grass Valley, CA 95945. Phone: (530) 478-1830. Fax: (530) 478-1832. E-mail: info@endes.com. Web Site: www.ensembledesigns.com. David S. Wood, pres; Cindy Zuelsdorf, mktg mgr.
Video, Audio conversion distribution, routing & embedding. Testing signal generators, frame synchronizers, TBC control, MAC/PC/SGI to serial digital interfaces

Enterprise Systems Group Inc.
See Encoda Systems Inc.

Entertainment Communications Network (ECN), 4370 Tujunga Ave., Studio City, CA 91604. Phone: (818) 752-1400. Fax: (818) 752-1443. E-mail: csd@ecnmedia.com. Web Site: www.ecnmedia.com. Barry Weintraub, chmn; Dennis Fitch, chmn.
Wall, NJ 07719, 1628 Dubac Rd. Phone: (732) 280-7107.
Bcst faxing to entertainment data bases, online resources, E-mail networks, digital graphics-delivery.

Equipment Technology Inc., 341 N.W. 122nd, Oklahoma City, OK 73114. Phone: (405) 748-3841. Fax: (405) 755-6829. Web Site: www.eti1.com. James Neuberger, pres.
Oklahoma City, OK 73114, 341 N.W. 122 No. Glenn Smith, VP mktg/sls.
Aerial buckets: articulating & telescoping; truck & van mounted; working height ranges 33 to 43 ft.

e-Studio Live!, 2 Highwood Dr., Suite 102, Tewksbury, MA 01876-1100. Phone: (978) 640-1853. Fax: (978) 640-1523. E-mail: jjones@echolab.com. Web Site: www.e-studiolive.com. Stephen Crummey, pres; Art Souza, mktg VP.
Color special effects generators with memory. Video Production switchers.

Euphonix Inc., 220 Portage Ave., Palo Alto, CA 94306. Phone: (650) 855-0400. Fax: (650) 855-0410. Web Site: www.euphonix.com. James Dobbie, dir.
North Hollywood, CA 91602. Euphonix Sales & Marketing, 10647B Riverside Dr. Phone: (818) 766-1666. Fax: (818) 766-3401. Andy Wild, VP sls & mktg.
Manufactures the Euphonix CSII digitally-controlled analog audio mixing system.

Eventide Inc., One Alsan Way, Little Ferry, NJ 07643. Phone: (201) 641-1200. Fax: (201) 641-1640. E-mail: audio@eventide.com. Web Site: www.eventide.com. Gordon Moore, gen mgr; Richard Factor, pres; Tony Agnello, CTO; Ray Maxwell, VP.
Audio & video delay lines, time compression/expansion, pitch change effects, digital reverb & effects processor, digital audio logger.

Evertz Microsystems Ltd., 5288 John Lucas Dr., Burlington, ON L7L 5Z9. Canada. Phone: (905) 335-3700. Fax: (905) 335-3573. E-mail: sales@evertz.com. Web Site: www.evertz.com.
Rayleigh, Essex, NO 556 75A United Kingdom, Unit 1, Alderhouse.
Burbank, CA 91506, 1612 W. Olive Ave, Suite 302.
Telecine reader head, HDTV 1.5Gb/s DA's, Telecine Keyer, Digital afterburner, Digital & HDTV Graticule Generator, GPS Receiver, Downstream Keyer, SID Decoder/Encoders, Routers, Audio Embedders, Fiber Converters.

The Express Group, 3360 Thorn St., San Diego, CA 92104. Phone: (619) 280-9061. Fax: (619) 280-9030. E-mail: egmail@theexpressgroup.com. Web Site: www.theexpressgroup.com. Byron Andrus, pres; George Andrus, consultant.
Design, fabrication, lighting of custom news sets, newsrooms, interview sets; custom & modular radio cabinetry.

F

F&F Productions, L.L.C., 14333 Myerlake Cir., Clearwater, FL 33760. Phone: (727) 535-6776. Fax: (727) 577-5011. George Orgera, pres; Connie Vizaro, VP sls & operations; Bill McKechney, engrg VP.
Remote production svcs & TV mobile units.

F-Conn Industries, (A division of ICM Corp.) 6260 Downing St., Denver, CO 80216. Phone: (303) 288-8107. Fax: (303) 288-4769. E-mail: sales@icmcorp.net. Web Site: www.icmcorp.net. Randy Holliday, pres; Susan Stockstill, sls VP.
Get the performance of a high end connector at a standard F-fitting cost.

FM Atlas—Publishing and Electronics, Box 336, Esko, MN 55733-0336. Phone: (218) 879-7676. Fax: (218) 879-7676. E-mail: fmatlas@aol.com. Web Site: www.user.aol.com/fmatlas. Bruce Elving, owner.
Tunable FM/SCS & SAP-modified TV audio radios, adaptor kits with LED display. Brailled radios for the blind.

FM Systems Inc., 3877 S. Main St., Santa Ana, CA 92707. Phone: (714) 979-3355. Phone: (800) 235-6960. Fax: (714) 979-0913. Web Site: www.fmsystems-inc.com. E-mail: fmsystemsinc@worldnet.att.net. Frank McClatchie, pres; Don McClatchie, COO.
Stereo performance meter, audio level masters, digital video volt meters, video & audio modulation meters, multichannel subcarriers & video gain controls (VM771).

FOR.A Corp. of America, 11125 Knott Ave., Suite A, Cypress, CA 90630. Phone: (714) 894-3311. Fax: (714) 894-5399. Web Site: www.for-a.com. Robert Browne, gen sls mgr.
Video & audio bcst & postproduction equipment; TBCs, color correctors, production switchers, de/encoders, complete video editing systems, virtual stoid, multiviewing.

FWT Inc., Box 8597, 5750 E. I-20, Fort Worth, TX 76124. Phone: (817) 255-3060. Fax: (817) 255-2957. Web Site: www.fwtinc.com.
Towers, communications bldgs, standby power systems, mobile communications bldgs, fiber optics, & splicing trailers.

Fairlight ESP Pty. Ltd., Box 6117, Frenchs Forest, Sydney NSW 1670. Australia. Phone: +612 8977 9909. Fax: +612 8977 9994. E-mail: jlancken@fairlightesp.com.au. Web Site: www.fairlightesp.com. David Hanney, CEO; Andrew Bell, product dir; Athal Warmer, CFO; John Lancken, sr VP sls; Gregg Sampson, mktg VP.
92100 Boulogne-Billancourt 92100. Fairlight France, 41-43 Rue des Peupliers. Phone: +33 (1) 4610 9292. Fax: +33 (1) 4610 9295. E-mail: mail@fairlight.fr. Joe Hammer.
London NW5 1LP. Fairlight ESP Ltd., Unit 12, Spectrum House, 32-34 Gordon House Rd. Phone: +44 171 267-3323. Fax: +44 171 267-0919. E-mail: sales@fairlightesp. Charles Rowden.

Potsdam-Babelsberg 14482. Fairlight Deutschland, 26-53 August-Bebel Strasse. Phone: +49 331 721 2930. Fax: +49 331 721 2933. Robert Trebus, Sales Mgr.,Ronnie Schreinzer, Product Mgr.

Toyko 154-0001. Fairlight Japan Inc., 3-3-11 Ikejiri, Setagaya-ku. Phone: +81 (3) 5432-4151. Fax: +81 (3) 5432-4533. E-mail: k.fukuda@fairlight.co.jp. Kenji Fukuda.

Hollywood, CA 90038. Fairlight USA - West Coast, 844 N. Seward St. Phone: (323) 465-0070. (800) 4 FAIRLIGHT. Fax: (323) 465-0080. www.fairlightusa.com. John Lancken, sr VP.

New York, NY 10036. Fairlight-East Coast, 2 W. 45th St, Suite 605. Phone: (212) 819-1289. (800) 4 FAIRLIGHT. Fax: (212) 819-0376. Michael Muller.

Manfacturer of digital audio recording, playback, editing & mixing systems for film, video & bcst audio postproduction.

Faraone Communications Inc., 75 West End Ave., Suite R-9A, New York, NY 10023. Phone: (212) 489-1313. E-mail: tfaraon@attglobal.net. Web Site: www.pr-agency.com. Ted Faraone, chmn.

Faroudja Laboratories, (A Division of Genesis Microchip). 750 Palomar Ave., Sunnyvale, CA 94085. Phone: (408) 735-1492. Fax: (408) 735-8571. Web Site: www.faroudja.com.

NTSC Encoder; NTSC & PAL/NTSC Decoder (RGB or D1 output); Bidirectional Transcoder; NTSC & PAL/NTSC Line Doublers & Line Quadruplers.

Farrtronics Ltd., 39 Kent Ave., Kitchener, ON N2G 3R2. Canada. Phone: (519) 741-1010. Fax: (519) 578-2044.

Audio & video patchfields; intercom systems, IFB systems, audio distribution amplifiers, beltpack party line systems, monitor packages.

Fast Forward Video, 18200-B W. McDurmott, Irvine, CA 92614. Phone: (949) 852-8404. Fax: (949) 852-1226. Web Site: www.ffv.com. E-mail: kevin@ffv.com. Paul Dekeyser, pres; Claudette Kay, mgr; Dennis Mallon, open mgr; Kevin McNally, VP/sls.

Bandit-digital playback/recorder F-30 & F-22. Time code generator/readers/character inserter.

Feldmar Watch and Clock Center, 9000 W. Pico Blvd., Los Angeles, CA 90035. Phone: (310) 274-8016. Fax: (310) 274-2081. E-mail: sales@feldmarwatch.com. Web Site: www.feldmarwatch.com. Sol Meller, pres.

Stopwatches, clocks, watches, timers, sls & repairs.

Fermont ACTS Co., (subsidiary of ESSI). 141 N. Ave., Bridgeport, CT 06606. Phone: (203) 366-5211. Fax: (203) 367-3642. Web Site: www.engineeredsupport.com. Thomas Santoro, pres.

Emergency standby power & diesel generator sets. Co-generation plant modules.

Ferno-Washington Inc., 70 Weil Way, Wilmington, OH 45177-9371. Phone: (937) 382-1451. Fax: (937) 382-1191. Web Site: www.ferno.com. Joe Bourgraf, CEO; Tim Schroeder, mktg mgr.

Carts designed to aid in the movement of heavy & bulky equipment.

Fiber Options, 4575 Research Way, Suite 250, Corvallis, OR 97333. Phone: (800) 469-1676. Phone: (541) 754-9134. Fax: (541) 752-9097. E-mail: cvovideosales@ge.com. John Collins, pres; Fred Scott, sls VP; Vic Milani, VP.

West Yorkshire L527 OLQ. Fiber Options Europe Ltd., Unit 7, Cliff Pk, Morley, Leeds. Phone: 44-1132-3816668. Fax: 44-1132-2588121. Steve Clarke, mgng dir.

Manufactures fiber-optic video, data, and audio transmission systems for security, bcst, educ, teleconferencing, ITS, and industrial markets.

Film/Video Equipment Service Co. Inc., 800 S. Jason St., Denver, CO 80223. Phone: (303) 778-8616. Fax: (303) 778-8657. E-mail: fvesco@fvesco.com. Web Site: www.fvesco.com. Dean D. Schneider, pres; Kay Baker, sls/mktg mgr.

Film & video equipment rental & sls-cameras, lenses, lighting, grip, pro audio, camera support, specialty gear for quality production.

FitzCo. Inc., 2600 W. Wall, Midland, TX 79701. Phone: (432) 684-0861. Fax: (432) 682-9978. Michael Fitz-Gerald, pres.

Speakers, recorders, amplifiers, mixers, tapes, microphones, & headphones; sound reinforcement & bcst equipment.

Flash Technology Corporation of America, 332 Nichol Mill Ln., Franklin, TN 37067. Phone: (615) 261-2000. Fax: (615) 261-2600. E-mail: info@flashtechnology.com. Web Site: www.flashtechnology.com. Mark Joss, VP.

Nashua, NH 03060, 55 Lake St. Phone: (603) 883-6500.

Aviation high-intensity obstruction lights for tall structures & medium intensity for structures up to 500 ft.

FloriCal Systems Inc., 4581 N.W. 6th St., Gainesville, FL 32609. Phone: (352) 372-8326. Fax: (352) 375-0859. E-mail: sales@florical.com. Web Site: www.florical.com. Jim Moneyhun, pres; Sunda Scanlon, VP/gen mgr.

TV Automation, on-air presentation, assset mgmt, material aquisition, meida prep, hi/lo resbrowsing, multi-ch monitoring/alarms & electronic progmg guides.

Fluke Corp., Box 9090, Everett, WA 98206-9090. Phone: (800) 443-5853. Fax: (206) 446-5116. E-mail: fluke-info@fluke.com. Web Site: www.fluke.com. George Sherman, pres/CEO; H. Lawrence Culp Jr., pres; Jim Lico, pres.

Electronic test, measurement & control instrumentation.

Focus Enhancements, 1370 Dell Ave., Campbell, CA 95008. Phone: (408) 866-8300. Fax: (408) 866-4859. E-mail: info@focusinfo.com. Web Site: www.focusinfo.com. Bret Moyer, CEO.

World class manufacturer of ASICs for scan conversion, internet & interavtive TV applications. Manufactures PC to TV scan converters, scalers, line quadruplers & DV video production equipment & effects generators.

Fostex Corp. of America, 15431 Blackburn Ave., Norwalk, CA 90650. Phone: (562) 921-1112. Fax: (562) 802-1964. E-mail: info@fostex.com. Web Site: www.fostex.com. Bob Schmidt, pres; Budd Johnson, mktg dir.

Multitrack tape recorders, audio-to-video synchronizers, speakers, microphones, headphones & digital audio recorders.

Four Seasons Solar Products Corp., 5005 Veterans Memorial Hwy., Holbrook, NY 11741. Phone: (631) 563-4000. Fax: (631) 563-4010. Web Site: www. oikos.com. David Ewing, pres.

Freeland Products Inc., 75412 Hwy. 25, Covington, LA 70435. Phone: (985) 893-1243. Phone: (800) 624-7626. Fax: (985) 892-7323. E-mail: freeland-inc.com @freeland-inc.com. Web Site: www.freeland-inc.com. Joel H. Freeland, pres.

Rebuilding of TV & radio transmitter tubes.

Frequency Measuring Service Inc., Box 353, Commerce City, CO 80037. Phone: (303) 288-1482. Fax: (303) 289-8006. Howard S. Eldridge, pres & dir.

Frequency measurements, modulation calibration, field intensity measurements, spectrum analysis.

Frezzolini Electronics Inc., 5-7 Valley St., Hawthorne, NJ 07506. Phone: (973) 427-1160. Fax: (973) 427-0934. E-mail: frezzi@frezzi.com. Web Site: www.frezzi.com. James J. Crawford, pres.

High-capacity NICAD/NIMH batteries for all professional cameras & camcorders; advanced power supplies; microcomputer control chargers; ENG lighting & accessories.

Frontline Communications, 12770 44th St. N., Clearwater, FL 33762. Phone: (727) 573-0400. Fax: (727) 571-3295. E-mail: dmckay@frontlinecomm.com. Web Site: www.frontlinecomm.com. Jonathan Sherr, gen mgr; Doug McKay, sls mgr; Bob King, international sls mgr.

Manufacturer of custom bcst vehicles for ENG microwave, analog & digital satellite uplink & remote field production applications.

Fuji Photo Film U.S.A. Inc., 200 Summit Lake Dr., Val Halla, NY 10595-1356. Phone: (914) 789-8100. Fax: (914) 789-8490. Web Site: www.fujiphotofilm.com. Stan Bauer, VP/gen mgr; George Tanaka, pres; Joe Visslailli, VP; Jim Hegadorn, mgr; Tom Daily, dir mktg; Tom Volpicella, VP bcst sls.

Cypress, CA 90630, 6200 Phyllis Dr. Phone: (714) 372-4200. Fax: (714) 372-4370. Jim Ghelfi, rgnl sls mgr.

Duluth, GA 30136, 2450 Satelite Blvd. Phone: (770) 813-5100. Fax: (770) 813-5166. Brett Mercurio, rgnl sls mgr.

Hanover Park, IL 60133, 850 Central Ave. Phone: (630) 259-7200. Fax: (630) 259-7879. Dave Perin, rgnl sls mgr.

Edison, NJ 08837, 1100 King George Post Road. Phone: (732) 857-3000. Fax: (732) 857-3495. Bob Currie, rgnl sls mgr.

Carrollton, TX 75006, 1628 W. Crosby Rd, Suite 100. Phone: (972) 466-9200. Fax: (972) 446-1329. Stan Risetter, rgnl sls mgr.

Professional videotape & audiocassettes for bcst, production, industrial, corporate & duplication applications.

Fujinon Inc., 10 High Point Dr., Wayne, NJ 07470. Phone: (973) 633-5600. Fax: (973) 633-5216. T. Nakamura, pres; John Newton, VP; Tom Calabro, natl sls mgr.

Redondo, CA 90278, West Bay Business Park, 2621A Manhattan Beach Blvd. Phone: (310) 536-0800. Miles Shozuya, West Coast sls mgr; Chuck Lee, mktg mgr.

Hollywood, FL 33021, 4101 N. 48th Terr. Phone: (954) 966-0484. Kelly Nelson, Southeast rgnl sls mgr.

Addison, TX 75001, 4951 Airport Pkwy, Suite 802A. Phone: (972) 385-8902. David Waddell, mktg mgr.

CTV, ENG, EFP lenses, optical systems, accessories.

Full Compass Systems Ltd., 8001 Terrace Ave., Middleton, WI 53562-3194. Phone: (800) 356-5844. Phone: (608) 831-7330. Fax: (608) 831-6330. E-mail: webmaster@fullcompass.com. Web Site: www.fullcompass.com. Jonathan Lipp, CEO.

Over 300 product lines for broadcast recording, entertainment, video & sound reinforcement industries.

Fuller Manufacturing, 695 S. Glenwood Pl., Burbank, CA 91506. Phone: (818) 500-0116. Fax: (818) 238-9959. Ron Fuller, engrg mgr.

IFB for news & satellite trunks.

Furman Sound Inc., 1997 S. McDowell Blvd., Petaluma, CA 94954. Phone: (707) 763-1010. Fax: (707) 763-1310. E-mail: info@furmansound.com. Web Site: www.furmansound.com. Joe Desmond, VP sls & mktg VP; John Humphrey, CFO.

Analog, digital, video monitor systems; power conditioning/distribution, mixers, equalizers, compressors, crossovers, patch bays,voltage regulators, headphone ampliflers & distribution sustems.

Future Productions Inc., 750 Huyler St., Teterboro, NJ 07608. Phone: (201) 727-0903. Fax: (201) 727-0908. Ken Washino, VP.

Manufactures & svcs audio/video distribution amplifiers, video duplication control systems, bcst camera control systems, computer graphic systems; & video duplication service.

G

GAMPRODUCTS Inc., 4975 W. Pico Blvd., Los Angeles, CA 90019. Phone: (323) 935-4975. Fax: (323) 935-2002. Web Site: www.gamonline.com. Joseph N. Tawil, owner/gen mgr; Harry Beard, opns mgr.

Lighting equipment, portable & studio special effects & projections, control console, dimming & color, correction & diffusion filters, patterns (gobos).

GKM Manufacturing Corp., 47 Bridgewater St., Brooklyn, NY 11222. Fax: (718) 384-1325. E-mail: gkmmanuf@aol.com. Web Site: www.gkmmanuf.com. John D'Augelli, gen mgr.

Standard & custom broadcast racks, cabinets, panels, etc. Standard sloped consoles (metal), & related job shop activities.

G Prime Ltd., Radio City Sn., Box 1525, New York, NY 10101. Phone: (212) 765-3415. Fax: (212) 581-8938. E-mail: info@gprime.com. Web Site: www.gprime.com. Russ O. Hamm, pres.

Importer & distributor of European professional audio equipment for the bcst & recording industries.

Gala, (A division of Paco Corp). 3185 First Street, St. Hubert, PQ J3Y 8Y6. Canada. Phone: (450) 678-7226. Fax: (450) 678-4060. E-mail: Info@pacocorp.com. Web Site: www.pacocorp.com.

Es Condido, CA 92025, 655 Calle Ladra. Phone: (760) 738-5555. Richard R. Haller.

Theatrical rigging, revolving stages & orchestra lifts.

Galaxy Audio Inc., (dba Valley Audio). Box 16285, Wichita, KS 67216-0285. Phone: (316) 263-2852. Fax: (316) 263-0642. Web Site: www.galaxyaudio.com. Brock Jabara, CEO; Yule Jabara, natl sls mgr.

Microphone preamplifiers, loudspeaker, powered amplifiers, combiners, splitters & test equipment.

Garner Products, (division of Audiolab Electronics Inc.). 620 Commerce Dr., Suite C, Roseville 95678. Phone: (926) 784- 0200. Fax: (916) 784-1425. E-mail: info@garner-products.com. Web Site: www.garner-products.com. Ronald A. Stofan, pres.

Professional line of bulk tape degaussers for all formats of tape including: Beta SP, DAT 2" reels up to 16" diameters, hard drives, DLT media & degaussing svc.

Geac Libra, 1193 W. 2400 South., Suite C, Salt Lake City, UT 84119. Phone: (800) 453-3827. Fax: (801) 974-1900. E-mail: info@geac.com. Web Site: www.gcs.geac.com. Eric Schlor, sls.

Accounting software for radio, including billing affidavits & sls analysis.

Broadcasting & Cable Yearbook 2006

F-13

Equipment Manufacturers and Distributors Alphabetical Index

Gefen Inc., 6265 Variel Ave., Woodland Hills, CA 91367. Phone: (800) 545-6900. Phone: (818) 884-6294. Fax: (818) 884-3108. E-mail: gsinfo@gefen.com. Web Site: www.gefen.com. Hagai Gefen, pres; John Guzman, tech & sls.
Manufacturer of computer peripherals that enhance the studio environment. HDTV, KVM, USB, CAT-5 DVI, ADC extenders, switchers, converters, adapters, distribution amplifiers & cable.

General Atomics, 4949 Greencraig Ln., San Diego, CA 92123. Phone: (858) 522-8300. Fax: (858) 522-8301. Web Site: www.ga-esi.com. Phil Arneson, pres.
Terminal automation products, radiation, monitoring system, triqq and manufacturer of Maxwell high voltage capacitors & power supplies.

General Cable, 4 Tesseneer Dr., Highland Heights, KY 41076. Phone: (859) 572-8000. Fax: (859) 572-8458. Web Site: www.generalcable.com.
Copper, aluminum and fiberoptic wire and cable products for communications, energy, and electrical markets.

General Electric Co., 3135 Easton Tpke., Fairfield, CT 06431. Phone: (800) 626-2004. Phone: (203)373-2039. Fax: (203) 373-3198. Web Site: www.ge.com. E-mail: geinfo@www.ge.com.
Fort Lee, NJ 07024. CNBC & MSNBC, 2200 Fletcher Ave. Bill Bolste, pres.
New York, NY 10020. NBC, 30 Rockefeller Plaza. Phone: (212) 664-4444. Robert C. Wright, pres.
Cleveland, OH 44112, 4338 Nela Park. Phone: (216) 362-5600. Fax: (216) 266-2310. Keith T.S. Ward, quartz-stage studio production mgr.
NBC bcstg; CNBC & MSNBC; lighting products; Americom satellite; electrical distribution & control; intercast; MSNBC desktop video.

General Electrodynamics Corp., 8000 Calendar Rd., Arlington, TX 76001. Phone: (817) 572-0366. Fax: (817) 572-0373. Web Site: www.gecscales.com. Dick Davis, pres.
Tubes, TV cameras, electronics, aircraft weighing equipment, contract weighing svcs, truck scales, load scales.

Geneva Aviation Inc., 20021 80th Ave. S., Kent, WA 98032. Phone: (253) 395-9105. Fax: (253) 395-9150. E-mail: info@genevaaviation.com. Web Site: www.genevaaviation.com. Gary Hasson, pres.
Design, manufacture & instal of E.N.G. & microwave equipment for news helicopters.

Gennum Corp., Box 489, Station A, Burlington, ON L7R 3Y3. Canada. Phone: (905) 632-2996. Fax: (905) 632-2055. Web Site: www.gennum.com.
High performance integrated circuits, including switches & processing functions, for analog & digital video applications.

Gepco International Inc., 1770 Birchwood Ave., Des Plaines, IL 60018. Phone: (847) 795-9555. Fax: (847) 795-8770. E-mail: gepco@gepco.com. Web Site: www.gepco.com. Gary R. Geppert, pres; David Mecklenburger, CFO; Greg Hansen, VP sls mktg; Ken Bernd, inside sls mgr.
Burbank, CA 91502, 826 N. Lake St. Phone: (818) 894-3446. Fax: (818) 569-5226. Jeff Shorsher, western rgnl sls.
Audio cable & video cable in bulk or cut to length. Assemblies, boxes, connectors, patchbays. ADC, kings neutrix, switchcraft

Glentronix, 90 Nolan Ct., Unit 7, Markham, ON L3R 4L9. Canada. Phone: (905) 475-8494. Fax: (905) 475-0955. Web Site: www.glentronix.com.
Studio video equipment, audio jackfield & test equipment.

Global Microwave Systems Inc., 4141 Avenida de la Plata, Oceanside, CA 92056-8031. Phone: (760) 631-8021. Fax: (760) 631-8031. E-mail: gms@gmsinc.com. Web Site: www.gmsinc.com. Sam Nasiri, pres; Wayne Rogers, sls agent.
Subminiature & compact microwave transmitters/receivers for portable applications, ENG, P.O.V., hidden camera, ant systems for helicopters, autotrackers & fixed or portable use.

Globecomm Systems Inc., 45 Oser Ave., Hauppauge, NY 11788-3816. Phone: (631) 231-9800. Fax: (631) 231-1557. Web Site: www.globecommsystems.com. David Hershberg, CEO; Kenneth Miller, pres; F. Dugourd, Contact.
Earth station ground segments. Video Broadcasting Service; Content Delivery Service.

Alan Gordon Enterprises Inc., 5625 Melrose Ave., Hollywood, CA 90038. Phone: (323) 466-3561. Fax: (323) 871-2193. E-mail: info@alangordon.com. Web Site: www.alangordon.com. Grant Loucks, pres; Wayne Loucks, gen mgr; Don Sahlein, exec VP.
Professional motion picture & video equipment sls mf & rental, & video equipment.

Gorman-Redlich Manufacturing Co., 257 W. Union St., Athens, OH 45701. Phone: (740) 593-3150. Fax: (740) 592-3898. Web Site: www.gorman-redlich.com. E-mail: jmg@gorman-redlich.com. James T. Gorman, owner.
EAS encoders, decoders, encoder-decoders & receivers, digital antennas monitors, NOAA weather radios.

Graham-Patten Systems Inc., 13366 Grass Valley Ave., Grass Valley, CA 95945-9098. Phone: (530) 273-8412. Phone: (800) 422-6662. Fax: (530) 273-7458. Web Site: www.gpsys.com.
Digital audio mixers, digital audio systemization products.

Grant Tower, Inc., 13064 Wisner Ave., Grant, MI 49327. Phone: (231) 834-5665. Fax: (231) 834-7870. Terry L. Sharp Jr., pres; Walter Knoch, office mgr.
Bcst tower erection & maintenance service.

Gray Engineering Laboratories Inc., 504 W. Chapman Ave., Suite O, Orange, CA 92668. Phone: (714) 997-4151. Fax: (714) 997-1939. Web Site: www.grayengineeringlabs.com. Scott R. Gray, pres.
SMPTE time-code generators & readers, safe area generators, video-assisted film editing components.

Great Lakes Data Systems, Inc., 5954 Priestly Dr., Carlsbad, CA 92008. Phone: (760) 753-1024. Fax: (760) 753-2538. E-mail: sales@cablebilling.com. Web Site: www.cablebilling.com. J. Alonzo Rosado, pres; Laura Rosado, VP sls/mktg.
Beaver Dam, WI 53916, Box 295. Phone: (920) 887-7651. Fax: (920) 887-7653.
Affordable PC/Network billing & subscriber mgmt systems. Addressable interface, PPV, ARU, ANI, Hotel PPV. Training, data conversion & toll-free support.

Greenberg Teleprompting, 115 S. Olive St., Orange, CA 92866. Phone: (818) 838-4437. Fax: (818) 838-0447. Web Site: www.greenprompt.com. Jim Estochin, owner.
Color computerized electronic teleprompting for all bcst & industrial uses.

Group One Ltd., 70 Sea Ln., Farmingdale, NY 11735. Phone: (561) 249-1399. Fax: (516) 249-8870. E-mail: jackk@g1limited.com. Web Site: www.g1limited.com.
Exclusive distributor for a number of prominent audio & lighting products including: MC2, Celestion, XTA Electronics, Elektralite, Pulsar, Blue Sky.

Gyrocams Systems, 8100 15th St. E., Sarasota, FL 34243. Phone: (941) 355-3206. Fax: (941) 355-3417. E-mail: info@gyrocamsystems.com. Web Site: www.gyrocamsystems.com. Ken Sanborn, pres/CEO; Joe Stark, VP sls; Stefanie Kowitt, exec VP.
Manufacturer of the Gyrocam-gyrostablized camera systems for aircraft, boats or vehicles. High Definition Cameras and V700 watt searchlight also available.

H

HM Electronics Inc., 14110 Stowe Dr., Poway, CA 92064-7147. Phone: (858) 535-6000. Fax: (858) 452-7207. Web Site: www.hme.com. H. Y. Miyahira, pres/CEO; J. M. Hughes, pres NSI division; Chuck Miyahira, VP mktg; Mitzi Dominguez, VP finance admin; Barnie Wallace, opns VP.
Intercom systems, security surveillance systems, nationwide field service & installation.

Hardigg Cases, (A division of Hardigg Industries Inc.). Box 201, 147 N. Main St., South Deerfield, MA 01373-0201. Phone: (413) 665-2163. Fax: (413) 665-8330. E-mail: cases@hardigg.com. Web Site: www.hardigg.com. James S. Hardigg, pres.
Reusable shipping cases. Rugged 19 rack, shock-mounted enclosures. Bcst equipment cases.

Harman International Industries Inc., (A subsidiary of JBL Professional). 8500 Balboa Blvd., Northridge, CA 91329. Phone: (818) 893-8411. Fax: (818) 892-9590. Web Site: www.harman.com. Dr. Sidney Harman, pres; Bernard Girod, CEO.
Manufacturer of audio signal processing equipment designed for sound reinforcement, recording & bcstg.

Harmonic Inc., 549 Baltic Way, Sunnyvale, CA 94089. Phone: (408) 542-2500. Fax: (408) 542-2510. Web Site: www.harmonicinc.com. Anthony J. Ley, pres.
Fiber-optic & digital transmission systems for cable TV, including transmitters, receivers, return path equipment & network mgmt hardware & software.

Harris Automation Solutions, 1134 E. Arques Ave., Sunnyvale, CA 94085. Phone: (408) 990-8200. Fax: (408) 990-8250. E-mail: sales@harris.com. Web Site: www.harris.com. Jim Wood, mgr.
Wantagh, NY 11793, Bos 3200. Phone: (516) 783-6026. Martin Frange, dir sls, northeast & southeast rgn.
Issaquah, WA 98027, 700 NW Gilman Blvd, 133-227. Phone: (425) 837-3799. Brian Lay, dir sls, western & central rgn.
Louth is a supplier of media management and automation system: for broadcast and cable television.

Harris Corp., Broadcast Communications Division, 4393 Digital Way, Mason, OH 45040. Phone: (513) 459-3400. Phone: (513) 459-3547 (Jackie Broo, mktg). Fax: (513) 701-5315. E-mail: broadcast@harris.com. Web Site: www.harris.com. Bruce Allen, pres/gen mgr.
Sunnyvale, CA 94086, 1134 E. Arques Ave. Phone: (408) 990-8200.
Quincy, IL 62305. Harris Corp., Broadcast Communications Division, Box 4290, 3200 Wismann Ln. Phone: (217) 222-8200. Fax: (217) 222-7041.
Supplier of products, systems, svc & automation solutions for the broadcast industry.

Harris Corp., Broadcast Division, Box 4290, 3200 Wismann Ln., Quincy, IL 62305-4290. Phone: (217) 222-8200. Fax: (217) 221-7085. Web Site: www.harris.com. Bob Weirather, dir TV product line; Jack O'Dear, dir international sls; Gaylen C. Evans, dir N.American field sls.
South Glens Falls, NY 12803, Box 1179, 10373 Saratoga Rd. Phone: (518) 793-2181. Fax: (518) 793-7423. Rich Redmond, sls mgr. (Northeast U.S. radio sls).
Federal Way, WA 98003, 33430 13th Pl. S, Suite 205A. Phone: (206) 874-7444. Fax: (206) 874-8866. Cal Vandegrift, sls rep. (Northwest U.S. radio sls).
Digital radio & TV transmission equipment, service, tower studies, training, turnkey RF systems.

Harris Corporation Co., 107 Gilbert Rd., Saratoga Springs, NY 12866. Phone: (518) 226-0918. Fax: (518) 226-0741. Web Site: www.harris.com. Brian Szewczyk, mgr.
Plano, TX 75023, Box 867717. Phone: (214) 612-2053. (800) 729-0494. Fax: (214) 612-2145. "Doc" Masoomian, pres.
Complete AM & FM bcst systems—equipment sls, service & instal. Bcst systems intergrators.

Harris-Farinon, 350 Twin Dolphin Dr., Redwood Shores, CA 94065. Phone: (650) 594-3000. Fax: (650) 594-3110. Web Site: www.harris.com.
Microwave for intercity relay & STLs.

Harrison by GLW, 1024 Firestone Pkwy., LaVergne, TN 37086. Phone: (615) 641-7200. Fax: (615) 641-7224. E-mail: info@glw.com. Web Site: www.glw.com. William B. Owen, pres; Gary Thielman, advanced product mgr.
Analog & digital audio mixing consoles for on-air bcst, production, video & film sound postproduction, live sound & music recording.

HAVE Inc., 309 Power Ave., Hudson, NY 12534-2448. Phone: (518) 828-2000. Phone: (800) 999-4283. Fax: (518) 828-2008. E-mail: have@haveinc.com. Web Site: www.haveinc.com. Nancy Gordon, pres; Paul Swedenburg, VP.
Professional audio & videotape, equipment, accessories & supplies. Belden, Canare, Mogami cable; connectors & adaptors. Duplication & postproduction service.

Henry Engineering, 503 Key Vista Dr., Sierra Madre, CA 91024. Phone: (626) 355-3656. Fax: (626) 355-0077. Web Site: www.henryeng.com. Hank Landsberg, pres.
The Matchbox & other audio interface, control interface & digital audio storage devices.

Hessler Enterprises Inc., 106 Susan Dr., #1, Elkins Park, PA 19027. Phone: (215) 379-2300. Fax: (215) 663-8839. Web Site: www.hessler.com. Ed Hessler, pres; Brian Hessler, VP.
Produces bcstg forms including script sets, contracts, program logs, invoices, labels, A/R statements & computer stock paper.

Hewlett Packard USA, 20555 State Highway 249, Houston, TX 77070. Phone: (281) 370-0670. Fax: (281) 514-1740. Web Site: www.hewlettpackard.com. Michael Capellas, chmn.
Manufactures interactive computer systems.

Equipment Manufacturers and Distributors Alphabetical Index

High Tech Industries, 298 N. Smith Ave., Corona, CA 91720. Phone: (909) 279-5770. Fax: (909) 279-5773. Web Site: www.customstudio.com. Douglas J. Kanczuzewski, gen mgr.

Custom & standard production, postproduction & computer racks for TV & radio.

Highway Information Systems, Inc., 4021 Stirrup Creek Dr., Suite 100, Durham, NC 27703. Phone: (919) 361-2479. Phone: (800) 849-4447. Fax: (800) 849-2947. E-mail: sales@high. Web Site: www.highwayinfo.com. Bruce Reimer, gen mgr; Mike Corbett, gen sls mgr.

Manufacturer of travelers information stations & highway advisory bcst systems on low-power AM radio for motorists.

Hignite Tower Service, 9945 Arkansas St., Bellflower, CA 90706. Phone: (562) 925-1951. Fax: (562) 925-6171. John Hignite, owner; Jackie Hignite, office mgr.

Tower engrg, erection, fabrication, maintenance & painting.

Hipotronics Inc., Box 414, 1650 Rt. 22, Brewster, NY 10509. Phone: (845) 279-8091. Fax: (845) 279-2467. Web Site: www.hipotronics.com. Gary Amato, gen mgr.

High-voltage DC power supplies & industrial grade voltage regulators for medium-to-high-power applications.

Hitachi Denshi America, Ltd., 150 Crossway Park Dr., Woodbury, NY 11797. Phone: (516) 921-7200. Fax: (516) 496-3718. E-mail: info@hdac.com. Web Site: www.hdal.com. M. Matsuhashi, pres; J. Breitenbucher, VP; S. Moran, rgnl sls mgr.

Torrance, CA 90501, 371 Van Ness Way. Phone: (310) 328-6116. David Morris, rgnl sls mgr.

Bcst, professional & industrial cameras, monitor, test & measurement equipment.

Hoagland Instrument, Inc., 78 Stone Pl., Melrose, MA 02176-0004. Phone: (781) 665-4428. Fax: (781) 665-3855. Web Site: www.hoagland-instrument.com. Debbie D'Ambrosio, pres.

Thermal & electronic time delay relays.

Hoffend & Sons Inc., 66 School St., Victor, NY 14564. Phone: (585) 924-5000. Fax: (585) 924-0545. Web Site: www.hoffend.net. Donald A. Hoffend, CEO; Peter Hoffend, pres.

Engrg, mfg & instal of studio rigging systems, motorized hoists, tracks, turntables & controls.

Hogg & Davis Inc., Box 405, 3800 Eagle Loop, Odell, OR 97044. Phone: (541) 354-1001. Fax: (541) 354-1080. E-mail: info@hoggdavis.com. Web Site: www.hoggdavis.com. F. Neil Hogg, pres.

Cable reels, cable reel trailers, pole tongs, cable sheaves, break-away reels, 36" & 52" tensioners underground puller, 4 drum puller.

Hollywood Rentals Production Services, 19731 Nordhoff St., North Ridge, CA 91324. Phone: (818) 407-7800. Fax: (818) 407-7875. Anil Sharma, pres.

Charlotte, NC 28216, 9100-C Perimeter Woods Dr. Phone: (740) 597-1308. Jeff Pentek.

Production equipment & vehicles for film & video (rental); sale of new equipment & expendable items.

Hollywood Vaults Inc., 742 N. Seward St., Hollywood, CA 90038. Phone: (323) 461-6464. Phone: (800) 569-5336. Fax: (323) 461-6479. Web Site: www.hollywoodvaults.com. David Wexler, pres; Julianna Wexler, VP.

Santa Barbara, CA 93103. (Corporate office of Hollywood Vaults Inc.), 1780 Prospect Ave. Phone: (805) 569-5336. Chris Robinson, exec admin.

State-of-the-art film & tape storage vault. Secure, climate-controlled, 24-hour self service access.

Homalite, 11 Brookside Dr., Wilmington, DE 19804. Phone: (302) 652-3686. Fax: (302) 652-4578. Web Site: www.homalite.com. Robert Cahill, pres.

Manufactures low-reflectance, contrast enhancement filters for use on CRTs, LEDs & other forms of info display.

Honeywell Airport Systems, 2162 Union Pl., Simi Valley, CA 93065. Phone: (805) 581-5591. Fax: (805) 581-5032. Ed Wheeler, VP opns; Steve Sortillion, dir opns.

Tower, obstruction lighting & controls.

Hoodman Corp., 20445 Gramercy Pl., Suite 201, Torrance, CA 90501. Phone: (310) 222-8608. Phone: (800) 818-3946 (US). Fax: (310) 222-8623. E-mail: lou@hoodmanusa.com. Web Site: www.hoodmanusa.com. Mike Schmidt, pres.

TV sun shades/monitor hoods for glare-free outdoor viewing & video carts.

Horita, Box 3993, Mission Viejo, CA 92690. Phone: (949) 489-0240. Fax: (949) 489-0242. E-mail: horita@horita.com. Web Site: www.horita.com. Gerald Hester, pres; Christopher Lovallo, sls.

SMPTE time code readers, generators, inserters, PC tape logging software; color bar, black, sync generators; titler, distribution amplifiers, audio meter, matte generator.

Hotbox Digital, 367 N. Hwy. 101, Solana Beach, CA 92075. Phone: (858) 292-8520. Fax: (858) 292-1812. Cam MacMillan, owner/exec produceer.

Design & production of bcst 3-D computer graphics. Logo animation, stn packages. All tape formats supported. Producers of Subito Studio Video Graphic Library.

Hotronic Inc., 1875 S. Winchester Blvd., Campbell, CA 95008. Phone: (408) 378-3883. Fax: (408) 378-3888. Web Site: www.hotronics.com. Andy Ho, pres; Linda Chang, sls & mktg mgr.

Time base corrector & frame synchronizer with freeze frame/field, digital effects, & 8x2 Asynchronized Router etc.

I

ICM (International Crystal Mfg.), 10 N. Lee Ave., Box 1768, Oklahoma City, OK 73101. Phone: (405) 236-3741. Fax: (405) 235-1904. E-mail: freeland@icmfg.com. Web Site: www.icmfg.com. Beth Freeland, pres; Royden Freeland, chief engr.

Precision electronic crystals, crystal filters, clock oscillators, TCXO's, VCXO's.

IMS (Interactive Market Systems Inc.), 770 Broadway, 15th Fl., New York, NY 10003. Phone: (646) 654-5900. Fax: (646) 654-5901. E-mail: sales@imsusa.com. Web Site: www.imsmediasolutions.com. Melissa Jacobson, VP.

Oslo, Norway N-0133, MMI Posst Boks 9143, Gronland. Phone: (011) 472-295-4700. Fax: (011) 472-217-1281.

Toronto, ON M5S 2Z7 Canada, 101 Bloor St. W, Suite 301. Phone: (416) 961-2840. Fax: (416) 644-3530.

Hong Kong Central Hongkong, 18/F, One International Finance Centre, 1 Harbour View St. Phone: (011) 852 2166 8683. Fax: (011) 852 2166 8875.

Johannesburg 2000 South Africa. Markanal, Suite 203 Willowbrook, Willowbrook Close, Melrose No. Phone: (011) 2711-447-7843. Fax: (011) 2411-447-7499.

London WC2 H8TJ United Kingdom, 189 Shaftesbury Avenue. Phone: (011) 44 20 7420 9200. Fax: (011) 44 20 7420 9222.

Los Angeles, CA 90028, 6255 Sunset Blvd., 19th Fl. Phone: (323) 817-1530. Fax: (323) 817-1536.

Chicago, IL 60606, 200 W. Jackson Blvd., 25th Fl, Suite 1600. Phone: (312) 583-5354. (312) 583-5354.

Sandy, UT 84070-2008, 49 W. 9000 S. Phone: (801) 352-1515. Fax: (801) 352-0707.

IMS is the leading international provider of information systems & solutions for the media industry. IMS systems & software form an integral part of media & marketing decisions around the world. Media professionals trust IMS for innovative technologies, an unparalled global perspective, & valuable insights.

IPITEK, 2330 Faraday Ave., Carlsbad, CA 92008. Phone: (760) 438-1010. Fax: (760) 438-2462. E-mail: sales@ipetk.com. Web Site: www.ipitek.com. Michael M. Salour, chmn/CEO; Horace Tsiang, VP sls.

IRIS Technologies Inc., R.R. 12, Box 36, Westmoreland Industrial Pk., Greensburg, PA 15601. Phone: (724) 832-9855. Fax: (724) 832-8999. Jerry Salandro, pres/CEO.

Bountiful, VT 84010, 563 W 500 South. Phone: (801) 296-8250. Fax: (801) 296-8248. (Engineering).

Video Commander icon based routing, iNED & SmartPort product lines which allow complete headend control from anywhere in the world.

ITI Electronics Inc., 214 Little Falls Road, Fairfield, NJ 07004-2637. Phone: (973) 890-7888. Fax: (973) 890-8774. E-mail: itielect@aol.com. Robert A Stein, pres.

Connectorized & Prewired jackfields; patch panels; telephone line amplifiers; and other series 400 and 10 line cards.

ITT Cannon Electric, 666 E. Dyer Rd., Santa Ana, CA 92707. Phone: (714) 557-4700. Fax: (714) 628-2142. Web Site: www.ittcannon.com.

Electronic connectors & interconnect systems & info card technology suppliers to a var of industries, including bcst & data communications companies.

Identix, 5600 Rowland Road, Minnetonka, MN 55343. Phone: (952) 932-0888. Fax: (952) 932-7181. Web Site: www.identix.com. Bob MacCashin, CEO.

Identix is a leading biometrics solutions provider with proven & cost-effective verification security for applications including banking, healthcare, government, & access control.

Ikegami Electronics (U.S.A.) Inc., 37 Brook Ave., Maywood, NJ 07607. Phone: (201) 368-9171. Fax: (201) 569-1626. Web Site: www.ikegami.com. E-mail: sales@ikegami.com. Alan Keil, engrg VP; Teri Zastrow, mktg dir & sls dir.

Ft. Lauderdale, FL 33309, 5200 N.W. 33rd Ave, Suite 111.

Manhattan Beach, CA 90273, 2631 Manhattan Beach Blvd. Phone: (310) 297-1900. Fax: (310) 536-9550.

Elmhurst, IL 60126, 747 Church Rd, Unit C1.

Waxahachie, TX 75167, 773 Bearden.

Bcst/professional video cameras, monitors, microwave equipment.

Illbruck Inc., 3800 Washington Ave. N., Minneapolis, MN 55412. Phone: (612) 520-3620. Phone: (800) 662-0032. Fax: (612) 521-5639. E-mail: sales@illbruck-sonex.com. Web Site: www.illbruck-sonex.com.

Sonex® accoustical products including wall panels & ceiling tiles.

Illumination Dynamics Inc., (A division of Arri, Inc.). 3823 Barringer Dr., Charlotte, NC 28217. Phone: (704) 679-9400. Fax: (704) 679-9420. Web Site: www.illuminationdynamics.com. Steve Hipsley, VP; Carly Barber, pres; Jeff Pentek, COO; Maria Carpenter, dir mktg.

Pacoima, CA 91331, 10232 Glenoaks Blvd. Phone: (818) 686-6400. Fax: (818) 686-6776. Craig Chiapuzio, Dir. of Operations.

Complete line of lighting, grip power distributors, generators for feature film, commercials, bcst & special events.

The Image Group Post, LLC, (Formerly MTI/The Image Group, Inc.). 885 2nd Ave., New York, NY 10017. Phone: (212) 548-7700. Fax: (212) 355-0523. Web Site: www.image-group.com. Charles Pontillo, chmn; Willie Sheehy, pres.

New York, NY 10017, 305 E. 46th St. Phone: (212) 548-4400.

Production & postproduction svcs, including remotes, computer animation, scenic svcs, satellite transmissions & networking.

Image Logic Corp., 6807 Brennon Ln., Chevy Chase, MD 20815. Phone: (301) 907-8891. Fax: (301) 652-6584. E-mail: info@imagelogic.com. Web Site: www.imagelogic.com. Woodrow Landay, pres.

Log producer, automated videotape logging system: Autocaption, automated desktop closed-captioning & sub-titling system.

Image Video, (A division of 1077541 Ontario Ltd). 1620 Midland Ave., Toronto, ON M1P 3C2. Canada. Phone: (416) 750-8872. Fax: (416) 750-8015. E-mail: sales@imagevideo.com. Web Site: www.imagevideo.com. Andy A. Vanags, pres; Dave Russell, VP.

Analog & digital audio & video routing switchers, master control, digital audio delay units & RGB clipper units, under monitor tally display systems, tally mappers, multi-video display systems.

Imagine Products Inc., 12220 N. Meridian St., Suite 130, Carmel, IN 46032-6936. Phone: (317) 843-0706. Fax: (317) 843-0807. E-mail: imagine@imagineproducts.com. Web Site: www.imagineproducts.com. Dan Montgomery, pres/CEO; M. Jane Montgomery, VP.

PC software/hardware for logging, video library, EDL transfers & tape libraries. Timecode readers & VTR controls.

Imaging Automation, 25 Constitution Dr., Bedford, NH 03110. Phone: (603) 471-9325. Fax: (603) 471-9326. Web Site: www.imaginguto.com. Bill Thalheimer, pres.

Supplier of optical-based systems for storing & retrieving documents & images.

Industrial Acoustics Co., Inc., 1160 Commerce Ave., Bronx, NY 10462. Phone: (718) 931-8000. Fax: (718) 863-1138. Web Site: www.industrialacoustics.com. Kenneth DeLasho, VP.

Staines, Middlesex TW18 4XB, Walton House, Central Trading Estate. Simon White, dir mktg.

Wanchai, Hopewell Centre, 183 Queen's Rd. E, Rm. 2501, 25/F. Phone: 557-8633. Alvin Leung Jr.

Complete accu-tone II acoustical environments for bcst industry plus noise-lock sound control doors, windows, walls & silencers.

Equipment Manufacturers and Distributors Alphabetical Index

Industrial Equipment Representatives (IER), 1685 Precision Park Ln., Suite E, San Diego, CA 92173. Phone: (619) 428-2261. Phone: (619) 428-2262. Fax: (619) 428-3483. Web Site: www.ier-broadcast.com. Alex Rodriguez, gen sls mgr; Juan Biosca, gen mgr.

Bcst, TV & recording studios equipment & supplies.

Industrial/Midwec Capacitor Corp., 100511 Airport Rd., Scottsbluff, NE 69361. Phone: (308) 632-4128. Fax: (308) 632-4128. Mike Farnett, plant mgr.

Film, oil & electrolytic capacitors; specialty toroids & filter networks.

Innovision Optics Inc., 1719 21st St., Santa Monica, CA 90404. Phone: (310) 453-4866. Fax: (310) 453-4677. E-mail: innovision@innovision-optics.com. Web Site: www.innovisionoptics.com. Mark Centkowski, pres.

Camera support & robotic camera shuttle systems aececones, spintec, charley & custom camera installations

Inovonics Inc., 1305 Fair Ave., Santa Cruz, CA 95060. Phone: (831) 458-0552. Fax: (831) 458-0554. E-mail: info@inovon.com. Web Site: www.inovon.com. James B. Wood,.

Manufacturers of bcst audio signal processing, encoding/decoding, sound recording & instrumentation equipment.

Inscriber Technology Corporation, 26 Peppler St., Waterloo, ON N2J 3C4. Canada. Phone: (519) 570-9111. Fax: (519) 570-9140. E-mail: info@inscriber.com. Web Site: www.inscriber.com. Dan Mance, pres; Mike Bernhardt, sls dir; Randy Fowlie, COO.

1431 EE Aalsmeer. Inscriber Technology-European Rep Office, Zijdsraat 72. Phone: +31-297-362030. Fax: +31-297-380939. David Hughes, dir European oper.

Chiyoda-ky, Tokyo 100-0005. Inscriber Technology-Asian Rep Office, Level 9, AIG Bldg, 1-1-3 Marunouchi. Phone: 81-3-5288-5237. Fax: 81-3-5288-5111. Doug Strable, dir oper - Asia Pacific.

Software for desktop and broadcast video markets, including Character generators, digital stores and Video Server/Sequencers

Insulated Wire Inc. Microwave Products Division, 20 E. Franklin St., Danbury, CT 06810. Phone: (203) 791-1999. Fax: (203) 748-5217. Saverio T. Bruno, pres.

High-frequency, low-loss microwave cable & cable assemblies featuring IW's Tuf-Flex Series to 60 GHz.

Integrys Holdings L.L.C., 770 Pelham Rd., Greenville, SC 29615. Phone: (864) 297-9290. Fax: (864) 297-9213. Web Site: www.integrysllc.com. William C. Cox, pres/CEO.

Subscriber mgmt and billing system.

Intelligent Media Technology, 9460 Delegates Dr., Suite 108, Orlando, FL 32837. Phone: (407) 855-8181. Fax: (407) 855-1653. Bob Proctor, engrg dir.

Digital audio snakes, A/D conversion & transmission, D/A conversion receiver/repeaters, multimedia fiber optic transmission systems (audio/video/voice/data).

Intelliprompt, 9037 Lucerne Ave., Culver City, CA 90232. Phone: (310) 837-0389. Fax: (310) 837-0806. E-mail: intelliprompt@attbi.com. Web Site: www.intelliprompt.com. Tony Finetti, W. coast opns; Ernest Boyden, pres.

Toronto, ON M5V 2R8 Canada, 44 Tecumseth St. Phone: (416) 504-9535. Ernest Boyden, pres.

New York, NY 10036, 630 9th Ave, Suite 970. Phone: (212) 765-0555. Ernest Boyden, pres.

Computerized color prompters for film, video, ENG, & live speaking situations. Quick editing, telephone transfers.

Interface Media Group, 1233 20th St. N.W., Washington, DC 20036. Phone: (202) 861-0500. Fax: (202) 296-4492. E-mail: info@interfacevideo.com. Web Site: www.interfacevideo.com. Tom Angell; Adam Hurst, VP.

FACILITY: film transfer/location/studio/motion control, Avid/interformat digital edit, audio, graphics, dubs, Vyvx/3D2/DGS/satellite, standards conversion.

Interlogix, 280 Huyler St., South Hackensack, NJ 07606. Phone: (201) 489-9595. Fax: (201) 489-0111.

Closed circuit TV cameras, monitors & accessories, specializing in covert surveillance cameras.

International Cinema Equipment, Division of Magna-Tech Electronic Co., Inc. 100 N.E. 39th St., Miami, FL 33147. Phone: (305) 573-7339. Fax: (305) 573-8101. E-mail: iceco@aol.com. Web Site: www.iceco.com. Steve Krams, pres; Dara Reusch, VP.

16mm, 35mm, 70mm film projection equipment, film-to-tape transfer equipment, sound systems, editing equipment.

International Datacasting Corp., 2680 Queensview Dr., Ottawa, ON K2B 8H6. Canada. Phone: (613) 596-4120. Fax: (613) 596-4863. Fax: (613) 596-9208. E-mail: corporate@intldata.ca. Web Site: www.intldata.ca. Ron W. Clifton, pres/CEO; Denzil Doyle, chmn.

Rsch, dev, manufacture & mktg of value added high speed digital data transmission network & svcs.

International Electro-Magnetics, 350 N. Eric Dr., Palatine, IL 60067. Phone: (847) 358-4622. Fax: (847) 358-4623. E-mail: mail@iemmag.com. Web Site: www.iemmag.com. Anthony Pretto, pres.

Standard replacement & custom recording heads for audio, video & film.

Intersil Corp. Headquarters, 675 Trade Zone Blvd., Milpitas, CA 95035. Phone: (408) 935-4300. Fax: (408) 945-9305. Web Site: www.intersil.com. Rich Beyer, pres/CEO; Dan Heneghan, CFO.

Tsimshatsui, Kowlon, NO Hongkong, The Gateway, 9 Canton Rd., Suite 1506, 15F Tower 6. Phone: +852 2709 7600.

Yokohama, NO 220-5820 Japan, Queen Tower A, 12F 2-3-1, Minato-Mirai, Nishi-ku. Phone: +81 45 682 5820. Fax: +81 45 682 5821.

Palm Bay, FL 32905, 2401 Palm Bay Rd. Phone: (321) 724-7000. (888) 486-3774. E-mail: investor@intersil.com. Web Site: www.intersil.com.

ICs for wireless networking, high performance analog-flat panel displays, optical storage (CD,DVD recordaable) & power mgmt.

Isaia & Co., 4650 Lankershim Blvd., North Hollywood, CA 91602. Phone: (818) 752-3104. Fax: (818) 752-3105. Web Site: www.isaia.com. Roy N. Isaia, pres.

Remote camera heads "Power-Pod," "Runford Baker" tripods & heads, camera cranes "Egripment"—"Cinerent carbon fiber," used cameras.

J

J and R Moviola Inc., 1135 N. Mansfield Ave., Los Angeles, CA 90038. Phone: (323) 467-3107. Fax: (213) 466-2201. Web Site: www.movieola.com. Joe Paskal, pres; Randy Paskal, exec VP.

Denver, CO 80238, 8000 E. 40th Ave. Phone: (303) 321-1099. Randy Urlik, exec VP.

Chicago, IL 60610, 416 W. Ontario. Phone: (312) 787-0622. Jeff McNeir, VP.

New York, NY 10036, 636 11th Ave. Phone: (212) 247-0972. Bob Herman, VP.

Film editing equipment, film & video shipping & storage, film-to-video transfer machine.

JBL Professional, Box 2200, 8500 Balboa Blvd., Northridge, CA 91329. Phone: (818) 894-8850. Fax: (818) 830-1220. Web Site: www.jblpro.com. E-mail: info@jblpro.com. Mark Gander, VP.

Manufacturers of loudspeaker systems for bcstg, recording studios, theaters, concerts, stadiums & other applications.

The J-Lab Co., Box 6530, Malibu, CA 90264. Phone: (310) 457-4090. Fax: (310) 457-4494. Web Site: www.j-lab.com. Jerry LaBarbera, pres.

Component accessories, battery-operated video, audio DAs, camera controls, variable speed shutter devices & portable switchers.

JNJ Industries Inc., 290 Beaver St., Suite 303, Franklin, MA 02038. Phone: (508) 553-0529. Fax: (508) 553-9973. E-mail: sales@jnj-industries.com. Web Site: www.jnj-industries.com. Jack Volpe, pres; Gail Howe, VP; Bob Enterkin, dir mktg.

CFC & HCFC free solvents, presaturated cloth wipes, spray bottles, dry cloth wipes, lens wipes; aqueous chemistries & ultra-sonic cleaning machines.

JOA Cartridge Service, 448 E. Hancock St., Lansdale, PA 19446. Phone: (215) 362-8796. Fax: (215) 368-2336. E-mail: mmolyneaux_joa@yahoo.com. Mark P. Molyneaux, owner.

Bcst audiotape cartridges, audio, videotape & cassettes, tape accessories, DAT tape & cassettes, data storage diskettes & cassettes, optical disks, recordable CDs & reloading service.

JSB Service Co., 204 S. Bayard Ave., Waynesboro, VA 22980. Phone: (540) 949-5899. Fax: (540) 949-5863. Web Site: www.jsbservice.com. Joseph S. Brumbelow, pres/CEO.

Repair, resale of microwave communication devices, receivers, transmitters, solid state sources, amplifiers. Manufacturer of microwave components & modules. Manufacturer of miniature dielectric resonant oscillators, & VCO.

JVC Professional Products Company, 1700 Valley Rd., Wayne, NJ 07470. Phone: (973) 317-5000. Fax: (973) 317-5030. Web Site: www.jvc.com/pro. E-mail: proinfo@jvc.com. Kirk Hirota, pres; Bob Mueller, CEO & exec VP.

Cypress, CA 90630, 5665 Corporate Ave. Phone: (714) 229-8024. Eric Rosenberg, rgnl sls mgr.

Aurora, IL 60504-8149, 705 Enterprise St. Phone: (630) 851-7809. Chris Dalaly, branch mgr.

Wayne, NJ 07470, 1700 Valley Rd. Phone: (973) 317-5000. Paul Kasparian, branch mgr.

Plasmas; full line of professional video equipment including digital VTRs cameras, monitors & projectors.

Jampro Antennas/RF Systems Inc., 6340 Skycreek Dr., Sacramento, CA 95828. Phone: (916) 383-1177. Fax: (916) 383-1182. E-mail: jampro@jampro.com. Web Site: www.jampro.com. Alex Perchevitch, pres; Doug McCabe, VP.

Manufacturers of TV & FM bcst antennas, combiners, filters & a complete line of rigid coaxial transmission line.

Jennings Technology Co., 970 McLaughlin Ave., San Jose, CA 95122. Phone: (408) 292-4025. Fax: (408) 286-1789. E-mail: sales@jenningstech.com. Web Site: www.jenningstech.com. Steve Randazzo, pres; J. Horton, controller.

High-voltage vacuum & gas capacitors; relays, switches, single- & three-phase contactors & instruments.

Jensen Tools, 7815 S. 46th St., Phoenix, AZ 85044. Phone: (602) 453-3169. Phone: (800) 366-9662. Fax: (602) 438-1690. E-mail: jensen@stanleyworks.com. Web Site: www.jensentools.com. Bridget Marnocha, pres.

Electronic tool kits & cases, tools, test equipment.

Jensen Transformers Inc., 7135 Hayvenhurst Ave., Van Nuys, CA 91406. Phone: (818) 374-5857. Fax: (818) 374-5856. E-mail: info@jensen-transformers.com. Web Site: www.jensen transformers.com. Bill Whitlock, pres.

Audio transformers, ISO-MAX audio & video ground isolation boxes

E.F. Johnson Co., (A division of Transcript International), 299 Johnson Ave., Waseca, MN 56093. Phone: (800) 328-3911. Phone: (507) 835-6222. Fax: (507) 835-6283. Web Site: www.efjohnson.com. Michael Jalbert, CEO.

Manufacturer, marketer of radio communication products, svcs & systems.

K

K&H Products Ltd (Porta-Brace), Box 249, North Bennington, VT 05257. Phone: (802) 442-8171. Fax: (802) 442-9118. E-mail: info@portabrace.com. Web Site: www.portabrace.com. Robert Howe, pres; John Fairley, plant mgr.

Soft carrying cases for professional portable video/audio equipment.

KES, 101 Merritt Ave., Iron Mountain, MI 49801. Phone: (906) 774-1755. Fax: (906) 774-6117. Web Site: www.cciinc.us. Bob Edberg, gen mgr; Randy Proudfit, tech sls rep.

Full line of broadband system supplies, including everything from the headend to converters, for fiber as well as coaxial.

Kahn Communications Inc., 501 Fifth Ave., Suite 2002, New York, NY 10017. Phone: (212) 983-6765. Leonard R. Kahn, pres.

Carle Place, NY 11514, 338 Westbury Ave. Phone: (516) 222-2221. Leonard R. Kahn, pres.

AM stereo; POWER-side(TM) & Flatterer(TM) systems & satellite system & Symmetra-Peak(TM); Cam-D (TM).

Kalun Communications Inc., 44 Larkfield Dr., Toronto, ON M3B 2H1. Canada. Phone: (416) 410-4138. Fax: (416) 410-4138. Paul Wong, engrg dir.

RF test equipment including wideband sweep generators, sweep comparator, switched attenuator, return loss bridge, detector & headend equipment for ATSC

Kangaroo Products Inc., 10845 Wheatlands Ave., Suite C, Santee, CA 92071-2856. Phone: (619) 562-9696. Fax: (619) 449-7244. E-mail: sales@kangarooproducts.com. Steve Leiserson, pres; Nancy Byrd, VP.

Custom contract carrying cases.

Kathrein Inc., Scala Division, Box 4580, Medford, OR 97501. Phone: (541) 779-6500. Fax: (541) 779-6575. E-mail: broadcast@kathrein.com. Web Site: www.kathrein-scala.com. Manfred Muenzel, pres; Judy Young, sls; Michael Bach, sls engr; Mike Johnson, sls engr.

Equipment Manufacturers and Distributors Alphabetical Index

Antennas & filters, low to full power, includes STL/TSL, LPTV, CATV, RPU, translator & FM/TV monitoring. Custom patterns our specialty.

Kay Industries Inc., 604 N. Hill St., South Bend, IN 46617. Phone: (574) 236-6220. Fax: (574) 289-5932. E-mail: phasemaster@kayind.com. Web Site: www.kayind.com. Larry Katz, natl sls mgr.

Rotary phase converters for single phase to three phase power.

Key West Technology, 14563 W. 96th Terr., Lenexa, KS 66215. Phone: (800) 331-2019. Phone: (913) 492-4666. Fax: (913) 322-1864. E-mail: sales@keywesttechnology.com. Web Site: www.keywesttechnology.com.

Manufacturer of titlers, character generators, Logo & ID inserters, automated display & control systems; graphic display generators; playback systems & emergency alert systems.

Kidde-Fenwal Inc., 400 Main St., Ashland, MA 01721. Phone: (508) 881-2000. Fax: (508) 881-6729. Web Site: www.fenwalcontrols.com. John Sullivan, pres; Kathleen Schoonmaker, VP.

High-speed fire protection systems.

Kings Electronics Co. Inc., 1685 Overview Dr., Rock Hill, SC 29730. Phone: (803) 909-5000. Fax: (803) 909-5092. Web Site: www.kingselectronics.com.

Video patch panels, patch cords, coaxial connectors, triaxial connectors, twinaxial connectors.

Kintronic Labs Inc., Box 845, Bristol, TN 37621-0845. Phone: (423) 878-3141. Fax: (423) 878-4224. E-mail: ktl@kintronic.com. Web Site: www.kintronic.com. Louis A. King, CEO; Gwen King, VP; Tom King, pres.

Phasers, ATUs, transmitter combiners & multiplexers, RF switches, attenuators, components & accessories; baluns, AM dummy loads, & isocouplers, rigid & open wire transmission line.

Kline Towers, 828 Williams Street, West Columbia, SC 29169. Phone: (803) 251-8000. Fax: (803) 251-6200. E-mail: raywhite@klinetowers.com. Web Site: www.klinetowers.com. J.C. Kline, pres; R.C. White, VP; Anthony J. Fronseca, sls.

Designers, fabricators & erectors of TV, FM & other bcst towers & specialty structures.

Knox Video, 8547 Grovemont Cir., Gaithersburg, MD 20877. Phone: (301) 840-5805. Fax: (301) 840-2946. Web Site: www.knoxvideo.com. Philip Edwards, pres; Stefan Seigel, production mgr; Roland Blood, exec VP.

Electronic bulletin bd for video messages. VCR control units. Full matrix routing switches.

Konica Minolta Corp., 725 Darlington Ave., Mahwah, NJ 07430. Phone: (201) 529-6060. Fax: (201) 529-6070. E-mail: isddisplay@minolta.com. Web Site: www.minoltausa.com.

CRT & LCD color analyzing instrumentation.

Kuhnel Co. Inc., 155 Harmony Rd., Mickleton, NJ 08056. Phone: (856) 423-4277. Fax: (856) 423-5105. Mary Kuhnel, pres.

Instal & maintenance of antennas & towers.

L

L-3 Communications Telemetry East, Box 729, Bristol, PA 19007-0729. Phone: (267) 545-7000. Fax: (267) 545-0100. Web Site: www.l-3com.com. Rod Oren, gen mgr & sr VP; William Wargo, VP business affrs.

Mfgr of satellite receiving systems, antennas, telemetry receiving systems & ancillary equipment. Mfgr of communications for aerospace & defense.

LARCAN, 228 Ambassador Dr., Mississauga, ON L5T 2J2. Canada. Phone: (905) 564-9222. Fax: (905) 564-9244. Web Site: www.larcan.com. E-mail: sales@larcan.com. Jim Adamson, pres; Steven Zakaib, VP mktg; Sean East, rgnl sls mgr.

Lafayette, CO 80026. LARCAN USA, 1390 Overlook Dr. Phone: (303) 665-8000. Fax: (303) 673-9900. Web Site: www.larcan.com. J.D. Adamson, pres.

LARCAN innovates, designs, and manufactures superior Analog and Digital television transmitters for broadcast standards worldwide. Product lines include LARCAN Solid State VHF, UHF, and high power IOT transmitters, as well as LP transmitters and translators. We offer transmitters from 1w to 100kW, and provide a wealth of broadcast solutions.

LARCAN USA, 1390 Overlook Dr., Lafayette, CO 80026. Phone: (303) 665-8000. Fax: (303) 673-9900. Web Site: www.larcan.com. David Hale, chmn & VP sls; Jim Adamson, pres.

Repair & sls of high power UHF TV transmitters, low power TV transmitters & translators, FM transmitters & translators & AC line surge protectors.

LBA Technology Inc., Box 8026, 3400 Tupper Dr., Greenville, NC 27835-8026. Phone: (800) 522-4464. Phone: (252) 757-0279. Fax: (252) 752-9155. E-mail: lbatech@lbagroup.com. Web Site: www.lbagroup.com. Lawrence Behr, CEO; Marcian Bouchard, pres; Javier Castillo, VP.

Design & manufacture medium wave antenna systems marketed worldwide, including folded unipole antennas, tuning units, transmitter combiners, diplexers, triplexers, RF components & collocation equiptment.

LEA International, 6520 Harney Rd., Tampa, FL 33610. Phone: (813) 621-1324. Fax: (813) 621-8980. Web Site: www.leaintl.com. Mike Everson, VP sls; Shawn Thompson, mgng dir.

Hayden Lake, ID 83835, 10701 Airport Dr. Phone: (800) 881-8506. Fax: (208) 762-6099.

Manufacturers of transient voltage surge suppression & power conditioning equipment.

LINK Electronics Inc., 2137 Rust Ave., Cape Girardeau, MO 63703. Phone: (573) 334-4433. Fax: (573) 334-9255. E-mail: link@linkelectronics.com. Web Site: www.linkelectronics.com. Bob Henson, pres; Ellen Henson, exec VP; James Timberlake, VP opns; Dave Aufdenberg, customer svc.

San Pedro, CA 90731. LINK Electronics Inc.-Western Rgnl Sls, 1035 W. 20th St. Phone: (310) 548-3925. Fax: (310) 548-3350. E-mail: philipburnslink@wmconnect.com. Phil Burns, rgnl mgr-Western rgn.

Lawrenceville, NJ 08648. LINK Electronics Inc.-Northeast & Southeast Rgnl Sls, 2 W. Laurelwood Dr. Phone: (609) 561-9551. E-mail: raybouchard@aol.com. Ray Bouchard, rgnl mgr-N.E. & S.W. rgns.

Manufacturer of Sync Generators, system timing, audio & video DAs, power amps, encoders, decoders, video processing, test equipment & video presence detectors, closed caption encoders, decoders, video switchers, digital distribution & conversion.

LTM Corp. of America, 7755 Haskell Ave., Van Nuys, CA 91406. Phone: (818) 780-9828. Fax: (818) 780-9848. E-mail: info@ltmlighting.com. Web Site: www.ltmlighting.com. Dennis Knopf, exec VP.

HMI & quartz lighting fixtures for film & video production; fresnels, open face, fiber optic, soft lights & fluorescents from 18w to 18,000 w. Also complete line of microphone poles, windscreens & muffs.

Laser Diode Inc., Fiber Optic Business Unit Tyco/Electronics. 2 Olsen Ave., Edison, NJ 08820. Phone: (732) 549-9001. Fax: (732) 906-1559. E-mail: sales@laserdiode.com. Web Site: www.laserdiode.com. Rollin Ball, dir; Peggy Scarillo, sls; Scott Grayman, production mgr; Steve Lerner, production mgr.

Manufacture FP, high power, & CW lasers along with high sensitivity detectors and FDDI/SONET modules for short/long haul transmission, test DWDM, military, and commercial fiber optic systems. Also offer Hi-Reliability custom packaging services.

The Laumic Rental Co., 432 W. 45th St., New York, NY 10036. Phone: (212) 586-6161. Fax: (212) 245-0974. Stuart Mann, gen mgr.

Sls, rental, svc, training for bcst, industrial equipment; systems designed & installed.

Leader Instruments Corp., 6484 Commerce Dr., Cypress, CA 90630. Phone: (714) 527-9300. Fax: (714) 527-7490. E-mail: lopez@leaderusa.com. Web Site: www.leaderusa.com. M. Sawa, pres.

Cypress, CA 90630, 6484 Commerce Dr. Phone: (714) 527-9300.

Electronic test equipment for video, audio, RF, microwave, oscilloscopes & gen use.

Leaming Industries, 3972 Barranca Pkwy., J 608, Irvine, CA 92606. Phone: (949) 743-5233. Fax: (949) 743-5233. E-mail: sales@leaming.com. Web Site: www.leaming.com. Robert F. Leaming, pres; Keith G. Rauch, sr engr.

BTSC Stereo/SAP encoders, modulators

The Leather Specialty Co., 2690 W. Airport Blvd., Sanford, FL 32771. Phone: (407) 323-1830. Fax: (407) 330-1317.

Transit/shipping cases, custom manufactured to specifications & tool cases.

Lectrosonics Inc., 581 Laser Rd. NE, Rio Rancho, NM 87124. Phone: (505) 892-4501. Fax: (505) 892-6243. E-mail: sales@lectrosonics.com. Web Site: www.lectrosonics.com. Larry E. Fisher, pres; Bruce C. Jones, mktg VP; Gordon Moore, sls VP; Bob Cunnings, engrg VP.

Wireless microphone systems for bcst, motion picture & tele-product applications. Automatic sound system mixing & control.

Leightronix Inc., 2330 Jarco Dr., Holt, MI 48842. Phone: (517) 694-8000. Fax: (517) 694-1600. E-mail: info@leightronix.com. Web Site: www.leightronix.com. Jeff Possanza,.

Real time event controllers for VCR & switcher automation. Telephone remote equipment control.

Leitch Inc., 4400 Vanowen Street, Burbank, CA 91505. Phone: (757) 548-2300. Phone: (800) 231-9673. Fax: (757) 548-0019. E-mail: leitch@leitch.com. Web Site: www.leitch.com. Paula Moore, gen mgr; Tom Jordan, sls VP; Don Thompson, dir mktg.

Toronto, ON M3C 3E5 Canada. Leitch Technology Corp., 150 Ferrand Dr, Suite 700. Phone: (416) 445-9640. (800) 387-0233. John Nielson, South Central rgnl sls mgr.

Audio & video distribution amplifiers, sync generators, clock systems & timers, synchronizers, test equipment, still storage, scramblers & descramblers. Audio, video, digital & data routing switchers, terminations, serial digital products.

Lemco Tool Corp., 1850 Metzgear Ave., Cogan Station, PA 17728. Phone: (570) 494-0620. Fax: (570) 494-0860. E-mail: toolinfo@lemco-tool.com. Web Site: www.lemco-tool.com. Glenn G. Miller, pres.

Designers & manufacturers of mechanical tools, equipment & materials for the construction & maintenance of CATV systems.

Lemo U.S.A. Inc., Box 2408, Rohnert Park, CA 94927-2408. Phone: (707) 578-8811. Fax: (707) 578-0869. E-mail: toolinfo@lemo-tool.com. Web Site: www.lemousa.com. Peter Mueller, gen mgr; Carol Taylor, natl sls & mktg mgr.

High quality, self latching circular connectors including single, multi & mixed contact arrangements. Fiber optic hybrid camera connectors, a/v patch panels. Custom designs & cable assemblies welcome.

Leviton NSI Colortran, (A division of NSI Corp.). 20497 S.W. Teton, Tualatin, OR 97062. Phone: (503) 404-5500. Phone: (800) 576-6060. Fax: (503) 404-5600. E-mail: pauls@leviton.com. Harold Leviton, pres; Paul Sherbo, VP sls & mktg.

Lighting fixtures & control devices for theater, TV & architectural applications.

Lightning Eliminators & Consultants Inc., 6687 Arapahoe Rd., Boulder, CO 80303. Phone: (303) 447-2828 ext.100. Fax: (303) 447-8122. E-mail: info@lightningeliminators.com. Web Site: www.lightningeliminators.com. Roy B. Carpenter Jr., chief technologist; Peter A. Carpenter, exec VP; Rob Harmon, sls dir.

Designers & manufacturers of lightning strike prevention, grounding & power conditioning systems.

Lightning Master Corp., Box 6017, 1351 N. Arcturas Ave., Clearwater, FL 33765. Phone: (727) 447-6800. Fax: (727) 461-3177. E-mail: bak@lightningmaster.com. Web Site: www.lightningmaster.com. Bruce A. Kaiser, pres; Ed Walker, gen sls mgr; Wayne DeGurshl, opns mgr.

Gwangju City 500-827 Korea, Democratic People's Republic Of, 3F 12 1-2 Sinan-Dong, Buk-Gu. Phone: 826 252 162 16. Sang Su Lee, gen mgr.

Structural lightning protection equipment, transient voltage surge suppression, bonding & grounding products, consulting svcs; site survey, analysis & training.

Lightning Prevention Systems, 424-A Kelley Dr., W. Berlin, NJ 08091. Phone: (856) 767-7806. Phone: (888) 667-8745. Fax: (856) 767-7547. E-mail: info@lpsnet.com. Web Site: www.lpsnet.com. Ian E. Fawthrop, pres.

Manufactures equipment utilizing point discharge technology to remove the lightning attractive static charge on towers or structures that they're on, preventing lightning strikes.

Lindsay Electronics, 50 Mary St. W., Lindsay, ON K9V 4S7. Canada. Phone: (705) 324-2196. Fax: (705) 324-5474. E-mail: sales@hq.lindsayelec.com. Web Site: www.lindsayelec.com. Meinrad Machler, pres; D. T. Atman, mktg dir; Brian Ward, key account mgr.

Full line of CATV actives & passives, Digital receive antennas, LPTV transmit antennas, & 2-way communications antennas.

Equipment Manufacturers and Distributors Alphabetical Index

Linear Acoustic Inc., 354 N. Prince St., Lancaster, PA 17603. Phone: (717) 735-3611. Fax: (717) 735-3612. E-mail: tim@linearacoustic.com. Web Site: www.linearacoustic.com. Tim Carroll, pres; Steven Strassberg, VP sls & mktg.

Lipsner Smith Co., 4700 Chase Ave., Lincolnwood, IL 60712. Phone: (847) 677-3000. Phone: (800) 323-7520. Fax: (847) 677-1311. Fax: (800) 784-6733. E-mail: sales@lipsner.com. Web Site: www.lipsner.com.
Motion Picture Film Laboratory Equipment.

Listec Video Corp., 2001 Palm Beach Lakes Blvd., Suite 411, West Palm Beach, FL 33409. Phone: (561) 683-3002. Fax: (561) 683-7336. E-mail: sales@listec.com. Web Site: www.listec.com. Joanne Camarda, pres.
Hauppauge, NY 11788, 40-3 Oser Ave. Phone: (631) 273-3029. Fax: (631) 435-4544. Bob Lorello, sls & product support.
Fully professional range of flat-panel and monitor prompters for studio, field and conferencing applications complemented by Windows prompting software.

Location Sound Corp., 10639 Riverside Dr., North Hollywood, CA 91602. Phone: (818) 980-9891. Fax: (818) 980-9911. E-mail: information@locationsound.com. Web Site: www.locationsound.com. David Panfili, pres.
Dealer of professional audio and communications solutions for film, video, broadcast, business, institutional and recording applications. Over 25 years experience.

Logica Inc., 655 3rd Ave., Suite 700, New York, NY 10017. Phone: (212) 682-7411. Fax: (212) 682-0715.
Consulting.

Logitek, 5622 Edgemoor Dr., Houston, TX 77081. Phone: (713) 664-4470. Phone: (800) 231-5870. Fax: (713) 664-4479. E-mail: info@logitekaudio.com. Web Site: www.logitekaudio.com. Tag Borland, pres; Cam Eicher, sls dir.
Digital audio consoles, digital audio routers & audio level indicators (meters).

Lowel-Light Manufacturing Inc., 140 58th St., Brooklyn, NY 11220. Phone: (718) 921-0600. Fax: (718) 921-0303. E-mail: info@lowel.com. Web Site: www.lowel.com. Don Youngberg, midwest sls; Dale Marks, sls rep; Toni Pearl, dealer liaison; Eric Drucker, eastern sls mgr.
Lights, controls, mounts & kits for imaging professionals, innovatively designed & built for rugged dependable use, ease of operation and portability.

Luxor, 2245 Delany Rd., Waukegan, IL 60087. Phone: (847) 244-1800. Fax: (800) 327-1698. E-mail: luxorfurn@ameritech.net. Web Site: www.luxorfurn.com. Robert T. Raw, gen mgr; Robert White, sls & mktg mgr.
Computer stands, A/V equipment stands, conference room furniture, TV stands, library & office furniture.

M

M/A-COM, (A division of AMP Incorporated). 1011 Pawtucket Blvd., Lowell, MA 01853. Phone: (978) 442-5000. Phone: (800) 366-2266. Fax: (978) 442-5350. Web Site: www.macom.com. Rick P. Hess, pres/CEO; Tim Emery, dir.
RF microwave & mm wave components & subsystems.

MATCO Inc., 15000 Stetson Rd., Los Gatos, CA 95033-9770. Phone: (408) 353-2670. Phone: (800) 348-1843. Fax: (408) 353-8781. E-mail: sales@matco.video.com. Web Site: www.matco-video.com. David Harbert, pres; Rita Harbert, gen mgr; William Meyer, dir.
Playback automation, coml insertion, & machine control systems for bcst, cable & coml, industrial & medical. MPEG 2 video servers with automation software options.

MCG Surge Protection, 12 Burt Dr., Deer Park, NY 11729. Phone: (631) 586-5125. Fax: (631) 586-5120. E-mail: info@mcgsurge.com. Web Site: www.mcgsurge.com. Christine Jelley, CEO; Diane Lanciotti, CFO; Sue Baron, gen sls mgr.
Surge protectors for AC power lines, telephone/signal & data lines. Protecting industry since 1967.

MCL Inc., 501 S. Woodcreek Rd., Bolingbrook, IL 60440-4999. Phone: (630) 759-9500. Fax: (630) 759-5018. E-mail: sales@mcl.com. Web Site: www.mcl.com. Frank P. Morgan, VP mktg; Art Faverio, pres/CEO; Frank Morgan, VP sls.
Satellite communication fixed & mobile High Power Amplifiers in C-band, X-Band, Ku-band, DBS, V-Band, Ka-Band & Multi-Band.

MGE UPS SYSTEMS Inc., 1660 Scenic Ave., Costa Mesa, CA 92626. Phone: (714) 557-1636. Fax: (714) 557-9788. E-mail: info@mgeups.com. Web Site: www.mgeups.com. Mike Chmura, VP; Ray Prince, pres.
Hoffman Estates, IL 60195, 2895 Greenspoint Pkwy. #350. Phone: (847) 585-1113. Fax: (847) 585 1125. Mike Chmura, VP sls & mktg.
New York, NY 10018, 520 8th Ave., 21st Fl. Phone: (212) 594-9333. Fax: (212) 594-3691.
Manufacturers of uninterruptible power systems (UPS) power conditioners & inverters that protect equipment from power related problems.

MODCOMP Inc., 1650 W. McNab Rd., Fort Lauderdale, FL 33309. Phone: (954) 974-1380. Fax: (954) 977-1900. E-mail: info@modcomp.com. Web Site: www.modcomp.com. Alex Lupinetti, pres; Ron Cook, opns VP.
Minicomputer systems, hardware & software for ground stn monitoring & control. SCADA applications & website enabling software.

MRPP Inc., 201 W. Chatham St., Suite 202, Cary, NC 27511. Phone: (919) 468-1000. Fax: (919) 468-1956. Web Site: www.mrppinc.com. Sheila Ogle, CEO; Sue Toth, pres.
Procuring, servicing, instal, & sale of bcstg & satellite equipment. Leasing plans available.

M2 America, 470 Riverside St., Portland, ME 04103. Phone: (207) 797-2600. Fax: (207) 797-2604. E-mail: info@m2america.com. Web Site: www.m2america.com.
CD, CD-R, DVD-R, optical disk duplicators.

MUSICAM U.S.A., Bldg. 4, 670 N. Beers St., Holmdel, NJ 07733. Phone: (732) 739-5600. Fax: (732) 739-1818. E-mail: sales@musicamusa.com. Web Site: www.musicamusa.com.
Digital Audio codecs for remote bcstg with Bandwidth up to 20 khz for ISDN, POTS or IP.

MYAT Inc., Box 425, 380 Chestnut St., Norwood, NJ 07648-0425. Phone: (201) 767-5380. Fax: (201) 767-4147. Web Site: www.myat.com. E-mail: sales@myat.com. Philip Cindrich, pres.
Falmouth, ME 04105, 60 Gray Rd. Phone: (207) 878-7807. (207) 767-7806.
Transmission line systems, filters, combiners. All-band UHF transmission line systems, component & accessories.

Macrovision Corp., 2830 De La Cruz Blvd., Santa Clara, CA 95050-2619. Phone: (408) 743-8600. Fax: (408) 743-8610. Web Site: www.macrovision.com. E-mail: info@macrovision.com. John Ryan, chmn; Bill Krepick, pres/CEO.
Tokyo 150-0001 Japan. Macrovision Japan K.K., Takaba Bldg. 2F, 6-18-5, Jingumae, Shibuya-Ku. Phone: 81-35-774-6253. Masao Kumei.
Beeshire SL 61 BR United Kingdom. Macrovision UK Ltd., 14-18 Bell St, Maiden Head. Phone: (44) 870 871 1111. Martin Brooker.
Copy protection & rights management for videocassettes, pay-per-view cable, satellite TV, & video conferencing.

Magna-Tech Electronic Co. Inc., 100 N.E. 39th St., Miami, FL 33137. Phone: (305) 573-7339. Fax: (305) 573-8101. E-mail: iceco@aol.com. Web Site: www.iceo.com. Steve Krams, owner/pres; Dara Reusch, VP.
Film recorders & reproducers; 16 & 35mm projectors, telecine film followers, time code generators/readers.

Magni Systems Inc., 22965 N.W. Evergreen Pkwy., Hillsboro, OR 97124. Phone: (503) 615-1900. Fax: (503) 615-1999. E-mail: sales@magnisystems.com. Web Site: www.magnisystems.com. Victor L. Kong, CEO; Chuck Barrows, VP sls.
Video Test Equipment and Scan Converters. Automated video test & monitoring equipment, waveform monitors, vectorscopes, test signal generators, VIT inserter, PC graphics to video encoders & video overlay scan converters.

Magnum Towers Inc., 9370 Elder Creek Rd., Sacramento, CA 95829. Phone: (916) 381-5053. Fax: (916) 381-2144. E-mail: magnumtowers@speedlink.com. Lawrence Smith, pres.
Radio, TV & microwave towers.

Marathon Norco Aerospace, Inc., 8301 Imperial Dr, Waco, TX 76712. Phone: (254) 776-0650. Fax: (254) 776-6558. Web Site: www.mptc.com. Al Rodriquez, pres.
CASP universal battery support systems & AC/DC power supplies.

Marcom, 540 Hauer Apple Way, Aptos, CA 95003-9501. Phone: (831) 768-8668. Fax: (831) 768-7810. E-mail: marty@mar-com.com. Web Site: www.mar-com.com. Martin Jackson, pres.
FM, AM, TV & microwave transmitting equipment; sls engrg, instal & maintenance.

Marconi Communications, 4350 Weaver Pkwy., Warrenville, IL 60555. Phone: (630) 579-5000. Fax: (630) 579-5050. Web Site: www.marconi.com. Dusty Becker, VP; David Smith, VP.
London WIK2HD United Kingdom, 34 Grosvenor. Phone: 44 (0) 20 7493 8484. Fax: 44 (0) 20 7493 1974.
CATV enclosures, security enclosures, protection devices, pole line hardware & connectors.

Marietta Design Group, 82 Plantation Point, Suite 200, Fairhope, AL 36532. Phone: (251) 990-3558. Fax: (360) 838-9046. E-mail: support@mariettadesign.com. Web Site: www.mariettadesign.com.
AccuPrompt— & QuickPrompt— teleprompting software for MacIntosh.
QuickPrompt 1.7.2—for professional video prompting.

Maritz Inc., 1375 North Highway Dr., Fenton, MO 63099. Phone: (877) 462-7489. Web Site: www.maritz.com.
Communications, film/video training, business meetings, marketing.

Marketron International, 411 Airport Blvd., Burlingame, CA 94010-2001. Phone: (800) 788-9245. Fax: (650) 548-2295. E-mail: lcarpenter@marketron.com. Web Site: www.marketron.com.
Toronto, ON M2N 6C6 Canada, 5075 Yonge St, Suite 404. Phone: (416) 221-9944. Bill Cross, gen mgr.
Birmingham, AL 35244, 3000 Riverchase Galleria, 8th Fl. Phone: (205) 987-7456. Fax: (205) 733-4535. E-mail: tvsales@marketron.com. Michael Hunter, gen mgr.
Hailey, ID 83333, 101 Empty Saddle Trail. Phone: (208) 788-6272. Gary Coats, gen mgr.
Software applications for radio, TV, networks, syndicators, traffic, accounting, mgmt, demand pricing, inventory control, rsch & proposals.

Marshall Electronics, 1910 E. Maple Ave., El Segundo, CA 90245. Phone: (310) 333-0606. Phone: (800) 800-6608. Fax: (310) 333-0688. E-mail: sales@lcdracks.com. Web Site: www.lcdracks.com. Thom Belford, dir mktg; Leonard Marshall, CEO.
Wire cable & connectors—Mogami superflex wire and cable, Tajimi, connectors & LCD bcst monitors. Marshall provides the highest quality products to the bcst, vidio & music recording mkts. Marshall specializes in manufacturing optics, LCD panels, microphones & mogami wire.

Marti Electronics, 4100 N. 24th St., Quincy, IL 62305. Phone: (217) 224-9600. Fax: (217) 224-9607. E-mail: sales@martielectronics.com. Web Site: www.martielectronics.com. John Lackness, sls.
Composite, dual mono & digital STL systems, remote pickup systems, telemetry links, studio to transmitter links, FM exciters, transmitters & pots remote pickup systems.

Martinsound Inc., 1151 W. Valley Blvd., Alhambra, CA 91803-2440. Phone: (626) 281-3555. Fax: (626) 284-3092. E-mail: info@martinsound.com. Web Site: www.martinsound.com. Joe Martinson, pres; Doug Osborne, dir & sls & mktg.
Complete line of audio control consoles for music recording, bcst, & video postproduction applications. MultiMax surround monitor control system, flying faders console automation, Martech MSS-10 precision microphone preamplifier.

Masterclock Inc., 2484 W. Clay St., St. Charles, MO 63301. Phone: (800) 940-2248. Fax: (636) 724-3776. Web Site: www.massterclock.com. William J. Clark, pres.
Masterclock systems, clock displays & time code products mfg & distribution.

Matrox Video Products Grp, 1055 St. Regis Blvd., Dorval, PQ H9P 2T4. Canada. Phone: (514) 685-2630, EXT. 2636. Fax: (514) 685-2853. E-mail: video.info@matrox.com. Web Site: www.matrox.com/video. Lorne Trottier, pres; Spiro Plagakis, VP sls & mktg.
Emmy award-winning technology & mktg leader in the field of digital video hardware for reeltime editing, DVD authoring & web streaming.

Matthews Studio Equipment Inc. (MSE), 2405 Empire Ave., Burbank, CA 91504-3399. Phone: (818) 843-6715. Fax: (323) 849-1525. E-mail: info@msegrip.com. Web Site: www.msegrip.com. Robert Kulesh, VP sls & mktg.
TV camera support dollies, land tripods, studio pedestals, pan/tilt heads, cases.

Equipment Manufacturers and Distributors Alphabetical Index

Maxell Corp. of America, 2208 Rt. 208, Fairlawn, NJ 07410. Phone: (201) 794-5900. Fax: (201) 796-8790. Web Site: www.maxellpromedia.com.
Blank audio & video recording tape for professional bcstrs & duplicators.

Maze Corporation, Box 100186, Birmingham, AL 35210. Phone: (205) 706-2080. Fax: (205) 956-5027. E-mail: maze@mazecorp.com. Web Site: www.mazecorp.com. Vira J. Maze, pres.
Remarketers of TV & video equipment.

McCurdy Radio Industries Ltd., 30 Kelfield St., Toronto, ON M9W 5A2. Canada. Phone: (416) 248-6155. Fax: (416) 248-6755. Web Site: www.mcradio.com.
Buffalo, NY 14206, 1051 Clinton St.
TV Automation systems, controlled robotic library cassette machines, video disc storage systems, near video on demand, audio monitors & meters.

Media Computing Inc., Box 4169, Cave Creek, AZ 85327-4169. Phone: (480) 575-7281. E-mail: info@mediacomputing.com. Web Site: www.mediacomputing.com. Michael Rich, CEO; Kathryn A. Hulka, treas; Larry L. Baum, mgr.
ANGIS-PC-based software automatically updates displays on characters generators & web pages with real-time data like elections, news tickers, closing.

Media Concepts Inc., 200 Spring Garden, Unit B, Philadelphia, PA 19123. Phone: (215) 923-2545. Fax: (215) 928-0750. E-mail: mediacon@libertynet.org. Bob Weissman, pres.
Video duplication, international video standards conversion, CD-Rom duplication, DVD duplication authoring. Macrovision copy-protection.

Mediasoft Inc., 7200 N. Broadway Ext., Oklahoma City, OK 73116. Phone: (405) 607-2000. Fax: (405) 607-2071. E-mail: info@mediafusa.com. Web Site: www.mediasoftusa.com. Bob Alfson, pres.
Microcomputer products & svcs.

Mega Hertz, 4100 International Plaza, Suite 150, Fort Worth, TX 76109. Phone: (800) 883-8839. Fax: (817) 529-0745. E-mail: sales@megahz.com. Web Site: www.megahz.com. Doug Sherar, gen sls mgr.
Mega Hertz is a Value-Added-Reseller of "Unique" Multi-Vendor System Solutions that support the deployment of advanced technologies in hybrid Fiber/Coax Braodband Networks.

Megastar Inc., 4709 Compass Bow Ln., Las Vegas, NV 89130. Phone: (702) 386-2844. Fax: (702) 388-1250. Nigel Macrae, pres.
Design & instal of integrated satellite networks. Reseller, earth stns, earth stn equip & microwave equipment & all support equipment.

MEGGER, 2621 Van Buren Ave., Norristown, PA 19403. Phone: (610) 676-8500. Fax: (610) 676-8610. E-mail: sales@megger.com. Web Site: www.megger.com.
Cable fault-locating equipment & other electrical testing instruments.

Memorex Products Inc., 17777 Center Court Dr., Suite 800, Cerritos, CA 90703. Phone: (562) 653-2800. Fax: (562) 653-2900. E-mail: generaling@memorex.com. Web Site: www.memorex.com. Scott Stroup, VP.
Memorex is a manufacture, marketer of consumer media & computer products.

Meridian Design Associates, Architects, 1140 Broadway, New York, NY 10001. Phone: (212) 431-8643. Fax: (212) 431-8775. E-mail: info@meridiandesign.com. Web Site: www.meridiandesign.com.
Miami, FL 33144, 907 S.W. 79th Ave. Phone: (305) 262-7663. Fax: (305) 262-7675. Antonio Argibay.
Architectural firm specializing in the design of bcst & media facilities.

Merlin Engineering Works Inc., 1888 Embarcadero Rd., Palo Alto, CA 94303. Phone: (650) 856-0900. Phone: (800) 227-1980. Fax: (650) 858-2302. E-mail: sales@merlineng.com. Web Site: www.merlineng.com. Debbie Dirickson, dir.
Bcst VTRs, custom VTRs & accessories, VTR automation systems, stereo audio encoders, standards converters.

Metz Engineering, 15684 Old Mormon Bridge Rd., Crescent, IA 51526-4138. Phone: (712) 545-3222. Fax: (712) 545-9111. Joanne M. Metz, owner; John P. Metz III, dir.
Machine & welding shop plus construction.

Mic Flags by Aladdin, Box 2186, Short Beach, CT 06405. Phone: (203) 488-4267. Fax: (203) 488-8548. E-mail: micflag@juno.com. Terry N. Parsons, pres.
Mic flags, camera plates of any size blank or with logo since 1969.

Michael Stevens & Partners Ltd., Invicta Works, Elliott Rd., Bromley, Kent BR2 9NT. Phone: 44(0)020-8460-7299. Fax: 44(0)020-8460-0499. E-mail: sales@michael-stevens.com. Web Site: www.michael-stevens.com. Michael Stevens, mgng dir.
Kingston Springs, TN 37082, 149 Dillard Ct, Suite E. Phone: (615) 952-2345. Fax: (615) 952-2342. Megan McCullough, sls office mgr.
Professional audio equipment for the audio & video bcst industries.

Micro Communications Inc., Box 4365, 438 Kelley Ave., Grenier Field, Manchester, NH 03108-4365. Phone: (603) 624-4351. Phone: (800) 545-0608. Fax: (603) 624-4822. E-mail: frank.malanga@mcibroadcast.com. Web Site: www.mcibroadcast.com. Al Kula, sls engr; Sam Matthews, mktg mgr; Paul Smith, CEO.
Waveguide & coaxial transmission line; complete RF system packages for UHF, VHF, FM & LPTV panel antennas; antennas for UHF, VHF & FM.

Micro Technology Unlimited, 6900 Six Forks Rd., Raleigh, NC 27615. Phone: (919) 870-0344. Fax: (919) 870-7163. E-mail: info@mtu.com. Web Site: www.mtu.com. David B. Cox, pres.
Karaoke software products & pro workstations.

Microlog Corp., 20270 Goldenrod Ln., Germantown, MD 20876. Phone: (301) 540-5500. Fax: (301) 540-5557. E-mail: info@mlog.com. Web Site: www.mlog.com. Joe Brookman, pres/CEO.
Automated outbound/inbound voice messaging systems & service bureau; interactive voice response to mainframe computer.

Micron Audio Products Ltd., 216 Little Falls Rd., Cedar Grove, NJ 07009. Phone: (973) 857-8150. Fax: (973) 857-3756. E-mail: micronaudio@cs.com. Paul Tepper, pres.
TRAM lavalier microphones, sls & svc.

Microspace Communications Corp., 3100 Highwoods Blvd., Raleigh, NC 27604. Phone: (919) 850-4500. Fax: (919) 850-4518. E-mail: uplink@microspace.com. Web Site: www.microspace.com. James Goodmon, pres/CEO; Joseph Amor III, VP/gen mgr; Greg Hurt, dir; Carolyn Newey, dir.
Providing video, data & audio transmission svcs designed for antennas as small as 30 inches. Operates on domestic satellites for coverage of North America. Also providing fixed C- & Ku-band uplink svcs for video transmissions supporting applications such as news, sports, program origination (live or taped); & business TV. Remote & studio production available. Turnaround svc to & from domestic & international satellites.

Microwave Filter Co. Inc., 6743 Kinne St., East Syracuse, NY 13057. Phone: (315) 438-4700. Phone: (800) 448-1666. Fax: (315) 463-1467. E-mail: mfcsales@microwavefilter.com. Web Site: www.microwavefilter.com. Carl Fahrenkrug, pres; Terry Owens, sls VP.
Filters, traps, combiners & custom networks for TV, radio, CATV, wireless cable, LAN & mobile radio.

Milestek Corp., 1506 I-35W, Denton, TX 76207-2402. Phone: (940) 484-9400. Phone: (800) 524-7444. Fax: (940) 484-9402. Web Site: www.milestek.com. E-mail: salesinfo@milestek.com. Brett Powers, pres.
Connectors including both 50 ohm & 75 ohm BNCs, cabling, patching & tools for coaxial cable.

Milestone Technologies Inc., Box 37145, Raleigh, NC 27627. Phone: (919) 773-1772. E-mail: info@milestonetechnologies.com. Web Site: www.milestonetechnologies.com. Miles Beam, pres.
Data bcstg file transfer software (SATX). Bcst binary files over one-way data nets (DBS, VSAT, TV, FM, VBI, RDS, MPEG2, etc.). Consulting & system integration svcs.

Miller Camera Support, L.L.C., 216 Little Falls Rd., Cedar Grove, NJ 07009. Phone: (973) 857-8300. Fax: (973) 857-8188. E-mail: info@millertripals.us. Web Site: www.millertripods.com. Art Kramer, pres; Gus Harilaou, gen sls mgr.
Pan & tilt fluid heads, tripods & camera support systems & accessories for ENG, EFP (OB) & motion picture production applications.

Miranda Technologies Inc., 3499 Douglas B. Floreani, Montreal, PQ H4S 2C6. Canada. Phone: (514) 333-1772. Phone: (800) 224-7882. Fax: (514) 333-9828. Web Site: www.miranda.com. Christian Tremblay, pres.
Glendale, CA 91202. Miranda MTI, 1101 N. Pacific Ave, Suite 204. Phone: (818) 550-8653. Fax: (818) 550-8614. E-mail: ussales@miranda.com.
Miami Lakes, FL 33014-2443. Miranda MTI, 6175 N.W. 153rd St, Suite 300. Phone: (305) 820-2990. Fax: (305) 820-2991.
Montreuil 93100 France. Miranda Europe, 222, 226 Rue De Rosny. Phone: +33 1 55 86 87 88. Fax: +33 1 55 86 00 29. E-mail: francesales@miranda.com.
Shibuya-Ku, Tokyo 151-0063 Japan. Miranda Asia, 2-2-5 Tomigaya, Neoba 303. Phone: 81-3-5452-1690. Fax: 81-3-5452-1695. E-mail: asiasales@miranda.com.
Wallingford Oxfordshire OX10 9DG United Kingdom. Miranda Technologies Ltd., Hithercroft Rd. Phone: +44 1491 820 000. Fax: +44 1491 820 001. E-mail: uksales@miranda.com.
Digital video interface products for bcstg & postproduction: serializers, digital-to-analog converters, NTSC encoders, computer video interfaces.

Mitsubishi Digital Electronics America Inc., 9351 Jeronimo Rd., Irvine, CA 92618. Phone: (949) 465-6000. Fax: (949) 465-6046. Web Site: www.mitsubishi-tv.com.
Portable videotape recorder systems, consumer VCR's & audio visual big screen TV's.

Mobile Video Services Ltd., 1620 Eye St. N.W., Washington, DC 20006. Phone: (202) 331-8882. Fax: (202) 331-9064. E-mail: Bookfeed@mobilevideo.net. Web Site: www.mobilevideo.net. Lawrence VanderVeen, pres; Jessica Carltin, opns mgr; Peter Rosenbaum, sls dir.
Complete EFP & ENG svcs, multi-camera remote packages, editing teleco & satellite transmission svcs available. CBS & CNN news feeds available.

Modulation Sciences Inc., 12A World's Fair Dr., Somerset, NJ 08873. Phone: (732) 320-3090. Fax: (732) 302-0206. E-mail: sales@modsci.com. Web Site: www.modsci.com. Eric Small, CEO; Judy Mueller, pres.
With 20 + years experience in the bcst industry, we manufacture full line of FM & TV equipment including: composite clipper, STL's distribution amplifiers, SteroMaxx—Spatial image englarger, modulation monitors, SCA & Data SCA equipment, TV stereo reference decoder, SAP & PRO generators, PRO ch receivers, SAP receivers, NTSC precision video demodulators.

Mohawk/CDT, 9 Mohawk Dr., Leominster, MA 01453. Phone: (978) 537-9961. Fax: (978) 537-4358. E-mail: info@mohawk-cdt.com. Web Site: www.mohawk-cdt.com. Mike Degnan, pres.
Mohawk/CDT is a major manufacturer of wire & cable to the bcst industry. Mohawk/CDT provides camera cable assemblies, both multi-core & fiber to all major OEM camera manufacturers. In addition, Mohawk/CDT has a full line of serial digital, high precision video & audio cable, video coax's, triaxial cables & fiber optic/copper composite cables. Also manufactures & distributes Kings, Lemo, ADC & Fischer connectors.

Mole-Richardson Co., 937 N. Sycamore Ave., Hollywood, CA 90038-2384. Phone: (323) 851-0111. Fax: (323) 851-5593. E-mail: info@mole.com. Web Site: www.mole.com. Michael C. Parker, pres; Don Phillips, VP sls; Larry Mole Parker, exec VP.
Lighting equipment for the motion picture, TV, video & still photographic industries.

Moseley Associates Inc., 111 Castilian Dr., Santa Barbara, CA 93117-3093. Phone: (805) 968-9621. Fax: (805) 685-9638. E-mail: info@moseleysb.com. Web Site: www.moseleysb.com. Jamal Hamdani, pres/CEO; Bruce Tarr, CFO.
Remote control systems, AM & FM stereo STLs, aural RPLs, data transmission systems & telecommunications, digital transmission system.

Motion Picture Enterprises Inc., Box 276, Tarrytown, NY 10591-0276. Phone: (212) 245-0969. Fax: (212) 245-0974. E-mail: mpeny@aol.com. Web Site: www.mpe.net. Neal R. Pilzer, pres.
Shipping cases, cabinets & cans for film & tape; custom made fibre cases, film & video equipment, supplies, sls, rental & repairs.

Motor Capacitors Inc., 6455 Avondale Ave., Chicago, IL 60631. Phone: (773) 774-6666. Fax: (773) 774-6690. E-mail: info@capacitorindustries.com. Web Site: www.capacitorindustries.com.
Motor-run, motor-start, metalized, oil-filtered, high voltage, film, electrolytic & power capacitors, & R.C. networks.

Motorola Broadband Communications Sector, 101 Tournament Dr., Horsham, PA 19044. Phone: (215) 323-1000. Fax: (215) 323-0242. E-mail: broadband@motorola.com. Web Site: www.motorola.com/broadband. Daniel M. Moloney, exec VP & pres/CEO.

Englewood, CO 80111, 6400 S. Fiddler-Green Cir. Phone: (303) 740-6118. Pete Wornski, VP.

Lewisville, TX 75057, 1330 Capital Pkwy. Phone: (972) 323-4100. Tim Roberti, rgnl mgr.

CATV headend & distribution equipment; sub terminals, addressable systems & interactive products.

Motorola Digital Media Systems, 55 Las Colinas Ln., San Jose, CA 95119. Phone: (408) 362-4800. Fax: (408) 362-4825. Web Site: www.motorola.com. Doug Means, VP/gen mgr.

San Jose, CA 95119. Motorola Digital Media Systems, 55 Las Colinas LN. Phone: (408) 362-4800. Fax: (408) 362-4851. (408) 362-4825. Web Site: www.motorola.com.

Fiber-optic video links for bcst & CATV use. 1550nm AM systems & AM return systems.

Moviola, (Formerly Videotape Distributors Inc.). 545 W. 45th St., New York, NY 10036. Phone: (212) 581-7111. Phone: (800) 327-3724. Fax: (212) 581-7977. Robert Schoenberg, VP/gen mgr.

Full-svc supplier of videotape, accessories & digital data storage products.

Multi-Image Network, 312 Otterson Dr., Suite F, Chico, CA 95928. Phone: (530) 345-4211. Fax: (530) 345-7737. Katheryn Schifferle, pres/CEO.

Multimedia production systems for cable TV, bcst, PE G training, education, & corporate TV. Pre- & post-launch consulting, training seminars, repair svcs.

Murphy Studio Furniture, 4153 N. Bonita St., Spring Valley, CA 91977. Phone: (619) 698-4658. Fax: (619) 698-1268. E-mail: dennismurphy@cox.net. Web Site: www.murphystudiofurniture.com. Dennis W. Murphy, pres.

Design/construction of studio furniture for radio, TV & production facilities. Five modular lines. Custom designs.

Murray Co., 1807 Park 270 Dr., Suite 460, St. Louis, MO 63146. Phone: (314) 576-2818. Fax: (314) 434-5780. Web Site: www.murray-company.com. John O'Hara, principal.

Kansas City, KS 66210, 7300 College, Suite 210. Phone: (913) 451 1884. Fax: (913) 451-3761.

General construction, design, program management, space planning, project budgeting, consolidation planning.

Murry Rosenblum Sound Assoc., Inc., Audio Limited U.S.A. 21-36 33rd Rd., Long Island City, NY 11106. Phone: (718) 728-2654. Fax: (718) 728-2654. E-mail: murryrosenblum2@nyc.rr.com. Murry Rosenblum, pres.

Audio limited wireless microphones—two switchable frequencies—small UHF standard or diversity receiver—pocket transmitter or handhold transmitter.

Musco Mobile Lighting Ltd., Box 808, 100 First Ave. W., Oskaloosa, IA 52577. Phone: (641) 673-0411. Fax: (641) 672-1996. Web Site: www.musco.com. Jerome Fynaardt, gen sls mgr.

Mobile location lighting utilizing 6K HMIs; remote control of pan, tilt & focus.

N

NEC America Inc., (Broadcast Equipment Dept.). 6555 N. State Hwy. 161, Irving, TX 75039. Phone: (214) 262-2000. Phone: (214) 262-6299. Fax: (972) 751-7001. Web Site: www.nec.com.

VUES on-line digital editing system (video).

NSI, 9050 Red Branch Rd., Columbia, MD 21045. Phone: (410) 964-8400. Fax: (410) 964-9661. Web Site: www.nsystems.com. E-mail: sales@nsystem.com. Stephen Neuberth, pres.

Microwave antennas & remote controls for ENG applications.

NTL Broadcast, Crawley Ct., Winchester, Hampshire S021 2QA. United Kingdom. Phone: 0-1962-824000. Fax: 0-1962-822553. Web Site: www.kftv.com. Peter Douglas, chmn.

Bcst transmission svcs & systems, satellite linking, telecommunications, turnkey bcst systems including digital.

NTV International Corporation, 50 Rockefeller Plaza, Suite 940, New York, NY 10020. Phone: (212) 489-8390. Fax: (212) 489-8395. Yoishi Shimada, VP.

TV News Gathering.

NUCOMM Inc., 101 Bilby Rd., Hackettstown, NJ 07840. Phone: (908) 852-3700. Fax: (908) 813-0399. Web Site: www.nucomm.com.

Microwave transmitters, receivers including digital video microwave systems & accessories for both portable & fixed line of sight applications. Modulators/demodulators & color bar generators.

NVISION Products, 125 Crown Point Ct., Grass Valley, CA 95945. Phone: (530) 265-1000. Fax: (530) 265-1021. E-mail: nvsales@nvision1.com. Web Site: www.nvision.tv. Charles S. Meyer, pres; Jay Kuca, dir.

Digital audio & data distribution, conversion, routing & transmission equipment for production/postproduction applications for bcstg industry.

NWL Capacitors, Box 10416, Riviera Beach, FL 33419-0416. Phone: (561) 848-9009. Fax: (561) 848-9011. Robert Scitz, gen mgr; Linda Nixon, VP.

Manufacturers.

Nady Systems Inc., 6701 Shellmound St., Emeryville, CA 94608. Phone: (510) 652-2411. Fax: (510) 652-5075. E-mail: ussales@nady.com. Web Site: www.nady.com. John Nady, pres/CEO; Scott Wunschel, sls dir.

Wireless VMP & AMF products for bcst, film, video, stage, fixed instals. Consumer audio & communication equipment.

Nakusa Inc., 1500 Olympic Blvd., Santa Monica, CA 90404. Phone: (310) 392-1155. Fax: (310) 392-1030. E-mail: sales@nakusa.com. Web Site: www.nakusa.com.

Professional cassette decks for bcst, production studio & duplication facilities; DAT also available. Audio, equipment home audio, mobile, home theater systems.

Nalpak, 1937 C Friendship Dr., El Cajon, CA 92020. Phone: (619) 258-1200. Fax: (619) 258-0925. E-mail: nalpaak@nalpak.com. Web Site: www.nalpakcom.com. Robert S. Kaplan, pres; Debra S. Kaplan, VP.

Packaging & Material Handling Products; teffpak,Torm, Magliner, Leatherman, Gerber, Buck, Surefire, Steamlight.

Narda Satellite Networks, 435 Moreland Road, Hauppauge, NY 11788. Phone: (631) 231-1700. Fax: (631) 272-5500. E-mail: sn.mktg@l-3com.com. Web Site: www.l-3com.com /satellitenetworks. Greg Federline, gen mgr.

Turnkey satellite earth stns & networks, SNG & Fly Away electronics, ground communications equipment & M&C systems. Manufactures & implements a full line of earth stn network monitors & control systems.

Nardal - An L-3 Communications Co., 435 Moreland Rd., Hauppauge, NY 11788. Phone: (631) 231-1700. Fax: (631) 231-1711. E-mail: nardaeast@l-3com.com. Web Site: nardamicrowave.com. John Mega, pres; Michael Sanatore, opns VP.

Portable RF/microwave test instruments, power density meters, coaxial power monitors & meters.

Narragansett Imaging, 51 Industrial Dr., North Smithfield, RI 02896. Phone: (401) 762-3800. Fax: (401) 767-4407. Web Site: www.nimaging.com. Donald Borwne, VP; Michael Halloran, VP.

Camera tubes, CCD camera modules.

National Audio Co. Inc., Box 3657, Glenstone Station, Springfield, MO 65808. Phone: (417) 863-1925. Fax: (417) 863-7825. E-mail: nac@nactape.com. Web Site: www.national -audiocompany.com. Steve Stepp, pres; Maxine Bass, sec/treas.

Quantegy audio & videotapes, Audio Pro-custom-loaded audio cassettes, Recordex Duplicators & Video Pro-professional video cassettes, Recordex equipment, CDL & DVD.

National Mobile Television, 2740 California St., Torrence, CA 90503. Phone: (800) 242-0642. Phone: (206) 782-9945. Fax: (206) 782-9949. Web Site: www.nmtv.com. Mark Howorth, chmn/CEO.

Equipment includes: 40' & 34' trailers. Philips LDK-26 cameras with 44X lenses, Ikegami HL-79EAL cameras, Grass Valley switchers, Sony BVH-2000 & BVH-3100 1" VTR's, Chyron 4100 EXB with CCM, Abekas A-53D, Yamaha audio mixers, RTS intercom & IFB, Sony BVE-900 edit on bd.

National Mobile TV - Houston, 10 Greenway Plaza, Houston, TX 77046. Phone: (713) 627-9270. Fax: (713) 871-9617. Bob Robinson, dir; Tim Jopplin, opns mgr.

Irving, TX 75039, 6 Communications Complex, 6221 N. O'Connor, Suite 117. Phone: (972) 556-1816. Fax: (972) 556-2543. (Dallas office).

Multi-camera location production company with 4-48' & 1-36' location production trucks. Eng Package & full-service offices in Houston & Dallas. Additional permanent facilities at the Summit in Houston.

National Steel Erectors Corp., Box 709, Muskogee, OK 74402. Phone: (918) 683-6511. Fax: (918) 683-0888. B.R. Bayless, pres; Neal Bayless, exec VP.

Erection of radio, TV & microwave towers, including turnkey construction, from design to completion.

National Video Services Inc., 18 Commerce Rd., Newtown, CT 06470. Phone: (203) 270-0677. Fax: (203) 270-9619. E-mail: sales@intermedvideo.com. Web Site: www.intermedvideo.com. Harry Davies, sec/treas.

Distribution of video equipment for corporate & industrial use; design & install of TV studios; manufacturing of video equipment; rsch & engrg.

National Video Tape Co. Inc., 6800 Sierra Ct., Suite D, Dublin, CA 94568. Phone: (925) 803-1440. Fax: (925) 803-0227. Jack E. Dixon, pres.

Seattle, WA 98199, 4200 23rd Ave. W. Phone: (206) 284-3340. Mari Scimeia.

Custom length VHS cassettes; Sony, Fuji, Maxell Panosanic video & data media products.

Nationwide Tower Company Inc., Box 1829, Henderson, KY 42419-1829. Phone: (270) 869-8000. Fax: (270) 869-8500. E-mail: hjohnston@nationwidetower.com. Web Site: www.nationwidetower.com. Kevin Roth, sls VP; Diane Pruitt, gen sls mgr.

Tower inspections, painting, repair re-guy, lighting, antennas, feedlines, analysis, erect, dismantle, line sweeping, site monitoring, and tower tracker svcs.

Nautel Ltd., 10089 Peggy's Cove Rd., Hackett's Cove, NS B3Z 3J4. Canada. Phone: (902) 823-2233. Fax: (902) 823-3183. E-mail: info@nautel.com. Web Site: www.nautel.com. Jorgen Jensen, mgr sls & mktg.

Bangor, ME 04401. Nautel Maine Inc., 201 Target Industrial Cir.

Solid state AM/FM bcst transmitters.

Navitar Inc., Buhl Optical Div. 200 Commerce Dr., Rochester, NY 14623. Phone: (585) 359-4000. Fax: (585) 359-4999. E-mail: info@navitar.com. Web Site: www.navitar.com.

Projection lenses, LCD, slide & overhead projectors.

L.E. Nelson Sales Corp., (Thorn-EMI Studio & Theatre Lamps). 4800 W. University Ave., Las Vegas, NV 89103. Phone: (702) 367-3656. Fax: (702) 367-7058. L.E. Nelson, pres; H.F. Nelson, VP western rgn; D.R. Imfeld, VP eastern rgn.

Fair Lawn, NJ 07410, 18-02 River Rd. Phone: (201) 794-6700. Dan Imfeld, VP eastern rgn.

Studio lamps, quartz (tungsten-halogen) from 25 w to 10 kw & projection lamps. Exculsive importer of Thorn Lamps.

Nemal Electronics International Inc., 12240 N.E. 14th Ave., North Miami, FL 33161. Phone: (305) 899-0900. Fax: (305) 895-8178. E-mail: info@nemal.com. Web Site: www.nemal.com. Benjamin L. Nemser, pres.

Sao Paulo, Av. Morumbi 7948. Phone: 011-5535-2368. Carlos Heckmann Jr., gen mgr.

Manufacturer of electronic cable, connectors, assemblies, & interconnect products for use in bcst applications.

Noise Control Corp., Box 81774, Bakersfield, CA 93380. Phone: (800) 606-6473. E-mail: ncc@noisecontrol.com. Web Site: www.noisecontrol.com.

Acoustical noise control products.

Neumade Products Corp., 30-40 Pecks Ln., Newtown, CT 06470. Phone: (203) 270-1100. Fax: (203) 270-7778. E-mail: neumadels@aol.com. Web Site: www.neumade.com. R.N. Jones, CEO; Gregory Jones, VP.

Film handling & editing equipment; storage facilities for film, slides, videotape, overhead & opaque projectors, motion picture projection systems.

Neutrik U.S.A. Inc., 195 Lehigh Ave., Lakewood, NJ 08701. Phone: (732) 901-9488. Fax: (732) 901-9608. E-mail: info@neutrikusa.com. Web Site: www.neutrikusa.com. James E. Cowan, pres; Julie Applegate, mgr.

Audio connectors, plugs & jacks, patch panels, patch cord assemblies, circular, industrial connectors & accessories, knobs, BNC jacks & plugs, RJ45, 3-5 mm plugs.

New York City Lites, 242 W. 27th St., 6th Floor, New York, NY 10001. Phone: (212) 366-9800. Fax: (212) 366-5040. E-mail: nycl@nycl.tv. Deke Hazirjian, pres.

Lighting design for video & TV.

Newark Electronics, (A Premier Co.). 4801 N. Ravenswood Ave., Chicago, IL 60640. Phone: (773) 784-5100. Fax: (888) 551-4801. Web Site: www.newark.com. Mike Ruprich, CEO.

Distributor of bcst cable, assemblies, connectors voice/data networking & electronic component parts. Branches throughout

Equipment Manufacturers and Distributors Alphabetical Index

the U.S., Canada, U.K. & Germany.

Nigel B. Furniture/Marketec, 4417 W. Magnolia Blvd., Burbank, CA 91505. Phone: (818) 557-2661. Fax: (818) 557-2665. E-mail: info@marketec.com. Web Site: www.nigelb.com. Penny Russell, owner.

Everything for rack mounting equipment, from vertical racks to desks, consoles, & workcenters for bcst & cable, post production, audio, & multimedia applications.

Norlight Telecommunications Inc., 13935 Bishops Dr., Brookfield, WI 53005. Phone: (262) 792-9700. Fax: (262) 792-7793. Web Site: www.norlight.com. James Ditter, pres; Robert Rogers, VP.

Skokie, IL 60076, 3617 Oakton St. Phone: (847) 674-7476. Dave Pritchard, dir.

Fiber-optic & microwave transmission of bcst level video.

Norpak Corporation, 10 Hearst Way, Kanata, ON K2L 2P4. Canada. Phone: (613) 592-4164. Fax: (613) 592-6560. E-mail: sales@nordak.ca. Web Site: www.norpak.ca. James Carruthers, pres.

TV Data Broadcast; Interactive TV; Financial, News, Weather Radar Information Broadcast; HDTV Data Encoding; Closed Captioning; V-Chip; NABTS

Norsat International Inc., 300-4401 Still Creek Dr., Burnaby, BC V5C 6G-9. Canada. Phone: (604) 292-9000. Phone: (800) 644-4562. Fax: (604) 292-9100. Web Site: www.norsat.com.

Beijing 100029P.R. Beijing Broadcasting Institute, 1704-A Union Plaza, 20 Chao Wai Plaza. Phone: (011) 86 10 65871281. Fax: (011) 86 10 65871081.

South Carlton, Lincoln LN1 2RL, The Old School. Phone: (011) 44 1522 730 800. Fax: 011- 44 1522 730 927. E-mail: smullery@noisat.com. Stan Mullery.

High speed, reliable data transmission products & networks, microware products & worldwide installations of opns STDs, DVB & SAT networks.

Nortel Networks, 8200 Dixie Rd., Suite 100, Brampton, ON L6T 5P6. Canada. Phone: (905) 863-0000. Web Site: www.northelworks.com. Frank A. Dunn, pres/CEO; Nicholas J. De Roma, chief legal off; Doug Beatty, CFO; Greg Munford, chief tech off; Chahram Bolouri, pres; William J. Donavan, sr VP; Albert Hitchock, CIO; Masood Tarig, pres.

Supplier of telecommunications equipment. Provides voice over packets, multimedia svcs & applications, wireless data, and broadband networking to public network carriers, wireless operators and multi-svc operators.

North American Cable Equipment Inc., 1085 Andrew Dr., Suite A, West Chester, PA 19380. E-mail: sales@northamericancable.com. Web Site: www.northamericancable.com. Aaron Starr, pres; Kirk Davies, gen sls mgr.

Manufacturer of CATV, RF modulators, demodulators and processors.

North Dakota Television L.L.C., (Formerly Sunrise Television). 200 N. Fourth St., Bismark, ND 58501. Phone: (701) 255-5757. Fax: (701) 255-8220. Web Site: www.kfyr.com. Jim Sande, progmg dir.

35' multi-camera bcst truck, Betacam SP VTRs, DVE, A/B roll edit, 24 ch audio bd, wireless IFB, 7kw generator, intercom systems.

North Hills Signal Processing, a PORTA Systems Co., 575 Underhill Blvd., Syosset, NY 11791. Phone: (516) 682-7740. Fax: (516) 682-7704. E-mail: info@northills-sp.com. Web Site: www.northhills-sp.com. Richard Schwarz, VP.

Video isolation transformers, humbuckers, baluns, impedance matching transformers, power splitters & data bus coupler (1553). Manufactures of MIL-STDT553 database products & wideband/video transformer.

Northeast Towers Inc., 199 Brickyard Rd., Farmington, CT 06032. Phone: (860) 677-1999. Fax: (860) 677-1300. E-mail: netowers@ctl.nai.net. Stephen Savino Jr., pres.

HDTV, TV, Cellular, PCS, AM, FM, CATV & microwave towers; ground systems; maintenance, materials, turnkey instals, specialty coatings, & strobes.

Northeastern Communications Concepts Inc., 40 Benford Dr., Princeton Junction, NJ 08550. Phone: (212) 972-1320. E-mail: webmaster@nccnewyork.com. Web Site: www.nccnewyork.com. Alfred W. D'Alessio, pres.

Bcst design svcs, studio furniture, custom audio equipment, custom data systems/components, cabinets, racks, panels, recording studios construction & prefab.

Northern Magnetics Inc., Bldg. 105, 9200 Nike Rd., Maple Plain, MN 55359-9572. Phone: (952) 446-1124. Fax: (952) 446-1387. Robert R. Rocheleau, VP.

Sls & service of magnetic recording heads.

Northern Power Systems, 182 Mad River Park, Waitsfield, VT 05673. Phone: (802) 496-2955. Fax: (802) 496-2953. E-mail: info@northernpower.com. Web Site: www.nothernpower.com. Clint Coleman, pres.

Remote power systems based on renewable energy inputs (wind/solar); hybrid power systems.

Northern Technologies Inc., Box 610, 23123 E. Mission Ave., Liberty Lake, WA 99019. Phone: (509) 927-0401. Fax: (509) 927-0435. E-mail: webmaster@northern-tech.com. Web Site: www.nothern-tech.com. Jarrod Goodwin, dir N. American sls.

Full line of transient control systems for AC, dataline & telephone, including UPS systems & regulators.

Northrop Grumman/Electronics & System Integration Division, South Oyster Bay Rd., Bethpage, NY 11714. Phone: (516) 575-0574. Fax: (516) 575-2311.

Ad insertion/program automation systems.

Northrup Grumman, 1840 Century Park E., Los Angeles, CA 90067. Phone: (310) 553-6262. Fax: (310) 553-2076. Kent Kresa, pres.

Film & video cameras for military; video-to-film recorders; optics & optical systems.

Northwest Monitoring Service, Box 70144, Eugene, OR 97401. Phone: (541) 345-2236. James C. Bradley, owner.

Monthly frequency measurements for AM-FM-TV. Mobile service includes California, Oregon, Washington, Idaho & Nevada.

Fred A. Nudd Corp., Box 577, 1743, Rt. 104, Ontario, NY 14519. Phone: (315) 524-2531. Fax: (315) 524-4249. Web Site: www.nuddtowers.com. Fred Nudd, VP; Tom Nudd, pres.

Design, manufacture, instal, maintenance & analysis of communication towers.

O

O'Connor Professional Camera Support Systems, 100 Kalmus Dr., Costa Mesa, CA 92626. Phone: (714) 979-3993. Fax: (714) 957-8138. E-mail: sales@ocon.com. Web site: www.ocon.com. Joel Johnson, VP/gen mgr; Robert Low, VP sls.

Manufacturer of camera support equipment including fluid heads, tripods & accessories.

Olesen, (A division of Entertainment Resources Inc.). 19731 Nordhoff St., North Ridge, CA 91324. Phone: (818) 407-7800. Fax: (818) 407-7868. Web Site: www.hollywoodrentals.com. Carlos DeMattos, CEO.

All production supplies, equipment for TV, theater, both live & taped.

Omicron Video, 22251 Roscoe Blvd., West Hills, CA 91304. Phone: (818) 704-0704. Fax: (818) 704-0475. E-mail: sales@omicronvideo.com. Web Site: www.omicronvideo.com. Kimiharu Akiyama, pres.

Video/audio distribution equipment. Computer graphics/HDTV distribution equipment.

Omnimount Systems, 8201 S. 48th St., Phoenix, AZ 85044. Phone: (480) 829-8000. Fax: (480) 756-9000. E-mail: info@omnimount.com. Web Site: www.omnimount.com. Garrett Weyand, CEO; Alexander Cyrell, pres.

Loudspeaker mounts-omnidirectional adjustability supporting ounces to hundreds of pounds. Also, flexible, refined mounting systems for TV's/computer monitors & peripherals.

180 Connect, 6365 N.W. 6th Way, Suite 200, Ft. Lauderdale, FL 33309. Phone: (800) 683-0253. Fax: (954) 671-8619. Dalia Rodborne, mgr.

Have been providing Turkey residential/commercial inside premise wiring & outside plant construction svcs for 20 yrs.

Opamp Labs Inc., 1033 N. Sycamore Ave., Los Angeles, CA 90038. Phone: (323) 934-3566. Fax: (323) 462-6490. E-mail: bel@opamplabs.com. Web Site: www.opamplabs.com. B. Losmandy, chief engr & pres.

Amplifiers: audio, video, microphone, line & power. Audio oscillators & transformers. Power supplies, network audio/video feed boxes, audio/video routing switches.

Optical Disc Corp., 12150 Mora Dr., Sante Fe Springs, CA 90670. Phone: (562) 946-3050. Fax: (562) 946-6030. Web Site: www.optical-disc.com. Richard Wilkinson, pres; Ken Shrimplin, sr VP; John Brown, VP.

Recordable laser video discs, videodisc recording systems & other auxiliary equipment. Compact disc & videodisc mastering systems.

Orban, (A Harman International Co.). 1525 Alvarado St., San Leandro, CA 94577. Phone: (510) 351-3500. Fax: (510) 351-0500. E-mail: info@orban.com. Web Site: www.orban.com. Jay Brentlinger, pres/CEO.

Orban manufacturers bcst audio equipment for radio & TV including processors for TV, FM, AM & HF & the Audicy digital audio workstation, & the Airtime digital audio delivery system.

Ortel, 2015 W. Chestnut St., Alhambra, CA 91803. Phone: (626) 293-3400. Fax: (626) 293-3428. E-mail: docmaster@agere.com. Web Site: www.emcore.com. Gyo Shinozaki, mgr.

Signal transmission products, specializing in opto electronics & RF electronics technologies.

Allen Osborne Associates Inc., 756 Lakefield Rd., Westlake Village, CA 91361. Phone: (805) 495-8420. Fax: (805) 373-6067. E-mail: j_osborne@aoa-gps.com. Web Site: www.aoa-gps.com. Jim Osborne, VP.

Pneumatic masts systems for remote E.N.G., fixed or mobile radio communications, etc.

Otari USA Sales Inc., 9420 Lurline Ave., Unit C, Chatsworth, CA 91311. Phone: (818) 731-1785. Fax: (818) 594-7208. Fax: (818) 734-1786. Web Site: www.otari.com.

Manufacturer of audio & video cassette loaders & duplicators. Manufacturer of audio mixing consoles, hard disk audio recorders, tape recorders, DAT recorders, minidisc recorders & players, CD changers, digital audio format converters.

P

PBI Media, 701 Westchester Ave., White Plains, NY 10604. Phone: (914) 328-9157. Fax: (914) 328-9093. E-mail: kipmktg@kipi.com. Web Site: www.kipinet.com. Don Pazour, chmn; John Nolan, vice chmn.

San Mateo, CA 94404. Knowledge Industry Publications, Inc., 1400 Fashion Island Blvd, Suite 600. Phone: (650) 524-1750.

Magazines, trade shows & seminars.

P.C.& E., 2235 Defoor Hills Rd., Atlanta, GA 30318. Phone: (404) 609-9001. Fax: (404) 609-9926. Web Site: www.pce-atlanta.com. Doug Smith, pres; Matt Timmons, gen mgr.

Equipment rental, grip & process trailers; rental & sls for lighting, expendables, camera.

PESA Switching Systems, Inc., 330 A Wynn Dr., Huntsville, AL 35805. Phone: (256) 726-9200. Fax: (256) 726-9271. Web Site: www.pesa.com. Dave Gass, CFO.

Melville, NY 11747, 35 Pinelawn Rd, Suite 99E. Phone: (800) 328-1008. Robert McAlpine.

Routing switchers.

PMTV Producers Management Television, 800 N. Henderson Ave., King of Prussia, PA 19406-3207. Phone: (610) 768-1770. Fax: (610) 768-1773. E-mail: mailto.pmtv@pmtv.com. Web Site: www.pmtv.com. Brian Powers, pres; Rob Schmoll, VP/gen mgr.

Full-svc mobile TV production company, providing mobile units, crews, satellite svcs, lighting, staging, etc. for sports, entertainment & teleconferences worldwide.

POA/Paul Olivier & Associates Ltd., Box 410, 626 Forest View Way, Palmer Lake, CO 80133. Phone: (719) 488-2270. Fax: (719) 488-2648. Paul Oliver, pres; Howard Phillips, engrg dir; Rick Brandon, controller.

TV bcst equipment, design engrg, fabrication, turnkey TV systems, bcst & cable consulting svcs, mobile units.

Pace Micro Technology P.L.C., Victoria Rd., Saltaire, Shipley, West Yorkshire BD18 3LF. United Kingdom. Phone: 44 (1274) 532000. Fax: 44 (1274) 532010. E-mail: info@pace.co.uk. Web Site: www.pace.co.uk. Michael Bett, chmn; John Dyson, dir & acting CEO; Neil Grydon, pres; Tim Fern, chief tech officer; Andrew Wallace, mktg dir.

Boca Raton, FL 33431, 3701 FAU Blvd, Suite 200. Phone: (561) 995-6000. Fax: (561) 995-6001. Tom O'Laughlin.

Analogue & digital set top boxes for the reception of satellite, cable & terrestrial TV transmissions.

Pacific Tower Co., 4334 N.E. 148th Ave., Portland, OR 97230. Phone: (503) 254-1055. Fax: (503) 254-1055. Gilbeert J. Nielsen, pres.

Tower sls & erection for TV, radio, microwave; obstruction lighting & ground systems.

Equipment Manufacturers and Distributors Alphabetical Index

Packaged Lighting Systems Inc., P.O. Box 285, 29 Grant St., Walden, NY 12586. Phone: (845) 778-3515. Phone: (800) 836-1024 (orders). Fax: (845) 778-1286. E-mail: info@packagedlighting.com. Web Site: www.packagedlighting.com. Lillian Hilzen, pres; Hy Hilzen, dir technology.
Factory prewired, self-contained TV studio systems complete with lighting/dimming/grid/power distribution.

Panasonic Broadcast & Television Systems Co., One Panasonic Way, Panazip 2E-7, Secaucus, NJ 07094. Phone: (201) 348-5300. Fax: (201) 348-5318. Web Site: www.panasonic.com/broadcast. Andy Takani, pres.
Los Angeles, CA 90068, 3330 Cahuenga Blvd. W. Phone: (323) 436-3500.
Secaucus, NJ 07094, One Panasonic Way, 4E-7. Phone: (201) 348-7621.
MII VCR, D3 digital VCRs, digital processed cameras, Carts (MARC) analog & digital, tapes, DVC pro, D5, Post Box, RAMJA products, monitors, projectors.

Panavision New York, 540 W. 36th St., New York, NY 10018. Phone: (212) 606-0700. Fax: (212) 244-4457. Web Site: www.panavisionnewyork.com. Peter Schnitzler, pres; Ira Goodman, VP.
16mm & 35mm motion picture & video equipment, lighting & grip equipment, generators, trucks, dollies & cranes.

Panel Authority Inc., 411 New Ave., Lockport, IL 60441. Phone: (815) 838-0488. Fax: (815) 838-7852. E-mail: preston@panelauthority.com. Web Site: www.panelauthority.com. Preston Wakeland, pres.
Custom made engraved aluminum connector panels & enclosures.

Parsons Audio, 192 Worcester St., Wellesley Hills, MA 02481. Phone: (781) 431-8708. Fax: (781) 431-8783. E-mail: sales@paudio.com. Web Site: www.paudio.com. Mark Parsons, owner; Les Arnold, sls; Rick Scott, sls.
Equipment sls for on-air & production Sony, Yamaha, Dolby, Digidesign, Lexicon, Denon, Tascam, etc.

Parsons Manufacturing Corp., 1055 O'Brien Dr., Menlo Park, CA 94025. Phone: (650) 324-4726. Fax: (650) 324-3051. E-mail: pmccase@aol.com. Web Site: www.pmccases.com. Alan R. Parsons, CEO; Alan Hall, controller.
Instrument carrying cases, shipping cases molded plastic, retracting wheels & recessed hardware.

Paulmar Industries Inc., Box 638, Antioch, IL 60002. Phone: (847) 395-2080. Fax: (847) 395-2475. Web Site: www.paulmar.com. E-mail: sales@paulmar.com. Robert F. Menary, pres.
Automatic film, video inspection machines, film & video supplies.

Peavey Electronics, 711 A St., Meridian, MS 39301-2898. Phone: (601) 483-5365. Fax: (601) 486-1278. Web Site: www.peavey.com. Hartley Peavey, CEO.
Recording & audio products, SMPTE/MIDI synchronization signal processing, reference monitors, microphones & production mixing consoles.

Peerless Industries Inc., 3215 W. North Ave., Melrose Park, IL 60160. Phone: (708) 865-8870. Fax: (708) 865-0760. Web Site: www.peerlessindustries.com. E-mail: info@peerlessindustries.com. Ken Dillon, CEO.
Video Mounting hardware including stands, carts & brackets for floor, furniture, wall & ceiling applications.

Penn Elcom Inc., 12691 Monarch St., Garden Grove, CA 92841. Phone: (714) 230-6200. Fax: (714) 230-6222. E-mail: california@penn-elcom.com. Web Site: www.penn-elcom.com. Frank McCourt, pres; Phil Strafford, dir.
Windsor, ON N9A 6J3 Canada, 2020 Halford Dr. Phone: (519) 737-9494. Mark Dryden, pres.
Pompton Plains, NJ 07444, 230 W. Pkwy, Unit 8. Phone: (201) 839-7777. Richard Stratford.
Houston, TX 77095, 9772 Whithorn Dr. Phone: (281) 855-9772. Andrew Lawson.
Hardware & accessories for flightcases, racks, speaker cabinets, stagelights & trussing.

Penny & Giles Inc., 1100 E. Woodfield Rd., Suite 140, Schaumburg, IL 60173-5116. Phone: (847) 995-0840. Fax: (847) 995-0838. E-mail: u.s.sales@controls.com. Web Site: www.pgcontrols.com.
Cwmfelinfach, Gwent NP1 7HZ Phone: (44) 1495-202024.
Studio faders; joystick controllers; T-Bar controllers for video effects generators; MIDI mgr & D.A.W. interface.

Penta Laboratories, 9740 Cozycroft Ave., Chatsworth, CA 91311. Phone: (818) 882-3872. Phone: (800) 421-4219. Fax: (818) 882-3968. Web Site: www.pentalabs.com. Steve Sanett, pres; Peter Russell, VP; Stacey Romm, CFO; Veronica Calderon, mgr.
Electron tubes distribution & mfg.

Pentax Imaging Co., 600 12th St., Suite 300, Golden, CO 80401. Phone: (303) 799-8000. Fax: (303) 728-0226. Web Site: www.pentaxusa.com. Robert Bender, pres.
Manufacture camera lens.

Performance Power Technologies, Box 947, Roswell, GA 30077. Phone: (770) 475-3192. E-mail: poweringcatv@yahoo.com. Web Site: www.performance-power.com. Jud Williams, pres.
Standby power supplies, AC power supplies & battery testers.

PerkinElmer, 35 Congress St., Salem, MA 01970. Phone: (978) 745-3200. Fax: (978) 745-0894. Web Site: www.perkinelmer.com. John Pautler, opns mgr.
High-medium-intensity aviation obstruction lighting & beacons. FAA-approved; StrobeGuard & FlashGuard.

Phasetek Inc., 550 California Rd., Unit 11, Quakertown, PA 18951. Phone: (215) 536-6648. Fax: (215) 536-7180. E-mail: phasetekinc1@earthlink.net. Web Site: www.phasetekinc.com. Kurt Gorman, pres; David Gorman, mktg VP.
Manufactures AM/MW antenna, phasing equipment, antenna tuning units, diplexers, dummy loads, RF inducters & components.

Philip-Cooke Co., 132 N. 11th St., Allentown, PA 18102. Phone: (800) 887-0950. Phone: (610) 437-2251. Fax: (610) 437-1610. E-mail: kentk@philipcooke.com. Web Site: www.philipcooke.com. Kent Kjellgren, pres.
Distribute video cassette duplications equipment & CD's.

Phillystran Inc., 151 Commerce Dr., Montgomeryville, PA 18936. Phone: (215) 368-6611. Fax: (215) 362-7956. E-mail: rstronski@phillystran.com. Web Site: www.phillystran.com. Wayne Wister III, pres; Kenneth A. Knight, sls.
Phillystran HPTG; electrically transparent, maintenance free tower guy system; specially designed systems for high-power applications.

Phoenix E N G, Inc., 6832 Foxhill Ln., Cincinnati, OH 45236. Phone: (513) 891-1444. Fax: (513) 891-3453. E-mail: engphoenix@aol.com. Jennifer Braun; Kevin Jordan, pres; Bob Braun, VP mktg.
"One man band" live trucks, vans, 4-wheel-drive. On-location radio vehicles & production trucks.

Photo Research, 9731 Topanga Canyon Pl., Chatsworth, CA 91311. Phone: (818) 341-5151. Fax: (818) 341-7070. Web Site: www.photoresearch.com. Francis Dominic, pres.
Brightness photometers, footcandle meters, telephotometers, spectroradiometers, spectral & spatial scanners.

Photomart Cine-Video Inc., 6327 S. Orange Ave., Orlando, FL 32809. Phone: (407) 851-2780. Phone: (800) 443-2901. Fax: (407) 851-2553. E-mail: info@photomartusa.com. Web Site: www.photomartusa.com. Cloyd Taylor, pres.
Sales, service, of professional support equipment and supplies for video, film and still photography.

Pinnacle Systems Inc., 280 N. Bernardo Ave., Mountain View, CA 94043. Phone: (650) 526-1600. Fax: (650) 526-1601. Web Site: www.pinnaclesys.com. E-mail: sales@pinnaclesys.com. Mark L. Sanders, chmn; Charles J. Vaughan, pres/CEO; Ajay Chopra, dir.
Manufacturer digital video effects & graphics work stns. Digital video effects & graphics.

Pinzone Engineering Group Inc., 10142 Fairmount Rd., Newbury, OH 44065. Phone: (304) 368-7950. Fax: (304) 729-5591. Basil F. Pinzone Jr., pres.
Turnkey satellite uplink/downlink systems & networks; Pinzone CORUM AM Anti-Skywave antenna.

Pioneer New Media Technologies Inc., 2265 E. 220th St., Long Beach, CA 90810. Phone: (310) 952-2000. Fax: (310) 952-2100. Web Site: www.pioneerbroadband.com. Paul Dempsey, pres.
Columbus, OH 43228, 2200 Dividend Dr. Phone: (614) 876-0771. John Unverzagt, dir engrg. (Engrg office).
Set-top & remote-controlled tunable converters; one- & two way addressable converters & control systems.

Pirelli Cables North America—Communications Division, 700 Industrial Dr., Lexington, SC 29072-3799. Phone: (803) 951-4800. Fax: (803) 951-1002. Web Site: www.us.pirelli.com. Raymond Robinson, VP/gen mgr; Charlie Carson, mktg mgr; Robert Hauptner, natl sls mgr.
Surrey, BC V3W 2WI Canada Phone: (604) 591-3311. Lynette Yakimovitch, customer svc mgr.
ISO 9001-registered manufacturer of fiber-optic cables & supplier of optical amplifier products for the cable TV industry.

Pirod Inc., Box 128, 1545 Pidco Dr., Plymouth, IN 46563. Phone: (574) 936-4221. Fax: (574) 936-6796. E-mail: pirod@pirod.com. Web Site: www.pirod.com. Myron C. Noble, CEO; Hillary Asher, sls VP.
Solid-rod towers, monopoles & tower accessories for cellular, PCs, bdcst, microwave & two-way communication.

Pixel Instruments Corp., 160-B Albright Way, Los Gatos, CA 95032. Phone: (408) 871-1975. Fax: (408) 871-1976. E-mail: info@pixelinstruments.tv. Web Site: www.pixelinstruments.tv. J. Carl Cooper, pres; Mirko Vojnovic, engrg dir.
Audio & video signals processing equipment including audio synchronizers, video frame synchronizers, audio delays & video delay detectors.

Plastic Reel Corp. of America, 40 Triangle Blvd., Carlstadt, NJ 07072. Fax: (201) 933-9468. Benjamin Zuk, pres; Pat Baccarella, exec VP; Carole Pinker, pres.
North Hollywood, CA 91605, 8140 Webb Ave. Phone: (818) 504-0400. Carole Pinker, VP.
Chicago, IL 60644, 5410 W. Roosevelt Rd. Phone: (800) 929-0356. Edwin Santani, office mgr.
Videotape, audiotape reels, boxes, video cassette mailing, storage boxes, video supplies, recording media, video & audio.

Polyline Corp., 1401 Estes Ave., Elk Grove Village, IL 60007-5405. Phone: (800) 701-7689. Phone: (847) 357-1266. Fax: (800) 816-3330. Web Site: www.polylinecorp.com. Ed Kaiser, pres.
Irwindale, CA 91702, 16018 Adelante, Unit C. Phone: (800) 701-7689.
Recording, duplicating & packaging supplies for audio, video & CD from stock.

Potomac Instruments Inc., 932 Philadelphia Ave., Silver Spring, MD 20910. Phone: (301) 589-2662. Fax: (301) 589-2665. E-mail: sales@pi-usa.com. Web Site: www.pi-usa.com. David G. Harry, COO; Guy E. Berry, mgr.
Antenna monitors, field strength meters, audio test equipment.

Power & Telephone Supply Co., 2673 Yale Ave., Memphis, TN 38112. Phone: (901) 324-6116. Fax: (901) 320-3082. Web Site: www.ptsupply.com. Jim Pentecost, pres; Laburn Dye, VP; Larry Smith, VP.
Los Angeles, CA 90670, 12314 Bell Ranch Rd. Phone: (310) 903-1701. Fax: (310) 903-1705. Sonny Dickinson.
Miami, FL 33166, 7535 N.W. 52nd St. Phone: (305) 597-0091; 597-0262. Tommy Browder.
Des Moines, IA 50321, 3107 S.W. 61st St, Bldg. D. Phone: (515) 244-4375. Fax: (515) 244-4757. Doug McPhee.
Lexington, NC 27292, Box 1856, 2950 Greensboro St. Phone: (704) 249-0256. Fax: (704) 249-7475. Don Skinner.
Tigard, OR 97224, 16666 S.W. 72nd, Bldg. 12. Phone: (503) 620-4909. Fax: (503) 620-9074. Andy Baker. (Portland branch).
Reamstown, PA 17567, Box 244, Rt. 272. Phone: (215) 267-4991. Fax: (215) 267-4367. Don Skinner.
Memphis, TN 38112, Box 12383, 2673 Yale Ave. Phone: (901) 324-6116. Fax: (901) 320-3082. Dale Stevenson.
Dallas, TX 76063, 1456 S. 2nd Ave. Phone: (817) 477-1556. Fax: (817) 477-1557. Ray Morrison.
Neenah, WI 54956, 987 Ehlers Rd. Phone: (414) 725-5454. Fax: (414) 725-6162. Roger Rademacher.
Full-line supplier of communication products, including telecom, data & cable TV.

Powr-Ups Corp., One Roned Rd., Shirley, NY 11967. Phone: (631) 345-5700. Fax: (631) 345-0060. Steven E. Summer, pres.
DC-motor controls.

Precision Microproducts of America, #1 Comac Loop, Unit 13, Ronkonkoma, NY 11779. Phone: (631) 580-3456. Fax: (631) 580-3003. E-mail: sales@p-m-a.com. Web Site: www.p-m-a.com. Jerry Wasserman, pres.
Photographic processing machines & accessories.

Equipment Manufacturers and Distributors Alphabetical Index

Prime Image Inc., 662 Giguere Ct., Suite C, San Jose, CA 95133-1742. Phone: (408) 867-6519. Fax: (408) 926-7294. E-mail: primeimageinc@earthlink.net. Web Site: www.primeimageinc.com. William B. Hendershot III, pres; Roberta Hendershot, exec VP; Keith Moeller, VP engrg; James Aldrich, VP.

Designs & manufactures video time base correctors, synchronizers, electronic still stores, audio/video delays, standards converters & time reduction devices.

PrismaGraphics Inc., Box 703, Milwaukee, WI 53201. Phone: (414) 342-6464. Phone: (800) 325-1089. Fax: (414) 342-0932. E-mail: info@prismapkg.com. Web Site: www.prismapkg.com. Richard Schmaelzle, pres.

Printer manufacturer specializing in presentation folders, media kits, sls kits & videocassette packaging.

Pro Video & Film Equipment Co. Inc., 11425 Mathis Ave., Dallas, TX 75234. Phone: (972) 869-9990. Phone: (888) 869-9998. Fax: (972) 869-0145. E-mail: providfilm@aol.com. Web Site: www.provideofilm.com. Bill Reiter, pres.

Used equipment dealer specializing in video, bcst, film, lighting, audio. Consignment, sales, leasing & appraisal svcs available. Service & repairs.

Production Consultants & Equipment, Inc. (PC&E), 2235 Defoor Hills Rd., Atlanta, GA 30318. Phone: (404) 609-9001. Phone: (800) 537-4021. Fax: (404) 609-9926. E-mail: mail@pce-atlanta.com. Web Site: www.pce-atlanta.com. Doug Smith, pres; Randy Nappier, mgr; Steve Samsini, mgr; Matt Timmons, gen mgr.

Atlanta, GA 30319. PC&E Briarwood Stage, 1842 Briarwood Rd. Phone: (404) 609-9001. Jeff Funderburk, stage mgr.

Maintains a 60,000-sq.-ft. facility. Motion picture equipment rental; Arriflex cameras; lighting & grip truck fleet; camera cars; sls showroom; three sound stages.

Production Intercom Inc., Box 3247, Barrington, IL 60011-3247. Phone: (800) 562-5872. Fax: (847) 381-4360. E-mail: info@beltpack.com. Web Site: www.beltpack.com. Glenn mullis, pres; Sibbelina Mullis, sec.

Unique talent receiver (IFB), small to large intercom systems, headsets for cameras & new half-duplex wireless system.

Products International Inc., 9893 Brewers Ct., Laurel, MD 20723. Phone: (240) 568-3940. Fax: (240) 568-3948. E-mail: sales@prodintl.com. Web Site: www.prodintl.com.

Equipment, instruments, tools, supplies for electronic production, maintenance & svc.

Professional Communications Systems, (A division of Media General Broadcasting, Inc). 5426 Beaumont Center Blvd., Suite 350, Tampa, FL 33634. Phone: (800) 447-4714. Fax: (813) 886-9477. Web Site: www.pcomsys.com. Ray A. Stephens, pres.

Pensacola, FL 32507, 2001 Augusta Ave. Phone: (850) 455-9800. Hardy Morris.

Jacksonville, FL 32216, 4110 Southpoint Blvd, Suite 129. Phone: (904) 281-0650. Fax: (904) 281-0309. Ed Kothera.

Miami, FL 33186, 11921 S.W. 144th St. Phone: (305) 253-4900. Fax: (305) 253-2551. Lloyd Hicks.

Plantation, FL 32792, 7860 Peters Rd, F-104. Phone: (954) 472-9400. Fax: (954) 424-6065. Charles Ross.

West Palm Beach, FL 33409, 931 Village Blvd, Suite 905A. Phone: (561) 753-3666. Fax: (561) 753-9387. Mike Marlow.

Winter Park, FL 32792, 7051 University Blvd, Suite 310. Phone: (407) 657-6421. Fax: (407) 657-0475.

Consulting, design, procurement, integration, training & support.

Professional Sound Corp., 28085 Smyth Dr., Valencia, CA 91355. Phone: (661) 295-9395. Fax: (661) 295-8398. E-mail: sales@professionalsales.com. Web Site: www.professionalsound.com. Ron Meyer, pres.

Design, manufacture of portable sound recording products for film & video industries

Professional Sound Services Inc., 311 W. 43rd St., Suite 1100, New York, NY 10036. Phone: (212) 586-1033. Fax: (212) 586-0970. Web Site: www.pro-sound.com. Rich Topham, pres.

Wireless microphones, wireless & wired intercoms, IFB, telephone interfaces, analog & digital recorders, mixers, lavaliers, boompoles.Sls, rentals & service.

Prophet Systems Innovations, 111 W. Third St., Ogallala, NE 69153. Phone: (877) 774-1010. Fax: (308) 284-4181. E-mail: prophetsales@prophetsys.com. Web Site: www.prophetsys.com. Kevin Lockhart, pres.

Protech Audio Corp., 192 Cedar Rd., Indian Lake, NY 12842. Phone: (518) 648-6410. Fax: (518) 648-6395. E-mail: sales@protechaudio.com. William Murphy, gen sls mgr.

Professional audio preamps, power amps & signal processors, Dugan Automixers.

Q

QEI Corporation, One Airport Dr., Box 805, Williamstown, NJ 08094. Phone: (856) 728-2020. Phone: (800) 334-9154. Fax: (856) 629-1751. E-mail: qeisales@qei-broadcast.com. Web Site: www.qei-broadcast.com. Charles H. Haubrich, pres; Edwin Etschman, opns VP; John J. Pilman, engrg VP.

FM transmitters 10 w to 60 kw, Cat-Link digital STL/TSL, digital stereo generator, 691 FM modulation monitor/test set. Digital RPU. System, custom remote control and monitoring systems

QSC Audio Products Inc., 1675 MacArthur Blvd., Costa Mesa, CA 92626-1440. Phone: (714) 754-6175. Fax: (714) 754-6174. Web Site: www.qscaudio.com. Barry Andrews, CEO; Pat N. Quilter, VP engrg; John Andrews, COO; Pete Kalmen, natl sls mgr.

Professional power amplifiers, dual monaural power amplifiers, plug-in accessory products, integrated amplifiers, music & paging system.

QTV, 208 Harbor Dr., Stamford, CT 06902. Phone: (203) 406-1400. Fax: (203) 323-3394. E-mail: sales@qtv.com. Web Site: www.qtv.com. Michael Accardi, VP sls.

New York, NY 10010, 19 W. 21st St. Phone: (212) 929-7755. Fax: (212) 929-2105. Steve Carofalo, gen mgr.

Los Angeles, CA 90036, 5919 W. 3rd St. Phone: (213) 936-6195. Steve Hulkower, gen mgr.

Computer prompter software. 9", 12" & 15" on-camera prompters. Lightweight flat panel prompters.

Qintar Technologies Inc., 31352 Via Colinas, Suite 104, West Lake Village, CA 91362. Phone: (818) 991-7300. Fax: (818) 889-7400. E-mail: sales@qintar.com. Web Site: www.qintar.com. Randall Tishkoff, pres.

Active & passive devices for CATV, amplifiers, filters, connectors, wall plates & wiring products.

Quality Tower Erectors Inc., 2280 10th St. S.E., Largo, FL 33771. Phone: (727) 585-6176. Fax: (727) 581-3277. Robert F. Diamond, pres.

Maintenance, erection, antenna systems, microwave, cellular, painting, turnkey service & tower site rental.

Quantel Inc., 199 Elm St., New Canaan, CT 06840. Phone: (203)972-3199. Fax: (203) 972-3189. Web Site: www.quantel.com. Ken Ellis, CEO.

Toronto, ON M5E 1E5 Canada, 1Yonge St, Suite 1100. Phone: (416) 362-9522. Mark Northeast.

Los Angeles, CA 90212, 8501 Wilshire Blvd, Suite 340. Phone: (310) 652-9227. Fax: (310) 657-8869. Mark Grasso.

San Francisco, CA 94104, 100 Bush St, Suite 1910. Phone: (650) 225-9036. (415) 263-1300. Fax: (650) 225-9091. Tom McGowan.

Atlanta, GA 30338, 5 Concourse Pkwy, Suite 330. Phone: (770) 804-5470. Fax: (770) 804-5479. Dan Wingard.

Chicago, IL 60611, 541 N. Fairbanks, Suite 1225. Phone: (312) 755-1766. Fax: (312) 755-1767.

New York, NY 10019, 111 W. 57th St., 10th Fl. Phone: (212) 977-4877. Fax: (212) 977-6539. Dave Saadatmandi.

Irving, TX 75038, 1425 Greenway Dr, Suite 470. Phone: (972) 751-1818. Fax: (752) 756-0006. Mike Rucker.

Quantel is the world's leading designer & manufacturer of digital image processing & manipulation products for video, film & print.

Quick-Set International Inc., 3650 Woodhead Dr., Northbrook, IL 60062-1895. Phone: (847) 498-0700. Fax: (847) 498-1258. E-mail: sales@tripods.com. Web Site: www.tripods.com. Jim Fenning, VP sls.

Instrument positioning equipment. Tripods, pan & tilts.

R

R-Columbia Products Co. Inc., 2008 St. Johns Ave., Highland Park, IL 60035. Phone: (847) 432-7915. Fax: (847) 432-9181. E-mail: sales@rcolumbia.com. Web Site: www.rcolumbia.com. I. Rozak, pres; Ed Hill, sls.

Headphones with & without microphone; cameraman headphones, wired & wireless intercom systems, ultralight headphones & IFB/ENG telephones.

RF Specialties Group, (RF Specialties of Missouri). 22406 N.E. 159th St., Kearney, MO 64060. Phone: (800) 467-7373. Fax: (816) 628-4508. Web Site: www.rfspec.com. Chris Kreger, CEO; John Sims, sls.

Makati City, Metro Manila, NO 15239 Philippines. RF Specialties of Asia Corporation, 4958 Guerrero St, Poblacion. Phone: +63-2-412-4327. Fax: +63-2-895-6509. E-mail: eedmiston@rfsasia.com. Ed Edmiston.

Santa Barbara, CA 93105. RF Specialties of California, 3463 State St, Suite 229. Phone: (805) 682-9429. (800) 346-6434. Fax: (805) 682-5170. E-mail: rfsca@aol.com. Sam Lane.

Crestview, FL 32539. RF Specialties of Florida, 4706 Young Rd. Phone: (850) 423-7335. (800) 476-8943. Fax: (850) 423-7331. E-mail: rfoffl@aol.com. William Hoisington. Cell (850) 621-3680.

Richmond, IN 47374-1501. RF Specialties of Missouri, Inc., 1651 Capri Lane. Phone: 888-966-1990. Fax: 800-859-5481. E-mail: rf@insightbb.com. Rick Funk. Cell: 765-914-7778.

Kearney, MO 64060. RF Specialties of Missouri, Inc., 22406 N.E. 159th St. Phone: (800) 467-7373. (816) 628-5959. Fax: (816) 628-4508. E-mail: rfmo@uniteone.net. Chris Kreger; John Sims. Chris Cell: 816-506-7473.

New Ipswich, NH 03071. RF Specialties of Pennsylvania, Inc., 40 Settlement Hill. Phone: (603) 878-0618. (800) 485-8684. Fax: (603) 878-1527. E-mail: sam_on_the_hill@Monad.net. S.A. Matthews. Cell: (603) 801- 8466.

Las Vegas, NV 89129. RF Specialties of California, 3416 Lacebark Pine Street. Phone: 888-737-7321. Fax: 866-737-7321. E-mail: newbro@ix.netcom.com. Bill Newbrough.

Ebensburg, PA 15931. RF Specialties of Pennsylvania, Inc., 619 Industrial Park Road, Ste 200. Phone: (814) 472-2000. Fax: (814) 472-2230. E-mail: rfofpa@aol.com. Dave Edmiston. Cell: (814) 659-6575.

Monroeville, PA 15146-0002. RF Specialties of Pennsylvania, Inc., Box 2. Phone: (866) 412-7373. Fax: (412) 291-1135. E-mail: edrfofpa@nb.net. Pittsburgh office - Ed Young.

Southampton, PA 18966. RF Specialties of Pennsylvania Inc., Box 477. Phone: (888) 260-9298. (215) 322-2410. Fax: (215) 322-4585. E-mail: harrynlarkin@cs.com. Harry Larkin. (Philadelphia Office).

Amarillo, TX 79114. RF Specialties of Texas, Box 7630. Phone: (800) 537-1801. (806) 372-4518. Fax: (806) 373-8036. E-mail: rfstx@swbell.net. Don Jones. Cell (817) 312-7489.

Fort Worth, TX 76119. RF Specialties of Texas (Fort Worth Sales Office), 3528 Fairfax. Phone: (888) 839-7373. (817) 535-1979. Fax: (817) 535-0784. E-mail: rfstxftw@charter.net. Wray Reed.

Mukilteo, WA 98275-2226. RF Specialties of Washington, Inc., 885 18th Street. Phone: 425-210-9196. Fax: 925-476-7886. E-mail: waltlowery@msn.com. Walt Lowery.

Vancouver, WA 98687. RF Specialties of Washington Inc., Box 87571. Phone: (800) 735-7051. (360) 828-5992. Fax: (360) 883-4940. E-mail: rfswa@bobtheitguy.com. Bob Trimble.

Full-line radio bcst equipment suppliers. AM & FM transmitters, towers, lines, antenna systems, studios, microwave & digital systems.

RF Technologies Corp., 12 Foss Rd., Lewiston, ME 04240. Phone: (207) 777-7778. Fax: (207) 777-7784. Web Site: www.rftechnologies.net. George M. Harris, CEO.

Designs & manufactures high-power bcst RF nets, components for FM & TV bcstrs. Products include antennas, diplexers, combiners, filters, switches, coax, waveguides & coaxal.

RTS Systems Telex Communications Inc, /. 2550 N. Hollywood Way, Suite 207, Burbank, CA 91505-1055. Phone: (818) 566-6700. Fax: (818) 843-7953. Web Site: www.telex.com. Ralph Strader, VP; Murray Porteous, natl sls mgr; Dave Richardson, rgnl sls mgr.

Destin, FL 32541, 311 Stillwater Cove. Phone: (850) 654-4058. Rick Fisher, sls regl mgr.

Butler, NJ 07405, Box 866, 10 Park Pl. Bldg. 1. Phone: (973) 283-6200. Ken Smalley, rgnl sls.

Milford, PA 18337, 3807 Sunrise Lakes. Phone: (570) 686-5444. Chuck Roberts, tech support/engrg.

Terrell, TX 75160, 10927 FM 1565. Phone: (972) 524-6047. Britt Bowers, rgnl sls.

Centerville, VA 20120, 15463 Waters Creek. Phone: (703) 867-8333. Michael Brown, sls regnl.

Intercommunication systems, IFB systems, pro-audio amplifiers, microphones & phono preamplifiers.

Radamec Inc., 100 Jersey Ave., Bldg. D, New Brunswick, NJ 08901. Phone: (732) 846-0500. Fax: (732) 846-0544. E-mail: bret@radamecbroadcast.com. Web Site: www.radamecbroadcast.com. Bret Lukezic, VP.

Bcst quality studio camera robotics, Parliamentary camera robotics & virtual sets.

Radian Communication Services Inc, 2700 Matheson Blvd. E., Suite 800 West Tower, Mississauga, ON L4W 4V9. Canada. Phone: (905) 212-8200. Fax: (905) 212-8250. Web Site: www.radiancorp.com.

Broadcasting & Cable Yearbook 2006

F-23

Equipment Manufacturers and Distributors Alphabetical Index

Design, supply, instal of bcst transmitters, antennas & towers.

Radio Aids Inc., 313 Kintzele Rd., Michigan City, IN 46350. Phone: (219) 879-2215. Fax: (219) 874-8239. John M. Carpenter, pres.

Measurement of occupied bandwidth, TV aural & visual, radio carriers, subcarriers, pilots, STL/TSL links.

Radio Computing Services (RCS), 12 Water St., White Plains, NY 10601. Phone: (914) 428-4600. Fax: (914) 428-5922. E-mail: info@rcsworks.com. Web Site: www.rcsworks.com. Philippe Generali, pres; Mike Powell, VP; Richard Darr, sls VP.

Frankfurt 60388, Borsigallee 37. Phone: 49-610-973-4450. Fax: 49-610-973-4499. E-mail: info@rcseurope.de. Karl Kessler, gen mgr.

Richmond, BC V6X 3R9 Canada, Box 32060, 410 #5 Rd. Phone: (604) 986-4468. Fax: (604) 986-4469. Ross Langbell.

Paris 75011 France, 83 Ave. Philippe Auguste. Phone: 33-1-53-27-36-36. Fax: 33- 1-53- 27- 36-60. Eric Vanryckeghem.

Bandra Mumboi (West), NO 400050 India, 262 Hart Niwas, 30th Rd. Phone: +91 22 697 1600. Fax: +91 22 695 5760. Elliot Stechman.

Christchurch, NO 8005 New Zealand. RCS (NZ) Ltd., 33 Sir William Pickering Dr. Phone: +64.3.358.4333. Fax: +64.3.358.4330. E-mail: info@rcs.co.nz. Web Site: www.rsc.co.nz. Ian Campbell.

Singapore 079903 Singapore, 10 Anson Rd, 10-10 International Plaza. Phone: +65 6324 6658. Fax: 65-6324-6659. E-mail: cfawell@attglobel.net. Colin Fawell, gen mgr.

Bergbron, Johannesburg, NO 1709 South Africa. RCS Africa, Leephy Studios, 11 Jonkershoek Rd. Phone: +27.11.477.1229. Fax: +27.11.673.3948. E-mail: hayden@rscafrica.co.za. Hayden Beetar.

Malmo SE-211 35 Sweden. RCS Scandinavia, Kalendgatan 26. Phone: +46.40.66.55.880. Fax: +46.40.66.55.888. E-mail: info@rcs.se. Web Site: www.rcs.se. Sven Andrae.

London, NO W1N 5FD United Kingdom. RCS United Kingdom, 167-169 Great Portland St. Phone: 44.20.7636.9636. Fax: 44.20.7636.7766. E-mail: info@rcsuk.com. Web Site: www.rcsuk.com. Sebastian Holmes.

Live Oak, CA 95953, 6018 Madden Ave. Phone: (530) 695-3997. Fax: (530) 674-5780. E-mail: hshaw@rcsworks.com. Dean Cull, western sls; Jennifer Cull, govt.

Miami, FL 33145, 1385 Carol Way, #202. Phone: (305) 860-5870. Fax: (305) 860-5832. Candice Castillo.

Digital studio automation & digital audio ripping/analysis, music scheduling, traf, sls, newsroom & talk show software/hardware, internet/streaming tools.

Radio Design Labs. (RDL), Box 1286, Carpinteria, CA 93014. Phone: (805) 684-5415. Fax: (805) 684-9316. E-mail: sales@rdlnet.com. Web Site: www.rdlnet. Joel Bump, pres; Jerry Clements, VP.

Full line of microphone & line level amplifiers, mixers, DAs & processors.

Radio Detection/Riser Bond, 154 Portland Rd., Bridgton, ME 04009. Phone: (207) 647-9495. Fax: (207) 647-9496. E-mail: bridgton@radiodetection.spx.com. Web Site: www.riserbond.com. Jim Walton, sls VP.

Electronic test equipment; cable fault locators; time domain reflectometer.

Radio Engineering Industries Inc., 6534 L St., Omaha, NE 68117. Phone: (402) 339-2200. Fax: (402) 339-1704. E-mail: sales@radioeng.com. Web Site: www.radioeng.com. Terry Jukes, chmn.

Sls, svc of bcst equipment, amplifiers, paging systems, SCA & coml sound equipment.

Radio Frequency Systems, 200 Pondview Dr., Meriden, CT 06450. Phone: (203) 630-3311. Fax: (203) 634-2272. E-mail: sales.americas@rfsworld.com. Bill Bayne, pres.

Rigid coaxial line (7/8" to 9 3/16"), FM antennas, FM, VHF/UHF IFTS, MMDS, TV antennas, dehydrators, instal accesories, RF, microwave antenna subsystems, instal & field svc.

Radio Photo Antennas Inc., 48 Mountain Rd., Farmington, CT 06032. Phone: (860) 676-0051. Fax: (860) 677-9639. E-mail: cfaricher@snet.net. Robert E. Richter, pres; Professor Maurice Hately, chief tech off; Alec Thomas, head engr.

Hansworth, Middlesex. NO TW13 7 DW United Kingdom, 97 Foxwood Close. Phone: (1) 44 0797 085. Fax: 8175. Alex Thomas, head engrg.

Company mkts medium wave & long wave antenna.

Radio Research Instrument Co. Inc., 584 N. Main St., Waterbury, CT 06704. Phone: (203) 753-5840. Fax: (203) 754-2567. E-mail: radiores@prodigy.net. Web Site: www.radioresearch.thomasregister.com. P. J. Plishner, pres; E. B. Doyle, exec VP.

Provides radar systems, threat emitters & spare parts; complete maintenance facility for repair.

Radio Systems Inc., 601 Heron Dr., Logan Township, NJ 08085-1741. Phone: (856) 467-8000. Fax: (856) 467-3044. E-mail: sales@radiosystems.com. Web Site: www.radiosystems.com. Daniel Braverman, pres; Gerrett Conover, VP.

Audio consoles, distribution amplifiers, low-power AM transmitters, clock, timer systems, telephone hybrids & studio wiring systems.

Radiogear Inc., 8746 Gerst Ave., Perry Hall, MD 21128. Phone: (410) 933-8445. Fax: (410) 933-8352. E-mail: email@radiogearinc.com. Web Site: www.radiogearinc.com. Charles Spencer, pres.

Radio bcst equipment, audio supplies (RF, audio) & quality pre-owned radio bcst equipment.

Radyne ComStream Corp., 3138 E. Elwood St., Phoenix, AZ 85034. Phone: (602) 437-9620. Fax: (602) 437-4811. E-mail: sales@radynecomstream.com. Web Site: www.radynecomstream.com. Brian Duggan, pres; Robert C. Fitting, CEO; Steve Eymann, VP engrg; David Koblanski, gen mgr.

Singapore 069045, 12-04 Natwest Centre, 15 McCallum St. Phone: (65) 2254016. Fax: (65) 3251950. Mike Lee.

Beijing 100045 China. China, Canway Bldg. Rm. 1501, N. 66 LanLishi Rd. Phone: (86) 10 68042542. Fax: (86) 10 68042524. (Xicheng district).

Godalming, Surrey GU7 1EY United Kingdom. Europe/Middle East/Africa, Mill Pool House, Mill Ln., Dunsfold Suite, 2nd Fl. Phone: (44) 1483 421 302. Fax: (44) 1483 421 303. Neil Pole.

San Diego, CA 92121, 6340 Sequence Dr. Phone: (619) 458-1800. Fax: (619) 657-5400. (U.S. & Canada).

Boca Raton, FL 33487. Latin America, 6413 Congress Ave, Suite 220. Phone: (561) 988-1210. Fax: (561) 988-8290.

Complete digital audio bcst network for compressed CD quality audio over satellite.

Digital data distribution products for the financial industry.

Railway Systems Design, Inc., Valley Forge Corporate Center, 1010 Adams Ave., Audubon, PA 19403-2402. Phone: (610) 650-7730. Fax: (610) 650-8190. Web Site: www.rsdconsulting.com. Walter J. Clarke, ptnr; Terry A. Shantz, ptnr.

Consulting engrs, tower engrg, design & construction mgmt.

Ram Broadcast Systems, Box 277, Wauconda, IL 60084-0277. Phone: (800) 779-7575. Phone: (847) 487-7575. Fax: (847) 487-2440. Web Site: www.ramsyscom.com. Ron Mitchell, pres.

Switchers (audio & video) mixers, intercom systems, audio/video DAs, systems engrg & custom cabinetry.

Rangertone Research Inc., 40 Entin Rd., Clifton, NJ 07014. Phone: (973) 594-8722. Fax: (973) 594-8724. George P. Zazzali, pres; Daniel J. Zazzali, VP.

Audiovisual equipment.

Raven Screen Corp., 112 Spring St., Monroe, NY 10950. Phone: (212) 534-8408. Fax: (845) 782-1840. Martin Soss, pres.

Manual, motorized & custom projection screens & materials.

Record/Play Tek Inc., Box 790, 110 E. Vistula St., Bristol, IN 46507-0790. Phone: (574) 848-5233. Fax: (574) 848-5333. E-mail: stoll@recordplaytek.com. Web Site: www.recordplaytek.com. Michael Stoll, CEO.

Voice logging recorders "911," cassette, reel-to-reel, VHS, computer CDR & DVD RAM.

Recortec Inc., 1620-A Berryessa Rd., San Jose, CA 95133-1026. Phone: (408) 928-1480. Fax: (408) 729-3661. E-mail: sales@recortec.com. Web Site: www.recortec.com. Dr. Lester H. Lee, pres.

Manufacturer of commercial disc players & LCD players.

Recoton Corp., 145 E. 57th St., New York, NY 10022. Phone: (212) 644-0220. Fax: (212) 644-8205. E-mail: ildau@recoton.com. Web Site: www.recoton.com. Robert Borcharbt, pres; Peter Ildau, exec VP.

MTS stereo & SAP decoders to convert monaural TV & VCRs to receive stereo TV & bilingual bcsts.

Reel-O-Matic Inc., Box 95309, Oklahoma City, OK 73143. Phone: (405) 672-0000. Fax: (405) 672-7200. Web Site: www.reel-o-matic.com. Terry Simmons, pres.

Equipment to re-spool, coil, measure & distribute cable.

Rees Associates Inc., 9211 Lake Hefner Pkwy., Oklahoma City, OK 73120. Phone: (405) 942-7337. Fax: (405) 948-1261. Web Site: www.rees-associates.com. Frank W. Rees Jr., pres; C. Leroy James, exec VP; William H. Yost, VP mktg.

Dallas, TX 75219-4341, 3102 Oak Lawn, Suite 200. Phone: (214) 522-7337. Frank W. Rees Jr., pres.

Bcst & production facility design; architectural svcs; studio design; equipment planning; facility business plans; interior design; consulting.

Register Data Systems, 1691 Forsyth St., Macon, GA 31201. Phone: (478) 745-5500. Fax: (478) 745-0500. E-mail: sales@registerdata.com. Web Site: www.registerdata.com. Lowell L. Register, pres; Ricky Lockerman, sls.

Digital audio automation systems for live assist, satellite, traf & billing software packages for radio & TV.

Renkus-Heinz Inc., 19201 Cook St., Foothill Ranch, CA 92610-3510. Phone: (949) 588-9997. Fax: (949) 588-9514. E-mail: sales@renkus-heinz.com. Web Site: www.renkus-heinz.com. Harro K. Heinz, pres; Carl Dorwaldt, mktg mgr.

Reference point arrays, powered network loudspeakers, R-control remote supervision network. Reference point arrays, powered network loudspeakers.

Research Technology International Inc., 4700 Chase Ave., Lincolnwood, IL 60712-1689. Phone: (847) 677-3000. Phone: (800) 323-7520. Fax: (847) 677-1311. E-mail: sales@rtico.com. Web Site: www.rtico.com. Ray L. Short Jr., pres; Thomas W. Boyle, sr VP; Bill Wolavka, sls VP.

Videotape evaluator/cleaners; degaussers; storage & care, supplies, film cleaners. CD/DVD cleaners-restorers inspectors.

Reuters American Inc., 199 Water St., New York, NY 10038. Phone: (646) 223-4000. Web Site: www.reuters.com.

Ottawa, ON K1P 5P8 Canada, 165 Sparks St., Booth Bldg. Phone: (613) 235-6745. Antony Parry, financial correspondent; John Rogers, gen news.

Toronto, ON M5H 3T9 Canada, Standard Life Centre, 121 King St. W., 20th Fl. Phone: (416) 869-3600. Peter Thomas, mgr Canada.

Montreal, PQ H3A 2A5 Canada, 2020 Rue Universite, Suite 1020. Phone: (514) 282-0705. William Miller.

Los Angeles, CA 90071, 445 S. Figueroa, Suite 2100. Phone: (213) 380-2014. Ronald Clarke, chief.

Washington, DC 20005, 1333 H St. N.W, Suite 410. Phone: (202) 898-8300. Bruce Russell, chief.

Chicago, IL 60606, 311 S. Wacker Dr, Suite 1100. Phone: (312) 922-6038. Geoffrey Atkins, chief.

Kansas City, MO 64112, 4800 Main. Phone: (816) 561-8671. Bob Martin.

Supplier of natl, world, business news, info to media & professionals.

Richardson Electronics, (A division of Broadcast Richardson). PO Box 393, 40W267 Keslinger Rd., LaFox, IL 60147. Phone: (630) 208-2200. Fax: (630) 208-2662. E-mail: broadcast@rell.com. Web Site: broadcast.rell.com. Edward Richardson, CEO; Dario Sacomani, CFO; Robert Prince, VP.

LaFox, IL 60147-0393, Box 393, 40W267 Keslinger Rd. Phone: (630) 208-2200. (800) 882-3872. Fax: (630) 208-2550. E-mail: broadcast@rell.com. Web Site: broadcast.rell.com.

Global provider of power tubes, TV, radio transmitters, IP, digital satellite systems, NLE video systems & studio pakages.

Richmond Sound Design Ltd., Box 19523, Vancouver, BC V5T 4E7. Canada. Phone: (604) 715-9441. Fax: (250) 414-5205. E-mail: sales@richmondsounddesign.com. Web Site: www.richmondsounddesign.com. C.B. Richmond, pres; M. Williams, mgr.

London, ON EC2A 3PB United Kingdom, 23 Charlotte Rd. Phone: +44 20 7613 3305. John Leonard.

Automated multichannel audio for live shows & theatre; show controllers.

Ripley Company, 46 Nooks Hill Rd., Cromwell, CT 06416. Phone: (860) 635-2200. Phone: (800) 528-8665. Fax: (860) 635-3631. E-mail: info@ripley-tools.com. Web Site: www.ripley-tools.com. Rick Salvas, sls dir; Keith D'Amato, sls dir.

Ripley's Cablematic, Miller, Claussana Utility tool lines offer manufacturers cable preparation tools for CATV telecomm data & electric utiliy.

Broadcasting & Cable Yearbook 2006

Rodelco Electronics Corp., 111 Haynes Ct., Ronkonkoma, NY 11779. Phone: (631) 981-0900. Fax: (631) 981-1792. E-mail: rodelco@erols.com. Joseph M. Rodgers, gen mgr.

TV translators, VHF & UHF.

Rohn Industries Inc., 6718 W. Plank Rd., Peoria, IL 61604. Phone: (309) 697-4400. Fax: (309) 697-5612. E-mail: mail@rohnnet.com. Web Site: www.rohnnet.com. Horace Ward, pres/CEO; Craig Ahlstrom, VP sls.

Towers (up to 2,000 feet) monopoles, antenna mounts for communication industry. Turnkey construction & installation avaible worldwide.

Roland Corp. U.S., Box 910921, 5100 S. Eastern Ave., Los Angeles, CA 90091-0921. Phone: (323) 890-3700. Fax: (323) 890-3701. Web Site: www.rolandus.com. Dennis Houlihan, pres; Mark Malbon, exec VP.

Electronic musical instruments, signal processors, sound reinforcement, hard disk editors, noise eliminators, bcst production equipment & post production equipment.

Rosco Laboratories Inc., 52 Harbor View Ave., Stamford, CT 06902. Phone: (203) 708-8900. Fax: (203) 708-8919. E-mail: info@rosco.com. Web Site: www.rosco.com. Stan Miller, pres; Stan Schwartz, exec VP.

Hollywood, CA 90038, 1120 N. Citrus Ave. Phone: (323) 462-2233. Fax: (323) 462-3338. Jim Meyer, mgr.

Lighting filters & diffusers, studio floor covering, connectors & digital (or rental & custom) backdrops.

Roscor Corp., 1061 Feehanville Dr., Mount Prospect, IL 60056. Phone: (847) 299-8080. Fax: (847) 299-4206. Fax: (847) 803-8089. E-mail: mroston@roscor.com. Web Site: www.roscor.com. Paul Roston, pres; Mitch Roston, exec VP; Howard Ellman, sls VP; Edward Jones, VP finance.

Cincinnati, OH 45241, 2868 E. Kemper Rd. Phone: (513) 772-3393. Tim Navaro, branch mgr.

Farmington Hills, MI 48331, 27280 Haggerty Rd, Suite C2. Phone: (248) 489-0090. Devon Tiderington, branch mgr.

Milwaukee, WI 53204, 600 W. Virginia St. Phone: (414) 223-2600. Marshall Carlson, branch mgr.

Professional audio/video/RF/presentation equipment. Turnkey engrg & instal svcs.

Ross Video Ltd., Box 220, 8 John St., Iroquois, ON K0E 1K0. Canada. Phone: (613) 652-4886. Fax: (613) 652-4425. E-mail: solutions@rossvideo.com. Web Site: www.rossvideo.com.

Video production switchers, analog & digital terminal gear, video keyers, encoders & decoders, mini master control & telecine switchers.

Royal Consumer Information Products, 379 Campus Dr., Somerset, NJ 08875. Phone: (732) 627-9977. Web Site: www.olivettiofficeusa.com. Salomon Suwalsky, pres; Todd Althoff, VP mktg.

S

SAIC, 1710 Saic Dr., Mclean, VA 22102. Phone: (703) 821-4300. Web Site: www.saic.com.

Eidophor large screen projectors. Rental source & sole North American distributor.

S&L Plastics Inc., 2860 Bath Pike, Nazareth, PA 18064. Phone: (610) 759-0280. Fax: (610) 759-0650. Web Site: www.slpinc.cc. John Bungert, pres.

Thermo plastic products.

SES Americom, 4 Research Way, Princeton, NJ 08540-6684. Phone: (609) 987-4000. Fax: (609) 987-4495. Web Site: www.ses-americom.com. Andreas Georghiou, sr VP.

Satellite distribution svcs for coml bcst & cable TV; prog syndicators, SNG & bcst radio distribution svcs.

S W R Inc., (Systems with Reliability.). 619 Industrial Park Rd., Ebensburg, PA 15931. Phone: (814) 472-5436. Fax: (814) 472-5552. Web Site: www.swr-rf.com. Edward J. Edmiston, pres; David K. Edmiston, gen sls mgr.

Timog, Quezon City, 31-E Scout Bayoran. Phone: 011-632-411-0068. Edward J. Edmiston, pres.

Manufacturers of TV & FM transmit antennas, rigid coax, waveguide & associated accessories.

Sabine Inc., 13301 Hwy. 441, Alachua, FL 32615. Phone: (386) 418-2000. Fax: (386) 418-2001. E-mail: sabine@sabine.com. Web Site: www.sabine.com. Doran Oster, pres.

Manufacturers of digital signal processing equipment for sound systems. Makers of the patented FBX Feedback Exterminator & True MobilityTM wireless microphones.

Sachtler Corp. of America, 55 N. Main St., Freeport, NY 11520. Phone: (516) 867-4900. Fax: (516) 623-6844. E-mail: sales@sachtler.com. Web Site: www.sachtler.com. Robert Carr, VP; Eric Falkenberg, pres.

Burbank, CA 91505, 3316 W. Victory Blvd. Phone: (818) 854-4446.

Complete line of camera support equipment for ENG, EFP, O.B. & the new generation of studio cameras. Lighting for news, production & studio open-face technology & fresnel.

Sacramento Theatrical Lighting (STL), 950 Richards Blvd., Sacramento, CA 95814. Phone: (800) 283-2785. Fax: (916) 447-5012. E-mail: saclight@aol.com. Steve Odehnal, mgr.

Specialists in studio & location lighting, grip equipment, draperies, rigging & grid work. Consultation & production svcs. Sls, rentals & svcs.

Sadelco Inc., 75 W. Forest Ave., Englewood, NJ 07631. Phone: (201) 569-3323. Fax: (201) 569-6285. E-mail: sadelco@aol.com. Web Site: www.sadelco.com. Les Kaplan, pres.

Signal level meters, calibrators & leakage detectors.

Samson Technologies Corp., Box 9031, Syosset, NY 11791. Phone: (516) 364-2244. Fax: (516) 364-3888. E-mail: sales@samsontech.com. Web Site: www.samsontech.com. Douglas Bryant, pres; Scott Goodman, CEO; Jack Knight, VP opns; Bob Caputo, VP sls; Pete Moe, VP mktg.

Manufacturer of wireless microphones, mixing consoles, power amplifiers & audio products. Behringer audio processing, Hartke speakers & Zoom effects processors.

Sanyo Fisher Co., 21605 Plummer St., Chatsworth, CA 91311. Phone: (818) 998-7322. Fax: (818) 998-3533. Web Site: www.sanyo.com. Paul W. D'Arcy, VP.

Audio amplifiers & receivers, CD players, audiotape recorders, turntables, dictation machines, cordless telephones, TVs, VTRs & LCD projectors.

Sarnoff Corp., (A Subsidiary of SRI International). 201 Washington Rd., Princeton, NJ 08543-5300. Phone: (609) 734-2000. Fax: (609) 734-2221. Web Site: www.sarnoff.com. Satyam C. Cherukuri, pres.

Contract rsch & dev facility for electronic, biomedical, & information technologies, specializing in digital video.

Sascom Marketing Group, 34 Nelson St., Oakville, ON L6L 3H6. Canada. Phone: (905) 469-8080. Fax: (905) 469-1129. E-mail: sales@sascom.com. Web Site: www.sascom.com. Curt Smith, pres.

Sascom Represents: Adgil, Audio Cube, Digital Audio Denmark, Doremi, Junger, Msoft Server Sound, Lafont & Stage Tec.

Satellite Systems Corp., 101 Malibu Dr., Virginia Beach, VA 23452. Phone: (757) 463-3553. Fax: (757) 463-3891. Web Site: www.satsyscorp.com. Bob Kite, pres.

SCPC & video subcarrier satellite systems for radio, SNG & data bcst networks.

Schafer International, 220 Surrey Dr., Bonita, CA 91902. Phone: (619) 267-9000. Fax: (619) 267-9003. E-mail: patty@schaferinternational.com. Web Site: www.schaferinternational.com. Paul C. Schafer, pres.

Equipment & parts, for radio & TV stns, primarily in Mexico.

Schafer World Communications Corp., Box 1047, Marion, VA 24354-1047. Phone: (276) 783-2000. Fax: (276) 783-2064. Bob Dix, pres; Ann Dix, VP; Kevin Soos, mktg.

Schafer offers two levels of sophistication in hard disk audio systems, "GENESIS" Digital Studio: touch screen & remote control interface; excellent live assist & full automation capability (complete music scheduling software included); cut-to-cut mixing on hard disk including editing; simultaneous record/playback from hard disk; can connect to external machines & CD multi-players.

Schneider Optics Inc., 285 Oser Ave., Hauppauge, NY 11788. Phone: (631) 761-5000. Fax: (631) 761-5090. E-mail: info@schneideroptics.com. Web Site: www.schneideroptics.com. Ron Leven, sr VP; Dwight Lindsay, sr VP.

Manufacturer/distributor of high quality optical filters for video, still photography & motion picture. Product line also includes a wide range of lenses for CCTV, large format photography, darkroom enlarging & slide & film projection.

Scientific-Atlanta, 5030 Sugarloaf Pkwy., Lawrenceville, GA 30044. Phone: (770) 236-5000. Fax: (770) 902-2591. E-mail: gregg.echols@sciatl.com. Web Site: www.sciatl.com. James McDonald, chmn/CEO; Patrick Tylka, pres; Dwight Duke, pres; Michael Harney, pres.

A complete line of cable TV & broadband communications systems, products. and professional services.

Scientific-Atlanta Canada Inc. Nexus Division, Satellite TV Networks, 120 Middlefield Rd. Unit 1, Scarborough, Ontario, BC MIS4-M6. Canada. Phone: (416) 299-6888. Fax: (416) 299-7145. Web Site: www.scientificatlanta.com.

TV RF signal processing equipment, transmission products & cable TV amplifiers.

Scott Studios Corp., 13375 Stemmons Fwy., Suite 400, Dallas, TX 75234. Phone: (972) 620-0070. Web Site: www.scottsstudios.com. David Scott, pres.

Radio automation systems; digital audio.

ScreenLight & Grip, 502 Sprague St., Dedham, MA 02026. Phone: (781) 326-5088. Fax: (781) 326-4751. E-mail: lightsne@aol.com. Web Site: www.screenlightandgrip.com. Guy Holt, pres.

Location lighting & production svcs, equipment rental, trucks, vans, etc.

Second Chance Body Armor Inc., 7915 Cameron St., Central Lake, MI 49622-0573. Phone: (231) 544-5721. Phone: (800) 253-7090. Fax: (231) 544-9824. E-mail: email@secondchance.com. Web Site: www.secondchance.com. Paul J. Banducci, VP/gen mgr.

Leading body armor manufacturer now offering ballistic protection for news media reporters & photographers.

Seger Electronics, 97 Libbey Pkwy, Weymouth, MA 02189. Phone: (781) 682-4844. Web Site: www.seger.com. Frank Flynn, pres; Ray Norton, CEO.

Carson, CA 90746-1313, 1010 Sandhill Ave. Phil Spinosa, Southern CA rgnl mgr; Elaine Fleischer, Karen Wamboldt.

Cupertino, CA 95014, 19925 Stevens Creek Blvd, Suite 126. Phone: (415) 621-7386 (Fresno). (415) 621-7386 (San Jose). Jan Wilcock, Northern CA rgnl mgr; Jan Wilcock, Larry Dickey.

San Diego, CA 92121, 6540 Lusk Blvd, Suite 138B. Phone: (619) 231-6740. (714) 525-6606. Gail Usher; Bill Zangger.

Aurora, CO 80014, 10730 E. Bethany Dr, Suite 107. Phone: (303) 773-1432 (CO). (801) 532-2832 (UT). Cathy Gauman, north central rgnl mgr.

Boca Raton, FL 33432, 499 E. Palmetto Park Rd. Phone: (561) 417-0224.

Franklin, MA 02038, Franklin Office Park W., 38 Pond St., Suite 104. Phone: (508) 553-9813 (Boston). Richard Hayes.

Concord, OH 44060, 9853 Johnnycake Ridge Rd, Suite 202. Phone: (216) 639-1796 Cleveland. Ed Koshinski, natl sls mgr.

Dallas, TX 75206, 6060 N. Central Expwy, Suite 560. Phone: (214) 234-6227. Brett Keller.

Stafford, TX 77477, 3727 Greenbriar, Suite 107, Unit 2021. Phone: (713) 222-0100 (Houston). (512) 474-9285 (Austin). Peggy Nowlin.

Kent, WA 98032, 23830 Pacific Hwy. S, Suite 300. Phone: (206) 343-9049 (WA). (503) 223-7110 (OR). Rick Fritz.

Largest inventory of electromechanical components. No mimimums. Liberal sampling. 24-hour order check. Custom assembly, engraving & printing.

Selco Products Co., 605 S. East Street, Anaheim, CA 92805. Phone: (714) 717-1333. Fax: (714) 917-1355. E-mail: sales@selcoproducts.com. Web Site: www.selcoproducts.com. Tim Wilkinson, pres; Michelle Blakeslee, mktg.

A full range of product lines are offered by selco including thermal products, control knobs, electronic controls and digital panel meters.

Sencore Inc./AAVS, 3200 Sencore Dr., Sioux Falls, SD 57107. Phone: (605) 339-0100. Fax: (605) 339-0317. Fax: (605) 335-6379. Web Site: www.sencore.com. Doug Bowden, VP.

Electronic test equipment for servicing & performance testing of consumer electronics & CATV/MATV equipment.

Senior Aerospace, Ketema Division. 790 Greenfield Dr., El Cajon, CA 92021. Phone: (619) 442-3451. Fax: (619) 440-1456. Ron Case, gen mgr.

Design build-to-print aerospace products, cryogenic lines, valves, burst discs, electric motors, actuators.

Sennheiser Electronic Corp., One Enterprise Dr., Old Lyme, CT 06371. Phone: (860) 434-9190. Fax: (860) 434-1759. E-mail: info@sennheiserusa.com. Web Site: www.sennheiserusa.com. John Falcone, pres/CEO; Scott Schumer, VP sls.

Col. Del Valle, D.F. Mexico 03100, Av. Xola No. 613 PH6. Phone: (525) 639-0956. Fax: (525) 639-9482.

Burbank, CA 91505, 4116 W. Magnolia Blvd, Suite 100. Phone: (818) 845-7366. Fax: (818) 845-7140.

Broadcasting & Cable Yearbook 2006

F-25

Equipment Manufacturers and Distributors Alphabetical Index

Microphones, headphones, boomsets, wireless microphones & infrared products as well as DAS audio loudspeakers & Chevin research amplifiers.

Servoreeler Systems, (Xedit Corp.). 218-31 97th Ave., Queens Village, NY 11429. Phone: (718) 464-9400. Fax: (718) 464-9435. E-mail: srsystems@servoreelers.com. Web Site: www.servoreelers.com. Claude M. Karczmer, pres; Eileen Karczmer, sls dir.

SUSPENDED MICROPHONE SERVOREELERS - deploy, retract and position suspended microphones by remote pushbutton or computer control. ex-teleconferencing, corp board rooms, churches, concert halls, sports arenas & universities.

Sescom Inc., 608 Main St., wellsville, KS 66092. Phone: (785) 883-3009. Fax: (785) 883-4422. E-mail: sescom@sescom.com. Web Site: www.sescom.com.

Audio interfacing equipment, audio transformers & modules.

Setcom Corp., 1400 N. Shoreline Blvd., Mountain View, CA 94043-1385. E-mail: rvb@setcomcorp.com. Web Site: www.setcomcorp.com. L. Kent Schwartzman, pres; Bob Von Buelow, mktg mgr.

Portable & fixed position intercom systems, bcst intercom & portable radio headsets.

Seton Identification Products, Box 819, Branford, CT 06405. Phone: (203) 488-8059. Fax: (203) 488-7259. Web Site: www.seton.com. E-mail: comments@seton.com. Richard L. Fisk, pres.

Signs, tags, labels, pipe markers, valve tags, & nameplates to meet OSHA/ANSI specifications.

Shallco Inc., Box 1089, 308 Components Dr., Smithfield, NC 27577. Phone: (800) 876-3135 (USA only). Phone: (919) 934-3298 (outside USA). Fax: (919) 934-3135 (outside USA only). E-mail: sales@shallco.com. Web Site: www.shallco.com. John Shallcross Sr.; chmn; Jason S. Shallcross, pres.

Variable & fixed audio attenuators.

Sharp Electronics Corp., CCD Products Div., (LCD Products Group). Sharp Plaza, Mail Stop One, Mahwah, NJ 07430-2135. Phone: (201) 529-8200. Phone: (866) 4-VISUAL. Fax: (201) 529-9636. E-mail: ProLCD@SharpSEC.com. Web Site: www.SharpLCD.com. Ron Colgan, VP; Fred Krazeisze, Dir. Strategic Marketing; Bruce Pollack, Assoc. Dir. Marketing; Bob Soucy, sls dir.

Data/video projection systems for portable and permanent installation applications; LCD video monitors, TVs, VCRs, TV/VCRs and Viewcam Camcorders.

Shively Labs, Box 389, Bridgton, ME 04009. Phone: (207) 647-3327. Fax: (207) 647-8273. E-mail: sales@shively.com. Web Site: www.shively.com. Robert A. Surette; Gail Merrill, TV adv coord; David G. Allen, sls; Joe Rohrer, sls; Edd Forke, sls.

FM antennas, FM translators, branched & balanced combiners, coax, patch panels, filters, compressor dehydrators, & related RF equipment, pattern work & field svcs.

Shook Mobile Technology, LP, 7451 FM 3009, Schertz, TX 78154. Phone: (210) 651-5700. Fax: (210) 651-5220. E-mail: shook@shook-usa.com. Web Site: www.shook-usa.com. John Heaney, CEO; Ronald Crockett, pres & dir mktg.

Mobile TV production, ENG, SNV vehicles. Rack ready or turnkey delivery. HD/SD Systems integration.

Shure Inc., 222 Hartrey Ave., Evanston, IL 60202. Phone: (847) 600-8699. Fax: (847) 866-5725. Web Site: www.shure.com. E-mail: info@shur.com. R.L. Shure, chmn; S. LaMantia, pres.

Cabled & wireless microphones, automatic microphone systems, field production equipment, sound reinforcement systems.

Siemens Dematic Limited, 167 Hunt St., Ajax, ON L1S 1P6. Canada. Phone: (905) 683-8200. Fax: (905) 683-0186. Web Site: www.siemens.ca.

Solid state FM transmitters to 5 kw, automatic coaxial changeover units, shortwave transmitters.

Sierra Automated Systems & Engineering Corp., 2625 N. San Fernando Blvd., Burbank, CA 91504. Phone: (818) 840-6749. Fax: (818) 840-6751. Web Site: www.sasaudio.com. Edward O. Fritz, pres; Al Salci, VP; Giovanni Morales, gen mgr.

Audio switching & mixing systems maunufacturer. Mix-Minus/IFB, satellite distribution/switching, automated switching & distribution, studio intercom, on-air routing, teleconferencing.

Sifford Video Services, 802 Ewing Ave., Nashville, TN 37203. Phone: (615) 248-1010. Fax: (615) 244-5712. Joel Covington, pres.

DVD, CD & videotape duplication; standards conversion, distribution; specialized packaging; custom work.

Sigma Electronics Inc., 1027 Commercial Ave., Box 448, East Petersburg, PA 17520-0448. Phone: (717) 569-2681. Fax: (717) 569-4056. E-mail: eric@sigmaelectronics.com. Web Site: www.sigmaelectronics.com. Nigel Spratling, pres.

Santa Rosa, CA. Western rgnl office Phone: (707)539-5314. Randy Smith, western rgnl sls mgr.

E Greenville, PA. eastern rgnl office Phone: (215) 541-4953. Barry Gardner, international sls mgr.

Routing switchers for audio & video; distribution amplifiers; sync & test signal generators; encoders, decoders, transcoders, converters.

Signal Monitoring Service, 773 Upper Fredricktown Rd., Mt. Vernon, OH 43050. Phone: (888) 449-5643. Fax: (740) 397-2769. Robert (Bob) Bowman, owner.

AM/FM/TV frequency & modulation documentation - NRSC proof for AM.

Sinar Bron Inc., 17 Progress St., Edison, NJ 08820. Phone: (908) 754-5800. Fax: (908) 754-5807. Web Site: www.sinarbron.com. James Bellina, pres; William D. Andrews, VP.

Pro-Cyc prefabricated coves for infiniti walls in video & photo studios; & studio lighting/HMI.

Sitco Antenna Company, Box 20456, 10330 N.E. Marx St., Portland, OR 97220-1139. Phone: (503) 253-2000. Fax: (503) 253-2009. E-mail: sitco@simplicitytool.com. Web Site: www.simplicitytool.com. Gustave Berliner, CEO; Markus Burcker, pres.

CATV, MATV antennas.

SiteSafe Inc., 200 N. Glebe Rd., Suite 1000, Arlington, VA 22203. Phone: (703) 276-1100. Fax: (703) 276-1169. Web Site: www.sitesafe.com. Wesley O. McGee, pres.

Engrg software & wireless telecom engrg consulting svcs.

Skotel Corp., 92094-7400 Taschereau, Brossard, PQ J4W 3K8. Canada. Phone: (514) 806-2340. Fax: (514) 221-2338. E-mail: stephenscott@videotron.ca. Stephen Scott, pres.

Time code readers & generators, reference signal generators.

Snell & Wilcox Inc., 2225-I Martin Ave., Santa Clara, CA 95050. Phone: (408) 260-1000. Phone: (800) 827-4544. Fax: (408) 260-2800. E-mail: snellcal@aol.com. Web Site: www.snellwilcox.com. Dick Crippa, pres.

Havant, Harts P09 2PE. Smith & Wilcox Ltd., Southleigh Park House, Eastleigh Rd.

Petersfield, Hampshire GU33 5AZ. Snell & Wilcox Ltd., Durford Mill. Phone: 44-0-730-821-188. 44-0-730-821-199. David Youlton, chmn.

Snell & Wilcox is one of the world's largest manufacturers of bcst electronics. The complete product family includes a full range of video & audio processing equipment consisting of Decoding, Encoding, High Definition Format Conversion, MPEG Compression & Pre-processing, Display, Noise Reduction, Post Production Switchers (both SDTV & HDTV), Standards Conversion, Synchronization, Test & Measurement & IQ Modular products.

Solid State Logic Inc., 320 W. 46th St., New York, NY 10036. Phone: (212) 315-1111. Fax: (212) 315-0251. E-mail: nysales@solid-state-logic.com. Web Site: www.solid-state-logic.com. Rick Plushner, pres.

Los Angeles, CA 90036, 5757 Wilshire Blvd. Phone: (323) 549-9090. Phil Wagner, VP/western opns.

SSL C100 digital bcst console is perfect for on-air, live to tape.

Solutec Ltd. (HA), 4360 D'Iberville, Montreal, PQ 437 8572. Canada. Phone: (514) 522-8960. Fax: (450) 437-8572.

Closed Caption encoders (analog &SDI) & software.

Sound Designers Studio, 424 W. 45th St., New York, NY 10036-3565. Phone: (212) 757-5679. Fax: (212) 265-1250.

Electronic equipment racking systems, console automation systems, digital recording facilities.

Soundcraft U.S.A., 8500 Balboa Blvd., Northridge, CA 91329. Phone: (818) 920-3212. Fax: (818) 920-3208. E-mail: soundcraft-usa@harman.com. Web Site: www.soundcraft.com. Dave Neal, mktg; Tom Der, natl sls mgr.

Audio mixing consoles for recording, theater, concert sound reinforcement & bcstg.

Southern Broadcast Services, 80 Commerce Dr., Suite B, Pelham, AL 35124. Phone: (800) 256-9235. Fax: (205) 663-7108. Web Site: www.southernbroadcastservices.com. Jim Coleman, pres.

Tower erection, antenna instal, maintenance svcs.

Spacenet Services Inc., 1750 Old Meadow Rd., McLean, VA 22102. Phone: (703) 848-1000. Fax: (703) 848-1010. Web Site: www.spacenet.com. David Shiff, VP mktg.

Satellite-based interactive data, bcst data & bcst video for coml companies worldwide.

Specialized Communications, 20940 Twin Springs Dr., Smithsburg, MD 21783-1510. Phone: (800) 359-1858. Fax: (301) 790-0173. E-mail: service@spec-comm.com. Web Site: www.spec-comm.com. David Linetsky, pres; Beth A. Linetsky, mktg dir.

Factory Authorized Service Center providing repair & maintenance of bcst video equipment. Factory Integrator & Dealer for distinctive industry brands.

Spectra Sonics, 3750 Airport Rd., Ogden, UT 84405. Phone: (801) 392-7531. Fax: (801) 392-7531. Jean Dilley, controller; Gregory D. Dilley, pres.

Professional audio production, including power amps, compressor/limiters, portable speaker system, mixers, & line/distribution amps.

Spotcat Software, Box 1538, Havertown, PA 19083. Phone: (800) 536-1515. Phone: (610) 446-1515. Fax: (610) 789-4353. E-mail: support@spotcat.com. Saul Meyer, pres.

Traf & billing software for the one-person traf dept.

Sprague Magnetics Inc., 12806 Bradley Ave., Sylmar, CA 91342. Phone: (818) 364-1800. Phone: (800) 553-8712. Fax: (818) 364-1810. E-mail: smiav@spraguemagnetics.com. Web Site: www.spraguemagnetics.com. Dorothy Sprague, pres; John Austin, mgr.

Long-wearing cart, film, reel-to-reel tape heads, refurbishment svcs, replacement parts, alignment tapes, accessories.

Stage Equipment & Lighting Inc., 12250 N.E. 13th Ct., North Miami, FL 33161. Phone: (305) 891-2010. Fax: (305) 893-2828. Fax: (800) 597-2010. E-mail: mail@seal-fla.com. Web Site: www.seal-fla.com. Vivian Gill, pres; Michael Grosz, VP; Rick Rudolph, VP.

Orlando, FL 32811, 4600 S.W. 36th St. Phone: (407) 425-2010. Fax: (407) 648-2604. Mike Collins, tech consultant.

Tampa, FL 33619, 9207 Palm River Rd, Suite 108. Phone: (813) 626-8500. Fax: (813) 620-1404.

Film, video & theatrical lighting & grip, & related support equipment.

Stahl, A Scott & Fetzer Co., 3201 Old Lincoln Way, Wooster, OH 44691. Phone: (330) 264-7441. Fax: (330) 264-3319. Web Site: www.stahl.cc. Bob McBride, pres; Tom Cole, sls dir.

Merced, CA 95340 Phone: (209) 383-4336.

Cardington, OH 43315 Phone: (419) 864-6871. Eric McNaly, plant mgr.

Durant, OK 74701 Phone: (405) 924-5575. Steve Shepard, plant mgr.

Stainless LLC, 1140 Welsh Rd., Suite 250, North Wales, PA 19454. Phone: (215) 631-1400. Fax: (215) 631-1427. E-mail: ssales@stainlessllc.com. Web Site: www.stainlessllc.com. Don Doty, pres; Patrick Moore, VP; Tom Hoenninger, chief engr & VP opns; Les Kutasi, gen sls mgr.

Design, engrg and fabrication of communications and broadcast towers. Existing tower engrg studies and DTV analysis.

Stancil Corp., 2644 S. Croddy Way, Santa Ana, CA 92704. Phone: (714) 546-2002 ext. 4316. Phone: (800) 782-6245. Fax: (714) 546-2092. E-mail: guy.churchouse @stancilcorp.com. Web Site: www.stancilcorp.com. Michael Custer, CEO.

Voice logging recorders, multichannel, 4-144 channels, 24-hour recording time; digital format, instant recall recorders, windows 2000 voiceXP.

Standard Communications Corp., 1111 Knox Street, Torrance, CA 90502. Phone: (310) 532-5300. Fax: (310) 532-0397. E-mail: SatcommSales@stdcom.com. Web Site: www.standardcom.com. Ron Blanchard, pres/CEO.

Broadband TV receivers & cable headend products for broadcast and CATV.

Equipment Manufacturers and Distributors Alphabetical Index

Stanton Group, 3000 S.W. 42nd St., Ft. Lauderdale, FL 33312. Phone: (954) 689-8833. Fax: (954) 689-8460. Web Site: www.stantonmagnetics.com. E-mail: info@stantonmagnetics.com. Henri Cohen, sls dir.

Huntington, CA 92649. KRK, 5242 Business Dr. Phone: (714) 373-4600. (714) 373-0421.

Simi Valley, CA 93065. Kerwin Vega, 555 Fast Easy Street.

Turntables, professional cartridges, CD players, final scratch, monitors, speakers.

Star Case Manufacturing Co. Inc., 648 Superior Ave., Munster, IN 46321. Phone: (219) 922-4440. Phone: (800) 822-STAR. Fax: (219) 922-4442. E-mail: starcase@starcase.com. Web Site: www.starcase.com. Dennis Toma, pres; Ralph G. Hoopes, VP.

Flight cases (protective casement)—Carry Star, ATA Star, Super Star, Ultra Star, Star Light.

StarGuide Digital Networks Inc., 750 W. John Carpenter Fwy., Suite 700, Irving, TX 75039. Phone: (972) 581-2000. Fax: (972) 581-2001. Web Site: www.starguidedigital.com. E-mail: hq@starguidedigital.com.

High speed internet networking of digital audio, video & web. Software, satellite, terrestrial & DSL systems.

Storeel Corp., Box 80523, Atlanta, GA 30366. Phone: (770) 458-3280. Fax: (770) 457-5585. E-mail: reely@mindspring.com. Carolyn S. Galvin, pres; Michael Valerio, gen sls mgr; Elizabeth Galvin, VP sls.

Space-efficient storage for all formats of tape & film; double-drive systems for longer lengths; set-up trucks; CD storage.

Peter Storer & Associates Inc., 1361 W. Towne Square Rd., Mequon, WI 53092. Phone: (262) 241-9005. Fax: (262) 241-9036. E-mail: storer@storertv.com. Web Site: www.storertv.com. Peter Storer, pres; Doug Knight, sls VP.

The Program Management System - Multi-channel, multi-user, PC-based television program schedule, amortization and liability system.

Straight Line, 13410 S, E. 32nd St., Suite 3B, Bellingham, WA 98005. Phone: (425) 865-8314.

Bldg automated tape library for data storage & retrival.

Strand Lighting Inc., 6603 Darin Way, Cypress, CA 90630. Phone: (714) 230-8200. Fax: (714) 899-0042. E-mail: sales@strandlight.com. Web Site: www.strandlight.com. Bill King, pres.

New York, NY, 928 Broadway. Phone: (212) 242-1042.

Studio & remote lighting, & control equipment.

Strata Marketing Inc., 30 W. Monroe, Suite 1900, Chicago, IL 60603. Phone: (312) 222-1555. Fax: (312) 222-2510. Web Site: www.stratag.com. John Shelton, pres.

Computer software for quantitative & qualitative radio, TV & nwspr media, cable.

Strong International, c/o Ballantyne of Omaha Inc., 4350 McKinley St., Omaha, NE 68112. Phone: (402) 453-4444. Fax: (402) 453-7238. Web Site: www.ballantyne-omaha.com. John P. Wilmers, pres; Ray Boegner, sr VP.

35/70mm projection equipment, Xenon lamphouse systems, platters, Xenon bulbs, follow spotlights.

Structural System Technology Inc., 6867 Elm St., McLean, VA 22101. Phone: (703) 356-9765. Fax: (703) 448-0979.

Structural engrg studies, analysis, design, modifications, inspections, fabrication & erection of towers & antenna.

Studio Technologies Inc., 5520 W. Touhy Ave., Skokie, IL 60077. Phone: (847) 676-9177. Fax: (847) 982-0747. E-mail: stisales@studio-tech.com. Web Site: www.studio-tech.com. Gordon Kapes, pres; Carrie Loving, mgr.

Microphone pre-amplifiers, stereo simulators & recognition units, telephone & hard-wired IFB communications systems on-air announcer's consoles. Accessories for digital audio workstations.

Studio Technology, 529 Rosedale Rd., Suite #103, Kenneth Square, PA 19348. Phone: (610) 925-2785. Fax: (610) 925-2787. E-mail: sales@studiotechnology.com. Web Site: www.studiotechnology.com. Vince Fiola, owner.

Bcst furniture, design & instal svcs.

Summit Software Systems Inc., 555 Camino del Rio, Unit A1, Durango, CO 81303. Phone: (970) 385-4411. Fax: (970) 385-4734. E-mail: sales@summitsoft. Web Site: www.summitsoftware.com. Paul Adams, pres.

PC-based traf, sls, billing, accounts receivable, accounts payable, payroll & gen ledger for single or multi-stns & single or multi-users.

SUNDANCE DIGITAL

Sundance Digital Inc., 545 E. John Carpenter Fwy., Suite 200, Irving, TX 75062. Phone: (972) 444-8442. Fax: (972) 444-8450. E-mail: sales@sundig.com. Web Site: www.sundancedigital.com. Robert C. Johnson, pres; Steve Krant, Vp sls & mktg; Fred Schultz, news automation.

Sundance Digital is an award-winning leader in television automation solutions for individual, as well as multistation & central-casting broadcasters.

Superior Satellite Engineers Inc., 1743 Middle Rd., Columbia Falls, MT 59912. Phone: (406) 257-9590. Fax: (406) 257-9599. E-mail: superior@digisys.net. Web Site: www.superiorsatelliteusa.com. Ron Catlett, mgr.

Complete satellite antenna systems/svc for cable & bcst TV.

Superior Tower Services Inc., 5757 FM 1696, Iola, TX 77861. Phone: (936) 394-9925. Phone: (800) 306-4504. Fax: (936) 394-4020. Edward Carter, pres.

For all your tower & antenna needs: antenna, transmission line analysis, emergency repairs, two way, microwave, cellular, AM/FM, installations, tower erections, inspections, & maintenance.

Superscope Technologies Professionals, 2640 White Oaks Circle, Suite A, Aurora, IL 60504. Phone: (630) 820-4800. Fax: (630) 820-8103. Web Site: www.superscopetechnologies.com. Fred Hackendahl, pres.

Products include portable cassette recorders, single & dual cassette recorders, CD players, multi-track recorders, compact recorders, portable, & rackmount.

Swager Communications Inc., Box 656, Fremont, IN 46737. Phone: (260) 495-2515. Fax: (260) 495-4205. E-mail: bswager@dmci.net. Web Site: www.swager.com. Dan J. Swager, pres; Lee Swager, VP; Tim Swager, sec/treas.

Designs, fabricates, installs & maintains AM/FM, TV/CATV & microwave communication towers.

Swintek Enterprises Inc., 965 Shulman Ave., Santa Clara, CA 95050. Phone: (408) 727-4889. Phone: (408) 727-7544. Fax: (408) 727-3025. E-mail: ssales@swintek.com. Web Site: www.swintek.com. William P. Swintek, pres.

18 ch wireless intercom, 1 w IFB with wireless EAR piece receiver, complete linear headsets.

Switchcraft Inc., 5555 N. Elston Ave., Chicago, IL 60630. Phone: (773) 792-2700. Fax: (773) 792-2129. Web Site: www.switchcraft.com. Keith A. Bandolik, pres.

Offers a variety of products including audio patchbays, connectors, adapters, jacks & plugs, and video patchbays.

Symetrix Inc., 6408 216th St. S.W., Mountlake Terrace, WA 98043. Phone: (425) 778-7728. Fax: (425) 778-7727. E-mail: symetrix@symetrixaudio.com. Web Site: www.symetrixaudio.com. Dane Butcher, pres; Jim Latimer, sls dir.

Digital & analog audio signal processing.

Symmetricom, 3750 Westwind Blvd, Santa Rosa, CA 95403. Phone: (707) 528-1230. Fax: (707) 527-6640. Web Site: www.symmetricom.com.

Time & frequency receivers traceable to NIST & USNO. Complete line of time code instrumentation.

Symmetricom, 2300 Orchard Pkwy., San Jose, CA 95131. Phone: (949) 598-7500. Fax: (949) 598-7524. Erik Van derKay, pres; Bob Krist, VP.

Irvine, CA 92718. Datum-Irvine, 3 Parker. Phone: (714) 770-5000. Heinz Badura, pres.

Austin, TX 78761. Datum-Austin, Box 14766. Phone: (512) 251-2341. Jack Rice, pres.

Time code generators, readers, displays, encoders, search systems, distribution amplifiers, transmitters & receivers; design & manufacture of precision frequency products & timing instruments.

Syntellect Inc., 16610 N. Black Canyon Hwy., Suite 100, Phoenix, AZ 85053. Phone: (770) 587-0700. Phone: (800) 347-9907. Fax: (770) 587-0589. Web Site: www.syntellect.com.

Phoenix AZ 85027, 20401 N. 29th Ave. Phone: (602) 789-2800. Scott Coleman, pres.

ARUs for automated customer service, ANI svcs for PPV order processing & predictive dialing systems for telemarketing & collections.

SyntheSys Research Inc., 3475-D Edison Way, Menlo Park, CA 94025. Phone: (650) 364-1853. Fax: (650) 364-5716. E-mail: info@synthesysresearch.com. Web Site: www.synthesysresearch.com. Jim Waschura, pres; John Ryan, gen sls mgr.

SyntheSys is a leading manufacturer of test & measurement specializing in serial digital video analyzers for SDI & high definition.

System Associates, Box 5925, 4848 W. Seldon Ln., Glendale, AZ 85312. Phone: (866) 937-0209. Fax: (866) 435-0160. Web Site: www.systemassociates.com. Mike Ferguson, pres.

Used bcst TV equipment.

Systems Wireless Ltd., 555 Herndon Pkwy., Ste. 135, Herndon, VA 20170. Phone: (800) 542-3332. Fax: (703) 437-1107. E-mail: sales@swl.com. Web Site: www.swl.com. Bill Sien, sls.

Sls, service & rental of wireless microphones, wireless intercom, wireless listening devices, wireless video & Clear Com cabled intercom systems.

T

TAI Audio, 5828 Old Winter Garden Rd., Orlando, FL 32835. Phone: (407) 296-9959. Fax: (407) 648-1352. E-mail: taiaudio@aol.com. Web Site: www.taiaudio.com. Joseph Guzzi, pres.

Rental, sls & svc of professional audio for film, video, TV & postproduction. Specializes in wireless communication equipment.

TALX Corp., 1850 Borman Ct., St. Louis, MO 63146. Phone: (314) 214-7000. Fax: (314) 214-7588. Web Site: www.talx.com. William W. Canfield, pres; Michael E. Smith, VP.

Interactive communications; more specific svc; Interactive voice response, Interactive web, employment verification (work # for everyone) & Outsource svc.

TC Electronic, 5706 Lorsa Ave., Suite 107, Westlake Village, CA 91362. Phone: (818) 665-4900. Fax: (818) 665-4901. E-mail: infous@tcelectronic.com. Web Site: www.tcelectronic.com. John Maier, CEO; Ed Simeone, chmn.

Digital compressor/limiter expander, digital signal processors, DTV audio processors & high-resolution digital delays.

T-C Specialties Co., Box 192, Coudersport, PA 16915. Phone: (814) 274-8060. Phone: (800) 458-6074. Fax: (814) 274-0690. E-mail: tcsmail@adelphia.net. Web Site: www.tcspecialties.com. Daniel C. Major, pres; Bill Crown, VP production; Judi Tucker, sec; Mike Harris, VP opns.

Coupon billing systems & related forms; large volume dir mail inkjetting, presort/barcoding mailing

TDK Electronics Corp., 901 Franklin Ave., Garden City, NY 11530. Phone: (516) 535-2600. Fax: (516) 294-9318. Web Site: www.tdk.com. Hajime Sawabe, pres.

Gardena, CA 90248, 1411 W. 190 St. Phone: (310) 538-5259. Doug Booth, natl industrial sls mgr.

Irvine, CA 92614, 17871 Van Karman.

Full line of optical, magnetic, magneto optical products, audio & video pancake.

TEAC America Inc., 7733 Telegraph Rd., Montebello, CA 90640. Phone: (323) 726-0303. Fax: (323) 727-7656. Hajime Yamaguchi, pres; Gary S. Beckerman, exec VP.

Consumer audio/video & professional recording equipment, airborne video recorder, instrumentation data recorders, computer peripherals/floppy disks, tape backup & industrial optical disk recorders & playback.

TFT Inc., 1953 Concourse Dr., San Jose, CA 95131-1708. Phone: (408) 943-9323. Fax: (408) 432-9218. E-mail: info@tftinc.com. Web Site: www.tftinc.com. Darryl E. Parker, VP.

Digital, analog STLs, Reciters, synchronous boosters, modulation monitors & emergency alert systems.

TOA Electronics Inc., 601 Gateway Blvd., Suite 300, South San Francisco, CA 94080. Phone: (650) 588-2538. Fax: (650) 588-3349. Jeff Pallin, sr VP & COO.

Sound, communication equipment for coml sound & audio/video industries.

Equipment Manufacturers and Distributors Alphabetical Index

TTE Inc., 11652 W. Olympic Blvd., Los Angeles, CA 90064. Phone: (310) 478-8224. Fax: (800) 473-2791. E-mail: sls@tte.com. Web Site: www.tte.com. Stephen J. Sodaro, sls VP & mktg VP.

LC filters to 18 GHz, balun, matching transformers, combiners, active filters to 1 MHz. RF, microwave filters DC-18ghz & video splitters.

T.T. Technologies Inc., 2020 E. New York St., Aurora, IL 60504. Phone: (800) 533-2078. Phone: (630) 851-8200. Fax: (630) 851-8299. E-mail: info@tttechnologies.com. Web Site: www.tttechnologies.com. Chris Brahler, pres; Dave Holcomb, VP.

Ocala, FL 34479, 3701 N.E. 36th Ave, Suite C. Phone: (352) 622-2077. Tom Garner, gen mgr.

Grundomat pneumatic piercing tools, Grundoram pipe ramming system & Grundocrack pipe bursting systems.

TWR Lighting, (Division of 02 Wireless Solutions). 4300 Windfern, Suite 100, Houston, TX 77041-0943. Phone: (713) 973-6905. Fax: (713) 973-9352. Web Site: www.twrlighting.com. Ken Meador, pres/CEO; Raymond Kraemer, VP sls & mktg; Jeff Huchlefeld, VP opns.

Aviation obstruction lighting manufacturer, sls & service of low, medium, LED products and High Intensity systems.

Talk-A-Phone Co., 5013 N. Kedzie Ave., Chicago, IL 60625. Phone: (773) 539-1100. Fax: (773) 539-1241. E-mail: info@talkaphone.com. Web Site: www.talkaphone.com. S. Shanes, exec VP; Robert Shanes, VP sls.

Intercommunication systems, ADA compliant emergency phones, ADA areas of rescue, apartment access systems.

Tamron U.S.A. Inc., 10 Austin Blvd., Commack, NY 11725. Phone: (631) 858-8400. Fax: (631) 543-5666. Web Site: www.tamron.com. E-mail: feedback@tamron.com. Tak Move, pres; Bert Krank, western sls mgr; John Steenberg, sls; Stacie Errera, mktg comm dir; Gregg Maniaci, eastern sls mgr.

Lenses for 35mm SLR cameras, Bronica medium format cameras and CCTV lenses.

Tandberg Television Inc., 12633 Challenger Pkwy., Suite 250, Orlando, FL 32826. Phone: (407) 380-7055. Fax: (407) 380-6691. Web Site: www.tandbergtv.com.

MPEG-2 & ATSC digital compression systems for the bcst industry.

Tannoy North America Inc., 335 Gage Ave., Suite 1, Kitchener, ON N2M 5E1. Canada. Phone: (519) 745-1158. Fax: (519) 745-2364. E-mail: inquiries@tannoy.com. Web Site: www.tannoy.com. Marc Bertrand, mgng dir.

Tannoy is a leading innovator of premium audio solutions utilizing cutting edge acoustic, electronic and digital expertise.

Tapeswitch Corp., 100 Schmitt Blvd., Farmingdale, NY 11735. Phone: (631) 630-0442. Fax: (631) 630-0454. E-mail: sales@tapes.com. Web Site: www.tapeswitch.com.

Mission, CA 92692 Phone: (949) 588-9387. Jeff Johnson, rgnl sls mgr.

Fishers, IN 46038 Phone: (317) 570-6178. Tom Bertellotti, rgnl sls mgr.

New Bern, NC 28562 Phone: (252) 637-7728. Vinnie Colucci, rgnl sls mgr.

Franklin, TN 37064 Phone: (615) 591 7399. Tim DePeri, rgnl sls mgr.

Safety light curtains, sensing mats, edges, ribbon switches, electronic zone controllers, sensing bumpers, safety & protection equipment.

J.A. Taylor & Associates, Box 331, Boyertown, PA 19512-0331. Phone: (610) 754-6800. Fax: (610) 754-9766. E-mail: jataylor@broadcastassociates.com. Web Site: www.broadcastassociates.com.

Appraisers & brokers of TV production equipment. Serves video production companies, TV stns & financial institutions.

Teatronics/Entertainment Lighting Control, P.O. Box 508, Santa Mangarita, CA 93353. Phone: (805) 438-4000. Fax: (805) 438-5400. E-mail: sales@teatronics.com. Web Site: www.teatronics.com.

Lighting control & power distribution systems for stage, studio & remote applications.

Tech Laboratories Inc., 955 Belmont Ave., North Haledon, NJ 07508. Phone: (973) 427-5333. Fax: (973) 427-5455. E-mail: corporate@techlabs.com. Web Site: www.techlabsinc.com. Bernard M. Ciongoli, pres; Earl R. Bjorndal, VP.

Rotary switches; electrical/electronic subcontract, attenuators, transformers, pcb assembly, infrared security systems.

TECH-SA-PORT, Box 5372, 120 S. Whitfield St., Pittsburgh, PA 15206-0372. Phone: (412) 661-1620. Phone: (800) 543-2233. E-mail: tech-sa-port@juno.com. Web Site: www.tech-sa-port.com. Lewis J. Scheinman, pres.

Computer & electronic equipment cleaning supplies, including lint-free wipers, contamination-free chemicals, & spray dusters. All types of wiping materials.

Technet Systems Group, (A Division of Steve Vanni Associates Inc). Box 422, Auburn, NH 03032. Phone: (603) 483-5365. Fax: (603) 483-0512. E-mail: svanni@technetsystems.com. Web Site: www.technetsystems.com. Steve Vanni, pres.

Bcst equipment supplier & distributor for radio & TV, specializing in complete turnkey packages including planning, design, equipment, instal, towers & FCC licensing.

Techni-Tool Inc., 1547 N. Trooper Rd., Worcester, PA 19490-1117. Phone: (800) 832-4866. Phone: (610) 825-4990. Fax: (610) 828-5623. Fax: (800) 854-8665. E-mail: sales@techni-tool.com. Web Site: www.techni-tool.com. Paul Weiss, pres; David Weitner, mktg dir; Stuart Weiss, VP; Michael T. Ryan, sls dir.

Master distributor of hand tools/kits & shipping cases, solder/desolder equipment, ESD products, cleanroom products, test equipment & telecommunications products for the Broadcast Industry.

Technologies for Worship, 3891 Holburn Rd., Queensville, ON L0G 1R0. Canada. Phone: (905) 473-9822. Fax: (905) 473-9928. E-mail: bc@tfwm.com. Web Site: www.tfwm.com.

Trade magazine & tech directory for houses of worship involved in audio, AV, bcst, computers, film, video & music. Owner of "Inspiration Conferences & Expositions."

Tekskil Industries Inc., 108-15290-103A Ave., Surrey, BC V3R 7A2. Canada. Phone: (604) 589-1100. Fax: (604) 589-1185. E-mail: inquiries@tekskil.com. Web Site: www.tekskil.com. John Veenstra, pres; Rick Anselmo, product dev.

Cumming, GA 30040, 2145 Robin Hood Tr. Phone: (770) 844-0457. Dave Comstock.

New Orleans, LA 70118, 2101 S Carrollton Ave. Phone: (504) 865-7714.

Manufacturer of video, speech, computer teleprompting equipment, specializing in bright flat panel technology. Fold down portability & podium conversion packages.

Tektronix Inc., Box 4600, Beaverton, OR 97077. Phone: (800) 426-2200. Web Site: www.tektronix.com. Richard Willis, pres/CEO; Rich McBee, VP sls; Bob Agnes, VP/gen mgr.

Manufacturers of test, measurement & monitoring equipment for audio, bcst cable, telecommunications & equipment mf industries.

Telcom Research, 3375 N. Service Rd., A7, Burlington, ON L7N 3G2. Canada. Phone: (905) 336-2450. Fax: (905) 336-1487. E-mail: dougl@tecomresearch.com. Web Site: www.timecode.com. Tom Banting, pres.

SMPTE/EBU time code generators, readers; character inserters, LTC-VITC & VITC-LTC trans. Logging/offline/EDL software.

Tele-Measurements Inc., 145 Main Ave., Clifton, NJ 07014-1078. Phone: (973) 473-8822. Fax: (973) 473-0521. E-mail: tmcorp@aol.com. Web Site: www.tele-measurements.com. William E. Endres, pres; W. Chris Endres, gen mgr.

Bcst video equipment, tapes TV systems, teleconferencing, maintenance support, CCTV & rentals, distance learning.

Telecast Fiber Systems Inc., 102 Grove St., Worcester, MA 01605. Phone: (508) 754-4858. Fax: (508) 752-1520. E-mail: sales@telecast-fiber.com. Web Site: www.telecast-fiber.com. Richard A. Cerny, pres; Eugene E. Baker, VP.

Mill Valley, CA 94941, 835 Autumn Ln. Phone: (415) 383-5388. Fax: (650) 745-3711. James Hurwitz, mgr Western U.S.

Saco, ME 04072, 280 Ferry Rd. Phone: (207) 282-9772. Fax: (207) 282-8666.

Fuquay-Varina, NC 27526, 3009 Bentwillow Dr. Phone: (919) 557-6059. Fax: (919) 557-5206. Bryan Keen, sr sls engr.

Dallas, TX 75231, 8712 Lacrosse Dr. Phone: (214) 553-1366. Fax: (241) 553-1367.

Fiber-optic video & audio systems for TV bcst production.

Telecrafter Products, 12687 W. Cedar Dr., Suite 100, Lakewood, CO 80228-2031. Phone: (303) 986-0086. Fax: (303) 986-1042. E-mail: mail@telecrafter.com. Web Site: www.telecrafter.com. Jim Marzano, sls; Ronnie Cox, sls.

Drop installation products for broadband telecommunications delivery svc, including cable chips, cablemakers, cable guard, house boxes, fitting savers, & more.

TELEMETRICS Inc., 6 Leighton Pl., Mahwah, NJ 07430. Phone: (201) 848-9818. Fax: (201) 848-9819. Web Site: www.telemetricsinc.com. Anthony C. Cuomo, pres; Anthony E. Cuomo, mgr.

Camera pan & tilt systems & triax camera control systems.

Telenium Mobile, 525 Mildred Ave., Primos, PA 19018. Phone: (610) 626-6500. Fax: (610) 626-2638. Web Site: www.telenium.com. Tod Strine, pres.

48-foot mobile unit with Ikegami cameras; Chyron 4100EXB; Chyron Infinity A42 & A53 & Sony 1" VTRs; & BVW 75's. Available in United States & Canada.

Teleplex Inc., (Alford Division). 4801 Industrial Pkwy., Indianapolis, IN 46226. Phone: (317) 895-8800. Fax: (317) 895-2900. Tom L. Fitch, pres/CEO; Lois E. Clark, VP.

Produces precision electronics, components, FM stn combiners, custom FM radio antenna arrays, TV antenna systems, & HDTV monitor antennas. Supports all Alford products & antenna products.

Telescript Inc., 445 Livingston St., Norwood, NJ 07648. Phone: (201) 767-6733. Fax: (201) 784-0323. E-mail: info@telescript.com. Web Site: www.telescript.com. John McGrath, mgng dir.

Austin, TX 78752. Telescript West, 7801 N. Lamar Blvd. Phone: (512) 302-0766. Jim Stringer, mgr.

IBM & compatibles prompting programs & equipment. Lightweight, high-resolution 12" & 17" monitor prompters. Flat panel prompters, window based prompting software for bcst & video productions applications, comprehensive line of LCD prompters.

Teletech Inc., 38235 Executive Drive, Westland, MI 48185. Phone: (734) 641-2300. Fax: (734) 641-2323. Web Site: www.teletech-inc.com.

Facility construction, antenna instal for AM, FM, TV, LPTV & microwave; antenna site mgmt.

teletech.ca 211 Telson Rd., Unit 3, Markham, ON L3R 1E7. Canada. Phone: (905) 475-5646. Fax: (905) 475-5684. E-mail: jacksrwld@rogers.com. Web Site: www.teletech.ca. Jack Kirkpatrick, pres.

London, ON N5Z 3M7 Canada, 931 Leathorne St. Brad Rose, mgr.

Total bcst, postproduction, audio & video sls, service, & rentals of equipment & supplies.

Televideo San Diego, 4783 Ruffner St., San Diego, CA 92111. Phone: (858) 268-1100. Fax: (858) 268-1790. Web Site: www.televideosd.com. Linda Stepp, CFO; David Stepp, pres.

Televideo designs, installs, svcs video production, training, distance learning & videoconferencing systems.

Television Engineering Corp., 101 Industrial Dr., Sullivan, MO 63080. Phone: (573) 860-4700. Fax: (573) 860-4600. Web Site: www.tvengineering.com. Jack Vines Jr., gen sls mgr; Jack Vines Sr., design engr.

Manufacturer of news vans, satellite vehicles, Eagle Eye camera, IFB controller & turnkey systems.

Television Equipment Assoc. Inc./Matthey, Box 404, Brewster, NY 10509-0404. Phone: (845) 278-0960. Fax: (845) 278-0964. Bill Pegler, pres; Joseph Tocidlowski, mgr.

Serial digital interface products, NTSC/PAL Decoders, analog & digital DAs, video & pulse delays, video filters, A/D & D/A converters, headsets, serial digital/Fiberoptic links, Routing switches for digital video and radio.

Telex Communications Inc., 12000 Portland Ave. S., Burnsville, MN 55337. Phone: (952) 884-4051. Fax: (952) 884-0043. E-mail: prosound@telex.com. Web Site: www.telex.com. Ned Jackson, CEO.

Burbank, CA 91505, 2550 Hollywood Way, Suite 207. Phone: (818) 566-6700.

Wired & wireless microphones; headphones/headsets; wired & wireless intercoms; audio duplicators/copiers.

TELLABS, 1415 W. Diehl Rd., Naperville, IL 60563. Phone: (630) 798-8800. Fax: (630) 798-2000. Web Site: www.tellabs.com.

Abingdon, Oxfordshire OX14 3Y3, 29 The Quandrant. Phone: 011-44-235-524-400.

Hauppauge, NY 11788, 60 Commerce Dr. Phone: (516) 231-1550.

Teleconferencing systems, digital echo cancellers, data over voice multiplexers, signaling systems, video conferencing, audio systems.

Broadcasting & Cable Yearbook 2006

Telos Systems, 2101 Superior Ave., Cleveland, OH 44114. Phone: (216) 241-7225. Fax: (216) 241-4103. Web Site: www.telos-systems.com. Steve Church, pres/CEO; Frank Foti, pres; Michael Dosch, mgng dir.

Manufacturer of MP 3 ISDN codecs, digital network, telephone interfaces (e.g. hybrids), MP 3 internet hardware & software for webcasting.

Teltron Technologies Inc., 2 Riga Ln., Birdsboro, PA 19508. Phone: (610) 582-9450. Phone: (800) 835-8766. Fax: (610) 582-0851. E-mail: teltron@ptdprolog.net. Web Site: www.teltrontech.com.

Camera tubes for monochrome, color, special purpose applications & view finder CRTs.

Tenco Tower Co., 9647 Folsom Blvd., Sacramento, CA 95827-1326. Phone: (916) 638-8833. Fax: (916) 362-6846. E-mail: donald.tenn@towerguys.com. Donald Joseph Tenn, pres/CEO.

Instal, maintenance, sls of towers, antennas, hardware for the bcst, cable & communications industry.

Tentel, 4921 Robert J. Matthews Pkwy. # 4, El Dorado Hills, CA 95762. Phone: (916) 939-4005. Fax: (916) 939-4114. Web Site: www.tentel.com. E-mail: info@tentel.com. John Chavers, gen mgr.

Tape tension, torque,head protrusion, and spindle height gauges for tape Transports. Betacam & DVCPro training classes. DVCPro tool kit. Tape Transport Parts.

Texas Electronics Inc., Box 7225, Dallas, TX 75209. Phone: (214) 631-2490. Fax: (214) 631-4218. E-mail: info@texaselectronics.com. Web Site: www.texaselectronics.com. Carol Westlund, pres; Jane Hansen, VP; Jason Burson, sls.

Manufacturer of meteorological instruments & controls.

Texscan MSI, 2210 W. Alexander Street Ste. A, Salt Lake City, UT 84119. Phone: (801) 956-0000. Fax: (801) 956-0750. Web Site: www.texscan.com. Leonard J. Fabiano, pres.

Character generators, digital, analog commercial insertion systems, audio/video playback systems, weather data svc, multimedia graphics production systems & VCR controllers.

Thales, Box 69, 395 Oakhill Rd., Mountaintop, PA 18707. Phone: (570) 821-5000. Fax: (570) 474-5469.

Thomcast Communications Comwave Division engineers systems & solutions for the 1.8-3.6 GH2 frequency range.

Thales Broadcast & Multimedia Inc., 104 Feeding Hills Rd., Southwick, MA 01077. Phone: (413) 998-1100. Fax: (413) 569-0679. E-mail: joe.turbolski@us.thales.bm.com. Web Site: www.hales-bm.com. Mark Kearns, CEO; Richard E. Fiore Jr., sr VP.

Coral Gables, FL 33146, Gables One Tower, Suite 780. Phone: (305) 665-0067. Perry Priestley, sls dir Canada & Latin America.

Thales B&M desugbs devekios, manufactures & markets equipment sytems and solutions in the fields of terrestrial transmission, digital videl processing & multimedia distribution.

Thales Broadcast & Multimedia S.A., One rue de L'Hautil, Box150, ConFlans-Ste. Honorine F-78702. France. Phone: +33 1 34 90 31 00. Fax: +33 1 34 90 30 00. Web Site: www.thomcast.thanson-csf.con.

Provides TV, AM & FM transmitters.

Thales Components Corp., 40 G Commerce Way, Totowa, NJ 07511. Phone: (973) 812-9000. Fax: (973) 812-9050. Web Site: www.tccus.com. S. Shpock, CEO.

Power grid triodes & tetrodes, cavities, klystrons travel wave tubes & I.O.T.s.

Theatre Service & Supply Corp., 1792 Union Ave., Baltimore, MD 21211. Phone: (410) 467-1225. Fax: (410) 467-1289. E-mail: sales@stage-n-studio.com. Web Site: www.stage-n-studio.com. Richard A. Antisdel, pres; Jacauelin Keleman, sls.

Manufacturer of studio, theatrical curtains, track systems, distributor of lighting & theatrical hardware.

Theatrical Services Inc., 128 S. Washington, Wichita, KS 67202. Phone: (316) 263-4415. Fax: (316) 263-9927. Web Site: www.theatricalservices.com. E-mail: tsi@theatricalservices.com. Stephen A. Wolf, pres.

Manufacturers & distributors of studio lighting & control equipment, studio cycloramas, curtains & track.

Thermodyne International Ltd., 1841 Business Pkwy., Ontario, CA 91761. Phone: (909) 923-9945. Fax: (909) 923-7505. Web Site: www.shokstop.com. Gary S. Ackerman, pres.

Reusable shipping cases; rack-mounted operating cases. Provides protection for all electronic equipment during transit.

Thomas & Betts, 745 Avoca Ave., Dorval, PQ H9P 1G4. Canada. Phone: (514) 636-6560. Fax: (514) 631-4306. Web Site: www.t&b.com.

Manufacturer of quality products for aerial construction & subscriber instal hardware for the Cable TV & telephone industry.

Thomas & Betts Corp., 8155 T&B Blvd., Memphis, TN 38120. Phone: (800) 920-0328. Fax: (800) 283-6756.

Manufacturer of Poleline hardware aerial & drop systems, fiber-optic hand holes, MMDS antenna mounting hardware.

James Thomas Engineering, 10240 Caneel Dr., Knoxville, TN 37931. Phone: (865) 692-3060. Fax: (865) 692-9020. Web Site: www.jthomaseng.com. Mike Garl, pres.

Worcestershire WR10 2DB, Station Approach, Pershore Trading Estate, NR Pershore. Fax: (0386) 553002. Graham Thomas, pres.

Manufactures & distributes spun aluminum PAR fixtures, modular aluminum trussing, ground support, pre-wired lamp bars, spot banks & lighting accessories. Distributes Socapex & VEAM multipin connectors & cable. Assembles custom multicables, breakouts & distributes boxes to specifications. Distributor of olflex cables.

Thomson Broadcast & Media Solutions, Box 599000, Nevada City, CA 95959-5900. Phone: (800) 824-5127. Fax: (530) 478-3166. Web Site: www.thomsongrassvalley.com. Tim Thorsteinson, pres/CEO; Russ Johnson, the Americas sls; Stephen Wong, Pacific rgn sls.

Tokyo 170, Seiko Sunshine Bldg. XII, 1-30-6 Higashi-Ikebukuro Toshima-ku. Phone: 813-5992-0621.

Winchester, Hampshire S023-9HE. GVG International Ltd., St. Thomas House, 7 St. Thomas St. Phone: 44-256-817817.

Rohnert Park, CA 94928, 613 Martin Ave, Suite 100 A. Phone: (707) 585-8905.

Woodland Hills, CA 91364, 21243 Ventura Blvd, Suite 143. Phone: (818) 999-2303.

Granby, CT 06035, Box 839. Phone: (203) 653-3104.

Miami, FL 33172. The Grass Valley Group Sud America, 8880 N.W. 20th St, Suite I. Phone: (305) 477-5583. (305) 477-5488.

Tampa, FL 33634, 3929 Eden Roc Cir. E. Phone: (813) 884-0047.

Tucker, GA 30084, 3554 Habersham at Northlake. Phone: (404) 493-1255.

Arlington Heights, IL 60005, 515 W. Algonquin Rd, Suite 100. Phone: (847) 364-0022.

Elkhart, IN 46514, 810 W. Bristol St. Phone: (219) 264-0931.

Silver Spring, MD 20904, 12520 Prosperity Dr, Suite 110. Phone: (301) 622-6313.

Arden Hills, MN 55112, 8 Pine Tree Dr, Suite 140. Phone: (651) 481-3297.

Paramus, NJ 07652, 6 Forest Ave. Phone: (201) 845-7988.

Arlington, TX 76017, 5628 Green Oaks Blvd. S.W, Suite A. Phone: (817) 483-7447.

Maple Valley, WA 98038, 26326 S.E. 237th.

Video servers/disk recorders, media platforms, video production centers (switchers), signal mgmt systems (routers, modular), DVEs, HDTV equipment.

Thomson, Inc, (RCA/GE), 10330 N. Meridian St., Indianapolis, IN 46290. Phone: (317) 587-3000. Fax: (317) 587-6708. E-mail: dave.arland@thomson.net. Web Site: www.rca.com. Michael D. O'Hara, exec VP.

Boulogne, Cedex 92045. Thomson S.A. (parent co.), 46 Quai Alphonse Le Gallo. Phone: 3301-418650.

Manufactures mkt audio, video communications & accessories products.

Thomson Multi Media, 2300 S. Decker Lake Blvd., Salt Lake City, UT 84119. Phone: (801) 972-8000. Fax: (801) 972-6304. Web Site: www.thomsonmultimedia.com. Martin Fry, CEO.

Wyomissing, PA 19610, 13 Kevin Ct. Phone: (215) 678-8711. Fax: (215) 678-8784. Jeff Rosica, sls mgr.

Thorn-EMI Studio Lamps/L.C., 4800 W. Univ. Ave., Las Vegas, NV 89103. Phone: (702) 367-3656. Fax: (702) 367-7058. L.E. Nelson, pres; H.F. Dowd, VP; D.R. Imfeld, VP.

Fair Lawn, NJ 07410, 18-02 River Rd. Phone: (201) 794-6700. Fax: (201) 794-1488. Dan Imfeld, VP eastern rgn.

Thorn-EMI studio lamps and lamps from: G.E., Philips, Osram, Ushio.

360 Systems, 5321 Sterling Ctr. Dr., Westlake Village, CA 91361. Phone: (818) 991-0360. Fax: (818) 991-1360. E-mail: info@360systems.com. Web Site: www.360systems.com. Robert Easton, pres.

Image Server Video & Graphics servers, Progm Time Delays, Content Mirroring Systems, DigiCart, Instant Replay and ShortCut audio editors and players.

3M, 3M Center, St. Paul, MN 55144-1000. Phone: (651) 733-1110. Fax: (651) 733-9973. Web Site: www.3m.com. David Powell, VP mktg.

Stormscope Weather Mapping Systems—passive thunderstorm detection & avoidance instrument.

The Tiffen Company, 90 Oser Ave., Hauppauge, NY 11788. Phone: (631) 273-2500. Phone: (800) 645-2522. Fax: (631) 273-2557. Steve Tiffen, pres/CEO; Ira Tiffen, sr VP; Jeff Cohen, VP; Michael Cannatta, COO.

Photographic filters, lens accessories for motion picture, still photography, digital video, Davis & Sanford tripods, Domke Bags, support systems; steadicam camera stabilizing systems.

Time Logic Inc., 1914 Palomar Oaks Way, Suite 150, Carlsbad, CA 92008. Phone: (760) 517-0445. Fax: (760) 431-1351. E-mail: jiml@timelogic.com. Web Site: www.timelogic.com. Jim Lindelien, pres.

Automation systems for TV bcstrs & radio stns. Custom software dev for Tektronix Profile disks, HDTV time delay systems, using disk or tape.

Time Manufacturing Co., Box 20368, Waco, TX 76702-0368. Phone: (254) 399-2100. Fax: (254) 399-2651. E-mail: renees@timemfg.com. Web Site: www.timemfg.com.

Truck mounted aerial lifts ranging from 29' to 210' in height.

Times Fiber Communications Inc., 358 Hall Ave., Wallingford, CT 06492. Phone: (203) 265-8500. Fax: (203) 265-8422. Web Site: www.timesfiber.com. Timothy F. Cohane, pres/COO; Stan VonFeldt, VP sls; Chris Huffman, dir mktg.

Renfrew, ON Canada, Box 430. Phone: (613) 432-8557.

Phoenix, AZ 85063, Box 14975. Phone: (602) 278-5576. Les Judd.

Chatham, VA 24531, Box 119A, Rt. 2. Phone: (804) 432-1800.

Coaxial, twisted pair composite cables for broadband, cellular/PCS applications, semiflex, svc entry, drop cables & connectors.

Tinsley Laboratory Inc., (A division of Silicon Valley Group). 4040 Lakeside Dr., Richmond, CA 94806. Phone: (510) 222-8110. Fax: (510) 223-4534. Dan Desmond, pres.

Gyrozoom image stabilizing lens, GX3 integrated CCD camera/stabilizing system.

Toner Cable Equipment Inc., 969 Horsham Rd., Horsham, PA 19044. Phone: (215) 675-2053. Phone: (800) 523-5947. Fax: (215) 675-7543. E-mail: info@tonercable.com. Web Site: www.tonercable.com. Robert L. Toner, pres; B.J. Toner, VP.

International distributor & manufacturer of a complete line of cable TV & wireless cable equipment.

Torpey Time, 98-2220 Midland Ave., Scarborough, ON M1P 3E6. Canada. Phone: (416) 298-7788. Phone: (800) 387-6141. Fax: (416) 298-7789. E-mail: sales@torpeytime.com. Web Site: www.torpeytime.com. Bob Torpey, pres.

Master clock systems, digital & analog slave clocks, timers, video time & temperature equipment.

Toshiba America Consumer Products, 1420 Toshiba Dr., Lebanon, TN 37087. Phone: (615) 444-8501. Fax: (615) 443-3810. Web Site: www.toshiba.com. Robert Arnett, sr VP.

Wayne, NJ 07470, 82 Totowa Rd. Phone: (973) 628-8000. Fax: (973) 628-1875. (New Jersey office).

HDTV products: HD-VCR (Analog-UniHi), HD monitor (projection & CRT), NTSC to HDTV upconverter, HD-CCD color camera, HD horizon system.

Tower Inspection Inc., Box 709, Muskogee, OK 74402-0709. Phone: (918) 683-8915. Fax: (918) 683-0888. E-mail: sales@towerinspection.com. Web Site: www.towerinspection.com. Barry R. Bayless, pres; Gary G. Lehman, VP.

Inspection svcs during construction; maintenance inspection, painting, repairs of radio, microwave & TV towers.

Tower Network Services, 16205 Old US 41, Fort Myers, FL 33912. Phone: (954) 771-7180. Fax: (239) 267-4489. Web Site: www.towernetwork.com.

Svc tower, antenna. RF testing & tower structural analysis. Tower elevator repair and upgrading.

Tower Structures Inc., 2567 Business Pkwy., Minden, NV 89423. Phone: (888) 219-0299. Fax: (775) 267-1308. Web Site: www.towerstructures.com. Steven Hopkins, pres; Donald G. Weirauch, VP; Tony Lyerly, VP.

Vista, CA 92083, 430 Olive. Phone: (760) 631-4577. Tony Sierra, rgnl mgr.

Equipment Manufacturers and Distributors Alphabetical Index

Towers, design & construction of transmitter bldgs, instal of bcst, microwave & satellite antennas.

Transcom Corp., Box 26744, Elkins Park, PA 19027. Phone: (215) 938-7304. Fax: (215) 938-7361. E-mail: transcom@fmamtv.com. Web Site: www.fmamtv.com. Martin Cooper, pres.

Huntington Valley, PA 19006, 2655 Philmont Ave, Suite 200. Phone: (215) 938-7304. (800) 441-8454. Fax: (215) 938-7361. Martin Cooper, pres.

Provide used AM, FM transmitters, new bcst equipment packages & new TV transmitters to 10kw.

Transcrypt International, 4800 N.W. 1st St., Suite 100, Lincoln 68521. Phone: (402) 474-4800. Fax: (402) 479-8482. Mike Kelley, gen mgr.

Encryption products for secure communications, decoders & scramblers, serves radio.

Transtector Systems Inc., 10701 N. Airport Rd., Hayden, ID 83835. Phone: (800) 882-9110. Phone: (208) 772-8515. Fax: (208) 762-6133. E-mail: sales@transtector.com. Web Site: www.transtector.com. Shawn Thompson, mgng dir.

Transient overvoltage protective devices, power quality consulting svcs; college-accredited, power-quality assurance education courses.

Transvision/Vision Accomplished Inc., 550 Maulhardt Ave., Oxnard, CA 93030. Phone: (805) 981-8740. Fax: (805) 981-8738. E-mail: info@txvision.com. Web Site: www.txvision.com. Kimithy Vaughan, pres.

Transportable, flyaway satellite transmission; mobile/TVROs; studio/remote production & transmission mgmt.

Tribune Media Services, 333 Glen St., Glens Falls, NY 12801. Phone: (800) 833-9581. Phone: (518) 792-9914. Fax: (518) 761-7118. E-mail: tvdata@tvdata.com. Web Site: www.tvdata.com. James McCormick, VP opns; Kathleen Tolstrup, VP sls; Lanna Langlois, VP finance.

International source for TV info. Clients include interactive on-screen & on-line guides, nwsprs, print publications, cable companies, telephone companies, rsch organizations, producers, syndicators of TV programs & advertisers.

Trident Media Group/ Spector Entertainment Group Inc., 2441 Impala Dr., Carlsbad, CA 92008. Phone: (760) 438-9080. Fax: (760) 438-0968. Eric M. Spector, exec VP; Evan M. Spector, pres.

International audio, video, data & telephone communications svcs between United States/Canada & Mexico/Latin America; private TV networks; 12 C-band uplinks; teleports; satellite space segment; encryption; organization svcs; closed circuit TV & security systems.

Trilogy Communications Inc., 2910 Hwy. 80 E., Pearl, MS 39208. Phone: (601) 932-4461. Phone: (800) 874-5649. Fax: (601) 939-6637. E-mail: info@trilogycoax.com. Web Site: www.trilogycoax.com. Shinn Lee, chmn/pres/CEO; John Kaye, vice chmn; Gary Cohen, CFO; Grace Lee, VP; Dennis Park, VP; Bill Lee, VP International opns.

World leading manufacturer of advanced technology coaxial cables for CATV, cellular, paging, PCS, SMR and in-building networking applications. ISO-9001 certified.

Trimm Inc., 407 Railroad St., Butner, NC 27509. Phone: (847) 362-3700. Fax: (847) 680-3888. E-mail: trimminc@frontiernet.net. Web Site: www.trimminc.com.

Manufacturer of fuse panel s& terminal blocks.

Triplett Corp., One Triplett Dr., Bluffton, OH 45817. Phone: (419) 358-5015. Phone: (800) 874-7538. Fax: (419) 358-7956. Fax: (888) trip-fax. E-mail: wjh@triplett.com. Web Site: www.triplett.com. Warren Hess, pres/CEO.

Panel instruments & test equipment. Electrical, electronic, telecommunication & railroad testers.

Trompeter Electronics Inc., 31194 La Baya Dr., Suite 202, Westlake Village, CA 91362-4047. Phone: (818) 707-2020. Fax: (818) 706-1040. Web Site: www.trompeter.com. Joe Norwood, pres.

DS3 interconnection & DSX products for central office.

Tulsat/An Addvantage Technologies Co., 1605 E. Iola, Broken Arrow, OK 74012. Phone: (918) 251-2887. Phone: (800) 331-5997. Fax: (918) 251-1138. E-mail: tulsat@tulsat.com. Web Site: www.tulsat.com. David Chymiak, pres; Mark Schumacher, gen sls mgr; Ken Chymick, sr VP; Ken Chymiak, CEO.

Suwanee, GA 30024. Tulsat Atlanta, 49 Buford Hwy. Phone: (866) 714-3214. Fax: (678) 714-2313.

Sedalia, MO 65301. ComTech Services, Box 255 B, RR6. Phone: (800) 467-2588. Fax: (660) 826-8461. Nickolas Ferolito, sls assoc.

Deshler, NE 68340. Lee Enterprise, 701 3rd St. Phone: (800) 551-0096. Fax: (402) 365-7856. John Noojin, sls mgr, pres; John Denne, svc mgr.

Warminster, PA 98974. NCS Industries, 375 Ivyland Rd, Suite 11. Phone: (800) 523-2342. Fax: (215) 657-0840. Fred Baker, gen mgr; Joan Walls, Harry Williams, & Mike Moran, sls assocs.

New Boston, TX 75570. Tulsat-Texas, Rt. 2, Box 378. Phone: (800) 235-2288. Fax: (903) 628-5074. Johnny Lopez, gen mgr.

Authorized Scientific Atlanta distributor of headend products & passives. Large inventory of remanufactured headend equipment & line gear in the U.S. repair facility.

Turner Studios Field Operations, 1020 Techwood Dr., Atlanta, GA 30318. Phone: (404) 885-4746. Fax: (404) 885-2175. E-mail: charli.whitfield@turner.com. Bob McGee, dir; Scott Marks, VP; Charli Whitfield, opns mgr.

Two 53 ft expandable mobile units with or without crews; 12 cams, 9 VTRs, EVS, DVEous, Infinit & Deko; FFV Omega DDRs.

Tyco Electronics, 300 Constitution Dr., Menlo Park, CA 94025. Phone: (650) 361-3333. Fax: (650) 361-2288. Web Site: www.tycoelectronics.com. Jackie Heisse, CEO.

Coaxial connectors, environmental sealing products, antenna de-icers.

U

U.S. Electronics Components Corp., 585 N. Bicycle Path, Suite 10, Port Jefferson Station, NY 11776. Phone: (631) 331-2552. Phone: (800) 283-1792. Fax: (631) 331-1833. Web Site: www.uselectronics.com. Robert Ackerman, pres; Mike Fruth, sls dir.

Amherst, NY 14226, 3960 Harlem Rd. Phone: (716) 839-3803.

Manufacturer & distributor of cable TV equipment.

U.S. Tape & Label Corp., 2092 Westport Ctr. Dr., St. Louis, MO 63146. Phone: (314) 824-4444. Fax: (314) 824-4400. Web Site: www.ustl.com. Jim Eiseman, pres.

Custom printed bumper strips & window labels for the bcst industry. Industrial labels, direct mail printing & label-aire equipment.

U.S. Traffic & Display Solutions, 9603 John St., Santa Fe Springs, CA 90670. Phone: (562) 923-9600. Fax: (562) 923-7555. E-mail: dsi@dsiusa.com. Web Site: www.displaysolutionsinc.com.

Changeable outdoor electronic adv displays.

Ultimate Support Systems Inc., Box 470, Fort Collins, CO 80522. Phone: (970) 493-4488. Fax: (970) 221-2274. E-mail: custserv@ultimatesupport.com. Jim Dismore, chmn/CEO.

Strong, lightweight speaker & lighting tripods. Microphone stands for nearly any application.

Ultimatte Corp., 20945 Plummer St., Chatsworth, CA 91311. Phone: (818) 993-8007. Fax: (818) 993-3762. Web Site: www.ultimatte.com. Reid Baker, bussiness dev; Alan Dadourian, chief engr; Lynne Sauve, pres.

Video compositing devices for comls, live bcst, production, postproduction & computerized tripod head.

Uni-Set Corp., 449 Ave. A, Rochester, NY 14621. Phone: (585) 544-3820. Fax: (585) 544-1110. Web Site: www.unisetcorp.com. Ronald D. Kniffin, pres.

Modular studio staging systems for studio settings; news setting riser/tops/ramp system; uni-set system. UNI-CYC portable cyclorama-hard cycs.

Union Connector Co., 40 Dale St., West Babylon, NY 11704-1104. Phone: (631) 753-9550. Fax: (631) 753-9560. Web Site: www.unionconnector.com. Richard A. Wolpert, pres; Alan T. Wolpert, VP.

Electrical connectors, power distribution systems, portable power cabinets & custom switchgear, cases, carts and grip equipment.

Unique Business Systems, 2901 Ocean Park Blvd., Suite 215, Santa Monica, CA 90405. Phone: (310) 396-3929. Fax: (310) 396-6114. E-mail: pbatra@unibiz.com. Web Site: www.unibiz.com. Pradeep Batra, pres.

Langhorne, PA 19047, 3000 Cabot Blvd. W, Suite 220E. Phone: (215) 702-3530.

RentTrace-asset mgmt software to track rental equipment. Handles quotes, reservation, contracts, inventory control, invoicing & accounts receivable. Completely barcode compatible.

Unisys Corp., Unisys Way, Blue Bell, PA 19424. Phone: (215) 986-4011. Web Site: www.unisys.com. George Gazerwitz, pres.

Cable info business systems. Unisys hardware: A1, A4, A6, A10, A12, A17 & IBM PC compatibles.

United Media Inc., 4771 E. Hunter, Anaheim, CA 92807. Phone: (714) 777-4510. Fax: (714) 777-2434. E-mail: umi@unitedmediainc.com. Web Site: www.unitedmediainc.com.

United Media Inc is a developer & manufacturer which recognizes the ongoing need for high quality, affordable professional video equipment, developer of the On-Line Express non-linear editing system for Windows NT and multicom. The On-Line Express offers uncompromised digital editing, compositing, digital audio editing, titling, 2D & 3D realtime effects & sophisticated media mgmt.

United States Broadcast, 1371 Production Dr., Burlington, KY 41005. Phone: (859) 282-1802. Fax: (859) 282-1804. E-mail: genmgr@usbroadcast.com.

New, used TV, audio equipment, bcst batteries & chargers.

UniVision Inc., 2801 S. Russell, Missoula, MT 59801. Phone: (406) 721-8876. Fax: (406) 721-0810. E-mail: sales@univision-computers.com. Web Site: www.univision-computers.com. Jim Green, pres.

Sell & repair computers. Program software, fiberoptics & wiring.

Utah Scientific Inc., 4750 Wiley Post Way, Suite 150, Salt Lake City, UT 84116. Phone: (801) 575-8801. Fax: (801) 537-3099. Web Site: www.utahscientific.com.

Celebrating 25th yr serving bcst industry's requirement for signal distribution equipment. Routing, master control switches & control systems.

Utility Tower Company, Box 12369, 3200 N.W. 38th, Oklahoma City, OK 73157. Phone: (405) 946-5551. Fax: (405) 947-8466. E-mail: utctower@aol.com. Gloria Nelson, pres; Ron Nelson Jr., VP; Joe James, production mgr.

Tower structures, accessories for bcstg & wireless applications; tower design, engrg analysis, turnkey instals; modifications, maintenance & inspections.

V

VCI-Video Communications Inc., 146 Chestnut St., Springfield, MA 01103. Phone: (413) 272-7200. Fax: (413) 272-7201. Web Site: www.vcisolutions.com. W. Lowell Putnam, CEO; Claude P. Morris, VP; Skip Sawyer, gen sls mgr.

Trafficing software system for the bcst television & cable industries that manage revenue and provide extensive sls & financial reporting.

VRI (Video Rentals Inc.), 100 Stonehurst Ct., Northvale, NJ 07647. Phone: (800) 255-2874. Phone: (201) 750-3206. Fax: (201) 784-2795. E-mail: info@renturi.com. Alan Schneider, VP/gen mgr.

Burbank, CA 91502, 200 S Flower St. Phone: (877) 736-8874. Fax: (818) 729-0073.

New York, NY 10019, 423 W. 55th St. Phone: (212) 582-4400.

Full-svc rental facility with a complete inventory of bcst & industrial video equipment.

V-Soft Communications, 721 W. 1st St., Suite A., Cedar Falls, IA 50613. Phone: (319) 266-8402. Phone: (800) 743-3684. Fax: (319) 266-9212. E-mail: dvernier@v-soft.com. Web Site: www.v-soft.com. Doug Vernier, pres; John Gray, rsch dir & dev dir; Gayle Vernier, mgr; Kate Michler, assoc; Jake Byers, mktg.

Bcst engrg computer software for AM, FM, TV & DTV. Longley-Rice Propagation, frequency search, path profiles & RFHaz progms.

VTECH Communications, 9590 S.W. Gemini Dr., Suite 120, Beaverton, OR 97008-7109. Phone: (503) 643-8981. Fax: (503) 644-9887. Web Site: www.vtechphones.com.

900 mhz cordless analog digital telephones.

Valmont Communications Inc., (Formerly Microflect Co. Inc.) 3575 25th St. S.E., Salem, OR 97302-1190. Phone: (503) 363-9267. Phone: (800) 547-2151. Fax: (503) 363-4613. E-mail: custoinfo@microflect.com. Web Site: www.valmont.com. Doug Kochenderfer, pres.

Towers, microwave passive repeaters, waveguide support systems & tech svcs.

Van Nostrand Radio Engineering Service, 256 Strickland Pasture Rd., Jackson, GA 30233-3928. Phone: (770) 775-7575. E-mail: vnres@yahoo.com. W.L. Van Nostrand,. Melbourne Beach, FL 32951-0458, Box 510458. Phone: (321) 723-1250. Samuel B. Boor, co-owner.

Frequency measurements up to 26 ghz.

Equipment Manufacturers and Distributors Alphabetical Index

Vantage Lighting Inc., 175 Paul Dr., San Rafael, CA 94903. Phone: (800) 445-2677. Phone: (415) 507-0402. Fax: (415) 507-0502. E-mail: eight@vanltg.com. Web Site: www.vanltg.com. Marc Allsman, pres; Peter Allsman, sec/treas.

Replacement lamps including stage, studio, projection audiovisual, HMI, Xenon, 3D video & laser system. Electronic ballasts for HID lighting.

Veetronix Inc., Box 480, 1311 W. Pacific, Lexington, NE 68850. Phone: (308) 324-6661. Fax: (308) 324-4985. E-mail: sales@veetronix.com. Web Site: www.veetronix.com. Roger Teeters, gen sls mgr.

Keyboard & panel reed switches & keycaps with in-house tooling.

Vega, (A Telex Company). 8601 Cornhusker E. Hwy., Lincoln, NE 68505-5321. Phone: (402) 467-5324. Fax: (402) 467-3279. E-mail: vega@telex.com. Web Site: www.vega-signaling.com. Don Poysa, sls.

Dispatch control consoles, amplifiers & monitoring products.

Veriad, 650 Columbia St., Brea, CA 92821. Phone: (800) 423-4643. Phone: (714) 990-2700. Fax: (800) 962-0658. Web Site: www.veriad.com. E-mail: info@veriad.com.

Videotape & audiotape format labels, CD & DVD labels tape mgmt labels, labeling software, packaging products & production supplies.

Vermeer Manufacturing Co., 1210 Vermeer Rd. E., Pella, IA 50219. Phone: (515) 628-3141. Phone: (888) 837-6337. Fax: (621) 621-7734. E-mail: salesinfo@vermeermfg.com. Web Site: www.vermeer.com. Robert Vermeer, chmn/CEO; Mary Andringa, pres/COO.

Cable plows, trenchers, backhoes, stump cutters, hyraulic boring equip.

Vertex Communications Corp., 2600 N. Longview St., Kilgore, TX 75662-6842. Phone: (903) 984-0555. Fax: (903) 984-1826. E-mail: info@vertexcomm.com. Gary Kanipe, VP.

Beijing 100005. Vertex Beijing Office, COFCO Plaza, Suite 411, Tower B, N. 8 Jian Guo Men Nei Ave. Phone: (+86-10) 6528-7258. Fax: (+86-10) 6528-7261. E-mail: info@vertex.com.cn.

Burntisland, Fife KY3 9EA. Vertex International Ltd., 37 Kinghorn Rd. Phone: 44-1592-873-956. E-mail: vertes@mbox3.singnet.com.sg.

Duisburg D-47198. Vertex Antennentechnik GmbH, Baumstr. 50. Phone: 49-2066-20960. Fax: 49-2066-209611. E-mail: info@vertexant.com.

Singapore 038987. Vertex Asia (Singapore Representative Office), 21-03 Suntec Tower One, 7 Temasek Blvd. Phone: 65-430-9524. Fax: 65-430-9516. E-mail: vertex@pacific.net.sg.

Santa Clara, CA 95054. Vertex Antenna Systems LLC, 2211 Lawson Ln. Phone: (408) 654-5600. Fax: (408) 654-5613/5614. E-mail: bernard@tiw.com.

Torrance, CA 90505. Vertex Microwave Products Inc., 3111 Fujita St. Phone: (310) 539-6704. Fax: (310) 539-7463. E-mail: info@vertexmpi.com.

West Melbourne, FL 32904. Vertex Florida Office, 255 East Dr, Suite F. Phone: (407) 956-8999. Fax: (407) 956-7999. E-mail: vertexflorida@ibm.net.

Albuquerque, NM 87121. Vertex-New Mexico Inc., 1255 Old Coors Rd. S.W. Phone: (505) 242-5251. Fax: (505)243-5630. E-mail: vnm@abq.com.

State College, PA 16803. Vertex Electronic Products Inc., 2120 Old Gatesburg Rd. Phone: (814) 238-2700. Fax: (814) 238-6589. E-mail: sales@vertexepi.com.

Kilgore, TX 75662-6842. Vertex Antenna Products Division, 2600 N. Longview St. Phone: (903) 984-0555. (903) 984-1826. E-mail: vapdmktg@vertexcomm.com.

Longview, TX 75604. Vertex Control Systems Division, 1915 Harrison Rd. Phone: (903) 295-1480. Fax: (903) 295-1479. E-mail: sales@vcsd.com.

Richardson, TX 75081. Vertex Special Projects Division, 101 W. Buckingham Rd. Phone: (972) 643-1869. Fax: (972) 643-1870. E-mail: sales@vertexdallas.com.

Antennas, control systems, passive microwave devices, field svcs, satcom net equipment, custom engrg solutions, SSPAs, LNAs, RF components/subsystems.

Vertigo Technology Inc., 1255 W. Pender St., Vancouver, BC V6E 2V1. Canada. Phone: (604) 684-2113. Fax: (604) 684-2108.

Plug-ins Adobe, PhotoShop, & Illustrator.

Vicon Industries Inc., 89 Arkay Dr., Hauppauge, NY 11788. Phone: (631) 952-2288. Fax: (631) 951-2288. Web Site: www.vicon-cctv.com. Ken Darby, pres/CEO; John Badke, VP.

Closed circuit television equipment and systems for the security and surveillance industry.

VidCAD Documentation Programs (VDP Inc.), 755 South Telshor Blvd., Suite D9, Las Cruces, NM 88011. Phone: (505) 522-0003. Fax: (505) 522-0009. E-mail: sales@vidcad.com. Web Site: www.vidcad.com. Dr. Walter Black, CEO.

VidCAD software connects your idea from diagram design & rack planning to installation, maintenance & rebuilds-on time & on budget.

Video Accessory Corp., 2450 Central Ave., Suite G, Boulder, CO 80301. Phone: (800) 821-0426. Fax: (303) 440-8878. E-mail: vac@vac-brick.com. Web Site: www.vac-brick.com. Richard Frey, chief technical officer; Amy Barnes Frey, dir; Frank S. Barnes, pres.

Black Burst generators, video & audio distribution amplifiers, video line isolators, video & audio switches.

Video International Development Corp., 65-15 Brook Ave., Deer Park, NY 11729. Phone: (631) 243-5414. Fax: (631) 243-4314. E-mail: info@videointernational.com. Web Site: www.videointernational.com. Bernard Bressel, pres.

Barsinghausen 30890, Ulmenweg II. Phone: (05105) 81144. S. Freitag, VP.

Digital TV standards converters with four-field/four-line interpolation for bcst & industrial use as well as noise reducers, analog to digital converters, audio delay lines & transcoders.

Videomagnetics Inc., 3970 Clearview Frontage Rd., Colorado Springs, CO 80911. Phone: (719) 390-1313. Fax: (719) 390-1316. E-mail: vmi@csprings.com. Web Site: www.videomagnetics.com. Jane Pennie, sls VP; Tony B. Korte, pres.

Full service specialists in betacam camera & recorders. Refurbished video heads & scanners.

Videotek, A Division of Leitch Technology. 243 Shoemaker Rd., Pottstown, PA 19464-6433. Phone: (800) 800-5719. Fax: (610) 327-9295. E-mail: sales@videotek.com. Web Site: www.videotek.com. Philip Steyaert, pres; Richard R. Hollowbush, VP; Bob Landingham, VP sls; Jeff Viola, dev VP.

Manufacturer of test/measurement equipment, video demodulators, routing switchers, color correctors/processors, related equipment for professional video/TV bcst markets.

Videotron Ltee, 300 Viger Ave. E., Montreal, PQ H28 3W4. Canada. Phone: (514) 281-1711. Fax: (514) 985-8652.

Montreal, PQ H2X 3W4 Canada. LeGroupe Videotron Ltee., 300 ave Viger est.

Cable TV, digital TV, interactive TV and telecommunications.

Videssence L.L.C., 10768 Lower Azusa Rd., El Monte, CA 91731. Phone: (626) 579-0943. Fax: (626) 579-6803. E-mail: contact@videssence.tv. Web Site: www.videssence.tv. Toni Swarens, pres; Lauri Maines, VP.

Energy-efficient floorescent, studio lighting products for TV, film, stage & industrial communications applications.

Viewsonics Inc., 3103 N. Andrews Ave. Ext, Pompano Beach, FL 33064-2118. Phone: (954) 971-8439. Fax: (954) 971-4422. E-mail: viewsonics@viewsonics.com. Web Site: www.viewsonics.com.

One GHz amplifiers, security systems, apartment boxes, combiners, LAN, CATV, one GHz splitters, taps, custom design systems & products, head end signal couplor/splitter system.

Viking Cases, 10480 Oak St. N.E., St. Petersburg, FL 33716. Phone: (800) 237-8560. Fax: (727) 577-2082. E-mail: sales@vikingcases.com. Web Site: www.vikingcases.com. Arthur W. Stemler, CEO; Bruce S. Stemler, pres; Reese Autry, VP.

Heavy-duty reusable shipping cases, lightweight carrying cases & EIA rack cases.

Vinten Inc., 709 Executive Blvd., Valley Cottage, NY 10989. Phone: (845) 268-0100. Fax: (845) 268-0113. E-mail: mike.denicola@vinten.com. Web Site: www.vinten.com. Michael DeNicola, pres.

Toronto M4CC 2B1 Canada, 50 Moberly Ave. Phone: (416) 693-8578. Fax: (416) 693-9489. Sam Duncan, Canadian rgnl sls mgr.

Burbank, CA 91506, G 95 S. Glenwood, Suite B. Phone: (818) 843-5244. Fax: (818) 843-5176. Mark Playdon, west rgn sls mgr.

Sunrise, FL 33351, 10208 N.W. 47th St. Phone: (945) 572-4344. Fax: (945) 572-4565. Joseph Lantowski, southern rgnl sls mgr.

Shamong, NJ 08088, 4 Birch Ct. Phone: (609) 268-2405. Fax: 609-268-3204. Len Donovan, northeast rgnl sls mgr.

Remote control camera systems. Pneumatic studio pedestals, pan & tilt heads, lightweight tripods & heads.

Vision Database Systems, 1095 Jupiter Park Dr., Suite 3, Jupiter, FL 33458. Phone: (561) 748-0711. Fax: (561) 748-0712. Web Site: www.visiondatabase.com. Emil Bonaduce, pres.

Photo image software.

Visual Sound Inc., 485 Pkwy. S., Broomall, PA 19008. Phone: (610) 544-8700. Phone: (800) 523-7525. Fax: (610) 544-3385. Web Site: www.visualsound.com. John Bogosian, pres.

Beltsville, MD 20705-4220, 1000 Virginia Manor Rd, Suite 350. Phone: (301) 419-7646. (800) 648-5266. Fax: (301) 948-9747.

Camp Hill, PA 17011, 490 S. St. John's Church Rd. Phone: (717) 730-6651. (800) 382-1301. Fax: (717) 761-0874.

Audio-video sls & svcs; installation & maintainance of teleconferencing rooms; ENG, production vans & studios.

W

WIREMAX Ltd., Box 3336, 705 Wamba Ave., Toledo 43607. Phone: (800) 843-9479. Fax: (419) 531-9503. Al Mocek, pres; Mark Robinson, gen mgr; Tom Ricketts, VP.

Manufacturer of high temp, wire, cable, high voltage wire & cable.

WOIO & WUAB TV, 1717 E. 12th St., Cleveland, OH 44114. Phone: (216) 771-1943. Fax: (216) 515-7152. Web Site: www.hometeam19.com. Jim Stunek, mgr; Sharon Ohlson, product coord.

Full studio facilities; GVG 300 switcher, CMX 3100B edit, 1-inch, 3/4-inch, Beta formats; Abekas digital F/X; Artstar graphics; remote packages.

Ward-Beck Systems Ltd., Unit 10, 455 Milner Ave., Toronto, ON M1B 2K4. Canada. Phone: (416) 335-5999. Fax: (416) 335-5202. E-mail: michael@ward-beck.com. Web Site: ward-beck.com. Eugene L. Johnson, mgng dir; Michael Jordan, sls dir; Doug Bascombe, engrg dir.

Distribution metering, monitoring, conversion of AES & analog audio, video & serial digital bcstg signals. Radio consoles.

Wave: Space Inc., 26741 Portola Pkwy., Suite 1E, Foothill Ranch, CA 92610-1713. Phone: (949) 770-6601. Fax: (949) 770-6575. E-mail: info@wave-space.com. Web Site: www.wave-space.com. Carl J. Yanchar, pres.

Acoustical design, facility design, consultation, systems design, studio construction, instal.

Wearguard, 141 Longwater Dr., Norwell, MA 02061. Fax: (800) 867-7160. Web Site: www.wearguard.com. David Gold, pres.

Offers a comprehensive line of work clothing & identity apparel serving the cable industry.

WeatherBank Inc., 1015 Waterwood Pkwy., Suite J, Edmond, OK 73034. Phone: (405) 359-0773. Phone: (800) 687-3562. Fax: (405) 341-0115. E-mail: sroot@weatherbank.com. Web Site: www.weatherbank.com. Steven A. Root, pres/CEO.

Satellite-delivered weather info, audio forecasting svcs, consulting to all industries.

Wegener Communications Inc., 11350 Technology Cir., Duluth, GA 30097. Phone: (770) 814-4000. Fax: (770) 623-0698. E-mail: info@wegener.com. Web Site: www.wegener.com. Robert Placek, CEO; Ned Mountain, exec VP.

Provider of digital solutions for IP data, video and audio networks, broadcast TV, cable TV, radio networks, dist. ed., compel network control for regionalized progmg, and commercial insertion.

Wescam Inc., 649 N. Service Rd. W., Burlington, ON L7P 5B9. Canada. Phone: (905) 633-4000. Fax: (905) 633-4100. Web Site: www.wescam.com.

Van Nuys, CA 91406-3823, 7150 Hayvenhurst Ave. Phone: (818) 785-9282. Fax: (818) 785-9787. Chris White.

Featuring Wescam Helicopter film, video, HD system, new & ultimately stable XR for all group applications.

Weschler Instruments, Weshler Instruments Division of Hughes Corporation. 16900 Foltz Pkwy., Cleveland, OH 44149. Phone: (440) 238-2550. Fax: (440) 238-0660. E-mail: sales@weschler.com. Web Site: www.weschler.com. Jerry Lucak, gen sls mgr.

Hunt Valley, MD 21032, 10946 Golden West Dr. Phone: (410) 584-9770. Fax: (410) 584-0666.

Rochester, NY 14611, 803 West Ave. Phone: (800) 903-9870. Fax: (800) 903-9500.

Volt-Pac auto-transformers, voltage controllers and regulators; analog meters, digital instruments; voltage,

Equipment Manufacturers and Distributors Alphabetical Index

current, watts, vars, frequency, temperature measuring devices.

Westcott, 1447 Summit St., Toledo, OH 43603. Phone: (419) 243-7311. Fax: (419) 243-8401. Web Site: www.fjwestcott.com. E-mail: info@fjwestcott.com. Thomas A. Waltz, pres.

Lightweight, portable & collapsible light control equipment: silks & solids, scrims, Illuminator® reflectors, umbrellas, light modifiers, & Scrim Jim modular light panels.

Westlake Audio, Professional Products Manufacturing Group, 2696 Lavery Ct., Unit 18, Newbury Park, CA 91320. Phone: (805) 499-3686. Fax: (805) 498-2571. Web Site: www.westakeaudio.com. Glenn Phoenix, pres; Sherwood Davies, mktg.

Audio monitors & accessories.

Westlake Audio, Professional Sales Group, 7265 Santa Monica Blvd., Los Angeles, CA 90046. Phone: (323) 851-9800. Fax: (323) 851-0182. Web Site: www.westlakeaudio.com. Deborah Rally, gen mgr; David Logan, gen sls mgr; Steve Burdick, VP.

Los Angeles, CA 90048, 8447 Beverly Blvd. Phone: (323) 654-2155. Fax: (323) 655-0478.

Newbury Park, CA 91320, 2696 Lavery Ct, Unit 18. Phone: (805) 499-3686. Fax: (805) 498-2571. Glenn Phoenix, pres.

Professional audio equipment repairs, professional recording equipment sales, rentals, studio design. Westlake can provide all your Pro Audio needs, from Pro Audio equipment sls to full tracking & mixing.

Wheatstone Corp., 600 Industrial Dr., New Bern, NC 28562. Phone: (252) 638-7000. Fax: (252) 635-4857. E-mail: sales@wheatstone.com. Web Site: www.wheatstone.com. Gary C. Snow, pres; Andrew Calvanese, VP; Yvette Sullivan, CFO; Brad Harrison, sls dir.

Manufacturer of analog, digital bcst audio mixing consoles, processing equipment, radio & TV products since 1976.

Wheelit Inc., 440 Arco Dr, Toledo, OH 43635-2800. Phone: (419) 531-4900. Fax: (419) 531-6415. E-mail: wheelit@solarstop.net. Web Site: www.wheelitinc.com. John M. Skilliter, pres.

Video production carts (folding & non-folding), video display stands, computer carts.

Whirlwind, 99 Ling Rd., Rochester, NY 14612. Phone: (585) 663-8820. Fax: (585) 865-8930. Fax: (888) 733-4396. E-mail: sales@whirlwindusa.com. Web Site: www.whirlwindusa.com. Michael Laiacona, pres.

Mix-6 audio mixers, presspower 2 active pressbox, active splitters; P-12 & power amplifiers, MD-1 MIC/line driver.

Wicks Broadcast Solutions, Box 3078, 508 S. 7th St., Opelika, AL 36803. Phone: (334) 749-5641. Fax: (334) 749-5666. E-mail: sales@datacount.com. Web Site: www.datacount.com. Bill Price, gen mgr.

Datacount produces a bcst traf system for radio, called Darts. In addition to single user, Darts is available for multi-user as well as multi-stn groups. Datacount is one of the largest supplier of vcstg software in the world. PC and window based system encompassing all aspects of logging, traf, co-op, billing, accts receivable & sls mgmt.

Wicks Broadcast Solutions L.L.C., Box 67, 1950 Winchester Ave., Reedsport, OR 97467. Phone: (800) 547-3930. Phone: (541) 271-3681. Fax: (541) 271-5721. Web Site: www.wicksbroadcastsolutions.com. Bob Richardson, pres; Jeffrey Kimmel, sls dir; Bob Leighton, dev dir.

Windows-based software for radio operations, traf, billing, sls, analysis functions. Digital Universe system for uncompressed audio in live assist/automation applications.

Wil-Can Electronics Ltd., 8560 Torbram Rd., Unit #35, Brampton, ON L6T 5C9. Canada. Phone: (888) 596-2020. Fax: (888) 866-7775. E-mail: wilcan@lightningtvss.com. Web Site: www.powersurges.com. William J. Black, pres; Gregory J. Black, gen mgr.

Buffalo, NY 14216, 2316 Delaware Ave, Suite 285. Phone: (888) 596-2020. Fax: (888) 866-7775. Gregory J. Black, gen mgr/sec treas.

Designers, manufacturers & consultants. Lightning & high energy transient control including protection for telephone, signal & data lines.

WILL-BURT Co., Box 900, Orrville, OH 44667. Phone: (330) 682-7015. Fax: (330) 684-1190. Web Site: www.willburt.com. Jeff Evans, CEO; Steven Pinkley, gen sls mgr.

Telescoping mast used to position antennas, lights & cameras to heights of 20 to 134 ft.

Wiltronix Inc., Box 364, 16850 Oakmont Ave., Washington Grove, MD 20880. Phone: (301) 258-7676. Fax: (301) 963-8624. E-mail: sales@wiltronix.com. Web Site: www.wiltronix.com. Dwight Wilcox, pres; Ellen Packard, sls.

Sls force under contract to sell for manufacturers of these products. Bcst, production post (analog ditigal, video, audio) & transmission.

Winsted Corp., 10901 Hampshire Ave. S., Minneapolis, MN 55438. Phone: (952) 944-9050. Fax: (952) 944-1546. E-mail: racks@winsted.com. Web Site: www.winsted.com. G.R. Hoska, CEO; Randy Smith, pres.

Editing & production consoles, space saving tape & film storage systems. Multimedia & Lan/Wan server workstations.

Wireless Accessories Group, 1840 County Line Rd., Suite 301, Huntingdon Valley, PA 19006. Phone: (888) 233-0202. Phone: (215) 322-4600. Fax: (215) 322-4606. Web Site: www.wirexgroupl.com.

Two-way radio equipment.

WireReady NSI, 56 Hudson St., Northboro, MA 01532. Phone: (800) 833-4459. Phone: (508) 393-0200. Fax: (508) 393-0255. E-mail: sales@wireready.com. Web Site: www.wireready.com. David Gerstmann, pres.

NewsReady 32, CartReady, ControlReady, NewsReady, StormReady & SalesReady software. Cart replacement, satellite, music on HD, newsrooms & sls automation. All windows/pc.

Wireworks Corp., 380 Hillside Ave., Hillside, NJ 07205. Phone: (908) 686-7400. Phone: (800) 642-9473. Fax: (908) 686-0483. E-mail: sales@wireworks.com. Web Site: www.wireworks.com. Gerald J. Krulewicz, pres; Larry J. Williams, controller.

Audio, video, & audio/video combination cabling assemblies for bcst market; cable testers, transformer isolated mic splitters; perfect custom panels.

Wohler Technologies Inc., 713 Grandview Dr., South San Francisco, CA 94080. Phone: (650) 589-5676. Fax: (650) 589-1355. Web Site: www.wohler.com. Will C. Wohler, pres; Carl J. Dempsey, VP; Chris Shaw, sls dir.

Single rackspace, self-powered stereo, audio monitor speaker systems & other related audio products. Dolby Digital & Digital E monitoring.

Wolf Coach Inc., 7 B St., Auburn Industrial Park, Auburn, MA 01501. Phone: (508) 791-1950. Fax: (508) 799-2384. E-mail: sales@wolfcoach.com. Web Site: www.wolfcoach.com. Richard Wolf, VP; Mark A. Leonard, natl sls reps; Thomas P. Jennings, natl sls reps; Emeric Feldmar, mgr.

Salt Lake City, UT 84115, 2451 South 600 W, 200. Phone: (801) 977-9533. Rex A. Reed, systems mgr/engr, Wesley K. Gordon, chief engr.

News vans, satellite vehicles, production trailers, vehicle based microwave, satellite uplink, digital SNG, audio/video systems & turnkey systems.

Frank Woolley & Co. Inc., 529 Franklin St., Reading, PA 19602. Phone: (610) 374-8335. Fax: (610) 374-3214. Web Site: www.frankwooleyandco.com. Alison M. Whalen, VP.

Video animation system.

World Tower Co. Inc., Box 508, 1213 Compressor Dr., Mayfield, KY 42066. Phone: (270) 247-3642. Fax: (270) 247-0909. E-mail: worldtow@ldd.net. Web Site: www.worldtower.com. Doug Walker, pres.

Manufactures & erects bcst & CATV towers, microwave & cellular.

World Video Sales Co., Box 331, Boyertown, PA 19512. Phone: (610) 754-6800. Fax: (610) 754-9766. E-mail: sales@mivs.com. John A. Taylor, pres.

Manufacturers of: video timers/titlers; screen splitters; pattern generators, routing systems, distribution amplifiers & other special purpose video equipment.

X

Xintekvideo Inc., 56 W. Broad St., Stamford, CT 06902. Phone: (203) 348-9229. Fax: (203) 348-9266. E-mail: john@xintekvideo.com. Web Site: www.xintekvideo.com. John Rossi, pres.

Video processing equipment, including transcoders, color correctors, image enhancers, noise reducers, co-channel filters, ghost removers, impulse noise eliminators.

Y

Yamaha Corp. of America, 6600 Orangethorpe Ave., Buena Park, CA 90620. Phone: (714) 522-9015. Fax: (714) 522-4023. Fax: (714) 739-2680. Web Site: www.yamaha.com.

Portable keyboards, synthesizers & drums. Manufactures a complete line of professional audio products targeted to the project studio, commercial studio, postproduction, bcst & sound reinforcement markets.

Z

Zack Electronics Inc., 1070 Hamilton Rd., Duarte, CA 91010. Phone: (626) 303-0655. Fax: (626) 303-8694. E-mail: jlomas@zackinc.com. Web Site: www.zackinc.com. Judi Lomas, mgr.

Cable, connectors, & comprehensive core products for the bcst industry, plus HOT LEADS standard & custom audio/video/data cable assemblies.

Zenith Electronics Corp., 2000 Millbrook Dr., Lincolnshire, IL 60069. Phone: (847) 391-7000. Fax: (847) 941-9200. Web Site: www.zenith.com. T.J. Lee, pres/CEO.

Full line of CATV converters; MMDS systems; cable & pay TV systems for PAL & SECAM international markets; PC-based system controllers; accessories.

Ziehl Electronic Service, 8611 Dale Rd., Gasport, NY 14067. Phone: (716) 772-7800. Fax: (716) 772-7985. Richard F. Ziehl, owner.

Frequency measurement svc.

Zomax Inc., 800 Corporate Way, Fremont, CA 94539. Phone: (510) 657-8425. Fax: (510) 657-8427. Web Site: www.zomax.com.

CD manufacturer specializing in printing fulfillment svcs, & custom work in CD entertainment & CD-ROM.

Equipment Manufacturers and Distributors Subject Index

Acoustic Equipment
Acoustic Systems, a div. of ETS-LINDEREN
Acoustical Solutions Inc.

Acoustical Panels and Treatment
Acoustical Solutions Inc.
Illbruck Inc.
Industrial Acoustics Co., Inc.
Noise Control Corp.

Aerial Buckets
Equipment Technology Inc.
Time Manufacturing Co.

Aerial Stereo Exciters
Delta Electronics Inc.

Amplifiers
Amplifier Technologies, Inc.
Communication & Power Industries, EIMAC Division
Electroline Equipment Inc.
Farrtronics Ltd.
FitzCo. Inc.
Harris Corporation Co.
Henry Engineering
Lindsay Electronics
M/A-COM
Megastar Inc.
Miranda Technologies Inc.
Opamp Labs Inc.
Peavey Electronics
Pirelli Cables North America—Communications Division
QSC Audio Products Inc.
Radio Design Labs. (RDL)
Ram Broadcast Systems
Recoton Corp.
Spectra Sonics
Symmetricom
TOA Electronics Inc.
Viewsonics Inc.
Whirlwind

Amplifiers, Audio
A R T Applied Research and Technology
ATI-Audio Technologies Inc.
Amplifier Technologies, Inc.
Audio Implements/GKC
Benchmark Media Systems Inc.
Bogen Communications Inc.
Bryston Ltd.
Cablynx, Inc.
DBX Professional Products
ESE
Galaxy Audio Inc.
Harman International Industries Inc.
Henry Engineering
Image Video
JBL Professional
LINK Electronics Inc.
Michael Stevens & Partners Ltd.
Motorola Broadband Communications Sector
Opamp Labs Inc.
Philip-Cooke Co.
RTS Systems Telex Communications Inc
Radio Engineering Industries Inc.
Sescom Inc.
Video Accessory Corp.

Amplifiers, RF
Advent Communications Ltd.
Andrew Corp.
Bauer Transmitters
Blonder Tongue Laboratories Inc.
C-COR
Communication & Power Industries

Communication & Power Industries, EIMAC Division
e2v technologies Inc.
Energy-Onix Broadcast Equipment Co. Inc.
Global Microwave Systems Inc.
JSB Service Co.
KES
LARCAN
Lindsay Electronics
MCL Inc.
North American Cable Equipment Inc.
QEI Corporation
Qintar Technologies Inc.
Toner Cable Equipment Inc.
Tulsat/AN Addvantage Technology Co.
Vertex Communications Corp.
Viewsonics Inc.

Amplifiers, Video
Cablynx, Inc.
Comprehensive Video Group
ESE
Image Video
Interlogix
Intersil Corp. Headquarters
LINK Electronics Inc.
Opamp Labs Inc.
Philip-Cooke Co.
Radio Engineering Industries Inc.
Video Accessory Corp.

Analyzers, Distortion, Intermodulation
Audio Precision Inc.
Boonton Electronics Corp.
Electro Rent Corp.
Potomac Instruments Inc.
Radio Detection/Riser Bond
SyntheSys Research Inc.

Animation Systems
AccuWeather Inc.
Alias/WaveFront Inc.
Fast Forward Video
Hotbox Digital
Vertigo Technology Inc.

Announcement Systems
Amerivox Corp.
Bogen Communications Inc.
Interface Media Group
Protech Audio Corp.

Antennas and Accessories
ATCI/Antenna Technology Communications Inc.
American Antenna Inc.
Antenna Concepts Inc.
BEXT Inc.
California Amplifier
Channel Master L.L.C.
Cortland Cable Co. Inc.
ERI-Installations Inc.
Global Microwave Systems Inc.
Harris Corp., Broadcast Division
Harris Corporation Co.
Jampro Antennas/RF Systems Inc.
Kathrein Inc., Scala Division
Kintronic Labs Inc.
LBA Technology Inc.
Lindsay Electronics
M/A-COM
NSI
Radio Engineering Industries Inc.
Radio Frequency Systems
S W R Inc.
Sitco Antenna Company
Thales

Times Fiber Communications Inc.
Tyco Electronics

Antennas, Broadcast
ATCI/Antenna Technology Communications Inc.
American Antenna Inc.
Andrew Corp.
Antenna Concepts Inc.
Broadcast Equipment Surplus Inc.
Dielectric Communications
DMT USA, Inc.
DRS Broadcast Technology
Kathrein Inc., Scala Division
LARCAN USA
Marcom
Micro Communications Inc.
Allen Osborne Associates Inc.
Phasetek Inc.
RF Specialties Group
Radio Frequency Systems
Radio Photo Antennas Inc.
Recoton Corp.
S W R Inc.
Shively Labs
Superior Satellite Engineers Inc.
Teleplex Inc.
Thales Broadcast & Multimedia S.A.
Tower Network Services
Transcom Corp.
WILL-BURT Co.

Antennas, Earth Station
ATCI/Antenna Technology Communications Inc.
Advent Communications Ltd.
All Mobile Video Inc.
American Antenna Inc.
Andrew Corp.
Channel Master L.L.C.
Comex Worldwide Corp.
D.H. Satellite
Radio Research Instrument Co. Inc.
Superior Satellite Engineers Inc.
Vertex Communications Corp.

Antennas, Installation
Abroyd Communications Ltd.
Cygnal Technology
Doty-Moore Tower Services
EDX Wireless LLC
National Steel Erectors Corp.
Fred A. Nudd Corp.
S W R Inc.
Southern Broadcast Services
Stainless LLC
Structural System Technology Inc.
Swager Communications Inc.
Teletech Inc.
Tenco Tower Co.
Tower Network Services
Tower Structures Inc.

Antennas, Satellite
ATCI/Antenna Technology Communications Inc.
American Antenna Inc.
California Amplifier
Channel Master L.L.C.
Comtech Antenna Systems Inc.
D.H. Satellite
MRPP Inc.
North American Cable Equipment Inc.
Superior Satellite Engineers Inc.

Antennas, TVRO
American Antenna Inc.
California Amplifier
D.H. Satellite
Mega Hertz

Broadcasting & Cable Yearbook 2006

F-33

Equipment Manufacturers and Distributors Subject Index

North American Cable Equipment Inc.
Superior Satellite Engineers Inc.

Attenuators and Equalizers

Allen Avionics, Inc.
BEI Duncan
Motorola Broadband Communications Sector
Nardal - An L-3 Communications Co.
North American Cable Equipment Inc.
Penny & Giles Inc.
Shallco Inc.
Tech Laboratories Inc.
Viewsonics Inc.

Audio Accessories

AKG Acoustics, U.S.
Allsop Inc.
Amek U.S.A.
Amerivox Corp.
Aphex Systems Ltd.
Audico Labels
Audio Implements/GKC
Black Audio
Bogen Communications Inc.
Dorrough Electronics
Edcor Electronics Corp.
HAVE Inc.
Henry Engineering
The J-Lab Co.
Jensen Transformers Inc.
Mic Flags by Aladdin
Neutrik U.S.A. Inc.
Peavey Electronics
Polyline Corp.
Professional Sound Corp.
Radio Design Labs. (RDL)
Seger Electronics
Sescom Inc.
Sprague Magnetics Inc.
Star Case Manufacturing Co. Inc.
TAI Audio
Trimm Inc.
Video Accessory Corp.
Westlake Audio, Professional Products Manufacturing Group
Wireworks Corp.
Zack Electronics Inc.

Audio Amps, AGC & Limiters

Professional Sound Corp.
Renkus-Heinz Inc.
Samson Technologies Corp.
Sescom Inc.
Spectra Sonics

Audio Cartridge Library Labels

GKM Manufacturing Corp.
Veriad

Audio Cartridges

JOA Cartridge Service
Spectra Sonics
Stanton Group

Audio Compressors

Alesis
Circuit Research Labs Inc. (CRL Systems, Inc.)
Furman Sound Inc.
Sascom Marketing Group
Sescom Inc.
Spectra Sonics
TC Electronic

Audio Consoles

Autogram Corp.
DiGi Co. U.K. LTD.
Harris Corp., Broadcast Communications Division
Logitek
North American Cable Equipment Inc.
Ward-Beck Systems Ltd.
Wheatstone Corp.

Audio Equipment

AMS Neve Inc.
AVI Systems
Audio Implements/GKC
Audio Precision Inc.
BBE Sound Inc.
Black Audio
Bogen Communications Inc.
Broadcast Store Inc.
Burlington A/V Recording Media Inc.
Comprehensive Video Group
Comrex Corp.
Countryman Associates Inc.
Crouse-Kimzey Co.
DBX Professional Products
DiGi Co. U.K. LTD.
Dorrough Electronics
Film/Video Equipment Service Co. Inc.
FitzCo. Inc.
Fostex Corp. of America
Full Compass Systems Ltd.
Galaxy Audio Inc.
Geneva Aviation Inc.
Group One Ltd.
Harris Corporation Co.
Industrial Equipment Representatives (IER)
Jensen Transformers Inc.
Lectrosonics Inc.
Location Sound Corp.
Memorex Products Inc.
Microspace Communications Corp.
Nady Systems Inc.
Nakusa Inc.
National Video Services Inc.
Opamp Labs Inc.
PBI Media
Peavey Electronics
Photomart Cine-Video Inc.
Professional Sound Corp.
Protech Audio Corp.
QSC Audio Products Inc.
Ram Broadcast Systems
Rangertone Research Inc.
Samson Technologies Corp.
Sanyo Fisher Co.
Sascom Marketing Group
Sennheiser Electronic Corp.
Spectra Sonics
Systems Wireless Ltd.
TAI Audio
TEAC America Inc.
Thomson, Inc, (RCA/GE)
Visual Sound Inc.
Whirlwind

Audio Jackfields, Pre-Wired

Audio Accessories Inc.
Farrtronics Ltd.
Fostex Corp. of America
Furman Sound Inc.
Gepco International Inc.
Glentronix
Milestek Corp.
Penny & Giles Inc.
Seger Electronics
Switchcraft Inc.

Audio Limiters

Amek U.S.A.
Circuit Research Labs Inc. (CRL Systems, Inc.)
Harman International Industries Inc.
Spectra Sonics
Symetrix Inc.

Audio Mixers and Recorders

ATI-Audio Technologies Inc.
Alesis
Allen & Heath USA
Amek U.S.A.
Audio-Technica U.S., Inc.
Cooper Sound Systems Inc.
Edcor Electronics Corp.
Fairlight ESP Pty. Ltd.
Graham-Patten Systems Inc.
Harrison by GLW
Henry Engineering
The Image Group Post, LLC.
Martinsound Inc.
Micro Technology Unlimited

Nady Systems Inc.
Otari USA Sales Inc.
Penny & Giles Inc.
Professional Sound Corp.
Professional Sound Services Inc.
Protech Audio Corp.
Radio Design Labs. (RDL)
Sascom Marketing Group
Shure Inc.
Superscope Technologies Professionals
TAI Audio
United States Broadcast

Audio Monitoring Systems

AKG Acoustics, U.S.
Auratone Corp.
B&B Systems
Furman Sound Inc.
IRIS Technologies Inc.
Image Video
Martinsound Inc.
McCurdy Radio Industries Ltd.
Michael Stevens & Partners Ltd.
Renkus-Heinz Inc.
Solutec Ltd. (HA)
Tannoy North America Inc.
Tektronix Inc.
Westlake Audio, Professional Products Manufacturing Group
Wohler Technologies Inc.

Audio Noise Reduction Systems

Digidesign
Dolby Laboratories Inc.
Noise Control Corp.
Recoton Corp.
Symetrix Inc.

Audio Processors

Audioarts Engineering
BBE Sound Inc.
Delta Electronics Inc.
Inovonics Inc.
Linear Acoustic Inc.
Modulation Sciences Inc.
Nady Systems Inc.
Peavey Electronics
Samson Technologies Corp.
Sascom Marketing Group
Symetrix Inc.

Audio Replacement Heads

International Electro-Magnetics
Northern Magnetics Inc.
Sprague Magnetics Inc.

Audio Routing Switches

Burk Technology
Datatek Corp.
Electronology, Inc.
Harrison by GLW
Image Video
Logitek
NTV International Corporation
NVISION Products
Omicron Video
Radio Design Labs. (RDL)
Richmond Sound Design Ltd.
Sierra Automated Systems & Engineering Corp.
Sigma Electronics Inc.
Wohler Technologies Inc.

Audio Signal Processing Systems

Alesis
Aphex Systems Ltd.
BBE Sound Inc.
Broadcasters General Store Inc.
Circuit Research Labs Inc. (CRL Systems, Inc.)
Communications Specialties Inc.
Dolby Laboratories Inc.
Eventide Inc.
G Prime Ltd.
Graham-Patten Systems Inc.
Group One Ltd.

Equipment Manufacturers and Distributors Subject Index

International Datacasting Corp.
Lectrosonics Inc.
Pixel Instruments Corp.
Sabine Inc.
Shure Inc.
Symetrix Inc.
TC Electronic

Audio Systems and Components

Audio Implements/GKC
Commercial Electronics Ltd.
Gefen Inc.
Parsons Audio
Protech Audio Corp.
TAI Audio
Tannoy North America Inc.
VidCAD Documentation Programs (VDP Inc.)
Visual Sound Inc.

Audio Test Tapes, Gauges & Equipment

Audio Precision Inc.
Leader Instruments Corp.
Microspace Communications Corp.
Tentel

Audio Transmission Equipment

Advent Communications Ltd.
Audio Processing Technology Ltd.
Fiber Options
Intelligent Media Technology
International Datacasting Corp.
Leaming Industries
MUSICAM U.S.A.
Microspace Communications Corp.

Audio/Video Cartridges

CoarcVideo
Memorex Products Inc.

Audiotape

BMG
Burlington A/V Recording Media Inc.
CoarcVideo
Fuji Photo Film U.S.A. Inc.
JOA Cartridge Service
Maxell Corp. of America
Memorex Products Inc.
Moviola
National Audio Co. Inc.
National Video Services Inc.

Audiotape Cartridge Machines

A.C.C. Electronix, Inc.

Automated Newsroom Systems

Avid Broadcast
BDL-Autoscript
CEA-Computer Engineering Associates
Comprompter Inc.
Computer Concepts Corp.
Dalet Digital Media Systems
FloriCal Systems Inc.
Harris Automation Solutions
Media Computing Inc.
Reuters American Inc.
Scott Studios Corp.
Sundance Digital Inc.
WireReady NSI

Automated Radio

Dalet Digital Media Systems
Encoda Systems Inc.
Marketron International
McCurdy Radio Industries Ltd.
Radio Computing Services (RCS)
Register Data Systems
Scott Studios Corp.
Spotcat Software
Wicks Broadcast Solutions L.L.C.
WireReady NSI

Automated Tape Winders

Otari USA Sales Inc.

Automated Telephone & Voice Mail

Concerto Software
Microlog Corp.
TALX Corp.

Automatic Cassette Loaders

Otari USA Sales Inc.

Automatic Transmission Systems

Encoda Systems Inc.
Harris Automation Solutions

Automation Systems

ADTEC Inc.
Arrakis Systems Inc.
Broadcast Electronics Inc.
CEA-Computer Engineering Associates
Computer Concepts Corp.
Dalet Digital Media Systems
ENCO Systems Inc.
Encoda Systems Inc.
Harris Automation Solutions
Harris Corp., Broadcast Communications Division
MATCO Inc.
Marketron International
Media Computing Inc.
Orban
Radio Computing Services (RCS)
Register Data Systems
Scott Studios Corp.
Solutec Ltd. (HA)
Spotcat Software
Sundance Digital Inc.
Thomson Multi Media
Time Logic Inc.
Wicks Broadcast Solutions L.L.C.
WireReady NSI

Automation, Switching and Control

ADTEC Inc.
Digitel Corp.
FloriCal Systems Inc.
Harris Automation Solutions
Image Video
Leightronix Inc.
MATCO Inc.
Northrop Grumman/Electronics & System Integration Division
Register Data Systems
Richmond Sound Design Ltd.
Sierra Automated Systems & Engineering Corp.
Sundance Digital Inc.
Texscan MSI
Thomson Multi Media

Automation, TV Station

Avid Broadcast
Encoda Systems Inc.
FloriCal Systems Inc.
Harris Automation Solutions
MATCO Inc.
Marketron International
McCurdy Radio Industries Ltd.
Media Computing Inc.
Peter Storer & Associates Inc.
Sundance Digital Inc.
Thomson Multi Media
Time Logic Inc.
VCI-Video Communications Inc.
Videotron Ltee
WireReady NSI

Base Insulators

Utility Tower Company

Batteries and Accessories

ADCOUR
Acme Electric Corp., Aerospace Division
Alexander Technology
Alpha Technologies Inc.
Anton/Bauer Inc.
Arri Canada Ltd.
Battery Pros Inc.
Burlington A/V Recording Media Inc.
Cine 60 Inc.
Frezzolini Electronics Inc.
Alan Gordon Enterprises Inc.
Marathon Norco Aerospace, Inc.
North American Cable Equipment Inc.
Performance Power Technologies

Blimps

Blimpy Floating Signs/Bend-A-Lite

Blowers and Fans

Allied Electronics Inc.
Bud Industries Inc.
CMP Enclosures Inc.
Condux International
EMCOR Enclosures
Seger Electronics

Booms and Cameras

Alan Gordon Enterprises Inc.

Boosters, TV

Axcera

Broadcast & Program Logging Recorders

Dictaphone Corp.
Eventide Inc.
Fast Forward Video
Wicks Broadcast Solutions

Broadcast Audio Products

A.C.C. Electronix, Inc.
ADC
AKG Acoustics, U.S.
AMS Neve Inc.
AheadTek
Aphex Systems Ltd.
Audio Implements/GKC
Audio Processing Technology Ltd.
Autogram Corp.
Belden Electronics Divison
Benchmark Media Systems Inc.
Comrex Corp.
DBX Professional Products
Dolby Laboratories Inc.
Dorrough Electronics
Eventide Inc.
FM Systems Inc.
Fairlight ESP Pty. Ltd.
Farrtronics Ltd.
Fiber Options
Full Compass Systems Ltd.
Furman Sound Inc.
Galaxy Audio Inc.
Gefen Inc.
Harrison by GLW
Image Video
Kahn Communications Inc.
Lectrosonics Inc.
Logitek
MUSICAM U.S.A.
Michael Stevens & Partners Ltd.
Mohawk/CDT
Orban
Parsons Audio
Polyline Corp.
Sennheiser Electronic Corp.
Telecast Fiber Systems Inc.
teletech.ca
Telex Communications Inc.
360 Systems
Wegener Communications Inc.
Wheatstone Corp.
Wicks Broadcast Solutions L.L.C.

Broadcasting & Cable Yearbook 2006

Equipment Manufacturers and Distributors Subject Index

Yamaha Corp. of America
Zack Electronics Inc.

Broadcast Equipment

Advanced Media Technologies, Inc.
Advanced Research Technology Inc.
Allison Payments Systems L.L.C.
Analog Digital International Inc.
Atlantic Sound Systems
Audio Implements/GKC
Bexel, Inc.
Broadcast Store Inc.
Broadcast Supply Worldwide
C-COR
CamMate Studios/Systems
Camplex Corporation
Crouse-Kimzey Co.
Digitel Corp.
DMT USA, Inc.
Dorrough Electronics
ENCO Systems Inc.
Energy-Onix Broadcast Equipment Co. Inc.
FitzCo. Inc.
GKM Manufacturing Corp.
Harris Corporation Co.
Henry Engineering
Ikegami Electronics (U.S.A.) Inc.
Image Video
Industrial Equipment Representatives (IER)
Inscriber Technology Corporation
JVC Professional Products Company
Kahn Communications Inc.
Kay Industries Inc.
Konica Minolta Corp.
The Laumic Rental Co.
MRPP Inc.
MUSICAM U.S.A.
Marshall Electronics
Megastar Inc.
Merlin Engineering Works Inc.
Modulation Sciences Inc.
NVISION Products
National Video Services Inc.
Nautel Ltd.
Allen Osborne Associates Inc.
POA/Paul Olivier & Associates Ltd.
Panasonic Broadcast & Television Systems Co.
Phasetek Inc.
RF Specialties Group
Schafer International
Scientific-Atlanta Canada Inc. Nexus Division
Tannoy North America Inc.
J.A. Taylor & Associates
Technet Systems Group
Thales Broadcast & Multimedia Inc.
Transcom Corp.
Westcott

Broadcast Radio Equipment

Arrakis Systems Inc.
Belar Electronics Laboratory Inc.
Bradley Broadcast Sales
Broadcast Electronics Inc.
Broadcasters General Store Inc.
Comrex Corp.
DBX Professional Products
DPA Microphones, Inc.
Dalet Digital Media Systems
Dorrough Electronics
DRS Broadcast Technology
Henry Engineering
Highway Information Systems, Inc.
Industrial Equipment Representatives (IER)
Inovonics Inc.
Jampro Antennas/RF Systems Inc.
Kintronic Labs Inc.
Lindsay Electronics
Nautel Ltd.
Prime Image Inc.
QEI Corporation
Radiogear Inc.
Schafer International
Swintek Enterprises Inc.
TFT Inc.
Wicks Broadcast Solutions L.L.C.

Broadcast RF Equipment

Antenna Concepts Inc.
Bauer Transmitters
Belar Electronics Laboratory Inc.
Bird Electronic Corp.
Broadcast Microwave Services Inc.
CED
Communication & Power Industries
Communication & Power Industries, EIMAC Division
Crown Broadcast IREC
Dielectric Communications
DMT USA, Inc.
DRS Broadcast Technology
e2v technologies Inc.
Industrial Equipment Representatives (IER)
Jampro Antennas/RF Systems Inc.
Kahn Communications Inc.
Kathrein Inc., Scala Division
LARCAN USA
Micro Communications Inc.
Nautel Ltd.
Radiogear Inc.
Shively Labs
Swintek Enterprises Inc.
TFT Inc.
Teleplex Inc.
Televideo San Diego
Thales

Broadcast Studio Construction, Prefab

Acoustic Systems, a div. of ETS-LINDEREN
Devlin Design Group Inc.
Industrial Acoustics Co., Inc.
Northeastern Communications Concepts Inc.

Broadcast Studio Equipment

A.C.C. Electronix, Inc.
ADC
AKG Acoustics, U.S.
Audioarts Engineering
Auratone Corp.
BDL-Autoscript
Barco Visual Solutions, LLC
Bradley Broadcast Sales
Broadcast Electronic Services
Broadcasters General Store Inc.
Canon U.S.A. Inc.
Digidesign
e-Studio Live!
Furman Sound Inc.
Harris Corp., Broadcast Division
Image Video
Inscriber Technology Corporation
JOA Cartridge Service
MUSICAM U.S.A.
Marshall Electronics
O'Connor Professional Camera Support Systems
Parsons Audio
Radamec Inc.
Radiogear Inc.
Richardson Electronics
Rosco Laboratories Inc.
J.A. Taylor & Associates
Thales Broadcast & Multimedia Inc.
Theatre Service & Supply Corp.
Transcom Corp.
United States Broadcast
Utah Scientific Inc.
Videotron Ltee

Broadcast TV Equipment

AKG Acoustics, U.S.
AVS Graphics & Media Inc.
AZCAR U.S.A. Inc.
Accom Inc.
All Mobile Video Inc.
Alpine Optics Inc.
Artel Video Systems
Belar Electronics Laboratory Inc.
Bexel Corp.
Bexel, Inc.
Broadcast Electronic Services
Broadcast International Group
Canon U.S.A. Inc.
DPA Microphones, Inc.
DeSisti Lighting
DMT USA, Inc.
e2v technologies Inc.
Fast Forward Video
Fiber Options
Freeland Products Inc.
Full Compass Systems Ltd.
Hitachi Denshi America, Ltd.
Image Video
Jampro Antennas/RF Systems Inc.
LARCAN
Maze Corporation
Allen Osborne Associates Inc.
POA/Paul Olivier & Associates Ltd.
Schafer International
Snell & Wilcox Inc.
Solutec Ltd. (HA)
Standard Communications Corp.
Thales Broadcast & Multimedia Inc.
Toshiba America Consumer Products
VCI-Video Communications Inc.
Wegener Communications Inc.
Wescam Inc.
Wiltronix Inc.

Broadcast Video Products

ADC
Accom Inc.
Alpine Optics Inc.
Analog Digital International Inc.
Battery Pros Inc.
Belden Electronics Divison
Broadcast Electronic Services
Camplex Corporation
Canon U.S.A. Inc.
Dorrough Electronics
Fast Forward Video
Glentronix
Image Video
LINK Electronics Inc.
MATCO Inc.
Marshall Electronics
Matrox Video Products Grp
Maxell Corp. of America
Miranda Technologies Inc.
Prime Image Inc.
Roscor Corp.
Snell & Wilcox Inc.
Solutec Ltd. (HA)
J.A. Taylor & Associates
Telecast Fiber Systems Inc.
TELEMETRICS Inc.
teletech.ca
360 Systems
TheTiffen Company
Utah Scientific Inc.
Videomagnetics Inc.
Wegener Communications Inc.
Zack Electronics Inc.

Bulktape DeGausser

Audiolab Electronics Inc.
Data Security Inc.
Garner Products
Glentronix
Paulmar Industries Inc.
Sprague Magnetics Inc.

Bulktape, Audio Cassette

CoarcVideo

Cabinets, Racks, Panels

A & S Case Co. Inc.
ADTEC Inc.
AMCO Engineering Co.
APW Enclosure Products
Allied Electronics Inc.
Atlas Sound
Benner-Nawman Inc.
Bud Industries Inc.
CMP Enclosures Inc.
Calzone Case Co.
EMCOR Enclosures
GKM Manufacturing Corp.
Hardigg Cases
High Tech Industries
Murphy Studio Furniture
National Video Services Inc.
Neumade Products Corp.
Newark Electronics
North American Cable Equipment Inc.
Northern Technologies Inc.
Parsons Manufacturing Corp.
Penn Elcom Inc.
Performance Power Technologies

Broadcasting & Cable Yearbook 2006

Equipment Manufacturers and Distributors Subject Index

Ram Broadcast Systems
Seger Electronics
Seton Identification Products
Stahl, A Scott & Fetzer Co.
Star Case Manufacturing Co. Inc.
Storeel Corp.
Thermodyne International Ltd.
Winsted Corp.
Zack Electronics Inc.

Cable and Accessories

Allied Electronics Inc.
Belden Electronics Divison
Canare Corp.
Communications Specialties Inc.
Comprehensive Video Group
Cortland Cable Co. Inc.
DBS Direct
Gefen Inc.
General Cable
Gepco International Inc.
HAVE Inc.
Insulated Wire Inc. Microwave Products Division
Jensen Tools
KES
Lemo U.S.A. Inc.
M/A-COM
Marshall Electronics
Mic Flags by Aladdin
Milestek Corp.
Mohawk/CDT
Nemal Electronics International Inc.
Neutrik U.S.A. Inc.
Newark Electronics
North American Cable Equipment Inc.
Phillystran Inc.
Pirelli Cables North America—Communications Division
Radio Frequency Systems
Servoreeler Systems
Stage Equipment & Lighting Inc.
Telecast Fiber Systems Inc.
James Thomas Engineering
Times Fiber Communications Inc.
Trilogy Communications Inc.
Trompeter Electronics Inc.
U.S. Electronics Components Corp.
WIREMAX Ltd.
Whirlwind
Wireworks Corp.
Zack Electronics Inc.

Cable Security Systems

Electroline Equipment Inc.
Marshall Electronics
North American Cable Equipment Inc.
Viewsonics Inc.

Cable Termination Equipment, A/V

Clark Wire & Cable Co. Inc.
North American Cable Equipment Inc.
Ripley Company
Videotron Ltee

Calibrators, TV Cameras/Monitors

Commercial Radio Monitoring Co.
Dage-MTI Inc.
Sadelco Inc.

Camera Mounts

Alpha Video & Electronics Co. (AVEC)
Band Pro Film/Video Inc.
Birns and Sawyer Inc.
CSI-Camera Support International
CamMate Studios/Systems
Coptervision
Alan Gordon Enterprises Inc.
Interlogix
Matthews Studio Equipment Inc. (MSE)
Production Consultants & Equipment, Inc. (PC&E)
Sachtler Corp. of America
Vicon Industries Inc.
Wescam Inc.

Camera Pan/Tilt Heads

Arri Canada Ltd.
Arri, Inc.
Avtech Systems Inc.
Bogen Imaging Inc.
Broadcast Sports Technologies
CSI-Camera Support International
CamMate Studios/Systems
Canon U.S.A. Inc.
Coptervision
Alan Gordon Enterprises Inc.
Innovision Optics Inc.
Isaia & Co.
Miller Camera Support, L.L.C.
O'Connor Professional Camera Support Systems
Allen Osborne Associates Inc.
Quick-Set International Inc.
Radamec Inc.
TELEMETRICS Inc.
Vicon Industries Inc.
Vinten Inc.

Camera Tubes

Daily Electronics Corp.
Narragansett Imaging
Teltron Technologies Inc.

Cameras, Projectors & Accessories

Arri Canada Ltd.
Band Pro Film/Video Inc.
Broadcast Store Inc.
Camera Service Center
Coptervision
Eastman Kodak Co.
General Electrodynamics Corp.
Alan Gordon Enterprises Inc.
Ikegami Electronics (U.S.A.) Inc.
Innovision Optics Inc.
International Cinema Equipment
The J-Lab Co.
JVC Professional Products Company
Northrup Grumman
Production Consultants & Equipment, Inc. (PC&E)
Schneider Optics Inc.
Tamron U.S.A. Inc.
Television Engineering Corp.
The Tiffen Company
Toshiba America Consumer Products

Capacitors

Allied Electronics Inc.
Chicago Condenser Corp.
Peter W. Dahl Co. Inc.
Industrial/Midwec Capacitor Corp.
Jennings Technology Co.
Motor Capacitors Inc.
NWL Capacitors

Captioning Equipment

Broadcast Video Systems Corp.
Cheetah International
Evertz Microsystems Ltd.
Image Logic Corp.

Cartridge Automatic Tape

Electronology, Inc.
National Video Tape Co. Inc.

Cartridge Storage Racks

Russ Bassett
Murphy Studio Furniture

Cases

A & S Case Co. Inc.
Alpack Associates, Inc.
Anvil Cases
Atlas Case Corp.
Band Pro Film/Video Inc.
CSI-Camera Support International
Calzone Case Co.
Hardigg Cases
K&H Products Ltd (Porta-Brace)
Kangaroo Products Inc.
The Leather Specialty Co.
Motion Picture Enterprises Inc.
Nalpak
Parsons Manufacturing Corp.
Photomart Cine-Video Inc.
Plastic Reel Corp. of America
Star Case Manufacturing Co. Inc.
Thermodyne International Ltd.
Union Connector Co.
Viking Cases

Cassette Duplication, Audio/Video

Accurate Sound Corp.
Atlantic Sound Systems
Atlantic Video Inc.
CoarcVideo
HAVE Inc.
Leightronix Inc.
M2 America
Media Concepts Inc.

Cassette, Audiotape Equip. & Access.

Audiolab Electronics Inc.
Burlington A/V Recording Media Inc.
Garner Products
JOA Cartridge Service
Moviola
National Video Services Inc.
Veriad

Cassette, Videotape Equip. & Access.

Audiolab Electronics Inc.
Burlington A/V Recording Media Inc.
CoarcVideo
Data Security Inc.
Garner Products
Moviola
Plastic Reel Corp. of America
Veriad

Cassettes

BMG
Burlington A/V Recording Media Inc.
CoarcVideo
Fuji Photo Film U.S.A. Inc.
Future Productions Inc.
Memorex Products Inc.
Moviola
National Audio Co. Inc.
National Video Tape Co. Inc.
Polyline Corp.

CATV Equipment and Supplies

ADSCO Line Products Inc.
ARRIS Telewire Supply
AVCOM of Virginia Inc.
Acterna
Advanced Media Technologies, Inc.
Alpha Technologies Inc.
Andrew Corp.
Arista Information Systems
Artel Video Systems
Benner-Nawman Inc.
Blonder Tongue Laboratories Inc.
CADCO Systems Inc.
CATV Services Inc.
C-COR
C I S Inc.
CONTEC Corp.
Cable Prep
Cable Services Company Inc.
Cable Technologies International
CablePro
Channell Commercial Corp.
Charles Industries Ltd.
Condux International
Convergys Inc.
DBS Direct
DST Innovis
Ditch Witch
R.L. Drake Co.
Eagle Comtronics Inc.
Electroline Equipment Inc.

Broadcasting & Cable Yearbook 2006

Equipment Manufacturers and Distributors Subject Index

FM Systems Inc.
Gefen Inc.
General Atomics
Harmonic Inc.
Hogg & Davis Inc.
KES
Kalun Communications Inc.
Lemco Tool Corp.
Marconi Communications
Mega Hertz
Motorola Broadband Communications Sector
Motorola Digital Media Systems
North American Cable Equipment Inc.
Ortel
Performance Power Technologies
Qintar Technologies Inc.
Ripley Company
Scientific-Atlanta
Sencore Inc./AAVS
Telecrafter Products
Texscan MSI
Thomas & Betts
Thomas & Betts Corp.
Times Fiber Communications Inc.
Toner Cable Equipment Inc.
Transtector Systems Inc.
Trilogy Communications Inc.
U.S. Electronics Components Corp.
VCI-Video Communications Inc.
Vermeer Manufacturing Co.
Viewsonics Inc.
Wegener Communications Inc.
Zenith Electronics Corp.

CATV Hybrid Modules

KES
Narragansett Imaging
North American Cable Equipment Inc.
U.S. Electronics Components Corp.
Viewsonics Inc.

CATV Power Supplies

ARRIS Telewire Supply
Alpha Technologies Inc.
DBS Direct
Electroline Equipment Inc.
North American Cable Equipment Inc.
Performance Power Technologies
U.S. Electronics Components Corp.

CD Players

aeco Ltd.
PBI Media
Sanyo Fisher Co.
Stanton Group
Superscope Technologies Professionals

Cellular Mobile Telephones

TDK Electronics Corp.

Character Generators

ADTEC Inc.
AVS Graphics & Media Inc.
Burst Electronics Inc.
Comprehensive Video Group
Display Systems International Inc.
Focus Enhancements
Gorman-Redlich Manufacturing Co.
Inscriber Technology Corporation
Key West Technology
Knox Video
Matrox Video Products Grp
Mega Hertz
Pinnacle Systems Inc.
Texscan MSI

Chroma Keyers

Broadcast Video Systems Corp.
Focus Enhancements
Ultimatte Corp.

Chronometers, Clocks

Autogram Corp.
Chrono-Log Corp.
ESE
Feldmar Watch and Clock Center
Radio Systems Inc.
Torpey Time

Cleaning Accessories, Audio/Video

Data Security Inc.
HAVE Inc.
JNJ Industries Inc.
Research Technology International Inc.
Sprague Magnetics Inc.
TECH-SA-PORT

Closed Captioning Systems

CPC-Computer Prompting & Captioning Co.
Cheetah International
EEG Enterprises Inc.
Image Logic Corp.
LINK Electronics Inc.
Norpak Corporation

Closed Circuit Systems

Aries Industries Inc.
Avtech Systems Inc.
Cohu Inc.
Interlogix
Marshall Electronics
Trident Media Group/ Spector Entertainment Group Inc.

Coaxial Cables

Andrew Corp.
Belden Electronics Divison
Broadcast Equipment Surplus Inc.
Comm Scope Inc.
Connectronics Corp.
General Cable
Gepco International Inc.
Jensen Tools
Kathrein Inc., Scala Division
MYAT Inc.
Marcom
Milestek Corp.
Mohawk/CDT
Nemal Electronics International Inc.
Nortel Networks
North American Cable Equipment Inc.
Power & Telephone Supply Co.
Seger Electronics
Teleplex Inc.
Times Fiber Communications Inc.
Trilogy Communications Inc.
Trompeter Electronics Inc.
Videotron Ltee

Coaxial Changeover Units, Automatic

North American Cable Equipment Inc.
Siemens Dematic Limited
Video Accessory Corp.

Coaxial Connectors

ARRIS Telewire Supply
Cable Technologies International
CablePro
Canare Corp.
Clark Wire & Cable Co. Inc.
Corning Gilbert Inc.
F-Conn Industries
Kings Electronics Co. Inc.
Lemo U.S.A. Inc.
Milestek Corp.
Mohawk/CDT
Nemal Electronics International Inc.
North American Cable Equipment Inc.
Power & Telephone Supply Co.
Qintar Technologies Inc.
Trilogy Communications Inc.
Trimm Inc.
Trompeter Electronics Inc.
Tyco Electronics
Viewsonics Inc.

Coaxial Patch Panels

Canare Corp.
Clark Wire & Cable Co. Inc.
Connectronics Corp.
Glentronix
LARCAN
Milestek Corp.
Mohawk/CDT
North American Cable Equipment Inc.
Trompeter Electronics Inc.

Coils

Audio-Video Engineering Co.
LBA Technology Inc.

Combiners

Andrew Corp.
Bauer Transmitters
R.L. Drake Co.
Galaxy Audio Inc.
Jampro Antennas/RF Systems Inc.
Kathrein Inc., Scala Division
LARCAN
MYAT Inc.
Microwave Filter Co. Inc.
Nardal - An L-3 Communications Co.
Shively Labs
Viewsonics Inc.

Commercial Compilation

Spotcat Software
Thomson Multi Media

Communications Systems

Advent Communications Ltd.
Anchor Audio Inc.
Clear-Com Communication Systems
Computer Concepts Corp.
DST Innovis
EDX Wireless LLC
Entertainment Communications Network (ECN)
Global Microwave Systems Inc.
IMS (Interactive Market Systems Inc.)
E.F. Johnson Co.
MODCOMP Inc.
MRPP Inc.
Ortel
Production Intercom Inc.
Radyne ComStream Corp.
Roscor Inc.
Studio Technologies Inc.
TDK Electronics Corp.
Talk-A-Phone Co.
Thomas & Betts
V-Soft Communications
Visual Sound Inc.
Wegener Communications Inc.

Compact Disc Equipment

Accurate Sound Corp.
Burlington A/V Recording Media Inc.
Micro Technology Unlimited
Optical Disc Corp.
Products International Inc.
Research Technology International Inc.

Compact Disc Manufacturers

BMG

Computer Desks

High Tech Industries
Luxor
TEAC America Inc.

Computer Floppy Disks

Maxell Corp. of America
Memorex Products Inc.

Broadcasting & Cable Yearbook 2006

Equipment Manufacturers and Distributors Subject Index

Computers and Peripherals

Amerivox Corp.
Ampex Data Systems Corp.
AVerMedia Technologies Inc.
Broadcast Data Consultants
CEA-Computer Engineering Associates
C I S Inc.
CSG Systems
Computer Resolutions
DST Innovis
Dynamic Solutions 2000
ENCO Systems Inc.
Encoda Systems Inc.
Enghouse Systems Limited
Gefen Inc.
Great Lakes Data Systems, Inc.
Greenberg Teleprompting
Hewlett Packard USA
IMS (Interactive Market Systems Inc.)
MCG Surge Protection
MGE UPS SYSTEMS Inc.
MODCOMP Inc.
Marketron International
Mediasoft Inc.
Memorex Products Inc.
Radio Computing Services (RCS)
Peter Storer & Associates Inc.
Strata Marketing Inc.
Summit Software Systems Inc.
Unique Business Systems
Unisys Corp.
UniVision Inc.
Vision Database Systems
Wicks Broadcast Solutions

Computers/Broadcast Equipment Control

Adrienne Electronics Corp.
CEA-Computer Engineering Associates
CS Communications Inc.
Computer Concepts Corp.
ENCO Systems Inc.
Fast Forward Video
Hotbox Digital
Identix
Imagine Products Inc.
MATCO Inc.
MODCOMP Inc.
Marketron International
Media Computing Inc.
Radio Computing Services (RCS)
Register Data Systems
Time Logic Inc.
VCI-Video Communications Inc.
Wicks Broadcast Solutions L.L.C.

Connectors

Allied Electronics Inc.
CATV Services Inc.
Clark Wire & Cable Co. Inc.
Connectronics Corp.
ITT Cannon Electric
Lemo U.S.A. Inc.
Marshall Electronics
Neutrik U.S.A. Inc.
Sacramento Theatrical Lighting (STL)
Switchcraft Inc.
Union Connector Co.
Wireworks Corp.

Console Equipment

AMCO Engineering Co.
Audioarts Engineering
Broadcast Supply Worldwide
GKM Manufacturing Corp.
Teatronics/Entertainment Lighting Control

Consoles

AMCO Engineering Co.
AMS Neve Inc.
AVI Systems
Arrakis Systems Inc.
Audioarts Engineering
Bud Industries Inc.
CMP Enclosures Inc.
DiGi Co. U.K. LTD.
EMCOR Enclosures
High Tech Industries
Martinsound Inc.
Nigel B. Furniture/Marketec
North American Cable Equipment Inc.
Otari USA Sales Inc.
Peavey Electronics
Solid State Logic Inc.
Soundcraft U.S.A.
Vega
Wheatstone Corp.
Winsted Corp.

Consoles, On-Air

AMCO Engineering Co.
Audioarts Engineering
Autogram Corp.
Broadcast Equipment Surplus Inc.
Crouse-Kimzey Co.
DiGi Co. U.K. LTD.
Logitek
North American Cable Equipment Inc.
Radio Systems Inc.
Soundcraft U.S.A.
Wheatstone Corp.
Yamaha Corp. of America

Construction Services

Cygnal Technology
180 Connect
T.T. Technologies Inc.
Teletech Inc.
Tenco Tower Co.

Control Systems

Fast Forward Video
Identix
Image Logic Corp.
Image Video
Knox Video
Leightronix Inc.
MATCO Inc.
NSI
Richmond Sound Design Ltd.
Sacramento Theatrical Lighting (STL)
Teatronics/Entertainment Lighting Control
Vega
Vertex Communications Corp.

Converters and Switchers (CATV)

CONTEC Corp.
Ensemble Designs
Gefen Inc.

Converters, Standards

CATV Services Inc.
Evertz Microsystems Ltd.
Ikegami Electronics (U.S.A.) Inc.
The Image Group Post, LLC.
Kay Industries Inc.
Merlin Engineering Works Inc.
Miranda Technologies Inc.
Sifford Video Services
Snell & Wilcox Inc.
Video International Development Corp.

Converters, TV

Kay Industries Inc.
Miranda Technologies Inc.
Pioneer New Media Technologies Inc.
Scientific-Atlanta
Wiltronix Inc.

Copy Stands

Murphy Studio Furniture

Costumes and Properties

Costume Armour Inc./Christo Vac

Crystal Units

ICM (International Crystal Mfg.)

Cue Systems

COMTEK Inc.
Greenberg Teleprompting
Studio Technologies Inc.

Custom Consoles

CMP Enclosures Inc.
Calzone Case Co.
High Tech Industries
Northeastern Communications Concepts Inc.
Studio Technology
Winsted Corp.

Custom Studios

Channel One Lighting Systems Inc.
Industrial Acoustics Co., Inc.
Murphy Studio Furniture
POA/Paul Olivier & Associates Ltd.
Studio Technology
Wave: Space Inc.

Cyclorama Tracks

Peter Albrecht Company Inc.
Automatic Devices Company
Channel One Lighting Systems Inc.
Olesen
Theatre Service & Supply Corp.
Theatrical Services Inc.

Data Communications Systems

Canon U.S.A. Inc.
Dynamic Solutions 2000
EEG Enterprises Inc.
Entertainment Communications Network (ECN)
FM Systems Inc.
Great Lakes Data Systems, Inc.
E.F. Johnson Co.
MCG Surge Protection
MODCOMP Inc.
Microspace Communications Corp.
Milestone Technologies Inc.
Modulation Sciences Inc.
Norpak Corporation
180 Connect
Spacenet Services Inc.
Trident Media Group/ Spector Entertainment Group Inc.

Data Transmission Equipment

Broadcast Video Systems Corp.
Canon U.S.A. Inc.
Fiber Options
IPITEK
Inovonics Inc.
Intelligent Media Technology
International Datacasting Corp.
MCL Inc.
Microspace Communications Corp.
Moseley Associates Inc.
Norpak Corporation
Nortel Networks
Radyne ComStream Corp.
Spacenet Services Inc.
TELLABS
Thales
Wegener Communications Inc.

Decals

Seton Identification Products

Decoders

Audio Processing Technology Ltd.
Belar Electronics Laboratory Inc.
EEG Enterprises Inc.
Faroudja Laboratories
Macrovision Corp.
Pixel Instruments Corp.
Sarnoff Corp.
Snell & Wilcox Inc.
Tandberg Television Inc.
Television Equipment Assoc. Inc./Matthey
Transcrypt International

Equipment Manufacturers and Distributors Subject Index

Trident Media Group/ Spector Entertainment Group Inc.
Vega
Video International Development Corp.

Dehydrators and Accessories

Dielectric Communications
Radio Frequency Systems
Shively Labs

Demodulators and Modulators

CADCO Systems Inc.
Cable Serv Inc.
FM Systems Inc.
General Atomics
L-3 Communications Telemetry East
NUCOMM Inc.
North American Cable Equipment Inc.
Tektronix Inc.
Tulsat/AN Addvantage Technology Co.
Videotek
Videotron Ltee

Descramblers, Pay TV

CONTEC Corp.
Macrovision Corp.
Motorola Broadband Communications Sector
North American Cable Equipment Inc.

Design Services, Broadcast

Cadix International Inc.
Cygnal Technology
DeSisti Lighting
Meridian Design Associates, Architects
Murphy Studio Furniture
Northeastern Communications Concepts Inc.
Professional Communications Systems
Rees Associates Inc.
Studio Technology
VidCAD Documentation Programs (VDP Inc.)
Wave: Space Inc.

Designers, Production Facilities

CBT Systems
Four Seasons Solar Products Corp.
Meridian Design Associates, Architects
Northeastern Communications Concepts Inc.
POA/Paul Olivier & Associates Ltd.
Rees Associates Inc.
Wave: Space Inc.

Digital Audio Processing Equipment

Aphex Systems Ltd.
Audio Processing Technology Ltd.
Benchmark Media Systems Inc.
Broadcast Supply Worldwide
COASTCOM
Circuit Research Labs Inc. (CRL Systems, Inc.)
Dalet Digital Media Systems
Dialogic Communications Corp.
ENCO Systems Inc.
Eventide Inc.
G Prime Ltd.
Graham-Patten Systems Inc.
Linear Acoustic Inc.
Logitek
Micro Technology Unlimited
NVISION Products
Nortel Networks
Orban
Penny & Giles Inc.
QEI Corporation
Radio Computing Services (RCS)
Roland Corp. U.S.
Sabine Inc.
Symetrix Inc.
TC Electronic
Ward-Beck Systems Ltd.
Yamaha Corp. of America

Digital Audio Recorders

Alesis
Electronology, Inc.
Fostex Corp. of America
Location Sound Corp.
Magna-Tech Electronic Co. Inc.
Micro Technology Unlimited
Roland Corp. U.S.
Sascom Marketing Group
Scott Studios Corp.
Stancil Corp.
Superscope Technologies Professionals
360 Systems

Digital Audio Recording & Editing Station

AMS Neve Inc.
Avid Broadcast
Computer Concepts Corp.
Dalet Digital Media Systems
Digidesign
ENCO Systems Inc.
Electronology, Inc.
Fairlight ESP Pty. Ltd.
McCurdy Radio Industries Ltd.
Micro Technology Unlimited
Orban
Parsons Audio
Penny & Giles Inc.
Radio Computing Services (RCS)
Scott Studios Corp.
360 Systems
Visual Sound Inc.
WireReady NSI
Yamaha Corp. of America

Digital Broadcast Equipment

ADTEC Inc.
AMS Neve Inc.
ATCI/Antenna Technology Communications Inc.
ATI-Audio Technologies Inc.
Accom Inc.
Acterna
Arrakis Systems Inc.
Artel Video Systems
Axcera
Belar Electronics Laboratory Inc.
Bexel Corp.
Bexel, Inc.
Broadcast Electronics Inc.
Broadcast Store Inc.
Broadcast Supply Worldwide
COASTCOM
CORPLEX Inc.
Computer Concepts Corp.
Datatek Corp.
DiGi Co. U.K. LTD.
R.L. Drake Co.
Dubner International Inc.
General Atomics
Harris Corp., Broadcast Communications Division
Harris Corp., Broadcast Division
Hitachi Denshi America, Ltd.
IPITEK
Image Video
International Datacasting Corp.
JVC Professional Products Company
Kahn Communications Inc.
MATCO Inc.
MUSICAM U.S.A.
Marshall Electronics
Panasonic Broadcast & Television Systems Co.
Pinnacle Systems Inc.
QEI Corporation
Radyne ComStream Corp.
Register Data Systems
Tandberg Television Inc.
Tektronix Inc.
Telos Systems
Thales
VCI-Video Communications Inc.
Visual Sound Inc.

Digital Image Processors

Barco Visual Solutions, LLC
Discreet
Eigen

Multi-Image Network
Xintekvideo Inc.

Digital Special Effects Systems

Alias/WaveFront Inc.
Chyron Corp.
Cintel Inc.
Discreet
Eastman Kodak Co.
e-Studio Live!
FOR.A Corp. of America
Focus Enhancements
Pinnacle Systems Inc.
Quantel Inc.
Toshiba America Consumer Products

Digital Video Graphics and Animation

Alias/WaveFront Inc.
Commercial Electronics Ltd.
Discreet
Key West Technology
Matrox Video Products Grp
Multi-Image Network
Quantel Inc.
Vertigo Technology Inc.

Digital Video Processing Equipment

Burst Electronics Inc.
Dubner International Inc.
FOR.A Corp. of America
Focus Enhancements
Gennum Corp.
LINK Electronics Inc.
Leitch Inc.
NTV International Corporation
NVISION Products
Prime Image Inc.
Scientific-Atlanta
Television Equipment Assoc. Inc./Matthey
Visual Sound Inc.
Ward-Beck Systems Ltd.
Wiltronix Inc.
Xintekvideo Inc.

Digital Video Production Systems

Commercial Electronics Ltd.
Matrox Video Products Grp
Multi-Image Network
NVISION Products
Thomson Broadcast & Media Solutions

Distortion Analyzers

Audio Precision Inc.
Boonton Electronics Corp.
Electro Rent Corp.
SyntheSys Research Inc.

Distribution Amplifiers

ATI-Audio Technologies Inc.
Autogram Corp.
Benchmark Media Systems Inc.
Burst Electronics Inc.
Cablynx, Inc.
Datatek Corp.
ESE
Farrtronics Ltd.
Horita
Image Video
Intersil Corp. Headquarters
Leitch Inc.
North American Cable Equipment Inc.
Omicron Video
Philip-Cooke Co.
Qintar Technologies Inc.
Radio Systems Inc.
Ross Video Ltd.
Sigma Electronics Inc.
Solutec Ltd. (HA)
Studio Technologies Inc.
Symmetricom
Symmetricom
Television Equipment Assoc. Inc./Matthey
Video Accessory Corp.

Equipment Manufacturers and Distributors Subject Index

Videotek
Ward-Beck Systems Ltd.
World Video Sales Co.

Distribution Systems

Datatek Corp.
Enghouse Systems Limited
IPITEK
Motorola Digital Media Systems
North American Cable Equipment Inc.
Philip-Cooke Co.
Scientific-Atlanta
StarGuide Digital Networks Inc.

Dollies, Instrument Carts, Etc.

Ferno-Washington Inc.
Hogg & Davis Inc.
Matthews Studio Equipment Inc. (MSE)
Panavision New York
Wheelit Inc.

Dummy Loads

Altronic Research Inc.
Electro Impulse Laboratory Inc.
Kintronic Labs Inc.
Lindsay Electronics
Nardal - An L-3 Communications Co.
Phasetek Inc.
Sencore Inc./AAVS

Duplicators

Accurate Sound Corp.
Ascent Media Management Services
Interface Media Group
M2 America
National Audio Co. Inc.
Sifford Video Services

Earth Stations

Ascent Media Services
BitCentral Inc.
D.H. Satellite
General Electric Co.
Maze Corporation
Megastar Inc.
NTL Broadcast
Narda Satellite Networks
Pinzone Engineering Group Inc.
TDK Electronics Corp.
Trident Media Group/ Spector Entertainment Group Inc.
Vertex Communications Corp.

Editing Equipment, Sales-Rental-Service

Adcom
Commercial Electronics Ltd.
Dubner International Inc.
International Cinema Equipment
Neumade Products Corp.
Plastic Reel Corp. of America
TDK Electronics Corp.
United Media Inc.
VRI (Video Rentals Inc.)

Editing Film and Tape

Ascent Media Management Services
Atlantic Video Inc.
Avid Broadcast
Center City Film & Video
Chyron Corp.
The Image Group Post, LLC.
J and R Moviola Inc.
Paulmar Industries Inc.
Servoreeler Systems
Skotel Corp.
TDK Electronics Corp.

EFP (Electronic Field Production)

Band Pro Film/Video Inc.
Bexel Corp.
Mobile Video Services Ltd.
PMTV Producers Management Television
Panasonic Broadcast & Television Systems Co.
Shook Mobile Technology, LP
TDK Electronics Corp.

Electronic Advertising Displays

U.S. Traffic & Display Solutions

Electronic Components

ADCOUR
Communication & Power Industries, EIMAC Division
Dow-Key Microwave Corp.
Jennings Technology Co.
E.F. Johnson Co.
Kay Industries Inc.
Laser Diode Inc.
M/A-COM
Nardal - An L-3 Communications Co.
Newark Electronics
Selco Products Co.
TTE Inc.
Westlake Audio, Professional Sales Group

Electronic Equipment

Adrienne Electronics Corp.
Boonton Electronics Corp.
Cable Leakage Technologies
Cable Technologies International
Condor D C Power Supplies Inc.
Marconi Communications
Narda Satellite Networks
Power & Telephone Supply Co.
Sencore Inc./AAVS
Teleplex Inc.
Thomson, Inc, (RCA/GE)
Whirlwind

Electronic Protection Equipment

Condor D C Power Supplies Inc.
Control Concepts Corp.
EFI Electronics Corp.
General Electric Co.
LEA International
MCG Surge Protection
Marconi Communications
Tapeswitch Corp.
Transtector Systems Inc.
Wil-Can Electronics Ltd.

Emergency Alerting Systems

Gorman-Redlich Manufacturing Co.
Key West Technology
Mega Hertz
TFT Inc.

Emergency Broadcast Equipment

Gorman-Redlich Manufacturing Co.
Highway Information Systems, Inc.

EMI Cabinets

AMCO Engineering Co.
EMCOR Enclosures
Ross Video Ltd.

Encoders

Audio Processing Technology Ltd.
Broadcast Video Systems Corp.
Cheetah International
Dolby Laboratories Inc.
EEG Enterprises Inc.
Evertz Microsystems Ltd.
Faroudja Laboratories
Gorman-Redlich Manufacturing Co.
L-3 Communications Telemetry East
Macrovision Corp.
Merlin Engineering Works Inc.
Pixel Instruments Corp.

Sarnoff Corp.
Sigma Electronics Inc.
StarGuide Digital Networks Inc.
Symmetricom
Tandberg Television Inc.
Vega
World Video Sales Co.

ENG Equipment and Accessories

AKG Acoustics, U.S.
Ampex Data Systems Corp.
Band Pro Film/Video Inc.
Battery Pros Inc.
Bexel Corp.
Broadcast Microwave Services Inc.
COMTEK Inc.
CSI-Camera Support International
Comrex Corp.
Cooper Sound Systems Inc.
e2v technologies Inc.
E-N-G Mobile Systems Inc.
Gyrocam Systems
Ikegami Electronics (U.S.A.) Inc.
Location Sound Corp.
Marathon Norco Aerospace, Inc.
Marti Electronics
Modulation Sciences Inc.
NSI
NUCOMM Inc.
Photomart Cine-Video Inc.
Professional Sound Services Inc.
Swintek Enterprises Inc.
Tandberg Television Inc.
Television Engineering Corp.
Telex Communications Inc.
Telos Systems

ENG Vans

Alpha Video & Electronics Co. (AVEC)
E-N-G Mobile Systems Inc.
Frontline Communications
Mobile Video Services Ltd.
Phoenix E N G, Inc.
Shook Mobile Technology, LP
Television Engineering Corp.
Wolf Coach Inc.

Engineering Systems

AZCAR U.S.A. Inc.
CBT Systems
C I S Inc.
CS Communications Inc.
Cadix International Inc.
Cygnal Technology
EDX Wireless LLC
Enghouse Systems Limited
Freeland Products Inc.
Professional Communications Systems
V-Soft Communications

Equalizers

A R T Applied Research and Technology
Alesis
Allen Avionics, Inc.
BEI Duncan
Furman Sound Inc.
G Prime Ltd.
Group One Ltd.
Harman International Industries Inc.
Sabine Inc.
TC Electronic

Equipment Maintenance and Repair

Alpine Optics Inc.
CORPLEX Inc.
Feldmar Watch and Clock Center
Film/Video Equipment Service Co. Inc.
LARCAN USA
Tech Laboratories Inc.
Televideo San Diego
Tentel

Broadcasting & Cable Yearbook 2006

Equipment Manufacturers and Distributors Subject Index

Erasers, Magnetic Tape
Audiolab Electronics Inc.
Data Security Inc.
Paulmar Industries Inc.
Research Technology International Inc.

Exciters
Acrodyne Industries Inc.
Advent Communications Ltd.
Axcera
BEXT Inc.
Bauer Transmitters
Delta Electronics Inc.
Marti Electronics
Nautel Ltd.

Facilities Planning
CBT Systems
Devlin Design Group Inc.
The Express Group
Hollywood Vaults Inc.
Rees Associates Inc.
Technet Systems Group
V-Soft Communications
VidCAD Documentation Programs (VDP Inc.)
Wave: Space Inc.

Fiber Optic Cable and Accessories
ADC
ADSCO Line Products Inc.
ARRIS Telewire Supply
Channell Commercial Corp.
Comm Scope Inc.
Communications Specialties Inc.
Condux International
Corning Cable Systems
Corning Inc.
Cortland Cable Co. Inc.
Direct Broadcast Services Inc.
Evertz Microsystems Ltd.
General Cable
Jensen Tools
KES
Laser Diode Inc.
Lemo U.S.A. Inc.
Mohawk/CDT
Newark Electronics
Nortel Networks
North American Cable Equipment Inc.
Pirelli Cables North America—Communications Division
Telecast Fiber Systems Inc.
Thomas & Betts Corp.
Whirlwind

Fiber Optic Transmission Systems
Artel Video Systems
Ascent Media Services
C-COR
Cable Services Company Inc.
Cadix International Inc.
Communications Specialties Inc.
Direct Broadcast Services Inc.
Fiber Options
General Atomics
Harmonic Inc.
IPITEK
Intelligent Media Technology
KES
Laser Diode Inc.
Motorola Digital Media Systems
NTV International Corporation
Norlight Telecommunications Inc.
North American Cable Equipment Inc.
180 Connect
Ortel
Pirelli Cables North America—Communications Division
Standard Communications Corp.
StarGuide Digital Networks Inc.
Telecast Fiber Systems Inc.
Toner Cable Equipment Inc.
V-Soft Communications
Videotron Ltee

Field Strength Meters
ETS-Lindgren
Nardal - An L-3 Communications Co.
North American Cable Equipment Inc.
Potomac Instruments Inc.
Products International Inc.
Sadelco Inc.
Sencore Inc./AAVS
Toner Cable Equipment Inc.

Film Equipment
Arri Canada Ltd.
BDL-Autoscript
BHP Inc.
Birns and Sawyer Inc.
CECO International Corp.
Camera Service Center
Dimension 3
Eastman Kodak Co.
Film/Video Equipment Service Co. Inc.
International Cinema Equipment
J and R Moviola Inc.
Lipsner Smith Co.
Motion Picture Enterprises Inc.
Neumade Products Corp.
Paulmar Industries Inc.
Pro Video & Film Equipment Co. Inc.
Production Consultants & Equipment, Inc. (PC&E)
ScreenLight & Grip
Wescam Inc.
Westcott

Film Printers, Motion Pictures
BHP Inc.
Eastman Kodak Co.

Film Processors
Eastman Kodak Co.
Lipsner Smith Co.
Precision Microproducts of America

Film Scanners
Cintel Inc.

Film-to-Tape Transfer Equipment
International Cinema Equipment
J and R Moviola Inc.
Lipsner Smith Co.

Filters and Delay Lines
Allen Avionics, Inc.
Electroline Equipment Inc.
Industrial/Midwec Capacitor Corp.
MYAT Inc.
Microwave Filter Co. Inc.
Motorola Broadband Communications Sector
Schneider Optics Inc.
TTE Inc.
Television Equipment Assoc. Inc./Matthey
The Tiffen Company

Fire Detection System
Kidde-Fenwal Inc.

Floor Covering Stages
Eddie Egan & Associates
Rosco Laboratories Inc.

Frame Synchronizers
Cablynx, Inc.
Ensemble Designs
Evertz Microsystems Ltd.
Hotronic Inc.
Leitch Inc.
Miranda Technologies Inc.
Pixel Instruments Corp.
Prime Image Inc.
Videotek

Frequency Measuring Services
Antenna Concepts Inc.
Commercial Radio Monitoring Co.
Communications General Corp.
Frequency Measuring Service Inc.
Northwest Monitoring Service
Radio Aids Inc.
Sencore Inc./AAVS
Signal Monitoring Service
Symmetricom
Van Nostrand Radio Engineering Service
Ziehl Electronic Service

Frequency Monitors
Symmetricom

Generators, Electric
CECO International Corp.
Elan Enterprises Ltd.
FWT Inc.
Hollywood Rentals Production Services
PMTV Producers Management Television
Panavision New York
ScreenLight & Grip

Generators, Signal
Kalun Communications Inc.
Magni Systems Inc.
Sencore Inc./AAVS
Video Accessory Corp.

Graphics
AccuWeather Inc.
Alias/WaveFront Inc.
All Mobile Video Inc.
Atlantic Video Inc.
Chyron Corp.
The Image Group Post, LLC.
Inscriber Technology Corporation
Interface Media Group
Multi-Image Network
Vertigo Technology Inc.
Frank Woolley & Co. Inc.

HDTV Equipment
Accom Inc.
Acrodyne Industries Inc.
Antenna Concepts Inc.
Band Pro Film/Video Inc.
Bexel Corp.
Birns and Sawyer Inc.
Canon U.S.A. Inc.
Communication & Power Industries
Dielectric Communications
Enghouse Systems Limited
Frequency Measuring Service Inc.
Harris Corp., Broadcast Division
Hitachi Denshi America, Ltd.
JVC Professional Products Company
Kalun Communications Inc.
Marshall Electronics
Mega Hertz
Milestone Technologies Inc.
O'Connor Professional Camera Support Systems
Panasonic Broadcast & Television Systems Co.
Professional Communications Systems
Radyne ComStream Corp.
Sarnoff Corp.
Sharp Electronics Corp., CCD Products Div.
SyntheSys Research Inc.
Tandberg Television Inc.
Tektronix Inc.
Teleplex Inc.
Thomson Broadcast & Media Solutions
Toshiba America Consumer Products
Ward-Beck Systems Ltd.
Wiltronix Inc.

Headend Systems
ADC
Alpha Technologies Inc.
Blonder Tongue Laboratories Inc.
C-COR
Comex Worldwide Corp.

Equipment Manufacturers and Distributors Subject Index

ComSonics Inc.
Corning Cable Systems
DBS Direct
D.H. Satellite
General Atomics
Kalun Communications Inc.
Norsat International Inc.
North American Cable Equipment Inc.
Ortel
Scientific-Atlanta
Sitco Antenna Company
Standard Communications Corp.
Toner Cable Equipment Inc.
Tulsat/AN Addvantage Technology Co.
Viewsonics Inc.

Heads, Magnetic Film & Tape, Disk

AheadTek
Northern Magnetics Inc.
Sprague Magnetics Inc.

Heads, Refurbishing

Northern Magnetics Inc.
Sprague Magnetics Inc.
Videomagnetics Inc.

Headset Amplifiers

Fostex Corp. of America
R-Columbia Products Co. Inc.

Headsets, Headphones

AKG Acoustics, U.S.
Anchor Audio Inc.
Audio-Technica U.S., Inc.
COMTEK Inc.
Clear-Com Communication Systems
Fostex Corp. of America
Production Intercom Inc.
R-Columbia Products Co. Inc.
RTS Systems Telex Communications Inc
Sacramento Theatrical Lighting (STL)
Sennheiser Electronic Corp.
Setcom Corp.
Stanton Group
Telex Communications Inc.

Helicopters

American Eurocopter Corp.
Geneva Aviation Inc.
Gyrocam Systems
Wescam Inc.

High Definition Television (HDTV)

Cintel Inc.
LARCAN USA
Leitch Inc.
Sarnoff Corp.
Toshiba America Consumer Products

Image Enhancers, TV

Colorado Video Inc.
Xintekvideo Inc.

Infrared Transmission Systems

Sennheiser Electronic Corp.
Sound Designers Studio

Installation Services

American Antenna Inc.
B&B Systems
Broadcast Store Inc.
CBT Systems
Cadix International Inc.
Corning Cable Systems
e2v technologies Inc.
Harris Corporation Co.
180 Connect
Professional Communications Systems
Superior Tower Services Inc.

Teletech Inc.
VidCAD Documentation Programs (VDP Inc.)

Instruments Cases

A & S Case Co. Inc.
Atlas Case Corp.
Calzone Case Co.
Hardigg Cases
Jensen Tools
Penn Elcom Inc.
Star Case Manufacturing Co. Inc.

Interactive Television

Avid Broadcast
Tribune Media Services

Intercom Systems

Anchor Audio Inc.
Clear-Com Communication Systems
Farrtronics Ltd.
Fuller Manufacturing
HM Electronics Inc.
ITI Electronics Inc.
Olesen
Production Intercom Inc.
R-Columbia Products Co. Inc.
RTS Systems Telex Communications Inc
Ram Broadcast Systems
Sacramento Theatrical Lighting (STL)
Setcom Corp.
Sierra Automated Systems & Engineering Corp.
Studio Technologies Inc.
Swintek Enterprises Inc.
Systems Wireless Ltd.
Talk-A-Phone Co.
Telex Communications Inc.
Wiltronix Inc.

ISO Couplers (AM & FM)

Kintronic Labs Inc.
Lindsay Electronics
Phasetek Inc.

Jack Panels and Accessories

ADC
Amplifier Technologies, Inc.
Audio Accessories Inc.
Clark Wire & Cable Co. Inc.
Gepco International Inc.
ITI Electronics Inc.
Kings Electronics Co. Inc.
NVISION Products
Nemal Electronics International Inc.
Neutrik U.S.A. Inc.
Penn Elcom Inc.
Penny & Giles Inc.
Trimm Inc.

Klystron Amplifiers/Lead Oxide Vidicon

Daily Electronics Corp.
e2v technologies Inc.
Penta Laboratories

Klystrons

Communication & Power Industries
Daily Electronics Corp.
e2v technologies Inc.
LARCAN USA
MRPP Inc.
Megastar Inc.
Penta Laboratories
Thales Components Corp.

Labels

Audico Labels
Memorex Products Inc.
National Audio Co. Inc.
Seton Identification Products
U.S. Tape & Label Corp.
Veriad

LED, VU and S Panel Meters

ATI-Audio Technologies Inc.
Dorrough Electronics
Image Video
Logitek
Sescom Inc.
Weschler Instruments
Wohler Technologies Inc.

Lenses, Optical and Camera

Alpine Optics Inc.
Canon U.S.A. Inc.
Century Precision Optics
Dimension 3
Film/Video Equipment Service Co. Inc.
Fujinon Inc.
Homalite
Innovision Optics Inc.
Marshall Electronics
Navitar Inc.
Pentax Imaging Co.
Production Consultants & Equipment, Inc. (PC&E)
Schneider Optics Inc.
Tamron U.S.A. Inc.

Library Storage Systems

Hollywood Vaults Inc.
Imagine Products Inc.
McCurdy Radio Industries Ltd.
Neumade Products Corp.
Paulmar Industries Inc.
Winsted Corp.

Lighting Design

DeSisti Lighting
Devlin Design Group Inc.
The Express Group
Mole-Richardson Co.
L.E. Nelson Sales Corp.
New York City Lites
Packaged Lighting Systems Inc.
Sachtler Corp. of America
Teatronics/Entertainment Lighting Control
Thorn-EMI Studio Lamps/L.C.
Videssence L.L.C.

Lighting Equipment

AVAB America Inc.
Peter Albrecht Company Inc.
Anton/Bauer Inc.
Arri Canada Ltd.
Arri, Inc.
Atlantic Sound Systems
Automatic Devices Company
Bend-A-Lite Flexible Neon
Birns and Sawyer Inc.
CECO International Corp.
Camera Service Center
Channel One Lighting Systems Inc.
Comprehensive Video Group
Control Concepts Corp.
DEDOTEC USA Inc.
DeSisti Lighting
Dove Systems
Electronic Theatre Controls Inc.
Film/Video Equipment Service Co. Inc.
Flash Technology Corporation of America
Frezzolini Electronics Inc.
Full Compass Systems Ltd.
GAMPRODUCTS Inc.
Group One Ltd.
Honeywell Airport Systems
LTM Corp. of America
Leviton NSI Colortran
Lowel-Light Manufacturing Inc.
Matthews Studio Equipment Inc. (MSE)
Mole-Richardson Co.
Musco Mobile Lighting Ltd.
L.E. Nelson Sales Corp.
Olesen
Allen Osborne Associates Inc.
P.C.& E.
Packaged Lighting Systems Inc.
Panavision New York
Photomart Cine-Video Inc.
Pro Video & Film Equipment Co. Inc.
Production Consultants & Equipment, Inc. (PC&E)
Rosco Laboratories Inc.

Equipment Manufacturers and Distributors Subject Index

Sachtler Corp. of America
ScreenLight & Grip
Sinar Bron Inc.
Stage Equipment & Lighting Inc.
Strand Lighting Inc.
Strong International
Teatronics/Entertainment Lighting Control
Theatre Service & Supply Corp.
Theatrical Services Inc.
James Thomas Engineering
Thorn-EMI Studio Lamps/L.C.
Ultimate Support Systems Inc.
Union Connector Co.
Vantage Lighting Inc.
Videssence L.L.C.
Westcott
WILL-BURT Co.

Lightning Protection Equip. & Systems

Abroyd Communications Ltd.
Cortana Corp.
EFI Electronics Corp.
LBA Technology Inc.
LEA International
Lightning Eliminators & Consultants Inc.
Lightning Master Corp.
Lightning Prevention Systems
MCG Surge Protection
Neumade Products Corp.
Northern Technologies Inc.
Pacific Tower Co.
Stage Equipment & Lighting Inc.
Thorn-EMI Studio Lamps/L.C.
Transtector Systems Inc.
Wil-Can Electronics Ltd.

Lights, On-Air

Electronic Theatre Controls Inc.
General Electric Co.
Sachtler Corp. of America
Sinar Bron Inc.
Teatronics/Entertainment Lighting Control

Lights, Recording

Electronic Theatre Controls Inc.
General Electric Co.
Sinar Bron Inc.

Lights, Stage

AVAB America Inc.
Bend-A-Lite Flexible Neon
Channel One Lighting Systems Inc.
Electronic Theatre Controls Inc.
GAMPRODUCTS Inc.
General Electric Co.
Hollywood Rentals Production Services
Mole-Richardson Co.
L.E. Nelson Sales Corp.
Olesen
Packaged Lighting Systems Inc.
Sacramento Theatrical Lighting (STL)
Stage Equipment & Lighting Inc.
Strong International
Theatre Service & Supply Corp.
James Thomas Engineering
Thorn-EMI Studio Lamps/L.C.
Vantage Lighting Inc.

Line Conditioning

ADCOUR
Control Concepts Corp.
Furman Sound Inc.
LEA International
MCG Surge Protection
MGE UPS SYSTEMS Inc.
Newark Electronics
Nigel B. Furniture/Marketec
Northern Technologies Inc.
Wil-Can Electronics Ltd.

Line Surge Protectors

ADCOUR
Control Concepts Corp.
EFI Electronics Corp.
LEA International
Lightning Master Corp.
MCG Surge Protection
MGE UPS SYSTEMS Inc.
Northern Technologies Inc.
Transtector Systems Inc.
Wil-Can Electronics Ltd.

Locks

CableTek Wiring Products Inc.
Penn Elcom Inc.

Logging System

Accurate Sound Corp.
Dubner International Inc.
Eventide Inc.
Geac Libra
Horita
Image Logic Corp.
Imagine Products Inc.
Spotcat Software
Telcom Research

Loudspeakers and Accessories

Atlas Sound
Auernheimer Labs Corp.
Auratone Corp.
JBL Professional
Recoton Corp.
Sennheiser Electronic Corp.
Ultimate Support Systems Inc.
Wave: Space Inc.
Yamaha Corp. of America

Machine Control Systems

ADTEC Inc.
Peter Albrecht Company Inc.
Focus Enhancements
General Electric Co.
Leightronix Inc.
MATCO Inc.
Media Computing Inc.
Micro Technology Unlimited
Philip-Cooke Co.
Tapeswitch Corp.

Master Control Switches

Image Video
Leitch Inc.
Tapeswitch Corp.

Meters

Aeroflex
B&B Systems
Benchmark Media Systems Inc.
ComSonics Inc.
Electro Rent Corp.
G Prime Ltd.
Jennings Technology Co.
Konica Minolta Corp.
Photo Research
Radio Detection/Riser Bond
Techni-Tool Inc.
Tentel
Triplett Corp.
Weschler Instruments
Wohler Technologies Inc.

Microphones and Accessories

AKG Acoustics, U.S.
AVI Systems
Amplivox Portable Sound Systems
Audio-Technica U.S., Inc.
Black Audio
Bogen Communications Inc.
COMTEK Inc.
Countryman Associates Inc.
DPA Microphones, Inc.
FitzCo. Inc.
G Prime Ltd.
Group One Ltd.
LTM Corp. of America
Marshall Electronics
Mic Flags by Aladdin
Micron Audio Products Ltd.
Nady Systems Inc.
Professional Sound Corp.
R-Columbia Products Co. Inc.
RTS Systems Telex Communications Inc
Sennheiser Electronic Corp.
Servoreeler Systems
Sescom Inc.
Shure Inc.
Systems Wireless Ltd.
TAI Audio
Telex Communications Inc.
Ultimate Support Systems Inc.

Microwave

Ascent Media Services
Broadcast Microwave Services Inc.
Broadcast Sports Technologies
Comsearch
Direct Broadcast Services Inc.
Ensat Broadcast Services Inc.
Global Microwave Systems Inc.
Harris-Farinon
M/A-COM
Marcom
NSI
PMTV Producers Management Television
RF Specialties Group
TFT Inc.

Microwave Amplifiers

Harris-Farinon
JSB Service Co.
NUCOMM Inc.

Microwave Antennas

Broadcast Microwave Services Inc.
Broadcast Sports Technologies
Comex Worldwide Corp.
D.H. Satellite
NSI
NUCOMM Inc.
Radio Frequency Systems
Radio Research Instrument Co. Inc.
Southern Broadcast Services

Microwave Equipment

AVCOM of Virginia Inc.
BEXT Inc.
Blonder Tongue Laboratories Inc.
Broadcast Equipment Surplus Inc.
Broadcast Microwave Services Inc.
Broadcast Sports Technologies
Comex Worldwide Corp.
Dow-Key Microwave Corp.
E-N-G Mobile Systems Inc.
Frontline Communications
Geneva Aviation Inc.
Hitachi Denshi America, Ltd.
JSB Service Co.
Marti Electronics
Moseley Associates Inc.
NUCOMM Inc.
Norsat International Inc.
Ortel
Radio Research Instrument Co. Inc.
U.S. Electronics Components Corp.

Microwave Transmitters

Broadcast Microwave Services Inc.
Broadcast Sports Technologies
CED
Global Microwave Systems Inc.
NUCOMM Inc.
Norlight Telecommunications Inc.
Thales

Equipment Manufacturers and Distributors Subject Index

Mobile Communications

Aluma Tower Company Inc.
CSG Systems
Comtech Antenna Systems Inc.
DST Innovis
Ensat Broadcast Services Inc.
Geneva Aviation Inc.
Hardigg Cases
ICM (International Crystal Mfg.)
E.F. Johnson Co.
MCL Inc.
Recoton Corp.
Thermodyne International Ltd.

Mobile Studio Equipment

Calzone Case Co.
F&F Productions, L.L.C.
Ferno-Washington Inc.
Harrison by GLW
Hollywood Rentals Production Services
National Mobile Television
National Mobile TV - Houston
North Dakota Television L.L.C.
Packaged Lighting Systems Inc.
Telos Systems
United States Broadcast

Mobile Units-Sales/Rental

All Mobile Video Inc.
Frontline Communications
PMTV Producers Management Television
J.A. Taylor & Associates
Telenium Mobile
Turner Studios Field Operations

Mobile Vans

Alpha Video & Electronics Co. (AVEC)
E-N-G Mobile Systems Inc.
Frontline Communications
North Dakota Television L.L.C.
Panavision New York
Phoenix E N G, Inc.
Roscor Corp.
ScreenLight & Grip
Shook Mobile Technology, LP
Television Engineering Corp.

Modular Set Design System

The Display & Exhibit Source
Uni-Set Corp.

Modulators

Advanced Media Technologies, Inc.
Blonder Tongue Laboratories Inc.
CADCO Systems Inc.
Cable Serv Inc.
Cable Technologies International
R.L. Drake Co.
Leaming Industries
Radyne ComStream Corp.
Standard Communications Corp.
Toner Cable Equipment Inc.

Moldings

CablePro
CableReady Inc.
The Display & Exhibit Source

Monitor Amplifiers

ATI-Audio Technologies Inc.
Alesis
Amplifier Technologies, Inc.
Image Video
Ross Video Ltd.

Monitor Speakers

Auratone Corp.
Group One Ltd.
Harman International Industries Inc.
JBL Professional
Stanton Group

Wave: Space Inc.
Westlake Audio, Professional Sales Group
Wohler Technologies Inc.

Monitors, Audio and Video

AVI Systems
Birns and Sawyer Inc.
Conrac Systems Inc.
Delta Electronics Inc.
Dorrough Electronics
Evertz Microsystems Ltd.
Farrtronics Ltd.
Furman Sound Inc.
Hoodman Corp.
Ikegami Electronics (U.S.A.) Inc.
Image Video
Interlogix
JVC Professional Products Company
Magni Systems Inc.
Marshall Electronics
Sharp Electronics Corp., CCD Products Div.

Monitors, Frequency, Modulation Phase

Belar Electronics Laboratory Inc.
Commercial Radio Monitoring Co.
Frequency Measuring Service Inc.
Gorman-Redlich Manufacturing Co.
Inovonics Inc.
Nardal - An L-3 Communications Co.
QEI Corporation
TFT Inc.

Monopoles

FWT Inc.
Fred A. Nudd Corp.
Pirod Inc.
Rohn Industries Inc.
Tower Structures Inc.

Motion Control Equipment

Innovision Optics Inc.
Richmond Sound Design Ltd.
Tapeswitch Corp.
Vinten Inc.

Motion Picture Equipment

Arri, Inc.
BHP Inc.
Birns and Sawyer Inc.
CECO International Corp.
Celco
Dimension 3
Eastman Kodak Co.
Alan Gordon Enterprises Inc.
Hollywood Rentals Production Services
Magna-Tech Electronic Co. Inc.
Motion Picture Enterprises Inc.
O'Connor Professional Camera Support Systems
P.C.& E.
Panavision New York
Pro Video & Film Equipment Co. Inc.
Production Consultants & Equipment, Inc. (PC&E)

Motors

Powr-Ups Corp.
Senior Aerospace

Mounting Products

Advance Products Co. Inc.
California Amplifier
Omnimount Systems
Peerless Industries Inc.
Penn Elcom Inc.

Multiplexers

COASTCOM

Multiplexing

Camplex Corporation
Colorado Video Inc.
L-3 Communications Telemetry East

Multistandard TV, VCR Camcorders

Analog Digital International Inc.

Music Equipment

Whirlwind

Name Plates

Seton Identification Products

Neon Lighting

Bend-A-Lite Flexible Neon

Network Delay Systems

StarGuide Digital Networks Inc.

Noise Reduction Systems, Video

Noise Control Corp.
North Hills Signal Processing, a PORTA Systems Co.
Video International Development Corp.
Xintekvideo Inc.

Office Equipment

Luxor
Royal Consumer Information Products

Office Supplies and Forms

Hessler Enterprises Inc.
Veriad

Optical Disk Systems

aeco Ltd.
Identix
Imaging Automation
TEAC America Inc.

Oscillators

ICM (International Crystal Mfg.)
Opamp Labs Inc.
Potomac Instruments Inc.

Panels

APW Enclosure Products
Acoustic Systems, a div. of ETS-LINDEREN
Amplifier Technologies, Inc.
Benner-Nawman Inc.
Bud Industries Inc.
GKM Manufacturing Corp.
High Tech Industries
Kings Electronics Co. Inc.
Panel Authority Inc.
Servoreeler Systems
Wireworks Corp.

Passive Components

Connectronics Corp.
Peter W. Dahl Co. Inc.
Elcom Systems Inc.
IPITEK
MYAT Inc.
Micro Communications Inc.
Microwave Filter Co. Inc.
Nemal Electronics International Inc.
Power & Telephone Supply Co.
Qintar Technologies Inc.
S W R Inc.
Thales Components Corp.
Tulsat/AN Addvantage Technology Co.

Equipment Manufacturers and Distributors Subject Index

Patch Cords
Audio Accessories Inc.
Canare Corp.
Kings Electronics Co. Inc.
Nemal Electronics International Inc.
Neutrik U.S.A. Inc.
Switchcraft Inc.
Trompeter Electronics Inc.

Pay TV Equipment and Services
Comex Worldwide Corp.
DST Innovis
Electroline Equipment Inc.
Great Lakes Data Systems, Inc.
Macrovision Corp.
Syntellect Inc.
T-C Specialties Co.
Tandberg Television Inc.
Zenith Electronics Corp.

Pedestals
Argraph Corp.
CSI-Camera Support International
Channell Commercial Corp.
Charles Industries Ltd.
Matthews Studio Equipment Inc. (MSE)
Miller Camera Support, L.L.C.
Sachtler Corp. of America
Thomas & Betts Corp.
Vinten Inc.

Phasing Equipment
Intersil Corp. Headquarters
Kay Industries Inc.
Phasetek Inc.

Phono Equipment and E Micro-Trak
Audio-Technica U.S., Inc.

Photographic Equipment
Bencher Inc.
Calumet Photographic
Precision Microproducts of America
Sinar Bron Inc.
Tamron U.S.A. Inc.
The Tiffen Company
Tinsley Laboratory Inc.
Westcott

Photographic Processing Machines
Precision Microproducts of America

Plastics and Injection Molders
S&L Plastics Inc.

Plugs and Connectors
Canare Corp.
Condor D C Power Supplies Inc.
Connectronics Corp.
DBS Direct
Gepco International Inc.
Kings Electronics Co. Inc.
Marconi Communications
Neutrik U.S.A. Inc.
Olesen
Selco Products Co.
Switchcraft Inc.

Pole Line Hardware
ARRIS Telewire Supply
Condux International
Hogg & Davis Inc.
Marconi Communications
Power & Telephone Supply Co.
Thomas & Betts Corp.

Portable Light Plants
Mole-Richardson Co.

Portable Power Supplies
Fermont ACTS Co.
Frezzolini Electronics Inc.
Hollywood Rentals Production Services
Northern Power Systems

Portable Video Tape Recorder Systems
Mitsubishi Digital Electronics America Inc.

Postproduction Systems
Accom Inc.
Adcom
Analog Digital International Inc.
Ascent Media Services
B&B Systems
CORPLEX Inc.
Cheetah International
Interface Media Group
Magna-Tech Electronic Co. Inc.

Power Meters
Boonton Electronics Corp.
Coaxial Dynamics
Dorrough Electronics
Products International Inc.
Viewsonics Inc.
Weschler Instruments

Power Supplies and Accessories
ADCOUR
Alpha Technologies Inc.
CableReady Inc.
Kay Industries Inc.
Leader Instruments Corp.
MGE UPS SYSTEMS Inc.
Mole-Richardson Co.
Northern Power Systems
Northern Technologies Inc.
Products International Inc.
Transtector Systems Inc.

Pre-Amps, Microphone
Benchmark Media Systems Inc.
Beyerdynamic
Bryston Ltd.
Edcor Electronics Corp.
Martinsound Inc.
Sascom Marketing Group
Stanton Group
Studio Technologies Inc.
Symetrix Inc.

Pressurizing Equipment and Accessories
Andrew Corp.
Radio Frequency Systems

Professional Audio Equipment
BBE Sound Inc.
Countryman Associates Inc.
DBX Professional Products
Dolby Laboratories Inc.
Electronology, Inc.
Jensen Transformers Inc.
Lectrosonics Inc.
Michael Stevens & Partners Ltd.
Nakusa Inc.
Parsons Audio
Professional Sound Services Inc.
QSC Audio Products Inc.
Radio Design Labs. (RDL)
Roland Corp. U.S.
Roscor Corp.
Sabine Inc.
Shure Inc.
Sound Designers Studio
TC Electronic
Thermodyne International Ltd.
Westlake Audio, Professional Sales Group

Professional Recording Equipment
Aphex Systems Ltd.
DiGi Co. U.K. LTD.
Digidesign
Fairlight ESP Pty. Ltd.
Harman International Industries Inc.
Professional Sound Services Inc.
Roland Corp. U.S.
Soundcraft U.S.A.
Superscope Technologies Professionals
TEAC America Inc.
Westlake Audio, Professional Sales Group

Professional Sound Equipment
A R T Applied Research and Technology
BBE Sound Inc.
Bradley Broadcast Sales
Broadcasters General Store Inc.
Cooper Sound Systems Inc.
Countryman Associates Inc.
Crouse-Kimzey Co.
DiGi Co. U.K. LTD.
JBL Professional
Magna-Tech Electronic Co. Inc.
Professional Sound Services Inc.
Sound Designers Studio

Professional Video Equipment
AVS Graphics & Media Inc.
Alpine Optics Inc.
BDL-Autoscript
Bexel, Inc.
Bogen Imaging Inc.
CamMate Studios/Systems
Dubner International Inc.
Ensemble Designs
Gray Engineering Laboratories Inc.
MATCO Inc.
Merlin Engineering Works Inc.
Pinnacle Systems Inc.
Prime Image Inc.
Roscor Corp.
Televideo San Diego
Thermodyne International Ltd.
Videomagnetics Inc.

Projectors, Projection Systems
Barco Visual Solutions, LLC
International Cinema Equipment
Magna-Tech Electronic Co. Inc.
Motion Picture Enterprises Inc.
Navitar Inc.
Raven Screen Corp.
SAIC
Sharp Electronics Corp., CCD Products Div.
Strong International
Theatre Service & Supply Corp.

Promotion Products
Blimpy Floating Signs/Bend-A-Lite
Communication Graphics, Inc.
Mic Flags by Aladdin
PrismaGraphics Inc.

Prompting Equipment
BDL-Autoscript
COMTEK Inc.
CPC-Computer Prompting & Captioning Co.
Comprompter Inc.
Electronic Script Prompting
Intelliprompt
Listec Video Corp.
Marietta Design Group
QTV
Tekskil Industries Inc.

Protective Apparel
Second Chance Body Armor Inc.

Public Address Systems
Amplivox Portable Sound Systems
Atlantic Sound Systems
Greenberg Teleprompting

Broadcasting & Cable Yearbook 2006

Equipment Manufacturers and Distributors Subject Index

TOA Electronics Inc.
Talk-A-Phone Co.

Publications, Broadcast

Broadcast Engineering
Cable Yellow Pages
FM Atlas—Publishing and Electronics
Tribune Media Services

Racks

A & S Case Co. Inc.
AMCO Engineering Co.
APW Enclosure Products
Atlas Case Corp.
Atlas Sound
Benner-Nawman Inc.
Bud Industries Inc.
CMP Enclosures Inc.
EMCOR Enclosures
GKM Manufacturing Corp.
Nigel B. Furniture/Marketec
Packaged Lighting Systems Inc.
Panel Authority Inc.
Parsons Manufacturing Corp.
Penn Elcom Inc.
Sound Designers Studio
Star Case Manufacturing Co. Inc.
Storeel Corp.
Viking Cases
Winsted Corp.

Radar Systems

Advanced Designs Corp.
Radio Research Instrument Co. Inc.

Radio Control Equipment

Motor Capacitors Inc.

Radio Equipment

Motor Capacitors Inc.
RF Specialties Group
Schafer International
Wicks Broadcast Solutions L.L.C.
Wireless Accessories Group

Radio Equipment, 2-Way

ICM (International Crystal Mfg.)
E.F. Johnson Co.
Nady Systems Inc.
R-Columbia Products Co. Inc.
Systems Wireless Ltd.
TAI Audio
Wireless Accessories Group

Receivers, Shortwave, AM-FM-TV, Multiplex

R.L. Drake Co.
FM Atlas—Publishing and Electronics
Freeland Products Inc.
JSB Service Co.
Samson Technologies Corp.
Symmetricom

Recorders, Accessories

Electronology, Inc.
Record/Play Tek Inc.
Stancil Corp.
360 Systems

Recorders, Audio

Bradley Broadcast Sales
Magna-Tech Electronic Co. Inc.
National Audio Co. Inc.
Otari USA Sales Inc.
Record/Play Tek Inc.
Sanyo Fisher Co.
Stancil Corp.
Superscope Technologies Professionals

Recorders, Cassette Audio Logging

International Electro-Magnetics
Stancil Corp.

Recorders, Video

Accom Inc.
Eigen
JVC Professional Products Company
MATCO Inc.
Merlin Engineering Works Inc.
Northrup Grumman
Optical Disc Corp.
Sanyo Fisher Co.
TEAC America Inc.
Thomson, Inc, (RCA/GE)
Videomagnetics Inc.

Recording Studios

Acoustic Systems, a div. of ETS-LINDEREN
Cole Stages
Sound Designers Studio
Wave: Space Inc.
Westlake Audio, Professional Sales Group

Recording Studios Construction, Prefab

Acoustic Systems, a div. of ETS-LINDEREN
Industrial Acoustics Co., Inc.
Northeastern Communications Concepts Inc.

Reels, Magnetic Tape

JOA Cartridge Service
Motion Picture Enterprises Inc.
Polyline Corp.
Stancil Corp.

Remote Broadcast Equipment

Aluma Tower Company Inc.
Broadcast Supply Worldwide
Comrex Corp.
Digitel Corp.
Global Microwave Systems Inc.
LBA Technology Inc.
MUSICAM U.S.A.
Marti Electronics
PMTV Producers Management Television
Radamec Inc.
StarGuide Digital Networks Inc.
Telecast Fiber Systems Inc.
Telos Systems
Wescam Inc.

Remote Control

AVI Systems
Broadcast Equipment Surplus Inc.
Broadcast Sports Technologies
Burk Technology
CONTEC Corp.
Innovision Optics Inc.
Leightronix Inc.
Moseley Associates Inc.
Motorola Broadband Communications Sector
NSI
Nigel B. Furniture/Marketec
Quick-Set International Inc.
Radamec Inc.
Vinten Inc.
Wescam Inc.

Remote Control for VTRs

Imagine Products Inc.
Leightronix Inc.

Remote Control Systems for TV Cameras

Avtech Systems Inc.
Camplex Corporation
Interlogix
Quick-Set International Inc.

Radamec Inc.
TELEMETRICS Inc.

Rental Equipment (Broadcast and Cable)

Analog Digital International Inc.
Bexel Corp.
Bexel, Inc.
CORPLEX Inc.
CamMate Studios/Systems
Direct Broadcast Services Inc.
e2v technologies Inc.
Ensat Broadcast Services Inc.
Greenberg Teleprompting
The Laumic Rental Co.
P.C.& E.
ScreenLight & Grip
Systems Wireless Ltd.
Tele-Measurements Inc.
Unique Business Systems
VRI (Video Rentals Inc.)

Repair

CONTEC Corp.
ComSonics Inc.
Feldmar Watch and Clock Center
Flash Technology Corporation of America
JSB Service Co.
Multi-Image Network
Swintek Enterprises Inc.
Tele-Measurements Inc.
Tentel

Research and Equipment

aeco Ltd.
Future Productions Inc.
IMS (Interactive Market Systems Inc.)
National Video Services Inc.
Sarnoff Corp.
Tech Laboratories Inc.
Teleplex Inc.
Tribune Media Services

Reverberation Chambers

Industrial Acoustics Co., Inc.

RF Bridging Equipment

Potomac Instruments Inc.

RF Coaxial Load Resistors

Altronic Research Inc.
Bird Electronic Corp.
Coaxial Dynamics
LARCAN USA
Trompeter Electronics Inc.

RF Instrumentation & Components

Bird Electronic Corp.
Boonton Electronics Corp.
Coaxial Dynamics
Dow-Key Microwave Corp.
Jennings Technology Co.
LBA Technology Inc.
Phasetek Inc.
Potomac Instruments Inc.
RF Specialties Group
Sadelco Inc.
Shively Labs
TTE Inc.
Viewsonics Inc.

RF Power Attenuators

Bird Electronic Corp.
Kalun Communications Inc.

Rigging Systems

Peter Albrecht Company Inc.
Channel One Lighting Systems Inc.
DeSisti Lighting

Broadcasting & Cable Yearbook 2006

Equipment Manufacturers and Distributors Subject Index

Gala
Hoffend & Sons Inc.
Hollywood Rentals Production Services
Olesen
Packaged Lighting Systems Inc.
Sacramento Theatrical Lighting (STL)
Superior Tower Services Inc.
James Thomas Engineering

Robotics

CSI-Camera Support International
DeSisti Lighting
Frezzolini Electronics Inc.
Fujinon Inc.
O'Connor Professional Camera Support Systems
Radamec Inc.
TELEMETRICS Inc.
Vinten Inc.

Routing Switchers

Adrienne Electronics Corp.
Amek U.S.A.
Cablynx, Inc.
General Atomics
IRIS Technologies Inc.
Image Video
Knox Video
Leitch Inc.
NTV International Corporation
PESA Switching Systems, Inc.
Richmond Sound Design Ltd.
Sierra Automated Systems & Engineering Corp.
Sigma Electronics Inc.
Thomson Broadcast & Media Solutions
Utah Scientific Inc.
Video Accessory Corp.
Wheatstone Corp.
Wiltronix Inc.

Satellite Audio Systems

International Datacasting Corp.
Register Data Systems
Standard Communications Corp.
StarGuide Digital Networks Inc.

Satellite Communications Systems

ATCI/Antenna Technology Communications Inc.
Advent Communications Ltd.
Andrew Corp.
Ascent Media Services
Channel Master L.L.C.
Communication & Power Industries
Kahn Communications Inc.
MCL Inc.
MRPP Inc.
Maze Corporation
Megastar Inc.
Microspace Communications Corp.
Milestone Technologies Inc.
Narda Satellite Networks
Norsat International Inc.
Pinzone Engineering Group Inc.
Richardson Electronics
Rodelco Electronics Corp.
Roscor Corp.
Satellite Systems Corp.
Spacenet Services Inc.
Superior Satellite Engineers Inc.

Satellite News Vehicle

Direct Broadcast Services Inc.
E-N-G Mobile Systems Inc.
Ensat Broadcast Services Inc.
Frontline Communications
Shook Mobile Technology, LP
J.A. Taylor & Associates
Television Engineering Corp.
Wolf Coach Inc.

Satellite Receiver

AVCOM of Virginia Inc.
Advanced Media Technologies, Inc.
Blonder Tongue Laboratories Inc.
Cable Serv Inc.
Chrono-Log Corp.

R.L. Drake Co.
International Datacasting Corp.
L-3 Communications Telemetry East
Pace Micro Technology P.L.C.
Standard Communications Corp.
Tulsat/AN Addvantage Technology Co.
U.S. Electronics Components Corp.

Satellite Resale and Common Carriers

Ascent Media Services
Norlight Telecommunications Inc.
SES Americom
Trident Media Group/ Spector Entertainment Group Inc.

Satellite Services

Ascent Media Management Services
Ascent Media Services
Ascent Media Services
Comsearch
Direct Broadcast Services Inc.
Ensat Broadcast Services Inc.
Milestone Technologies Inc.
Mobile Video Services Ltd.
NTL Broadcast
PMTV Producers Management Television
SES Americom
Trident Media Group/ Spector Entertainment Group Inc.

Satellite Terminals

Channel Master L.L.C.

Scan Converters

AVerMedia Technologies Inc.
Communications Specialties Inc.
Faroudja Laboratories
Focus Enhancements
Magni Systems Inc.

Scramblers, Pay TV

CED
Macrovision Corp.

Security Surveillance

AVCOM of Virginia Inc.
Avtech Systems Inc.
Cablynx, Inc.
Colorado Video Inc.
HM Electronics Inc.
Macrovision Corp.
Tele-Measurements Inc.
Vicon Industries Inc.

Security Systems

Avtech Systems Inc.
Imaging Automation
Tech Laboratories Inc.

Service, Repair and Maintenance

Alpine Optics Inc.
Arri Canada Ltd.
C-COR
ComSonics Inc.
Cygnal Technology
Flash Technology Corporation of America
HM Electronics Inc.
Signal Monitoring Service
Specialized Communications
Tulsat/AN Addvantage Technology Co.
United States Broadcast
Videomagnetics Inc.
Westlake Audio, Professional Sales Group

Signal Generators

AVCOM of Virginia Inc.
Condux International
Image Video
Leader Instruments Corp.

Magni Systems Inc.
Sadelco Inc.
Techni-Tool Inc.
Video Accessory Corp.
World Video Sales Co.

Signal Processor

A R T Applied Research and Technology
BBE Sound Inc.
CADCO Systems Inc.
Eventide Inc.
G Prime Ltd.
LINK Electronics Inc.
Renkus-Heinz Inc.
Roland Corp. U.S.
Ross Video Ltd.
Sabine Inc.
Scientific-Atlanta Canada Inc. Nexus Division
TC Electronic
TOA Electronics Inc.
Tulsat/AN Addvantage Technology Co.

Signs, Engraved, Plastic

Blimpy Floating Signs/Bend-A-Lite
The Display & Exhibit Source
Seton Identification Products

Sound Editing

Ascent Media Management Services

Sound Equipment

Amplivox Portable Sound Systems
Atlantic Sound Systems
Atlas Sound
Cooper Sound Systems Inc.
International Cinema Equipment
Location Sound Corp.
Radio Design Labs. (RDL)
Renkus-Heinz Inc.
TOA Electronics Inc.

Sound Mixers

Amplivox Portable Sound Systems
Cooper Sound Systems Inc.
DiGi Co. U.K. LTD.
Harrison by GLW
Professional Sound Corp.

Sound Recording Equipment

A R T Applied Research and Technology
Atlantic Sound Systems
Bradley Broadcast Sales
Cooper Sound Systems Inc.
Countryman Associates Inc.
Digidesign
Location Sound Corp.
Roland Corp. U.S.

Sound Systems

Amplivox Portable Sound Systems
Auratone Corp.
Full Compass Systems Ltd.
JBL Professional
Renkus-Heinz Inc.

Speakers

Amplifier Technologies, Inc.
Amplivox Portable Sound Systems
Atlas Sound
Auernheimer Labs Corp.
Auratone Corp.
FitzCo. Inc.
Galaxy Audio Inc.
JBL Professional
QSC Audio Products Inc.
Renkus-Heinz Inc.
Stanton Group
TOA Electronics Inc.
Wohler Technologies Inc.

Broadcasting & Cable Yearbook 2006

Equipment Manufacturers and Distributors Subject Index

Special Effects Generators
Alias/WaveFront Inc.
e-Studio Live!

Special Effects, Audiovisual
Ampex Data Systems Corp.
Chyron Corp.
Dimension 3
Richmond Sound Design Ltd.

Spectrum Analyzers
AVCOM of Virginia Inc.
Frequency Measuring Service Inc.
Products International Inc.
SyntheSys Research Inc.
Tektronix Inc.

Splicing Equipment, Film, Tape
Amek U.S.A.
Neumade Products Corp.
Servoreeler Systems

Standards Converters
Glentronix
Interface Media Group
Merlin Engineering Works Inc.
Sifford Video Services
Snell & Wilcox Inc.
Video International Development Corp.

Standby Power
ADCOUR
Alpha Technologies Inc.
LEA International
MGE UPS SYSTEMS Inc.
Northern Technologies Inc.
Performance Power Technologies

Stands, Computer, A/V, TV Etc.
Advance Products Co. Inc.
Calzone Case Co.
Luxor
Matthews Studio Equipment Inc. (MSE)
Peerless Industries Inc.
Wheelit Inc.
Winsted Corp.

Stands, Microphone
Atlas Sound
Mic Flags by Aladdin
Ultimate Support Systems Inc.

Station Automation
CEA-Computer Engineering Associates
Encoda Systems Inc.
FloriCal Systems Inc.
Key West Technology
Media Computing Inc.
Professional Communications Systems
Scott Studios Corp.
Spotcat Software
VCI-Video Communications Inc.
WireReady NSI

Status Monitoring
Acterna
C I S Inc.
Flash Technology Corporation of America

Stereo Equipment, Audio
Advanced Media Technologies, Inc.
Learning Industries

Stereo Generation Equipment
Aphex Systems Ltd.
Circuit Research Labs Inc. (CRL Systems, Inc.)
Inovonics Inc.
Kahn Communications Inc.
Learning Industries
Modulation Sciences Inc.

Stereo Simulation
Studio Technologies Inc.

Still Stores
AVS Graphics & Media Inc.
Inscriber Technology Corporation

Still Stores-Digital
AVS Graphics & Media Inc.
Multi-Image Network

Stopwatches
M. Ducommun Co.
Feldmar Watch and Clock Center

Storage Facilities
Atlantic Inc.
Hollywood Vaults Inc.
Research Technology International Inc.

Studio Equipment
Peter Albrecht Company Inc.
Bradley Broadcast Sales
Channel One Lighting Systems Inc.
DBX Professional Products
Ferno-Washington Inc.
Matthews Studio Equipment Inc. (MSE)
P.C.& E.
Parsons Audio
Shure Inc.
Stage Equipment & Lighting Inc.
Theatre Service & Supply Corp.

Studio Facilities
Acoustic Systems, a div. of ETS-LINDEREN
All Mobile Video Inc.
Ascent Media Services
Atlantic Video Inc.
CECO International Corp.
Center City Film & Video
Devlin Design Group Inc.
The Image Group Post, LLC.
Interface Media Group
Technet Systems Group

Studio Furniture
Devlin Design Group Inc.
The Express Group
Murphy Studio Furniture
Nigel B. Furniture/Marketec
Northeastern Communications Concepts Inc.
Studio Technology
Wheatstone Corp.

Studio Sets, Custom
Devlin Design Group Inc.
The Express Group
Studio Technology
Uni-Set Corp.

Sub-Carrier Generators
Marti Electronics

Switches and Accessories
Communications Specialties Inc.
Dow-Key Microwave Corp.
IRIS Technologies Inc.
Nortel Networks

Qintar Technologies Inc.
Seger Electronics
Selco Products Co.
Tapeswitch Corp.
Tech Laboratories Inc.
Veetronix Inc.

Switching Equipment, Audio
Autogram Corp.
Broadcast Electronic Services
IRIS Technologies Inc.
Image Video
NTV International Corporation
Ram Broadcast Systems
Sierra Automated Systems & Engineering Corp.
Utah Scientific Inc.
Veetronix Inc.
Video Accessory Corp.

Switching Equipment, Video
Ampex Data Systems Corp.
Broadcast Electronic Services
e-Studio Live!
Gennum Corp.
Hotronic Inc.
IRIS Technologies Inc.
Ikegami Electronics (U.S.A.) Inc.
Image Video
Ross Video Ltd.
Utah Scientific Inc.
Veetronix Inc.
Video Accessory Corp.
World Video Sales Co.

Tape Conditioner, Audio/Video
Data Security Inc.

Tape Duplicators
Accurate Sound Corp.
Ascent Media Management Services
Future Productions Inc.
IRIS Technologies Inc.
M2 America
Sifford Video Services

Tape Equipment and Accessories
Audiolab Electronics Inc.
Plastic Reel Corp. of America
Record/Play Tek Inc.
Research Technology International Inc.
Tentel

Tape Heads, Audio
AheadTek
Northern Magnetics Inc.
Record/Play Tek Inc.

Tape Recorders
National Audio Co. Inc.
Northrup Grumman
PBI Media
Record/Play Tek Inc.
Sanyo Fisher Co.
Superscope Technologies Professionals
TEAC America Inc.
Thomson, Inc, (RCA/GE)

Tape Synchronizers
Adcom

Tape, Audio and Video
BMG
Fuji Photo Film U.S.A. Inc.
HAVE Inc.
JOA Cartridge Service
Maxell Corp. of America
Memorex Products Inc.
Motion Picture Enterprises Inc.
Moviola
National Video Tape Co. Inc.

Broadcasting & Cable Yearbook 2006

Equipment Manufacturers and Distributors Subject Index

Panasonic Broadcast & Television Systems Co.
Plastic Reel Corp. of America
Polyline Corp.
Record/Play Tek Inc.
Recoton Corp.

Tap-Offs (CATV)

ARRIS Telewire Supply
Viewsonics Inc.

Telecine

Accom Inc.
Ascent Media Management Services
Atlantic Video Inc.
B&B Systems
Cintel Inc.

Telecommunications Products

Aluma Tower Company Inc.
Artel Video Systems
Audio Processing Technology Ltd.
CSG Systems
Cable Technologies International
Cadix International Inc.
Concerto Software
Corning Cable Systems
DST Innovis
Dolby Laboratories Inc.
EDX Wireless LLC
Enghouse Systems Limited
Hogg & Davis Inc.
ICM (International Crystal Mfg.)
IPITEK
ITI Electronics Inc.
Intersil Corp. Headquarters
MODCOMP Inc.
MEGGER
Milestone Technologies Inc.
Newark Electronics
Nortel Networks
Northern Power Systems
Ortel
Pirelli Cables North America—Communications Division
Power & Telephone Supply Co.
Ripley Company
Sierra Automated Systems & Engineering Corp.
SiteSafe Inc.
Syntellect Inc.
T-C Specialties Co.
Techni-Tool Inc.
Telecrafter Products
TELLABS
Telos Systems
Thomas & Betts Corp.
V-Soft Communications
VTECH Communications

Teleconferencing

Artesia Technologies
Atlantic Video Inc.
Burst Electronics Inc.
Canon U.S.A. Inc.
Lectrosonics Inc.
MODCOMP Inc.
Servoreeler Systems
Tamron U.S.A. Inc.
Tele-Measurements Inc.
Televideo San Diego
TELLABS
VidCAD Documentation Programs (VDP Inc.)

Telemetry Receiving Systems

L-3 Communications Telemetry East

Telemetry Transmission Links

Burk Technology
Crouse-Kimzey Co.
Marti Electronics

Telephone Control Systems

Inovonics Inc.

Telephone Interface Equipment

Broadcasters General Store Inc.
Comrex Corp.
Crouse-Kimzey Co.
Radio Systems Inc.
Syntellect Inc.
Telos Systems

Telephone Line Amplifiers

ITI Electronics Inc.
Pirelli Cables North America—Communications Division

Teleprompters

BDL-Autoscript
CPC-Computer Prompting & Captioning Co.
Electronic Script Prompting
Greenberg Teleprompting
Intelliprompt
QTV
Telescript Inc.

Test Equipment

aeco Ltd.
Acterna
Aeroflex
Audio Precision Inc.
Bird Electronic Corp.
Boonton Electronics Corp.
Broadcast Video Systems Corp.
Cable Leakage Technologies
Coaxial Dynamics
Comprehensive Video Group
ComSonics Inc.
Corning Cable Systems
DBS Direct
DSC Laboratories
ETS-Lindgren
Electro Rent Corp.
FM Systems Inc.
Fluke Corp.
Galaxy Audio Inc.
Horita
Jennings Technology Co.
Jensen Tools
Kalun Communications Inc.
Kathrein Inc., Scala Division
Leader Instruments Corp.
Magni Systems Inc.
Megastar Inc.
MEGGER
Modulation Sciences Inc.
Products International Inc.
Radio Detection/Riser Bond
Sadelco Inc.
Sarnoff Corp.
Shallco Inc.
Techni-Tool Inc.
Tektronix Inc.
Tentel
Thales Broadcast & Multimedia Inc.
Triplett Corp.
Videotek
Weschler Instruments
Wireworks Corp.

Time Base Correctors

Broadcast Electronic Services
FOR.A Corp. of America
Glentronix
Hotronic Inc.
Symmetricom

Time Code Equipment

Adrienne Electronics Corp.
Analog Digital International Inc.
Burst Electronics Inc.
Calculated Industries Inc.
Chrono-Log Corp.
Digidesign
ESE
Electronic Theatre Controls Inc.
Gray Engineering Laboratories Inc.
Horita
Image Logic Corp.
Imagine Products Inc.

Miranda Technologies Inc.
Skotel Corp.
Symmetricom
Symmetricom
SyntheSys Research Inc.
Telcom Research

Time Delay Units, Audio

Allen Avionics, Inc.
Hoagland Instrument, Inc.
Michael Stevens & Partners Ltd.
Pixel Instruments Corp.

Timers

Chrono-Log Corp.
ESE
Feldmar Watch and Clock Center
Symmetricom
Torpey Time
World Video Sales Co.

Tone Generator and Detectors

Image Video
MATCO Inc.
Techni-Tool Inc.
Texscan MSI
Vega

Tools and Accessories

Benner-Nawman Inc.
Cable Prep
CablePro
Canare Corp.
E-Z Trench Manufacturing Co. Inc.
F-Conn Industries
Hogg & Davis Inc.
Jensen Tools
Lemco Tool Corp.
Milestek Corp.
Ripley Company
Telecrafter Products

Tower Design, Manufacture

Abroyd Communications Ltd.
Allied Tower Co. Inc.
Aluma Tower Company Inc.
Baron Telecom
Central Tower
Communications Structures & Services
Doty-Moore Tower Services
FWT Inc.
Hignite Tower Service
Kline Towers
Magnum Towers Inc.
Nationwide Tower Company Inc.
Fred A. Nudd Corp.
Pirod Inc.
Railway Systems Design, Inc.
Rohn Industries Inc.
Stainless LLC
Swager Communications Inc.
Tower Inspection Inc.
Tower Structures Inc.
Utility Tower Company
Valmont Communications Inc.
WILL-BURT Co.
World Tower Co. Inc.

Tower Erection

Abroyd Communications Ltd.
Allied Tower Co. Inc.
Baron Telecom
Central Tower
Communications Structures & Services
Doty-Moore Tower Services
ERI-Installations Inc.
FWT Inc.
Grant Tower, Inc.
Hignite Tower Service
Kline Towers
Kuhnel Co. Inc.
National Steel Erectors Corp.
Northeast Towers Inc.
Fred A. Nudd Corp.
Pacific Tower Co.

Equipment Manufacturers and Distributors Subject Index

Quality Tower Erectors Inc.
Radian Communication Services Inc
Rohn Industries Inc.
Southern Broadcast Services
Stainless LLC
Structural System Technology Inc.
Superior Tower Services Inc.
Swager Communications Inc.
Tenco Tower Co.
Tower Inspection Inc.
Utility Tower Company
Valmont Communications Inc.
World Tower Co. Inc.

Tower Inspections

Baron Telecom
Central Tower
Communications Structures & Services
Doty-Moore Tower Services
ERI-Installations Inc.
Grant Tower, Inc.
Kline Towers
National Steel Erectors Corp.
Nationwide Tower Company Inc.
Northeast Towers Inc.
Quality Tower Erectors Inc.
Radian Communication Services Inc
Southern Broadcast Services
Stainless LLC
Superior Tower Services Inc.
Swager Communications Inc.
Tenco Tower Co.
Tower Inspection Inc.
Tower Network Services
Valmont Communications Inc.
World Tower Co. Inc.

Tower Maintenance

Baron Telecom
Central Tower
Communications Structures & Services
Doty-Moore Tower Services
ERI-Installations Inc.
Grant Tower, Inc.
Hignite Tower Service
Kuhnel Co. Inc.
Metz Engineering
National Steel Erectors Corp.
Nationwide Tower Company Inc.
Northeast Towers Inc.
Quality Tower Erectors Inc.
Radian Communication Services Inc
Railway Systems Design, Inc.
Southern Broadcast Services
Stainless LLC
Structural System Technology Inc.
Superior Tower Services Inc.
Swager Communications Inc.
Teletech Inc.
Tenco Tower Co.
Tower Inspection Inc.
Tower Network Services
Valmont Communications Inc.

Tower Obstruction Lighting and Controls

Allied Tower Co. Inc.
Austin Insulators Inc.
Peter W. Dahl Co. Inc.
Doty-Moore Tower Services
ERI-Installations Inc.
Flash Technology Corporation of America
Honeywell Airport Systems
Nationwide Tower Company Inc.
Northeast Towers Inc.
PerkinElmer
Quality Tower Erectors Inc.
Railway Systems Design, Inc.
Rohn Industries Inc.
TWR Lighting
Tower Inspection Inc.
Tower Network Services
Utility Tower Company
Valmont Communications Inc.
World Tower Co. Inc.

Tower Structural Analysis

Baron Telecom
Central Tower
Communications Structures & Services
FWT Inc.
Kline Towers
National Steel Erectors Corp.
Nationwide Tower Company Inc.
Fred A. Nudd Corp.
Radian Communication Services Inc
Rohn Industries Inc.
Stainless LLC
Superior Tower Services Inc.
Tower Inspection Inc.
Tower Network Services
Tower Structures Inc.
Utility Tower Company
Valmont Communications Inc.
World Tower Co. Inc.

Towers, Accessories and Service

Abroyd Communications Ltd.
Allied Tower Co. Inc.
Austin Insulators Inc.
Baron Telecom
Central Tower
Communications Structures & Services
Condux International
ERI-Installations Inc.
FWT Inc.
Flash Technology Corporation of America
Jampro Antennas/RF Systems Inc.
Kline Towers
Lightning Prevention Systems
Magnum Towers Inc.
Nationwide Tower Company Inc.
Northeast Towers Inc.
Fred A. Nudd Corp.
Pacific Tower Co.
Phillystran Inc.
Quality Tower Erectors Inc.
Railway Systems Design, Inc.
Rohn Industries Inc.
Southern Broadcast Services
Swager Communications Inc.
Technet Systems Group
Tenco Tower Co.
Tower Structures Inc.
Utility Tower Company
WILL-BURT Co.
World Tower Co. Inc.

Towers, Used

Abroyd Communications Ltd.
Communications Structures & Services
Northeast Towers Inc.
Quality Tower Erectors Inc.

Traffic Advisory System

Highway Information Systems, Inc.
Hitachi Denshi America, Ltd.
Seton Identification Products
Spotcat Software
VCI-Video Communications Inc.

Transcoders

Faroudja Laboratories
Magni Systems Inc.
Sigma Electronics Inc.
Xintekvideo Inc.

Transformers

Allied Electronics Inc.
Cable Technologies International
Peter W. Dahl Co. Inc.
Edcor Electronics Corp.
Jensen Transformers Inc.
MGE UPS SYSTEMS Inc.
North Hills Signal Processing, a PORTA Systems Co.
TTE Inc.
Tech Laboratories Inc.
Weschler Instruments

Translators and Accessories

Axcera
BEXT Inc.
CADCO Systems Inc.
Energy-Onix Broadcast Equipment Co. Inc.
Rodelco Electronics Corp.

Transmission Lines

Andrew Corp.
Ascent Media Services
Belden Electronics Divison
Dielectric Communications
Industrial Equipment Representatives (IER)
MYAT Inc.
S W R Inc.
Transcom Corp.

Transmitter Building

Allied Tower Co. Inc.
Rees Associates Inc.
Tower Structures Inc.

Transmitter Systems

Acrodyne Industries Inc.
Axcera
B&B Systems
Broadcasters General Store Inc.
Colorado Video Inc.
DRS Broadcast Technology
Energy-Onix Broadcast Equipment Co. Inc.
Marcom
NTL Broadcast
Nautel Ltd.
RF Specialties Group
Scientific-Atlanta Canada Inc. Nexus Division
Siemens Dematic Limited
Swintek Enterprises Inc.
Technet Systems Group

Transmitters

Acrodyne Industries Inc.
Broadcast Supply Worldwide
CED
Colorado Video Inc.
DMT USA, Inc.
DRS Broadcast Technology
Energy-Onix Broadcast Equipment Co. Inc.
JSB Service Co.
L-3 Communications Telemetry East
Laser Diode Inc.
Norsat International Inc.
QEI Corporation
Samson Technologies Corp.
Scientific-Atlanta Canada Inc. Nexus Division
Thales
Thales Broadcast & Multimedia Inc.

Transmitters, Radio

BEXT Inc.
Bauer Transmitters
Broadcast Electronics Inc.
Broadcast Equipment Surplus Inc.
Crown Broadcast IREC
DRS Broadcast Technology
Energy-Onix Broadcast Equipment Co. Inc.
Harris Corp., Broadcast Communications Division
Harris Corp., Broadcast Division
Industrial Equipment Representatives (IER)
Marcom
Nautel Ltd.
Richardson Electronics
TFT Inc.
Thales Broadcast & Multimedia S.A.
Transcom Corp.

Transmitters, TV

Acrodyne Industries Inc.
Axcera
BEXT Inc.
CED
DMT USA, Inc.
Harris Corp., Broadcast Communications Division
Harris Corp., Broadcast Division
Kalun Communications Inc.

Equipment Manufacturers and Distributors Subject Index

LARCAN
MRPP Inc.
Marcom
Radian Communication Services Inc
Scientific-Atlanta Canada Inc. Nexus Division
Thales Broadcast & Multimedia S.A.
Transcom Corp.

Traveling Wave Tubes

Communication & Power Industries
Daily Electronics Corp.
e2v technologies Inc.
Penta Laboratories
Thales Components Corp.

Tripods, Pedestals and Accessories

Argraph Corp.
Bogen Imaging Inc.
Isaia & Co.
Miller Camera Support, L.L.C.
O'Connor Professional Camera Support Systems
Photomart Cine-Video Inc.
Pro Video & Film Equipment Co. Inc.
Quick-Set International Inc.
Sachtler Corp. of America
Sinar Bron Inc.
Stage Equipment & Lighting Inc.
Thomas & Betts Corp.
The Tiffen Company
Ultimate Support Systems Inc.
Vinten Inc.

Tubes and Tube Rebuilding

Burle Industries Inc.
Communication & Power Industries, EIMAC Division
Daily Electronics Corp.
e2v technologies Inc.
Freeland Products Inc.
General Electrodynamics Corp.
Narragansett Imaging
Penta Laboratories
Richardson Electronics
Thales Components Corp.

Tuning and Phasing Units

Kintronic Labs Inc.
LBA Technology Inc.
Lindsay Electronics
SES Americom

Turnkey Studio Systems

Peter Albrecht Company Inc.
Alpha Video & Electronics Co. (AVEC)
CBT Systems
Cygnal Technology
Harris Corp., Broadcast Communications Division
NTL Broadcast
POA/Paul Olivier & Associates Ltd.
Radio Systems Inc.
Technet Systems Group

TV Equipment

Advanced Research Technology Inc.
AVerMedia Technologies Inc.
Broadcast Electronic Services
CECO International Corp.
CED
Cable Serv Inc.
Freeland Products Inc.
Hitachi Denshi America, Ltd.
LARCAN
POA/Paul Olivier & Associates Ltd.
Schafer International
Sharp Electronics Corp., CCD Products Div.
Solutec Ltd. (HA)
Zenith Electronics Corp.

TV Standards Converter

Prime Image Inc.
Sifford Video Services
Snell & Wilcox Inc.
Video International Development Corp.

TV Terminal Equipment

Hoodman Corp.

Used Broadcast Equipment

Intersil Corp. Headquarters
Maze Corporation
Pro Video & Film Equipment Co. Inc.
Radiogear Inc.
System Associates
United States Broadcast

Vacuum Capacitors

Jennings Technology Co.
Kintronic Labs Inc.
Lindsay Electronics
Penta Laboratories
Richardson Electronics

Vans and Mobile Units

Alpha Video & Electronics Co. (AVEC)
CBT Systems
E-N-G Mobile Systems Inc.
F&F Productions, L.L.C.
Frontline Communications
Maze Corporation
Panavision New York
Phoenix E N G, Inc.
Shook Mobile Technology, LP
Television Engineering Corp.
WOIO & WUAB TV

VBI Equipment

Broadcast Video Systems Corp.
CPC-Computer Prompting & Captioning Co.
Milestone Technologies Inc.
Norpak Corporation

Video Accessories

APW Enclosure Products
Adrienne Electronics Corp.
Audiolab Electronics Inc.
AVerMedia Technologies Inc.
Battery Pros Inc.
Bencher Inc.
Broadcast Electronic Services
The J-Lab Co.
Jensen Transformers Inc.
Kings Electronics Co. Inc.
Mic Flags by Aladdin
North Hills Signal Processing, a PORTA Systems Co.
Peerless Industries Inc.
Plastic Reel Corp. of America
Polyline Corp.
Research Technology International Inc.
Star Case Manufacturing Co. Inc.
Switchcraft Inc.
The Tiffen Company
Veriad
Vicon Industries Inc.
Video Accessory Corp.
Westcott
Zack Electronics Inc.

Video Character Generators

Display Systems International Inc.
EEG Enterprises Inc.
FOR.A Corp. of America
Horita
Hotbox Digital
Inscriber Technology Corporation
Key West Technology

Video Delay Lines

Allen Avionics, Inc.
Camplex Corporation
Television Equipment Assoc. Inc./Matthey

Video Delay Subsystems

Television Equipment Assoc. Inc./Matthey

Video Disc Recorders

Accom Inc.
MATCO Inc.
McCurdy Radio Industries Ltd.
Optical Disc Corp.
Pinnacle Systems Inc.

Video Editing Equipment

Accom Inc.
Audio Video Systems International
Avid Broadcast
Broadcast Electronic Services
CORPLEX Inc.
Commercial Electronics Ltd.
Dubner International Inc.
Ensemble Designs
Focus Enhancements
The Image Group Post, LLC.
Imagine Products Inc.
Matrox Video Products Grp
NEC America Inc.
PBI Media
Paulmar Industries Inc.
Pinnacle Systems Inc.
Richardson Electronics
Specialized Communications
Tele-Measurements Inc.
United Media Inc.
United States Broadcast

Video Effects Generators and Accessories

Cintel Inc.
e-Studio Live!
FOR.A Corp. of America

Video Equipment

All Mobile Video Inc.
Allen Avionics, Inc.
AVerMedia Technologies Inc.
Bencher Inc.
Bexel, Inc.
Broadcast Store Inc.
CORPLEX Inc.
Dage-MTI Inc.
Dimension 3
Fiber Options
Film/Video Equipment Service Co. Inc.
Full Compass Systems Ltd.
Geneva Aviation Inc.
HAVE Inc.
Horita
Image Video
Innovision Optics Inc.
MATCO Inc.
Maze Corporation
National Mobile Television
PBI Media
Photomart Cine-Video Inc.
Pro Video & Film Equipment Co. Inc.
Professional Communications Systems
Switchcraft Inc.
J.A. Taylor & Associates
Telcom Research
Televideo San Diego
Thermodyne International Ltd.
United Media Inc.
Vicon Industries Inc.
Westcott
World Video Sales Co.

Video Graphics Systems

Accom Inc.
Alias/WaveFront Inc.
Chyron Corp.
Commercial Electronics Ltd.
Hotbox Digital
Vertigo Technology Inc.
Frank Woolley & Co. Inc.

Video Processing Equipment

FM Systems Inc.
Pixel Instruments Corp.
Thomson Broadcast & Media Solutions
Xintekvideo Inc.

Broadcasting & Cable Yearbook 2006

Equipment Manufacturers and Distributors Subject Index

Video Production Switchers

Ensemble Designs
FOR.A Corp. of America
Focus Enhancements
Ross Video Ltd.
Thomson Broadcast & Media Solutions
Vicon Industries Inc.
Videotek

Video Projection System, Large Screen

Barco Visual Solutions, LLC
SAIC
Sharp Electronics Corp., CCD Products Div.

Video Routing Switchers

Adrienne Electronics Corp.
Broadcast Electronic Services
Burst Electronics Inc.
Datatek Corp.
Image Video
MATCO Inc.
NTV International Corporation
Omicron Video
Sigma Electronics Inc.
Utah Scientific Inc.
Videotek

Video Special Effects Systems

Accom Inc.
Chyron Corp.
e-Studio Live!
Image Logic Corp.
Matrox Video Products Grp
PBI Media
Ultimatte Corp.
Vertigo Technology Inc.

Videotape Recorders

Audio Video Systems International
Northrup Grumman
Sanyo Fisher Co.
Sharp Electronics Corp., CCD Products Div.
Thomson, Inc, (RCA/GE)
Toshiba America Consumer Products

Videotape Suppliers

BMG
Carpel Video Inc.
Fuji Photo Film U.S.A. Inc.
Maxell Corp. of America
Memorex Products Inc.
Moviola
National Video Tape Co. Inc.
Plastic Reel Corp. of America
Tele-Measurements Inc.

Voltage Regulators

Furman Sound Inc.
Hipotronics Inc.
LEA International
Weschler Instruments

Watt Meters

Bird Electronic Corp.
Coaxial Dynamics

Wave Guides

Dielectric Communications
MYAT Inc.
Radio Research Instrument Co. Inc.
S W R Inc.

Weather Data Display Systems (WDDS)

AccuWeather Inc.
Advanced Designs Corp.
DRS Technologies
Key West Technology
Norpak Corporation
Texscan MSI
Ultimatte Corp.
WeatherBank Inc.

Weather Forecasting

AccuWeather Inc.
DRS Technologies
WeatherBank Inc.

Weather Instruments

AccuWeather Inc.
DRS Technologies
Gorman-Redlich Manufacturing Co.
Texas Electronics Inc.
Texscan MSI
3M
WeatherBank Inc.

Weather Radar & Graphic Displays, Color

AccuWeather Inc.
Advanced Designs Corp.
DRS Technologies
Norpak Corporation
Radio Research Instrument Co. Inc.
WeatherBank Inc.

Weighing Equipment

General Electrodynamics Corp.

Wireless Microphones

Audio-Technica U.S., Inc.
Beyerdynamic
COMTEK Inc.
Countryman Associates Inc.
Lectrosonics Inc.
Murry Rosenblum Sound Assoc., Inc.
Nady Systems Inc.
Professional Sound Services Inc.
R-Columbia Products Co. Inc.
Radio Engineering Industries Inc.
Sabine Inc.
Shure Inc.
Systems Wireless Ltd.
TOA Electronics Inc.
Telex Communications Inc.
Vega

Wiring Products

AKG Acoustics, U.S.
Belden Electronics Divison
CableTek Wiring Products Inc.
Clark Wire & Cable Co. Inc.
Condux International
Connectronics Corp.
Copperweld Fayetteville Division
General Cable
Gepco International Inc.
Radio Systems Inc.
Ripley Company
Techni-Tool Inc.
Telecrafter Products
WIREMAX Ltd.
Wireworks Corp.

Satellite Owners and Transmission Services

ABC Family Worldwide, (a subsidiary of International Family Entertainment Inc.). 500 S. Buena Vista, Burbank, CA 91521-0001. Phone: (818) 560-1000. Haim Saban, chmn/CEO; Maureen Smith, exec VP.

Studio City, CA 91604, 12700 Ventura Blvd. Phone: (818) 755-2400. Tony Thomopoulos, CEO MTM Entertainment.

New York, NY 10036, 1133 Ave. of the Americas, 37th Fl. Phone: (212) 782-0600. Rick Sirvaitis, pres adv sls; Barbara Bekkedahl, exec VP/ adv sls.

Basic cable network available in over 76 million homes nationwide; delivers a dynamic mix of quality entertainment with original movies, specials & series in prime time & a fun-filled daytime lineup of newly produced and classic series for kids.

AMV Gateway, Williams Communications Group. Box 420, 27 Randolph St., Carteret, NJ 07008. Phone: (732) 969-3191. Fax: (732) 541-2007. Michael Carberry, gen mgr.

Operates teleport facilities serving New York City. Videotape svcs; satellite transmission for the bcst, CATV & videoconferencing industries. International wideband voice, data & videoconferencing svcs overseas.

AT&T Alascom, 505 E. Bluff Dr., Anchorage, AK 99501-1100. Phone: (907) 264-7274. Fax: (907) 274-5029. Mike Felix, pres.

Telecommunications, long-distance telephone carrier for the state of Alaska offering bcst, voice, data, WATS, Alaskanet & dedicated private line long-distance svcs.

Agri Net Ray Communications Inc., 104 Radio Rd., Powells Point, NC 27966-9601. Phone: (252) 491-2414. Fax: (252) 491-2939. E-mail: info@agrinetradio.com. Web Site: www.agrinetradio.com. William S. Ray, pres; Lisa Ray, sls.

Turnkey satellite transmission service for radio news, sports, syndicated program distribution, audio conferencing; transportable bcst studio/uplinks for remote bcsts & domestic back hauling; network coord svcs & space segment bookings available.

American Microwave & Communications, (A division of Western Tele-Communications). 4616 N. Grand River Ave., Suite D, Lansing, MI 48906-2576. Phone: (517) 327-3000. Fax: (517) 327-4706. E-mail: albronson@sbcglobal.net.

Microwave delivery of distant signals to cable systems; net TV & radio service to bcst stns; networking among TV stations.

Arch Wireless, 1800 West Park Dr., Suite 250, West Borough, MA 01581. Phone: (508) 870-6700. Fax: (508) 870-6069. Web Site: www.arch.com. Ed Baker, CEO.

Holds construction permit for DBS satellite, has radio paging business & two cellular telephone partnerships, & serves the corporate syndicate communications needs of the investment banking community.

Ascent Media Network Services, 250 Harbor Dr., Stamford, CT 06904. Phone: (203) 965-6800. Fax: (203) 965-6320. Web Site: www.ascentmedia.com. Scott Davis, pres; Matt Armstrong, sr VP.

Minneapolis, MN 55403. Teleport Minnesota, 90 S. 11th St. Phone: (612) 330-2433. Fax: (612) 330-2603. Mark Durenberger, gen mgr.

C- & Ku-band domestic & international transmission service; fiber-optic connectivity to metropolitan New York. Cable origination, bcst, business TV, transponder availability, studio & postproduction.

BAF Satellite & Technology Corp., 200 S. Harbor City Blvd., Suite 201, Melbourne, FL 32901. Phone: (800) 966-3822. Phone: (800) 223-1860 (24 hr). Fax: (800) 486-5983. Fax: (800) 223-1866 (24 hr). E-mail: info@bafsat.com. Web Site: www.bafsat.com. James Vautrot, pres/CEO.

Long-term, short-term & occasional analog & digital KU & C band satellite space, full or partial transponder or transponders for domestic or international video, voice or data transmissions.

BT North America, Broadcast Services, 2025 M St. N.W., Washington, DC 20036. Phone: (202) 721-8598. Fax: (202) 721-8595. Fax: (202) 721-8596. Web Site: www.broadcast.bt.com. Jon Romm, gen mgr; Andrew Cassells, opns mgr; Lisa Fanning, mktg mgr.

Operates international bcst center; 24-hour satellite rooftop teleport, digital compression & encryption svcs.

CATV Services Inc., (Penn Service Microwave Co. Inc.). 115 Mill St., Danville, PA 17821. Phone: (570) 275-1431. Fax: (570) 275-3888. Samuel Haulman, gen mgr.

Video distribution of TV signals to various CATV companies in Pennsylvania.

CONUS Communications Inc., 3415 University Ave., St. Paul, MN 55114. Phone: (651) 642-4645. Phone: (651) 642-4644. Web Site: www.conus.com. Charles H. Dutcher III, pres; Terry O'Reilly, VP/gen mgr.

Washington, DC 20006, 1825 K St. N.W. Phone: (202) 467-5600. Fax: (202) 467-5610. Tim Rudell, sr VP/bureau chief.

Provider of television production & transmission svcs to loc, natl & international bcstrs & corporate clients.

Communications III, 1156 Dublin Rd., Suite 101, Columbus, OH 43215. Phone: (614) 485-4500. Fax: (614) 485-4512. E-mail: shalliday@comiii.com. Web Site: www.comiii.com. Scott Halliday, pres.

Common carrier/C-band uplink svcs. ISDN, IP, & Satellite videoconferencing, Polycom & First Virtual.

Crawford Satellite Services, 3845 Pleasantdale Rd., Atlanta, GA 30340. Phone: (404) 876-7149. Fax: (678) 421-6717. Web Site: www.crawford.com. Jesse Crawford, owner; Paul Hansil, pres.

Teleport C- & Ku-band, satellite networking, special event bcstg, ad-hoc teleconferencing, news feeds, private networking, satellite time, program distribution, & transportable uplinks. Postproduction svcs include Crawford Audio.

DCT Transmission L.L.C., 10040 E. Happy Valley Rd., Unit 454, Scottsdale, AR 85255. Phone: (480) 515-0913. Fax: (480) 515-4632. E-mail: wiesenberg@spacedata.net. Jim Wiesenberg, dir.

Broadband microwave provider for metro-wide analog, digital, data voice or video delivery to end users or as interconnect —2-38 ghz.

DIRECTV Latin America, (formerly-Galaxy Latin America). 2400 E. Commerical Blvd., Fort Lauderdale, FL 33308. Phone: (954) 958-3200. Fax: (954) 958-3374. Web Site: www.directvla.com. Kevin McGrath, chmn.

Provides direct TV for Latin America.

GlobeCast America, 10525 Washington Blvd., Culver City, CA 90232. Phone: (310) 845-3900. Fax: (310) 845-3904. Web Site: www.globecastamerica.com. David Sprechman, CEO.

Miami, FL 33166. GlobeCast Hero Productions, 7291 N.W. 74 St. Phone: (305) 887-1600. Fax: (305) 391-4424. (Corporate hqtrs).

GlobeCast America provides the bcstg industry with a unique combination of both recognized expertise & extensive inter-continental svcs. Through GlobeCast's vast global infrastructure of over 100 transponders, 30 teleports & interconnect facilities, the company provides instant access to the world's major media markets. GlobeCast America is part of France Telecom, one of the world's largest telecommunications companies.

Grace Digital Media, 1919 M St. N.W., Suite 200, Washington, DC 20036. Phone: (202) 775-0894. Fax: (202) 775-1288. Web Site: www.gracedigitalmedia.com. Shirl Reagan, owner.

TV & production studios, multi-format edit suites, computer avid rentals, avid 800 editing, graphics, Ku-band truck, satellite, production, dubbing & standards conversion, transponder services, camera crews & equipment rentals.

Home Shopping Network, 1 HSN Dr., St. Petersburg, FL 33729. Phone: (727) 872-1000. Fax: (727) 872-6615. Web Site: www.hsn.com. Tom McInerney, pres/CEO.

Svcs include C- & Ku-band transmissions from Tampa, FL, C-band transmissions from New York, NY, & Los Angeles, CA, & postproduction.

International Telecommunications Satellite Organization (INTELSAT), 3400 International Dr. N.W., Washington, DC 20008-3098. Phone: (202) 944-6800. Fax: (202) 944-8125. Web Site: www.intelsat.com. Conny Killman, dir; Romu Potarazu, VP opns.

Provider of international & domestic satellite telecommunications svcs serving more than 130 nations. Operates a global net of more than 20 satellites.

Kaufman Broadcast Services, 3655 Olive St., St. Louis, MO 63108. Phone: (314) 533-6633. Fax: (314) 533-1113. E-mail: mail@kaufmanbroadcast.com. Web Site: www.kaufmanbroadcast.com. Bill Kaufman, pres.

Transmission svcs via satellite or fiber optics, production & editing facilities.

Kingston inmedia, Box 2287, Gerrards Cross SL9 8BF. United Kingdom. Phone: 44-8708-79-8787. E-mail: inmedia@kcom.com. Web Site: www.kingstoninmedia.com.

Satellite svcs company providing data bcst, business TV, international VSAT nets & uplink facilities.

Loral Skynet, (A subsidiary of Loral Space & Communications). 500 Hills Dr., Bedminster, NJ 07921. Phone: (908) 470-2300. Fax: (908) 470-2459. E-mail: info@loralskynet.com. Web Site: www.loralskynet.com. Patrick K. Brant, pres.

Miami, FL 33126, 7820 N.W. LeJeune Rd. Phone: (305) 476-0503. Fax: (305) 476-0722. (Parent Company).

Full- & part-time C- & Ku-band transponder svcs on Telstar 4, 5, 6 & 7. Provides service on both C-band & Ku-band transponders on Telstar satellites & other satellites, in addition to tech consulting & tracking, telemetry & control of satellite fleets for other customers. Applications include: coml & pub TV bcst, syndication, satellite news gathering, distance learning, videoconferencing, data networking, & occasional use. The company operates two state-of-the-art satellite earth stns in Hawley, PA, & Three Peaks, CA. The main Satellite Operations Center & the Transponder Booking Center reside at Hawley.

MCI Tampa, 3608 Queen Palm Dr., Tampa, FL 33619-1311. Phone: (813) 829-0011. Web Site: www.mci.com. Michael Capellas, pres/CEO.

Serves Pennsylvania Public Television Network, Pennsylvania, Ohio, New Jersey, Vermont, New Hampshire, New York & Massachusetts. CATV systems with a variety of svcs.

MCI, 500 Clinton Ctr. Dr., Clinton, MS 39056. Phone: (601) 460-5600. Phone: (800) 644-news. Web Site: www.mci.com. Nicholas Katzenbach, chmn.

Data, internet, international long distance & telecom svcs throughout the United States.

Megastar Inc., 4709 Compass Bow Ln., Las Vegas, NV 89130. Phone: (702) 386-2844. Fax: (702) 388-1250. Nigel Macrae, pres.

Houston, TX Teleport svcs, C-band & Ku-band, fiber-optic & microwave interconnect. 11M Intelsat antenna, PanAmSat, etc. Other svcs available.

Microwave Networks Inc., 4000 Greenbriar St. #100A, Stafford, TX 77477-3921. Phone: (281) 263-6500. Fax: (281) 263-6400. Web Site: www.microwavenetworks.com.

Microwave Service Co., 1359 Rd. 681, Tupelo, MS 38802. Phone: (662) 842-7620. Fax: (662) 844-7061. Frank K. Spain, owner.

Point-to-point transmission of video by microwave.

Multicomm Sciences International Inc. (MSI), 266 W. Main St., Denville, NJ 07834. Phone: (973) 627-7400. Fax: (973) 625-1002. E-mail: mail@multicommsciences.com. Web Site: www.multicommsciences.com. Victor J. Nexon, Jr., pres.

Serves satellite, microwave, lightwave, radio & cable industries. Market info, field surveys, system design, feasibility studies, frequency coordination & project mgmt.

NPR Satellite Services, 635 Massachusetts Ave. N.W., Washington, DC 20001. Phone: (202) 513-2626. Fax: (202) 513-3035. E-mail: linkup@npr.org. Web Site: www.nprss.org. George Gimourginas, dir.

Provides full-time wideband chs for stereo audio transmission & narrow-band chs for voice networks. Audio distribution via analog or digital transponders.

NTL Broadcast, Crawley Ct., Winchester, Hampshire S021 2QA. United Kingdom. Phone: 0-1962-824000. Fax: 0-1962-822553. Web Site: www.kftv.com. Peter Douglas, chmn.

Bcst transmission svcs & systems, satellite linking, telecommunications, turnkey bcst systems including digital.

Norlight Telecommunications, 13935 Bishops Drive, Brookfield, WI 53005. Fax: (262) 792-7660. Web Site: www.norlight.com.

Design, installation & maintenance of custom network solutions, including HDTV transport, on-site data center - secure co-location svc, off-site video file servers & managed router svc.

Novanet Communications Ltd., 725 Westney Rd. S., Suite 4, Ajax, ON L1J 7J7. Canada. Phone: (905) 686-6666. Fax: (905) 619-1053. E-mail: getinfo@novanetcomm.com. Web Site: www.novanetcomm.com. Joseph Uyede, pres/CEO.

Provides info distribution svcs; audio svcs from 3.5 khz to 20 khz in analog or digital formats, also a line of data bcst offerings ranging in speed from 75 baud to T-1; & "Satpac," a packet-switched data net using receiver technology.

PMTV Producers Management Television, 800 N. Henderson Rd., King of Prussia, PA 19406-3207. Phone: (610) 768-1770. Fax: (610) 768-1773. E-mail: mailto.pmtv@pmtv.com. Web Site: www.pmtv.com. Brian Powers, pres; Rob Schmoll, VP/gen mgr.

Full-svc mobile TV production company, providing mobile units, crews, satellite svcs, lighting, staging, etc. for sports, entertainment & teleconferences worldwide.

PROSTAR, 12831 Royal Dr., Stafford, TX 77477. Phone: (281) 240-2800. Fax: (281) 240-1447. E-mail: prostar@prostar-inc.com. Web Site: www.prostar-inc.com. John C. Parks, pres; D. Scott Hofmann, VP; Steve Santini, natl sls.

Provides satellite VP links encryption services for business, entertainment & sports use. Natl promoter for live boxing & soccer events.

Pacific Microwave, 620 Parsons Dr., Medford, OR 97501. Phone: (541) 773-4171.

Common carrier microwave svc for cable systems & bcst TV.

PanAmSat, 20 Westport Rd., Suite 270, Wilton, CT 06897. Phone: (203) 210-8000. Fax: (203) 210-8001. Web Site: www.panamsat.com. Mike Antonovich, exec VP.

Long Beach, CA 90810, 1600 Forbes Way. Phone: (310) 525-5500. Fax: (310) 525-5505. Kurt Riegelman. (North America office).

Coral Gables, FL 33134, One Alhambra Plaza, Suite 100. Phone: (305) 445-5536. Fax: (305) 445-5315. Estevao Ghizoni, sr dir. (Latin America office).

Owns & operates private global network of communications satellites providing bcst, business communications, telephony & data svcs to customers worldwide.

Production & Satellite Services Inc. (PSSI), 11860 Mississippi Ave., Los Angeles, CA 90025. Phone: (310) 575-4400. Fax: (310) 575-4451. E-mail: pssi@800satlink.com. Web Site: www.pssi-usa.com. Brian Nellis, VP.

Full service production & satellite transmission company specializing in coordination, production & transmission of international live-event progmg. Own & operate 12 fully redundant transportable upling/production trucks which are maintained in Los Angeles, San Francisco, Seattle, Las Vegas, Denver, Phoenix & Chicago. Entire Western region of the United States is covered including Albuquerque, Salt Lake City & Portland. Also subcontract with vendors throughout U.S. to provide uplink, downlink & production svcs and production svcs for teleconferences & other events.

Pyramid NewsPort, 480 National Press Bldg., Washington, DC 20001. Phone: (202) 783-5030. Fax: (202) 628-7228. E-mail: tmurasev@ptpngroup.com. Web Site: www.ptpngroup.com. Nicholas J. Chiaia Jr., pres; Tina Murasev, opns mgr.

TV production facilities include studios, on-line & non-linear editing & transmission facilities to Ku-band & C-band satellites. Interconnect to major news-gathering points in Washington, DC, at the National Press Bldg.

Radio Sound Network, 770 Twin Rivers Dr., Columbus, OH 43215. Phone: (614) 621-5600. Fax: (614) 621-5620. E-mail: sclawson@radiohio.com. Web Site: www.radiohio.com. Steve Clawson, engrg dir; Tony Miller, dir.

Columbus, OH 43215, 175 S. 3rd St. Phone: (614) 460-3850.

Full-svc digital satellite audio & data distribution, including affil rel & network bldg for new & existing sports, news/talk, music & specialty networks.

Reuters Television Internationale, 3 Times Sq., 4th Fl., New York, NY 10036. Phone: (646) 223-6600. Fax: (646) 223-6615. Web Site: www.reuters.com. Bob LaGrasso, dir client svcs.

Satellite svcs for news departments. Satellite production & communication departments handle satellite feed requirements from anywhere in the world. Satellite coordinates, video crews & major studios on six continents. Standards conversion.

SES Americom, 4 Research Way, Princeton, NJ 08540. Phone: (609) 987-4000. Fax: (609) 987-4517. Web Site: www.ses-americom.com. Edward D. Horowitz, pres/CEO.

Operates GE-1-3, SATCOM, GSTAR & SPACENET domestic satellites (C-band & six Ku-band). The fleet svcs the cable TV, bcst, radio & educ market & govt businesses. Supports net of earth stns, central terminal offices & TT&C facilities.

SpaceCom Systems, A TV Guide Company. 1950 E. 71st St., Tulsa, OK 74136-5422. Phone: (800) 950-6690. Fax: (918) 499-6060. Web Site: www.spacecom.com. Dick Ellis, VP/gen mgr.

Satellite transmission svcs, equipment & space segment on C- & Ku-Band for point-to-multipoint applications. Also two-way high-speed Satellite Broadband for remote locations, quick connects, disaster recovery, Internet.

Spacenet Services Inc., 1750 Old Meadow Rd., McLean, VA 22102. Phone: (703) 848-1000. Web Site: www.spacenet.com. Bill Gerety, CEO; Glenn Katz, COO.

Comprehensive range of satellite-based communication svcs for video & data; digital video networks for business applications.

StarNet, 3417 N. First St., Abilene, TX 79603. Phone: (888) 828-7352. Phone: (915) 672-9618. Glenda Mathis, owner.

Ku-band distance learning, Ku-band transponder time, & program/production svcs.

Teleglobe, 1555 RUE CARRIE-DERICK, Montreal, PQ H3C 6W2. Canada. Phone: (514) 868-7272. Fax: (514) 868-7234. Web Site: www.teleglobe.com. Liam Strong, CEO.

Hong Kong 02508, Two Pacifco Place, 88 Queensway. Phone: 852-2530-8500. Fax: 852-2-537-7417. Andrew Kwok, dir.

International satellite transmission svcs from Lawrentides/Lake Cowichan earth stns in Canada. Signatory on Intelsat, Immarsat. Full range of svcs to world satellite systems.

Telemundo Network, 2470 W. 8th Ave, Hialeah, FL 33010. Phone: (305) 884-8200. Web Site: www.telemundo.com. James McNammara, pres.

Production capabilities & svcs. Uplink & video transmission. C- & Ku-band uplink & downlink. Fiber & microwave also available.

Telenor Satellite Services, Snaroyvein 30, M6, N-1331 Fornebu Norway. Phone: (301) 838-7800. Phone: 47 67-89-40-41. Fax: 47 67-89-00-00. E-mail: customer.care@telenor.com. Web Site: www.telenor.com/satellite. Tore Hilde, CEO.

Rockville, MD 20852. Telenor Satellite Services, Inc., 1101 Wootton Pkwy., 4th Fl. Phone: (301) 838-7800. Fax: (301) 838-7701.

Telenor is a global provider of satellite svcs, inmarsat, intelsat, new skies, satmex, digital networking svcs & technology.

Teleport Chicago, 3617 Oakton St.-rear, Skokie, IL 60076. Phone: (800) 875-4657. Phone: (888) 255-8755. Fax: (847) 674-7485. E-mail: sales@norlight.com. Web Site: www.norlight.com. Jim Ditter, pres; Robert E. Rogers, sr VP; Dave Pritchard, dir.

A full-svc teleport serving the upper Midwest via the Norlight Telecommunications microwave & fiber-optic transmission system.

Telesat Canada, 1601 Telesat Ct., Gloucester, ON K1B 5P4. Canada. Phone: (613) 748-0123. Fax: (613) 748-8712. E-mail: info@telesat.ca. Web Site: www.telesat.ca. Larry Boisvert, pres/CEO; Paul Bush, dir.

Calgary, AB T2E 0A6 Canada, 1780 Centre Ave. N.E. Phone: (403) 235-5751. Fax: (403) 273-3337. (Calgary rgnl office).

Montreal, PQ H2K 4R5 Canada, 1200 Papineau Ave, Suite 140. Phone: (514) 521-7862. Fax: (514) 527-6429. (Montreal rgnl office).

Communications via satellite, consulting, & satellite earth stn nets.

Time Warner Cable, Box 85100, Austin, TX 78708.

Common carrier & other loc area net svcs in California, Washington, Minnesota, Virginia, North Carolina & South Carolina.

Transvision Inc., 550 Maulhardt Ave., Oxnard, CA 93030. Phone: (805) 981-8740. Fax: (805) 981-8738. E-mail: info@txvision.com. Web Site: www.txvision.com. Kimithy Vaughan, sls & mktg; Scott Husband, engr; Steve Browneller, engr.

Twelve transportable & satellite transmission facilities (video, audio, voice, data); flypack production & SNG svcs; digital compression; domestic & international.

TV Guide Inc., One TV Guide Plaza, 7140 S. Lewis Ave., Tulsa, OK 74136-5422. Phone: (918) 488-4000. Fax: (918) 488-4979. Web Site: www.tvguide.com. Jeff Shell, CEO.

Diversified communications company serving cable, home satellite TV, radio/data networks, private businesses; operating companies: UVTV, Prevue Networks, Superstar Satellite Entertainment, SpaceCom Systems.

Verestar Inc., 3040 Williams Dr., Suite 600, Fairfax, VA 22031. Phone: (703) 206-9000. Fax: (703) 573-3293. E-mail: info@verestar.com. Web Site: www.verestar.com. Raymond J. O'Brien, pres/COO.

Hagerstown, MD 21740. Hagerstown, 20140 Scholar Dr., Suite 311. Phone: (301) 739-8993. Fax: (301) 739-8994. David Fields, exec.

Holmdel, NJ 07733. Holmdel, 200 Telegraph Hill Rd. Phone: (732) 739-2874. Fax: (732) 739-2978. Mark DeSantis, exec.

Cedar Hill, TX 75104. Cedar Hill, 777 Westar Rd. Phone: (972) 299-5091. Bob Vaile, exec.

Alexandria, VA 22312. Alexandria, 6461 Stephenson Way. Phone: (703) 941-4312. Fax: (703) 914-2152. Rick Minter, exec.

Brewster, WA 98812. Brewster, 66C Verestar Dr, Box 430. Phone: (509) 689-6000. Fax: (509) 689-3798. Chris Harlow, exec.

Singapore 38989 Singapore. Singapore, 9 Temasek Blvd, Suntec Tower Two #22-02. Phone: 65-333-0066. Fax: 65-338-1033. Yew Weng Soo, exec.

Leuk-stadt 3953 Switzerland. Switzerland/Leuk, Satellitenbodenstation Leuk. Phone: 41 (27) 474-92-12. Fax: 41 (27) 473-31-36. Alfred Kuonen, exec.

Amersham, Bucks HP7 OUT United Kingdom. UK, St. Mary's Court, The Broadway. Phone: 44 (1494) 582094. Fax: 44 (1494) 582474. Mark Guthrie, exec.

Verestar, a global service provider, delivers integrated satellite, terrestrial, and Internet solutions to customers around the globe. With an unparalleled infrastructure including teleports in the US and Europe, more than 150 antennas and extensive space and terrestrial capacity, Verestar seamlessly manages customers' communications with end-to-end solutions and flexible service options.

Videocom Media Services, LLC, Box 212, Boston, MA 02137. Phone: (781) 329-4080. Fax: (781) 329-8534. E-mail: traffic@videocom.com. Web Site: www.videocom.com. Bob Hanson, opns mgr; Daniel V. Swartz, pres/CEO.

Videocom Teleport Boston. Steerable C- & Ku-band antennas interconnected via private microwave & telco loops co-located with single- & multiple-camera program origination facility. Receives & transmits all formats of videotape; transportable uplinks; bcst news distribution; link with Canadian satellites. Digital video transmission & net mgmt svcs. Videocam Teleport Rio de Janerio & Videocam Teleport Sao Paulo.

Vision Accomplished/Hawaii Overseas Teleport, 91-110 Hanua St., Suite 31, Barbers Point, HI 96862. Phone: (808) 682-0032. Craig Landis, pres.

Portable uplink & downlink systems plus full-svc teleport facility on Honolulu. Studio & tape svcs plus fiber connections.

WGVU-TV, 301 W. Fulton, Grand Rapids, MI 49504-6492. Phone: (616) 331-6666. Fax: (616) 331-6625. E-mail: wgvu@gvsu.edu. Web Site: www.wgvu.org. Michael Walenta, gen mgr; Ken Kolbe, opns mgr; Bob Lumbert, engrg dir.

Provides multiple studio post production, teleconferencing & satellite uplink svcs.

WHYY Inc., Independence Mall W., 150 N. 6th St., Philadelphia, PA 19106. Phone: (215) 351-1200. Fax: (215) 351-0398. Web Site: www.whyy.org. William J. Marrazzo, pres/CEO.

Occasional video, encryption svcs, transponder time available. Interconnect with Telco, on-site production facilities, & teleconferencing for up to 1,000 people. Transportable Ku-band earth stn; C- or Ku-band uplinking.

WRS Motion Picture & Video Laboratory, 1000 Napor Blvd., Pittsburgh, PA 15205. Phone: (412) 937-7700. E-mail: jackn@wrslabs.com. F. Jack Napor, pres.

Videotape & satellite distribution service; uplinking & downlinking. Tape duplication in all formats, film-to-tape transfer & standard conversions.

Satellite Owners and Transmission Services

WSAC, 9601 South Meridian, Englewood, CO 80112. Phone: (800) 367-3193.
The premiere provider of digital satellite progmg, mktg support & informational svcs to the private cable & wireless cable industry serving multi dwelling units (MDVs).

WTVS-Analog 56 & Digital 43 Detroit Public Television, 7441 Second Ave., Detroit, MI 48202. Phone: (313) 873-7200. Fax: (313) 876-8118. E-mail: email@dptv.org. Web Site: www.detroitpublictv.org. John Wenzel, CFO; Steven R. Antoiotti, pres; Daniel Alpert, COO.
Offers Ku-band uplinking to any satellite; uplink, fiberlink, downlink, production, postproduction & teleconference svcs available.

Warren Only Media Group, 19 West Almond Street, Vineland, NJ 08360. Phone: (856) 507-9368. Fax: (856) 507-9368. E-mail: warren@warrenonly.com. Web Site: www.warrenonly.com. Warren Only, pres.
New York, NY 10036, Box 2372. Phone: (917) 339-0036.
Program playout, turnarounds, uplink services.

Williams Communications, 111 E. 1st St., Vyvx Services, Tulsa, OK 74103. Phone: (918) 547-5760. Jeff Storey, CEO.
Long Beach, CA 90802, 200 Oceangate, Suite 570. Phone: (800) 747-7074.
Atlanta, GA 30329, 1802 Briarcliff Rd. Phone: (800) 648-3333.
Park Ridge, NJ 07656, One Maynard Dr. Phone: (800) 746-3019.
Provider of integrated fiber-optic, satellite & teleport multimedia and data gathering, management and transmission services.

Wiltel Communications - VYVX, One Technology Center, Tulsa, OK 74103. Phone: (866) 945-8351. E-mail: info@vyvx.com. Web Site: www.wiltel.com.
F/T K2 lease, time available. Two SNV units. C- & Ku-band earth stns, turnaround. Complete production facility, multi-format duplication.

Teleports

Alexandria, VA—Verestar Inc., 3040 Williams Dr., Suite 600, Fairfax, VA 22031. Phone: (703) 206-9000. Fax: (703) 573-3293. E-mail: info@verestar.com. Web Site: www.verestar.com. Raymond J. O'Brien, pres/COO.

Hagerstown, MD 21740. Hagerstown, 20140 Scholar Dr., Suite 311. Phone: (301) 739-8993. Fax: (301) 739-8994. David Fields, exec.

Holmdel, NJ 07733. Holmdel, 200 Telegraph Hill Rd. Phone: (732) 739-2874. Fax: (732) 739-2978. Mark DeSantis, exec.

Cedar Hill, TX 75104. Cedar Hill, 777 Westar Rd. Phone: (972) 299-5091. Bob Vaile, exec.

Alexandria, VA 22312. Alexandria, 6461 Stephenson Way. Phone: (703) 941-4312. Fax: (703) 914-2152. Rick Minter, exec.

Brewster, WA 98812. Brewster, 66C Verestar Dr., Box 430. Phone: (509) 689-6000. Fax: (509) 689-3798. Chris Harlow, exec.

Singapore 38989 Singapore. Singapore, 9 Temasek Blvd, Suntec Tower Two #22-02. Phone: 65-333-0066. Fax: 65-338-1033. Yew Weng Soo, exec.

Leuk-stadt 3953 Switzerland. Switzerland/Leuk, Satellitenbodenstation Leuk. Phone: 41 (27) 474-92-12. Fax: 41 (27) 473-31-36. Alfred Kuonen, exec.

Amersham, Bucks HP7 OUT United Kingdom. UK, St. Mary's Court, The Broadway. Phone: 44 (1494) 582094. Fax: 44 (1494) 582474. Mark Guthrie, exec.

Verestar, a global service provider, delivers integrated satellite, terrestrial, and Internet solutions to customers around the globe. With an unparalleled infrastructure including teleports in the US and Europe, more than 150 antennas and extensive space and terrestrial capacity, Verestar seamlessly manages customers' communications with end-to-end solutions and flexible service options.

Atlanta, GA—Atlanta International Teleport, 3530 Bomar Rd., Douglasville, GA 30135. Phone: (770) 949-6600. Fax: (770) 942-6653. E-mail: sales@atlanteleport.com. Web Site: www.atlanteleport.com.

Internet, private business networks, VSAT Hub, C/Ku Up/down, audio, video, data, telephony, TDMA, SCPC, VCII+, fiber, standards conversion, Intelsat-B Station.

Atlanta, GA—Crawford Satellite Services, 3845 Pleasantdale Rd., Atlanta, GA 30340. Phone: (404) 876-7149. Phone: (800) 831-8027. Fax: (678) 421-6717. Web Site: www.crawford.com. Thomas W. Crawford, CEO; Jesse Crawford, chmn.

On-line, net origination, transportables, & transponder brokerage.

Atlanta, GA—Turner Teleport Inc., Box 105366, One CNN Ctr., Atlanta, GA 30348-5366. Phone: (404) 827-1500.

Satellite uplink & downlink svcs for Turner Broadcasting Services.

Atlanta, GA—VYVX Teleport Atlanta, 1802 Briarcliff Rd., Atlanta, GA 30329. Phone: (404) 325-0818. Fax: (404) 325-3949. Jeff Huffman, gen mgr; Steve Smith, opns mgr.

VYVX's UpSouth Teleport offers domestic U.S. & international uplink, downlink & transponder service for video (analog or compressed), data, & voice telecommunication. Fiber-optic & microwave links to points of presence for major bcst & telco locations in the Atlanta, GA, metropolitan area. Direct access to all C- & Ku-band satellites in domestic U.S. arc & AOR. Svcs include program origination; tape playback, recording & editing; standards conversion; encryption; & turnarounds.

Boston, MA—Videocom Media Services, LLC, Box 212, Boston, MA 02137. Phone: (781) 329-4080. Fax: (781) 329-8534. E-mail: traffic@videocom.com. Web Site: www.videocom.com. Bob Hanson, opns mgr; Daniel V. Swartz, pres/CEO. Ownership: Private.

Videocom Teleport Boston. Steerable C- & Ku-band antennas interconnected via private microwave & telco loops co-located with single- & multiple-camera program origination facility. Receives & transmits all formats of videotape; transportable uplinks; bcst news distribution; link with Canadian satellites. Digital video transmission & net mgmt svcs. Videocam Teleport Rio de Janerio & Videocam Teleport Sao Paulo.

Catawissa, PA—Roaring Creek International Teleport/AT&T, 311 Earth Station Rd., Catawissa, PA 17820. Phone: (570) 799-1000. Phone: (570) 799-1012. Fax: (570) 799-1042.

Ant 1, 2, 3, 4, 5. G/T 40.91 international voice, data, video to primary path, major path 1 & 2, international satellites, Fuji fiber, connectivity. Facilities are available for transportable interconnect or permanent transmission space. All C-band ants are Intelesat standard meters & all Ku-band ants are standard C meters.

Chicago, IL—Norlight Teleport Chicago, 3617 Oakton St., Skokie, IL 60076. Phone: (847) 568-7195. Fax: (847) 674-7485. E-mail: drp@norlight.com. Web Site: www.norlight.com. Jim Ditter, pres; Robert E. Rogers, VP; Dave Pritchard, dir.

Brookfield, WI 53045, 275 N. Corporate.

Full-svc teleport, domestic & international, satellite uplink, downlink, turnaround, encryption, rgn access on Norlight Telecommunications Interstate Network, VYVX and AT&T fiber access.

Chicago, IL—SpaceCom Systems' Chicago International Teleport, 6723 W. Steger Rd., Monee, IL 60449. Phone: (708) 534-2400. Fax: (708) 534-0060. E-mail: daves@spacecom.com. Christina Sips, gen mgr. Ownership: Chicago, IL.

C- & Ku-band satellite transmission svcs. Audio, video, data, uplink/downlink communication.

Cincinnati, OH—WLWT-TV, 1700 Young St., Cincinnati, OH 45202. Phone: (513) 412-5000. Fax: (513) 412-6100. Web Site: www.channelcincinnati.com. Richard Dyer, gen mgr.

On-line. Provides occasional C-band uplinking svcs.

Culver City, CA—GlobeCast North America, 3872 Keystone Ave. S., 10525 W. Washington Blvd., Culver City, CA 90232. Phone: (310) 845-3900 (sales). Phone: (310) 845-3939. Fax: (310) 845-3904. E-mail: rmarking@globecastna.com. Web Site: www.globecastna.com.

Washington, DC 20006, 1825 K St. N.W., 9th Fl. Phone: (202) 861-0894. Fax: (202) 861-3107.

Washington, DC 20001, 400 North Capitol St. N.W, Suite 880. Phone: (202) 737-4440. Fax: (202) 737-1476. (International Sales).

Miami, FL 33166. GlobeCast Hero Productions, 7291 N.W. 74 St. Phone: (305) 887-1600. Fax: (305) 887-7076. (Corporate Headquarters).

New York, NY 10017, 110 E. 42nd St., 11th Fl. Phone: (212) 885-8700. Fax: (212) 885-8701. (Eastern Region office).

Keystone's Los Angeles International Teleport, in Culver City, CA & Sylmar, offers a transmission network of domestic & international satellite transponders providing video & audio origination svcs for over 1,000 united states & international clients, including news, sports, program distribution & business TV clientele. The company utilizes its extensive worldwide network of space & terrestrial facilities in the united states, as well as through its international parternships.

Dallas, TX—Megastar Inc., 4709 Compass Bow Ln., Las Vegas, NV 89130. Phone: (702) 386-2844. Fax: (702) 388-1250. Nigel Macrae, pres. Ownership: Dallas.

Texas teleport offering full svc Ku & C-band svcs to Europe, Africa, Canada, US, Mexico & the Caribbean.

Denver, CO—VYVX Teleport Denver, 9174 S. Jamaica St., Englewood, CO 80112. Phone: (303) 397-4100. Fax: (303) 799-8325. Theran Davis, opns mgr. Ownership: Denver.

Domestic & international uplink, downlink & transponder service for video & date communications. Regional Fiber & microwave interconnectivity to broadcast affiliates, PoPs & sports venues

Edmonton, AB—Edmonton Teleport. Telesat Canada, 5311 Allard Way, Edmonton, AB T6H 5B8. Canada. Phone: (780) 437-6167. Fax: (780) 436-5667. L.J. Boisvert, pres/COO; Dave Lahey, VP network svcs.

Major bcst teleport offering full North American arc at C-band, & Anik E1 & E2 at Ku-band for occasional use needs.

Jackson, MS—Jackson Teleport Inc., 916 Foley St., Jackson, MS 39202. Phone: (800) 353-9177. Phone: (61) 352-6673. Fax: (601) 948-6052. Web Site: www.weathervision.com. E-mail: edward@nwnstudios.com. Edward St. Pe, pres; Jason McCleave, VP; Cindy Snell, admin.

Fixed 7-meter earth stn on site. Video satellite transmission & reception. Videoconferencing, business TV, news, sports & weathercast feed, origination, program distribution & syndication svcs.

Los Angeles, CA—Willliams Services/VYVX Steele Valley Teleports, 20021 Santa Rosa Mine Rd., Perris, CA 92570. Phone: (909) 943-5399. Fax: (909) 943-3459. E-mail: gene.brookhart@wcg.com. Gene Brookhart, gen mgr.

Englewood, CO 80112, 58 Inverness Dr. E. Phone: (303) 397-4100. (800) 424-9757 (full-time svcs).

Steele Valley Teleports offers domestic U.S. & international uplink, downlink & transponder service for video (analog or compressed), image, data & voice telecommunication. Fiber-optic & microwave links to points of presence for major bcst & telco locations in the Los Angeles metropolitan area. Direct access to all C- & Ku-band satellites in domestic U.S. arc & POR. Svcs include program origination; tape playback, recording & editing; standards conversion; encryption; & turnarounds. Williams Services/VYVX Steele Valley Teleports coast-to-coast teleport locations, which include Los Angeles, CA; New York, NY; Denver, CO; & Atlanta, GA, are interconnected via fiber-optic backbone.

Montreal, PQ—Montreal Teleport. Telesat Canada, 1601 Telesat Ct., Gloucester, ON K1B 5P4. Canada. Phone: (613) 748-0123. Fax: (613) 748-8712. E-mail: info@telesat.ca. Web Site: www.telesat.ca. Larry Boisvert, pres; Dennis Billard, VP business dev. Ownership: Montreal.

Access to all Telesat Anik and Nimiq satellites & most U.S. domestic satellites.

New Orleans, LA—Network Teleports Inc., 3200 Chartres St., New Orleans, LA 70117. Phone: (504) 942-9200. Fax: (504) 942-9204. E-mail: uplink@networkteleports.com. Web Site: www.networkteleports.com. Barbara Lamont, pres; Ludwig Gelobter, VP; C.E. Feltner, chmn of bd; Nolly Paul, VP opns. Ownership: New Orleans.

C-band voice/video & data, Ku-band data/voice, B-MAC encryption, newsfeeds, production, fiber-optic links, audio-subcarrier & C- & Ku-band 5CPC, satellite telephones, IP multicasting, webcasting.

New York, NY—GlobeCast Communications Corp., 5 Teleport Dr., Staten Island, NY 10311. Phone: (718) 983-2600. Fax: (718) 983-2615.

Keystone's New York Teleport in Staten Island, NY, offers a transmission network of leased domestic & international satellite transponders providing radio & TV origination svcs for more than 1,000 U.S. & international clients every year, including news, sports, program distribution & business TV clientele. Bob Bechar, pres.

Oakland, CA—ICG Telecom Group, 161 Inverness Dr., West Englewood, CO 80112.

Alternative Access Carrier. Bay Area Teleport provides communications svcs at DS0, T1 or T3 levels for primary or alternative access applications. Bay Area Teleport's system connects 12 counties in northern California. Includes a fiber-optic network in San Francisco, CA & across to Oakland, CA, as well as access to satellite svcs through its earth stn complex in Niles Canyon.

Pittsburgh, PA—Pittsburgh Telecommunications, Box 14070, Pittsburgh, PA 15239. Phone: (724) 337-1888. Fax: (724) 337-1754. E-mail: info@pitcomm.com. Web Site: www.pitcomm.com. Robert R. Linden, engrg mgr.

Fixed & remote uplinking & downlinking, turnarounds, space segment, microwave & fiber-optic interconnects, point-to-point & VSAT svcs.

Stamford, CT—Ascent Media Network Services, 250 Harbor Dr., Stamford, CT 06902. Phone: (888) 826-4016. Fax: (203) 965-6405. Web Site: www.ascentmedia.com. Frances G. Luperella, sr VP; Matt Armstrong, mktg VP. Ownership: Stamford

C- & Ku-band domestic & international transmission service; connectivity to metro New York via proprietary fiber origination, bcst, business TV, transponder availability; studio & postproduction svcs.

Toronto, ON—Toronto Teleport. Telesat Canada, 1601 Telesat Ct., Gloucester, ON K1B 5P4. Canada. Phone: (613) 748-0123. Fax: (613) 748-8712. E-mail: info@telesat.ca. Web Site: www.telesat.ca. Larry Boisvert, pres; Dennis Billard, VP business dev. Ownership: Toronto.

Access to all Telesat Anik & Nimiq satellites & most united states domestic satellites.

Teleports

Vancouver, BC—Vancouver Teleport. Telesat Canada, 1601 Telesat Ct., Gloucester, ON K1B 5P4. Canada. Phone: (613) 748-0123. Fax: (613) 748-8712. E-mail: info@telesat.ca. Web Site: www.telesat.ca. Larry Boisvert, pres; Dennis Billard, VP business dev. Ownership: Vancouver.

Access to all Telesat Anik & Nimiq satellites & most North American satellites.

Washington, DC—Diversified Communications Inc. (DCI), 2000 M St. N.W., 3rd Fl., Washington, DC 20036. Phone: (202) 775-4300. Phone: (800) 333-0010. Fax: (202) 775-4363. E-mail: levin@dciteleport.com. Web Site: www.dciteleport.com.

DCI offers full teleport services with a large fleet of ku-Band trucks with production, air transportable units and Internet services. ToC 24x7

Washington, DC—Pyramid NewsPort, 480 National Press Bldg., Washington, DC 20001. Phone: (202) 783-5030. Fax: (202) 628-7228. E-mail: tmurasev@ptpngroup.com. Web Site: www.ptpngroup.com. Nicholas J. Chiaia Jr., pres; Tina Murasev, opns mgr.

TV production facilities include studios, on-line & non-linear editing & transmission facilities to Ku-band & C-band satellites. Interconnect to major news-gathering points in Washington, DC, at the National Press Bldg.

Woodbury, NY—Rainbow Network Communications, 620 Hicksville Rd., Bethpage, NY 11714. Phone: (516) 803-0355. Fax: (516) 803-4924. E-mail: togreco@rainbow-media.com. Web Site: www.rncnetwork.com.

Multiple 11-meter & 9-meter uplinking antennas, multiple downlinking ants, both servicing the entire satellite arc. Connectivity in & out of New York & metropolitan area, Ku-band transportable, origination/editing svcs, & full, longterm & occasional transponder leasing. Compression svcs.

Section G
Professional Services

Section G
Professional Services

Station and Cable System Brokers	G-2
Management and Marketing Consultants	G-6
Station Financing Services	G-14
Research Services	G-16
Engineering and Technical Consultants	G-20
Law Firms	G-24
Talent Agents and Managers	G-33
Employment and Executive Search Services	G-34
Professional Cards Engineering & Technical Consultants	G-35

Station and Cable System Brokers

American Media Services L.L.C. Box 20696, Charleston, SC 29413. Phone: (843) 972-2200. Fax: (843) 881-4436. E-mail: ams@ams.fm. Web Site: www.americanmediaservices.com. Edward F. Seeger, pres/CEO; Andrew J. Guest, sr VP/COO; W. David Chandler, exec VP & development; Todd W. Fowler, exec VP/Brokerage.

Bonham, TX 75418. Dallas office: 9208 Timbercreek Dr. Phone: (903) 640-5857. Fax: (903) 640-5859. David Reeder, regional broker.

Forest Lake, IL 60047. Chicago office: 24180 N. Forest Dr. Phone: (847) 540-5410. Frank McCoy, exec VP/engineering.

Marble Falls, TX 78654. Austin office: 303 Avenue Q. Phone: (877) 267-2636. Patrick McNamara, regional broker.

Developers & brokers of radio properties. Also appraisals, search svcs (buyer's agent), upgrade studies.

Associated Broadcasters Station Brokers
Appraisals — Consulting
Irv Schwartz, Managing Director
PO Box 42566, Cincinnati, OH 45242
(513) 791-5982 Fax: (513) 891-5727

Associated Broadcasters, Inc. Box 42566, Cincinnati, OH 45242. Phone: (513) 791-5982. Fax: (513) 891-5727. Irv Schwartz, mngg dir; R. Galen, rsch admin.

Legal & filing svcs in turnkey packages; consulting & appraisal svcs available.

Ohio Broadcast Properties Specialists.

Barger Broadcast Brokerage, Ltd., 8023 Vantage Dr., Suite 840, San Antonio, TX 78230. Phone: (210) 340-7080. Fax: (210) 341-1777. John W. Barger, pres.

Media brokerage, local mktg agreements, financial placements, appraisals & mgmt/financial consulting.

Blackburn & Co. Inc., 201 N. Union St., Suite 340, Alexandria, VA 22314. Phone: (703) 519-3703. Fax: (703) 519-9756. James W. Blackburn Jr., chmn; Richard F. Blackburn, pres; Jack V. Harvey, assoc; Tony Rizzo, assoc; Bruce Houston, assoc.

Radio & TV stations and communications tower brokerage, financing and appraisals.

Frank Boyle & Co., L.L.C., 24 Stag Ln., Greenwich, CT 06831. Phone: (203) 661-8879. Phone: (203) 969-2020. Fax: (203) 316-0800. E-mail: fboylebrkr@aol.com. Frank Boyle, pres; Mary C. Downey, VP opns.

Radio & TV media brokerage, mergers & acquisitions/appraisals.

Broadcast Media Associates, P.O. 1233, Santa Maria, CA 93456. Phone: (805) 937-1553. Fax: (805) 937 1553. Web Site: broadcastmediabroker.com. Clifford M. Hunter, pres.

Radio/TV/cable brokerage in the western states. Confidential mktg for radio, TV & LPTV properties; valuation packages & financial analysis; consultants to sellers & buyers.

Broadcast Media Partners, 8216 N. 54th St., Scottsdale, AZ 85253. Phone: (480) 951-1897. Fax: (480) 596-8385. E-mail: ted@nicholsoncompany.com. Ted Nicholson, ptnr.

Murrieta, CA 92562, 3855 Lochinvar Ct. Phone: (909) 698-1131. Fax: (909) 696-0998. F. Patrick Nugent, ptnr. (Los Angeles office).

Brokerage svcs, valuations, due diligence, Far East consulting, court-approved takeover specialists.

BroadcastStations4Sale.com, 905 N. Gilbreath St., Graham, NC 27253. Phone: (336) 570-9133. Fax: (336) 570-3464. E-mail: tedjgray@netzero.net. Web Site: www.broadcaststations4sale.com. Ted J. Gray, pres; Dave Hedrick, VP.

Buy or sell radio stns or TV stns. List to sell yourself or let BroadcastStations4Sale.com sell it for you.

Broadcasting Asset Management Corp., 1323 Forest Glen, Winnetka, IL 60093. Phone: (847) 446-8882. Fax: (847) 446-4855. Jack Minkow, pres.

Radio stn & group stn brokerage, mergers, acquisition analysis, appraisals, feasibility studies; subdebt & equity placement.

The Jesse Neal Browder Co., 1270 County Club Ln., Elberton, GA 30635. Phone: (706) 283-3016. Fax: (706) 283-3016. E-mail: fly4fun@elberton.net.

Stn brokerage & appraisals specializing in the southeast market.

Bulkley Capital, L.P., 5949 Sherry Ln., #1370, Dallas, TX 75225. Phone: (214) 692-5476. Fax: (214) 692-9309. E-mail: info@bulkleycapital.com. Web Site: www.bulkleycapital.com. G. Bradford Bulkey, pres/CEO; John A. McKay, dir; Martin Greenberg, dir; Richard Gilbert, mngg dir; Oliver Cone, Inv. Officer; Lisa Bulkley, Inv. Officer.

Chicago, IL 60606 Phone: (312) 726-1220. Richard W. Gilbert, dir; Gail Quick, VP.

Investment banking: mergers, acquisitions & private placements of debt & equity capital. Also, direct investment activities of certain institutional equity investors.

Business Broker Associates, 114 N. Cliff Lane, Chattanooga, TN 37415. Phone: (423) 756-7635. Fax: (423) 870-9036. E-mail: bba@cdc.net. Web Site: www.cdc.net/~bba. Alfred C. Dick, owner & broker.

Media broker & consultant for radio, TV & cable systems.

Chaisson & Company Inc., 154 Indian Waters Dr., New Canaan, CT 06840. Phone: (203) 966-6333. Fax: (203) 966-1298. E-mail: rchaisco@aol.com. Robert A. Chaisson, pres.

Brokerage of radio/TV sls & acquisitions.

S.R. Chanen & Co. Inc./Media Technology Capital Corp., 3300 N. 3rd Ave., Phoenix, AZ 85013. Phone: (602) 234-1411. Fax: (602) 285-9268. Steven R. Chanen, chmn; Donald E. New, pres acquisitions & investments.

Investment banking, brokerage & financial advisory svcs for the communications & entertainment industries.

Chapin Enterprises, 751 Wells Fargo Ctr., Lincoln, NE 68508. Phone: (402) 475-5285. Fax: (402) 475-5293. R.W. Chapin, pres.

Stn sls, consulting, financial counseling, per location & receiver.

Cobb Corp. LLC 800 Laurel Oak Dr., Suite 210, Naples, FL 34108. Phone: (202) 478-3737. Fax: (239) 596-0660. E-mail: briancobb@cobbcorp.tv. Web Site: www.cobbcorp.tv. Brian E. Cobb, pres; Susan W. Cook, mktg dir; Dan Graves, mngg dir; Denis LeClair, VP; Jeanette Kuszlyk, controller; Joel Day, assoc.

Vero Beach, FL 32963, 4702 Sunset Drive. Phone: (202) 478-3737. Fax: (239) 596-0660. Joel Day, Associate.

Brokerage, mergers, acquisitions, appraisals, merchant banking.

Communication Resources Media Brokers, 5343 E. 22nd St., Tulsa, OK 74114. Phone: (918) 743-8300. Fax: (918) 749-3348. E-mail: tbelc@cox.net. Tom Belcher, pres.

Brokerage service to radio & TV stns, cable TV companies, & ind telephone companies.

Communications Equity Associates Inc., 101 E. Kennedy Blvd., Suite 3300, Tampa, FL 33602. Phone: (813) 226-8844. Fax: (813) 225-1513. Web Site: www.ceaworldwide.com. J. Patrick Michaels Jr., chmn/CEO.

Praha 1, NO 11000 Czech Republic, Melantrichova 17. Phone: 420-2-216-32 451. Fax: 420-2-242 29 412. Vaclav Matatko, mngg dir.

Paris 75008 France. CEA France, SAS, 9, Rue Royale. Phone: 33-1-53-30-86-07. Fax: 33-1-47-42-32-14. Frank Portais, mngg dir.

Munich D-80539 Germany. CEA GMBH, Prinzregentenstrasse 56. Phone: 49- (0)89-290-725 0. Fax: 49-(0)89-290 725 200. Jose Kabana, mngg dir.

Madrid 28006 Spain. CEA Madrid, Serrano 93, Oficina 6E. Phone: 34-91-745-13 13. Fax: 34-91-56338 62. Jose Cabrera-Kabana Sartorius, mngg dir.

London, NO WIG OPW United Kingdom. London, 33 Cavendish Square. Phone: 44-207-647-7700. Fax: 44-207-647-7710. Dr. Stephan Goetz; mngg Dir/E VP; Hak Yeung, Dir.

Westport, CT 06880. Principal Advisors Group, LLC, 191 Post Road West. Phone: (203) 221-26622. Fax: (203) 221-2663. Dave Moyer, Pres..

Miami, FL 33131, 150 S.E. 2nd Ave. Phone: (305) 810-2740. Fax: (305) 810-2741. Fernando Polar, VP.

Tampa, FL 33602, 101 E. Kennedy Blvd., Ste. 3300. Phone: (813) 226-8844. Fax: (813) 225-1513. J. Patrick Michaels, Jr., chmn/CEO.

New York, NY 10020, 1270 Ave of the Americas, Ste. 1818. Phone: (212) 218-5085. Fax: (212) 218-5099. Alexander Rossi, mngg dir.

Investment banking and private equity firm specializing in the cable, broadcasting, telecommunications, media, and entertainment industries.

The Connelly Co., 17909 Holly Brook Dr., Tampa, FL 33647-2245. Phone: (813) 991-9494. E-mail: connellyradiotv@verizon.net. Robert J. Connelly, broker; Robert J. (Rob) Connelly, broker.

New Market, NH 03857, 198 S. Main St. Phone: (603) 659-3648.

South Effingham, NH 03882, Bailey Rd. (Summer only). Phone: (603) 522-6462. Fax: (603) 522-6462.

Brokers, consultants & recovery unit to assist banks & financial institutions.

The Media Brokerage Firm of
COX & COX
A Limited Liability Company

Cox & Cox L.L.C. 2454 Shiva Ct., St. Louis, MO 63011. Phone: (636) 458-4780. Fax: (636) 458-6323. E-mail: bc@coxandcoxllc.com. Web Site: www.coxandcoxllc.com. Bob Cox, pres.

Mergers & acquisitions, appraisals, consulting & expert testimony.

Daniels & Associates, 3200 Cherry Creek Dr. S., Suite 500, Denver, CO 80209. Phone: (303) 778-5555. Fax: (303) 778-5599. Web Site: www.danielsonline.com. E-mail: info@danielsonline.com. Brian Deevy, CEO; Brad Busse, pres/COO.

New York, NY 10022, 711 Fifth Ave, Suite 405. Phone: (212) 935-5900. Fax: (212) 863-4859. Greg Ainsworth, sr mngg dir; David Tolliver, mngg dir.

Provides mergers & acquisitions, corporate finance & financial advisory svcs to the telecommunications industry.

Diversified Investment Services, Inc., 1500 S.W. 5th Ave., Suite 2602, Portland, OR 97201. Phone: (503) 221-1122. Phone: (800) 635-1772. Fax: (503) 525-9241. E-mail: sharmie@aol.com. Armand J. Santilli, pres.

Media brokers/finders, real estate investment bankers & brokers.

Earl Reilly Enterprises, 550 Aloha St., Suite 404, Seattle, WA 98019. Phone: (206) 282-6914. Fax: (206) 285-2765. Web Site: www.tvspotnet.com. Earl F. Reilly, pres; J. M. Reilly, sls mgr.

Freeland, WA 98249, Box 1300. Phone: (206) 331-7223. Fax: (206) 331-7223.

Bcst rep, representing U.S. TV stns in Canada. Also licensed bcst stn brokers.

Edwin Tornberg & Co. Inc., 8917 Cherbourg Dr., Potomac, MD 20854. Phone: (301) 983-8700. Fax: (301) 299-2297. Edwin Tornberg, pres.

Appraisals, brokerage, financial & mgmt consulting for radio, TV & cable.

Station and Cable System Brokers

EnVest Media, LLC, 6802 Patterson Ave., Richmond, VA 23226. Phone: (804) 282-5561. Fax: (804) 282-5703. E-mail: mittyounts@cs.com. Web Site: www.envestmedia.com. Mitt S. Younts, mgr.

Alpharetta, GA 30004, 11770 Haynes Bridge Rd, #205. Phone: (770) 753-9650. Fax: (770) 753-0089. E-mail: jswnet@aol.com. Jesse Weatherby, member, manager.

Envest Media is a nationwide radio & TV acquisition, valuation, financing & consulting firm. The company provides brokerage svcs to stn transaction, appraisal svcs to stn owners & financial institutions. The group secures debt & equity acquisition financing, offers consulting & asset mgmt svcs, acting as court appointed receivers or trustees for bcst stations.

The Exline Company 4340 Redwood Hwy., Suite F-230, San Rafael, CA 94903. Phone: (415) 479-3484. Fax: (415) 479-1574. E-mail: exline@pacbell.net. Andrew P. McClure, pres; W. Dean LeGras, VP.

Complete brokerage, consulting & appraisal svcs for radio & TV properties.

Explorer Communications Inc., 9606 Sea Turtle Terr., Suite 101, Bradenton, FL 34212. Phone: (941) 708-5440. Fax: (941) 708-5450. E-mail: jfhoff@att.net. Jim Hoffman, pres.

Alto, NM 88312, Box 2209. Phone: (505) 336-1231. Jim Hoffman, pres.

Bcst media brokerage svcs. Specialists in medium & small market entrepreneurial transactions.

Norman Fischer & Associates Inc., P.O. Box 5308, Austin, TX 78763-5308. Phone: (512) 476-9457. Fax: (512) 476-0540. E-mail: terrill@nfainc.com. Web Site: www.nfainc.com. Terrill Fischer, pres.

Brokerage in radio, TV & cable. Consultation in mgmt & opns, appraisals, feasibility studies, expert testimony, financial planning & assistance.

Richard A. Foreman Associates, Inc., 330 Emery Dr. E., Stamford, CT 06902-2210. Phone: (203) 327-2800. Fax: (203) 967-9393. E-mail: rafamedia@compuserve.com. Web Site: www.rafamenia.com. Richard A. Foreman, pres.

Specializing in cash-positive radio & TV stns in major growth mkts.

Michael Fox International, Inc., 11425 Cronhill Dr., Owings Mills, MD 21117. Phone: (410) 654-7500. Fax: (410) 654-5876. E-mail: info@michaelfox.com. Web Site: www.michaelfox.com. William Z. Fox, chmn; David S. Fox, CEO.

Beverly Hills, CA 90212, 9454 Wilshire Blvd, Penthouse. Phone: (310) 248-2821. Adam Reich, co-pres.

Baltimore, MD 21117, 11425 Cronhill Dr. Phone: (410) 654-7500. Gilbert Schwartzman, sr VP.

New York, NY 10601, 75 S. Broadway, 4th Fl. Phone: (914) 723-7600. Jonathan Reich, pres.

Auction sls of bcst properties.

Fugatt Media Services, 9214 Butternut Dr., Crystal Lake, IL 60014. Phone: (815) 788-7481. Fax: (815) 788-7482. E-mail: fugattmediaservices@comcast.net. Michael L. Fugatt, pres.

Media brokerage firm specialing in radio and cable services including appraisals.

Gammon Media Brokers L.L.C., 5219 N. Casa Blanca Dr., #16, Scottsdale, AZ 85253. Phone: (480) 614-6612. Fax: (480) 614-6613. E-mail: cmiller@gmbi.com. Web Site: www.gmbi.com. Christopher D. Miller, pres/CEO.

Chevy Chase, MD 20815, 5600 Wisconsin Ave, Suite 308. Phone: (301) 332-0940. Fax: (301) 654-8123. James A. Gammon, chmn.

Brokerage & strategy advice to sellers & buyers of radio stns & TV stns; nwspr and cable TV systems.

Clifton Gardiner & Company, L.L.C., 2437 S. Chase Ln., Lakewood, CO 80227. Phone: (303) 758-6900. Fax: (303) 479-9210. E-mail: cliff@cliftongardiner.com. Web Site: www.cliftongardner.com. Clifton H. Gardiner, pres.

Brokerage & financial svcs for the bcst & cable industries.

Dave Garland Media Brokerage, 1110 Hackney St., Houston, TX 77023. Phone: (713) 921-9603. Fax: (713) 926-2694. E-mail: garland@radiobroker.com. Web Site: www.radiobroker.com. David Garland, owner.

Broker of radio stn properties in Texas & surrounding states.

HPC Puckett & Co., Box 9063, Rancho Santa Fe, CA 92130. Phone: (858) 756-4915. Fax: (858) 756-4534. Thomas F. Puckett, chmn; Hiram H. Powell, exec VP.

Topeka, KS 66614, 2921 S.W. Wanamaker Dr, Suite 104. Phone: (913) 273-0017.

Communications brokerage & investment banking.

Hadden & Associates, Media Brokers - Orlando. 100 Seville Chase Dr., Winter Springs, FL 32708. Phone: (407) 699-6069. Fax: (407) 699-1444. E-mail: haddenws@aol.com. Web Site: www.haddenonline.com. Doyle Hadden, pres/CEO; Ryan P. Hadden, VP.

Communications broker, acquisitions, divestitures; financial assistance and appraisal to the broadcasting industry.

Margret Haney Media Brokerage & Consultants, 2995 Woodside Rd., Bldg. 400, Woodside, CA 94062-2446. Phone: (650) 324-8262. Fax: (650) 324-8261. E-mail: www.hhmargret@yahoo.com. Web Site: www.margret@margrethaney.com. Sondralyn Carver, consultant; Margret Haney, pres.

Media brokerage/consulting, adv, media buyers.

Hardesty & Associates, 500 East Balboa, Newport Beach, CA 92661. Phone: (949) 723-2230. Fax: (949) 723-2240. Bill Hardesty, pres; Lillian Barnhart, office mgr.

Acquisitions, divestitures, appraisals, financing & consulting.

Hawkeye Radio Properties Inc., 3325 Conservancy Ln., Middleton, WI 53562. Phone: (608) 831-8708. Fax: (608) 831-6100. E-mail: dganske@charter.net. Dale A. Ganske, pres.

Complete radio/TV, consulting, FCC rules & regulations.

Henson Media Inc., 455 S. Fourth Ave., Suite 427, Louisville, KY 40202-2508. Phone: (502) 589-0060. Fax: (502) 589-0058. E-mail: edhenson1@cs.com. Ed Henson, pres.

Radio & TV brokers specializing in Midwest & Southeast.

The Ted Hepburn Co., 325 Garden Rd., Palm Beach, FL 33480. Phone: (561) 863-8995. Fax: (561) 863-8997. E-mail: tedhep@aol.com. Ted Hepburn, mng dir.

Radio, TV & cable brokerage; appraisals.

R. Miller Hicks & Co., 1011 W. 11th St., Austin, TX 78703. Phone: (512) 477-7000. Fax: (512) 477-9697. E-mail: millerhicks@rmhicks.com. R. Miller Hicks, pres.

Business dev & consulting svcs since 1957.

Mel Hodell, Media Broker Inc., 1388 N. Euclid Ave., Upland, CA 91786-3206. Phone: (909) 982-0424. Fax: (909) 982-3455. E-mail: melhodell@verizon.net. Mel Hodell, pres.

Newspaper Broker-Sales, Consultation.

Holt Media Group, 2178 Industrial Dr., Suite 914, Bethlehem, PA 18017. Phone: (610) 814-2821. Fax: (610) 814-2826. E-mail: artholt@holtmedia.com. Web Site: www.holtmedia.com. Christine E. Borger, exec VP.

Macon, GA 31220-5260, 6826 Bay Point Dr. Phone: (478) 474-8161. Fax: (610) 814-2826. Carl Strandell, assoc.

Brokerage, consulting, appraisals.

Bruce Houston Associates, Inc., 2251 Hunter Mill Rd., Vienna, VA 22181. Phone: (703) 938-1016. Fax: (703) 938-6078. Web Site: bruceahouston@aol.com. Bruce Houston, pres.

Media brokers for radio & TV.

International Media Consulting, 48 Mountain Rd., Farmington, CT 06032-2341. Phone: (860) 677-9688. Fax: (860) 677-9639. E-mail: robert.richer@snet.net. Robert E. Richer, owner.

Broker specializing in the sale of overseas media properties.

Johnson Communication Properties Inc., 880 Old Crystal Bay Rd., Minneapolis, MN 55391. Phone: (952) 4041-1104. Fax: (952) 404-1102. E-mail: johncomm88@aol.com. Jerry Johnson, pres.

Radio & TV broker for 20 years.

Jorgenson Broadcast Brokerage Inc., 11521 Innfields Dr., Odessa, FL 33556. Phone: (813) 926-9260. Fax: (813) 926-9001. E-mail: goradiotv@aol.com. Mark W. Jorgenson, pres.

Cupertino, CA 95014, 21801 Stevens Creek Blvd, Suite 2B. Phone: (408) 996-0496. Fax: (408) 516-9526. Peter Mieuli.

Confidential, nationwide brokerage of bcst properties.

Kalil & Co. Inc., 3444 N. Country Club, Suite 200, Tucson, AZ 85716. Phone: (520) 795-1050. Fax: (520) 322-0584. E-mail: kalil@kalilco.com.

Media brokerage firm dealing in radio, TV & cable. Handles exclusive listings, confidential searches.

Kempff Communications Co., 3301 Bayshore Blvd., Suite 1407, Tampa, FL 33629. Phone: (813) 258-3433. Fax: (813) 902-1360. E-mail: kempffcc@aol.com. Ron Kempff, pres; Aurelia Serna, VP.

Broker and consultant also offering financial and management svcs, court ordered sale of stations.

Kepper, Tupper & Company, 112 High Ridge Ave., Ridgefield, CT 06877. Phone: (203) 431-3366. Fax: (203) 431-3864. E-mail: keppertup@aol.com. Web Site: kepper-tupper.com. John B. Tupper, pres.

Brokerage & investment banking svcs for the cable & bcst TV industries. Please visit our website kepper-tupper.com.

Knowles Media Brokerage Services, Box 9698, Bakersfield, CA 93389. Phone: (661) 833-3834. Fax: (661) 833-3845. E-mail: gregg.knowles@netzero.net. Web Site: www.media-broker.com. Gregg K. Knowles, pres.

Daily & wkly nwsprs, print publications/sls, consultation. Sales, mergers, acquistions, appraisals.

Kozacko Media Services, Box 948, Elmira, NY 14902. Phone: (607) 733-7138. Fax: (607) 733-1212. E-mail: rkozacko@stny.rr.com. Web Site: www.kozackomediaservices.com. Richard L. Kozacko, pres; John C. Clancy, assoc.

Tucson, AZ 85750, 6890 E. Sunrise Dr, Box120-40. Phone: (520) 456-4302. Fax: (520) 299-1786. George W. Kimble, assoc.

Keswick, VA 22947, 1071 Club Dr. Phone: (434) 244-2653. Fax: (434) 244-2666. W. Donald Roberts Jr., assoc.

Appraisals & current market evaluations of radio & TV stns; bcst stn acquisition brokers.

The LPTV Store.Com, LLC., Box 250813, Milwaukee, WI 53225-6513. Phone: (262) 781-0188. Fax: (262) 781-5313. E-mail: kompasgroup@toast.net. Web Site: www.thelptvstore.com. John Kompas, ptnr; Burt Sherwood, ptnr.

Sarasota, FL 34242, 5053 Ocean Blvd., Suite 14. Phone: (941) 349-2165. Fax: (941) 312-0974.

Financial & mktg svcs for LPTV; audience demographic reports; stn coverage maps; appraisals/brokerage; financial & strategic planning.

H.B. LaRue, Media Brokers 9454 Wilshire Blvd., Suite 628, Beverly Hills, CA 90212. Phone: (310) 275-9266. Fax: (310) 274-4076. E-mail: hblarue@sbcglobal.net.

New York, NY 10021, 500 E. 77th St, Suite 1909. Phone: (212) 288-0737. Hugh Ben LaRue, pres; Joy Thomas, VP.

Media brokerage; TV, radio & CATV. Appraisals & feasibility studies.

Lattice Communications, L.L.C., 441 Vine St., Suite 3900, Cincinnati, OH 45202. Phone: (513) 381-7775. Fax: (513) 381-8808. Web Site: www.latticecommunications.com. R. Dean Merger, pres; Stephen E. Kaufmann, VP.

Acquisition, merger, appraisal & financial svcs to radio, TV, nwspr, cable & other media-related industries.

Lazard L.L.C., 30 Rockefeller Plaza, New York, NY 10020. Phone: (212) 632-6000. Web Site: www.lazard.com. David Braunschvig, mng dir; Robert Hougie, mng dir; Peter Shawn, VP.

Lazard's broad range of svcs includes: general financial advice; domestic & cross-border mergers & acquisitions; divestitures; privatizations; special committee assignments; takeover defenses; corporate restructurings; strategic partnerships/joint ventures; & debt/equity underwriting.

Legacy Securities Corp., 3340 Peachtree Rd., Suite 1560, Suite 1210, Atlanta, GA 30326. Phone: (404) 965-2420. Fax: (404) 965-2421. E-mail: treich@legacysecurities.com. Web Site: www.legacysecurities.com. Michael D. Easterly, CEO; Christopher F. Battel, pres; Carol H. Langendorfer, mng dir.

Full-svc investment banking boutique offering buyers agent & capital raising svcs to small/middle-market owners.

Joe M. Leonard Jr. & Associates Inc., Box 222, Gainesville, TX 76241. Phone: (940) 665-4076. E-mail: lin45@ntin.net. Web Site: www.rockabillyhall.com/joeleonard.html. Joe M. Leonard Jr., pres.

Brokerage of radio & TV.

Broadcasting & Cable Yearbook 2006

Station and Cable System Brokers

Jack Maloney Inc., 28 Shore Dr., Huntington, NY 11743. Phone: (631) 549-2656. Fax: (631) 549-2656. Jack Maloney, pres.
   Provides confidential svcs to buyers & sellers in the radio & TV business.

Mayo Communications Inc., Box 82784, Tampa, FL 33682. Phone: (813) 971-2061. Fax: (813) 977-1947. Lincoln A. Mayo, pres.
   Media brokerage, & appraisals for bcst & print. Consulting concerning media sls & acquisitions.

Edward R. McKenna Communications, Box 71084, Bethesda, MD 20813. Phone: (301) 986-1118. Edward R. McKenna, owner.
   Radio brokerage & consulting.

R.E. Meador & Associates, Inc., Box 36, Lexington, MO 64067. Phone: (660) 259-2544. Fax: (660) 259-6424. Ralph E. Meador, pres.
   Acquisitions, sls, mktg studies & appraisal svcs in central & midwestern states.

Media Services Group Inc., 3948 S. Third St. #191, Jacksonville Beach, FL 32250. Phone: (904) 285-3239. Fax: (904) 285-5618. E-mail: REEDmsconsulting@cs.com. Web Site: www.mediaservicesgroup.com.
   San Francisco, CA 94123. San Francisco, South, 2269 Chestnut St., #270. Phone: (415) 924-2515. Fax: (415) 924-2649. E-mail: RTMcK2515@cs.com. Tom McKinley, dir.
   Colorado Springs, CO 80906-1073. Colorado Springs, CO, 2910 Electra Drive. Phone: (719) 630-3111. Fax: (719) 630-1871. E-mail: jbmccoy@adelphia.net. Jody McCoy, dir.
   St. Simons Island, GA 31522. St. Simons Island, GA, 507 Ocean Blvd., Ste. 201-5. Phone: (912) 634-6575. Fax: (912) 634-5770. E-mail: edwesser@bellsouth.net. Eddie Esserman, assoc.
   Overland Park, KS 66209. Kansas City, KS, 5225 W. 122nd Street. Phone: (913) 498-0040. Fax: (913) 498-0041. E-mail: 75767.3151@compuserve.com. Bill Lytle, dir.
   Providence, RI 02903. Providence, RI, 170 Westminster St., Suite 701. Phone: (401) 454-3130. Fax: (401) 454-3131. E-mail: scs@scsloan.com. Stephan Sloan, assoc; Ted Clark, analyst.
   Greenville, SC 29607. Greenville, SC, 100 Tower Drive, Unit 4, Box 9. Phone: (864) 233-9530. Fax: (864) 233-9565. E-mail: smknob@cs.com. Scott Knoblauch, assoc.
   Richardson, TX 75080. Dallas, TX, 1131 Rockingham Dr, Suite 209. Phone: (972) 231-4500. Fax: (972) 231-4509. E-mail: whitelytx@cs.com. Bill Whitley, dir.
   Logan, UT 84341. Salt Lake City, 1289 North 1500 East. Phone: (435) 753-8090. Fax: (435) 753-2980. E-mail: ggm@cache.net. Greg Merrill, dir.
   One of the nation's leading full service Media Brokerage, Valuation and Consulting firms with in-depth industry knowledge and market expertise.

Media Venture Partners, 2 Jackson St., Suite 100, San Francisco, CA 94111. Phone: (415) 391-4877. Web Site: www.mediaventurepartners.com. Elliot B. Evers, mgng dir; Charles E. Giddens, mgng dir; Greg D. Widroe, mgng dir; Jason D. Hill, VP; Brian E. Cobb, mgng dir.
   Radio & TV brokerage svcs; mergers & acquisitions; telecom; investment banking.

Mitchell & Associates, 7308 Old River Dr., Shreveport, LA 71105. Phone: (318) 798-7816. Fax: (318) 798-6084. Fax: (318) 797-5987. John Mitchell, pres.
   Media brokers, appraisers, consultants.

Montcalm, Box 4608, Rolling Bay, WA 98061-0608. Phone: (206) 780-1700. Fax: (206) 842-7151. E-mail: jerden@aol.com. Jerry Dennon, pres.
   Radio & TV brokerage svcs, mergers & acquisitions, & investment banking.

George Moore & Associates Inc., 6918 Wildglen Dr., Suite 100 W, Dallas, TX 75230. Phone: (214) 369-5665. Fax: (214) 369-5667. W. James Moore, pres.
   Brokerage of radio & TV; asset & market appraisals prepared for owners, buyers & lenders.

Gordon P. Moul & Associates Inc., Box 42, York Haven, PA 17370. Phone: (717) 266-4212. Fax: (717) 266-0780. Gordon Moul, pres/CEO.
   Bcst broker & consultant. Specializing in East Coast AM-FM & TV.

MyMediaBroker.com, 407 Broadmoor Acres, Portales, NM 88130. Phone: (505) 356-2000. Fax: (505) 356-2003. E-mail: Sandi@mymediabroker.com. Web Site: www.mymediabroker.com. Sandi Bergman, pres.
   Full service media brokerage firm.

New England Media L.L.C., Box 594, Willimantic, CT 06226. Phone: (860) 456-1111. Fax: (860) 456-9501. E-mail: mcrice@prodigy.net.com. Web Site: www.expage.com/pagenemedia. Michael C. Rice, mgng ptnr.
   Mansfield Center, CT 06250, 50 Kaya Lane. Phone: (860) 455-1414. Michael Rice, mgng ptnr.
   Media brokers, consultants & appraisers specializing in radio in the Northeast.

O'Grady & Associates, 8431 Sabal Palm Ct., Vero Beach, FL 32963-4296. Phone: (772) 234-4177. Fax: (772) 231-9819. E-mail: jfogjr@juno.com. James F. O'Grady, pres.
   Confidential media brokerage svcs, consultants & appraisals.

Patrick Communications L.L.C. 5074 Dorsey Hall Dr., Suite 205, Ellicott City, MD 21042. Phone: (410) 740-0250. Fax: (410) 740-7222. E-mail: patrick@patcomm.com. Web Site: www.patcomm.com. Larry Patrick, pres.
   Stn brokerage, investment banking, mgmt consulting svcs, appraisals & opns consulting.

John Pierce & Company L.L.C., 11 Spiral Dr., Suite 3, Florence, KY 41042. Phone: (859) 647-0101. Fax: (859) 647-2616. E-mail: jpierce@johnpierceco.com. Web Site: www.johnpierceco.com.
   Radio, TV, & cable sls & appraisals.

Questcom Media Brokerage Inc., 10925 David Taylor Dr., Suite 100, Charlotte, NC 28262. Phone: (704) 948-9800. Fax: (704) 948-9888. E-mail: drbussell@aol.com. Donald R. Bussell, pres.
   Radio & TV stn brokerage specialists concentrating in top 150 markets; offering assistance with mergers & consolidations. Registered FDIC & RTC broker/appraiser.

Stan Raymond & Associates Inc., Box 8231, Longboat Key, FL 34228. Phone: (941) 383-9404. Fax: (941) 383-9132. E-mail: StnRay@aol.com. Stan Raymond, pres.
   Financial svcs, media brokers, appraisers & consultants specializing in the Southeast.

Gordon Rice Associates, Box 20398, Charleston, SC 29413. Phone: (843) 884-3590. Fax: (843) 881-0358. E-mail: gordon@gordonriceassociates.com. Gordon Rice, broker.
   Brokerage svcs, appraisals & investment analysis for radio & TV.

Riley Representatives, 240 Lakeland Dr., Highland Village, TX 75077. Phone: (972) 966-1715. Fax: (972) 966-1015. Jack Riley, owner.

Roehling Broadcast Services Ltd., 7340 Oak Knoll Dr., Indianapolis, IN 46217. Phone: (317) 887-1945. Fax: (317) 887-1947. E-mail: edradiobr@aol.com. Web Site: roehlingbroadcast.com. Edward W. Roehling, pres; Sandra Roehling, VP & treas.
   Broadcast appraisers, brokers, consultants, financing negotiators, also narration of audio and video.

Ray H. Rosenblum, Media Broker / Appraiser / Consultant, Box 38296, Pittsburgh, PA 15238. Phone: (412) 362-6311. Fax: (412) 362-6317. Ray H. Rosenblum, pres.
   Media brokering, appraising, financing & consulting for radio & TV stns in 50 states plus territories.

Rumbaut & Company, 1060 Stillwater Dr., Tower Suites, Miami Beach, FL 33141-1024. Phone: (305) 868-0000. Fax: (305) 868-7000. E-mail: julio@rumbaut.com. Web Site: www.rumbaut.com. Julio Rumbaut, pres.
   Media brokers & consultants in all facets of the TV & radio industries.

Sailors & Associates, 150 Executive Center Dr., Suite 4, Box 67, Greenville, SC 29615. Phone: (864) 297-0530. Fax: (864) 297-0595. Don F. Sailors, owner.
   Media brokerage & specializing in radio, TV & cable.

SalesGroup, 41 Herbert Rd., Boston, MA 02184-5507. Phone: (781) 848-4201. Fax: (781) 848-4715. E-mail: salesgroup@beld.net. Harold Bausemer, pres.
   Stn brokers, Northeast.

Satterfield & Perry Inc., 7211 Fourth Ave. S., St. Petersburg, FL 33707. Phone: (727) 345-7338. Fax: (727) 345-3809. Bob Austin, pres.
   Wetumpka, AL 36093, 169 Mountain Meadows La. Phone: (334) 514-2241. Fax: (334) 514-2291. Ken Hawkins, VP.
   Denver, CO 80215-7067, 3062 Robb Cir. Phone: (303) 239-6670. Fax: (303) 231-9562. Al Perry, chmn emeritus.
   Littleton, CO 80120, 7420 S. Curtice Ct. Phone: (720) 283-7980. Fax: (720) 283-7980.
   Coos Bay, OR 97420, PO Box 362. Phone: (541) 751-0043. Fax: (541) 751-0043. Dick McMahon, VP.
   Overland Park, KS 66207, 4918 W. 101st Terr. Phone: (913) 649-5103. Fax: (913) 649-5103. Douglas Stephens, sr VP.
   Aiken, SC 29803, 131 Inwood Dr. Phone: (803) 649-0031. Fax: (803) 649-7786. John Willis, VP.
   Radio & TV broker, mgmt & sls consultant, FDIC-approved appraiser & expert witness.

John W. Saunders, Media Broker, 1207 Woodhollow Dr., Suite 3101, Houston, TX 77057. Phone: (713) 789-4222. Fax: (713) 789-4322. E-mail: theradiobroker@aol.com. Web Site: www.theradiobroker.com. John W. Saunders, owner.
   Nationwide radio brokerage & appraisals. Buyers or sellers represented on a confidential, professional & personal basis. Top 10 to small markets.

Serafin Bros. Inc., Box 262888, Tampa, FL 33685. Phone: (813) 885-6060. Fax: (813) 885-6857. E-mail: gserafin@compuserve.com. Glenn Serafin, pres.
   Tampa, FL 33615, 4212 Deepwater Ln.
   Bcst brokerage, finance & valuation svcs.

Burt Sherwood & Associates Inc., 6415 Midnight Pass Rd., Suite 206, Sarasota, FL 34242. Phone: (941) 349-2165. Fax: (941) 312-0974. E-mail: BOHICA1@comcast.net. Burt Sherwood, pres; Ellen Lyle, VP; Jason Sherwood, VP.
   Brokerage radio, TV & LPTV; appraisals.

Barry Skidelsky, Esq., 185 E. 85th St., 23D, New York, NY 10028. Phone: (212) 832-4800. Barry Skidelsky.
   Acquisitions, divestitures, mergers, time brokerage, financing.

Snowden Associates, Box 1966, One Commerce Sq., Suite 200, Washington, NC 27889. Phone: (252) 940-1680. Fax: (252) 940-1682. E-mail: zophsnowden@earthlink.net. C. Zoph Potts, chmn; Ray Bergevin, pres.
   Brokers, consultants & appraisers to the bcst industry in the Southeast.

Howard E. Stark, 575 Madison Ave., 10th Fl., New York, NY 10022. Phone: (212) 355-0405. Howard E. Stark, pres.
   Media broker; mergers & acquisitions in the communications field.

John D. Stebbins Co., Box 30, Lake Forest, IL 60045. Phone: (847) 234-4534. John D. Stebbins, pres.
   Represents sellers & buyers in the bcst media. Financing.

Gary Stevens & Co., 49 Locust Ave., Suite 107, New Canaan, CT 06840. Phone: (203) 966-6465. Fax: (203) 966-6522. E-mail: deelmakur@aol.com. Gary Stevens, pres.
   Bcst mergers, acquisitions, investment banking svcs.

Stonemark Inc., Box 21305, Seattle, WA 98111. Phone: (206) 343-7777. Fax: (206) 628-0839. E-mail: info@stonemark.net. Web Site: www.stonemark.net. William V. May, pres.
   Specializing in business brokerage, acquisition searches, capital arrangement & debt placement for bcst properties as well as other industries.

The Thorburn Co., 6625 Hwy. 53 E., Suite 410-72, Dawsonville, GA 30534. Phone: (678) 513-1363. Fax: (678) 513-1615. E-mail: thorburnco@aol.com. Web Site: www.thorburncompany.com. Robert M. Thorburn, pres.
   Appraisals, brokerage, & financial & mgmt consulting for radio, TV & cable.

Station and Cable System Brokers

Van Huss Media Services, Inc., 4239 Heyward Pl., Indianapolis, IN 46250. Phone: (317) 813-0106. Fax: (317) 813-0107. E-mail: vanhussmediaservices@aol.com. William "Bill" Van Huss, pres.

Brokerage, financial consulting & appraisals for radio, TV & cable.

The Venture Group, 415 Discovery Rd., Virginia Beach, VA 23451. Phone: (757) 491-5444. Fax: (757) 422-0727. E-mail: hhurst@hrfn.net. Herbert M. Hurst, pres.

Intermediaries in the sale, merger & acquisition of radio & TV stns.

Ed Walters & Associates, Box 3697, Barrington, IL 60011. Phone: (847) 304-8993. Fax: (847) 359-6167. E-mail: radiobroker@msn.com. Web Site: www.edwaltersandassoc.com. Ed Walters, pres; Michael Walters, VP; Karrol Walters, sec.

Waukesha, WI 53186, 1801 Coral D. Phone: (414) 544-6800. Fax: (414) 544-1705. Ed Walters, pres.

Nationwide brokers, specializing in radio-TV & cable systems, acquisition searches with confidentiality ensured.

The Whittle Agency, 12716 Lindley Dr., Raleigh, NC 27614. Phone: (919) 848-3596. Fax: (919) 848-0519. E-mail: thewhittleagency@mindspring.com. Gary L. Whittle, pres.

Total media brokerage svcs, including sls/appraisals of radio stns in the Carolinas, Virginia & Southeast.

Willis Broadcasting, 645 Church St., Suite 400, Norfolk, VA 23510. Phone: (757) 624-6500. Fax: (757) 624-6515. L. E. Willis Sr., pres.

Wood & Co. Inc., 431 Ohio Pike, Suite 200 N, Cincinnati, OH 45255. Phone: (513) 528-7373. Fax: (513) 528-7374. Larry C. Wood, pres.

Nationwide brokerage service to buyers & sellers of TV & radio properties.

Management and Marketing Consultants

AVI Communications Inc., 6200 W. Northwest Hwy., Suite 253 D, Dallas, TX 75225. Phone: (214) 637-5464. Fax: (214) 637-6285. E-mail: avi@avi-communications.com. Web Site: www.avi-communications.com. Patrick Shaughnessy, pres/CEO.
TV sls training, new business dev svcs & Butch Harmon golf tips for TV & radio.

Abt Associates Inc., 55 Wheeler St., Cambridge, MA 02138. Phone: (617) 492-7100. Fax: (617) 492-5219. Web Site: www.abtassoc.com. Peg Laplan, pres/CEO.
Washington, DC 20005, 1110 Vermont Ave. N.W. Phone: (202) 263-1800. (202) 263-1801.
Chicago, IL 60610, 640 N. LaSalle. Phone: (312) 867-4000. Fax: (312) 867-4200.
Bethesda, MD 20814, 4800 Montgomery Ln, Suite 600. Phone: (301) 913-0500. Fax: (301) 652-3618.
Mktg rsch, strategic planning, mgmt consulting, audience rsch & segmentation; customer satisfaction programs, quality of service programs, social science survey rsch, pub policy rsch, economical rsch.

John P. Allen Airspace Consultants Inc., 290 Marsh Lakes Dr., Fernandina Beach, FL 32034. Phone: (904) 261-6523. Fax: (904) 277-3651. E-mail: maryjpa@bellsouth.net. Web Site: johnpallenairspace.com. Mary C. Lowe, pres.
Conducts FAA aeronautical evaluations as specified in Subpart C of Part 77 of the Federal Aviation Regulations.

American Radio Brokers Inc./SFO, Cathedral Hill Hotel Office Bldg., 1255 Post St., Suite 1011, San Francisco, CA 94109. Phone: (415) 441-3377. Fax: (415) 441-3738. Chester P. Coleman, pres; Richard Julio Haskey, tech dir; Warren Earl, consultant.
Anchorage, AK 99507. c/o KABN, KAXX, KADX-FM Radio Facilities, 2509 Eide St, Suite 6. Phone: (907) 277-5652. Fax: (907) 344-5728. Susan Richards, dir Alaskan opns.
Stn reviews, mgmt consulting, valuations, market analysis & assistance for new, nonbcst owners. Duopolies & group strategies for the new millennium.

Anderson Productions Ltd., 37 W. 20th St., Suite 904, New York, NY 10011. Phone: (212) 414-9220. Fax: (212) 206-0279. E-mail: andersontv@aol.com. Steven C.F. Anderson, pres & exec producer.
TV program production & consulting firm specializing in info progmg for cable & bcstg TV.

Nick Anthony & Associates Inc., 1795 W. Market St., Akron, OH 44313. Phone: (330) 864-2268. Fax: (330) 864-2261. E-mail: nick@nickanthony.com. Web Site: www.nickanthony.com. Nick Anthony, pres; Diane Agnesi, office mgr.
Mktg, progmg & motivational consultant.

The Aspen Institute Communications & Society Program, 1 Dupont Circle N.W., Suite 700, Washington, DC 20036. Phone: (202) 736-5818. Fax: (202) 467-0790. E-mail: firestone@aspeninstitute.org. Web Site: www.aspeninstitute.org/c&s. Charles M. Firestone, exec dir; Patricia K. Kelly, asst dir.
Pub policy seminars & reports.

Associated Broadcasters, Inc., Box 42566, Cincinnati, OH 45242. Phone: (513) 791-5982. Fax: (513) 891-5727. Irv Schwartz, mngng dir; R. Galen, rsch admin.
Legal & filing svcs in turnkey packages; consulting & appraisal svcs available.
Ohio Broadcast Properties Specialists.

Audience Research & Development (AR&D), 8828 Stemmons Fwy., Suite 500, Dallas, TX 75247. Phone: (214) 630-5097. Fax: (214) 630-4951. Web Site: www.ar-d.com. Willis Duff, CEO; Jim Willi, pres.
Rsch-based, full-svc, new media consulting firm serving TV stns, cable systems, internet companies, nwsprs & program syndicators.

The Austin Company 6095 Parkland Blvd., Cleveland, OH 44124. Phone: (440) 544-2600. Fax: (440) 544-2690. E-mail: broadcastgroup@theaustin.com. Web Site: www.theaustin.com. Michael G. Pierce, sr VP sls & mktg; Patrick B. Flanagan, pres/COO.
Other Branches: Atlanta, GA; Cleveland, OH; Kansas City, MO; Irvine, CA.
Consulting, architectural design, engrg & construction svcs for TV, cable & radio bcstg facilities.

AZCAR, 121 Hillpointe Dr., Suite 700, Canonsburg, PA 15317. Phone: (724) 873-0800. Fax: (724) 873-4770. Richard Bisignano, pres; Mary Nahra, VP.
Video & audio system consultation, systems integration, design, instal & training; serving cable systems, cable mfg, corporate, bcst & teleproduction facilities & engineering.

BIA Financial Network, 15120 Enterprise Ct., Suite 100, Chantilly, VA 20151. Phone: (703) 818-2425. Fax: (703) 803-3299. E-mail: pubs@bia.com. Web Site: www.bia.com. Thomas J. Buono, chmn/CEO; Mark Giannini, VP; Mark Fratrik, VP.
Financial & strategic consultants to communications industries offering fair market valuations, expert tax appraisals, due diligence, acquisition consulting, business plans, internal operational audits, litigation support, investment banking, venture funding, capital, industry research & analysis publications & software.

BTMI (Broadcast Trustee Management Inc.), 1090 Vermont Ave. N.W., Suite 800, Washington, DC 20005. Phone: (202) 408-7036. Fax: (202) 408-1590. E-mail: Probinson@aol.cin. Web Site: www.btmi.com.
Financial-asset mgmt, valuation, mktg, restructuring & recovery consultation svcs.

The John Bayliss Broadcast Foundation, Box 51126, Pacific Grove, CA 93950. Phone: (831) 655-5229. Fax: (831) 655-5228. E-mail: khfranke@baylissfoundation.org. Web Site: www.baylissfoundation.org. Kit Hunter Franke, exec dir; Carl Butrum, pres.
Bayliss Radio Roast proceeds & individual donations to the scholarship fund are awarded to college students desiring a radio career. Contact foundation for more information & an application form.

The Benchmark Co., 907 S. Congress, Suite 207, Austin, TX 78701-1700. Phone: (512) 707-7500. E-mail: Benchmark@aol.com. Web Site: www.Benchmarkresearch.com. Rob Balon, pres.
Full-svc bcst consulting & rsch company featuring benchmark perceptual phone surveys & the Focus 100 system, which replaces focus groups.

The Benton Group, Box 5076, Vancouver, WA 98668. Phone: (360) 574-7369. Fax: (360) 576-6866. Web Site: www.thebentongroup.net. Donald Benton, pres.
Yellow-page & nwspr conversion, specialized sls training programs & seminars.

Beveridge Institute of Sales & Sales Management, 113 North Grant St., Barringto, IL 60010. Phone: (847) 381-7797. Phone: (800) 227-4332. Fax: (847) 381-7301. Web Site: www.beveridgeinc.com.
Sls & sls mgmt performance & productivity improvement programs; training workshops.

Big Blue Dot, 63 Pleasant St., Watertown, MA 02472. Phone: (617) 923-2583. Fax: (617) 923-8014. E-mail: bigbluedot@bigblue.com. Web Site: www.bigblue.com. Jan Craige Singer, pres.
Trend tracking resources for the kids' market, consulting, & newsletter via e-mail; creative svcs.

Blackburn & Co. Inc., 201 N. Union St., Suite 340, Alexandria, VA 22314. Phone: (703) 519-3703. Fax: (703) 519-9756. James W. Blackburn Jr., chmn; Richard F. Blackburn, pres.
Acquisition svcs of all kinds including appraisals, brokerage & financing for radio & TV stations and communications towers.

Blair Productions, Box 42513, Washington, DC 20015. Phone: (202) 364-1019. Fax: (202) 363-5524.
Full-svc mgmt & financial counseling to the bcst industry with emphasis on radio turnarounds, problems & start-ups; investment banking service.

Mark Blinoff Inc., 1837 S.E. Harold St., Portland, OR 97202-4932. Phone: (503) 232-9787. Phone: (800) 929-5119. Fax: (503) 232-9787. Fax: (800) 929-5119. E-mail: acmrl@myexcel.com. Mark Blinoff, gen mgr; Eric Norberg, progmg VP.
Consulting firm for radio bcstrs, including sls dev, mgmt training & progmg.

Block Communications Group Inc., 2910 Neilson Way, Suite 503, Santa Monica, CA 90405-5368. Phone: (310) 452-3355. Fax: (310) 452-4077. E-mail: dblock@earthlink.net. Web Site: www.blockcommunicationsgroup.com. Richard C. Block, pres.
Consultants specializing in new cable svcs, bcstg stns, syndicated progmg, distribution & mktg serving U.S. & international clients since 1974.

Bond & Pecaro Inc. 1920 N St. N.W., Suite 350, Washington, DC 20036. Phone: (202) 775-8870. Fax: (202) 775-0175. E-mail: bp@bondpecaro.com. Web Site: www.bondpecaro.com. James R. Bond Jr, dir; Timothy S. Pecaro, principals; John S. Sanders, principals; Jeffrey P. Anderson, principals.
Economic and financial consulting, valuation studies, asset allocations, appraisals, feasibility studies, fairness opinions, Internet valuations, expert testimony.

Bortz Media & Sports Group, 4582 S. Ulster St., Ste 1450, Denver, CO 80237. Phone: (303) 893-9902. Fax: (303) 893-9913. E-mail: info@bortz.com. Web Site: www.bortz.com. James M. Trautman, mgng dir; Mark C. Wyche, mgng dir; Stephen B. Lehan, sr VP; Brian Broderick, VP; Dean Ericson, sr VP.
TV stn mgmt consulting, cable financial & market analysis; corporate strategic planning.

Frank Boyle & Co., L.L.C., 24 Stag Ln., Greenwich, CT 06831. Phone: (203) 661-8879. Phone: (203) 969-2020. Fax: (203) 316-0800. E-mail: fboylebrkr@aol.com. Frank Boyle, pres; Mary C. Downey, VP opns.
Radio & TV media brokerage, mergers & acquisitions/appraisals.

Broad Street Communications, L.L.C., 37 Tower Rd., Riverside, CT 06878. Phone: (203) 637-4605. Fax: (203) 637-4605. E-mail: daddick37@aol.com. Richard L. Geismar, pres.
Financial & mgmt consulting for bcst industries, electronic communications.

Broadcast Media Associates, Box 1233, Santa Maria, CA 93456. Phone: (805) 937-1553. Fax: (805) 937-1553. Web Site: broadcastmediabroker.com. Clifford M. Hunter, pres.
Mgmt consulting, mktg studies, bcst investment analysis.

Broadcast Services Inc., Box 6418, Brattleboro, VT 05302-6418. Phone: (802) 258-3000. Phone: (802) 258-4500 svc. Fax: (802) 258-2500. E-mail: mh@markhutchins.com. Web Site: www.markhutchins.com. Mark F. Hutchins, pres.
Predicted-coverage mapping, signal-improvement studies, interference mitigation, satellite & microwave facilities inter-connection, RF radiation safety/compliance.

Broadcasting Asset Management Corp., 1323 Forest Glen Dr. N., Winnetka, IL 60093. Phone: (847) 446-8882. Fax: (847) 446-4855. Jack Minkow, pres.
Merger & feasibility studies; acquisition analyses; capital structuring, brokerage, mgmt procurement & consulting; sr, subordinated & equity placement.

Broadcasting Unlimited Inc., 35 Main St., Wayland, MA 01778. Phone: (508) 653-7200. Fax: (508) 653-4088. E-mail: jwilliams@dmrinteractive.com. Jay Williams Jr., pres; Kathy O'Neill, asst.
Strategic planning & execution of direct mktg, telemarketing, & e-marketing promotion svcs for radio bcstr.

Broward Alliance, 300 S.E. 2nd St., Suite 780, Fort Lauderdale, FL 33301-2248. Phone: (954) 524-3127. Phone: (800) 741-1420. Fax: (954) 524-3167. E-mail: info@browardalliance.org. Web Site: www.browardalliance.org/film. Elizabeth Wentworth, film commissioner.
Resource for film, TV & print industry production and business relocation.

Broadcasting & Cable Yearbook 2006

Management and Marketing Consultants

Howard Burkat Communications, 16 Drake Rd., Scarsdale, NY 10583. Phone: (914) 723-2657. E-mail: hburkat@burkat.com.

Sls, mktg & mgmt consulting for TV, cable, radio, domestic & international. Planning analysis, research & recruiting.

Kent Burkhart's Office Inc., Box 345, Key Biscayne, FL 33149. Phone: (305) 361-5035. Phone: (305) 439-8871. Fax: (305) 361-0650. E-mail: radiokent@aol.com. Kent Burkhart, chmn.

Media consultant to radio stns & networks, the Internet, cable TV, & audio & product mktg. LMA liaisons & negotiators.

Alan Burns & Associates, 11705 Sumacs St., Oakton, VA 22124. Phone: (703) 648-0000. Fax: (703) 264-1710. Web Site: www.burnsradio.com.

Progmg & mktg consultants.

CLC Consulting, 9519 Mount Vernon Landing, Alexandria, VA 22309. Phone: (703) 799-8000. Web Site: www.communcationlaw.org. Chase Libbey, consultant.

Cable Audit Associates Inc., 5340 So. Quebec St., Ste 100, Greenwood Village, CO 80111. Phone: (303) 694-0444. Fax: (303) 694-2559. E-mail: blazarus@cableaudit.com. Bruce N. Lazarus, CEO.

Progmg license fee audits of cable operators, MMDS, SMATVs & TVRO middlemen.

Carolina Media Professionals Inc., Box 3325, Spartanburg, SC 29304. Phone: (864) 597-1301. Fax: (864) 596-7539. E-mail: rachel@upstate.net. Web Site: www.carolinamedia.com.

Specializes in the placement of national advertising through radio, television for products, services and programs. Print: national advertising. Production: audio and video.

Cashdollar Inc., 4409 W. Kings Row, Muncie, IN 47304. Phone: (765) 254-1564.

Sls training, sls seminars & consulting advisory svcs.

The Center for Sales Strategy, (formerly NewCity Associates Inc.). 610 W. DeLeon St., Tampa, FL 33606-2720. Phone: (813) 254-2222. Fax: (813) 254-9222. Web Site: www.csscenter.com. Steve Marx, chmn; John Henley, exec VP; Jim Prain, sr VP; Alan Farr, rsch dir.

Comprehensive consulting & training svcs for radio & TV, cable, and newspaper, in sls, mktg & mgmt, exclusively on a long-term, multi-year basis.

Chenevert Songy Rodi Soderberg, (An Engineering/Architectural Corp.). 6767 Perkins Rd., Suite 200, Baton Rouge, LA 70808. Phone: (225) 769-0546. Fax: (225) 767-0060. E-mail: csrs@csrsonline.com. Web Site: www.csrsonline.com.

Architects, planners & tech designers specializing in new & renovated bcst/cable production facilities.

Christian TV Services, 18 Elizabeth St., P.O. Box 209, Ellicottville, NY 14731-0209. Phone: (716) 699-2549. Fax: (716) 699-2590. E-mail: george@christianservices.com. Web Site: www.christiantvservices.com. Russ Thayer, prom; Roger A. Thayer, progmg; Randy Thayer, production mgr.

TVRO consultant for Christian media started: 1974; affil: TBN/TCT/CTS ministering to Ministries, listing media links & Internet places of worship. (800) 982-8823.

Christian Television Services, 6538 Collins Ave., Miami Beach, FL 33141. Phone: (305) 867-3250. Fax: (305) 867-3251. E-mail: media@russ.com. Russell Thorne, CEO.

Religious media buying.

Chubb Group of Insurance Companies, 15 Mountain View Rd., Warren, NJ 07059. Phone: (908) 903-3354. Fax: (908) 903-2027. E-mail: info@chubb.com. Web Site: www.chubb.com.

Endorsed multi-national property/casualty carrier by the Broadcast Financial Managers Assns.

Branches in more than 115 offices in 30 countries.

Claritas Inc., 1525 Wilson Blvd., Suite 1000, Arlington, VA 22209. Phone: (703) 812-2700. Fax: (703) 812-2701. Web Site: www.claritas.com.

Chicago, IL 60604-4302, 332 S. Michigan Ave, Suite 200. Phone: (312) 986-2650. Margie Lymperis, VP electronic media.

Mktg data, software & consulting designed for cable, TV, radio & other new media companies.

Clark-Mann & Associates, 203 Columbus Ave., San Francisco, CA 94133. Phone: (415) 421-0220. Fax: (415) 421-0417. E-mail: wclarkmannz@msn.net.

London WIR 51A, 500 Chesham House, 150 Regent St. Phone: (071) 439-6228. Fax: (071) 734-4166. William D. Clark, pres.

Full-svc adv agency & PR firm with background in bcst & print.

Clear Channel Satellite, 7042 South Revere Parkway, Suite 450, Centennial, CO 80112. Phone: (303) 925-1708. Fax: (303) 209-0001. E-mail: sales@clearchannelsatellite.com. Web Site: www.clearchannelsatellite.com. Don Harms, gen mgr.

Satellite Space-time; Audio Distribution via Satellite; WAN Protection Services; DSNG Services; Satellite Equipment Sales; Satellite Installation Services.

Cole & Bowman, LLC, 800 Third St., Suite140, Herndon, VA 20170. Phone: (703) 471-2177. Fax: (703) 471-5075. E-mail: pbowman@colebowman.com. David Cole, ptnr; Peter Bowman, ptnr.

Appraisals, asset allocations, specialized studies.

Colombia Management Advisors, One S. Wacker Dr., Chicago, IL 60606. Phone: (312) 443-4000. Fax: (312) 855-2552. William Rarkin, pres.

Investment counsel & mutual fund mgmt. Offices in Chicago, IL; Cleveland, OH; New York, NY; San Francisco, CA; & Puerto Rico.

Colorado Springs Film Commission, 515 S. Cascade Ave., Colorado Springs, CO 80903. Fax: (719) 635-4968. E-mail: eforeman@filmcoloradosprings.com. Web Site: www.filmcoloradosprings.com. Edwina A. Foreman, fillm coord.

Free location svcs, Production Resource Guide, location guide available for the Colorado Springs, CO area; help with crews, hotels & permits.

Coltrin & Associates Inc., 1212 Ave. of the Americas, 10th Fl., New York, NY 10036. Phone: (212) 221-1616. Fax: (212) 221-7718. E-mail: steve_coltrin@coltrin.com. Web Site: www.coltrin.com.

Yardley, PA 19067, 801 Floral Vale Blvd. Phone: (215) 497-3188. Gwen Coltrin, COO.

Singapore 048623 Indonesia, 50 Raffles Pl. Phone: +65 6320 8358. Chan Chee Pong, VP.

London W1J0DW United Kingdom, 35 Picadilly, 3rd Fl. Phone: +44 20 7494 4748.

BOND & PECARO

PROVIDING APPRAISALS, FEASIBILITY STUDIES,

EXPERT TESTIMONY, AND RELATED FINANCIAL SERVICES

TO THE COMMUNICATIONS INDUSTRY.

1920 N Street, N.W.

Suite 350

Washington, D.C. 20036

(202) 775-8870 • FAX (202) 775-0175

email: bp@bondpecaro.com • www.bondpecaro.com

Burlingame, CA 94010, 433 Airport Blvd, Suite 432. Phone: (650) 373-2005. Benoit Rungeard, dir. (San Francisco office).

Celebration, FL 344747, 215 Celebration Pl, Suite 500. Phone: (321) 559-1112.

Salt Lake City, UT 84111, 215 S. State St, Suite 675. Phone: (801) 350-9412.

Consultant svcs to bcst mgmt, mktg sls, promotional rsch; New York, NY, & Washington, DC representation in corporate, govt & PR.

ComBridges, 754 Sir Francis Drake Blvd., San Anselmo, CA 94960. Phone: (415) 454-5505. Fax: (415) 454-1941. E-mail: info@Combridges.com. Web Site: www.combridges.com.

Complete creative & production svcs including: animation, special effects, video production & video streaming, web site design, & computer-based production system design. Experience with creative service departments & corporate communications.

CommNOW, 15 Random Farm Rd., Chappaqua, NY 10514. Phone: (203) 440-3636. Web Site: www.commnow.com. Robert Daigle, VP mktg & VP sls.

Telecommunications, high-technology, mkt. research.

Communication Trends Inc., 5871 Glenridge Dr., Suite 300, Atlanta, GA 30328. Phone: (404) 843-8717. Fax: (404) 843-6869. Toni Dwyer, chmn/CEO; Arthur A. Dwyer, pres/COO; Elizabeth Maury, VP/business mgr.

Mktg & adv for cable, direct bcst, & bcst communications industries & related technologies.

Communications Design Associates Inc., 1410 Providence Hwy., Norwood, MA 02062. Phone: (781) 551-8490. Fax: (781) 551-8491. Web Site: www.cdaconsultants.com.

Independent consultants to radio, TV, corp & govt clients. Designers of studios, production, presentation & multi-media facilities.

Communications Equity Associates, LLC, 101 E. Kennedy Blvd., Suite 3300, Tampa, FL 33602. Phone: (813) 226-8844. Fax: (813) 225-1513. Web Site: www.ceaworldwide.com.

London W1M OBQ, 33 Cavendish Sq. Phone: 44-207-647-7700. Fax: 44-207-647-7710. E-mail: london@cea-europe.com.

Madrid 28006, Serrano 93, 6E. Phone: 34-91-745 13 13. Fax: 34-91-563 38 62. E-mail: madrid@cea-europe.com.

Munich D-80538, Prinzregentenstrasse 56. Phone: 49-(0)89-290 725 0. Fax: 49-(0)89-290 725 200. Dr. Stephan Goetz, exec VP international opns/mgng dir.

Paris 75008, 9, Rue Royale. Phone: 33 153 308607. Fax: 33 142 42 3214. Frank Portais, mgng dir.

Tampa, FL 33602, 101 E. Kennedy Blvd. Phone: (813) 226-8844. Fax: (813) 225-1513.

Praha 1 110 00 Czech Republic, Melantrichova 17. Phone: 420-2-216-32451. Fax: 420-2-242 29 412. E-mail: prague@cea-europe.com. Vaclav Matatko, mgng dir CEA Prague.

Westport, CT 06880, 191 Post Rd W. Phone: (203) 221-2662. Fax: (203) 221-2663. E-mail: dmoyer@ceaworldwide.com. Dave Moyer, mgng dir-CEA Principal Advisors.

Miami, FL 33131, 150 S.E. 2nd Ave. Phone: (305) 810-2740. Fax: (305) 810-2741. Scot Fischer, mgng dir.

New York, NY 10020, 1270 Ave of the Americas, Suite 1818. Phone: (212) 218-5085. Fax: (212) 218-5099.

Wayne, PA 19087, 997 Old Eagle School Rd, Suite 219. Phone: (610) 341-9300. Fax: (610) 341-1920. Tony Parisi, VP communications div.

Provides investment banking, brokerage, regulatory affrs & mgmt svcs for bcst, CATV & related communications industries.

Communications Resources Inc., 152 West 57th St., 46th Fl, New York, NY 10019. Phone: (212) 277-5670. Fax: (212) 245-3456. E-mail: ebgibbs@crimediapartners.com. Ellen Berland Gibbs, pres.

Strategic planning & financial consulting to bcst, cable & nwspr companies, including merger & acquisition, investment banking & investment mgmt.

Comsearch, 19700 Janelia Farm Blvd., Ashburn, VA 20147. Phone: (703) 726-5500. Fax: (703) 726-5600. E-mail: info@comsearch.com. Web Site: www.comsearch.com. Douglass R. Hall, pres.

Provides frequency coord, site selection, RFI measurements, path surveys, protection for satellite earth stn dishes & terrestrial microwave facilities & wireless engrg svcs & data.

Conley & Associates, LLC, 1459 Interstate Loop, Bismarck, ND 58503-5560. Phone: (701) 222-3902. Fax: (701) 222-4815. E-mail: info@conleyassociates.net. Web Site: www.conleyassociates.net. Christopher J. Conley, gen ptnr; Candace Christianson, gen ptnr.

Consultants in the areas of strategic planning, appraisals, finance, opns, engrg, mktg, human resources & pub/govt rel.

Connecticut Film Video & Media Office, 805 Brook St., Bldg 4, Rocky Hill, CT 06067 3405. Phone: (800) 392-2122. Phone: (860) 571-7130. Fax: (860) 721-7088. E-mail: info@ctfilm.com. Web Site: www.CTfilm.com. Guy Ortoleva, exec dir; Judy Schultz, project mgr; Mark Dixon, asst dir.

A film commission eager to respond to any situation or need.

Connelly Co. Inc., 17909 Holly Brook Dr., Tampa, FL 33647-2245. Phone: (813) 991-9494. E-mail: connellyradiotv@verizon.net. Robert J. Connelly, broker; Charlotte A. Connelly, VP; Rob Connelly, broker.

New Market, NH 03857, 198 S. Main St. Phone: (603) 659-3648. Fax: (603) 659-3681. Rob Connelly.

South Effingham, NH 03882, Bailey Rd. Phone: (603) 522-6462. Fax: (603) 522-6348. R.J. Connelly, pres. (Summer only).

Brokers, consultants & recovery units to assist banks & financial institutions.

Consolidated Communications Consultants, 1837 S.E. Harold St., Portland, OR 97202-4932. Phone: (503) 232-9787. Phone: (800) 929-5119. Fax: (503) 232-9787. Fax: (800) 929-5119. E-mail: acmrl@myexcel.com. Web Site: www.acmusicresearch.com. Eric G. Norberg, VP & gen mgr.

Provide progmg, sls & mktg assistance for radio stns (AM mass-appeal, A/C stns a specialty).

Contemporary Communications, 9408 Grand Gate St., Las Vegas, NV 89143. Phone: (702) 898-4669. Fax: (208) 567-6865. E-mail: lfuss@cox.net. Larry G. Fuss, pres.

Progmg, opns & mgmt consulting for small- & medium-market radio stns; tech svcs; FCC compliance; computer software svcs.

Convergent Media Systems, 190 Bluegrass Valley Pky., Suite 800, Alpharetta, GA 30305. Phone: (770) 369-9000. Fax: (770) 369-9100. E-mail: convergent@convergent.com. Web Site: www.convergent.com.

Provider of video & data technologies to support the communication & training needs of companies. Svcs include consultation, design, instal, net & systems mgmt; systems integration in the following areas: special event TV, business TV, desktop video, video production, videoconferencing, & interactive multimedia.

Cox & Cox L.L.C., 2454 Shiva Ct., St. Louis, MO 63011. Phone: (636) 458-4780. Fax: (636) 458-6323. E-mail: bc@coxandcoxllc.com. Web Site: www.coxandcoxllc.com. Bob Cox, pres.

Mergers & acquisitions, appraisals, consulting & expert testimony.

Cross-Country Communications Inc., Box 535, Suffern, NY 10901. Phone: (845) 368-1720. Fax: (845) 368-2012. E-mail: cccomm@aol.com. Web Site: www.cross-country.com. Joe Capobianco, pres.

Strategic planning, business development and new product launches in media/entertainment, production for Radio-TV-Web.

DDS Sales Training, 6904 W. Sagamore Cir., Sioux Falls, SD 57106. Phone: (605) 361-9923. Fax: (605) 361-1828. E-mail: ddssales@sio.mideo.net. Darrell Solberg, pres.

Radio sls training & consulting; mgmt training & consulting; mktg/adv seminars for businesses.

DIS Consulting Corp., 10 Waterside Plaza, #33D, New York, NY 10010-2608. Phone: (212) 213-6872. Fax: (212) 213-6876. E-mail: dougsheer@aol.com. Web Site: www.sheerconsulting.com. Douglas I. Sheer, CEO.

Mktg consultants to 900 equipment manufacturers since 1982. Mktg consultation, business plan writing, financial & market research, mktg & distribution plans.

DST Innovis, 1104 Investment Blvd., Eldorado Hills, CA 95762. Phone: (800) 835-8389. Fax: (916) 934-7054. Web Site: www.dstinnovis.com. Michael McGrail, pres; Robert McKenzie, VP mktg.

North Sydney NSW 2061. CableData (Asia Pacific), Level 4, 44 Miller St, Suite 404. Phone: +61 29.460.2250. Fax: +61 29.460.2238.

Sao Paulo 04571-010. CableData (Latin America), Andar, Suite 81, Ave. Eng Luis Carlos Berrini, 1297. Phone: +55 11.5505.6799. Fax: +55 11.5505.8691.

Customer mgmt & billing solutions for communications & utilities industries. Clients include providers of CATV, telephony, DBS, wireless, electricity, water, gas, waste mgmt, utility & multi-services in over 20 countries.

Daniels & Associates, 3200 Cherry Creek S. Dr., Suite 500, Denver, CO 80209. Phone: (303) 778-5555. Fax: (303) 778-5599. E-mail: www.daniels@online.com. Web Site: www.danielsonline.com. Brian Deevy, chmn/CEO; Brad Busse, pres/COO; Robert Russo, exec VP.

New York, NY 10022, 711 5th Ave, Suite 405. Phone: (212) 935-5900. Fax: (212) 863-4859. Greg Ainsworth, exec VP/sr mgng dir; Robert Russo, exec VP.

Provides both mergers & acquisitions, & corporate financial svcs to the telecommunications industries.

David Tait Appraisal, 1848 Laurel Canyon Rd, Los Angeles, CA 90046-2029. Phone: (323) 654-8420. Fax: (323) 656-1854. E-mail: dta@altavista.net. David Tait, BCBA/MSA; Mel Fineberg, assoc.

Fair market value appraisals of radio/TV/CATV for purchase allocation, finance, estate planning, ESOPs, bankruptcy.

E. Alvin Davis & Associates Inc., 35 Hampton Ln., Cincinnati, OH 45208. Phone: (513) 325-5600. Fax: (513) 272-2303. E-mail: ealvin@ealvin.com. Web Site: www.ealvin.com. E. Alvin Davis, pres; Ted McAllister, VP.

Provides expert counsel to oldies stns.

Direct Mail Express Inc., 2441 Bellevue Ave., Daytona Beach, FL 32114. Phone: (386) 257-2500. Fax: (386) 271-3001. E-mail: tpanaggio@dmenet.com. Web Site: www.dmenet.com.

High-impact, direct-mail campaigns, data base mgmt, audience rsch via cluster-targeted mktg, market exclusive.

Ditingo Media Enterprises, 100 Park Ave., 6th Fl., New York, NY 10017. Phone: (212) 308-8810. Fax: (212) 916-0772. E-mail: vditingo@aol.com. Vincent M. Ditingo, pres.

Media & mktg consulting, training, corporate writing, books, profiles, articles, speeches, news announcements, brochures, web site content & newsletters for bcstg & cable.

Electronicast Corp., 800 S. Claremont St., Suite 105, San Mateo, CA 94402. Phone: (650) 343-1398. Fax: (650) 343-1698. E-mail: mail@electronicast.com. Web Site: www.electronicast.com.

Market forecast consulting concern for the fiber-optic, optoelectronic, telecommunication & CATV industries. Multi-client & custom reports available.

Enterprise Appraisal Co., 489 Devon Park Dr., Suite 320, Wayne, PA 19087. Phone: (610) 687-5855. Fax: (610) 971-0760.

Washington, DC Phone: (202) 887-0948.

New York, NY Phone: (212) 517-8037.

Evaluates communications-oriented assets, such as equipment & real estate, for TV, CATV, radio, cellular systems, & satellites.

EnVest Media, LLC, 6802 Patterson Ave., Richmond, VA 23226. Phone: (804) 282-5561. Fax: (804) 282-5703. E-mail: mittyounts@cs.com. Web Site: www.envestmedia.com. Mitt S. Younts, mgr.

Alpharetta, GA 30004, 11770 Haynes Bridge Rd, #205. Phone: (770) 753-9650. Fax: (770) 753-0089. E-mail: jswnet@aol.com. Jesse Weatherby, member, manager.

Envest Media is a nationwide radio & TV acquisition, valuation, financing & consulting firm. The company provides brokerage svcs to stn transaction, appraisal svcs to stn owners & financial institutions. The group secures debt & equity acquisition financing, offers consulting & asset mgmt svcs, acting as court appointed receivers or trustees for bcst stations.

Equidata, 724 Thimble Shoals Blvd., Newport News, VA 23606. Phone: (757) 873-3395. Phone: (757) 873-0519. Fax: (800) 873-9752. Fax: (757) 873-1224. Thomas E. Cucuel, exec VP & gen mgr.

Nationwide collection agency/credit reporting agency.

Evalueserve, 15 Random Farm Rd., Chappaqua, NY 10514. Phone: (203) 440-3636. Web Site: evalueserve.com.

Telecommunications, high-technology, mkt. research.

Executive Broadcast Services, 5015 Farthing Dr., Colorado Springs, CO 80906. Phone: (719) 579-6676. Fax: (719) 579-6664. E-mail: skip@executivebroadcast.com. Skip Joeckel, pres.

Offers talk progmg & sports guides.

Executive Decision Systems Inc., 6421 W. Weaver Dr., Littleton, CO 80123-3815. Phone: (303) 795-9090. E-mail: donnale@aol.com. Web Site: www.retailinsights.com.

Provide sls & mgmt training, focusing on generating long-term, loc direct revenues. Provides academic approach to media mktg to stns around the United States & abroad. System 21 is guaranteed to return 12 times the revenues within 150 days or your money is refunded.

Management and Marketing Consultants

Executive Media Services, 138 E. Waterford Dr., Seneca, SC 299672. Phone: (864) 985-1133. Fax: (864) 985-1137. Web Site: www.executivecomm.com. E-mail: ron@executivecomm.com.

Loc sls consulting for TV & radio stns, cable TV systems. Provides source for sls strategy & sls support, sls seminars; start-up & turnaround specialists. New revenue dev & sls, training, using the internet, the home of one-on-one sls & training.

The Exline Company, 4340 Redwood Hwy., Suite F230, San Rafael, CA 94903. Phone: (415) 479-3484. Fax: (415) 479-1574. E-mail: exline@pacbell.net. Andrew P. McClure, pres; W. Dean LeGras, VP.

Mgmt, financial rsch, appraisal, receiverships & bankruptcies.

The Express Group, 2231 Westland Ave., San Diego, CA 92104. Phone: (619) 280-9061. Fax: (619) 280-9030. E-mail: egmail@theexpressgroup.com. Web Site: www.theexpressgroup.com. Byron Andrus, pres.

Design, fabrication, instal & lighting of news environments, newsrooms, interview & talkshow sets.

Eyewitness Newservice Inc., Box 116, 182 Sound Beach Ave., Old Greenwich, CT 06870-0116. Phone: (203) 637-0044. Fax: (203) 698-0812. E-mail: primonews@aol.com. Web Site: www.teenkidsnews.com. Albert T. Primo, pres.

New York, NY 10019, 355 W. 52nd St.

TV news strategic planning, focus group rsch talent & management, coaching. Cable news training; Internet Broadband Service; TV Production.

FM Atlas - Publishing and Electronics, Box 336, Esko, MN 55733-0336. Phone: (218) 879-7676. Fax: (218) 879-7676. E-mail: FmAtlas@aol.com. Web Site: users.aol.com/fmatlas. Bruce F. Elving, owner; Carol J. Elving, office mgr.

FM radio directory, rsch on FM-SCS & FM trans, FM-SCS receivers, *FMedia!* newsletter.

Fair West Direct, 9815 Carroll Canyon Rd., Suite 206, San Diego, CA 92131. Phone: (858) 578-9100. Fax: (858) 578-9130. Web Site: www.fairwestdirect.com.

Direct & data base mktg systems for bcstg.

Faraone Communications Inc., 75 West End Ave., Suite R-9A, New York, NY 10023. Phone: (212) 489-1313. Fax: (212) 489-8978. E-mail: ted@pr-agency.com. Web Site: www.pr-agency.com. Ted Faraone, principal.

Media, press rels, & image building for TV, cable, radio, home video, & new media.

David A. Faries & Associates, 67 Central Ave., Los Gatos, CA 95030. Phone: (408) 354-7308. Fax: (408) 395-6670. Web Site: ww.fariesinc.com. David A. Faries, ptnr.

Corporate PR, business info advisory.

Federal Engineering Inc., Redwood Plaza II, 10600 Arrowhead Dr., Fairfax, VA 22030. Phone: (703) 359-8200. Fax: (703) 359-8204. E-mail: info@fedeng.com. Web Site: www.fedeng.com. Ronald F. Bosco, pres; John E. Murray, sr VP.

Strategic planning, coverage analysis, new product definition, market rsch, competitive analysis, rates & tariffs, bcst stn design, mergers & acquisitions, expert testimony, regulatory support.

Ferraro Communications Inc., 39 Byron Rd., Weston, MA 02193. Phone: (781) 235-5556. Fax: (781) 235-5558. Tom Ferraro, pres.

Concept, script & production/direction for coml, radio, film & videotape productions.

Norman Fischer & Associates Inc., Box 5308, Austin, TX 78763. Phone: (512) 476-9457. Fax: (512) 476-0540. E-mail: terrill@nfainc.com. Web Site: www.nfainc.com. Terrill Fischer, pres.

Brokerage in radio, TV & cable, consultation in mgmt & opns, appraisals, feasibility studies, expert testimony, financial planning & assistance.

William Fleming & Associates, 176 N. Beacon St., Hartford, CT 06105. Phone: (860) 236-4453. Fax: (860) 236-2982. E-mail: wfleming@comcast.net. William L. Fleming, Principal.

Investment banking & financial consultant to bcstrs; assists in structuring mergers, acquisitions & refinancings; arranges equity, debt or other funds needed.

Florical Systems, 4581 N. W. 6th St., Gainesville, FL 32609. Phone: (352) 372-8326. Fax: (352) 375-0859. E-mail: sales@florical.com. Web Site: www.florical.com. Jim Moneyhun, pres.

Manufacturer of TV automations, controls & effects.

Focal Press, 200 Wheeler Road, 6th Fl, Burlington, MA 01803. Phone: (781) 313-4700. Fax: (781) 221-1615. E-mail: j.tracy@elsevier.com. Web Site: www.focalpress.com. Chris Mebegon, mktg mgr.

Oxford OX2 8DP, Linacre House, Jordan Hill. Phone: 011-44-1-865-310366. Jennifer Welham.

Publishes professional tech books in bcstg, film, video, multimedia, theatre & photography.

Ford Foundation, Media, Arts, & Culture, 320 E. 43rd St., New York, NY 10017. Phone: (212) 573-4951. Fax: (212) 351-3649. Web Site: www.fordfound.org.

Richard A. Foreman Associates Inc., 330 Emery Dr. E., Stamford, CT 06902. Phone: (203) 327-2800. Fax: (203) 967-9393. E-mail: raf@rafmedia.com. Web Site: rafamedia.om. Richard A. Foreman, pres.

Fair market evaluations & asset appraisals, media brokerage, stn financing, & mgmt/production consultation.

Franey, Maha & Allianet Inc., 9901 Business Pkwy., Suite B, Lanham, MD 20706. Phone: (301) 459-0055. Fax: (301) 459-5405. Web Site: www.franeymahaallianet.com. Bill Franey, CEO.

Herndon, VA 20171, 13921 Park Central Rd, Suite160. Phone: (703) 397-0977. Fax: (703) 397-0995. John Muha.

Insurance, bonding & benefits admin.

Clifton Gardiner & Company, L.L.C., 2437 S. Chase Ln., Denver, CO 80227. Phone: (303) 758-6900. Fax: (303) 479-9210. E-mail: cliff@cliftongardiner.com. Web Site: www.cliftongardiner.com. Clifton Gardiner, pres.

Brokerage, consulting & financial svcs for the bcst & cable TV industries.

Georgia Film, Video & Music Office, 285 Peachtree Ctr. Ave., Suite 1000, Atlanta, GA 30303. Phone: (404) 656-3591. Fax: (404) 656-3565. E-mail: film@georgia.org. Web Site: www.filmgeorgia.org. Greg Torre, dir.

Mailing address: Box 1776, Atlanta, GA 30301-1776.

Location scouting & preproduction svcs provided to feature film, TV movie, coml & multimedia production companies.

Getty Images, 601 N. 34th St., Seattle, WA 98103. Phone: (206) 925-5000. Fax: (206) 925-5001. Web Site: www.gettyimages.com. Jonathan Klein, CEO.

Business & mgmt consulting, training, long-term strategic planning, organizations analysis, mktg positioning; seminars on goal setting, leadership, mgmt skills, sls training. Retail training.

Dave Gifford International, Box 31940, Santa Fe, NM 87594-1940. Phone: (505) 989-7007. Fax: (505) 988-1991. E-mail: giff@talkgiff.com.

Sls & sls management training, sls turnarounds & troubleshooting. Sls, mgmt & adv seminars. New account sls & client dev., creator of graduate school of sls.

Gilbert Communications, 4101 Legends Way, Maryville, TN 37801. Phone: (865) 982-2889. Fax: (865) 977-6633. E-mail: rgilbert63090@mindspring.com. Robert W. Gilbert, consultant.

Full-svc radio/TV news consulting, writing seminars, staff motivation, news policy formulation, profit center strategy, *Broadcast News Handbook*.

Greenwood Performance Systems, Inc., 907 S. Detroit, Suite 720, Tulsa, OK 74120. Phone: (800) 331-9115. Fax: (918) 665-7252. Fax: (918) 665-7233. E-mail: info@greenwoodperformance.com. Web Site: www.greenwoodperformance.com. Jim Rhea, CEO; Jena Rhea, pres; Hoyit Bacon, VP.

Odessa, FL 33556, 15646 Indian Queen Dr. Phone: (813) 926-8222. Tim Menowsky, VP.

Ellicott City, MD 21042, 5074 Dorsey Hall Dr, Suite 205. Phone: (410) 740-0250. Larry Patrick, VP.

Bcst-specific sls & mgmt training, seminars & courses including sls mgmt consultation, strategic planning, compensation, selection & evaluation.

Guidestar Corp., 10600 Arrowhead Dr., Fairfax, VA 22030. Phone: (703) 352-5700. Fax: (703) 359-8204. Web Site: www.fedeng.com. Ronald F. Bosco, dir.

Mktg communications & PR specifically tailored to serve the telecommunications & info processing marketplaces.

Halper & Associates, 304 Newbury St., # 506, Boston, MA 02115. Phone: (617) 786-0666. Fax: (617) 786-1809. E-mail: dlh@donnahalper.com. Web Site: www.donnahalper.com. Donna L. Halper, pres; Jon Jacobik, computer consultant.

Radio progmg & mgmt consulting, market studies, format changes, music library software. Staff training, motivation. Specialize in small & medium markets, new owners, turnarounds. Also bcst historian.

Margret Haney Media Brokerage & Consultants, 2995 Woodside Rd., Bldg. 400, Woodside, CA 94062-2446. Phone: (650) 324-8262. Fax: (650) 324-8261. E-mail: www.hhmargret@yahoo.com. Web Site: www.margret @margrethaney.com. Sondralyn Carver, consultant; Margret Haney, pres.

Media brokerage/consulting, adv, media buyers.

Happi Associates, Sales/Programming/Management Consultants. Box 110892, Nashville, TN 37222. Phone: (615) 220-6050. Fax: (615) 331-8571. Skeeter Dodd, VP/gen mgr.

Sls & mgmt assistance & motivation for radio, cable TV & business; progmg & format; AM specialist.

Bill Hennes & Associates, 5009 Crosswinds Dr., Wilmington, NC 28409. Phone: (910) 313-2491. Fax: (910) 313-0228. E-mail: bhennes105@aol.com. Web Site: www.allaboutcountry.com. Bill Hennes, pres; Kim Hennes, mktg VP.

Progmg & mgmt consulting.

The Ted Hepburn Co., 325 Garden Rd., Palm Beach, FL 33480. Phone: (561) 863-8995. Fax: (561) 863-8997. E-mail: tedhep@aol.com. Ted Hepburn, mgng dir.

Radio, TV & cable brokerage; appraisals.

R. Miller Hicks & Co., 1011 W. 11th St., Austin, TX 78703. Phone: (512) 477-7000. Fax: (512) 477-9697. R. Miller Hicks, pres.

Brokerage, financing, mgmt consulting.

Hoffman Schutz Media Capital Inc., 2044 West California St., San Diego, CA 92110. Phone: (619) 291-7070. Web Site: www.hs-media.com. Anthony M. Hoffman, pres; David E. Schutz, VP.

Strategic planning for lender & investor appraisals & litigation support.

Host Communications, 546 E. Main St., Lexington, KY 40508. Phone: (859) 226-4678. Fax: (859) 226-4391. E-mail: debra.locker@hostcommunication.com. Web Site: www.hostcommunications.com. W. James Host, CEO.

Roswell, GA 30075, 1255 Canton St. E. Phone: (770) 645-7780. Kevin Bryant, VP natl sls.

Dallas, TX 75248, 17300 Dallas Pkwy, Suite 1000. Phone: (972) 392-5700. Marc Kidd, sports pres.

College sports bcstg & TV syndications; publishing & sports mktg.

The Howard-Sloan-Koller Group, 300 E. 42nd St., New York, NY 10016. Phone: (212) 661-5250. Fax: (212) 557-9178. E-mail: ekoller@hsksearch.com. Web Site: www.hsksearch.com. Edward R. Koller Jr., pres; Karen Danziger, exec VP.

Exec search & consulting in the cable, infotechnology, entertainment, new media & publishing industries.

The Image Generators, (A division of Voicelines Inc.). 18156 Darnell Dr., Olney, MD 20832. Phone: (301) 924-5700. Fax: (301) 570-8916. E-mail: mweiner@imagegenerators.com. Web Site: www.imagegenerators.com. Michael J. Weiner, pres/CEO.

Mktg & mgmt issues; talent training workshops & coaching.

Innovative Audience Research, 119 La Colima, Pismo Beach, CA 93449. Phone: (805) 556-0772. Fax: (805) 556-0772. E-mail: iarinc@charter.net. Mike Silverstein, pres; Susan B. Silverstein, exec VP.

Strategic planning in news, progmg & promotion, impacting sweep book ratings in TV metered markets.

International Media Consulting, Inc., 48 Mountain Rd., Farmington, CT 06032-2341. Phone: (860) 677-9688. Fax: (860) 677-9639. E-mail: robert.richer@snet.net. Robert E. Richer, owner.

International brokerage firm dealing exclusively with the buying & selling of media properties located outside of the United States.

IPI Report, The International Journalism Magazine. 320 Lee Hills Hall, Columbia, MO 65211. Phone: (573) 884-7542. Fax: (573) 884-1870. E-mail: ipi-report@jmail.jour.missouri.edu. Dean Mills, publisher; Stuart H. Loory, editor; Danita Allen, editorial dir.

Columbia, MO 65211, 132A Neff Annex. Phone: (573) 884-7542. Stuart H. Loory, editor.

IPI Report defends, celebrates, relects & explores the international media & freedom of expression.

KEENE Management Group Inc., 508 Sparrow Rd., Greenwood, SC 29649. Phone: (864) 227-8500. Fax: (864) 227-2342.

Radio consulting.

Broadcasting & Cable Yearbook 2006

KSL Television, 55 N. 300 W., Salt Lake City, UT 84110-1160. Phone: (801) 575-5555. Fax: (801) 575-5857. Web Site: www.ksl.com. Bruce Reese, exec VP.

An advertiser-supported NABTS news & info service available through TV decoders or personal computers equipped with modems. Modem number is (801) 575-5911.

Kagan Media Appraisals, a division of Media Central/Primedia, 126 Clock Tower Pl., Carmel, CA 93923-8734. Phone: (831) 624-1536. Fax: (831) 624-3105. E-mail: info@kagan.com. Web Site: www.Kagan.com. Robin Flynn, VP bcstg.

Specializes in the valuation & appraisal of media & communications properties. As part of the Media Central Group of Companies, we maintain the industry's most comprehensive data base of stn values, so we know what yesterday's stns sold for, what buyers are paying today & what they are likely to pay tomorrow. Svcs include: Fair market valuations, expert witness testimony, asset appraisals, ESOP valuations, fairness opinions, minority interest valuations, financial feasibility studies, strategic planning, custom rsch & reports & consulting.

Kagan World Media/Primedia, Inc., 126 Clock Tower Pl., Carmel, CA 93923-8734. Phone: (831) 624-1536. Fax: (831) 625-3225. Web Site: www.kagan.com. Larry Gerbrandt, COO; Sandie Borthwick, dir opns.

Strategic conferences on media & communications topics, including interactive, multimedia, telecommunications, entertainment deals & financing.

Kalba International Inc., 23 Sandy Pond Rd., Lincoln, MA 01773. Phone: (781) 259-9589. Fax: (781) 259-1460. E-mail: info@kalbainternational.com. Web Site: www.kalbainternational.com. Kas Kalba, pres; Pat Kalba, VP; F. Roberts, VP.

Consulting & advisory svcs on telecommunications, bcstg & cable TV, including international ventures, due diligence, litigation support.

Kane Reece Associates Inc., 822 South Ave. W., Westfield, NJ 07090-1460. Phone: (908) 317-5757. Fax: (908) 317-4434. E-mail: info@kanereece.com. Web Site: www.kanereece.com. John "Jack" E. Kane, principal; Norval D. Reece, principal; Robert E. Ott, principal; Frederick H. Bliss, principal.

Asset appraisals, business valuations, due diligence, expert testimony, property tax compliance & control, system mgmt & mgmt/engrg consulting.

Kempff Communications Co., 3301 Bayshore Blvd., Suite 1407, Tampa, FL 33629. Phone: (813) 258-3433. Fax: (813) 902-1360. E-mail: kempffcc@aol.com. Ron Kempff, pres; Aurelia Serna, VP.

Broker and consultant also offering financial and management svcs, court ordered sale of stations.

Kovsky & Miller Research, 37 Sawmill River Rd., Hawthorne, NY 10532. Phone: (914) 347-3606. Fax: (914) 347-3976. E-mail: hkkmrresearch@aol.com. Harry Kovsky, pres.

Specialists in content & format analysis of loc & network TV news & entertainment programs, promotional analysis, ratings analysis, audience promotional rsch & audience survey rsch.

Kozacko Media Services, Box 948, Elmira, NY 14902. Phone: (607) 733-7138. Fax: (607) 733-1212. E-mail: rkozacko@stny.rr.com. Web Site: www.kozackomediaservices.com. Richard L. Kozacko, pres; John C. Clancy, assoc.

Tucson, AZ 85750, 6890 E. Sunrise Dr, Box 120-40. Phone: (520) 299-1786. Fax: (520) 299-1786. George W. Kimble, assoc.

Keswick, VA 22947, 1071 Club Dr. Phone: (434) 244-2653. Fax: (434) 244-2666. W. Donald Roberts Jr., assoc.

Appraisals & current market evaluations of radio & TV stns. Bcst acquisition planning.

The LPTV Store.Com, LLC., Box 250813, Milwaukee, WI 53225-6513. Phone: (262) 781-0188. Fax: (262) 781-5313. E-mail: kompasgroup@toast.net. Web Site: www.thelptvstore.com. John Kompas, ptnr; Burt Sherwood, ptnr.

Sarasota, FL 34242, 5053 Ocean Blvd., Suite 14. Phone: (941) 349-2165. Fax: (941) 312-0974.

Financial & mktg svcs for LPTV; audience demographic reports; stn coverage maps; appraisals/brokerage; financial & strategic planning.

Lawson & Associates Architects, 8520 Connecticut Ave., Suite 240, Chevy Chase, MD 20815. Phone: (301) 654-1600. Fax: (301) 654-1601. E-mail: blarchitect@aol.com. Web Site: www.lawsonarch.com. Bruce Lawson,.

Consulting architectural design & construction mgmt svcs for the TV & cable industry; facility planning, design & coordination of construction svcs.

Tony Lease Incentive Tours, 4900 S.W. Griffith Dr., Suite 110, Beaverton, OR 97005. Phone: (800) 545-1010. Phone: (503) 574-3500. Fax: (503) 574-3400. E-mail: tlit@msn.com. Web Site: www.tonylease.com. Tony Lease, pres; June Hope Lease, exec VP.

Laguna Niguel, CA 92677, Box 7531. Phone: (949) 249-6867. Becky Cerato, exec asst mgr.

Five star sls incentive tours for media. Also has Media Sports Tours for Superbowl, Final Four & Olympic packages. Forty years experience; world wide contacts.

Liberty Hill Corp., Box 253003, West Bloomfield, MI 48325. Phone: (248) 737-3000. Fax: (248) 737-3555. E-mail: barryzate@aol.com. Barry Zate, sr VP; Ronald Zate, sr VP.

Consulting for radio progmg, talent & admin svcs; on-site seminars, problem targeting & complete strategic planning for the communications industry.

Lipson & Co., 1900 Ave. of the Stars, Suite 2810, Los Angeles, CA 90067. Phone: (310) 277-4646. Fax: (310) 277-8585. E-mail: howard@lipsonco.com. Howard R. Lipson, pres; Harriet L. Lipson, VP.

Specializes in recruiting for international & domestic bcstg, cable, entertainment, adv, mktg, finance, mdse & licensing.

Locations Tasmania Pty. Ltd., Box 537, Sandy Bay, Tasmania 07005. Phone: 61-362-243578. Fax: 61-362-24248211. E-mail: wildangels@bigpond.com.

Coordination svcs for international film & TV production. Second unit svcs stock footage library.

Loral Skynet, 2400 Research Blvd., Suite 200, Rockville, MD 20850. Phone: (301) 258-8101. Fax: (301) 258-8119. Web Site: www.loralorion.com. Terry Hart, pres/CEO.

International telecommunication svcs in Asia Pacific rgn, specializing in private networks via satellite.

Lund Consultants to Broadcast Management Inc., 840 Hinckley Rd., Suite 123, Burlingame, CA 94010-1505. Phone: (650) 692-7777. Fax: (650) 692-7799. E-mail: lundradio@aol.com. Web Site: www.lundradio.com. John C. Lund, pres.

Experts in progmg consulting; multiopoly strategy. AC, Country, Top 40, Rock, Classic Rock, Oldies, News-Talk. Music, formatics, promotions, talent dev, perceptual rsch.

Frank N. Magid Associates Inc., One Research Ctr., Marion, IA 52302. Phone: (319) 377-7345. Fax: (319) 377-5861. E-mail: mailia@magid.com. Web Site: www.magid.com. Brent Magid, pres/CEO; Joe George, exec VP; Steve Ridge, exec VP.

Sherman Oaks, CA 91403, 15260 Ventura Blvd, Suite 2130. Phone: (818) 263-3300. Fax: (818) 263-3311. Jack Mackenzie, SVP, entertainment.

New York, NY 10019, 1775 Broadway, Suite 1401. Phone: (212) 974-2310. Fax: (212) 515-4540. Vicki Cohen, SVP, entertainment.

Specialists in rsch-driven consultation to traditional & new media firms; svcs include strategic planning, web site evaluation & development, program evaluation, talent search, coaching, TMI, & the Magid Network.

Mahlum Architects, 71 Columbia, Suite 400, Seattle, WA 98104. Phone: (206) 441-4151. Fax: (206) 441-0478. Web Site: www.mahlum.com.

Design; tech consulting; feasibility & facilities studies; cost analysis & construction admin for TV/radio stns, production & equipment storage facilities, & film studios.

Marketing & Creative Services, (Division of Frank N. Magid Associates Inc.). One Research Ctr., Marion, IA 52302. Phone: (319) 377-7345. Fax: (319) 377-5861. E-mail: info@magid.com. Web Site: www.magid.com. Frank N. Magid, chmn/CEO; Steve Ridge, sr VP; Joe George, sr VP; Brent Magid, pres domestic TV.

Rsch & consultation.

Marshall & Stevens Inc., 707 Wilshire Blvd., Suite 5200, Los Angeles, CA 90017. Phone: (213) 612-8000. Fax: (213) 612-8010. E-mail: info@marshall-stevens.com. Web Site: www.marshall-stevens.com. Fred Thomas, VP.

St. Louis, MO 63101, 720 Olive St. Phone: (314) 621-7025. (800)-325-7337. Raymond Essma, VP Central div.

New York, NY 10006-3007, 45 Broadway Atrium. Phone: (212) 425-4300. Wiley Scott, VP sls.

Natl appraisal firm with extensive bcstg client base. Value real estate, equipment, intangible assets & overall business valuations. Assist in financing sls, purchase price allocation, & cast segregation.

Maxagrid, 3939 Belt Line Rd., Suite 250, Addison, TX 75001. Phone: (972) 241-2110. Fax: (972) 241-2174. E-mail: maxagrid@maxagrid.com. Web Site: www.maxagrid.com. Jim Tiller, pres/CEO.

Yield Management Systems for broadcast in USA, Australia, and Canada. Systems and strategies that help managers improve yields on ad revenues.

Maxwell Media Group, 6053 Bunker Hill, Pittsburgh, PA 15206. Phone: (412) 441-2020. Fax: (412) 661-9377. Bill Maxwell, pres.

Consultant.

Mayo Communications Inc., Box 82784, Tampa, FL 33682. Phone: (813) 971-2061. Fax: (813) 977-1947. Lincoln A. Mayo, pres.

Media brokerage, appraisals for bcst & print. Consulting, concerning media sls & acquisitions.

Mazer & Associates, 3452 Grayton Rd., Detroit, MI 48224. Phone: (313) 885-5686. John Mazer Jr., pres.

Radio & TV progmg svcs, market rsch, format design, talent evaluation, license renewal preparation, labor rel, mgmt & admin consulting.

Edward R. McKenna Communications, Box 71084, Bethesda, MD 20813. Phone: (301) 986-1118. Edward R. McKenna, owner.

Radio brokerage & consulting.

McNulty Consultants, 1926 E. 34th Ave., Spokane, WA 99203. Phone: (509) 535-5168. Wayne F. McNulty, pres.

Scottsdale, AZ 95258, 7819 Via Rio. Phone: (480) 922-9546. Wayne F. McNulty, pres.

Mgmt & financial assistance in purchasing & operating TV & radio stns. Effective bottom-line mgmt, all phases of stn & group opns.

McVay Media, 2001 Crocker Rd., Suite 260, Cleveland, OH 44145. Phone: (440) 892-1910. Web Site: www.mcvaymedia.com. Mike McVay, pres; Doris McVay, gen mgr; Jerry King, VP; Daniel Arstandis, AC/Interactive.

Atlanta, GA 30101. Atlanta, 628 Braidwood Dr. Fax: (770) 795-1022.

Consultant radio stns in progmg various formats.

Media & Marketing, 4245 Sarah St., Suite 462, Burbank, CA 91505. Phone: (818) 753-9510. E-mail: mediapr@earthlink.net. Web Site: www.mediaandmarketing.com. Mel Lambert, Creative director.

Consulting service for the audio & multimedia industries.

Media Communications Group Inc., 11 Spiral Dr., Suite 3, Florence, KY 41042. Phone: (859) 647-0055. Fax: (859) 647-2611. Web Site: www.paragoncomm.com. Dan Hubbard, sr VP; Rebecca Neal, chief of opns; John L. Pierce, pres.

Representing, consulting & mgmt svcs to radio stns nationwide.

Media Economics, 69 N. Sheridan Ave., Bethpage, NY 11714. Phone: (516) 931-0248. E-mail: beconomist@aol.com. Layton W. Franko PhD., pres.

Market analysis, forecasting, pricing, planning, sports economics & business rsch for TV, cable & radio industries.

Media Perspectives, 127 Greensward Ln., Cherry Hill, NJ 08002. Phone: (856) 482-7979. Fax: (856) 482-0957. Steven G. Apel, pres.

Progmg & mktg counseling through applied audience & advertiser rsch.

Media Sales Management, Potsdamer Strasse 31, Berlin 10783. Phone: 49-30-215-30300. Fax: 49-30-215-1182.

Hamburg D-22397, Sthamerstrasse 58. Phone: 49-40-605-2114. Fax: 49-40-605-1762. Norbert Schmidt, pres.

Offers a complete package of bcst svcs, finance, acquisition, progmg sls mgmt, rsch & valuations. German & European specialists.

The Mediacenter, 1500 Harbor Blvd., Weehawken, NJ 07086. Phone: (866) 622-7587. Fax: (201) 348-1761. E-mail: sales@mediacenteronline.com. Web Site: www.mediacenteronline.com. Barbara Ann Zeiger, pres; Russell Sands, gen mgr.

Promote increased mktg professionalism among TV execs & mgrs; provide sls support tools that identify & dev new adv budgets.

Mercer Capital Management Inc., 5860 Ridgeway Center Parkway, 4th Fl, Memphis, TN 38120. Phone: (901) 685-2120. Fax: (901) 685-2199. E-mail: mcm@mercercapital.com. Web Site: www.mercercapital.com.

Louisville, KY 40202, 206 Kentuckey Towers. Phone: (502) 585-6340. James E. Graves, VP.

Mercer Capital provides high-quality independent business appraisals, and other financial advisory services for all types of media including radio.

Management and Marketing Consultants

Metro Orlando Film & Television Commission, 301 E. Pine St., Suite 900, Orlando, FL 32801. Phone: (407) 422-7159. Fax: (407) 841-9069. E-mail: suzy.allen @filmorlando.com. Web Site: www.filmorland.com. Suzy Allen, Orlando & film commissioner/sr VP.

One stop permitting, locations library, location scouting, community familiarization tours, Filmbook with complete listings of crews, technicians & production support vendors.

Jack Myers Reports, 20 E. 68th St., New York, NY 10021. Phone: (212) 794-4926. Fax: (212) 794-5160. E-mail: jack@jackmyers.com. Web Site: www.jackmyers.com. Jack Myers, chmn/CEO; Mark Bonilla, CEO; Craig Geddy, sr VP; Ann Roed, sr VP; Joe Mandese, editor; Mark Altschuler, exec VP.

Daily behind-the-scenes newsletter or media economics, advertising, content. Syndicated rsch & evaluation for media companies, advertisers & adv agencies. Publishes *The Jack Myers Report Newsletter*.

Michael Davis & Co., 207 S. State Rd., Upper Darby, PA 19082. Phone: (610) 668-1771. Fax: (610) 668-2287. Michael Davis, pres.

Consulting on both news product & topical promotion. Branding, stratetgic mktg, creating & producing image campaigns. Twenty-five years of success.

J.M. Miller, Box 190, Ashburn, VA 20146. Phone: 703-729-7745. Fax: 703-729-7745. E-mail: broadcastappraisal@yahoo.com. Jan M. Miller, owner.

Broadcast TV, DTV, AM, FM, production, satellite, microwave facility and equipment inspection, asset appraisal reports, engineering evaluation overviews and consulting services. For valuation, acquisition, finance, purchase price allocation, ad valorem tax, insurance, leasing, liquidation and litigation.

Jay Mitchell Associates Inc., Box 1285, Fairfield, IA 52556. Phone: (641) 472-4087. Fax: (641) 472-2071. E-mail: jay@ffradio.com. Web Site: www.smallmarketradio.com. Jay Mitchell, pres.

Mgmt, mktg, progmg & promotions consulting; market analysis, web site design & consulting.

George Moore & Associates Inc., 6918 Wildglen Dr., Suite 100 W, Dallas, TX 75230. Phone: (214) 369-5665. Fax: (214) 369-5667. W. James Moore, pres.

Brokerage of radio, TV & CATV properties; asset & market appraisals; introduction to institutional financing sources.

Nashville Mayor's Office of Film, 222 2nd Ave, Suite 418, Nashville, TN 37201. Phone: (615) 880-1827. Fax: (615) 862-6025. E-mail: jennifer.andrews@nashville.gov. Web Site: www.filmnashville.com. Jennifer Andrews, film coord.

Location scouting, permits, produce annual production directory, assist with all logistics of TV/film/video projects, liaison to media & government.

National Strategies Inc., 888 17th St. N.W., 12th Fl., Washington, DC 20006. Phone: (202) 429-8744. Fax: (202) 296-2962. E-mail: daylward@natstrat.com. Web Site: www.natstrat.com. David Aylward, pres.

Pub policy strategies & implementation, business & investment dev.

Navigant International, 947 Hornet Drive,Ste.101, Hazelwood, MO 63042. Phone: (314) 592-3800. Fax: (314) 592-3900. Mike Million, dir opns.

Corporate & leisure travel, specializes in promotional packages & incentive programs.

New England Media L.L.C., Box 594, Willimantic, CT 06226. Phone: (860) 456-1111. Fax: (860) 456-9501. E-mail: mcrice@prodigy.net. Michael Rice, mgng ptnr.

Mansfield Center, CT 06250, 50 Kaya Lane. Phone: (860) 455-1414. Michael Rice, mgng ptnr.

Media brokers, consultants & appraisers specializing in radio in the Northeast.

New York Communications, 450 N. Narbereth Ave., Ste. 105, Narbereth, PA 19072. Phone: (610) 668-1771. Fax: (610) 668-2287. E-mail: nycomm@aol.com. Michael Davis, pres.

Consulting on news promotion. Branding, strategic mktg, creating & producing image campaigns. Twenty-seven years of success.

Newbrough Associates Inc., Box 1822, Des Moines, IA 50306-1822. Phone: (515) 244-8909. Fax: (515) 244-8909. E-mail: wbn@att.net. Bill Newbrough, pres.

Gen mgmt consulting & episodic mgmt svcs for mass communications organizations. Specialties: electronic journalism, music radio, organizational dev & telephone interactivity.

NEWSDirections, 935 Pebblestone Ct., Alpharetta, GA 30004-6824. Phone: (770) 569- 2277. E-mail: tony@news-direction.com. Web Site: www.news-directions.com. Tony Windsor, pres.

Professional dev & career mktg for TV news reporters, anchors & producers.

Nathan M. Nickolaus, 320 E. McCarthy St., Jefferson City, MO 65101-3115. Phone: (573) 634-6313. Fax: (573) 634-6504. Web Site: nnickolaus@jeffcitymo.org.

Noll & Associates, 475 Gate Five Rd., Suite 211, Sausalito, CA 94965. Phone: (415) 332-2254. Fax: (415) 332-5519. E-mail: kennen@nollmedia.com. Web Site: www.nollmedia.com. Kennen Williams, pres.

Bcst mktg/sls training, new business dev & organizational dev.

Northwest Broadcasting Co., Box 332, Dallastown, PA 17313-0332. Phone: (717) 887-8864. E-mail: mkrafcisin@suscom.net.

Mgmt, progmg, production, scriptwriting, talent, voice-over svcs, opns & engrg consultation

The Omnia Group, 601 South Blvd., Tampa, FL 33606. Phone: (800) 525-7117. Fax: (813) 254-8558. E-mail: jthiessen@omniagroup.com. Web Site: www.omniagroup.com. Fleming Ford, VP sls.

Same-day response on best industry-validated selection tools that help hire the right person the first time.

Ott & Associates, 9225 Chatham Grove Ln., Suite D, Richmond, VA 23236. Phone: (804) 276-7202. Fax: (804) 745-7778. E-mail: rick@aol.com. Web Site: www.rickott.com. Rick Ott, pres.

Problem solving, consultation in complete confidentiality. Mgmt consulting.

PMA Marketing Inc., 4359 S. Howell, Suite 106, Milwaukee, WI 53207. Phone: (414) 482-2638. Fax: (414) 483-1980. E-mail: pma@execpc.com. Web Site: www.amfmtv.com. Pat Martin, pres.

Buy & sell new & used bcst equipment, radio stn start-ups & turnarounds, problem solving for difficult bcst situations.

PR/PR, 775 S. Kirkman Rd., Suite 104, Orlando, FL 32811. Phone: (407) 299-6128. Fax: (407) 299-2166. E-mail: pam@prpr.net. Web Site: www.prpr.net. Pam Lontos, pres.

Publicity in Radio, TV, print for speakers & authors.

Palazzo Intercreative, 308 Occidental Ave. South, Suite 200, Seattle, WA 98104. Phone: (206) 328-5555. Fax: (206) 324-4348. E-mail: palazzo@palazzo.com. Web Site: www.palazzo.com. Richard Roberts, pres.

Stn identity design & consultation svcs, including on-air, print, outdoor, graphics, syndicated animation packages, movie & news opns, & radio spots.

Paragon Media Strategies, 550 S. Wadsworth Blvd., Suite 401, Denver, CO 80226. Phone: (303) 922-5600. Fax: (303) 922-1589. E-mail: mhenry@paragonmediastrategies.com. Web Site: www.paragonmediastrategies.com. Mike Henry, CEO.

Monterey, CA 93940, 2511 Garden Rd, Suite 104, Bldg. A. Phone: (831) 655-5036. Fax: (831) 655-5037. Larry Johnson, pres.

Custom rsch: focus groups, auditorium music tests, perceptual studies, tracking, auditorium format analysis.

Patrick Communications L.L.C. 5074 Dorsey Hall Dr., Suite 205, Ellicott City, MD 21042. Phone: (410) 740-0250. Fax: (410) 740-7222. E-mail: patrick@patcomm.com. Web Site: www.patcomm.com. Larry Patrick, pres.

Stn brokerage, investment banking, mgmt consulting svcs, appraisals & opns consulting.

Donald A Perry & Associates Inc., Box 1275, Newport News, VA 23601. Phone: (757) 877-4367. Fax: (757) 693-2885. E-mail: dperry@cablefirst.net. Donald A. Perry, pres.

Mgmt, brokerage & appraisal svcs to the cable TV industry.

Peters Communications, 1555 Berenda Pl., El Cajon, CA 92020. Phone: (858) 565-8511. Fax: (619) 440-1481. E-mail: ppiep@cox.net. Edward J. Peters, pres.

Media mktg consultants, providing rsch, concept, mktg plan, music, graphics & animation.

Point Broadcasting Company, Point 3G. 715 Broadway, Suite 320, Santa Monica, CA 90401. Phone: (310) 451-4430. Fax: (310) 451-1423. John Hearne, pres.

Operating, technical & financial management.

Pollack Media Group Inc., 860 Via De La Paz, Suite D2, Pacific Palisades, CA 90272. Phone: (310) 459-8556. Fax: (310) 454-5046. E-mail: hq@pollackmedia.com. Web Site: www.pollackmedia.com. Jeff Pollack, chmn/CEO; Tommy Hadges, pres.

Worldwide bcst progmg advisory firm, all facets of progmg, positioning, mktg, adv, rsch, music. All formats.

Poorman & Group, 143-147 E. Main St., Suite 2C, Lock Haven, PA 17745. Phone: (570) 748-7000. Fax: (570) 748-7700. Web Site: www.lockhaven.com. Stephen P. Poorman, pres.

Pennsylvania & Texas-based mgmt consulting firm offers "no-charge" interviews to radio & TV stns relating to business & real estate issues. Specializes in organizing & mgng financially distressed businesses.

Price Waterhouse Coopers, 1 North Wacker Drive, Chicago, IL 60606. Phone: (312) 298-2000. Fax: (312) 298-2001. Web Site: www.pwc.com.

Provides valuation consulting svcs for acquisitions, swaps, estate planning & litigation.

W.L. Pritchard & Co. L.C., 4405 E.W. Hwy., Suite 501, Bethesda, MD 20814. Phone: (301) 654-1144. Fax: (301) 654-1814. E-mail: wlpco@wlpco.com. Web Site: www.wlpco.com.

Professional engrg and business problem solving in telecommunications, competitor analysis, satellite communications, earth stns, and launch vehicles.

PROSTAR, 12831 Royal Dr., Stafford, TX 77477. Phone: (281) 240-2800. Fax: (281) 240-1447. E-mail: prostar@prostar-inc.com. Web Site: www.prostar-inc.com. John C. Parks, pres.

Provides leased & ad-hoc satellite encryption systems for business, entertainment & sports usage.

The Ward L. Quaal Co., Box 368, Winnetka, IL 60093. Phone: (312) 644-6066. Fax: (312) 644-3733. Ward L. Quaal, owner; Rondi L. Carlsen, admin asst.

Mgmt consultants specializing in svcs to bcstg & allied arts.

The R Corp., 2477 Stickney Point Rd., Suite 201 Bldg. B, Sarasota, FL 34231. Phone: (941) 924-2400. Fax: (941) 924-1650. E-mail: rcorp@comcast.net.

Consulting to electronic media, cable, wireless, & bcstg.

R.F. Technologies Corp., 12 Foss Rd., Lewiston, ME 04240. Phone: (207) 777-7778. Phone: (480) 496-0165 (Phoenix, AZ sls office). Fax: (207) 777-7784. Web Site: www.rftechnologies.net. George M. Harris, P.E. & principal; Deepay Mukerjee, pres; Bill Ammons, dir bcst sls.

Provides file engrg & service for TV & FM antennas, transmission lines, diplexers & combiners.

RPM Radio Programming & Management, 1133 W. Longlake Rd., Suite 200, Bloomfield Hills, MI 48302. Phone: (248) 647-1068. Fax: (248) 647-2663. E-mail: rpmorlk@aol.com. Web Site: www.tophitsusa.com. Thomas M. Krikorian, pres.

Top Hits U.S. weekly CD service & CD libraries including Solid Gold, Spectrum A/C & Country One; CD Christmas library.

The Radio-Studio Network, Box 683, Times Square Station, New York, NY 10108-0683. Phone: (800) 608-5835. Fax: (212) 868-5663. E-mail: programming@radio-studio.net. Web Site: www.radio-studio.net. Steve Warren, pres.

Multi-Format Network Programming by MP3 download. Music, News, Talk, Infomercials.

Rattigan Resources, 3409 Wilshire Rd., Portsmouth, VA 23703. Phone: (757) 484-3017. Fax: (757) 484-0336. E-mail: rattiganjack@aol.com. Jack M. Rattigan CRMC, CEO.

Specializes in "Marketing to the 50+ Demographic" (Baby Boomers and Beyond). Customized sls training & seminars for stations programmed to the Mature and Wealthiest Audience.

Rees Associates Inc., Rees Plaza at East Wharf, 9211 Lake Hefner Pkwy, Suite 300, Oklahoma City, OK 73120. Phone: (405) 942-7337. Phone: (888) 942-7337. Fax: (405) 948-1261. E-mail: rees@rees-associates.com. Web Site: www.rees-associates.com. Frank W. Rees Jr., pres; Leroy James, exec VP; William H. Yost, VP mktg; Ralph S. Blackmon, VP; Walter L. Gregg, VP.

Dallas, TX 75219-4341, 3102 Oak Lawn, Suite 200. Phone: (214) 522-7337. Fax: (214) 522-0444. Frank Rees Jr., pres.

Bcst & production facility design; architectural svcs; facility business plans; interior design; studio design; equipment planning, consulting.

Management and Marketing Consultants

Restivo Communications, 73 Widdicombe Hill Blvd., Suite 1515, Toronto, ON M9R 4B3. Canada. Phone: (416) 242-7009. Peter J. Restivo, pres.
Bcst & media consultants; media training, MOW development.

George Rodman Associates, 26303 Ocean View Dr., Carmel, CA 93923. Phone: (831) 626-1630. Fax: (831) 626-8662. E-mail: grodman@viaworldwide.com. George T. Rodman, pres; Sally M. Rodman, VP.
Provides stns, networks, groups & program suppliers with mktg counseling & promotional materials, including adv campaigns, logos, on-air design, TV spots & animation.

Roehling Broadcast Services Ltd., 7340 Oak Knoll Dr., Indianapolis, IN 46217. Phone: (317) 887-1945. Fax: (317) 887-1947. E-mail: edradiobr@aol.com. Web Site: roehlingbroadcast.com. Edward W. Roehling, pres; Sandra Roehling, VP & treas.
Broadcast appraisers, brokers, consultants, financing negotiators, also narration of audio and video.

Ray H. Rosenblum Sales & Management Consultant, Box 38296, Pittsburgh, PA 15238. Phone: (412) 362-6311. Fax: (412) 362-6317. E-mail: rayhrosenblum@hotmail.com. Ray H. Rosenblum, pres; Helen Faye Rosenblum, VP.
Consultant & appraiser for radio & TV stns & political candidates, with focus on mgmt, sls, proms, news & PR.

Rumbaut & Co., 1060 Stillwater Dr., Tower Suites, Miami Beach, FL 33141-1024. Phone: (305) 868-0000. Fax: (305) 868-7000. E-mail: julio@rumbaut.com. Web Site: www.rumbaut.com. Julio Rumbaut, pres.
Media brokers & consultants in all facets of the TV & radio industries.

William Russell & Associates Inc., 305 W. Masonic View Ave., Alexandria, VA 22301. Phone: (703) 739-6277. Fax: (703) 739-6277. E-mail: bill32394@netzero.net. William A. Russell Jr., pres.
Govt rel & mktg consultants specializing in telecommunications & international trade issues. Telecommunications svcs to bcst stns.

SB Management, 890 Monterey St., Suite G, San Luis Obispo, CA 93401. Phone: (805) 543-9214. Fax: (805) 543-9243. E-mail: Michael@mikehesser.com. Michael Hesser, pres.
Assist in finding, evaluating, financing & structuring acquisitions. Also, consult mgmt & sls.

S C Research International Inc., 1317 Third Ave., Suite 100, New York, NY 10021. Phone: (212) 867-6060. Fax: (212) 867-6579. E-mail: info@scri.com. Web Site: www.scri.com. Desmond C. Chaskelson, dir.
Syndicated reports & custom rsch for manufacturers & investors in bcstg, professional video & audio; publishers of Broadcast Equipment Marketplace (BEM), Professional Video Marketplace (PFM), Professional Multi-Media Marketplace (PMM), European Telemedia Marketplace (ETM), Asian Telemedia Marketplace (ATM).

SRCS/Markits, 17 Royal Rd., Bangor, ME 04401. Phone: (207) 942-5548. Fax: (207) 942-9164. J. Stephen Robbins, pres.
Client-directed mktg program for coml bcst properties (radio & TV).

San Antonio Film Commission, 203 S. St. Mary's St., 2nd Floor, San Antonio, TX 78298. Phone: (210) 207-6730. Fax: (210) 207-6843. E-mail: filmsa@filmsanantonio.com. Web Site: www.filmsanantonio.com.
City film commission. Photo Library. Liaison with all city offices. Filming permits. Parking assistance.

SatNews Publishers, (International Satellite Directory). 800 Siesta Way, Sonoma, CA 95476. Phone: (707) 939-9306. Fax: (707) 939-9235. E-mail: design@satnews.com. Web Site: www.satnews.com. Silvano Payne, CEO.
Publishers of the 1,500-page International Satellite Directory, the complete source for all info on the satellite industry. Also available on a CD-ROM & through the web at http://www.satnews.com.

Satterfield & Perry Inc., 7211 Fourth Ave. S., St. Petersburg, FL 33707. Phone: (727) 345-7338. Fax: (727) 345-3809. Bob Austin, pres.
Wetumpka, AL 36093, 169 Mountain Meadows La. Phone: (334) 514-2241. Fax: (334) 514-2291. Ken Hawkins, VP.
Denver, CO 80215-7067, 3062 Robb Cir. Phone: (303) 239-6670. Fax: (303) 231-9562. Al Perry, chmn emeritus.
Coos Bay, OR 97420, PO Box 362. Phone: (541) 751-0043. Fax: (541) 751-0043. Dick McMahon, VP.
Littleton, CO 80120, 7420 S. Curtice Ct. Phone: (720) 283-7980. Fax: (720) 283-7980. Jim Ortega, VP.

Overland Park, KS 66207, 4918 W. 101st Terr. Phone: (913) 649-5103. Fax: (913) 649-5103. Douglas Stevens, VP.
Aiken, SC 29803, 131 Inwood Dr. Phone: (803) 649-0031. Fax: (803) 649-7786. John Willis, VP.
Radio & TV, broker; mgmt & sls consultant, FDIC-approved appraiser & expert witness.

Seabrook Travel Consultants, 4225 Sawgrass Dr., Summerville, SC 29420. Phone: (843) 552-0702. Fax: (843) 552-3717. E-mail: larry@thekirbycompanies.com. Larry Kirby, CEO.
Bcst incentive trips worldwide; all major sporting events; owned & operated by bcstrs.

Shane Media Services, 2500 Tanglewilde, Suite 106, Houston, TX 77063. Phone: (713) 952-9221. Fax: (713) 952-1207. E-mail: smsofc@shanemedia.com. Web Site: www.shanemedia.com. Ed Shane, CEO.
Radio progmg and mgmt consultation, custom designed perceptual and qualitative research for electronic media outlets.

Shotmakers, Inc., One Horizon Rd., Fort Lee, NJ 07024. Phone: (201) 886-0287. Fax: (201) 886-0287. E-mail: danjo@bellatlantic.net. Web Site: www.shotmakers.org. Dan Robinson, pres.
Media consultant, original film & TV productions; novelist. Represent historic photos & film of New York City & Atlanta.

Barry Skidelsky, Esq., 185 E. 85th St., # 23D, New York, NY 10028. Phone: (212) 832-4800. Barry Skidelsky, consultant.
Full-svc assistance to investors, owners & mgmt, e.g., acquisition, divestiture, start-up, improvement, trustee (bankruptcy & FCC ownership), expert witness, Arbitrator.

Skywatch Weather Center, 347 Prestley Rd., Bridgeville, PA 15017. Phone: (412) 221-6000. Phone: (800) SKY-WATCH. Fax: (412) 221-3160. E-mail: airsci@skywatchweather.com. Web Site: www.skywatchweather.com. Dr. Stanley J. Penkala, pres.
Specially formatted weathercasts from the Skywatch Weather Center.®

Bill Slatter & Associates, 423 Main St., Natchez, MS 39120. Phone: (601) 442-1828. Fax: (601) 442-1828. E-mail: slatterb@bkbank.com.
Talent coaching.

Smart Target Marketing, 6800 Southwest 40th St., #304, Miami, FL 33155. Phone: (305) 443-4995. Fax: (305) 443-1822. Web Site: www.smarttarget.com.
Denver, CO Phone: (303) 594-8000.
Custom strategic direct-mktg programs; complete promotional & adv svcs including direct mail/targeted mailing lists, telemarketing, data base, custom publishing, sls training, & interactive phone/prom, smart targets & prizm targeting services.

Soundtrack, 162 Columbus Ave., Boston, MA 02116-5222. Phone: (617) 303-7500. Fax: (617) 303-7515. Web Site: www.soundtrackgroup.com. Jeannie Lombardi, COO.
New York, NY 10010, 936 Broadway. Phone: (212) 420-6010. Chris Rich, opns mgr.
Production, postproduction & custom music of all kinds; specializing in sound designs.

Southern Surveys, 1551 Olde Mill Pl., Marietta, GA 30066. Phone: (770) 924-3584. Fax: (770) 924-3584. Rick Phillips, pres.
Natl qualitative moderator for one-on-one rsch. Nationwide recruiting for auditorium music tests since 1986.

Wayne A. Stacey & Assoc. Ltd., 5B-1420 Youville Dr., Ottawa, ON K1C 7B3. Canada. Phone: (613) 830-6985. Fax: (613) 830-8124. E-mail: wstacey@stacey.ca. W.A. Stacey, pres.
Govt rels, CRTC/IC applications, bcst rsch, bcst consulting, engrg svcs, demographic studies.

Gary Stevens & Co., 49 Locust Ave., Suite 107, New Canaan, CT 06840. Phone: (203) 966-6465. Fax: (203) 966-6522. E-mail: deelmakur@aol.com. Gary Stevens, pres.
Bcst mergers, acquistions & investment banking svcs.

Stonick Recruitment Inc., 2504 Hunter's Run Way, Weston, FL 33327. Phone: (954) 217-0068. Fax: (954) 217-0161. E-mail: stonick@gate.net. Web Site: www.stonickrecruitment.com. Chris Stonick, pres.
A natl radio sls consulting firm bringing "recruitment adv" to radio (strictly new business dev).

Peter Storer & Associates Inc., 1361 W. Towne Sq. Rd., Mequon, WI 53092. Phone: (262) 241-9005. Fax: (262) 241-9036. E-mail: doug@storertv.com. Web Site: www.storertv.com. Doug Knight, sls VP; Peter Storer Jr., pres.
Storer Information System (SIMS): Multi-ch, multi-user, PC based TV program schedule, amortization & liability system.

Structural System Technology Inc., 6867 Elm St., McLean, VA 22101. Phone: (703) 356-9765. Fax: (703) 448-0979. Fred Purdy, pres; Kaveh Mehrnama, VP engrg.
Structural engrg studies, analysis, design, modifications, inspections, fabrication & erection of towers & antenna structures.

Joe Sullivan Executive Search & Recruiting, Box 178,, 1202 Lexington Ave., New York, NY 10028. Phone: (212) 734-7890. Fax: (212) 734-0631. E-mail: jsa6@aol.com. Web Site: www.joesullivanexecutivesearch.com. Joseph J. Sullivan Jr., pres; Shane P. Sullivan, VP; Barbara Sullivan, CFO; Jana Heffernan, rsch dir.
Retain exec recruitment in media & academia for positions in middle & sr mgmt with incomes in excess of $120,000 per year.

Synovate, 8600 N.W. 17th St., Suite 100, Miami, FL 33126. Phone: (305) 716-6800. Fax: (305) 716-6756. Web Site: www.synovate.com. Richard Tobin, pres.
Laguna Hills, CA 92653, 23151 Alde Dr, Suite C4. Phone: (714) 598-9055. Dave Thomas, VP/gen mgr. (Los Angeles office).
Full-svc mktg rsch company, specializing in the Hispanic market; focus group testing, awareness usage tracking studies, media ratings.

Szabo Associates Inc., Media Collection Professionals, 3355 Lenox Rd. NE, 9th Fl., Atlanta, GA 30326. Phone: (404) 266-2464. Fax: (404) 266-2165. E-mail: info@szabo.com. Web Site: www.szabo.com. Peter F. Szabo, pres; C. Robin Szabo, VP.
Experts in creditor & debtor rights; consulting media properties in the accounts receivable process; domestic & international collections.

TM Century Inc., 2002 Academy, Dallas, TX 75234. Phone: (972) 406-6800. Fax: (972) 406-6890. E-mail: tmci@tmcentury.com. Web Site: www.tmcentury.com. David Graupner, CEO.
The world's leading supplier of jingles, production & imaging libraries, wkly music service & music libraries on hard drive.

TalentTrainers, 10807 Waring Pl., Charlotte, NC 28277. Phone: (704) 541-0892. Fax: 1-800-787-4284. E-mail: brice@talenttrainers.com. Web Site: www.talenttrainers.com. Shirley Brice, pres.
Talent coaching for tv stns and newspapers. Media trainer for corporate executives. One-on-one sessions, small workshops & individual critiques. Weekly "live" coaching chat on www.talent trainers.com.

J.A. Taylor & Associates, Box 331, Boyertown, PA 19512-0331. Phone: (610) 754-6800. Fax: (610) 754-9766. E-mail: jataylor@broadcastassociates.com. Web Site: www.broadcastassociates.com.
Appraisers & brokers of TV production equipment. Serves video production companies, TV stns & financial institutions.

Tele-Measurements Inc., 145 Main Ave., Clifton, NJ 07014-1078. Phone: (973) 473-8822. Fax: (973) 473-0521. Web Site: www.tele-measurements.com. William E. Endres, pres; Douglas W. Cook, VP sls.
Bcst, professional video equipment, videotape, TV systems, teleconferencing, ongoing maintenance support, CCTV, equipment rentals.

Teletech Inc., Box 85567, Westland, MI 48185. Phone: (734) 641-2300. Keith Johnson, VP.
Scottsdale, AZ 85261, Box 4221. Phone: (480) 367-1500.
Antenna site mgmt; tower, studio & antenna construction & maintenance; frequency searches; FCC application preparation; EMI, radiation & microwave studies.

Television by Design Inc., 3277 Roswell Rd., Suite 714, Atlanta, GA 30305. Phone: (404) 873-3277. Fax: (404) 873-7900. E-mail: jay@tvbd.com. Web Site: www.tvbd.com. Jay Antzakas, pres; Melanie Goux, dir design.
Creators of electronic graphic design; consultants on visual design, equipment & operations for TV stns.

Management and Marketing Consultants

Television Consulting Services, 950 N. Kings Rd. 122, Los Angeles, CA 90069-4397. Phone: (323) 654-1512. Fax: (323) 654-1588. E-mail: hollyentron@lanset.com. Ron Krueger, pres.

Bcst consultants to TV stns, productions, cable TV, group owners & operators, both domestic & international.

Tenner & Associates Inc., 121 Quail Run Rd., Henderson, NV 89014. Phone: (702) 792-9430. Fax: (702) 792-5748. Web Site: www.tennerassoc.com. Lisa Tenner, ptnr.

Event & conference producers for the entertainment industry.

3-H Cable Communications Consultants, 504 Main St., Auburn, WA 98002-5502. Phone: (253) 833-8380. Fax: (253) 833-8430.

Cable franchise admin, negotiation, renewal, tech evaluation, community needs assessment & franchise fee audits.

Edwin Tornberg & Co. Inc., 8917 Cherbourg Dr., Potomac, MD 20854. Phone: (301) 983-8700. Fax: (301) 299-2297. Edwin Tornberg, pres.

Negotiators for purchase & sale of radio, TV stns & CATV systems; appraisers & financial advisers; mgmt consultants.

Transcomm Inc., Box 2845, Fairfax, VA 22031. Phone: (703) 323-5150. Fax: (703) 426-4527. E-mail: transcommusa@msn.com. Web Site: www.transcommusa.com. Dr. Norman C. Lerner, pres.

Financial/economic analysis, market rsch, pricing studies & regulatory economics.

24 Karat Productions Inc., 1717 W. Sanderling Ln., Ft. Pierce, FL 34982. Phone: (772) 465-5511. Mark Prichard, pres/CEO; Gloria Prichard, exec VP.

Music-1 Mix: over 10,000 key stereo selections plus monthly updates, complete consultant svcs delivered on CD or tape.

Jon Ulmer & Associates, 2176 Highpoint Rd., Snellville, GA 30078. Phone: (770) 979-3031. Fax: (770) 979-3789. John R. Ulmer, C.P.A.

Accounting, computer & financial mgmt consulting.

VIP Research Inc., 5700 Broadmoor, Suite 710, Mission, KS 66202. Phone: (888) 384-9494. Fax: (913) 677-2727. E-mail: mike@viprresearch.net. Web Site: www.vipresearch.net. C. C. McCartney, pres; Clark Roberts, VP.

Provides hook-tape production, listener screening, fielding & tabulation for all music testing, perceptual studies, focus groups & promotional telemarketing.

Vanguard Media Corp., 370 N. Westlake Blvd., Suite 100, Westlake Village, CA 91362. Phone: (805) 446-4100. Fax: (805) 446-4111. Rick Newberger, pres.

Advisory firm to media companies, specializing in planning, & dev of new progmg svcs (e.g., The Golf Channel) & distribution systems (e.g., DBS).

Veronis, Suhler, 350 Park Ave., New York, NY 10022. Phone: (212) 935-4990. Fax: (212) 381-8168. E-mail: lesperancef@veronissuhler.com. Web Site: www.veronissuhler.com. John J. Veronis, chmn/CEO; John S. Suhler, pres/CEO; Jeffrey T. Stevenson, gen ptnr; James P. Rutherfurd, exec VP; Kevin Waldman, dir.

Merchant bankers to media, communications & info industries, with focus on mergers & acquisitions, valuations, joint ventures & private equity.

A.G. Visk, 2973 Evans Oaks Ct., Atlanta, GA 30340. Phone: (770) 939-5657. E-mail: tuisk@yahoo.com.

Promotional concepts, scripts & publications for the bcstg & entertainment industries.

WW Associates, 10040 East Happy Valley Rd. unit 454, Scottsdale, AZ 85225. Phone: (480) 515-0913. Fax: (480) 515-4632. E-mail: jwiesenberg@mba1977.hbs.edu. Jim Wiesenberg,.

International new media dev, strategic planning & acquisition assistance, cable & wireless MMDS expertise, PPV event & movie studio liaison.

Warren Only Media Group, 19 W. Almond St., Vineland, NJ 08360. Phone: (856) 507-9368. Fax: (856) 507-9368. E-mail: warrenonly@msn.com. Web Site: www.warrenonly.com. Warren Only, consultant.

Broadcasting radio & TV consultants, telecommunications, FCC applications.

Washington DC Media Site/Facilities Selection Group, (National-International). 1666 K St. N.W., Suite 1200, Washington, DC 20006. Phone: (202) 833-5801. Fax: (202) 457-1702.

Consulting coml real estate svcs, tenant/client representation, construction/financial analysis, turnkey lease/sale assumptions; roof & bldg zoning surveys, serving metropolitan Washington, DC.

Washington Information Group Ltd., 1655 N. Ft. Meyer Dr., Suite 800, Arlington, VA 22209. Phone: (202) 463-7334. Fax: (703) 527-4586. Web Site: www.winfogroup.com. Douglas House, pres.

Customized business rsch. Competitive intelligence, pub & private company rsch, industry & market studies. Strictly confidential; free consultation.

"The Weather Center", (A broadcast service of Aviation Weather Inc.). 701 Gervais St., Suite 150-224, Columbia, SC 29201. Phone: (803) 739-2827. E-mail: wxcenter@aviationweatherinc.com. Web Site: www.aviationweatherinc.com. L.R. Ferguson, pres.

"Regional Radio Broadcast/Weathercast Network" across the Carolinas and Georgia in over 20 broadcast markets. Weather forecasting, site-specific broadcast svcs for stns all across America. 100% barter.

The Wexler Group, 1317 F St. N.W., Suite 600, Washington, DC 20004. Phone: (202) 638-2121. Fax: (202) 638-7045. Web Site: www.wexlergroup.com. Anne Wexler, chmn.

Consulting firm, specializing in govt rel & pub affrs with strong emphasis on mass media, telecommunications, copyright, trade.

Wind River Broadcast Center, 117 E. 11th St., Loveland, CO 80537. Phone: (800) 669-3993. Phone: (970) 669-3442. Fax: (970) 663-6081. E-mail: info@windriverbroadcast.com. Web Site: www.windriverbroadcast.com. Jim McDonald, gen mgr/CEO; Nancy McDonald, Bigbook Project publisher.

TV/FM/AM tech & regulatory consulting; publishers of *The Bigbook Project*, a radio/TV stn tech & regulatory workbook system. FCC applications, exhibits.

Wishnow Group Inc., 82 Bubier Rd., Marblehead, MA 01945-3640. Phone: (781) 631-2444. Fax: (781) 639-1346. E-mail: jwishnow@yahoo.com. Jerrold D. Wishnow, pres.

Position bcst clients as community service leaders.

Wolfe Media, 10755-F Scripps Poway Pkwy, #612, San Diego, CA 92131. Phone: (858) 530-8787. Fax: (858) 530-9974. E-mail: dw@wolfemedia.com. Web Site: www.wolfemedia.com. David Wolfe, pres.

Walter Wulff & Associates, FAA Consultants. Box 914, Point Clear, AL 36564. Phone: (251) 990-2502. Fax: (334) 990-2503. E-mail: wulff@zebra.net. Walter H. Wulff, CEO.

Conducts FAA tower studies & EMI evaluations.

Station Financing Services

ABN AMRO, Park Ave. Plaza 55 E. 52nd St., New York, NY 10055. Phone: (212) 409-1000. Fax: (212) 409-7291.

Allied Capital Corp., 1919 Pennsylvania Ave. N.W., 3rd Fl., Washington, DC 20006. Phone: (202) 331-1112. Fax: (202) 659-2053. Web Site: www.alliedcapital.com.
Subordinated debt, deal size $3 million to $8 million, natl & international.

Alta Communications, 200 Clarendon St., 51st Fl., Boston, MA 02116. Phone: (617) 262-7770. Fax: (617) 262-9779. Web Site: www.altacomm.com. William P. Egan, gen ptnr; Brian W. McNeill, gen ptnr; Timothy L. Dibble, gen ptnr; Robert Y. Emmert, gen ptnr; B. Lane MacDonald, gen ptnr; Philip L. Thompson, gen ptnr; Patrick D. Brubaker, gen ptnr; Eileen A. McCarthy, gen ptnr; Andrew Mulderry, gen ptnr.
Provide equity & subordinated debt for acquisitions, buyouts, recapitalizations, etc. for companies in radio, TV, cable TV & related industries.

BIA Capital Corp., 15120 Enterprise Ct., Suite 100, Chantilly, VA 20151. Phone: (703) 818-8115. Fax: (703) 803-3299. E-mail: cwiebe@bia.com. Web Site: www.bia.com.
Investment banking service, including placement of debt & equity, advice in capital structure & merger, & acquisition issues.

BIA Digital Partners, L.P., 15120 Enterprise Ct., Suite 200, Chantilly, VA 20151. Phone: (703) 227-9600. Fax: (703) 803-3299. E-mail: gjohnson@bia.com. Web Site: www.bia.com.
Provides subordinated debt and preferred equity for communications companies in amounts from $3 to $25 million.

BIA Financial Network, 15120 Enterprise Ct., Chantilly, VA 20151-1102. Phone: (703) 818-2425. Fax: (703) 803-3299. E-mail: consulting@bia.com. Web Site: www.bia.com. Thomas J. Buono, pres/CEO; Mark Giannini, exec VP; Mark O'Brien, VP; Cary Kelly, VP.
Financial consultants to the communications industry; fair market valuations, tax appraisals, acquisition consulting, business plans, internal operational audits, litigation support, investment, publications, & database software, venture funding, capital.

BMO Nesbitt Burns (Bank of Montreal), 3 Times Sq., New York, NY 10036. Phone: (212) 605-1424. Fax: (212) 605-1648. E-mail: yvonne.bos@bmo.com. Web Site: www.bmo.com.
Provides lending & other capital raising svcs, derivatives, & cash mgmt to the bcst & cable industries.

BNP Paribas, 787 Seventh Ave., New York, NY 10019. Phone: (212) 841-2595. Fax: (212) 841-2369. E-mail: lynne.randall@americas.bnpparibas.
Leading underwriting & syndicating time-sensitive, non-investment grade debt financing; often requiring complex & creative capital structures; also financing & equity co-investments.
Branch offices located in Los Angeles, London, New York, & Paris.

BTMI, 1090 Vermont Ave. N.W., Suite 800, Washington, DC 20005. Phone: (202) 408-7036. Fax: (202) 408-1590. E-mail: probinson@btmiconsulting.com. Web Site: www.btmiconsulting.com. Paul Robinson, pres; Robert Long, ptnr; Peter Michaud, ptnr.
Due diligence svcs, valuation svcs, investment counseling & recovery svcs.

BancBoston Capital Inc., 175 Federal St. 10th floor, Boston, MA 02110. Phone: (617) 434-2509. Fax: (617) 434-1153.
Active, experienced financing source of equity & mezzanine capital for media companies with over $150 million invested in these businesses.

Bank of America Illinois, 231 S. LaSalle St., Chicago, IL 60697. Phone: (312) 828-2345. Fax: (312) 987-7148. Web Site: www.bankofamerica.com. Terry Perucca, chmn.

Bank One, One Bank One Plaza, IL1-0629, Chicago, IL 60670. Phone: (312) 732-4000. Fax: (312) 732-8587. Web Site: www.bankone.com.
Industry specialists committed to serving the financial needs of cable & bcst companies, including loans, derivatives, capital raising & cash mgmt.

The Barclays Group, 200 Park Ave., New York, NY 10166. Phone: (212) 412-4000. Fax: (212) 412-7300. Web Site: www.barcap.com.
San Francisco, CA 94111, 388 Market St. Phone: (415) 765-4700. Fax: (415) 765-4760. Andrew Wynns, mgr.

Berkery, Noyes & Co., 50 Broad St., New York, NY 10004. Phone: (212) 668-3022. Fax: (212) 747-9092. Web Site: www.berkerynoyes.com. Joseph W. Berkery, pres; John T. Shea, COO; Peter B. Ognibene, mgng dir.
San Francisco, CA 94104, 580 California St., 5th Fl. Phone: (415) 440-5001.
Newton, MA 02460, 40 Kirkstall Rd. Phone: (617) 969-7935. Marlowe G. Teig, mgng dir.
Assists with mergers, acquisitions, divestitures; financial analysis & counsel; debt or equity financing through private or pub chs, including LBOs, ESOPs & valuations.

Blackburn & Co. Capital Markets Group, 201 N. Union St., Suite 340, Alexandria, VA 22314. Phone: (703) 519-3703. Fax: (703) 519-9756.
Brokerage of radio & TV stns.

Bulkley Capital L.P., 5949 Sherry Lane, Suite 1370, Dallas, TX 75225. Phone: (214) 692-5476. Fax: (214) 692-9309. E-mail: info@bulkleycapital.com. Web Site: www.bulkleycapital.com. Lisa Bulkley, investment off.
Investment banking; mergers, acquisitions, private placements of debt & equity capital.

CEA Inc., 1270 Ave. of the Americas, Suite 1818, New York, NY 10020. Phone: (212) 218-5085. Fax: (212) 218-5099. Web Site: www.ceaworldwide.com.
Investment banking & brokerage.

CIBC World Markets, 425 Lexington Ave., New York, NY 10017. Phone: (212) 856-4000. Fax: (212) 856-3996. Web Site: www.cibcwm.com.
Investment banking & asset mgmt.

CIT Equipment Rental and Finance, 900 Ashwood Pkwy., Suite 170, Atlanta, GA 30338. Phone: (770) 551-7847. Fax: (770) 206-9295.
CIT Equipment Rental and Finance provides senior debt capital for equipment, expansion, and modernization.

Chaisson & Company Inc., 154 Indian Waters Dr., New Canaan, CT 06840. Phone: (203) 966-6333. Fax: (203) 966-1298. E-mail: rchaisco@aol.com. Robert A. Chaisson, pres.
Brokerage of radio/TV sls & acquisitions.

ComCapital Group, Box 1950, Cathedral Station, New York, NY 10025. Phone: (212) 663-3068. Fax: (212) 663-6512. E-mail: paulraeder@comcapitalgroup.com. Paul C. Raeder, pres.
Investment banking svcs for bcstrs, private placement of equity & subordinated debt, sr bank financing, capital restructuring & refinancing.

Communications Equity Associates, L.L.C., 101 E. Kennedy Blvd., Suite 3300, Tampa, FL 33602. Phone: (813) 226-8844. Fax: (813) 225-1513. Web Site: www.ceaworldwide.com. J. Patrick Michaels, Jr., chmn/CEO; Brad Gordon, CFO.
Muenchen D-80538, Prinzregentenstrasse 56. Phone: 49-89-290-7250. Dr. Stephan Goetz, mgng dir/exec VP international opns CEA GMBH.
Praha 1 11000, Melantrichova 17. Phone: 420-2-216-32451. Vaclav Matatko, mgng dir CEA Prague.
Paris, NO 75008 France. CEA France, 9, Rue Royale. Phone: 33 153 308607. Fax: 33 147 423214. Franck Portais, mgng dir.
Madrid 28006 Spain. CEA Spain, Serrano 93, 6 E. Jose Kabana.
London, NO W1G 0PW United Kingdom, 33 Cavendish Sq. Phone: 44-207-647-7700. Hank Young, mgng dir Communications Equity Associates Internat.
Investment & merchant banking firm specializing in cable, bcstg, new media & entertainment industries.

Cox & Cox L.L.C., 2454 Shiva Ct., St. Louis, MO 63011. Phone: (636) 458-4780. Fax: (636) 458-6323. E-mail: bc@coxandcoxllc.com. Web Site: www.coxandcoxllc.com. Bob Cox, pres.
Mergers & acquisitions, appraisals, consulting & expert testimony.

Daniels & Associates, 3200 Cherry Creek S. Dr., Suite 500, Denver, CO 80209. Phone: (303) 778-5555. Fax: (303) 778-5599. Web Site: www.danielsonline.com. E-mail: info@danielsonline.com. Brian Deevy, chmn/CEO; Brad Busse, pres/COO.
New York, NY 10022, 711 5th Ave, Suite 405. Phone: (212) 935-5900. Fax: (212) 8634859. David Tolliver, VP.
Provides mergers, acquisitions, corporate finance & financial advisory svcs to the tcable, telecom, media & internet industries.

The Deer River Group, 800 17th St., N.W., 11th Fl., Washington, DC 20006. Phone: (202) 939-9090. Fax: (202) 939-9091. E-mail: robin.martin@earthlink.net. Robin B. Martin, pres/CEO; Erwin G. Krasnow, gen counsel.
Assist bcst execs in acquiring stns, securing financing; financial consultant to single stns & group owners; investment banking svcs.

Dresdner Kleinwort Wasserstein, 1301 Ave. of the Americas, New York, NY 10019. Phone: (212) 969-2700. John Fieseler, sr VP; Laura Fazio, first VP; Jane Majeski, first VP.
Integrated investment bank offering premier mergers & acquisitions advising as well as private equity investment & placement, structuring, underwriting & advisory for global debt & equity.

EnVest Media, LLC, 6802 Patterson Ave., Richmond, VA 23226. Phone: (804) 282-5561. Fax: (804) 282-5703. E-mail: mittyounts@cs.com. Web Site: www.envestmedia.com. Mitt S. Younts, mgr.
Alpharetta, GA 30004, 11770 Haynes Bridge Rd, #205. Phone: (770) 753-9650. Fax: (770) 753-0089. E-mail: jswnet@aol.com. Jesse Weatherby, member, manager.
Envest Media is a nationwide radio & TV acquisition, valuation, financing & consulting firm. The company provides brokerage svcs to stn transaction, appraisal svcs to stn owners & financial institutions. The group secures debt & equity acquisition financing, offers consulting & asset mgmt svcs, acting as court appointed receivers or trustees for bcst stations.

First Union National Bank, Wachovia Securities, 301 S. College St., Charlotte, NC 28288. Phone: (704) 715-6065. Fax: (704) 715-1997. Web Site: www.wachovia.com. Gregory J. Attori, mgng dir.
Secured financing for acquisition &/or recapitalization of bcst properties.

Norman Fischer & Associates Inc., Box 5308, Austin, TX 78763. Phone: (512) 476-9457. Fax: (512) 476-0504. E-mail: terrille@nfainc.com. Web Site: www.nfainc.com. Terrill Fischer, pres.
Bethlehem, PA 18017, 1330 Biafore Ave. Phone: (610) 317-2424. Bernhard Fuhrmann, East Coast/Atlantic assoc.
Brokerage in radio, TV & cable; consultation in mgmt & opns; appraisals; feasibility studies; expert testimony; financial planning & assistance.

William Fleming & Associates, 176 N. Beacon St., Hartford, CT 06105. Phone: (860) 236-4453. Fax: (860) 236-2982. E-mail: wlfleming@comcast.net. William L. Fleming, Principal.
Investment banking & financial consultant to bcstrs; assists in structuring mergers, acquisitions & refinancings; arranges equity, debt or other funds needed.

Richard A. Foreman Associates Inc., 330 Emery Dr. E., Stamford, CT 06902-2210. Phone: (203) 327-2800. Fax: (203) 967-9393. E-mail: rafamedia@compuserve.com. Web Site: www.rafamedia.com. Richard A. Foreman, pres.
Debt & equity placement for radio & TV stn acquisitions in major growth markets.

GE Capital Inc., 500 W. Monroe St., Chicago, IL 60661. Phone: (312) 441-7000. Fax: (312) 441-6728. Web Site: www.gecapital.com. Kim Gutierrez, dir mktg.
Coml financial svcs.

GE Commercial Finance Global Media and Communications, 201 Merritt 7, 4th fl, Norwalk, CT 06851. Phone: (203) 956-4000. Fax: (203) 956-4528. Web Site: www.geglobalmediacomm.com. Robert V. Stefanowski, mgng dir.
Leading provider of capital to the broadcasting, cable, entertainment, movie theater, outdoor advertising, publishing, technology, towers, wireless, and wireline industries. Locations in Atlanta, Chicago, Delhi, London, New York, Norwalk, and San Francisco.

Broadcasting & Cable Yearbook 2006

Station Financing Services

Clifton Gardiner & Company L.L.C., 2437 S. Chase Ln., Denver, CO 80227. Phone: (303) 758-6900. Fax: (303) 479-9210. E-mail: cliff@cliftongardiner.com. Web Site: www.cliftongardiner.com. Clifton H. Gardiner, pres.

Consulting svcs on debt & equity placements.

Gleacher & Co., 660 Madison Ave., New York, NY 10021. Phone: (212) 418-4200. Fax: (212) 752-2711. Web Site: www.gleacher.com.

Provide advice & capital to companies in the media & telecommunications industries.

Great Hill Partners, One Liberty Sq., Boston, MA 02109. Phone: (617) 790-9400. Fax: (617) 790-9401. Web Site: www.greathillpartners.com.

Private equity for media and communications companies.

HSBC, One HSBC Center., Buffalo, NY 14203. Fax: (716) 854-2751. Web Site: www.ushsbc.com.

Postproduction & radio/TV equipment financing.

R. Miller Hicks & Co., 1011 W. 11th St., Austin, TX 78703. Phone: (512) 477-7000. Fax: (512) 477-9697. E-mail: millerhicks@rmhicks.com.

Business consultant & dev firm.

Hoffman Schutz Media Capital Inc., 2044 W. California St., San Diego, CA 92110. Phone: (619) 291-7070. E-mail: dave@hs-media.com. Web Site: www.hs-media.com. David E. Schutz, pres.

Peru, VT 05152, Rock Bottom Lane. Phone: (802) 824-6544. Anthony Hoffman.

Appraisals, restructurings & litigation support.

Hungerford, Aldrin, Nichols & Carter, CPAs, 2910 Lucerne Dr. S.E., Grand Rapids, MI 49546. Phone: (616) 949-3200. Fax: (616) 949-7720. E-mail: caldrin@hanc.com. Web Site: www.hanc.com.

Confidential radio & TV market revenue share reports for the bcst industry.

J P Morgan and Co. Inc., 60 Wall St., New York, NY 10260. Phone: (212) 483-2323. Web Site: www.jpmorgan.com.

Los Angeles, CA 90071, 333 S. Hope St, 35th Fl. Phone: (213) 437-9300.

San Francisco, CA 94111, 101 California St, 38th Fl. Phone: (415) 954-3200.

Chicago, IL 60606, 227 W. Monroe St, Suite 2800m. Phone: (312) 541-3300.

Mergers & acquisitions; debt & equity capital raising; swaps & derivatives; credit arrangement & loan syndication; securities sls & trading; asset mgmt.

Kagan World Media, 126 Clock Tower Pl., Carmel, CA 93923-8734. Phone: (831) 624-1536. Fax: (831) 625-3225. E-mail: info@kagan.com. Web Site: www.kagan.com. Sandie Borthwick, dir opns.

Specializing in financial & investment rsch. Media financial newsletters & database reports. Strategic consulting, seminars & conferences.

Key Corporate Capital Inc./KeyCorp, 127 Public Sq., 6th Fl., Cleveland, OH 44114-1306. Phone: (216) 689-5787. Fax: (216) 689-4666. E-mail: kathleen_mayher@key.com. Web Site: www.key.com/media. Kathleen Mayher, exec VP & mgr.

Financing for media—TV, radio, cable, nwsprs, bcstg & telecommunications.

M/C Venture Partners, 75 State St., Suite 2500, Boston, MA 02109. Phone: (617) 345-7200. Fax: (617) 345-7201. Web Site: www.mcventurepartners.com. Gillis S. Cashman, VP; Joseph S. Monaco, CFO.

Provides equity financing & strategic guidance to entrepreneurial ventures in the media & telecommunications industries.

The MFR Group, Box 1184, Rancho Mirage, CA 92270. Fax: (800) 540-0335. E-mail: info@mfrgroup.net. Web Site: www.mfrgroup.com. Bart Fenmore, pres.

Accounts receivable funding for radio/TV stns.

Media Capital Inc., 890 Monterey St., Suite G, San Luis Obispo, CA 93401. Phone: (805) 543-9214. Fax: (805) 543-9243. E-mail: michael@mikehesser.com. Web Site: www.mikehesser.com. Michael B. Hesser, pres.

Assist in finding, evaluating, financing & structuring acquisitions. Also, consult mgmt & sls.

Multimedia Broadcast Investment Corp., 3101 South St. N.W., Washington, DC 20007. Phone: (202) 293-1166. Fax: (202) 293-1181. Walter Threadgill, pres.

Provides sr, subordinated deb, equity for telecommunications & bcst ventures.

National Broadcast Finance Corp., Box 3167, 27 Harrison St., New Haven, CT 06515. Phone: (203) 389-6000. Fax: (203) 389-6020. David C. Cherhoniak, pres.

Specialized investment banking & financial consulting, including raising debt & equity for bcst acquisitions & refinancings; also brokerage for acquisitions & divestitures.

Nautic Partners, 50 Kennedy Plaza, Providence, RI 02903. Phone: (401) 278-6770. Fax: (401) 278-6387. Web Site: www.nauticpartners.com. Cynthia L. Balasco, ptnr; Gregory M. Barr, ptnr; Bernard V. Buonanno, ptnr; Habib Y. Gorgi, ptnr; Scott F. Hilinski, ptnr; Robert M. Van Degna, ptnr; Michael W. Joe, ptnr; Rory B. Smith, ptnr.

Source of equity capital to well-managed, positive cash flowing companies.

Patrick Communications L.L.C. 5074 Dorsey Hall Dr., Suite 205, Ellicott City, MD 21042. Phone: (410) 740-0250. Fax: (410) 740-7222. E-mail: patrick@patcomm.com. Web Site: www.patcomm.com. Larry Patrick, pres.

Stn brokerage, investment banking, mgmt consulting svcs, appraisals & opns consulting.

Phoenix Cable Inc., 17 S. Franklin Tpke., Ramsey, NJ 07446. Phone: (201) 825-9090. Fax: (201) 825-8794.

San Rafael, CA 94901, 2401 Kerner Blvd. Phone: (415) 485-4500. Gus Constantin, pres.

Cable TV systems ownership, system mgmt svcs, lease & debt financing svcs.

Premier Capital Group, 1308 8th St., Suite 5, West Des Moines, IA 50265. Phone: (515) 698-9600. Fax: (515) 698-9699.

The Proctor Group, Inc., 137 Magnolia Bend Dr., Livingston, TX 77351. Phone: (936) 328-5960. Fax: (936) 328-5970. E-mail: tvbroker@livingston.net. Web Site: www.thelptvstore.com. Gerald R. Proctor, pres.

Brokerage & financial svcs to the bcst, cable & communications industries.

Rodgers Broadcasting, Box 1646, Richmond, IN 47375. Phone: (765) 962-6533. Fax: (765) 966-1499. David A. Rodgers, pres.

Financeing particulary for small operators.

Sanders & Co., 2741 Margaret Mitchell Dr. N.W., Atlanta, GA 30327. Phone: (404) 367-0850. Fax: (404) 367-0580.

Private placements of debt & equity for bcstrs & cable operators.

Schroder Investment Management, Equitable Ctr., 875 Third Ave., New York, NY 10022. Phone: (212) 641-3800.

Silicon Valley Bank, 185 Berry St., Suite 190, San Francisco, CA 94107. Phone: (415) 512-4227. Fax: (415) 348-0259. E-mail: jbrooks@svbank.com. Web Site: www.svb.com. John R. Brooks, mgr.

Comprehensive finance svcs for middle market bcst & cable operators.

Barry Skidelsky, Esq., 185 E. 85th St., 23 D, New York, NY 10028. Phone: (212) 832-4800. Barry Skidelsky, owner.

Full svc assistance to investors, owners, mgmt, aquisition, divestiture, start-up, improvement, trustee (bankruptcy & FCC ownership), expert witness & arbitrator.

Stonemark Media Brokers, P.O. Box 21305, Seattle, WA 98111-3305. Phone: (206) 628-8989. Fax: (206) 628-0839. Web Site: www.radiobrokers.com. William Victor May, pres.

Specializing in business brokerage, debt placement & equity arrangement related to bcst properties as well as other industries.

Syndicated Communications Inc. (SYNCOM), 8401 Colesville Rd., Suite 300, Silver Spring, MD 20910. Phone: (301) 608-3203. Fax: (301) 608-3307. Terry L. Jones, pres; Duane C. Mcknight, VP.

Edwin Tornberg & Co. Inc., 8917 Cherbourg Dr., Potomac, MD 20854. Phone: (301) 299-6661. Fax: (301) 299-2297. Edwin Tornberg, pres.

Veronis Suhler Stevenson, 350 Park Ave, New York, NY 10022. Phone: (212) 935-4990. Fax: (212) 381-8168. E-mail: stevenson@veronissuhler.com. Web Site: www.veronissuhler.com. Jeffrey T. Stevenson; Marco Sodi, mgng dir international; Marv Shapiro, mgng dir.

London SW1 Y4J0 United Kingdom. London, St. James Square, Buchanan House, 8th Fl. Phone: 44-207-484-1440. Fax: 44-207-484-1415. Nigel Stapleton, chmn Veloms Schler International.

Private equity/media buyout affil of Veronis, Suhler, established in 1987 & investing in companies across the spectrum of communications industry segments.

Waller Capital Corp., 30 Rockefeller Plaza, Suite 4350, New York, NY 10112. Phone: (212) 632-3600. Fax: (212) 632-3607. Web Site: www.wallercc.com. Townsend Deveraux, sr VP.

Financing & investment svcs to cable TV industry, specializing in cable TV mergers & acquisitions, buyout financing, raising debt & equity.

Wells Fargo Equipment Finance Inc., 530 Fifth Ave., 15th Fl., New York, NY 10036. Phone: (212) 805-1000. Fax: (212) 805-1050. Henry Frommer, sr VP.

Tustin, CA 92780, 14081 Yorba St, Suite 205. Phone: (714) 544-4190. Deborah Anderson, VP.

Danbury, CT 06811, 100 Mill Plain Rd., 3rd Fl. Phone: (203) 791-3944. Brian Rodden, VP.

Wilsonville, OR 97070, 11025 S.W. Matzen Dr. Phone: (888) 325-8100. Ross Guilford, VP.

Leading provider of equipment leasing & financing, intermediate term lending & specialty finance products to the bcst industry.

Wellsprings Financial Corp., 226 Sussex Ave., Morristown, NJ 07960. Phone: (973) 984-8822. Fax: (973) 984-8822.

Investment banking svcs acquisitions, refinancing, equipment leasing, advisory consulting.

Wood & Co. Inc., 431 Ohio Pike, Suite 200, Cincinnati, OH 45255. Phone: (513) 528-7373. Fax: (513) 528-7374. Larry C. Wood, pres; M.A. Dennis, rsch analyst; S.L. Kabbes, rsch analyst.

Research Services

A & A Research, 690 Sunset Blvd., Kalispell, MT 59901. Phone: (406) 752-7857. Fax: (406) 752-0194. E-mail: fireowl@in-tch.com. Judith Doonan, pres; Dr. E. B. Eiselein, rsch dir.

Qualitative & quantitative audience surveys for small- & medium-market radio stns, TV stns, cable. Experience with minority stns.

The ARS Group, 110 Walnut St., Evansville, IN 47708. Phone: (812) 425-4562. Fax: (812) 425-2844. E-mail: info@ars-group.com. Web Site: www.ars-group.com. Dr. Margaret Blair, CEO; John Walling, pres.

Ad mgmt & dev tools: ARS Copytest, Firstep Proposition test, Outlook Advertising planner, StarBoard Story Board reviewer. WOWWW Competitive Intelligence system.

Abt Associates Inc., 55 Wheeler St., Cambridge, MA 02138. Phone: (617) 492-7100. Fax: (617) 492-5219. Web Site: www.abtassoc.com. Peg Laplan, pres/CEO.

Washington, DC 20005, 1110 Vermont Ave. N.W. Phone: (202) 263-1800. (202) 263-1801.

Chicago, IL 60610, 640 N. LaSalle. Phone: (312) 867-4000. Fax: (312) 867-4200.

Bethesda, MD 20814, 4800 Montgomery Ln, Suite 600. Phone: (301) 913-0500. Fax: (301) 652-3618.

Mktg rsch, strategic planning, mgmt consulting, audience rsch & segmentation; customer satisfaction programs, quality of service programs, social science survey rsch, pub policy rsch, economical rsch.

ADcom Information Services Inc., 700 W. Hillsboro Blvd., Suite 201, Bldg. 3, Deerfield Beach, FL 33441. Phone: (954) 481-8380. Fax: (954) 427-8950. E-mail: dickspooner@cableratings.com. Web Site: www.cableratings.com. Bill Livek, pres/CEO; Dick Spooner, exec VP sls.

New York, NY 10003, 230 Park Ave. South. Phone: (212) 598-5400. Alan Trugman, VP agency svcs.

Viewership rsch systems designed for multi-ch systems, with emphasis on cable ratings & qualitative data.

Admar Group, Inc., Box 1098, 87 Ruckman Road, Alpine, NJ 07620-1098. Phone: (201) 767-8000. Fax: (201) 767-8006. Henry D. Ostberg, chmn.

Adv rsch, concept evaluation, product testing & tracking studies; specializes in rsch for legal purposes.

The Adult Contemporary Music Research Letter, 1837 S.E. Harold St., Portland, OR 97202-4932. Phone: (503) 232-9787. Phone: (800) 929-5119. Fax: (503) 232-9787. Fax: (800) 929-5119. E-mail: acmrl@myexcel.com. Web Site: www.acmusicresearch.com. Eric G. Norberg, editor.

Rsch audience appeal of current adult contemp mus, reported in wkly newsletter. Book of oldies rsch also available.

Advanced Television Technology Center, 1330 Braddock Pl., Suite 200, Alexandria, VA 22314. Phone: (703) 739-3850. Fax: (703) 739-3230. Web Site: www.attc.org. Paul K. DeGonia, exec dir; Charles W. Elnolf, deputy exec dir.

Testing/evaluation of digital transmission systems, RF bcst systems; video codes, quality (up to MDTV); TV design, consulting engrg.

Arbitron Inc., 142 W. 57th St., New York, NY 10019. Phone: (212) 887-1300. Fax: (212) 887-1401. Web Site: www.arbitron.com. Stephen B. Morris, pres/CEO; Pierre Bouvard, pres; E. Owen Charlebois, pres; William J. Walsh, exec VP; Dolores L. Cpody, exec VP; Janice M. Giannini, exec VP; Claire L. Kummer, exec VP; David A. Lapovsky, engrg VP; Kathleen T. Ross, exec VP.

Los Angeles, CA 90024, 10877 Wilshire Blvd. Phone: (310) 824-6600. Fax: (310) 824-6651. Tony Belzer-Western Div Mgr.- radio stn svcs; John Hegelmeyer, adv & Agency svcs. (Western office).

Atlanta, GA 30328, 9000 Central Pkwy. Phone: (770) 668-5400. Fax: (770) 688-5417. Jim Remeny, radio stn svcs; Dan Griffin, mgr adv/agency svcs. (Southeastern office).

Chicago, IL 60606, 222 Riverside Plaza. Phone: (312) 542-1900. Fax: (312) 542-1901. John Nolan-Radio stn svcs, James Tobolski-Agency & adv svcs. (Midwestern office).

Columbia, MD 21046, 9705 Patuxent Woods Dr. Phone: (410) 312-8000. Tom O'Sullivan RSS eastern div mgr-Rad Sta svcs; Julie Ellis- agency & adv svcs. (Eastern office).

New York, NY 10019, 142 W. 57th St., 12th Fl. Phone: (212) 887-1300. Fax: (212) 887-1401. Tom O'Sullivan-RSS Eastern Div Mgr-Rad Sta Servs; Julie Ellis-agency & adv svcs.

Dallas, TX 75240, One Galleria Tower. Phone: (972) 385-5388. Fax: (972) 385-5377. Harry Clark, radio stn svcs; Becky Burkett, adv agency svcs. (Southwestern office).

Loc radio audience measurement in 286 markets, qualitative service through RetailDirect, Scarborough & the Qualitative Diary service in 260+ markets; Arbitron NewMedia; rsch based info svcs for the new electronic media.

Audience Research & Development (AR&D), 2440 Lofton Terrace, Ft. Worth, TX 76109. Phone: (817) 924-6922. Fax: (817) 924-7539. Web Site: www.ar-d.com. E-mail: jgumbert@ar-d.com. Jim Willi, dir; Fred Ertz, dir; Jerry Florence, dir; Jerry Gumbert, mgng dir; Bob Kaplitz, dir.

Rsch & consultation in loc & natl TV progmg, specializing in news. Program dev, prom, strategic planning, mktg & sls rsch for bcst TV.

BBM Canada, 1500 Don Mills Rd., Suite 305, Toronto, ON M3B 3L7. Canada. Phone: (416) 445-9800. Fax: (416) 445-8644. Web Site: www.bbm.ca. Jim MacLeod, pres/CEO; Mark Johnston, VP; Don Easter, VP; Ron Bremner, VP; Pat Pelligrini, VP; Tom Saint, VP; Randy Missen, VP; Kathy Carson, dir; Jeff Osborne, pres.

Richmond, BC V6X 3C6 Canada, 10991 Shellbridge Way, 2nd Fl. Phone: (604) 249-3500. Fax: (604) 214-9648. Catherine Kelly, VP Western svcs.

Moncton, NB E1C 817 Canada, 1234 Main St, Suite 3000. Phone: (506) 859-7700. Fax: (506) 852-4445.

Montreal, PQ H3A 1V4 Canada, 2055 Peel St., 11th Fl. Phone: (514) 878-9711. Fax: (514) 878-4210. Robert Langlois, VP Quebec svcs.

Media rsch for radio & TV, & custom rsch through ComQuest Division.

BDS Radio, One N. Lexington Ave., White Plains, NY 10601. Phone: (914) 684-5579.

Los Angeles, CA 90036, 5055 Wilshire Blvd, 7th Floor. Phone: (323) 525-2252. Fax: (323) 525-2373. Mark Tindle, gen mgr.

Radio Track electronically monitors airplay of stns nationwide. Data available on-line within hours of actual bcst.

BIA Financial Network, 15120 Enterprise Ct., Chantilly, VA 20151-1102. Phone: (703) 818-2425. Fax: (703) 803-3299. E-mail: consulting@bia.com. Web Site: www.bia.com. Thomas J. Buono, pres/CEO; Mark Giannini, exec VP; Mark O'Brien, VP; Cary Kelly, VP.

Financial consultants to the communications industry; fair market valuations, tax appraisals, acquisition consulting, business plans, internal operational audits, litigation support, investment, publications, & database software; venture funding, capital.

The Benchmark Co., 907 S. Congress, Suite 7, Austin, TX 78704. Phone: (512) 707-7500. Fax: (512) 707-7757. E-mail: benchmarkr@aol.com. Web Site: www.thebenchmarkcompany.net. Rob Balon, pres/CEO; Holly Brown, rsch dir.

Rsch & mktg for the bcst industry.

Berry Best Services Ltd., 1990 M St. N.W., Suite 740, Washington, DC 20036. Phone: (202) 293-4964. Fax: (202) 293-0287. E-mail: admin@berrybest.com. Web Site: www.berrybest.com. Thomas L. Berry, pres.

FCC rsch, hard-copy & full electronic distribution of FCC news releases, pub notices & texts; web based FCC data bases.

Big Blue Dot, 63 Pleasant St., Watertown, MA 02472. Phone: (617) 923-2583. Fax: (617) 923-8014. E-mail: bigbluedot@bigblue.com. Web Site: www.bigblue.com. Jan Craige Singer, pres.

Trend tracking resources for the kids' market, consulting, & newsletter via e-mail; creative svcs.

Bolton Research Corporation, 2709 S.W. 22nd Ave., Miami, FL 33133. Phone: (305) 854-3887. Fax: (305) 854-3807. E-mail: brct@aol.com. Web Site: www.boltonresearch.com. Ted Bolton, pres.

Perceptual rsch studies; marketplace positioning; mus rsch; format opportunity studies; focus groups.

Broadcast News Service, Box 919, Norwood, MA 02062-0919. Phone: (781) 344-6988. Fax: (781) 344-8928. E-mail: pjrbroadcasting@aol.com. P.J. Romano, dir.

Recording & bcst svcs.

Broadcast Research & Consulting Inc., Box 728, Port Washington, NY 11050. Phone: (516) 883-8486. Fax: (516) 883-3090. E-mail: jaltman752@aol.com. Herbert Altman, pres.

Syndicated svcs include news & entertainment talent search, net anchor index. Natl & loc market rsch studies & consultation for bcstrs covering programs, movies, news, prom, stn image & new electronic media. Determined the nominees & winners for the annual American Music Awards for 31 consecutive years.

CRI Research / Center for Radio Information, 18 Fair St., Cold Spring, NY 10516. Phone: (845) 265-4459. Phone: (800) 359-9898. Fax: (845) 265-2715. E-mail: info@the-cri.com. Web Site: www.the-cri.com. Scott Webster, pres.

Radioscan, market/probe, radio/link, mailing labels, phone lists, mktg file, net analysis, group owner, cp reports, radio/TV data bases, available calls.

Carolina Map Distributors, Box 1556, Waynesville, NC 28786. Phone: (828) 454-0112. Fax: (828) 454-0232. E-mail: sales@carolinamapdistributors.com. Web Site: www.carolinamapdistributors.com. Chuck Cotherman, owner.

All USGS & DMA digital & paper maps. All NOS/NOAA charts, international topographic series, aerial photography, raised relief maps, digital products, business & mktg maps, travel maps, globes, etc.

Mark Clements Research Inc., 516 Fifth Ave., New York, NY 10036. Phone: (212) 221-2470. Fax: (212) 221-7628. E-mail: mcresearch@aol.com. Mark Clements, pres; E.L. Reiter, exec VP.

Mktg, mgmt & product rsch; economic & progmg studies for TV & radio.

Coleman Research Inc., P.O. Box 13829, Research Triangle Park, NC 27709. Phone: (919) 571-0000. Fax: (919) 468-9380. E-mail: coleman@colemanres.com. Web Site: www.colemaninsights.com. Jon Coleman, pres; Chris Ackerman, sls VP.

Perceptual rsch, including progmg, mktg & sls studies; continuing consultation.

Commtek Communications, 9302 Lee Hwy., Fairfax, VA 22031. Phone: (703) 251-3000. Fax: (703) 251-3010. E-mail: satdirect@aol.com. Web Site: www.satelliteguide.com.

Mesa, AZ 85210, Dealer Program Division, 1660 S. Alma School Rd, 225. Phone: (602) 456-1540.

Publisher of *Satellite Orbit* and *Satellite Direct*. The number one publisher of TV listing guides for C-Band & DSS systems.

Comsearch, 19700 Janelia Farm Blvd., Ashburn, VA 20147. Phone: (703) 726-5500. Fax: (703) 726-5600. Web Site: www.comsearch.com. Doug Hall, chmn/pres.

Computerized allocation studies, ch analysis, transinterference analysis, system design, detailed coverage prediction, FCC application preparation, site location, mktg rsch.

Core Research, 2161 N.W. Military Hwy., Suite 202, San Antonio, TX 78213. Phone: (210) 366-4210. Fax: (210) 366-4323. E-mail: korbel@world-net.net. Web Site: www.coreresearch.biz. Susan Korbel, owner.

Critical Mass Media, 3857 Ivanhoe Ave., Cincinnati, OH 45212. Phone: (513) 631-4266. Fax: (513) 631-4329. E-mail: help@criticalmassmedia.com. Web Site: www.criticalmassmedia.com. Carolyn Gilbert, pres.

Rsch, telemarketing, direct mail, data mgmt & strategic planning for the radio & TV industry.

Dataworld Inc., Box 30730, Bethesda, MD 20824. Phone: (301) 652-8822. Fax: (301) 656-5341. E-mail: info@dataworld.com. Web Site: www.dataworld.com. David J. Doherty, pres; Nancy McCall, mgr.

Internet access to feasibility studies and subscription services for Flag & DataXpert; FM Explorer; visual on-line allocation tool; custom mapping; broadcast facilities database.

Eastlan Resources, Box 3500-404, Sisters, OR 97759-3500. Phone: (877) 886-3320. Fax: (541) 318-4646. E-mail: info@eastlan.com. Web Site: www.eastlan.com. Mike Gould, pres; Bert Hambleton, VP.

The second largest radio audience measurement company in the US.

Research Services

Edison Media Research, 6 W. Cliff St., Somerville, NJ 08876. Phone: (908) 707-4707. Fax: (908) 707-4740. E-mail: rfarbman@edisonresearch.com. Web Site: www.edisonresearch.com. Larry Rosin, pres; Joe Lenski, exec VP; Rob Farbman, sr VP.

Complete market surveys with fast turn-around. Telephone surveys, music testing, focus groups, exit polling.

Entertainment Partners, 2835 N. Naomi, Burbank, CA 91504. Phone: (818) 955-6000. Fax: (818) 845-6507. Web Site: www.entertainmentpartners.com. Mark Goldstein, pres/CEO; John Minton, exec VP; Joe Giarrusso, exec VP mktg/sls.

Orlando, FL 32819, 2000 Universal Studios Plaza. Phone: (407) 354-5900. Joy Ellis.

New York, NY 10001, 875 6th Ave., 15th Fl. Phone: (646) 473-9000. Myfa Cirinna, VP/gen mgr.

Production payroll software, residual, commercials, music & casting svcs, The Paymaster Industry Guide. Branches in New York, Los Angeles, Florida, London, Toronto, Vancouver, Australia, Japan.

FM Atlas Publishing, PO Box 336, Esko, MN 55733-0336. Phone: (218) 879-7676. E-mail: FmAtlas@aol.com. Bruce F. Elving PhD., owner; Carol Elving, office mgr; Don Johnson, technician.

FM radio directory & *FMedia!* newsletter; rsch on utilization of FM/SCA & FM translators.

FMR Associates Inc., 6045 E. Grant Rd., Tucson, AZ 85712. Phone: (520) 886-5548. Fax: (520) 886-9307. Web Site: www.FMRassociates.com.

Perceptual progmg studies, wkly callout, EARS Music Studies, format opportunity & vulnerability positioning studies; TV coml testing. Electronic progmg simulation tests.

First Amendment Center, (An operating program of The Freedom Forum). 1207 18th Ave. S., Nashville, TN 37212. Phone: (615) 727-1600. Fax: (615) 727-1309. E-mail: info@fac.org. Web Site: www.firstamendmentcenter.org.

Arlington, VA 22209, 1101 Wilson Blvd. Phone: (703) 528-0800. Gene Policinski.

Rsch & commentary on media issues. The center is devoted to improving the understanding of media issues by the press & the public.

Gallup Organization, 1001 Gallup Drive, Omaha, NE 68102. Phone: (402) 951-2003. Web Site: www.gallup.com. James K. Clifton, pres/CEO; Jane Miller, COO.

Mgmt consulting.

Global Research Institute, 747 Wire Rd., Auburn, AL 36832. Phone: (334) 826-0390. Fax: (334) 826-0390. H.D. Norman, pres; Enrico Valdez, VP; Cherry Foster, gen mgr.

Mktg, data & media studies. International radio & TV audience measurement & progmg consultants.

Hagen Media Research, Box 40542, Washington, DC 20016-0542. Phone: (703) 534-3003. Fax: (703) 534-3073. E-mail: DonHagen@aol.com. Web Site: www.hagenmedia.com. Don Hagen, pres.

Perceptual rsch for radio. Designs, conducts & analyzes qualitative & quantitative studies. Focus groups, telephone surveys, one-on-one sessions, mus tests.

Hamilton Beattie & Staff Inc., 4201 Connecticut Ave. N.W., Suite 212, Washington, DC 20008. Phone: (202) 686-5900. Fax: (202) 686-7080. E-mail: dave@hbstaff.com. Web Site: www.hbstaff.com. David Beattie, pres.

Fernandina Beach, FL 32034, 102 South 10th St. Phone: (904) 491-0591. Fax: (904) 491-0594. David Beattie, pres.

News rsch, mktg rsch & pub opinion surveys relating to program evaluation, licensing, new products, & high-tech telecommunications.

Peter D. Hart Research Associates, 1724 Connecticut Ave. N.W., Washington, DC 20009. Phone: (202) 234-5570. Fax: (202) 232-8134. E-mail: info@hartresearch.com. Web Site: www.hartresearch.com. Geoffrey Garin, pres; Peter D. Hart, CEO; Frederick Yang, sr VP.

Audience rsch; polling for on-air use; bcst, cable, ETV, radio rsch svcs, including mkt surveys, political communication & cable referenda rsch.

Hartford Gunn Institute, 5807 Massachusetts Ave., Bethesda, MD 20816. Phone: (301) 229-8130. Fax: (301) 229-9039. E-mail: jfellows@atgonline.org. James Fellows, pres; Michael Hobbs, sr fellow.

Policy rsch & dev for pub telecommunications.

Norman Hecht Research Inc., 33 Queens St., 3rd Fl., Syosset, NY 11791. Phone: (516) 496-8866. Fax: (516) 496-8165. E-mail: nhr@normanhechtresearch.com. Web Site: www.normanhechtresearch.com.

Market rsch & consulting, specializing in progmg, news & talent rsch, image studies, ratings analysis, adv effectiveness, cable MSO & cable network rsch, sales force assessmt.

Kenneth Hollander Associates Inc., Box 49625, Atlanta, GA 30359. Phone: (404) 231-4077. Fax: (770) 729-9375. Kenneth Hollander, pres.

Mendocino, CA 95460, 45431 Greenling Cir. Phone: (707) 962-1648. (707) 962-1635.

Hungerford, Aldrin, Nichols & Carter, CPAs, 2910 Lucerne Dr. S.E., Grand Rapids, MI 49546. Phone: (616) 949-3200. Fax: (616) 949-7720. E-mail: caldrin@hanc.com. Web Site: www.hanc.com. Clifford A. Aldrin C.P.A., ptnr bcst svcs.

Hungerford radio & TV revenue report preparation & year-end accounting/auditing.

Innovative Audience Research, 119 LaColima, Pismo Beach, CA 93449. Phone: (805) 556-0772. Fax: (805) 556-0772. E-mail: lavinc@charter.net. Mike Silverstein, pres; Susan B. Silverstein, exec VP.

Strategic planning in news, progmg & prom, impacting sweep book ratings in TV metered markets.

Insite Media Research, 31510 Anacapa View Dr., Mailbu, CA 90265. Phone: (310) 589-0223. E-mail: scott@tvsurveys.com. Web Site: www.tvsurveys.com. Scott V. Tallel, pres.

Full-svc audience rsch firm specializing in voice capture telephone surveys online interviewing and program testing focus groups for television & the internet

Institute For Research On Public Policy, 1470 Peel St., Suite 200, Montreal, PQ H3A 1T1. Canada. Phone: (514) 985-2461. Fax: (514) 985-2559. E-mail: irpp@irpp.org. Web Site: www.irpp.org.

Social policy, pub finance, governance, city-regions, educ, structural change, pub security labor mkt.

Intermedia Analyses Inc., 8 Shadow Rd., Upper Saddle River, NJ 07458. Phone: (201) 327-6223. Fax: (201) 934-0192. Carol G. Mayberry, pres.

Strategies/analyses for buying and/or selling radio, optimizing revenue or investment. Broker bcst equipment.

Kagan World Media, 126 Clock Tower Pl., Carmel, CA 93923-8734. Phone: (831) 624-1536. Fax: (831) 625-3225. E-mail: info@kagan.com. Web Site: www.kagan.com.

Specializing in financial & investment rsch. Media financial newsletters & data base reports.

Mark Kassof & Co., 527 E. Liberty St., Suite 202, Ann Arbor, MI 48104. Phone: (734) 662-5700. Fax: (734) 662-3255. E-mail: info@kassof.com. Web Site: www.kassof.com. Mark Kassof, pres.

Strategic audience rsch to pinpoint a radio stn's most profitable format strategy; focus groups, auditorium mus testing & promotional testing.

KIDSNET, 6856 Eastern Ave. N.W., Suite 208, Washington, DC 20012. Phone: (202) 291-1400. Fax: (202) 882-7315. E-mail: kidsnet@kidsnet.org. Web Site: www.kidsnet.org. Karen W. Jaffe, exec dir; Matthew Smith, rsch mgr; Tracy Kondga, project dir.

Natl resource of TV, radio, audio & video for children & educ multimedia; program-related study guides; mthy print & electronic publications.

Knowledge Networks/SRI, 570 South Ave. E, Cranford, NJ 07016. Phone: (908) 497-8000. Fax: (908) 497-8001. Web Site: www.knowledgenetworks.com. E-mail: info@knowledgenetworks.com. Gale D. Metzger, gen mgr; Maura Clancey, VP.

Specialists in cross-media allocation strategies, consumer media technologies. How Peope Use media.

The LPTV Store.Com, LLC., Box 250813, Milwaukee, WI 53225-6513. Phone: (262) 781-0188. Fax: (262) 781-5313. E-mail: kompasgroup@toast.net. Web Site: www.thelptvstore.com. John Kompas, ptnr; Burt Sherwood, ptnr.

Sarasota, FL 34242, 5053 Ocean Blvd., Suite 14. Phone: (941) 349-2165. Fax: (941) 312-0974.

Financial & mktg svcs for LPTV; audience demographic reports; stn coverage maps; appraisals/brokerage; financial & strategic planning.

Lincoln Property Company, 101 Constitution Ave. N.W., Suite 600 E., Washington, DC 20001. Phone: (202) 513-6700. Fax: (202) 898-2001. E-mail: jconnelly@lpc.com. Web Site: www.smithcommercialreality.com. James M. Connelly, VP.

Consulting coml real estate svcs, tenant/client representation, construction/financial analysis, turnkey lease/sale assumptions; roof & building zoning surveys.

Lund Media Research, 840 Hinckley Rd., Suite 123, Burlingame, CA 94010-1505. Phone: (650) 692-7777. Fax: (650) 692-7799. E-mail: lundradio@aol.com. Web Site: www.lundradio.com. John C. Lund, pres.

Perceptual, focus group, mus rsch; customized Radio Marketing Ascertainment evaluates stn & competitive progmg; implementation & progmg consultation; format design & multiopoly strategy.

M Street Journal, PO Box 442, Littleton, NH 03561. Phone: (603) 444-5720. Fax: (603) 444-2872. E-mail: genemckay@insideradio.com. Web Site: www.insideradio.com. Pat McCrummen, adv; Gene McKay, gen mgr; Tom Taylor, editor.

Summary of FCC data & format changes. Publishes the *M Street Journal* & *M Street Radio Directory*, & M Street daily fax.

Magazine Publishers of America, 919 Third Ave. 22nd Fl., New York, NY 10022. Phone: (212) 872-3700. Fax: (212) 888-4217. E-mail: infocenter@magazine.org. Web Site: www.magazine.org. Nina B. Link, pres/CEO; Ellen Oppenheim, EVP chief mktg off; Michael Pashby, gen mgr.

Washington, DC 20036, 1211 Connecticut Ave. N.W. Phone: (202) 296-7277. Jim Cregan, exec VP govt affrs.

Educ seminars; surveys members on various topics; extensive library on magazine publishing; monitors issues in the magazine industry. Publications: *Newsletter of Research, Newsletter of International Publishing, Washington Newsletter & Magazine Newsletter.*

Frank N. Magid Associates Inc., One Research Ctr., Marion, IA 52302. Phone: (319) 377-7345. Fax: (319) 377-5861. E-mail: mailia@magid.com. Web Site: www.magid.com. Brent Magid, pres/CEO; Steve Ridge, exec VP; Joe George, exec VP.

Sherman Oaks, CA 91403, 15260 Ventura Blvd, Suite 2130. Phone: (818) 263-3300. Fax: (818) 263-3311. Jack MacKenzie, sr VP entertainment.

New York, NY 10019, 1775 Broadway, Suite 1401. Phone: (212) 974-2310. Fax: (212) 515-4540. Vicki Cohen, sr VP entertainment.

Strategic rsch applications for traditional & new media companies, including Executive Telefocus, Magid Media Futures, INstant-STUDIO, Magid Performance Predictor, Magid Revenue Enhancer.

Marketing Evaluations Inc. The Q Scores Company, (A division of Marketing Evaluations Inc.). 1615 Northern Blvd., Manhasset, NY 11030. Phone: (516) 365-7979. Fax: (516) 365-9351. E-mail: info@qscores.com. Web Site: www.qscores.com. Steven Levitt, pres; Henry Schafer, exec VP; Francine Purcell, VP.

Syndicated market rsch surveys measuring familiarity & appeal of TV programs, cable programs, performers, characters, company & brand names, sports personalities.

Marketron International, 411 Airport Blvd., Burlingame, CA 94010-2001. Phone: (800) 788-9245. Fax: (650) 548-2295. E-mail: lcarpenter@marketron.com. Web Site: www.marketron.com.

Toronto, ON M2N 6C6 Canada, 5075 Yonge St, Suite 404. Phone: (416) 221-9944. Bill Cross, gen mgr.

Birmingham, AL 35244, 3000 Riverchase Galleria, 8th Fl. Phone: (205) 987-7456. Fax: (205) 733-4535. E-mail: tvsales@marketron.com. Michael Hunter, gen mgr.

Hailey, ID 83333, 101 Empty Saddle Trail. Phone: (208) 788-6272. Gary Coats, gen mgr.

Software applications for radio, TV, networks, syndicators, traffic, accounting, mgmt, demand pricing, inventory control, rsch & proposals.

MarketVision Research Inc., 10300 Alliance Rd., Cincinnati, OH 45242-5617. Phone: (513) 791-3100. Fax: (513) 794-3500. Web Site: www.mv-research.com. Jon Pinnell, pres.

Charlotte, NC 28210, 6805-A Fairview Rd. Phone: (704) 442-0444. Ronald Miller, exec VP.

Flower Mound, TX 75028, 2670 Firewheel Dr, Suite D. Phone: (972) 355-4495.

Full-svc rsch firm. Specialized division for design, execution & analysis of audience & entertainment rsch.

Marquest Research, 314 Orange Street, Beaufort, NC 28516-1821. Phone: (252) 729-1100. E-mail: paul.rule@marquest.net. Web Site: www.marquest.net. Paul Rule, pres; Tyrus C. Ragland, VP.

Loc & natl cable, bcst & print surveys. Coincidentals, audience ratings & profiles, subscriber surveys, focus groups, & interviewing/tabulation svcs.

Marshall Marketing & Communications Inc., 2600 Boyce Plaza Rd, Suite 210, Pittsburgh, PA 15241-3949. Phone: (412) 914-0970. Fax: (412) 914-0971. E-mail: info@mm-c.com. Web Site: www.mm-c.com. Craig A. Marshall, chmn/CEO; Richard Kinzler, pres/COO.

Orlando, FL 32835, 1445 Saddleridge Dr. Phone: (407) 299-3510. Bruce Hahn, research & sales consultant.

Cary, NC 27513, 102 Silver Lining Lane. Phone: (919) 388-7622. James Filippi, research & sales consultant.

Langley, WA 98260, 5280 Lakeside Dr. Phone: (360) 321-2139. Lori West, research & sales consultant.

Spokane, WA 99223, 3021 E. 62nd Ave. Phone: (509) 443-1362. Rick Hamm, research & sales consultant.

Sls dev rsch; custom-designed, consumer market-specific data; demographics; media usage & Risc Amerisan program. Leading-Edge software: exclusive & non-exclusive mktg programs.

Media Market Resources, 81 Main St., Littleton, NH 03561. Phone: (603) 444-5720. Fax: (603) 444-2872. Web Site: www.mediamarket.com. Gene McKay, gen mgr; Cathy Devine, VP rsch.

Produces multimedia profile reports, printed & electronic bcst directories & software.

Media Monitors Inc., 6535 E. 82nd St., Suite 102, Indianapolis, IN 46250-4518. Phone: (317) 547-1362. Fax: (317) 549-0331. E-mail: jselig@mediamonitors.com. Web Site: www.mediamonitors.com. John L. Selig, pres; Anita Selig, VP.

Radio, nwspr & magazine monitoring company. Creative review for natl & loc advertisers' radio spots.

Media Perspectives, 127 Greensward Ln., Cherry Hill, NJ 08002. Phone: (856) 482-7979. Fax: (856) 482-0957. E-mail: steve@apels.net. Steven G. Apels, pres.

Rschs audience tastes & perceptions, employs advanced analytical techniques to guide bcstrs in constructing strategic progmg & mktg plans.

Media Rating Council, Inc., 370 Lexington Ave., Suite 902, New York, NY 10017. Phone: (212) 972-0300. Fax: (212) 972-2786. George W. Ivie, exec dir.

Determines criteria & standards & administers an audit system for accreditation of audience measurement svcs to assure conformance with criteria, standards & procedures developed.

Mediamark Research Inc., 75 Ninth Avenue, 5th Floor, New York, NY 10011. Phone: (212) 884-9200. Fax: (212) 884-9339. Web Site: www.mediamark.com. Alain J. Tessier, chmn; Kathi Love, pres/CEO; Ian Jack, exec VP/COO.

Los Angeles, CA 90068, 3575 Cahuenga Blvd. W, Suite 223. Phone: (232) 882-6325. Chetan Shah, western rgnl mgr.

Chicago, IL 60611, 444 N. Michigan Ave, Suite 2050. Phone: (312) 329-0901. Scott Turner, VP.

Syndicated rsch—product, demographics for TV, radio, cable, new media & print. Custom recontact surveys.

Miller, Kaplan, Arase & Co., 4123 Lankershim Blvd., North Hollywood, CA 91602. Phone: (818) 769-2010. Fax: (818) 769-3100. Web Site: www.millerkaplan.com. George Nadel Rivin C.P.A., ptnr in charge of bcst svcs.

San Francisco, CA 94104, 180 Montgomery St, Suite 1840. Phone: (415) 956-3600. Catherine C. Gardner, C.P.A., ptnr.

Financial consulting, accounting & tax svcs, computer consulting, market revenue report, & revenue forecast software, market x-ray.

Jay Mitchell Associates Inc., Box 1285, Fairfield, IA 52556. Phone: (641) 472-4087. Fax: (425) 871-7574. E-mail: jay@jaymitchell.com. Web Site: www.smallmarketradio.com. Jay Mitchell, pres; Greg Baum, mgmg editor.

Mgmt, mktg & progmg consulting; market analysis & rsch. Web Site consulting, design & dev.

MORPACE International, 31700 Middlebelt, Suite 200, Farmington Hills, MI 48334. Phone: (248) 737-5300. Fax: (248) 737-5326. E-mail: info@morpace.com. Web Site: www.morpace.com. Jim Leiman, media studies.

Market rsch, strategic planning, viewer satisfaction, economic modeling, audience analysis, data base mapping for TV & radio stns, cable TV franchises.

Multimedia Research Group Inc. (MRG, Inc.), 1095 E. Duane Ave., Suite 106, Sunnyvale, CA 94085. Phone: (408) 524-9767. Fax: (408) 524-9770. E-mail: info@mrgco.com. Web Site: www.mrgco.com. Gary Schultz, pres/principal analyst.

Provides strategic consulting & published market intelligence on content dev, content distribution, channels & networks.

Jack Myers LLC, 20 E. 68 St., Suite 7B, New York, NY 10021. Phone: (212) 794-4926. Fax: (212) 794-5160. E-mail: jack@jackmyers.com. Web Site: www.jackmyers.com. Jack Myers, pres.

Syndicated & proprietary rsch, consulting, & evaluation for media companies, advertisers, & adv agencies. Publishes *Jack Myers Report* industry newsletter.

NOP World, 1060 State Rd., Princeton, NJ 08540. Phone: (609) 683-6100. Fax: (609) 683-6255. Bruce Barr, exec VP; Jim Timony, sr VP.

Custom-designed surveys for bcst industry on loc, rgnl & natl basis; loc & net radio & TV, cable/pay TV/DBS, videocassette & videodisc; natl omnibus studies; overnight custom rsch.

National Broadcast Finance Corp., Box 3167, 27 Harrison St., New Haven, CT 06515-0267. Phone: (203) 389-6000. Fax: (203) 389-6020. E-mail: cheerhoniak@sbcglobal.net. David C. Cherhoniak, pres.

Financial advisory & investment banking svcs to bcstg industry & brokerage.

National Economic Research Associates Inc. (NERA), 50 Main St., White Plains, NY 10606. Phone: (914) 448-4000. Fax: (914) 448-4040. Web Site: www.nera.com. Richard Rapp, pres.

San Francisco, CA 94111, One Front St. Phone: (415) 291-1000. Gregory Duncan, sr VP.

Sydney NSW 2000 Australia, Level 6, 50 Bridge St. Fax: 2-8272-6500. Greg Houston, dir.

Brussels, NO B-1040 Belgium, rue de la Loi, 23 Wetstraat. Phone: 32-2282-4340. Mark Williams, dir.

Madrid 28046 Spain, Paseo de la Castellana, 13. Phone: 91-212-6400. David Robinson, dir.

London W1C 1BE United Kingdom, 15 Stratford Pl. Phone: 20-7659-8500. John Rhys, dir.

Los Angeles, CA 90017, 777 S. Figueroa St. Phone: (213) 346-3000. Gary Dorman, sr VP.

Washington, DC 20037, 1255 23rd St. N.W. Phone: (202) 466-3510. Andrew Joskow, VP.

Chicago, IL 60611, 875 N. Michigan Ave. Phone: (312) 573-2800. David Evans, sr VP.

Cambridge, MA 02142, One Main St. Phone: (617) 621-0444. William Taylor, sr VP.

Ithaca, NY 14850, 308 N. Cayuga St. Phone: (607) 277-3007. Alfred E. Kahn, special consultant.

New York, NY 10036, 1166 Ave. of the Americas, 31st Fl. Phone: (212) 345-3000. Linda McLaughlin, sr VP.

Philadelphia, PA 19103, Two Logan Sq. Phone: (215) 864-3880. Eugene Ericksen, special consultant.

Economic consultant to bcst & cable TV companies on economic, pub policy & business strategy issues.

Nielsen Media Research, 770 Broadway, New York, NY 10003. Phone: (646) 654-5300. Fax: (646) 654-8990. E-mail: info@nielsenmedia.com. Web Site: www.nielsenmedia.com. Jim O'Hara, CFO; John A. Loftus, sr VP; Betsy Williams, sr VP; Susan D. Whiting, pres/CEO; Susan S. Buchanan, gen mgr opns; Sara Erichson, natl svcs; Jack Oken, gen mgr loc scvs; Dave Thomas, gen mgr natl svcs; David Schwartz-Leeper, sr VP; David H. Harkness, sr VP; Paul Donato, sr VP.

Los Angeles, CA 90028, 6255 Sunset Blvd. Phone: (323) 817-1200. Julie Girocco, VP, regional mgr..

San Francisco, CA 94111, 2 Embarcadero Center. Phone: (415) 249-6000. Colleen Hall, VP, NSI regional mgr..

Dallas, TX 75201, 1717 Main St. Phone: (214) 290-9200. Lucinda Nobles, VP; South Central NSI regional mgr..

Atlanta, GA 30339-5916, 300 Galleria Pkwy, NW. Phone: (770) 763-9100. Stephen Posnock, VP, Southeastern NSI rgnl mgr..

Chicago, IL 60606, 200 W. Jackson Blvd. Phone: (312) 385-6601. Jane Ryan, sr VP sls & mktg NSI.

Nielsen offers TV audience measurement for network, local, syndication, cable and Sp-language networks & stns; metered market & individual loc market reports in all markets; natl sydicated prog ratings; loc syndicated prog ratings; daily, wkly, & monthly network prog ratings; telephone coincidentals; & competitive adv intelligence.

Paragon Media Strategies, 550 S. Wadsworth Blvd., Suite 401, Denver, CO 80226. Phone: (303) 922-5600. Fax: (303) 922-1589. E-mail: mhenry@paragonmediastrategies.com. Web Site: www.paragonmediastrategies.com. Mike Henry, CEO.

Monterey, CA 93940, 2511 Garden Rd, Suite 104, Bldg. A. Phone: (831) 655-5036. Fax: (831) 655-5037. Larry Johnson, pres.

Custom rsch: focus groups, auditorium music tests, perceptual studies, tracking, auditorium format analysis.

Peters Communications, 1555 Berenda Pl., El Cajon, CA 92020. Phone: (858) 565-8511. Fax: (619) 440-1481. E-mail: ppiep@cox.net. Edward J. Peters, pres.

Media mktg consultants, providing rsch, concept, mktg plan, music, graphics & animation.

Pike & Fischer Inc., 1010 Wayne Ave., Suite 1400, Silver Spring, MD 20910. Phone: (301) 562-1530. Fax: (301) 562-1521. E-mail: pike@pf.com. Web Site: www.pf.com. Paul Wojcik, chmn; Meg Hargreaves, pres; Robert E. Emeritz, VP; Carol Bram, dir mktg.

Publishers of communications print and eletronic information services including; Broadcast Rules Service, Cable TV Rules Service, Communications Regulation and U.S. Spectrum Report.

RAD Marketing & CableTowns, 167 Crary-on-the-Park, Mount Vernon, NY 10550-0572. Phone: (914) 668-3563. Fax: (914) 668-4247. Robert Dadarria, pres.

Cable subs, or TV buyers, MOB buyers- Mailing lists provided to marketers largest most ideal cable TV H/H audience available. Phone numbers; data base by age, gender, MOBs, and direct marketing responses.

Radio Computing Services Inc., 12 Water St., White Plains, NY 10601. Phone: (914) 428-4600. Fax: (914) 428-5922. Web Site: www.rcsworks.com. Andrew M. Economos, chmn; Philippe Generali, pres; Ted Nygreen, gen mgr.

Computer software for bcstrs, mus scheduling, rsch, data bases, yield mgmt, audio logging, digital audio systems.

Research Communications Ltd., 220 Forbes Rd., Braintree, MA 02184. Phone: (781) 794-3031. Fax: (781) 794-1280. E-mail: cranev@aol.com. Web Site: www.researchcommunications.com. Dr. Valerie Crane, pres.

Full-svc media rsch company specializing in quantitative/qualitative news mktg, & progmg rsch for bcst, cable, radio & adv.

Research International U.S.A., The John Hancock Center, 875 North Michigan Ave., Suite 2511, Chicago, IL 60611. Phone: (312) 787-4060. Fax: (312) 787-4156. E-mail: info@riusa.com. Web Site: www.riusa.com. Mary Vallender, exec VP; Diane Frederick, exec VP; Mark Willard, exec VP; Bruce E. Lervoog, exec VP.

Phoenix, AZ 85021-4258. Phoenix, 8800 North 22nd Ave. Phone: (602) 735-8800. Fax: (602) 735-3270. Diane Frederick, exec VP.

San Francisco, CA 94107. San Francisco, 303 2nd St., 9th Fl. S. Phone: (415) 281-2760. Fax: (415) 281-2799. Bruce Lervoog, exec VP.

Stamford, CT 06901, 3 Landmark Sq. Phone: (203) 358-0900. Fax: (203) 353-0883. Mark Willard, exec VP.

Cambridge, MA 02139. Cambridge, 955 Massachusetts Ave. Phone: (617) 661-0110. Fax: (617) 661-3575. Mark Willard, exec VP.

Full-svc custom rsch design through analysis. Facilities include 300-position WATS phones with CRTs & complete computer capabilities.

Rules Service, (a division of Pike & Fischer Inc.). c/o Pike & Fischer Inc., 1010 Wayne Ave., Suite 1400, Silver Spring, MD 20910. Phone: (301) 562-1530. Fax: (301) 562-1521. E-mail: ruletwo@starpower.net. Web Site: www.ruleserv.com. Zachary Wheat, group publisher; Barbara Vaszil, editor.

FCC rules & regulations updated in loose-leaf & disk svcs, includes 0, 1, 2, 5, 11, 13, 15, 17, 18, 19, 20, 21, 22, 24, 25, 27, 73, 74, 76, 78, 79, 80, 87, 90, 95, 97, 100 & 101.

SatNews Publishers, 800 Siesta Way, Sonoma, CA 95476. Phone: (707) 939-9306. Fax: (707) 939-9235. E-mail: design@satnews.com. Web Site: www.satnews.com. Kathryn Sanderson, pres; Silvano Payne, publisher.

Publishes the *International Satellite Directory*, the complete guide to the satellite communications industry.

Scarborough Research, 770 Broadway, 13th Fl., New York, NY 10003-9595. Phone: (646) 654-8400. Fax: (646) 654-8450. Fax: (646) 654-8440. E-mail: info@scarborough.com. Web Site: www.scarborough.com. Robert L. Cohen PhD., pres; Cheryl Greenblatt, sr VP.

Chicago, IL 60606, 200 W. Jackson Blvd, Suite 1822. Phone: (312) 385-6700. Howard Goldberg, sr VP Radio/Sports marketing.

Specializes in loc market & multimedia consumer studies; hundreds of consumer categories & media behavior, all specific to the individual market.

Paul A. Scipione, Ph.D., P.A., Marketing Research & Consumer Psychology. 5 Burr Dr., Metuchen, NJ 08840-2617. Phone: (732) 548-8096. Fax: (732) 548-8871. E-mail: scipion@mail.montclair.edu. Dr. Paul Scipione, sr ptnr.

Loc market profiles; acquisition analysis; pub opinion surveys; listener profiles for advertisers & agencies; progmg & talent surveys.

Shane Media Services, 2500 Tanglewilde, Suite 106, Houston, TX 77063. Phone: (713) 952-9221. Fax: (713) 952-1207. E-mail: smsofc@shanemedia.com. Web Site: www.shanemedia.com. Ed Shane, CEO.

Radio progmg and mgmt consultation, custom designed perceptual and qualitative research for electronic media outlets.

Research Services

The Shosteck Group, 11160 Viers Mill Rd., Suite 709, Wheaton, MD 20902-2538. Phone: (301) 589-2259. Fax: (301) 588-3311. E-mail: jzweig@shosteck.com. Web Site: www.shosteck.com. Dr. Herschel Shosteck, chmn; Jane Zweig, CEO.

Telecommunication economics & market analysis emphasizing cellular. International consultation on demand, svc & equipment competition, distribution chns, economic & market effects of privatization, liberalization, competition, deregulation & market acceptance. Newly published studies on wireless and wireless internet.

Simmons Market Research Bureau, Inc., 230 Park Ave. S., 3rd Floor, New York, NY 10003-1502. Phone: (212) 598-5400. Fax: (212) 598-5401. Web Site: www.smrb.com. Christopher T. Wilson, pres/COO; Bill Livek, CEO; Bill Engel, CEO.

Deerfield Beach, FL 33441, 700 W. Hillsboro Blvd., Bldg 4, Suite 201. Phone: (954) 427-4104. Fax: (954) 427-4104. Bill Livek, CEO; Bill Engel, CEO.

Schaumburg, IL 60173, 955 American Ln. Phone: (224) 698-8142. Fax: (224) 698-4139. Mary Kay Petrella, dir of clients.

Study of media & markets; comprehensive measurement of media & product usage. Other studies include kids, teens, Hispanic & the Internet.

Sindlinger & Co. Inc., 405 Osborne St., Wallingford, PA 19086. Phone: (610) 565-0247. Fax: (610) 565-7174. E-mail: nelsind@aol.com. Albert E. Sindlinger, chmn/pres.

Daily polling to determine consumer attitudes; microeconomic forecasting.

Spectrum Research, 14 Equestrian Ln., Cherry Hill, NJ 08003-5161. Phone: (856) 795-7990. Fax: (708) 570-7553. E-mail: peter@spectrumresearch.com.

Focus groups, lifestyle studies, & strategic market studies. Custom rsch for radio & TV.

SQAD Inc., 303 S. Broadway, Suite 108, Tarrytown, NY 10591-5410. Phone: (914) 524-7600. Fax: (914) 524-7650. E-mail: info@sqad.com. Web Site: www.sqad.com. Neil Klar, pres/CEO.

Cost projections for National broadcast, cable and syndication (Net Costs), local CPP/CPM projections for Spot TV, Radio & Hispanic TV. SNAP software for Sweeps and Overnights.

Strata Marketing Inc., One E. Wacker Dr., Suite 2304, Chicago, IL 60601. Phone: (312) 222-1555. Fax: (312) 222-2510. E-mail: rsparks@stratag.com. Web Site: www.stratag.com. Bruce W. Johnson, pres.

TV, radio & media ratings analysis. Microsoft Windows-based software systems for cable systems & broadcast TV stations.

Super Ratings Research Corporation, 410 W. Badillo St., 2nd Fl., Covina, CA 91723. Phone: (626) 339-3333. E-mail: markolson@superratings.com. Web Site: www.superratings.com. Mark Olson, pres.

Specialized ratings analysis & audience measurement for radio, TV & corporate mgmt. Exclusive provider of Synchronous Statistics & Pattern Research tracking more than 395,000 audience trends. Other expertise includes longitudinal studies of upscale consumers with high disposable incomes.

Synovate-Americas, 8600 NW 17th St., Suite 100, Miami, FL 33126. Phone: (305) 716-6800. Fax: (305) 716-6756. Web Site: www.synovate.com. Richard Tobin, pres.

Laguna Hills, CA 92653, 23151 Alcalbe Dr, Suite C-4. Phone: (949) 598-9055. Dave Thomas, VP/gen mgr. (Los Angeles office).

Radio/TV Hispanic audience ratings, natl & loc; market studies, stn profiles, focus groups, product usage/awareness, progmg/format rsch, copy testing. Specialization in ethnic rsch.

TNS Canadian Facts, 1075 Bay St., Toronto, ON M5S 2X5. Canada. Phone: (416) 924-5751. Fax: (416) 923-7085. E-mail: info@nfocfgroup.com. Web Site: www.tns-global.com. Michael LoPresti, pres/CEO; David Stark, pub affairs dir.

Vancouver, BC V6E 4A4 Canada, 1130 W. Pender St, Suite 600. Phone: (604) 668-3344. Fax: (604) 668-3333. Diana Tindall, rsch dir.

Ottawa, ON K1P 5W6 Canada, Place de Ville Tower B, 112 Kent St, Suite 2010A. Phone: (613) 232-4408. Fax: (613) 232-7102. Bente Nielsen, VP.

Montreal, PQ H3G 2B3 Canada, 1250 Guy St, Suite 1030. Phone: (514) 935-7666. Fax: (514) 935-6770. Michel Gauvreau, VP.

Full range of custom-designed & syndicated market rsch svcs.

The Tarrance Group, 201 N. Union St., Suite 410, Alexandria, VA 22314. Phone: (703) 684-6688. Fax: (703) 836-8256. Web Site: www.tarrance.com. David Sackett, partner.

Audience rsch svcs for radio, TV & cable. News, progmg, positioning, survey & promotional rsch.

Teen-age Research Unlimited, 707 Skokie Blvd., 7th Flr., Northbrook, IL 60062. Phone: (847) 564-3440. Fax: (847) 564-0825. Web Site: www.teenresearch.com. Peter Zollo, pres.

Twice annually, syndicated study of the teen market with optional custom/proprietary questions. Custom rsch in teenage markets.

Telecommunications Research Inc., (A division of Nathan Associates Inc.). 2101 Wilson Blvd., Suite 1200, Arlington, VA 22201. Phone: (703) 516-7700. Fax: (703) 351-6162. E-mail: info@triresearch.com. Web Site: www.triresearch.com.

Economic & mgmt consultants specializing in mktg & survey rsch, business & property valuation & financial viability analysis.

VIP Research Inc., 5700 Broadmoor, Suite 710, Mission, KS 66202. Phone: (913) 384-9494. Fax: (913) 677-2727. E-mail: mike@mjmresearch.com. Web Site: www.mjmresearch.com. Clark D. Roberts, sls VP; Mike Heydman, pres.

Provides hook-tape production, listener screening, fielding, & tabulation for all mus testing, perceptual studies, focus groups & promotional telemarketing.

VNU Consumer Research Services, Inc., 12350 N.W. 39th St., Coral Springs, FL 33065. Phone: (954) 753-6043. Fax: (954) 346-8869. Kathy Pilhuj, VP; Mary Glover, VP; Mark Manders, VP.

Tuczon, AZ 85710, 6339 Speedway, Suite 200. Phone: (520) 751-2223. Barbara Garvin, mgr.

Sarasota, FL 34236, 1751 Mound St, Suite 205. Phone: (941) 955-9877. Kathleen Goodwin, mgr.

San Antonio, TX 78229, 4801 N.W. Loop 410, Suite 125. Phone: (210) 647-3198. Juan Hernandez, mgr.

Data collection for Survey Research, production of The Scarborough Report and The Market Audit Report.

Vallie-Richards Consulting Inc., 2175 Bent Creek Manor, Alpharetta, GA 30005. Phone: (770) 346-0026. Fax: (770) 346-0028. Web Site: www.vallierichards.com. Dan Vallie, CEO; Jim Richards, pres.

America's premier contemp radio consultancy specializing in all variations of contemp radio balancing art & science to create ratings & revenue success.

Ventures in Media Inc., 32488 Saddle Mountain Dr., Westlake Village, CA 91361. Phone: (818) 991-1648. Morrie Gelman, pres; Adam Gelman, VP/sec; Gene Accas, assoc.

Market rsch info packaging & consulting.

Video Monitoring Services, 330 W. 42nd St., New York, NY 10036. Phone: (212) 736-2010. Fax: (212) 736-8206. Web Site: www.vmsinfo.com. Jeff Tidyman, gen mgr.

Los Angeles, CA 90028, 6430 W. Sunset Blvd, Suite 400. Phone: (323) 993-0111. Fax: (323) 467-7540. Ashley Griffin.

Washington, DC 20045, 1066 National Press Bldg. Phone: (202) 393-7110. Fax: (202) 393-5451. Meredith Imwalle.

Chicago, IL 60610, 212 W. Superior St. Phone: (312) 649-1131. Fax: (312) 649-1527. Jack Monson.

Provides transcripts, digests & analysis of radio & TV news & commentary; surveys of program content; monitoring of comls; tape & cassette recordings; photoboards; film conversions.

Mona Wargo, 1600 N. Oak St., Suite 1401, Arlington, VA 22209. Phone: (703) 243-9352. Fax: (703) 243-5795. E-mail: mwrsrch@erols.com. Mona Wargo, MS-IT/TS; rsch analyst.

Ind rsch analyst in bcst & telecommunications, FCC regulatory policy, legal & enginering research, and consultant.

Washington Information Group Ltd., 1655 N. Fort Myer Dr., Suite 825, Arlington, VA 22209. Phone: (703) 312-6004. Fax: (703) 527-4586. Doug House, pres.

Customized business rsch on client-specified aspects of the bcstg industry, including competitor intelligence on companies, products, svcs & markets.

World Information Technologies Inc., 70 Carley Ave., Huntington, NY 11743. Phone: (631) 549-3629. Fax: (631) 549-7527. Amadee Bender, pres.

Telecommunications market rsch.

Your Personal Researcher, 22848 Mesa Way, Lake Forest, CA 92630-4643. Phone: (949) 472-8538. E-mail: dlbraunstein@prodigy.net. Donna Lee Braunstein, owner.

Script & documentary rsch.

Engineering and Technical Consultants

AF Associates Inc., 100 Stonehurst Ct., Northvale, NJ 07647. Phone: (201) 750-1200. Fax: (201) 784-8637. Web Site: www.afassoc.com. Tom Canavan, pres; Jack Dawson, sr VP; Chris Summey, sr VP.

AFA is a worldwide leader in technology consulting, systems integration and engineering svcs for broadcast, cable & entertainment industries.

AZCAR U.S.A. Inc., 121 Hillpointe Dr., Canonsburg, PA 15317. Phone: (724) 873-0800. Fax: (724) 873-4770. Web Site: www.azcar.com. Stephen Pumple, pres/CEO.

Bcst, video & audio system consultation, design, instal & training; serving cable systems, corporate & teleproduction facilities.

Advanced Technology Systems Inc., 7915 Jones Branch Dr., McLean, VA 22102. Phone: (703) 506-0088. Fax: (703) 903-0415. Web Site: www.atsva.com. Claude Rumsey, owner.

Engrg & cost analyses pertinent to planning, evaluation, regulation & purchase of telecommunications networks & svcs.

Advanced Television Technology Center, 1330 Braddock Pl., Suite 200, Alexandria, VA 22314. Phone: (703) 739-3850. Fax: (703) 739-3230. Web site: www.attc.org. Paul K. DeGonia, exec dir; Charles W. Elnolf, deputy exec dir.

Testing/evaluation of digital transmission systems, RF bcst systems; video codes, quality (up to MDTV); TV design, consulting engrg.

Munn-Reese, Inc.
Broadcast Engineering Consultants
P.O. Box 220
Coldwater, Michigan 49036
Phone: 517-278-7339
wayne@munn-reese.com

John H. Battison, P.E. & Associates, Consulting Radio Engineers. 2684 State Rt. 60, Loudonville, OH 44842. Phone: (419) 994-3849. Fax: (419) 994-5419. E-mail: batcom@bright.net. John H. Battison, P.E.; S. Bennett, VP.

All FCC svcs: AM, FM, TV, LPTV, applications, licensing, DA-proofs, ITFS & MMDS expert witness svcs.

Richard S. Becker & Associates, Chartered, 7128 Fair Fax Rd., Bethesda, MD 20814. Phone: (301) 986-9005. Fax: (301) 986-8496. E-mail: beckereng@aol.com. Richard Becker, pres; Siamak Harandi, assoc; Christopher Fedeli, assoc.

Legal & engrg svc for bcstg, cable TV, cellular, paging, microwave & private radio.

Lawrence Behr Associates Inc., Box 8026, Greenville, NC 27835-8026. Phone: (252) 757-0279. Fax: (252) 752-9155. E-mail: lbagrp@lbagroup.com. Web site: www.lbagroup.com. Lawrence Behr, CEO; Win Donat, pres; Mike Britner, VP business dev; Chuck Martin, VP site services.

Provides wireless svcs: site acquisition, construction mgmt, AM detuning, AM tower colocation, RF hazard mgmt, RF shielding, due diligence, facility mgmt, dev, maintenance, support svcs.

Serge Bergen, P.E., 7503 Amkin Ct., Clifton, VA 22024. Phone: (703) 250-2691. E-mail: wtranavitch@cox.net. William V. Tranavitch Jr., ptnr.

Engrg svcs: AM, FM, TV, translators, LPTV.

Bernard Associates, 143 Palmers Hill Rd., Stamford, CT 06902-2111. Phone: (203) 348-0804. Fax: (203) 921-1016. Bernard Eishwald, P.E.

Broadcast Engineering & Equipment Maintenance Co., (BEEM Co.). 2322 S. 2nd Ave., Arcadia, CA 91006. Phone: (626) 446-3468. Fax: (626) 445-8028. E-mail: joel@beemco.com. Web Site: www.beemco.com. Joel T. Saxberg, owner.

Site studies, applications, AM directional arrays, allocation studies, field work, mobile signal analysis, broadcast consulting, radiofrequency electromagnetic field measurements.

Broadcast Services Inc., Box 6418, Brattleboro, VT 05302-6418. Phone: (802) 258-3000. Phone: (802) 258-4500 Svc. Fax: (802) 258-2500. E-mail: mh@markhutchins.com. Web Site: www.markhutchins.com. Mark F. Hutchins, pres.

Field studies: Spectrum analysis, NRSC/RFR compliance. Propagation analysis, coverage maps, path profiles & shadowing studies.

Broadcast Signal Lab, LLP, 64 Richdale Ave., Cambridge, MA 02140-2629. Phone: (617) 864-4298. Fax: (617) 661-1345. E-mail: information@broadcastsignallab.com. Web Site: www.broadcastsignallab.com.

RF safety evaluation, expert testimony, coverage analysis, license engineering & applications, interference & spectrum analysis, frequency monitoring, technical due diligence.

Bromo Communications Inc., Box 191747, Atlanta, GA 31117-1747. Phone: (404) 266-2257. Fax: (404) 842-9535. E-mail: bill@bromocom.com. Web Site: www.bromocom.com.

Washington, DC Phone: (202) 429-0600.

Consulting engrg for bcst stns. AM/FM & TV allocations, including field instals.

John F.X. Browne & Associates P.C. 38500 N. Woodward Ave., Suite 350, Bloomfield Hills, MI 48304. Phone: (248) 642-6226. Fax: (248) 642-6027. E-mail: consultants@jfxb.com. Web Site: www.jfxb.com. *John F.X. Browne, P.E., pres; John Fleming, engr; Leonard W. Eden, engr.

Bcst consulting AM/FM/TV/DTV, MMDS/ITFS, PCS & satellite systems. FCC/FAA applications, filings & studies. Field measurement vehicle AM/FM/TV/DTV.

Richard W. Burden Associates, 20944 Sherman Way, Suite 213, Canoga Park, CA 91303. Phone: (818) 340-4590. Fax: (818) 884-8840. Richard W. Burden, Principal.

Bcst tech svcs, facilities design, Traveller's Information Service (TIS) & Educational FM (EDFM) FCC applications, Part 15 AM & FM bcst systems engrg.

C.S.I. Telecommunications, Box 29002, San Francisco, CA 94129-0002. Phone: (415) 751-8845. Fax: (415) 292-9981. E-mail: info@csitele.com. M.S. Newman, VP engrg.

Telecommunications, radio & microwave engrg, feasibility studies, FCC applications, systems engrg; equipment specifications, project mgmt, lab measurements.

Carolina Map Distributors, Box 1556, Waynesville, NC 28786. Phone: (828) 454-0112. Fax: (828) 454-0232. E-mail: sales@carolinamapdistributors.com. Web Site: www.carolinamapdistributors.com. Chuck Cotherman, owner.

All USGS & DMA digital & paper maps. All NOS/NOAA charts, international topographic series, aerial photography, raised relief maps, digital products, business & mktg maps, travel maps, globes, etc.

Cavell, Mertz & Davis, Inc. 7839 Ashton Ave., Manassas, VA 20109. Phone: (703) 392-9090. Fax: (703) 392-9559. E-mail: office@cmdconsulting.com. Web Site: www.cmdconsulting.com. Garrison C. Cavell, pres; Richard H. Mertz, VP; *Joseph M. Davis, P.E., VP; Michael D. Rhodes, P.E., sr. engr.; Daniel G. Ryson, sr. engr.; Robert J. Clinton, sr. engr.

Consultants in engineering; new technologies; systems design & integration; communications; facility design, project implementation & mgmt svcs. Experts in studio, transmission, RF exposure, coverage & strategic planning, both bcst (radio, TV, digital TV) & industrial; channel searches, upgrades, FCC application support. Ability to design, develop & organize large projects. Assist with equipment procurement (package purchases), price negotiations & implementation of projects. Able to provide high level personnel management & assessment svcs for existing operations or staff changes.

Chenevert Architects LLC, 6767 Perkins Rd., Suite 100, Baton Rouge, LA 70808. Phone: (225) 757-0955. Fax: (225) 757-0765. E-mail: chenevert@architects.com. Web Site: chenevertarchitects.com. Norman J. Chenevert, AIA, sole member.

Architects, planners, & technical designers, specializing in new & renovated bcst/cable production facilities.

Chevalier Aviation Associates, LLC, 928 Via Panorama, Palos Verdes, CA 90274. Phone: (310) 375-2979. Fax: (310) 791-7181. E-mail: jack.chevalier@verizon.net.

Part 77 studies, FCC registrations, EMI analysis, legal assistance & representation before FAA, state & loc aeronautical & zoning agencies.

Clear Channel Communications, 1834 Lisenby Ave., Panama City, FL 32401. Phone: (850) 769-1408. Fax: (850) 769-0659. Web Site: www.clearchannel.com.

Turnkey installations (AM, FM studios & transmitters), tech appraisals, emergency repairs, upgrades. International startups & upgrades.

Cohen, Dippell and Everist, P.C. 1300 L St. N.W., Suite 1100, Washington, DC 20005. Phone: (202) 898-0111. Fax: (202) 898-0895. E-mail: cde@attgobal.net. Web Site: http://www.broadcast-consulting-engineers.com. *Donald G. Everist, P.E., pres.

Professional engrg svcs to the bcstg industry, United States & worldwide.

Commercial Radio Co., One Duttonsville School Dr., Cavendish, VT 05142. Phone: (802) 226-7582. Fax: (802) 226-7738. Web Site: commercialradiocompany.com. Daniel W. Churchill, P.E., pres; Centura L. Churchill, VP; Andre S. LaPlante, gen sls mgr.

Custom bcst engrg; AM, FM & shortwave bcst equipment sls & service, specializing in transmitting components.

Communications Design Associates Inc., 1410 Providence Hwy., Norwood, MA 02062. Phone: (781) 551-8490. Fax: (781) 551-8491. E-mail: info@cdaconsultants.com. Web Site: www.cdaconsultants.com. Robert Hemenway, ptnr; Stewart Randall, ptnr; Greg Vincent, ptnr.

Ind consultants to radio, TV, corporate & govt clients. Designers of studios, production, presentation & multimedia facilities.

Communications General Corp., 2685 Alta Vista Dr., Fallbrook, CA 92028-9739. Phone: (760) 723-2700. Robert F. Gonsett, pres.

Bcst engrg consulting, AM/FM/TV applications & field engrg. Specializes in southwest United States, Hawaii & Mexico.

Communications Technologies Inc. Box 1130, 65 Country Club Ln., Marlton, NJ 08053. Phone: (856) 985-0077. Fax: (856) 985-8124. E-mail: info@commtechrf.com. Web Site: www.commtechrf.com. Clarence M. Beverage, pres; Laura M. Mizrahi, VP; James W. Pollock, engr.

Bcst engrg consulting svcs with emphasis on AM, FM & TV RF systems design & FCC application preparation consistent with FCC rules & policies.

Comsearch, 19700 Janellia Farm Blvd., Ashburn, VA 20147. Phone: (703) 726-5500. Fax: (703) 726-5600. Web Site: www.comsearch.com. Doug Hall, pres.

A complete communications engrg service organization, specializing in frequency mgmt & propagation engrg.

ComSonics Inc., 1350 Port Republic Rd., Harrisonburg, VA 22801. Phone: (540) 434-5965. Fax: (540) 432-9794. E-mail: marketing@comsonics.com. Web Site: www.comsonics.com. Dennis A. Zimmerman, pres/CEO; Donn E. Meyerhoeffer, dir opns; Don J. Sommerville, dir mktg & sls.

Microprocessor controlled signal level meters, RF leakage detection & CATV repair facility.

Contemporary Communications, 9408 Grand Gate St., Las Vegas, NV 89143. Phone: (702) 898-4669. Fax: (208) 567-6865. E-mail: lfuss@cox.net. Larry G. Fuss, pres.

FM, TV, STL & RPU applications; FM upgrades; computerized frequency searches; site selection assistance.

C.P. Crossno & Associates, Consulting Engineers. Box 180312, Dallas, TX 75218. Phone: (214) 321-9140. Fax: (214) 321-9146. E-mail: c.crossno@ieee.org. Charles Paul Crossno, owner.

Aeronautical issues; antenna design.

Crown Castle, 2000 Corporate Dr., Cannonsburg, PA 15317. Phone: (724) 416-2000. Fax: (724) 416-2200. Web Site: www.crowncastle.com.

Communications engrg consultants & site/tower mgrs.

William Culpepper & Associates Inc., 900 Jefferson Dr., Charlotte, NC 28270. Phone: (704) 365-9995. Fax: (704) 364-4823. *William A. Culpepper, pres.

AM & FM applications & feasibility studies, specializing in applications for AM power increases and transmitter relocation.

DSI RF Systems Inc., 26H World's Fair Dr., Somerset, NJ 08873. Phone: (732) 563-1144. Fax: (732) 563-1818. E-mail: tcarroll@dsirf.com. Web Site: www.dsirf.com. Joseph Giardina, chief engr; Herb Squire, VP engrg.

Radio & TV system design, transmitter & studio instal, microwave & satellite engrg & instal, remote control camera systems.

Broadcasting & Cable Yearbook 2006

Engineering and Technical Consultants

John J. Davis & Associates, Box 128, Sierra Madre, CA 91025-0128. Phone: (626) 355-6909. Fax: (626) 355-4890. E-mail: johnjdavis@adelphia.net. *John J. Davis, pres.
Primary focus on FM & TV ch allocation studies & applications; facility upgrades, FM & TV translator applications, tower site mgmt.

Denny & Associates, P.C., 6444 Bock Rd., Oxon Hill, MD 20745-3001. Phone: (301) 686-1800. Fax: (301) 686-1820. E-mail: info@denny.com. Web Site: www.denny.com. *Jules Cohen, P.E., engr; *Robert W. Denny, Jr., P.E., pres; Tiffany E. Ligon, engr; Bernard R. Segal, P.E., engr; Alfred S. Kenyon, III, sr tech consultant.
AM, FM, TV, DTV, IBOC, ITFS, MMDS, channel studies; proofs; RFR surveys; FCC applications; facility design; project mgmt.

Dettra Communications Inc., 7906 Fox Hound Rd., McLean, VA 22102. Phone: (703) 790-1427. Fax: (703) 790-0497. John E. Dettra Jr., pres.
Applications & hearing exhibits for bcst, paging, mobile telephone, cellular, microwave & private radio svcs; MMDS/ITFS; FCC rsch & consulting.

Devlin Design Group Inc., 12526 High Bluff Dr., Suite 300, San Diego, CA 92130. Phone: (760) 634-6514. E-mail: ddevlin@ddgtv.com. Web Site: www.ddgtv.com. Dan Devlin, CEO.
News sets, softset, virtual set environments, promotions, newsrooms, facility planning, lighting direction, consultation, Videssence Integration & softset (Virtual Reality Sets).

Diversified Systems Inc., 385 Market St., Kenilworth, NJ 07033. Phone: (908) 245-4833. Fax: (908) 245-0011. E-mail: info@divsysinc.com. Web Site: www.divsysinc.com. Alfred D'Alessandro, pres.
Full-svc engrg, specializing in video & RF systems.

The Downtown Group, 236 W. 27th St., New York, NY 10001. Phone: (212) 675-9506. Fax: (212) 675-3276. E-mail: info@downtowngroup.com. Web Site: www.downtowngroup.com. Peter Wilcox, ptnr; Mark Winkelman, ptnr.
Design of tech facilities: architecture, acoustics, engrg, testing. Typical projects include edit rooms, stages, recording studios & support facilities.

du Treil, Lundin & Rackley Inc., 201 Fletcher Ave., Sarasota, FL 34237-6019. Phone: (941) 329-6000. Fax: (941) 329-6030. E-mail: bobjr@dlr.com. Web Site: www.dlr.com. *Ronald D. Rackley, VP; *John A. Lundin, treas; *L. Robert du Treil, CEO.
Tech consulting for the communications industry.

ERI - Electronics Research Inc., 7777 Gardner Rd., Chandler, IN 47610. Phone: (812) 925-6000. Fax: (812) 925-4030. Web site: www.eriinc.com. *Thomas B. Sillman, pres; Bill Elmer, sls; Ernest R. Jones, P.E./structural engrg; David Davies, mktg & B.S.M.E.; Robert Rose, rsch & dev & B.S.M.E.; Jim Kemman, B.S.M.E.; Dan Dowdle, B.S.M.E.; John Robinson, P.E.; Eric Wandel, engr.
Mfg & instal FM antennas, towers, filters, combiners, lightning protection & grounding systems. Structural analysis also available.

Evans Associates Consulting, 210 S. Main St., Thiensville, WI 53092. Phone: (262) 242-6000. Fax: (262) 242-6045. E-mail: info@evansassoc.com. Web Site: www.evansassoc.com. *Ralph E. Evans Sr., ptnr; *B. Benjamin Evans, P.E., ptnr; *Ralph E. Evans, Sr., ptnr.
Telecommunications consulting engrs, net design, FCC applications, digital bcstg strategic planning, fieldwork for AM, FM, TV, CATV, ITFS, microwave relay facilities & fiber, wireless, & PCS networks.

Federal Engineering Inc., Redwood Plaza II, 10600 Arrowhead Dr., Fairfax, VA 22030. Phone: (703) 359-8200. Fax: (703) 359-8204. E-mail: info@fedeng.com. Web Site: www.fedeng.com. Ronald F. Bosco, pres; John E. Murray, sr VP.
Strategic planning, coverage analysis, new product definition, market rsch, competitive analysis, rates & tariffs, bcst stn design, mergers & acquisitions, expert testimony, regulatory support.

Charles S. Fitch, P.E., 45 Sarah Dr., Avon, CT 06001. Phone: (860) 673-7260. Fax: (860) 673-7260. E-mail: fitchpe@comcast.net. *Charles S. Fitch, P.E., engr.
FCC allocations & applications, facility design, system design, construction supervision, field surveys, facility appraisals & inspections, computer progmg.

Paul Dean Ford, Broadcast Engineering Consultant. 18889 N.2350th St., Dennison, IL 62423. Phone: (217) 826-9673. E-mail: wkzi@rr1.net. Paul Dean Ford, P.E., owner.
Engineering consultant.

Freedman, Mel, 2612 Portsmouth Ln., Modesto, CA 95355. Phone: (209) 522-1180. Fax: (209) 522-1750. E-mail: melengr@sbcglobal.net. Mel Freeman, engr.

George M. Frese, P.E., 1011 Denis Ct., East Wenatchee, WA 98802. Phone: (509) 884-4558. Fax: (509) 884-9170. E-mail: frese@crcwnet.com. *George M. Frese, owner.
AM, FM, TV, FM tran, & TV tran applications. AM special, diplexing & DA ant design.

Graphic Enterprises Inc., 3874 Highland Park N.W., North Canton, OH 44720. Web Site: www.geiworldwide.com. Austin Vanchieri, pres.
Large-format digital printing systems.

Hammett & Edison Inc. Box 280068, San Francisco, CA 94128-0068. Phone: (707) 996-5200. Phone: (202) 396-5200 (DC). Fax: (707) 996-5280. E-mail: engr@h-e.com. Web Site: www.h-e.com. *William F. Hammett, P.E.; Dane E. Ericksen, P.E.; *Stanley Salek, P.E.; *Robert D. Weller, P.E.; Mark D. Neumann, P.E.
Design & FCC filings: AM, FM, TV, STL, wireless cable. Specialties: computerized coverage studies, AM directionals / diplexers, RF radiation predictions / measurements / mitigations, field strength measurements, due diligence technical surveys, FAA EMI analysis.

Hatfield & Dawson, Consulting Engineers L.L.C. 9500 Greenwood Ave. N., Seattle, WA 98103. Phone: (206) 783-9151. Fax: (206) 789-9834. E-mail: hatdaw@hatdaw.com. Web Site: www.hatdaw.com. B. F. Dawson III, pres; J. B. Hatfield, sec/treas; T.M. Eckels, VP; *Stephen S. Lockwood, ptnr; *James B. Hatfield, P.E.; *Benj. F. Dawson III, P.E.; *Thomas M. Eckels, P.E.; Paul W. Leonard, P.E.; Thomas Gordon, P.E.; *Erik C. Swanson, staff engr.
Telecommunications & radio physics engrg, including bcst, electromagnetic compatibility, NIER measurement & analysis, antenna & propagation analysis, & design.

Charles A. Hecht & Associates Inc., 16 Doe Run, Pittstown, NJ 08867. Phone: (908) 730-7959. Fax: (908) 730-7408. E-mail: hechtassoc@sprintmail.com. Charles A. Hecht, pres; William L. Smith, engr; C.J. Hecht, engr.
Bcst engrg svcs including FCC studies & applications, directional antenna design, fieldwork, tech litigation; specialists in AM studies for telecommunications companies.

Hilding Communications, Box 1700, Morgan Hill, CA 95038-2222. Phone: (408) 842-2222. E-mail: eric@hilding.com. Eric Hilding, owner.
FM ch studies, complex FM substitution proposals, site locations, 301 applications engrg, gen bcst consulting.

HN Telecom Inc., 1160 Douglas Rd., Burnaby, BC V5C 4Z6. Canada. Phone: (604) 294-3401. Fax: (604) 299-6712. E-mail: contact@hntelecom.com. Web Site: www.hntelecom.com. P. Hostinsky, principal; Bruce W. Grantholm, sr VP engrg/opns.
Telecommunications tech consulting svcs for AM, FM, TV bcst & CATV systems, studio-to-transmitter links & studio systems.

Doug Holland Inc., 1871 Sweet Briar Ln., Birmingham, AL 35235-3357. Phone: (205) 229-5628. Fax: (205) 655-4092. E-mail: doug@dougholland.com. Web Site: www.dougholland.com. Doug Holland, pres.
Turnkey opns, allocation studies, due diligence, transmitter installations, upgrades & coverage maps

R.L. Hoover Consulting Telecommunications, Consulting Telecommunications Engineer. 11704 Seven Locks Rd., Potomac, MD 20854. Phone: (301) 983-0054. *Robert Lloyd Hoover, P.E., owner.
Professional engrg consulting for AM, FM & TV applications & testimony. Radiation hazard analyses & testimony. Ex-owner AM & FM stns. Patent agent.

Independent Broadcast Consultants Inc., 110 County Rd. 146, Trumansburg, NY 14886-9721. Phone: (607) 273-2970. Fax: (607) 273-5125. E-mail: ibcengineering@juno.com. Web Site: www.trumansburgchamber.com. William J. Sitzman, pres; M.F. Sitzman, VP; George Soltysik, P.E., engr; N.L. Hollenback, engr; R.A. Lynch, engr.
AM, FM & SW applications, specializing in AM allocation studies & broadband AM directional antenna design & AM diplexer design.

J. Boyd Ingram & Associates, Box 1528, Batesville, MS 38606. Phone: (662) 563-4007. Fax: (601) 563-9002. J. Boyd Ingram, A.E., pres; A.E. Jennings, VP.
Tech consultation, facility construction & repair.

George Jacobs & Associates Inc., Box 12298, Silver Spring, MD 20908-0298. Phone: (301) 598-1283. Fax: (301) 598-7788. E-mail: gja@gjainc.com. Web Site: www.gjainc.com. George Jacobs, pres; Anne Case, engr; Robert German, engr.
Specialists in conceptional design, application filing & frequency mgmt for FCC-licensed International Broadcast Stations (shortwave). Consultative liaison with foreign bcst stns & organizations.

Vir James, P.C., 965 S. Irving St., Denver, CO 80219. Phone: (303) 937-1900. Fax: (303) 937-1902. *Timothy C. Cutforth, pres.
AM/FM/TV allocation studies & applications, AM directional ant design & tune-up, conductivity measurements.

Jenel Systems and Design Inc./Smalling Systems, 6700 Spokane, Plano, TX 75023. Phone: (972) 491-1442. Fax: (972) 491-1442. E-mail: smalling@smallingsystems.com. Web Site: www.smallingsystems.com. Elmer Smalling III, pres/CEO; Howard Halcomb, sls VP; Erin Day Loyd, VP mktg.
Digital bcstg solutions; studio, post, acoustic & earth stn, design; trucks; TV system design from planning to turnkey construction.

Carl T. Jones Corp., 7901 Yarnwood Ct., Springfield, VA 22153. Phone: (703) 569-7704. Fax: (703) 569-6417. Web site: www.ctjc.com. *Carl T. Jones Jr., pres; Hernab E. Hurst Jr., communications svcs mgr; Zar B. Aung, engr; William J. Getz, engr; David W. Goldsworthy, engr; *John E. Hidle, engr; John E. Hidle Jr., engr; Peter Huang, engr; *Cynthia M. Jacobson, engr; Brian D. Parrish, engr; Paul M. Piccione, engr; *Alfred E. Resnick, engr; Patrick W. Rio, engr; James D. Sadler, engr.
Consulting engrs specializing in bcstg & CATV tech design & regulatory filings. Maintain EMC/EMI testing laboratory.

KCI Technologies Inc., 4601 Six Forks Rd., Suite 200, Raleigh, NC 27609. Phone: (919) 783-9214. Fax: (919) 783-9266. Tom Donohue, P.E., sr VP; James Blake, engrg mgr.
Full engrg svcs to the communications industry, including tower analysis & remediation, design of standard &

COHEN, DIPPELL AND EVERIST, P.C.

Communications Consulting Engineers
(Serving the Broadcast Industry since 1937)

- Radio and TV RF System Designs
- STL and Microwave System Design
- NTSC/DTV Coverage and Interference Studies Using FCC Traditional and Longley-Rice Methodologies
- Expert Testimony on FCC Matters
- Radio Frequency Field Level Assessment
- AM and FM Coverage and Interference Studies
- Field Measurements
- Technical Reports and Exhibits in Support of FCC Applications
- FAA and Zoning Appeals

1300 L Street, N.W., Suite 1100
Washington, D.C. 20005
(202) 898-0111
Fax (202) 898-0895
www.broadcast-consulting-engineers.com
E-Mail: dgeverist@covad.net
E-Mail: cde@attglobal.net

Donald G. Everist, P.E., President
Resumé Available Upon Request

Member AFCCE

Engineering and Technical Consultants

non-standard sites, "stealth" engrg, photo realistic renderings & turnkey construction.

Kessler & Gehman Associates Inc., 507 N.W. 60th St., Suite C, Gainesville, FL 32607. Phone: (352) 332-3157. Fax: (352) 332-7481. E-mail: rgehman@bellsouth.net; ryanw@mindspring.com. *Robert Gehman, P.E. Jr., pres; William Kessler, P.E., VP; Jeffrey C. Gehman, engr; Ryan C. Wilhour, engr; William T. Godfrey, P.E.

Studies, system design, FCC applications, bidding documents & contract monitoring for bcst, ITFS, wireless cable, microwave & mobile communications systems & digital TV.

Lightning Eliminators & Consultants Inc., 6687 Arapahoe Rd., Boulder, CO 80303. Phone: (303) 447-2828 ext 100. Fax: (303) 447-8122. E-mail: info@lightingeliminators.com. Web Site: www.lightningeliminators.com. Roy B. Carpenter Jr, dir; Jerry Kerr, VP mktg & sls; Darwin N. Sletten, chief engr.

Consulting & engrg svcs in lightning prevention, grounding & power / signal / telephone / data line conditioning.

Lohnes and Culver, 8309 Cherry Ln., Laurel, MD 20707-4830. Phone: (301) 776-4488. Fax: (301) 776-4499. E-mail: locul@locul.com. *Robert D. Culver, P.E., ptnr; Frederick D. Veihmeyer, ptnr.

Communication consulting engrg svc for bcst & related fields. Design, application, optimization, system evaluation & expert representation svcs.

Cecil Lynch Consulting Engineers, 2460 Illinois Ave., Modesto, CA 95358. Phone: (209) 523-3955. Fax: (209) 522-5287. Cecil Lynch, CEO; Gerald L. Moore, ptnr.

Bcst engrg, stn appraisals, customized computer progmg svc, GPS surveying & RFR measurements.

MLJ Wireless Engineering Inc., (formerly JMS/MLJ Worldwide Inc.). 111M Carpenter Dr., Suite 150, Stirling, VA 20164. Phone: (703) 481-4500 (technical questions & sls). Web Site: www.jms.com. E-mail: skowdley@wse-mlj.com. Sridhar Kowdley, technical support & sls.

International wireless engrg firm specializing in PCS, CDMA, LMDS, bcst & wireless.

Magnusson Klemencic, 1301 Fifth Ave., Suite 3200, Seattle, WA 98101-2699. Phone: (206) 292-1200. Fax: (206) 292-1201. Web Site: www.mka.com. Jon D. Magnusson, CEO; Brian McIntyre, sr VP.

Tower inspection, wind rating, tower retrofit, concept studies, design, contract documents & construction mgmt.

Mahlum Architects, 71 Columbia, Suite 400, Seattle, WA 98104. Phone: (206) 441-4151. Fax: (206) 441-0478. Web Site: www.mahlum.com. John Mahlum, pres.

D.L. Markley & Associates Inc., 2104 W. Moss Ave., Peoria, IL 61604. Phone: (309) 673-7511. Fax: (309) 673-8128. E-mail: dlm@dlmarkley.com. Web Site: www.dlmarkley.com. *Donald L. Markley, P.E., pres; Jeremy Ruck, engr.

AM, FM, TV & microwave applications, construction & measurements. Allocation studies, non-ionizing radiation measurements.

Marsand Inc., Box 485, 6100 IH-35W, Alvarado, TX 76009. Phone: (817) 783-5566. Fax: (817) 783-5577. E-mail: tvcowboy@marsand.com. Web Site: www.marsand.com. *Matthew A. Sanderford, Jr., P.E., pres; David Sanderford, VP.

Turnkey installation svcs, CAD-VIDCAD wiring documentation, FM & TV proof-of-performance, analog &

digital, FCC consulting & applications, RF troubleshooting, installations & conversions.

Frank J. Maynard, 44683 Mansfield Dr., Novi, MI 48375. Phone: (248) 344-2965. E-mail: info@fmaynard.com. Web Site: www.fmaynard.com. Frank J. Maynard, owner.

Radio & TV engrg svcs & applications.

McClanathan & Associates Inc., Box 939, Portland, OR 97207. Phone: (503) 246-8080. Fax: (503) 246-6304. *Robert A. McClanathan P.E., pres.

Professional electrical engrs for radio & TV FCC applications, computer svcs, field engrg & construction svcs.

Meintel, Sgrignoli, & Wallace, 1282 Smallwood Dr., Suite 372, Waldorf, MD 20603. Phone: (202) 251-7589. E-mail: wallacedtv@aol.com. Dennis Wallace, pres.

Specializing in digital television.

MidAmerica Electronics Service Inc., 410 Mt. Tabor Rd., New Albany, IN 47150. Phone: (812) 945-1209. Fax: (812) 945-1859. E-mail: peterclb@aol.com.

AM & FM field engrg svcs, antenna measurements, AM stereo instal & proof of performance, AM & FM spectrum analysis, NRSC compliance measurement, new construction & rebuilding.

Lawrence L. Morton Associates, 2867 Belden Dr., Hollywood Hills, CA 90068-1901. Phone: (323) 467-5010. Fax: (323) 467-5848. E-mail: larry@radiotv.biz. *Lawrence L. Morton, P.E., owner.

Telecommunications engrg consulting svcs for AM, FM, TV & LPTV. Computerized engrg svcs, field svcs, FCC applications.

Mueller Broadcast Design, 613 S. La Grange Rd., La Grange, IL 60525. Phone: (708) 352-2166. Fax: (708) 352-2170. E-mail: mark@muellerbroadcastdesign.com. Web Site: www.muellerbroadcastdesign.com. Mark A. Mueller, owner.

AM/FM tech consultant, AM directional systems.

Mullaney Engineering Inc., 9049 Shady Grove Ct., Gaithersburg, MD 20877. Phone: (301) 921-0115. Fax: (301) 590-9757. E-mail: jmullaney@mullengr.com. *John J. Mullaney, pres/engr; *Alan E. Gearing, P.E.; Tim Z. Sawyer.

Consulting communications engrs providing: design & optimization of AM directional arrays; analysis for new allocation, site relocation & upgrades AM FM TV LPTV wireless cable (MDS/MMDS/ITFS/OFS); environmental radiation analysis; fieldwork; expert testimony.

Multicomm Sciences International Inc., 266 W. Main St., Denville, NJ 07834. Phone: (973) 627-7400. Fax: (973) 625-1002. E-mail: mail@multicommsciences.com. Web Site: www.multicommsciences.com. Victor J. Nexon Jr., pres.

Frequency coordination, site surveys, earth stn interference studies, FCC license, radiation hazard testing.

Munn-Reese, Inc.
Broadcast Engineering Consultants
P.O. Box 220
Coldwater, Michigan 49036
Phone: 517-278-7339
wayne@munn-reese.com

Munn-Reese Inc. Box 220, 385 Airport Dr., Coldwater, MI 49036-0220. Phone: (517) 278-7339. Fax: (517) 278-6973. E-mail: wayne@munn-reese.com. Web Site: www.munn-reese.com. Christine Reese, VP; Wayne S. Reese, pres.

AM, FM, TV, low power TV & engrg consulting service, including applications, field tuning & problem solving.

Nationwide Tower Company Inc., Box 1829, Henderson, KY 42419-1829. Phone: (270) 869-8000. Fax: (270) 869-8500. E-mail: hjohnston@nationwidetower.com. Web Site: www.nationwidetower.com. Kevin Roth, sls VP; Diane Pruitt, gen sls mgr.

Tower inspections, painting, repair re-guy, lighting, antennas, feedlines, analysis, erect, dismantle, line sweeping, site monitoring, and tower tracker svcs.

Newman-Kees Frequency Measurements, Engineering, & Installations, 8611 Slate Rd., Evansville, IN 47720. Phone: (812) 963-3294. E-mail: nkeng@insightbb.com. Frank Hertel, owner.

RF & frequency measurements for AM-FM-TV coml

users via air or on location. Audio/video service & instals.

Owl Engineering & EMC Test Labs, Inc., 5844 Avenue N., Shoreview, MN 55126. Phone: (651) 784-7445. Fax: (763) 784-4541. E-mail: info@owleng.com. Web Site: www.owleng.com. *Garrett G. Lysiak, P.E., ptnr; Diane Stewart Lysiak, ptnr.

Telecommunications consulting engrg svcs, applications, facilities specifications svcs, field engrg svcs, maintenance & FCC compliance svcs, EMC testing.

Pacific Radio Electronics, 969 N. La Brea, Los Angeles, CA 90038. Phone: (323) 969-2035. Phone: (800) 634-9476. Fax: (323) 969-2053. E-mail: info@pacrad.com. Web Site: www.pacrad.com. Joseph Phillips, pres.

Distributor of racks, patch bays, cable, adaptors, connectors, handtools, outlet strips & many other products for the bcst industry.

William F. Pohts Telecommunications, 225 Denfield Dr., Alexandria, VA 22309. Phone: (703) 360-7193. Fax: (703) 360-0309. E-mail: bill@pohts.com. *William F. Pohts, consulting engr.

Consulting engr specializing in the emerging technologies in telecommunications & electronic systems.

Rimma Posin, 3712 Carmel Ave., Irvine, CA 92606. Phone: (949) 857-9639. Fax: (949) 857-9639. Rimma Posin, owner.

Consulting for cable; FCC applications.

W.L. Pritchard & Co. L.C., 4405 E.W. Hwy., Suite 501, Bethesda, MD 20814. Phone: (301) 654-1144. Fax: (301) 654-1814. E-mail: wlpco@wlpco.com. Web Site: www.wlpco.com.

Professional engrg and business problem solving in telecommunications, competitor analysis, satellite communications, earth stns, and launch vehicles.

RFK Engineering, LLC, 1229 19th St., N.W., Washington, DC 20036. Phone: (202) 463-1565. E-mail: prubin@satpar.com. Web Site: www.rfkengineering. *Philip A. Rubin, pres; Ted Kaplan, VP engrg; Jeffrey Freedman, CFO.

Communication and Direct Broadcast satellite experts TV & radio cellular & other new media technologies. Experts in FCC rules & regulations. International experience, experts in ITU regulation. Software developers, simulation & modeling. In business over 20 years.

RF Technologies Corp., 12 Foss Rd., Lewiston, ME 04240. Phone: (207) 777-7778. Fax: (207) 777-7784. Web Site: www.rftechnologies.net.

Designs & manufactures high-power bcst RF networks & components for FM & TV bcstrs. Products include ants, diplexers, combiners, filters, switches, coaxial & waveguides.

Radio/TV Engineering Co., 1416 Hollister Ln., Los Osos, CA 93402. Phone: (805) 528-1996. Fax: (805) 528-1982. Norwood J. Patterson, pres; G. Dawn Patterson, exec sec/asst engrg.

AM, FM, FCC applications, directional ant design. Serving bcstrs for over 35 years.

Radiotechniques Engineering, LLC, Box 367, 402 10th Ave., Haddon Heights, NJ 08035-0367. Phone: (856) 546-8008. Fax: (856) 546-1841. E-mail: ted@radiotechniques.com. *Edward A. Schober, P.E., VP.

AM, FM, TV, digital bcst, boosters, FCC, equipment, field, & systems engrg. RF, financial, opns, & acoustical design.

Rogers Cable Systems, 35-73 Wolfdale, Mississauga, ON L5C 3T6. Canada. Phone: (905) 273-8000. Fax: (905) 273-9661. Web Site: www.rogers.com.

Consulting engrg svcs with emphasis on design, instal & testing of CATV systems, fiber-optic nets.

D.W. Sargent Broadcast Service Inc., 804 Richard Rd., Cherry Hill, NJ 08034. Phone: (856) 667-8573. Fax: (856) 667-1409. Dean W. Sargent, pres.

Ant system design & measurements for FM & TV. FM & TV master ant system design.

T.Z. Sawyer Technical Consultants, Box 70696, Chevy Chase, MD 20816. Phone: (301) 921-0115. Fax: (301) 590-9757. E-mail: info@sawyer.com. Web Site: www.sawyer.com. Timothy Z. Sawyer, pres; Trisha E. Ford, admin asst.

FCC applications for AM, FM, TV, LPTV & aux svcs; AM directional ant design; AM, FM, & TV ant measurements; allocation studies; site surveys & inspections.

Engineering and Technical Consultants

Sellmeyer Engineering, Box 356, McKinney, TX 75070. Phone: (214) 495-9764. Fax: (214) 495-9764. *J.S. Sellmeyer, P.E., owner.

AM, FM, TV applications, hearing support, directional ant design & adjustment; facilities planning & specialized equipment design.

Shortwave Engineering, 1300 WWCR Ave., Nashville, TN 37218. Phone: (615) 255-1300. Fax: (615) 255-1311. E-mail: k4bty@arrl.net. George McClintock, pres; William Hair, engr.

Consulting & emergency repair for AM, FM & shortwave radio.

SiteSafe Inc., 200 N. Glebe Rd., Suite 1000, Arlington, VA 22203. Phone: (703) 276-1100. Fax: (703) 276-1169. E-mail: info@sitesafe.com. Web Site: www.sitesafe.com. Wesley McGee, pres.

Bcst & land mobile & wireless engrg consulting svcs.

Smith and Fisher, 2237 Tackett's Mill Dr., Suite A, Woodbridge, VA 22192. Phone: (703) 494-2101. Fax: (703) 494-2132. E-mail: kevin@smithandfisher.com. Web Site: www.smithandfisher.com. Neil Smith, ptnr; Kevin Fisher, ptnr.

Tech consultants to AM, FM, TV, & LPTV stns; FCC applications; allocations studies; RF measurements; expert witness testimony.

Carl E. Smith, Consulting Engineers. Box 807, 2324 N. Cleveland-Massilon Rd., Bath, OH 44210-0807. Phone: (330) 659-4440. Fax: (330) 659-9234.

AM, FM, TV & LPTV engrg, FCC applications, ant systems adjustments. Sls: towers, ants, transmission line, phasing equipment. Turnkey instal.

Frederick A. Smith Engineers, 1123 Old River Rd., Elloree, SC 29047. Phone: (803) 897-2815. Fax: (803) 897-2816. Frederick A. Smith, P.E., chief engr.

Communications systems design, microwave path surveys, ant impedance measurements. United States & foreign.

Southern Broadcast Services, 80 Commerce Dr., Suite B, Pelham, AL 35124. Phone: (205) 663-3709. Fax: (205) 663-7108. E-mail: jwcoleman@southernbroadcastservices.com. Web Site: www.southernbroadcastservices.com. Jim Coleman, pres.

Tower erection, ant & line instal, cellular & maintenance svcs.

Southwest Frequency Measurements, 11508 Big Trail, Austin, TX 78759. Phone: (512) 345-5931. Fax: (512) 345-5931. Ben F. Green, owner; Frieda M. Green, sec.

AM, FM, & TV bcst carriers; pilot, SCA, & color subcarrier measurements. Current capability to 3GHZ.

Sparling, 720 Olive Way, Suite 1400, Seattle, WA 98101-0554. Phone: (206) 667-0555. Fax: (206) 667-0554. E-mail: connect@sparling.com. Web Site: www.sparling.com. James R. Duncan, CEO; Tom Leonidas Jr., VP; Eric Overton, VP.

Combining cutting-edge technology with professional expertise, Sparling's TV bcst design team delivers state-of-the-art facilities equipped for the DTV transition.

Standard Frequency Measuring Service, 2092 Arrowood Pl., Cincinnati, OH 45231. Phone: (513) 851-4964. E-mail: lawilliams@alum.mit.edu. *Louis A. Williams, P.E, Jr., consulting engr; Pat Williams, office mgr.

Frequency, modulation, subcarrier measurements on AM, FM, TV, STL, & microwave. RFR, spurious & harmonic & field strength measurements.

J.M. Stitt & Associates Inc., 621 Mehring Way, Suite 1907, Cincinnati, OH 45202. Phone: (513) 621-9292. Fax: (513) 651-9622. E-mail: towerjim@aol.com. Web Site: www.jmstittassociates.com. James Stitt, pres.

Engrg consultants, facility design & instal, contract engrg svcs, acoustical consultants, tower site mgmt.

Structural Systems Technology Inc., 6867 Elm St., McLean, VA 22101. Phone: (703) 356-9765. Fax: (703) 448-0979. Fred W. Purdy, P.E., pres; Keveh Mehrnama, P.E., engrg VP.

Structural engrg studies, analysis, design, modifications, inspections, fabrication & erection of towers & ant structures.

Superior Satellite Engineers, 1743 Middle Rd., Columbia Falls, MT 59912. Phone: (406) 257-9590. Fax: (406) 257-9599. E-mail: superior@superiorsatelliteusa.com. Web Site: www.superiorsatelliteusa.com. Doyle Catlett, pres; Ron Catlett, gen mgr; Ed Catlett, sls.

Manufacturer of multi-beam retro fit feed systems for coml ants & complete ant systems from 2.8 meters to 7 meters.

Technet Systems Group, (A division of Steve Vanni Associates Inc). Box 422, Auburn, NH 03032. Phone: (603) 483-5365. Fax: (603) 483-0512. E-mail: sales@technetsystems.com. Web Site: www.technetsystems.com. Steve Vanni, pres; Bob Smith, mgr instal div; Kim Meisinger, mgr tower div; Criss Onan, mgr equip sls.

Bcst equipment supplier/distributor for radio & TV, specializing in complete "turnkeyed" packages including planning, design, equipment, instal, towers & FCC licensing.

Teletech Inc., Box 85567, Westland, MI 48185. Phone: (734) 641-2300. Keith Johnson, gen mgr.

Scottsdale, AZ 85261, Box 4221. Phone: (480) 367-1500.

Engrg consultants: AM, FM, TV, LPTV; FCC applications/filings; FAA filings, aeronautical studies; tower erection, maintenance & inspections; antenna site dev & mgmt; directional antenna design & proof of performance; contract engrg svcs.

Cullen B. Tendick Consulting Radio Engineer, 11753 N. Cassiopeia Dr., Tucson, AZ 85737. Phone: (520) 575-8265. Fax: (520) 498-0156. E-mail: cullen3@juno.com. Cullen B. Tendick, consulting radio engr.

AM, FM & TV measurements & allocations.

TransVision, 550 Maulhardt Ave., Oxnard, CA 93030. Phone: (805) 981-8740. Fax: (805) 981-8738. E-mail: info@txvision.com. Web Site: www.txvision.com. Kimithy Vaughn, mngng dir.

Twelve transportable & satellite transmission facilities (video, audio, voice, data). Flypack production & SNG svcs.

Steve Vanni Associates Inc., Box 422, Auburn, NH 03032. Phone: (603) 483-5365. Fax: (603) 483-0512. Steve Vanni, pres.

Tech consulting, systems design, project mgmt; complete turnkey svcs including equipment & towers through Technet Systems Group.

The Richard L. Vega Group Inc., 1245 W. Fairbanks Ave., Suite 380, Winter Park, FL 32789-4878. Phone: (407) 539-6540. Fax: (407) 539-6547. E-mail: vega@magicnet.net. Richard L. Vega Jr., chmn.

Tech consulting svcs for all telecommunications svcs including FCC applications, allocation studies, site acquisition.

Vernier, Doug, Telecommunications Consultants, 721 W. 1st St., Suite A, Cedar Falls, IA 50613. Phone: (319) 266-8402. Fax: (319) 266-9212. E-mail: dvernier@v-soft.com. Web Site: www.v-soft.com. Doug Vernier, pres/engr; Kate Michler, assoc; John Gray, dir rsch & dev; Jake Vernier, assoc; Gayle Vernier, business mgr.

Bcst engrg & consultation, ch searches, FCC applications, allocations, custom mapping, coverage analysis. V-Soft Communications broadcast eng software.

D.C. Williams Ph.D, P.E., Consulting Radio Engineer. Box 1888, Carson City, NV 89702. Phone: (775) 885-2400. Fax: (775) 885-8705. *D.C. Williams, P.E. PhD., pres.

Registered professional engr, specializing in allocations, antenna system design, applications, construction, evaluation & measurement of AM & FM directional facilities.

Louis A. Williams Jr. & Associates, 2092 Arrowood Pl., Cincinnati, OH 45231. Phone: (513) 851-4964. E-mail: lawilliams@alum.mit.edu. Pat Williams, office mgr.

FCC filings, frequency searches, RFR hazard measurements & analysis, field strength measurements, tech assistance, & other measurement svcs.

Willoughby & Voss, Box 701190, San Antonio, TX 78270-1190. Phone: (210) 490-2778. Fax: (210) 525-1111. Fax: (210) 490-2779. Lyndon H. Willoughby, owner.

AM, FM, TV, STL, trans applications, directional ant design, field svcs, allocations, site studies, system planning, frequency searches, facility inspection & non-ionized radiation studies.

Walter Wulff & Associates, FAA Consultants. Box 914, Pt. Clear, AL 36564. Phone: (251) 990-2502. Fax: (251) 990-2503. E-mail: wulff@zebra.net. Walter H. Wulff, pres.

Conducts FAA obstruction evaluation studies, FM electro magnetic interference analysis & communications consulting engrs.

Law Firms

Abdo, Abdo, Broady & Satorius, P. A., 710 Northstar W., 625 Marquette Ave., Minneapolis, MN 55402. Phone: (612) 333-1526. Fax: (612) 342-2608. E-mail: kabdo@abdoabdo.com. Web Site: www.abdoabdo.com. Kenneth J. Abdo, Daniel M. Satorius.

Akerman & Senterfitt, Citrus Center, 255 South Orange Ave. 17th fl., Orlando, FL 32801. Phone: (407) 843-7860. Fax: (407) 843-6610. Tom Cardwell.

Akin, Gump, Strauss, Hauer & Feld, 1333 New Hampshire Ave. N.W., Suite 400, Washington, DC 20036. Phone: (202) 887-4000. Fax: (202) 887-4288.

Alan Vogl & Bryant Young, 44 Montgomery St., Suite 4020, San Francisco, CA 94104. Phone: (415) 291-1970. Fax: (415) 291-1984. Mark Rosenthal, Bryant Young, Alan Vogl.

Anderson, Kill & Olick L.L.P., 2100 M St. N.W., Suite 650, Washington, DC 20037. Phone: (202) 218-0040. Fax: (202) 218-0055. Web Site: www.andersonkill.com.

Ardi, Dennis, 340 N. Camden Dr., Third Fl., Beverly Hills, CA 90210. Phone: (310) 271-6900. Fax: (310) 271-6963.

Arent & Fox, PLLC, 1050 Connecticut Ave. N.W., Washington, DC 20036-5339. Phone: (202) 857-6000. Fax: (202) 857-6395. Web Site: www.arentfox.com.

Arnold & Porter LLP, 555 12th St. N.W., Washington, DC 20004-1206. Phone: (202) 942-5000. Fax: (202) 942-5999. E-mail: norman_sinel@aporter.com. Web Site: www.arnoldporter.com. Phillip W. Horton, Richard L. Rosen, Norman M. Sinel, Richard M. Firestone, Stephanie M. Phillipps, Patrick J. Grant, Marcia Cranbeg, William E. Cook, Theodore D. Frank, P. Scott Feira, Maureen Jeffreys, Peter Schildkraut, Michael Ryan, Donald T. Stepka, Emma Wright.

Asbury, Philip S., 309 S. Broad St., Philadelphia, PA 19107-5813. Phone: (215) 985-0911. Fax: (215) 985-1195.

Ausley & McMullen, Box 391, 227 S. Calhoun St., Tallahassee, FL 32302. Phone: (850) 224-9115. Fax: (850) 222-7560.

Baker & Hostetler LLP, 1050 Connecticut Ave. N.W., Suite 1100, Washington, DC 20036. Phone: (202) 861-1500. Fax: (202) 861-1783. E-mail: khoward@bakerlaw.com. Web Site: www.bakerlaw.com. Kenneth C. Howard Jr., Bruce W. Sanford, Malena F. Barzilai, Mark I. Bailen.

Law Offices of Ruth S. Baker-Battist, 5600 Wisconsin Ave., Chevy Chase, MD 20815. Phone: (301) 718-0955. Fax: (301) 718-8867. E-mail: rbattist@aol.com.

Baker Botts L.L.P., 1299 Pennsylvania Ave. N.W., Washington, DC 20004. Phone: (202) 639-7700. Fax: (202) 639-7890. Herbert J. Miller Jr., John Joseph Cassidy.

Baker, Ravenel & Bender, Box 8057, 1730 Main St., Columbia, SC 20292. Phone: (803) 799-9091. Fax: (803) 779-3423. Charles E. Baker, Jay Bender, ptnrs.

Law Office of Martin J. Barab, 9606 Santa Monica Blvd., 3rd Fl., Beverly Hills, CA 90210. Phone: (310) 859-6644. Fax: (310) 859-6650. E-mail: mjbarab@barablaw.com. Martin J. Barab, Sean M. Fawcett.

Barron & Newburger, P.C., 811 Baron Springs, Austin, TX 78704. Phone: (512) 476-9103. Fax: (512) 476-9253. E-mail: bbarron@bnpdaw.com. Barbara M. Barron.

Bass, Berry & Sims, 315 Deaderick St., South Center Suite 2700, Nashville, TN 37238-0002. Phone: (615) 742-6200. Fax: (615) 742-6293.

Richard S. Becker & Associates, 7128 Fairfax Rd., Bethesda, MD 20814. Phone: (301) 986-9005. Fax: (301) 986-8456. Richard S. Becker, James S. Finerfrock.

Beitchman & Hudson, 215 14th St. N.W., Atlanta, GA 30318. Phone: (404) 897-5252. Fax: (404) 874-4270. E-mail: leebeebee@aol.com. Lee B. Beitchman.

Bell, Boyd & Lloyd, 1615 L St. N.W., Suite 1200, Washington, DC 20036. Phone: (202) 466-6300. Fax: (202) 463-0678.

BellSouth Corp., 1155 Peachtree St. N.E., Atlanta, GA 30309-3610. Phone: (404) 249-2000. Fax: (404) 249-3839. Web Site: www.bellsouth.com. William B. Barfield, assoc gen counsel.

Law Offices of Jeff Berke, 12400 Wilshire Blvd., Suite 1500, Los Angeles, CA 90025-6538. Phone: (310) 571-2808. Jeff Berke. Esq.

Berkowitz, Trager & Trager, P.C., 8 Wright Street, Westport, CT 06880. Phone: (203) 226-1001. Fax: (203) 226-3801.

Law Offices of Lawrence Bernstein, 1818 N St. N.W., Suite 700, Washington, DC 20036. Phone: (202) 296-1800. Fax: (202) 331-9306. E-mail: lawberns@erols.com. Lawrence Bernstein.

Birch, Horton, Bittner & Cherot, 1155 Connecticut Ave. N.W., Suite 1200, Washington, DC 20036. Phone: (202) 659-5800. Fax: (202) 659-1027. Elisabeth H. Ross, Thomas L. Albert, Ronald Birch, William Horn.

Bishop, Payne, Harvard & Kaitcer, L.L.P., 500 W. Seventh St., Suite 1800, Fort Worth, TX 76102-4782. Phone: (817) 335-4911. Fax: (817) 870-2631.

Blank, Rome, LLP, 405 Lexington Ave., 23rd Floor, New York, NY 10174. Phone: (212) 885-5000. Fax: (212) 885-5001. Web Site: www.blankrome.com.

Bleiweiss, Irene, U.S. FCC, Audio Services Division, 445 12th St. S.W., Rm. 2B450, Washington, DC 20554. Phone: (202) 418-2700. Fax: (202) 418-1411. Web Site: www.fcc.gov/mb/audio. Irene Bleiweiss.

Blooston, Mordkofsky, Dickens, Duffy & Prendergast, 2120 L St. N.W., Suite 300, Washington, DC 20037. Phone: (202) 659-0830. Fax: (202) 828-5568. Web Site: www.bloostonlaw.com. Harold Mordkofsky, Benjamin H. Dickens Jr., John A. Prendergast, Gerald J. Duffy, Richard Rubino, Mary J. Sisak, D. Cary Mitchell.

Blumberg, Grace Ganz, UCLA School of Law, 405 Hilgard Ave., Los Angeles, CA 90095. Phone: (310) 825-1334. Fax: (310) 206-6489.

Blume & Associates LLC, 10 Ellsworth Rd., Suite 209, West Hartford, CT 06107. Phone: (860) 231-8777. Fax: (860) 231-7763. E-mail: dblume@cowparade.net. Daniel Blume.

Bobbitt & Roberts, 6601 Center Drive West, Ste 500, Los Angeles, CA 90045. Phone: (310) 315-7150. Fax: (310) 315-7159. Leroy Bobbitt, Virgil Roberts.

Boelter & Perry, 330 Washington Blvd., Suite 400, Marina Del Rey, CA 90292. Phone: (310) 822-5037. Fax: (310) 823-4325. E-mail: boltperr@comcast.net.

Boies, Schiller & Flexner, LLP, 100 S.E. 2nd St., Suite 2800, Miami, FL 33131. Phone: (305) 539-8400. Fax: (305) 539-1307. Web Site: www.bsfllp.com.

Bone McAllester Norten PLLC, 511 Union St., Suite 1600, Nashville, TN 37219. Phone: (615) 238-6330. Fax: (615) 238-6301. Web Site: www.bonelaw.com. C. Michael Norton.

William R. Booker III, 4641 N. 20th R.D. #3, Arlington, VA 22207-2239. Phone: (703) 351-7836. Fax: (703) 351-7954.

Boose, Casey, Ciklin, Lubitz, Martens, McBane & O'Connell, Northbridge Tower, 515 N. Flagler Dr., Suite 1900, West Palm Beach, FL 33401. Phone: (561) 832-5900. Fax: (561) 833-4209. Patrick J. Casey.

Booth, Freret, Imlay & Tepper P.C., 14356 Cape May Rd., Silver Spring, MD 20904-6011. Phone: (301) 384-5525. Fax: (301) 384-6384. E-mail: bfitpc@aol.com. Christopher D. Imlay, Cary S. Tepper.

Bordelon, Hamlin & Theriot, 701 S. Peters St., New Orleans, LA 70130. Phone: (504) 524-5328. Fax: (504) 523-1071. E-mail: rwedig@bh-t.com.

Borsari and Assoc., P.L.C., P.O. Box 29, Arlington, VA 22210. Phone: (703) 524-5800. Fax: (703) 524-4329. E-mail: John@borsari.com. Web Site: www.borsari.com. John A. Borsari.

Borsari & Paxson, 4000 Albemarle St. N.W., Suite 100, Washington, DC 20016. Phone: (202) 296-4800. Fax: (202) 296-4460. E-mail: bap@baplaw.com. Web Site: www.baplaw.com. George R. Borsari Jr., Anne Thomas Paxson.

Boult, Cummings, Conners & Berry, Box 198062, 414 Union St., Suite 1600, Nashville, TN 37219. Phone: (615) 244-2582. Fax: (615) 252-6380. Web Site: www.boultcummings.com.

Law Offices of Timothy K. Brady, Box 71309, Newnan, GA 30271-1309. Phone: (770) 252-2620. E-mail: tkbrady@bellsouth.net. Timothy K. Brady.

Golob, Bragin & Sassoe, 1990 S. Bundy Dr., Suite 540, Los Angeles, CA 90025-5245. Phone: (310) 979-0321. Fax: (310) 979-0366.

Bramson, Plutzik, Mahler, Birkhaeuser, LLP, 2125 Oak Grove Rd., Suite 120, Walnut Creek, CA 94598. Phone: (925) 945-0200. Fax: (925) 945-8792. Robert M. Branson, Alan Plutzik.

Brann & Isaacson, Box 3070, 184 Main St., Lewiston, ME 04243. Phone: (207) 786-3566. Fax: (207) 783-9325. Web Site: www.brannlaw.com. George Isaacson.

Brenner, Daniel L., National Cable Telecommunications Association, 1724 Massachusetts Ave. N.W., Washington, DC 20036. Phone: (202) 775-3664. Fax: (202) 775-3603. Web Site: www.ncta.com. Daniel L. Brenner, sr VP.

Brickfield, Burchette, Ritts & Stone, 1025 Thomas Jefferson St. N.W., Suite 800 West Tower, 8th Fl., Washington, DC 20007. Phone: (202) 342-0800. Fax: (202) 342-0807. Peter Mattheis.

Brighton & Runyon, 45 Main St., Suite 22, Peterborough, NH 03458-0674. Phone: (603) 924-7276. Fax: (603) 924-9764. L. Phillips Runyon III, sr ptnr.

Brooks, Pierce, McLendon, Humphrey & Leonard, Box 1800, Wachovia Capitol Center, 150 Fayetteville St. Mall Ste 1600, Raleigh, NC 27602. Phone: (919) 839-0300. Fax: (919) 839-0304. E-mail: whargrove@brookspierce.com. Web Site: www.brookspierce.com. Wade H. Hargrove, Mark J. Prak, Marcus W. Trathen, Ed Turlington, Kathy Thornton, David Kushner, Coe Ramsey, Charles Coble, Stephen Hartzell-Jordan, Charles Marshall.

Brown, Dean, Wiseman, Lisert, Proctor & Hart, L.L.P., 200 Fort Worth Club Bldg., 306 W. 7th St., Fort Worth, TX 76102-4905. Phone: (817) 332-1391. Fax: (817) 870-2427. Web Site: www.browndean.com. Beale Dean.

Frederic E. Brown, Attorney at Law, Box 71718, Fairbanks, AK 99707. Phone: (907) 452-3452. Fax: (907) 452-3733. E-mail: fbrown@mosquitonet.com. Frederic E. Brown.

Brown, Nietert, & Kaufman, Chartered, 2000 L St. N.W., Suite 817, Washington, DC 20036. Phone: (202) 887-0600. Fax: (202) 457-0126. Richard L. Brown, Robyn G. Nietert, David J. Kaufman, Lorretta K. Tobin.

Brown, Steven Ames, 69 Grand View Ave., San Francisco, CA 94114-2741. Phone: (415) 647-7700. Fax: (415) 285-3048. E-mail: sabrown@entertainmentlaw.com.

Law Offices of Tom Watson Brown, 2859 Paces Ferry Rd., Suite 2150, Atlanta, GA 30339. Phone: (770) 434-8100. Fax: (770) 434-9998. Tom Watson Brown, ptnr.

Bubar, James S., Attorney at Law, 1776 K St. N.W., Suite 800, Washington, DC 20006. Phone: (202) 223-2060. Fax: (202) 223-2061. E-mail: jbubar@aol.com. James S. Bubar.

Dan Buchwald & Associates, 10 E. 44 St., 7th Fl., New York, NY 10017-3606. Phone: (212) 867-1200. Fax: (212) 972-3209. E-mail: dan@buchwald.com.

Law Offices of Robert J. Buenzle, 11710 Plaza America Dr., Suite 2000, Reston, VA 20190. Phone: (703) 430-6751. Fax: (703) 430-4994. E-mail: buenzle@buenzlelaw.com. Robert J. Buenzle.

Law Firms

Bullivant, Houser, & Bailey, 300 Pioneer Tower, 888 S.W. 5th Ave., Suite 300, Portland, OR 97204. Phone: (503) 228-6351. Fax: (503) 295-0915. Web Site: www.bullivant.com.

Byelas & Neigher, 1804 Post Rd. E., Westport, CT 06880. Phone: (203) 259-0599. Fax: (203) 255-2570.

Cades Schutte, 1000 Bishop St., Honolulu, HI 96813. Phone: (808) 521-9221. Fax: (808) 540-5040. E-mail: jportney@cads.com. Jeffrey S. Portnoy.

Cahill, Gordon & Reindel LLP, 1990 K St. N.W., Suite 950, Washington, DC 20006. Phone: (202) 862-8900. Fax: (202) 862-8958. E-mail: mulvid@cgrdc.com. Kathy Silberthau Strom, assoc.
New York, NY 10005, 80 Pine St. Phone: (212) 701-3000. Floyd Abrams.

Calfee, Halter & Griswold, 800 Superior Ave., Suite 1400 MacDonald Investment Ctr., Cleveland, OH 44114. Phone: (216) 622-8200. Fax: (216) 241-0816.

Callister, Nebeker & McCullough, Gateway Tower E., Suite 900, Salt Lake City, UT 84133. Phone: (801) 530-7300. Fax: (801) 364-9127. Web Site: www.cnmlaw.com. Laurie S. Hart, Randall D. Benson, Jennifer Ward.

Cameron & Mittleman, 56 Exchange Terr., Providence, RI 02903-1766. Phone: (401) 331-5700. Fax: (401) 331-5787.

Caridi, Carmella, Esq., Caridi Entertainment, 250 W. 57th St., Suite 1326, New York, NY 10107-1722. Phone: (212) 581-2277. Fax: (212) 581-2278.

Carr, Morris & Graeff, 1120 G St. N.W., Suite 930, Washington, DC 20005. Phone: (202) 789-1000. Fax: (202) 628-3834.

Carter Ledyard & Milburn LLP, 1401 I St. N.W., Suite 300, Washington, DC 20005. Phone: (202) 898-1515. Fax: (202) 898-1521. E-mail: hoegle@clm.com. Web Site: www.clm.com. Thomas F. Bardo, Mary S. Diemer, Bradley A. Farrell, Peter K. Killough, Timothy J. Fitzgibbon, Jennifer E. Wagman, Robert L. Hoegle.

Peter A. Casciato P.C., 335 Bryant St., Suite 410, Suite 701, San Francisco, CA 94107. Phone: (415) 291-8661. Fax: (415) 291-8165. E-mail: pcasciato@sbcglobal.net. Peter A. Casciato.

Cavallo, Robert M., 400 Park Ave., 21st Fl., New York, NY 10022-2049. Phone: (212) 753-2224. Fax: (212) 753-7113. E-mail: rcavallo@jtjsys.com. Robert Cavallo, Esq.

Bryan Cave L.L.P., 700 13th St. N.W., Suite 700, Washington, DC 20005. Phone: (202) 508-6000. Fax: (202) 508-6200. John R. Wilner.
Kansas City, MO 64105, 3500 One Kansas City Pl. Phone: (816) 474-7400. Fax: (816) 374-3300. Web Site: www.bryancave.com. John R. Wilner.
New York, NY 10104, 1290 Ave. of the Americas. Phone: (212) 541-2000. Fax: (212) 541-4630. Web Site: www.bryancave.com. Jerome S. Boros, Renee E. Frost, Andrew Irving, Alan Pearce, Michael Rosen.

Edward de R. Cayia, P.A., 432 N.E. 3rd Ave., Fort Lauderdale, FL 33301. Phone: (954) 765-1400. Fax: (954) 765-1421.

Chadbourne & Parke, 1200 New Hampshire Ave. N.W., Suite 300, Washington, DC 20036. Phone: (202) 974-5600. Fax: (202) 974-5602. Web Site: www.chadbourne.com. Keith Martin, ptnr.
Los Angeles, CA 90017, 601 S. Figueroa St. Phone: (213) 892-1000.
New York, NY 10112, 30 Rockefeller Plaza. Phone: (212) 408-5100.

Chetkof, Gary H., Box 367, 293 Tinker St., Woodstock, NY 12498. Phone: (845) 679-7600. Fax: (845) 679-5395.

Clark Hill P.L.C., 500 Woodward Ave., Suite 3500, Detroit, MI 48226-3435. Phone: (313) 965-8300. Fax: (313) 962-4348. Fax: (313) 965-8252. E-mail: email@clarkhill.com. Web Site: www.clarkhill.com. David E. Nims III, Roderick S. Coy, Haran C. Rashes.

Richard N. Clarvit, P.A., 1313 N.E. 125th St., North Miami, FL 33161. Phone: (305) 893-4135. Fax: (305) 893-4173. E-mail: richsongs@aol.com. Richard N. Clarvit.

Clifford, Chance, LLP, 200 Park Ave., New York, NY 10166. Phone: (212) 878-8000. Fax: (212) 878-8375. Web Site: www.cliffordchance.com.

Cohn and Marks LLP, 1920 N St. N.W., Suite 300, Washington, DC 20036-1622. Phone: (202) 293-3860. Fax: (202) 293-4827. E-mail: roy.russo@cohnmarks.com. Web Site: www.cohnmarks.com. Lawrence N. Cohn, Richard A. Helmick, Robert B. Jacobi, Roy R. Russo, J. Brian DeBoice, Kevin M. Goldberg, Joseph M. DiScipo, Jerold L. Jacobs.

Colby, Lauren A. Box 113, 10 E. 4th St., Frederick, MD 21705-0113. Phone: (301) 663-1086. Fax: (301) 695-8734. E-mail: lac@lcolby.com. Web Site: www.lcolby.com. Lauren A. Colby.

Cole, Raywid & Braverman, L.L.P., 1919 Pennsylvania Ave. N.W., Suite 200, Washington, DC 20006. Phone: (202) 659-9750. Fax: (202) 452-0067. E-mail: crblaw@cais.com. Web Site: www.crblaw.com. John P. Cole Jr., Wesley R. Heppler, James F. Ireland III, Robert L. James, David M. Silverman, Burt A. Braverman, Frances J. Chetwynd, Paul Glist, Steven J. Horvitz, Robert G. Scott, Susan W. Westfall, Zeterberg Cavanaugh, John D. Thomas, Maria T. Browne, T. Scott Thompson, Fred Giroux, John C. Dodge, Christopher Savage, John D. Seiver, Ann Flowers, Adrienne Byrd, Adam Caldwell, Erik Cecil, Maurita Coley, Geoff Cook, Terence Cooke, Edward Donohue, Racheal Galoob, K.C. Halm, Brian Josef, Gerie Miller, Heidi Pearlman, Genevieve Sapir, Laura Schloss, Karlyn Stanley.

Collier, Shannon & Scott PLLC, 3050 K St. N.W., Washington, DC 20007. Phone: (202) 342-8400. Fax: (202) 342-8451.

Cooper, White & Cooper, L.L.P., 201 California St., 17th Fl., San Francisco, CA 94111. Phone: (415) 433-1900. Fax: (415) 433-5530. E-mail: whansell@cwclaw.com. Web Site: www.cwclaw.com. Walter W. Hansell, Mark P. Schreiber, Jed E. Solomon, Jed Solomon, E. Garth Black, Sean P. Beatty, Patrick M. Rosvall, Liana C. Epperson, Jamie Chou.

Cooter, Mangold, Tompert & Wayson, 5301 Wisconsin Ave N.W., Suite 500, Washington, DC 20015. Phone: (202) 537-0700. Fax: (202) 364-3664.

Corberlaw, Box 44212, Panorama City, CA 91412-0212. Phone: (818) 786-7133. E-mail: corberlaw@aol.com. Brian L. Corber, owner.

Law Offices of Bernard R. Corbett, 123 S. Royal St., Alexandria, VA 22314. Phone: (703) 549-4700. Fax: (703) 549-5290.

Corn-Revere, Robert L., Davis Wright Tremaine LLP, 1500 K St. N.W., Suite 4, Washington, DC 20005-1272. Phone: (202) 508-6600. Fax: (202) 508-6699. E-mail: bobcornrevere@dwt.com. Web Site: www.dwt.com.

Couzens, Michael, Box 3642, Oakland, CA 94609. Phone: (510) 658-7654. Fax: (510) 654-6741. Web Site: www.lptv.tv.

Covington & Burling, 1201 Pennsylvania Ave. N.W., Washington, DC 20004. Phone: (202) 662-6000. Fax: (202) 662-6291. E-mail: jblake@cov.com. Web Site: www.cov.com. Jonathan Blake, John Blevins, Aaron Cooper, Matthew S. DelNero, Heidi C. Doerhoff, Erin M. Egan, Christine E. Enemark, David H. Engvall, David N. Fagan, William A. Fitz, Ellen P. Goodman, Eric Dodson Greenberg, Darrin Hurwitz, Jennifer A. Johnson, Timothy L. Jucovy, Theodore P. Lazarus, Robert A. Long, David M. Marchick, Louise Nash, Gina L. Paik, B.J. Sanford, Robert M. Sherman, Brian D. Smith, Lee J. Tiedrich, Ralph C. Voltmer, Gerard J. Waldron, Stephen A. Weiswasser, Mary Newcomer Williams, Kurt A. Wimmer.

Craven Law Office, 1005 N. 7th St., Springfield, IL 62702. Phone: (217) 544-1777. Fax: (217) 544-0713. E-mail: presslaw@aol.com. Donald M. Craven.

Crowell & Moring, 1001 Pennsylvania Ave. N.W., Washington, DC 20004-2595. Phone: (202) 624-2500. Fax: (202) 628-5116. John I. Stewart Jr., Robert M. Halperin, William D. Wallace.

Cuni, Ferguson & Levay Company, L.P.A., 10655 Springfield Pike, Cincinnati, OH 45215. Phone: (513) 771-6768. Fax: (513) 771-6781. Thomas Cuni.

DLA Piper Rudnick Gray Cary US LLP, 1200 19th St. N.W., Suite 700, Washington, DC 20036. Phone: (202) 861-3913. Fax: (202) 689-7626. Web Site: www.dlapiper.com. Mark J. Tauber, E. Ashton Johnston.
New York, NY 10020-1104, 1251 Ave. of the Americas. Phone: (212) 835-6000. Fax: (212) 835-6001. E-mail: mmccabe@piperrudnick.com. Monica McCabe.

LAUREN A. COLBY
Attorney

Special attention to difficult cases.

301-663-1086
www.lcolby.com

e-mail:
lac@lcolby.com

Contact me today!

Law Firms

Law Offices of George E. Darby, Box 893010, Mililani, HI 96789-3010. Phone: (808) 626-1300. Fax: (808) 626-1350. E-mail: darbylaw@teleport-asia.com. Web Site: www.teleport-asia.com. George Darby.

Davis Wright Tremaine P.C., 1500 K St. N.W., Suite 450, Washington, DC 20005. Phone: (202) 508-6600. Fax: (202) 508-6699. Lawrence Roberts, James S. Blitz, Mary L. Plantamura, Pamela C. Cooper, Rebecca R. Reed, Robert S. Tanner, Richard L. Cys.

Davis Wright Tremaine L.L.P., 2600 Century Sq., 1501 4th Ave., Seattle, WA 98101-1688. Phone: (206) 622-3150. Fax: (206) 628-7699. Web Site: www.dwt.com.
  Los Angeles, CA 90017, 1000 Wilshire Blvd, Suite 600. Phone: (213) 633-6800. Fax: (213) 633-6899. Kelli L. Sager.
  Washington, DC 20036, 1155 Connecticut Ave. N.W. Phone: (202) 508-6600. Fax: (202) 508-6699.
  Boise, ID 83702, 999 Main St, Suite 911. Phone: (208) 338-8200. Fax: (208) 338-8299. Deborah Kristensen.
  Portland, OR 97201, 2300 First Interstate Tower, 1300 S.W. 5th Ave. Phone: (503) 241-2300. Fax: (503) 778-5299. Duane A. Bosworth.

Day & Associates, 1812 Waterfront Plaza, 325 W. Main, Louisville, KY 40202-4251. Phone: (502) 585-4131. Fax: (502) 581-1210. E-mail: dayandassociates@bellsouth.net. Joe Day, owner.

Day, Berry & Howard L.L.P., CityPlace I, Hartford, CT 06103-3499. Phone: (860) 275-0122. Fax: (860) 275-0343. E-mail: rpknickerbocker@dbh.com. Web Site: www.dbh.com. Robert P. Knickerbocker Jr., Paul N. Belval, Michael F. Halloran, William A. Hunter, Ross A. Pascal, David A. Swerdloff, Sabino Rodriguez, David T. Doot.

Debevoise & Plimpton LLP, 919 3rd Ave., New York, NY 10022. Phone: (212) 909-6000. Fax: (212) 909-6836. E-mail: RDBOHM@Debevoise.com. Web Site: www.Debevoise.com. Richard D. Bohm, Bruce Keller.
  Hong Kong, 13/F Entertainment Bldg, 30 Queen's Rd. Central. Phone: 852-2810-7918. Jeffrey S. Wood.
  London EC2N 1HQ, The International Financial Centre, 25 Old Broad St. Phone: 44-171-786-9000. Robert R. Bruce.
  Moscow 103104, Bolshoi Palashevsky Per 13/2. Phone: 7503-956-3858. Dmitri V. Nikiforov.
  Paris 75008, 21 Ave. George V. Phone: 33-1-40-73-12-12. James A. Kiernan III, Antoine F. Kirry.
  Washington, DC 20004, 555 13th St. N.W, Suite 1100-E. Phone: (202) 383-8000. Jeffrey P. Cunard.

Decker, Jones, McMackin, McClane, Hall & Bates, 801 Cherry St., Suite 2000, Unit 46, Fort Worth, TX 76102. Phone: (817) 336-2400. Fax: (817) 332-3043.

Del, Shaw, Moonves, Tanaka & Finkelstein, 2120 Colorado Ave., Suite 200, Santa Monica, CA 90404. Phone: (310) 979-7900. Fax: (310) 979-7999.

Denechaud & Denechaud, 210 Baronne St. Ste 1207, New Orleans, LA 70112. Phone: (504) 522-4756. Fax: (504) 568-0783. E-mail: cidlaw@bellsouth.net.

Robert A. DePont, Attorney at Law, 140 South St., Annapolis, MD 21401. Phone: (410) 263-0632. Fax: (410) 280-8624. E-mail: robertade@msn.com. Robert A. DePont.

Devine & Millimet, Box 719, 111 Amherst St., Manchester, NH 03101. Phone: (603) 669-1000. Fax: (603) 669-8547. E-mail: kmcginley@dm.com. Web Site: www.devinemillimet.com.

LAUREN A. COLBY
301-663-1086
www.lcolby.com

ATTORNEY
Special Attention to Difficult Cases

DeWitt, Ross & Stevens, 2 E. Mifflin St., Suite 600, Madison, WI 53703. Phone: (608) 255-8891. Fax: (608) 252-9243. Todd E. Palmer, Dennis P. Birke, Donald Leo Bach.

Dickstein Shapiro Morin & Oshinsky LLP, 2101 L St., N.W., Washington, DC 20037-1526. Phone: (202) 785-9700. Fax: (202) 887-0689. E-mail: info@dsmo.com. Web Site: www.dicksteinshapiro.com. Walter J. Walvick, counsel; Robert F. Aldrich, Jacob S. Farber, Robert Felger, Valerie M. Furman, Allan C. Hubbard, Andrew S. Kersting, Adam Kirschenbaum, Albert H. Kramer, Gregory D. Kwan, Edward Modell, Lewis J. Paper.
  New York, NY 10036-2714, 1177 Ave. of the Americas, 41st Fl.

Dieguez, Richard P., 192 Garden St.,, Suite 2, Roslyn Heights, NY 11577-1012. Phone: (516) 621-6424. Fax: (516) 621-6508. E-mail: rpdieguez@rpdieguez.com. Web Site: www.rpdieguez.com. Richard P. Dieguez.

Dorsey & Whitney, L L P, 50 S. 6th St., Suite 1500, Minneapolis, MN 55402-1498. Phone: (612) 340-2600. Fax: (612) 340-2868. Web Site: www.dorsey.com.
  London EC2A INQ, Veritas House, 125 Finsbury Pavement. Phone: 011-44-171-588-0800. Fax: 011-44-171-588-0555.
  Vancouver, BC V6C 3J8 Canada, 666 Burrard St., Suite 1300, Park Pl. Phone: (604) 687-5151. Fax: (604) 687-8504.
  Anchorage, AK 99501, 1031 West 4th Ave, Suite 600. Phone: (907) 276-4557. Fax: (907) 276-4152.
  Irvine, CA 92618-5310, 38 Technology Dr. Phone: (714) 424-5555. Fax: (714) 424-5554.
  Denver, CO 80202-5644, Republic Plaza Bldg., Suite 4400, 370 Seventeenth St. Phone: (303) 629-3400. Fax: (303) 629-3450.
  Washington, DC 20004, 1001 Pennsylvania Ave. N.W. Suite 200 Soutth. Phone: (202) 824-8800. Fax: (202) 824-8990.
  Minneapolis, MN 55402-1498, 50 S. Sixth St. Phone: (612) 340-2600. Fax: (612) 340-2868.
  Great Falls, MO 59401, 507 Davidson Bldg., 8 Third St. Phone: (406) 727-3632. Fax: (406) 727-3638.
  Missoula, MO 59802-4407, 125 Bank St., Suite 600. Phone: (406) 721-6025. Fax: (406) 543-0863.
  Fargo, ND 58107-1344, Dakota Ctr., 51 N. Broadway, Suite 402. Phone: (701) 235-6000. Fax: (701) 235-9969.
  New York, NY 10177, 250 Park Ave. Phone: (212) 415-9200. Fax: (212) 953-7201.
  Salt Lake City, UT 84101, Wells Fargo Plaza, 170 S. Main St., Suite 925. Phone: (801) 350-3581. Fax: (801) 350-3585.
  Seattle, WA 98101, US Bank Building Centre, 1420 Fifth Ave., Suite 400. Phone: (206) 654-5400. Fax: (206) 654-5500.

Dow, Lohnes & Albertson, PLLC, 1200 New Hampshire Ave. N.W., Suite 800, Washington, DC 20036. Phone: (202) 776-2000. Fax: (202) 776-2222. Web Site: www.dowlohnes.com. E-mail: info@dowlohnes.com. Michael D. Basile, Raymond G. Bender, James M. Burger, Christina H. Burrow, Peter H. Feinberg, John R. Feore Jr., Jeffrey L. Gee, Todd D. Gray, J.G. Harrington, Nam E. Kim, Kevin P. Latek, John S. Logan, Gary S. Lutzker, Melissa A. Marshall, Elizabeth A. McFadden, Margaret L. Miller, Edward J. Palmieri, Scott S. Patrick, Barry S. Persh, Jason E. Rademacher, Christopher J. Redding, Kevin F. Reed, Kenneth D. Salomon, M. Anne Swanson, To-Quyen T. Truong.
  Atlanta, GA 30346, One Ravinia Dr., Suite 1600. Phone: (770) 901-8800.

Downs, Bertis E., 170 College Ave., Athens, GA 30601. Phone: (706) 353-6689. Fax: (706) 546-6069.

Drinker Biddle & Reath L.L.P., 1500 K St. N.W., Suite 1100, Washington, DC 20005-1209. Phone: (202) 842-8800. Fax: (202) 842-8465. Web Site: www.dbr.com. Joe Dixon Edge, Mark L. Pelesh, Richard M. Singer, Joaquin A. Marquez, Philip J. Mause, Timothy R. Hughes, Tina M. Pidgeon, John R. Przypyszny.

Law Office of David M. Drucker, 795 S. Cielo Lane, Evergreen, CO 80439. Phone: (303) 670-5103. Fax: (303) 670-5103. David M. Drucker.

Duane Morris LLP, 1 Liberty Pl., Philadelphia, PA 19103. Phone: (215) 979-1000. Fax: (215) 979-1020. Web Site: www.duanemorris.com. Abraham Frumkin, ptnr.

Dunham, Corydon B. Counsel, Cahill Gordon & Reindel, 80 Pine St., New York, NY 10005. Phone: (212) 701-3776. Fax: (212) 269-5420. Web Site: www.cahill.com. Corydon B. Dunham.

Joseph E. Dunne III, Attorney at Law, P.O. Box 9203, Durango, CO 81302-9203. Phone: (970) 385-7312. Fax: (970) 385-7343. E-mail: lawman@animas.net. Joseph E. Dunne III.

Ross Eatman, Esq., Box 102, Bedford, NY 10506-0102. Phone: (914) 234-4748. Fax: (914) 234-4750. E-mail: emstalent@aol.com. Ross Eatman, Esq.

Eaton, Peabody, Box 1210, 80 Excahange St., Bangor, ME 04402-1210. Phone: (207) 947-0111. Fax: (207) 942-3040. E-mail: eaton@eatonpeabody.com. Web Site: www.eatonpeabody.com.

Eckert, Seamans, Cherin & Mellott, 1515 Market St. 9th Fl., Philadelphia, PA 19102. Phone: (215) 851-8400. Fax: (215) 851-8383. Web Site: www.escm.com.

Edelstein, Laird & Sobel, L.L.P., 9255 Sunset Blvd., Suite 800, Los Angeles, CA 90069. Phone: (310) 274-6184. Fax: (310) 271-2664.

Edwards & Angell, L.L.P., 101 Federal St., Boston, MA 02110-1810. Phone: (617) 439-4444. Fax: (617) 439-4170. E-mail: smeredith@ealaw.com. Web Site: www.ealaw.com. Elizabeth H. Munnell, Stephen O. Meredith, Leonard Q. Slap, David K. Duffell, Andrea A. Jacobs, Sarah N.A. Camouglis, Walter G. D. Reed, Andrew J. Chlebus, Peter J. Barrett.

Elam & Burke, P.A., 251 E. Front St., Suite 300, Boise, ID 83702-7311. Phone: (208) 343-5454. Fax: (208) 384-5844. E-mail: eblaw@elamburke.com.

Epstein, Levinsohn, Bodine, Hurwitz & Weinstein, P.C., 1790 Broadway, 10th Fl., New York, NY 10019. Phone: (212) 262-1000. Fax: (212) 262-5022.

Ezor, A. Edward, 201 S. Lake Ave., Suite 505, Pasadena, CA 91101. Phone: (626) 568-8098. Fax: (626) 568-8475.

Faegre & Benson, L.L.P., 801 Grand, Suite 3100, Des Moines, IA 50309-8002. Phone: (515) 248-9000. Fax: (515) 248-9010. E-mail: mgiudicessi@faegre.com. Web Site: www.faegre.com. Michael A. Giudicessi.

Farmer, Shirley Stewart, One Lincoln Plaza, Suite 19S, New York, NY 10023-7149. Phone: (212) 787-6566. Fax: (212) 787-6567. E-mail: stewfar@rcn.com.

Farrand, Cooper P.C., 235 Montgomery St., Suite 1035, San Francisco, CA 94104. Phone: (415) 399-0600. Fax: (415) 677-2950. Web Site: www.fcblaw.com. Wayne B. Cooper, Stephen R. Farrand.

Federal Communications Communications Wireless Telecommunications Bureau, Public Safety & Critical Infrastructure Division, 445 12th St., S.W., Washington, DC 20554. Phone: (202) 418-0680. Fax: (202) 418-2643. E-mail: mwilhelm@fcc.gov. Web Site: www.fcc.gov. Michael J. Wilhelm.

Lindsey S. Feldman, Attorney at Law, c/o Berger Kahn, 4215 Glencoe Ave., 2nd Fl., Marina del Rey, CA 90292-5634. Phone: (310) 821-9000. Fax: (310) 578-6178. E-mail: lfeldman@la.bergerkahn.com. Lindsey S. Feldman.

Ferris & Britton, 401 West A St., Suite 1600, San Diego, CA 92101. Phone: (619) 233-3131. Fax: (619) 232-9316. E-mail: aferris@ferrisbritton.com. Web Site: www.ferrisbritton.com. Alfred G. Ferris, Christopher Q. Britton, Lee Austin, Michael Weinstein.

Fine & Associates, P.L.C., 335-337 Decatur St., Vieux Carre, New Orleans, LA 70130-1023. Phone: (504) 581-5152. Fax: (504) 581-5152, EXT. 124.

Fine & Block, 2060 Mt. Paran Rd. N.W., Suite 106, Atlanta, GA 30327. Phone: (404) 261-6800. Fax: (404) 261-6960. Web Site: www.fineandblock.com. A. J. Block Jr.

Finkelstein, Thompson & Loughran, 1050 30th St. N.W., Washington, DC 20007. Phone: (202) 337-8000. Phone: (866) 592-1960. Fax: (202) 337-8090. Web Site: www.ftlaw.com. Douglas G. Thompson Jr., L. Kendall Satterfield.

Fleischman & Walsh, L.L.P., 1919 Pennsylvania Ave. N.W., 6th Fl., Washington, DC 20006. Phone: (202) 939-7900. Fax: (202) 745-0916. E-mail: fw@fw-law.com. Web Site: www.fw-law.com. Aaron I. Fleischman, Charles S. Walsh, Arthur H. Harding, Stuart F. Feldstein, Jeffrey L. Hardin, Stephen A. Bouchard, R. Bruce Beckner, Christopher G. Wood, Seth A. Davidson, James F. Moriarty, Matthew D. Emmer, Jill Kleppe McClelland, Regina Famiglietti Pace,

Law Firms

Craig A. Gilley, Mark D. Pihlstrom, Brian C. Malady, Seth M. Warner, Larry Freedman, Richard Davis, Mark Denbro, Steven Hamrick, David Konuch, James Moskowitz.

Fletcher, Heald & Hildreth, P.L.C., 1300 N. 17th St., 11th Fl., Arlington, VA 22209. Phone: (703) 812-0400. Fax: (703) 812-0486. E-mail: office@fhh-telecomlaw.com. Web Site: www.fhh-telcomlaw.com. Vincent J. Curtis Jr., Frank R. Jazzo, James P. Riley, Howard M. Weiss, Paul J. Feldman, Kathleen Victory, Harry Martin, Mitchel Lazarus, Susan Marshall, Harry F. Cole, Scott M. Johnson, ptnrs; Ann Bavender, Anne G. Crump, sr. counsel; Donal J. Evans, Robert M. Gurss, Eugene M. Lawson, Francisco R. Montero, Edwards O'Neil, of counsel.

Foley & Lardner, 150 E. Gilman St., Madison 53703. Phone: (608) 257-5035. Fax: (608) 258-4258. E-mail: dwalsh@foleylaw.com. David G. Walsh.

Forrest, Herbert E., Federal Programs Br., Civil Division, Rm. 7112, U.S. Dept. of Justice, 20 Massachusetts Ave. N.W., Washington, DC 20530. Phone: (202) 514-2809. Fax: (202) 616-8470. E-mail: herbert.forest@usdos.gov. Herbert E. Forrest, trial atty, Federal Programs Br., Civil Divison, U.S. Dept of Justice.

Fowler, Measle & Bell, 300 W. Vine St., Suite 600, Lexington, KY 40507-1660. Phone: (859) 252-6700. Fax: (859) 255-3735. E-mail: fmb@fmb.com. Web Site: www.fmblaw.com.

Fox & Film Entertainment, 10201 W. Pico Blvd., Los Angeles, CA 90035. Phone: (310) 369-1000. Fax: (310) 369-3333. Gregory Gelfan, Esq., exec VP.

Frost, Mark E., Box 153, Glens Falls, NY 12801-0153. Phone: (518) 792-1126. Fax: (518) 793-1587. Mark E. Frost.

Gammon & Grange, P.C., 8280 Greensboro Dr., 7th Fl., McLean, VA 22102-3807. Phone: (703) 761-5000. Fax: (703) 761-5023. E-mail: awf@gandglaw.com. Web Site: www.gandglaw.com. A. Wray Fiitch III, Timothy R. Obitts, Stephen M. Clarke.

Ganz & Hollinger, 1394 3rd Ave., New York, NY 10021. Phone: (212) 517-5500. Fax: (212) 772-2720. Web Site: www.ganzhollinger.com.

Gardere Attorneys and Counselors, Thanksgiving Tower, 1601 Elm St., Suite 3000, Dallas, TX 75201-4761. Phone: (214) 999-3000. Fax: (214) 999-4667. Web Site: www.gardere.com.

Gardner, Carton & Douglas, 1301 K St. N.W., Suite 900 E. Tower, Washington, DC 20005. Phone: (202) 230-5000. Fax: (202) 230-5300. Web Site: www.gcd.com. Francis E. Fletcher Jr., M. Scott Johnson, Thomas Dougherty, Laura Mow, Lee Petro, Jennifer Lewis.

Law Offices of Michael R. Gardner, P.C., 1150 Connecticut Ave. N.W., Suite 710, Washington, DC 20036. Phone: (202) 785-2828. Fax: (202) 785-1504. E-mail: mrgpc@aol.com. Michael R. Gardner, mgng ptnr.

Garvey, Schubert & Barer, 1191 2nd Ave., 18th Fl., Seattle, WA 98101-2939. Phone: (206) 464-3939. Fax: (206) 464-0125. Web Site: www.gsblaw.com.
 Washington, DC 20007-3501, 1000 Potomac St. N.W., 5th Fl. Phone: (202) 965-7880. Fax: (202) 965-1729. E-mail: jking@gsblaw.com. Web Site: www.gsblaw. Matthew R. Schneider, D.C. ofc mgng dir. Contact: John Wells King, counsel.
 New York, NY 10012-3235, 599 Broadway, 10th Fl. Phone: (212) 431-8700. Fax: (212) 334-1278. Web Site: www.gsblaw.com. Matthew R. Schneider, NY ofc mgng dir.
 Portland, OR 97204-3141, 121 S. W. Morrison St. Phone: (503) 228-3939. Fax: (503) 226-0259. Web Site: www.gsblaw.com. Larry Brant, Steve Connolly, Bob Weaver, Portland ofc mgmt comm.

Gerry & Sapronov L.L.P., 3 Ravinia Dr., Suite 1455, Atlanta, GA 30346. Phone: (770) 399-9100. Fax: (770) 395-0505. E-mail: info@gstelecomlaw.com. Web Site: www.gstelecomlaw.com. Walt Sapronov, William D. Friend, Charles A. Hudak, Chip Gerry, Michael Stewart, Ronald Jackson, Timothy Geraghty.

Thomas G. Gherardi, P.C., 1229 19th St. N.W., Washington, DC 20036. Phone: (202) 223-1535. Fax: (703) 243-9366. E-mail: tomg@counsellor.com. Thomas Gherardi.

Gibbs & Associates, P.C., 1700 Broadway, New York, NY 10019. Phone: (212) 765-0888. Fax: (212) 765-7189. E-mail: bhg1cg2@aol.com. Bud H. Gibbs.

Gibson, Dunn & Crutcher, 333 S. Grand Ave., Suite 4600, Los Angeles, CA 90071-3197. Phone: (213) 229-7000. Fax: (213) 229-7520. Web Site: www.gdclaw.com.
 Washington, DC 20036, 1050 Connecticut Ave. N.W, Suite 900. Phone: (202) 955-8500. Jill Sterner.

Gold & Pyle, 526 Superior Ave. E.,, 1140 Leader Bldg., Cleveland, OH 44114. Phone: (216) 696-6122. Fax: (216) 696-3214.

Goldberg, Godles, Wiener & Wright, 1229 19th St. N.W., Washington, DC 20036. Phone: (202) 429-4900. Fax: (202) 429-4912. E-mail: general@g2w2.com. Web Site: g2w2.com. Henry Goldberg, Joseph A. Godles, Jonathan L. Wiener, Henrietta Wright, Laura Stefani, Brita D. Strandberg, Thomas G. Gherardi.

Golden & Golden, P.C., 10627 Jones St., Suite 101B, Fairfax, VA 22030. Phone: (703) 691-0117. E-mail: k8los@aol.com. Richard A. Golden.

Glenn A. Goldstein, Attorney at Law, 1650 Market St., Suite 4900, Philadelphia, PA 19103. Phone: (215) 981-5922. Fax: (215) 981-5959. E-mail: glenn802@aol.com. Glenn A. Goldstein, Esq.

Goodkind, Labaton, Rudoff & Sucharow, L.L.P., 100 Park Ave., New York, NY 10017. Phone: (212) 907-0700. Fax: (212) 818-0477. Web Site: www.glrs.com.

Law Offices of Jeffrey L. Graubart, 350 W. Colorado Blvd.,, Suite 200, Pasadena, CA 91105. Phone: (310) 788-2650. Fax: (310) 788-2657. E-mail: graubart@gte.net. Web Site: www.lawyers.com. Jeffrey L. Graubart.

Gray & Robinson, 301 E. Pine St., Suite 1400, Orlando, FL 32802. Phone: (407) 843-8880. Fax: (407) 244-5690. Web Site: www.gray-robinson.com. J. Charles Gray, Richard M. Robinson, founding ptnrs.

Gray Cary, Blumenfeld and Cohen. 1625 Massachusetts Ave. N.W., Suite 300, Washington, DC 20036. Phone: (202) 238-7700. Fax: (202) 238-7701. Web Site: www.graycary.com. Jeffrey Blumenfeld, Christy C. Kunin, Michael McNeely, Larry Blosser.

Graybill & English, L.L.C., 1875 Connecticut Ave. N.W.,, Suite 712, Washington, DC 20009. Phone: (202) 588-9798. Fax: (202) 457-0662. Web Site: www.graybillandenglish.com. Nina Graybill, Elaine English.

Greensfelder, Hemker & Gale, P.C., 2000 Equitable Bldg., 10 S. Broadway, St. Louis, MO 63102-1774. Phone: (314) 241-9090. Fax: (314) 241-8624. E-mail: mlw@greensfelder.com. Web Site: www.greensfelder.com. Sheldon K. Stock, Mary Ann L. Wymore, Jason L. Ross.

Greiter, Pegger, Kofler & Partner, Maria Theresien-Strasse 24, A-6020, Innsbruck Phone: 43 512-57-1811. Fax: 43 512-5849-25. Fax: 43 512-5711-52.

Groveman, Amy S., Cablevision Systems Corp., 111 Stewart Ave., Bethpage, NY 11714. Phone: (516) 803-2300. Fax: (516) 803-2575. Web Site: www.cablevision.com.

Grubb, Jay G., 2718 Greene Rd., Baldwin, MD 21013. Phone: (410) 329-2108. Fax: (410) 329-2109. Jay G. Grubb.

Grubman, Indursky & Schindler, P.C., 152 W. 57th St., 31st Fl., New York, NY 10019. Phone: (212) 554-0400. Fax: (212) 554-0444.

Gullett, Sanford, Robinson & Martin, 315 Deadrick St., Suite 1100, Nashville, TN 37238. Phone: (615) 244-4994. Fax: (615) 256-6339. John D. Lentz.

Gurman, Blask & Freedman, Chartered, 1400 16th St. N.W., Suite 500, Washington, DC 20036. Phone: (202) 328-8200. Fax: (202) 462-1786. E-mail: wfreedman@gurmon.com. Louis Gurman, Jerome K. Blask, William D. Freedman, Doane Kiechel, Nadja Sodos-Wallace, Dan Smith, Brenda Boykin.

Hall, Dickler, Kent, Goldstein & Wood, 909 3rd Ave., 27th Fl., New York, NY 10022. Phone: (212) 339-5400. Fax: (212) 935-3121. Web Site: www.halldickler.com. Jeffrey S. Edelstein.

Halpern, Steven J., Box 5948, Beverly Hills, CA 90209-0677. Phone: (310) 456-3316. Fax: (310) 456-6627. E-mail: sjhalpern@aol.com.

Handman, Stanley H., 10160 Cielo Dr., Beverly Hills, CA 90210-2037. Phone: (310) 276-7503. Fax: (310) 276-1559. E-mail: stanhandman@yahoo.com. Stanley H. Handman.

Hansen, Jacobson, Teller, Hoberman, Newman, Warren & Sloan, L.L.P., 450 N. Roxbury Dr., 8th Fl., Beverly Hills, CA 90210-4222. Phone: (310) 248-3105/248-3101. Fax: (310) 275-2329/550-5209. Gretchen Bruggeman, John Farrell, Tom Hanson, Jason Hendler, Tom Hoberman, Craig Jacobson, Tom McGuire, Jeanne Newman, Ken Richman, Jason Sloane, Don Steele, Walter Teller, Steve Warren.

Law Offices of Douglas W. Harold Jr., 5413 Main St., Stephens City, VA 22655. Phone: (540) 869-0040. Fax: (540) 869-0041. E-mail: douglash@visuallink.com. Douglas W. Harold Jr.

Harris, Barrett, Mann & Dew, 1700 66th St. N., Suite 403, St. Petersburg, FL 33710. Phone: (727) 892-3100. Fax: (727) 898-0227. Web Site: www.harrisbarrett.com.

Harris, Beach L.L.P., 1776 K St. N.W. Ste. 300, Washington, DC 20006. Phone: (202) 861-0001. Fax: (202) 861-0011. E-mail: jcooke@harrisbeach.com. Web Site: www.harrisbeach.com. James R. Cooke, sr ptnr.
 Hackensack, NJ 07601, 2 University Plaza, 2nd Fl. Phone: (201) 488-2200. Fax: (201) 342-6677. Vincenzo Taparo.
 Albany, NY 12211, 20 Corporate Woods Blvd. Phone: (518) 427-9706. Fax: (518) 427-0235. Terence Burke.
 Hamburg, NY 14075, One Grimsby Dr. Phone: (716) 646-5050. Fax: (716) 648-8204. Raymond Stapell, mgng ptnr.
 Ithaca, NY 14850, 119 E. Seneca St. Phone: (607) 273-6444. Fax: (607) 273-6802. Mark Wheeler.
 New York, NY 10036, 530 Fifth Ave. Phone: (212) 687-0100. Fax: (212) 997-7868. William O'Connor.
 Rochester, NY 14604, 130 E. Main St. Phone: (716) 232-4440. Fax: (716) 232-1925. Gunther Buerman, mgng ptnr.
 Syracuse, NY 13202, 300 S. State St., 4th Fl. Phone: (315) 423-7100. Fax: (315) 426-9331. Thomas E. Taylor.

Harris, Wiltshire & Grannis, L.L.P., 1200 Eighteenth St. N.W., Washington, DC 20036. Phone: (202) 730-1300. Fax: (202) 730-1301. E-mail: sharris@harris. Web Site: www.harriswiltshire.com. Mark A. Grannis, William M. Wiltshire, Kent D. Bressie, Jonathan B. Mirsky, John T. Nakahata.

Hasse / Molesky P.C., 526 Columbus Ave., 2nd Fl., San Francisco, CA 94133. Phone: (415) 433-4380. Fax: (415) 433-6580. E-mail: jmolesky@molesky.com. Web Site: www.entertainmentlaw.leadcounsel.com.

James A. Hatcher, Cox Communications Inc., 1400 Lake Hearn Dr. N.E., Atlanta, GA 30319. Phone: (404) 843-5000. Fax: (404) 843-5845. James Hatcher, sr VP/gen counsel; John P. Spalding, VP/asst gen counsel; Robin H. Sangston, VP/asst gen counsel; Teresa T. Kennedy; Jennifer W. Hightower, sr counsel; Joseph M. Freeman, asst gen counsel; Carrington Phillip, VP/asst gen counsel.

Law Offices of Richard J. Hayes, 8404 Lee's Ridge Rd., Warrenton, VA 20186. Phone: (540) 349-9970. Fax: (202) 478-0048. E-mail: fcclaw@rjhayes.com. Web Site: www.rjhayes.com. Richard J. Hayes.

Head, Johnson & Kachigian, 228 W. 17th Pl., Tulsa, OK 74119. Phone: (918) 587-2000. Fax: (918) 587-5603. E-mail: hjk@law.com. Mark G. Kachigian.

Hearn, Edward R., 84 W. Santa Clara St., Suite 660, San Jose, CA 95113. Phone: (408) 998-3400. Fax: (408) 297-1104. E-mail: nedhearnml@aol.com.

John Hearne, 715 Broadway, Suite 320, Santa Monica, CA 90401. Phone: (310) 451-4430. Fax: (310) 451-1423. John Hearne, owner.

Hebert, Spencer, Cusimano & Fry, LLP, 701 Laurel St., Baton Rouge, LA 70802. Phone: (225) 344-2601. Fax: (225) 387-1714. E-mail: clsatty@aol.com. Charles L. Spencer.

Heller, Ehrman, White & McAuliffe, 275 Middlefield Rd., Menlo Park, CA 94025. Phone: (650) 324-7000. Fax: (650) 324-0638. Web Site: www.hewm.com. Daniel L. Appelman.

Hendrickson, Thomas, 203 Alderwood Dr., N. Potomac, MD 20878. Phone: (301) 519-0085. E-mail: thomashendrickson@yahoo.com.

Law Firms

Hewitt Katz Stepp and Wright Attorney at Law, 945 E. Paces Ferry Rd., Resurgens Plaza Ste. 2610, Atlanta, GA 30326. Phone: (404) 240-0400. Fax: (404) 240-0401. E-mail: khewitt@atllawofc.com. Web Site: www.robertnkatz.com.

Hill & Welch, 1330 New Hampshire Ave. N.W., Suite 113, Washington, DC 20036. Phone: (202) 775-0070. Fax: (202) 775-9026. E-mail: welchlaw@earthlink.net.

Hillman, Adria S., 41 E. 57th St., 15th Fl., New York, NY 10022. Phone: (212) 593-5223. Fax: (212) 593-4633. Adria S. Hillman.

Hinshaw & Culbertson, 3100 Campbell Mithun Tower, 222 S. 9th St., Minneapolis, MN 55402. Phone: (612) 333-3434. Fax: (612) 334-8888. Web Site: www.hinshawculbertson.com. Thomas J. Barrett, Roger Schnobrich.

Hirst & Applegate, Box 1083, 1720 Carey Ave., Suite 200, Cheyenne, WY 82003-1083. Phone: (307) 632-0541. Fax: (307) 632-4999. E-mail: attorneys@hirstapplegate.com. Web Site: www.hirstapplegate.com.

Hogan & Hartson, Columbia Sq., 555 13th St. N.W., Washington, DC 20004. Phone: (202) 637-5600. Fax: (202) 637-5910. Web Site: www.hhlaw.com. Ptnrs: Robert Corn-Revere, Marvin J. Diamond, Gardner F. Gillespie III, William S. Reyner Jr., Richard S. Rodin, Peter A. Rohrbach, Mace J. Rosenstein, David J. Saylor, Joel S. Winnik, Gerald E. Oberst, Linda Oliver, Marissa G. Repp, Edgar W. Holtz. Associates: Jacqueline P. Cleary, Karis A. Hastings.
   1040 Brussels, Ave. Des Arts 41. Phone: (32.2) 505.09.11. Fax: (32.2) 505.09.96.
   Budapest, Szabadsag ter 7 01944, Bank Center, Granite Tower, 9th Floor. Phone: 36-1-302-9050. Fax: 36-1-302-9060.
   London EC4V 2AU, 21 Garlick Hill. Phone: (44 171) 815.1200. Fax: (44 171) 329.0299.
   Moscow 119048, Bldg. 3, 33/2 Usacheva Street. Phone: 7095-245-5190. Fax: 7095-245-5192.
   Paris 75002, 12, rue de la Paix. Phone: (33-1) 42.61.57.71. Fax: (33-1) 42.61.79.21.
   Prague 1 110 00. Hogan & Hogan Praha, Opletalova 37. Phone: (40-2) 2411-7111. Fax: (40-2) 2421-5105.
   Warsaw 00-854. Hogan & Hartson, Sp ZO.O., Atrium Tower, Al. Jana Pawla II 25. Phone: (48-22) 653 4200. Fax: (48-22) 653 4250.
   Los Angeles, CA 90071, Biltmore Tower, 500 S. Grand Ave., Suite 1900. Phone: (213) 337-6700. Fax: (213) 337-6701.
   Newport Beach, CA 92660, 46-75 MacArthur, Suite 670. Phone: (949) 250-4550. Fax: (949) 833-0976.
   Colorado Springs, CO 80903, 2 N. Cascade Ave, Suite 1300. Phone: (719) 448-5900. Fax: (719) 448-5922.
   Denver, CO 80202, One Tabor Ctr., 1200 17th St., Suite 1500. Phone: (303) 899-7300. Fax: (303) 899-7333.
   Baltimore, MD 21202, 111 S. Calvert St. Phone: (410) 659-2700. Fax: (410) 539-6981.
   McLean, VA 22102, 8300 Greensboro Dr. Phone: (703) 610-6100. Fax: (703) 610-6200.

Holland & Knight LLC, 131 S. Dearborn St., 30 Fl., Chicago, IL 60603. Phone: (312) 263-3600. Fax: (312) 578-6666. Web Site: www.hklaw.com.

Holland & Knight LLP, 2099 Pennsylvania Ave. N.W., Suite 100, Washington, DC 20006. Phone: (202) 955-3000. Fax: (202) 955-5564. Web Site: www.hklaw.com. Janet R. Studley, Edward W. Hummers Jr., Marvin Rosenberg, Charles Naftalin, Peter Connolly, George Wheeler, Alan Naftalin, Xiaohau Zhan.

Law Office of David Honig, 3636 16th St. N.W., Suite B-366, Washington, DC 20010. Phone: (202) 332-7005. Fax: (202) 332-7511. David Honig.

Horgan, Michael Owen, 407 E. Robert Toomb Ave., Washington, GA 30673. Phone: (706) 678-1987. Fax: (706) 678-1999. E-mail: mhorgan@nu-z.net. Michael O. Horgan.

Howrey, Simon, Arnold & White, 1299 Pennsylvania Ave. N.W., Washington, DC 20006. Phone: (202) 783-0800. Fax: (202) 383-6610. E-mail: henneberrye@howrey.com. Web Site: www.howrey.com. Edward P. Henneberry, Rosemary H. McEnery, James Olson.

Ice Miller, One American Sq., Box 82001, Indianapolis, IN 46282-0002. Phone: (317) 236-2100. Fax: (317) 236-2219. E-mail: info@icemiller.com. Web Site: www.icemiller.com. Thomas H. Ristine.

Inghram & Inghram, 529 Hampshire, Suite 409, Bank of America Bldg., Quincy, IL 62301. Phone: (217) 222-7420. Fax: (217) 222-1653. E-mail: inghram@rnet.com. John T. Inghram IV, James R. Inghram.

Irwin, Campbell & Tannenwald, 1730 Rhode Island Ave. N.W. #200, Washington, DC 20036-3101. Phone: (202) 728-0400. Fax: (202) 728-0354. Web Site: www.ictpc.com. Peter Tannenwald, Alan Campbell, David Irwin, Richard Swift, Kevin Walsh, Jason Roberts, Michelle McClure, Ramsey Woodworth, Nathaniel Hardy, Gregory Haledjian, Tara Shostek.

Isaacman, Kaufman & Painter, 8484 Wilshire Blvd., Suite 850, Beverly Hills, CA 90211. Phone: (323) 782-7700. Fax: (323) 782-7744.

Jackson & Campbell, P.C., 1120 20th St. N.W., Suite 300-S, Washington, DC 20036. Phone: (202) 457-1600. Fax: (202) 457-1678. James R. Michal, Esq.

Jacobs & Associates, 2300 M St. N.W., Suite 800, Washington, DC 20037. Phone: (202) 457-0100. Fax: (202) 457-0186. Web Site: www.internet-law-firm.com.

Jeffer, Mangels, Butler & Marmaro, 1900 Ave. of the Stars, 7th Fl., Los Angeles, CA 90067-5010. Phone: (310) 203-8080. Fax: (310) 203-0567. Web Site: www.jmbm.com. Michael S. Sherman.

Jenner & Block, 601 13th St. N.W., 12th Fl., Washington, DC 20005. Phone: (202) 639-6000. Fax: (202) 639-6066. Web Site: www.jenner.com. Donald B. Verrilli Jr., Mark D. Schneider, Paul M. Smith, Jerome Epstein.

Johnson, Andrea L., California Western School of Law, 225 Cedar St., San Diego, CA 92101. Phone: (800) 255-4252, EXT. 1474. Fax: (619) 696-9999. E-mail: ajohnson@cwsl.edu.

Johnston & Buchan LLP, 275 Slater St., Suite 1700, Ottawa, ON K1P 5H9. Canada. Phone: (613) 236-3882. Fax: (613) 230-6423/230-6762. Fax: (613) 230-6762. Web Site: www.johnstonbuchan.com.

Jones, Day, 51 Louisiana Ave. N. W., Washington, DC 20001. Phone: (202) 879-3939. Fax: (202) 626-1700. Web Site: www.jonesday.com.

Julian & Associates, 1038 N. LaSalle Dr., Chicago, IL 60610. Phone: (312) 266-1500. Fax: (312) 337-1972.

Julien, Jay I., 1501 Broadway, Suite 2600, New York, NY 10036-5503. Phone: (212) 221-7575. Fax: (212) 221-7386. E-mail: jijulien@aol.com.

Kass, Mitek & Kass, 1050 17th St. N.W., Suite 1100, Washington, DC 20036. Phone: (202) 659-6500. Fax: (202) 293-2608. Web Site: www.kmklawyers.com.

Katten Muchin Rosenman LLP, 1025 Thomas Jefferson St. NW, 700 East Lobby, Washington, DC 20007. Phone: (202) 625-3500. Fax: (202) 298-7570. E-mail: howard.braun@kattenlaw.com. Web Site: www.kattenlaw.com. Lee W. Shubert, Shelley Sadowsky, Howard Braun.

Kay, Sheldon L., 30445 Northwestern Hwy., Suite 320, Farmington Hills, MI 48334. Phone: (248) 539-1111. Fax: (248) 539-1114. E-mail: sllaw@hotmail.com.

Kaye, Scholer, L.L.P., 901 15th St. N.W., Suite 1100, Washington, DC 20005. Phone: (202) 682-3500. Fax: (202) 682-3580. E-mail: jsheinsky@kayescholer.com. Web Site: kayescholer.com.

Keller & Heckman, 1001 G St. N.W., Suite 500 W, Washington, DC 20001. Phone: (202) 434-4100. Fax: (202) 434-4646. Web Site: www.khlaw.com. Wayne V. Black, Martin W. Bercovici, Michael F. Morrone, John B. Richards, C. Douglas Jarrett, Richard J. Leighton, Richard F. Mann, ptnrs.

Law Office of Dennis J. Kelly, Box 41177, Washington, DC 20018. Phone: (202) 293-2300. Phone: 888-FCC-LAW-1. Fax: (410) 626-1794. E-mail: dkellyfcclaw1@comcast.net. Dennis J. Kelly.

Law Office of Edward M. Kelman, 100 Park Ave., 20th Fl., New York, NY 10017. Phone: (212) 371-9490. Fax: (212) 750-1356. E-mail: emknyc@aol.com.

Kenkel & Associates, 9908 Sorrel Ave., Potomac, MD 20854. Phone: (301) 299-6260. Fax: (301) 299-0720. E-mail: jngkenkel@aol.com. John B. Kenkel.

Kilpatrick & Stockton L.L.P., 1100 Peach Tree St., Suite 2800, Atlanta, GA 30309. Phone: (404) 815-6500. Fax: (404) 815-6555. Web Site: www.kilpatrickstockton.com.

King & Ballow, 1100 Union St. Plaza, 315 Union St., Nashville, TN 37201. Phone: (615) 259-3456. Fax: (615) 254-7907. E-mail: lawfirm@kingballow.com. Web Site: www.kingballow.com. Douglas R. Pierce, Mark E. Hunt.

Kirkpatrick & Lockhart L.L.P., 75 State St., Boston, MA 02109. Phone: (617) 261-3100. Fax: (617) 261-3175. Web Site: www.kl.com. Stephen L. Palmer, Esq..

Harold S. Klein, Esq., 36 W. 44th St.,Ste.908, New York, NY 10036-8102. Phone: (212) 575-2345. Fax: (212) 869-1091. Harold S. Klein, Esq.

Kleinberg, Lopez, Lange, Cuddy & Edel L.L.P., 2049 Century Park E., Suite 3180, Los Angeles, CA 90067-3205. Phone: (310) 286-9696. Fax: (310) 277-7145. Fax: (310) 286-6445. E-mail: lawyers@kllce.com. Kenneth Kleinberg.

Kletter, Matthew L., 183 Madison Ave., Penthouse, New York, NY 10016. Phone: (212) 726-0090. Fax: (212) 447-6677.

Klitzman, Stephen, Office of Legislative & Inter-Govt Affairs. U.S. Federal Communications Commission, 445 12th St., SW, Office of General Counsel, Washington, DC 20554. Phone: (202) 418-1763. Fax: (202) 418-7540. E-mail: steve.klitzma@fcc.gov. Stephen Klitzman.

Koerner & Olender, P.C., 5809 Nicholson Lane, Suite 124, North Bethesda, MD 20852. Phone: (301) 468-3336. Fax: (301) 468-3343. E-mail: bkofeelaw@erols.com. James A. Koerner, Robert L. Olender.

Kraditor & Haber, P.C., 1212 Ave. of the Americas 3rd Fl., New York, NY 10036. Phone: (212) 768-2100. Fax: (212) 768-2450.

Krech, David H., Wireless Telecommunications Bureau, FCC, 445 12th St. S.W., Rm. 4C216, Washington, DC 20554. Phone: (202) 418-7240. Fax: (202) 418-7224. E-mail: dkrech@fcc.gov.

Lang, Richert & Patch, 5200 N. Palm Ave., Suite 401, Fresno, CA 93704-2225. Phone: (559) 228-6700. Fax: (559) 228-6727. Web Site: www.lrp.org.

Latham & Watkins, 555 11th St. N.W., Suite 1000, Washington, DC 20004. Phone: (202) 637-2200. Fax: (202) 637-2201. Web Site: www.lw.com.

Law Office of Dan J. Alpert, 2120 N. 21st Rd., Arlington, VA 22201. Phone: (703) 243-8690. Fax: (703) 243-8692. E-mail: dja@commlaw.tv. Dan J. Alpert; Washington DC: (202) 371-7200 John C. Quale, Antoinette Cook Bush, Kenneth M. Kaufman, Lawrence Roberts, Ivan A. Schlager, Richard A. Hindman, Brian D. Weimer, David H. Pawlik, Margaret E. Lancaster, John M. Beahn, Malcolm J. Tuesley, Jared S. Sher; Chicago Office: Warren Lavey, David S. Prohofsky.

Law Offices of Henry W. Root, P.C., 1541 Ocean Ave., Suite 200, Santa Monica, CA 90401-2104. Phone: (310) 395-6800. Fax: (310) 393-7777. E-mail: henry@grrlaw.com. Henry W. Root Esq., Bruce Grakal Esq., Richard Rosenthal Esq.

Lawrence & Eason, 4900 Richmond Sq.,, Suite 200, Oklahoma City, OK 73118. Phone: (405) 948-6000. Fax: (405) 841-6006.

LeBoeuf, Lamb, Greene & MacRae, 1875 Connecticut Ave. N.W., Suite 1200, Washington, DC 20009. Phone: (202) 986-8000. Fax: (202) 986-8102. Web Site: www.llgm.com. David R. Poe, Lawrence G. Acker, Catherine P. McCarthy, Yvonne Coviello.
   San Francisco, CA 94111, One Embarcadero Ctr. Phone: (415) 951-1100. Fax: (415) 951-1180. Thomas McDonald, R. Scott Puddy.
   Boston, MA 02110, 260 Franklin St. Phone: (617) 439-9500. Fax: (617) 439-0341. Paul Connolly, Meab Purcell.
   Newark, NJ 07102-5311, One Gateway Ctr, Suite 603. Phone: (201) 643-8000. Hon. Fredrick B. Lacey.
   Albany, NY 12210, One Commerce Plaza, 99 Washington Ave. Phone: (518) 465-1500. Brian Fitzgerald.
   New York, NY 10019, 125 W. 55th St. Phone: (212) 424-8000. Fax: (212) 424-8500. Vivian Polak.
   Harrisburg, PA 17108, Box 12105, Strawberry Sq, 320 Market St, Suite E-400. Phone: (717) 232-8199. Jim Cawley.
   Pittsburgh, PA 15219, 601 Grant St. Phone: (412) 594-2300. Fax: (412) 594-5237.

Law Firms

Leibowitz & Associates, P.A., One S.E. 3rd Ave., Suite 1450, Miami, FL 33131-1715. Phone: (305) 530-1322. Fax: (305) 530-9417. E-mail: firm@broadlaw.com. Matthew L. Leibowitz, Joseph A. Belisle, Ila L. Feld, Nicki J. Fernandez.

Leopold, Petrich & Smith, 2049 Century Park E., Suite 3110, Los Angeles, CA 90067-3274. Phone: (310) 277-3333. Fax: (310) 277-7444. E-mail: dmayed@lpsla.com. Web Site: www.lpsla.com. Daniel M. Mayeda.

Leventhal, Senter & Lerman, P.L.L.C., 2000 K St. N.W., Suite 600, Washington, DC 20006-1809. Phone: (202) 429-8970. Fax: (202) 293-7783. Web Site: www.lsl-law.com. Norman P. Leventhal, Meredith S. Senter Jr., Steven Alman Lerman, Raul R. Rodriguez, Dennis P. Corbett, Barbara K. Gardner, Stephen D. Baruch, Sally A. Buckman, Brian M. Madden, David S. Keir, Nancy L. Wolf, Deborah R. Coleman, Nancy A. Ory, John D. Poutasse, Christopher J. Sova, Philip A. Bonomo, Howard A. Topel, Linda D. Feldmann, S. Jenell Trigg, Beth-Sherri Akyereko, Peter M. Gould, Jean F. Walker, John W. Bagwell, Jessica L. Davidson, Suzanne E. Head, Louis J. Levy, Linda G. Morrison.

Lewis, Lewis & Ferraro, 28 N. Main St., West Hartford, CT 06107-1928. Phone: (860) 521-1500. Fax: (860) 521-4500.

Law Firm of Rosalind Lichter, Tribeca Film Ctr., 375 Greenwich St., New York, NY 10013. Phone: (212) 941-4075. Fax: (212) 941-4076. Rosalind Lichter.

Loeb & Loeb L.L.P., 345 Park Ave., New York, NY 10154. Phone: (212) 407-4000. Phone: (212) 407-4987. Fax: (212) 407-4990. Web Site: www.loeb.com. Donald L. B. Baraf, Marc Chamlin.
  Los Angeles, CA 90067-4164, 10100 Santa Monica Blvd. Phone: (310) 282-2475. Fax: (310) 282-2192. Mickey Mayerson.
  Los Angeles, CA 90017-2475, 1000 Wilshire Blvd. Phone: (213) 688-3400. Fax: (213) 688-3460.

Loftus & Borgstrom, One Court St., Suite 320, Lebanon, NH 03766. Phone: (603) 448-6420. Fax: (603) 448-6147. E-mail: wrlpc@valley.net. William R. Loftus, Esq.; Karen J. Borgstrom, Esq.

London, Michael B., 10452 Oletha Ln., Los Angeles, CA 90077-2420. Phone: (310) 474-0577. Fax: (310) 474-5413.

Lowndes, Drosdick, Doster, Kantor & Reed, P.A., Box 2809, 215 N. Eola Dr., Orlando, FL 32801. Phone: (407) 843-4600. Fax: (407) 843-4444. Julia L. Frey, Louis Frey Jr.

Lukas, Nace, Gutierrez & Sachs Chartered, 1111 19th St. N.W., Suite 1200, Washington, DC 20036. Phone: (202) 857-3500. Fax: (202) 857-5747. Russell D. Lukas, David L. Nace, Thomas Gutierrez, George L. Lyon Jr., Elizabeth R. Sachs, Pamela L. Gist, David A. LaFuria, Marilyn Suchecki.

Law Offices of Patrice Lyons, Chartered, 910 17th St. N.W., Suite 800, Washington, DC 20006. Phone: (202) 293-5990. Fax: (202) 293-5121. E-mail: palyons@bellatlantic.net. Patrice Lyons.

David L. Maddox & Associates, P.C., 1207 17 Ave. S., Suite 300, Nashville, TN 37212. Phone: (615) 329-0086. Fax: (615) 320-7150. E-mail: david@dmaddox.com.

Madigan & Getzendanner, 30 N. LaSalle St., Suite 3906, Chicago, IL 60602. Phone: (312) 346-4321. Fax: (312) 346-5619. Michael J. Madigan, Vincent J. Getzendanner.

Magee Law Firm, PLLC, 6845 Elm St., Suite 205, McLean, VA 22101. Phone: (703) 356-7500. Fax: (703) 356-6863. E-mail: jmagee@mageelawfirm.com. James E. Magee, Kristie S. Hassett, Jennifer A. Newberry.

Margolin Law Firm, 4520 Madison Ave., Suite 220, Kansas City, MO 64111. Phone: (816) 753-3838. Fax: (816) 753-3842. James S. Margolin.

The Marshall Firm, 1065 Ave. of the Americas, 11th Fl., New York, NY 10018. Phone: (212) 382-2044. Fax: (212) 382-3610. E-mail: tmf@marshallfirm.com. Paul Marshall.

Donald E. Martin, P.C., Box 8433, Falls Church, VA 22041. Phone: (703) 642-2344. Fax: (703) 642-2357. E-mail: dempc@prodigy.net. Donald E. Martin.

McCampbell & Young, P.C., Box 550, First Tennessee Plaza, Suite 2021, Knoxville, TN 37901-0550. Phone: (865) 637-1440. Fax: (865) 546-9808. E-mail: stone@mcylaw.com. Robert S. Stone.

McDonald, Hopkins, L.P.A., 2100 Bank One Ctr., 600 Superior Ave. E., Cleveland, OH 44114-2653. Phone: (216) 348-5400. Fax: (216) 348-5474. E-mail: attorneys@mhbh.com. Web Site: www.mhbh.com. Brian M. O'Neil.

Mary A. McReynolds, P.C., 1701 Pennsylvania Ave. N.W., Suite 300, Washington, DC 20006. Phone: (202) 879-2695. Fax: (202) 879-2696. Mary A. McReynolds, Esq.

Mensch, Linda Susan, 200 S. Michigan Ave., Suite 1240, Chicago, IL 60604. Phone: (312) 922-2910. Fax: (312) 922-1865. E-mail: menshlaw@yahoo.com. Web Site: menschlaw@yahoo.com. Linda Mensch.

Messerli & Kramer, 150 S. 5th St., Suite 1800, Minneapolis, MN 55402-4246. Phone: (612) 672-3600. Fax: (612) 672-3777. Web Site: www.messerlikramer.com. William F. Messerli.

Meyers & Meyers, 360 E. Randolph St., Suite 3104, Chicago, IL 60601. Phone: (312) 616-1500. Fax: (312) 616-1737. E-mail: peterarbme@aol.com. Therese Zaller, Peter R. Meyers, Irving Meyers.

Midlen Law Center, 7618 Lynn, Chevy Chase, MD 20815-6043. Phone: (301) 656-3000. Fax: (301) 656-8262. E-mail: john@midlen.com. Web Site: www.midlen.com. John H. Midlen Jr.

Miller & Neely, P.C., 6900 Wisconsin Ave., Suite 704, Bethesda, MD 20815. Phone: (301) 986-4160. Fax: (301) 986-4162. E-mail: millaw@netkonnect.net. Jerrold D. Miller, John S. Neely.

Miller & Van Eaton, P.L.L.C., 1155 Connecticut Ave. N.W., Suite 1000, Washington, DC 20036. Phone: (202) 785-0600. Fax: (202) 785-1234. E-mail: info2@millervaneaton.com. Web Site: www.millervaneaton.com.

Miller, Canfield, Paddock & Stone, P.L.C., 150 W Jefferson Ave.,, Suite 2500, Detroit, MI 48226. Phone: (313) 963-6420. Fax: (313) 496-7500. E-mail: lay@millercanfield.com. Web Site: www.millercanfield.com. Tillman L. Lay.

Miller, Balis and O'Neil, 1140 19th St. N.W., Suite 700, Washington, DC 20006. Phone: (202) 296-2960. Fax: (202) 296-0166. E-mail: mgrossman@mbolaw.com. Milton J. Grossman.

Mintz, Levin, Cohn, Ferris, Glovsky & Popeo, P.C., 701 Pennsylvania Ave. N.W., Suite 900, Washington, DC 20004. Phone: (202) 434-7300. Fax: (202) 434-7400. Web Site: www.mintzlevin.com. Charles D. Ferris, Frank W. Lloyd, Bruce D. Sokler, Howard J. Symons.
  Boston, MA 02111, One Financial Center. Phone: (617) 542-6000. Fax: (617) 542-2241. Irwin Heller.

Mirowski & Associates, 757 W. Ivy St., San Diego, CA 92101. Phone: (619) 702-5300. Fax: (619) 702-4666. E-mail: pmirowski@mirlaw.com. Web Site: www.mirlaw.com. Paul J. Mirowski..

Mitchell, Charles D., 1601 N. Frontage Rd., Suite F, Vicksburg, MS 39180. Phone: (601) 636-4545, EXT. 123. Fax: (601) 634-0897. E-mail: fysadm@vicksburgpost.net. Web Site: www.vicksburgpost.com. Charles D. Mitchell.

Mitchell Silberberg & Knupp, 11377 W. Olympic Blvd., Los Angeles, CA 90064. Phone: (310) 312-2000. Fax: (310) 312-3100. E-mail: info@msk.com. Web Site: www.msk.com. Bernard Donnenfeld.

Mizrack & Gantt, 555 11th St. N.W., Suite 850, Washington, DC 20004. Phone: (202) 628-1717. Fax: (202) 628-1919.

Moir & Hardman, 1015 18th St. N.W., Suite 800, Washington, DC 20036-5204. Phone: (202) 223-3772. Fax: (202) 833-2416. Brian R. Moir, Kenneth E. Hardman.

Morris, Rathnau & De La Rosa, 100 W. Monroe St.,, Suite 2101, Chicago, IL 60603. Phone: (312) 606-0876. Fax: (312) 606-0879. E-mail: mdlrlawchicago@aol.com. Joseph A. Morris, ptnr.

Morrison & Foerster L.L.P., 2000 Pennsylvania Ave. N.W., Suite 5500, Washington, DC 20006. Phone: (202) 887-1500. Fax: (202) 887-0763. Web Site: www.mofo.com. Cheryl A.Tritt, Joan E. Neal, Charles H. Kennedy, Margaret L. Tobey, Frank W. Krogh, Stuart L. Crenshaw, William D. Freedman, Doane Kiechal, Jennifer Kostyu, Christa M. McAndrew, David Munson, Phuong N. Pham, Jennifer L. Richter, Jennifer Cetta.

Moss & Barnett, A Professional Assn, 4800 Wells Fargo Ctr., 90 S. 7th St., Minneapolis, MN 55402-4129. Phone: (612) 347-0300. Fax: (612) 339-6686. Web Site: www.moss-barnett.com. Brian T. Grogan, Esq.

Todd W. Musburger, Ltd., 142 E. Ontario St., Suite 500, Chicago, IL 60611. Phone: (312) 664-2600. Fax: (312) 664-4137. E-mail: todd@musburger.com. Todd W. Musburger.

Myman, Abell, Fineman, Greenspan & Light, 11601 Wilshire Blvd., Suite 2200, Los Angeles, CA 90025. Phone: (310) 820-7717. Fax: (310) 207-2680. Robert M. Myman.

Nadel, Mark S., U.S. Federal Communications Commission, 445 12th St. S.W., Rm. 5B 551, Washington, DC 20554. Phone: (202) 418-7385. Fax: (202) 418-7361. E-mail: mnadel@fcc.gov. Web Site: www.fcc.gov.

Naphtali, Ashirah S., 130-33 217 St.,, Suite B, Laurelton, NY 11413-1230. Phone: (718) 481-7236. Fax: (718) 481-7236. E-mail: anaphml@aol.com. Ashirah S. Naphtali, Esq., MBA.

National Exchange Carrier Association, N.E.C.A., 80 S. Jefferson Rd., Whippany, NJ 07981-1009. Phone: (973) 884-8000. Phone: (800) 228-8597. Fax: (973) 884-8469. Web Site: www.neca.org.

Nemeth, Valerie A., Attorney at Law, 619 S. Vulcan Ave., Suite 215, Encinitas, CA 92024-3652. Phone: (760) 944-4130 ext 130. Fax: (760) 942-6043. E-mail: vanemeth@cs.com. Web Site: www.entlawyer.com. Valerie Nemeth.

Neuland, Nordberg & Andrews, 22502 Avenida Empresa, Rancho Santa Margarita, CA 92688. Phone: (949) 766-4700. Fax: (949) 766-4712.

Nathan M. Nickolaus, 320 E. McCarthy St., Jefferson City, MO 65101-3115. Phone: (573) 634-6313. Fax: (573) 634-6504. Web Site: nnickolaus@jeffcitymo.org.

Nilsson, Kent R., U.S. Federal Communications Commission, 445 12th St. S.W., Washington, DC 20554. Phone: (202) 418-2478. Fax: (202) 418-2345.

Nixon Peabody L.L.P., 401 9th St. NW, Suite 900, Washington, DC 20004. Phone: (202) 585-8000. Fax: (202) 585-8080. Web Site: www.nixonpeabody.com. Veronica M. Ahern, William S. Andrews.
  Rochester, NY 14603, Box 1051, Clinton Sq. Phone: (716) 263-1000. Richard D. Rochford Jr.

Nixon, Wilbert E. Jr., Wireless Telecommunications Bureau, Police & Rules Branch. Federal Communications Commission, 445 12th St. S.W. Rm. 4-A207, Washington, DC 20554. Phone: (202) 418-7240. Fax: (202) 418-7447. Web Site: www.fcc.gov.

Nossaman, Guthner, Knox & Elliott, L.L.P., 50 California St., 34th Fl., San Francisco, CA 94111. Phone: (415) 398-3600. Fax: (415) 398-2438. E-mail: mmattes@nossaman.com. Web Site: www.nossaman.com. Martin A. Mattes, Jose E. Guzman.

OPASTCO, 21 Dupont Cir. N.W., Suite 700, Washington, DC 20036. Phone: (202) 659-5990. Fax: (202) 659-4619. Web Site: www.opastco.org.

O'Connell & Aronowitz PC, 54 State St., Albany, NY 12207. Phone: (518) 462-5601. Fax: (518) 462-2670. E-mail: o'connell@albany.net. Web Site: www.oalaw.com. Peter Danziger, Neil H. Rivchin.

O'Connell, Susan Lee, U.S. Federal Communications Commission, 445 12th St. S.W., Rm. 6A847, Washington, DC 20554. Phone: (202) 418-1484. Fax: (202) 418-2824.

O'Connor & Hannan, 1666 K St. N.W., Suite 500, Washington, DC 20006. Phone: (202) 887-1400. Fax: (202) 466-2198. Gary Adler.

Ogden Murphy Wallace, P.L.L.C., 2100 Westlake Ctr. Tower, 1601 5th Ave., Seattle, WA 98101-1686. Phone: (206) 447-7000. Fax: (206) 447-0215. Web Site: www.omwlaw.com.

O'Melveny & Myers, 1625 Eye St. NW, Washington, DC 20006. Phone: (202) 383-5300. Fax: (202) 383-5414. Web Site: www.omm.com. John H. Beisner, Donald T. Bliss, John Rogovin, Jessica Davidson-Miller, Carl R. Schenker Jr., Charles Read, Paul McNamara, Martine Apollon, Todd Rosenberg.

Broadcasting & Cable Yearbook 2006

Law Firms

O'Neil, Cannon, Hollman, Dejong, Bank One Plaza, 111 E. Wisconsin Ave., Suite 1400, Milwaukee, WI 53202-4803. Phone: (414) 276-5000. Fax: (414) 276-6581. Carl Holborn.

O'Neill, Athy & Casey, P.C., 1310 19th St. N.W., Washington, DC 20036. Phone: (202) 466-6555. Fax: (202) 466-6596. E-mail: croneill@oacpc.com. Christopher R. O'Neill.

O'Reilly, Rancilio, Nitz, Andrews, Turnbull, & Scott P.C., 12900 Hall Rd., Suite 350, Sterling Heights, MI 48313-1151. Phone: (586) 726-1000. Fax: (586) 726-1560. E-mail: nlehto@ornats.net. Web Site: www.orlaw.com. Neil J. Lehto, Donald DeNault.

Orr & Reno, Box 3550, One Eagle Sq., Concord, NH 03302-3550. Phone: (603) 224-2381. Fax: (603) 224-2318. William L. Chapman.

Overton, John B., 302 Caladonia, Sausalito, CA 94965. Phone: (415) 331-2889.

Law Offices of James L. Oyster, 108 Oyster Ln., Castleton, VA 22716. Phone: (540) 937-4800. Fax: (540) 937-2148. E-mail: joyster@crosslink.net. James L. Oyster.

Pankopf, Arthur, 7819 Hampden Ln., Bethesda, MD 20814-1108. Phone: (301) 657-8790. Fax: (301) 657-3296. E-mail: apankopf@worldnet.att.net. Arthur Pankopf.

Pardo & Pardo P.A., Box 398646, Miami Beach, FL 33239. Phone: (305) 673-1515. Fax: (305) 673-9359.

Patton Boggs L.L.P., 2550 M St. N.W., Suite 900, Washington, DC 20037. Phone: (202) 457-6000. Fax: (202) 457-6315. Web Site: www.pattonboggs.com. Thomas H. Boggs Jr., Stephen Diaz Gavin, Paul C. Besozzi, J. Jeffrey Craven, John F. Fithian, Penelope S. Farthing, Janet Fitzpatrick, Jeffrey L. Ross. Dallas: Charles Miller, Jennifer Boudreau.

Pauker, Molly, Fox Television Stations Inc., 5151 Wisconsin Ave. N.W., Washington, DC 20016-4124. Phone: (202) 895-3088. Fax: (202) 895-3222. E-mail: mollyp@fox.com.

Paul, Hastings, Janofsky & Walker LLP, 1299 Pennsylvania Ave. N.W., 10th Fl., Washington, DC 20004-2400. Phone: (202) 508-9500. Fax: (202) 508-9700. Web Site: www.paulhastings.com. Ralph B. Everett, Bruce D. Ryan, Michelle Cohen, Carl W. Northrop, John G. Johnson, William D. DeGrandis, David Burns, Christine Crowe, G. Hamilton Loeb.

Paul, Weiss, Rifkind, Wharton & Garrison, L.L.P., 1615 L St. N.W., Suite 1300, Washington, DC 20036. Phone: (202) 223-7300. Fax: (202) 223-7420. Phillip L. Spector, Jeffrey H. Olson, Patrick S. Campbell.

Pearce & Durick, Box 400, 314 E. Thayer Ave., Bismarck, ND 58502-0400. Phone: (701) 223-2890. Fax: (701) 223-7865. E-mail: law.office@pearce-durick.com. Web Site: www.pearce-durick.com. Patrick W. Durick, Larry L. Boschee, Jerome C. Kettleson, Gary R. Thune, Jonathan P. Sanstead.

John D. Pellegrin P.C., 9306 Old Keene Mill Rd., Burke, VA 22015. Phone: (703) 455-6101. Fax: (703) 455-6106. E-mail: jdpc@erols.com. Web Site: www.pellegrin-law.com. John D. Pellegrin.

Pepper Hamilton LLP, 3000 Two Logan Sq., Eighteenth & Arch St., Philadelphia, PA 19103-2799. Phone: (215) 981-4000. Fax: (215) 981-4750. E-mail: phinfo@pepperlaw.com. Web Site: www.pepperlaw.com. Pepper Hamilton LLP, David A. Wormser.
   Washington, DC 20005-2004, 600 14th St. N.W. Phone: (202) 220-1200. Fax: (202) 220-1665. David A. Wormser.

Perez, Benjamin, Abacus Communications Co., 1801 Columbus Rd. N.W., Suite 101, Washington, DC 20009-2031. Phone: (202) 462-3680. Fax: (202) 462-3781. E-mail: abacus@erols.com. Benjamin Perez.

Perkins, Jr., Roy F., 1724 Whitewood Ln., Herndon, VA 20170. Phone: (703) 435-9700. Fax: (703) 435-9701. Roy F. Perkins Jr.

Larry D. Perry, Attorney at Law, 11464 Saga Ln., Suite 110, Knoxville, TN 37931-2819. Phone: (865) 927-8474. Fax: (865) 927-4912. E-mail: larryperry@worldnet.att.net. Larry D. Perry, Esq.

Peterson Law Firm, 2033 Walnut St., Philadelphia, PA 19103. Phone: (215) 557-9001. Fax: (215) 557-9108.

Phillips Nizer LLP, 666 5th Ave., New York, NY 10103-0084. Phone: (212) 977-9700. Fax: (212) 262-5152. Web Site: www.phillipsnizer.com.

Pierce, Robinson & Greene P A, 600 W. 4th St., North Little Rock, AR 72114-5360. Phone: (501) 372-3131. Fax: (501) 372-3825. Web Site: www.prg-law.com. William Robinson.

Pike & Fischer Inc., 1010 Wayne Ave, Suite 1400, Silver Spring, MD 20910-5600. Phone: (301) 562-1530, Ext. 237. Fax: (301) 562-1521. E-mail: customercare@pf.com. Web Site: www.pf.com.

Pillsbury, Winthrop, Box 7880, San Francisco, CA 94120-7880. Phone: (415) 983-1000. Fax: (415) 983-1200. Gregg F. Vignos.

Law Offices of Dean George Popps, Box 3274, West McLean, VA 22103-3274. Phone: (703) 734-0159. Fax: (703) 448-9843. E-mail: deanpoppsol@aol.com. Dean George Popps.

Powell, Goldstein, Frazer & Murphy, 191 Peachtree St. N.E., 16th Fl., Atlanta, GA 30303. Phone: (404) 572-6600. Fax: (404) 572-6999. E-mail: wmoeling@pgfm.com. Web Site: www.pgfm.com.
   Washington, DC 20004, 1001 Pennsylvania Ave. N.W, 6th Fl. Phone: (202) 347-0066. Fax: (202) 624-7222. Jerome S. Breed.

Pratcher & Associates P.C., 1133 Kensington Ave., Buffalo, NY 14215-1611. Phone: (716) 838-4612. Fax: (716) 838-4828. E-mail: frpratcher@pratcher.com. Franklin Pratcher.
   Buffalo, NY 14204, Town Gardens Plaza, 447 Williams St, Suite H. Phone: (716) 847-0145.

Preston, Gates, Ellis & Rouvelas Meeds L.L.P., 1735 New York Ave. N.W., Suite 500, Washington, DC 20006. Phone: (202) 628-1700. Fax: (202) 331-1024. E-mail: gregm@prestongates.com. Web Site: www.prestongates.com. Martin L. Stern.

Proskauer Rose L.L.P., 1585 Broadway, New York, NY 10036. Phone: (212) 969-3000. Fax: (212) 969-2900. E-mail: lbudish@proskauer.com. Web Site: www.proskauer.com. Bertram A. Abrams, Lawrence H. Budish.

Provosty, Sadler Delaunay, Fiorenza & Sobel, Box 1791, Hibernia National Bank, 8th Fl., Alexandria, LA 71309-1791. Phone: (318) 445-3631. Fax: (318) 445-9377. David Sobel.

Pulis, Gregory M., (Creative Artists Agency). 9830 Wilshire Blvd., Beverly Hills, CA 90212. Phone: (310) 288-4545.

Putbrese, Hunsaker & Trent, P.C., 200 S. Church St., Woodstock, VA 22664. Phone: (540) 459-7649. Fax: (540) 459-7656. E-mail: phtlaw@mindspring.com. Web Site: www.pht-law.com. John C. Trent.

Reddy, Begley & McCormick, L.L.P., 1156 15th St. N.W., Suite 610, Washington, DC 20005-1770. Phone: (202) 659-5700. Fax: (202) 659-5711. E-mail: rbm@rbmfcclaw.com. Web Site: www.rbmfcclaw.com. Dennis F. Begley, Matthew E. McCormick.

Rees, Broome & Diaz, 8133 Leesburg Pike, 9th Fl., Vienna, VA 22182. Phone: (703) 790-1911. Fax: (703) 848-2530. Web Site: www.rbdlaw.com. Peter S. Philbin.

The Law Offices of George Edward Regis, 121 W. 27th St., Suite 1001, New York, NY 10001-6207. Phone: (212) 645-8800. Fax: (212) 645-7900. George Edward Regis.

Renouf & Polivy, 1532 16th St. N.W., Washington, DC 20036. Phone: (202) 265-1807. Fax: (202) 265-1810. E-mail: thamber@aol.com. Katrina Renouf, Margot Polivy.

Resnick, Bernard Max, Esq, P.C., Two Bala Plaza, Suite 300, Bala Cynwyd, PA 19004-1501. Phone: (610) 660-7774. Fax: (610) 668-0574. E-mail: bmresnick@aol.com. Web Site: www.bernardresnick.com. Bernard Max Resnick, Priscilla J. Mattison.

Reynolds & Manning, P.A., Box 2809, Prince Frederick, MD 20678. Phone: (410) 535-9220. Fax: (410) 535-9171. E-mail: calvertlawyer@comcast.net. Web Site: www.lawyers.com/reynoldsandmanning. Christopher J. Reynolds, pres.

Rich, Tracy S., NBC Inc., 330 Bob Hope Dr., C205, Burbank, CA 91523. Phone: (818) 840-3510. Fax: (818) 840-3495. E-mail: tracy.rich@nbc.com.

Richards, Mary Beth, U.S. Federal Communications Commission, 445 12th St. S.W., Rm. 8-C750, Washington, DC 20554. Phone: (202) 418-1000. Fax: (202) 418-2801. Web Site: www.marybeth.richards@fcc.gov.

Riezman & Berger, 7700 Bonhomme Ave., 7th Fl., St. Louis, MO 63105. Phone: (314) 727-0101. Fax: (314) 727-6458. Web Site: www.riezmanberger.com. Bob Jacobs.

Riker, Danzig, Scherer, Hyland & Perretti LLP, One Speedwell Ave., Headquarters Plaza, Morristown, NJ 07962-1981. Phone: (973) 538-0800. Fax: (973) 538-1984. E-mail: info@riker.com. Web Site: www.riker.com. Sidney M. Schreiber, Vincent J. Sharkey Jr., Edward K. DeHope, James C. Meyer, Michael A. Schmerling, Mark T. Pasko.
   Trenton, NJ 08608-1220, 50 W. State St, Suite 1010.

Robins, Kaplan, Miller & Ciresi, 2800 LaSalle Plaza, 800 LaSalle Ave., Minneapolis, MN 55402-2015. Phone: (612) 349-8500. Fax: (612) 339-4181. E-mail: kamarron@rkmc.com. Web Site: www.rkmc.com. Timothy Block, Doug Boettge, John F. Gibbs, Todd Hartman, Lisa Heller, Rebecca Liethen, Kathleen A. Marron, Edward Muramoto, Thomas A. Miller, Ed Muramoto, Sara A. Poulos, Steven Safvanski.

Romano, B. Alan, U.S. Federal Communications Commission, 445 12th St. S.W. Rm. 2-C267, Washington, DC 20554. Phone: (202) 418-2120. Fax: (202) 418-2053. Web Site: www.fcc.gov.

Gust Rosenfeld P.L.C., 201 E. Washington, Suite 800, Phoenix, AZ 85004-2327. Phone: (602) 257-7422. Fax: (602) 254-4878. E-mail: chauncey@gustlaw.com. Web Site: www.gustlaw.com. Tom Chauncey II.

Rosenfeld, Meyer & Susman L.L.P., 9601 Wilshire Blvd., 4th Fl., Beverly Hills, CA 90210-5288. Phone: (310) 858-7700. Fax: (310) 860-2430. Web Site: www.rmslaw.com. Debbie Mograw.

Rothman, Gordon P.C., 300 Grant Bldg., Pittsburgh, PA 15219. Phone: (412) 338-1100. Fax: (412) 281-7304. Frederick A. Polner, Esq.

Rourke, Gerald S., 76 Northwood Rd., Madison, CT 06443. Phone: (203) 421-3424. Fax: (203) 421-8683. E-mail: gsrourke1@cs.com. Gerald S. Rourke.

Rubin, Winston, Diercks, Harris & Cooke, L.L.P., 1155 Connecticut Ave. N.W., 6th Fl, Washington, DC 20036. Phone: (202) 861-0870. Fax: (202) 429-0657. E-mail: jwinston@rwdhc.com. James L. Winston, Eric M. Rubin, Steven Stone, Walter E. Diercks.

Ryan, Swanson & Cleveland P.L.L.C., 1201 3rd Ave., Suite 3400, Seattle, WA 98101-3034. Phone: (206) 464-4224. Phone: (800) 458-5973. Fax: (206) 583-0359. Web Site: www.ryanlaw.com.

SBC Telecommunications Inc., 1401 I St. N.W., Suite 400, Washington, DC 20005. Phone: (202) 326-8800. Web Site: www.fcc.com.

Law Offices of Lee Sacks, 100 Wilshire Blvd. Wilshire Bldg. Suite 1300, Santa Monica, CA 90401. Phone: (310) 451-3113. Fax: (310) 451-0089. E-mail: office@sacksapclaw.com. Lee Sacks.

Sahl, Jack, School of Law, University of Akron, Akron, OH 44325-2901. Phone: (330) 972-6753. Fax: (330) 258-2343. E-mail: jps@uakron.edu.

Sanchez Law Firm, 2300 M St., N.W., Suite 800, Washington, DC 20037. Phone: (202) 237-2814. Fax: (202) 237-5614. E-mail: esanchez@bellatlantic.net. Ernest T. Sanchez, Susan M. Jenkins.

Gary P. Schonman, Federal Communications Commission, 445 12th St. S.W. Rm. 3A660, Washington, DC 20554. Phone: (202) 418-1795. Fax: (202) 418-2080. Web Site: www.fcc.gov. Gary P. Schonman.

Schuman, Felts, Chartered, 4804 Moorland Ln., Bethesda, MD 20814. Phone: (301) 986-0200. Fax: (301) 986-7960. Sheldon Paul Schuman.

Schuster & Associates, 3594 Armourdale Ave., Long Beach, CA 90808. Phone: (562) 596-5900. Fax: (562) 431-4540. E-mail: attorney@flightlaw.com. Web Site: www.flightlaw.com.

Schwaninger & Associates, P.C., 1331 H St. N.W., Suite 500, Washington, DC 20005. Phone: (202) 347-8580. Fax: (202) 347-8607/347-8643. E-mail: rschwaninger@sa-lawyers.net. Web Site: www.sa-lawyers.net. Richard P. Hanno.

Law Firms

Schwartz, Woods & Miller, 1123 20th St., N.W., Suite 610, Washington, DC 20036. Phone: (202) 833-1700. Fax: (202) 833-2351. E-mail: [last name]@swmlaw.com. Web Site: www.swmlaw.com. Lawrence M. Miller, Steven C. Schaffer, Malcolm G. Stevenson.

Law Offices of Philip L. Schwartz PA, 2000 Glades Rd., Suite 208, Boca Raton, FL 33431. Phone: (954) 760-7770. Fax: (954) 524-4169. E-mail: phil@philipschwartz.com. Philip L. Schwartz, Esq.

The Seale Law Firm, Bryton Tower, 1271 Poplar Ave., Suite 101, Memphis, TN 38104. Phone: (901) 722-8188. Fax: (901) 278-7126. E-mail: artslaw@bellsouth.net. William B. Seale, Lisa A. Maniseali.

Sell & Melton, Box 229, 577 Mulberry St., Suite 1400, Macon, GA 31202-0229. Phone: (478) 746-8521. Fax: (478) 745-6426. E-mail: eds@sell-melton.com. Web Site: www.sell-melton.com. Ed S. Sell III, Jeffrey B. Hanson.

Severaid, Ronald H., 1805 Tribute Rd.,, Suite J, Sacramento, CA 95815. Phone: (916) 929-9383. Fax: (916) 925-4763. E-mail: rhseveraid@earthlink.net.

Seyfarth Shaw, 2029 Century Park E., 33rd Fl., Los Angeles, CA 90067-3063. Phone: (310) 277-7200. Fax: (310) 201-5219. Web Site: www.seyfarth.com. Mitchell Whitehead, ptnr.

Seyfarth Shaw LLP, 55 E. Monroe St., Chicago, IL 60603. Phone: (312) 781-8655. Fax: (312) 269-8869. Web Site: www.seyfarth.com. Paul H. Vishny, Joel D. Rubin.

Law Offices of Thomas G. Shack Jr., 1150 Connecticut Ave. N.W., Suite 900, Washington, DC 20036. Phone: (202) 293-5900. Fax: (202) 659-3493. Thomas G. Shack Jr.

Shapiro, Burton J., 2147 N. Beachwood Dr., Los Angeles, CA 90068-3462. Phone: (323) 469-9452. Fax: (603) 710-8109. E-mail: burtjay@mail.com. Web Site: www.burtshaprio.com.

Shaw Pittman L.L.P., Communications Practice Group, 2300 N St. N.W., Washington, DC 20037-1128. Phone: (202) 663-8000. Fax: (202) 663-8007. E-mail: info@shawpittman.com. Web Site: www.shawpittman.com. Ben C. Fisher, Richard R. Zaragoza, Clifford M. Harrington, Kathryn R. Schmeltzer, David D. Oxenford, Bruce D. Jacobs, Barry H. Gottfried, Glenn S. Richards, Scott R. Flick, Lauren Lynch Flick, Miles S. Mason, Carroll John Yung, Jane Sullivan Roberts, Dawn M. Sciarrino, Bryan T. McGinnis, Cynthia D. Greer, Susan M. Hafeli, Brendan Holland, David S. Konczal, Tony Lin, Veronica D. McLaughlin, Tina R. Reynolds, Christopher J. Sadowski, Katherine T. Suh, Amy L. Van de Kerckhove.

Shine and Hardin L.L.P., 2810 Beaver Ave., Fort Wayne, IN 46807. Phone: (260) 745-1970. Fax: (260) 744-5411. E-mail: sshine@shineandhardin.com.

Shukat, Arrow, Hafer & Weber, L.L.P., 111 W. 57th St., Suite 1120, New York, NY 10019-2211. Phone: (212) 245-4580. Fax: (212) 956-6471. E-mail: Peter@musiclaw.com. Peter Shukat.

Shulman, Rogers, Gandal, Pordy & Ecker, P.A., 11921 Rockville Pike, 3rd Fl., Rockville, MD 20852. Phone: (301) 230-5200. Fax: (301) 230-2891.

Siegal, Joel H., 703 Market St., San Francisco, CA 94103. Phone: (415) 777-5547.

Siegel, Kelleher & Kahn, 420 Franklin St., Buffalo, NY 14202. Phone: (716) 881-5800. Fax: (716) 885-3369. LeRoi Johnson.

Law Offices of William D. Silva, 5335 Wisconsin Ave. N.W., Suite 400, Washington, DC 20015-2003. Phone: (202) 362-1711. Fax: (202) 686-8282. E-mail: bill@luselaw.com. Web Site: wmmsilva.com. William D. Silva.

Silver, Garvett & Henkel, 1110 Brickell Ave. Penthouse 1, Miami, FL 33131. Phone: (305) 377-8802. Fax: (305) 377-8804.

Law Office of Steven Simenowitz, c/o Morici & Morici, P.C., 1001 Franklin Ave., Suite 201, Garden City, NY 11530. Phone: (631) 232-3117. Fax: (802) 423-8244. E-mail: swfarms@together.net. Steven H. Simenowitz.

Skadden, Arps, Slate, Meagher & Flom L.L.P., 1440 New York Ave. N.W., Washington, DC 20005. Phone: (202) 371-7000. Fax: (202) 661-8233. Richard A. Hindman, David H. Pawlik, Brian D. Weimer, John C. Quale, John M. Beahn, Antoinette C. Bush, Margaret E. Lancaster, Ivan A. Schlager, Jennifer B. Irvin, Lawrence Roberts, Jared S. Sher, Malcom J. Tuesley, (Washington DC); Warren G. Lavey, David S. Prohofsky, (Chicago).

Barry Skidelsky, Esq., 185 E. 85th St., 23 D, New York, NY 10028. Phone: (212) 832-4800. Barry Skidelsky (New York & Washington DC).

Smith & Metalitz LLP, 1747 Pennsylvania Ave. N.W., Suite 825, Washington, DC 20006. Phone: (202) 833-4198. Fax: (202) 872-0546. E-mail: info@smimetlaw.com. Web Site: www.smimetlaw.com.

Reed Smith LLP, 3110 Fairview Park Dr., Suite 1400, Falls Church, VA 22042-4503. Phone: (703) 641-4200. Fax: (703) 641-4340. E-mail: reedsmith@reedsmith.com. Web Site: www.reedsmith.com.

Smithwick & Belendiuk, P.C., Suite 301, 5028 Wisconsin Ave. N.W., Washington, DC 20016. Phone: (202) 363-4050. Fax: (202) 363-4266. Gary S, Smithwick, Arthur V. Belendiuk, William M. Bernard.

Sodos & Kafkas, 16985 Bluemount Rd., Suite 202, Brookfield, WI 53005. Phone: (414) 785-5500. Fax: (414) 785-1100. E-mail: office@sodos.com.

Solomon, Elise, Lifetime Television. Lifetime Television, 309 W. 49th St., New York, NY 10019. Phone: (212) 424-7112. Fax: (212) 957-4447. E-mail: solomon@lifetimetv.com. Web Site: www.lifetimetv.com. Elise Soloman.

Sommers, Schwartz, Silver & Schwartz, P.C., 2000 Town Ctr., Suite 900, Southfield, MI 48075. Phone: (248) 355-0300. Fax: (248) 746-4001. Patrick B. McCauley.

Sonneman & Sonneman, P.A., 111 Riverfront, Suite 202, Winona, MN 55987. Phone: (507) 454-8885. Fax: (507) 454-8887. E-mail: sonneman@luminet.net. Karl W. Sonneman, VP.

Sonnenschein, Nath & Rosenthal LLP, 8000 Sears Tower, 233 S. Wacker Dr., Chicago, IL 60606. Phone: (312) 876-3114. Fax: (312) 876-7934. E-mail: sfifer@sonnenschein.com. Web Site: www.sonnenschein.com. David W. Maher, Samuel Fifer.

Southmayd & Miller, 1220 19th St. N.W., Suite 400, Washington, DC 20036. Phone: (202) 331-4100. Fax: (202) 331-4123. E-mail: jdsouthmayd@msn.com. Jeffrey D. Southmayd, Michael R. Miller.

Spawn, Coy U., 1815 Bering Dr., Houston, TX 77057-3109. Phone: (713) 782-2977. Fax: (713) 782-2977.

Spiegel & McDiarmid, 1333 New Hampshire Ave. N.W., Washington, DC 20036. Phone: (202) 879-4000. Fax: (202) 393-2866. E-mail: jim.horwood@spiegelmcd.com. Web Site: www.spiegelmcd.com.

Springman, Braden, Wilson & Pontius, P.C., 1022 Bannock St., Denver, CO 80204. Phone: (303) 685-4897/685-4633. Fax: (303) 685-4627. E-mail: sbwp@indra.com.

Squire, Sanders & Dempsey, Box 407, 1201 Pennsylvania Ave. N.W., Washington, DC 20044-0407. Phone: (202) 626-6600. Fax: (202) 626-6780. Web Site: www.ssd.com. Thomas J. Ramsey, Herbert E. Marks, Joseph P. Markoski, Jonathan J. Nadler.

Cleveland, OH 44114-1304, 4900 Key Tower, 127 Public Sq. Phone: (216) 479-8500. Fax: (216) 479-8780. Terrence J. Clark, ptnr.

Stennett, Wilkinson & Peden, Box 13308, Jackson, MS 39236-3308. Phone: (601) 982-3330. Fax: (601) 982-3331. E-mail: swplaw@attorney.net. Web Site: www.swplaw.com. Gene Wilkinson.

Stephens Media Group, P.O. Box 70, Las Vegas, NV 89125. Phone: (702) 477-3830. Fax: (702) 383-0230. Web Site: www.stephensmedia.com.

Steptoe & Johnson, 1330 Connecticut Ave. N.W., Washington, DC 20036. Phone: (202) 429-3000. Fax: (202) 429-3902. E-mail: amamlet@steptoe.com. Web Site: www.steptoe.com.

Stevens, Sally L., Box 41, Lumberville, PA 18933. Phone: (215) 297-8245. Fax: (215) 297-5106.

Stewart & Irwin P.C., 251 E. Ohio St., Suite 1100, Indianapolis, IN 46204. Phone: (317) 639-5454. Fax: (317) 632-1319. Web Site: www.stewart-irwin.com. Richard E. Aikman.

Stewart, Estes & Donnell, 424 Church St. Suntrust Ctr., Suite 1401, Nashville, TN 37219. Phone: (615) 244-6538. Fax: (615) 256-8386. Web Site: www.sedlaw.com. Stephen Heard.

Law Offices of Richard Augustin Storm III, P.C., 1037 22nd St. S, Suite 210, Birmingham, AL 35205. Phone: (205) 252-5725. Fax: (205) 252-0010. E-mail: stormlaw@bellsouth.net. R.A.Storm III.

Strichartz, James L., 201 Queenanne Ave. North, Ste 400, Seattle, WA 98109. Phone: (206) 282-8020. Fax: (206) 286-2050.

Stroock, Stroock & Lavin, 180 Maiden Lane, New York, NY 10038-4982. Phone: (212) 806-5400. Fax: (212) 806-6006. Web Site: www.stroock.com.

Stryker, Tams & Dill LLP, 2 Penn Plaza E., Newark, NJ 07105-2293. Phone: (973) 491-9500. Fax: (973) 491-9692. E-mail: dlinken@strykertams.com. Web Site: www.stryker.com. Dennis C. Linken, Richard P. De Angelis Jr.

Suffness, Michael, 2325 Coit Rd., Suite B, Plano, TX 75075. Phone: (972) 985-1331. Fax: (972) 985-1315.

Swindler Berlin Shereff Friedman, LLP, 3000 K St. N.W., Suite 300, Washington, DC 20007. Phone: (202) 424-7833. Fax: (202) 424-7645. Andy Lipman, Jean Kiddoo, Russell Blau, Helen Disenhaus, Catherine Wang, Richard Rindler, Kathy Cooper, William Wilhelm, Nancy Spooner, Paul Gagnier, Tamar Finn, Priscilla Whitehead, Eric Branfman, Jeff Karp.

Taylor, Jack, 1289 Lincoln Rd., Yuba City, CA 95991. Phone: (530) 671-6800. Fax: (530) 671-6447.

Leslie Taylor Associates, 6800 Carlynn Ct., Bethesda, MD 20817-4302. Phone: (301) 229-9410. Fax: (301) 229-3148. E-mail: ltaylor@lta.com. Web Site: www.lta.com. Leslie Taylor.

Taylor, Ray L., 11608 Chayote St., Los Angeles, CA 90049. Phone: (310) 476-6493. Fax: (310) 471-2763.

Technology Law Group L.L.C., 5335 Wisconsin Ave. N.W., Suite 440, Washington, DC 20015. Phone: (202) 895-1707. Fax: (202) 244-8257.

Teitelbaum, Israel, 11301 Amherst Ave., Suite 202, Silver Spring, MD 20902. Phone: (301) 933-3373. Fax: (301) 933-3651. Israel Teitelbaum.

Thelen Reid & Priest LLP, Washington, D.C. 701 Pennsylvania Ave. N.W., Suite 800, Washington, DC 20004. Phone: (202) 508-4000. Fax: (202) 508-4321. Web Site: www.thelenreid.com.

San Francisco, CA 94105, 101 2nd St, Suite 1800. Phone: (415) 371-1200. Fax: (415) 371-1211.

Thiemann, Aitken & Vohra, 908 King St., Suite 300, Alexandria, VA 22314. Phone: (703) 836-9400. Fax: (703) 836-9410. E-mail: rlt4fcc@erols.com. Russell C. Powell, Robert Lewis Thompson.

Thomas, Ballenger, Vogelman & Turner, 124 S. Royal St., Alexandria, VA 22314. Phone: (703) 836-3400. Fax: (703) 836-3549. John M. Ballenger.

Thompson Hine LLP, 1920 N St. N.W., Suite 800, Washington, DC 20036. Phone: (202) 331-8800. Fax: (202) 331-8330. E-mail: barry.friedman@thompsonhine.com. Web Site: www.thompsonhine.com. Barry A. Friedman, Stephen T. Lovelady, John C. Butcher.

Columbus, OH 43215, 10 W. Broad St, Suite 700. Phone: (614) 469-3200. Fax: (614) 469-3361. E-mail: tom.lodge@thompsonhine.com. Web Site: www.thompsonhine.com. Thomas E. Lodge.

Thrasher, Dinsmore & Dolan, 100 7th Ave., Suite 150, Chardon, OH 44024-1079. Phone: (440) 285-2242. Fax: (440) 285-9423. Matthew Dolan.

Troutman Sanders L.L.P., 600 Peachtree St., Suite 5200, Atlanta, GA 30308. Phone: (404) 885-3000. Fax: (404) 885-3900. Web Site: www.troutmansanders.com. Robert W. Webb, Richard H. Brody, Alan E. Serby.

Law Firms

Troy & Gould, 1801 Century Park E.,, 16th Fl., Los Angeles, CA 90067. Phone: (310) 553-4441. Fax: (310) 201-4746. Web Site: www.troygould.com.

Trugman, Richard S., 9200 Sunset Blvd., Suite 808, Los Angeles, CA 90069. Phone: (310) 273-8834. Fax: (310) 273-8345. E-mail: trulaw@sbcglobal.net.

Edmund W. Turnley III, 30 Music Square W., Suite 302, Nashville, TN 37203. Phone: (615) 321-8600. Fax: (615) 321-8602. Edmund W. Turnley.

Turtle, Joel S., 55 Santa Clara Ave., Suite 120, Oakland, CA 94610. Phone: (510) 763-7600. Fax: (510) 763-7894. E-mail: joelturtle@yahoo.com. Web Site: www.riotmedia.com.

Umansky, Barry D., Irwin, Campbell & Tannerwald, 1730 Rhode Island Ave. N.W., Suite 200, Washington, DC 20036-3101. Phone: (202) 728-0400. Fax: (202) 728-0354. Web Site: www.ictpc.com.

Van Cott, Bagley, Cornwall & McCarthy, 50 S. Main St.,, Suite 1600, Salt Lake City, UT 84144-0103. Phone: (801) 532-3333. Fax: (801) 534-0058. E-mail: info@vancott.com. Web Site: www.vancott.com. Robert M. Anderson, Jennifer K. Anderson.

A. Chavis Vanias, Attorney at Law, P.O. Box 9612, Columbia, SC 29209. Phone: (803) 783-8320. Fax: (803) 695-0707.

Varnum, Riddering, Schmidt & Howlett L.L.P., Box 352, Bridgewater Pl., Grand Rapids, MI 49501-0352. Phone: (616) 336-6000. Fax: (616) 336-7000. Web Site: www.varnumlaw.com. John W. Pestle.

Venable LLP, 1800 Mercantile Bank Bldg., 2 Hopkins Plaza, Baltimore, MD 21201. Phone: (410) 244-7400. Fax: (410) 244-7742.

Washington, DC 20005, 1201 New York Ave. N.W, Suite 1000. Phone: (202) 962-4800. (202) 962-8300.

Vorys, Sater, Seymour and Pease LLP, Box 1008, 52 E. Gay St., Columbus, OH 43216-1008. Phone: (614) 464-6400. Fax: (614) 464-6350. E-mail: jhgross@vssp.com. Web Site: www.vssp.com. Sheldon A. Taft, M. Howard Petricoff, Stephen M. Howard, James H. Gross, William D. Kloss, C. William O'Neill, William S. Newcomb Jr., Benita A. Kahn, Robert N. Webner.

Washington, DC 20036-5109, 1828 L St. N.W, Suite 1111. Phone: (202) 467-8800. Fax: (202) 467-8900. Mark J. Palchick, Robert E. Levine.

WGBH Educational Foundation, 125 Western Ave., Boston, MA 02134-1098. Phone: (617) 300-2000. Fax: (617) 300-1014. Web Site: www.wgbh.org. Eric A. Brass.

WTTW Channel 11/Chicago, 5400 N. St. Louis Ave., Chicago, IL 60625. Phone: (773) 583-5000. Fax: (773) 583-3046. Web Site: www.wttw.com. Jerry Glover.

Wagner, Michael Francis, Mass Media Bureau, 445 12th St. S.W., Rm. 2-A523, Washington, DC 20554. Phone: (202) 418-2700. Fax: (202) 418-1410. Web Site: www.fcc.gov/mb/audio.

Waller Lansden Dortch & Davis, PLLC, 511 Union St., Suite 2700, Nashville, TN 37219. Phone: (615) 244-6380. Fax: (615) 244-6804. Web Site: www.wallerlaw.com. Robb S. Harvey.

Jon M. Waxman Associates, 302 W. 12th St., New York, NY 10014. Phone: (212) 929-2562. Fax: (212) 229-1625.

Law Offices of Edward L. Weidenfeld, 1828 L St. N.W., Suite 500, Washington, DC 20036. Phone: (202) 785-2143. Fax: (202) 452-8938.

Weil, Gotshal & Manges, L.L.P., 1501 K St. N.W., Suite 100, Washington, DC 20036. Phone: (202) 682-7000. Fax: (202) 857-0940. Bruce H. Turnbull, ptnr.

Law Offices of Joel Weisman, P.C., 1901 Raymond Dr., Suite 6, Northbrook, IL 60062. Phone: (847) 400-5900. Fax: (847) 400-5534. Web Site: weismanmedia.com. Joel Weisman, David Rosenberg, Keith M. Kanter, Scott A. Weisman.

Weissmann, Wolff, Bergman, Coleman, Grodin & Evall, 9665 Wilshire Blvd., Suite 900, Beverly Hills, CA 90212-2345. Phone: (310) 858-7888. Fax: (310) 550-7191. E-mail: wwbcsh@wwllp.com. Eric Weissman.

Westervelt, Johnson, Nicholl & Keller, LLC, Associated Bank Bldg., 411 Hamilton Blvd., 14th Fl., Peoria, IL 61602. Phone: (309) 671-3550. Fax: (309) 671-3588. E-mail: westervelt@westerveltlaw.com.

Wheeler Wolf Law Firm, Box 2056, 220 N. 4th. St., Bismarck, ND 58502-2056. Phone: (701) 223-5300. Fax: (701) 223-5366. E-mail: jackmcdonald@wheelerwolf.com. Jack McDonald.

John P. Whitesell, Box 308, Iowa Falls, IA 50126. Phone: (641) 648-3160. Fax: (641) 648-3283.

Joan Wilbon & Associates, 1120 Conneticut Ave. N.W., Suite 1020, Washington, DC 20036. Phone: (202) 737-7458. Fax: (202) 347-5845.

Wildman, Harrold, Allen & Dixon, 225 W. Wacker Dr., Suite 3000, Chicago, IL 60606. Phone: (312) 201-2000. Fax: (312) 201-2555. Web Site: www.wildmanharrold.com.

Wiley, Rein & Fielding, 1776 K St. N.W., Washington, DC 20006. Phone: (202) 719-7000. Fax: (202) 719/7049/719-7207. E-mail: wr&fmarketing@wrf.com. Web Site: www.wrf.com.

Wilkinson Barker Knauer, L.L.P., 2300 N St. N.W., Suite 700, Washington, DC 20037. Phone: (202) 783-4141. Fax: (202) 783-5851.Leon T. Knauer, L. Andrew Tollin, Michael D. Sullivan, Kenneth E. Satten, F. Thomas Moran, Kenneth D. Patrich, Kathryn A. Zachem, Lawrence J. Movshin, Robert Kirk, Carolyn Groves, Paul J. Sinderbrand, William J. Sill, Robert D. Primosch, J. Wade Lindsay, Timothy J. Cooney, Jonathan V. Cohen, Jeffrey S. Cohen, Craig E. Gilmore, Linda M. Wellstein, Barry P. Miller, L. Charles Keller, Stephen L. Goodman, Adam D. Krinsky, Mary N. O'Connor, Georgina L. O. Feigen, David K. Judelsohn, Lynn H. Johanson, Paige N. Fronabarger, Robert G. Morse, Brian W. Higgins, Catherine C. Butcher, Kevin M. Jordan, William R. Layton, Anne H. Sullivan, Kathryn P. Wildrick, Christopher D. Ornelas, Elizabeth R. Braman, Lee J. Rosen, Rebecca A. Schillings.

Willcox & Savage, P.C., One Commercial Place, Suite 1800, Norfolk, VA 23510. Phone: (757) 628-5500. Fax: (757) 628-5566. Web Site: www.willsav.com.

Virginia Beach, VA 23466-1888, Box 61888, One Columbus Ctr, Suite 1010. Fax: (757) 628-5659. Jeffrey H. Gray.

William Morris Agency, 151 El Camino Dr., Beverly Hills, CA 90212-2704. Phone: (310) 274-7451. Fax: (310) 859-4176.

Willkie Farr & Gallagher, 1875 K St. N.W., Washington, DC 20006. Phone: (202) 303-1000. Fax: (202) 303-2000. Web Site: www.willkie.com. Sue D. Blumenfeld, John L. McGrew, Philip Verveer, Theodore Whitehouse, Brian Conboy, Michael Hammer, Frank Buono, Demetrios Eleftheriou, Michael Jones, Thomas Jones, David Don, Gunnar Halley, Angie Kronenberg, Stephen Bell, Pamela Strauss, Ryan Wallach, Sophie Keefer, Jennifer Desmond McCarthy, Jonathan Friedman, Kasey Chappelle, Jeneba Ghatt, Robert Millar, Stephanie Podey, Jennifer Ashworth, James L. Casserly, McLean Sieverding, Patrick Sullivan.

Wilmer, Cutler, Pickering, Hale and Dorr LLP, 2445 M St. N.W., Washington, DC 20037-1420. Phone: (202) 663-6000. Fax: (202) 663-6363. E-mail: william.richardson@wilmerhale.com.Bradford Berry, Beckwith Burr, Patrick Carome, Lynn Charytan, Jonathan Frankel, John Hardwood, Samir Jain, William Lake, Eric Mahr, David Medine, Jonathan Nuechterlein, Thomas Olson, William Richardson, John Rogovin, Catherine Ronis, John Flynn, Jack Goodman, Janis Kestenbaum, David Mendel, Josh Roland, Amit Agarwal, Will DeVries, Michael Grynberg, Meredith Halama, Anne Harden, Aaron Hurowitz, Marina Mazor, Daniel McCuaig, Nathan Mitchler, Brian Murray, Stephen Obenski, Jonathan Siegelbaum, Catherine Sircy, Polly Smothergill, Alison Southall, Robert Strayer, Kenny Wright, Heather Zachary, Daniel Zibel.

Winkler, Bevacqua & Simmons, P.C., 60 Park Pl.,, 19th Fl., Newark, NJ 07102. Phone: (973) 676-1200. Fax: (973) 624-5980. Maury R. Winkler.

Winston & Strawn, 35 W. Wacker Dr., Chicago, IL 60601-9703. Phone: (312) 558-5600. Fax: (312) 558-5700. Web Site: www.winston.com.

Washington, DC 20005, 1400 L St. N.W, 8th Fl. Phone: (202) 371-5700. Fax: (202) 371-5950. Deborah C. Costlow.

Wolf & Wolf, P.C., 9000 Sunset Blvd., Suite 1005, Los Angeles, CA 90069-5810. Phone: (310) 278-6060. Fax: (310) 278-6064. E-mail: wolf90210@msn.com. David M. Wolf, Joseph Wolf.

Wolf, Block, Schorr, & Solis-Cohen, 250 Park Ave., New York, NY 10177-0030. Phone: (212) 986-1116. Fax: (212) 986-0604. Web Site: www.wolfblock.com. Stuart A. Shorenstein, David E. Bronston.

Womble, Carlyle, Sandridge & Rice, PLLC, 1401 I St. N.W., 7th Fl., Washington, DC 20005. Phone: (202) 467-6900. Fax: (202) 467-6910. Web Site: www.wcsr.com. Howard J. Barr, Patricia M. Chuh, John F. Garziglia, Peter Gutmann, Vicent A. Pepper, Gregg P Skall, Joan D. Stewart, Mark Blackwell.

Wood, Maines & Brown, Chartered, 1827 Jefferson Pl. N.W., Washington, DC 20036. Phone: (202) 293-5333. Fax: (202) 293-9811. E-mail: wmb@legalcompass.com. Web Site: legalcompass.com. Barry B. Wood, Paul H. Brown, Ronald B. Maines, Stuart W. Nolan.

Wright & Talisman, P.C., 1200 G St. N.W., Suite 600, Washington, DC 20005. Phone: (202) 393-1200. Fax: (202) 393-1240. Web Site: www.wright.com.

Young, Clement, & Rivers, 28 Broad St., Charleston, SC 29401. Phone: (843) 577-4000. Fax: (843) 724-6600. E-mail: ycrt@ycrt.com. Web Site: www.ycrt.com. Thomas S. Tisdale.

Zuckman, Harvey L./Professor at Law School, Cardinal Station, Columbus School of Law/Catholic Univ. America, Washington, DC 20064. Phone: (202) 319-5140. Fax: (202) 319-4459. E-mail: zuckman@law.edu.

Talent Agents and Managers

Abrams Artists Agency, 9200 Sunset Blvd., 11th Fl., Los Angeles, CA 90069. Phone: (310) 859-0625. Fax: (310) 276-6193. E-mail: harry.abrams@abramsart.com. Harry Abrams, pres.
New York, NY 10001. Abrams Artists Agency, 275 7th Ave. Phone: (646) 486-4600. Fax:. (646) 486-0100. Neal Altman, sr VP.
Performing artists reps-talent agency.

Abrams-Rubaloff & Lawrence, Inc., 8075 W. Third St., Suite 303, Los Angeles, CA 90048. Phone: (323) 935-1700. Fax: (323) 932-9901. E-mail: rlawre8075@aol.com. Web Site: www.arltalent.com. Richard Lawrence, pres; Debra Goldfarb, VP.
Talent placement & TV show packaging.

N S Bienstock Inc., 1740 Broadway, 24th Fl., New York, NY 10019. Phone: (212) 765-3040. Fax: (212) 757-6411. E-mail: nsb@nsbienstock.com. Web Site: www.nsbienstock.com. Richard A. Leibner, agent; Carole Cooper, agent; Stuart Witt, agent; Peter Goldberg, agent; Nancy Kay, agent; Adam Leibner, agent; George Hiltzik, agent; Steve Sadicrio, agent; Ezra Marcus, agent; Eric Wattenberg, agent; Robert Miller, agent; Myles Hazleton, agent.
News & syndication talent specialists—loc & net—on & off camera. Packager of talk & reality progmg—MOWs.

Eatman Media Services Inc. 5901 N. Cicero Ave., Suite 307, Chicago, IL 60646. Phone: (773) 777-5463. Fax: (773) 777-7106. E-mail: emstalent@aol.com. Robert Eatman, pres; Ross Eatman, sec.
Pacific Palisades, CA 90272, Box 853. Phone: (310) 459-3728. Robert Eatman, pres.
Bedford, NY 10506, Box 102. Phone: (914) 234-4748. Ross Eatman, Esq.
Representation of TV newspersons, TV personalities, & radio talent in job placement & contract negotiation.

Ephraim & Associates, P.C., 108 W. Grand Ave., Chicago, IL 60610-4206. Phone: (312) 321-9700. Fax: (312) 321-3655. E-mail: eliot@ephraim-associates.com. Donald M. Ephraim, pres; Joseph F. Coyne, VP; Eliot S. Ephraim, VP; David M. Ephraim, VP.
Talent representation, including contract negotiation, legal & career consulation, tax, estate & pension planning.

Ken Fishkin & Associates, 50 Milk St., 20th Fl., Boston, MA 02109-5002. Phone: (617) 423-5800. Fax: (617) 426-2674. E-mail: cjwatkfa@aol.com. Kenneth R. Fishkin, pres; Cindy Williams, dir pub affrs.
Contract negotiation & job placement, TV & radio.

Goldstein Management Group, Inc., 1601 N. Sepulveda Blvd. Suite 357, Manhattan Beach, CA 90266. Phone: (310) 545-8530. Fax: (310) 943-1569. E-mail: glenn802@aol.com. Glenn A. Goldstein, pres.
Full-svc representation of bcst talent & bcst journalists.

Reece Halsey Agency, 8733 Sunset Blvd., Suite 101, West Hollywood, CA 90069. Phone: (310) 652-2409. Fax: (310) 652-7595. Dorris Halsey, owner; Kimberly Cameron, assoc literary representation.
Tiburon, CA 99920. Reece Halsey Agency, P.O. Box 704., 98 Main St. Phone: (415) 789-9191. Kimberly Cameron.

Shirley Hamilton Inc., 333 E. Ontario, Chicago, IL 60611. Phone: (312) 787-4700. Fax: (312) 787-8456. Web Site: www.shirleyhamilton.com. Shirley Hamilton, pres; Lynne S. Hamilton, VP.
Representing talent for TV, PRINT, RADIO, ON CAMERA, FILM, LIVE, THEATRICAL, VOICEOVER, INDUSTRIALS. Audition facilities for OnCamera, Digital voiceover, Print.

International Creative Management Inc., 40 W. 57th St., 18th Fl., New York, NY 10019. Phone: (212) 556-5600. Fax: (212) 556-5665. Web Site: www.ICMtalent.com. Jeff Berg, pres/CEO; Sam Cohn, vice chmn.
London W1R 1RB, 76 Oxford St.-OAX. Phone: (011) 44-1-81-743-0558. Fax:. (011) 44-1-81-743-6598.
Beverly Hills, CA 90211, 8942 Wilshire Blvd. Phone: (310) 550-4000. Fax:. (310) 550-4100.

Jennifer Jones Booking Agency, 523 Dumaine, Suite 6, New Orleans, LA 70116. Phone: (504) 529-2543. E-mail: jenjones@yahoo.com.
Booking agency, promotion mgmt, PR, business mgmt, event planning.

Media Alliance, 6017 Pine Ridge Rd. #247, Naples, FL 34119-3956. Phone: (239) 352-3123. Fax: (239) 352-3134. E-mail: mediaalliance@cs.com. Web Site: www.mediaalliance.com. Bill LaPlante II, exec dir; Guy LaPlante, sr exec VP.; Lauren LaPlante, Director & Talent Dev.
Sober Island, Nova Scotia B0J 3B0 W.F. LaPlante II.
Talent mgmt, placement, mktg, presentation coaching & financial organization options. Providing "Good Jobs for Good People," in broadcasting & cable since being founded three decades ago by network news multiple Emmy-winners.

Miller Broadcast Management Inc., 616 W. Fulton St., Suite 516, Chicago, IL 60661. Phone: (312) 454-1111. Fax: (312) 454-0044. E-mail: info@millerbroadcast.com. Web Site: www.millerbroadcast.com. Lisa Miller, pres; Matt Miller, VP.
Representing radio & TV personalities.

William Morris Agency Inc., 1325 Ave. of the Americas, New York, NY 10019. Phone: (212) 586-5100. Fax: (212) 246-3583. Web Site: www.wma.com. Norman Brokaw, chmn; Jerry Katzman, vice-chmn; Lou Weiss, chmn emeritus; Walter Zifkin, CO-CEO; Jim Griffin, exec VP & head TV East Coast; Jim Wiatt, pres.
London W1V 5DG, 31/32 Soho Sq. Phone: (71) 434-2191. Steve Kenis, dir.
Beverly Hills, CA 90212, 151 El Camino Dr. Phone: (310) 859-4000. Fax:. (310) 859-4440. E-mail: bgoodman@wma.com. Brad Goodman.
Nashville, TN 37203, 2100 West End Ave. Phone: (615) 385-0310. Rick Shipp.

Navarro-Bertoni Casting Co., 875 Avenue of the Americas, Suite 1707, New York, NY 10001. Phone: (212) 736-9272. Fax: (212) 465-2064. Riccardo Bertoni, pres; Ester Navarro, VP.
Casting of principals & extras for films, comls, etc.

Paradigm, 10100 Santa Monica Blvd., Suite 2500, Los Angeles, CA 90067. Phone: (310) 277-4400. Fax: (310) 277-7820. E-mail: info@paradigm-agency.com. Sam Gores, pres; Debbee Klein, ptnr; Lucy Stille, ptnr.
New York, NY 10110, 500 5th Ave.., 37th Floor. Phone: (212) 703-7540. Fax:. (212) 764-8941.
Talent & Literary Agency.

Screen Children's Casting, 4000 Riverside Dr., Suite A, Burbank, CA 91505. Phone: (818) 846-4300. Fax: (818) 846-3745. Irene B. Gallagher, casting dir & owner.
Full-svc children's casting representing babies (especially twins), children & teenagers up to age 18, extra work.

Burt Shapiro Management, 2147 N. Beachwood Dr., Los Angeles, CA 90068. Phone: (323) 469-9452. Fax: (603) 710-8019. E-mail: burtjay@mail.com. Web Site: www.burtshaprio.com. Burt Shapiro, pres.
Represents on-air talent including anchors, reporters, hosts, & sports anchor/reporters, as well as producers and news directors.

Barry Skidelsky, Esq., 185 East 85th St., 23D, New York, NY 10028. Phone: (212) 832-4800. Barry Skidelsky, Esq., pres.
Personal management & representation. Contract negotiations, counsel, etc.

The Voicecaster, 1832 W. Burbank Blvd., Burbank, CA 91506. Phone: (818) 841-5300. Fax: (818) 841-2085. E-mail: casting@voicecaster.com. Web Site: www.voicecaster.com. Huck Liggett, owner.
Voice casting for comls, films, animation, theme parks, audiovisual projects, etc.

Voiceline.com Voiceover Talent, Box 742, Olney, MD 20830. Phone: (301) 924-4327. Fax: (301) 570-8916. E-mail: mweiner@voiceline.com. Web Site: www.voiceline.com. Michael J. Weiner, pres/CEO.
Voice over talent, audition service, online demos of pro voices.

Weisman Media, Joel Weisman, P.C., 1901 Raymond Dr., North Brook, IL 60062. Phone: (847) 400-5900. Fax: (847) 400-5534. E-mail: joel@weismanmedia.com. Web Site: www.weismanmedia.com. Joel Weisman, pres; David Rosenberg, attorney/agent.
Bcst contract drafting & negotiation; career & performance counseling; job search & market placement for on-air producers.

TALENT REPRESENTATION

EATMAN MEDIA SERVICES INC.

Specializing in job placement and contract negotiations for television news, sports, and weather talent and program hosts. Serving all markets, with offices in Los Angeles, Chicago, and New York.

For further information, contact: **Ross Eatman, Esq. (914.234.4748)** (e-mail: EMSTALENT@aol.com) or **Robert Eatman, Esq. (310.459.3728).**

Employment and Executive Search Services

Bishop Partners, 708 Third Ave., Suite 2200, New York, NY 10017. Phone: (212) 986-3419. Fax: (212) 986-3350. E-mail: info@bishoppartners.com. Web Site: www.bishoppartners.com. Susan Bishop, pres/CEO.

A retained exec search firm specializing in cable, bcst, telecommunications, wireless, entertainment, publishing & multimedia.

California Broadcasters Association, 915 L St., Sacramento, CA 95814. Phone: (916) 444-2237. Fax: (916) 444-2043. E-mail: cbaberry@aol.com. Web Site: www.cabroadcasters.org. Stan Statham, pres; Lillie Player, exec asst; Mark Powers, dir govt affrs; Joe Berry, dir special projects.

Lobbyist for coml radio & TV for the state of California & other legal issues.

Eatman Media Services Inc., 5901 N. Cicero Ave., Suite 307, Chicago, IL 60646. Phone: (773) 777-5463. Fax: (773) 777-7106. E-mail: emstalent@aol.com. Robert Eatman, pres; Ross Eatman, sec.

Pacific Palisades, CA 90272, Box 853. Phone: (310) 459-3728. Robert Eatman, pres.

Bedford, NY 10506, Box 102. Phone: (914) 234-4748. Ross Eatman, Esq.

Representation of TV newspersons, TV personalities, & radio talent in job placement & contract negotiation.

Entertainment Employment Journal (T.M.), 5632 Van Nuys Blvd., Suite 320, Van Nuys, CA 91401. Phone: (800) 335-4335. E-mail: sales@eej.com. Web Site: www.eej.com.

Bimonthly magazine providing career information & job listings with major & independent motion picture, TV & cable companies.

The Howard-Sloan-Koller Group, 300 E. 42nd St., New York, NY 10017. Phone: (212) 661-5250. Fax: (212) 490-5322. E-mail: ekoller@hsksearch.com. Web Site: www.hsksearch.com. Edward T. Koller Jr., pres; Karen Danziger, exec VP.

Exec search & consulting in the cable, digital, entertainment & publishing industries.

JOBPHONE, Box 5048, Newport Beach, CA 92662. Phone: (949) 721-9280. Fax: (949) 721-8478. E-mail: jobphone@aol.com. Web Site: www.infoguru.com. Keith Mueller, gen mgr.

Natl TV/radio employment hotline. To hear job openings nationwide: (900) 726-5627 (JOBS), $1.99 per minute.

Keystone America (Div Keystone Int'l, Inc.), 298 Yates St., Suite 3, Pittston, PA 18640. Phone: (570) 655-7143. Fax: (570) 654-5765. E-mail: usmail@keystoneamerica.com. Web Site: keystoneamerica.com. Alan Kornish, VP opns.

National Employment Service for Broadcast employers and candidates. Serving all USA states.

Keystone International Inc., Dime Bank Bldg., 49 S. Main St., Pittston, PA 18640. Phone: (570) 655-7143. Fax: (570) 654-5765. E-mail: mail@keystoneint.com. Web Site: www.keystoneint.com. Alan X. Cornish, gen mgr; Mark Kelly, opns VP.

Employment search svcs, placement of engrs with TV, teleproduction, satellite, video & mfg.

Korn/Ferry International, 1800 Century Park E., Suite 900, Los Angeles, CA 90067. Phone: (310) 552-1834. Fax: (310) 553-6452. Web Site: www.kornferry.com. William D. Simon, mgng dir entertainment; Roysi Erbes, sr assoc.

Hong Kong, The Landmark, Central, 2104-2106 Gloucester Tower. Phone: (852) 2521-5457. Lynn Ogden, mgng dir.

London WIR 5DA, Regent Arcade House, 252 Regent St. Phone: 44-171-312-3100. Tim Vigholes, mgng dir; Ben Ward, sr assoc.

New York, NY 10016, 200 Park Ave. Phone: (212) 687-1834. Michelle James, partner/VP; James Celentano, sr assoc entertainment.

Worldwide sr level mgmt exec search firm servicing all sectors of the entertainment industry.

Lipson & Co., 1900 Ave. of the Stars,, Suite 2810, Los Angeles, CA 90067. Phone: (310) 277-4646. Fax: (310) 277-8585. E-mail: inquiries@lipsonco.com. Web Site: www.lipsonco.com. Howard R. Lipson, pres; Harriet L. Lipson, exec VP.

Specialists in international & domestic bcstg (TV & radio), cable & entertainment, & related financial, professional audio/video & electronic recruiting. Svcs also for TV & film production, merchandising, licensing, & computers.

Management Recruiters Rocky Mount S.W., Box 4139, Rocky Mount, NC 27803-0139. Phone: (252) 442-8000. Fax: (252) 442-9000. E-mail: bob@mrigreatjobs.com. Bob Manning, owner.

Nationwide exec search for mgmt, sls mgmt, financial & mktg positions.

Brad Marks International, 15233 Ventura Blvd.,, PH 16, Sherman Oaks, CA 91403. Phone: (818) 382-6300. Fax: (818) 386-0050. E-mail: bodysnatcher@bradmarks.com. Web Site: www.bradmarks.com. Brad Marks, chmn/CEO.

Exec search at sr mgmt levels for communications, bcst, cable & multimedia companies. Areas include TV & film production, progmg, sls, mktg, news, gen mgmt, financial svcs, postproduction & adv/promotion.

Maslow Media Group Inc., 2134 Wisconsin Ave. N.W., Washington, DC 20007. Phone: (202) 965-1100. Fax: (202) 965-6171. E-mail: lmaslow@maslowmedia.com. Web Site: www.maslowmedia.com. Linda Maslow, CEO.

Freelance & fulltime staffing, crewing & payroll svcs for bcst, corporate, & federal govt. Find a job @ www.tvgigsonline.com

Media Management Resources Inc., 6890 S. Tuscon Way, Englewood, CO 80112. Phone: (303) 290-9800. Fax: (303) 290-9596. E-mail: bwein@mediamanagement.com. Michael S. Wein, pres; Bill Wein, VP.

Gulf Breeze, FL 32561. Media Management Resources Inc., 31-B Gulf Breeze Pkwy. Phone: (850) 934-4880. Fax: (850) 934-4756.

Full-svc consulting practice providing business support & technology svcs to select media & technology companies.

Media Staffing Network, 150 E. Huron,, Suite 1305, Chicago, IL 60611. Phone: (312) 944-9194. Fax: (312) 944-9195. E-mail: tracey@mediastaffingnetwork.com. Web Site: www.mediastaffingnetwork.com. Tracey Norton, mktg VP.

Media Staffing Network the only full-service staffing company that specializes in media adv sls & associated departments, offering both temporary & full-time positions nationwide. Clients include radio & TV stns, rep firms, Internet, cable systems, networks, syndication, magazines & adv agencies. Openings range from entry-level support to sr mgmt positions in sls, prom, buying, planning, traf, continuity, customer service & rsch.

MediaLine, Box 51909, 542 Lighthouse Ave, Pacific Grove, CA 93950. Phone: (800) 237-8073. Fax: (831) 648-5204. E-mail: medialine@medialine.com. Web Site: www.medialine.com. Adrienne Laurent, pres.

Job listings for TV news, production & promotions; streaming video of resume tapes on the Internet; daily eletronic newsletter.

Miller Broadcast Management Inc., 616 W. Fulton St., Suite 516, Chicago, IL 60661. Phone: (312) 454-1111. Fax: (312) 454-0044. E-mail: info@millerbroadcast.com. Lisa Miller, pres; Matt Miller, VP.

Representing radio personalities.

Promotion Recruiters Inc., 16 Drake Rd., Scarsdale, NY 10583. Phone: (914) 723-2657. Howard Burkat, pres.

Search for stn, net & cable promotion, mktg execs & producers exclusively.

RTNDA Job Services, 1600 K St. N.W., Suite 700, Washington, DC 20006. Phone: (202) 659-6510. Fax: (202) 223-4007. E-mail: rtnda@rtnda.org. Web Site: www.rtnda.org. Barbara Cochran, pres; Bob Priddy, chmn.

Job bulletin.

Screen Children's Casting, 4000 Riverside Dr., Suite A, Burbank, CA 91505. Phone: (818) 846-4300. Fax: (818) 846-3745. Irene B. Gallagher, talent agent/owner.

Full-svc children's agency, representing babies (twins) to age 18.

Search Source Inc., 2945 Madison Ave., Granite City, IL 62040. Phone: (618) 876-6060. Fax: (618) 876-6071. E-mail: search@norcom2000.com. James R. McKechan, pres.

Search & recruitment of bcst professionals.

Search West Inc., 2049 Century Park E., Suite 650, Los Angeles, CA 90067. Phone: (310) 284-8888. Fax: (310) 284-3409. E-mail: mgsi@earthlink.net. Web Site: www.searchwest.com. Don Dreifus, VP.

Exec search firm providing svcs to the upper-middle mgmt & tech community.

Barry Skidelsky, Esq., 185 E. 85th St., 23 D, New York, NY 10028. Phone: (212) 832-4800. Barry Skidelsky, atty/consultant.

Personal management & representation. Contract negotiations, counsel, etc.

Stone & Youngblood/Target Search, 304 Newbury St., Boston, MA 02115. Phone: (781) 647-0070. Fax: (781) 647-0460. Stephen Sarkis, pres.

R.A. Stone & Associates, 5495 Beltline Rd.,, Suite 325, Dallas, TX 75254. Phone: (972) 233-0483. Fax: (972) 991-4995. E-mail: stonesearch@aol.com. Robert Stone, pres.

Retainer based exec search svcs for the domestic & international TV, radio, cable, multimedia, production & related communications/entertainment industries.

Joe Sullivan Executive Search & Recruiting, Box 178,, 1202 Lexington Ave., New York, NY 10028. Phone: (212) 734-7890. Fax: (212) 734-0631. E-mail: jsa6@aol.com. Web Site: www.joesullivanexecutivesearch.com. Joseph J. Sullivan Jr., pres; Shane P. Sullivan, VP; Barbara Sullivan, CFO; Jana Heffernan, rsch dir.

Retain exec recruitment in media & academia for positions in middle & sr mgmt with incomes in excess of $120,000 per year.

Ron Sunshine Associates, 10021 Dryden Ln., Plano, TX 75025. Phone: (972) 618-3670. Fax: (972) 599-9583. E-mail: Ron@Ronsunshineassociates.com. Ron Sunshine, pres; Barbara Blake, VP.

Radio, TV & cable middle & upper mgmt.

Warren & Morris Ltd., 2190 Carmel Valley Rd., Del Mar, CA 92014. Phone: (858) 481-3388. Fax: (858) 481-6221. E-mail: info@wmmltd.com. Web Site: www.warrenmorrisltd.com. Charles C. Morris, chmn; Scott C. Warren, pres.

Portsmouth, NH 03801, 132 Chapel St. Phone: (603) 431-7929. Fax: (603) 431-3460.

Natl & international exec/mgmt-level recruitment svcs in the cable TV, wireless communications, competitive telephone & multimedia industries.

Steve Wyman & Associates Inc., 4201 Fairgreen Terr., Marietta, GA 30068. Phone: (770) 977-4410. Fax: (770) 578-0883. Steve Wyman, pres.

Exec search for bcst industry.

Youngs, Walker & Co., 1605 Colonial Pkwy., Inverness, IL 60067. Phone: (847) 991-6900. Fax: (847) 934-6607. E-mail: info@youngswalker.com. Web Site: www.youngswalker.com. Carl Youngs, pres; Mike Walker, VP; Robert Epperly, consultant.

Exec recruitment on a retained basis for TV & radio stn mgmt levels & corporate positions.

Professional Cards
Engineering & Technical Consultants

MARY C. LOWE

JOHN P. ALLEN AIRSPACE CONSULTANTS, INC.
290 MARSH LAKES DRIVE, FERNANDINA BEACH, FL 32034
Ph: (904) 261-6523 Fax: (904) 277-3651
maryjpa@bellsouth.net

John F.X. Browne & Associates
A Professional Corporation
Member AFCCE
BROADCAST/TELECOMMUNICATIONS
Bloomfield Hills, MI   Washington, DC
248.642.6226   (TEL)   202.293.2020
248.642.6027   (FAX)   202.293.2021
www.jfxb.com

Broadcast and Communications Consulting Engineers
7839 Ashton Avenue
Manassas, VA 20109
703-392-9090
www.CMDconsulting.com
www.FCCinfo.com
Member AFCCE

Communications Technologies, Inc.
Radio Frequency / Broadcast
Engineering Consultants
P.O. Box 1130 ⊁ Marlton, NJ 08053
Tel: 856/985-0077
Fax: 856/985-8124
web: commtechrf.com

Clarence M. Beverage
Laura M. Mizrahi

301-686-1800 tel
301-686-1820 fax
www.denny.com
Denny & Associates, P.C.
Consulting Engineers
Member AFCCE

---

du Treil, Lundin & Rackley, Inc.
CONSULTING ENGINEERS

201 Fletcher Avenue
Sarasota, Florida 34237
(941) 329-6000
www.DLR.com
Member AFCCE

 **EVANS** Consulting Communications Engineers
FOR ALL YOUR BROADCAST NEEDS
♦ Field Services/New Construction
♦ FCC Applications
♦ Upgrade Studies & Technical Negotiations
210 S. Main St., Thiensville, WI 53092
(262) 242-6000; FAX (262) 242-6045
http://www.evansassoc.com

HAMMETT & EDISON, INC.
CONSULTING ENGINEERS
Box 280068
San Francisco, California 94128
H&E   707/996-5200
         202/396-5200
www.h-e.com

HATFIELD & DAWSON
CONSULTING ENGINEERS
9500 GREENWOOD AVE. N.
SEATTLE, WA 98103

(206) 783-9151   (206) 789-9834 Fax
e-mail: hatdaw@hatdaw.com
Member AFCCE

WILLIAM J. SITZMAN
PRESIDENT
INDEPENDENT BROADCAST CONSULTANTS, INC.
CONSULTING COMMUNICATIONS ENGINEERS
110 COUNTY RD. 146,
TRUMANSBURG, N.Y. 14886 9721
(607) 273-2970 / FAX (607) 273-5125

 **CARL T. JONES**
CORPORATION
Consulting Engineers
7901 Yarnwood Ct.
Springfield, Virginia 22153
(703) 569-7704   fax (703) 569-6417
Member AFCCE   www.ctjc.com

 **MARSAND, INC.**
Consulting Engineer AFCCE
                     SBE-PBE
Matthew A. Sanderford, Jr., P.E.
President

tvcowboy@marsand.com   www.marsand.com
6100 IH-35W / PO Box 485   Office: 817-783-5566
Alvarado, Texas 76009-0485   Fax: 817-783-5577

• Digital & Analog Broadcasting • Technical Software
• Consumer & Professional Electronics

William Meintel: (540) 428-2308
Gary Sgrignoli: (847) 259-3352
Dennis Wallace: (202) 251-7589
www.MSWDTV.com

Mullaney Engineering, Inc.
Member AFCCE

Serving Broadcasters Since 1948
9049 Shady Grove Court
Gaithersburg, MD 20877
(301) 921-0115
Fax (301) 590-9757
mullaney@mullengr.com

Munn-Reese, Inc.
Broadcast Engineering Consultants
P.O. Box 220
Coldwater, Michigan 49036
Phone: 517-278-7339
wayne@munn-reese.com

CARL E. SMITH CONSULTING ENGINEERS
AM FM TV Engineering Consultants
Complete Tower and Rigging Services
"Serving the Broadcast Industry for over 60 years"
Box 807 Bath, Ohio 44210
(330) 659-4440

SMITH AND FISHER
BROADCASTING AND
TELECOMMUNICATIONS CONSULTANTS

SUITE A
2237 TACKETT'S MILL DRIVE
LAKE RIDGE, VA 22192
PHONE: (703)494-2101   FAX: (703)494-2132

AM FM TV   Phone (303) 937-1900
APPLICATIONS   FIELD MEASUREMENTS
PROOFS   AUDIO AND RF ENGINEERING
DIRECTIONAL ANTENNAS   EMERGENCY REPAIR

VIR JAMES P. C.
BROADCAST ENGINEERING CONSULTANTS

TIMOTHY C. CUTFORTH, P.E.   965 S. IRVING ST.
President   DENVER, CO 80219
Director of Engineering   Member AFCCE & SBE

Section H
Associations, Events, Education, and Awards

Associations
Major National Associations H-2
National Associations H-5
State and Regional Broadcast Associations H-9
State and Regional Cable Associations H-11
Union/Labor Groups H-12

Events
Trade Shows H-14

Education
Vocational and Career Development Schools H-16
Universities and Colleges with Broadcasting or Journalism Programs . H-18

Awards
Major Broadcasting and Cable Awards H-23

Major National Associations

Academy of Television Arts & Sciences

Headquarters: 5220 Lankershim Blvd., North Hollywood, CA 91601-3109. (818) 754-2800. FAX: (818) 761-2827. Web Site: http://www.emmys.org.

Executives: Dick Askin, chmn & CEO; Tom Sarnoff, Academy Foundation chmn & CEO; Todd Leavitt, pres/COO; Frank Kohler, CFO; Laurel Whitcomb, VP mktg; Dan Birman, sec; Leo Chaloukian, CAS treas.

Mission Statement: The mission of the Academy is to promote creativity, diversity, innovation and excellence through recognition, education and leadership in the advancement of the telecommunications arts and sciences.

Cabletelevision Advertising Bureau Inc. (CAB)

Headquarters: 830 3rd Ave., New York, NY 10022. (212) 508-1200. FAX: (212) 832-3268. Web Site: www.onetvworld.org.

Executives: Steven J. Heyer, chmn; Joseph W. Ostrow, pres/CEO; Robert H. Alter, vice-chmn; Kim Kelly, vice-chmn; George Bodenheimer, treas; Curtis Symonds, sec; Ken Damsky, VP finance & admin; Jerry Dominus, VP network sls & mktg; Kevin Barry, VP local sls & mktg; Jonathan B. Sims, VP rsch; Lynne Nordone, VP member svcs; Steve Raddock, VP creative svcs.

Mission Statement: The CAB is dedicated to providing advertisers & agencies with the most current, complete actionable cable TV media insights at the national DMA & loc levels.

Board of Directors: Jack Olson, VP media dev, Adelphia Communications; Louis Carr, exec VP, BET; Robert H. Alter, vice-chmn, CAB; Joseph Abruzzese, pres ad sls, Discovery Networks; Robert Bakish, exec VP opns, Viacom, Inc.; Lawrence Fischer, Time Warner City Cable; Phil Kent, chmn/CEO, Turner Broadcasting Systems Inc.; Paul Iaffaldano, sr VP ad sls, The Weather Channel; Lynn Picard, exec VP sls, Lifetime Entertainment; Lou La Torre, pres ad sls/corporate, Fox Channel Group; Sonja Farrand, group VP/ad sls, On Media; David Cassaro, exec VP, E! Entertainment Television; David Kline, pres/COO, Rainbow Advertising; Edward R. Erhardt, pres ad sls, ESPN; William Farina, VP ad sls, Cox Communications; Jim Heneghan, corporate VP/ad, Charter Communication; Whitney Goit, exec VP sls/mktg, A&E Networks; Kevin Dowell, VP ad sls, Insight Communications; Michael Bowker, VP ad, Cable ONE; Charlie Thurston, pres ad sls, Comcast Communications; Jeffrey C. Wayne, pres, Jones Media Networks.

Canadian Cable Television Association (CCTA)

Headquarters: 360 Albert St., Suite 1010, Ottawa, ON, Canada K1R 7X7. (613) 232-2631. FAX: (613) 232-2137. Web Site: www.ccta.ca. Contact: Victoria Pigeon, admin asst to external affrs & communications. (613) 688-5564.

Executive Staff: Janet Yale, pres/CEO; Rob Moulson, controller; Elizabeth Roscoe, sr VP/external affrs and communications; Nick Masciantonio, VP govt rel; Harris Boyd, sr VP industry affrs/office of small systems; Shauna McCaffrey, dir industry affrs; Michael Hennessy, sr VP policy/regulatory affrs; Suzanne Blackwell, VP economic research; Lori Assheton-Smith, sr VP/gen counsel; Jay Kerr-Wilson, sr counsel; Rachelle Frenette, counsel, pub law; Michele Beck, VP regulatory engrg.

Mission Statement: CCTA's primary role is to communicate the industry views to regulatory bodies, govt, and other stakeholders. CCTA also works with its members to promote standards of excellence, assess new technology & business opportunities, as well as advance the dev of services to Canadian consumers.

Board of Directors: Dean MacDonald, (chmn), pres/CEO Persona Communications; Louis Audet, pres/CEO COGECO Inc.; John Bragg, sec/pres EastLink Cable Systems; Michael Adams, exec VP/COO Rogers Cable Inc.; Edward S. (Ted) Rogers, pres/CEO Rogers Communications Inc.; Jim Shaw, CEO Shaw Communications Inc.; Ken Stein, sr VP corporate/regulatory affrs Shaw Communications Inc.; David Baxter, pres/CEO Westman Communications Group; Warren Ritchie, gen mgr Norcom Television.

Small Systems: *Eastern*—Jacques Perron, gen mgr Cooperative de Cablodistribution de l'Arriere-Pays; *Central*Warren Richie, gen mgr Norcom Telecommunications Ltd.; *Western*—David Baxter, pres/CEO Western Communications Group.

Media Rating Council

Headquarters: 370 Lexington Ave., Suite 902, New York, NY 10017. (212) 972-0300. FAX: (212) 972-2786. E-mail: albana.mrc@inctools.com. Web site: www.mrchtsp.com

Officers: Richard Weinstein, exec dir/CEO; Tim Brooks (chmn of bd MRC), USA Network, New York, NY; David Poltrack (ex officio MRC), CBS, New York, NY; Ron Werth (chmn Radio Committee), Westwood One, New York, NY; Barry Kresch (chmn Cable Committee), Lifetime Television, New York, NY; Leigh Graham (chmn TV Committee), Allbritton-KATV Little Rock, AR; Susan Nathan (chmn Print Committee); McCann Ericson, New York, NY.

National Association of Broadcasters (NAB)

Headquarters: 1771 N St. N.W., Washington, DC 20036. Phone: (202) 429-5300. FAX: (202) 429-4199. E-mail: nab@nab.org. Web Site: www.nab.org.

NAB Officers and Staff

NAB Executive Committee: Bruce T. Reese (chair), pres/CEO, Bonneville International Corp., Salt Lake City, UT; Philip J. Lombardo, (past chair), CEO, Citadel Communications Co. Ltd., Bronxville, NY; Robert V. Cahill, (vice chair), Univision Communications Inc., Los Angeles, CA; Jim Conschafter, sr VP/bcst stns, Media General Broadcast Group, Richmond, VA; David J. Field, CEO/pres, Entercom Communications Corp., Bala Cynwyd, PA; Andrew S. Fisher, pres, Cox Television, Atlanta, GA; Edward O. Fritts, pres/CEO, NAB exec offices, Washington, DC; Jerry T. Hanszen, owner/gen mgr, Hanszen Broadcasting, Carthage, TX; Benjamin W. Tucker Jr., acting pres/CEO, Fisher Communications, Inc., Seattle, WA; W. Russell Withers Jr., owner, Broadcasting Companies, Mount Vernon, IL.

NAB Radio Board of Directors: David J. Field, (chair), Entercom Communications Corp., Bala Cynwyd, PA; W. Russell Withers Jr., (first vice chair), WMIX AM-FM Withers Broadcasting Companies, Mount Vernon, IL; Jerry T. Henszen (second vice chair), Henszen Broadcasting, Carthage, TX.

NAB District Representatives: Howard B. Anderson, KHWY, Inc., district: 24 (S.CA-GU-HI) Los Angeles, CA; John W. Warger, VictoriaRadio Works, Ltd., KVIC/KEPG/KITE/KRNX/KNAL, District: 18 (SO. TX) San Antonia, TX; Pete Benedetti, New Northwest Broadcasters, district: 25 (OR-WA), Seattle, WA; Joseph M. Bilotta, Buckley Radio, district: 2 (NY-NJ), Greenwich, CT; Robert L. Bundgaard, KLKS, Lakes Broadcasting, district: 21 (MN-SD-ND), Breezy Point, MN; Bobby Caldwell, KWYN, East Arkansas Broadcasters, district: 15 (TN-AR), Wynne, AR; Rodney P. Chambers, KSUE/KJDZ/KHJQ, Sierra Broadcasting Corp., district: 23 (N.CA-AK) Susanville, CA; W. Bradford Eure, The Charlottesville Radio Group, district: 4 (DE-DC-MD-VA), Charlottesville, VA; Paul G. Gardner, Elko Broadcasters Co., district: 22 (AZ-NV-NM-UT), Elko, NV; Robert L. Bundgaard, KLKS, Lakes Broadcasting, district: 21 (MN-SD-ND), Breezy Point, MN; Bruce Goldsen, WKHM AM/FM, WIBM Jackson Radio Works, Inc., district: 13 (MI) Jackson, MI; Alene Grevey, Clear Channel Radio, district: 9 (GA-AL), Mt Pleasant, SC; Alan W. Harris, Wagonwheel Communications KUGR/KYCS/KFRZ, district: 20 (MT-ID-WY) Green River, WY; Bill Hendrich, WDBO/WWKA, Cox Radio, district: 7 (FL-PR-VI) Orlando, FL; James (Bud) E. Janes, Bick Broadcasting/KHMO/KICK, district: 12 (MO-KS), Hannibal, MO; Rolland "Rollie" C. Johnson, Three Eagles Communications, district: 16 (CO-NE), Larkspur, CO; Jerry Lee, WBEB FM Radio district: 3 (PA) Bala Cynwyd, PA; Stephen Levet, WCKWQ-AM/River Parish Radio LLC, district: 8 (LA-MS) Mandeville, LA; Gunther S. Meisse, WVNO/WRGM, district: 11 (OH) Mansfield, OH; Matt Mills, Greater Media Boston, district: 1 (New England), Boston, MA; Steven W. Newberry, Commonwealth Broadcasting Corp, district: 5 (WV-KY), Glasgow, KY; Mary Quass, NRG Media, LLC, district: 14 (IA-WI) Cedar Rapids, IA; Jeffrey H. Smulyan, Emmis Communications Corp., district: 10 (IN) Indianapolis, IN; Alex Snipe Jr., Glory Communications, Inc., district: 6 (NC-SC) Columbia, SC.

NAB Designated Board Seats: Edward K. Christian, Sage Communications, Grosse Pointe Farms, MI; Lew Dickey Jr., Cumulus Media, Inc., Atlanta, GA; Susan Davenport Austin, Sheridan Broadcasting Corp.; Alfred Liggins, Radio One Inc., Lanham, MD; Mark P. Mays, Clear Channel Worldwide, San Antonio, TX; Susan K. Patrick, Legend Communications, Ellicott City, MD; Miguel Villarreal Jr., Border Media Partners, Laredo, TX; Charles Warfield, ICBC Broadcast Holding, Inc.

NAB TV Broad of Directors: Benjamin W. Tucker Jr., (chair), acting pres Fisher Communications, Inc., Seattle, WA; Jim Conschafter, (first vice chair), sr VP/bcst stns, Media General Broadcast Croup, Richmond, VA; Andrew S. Fisher, (second vice chair), pres, Cox Television, Atlanta, GA.

NAB Elected Representatives: Elizabeth Murphy Burns, pres, Morgan Murphy Stations; Craig A. Dubow, pres/CEO, Gannett Broadcasting, McLean, VA; Michael J. Fiorile, pre/CEO, Dispatch Broadcast Group, Columbus, OH; Alan W. Frank, pres/CEO Post-Newsweek Stations, Inc., Detroit, MI; James M. Keelor, pres/COO Liberty Corp., Greenville, SC; John C. Kueneke, pres, New-Press & Gazette Broadcasting, St. Louis, MO; Michael D. McKinnon Sr., pres, McKinnon Broadcasting Co., San Diego, CA; Patrick J. Mullen, pres, Tribune Broadcasting Co., Chicago, IL; Edward L. Munson Jr., co-VP, Television WAVY-TV/LIN TV Corp., Portsmouth, VA; William B. Peterson; sr VP/Television, The E.W. Scripps Co., Cincinnati, OH; Doreen Wade, pres, Freedom Broadcasting, Inc., West Palm Beach, FL; K. James Yager, CEO, Barrington Broadcasting Co., LLC, Hoffman Estates, IL.

NAB Designated Broad Seats: Lyle Banks, pres/CEO Banks Broadcasting, Inc., Winnetka, IL; Robert G. Lee, pres/gen mgr WDBJ Television Inc., Roanoke, VA; Madelyn Bonnot Griffin, VP/opns, National Communications, Lake Charles, LA; John L. Sander, pres/media opns, Belo Corp., Dallas, TX; David Woods, pres, WCOV-TV, Montgomery, AL.

NAB Network Representative: Robert V. Cahill, (vice chair), Univision Communications Inc., Los Angeles, CA; Dean Goodman, pres/COO Paxson Communications Corp., West Palm Beach, FL.

National Association of Farm Broadcasters

Headquarters: Box 500, Platte City, MO 64079. (816) 431-4032. FAX: (816) 431-4087. E-mail: info@nafb.com. Web Site: www.nafb.com.

Officers: Emery Kleven, pres; Danny Waddle, (ex-officio); Kevin Morse, VP; Dix Harper, historian*CHATS*.

Executive Director: Gene Millard, exec dir.

National Association of Television Program Executives (NATPE)

Headquarters: 5757 Wilshire Blvd., Penthouse 10, Los Angeles, CA 90036. (310) 453-4440. FAX: (310) 453-3398. Web Site: www.natpe.org.

Broadcasting & Cable Yearbook 2006

Major National Associations

Mission Statement: Best known for the annual program conference & exhibition held every January, NATPE has become the voice of our industry, offering a global perspective through loc resources. Corporate members range from loc TV stns & cable systems to U.S. & international program distributors, networks, stn group owners & decision-makers from adv, finance & production companies. NATPE is the world's leading nonprofit TV prgmg & software assn dedicated to the continued growth & success of the global TV marketplace.

Staff & Consultants: Rick Feldman, pres/CEO; Nick Orfanopoulos, sr VP conferences, opns/sls; Beth Braen, sr VP mktg; Jon Dobkin, CFO; Chris Blackledge, mktg mgr; Lew Klein, pres NATPE Educational Foundation.

Publications: *The NATPE Monthly; Programmer's Guide; Station Listening Guide; Reps, Groups, Distributors, Networks, Ad Agencies, Telco-DBS Guide, NATPE News & NATPE Daily Lead.*

International Representatives

European Director: Pam Smithard, mgng dir, 452 Oakleigh Rd. N., London, England, UK N2O 0RZ (44 20) 8361-3793. FAX: (44 20) 8368-3824.

French Representative: Sylvie Brauns, SBC & Associates, 7 rue Sainte Claude, 75003 Paris, France (33 1) 42 71 12 79. FAX: (33 1) 42 71 80 24.

Pacific Rim Representative: Nick McMahon, Crawford Productions Group, 259 Middleborough Rd., Box Hill 3128, Victoria, Australia. 61 398 95 2211. FAX: 61 398 90 5732.

Japanese Representative: Akio Taniguchi, Act International, Inc., 2-6-2 Shinkawa, Ishibashi Bldg., #502, Chuo-Ku, Tokyo 104, Japan (813) 3206-9788. FAX: (813) 3206-1636.

Indian Representative: Bhuvan Lall, Empire Entertainment Private Ltd., B 157 Shivalik, New Delhi 110017, India (91) 11 669 3472. FAX: (91) 11 699-1078. E-mail: bhuvanlall@vsnl.com

Chinese Consultant: Grace Ip, Neutral Distributing Services Inc., 347 W. Arbor Vitae St., Inglewood, CA 90301 (310) 330-7888. FAX: (310) 330-7889.

National Cable and Telecommunications Association (NCTA)

Headquarters: 1724 Massachusetts Ave. N.W., Washington, DC 20036. (202) 775-3550. E-mail: webmaster@ncta.com. Web Site: www.ncta.com

NCTA Officer

Kyle McSlarrow, pres/CEO.

NCTA Board of Directors

Blair Sadler, (chair); Nancy Chandler, (vice chair); Victoria Nugent, treas; Marvin Ventrell, sec.

National Cable Television Cooperative Inc.

Headquarters: 11200 Corporate Ave., Lenexa, KS 66219. (913) 599-5900. FAX: (913) 599-5903. Web Site: www.cabletvcoop.org.

Executives: Neil Wilkin, (pres elect), pres/CEO, Optical Cable Corp.; Ted Melnik, pres, Novozymes Biogicals; Ken Ferris, (past pres), Pres, IHS iMonitoring; Mary Miller, sec, Interactive Design & Development; Mary Anne McElmurray, Tax Services Director, Brown, Edwards & Co.

NCTC Board Members: Doyle Edgerton, CEO, Rev.Net; Greg Feldmann, pres, FNB Salem; Leon Harris, pres, Keltech; Roger Baiers, gen mgr, Cox Business Services; Henry Bass, dir; David Poteet, dir.

Radio Advertising Bureau

Headquarters: 261 Madison Ave., 23rd Fl., New York, NY 10016. (212) 681-7200. FAX: (212) 681-7223. Web Site: www.rab.com.

Services and Administration Center: 1320 Greenway Dr., Suite 500, Irving, TX 75038. (972) 753-6750. FAX: (972) 753-6727.

Chicago Office: 30 South Wacker Dr., 22nd Fl., Chicago, IL 60606. (312) 466-5639.

Los Angeles Office: 5670 Wilshire Blvd., Suite 1365, Los Angeles, CA 90036. (213) 938-3228. FAX: (213) 938-8174. Bob Griffith, SVP/stations.

Officers

Joe Bilotta (chair); Herb McCord (chair); Peter Smyth (vice chair).

Officers of the Corporation

Gary Fries, pres/CEO; Van Allen, ex VP/CFO; Mary Bennett, exec VP mktg; George Hyde, exec VP/training; Mike Mahone, exec VP/svcs; Ron Ruth, exec VP/stns; Lynn Anderson, sr VP/training; Dave Casper, sr VP/internet svcs; Howell Cohen, sr VP/mktg; Roger Dodson, sr VP/training; Bob Griffith, sr VP/stns; Richard Rakovan, sr VP/stns; Thomas Barnhardt, VP/tech svcs; Brandeis Hall, VP/Co-op-NTR; Renee Cassis, VP/corporate mktg; Clint Culp, sr VP/stns; Christa Dahlander, sr VP/communications; Beverly Fraser, sr VP/controller; Wendy French, VP/mktg; Mary Malone, VP educ svcs; Dolores Nolan, VP/stns; Andy Rainey, sr VP/rsch.

Board of Directors: David Kennedy, pres/COO, Susquehanna Radio Corp., York, PA (717) 852-2139. FAX: (717) 771-1436. E-mail: dkennedy@suscom.com; David Pearlman, Pearlman Advisors, Lexington, MA Cell: (617) 529 8500. FAX: (781) 674-1434. E-mail: david@pearlmanadvisors.com; Joe Bilotta, pres/CEO, Buckley Broadcasting, Greenwich CT (203) 661-4307. FAX: (203) 662-7341. E-mail: jbilotta@buckleyradio.com; Herb McCord, pres/CEO, Granum Communications Corp, Red Bank, NJ (732) 933-2626. FAX: (732) 933-2626; Gary Fries, pres/CEO Radio Advertising Bureau, Inc., New York, NY (212) 681-7210. FAX: (212) 681-7217. E-mail: gfries@rab.com; Bruce Beasley, pres, Beasley Broadcast Group, Estero, FL (941) 495-2100. FAX: (941) 992-0349; Charles (Chuck) Bortnick, COO, Westwood One, New York, NY (212) 641-2181. E-mail: chuck_bortnick@metronetworks.com; Carl Gardner, pres/radio, Journal Co.; Clarke Brown, pres/radio div, Jefferson-Pilot Communications, Atlanta, GA (404) 261-2970. FAX: (404) 237-8769. E-mail: cbrown@jpc.com; Ginny Morris, pres/radio, Hubbard Broadcasting; Gary Buchanan, pres/COO, Three Eagles Communications, Inc., Lincoln, NE (402) 483-0489. FAX: (402) 489-0963. E-mail: gbuchanan@lincnet.com; Michael Carter, pres, Carter Broadcast Group, Inc., (816)763-2040. FAX: (816) 765-1251. mic@kprs.com; Rick Cummings, pres/radio, Emmis Communications, Encino, CA (818) 817-8521. FAX: (818) 784-4059. rcummings@emmis.com; Lee Davis, pres/gen mgr, Cub Radio, Inc., (920) 683-6800. FAX: (708) 799-1663. E-mail: ldavis@cubradio.com; Tom Dobrez, pres, State Nets Radio, (708) 799-6676. FAX: (708) 799-1663; John Douglas, pres, AIM Broadcasting; Glenn Cherry, pres/CEO, Tama Broadcasting Inc.; David Field, pres/CEO, Entercom Communications Corp., Bala Cynwyd, PA (610) 660-5633. FAX: (610) 660-5693. djfield@entercom.com; Marcus Forsell, pres, SBS Radio AB; Steffen Mueller, CEO, RundfunkGmbh; Laura Hagan, pres, Univision Radio National Sales; David Kantor, CEO, Reach Media, Longboat Key, FL (941) 387-7275. FAX: (941) 387-0357. dk511@aol.com; Traug Keller, sr VP, ESPN Radio; Scott Knight, pres/CEO, Knight Quality Stations, Boston, MA (617) 262-1950, x11. FAX: (617) 267-5160. sknight99@aol.com; Weezie Kramer, rgnl VP, Entercom, Chicago, IL (773) 832-0419. FAX: (773) 832-0417. E-mail: wkramer@entercom.com; Jerry Lee, pres, WBEB Radio, Bala Cynwyd, PA (610) 667-8400. FAX: (610) 538-8420. E-mail: jerryl@101-fm.com; Glenn Mahone, Esq., (RAB Counsel), Reed, Smith LLP, Pittsburgh, PA (412) 288-4240. FAX: (412) 288-3063. E-mail: gmahone@reedsmith.com; Gunther Meisse, pres, Johnny Appleseed Broadcasting, Inc., Mansfield, OH (419) 529-5900, x205. FAX: (419) 529-2319. E-mail: gogm@wmfd.com; Jay Meyers, sr VP, Clear Channel Communications, Covington, KY (859) 655-6518. FAX: (859) 655-9356. E-mail: jaymeyers@clearchannel.com; Marc Morgan, exec VP/COO, Cox Radio, Inc., Cox Radio, Inc., Atlanta, GA (404) 897-6230. (404) 897-7361. marc.morgan@cox.com; Stuart (Stu) Olds, CEO, Katz Media Group, Inc., New York, NY (212) 424-6780. FAX: (212) 424-6769. E-mail: stu.olds@katu-media.com; Michael Osterhout,

COO, Morris Radio LLC, Augusta, GA (706) 828-3331. FAX: (706) 828-3644. E-mail: mosterhout@morris.com; Norman D. Rau, pres, Sandusky Radio, New York, NY (212) 355-3074. FAX: (212) 355-3075. E-mail: ndrau@aol.com; Bruce Reese, pres/CEO, Bonneville International, Salt Lake City, UT (801) 575-7565. FAX: (801) 575-7567. E-mail: breese@bonnint.com; Art Rowbotham, pres, Hall Communications, Inc. Lakeland, FL (863) 682-8184. E-mail: arowbotham@hallradio.com; Allen Shaw, vice-chmn/COO, Beasley Broadcast Group, Winston-Salem, NC (336) 774-3186. FAX: (336) 774-3192. E-mail: allenshaw@msn.com; Cary H. Simpson, (RAB sec), pres, Allegheny Mountain Network, Tyrone, PA (814) 684-3200. FAX: (814) 684-1220. E-mail: amnnet@aol.com; Thomas E. Sly, COO, Marathon Media, Park City, UT (801) 824-7000. E-mail: tesly@aol.com; Peter Smyth, pres/CEO, Greater Media, Braintree, MA (781) 348-8605. FAX: (775) 806-2661. E-mail: pswmjx@aol.com; Dean Sorenson, CRMC. Pres, Sorenson Broadcasting, Sioux Falls, SD (605) 334-1117. FAX: (775) 806-2661. E-mail: sorenson@sbcradio.com; William L. Stakelin, pres/COO, Regent Communications, Covington, KY (859) 292-0030. FAX: (859) 292-0352. E-mail: wstakelin@regentcomm.com; Mark S. Steinmetz, VP, American Media Services, LLC, Mt. Pleasant, SC (843) 972-2200. FAX: (843) 216-7782. E-mail: ms@ams.fm; Pierre (Pepe) Sutton, (chmn), Inner City Broadcasting Corp., New York, NY (212) 447-1000. FAX: (212) 447-5292. E-mail: pmsutton@wlib.com; Al Vicente, pres, Archway Broadcasting Group, East Point, GA (404) 762-9942. E-mail: avicente@archwaybroadcasting.com; Bayard (Bud) Walters, pres, Cromwell Group, Inc., Nashville, TN (615) 361-7560. FAX: (615) 366-4313. E-mail: bwalters@cromwellradio.com; Samuel (Skip) Weller, pres/COO, Radio Division NextMedia Group, Inc., Englewood, CO (303) 694-9118. FAX: (303) 694-4940. E-mail: sweller@nectmediagroup.net, cc: srabern@nextmediagroup.net; E.J. (Jay) Williams, Jr., pres, American Urban Radio Networks, New York, NY (212) 883-2100. FAX: (212) 557-5706. E-mail: presaurn@aol.com; Peter Doyle, sr VP/media, Traffic Pulse Network; Marc Guild, pres/mktg, Interep Radio Sales; Scott Herman, exec VP, Infinity Broadcasting Corp.; Warren Lada, sr VP/opns, Saga Communications; George Pine, pres/COO, Interep; Tony Renda, pres, Renda Broadcasting Corp.; James Robinson, pres, ABC Radio Networks; Art Rowbotham, pres, Hall Communications Inc.; Richard Chapin (past chmn), pres, Chapin Enterprises; Jeff Smulyan (chmn), Emmis Communications Corp.; William L. Stakelin, pres/COO; Mark S. Steinmetz, sr VP/mktg mgr, Infinity Broadcasting Phoenix; Gary Stone, COO, Univision; Roger Utnehmer, pres, Nicolet Broadcasting (WBDK Radio); Nancy Vaeth, pres/COO, Susquehanna Radio Corp.; Charles Warfield, pres/COO, ICBC Broadcasting Holding Inc.; Richard Buckley (past chmn), pres, Buckley Broadcasting, Greenwich, CT (203) 661-4307. (203) 622-7341. E-mail: rbuckley@buckleyradio.com; David Crowl, sr VP/radio, Clear Channel Communications, Covington, KY (859) 655-6555. FAX: (859) 655-9356. E-mail: davecrowl@clearchannel.com; John Dille (past chmn), pres, Federation Media, Elkhart, IN (219) 295-2500. FAX: (219) 294-4014. E-mail: jdille@fedmed.com; Paul Fiddick (past chmn), pres, Emmis International, Arlington, VA (703) 248-8081. FAX: (703) 248-0647. E-mail: pfiddick@emmis.com; Skip Finley (vice chmn), Inner City Broadcasting Corp; .

Executive Committee: Lee Davis; Kraig Kitchin; Gunther Meisse; Cary H. Simpson; Bayard "Bud" Walters; John Douglas.

Past Chairmen Advisory Committee: David Crowl; Jeffrey Smulyan; John Dille; Arthur Carlson; Richard Chapin; Skip Finley.

Finance Committee: Herb McCord; John Douglas.

Radio-Television News Directors Association Foundation

Headquarters: 1600 K St. N.W. Suite 700, Washington, DC 20006-2838. (202) 659-6510. FAX: (202) 223-4007. E-mail: rtnda@rtnda.org. Web Site: www.rtnda.org

Officers: Bob Salsberg, Associated Press, Boston; Dan Shelly (chair), WTMJ-AM, Wilwaukee; Bob Priddy, (chmn) MissouriNet, Jefferson City, MO. E-mail: bpriddy@learfield.com; Loren Tobia, AccuWeather, Syracuse, NY. E-mail: ltobia@wtvh.com.

Major National Associations

Directors-at-Large: Janice Gin, KTVU-TV Oakland, CA. E-mail: janice.gin@ktvu.com; Princell Hair, CNN News/US, Atlanta. E-mail: princellhair@turner.com; Ed Tobias, Associated Press, Washington. E-mail: ed_tobias@ap.org; Derrick Hinds, KEYC-TV, Mankato, MN. E-mail: derrick@keyc.com; Paula Pendarvis, WGNO-TV, New Orleans. E-mail: ppendarvis@tribune.com; Susana Schuler, Nexstar Broadcasting Group, Irving, TX. E-mail: sschuler@nexstar.tv; Brian Trauring, WTVG-TV, Toledo, OH. E-mail: brian.trauning@abc.com.

Staff: Barbara Cochran, pres, (202) 467-5205. E-mail: barbarac@rtnda.org; Stacey Staniak, asst to pres, (202) 467-5214. E-mail: staceys@rtnda.org; Rick Osmanski, CMP, VP/convention & special project, (202) 467-5200; Danielle Browne, mgr convention opns, (202) 467-5254. E-mail: danib@rtnda.org; Jane Nassiri, VP finance/admin, (202) 467-5251. E-mail: janen@rtnda.org; Noreen Welle, VP/communications, mktg & membership, (202) 467-5203. E-mail: noreenw@rtnda.org; Bryan Moffett, editorial dir, (202) 467-5256; Nicole Newsome, awards/products mgr, (202) 467-5208.

Active Members: About 1,100 radio & TV news directors.

Television Bureau of Advertising (TVB)

Headquarters: 3 E. 54th St., 10th Fl., New York, NY 10022-3108. (212) 486-1111. FAX: (212) 935-5631. E-mail: info@tvb.org. Web Site: www.tvb.org.

Officers

Christopher Rohrs, pres; Abby Auerbach, exec VP; John Catanese, dir mktg research; Hope Etheridge, VP/fin and admin; Janice Garjian, VP member svcs; Peter Schmid, sr VP mktg and sls dev; Joseph C. Tirinato, sr VP/mktg and membership; Gary Belis, VP communications.

Board of Directors: Tom Arnost, co-pres Univision Television Group, Inc.; Bruce Baker, exec VP Cox Television; Jim Beloyianis, pres KTVG Companies, Katz Media Group, Inc., New York, NY; Frank Comerford, pres/gen mgr WNBC-TV, New York, NY; John Cottingham, VP/gen mgr WSPA-TV, Spartanburg, SC; Dick Robertson, pres domestic TV distribution Warner Brothers, Burbank, CA; Andrew S. Fisher, pres Cox Television, Inc.; Alan Frank, pres Post-Newsweek Stations Inc.; Grace M. Gilchrist, VP/gen mgr WXYZ-TV, Southfield, MI; Ibra Morales, pres Telemundo Group, Inc.; Julio Marenghi, pres/gen mgr WBZT-TV; Boston, MA; Kathleen Keefe, VP sls Hearst-Argyle Television; Paul Karpowicz, pres Meredith Broadcasting; Michael Hugger, pres Eagle Television Sales; Louis Wall, pres Sagamore Hill Broadcasting; Jay Ireland, pres Television Station Division, NBC; Paul Kalpavitz, VP of Television LIN Television Corp.; John Reardon, group VP Tribune Co.; John Weiser, pres/distribution Sony Pictures Television; James M. Keelor, pres Liberty Corporation; Rick Keilty, sr VP Television Group Belo Corporation; Walter Liss, pres ABC Owned Television Stations, Inc.; Leo MacCourtney, pres/CEO Blair Television; Paul McTear, CEO/pres Raycom Media, Inc.; Jim Monohan, exec VP TeleRep, Inc.; I. Morcles, pres Telemundo Group Inc.; Patrick Mullen, pres Tribune Television, Tribune Company; Frank Comeford, pres/gen mgr, WNBC-TV, New York, NY; Ted Pearse, gen sls mgr WDIV-TV, Detroit, MI; Christopher J. Rohrs, pres Television Bureau of Advertising; Raymond Schonbak, sr VP/opns Emmis Communications; Rich Sheingold; Perry Sook, pres/CEO Nexstar Broadcasting Group; Dennis Swanson, exec VP/COO VICDM Television Stations Group; Paul Trelstad, sr VP Gannet Broadcasting; John Watkins, pres ABC National Television Sales, Inc., New York, NY.

National Sales Advisory Committee: Murray Berkowitz, pres HRP, Inc., New York, NY; Craig Broitman, pres Millennium Sales & Marketing; Michael Hugger, pres Eagle Television Sales; Chris Jordan, sr VP/COO Continental Television Sales; Mike Kronefeld, pres/CEO Adam Young, Inc., New York, NY; Leo MacCourtney, pres/CEO Blair Television; Jim Monahan, exec VP TeleRep, Inc.; Val Napolitano, pres/CEO Petry Television; Larry Strumwasser, pres MMT Sales, Inc.; Charlie Stuart, VP/national sls Univision Television Group, Inc.; John Watkins, pres ABC National Television Sales, Inc., New York, NY; Tom Kane, pres/sls Viacom Television; Alan Brittain, sr VP/national sls organization NBC Universal Television.

Sales Advisory Committee: Lynn Bailie, VP/sls & mktg WCNC-TV, Charlotte, NC; Michael Chico, sr VP/NSO East NBC, NY; Nancy Dodson, VP sls/West Coast, Blair Television, Los Angeles, CA; Cathy Egan, sr VP/new business & mktg, ABC National Television Sales, Inc., New York, NY; Patty Golden, VP sls WMAQ-TV, Chicago, IL; Joe Fazio, dir sls WHEC TV, Rochester, NY; Scott Heath, gen sls mgr KSWB-TV, San Diego, CA; Jim Hughes, sr VP/dir of sls TeleRep, Inc.; Mike Kronenfeld, pres/CEO Adam Young, Inc., New York, NY; Kristin Long, sr VP ABC National Television Sales, Inc.; Robert D. Silva, VP/dir of sls E.W. Scripps Co.; Lou Abitabilo, gen sls mgr WNEP-TV, Moosic, PA; Michelle Harper, natl sls mgr WTVD-TV, Durham, NC; Tim Bush, sr VP/ rgnl mgr Nexstar Broadcasting Group; Robert Fein, stn mgr KYW-TV, Philadelphia, PA; Roger Hess, gen sls mgr WTNH-TV, New Haven, CT; Brooks Hogg, VP/gen mgr WOAI-TV, San Antonio, TX; Nick Ulmer, gen sls mgr WAVE-TV Louisville, KY; Arika Zink, gen sls mgr WYFF-TV, Greenville, SC; Enrique Perez, sr VP Telemundo Sales; Thomas Stemlar, sr VP/sls Emmis Communications; Jill Saarela, gen sls mgr KVVU-TV, Henderson, NV; Peter Russell, gen sls mgr WEEK-TV, East Peoria, IL.

NSAC Research Committee: Amber Bell, dir/ rsch & mktg; Patti Cohen, VP/ rsch Viacom Television Stations Group; David Daniels, VP/sls mgr ABC National Television Sales, Inc.; Melinda Maidhof, VP/mktg & rsch Univision Television Group, Inc.; John McMorrow sr VP/progmg & rsch HRP, Inc.; Darrylanne Oliva, VP/rsch & progmg MMT Sales, Inc.; Richard Pollina, VP/rsch dir Millennium Sales & Marketing; Michael Steinberg, VP/sls rsch dir Continental Television Sales; Rob Murray, VP/rsch mktg Eagle Television Sales; Alan Picozzi, VP/dir rsch Petry Media Corp.; Fred Gold, dir rsch TeleRep, Inc.

National Associations

AFCEA, 4400 Fair Lakes Ct., Fairfax, VA 22033-3899. Phone: (703) 631-6100. Phone: (800) 336-4583. Fax: (703) 631-4693. E-mail: plans@afcea.org. Web Site: www.afcea.org.

AFMA, 10850 Wilshire Blvd., 9th Fl., Los Angeles, CA 90024-4321. Phone: (310) 446-1000. Fax: (310) 446-1600. E-mail: info@afma.com. Web Site: www.afma.com.
Directors: Wouter Barendrecht, Patrick Binet, Ehud Bleiberg, Michael Weiser, Nicholas Chartier, Robert Hayward, Paul Hertzberg, David Linde, Lewis Horwitz, Mark Lindsay, Robert Little, Lisa Wilson, Nick Meyer, Charlotte Mickie, Andrew Stevens, Kathy Morgan, Lloyd Kaufman, Antonia Nava, Kirk D'amico & Alison Thompson.

ANEPA, C/Costello, 59 bis, 28001, Madrid Spain. Phone: 91 575 53 81. Fax: 91 435 66 53. E-mail: anepa@anepa.net. Web Site: www.anepa.net.

Academy of Canadian Cinema & Television, 172 King St. E., Toronto, ON M5A 1J3. Canada. Phone: (416) 366-2227. Fax: (416) 366-8454. Web Site: www.academy.ca.
Directors: Cynthia Dron, Carmen Celestini, Jeanette Slinger & Joanne Kovich Robinson.
Vancouver, BC V6B 5M9, 1385 Homer St. Phone: (604) 684-4528. Fax: (604) 684-4574. Judy Jackson-Rink, mgr.
Montreal, PQ HZW 1M5, 225 rue Roy, Est # 106. Phone: (514) 849-7448. Fax: (514) 849-5069. Patrice Lachance, dir.

Acoustical Society of America, 2 Huntington Quadrayle, Suite 1N01, Melville, NY 11747-4502. Phone: (516) 576-2360. Fax: (516) 576-2377. E-mail: asa@aip.org. Web Site: asa.aip.org.

Advanced Television Systems Committee (ATSC), 1750 K St. N.W., Suite 1200, Washington, DC 20006. Phone: (202) 872-9160. Fax: (202) 872-9161. E-mail: atsc@atsc.org. Web Site: www.atsc.org.
More than 130 members representing TV networks, mfg assns & others. International voluntary tech standards-setting organization for advanced TV.

The Advertising Council Inc., 261 Madison Ave., New York, NY 10016-2303. Phone: (212) 922-1500. Fax: (212) 922-1676. E-mail: info@adcouncil.org. Web Site: www.adcouncil.org.
Washington, DC 20036, 1203 19th St. N.W., 4th Fl.. Phone: (202) 331-9153. Fax: (202) 331-9790.

Advertising Research Foundation Inc., 641 Lexington Ave., New York, NY 10022. Phone: (212) 751-5656. Fax: (212) 319-5265. Web Site: www.thearf.org.

Alliance for Community Media, 666 11th St. N.W., Suite 740, Washington, DC 20001-4542. Phone: (202) 393-2650. Fax: (202) 393-2653. E-mail: acm@alliancecm.org. Web Site: www.alliancecm.org.
Directors: Rob Brading.

Alliance of Motion Picture and Television Producers, 15503 Ventura Blvd., Encino, CA 91436. Phone: (818) 995-3600. Fax: (818) 382-1793. Web Site: www.amptp.org.

American Advertising Federation, 1101 Vermont Ave. N.W., Suite 500, Washington, DC 20005-6306. Phone: (202) 898-0089. Fax: (202) 898-0159. E-mail: aaf@aaf.org. Web Site: www.aaf.org.

American Association of Advertising Agencies (AAAA), 405 Lexington Ave., 18th Fl., New York, NY 10174-1801. Phone: (212) 682-2500. Fax: (212) 682-8391. Web Site: www.aaaa.org.
Phil Dusenberry, chmn of bd. Directors: James C. Martucci Jr., William Nicholson, JoAnn Kessler, Kathleen Quinn, J. Brown, Joanne Rotella, David Perry, Barbara Badyna, Daisy Sinclair, Sara Sax & Gloria Anderson.
Broadcast Administration Policy Committee: JoAnn Kessler (Grey Advertising Inc.), chmn; Kathleen Quinn, AAAA staff rep.
Broadcast Administration Policy Subcommittee—Central: Phila Broich, chmn; J. Brown (LMC Group, Chi).
Broadcast Administration Policy Subcommittee—South: Scott Radick (Focus-Dallas), chmn.
Broadcast Administration Policy Subcommittee—Los Angeles: Joanne Rotells (BBDO, LA), chmn.
Broadcast Administration Policy Subcommittee—San Francisco: Sharon Rundberg (Goldberg Moser O'Neill, SF), chmn.
Broadcast Production Committee: David Perry (Saatchi & Saatchi, NY).
Broadcast Administration Policy Subcommittee on Casting & Talent Agent Relations: Barbara Badyna (Young & Rubicam, NY), chmn.

American Center for Children and Media, 5400 N. St. Louis Ave., Chicago, IL 60625. Phone: (847) 390-6499. Fax: (847) 390-9435. E-mail: dkleeman@atgonline.org.
Directors: Juliet Blake, Robert Coonrod, Deborah Forte, Donna Friedman Meir, Pat Mitchell, Anne Sweeney, Jocelyn Stevenson, Marjorie Kaplan, Ame Simon, Herb Scannell, Sterling C. Quinlan, Dolores Morris & Donna Mitroff.

American Cinema Editors Inc., 100 Universal City Plaza, Bldg. 2282, Rm. 234, Universal City, CA 91608. Phone: (818) 777-2900. Fax: (818) 733-5023. E-mail: americancinema@earthlink.com. Web Site: www.ace-filmeditors.org.

American Composers Alliance (ACA), 73 Spring St., Rm. 505, New York, NY 10012. Phone: (212) 362-8900. Fax: (212) 925-6798. E-mail: info@composers.com. Web Site: www.composers.com.

American Electronics Association, 5201 Great America Pkwy., Suite 520, Santa Clara, CA 95054. Phone: (408) 987-4200. Fax: (408) 970-8565. Web Site: www.aeanet.org.
Washington, DC 20005, 601 Pennsylvania Ave Phone: (202) 682-9110. Fax: (202) 682-9111. William Archey, pres.

American Marketing Association, 311 S. Wacker Dr., Suite 5800, Chicago, IL 60606. Phone: (312) 542-9000. Fax: (312) 542-9001. Web Site: www.marketingpower.com. E-mail: info@ama.org.

American Meteorological Society, 45 Beacon St., Boston, MA 02108-3693. Phone: (617) 227-2425. Fax: (617) 742-8718. E-mail: amsinfo@ametsoc.org. Web Site: www.ametsoc.org/ams.

American Radio Relay League, 225 Main St., Newington, CT 06111. Phone: (860) 594-0200. Fax: (860) 594-0259. E-mail: hg@arrl.org. Web Site: www.arrl.org.
Joel Harrison, 1st VP.

American Society of Composers, Authors & Publishers (ASCAP), One Lincoln Plaza, New York, NY 10023. Phone: (212) 621-6000. Fax: (212) 721-0955. E-mail: info@ascap.com. Web Site: www.ascap.com.
Atlanta, GA 30339, 2690 Cumberland Pkwy, Suite 490. Phone: (800 505-4052). Fax: (770) 805-3410.
Nashville, TN 37203, 2 Music Square West Phone: (615) 742-5000. Fax: (615) 742-5020. Vincent Candilora, sr VP of licensing.
(See listing under Music Licensing, Section E.)

American Society of Media Photographers (ASMP), 150 N. Second St., Philadelphia, PA 19106. Phone: (215) 451-2767. Fax: (215) 451-0880. E-mail: info@asmp.org. Web Site: www.asmp.org.
Robert Wilex, 1st VP. Directors: Susan Carr, Judy Herrman & Clem Spalding.

American Society of TV Cameramen Inc., (U.S. affiliate of International Society of Videographers.). 2520 Lotus Hill Dr., Las Vegas, NV 89134-7855. Phone: (702) 228-6704. Fax: (702) 228-6714. E-mail: rzweck@mymailstation.com.
Directors: V.T. Jocelyn, F. Melchiorre, P. Basil & S. Bress.
Las Vegas, NV 89117. International Society of Videographers, c/o ASTVC, Inc., (U.S. Liaison Organization)., 4314 Hilary St.

American Sportscasters Association, 225 Broadway, Suite 2030, New York, NY 10007. Phone: (212) 227-8080. Fax: (212) 571-0556. E-mail: lschwa8918@aol.com. Web Site: americansportscastersonline.com.
Dick Enberg, chmn of bd. Directors: Curt Gowdy, Louis O. Schwartz, Jon Miller & Jim Nantz.

American Sportscasters Hall of Fame Trust, 225 Broadway, Suite 2030, New York, NY 10007. Phone: (212) 227-8080. Fax: (212) 571-0556. E-mail: lschwa8918@aol.com. Web Site: www.americansportscasters.com.

American Women in Radio and Television Inc., 8405 Greenboro Dr., Suite 800, McLean, VA 22102. Phone: (703) 506-3290. Fax: (703) 506-3266. Web Site: www.awrt.org. E-mail: info@awrt.org.

Association for Education in Journalism & Mass Communication (AEJMC), 234 Outlet Point Blvd., Suite A, Columbia, SC 29210. Phone: (803) 798-0271. Fax: (803) 772-3509. E-mail: aejmc@aejmc.org. Web Site: www.aejmc.org.

Association for Interactive Marketing, (AIM). 1430 Broadway 8th floor, NY, NY 10018. Phone: (888) 337-0008. Fax: (212) 391-9233. E-mail: info@imarketing.org. Web Site: www.imarketing.org.
AIM brings together companies involved in ITV, the Internet, Intranets, broadband modems & other new media in an effort to establish industry standards & hasten the dev & deployment of high speed svcs through cooperative & joint ventures. Companies enjoy a variety of membership svcs, publications, opportunities to serve on high profile leadership councils, access to speakers bureaus & other PR & promotional svcs & market rsch.

The Association for International Broadcasting, Box 990, London SE3 9XL. Phone: (44) 181-852-6347. Phone: (44) 1255 676 996. Fax: (44) 181 852 0853.
Directors: Tom Walters, mktg; Tim Keeler, pub affrs.

Association for Maximum Service Television Inc., (MSTV, Inc.). Box 9897, 4100 Wisconsin Ave., N.W., Washington, DC 20016. Phone: (202) 966-1956. Fax: (202) 96617. Web Site: www.mstv.org.

The Association for Women In Communications, 780 Ritchie Hwy., Suite 28 S, Severna Park, MD 21146. Phone: (410) 544-7442. Fax: (410) 544-4640. E-mail: info@womcom.com. Web Site: www.womcom.org.
Directors: Lucy Harr, Nancy Tack, Betty Parker Ellis, Helene O'Haver, Mary Ann Edwards, Tina Steger-Gratz, Mary Kay Switzer, Jane Hardy & Lucia Libretti.

Association of American Railroads, American Railroads Bldg., 50 F St. N.W., Washington, DC 20001. Phone: (202) 639-2556. Fax: (202) 639-2558. E-mail: twhite@www.aar.org. Web Site: www.aar.org.

Association of Canadian Advertisers Inc., 175 Bloor St. E., South Tower, Suite 307, Toronto, ON M4W 3R8. Canada. Phone: (416) 964-3805. Phone: (800) 565-0109 (CA). Fax: (416) 964-0771. E-mail: info@aca-online.com. Web Site: www.aca-online.com.
Montreal, PQ H7A 3C6, 500 Sherbrooke St. W. Phone: (514) 842-6422. (800) 883-0422. Fax: (514) 842-6223. Roger Sirard, VP/member svcs.

Association of Federal Communications Consulting Engineers, Box 19333, Washington, DC 20036-0333. Phone: (941) 329-6000. Fax: (941) 329-6030. Web Site: www.afcce.org.

Association of National Advertisers Inc. (ANA), 708 Third Ave., New York, NY 10017. Phone: (212) 697-5950. Fax: (212) 661-8057. Web Site: www.ana.net.
Directors: Donald F. Calhoon, Jocelyn Carter-Miller, J. Andrea Alstrup, Catherine D. Constable, Christopher Fraleigh, James J. Garrity, David B. Green, John D. Hayes, Stephen C. Jones, Dawn Hudson, David N. Iauco, Abby F. Kohnstamm, Ann Lewnes, Eric W. Leininger, Robert D. Liodice, Paula S. Sneed, Gary E. McCullough, James R. Stengel, James D. Speros, Allan H. Stefl, Stephen G. Sullivan, Joseph V. Tripodi, Rebecca Saeger, James L. McDowell, Nancy J. Wiese, Robert J. Gamgort & Robert C Lachky.
Washington, DC 20036. Washington Office, 1120 20th St. N.W., Suite 5206. Phone: (202) 296-1883. Fax: (202) 296-1430.

Association of Public Television Stations, 666 11th St. NW, Suite 200, Washington, DC 20001. Phone: (202) 654-4200. Fax: (202) 654-4237. Web Site: www.apts.org.
Directors: Meegan White.

The Audio Engineering Society Inc., 60 E. 42nd St., Rm. 2520, New York, NY 10165. Phone: (212) 661-8528. Fax: (212) 682-0477. E-mail: hq@aes.org. Web Site: www.aes.org.

BMI Broadcast Music Inc. 320 W. 57th St., New York, NY 10019-3790. Phone: (212) 586-2000. Fax: (212) 246-2163. E-mail: abooth@bmi.com. Web Site: www.bmi.com.
Directors: Philip A. Jones, Frances W. Preston, James G. Babb, Harold C. Crump, N. John Douglas, Frank E. Melton, George V. Willoughby, K. James Yager, G. Neil Smith, David Sherman, Donald A. Thurston, Cecil L. Walker, Catherine L. Hughes, Craig A. Dubow, Amador Bustos & John L. Sander.
West Hollywood, CA 90069-2211, 8730 Sunset Blvd, 3rd Fl. W.. Phone: (310) 659-9109.

National Associations

Nashville, TN 37203-4399, 10 Music Sq. E Phone: (615) 401-2000.

Broadcast Cable Credit Association Inc. (BCCA), 550 W. Frontage Rd., Suite 3600, Northfield, IL 60093. Phone: (847) 881-8059. Fax: (847) 784-8059. E-mail: info@bccacredit.com. Web Site: www.bccacredit.com.

Directors: Joseph Barlek, Tim Pecaro & Leslie Hartmann.

Broadcast Cable Financial Management Association (BCFM), 932 Lee St., Suite 204, Des Plaines, IL 60016. Phone: (847) 296-0200. Fax: (847) 296-7510. E-mail: info@bcfm.com. Web Site: www.bcfm.com.

Directors: Timothy Pecaro, Leslie Hartman & Joseph Barlek.

Broadcast Education Association, 1771 N St. N.W., Washington, DC 20036-2891. Phone: (202) 429-5355. Phone: (888) 380-7222. Fax: (202) 775-2981. E-mail: beainfo@beaweb.org. Web Site: www.beaweb.org.

Directors: Mary Alice Molgard, Thomas R. Berg, Rustin Greene, Joe Misiewicz, David Byland, Robert K. Avery, Gary Martin, Greg Luft, D'Artagnan Bebel, Stephen J. Cohen, Larry Patrick, Alan R. Albarran, Gary Corbitt, Steven Anderson, Norman Pattiz & Jannette L. Dates.

Broadcasters' Foundation Inc., 7 Lincoln Ave., Greenwich, CT 06830. Phone: (203) 862-8577. Fax: (203) 629-5739. E-mail: ghhbcast@aol.com.

Gordon H. Hastings, pres/CEO. Directors: Edward F. McLaughlin, David Abramson, Arthur M. Angstreich, Martin F. Beck, Philip R. Beuth, Arthur W. Carlson, James E. Champlin, Vincent J. Curtis, Aaron Daniels, Erica Farber, Richard A. Foreman, Gary Fries, Edward Fritts, Ragan A. Henry, Catherine Hughes, John A. Knebel, N. Scott Knight, Jerry Lee, Philip J. Lombardo, Lucille F. Luongo, Tony Malara, William McGorry, Stanley H. Moger, Dawson Nail, Deborah Norville, William O'Shaughnessy, Frances Preston, Joseph Reilly, Dennis Swanson, Sherril Taylor, Nicholas J. Verbitsky, Arthur Liu, William G. Moll, Diane Linen Powell & Edward T. Reilly.

Broadcasters Hall of Fame, 1240 Ashford Ln. #1A, Akron, OH 44313. Phone: (330) 836-4864.

Directors: Kelly Bolles, Ralph Gillman, Lucille Hageman, Brenda M. Abrams, Sue Duncan, Melvin L. Brown, Charles Short, Cherie McGregor & Jack Bennett.

Akron, OH 044320, Box 8192 Henry Dunn, treas. (Broadcaster's Hall of Fame).

CTAM, Cable & Telecommunications Association. 201 N. Union St., Suite 440, Alexandria, VA 22314. Phone: (703) 549-4200. Fax: (703) 684-1167. E-mail: info@ctam.com. Web Site: www.ctam.com.

Kevin Leddy, vice chmn; Len Fogge, sec. Directors: Douglas Holloway, Dave Watson, James O'Brien, Pamela Euler Halling, Sean Bratches, John Dyer, Eric Kesler, Coleman Breland, Betsy Frank, Bill Goodwyn & Gregg Graff.

The Cable Center, 2000 Buchtel Blvd., Denver, CO 80210. Phone: (303) 871-4885. Fax: (303) 871-4514. E-mail: info@cablecenter.org. Web Site: www.cablecenter.org.

Directors: Lisa Barkman & Nora Feeley.

Cable in the Classroom, 1724 Massachusetts Ave. N.W., Washington, DC 20036. Phone: (202) 775-1040. Fax: (202) 775-1047. Web Site: www.ciconline.org.

Cable Television Laboratories, 858 Coal Creek Cir., Louisville, CO 80027-9750. Phone: (303) 661-9100. Fax: (303) 661-9199. Web Site: www.cablelabs.com.

Cable TV Public Affairs Association, Box 33697, Washington, DC 20033. Phone: (202) 775-1081. Fax: (202) 955-1134. E-mail: services@ctpaa.org. Web Site: www.ctpaa.org.

Portia Badham, pres; Mark Harrad, VP; Christine Levesque, VP; Steve Raddock, VP; Charles Schueler, sr VP; Mike Schwartz, sr VP; Jim Ewalt, VP; Mark Hotz, sr VP; Directors: Jenni Moyer, Scoot MacPherson, Rosa Gatti, Libby O'Connell, Anthony W. Accamando Jr. & Anita Lamont.

Cabletelevision Advertising Bureau Inc. (CAB),

See listing under Major National Associations, this section.

Can-West Media Sales, 333 King St. E., Toronto, ON M5A 4R7. Canada. Phone: (416) 350-6002. Fax: (416) 442-2209. E-mail: queries@nationalpost.com. Web Site: www.canada.com.

Canadian Association of Broadcast Consultants, 275 rue High, Sherbrooke, PQ J1H 3W2. Canada. Phone: (819) 346-1556. Fax: (819) 346-7174. E-mail: info@enondes.net.

The Canadian Association of Broadcasters, Box 627, Station B, 306-350 Sparks St., Ottawa, ON K1P 5S2. Canada. Phone: (613) 233-4035. Fax: (613) 233-6961. E-mail: cab@cab-acr.ca. Web Site: www.cab-arc.ca.

Ottawa, ON K1R 7S8 Canada, 306-350 Sparks St Phone: (613) 233-4035.

Canadian Association of Ethnic (Radio) Broadcasters, 622 College St., Toronto, ON M6G 1B6. Canada. Phone: (416) 531-9991. Fax: (416) 531-5274. E-mail: info@chinradio.com. Web Site: www.chinradio.com.

Canadian Cable Television Association (CCTA),

See listing under Major National Associations, this section.

Canadian Film and Television Production Association (CFTPA), 160 John St., Toronto, ON M5C 2E5. Canada. Phone: (416) 304-0280. Fax: (416) 304-0499. E-mail: toronto@cftpa.ca. Web Site: www.cftpa.ca.

Directors: Cara Martin.

Ottawa, ON K1P 5H3, 151 Slater St., Suite 605. Phone: (613)-233-1444. Fax: (613)-233-0073.

Caribbean Broadcasting Union (CBU), Waterford Main House, Waterford, St. Michael Barbados. Phone: (246) 430-1006. Fax: (246) 228-7756. Fax: (246) 228-9524. E-mail: jpc@inaccs.com.bb. Web Site: www.caribunion.com.

Directors: Mr. Vic Fernandes, Mr. Guno Cooman, Mrs. Melba Smith, Mr. Anthony Vieira & Mr. Edwin Lightbourne.

Catholic Academy for Communication Arts Professionals, 901 Irving Ave., Dayton, OH 45409-2316. Phone: (937) 229-2303. Fax: (937) 229-2300. E-mail: admin@catholicacademy.org. Web Site: www.catholicacademy.org.

Jeanean Merkel, 1st VP; Vicki Bedard, 2nd VP.

Center for Communication Inc., 561 Broadway, Suite 12 B, New York, NY 10012. Phone: (212) 686-5005. Fax: (212) 686-6393. E-mail: info@cencom.org. Web Site: www.cencom.org.

Edward Bleier, chmn; Frank Stanton, dir emeritus. Directors: Timothy Barry, William F. Baker, Robert M. Batscha, Patricia T. Carbine, Antoinette Cook Bush, John A. Dimling, David R. Drobis, Michael Eigner, Peter R. Ezersky, Charles B. Fruit, Ralph Guild, Andrew Heyward, Peter Jennings, Gerald M. Levin, Kate McEnroe, Martin Nisenholtz, Herbert Scannell, Alan Siegel, Alfred C. Sikes, Kenneth Stoddard, Howard Stringer, Alberto Vitale, Stephen A. Weiswasser, David Westin, Bob Wright, Lois Wyse, Mortimer B. Zuckerman, Simon Michael Bessie, Louis D. Boccardi, David W. Burke, Henry A. Grunwald, Irwin Segelstein, Burton B. Staniar & Loet A. Velmans.

Commercial Television Australia Limited, 44 Avenue Rd., Mosman, N.S.W 02088. Australia. Phone: (612) 9960 2622. Fax: (612) 9960 3520. Web Site: www.ctva.com.au.

John Mc Alpine, chmn.

Commonwealth Broadcasting Assn, CBA Secretariat, 17 Fleet St., London EC4Y 1AA. United Kingdom. Phone: 011-44-171-5835550. Fax: 011-44-171-5835549. E-mail: cba@cba.org.uk.

Directors: George Valarino, Ronald Abraham, Roger Grant, Robert O'Rielly, Tombong Saidy, Sharon Crosbie & Cecilia Khuzwayo.

Community Broadcasters Association (CBA), 515 King St., Suite 420, Alexandria, VA 22314. Phone: (703) 562-3588. Fax: (703) 684-6048. Web Site: www.communitybroadcasters.com.

Directors: Gary Co Cola, Larry Morton, Eleanor St. John, Warren Trumbly, Doug Williams, Sandra Woodworth & Lou Zanoni.

Produces major country radio convention; rgnl radio seminar; Country DJ Hall of Fame

Council of Better Business Bureaus Inc., 4200 Wilson Blvd., 8th Fl., Arlington, VA 22203-1838. Phone: (703) 276-0100. Fax: (703) 525-8277. E-mail: bbb@bbb.org. Web Site: www.bbb.org.

Ottawa, ON K1N 7A2 Canada, 44 Byward Market Sq., Suite 220.

Country Music Association Inc., One Music Cir. S., Nashville, TN 37203. Phone: (615) 244-2840. Fax: (615) 726-0314. Web Site: www.cnaworld.com.

Country Radio Broadcasters Inc., 819 18th Ave. S., Nashville, TN 37203. Phone: (615) 327-4487. Fax: (615) 329-4492. Web Site: www.crb.org.

This non-profit organization is the only assn specifically serving country radio. Holds annual Country Radio Seminar; rgnl conventions; trustee of Country DJ Hall of Fame &Country Radio Hall of Fame.

Electro Federation Canada, 5800 Explorer Dr., Suite 200, Mississauga, ON L4W 5K9. Canada. Phone: (905) 602-8877. Fax: (905) 602-5686. E-mail: info@electrofed.com. Web Site: www.electrofed.com.

Electronic Industries Alliance (EIA), 2500 Wilson Blvd., Arlington, VA 22201. Phone: (703) 907-7500. Fax: (703) 907-7501. Web Site: www.eia.org.

Electronic Retailing Association (ERA), 2101 Wilson Blvd., Suite 1002, Arlington, VA 22201. Phone: (703) 841-1751. Fax: (703) 841-1750. E-mail: contact@retailing.org. Web Site: www.retailing.org.

Stephen F. Breimer, Esq.; Jeffrey Knowles, Esq.. Directors: Linda Goldstein, Mike Ackerman, Rick Cesari, Dan Danielson, Denise Dubarry Hay, Rollie Froehlig, Larry Jellen, Jack Kirby, Mark Lavin, Shigeru Ohashi, Rick Petry, Steve Pittenridgh, Richard Prochnow, Randy Ronning, Robert Rosenblatt, Bret Saxton, Mark Thornton & Reiner Weihofen.

Electronic Service Dealers Association, 4927 W. Irving Park Rd., Chicago, IL 60641. Phone: (773) 282-9400.

Electronics Representatives Association, 444 N. Michigan Ave., Suite 1960, Chicago, IL 60611. Phone: (312) 527-3050. Fax: (312) 527-3783. E-mail: info@era.org. Web Site: www.era.org.

FCBA (Federal Communications Bar Association), 1020 19th St. N.W., Suite 325, Washington, DC 20036-6101. Phone: (202) 293-4000. Fax: (202) 293-4317. E-mail: fcba@fcba.org. Web Site: www.fcba.org.

Festival international du nouveau Cinema et des nouveaux Medias de Montreal, 3530 St. Laurent Blvd., Ste. Bureau 304, Montreal, PQ H2X 2v1. Canada. Phone: (514) 847-9272. Fax: (514) 847-0732. E-mail: info@fcmm.com. Web Site: www.fcmm.com.

Foundation for American Communications (FACS), 85 South Grand Ave., Pasadena, CA 91105. Phone: (626) 584-0010. Fax: (626) 584-0627. E-mail: facs@facsnet.org. Web Site: www.facsnet.org.

Leesburg, VA 20176, 3 Wirt St. N.W. Phone: (703) 737-3570. (888) 739-7865.

Hollywood Radio & Television Society, 13701 Riverside Dr., Suite 205, Sherman Oaks, CA 91423. Phone: (818) 789-1182. Fax: (818) 789-1210. E-mail: info@hrts.org. Web Site: www.hrts.org.

IEEE, 445 Hoes Ln., Piscataway, NJ 08854-1331. Phone: (732) 981-0060. Fax: (732) 981-1721. Web Site: www.ieee.org.

Directors: Cecelia Jankowski, Pete Lewis, Helen Horwitz, Mary Ward-Callan, John Witsken, Tom Suttle, Judy Gorman, Henry Shein & Don Curtis.

New York, NY 10016-5997, 3 Park Ave. 17th Fl. Phone: (212) 419-7900. Fax: (212) 752-4929.

Intercollegiate Broadcasting System Inc., 367 Windsor Hwy., New Windsor, NY 12553-7900. Phone: (845) 565-0003. Fax: (845) 565-7446. E-mail: ibs@ibsradio.org. Web Site: www.ibsradio.org.

Directors: John Murphy, Fritz Kass, Norm Prusslin & Chuck Platt.

The International Academy of Television Arts & Sciences, 142 W. 57th St., 16th Fl., New York, NY 10019. Phone: (212) 489-6969. Fax: (212) 489-6557. Web Site: www.jemmys.com.

International Advertising Association, (The global partnership of advertisers, agencies & media.). 521 Fifth Ave., Suite 1807, New York, NY 10175. Phone: (212) 557-1133. Fax: (212) 983-0455. E-mail: iaa@iaaglobal.org. Web Site: www.iaaglobal.org.

Wendy Burrell, mgng dir. Directors: Richard Corner.

International Animated Film Society, ASIFA-Hollywood, 721 S. Victory Blvd., Burbank, CA 91502. Phone: (818) 842-8330. Fax: (818) 842-5645. E-mail: info@asifa-hollywood.org. Web Site: www.asifa-hollywood.org.

Directors: Jerry Beck, Stephen Worth, Bob Miller, Tom Knott, Frank Gladstone, David Derks, Margaret Kerry-Wilcox, Larry Loc & Will Ryan.

International Association of Audio Information Services, c/o WVTF Public Radio, 4235 Electric Rd., Suite 105, Roanoke, VA 24014. Phone: (800) 280-5325. Fax: (540) 776-2727. E-mail: benm@vt.edu. Web Site: www.iaais.org.

Directors: Lynne Koral, Mike Duke, David Andrews, Heather Lusignan, Allen Little, Lehy Graham-Corona, Glenn Sabatka, Kim Walsh, Linda Ornt, Kathy Garver, Carl Matthusen, Paul McLane, Mike Starling & Hal Kneller.

National Associations

International Communication Agency Network (ICOM), Box 490, Rollinsville, CO 80474. Phone: (303) 258-9511. Fax: (303) 258-3090. E-mail: info@icomagencies.com.

Directors: Frank G. Weyforth.

International Institute of Communications, 35 Porland Pl., 3rd. Fl., Westcott, London WIB IAE. Phone: (44) 207-323-9622. Fax: (44) 207-323-9623. E-mail: enquiries@iicom.org. Web Site: www.iicom.org.

International Radio & Television Society Foundation Inc., 420 Lexington Ave., Suite 1601, New York, NY 10170. Phone: (212) 867-6650. Fax: (212) 867-6653. Web Site: www.irts.org.

International Recording Media Association, 182 Nassau St., Suite 204, Princeton, NJ 08542. Phone: (609) 279-1700. Fax: (609) 279-1999. E-mail: info@recordingmedia.org. Web Site: www.recordingmedia.org.

Directors: Tony Perez.

KOBI-TV (NBC Affiliate), (An affiliate of California & Oregon Broadcasting Inc.). 125 S. Fir St., Medford, OR 97501. Phone: (541) 779-5555. Fax: (541) 779-1151. Web Site: www.localnewscomesfirst.com. E-mail: kobi@kobi5.com.

Klamath Falls, OR 97601. KOTI-TV, 222 S. 7th St.

League of Advertising Agencies, 915 Clifton Ave., Clifton, NJ 07013. Phone: (973) 473-6643. Fax: (943) 473-0685. E-mail: info@weinrichadv.com. Web Site: www.weinrichadv.com.

Library of American Broadcasting Foundtion Inc., 21 Seven Bridges Rd., Chappaqua, NY 10514. Phone: (914) 238-8292. Fax: (914) 238-9187. E-mail: broadcastlibrary@aol.com.

Directors: James L. Greenwald, Vincent Curtis, Arthur W. Carlson, Erwin Krasnow, Jerry Lee, Larry Taishoff, Jim Morley, Susan Ness, Don West, Richard Buckley, Judy Kuriansky, Russ Withers & Pier Mapes.

Maryland, NO, University of Maryland, College Park. Phone: (301) 405-9160. Fax: (301) 314-2634. Web Site: www.lib.umd.edu/UMCP/LAB.

Los Angeles Advertising Agencies Association, 5670 Wilshire Blvd., Suite 1550, Los Angeles, CA 90036. Phone: (323) 857-5301. Fax: (323) 857-5302. E-mail: submissions@aaaa.com. Web Site: www.laaaa.com.

Magazine Publishers of America, 810 7th Ave, 24th Fl., New York, NY 10019. Phone: (212) 872-3700. Fax: (212) 888-4217. E-mail: mpa@magazine.org. Web Site: www.magazine.org.

Directors: Galit Rich & Wayne Eadie.

Media Access Group, WGBH, Box 200, Boston, MA 02134. Phone: (617) 300-2000. Fax: (617) 300-1020. Fax: (617) 300-1026. E-mail: access@wgbh.org. Web Site: access.wgbh.org.

Directors: Lori Kay, Tom Apone & Susan Schneider.

The Media Institute, 1000 Potomac St. N.W., Suite 301, Washington, DC 20007. Phone: (202) 298-7512. Fax: (202) 337-7092. E-mail: info@mediainstitute.org. Web Site: www.mediainstitute.org.

Minority Media and Telecommunications Council, 3636 16th St. N.W., B-366, Washington, DC 20010. Phone: (202) 332-0500. Fax: (202) 332-0503.

Mortgage Bankers Association of America (MBA), 1919 Pennsylvania Ave. N.W., Washington, DC 20006-3404. Phone: (202) 557-2700 (hqtrs). Phone: (202) 557-2752 (membership). E-mail: communications@mbaa.org. Web Site: www.mbaa.org.

Motion Picture Association of America, 15503 Ventura Blvd., Encino, CA 91436. Phone: (818) 995-6600. Fax: (818) 382-1799. Web Site: www.mpaa.org.

Encino, CA 91436, 15503 Ventura Blvd Phone: (818) 995-6600. Fax: (818) 382-1778.

The Museum of Broadcast Communications, 400 N. State St., Suite 240, Chicago, IL 60610-4624. Phone: (312) 396-0101. Fax: (312) 396-0103. Web Site: www.museum.tv.

Museum is free to public. Hours: 10 AM-4:30PM (M-S); Noon-5PM (Su).

The Museum of Television & Radio, 25 W. 52nd St., New York, NY 10019-6101. Phone: (212) 621-6600. Fax: (212) 621-6700. Web Site: www.mtr.org. E-mail: publicrelations@mtr.org.

Directors: Barbara Dixon.

NCTI, 8022 Couthpark Circle, Suite 100, Littleton, CO 80120-5658. Phone: (303) 797-9393. Fax: (303) 797-9394. Web Site: www.ncti.com.

The National Academy of Television Arts & Sciences, 111 W. 57th St., Suite 600, New York, NY 10019. Phone: (212) 586-8424. Fax: (212) 246-8129. Web Site: www.emmyonline.org.

The National Academy of Television Journalists Inc., Box 31, Salisbury, MD 21803. Phone: (410) 548-5343. Fax: (410) 543-0658. E-mail: infi@goldenviddyawards.com. Web Site: www.goldenviddyawards.com.

Directors: Dr. Catherine North & Cathy Roche.

National Association of Black Journalists (NABJ), 8701-A Adelphi Road, Adelphi, MD 20783-1716. Phone: (301) 445-7100. Fax: (301) 445-7101. E-mail: nabj@nabj.org. Web Site: www.nabj.org.

Directors: Ernie Suggs, Jerry McClendon, Stephanie Jones, Rachelle Dickerson Christie, Elliott Lewis, Marsha J. Eaglin, Victor W. Vaughan, Russell Lacour & Neal T. Scarbrough.

National Association of Black Owned Broadcasters Inc. (NABOB), 1155 Connecticut Ave., N.W., 6th Fl., Washington, DC 20036. Phone: (202) 463-8970. Fax: (202) 429-0657. E-mail: info@nabob.org. Web Site: www.nabob.org.

Directors: Pierre M. Sutton, Bennie Turner, Sydney L Small, Lois E. Wright, Michael Carter, Alfred Liggins, James Wolfe, Michael Roberts, Karen Slade & Carol Moore Cutting.

National Association of Broadcasters,

See listing under Major National Associations, this section.

National Association of College Broadcasters (NACB), 71 George St., Providence, RI 02912-1824. Phone: (401) 863-2225. Fax: (401) 863-2221. E-mail: nacb@brown.edu.

National Association of Hispanic Journalists, 1000 National Press Bldg., 529 14th St. N.W., Washington, DC 20045-2001. Phone: (202) 662-7145. Phone: (888) 346-nahj. Fax: (202) 662-7144. E-mail: nahj@nahj.org. Web Site: www.nahj.org.

National Association of Telecommunications Officers and Advisors, 1800 Diagonal Rd., Suite 495, Alexandria, VA 22314. Phone: (703) 519-8035. Fax: (703) 519-8036. E-mail: info@natoa.org. Web Site: www.natoa.org.

National Association of Television Program Executives International,

See listing under Major National Associations, this section.

National Association of Theatre Owners Inc. (NATO), 750 1st St. N.E., Suite 1130, Washington, DC 20002. Phone: (202) 962-0054. Fax: (202) 962-0370. E-mail: nato@natodc.com. Web Site: www.natoonline.org.

North Hollywood, CA 91602. NATO Communications (In Focus), 4605 Lankershim Blvd., #340. Phone: (818) 506-1778.

National Black Media Coalition, 1738 Elton Rd., Suite 314, Silver Springs, MD 20903. Phone: (301) 445-2600. Fax: (301) 445-1693. E-mail: nbmc2000@aol.com. Web Site: www.nbmc.org.

National Cable and Television Association Inc. (NCTA),

See listing under Major National Associations, this section.

National Cable Television Cooperative Inc.,

See listing under Major National Associations, this section.

National Captioning Institute (NCI), 1900 Gallows Rd., Suite 3000, Vienna, VA 22182. Phone: (703) 917-7600. Fax: (703) 917-9878. E-mail: mail@ncicap.org. Web Site: www.ncicap.org.

Directors: Karen O' Connor, Marc Okrand, Beth Nubbe & Stephanie Gray.

Burbank, CA 91502, 303 N. Glenoaks Blvd., Suite 200. Phone: (818) 238-0068. (818) 238-4255.

Dallas, TX 75247, 7610 N. Stemmons Fwy., Suite 200. Phone: (214) 647-4360. (214) 647-4386.

National Council for Families & Television, 6500 Wilshire Blvd., Suite 1950, Los Angeles, CA 90048. Phone: (323) 866-6020. Fax: (310) 208-5984. E-mail: ncft@yahoo.com.

Directors: Garth Ancier, Marcy Carsey, Bill Nielsen, Geraldine Laybourne, Marian Rees, Leslie Moonves & Teresa Heinz.

National Education Association, 1201 16th St. N.W., Washington, DC 20036-3290. Phone: (202) 833-4000. Fax: (202) 822-7974. Web Site: www.nea.org.

National Electrical Manufacturers Association (NEMA), 1300 N. 17th St., Suite 1847, Rosslyn, VA 22209. Phone: (703) 841-3200. Fax: (703) 841-3300. E-mail: webmaster@nema.org. Web Site: www.nema.org.

National Federation of Community Broadcasters (NFCB), 1970 Broadway, Suite 1000, Oakland, CA 94612. Phone: (510) 451-8200. Fax: (510) 451-8208. E-mail: nfcb@nfcb.org. Web Site: www.nfcb.org.

National Federation of Press Women Inc.-NFPW, Box 5556, Arlington, VA 22205. Phone: (703) 534-2500. Phone: (800) 780-2715. Fax: (703) 534-5751. E-mail: presswomen@aol.com. Web Site: www.nfpw.org.

Donna Penticuff, 1st VP; Meg Hunt, 2nd VP.

Programs, svcs & contest categories for female & male professionals in all media.

National League of Cities, 1301 Pennsylvania Ave. N.W., Suite 550, Washington, DC 20004. Phone: (202) 626-3000. Fax: (202) 626-3043. E-mail: reinemer@nlc.org. Web Site: www.nlc.org.

Directors: Sherry Conway, Marilyn Mohrman & William Barnes.

National Museum of Communications Inc., 2001 Plymouth Rock Dr., Richardson, TX 75081. Phone: (214) 616-6562. Fax: (972) 889-2329. E-mail: bill@yesterdayusa.com. Web Site: www.yesterdayusa.com.

National Newspaper Association, Box 7540, Columbia, MO 65205-7540. Phone: (573) 882-5800. Fax: (573) 884-5490. E-mail: info@nna.org. Web Site: www.nna.org.

Directors: Robert Sweeney, Mike Buffington & Jerry Reppert.

Arlington, VA 22205, Box 5737 Phone: (703) 534-1278.

National Press Club, 529 14th St. N.W., Washington, DC 20045. Phone: (202) 662-7500. Fax: (202) 662-7512. E-mail: info@npcpress.org. Web Site: www.press.org.

Joe Anselmo, chmn of bd. Directors: Tom Glad.

National Religious Broadcasters (NRB), 9510 Technology Dr., Manassas, VA 20110. Phone: (703) 330-7000. Fax: (703) 330-7100. E-mail: fwright@nrb.org. Web Site: www.nrb.org/nrb.

National Retail Federation, 325 7th St. N.W., Suite 1100, Washington, DC 20004. Phone: (202) 783-7971. Phone: (800) nrf-how2. Fax: (202) 737-2849. Web Site: www.nrf.com.

National Statenets of State Radio Networks Inc., 17911 Harwood Ave., Homewood, IL 60430. Phone: (708) 799-6676. Fax: (708) 799-6698. Fax: (708) 799-1163. E-mail: tdobrez@statenets.com. Web Site: www.statenets.com.

Directors: Carolyn Martin, Thomas Dobrez & Darren Smith.

National Telemedia Council Inc., 1922 University Ave., Madison, WI 53726. Phone: (608) 218-1182. Fax: (608) 218-1183. E-mail: ntelemedia@aol.com. Web Site: nationaltelemediacouncil.org.

Rev. Stephen Umhoefer, treas.

Newseum, 1101 Wilson Blvd., Arlington, VA 22209. Phone: (703) 284-3544. Phone: (888) new-seum. E-mail: newseum@freedomforum.org. Web Site: www.newseum.org.

Newspaper Association of America, 1921 Gallows Rd., Suite 600, Vienna, VA 22182-3900. Phone: (703) 902-1600. Fax: (703) 719-0636. Web Site: www.naa.org.

Directors: R. Gene Bell, William Blocl Jr., R. Bruce Bradley, J. Stewart Bryan III, Susan Clark-Johnson, Jean B. Clifton, Mark G. Contreras, W. Stacey Cowles, James C. Currow, R. Jack Fishman, Dennis J. Fitzsimons, Caroline D. Harrison, Alan M. Horton, Alberto Ibarguen, Julie Inskeep, George B. Irish, Boisfeuillet Jones Jr. & Robert C. Woodworth.

North American Broadcasters Association (NABA), Box 500, Stn A, Rm. 6C 300, Toronto, ON M5W 1E6. Canada. Phone: (416) 598-9877. Fax: (416) 598-9774. E-mail: info@nabanet.com. Web Site: www.nabanet.com.

Directors: Joseph Flaherty, Felix Arauji Ramirez, Ignacio Suarez, Andy Setos & Peter Smith.

North American Retail Dealers Association, 10 E. 22nd St., Suite 310, Lombard, IL 60148-6191. Phone: (630) 953-8950. Phone: (800) 621-0298. Fax: (630) 953-8957. E-mail: nardahdq@narda.com. Web Site: www.narda.com.

Michael Fischer, chmn of bd; Andy Whitehead, 1st VP. Directors: Timothy Seavey, Michael Corder, Ivans Popkin, Kent Reiner, Ben Benson & Larry Clark.

Pacific Pioneer Broadcasters, Box 4866, Valley Village, CA 91617-4866. Phone: (323) 461-2121. Fax: (818) 768-8251. Web Site: ppbwebsite.org.

Broadcasting & Cable Yearbook 2006

National Associations

PROMAX&BDA, 2029 Century Park E., Suite 555, Los Angeles, CA 90067-2906. Phone: (310) 788-7600. Phone: (800) 977-6629. Fax: (310) 788-7616. Web Site: www.promax.tv. E-mail: jim@promax.tv.

Directors: David Snapp, George Pierson, Lisa Fengler, Leslie Celia, Jeannine Chanin, Tony Cleave, Ann Epstein-Cohen, Steve Delaney, Miguel Muelle, Karen Olcott, Jan Phillips, Abel Sanchez, Robin Skirboll, Anne White, Mark Stroman, Glynn Brailsford, Brian Blum, Judy Braune, Alan Cohen, Scott Danielson, C.J. Fredricksen, Lee Hunt, Kay Hutchison, Tony Lakin, Vince Manze, Brigitte McCray, Rob Middleton, Nick Miller, Michael Mischler, David Muscari, Billy Pittard, Sal Sardo, George Schweitzer, Curtis Symonds & Donna Weston.

Hong Kong China. Synapse Pacific LTD, 49 Hollywood Rd., 19th Fl..

London, NO SE1 0RF United Kingdom. Promax & BDA Europe, 61 Webber St.

Promotion Marketing Association Inc., 257 Park Ave. S., Suite 1102, New York, NY 10010. Phone: (212) 420-1100. Fax: (212) 533-7622. E-mail: pma@pmalink.org. Web Site: www.pmalink.org.

Public Radio in Mid-America (PRIMA), c/o KWMU-FM One University Blvd., University of Missouri, St. Louis, MO 63121-4499. Phone: (314) 516-5968. Fax: (314) 516-5993. E-mail: pwente@kwmu.org. Web Site: www.prima.org.

Directors: Bill McGinley, Christina Kuzmych, Tim Emmons & Jon Schwartz.

Public Radio News Directors Incorporated, 821 University Ave., Madison, NY 53706. Phone: (608) 265-3378. Fax: (608) 263-5838. E-mail: walker@wpr.org.

Directors: Dave Piznanelli, Martha Foley, Jonathan Ahl & Christine Paige-Diers.

Public Relations Society of America, 33 Maiden Ln., 11th Fl., New York, NY 10038. Phone: (212) 460-1400. Fax: (212) 995-0757. E-mail: hq@prsa.org. Web Site: www.prsa.org.

Cheryl Procter-Rogers, pres. Directors: Janet Troy.

Radio Advertising Bureau,

See listing under Major National Associations, this section.

Radio and Television Museum, 2608 Mitchellville Rd., Bowie, MD 20716. Phone: (301) 390-1020. Web Site: www.radiohistory.org.

Radio & Television News Directors Foundation, 1600 K St. NW, Suite 700, Washington, DC 20006. Phone: (202) 659-6510. Fax: (202) 223-4007. E-mail: rtndf@rtndf.org. Web Site: www.rtndf.org.

Radio & Television Research Council, c/o MSA, Attn: R. Sharpe, 234 5th Ave., Suite 417, New York, NY 10001. Phone: (212) 481-3038. Fax: (212) 481-3071. E-mail: rtrcny@aol.com.

Radio Marketing Bureau, 175 Bloor St. E., Suite 316 North Tower, Toronto, ON MRW 3R8. Canada. Phone: (416) 922-5757. Fax: (416) 922-6542. E-mail: info@rmb.ca. Web Site: www.rmb.ca.

Directors: Bill Herz, Tom Manton, Elmer Hildebrand, Ross Tirrell, Patrick Grierson, John Hayes, Jim MacLeod, Mark Olsen, Chris Pandoff, Luc Sabbatini, Gerry Siemens, Dick Sienko, Jim Blundell, Richard Cavanaugh, Lesley Conway-Kelley, Glenn Chalmers & Ron Hutchinson.

Radio-Television Correspondents' Association, S-325, U.S. Capitol, Washington, DC 20510. Phone: (202) 224-6421. Fax: (202) 224-4882. Web Site: www.senate.gov/galleries.radiotv.com.

Directors: Jerry Bodlander, Bob Fuss, Edward O'Keefe, Dave McConnell, Richard Tillery & David Welna.

Radio Television News Directors Association (Canada), 2175 Shephard Ave. E., Suite 310, Toronto, ON M2J 1W8. Canada. Phone: (416) 756-2213. Fax: (416) 491-1670. E-mail: rtnda@taylorenterprises.com. Web Site: www.rtndacanada.com.

Radio-Television News Directors Association,

See listing under Major National Associations, this section.

Recording Industry Association of America Inc. (RIAA), 1330 Connecticut Ave. N.W., Suite 300, Washington, DC 20036. Phone: (202) 775-0101. Fax: (202) 775-7253. Web Site: www.riaa.org.

Royal Television Society, North America Inc., Box 870501, Arizona State University, Tempe, AZ 85287-0501. Phone: (480) 965-7661. Fax: (480) 965-1371. E-mail: royaltv@asu.edu. Web Site: www.royaltv.pp.asu.edu.

SPTV, 74 Hartzel Rd., CBC Newsworld, St. Catherines, ON M5W 1E6. Canada. Phone: (416) 682-9924. E-mail: streyn@iaw.on.ca.

Satellite Broadcasting & Communications Assn. of America (SBCA), 225 Reinekers Ln., Suite 600, Alexandria, VA 22314. Phone: (703) 549-6990. Phone: (800) 541-5981. Fax: (703) 549-7640. E-mail: info@sbca.org. Web Site: www.sbca.com.

Society of Broadcast Engineers Inc., 9247 N. Meridian St., Suite 305, Indianapolis, IN 46260. Phone: (317) 846-9000. Fax: (317) 846-9120. E-mail: jporay@sbe.org. Web Site: www.sbe.org.

Society of Cable Telecommunications Engineers Inc., 140 Philips Rd., Exton, PA 19341-1318. Phone: (610) 363-6888. Fax: (610) 363-5898. E-mail: scte@scte.org. Web Site: www.scte.org.

Directors: Joel E. Welch, Thomas Russell & Joan Hagelin.

Professional membership assn offering information, professional dev resources, standards to cable telecommunications engineers & other professional.

Society of Environmental Journalists (SEJ), PO Box 2492, Jenkintown, PA 19046. Phone: (215) 884-8174. Fax: (215) 884-8175. E-mail: sej@sej.org. Web Site: www.sej.org.

Christine Rigel, assoc dir. Directors: Mark Schleifstein.

Society of Motion Picture & Television Engineers (SMPTE), 595 W. Hartdale Ave., White Plains, NY 10607. Phone: (914) 761-1100. Fax: (914) 761-3115. E-mail: smpte@smpte.org. Web Site: www.smpte.org.

Society of Professional Journalists, 3909 N. Meridian St., Indianapolis, IN 46208-4011. Phone: (317) 927-8000. Fax: (317) 920-4789. E-mail: tharper@spj.org. Web Site: www.spj.org.

Robert Leger, sec/treas; David Carlson, VP. Directors: Alvin Cross.

Twelve rgnl dirs, natl officers elected annually, two students reps, two dirs, at-large & two campus advisors at-large.

Society of Satellite Professionals International, 55 Broad St., 14th Fl., New York, NY 10004. Phone: (212) 809-5199. Fax: (212) 825-0075. Web Site: www.sspi.org.

The Songwriters Guild of America, 1560 Broadway, Suite 1306, New York, NY 10036. Phone: (212) 768-7902. Fax: (212) 768-9048. E-mail: ny@songwriters.com. Web Site: www.songwriters.org.

Hollywood, CA 90028, 6430 Sunset Blvd Phone: (213) 462-1108. Aaron Meza, rgnl dir.

Los Angeles, CA, 6430 Sunset Blvd.

Nashville, TN 37212, 1222 16th Ave. St, Suite 25. Phone: (615) 329-1782. Rondi Regan, rgnl dir.

Syndicated Network Television Association, 630 Fifth Ave., Suite 2320, New York, NY 10111. Phone: (212) 259-3740. Fax: (212) 259-3770. E-mail: mburg@snta.com. Web Site: www.snta.com.

Telecommunications Industry Association, 2500 Wilson Blvd., Arlington, VA 22201. Phone: (703) 907-7700. Fax: (703) 907-7727. E-mail: tia@tiaonline.org. Web Site: www.tiaonline.org.

Directors: Grant Seiffert, Bill Belt, John Derr, Derek Khlopin, Jason Leuck, Anna Amselle, Henry Wieland, Maryann Lesso, David Smith, Dan Bart & Henry Cuschieri.

Beijing 100004 China. USITO, Rm. 332, 3/f Lido Office Tower, Lido Place, Jichang Rd.., Jiang Tai Rd.. Phone: (8610) 6430-1368/69/70/71/72. Fax: (8610) 6430-1367. E-mail: usito@usito.org. Web Site: www.usito.org. Anne Stevenson-Yang, mgng dir.

Telecommunications Research and Action Center (TRAC), Box 27279, Washington, DC 20005. Phone: (202) 263-2950. Fax: (202) 263-2960. E-mail: trac@trac.org. Web Site: www.trac.org.

Television Bureau of Advertising (TVB),

See listing under Major National Associations, this section.

Television Bureau of Canada, 160 Bloor St. E, Suite 1005, Toronto, ON M4W 1B9. Canada. Phone: (416) 923-8813. Fax: (416) 413-3879. E-mail: tvb@tvb.ca. Web Site: www.tvb.ca.

Television Critics Association, The Wichita Eagle, 825 E. Douglas Ave., Witchita, KS 67202. Phone: (316) 268-6394. Fax: (316) 268-6627. E-mail: tca@tvcritics.org. Web Site: www.tvcritics.org.

Television Operators Caucus, 1776 K Street NW, Washington, DC 20006. Phone: (202) 719-7090. Fax: (202) 719-7546.

U.S. Catholic Conference, Dept. of Communications, 3211 4th St. N.E., Washington, DC 20017-1194. Phone: (202) 541-3320. Fax: (202) 541-3129. Web Site: www.usccb.org.

Veteran Wireless Operators Association Inc., Office of the Secretary, 46 Murdock St., Fords, NJ 08863-1224. Phone: (908) 225-2539. E-mail: vwoa@interactive.net. Web Site: www.vwoa.org.

Directors: Richard T. Kenney, Jerome Mulberg, Dr. R. J. Mullin, B. C. Flatom, M. D. MacMahon, N. Mills, D. I. Temple, F.T. Cassidy, P. Anselmo, Herman Arond, W.R. Benson & J. Chooljian.

Veterans Bedside Network, (The Veterans Hospital Radio & TV Guild.). 10 Fiske Pl., Rm. 301, Mount Vernon, NY 10550. Phone: (914) 699-6069. Fax: (914) 667-0405.

Wireless Communications Association International, Inc., 1333 H St. N.W., Suite 700, Washington, DC 20005-4754. Phone: (202) 452-7823. Fax: (202) 452-0041. E-mail: sonu@wcai.com. Web Site: www.wcai.com.

Directors: John T. von Harz III, William Andrle Jr., T. Lauriston Hardin, Chris Farnworth & Patrick J. Gossman.

Women in Cable & Telecommunications, 14555 Avion Pkwy., Suite 250, Chantilly, VA 20151. Phone: (703) 234-9810. Fax: (703) 817-1595. E-mail: info@wict.org. Web Site: www.wict.org.

Women In Film, 8857 W. Olympic Blvd., Suite 201, Beverly Hills, CA 90211. Phone: (310) 657-5144. Fax: (310) 657-5154. E-mail: info@wif.org. Web Site: www.wif.org.

World Broadcasting Unions (WBU), Box 500, Stn A, Rm. 6C 300, Toronto, ON M5W 1E6. Canada. Phone: (416) 598-9877. Fax: (416) 598-9774. E-mail: info@nabanet.org. Web Site: www.nabanet.com/wbu.

World Teleport Association, 55 Broad St., 14th Fl., New York, NY 10004. Phone: (212) 825-0218. Fax: (212) 825-0075. E-mail: wta@worldteleport.org. Web Site: www.worldteleport.org.

State and Regional Broadcast Associations

Alabama Broadcasters Association, 1316 Alford Ave., Suite 201, Birmingham, AL 35226. Phone: (205) 979-1690. Fax: (205) 979-9981. Web Site: www.al-broadcasters.org.

Alaska Broadcasters Association, Box 102424, Anchorage, AK 99510. Phone: (907) 258-2424. Fax: (907) 258-2414. Web Site: www.akbroadcasters.org.

Directors: Dennis Egan, Chrys Castle, Molly Glasoe, Bill Legere, Jeff Glaser, Don Rinker, Elizabeth Ruccio.

Arizona Broadcasters Association, 2302 N. 3rd St., Phoenix, AZ 85004. Phone: (602) 252-4833. Fax: (602) 252-5265. E-mail: aba3@mindsprime.com. Web Site: www.azbroadcasters.org.

J. D. Freeman, chmn; Diane Frisch, vice chmn.

Arkansas Broadcasters Association, 2024 Arkansas Valley Dr., Suite 403, Little Rock, AR 72212. Phone: (501) 227-7564. Fax: (501) 223-9798. E-mail: mail@arkbroadcasters.org. Web Site: www.arkbroadcasters.org.

Directors: Gordon Heiges, Jim Beard, Jamie Holt, Dina Mason, Bob Knight, Ken Madden, Chuck Spohn, Jay Bunyard, Gary Bridgman, Bill Cate, Bob Connell, Trey Stafford, Bobby Caldwell, Sandy Sanford, Rob Roedel, Gregg Fess, Donna Stweart, Ted Fortenberry.

California Broadcasters Association, 915 L St., Suite 1150, Sacramento, CA 95814. Phone: (916) 444-2237. Fax: (916) 444-2043. E-mail: info@cabroadcasters.org. Web Site: www.cabroadcasters.org.

Kathy Baker, chmn.

Colorado Broadcasters Association, Box 2369, Breckenridge, CO 80424. Phone: (970) 547-1388. Fax: (970) 547-1384. Web Site: www.e-cba.org. E-mail: cobroadcasters@earthlink.net.

Connecticut Broadcasters Association, Box 678, Glastonbury, CT 06033. Phone: (860) 633-5031. Fax: (860) 657-2491. E-mail: mcrice@prodigy.net. Web Site: www.ctba.org.

Florida Association of Broadcasters, 800 N. Calhoun St., Tallahassee, FL 32303. Phone: (850) 681-6444. Fax: (850) 222-3957. Web Site: www.fab.org.

Georgia Association of Broadcasters Inc., 8010 Roswell Rd., Suite 150, Atlanta, GA 30350. Phone: (770) 395-7200. Fax: (770) 395-7235. E-mail: finch@gab.org. Web Site: www.gab.org.

Idaho State Broadcasters Association, 270 N. 27th St., Suite B, Boise, ID 83702-3167. Phone: (208) 345-3072. Fax: (208) 343-8046. E-mail: connies@rmci.net. Web Site: www.isdahobroadcasters.org.

Connie Searles, exec dir.

Illinois Broadcasters Association, 300 N. Pershing St., Suite B, Enery, IL 62933. Phone: (618) 942-2139. Fax: (618) 988-9056. E-mail: ilbrdcst@neondsl.com. Web Site: www.ilba.org.

Indiana Broadcasters Association Inc., 3003 E. 98th St.,, Suite 161, Indianapolis, IN 46280. Phone: (317) 573-0119. Fax: (317) 573-0895. E-mail: indba@aol.com. Web Site: www.indianabroadcasters.org.

Directors: Ron Miller, Todd Schurz, Chris Fedele, Arthur Angotti III, ChristopherJ. Wheat, Tasha Mann, Lundy, James Conner, Earl Metzger. Directors at Large: Marty Pieratt, Steve Lindell, John Dawson, Jeff Smulyan, Dr. Joe Misiewicz Fred Berger, William Van Huss.

Iowa Broadcasters Association, Box 71186, Des Moines, IA 50325. Phone: (515) 224-7237. Fax: (515) 224-6560. E-mail: iowaiba@dwx.com. Web Site: www.iowabroadcasters.com.

Kansas Assn of Broadcasters, 1916 S.W. Sieben Ct., Topeka, KS 66611-1656. Phone: (785) 235-1307. Fax: (785) 233-3052. E-mail: harriet@kab.net. Web Site: www.kab.net.

Kentucky Broadcasters Association, 101 Enterprise Dr., Frankfort, KY 40601. Phone: (502) 848-0426. Fax: (502) 845-5710. E-mail: kba@mis.net. Web Site: www.kba.org.

Directors: David Jernigan, Lori Morgan, Steve Langford, Beth Mann, Corky Norcia, Mark Thomas, Bryan McFarland, Ray Holbrook, Jeff Ray, Randy Thompson, Roger Chesser, Jerry Barnaby, Mike Feldhaus, assoc dir, Ed Mastrean, at large dir.

Louisiana Association of Broadcasters, 660 Florida St., Baton Rouge, LA 70801. Phone: (225) 267-4522. Fax: (225) 267-4329. E-mail: lab@broadcasters.org. Web Site: www.broadcasters.org.

Directors: Les Golmon, chmn; Barry Thompson, chmn-elect; Louise Munson, press/CEO; Patrick Bonin, vice chmn radio; George Sirven, vice chmn TV; Rebecca Breeding, sec/treas; Mike Grimsley, past chmn; Charles Spencer, legal counsel; Mike Barras; Tom Gay; J.R. Greeley; Bob Holladay; Stephen Levet; Irene Robinson; Nick Simonette. Associate Directors: Robbie Morrisette; Bill Benedetto.

Maine Assn of Broadcasters, 128 State St., Augusta, ME 04330. Phone: (207) 623-3870. Fax: (207) 621-0585. E-mail: suzanne@mab.org. Web Site: www.mab.org.

Maryland-District of Columbia-Delaware Broadcasters Association, One E. Chase St., Suite 1129, Baltimore, MD 21202. Phone: (410) 653-4122. E-mail: cweinman@mdcd.com.

Massachusetts Broadcasters Association Inc., PMB 401, 43 Riverside Ave., Medford, MA 02155. Phone: (800) 471-1875. Fax: (800) 471-1876. E-mail: info@massbroadcasters.org. Web Site: www.massbroadcasters.org.

Directors: Donna Griffin.

Michigan Association of Broadcasters, 819 N. Washington Ave., Lansing, MI 48906. Phone: (517) 484-7444. Fax: (517) 484-5810. E-mail: mab@michmab.com. Web Site: www.michmab.com.

Minnesota Broadcasters Association, 3033 Excelsior Blvd., Suite 301, Minneapolis, MN 55416. Phone: (612) 926-8123. Fax: (612) 926-9761. E-mail: jdubois@minnesotabroadcasters.com. Web Site: www.minnesotabroadcasters.com.

Directors: Mike Neudecker, chmn; Robert Willmers, chmn elect; Mike Pederson, vice chmn; Frank Hanford, sec; George Couture, treas; Bob Bundgaard, past chmn; Rosanne Rybak; Steve Woodbury; Brett Paradis; John J. Sowada; Dan Seeman; Mike Iazzo; Dennis Wahlstrom; Ed Smith; Terry Moore; Gregg Skall.

Mississippi Association of Broadcasters, 855 S. Pear Orchard Rd., Suite 403, Ridgeland, MS 39157. Phone: (601) 957-9121. Fax: (601) 957-9175. E-mail: jlett2@earthlink.net.

Missouri Broadcasters Association, Box 104445, Jefferson City, MO 65110-4445. Phone: (573) 636-6692. Fax: (573) 634-8258. E-mail: dhicks@mbaweb.org. Web Site: www.mbaweb.org.

Directors: Beth Davis, Herndon Hasty, Mike Meara, Wayne Godsey, Randy Wright, Dan Leatherman, Mike Harbit, Rick McCoy, Richard Womack.

Montana Broadcasters Association, HC 70 Box 98, Bonner, MT 59823. Phone: (406) 244-4622. Fax: (406) 244-5518. E-mail: mba@mtbroadcasters.org. Web Site: www.mtbroadcasters.org.

Nebraska Broadcasters Association, 12020 Shamrock Plaza, Suite 200, Omaha, NE 68154. Phone: (402) 778-5178. E-mail: marty@ne-ba.org. Web Site: www.ne-ba.org.

Nevada Broadcasters Association, 1050 E. Flamingo Rd., Suite S-110, Las Vegas, NV 89119. Phone: (702) 794-4994. Fax: (702) 794-4997. E-mail: rdfnba@aol.com. Web Site: www.nevadabroadcasters.org.

Mary Ozer, chmn; Tony Bonnici, chmn elect.

New Hampshire Association of Broadcasters, 707 Chestnut St., Manchester, NH 03104. Phone: (603) 627-9600. Fax: (603) 627-9603. E-mail: info@nhab.org. Web Site: www.nhab.org.

New Jersey Broadcasters Association, 348 Applegarth Rd., Monroe Twp., NJ 08831. Phone: (609) 860-0111. Fax: (609) 860-0110. E-mail: njba@njba.com. Web Site: www.njba.com.

Arthur Camido (WMGG, Philidelphia), sec; Don Brooks, chmn; Robert McAllam, vice chmn; Joan Gerberding, vice chmn; Dave Finn, treas.

New Mexico Broadcasters Association, 8014 Menaul N.E., Albuquerque, NM 87110. Phone: (505) 881-4444. Fax: (505) 881-5353. E-mail: nmbroadcasters@aol.com. Web Site: www.nmba.org.

New York Market Radio Broadcasters Association (NYMRAD), 261 Madison Ave., 23rd Fl., New York, NY 10016. Phone: (646) 254-4493. Fax: (646) 254-4498. E-mail: db@nymrad.org. Web Site: www.nymrad.org.

New York State Broadcasters Association Inc., 1805 Western Ave., Albany, NY 12203. Phone: (518) 456-8888. Fax: (518) 456-8943. Web Site: www.nysbroadcastersassn.org.

North Carolina Assoc of Broadcasters, Box 627, Raleigh, NC 27602. Phone: (919) 821-7300. Fax: (919) 839-0304. E-mail: ncbrdcast@aol.com. Web Site: www.ncbroadcast.com.

Directors: Don Curtis, Bruce Wheeler, James Carson, Lee Armstrong, Brian Beasley, Dan Berman, Henry Hinton, Brent Miller, Michael Ward, Mike Weeks, Gary Weiss, Tom Howe, affil dir.

North Dakota Broadcasters Association, Box 3178, Bismarck, ND 58502-3178. Phone: (701) 258-1332. Fax: (701) 250-6372. E-mail: bethh@ndba.org. Web Site: www.ndba.org.

Directors: Syd Stewart, Barry Schumaier, Larry Timpe, Tim Ost, Carol Anhorn, Darren Lenertz, George Smith.

Northern California Broadcasters Association, 900 N, Point, Suite C406, San Francisco, CA 94109. Phone: (415) 292-5700. Fax: (415) 292-5790. Web Site: www.ncradio.com.

Ohio Association of Broadcasters Inc., 88 E. Broad St., Suite 1180, Columbus, OH 43215-3525. Phone: (614) 228-4052. Fax: (614) 228-8133. E-mail: oab@oab.org. Web Site: www.oab.org.

Oklahoma Association of Broadcasters, 6520 N. Western, Suite 104, Oklahoma City, OK 73116. Phone: (405) 848-0771. Fax: (405) 848-0772. E-mail: smith@oakok.org. Web Site: www.oabok.org.

Oregon Assn of Broadcasters, 7150 S.W. Hampton St., Suite 240, Portland, OR 97223-8366. Phone: (503) 443-2299. Fax: (503) 443-2488. E-mail: theoab@theoab.org. Web Site: www.theoab.org.

Directors: J. Dominic Monahan, legal counsel; Ron Hren, Kenn Brown, Rick Stevens, David Lippoff, Dan Manciu, Angela Pursel, Joe Costello, John Rice, Paul Steinle.

Pennsylvania Association of Broadcasters, 8501 Paxton St., Hummelstown, PA 17036. Phone: (717) 482-4820. Fax: (717) 482-1111. E-mail: rwyckoff@pab.org. Web Site: www.pab.org.

Rhode Island Broadcasters Association, c/o WNRI Radio, 786 Diamond Hill Rd., Woonsocket, RI 02895. Phone: (401) 769-6925. Fax: (401) 762-0442. Web Site: www.wnri.com.

South Carolina Broadcasters Association, One Harbison Way, Suite 112, Columbia, SC 29212. Phone: (803) 732-1186. Fax: (803) 732-4085. E-mail: scba@scba.net. Web Site: www.scba.net.

South Dakota Broadcasters Association, Box 1037, 106 W. Capital Ave., Pierre, SD 57501. Phone: (605) 224-1034. Fax: (605) 224-7426. Web Site: www.sdba.org.

Directors: Lee Axdahl (KSOB/KQOB, Sioux Falls); Gary Bolton (KDLT-TV, Sioux Falls); David J. Law (KWAT/KDLO/KIXX, Watertown); Monte Loos (KOTA-TV, Rapid City); Linda Marcus (KOKK/KZKK, Huron); Lia Green (Rushmore Radio, Rapid City); Lorin Larsen (KJAM, Madison); Rob Feller (Clear Channel Communications, Aberdeen).

Tennessee Association of Broadcasters, Box 101015, Nashville, TN 37224-1015. Phone: (615) 399-3791. Fax: (615) 361-3488. E-mail: tabtn@bellsouth.net. Web Site: www.tabtn.org.

Texas Association of Broadcasters, 502 E. 11th St., Suite 200, Austin, TX 78701. Phone: (512) 322-9944. Fax: (512) 322-0522. E-mail: tab@tab.org. Web Site: www.tab.org.

Directors: Ann Arnold, exec dir; Ben Downs, pres; Don Perry, VP; Bob Cohen, sec; Patti Smith, treas; Benny Springer, past pres; Jeff Cook, past pres; Danny Baker;

State and Regional Broadcast Associations

Dusty Black; Jerry Bobo; Frank Carter; Tom Ehlmann; Steve Guist; Jason Hightower; Brian Jones; John Kerr; Ken Lane; Mike Lee; Mark Masepohl; Mark McKay; Becky Munoz-Diaz; Tom O'Brien; Michael Oppenheimer; Jim Ray; Jackie Rutledge; Bill Struck; Mac Tichenor; Tommy Vascocu; Amy Villarreal; Ted Wernn; Stephen Yates; Rodney Zent. Associate Representatives: Britt Bowers, Gene Fondren, Lucinda Nobles.

Utah Broadcasters Association, 1600 S. Main St., Salt Lake City, UT 84115. Phone: (801) 486-9521. Fax: (801) 484-7294. Web Site: www.utahbroadcasters.com.

Vermont Association of Broadcasters, Box 4489, Burlington, VT 05406. Phone: (802) 476-8789. Fax: (802) 479-5893. Web Site: www.vab.org.

Virginia Association of Broadcasters, 630 Country Green Ln., Charlottesville, VA 22902. Phone: (434) 977-3716. Fax: (434) 979-2439. E-mail: doug@easterassociates.com. Web Site: www.vab.net.

Directors: Edward L. Munson, Michael Guld, Francis Wood, Robert G. Lee, Michael Slenski, Leonard Wheeler, John Schick, Doris Newcomb, Kenneth Hill, Harrison Pittman & Bob Peterson.

Directors: Brad Eure, pres; Randy Smith, pres elect; David Paulus, sec/treas; Joe Macione, past pres; Mario Hewitt; Lisa Sinclair; Danny Wadsworth; Steve McCall; Donald Richards; Michael Guld; Denny Royer; Tony Kahl; Herm Reavis; Chris Clendenen; Tracey Jones; Arthur D. Stamler; Gary Hagerich; Mitt Younts.

Virginia Public Radio Association, c/o WCVE, 23 Sesame St., Richmond, VA 23235. Phone: (804) 320-1301. Fax: (804) 320-8729. E-mail: bmiller@ideastations.org.

Washington State Association of Broadcasters, 724 Columbia St., Suite 310, Olympia, WA 98501-1249. Phone: (360) 705-0774. Fax: (360) 705-0873. E-mail: wa-broadcasters@earthlink.net. Web Site: www.wsab.org.

West Virginia Broadcasters Association, 140 Seventh Ave., South Charleston, WV 25303-1452. Phone: (304) 744-2143. Fax: (304) 744-1764. E-mail: wvba@citynet.net. Web Site: www.wvba.com.

Directors: Jay Phillipone, treas; Mike Smith, past pres, WOAY-TV

Wisconsin Broadcasters Association, 44 E. Mifflin St., Suite 900, Madison, WI 53703. Phone: (608) 255-2600. Phone: (800) 236-1922. Fax: (608) 256-3986. E-mail: jlaabs@aol.com. Web Site: www.wi-broadcasters.org.

Directors: Edward Allen III, Ellis Bromberg, Juli Buehler, Jim Hall, Bill Hurwitz, Tom Koser, Al Lancaster, Dean Maytag, Wendy Oberg & Jeff Tyler.

Wausau, WI 54403, 1908 Grand Ave. Laurin Jorstad, WAOW-TV.

Wausau, WI 54402, Box 2048. Bob Jung, Midwest Communications.

West Bend, WI 53095, Box 933. Jim Hodges, WBKV/WBWI.

Directors: Jim Hall, Jim Hodges, Laurin Jorstad, Tom Koser, Dave Magnum, Charlie Peterson, Jesse Mix, Greg Schnirring, Jon Schweitzer, Bob Smith, Jeff Tyler, Jay Zollar.

Wyoming Association of Broadcasters, 7217 Hawthorne Dr., Cheyenne, WY 82009. Phone: (307) 632-7622. Fax: (307) 638-3469. E-mail: grottski@aol.com. Web Site: www.wyomingbroadcasting.org.

Directors: Dave Montgomery, Bob Grammens, Kent Smith.

State and Regional Cable Associations

Alabama Cable Telecommunications Association, Box 20683, Montgomery, AL 36120. Phone: (334) 271-2281. Fax: (334) 271-2260. E-mail: alacable@aol.com. Web Site: www.alacta.com.

Arizona Cable Telecommunications Association, 3610 N. 44th St., Suite 240, Phoenix, AZ 85018. Phone: (602) 955-4122. Fax: (602) 955-4505. E-mail: info@azcable.org. Web Site: www.azcta.org.

Directors: Susan Bitter Smith, exec dir; Steve Brideau, pres.

Arkansas Cable Telecommunications Association, Box 1468, 3001 J.F.K. Blvd. Suite B, North Little Rock, AR 72115. Phone: (501) 791-7344. Fax: (501) 791-7345. E-mail: arkcable@comcast.net. Web Site: www.arcta.org.

Directors: Mike Wilson, Dennis Yocum, Garry Bowman, Harold Kimmel, Rick Smith, Harvey Oxner, Jay Butler, Doug Martin.

Broadband Communications Association of Washington, 216 First Ave. S., Suite 260, Seattle, WA 98104. Phone: (206) 652-9303. Fax: (206) 652-8297. E-mail: sena@broadbandwashington.org. Web Site: www.broadbandwashington.org.

Directors: Janet Turpen, Steve Kipp, Jerry Rotondo, Jim Elliott, Matt Zavala, Bruce Gladner & Randy Lee.

Cable Telecommunications Association of Maryland, Delaware & District of Columbia, 2530 Riva Rd., #316, Annapolis, MD 21401. Phone: (410) 266-9111. Fax: (410) 266-6133. E-mail: ctaofmd-de-dc@msn.com.

Cable Telecommunications Association of New York Inc., 80 State St., 10th Fl., Albany, NY 12207. Phone: (518) 463-6676. Fax: (518) 463-0574. E-mail: cttany@ny.rr.com. Web Site: www.cabletvny.com.

Cable Television & Communications Association of Illinois, 2400 E. Devon, Suite 317, Des Plaines, IL 60018. Phone: (847) 297-4520. Fax: (847) 297-3865. E-mail: ctc2400@aol.com.

Cable Television Association of Georgia, 6175 Barfield Rd., Suite 220, Atlanta, GA 30328. Phone: (404) 252-4371. Fax: (404) 252-0215. E-mail: ctag@scta.com. Web Site: www.gacable.com.

Directors: Tom Autry (Jones Communications); Alsion Jenkin (Comcast Cable Communications, Inc.); Danny Jobe (InterMedia); Don Karell (Cox Communications); Dick Kirby (TCI, Southeast); Claus Kroeger (Cox Communications, Inc.); Dennis Lopach (MediaOne); Dale Ordoyne (MediaOne, Inc.); Dave Scott (Comcast, South Central Region); Melani Griffith (Discovery Communications), assoc dir; Michael Clemons (Key Marketing & Cable Connect), assoc dir elect; Mark Williams (Cox Communications, Inc.), dir engrg.

California Cable & Telecommunications Assn., Box 11080, Oakland, CA 94611. Phone: (510) 428-2225. Fax: (510) 428-0151. E-mail: frank@calcable.org. Web Site: www.calcable.org.

Sacramento, CA 95814, 1121 L St., Suite 400. Phone: (916) 446-7732. Fax: (916) 446-1605.

Directors: Leo Brennan, chmn; Don Schena, sect; Jeffrey Schwall, treas.

Colorado Cable TV Association, 1512 Larimer St., Suite 700, Henderson, CO 80202. Phone: (303) 607-0486. Fax: (303) 436-1191.

Florida Cable Telecommunications Association, 246 East 6th Ave., Suite 100, Tallahassee, FL 32303. Phone: (850) 681-1990. Fax: (850) 681-9676. E-mail: fcta@fcta.com. Web Site: www.fcta.com.

Hawaii Cable Television Association, 200 Akamainui St., Mililani, HI 96789. Phone: (808) 625-8359. Fax: (808) 625-5888. E-mail: kbeuret@oceanic.com.

Idaho Cable Telecommunications Association, 1015 W. Hays Street, Boise, ID 83702. Phone: (208) 344-6633. Fax: (208) 344-0077. E-mail: ron.williams@rmci.net. Web Site: www.idahocable.com.

Directors: Russ Young, pres; Dan Clark, past pres.

Indiana Cable Telecommunications Association Inc., 201 N. Illinois, Suite 1560, Indianapolis, IN 46204. Phone: (317) 237-2288. Fax: (317) 237-2290. Web Site: www.incable.org.

Iowa Cable & Telecommunications Association, Box 41457, 2300 University, Des Moines, IA 50311. Phone: (515) 276-0006. E-mail: tomgraves@mchsi.com.

Directors: Jerry Kittelson, pres; Jeff Olson, VP.

Kansas Cable Telecommunications Association, 815 S.W. Topeka Blvd., 2nd Floor, Topeka, KS 66612. Phone: (785) 290-0018. Fax: (785) 232-1703. E-mail: johnfed@cox.net.

Directors: Gary Shorman, pres; Joe Michael, VP; Jay Allbaugh, treas; Mike Flood; Pat James; Linda Jurgensen; Don Karell; Patrick Knorr; Tom Krewson; Clarence Matlock; Rob Moel; Carol Rothwell.

Kentucky Cable Telecommunications Association, Box 415, Burkesville, KY 42717. Phone: (270) 864-5352. Fax: (270) 864-3110. E-mail: juddph@mchsi.com. Web Site: www.kycable.com.

Jim Finch, assoc dir; Jim Hays III, assoc dir; Robert Thacker, assoc dir.

Louisiana Cable & Telecommunications Association, 763 North St., Baton Rouge, LA 70802. Phone: (225) 387-5960. Fax: (225) 383-6705. E-mail: lcta@lacable.com. Web Site: www.lacable.com.

Michigan Cable Telecommunications Association, 412 W. Ionia St., Lansing, MI 48933. Phone: (517) 482-2622. Fax: (517) 482-1819. Web Site: www.michcable.org.

Directors: Colleen M. McNamara, exec dir; Mike Cleland, pres; Gary Mizga, VP; Bob McCann, sect; Rick Clark, treas; Tim Collins; Jon Kreucher; Tim Ransberger.

Mid-America Cable Telecommunications Association, 223 E. Capitol Ave., Jefferson City, MO 65102. Phone: (573) 635-5588. Fax: (573) 635-1778. E-mail: cabletv@sun flower.net. Web Site: www.midamericacable.com.

Directors: Charlotte McClure, chmn; Tom Krewson, first VP; Brian Thompson, second VP; Vic Davis, sect/treas; Richard Bates, LeaAnn Quist; Carol Rothwell; Chance Russell; Bill Severn, assoc dir: Debby Exon; Kim Francis; David Headley; Deirdre LaVerdiere; Tyler Leach; Blake Miller; Rick Moravec; Oscar Ordaz; Joe Scott; Larry Stiffelman; Wendy Tobias. Ex-Officio Dir: mary Campbell; Greg Harrison; Rob Marshall; Emeritus: Ron Marnell.

Minnesota Cable Communications Association, 1885 University Ave, Suite 320, St. Paul, MN 55104. Phone: (651) 641-0268. Fax: (651) 641-0319. E-mail: mncca@msn.com. Web Site: www.mncca.com.

Mississippi Cable Telecommunications Association, 1501 Lakeland Dr., Suite 301, Jackson, MS 39216. Phone: (601) 981-3646. Fax: (601) 981-5547. E-mail: mcta@bellsouth.net. Web Site: www.mctaweb.com.

Missouri Cable Telecommunications Association, 223 E. Capitol Ave., Box 1895, Jefferson City, MO 65102-1895. Phone: (573) 635-1915. Fax: (573) 635-1778. E-mail: gpharrison@mchsi.com. Web Site: www.missouricabletv.com.

Nebraska Cable Communications Association, 635 S. 14th St., Suite 315, Lincoln, NE 68508. Phone: (402) 476-1177. Fax: (402) 476-4890. E-mail: mary@campbellassociates.net.

Directors: Mary Campbell, exec dir; Bridgit Farley, assoc dir; John Fullenkamp, legal counsel; Randy Bang, Valerie Kramer, Dick Bates, Mike Kohler, Gerald Lampe, Greg Harrison, LeaAnn Quist.

Nevada State Cable Telecommunications Association, Box 1802, Carson City, NV 89702. Phone: (775) 852-2253. Fax: (775) 852-2403.

Directors: Steve Schorr; Rick Steele, Carol Eure, Valerie Castellana, Susan Watters, John Ortiz.

New England Cable Telecommunications Association Inc., 100 Grandview Rd., Suite 310, Braintree, MA 02184. Phone: (781) 843-3418. Fax: (781) 849-6267.

New Jersey Cable Telecommunications Association, 124 W. State St., Trenton, NJ 08608. Phone: (609) 392-3223. Fax: (609) 394-0074. Web Site: www.cablenj.org.

Directors: William J. Kettleson, chmn of board; Liz Murray, vice chmn.

New Mexico Cable Communications Association, Box 2264, Santa Fe, NM 87504. Phone: (505) 988-7529. Fax: (505) 986-0442. E-mail: davenport@aol.com. Web Site: www.nmcca.com.

Directors: Kevin Bethke, John Christopher, Dennis Jones, Tony Hotten, Ben Hernandez.

North Carolina Cable Telecommunications Association, Box 1347, Raleigh, NC 27602. Phone: (919) 834-7113. Fax: (919) 839-0304. E-mail: nccable@aol.com. Web Site: www.nccta.com.

Directors: Landon Barefoot, pres; D.K. McLaughlin, VP; Maggie Blythe, sect; Brad Phillips, treas; Randy Fraser, immed past pres; JoAnn Davis, exec mgr; Wade Hargrove, gen counsel; David Auger; Anthony Barlage; Janet Cloyde; Brenda McNutt; Larry Ott; Bill Paramore; Tom Smith. Assoc Dir: Bill McCall; Paula Silas.

North Central Cable Television Association, 1885 University Ave., Suite 320, St. Paul, MN 55104. Phone: (651) 641-0268. Fax: (651) 641-0319. E-mail: mncca@msn.com.

Director: Mark Hammerstrom, pres.

Ohio Cable Telecommunications Association, 50 W. Broad St., Suite 1118, Columbus, OH 43215. Phone: (614) 461-4014. Fax: (614) 461-9326. E-mail: octa@octa.org. Web Site: www.octa.org.

Directors: Dex Sedwick, Pres., Jim Hires, Virgil Reed, Tom Dawson, Jerry DeGrazia, Kevin Flanigan, Bob Gessner, Kevin Haynes, Zakee Rashid, Steve Trippe. Associate Directors: Monica Carriedo, Rich Baudo.

Oklahoma Cable and Telecommunications Association, 301 N.W. 63rd, Suite 400, Oklahoma City, OK 73116. Phone: (405) 843-8855. Fax: (405) 843-8934. E-mail: octa@coxatwork.com. Web Site: www.okcable.net.

Directors: Dave Bialis, chmn; Andy Dearth, vice chmn; George Wilburn, sect/treas; Jay Allbaugh; Mike Franke; Danny Thompson; Bill Drewry; Brook McDonald; Bobby Story; Johnny Bowen; Ken Crouch; David Wall; Leon Pfeifer; Tim Easley; Wendy Tobias; Dane Huston; Jim Walker.

Oregon Cable Telecommunications Association, 1249 Commercial St. S.E., Salem, OR 97302. Phone: (503) 362-8838. Fax: (503) 399-1029. E-mail: heidi@oregoncable.com. Web Site: www.oregoncable.com.

Director: Mike Dewey, exec dir.

Pennsylvania Cable & Telecommunications Association, 127 State St., Harrisburg, PA 17101. Phone: (717) 214-2000. Fax: (717) 214-2020. E-mail: pacable@pcta.com. Web Site: www.pcta.com.

Southern Cable Television Association, 6175 Barfield Rd., Suite 220, Atlanta, GA 30328. Phone: (404) 255-1608. Fax: (404) 252-0215. Web Site: www.scta.com.

Tennessee Cable Telecommunications Association, 611 Commerce St., Suite 2706, Nashville, TN 37203. Phone: (615) 256-7037. Fax: (615) 254-9710. E-mail: sbtcta@aol.com. Web Site: www.tcta.net.

Texas Cable & Telecommunications Association, Box 13518, Austin, TX 78711. Phone: (512) 474-2082. Fax: (512) 474-0966. Web Site: www.txcable.com.

Directors: Amanda Davis Batson, pres; Kathy Grant, VP govt relations.

Utah Cable Telecommunications Association, 1350 N. 200 West, Logan, UT 84341. Phone: (801) 401-3250.

Director: Shane Baggs, pres.

Virginia Cable Telecommunications Association, 1001 E. Broad St., Suite 210, Richmond, VA 23219. Phone: (804) 780-1776. Fax: (804) 225-8036. E-mail: kfalk@vcta.com. Web Site: www.vcta.com.

Director: Ken Dye, chmn.

West Virginia Cable Telecommunications Association, 117 Summers St., Charleston, WV 25301. Phone: (304) 345-2917. Fax: (304) 342-1285. Web Site: www.wvcta.com.

Directors: Mark Polen, Emily White Midea, Michael Kelemen (Capital Cablecomm, Charleston, WV), Joel Patten (Harnon Cable Communications, St. Albans, WV), Jim Uncerwood (TCI of West Virginia, Parkersburg, WV).

Wisconsin Cable Communications Association, 22 East Mifflin Street, Suite 1010, Madison, WI 53703. Phone: (608) 256-1683. Fax: (608) 256-6222.

Directors: Shirley Hehn Weibel, John Miller, Robert Ryan, Bob Steichen, Kent Reeves, Randy Scott. Directors at large: Joe Browning, Bob Lunda Associate Directors: Kate Schroeder, Teri Lenth. Executive Director: Thomas Hanson. Director of Regulatory Affairs: Thomas Moore

Wyoming CATV Association, Box 6281, Cheyenne, WY 82003. Phone: (307) 637-3933. Phone: (307) 733-3081. Fax: (307) 637-5399.

Board Members: Clint Rodeman, pres; David Alexanderson, VP; Jeff Frankenberger, sect/treas; John Nickle, past pres; Jim Wilhelm; Marty Carollo; Curtis Syme; Jack Harrison. Assoc Board Members: Kristen Doyle; Todd Shimirak; Takashi Nakano.

Union/Labor Groups

Actors' Equity Association (AEA), (AFL-CIO). 165 W. 46th St., New York, NY 10036. Phone: (212) 869-8530. Fax: (212) 719-9815. Web Site: www.actorsequity.org. Patrick Quinn, pres.

Los Angeles, CA 90036, 5757 Wilshire Blvd, Suite 1. Phone: (323) 634-1750. Fax: (323) 634-1777. John Holly, western rgnl dir.

San Francisco, CA 94104, 350 Sansome St., Ste 900. Phone: (415) 391-3838. Fax: (415) 391-0102. Jane Shaffer, business rep.

Orlando, FL 32821, 10319 Orangewood Blvd. Phone: (407) 345-8600. Fax: (407) 345-1522.

Chicago, IL 60603, 1255 Clark St. Phone: (312) 641-0393. Fax: (312) 641-6365. Kathryn Lamkey, central rgnl dir.

Labor Union for Theatrical Actors & Stage mgrs.

Affiliated Property Craftsperson (IATSE Local 44), (IATSE, AFL-CIO). 12021 Riverside Dr., North Hollywood, CA 91607. Phone: (818) 769-2500. Fax: (818) 769-3111. Web Site: www.local44.org. Erik Nelson, pres.

American Federation of Labor-Congress of Industrial Organizations (AFL-CIO), 815 16th St. N.W., Washington, DC 20006. Phone: (202) 637-5000. Fax: (202) 637-5058. Web Site: www.aflcio.org. John Sweeney, pres.

American Federation of Musicians, United States & Canada, 1501 Broadway, Suite 600, New York, NY 10036. Phone: (212) 869-1330. Fax: (212) 764-6134. Web Site: www.afm.org. Thomas F. Lee, pres.

Washington, DC 20036, 1717 K St. NW, Suite 500. Phone: (202) 463-0772. Fax: (202) 466-9009. Hal Ponder.

Don Mills, ON M3C 2E9 Canada, 75 The Donway W, Suite 1010. Phone: (416) 391-5161. Fax: (416) 391-5165. Bobby Herriot.

Los Angeles, CA 90010. Los Angeles, 3550 Wilshire Blvd., Suite 1900. Phone: (213) 251-4510. Fax: (213) 251-4520.

Representing 110,000 professional musicians throughout the United States & Canada.

American Federation of Television & Radio Artists (AFTRA), (AFL-CIO). 260 Madison Ave., New York, NY 10016. Phone: (212) 532-0800. Fax: (212) 532-2242. Web Site: www.aftra.com. Kim Roberts Hedgpeth, exec dir.

Los Angeles, CA 90036, 5757 Wilshire Blvd., 9th Fl. Phone: (323) 634-8100. Fax: (323) 634-8194. John Russum.

AFTRA represents 77,000 professional actors, singers, dancers, announcers, newspersons, sportscasters & disc jockeys throughout the country who work in TV, radio, comls, industrial & educ videos, interactive media & the recording industry.

American Guild of Musical Artists, 1430 Broadway, 14th Fl, New York, NY 10018-3308. Phone: (212) 265-3687. Fax: (212) 262-9088. E-mail: agma@musicalartists.org. Web Site: www.musicalartists.org. Linda Mays, pres; Alan S. Gordon, natl exec dir.

Branch offices in Los Angeles, CA; Chicago, IL; San Francisco, CA; New Orleans, LA; Seattle, WA; Dallas, TX; Washington, DC; Boston, MA; Philadelphia, PA & Toronto, ON, Canada.

American Guild of Variety Artists, (AFL-CIO). 363 7th Ave 17th Fl., New York, NY 10001. Phone: (212) 675-1003. Fax: (212) 633-0097. E-mail: agva@aol.com. Rod McKuen; Frances Gaar, exec sec & treas.

Los Angeles, CA 91607, 4741 Laurel Canyon Blvd. Phone: (818) 508-9984. Fax: (818) 508-3029.

Labor Union for performers in live venues.

The Animation Guild (IATSE Local 839), 4729 Lankershim Blvd., North Hollywood, CA 91602. Phone: (818) 766-7151. Fax: (818) 506-4805. E-mail: mpsc839@mindspring.com. Web Site: www.mpsc839.org. Earl Kress, VP; Kevin Koch, pres.

Art Directors Guild & Scenic Title and Graphic Artists (IATSE Local 800), 11969 Ventura Blvd., Suite 200, Studio City, CA 91604. Phone: (818) 762-9995. Fax: (818) 762-9997. E-mail: lydia@artdirectors.org. Web Site: www.artdirectors.org. Scott Roth, exec dir; Tom Walsh, pres.

Broadcast-Television Recording Engineers (IBEW Local 45), 6255 Sunset Blvd., Suite 721, Hollywood, CA 90028. Phone: (323) 851-5515. Fax: (323) 466-1793. E-mail: feedback@ibew45.org. Web Site: www.ibew45.org. Victor Marrero, pres; Chuck Guzzi, VP.

Represents Radio, TV, Cable Engineers, Federal, County, City Electronic Tech.

Communications Workers of America (CWA), (AFL-CIO). 501 3rd St. N.W., Washington, DC 20001-2797. Phone: (202) 434-1100. Fax: (202) 434-1279. Web Site: www.cwa-union.org. Larry Cohen, pres; Jeff Rechenbach, exec VP.

Directors Guild of America Inc. (DGA), 7920 Sunset Blvd., Los Angeles, CA 90046. Phone: (310) 289-2000. Fax: (310) 289-2029. Web Site: www.dga.org. Michael Apted, pres; Steven Soderbergh, VP.

Chicago, IL 60611, 400 N. Michigan Ave, Suite 307. Phone: (312) 644-5050. Fax: (312) 644-5775.

New York, NY 10019, 110 W. 57th St. Phone: (212) 581-0370. Fax: (212) 581-1441. Chris Lomdino, eastern exec dir.

Illustrators & Matte Artists (IATSE Local 790), 13245 Riverside Dr., Suite 300-A, Sherman Oaks, CA 91423. Phone: (818) 784-6555. Fax: (818) 784-2004. Joseph Musso, pres; Marty Kline, VP; Camille Abbott, sec & treas; Marjo Bernay, business rep.

International Alliance of Theatrical Stage Employees, Moving Picture (IATSE), 1515 Broadway, Suite 601, New York, NY 10036. Phone: (212) 730-1770. Fax: (212) 730-7809. Web Site: www.iatse-intl.org. Thomas Short, intl pres.

Toronto, ON M5A 1N1 Canada, 258 Adelaide St E, Suite 403. Phone: (416) 362-3569. Fax: (416) 362-3483.

Toluca Lake, CA 91602, 10045 Riverside Dr. Phone: (818) 980-3499. Fax: (818) 980-3496. Joseph Aredas.

International Association of Machinists and Aerospace Workers (IAM), 9000 Machinists Pl, Upper Marlboro, MD 20772-2687. Phone: (301) 967-4500. E-mail: websteward@goiam.org. Web Site: www.iamaw.org.

International Brotherhood of Electrical Workers (IBEW), (AFL-CIO). 900 7th St NW, Washington, DC 20001. Phone: (202) 833-7000. Fax: (202) 728-7676. E-mail: broadcasting@ibew.org. Web Site: www.ibew.org. Edwin D. Hill, pres; Jon F. Walters, sec/treas.

International Cinematographers Guild, 7715 Sunset Blvd., Suite 300, Los Angeles, CA 90046. Phone: (323) 876-0160. Fax: (323) 876-6383. Web Site: www.cameraguild.com. Gary Dunham, pres; Bruce C. Doering, exec dir.

Orlando, FL 32835, 7463 Conroy-Windermere Rd, Suite A. Phone: (407) 295-5577. Fax: (407) 295-5335.

Park Ridge, IL 60068, 1411 Peterson Ave, Suite 102. Phone: (847) 692-9900. Fax: (847) 692-5607.

New York, NY 10011, 80 Either Ave, 14th Fl. Phone: (212) 647-7300. Fax: (212) 647-7317.

Represents our members' contracts & activities.

International Sound Technicians (IATSE Local 695), (IATSE, MPMO). 5439 Cahuenga Blvd., North Hollywood, CA 91601. Phone: (818) 985-9204. Phone: (323) 877-1052. Fax: (818) 760-4681. E-mail: local695@695.com. Web Site: www.695.com. James A. Osburn, & exec dir.

International Union of Electronic, Electrical, Technical, Salaried Machine & Furniture Workers AFL-CIO, 1275 "K" N.W., Washington, DC 20005. Phone: (202) 513-6300. Fax: (202) 513-6357. Web Site: iue-cwa.org. James Clark, pres.

Little Rock, AR 72209, 8803 Oman Rd. Phone: (501) 565-3488. George Clark, district pres.

Fort Wayne, IN 46825, 9006 Coldwater Rd. Phone: (219) 489-7092. Bruce Van Ess, district pres; Rich Chapman, asst to the pres.

Saugus, MA 01906, 335 Central St. Phone: (617) 233-4807. Robert Scott, district pres.

East Rutherford, NJ 07073, 355 Murray Hill Pkwy. Phone: (201) 933-9494. Sal Ingrassia, district pres.

Dayton, OH 45439, 3461 Office Park Dr. Phone: (513) 294-1491. Michael Bindas, district pres.

Elkins Park, PA 19027, 8117 Old York Rd. Phone: (215) 886-9860. Michael Giardino, district pres.

Laboratory Film/Video Technicians & Cinetechnicians (IATSE Local 683), Box 7429, Burbank, CA 91510-7429. Phone: (818) 252-5628. Fax: (818) 252-4962.

New York, NY 10036-5741. IATSE, 1515 Broadway, Suite 601.

Serves the Labor Union.

Make-Up Artist & Hairstylists Guild (IATSE Local 706), 828 N. Hollywood Way, Burbank, CA 91505. Phone: (818) 295-3933. Fax: (818) 295-3930. E-mail: info@ialocal706.org. Web Site: www.local706.com. Susan Cabral, pres.

Motion Picture Costumers (IATSE Local 705), 4731 Laurel Canyon Blvd. Suite 201, Valley Village, CA 91607. Phone: (818) 487-5655. Fax: (818) 487-5663. E-mail: mpc705@aol.com. Web Site: www.motionpicturecostumers.org. Sandra Berke Jordan, pres; Rudolph Garcia, business rep.

The gathering (by rental or puchase) of costumes for film & TV. The construction of new costumes (wardrobe). The fitting & handling of costumes (wardrobe) during filming.

Motion Picture Editors Guild (IATSE Local 700), 7715 W. Sunset Blvd., Suite 200, Hollywood, CA 90046. Phone: (323) 876-4770. Fax: (323) 876-0861. E-mail: mail@editorsguild.com. Web Site: www.editorsguild.com. Lisa Zeno Churgin, pres.

Chicago, IL 60631. Chicago, 6317 N. Northwest Hwy. Phone: (773) 594-6598. Fax: (773) 594-6599.

New York, NY 10013. New York, 145 Hudson St., Suite 201. Phone: (212) 302-0700. Fax: (212) 302-1091.

Labor union representin post-production employees.

Motion Picture Set Painters & Sign Writers (IATSE Local 729), 1811 W. Burbank Blvd., Burbank, CA 91506-1314. Phone: (818) 842-7729. Fax: (818) 846-3729. Web Site: www.ialocal729.com. Kirk D. Hansen, pres.

National Association of Broadcast Employees & Technicians, (Communications Workers of America, AFL-CIO). 501 3rd St., 8th Fl., Washington, DC 20001. Phone: (202) 434-1254. Fax: (202) 434-1426. E-mail: nabet@cwa-union.org. Web Site: www.nabetcwa.org. Alex Grossman, pres.

New York, NY 10106, Local 11, 888 7th Ave., Suite 4511. Phone: (212) 757-3065. John S. Clark, pres NABET-CWA.

Representing employees in the bcstg, cable TV & related industries.

The Newspaper Guild, (CWA). 501 3rd St. N.W., Suite 250, Washington, DC 20001. Phone: (202) 434-7177. Fax: (202) 434-1472. Web Site: www.newsguild.org. E-mail: guild@cwa-union.org. Linda K. Foley, pres.

Ottawa, ON K2C 3P1 Canada, Baxter Centre, 1050 Baxter Rd, Unit 7B. Phone: (613) 820-9777. Arnold Amber, Canadian dir.

Office & Professional Employees International Union, 265 W 14th St, 6th Fl, New York, NY 10011. Michael Goodwin, pres.

Professional Musicians (AFM Local 47), 817 N. Vine St., Hollywood, CA 90038-3779. Phone: (323) 462-2161. Fax: (323) 461-5260. Web Site: www.promusic.com. Hal Espinosa, pres.

Musicians, vocalists, orchestrators, copyists, composers, conductors, contractors & librarians, referral service & recording studio.

Screen Actors Guild, 5757 Wilshire Blvd., Los Angeles, CA 90036. Phone: (323) 954-1600. Fax: (323) 549-6656. Web Site: www.sag.org. Melissa Gilbert, pres.

Wilmington, NC 28405, 1319 CC Military Cut-of Road #152. Phone: (305) 670-7677. Fax: (305) 670-1813. Brad Karl.

Phoenix, AZ 85016, 3131 E Camelback Rd, Suite 200, Suite 330. Phone: (602) 383-3780. Fax: (602) 838-3781. Don Livesay.

San Francisco, CA 94104, 350 Sansome St., Suite 900. Phone: (415) 391-7510. Fax: (415) 391-1108.

Denver, CO 80202, Market Square Center, 1400 16th St. #400. Phone: (720) 932-8193. Fax: (702) 932-8194. Julie Crane.

Apopka, FL 32703, 522 Hunt Club Blvd, #410. Phone: (407) 788-3020. Fax: (407) 788-3080. David A. Fazekes.

Miami, FL 33156, 7300 N. Kendall Dr, Suite 620. Phone: (305) 670-7677. Fax: (305) 670-1813. (rgnl office).

Atlanta, GA 30305, 455 E. Paces Ferry Rd. N.E, Suite 334. Phone: (404) 239-0131. Fax: (404) 239-0137. Melissa Goodman.

Honolulu, HI 96814, 949 Kapiolani Blvd #105. Phone: (808) 596-0388. Fax: (808) 593-2636. Brenda Ching.

Chicago, IL 60611, One E. Erie St, Suite 650. Phone: (312) 573-8081. Fax: (312) 573-0318. Eileen Willenborg.

Boston, MA 02116, 535 Boylston St. Phone: (617) 262-8001. Fax: (617) 262-3006. Dona Summers.

Bethesda, MD 20814. Baltimore/Washington Office, 4340

Union/Labor Groups

East West Hwy, Suite 204. Phone: (301) 657-2560. Fax: (301) 656-3615. Patricia O'Donnell. (Washington-Baltimore office).

Southfield, MI 48034-2352, 27777 Franklin Rd, Suite 300. Phone: (248) 213-0272. Fax: (248) 213-0273. (Detroit office).

New York, NY 10017, 360 Madison Ave., 12th Fl. Phone: (212) 944-1030. Fax: (212) 944-6774. Jae Je Simmons.

Dallas, TX 75248, 15950 N. Dallas Pkwy, Suite 400. Phone: (972) 361-8185. Fax: (972) 361-8186. Linda Dowell.

Contract administration, negotiation and enforcement, residual payment processing, regulation franchising of talent agents, membership, record-keeping and communication.

Script Supervisors/Continuity & Allied Prodution Specialists Guild Local 871, (IATSE). 11519 Chandler Blvd., North Hollywood, CA 91601. Phone: (818) 509-7871. Fax: (818) 506-1555. E-mail: ialocal871@aol.com. Web Site: www.ialocal871.org.

"We think for a living." Script Supervisors/Continuity, Teleprompter Operators, Production Office Coordinator, Art Department Coordinator, Production Accountants & Assistants.

Service Employees International Union (SEIU), 1313 L St NW, Washington, DC 20005. Phone: (202) 898-3200. Web Site: www.seiu.org. Andrew L. Stern, pres.

Set Designers & Model Makers (IATSE Local 847), 13245 Riverside Dr., Ste 300-A, Sherman Oaks, CA 91423. Phone: (818) 784-6555. Fax: (818) 784-2004. Suzanne Feller-Otto, sec; Marjo Bernay, business rep.

Studio Electrical Lighting Technicians (IATSE Local 728), 14629 Nordhoff St., Panorama City, CA 91402. Fax: (818) 891-5288. E-mail: loc728@iatse728.org. Web Site: www.iatse728.org. Patric J. Abaravich, pres.

United Electrical, Radio & Machine Workers of America (UE), One Gateway Ctr., Suite 1400, Pittsburgh, PA 15222-1416. Phone: (412) 471-8919. Fax: (412) 471-8999. Web Site: www.ranknfile-ue.org. E-mail: ue@ranknfile-ue.org.

United Scenic Artists (IATSE Local 829) 29 W. 38th St. 15th Fl., New York, NY 10018. Phone: (212) 581-0300. Fax: (212) 977-2011. E-mail: administrator@usa829.org. Web Site: www.usa829.org. Michael McBride, business mgr.

Los Angeles, CA 90036, 5225 Wilshire Blvd, Suite 506. Phone: (323) 965-0957. Fax: (323) 965-0958. Charles Berliner, rgnl business rep.

Miami, FL 33173, 10459 SW 78th St. Phone: (305) 596-4772. Fax: (305) 596-6095. David Goodman, rgnl business rep.

Chicago, IL 60601, 203 N. Wabash, Suite 1210. Phone: (312) 857-0829. Fax: (312) 857-0819. Chris Phillips, rgnl business rep.

Representing designers of set, costume, lighting, sound, scenic artists, computer arts and art dept coordinators in the entertainment industry.

Writers Guild of America, East Inc. (WGAE), 555 W. 57th St., Suite 1230, New York, NY 10019. Phone: (212) 767-7800. Fax: (212) 582-1909. E-mail: info@wgaeast.org. Web Site: www.wgaeast.org. Warren Leight, pres.

Writers Guild of America, West Inc. (WGAW), 7000 W. Third St., Los Angeles, CA 90048-4329. Phone: (323) 951-4000. Fax: (323) 782-4800. Web Site: www.wga.org. Daniel Petrie Jr., pres.

WGAW represents writers primarily for the purpose of collective bargaining in the motion picture, bcst, cable & new technologies industries.

Trade Shows

Arizona Cable Telecommunication Association Annual Meeting. SHOW MANAGEMENT: Arizona Cable Telecommunication Association. ASSOCIATION ADDRESS: 3610 N. 44th St., Suite 240, Phoenix, AZ 85018. Contact: Susan Bitter Smith, executive dir. (602) 955-4122. FAX: (602) 955-4505. www.azcable.org. E-mail: info@azcable.org.

Audio Engineering Society Convention (Public/Trade). SHOW DATE: May 2006. SHOW MANAGEMENT: Audio Engineering Society (AES), 60 E. 42nd St., New York, NY 10165. Contact: Roger Furness, exec dir. (212) 661-8528. FAX: (212) 682-0477. Web site: http://www.aes.org. SHOW MANAGEMENT STATEMENT: This show provides an annual marketplace for professional audio equipment engineers. PROFILE OF ATTENDEES: Audio engineers.

Broadcast Cable Financial Management Association. SHOW DATE: June 11-13, 2006, Wyndham Palace, Orlando, FL, May 22-24 2007, Rio Suites Hotel, Las Vegas. SHOW MANAGEMENT: BCFM, 550 Frontage Rd., Suite 3600, Northfield, IL 60093. Contact: Mary M. Collins, pres/CEO. (847) 716-7000. FAX: (847) 716-7004. Web: www.bcfm.com. SHOW MANAGEMENT STATEMENT: BCFM sponsors an annual conference with exhibits targeting financial, HR, MIS, executive mgmt from TV, radio & cable plus association in auditing data processing, credit & collections. SHOW HISTORY: Annual. First Year of Show: 1960.

Broadcasting 2006 (Public/Trade). SHOW MANAGEMENT: Canadian Association of Broadcasters, 350 Sparks St., Suite 306, Ottawa, ON, Canada K1R 7S8. Contact: Marye Menard-Bos, senior dir. (613) 233-4035. FAX: (613) 233-6961. E-mail: cab@cab-acr.ca. PROFILE OF EXHIBITORS: Companies who provide products or svcs to Canadian bcst (radio-TV) operators. PROFILE ATTENDEES: Senior mgmt, owners, engineers & new directors. SHOW HISTORY: Set Rotation Pattern: East/West rotation.

CAB Sales Management Conference. SHOW DATE: May 23-24, 2006, Hyatt Regency, Chicago, IL. SHOW MANAGEMENT: Cabletelevision Advertising Bureau, Inc., 830 Third Ave., 2nd Fl., New York, NY 10022. Contact: Nancy Lagos. (212) 508-1200. FAX: (212) 832-3268.

Cable-Tec Expo. SHOW DATE: June 21-23, 2006, Denver. SHOW MANAGEMENT: Society of Cable Television Engineers, 140 Phillips Rd., Exton, PA 19341. Contact: Lori Bower. (610) 363-6888. FAX: (610) 363-5898. SHOW SPONSOR: Same as show management. SHOW MANAGEMENT STATEMENT: The SCTE Cable-Tec Expo brings together engineers, technicians & technical executives from the United States who represent cable systems, MSOs & independent operators. A fulfillment to the growing need to address the technical end of the cable TV industry. PROFILE OF EXHIBITORS: Construction equipment, signal distribution, cable casting, transmission/receiving, test equipment, microware/mds, digital systems, system testing quality control & other related hardware. PROFILE OF ATTENDEES: Engineers, technicians, executives of MSOs & independent operators. SHOW HISTORY: Concurrent with rotating Annual Engineering Conference. First Year of Show: 1983.

Forum 2006. SHOW DATE: March 19-22, 2006, JW Marriot Hotel, Washington, DC. SHOW MANAGEMENT: CTPAA. ASSOCIATION ADDRESS: Box 33697, Washington, DC 20033-0697.(202) 775-1081. FAX: (202) 955-1134. E-mail: services@ctpaa.org. Web site: http://www.ctpaa.org. SHOW MANAGEMENT STATEMENT: Educational conference for cable pub affrs professionals. PROFILE OF ATTENDEES; Programmers, MSO, & loc system personnel. SHOW FREQUENCY: Annual. First Year of Show: 1985.

Great Lakes Broadcasting Conference & Expo (Public/Trade). SHOW MANAGEMENT: Michigan Association of Broadcasters, 819 N. Washington Ave., Lansing, MI 48906. (517) 484-7444. FAX: (517) 484-5810. E-mail: michmab@aol.com. SHOW SPONSOR: Same as show management. SHOW MANAGEMENT STATEMENT: Regional bcstg trade show which provides speakers & seminars to educate members while showcasing bcst equipment & svcs. PROFILE OF EXHIBITORS: Broadcast equipment, products & svcs. PROFILE OF ATTENDEES: General mgrs, engineers, sls mgrs, account executives, news directors & anybody involved in the audio, video or bcst industries. SHOW HISTORY: Annual.

INFOCOMM International. SHOW DATE: June 2006. SHOW MANAGEMENT: International Communications Industries Association Inc., 11242 Waples Mill Rd., Suite 200, Fairfax, VA 22030. Contact: Jason C. McGraw, senior VP. (703) 273-7200. FAX: (703) 278-8082. SHOW SPONSOR: Same as show management. SHOW MANAGEMENT STATEMENT: INFOCOMM International is the exposition of the video, computer, audiovisual, presentation & multimedia communications industries. It is sponsored by the International Communications Industries Association (ICIA). ICIA brings together more than 1,400 firms selling video, audiovisual & computer products & svcs. Members are dealers, software producers, independent representatives, rental companies & others serving users in communications, training, business, govt & education. In addition to the trade show, there are annual conventions, meetings, seminars, courses & institutes of many organizations who bring their members & interested associates to the event. PROFILE OF EXHIBITORS: Manufacturers & producers of video, computer & audiovisual-based communications & information products & producers of software programs for all technologies represented. PROFILE OF ATTENDEES: Dealers who sell video, audio, presentation systems & installations to professional users of these media; production & post-production companies, adv & PR agencies, laboratories & other users of video & related technologies. SHOW HISTORY: Annual. First Year of Show: 1983.

Interwire Trade Exposition. SHOW DATE: May 20-24, 2006, Hynes Convention Center, Boston, MA. SHOW MANAGEMENT: Wire Association International, 1570 Boston Post Rd., Box 578, Guilford, CT 06437. Contact: Steve Fetteroll, exec dir. (203) 453-2777. FAX: (203) 453-8384. SHOW SPONSOR: Same as show management. SHOW MANAGEMENT STATEMENT: Interwire provides a marketplace for the wire & cable industry. It is a trade show for wire manufacturers, fabricators, suppliers, other buyers & users with admin, engrg, tech & purchasing personnel in attendance from the United States, Europe, Asia, South & Central Americas. Product classifications include wire machinery, spring machinery, fasteners, fabricators, fiber optics, chemical coatings, accessories & other wire-related products. PROFILE OF EXHIBITORS: Machinery & accessories; fiber optics, chemicals, coatings, lubricants, dies, compounds, spools, reels, packaging, measuring, testing equipment, wire, cable, fasteners & fabricated wire products. PROFILE OF ATTENDEES: Gen & admin mgmt; engrg, opns, production; tech, rsch & dev, quality control; purchasing; sls & mktg concerned with wire industry. SHOW HISTORY: Biennial. First Year of Show: 1981.

Kentucky Broadcasters Association Fall Convention. SHOW MANAGEMENT: Kentucky Broadcasters Association, 101 Enterprise Dr., Frankfort, KY 40601. Contact: Gary White, pres. (888) 843-5221. FAX: (502) 843-5710. SHOW MANAGEMENT STATEMENT: This convention's purpose is to further train bcstrs on both legal aspects of bcstrs as well as sls & mgmt. PROFILE OF EXHIBITORS: Electronics, computers, program syndications, bcst suppliers (radio & TV). PROFILE OF ATTENDEES: Owners & mgmt throughout the state of Kentucky. SHOW HISTORY: First Year of Show: 1953.

Louisiana Krewe of Cable Show. SHOW DATES: February 22-23, 2006, February 14-15, 2007, January 30-31, 2008, February 18-19, 2009, New Orleans, LA. SHOW MANAGEMENT: Louisiana Cable & Telecommunications Association, 763 North St., Baton Rouge, LA 70802. (225) 387-5960. FAX: (225) 383-6705. E-mail: lacable.com. SHOW FREQUENCY: Annual.

Minnesota Broadcasters Association Annual Conference & Expo (Public/Trade). SHOW MANAGEMENT: Minnesota Broadcasters Association, 3033 Excelsier Blvd., Suite 301, Minneapolis, MN 55416. Contact: Jim DuBois, pres/CEO. (612) 926-8123. FAX: (612) 926-9761. E-mail: jdubois@minnesotabroadcasters.com. SHOW MANAGEMENT STATEMENT: The show includes exhibits for bcstg, cable, production, & other electronic media.

NAB 2006. SHOW DATE: April 22-27, 2006, Las Vegas Convention Center, Las Vegas, NV. SHOW MANAGEMENT: National Association of Broadcasters, 1771 N St. N.W., Washington, DC 20036. (202) 429-5300. FAX: (202) 429-7427. SHOW MANAGEMENT STATEMENT: The Convention is an annual gathering of radio, TV, video, post-production, multimedia & telecommunications professionals worldwide. Sessions cover aspects of electronic media, both tech & management-oriented. PROFILE OF EXHIBITORS: Manufacturers, distributors of products, equipment & svcs for the radio, TV, video, post-production, film multimedia & telecommunications industries. PROFILE OF ATTENDEES: Owners & managers of radio, TV, video, post-production & users of multimedia & telecommunications products & svcs. SHOW HISTORY: First Year of Show: 1922.

NATPE 2006. SHOW DATE: January 24-26, 2006, Mandalay Bay Resort Convention Center, Las Vegas, CA. SHOW MANAGEMENT: National Association of Television Program Executives, 5757 Wilshire Blvd., Penthouse 10, Los Angeles, CA 90036. Contact: Nick Orfanopoulos, sr VP Conferences/Special Events. (310) 453-4440. FAX: (310) 453-5258. E-mail: orfan@aol.com. SHOW SPONSOR: Same as show management. SHOW MANAGEMENT STATEMENT: This show provides an annual marketplace for syndicated TV programs, first-run &/or off-network programs, as well as aspects of the TV business. PROFILE OF EXHIBITORS: Major studios, independent producers, marketers, cable networks, electronic retailers, new media producers, United States & intl program distributors. PROFILE OF ATTENDEES: Advertisers, cable MSOs, bcst stns & networks, producers, marketers, bankers, merchandisers, talent agents, new media, United States & overseas program distributors & TV programmers. SHOW HISTORY: First Year of Show: 1984.

National Religious Broadcasters Convention and Exposition (Public/Trade). SHOW DATE: February 17-22, 2006, Gaylord Texan Resort, Dallas TX, CA. SHOW MANAGEMENT: National Religious Broadcasters Association, 9510 Technology Dr., Manassas, VA 20110. Contact: David Keith. (703) 330-7000. FAX: (703) 330-7100. Website: www.nrb.org. SHOW SPONSOR: Same as show management. SHOW MANAGEMENT STATEMENT: The NRB Convention and Exposition is an annual gathering of manufacturers & distributors of bcst equipment, computers, radio & TV programs, consultant svcs, gospel music, publishing & other related items to the religious communications industry. PROFILE OF EXHIBITORS: Manufacturers & distributors of consumer & bcst audio & video equipment, computers, radio & TV programs, publishers, & miscellaneous items relating to the religious field. PROFILE OF ATTENDEES: Radio & TV executives, ministers, denominational executives, musicians, adv executives, educators & Christian bookstore owners. SHOW HISTORY: Annual. First Year of Show: 1944.

NCTA. SHOW DATES: May 21-23, 2006, New Orleans, LA; May 6-9, 2007, Las Vegas, NV. SHOW SPONSOR: National Cable Television Association, 1724 Massachusetts Ave., N.W., Washington, DC 20036. Contact: Barbara York. (202) 775-3669. FAX: (202) 775-3692. Web site: http://www.thenationalshow.com. SPONSOR STATEMENT: NCTA's Annual Convention and International Exposition provides the industry's largest, most comprehensive showcase for equipment, progmg & enhanced svcs for cable TV, broadband & telecommunications systems. PROFILE OF EXHIBITORS: All industries related to cable TV & broadband svcs including hardware manufacturers, equipment suppliers, programming networks, enhanced svcs including VOD, PVR, software & technology providers. PROFILE OF ATTENDEES: Includes multiple system operators, independent operators, program networks, media & entertainment companies, investment & financial institutions, telecommunications providers, enhanced svc providers & the press. SHOW HISTORY: Annual. First Year of Show: 1950.

Broadcasting & Cable Yearbook 2006

Trade Shows

Promax & BDA 2006 International (Trade). SHOW MANAGEMENT: Promax & BDA, 9000 W. Sunset Blvd., Suite 900, Los Angeles, CA 90069. Contact: Gregg Balko. (310) 788-7600. FAX: (310) 788-7676. SHOW SPONSOR: Same as show management. SHOW MANAGEMENT STATEMENT: The purpose of the show is to bring together bcst promoters & designers in the electronic media, all incorporated in one show. PROFILE OF EXHIBITORS: Music video production; computer animation & graphics hardware; stn design & image packages; adv premiums & incentives. PROFILE OF ATTENDEES: Promax International serves those individuals responsible for the mktg, adv, promotion & publicizing of TV stns, networks, production companies, radio stns & cable system on a national & international level. BDA consists of an international membership of art directors, designers & graphics artists.

RAB 2006 Marketing Leadership Conference. SHOW DATE: February 9-12, 2006, Hyatt Regency New Orleans, LA. SHOW MANAGEMENT: Radio Advertising Bureau, 261 Madison Ave., 23rd Fl., New York, NY 10016. Contact: Dana Honors. (972) 753-6740. FAX: (972) 753-6802. SHOW SPONSOR: Same as show management. SHOW MANAGEMENT STATEMENT: RAB, the largest gathering of sls and mgmt professionals in the radio industry. The Conference represents more than 5,000 members radio stns, radio stn sls managers, bcst groups, radio networks, stn representatives, network executives & associated industry organizations from the 50 states and 23 foreign countries. To educate, train radio sls & mktg professionals. The goal is to raise the lever of professionalism in radio sls & mktg. PROFILE OF EXHIBITORS: Manufacturers, distributors or suppliers of a product or svc for any of the following categories: computer/software programs; radio & TV products; radio networks; specialty adv; program syndication; sls & mktg rsch; sls consulting. PROFILE OF ATTENDEES: Radio stn sls mgrs, gen mgrs, network executives & group heads from throughout the United States. SHOW HISTORY: First Year of Show: 1980.

SATELLITE 2006. SHOW DATE: February 4-6, 2006, The Washington Convention Center, Washington, DC. SHOW MANAGEMENT: Access Intelligence, LLC. SHOW SPONSOR: Via Satellite Magazine. ASSOCIATION ADDRESS: 1201 Seven Locks Rd., Suite 300, Potomac, MD 20854. (301) 354-2000. FAX (301) 354-2315. www.satelliteshow.net. SHOW MANAGEMENT STATEMENT: This is the largest Satellite specific conference & exhibition in the world. SATELLITE 2006 provides you with an unequalled opportunity to meet key, senior satellite company executives from the United States, Europe, the Pacific Rim, South America and Africa. This is your chance to strengthen existing professional and business relationships as well as initiate new ones. Before, during and after the conference sessions and throughout our expansive exhibit hall. PROFILE OF EXHIBITORS: Satellite operators, end users, manufactures, svc providers, launch vehicle operators teleports, consumer svc providers. PROFILE OF ATTENDEES: Distributors bcsters, programmergers, VSAI network providers, satellite operators, launch vehicle svc providers & manufacturers. SHOW FREQUENCY: Annual. First Year of Show: 1976.

Society of Motion Picture and Television Engineers Annual Technical Conference and Exhibition (Public/Trade). SHOW MANAGEMENT: Society of Motion Picture and Television Engineers, 595 W. Hartsdale Ave., White Plains, NY 10607. Contact: Dianne Gabriele. (914) 761-1100. FAX: (914) 761-3115. SHOW SPONSOR: Same as show management. SHOW MANAGEMENT STATEMENT: The show provides an annual marketplace for equipment & supplies for production, engrg & purchasing personnel in worldwide professional motion-picture & bcst-TV industries. Product classifications includes TV, cable, production, postproduction, laboratory & field-production equipment. PROFILE OF EXHIBITORS: Manufacturers, dealers & distributors of professional TV-bcst & motion-picture equipment. PROFILE OF ATTENDEES: Senior bcst & film-engineering personnel from the motion-picture & bcst-TV industries. SHOW HISTORY: Annual. Set Rotation Pattern: East coast odd-numbered years, west coast even-numbered years.

Texas Show 2006. SHOW DATE: February 2006. SHOW MANAGEMENT: Texas Cable & Telecommunications Association, 506 W. 16th St., Austin, TX 78701. Contact: William D. Arnold. (512) 474-2082. FAX: (512) 474-0966. SHOW SPONSOR: Same as show management. SHOW MANAGEMENT STATEMENT: This is a trade show & convention for the cable TV industry. PROFILE OF EXHIBITORS: Those associated with cable TV, hardware & software. PROFILE OF ATTENDEES: Cable operators, trade press, persons interested in cable TV. SHOW HISTORY: Annual show held in February. First Year of Show: 1960.

WCA Technical Symposium and Business Expo. SHOW DATE: January 18-20, 2006, Fairmont Hotel, San Jose, CA. SHOW MANAGEMENT: Carl Berndtson. SHOW SPONSOR: Wireless Communications Association International. ASSOCIATION ADDRESS: 1333 H St. N.W., Suite 700 W., Washington, DC 20005. (202) 452-7823. FAX (202) 452-0041. wwww.wcai.com. Contact: Carl Berndton (978) 371-1792. PROFILE OF EXHIBITORS: Excellent mix of wireless broadband operators, vendors and integrators. PROFILE OF ATTENDEES: Executive and upper management; CTOs from wireless broadband industry. SHOW FREQUENCY: Annual. First Year of Show: 1983.

Vocational and Career Development Schools

The Art Institute of Pittsburgh, 420 Blvd. of the Allies, Pittsburgh, PA 15219. Phone: (412) 263-6600. Fax: (412) 263-3715. E-mail: admissions-aip@aii.edu. Web Site: www.aip.aii.edu. George Pry, pres; Hans Westman, media arts & animation.

Courses offered include audio recording & production, engrg, EFP video production, bcst media, feature writing, scriptwriting, legal issues, non-linear editing, image manipulation, filmmaking & multicamera field production.

Broadcast Center, 2360 Hampton Ave., St. Louis, MO 63139. Phone: (314) 647-8181. Fax: (314) 647-1575. E-mail: bcinfo@broadcastcenterinfo.com. Web Site: www.broadcastcenterinfo.com. Linda Hauhe, VP.

Training in mktg & time sls, coml & program production, bcst journalism & bcst performance. Training includes voice training & dev for bcstg; announcing training including news, comls, DJ & sportscasting; news & coml copywriting.

Broadcasting Institute of Maryland, 7200 Harford Rd., Baltimore, MD 21234. Phone: (410) 254-2770. Phone: (800) 942-9246. Fax: (410) 254-5357. E-mail: aw@bim.org. Web Site: www.bim.org. John C. Jeppi Sr., pres; John I. Perry, business mgr; Dean R. Kendall, dir education; Angela Whaples, admissions dir.

Courses offered include comprehensive course in radio & TV bcstg; majors available in radio, TV production, news & sports.

Brown College, 1440 Northland Dr., Mendota Heights, MN 55120. Phone: (651) 905-3400. Fax: (651) 905-3550. Web Site: www.browncollege.edu. Rachel Tepfer, dept chair bcstng & comm; Colleen McDermott, pres; Tami Hansen, dir career svcs; Kevin Sanderson, opns VP.

Courses offered include RTV announcing, sls, bcst adv, bcst journalism, audio production, TV production, TV engrg & editing, sports announcing & audio engrg. Assoc of applied science degree in radio-bcstg. Assoc degrees in radio-bcstg & TV production. BA in communications.

Carolina School of Broadcasting, 3435 Performance Rd., Charlotte, NC 28214. Phone: (704) 395-9272. Fax: (704) 395-9698. E-mail: csbnc@bellsouth.net. Web Site: www.csbradiotv.com. Ken D. FuQuay, dir; Alyson M. Young, assit dir; Christine Remme, assit dir.

Courses offered include a non-tech bcstg group session & an in-stn training lab course; announcing, production, copywriting, news, digital coml production, sls & administration. Day & night sessions. In-stn training, full- or part-time as determined by stn & student. TV facilities & stereo control room; resident training in studio & stn opns at coml radio & TV stns worldwide. Digital audio & non-linear editing for TV.

Cleveland Institute of Electronics, 1776 E. 17th St., Cleveland, OH 44114. Phone: (216) 781-9400. Fax: (216) 781-0331. Web Site: www.cie-wc.edu. E-mail: instruct@cie-wc.edu. John R. Drinko, pres; Scott D. Katzenmeyer, industrial account mgr.

Offers associate in applied science degree in electronics engrg technology, bsct engrg. FCC license preparation & cable technician training.

Clover Park Technical College, 4500 Steilacoom Blvd. S.W., Lakewood, WA 98499-4098. Phone: (253) 589-5800. Fax: (253) 589-5797. Web Site: www.cptc.edu. Dr. Sharon McKavick, pres; John L. Mangan, radio bcstg instructor.

Bcst training since 1954. Comprehensive Associate degree program in all aspects of radio stn opn prepares students for entry-level employment. Course includes staff experience at 51-kw *KVTI(FM). A two-year state college. Assoc of Applied Technology degree programs.

Columbia College Hollywood, 18618 Oxnard St., Tarzana, CA 91356-1411. Phone: (818) 345-8414. Fax: (818) 345-9053. E-mail: info@columbiacollege.edu. Web Site: www.columbiacollege.edu. Jan Stanley Mason, pres; Mark J. Stratton, admin dir.

Courses offered in TV/video production & cinema; degree program includes classes in directing, studio lighting, camera opns, videotape editing, scriptwriting, film editing, sound mixing, asst camera & script supervision. A.A. degree in TV/video production; B.A. degree in TV/video, cinema, and cinema/TV combination.

Columbia School of Broadcasting, (Washington, DC Metro Area). 3947 University Dr., 2nd Fl., Fairfax, VA 22030-2506. Phone: (703) 591-6000. Fax: (703) 591-6147. E-mail: djtrain@columbiaschoolbroadcas.com. Web Site: www.columbiaschoolbroadcas.com. Bill Butler, pres; Ron MacDonald, dir of admissions & mktg.

Courses offered include English/Sp radio announcing (voice-over, newscaster, DJ, sportscaster, traffic/weather reporter & interviews/talk show host), TV announcing, radio play-by-play sportscasting & basic radio production. Distance education & resident courses offer comprehensive training for entry-level bcstg positions. Founded in 1964.

Columbia School of Broadcasting, 46-001 Kam Hwy., Suite 216, Kaneohe, HI 96744. Phone: (808) 236-7333. Dennis McCann, dir.

Courses offered include radio/TV announcing.

Columbia School of Broadcasting, 3080 Stage Rd., Suite 8, Bartlett, TN 38134. Phone: (901) 377-5747. E-mail: enrollmentinfo@csbmemphis.com. Web Site: www.csbmemphis.com. Bill Bannister, dir.

Connecticut School of Broadcasting, Inc., Media Park, 130 Birdseye Rd., Farmington, CT 06032. Phone: (800) 887-2346. Phone: (860) 677-7577. Fax: (860) 677-1141. E-mail: farmcsb@aol.com. Web Site: www.800tvradio.com. Dick Robinson, pres; Jill Robinson, VP; Missy Robinson, VP; Jim Robinson, VP.

Pawcatuck, CT 06379, 185 S. Broad St., 3rd Fl. #303. Phone: (860) 599-1108. Hank Tenney, exec dir; Jesse Guralnick, dir.

Tampa, FL 33619. Sabal Business Center II, 3901 Coconut Palm Dr, Suite 105. Phone: (813) 740-0990. Ron Gannon, Dir..

Westbury, LI, NY 11590, 1400 Old Country Rd, Suite 211. Marty Herstein, dir.

Farmington, CT 06032. Campus, Media Park 130 Birdseye Rd. Phone: (860) 677-7577. Hank Tenney, exec dir; Renee Falcone, dir.

Stratford, CT 06615. Campus, 80 Ferry Blvd. Phone: (203) 378-5155. Hank Tenney, exec dir; Frank Marro, dir.

Davie, FL 33328. Campus, University Plaza, 3538 S. University Dr. Phone: (954) 474-3700. David Banner, exec dir; Chris Hudspeth, dir. (Fort Lauderdale area).

Palm Beach Gardens, FL 33403. Campus, 3450 Northlake Blvd., Ste. 110. Phone: (561) 842-2000. David Banner, exec dir; Dave Duran, dir.

Atlanta, GA 30338, 1117 Perimeter Center West, Ste. N-301. Phone: (770) 522-8803. Jordan Walsh, Dir.

Wellesley Hills, MA 02481. Campus, 49 Walnut Park. Phone: (781) 235-2050. Hank Tenney, exec. dir; Steve Williams, dir.

Cherry Hill, NJ 08002. Campus, One Cherry Hill, #201. Phone: (856) 755-1200. Tom DeFranco, dir. (Philadelphia area).

Hasbrouck Heights, NJ 07604. Campus, 377 Rt. 17 S, Penthouse. Phone: (201) 288-5800. Janet Hutsebaut, dir. (NYC area).

Arlington, VA 22202. Campus, 2170 Crystal Plaza Arcade. Phone: (703) 415-7600. R.J. Narsavage, dir.

Courses (day & evening): On-air performance: Radio, TV, Internet broadcast. Production courses: Digital audio & video, linear & non-linear avid editing. Other communications courses: Sports, voice-overs, sls, promotions, mktg, wireless & multi-media technology.

Dunwoody College of Technology, 818 Dunwoody Blvd., Minneapolis, MN 55403. Phone: (612) 374-5800. Fax: (612) 374-4128. E-mail: info@dunwoody.edu. Web Site: www.dunwoody.edu. R. Dettmann, pres.

Courses offered include assoc in electronics tech degree, computer technician, radio-TV, industrial electronics technician, digital electronics specialists, electronics technician, TV specialists, certificate programs, aviation electronics, & info mgmt systems.

Education Direct, 925 Oak St., Box 1900, Scranton, PA 18501. Phone: (570) 342-7701. Fax: (570) 961-4888. Web Site: www.educationdirect.com. E-mail: info@educationdirect.com. Connie Dempsey, education dir; David Beach, exec dir.

Diploma courses include basic electronics, electronics technology, basic computer progmg, TV/VCR repair or personal computer repair, Java progmg, internet web page design, electricians, telecommunications technician. Center for Degree Studies: specialized assoc degree in electronics technology & electrical, mechanical, civil & industrial engrg technology; specialized assoc degree in business mgmt, mktg, finance, accounting or applied computer science; Internet technology in web programming, Internet technology multimedia, Internet technology in e-commerce administration, graphic design, DC maintenance technology.

Grantham University, 2101 Wilson Blvd, Suite 110, Arlington, VA 22201. Fax: (703) 465-1273. E-mail: info@grantham.edu. Web Site: www.grantham.edu. Roy Winter, pres; Joanna Boldt, dir of student affairs.

Courses offered include computer science, electronics engrg tech & computer engrg tech by correspondence, leading to A.S. & B.S. degrees.

The Illinois Center for Broadcasting, 55 West 22nd St., Suite 240, Lombard, IL 60148. Phone: (630) 916-1700. Fax: (630) 916-1764. Web Site: www.beonair.com. Robert Mills, pres; Bruce Ryan, corporate dir of education; Patrick Johnson, school dir; Chris Hunter, natl placement dir.

10-month, hands-on course in radio and television broadcasting procedures and techniques.

International College of Broadcasting, 6 S. Smithville Rd., Dayton, OH 45431. Phone: (937) 258-8251. Fax: (937) 258-8714. Web Site: www.icbcollege.com. E-mail: admissions@icbcollege.com. Michael A. LeMaster, pres; J. Michael LeMaster, VP opns.

Courses offered include radio, TV, cameraman, CATV, disc jockey, news, sports & audio/recording engrg. Assoc degree in communication arts available in radio/TV & video production/recording audio engrg. Diploma programs offered in audio/recording engrg & bcstg.

Madison Media Institute, 2702 Agriculture Dr., Madison, WI 53718. Phone: (608) 663-2000. Fax: (608) 442-0141. E-mail: broadcast@madisonmedia.com. Web Site: www.madisonmedia.com. Ed Hutchings, pres; Chris Hutchings, dir.

Courses offered include audio production, recording & mus technology, TV production, & multimedia technologies. Accredited by Accrediting Commission of Career Schools and Colleges of Technology.

The New England Institute of Art, 10 Brookline Pl. W., Boston, MA 02445. Fax: (617) 582-4520. Web Site: www.neia.aii.edu. E-mail: neia_admissions@aii.edu. Stacy Sweeney, pres; Deborah Brent, Dir. of admissions; Tom Dyer, Dean of Academic Affairs; Deana Coady, Dir. of Financial Aid; Laura Cioffi, Contact.

Programs offered: Bachelor's degree in Graphic Design, multimedia & web design, Media Arts & Animation, Digital Media Production, Interior Design, and audio & media technology. Associate's degrees in Audio Production, Broadcasting Radio and Broadcasting TV. Broadcasting.

New England School of Communications, One College Cir., Bangor, ME 04401. Phone: (207) 941-7176. Fax: (207) 947-3987. E-mail: info@nescom.edu. Web Site: www.nescom.edu. Ben Haskell, dir; Nelson Jewell, admissions dir; Kim Nason, administrator.

Courses offered include announcing, bcst sls, writing for bcst, TV production, sound recording, voice & diction, news & sports reporting, adv & PR, pub speaking, video graphics, desktop publishing.

New School University, 2 W. 13th St., New York, NY 10011. Phone: (212) 229-8903. Fax: (212) 229-5357. E-mail: webmaster@newschool.edu. Web Site: www.newschool.edu. Carol Wilder, chmn communication dept; Bob Kerrey, pres.

Courses offered include TV writing workshop; writing for TV, films & radio; TV production workshop; voice & speech for theater & TV; seminars on TV comls; writing TV comls. Offers certificate in film/TV studies, B.A., B.A./M.A., M.A. in media studies.

Northland Community & Technical College (KSRQ-FM), 1101 Hwy. 1 E., Thief River Falls, MN 56701. Phone: (218) 681-0701. Phone: (800) 959-6282. Fax: (218) 681-0774. Web Site: www.northlandcollege.edu. Orley Gunderson, dir; Mark Johnson, instructor; Don Howe, gen mgr.

Courses offered include a diploma-earning program in radio bcstg working on a 24,000 kw educ FM stn.

The Ohio Center for Broadcasting-Cincinnati, 6703 Madison Rd., Cincinnati, OH 43227. Phone: (513) 271-6060. Fax: (513) 271-6135. Web Site: www.beonair.com.

10-month, hands-on course in Radio and Television procedures and techniques.

The Ohio Center for Broadcasting-Cleveland, 9000 Sweet Valley Drive, Valley View, OH 44125. Phone: (216) 447-9117. Fax: (216) 642-9232. E-mail: ocb@beonair.com. Web Site: www.beonair.com. Kathy Hartman, dir admissions; Jean Salada, dir financial aid; Bruce Ryan, dir of education; Gary James, placement dir.

10-month, hands-on course on radio and television broadcasting and techniques. Fully accredited by state of Ohio. Graduates earn 36 quarter college credit hrs with diploma. Instructors are professional broadcasters.

Vocational and Career Development Schools

The Poynter Institute for Media Studies, 801 3rd St. S., St. Petersburg, FL 33701. Phone: (727) 821-9494. Fax: (727) 821-0583. E-mail: oseifert@poynter.org. Web Site: www.poynter.org. Karen Brown Dunlap, pres; Keith Woods, dean; Andrew E. Barnes, chmn.

Seminars & conferences for print & bcst & online journalists. Courses for TV/radio include stn leadership, new leaders in the newsroom, newsroom mgmt, ethical decision-making, anchors as newsroom leaders investigative reporting, power reporting, computer-assisted journalism, visual storytelling & ethics, & producing newscasts.

Specs Howard School of Broadcast Arts Inc., 19900 W. Nine Mile Rd., Southfield, MI 48075-3953. Phone: (248) 358-9000. Fax: (248) 746-9772. E-mail: info@specshoward.edu. Web Site: www.specshoward.edu. Dick Kemen, VP; Jonathan Liebman, pres/CEO; Lisa Zahodne, dir; Donnie Hopps, dir education.

Courses offered include radio & TV bcstg & production. Accredited by ACCSCT.

Technical Career Institutes, 320 W. 31st St., New York, NY 10001. Phone: (212) 594-4000. Fax: (212) 629-3937. Web Site: www.tcicollege.net. E-mail: admissions@tcicollege.edu. Thomas M. Coleman, pres.

Technical courses offered include electronics engrg, EETT & IETC office technology, computerized accounting, building maintenance, air conditioning, heating & refrigeration technology. Assoc degree available.

Western Wisconsin Technical College, 304 6th St. N., La Crosse, WI 54601. Phone: (608) 785-9107. Fax: (608) 785-9407. E-mail: jennerjahnj@wwtc.edu. Web Site: www.wwtc.edu. Jack Jennerjahn; Richard Westpfahl, assoc dean visual communications.

Courses offered include photography, computer graphics, TV production, video editing, operation & maintenance of media equipment, audio production & all parts of the assoc degree in visual communications science.

Universities and Colleges with Broadcasting or Journalism Programs

Universities and Colleges Offering Degrees in Broadcasting

Alabama
Alabama, U. of; Tuscaloosa 35487-0152.

Arizona
Arizona State U.; Tempe 85287-1305. BA.
Northern Arizona U.; Flagstaff 86011. BA-BS-BFA.

Arkansas
Arkansas State U.; State University 72467-2160. BS-MS.
Arkansas, U. of; Fayetteville 72701. BA-MA.
Harding U.; Searcy 72149. BA-BS.
John Brown U.; Siloam Springs 72761-2121.
Ozarks U. of; Clarksville 72830.

California
Azusa Pacific U.; Azusa 91702.
California State U., Chico; Chico 95929. BA-BS-MS.
California State U., Fresno; Fresno 93740-8029. BA-MA.
California State U., Fullerton; Fullerton 92831-3599. BA.
California State U., Northridge; Northridge 91330-8137. BA-MA.
Golden West College; Huntington Beach 92647-2581.
Humboldt State U.; Arcata 95521.
Palomar College; San Marcos 92069-1487.
Pepperdine U.; Malibu 90263.
Point Loma Nazarene U.; San Diego 92106.
San Francisco State U.; San Francisco 94132. BA-MA.
San Jose State U.; San Jose 95192-0098. BA-MA.
LaVerne, U. of; La Verne 91750.
San Francisco, U. of; San Francisco 94117-1030.
Southern California, U. of; Los Angeles 90089-0281.

Colorado
Aims Community College; Greeley 80634.
Colorado State U.; Fort Collins 80523-1783.
Colorado, Boulder U. of; Boulder 80309-0478. BS-MA-PhD.
Denver, U. of; Denver 80208. BA.

District of Columbia
American U.; Washington 20016. BS-MA-MFA.
George Washington U.; Washington 20052. BA-MA.
Howard U.; Washington 20059. BA-BS-MA-MS-MFA-PhD.

Florida
Art Institute of Fort Lauderdale; Fort Lauderdale 33316-3000. AS-BS.
Barry U.; Miami Shores 33161. BA-MA-MS.
Central Florida, U. of; Orlando 32816-1344. BA-MA.
City College; Fort Lauderdale 33309. AS-BA.
Florida A&M U.; Tallahassee 32307-4800. BS-MS.
Florida International U.; North Miami 33181-3600. BS-MS.
Florida State U.; Tallahassee 32306-2350. BFA-MFA.
Central Florida, U. of; Orlando 32816-1344. BS-MA.
Miami, U. of; Coral Gables 33124. BA-BFA-MA-MFA-PhD.

Georgia
Augusta State U.; Augusta 30904.
Georgia, U. of; Athens 30602. BA-MA-PhD-MMC.
Valdosta State U.; Valdosta 31698. BFA.

Hawaii
Hawaii, U. of; Honolulu 96822-5396. BA-MA-PhD.

Idaho
Brigham Young Idaho, U.; Rexburg 83460-0708.

Illinois
Bradley U.; Peoria 61625. BA-BS.
College of St. Francis; Joliet 60435.
Eastern Illinois U.; Charleston 61920. BA-MA.
Illinois Institute of Technology; Chicago 60616-3796.
Illinois State U.; Normal 61790-4480. BA-BS-MA-MS.
North Central College; Naperville 60566-4690. BA.
Northwestern U.; Evanston 60208. BA-BS-MFA-PhD.
Prairie State College; Chicago Heights 60411.
Principia College; Elsah 62028-9799. BA-BS.
Rock Valley College; Rockford 61114-5699. AA.
Roosevelt U.; Chicago 60605. BA-MS.
Saint Xavier U.; Chicago 60655.
Southern Illinois, Edwardsville U. of; Edwardsville 62026.
Western Illinois U.; Macomb 61455. BA-MA.

Indiana
Ball State U.; Muncie 47306. MA.
Butler U.; Indianapolis 46208. BS.
DePauw U.; Greencastle 46135. BA.
Indiana State U.; Terre Haute 47809. BA-BS-MA-MS.
Indiana U., Bloomington; Bloomington 47405. BA-MA-MS-PhD.
Indianapolis, U. of; Indianapolis 46227. BA-BS.
Manchester College; North Manchester 46962. AA-BA-BS.
Purdue U., Hammond; Hammond 46323.

Iowa
Dordt College; Sioux Center 51250.
Drake U.; Des Moines 50311. BA.
Iowa, U. of; Iowa City 52242. BA-BS-MA-PhD.
Northern Iowa, U. of; Cedar Falls 50614-0139. BA-MA.
Wartburg College; Waverly 50677-0903. BA.

Kansas
Fort Hays State U.; Hays 67601-4099. BS.
Kansas State U.; Manhattan 66505-1501.
Pittsburg State U.; Pittsburg 66762. BA-BSEd-MA.
Washburn U.; Topeka 66621. BA.

Kentucky
Kentucky, U. of; Lexington 40506-0042. BA-BS-MA-PhD.
Morehead State U.; Morehead 40351. BA-MA.
Murray State U.; Murray 42071-3311. BA-BS.

Louisiana
Grambling State U.; Grambling 71245-0045. BA-MA.
Louisiana at Monroe, U. of; Monroe 71209-0322. BA-MA.
Louisiana College; Pineville 71359. BA.
Louisiana State U.; Baton Rouge 70803. BAMC-PhD-MMC.
Loyola U.; New Orleans 70118. BA-MA.
McNeese State U.; Lake Charles 70609-0335. BS.

Maine
St. Joseph's College; Standish 04084. BA.

Maryland
Columbia Union College; Takoma Park 20912. BA.
Towson U.; Towson 21252.

Massachusetts
Boston U.; Boston 02215-2422.
Emerson College; Boston 02116. BA-BS-MA-MS.
Mount Ida College; Newton Center 02459.
Massachusetts, U. of; Amherst 01003. BA-MA-PhD.

Michigan
Central Michigan U.; Mt. Pleasant 48859. BA-BS-BFA-BAA-BS in Ed-MA.
Eastern Michigan U.; Ypsilanti 48197.
Ferris State U.; Big Rapids 49307. BS.
Michigan State U.; East Lansing 48824-1212.
Wayne State U.; Detroit 48201. BA-MA-PhD.

Minnesota
Bethany Lutheran College; Mankato 56001. AA-BA.
Normandale Community College; Minneapolis 55431.
Minnesota, U. of; Minneapolis 55455. BA-MA-PhD.
St. Thomas, U. of; St. Paul 55105. BA.

Mississippi
Meridian Community College; Meridian 39307.
Mississippi State U.; Mississippi State 39762.
Southern Mississippi, U. of; Hattiesburg 39406. BA-MA-MS-PhD.

Missouri
Evangel College; Springfield 65802. BA-BS.
Missouri Southern State U. at Joplin; Joplin 64801-1595. BA.
Southeast Missouri State U.; Cape Girardeau 63701. BA-BS.
Southwest Missouri State U.; Springfield 65804. BA-BS.
Stephens College; Columbia 65215. BA-BS.
Truman State U.; Kirksville 63501.
Webster U.; Saint Louis 63119.

Montana
Montana, U. of; Missoula 59812-6480.

Universities and Colleges with Broadcasting or Journalism Programs

Nebraska
Creighton U.; Omaha 68178.
Nebraska at Kearney, U. of; Kearney 68849. BA-BS.
Nebraska at Omaha, U. of; Omaha 68182-0112. BA-BS-MA.

Nevada
Nevada, Las Vegas U. of; Las Vegas 89154-5007. BA-MA.
Nevada, Reno U. of; Reno 89557-0040. BA-MA.

New Jersey
Montclair State U.; Upper Montclair 07043.
Rowan U.; Glassboro.

New York
Brooklyn College, CUNY; Brooklyn 11210-2889. BA-BS-MS-MFA.
Buffalo State College; Buffalo 14222. BA.
C.W. Post Campus, Long Island U.; Brookville 11548. BFA-MA.
Hofstra U.; Hempstead 11549. BA-BS.
Marist College; Poughkeepsie 12601. BA.
St. Bonaventure U.; Saint Bonaventure 14778-2289.
St John'S U.; Jamaica 11439. AS-BS.
SUNY, Brockport; Brockport 14420-2978. BA-BS-MA.
Syracuse U.; Syracuse 13244. BA-BS-MA-MS-PhD.

North Carolina
Appalachian State U.; Boone 28608-2039. BS.
North Carolina at Greensboro, U. of; Greensboro 27402-6170.
North Carolina at Wilmington, U. of; Wilmington 28403-5933. BA.
Wake Forest U.; Winston Salem 27109.

North Dakota
North Dakota, U. of; Grand Forks 58202-7169. MA.

Ohio
Akron, The U. of; Akron 44325-1003. BA-MA.
Bowling Green State U.; Bowling Green 43403.
Case Western Reserve U.; Cleveland 44106. BA.
Cincinnati, U. of; Cincinnati 45221-0003. BFA.
Dayton, U. of; Dayton 45469-1410. BA-MA.
Franciscan Steubenville, U. of; Steubenville 43952.
International College of Broadcasting; Dayton 45431.
John Carroll U.; University Heights 44118. BA-MA.
Muskingum College; New Concord 43762-1199. BA.
Ohio U.; Athens 45701. BS-MA-PhD.
Otterbein College; Westerville 43081. BA.
Xavier U.; Cincinnati 45207-5171. BA.

Oklahoma
Cameron U.; Lawton 73505. BA.
Central Oklahoma, U. of;Edmond 73034. BA.
Northwestern Oklahoma State U.; Alva 73717. BA.
Oklahoma, U. of;Norman 73019-0270. BA-MA.
Oklahoma Baptist U.; Shawnee 74804. BA.
Oklahoma City U.; Oklahoma 73106.
Oklahoma State U.; Stillwater 74078. BA-BS-MS.
Oral Roberts U.; Tulsa 74171. BS
Southeastern Oklahoma State U.;Durant 74701-0609.

Pennsylvania
College Misericordia; Dallas 18612. BA.
Duquesne U.; Pittsburgh 15282.
La Salle U.; Philadelphia 19141-1199. BA-MA.
Pennsylvania State U.; University Park 16802.
Shippensburg U.; Shippensburg 17257. BA-MS.
Slippery Rock U.; Slippery Rock 16057. BA-BS.

Susquehanna U.; Selinsgrove 17870. BA.
Temple U.; Philadelphia 19122-6080. BA-MA.
Westminster College; New Wilmington 16172.
Wilkes U.; Wilkes-Barre 18766.

South Carolina
South Carolina, U. of; Columbia 29208. BA-MA-PhD-MMC.
Winthrop U.; Rock Hill 29733-0001. BA-BS.

South Dakota
South Dakota, U. of; Vermillion 57069-2390.

Tennessee
Belmont U.; Nashville 37212. BA-BS.
Lee U.; Cleveland 37311.
Middle Tennessee State U.; Murfreesboro 37032. BS-MS.
Tennessee State U.; Nashville 37221.
Tennessee at Chattanooga, U. of; Chattanooga 37403. BA.
Tennessee at Knoxville, U. of; Knoxville 37996. BS-MS-PhD.
Tennessee at Martin, U. of; Martin 38238.

Texas
Baylor U.; Waco 76798-7368. BA-MA.
Central Texas College; Killeen 76540-9990. AS.
Houston, U. of; Houston 77204-3786. BA-MA.
Navarro College; Corsicana 75110.
North Texas, U. of; Denton 76203. BA-MA-MMS.
Prairie View A&M U.; Prairie View 77446.
Sam Houston State U.; Huntsville 77341.
San Antonio College; San Antonio 78212-4299. AA-AAS.
Stephen F. Austin State U.; Nacogdoches 75962. BA-BS-MA.
Texas A&M U.; College Station 77843-4111. BA-BS-MA.
Texas at Arlington U. of; Arlington 76019. BA.
Texas at Austin, U. of; Austin. BJ-MA-PhD.
Texas at El Paso, U. of; El Paso 79968. BA.
Texas Christian U.; Fort Worth 76129.
Texas State U. at San Marcos; San Marcos 78666. BA-MA.
Texas Tech U.; Lubbock 79409-3082. BA.
The Incarnate Word, U. of; San Antonio 78209. AA-BA-MA.
Trinity U.; San Antonio 78212-7200. BA.

Utah
Brigham Young U.; Provo 84602. BA.
Utah, U. of; Salt Lake City 84112. BA-BS-MA-MS-PhD
Utah State U.; Logan 84322-4605. BA-BS-MA-MS.

Virginia
Hampton U.; Hampton 23668.
James Madison U.; Harrisonburg 22807.

Washington
Clover Park Technical College; Lakewood 98499-4098.
Pacific Lutheran U.; Tacoma 98447.
Washington State U.; Pullman 99165.

West Virginia
Marshall U.; Huntington 25755-2622. BA-MA.

Wisconsin
Madison Media Institute; Madison 53719. AA.
Marquette U.; Milwaukee 53201-1881. BA-MA.
Wisconsin Eau Claire, U. of; Eau Claire 54702-4004. BA-BS.
Wisconsin La Crosse, U. of; La Crosse 54601. AA-BA-BS.

Wisconsin-Platteville, U. of; Platteville 53818-3099. BA-BS.
Wisconsin Stevens Point, U. of; Stevens Point 54481. BA-BS-MA.

Wyoming
Wyoming, U. of; Laramie 82071.

Two-Year Colleges Offering Programs in Broadcasting

Alabama
Gadsden State Community College; Gadsden 35902-0227. AA.

Arizona
Yavapai College Sedona Center for Arts & Technology; Sedona 86336. AA-AS-AAS.

California
Citrus College; Glendora 91741.
City College of San Francisco; San Francisco 94112. AA.
Cosumnes River College; Sacramento 95823. AA.
Mount San Antonio College; Walnut 91789.
Pasadena Area Community College; Pasadena 91106. AA-AS.
Santa Ana/Santiago Canyon College; Santa Ana 92706. AA.

Florida
Florida Community College at Jacksonville; Jacksonville 32256. AA-AS.
Hillsborough Community College; Tampa 33675-5096. AS.

Illinois
South Suburban College; South Holland 60473. AA.

Indiana
Vincennes U.; Vincennes 47591. AA-AS.

Iowa
Iowa Lakes Community College; Estherville. AA-AS.

Louisiana
Bossier Parish Community College; Bossier City 71111-5808. AA-AAS.

Maine
Southern Maine Technical College; South Portland 04106. AS.

Maryland
Montgomery College; Rockville 20850. AA-AS.

Massachusetts
Mount Wachusett Community College; Gardner 01440-1000. AS.

Michigan
Lansing Community College; Lansing 48933.

Universities and Colleges with Broadcasting or Journalism Programs

New Jersey
Bergen Community College; Paramus 07652. AAS.
Morris County College; Randolph 07869. AA-AS.

New York
Cayuga Community College; Auburn 13021. AAS.
Finger Lakes Community College; Canandaigua 14424.
Hudson Valley Community College; Troy 12180. AA-AAS.
Monroe Community College; Rochester 14623-5780.
Onondaga Community College; Syracuse 13215. AAS.

North Carolina
Isothermal Community College; Spindale 28160. AAS.

Ohio
Washington State Community College; Marietta 45750.

Oregon
Treasure Valley Community College; Ontario 97914. AA-AS.

Texas
Austin Community College; Austin 78736.
Central Texas College; Killeen 76540-9990. AS.
Houston Community College Southwest; Stafford 77477.

Virginia
Virginia Western Community College; Roanoke 24038-4007.

Washington
Green River Community College; Auburn 98092.

Universities and Colleges Offering Degrees in Journalism and Mass Communication

Alabama
Alabama, U. of; Tuscaloosa 35487-0152. BA, MA, MLIS, PhD.
Alabama State U.; Montgomery 36104-0271. BA.
Auburn U.; Auburn 36849-5211. BA, MA.
Jacksonville State, U.; Jacksonville 36265. BA.
Samford U.; Birmingham 35229. BA.
South Alabama, U. of; Mobile 36688. BA, MA.
Spring Hill College; Mobile 36608.
Troy State U.; Troy 36082.

Alaska
Alaska Anchorage, U. of; Anchorage 99508. BA.
Alaska at Fairbanks, U. of; Fairbanks 99775-6120.

Arizona
Arizona, U. of; Tucson 85721. BA, MA.
Arizona State U.; Tempe 85287-1305. BA, MMC.
North Arizona U.; Flagstaff 86011-5619.

Arkansas
Arkansas, U. of; Fayetteville 72701. BA, MA.
Arkansas at Little Rock, U. of; Little Rock 72204. BA, MA.
Arkansas State U.; State University 72467. BS, MSMC.
Arkansas Tech U.; Russellville 72801. BA, MA.
Central Arkansas, U. of; Conway 72035.
Harding U.; Searcy 72149. BA, BS.
Henderson State U.; Arkadelphia 71999. BA, MA.
John Brown U.; Siloam Springs 72761.

California
California at Berkeley, U. of; Berkeley 94720. MJ.
California Lutheran U.; Thousand Oaks 91360-2787.
California State Polytechnic U.; Pomona 91768-4007.
California State U., Chico; Chico 95929-0145. BA, MA.
California State U., Dominguez Hills; Dominguez Hills 90747. BA.
California State U., Fresno; Fresno 93740-8029. BA, MA.
California State U., Fullerton; Fullerton 92834-6846. BA, MA.
California State U., Hayward; Hayward 94542.
California State U., Long Beach; Long Beach 90840-4601. BA.
California State U., Los Angeles; Los Angeles 90032.
California State U., Northridge; Northridge 91330-8311. BA, MA.
California State U., Sacramento; Sacramento 95819-6070. BA.
Humboldt State U.; Arcata 95521. BA.
Menlo College; Atherton 94027-4185.
Pacific U. of the; Stockton 95211.
Pacific Union College; Angwin (Napa County) 94508.
Pepperdine U.; Malibu 90263. BA, MA.
Point Loma Nazarene U; San Diego 92106.
Saint Mary's College of California; Moraga 94575.
San Diego State U.; San Diego 92182-4561. BA, MA.
San Francisco, U. of; San Francisco 94117-1080.
San Francisco State U.; San Francisco 94132. BA.
San Jose State U.; San Jose 95192-0055. BS.
Santa Clara U.; Santa Clara 95053.
Southern California, U. of; Los Angeles 90089-0281. B.A., B.A./M.A., M.A.
Stanford U.; Stanford 94305. BA, MA, PhD.

Colorado
Adams State U.; Alamosa 81102.
Colorado, U. of; Boulder 80309-0478. BS JR, MA, PhD.
Colorado State U.; Fort Collins 80523. BA, MS.
Denver, U. of; Denver 80208. BA, MA, MS.
Mesa State College; Grand Junction 81502. BA.
Metropolitan State College of Denver; Denver 80217-3362.
Northern Colorado, U. of; Greeley 80639. BA.
Southern Colorado, U. of; Pueblo 81001-4901.

Connecticut
Bridgeport, U. of; Bridgeport 06601.
Connecticut, U. of; Storrs 06269. BA, MA, PhD.
Hartford, U. of; West Hartford 06117-1599.
Quinnipiac U.; Hamden 06518. BA, MS.
Southern Connecticut State U.; New Haven 06515. BA, BS.

Delaware
Delaware, U. of; Newark 19716.

District of Columbia
American U.; Washington 20016. BA, BS, MA, MFA.
Catholic U. School of Law; Washington 20064.
George Washington U.; Washington 20052. BA, MA.
Howard U.; Washington 20059. BA, BS, MA, MS, MFA, PhD.

Florida
Central Florida, U. of; Orlando 32816-1344. BA, MA.
Edward Waters College; Jacksonville 32218. BA.
Flagler College; St. Augustine 32085-1027. BA.
Florida, U. of; Gainesville 32611-8400. BS, MA, PhD.
Florida A&M U.; Tallahassee 32307-4800. BSJ, BS, MS.
Florida International U.; North Miami 33181. BS, MS.
Florida Southern College; Lakeland 33801-5698.
Jacksonville U.; Jacksonville 32211.
Miami, U. of; Coral Gables 33124. BSC, BFA, MA, MFA, PhD.
North Florida, U. of; Jacksonville 32224-2645. BA, BS, BFA.
South Florida, U. of; Tampa 33620-7800. BA, MA.
West Florida, U. of; Pensacola 32514. BA, MA.

Georgia
Berry College; Mount Berry. 30149-0299. BA.
Brenau U.; Gainesville 30501.
Clark Atlanta U.; Atlanta 30314. BA.
Georgia, U. of; Athens. 30602-3018. ABJ (BA in Jour.), MA, MMC, PhD.
Georgia State U.; Atlanta 30303. BA, MA.
Mercer U. at Macon ; Macon 31207.
Toccoa Falls College; Toccoa Falls 30598. BA, BS.

Hawaii
Chaminade, U. of Honolulu; Honolulu 96816. BA.
Hawaii at Manoa, U. of; Honolulu 96822. BA.
Hawaii Pacific U.; Honolulu 96813-2807. BA, MA/COM.

Idaho
Boise State U.; Boise 83725. BA, MA.
Idaho, U. of; Moscow 83744. BA, BS.
Idaho State U.; Pocatello 83709.

Illinois
Bradley U.; Peoria 61625. BA, BS.
Columbia College Chicago; Chicago 60605-1996.
DePaul U.; Chicago 60614. B.A., M.A.
Eastern Illinois U.; Charleston 61920-3099. BA.
Governors State U.; University Park 60466-0975. BA, BS, MA, MS.
Illinois College; Jacksonville 62650.
Illinois, U. of; Urbana 61801. BS, MS, PhD.
Illinois State U.; Normal 61790. BA, BS, MA, MS.
Loyola U. of Chicago; Chicago 60626.
MacMurray College; Jacksonville 62650.
Northern Illinois U.; DeKalb 60115. BA, BS.
Northwestern U.; Evanston 60208-2101. BSJ, MSJ, MSIMC.
Roosevelt U.; Chicago 60605.
Southern Illinois U. at Carbondale; Carbondale 62901-6606. BA, BS, MA, MFA, PhD.
Southern Illinois U.; Edwardsville 62026-1775. BA, BS, MS.
St Francis, U. of; Joliet 60435.
Western Illinois U.; Macomb 61455. BA.

Indiana
Anderson U.; Anderson 46012.
Ball State U.; Muncie 47306. BA, BS, MA.
Butler U.; Indianapolis 46208.
Calumet College; Whiting 46394. BA.
DePauw U.; Greencastle 46135.
Evansville, U. of; Evansville 47722. BA, BS.
Franklin College; Franklin 46131. BA.
Goshen College; Goshen 46526-4798.
Indiana State U.; Terre Haute 47809. BA,BS.
Indiana U.; Bloomington 47405. BAJ, MA, PhD.
Indianapolis, U. of; Indianapolis 46227.
Notre Dame, U. of; Notre Dame 46556.
Purdue U.; West Lafayette 47907-1366. MA, PhD.
Saint Mary-of-the-Woods College; Saint Mary-of-the-Woods 47876.
Southern Indiana, U. of; Evansville 47712-3596. BA, BS, AS.

Universities and Colleges with Broadcasting or Journalism Programs

Taylor U., Fort Wayne Campus; Fort Wayne 46807-2197.
Valparaiso U.; Valparaiso 46383.
Vincennes U.; Vincennes 47591.

Iowa
Clarke College; Dubuque 52001.
Drake U.; Des Moines 50311. BA.
Grand View College; Des Moines 50316.
Iowa, U. of; Iowa City 52242. BA, BS, MA, PhD.
Iowa State U. Science and Technology of; Ames 50011-1180. BA, BS, MS.
Marycrest College; Davenport 52804.
Northern Iowa, U. of; Cedar Falls 50614.

Kansas
Baker U.; Baldwin City 66066-0065.
Fort Hays State U.; Hays 67601.
Kansas, U. of; Lawrence 66045-7575. BS, MS.
Kansas State U.; Manhattan 66506-1501. BS, BA, MS.
Pittsburg State U.; Pittsburg 66762. BA/BSEd, MA.
Washburn U.; Topeka 66621.
Wichita State U.; Wichita 67260-0031. BA, MA.

Kentucky
Asbury College; Wilmore 40390-1198.
Eastern Kentucky U.; Richmond 40475-3102. BA.
Kentucky, U. of; Lexington 40506-0042. BA, BGS, BS.
Louisville, U. of; Louisville 40292.
Morehead State U.; Morehead 40351.
Murray State U.; Murray 42071. BS, BA, MS, MA.
Northern Kentucky U.; Highland Heights 41076. BA.
Western Kentucky U.; Bowling Green 42101-3576. BA.

Louisiana
Grambling State U.; Grambling 71254. BA, MA.
Louisiana State U.; Baton Rouge 70803-7202. BMC, MMC, PhD.
Louisiana State U. in Shreveport; Shreveport 71115. BA.
Louisiana Tech U.; Ruston 71272-0045. BA.
Louisiana at Lafayette, U. of; Lafayette 70503. BA, MS.
Louisiana at Monroe, U. of; Monroe 71209-0322. BA, MA.
Loyola U.; New Orleans 70118. BA, MA, MA/JD.
McNeese State U.; Lake Charles 70609. BS.
New Orleans, U. of; New Orleans 70148.
Nicholls State U.; Thibodaux 70310. BA.
Northwestern State U. of Louisiana; Natchitoches 71497. BA.
Southern U. and A&M College; Baton Rouge 70813. BA, MA.
Southeastern Louisiana U.; Hammond 70402. BA.
Xavier U. of Louisiana; New Orleans 70125.

Maine
Maine, U. of; Orono 04469-5724. BA.

Maryland
Bowie State U.; Bowie 20715.
Defense Information School; Ft. George G. Meade 20755-5620.
Goucher College; Baltimore 21204.
Hood College; Frederick 21701. BA.
Loyola College; Baltimore 21210-2601. BA.
Maryland, U. of; College Park 20742. BA, MA, PhD.
Towson U.; Towson 21252. BA, BS.

Massachusetts
Boston U.; Boston 02215.
Emerson College; Boston 02116. BA, BFA, BS, MA.
Hampshire College; Amherst 01002.
Massachusetts, U. of; Amherst 01003-0520. BA.
Northeastern U.; Boston 02115. BA, BS, MA.

Simmons College; Boston 02115.
Stonehill College; Easton 02357. BA.
Suffolk U.; Boston 02114.

Michigan
Alma College; Alma 48801.
Calvin College; Grand Rapids 49546. BA.
Central Michigan U.; Mt. Pleasant 48859. BA, BS.
Detroit Mercy, U. of; Detroit 48219-0900.
Eastern Michigan U.; Ypsilanti 48197-4210.
Grand Valley State U.; Allendale 49401. BA, BS.
Madonna U.; Livonia 48150.
Michigan, U. of; Ann Arbor 48109-1285. BA, PhD.
Michigan State U.; East Lansing 48824-1212. BA, MA, PhD.
Oakland U.; Rochester 48309.
Wayne State U.; Detroit 48201. BA.
Western Michigan U.; Kalamazoo 49008-3805. BA.

Minnesota
Bemidji State U.; Bemidji 56601. BS.
Minnesota State U.; Mankato 56001. BA, BS.
Minnesota, U. of; Minneapolis 55455-0418. BA, MA, PhD.
Minnesota State U.; Moorehead 56563. BS,BA.
St. Cloud State U.; St Cloud 56301. BS, MS.
St. Mary's U.; Winona 55987.
St. Thomas, U. of; St. Paul 55105. BA.
Winona State U.; Winona 55987. BA.

Mississippi
Alcorn State U.; Alcorn State 39096-7500. BA.
Jackson State U.; Jackson 39217. BS, MS.
Mississippi, U. of; University 38677-1848. BA, MA.
Mississippi State U.; Mississippi State 39762.
Mississippi State U. for Women; Columbus 39701. BS/BA.
Mississippi Valley State U.; Itta Bena 38941-1400. BA.
Rust College; Holly Springs 38635.
Southern Mississippi, U. of; Hattiesburg 39406-5121. BA, MA, MS.
Tougaloo College; Tougaloo 39174.

Missouri
Central Missouri State U.; Warrensburg 64093. BA, BS, BSE, MA.
Culver-Stockton College; Canton 63435.
Evangel U.; Springfield 65802.
Lincoln U.; Jefferson City 65102. BA, BS.
Lindenwood U.; St Charles 63301.
Maryville U.; St. Louis 63141.
Missouri, U. of; Columbia 65211. BJ, MA, PhD.
Missouri-Kansas City, U. of; Kansas City 64110. BA, MA.
Missouri Southern State College; Joplin 64801-1595.
Missouri-St. Louis, U. of; St. Louis 63121.
Missouri Western State College; St. Joseph 64507.
Northwest Missouri State U.; Maryville 64468.
Saint Louis U.; St. Louis 63108. BA, MA.
Southeast Missouri State U.; Cape Girardeau 63701. BA, BS.
Southwest Missouri State U.; Springfield 65804. BA, BS.
Stephens College; Columbia 65215.
Truman State U.; Kirksville 63501. BA.
Webster U.; St. Louis 63119.

Montana
Montana, The U. of; Missoula 59812-0648. BA, MA.

Nebraska
Creighton U.; Omaha 68178-0119. BA, BS.
Hasting College; Hasting 68902.
Midland Lutheran College; Fremont 68025.
Nebraska-Kearney, U. of; Kearney 68849.
Nebraska-Lincoln, U. of; Lincoln 68588-0443. BJ, MA.

Nebraska at Omaha, U. of; Omaha 68182. BA, BS, MA.

Nevada
Nevada, Las Vegas, U. of; Las Vegas 89154-5007. BA, MA.
Nevada-Reno, U. of; Reno 89557-0040. BA, MA.

New Hampshire
Keene State College of the U. System of New Hampshire; Keene 03435. BA.
New Hampshire, U. of; Durham 03824.

New Jersey
Fairleigh Dickinson U.; Teaneck 07666. BA, MA.
Rider U.; Lawrenceville 08648.
Rowan U.; Glassboro 08028-1701. BA, MA.
Rutgers U.; New Brunswick 08903. BA.
Rutgers U. Newark; Newark 07102.
Seton Hall U.; South Orange 07079. BA.
William Paterson U.; Wayne 07470.

New Mexico
Eastern New Mexico U.; Portales 88130.
New Mexico, U. of; Albuquerque 87131. BA.
New Mexico Highlands U.; Las Vegas 87701.
New Mexico State U.; Las Cruces 88003. BA.

New York
Albany, State U. of New York at; Albany 1222.
Buffalo, State U. College at; Buffalo 14222. BA.
Canisius College; Buffalo 14208. BS, BA.
Columbia U.; New York 10027. MSJ, PhD.
Cornell U.; Ithaca 14853-4203. BS, MS, PhD.
Empire State College of SUNY; Rochester 14607.
Fordham U.; Bronx 10458. MA.
Hofstra U.; Hempstead 11549-1110. BA.
Iona College; New Rochelle 10801-1890. BA, BS, MA, MSJ.
Ithaca College; Ithaca 14850. BS, BA, BFA, MS.
Long Island University-The Brooklyn Campus; Brooklyn 11201. BA.
Marist College; Poughkeepsie 12601. BA.
New York U.; New York 10003. BA, MA.
Niagara U.; Niagara 14109. BA.
Pace U.; New York 10038.
Pace U. (Pleasantville); Pleasantville 10570. BA.
Rochester Institute of Technology; Rochester 14623. BFA.
St. Bonaventure U.; St. Bonaventure 14778-2289. BA.
St. John Fisher College; Rochester 14618.
SUNDY College at New Paltz; New Paltz 12561.
Syracuse U.; Syracuse 13244-2100. BS, MA, MS, PhD.
Utica College of Syracuse U.; Utica 13502. BA, BS.

North Carolina
Appalachian State U.; Boone 28608. BS.
Campbell U.; Buies Creek 27506. BA.
East Carolina U.; Greenville 27858-4353.
Elon U.; Elon 27244. BA.
Johnson C. Smith U.; Charlotte 28216.
Lenoir-Rhyne College; Hickory 28303. BA.
North Carolina, U. of; Chapel Hill 27599-3365. AB, MA, PhD.
North Carolina-Asheville, U. of; Asheville 28804.
North Carolina A&T State U.; Greensboro 27411. BS.
North Carolina-Pembroke, U. of; Pembroke 28372-1510.
Wingate U.; Wingate 28174.

North Dakota
North Dakota, U. of; Grand Forks 58202. BA, BS, Ed, MA, MS, PhD.
North Dakota State U.; Fargo 58105.

Universities and Colleges with Broadcasting or Journalism Programs

Ohio
Akron, U. of; Akron 44325.
Bowling Green State U.; Bowling Green 43403. BS, MA, PhD.
Cincinnati, U. of; Cincinnati 45221-0003.
Cleveland U.; Cleveland 44115-2212. BA
Dayton, U. of; Dayton 45469-1410.
Franciscan U.; Steubenville 43952.
John Carroll U.; University Heights 44118. BA, MA.
Kent State U.; Kent 44242. BS, MA.
Marietta College; Marietta 45750. BA.
Ohio State U.; Columbus 43210-1339. BAJ, BA, MA, PhD.
Ohio U.; Athens 45701. BSJ, MSJ, PhD.
Ohio Wesleyan U.; Delaware 43015. BA.
Otterbein College; Westerville 43081. BA.
Toledo, U. of; Toledo 43606. BA.
Wright State U.; Dayton 45435.
Xavier U.; Cincinnati 45207-5171. BA.
Youngstown State U.; Youngstown 4455-3415.

Oklahoma
Central Oklahoma, U. of; Edmond 73034.
East Central U.; Ada 74820.
Northeastern State U.; Tahlequah 74464.
Oklahoma, U. of; Norman 73019. BAJ, MA.
Oklahoma Baptist U.; Shawnee 74804. BA.
Oklahoma Christian, U.; Oklahoma City 73136. BA.
Oklahoma State U.; Stillwater 74078-0195. BA, BS, MS, EdD.
Southern Nazarene U.; Bethany 73008.
Tulsa, U. of; Tulsa 74104. BA.

Oregon
Linfield College; McMinnville 97128-6894. BA.
Oregon, U. of; Eugene 97403-1275. BA, BS, MA, MS, PhD.
Portland, U. of; Portland 97203-5798. BS, MA, MS.
Southern Oregon U.; Ashland 97520.

Pennsylvania
Bloomsburg U.; Bloomsburg 17815. BA.
Cabrini College; Radnor 19087-3698. BA.
Duquesne U.; Pittsburgh 15282. BA, MA, PhD.
Elizabethtown College; Elizabethtown 17022. BA.
Indiana U. of Pennsylvania; Indiana 15705. BA
La Salle U.; Philadelphia 19141-1199.
Lehigh U.; Bethlehem 18015.
Lock Haven U.; Lock Heaven 17745-2390.
Lycoming College; Williamsport 17701.
Millersville U.; Millersville 17551-0302.
Pennsylvania, U. of (Annenberg School for Communication); Philadelphia 19104-6220.
Pennsylvania State U., The; University Park 16802. BA, MA, PhD.
Pittsburgh, U. of; Pittsburgh 15260.
Point Park U.; Pittsburgh 15222-1984. AA, BA, MA.
Shippensburg U.; Shippensburg 17257. BA, MS.
Susquehanna U.; Sellingsgrove 17870-1001.
Temple U.; Philadelphia 19122-6080. BA, MA, MJ, PhD.
Ursinus College; Collegeville 19426-1000.

Rhode Island
Rhode Island, U. of; Kingston 02881. BA.

South Carolina
Benedict College; Columbia 29204.
College of Charleston; Charleston 29424-0001. BA.
Francis Marion U.; Florence 29501-0547.
South Carolina, U. of; Columbia 29208. BA, MA, MMC, PhD.
South Carolina Aiken, U. of; Aiken 29801. BA.
Winthrop U.; Rock Hill 29733. BA, BS.

South Dakota
Black Hills State U.; Spearfish 57799-9003.
Mount Marty College; Yankton 57078. BA.
South Dakota, U. of; Vermillion 57069. BA, BS, MA.
South Dakota State U.; Brookings 57007-0596. BS, BA, MS.

Tennessee
Austin Peay State U.; Clarksville 37044. BA, BS, MA.
Christian Brothers U.; Memphis 38104. BA.
East Tennessee State U.; Johnson City 37614. BS, BA.
Memphis, U. of; Memphis 38152. BA, MA.
Middle Tennessee State U.; Murfreesboro 37132. BS, MS.
Milligan College; Milligan College 37682. BA, BS.
Tennessee, The U. of; Knoxville 37996-0332. BS, MS, PhD.
Tennessee at Chattanooga, U. of; Chattanooga 37403-2598. BA.
Tennessee at Martin, U. of; Martin 38238. BA. BS.
Tennessee Technological U.; Cookeville 38505. BS.

Texas
Abilene Christian U.; Abilene 79699. BS.
Angelo State U.; San Angelo 76909.
Baylor U.; Waco 76798-7353. BA, MA, MIJ.
Hardin-Simmons U.; Abilene 79698.
Houston, U. of; Houston 77204. BA, MA.
Houston Baptist U.; Houston 77074. BA, BS.
Lamar University-Beaumont; Beaumont 77710. BS.
Midwestern State U.; Wichita Falls 76308. BA.
North Texas, U. of; Denton 76203. BA, BS, MA, MJ.
Prairie View A&M U.; Prairie 77446-0156. BA.
Sam Houston State U.; Huntsville 77341-2299.
Southern Methodist U.; Dallas 75205. BA.
Stephen F. Austin State U.; Nacogdoches 75962.
Texas A&M U.; College Station 77843-4111. BA, BS, MS.
Texas A&M University-Commerce; Commerce 75429. BA, BS, MA, MS.
Texas A&M University-Kingsville; Kingsville 78363. BA.
Texas A&M University-Texarkana; Texarkana 75505-5518. BS.
Texas at Arlington, U. of; Arlington 76019. BA.
Texas at Austin, U. of; Austin 78712. BJ, MA, PhD.
Texas at El Paso, U. of; El Paso 79968-0550. BA, MA.
Texas Christian U.; fort Worth 76129. BA, BS, MS.
Texas Lutheran U.; Seguin 78155.
Texas-Pan American, U. of; Edinburg 78539-2999.
Texas of The Permian Basin, U. of; Odessa 79762.
Texas Southern U.; Houston 77004. BA, MA.
Texas State University-San Marcos; San Marcos 78664-4616. BA, MA.
Texas Tech U.; Lubbock 79409-3082. BA, MA.
Texas Wesleyan U.; Forth 76105.
Texas Women's U.; Denton 76204-5828. BS, BA.
Trinity U.; San Antonio 78212-7200. BA.
West Texas A&M U.; Canyon 79016. BA, BS.

Utah
Brigham Young U.; Provo 84602. BA, MA.
Southern Utah U.; Cedar City 84720. BA, BS.
Utah, U. of; Salt Lake City 84112-0491. BS, BA, MS, MA, PhD.
Utah State U.; Logan 84322-4605. BA, BS, MA, MS.
Weber State U.; Ogden 84408. BA.

Vermont
St. Michael's College; Colchester 05439. BA.

Virginia
Emory and Henry College; Emory 24327.
Hampton U.; Hampton 23668. BA.
James Madison U.; Harrisonburg 22807.
Liberty U.; Lynchburg 24506. BS.
Lynchburg College; Lynchburg 24501.
Mary Baldwin College; Staunton 24401.
Marymount U.; Arlington 22207. BA.
Norfolk State U.; Norfolk 23504. BA, BS, MA.
Radford U.; Radford 24142. BS, BA, MS.
Regent U.; Virginia Beach 23464-9800. MA, PhD.
Richmond, U. of; Richmond 23173.
Virginia Commonwealth U.; Richmond 23284-2034. BS, MS.
Virginia Polytechnic Institute and State U.; Blacksburg 24061. BA, MA.
Virginia Union U.; Richmond 23220. BA.
Washington and Lee U.; Lexington 24450. BA.

Washington
Central Washington U.; Ellensburg 98926.
Eastern Washington U.; Spokane 99201-3900. BA.
Gonzaga U.; Spokane 99258. BA.
Pacific Lutheran U.; Tacoma 98447.
Seattle U.; Seattle 98122.
Walla Walla College; College Place 99324. BA.
Washington, U. of; Seattle 98195-3740. BA, MA, MC, PhD.
Washington State U.; Pullman 99164-2520. BA, MA, PhD.
Western Washington U.; Bellingham 98225-9101. BA.
Whitworth College; Spokane 99251.

West Virginia
Bethany College; Bethany 26032. BA.
Marshall U.; Huntington 25755. BA, MAJ.
West Virginia U.; Morgantown 26506. BSJ, MSJ.

Wisconsin
Marquette U.; Milwaukee 53201. BA, MA.
Wisconsin-Eau Claire, U. of; Eau Claire 54702. BA, BS.
Wisconsin-La Crosse, U. of; La Crosse 54601. BA, BS.
Wisconsin-Madison, U. of; Madison 53706-1497. BA, BS, MA, PhD.
Wisconsin-Madison, U. of; Madison 53706-1563. BS, MS, PhD.
Wisconsin-Milwaukee, U. of; Milwaukee 53201. BA, MA.
Wisconsin-Oshkosh, U. of; Oshkosh 54901. BA, BS.
Wisconsin-River Falls, U. of; River Falls 54022. BS, BA.
Wisconsin-Stevens Point, U. of; Stevens Point 54481.
Wisconsin-Whitewater, U. of; Whitewater 53190.

Wyoming
Wyoming, U. of; Laramie 82071-3904. BA, BS, MA.

Major Broadcasting and Cable Awards

AAAS Science Journalism Awards, 1200 New York Ave. N.W., Washington, DC 20005. Phone: (202) 326-6440. Fax: (202) 789-0455. E-mail: gpinhols@aaas.org. Web Site: www.aaas.org.

Since 1946, the AAAS Science Journalism Awards honors individual professional journalists for their coverage of sciences, engineering & mathematics. Contact: Ginger Pinholster, AAAS Science Journalism Awards, 1200 New York Ave. N.W. Washington, DC 20005.

AOPA Max Karant Awards for Excellence in Gerneral Aviation Journalism, Aircraft Owners & Pilots Assn, 421 Aviation Way, Frederick, MD 21701. Phone: (301) 695-2157. Fax: (301) 695-2309. E-mail: pat.rishel@aopa.org. Web Site: www.aopa.org/special/karant/.For 16 years, the Aircraft Owners & Pilots Assn has honored news professionals who have made a positive contribution to general aviation - all aviation except the military & commercial airlines - through their enlighteded coverage. Named after the legendary founding editor of AOPA PILOT magazine, the 2005 Max Karant Awards for Excellence in General Aviation Journalism are aviation journalism's most prestigious honors and are open to any journalist-not part of the aviation trade industry-who created an enlightening story about general aviation during calendar year 2005. Four $1,000 awards are given for Print, TV-news or short feature, TV-program length, and radio categories. Works published or bcst between Jan 1- Dec 31, 2005 will be judged by a panel of aviation & media professionals. Awards are presented at AOPA EXPO in Palm Springs, CA on Nov 9,2006. There is no entry fee. Eligibility Period: Jan 1-Dec 31, 2005. Deadline for entries: Postmark deadline: April 15, 2006. Contact: Pat Rishel, 301-695-2157, Aircraft Owners & Pilots Association, 421 Aviation Way, Frederick, MD 21701.

Academy of Television Arts and Sciences Emmy Awards, Academy of Television Arts & Sciences, 5220 Lankershim Blvd., North Hollywood, CA 91601. Phone: (818) 754-2800. Fax: (818) 761-2827. E-mail: leverence@emmys.org. Web Site: www.emmys.org.

Annual awards covering a broad range of TV primetime. Eligibility Period: June 1-May 31. Deadline for entries: Late March. Contact: John Leverence, Awards Director, Academy of Television Arts & Sciences, 5220 Lankershim Blvd., North Hollywood, CA 91601.

Alliance for Community Media Hometown Video Festival Awards, 666 11th St. N.W., Suite 740, Washington, DC 20001-4542. Phone: (202) 393-2650. Fax: (202) 393-2653. E-mail: acm@alliance.org. Web Site: www.alliancecm.org.

Awards those who have made outstanding contributions to humanistic community communications, demonstrated leadership & encouraged cultural diversity in community media. Eligibility Period: January 1-December 31. Deadline for entries: Postmark March 1. Contact: Bunnie Riedel, Exec Dir, 666 11th St. N.W., Suite 740, Washington, DC 20001-4542.

The American Legion Fourth Estate Award, ATTN: Public Relations, The American Legion National Hqtrs., 700 N Pennslyvania St., Indianapolis, IN 46204. Phone: (317) 630-1253. Fax: (317) 630-1368. E-mail: pr@legion.org. Web Site: www.legion.org.The Fourth Estate Award is presented annually by The American Legion's National Public Relations Commission to an individual, publication or bcst organization for outstanding achievement in the field of journalism. A $2,000 stipend accompanies the award to defray expenses of recipient accepting the award at The American Legion National Convention in August & September. Eligibility Period: Entries must have been aired or published for bcst during the calendar year. Deadline for entries: January 31 of the year the award is presented. Contact: Public Relations, The American Legion National Headquarters, 700 N. Pennsylvania St., Indianapolis, IN 46204.

American Women in Radio and Television Inc. Awards, 8405 Greensboro Dr., Suite 800, McLean, VA 22102. Phone: (703) 506-3260. Fax: (703) 506-3266. E-mail: info@awrt.org. Web Site: www.awrt.org.

The Gracie Allen Awards strive to encourage the positive, realistic portrayal of women in entertainment, news, commercials, features & other progmg. Deadline for entries: See Website. Contact: Amy Lotz, Mgr, AWRT, 1595 Spring Hill Road, Ste 330, Vienna, VA 22182.

Armstrong Awards, S.W. Mudd Bldg., Armstrong Foundation, Columbia Univ., 500 W. 120th St., Rm. 1311-Seeley Mudd, New York, NY 10027. Phone: (212) 854-4718. Phone: (212) 854-3121. Fax: (212) 854-7837. E-mail: kkg1@columbia.edu. Web Site: www.armstrongfoundation.org.

Awards to electrical engrg students, rsch scientists in the field of communications, AM, FM radio stns for excellence & originality in bcstg. Eligibility Period: The annual awards program covers the period from January-December 31. Deadline for entries: September 1. Contact: Ken Goldstein, pres, Armstrong Foundation, Columbia University, S.W. Mudd Hall, 500 W. 120th St., Room 1311, New York, NY 10027.

The Association for Women in Communications, River Reach Ctr., 780 Ritchie Hwy., Suite 28S, Severna Park, MD 21146. Phone: (410) 544-7442. Fax: (410) 544-4640. E-mail: clarion@womcom.org. Web Site: www.womcom.org.

A series of annual awards recognizing excellence in communication fields. Eligibility Period: January 1-December 31. Deadline for entries: April

BDA International Design Award, BDA International, 2029 Century Park E., Suite 555, Los Angeles, CA 90067. Phone: (310) 712-0040. Fax: (310) 712-0039. Web Site: www.bda.tv. E-mail: adrienne@promax.tv.

Acknowledges outstanding contributions in design for the screen & its associated promotions. Eligibility Period: January 1-December 31. Deadline for entries: January. Contact: Adrienne Alwag, BDA Design-awards cordinator, 2029 Century Park E., Suite 555, Los Angeles, CA 90067.

Batten Fellows Program, Box 6550, The Darden School, University of Virginia, Charlottesville, VA 22906. Phone: (434) 924-7739. Fax: (434) 243-8708. E-mail: ahs4c@virginia.edu. Web Site: www.darden.virginia.edu.

Brings high-potential young professionals & prominant thought leaders to the Darden School to dev new intellectual capital. Eligibility Period: Fall. Deadline for entries: April 1. Contact: Director of Financial Aid, The Darden School, University of Virginia, Box 6550, Charlottesville, VA 22906.

The John Bayliss Broadcast Foundation Internships, Scholarships Programs, Box 51126, Pacific Grove, CA 93950. Phone: (831) 655-5229. Fax: (831) 655-5228. E-mail: info@baylissfoundation.org. Web Site: www.baylissfoundation.org.

Application & information available on website. Deadline for entries: Apr 30

Broadcast Cable Financial Management Assn. "Avatar" Award, 932 Lee St., Suite 204, Des Plaines, IL 60016. Phone: (847) 296-0200. Fax: (847) 296-7510. E-mail: info@bcfm.com. Web Site: www.bcfm.com.

Awarded to persons who have made outstanding contributions to the communications industry and are committed to community affairs projects and/or service. Eligibility Period: Annually. Deadline for entries: Feb. Contact: BCFM, Buz Buzogany, pres, Broadcast Cable Financial Management Association, 701 Lee St., Suite 640, Des Plaines, IL 60016.

Broadcast Education Association, 1771 N St. N.W., Washington, DC 20036-2891. Phone: 202-429-5355. Fax: (202) 775-2981. E-mail: beainfo@beaweb.org. Web Site: www.beaweb.org.

BEA is the professional development association for professors, industry professionals, students involved in teaching & rsch related to radio, TV, & electronic media. BEA administers 16 scholarships annually, to honor bcstrs & the bcst industry. The BEA 2 yr Scholarship is for study at schools offering only freshman & sophomore instruction. All other scholarships are awarded to juniors,seniors & graduate students at BEA Member Universities. Scholarships offered are as follows: The Broadcasters' Foundation Helen J. Sioussat/Fay Wells, 2 scholarships of $1,250 each for study in any area of bcstg. Philo T. Farnsworth, one scholarship of $1,500. Graduate and undergrad applicants encouraged; Andrew M. Economos, one scholarship of $3,500 for study toward a career in radio presented by the RCS Charitable Foundation; Harold E. Fellows Memorial Scholarships, four scholarships of $1,250 each for study in any area of bcstg presented by the NAB, Washington, DC; Joseph and Marcia Silbergleid, One (1) scholarship; $1,500. Study in digital television presented by the SilverKnight Group, West Palm Beach, FL; Graduate students only. Walter Patterson Scholarships, two scholarships of $1,250 each awarded to students working for a career in radio; Sponsored by the National Association of Broadcasters, Alexander M. Tanger, one scholarship of $5,000 each for study in any area of bcstg; Two Year/Community College BEA Award, 2 scholarships of $1,500 each. For study at a BEA 2-year/community college; Abe Veron, one scholarship of $5,000 for study toward a career in radio presented by the Abe Veron Committee; Vincent T. Wasilewski Scholarship, one scholarship of $2,500 awarded to graduate students only studying any area of bcstg, presented by Patrick Communications, LLC, Ellicott City , MD. Scholarships will be awarded for full-time degree work FOR THE FULL ACADEMIC YEAR. Scholarships must be used exclusively for tuition, student fees, university bookstore course purchases and university dormitory (room and board). Current scholarship holders are not eligible for reappointment in the year following their award. All scholarships must be applied to study at a campus where a least one department is a BEA institutional member (BEA Member Institutions located at http://www.beaweb.org, "institutional listings," or ask your department). BEA is the professional dev assoc for professors, industry professionals, students involved in teaching, rsch related to radio, TV & electronic media. BEA administers fifteen scholarships annually to honor bcstrs & the bcst industry. The Two-Year Award $1,500 is for study at schools offering only freshman & sophomore instruction or for use at a four-year school by a graduate of a BEA two-year campus. All others scholarships are awarded to juniors, seniors & graduate students at BEA Member institutions. Eligibility Period: 2005-2006 School Year. Deadline for entries: Sept 15, 2004. Contact: BEA Scholarships, 1771 N. St. N.W., Washington, DC 20036.

Heywood Broun Award, The Newspaper Guild-CWA, 501 Third St. N.W., Washington, DC 20001. Phone: (202) 434-7177. Fax: (202) 434-1472. Web Site: www.newsguild.org. E-mail: guid@cwa-union.org.

Recognizes individual achievement by members of the working media, particularly if it helps right a wrong or correct an injustice. Eligibility Period: Preceding calendar year. Deadline for entries: January. Contact: Andy Zipser, Editor of the Guild Reporter, The Newspaper Guild.

The CLIO Awards Ltd., 220 5th Ave., Suite 1500, New York, NY 10001. Phone: (212) 683-4300. Fax: (212) 683-4796. Web Site: www.clioawards.com.

Awards honoring advertising & design excellence worldwide. Eligibility Period: 12 month calendar year. Deadline for entries: call for details, they vary per medium. Contact: Andrew Jaffe, exec dir, 220 5th Ave., Suite 1500, New York, NY 10001.

Cable Television Public Affairs Association, Beacon Awards, 1724 Massachusetts Ave. N. W., Washington, DC 20036. Phone: (202) 775-1081. Fax: (202) 955-1134. E-mail: services@ctpaa.org. Web Site: www.ctpaa.org.

Honors excellence in pub affrs throughout the cable industry in the areas of PR, community outreach, customer service, edu & govt affrs. Deadline for entries: Call for specific deadline. Contact: Steve Jones.

Christopher Video Contest for College Students, The Christophers, 12 E. 48th St., New York, NY 10017. Phone: (212) 759-4050. Fax: (212) 838-5073. E-mail: youth@christophers.org. Web Site: www.christophers.org/contests.html.

Students are invited to interpret the theme "One Person Can Make A Difference" in a short film of 5 minutes or less. Please contact for more details. Contact: Jonathan Englert

Corporation for Public Broadcasting, 401 9th St. N.W., Washington, DC 20004. Phone: (202) 879-9600. Fax: (202) 879-9700. Web Site: www.cpb.org.

The Edward R. Murrow Award recognizes individual whose work has fostered the growth, quality & image of public radio. Contact: Systems & Station Development, CPB, 901 E St. N.W., Washington, DC 20004-2006.

DGA Awards, Directors Guild of America Inc., 7920 Sunset Blvd., Los Angeles, CA 90046. Phone: (310) 289-5333. Fax: (310) 289-5384. E-mail: allisonh@dga.org. Web Site: www.dga.org.

Outstanding Directorial Achievement. Eligibility Period: Calendar year. Deadline for entries: Nov 2005. Contact: Directors Guild of America Inc., 7920 Sunset Blvd., Los Angeles, CA 90046.

Alfred I. duPont-Columbia University Awards, duPont Center for Broadcast Journalism. Columbia Univ Grad School of Journalism, 2950 Broadway, Rm. 709B, New York, NY 10027. Phone: (212) 854-5047. Fax: (212) 854-3148. E-mail: dupontawards@jrn.columbia.edu. Web Site: www.dupont.org.

Honoring the best in TV & Radio News and Public Affrs progmg. Eligibility Period: Programs that have aired for the first time between July 1, 2004 & June 30, 2005. Deadline for entries: Postmarked by June 15. Contact: Rosemary Culver, admin asst, Alfred I. duPont Center for Broadcast Journalism, Columbia University Graduate School of Journalism, 2950 Broadway, New York, NY 10027 OR phone or use website.

Freedoms Foundation National Awards, Freedoms Foundation at Valley Forge, 1601 Valley Forge Rd., Valley Forge, PA 19482-0706. Phone: (610) 933-8825. Fax: (610) 935-0522. E-mail: challman@ffvf.org. Web Site: www.ffvf.org.

George Washington Honor Metdal for exceptional radio,

television or movie which promotes the American Way of Life. Given annually. Eligibility Period: June 1-May 31 each year. Deadline for entries: June 1. Contact: Freedoms Foundation at Valley Forge, Awards Department, Rt. 23, 1601 Valley Forge Rd., Valley Forge, PA 19482-0706.

Gabriel Awards, Catholic Academy for Communications Arts Professionals, 901 Irving Ave., Dayton, OH 45409-2316. Phone: (937) 229-2303. Fax: (937) 229-2300. E-mail: admin@catholicacademy.org. Web Site: www.catholicacademy.org.The Gabriel Awards are designed to honor works of excellence in film, bcst programs, features, spots & stns which serve viewers & listeners through the positive, creative treatment of concerns to humankind. Presented by the Catholic Academy, the National Catholic Assn for Communicators. Eligibility Period: Calendar year 2005. Deadline for entries: Mar 2006. Contact: Unda-USA, National Catholic Assn for Communicators, 901 Irving Ave., Dayton, OH 45409-2316.

Global Media Awards, (For Excellence in Population Reporting). The Population Institute, 107 2nd St. N.E., Washington, DC 20002. Phone: (202) 544-3300. Fax: (202) 544-0068. E-mail: web@populationinstitute.org. Web Site: www.populationinstitute.org.

Awards honors those who have contributed to creating awareness of population related issues through their journalistic endeavors. Eligibility Period: September-August. Deadline for entries: September 1. Contact: Global Media Awards Coord. The Population Institute, 107 2nd St. N.E., Washington, DC 20002.

Golden Mike Award, Broadcast Foundation, 7 Lincoln Ave., Greenwich, CT 06830. Phone: (203) 862-8577. Fax: (203) 629-5739. E-mail: ghhbcast@aol.com. Web Site: www.broadcastersfoundation.org.

Presented annually for excellence in loc bcst journalism. Eligibility Period: Annually. Deadline for entries: Year round. Contact: Gordon Hastings, pres/CEO, Broadcast Foundation, 296 Old Church Rd., Greenwich, CT 06830.

Golden Viddy Award, Box 31, National Academy of TV Journalists Inc., Salisbury, MD 21803. Phone: (410) 548-5343. Fax: (410) 543-0658. E-mail: nbayne@shore.intercom.net.

Award: Gold Statuette. Eligibility Period: Year before. Deadline for entries: Third week of April. Contact: Neil Bayne, The National Academy of Television Journalists Inc., Box 31, Salisbury, MD 21803.

Hugo Awards, Chicago International TV Competition, 32 W. Randolph St.,Suite 600, Chicago, IL 60601. Phone: (312) 425-9400. Fax: (312) 425-0944. E-mail: info@chicagofilmfestival.com. Web Site: www.chicagofilmfestival.com.

Gold HUGO to best overall production. Silver HUGO, Gold Plaque, Silver Plaque, certificate of Merit to best production with a specific category. Eligibility Period: Screening date in 2004 or a scheduled date in 2005. Deadline for entries: January 31, 2005. Contact: Entry Coordinator, Chicago International Television Competition, 32 W. Randolph St., Suite 600, Chicago, IL 60610.

IRE Annual Awards for Investigative Reporting, 138 Neff Annex, Missouri School of Journalism, Columbia, MO 65211. Phone: (573) 882-6668. Fax: (573) 884-8151. E-mail: beth@ire.org. Web Site: www.ire.org/contest.The IRE Awards is the annual contest of Investigative Reporters & Editors Inc. recognizing the best in investigative reporting by print, bcst and online media. After judging, all entries are placed in IRE's Resource Ctr. story library so that IRE members may learn from others' triumphs & troubles. The contest helps identify techniques & resources used by the entrants. Eligibility Period: Any work produced during the calendar year (Jan-Dec). Deadline for entries: Early Jan. Contact: Carolyn Edds, Research Dir, IRE, 138 Neff Annex, UMC-Journalism, Columbia, MO 65211.

IRE Tom Renner Award for Crime Reporting, 138 Neff Annex, UMC-Journalism, Columbia, MO 65211. Phone: (573) 882-2042. Fax: (573) 882-5431. E-mail: info@ire.org. Web Site: www.ire.org.

For the best investigative crime reporting. Eligibility Period: Open. Deadline for entries: January. Contact: Len Bruzzese, Dept Dir, IRE, 138 Neff Annex, UMC-Journalism, Columbia, MO 65211.

International Broadcasting Awards, Hollywood Radio & TV Society, 13701 Riverside Dr., Suite 205, Sherman Oaks, CA 91423. Phone: (818) 789-1182. Fax: (818) 789-1210. E-mail: info@hrts.org. Web Site: www.hrts-iba.org.

Currently on hiatus. Eligibility Period: Commercials: Must have been transmitted in previous year. Deadline for entries: Dec. 6. Contact: Dave Ferrara, exec dir, Hollywood Radio & TV Society, 13701 Riverside Drive, Suite 205, Sherman Oaks, CA 91423.

International Emmy Awards, The International Academy of Television Arts & Sciences, 888 7th Ave., Suite 506, New York, NY 10019. Phone: (212) 489-6969. Fax: (212) 489-6557. E-mail: info@iemmys.tv. Web Site: www.iemmys.tv.

The International Emmy Award recognites excellence in programming produced outside of the US. Deadline for entries: April 1

International Radio & Television Society Foundation Gold Medal, 420 Lexington Ave., Suite 1601, New York, NY 10170. Phone: (212) 867-6650. Fax: (212) 867-6653. Web Site: www.irts.org.

A gold medal is presented annually for significant career long contributions to the integrity, health & success of the electronic media industry. Eligibility Period: Nominations accepted until September of previous year. Contact: Joyce Tudryn, pres, International Radio & TV Society Foundation, 420 Lexington Ave., New York, NY 10170.

Robert F. Kennedy Journalism Awards, 1367 Connecticut Ave. N.W., Suite 200, Washington, DC 20036. Phone: (202) 463-7575. Fax: (202) 463-6606. E-mail: info@rfkmemorial.org. Web Site: www.rfkmemorial.org.

Awards honoring outstanding reporting of problems of the disavantaged. Eligibility Period: Calendar year. Deadline for entries: January. Contact: Robert F. Kennedy Journalism Awards, 1367 Connecticut Ave. N.W., Suite 200, Washington, DC 20036.

Knight-Wallace Journalism Fellows, Wallace House, 620 Oxford Rd., Ann Arbor, MI 48104. Phone: (734) 998-7666. Fax: (734) 998-7979. E-mail: wpalms@umich.edu. Web Site: www.kwfellows.org.

Provides outstanding mid-career professionals the opportunity to indulge in a sabbatical year of study & reflection. Eligibility Period: academic year (September-April). Deadline for entries: February 1. Contact: Charles R. Eisendrath, Michigan Journalism Fellows, Wallace House, 620 Oxford Rd., Ann Arbor, MI 48104.

The Livingston Awards for Young Journalists, Wallace House, 620 Oxford Rd., Ann Arbor, MI 48104. Phone: (734) 998-7575. Fax: (734) 998-7979. Web Site: www.livawards.org. E-mail: LivingstonAwards@umich.edu.

The largest all media, gen reporting prizes in American journalism, honoring excellence by professionals aged 34 or younger. Eligibility Period: January 1-December 31. Deadline for entries: February 1. Contact: Charles R. Eisendrath, The Livingston Awards, Wallace House, 620 Oxford Rd., Ann Arbor, MI 48104.

Mark of Excellence, 3909 N. Meridian St., Society of Professional Journalists, Indianapolis, IN 46208-4011. Phone: (317) 927-8000. Fax: (317) 920-4789. E-mail: awards@spj.org. Web Site: www.spj.org.

Honors the best in student journalism. Open to all students enrolled in a college or university & studying for an academic degree. Eligibility Period: Entries must have been bcst in the calendar year. Deadline for entries: January 31. Contact: MOE Awards Coord, SPJ, 3909 N. Meridian St., Indianapolis, IN 46208.

Paul Miller Washington Reporting Fellowships, National Press Foundation, 1211 Connectiuct Ave NW, Suite 310, Washington, DC 20036. Phone: (202) 663-7280. Fax: (202) 530-2855. E-mail: nolan@nationalpress.org. Web Site: www.nationalpress.org.

A unique program to help journalists assigned to cover Washington on behalf of rgnl news organizations, involving intensive study sessions. Eligibility Period: Seminars from September-May. Deadline for entries: Applications accepted in the spring. Contact: Nolan Walters, 1211 Connecticut Ave NW, Suite 310, Washington, DC 20036.

Missouri Honor Medal, Univ. of Missouri School of Journalism, 102 Neff Hall, Columbia, MO 65211. Phone: (573) 882-6686. Fax: (573) 884-5400. E-mail: raur@missouri.edu. Web Site: www.missouri.edu.

The Missouri Honor Metal for Distinguished Service in Journalism is given to recognize the highest standards of excellence. Eligibility Period: Open. Deadline for entries: March of each year. Contact: Dean, School of Journalism, 103 Neff Hall, University of Missouri-Columbia, Columbia, MO 65211.

The Mobius Advertising Awards, 713 S. Pacific Coast Hwy., Suite A, Redondo Beach, CA 90277-4233. Phone: (310) 540-0959. Fax: (310) 316-8905. E-mail: mobiusinfo @mobiusawards.com. Web Site: www.mobiusawards.com.

The Mobius Award - La Fold Statuette with marble base. Eligibility Period: Oct 1, 2004 - Oct 1, 2005. Deadline for entries: Oct 1 yearly. Contact: J.W. Anderson, chmn; Patricia Meyer, exec dir, 841 N. Addison Ave., Elmhurst, IL 60126-1291.

NAB Crystal Radio Awards, NAB Radio, 1771 N St. N.W., Washington, DC 20036-2891. Phone: (202) 775-3511. Fax: (202) 775-3523. E-mail: csuever@nab.org. Web Site: www.nab.org.

Given to radio stn for ongoing commitment to community service. Eligibility Period: Jan 1-Dec 31, 2005. Deadline for entries: Feb 1, 2006. Contact: Chris Suever, NAB Radio, 1771 N St. N.W., Washington, DC 20036-2891.

NAB Marconi Radio Awards, NAB Radio, 1771 N St. N.W., Washington, DC 20036. Phone: (202) 775-3511. Fax: (202) 775-3523. E-mail: csuever@nab.org. Web Site: www.nab.org.

Given to stns & personalities for excellence in bcsting. Eligibility Period: Jan 1-Dec 31. Contact: NAB Radio, 1771 N St. N.W., Washington, DC 20036.

NFCB Golden Reel Award, National Federation of Community Bcstrs., 1970 Broadway, suite 1000, Oakland, CA 94612. Phone: (510) 451-8200. Fax: (510) 451-8208. E-mail: nfcb@aol.com. Web Site: www.nfcb.org.

The Awards honor the best programs on non-commercial community & public radio. Eligibility Period: Nov-Oct to abe awarded the following Apr. Contact: National Federation of Community Broadcasters, Fort Mason Ctr., Bldg. D, San Francisco, CA 94123.

NPPA Annual TV News Photography & Editing Competition, c/o Rich Murphy, WTSP - TV 10, 11450 Gandy Blvd., St. Petersburg, FL 33702. Phone: (727) 577-8582. Fax: (727) 576-6924. E-mail: rmurphy@tampabays10.com. Web Site: www.nppa.org.

Contest showcases the best news photography, editing in print, TV & on the website. Eligibility Period: January 1-December 31 (annually). Deadline for entries: January 31, postmarked by midnight. Contact: Rich Murphy, contest chmn, WFLA, 200 South Parker St, Tampa, FL 33606; rmurphy@wfla.com.

National Academy of Television Arts and Sciences "Emmy" Awards, 111 W. 57th St., Suite 600, New York, NY 10019. Phone: (212) 586-8424. Fax: (212) 246-8129. Web Site: www.emmyonline.org.Recognizes outstanding achievements in all phases of TV, including progmg, directing, writing, performing, etc. The National Academy of TV Arts & Sciences also presents the Sports Emmy & the tech achievement awards, news & documentary awards, & community service awards covering the entire previous year. Contact: Allan Benish, exec VP, 111 W. 57th St., Suite 1020, New York, NY 10019.

National Association of Broadcasters (NAB) Engineering Achievement Awards, 532249. 1771 N St. N.W., Washington, DC 20036-2891. Phone: (202) 429-5360. Fax: (202) 429-5461. E-mail: edorey@nab.org. Web Site: www.nab.org.

Given to industry leaders for significant contributions that have advanced bcst engrg.

National Association of Broadcasters (NAB) Broadcasting Excellence Award, 1771 N St., N.W., Washington, DC 20036-2891. Phone: (202) 429-5360. Fax: (202) 429-5461. E-mail: edorey@nab.org. Web Site: www.nab.org/lag /international/award.asp.The NAB International Broadcasting Excellence Award was established in 1995 to recognized NAB International Broadcaster (terrestrial, satellite & cable) members who have demonstrated exceptional leadership & uniqueness in successfully serving their lstng or viewing audience through bcst innovation or service to community. Deadline for entries: February each year, check website www.nab.org, for details. Contact: Emily Dorey at the address listed above.

National Association of Broadcasters (NAB) Distinguished Service Award, 1771 N St. N.W., Washington, DC 20036. Phone: (202) 429-5368. Fax: (202) 775-3516. E-mail: tguerra@nab.org. Web Site: www.nab.org.DSA Award given annually to any bcstr, whether or not actively engaged in the operations end of the bcstg industry, who has made a significant & lasting contribution to the American system of bcstg by virtue of singular achievement or continuing service for, or on behalf of, the industry. The recipient is required to be present at the convention to receive the award. Established in 1953, the award is presented at the annual convention. Deadline for entries: Dec. 2. Contact: NAB Distinguished Service Award, 1771 N St. N.W., Washington, DC 20036.

National Association of Broadcasters (NAB) National Radio Award, 1771 N St. N.W., Washington, DC 20036-2891. Phone: (202) 775-3511. Fax: (202) 775-3523. E-mail: csuever@nab.org. Web Site: www.nab.org.

Created to recognize individuals who have made a significant or on-going contribution to radio in at leadership capacity. Contact: Chris Suever, NAB Radio, 1771 N St. N.W., Washington, DC 20036-2891.

National Awards for Education Reporting, Education Writers Association, 2122 P St. N. W. # 201, Washington, DC 20037. Phone: (202) 452-9830. Fax: (202) 452-9837. E-mail: ewa@ewa.org. Web Site: www.ewa.org.

Prestigious national competition for education writing. Honors the best education reporting in the print & bcst media. Eligibility Period: Entries must have been published or bcst for the first time during the contest's calendar year. Deadline for entries: Mid-January. Contact: Education Writers Assn, 1331 H St. N.W., Suite 307, Washington, DC 20005.

National Headliner Awards, Box 239, 226 Mt. Vernon Ave., Northfield, NJ 08225. Phone: (609) 646-8896. Fax: (609) 646-8826. Web Site: www.nationalheadlinerawards.com. E-mail: infoheadliners@aol.com.

One of the oldest & largest contests recognizing journalist merit in the communications industry. Deadline for entries: January 11. Contact: Michael Schurman, exec dir, National Headliners Club, Box 239, Northfield, NJ 08225.

The New York Festivals International Radio Programming & Promotion Awards, 7 W. 36 St., 14th Fl., New York, NY 10018. Phone: (212) 643-4800. Fax: (212) 643-0170. E-mail: info@newyorkfestivals.com. Web Site: www.newyorkfestivals.com.

Recognizes the world's best work in radio progmg & promotion. Eligibility Period: March-March. Deadline for entries: February-March. Contact: Bilha Goldberg, festival Director, The New York Festivals, 186 5th Ave, New York, NY 10010.

The New York Festivals International TV, Cinema & Radio Advertising Awards, 7 W. 36 St., 14th Fl., New York, NY 10018. Phone: (212) 643-4800. Fax: (212) 643-0170. Web Site: www.newyorkfestivals.com. E-mail: info@newyorkfestivals.com.

Recognizes the world's best work in TV, radio consumer advertising & pub service announcements. Eligibility Period: June-June. Deadline for entries: June 30-USA / September 15-overseas. Contact: Bilha Goldberg, festivel dir, The New York Festivals, 186 Fifth Ave., New York, NY 10010.

The Ollie Awards, American Center for Children and Media, 5400 N. Saint Louis Ave., Chicago, IL 60625. Phone: (773) 509-5510. Fax: (773) 509-5303. E-mail: dkleeman@atgonline.org.

Award for excellence in children's TV. Eligibility Period: To be announced. Deadline for entries: To be announced. Contact: David Kleeman, exec dir, American Center for Children and Media, 5400 N. Saint Louis Ave., Chicago, IL 60625.

Overseas Press Club Awards, 40 W. 45th St., New York, NY 10036. Phone: (212) 626-9220. Fax: (212) 626-9210. Web Site: www.opcofamerica.org.

A series of annual awards recognizing the best reporting & photography from abroad or on an intl theme. Eligibility Period: Covers entries from January 1-December 31, of award year. Deadline for entries: End of January for previous year's work. Contact: Sonya K. Fry, exec dir, Overseas Press Club Awards, 320 E. 42nd St., New York, NY 10017.

PRISM Awards, Entertainment Industries Council Inc., PRISM Awards, Entertainment Industries Council Inc., 1760 Reston Pkwy., Suite 415, Reston, VA 20190-3303. Phone: (703) 481-1414. Fax: (703) 481-1418. Fax: (818) 955-6845 (West Coast). E-mail: eiceast@eiconline.org. Web Site: www.prismawards.com.

The PRISM Awards honor the accurate depiction of drug, alcohol, tobacco use & addiction in comic book, music & interactive media. Eligibility Period: All submissions must have had initial public exhibition between Jan1-Dec 31. Deadline for entries: January 14.

PROMAX & BDA Awards, PROMAX & BDA, 2029 Century Park E., Suite 555, Los Angeles, CA 90067-2906. Phone: (310) 788-7600. Fax: (310) 788-7616. Web Site: www.promax.tv. E-mail: awards@bda.tv.

Recognizes the best in promotion & mktg. Eligibility Period: Previous calender year. Deadline for entries: January & March. Contact: PROMAX & BDA, 2029 Century Park E., Suite 555, Los Angeles, CA 90067-2906.

George Foster Peabody Award, H.W. Grady College of Journalism, University of Georgia, Athens, GA 30602-3018. Phone: (706) 542-3787. Fax: (706) 542-9273. E-mail: peabody@uga.edu. Web Site: www.peabody.uga.edu.

Awarded for excellence in electronic media including bcst, cable TV, radio & internet. Eligibility Period: Jan 1, 2004-Dec 31, 2004. Deadline for entries: Jan 17, 2005. Contact: Dr. Louise M. Benjamin, interim dir Peabody Awards, Henry W. Grady College of Journalism, University of Georgia, Athens, GA 30602-3018.

George Polk Awards, Long Island University,The English Dept, University Plaza, Brooklyn, NY 11201. Phone: (718) 488-1115. Fax: (718) 243-0766. Fax: (718) 246-6302. Web Site: www.liu.edu/cwis/bklyn/polk/polk.html.

Award for outstanding achievements in investigative journalism. Eligibility Period: 2002. Deadline for entries: End of First complete week in January. Contact: c/o The English Dept. Robert Spector PhD., Curator, George Polk Awards, Long Island University, The Brooklyn Center, University Plaza, Brooklyn, NY 11201.

RTNDA Edward R. Murrow Awards, 1600 K St., Suite 700, Washington, DC 20006-2838. Phone: (202) 659-6510. Phone: 800-80-RTNDA. Fax: (202) 223-4007. E-mail: rtnda@rtnda.org. Web Site: www.rtnda.org.

Honors those whose work has fostered the growth, quality & positive image of public radio. Eligibility Period: Previous calendar year. Deadline for entries: January 31. Contact: RTNDA, 1000 Connecticut Ave. N.W., Suite 615, Washington, DC 20036.

Radio-Mercury Awards, 261 Madison Ave, 23rd Fl., New York, NY 10016. Phone: (212) 681-7207. Fax: (212) 681-7223. E-mail: mercury@rab.com. Web Site: www.radiomercuryaward.com.Since the first Radio-Mercury Awards competition and awards ceremony in 1992, close to $2 million has been awarded to honor the writers and producers in the finest radio commercials in America. A Mercury Award is recognized as the highest honor a radio commercial can achieve. The Radio-Mercury Awards is the richest nationwide competition devoted exclusively to honoring & rewarding excellence in Radio creative. Prizes consist of the $100,000 Grand Prize, plus cash prizes in gen station produced & spanish-lanuage categories. In addition, a charitable donation is awarded in conjuction with the Public Service Announcement Award & the Radio-Mercury Student competition awards a cash prize to the winning school. The awards are presented annually at a gala luncheon ceremony in New York City, and are governed by the Radio Creative Fund, a non-profit corporation funded by the Radio industry. Eligibility Period: Paid radio advertisements that aired on a U.S. radio stn during the calendar year are eligible. Deadline for entries: February. Contact: Wendy Frech, Radio-Mercury Awards, 261 Madison Ave., 23rd Fl., New York, NY 10016 or E-mail: mercury@rab.com.

Bart Richards Award for Media Criticism, 302 James Bldg., Pennsylvania State University, University Park, PA 16801-3867. Phone: (814) 865-8801. Fax: (814) 863-6134. E-mail: sws102@psu.edu. Web Site: www.comm.psu.edu.Work nominated for the award evaluates new media coverage of significant subjects and issues. Winner receives $1,000 and is expected to attend the awards ceremony and talk on the subject for which he or she is being honored. Eligibility Period: Calendar year. Deadline for entries: January 31. Contact: The Bart Richards Award for Media Criticism, The Pennsylvania State University, College of Communications, 302 James Bldg., University Park, PA 16801-3867.

Scripps Howard Foundation - Jack R. Howard Awards, Scripps Howard Foundation, 312 Walnut St., Cincinnati, OH 45202-4067. Phone: (513) 977-3035. Fax: (513) 977-3800. E-mail: cottingham@scripps.com. Web Site: www.scripps.com/foundation.

Honors journalistic excellence in electronic media; the best investigative or in-depth reporting of events covered by TV & radio stns or cable systems. Eligibility Period: The preceding calendar year. Deadline for entries: January 31. Entry form required. $50.entry fee. Contact: Patty Cottingham, exec dir, Scripps Howard Foundation, Box 5380, Cincinnati, OH 45201.

Sigma Delta Chi Distinguished Service Awards Society of Professional Journalists, 3909 N. Meridian St., Indianapolis, IN 46208. Phone: (317) 927-8000. Fax: (317) 920-4789. E-mail: awards@spj.org. Web Site: www.spj.org.

A series of annual awards recognizing excellence in many categories of professional journalism. Eligibility Period: Work published in the previous calendar year. Deadline for entries: February 9, SDX; July 6, Pulliam Fellowship. Contact: SDX Awards coord, SPJ, 3909 N. Meridian St., Indianapolis, In 46208.

Silver Anvil Awards, Public Relations Society of America Inc., 33 Maiden Ln., 11th Fl., New York, NY 10003-5150. Phone: (212) 460-1400. Fax: (212) 995-0757. E-mail: hq@prsa.org. Web Site: www.prsa.org.

Best public relations practices. Deadline for entries: Varies - check website. Contact: Carla Voth, Public Relations Society of America Inc., 33 Irving Pl., 3rd Fl., New York, NY 10003.

Silver Gavel Awards, American Bar Association, Div for Pub Education, 541 N. Fairbanks Ct., Chicago, IL 60611. Phone: (312) 988-5738. Fax: (312) 988-5494. E-mail: craytonw@staff.abanet.org. Web Site: www.abanet.org /publiced/gavel.

Annually recognizes eligible entries from communications media that have been exemplary in fostering pub understanding of the law & legal system. Eligibility Period: Eligible radio & TV programs (including network, cable, syndicated, loc & ind productions) for the competition must have been originally bcst or presented between Jan. 1 & Dec. 31 of the same year. Deadline for entries: Mid January annually. Contact: The Gavel Awards Program, American Bar Association, Division for Public Education, 541 N. Fairbanks Ct, Chicago, IL 60611.

Society of Motion Picture & Television Engineers Awards, 595 W. Hartsdale Ave., White Plains, NY 10607. Phone: (914) 761-1100. Phone: smpte@smpte.org. Fax: (914) 761-3115. Web Site: www.smpte.org.Citation for Outstanding Service to the Society recognizes individuals for dedicated service to the society. The Presidential Proclamation recognizes individuals of established & outstanding status & reputation in the motion picture & TV industries worldwide. Eastman Kodak Medal Award recognizes outstanding contributions that lead to new or unique educ programs using motion pictures, TV, high-speed & instrumental photography or other photographic sciences. The award recognizes dev in equipment, systems or instructional applications that advance the educ process at any or all levels. The John Grierson International Gold Medal Award recognizes significant tech achievements related to the production of documentary motion picture films. The Journal Award recognizes the outstanding paper originally published in the Journal of the Society during the previous calendar year. The Technicolor/Herbert T. Kalmus Gold medal Award recognizes outstanding contributions in the dev of color films, processing, techniques or equipment useful in making color motion pictures for theater or TV use. The Fuji Gold Medal Award recognizes outstanding engrg achievements in the design & dev of new or enhanced techniques &/or equipment that have contributed significantly to the advancement of photographic or electronic image origination . Deadline for entries: January 15. Contact: Fred Motts, exec dir, Society of Motion Pictures & TV Engineers, 595 W. Hartsdale Ave., White Plains, NY, 10607.

Voice of Democracy Scholarship Program, VFW National Hqtrs., 406 W. 34th St., Kansas City, MO 64111. Phone: (816) 968-1117. Fax: (816) 968-1149. E-mail: kharmer@vfw.org. Web Site: www.vfw.org.

An annual national audio essay contest designed to foster patriotism in high school students. Eligibility Period: 9th-12th grade. Deadline for entries: November 1. Contact: Your high school counselor, local VFW Post, or Voice of Democracy Scholarship Program, VFW National Hqtrs, 406 W. 34th St., Kansas City, MO 64111.

Ida B. Wells Award, Northwestern University, Medill School of Journalism, 1845 Sheridan Rd., Evanston, IL 60208. Phone: (847) 467-2579. Fax: (847) 491-2370. E-mail: m-awards@northwestern.edu. Web Site: www.medill.northwestern.edu/inside/2003/wellstory.html.

Lawrence, KS 66647. Sam Adams (Curator), Ida B.Wells Award, 1552 Alvamar Dr.

Award horors media executives whose actions demonstrate a commitment to a diverse newsroomer coverage of minorities in American Journalism. Deadline for entries: Apr 1 each yr. Ava Greenwell, Assoc Dean, William Allen White School of Journalism & Mass Communication, University of Kansas, 200 Stauffer-Flint Hall, Lawrence, KS 66045-2350 OR Sam Adams (Curator), Ida B. Wells Award, 1304 McDonald St, Waycross, GA 31501.

Western Heritage Awards-The Wrangler, National Cowboy & Western Heritage Museum, 1700 N.E. 63rd St., Oklahoma City, OK 73111. Phone: (405) 478-2250. Fax: (405) 478-4714. E-mail: lyndahaller@nationalcowboymuseum.org. Web Site: www.nationalcowboymuseum.org.

Honors principal creators of the winning entries in specified categories of Western literature, music, film & TV. Eligibility Period: Must be aired/released within the calendar yr of the entry. Deadline for entries: Music, film, & TV due Dec 31, 2005; Literary due Nov 30, 2005. Contact: Lynda Haller, dir PR, National Cowboy Hall of Fame, 1700 N.E. 63rd St., Oklahoma City, OK 73111.

Section I
Government

Federal Communications Commission Executives and Staff I-2
U.S. Government Agencies I-8
U.S. State Cable Regulatory Agencies I-9

Federal Communications Commission Executives and Staff

Headquarters: The Portals, 445 12th St. S.W., Washington, DC 20554. (888) 225-5322.

CHAIRMAN

Kevin J. Martin (202) 418-1000 8 B201; Confidential Assistant Lori Alexiou (202) 418-1000; Chief of Staff Daniel Gonzalez (Acting) (202) 418-1000; Special Advisor/Deputy Chief of Staff/Emily Willeford (202) 418-1000; Staff Assistant/Vivette Hart (202) 418-1000; Senior Legal Advisor/ Catherine Bohigian (Acting) (202) 418-1000; Special Assistant/Susan Fisenne (Detail) (202) 418-1000; Legal Advisor/Michelle Carey (Detail) (202) 418-1000; Staff Assistant/Shandria Dixon (202) 418-1000; Attorney Advisor/Fred Campbell (Detail) (202) 418-1000; Administrative Management Specialist Tommi Greely (202) 418-1000.

COMMISSIONERS

COMMISSIONER Kathleen Q. Abernathy (202) 418-2400 8 B115; Confidential Assistant Ann Monahan (Detail) 202) 418-2400; Legal Advisor Lauren "Pete" Belvin (Detail) (202) 418-2400; Senior Legal Advisor Russell Hanser (Detail) (202) 418-2400; Legal Advisor John Branscome (Detail) (202) 418-2400; Staff Assistant Teri Swinton (202) 418-2400.

COMMISSIONER Michael J. Copps (202) 418-2000 8 A302; Confidential Assistant Carolyn Conyers (202) 418-2000; Senior Legal Advisor Jordan Goldstein (202) 418-2000; Legal Advisor Paul Margie (202) 418-2000; Legal Advisor Jessica Rosenworcel (202) 418-2000; Staff Assistant Betty Morris (202) 418-2000.

COMMISSIONER Jonathan S. Adelstein (202) 418-2300 8 C302; Confidential Assistant Amber Danter (202) 418-2300; Senior Legal Advisor Barry Ohlson (202) 418-2300; Legal Advisor Scott Bergmann (202) 418-2300; Legal Advisor Rudy Brioche (202) 418-2300; Staff Assistant Tajuana Dill (202) 418-2300.

OFFICE OF ADMINISTRATIVE LAW JUDGES

Richard L. Sippel/Chief Administrative Law Judge (202) 418-2280 1 C768;

Arthur I. Steinberg/Administrative Law Judge (202) 418-2255 1 C861.

OFFICE OF COMMUNICATIONS BUSINESS OPPORTUNITIES

Carolyn Fleming Williams/Director (202) 418-0990 7 C204.

OFFICE OF ENGINEERING AND TECHNOLOGY

Vacant/Chief (202) 418-2470 7 C155; Bruce A. Franca/Acting Chief (202) 418-2470 7 C153; Julius P. Knapp/Deputy Chief (202) 418-2470 7 C250; Jim Schlichting/Deputy Chief (202) 418-2470 7 C252; Fred Thomas/Chief of Staff (202) 418-2470 7 C140; Kenneth P. Moran/Director of Defense and Security (202) 418-2470 7 C161; Vacant/Director of National Defense (202) 418-2470 6 A324; R. Alan Stillwell/Senior Associate Chief (202) 418-2470 7 C210; Bruce A. Romano/Associate Chief (202) 418-7293 7 A164; Lauren Van Wazer/Special Counsel & Associate Chief (202) 418-2470 7 C257; Timothy Peterson/Special Counsel, Defense & Security (202) 418-2470 6 C363.

Administrative and Management Office

Xenia Hajicosti/Assistant Chief for Management (202) 418-2461 7 B113.

Policy and Rules Division

Alan Scrime/Division Chief (202) 418-2472 7 B133; Geraldine Matise/Deputy Division Chief (202) 418-2472 7 A260; Ronald Repasi/Deputy Division Chief (202) 418-2472 7 A265; William Lane/Associate Chief (202) 418-2472 7 C115.

Spectrum Policy Branch

Jamison Prime/Branch Chief (202) 418-2472 7 A132.

Technical Rules Branch

Karen Rackley/Branch Chief (202) 418-2472 7 A161.

Spectrum Coordination Branch

Kathryn Hosford/Branch Chief (202) 418-2472 7 B438.

Electromagnetic Compatibility Division

Ira Keltz/Division Chief (202) 418-2475 7 A224; Charles Iseman/Deputy Division Chief (202) 418-2475 7 A363.

Technical Analysis Branch

Ronald Chase/Branch Chief (202) 418-2475 7 A364.

Experimental Licensing Branch

James R. Burtle/Branch Chief (202) 418-2477 7 A267.

Network Technology Division

Jeffery Goldthorp/Division Chief (202) 418-2478 7 A325; Kent Nilsson/Deputy Division Chief (202) 418-2478 7 B452.

Laboratory (Columbia, MD)

Rashmi Doshi/Chief (301) 362-3000 LAB; Vacant/Deputy Chief (301) 362-3000 LAB.

Equipment Authorization Branch

Vacant/Branch Chief (301) 362-3000 LAB.

Technical Research Branch

William Hurst/Branch Chief (301) 362-3000 LAB.

Auditing and Compliance Branch

Raymond LaForge/Branch Chief (301) 362-3000 LAB.

Customer Service Branch

Sandra Haase/Branch Chief (301) 362-3013 LAB.

OFFICE OF GENERAL COUNSEL

Samuel Feder/Acting General Counsel (202) 418-1700 8 C723; Matthew Berry/Acting Deputy General Counsel (202) 418-1700; P. Michele Ellison/Deputy General Counsel (202) 418-1700; Linda I. Kinney/Deputy General Counsel (202) 418-1700; Diane Griffin/Assistant GC/Chief of Staff (Detail) (202) 418-1700; Richard K. Welch/Associate General Counsel (202) 418-1700; Jacob Lewis/Associate General Counsel (Counselor to the General Counsel) (202) 418-1700; James R. Bird/Senior Counsel (202) 418-1700; Karen E. Onyeije/Special Counsel (202) 418-1700.

Administrative and Management Office

Charmayne C. Keene/Assistant Chief for Management (202) 418-1701.

Litigation Division

Daniel M. Armstrong/Assoc. General Counsel-Litigation (202) 418-1740 8 B724; John E. Ingle/Deputy Assoc. General Counsel-Litigation (202) 418-1740; Susan L. Launer/Deputy Assoc. GC-Trial & Enforcement (202) 418-1740.

Administrative Law Division

Vacant/Assoc. General Counsel-Administrative Law (202) 418-1720 8 B616; Joel Kaufman/Deputy Assoc. General Counsel-Administrati(202) 418-1720; Patrick J. Carney/Assistant General Counsel-Administrat(202) 418-1720; Maureen Duignan/Assistant General Counsel-Administrativ(202) 418-1720; Debra A. Weiner/Assistant General Counsel-Administrativ(202) 418-1720; Marilyn Sonn/Assistant General Counsel-Administrative L(202) 418-1720; David E. Horowitz/Assistant General Counsel-Administrat(202) 418-1720; Christopher Killion/Assistant General Counsel-Administr(202) 418-1720; Mary McManus/Special Counsel (202) 418-1720.

OFFICE OF INSPECTOR GENERAL

H. Walker Feaster/Inspector General (202) 418-0476 2 C762; Kent Nilsson/Acting Deputy Inspector General (202) 418-; Thomas D. Bennett/Assistant IG - Universal Service Fund(202) 418-0477; Vacant/Assistant IG - Investigations (202) 418-0472; Thomas M. Holleran/Assistant IG - Management (202) 418-1923; Thomas Cline/Assistant IG - Policy and Planning (202) 418-7890; Steven Rickrode/Assistant IG - Audits (202) 418-0478.

OFFICE OF LEGISLATIVE AFFAIRS

Anthony J. Dale/Acting Director (202) 418-1900 8 C432; Congressional Correspondence Team (202) 418-1900.

OFFICE OF MANAGING DIRECTOR

Andrew S. Fishel/Managing Director (202) 418-1919 1 C144; Vacant/Deputy Managing Director (202) 418-1919; William Spencer/Deputy Managing Director (202) 418-1919.

Administrative and Management Office

Eileen Devan/Assistant Bureau Chief for Management (202) 418-1927 1 C120. Valerie Brock/Deputy Assistant Bureau Chief for Management, OMD; & Policy/Support Offices (202) 418-0118 1 C110.

Office of The Secretary

Marlene Dortch/Secretary (202) 418-0300 TW B204; William F. Caton/Deputy Secretary (202) 418-0304; Ruth Dancey/Associate Secretary (202) 418-7085.

Organizational Chart

Commissioners
- Kathleen Q. Abernathy
- Kevin J. Martin, Chairman
- Michael J. Copps
- Jonathan S. Adelstein

Office of Inspector General

Offices reporting to Commissioners

Office of Engineering & Technology
- Electromagnetic Compatibility Div.
- Laboratory Div.
- Network Technology Div.
- Policy & Rules Div.
- Administrative Staff

Office of General Counsel
- Administrative Law Div.
- Litigation Div.

Office of Managing Director
- Human Resources Management
- Information Technology Center
- Financial Operations
- Administrative Operations
- Performance Eval. & Records Mgmt
- Secretary

Office of Media Relations
- Media Services Staff
- Internet Services Staff
- Audio-Visual Services Staff

Office of Legislative Affairs

Office of Administrative Law Judges

Office of Strategic Planning & Policy Analysis

Office of Communications Business Opportunities

Office of Workplace Diversity

Bureaus

Wireline Competition Bureau
- Admin. & Mgmt. Office
- Competition Policy Div.
- Pricing Policy Div.
- Telecommunications Access Policy Div.
- Industry Analysis & Technology Div.

Enforcement Bureau
- Office of Management & Resources
- Office of Homeland Security
- Telecommunications Consumers Div.
- Spectrum Enforcement Div.
- Market Disputes Resolution Div.
- Investigations & Hearings Div.
- Regional & Field Offices

Wireless Telecommunications Bureau
- Management & Resources Staff
- Auctions & Spectrum Access Div.
- Spectrum Mgmt. Resources & Technologies Div.
- Spectrum & Competition Policy Div.
- Public Safety & Critical Infrastructure Div.
- Mobility Div.
- Broadband Div.

Media Bureau
- Mgmt. & Resources Staff
- Office of Com. & Industry Info.
- Policy Div.
- Industry Analysis Div.
- Engineering Div.
- Office of Broadcast License Policy
- Audio Div.
- Video Div.

Consumer & Governmental Affairs Bureau
- Admin & Mgmt. Office
- Systems Support Office
- Information Access & Privacy Office
- Consumer Inquiries & Complaints Div.
- Policy Div.
- Disabilities Rights Office
- Consumer Affairs & Outreach Div.
- Reference Information Center

International Bureau
- Management & Administrative Staff
- Policy Div.
- Satellite Div.
- Strategic Analysis & Negotiations Div.

Federal Communications Commission Executives and Staff

Information Resources Group
Sheryl A. Segal/Associate Secretary/Information Resourc(202) 418-0234 TW B204; Agenda & Publications Group; Jacqueline Coles/Manager (202) 418-0320 TW B204.

Library
(202) 418-0450 TW B505.

Associate Managing Director - Human Resources Management
Kent Baum/Chief Human Capital Officer (202) 418-0100 1 A100; Carol Nichols/Deputy Chief Human Capital Officer (202) 418-0100 1 A130; Thomas Green/Senior Policy Adviser (202) 418-0116 1 A161; Michelle Scott/HR Funds Manager (202) 418-1375 1 A734; Human Resources TTY (202) 418-0126; Employment Verification (202) 418-0150.

Recruitment and Staffing Service Center
Bonita Tingley/Chief (202) 418-0293 1 A265; Employee Assistance Program (EAP) Phyllis White/EAP Counselor 1-800-462-1812 x72780; 24 Hour Service Number 1-800-222-0364; Health Unit on Fridays (202) 418-0915; Payroll and Benefits Service Center (202) 418-0150 1 A227; Pearlena Butler/Chief (202) 418-0152.

Labor Relations and Performance Management Service Center
Gary McLean/Chief (202) 418-0117 1 B115.

Learning and Development Service Center
Jerry Liebes/Chief (202) 418-1582 1 A124.

Information Technology Center
Ronald Stone/Director and Chief Information Officer (202) 418-2022 1 C264; Wanda M. Sims/Deputy CIO for Customer Services (202) 418-2990 1 C266; Kimberly Hancher/Deputy CIO for E-Government (202) 418-2030 1 C233; Joseph Salama/Deputy CIO for Infrastructure & Operation(202) 418-7003 1 C226; Marc Noble/Acting Computer Security Officer (202) 418-0588 1 C486.

Associate Chief Information Officers
Carl Heise/Associate CIO for Technologies (202) 418-1814 1 C261; Paul Mocko/Associate CIO for Mobile Computing (202) 418-7835 1 C220; James Greening/Associate CIO for Consumer Systems (202) 418-4137 1 C214; Rosalind Singleton/Associate CIO for Assistive Technolo(202) 418-2850 1 C224; Stephen Miller/Associate CIO for Remote Operations (717) 338-2623 Gettysburg.

Network Development Group
Spencer Hyndman/Chief (202) 418-1823 1 C360; Debbie Wheeler/Deputy Chief and Telecom Manager (202) 418-1801 1 C361.

Planning and Support Group
David Reed/Chief (202) 418-1812 1 A322.

Applications Integration Group
Robert Snow/Chief (202) 418-0564 1 A317; Michael Kemper/Deputy Chief (202) 418-0595 1 B441.

Operations Group
Rick Kanner/Acting Chief (202) 418-1830 1 C734; Charles Davis/Deputy Chief (202) 418-1856 1 C764.

Associate Managing Director - Financial Operations
Mark Reger/Chief Financial Officer (202) 418-1924 1 A623; Regina Dorsey/Special Assistant to Chief Financial Offi(202) 418-1993 1 A660.

Financial Systems Development
Tim Taylor/Chief (202) 418-0717 TW A626.

Contract Oversight
Andrew Cox/Chief (202) 418-0617 1 C823.

Budget Center
Donald Hartline/Deputy CFO/Chief (202) 418-1963 1 B521; Mary Maldonaldo/Deputy Chief (202) 418-1968 1 B522.

Financial Operations Center
Patricia Cappello/Deputy CFO/Chief (202) 418-1970 1 A663; Clara Boykin/Operations Manager (202) 418-2943 1 A728; Marvin Washington/Credit Manager (202) 418-7550 1 A820.

Financial Systems Operations
Norman Bowden/Chief (202) 418-1986 1 A636.

Auctions Accounting
Gail Glasser/Acting Chief (202) 418-0578 1 C863.

Research Reconciliation & Reporting
Jeanne McDonald/Chief (202) 418-1977 1 C866.

Travel Operations
Cheryl Walton/Chief (202) 418-1375 1 A734.

Revenue and Receivables Operations
Vacant/Chief (202) 418-1996 1 A821.

International Telecommunications Team
Tim Dates/Chief (202) 418-0496 1 A824.

Financial Statement and Policy
Mike Smith/Chief (202) 418-1970 1 C844.

Associate Managing Director - Administrative Operations
Jeffrey R. Ryan/Associate Managing Director-AO (202) 418-1953 1 A402; Sonna Stampone/Deputy Associate Managing Director-AO (202) 418-0992 1 A411.

Security Operations Center
Eric Botker/Manager (202) 418-7884 1 B458; Mary Long/Deputy Manager (202) 418-7884.

Space Management Center
Mary Kay Welch/Manager (202) 418-1957 1 A434.

Contracts and Purchasing Center
Dennis Dorsey/Manager (202) 418-1952 1 A524; Randi Bettencourt/Deputy Manager (202) 418-0932 1 A511.

Administrative Services Center
Ginger Weasenforth/Manager (202) 418-0330 TW B230G; Daniel Walker/Deputy Manager (202) 418-0356 TW C201D. John Zentner/Safety and Health Officer (202) 418-0119 TW C201; Health Center (Nurse, Helene Frank) (202) 418-0911 MA A626.

Printing and Graphics Center
Toby Brown/Manager (202) 418-0350 TW A822; Carlyn Walker/Printing Specialist (202) 418-0350.

Associate Managing Director - Performance Evaluation and Records Management
Karen Wheeless /Associate Managing Director-PERM (202) 418-2910 1 A838; Yvette Barrett /Acting Deputy Associate Managing Direct(202) 418-0603 1 C828.

OFFICE OF MEDIA RELATIONS
David H. Fiske/Director (202) 418-0513 CY C314; Richard Diamond/Deputy Director (202) 418-0506; Audrey Spivack/Associate Director (202) 418-0512; Meribeth McCarrick/Associate Director (202) 418-0654.

Audio Visual Center
Dann Oliver/Manager (202) 418-0460 TW A206A.

OFFICE OF STRATEGIC PLANNING AND POLICY ANALYSIS
Timothy Peterson/Acting Chief (202) 418-2030 7 C347; Vacant/Deputy Chief (202) 418-2030; Maureen McLaughlin/Chief of Staff (202) 418-2030; Sarah Whitesell/Associate Office Chief (202) 418-2030; Chief Economist/Vacant (202) 418-2030.

OFFICE OF WORKPLACE DIVERSITY
June Taylor/Acting Director (202) 418-1799 5 C750; Vacant/Deputy Director (202) 418-1799 5 C751.

CONSUMER & GOVERNMENTAL AFFAIRS BUREAU
Monica DeSai/Acting Bureau Chief (202) 418-1400 5 C754; Erica McMahon/Acting Chief of Staff (202) 418-1400 5 C739; Thomas D. Wyatt/Deputy Bureau Chief (Inquiries and Comp(202) 418-1400 5 A844; Jay Keithley/Deputy Bureau Chief (Policy) (202) 418-1400 5 C754; Sue McNeil/Acting Deputy Bureau Chief.

(Consumer Outreach & Intergovernmental Affairs)
(202) 418-1400 5 A660; Vacant/Associate Bureau Chief (202) 418-1400 5 C831; Genaro Fullano/Legal Advisor (202) 418-1400 5 C737; Leon Jackler/Legal Advisor (202) 418-1400 5 C736; Jeffrey H. Tignor/Legal Advisor (202) 418-1400 5 C738.

Federal Communications Commission Executives and Staff

Administrative and Management Office

Patricia Green/Assistant Bureau Chief for Management (202) 418-1571 5 A848 Gwendolyn Inge/Deputy Assistant Bureau Chief for Manage(202) 418-1376 5 C848

Office of Intergovernmental Affairs

Sue McNeil (202) 418-7619 5 A660.

Office of Information Resource Management

Stephen Ebner Chief (202) 418-2147 4 A525; Roger Goldblatt/Deputy Chief (202) 418-1035 4 A523.

Consumer Inquiries and Complaints Division

Martha Contee/Division Chief (202) 418-2516 4 C763; Sharon Bowers/Deputy Division Chief.

(Gettysburg Consumer Center)

(717) 338-2531; Suzanne Perrin/Deputy Division Chief; (Washington Consumer Center) (202) 418-2516 4 B522; Cynthia D. Brown/Associate Division Chief (202) 418-2516 4 B511.

Information Access and Privacy Office

Sumita Mukhoty/Director (202) 418-1110 4 A663.

Consumer Policy Division

Vacant/Division Chief (202) 418-xxxx; Erica H. McMahon/Associate Division Chief (202) 418-0346 5 A803; Nancy Stevenson/ Deputy Division Chief (202) 418-7039 5 A823.

Disability Rights Office

Thomas E. Chandler/Chief (202) 418-1475 CY B523; Cheryl J. King/Deputy Chief (202) 418-2284 CY A636; Pamela Gregory/Special Advisor (202) 418-2517 CY C428.

Reference Information Center

Bill Cline/Director (202) 418-0267 CY B533.

Consumer Affairs and Outreach Division

Louis Sigalos/Division Chief (202) 418-0614 3 A662; Sherry Dawson/Deputy Chief (202) 418-7401 3 A660.

Consumer Publications Branch

Stacey Reuben-Mesa/Branch Chief (202) 418-0254 3 A633.

Consumer Advisory Committee

Scott Marshall/Designated Federal Officer (202) 418-2809 5 A824.

ENFORCEMENT BUREAU

Kris Monteith/Acting Bureau Chief (202) 418-7450 7 C485; Michael Carowitz/Acting Chief of Staff/Associate Bureau (202) 418-0026 7 C735; Linda Blair/Deputy Bureau Chief (202) 418-7450 7 C751; Mary Beth Richards/Deputy Bureau Chief (202) 418-7450 7 C745; Christopher Olsen/Deputy Bureau Chief (202) 418-7450 7 C753; Lisa Fowlkes/Assistant Bureau Chief (202) 418-7450 7 C738; George R. Dillon/Assistant Bureau Chief (202) 418-1215 7 C830.

Office of Management and Resources

Sharon Agee/Assistant Bureau Chief for Management (202) 418-1136 7 C838; Joan Sames/Acting Deputy Assistant Bureau Chief for Man(202) 418-1130 7 C804.

Office of Homeland Security

Kenneth Moran/Acting Director (202) 418-0802 7 C161; Gregory M. Cooke/Deputy Director (202) 418-2351 7 C831; Dan Emrick/Assistant Director (202) 418-1175 7 A727; Jeanne Kowalski/Assistant Director (202) 418-1897 7 C841.

Communications and Crisis Management Center

David T. Prescott/Director (202) 418-1190 7 C404.

Investigations and Hearing Division

(202) 418-1420; William Davenport /Division Chief (202) 418-1034 4 C321; William D. Freedman/Deputy Division Chief (202) 418-1415 4 A465; Hillary DeNigro/Deputy Division Chief (202) 418-7334 4 C322; David Brown/Assistant Division Chief (202) 418-1645 4 A462; Trent Harkrader/Assistant Division Chief (202) 418-2955 4 A361; Eric Bash/Assistant Division Chief (202) 418-1188 4 A236; Thomas Hutton/Assistant Division Chief (202) 418-7266 4 A336; Hugh Boyle/Chief Auditor (202) 418-1420 4 C431; Gary Schonman/Special Counsel (202) 418-1795 4 C237.

Market Disputes Resolution Division

(202) 418-7330 Alexander Starr/Division Chief (202) 418-7284 4 C342; Lisa Griffin/Deputy Division Chief (202) 418-7273 4 C324; Rosemary McEnery/Deputy Division Chief (202) 418-7336 4 C121; Lisa Saks/Assistant Division Chief (202) 418-7335 4 C124; Tracy Bridgham/Special Counsel (202) 418-0967 5 A664; Lia Royle/Special Counsel (202) 418-7391 4 C264.

Spectrum Enforcement Division

(202) 418-1160; Joseph P. Casey/Division Chief (202) 418-1111 7 A843; Ricardo M. Durham/Deputy Division Chief (202) 418-1160 7 A744; Kathryn Berthot/Deputy Division Chief (202) 418-7454 7 C802; Thomas Spavins/Assistant Division Chief for Economics (202) 418-1739 2 C423; Brian Butler/Assistant Division Chief (202) 418-2702 7 A629; Norman Goldstein/Special Counsel (202) 418-1424 7 A846; Riley Hollingsworth/Special Counsel (Gettysburg, PA) (717) 338-2502.

Equipment Development Group (Powder Springs, GA)

Scott Parker/Acting Director (770) 222-4234.

Telecommunications Consumers Division

(202) 418-7320; Colleen Heitkamp/Division Chief (202) 418-0974 4 C224; Kurt Schroeder/Deputy Division Chief (202) 418-0966 4 C222; Mark Stone/Deputy Division Chief (202) 418-0816 4 C220; Sharon D. Lee/Associate Division Chief (202) 418-7534 4 A222; Emmitt Carlton/Assistant Division Chief (202) 418-7321 4 A223; Mary Romano/Special Advisor (202) 418-0975 4 A260.

North East Region

Russell (Joe) D. Monie/Regional Director (Chicago, IL) (847) 813-4670; Barry A. Bohac/Deputy Regional Director (Chicago,IL) (847) 813-4670.

South Central Region

Dennis (Denny) P. Carlton/Director (816) 316-1243; Loyd P. Perry/Deputy Regional Director (Houston, TX) (713) 983-6104.

Western Region

Rebecca L. Dorch/Regional Director (Denver, CO) (925) 416-9661; Leo Cirbo/Deputy Regional Director (Denver, CO) (925) 416-9661.

INTERNATIONAL BUREAU

Donald Abelson/Bureau Chief (202) 418-0437 6 C750; Anna Gomez/Deputy Bureau Chief (202) 418-0438 6 C475; Roderick K. Porter/Deputy Bureau Chief (202) 418-0438 6 C752; Jacqueline Ponti/Associate Bureau Chief (202) 418-0437 6 C747; Linda Haller/Associate Bureau Chief (202) 418-0438 6 C767; Breck Blalock/Chief of Staff (202) 418-8191 6 C749; John V. Giusti/Assistant Bureau Chief (202) 418-0437 6 C746; Richard B. Engelman/Chief Engineer (202) 418-0438 6 A668; Jerry B. Duvall/Chief Economist (Acting) (202) 418-0437 6 C730; Gardner Foster/Legal Advisor/Satellite Division (202) 418-1990 6 C477; Brad Lerner/Legal Advisor/Policy Division (202) 418-7066 6 C769.

Administrative and Management Staff

Thomas Sullivan/Assistant Bureau Chief for Management (202) 418-0411 6 C841; Sarah Y. Van Valzah/Deputy Assistant Bureau Chief, Mgmt(202) 418-0409 6 C860.

Policy Division

James L. Ball/Division Chief (202) 418-1460 7 A760; Claudia Fox/Deputy Division Chief (202) 418-1460 7 A761; George S. Li/Deputy Division Chief (Operations) (202) 418-1460 7 A669; Joann Ekblad/Assistant Division Chief (202) 418-1372 7 A660; Howard Griboff/Assistant Division Chief (202) 418-0657 7 A662; David Krech/Assistant Division Chief (202) 418-7443 7 A664; Paul Locke/Assistant Division Chief (Engineering) (202) 418-0756 7 A666; David Strickland/Assistant Division Chief (202) 418-0977 7 A633.

Satellite Division

Vacant/Division Chief (202) 418-0719 6 A665; Cassandra Thomas/Deputy Division Chief (202) 418-0719 6 A666; Fern Jarmulnek/Deputy Division Chief (202) 418-0719 6 A760; Joann Lucanik/Associate Division Chief (202) 418-0873 6 A660 Karl Kensinger/Associate Division Chief (202) 418-0773 6 A663; Steven Spaeth/Assistant Division Chief (202) 418-1539 6 C407; John Martin/Senior Engineer (202) 418-7281 6 A426; Marilyn Simon/Senior Economist (202) 418-2044 6 A633.

Policy Branch

Andrea Kelly/Branch Chief (202) 418-7877 6 A521.

Systems Analysis Branch

Scott Kotler/Branch Chief (202) 418-0596 6 C411

Engineering Branch

Robert Nelson/Branch Chief (202) 418-2341 6 B554.

Broadcasting & Cable Yearbook 2006

Federal Communications Commission Executives and Staff

Strategic Analysis and Negotiations Division

Kathryn O'Brien/Division Chief (202) 418-2150 6 A763; Linda Dubroof/Deputy Division Chief (202) 418-2150 6 A764; Jennifer Gilsenan/Deputy Division Chief (202) 418-2150 6 A761; Alexander Royblat/Assistant Division Chief (202) 418-7501 6 A865; Julie Barrie Buchanan /Assistant Division Chief (202) 418-2150 6 B411; Larry Olson/Senior Engineer (202) 418-2142 6 A866.

Cross Border Negotiations & Treaty Compliance Branch

James Ballis/Branch Chief (202) 418-2141 6 A404.

Regional & Bilateral Affairs Branch

Patricia Cooper/Branch Chief (202) 418-0723 6 A844.

Multilateral Negotiations & Industry Analysis Branch

Christopher Murphy/Division Chief (202) 418-2373 6 C866.

International Radiocommunications Branch

William A. Luther/Branch Chief (202) 418-0729 6 A814.

MEDIA BUREAU

Donna Gregg/Acting Bureau Chief (202) 418-7200 3 C740; Roy Stewart/Senior Deputy Bureau Chief (202) 418-2600 2 C347; Deborah Klein/Deputy Bureau Chief (202) 418-7200 3 C478; William H. Johnson/Deputy Bureau Chief (202) 418-7200 3 C742; Robert H. Ratcliffe/Deputy Bureau Chief (202) 418-7200 3 C486; Vacant/Associate Bureau Chief (202) 418-7200 3 C838; Rick Chessen/Associate Bureau Chief (202) 418-7200 3 C726; Barbara S. Esbin/Associate Bureau Chief (202) 418-7200 3 C458; Tracy Waldon/Chief Economist (202) 418-7200 3 C488; Jerry B. Duvall/Asst. Bureau Chief/ Dir of Media Economic Research (202) 418-2600 2 C463; Keith A. Larson/Chief Engineer (202) 418-2600 2 C420; Thomas Horan/Senior Legal Advisor (202) 418-7200 3 C736; Erin Dozier/Special Advisor (Ownership) (202) 418-7200 3 C438; Rebecca Fisher/Special Advisor (Media Relations) (202) 418-7200 3 C738.

Management and Resources Staff

Janet S. Amaya/Assistant Bureau Chief for Management (202) 418-2614 3 C830; Michael E. Teaney/Deputy Assistant Chief for Management(202) 418-2619 3 A866.

Office of Communications and Industry Information

Michael S. Perko/Chief (202) 418-7200 3 C831; Margo Domon Davenport/Senior Legal Advisor (202) 418-7200 3 A729;

Office of Broadcast License Policy

Roy J. Stewart/Chief (202) 418-2600 2 C347.

Audio Division

Peter H. Doyle/Division Chief (202) 418-2700 2 A360; Nina Shafran/Deputy Division Chief (Law) (202) 418-2700 2 A267; James Bradshaw/Deputy Division Chief (Engineering) (202) 418-2700 2 A262; Rudolfo Bonacci/Assistant Chief (202) 418-2700 2 A234; Susan Crawford/Assistant Chief (202) 418-2700 2 A333; John A. Karousos/Assistant Chief (202) 418-2180 2 A465; Lisa Scanlan/Assistant Chief (202) 418-2700 2 A427; Michael Wagner/Assistant Chief (202) 418-2700 2 A523; Andrew J. Rhodes/Senior Counsel, Allocations (202) 418-2180 2 A461.

Video Division

Barbara A. Kreisman/Division Chief (202) 418-1600 2 A666; James J. Brown/Deputy Division Chief (202) 418-1600 2 A663; Hossein Hashemzadeh/Associate Chief (202) 418-1600 2 C866; Clay C. Pendarvis/Associate Chief (202) 418-1600 2 A662; Mary M. Fitzgerald/Assistant Chief (202) 418-1600 2 A660.

Policy Division

Mary Beth Murphy/Division Chief (202) 418-2120 4 A766; Steven A. Broeckaert/Deputy Division Chief (202) 418-7200 4 A865; John B. Norton/Deputy Division Chief (202) 418-7034 4 C764; Robert Baker/Assistant Chief (202) 418-1440 3 A832; Eloise Gore/Assistant Chief (202) 418-2120 4 A726; Ronald Parver/Assistant Chief (202) 418-7200 4 A822; Lewis Pulley/Assistant Chief (202) 418-1450 3 A738.

Industry Analysis Division

Royce D. Sherlock/Division Chief (202) 418-2330 2 C360; Mania K. Baghdadi/Deputy Division Chief (202) 418-2120 2 C267; Marcia A. Glauberman/Deputy Division Chief (202) 418-2330 2 C264; Judith Herman/Assistant Chief (202) 418-2330 2 C160; Daniel Hodes/Senior Economic Advisor (202) 418-2330 2 C164.

Engineering Division

John P. Wong/Division Chief (202) 418-7200 4 C838; Michael L. Lance/Deputy Division Chief (202) 418-7200 4 C818; Wayne T. McKee/Assistant Chief (202) 418-7200 4 C737.

WIRELESS TELECOMMUNICATIONS BUREAU

Vacant/Bureau Chief (202) 418-0600 3 C252; Catherine W. Seidel/Acting Bureau Chief (202) 418-0600 3 C255; Scott Delacourt/Deputy Bureau Chief (202) 418-0600 3 C250; Peter A. Tenhula/Acting Deputy Bureau Chief (202) 418-0600 3 C254; David Furth/Associate Bureau Chief/Counsel (202) 418-0600 3 C162; D'wana Terry/Chief of Staff (202) 418-0600 3 C220; Thomas Stanley/WTB Chief Engineer (202) 418-0600 3 C222; Walter Strack/WTB Chief Economist (202) 418-0600 3 C204; Blaise Scinto/Special Counsel for Spectrum Policy (202) 418-0600 3 C163 Harry Wingo/Legal Advisor (Detailed) (202) 418-0600 3 C277; Uzoma C. Onyeije/Legal Advisor (202) 418-0600 3 C217; John Branscome/Legal Advisor (Detail) (202) 418-0600 3 C224; Aaron Goldberger/Legal Advisor (Detail) (202) 418-0600 3 C310; Nicole McGinnis/Legal Advisor (202) 418-0600 3 C300; Zenji Nakazawa/Acting Legal Advisor (Detail) (202) 418-0600 3 C401; Paul Murray/Acting Legal Advisor (Detail) (202) 418-0600 3 C224; Vacant/Special Counsel For Media & Public Affairs (202) 418-7944 3 C313.

Management and Resources Staff

Vacant/Assistant Bureau Chief for Management (202) 418-1469 3 C362; Diane Scott/Deputy Assistant Bureau Chief for Managemen(202) 418-2049 3 C367; Sam Francis/Chief, Auctions Expenditures and Budget Gro (202) 418-0796 6-6100; Gail Calhoun/Deputy Chief, Auctions Expenditures& Budge (202) 418-0671 6-6101;

Auctions and Spectrum Access Division

(202) 418-0660; Margaret Wiener/Division Chief (202) 418-0660 6-6419; Kathryn Garland/Deputy Division Chief (Auctions Analysis & Implementation)-(Gettysburg, PA) (202) 418-0660; Gary Michaels/Deputy Division Chief (Legal & Policy) (202) 418-0660 6-6604; Craig Bomberger/Associate Division Chief- (Auctions Analysis & Implementation) (202) 418-0660 6-6507; Bill Huber/Associate Division Chief (Legal & Policy) (202) 418-0660; Erik Salovaara/Assistant Division Chief (Chief Counsel) (202) 418-0660 6-6603; Kelly Quinn/Assistant Division Chief (Legal) (202) 418-0660 6-6417; S. Diane Conley/Assistant Division Chief (Policy) (202) 418-0660 6-6422; Brain Carter/Special Counsel (202) 418-0600; Rita Cookmeyer/Financial Policy Analyst (202) 418-0600 6-506.

Broadband Division

(202) 418-BITS; Joel Taubenblatt/Division Chief (202) 418-BITS 3 C124; Jennifer Tomchin/Deputy Div. Chief (Legal-Rulemakings-Mob(202) 418-BITS 3 C133; John Schauble/Deputy Div. Chief (Legal-Rulemakings-Fixed)(202) 418-BITS 3 C130; Mary Shultz/Deputy Division Chief (Gettysburg, PA) (202) 418-BITS; Linda C. Ray/Associate Div. Chief (Legal-Licensing-Mobile(202) 418-BITS 3 A160; Suzan Friedman/Associate Div. Chief (Legal-Licensing-Mobi(202) 418-BITS 3 A165; Stephen Buenzow/Associate Division Chief (Gettysburg, PA)(202) 418-BITS; Sandra Danner/Assistant Division Chief (202) 418-BITS 3 A266; Peter Daronco/Assistant Division Chief (202) 418-BITS 3 A264.

Mobility Division

(202) 418-0620; Roger Noel/Division Chief (202) 418-0620 6-6411; Lloyd Coward/Deputy Division Chief (Legal) (202) 418-0620 6-6329; Thomas Derenge/Deputy Division Chief (Technical Policy) (202) 418-0620 6-6339; Kathy Harris/Deputy Division Chief (Policy) (202) 418-0620 6-6409; Linda Chang/Associate Division Chief (Rules Pt. 22, 24 & (202) 418-0620 6-6402; Vacant/Associate Division Chief (Rule Pt. 90 & 95) (202) 418-0620 6-6320; Stephen Markendorff/Associate Division Chief-(Knowledge, Information, and Security Management) (202) 418-0620 6-6407; Michael Ferrante/Associate Division Chief- (Technical and Licensing under Parts 22, 24, and 27) (202) 418-0620 6-6327; Terry Fishel/Associate Division Chief- (Technical and Licensing under Parts 90 and 95) (Gettysbu(202) 418-0620; Cyndi Thomas/Assistant Chief (Licensing and Re-licensing (202) 418-0620 6-6319; James Gumbert/Assistant Div. Chief (Licensing technical m(202) 418-0620 6-6326; Erin McGrath/Assistant Chief (Post Auction/Transfer Appli(202) 418-0620 6-6338.

Public Safety & Critical Infrastructure Division

(202) 418-0680; Michael Wilhelm/Division Chief (202) 418-0680 4 C321; Herbert W. Zeiler/Deputy Division Chief- Engineering and Licensing Operations) (202) 418-0680 4 C343; Scot Stone/Deputy Division Chief (Legal) (202) 418-0680; Jeffrey Cohen/Deputy Division Chief (Spectrum Policy) (202) 418-0680; Brain Marenco/Associate Division Chief (Engineering)(202) 418-0680; Tracy Simmons/Associate Div. Chief (Licensing Operations (202) 418-0680; Ramona Melson/Associate Division Chief (Chief of Staff) (202) 418-0680 4 C322; Angela Giancarlo/Associate Division Chief (Spectrum Polic(202) 418-0680; Gregory Intoccia/Associate Division Chief (Legal) (202) 418-0680; Michael Regiec/Assistant Division Chief (Gettysburg) (202) 418-0680.

Spectrum & Competition Policy Division

(202) 418-1310; William Kunze/Division Chief (202) 418-7887 6-6411; Paul D'Ari/Deputy Division Chief (202) 418-1550 6-6326; Jeffrey Steinberg/Deputy Division Chief (202) 418-0896 6-6413; Nese Guendelsberger/Deputy Division Chief (202) 418-0634 6-6405; Rachel Kazan/Associate Chief (202) 418-0651 6-126; Dan Abeyta/Assistant Chief (202) 418-1538 6-6330; John Borkowski/Assistant Chief (202) 418-0626 4-C237; Aaron Goldschmidt/Assistant Chief (202) 418-7146 6215.

Broadcasting & Cable Yearbook 2006

Federal Communications Commission Executives and Staff

Spectrum Management Resource & Technology Division

1-888-225-5322; John Chudovan/Division Chief (Gettysburg, PA) (717) 338-2510; Judith Kassakatis/Deputy Division Chief (Licensing Support & Outreach)- (Gettysburg, PA) (717) 338-2511; Andrew Martin/Deputy Division Chief (Acting - (Auctions Support and Performance Measurement) (202) 418-7471 6-6119; Eddie Richardson/Associate Div. Chief (Performance Measur(202) 418-0573 4 B404; Sandra Eckenrode/Associate Division Chief (Licensing Supp(717) 338-2630; Pat Rinn/Associate Division Chief (Auction Support) (202) 414-1223 CY A723; Dorothy Conway/Associate Division Chief (Outreach) (202) 418-7349 6-6115; Andrew Martin/Assistant Division Chief- (Investment Oversight and Planning) (202) 418-7471 6-6119.

WIRELINE COMPETITION BUREAU

Tom Navin/Acting Bureau Chief (202) 418-1500 5 C450; Vacant//Deputy Bureau Chief (202) 418-1500 5 C356; Lisa Gelb/ Deputy Bureau Chief (202) 418-1500 5 C451; Jane Jackson/Associate Bureau Chief (202) 418-1500 5 C354; Richard Lerner/Associate Bureau Chief (202) 418-1500 5 C352; Diane L. Griffin/Associate Bureau Chief/Chief of Staff (202) 418-1500 5 C441; Robert Tanner/ Associate Bureau Chief (202) 418-1500 5 C433; Margaret Dailey/Legal Counsel to the Bureau Chief (202) 418-1500 5 C453; Pam Arluk/Legal Counsel to the Bureau Chief (202) 418-1500 5 C433; Jeremy Marcus/Legal Counsel to the Bureau Chief (202) 418-1500 5 C413; Mark Wigfield/Public Affairs Specialist (202) 418-1500 5 C424.

Administrative and Management Office

Joseph Hall/Assistant Bureau Chief (202) 418-1370 5 C455.

Competition Policy Division

Julie Veach/Acting Division Chief (202) 418-1580 5 B125; William Dever/Deputy Division Chief (202) 418-1580 6 A420; Julie Veach/Deputy Division Chief (202) 418-1580 5 B125; Renee Crittendon/Assistant Division Chief (202) 418-2352 6320; Ann Stevens/Associate Division Chief (202) 418-1580 5 C162; Jeremy Miller/Assistant Division Chief (202) 418-1580 5 C266; Terri Natoli/Assistant Division Chief (202) 418-1580 5 C124.

Pricing Policy Division

Tamara L. Preiss/Division Chief (202) 418-1520 5 A225; Clifford M. Rand/Deputy Division Chief (202) 418-1520 6 C464; Deena M. Shetler/Deputy Division Chief (202) 418-1520 5 A221; Steve Morris/Deputy Division Chief (202) 418-1520 5 A223; Jennifer McKee/Assistant Division Chief (202) 418-1520 5 A263; Judith A. Nitsche/Assistant Division Chief (202) 418-1520 5 A121; Len Smith/Assistant Division Chief (202) 418-1520 5 A461.

Telecommunications Access Policy Division

Narda Jones/Division Chief (202) 418-7400 5 A426; Tony Dale/Deputy Division Chief (202) 418-7400 5 A423; Cathy Carpino/Deputy Division Chief (202) 418-7400 5 A425; Cheryl Callahan/Assistant Division Chief (202) 418-7400 6 A431; Gina Spade/Assistant Division Chief (202) 418-7400 5 B550; Mark Seifert/Assistant Division Chief (202) 418-7400 5 A523.

Industry Analysis and Technology Division

Rodger Woock/Division Chief (202) 418-0940 6 A224; Alan I. Feldman/Deputy Division Chief (202) 418-0940 6 A221; Thomas J. Beers/Deputy Division Chief (202) 418-0940 6 A225; Cathy H. Zima/Acting Deputy Division Chief (202) 418-0940 6 A326; Ellen Burton/Assistant Division Chief (202) 418-0940 6 A233; Fatina K. Franklin/Assistant Division Chief (202) 418-0840 6 B145. Last Updated: 07/11/05

U.S. Government Agencies

U.S. Government Agencies of Interest to TV and Radio

Department of Agriculture, 1400 Independence Ave. S.W., Washington, DC 20250. Phone: (202) 720-4623. Fax: (202) 720-5043. Web Site: www.usda.gov.

Wkly TV satellite newsfeed. Daily radio newsline. Wkly radio features on CD.

Department of Commerce, 1401 Constitution Ave. N.W., Suite 5040, Washington, DC 20230. Phone: (202) 219-3605. Fax: (202) 482-2639. E-mail: opaosec@doc.gov. Web Site: www.doc.gov/opa.

Department of Defense, Pentagon, Washington, DC 20301. Phone: (703) 545-6700. Fax: (703) 695-4299. Fax: (703) 695-9080. Web Site: www.defense.gov.

Department of Education, 400 Maryland Ave. S.W., Washington, DC 20202. Phone: (202) 401-2000. Fax: (202) 401-0689. E-mail: opa@ed.gov. Web Site: www.ed.gov.

Provides daily audio service for radio news; arranges bcst interviews with sr department officials.

Department of Energy, 1000 Independence Ave. S.W., Washington, DC 20585. Phone: (202) 586-5000. Phone: (202) 586-5806 (Press Off). Fax: (202) 586-9987 (Dir.). Fax: (202) 586-4403. Web Site: www.energy.gov.

Five business lines encompass everything that DOE does: energy, resouces, natl security, environmental quality, science & technology, & economic productivity.

Department of Health and Human Services, 200 Independence Ave. S.W., Washington, DC 20201. Phone: (202) 619-0257. Fax: (202) 690-7203. Web Site: www.hhs.gov.

Department of Justice, Office of Public Aff., 950 Pennsylvania Ave. N.W., Washington, DC 20530. Phone: (202) 514-2007. E-mail: AskDOJ@usdoj.gov. Web Site: www.justice.gov. Tasia Scolinos, dir.

Department of Labor, 200 Constitution Ave. N.W., Washington, DC 20210. Phone: (202) 693-5000. Phone: (202) 693-4650 (pub affrs). Fax: (202) 693-4674. Web Site: www.dol.gov. Elaine L. Chao, sec.

Fosters, promotes, & develops the welfare of working people.

Department of State, 2201 C St. N.W., Washington, DC 20520. Phone: (202) 647-4000. Web Site: www.state.gov.

Department of the Treasury, 1500 Pennsylvania Ave. N.W., 3442 MT, Washington, DC 20020. Phone: (202) 622-2000. Phone: (202) 622-2960 (press off.). Fax: (202) 622-6415. Web Site: www.treasury.gov. John W. Snow, sec; Christopher Smith, chief of staff.

Department of Transportation, 400 7th St. S.W., Washington, DC 20590. Phone: (202) 366-4000. Web Site: www.dot.gov. E-mail: dot.comments@ost.dot.gov. Norman Y. Mineta, sec.

Mission: To serve the United States by ensuring a fast, safe, efficient, accessible and convenient transportation system that meets our vital national interests and enhances the quality of life of the American people, today and into the future.

Executive Office of the President, The White House, 1600 Pennsylvania Ave. N.W., Washington, DC 20500. Phone: (202) 456-1414. Fax: (202) 456-2461. Web Site: www.whitehouse.gov. E-mail: comments@whitehouse.gov. Joe Lockhart; Barry Toiv.

Federal Communications Commission, 445 12th St. S.W., Washington, DC 20554. Web Site: www.fcc.gov. E-mail: fccinfo@fcc.gov. Kevin J. Martin, chmn.

(For full listing of commissioners & staff, see FCC Executives & Staff.)

Federal Emergency Management Agency, 500 C St. S.W., Washington, DC 20472. Phone: (202) 566-1600. E-mail: FEMAOPA@dhs.gov. Web Site: www.fema.gov. R. David Paulison, Acting Undersec.

Comprehensive info source on emergency preparedness & federal disaster response & recovery.

Federal Trade Commission, 600 Pennsylvania Ave. N.W., Washington, DC 20580. Phone: (202) 326-2222. Fax: (202) 326-3366. Web Site: www.ftc.gov. Deborah Platt Majoras, chmn.

House Appropriations Committee, Rm. H218, Capitol Bldg, Washington, DC 20515. Phone: (202) 225-2771. Phone: (202) 225-3351 (commerce/justice/state subcomm). Web Site: http://appropriations.house.gov/. Jerry Lewis, chmn.

Funds government agencies.

House Committee on Energy and Commerce, 2125 Rayburn House Office Bldg., Washington, DC 20515-6115. Phone: (202) 225-2927. Web Site: energycommerce.house.gov. Joe Barton, chmn.

The Committee, the oldest legislative standing committee in the U.S. House of Representatives, has served as the principal guide for the House in matters relating to the promotion of commerce and to the public's health and marketplace interests.

House Committee on the Judiciary, 2138 Rayburn House Office Bldg., Washington, DC 20515-6216. Phone: (202) 225-3951. Web Site: www.house.gov/judiciary. E-mail: judiciary@mail.house.gov. F. James Sensenbrenner, Jr., chmn.

The Committee on the Judiciary has been called the lawyer for the House of Representatives because of its jurisdiction over matters relating to the administration of justice in Federal courts, administrative bodies, and law enforcement agencies. Its infrequent but important role in impeachment proceedings has also brought it much attention.

National Aeronautics & Space Administration (NASA), 300 E St. S.W., Washington, DC 20546. Phone: (202) 358-0001. Fax: (202) 358-3469. E-mail: public-inquiries@hq.nasa.gov. Web Site: www.nasa.gov. Michael Griffin, admin.

National Labor Relations Board, 1099 14th St. N.W., Washington, DC 20570-0001. Phone: (202) 273-1991. Fax: (202) 208-3013. E-mail: dparker@nlrb.gov. Web Site: www.nlrb.gov. Robert J. Battista, chmn; Arthur F. Rosenfeld, gen counsel.

The NLRB adjudicates unfair labor practice charges & conducts union representation elections under the National Labor Relations Act.

National Science Foundation, 4201 Wilson Blvd., Arlington, VA 22230. Phone: (703) 292-5111. Fax: (703) 292-9087. E-mail: info@nsf.gov. Web Site: www.nsf.gov. Arden Bement, dir; Kathie L. Olsen, deputy dir.

National Telecommunications and Information Administration, 14th & Constitution N.W., Washington, DC 20230. Phone: (202) 482-7002. Web Site: www.ntia.doc.gov. Michael Gallagher, admin. & asst. sec.

NTIA serves as the principal advisor to the exec branch on domestic & international communication & info issues.

Securities and Exchange Commission, 450 5th St. N.W., Washington, DC 20549. Phone: (202) 942-8088. Phone: (202) 551-5400 (sec). Fax: (202) 942-9628. Web Site: www.sec.gov. Christopher Cox, chmn; Cynthia A. Glassman, commissioner; Paul S. Atkins, commissioner; Roel C. Campos, commissioner; Annette L. Nazareth, commissioner.

Administers federal securities laws that protect investors. These laws ensure that securities markets are fair & provide sanctions for enforcement.

Senate Appropriations Committee, Rm. SD-128, Dirksen Senate Office Bldg., Washington, DC 20510. Phone: (202) 224-3471. Web Site: http://appropriations.senate.gov/. Thad Cocharn, chmn.

Senate Committee on Commerce, Science, and Transportation, Dirksen Senate Office Bldg., Suite 508, Washington, DC 20510-6125. Phone: (202) 224-0411 (minority). Phone: (202) 224-1251 (majority). Fax: (202) 224-1259 (majority). Fax: (202) 228-0303 (minority). Web Site: http://commerce.senate.gov/. Ted Stevens, chmn.

Jurisdiction includes communications, aviation, consumer affairs, foreign commerce & tourism, oceans & fisheries, science, technolgy & space, surface transportion & merchant marine, manufactruring & competiveness.

Senate Judiciary Committee, 224 Dirksen Senate Office Bldg, Washington, DC 20510-6275. Phone: (202) 224-5225. Fax: (202) 224-9102. Web Site: http://judiciary.senate.gov/. Arlen Specter, chmn.

U.S. District Court for the District of Columbia, 333 Constitution Ave. N.W., Washington, DC 20001. Phone: (202) 354-3000. Web Site: www.dcd.uscourts.gov.

Hears civil & criminal cases that arise under federal law, cases involving the U.S. Constitution, disputes between two states, or cases in which the United States is a party.

U.S. Advisory Commission on Public Diplomacy, 301 4th St. S.W., Washington, DC 20547. Phone: (202) 203-7880. Fax: (202) 203-7886. Web Site: http://www.state.gov/r/adcompd/. Athena Katsoulos, exec dir.

A bipartisan presidentially appointed panel created by Congress to oversee U.S. government activities intended to understand, inform, & influence foreign publics.

U.S. Court of Appeals for the District of Columbia Circuit, 333 Constitution Ave. N.W., Washington, DC 20001-2866. Phone: (202) 216-7000. Fax: (202) 273-0988. Fax: (202) 219-8530. Web Site: www.cadc.uscourts.gov.

Appeals from District Court cases. Appeals from federal agency decisions.

U.S. Supreme Court, One First St. N.E, Washington, DC 20543. Phone: (202) 479-3211 (pub. info. off.). Phone: (202) 479-3030 (visitor info.). Web Site: www.supremecourtus.gov/. John Roberts, Chief Justice; John Paul Stevens, Associate Justice; Sandra Day O'Connor, Associate Justice; Antonin Scalia, Associate Justice; Anthony M. Kennedy, Associate Justice; David H. Souter, Associate Justice; Clarence Thomas, Associate Justice; Ruth Bader Ginsburg, Associate Justice; Stephen G. Breyer, Associate Justice.

U.S. State Cable Regulatory Agencies

Connecticut Department of Public Utility Control, 10 Franklin Sq., New Britain, CT 06051. Phone: (860) 827-1553. Fax: (860) 827-2613. E-mail: dpuc.information@po.state.ct.us. Web Site: www.state.ct.us/dpuc. Donald W. Downes, chmn.

Delaware Public Service Commission, 861 Silver Lake Blvd. Cannon Bldg., Suite 100, Dover, DE 19904. Phone: (302) 739-4247. Fax: (302) 739-4849. Web Site: www.state.de.us/delpsc. Bruce Burcat, exec dir.

Hawaii Cable Television Division, Box 541, Dept. of Commerce & Consumer Affairs, Honolulu, HI 96809. Phone: (808) 586-2620. Fax: (808) 586-2625. E-mail: cabletv@dcca.hawaii.gov. Web Site: www.state.hi.us/dcca. Mark E. Recktenwald, dir.

Massachusetts Department of Telecommunications & Energy, (Cable Television Division). One South Station, Boston, MA 02110. Phone: (617) 305-3580. Fax: (617) 478-2590. E-mail: cable.inquiry@state.ma.us. Web Site: www.state.ma.us/dpu/catv.

New Jersey Office of Cable Television, 2 Gateway Center, Newark, NJ 07102. Phone: (973) 648-2670. Fax: (973) 648-3135. Web Site: http://www.state.nj.us/bpu/home/cable.shtml. Celeste M. Fasone, dir.

New York State Department of Public Service, 3 Empire State Plaza, Albany, NY 12223-1350. Phone: (518) 474-1939. Fax: (518) 486-5727. Web Site: www.dps.state.ny.us. Chad G. Hume, deputy dir.-cable; Robert Mayer, dir.

Regulatory Commission of Alaska, 701 W. 8th Ave., Suite 300, Anchorage, AK 99501. Phone: (907) 276-6222. Fax: (907) 276-0160. E-mail: rca-mail@rca.state.ak.us. Web Site: www.state.ak.us/rca. G. Nanette Thompson, chmn/exec dir.

Rhode Island Division of Public Utilities and Carriers, 89 Jefferson Blvd., Warwick, RI 02888. Phone: (401) 941-4500. Fax: (401) 941-9248. E-mail: mary.kent@ripuc.org. Web Site: http://www.ripuc.org/.

Vermont Public Service Board, Chittenden Bank Bldg., 4th Fl., 112 State St., Drawer 20, Montpelier, VT 05620-2701. Phone: (802) 828-2358. Fax: (802) 828-3351. Web Site: www.state.vt.us/psb. James Volz, chmn.